Start professional backing

Consistently profitable over the last fifteen years, leading full time professional backer Steve Lewis Hamilton puts his success down to:

"Detailed analysis, accurate and exclusive information, proven staking methods and above all, sheer hard work"

Throughout the last National Hunt season Steve's select group of private clients greatly benefitted from his dedication, knowledge and ability by:-

- Amassing over £5,500 profit to just £25 per point invested through Steve's proven staking methods
- Backing a catalogue of big winners, including...
  - — Coome Hill Won 11/2
  - — Barna Boy Won 25/1
  - — Harwell Lad Won 16/1
  - — Cittadino Won 8/1
- Being part of a genuine and honest service
  - — Definite bets only
  - — No odds on
  - — No premium rate
  - — No 'last minute calls'
  - — All bets substantiated by the racing press in advance

'Steve is an honest, hard working professional with the drive and abilty to achieve outstanding results'

Peter Walwyn

As a reader of this publication you are demonstrating an above average understanding of racing. It is now time for you to progress and start backing alongside a true professional **PLUS** you qualify for an exclusive 20% saving on membership fees.

Call the racing office for further information and immediate membership

Tel: 0181 466 9817

Internet: www.slh.co.uk
Email: steve@slh.co.uk

Information pack and guaranteed 20% discount
Write to: Steve Lewis Hamilton, 602 The Cotton Exchange Buildings, Liverpool L3 9LQ
(Quote Ref. CF20 to qualify for bonus)

Chaseform

1996-97 JUMPS ANNUAL

The BHB's Official Form Book

Complete record of all Steeplechasing and Hurdling in Great Britain from June 6th, 1996 to May 31st, 1997

Sponsored by:

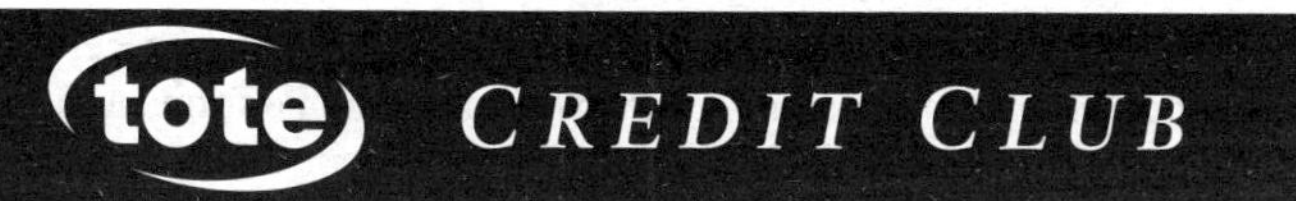

Published by Raceform Ltd
Compton, Newbury, Berkshire, RG20 6NL
Tel: 01635 578080
Fax: 01635 578101
Editorial: 01635 578643
Web http://www.raceform.co.uk
Email raceform@raceform.co.uk

Printed by BPC Wheatons Ltd, Hennock Road,
Exeter, DEVON EX2 8RP
Typeset by Raceform

Edited by Ashley Rumney

Registered as a newspaper at the Post Office

ISBN 1-901100-35-9

£24.00

CONTENTS

Chaseform, The Official Form Book, is updated weekly. Subscribers receive a binder including a front section, which contains the Index to Performances and many other features, together with all the early Summer racing. Weekly sections and a new index are threaded into the binder to keep it up to date.

The data contained in Chaseform 1996-97 Jumps Annual is available in paper form or on computer disk. The disk service contains the same data as Chaseform, The Form Book, and operates on any PC within a 'Windows' environment. The database is designed to allow you to access the information in a number of different ways, and is extremely quick and easy to use.

Full details of all Raceform services and publications are available from
Raceform, Compton, Newbury, Berkshire RG20 6NL.
Tel: 01635 578080 Fax: 01635 578101.

Cover Photo: Alan Johnson
Martha's Son heads Viking Flagship on his way to becoming
Champion Two-Mile Chaser

HOW TO READ CHASEFORM

CHASEFORM, THE OFFICIAL FORM BOOK, records comprehensive race details of every domestic race, principal races abroad, and every foreign event in which a British-trained runner participated. Extended notes are given to runners worthy of a mention, including all placed horses and all favourites. Generally speaking, the higher the class of race, the greater the number of runners noted.

MEETING BACK REFERENCE NUMBER is the Chaseform number of the last meeting run at the track and is shown to the left of the course name. Abandoned meetings are signified by a †.

THE OFFICIAL GOING, shown at the head of each meeting, is recorded as follows:
Hard; Firm; Good to firm; Good; Good to soft; Soft; Heavy.

THE WIND is included only if 'strong' or classified as unusual.

CHASEFORM GOING, which may differ from the Official Going, now appears against each race to allow for changing conditions of the ground. It takes into account the race times compared with the Raceform Standard Times, the wind and other elements, and is recorded in the following stages:
H (Hard); **F** (Firm); **GF** (Good to firm); **G** (Good);
GS (Good to soft); **S** (Soft); **Hvy** (Heavy).

THE RACE DISTANCE is given for all races and is followed by the number of obstacles.

PRIZE MONEY shows penalty values down to sixth place (where applicable).

WEIGHT-FOR-AGE allowances are given where applicable for mixed age races.

COMPETITIVE RACING CLASSIFICATIONS are shown on a scale from Class A to Class H.

RACE NUMBERS for Foreign races carry the suffix 'a'. Irish Races which do not appear in Chaseform can be found in Computer Raceform.

IN THE RACE RESULT, the figures to the left of each horse show the race number of its most recent listing in Chaseform. The superscript figure indicates its finishing position in that race and are coded as follows:
***** - winner
2, 8, 17 etc. - other finishing positions
b - brought down; **c** - carried out; **f** - fell; **p** - pulled up; **r** - refused (to race);
ro - ran out; **s** - slipped up; **u** - unseated rider; **v** - void race; **w** - withdrawn.
A figure to the left of the extended comment is the last race in which the horse warranted a *Note-Book* comment.

THE ADJUSTED OFFICIAL RATING is the figure in **bold type** directly after the horse's name in the race result. This figure indicates the Official BHB rating, at entry, after the following adjustments had been made:
(i) Overweight carried by the rider.
(ii) The number of pounds out of the handicap (if applicable).
(iii) Penalties incurred after the publication of the weights.
However, **no** adjustments have been made for:
(i) Weight-for-age.
(ii) Rider's allowances.

THE TRAINER is shown in parentheses for every runner.

THE HORSE'S AGE is shown immediately before the weight carried.

WEIGHTS shown are actual weights carried. A figure next to the weight with an 'ow' sign is the amount of overweight put up by the jockey, e.g. ^{ow4} Allowances are now shown after the weight carried and before the jockey name,
e.g. **11-1**$^{(7)}$LAspell

LONG HANDICAP WEIGHTS for runners allotted a lower-than-minimum weight at entry **(handicaps only)** are shown above the *Note-Book* comments.

CONDITIONAL ALLOWANCES The holders of conditional jockeys' licences under the provisions of Rule 60(iv) are permitted to claim the following allowances in Steeple Chases, Hurdle races and National Hunt flat races until the age of 25:
7lb until they have won 15 races run under the Rules of any recognised Turf Authority; thereafter 5lb until they have won 30 such races; thereafter 3lb until they have won 55 such races.
These allowances can be claimed in those Steeple Chases, Hurdle races and National Hunt Flat races that are open to professional jockeys set out below, with the exception of races confined to conditional jockeys:
(a) All handicaps, except the Grand National, and all selling races.
(b) All other races with guaranteed prize money of not more than £5000.
The same allowances can also be claimed in those Steeple Chases, Hurdle races and National Hunt Flat races that are confined to amateur riders set out below:
(a) All handicaps and selling races confined to amateur riders.
(b) All other races confined to amateur riders with guaranteed prize money of not more than £5000.

HEADGEAR is shown after the actual weight carried and expressed as: **b** (blinkers); **v** (visor); **h** (hood); **e** (eyeshield); **c** (eyecover). A horse sporting headgear for the first time under either code is shown thus; **b**^{1} **v**^{1} **h**^{1} **e**^{1} **c**^{1}

THE OFFICIAL DISTANCES are shown on the right-hand side immediately preceding the horse's finishing position.

STARTING PRICES (SP) appear to the right of the finishing position in the race result. The favourite indicator appears to the right of the Starting Price, 1 for favourite, 2 for second favourite and 3 for the third favourite. Joint-favourites will each display the number 1.

RACEFORM RATINGS (RR), which record the level of performance attained in this race for each horse, are given after the starting price. Reference to the *Raceform Ratings* section should be made for a full description of this feature.

SPEED FIGURES (SF) now appear for every horse that clocks a sufficiently fast time, and appear in the column to the right of the Raceform Ratings. The figures are adjusted to 12st 7lbs, and calculations made for going, wind, and distance behind the winner. To apply Speed Figures to future races, add 1 point for each 1lb below 12st 7lbs, and deduct 1 point for each 1lb above 12st 7lbs. The highest resultant figure is the best in that particular race.

WITHDRAWN horses that fail to come under orders after the jockey has weighed out, are included in the index to past racing (with W after the race number); side reference, odds at the time of withdrawal and the reason for withdrawal (if known) are shown in italics in the race comment for that horse.

RULE 4C TATTERSALL'S COMMITTEE RULES ON BETTING STATES:

In the case of bets made at a price on the day of the race, before it has been officially notified that a horse has been withdrawn before coming under Starter's Orders or has been declared "not to have started", the liability of a layer against any horse remaining in the race, win or place, will be reduced in accordance with the following scale depending on the odds current against the withdrawn horse at the time of such official notification:

(a) if the current odds are 30/100 or longer odds on by 75p in the £.
(b) if shorter odds on than 30/100 up to and including 2/5 by 70p in the £.
(c) if shorter odds on than 2/5 up to and including 8/15 by 65p in the £.
(d) if shorter odds on than 8/15 up to and including 8/13 by 60p in the £.
(e) if shorter odds on than 8/13 up to and including 4/5 by 55p in the £.
(f) if shorter odds on than 4/5 up to and including 20/21 by 50p in the £.
(g) if shorter odds on than 20/21 up to and including 6/5 by 45p in the £.
(h) if over 6/5 up to and including 6/4 by 40p in the £.
(i) if over 6/4 up to and including 7/4 by 35p in the £.
(j) if over 7/4 up to and including 9/4 by 30p in the £.
(k) if over 9/4 up to and including 3/1 by 25p in the £.
(l) if over 3/1 up to and including 4/1 by 20p in the £.
(m) if over 4/1 up to and including 11/2 by 15p in the £.
(n) if over 11/2 up to and including 9/1 by 10p in the £.
(o) if over 9/1 up to and including 14/1 by 5p in the £.
(p) if over 14/1 the liability would be unchanged.
(q) in the case of two or more horses being withdrawn the total deduction shall not exceed 75p in the £.

Ante-post bets are not affected and SP bets are also not affected, except in cases where insufficient time arises for a fresh market to be formed, when the above named scale reductions will apply.

STEWARDS' ENQUIRY, except in special circumstances, is included only if it concerns a prize winner or an objection. All suspensions are listed.

OFFICIAL EXPLANATIONS are included where given.

RACE TIMES in Great Britain are clocked by Raceform's own watch-holders. Figures in parentheses following the time show the number of seconds slower than the Raceform Standard Time for the course and distance.

RACEFORM STANDARD TIMES were originally compiled from times recorded on good to firm going after adjustments had been made for weights carried above or below a norm of 12st 7lbs. Times equal to the standard are shown thus (equals standard). Times under the standard are preceded by a - for instance, 1.8 seconds under the standard would be shown as (-1.8). Record times would be shown as (1.2 under best; -2.3). The Standard Times are subject to ongoing revision and may be different from those published in Chaseform 1996/97.

STARTING PRICE PERCENTAGE can be found below the SP of the final finisher and gives the total SP percentage of all runners that competed.

TOTE prices include £1 stake. Dual Forecast dividends are shown in brackets. The Tote Trio dividend is preceded by the word Trio. Jackpot, Placepot and Quadpot details appear at the end of the meeting to which they refer.

THE OWNER of the winner is shown immediately after the Tote returns together with the location of the trainer (in parentheses), the name of the breeder, result of the auction for sellers and details regarding any claimed horse. Friendly claims are not detailed.

Abbreviations and their meanings

Paddock comments

gd sort	- well made, above average on looks
h.d.w	- has done well, improved in looks
wl grwn	- well grown, has filled to its frame
lengthy	- longer than average for its height
tall	- tall
rangy	- lengthy and tall but in proportion, covers a deal of ground
scope	- scope for physical development
str	- strong, powerful looking
w'like	- workmanlike, ordinary in looks
lt-f	- light-framed, not much substance
neat	- smallish, well put together
leggy	- long legs compared to body
angular	- unfurnished behind the saddle, not filled to frame
unf	- unfurnished in the midriff, not filled to frame
narrow	- not as wide as side appearance would suggest
small	- lacks any physical scope
nt grwn	- not grown
lw	- looked fit and well
bkwd	- backward in condition
t	- tubed
swtg	- sweating
b.(off fore or nr fore)	- bandaged in front
b.hind (off or nr)	- bandaged behind

At the start

stdd s	- jockey purposely reins back the horse
dwlt	- missed the break and left for a short time
s.s	- slow to start, left longer than a horse that dwelt
s.i.s	- started on terms but took time to get going
ref to r	- either does not jump off, or travels a few yards and then stops
rel to r	- tries to pull itself up in mid-race

Position in the race

led	- in lead on its own
disp ld	- upsides the leader
w ldr	- almost upsides the leader
w ldrs	- in a line of three or more disputing the lead
prom	- on the heels of the leaders, in the front third of the field
trckd ldr(s)	- just in behind the leaders giving impression that it could lead if asked
chsd ldr	- horse in second place
chsd clr ldrs	- horse heads main body of field behind two clear leaders
chsd ldrs	- horse is in the first four or five but making more of an effort to stay close to the pace than if it were tracking the leaders.
in tch	- close enough to have a chance
hdwy	- making ground on the leader
gd hdwy	- making ground quickly on the leader, could be a deliberate move

sme hdwy - making some ground but no real impact on the race
stdy hdwy - gradually making ground
ev ch - upsides the leaders when the race starts in earnest
rr - last of main group but not detached
bhd - detached from the main body of runners
hld up - restrained as a deliberate tactical move
nt rcvr - lost all chance after interference, mistake etc.
wknd - stride shortened as it began to tire
lost tch - had been in the main body but a gap appeared as it tired
lost pl - remains in main body of runners but lost several positions quickly

Riding

effrt - short-lived effort
pushed along - received urgings with hands only, jockey not using legs
rdn - received urgings from the saddle, including use of the whip
hrd rdn - received maximum assistance from the saddle including use of whip
drvn - received forceful urgings, jockey putting in a lot of effort and using whip
hrd drvn - jockey very animated, plenty of kicking, pushing and reminders

Finishing Comments

jst failed - closing rapidly on the winner and probably would have led a stride after the line
r.o - jockey's efforts usually involved to produce an increase in pace without finding an appreciable turn of speed
r.o wl - jockey's efforts usually involved to produce an obvious increase in pace without finding an appreciable turn of speed
unable qckn - not visibly tiring but does not possess a sufficient change of pace
one pce - not tiring but does not find a turn of speed, from a position further out than unable qckn
nt r.o - did not consent to respond to pressure
styd on - going on well towards the end, utilising stamina
nvr plcd to chal - never apparently given the chance to make a challenge
nvr able to chal - unable to produce a challenge without a specific reason
nvr nr to chal - unable to produce a challenge, normally due to a slow start, stumbling etc.
nrst fin - nearer to the winner in distance beaten than at any time since the race had begun in earnest
nvr nrr - nearer to the winner position wise than at any time since the race had begun in earnest
rallied - responded to pressure to come back with a chance having lost its place
no ex - unable to sustain its run due to lack of strength or effort from the saddle, enthusiasm etc.
bttr for r - likely to improve for the run and experience
rn green - inclined to wander and falter through inexperience
too much to do - left with too much leeway to make up

Winning Comments

v.easily - a great deal in hand
easily - plenty in hand
comf - something in hand, always holding the others

pushed out	- kept up to its work with hands and heels without jockey resorting to whip or kicking along and wins fairly comfortably
rdn out	- pushed and kicked out to the line
drvn out	- pushed and kicked out to the line, with the whip employed
all out	- nothing to spare, could not have found any more
jst hld on	- holding on to a rapidly diminishing lead, could not have found any more if passed
unchal	- must either make all or a majority of the running and not be challenged from an early stage

Complete list of abbreviations

a - always
a.p - always prominent
abt - about
appr - approaching
awrdd - awarded
b.b.v - broke blood-vessel
b.d - brought down
bdly - badly
bef - before
bhd - behind
bk - back
blkd - baulked
bmpd - bumped
bnd - bend
btn - beaten
bttr - better
c - came
ch - chance
chal - challenged
chsd - chased
circ - circuit
cl - close
clr - clear
comf - comfortably
cpld - coupled
crse - course
ct - caught
dismntd - dismounted
disp - disputed
dist - distance
div - division
drvn - driven
dwlt - dwelt
edgd - edged
effrt - effort
ent - entering
ev ch - every chance
ex - extra
f - furlong
fin - finished
fnd - found
fnl - final
fr - from
gd - good
gng - going
grad - gradually
grnd - ground
hd - head
hdd - headed
hdwy - headway
hld - held
hmpd - hampered
imp - impression
ins - inside
j.b - jumped badly
j.w - jumped well
jnd - joined
jst - just
kpt - kept
l - length
ld - lead
ldr - leader
lft - left
m - mile
m.n.s - made no show
mde - made
mid div - mid division
n.d - never dangerous
n.g.t - not go through
n.m.r - not much room
nk - neck
no ex - no extra
nr - near
nrr - nearer
nrst fin - nearest finish
nt - not
nvr - never
one pce - one pace
out - from finish
outpcd - outpaced
p.u - pulled up
pce - pace
pl - place
plcd - placed
plld - pulled
press - pressure
prog - progress
prom - prominent
qckly - quickly
qckn - quicken
r - race
racd - raced
rch - reach
rcvr - recover
rdn - ridden
rdr - rider
reard - reared
ref - refused
rn - ran
rnd - round
r.o - ran on
rr - rear
rspnse - response
rt - right
s - start
slt - slight
sme - some
sn - soon
spd - speed
st - straight
stdd - steadied
stdy - steady
styd - stayed
swtchd - switched
swvd - swerved
t.o - tailed off
tch - touch
thrght - throughout
trckd - tracked
u.p - under pressure
w - with
w.r.s - whipped round start
wd - wide
whn - when
wknd - weakened
wl - well
wnr - winner
wnt - went
½-wy - halfway

RACEFORM PRIVATE HANDICAP RATINGS

Raceform Ratings for each horse are listed after the Starting Price and indicate the actual level of performance attained in that race. The figure in the back index represents the BEST public form that Raceform's Handicappers still believe the horse capable of reproducing.

To use the ratings constructively in determining those horses *best-in* in future events, the following procedure should be followed:

(i) In races where all runners are the same age and are set to carry the same weight, no calculations are necessary. The horse with the highest rating is *best-in.*

(ii) In races where all runners are the same age but are set to carry different weights, add one point to the Raceform Rating for every pound less than 12 st 7lbs to be carried; deduct one point for every pound more than 12 st 7lbs.

For example,

Horse	Age & Weight	Adjustment from 10st	RR base rating	Adjusted rating
Fouroutoffive	4-12-0	+7	88	95
Nodefence	4-11-10	+11	82	93
French Artillery	4-11-7	+14	75	89
Butterfingers	4-11-7	+14	77	91

Therefore Fouroutoffive is top-rated (best-in)

(iii) In races concerning horses of different ages the procedure in example (ii) should again be followed, but reference must also be made to the Official Scale of Weight-For-Age (Jumping).

For example,

2m Hurdle January 15th

Horse	Age & Weight	Adjusted from 12-7	RR base rating	Adjusted rating	W-F-A deduct	Final rating
Goodysun	6-11-3	+18	89	107	Nil	107
Edgar Street	5-11-0	+21	78	99	Nil	99
Minchery Farm	4-10-7	+28	82	110	-12	98
On The Move	4-10-7	+28	90	118	-12	106

Therefore Goodysun is top-rated (best-in)

(A 4-y-o is deemed 12lb less mature than a 5-y-o or older horse on 15th January over 2m. Therefore, the deduction of 12 points is necessary.)

The following symbols are used in conjunction with the ratings:

++ almost certain to prove better
d disappointing (has run well below best recently)
t tentative rating based on race-time
\+ likely to prove better
? form hard to evaluate- may prove unreliable

Weight adjusted ratings for every race are published daily in Raceform Private Handicap. For subscription terms please contact the Subscription Department on (01635) 578080.

SCALE OF WEIGHT-FOR-AGE (JUMPING)

The Stewards of the Jockey Club recommend the following revised Scale of weight for age should be used as a guide.

HURDLE RACES

ALLOWANCE, ASSESSED IN LBS WHICH 3 YEAR OLDS AND 4 YEAR OLDS WILL RECEIVE FROM 5 YEAR OLDS AND UPWARDS

		J	**F**	**M**	**A**	**M**	**J**	**J**	**A**	**S**	**O**	**N**	**D**
2M	3							20	20	18	17	16	14
	4	12	10	8	6	5	5	3	3	2	1	-	-
2½M	3							21	21	19	18	17	15
	4	13	11	9	7	6	6	3	3	2	1	-	-
3M	3							23	23	21	19	18	16
	4	14	12	10	8	7	7	4	4	3	2	1	-

STEEPLECHASES

ALLOWANCE, ASSESSED IN LBS WHICH 4 YEAR OLDS AND 5 YEAR OLDS WILL RECEIVE FROM 6 YEAR OLDS AND UPWARDS

		J	**F**	**M**	**A**	**M**	**J**	**J**	**A**	**S**	**O**	**N**	**D**
2M	4							15	15	14	13	12	11
	5	10	9	8	7	6	6	3	3	2	1	-	-
2½M	4							16	16	15	14	13	12
	5	11	10	9	8	7	7	4	4	3	2	1	-
3M	4							17	17	16	15	14	13
	5	12	11	10	9	8	8	5	5	4	3	2	1

The letters in **bold** along the top relate to the month of the race.
A 4-y.o running in a two-mile hurdle is considered 3lb less mature than a horse of 5-y.o or above. Were this 4-y.o to run in a steeplechase it would be considered 15lb less mature than any horse of 6-y.o and above.

PERTH (R-H) (Good to firm, Good patches becoming Good to firm)
Thursday June 6th
WEATHER: fine WIND: almost nil

1 JOLLY MILLER NOVICES' HURDLE (4-Y.O+) (Class D)
7-00 (7-00) **2m 4f 110y (10 hdls)** £2,788.00 (£844.00: £412.00: £196.00) GOING minus 0.32 sec per fur (GF)

Horse	Dist	Pos	SP	RR	SF
Muzrak (CAN) (96) (MDHammond) **5-11-1** RGarritty (lw: a.p: led appr 2 out: sn pushed clr)	—	1	Evens[1]	76	14
Birequest (80) (DMoffatt) **5-11-1** DJMoffatt (led tl hdd appr 2 out: sn btn)	18	2	20/1	62	—
Ballyallia Castle (IRE) (72) (RFFisher) **7-11-1b[1]** PNiven (hdwy & prom 5th: effrt appr 3 out: sn outpcd)	14	3	14/1	51	—
Excuse Me (IRE) (IRFerguson,Ireland) **7-11-1b[1]** PCarberry (lw: hdwy & prom ½-wy: outpcd fr 4 out)	16	4	33/1	39	—
Kitzberg (IRE) (WRock,Ireland) **5-10-10** APMcCoy (cl up tl wknd 4 out)	dist	5	9/1[3]	—	—
Gawn Inn (IRE) (WPatton,Ireland) **6-11-7** MrRJPatton (chsd ldrs to 5th: p.u bef next)		P	9/4[2]	—	—
Just A Guess (IRE) (JJO'Neill) **5-10-12b[1](3)** ARoche (nt j.w: t.o fr 6th: p.u bef 3 out)		P	50/1	—	—
			(SP 107.1%)		**7 Rn**

4m 55.0 (7.00) CSF £16.51 TOTE £1.80: £1.10 £5.10 (£12.20) OWNER The Gemini Partnership (MIDDLEHAM) BRED Windfields Farm
3576 **Muzrak (CAN)** had to work to win this but, once in front, soon had the opposition spreadeagled. (Evens)
Birequest tried new tactics here and ran better, but was well outpointed by the winner from the second last. (20/1)
3419 **Ballyallia Castle (IRE)** looked pretty slow here and is probably better on soft ground. (14/1)
Excuse Me (IRE), in blinkers for the first time, found nothing once pressure was applied four out. (33/1)
Gawn Inn (IRE) (9/4: op 6/4)

2 RIVERBOAT CASINO H'CAP CHASE (0-125) (5-Y.O+) (Class D)
7-30 (7-30) **3m (18 fncs)** £4,052.00 (£1,226.00: £598.00: £284.00) GOING minus 0.32 sec per fur (GF)

Horse	Dist	Pos	SP	RR	SF
Hillwalk (110) (RCurtis) **10-11-4** DMorris (bhd: hdwy 14th: chsng ldrs 3 out: styd on to ld fnl 100y)	—	1	11/2[3]	119	36
The Yank (97) (MDHammond) **10-10-2v(3)** MrCBonner (a.p: led 4 out: wknd flat: ct fnl 100y)	1¼	2	25/1	105	22
East Houston (96) (JJO'Neill) **7-10-4** APMcCoy (a in tch: hdwy 4 out: ch 2 out: no ex flat)	3	3	9/2[2]	102	19
Rocket Run (IRE) (107) (MissLucindaRussell) **8-11-1** AThornton (lw: led tl hdd 4 out: disp 2nd & struggling whn blnd 2 out)	11	4	9/4[1]	106	23
Bald Joker (92) (DMcBratney,Ireland) **11-10-0** PCarberry (chsd ldrs tl wknd appr 4 out)	24	5	14/1	75	—
Sword Beach (112) (MrsMReveley) **12-11-6** PNiven (bhd: effrt 12th: outpcd fr 14th)	20	6	14/1	82	—
Positive Action (92) (MABarnes) **10-10-0b[1]** ADobbin (prom tl wknd qckly 13th)	10	7	50/1	55	—
Cross Cannon (115) (JAHellens) **10-11-9** BStorey (lw: trckd ldrs: ev ch whn fell 11th)		F	9/1	—	—
Off The Bru (104) (MrsSCBradburne) **11-10-5(7)ow10** MrMBradburne (nt j.w: a bhd: t.o whn p.u bef 13th)		P	8/1	—	—
Jims Choice (94) (WPatton,Ireland) **9-10-2** RDavis (chsd ldrs: rdn fr 13th: p.u lame appr 4 out)		P	12/1	—	—
Ceilidh Boy (120) (MrsJDGoodfellow) **10-11-11(3)** GCahill (mstkes: sn bhd: t.o whn p.u bef 4 out)		P	14/1	—	—
			(SP 118.9%)		**11 Rn**

6m 0.4 (2.40) CSF £110.06 CT £615.67 TOTE £6.00: £1.80 £4.20 £1.80 (£57.80) Trio £181.00; £50.99 to 8/6/96 OWNER Mr M. L. Shone (LAMBOURN) BRED Martin Ryan
LONG HANDICAP Positive Action 9-12 Bald Joker 9-6
OFFICIAL EXPLANATION **Rocket Run (IRE): pulled up sore.**
3662* **Hillwalk** just stays and is honest, and that gained him the day after looking in trouble. (11/2)
The Yank, having his first run for over thirteen months, put in a tremendous effort but just ran out of petrol after the last. (25/1)
3672 **East Houston** had his chances and had the right man on board, but was still not doing enough when it mattered. (9/2)
3322 **Rocket Run (IRE)**, who only just gets this trip, was found out this time and was beaten when a blunder finished his hopes of a place two out. (9/4)
1766 **Sword Beach** (14/1: 10/1-16/1)
3560 **Cross Cannon** (9/1: 6/1-10/1)
3320 **Ceilidh Boy** was never jumping or going at any stage. (14/1: 10/1-16/1)

3 BRUCE WILSON SPORTS AND LEISURE H'CAP HURDLE (0-110) (5-Y.O+) (Class E)
8-00 (8-00) **2m 4f 110y (10 hdls)** £2,723.00 (£824.00: £402.00: £191.00) GOING minus 0.32 sec per fur (GF)

Horse	Dist	Pos	SP	RR	SF
Tabu Lady (IRE) (90) (WRock,Ireland) **5-10-12b** APMcCoy (mde all: clr fr ½-wy: kpt on u.p)	—	1	7/1[3]	82	15
Level Edge (86) (HAlexander) **5-10-3(5)** RMcGrath (lw: in tch: hit 6th: chsd wnr fr 3 out: hrd rdn & no imp)	8	2	11/8[1]	72	5
Master Ofthe House (90) (MDHammond) **10-10-12** RGarritty (hld up: effrt 3 out: rdn & no imp)	14	3	5/2[2]	65	—
Dalusman (IRE) (79) (JJBirkett) **8-10-1** LO'Hara (chsd wnr tl rdn & wknd fr 4 out)	10	4	12/1	46	—
Candid Lad (82) (FSStorey) **9-10-4 7x** BStorey (prom tl outpcd 4 out: bhd whn blnd 3 out: p.u bef next)		P	7/1[3]	—	—
Sylvan Celebration (78) (JSGoldie) **5-9-11(3)** GCahill (mstkes: a bhd: hmpd 3 out: p.u bef next)		P	25/1	—	—
			(SP 107.2%)		**6 Rn**

4m 54.1 (6.10) CSF £15.85 TOTE £5.70: £2.30 £1.60 (£3.90) OWNER Mr P. McWilliams (CULLYBACKEY) BRED Paul McWilliams
LONG HANDICAP Sylvan Celebration 9-1
12* **Tabu Lady (IRE)** won at this meeting last year and now wears blinkers. She certainly needed both them and all McCoy's skill. (7/1: 4/1-8/1)
3751 **Level Edge** is in good form and had her chances, but found the struggle too much from three out. (11/8)
3668 **Master Ofthe House** was quite happy when held up off the pace but, once asked a serious question three out, soon gave up. (5/2)
3079* **Dalusman (IRE)**, after chasing the winner, found nothing when put under pressure four out. (12/1)
3724* **Candid Lad** has two ways of running and was never in the right mood this time. (7/1: 5/1-8/1)

4 EARL GREY NOVICES' CHASE (5-Y.O+) (Class D)
8-30 (8-31) **2m (12 fncs)** £3,761.25 (£1,140.00: £557.50: £266.25) GOING minus 0.32 sec per fur (GF)

Horse	Dist	Pos	SP	RR	SF
Secretary of State (DWPArbuthnot) **10-11-2** APMcCoy (led fr 4th: clr 4 out: styd on wl)	—	1	9/2[2]	91	31
Movac (IRE) (82) (MissLucindaRussell) **7-11-9** AThornton (lw: in tch: hdwy 6th: chsd wnr fr 4 out: nvr able to chal)	11	2	8/11[1]	87	27
Boring (USA) (80) (WStorey) **7-10-11(5)** RMcGrath (hld up: effrt 7th: blnd 4 out: no imp after)	25	3	10/1	55	—
Reve de Valse (USA) (81) (RJohnson) **9-11-2** MrPJohnson (led to 4th: chsd ldrs tl wknd 4 out)	3½	4	12/1	52	—

Horse			SP	RR	SF
Mister Black (IRE) (PFGraffin,Ireland) **8-11-2** PCarberry (lw: mstkes: lost tch ½-wy: t.o)	dist	5	9/1 3	—	—
Excise Man (81) (FTWalton) **8-11-9** BStorey (lw: chsd ldrs: 5th & wl btn whn fell 3 out)		F	12/1	—	—
Le Denstan (70) (MrsDThomson) **9-11-2** RDavis (lw: unruly s: s.s: nt j.w: a t.o: p.u bef 8th)		P	16/1	—	—
Boethius (USA) (80) (MABarnes) **7-11-2** ADobbin (in tch to 6th: t.o whn p.u bef 4 out)		P	25/1	—	—
Pop In There (IRE) (JJBirkett) **8-11-2** LO'Hara (nt j.w: sn t.o: p.u bef 8th)		P	100/1	—	—

(SP 121.3%) **9 Rn**

3m 53.1 (2.10) CSF £8.29 TOTE £4.20: £1.30 £1.10 £2.80 (£3.30) Trio £12.40 OWNER Mr W. H. Ponsonby (COMPTON) BRED Greenville House Stud

3517* Secretary of State won this really well, but was inclined to hurdle his fences and, on a stiffer track, he might be in trouble. (9/2)

3717* Movac (IRE), over this shorter trip, was always finding things happening too quickly and, although keeping on well, could never get near the winner. (8/11)

3675 Boring (USA) has plenty of ability but has also got his own ideas and a blunder four out soon put him off. (10/1)

3681 Reve de Valse (USA) looked too slow to offer any sort of threat at the business end. (12/1: op 8/1)

3675* Excise Man had his limitations exposed here and was well out of it when falling three from home. (12/1)

3717 Le Denstan was in a most awkward mood and gave the field a big start and, never jumping at all, was wisely pulled up. (16/1)

5 SNUGGLES BREAK NOVICES' H'CAP HURDLE (0-100) (4-Y.O+) (Class E)

9-00 (9-01) **2m 110y (8 hdls)** £2,388.00 (£668.00: £324.00) GOING minus 0.32 sec per fur (GF)

Horse			SP	RR	SF
Bourdonner (75) (MDHammond) **4-10-2** PCarberry (lw: mde all: clr fr 5th: eased flat)	—	1	13/2 3	63+	16
Teejay'n'aitch (IRE) (77) (JSGoldie) **4-10-1**(3) GCahill (a.p: chsd wnr fr 3 out: nvr able to chal)	7	2	9/2 2	58	11
Charlistiona (68) (JPDodds) **5-9-11**(3) BFenton (a.p: effrt 5th & no imp)	11	3	16/1	39	—
Triennium (USA) (81) (RAllan) **7-10-6**(7) SMelrose (hld up: effrt appr 3 out: sn rdn & no imp)	8	4	9/4 1	44	2
Lac de Gras (IRE) (68) (RCurtis) **5-10-0** DMorris (unruly s: dwlt: mstke 2nd: sme hdwy fr 3 out: hit 2 out: n.d)	8	5	25/1	23	—
Mister Casual (72) (WGReed) **7-9-13**(5) RMcGrath (a in tch: rdn & one pce fr 5th)	1¾	6	12/1	25	—
Pats Cross (IRE) (92) (IRFerguson,Ireland) **7-11-10b1** APMcCoy (chsd ldrs: hit 2nd & reminders: wl outpcd fr 5th)	7	7	9/2 2	39	—
Coquet Gold (68) (FTWalton) **5-10-0** BStorey (nvr nr ldrs)	4	8	10/1	11	—
Daytime Dawn (IRE) (77) (DMoffatt) **5-10-9** DJMoffatt (lw: n.d)	14	9	50/1	6	—
Melody Dancer (75) (JackAndrews) **5-10-0**(7)ow7 RMurphy (chsd ldrs tl rdn & wknd appr 3 out)	1¾	10	66/1	2	—
Grinnell (70) (DMcCune) **6-10-2** RDavis (sn t.o)	dist	11	50/1	—	—
On The Move (76) (JRTurner) **5-10-8** WFry (lw: in tch to 5th: p.u bef 2 out)		P	20/1	—	—

(SP 117.2%) **12 Rn**

3m 48.3 (2.30) CSF £33.21 CT £412.64 TOTE £11.00: £2.60 £1.80 £6.90 (£22.80) Trio £173.00; £114.55 to 8/6/96 OWNER Mr Cornelius Lysaght (MIDDLEHAM) BRED The Overbury Stud

LONG HANDICAP Charlistiona 9-9 Melody Dancer 9-6 Coquet Gold 9-6 Lac de Gras (IRE) 9-11

WEIGHT FOR AGE 4yo-5lb

Bourdonner, given a most aggressive ride, was a bit novicey and slow at some hurdles but was kept up to his work in great style and was allowed to coast home after the last. (13/2: 9/2-7/1)

3577 Teejay'n'aitch (IRE) keeps running reasonably under both codes, but never quite comes up with the goods. (9/2: op 3/1)

1098 Charlistiona reached the frame here for the first time but lacked the pace to ever make any impression. (16/1)

3718 Triennium (USA) travelled quite well when held up but, once asked for an effort three out, he soon decided it was not for him. (9/4)

Lac de Gras (IRE), who showed signs of temperament, did not jump at all well and never got into it. (25/1)

6 GLASGOW WEST END CONDITIONAL H'CAP HURDLE (0-110) (4-Y.O+) (Class E)

9-30 (9-30) **3m 110y (12 hdls)** £2,786.25 (£840.00: £407.50: £191.25) GOING minus 0.32 sec per fur (GF)

Horse			SP	RR	SF
Tough Test (IRE) (93) (MrsJDGoodfellow) **6-11-8** BFenton (trckd ldrs: rdn to ld 3 out: clr whn hit next: eased flat)	—	1	3/1 2	74+	14
Nicholas Plant (92) (JSGoldie) **7-11-7** GCahill (disp ld tl led 8th: hdd 3 out: hrd rdn & one pce)	12	2	4/1 3	65	5
Scrabo View (IRE) (99) (PBeaumont) **8-11-8**(6) BGrattan (lw: hld up: effrt 4 out: sn hrd rdn & no imp)	8	3	10/1	67	7
Slaught Son (IRE) (91) (MartinTodhunter) **8-11-6** FLeahy (lw: hld up: effrt 4 out: sn rdn & btn)	dist	4	2/1 1	—	—
Classic Statement (81) (JAHellens) **10-10-7b**(3) STaylor (lw: disp ld to 8th: sn hrd rdn & wknd: p.u bef 2 out)		P	4/1 3	—	—

(SP 107.4%) **5 Rn**

5m 56.9 (10.90) CSF £13.25 TOTE £4.40: £1.80 £1.90 (£7.50) OWNER Mr J. D. Goodfellow (EARLSTON) BRED Liam Burke

3580 Tough Test (IRE) always looked to be going best but had to work to get on top from three out. He had it well sewn up after the last and was allowed to take things easily. (3/1)

3676* Nicholas Plant went too fast early on and had a real tussle for the lead with Classic Statement, but was then not surprisingly picked off by the winner. (4/1)

3462 Scrabo View (IRE), happy to sit off the strong early pace, was suddenly struggling four out and could never get into it. (10/1)

3670 Slaught Son (IRE) ran a stinker, coming off the bit a long way out and trailing in tailed off. (2/1)

1287 Classic Statement tried to gain the initiative but was always being taken on by Nicholas Plant and threw in the towel setting out on the final circuit. (4/1: op 10/1)

T/Plpt: £53.10 (228.78 Tckts). T/Qdpt: £16.60 (53.85 Tckts). AA

1-PERTH (R-H) (Good to firm)

Friday June 7th

water jump omitted

WEATHER: fine

7 WETTER BETTER PEOPLE NOVICES' HURDLE (4-Y.O+) (Class E)

2-30 (2-30) **2m 110y (8 hdls)** £2,332.00 (£652.00: £316.00) GOING minus 0.56 sec per fur (F)

Horse			SP	RR	SF
Tukano (CAN) (93) (JRJenkins) **5-10-12** APMcCoy (chsd ldr: lft clr after 3rd: kpt on u.p fr 2 out)	—	1	11/10 1	75	7
Forgotten Empress (AHarrison) **4-10-2** PCarberry (hld up: hdwy & prom 5th: ev ch appr last: nt run on)	2	2	33/1	68?	—

Form	Horse	Dist	Pos	SP	RR	SF
	Mullins (IRE) (DMoffatt) **5-10-12** DJMoffatt (a chsng ldrs: rdn & one pce fr 3 out)	16	3	6/1	58	—
	Saracen Prince (USA) (90) (HAlexander) **4-10-7v** PNiven (chsd ldrs: blnd 3 out: no imp after)	1¼	4	5/1[3]	56	—
	Mac's Taxi (PCHaslam) **4-10-7** MFoster (outpcd fr ½-wy)	dist	5	12/1	—	—
5[11]	**Grinnell (70)** (DMcCune) **6-10-12** RDavis (t.o fr 4th)	dist	6	100/1	—	—
	Drakewrath (IRE) (IRFerguson,Ireland) **6-10-9**(3) DParker (lw: chsd lrs tl wknd 3 out: p.u bef next)		P	9/2[2]	—	—
	Gorodenka Boy (MrsJJordan) **6-10-12** DMorris (swtg: sn t.o: p.u bef 3 out)		P	100/1	—	—
	Balmaha (MrsPGrainger) **5-10-7** MrAPhillips (prom to ½-wy: t.o whn p.u bef 3 out)		P	9/1	—	—
	Patter Merchant (MrsDThomson) **7-10-12** BStorey (led tl rn out paddock bnd after 3rd)		R	50/1	—	—

(SP 121.3%) **10 Rn**

3m 48.5 (2.50) CSF £33.64 TOTE £1.90: £1.20 £5.70 £2.10 (£26.90) Trio £66.80 OWNER Mrs T. McCoubrey (ROYSTON) BRED Windfields Farm

WEIGHT FOR AGE 4yo-5lb

OFFICIAL EXPLANATION **Patter Merchant: the trainer reported that the gelding would not run again from her yard.**

Tukano (CAN) certainly has his own ideas about the game, but his jockey made it up for him this time, and his only serious rival looked none too keen. (11/10)

Forgotten Empress put in a decent first run over hurdles here but, when the pressure was on going to the last, she did not seem to relish the struggle. (33/1)

Mullins (IRE) had his chances, but is basically not very good. (6/1: op 4/1)

Saracen Prince (USA) looked a danger until a very clumsy jump stopped him three out. (5/1: 7/2-6/1)

Drakewrath (IRE) (9/2: 3/1-5/1)

8 WATER OPTIONS FOR GROWTH NOVICES' CHASE (5-Y.O+) (Class E)

3-00 (3-01) **3m (16 fncs)** £3,178.00 (£964.00: £472.00: £226.00) GOING minus 0.56 sec per fur (F)

Form	Horse	Dist	Pos	SP	RR	SF
	Temple Garth (88) (PBeaumont) **7-12-1** RSupple (lw: led tl after 2nd: chsd ldr: led 4 out: clr whn blnd last)	—	1	6/4[1]	118	27
	Cabbery Rose (IRE) (PFGraffin,Ireland) **8-10-10** PCarberry (chsd ldrs: chal 4 out: hrd rdn & one pce fr next)	10	2	11/4[3]	92	1
	White Diamond (84) (MissLucindaRussell) **8-11-1b[1]** MFoster (led after 2nd & sn clr: j.lft 12th: j.lft & hdd 4 out: sn btn)	14	3	9/4[2]	88	—
5[6]	**Mister Casual (72)** (WGReed) **7-10-10**(5) RMcGrath (mstke 8th: lost tch 10th)	16	4	20/1	77	—
	Beccy Brown (FTWalton) **8-10-7**(3) DParker (prom: hit 9th: sn lost tch)	15	5	50/1	62	—
	Establish (IRE) (86) (JPDodds) **8-10-10** AThornton (swtg: mstkes: sn t.o: p.u bef 7th)		P	20/1	—	—

(SP 108.9%) **6 Rn**

6m 1.4 (3.40) CSF £5.62 TOTE £2.40: £1.10 £2.20 (£4.40) OWNER Mrs Jos Wilson (BRANDSBY) BRED Mrs J. Wilson

Temple Garth is making up into a useful chaser, but he did give supporters a heart-stopping moment when belting the last as he did on his previous win here. (6/4)

Cabbery Rose (IRE) never looked to be going all that well, but was given some fine assistance, although she had to admit she had met one too good in the home straight. (11/4)

White Diamond, in blinkers for the first time, looked as unenthusiastic as ever. (9/4)

Mister Casual has gone backwards of late. (20/1)

9 IRRIGATION BY DESIGN H'CAP CHASE (0-115) (5-Y.O+) (Class E)

3-30 (3-31) **2m 4f 110y (14 fncs)** £3,590.50 (£1,084.00: £527.00: £248.50) GOING minus 0.56 sec per fur (F)

Form	Horse	Dist	Pos	SP	RR	SF
	Unor (FR) (101) (PMonteith) **10-11-4** ADobbin (a.p: led 4 out: drew clr fr next: eased considerably flat)	—	1	5/2[1]	108+	29
	Bitacrack (83) (JJBirkett) **9-10-0** LO'Hara (a.p: outpcd 10th: styd on fr 3 out: no ch w wnr)	1¾	2	10/1	89	10
	Blazing Dawn (83) (JSHubbuck) **9-10-0** [6x] BStorey (led tl hdd 4 out: outpcd fr next)	1¼	3	6/1	88	9
2[5]	**Bald Joker (84)** (DMcBratney,Ireland) **11-9-12**(3) BFenton (in tch: effrt 9th: outpcd fr next)	dist	4	25/1	—	—
	Charming Gale (92) (MrsSCBradburne) **9-10-9** PCarberry (prom tl outpcd fr 9th)	12	5	10/1	—	—
	Old Money (83) (SEKettlewell) **10-10-0** [6x] APMcCoy (lw: wl bhd fr 10th)	17	6	5/1[3]	—	—
	Wise Advice (IRE) (104) (MDHammond) **6-11-7b[1]** RGarritty (lw: cl up to 7th: sn rdn & wknd: hit 9th)	4	7	7/1	—	—
	Willchris (107) (DMcBratney,Ireland) **9-11-10** TPRudd (bolted gng to s: t.o fr 5th: p.u bef 8th)		P	9/2[2]	—	—
	Funny Old Game (83) (DMcCune) **9-10-0** RDavis (sn wl t.o: p.u bef 8th)		P	20/1	—	—

(SP 117.0%) **9 Rn**

4m 58.1 (-0.90) CSF £25.47 CT £125.63 TOTE £3.20: £1.50 £1.80 £2.40 (£47.80) Trio £47.00 OWNER Miss H. B. Hamilton (ROSEWELL) BRED Roger Chaignon

LONG HANDICAP Old Money 9-4 Bitacrack 9-13 Funny Old Game 9-9

Unor (FR) needs further than this, but the strong pace set the race up for him and, in the end, he won pulling up. He is certainly in top form just now. (5/2)

Bitacrack was tapped for toe six out and then struggled on in the closing stages, but without having a chance with the winner. (10/1)

Blazing Dawn again tried front-running tactics, but he was continually being taken on and, in the end, this trip probably found him out. (6/1)

Charming Gale needs things to go just right and found this too competitive. (10/1: op 6/1)

Wise Advice (IRE), in blinkers for the first time, could never get his own way, and threw in the towel a long way from home. (7/1: 5/1-8/1)

10 SPRINKLED EXCELLENCE NOVICES' HURDLE (4-Y.O+) (Class E)

4-00 (4-00) **3m 110y (12 hdls)** £2,332.00 (£652.00: £316.00) GOING minus 0.56 sec per fur (F)

Form	Horse	Dist	Pos	SP	RR	SF
	Blooming Spring (IRE) (69) (MrsDThomson) **7-10-9** LO'Hara (chsd ldrs: reminders 6th: led after 4 out: rdn clr: eased flat)	—	1	7/2[2]	64?	—
	Micksdilemma (MrsPGrainger) **9-11-0** MrAPhillips (prom: led 7th: blnd 4 out: sn hdd & one pce)	13	2	4/1[3]	61	—
	Vilprano (84) (DMoffatt) **5-11-7** DJMoffatt (a.p: ev ch 4 out: wl outpcd fr next)	16	3	4/7[1]	57	—
1[P]	**Just A Guess (IRE)** (JJO'Neill) **5-11-0b** APMcCoy (mstkes: led to 7th: sn t.o)	dist	4	33/1	—	—
	Sally Smith (WGReed) **7-10-4**(5) RMcGrath (mstkes: t.o whn p.u after 7th)		P	33/1	—	—

(SP 111.7%) **5 Rn**

5m 56.0 (10.00) CSF £15.90 TOTE £4.30: £1.80 £2.30 (£7.60) OWNER Capt Ben Coutts (MILNATHORT)

Blooming Spring (IRE) at last found a race bad enough, but she will have to go a long way to find such a bad event again. (7/2)

Micksdilemma, despite struggling, was there to be beaten until a blunder four out stopped him. (4/1)

Vilprano must have been a very lucky winner last time, as this was an extremely poor event in which he was beaten fully three out. (4/7)

Just A Guess (IRE) does not want to know about the game. (33/1)

11 GIVING NATURE A HAND H'CAP CHASE (0-115) (5-Y.O+) (Class E)

4-30 (4-30) **2m (11 fncs)** £3,403.75 (£1,030.00: £502.50: £238.75) GOING minus 0.56 sec per fur (F)

Horse		Pos	SP	RR	SF
Grouse-N-Heather (89) (PMonteith) **7-10-7** ADobbin (lw: trckd ldrs: led appr 4 out: r.o u.p fr 2 out)	—	1	2/1 2	95	2
Gone by (IRE) (82) (JRJenkins) **8-10-0** APMcCoy (lw: hld up: hit 3rd & 6th: hdwy u.p 3 out: ev ch flat: nt qckn)	¾	2	5/4 1	87	—
Lochnagrain (IRE) (110) (MrsMReveley) **8-12-0** PNiven (led to 4th: outpcd ½-wy: kpt on u.p fr 3 out: no imp)	4	3	5/2 3	111	18
Cardenden (IRE) (82) (JBarclay) **8-10-0** BStorey (led 4th tl appr 4 out: outpcd fr next)	14	4	33/1	69	—
			(SP 109.3%)		**4 Rn**

3m 54.0 (3.00) CSF £4.72 TOTE £2.40 (£2.70) OWNER Mr D. J. Fairbairn (ROSEWELL) BRED R. A. Cameron
LONG HANDICAP Gone by (IRE) 9-12 Cardenden (IRE) 9-10
STEWARDS' ENQUIRY McCoy susp. 19, 20 & 22/6/96 (excessive use of whip).
Grouse-N-Heather is game and that was all that was needed to win this. (2/1)
Gone by (IRE) has ability but does have his own ideas and, but for some brilliant assistance, would never have been so close. (5/4)
Lochnagrain (IRE) always found this trip a bit sharp, and would not have a real cut at his fences but, to his credit, he was keeping on towards the finish. (5/2: op 6/4)
Cardenden (IRE) ran his best race for some time. (33/1)

12 DROPS EQUAL GOOD CROPS H'CAP HURDLE (0-115) (4-Y.O+) (Class E)

5-00 (5-01) **2m 110y (8 hdls)** £2,762.00 (£836.00: £408.00: £194.00) GOING minus 0.56 sec per fur (F)

Horse		Pos	SP	RR	SF
Keep Battling (88) (JSGoldie) **6-10-11**(3) GCahill (hld up: stdy hdwy 3 out: led flat: rdn & qcknd)	—	1	6/1 3	74	31
Sarmatian (USA) (91) (MDHammond) **5-11-3** RGarritty (lw: hld up: smooth hdwy 3 out: led last: sn hdd & nt qckn)	3½	2	11/8 1	74	31
3* **Tabu Lady (IRE) (96)** (WRock,Ireland) **5-11-8b** 6x APMcCoy (led & sn clr: rdn 3 out: hdd last: no ex)	hd	3	6/1 3	79	30
Flintlock (IRE) (87) (HAlexander) **6-10-8**(5) RMcGrath (chsd ldrs: ev ch 2 out: 4th & btn whn hit last)	12	4	9/2 2	58	15
Well Appointed (IRE) (98) (BMactaggart) **7-11-10** BStorey (in tch tl outpcd fr 5th)	dist	5	9/2 2	—	—
Liability Order (85) (JJBirkett) **7-10-11b** MMoloney (chsd ldrs to 4th: sn wknd)	8	6	100/1	—	—
			(SP 108.0%)		**6 Rn**

3m 43.4 (-2.60) CSF £13.74 TOTE £5.90: £1.80 £1.30 (£2.90) OWNER Mr J. S. Goldie (GLASGOW) BRED Mrs E. Campbell
Keep Battling was again given a superb ride and settled it after the last, despite running with his ears absolutely flat. (6/1)
Sarmatian (USA) looked to have this when making stealthy progress to lead going to the last but, soon asked for an effort, his response was extremely disappointing (11/8)
3* Tabu Lady (IRE) tried the same tactics as the previous evening, but was well outpointed from the last. To her credit though, she did battle on. (6/1)
Flintlock (IRE), who has looked at his best when allowed to go out in front, had to sit in behind this time and, after having his chance two out, he was soon beaten. (9/2)

T/Plpt: £61.10 (114.53 Tckts). T/Qdpt: £24.10 (15.16 Tckts). AA

SOUTHWELL (L-H) (Good to firm)

Saturday June 8th

WEATHER: fine WIND: almost nil

13 SUMMER JUMPING NOVICES' CHASE (5-Y.O+) (Class D)

6-50 (6-50) **2m 4f 110y (16 fncs)** £4,253.25 (£1,272.00: £609.50: £278.25) GOING: 0.25 sec per fur (GS)

Horse		Pos	SP	RR	SF
Tuffnut George (97) (MrsPGrainger) **9-11-7** MrAPhillips (lw: wnt prom 7th: led 10th: clr 4 out: all out)	—	1	11/4 2	95	21
Call Me Albi (IRE) (MrsLRichards) **5-10-7** MRichards (a.p: rdn & wnt 2nd after 4 out: blnd 2 out: styd on flat)	2½	2	11/1	86	5
Top Spin (JRJenkins) **7-11-0** JOsborne (j.slowly: sn bhd: reminders 10th: styd on fr 3 out: nt rch ldrs)	6	3	6/4 1	81	7
Hizal (60) (HJManners) **7-11-0** MrACharles-Jones (bhd: blnd 7th: hdwy 4 out: styd on fr 2 out)	½	4	50/1	81	7
Mariners Cove (81) (CDBroad) **8-11-0** RFarrant (lw: hdwy to chse ldrs 9th: wknd 12th)	14	5	7/1 3	70	—
Golden Savannah (75) (MESowersby) **6-11-0b** AThornton (led to 10th: wknd next)	6	6	10/1	65	—
Bit of A Dream (IRE) (MrsSJSmith) **6-11-0** RichardGuest (mstke 1st: wnt prom 6th: rdn 4 out: poor 3rd whn blnd next: wknd)	7	7	25/1	60	—
Dormston Boyo (74) (TWall) **6-10-11**(3) RMassey (prom tl reminders & lost pl 7th: t.o 10th)	13	8	33/1	50	—
Without a Flag (USA) (71) (JWhite) **6-11-0** WMcFarland (mstkes: t.o fr 10th)	22	9	14/1	33	—
Prince Rockaway (IRE) (NMLampard) **8-10-11**(3) GuyLewis (chsd ldrs tl wknd 10th: t.o whn p.u bef 3 out)		P	50/1	—	—
Rushhome (60) (PRRodford) **9-10-9** SBurrough (sme hdwy 10th: sn wknd: bhd whn ref 3 out)		R	50/1	—	—
			(SP 115.9%)		**11 Rn**

5m 23.0 (19.00) CSF £29.89 TOTE £3.50: £1.30 £3.10 £1.70 (£11.00) Trio £8.10 OWNER Mr P. T. Cartridge (KIDDERMINSTER) BRED F. C. Harvey
WEIGHT FOR AGE 5yo-7lb
Tuffnut George, a winner of five of his ten outings in point-to-points, made it two out of fourteen under Rules but, at the line, there was nothing at all left in the tank. (11/4)
Call Me Albi (IRE) showed the benefit of his latest outing twelve days earlier, his first for six months and, had he not ploughed through the second last, he might have given the winner plenty to do. (11/1)
Top Spin, a winner six times over hurdles, would not have a cut at his fences on this chasing bow, and it was only his rider's perseverance over the final three fences that enabled him to get so close. (6/4)
Hizal, pulled up on his last three outings in hunter chases, was staying on when it was all over. (50/1)
Mariners Cove (7/1: op 9/2)

14 J.T.F. WHOLESALE DISTRIBUTION H'CAP CHASE (0-100) (5-Y.O+) (Class F)

7-15 (7-17) **3m 110y (19 fncs)** £3,980.00 (£1,190.00: £570.00: £260.00) GOING: 0.25 sec per fur (GS)

Horse		Pos	SP	RR	SF
Royal Vacation (95) (GMMoore) **7-11-10** NBentley (lw: gd hdwy 12th: rdn to ld 3 out: styd on wl flat)	—	1	6/1 3	106	38

Runner	Dist	Pl	SP	RR	SF
Sea Breaker (IRE) (92) (DECantillon) **8-11-7** RichardGuest (lw: hld up: stdy hdwy 4 out: chal last: sn rdn & nt run on)	2	**2**	7/2[1]	102	34
Albert Blake (92) (TRKinsey) **9-11-7** APMcCoy (led: reminders 12th: hdd 3 out: hung lft & one pce flat)	3	**3**	13/2	100	32
Miss Enrico (89) (MissLucindaRussell) **10-11-4** AThornton (lw: hld up: effrt 13th: wknd 4 out)	16	**4**	14/1	86	18
Brindley House (82) (JWhite) **9-10-11** WMcFarland (mstkes: hdwy 8th: sn chsng ldrs: 4th whn blnd 14th: wknd after 4 out)	3	**5**	14/1	77	9
Tenbit (IRE) (73) (NATwiston-Davies) **6-10-2** CLlewellyn (chsd ldr: mstke 6th: wknd 15th)	1	**6**	11/2[2]	68	—
Two Step Rhythm (82) (JCMcConnochie) **12-10-11** MSharratt (mstkes: hdwy & in tch 10th: rdn & lost pl 12th: t.o 4 out)	dist	**7**	33/1	—	—
Truss (85) (JohnUpson) **9-11-0** RSupple (in tch: 5th whn fell 13th)		**F**	7/1	—	—
Hawaiian Goddess (USA) (77) (SWCampion) **9-10-6** DLeahy (sn bhd: t.o 12th: p.u bef 3 out)		**P**	33/1	—	—
Royal Mile (75) (FSJackson) **11-10-4**[ow1] MrNKent (hit 11th: sn t.o: p.u bef 14th)		**P**	33/1	—	—
Lady Blakeney (86) (BSRothwell) **10-11-1** JOsborne (chsd ldrs tl p.u lame after 12th)		**P**	7/2[1]	—	—
			(SP 122.1%)		**11 Rn**

6m 24.7 (17.70) CSF £26.82 CT £129.27 TOTE £8.80: £2.60 £1.60 £2.00 (£46.20) Trio £13.00 OWNER Mr G. P. Edwards (MIDDLEHAM) BRED Small Breeders' Group

Royal Vacation, who loves fast ground, bounced right back to his very best. (6/1)

Sea Breaker (IRE), from a 7lb higher mark, came there to challenge at the last looking all over a winner but, when asked to go on and win his race, he stuck his head in the air, swished his tail, and would not go past. (7/2)

Albert Blake, who is by no means a consistent individual, had been raised 6lb after finishing runner-up at Cartmel. Racing with his tongue tied down, he gave problems by persisting in hanging left. (13/2)

Miss Enrico, out of sorts in point-to-points, gave no immediate signs of a return to her best. (14/1)

15 MAUN MOTORS H'CAP CHASE (0-115) (5-Y.O+) (Class E)

7-45 (7-47) **2m (13 fncs)** £4,230.00 (£1,260.00: £600.00: £270.00) GOING: 0.25 sec per fur (GS)

Runner	Dist	Pl	SP	RR	SF
Saskia's Hero (104) (JFBottomley) **9-11-10** DerekByrne (lw: hld up: smooth hdwy 5th: led 8th: clr last: drvn out)	—	**1**	5/2[1]	116	47
Gesnera (88) (JGMO'Shea) **8-10-1**(7) MichaelBrennan (bit bkwd: chsd ldrs: kpt on u.p fr 3 out: no imp)	3	**2**	7/1	97	28
Dr Rocket (86) (RDickin) **11-10-3b**(3) JCulloty (trckd ldrs: rdn 4 out: wknd between last two)	7	**3**	5/1[3]	88	19
Emerald Moon (82) (PRRodford) **9-10-2**[ow2] SBurrough (wnt prom 5th: outpcd 4 out: btn whn hit next)	7	**4**	25/1	77	6
Ramstar (99) (PJHobbs) **8-11-5** APMcCoy (led to 8th: wknd 4 out: eased)	10	**5**	5/2[1]	84	15
Full O'Praise (NZ) (108) (PCalver) **9-12-0** GaryLyons (plld hrd: trckd ldrs: reminders 6th: sn lost pl: t.o 4 out)	14	**6**	4/1[2]	79	10
Master Salesman (80) (MrsVCWard) **13-9-11**(3) DParker (blnd 5th: sn bhd: t.o 7th: p.u bef 3 out)		**P**	16/1	—	—
			(SP 116.0%)		**7 Rn**

4m 2.4 (9.40) CSF £18.81 TOTE £3.30: £1.50 £3.00 (£15.80) OWNER Qualitair Holdings Ltd (MALTON) BRED Qualitair Stud Ltd

LONG HANDICAP Emerald Moon 9-2 Master Salesman 9-11

Saskia's Hero, raised 6lb for his Huntingdon win, made it four wins from his last five starts. Pulled up on his other outing, he was found to be suffering from a viral infection. After travelling best from a long way out, he had only to be kept up to his work. (5/2)

Gesnera, having her first outing since November, kept on grimly in pursuit, but her cause was a hopeless one. (7/1)

Dr Rocket, who had the blinkers back on, was very leg weary between the last two. (5/1)

Emerald Moon ran as well as could be expected considering he was 12lb wrong at the weights. (25/1)

Ramstar seems to have lost his way, and his rider gave up a long way out. (5/2)

Full O'Praise (NZ) seemed to resent not being able to dominate, and spat the dummy out with a circuit to go. (4/1)

16 NOTTINGHAM EVENING POST H'CAP HURDLE (0-125) (4-Y.O+) (Class D)

8-15 (8-15) **2m 4f 110y (11 hdls)** £2,976.50 (£824.00: £393.50) GOING: 0.25 sec per fur (GS)

Runner	Dist	Pl	SP	RR	SF
Eid (USA) (118) (MrsSJSmith) **7-12-0** RichardGuest (lw: hld up: hdwy 5th: led between last two: hrd rdn flat: jst hld on)	—	**1**	9/2[3]	96	29
Red Valerian (111) (JGMO'Shea) **5-11-0v**(7) MichaelBrennan (trckd ldrs: mstke 5th: hit 3 out & 2 out: ev ch between last two: hrd rdn & rallied towards fin)	hd	**2**	7/2[2]	89	22
Blue Raven (90) (PJHobbs) **5-10-0** APMcCoy (j.rt & mstke 1st: chsd ldrs: rdn to ld appr 2 out: blnd: hdd between last 2: sn wknd)	5	**3**	9/2[3]	64	—
Dibloom (90) (JNeville) **8-10-0** RJohnson (led tl appr 2 out: sn wknd: virtually p.u towards fin)	14	**4**	16/1	53	—
Topformer (90) (FWatson) **9-10-0** RSupple (j.rt: sn bhd: lost tch 7th)	12	**5**	25/1	44	—
Circus Colours (98) (JRJenkins) **6-10-8** JOsborne (sn bhd: reminders 6th: t.o 3 out)	dist	**6**	6/1	—	—
Mr Geneaology (USA) (96) (TPMcGovern) **6-10-6** AThornton (sn rdn along: mstke & lost pl 6th: sn t.o)	dist	**7**	7/1	—	—
All On (110) (JHetherton) **5-11-6** RMarley (mstke, bmpd & uns rdr 1st)		**U**	100/30[1]	—	—
			(SP 118.2%)		**8 Rn**

5m 3.8 (17.80) CSF £20.16 CT £68.96 TOTE £5.00: £1.90 £1.20 £1.40 (£13.80) OWNER Mr N. Wilby (BINGLEY) BRED Ralph C. Wilson, Jr.

LONG HANDICAP Topformer 9-5 Dibloom 9-9

Eid (USA), a fast-ground specialist, came there travelling strongly but, in the end, scraped home by the skin of his teeth. His rider dismounted after the post, but hopefully he is none the worse. (9/2)

Red Valerian, fitted with a visor for the first time, would have won if he had jumped the last three flights better. Slowly away from the last, he just failed to get back up. (7/2)

Blue Raven put a poor effort a week earlier behind him. Had he jumped better, he would have finished on the heels of the first two. (9/2)

Circus Colours (6/1: op 4/1)

All On, who has shot up in the weights, collided with Blue Raven at the first and gave her rider little chance. (100/30)

17 TOP OF THE GROUND (S) H'CAP HURDLE (0-90) (4,5,6 & 7-Y.O) (Class G)

8-45 (8-47) **2m (9 hdls)** £2,027.00 (£562.00: £269.00) GOING: 0.25 sec per fur (GS)

Runner	Dist	Pl	SP	RR	SF
Nocatchim (85) (KAMorgan) **7-11-7**(3) RMassey (led to 3 out: led 2 out: lft clr last)	—	**1**	11/2[2]	79	21
Parish Walk (IRE) (85) (KJDrewry) **5-11-10** SWynne (prom: outpcd 6th: rallied 2 out: 3rd & one pce whn blnd last)	6	**2**	100/30[1]	73	15
Against The Clock (70) (JWMullins) **4-10-4** RGreene (bhd: hdwy 5th: styd on one pce fr 3 out)	3	**3**	11/1	55	—
High Flown (USA) (79) (RonaldThompson) **4-10-13** APMcCoy (chsd ldrs: rdn 6th: wknd 3 out)	11	**4**	7/1	53	—

Classic Image (IRE) (72) (HJManners) **6-10-11** MrACharles-Jones (chsd ldrs: rdn 3 out: sn wknd)	2½	**5**	16/1	44	—
Speaker's House (USA) (89) (MissLucindaRussell) **7-12-0** AThornton (in tch to 6th: sn wknd)	2	**6**	6/1[3]	59	1
Legal Drama (USA) (71) (JohnBerry) **4-9-12**(7)ow1 CRae (hdwy 5th: rdn & wknd next)	hd	**7**	20/1	40	—
Woodlands Energy (61) (PAPritchard) **5-10-0** RDavis (trckd ldrs: effrt 6th: wknd next)	11	**8**	8/1	19	—
Night Boat (76) (WClay) **5-10-12v1**(3) GuyLewis (lw: bhd fr 3 out)	s.h	**9**	8/1	34	—
Siesta Time (USA) (64) (RJO'Sullivan) **6-10-3b1**ow3 DO'Sullivan (hld up & plld hrd: sme hdwy whn mstke 5th: sn wknd)	6	**10**	25/1	16	—
Sakbah (USA) (65) (JAPickering) **7-10-1**(3) TDascombe (bhd: reminders 3rd: sme hdwy 5th: outpcd whn fell 3 out)		**F**	14/1	—	—
Set-Em-Alight (65) (BSmart) **6-10-4** ILawrence (plld hrd: trckd ldrs: led 3 out: hrd rdn & hdd next: 5l 2nd & btn whn fell last)		**F**	12/1	—	—
			(SP 124.7%)	**12 Rn**	

3m 56.8 (14.80) CSF £24.09 CT £186.28 TOTE £7.30: £2.10 £1.60 £3.60 (£12.60) Trio £37.30 OWNER Mr R. E. Gray (MELTON MOWBRAY) BRED Charlton Down Stud
LONG HANDICAP Siesta Time (USA) 9-13 Woodlands Energy 9-8
WEIGHT FOR AGE 4yo-5lb
No bid

Nocatchim, with the blinkers left off, was firmly in command when left clear at the last. (11/2)
Parish Walk (IRE), who looked very fit, was third and well held when he ploughed through the last. (100/30)
Against The Clock struggled to go the pace, but stayed on over the last three. He needs a stiffer test. (11/1: op 7/1)
Woodlands Energy (8/1: op 16/1)
Set-Em-Alight, a really keen sort, was well held when he fell at the final obstacle. (12/1)

18 FAST GROUND MAIDEN HURDLE (4-Y.O+) (Class E)

9-15 (9-15) **2m (9 hdls)** £2,511.00 (£696.00: £333.00) GOING: 0.25 sec per fur (GS)

			SP	RR	SF
Zahid (USA) (78) (KRBurke) **5-11-5** RJohnson (hld up: stdy hdwy 5th: chal on bit last: hrd rdn to ld nr fin)	—	**1**	9/2[3]	73	18
Ordog Mor (IRE) (92) (MGMeagher) **7-11-5** APMcCoy (lw: j.w: led 3rd: rdn appr 2 out: jst ct)	½	**2**	11/4[1]	73	18
Scamallach (IRE) (89) (JRJenkins) **6-11-0b** JOsborne (trckd ldrs: rdn 3 out: one pce fr next)	4	**3**	3/1[2]	64	9
Just Bruce (88) (MrsEHHeath) **7-11-5** AThornton (led to 3rd: drvn along 5th: wknd 2 out)	10	**4**	9/2[3]	59	4
Pegasus Bay (86) (WWHaigh) **5-11-5** RGarritty (trckd ldrs: blnd 6th: wknd next)	10	**5**	8/1	49	—
Deep Fair (83) (MrsSJSmith) **9-11-5** RichardGuest (in tch: drvn along 4th: lost pl 6th)	8	**6**	14/1	41	—
Papa's Boy (IRE) (96) (HowardJohnson) **5-11-5** MFoster (chsd ldrs: effrt 6th: outpcd fr next)	2	**7**	11/2	39	—
Never Say so (MrsSLamyman) **4-10-9** MrNKent (prom tl lost pl 5th: t.o whn p.u bef 2 out)		**P**	50/1	—	—
			(SP 123.2%)	**8 Rn**	

3m 56.5 (14.50) CSF £17.84 TOTE £3.00: £1.10 £1.60 £1.90 (£6.50) OWNER Mr Keith Booth (WANTAGE) BRED Dr. Murray West, Nicholas Lotz & Overbrook Farm
WEIGHT FOR AGE 4yo-5lb

Zahid (USA) appreciated the sharp track and fast ground but, after challenging on the bit at the final flight, it took all his rider's brilliance to get him up near the line. (9/2)
Ordog Mor (IRE) jumped these obstacles particularly well. Despite every assistance from the champion, he was shaded in the final strides and is probably better suited by two and a half miles. (11/4)
Scamallach (IRE) came under pressure at the third last and found the first two simply too good. (3/1)
Just Bruce, an excitable type, was on his toes beforehand and is not running up to his best at present. (9/2: 3/1-5/1)

T/Plpt: £32.90 (234.99 Tckts). T/Qdpt: £12.90 (32.44 Tckts). WG

WORCESTER (L-H) (Good)

Saturday June 8th

WEATHER: fine

19 BRANSFORD NOVICES' H'CAP HURDLE (0-95) (5-Y.O+) (Class F)

3-00 (3-00) **3m (12 hdls)** £2,143.00 (£598.00: £289.00) GOING: 0.03 sec per fur (G)

			SP	RR	SF
Valisky (75) (RLee) **6-11-0** CLlewellyn (stdy hdwy 4 out: chal last: led flat: drvn out)	—	**1**	12/1	58	23
High Post (75) (GAHam) **7-10-11**(3) RMassey (hdwy 6th: led appr 3 out tl flat: r.o)	1¼	**2**	10/1	57	22
Wynberg (89) (CaptTAForster) **5-11-9**(5) LAspell (hdwy 6th: led 8th tl appr 3 out: r.o one pce)	3½	**3**	8/1	69	34
Palace Parade (USA) (65) (GAHam) **6-10-4** SBurrough (hdwy 6th: wknd appr 2 out)	7	**4**	33/1	40	5
Limosa (81) (MrsLRichards) **5-11-6** MRichards (hdwy 6th: ev ch appr 3 out: wknd 2 out)	6	**5**	7/1[3]	52	17
Mr Poppleton (71) (RBrotherton) **7-10-7b1**(3) GuyLewis (prom tl wknd appr 3 out)	17	**6**	14/1	31	—
Spanish Blaze (IRE) (68) (MrsMerritaJones) **8-10-7** DerekByrne (hdwy 6th: rdn & wknd appr 3 out)	3	**7**	2/1[1]	26	—
Little Court (61) (EGBevan) **5-10-0** RJohnson (wl bhd fr 4 out)	3½	**8**	33/1	17	—
Akiymann (USA) (87) (MCPipe) **6-11-12** DBridgwater (t.o fr 5th: p.u bef 3 out)		**P**	6/1[2]	—	—
Red Eikon (72) (GHolmes) **5-10-11b** APMcCoy (chsd ldr: led 7th to 8th: wknd qckly: p.u bef 3 out)		**P**	9/1	—	—
Stonecrop (79) (JWhite) **5-11-4** JRKavanagh (t.o fr 5th: p.u bef 4 out)		**P**	20/1	—	—
Up the Tempo (IRE) (72) (PaddyFarrell) **7-10-11** RGreene (t.o fr 7th: p.u bef 4 out: b.b.v)		**P**	12/1	—	—
Van Der Grass (63) (PCalver) **7-10-2**ow2 GaryLyons (bhd fr 8th: t.o whn p.u bef 3 out)		**P**	33/1	—	—
Winter Rose (75) (MSheppard) **5-11-0** BPowell (t.o fr 5th: p.u bef 4 out)		**P**	10/1	—	—
Hidden Flower (61) (HSHowe) **7-9-11v1**(3) BFenton (led tl wknd 7th: t.o whn p.u bef 3 out)		**P**	50/1	—	—
			(SP 137.0%)	**15 Rn**	

5m 49.4 (13.40) CSF £129.22 CT £964.90 TOTE £9.30: £2.90 £3.40 £3.90 (£36.70) Trio £72.70; £64.56 to Epsom Downs 9/6/96 OWNER Risk Another Partnership (PRESTEIGNE)
LONG HANDICAP Van Der Grass 9-13 Little Court 9-13 Hidden Flower 9-4
OFFICIAL EXPLANATION **Spanish Blaze (IRE): had suffered an overreach and lost a shoe during the race, and was found to be sore the next morning.**

Valisky, patiently ridden in a strongly-run race, came through steadily to challenge at the last hurdle. Staying on well, she gained the upper hand in the final 100 yards. (12/1)

High Post went for home approaching the third last but, after finally shaking off the attentions of the third, could not hold the winner in the last 100 yards. (10/1)
Wynberg went to the front at the eighth. Although headed on the home turn, he kept battling on and did not give best until the final furlong. (8/1: 5/1-9/1)
Palace Parade (USA) moved up at halfway, but his effort petered out approaching the second last. (33/1)
Limosa looked very dangerous on the home turn, but appeared not to get the trip in a strongly-run race. (7/1)
Spanish Blaze (IRE) (2/1: op 7/1)
Akiymann (USA) (6/1: 7/2-7/1)

20 REDHILL H'CAP CHASE (0-120) (5-Y.O+) (Class D)

3-30 (3-30) **2m 4f 110y (15 fncs)** £4,500.00 (£1,350.00: £650.00: £300.00) GOING: 0.03 sec per fur (G)

Horse		Pos	SP	RR	SF
Sartorius (100) (TThomsonJones) **10-10-9v** BPowell (led to 2nd: led 7th: hld on wl)	—	1	10/1	108	25
Polden Pride (112) (GBBalding) **8-11-4**(3) BFenton (hdwy 11th: ev ch flat: r.o)	½	2	7/2 2	120	37
Henley Regatta (94) (PRRodford) **8-10-3**ow3 SBurrough (hdwy 4 out: styd on wl fr last: nrst fin)	¾	3	20/1	101	15
Monks Jay (IRE) (91) (GThorner) **7-10-0** ILawrence (chsd ldrs: one pce fr 4 out)	12	4	10/1	89	6
Muskora (IRE) (119) (PJHobbs) **7-12-0b** RDunwoody (nt j.w: led 2nd to 7th: wknd appr 4 out)	1	5	7/4 1	116	33
Black Church (100) (RRowe) **10-10-9** DO'Sullivan (hdwy 5th: blnd & wknd 10th)	9	6	12/1	90	7
Castle King (119) (PRHedger) **9-12-0** MRichards (prom tl wknd 4 out: bhd whn p.u bef 2 out)		P	10/1	—	—
Rather Sharp (91) (CLPopham) **10-9-11**(3) TDascombe (hdwy 9th: wknd appr 4 out: bhd whn p.u bef last)		P	33/1	—	—
Nadjati (USA) (100) (DRGandolfo) **7-10-9** GUpton (hld up in rr: mstke 4 out: bhd whn p.u flat)		P	10/1	—	—
Pontynyswen (111) (DBurchell) **8-11-6v** DJBurchell (hdwy 9th: ev ch 2 out: 3rd & wkng whn blnd & uns rdr last)		U	5/1 3	—	—

(SP 127.0%) **10 Rn**

5m 10.8 (9.80) CSF £46.10 CT £659.54 TOTE £13.00: £2.70 £2.00 £4.90 (£19.00) Trio £61.60; £11.30 to Epsom Downs 9/6/96 OWNER Mr M. Popham (UPPER LAMBOURN) BRED Airlie Stud and Societe d'Elevage Agricoles
LONG HANDICAP Henley Regatta 9-12 Rather Sharp 9-2 Monks Jay (IRE) 9-11
Sartorius, always in the leading pair, made the best of his way home in the straight and found extra when challenged. (10/1)
Polden Pride moved up steadily to challenge at the last fence but, after looking likely to catch the winner, could not find that little bit extra close home. (7/2)
Henley Regatta was under pressure some way out, but did not make any ground until too late. (20/1)
Monks Jay (IRE) was on the heels of the leaders until chopped for foot at the fourth last. (10/1)
Muskora (IRE) jumped indifferently from the start and was never travelling really well. (7/4)

21 BOXFOLDIA JUBILEE H'CAP HURDLE (0-105) (4-Y.O+) (Class F)

4-00 (4-00) **2m (8 hdls)** £2,512.50 (£700.00: £337.50) GOING: 0.03 sec per fur (G)

Horse		Pos	SP	RR	SF
Phalarope (IRE) (84) (KAMorgan) **8-10-10** RDunwoody (stdy hdwy 5th: led 2 out: drvn out)	—	1	9/4 1	65	28
Call the Guv'nor (90) (NJHenderson) **7-11-2** JRKavanagh (hdwy appr 3 out: mstke 2 out: ev ch last: hung bdly lft flat: nt rcvr)	2	2	6/1 2	69	32
Boltrose (92) (RJPrice) **6-11-4** RDavis (hdwy 3 out: styd on fr next)	7	3	16/1	64	27
Legatee (85) (AStreeter) **5-10-11v** TEley (wnt 2nd & hrd rdn 5th: one pce fr 2 out: lame)	4	4	11/1	53	16
How's it Goin (IRE) (98) (WRMuir) **5-11-10** MRichards (lost pl 4th: sme hdwy fr 2 out)	5	5	10/1	61	24
Eleanora Muse (74) (PaddyFarrell) **6-9-9**(5) ChrisWebb (prom tl wknd 3 out)	1¼	6	8/1 3	36	—
Buglet (90) (MCPipe) **6-11-2** DBridgwater (wl bhd fr 5th: t.o)	28	7	6/1 2	24	—
Whistling Buck (IRE) (80) (RRowe) **8-10-6** DO'Sullivan (prom tl wknd 5th: t.o)	8	8	10/1	6	—
Java Shrine (USA) (76) (JCTuck) **5-10-2b** SMcNeill (led 3rd: clr 5th: hdd 2 out: 4th & btn whn fell last)		F	20/1	—	—
Frontier Flight (USA) (88) (MissLCSiddall) **6-10-11**(3) EHusband (wl bhd tl hdwy appr 3 out: 6th whn fell 2 out)		F	10/1	—	—
Will James (80) (CJDrewe) **10-10-3b**(3) JCulloty (t.o fr 3 out: p.u bef last)		P	16/1	—	—
Have a Nightcap (102) (NPLittmoden) **7-12-0b** BPowell (led to 3rd: wknd 4th: t.o whn p.u bef 3 out)		P	20/1	—	—

(SP 127.3%) **12 Rn**

3m 46.9 (6.90) CSF £16.88 CT £166.61 TOTE £2.70: £1.30 £2.30 £3.50 (£9.50) Trio £34.60 OWNER Foreneish Racing (MELTON MOWBRAY) BRED Paul Maguire
LONG HANDICAP Eleanora Muse 9-10
Phalarope (IRE), patiently ridden, came through to lead at the second last and stayed on under pressure. (9/4)
Call the Guv'nor moved up approaching the straight. Despite a mistake at the second last, he was almost level at the final flight, only to ruin his chance by veering badly to the left. (6/1)
Boltrose made a forward move three out, and stayed on at one pace from the next without causing the first two any concern. (16/1)
Legatee took second place approaching the straight, but was soon under maximum pressure and could find no more. (11/1)
How's it Goin (IRE) dropped right out at halfway but stayed on again at the finish. (10/1)
Eleanora Muse was on the heels of the leaders until weakening three out. (8/1)

22 HOLT NOVICES' HURDLE (4-Y.O+) (Class E)

4-30 (4-31) **2m (8 hdls)** £2,617.50 (£730.00: £352.50) GOING: 0.03 sec per fur (G)

Horse		Pos	SP	RR	SF
Brave Patriarch (IRE) (NJHenderson) **5-10-12** JRKavanagh (a.p: led 3 out: edgd lft flat: drvn out)	—	1	Evens 1	71	13
Born to Please (IRE) (PJHobbs) **4-10-7** APMcCoy (led to 4th: led after 5th to 3 out: rallied flat: r.o)	2½	2	4/1 2	69	6
Bramley May (RJRWilliams) **6-10-12** BPowell (wl in rr to 4th: gd hdwy 5th: ev ch 2 out: nt qckn)	1	3	11/2 3	68	10
General Shirley (IRE) (80) (PRHedger) **5-10-12**(7) MClinton (hdwy 5th: ev ch 3 out: one pce)	6	4	15/2	69	11
Out For A Duck (HEHaynes) **5-10-12** RDavis (nvr nr to chal)	14	5	50/1	48	—
Manaboutthehouse (94) (GThorner) **9-10-12** LHarvey (prom tl wknd 5th)	5	6	25/1	43	—
Mafuta (IRE) (CLPopham) **4-9-13b**(3) TDascombe (wl bhd fr 5th)	8	7	25/1	30	—
Laser Light Lady (NPLittmoden) **4-10-2** SWynne (prom tl wknd appr 5th)	3½	8	150/1	26	—
Frankie Harry (AWCarroll) **4-10-7** TEley (bhd most of way)	6	9	150/1	25	—
Kutan (IRE) (65) (MrsBarbaraWaring) **6-10-12b** EByrne (led 4th tl after 5th: wknd qckly: bhd whn fell 2 out)		F	33/1	—	—

(SP 111.1%) **10 Rn**

3m 50.6 (10.60) CSF £4.99 TOTE £2.10: £1.40 £1.30 £1.40 (£3.40) Trio £3.60 OWNER Mr Peter Winfield (LAMBOURN) BRED Peter Winfield in Ireland
WEIGHT FOR AGE 4yo-5lb

Brave Patriarch (IRE), always travelling well, took up the running at the third last. Always in control thereafter, he did have to be driven out though. (Evens)
Born to Please (IRE) ran very green, continually ducking and diving going to his hurdles. Sent on, he looked beaten when headed three out but rallied strongly to regain second on the run-in. (4/1: 3/1-9/2)
Bramley May was dropped out last, many lengths behind his rivals. He made smooth headway at halfway and was almost level at the second last. The effort of making up so much ground cost him dear, but he will be hard to beat next time. (11/2)
General Shirley (IRE) moved into contention on the home turn but, after having every chance, could find no extra from the second last. (15/2)
Out For A Duck stayed on to finish a distant fifth, but was never in the race with a chance. (50/1)

23 P & O H'CAP CHASE (0-110) (5-Y.O+) (Class E)

5-05 (5-05) **2m 7f (18 fncs)** £3,104.50 (£931.00: £448.00: £206.50) GOING: 0.03 sec per fur (G)

			SP	RR	SF
Funcheon Gale (85) (RCurtis) **9-10-3** DMorris (hdwy 9th: led 14th: easily)	—	**1**	5/2[1]	97+	4
Howgill (94) (CaptTAForster) **10-10-12b** SWynne (w ldr: led 8th to 11th: ev ch 4 out: one pce fr next)	12	**2**	8/1[3]	98	5
Charged (97) (PJHobbs) **7-11-1** APMcCoy (chsd ldrs: ev ch 14th: wkng whn blnd 4 out)	30	**3**	5/2[1]	80	—
Bravo Star (USA) (82) (PaddyFarrell) **11-9-9**(5) ChrisWebb (prom tl wknd 12th)	2½	**4**	16/1	63	—
Artful Arthur (82) (LPGrassick) **10-10-0** MrJGrassick (t.o tl sme late hdwy)	s.h	**5**	50/1	63	—
Victory Anthem (82) (PCClarke) **10-9-11**(3) BFenton (led to 8th: led 11th to 14th: wknd qckly: t.o)	dist	**6**	16/1	—	—
The Blue Boy (IRE) (100) (PBowen) **8-11-4b** RJohnson (prom tl wknd 9th: t.o whn p.u flat)		**P**	10/1	—	—
Vicar of Bray (90) (GBBalding) **9-10-8** JRKavanagh (s.s: t.o whn bef 4 out)		**P**	9/1	—	—
Merivel (110) (RRowe) **9-12-0** DO'Sullivan (t.o whn p.u bef 4 out)		**P**	13/2[2]	—	—
			(SP 114.4%)		**9 Rn**

5m 54.5 (16.50) CSF £20.84 CT £49.16 TOTE £3.90: £1.90 £2.20 £1.20 (£20.00) Trio £10.50 OWNER Kings Of The Road Partnership (LAMBOURN) BRED Patrick Moakley
LONG HANDICAP Victory Anthem 9-12 Artful Arthur 9-5 Bravo Star (USA) 9-12
STEWARDS' ENQUIRY Grassick susp. 19-20/6/96 (excessive use of whip).
Funcheon Gale treated this field with complete contempt. He went to the front five from home and readily drew clear to win with his head in his chest. Further success looks assured. (5/2)
Howgill helped make the running, and gallantly struggled to stay in touch with the winner from four out, but it was in vain. (8/1: op 5/1)
Charged travelled well on the heels of the leaders for much of the race, though his jumping did not inspire confidence. He appeared to be struggling when a bad blunder at the fourth last brought him almost to a standstill. (5/2)
The Blue Boy (IRE) (10/1: op 6/1)
Vicar of Bray (9/1: 6/1-10/1)

24 GRIMLEY STANDARD N.H. FLAT RACE (I) (4, 5 & 6-Y.O) (Class H)

5-40 (5-42) **2m** £1,280.00 (£355.00: £170.00)

			SP	RR	SF
Regal Gem (IRE) (CRBarwell) **5-11-0**(3) BFenton (hdwy 5f out: led over 2 out: drvn out)	—	**1**	4/5[1]	—	—
Oh Dear Me (RMFlower) **5-10-10** DO'Sullivan (hld up: jnd ldrs 4f out: ev ch fnl f: r.o)	½	**2**	25/1	—	—
Boundtohonour (IRE) (HOliver) **4-10-10** JacquiOliver (hld up: smooth hdwy 4f out: ev ch 2f out: nt qckn fnl f)	1½	**3**	12/1	—	—
Seven Wells (JHPeacock) **4-10-10** RGreene (chsd ldrs: one pce fnl 3f)	11	**4**	33/1	—	—
Roc Age (GWDavies) **5-10-10** RDavis (a.p: led 5f out tl over 2f out)	2	**5**	33/1	—	—
Fools Nook (CLPopham) **5-10-12**(3) TDascombe (prom tl rdn & wknd 3f out)	9	**6**	4/1[2]	—	—
Blue Havana (GraemeRoe) **4-9-12**(7) ShaunGraham (hdwy 6f out: wknd 3f out)	1¼	**7**	33/1	—	—
Jackamus (IRE) (GAHam) **5-10-8**(7) MrMFrith (nvr nr to chal)	12	**8**	33/1	—	—
Future Health (HJCollingridge) **6-11-1** VSmith (chsd ldrs: wkng whn ran v.wd over 4f out)	8	**9**	10/1	—	—
Tiger Bee (NRMitchell) **5-10-5**(5) SophieMitchell (led tl wknd qckly 5f out)	2	**10**	25/1	—	—
Sonrisa (IRE) (JWhite) **4-10-10** JRKavanagh (a bhd: t.o)	16	**11**	7/1[3]	—	—
Aber Glen (NASmith) **6-10-10** MrMRodda (prom tl wknd 6f out: t.o)	6	**12**	33/1	—	—
Another Bula (IRE) (HSHowe) **5-11-1** BPowell (a bhd: t.o)	10	**13**	20/1	—	—
Derring Court (EGBevan) **6-10-10** GUpton (chsd ldr tl wknd qckly 6f out: t.o)	dist	**14**	33/1	—	—
			(SP 134.9%)		**14 Rn**

3m 43.6 CSF £23.13 TOTE £1.50: £1.20 £4.90 £3.10 (£16.40) Trio £111.90; £143.44 to Epsom Downs 9/6/96 OWNER Mr D. W. E. Coombs (TIVERTON) BRED Mrs M. T. Ward
WEIGHT FOR AGE 4yo-5lb
Regal Gem (IRE) had to work very hard for this. She moved up approaching the straight and, after taking up the running over two furlongs from home, was driven all the way to the line. (4/5)
Oh Dear Me joined the leaders on the home turn. She had every chance and, though running on, could not find quite enough. (25/1)
Boundtohonour (IRE) looked very much like the winner and moved up to challenge over two furlongs from home. With a little more assistance from the saddle, he would probably have beaten his rivals and should certainly be able to pick up a similar event. (12/1)
Seven Wells, always on the heels of the leading group, lacked a turn of foot from the three-furlong marker. (33/1)
Roc Age took up the running five furlongs from home and did not drop right out of it when headed approaching the two-furlong pole. Improvement can follow. (33/1)
Fools Nook was on the heels of the leaders until weakening early in the straight. (4/1: 3/1-9/2)
Future Health (10/1: 6/1-12/1)

25 GRIMLEY STANDARD N.H. FLAT RACE (II) (4, 5 & 6-Y.O) (Class H)

6-10 (6-15) **2m** £1,269.50 (£352.00: £168.50)

			SP	RR	SF
Kailash (USA) (MCPipe) **5-11-8** DBridgwater (a.p: led over 4f out: sn clr: hrd rdn fnl f: all out)	—	**1**	5/2[2]	—	—
Tanglefoot Tipple (DRCElsworth) **5-11-1** PHolley (hdwy 8f out: wnt 2nd 4f out: hung lft over 1f out: ev ch fnl f: r.o nr fin)	hd	**2**	12/1	—	—
Popsi's Cloggs (RCurtis) **4-10-10** DMorris (hdwy 6f out: hung lft over 2f out: nt rch first two)	16	**3**	33/1	—	—
Profit And Loss (FMurphy) **5-10-10** RDunwoody (a.p: hrd rdn & btn 3f out)	1½	**4**	7/4[1]	—	—
Carnival Clown (KBishop) **4-10-10** RGreene (nrst fin)	¾	**5**	50/1	—	—
Sarenacare (IRE) (PJHobbs) **4-10-10** BPowell (chsd ldrs: rdn over 3f out: one pce)	3	**6**	16/1	—	—
Suffolk Girl (MrsMReveley) **4-10-9**(3) GCahill (nvr nr ldrs)	8	**7**	11/4[3]	—	—

			SP	RR	SF
Derrybelle (DLWilliams) **5-10-7**(3) TDascombe (chsd ldr: led 7f out tl over 4f out: sn wknd)	2	**8**	16/1	—	—
Arctic Chanter (BRMillman) **4-10-10** JRKavanagh (a wl bhd)	12	**9**	33/1	—	—
Rosslayne Serenade (RJWeaver) **5-10-10** PMcLoughlin (bhd fnl 8f: t.o)	dist	**10**	50/1	—	—
Wotanite (OO'Neill) **6-11-1** VSlattery (led tl wknd 7f out: t.o)	¾	**11**	50/1	—	—
Barton Bulldozer (IRE) (GBBalding) **6-10-12**(3) BFenton (prom tl wknd 7f out: t.o)	7	**12**	50/1	—	—
Magnum Force (IRE) (MissLCSiddall) **5-11-1** TEley (mid div tl p.u & dismntd 7f out)		**P**	40/1	—	—
Sweet Talker (IRE) (MrsPGrainger) **4-10-10** MrMRimell (Withdrawn not under Starter's orders: uns rdr & bolted bef s)		**W**	33/1	—	—
			(SP 130.2%)		**13 Rn**

3m 42.0 CSF £32.24 TOTE £3.50: £1.50 £3.40 £5.10 (£12.20) OWNER Mr Mick Fletcher (WELLINGTON) BRED William C. Miller
WEIGHT FOR AGE 4yo-5lb
Kailash (USA), always in the first three, went to the front over four furlongs from home and had all but the second in trouble within 100 yards. He had to be kept up to his work all the way to the post. (5/2)
Tanglefoot Tipple should have won. He moved up at halfway and went in pursuit of the winner from the four-furlong marker. Very green under pressure below the distance, he looked held, but suddenly realised what was required near the finish. (12/1)
Popsi's Cloggs made ground approaching the straight, but was inclined to hang to the left under pressure, and never promised to get near the leading pair. (33/1)
Profit And Loss chased the leaders until weakening under strong pressure at the three-furlong marker. (7/4)
Carnival Clown made some late headway, but was never in the race with a chance. (50/1)
Sarenacare (IRE), close enough on the home turn, was ridden and beaten with more than three furlongs to race. (16/1)
Suffolk Girl (11/4: 6/4-3/1)

T/Plpt: £54.00 (105.27 Tckts). T/Qdpt: £12.30 (101.27 Tckts). Hn

UTTOXETER (L-H) (Good to firm, Good patches)

Sunday June 9th

WEATHER: fine but cloudy

26 JANERITE SERVICES 'MILITARY' MAIDEN HURDLE (4-Y.O+) (Class D)

2-15 (2-16) **2m (9 hdls)** £3,048.00 (£924.00: £452.00: £216.00) GOING minus 0.60 sec per fur (F)

			SP	RR	SF
Birthday Boy (IRE) (94) (JRJenkins) **4-11-0v** JOsborne (hld up in tch: chal 2 out: slt ld last: rdn out)	—	**1**	7/2[1]	67	17
Imlak (IRE) (JLHarris) **4-11-0** RDunwoody (a.p: led appr 3 out to last: kpt on u.p flat)	½	**2**	4/1[2]	67	17
Efharisto (JWhite) **7-11-5b** DBridgwater (hld up: hdwy appr 6th: rdn & one pce fr 2 out)	6	**3**	7/2[1]	61	16
Double Pendant (IRE) (PJHobbs) **5-11-5** APMcCoy (hdwy 4th: hrd rdn & hld whn mstke last)	7	**4**	9/1	54	9
Ilewin Janine (IRE) (PCRitchens) **5-11-0** CMaude (hld up: gd hdwy appr 6th: ev ch 3 out: sn rdn: wknd appr last)	1¾	**5**	10/1	47	2
Tom's Gemini Star (OJCarter) **8-11-5** RichardGuest (bkwd: wl bhd tl styd on fr 3 out)	18	**6**	50/1	34	—
Pot Blackbird (RLee) **7-11-0** RJohnson (nvr bttr than mid div: t.o fr 3 out)	9	**7**	14/1	20	—
Kama Simba (JWhite) **4-11-0** WMcFarland (bit bkwd: hit 1st: nvr nr ldrs: t.o)	4	**8**	16/1	21	—
Dancing At Laharn (IRE) (85) (MissSJWilton) **6-10-12v**[1](7) NWillmington (led 2nd: clr 5th: hdd appr 3 out: sn wknd: t.o)	1¾	**9**	15/2[3]	19	—
Hatta River (USA) (PTDalton) **6-11-5** TEley (trckd ldrs: rdn 6th: sn wknd: t.o)	1½	**10**	14/1	18	—
Trina's Cottage (IRE) (JohnUpson) **4-11-0** RSupple (s.s: a bhd: t.o)	1¼	**11**	50/1	16	—
Watch Sooty (RJWeaver) **5-10-7**(7) DFinnegan (swtg: plld hrd: led to 2nd: wknd 6th: t.o)	2½	**12**	66/1	9	—
Aws Contracts (CJHemsley) **5-11-2**(3) BFenton (mstke 4th: a bhd: virtually p.u flat: lame)	20	**13**	33/1	—	—
Fern Grove (ABarrow) **4-11-0** AThornton (a bhd: j.slowly 5th: t.o whn p.u bef next)		**P**	50/1	—	—
Sister Jim (RJPrice) **6-11-0** RDavis (mstke 2nd: sn t.o: p.u bef 3 out)		**P**	100/1	—	—
Winter Gem (RJPrice) **7-11-0** PMcLoughlin (a bhd: t.o whn p.u bef 6th)		**P**	100/1	—	—
			(SP 126.8%)		**16 Rn**

3m 40.9 (-0.10) CSF £17.61 TOTE £4.20: £1.40 £1.70 £2.20 (£5.40) Trio £5.40 OWNER Mr T. R. Pearson (ROYSTON) BRED P. J. Maher
WEIGHT FOR AGE 4yo-5lb
Birthday Boy (IRE), not winning out of turn, needed to dig deep to get the better of the persistent runner-up, and his first success was thoroughly deserved. (7/2)
Imlak (IRE), running by far his best race over hurdles, did not give in without a hard fight and, on this showing, he would appear to be on the upgrade. (4/1)
Efharisto looked to be the one to beat when he joined issue three out, but he did not find much when shown the whip and could only stay on at the one pace. (7/2)
Double Pendant (IRE), a winner on the Flat in Ireland, did not fire on his hurdling debut but performed much better this time and was still fighting for places when he landed awkwardly at the last. (9/1)
Dancing At Laharn (IRE) (15/2: 5/1-8/1)

27 SENATE CONDITIONAL (S) H'CAP HURDLE (0-90) (4-Y.O+) (Class G)

2-50 (2-50) **2m 4f 110y (10 hdls)** £2,134.00 (£599.00: £292.00) GOING minus 0.60 sec per fur (F)

			SP	RR	SF
Crazy Horse Dancer (USA) (77) (FJordan) **8-11-2** LAspell (trckd ldrs: led appr 3 out: rdn out)	—	**1**	8/1	54	6
Sovereign Niche (IRE) (84) (MCPipe) **8-11-9v** EHusband (s.i.s: sn chsng ldrs: led 7th tl appr next: rallied u.p flat)	1¼	**2**	4/1[1]	60	12
Whistling Gipsy (66) (HOliver) **11-10-5** ChrisWebb (hld up: hdwy 5th: ev ch 2 out: rdn whn mstke last: one pce)	5	**3**	10/1	38	—
Sweet Noble (IRE) (85) (KJDrewry) **7-11-7**(3) BGrattan (lw: led: clr ½-wy: hdd 7th: hrd rdn 2 out: sn btn)	3	**4**	33/1	55	7
Antarcticern (USA) (78) (GROldroyd) **6-11-3** PMidgley (lw: hld up: hdwy 6th: wknd after 3 out)	1¼	**5**	7/1[3]	47	—
Miss Pimpernel (77) (ABarrow) **6-11-2b** SophieMitchell (prom tl wknd appr 2 out)	9	**6**	12/1	39	—
Jobber's Fiddle (72) (DLWilliams) **4-10-5** TDascombe (prom tl wknd 3 out)	2½	**7**	12/1	32	—
Tudor Flight (63) (AGNewcombe) **5-10-2** BFenton (lw: hld up: effrt 6th: wknd after next)	½	**8**	5/1[2]	22	—
Station Express (IRE) (61) (BJLlewellyn) **8-10-0** FLeahy (a in rr: t.o)	16	**9**	25/1	16	—
The Secret Seven (65) (JKCresswell) **6-10-4** RMassey (a bhd: t.o fr 7th)	6	**10**	20/1	15	—
Lady Lois (61) (BPreece) **5-9-11**(3) DFinnegan (mstke 4th: a bhd: t.o)	4	**11**	7/1[3]	8	—

Horse	Dist	Pos	SP	RR	SF
Miniture Melody (IRE) (63) (PCRitchens) **8-9-11**(5)ow2 MKeighley (mid div tl wknd 6th: sn t.o)	5	**12**	33/1	6	—
Lovelark (61) (RLee) **7-10-0** SRyan (a bhd: t.o fr ½-wy)	2½	**13**	20/1	2	—
Skittle Alley (82) (WClay) **10-11-7** GuyLewis (a bhd: rdn 6th: t.o)	27	**14**	16/1	2	—
Mason Dixon (74) (JAPickering) **7-10-10**(3) CRae (hld up: hdwy appr 5th: wknd qckly after 7th: p.u bef next)		**P**	8/1	—	—
Roscommon Lad (IRE) (67) (RHollinshead) **4-10-0** DParker (sn bhd: t.o: p.u bef 3 out)		**P**	25/1	—	—
			(SP 137.3%)		**16 Rn**

4m 47.8 (3.80) CSF £42.11 CT £317.04 TOTE £11.00: £2.20 £1.40 £3.90 £10.40 (£38.80) Trio £187.90; £116.47 to Windsor 10/6/96 OWNER Mrs A. Roddis (LEOMINSTER) BRED Paul R. Denes, Trustee for Dustin M. Denes
LONG HANDICAP Lovelark 9-12 Station Express (IRE) 9-7 Miniture Melody (IRE) 9-5 Roscommon Lad (IRE) 9-6
WEIGHT FOR AGE 4yo-6lb
No bid

Crazy Horse Dancer (USA), winning for the first time in over two years, kicked on early in the straight and, soon gaining a healthy cushion, was always holding the hard-ridden favourite. (8/1)
Sovereign Niche (IRE), sharing the lead at the end of the back straight, could not quicken up when the winner threw down his challenge, but he did rally on the run-in and would have got there with a bit further to travel. (4/1)
Whistling Gipsy delivered a determined challenge at the penultimate flight, but the winner was not stopping and he had shot his bolt when making a mistake at the last. (10/1)

28 LADBROKE H'CAP CHASE (0-120) (5-Y.O+) (Class D)

3-25 (3-25) **2m 7f (16 fncs)** £4,221.00 (£1,278.00: £624.00: £297.00) GOING minus 0.60 sec per fur (F)

Horse	Dist	Pos	SP	RR	SF
Certain Angle (105) (PJHobbs) **7-10-13** APMcCoy (lw: chsd ldr: led 7th: wandered & collided 2 out: hdd & bmpd last: styd on u.p to ld flat)	—	**1**	9/4[2]	114	46
Lemon's Mill (USA) (120) (MCPipe) **7-12-0b** DBridgwater (reminders 6th: hdwy next: rdn to chal & collided 2 out: led & j.rt last: hdd flat)	hd	**2**	5/6[1]	129	61
Counterbalance (99) (JCMcConnochie) **9-10-7** SMcNeill (lw: trckd ldrs tl outpcd appr 3 out)	16	**3**	10/1[3]	97	29
Abbotsham (98) (OJCarter) **11-10-6** AThornton (a bhd: t.o fr 11th)	dist	**4**	14/1	—	—
Shannon Glen (102) (MSmith) **10-10-10b** RSupple (chsd ldrs tl rdn & lost tch ½-wy: sn bhd: t.o)	½	**5**	14/1	—	—
Mutual Trust (112) (PBowen) **12-11-6** RJohnson (led to 7th: btn whn mstke 11th: p.u bef next)		**P**	20/1	—	—
Hurryup (96) (RDickin) **9-10-4** BPowell (lw: sn bhd & outpcd: t.o: p.u bef 12th)		**P**	20/1	—	—
			(SP 117.3%)		**7 Rn**

5m 26.8 (8.60 under best) (-9.20) CSF £4.56 TOTE £3.50: £1.40 £1.40 (£1.90) OWNER The Plyform Syndicate (MINEHEAD) BRED J. Thompson

Certain Angle helped set a furious pace and went on before halfway. He was out on his feet when he did threaten to run out at the second last but, answering his rider's every call, somehow had the strength to thrust his head in front again near the line. Knocking 7.2 seconds off the track record was testament itself to what a true test this really was. (9/4)
Lemon's Mill (USA) struggled with the pace in the early stages but responded to a forceful ride to put in her bid at the penultimate fence where she looked likely to gain the spoils. The winner would not be denied though and worried her out of it on the run-in. Both she and the winner will not forget this race in a hurry. (5/6)
Abbotsham (14/1: op 9/1)
Shannon Glen (14/1: 10/1-16/1)

29 SENATE H'CAP HURDLE (0-125) (4-Y.O+) (Class D)

3-55 (3-56) **3m 110y (12 hdls)** £3,204.00 (£972.00: £476.00: £228.00) GOING minus 0.60 sec per fur (F)

Horse	Dist	Pos	SP	RR	SF
Morning Blush (IRE) (95) (MCPipe) **6-10-0** DBridgwater (mde all: clr 9th: styd on strly)	—	**1**	6/1[3]	82	14
South Westerly (IRE) (111) (MrsMReveley) **8-11-2** PNiven (hld up: hdwy 7th: chsd wnr 2 out: no imp)	8	**2**	5/1[2]	93	25
Cats Run (IRE) (118) (JohnUpson) **8-11-9** RSupple (lw: chsd wnr to 2 out: rdn & kpt on one pce)	1	**3**	5/1[2]	99	31
Tallywagger (118) (GMMoore) **9-11-2**(7) THogg (lw: hld up in rr: hdwy appr 3 out: nvr nrr)	12	**4**	9/4[1]	91	23
Able Player (USA) (95) (KJDrewry) **9-10-0** MSharratt (trckd ldrs tl wknd appr 3 out)	1¾	**5**	14/1	67	—
La Fontainbleau (IRE) (97) (DHBrown) **8-10-2** APMcCoy (trckd ldng pair: outpcd 4th: lost tch 9th: t.o)	25	**6**	9/1	53	—
Macedonas (95) (GThorner) **8-10-0** BPowell (hld up mid div: wknd appr 8th: t.o)	18	**7**	33/1	39	—
First Crack (95) (FJordan) **11-10-0** RGreene (mstke 5th: a bhd: t.o)	18	**8**	14/1	27	—
Far Out (95) (OBrennan) **10-10-0v** MBrennan (lw: hld up: hdwy 8th: poor 4th whn p.u lame appr 3 out)		**P**	9/1	—	—
			(SP 114.7%)		**9 Rn**

5m 38.7 (-3.30) CSF £33.25 CT £146.48 TOTE £10.40: £2.70 £1.90 £2.20 (£24.00) Trio £26.60 OWNER Bisgrove Partnership (WELLINGTON) BRED R. N. Clay and Airlie Stud
LONG HANDICAP Morning Blush (IRE) 9-9 Macedonas 8-11 First Crack 9-10 Far Out 9-9
OFFICIAL EXPLANATION **Tallywagger: finished distressed.**

Morning Blush (IRE), fresh and well after a six-month break, galloped the opposition into the ground and her trainer intends to keep her going while she is in good heart. (6/1)
South Westerly (IRE) stayed extremely well and promised to prove the stronger when mounting a challenge at the second last, but the boot was on the other foot as the winner lengthened to draw clear. (5/1)
Cats Run (IRE), on the heels of the winner for most of the way, was the first to crack approaching the second last as the weight concession took its toll. (5/1)
Tallywagger could not cope with the strong gallop on this flat track, and was always a long way adrift of the principals. (9/4)

30 CITY OF STOKE ON TRENT CELEBRATION PLATE NOVICES' CHASE (5-Y.O+) (Class C)

4-25 (4-25) **2m 5f (16 fncs)** £5,174.75 (£1,568.00: £766.50: £365.75) GOING minus 0.60 sec per fur (F)

Horse	Dist	Pos	SP	RR	SF
Factor Ten (IRE) (113) (MissHCKnight) **8-12-0** JFTitley (hld up: chsd ldr fr 8th: rdn to ld appr last: r.o wl)	—	**1**	8/11[1]	100	30
Ballyline (IRE) (WTKemp) **5-10-7** RSupple (j.w: led 3rd: sn clr: hdd appr last: one pce)	4	**2**	14/1	83	6
Nescaf (NZ) (CJMann) **6-11-0** RDunwoody (lw: a.p: blnd 4th: rdn & wknd 3 out)	11	**3**	100/30[2]	75	5
Music Score (82) (MrsLCTaylor) **10-11-0** AThornton (led to 3rd: no hdwy fr 12th)	4	**4**	20/1	72	2
Manor Rhyme (74) (JCMcConnochie) **9-11-0** SMcNeill (lw: mid div tl outpcd fr 12th)	9	**5**	12/1[3]	65	—
And Why Not (74) (MrsSJSmith) **8-11-0** RichardGuest (a bhd: rdn 10th: sn t.o)	1½	**6**	33/1	64	—
Tristan's Comet (JLHarris) **9-11-0** BDalton (a bhd: t.o fr 10th)	1½	**7**	16/1	62	—
Welsh's Gamble (60) (RHAlner) **7-11-0** WMcFarland (lw: hld up: hdwy 11th: mstke next: sn wknd: t.o)	2½	**8**	50/1	61	—
Misty Grey (76) (GFierro) **7-10-8**(7)ow1 SLycett (trckd ldrs: mstke 4th: lost pl ½-wy: t.o)	21	**9**	50/1	46	—

Horse	Pos	SP	RR	SF
Precis (62) (OJCarter) **8-10-9** RDavis (sn t.o: p.u after 8th)	**P**	50/1	—	—
		(SP 114.8%)		**10 Rn**

5m 5.6 (0.60) CSF £11.28 TOTE £1.60: £1.30 £3.40 £1.10 (£6.60) Trio £9.80 OWNER Premier Crops Ltd (WANTAGE) BRED Mrs F. J. Maxwell
WEIGHT FOR AGE 5yo-7lb
Factor Ten (IRE) had to work very hard indeed to maintain his winning sequence, but he was conceding a lot of weight all round, and it goes to show how much he has improved since the turn of the year. (8/11)
Ballyline (IRE), a point winner in Ireland but a faller on his debut under Rules, turned in a most impressive display of jumping here and gave supporters of the favourite a very worrying time, before being forced to give best. Still only five, he looks to have a future. (14/1)
Nescaf (NZ), making his chasing debut, survived an early mistake but jumped well in the main and held a live chance until calling enough at the third last. (100/30)

31 BET WITH THE TOTE NOVICES' HURDLE (4-Y.O+) (Class C)

4-55 (4-55) **2m 4f 110y (10 hdls)** £4,494.00 (£1,362.00: £666.00: £318.00) GOING minus 0.60 sec per fur (F)

Horse	Dist	Pos	SP	RR	SF
Rolfe (NZ) (104) (DNicholson) **6-11-12b** RJohnson (hld up in tch: hdwy to ld 2 out: clr last)	—	**1**	2/1 [1]	84+	31
Pembridge Place (94) (GFJohnsonHoughton) **5-11-0** AThornton (led to 2 out: rallied u.p flat)	4	**2**	6/1	69	16
Amercius (JLHarris) **4-10-8b** RDunwoody (lw: chsd ldr to 7th: outpcd appr 3 out: n.d after)	nk	**3**	4/1 [3]	69	10
Supermodel (MrsNMacauley) **4-10-9** PHide (a.p: chsd ldr fr 7th: wknd appr last)	1	**4**	9/4 [2]	69	10
Mrs Robinson (IRE) (JMackie) **5-10-6**(3) EHusband (a in rr: t.o)	dist	**5**	20/1	—	—
Leap in the Dark (IRE) (71) (MissLCSiddall) **7-11-0** MRichards (trckd ldrs tl rdn & wknd 6th: t.o)	1½	**6**	33/1	—	—
Rah Wan (USA) (CTNash) **10-11-0** BPowell (hld up: hdwy 5th: wknd appr 7th: t.o)	1	**7**	33/1	—	—
Crown Ivory (NZ) (PCRitchens) **8-11-0** SFox (bkwd: bhd: effrt 6th: wknd next: t.o)	18	**8**	33/1	—	—
Shers Delight (IRE) (91) (OBrennan) **6-11-12v** MBrennan (a bhd: t.o)	10	**9**	12/1	—	—
True Rhyme (CASmith) **6-10-9** VSlattery (lost pl ½-wy: t.o whn p.u bef 3 out)		**P**	50/1	—	—
Matachon (MSmith) **6-11-0** RSupple (a bhd: t.o ½-wy: p.u bef 3 out)		**P**	50/1	—	—
			(SP 123.6%)		**11 Rn**

4m 43.1 (-0.90) CSF £14.75 TOTE £2.90: £1.50 £1.80 £1.20 (£7.50) Trio £7.40 OWNER Mr Stanley Clarke (TEMPLE GUITING) BRED Est. Late C. A. Young
WEIGHT FOR AGE 4yo-6lb
Rolfe (NZ) goes from strength to strength and, in completing his hat-trick, could now be aimed at a novice in Galway. (2/1: 6/4-9/4)
Pembridge Place is gradually getting his act together and, though he was forced to give best here, he performed with credit and his turn will come. (6/1)
Amercius lost his pitch turning in, but was galvanized into action again and staying on best of all at the finish. (4/1)
Supermodel could never get to the front but she pushed the pace and had every chance until feeling the strain on the approach the last flight. (9/4)

32 SENATE ELECTRICAL H'CAP HURDLE (0-115) (4-Y.O+) (Class E)

5-25 (5-25) **2m (9 hdls)** £2,284.50 (£642.00: £313.50) GOING minus 0.60 sec per fur (F)

Horse	Dist	Pos	SP	RR	SF
Lady Confess (87) (JohnUpson) **6-10-1** RSupple (led 3rd: clr appr 3 out: rdn & drifted lft flat: r.o)	—	**1**	11/1	65	21
Kalzari (USA) (86) (AWCarroll) **11-10-0** APMcCoy (lw: plld hrd: hld up: hdwy appr 6th: chsd wnr 3 out: kpt on u.p)	2½	**2**	12/1	62	18
Toute Bagaille (FR) (98) (MCPipe) **4-10-7** DBridgwater (lw: prom tl outpcd 6th: styd on again fr 2 out)	14	**3**	11/4 [1]	60	11
Naiysari (IRE) (114) (PMRich) **8-11-7**(7) DFinnegan (a.p: rdn appr 2 out: one pce)	hd	**4**	9/2 [3]	75	31
Coast Along (IRE) (91) (PJBevan) **4-10-0** WWorthington (trckd ldrs tl rdn & wknd 3 out)	1¼	**5**	6/1	51	2
Northern Trial (USA) (95) (KRBurke) **8-10-9** RDunwoody (lw: hld up: outpcd 5th: reminders & effrt next: nt rch ldrs)	5	**6**	4/1 [2]	50	6
Marsh's Law (89) (OBrennan) **9-10-3v** MBrennan (a bhd: t.o)	1	**7**	9/1	43	—
Wordsmith (IRE) (92) (JLHarris) **6-10-6** BDalton (a in rr: t.o)	2½	**8**	9/1	44	—
Bud's Bet (IRE) (86) (MissJFCraze) **8-10-0** RJohnson (led to 3rd: wknd appr 3 out: t.o)	3	**9**	14/1	35	—
			(SP 121.8%)		**9 Rn**

3m 37.5 (-3.50) CSF £120.20 CT £429.89 TOTE £15.60: £2.70 £2.80 £1.60 (£47.60) Trio £304.60; £343.30 to Windsor 10/6/96 OWNER Mrs R. E. Tate (TOWCESTER) BRED Mrs B. Tate
LONG HANDICAP Coast Along (IRE) 9-12 Bud's Bet (IRE) 9-7
WEIGHT FOR AGE 4yo-5lb
STEWARDS' ENQUIRY Finnegan susp. 19-20 & 22/6/96 (failure to obtain best possible placing).
Lady Confess stepped up the pace to draw clear turning in and, though she had a fight on her hands on the flat, always looked to be in charge. (11/1)
Kalzari (USA) is long overdue another success and he fought long and hard here, but had to admit his younger rival just that bit too fleet-footed for him. (12/1: 8/1-14/1)
Toute Bagaille (FR) dropped to the rear entering the straight, but found stamina coming into play in the latter stages and stuck on strongly to gain the minor prize right on the line. (11/4)
Marsh's Law (9/1: op 6/1)

T/Plpt: £15.30 (795.24 Tckts). T/Qdpt: £4.00 (187.34 Tckts). IM

33a-48a **(Irish Racing)** - See Computer Raceform

AUTEUIL (Paris, France) (L-H) (Very Soft)

Tuesday May 28th

49a PRIX MILLIONNAIRE II CHASE (5-Y.O+)

3-20 (3-20) **2m 6f** £39,526.00 GOING: 0.00 sec per fur (G)

Horse	Dist	Pos	SP	RR	SF
Arenice (FR) (GMacaire,France) **8-10-3** PSourzac	—	**1**		—	—
Chamberko (FR) (France) **8-10-12** CPieux	5	**2**		—	—
Al Capone II (FR) (BSecly,France) **8-10-7** JYBeaurain	6	**3**		—	—
As des Carres (FR) (France) **9-10-3** CGombeau	8	**4**		—	—

		SP	RR	SF
Algan (FR) (FDoumen,France) **8-10-5** PChevalier (btn over 34l)	7		—	—

7 Rn

5m 28.0 P-M 20.90F: 2.80F 1.20F (55.30F) OWNER Mme F. Montauban BRED Mme Annick Deliberos

BADEN-BADEN (Germany) (L-H) (Good to soft)
Tuesday June 4th

50a BADENER ROULETTE-PREIS HURDLE (4-Y.O)
5-10 (5-13) **2m 110y** £11,261.00 (£4,505.00: £2,928.00) GOING: 0.00 sec per fur (G)

			SP	RR	SF
Last Corner (CvonderRecke,Germany) **4-10-8** KlausHviid	—	1		88	—
Multy (IRE) (CJMann) **4-10-12** RDunwoody	4½	2		88	—
Reveillon (GER) (CvonderRecke,Germany) **4-11-0** SHickey	4½	3		85	—

8 Rn

3m 53.5 TOTE 94DM: 17DM 17DM 16DM (334DM) OWNER Mr B. Raber BRED Aston Park Stud
3566 Multy (IRE) ran a sound race on ground softer than he likes. Making headway to join issue two out, he was unable to match the winner's turn of foot, but kept on well to secure the sizeable second prize. He could come back here for a similar event at the August meeting.

BADEN-BADEN (Germany) (L-H) (Good)
Wednesday June 5th

51a BADER-PREIS-HURDENRENNEN HURDLE (5-Y.O+)
3-25 (3-42) **2m 4f 165y** £15,766.00 GOING: 0.00 sec per fur (G)

			SP	RR	SF
Registano (GER) (UweStoltefuss,Germany) **9-10-6** DFuhrmann	—	1		—?	—
Weissenstein (IRE) (HBlume,Germany) **5-10-8** DerekByrne	4	2		—	—
Aconcagua (GER) (EPils,Germany) **9-10-11** MrPGehm	2½	3		—	—
Decide Yourself (IRE) (TThomsonJones) **6-10-8** GBradley		P		—	—

12 Rn

4m 47.8 TOTE 44DM: 19DM 17DM 17DM (182DM) OWNER Gestut Sybille BRED Gestut Gorlsdorf
3586* Decide Yourself (IRE) began to lose touch soon after halfway and was tailed off when pulled up two out. He is better going right-handed.

49a-AUTEUIL (Paris, France) (L-H) (Good to soft)
Thursday June 6th

52a PRIX LA BARKA HURDLE (5-Y.O+)
3-25 (3-22) **2m 5f 110y** £39,526.00 (£19,763.00: £11,858.00) GOING: 0.00 sec per fur (G)

			SP	RR	SF
Montperle (FR) (JBertranDeBalanda,France) **7-10-2** YFouin	—	1		154	—
Mysilv (CREgerton) **6-10-0** JOsborne	1½	2		151	—
Earl Grant (FR) (France) **7-10-4** JYBeaurain	½	3		155	—

10 Rn

5m 22.0 P-M 17.80F: 3.20F 2.70F 1.70F (72.20F) OWNER Mme H. Carion BRED Hubert Carion
Montperle (FR) took this event after having a varied campaign this season, running over fences, hurdles and on the Flat.
2784 Mysilv overcame her inexperience of the track and once again put in a very brave effort. She looked in trouble in the back straight when Osborne took her over to the inside rail while the rest of the field went in search of the better ground. In fifth place on the final turn, she seemed to have no chance of reaching the prizes, but while most of her rivals were weakening in the sweltering heat, she kept plugging away and stayed on steadily from the last to take a well deserved second prize. Her sights are now set on the Grande Course de Haies, over an extra half a mile here at the end of June, where she will not be without a chance.

STROMSHOLM (Stockholm, Sweden) (R-H) (Good)
Sunday June 9th

53a SVENSKT GRAND NATIONAL CHASE (5-Y.O+)
2-45 **2m 5f** £9,718.00 GOING: 0.00 sec per fur (G)

			SP	RR	SF
Black Hero (FR) (MrsRNilsen,Norway) **7-10-10** JTwomey	—	1		109	—
Serafin (POL) (NPBogen,Norway) **12-11-0** JMcLaughlin	2	2		112	—
Horrible Hatta (IRE) (BHelander,Sweden) **8-10-3** MrAGammell	5	3		97	—
Raglan Road (MissAEEmbiricos) **12-10-3** JRyan (btn 15l)		6		91	—

9 Rn

5m 4.3 TOTE 23.70KR: 13.80KR 15.30KR 47.30KR (56.70KR) OWNER Stall Nor BRED F. Geffroy
Black Hero (FR) started as favourite and justified his support by denying the runner-up a fifth win in this race.
Raglan Road jumped well in the rear. He made headway to take a distant fourth position with under a mile to race, but could only plug on at one pace on the final circuit.

MARKET RASEN (R-H) (Good to firm, Good patches)
Friday June 14th
WEATHER: fine & sunny

54 PROMOTA 'JOCKEYS TITLE' (S) HURDLE (4-Y.O+) (Class G)
6-50 (6-50) **2m 1f 110y (8 hdls)** £2,057.50 (£570.00: £272.50) GOING minus 0.17 sec per fur (G)

			SP	RR	SF
Sian Wyn (80) (KRBurke) **6-11-1** RDunwoody (lw: trckd ldrs fr 3rd: led between last 2: rdn out)	—	1	5/2[1]	59	26

	Horse / details	Dist	Pos	SP	RR	SF
	Elite Justice (85) (SGollings) **4-11-1b** APMcCoy (lw: led: clr 3rd: hdd between last 2: kpt on wl)	2½	**2**	7/1	62	24
	Swiss Mountain (69) (PJBevan) **6-10-8** WWorthington (a in tch: rdn 3 out: styd on one pce)	2	**3**	4/1[3]	48	15
	Eastern Charly (BEL) (MrsSJSmith) **6-10-13** RichardGuest (hdwy 5th: styd on one pce fr 3 out)	1¼	**4**	10/1	52	19
	Nandura (65) (MissAEEmbiricos) **5-10-8** JRyan (bhd: sme hdwy 3 out: nvr nr ldrs)	10	**5**	16/1	38	5
	Lago Lago (IRE) (85) (WMcKeown) **4-10-7**(3) GCahill (mid div: effrt u.p 5th: nvr nr to chal)	2	**6**	11/4[2]	43	5
	Mendip Son (90) (MrsPGrainger) **6-10-13b[1]** MrAPhillips (sn bhd)	14	**7**	25/1	28	—
	Surgical Spirit (55) (JRPoulton) **6-10-5b**(3) KGaule (chsd ldrs: rdn 4th: sn lost pl)	22	**8**	25/1	3	—
	Normead Lass (65) (CSmith) **8-10-8** MRanger (bhd: sme hdwy 5th: sn wknd)	hd	**9**	16/1	3	—
	Needwood Cube (TWall) **5-10-10**(3) RMassey (bhd & rdn 4th)	15	**10**	20/1	—	—
	Free Tyson (59) (OBrennan) **5-10-13** MBrennan (bhd fr 4th)	1½	**11**	25/1	—	—
	Jungle Highway (54) (PWHiatt) **7-10-1b**(7) MrRThornton (chsd ldrs tl wknd 3rd: blnd next: sn t.o)	11	**12**	25/1	—	—
				(SP 128.7%)		**12 Rn**

4m 8.5 (5.50) CSF £20.73 TOTE £3.30: £1.40 £1.60 £2.80 (£7.30) Trio £14.00 OWNER D G & D J Robinson (WANTAGE) BRED D. Robinson
WEIGHT FOR AGE 4yo-5lb
Bt in 3,600gns

Sian Wyn, who had struggled when winning in lesser company on soft ground at Cartmel, looked to be running away after three out but, in the end, there was nothing to spare. (5/2)
Elite Justice, in blinkers for the first time, was given a terrific attacking ride and, to his credit, he kept on all the way to the line. (7/1)
Swiss Mountain is running as well as she can at present. (4/1)
Eastern Charly (BEL), who is said to have won on the Flat in France, was warm beforehand. Staying on at the finish, he might be capable of better with this behind him. (10/1: 7/1-12/1)

55 ROSELAND GROUP H'CAP HURDLE (0-110) (4-Y.O+) (Class E)

7-20 (7-23) **2m 3f 110y (10 hdls)** £2,990.75 (£896.00: £430.50: £197.75) GOING minus 0.17 sec per fur (G)

	Horse / details	Dist	Pos	SP	RR	SF
	Superhoo (86) (RCraggs) **5-11-3**(3) BFenton (wnt prom 6th: chal & lft clr 2 out: rdn out)	—	**1**	6/1[3]	70	23
	Pasja (IRE) (88) (SGollings) **5-11-8v** JOsborne (led to 3 out: sn outpcd: rallied next: styd on flat)	5	**2**	3/1[1]	68	21
	Jennyellen (IRE) (90) (FMurphy) **7-11-10** MFoster (hdwy 5th: outpcd after 3 out: styd on fr next)	3½	**3**	12/1	67	20
21*	**Phalarope (IRE) (90)** (KAMorgan) **8-11-10**[6x] RDunwoody (chsd ldrs: rdn & outpcd 3 out: kpt on)	3	**4**	3/1[1]	65	18
	Easy Over (USA) (70) (JRJenkins) **10-10-4** SFox (bhd: rdn along 6th: sme hdwy 2 out: nvr nr to chal)	3	**5**	25/1	42	—
	Cromaboo Crown (78) (PJBevan) **5-10-12** WWorthington (prom to 5th: bhd & rdn 7th:)	20	**6**	10/1	34	—
	Chris's Glen (84) (JMBradley) **7-11-4v** APMcCoy (chsd ldrs tl wknd appr 2 out: virtually p.u run in)	dist	**7**	6/1[3]	—	—
	Dark Silhouette (IRE) (75) (OBrennan) **7-10-9** MBrennan (trckd ldrs: led 3 out tl fell next)		**F**	5/1[2]	—	—
				(SP 115.9%)		**8 Rn**

4m 41.5 (8.50) CSF £23.37 CT £191.80 TOTE £7.20: £1.90 £1.40 £4.20 (£17.20) OWNER Prince Bishop Racing (SEDGEFIELD) BRED G. Reed

Superhoo, raised 6lb for his Southwell success, looked to be holding the aces when left clear. (6/1: op 4/1)
Pasja (IRE), outpaced starting the home turn, was sticking on at the finish, and is worth a try over three. (3/1)
Jennyellen (IRE), who had just two outings last season, ran well enough under joint topweight. (12/1: op 8/1)
21* Phalarope (IRE), with a 6lb penalty, was in trouble three out. (3/1)
Dark Silhouette (IRE), looked to have had his measure taken when taking a crashing fall. (5/1)

56 TOTE BOOKMAKERS SUMMER FESTIVAL H'CAP CHASE (0-130) (5-Y.O+) (Class C)

7-50 (7-53) **2m 4f (15 fncs)** £8,689.00 (£2,632.00: £1,286.00: £613.00) GOING minus 0.17 sec per fur (G)

	Horse / details	Dist	Pos	SP	RR	SF
	Bobby Socks (110) (RLee) **10-10-8** RJohnson (w ldrs: led 11th: blnd 2 out: styd on flat)	—	**1**	4/1[2]	121	42
	Wise Approach (130) (KCBailey) **9-12-0** SMcNeill (lw: mde most to 11th: nt qckn appr last)	6	**2**	6/1[3]	136	57
2[6]	**Sword Beach (112)** (MrsMReveley) **12-10-10** PNiven (lw: bhd fr 9th: styd on fr 3 out: nt rch ldrs)	2	**3**	16/1	117	38
	Channel Pastime (102) (DBurchell) **12-9-11**(3) GuyLewis (chsd ldrs: one pce fr 4 out)	1	**4**	16/1	106	27
	Bally Parson (116) (RDickin) **10-10-11**(3) JCulloty (bhd: sme hdwy 4 out: nvr nr to chal)	1½	**5**	11/1	119	40
	Postage Stamp (126) (FMurphy) **9-11-10** PCarberry (prom: rdn & outpcd 4 out: n.d after)	½	**6**	7/2[1]	128	49
2[F]	**Cross Cannon (115)** (JAHellens) **10-10-13** RDunwoody (jnd ldrs 10th: wknd appr 2 out)	hd	**7**	7/1	117	38
	Strong Sound (103) (PCheesbrough) **9-9-12**(3) GCahill (lw: w ldrs tl stirrup leather broke bef 9th: p.u bef next)		**P**	8/1	—	—
	Shaarid (USA) (112) (IABalding) **8-10-10** JOsborne (in tch tl wknd 10th: bhd whn p.u bef 3 out)		**P**	4/1[2]	—	—
				(SP 120.2%)		**9 Rn**

4m 51.4 (2.70 under best) (0.40) CSF £27.27 CT £322.18 TOTE £4.50: £1.70 £2.40 £3.10 (£12.10) Trio £113.20 OWNER Risk Factor Partnership (PRESTEIGNE)
LONG HANDICAP Channel Pastime 9-5

Bobby Socks, raised 7lb for his win here on his only outing last term, survived a blunder at the second last and seems at least as good as ever. (4/1: op 6/1)
Wise Approach ran well under topweight, but his high rating means he will struggle to find opportunities through the summer. (6/1: op 4/1)
Sword Beach dropped himself out down the back straight. Ridden with a view to regaining his confidence, he was staying on in good style at the death. (16/1)
Postage Stamp did not show much sparkle. (7/2)
Strong Sound, turned out in tremendous shape, had no option but to pull up when a leather broke. (8/1)

57 LINCOLNSHIRE ECHO H'CAP CHASE (0-110) (5-Y.O+) (Class E)

8-20 (8-22) **3m 1f (19 fncs)** £4,703.25 (£1,416.00: £685.50: £320.25) GOING minus 0.17 sec per fur (G)

	Horse / details	Dist	Pos	SP	RR	SF
2[3]	**East Houston (96)** (JJO'Neill) **7-11-5** APMcCoy (trckd ldrs: led 3 out: sn rdn clr: eased towards fin)	—	**1**	3/1[2]	107	39
	Knockumshin (84) (JohnUpson) **13-10-7** RSupple (hdwy 13th: sn chsng ldrs: kpt on sme pce fr 3 out)	8	**2**	10/1	90	22
	Cosmic Force (NZ) (83) (HOliver) **12-10-6v** JacquiOliver (j.rt: prom tl lost pl 11th: hdwy to chse ldrs 14th: led next to 3 out: wandered: one pce)	1½	**3**	25/1	88	20
	Storm Warrior (77) (TWall) **11-9-11b**(3) RMassey (chsd ldrs: blnd 14th: mstke 3 out: one pce)	3	**4**	25/1	80	12
	Maggots Green (77) (JMBradley) **9-10-0** RJohnson (led to 15th: wkng whn hit 2 out)	13	**5**	16/1	72	4
	Adrien (FR) (103) (FMurphy) **8-11-12b** PCarberry (nt j.w: hld up & bhd: effrt 15th: sn rdn: nvr nr to chal)	7	**6**	11/4[1]	93	25
	K C'S Dancer (83) (RDickin) **11-10-3**(3) JCulloty (chsd ldrs: rdn 12th: wknd 15th)	9	**7**	16/1	67	—
	Gale Ahead (IRE) (104) (GMMoore) **6-11-13** NBentley (hld up: rdn & lost tch 14th: t.o)	dist	**8**	4/1[3]	—	—
	Regardless (77) (JPLeigh) **14-9-11**(3) KGaule (chsd ldrs: drvn along 13th: hit next: blnd 15th: sn wknd: t.o)	14	**9**	25/1	—	—

	Horse	Dist	Pos	SP	RR	SF
	Winnie Lorraine (99) (RHAlner) **11-11-3**(5) PHenley (wnt prom 10th: wknd 15th: bhd whn p.u bef 3 out)		**P**	6/1	—	—
	Romany King (102) (KCBailey) **12-11-11** JOsborne (pushed along & lost pl 7th: bhd whn p.u bef 4 out)		**P**	8/1	—	—
				(SP 129.5%)	**11 Rn**	

6m 16.3 (5.30) CSF £33.86 CT £594.05 TOTE £3.60: £1.10 £2.50 £9.40 (£18.30) Trio £102.20 OWNER Highgreen Partnership (PENRITH) BRED J. R. Mitchell

LONG HANDICAP Storm Warrior 9-9 Maggots Green 9-7

OFFICIAL EXPLANATION **Adrien (FR): made several jumping errors and lost interest.**

2 **East Houston** came here on the back of a losing sequence stretching to nine, but the Champion soon made his mind up for him in this weak contest. (3/1)

Knockumshin, now a veteran, ran his heart out. (10/1: 8/1-12/1)

Cosmic Force (NZ), lightly-raced and out of form for a long time, wandered about badly under pressure. (25/1)

Adrien (FR) lacked confidence in his jumping. (11/4: 7/4-3/1)

Gale Ahead (IRE) did not take the eye in the paddock and was in trouble a long way out. (4/1)

58 ROTARY CLUB NOVICES' HURDLE (4-Y.O+) (Class D)

8-50 (8-54) **2m 3f 110y (10 hdls)** £2,924.00 (£872.00: £416.00: £188.00) GOING minus 0.17 sec per fur (G)

	Horse	Dist	Pos	SP	RR	SF
	River Room (KCBailey) **6-11-0** JOsborne (led to 3 out: styd on u.p to ld towards fin)	—	**1**	10/1 3	70	11
1*	**Muzrak (CAN) (96)** (MDHammond) **5-11-6** RGarritty (trckd ldr: rdn to ld 3 out: hrd rdn flat: just ct)	hd	**2**	Evens 1	76	17
7*	**Tukano (CAN) (93)** (JRJenkins) **5-11-6** APMcCoy (chsd ldrs: n.m.r after 3 out: hrd rdn & one pce between last 2)	2	**3**	13/8 2	74	15
	Simon Says (RCraggs) **6-10-11**(3) BFenton (bit bkwd: rn green: wnt prom 6th: wknd appr 3 out)	dist	**4**	25/1	—	—
	Irbee (MrsPGrainger) **4-10-1**(7) MichaelBrennan (chsd ldrs: outpcd 6th: sn wknd)	1¼	**5**	33/1	—	—
	Oakbury (IRE) (MissLCSiddall) **4-10-8** AThornton (prom: pushed along 6th: sn lost pl)	28	**6**	16/1	—	—
	Clashawan (IRE) (OBrennan) **6-10-9** RichardGuest (bit bkwd: bhd fr 7th: t.o whn p.u bef last)		**P**	25/1	—	—
				(SP 113.7%)	**7 Rn**	

4m 43.3 (10.30) CSF £20.08 TOTE £7.90: £2.40 £1.60 (£5.80) OWNER Mr Douglas Allum (UPPER LAMBOURN) BRED E. Stuart Knape

WEIGHT FOR AGE 4yo-5lb

River Room, a three-parts brother to Royal Gait, looked as if the outing would do him good. Showing the right sort of spirit, he regained the advantage nearing the line. (10/1)

1* Muzrak (CAN), now wearing a tongue-strap after apparently making a noise when winning at Perth, was just outbattled. (Evens)

7* Tukano (CAN), who is not as consistent as his form figures would suggest, does not look 100% in love with the game. (13/8)

59 PROMOTA SUMMER FESTIVAL STANDARD N.H. FLAT RACE (4, 5 & 6-Y.O) (Class H)

9-20 (9-24) **1m 5f 110y** £1,273.00 (£353.00: £169.00)

	Horse	Dist	Pos	SP	RR	SF
	Petit Flora (GHolmes) **4-10-7** RGarritty (lw: hld up: gd hdwy on outside 3f out: led 1f out: hung rt: styd on)	—	**1**	5/2 2	—	—
	Supreme Comfort (IRE) (EMCaine) **4-10-0**(7) MrRThornton (bit bkwd: hdwy 5f out: led 2f out to 1f out: nt qckn fnl f)	1½	**2**	33/1	—	—
	Rocket Ron (OBrennan) **4-10-12** RichardGuest (prom tl lost pl 5f out: styd on again fnl 2f)	1¾	**3**	7/1 3	—	—
	General Monty (PatMitchell) **4-10-12** MissAEmbiricos (mde most to 2f out: kpt on sme pce)	½	**4**	10/1	—	—
	Flame of Dance (AStreeter) **5-11-3** TEley (hld up: hdwy 5f out: sn rdn: outpcd fnl 2f)	¾	**5**	7/1 3	—	—
	Saboteuse (JCPoulton) **4-10-7** LO'Hara (lw: swvd s: sn trckng ldrs: effrt 3f out: grad wknd)	1	**6**	20/1	—	—
	Ousefleet Boy (MissMKMilligan) **4-10-9**(3) GCahill (sn trckng ldrs: effrt over 3f out: wknd 2f out)	8	**7**	25/1	—	—
	Tamsin's Gem (MissJBower) **5-10-9**(3) TDascombe (chsd ldrs: outpcd 4f out: lost pl 3f out)	4	**8**	14/1	—	—
	Chief of Khorassan (FR) (SEKettlewell) **4-10-7**(5) STaylor (lw: plld hrd: jnd ldrs after 3f: rdn 3f out: sn btn)	nk	**9**	9/4 1	—	—
	Life of Brian (IRE) (MrsPGrainger) **5-11-3** MrAPhillips (chsd ldrs tl rdn & wknd over 2f out)	nk	**10**	20/1	—	—
	Bugsysiegel (TWall) **6-11-0**(3) RMassey (bhd & rn wd over 3f out: t.o)	16	**11**	25/1	—	—
				(SP 120.3%)	**11 Rn**	

3m 20.9 CSF £67.32 TOTE £2.90: £1.60 £5.60 £2.10 (£100.90) Trio Not won; £144.35 to 17/6/96 OWNER Mr G. W. Singleton (PICKERING) BRED G. W. and M. Singleton

OFFICIAL EXPLANATION **Chief of Khorassan (FR): pulled too hard and refused to settle.**

Petit Flora, who looked very fit, took this very moderate bumper, despite a marked tendency to hang right. (5/2)

Supreme Comfort (IRE) ran really well, despite looking burly, and this does not say much for those behind her. (33/1)

Rocket Ron, badly tapped for toe turning out of the back straight, was staying on again at the finish. (7/1)

General Monty (10/1: op 5/1)

Flame of Dance (7/1: 4/1-8/1)

Chief of Khorassan (FR) did not help his cause by refusing to settle. (9/4: op 6/4)

T/Plpt: £262.50 (40 Tckts). T/Qdpt: £120.40 (5.61 Tckts). WG

54-MARKET RASEN (R-H) (Good to firm)

Saturday June 15th

WEATHER: fine & sunny

60 TOTE BOOKMAKERS NOVICES' HURDLE (4-Y.O+) (Class D)

2-10 (2-10) **3m (12 hdls)** £2,974.50 (£891.00: £428.00: £196.50) GOING minus 0.29 sec per fur (GF)

	Horse	Dist	Pos	SP	RR	SF
	Santella Boy (USA) (90) (CJMann) **4-10-9** APMcCoy (trckd ldrs: led 2 out: drvn clr appr last)	—	**1**	7/2 2	77	—
	Tipping The Line (102) (MCPipe) **6-11-9** RJohnson (lw: w ldrs: led after 3 out: hdd 2 out: nt qckn)	6	**2**	9/2	80	—
	Big Treat (IRE) (78) (PWHiatt) **4-10-6**(3) EHusband (s.s: wnt prom 5th: one pce fr 2 out)	3	**3**	14/1	71	—
	Sujud (IRE) (MrsJRRamsden) **4-10-4** MDwyer (lw: blnd 2nd: shkn up 5th: hdwy u.p 9th: sn chsng ldrs: outpcd fr 2 out)	4	**4**	3/1 1	63	—
31 2	**Pembridge Place (94)** (GFJohnsonHoughton) **5-11-2** AThornton (lw: mde most: hit 9th: hdd after 3 out: wknd between last 2)	4	**5**	4/1 3	66	—
	Apache Raider (FMurphy) **4-10-9** PCarberry (bit bkwd: bhd: hdwy u.p 9th: nvr nr ldrs)	3½	**6**	20/1	63	—

Horse	Dist	Pos	SP	RR	SF
Young Kenny (99) (PBeaumont) **5-11-9** RSupple (hld up: bhd tl sme hdwy 7th: sn lost pl)	dist	**7**	8/1	—	—
Patscilla (65) (RDickin) **5-10-8**(3) JCulloty (mid div: drvn along 9th: sn wknd)	16	**8**	50/1	—	—
Classic Crest (IRE) (85) (GMMoore) **5-11-9v** NBentley (chsd ldrs to 6th: sn lost pl)	20	**9**	14/1	—	—
Tremble (MESowersby) **7-11-2** JOsborne (w ldrs: mstke & lost pl 8th: bhd whn p.u bef 2 out)		**P**	33/1	—	—
Timur's Star (JParkes) **7-10-11** RichardGuest (in tch tl lost pl 5th: t.o whn p.u bef 9th)		**P**	50/1	—	—
Swiss Comfort (IRE) (EMCaine) **5-10-4**(7) MrRThornton (unruly: blnd 2nd: bhd tl p.u bef 8th)		**P**	50/1	—	—
Political Skirmish (IPark) **7-10-11** LO'Hara (sn bhd: t.o whn p.u bef 2 out)		**P**	66/1	—	—

(SP 124.9%) **13 Rn**

5m 57.5 (18.50) CSF £19.54 TOTE £6.60: £1.10 £1.70 £3.20 (£18.60) Trio £48.40 OWNER The Link Leasing Partnership (UPPER LAMBOURN) BRED Galbreaph - Phillips Racing Partnership
WEIGHT FOR AGE 4yo-7lb

Santella Boy (USA) proved well suited by the step up in distance. (7/2)
Tipping The Line was another who appreciated three miles for the first time. (9/2)
Big Treat (IRE), stepped right up in distance, ran his best race for some time. (14/1)
Sujud (IRE) is beginning to look a disappointing type both over hurdles and on the Flat. (3/1)

61 LINCS FM NOVICES' CHASE (5-Y.O+) (Class D)

2-40 (2-42) **2m 1f 110y (13 fncs)** £4,323.00 (£1,299.00: £627.00: £291.00) GOING minus 0.29 sec per fur (GF)

Horse	Dist	Pos	SP	RR	SF
Robert's Toy (IRE) (116) (MCPipe) **5-11-3b** APMcCoy (chsd ldrs: hit 4th: led after 9th: wnt clr after next: eased flat)	—	**1**	6/4[1]	111	1
Micherado (FR) (92) (SABrookshaw) **6-11-9** PCarberry (j.b: led: blnd 9th: sn hdd & wknd)	16	**2**	6/1	96	—
Dear Emily (JESwiers) **8-10-11** RJohnson (hit 1st: sme hdwy whn blnd 8th: kpt on fr 3 out)	1¾	**3**	25/1	83	—
Lowawatha (103) (MrsEHHeath) **8-11-9** AThornton (lw: chsd ldrs: rdn 9th: sn wknd)	6	**4**	3/1[2]	89	—
Miss Dotty (MCPipe) **6-10-11** RFarrant (nt j.w: sn bhd: t.o 7th)	29	**5**	14/1	51	—
Colway Prince (IRE) (APJones) **8-11-2** SMcNeill (hdwy 8th: mod 4th whn fell 4 out)		**F**	20/1	—	—
Sherwood Boy (KCBailey) **7-11-2** JOsborne (blnd 2nd: wkng whn hmpd 8th: bhd whn p.u bef 3 out)		**P**	4/1[3]	—	—

(SP 114.6%) **7 Rn**

4m 25.8 (10.80) CSF £10.49 TOTE £2.00: £1.10 £3.30 (£9.70) OWNER Mr Clive Smith (WELLINGTON) BRED M. Conaghan
WEIGHT FOR AGE 5yo-6lb

Robert's Toy (IRE), with the blinkers on again, took a while to warm to his task, but he sprinted clear on the final turn and should continue to do well. (6/4)
Micherado (FR) hardly jumped a fence properly. (6/1)
Dear Emily, a maiden pointer, was making her debut over regulation fences. (25/1)
Lowawatha was unable to dominate and called it a day. (3/1)

62 SUMMER FESTIVAL H'CAP HURDLE (0-130) (4-Y.O+) (Class C)

3-10 (3-10) **2m 1f 110y (8 hdls)** £8,559.00 (£2,592.00: £1,266.00: £603.00) GOING minus 0.29 sec per fur (GF)

Horse	Dist	Pos	SP	RR	SF
Mister Drum (IRE) (120) (MJWilkinson) **7-11-4** MDwyer (trckd ldrs: stumbled bnd after 1st: led 5th: styd on u.p flat: all out)	—	**1**	3/1[1]	101	32
Suivez (123) (MrsNMacauley) **6-11-7** PHide (trckd ldrs: chal 2 out: nt qckn nr fin)	nk	**2**	4/1[2]	104	35
Magslad (112) (JJO'Neill) **6-10-10** APMcCoy (prom: hmpd bnd after 1st: rdn & outpcd 3 out: styd on wl appr last)	2	**3**	7/1	91	22
Non Vintage (IRE) (130) (MCChapman) **5-11-7**(7) GSupple (w ldrs: led 3rd to 5th: 5th & rdn whn blnd 2 out: styd on flat)	2½	**4**	11/2[3]	107	38
No Light (106) (MrsIMcKie) **9-10-4** LHarvey (hld up: hdwy 3 out: one pce fr next)	nk	**5**	8/1	82	13
Glenugie (104) (GMMoore) **5-10-2v** NBentley (chsd ldrs: lost pl 4th: styd on between last 2)	2½	**6**	9/1	78	9
Sassiver (USA) (102) (PAKelleway) **6-10-0b** PCarberry (chsd ldrs: rdn & outpcd 3 out: kpt on flat)	3	**7**	16/1	73	4
Sylvan Sabre (IRE) (112) (KAMorgan) **7-10-7**(3) RMassey (led to 3rd: wknd 2 out: fin lame)	7	**8**	10/1	77	8
Wamdha (IRE) (107) (KAMorgan) **6-10-5**ow2 AThornton (a in rr)	9	**9**	8/1	64	—
Bures (IRE) (122) (MHTompkins) **5-11-3v**(3) KGaule (in tch: rdn 5th: sn lost pl)	28	**10**	9/1	53	—

(SP 130.1%) **10 Rn**

4m 5.8 (2.80) CSF £16.67 CT £76.91 TOTE £3.50: £1.60 £2.40 £1.90 (£9.00) Trio £20.10 OWNER Mr Malcolm Batchelor (BANBURY)
LONG HANDICAP Sassiver (USA) 9-4

Mister Drum (IRE), 6lb higher than when winning impressively here two weeks ago in record time, had reportedly been held up in his preparation since. Racing keenly, he showed the right sort of spirit to hang on. He will probably be even better over an extra half-mile. (3/1)
Suivez settled well in a fast-run race. He battled on all the way to the line, but was always just going to come off second best. (4/1)
Magslad, badly tapped for toe starting the home turn, was staying on when it was all over and will be better over two and a half miles. (7/1)
Non Vintage (IRE) had much more use made of him than usual, but looks to be in the grip of the Handicapper at present. (11/2: 4/1-6/1)
No Light likes to come from off the pace and ran satisfactorily on ground faster than he prefers. (8/1)

63 SYSTEMATIC PRINTING H'CAP CHASE (0-125) (5-Y.O+) (Class D)

3-45 (3-45) **2m 1f 110y (13 fncs)** £4,618.75 (£1,390.00: £672.50: £313.75) GOING minus 0.29 sec per fur (GF)

Horse	Dist	Pos	SP	RR	SF
Rodeo Star (USA) (100) (NTinkler) **10-10-12b** RGarritty (hld up: trckd ldrs: hit 4 out: styd on wl to ld flat)	—	**1**	9/2[3]	113	34
15* **Saskia's Hero (110)** (JFBottomley) **9-11-8** DerekByrne (hld up: hdwy 8th: led 2 out tl flat: unable qckn)	4	**2**	100/30[2]	119	40
Rupples (88) (MCChapman) **9-10-0** WWorthington (in tch: drvn along & oufpcd 8th: hit 2 out: kpt on)	13	**3**	25/1	86	7
Super Sharp (NZ) (89) (HOliver) **8-10-1** JacquiOliver (mstkes: w ldrs: led 4 out: hdd & blnd 2 out: sn wknd)	½	**4**	14/1	86	7
Sydney Barry (NZ) (93) (RHBuckler) **11-10-5** BPowell (led to 4 out: wkng whn hmpd next)	14	**5**	10/1	77	—
Oscail An Doras (IRE) (110) (FMurphy) **7-11-8** PCarberry (dwlt s: mstkes: effrt 8th: btn whn hit 4 out)	20	**6**	11/4[1]	76	—
Persian Tactics (116) (KCBailey) **7-12-0** JOsborne (lw: nvr gng wl: bhd & pushed along 5th: t.o 4 out)	6	**7**	6/1	76	—
Strong Approach (108) (JIACharlton) **11-11-6** APMcCoy (lw: chsd ldrs: 3rd & ev ch whn fell 3 out: dead)		**F**	9/2[3]	—	—

(SP 120.0%) **8 Rn**

4m 16.1 (1.10) CSF £19.80 CT £313.54 TOTE £5.80: £1.60 £2.20 £2.60 (£8.80) OWNER Mr J. C. Bradbury (MALTON) BRED Tartan Farms Corp. in USA
LONG HANDICAP Rupples 9-13

Rodeo Star (USA), who hit the front far too soon last time, scored decisively here in the end. His rider dismounted at the line, but it turned out he had only rapped himself at the fourth last. (9/2)
15* Saskia's Hero, who had shot up in the weights, could not match the winner for toe on the run-in. (100/30)
Rupples, an inconsistent individual, ran one of his better races. (25/1)
Super Sharp (NZ), a headstrong type, was let down by his jumping. Wandering about badly under pressure, he was out on his feet when falling through the second last. (14/1)
Oscail An Doras (IRE), an excitable sort, gave away ground at the start. Taken off his legs, his jumping suffered. (11/4)
Persian Tactics, who looked to have been given more than his fair share of weight, was never going at any stage. (6/1: op 7/2)

64 SCUNTHORPE SLAG NOVICES' H'CAP CHASE (0-105) (5-Y.O+) (Class D)

4-15 (4-15) **2m 6f 110y (15 fncs)** £4,107.00 (£1,236.00: £598.00: £279.00) GOING minus 0.29 sec per fur (GF)

	Horse		Pos	SP	RR	SF
	Daringly (71) (RCurtis) **7-10-3** DMorris (hld up: jnd ldrs 11th: led appr 3 out: drvn out)	—	1	14/1	87	26
	Southerly Gale (94) (MCPipe) **9-11-7**(5) MrAFarrant (chsd ldrs: led 10th tl appr 3 out: no ch w wnr)	6	2	6/1^{3}	106	45
11^{2}	**Gone by (IRE) (86)** (JRJenkins) **8-11-4** APMcCoy (hld up: effrt 11th: outpcd appr 3 out)	10	3	3/1^{1}	91	30
	Gorby's Myth (73) (JPLeigh) **6-10-2**(3) KGaule (hld up: hdwy 10th: no imp appr 3 out)	3	4	5/1^{2}	76	15
	Tour Leader (NZ) (89) (RHBuckler) **7-11-7** BPowell (in tch: effrt 4 out: sn outpcd)	8	5	8/1	86	25
	Killy's Filly (68) (JMBradley) **6-9-11**(3) BFenton (lw: hld up: 4th & effrt whn blnd 4 out: no ch after)	16	6	25/1	53	—
	Little Thyne (68) (DrPPritchard) **11-10-0b1** DrPPritchard (s.s: a bhd: t.o 9th)	dist	7	33/1	—	—
	Its Grand (69) (JMBradley) **7-10-1** RJohnson (blnd 2nd & 5th: sn wl bhd: t.o whn p.u bef 4 out)		P	10/1	—	—
	Lo-Flying Missile (68) (RDickin) **8-9-11**(3) JCulloty (w ldrs: led 9th: hdd next: wknd 4 out: p.u bef next)		P	6/1^{3}	—	—
	Darleyfordbay (78) (KCBailey) **7-10-10** AThornton (p.u after 8th: sddle slipped)		P	11/1	—	—
	Willie Makeit (IRE) (72) (RTPhillips) **6-10-4** JOsborne (led to 9th: sn lost pl: bhd whn p.u bef 3 out)		P	10/1	—	—

(SP 121.3%) **11 Rn**

5m 28.3 (1.30) CSF £90.74 CT £298.45 TOTE £24.40: £4.80 £3.30 £1.50 (£70.00) Trio £110.60 OWNER Mr Michael Appleby (LAMBOURN) BRED R. Lloyd
LONG HANDICAP Lo-Flying Missile 9-13 Little Thyne 9-9
OFFICIAL EXPLANATION **Gorby's Myth: gurgled throughout the race.**
Daringly, a safe jumper - he finished ninth in the Fox Hunters' at Aintree - scored in decisive fashion. (14/1)
Southerly Gale did nothing wrong at all on this occasion. (6/1)
11 Gone by (IRE) is proving somewhat disappointing over fences. (3/1)
Gorby's Myth, whose jumping has apparently come under close scrutiny, looked to travel strongly but his rider reported that he was gurgling all the way round. (5/1)

65 PETER RHODES NOVICES' H'CAP HURDLE (0-100) (4-Y.O+) (Class E)

4-50 (4-50) **2m 1f 110y (8 hdls)** £2,425.00 (£675.00: £325.00) GOING minus 0.29 sec per fur (GF)

	Horse		Pos	SP	RR	SF
	Karinska (90) (MCChapman) **6-11-4** WWorthington (lw: hld up: hdwy 3 out: ev ch whn blnd 2 out: styd on u.p to ld last strides)	—	1	8/1	72	26
	Pickens (USA) (92) (NTinkler) **4-10-12**(3) EHusband (hld up: hdwy 3 out: rdn next: led after last tl nr fin)	hd	2	13/2^{3}	74	23
	Plinth (74) (NAGraham) **5-10-2** APMcCoy (sn chsng ldr: rdn to ld 5th: hdd after last: one pce)	2	3	3/1^{1}	54	8
5*	**Bourdonner (85)** (MDHammond) **4-10-8** RGarritty (mde most to 5th: 4th & ev ch whn blnd last: one pce)	1¼	4	3/1^{1}	64	13
	Little Tincture (IRE) (72) (MrsTJMcInnesSkinner) **6-10-0** DLeahy (sn bhd: rdn along 5th: styd on fr 2 out)	4	5	33/1	47	1
	Reefa's Mill (IRE) (86) (JNeville) **4-10-9v** PCarberry (prom: effrt 5th: sn chsng ldrs: wknd after 2 out)	2½	6	10/1	59	8
	Cavil (77) (WClay) **4-9-11**(3) GuyLewis (prom: drvn along 4th: lost pl next)	16	7	5/1^{2}	35	—
	Coneygree (77) (JWharton) **4-10-0** BDalton (chsd ldrs tl lost pl after 3 out: fin lame)	6	8	16/1	30	—
	Limited Liability (100) (PRWebber) **6-12-0** MDwyer (swtg: hld up & bhd: plld hrd: lost tch 5th: bhd whn p.u bef 2 out)		P	9/1	—	—
	Astrolabe (77) (JMBradley) **4-10-0** RJohnson (chsd ldrs: rdn 3rd: sn wl outpcd: bhd whn p.u bef 2 out)		P	20/1	—	—
	Red Light (88) (JRJenkins) **4-10-11v** JOsborne (bhd fr 3 out: p.u bef next)		P	12/1	—	—
	Crambella (IRE) (81) (GPKelly) **4-10-4**ow4 RichardGuest (sn bhd: t.o 4th: p.u bef 2 out)		P	50/1	—	—
	M'Bebe (72) (KOWarner) **6-10-0** RFarrant (nt j.w: sn bhd: p.u bef 2 out)		P	50/1	—	—

(SP 135.4%) **13 Rn**

4m 7.2 (4.20) CSF £62.14 CT £183.82 TOTE £13.10: £3.30 £2.80 £1.40 (£35.50) Trio £80.00 OWNER Mr Geoff Whiting (MARKET RASEN) BRED Sheikh Mohammed bin Rashid al Maktoum
LONG HANDICAP Cavil 9-11 Little Tincture (IRE) 9-7 Astrolabe 9-2 Coneygree 9-13 Crambella (IRE) 9-10 M'Bebe 8-8
WEIGHT FOR AGE 4yo-5lb
Karinska, out of luck on the Flat last time, jumped better than she had at Cartmel. Even so, she ploughed through the second last but, showing the right sort of spirit, she poked her head in front near the line. (8/1)
Pickens (USA), unlucky here last time, again wore a tongue-strap. After going the best part of a length up after the last, he seemed to slow up and was just caught. (13/2)
Plinth, given a fine attacking ride, lacks anything in the way of finishing speed. (3/1)
5* Bourdonner, raised 10lb for his seven-length win at Perth, was upsides the second and third but coming off the worst when he hit the last hard. (3/1: 2/1-7/2)
Little Tincture (IRE), 7lb out of the handicap, was staying on when it was all over and a modest race can be found for him. (33/1)
Limited Liability, even on a sunny day, was awash with sweat. Dropped out at the start, he is one to have reservations about. (9/1: 6/1-10/1)

T/Plpt: £31.30 (314.77 Tckts). T/Qdpt: £6.50 (74.15 Tckts). WG

19-WORCESTER (L-H) (Good to firm)

Wednesday June 19th

WEATHER: cloudy

66 ST MARTINS (S) H'CAP HURDLE (0-90) (4-Y.O+) (Class G)

6-45 (6-48) **2m (8 hdls)** £2,185.00 (£610.00: £295.00) GOING minus 0.19 sec per fur (G)

Horse		Pos	SP	RR	SF
Highly Reputable (IRE) (81) (GCBravery) **6-11-8** RDunwoody (a.p: led 3 out: drvn out)	—	1	6/1^{2}	63	29

Form	Horse	Dist	Pos	SP	RR	SF
	Fluidity (USA) (87) (JGMO'Shea) **8-12-0b** DBridgwater (prom: j.slowly 4th: led 5th to 3 out: r.o one pce flat)	2	**2**	5/1 [1]	67	33
	Milzig (USA) (69) (JJoseph) **7-10-10** CLlewellyn (hld up & bhd: hdwy 3 out: r.o flat)	1	**3**	9/1	48	14
	Most Interesting (64) (GHJones) **11-10-2**(3) BFenton (hld up & bhd: hdwy 3 out: r.o flat)	nk	**4**	20/1	43	9
	Mylordmayor (59) (PBowen) **9-9-7**(7) MrRThornton (a.p: ev ch whn mstke 3 out: btn whn mstke last)	2½	**5**	33/1	35	1
	The Executor (76) (JJoseph) **6-11-3** JFrost (hdwy 3 out: one pce flat)	hd	**6**	20/1	52	18
	Becky Boo (72) (DBurchell) **6-10-13** DJBurchell (hdwy 4th: ev ch 3 out: wknd appr last)	hd	**7**	7/1 [3]	48	14
	Stay Happy (FR) (65) (AGNewcombe) **7-10-6**[ow3] AThornton (lw: nvr nr to chal)	¾	**8**	11/1	40	3
17[3]	**Against The Clock (69)** (JWMullins) **4-10-5v[1]** RGreene (hld up & bhd: hdwy appr 3 out: wknd 2 out)	1	**9**	11/1	43	4
17[5]	**Classic Image (IRE) (69)** (HJManners) **6-10-10** MrACharles-Jones (hld up & bhd: sme hdwy 5th: n.d)	1¾	**10**	25/1	42	8
54[3]	**Swiss Mountain (69)** (PJBevan) **6-10-10** WWorthington (prom tl wknd appr 3 out)	5	**11**	8/1	37	3
22[F]	**Kutan (IRE) (65)** (MrsBarbaraWaring) **6-10-6** JRKavanagh (hdwy 5th: wknd 3 out)	2	**12**	12/1	31	—
17[2]	**Parish Walk (IRE) (85)** (KJDrewry) **5-11-12** SWynne (n.d)	2½	**13**	10/1	48	14
	Doctor-J (IRE) (84) (MJWilkinson) **5-11-11** RSupple (lw: a bhd)	5	**14**	14/1	42	8
	Celcius (74) (MCPipe) **12-11-1** CMaude (a bhd)	nk	**15**	16/1	32	—
	Side Bar (67) (KGWingrove) **6-10-3b**(5) PHenley (prom: rdn 3rd: wknd 4th)	18	**16**	20/1	7	—
	Hugh Daniels (76) (BPreece) **8-11-3** GaryLyons (prom tl wknd 3 out)	2	**17**	20/1	14	—
	Orchestral Designs (IRE) (59) (GAHam) **5-9-11**(3) RMassey (a bhd)	2	**18**	40/1	—	—
	Ardearned (59) (MrsJAYoung) **9-10-0** RDavis (a bhd: t.o)	27	**19**	50/1	—	—
	Waaza (USA) (72) (RTPhillips) **7-10-13** JOsborne (bit bkwd: prom: j.slowly 3rd: wknd qckly appr 5th: t.o)	24	**20**	14/1	—	—
	Paid Elation (59) (NRMitchell) **11-9-9**(5) SophieMitchell (led to 5th: wknd qckly: whn p.u bef 3 out)		**P**	50/1	—	—

(SP 149.4%) **21 Rn**

3m 45.4 (5.40) CSF £39.83 CT £272.29 TOTE £8.70: £2.80 £2.10 £4.20 £5.70 (£37.20) Trio £61.10 OWNER Mr Michael Whatley (NEWMARKET) BRED Seahorse Investments

LONG HANDICAP Orchestral Designs (IRE) 9-10 Ardearned 9-5 Paid Elation 9-5

WEIGHT FOR AGE 4yo-5lb

Bt in 5,000 gns

OFFICIAL EXPLANATION **Stay Happy (FR): had lost his confidence after being brought down on his previous run, jumped deliberately early on and ran on through beaten horses.**

Highly Reputable (IRE) was only 1lb higher than when finishing a good third in a similar event at Fakenham in April. (6/1)

Fluidity (USA) ran well following a pipe-opener on the Flat a fortnight ago. (5/1)

Milzig (USA) won over an extra quarter-mile on this course a year ago and found this trip short of his best. (9/1)

Most Interesting has obviously had her training problems but, having slipped down the ratings, ran her best race for a long time. (20/1)

67 WHITBOURNE NOVICES' CLAIMING HURDLE (4-Y.O+) (Class F)

7-15 (7-18) **2m (8 hdls)** £2,129.00 (£594.00: £287.00) GOING minus 0.19 sec per fur (G)

Form	Horse	Dist	Pos	SP	RR	SF
	Night Time (85) (AStreeter) **4-10-0**(5) LAspell (hld up & bhd: hdwy appr 3 out: led flat: r.o wl)	—	**1**	2/1 [1]	61	6
	Betabetcorbett (74) (BPJBaugh) **5-11-2** TEley (led: j.lft 2nd: hdd flat: unable qckn)	3½	**2**	25/1	64	14
	Minnesota Fats (IRE) (67) (MissMERowland) **4-10-5** GaryLyons (a.p: ev ch fr 3 out: one pce flat)	2	**3**	8/1 [3]	56	1
	Pleasant Surprise (FR) (98) (MCPipe) **4-11-11** DBridgwater (rdn 3rd: hdwy appr 3 out: ev ch whn blnd bdly & rdr lost irons last: nt rcvr: fin lame)	¾	**4**	2/1 [1]	75+	20
	Lancer (USA) (85) (RTJuckes) **4-11-3** RDunwoody (hld up: hdwy 5th: hrd rdn 3 out: one pce fr 2 out)	hd	**5**	4/1 [2]	67	12
	Midnight Jestor (IRE) (GEJones) **8-10-7** MSharratt (prom: ev ch 2 out: sn wknd)	8	**6**	33/1	44	—
17[8]	**Woodlands Energy (55)** (PAPritchard) **5-10-11** RDavis (hld up: stdy hdwy appr 3 out: wknd appr 2 out)	6	**7**	12/1	42	—
22[9]	**Frankie Harry** (AWCarroll) **4-10-5** DMorris (hld up & bhd: hdwy appr 3 out: wknd appr 2 out)	3	**8**	33/1	38	—
22[8]	**Laser Light Lady** (NPLittmoden) **4-10-0** BPowell (prom tl wknd 3 out)	18	**9**	40/1	15	—
	Really Neat (LWaring) **10-10-6**(5) SophieMitchell (chsd ldr tl wknd 3 out)	2½	**10**	40/1	18	—
	Pats Folly (FJYardley) **5-10-3** PMcLoughlin (plld hrd: prom tl wknd qckly appr 3 out: t.o whn tried to ref 2 out)	dist	**11**	33/1	—	—
	Bide Our Time (USA) (60) (GraemeRoe) **4-10-6**(7) ShaunGraham (t.o 5th: fell last)		**F**	40/1	—	—

(SP 125.5%) **12 Rn**

3m 47.0 (7.00) CSF £48.00 TOTE £2.90: £1.20 £2.70 £2.60 (£37.20) Trio £127.60; £129.44 to 21/6/96 OWNER Mr D. Bentley (HEDNESFORD) BRED Mrs J. Johnson

WEIGHT FOR AGE 4yo-5lb

Night Time clmd DPugh £3,000

Night Time was reported to have choked and failed to handle the give in the ground when pulled up last time. (2/1)

Betabetcorbett bounced into form and stuck on well up the home straight until failing to cope with the winner on the run-in. (25/1)

Minnesota Fats (IRE), challenging three out, finished much closer to the winner than when they met at Southwell a month ago. (8/1)

Pleasant Surprise (FR) lost all chance when his rider had to make a miraculous recovery at the final flight. (2/1)

68 OVERBURY CLUB ATHLETICA H'CAP CHASE (0-115) (5-Y.O+) (Class E)

7-45 (7-47) **2m 4f 110y (15 fncs)** £3,327.00 (£996.00: £478.00: £219.00) GOING minus 0.19 sec per fur (G)

Form	Horse	Dist	Pos	SP	RR	SF
	Comedy Road (90) (RLee) **12-10-3** RJohnson (hdwy 6th: led 8th to 9th: led after 3 out: hit 2 out: all out)	—	**1**	8/1	102	27
20[3]	**Henley Regatta (94)** (PRRodford) **8-10-7** SBurrough (hld up & bhd: hdwy 8th: led appr 11th: hit 3 out: sn hdd: one pce)	6	**2**	5/1 [3]	101	26
9[2]	**Bitacrack (87)** (JJBirkett) **9-10-0** LO'Hara (prom: lost pl 9th: rallied 11th: one pce fr 4 out)	6	**3**	9/2 [2]	90	15
	Final Pride (100) (PBowen) **10-10-6**(7) MrRThornton (hld up: hdwy to ld 9th: mstke 10th: sn hdd: wknd 4 out)	9	**4**	7/2 [1]	96	21
	Hamper (87) (NRMitchell) **13-9-11b**(3) KGaule (hdwy to ld appr 7th: hdd 8th: wknd 4 out)	1¾	**5**	16/1	81	6
	Drumstick (100) (KCBailey) **10-10-13** AThornton (prom: lost pl 7th: sme hdwy 11th: wknd 4 out)	1½	**6**	6/1	93	18
20[P]	**Castle King (115)** (PRHedger) **9-12-0** BPowell (bhd fr 9th: t.o whn p.u bef 4 out)		**P**	9/1	—	—
	Golden Madjambo (95) (FJordan) **10-10-8** RGreene (led tl appr 3rd: led 5th tl appr 7th: wknd 8th: t.o whn p.u bef 11th)		**P**	5/1 [3]	—	—
	The Lorryman (IRE) (97) (NRMitchell) **8-10-10** GUpton (led appr 3rd to 5th: wknd 8th: t.o whn p.u bef 11th)		**P**	14/1	—	—
	Salcombe Harbour (NZ) (87) (DrPPritchard) **12-10-0** DrPPritchard (a bhd: t.o whn p.u bef 8th)		**P**	33/1	—	—

(SP 124.6%) **10 Rn**

5m 3.9 (2.90) CSF £47.46 CT £191.15 TOTE £8.00: £2.10 £2.00 £1.40 (£30.90) Trio £32.20 OWNER Winsbury Livestock (PRESTEIGNE) BRED Miss G. Newall

LONG HANDICAP Bitacrack 9-9 Salcombe Harbour (NZ) 8-4

Comedy Road, pulled up on his only outing in the last eighteen months, scored off a mark 18lb lower than when he last won two years ago. (8/1)
20 **Henley Regatta**, 10lb higher than when registering his only success, was the only one to make a race of it over the final three fences. (5/1)
9 **Bitacrack**, 5lb wrong at the weights, was effectively running off a mark 11lb higher than when winning at Carlisle in March. (9/2: op 3/1)
Final Pride had a couple of pipe-openers over hurdles last month. (7/2)
Drumstick (6/1: op 4/1)

69 HEREFORD & WORCESTER CHAMBER OF COMMERCE NOVICES' HURDLE (4-Y.O+) (Class E)

8-15 (8-16) **2m 4f (10 hdls)** £2,547.50 (£710.00: £342.50) GOING minus 0.19 sec per fur (G)

	Horse	Dist	Pos	SP	RR	SF
	Sigma Wireless (IRE) (CaptTAForster) **7-11-2** SWynne (hdwy 4th: led 2 out: wnt rt appr last: drvn out)	—	1	5/1	·84	25
	Milngavie (IRE) (BSmart) **6-11-2** CLlewellyn (hit 4th: hdwy 6th: j.slowly 7th: chsd wnr & pckd last: no imp)	4	2	4/1[3]	81	22
	Damas (FR) (103) (MCPipe) **5-11-2v[1]** DBridgwater (hld up: hdwy 4th: wknd flat)	10	3	11/4[2]	73	14
	Dream Here (95) (JCFox) **8-11-2** SFox (hdwy 4th: wknd 2 out)	nk	4	9/4[1]	73	14
	Blennerville (IRE) (MissJBower) **6-10-8**(3) TDascombe (prom: led appr 5th to 2 out: wknd flat)	1¼	5	10/1	67	8
	I Don't Think So (MissKMGeorge) **5-10-11** PMcLoughlin (mstke 2nd: rdn appr 4th: t.o fr 6th)	dist	6	50/1	—	—
	Dickies Girl (NMBabbage) **6-10-8**(3) BFenton (a bhd: t.o fr 6th)	14	7	12/1	—	—
	Saxon Blade (RMStronge) **8-11-2** WMcFarland (plld hrd: led tl after 1st: rdn & wknd qckly after 4th: p.u bef 5th)		P	33/1	—	—
	Classic Jester (IRE) (RChampion) **5-11-2b[1]** BPowell (s.s: a bhd: t.o whn p.u bef 3 out)		P	33/1	—	—
	Mutley (64) (NJHawke) **6-11-2** CMaude (bhd fr 5th: p.u & dismntd flat)		P	25/1	—	—
	Rory'm (IRE) (LWaring) **7-11-2** DLeahy (rdn appr 4th: sn t.o: p.u bef 7th)		P	50/1	—	—
	Miss Spent Youth (JWDufosee) **5-10-6**(5) PHenley (mstke 2nd: bhd whn rdn 5th: t.o whn p.u bef 3 out)		P	50/1	—	—
	Sandford Thyne (IRE) (JNDalton) **6-10-4**(7) MrRThornton (plld hrd: led after 1st tl appr 5th: wknd appr 7th: t.o whn blnd & uns rdr 3 out)		U	50/1	—	—
				(SP 128.5%)	**13 Rn**	

4m 44.4 (6.40) CSF £25.67 TOTE £7.40: £1.50 £1.70 £2.40 (£12.60) Trio £7.20 OWNER Mrs Richard Strachan & Mrs David Lewis (LUDLOW) BRED Killarkin Stud
OFFICIAL EXPLANATION **Saxon Blade: finished distressed.**
Sigma Wireless (IRE) won a Navan bumper just over two years ago and finished a good second over this trip at Down Royal last month. (5/1)
Milngavie (IRE), a bit novicey at some of his hurdles, should stay further on his Flat form. (4/1)
Damas (FR) was tried in a visor on this return to timber. (11/4)
Dream Here found his measure taken at the penultimate hurdle. (9/4)
Blennerville (IRE) (10/1: op 50/1)
Dickies Girl (12/1: 8/1-14/1)

70 GREEN STREET NOVICES' CHASE (5-Y.O+) (Class E)

8-45 (8-46) **2m 7f (18 fncs)** £3,535.00 (£1,060.00: £510.00: £235.00) GOING minus 0.19 sec per fur (G)

	Horse	Dist	Pos	SP	RR	SF
	Fly the Wind (MCPipe) **11-10-11** DBridgwater (led 4th: clr 10th: mstke last: eased flat)	—	1	7/2[3]	91+	—
19P	**Red Eikon** (GHolmes) **5-10-8** RichardGuest (hld up: mstke 11th: gd hdwy appr last: r.o wl: no ch w wnr)	9	2	33/1	89	—
30[5]	**Manor Rhyme (74)** (JCMcConnochie) **9-11-2** SWynne (sn wl bhd: gd hdwy appr last: r.o wl)	hd	3	20/1	90	—
	Dustys Trail (IRE) (PBowen) **7-10-9**(7) MrRThornton (prom to 10th: n.d after)	7	4	10/1	85	—
	Spy Dessa (60) (AGNewcombe) **8-11-2** AThornton (prom to 9th)	4	5	33/1	82	—
13[4]	**Hizal (72)** (HJManners) **7-11-2** MrACharles-Jones (nvr nr ldrs)	¾	6	16/1	82	—
	Cracking Idea (IRE) (84) (JACEdwards) **8-11-9b** RDunwoody (prom tl wknd 11th)	¾	7	9/1	88	—
	Sea Search (87) (PBowen) **9-11-2** RJohnson (prom: blnd 9th: wknd 11th: bhd whn blnd 4 out)	3	8	8/1	79	—
30[2]	**Ballyline (IRE)** (WTKemp) **5-10-8** RSupple (led to 4th: wknd 11th: t.o)	24	9	3/1[1]	61	—
30[8]	**Welsh's Gamble** (RHAlner) **7-11-2** WMcFarland (bhd fr 10th: t.o)	11	10	33/1	55	—
23[5]	**Artful Arthur (73)** (LPGrassick) **10-11-2** MrJGrassick (a bhd: t.o whn fell 4 out)		F	50/1	—	—
	Pink Sunset (IRE) (CTNash) **8-11-2** CMaude (fell 2nd)		F	33/1	—	—
	Brora Rose (IRE) (64) (PRRodford) **8-10-11b** SBurrough (a bhd: t.o 9th: p.u bef 3 out)		P	33/1	—	—
14[5]	**Brindley House (82)** (JWhite) **9-11-2** DMorris (bhd fr 10th: t.o whn p.u bef 13th)		P	10/1	—	—
	Arr Eff Bee (JPSmith) **9-11-2b** TEley (t.o 9th: p.u bef 4 out)		P	50/1	—	—
13[3]	**Top Spin** (JRJenkins) **7-11-2** JOsborne (nt j.w: wl bhd fr 5th: t.o whn p.u bef 4 out)		P	100/30[2]	—	—
	Bengazee (IRE) (BShaw) **8-11-2** VSlattery (blnd & uns rdr 1st)		U	50/1	—	—
				(SP 140.8%)	**17 Rn**	

5m 54.5 (16.50) CSF £113.27 TOTE £6.40: £2.40 £8.40 £6.60 (£108.80) Trio Not won; £183.25 to 21/6/96 OWNER Mrs Pam Pengelly (WELLINGTON) BRED Miss P. E. Decker
WEIGHT FOR AGE 5yo-7lb
Fly the Wind has obviously benefited from the Pipe touch and was at least twenty-five lengths clear when eased to a walk on the flat. (7/2)
Red Eikon, on his debut over fences, finished with a flourish in the separate battle for the runner-up spot. (33/1)
Manor Rhyme appreciated this longer trip, and came from a long way back to contest the minor honours. (20/1)
Dustys Trail (IRE) (10/1: op 6/1)
30 **Ballyline (IRE)** could not go the pace on the final circuit. (3/1)
13 **Top Spin** (100/30: op 2/1)

71 HIGH GREEN H'CAP HURDLE (0-120) (4-Y.O+) (Class D)

9-15 (9-17) **2m 4f (10 hdls)** £3,965.50 (£1,189.00: £572.00: £263.50) GOING minus 0.19 sec per fur (G)

	Horse	Dist	Pos	SP	RR	SF
	Nine O Three (IRE) (96) (AGNewcombe) **7-10-9** AThornton (hld up: hdwy 7th: led 2 out: rdn out)	—	1	9/2[2]	79	35
	Shikaree (IRE) (111) (MCPipe) **5-11-10** DBridgwater (hdwy appr 5th: ev ch 2 out: no imp)	6	2	7/1	89	45
21[2]	**Call the Guv'nor (96)** (NJHenderson) **7-10-9** JRKavanagh (hld up: hdwy 6th: led 3 out tl mstke 2 out: sn wknd)	6	3	3/1[1]	69	25
	First Class (94) (GNAlford) **6-10-7** RGreene (hld up: hdwy 7th: one pce fr 3 out)	2½	4	14/1	65	21
	Ray River (93) (KGWingrove) **4-10-0** JRyan (hld up: hdwy 5th: led appr 3 out: sn hdd: wknd 2 out)	2	5	16/1	63	13
	Sticky Money (97) (MCPipe) **8-10-10** CMaude (led to 2nd: hrd rdn appr 5th: wknd 3 out)	11	6	9/1	58	14
	Kippanour (USA) (115) (CJMann) **4-11-8b** RDunwoody (prom: led 5th tl appr 3 out: sn wknd)	2	7	13/2[3]	74	24
	Admiralty Way (95) (RBrotherton) **10-10-8** LHarvey (hld up & bhd: hdwy 7th: wkng whn blnd 3 out)	18	8	33/1	40	—
	Holy Joe (105) (AJWilson) **14-11-4** DJBurchell (bhd fr 6th)	½	9	25/1	50	6

		Dist	Pos	SP	RR	SF
27^4	**Sweet Noble (IRE) (87)** (KJDrewry) **7-10-0** MSharratt (led 2nd to 5th: wknd 7th)	9	**10**	20/1	24	—
	Beam Me Up Scotty (IRE) (94) (NJHawke) **7-10-7** CLlewellyn (prom to 7th: t.o)	30	**11**	25/1	7	—
	Batty's Island (109) (BPreece) **7-11-8v^1** GaryLyons (bit bkwd: prom: rdn 5th: wknd qckly appr 7th: t.o)	dist	**12**	20/1	—	—
	Twice the Groom (IRE) (90) (RLee) **6-10-3** PMcLoughlin (s.i.s: mid div whn fell 3rd)		**F**	10/1	—	—
21^5	**How's it Goin (IRE) (98)** (WRMuir) **5-10-11** MRichards (dwlt: fell 4th)		**F**	12/1	—	—

(SP 128.5%) **14 Rn**

4m 39.9 (1.90) CSF £36.07 CT £104.63 TOTE £7.70: £2.80 £3.20 £2.30 (£100.30) Trio £94.90 OWNER Bideford Tool Ltd (BARNSTAPLE) BRED Edmond Cronin

LONG HANDICAP Ray River 9-11 Sweet Noble (IRE) 9-11

WEIGHT FOR AGE 4yo-6lb

Nine O Three (IRE), 9lb higher than when winning at Taunton in March, showed he does not need soft ground and was ridden to get the trip. (9/2)

Shikaree (IRE) probably had a tough task at the weights. (7/1: op 9/2)

21 Call the Guv'nor, 6lb higher than when throwing away his chance last time, did not seem so effective over this extra half-mile. (3/1)

Sticky Money (9/1: 6/1-10/1)

Twice the Groom (IRE) (10/1: 6/1-12/1)

T/Plpt: £161.50 (62.47 Tckts). T/Qdpt: £47.00 (17.82 Tckts). KH

STRATFORD-ON-AVON (L-H) (Good to firm, Good patches)

Thursday June 20th

WEATHER: overcast

72

DUDLEY CASTLE AND ZOO 'AS YOU LIKE IT' NOVICES' CHASE (5-Y.O+) (Class E)
6-45 (6-48) **2m 4f (15 fncs)** £3,324.00 (£1,002.00: £486.00: £228.00) GOING minus 0.12 sec per fur (G)

		Dist	Pos	SP	RR	SF
20^P	**Nadjati (USA) (96)** (DRGandolfo) **7-11-0v^1** RDunwoody (hld up: hdwy 9th: led 4 out tl flat: led last stride)	—	**1**	4/1^2	97	17
	Simply (IRE) (TPMcGovern) **7-11-0** PHide (led 3rd to 10th: led 11th to 4 out: led flat: hdd last stride)	s.h	**2**	11/4^1	97	17
	Legal Artist (IRE) (MissCJohnsey) **6-11-0** LHarvey (hld up: 4th & btn whn mstke 2 out)	13	**3**	12/1	87	7
	Beat The Rap (DMorris) **10-11-0v^1** RichardGuest (swtg: prom tl wknd appr 2 out)	3½	**4**	50/1	84	4
66^2	**Fluidity (USA)** (JGMO'Shea) **8-11-0b** DBridgwater (s.s: hld up & plld hrd: hdwy 9th: mstke 11th: wknd appr 2 out)	6	**5**	11/4^1	79	—
	Duke of Dreams (72) (RJBaker) **6-11-0** BPowell (prom: led 10th to 11th: wknd appr 2 out)	6	**6**	12/1	74	—
	The Foolish One (RHAlner) **9-10-9** RJohnson (swtg: hld up: hdwy appr 11th: wknd appr 3 out)	1½	**7**	9/1^3	68	—
61^5	**Miss Dotty** (MCPipe) **6-10-9** RFarrant (bhd fr 11th: t.o fr 3 out)	10	**8**	14/1	60	—
13^P	**Prince Rockaway (IRE)** (NMLampard) **8-10-11**(3) GuyLewis (led to 3rd: j.slowly 3rd: wknd 11th: t.o)	13	**9**	20/1	55	—
	April Cruise (LASnook) **9-10-9** GUpton (nt j.w: a bhd: t.o whn p.u bef 9th)		**P**	50/1	—	—
	Musical Vocation (IRE) (BPreece) **5-10-2b** GaryLyons (bhd: mstke 5th: t.o whn p.u bef 2 out)		**P**	50/1	—	—

(SP 116.0%) **11 Rn**

4m 59.0 (3.00) CSF £14.44 TOTE £3.20: £1.60 £1.30 £5.40 (£6.10) Trio £29.00 OWNER Mr T. J. Whitley (WANTAGE) BRED H. H. Aga Khan

WEIGHT FOR AGE 5yo-7lb

Nadjati (USA) usually wore blinkers over hurdles and jumped better in the first time visor. He really needs to be held up longer, but managed to get back up to win on the nod. (4/1: op 7/4)

Simply (IRE) lost his way over hurdles, and seemed to be set for a successful debut over fences when getting his head in front after the last. (11/4)

Legal Artist (IRE) never recovered from a bad blunder early on, when pulled up on his chasing bow last time. (12/1: op 8/1)

66 Fluidity (USA) was reverting to the larger obstacles after finishing second in a selling handicap hurdle the previous evening. (11/4)

73

BAGGERIDGE BRICKS SEDGLEY 'COMEDY OF ERRORS' NOVICES' HURDLE (4-Y.O+) (Class E)
7-15 (7-17) **2m 110y (9 hdls)** £2,416.00 (£676.00: £328.00) GOING minus 0.12 sec per fur (G)

		Dist	Pos	SP	RR	SF
	Coureur (93) (MDHammond) **7-10-12** RGarritty (hld up: hdwy appr 3 out: led last: drvn out)	—	**1**	11/4^2	77	26
22*	**Brave Patriarch (IRE)** (NJHenderson) **5-11-5** JRKavanagh (hld up & plld hrd: led 2 out to last: unable qckn)	2	**2**	2/1^1	82	31
	Zine Lane (MajorWRHern) **4-10-7** RFarrant (led to 5th: led 6th to 2 out: 3rd & wkng whn hit last)	8	**3**	11/2	67	11
	I'm a Dreamer (IRE) (103) (MissMERowland) **6-11-5** GaryLyons (a.p: ev ch 3 out: wknd 2 out)	10	**4**	4/1^3	65	14
	Irish Wildcard (NZ) (HOliver) **8-10-12** VSlattery (plld hrd: w ldr: led 5th to 6th: wknd appr 3 out)	18	**5**	6/1	40	—
	The Campdonian (IRE) (HOliver) **5-10-12** RDunwoody (a bhd)	3	**6**	14/1	37	—
	Seven Brooks (74) (JCFox) **6-10-12** SFox (a bhd)	1½	**7**	25/1	36	—
	Best of Bold (NAGraham) **4-10-7** PHide (a bhd: t.o)	22	**8**	33/1	15	—
	Well Suited (THind) **6-10-12** DO'Sullivan (a bhd: t.o)	7	**9**	50/1	8	—
	Sparts Fault (IRE) (68) (PEccles) **6-10-12b** RichardGuest (bhd fr 5th: t.o whn p.u bef 3 out)		**P**	33/1	—	—
	Sayitagain (JRJenkins) **4-10-7** JOsborne (prom tl wknd 5th: t.o whn p.u bef 3 out)		**P**	50/1	—	—
	Merely Mortal (BPreece) **5-10-12** RJohnson (lost pl after 4th: rallied after 5th: wknd 6th: t.o whn p.u bef 3 out)		**P**	33/1	—	—

(SP 132.9%) **12 Rn**

3m 52.3 (5.30) CSF £9.48 TOTE £3.70: £1.40 £1.60 £2.50 (£4.40) Trio £8.30 OWNER Mr Frank Hanson (MIDDLEHAM) BRED Gainsborough Stud Management Ltd

WEIGHT FOR AGE 4yo-5lb

Coureur, in good form on the Flat, travelled nicely through the race and came with a well-timed run. (11/4)

22* Brave Patriarch (IRE) ran too freely under restraint and could not defy a penalty. (2/1)

Zine Lane may be capable of winning a similar event with less use made of him. (11/2)

74

J. ROUND MACHINERY WEDNESBURY 'MIDSUMMER NIGHT'S DREAM' H'CAP CHASE (0-125) (5-Y.O+) (Class D) 7-45 (7-45) **3m (18 fncs)** £3,658.50 (£1,098.00: £529.00: £244.50) GOING minus 0.12 sec per fur (G)

		Dist	Pos	SP	RR	SF
	Change the Reign (103) (MissAEEmbiricos) **9-10-12** JRyan (a.p: led 8th: r.o wl)	—	**1**	11/4^2	110	29
2*	**Hillwalk (115)** (RCurtis) **10-11-10** DMorris (swtg: hld up: j.slowly 4th: rdn & hdwy 12th: ev ch 2 out: unable qckn flat)	1½	**2**	11/10^1	121	40

Doonloughan (104) (GBBalding) **11-10-10**(3) BFenton (led to 3rd: lft in ld 7th: hdd 8th: rdn appr 14th: ev ch 2 out: one pce flat)....4 **3** 5/1[3] 107 26

Donna Del Lago (107) (GMMcCourt) **10-10-9b**(7) RHobson (prom: mstke 3rd: rdn 12th: lost pl & hit 3 out: styd on flat)....nk **4** 10/1 110 29

Petty Bridge (96) (APJames) **12-10-5** BPowell (lw: led 3rd tl blnd bdly 7th: reminders after 10th: sn t.o: p.u bef 4 out).... **P** 11/1 — —

(SP 108.4%) **5 Rn**

5m 57.3 (5.30) CSF £5.89 TOTE £3.50: £1.50 £1.30 (£3.00) OWNER Mr E. D. Nicolson (NEWMARKET) BRED W. Gavin

Change the Reign, who needs regular treatment for a muscle problem in his back, is not over big and likes top of the ground. (11/4)

2* Hillwalk, raised 11lb for his last two wins, made a good race of it despite sweating up, but the winner was always travelling the better. (11/10)

Doonloughan has dropped to a mark 7lb lower than when he last won a year ago. (5/1)

Donna Del Lago was back in the blinkers having tried a visor last time. (10/1: 5/1-12/1)

75 JOHN DAVIES INTERIORS WEST BROMWICH GARRICK JUBILEE CHALLENGE CUP H'CAP HURDLE (0-120) (4-Y.O+) (Class D) 8-15 (8-15) **2m 110y (9 hdls)** £3,116.00 (£938.00: £454.00: £212.00) GOING minus 0.12 sec per fur (G)

	Horse			SP	RR	SF
	Fisio Sands (96) (TPMcGovern) **7-10-6** PHide (led to 2nd: led appr 3 out: easily)	—	**1**	14/1	77+	26
	Commanche Creek (90) (MissJduPlessis) **6-9-9**(5) SophieMitchell (hld up: hdwy appr 6th: chsd wnr fr 3 out: one pce fr 2 out)	6	**2**	16/1	65	14
32*	**Lady Confess (93)** (JohnUpson) **6-10-3** RSupple (hld up: mstke 5th: hdwy 6th: one pce fr 2 out)	3	**3**	7/1	65	14
	Classic Exhibit (96) (AStreeter) **7-10-6** TEley (hld up: hdwy 5th: wknd appr 2 out)	16	**4**	10/1	53	2
	Ham N'Eggs (110) (MDHammond) **5-11-6** RGarritty (hld up & bhd: mstke 4th: sme hdwy 6th: n.d)	1½	**5**	100/30[1]	65	14
	Yubralee (USA) (111) (MCPipe) **4-11-2** DBridgwater (prom: led 5th tl appr 3 out: wknd qckly)	nk	**6**	6/1[3]	66	10
	Ivy Edith (114) (TGMills) **6-11-10** DO'Sullivan (hld up: hdwy whn blnd 5th: nt rcvr)	22	**7**	11/1	48	—
62[5]	**No Light (106)** (MrsIMcKie) **9-11-2** LHarvey (hld up: stdy hdwy appr 6th: wknd appr 3 out)	1½	**8**	11/2[2]	38	—
	Yacht (95) (THind) **4-10-0b** PMcLoughlin (prom: rdn after 4th: wknd 5th)	1¾	**9**	16/1	26	—
	Hacketts Cross (IRE) (113) (PEccles) **8-11-9** RichardGuest (a bhd)	4	**10**	16/1	40	—
	Bungee Jumper (108) (CaptTAForster) **6-11-4b** RDunwoody (led 2nd to 5th: wknd qckly appr 6th)	8	**11**	11/2[2]	27	—
	Royal Glint (90) (HEHaynes) **7-9-7**(7) MissEJJones (a bhd: t.o whn p.u bef 3 out)		**P**	33/1	—	—
				(SP 125.3%)		**12 Rn**

3m 51.1 (4.10) CSF £198.19 CT £1,567.96 TOTE £20.60: £4.30 £5.10 £2.60 (£505.90) Trio £162.70 OWNER The Best Of Luck Partnership (LEWES) BRED Mrs S. A. Willis

LONG HANDICAP Yacht 9-11 Commanche Creek 9-8 Royal Glint 8-5

WEIGHT FOR AGE 4yo-5lb

Fisio Sands, who has cracked her pelvis and had a foal since winning on her only run for Josh Gifford, would have gone close when falling on her comeback last month. She scored in fine style and can win again. (14/1: 6/1-16/1)

Commanche Creek, 6lb out of the handicap, could not go with the winner from the penultimate hurdle. (16/1)

32* Lady Confess could not overcome a 6lb hike in the weights for a win last time. (7/1)

Ham N'Eggs did not move well to post and never threatened to take a hand. (100/30)

Bungee Jumper (11/2: op 7/2)

76 KPMG BIRMINGHAM 'TWELFTH NIGHT' H'CAP CHASE (0-115) (5-Y.O+) (Class E) 8-45 (8-46) **2m 1f 110y (13 fncs)** £3,031.50 (£912.00: £441.00: £205.50) GOING minus 0.12 sec per fur (G)

	Horse			SP	RR	SF
	Noblely (USA) (105) (NJHWalker) **9-11-12** RFarrant (led 1st to 6th: led 9th: hit 4 out: all out)	—	**1**	3/1[2]	112	42
	Flying Ziad (CAN) (82) (HJManners) **13-10-3**ow3 MrACharles-Jones (hld up: outpcd 7th: hdwy 4 out: rdn & r.o wl flat)	½	**2**	25/1	89	16
63[4]	**Super Sharp (NZ) (89)** (HOliver) **8-10-10** JacquiOliver (swtg: mstke 3rd: hdwy to ld 6th: hdd 9th: ev ch 3 out: wknd 2 out)	16	**3**	7/2[3]	81	11
	Tango's Delight (79) (RJBaker) **8-10-0** BPowell (mstke 5th: bhd fr 7th)	5	**4**	7/2[3]	66	—
	Fierce (92) (JRJenkins) **8-10-13v** JOsborne (led tl j.slowly 1st: j.slowly 2nd: outpcd 7th: t.o)	19	**5**	15/8[1]	62	—
	Striding Edge (79) (THind) **11-10-0b** PMcLoughlin (bhd fr 7th: sn t.o)	4	**6**	16/1	45	—
				(SP 114.0%)		**6 Rn**

4m 16.3 (7.30) CSF £45.39 TOTE £4.10: £1.90 £8.10 (£91.20) OWNER Mr D. H. Cowgill (WANTAGE) BRED Societe Aland

LONG HANDICAP Tango's Delight 9-10 Flying Ziad (CAN) 9-7 Striding Edge 9-9

Noblely (USA) found strength from the saddle tipping the scales in his favour. (3/1: 9/4-7/2)

Flying Ziad (CAN), 7lb wrong at the weights, was having his first run after rejoining Manners and may have prevailed had he been put under pressure a bit sooner. (25/1)

63 Super Sharp (NZ), due to drop 1lb in future handicaps, had run his race at the penultimate fence. (7/2)

Fierce is not one to take too short a price about. (15/8)

77 A.H.P. TRAILERS WOMBOURNE 'TROILUS AND CRESSIDA' NOVICES' H'CAP HURDLE (0-95) (4-Y.O+) (Class F) 9-15 (9-15) **2m 6f 110y (12 hdls)** £2,234.00 (£624.00: £302.00) GOING minus 0.12 sec per fur (G)

	Horse			SP	RR	SF
19[8]	**Little Court (61)** (EGBevan) **5-10-0** RJohnson (a.p: led after 9th tl blnd 3 out: lft in ld 2 out: all out)	—	**1**	33/1	40	—
18[3]	**Scamallach (IRE) (85)** (JRJenkins) **6-11-10b** JOsborne (hdwy to ld 8th: hdd after 9th: rallied last: r.o)	hd	**2**	8/1	64	—
19[2]	**High Post (81)** (GAHam) **7-11-3**(3) RMassey (hld up: 4th whn slipped bnd appr 9th: wknd appr 2 out)	7	**3**	2/1[1]	55	—
	One More Dime (IRE) (75) (JLNeedham) **6-10-11**(3) BFenton (led tl hdd & mstke 8th: wknd appr 3 out)	18	**4**	8/1	36	—
5[5]	**Lac de Gras (IRE) (63)** (RCurtis) **5-10-2** DMorris (lw: plld hrd: nt j.w: hdwy after 6th: wknd 9th: t.o whn p.u bef 2 out)		**P**	11/1	—	—
	Nick the Biscuit (83) (RTPhillips) **5-11-8v** RDunwoody (swtg: chsd ldr to 8th: hmpd bnd appr 9th: sn wknd: t.o whn p.u bef 3 out)		**P**	9/2[3]	—	—
19[7]	**Spanish Blaze (IRE) (67)** (MrsMerritaJones) **8-10-6** DerekByrne (hld up: blnd bdly & uns rdr 6th)		**U**	3/1[2]	—	—
26[9]	**Dancing At Laharn (IRE) (85)** (MissSJWilton) **6-11-3**(7) NWillmington (hld up: hdwy appr 5th: lft in ld 3 out: blnd & uns rdr 2 out)		**U**	10/1	—	—
				(SP 119.1%)		**8 Rn**

5m 32.8 (16.80) CSF £243.78 CT £716.59 TOTE £43.40: £4.70 £1.80 £1.20 (£94.70) OWNER Mr E. G. Bevan (HEREFORD) BRED E. G. Bevan

LONG HANDICAP Little Court 9-9

STEWARDS' ENQUIRY Johnson susp. 29/6, 3/7, 10/7 & 13/7/96 (excessive use of the whip).

Little Court, 5lb out of the handicap, found the ground too loose at Worcester last time and his trainer considered they had overwatered. He scraped home here in an eventful race. (33/1)
18 Scamallach (IRE) fought back well in a race of changing fortunes. (8/1: 5/1-9/1)
19 High Post, raised 2lb for his good second last time, was 11lb higher than when winning at Hereford. (2/1)
One More Dime (IRE) (8/1: 6/1-10/1)
Nick the Biscuit (9/2: 3/1-5/1)
Dancing At Laharn (IRE) ran too freely in the visor last time, and was just beginning to look leg weary when unshipping his rider two out. (10/1: op 6/1)

T/Plpt: £245.70 (42.64 Tckts). T/Qdpt: £53.60 (13.07 Tckts) KH

78a-91a (Irish Racing) - See Computer Raceform

52a-AUTEUIL (Paris, France) (L-H) (Soft)
Sunday June 16th

92a GRAND STEEPLE-CHASE DE PARIS (5-Y.O+)
4-35 (4-37) **3m 5f** £158,103.00 (£79,051.00: £47,431.00)

Horse	Dist	Pos	SP	RR	SF
Arenice (FR) (GMacaire,France) **8-10-1** PSourzac	—	1		—	—
Al Capone II (FR) (France) **8-10-1** JYBeaurain	2½	2		—	—
Bannkipour (IRE) (France) **7-10-1** CPieux	3	3		—	—
					7 Rn

7m 7.0 P-M 3.60F: 2.00F 1.70F 8.50F OWNER Mme F. Montauban BRED Mme Annick Deliberos
Arenice (FR), the winner of the Prix Millionnaire II, took this, the French equivalent of the Cheltenham Gold Cup in impressive style. Always travelling well, he took the lead with two to jump and ran on strongly.
Al Capone II (FR) was always up with the pace, but found nothing when challenged by the winner.

13-SOUTHWELL (L-H) (Good to firm)
Saturday June 22nd
WEATHER: overcast

93 WILL SCARLET NOVICES' CHASE (5-Y.O+) (Class D)
1-55 (1-55) **2m (13 fncs)** £4,092.00 (£1,221.00: £583.00: £264.00) GOING: 0.13 sec per fur (G)

Form	Horse	Dist	Pos	SP	RR	SF
15^{2}	**Gesnera (91)** (JGMO'Shea) **8-10-2**(7) MichaelBrennan (trckd ldrs: lft clr 4 out: eased flat: fin lame)	—	1	5/2 2	93+	—
	Morcat (GPKelly) **7-10-11**ow2 MrCMulhall (hdwy 6th: pckd 8th: hmpd next: wnt 2nd appr 3 out: r.o flat)	3½	2	50/1	92	—
4*	**Secretary of State (100)** (DWPArbuthnot) **10-11-7** JOsborne (led 3rd tl appr 7th: hit 8th: wkng whn lft 2nd 4 out)	11	3	100/30 3	91	—
15^{4}	**Emerald Moon (75)** (PRRodford) **9-11-0** SBurrough (lw: nt j.w: chsd ldr tl blnd 7th)	10	4	33/1	74	—
61*	**Robert's Toy (IRE) (116)** (MCPipe) **5-11-8b** DBridgwater (lw: prom: hit 4th: led appr 7th: fell 4 out)		F	Evens 1	—	—
	Spanish Money (MPBielby) **9-11-0** MrNKent (led to 3rd: fell next)		F	33/1	—	—
	Quick Decision (IRE) (JKCresswell) **5-10-5**(3) RMassey (sn t.o: blnd 6th: p.u bef last)		P	50/1	—	—
				(SP 111.5%)		**7 Rn**

4m 9.1 (16.10) CSF £61.27 TOTE £3.40: £1.10 £16.50 (£50.50) OWNER Catch-42 (WESTBURY-ON-SEVERN) BRED Pinfold Stud & Farms Ltd
WEIGHT FOR AGE 5yo-6lb
15 Gesnera was in complete control from the moment the favourite fell at the fourth last but appeared to break down jumping the last. (5/2)
Morcat has been pointing without success but had just gone third when hampered by the faller four out. Staying on to the line, she is flattered to have got so close to the winner. (50/1)
4* Secretary of State was never able to dominate and, taking on the favourite going down the back, the mistake six from home ended his chance. (100/30)
15 Emerald Moon jumped poorly and was no threat on the final circuit. (33/1)
61* Robert's Toy (IRE) looked in control but was taking off a stride too early and took a crashing fall at the last on the far side. (Evens)

94 ROBIN HOOD H'CAP CHASE (0-100) (5-Y.O+) (Class F)
2-25 (2-30) **3m 110y (19 fncs)** £4,962.75 (£1,482.00: £708.50: £321.75) GOING: 0.13 sec per fur (G)

Form	Horse	Dist	Pos	SP	RR	SF
64^{2}	**Southerly Gale (97)** (MCPipe) **9-11-11** BPowell (led 2nd: hit 2 out: rdn out)	—	1	7/2 1	111	16
14^{F}	**Truss (85)** (JohnUpson) **9-10-13** RSupple (hld up: hdwy 12th: chsd wnr appr 3 out: btn whn mstke last)	5	2	5/1 2	96	1
	Upwell (72) (RJohnson) **12-9-11**(3) GCahill (hld up & bhd: hdwy appr 3 out: nvr rchd ldrs)	12	3	20/1	75	—
57^{9}	**Regardless (72)** (JPLeigh) **14-9-11**(3) KGaule (hdwy 7th: ev ch whn hit 13th: wknd appr 3 out)	¾	4	33/1	74	—
	Rusty Bridge (91) (MrsSMJohnson) **9-11-5b** RJohnson (sn rdn & wl bhd: nvr nrr)	13	5	15/2	85	—
	Jimmy O'Dea (95) (TTBill) **9-11-9v** JOsborne (chsd ldrs to 12th)	5	6	7/1 3	86	—
	Drumcullen (IRE) (88) (KCBailey) **7-11-2** RDunwoody (led to 2nd: rdn 12th: j.rt 4 out: sn wknd)	6	7	5/1 2	75	—
	Vazon Express (86) (PTDalton) **10-10-11**(3) DParker (lw: hit 1st: a bhd: t.o whn p.u bef 15th)		P	20/1	—	—
	Magic Bloom (100) (JMJefferson) **10-12-0** MDwyer (bit bkwd: hld up: j.rt: lost tch 12th: p.u bef next)		P	8/1	—	—
14^{4}	**Miss Enrico (89)** (MissLucindaRussell) **10-11-3** AThornton (chsd ldrs: hit 5th: wknd 14th: p.u bef 3 out)		P	10/1	—	—
57^{4}	**Storm Warrior (72)** (TWall) **11-9-11b**(3) RMassey (lw: mstkes: chsd ldrs to 11th: t.o whn p.u bef last)		P	9/1	—	—
				(SP 122.5%)		**11 Rn**

6m 30.0 (23.00) CSF £21.12 CT £287.90 TOTE £3.00: £1.10 £1.70 £10.10 (£14.80) Trio £117.60; £74.58 to 4.45 Nottingham 24/6/96 OWNER 405200 Racing (WELLINGTON) BRED Michael O'Donovan
LONG HANDICAP Upwell 9-12 Regardless 9-12
64 Southerly Gale was able to make most of the running once again, having shaken off the other trail blazers in the first mile, and never looked like stopping. (7/2)
Truss bided his time until being sent in pursuit of the winner on the home turn. His effort had already petered out when he hit the last hard. (5/1)
Upwell, on his toes and looking quite fit despite being off since October, looked likely to finish tailed off until staying on strongly in the final mile. (20/1)

Regardless, very much a veteran now, is well handicapped on his old form and showed here that he does retain some of his old ability. (33/1)
Rusty Bridge walked round the paddock with his ears flat back and looked reluctant when scrubbed along, soon losing touch. He finally ran on past beaten rivals late in the day. (15/2)
Jimmy O'Dea looked in decent shape for his first run since November but was unable to adopt his favoured front running role. (7/1)
Magic Bloom, not wearing the tongue strap that improved her last year, was pulled up after losing her pitch passing the stands with a circuit to go. She is much better than this. (8/1: 6/1-9/1)
Storm Warrior (9/1: 12/1-8/1)

95 ALEXANDRA MOTORS H'CAP HURDLE (0-110) (4-Y.O+) (Class E)

2-55 (3-00) **3m 110y (13 hdls)** £3,054.20 (£846.20: £404.60) GOING: 0.13 sec per fur (G)

				SP	RR	SF
	Derring Bridge (85) (MrsSMJohnson) **6-10-10** RJohnson (in tch: rdn & hdwy 8th: led & hit 3 out: rdn clr appr next)	—	**1**	9/1	66	—
6^{4}	**Slaught Son (IRE) (91)** (MartinTodhunter) **8-11-2** MDwyer (lw: trckd ldrs: rdn appr 2 out: one pce)	6	**2**	$7/1^{3}$	68	—
55^{5}	**Easy Over (USA) (75)** (JRJenkins) **10-10-0** SFox (a.p: chsd wnr appr 2 out: no imp)	2½	**3**	20/1	50	—
27^{6}	**Miss Pimpernel (75)** (ABarrow) **6-10-0b** LO'Hara (lw: hld up: hit 2nd: hdwy 8th: led 10th to next: sn rdn & wknd)	8	**4**	16/1	45	—
29^{6}	**La Fontainbleau (IRE) (91)** (DHBrown) **8-11-2** WFry (blnd 6th: nvr trbld ldrs)	12	**5**	14/1	53	—
29^{5}	**Able Player (USA) (93)** (KJDrewry) **9-11-4** MSharratt (hdwy 6th: rdn & wknd appr 2 out)	3	**6**	20/1	53	—
6^{3}	**Scrabo View (IRE) (99)** (PBeaumont) **8-11-10** RSupple (a bhd)	1¼	**7**	15/2	59	—
	Court Circular (95) (WClay) **7-11-3**(3) GuyLewis (bit bkwd: prom to 8th)	19	**8**	16/1	42	—
30^{3}	**Nescaf (NZ) (92)** (CJMann) **6-11-3** RDunwoody (lw: rdn 7th: bhd fr 9th)	dist	**9**	$11/2^{2}$	—	—
	Moobakkr (USA) (100) (KAMorgan) **5-11-11** JOsborne (chsd ldrs: pushed along 6th: wkng whn p.u bef 9th)		**P**	$7/1^{3}$	—	—
29*	**Morning Blush (IRE) (103)** (MCPipe) **6-12-0** BPowell (led to 3rd: rdn 6th: led 9th to next: wknd qckly: p.u bef 2 out)		**P**	$5/2^{1}$	—	—
	Strong John (IRE) (90) (MESowersby) **8-10-12**(3) KGaule (w ldr: led 3rd to 9th: wknd qckly next: p.u bef last)		**P**	14/1	—	—

(SP 125.3%) **12 Rn**

6m 16.5 (30.50) CSF £68.74 CT £1133.77 TOTE £11.10: £2.20 £1.70 £6.30 (£40.50) Trio £73.10; £51.52 to 4.45 Nottingham 24/6/96 OWNER Mr I. K. Johnson (MADLEY) BRED J. I. Johnson
LONG HANDICAP Easy Over (USA) 9-6
Derring Bridge found stamina his trump card in a race that was run at a suicidal early pace. (9/1)
6 Slaught Son (IRE) travelled well on the bridle and looked sure to win turning for home but found little once let down. (7/1)
Easy Over (USA) is not in love with fences and, with an ideal trip on his second run back over hurdles, ran his best race in a very long time. (20/1)
Miss Pimpernel again ran well on this track but may not quite stay the trip. (16/1)
Able Player (USA) was struggling as soon as the pressure was applied on the home turn. (20/1)

96 DERBY BUILDING SERVICES NOVICES' HURDLE (4-Y.O+) (Class E)

3-30 (3-31) **2m (9 hdls)** £2,322.00 (£642.00: £306.00) GOING: 0.13 sec per fur (G)

				SP	RR	SF
18*	**Zahid (USA) (93)** (KRBurke) **5-11-7** RJohnson (hld up: hdwy 6th: led after 2 out: sn rdn clr)	—	**1**	$2/1^{1}$	73	—
	Cuban Nights (USA) (BJLlewellyn) **4-10-9** BPowell (lw: trckd ldrs: hit 4th: ev ch 2 out: one pce)	6	**2**	7/1	60	—
	Suas Leat (IRE) (JMJefferson) **6-11-0** MDwyer (chsd ldrs: led 5th to 2 out: sn hdd & btn)	16	**3**	$5/2^{2}$	44	—
	Prinzal (GMMcCourt) **9-10-7**(7) RHobson (lw: led tl appr 3rd: led 4th tl hdd & pckd next: led & pckd 2 out: sn hdd: btn whn blnd last)	1¾	**4**	$11/2^{3}$	42	—
	Hamadryad (IRE) (85) (MrsVCWard) **8-11-7** RDavis (lw: hld up: hdwy appr 2 out: no imp appr last)	3	**5**	7/1	46	—
	Pimsboy (GROldroyd) **9-10-11**(3) PMidgley (bkwd: mstke 4th: a bhd)	9	**6**	33/1	30	—
	Bold Look (PRWebber) **5-11-0** RBellamy (prom to 6th: sn wknd: p.u bef 2 out)		**P**	12/1	—	—
65^{P}	**M'Bebe (52)** (KOWarner) **6-11-0** TKent (a.p: ev ch 3 out: wkng whn p.u bef next)		**P**	25/1	—	—
18^{P}	**Never Say so** (MrsSLamyman) **4-10-1**(3) GCahill (led appr 3rd to 4th: sn wknd: t.o whn p.u bef 2 out)		**P**	33/1	—	—

(SP 119.7%) **9 Rn**

4m 1.1 (19.10) CSF £16.18 TOTE £2.40: £1.40 £2.20 £1.10 (£10.50) Trio £6.80 OWNER Mr Keith Booth (WANTAGE) BRED Dr. Murray West, Nicholas Lotz & Overbrook Farm
WEIGHT FOR AGE 4yo-5lb
STEWARDS' ENQUIRY Kent susp. 3 & 10/7/96 (careless riding).
18* Zahid (USA) has been called a few names in the past but was winning his fourth race of the year, and took a race which looked well above average for its type in impressive style. (2/1)
Cuban Nights (USA), in great form on the All Weather in the last few months, looked really well and will surely score in this grade before too long. (7/1)
Suas Leat (IRE), gambled on, was made to look onepaced once in line for home. Two miles on this ground looks to be on the short side for him. (5/2)
Prinzal, dropping in trip, could have been expected to take to Southwell's miniature fence style hurdles, but made a string of mistakes and was already held when his pilot did well to keep the partnership intact at the last, a mistake that cost him third place. (11/2)
Hamadryad (IRE) crept forward on the home turn but found nothing once the chips were down. (7/1)

97 MAID MARION H'CAP HURDLE (0-105) (4-Y.O+) (Class F)

4-00 (4-00) **2m (9 hdls)** £2,211.20 (£613.20: £293.60) GOING: 0.13 sec per fur (G)

				SP	RR	SF
17*	**Nocatchim (90)** (KAMorgan) **7-10-10**(3) RMassey (lw: hdwy 4th: led 6th tl j.rt & hdd last: unable qckn: fin 2nd, ½l: awrdd r)	—	**1**	13/2	79	45
16^{4}	**Dibloom (85)** (JNeville) **8-10-8** RJohnson (lw: prom: rdn appr 2 out: sn btn: fin 3rd, 18l: plcd 2nd)		**2**	12/1	56	22
	Playful Juliet (CAN) (80) (ABailey) **8-10-3**ow3 TKent (wl bhd tl r.o fr 3 out: fin 4th, 12l: plcd 3rd)		**3**	15/2	39	2
	Nordic Valley (IRE) (105) (MCPipe) **5-12-0** BPowell (lw: rdn 4th: nvr trbld ldrs: fin 5th, 8l: plcd 4th)		**4**	$6/1^{3}$	56	22
	Stay With Me (FR) (95) (CREgerton) **6-11-4** JOsborne (hld up: hdwy 3 out: nvr nr ldrs)	1¼	**6**	15/2	44	10
	Mcgillycuddy Reeks (IRE) (95) (NTinkler) **5-11-4** RDunwoody (lw: w ldr: led 3rd tl hdd & hit 6th: wknd next)	10	**7**	$6/1^{3}$	34	—
	Eriny (USA) (93) (JJQuinn) **7-11-2** MDwyer (hld up: hdwy 5th: 4th & wkng whn p.u bef 2 out)		**P**	$5/1^{2}$	—	—
	Northern Nation (89) (WClay) **8-10-9**(3) GuyLewis (bit bkwd: chsd ldrs to 4th: t.o whn p.u bef 2 out)		**P**	20/1	—	—

			SP	RR	SF
	Shellhouse (IRE) (94) (KCBailey) **8-11-3** AThornton (bit bkwd: led to 3rd: wknd 5th: t.o whn p.u bef 2 out)	P	7/1	—	—
	Island Vision (IRE) (90) (JGMO'Shea) **6-10-6b**(7) MichaelBrennan (chsd ldrs: carried rt & led last: drvn out: fin 1st: disq: plcd last (prohibited substances (phenylbutazone and oxyphenbutazone) found in urine)	D	9/2 1	79	45

(SP 125.2%) **10 Rn**

3m 57.4 (15.40) CSF £33.77 CT £311.71 TOTE £5.30: £1.60 £2.00 £4.90 (£20.20) Trio £80.30; £52.03 to 4.45 Nottingham 24/6/96 OWNER Mr R. E. Gray (MELTON MOWBRAY) BRED Charlton Down Stud

LONG HANDICAP Playful Juliet (CAN) 9-12

STEWARDS' ENQUIRY O'Shea fined £450 under Rule 180 (ii)

17* Nocatchim unusually let others cut each other's throats in the early stages before making his move as the pace slowed. He was tying up when jumping right at the last but stuck to his task as best he could. (13/2)

Dibloom looks to be coming to hand but made all when last winning and could certainly never dominate these. (12/1)

Playful Juliet (CAN) needs much further but the strong early pace ensured that her stamina came into play late in the race. (15/2)

Nordic Valley (IRE) had decided he didn't fancy this with fully a circuit left. (6/1: op 4/1)

Stay With Me (FR) won a couple of egg and spoon races last August but had been off the course since. Not knocked about, he showed enough to suggest he may be capable of further success. (15/2)

Island Vision (IRE), showing his form for the first time in this country, had to battle hard to gain the day. (9/2: 8/1-4/1)

98 SHERIFF OF NOTTINGHAM CONDITIONAL (S) H'CAP HURDLE (0-90) (4-Y.O+) (Class G)

4-35 (4-35) **2m 4f 110y (11 hdls)** £1,943.00 (£538.00: £257.00) GOING: 0.13 sec per fur (G)

			SP	RR	SF
	Rosie (IRE) (56) (CJHemsley) **6-10-0** BFenton (bhd: hdwy 7th: led after 2 out: drvn out) —	1	16/1	38	—
60P	**Tremble (63)** (MESowersby) **7-10-7** DParker (hdwy 5th: led 3 out to next: kpt on) 3½	2	16/1	42	4
546	**Lago Lago (IRE) (80)** (WMcKeown) **4-11-4** GCahill (trckd ldrs: led 2 out: sn hdd & btn) 7	3	7/4 1	54	10
	Wordy's Wind (70) (LWordingham) **7-10-11**(3) CRae (lw: hdwy 6th: no imp fr 3 out) 8	4	16/1	38	—
	Kingfisher Blues (IRE) (58) (MrsPGrainger) **8-9-13**(3)ow2 MichaelBrennan (prom to 7th) 5	5	33/1	22	—
	Tukum (84) (JParkes) **8-11-11**(3) BGrattan (hld up: hdwy 7th: ev ch whn p.u bef 2 out)	P	10/1 3	—	—
	Marketing Man (60) (JWhite) **6-10-4** GuyLewis (prom: rdn to ld after 6th: hdd & wknd next: p.u bef 2 out)	P	10/1 3	—	—
	Denomination (USA) (85) (MCPipe) **4-11-9** EHusband (prom: led 7th to 3 out: sn wknd: p.u bef last)	P	9/4 2	—	—
	Dan de Lyon (71) (BLlewellyn) **8-11-1** JMagee (led tl after 6th: wknd qckly: p.u after next)	P	10/1 3	—	—

(SP 115.0%) **9 Rn**

5m 15.9 (29.90) CSF £198.80 CT £614.63 TOTE £22.50: £3.20 £2.70 £1.40 (£60.40) Trio £52.70 OWNER Mr W. E. Dudley (WITNEY) BRED John O'Dowd

LONG HANDICAP Kingfisher Blues (IRE) 9-12 Rosie (IRE) 9-13

WEIGHT FOR AGE 4yo-6lb

Bt in 3,000gns

Rosie (IRE), having her first run for her new yard, won this with stamina, as she stayed on determinedly in the straight. (16/1)

Tremble showed this different style of hurdle a bit of respect, and ran his best race ever over hurdles as a result. His form in National Hunt Flat races suggests that he will stay further still. (16/1)

Lago Lago (IRE) looked likely to land the gamble on the home turn but she lost her action after the second last and stopped rather quickly. Lack of stamina may well have been the problem. (7/4: 7/2-13/8)

Wordy's Wind, back over hurdles after a fall over fences here, could never get competitive. (16/1)

Kingfisher Blues (IRE) was in the leading group for almost two miles before flagging. (33/1)

Denomination (USA) (9/4: op 5/4)

Dan de Lyon (10/1: 7/1-12/1)

99 KING JOHN INTERMEDIATE N.H. FLAT RACE (4, 5 & 6-Y.O) (Class H)

5-05 (5-06) **2m** £1,269.50 (£352.00: £168.50)

			SP	RR	SF
	Ultimate Smoothie (MCPipe) **4-10-11**(3) RMassey (plld hrd: trckd ldrs: led over 1f out: sn qcknd clr: easily) —	1	5/1 3	—	—
	Arrange (CWThornton) **4-10-7**(7) NHorrocks (reard s: sn prom: led 3f out tl appr fnl f: one pce) 5	2	15/2	—	—
	Nenagh Gunner (JJQuinn) **6-10-11**(3) BFenton (hdwy 6f out: kpt on fnl 2f) s.h	3	14/1	—	—
	Millennium Man (EWeymes) **5-11-5** MrJWeymes (in tch: hdwy 8f out: ev ch over 2f out: one pce appr fnl f) s.h	4	12/1	—	—
59*	**Petit Flora** (GHolmes) **4-10-13**(3) GCahill (hld up: hdwy 5f out: wknd fnl f) 3	5	5/2 1	—	—
	Oats For Notes (MissVenetiaWilliams) **6-11-0** MrMRimell (led 13f: sn btn) 11	6	20/1	—	—
	Crustygun (OO'Neill) **6-11-2**(3) JCulloty (hdwy 5f out: wknd over 2f out) 4	7	5/1 3	—	—
	Knighton (TJNaughton) **5-11-0**(5) SRyan (chsd ldr 10f) 4	8	14/1	—	—
	Robert Samuel (NJHenderson) **5-11-0**(5) MrCVigors (chsd ldrs 6f: lost tch 6f out: n.d after) ¾	9	9/2 2	—	—
	Alice Sheer Thorn (IRE) (JRJenkins) **6-10-7**(7) MissETomlinson (hdwy 11f out: wknd 5f out) 20	10	20/1	—	—
25W	**Sweet Talker (IRE)** (MrsPGrainger) **4-11-0** MrAPhillips (chsd ldrs 9f) 5	11	20/1	—	—
	Stormin Gift (FPMurtagh) **5-11-2**(3) ARoche (lw: a bhd: t.o fnl 3f) dist	12	16/1	—	—
	Greens Pride (MrsNMacauley) **4-10-11**(3) EHusband (lw: prom 6f: t.o fnl 6f) 4	13	14/1	—	—
	Little Derring (MrsSMJohnson) **5-10-7**(7) MrRThornton (t.o fnl 8f) 15	14	25/1	—	—

(SP 143.6%) **14 Rn**

3m 59.1 CSF £47.25 TOTE £6.50: £2.90 £4.30 £4.20 (£15.70) Trio Not won; £45.26 to 4.45 Nottingham 24/6/96 OWNER Isca Bloodstock (WELLINGTON) BRED Fares Stables Ltd

WEIGHT FOR AGE 4yo-5lb

Ultimate Smoothie, a Flat-bred gelding, took this in impressive style and should win more races. (5/1)

Arrange lost half a dozen lengths at the start but this barely mattered at the slow early pace. His limitations were exposed in the straight but he ought to find a race, particularly with a little cut in the ground. (15/2: 4/1-8/1)

Nenagh Gunner, a short-backed mare, stuck to her guns in the home straight and looks to stay well. (14/1: 10/1-16/1)

Millennium Man, a tall newcomer, may have led for a stride or two early in the home straight before being outpaced. (12/1)

59* Petit Flora, trying two miles for the first time, did not appear to stay, despite being restrained at the back of the field and even with the slow early pace. (5/2)

Oats For Notes tried to put her experience between the flags to good use, but was soon left struggling once headed. (20/1)

Robert Samuel (9/2: 3/1-5/1)

T/Plpt: £282.60 (24.46 Tckts). T/Qdpt: £15.30 (29.22 Tckts). Dk

26-UTTOXETER (L-H) (Good to firm)

Thursday June 27th

WEATHER: fine & warm

100 UTTOXETER ADVERTISER ASHBOURNE NEWS TELEGRAPH MAIDEN HURDLE (4-Y.O+) (Class E)

6-45 (6-45) **3m 110y (12 hdls)** £2,232.00 (£627.00: £306.00) GOING minus 0.56 sec per fur (F)

Form	Horse	Dist	Pos	SP	RR	SF
19^{3}	**Wynberg (91)** (CaptTAForster) **5-11-3** SWynne (a.p: rdn 2 out: led appr last: drvn out)	—	1	5/2 [1]	75	20
18^{2}	**Ordog Mor (IRE) (92)** (MGMeagher) **7-11-3** DerekByrne (led after 4th tl appr last: no ex flat)	3	2	13/2	73	18
69^{2}	**Milngavie (IRE)** (BSmart) **6-11-3** CLlewellyn (trckd ldrs: rdn & outpcd appr 2 out: sn btn)	10	3	7/2 [2]	67	12
77^{U}	**Dancing At Laharn (IRE) (85)** (MissSJWilton) **6-11-3** RDunwoody (hld up: hdwy 8th: ev ch 3 out: rdn appr next: one pce)	1¼	4	8/1	66	11
19^{5}	**Limosa (81)** (MrsLRichards) **5-10-12** MRichards (hld up: stdy hdwy 8th: wknd appr 2 out)	16	5	10/1	50	—
19^{P}	**Hidden Flower (51)** (HSHowe) **7-10-9v**(3) RMassey (bkwd: led tl after 2nd: lost pl 8th)	3	6	100/1	48	—
	Silver Bird (IRE) (67) (MJRyan) **4-10-2**(3) KGaule (led after 2nd tl after 4th: rdn & wknd 8th)	¾	7	33/1	48	—
	Wye Oats (MissVenetiaWilliams) **7-10-12** RJohnson (mstke 3rd: a bhd)	1½	8	50/1	47	—
	Storm Dance (RonaldThompson) **5-11-0**(3) JCulloty (bit bkwd: a bhd: btn whn hit 3 out)	8	9	12/1	47	—
69^{6}	**I Don't Think So** (MissKMGeorge) **5-10-12b**[1] PMcLoughlin (a bhd: rdn 5th: mstke 8th: sn t.o)	dist	10	100/1	—	—
	Broomhill Boy (91) (MrsJPitman) **7-11-3** JOsborne (lw: hld up in rr: fell 8th)		F	9/2 [3]	—	—
19^{P}	**Stonecrop (73)** (JWhite) **5-11-0b**[1](3) BFenton (hld up: blnd 8th: rdr lost irons: p.u bef next)		P	50/1	—	—

(SP 119.0%) **12 Rn**

5m 42.9 (0.90) CSF £18.27 TOTE £3.90: £1.50 £2.20 £1.30 (£9.80) Trio £6.50 OWNER Mrs D. Pridden (LUDLOW) BRED Cheveley Park Stud Ltd

WEIGHT FOR AGE 4yo-7lb

19 Wynberg has taken a long time to win over hurdles but, with this extended trip made to measure, finally reached his goal. (5/2)

18 Ordog Mor (IRE) travelled much better than the winner for most of the way, and did look likely to succeed at the penultimate flight, but this first experience of such a test of stamina proved beyond him in the closing stages. (13/2)

69 Milngavie (IRE) jumped better than he did on his debut and should have found this trip ideal, but was in trouble on the approach to the second last, and his chance had gone. (7/2)

77 Dancing At Laharn (IRE) put himself in with a live chance three out, but was tapped for toe on the run to the next and appeared not to see the trip out. (8/1)

101 SPRINGBANK INDUSTRIES STAFFORDSHIRE NEWSLETTER (S) H'CAP HURDLE (0-90) (4-Y.O+) (Class G)

7-15 (7-15) **2m 4f 110y (10 hdls)** £2,036.00 (£571.00: £278.00) GOING minus 0.56 sec per fur (F)

Form	Horse	Dist	Pos	SP	RR	SF
66^{3}	**Milzig (USA) (69)** (JJoseph) **7-10-9** CLlewellyn (hld up & bhd: stdy hdwy 7th: chal last: hrd rdn to ld cl home)	—	1	100/30 [1]	52	1
	Erlemo (76) (WClay) **7-11-2** RJohnson (mstke 1st: a.p: rdn 6th: led 2 out to last: led flat: drifted lft: hdd nr fin)	hd	2	14/1	59	8
27^{3}	**Whistling Gipsy (66)** (HOliver) **11-10-6** JacquiOliver (hld up: hdwy 6th: slt ld last: sn rdn & hdd: no ex)	5	3	9/1 [3]	45	—
	Miss Souter (70) (HSHowe) **7-10-10v** RDunwoody (a.p: effrt appr 2 out: sn rdn: no imp)	3	4	9/1 [3]	47	—
55^{6}	**Cromaboo Crown (76)** (PJBevan) **5-11-2** WWorthington (a.p: led 3 out to 2 out: rdn & wknd appr last)	¾	5	12/1	52	1
	Riva's Book (USA) (83) (MGMeagher) **5-11-9** DerekByrne (hld up: hdwy 3 out: nt rch ldrs)	2½	6	16/1	57	6
23^{4}	**Bravo Star (USA) (65)** (PaddyFarrell) **11-10-0**(5) ChrisWebb (bit bkwd: led after 1st to 3 out: sn rdn & btn)	4	7	16/1	36	—
	Maryjo (IRE) (73) (MissCJECaroe) **7-10-13** SWynne (bkwd: nvr trbld ldrs)	hd	8	33/1	44	—
66^{4}	**Most Interesting (64)** (GHJones) **11-10-4** RGreene (nvr nr to chal)	7	9	10/1	30	—
	They All Forgot Me (70) (AWCarroll) **9-10-10** MissCDyson (swtg: bkwd: led tl after 1st: wknd 6th)	7	10	33/1	30	—
27^{2}	**Sovereign Niche (IRE) (88)** (MCPipe) **8-12-0v** DBridgwater (prom: reminders 7th: lost pl appr 3 out: eased whn btn: t.o)	18	11	4/1 [2]	34	—
	Oliver-J (69) (JMackie) **5-10-9** RSupple (prom: rdn 5th: sn lost pl: t.o)	8	12	20/1	9	—
	Cardea Castle (IRE) (61) (JAHellens) **8-9-10**(5) STaylor (bkwd: bhd fr 6th: t.o)	10	13	25/1	—	—
	Injunction (IRE) (87) (SCoathup) **5-11-6b**(7) CRae (bit bkwd: a bhd: t.o)	28	14	9/1 [3]	—	—
72^{9}	**Prince Rockaway (IRE) (60)** (NMLampard) **8-9-11b**[1](3) BFenton (a bhd: t.o)	18	15	50/1	—	—
54^{5}	**Nandura (65)** (MissAEEmbiricos) **5-10-5** NMann (swtg: mid div: wknd 7th: t.o: p.u bef last)		P	20/1	—	—
	Arrogant Boy (62) (SBClark) **7-9-9**(7)ow2 MissRClark (swtg: bit bkwd: a bhd: t.o: p.u after 6th)		P	50/1	—	—
	Soupreme (71) (MrsMReveley) **4-10-2b**(3) GCahill (sn t.o: p.u after 6th)		P	10/1	—	—

(SP 140.6%) **18 Rn**

4m 48.1 (4.10) CSF £52.75 CT £386.40 TOTE £4.00: £1.30 £3.20 £2.20 £1.90 (£23.00) Trio £104.50 OWNER Mr Jack Joseph (AMERSHAM) BRED E. W. Thomas & Partners

LONG HANDICAP Arrogant Boy 9-6 Prince Rockaway (IRE) 9-5

WEIGHT FOR AGE 4yo-6lb

Bt in 3,000gns

66 Milzig (USA), back over a more suitable trip, had to pull out all the stops to put his head in front a few strides from the line. (100/30: 9/2-3/1)

Erlemo, unplaced on the Flat four days ago, is being made to work for his keep. In the firing-line all the way, he nosed ahead for a second time on the run-in and, despite wandering off a true line and tightening up the winner, was forced to give best in the dying strides. (14/1)

27 Whistling Gipsy worked hard to gain a slight lead at the last, but had nothing more to offer on the run-in and was brushed aside with ease, (9/1)

27 Sovereign Niche (IRE) was never happy on this lively ground and, though he did push the pace, needed to be kept up to his work, and was going in reverse on reaching the home straight. (4/1: op 6/1)

102 BURTON MAIL NOVICES' CHASE (5-Y.O+) (Class D)

7-45 (7-45) **2m 7f (16 fncs)** £3,517.50 (£1,065.00: £520.00: £247.50) GOING minus 0.56 sec per fur (F)

Form	Horse	Dist	Pos	SP	RR	SF
	Imperial Vintage (IRE) (79) (KCBailey) **6-11-2** RDunwoody (set str pce: mde all: mstke 9th: blnd 3 out: clr last)	—	1	11/2 [3]	96	40
70*	**Fly the Wind** (MCPipe) **11-11-3** DBridgwater (chsd wnr to 4 out: styd on again appr last)	9	2	6/4 [1]	91	35
	Menature (IRE) (69) (NJPomfret) **7-10-13**(3) JCulloty (trckd ldrs: hdwy to chse wnr 4 out: rdn & wknd appr last)	7	3	33/1	85	29

Form	Horse	Dist	Pos	SP	RR	SF
70^{4}	**Dustys Trail (IRE)** (PBowen) **7-10-9**(7) MrRThornton (bhd: rdn 6th: blnd 12th: sn t.o)	10	**4**	16/1	78	22
4^{2}	**Movac (IRE) (96)** (MissLucindaRussell) **7-11-8** AThornton (prom tl wknd after 11th: t.o)	1½	**5**	11/4 2	83	27
	Wakt (77) (JWhite) **6-10-8**(3) BFenton (hld up: hdwy 9th: 3rd & rdn & styng on whn fell 2 out)		**F**	10/1	—	—
70^{6}	**Hizal (72)** (HJManners) **7-11-2** MrACharles-Jones (a in rr: t.o whn p.u bef 2 out)		**P**	20/1	—	—
30^{4}	**Music Score (82)** (MrsLCTaylor) **10-11-2** RSupple (bhd: rdn 8th: sn t.o: p.u bef last)		**P**	25/1	—	—
13^{2}	**Call Me Albi (IRE) (92)** (MrsLRichards) **5-10-8** MRichards (a bhd: t.o: p.u bef 12th)		**P**	8/1	—	—

(SP 119.7%) **9 Rn**

5m 30.8 (-5.20) CSF £14.15 TOTE £4.50: £1.40 £1.40 £5.10 (£5.60) Trio £113.80 OWNER May We Never Be Foun Out (UPPER LAMBOURN) BRED W. J. Mernagh

WEIGHT FOR AGE 5yo-7lb

Imperial Vintage (IRE) does not bend over his fences and it needed all his rider's skill to enable him to make all at a hectic pace, which eventually broke the course record by several seconds. (11/2)

70* Fly the Wind was the one prepared to make a race of it with the winner, but she was feeling the strain four out and, though she did stay on again in the latter stages, was well and truly thrashed. (6/4)

Menature (IRE), a winner between the Flags earlier in the month, turned in possibly his best performance yet under Rules and should be able to make the grade. (33/1)

Wakt, still to get off the mark over fences, made relentless progress and was in with every chance, although under pressure, when she bit the dust at the penultimate fence. (10/1)

103 ADVERTISER GUINNESS GALWAY H'CAP HURDLE (0-130) (4-Y.O+) (Class C)

8-15 (8-15) **2m (9 hdls)** £3,371.25 (£1,020.00: £497.50: £236.25) GOING minus 0.56 sec per fur (F)

Form	Horse	Dist	Pos	SP	RR	SF
75^{7}	**Ivy Edith (114)** (TGMills) **6-11-3** DBridgwater (mde all: sn wl clr: hrd rdn flat: jst hld on)	—	**1**	10/1	93	37
62^{2}	**Suivez (125)** (MrsNMacauley) **6-12-0** RDunwoody (lw: chsd wnr: stumbled 3 out: sn rdn: str chal flat: jst failed)	nk	**2**	13/8 1	104	48
32^{2}	**Kalzari (USA) (97)** (AWCarroll) **11-9-7**(7) BMoore (hld up: hdwy 5th: hrd rdn appr last: wknd flat)	5	**3**	10/1	71	15
	Amazon Express (111) (PBowen) **7-11-0** RJohnson (bkwd: nvr nr ldrs)	8	**4**	33/1	77	21
75^{4}	**Classic Exhibit (97)** (AStreeter) **7-10-0** TEley (drvn along whn bdly hmpd 6th: sn bhd)	6	**5**	4/1 2	57	1
75^{10}	**Hacketts Cross (IRE) (113)** (PEccles) **8-11-2** RichardGuest (outpcd: a t.o)	10	**6**	25/1	63	7
	Green Lane (USA) (119) (JJoseph) **8-11-8** CLlewellyn (bkwd: a bhd: outpcd: t.o)	dist	**7**	20/1	—	—
62^{9}	**Wamdha (IRE) (103)** (KAMorgan) **6-10-6** AThornton (bit bkwd: trckd ldrs tl fell 6th)		**F**	10/1	—	—
	Djais (FR) (119) (JRJenkins) **7-11-5**(3) JCulloty (lost pl 4th: hrd rdn 2 out: 4th & btn whn fell last)		**F**	9/2 3	—	—

(SP 115.1%) **9 Rn**

3m 37.9 (-3.10) CSF £25.50 CT £156.99 TOTE £8.70: £1.90 £1.40 £3.00 (£10.30) Trio £42.60 OWNER Mr Glen Antill (EPSOM) BRED G. A. and Mrs Antill

LONG HANDICAP Classic Exhibit 9-13 Kalzari (USA) 9-5

Ivy Edith, in her element when allowed to dictate, was being reeled in in the closing stages but she gave of her all gamely, and deservedly held on. (10/1)

62 Suivez lost valuable ground and quite possibly the race when he stumbled on landing three out, and a spirited late challenge was never going to get him there. (13/8)

32 Kalzari (USA) did pose a threat when putting in his bid two out, but was flat to the boards between the last two and had to admit he had met his match. (10/1)

Wamdha (IRE) still had work to do, but was not out of it when she crumpled up on landing three out. (10/1)

104 LICHFIELD CATHEDRAL DIGITAL GALWAY PLATE TRIAL H'CAP CHASE (0-130) (5-Y.O+) (Class C)

8-45 (8-45) **2m 5f (16 fncs)** £4,667.00 (£1,312.00: £641.00) GOING minus 0.56 sec per fur (F)

Form	Horse	Dist	Pos	SP	RR	SF
63^{2}	**Saskia's Hero (111)** (JFBottomley) **9-11-5** DerekByrne (hld up & bhd: hdwy 11th: lft in ld 3 out: comf)	—	**1**	13/8 1	118	2
56^{3}	**Sword Beach (112)** (MrsMReveley) **12-11-6** PNiven (led: clr 6th: blnd & hdd 3 out: sn hrd rdn: one pce)	3	**2**	15/8 2	117	1
76^{2}	**Flying Ziad (CAN) (96)** (HJManners) **13-10-4**ow4 MrACharles-Jones (a.p: disp ld 9th: mstke & lost pl 12th: hit next: rallied u.p appr last)	1¼	**3**	10/1	58 t	—
	Crosula (120) (MCPipe) **8-12-0** DBridgwater (j.slowly: trckd ldrs: 2nd & ev ch whn fell 4 out: broke leg: dead)		**F**	3/1 3	—	—

(SP 107.0%) **4 Rn**

5m 12.7 (7.70) CSF £4.67 TOTE £2.10 (£2.20) OWNER Qualitair Holdings Ltd (MALTON) BRED Qualitair Stud Ltd

LONG HANDICAP Flying Ziad (CAN) 8-8

63 Saskia's Hero, ridden with restraint over this longer trip, was only waiting to pounce when he was left with the advantage three out. From then on, the race was his. (13/8)

56 Sword Beach adopted more forceful tactics and was still calling the tune when he missed out at the final ditch. That more or less put paid to what little chance remained. (15/8)

76 Flying Ziad (CAN), carrying 26lb more than his long-handicap weight, ran extremely well and, except for a mistake five out and at the next, might well have taken a hand in proceedings. (10/1)

Crosula, the winner of this race last year, had gone in pursuit of the leader when he departed four out with tragic consequences. (3/1: op 2/1)

105 BRINDLEY HONDA STAFFORDSHIRE LIFE NOVICES' HURDLE (4-Y.O+) (Class D)

9-15 (9-17) **2m (9 hdls)** £2,857.00 (£802.00: £391.00) GOING minus 0.56 sec per fur (F)

Form	Horse	Dist	Pos	SP	RR	SF
	Shahrani (MCPipe) **4-10-9** DBridgwater (mde all: j.b rt early: clr fr 2 out: unchal)	—	**1**	8/1	71	14
26*	**Birthday Boy (IRE) (98)** (JRJenkins) **4-11-2v** RSupple (lw: trckd ldrs: hrd rdn 2 out: kpt on flat: no ch w wnr)	6	**2**	7/2 3	72	15
	Prussia (95) (WClay) **5-11-0** RJohnson (lw: a chsng wnr: mstke 5th: hrd rdn 2 out: one pce)	s.h	**3**	3/1 2	65	13
	Governor Daniel (99) (JGMO'Shea) **5-11-7** RDunwoody (a.p: reminders 6th: styd on one pce fr 2 out)	4	**4**	7/4 1	68	16
18^{5}	**Pegasus Bay (86)** (WWHaigh) **5-11-0** RGarritty (hld up: hdwy 6th: nt rch ldrs)	13	**5**	16/1	48	—
	Little Rousillon (TRGreathead) **8-11-0** WHumphreys (bkwd: nvr nr to chal)	4	**6**	33/1	44	—
	Positivo (MissCJECaroe) **5-11-0** ILawrence (swtg: trckd ldrs tl wknd after 6th)	s.h	**7**	14/1	44	—
	Guards Brigade (JHetherton) **5-11-0** RMarley (prom tl wknd 3 out: t.o)	9	**8**	25/1	35	—
	Specialize (KRBurke) **4-10-9** ALarnach (bit bkwd: a rr div: t.o)	20	**9**	16/1	15	—
	Slightly Special (IRE) (68) (MrsPGrainger) **4-10-9** MrAPhillips (a bhd: t.o)	nk	**10**	25/1	15	—
	Boost (MrsNMacauley) **4-10-9b** SWynne (lw: a bhd: t.o fr 3 out)	¾	**11**	50/1	14	—
	Trouble's Brewing (PRWebber) **5-10-9** CLlewellyn (hld up & bhd: t.o)	dist	**12**	33/1	—	—
	Top Bank (RHollinshead) **8-11-0** MissSSharratt (bkwd: a bhd: t.o fr 6th)	6	**13**	50/1	—	—

				SP	RR	SF
	Come on Winn (MissSJWilton) **4-10-4** TEley (ref to r: t.n.p)		R	33/1	—	—
				(SP 133.6%)	**14 Rn**	

3m 41.2 (0.20) CSF £37.71 TOTE £8.30: £2.80 £1.50 £1.10 (£17.60) Trio £25.60 OWNER Mr A S Helaissi and Mr S Helaissi (WELLINGTON) BRED R. V. Young
WEIGHT FOR AGE 4yo-5lb
Shahrani, making his hurdling debut, gave away substantial ground by hanging away to the right in the early stages, but he was still able to make all and gallop his rivals into submission. (8/1)
26* Birthday Boy (IRE) opened his account at the previous outing here and was strongly fancied to follow up, but the winner proved much too good, and he was unable to land a blow. (7/2)
Prussia tried his best to keep tabs on the winner, but he made more than the odd jumping mistake and was unable to get on terms. (3/1)
Governor Daniel probably needs a much tougher test of stamina than he had here, for he was at full stretch on the turn into the straight, and was unable to make any impression. (7/4: op 11/4)

T/Plpt: £22.80 (618.05 Tckts). T/Qdpt: £10.80 (76.42 Tckts). IM

106a-127a (Irish Racing) - See Computer Raceform

66-WORCESTER (L-H) (Good to firm)
Saturday June 29th
WEATHER: overcast

128 HAWFORD CONDITIONAL H'CAP HURDLE (0-110) (4-Y.O+) (Class E)
2-35 (2-38) **2m (8 hdls)** £2,337.50 (£650.00: £312.50) GOING: 0.04 sec per fur (G)

				SP	RR	SF
	Courageous Knight (82) (PHayward) **7-10-9** BFenton (lw: hld up & bhd: hdwy u.p 3 out: led flat: all out)	—	1	100/30[1]	64	29
97[D]	**Island Vision (IRE) (97)** (JGMO'Shea) **6-11-7b**(3) MichaelBrennan (lw: hld up in tch: hdwy appr last: led flat: sn hdd: kpt on u.p)	nk	2	11/2[3]	79	44
	Stately Home (IRE) (95) (PBowen) **5-11-3**(5) BMoore (bit bkwd: led 2nd to 5th: led appr 3 out to last: one pce flat)	1¾	3	12/1	75	40
	Stapleford Lady (86) (JSMoore) **8-10-13** JMagee (hld up: rdn & hdwy 2 out: ev ch flat: no ex nr fin)	½	4	20/1	65	30
54*	**Sian Wyn (83)** (KRBurke) **6-10-10** GLee (lw: trckd ldrs: rdn & effrt 3 out: r.o one pce)	3	5	5/1[2]	59	24
75[2]	**Commanche Creek (84)** (MissJduPlessis) **6-10-11** SophieMitchell (led to 2nd: led 5th: sn hdd: ev ch last: rdn & edgd lft flat: sn btn)	½	6	5/1[2]	60	25
75[P]	**Royal Glint (73)** (HEHaynes) **7-9-9**(5) ADowling (prom tl wknd 3 out)	nk	7	20/1	49	14
	Lawnswood Junior (89) (JLSpearing) **9-11-2** DWalsh (hld up: hdwy 4th: wknd appr 3 out)	7	8	9/1	58	23
97[P]	**Shellhouse (IRE) (91)** (KCBailey) **8-11-4** TJMurphy (lw: hld up & bhd: hdwy 5th: rdn 3 out: sn btn)	¾	9	10/1	59	24
	Countrywide Lad (73) (MMadgwick) **7-9-11**(3) SRyan (hld up: rdn 3 out: no rspnse: t.o)	26	10	50/1	15	—
	Secret Castle (73) (TWall) **8-10-0b[1]** ChrisWebb (bit bkwd: bolted bef s: sn bhd: t.o: p.u bef 5th)		P	66/1	—	—
				(SP 111.6%)	**11 Rn**	

3m 46.6 (6.60) CSF £19.53 CT £171.00 TOTE £4.30: £2.40 £2.50 £4.30 (£11.70) Trio £121.20 OWNER Mr L. Kirkwood (NETHERAVON) BRED C. A. Blackwell
LONG HANDICAP Royal Glint 9-8 Countrywide Lad 9-7 Secret Castle 9-1
Courageous Knight, a faller when poised to challenge in his most recent race here, made up a tremendous amount of ground in the last half-mile and took advantage of a decent pull in the weights to outbattle the runner-up in an all-out duel to the finish. (100/30)
97 Island Vision (IRE), a drifter in the market, looked all over a winner when leading on the flat, but the winner proved the stronger when the chips were down. (11/2: 3/1-6/1)
Stately Home (IRE) made the majority of the running and was only tapped for toe on the run-in. He will strip fitter for this first outing in two months and should be kept in mind. (12/1: op 8/1)
Stapleford Lady, at her best when faced with a stiffer test of stamina, threw down a determined challenge on the flat but just failed to quicken enough to get to terms. (20/1)

129 FERRY MAIDEN HURDLE (4-Y.O+) (Class F)
3-05 (3-05) **2m 4f (10 hdls)** £2,339.00 (£654.00: £317.00) GOING: 0.04 sec per fur (G)

				SP	RR	SF
	Searchlight (IRE) (91) (TRWatson) **8-11-5** DBridgwater (trckd ldrs: led appr 7th: reminders 3 out: drew clr fr next)	—	1	9/2[3]	75	30
	Greycoat Boy (BJMeehan) **4-10-13** RDunwoody (chsd ldrs: wnt 2nd 6th: rdn & outpcd appr 2 out)	9	2	7/4[1]	68	17
	Murberry (IRE) (MrsIMcKie) **6-11-0** LHarvey (in tch: effrt after 7th: nvr nr to chal)	14	3	7/1	52	7
	Miramare (JWDufosee) **6-11-5** GUpton (bkwd: nvr nr ldrs)	8	4	50/1	50	5
	Pharrago (IRE) (DBurchell) **7-11-5** DJBurchell (bkwd: wl bhd tl sme late hdwy)	13	5	20/1	40	—
	Cheer's Baby (GraemeRoe) **6-11-5** RichardGuest (nvr trbld ldrs: t.o)	7	6	66/1	34	—
69[U]	**Sandford Thyne (IRE)** (JNDalton) **6-11-0** SWynne (lw: t.o)	9	7	66/1	22	—
67[9]	**Laser Light Lady** (NPLittmoden) **4-10-8** BPowell (mid div tl wknd appr 7th: t.o)	6	8	50/1	17	—
	Priesthill (IRE) (DLWilliams) **7-11-2**(3) KGaule (bkwd: prom: wkng whn mstke 5th: sn lost tch: t.o)	4	9	50/1	19	—
	Coolmoreen (IRE) (AJWilson) **8-11-0**(5) ChrisWebb (bkwd: a bhd: t.o)	1¼	10	66/1	18	—
	Daring Hen (IRE) (KCBailey) **6-11-0** APMcCoy (led: clr 4th: wknd & hdd appr 7th: t.o)	2	11	11/4[2]	11	—
	Dotterel (IRE) (RGBrazington) **8-11-5** WHumphreys (a bhd: t.o fr ½-wy)	¾	12	14/1	16	—
	Lord of The Mill (IRE) (MrsIMcKie) **5-11-5** WMcFarland (bhd fr ½-wy: t.o)	dist	13	50/1	—	—
	Pertemps Zola (KSBridgwater) **7-11-0** VSlattery (bkwd: mstke 2nd: sn t.o: p.u bef 7th)		P	50/1	—	—
66[18]	**Orchestral Designs (IRE) (53)** (GAHam) **5-11-5b[1]** SBurrough (prom to 4th: sn wknd: bhd whn p.u bef 7th)		P	50/1	—	—
26[6]	**Tom's Gemini Star** (OJCarter) **8-11-5** MrJJukes (a in rr: t.o whn p.u bef 3 out)		P	20/1	—	—
	Tropwen Marroy (BPreece) **7-11-0** GaryLyons (mstke 1st: t.o whn p.u bef 5th)		P	66/1	—	—
67[10]	**Really Neat** (LWaring) **10-10-9**(5) SophieMitchell (bhd whn p.u bef 6th)		P	66/1	—	—
	Brensham Folly (RBrotherton) **5-11-5** TEley (t.o whn blnd 5th: p.u bef next)		P	66/1	—	—
				(SP 130.6%)	**19 Rn**	

4m 48.4 (10.40) CSF £12.54 TOTE £5.90: £1.50 £1.10 £2.60 (£11.10) Trio £49.40 OWNER Mrs R. T. Watson (GAINSBOROUGH) BRED Patrick Smith
WEIGHT FOR AGE 4yo-6lb

Searchlight (IRE) won a very poor race very easily indeed and certainly proved the star turn in this company. (9/2)
Greycoat Boy, fit from the Flat for this hurdling debut, was upsides the winner turning in but could not respond when that rival was sent about his work. He may well need all of three miles at this game. (7/4)
Murberry (IRE), a recent winner between the Flags, was having her first look at hurdles and could not go the pace, but at least she did stay on to run into the prizes. (7/1)
Daring Hen (IRE) did her best to make this a true test of stamina but she only succeeded in beating herself, and went out like a light after being collared at the end of the back straight. (11/4)

130 M JOAN SWIFT H'CAP CHASE (0-125) (5-Y.O+) (Class D)

3-35 (3-35) **2m 7f (18 fncs)** £4,500.00 (£1,350.00: £650.00: £300.00) GOING: 0.04 sec per fur (G)

				SP	RR	SF
	Waterford Castle (103) (KCBailey) **9-10-3**(3) TJMurphy (lw: hdwy 8th: led 4 out: clr last)	—	1	$9/2^{3}$	95	—
	Father Dowling (97) (GBBalding) **9-9-11v**(3) BFenton (hld up: hdwy 10th: disp ld fr 4 out: rdn & btn appr last)	8	2	25/1	83	—
	Andrelot (115) (PBowen) **9-11-4b** RDunwoody (lw: trckd ldrs: rdn appr 4 out: wknd appr next)	4	3	10/1	99	—
28^{4}	**Abbotsham (99)** (OJCarter) **11-10-2**ow1 MrJJukes (led 8th to 11th: ev ch tl wknd appr 3 out)	22	4	50/1	67	—
70^{F}	**Artful Arthur (97)** (LPGrassick) **10-10-0** MrJGrassick (a bhd: t.o fr ½-wy)	1	5	66/1	65	—
28^{P}	**Hurryup (97)** (RDickin) **9-9-11b**1(3) JCulloty (lw: prom: blnd 10th: sn lost tch: t.o)	dist	6	25/1	—	—
74^{P}	**Petty Bridge (97)** (APJames) **12-10-0** BPowell (bhd: rdn 5th: t.o & p.u bef 4 out)		P	33/1	—	—
28^{2}	**Lemon's Mill (USA) (125)** (MCPipe) **7-12-0b** DBridgwater (hld up in tch: reminders 9th: led 11th tl appr 4 out: wknd & p.u bef 2f out)		P	$85/40^{1}$	—	—
	Seal King (97) (JMBradley) **11-10-0** VSlattery (led to 8th: wknd qckly 10th: t.o & p.u bef 4 out)		P	14/1	—	—
	Taurean Tycoon (97) (DLWilliams) **12-10-0** TEley (blnd 2nd: t.o tl p.u bef 4 out)		P	66/1	—	—
57^{2}	**Knockumshin (97)** (JohnUpson) **13-10-0** RSupple (lw: mid div tl lost tch 10th: t.o & p.u bef last)		P	25/1	—	—
	Ryton Guard (97) (GBBarlow) **11-10-0** SWynne (bkwd: prom early: lost tch 6th: blnd & p.u bef 4 out)		P	66/1	—	—
23^{*}	**Funcheon Gale (97)** (RCurtis) **9-10-0** DMorris (blnd & uns rdr 2nd)		U	$9/4^{2}$	—	—

(SP 117.6%) **13 Rn**

6m 4.7 (26.70) CSF £93.52 CT £968.66 TOTE £6.80: £2.00 £2.60 £2.30 (£30.10) Trio £155.30 OWNER Sybil Lady Joseph (UPPER LAMBOURN) BRED S. Neville
LONG HANDICAP Father Dowling 8-12 Hurryup 9-12 Petty Bridge 9-10 Artful Arthur 8-4 Seal King 9-7 Taurean Tycoon 9-3 Knockumshin 9-1 Ryton Guard 9-1 Funcheon Gale 9-11
Waterford Castle was able to take advantage of a very lenient handicap mark, and kept up his good recent run with another clear-cut success. (9/2)
Father Dowling has not won a race for quite some time, but is running consistently well and another success is long overdue. (25/1)
Andrelot performed with credit in this first run in almost six months and, if he has the stamina to win at this extended trip, will not be long in doing so. (10/1: op 6/1)
Abbotsham had probably not fully recovered from the punishing race he had earlier in the month, and stopped to nothing soon after reaching the straight. He was pulled up when his chance had gone. (50/1)
28 Lemon's Mill (USA) (85/40: 6/4-9/4)

131 MALVERN BLINDS H'CAP HURDLE (0-120) (4-Y.O+) (Class D)

4-10 (4-10) **3m (12 hdls)** £3,760.75 (£1,126.00: £540.50: £247.75) GOING: 0.04 sec per fur (G)

				SP	RR	SF
60^{2}	**Tipping The Line (100)** (MCPipe) **6-10-10** DBridgwater (prom: reminders 6th: led 8th to next: outpcd appr 3 out: rallied u.p last: led nr fin)	—	1	$5/1^{2}$	80	13
29^{3}	**Cats Run (IRE) (117)** (JohnUpson) **8-11-13** RSupple (lw: a.p: led 9th: sn hdd: led 3 out tl ct nr fin)	½	2	11/1	97	30
60^{*}	**Santella Boy (USA) (100)** (CJMann) **4-10-3** RDunwoody (hld up: hdwy 8th: chsd ldr 3 out: one pce appr last)	3	3	$15/8^{1}$	78	4
95^{4}	**Miss Pimpernel (90)** (ABarrow) **6-9-9**(5) SophieMitchell (bhd: rdn 7th: styd on fr 3 out)	13	4	50/1	59	—
	Johnny Will (104) (MissAEEmbiricos) **11-11-0** JRyan (bit bkwd: hld up in tch: hdwy 9th: mstke 3 out: wknd next: fin lame)	5	5	25/1	70	3
16^{U}	**All On (110)** (JHetherton) **5-11-6** RMarley (hld up: hdwy 6th: j.slowly next: led after 9th to 3 out: wknd 2 out)	3½	6	$9/1^{3}$	73	6
29^{2}	**South Westerly (IRE) (111)** (MrsMReveley) **8-11-7** PNiven (hld up: stdy hdwy fr ½-wy: wknd appr 3 out)	s.h	7	$5/1^{2}$	74	7
	Laughing Gas (IRE) (100) (MrsNMacauley) **7-10-10** SWynne (led to 8th: wknd qckly: t.o)	16	8	12/1	53	—
57^{*}	**East Houston (101)** (JJO'Neill) **7-10-11** APMcCoy (lw: hld up: a in rr: t.o)	16	9	$9/1^{3}$	43	—
	Khazari (USA) (90) (RBrotherton) **8-10-0** LHarvey (trckd ldrs tl wknd appr 9th: t.o: p.u flat)		P	50/1	—	—
95^{*}	**Derring Bridge (91)** (MrsSMJohnson) **6-9-12**(3) BFenton (trckd ldrs tl blnd & uns rdr 5th)		U	$9/1^{3}$	—	—

(SP 121.9%) **11 Rn**

5m 51.7 (15.70) CSF £54.96 CT £128.34 TOTE £6.70: £1.90 £2.90 £1.30 (£36.40) Trio £116.40 OWNER Mrs L. M. Sewell (WELLINGTON) BRED Barton Stallion Partnership
LONG HANDICAP Miss Pimpernel 8-11 Khazari (USA) 8-7
WEIGHT FOR AGE 4yo-7lb
OFFICIAL EXPLANATION Johnny Will: lost his action and finished sore.
60 Tipping The Line gained his revenge over Santella Boy on 7lb better terms, but this success was due to his jockey's determined driving and his luck in keeping his seat when he lost his balance soon after the last. (5/1)
29 Cats Run (IRE) took control for the second time three out and looked to have the measure of his rivals at the last, but a concession of 17lb swayed the issue on the long run-in. (11/1: 5/1-12/1)
60* Santella Boy (USA) put himself in with every chance early in the straight, but the leader was in no mood to give best and he could do little more than struggle on at the one pace. (15/8)
16 All On (9/1: op 5/1)
29 South Westerly (IRE) improved his position and it just looked a matter of when his jockey pressed the button, but he went from one extreme to the other when asked to quicken and was beaten in next to no time. (5/1: op 3/1)

132 BESFORD NOVICES' H'CAP CHASE (0-100) (5-Y.O+) (Class E)

4-45 (4-45) **2m (12 fncs)** £3,353.00 (£1,004.00: £482.00: £221.00) GOING: 0.04 sec per fur (G)

				SP	RR	SF
	Caspian Beluga (93) (SGKnight) **8-12-0** GUpton (lw: j.w: mde all: sn clr: unchal: fin lame)	—	1	$5/1^{1}$	110	33
64^{P}	**Willie Makeit (IRE) (69)** (RTPhillips) **6-10-1**(3) JCulloty (hdwy 8th: chsd wnr 3 out: kpt on flat)	4	2	8/1	82	5

	Horse	Dist	Pos	SP	RR	SF
	Quinta Royale (74) (LASnook) **9-10-9** RichardGuest (bit bkwd: hdwy 8th: nt rch ldrs)	10	**3**	25/1	77	—
72^{6}	**Duke of Dreams (72)** (RJBaker) **6-10-7** BPowell (chsd ldng pair: lft 2nd 5th: wknd 3 out)	8	**4**	8/1	67	—
	Telmar Systems (65) (JWhite) **7-9-11**(3) BFenton (nvr plcd to chal)	3	**5**	16/1	57	—
	Jameswick (68) (JWDufosee) **6-9-12**(5)ow3 PHenley (lw: a in rr)	1¼	**6**	20/1	59	—
13^{5}	**Mariners Cove (81)** (CDBroad) **8-10-13**(3) TJMurphy (a bhd)	nk	**7**	15/2 3	71	—
	Lofty Deed (USA) (65) (WJMusson) **6-9-11**(3) KGaule (a bhd)	1¼	**8**	16/1	54	—
	Exclusion (84) (JHetherton) **7-11-5** RMarley (hld up in tch: rdn & wknd appr 4 out: t.o)	13	**9**	12/1	60	—
	Our Nikki (70) (PRRodford) **6-10-5**ow5 SBurrough (bkwd: a bhd: t.o whn blnd last)	½	**10**	50/1	46	—
22^{6}	**Manaboutthehouse (86)** (GThorner) **9-11-7** LHarvey (bit bkwd: in tch: mstke 7th: sn wknd: t.o)	¾	**11**	7/1 2	61	—
	Gimme (IRE) (90) (JGMO'Shea) **6-11-11** APMcCoy (bkwd: chsd wnr tl fell 5th)		**F**	5/1 1	—	—
	George Lane (68) (FJordan) **8-10-3** RGreene (bit bkwd: blnd & uns rdr 5th)		**U**	12/1	—	—
66^{P}	***Paid Elation (65)*** (NRMitchell) **11-9-9**(5) SophieMitchell (Withdrawn not under Starter's orders: Veterinary advice)		**W**		—	—
				(SP 117.5%)	**13 Rn**	

4m 0.9 (9.90) CSF £40.71 CT £834.05 TOTE £4.40: £2.70 £2.90 £6.50 (£14.70) Trio £172.70 OWNER Mr L. J. Hawkings (TAUNTON) BRED Wretham Stud

LONG HANDICAP Our Nikki 9-7 Lofty Deed (USA) 9-9 Telmar Systems 9-13 Jameswick 9-9 Paid Elation 9-9

Caspian Beluga gave his rivals a lesson in fast and bold jumping and simply galloped them into the ground. He did tie up on the run-in and was found to be lame after the race. (5/1)

Willie Makeit (IRE) ran up to his best on this step down to the minimum trip and a repeat could see him getting off the mark. (8/1)

Quinta Royale ran promisingly after three months out of action and this second attempt at fences will stand him in good stead for the future. (25/1)

133 LULSLEY STANDARD N.H. FLAT RACE (4, 5 & 6-Y.O) (Class H)

5-15 (5-15) **2m** £1,322.00 (£367.00: £176.00)

	Horse	Dist	Pos	SP	RR	SF
24*	**Regal Gem (IRE)** (CRBarwell) **5-11-7**(3) BFenton (hld up & bhd: hdwy 6f out: led 2f out: rdn clr)	—	**1**	5/1 3	—	—
24^{2}	**Oh Dear Me** (RMFlower) **5-11-0** BPowell (trckd ldrs: hrd rdn over 3f out: styd on appr fnl f)	2½	**2**	7/2 2	—	—
	Smart Remark (MissKMGeorge) **4-11-0** PMcLoughlin (hld up: hdwy over 4f out: kpt on ins fnl f)	4	**3**	50/1	—	—
	Dragon Fly (IRE) (CRBarwell) **5-11-5** BClifford (bhd tl styd on fnl 3f)	4	**4**	33/1	—	—
	Irish Delight (RCurtis) **4-10-11**(3) DWalsh (lost pl ½-wy: styd on again fnl 2f)	¾	**5**	33/1	—	—
25^{5}	**Carnival Clown** (KBishop) **4-11-0** RGreene (nvr nrr)	4	**6**	20/1	—	—
	Double Trouble (DRGandolfo) **5-11-2**(3) DFortt (hld up & bhd: styd on fnl 2f: nrst fin)	hd	**7**	16/1	—	—
	Disco's Well (ABailey) **5-11-5** OPears (chsd ldr: lft in ld 7f out: hdd 2f out: sn wknd)	¾	**8**	50/1	—	—
59^{5}	**Flame of Dance** (AStreeter) **5-11-5** TEley (hld up: hdwy 6f out: wknd over 2f out)	1¼	**9**	10/1	—	—
24^{4}	**Seven Wells** (JHPeacock) **4-11-0** RBellamy (a rr div: t.o)	12	**10**	25/1	—	—
	The Bratpack (IRE) (JKirby) **6-11-0** GUpton (bkwd: dwlt: a in rr: t.o)	nk	**11**	20/1	—	—
	Final Score (IRE) (PaddyFarrell) **6-10-9**(5) ChrisWebb (trckd ldrs to ½-wy: sn lost pl: t.o)	24	**12**	33/1	—	—
	Tipsy Queen (MissHCKnight) **5-10-11**(3) JCulloty (a rr div: t.o)	20	**13**	11/1	—	—
	Mrs Molotoff (RJBaker) **5-11-0** VSlattery (prom: rdn over 7f out: sn wknd: t.o)	1¼	**14**	33/1	—	—
24^{8}	**Jackamus (IRE)** (GAHam) **5-10-12**(7) MrMFrith (a bhd: t.o)	20	**15**	33/1	—	—
	Lysander (MrsSLamyman) **4-10-11**(3) GCahill (a bhd: t.o)	dist	**16**	33/1	—	—
	Rare Spread (IRE) (MCPipe) **6-11-5** DBridgwater (led tl rn out 7f out)		**R**	2/1 1	—	—
25^{3}	**Popsi's Cloggs** (RCurtis) **4-11-0** DMorris (lw: a.p: 3rd & rdn whn rn out & uns rdr over 3f out)		**U**	9/1	—	—
				(SP 140.5%)	**18 Rn**	

3m 45.3 CSF £24.42 TOTE £4.00: £2.20 £2.10 £9.10 (£4.40) Trio Not won; £215.46 to Doncaster 30/6/96 OWNER Mr D. W. E. Coombs (TIVERTON) BRED Mrs M. T. Ward

WEIGHT FOR AGE 4yo-5lb

24* Regal Gem (IRE) kept up her winning sequence with an easily-gained success, but whether she would have done so had the favourite not run out is open to debate. (5/1: op 3/1)

24 Oh Dear Me could not get as close to the winner as she did here earlier in the month, but she was staying on best of all at the finish and could be coming to herself. (7/2)

Smart Remark showed plenty of knee-action on the way down, but ran a pleasing race on this debut and should be able to win races. (50/1)

Dragon Fly (IRE) improved on his debut run last month and would seem to be getting it together. (33/1)

Tipsy Queen (11/1: 8/1-12/1)

Rare Spread (IRE), a winner of two point-to-points in Ireland in the spring, was soon bowling along in a clear lead but his steering gave problems at the end of the back straight and he finished up amongst the horse-boxes. This wrong will soon be righted. (2/1)

25 Popsi's Cloggs, in the action from the start, was being nudged along but still held every chance when he ran the wrong side of a marker early in the straight and dislodged his pilot. He must not be written off yet. (9/1)

T/Plpt: £121.70 (91.08 Tckts). T/Qdpt: £37.50 (13.1 Tckts). IM

60-MARKET RASEN (R-H) (Good, Good to firm patches)

Wednesday July 3rd

WEATHER: unsettled

134 'SUMMER SEASON' CONDITIONAL (S) H'CAP HURDLE (0-90) (4-Y.O+) (Class G)

2-10 (2-10) **2m 5f 110y (10 hdls)** £1,993.40 (£552.40: £264.20) GOING: 0.07 sec per fur (G)

	Horse	Dist	Pos	SP	RR	SF
	Red Jam Jar (85) (SBBell) **11-11-12** GCahill (lw: trckd ldrs: led 3 out: sn clr)	—	**1**	11/1	70	10
	North Bannister (73) (TPMcGovern) **9-11-0** TJMurphy (a chsng ldrs: kpt on fr 3 out: no imp)	27	**2**	11/4 1	38	—
98^{2}	**Tremble (65)** (MESowersby) **7-10-6** DParker (lw: a chsng ldrs: drvn along 5th: one pce fr 3 out)	9	**3**	9/1	23	—
	Nordic Crown (IRE) (80) (MCPipe) **5-11-7b** EHusband (chsd ldrs: rdn 6th: wknd appr 3 out)	9	**4**	7/2 2	32	—
101^{11}	**Sovereign Niche (IRE) (86)** (MCPipe) **8-11-13b** DWalsh (led to 3 out: sn wknd)	2	**5**	8/1	36	—
100^{7}	**Silver Bird (IRE) (67)** (MJRyan) **4-10-5** KGaule (nt j.w: in tch to 7th: sn lost pl)	1¼	**6**	14/1	16	—
95^{3}	**Easy Over (USA) (73)** (JRJenkins) **10-11-0** DFortt (bhd & drvn along 5th: t.o 3 out)	9	**7**	13/2 3	15	—
66^{10}	**Classic Image (IRE) (68)** (HJManners) **6-10-4**(5) ADowling (hdwy 5th: wknd 7th)	20	**8**	7/1	—	—
	Joli's Great (69) (MJRyan) **8-10-10b** GuyLewis (hld up: effrt 6th: sn lost pl: t.o 3 out)	2½	**9**	9/1	—	—

				SP	RR	SF
101^{13}	**Cardea Castle (IRE) (59)** (JAHellens) **8-10-0** STaylor (prom to 2nd: rdn 4th: t.o 6th)	s.h	**10**	25/1	—	—

(SP 124.7%) **10 Rn**

5m 24.3 (20.30) CSF £41.94 CT £274.53 TOTE £11.30: £2.20 £1.40 £2.50 (£11.60) Trio £135.10 OWNER Mr C. H. P. Bell (DRIFFIELD) BRED Majors Racing International Ltd
LONG HANDICAP Cardea Castle (IRE) 9-11
WEIGHT FOR AGE 4yo-3lb
Bt in 3,300 gns

Red Jam Jar, on particularly good terms with himself beforehand, was clear with his race won in a matter of strides starting the final turn. (11/1)
North Bannister stuck on in pursuit of the winner, but was never going to get close enough to land a blow. (11/4)
98 Tremble, pushed along with a circuit to go, stuck on in his own time from three out. (9/1)
Nordic Crown (IRE), 5lb higher in the weights than when winning here a month ago, was driven along to keep up setting out early on the final circuit, before calling it a day going to three out. (7/2: op 2/1)
101 Sovereign Niche (IRE), who made the running, found nothing at all when challenged by the winner. (8/1)
Joli's Great (9/1: op 6/1)

135 'BAR-B-Q' NOVICES' H'CAP CHASE (0-100) (5-Y.O+) (Class E)

2-40 (2-46) **3m 1f (19 fncs)** £3,185.75 (£956.00: £460.50: £212.75) GOING: 0.07 sec per fur (G)

				SP	RR	SF
70^{3}	**Manor Rhyme (74)** (JCMcConnochie) **9-10-12** BPowell (chsd ldrs: hit 6th: drvn along 13th: styd on fr 3 out: led flat)	—	**1**	9/1	90	29
64^{*}	**Daringly (78)** (RCurtis) **7-11-2** DMorris (lw: a in tch: led 14th: clr 4 out: wknd & hdd flat)	3½	**2**	$2/1^{1}$	92	31
	Buckaneer Bay (69) (SIPittendrigh) **9-10-4**(3) GCahill (mstkes: effrt 13th: lost pl & blnd 4 out)	27	**3**	14/1	66	5
61^{3}	**Dear Emily (77)** (JESwiers) **8-11-1** APMcCoy (chsd ldrs: outpcd 4 out: sn wknd)	12	**4**	11/2	66	5
	Cuchullains Gold (IRE) (86) (JWhite) **8-11-10** RDunwoody (hld up: mstke 10th: effrt 15th: wknd & hit next)	20	**5**	$7/2^{2}$	62	1
64^{7}	**Little Thyne (63)** (DrPPritchard) **11-10-1b** DrPPritchard (chsd ldrs: rdn 13th: wkng whn fell next)		**F**	33/1	—	—
	Ruber (74) (RWThomson) **9-10-12** BStorey (sn bhd: t.o whn p.u bef 9th)		**P**	25/1	—	—
95^{P}	**Morning Blush (IRE) (86)** (MCPipe) **6-11-10** DBridgwater (mde most to 14th: wknd qckly after next: bhd whn p.u bef 3 out)		**P**	$5/1^{3}$	—	—
	Quixall Crossett (67) (EMCaine) **11-9-12**(7) MrMHNaughton (j.b: sn bhd: t.o whn p.u bef 9th)		**P**	33/1	—	—
70^{2}	**Red Eikon (75)** (GHolmes) **5-10-8** RichardGuest (nt j.w: hld up: rdn & mstke 12th: sn wknd: bhd whn p.u bef 4 out)		**P**	8/1	—	—

(SP 125.1%) **10 Rn**

6m 23.7 (12.70) CSF £28.06 CT £242.39 TOTE £10.20: £1.60 £1.40 £2.40 (£12.50) Trio £97.00 OWNER Major H. R. M. Porter (STRATFORD)
WEIGHT FOR AGE 5yo-5lb

70 Manor Rhyme owes a lot to his jockey. Recording his first win in twenty-eight attempts, he was kept right up to his work to show ahead on the run-in. (9/1)
64* Daringly, 7lb higher after a success here last time, looked like coming home along when going clear on the final turn but, tiring after the last, he found the winning partnership much too strong. (2/1)
Buckaneer Bay, who showed little form in seventeen previous outings in Ireland, came in for market support. Let down by his jumping, he was going nowhere when he fell through the fourth last. (14/1: 20/1-10/1)
29* Morning Blush (IRE) (5/1: op 3/1)

136 ROSELAND GROUP H'CAP CHASE (0-120) (5-Y.O+) (Class D)

3-10 (3-16) **2m 4f (15 fncs)** £3,822.50 (£1,145.00: £550.00: £252.50) GOING: 0.07 sec per fur (G)

				SP	RR	SF
	Nordic Sun (IRE) (110) (LRLloyd-James) **8-11-12** MDwyer (w ldrs: led last: styd on wl)	—	**1**	11/2	121	36
56^{4}	**Channel Pastime (94)** (DBurchell) **12-10-7**(3) GuyLewis (led 5th: hdd last: kpt on same pce)	7	**2**	$7/2^{1}$	99	14
68^{3}	**Bitacrack (84)** (JJBirkett) **9-10-0** LO'Hara (led to 5th: trckd ldrs: effrt 4 out: rdn & styd on one pce fr next)	½	**3**	8/1	89	4
104^{2}	**Sword Beach (112)** (MrsMReveley) **12-12-0** PNiven (trckd ldrs: rdn 4 out: wknd appr next)	4	**4**	$5/1^{3}$	114	29
56^{P}	**Strong Sound (103)** (PCheesbrough) **9-11-2**(3) GCahill (chsd ldrs: rdn & outpcd 11th: ev ch 3 out: wkng whn hit next)	13	**5**	$9/2^{2}$	94	9
	Its Unbelievable (90) (DJWintle) **6-10-6** PMcLoughlin (in tch: blnd 4th: rdn & wknd 4 out)	17	**6**	16/1	68	—
68^{6}	**Drumstick (96)** (KCBailey) **10-10-12** RDunwoody (reminders 8th: bhd & rdn 10th)	20	**7**	10/1	58	—
69^{3}	**Damas (FR) (110)** (MCPipe) **5-11-8b** DBridgwater (drvn along & lost tch 9th: nt r.o: t.o whn p.u bef 3 out)		**P**	$5/1^{3}$	—	—

(SP 115.2%) **8 Rn**

5m 2.6 (11.60) CSF £23.78 CT £139.74 TOTE £7.60: £3.10 £1.80 £1.40 (£13.80) OWNER Mr J. B. Slatcher (MALTON)
LONG HANDICAP Bitacrack 9-12
WEIGHT FOR AGE 5yo-4lb

Nordic Sun (IRE), produced to lead at the last, came away in the closing stages. (11/2)
Channel Pastime, meeting Sword Beach on much better terms, forced the pace, but lacked the winner's turn of speed on the run-in. (7/2)
68 Bitacrack, 2lb out of the handicap, was badly tapped for foot three out but, to his credit, he was staying on again at the finish. (8/1)
104 Sword Beach, meeting Channel Pastime on 8lb worse terms compared with Uttoxeter, travelled strongly but, suddenly coming under pressure four out, called it a day going to the next. (5/1: 7/2-11/2)
56 Strong Sound carried plenty of condition. Tapped for foot five out, he was soon bang in the firing-line, but was feeling the strain when he hit the second last. He probably needs three miles now. (9/2)

137 ROSELAND GROUP MAIDEN HURDLE (4-Y.O+) (Class E)

3-40 (3-44) **2m 1f 110y (8 hdls)** £2,477.50 (£690.00: £332.50) GOING: 0.07 sec per fur (G)

				SP	RR	SF
26^{3}	**Efharisto** (JWhite) **7-11-1b** RDunwoody (trckd ldrs: rdn to ld last: styd on wl)	—	**1**	$5/2^{1}$	75	14
	Sea God (MCChapman) **5-11-1** WWorthington (hld up: wnt prom 4th: led appr 2 out: hdd last: nt qckn)	1¾	**2**	$6/1^{2}$	73	12
	Elly Fleetfoot (IRE) (MJRyan) **4-10-7** JRyan (trckd ldrs: 3rd & btn whn mstke last)	6	**3**	20/1	63	—
105^{7}	**Positivo** (MissCJECaroe) **5-11-1** ILawrence (chsd ldrs: drvn along 4th: led 3 out: hdd appr next: one pce)	4	**4**	$12/1^{3}$	64	3
65^{2}	**Pickens (USA) (95)** (NTinkler) **4-10-12** JOsborne (lw: chsd ldrs: rdn & outpcd appr 2 out: n.d)	14	**5**	$5/2^{1}$	52	—
7^{4}	**Saracen Prince (USA) (90)** (HAlexander) **4-10-12** PNiven (mid div: effrt 5 out: wknd appr 2 out)	6	**6**	$12/1^{3}$	46	—
	Kindergarten Boy (IRE) (KCBailey) **5-10-12**(3) TJMurphy (led: j.lft 2nd: hdd 3 out: sn wknd)	1¼	**7**	20/1	45	—
	Instantaneous (TDEasterby) **4-10-7** RGarritty (lw: hld up: sme hdwy whn mstke 3 out: n.d)	hd	**8**	$6/1^{2}$	40	—
69^{5}	**Blennerville (IRE)** (MissJBower) **6-10-10** MFoster (chsd ldrs: drvn along 4th: wknd after next)	10	**9**	14/1	31	—

	Horse	Dist	Pos	SP	RR	SF
	Smocking (MissKMGeorge) **6-10-10** PMcLoughlin (bhd fr 3 out)	12	**10**	33/1	20	—
	Irie Mon (IRE) (MPBielby) **4-10-12** APMcCoy (lw: in tch: wnt prom 4th: wknd after next)	2½	**11**	16/1	22	—
	Woodbine (RDEWoodhouse) **6-11-1** DerekByrne (plld hrd: w ldrs: bmpd 2nd: wknd 4th: t.o whn fell 3 out)		**F**	25/1	—	—
	Malzoom (SEKettlewell) **4-10-12** BStorey (lw: hld up & bhd: t.o 5th: p.u bef 2 out)		**P**	25/1	—	—
96[6]	**Pimsboy** (GROldroyd) **9-10-12**(3) PMidgley (sn bhd: t.o whn p.u bef 2 out)		**P**	33/1	—	—
	On the Ledge (USA) (HJManners) **6-10-8**(7) ADowling (sn bhd: t.o whn p.u bef 2 out)		**P**	50/1	—	—
				(SP 138.7%)	**15 Rn**	

4m 16.1 (13.10) CSF £20.03 TOTE £4.70: £1.80 £1.40 £5.90 (£10.50) Trio £88.20 OWNER Mr Adrian Fitzpatrick (ASTON ROWANT)
WEIGHT FOR AGE 4yo-3lb
26 Efharisto had to work hard to gain the upper hand on the run-in. He will be better suited by two and a half miles. (5/2)
Sea God was held up off the pace this tirme. Taking charge going to two out, he found the winner too strong on the run-in. (6/1)
Elly Fleetfoot (IRE) was third and held when she made a mistake at the last. Her rider dismounted after the line, but she seemed none the worse. (20/1)
Positivo, driven along to keep up before halfway, went on three out, but his one pace was never going to see him get home. (12/1)
65 Pickens (USA), who as usual wore a tongue-strap, was badly tapped for foot going to two out. (5/2)

138 'STRAWBERRIES & CREAM' H'CAP CHASE (0-105) (5-Y.O+) (Class F)
4-10 (4-13) **2m 1f 110y (13 fncs)** £2,861.00 (£796.00: £383.00) GOING: 0.07 sec per fur (G)

	Horse	Dist	Pos	SP	RR	SF
	Rhossili Bay (97) (MrsMReveley) **8-11-6** PNiven (lw: chsd ldrs: led 2 out: r.o u.p flat: all out)	—	**1**	13/8 [1]	105	19
	The Toaster (97) (JJQuinn) **9-11-6** MDwyer (lw: trckd ldrs: outpcd 4 out: rallied 2 out: hrd rdn & ev ch flat: r.o)	hd	**2**	9/2 [2]	105	19
76*	**Noblely (USA) (105)** (NJHWalker) **9-12-0** RFarrant (led: hdd & mstke 2 out: wknd appr last)	10	**3**	5/1 [3]	104	18
	Forgetful (87) (DBurchell) **7-10-10** DJBurchell (chsd ldr: 3rd & wkng whn blnd 3 out)	12	**4**	9/2 [2]	75	—
63[3]	**Rupples (87)** (MCChapman) **9-10-10** WWorthington (hdwy 6th: rdn & outpcd 8th: sn wknd)	3½	**5**	12/1	72	—
	Shrewd John (102) (RDEWoodhouse) **10-11-11** DerekByrne (hld up: effrt 9th: sn rdn & btn)	12	**6**	8/1	76	—
	Old Mortality (78) (RWThomson) **10-10-1**ow1 BStorey (mstke 2nd: drvn along 6th: t.o whn p.u bef 4 out)		**P**	33/1	—	—
				(SP 112.9%)	**7 Rn**	

4m 28.3 (13.30) CSF £8.92 TOTE £2.70: £1.60 £2.00 (£4.30) OWNER Mrs M. Williams (SALTBURN) BRED G. W. Sivell
LONG HANDICAP Old Mortality 9-4
STEWARDS' ENQUIRY Dwyer susp. 13, 19 & 21/7/96 (excessive use of the whip).
Rhossili Bay just came off best in a tight finish. He is even better over two and a half miles. (13/8)
The Toaster looked out of it four from home. Rallying at the second last, he answered his rider's every call on the run-in, but was just denied. He too is better over another half a mile. (9/2)
76* Noblely (USA), who won a weak race at Stratford, was already in trouble when he fell through the second last. (5/1: op 3/1)

139 'ICE CREAM' NOVICES' HURDLE (4-Y.O+) (Class D)
4-40 (4-40) **2m 3f 110y (10 hdls)** £2,819.00 (£784.00: £377.00) GOING: 0.07 sec per fur (G)

	Horse	Dist	Pos	SP	RR	SF
58*	**River Room (95)** (KCBailey) **6-11-6** JOsborne (a in tch: hdwy to ld appr 2 out: clr last: drvn out)	—	**1**	7/2 [2]	84	14
	Clean Edge (USA) (90) (JMackie) **4-10-8**(3) EHusband (lw: bhd: hdwy 3 out: sn rdn: styd on wl flat)	5	**2**	9/1	74	1
	Political Panto (IRE) (110) (MCPipe) **5-11-6** DBridgwater (led: rn wd & hdd appr 2 out: wknd appr last)	9	**3**	2/1 [1]	73	3
31[4]	**Supermodel (103)** (MrsNMacauley) **4-10-12** RDunwoody (chsd ldr: n.m.r & stmbld bnd bef 6th: wknd 2 out)	3	**4**	7/2 [2]	65	—
31[3]	**Amercius** (JLHarris) **4-10-11b** DGallagher (effrt u.p: 6th: sn hrd rdn: n.d)	20	**5**	6/1 [3]	48	—
	Poplin (JWharton) **5-10-9** BDalton (3rd whn fell 5th)		**F**	20/1	—	—
3[2]	**Level Edge (89)** (HAlexander) **5-10-8**(7) MrRThornton (bhd whn hmpd 5th: no ch after: p.u bef 3 out)		**P**	9/1	—	—
93[F]	**Spanish Money** (MPBielby) **9-11-0** APMcCoy (sn bhd & reminders: hmpd 5th: t.o whn p.u bef next)		**P**	16/1	—	—
	Teeter The Peeth (MissKMGeorge) **6-11-0** PMcLoughlin (bit bkwd: bhd whn rn out bnd bef 6th)		**R**	33/1	—	—
				(SP 125.6%)	**9 Rn**	

4m 48.6 (15.60) CSF £34.42 TOTE £4.90: £2.50 £4.20 £1.40 (£15.20) Trio £30.90 OWNER Mr Douglas Allum (UPPER LAMBOURN) BRED E. Stuart Knape
WEIGHT FOR AGE 4yo-3lb
58* River Room looked to have done well since winning here over two weeks ago. After taking charge two out, his rider left nothing to chance on the run-in. (7/2: op 7/4)
Clean Edge (USA), who changed hands after winning a selling handicap at Uttoxeter last month, came from some way off the pace. Staying on grimly on the run-in, he had given the winner too much start. He will be better suited by three miles. (9/1)
Political Panto (IRE), a headstrong individual, ran slightly wide on the home turn and soon forfeited the advantage. His stride shortened dramatically going to the last, and he his without doubt his own worst enemy. (2/1)
31 Supermodel was on the heels of the leader when she stumbled on the bend turning into the back straight before the sixth. Fading two out, she seems best when able to dominate. (7/2: 5/2-4/1)

T/Plpt: £36.30 (258.03 Tckts). T/Qdpt: £18.40 (38.59 Tckts). WG

140a-153a (Irish Racing) - See Computer Raceform

PARDUBICE (Czech Republic) (Good to firm)
Friday June 28th

154a CENA IC PARDUBICE HURDLE (4-Y.O+)
1m 7f (8 hdls) £483.00 (£278.00: £205.00)

Horse	Dist	Pos	SP	RR	SF
Kreator (POL) (FHolcak,CzechRepublic) **4-10-3** VSnitkovskij	—	**1**		—	—
Habasha (IRE) (RSimpson) **6-10-11** CMaude	11	**2**		—	—
Jerevan (CZE) (TPechat,CzechRepublic) **7-10-11** DMoravec	½	**3**		—	—
					10 Rn

3m 28.0 OWNER Valstav Paschal Zlin
Habasha (IRE), the only one of Rod Simpson's three travellers in good enough shape to run, set off in front. She led until turning for home and was no match for the winner in the closing stages.

92a-AUTEUIL (Paris, France) (L-H) (Soft)
Saturday June 29th

155a GRANDE COURSE DE HAIES D'AUTEUIL HURDLE (5-Y.O+)
3-40 (3-43) **3m 1f 110y** £105,402.00 (£52,701.00: £31,621.00)

				SP	RR	SF
52a^3	**Earl Grant (FR)** (BSecly,France) **7-10-5** JYBeaurain	—	1		156	—
52a^2	**Mysilv** (CREgerton) **6-10-1** JOsborne	2	2		151	—
52a*	**Montperle (FR)** (JBertranDeBalanda,France) **7-10-5** DBressou	15	3		145	—
						10 Rn

6m 19.0 P-M 7.20F: 2.10F 1.60F 2.20F (11.60F) OWNER Mr L. Gautier BRED B. Boutboul
52a Mysilv ran a great race. Bowling along from the start and pinging all the obstacles, she was joined in the lead halfway up the back straight by the eventual winner, and came into the final hurdle with two lengths to find. Although she battled on, she could not peg back the winner. She will next be seen at the beginning of the English jumps season when a decision will be made as to whether she goes over fences.
DS

128-WORCESTER (L-H) (Good to firm)
Wednesday July 10th
Race 2: one flight omitted fnl circ
WEATHER: fine

156 HARPLEY NOVICES' CLAIMING HURDLE (4-Y.O+) (Class F)
6-45 (6-49) **2m 4f (10 hdls)** £2,087.00 (£582.00: £281.00) GOING minus 0.26 sec per fur (GF)

				SP	RR	SF
73^P	**Sparts Fault (IRE) (68)** (PEccles) **6-10-10** RichardGuest (hld up: hdwy 5th: led appr last: drvn out)	—	1	25/1	69	—
69^P	**Mutley (61)** (NJHawke) **6-10-7** CMaude (hld up & bhd: gd hdwy 3 out: hmpd & led 2 out: sn hdd: one pce)	6	2	14/1	61	—
137^5	**Pickens (USA) (95)** (NTinkler) **4-11-6** JOsborne (a.p: ev ch whn hung lft 2 out: btn whn j.rt last)	2½	3	3/1^2	75	—
137^3	**Elly Fleetfoot (IRE)** (MJRyan) **4-10-9** JRyan (a.p: j.slowly 6th & 7th: led 3 out tl hung rt & hdd 2 out: sn wknd)	1½	4	5/2^1	63	—
	Ewar Imperial (KOCunningham-Brown) **4-10-11** DGallagher (lw: hld up: hdwy 7th: ev ch 3 out: wknd 2 out: hit last)	14	5	33/1	54	—
	Coolegale (50) (LWells) **10-10-7** SMcNeill (bit bkwd: led tl appr 3 out: sn wknd)	2½	6	20/1	45	—
67^{11}	**Pats Folly** (FJYardley) **5-10-2** PMcLoughlin (hld up & plld hrd: hdwy 6th: mstke 7th: wknd 3 out)	4	7	50/1	37	—
	Admiral's Guest (IRE) (WClay) **4-10-11** TEley (hld up: hdwy 7th: wknd appr 2 out)	3	8	20/1	46	—
	Don Tocino (JWhite) **6-11-2** APMcCoy (bit bkwd: hld up: hdwy 3rd: led appr 3 out: sn hdd & wknd)	4	9	5/1	45	—
	Emperors Wood (PHayward) **5-10-10** BFenton (unruly s: a bhd: t.o)	15	10	33/1	27	—
	Saltis (IRE) (MrsPGrainger) **4-10-5** VSlattery (nt j.w: bhd: blnd & rdr lost irons 2nd: t.o fr 7th)	½	11	33/1	25	—
77^P	**Nick the Biscuit (83)** (RTPhillips) **5-10-13v** RDunwoody (swtg: prom tl hrd rdn & wknd 3 out: t.o)	2	12	9/2^3	28	—
129^P	**Brensham Folly** (RBrotherton) **5-10-7b^1** LHarvey (a bhd: t.o whn p.u bef 3 out)		P	50/1	—	—
66^{19}	**Ardearned (50)** (MrsJAYoung) **9-10-4**ow2 MrACharles-Jones (prom: j.slowly 1st: wknd qckly 5th: t.o whn p.u bef last: lame)		P	50/1	—	—
				(SP 123.2%)		**14 Rn**

4m 53.2 (15.20) CSF £303.98 TOTE £48.90: £6.70 £4.50 £1.10 (£540.50) Trio Not won; £180.36 to 12/7/96 OWNER Mr Brian Lewendon (LAMBOURN) BRED John Carolan
WEIGHT FOR AGE 4yo-3lb
OFFICIAL EXPLANATION **Sparts Fault (IRE): was running without the blinkers that upset him last time out and this was a slower-run race, which enabled him to settle.**
Sparts Fault (IRE) had shown signs of ability over two years ago when trained by Simon Sherwood but has been an indifferent jumper of both hurdles and fences since. (25/1)
Mutley has disappointed since finishing third at Wincanton in April. (14/1)
137 Pickens (USA) was dropped in class and trying a longer trip. (3/1)
137 Elly Fleetfoot (IRE) was novicey at a couple of hurdles at this longer distance. (5/2)
Nick the Biscuit (9/2: op 5/2)

157 PERSHORE NOVICES' H'CAP HURDLE (0-100) (4-Y.O+) (Class E)
7-15 (7-16) **3m (11 hdls)** £2,250.00 (£625.00: £300.00) GOING minus 0.26 sec per fur (GF)

				SP	RR	SF
65^5	**Little Tincture (IRE) (66)** (MrsTJMcInnesSkinner) **6-10-2**(5) SophieMitchell (prom: led appr 4th: hrd rdn appr last: all out)	—	1	5/1	47	—
19^4	**Palace Parade (USA) (65)** (AGNewcombe) **6-10-6** AThornton (a.p: ev ch last: hrd rdn: unable qckn)	1¼	2	5/2^2	45	—
	Mountain Leader (69) (DMHyde) **6-10-10** BPowell (w ldr: led 3rd: sn hdd: lost pl 6th: rallied 8th: outpcd 2 out: styd on flat)	¾	3	20/1	49	—
77*	**Little Court (62)** (EGBevan) **5-10-3** APMcCoy (led to 3rd: wknd appr 3 out: t.o)	dist	4	9/2^3	—	—
19*	**Valisky (85)** (RLee) **6-11-12** CLlewellyn (fell 2nd: dead)		F	9/4^1	—	—
	Rumi (72) (NTinkler) **5-10-13** JOsborne (hld up: hdwy & j.slowly 8th: wknd qckly: t.o whn p.u bef 3 out)		P	9/2^3	—	—
	Credit Call (IRE) (59) (RGBrazington) **8-10-0** WHumphreys (a bhd: t.o fr 8th: p.u bef last)		P	50/1	—	—
				(SP 119.1%)		**7 Rn**

5m 54.9 (18.90) CSF £17.99 TOTE £7.50: £1.90 £3.70 (£8.90) OWNER Mrs T. J. McInnesSkinner (MELTON MOWBRAY)
65 Little Tincture (IRE) was suited by this stamina test, but had to dig deep to hold on. (5/1)
19 Palace Parade (USA) who has changed stables, gave his all but it was not quite enough. (5/2)
Mountain Leader certainly does not find stamina a problem. (20/1)
19* Valisky, raised 10lb, took a fatal fall early on. (9/4)

158 WADHAM KENNING WORCESTER VAUXHALL H'CAP CHASE (0-105) (5-Y.O+) (Class F)
7-45 (7-46) **2m 7f (18 fncs)** £3,099.00 (£864.00: £417.00) GOING minus 0.26 sec per fur (GF)

				SP	RR	SF
	Evangelica (USA) (105) (MCPipe) **6-12-0** DBridgwater (hld up: gd hdwy appr 4 out: led last: drvn out)	—	1	6/1^3	117	—

	Horse	Dist	Pos	SP	RR	SF
23P	**The Blue Boy (IRE) (100)** (PBowen) **8-11-9b** RDunwoody (a.p: ev ch last: hrd rdn: r.o)	1¼	2	16/1	111	—
102³	**Menature (IRE) (77)** (NJPomfret) **7-9-11**(3) JCulloty (swtg: a.p: led 11th tl mstke last: wknd)	8	3	10/1	83	—
94⁵	**Rusty Bridge (88)** (MrsSMJohnson) **9-10-4**(7) MrRThornton (sn rdn along: blnd 10th: styd on fr 2 out: nrst fin)	12	4	20/1	85	—
	Jim Valentine (93) (DJWintle) **10-11-2** WMarston (dwlt: blnd bdly 2nd: nvr nrr)	½	5	14/1	90	—
	Manamour (82) (RLee) **9-10-5**ow2 RichardGuest (hld up: hdwy appr 4 out: wknd 3 out)	2	6	20/1	78	—
	Boxing Match (78) (JMBradley) **9-10-1** BFenton (prom tl wknd 4 out)	s.h	7	20/1	73	—
130U	**Funcheon Gale (94)** (RCurtis) **9-11-3** DMorris (hld up & bhd: hdwy 12th: wknd appr 4 out)	11	8	11/4 1	82	—
	Trust Deed (USA) (77) (SGKnight) **8-10-0b** MRichards (hit 1st: bhd tl hdwy 10th: hrd rdn 12th: sn wknd)	2	9	12/1	63	—
68⁵	**Hamper (83)** (NRMitchell) **13-10-3b**(3) KGaule (hld up: hdwy 9th: wknd 12th)	9	10	25/1	63	—
94²	**Truss (87)** (JohnUpson) **9-10-10** RSupple (led to 4th: mstke 14th: wknd 4 out)	1¼	11	11/1	66	—
68P	**The Lorryman (IRE) (97)** (NRMitchell) **8-11-6** GUpton (led 4th to 11th: wknd appr 4 out)	1½	12	33/1	75	—
130²	**Father Dowling (82)** (GBBalding) **9-10-5** APMcCoy (a bhd)	9	13	11/2 2	54	—
	Gilston Lass (101) (JSKing) **9-11-10** ASSmith (lw: hdwy 7th: wknd 14th: t.o)	14	14	25/1	63	—
130⁴	**Abbotsham (87)** (OJCarter) **11-10-3**(7) MissEJJones (swtg: fell 5th)		F	20/1	—	—
94⁶	**Jimmy O'Dea (95)** (TTBill) **9-11-4v** JOsborne (a bhd: t.o whn p.u bef 14th)		P	14/1	—	—
14⁶	**Tenbit (IRE) (81)** (NATwiston-Davies) **6-10-4**ow4 CMaude (lw: prom to 9th: bhd whn p.u & dismntd after 14th)		P	16/1	—	—
94P	**Storm Warrior (77)** (TWall) **11-9-11b**(3) RMassey (mstke 6th: bhd whn blnd 3 out: p.u bef 2 out)		P	33/1	—	—
72⁷	**The Foolish One (77)** (RHAlner) **9-10-0** DGallagher (bhd: hmpd 5th: t.o whn p.u bef 10th)		P	33/1	—	—
	Cantantivy (77) (CFCJackson) **11-9-7**(7) MrOMcPhail (prom to 11th: t.o whn p.u bef last)		P	50/1	—	—

(SP 144.1%) **20 Rn**

5m 58.9 (20.90) CSF £102.68 CT £917.52 TOTE £10.00: £3.40 £5.30 £3.70 £4.20 (£142.00) Trio £123.00; £26.01 to 12/7/96 OWNER Martin Pipe Racing Club (WELLINGTON) BRED Helen C Alexander

LONG HANDICAP Trust Deed (USA) 9-11 Tenbit (IRE) 9-10 Storm Warrior 9-9 The Foolish One 9-3 Cantantivy 9-10

Evangelica (USA) was 7lb higher than when winning at Stratford on the final day of last season. (6/1: op 4/1)

The Blue Boy (IRE) bounced back to form with his best effort for a some time.. (16/1)

102 Menature (IRE) certainly seems capable of getting off the mark back in novice company. (10/1)

23* Funcheon Gale, 9lb higher than when winning here a month ago, also had to contend with faster ground. (11/4)

159 RADIO WYVERN H'CAP HURDLE (0-115) (4-Y.O+) (Class E)

8-15 (8-18) **2m (8 hdls)** £2,512.50 (£700.00: £337.50) GOING minus 0.26 sec per fur (GF)

	Horse	Dist	Pos	SP	RR	SF
	Routing (102) (NGAyliffe) **8-11-5** CMaude (a gng wl: led & mstke 2 out: clr whn j.rt last: easily)	—	1	16/1	91+	46
	El Grando (83) (KOCunningham-Brown) **6-10-0** DGallagher (hld up & bhd: hdwy 4th: r.o flat: no ch w wnr)	8	2	20/1	64	19
	Out Ranking (FR) (100) (MCPipe) **4-11-0** DBridgwater (a.p: led appr 3 out tl mstke 2 out: one pce)	1½	3	13/2 3	80	32
103³	**Kalzari (USA) (90)** (AWCarroll) **11-10-7** BPowell (hld up: hdwy 5th: one pce fr 3 out)	1	4	10/1	69	24
75³	**Lady Confess (93)** (JohnUpson) **6-10-10** RSupple (led tl appr 3 out: wknd 2 out)	½	5	8/1	71	26
	King's Shilling (USA) (99) (HOliver) **9-11-2** RDavis (hld up & bhd: hdwy appr 3 out: one pce fr 2 out)	8	6	25/1	69	24
128*	**Courageous Knight (85)** (PHayward) **7-10-2** BFenton (a bhd)	6	7	3/1 2	49	4
103F	**Wamdha (IRE) (103)** (KAMorgan) **6-11-6** ASSmith (a bhd)	nk	8	10/1	67	22
	Cavo Greco (USA) (83) (JJoseph) **7-10-0** DSkyrme (plld hrd: prom to 5th: t.o)	22	9	33/1	25	—
	Moymet (83) (JSKing) **10-10-0** JOsborne (prom to 4th: t.o)	28	10	33/1	—	—
	Shifting Moon (98) (FJordan) **4-10-12** WMarston (bhd fr 5th: t.o)	10	11	14/1	2	—
103⁴	**Amazon Express (106)** (PBowen) **7-11-9** RDunwoody (prom tl mstke 5th: bhd whn fell 3 out)		F	10/1	—	—
75*	**Fisio Sands (103)** (TPMcGovern) **7-11-6** APMcCoy (prom to 3rd: bhd whn p.u bef 5th)		P	5/2 1	—	—

(SP 132.3%) **13 Rn**

3m 40.2 (0.20) CSF £277.67 CT £2,108.36 TOTE £24.90: £6.00 £4.80 £2.70 (£175.20) Trio Not won; £197.98 to 12/7/96 OWNER Mr Derek Jones (MINEHEAD) BRED Fonthill Stud

LONG HANDICAP Cavo Greco (USA) 9-13

WEIGHT FOR AGE 4yo-3lb

Routing had dropped to a mark 2lb lower than when he last won. (16/1)

El Grando, who has been slipping down the handicap, kept on to finish best of the rest. (20/1)

Out Ranking (FR) could not go with the winner from the penultimate flight. (13/2)

103 Wamdha (IRE) (10/1: 8/1-12/1)

75* Fisio Sands ran no race at all. (5/2)

160 PROMOTA NOVICES' CHASE (5-Y.O+) (Class E)

8-45 (8-53) **2m (12 fncs)** £3,036.25 (£910.00: £437.50: £201.25) GOING minus 0.26 sec per fur (GF)

	Horse	Dist	Pos	SP	RR	SF
128³	**Stately Home (IRE)** (PBowen) **5-10-8** APMcCoy (j.w: mde all: r.o wl fr 3 out)	—	1	4/1 3	93	16
	Pontoon Bridge (100) (GHarwood) **9-11-4** RDunwoody (chsd wnr: mstke 7th: ev ch 3 out: rdn appr 2 out: no imp)	5	2	8/11 1	95	21
97⁴	**Nordic Valley (IRE)** (MCPipe) **5-10-8** DBridgwater (hld up: hdwy 8th: 3rd & wkng whn j.rt 4 out & 3 out)	20	3	7/2 2	68	—
72³	**Legal Artist (IRE)** (MissCJohnsey) **6-10-11** LHarvey (hld up: hdwy 8th: wknd 4 out)	2½	4	8/1	66	—
	Master Art (JWDufosee) **6-10-6**(5) PHenley (bhd fr 6th: t.o fr 8th)	6	5	50/1	60	—
132W	**Paid Elation (60)** (NRMitchell) **11-10-1**(5) SophieMitchell (prom to 8th)	2	6	100/1	53	—
	Ballyranebow (IRE) (CFCJackson) **8-10-11**ow5 MrGBarfoot-Saunt (hld up & bhd: t.o fr 8th)	28	7	100/1	30	—

(SP 115.2%) **7 Rn**

3m 55.8 (4.80) CSF £7.26 TOTE £5.00: £1.40 £1.50 (£3.60) OWNER Mr P. Bowen (HAVERFORDWEST) BRED Ash Hill Stud

WEIGHT FOR AGE 5yo-3lb

128 Stately Home (IRE) jumped like an old hand on his chasing debut and can score again. (4/1)

Pontoon Bridge found the winner holding all the aces over this shorter trip. (8/11)

97 Nordic Valley (IRE) was making his chasing debut. (7/2: 5/2-4/1)

161 WORCESTER STANDARD N.H. FLAT RACE (4, 5 & 6-Y.O) (Class H)

9-15 (9-20) **2m** £1,259.00 (£349.00: £167.00)

	Horse	Dist	Pos	SP	RR	SF
25*	**Kailash (USA)** (MCPipe) **5-12-0** DBridgwater (hld up: stdy hdwy 10f out: led on bit 3f out: clr over 1f out: easily)	—	1	5/2 2	—	—

	Horse	Dist	Pos	SP	RR	SF
	Marlousion (IRE) (CPEBrooks) **4-10-10** DGallagher (hld up & bhd: hdwy 3f out: sn rdn: r.o ins fnl f: no ch w wnr)	4	**2**	10/1	—	—
	Powerful Spirit (JGMO'Shea) **4-10-10**(5) MichaelBrennan (hld up & plld hrd: hdwy 9f out: led 5f out to 3f out: one pce)	5	**3**	9/1	—	—
133^{2}	**Oh Dear Me** (RMFlower) **5-10-13** BPowell (a.p: one pce fnl 3f)	nk	**4**	5/1^{3}	—	—
	Swynford King (JFBottomley) **4-11-1** DerekByrne (hld up: hdwy 5f out: wknd over 2f out)	6	**5**	7/4^{1}	—	—
	Moreceva (IRE) (PaddyFarrell) **6-11-4** RGreene (nvr nr ldrs)	12	**6**	33/1	—	—
	Heading North (OJCarter) **5-10-11**(7) MissEJJones (bit bkwd: bhd fnl 5f)	2½	**7**	33/1	—	—
99^{6}	**Oats For Notes** (MissVenetiaWilliams) **6-10-13** MrMRimell (hld up: hdwy 10f out: wknd 4f out)	1¼	**8**	20/1	—	—
133^{9}	**Flame of Dance** (AStreeter) **5-11-4** TEley (lw: hdwy 4f out: eased whn btn over 2f out)	4	**9**	25/1	—	—
	No Sacrifice (GAHam) **4-10-5**(5) SophieMitchell (a bhd)	3	**10**	33/1	—	—
	Hildens Memory (SADouch) **6-10-13** SMcNeill (bit bkwd: plld hrd: prom tl wknd over 3f out: sn eased)	¾	**11**	10/1	—	—
	Mollie Silvers (JKCresswell) **4-10-7**(3) RMassey (led after 3f to 5f out: wkng whn rn wd bnd over 3f out)	14	**12**	33/1	—	—
25^{11}	**Wotanite** (OO'Neill) **6-11-4** VSlattery (led 3f: wknd 5f out)	6	**13**	33/1	—	—
	Katharine's Song (IRE) (DMHyde) **6-10-13** RDunwoody (bkwd: prom 12f)	4	**14**	16/1	—	—
	Overseas Invader (IRE) (RMStronge) **4-11-1** WMcFarland (a bhd: t.o fnl 4f)	dist	**15**	33/1	—	—

(SP 141.9%) **15 Rn**

3m 43.0 CSF £29.87 TOTE £4.10: £2.90 £2.80 £2.20 (£14.30) Trio £78.80 OWNER Mr Mick Fletcher (WELLINGTON) BRED William C. Miller
WEIGHT FOR AGE 4yo-3lb
25* Kailash (USA) found no difficulty in defying a double penalty. (5/2)
Marlousion (IRE), a half sister to Bradbury Star, showed promise for the future. (10/1: op 5/1)
Powerful Spirit took a strong hold and did well in the circumstances. (9/1: op 16/1)
Swynford King was found to have been suffering from a lung infection when a disappointing favourite on his debut back in March. (7/4)
Hildens Memory (10/1: op 33/1)

T/Plpt: £3,640.50 (3.5 Tckts). T/Qdpt: £73.10 (15.2 Tckts). KH

162a-178a (Irish Racing) - See Computer Raceform

93-SOUTHWELL (L-H) (Firm)

Saturday July 13th

WEATHER: fine

179 BBC RADIO LINCOLNSHIRE NOVICES' CHASE (5-Y.O+) (Class D)

6-40 (6-41) **3m 110y (19 fncs)** £4,354.00 (£1,312.00: £636.00: £298.00) GOING: 0.23 sec per fur (G)

	Horse	Dist	Pos	SP	RR	SF
	Notable Exception (91) (MrsMReveley) **7-11-0** PNiven (lw: trckd ldrs: led 10th: all out: fin lame)	—	**1**	3/1^{2}	95	8
135^{5}	**Cuchullains Gold (IRE) (80)** (JWhite) **8-11-0** RDunwoody (hld up: hdwy 8th: rdn 2 out: styd on same pce)	7	**2**	11/1	90	3
	The West's Asleep (67) (JFfitch-Heyes) **11-11-0** DMorris (chsd ldrs tl wknd appr 3 out)	5	**3**	12/1	87	—
102^{4}	**Dustys Trail (IRE)** (PBowen) **7-10-7**(7) MrRThornton (hld up: hdwy 6th: rdn 3 out: wkng whn blnd 2 out)	8	**4**	14/1	82	—
	Strong Case (IRE) (MCPipe) **8-11-0b** DBridgwater (bit bkwd: prom: blnd 4th: led & fell 6th)		**F**	5/4^{1}	—	—
	Pendil's Delight (MrsPGrainger) **7-10-9** CLlewellyn (a in rr: t.o whn p.u after 12th)		**P**	6/1^{3}	—	—
	The Gallopin'major (IRE) (75) (MrsMReveley) **6-11-0** NSmith (hld up: a bhd: p.u bef 4 out)		**P**	10/1	—	—
135^{3}	**Buckaneer Bay (69)** (SIPittendrigh) **9-11-0** JOsborne (hld up: hdwy 7th: wknd 14th: t.o & p.u bef 4 out)		**P**	20/1	—	—
	Pacific Power (APJames) **6-11-0** DerekByrne (a bhd: t.o fr 9th: p.u after 12th)		**P**	40/1	—	—
129^{9}	**Priesthill (IRE)** (DLWilliams) **7-10-7**(7) MissSHiggins (prom: lft in ld 6th: hdd 10th: rdn & wknd 3 out: t.o whn p.u bef last)		**P**	50/1	—	—
139^{P}	**Spanish Money** (MPBielby) **9-10-11b**1(3) KGaule (led & sn clr: hdd 6th: grad wknd: p.u bef 10th)		**P**	50/1	—	—

(SP 126.6%) **11 Rn**

6m 32.1 (25.10) CSF £35.69 TOTE £3.60: £1.30 £2.30 £2.80 (£15.10) Trio £83.10; £11.72 to Windsor 15/7/96. OWNER Mr Roland Hope (SALTBURN) BRED Cliveden Stud
Notable Exception, the pick of the paddock, was winning over his furthest trip to date. (3/1)
Cuchullains Gold (IRE) looked to be travelling just as well as the winner three out, but found nothing off the bridle. (11/1)
The West's Asleep is going to need a moderate event to get off the mark. (12/1)
Dustys Trail (IRE), a dual point-to-point winner, finds things tougher at this level. (14/1)

180 EAST MIDLANDS ELECTRICITY (LINCOLN) H'CAP CHASE (0-110) (5-Y.O+) (Class E)

7-10 (7-10) **2m 4f 110y (16 fncs)** £4,445.00 (£1,340.00: £650.00: £305.00) GOING: 0.23 sec per fur (G)

	Horse	Dist	Pos	SP	RR	SF
97*	**Nocatchim (90)** (KAMorgan) **7-10-8** ASSmith (lw: led 3rd to 7th: led 10th: clr appr 3 out: pushed out)	—	**1**	5/1^{3}	101	34
130^{3}	**Andrelot (110)** (PBowen) **9-12-0b** RDunwoody (prom: rdn & lost pl 8th: rallied appr 3 out: styd on u.p flat)	2	**2**	100/30^{1}	119	52
	Pims Gunner (IRE) (110) (MDHammond) **8-12-0** ADobbin (hld up: hdwy 10th: styd on same pce fr 2 out)	2½	**3**	6/1	118	51
	Arctic Life (IRE) (100) (JRJenkins) **7-11-4** JOsborne (led to 3rd: led 7th: mstke 9th: hdd 10th: wknd 3 out)	20	**4**	100/30^{1}	92	25
72^{4}	**Beat The Rap (82)** (DMorris) **10-10-0** BFenton (mstkes: a in rr: t.o)	24	**5**	33/1	55	—
136^{4}	**Sword Beach (105)** (MrsMReveley) **12-11-9** PNiven (lw: prom: lost pl 11th: sn bhd: t.o whn fell last)		**F**	4/1^{2}	—	—
158^{11}	**Truss (87)** (JohnUpson) **9-10-5** RSupple (hld up: a bhd: t.o whn p.u bef 3 out)		**P**	9/1	—	—
130^{P}	**Seal King (90)** (JMBradley) **11-10-8** APMcCoy (prom to 12th: t.o whn p.u bef 3 out)		**P**	11/1	—	—

(SP 118.4%) **8 Rn**

5m 15.1 (11.10) CSF £21.58 CT £94.50 TOTE £5.80: £1.60 £1.60 £2.20 (£12.50) Trio £17.10 OWNER Mr R. E. Gray (MELTON MOWBRAY) BRED Charlton Down Stud
LONG HANDICAP Beat The Rap 9-12
97* Nocatchim made the most of his opportunity to beat some reluctant rivals. (5/1)
130 Andrelot ran in snatches and only got going when it was too late. (100/30)
Pims Gunner (IRE) will benefit from the outing. (6/1)
Arctic Life (IRE) may well have found this ground far too lively. (100/30)

181 PROMOTA NOVICES' HURDLE (4-Y.O+) (Class E)

7-40 (7-40) **3m 110y (13 hdls)** £2,326.80 (£644.80: £308.40) GOING: 0.23 sec per fur (G)

	Horse	Dist	Pos	SP	RR	SF
100[2]	**Ordog Mor (IRE) (93)** (MGMeagher) **7-10-12** DerekByrne (hld up: hdwy to ld 5th: clr 7th: eased flat)	—	1	3/1[2]	73	—
139*	**River Room (107)** (KCBailey) **6-11-12** JOsborne (lw: led to 5th: rdn 3 out: no imp)	14	2	9/4[1]	78	—
100*	**Wynberg (95)** (CaptTAForster) **5-11-5** SWynne (trckd ldrs: rdn 3 out: sn outpcd)	9	3	3/1[2]	65	—
134[3]	**Tremble (64)** (MESowersby) **7-10-9**(3) DParker (prom: wkng whn j.slowly 9th: t.o)	30	4	25/1[3]	38	—
129[10]	**Coolmoreen (IRE)** (AJWilson) **8-10-7**(5) ChrisWebb (lw: hld up: mstke 3rd: bhd fr 8th: t.o)	dist	5	50/1	—	—
131*	**Tipping The Line (103)** (MCPipe) **6-11-12** DBridgwater (hld up in tch: bhd whn p.u bef 7th)		P	9/4[1]	—	—
135[P]	**Quixall Crossett** (EMCaine) **11-10-7**(5) MrMHNaughton (hld up: hmpd 3rd: t.o whn p.u after 8th)		P	50/1	—	—
99[11]	**Sweet Talker (IRE)** (MrsPGrainger) **4-10-8** DLeahy (in tch: mstke 4th: wknd 7th: t.o whn p.u after next)		P	50/1	—	—
				(SP 121.3%)		**8 Rn**

6m 14.4 (28.40) CSF £10.49 TOTE £3.90: £1.10 £1.50 £1.30 (£5.00) OWNER Mr M. R. Johnson (ORMSKIRK) BRED T. McKeever
WEIGHT FOR AGE 4yo-4lb
OFFICIAL EXPLANATION **Tipping The Line: was unable to go on the firm ground.**
100 Ordog Mor (IRE) got off the mark in fine style and won with any amount in hand. (3/1)
139* River Room, who will eventually jump fences, was labouring on this fast ground. (9/4)
100* Wynberg, who had the winner behind him last time, was struggling a long way out. (3/1)
131* Tipping The Line did not go on this firm ground. (9/4)

182 IAN LOFTUS PRINTING H'CAP HURDLE (0-125) (4-Y.O+) (Class D)

8-10 (8-10) **2m 4f 110y (11 hdls)** £2,835.00 (£785.00: £375.00) GOING: 0.23 sec per fur (G)

	Horse	Dist	Pos	SP	RR	SF
72[5]	**Fluidity (USA) (92)** (JGMO'Shea) **8-10-5** RSupple (hld up & bhd: hdwy 2 out: str run to ld nr fin)	—	1	14/1	71	—
55*	**Superhoo (91)** (RCraggs) **5-10-4** BFenton (led 3rd: clr 5th: hdd 2 out: rallied to ld flat: hdd nr fin)	nk	2	4/1[2]	70	—
71[2]	**Shikaree (IRE) (111)** (MCPipe) **5-11-10** DBridgwater (lw: hld up: j.slowly 2nd: hdwy 7th: led 2 out: hdd flat: r.o)	¾	3	9/4[1]	89	—
105[4]	**Governor Daniel (97)** (JGMO'Shea) **5-10-5**(5) MichaelBrennan (a.p: rdn appr 2 out: styd on same pce)	1½	4	9/2[3]	74	—
	Elflaa (IRE) (115) (NJHenderson) **5-12-0** RDunwoody (prom: chsd ldr 5th: ev ch whn mstke 2 out: sn hrd rdn: wknd flat)	12	5	5/1	83	—
64[3]	**Gone by (IRE) (104)** (JRJenkins) **8-11-3b** APMcCoy (hld up: drvn along 3 out: no imp)	6	6	11/2	67	—
	George Ashford (IRE) (91) (KAMorgan) **6-10-4** ASSmith (led to 3rd: bhd fr 6th)	20	7	14/1	38	—
103[6]	**Hacketts Cross (IRE) (108)** (PEccles) **8-11-7** RichardGuest (hld up: hdwy 7th: wknd 3 out: p.u bef next)		P	20/1	—	—
				(SP 119.1%)		**8 Rn**

5m 13.9 (27.90) CSF £66.56 CT £162.42 TOTE £16.70: £3.30 £1.60 £1.40 (£67.70) Trio £27.30 OWNER DSM (Demolition Services (Midlands) Ltd) (WELFORD-ON-AVON) BRED Derry Meeting Farm
72 Fluidity (USA) was given a superb ride. Ridden like a non-trier, he made stealthy progress to put his head in front virtually on the line. (14/1: 10/1-16/1)
55* Superhoo is running well at present. (4/1)
71 Shikaree (IRE), a dual course winner, lost nothing in defeat. (9/4)
105 Governor Daniel, tackling handicappers, showed enough to suggest he can add to his novice hurdle win. (9/2)

183 PAPER ROSE GREETING CARDS (S) H'CAP HURDLE (0-95) (4,5,6 & 7-Y.O) (Class G)

8-40 (8-41) **2m (9 hdls)** £2,419.80 (£672.80: £323.40) GOING: 0.23 sec per fur (G)

	Horse	Dist	Pos	SP	RR	SF
98[P]	**Denomination (USA) (81)** (MCPipe) **4-11-6** DBridgwater (hld up: hdwy 3 out: led last: comf)	—	1	9/1	66+	16
128[5]	**Sian Wyn (82)** (KRBurke) **6-11-10** RDunwoody (a.p: led 2 out: rdn & hdd last: r.o one pce)	2	2	9/4[1]	65	18
137[11]	**Irie Mon (IRE) (80)** (MPBielby) **4-11-2**(3) KGaule (hld up: styd on fr 2 out: nrst fin)	3½	3	16/1	60	10
67[3]	**Minnesota Fats (IRE) (67)** (MissMERowland) **4-10-6** GaryLyons (hld up: hdwy 5th: no ex appr last)	3	4	9/1	44	—
17[4]	**High Flown (USA) (77)** (RonaldThompson) **4-11-2** WFry (mid div: drvn along 3 out: nvr able to chal)	1	5	14/1	53	3
66[6]	**The Executor (76)** (JJoseph) **6-11-4** DSkyrme (hld up: hdwy 3 out: r.o one pce fr next)	nk	6	5/1[3]	51	4
105[11]	**Boost (65)** (MrsNMacauley) **4-10-4** SWynne (mid div: rdn 3 out: no imp)	3	7	33/1	37	—
	Heretical Miss (75) (JFfitch-Heyes) **6-11-3** APMcCoy (led to 2nd: led 5th: hdd & wknd 2 out)	1½	8	4/1[2]	46	—
	Pacific Overture (61) (GrahamRichards) **4-10-0** PMcLoughlin (hld up: nvr rchd ldrs)	2	9	33/1	30	—
67[2]	**Betabetcorbett (74)** (BPJBaugh) **5-11-2** TEley (led 3rd to 5th: wknd qckly appr last)	½	10	13/2	42	—
21[F]	**Java Shrine (USA) (76)** (JCTuck) **5-11-4b** SMcNeill (chsd ldrs: lost pl 4th: sn bhd)	dist	11	7/1	—	—
	Ragamuffin Romeo (68) (HSawyer) **7-10-7**(3) RMassey (hld up: a bhd: t.o whn p.u & dismntd bef last)		P	14/1	—	—
101[P]	**Arrogant Boy (60)** (SBClark) **7-9-9**(7)ow2 MissRClark (prom tl wknd 3 out: uns rdr appr next)		U	33/1	—	—
				(SP 141.3%)		**13 Rn**

3m 56.7 (14.70) CSF £33.11 CT £324.95 TOTE £18.30: £4.30 £1.30 £5.90 (£28.50) Trio £128.00; £37.87 to Windsor 15/7/96. OWNER Martin Pipe Racing Club (WELLINGTON) BRED The Queen
LONG HANDICAP Pacific Overture 9-11 Arrogant Boy 9-5
WEIGHT FOR AGE 4yo-3lb
Bt in 4,400gns
OFFICIAL EXPLANATION **Denomination (USA): explaining the improvement in form, the trainer's representative stated that the horse was running over a shorter trip this time, and was ridden differently, being held up to get the trip.**
Denomination (USA), ridden this way, looked good at this level. (9/1)
54* Sian Wyn is consistent in this grade. (9/4)
Irie Mon (IRE) may well be suited by stepping up in trip. (16/1)
67 Minnesota Fats (IRE) may be better served by a stiffer test. (9/1)
Heretical Miss (4/1: 8/1-7/2)
Java Shrine (USA) (7/1: op 7/2)

184 OAK H'CAP HURDLE (0-100) (4-Y.O+) (Class F)

9-10 (9-11) **3m 110y (13 hdls)** £2,558.40 (£712.40: £343.20) GOING: 0.23 sec per fur (G)

	Horse	Dist	Pos	SP	RR	SF
	Dawn Flight (87) (JRJenkins) **7-11-4b** JOsborne (hld up in tch: led 2 out: rdn out)	—	1	11/1	69	—
98[4]	**Wordy's Wind (69)** (LWordingham) **7-10-0** BFenton (hld up: hdwy 9th: styd on flat)	1¼	2	33/1	50	—

95[7] **Scrabo View (IRE) (96)** (PBeaumont) **8-11-13b** RSupple (lw: trckd ldrs: rdn & ev ch 2 out: no ex appr last).....4 **3** 8/1 75 —
Bahrain Queen (IRE) (89) (CSmith) **8-11-6** MRanger (hld up: nvr plcd to chal)....10 **4** 9/1 61 —
101[4] **Miss Souter (70)** (HSHowe) **7-10-1v** DBridgwater (swtg: prom tl wknd appr 3 out)....3½ **5** 11/1 40 —
131[U] **Derring Bridge (91)** (MrsSMJohnson) **6-11-8** APMcCoy (chsd ldrs: led 3 out: hdd next: sn btn)....¾ **6** 9/4[1] 60 —
101[10] **They All Forgot Me (69)** (AWCarroll) **9-10-0** MissCDyson (hld up: bhd fr 8th)....6 **7** 33/1 34 —
Gunmaker (82) (BJLlewellyn) **7-10-13** MrJLLlewellyn (hld up: hdwy 6th: wknd 9th)....s.h **8** 5/1[3] 47 —
101* **Milzig (USA) (74)** (JJoseph) **7-10-5** CLlewellyn (lw: hld up: t.o fr 8th)....1½ **9** 7/2[2] 38 —
101[6] **Riva's Book (USA) (82)** (MGMeagher) **5-10-13** DerekByrne (led to 9th: sn wknd)....8 **10** 9/1 41 —
95[P] **Strong John (IRE) (85)** (MESowersby) **8-10-13**(3) KGaule (swtg: trckd ldrs: led 9th: hdd & wknd 3 out)....1¼ **11** 14/1 43 —
(SP 130.0%) **11 Rn**

6m 16.5 (30.50) CSF £263.67 CT £2,799.44 TOTE £12.70: £3.10 £12.00 £3.00 (£240.90) Trio £180.90; £229.39 to Windsor 15/7/96. OWNER Mrs Carol Davis (ROYSTON) BRED Mrs R. A. Lomax
LONG HANDICAP They All Forgot Me 9-12 Wordy's Wind 9-13
Dawn Flight seems to reserve his best for here. (11/1)
98 Wordy's Wind stayed this trip well. (33/1)
6 Scrabo View (IRE), a course and distance winner, was easily shaken off on the run to the last. (8/1)
Bahrain Queen (IRE) can step up on this in due course. (9/1)

T/Plpt: £271.40 (50.91 Tckts). T/Qdpt: £123.40 (6.54 Tckts). CR

0156-WORCESTER (L-H) (Good to firm)
Thursday July 18th
WEATHER: sunny & warm

185 STEVE RHODES BENEFIT (S) H'CAP HURDLE (0-90) (4-Y.O+) (Class G)
6-00 (6-08) **2m 4f (10 hdls)** £2,129.00 (£594.00: £287.00) GOING minus 0.50 sec per fur (GF)

SP RR SF
55[3] **Jennyellen (IRE) (90)** (FMurphy) **7-12-0** PCarberry (trckd ldrs: mstke 5th: led appr 2 out: sn clr)....— **1** 5/2[1] 73 33
Yacht Club (77) (JLEyre) **14-11-1** OPears (a.p: jnd ldr 7th: led appr next tl appr 2 out: btn whn hit last)....8 **2** 9/1 54 14
66[5] **Mylordmayor (62)** (PBowen) **9-10-0** RFarrant (trckd ldrs: rdn 3 out: styd on one pce)....3½ **3** 13/2[3] 36 —
184[7] **They All Forgot Me (67)** (AWCarroll) **9-10-5** MissCDyson (led tl after 1st: lost pl 5th: styd on again fr 2 out)....8 **4** 33/1 34 —
134[4] **Nordic Crown (IRE) (78)** (MCPipe) **5-11-2b** DBridgwater (led after 1st to 6th: rdn 3 out: one pce)....¾ **5** 4/1[2] 45 5
Vexford Model (65) (VGGreenway) **6-10-3**ow3 WMcFarland (bkwd: nvr nr ldrs)....10 **6** 50/1 24 —
134[5] **Sovereign Niche (IRE) (83)** (MCPipe) **8-11-4**(3) DWalsh (sn pushed along: prom: led 6th tl appr 3 out: grad wknd)....2½ **7** 8/1 40 —
129[7] **Sandford Thyne (IRE) (70)** (JNDalton) **6-10-8** SWynne (mid div tl wknd after 6th)....3½ **8** 33/1 24 —
101[8] **Maryjo (IRE) (72)** (MissCJECaroe) **7-10-10** BFenton (bit bkwd: mid div tl wknd 7th)....nk **9** 14/1 26 —
105[10] **Slightly Special (IRE) (65)** (MrsPGrainger) **4-10-0** VSlattery (bit bkwd: a bhd: t.o)....10 **10** 20/1 11 —
Gort (63) (JHarriman) **8-9-8**(7) JPrior (bkwd: in tch: mstke 4th: sn lost pl: t.o)....21 **11** 16/1 — —
Coeur Battant (FR) (65) (RJBaker) **6-10-3** BPowell (a in rr: t.o)....2 **12** 14/1 — —
12[6] **Liability Order (72)** (JJBirkett) **7-10-10** MMoloney (trckd ldrs to 6th: t.o whn p.u bef 3 out).... **P** 33/1 — —
131[P] **Khazari (USA) (69)** (RBrotherton) **8-10-7** LHarvey (bkwd: bhd tl p.u bef 6th).... **P** 16/1 — —
(SP 123.7%) **14 Rn**

4m 39.2 (1.20) CSF £24.69 CT £126.33 TOTE £3.50: £1.30 £2.80 £2.60 (£11.30) Trio £29.20 OWNER Mr Liam Mulryan (MIDDLEHAM) BRED W. Maxwell Ervine
LONG HANDICAP Mylordmayor 9-11 Vexford Model 9-1
WEIGHT FOR AGE 4yo-3lb
Sold PBowen 6,000 gns
STEWARDS' ENQUIRY Bridgwater susp. 29-30/7/96 (failure to ensure best possible placing).
55 Jennyellen (IRE) took advantage of this step down to selling company and drew right away in the latter stages for a very comfortable success. (5/2)
Yacht Club is getting a bit long in the tooth, but he performed with credit on this first outing of 1996 and is still capable of winning at this level. (9/1: op 5/1)
Mylordmayor needs more cut in the ground than he had here, but he gave his best and this former point-to-point winner should be able to find another small race. (13/2)
134 Nordic Crown (IRE) (4/1: op 2/1)
134 Sovereign Niche (IRE) (8/1: op 9/2)

186 TOM MOODY CAPTAIN'S NOVICES' HURDLE (4-Y.O+) (Class E)
6-30 (6-36) **2m (8 hdls)** £2,442.50 (£680.00: £327.50) GOING minus 0.50 sec per fur (GF)

SP RR SF
105* **Shahrani** (MCPipe) **4-11-2** DBridgwater (lw: j.b rt: mde all: rdn out)....— **1** 11/8[1] 75 34
73[3] **Zine Lane** (MajorWRHern) **4-10-9** RFarrant (a.p: chsd wnr 5th: hrd rdn appr last: r.o wl)....¾ **2** 11/4[2] 67 26
Chancey Fella (HEHaynes) **5-10-12** RDavis (plld hrd: chsd wnr to 5th: outpcd appr 3 out)....14 **3** 20/1 53 15
Sorisky (BGubby) **4-10-9** RichardGuest (hld up & bhd: hdwy 5th: nt rch ldrs)....5 **4** 33/1 48 7
Backview (BJLlewellyn) **4-10-9** APMcCoy (prom: ev ch tl wknd appr 5th: t.o)....16 **5** 10/1[3] 32 —
22[4] **General Shirley (IRE) (90)** (PRHedger) **5-11-5** MRichards (lw: hld up: hdwy 4th: wknd appr 3 out: t.o)....19 **6** 10/1[3] 20 —
Fenwick's Brother (JLEyre) **6-10-12** OPears (bit bkwd: trckd ldrs to 5th: sn lost tch: t.o)....6 **7** 16/1 7 —
Rockange (IRE) (NMBabbage) **7-10-7** WMarston (bkwd: a bhd: mstke 5th: t.o)....3 **8** 33/1 — —
Hand of Straw (IRE) (PGMurphy) **4-10-6**(3) JCulloty (a bhd: t.o)....¾ **9** 14/1 4 —
Ketabi (USA) (RAkehurst) **5-10-7**(5) SRyan (swtg: hld up in tch: lost pl 5th: t.o)....dist **10** 10/1[3] — —
(SP 119.2%) **10 Rn**

3m 38.2 (-1.80) CSF £5.62 TOTE £2.60: £1.10 £1.40 £2.90 (£3.40) Trio £21.80 OWNER Mr A S Helaissi and Mr S Helaissi (WELLINGTON) BRED R. V. Young
WEIGHT FOR AGE 4yo-3lb
STEWARDS' ENQUIRY Farrant susp. 27, 31/7 & 2/8/96 (excessive use of whip).
105* Shahrani again jumped badly to the right and gave away lots of ground at almost every hurdle. He is a classy individual and still had the ability to hold off his only serious market rival. (11/8: 5/4-Evens)

73 Zine Lane, biding his time just behind the leaders, put in a determined challenge from the penultimate flight but the winner always kept his head in front and he was never going to make it. (11/4)
Chancey Fella, taken to post early, raced very freely and pressed the winner until the end of the back straight. Battling back after getting outpaced, he was unable to get himself into contention. (20/1)
Sorisky, a winner on the Flat having his first look at hurdles, improved as the race developed and should make the grade at this game. (33/1)
22 General Shirley (IRE) (10/1: op 6/1)
Hand of Straw (IRE) (14/1: op 7/1)
Ketabi (USA) (10/1: op 5/1)

187 TOM SHERVINGTON STAG H'CAP HURDLE (0-115) (4-Y.O+) (Class E)

7-00 (7-01) **2m 4f (10 hdls)** £2,798.00 (£778.00: £374.00) GOING minus 0.50 sec per fur (GF)

				SP	RR	SF
32^{5}	**Coast Along (IRE) (89)** (PJBevan) **4-10-10** WWorthington (hld up: hdwy to ld after 3 out: rdn & r.o wl flat)	—	**1**	8/1	74	5
	Hostile Witness (IRE) (98) (PRHedger) **6-11-8** RDunwoody (lw: a.p: chal last: rdn & unable qckn flat)	1¾	**2**	$9/2^{2}$	82	16
128^{4}	**Stapleford Lady (86)** (JSMoore) **8-10-10** WMcFarland (hld up: hit 5th: hdwy 7th: rdn & one pce fr 3 out)	6	**3**	$4/1^{1}$	65	—
29^{8}	**First Crack (85)** (FJordan) **11-10-9** PCarberry (hld up: hdwy 5th: wknd appr 2 out)	3½	**4**	16/1	61	—
	Ozzie Jones (87) (NMBabbage) **5-10-11** DBridgwater (trckd ldrs to 3 out: sn wknd)	1¼	**5**	$11/2^{3}$	62	—
71^{11}	**Beam Me Up Scotty (IRE) (88)** (NJHawke) **7-10-12** CLlewellyn (in tch: effrt 6th: wknd appr 3 out: t.o)	10	**6**	20/1	55	—
71^{3}	**Call the Guv'nor (96)** (NJHenderson) **7-11-6b** JOsborne (a bhd: rdn along: no rspnse: t.o)	2½	**7**	$4/1^{1}$	61	—
63^{5}	**Sydney Barry (NZ) (93)** (RHBuckler) **11-11-3b¹** BPowell (led & sn wl clr: wknd & hdd after 3 out: t.o)	20	**8**	14/1	42	—
131^{5}	**Johnny Will (104)** (MissAEEmbiricos) **11-12-0** JRyan (bit bkwd: prom: mstkes 4th & 5th: wknd 7th: wl bhd whn p.u flat: lame)		**P**	16/1	—	—
	Captain My Captain (IRE) (87) (RBrotherton) **8-10-11** LHarvey (bkwd: lost tch ½-wy: t.o whn p.u after 7th)		**P**	50/1	—	—
	Riva Rock (83) (TPMcGovern) **6-10-7** APMcCoy (swtg: in tch: effrt whn hit 3 out: bhd whn p.u bef last: lame)		**P**	6/1	—	—
				(SP 124.1%)		**11 Rn**

4m 42.5 (4.50) CSF £43.40 CT £156.56 TOTE £18.00: £3.70 £1.60 £1.40 (£15.00) Trio £37.60 OWNER Peter J Douglas Engineering (UTTOXETER) BRED John Poynton
WEIGHT FOR AGE 4yo-3lb
OFFICIAL EXPLANATION **Call the Guv'nor: would not face the first-time blinkers.**
Coast Along (IRE), ridden with restraint over this longer trip, always had the measure of the runner-up after leading early in the straight, and should have no trouble in defying a penalty. (8/1)
Hostile Witness (IRE) is not short on stamina and was in the firing-line all the way, but the concession of 12lb to a younger rival proved just too much in the duel to the finish. (9/2)
128 Stapleford Lady should have been in her element here, but she was unable to get in a blow at the leading pair. (4/1)
71 Call the Guv'nor would not face the first-time blinkers according to his jockey, and was hard at work and going nowhere at least a mile from home. (4/1)

188 TAYHIRE 10TH ANNIVERSARY NOVICES' H'CAP CHASE (0-100) (5-Y.O+) (Class E)

7-30 (7-30) **2m (12 fncs)** £3,585.25 (£1,072.00: £513.50: £234.25) GOING minus 0.50 sec per fur (GF)

				SP	RR	SF
132^{2}	**Willie Makeit (IRE) (71)** (RTPhillips) **6-10-10**(3) JCulloty (lw: hld up: hdwy 6th: led appr 2 out: drvn clr)	—	**1**	$11/4^{1}$	85	8
13^{7}	**Bit of A Dream (IRE) (62)** (MrsSJSmith) **6-10-4**ow2 RichardGuest (in tch: hdwy to jn ldr 4 out: outpcd fr 2 out)	14	**2**	12/1	62	—
132^{9}	**Exclusion (80)** (JHetherton) **7-11-8** RMarley (led 2nd tl after next: lft in ld 5th: hdd appr 2 out: sn btn)	3	**3**	11/1	77	—
	Aldington Chapple (77) (BPreece) **8-11-5** GaryLyons (mstkes: hdwy 5th: rdn whn blnd 4 out: sn bhd)	8	**4**	9/1	66	—
132^{4}	**Duke of Dreams (71)** (RJBaker) **6-10-13b¹** BPowell (prom: rdn 8th: wknd 3 out)	2½	**5**	$7/1^{2}$	58	—
138^{4}	**Forgetful (82)** (DBurchell) **7-11-10** DJBurchell (trckd ldrs tl blnd 7th: sn lost pl: t.o)	10	**6**	$11/4^{1}$	59	—
132^{8}	**Lofty Deed (USA) (60)** (WJMusson) **6-9-13**(3) KGaule (sn wl bhd: t.o)	27	**7**	12/1	10	—
	Warner Forpleasure (64) (DMcCain) **10-10-3**(3)ow2 DWalsh (bhd fr 6th: t.o)	dist	**8**	33/1	—	—
132^{U}	**George Lane (68)** (FJordan) **8-10-10** PCarberry (led to 2nd: led after next tl blnd & uns rdr 5th)		**U**	$8/1^{3}$	—	—
				(SP 113.6%)		**9 Rn**

3m 54.9 (3.90) CSF £30.99 CT £283.86 TOTE £3.00: £1.40 £2.30 £3.50 (£20.40) Trio £205.40 OWNER Old Berks Three (LAMBOURN) BRED Mitchelstown Stud
132 Willie Makeit (IRE) got off the mark with a clear-cut success and, though the company was not up to much, he has now got the hang of the game, and should go on from here. (11/4)
Bit of A Dream (IRE) was not at all happy on this lively ground, but he gave a good account of himself until having to admit the winner much too sharp for him in the closing stages. (12/1)
Exclusion is gradually improving over fences and, though he was left for dead between the last two, he must not be written off yet. (11/1)
Forgetful was settled behind the leaders and going well within herself, until a bad mistake towards the end of the back straight took the stuffing out of her. (11/4)

189 MAN WORCESTER TRUCK SERVICES NOVICES' HURDLE (4-Y.O+) (Class E)

8-00 (8-02) **2m 4f (10 hdls)** £2,425.00 (£675.00: £325.00) GOING minus 0.50 sec per fur (GF)

				SP	RR	SF
105^{3}	**Prussia (92)** (WClay) **5-10-12** APMcCoy (lw: a.p: led after 7th tl appr 2 out: rallied u.p to ld nr fin)	—	**1**	$3/1^{1}$	71	14
	Stage Fright (FMurphy) **5-10-12** PCarberry (a.p: led appr 2 out: hrd rdn flat: ct fnl strides)	nk	**2**	14/1	71	14
	Polish Consul (MajorWRHern) **5-10-9**(3) JCulloty (bit bkwd: hld up: mstke 4th: hdwy 6th: ev ch 3 out: rdn whn mstke next: rallied u.p)	3	**3**	9/1	68	11
129^{*}	**Searchlight (IRE) (99)** (TRWatson) **8-11-5b¹** DBridgwater (lw: led tl after 7th: rdn 3 out: kpt on one pce)	4	**4**	$7/2^{3}$	72	15
137^{4}	**Positivo** (MissCJECaroe) **5-10-12** ILawrence (hld up: rdn 6th: one pce appr 2 out)	1½	**5**	20/1	64	7
69^{*}	**Sigma Wireless (IRE)** (CaptTAForster) **7-11-5** SWynne (hld up: hdwy 5th: rdn appr 3 out: sn btn)	6	**6**	$100/30^{2}$	66	9
129^{4}	**Miramare** (JWDufosee) **6-10-12** GUpton (trckd ldrs tl wknd appr 3 out)	5	**7**	50/1	55	—
69^{7}	**Dickies Girl** (NMBabbage) **6-10-7** BFenton (a bhd: mstke 7th: sn t.o)	19	**8**	50/1	35	—
105^{2}	**Birthday Boy (IRE) (99)** (JRJenkins) **4-11-2v** JOsborne (hld up: lost tch 7th: t.o)	dist	**9**	4/1	—	—
	Goodnight Vienna (IRE) (MSheppard) **6-10-8**ow1 MrMMunrowd (bkwd: a bhd: t.o)	dist	**10**	33/1	—	—
	Our Barny (JLEyre) **4-10-9** OPears (swtg: trckd ldrs: mstke 5th: sn bhd: t.o whn p.u bef 3 out)		**P**	50/1	—	—

				SP	RR	SF
139[R]	**Teeter The Peeth** (MissKMGeorge) **6-10-12** PMcLoughlin (sn drvn along: mstke 5th: t.o whn p.u bef 3 out)		P	50/1	—	—

(SP 122.5%) **12 Rn**

4m 40.3 (2.30) CSF £41.22 TOTE £4.10: £1.40 £3.80 £3.10 (£57.50) Trio £44.50 OWNER The Prussia Partnership (STOKE-ON-TRENT) BRED The Woodhaven Stud

WEIGHT FOR AGE 4yo-3lb

OFFICIAL EXPLANATION **Birthday Boy (IRE): was never really travelling, and may have been feeing the effects of being recently campaigned over both hurdles and on the Flat.**

105 Prussia, not winning out of turn, came into his own over this longer trip and should now begin to pay his way. (3/1)

Stage Fright, who had a run on the Flat last month, is very short on experience at this game. Never far away, he kicked for home early in the straight and held the call until worn down in the shadow of the post. He looks a ready-made winner. (14/1: 10/1-16/1)

Polish Consul, far from fully wound up for this hurdling debut, would have gone very close indeed but for a mistake when in full flight at the second last. He will not remain a maiden for long. (9/1)

69* Sigma Wireless (IRE) proved a big disappointment, for he was cantering for most of the way, but found absolutely nothing when put to the test, and was beaten soon after entering the straight. (100/30)

190 WORCESTERSHIRE COUNTY CRICKET CLUB H'CAP CHASE (0-100) (5-Y.O+) (Class F)

8-30 (8-30) **2m 7f (18 fncs)** £3,057.50 (£920.00: £445.00: £207.50) GOING minus 0.50 sec per fur (GF)

				SP	RR	SF
130[6]	**Hurryup (90)** (RDickin) **9-11-1**(3) JCulloty (lft in ld 1st: hdd 5th: led 14th: clr next: hld on nr fin)	—	1	20/1	99	—
129[5]	**Pharrago (IRE) (72)** (DBurchell) **7-10-0** DJBurchell (trckd ldrs: effrt 3 out: r.o strly flat)	¾	2	20/1	81	—
158[2]	**The Blue Boy (IRE) (100)** (PBowen) **8-12-0b** RJohnson (w.r.s: hdwy to ld after 5th: hdd 10th: led next to 14th: rallied 2 out: r.o)	1½	3	3/1[1]	107	—
158[5]	**Jim Valentine (93)** (DJWintle) **10-11-7** WMarston (bit bkwd: hld up: hdwy appr 10th: rdn appr 4 out: one pce fr next)	3	4	10/1	98	—
	Evening Rain (80) (RJHodges) **10-10-8** RDunwoody (bit bkwd: hld up gng wl: effrt appr 4 out: one pce appr 2 out)	1½	5	12/1	84	—
158[13]	**Father Dowling (82)** (GBBalding) **9-10-10v** BFenton (nvr nr to chal)	5	6	10/1	83	—
158[4]	**Rusty Bridge (88)** (MrsSMJohnson) **9-10-9**(7) MrRThornton (led 5th: sn hdd: rdn 9th: wknd 13th)	½	7	14/1	89	—
136[3]	**Bitacrack (82)** (JJBirkett) **9-10-10** LO'Hara (prom to 12th: sn wknd)	3	8	8/1[3]	80	—
101[7]	**Bravo Star (USA) (80)** (PaddyFarrell) **11-10-8** RGreene (a in rr)	11	9	20/1	71	—
	Cool Character (IRE) (72) (RHBuckler) **8-10-0** BPowell (bkwd: a bhd: t.o)	9	10	12/1	57	—
130[5]	**Artful Arthur (73)** (LPGrassick) **10-10-1** RSupple (a bhd: t.o)	14	11	33/1	48	—
	Turpin's Green (72) (JSKing) **13-10-0** JOsborne (a bhd: t.o)	2½	12	16/1	45	—
	Magsood (95) (JWMullins) **11-11-9v** SCurran (bkwd: hld up: hdwy appr 10th: wknd after 14th: virtually p.u flat: t.o)	5	13	9/1	65	—
94[4]	**Regardless (72)** (JPLeigh) **14-9-11**(3) KGaule (trckd ldrs: blnd & lost tch 10th: sn t.o)	dist	14	20/1	—	—
76[4]	**Tango's Delight (75)** (RJBaker) **8-10-3** DLeahy (a bhd: t.o whn p.u bef 13th)		P	16/1	—	—
	Palace Yard (78) (MissAEEmbiricos) **14-10-6**ow6 MissAEmbiricos (mid div: wknd 10th: t.o whn p.u bef 14th)		P	33/1	—	—
135[P]	**Morning Blush (IRE) (86)** (MCPipe) **6-11-0b**1 DBridgwater (led tl blnd & uns rdr 1st)		U	13/2[2]	—	—

(SP 136.4%) **17 Rn**

5m 59.5 (21.50) CSF £353.66 CT £1,426.32 TOTE £32.70: £5.80 £8.90 £1.10 £2.30 (£170.60) Trio £213.20; £270.36 to 20/7/96 OWNER Mr Allan Bennett (STRATFORD) BRED C. Mitchell

LONG HANDICAP Regardless 9-11 Pharrago (IRE) 9-2 Turpin's Green 9-11

Hurryup, winning for the first time on such lively ground, did not sport the blinkers he wore on his previous outing. Forging clear on the home turn, he had to find extra when strongly pressed nearing the finish. (20/1)

Pharrago (IRE), a winner between the Flags who was falling out of the bottom of the handicap, produced a determined late challenge under the stands' rail and only just failed to get up. (20/1)

158 The Blue Boy (IRE) gave away a lot of ground by whipping round as the tape was released, but had pulled himself to the front at the end of the back straight. In and out of the lead, he stayed on relentlessly in the closing stages and must be classed an unlucky loser. (3/1)

Jim Valentine needs more yielding ground and was possibly still just short of peak-fitness, but he did show a little until feeling the strain from the penultimate fence. (10/1)

Evening Rain did not get home after looking to be going best turning in, and will need to return to a more suitable trip. (12/1)

191 DURHAM COUNTY CRICKET CLUB STANDARD N.H. FLAT RACE (4, 5 & 6-Y.O) (Class H)

9-00 (9-02) **2m** £1,269.50 (£352.00: £168.50)

				SP	RR	SF
99*	**Ultimate Smoothie** (MCPipe) **4-11-8** DBridgwater (hld up: hdwy ½-wy: led over 2f out: rdn & r.o wl nr fin)	—	1	2/1[2]	—	—
	Mr Lurpak (MrsMReveley) **4-11-1** PNiven (lw: hld up: hdwy over 5f out: ev ch appr fnl f: unable qckn)	¾	2	7/2[3]	—	—
	Pridewood Fuggle (RJPrice) **6-11-4** APMcCoy (set slow pce 4f: led 3f out: sn hdd: rallied u.p towards fin)	¾	3	25/1	—	—
161[8]	**Oats For Notes** (MissVenetiaWilliams) **6-10-13** MrMRimell (hld up & bhd: hdwy 3f out: kpt on one pce fnl 2f)	5	4	33/1	—	—
	Summerway Legend (DWPArbuthnot) **4-10-10** AProcter (hld up: hdwy over 6f out: one pce fnl 3f)	5	5	12/1	—	—
133*	**Regal Gem (IRE)** (CRBarwell) **5-11-13** BFenton (hld up: hdwy over 4f out: rdn 3f out: sn btn)	4	6	15/8[1]	—	—
	Two Hearts (JWDufosee) **4-10-10** GUpton (bit bkwd: prom tl wknd 4f out)	6	7	25/1	—	—
133[3]	**Smart Remark** (MissKMGeorge) **4-11-1** PMcLoughlin (bit bkwd: prom: rdn 6f out: wknd over 3f out)	4	8	10/1	—	—
	Wheres Sarah (JGMO'Shea) **6-10-8**(5) MichaelBrennan (led after 4f tl hdd & wknd 3f out)	¾	9	33/1	—	—
	Commando Dancer (IRE) (GraemeRoe) **4-10-8**(7) ShaunGraham (bkwd: a bhd)	1½	10	33/1	—	—
	Noble Act (IRE) (NJPomfret) **5-11-1**(3) JCulloty (prom tl wknd 6f out)	3	11	33/1	—	—
133[12]	**Final Score (IRE)** (PaddyFarrell) **6-10-13** RGreene (bkwd: unruly s: a in rr: t.o)	2½	12	33/1	—	—
	Princely Charm (IRE) (MrsPGrainger) **4-11-1** DLeahy (bkwd: trckd ldrs 10f: sn wknd: t.o)	dist	13	33/1	—	—

(SP 132.5%) **13 Rn**

3m 55.2 CSF £9.90 TOTE £3.10: £1.30 £1.70 £3.50 (£7.40) Trio £47.70 OWNER Isca Bloodstock (WELLINGTON) BRED Fares Stables Ltd

WEIGHT FOR AGE 4yo-3lb

99* Ultimate Smoothie followed up his Southwell success with another pleasing performance, but he did need to exert himself on the run-in. (2/1: 11/10-9/4)

Mr Lurpak comes from a good winning family and he looked fit enough to do himself justice on this racecourse debut. Buried in the pack, he delivered a sustained last-furlong challenge and should have little trouble in going one better. (7/2)

Pridewood Fuggle turned in a fine display on this debut and, with this experience under his belt, will soon be troubling the Judge. (25/1)

133* Regal Gem (IRE) was unable to defy a 10lb penalty in this better-class event and was a spent force soon after turning in. (15/8)

133 **Smart Remark** (10/1: op 6/1)

T/Plpt: £66.80 (209.33 Tckts). T/Qdpt: £22.20 (45.99 Tckts). IM

192a-205a (Irish Racing) - See Computer Raceform

0179-SOUTHWELL (L-H) (Good to firm)

Friday July 19th

Race 1: One fence omitted
WEATHER: fine & warm

206 FISHERTON NOVICES' H'CAP CHASE (0-100) (5-Y.O+) (Class E)

2-20 (2-20) **2m 4f 110y (14 fncs)** £4,425.00 (£1,320.00: £630.00: £285.00) GOING: 0.49 sec per fur (GS)

				SP	RR	SF
62[7]	**Sassiver (USA) (87)** (PAKelleway) **6-11-13** APMcCoy (led tl j.slowly & hdd 4th: disp ld whn j.slowly 11th: sn rdn: styd on strly to ld nr fin)	—	1	13/8 [1]	102	30
	Saxon Magic (64) (JABennett) **6-10-4** LHarvey (lw: hld up: led 12th: hit next: hrd rdn & hdd cl home)	½	2	5/1	79	7
	Saint Bene't (IRE) (65) (GProdromou) **8-10-5v** RFarrant (bit bkwd: prom tl rdn & wknd 4 out)	16	3	4/1 [2]	67	—
180[5]	**Beat The Rap (80)** (DMorris) **10-11-6v** RichardGuest (led 4th to 12th: sn wknd: t.o)	9	4	8/1	75	3
135[4]	**Dear Emily (77)** (JESwiers) **8-11-3v[1]** RJohnson (lw: hld up: ev ch 9th: wknd 11th: t.o)	1	5	9/2 [3]	71	—
	Mr Sox (64) (MissLShally) **5-10-0** RDavis (bkwd: fell 1st)		F	20/1	—	—
				(SP 108.8%)		**6 Rn**

5m 26.9 (22.90) CSF £9.13 TOTE £2.40: £1.10 £2.40 (£4.20) OWNER Mr P. A. Kelleway (NEWMARKET) BRED Juddmonte Farms Inc
LONG HANDICAP Mr Sox 9-10
WEIGHT FOR AGE 5yo-4lb
IN-FOCUS: Tragically, jockey Richard Davis died following his fall on Mr Sox.
Sassiver (USA) did not stride out with any freedom on this fast ground and looked the least likely to win from some way out, but McCoy is not the Champion for nothing, and backers can thank their lucky stars they had him on their side. (13/8: 11/10-7/4)
Saxon Magic jumped to the front at the end of the back straight and soon opened up a healthy lead, but lack of stamina caught her out, and she was worn down nearing the line. (5/1)

207 LEEDS H'CAP CHASE (0-110) (5-Y.O+) (Class E)

2-50 (2-54) **2m (13 fncs)** £4,498.00 (£1,339.00: £637.00: £286.00) GOING: 0.49 sec per fur (GS)

				SP	RR	SF
138[3]	**Noblely (USA) (100)** (NJHWalker) **9-11-6** RFarrant (swtg: j.w: led 7th: rdn & hdd 3 out: led last: r.o wl)	—	1	11/8 [1]	104	27
15[6]	**Full O'Praise (NZ) (108)** (PCalver) **9-12-0** APMcCoy (prom: hit 6th: sn rdn: led & j.lft 3 out: hdd last: no ex)	3½	2	11/8 [1]	109	32
57[5]	**Maggots Green (80)** (JMBradley) **9-10-0** RJohnson (led to 7th: outpcd whn hit 4 out: rallied appr last: fin lame)	2½	3	7/1 [2]	78	1
	Circulation (80) (DMcCain) **10-10-0** BHarding (bit bkwd: trckd ldrs to 8th: sn outpcd: t.o)	dist	4	10/1 [3]	—	—
				(SP 105.8%)		**4 Rn**

4m 9.8 (16.80) CSF £3.37 TOTE £2.10: (£2.00) OWNER Mr D. H. Cowgill (WANTAGE) BRED Societe Aland
LONG HANDICAP Maggots Green 9-4 Circulation 9-1
138 Noblely (USA) looked to have shot his bolt when collared three out, but he responded to strong pressure to gain control again at the last and was driven out firmly to the finish. (11/8: op 8/11)
15 Full O'Praise (NZ) needs a lot of driving, so he had the right man on top, but he had to admit the winner had the legs of him on the run-in. (11/8)
Maggots Green lost her pitch when clouting the fourth last, but she was staying on strongly again in the closing stages, and may have been unlucky, for she was unsound on pulling up. (7/1)

208 IGGESUND TIMBER HANDICAP H'CAP HURDLE (0-105) (4-Y.O+) (Class F)

3-20 (3-20) **2m 4f 110y (11 hdls)** £2,566.10 (£709.60: £338.30) GOING: 0.49 sec per fur (GS)

				SP	RR	SF
132[F]	**Gimme (IRE) (97)** (JGMO'Shea) **6-11-7v[1]**(5) MichaelBrennan (lw: led after 1st: sn clr: rdn out nr fin)	—	1	6/1	77	9
184[11]	**Strong John (IRE) (85)** (MESowersby) **8-10-11**(3) DParker (swtg: hld up: hdwy 8th: chsd wnr 2 out: kpt on u.p flat)	1½	2	10/1	64	—
	Lawful Love (IRE) (80) (TWDonnelly) **6-10-4**(5) MrMHNaughton (hld up in rr: effrt appr 2 out: rdn & wknd appr last)	11	3	4/1 [3]	50	—
180[4]	**Arctic Life (IRE) (94)** (JRJenkins) **7-11-9** JOsborne (swtg: led tl after 1st: prom tl wknd 3 out)	20	4	3/1 [2]	49	—
	Chieftain's Crown (USA) (91) (MissKMGeorge) **5-11-6** PMcLoughlin (swtg: hdwy 4th: chsd wnr 7th tl wknd appr 2 out)	s.h	5	2/1 [1]	46	—
139[P]	**Level Edge (89)** (HAlexander) **5-10-11**(7) MrRThornton (trckd ldrs tl outpcd 3 out: t.o)	6	6	4/1 [3]	39	—
				(SP 121.7%)		**6 Rn**

5m 13.8 (27.80) CSF £53.00 TOTE £9.50: £4.90 £5.10 (£52.10) OWNER Mr Brian O'Kane (WELFORD-ON-AVON) BRED J. Griffin
OFFICIAL EXPLANATION Chieftain's Crown (USA): finished distressed.
Gimme (IRE), brought back to hurdling, quickened and slowed the pace from the front and won with far more in hand than the margin suggests. (6/1)
Strong John (IRE), ridden from off the pace, ran much better than of late and another success could be near at hand. (10/1)
Chieftain's Crown (USA), who sweated up in the paddock, went after the winner going out into the country for the final time, but he was in deep trouble on the home turn. (2/1: 13/8-5/2)

209 QUALVIS PACKAGING MAIDEN HURDLE (4-Y.O+) (Class E)

3-50 (3-50) **2m (9 hdls)** £2,346.40 (£650.40: £311.20) GOING: 0.49 sec per fur (GS)

				SP	RR	SF
105[5]	**Pegasus Bay (85)** (WWHaigh) **5-11-5** RGarritty (hld up & bhd: hit 6th: hdwy appr 2 out: rdn to ld flat)	—	1	4/1 [2]	58	3
	War Whoop (CWThornton) **4-11-2** MFoster (bit bkwd: hld up gng wl: led appr 2 out: rdn & j.slowly last: hdd & no ex flat)	1½	2	9/4 [1]	57+	—
	The Little Ferret (AMoore) **6-11-5** RJohnson (plld hrd: led 4th tl hdd appr 2 out: one pce)	5	3	7/1 [3]	52	—

				SP	RR	SF
137[6]	**Saracen Prince (USA) (88)** (HAlexander) **4-11-2** PNiven (led to 3rd: dropped rr 6th: n.d afterwards)	6	**4**	4/1 2	46	—
137[10]	**Smocking** (MissKMGeorge) **6-11-0** PMcLoughlin (bkwd: j.slowly 1st: in rr & rdn 4th: lost tch after 3 out)	5	**5**	33/1	36	—
105[9]	**Specialize** (KRBurke) **4-11-2** APMcCoy (bit bkwd: chsd ldrs: rdn & wknd appr 2 out)	¾	**6**	7/1 3	40	—
	Tony's Delight (IRE) (JRJenkins) **8-11-5** JOsborne (prom: led 3rd to 4th: hit 6th: p.u after next)		**P**	4/1 2	—	—

(SP 118.7%) **7 Rn**

4m 3.6 (21.60) CSF £13.56 TOTE £4.80: £2.60 £1.30 (£6.80) OWNER Mr R. P. Dineen (MALTON) BRED R. P. Dineen
WEIGHT FOR AGE 4yo-3lb

Pegasus Bay, given a very patient ride, found what was needed when set alight after the last and opened his account with a bit to spare. (4/1)
War Whoop did not look fully wound up for this first outing in three months, but he made quite an impressive hurdling debut, and his inexperience at the last was probably the difference between winning and losing. (9/4: 11/8-5/2)
The Little Ferret ran much better than on his initial outing over hurdles in January, but he proved difficult to settle and had run himself out when the race began in earnest. (7/1)
Tony's Delight (IRE) (4/1: op 5/2)

210 B.M.I. THE PARK HOSPITAL (S) HURDLE (4-Y.O+) (Class G)

4-20 (4-20) **2m (9 hdls)** £2,012.40 (£556.40: £265.20) GOING: 0.49 sec per fur (GS)

				SP	RR	SF
	Trade Wind (90) (JGMO'Shea) **5-11-0v**(5) MichaelBrennan (trckd ldrs: chal & hmpd 2 out: rdn to ld last: all out)	—	**1**	3/1 2	73	1
67*	**Night Time (85)** (FJordan) **4-10-9**(7) MrGShenkin (lw: hld up in rr: hdwy 3 out: led appr last: sn hdd: one pce)	2	**2**	7/2 3	71	—
67[5]	**Lancer (USA) (85)** (RTJuckes) **4-10-9** WMarston (chsd ldr: led appr 3 out to 2 out: sn rdn: one pce)	5	**3**	9/4 1	59	—
	Kenyatta (USA) (AMoore) **7-10-5**(7) MBatchelor (swtg: nt j.w: in tch & effrt 3 out: lft in ld next: sn hdd & wknd)	3	**4**	10/1	56	—
	Pillow Talk (IRE) (SWCampion) **5-10-7b1** RichardGuest (a bhd: t.o fr 6th)	dist	**5**	8/1	—	—
	Dr Dave (IRE) (KMcAuliffe) **5-10-9**(3) TJMurphy (sn chsng ldrs: led & fell 2 out)		**F**	25/1	—	—
	Noble Society (94) (KGWingrove) **8-11-12** JRyan (hld up: hdwy 6th: sn rdn: bhd whn p.u flat)		**P**	5/1	—	—
105[13]	**Top Bank** (RHollinshead) **8-10-12** MissSSharratt (bit bkwd: prom: j.slowy 5th: sn bhd: t.o & p.u bef last)		**P**	33/1	—	—
	Kajostar (53) (SWCampion) **6-10-7** ASSmith (bkwd: swtg: a bhd: t.o whn p.u bef last)		**P**	33/1	—	—
	Fine Timing (KMcAuliffe) **9-10-12** MrMRimell (led tl appr 3 out: wknd qckly: bhd whn p.u bef last)		**P**	33/1	—	—

(SP 127.5%) **10 Rn**

4m 4.0 (22.00) CSF £14.77 TOTE £3.80: £1.80 £3.10 £1.10 (£7.40) Trio £7.10 OWNER Mr Gary Roberts (WESTBURY-ON-SEVERN) BRED Mrs M. H. Hunter
WEIGHT FOR AGE 4yo-3lb
No bid
STEWARDS' ENQUIRY Brennan susp. 31/7 & 2/8/96 (excessive use of whip).

Trade Wind must be as tough as old boots for he was not beaten far on the Flat at Bath the day before and, having spent several hours in the horse box, still gave these rivals a thrashing. (3/1)
67* Night Time was going every bit like a winner when produced to lead at the last, but the winner jumped the final flight best and had his measure on the run-in. (7/2: 5/2-4/1)
Lancer (USA) is finding it increasingly difficult to get off the mark, and his breeding would suggest he may need further or more use made of him. (9/4)
Dr Dave (IRE), taken steadily to the start, had just taken command when he bit the dust at the penultimate flight. He did look to be travelling well, and he deserves another chance. (25/1)

211 EDINGLEY H'CAP HURDLE (0-100) (4-Y.O+) (Class F)

4-50 (4-50) **2m (9 hdls)** £2,589.20 (£716.20: £341.60) GOING: 0.49 sec per fur (GS)

				SP	RR	SF
128[2]	**Island Vision (IRE) (99)** (JGMO'Shea) **6-11-9v1**(5) MichaelBrennan (hld up & bhd: hdwy on bit appr 2 out: led last: drvn out)	—	**1**	9/4 1	80	15
	Verde Luna (80) (DWPArbuthnot) **4-10-6** APMcCoy (bit bkwd: hld up & bhd: hdwy 3 out: rdn & r.o wl flat)	2	**2**	5/1	59	—
97[6]	**Stay With Me (FR) (95)** (CREgerton) **6-11-10** JOsborne (lw: a.p: led 5th to last: rdn & one pce flat)	1½	**3**	9/2 3	73	8
32[6]	**Northern Trial (USA) (93)** (KRBurke) **8-11-8v** ALarnach (trckd ldrs tl rdn & wknd appr 2 out)	8	**4**	4/1 2	63	—
71[5]	**Ray River (93)** (KGWingrove) **4-11-5** JRyan (hld up: hdwy 3 out: rdn appr next: sn btn)	1	**5**	11/1	62	—
128[9]	**Shellhouse (IRE) (88)** (KCBailey) **8-11-0**(3) TJMurphy (lw: plld hrd: led 3rd to 5th: rdn & wknd 2 out)	s.h	**6**	13/2	56	—
12[4]	**Flintlock (IRE) (84)** (HAlexander) **6-10-6**(7) MrRThornton (bkwd: swtg: led 2nd to 3rd: j.slowly 6th: sn bhd: t.o)	26	**7**	5/1	26	—
	Aide Memoire (IRE) (82) (MrsBKBroad) **7-10-11** ASSmith (bkwd: led to 2nd: wknd 5th: p.u bef 2 out)		**P**	16/1	—	—

(SP 129.8%) **8 Rn**

4m 2.8 (20.80) CSF £15.31 CT £47.25 TOTE £3.10: £1.70 £2.30 £1.10 (£4.10) OWNER Mr Gary Roberts (WESTBURY-ON-SEVERN) BRED D. P. McConnell
WEIGHT FOR AGE 4yo-3lb

128 Island Vision (IRE) completed a very rewarding day for both trainer and jockey, and they are making a habit of gaining the spoils at this track. (9/4)
Verde Luna won his only race over a longer trip, but he ran well here after being out of action for two and a half months, and there is more success in store. (5/1)
97 Stay With Me (FR) finished much closer to the winner than he had when they met here last month, and it would seem another success is in the pipeline. (9/2: op 3/1)

T/Plpt: £280.40 (17.98 Tckts). T/Qdpt: £94.30 (3.37 Tckts). IM

0072-STRATFORD-ON-AVON (L-H) (Good to firm)
Sunday July 21st

212 WEST MIDLAND TRAVEL (S) H'CAP HURDLE (0-90) (4,5,6 & 7-Y.O) (Class G)

2-10 (2-11) **2m 110y (9 hdls)** £1,982.00 (£552.00: £266.00) GOING minus 0.53 sec per fur (GF)

				SP	RR	SF
17[F]	**Set-Em-Alight (65)** (BSmart) **6-10-3** ILawrence (hld up & bhd: hdwy 5th: hrd rdn whn lft in ld 2 out: drvn out)	—	**1**	8/1	50	—

	Horse / details	Dist	Pos	SP	RR	SF
183^{4}	**Minnesota Fats (IRE) (67)** (MissMERowland) **4-10-2**^{ow1} GaryLyons (hld up & bhd: gd hdwy 3 out: rdn & ev ch 2 out: one pce flat)	6	**2**	8/1	46	—
	King of Babylon (IRE) (75) (FJordan) **4-10-10** PCarberry (led to 3 out: one pce)	6	**3**	8/1	48	—
	Clancy's Express (64) (JCFox) **5-10-2**^{ow2} SFox (lw: nvr nr to chal)	3	**4**	9/1	35	—
129^{8}	**Laser Light Lady (65)** (NPLittmoden) **4-10-0** BPowell (prom: wnt 2nd after 4th: wknd appr 3 out)	10	**5**	40/1	26	—
	Buyers Dream (IRE) (79) (BEllison) **6-11-3v**^{1} ADobbin (chsd ldr tl hit 4th: wknd 6th)	3	**6**	7/2 ^{2}	37	—
	Swedish Invader (86) (JWhite) **5-11-10** APMcCoy (hld up: t.o fr 6th)	23	**7**	5/1 ^{3}	22	—
66^{8}	**Stay Happy (FR) (62)** (AGNewcombe) **7-10-0** BFenton (hld up: hdwy 5th: led 3 out: hrd rdn whn fell 2 out: dead)		**F**	9/4 ^{1}	—	—
137^{P}	**On the Ledge (USA) (62)** (HJManners) **6-9-7**$^{(7)}$ ADowling (swtg: bhd most of wy: t.o whn fell 6th)		**F**	66/1	—	—
				(SP 116.9%)	**9 Rn**	

3m 53.4 (6.40) CSF £63.67 CT £485.16 TOTE £11.80: £2.90 £1.80 £2.60 (£36.40) Trio £46.10 OWNER Mr R. A. Hughes (LAMBOURN) BRED R. A. Hughes
LONG HANDICAP Clancy's Express 9-8 On the Ledge (USA) 9-2
WEIGHT FOR AGE 4yo-3lb
No bid

17 Set-Em-Alight was on the heels of the favourite when that rival departed at the penultimate hurdle. (8/1)
183 Minnesota Fats (IRE) could not cope with the winner after Stay Happy fell two out. (8/1: 6/1-9/1)
King of Babylon (IRE) ran his best race since leaving Lady Herries' stable after refusing to race at Worcester in April. (8/1)
Stay Happy (FR) went smoothly enough to the front three from home, but had just come under pressure, with the result back in the balance, when taking a fatal fall at the next. (9/4)

213 DTZ DEBENHAM THORPE NOVICES' CHASE (5-Y.O+) (Class D)

2-40 (2-40) **3m (18 fncs)** £4,029.00 (£1,212.00: £586.00: £273.00) GOING minus 0.53 sec per fur (GF)

	Horse / details	Dist	Pos	SP	RR	SF
71^{6}	**Sticky Money (92)** (MCPipe) **8-10-9** CMaude (prom: lft 2nd 5th: led 13th: sn clr: hit last: easily)	—	**1**	7/1	75+	15
102^{P}	**Hizal (72)** (HJManners) **7-11-0** MrACharles-Jones (a.p: 3rd whn mstke 2 out: rdn & styd on flat)	12	**2**	33/1	72	12
102^{F}	**Wakt (77)** (JWhite) **6-10-9** BFenton (bhd tl gd hdwy 13th: chsd wnr 14th: no imp whn mstkes 3 out & last)	1¼	**3**	6/1 ^{3}	66	6
	Abalene (TWDonnelly) **7-11-0** TEley (sme hdwy whn blnd 12th: styd on fr 2 out: n.d)	3	**4**	3/1 ^{2}	69	9
	Dino Malta (FR) (104) (DNicholson) **5-10-9** AMaguire (hld up: hdwy 11th: 4th & btn whn blnd 4 out)	1¼	**5**	5/4 ^{1}	68	3
190^{11}	**Artful Arthur (73)** (LPGrassick) **10-11-0** MrJGrassick (rdn & hdwy after 10th: wknd 13th)	11	**6**	66/1	61	1
179^{4}	**Dustys Trail (IRE)** (PBowen) **7-10-7**$^{(7)}$ MrRThornton (lw: nt j.w: a bhd: t.o fr 8th)	dist	**7**	20/1	—	—
179^{P}	**Priesthill (IRE)** (DLWilliams) **7-11-0** PHolley (prom tl fell 5th)		**F**	66/1	—	—
	Signe de Mars (FR) (MissZAGreen) **5-10-9** KJones (a bhd: t.o 9th: p.u bef 12th)		**P**	16/1	—	—
69^{P}	**Saxon Blade** (RMStronge) **8-11-0** WMcFarland (led to 13th: wknd qckly: p.u bef 2 out)		**P**	66/1	—	—
158^{P}	**Storm Warrior (72)** (TWall) **11-10-11b**$^{(3)}$ RMassey (chsd ldr tl blnd & uns rdr 5th)		**U**	66/1	—	—
				(SP 115.8%)	**11 Rn**	

5m 53.5 (1.50) CSF £155.84 TOTE £6.40: £1.50 £6.50 £1.50 (£220.30) Trio £130.90 OWNER Mrs D. Jenks (WELLINGTON) BRED Mrs D. Jenks
WEIGHT FOR AGE 5yo-5lb
STEWARDS' ENQUIRY Grassick susp. 30-31/7 &1-2/8/96 (excessive use of the whip).

Sticky Money, making her chasing debut, was in command from the moment she took up the running and made her only blemish at the last. She can defy a penalty. (7/1)
13 Hizal stayed on under pressure to win the separate race for the runner-up spot. (33/1)
102 Wakt was not helped by an error at the last in the battle for second. (6/1)
Dino Malta (FR) was already held when Maguire had to sit tight at the final ditch on his comeback ride. (5/4)

214 MILLENNIUM COPTHORNE HOTELS PLC STRATFORD SUMMER SALVER H'CAP HURDLE (0-125) (4-Y.O+) (Class D)

3-10 (3-10) **2m 110y (9 hdls)** £5,377.50 (£1,620.00: £785.00: £367.50) GOING minus 0.53 sec per fur (GF)

	Horse / details	Dist	Pos	SP	RR	SF
	Star Market (115) (JLSpearing) **6-12-0b** APMcCoy (a.p: led appr 6th: clr appr 2 out: drvn out)	—	**1**	14/1	98	16
12^{2}	**Sarmatian (USA) (92)** (MDHammond) **5-10-5** NWilliamson (hld up & bhd: hdwy appr 6th: hit 3 out: hrd rdn & ev ch last: unable qckn)	1	**2**	4/1 ^{3}	74	—
	Fieldridge (103) (MPMuggeridge) **7-11-2** BPowell (sn prom: one pce fr 2 out)	7	**3**	9/1	78	—
159^{5}	**Lady Confess (92)** (JohnUpson) **6-10-5** RSupple (led tl appr 6th: 3rd & wkng whn mstke last)	¾	**4**	11/1	67	—
31^{*}	**Rolfe (NZ) (114)** (DNicholson) **6-11-13b** AMaguire (hld up: hdwy appr 5th: 2nd whn mstke 3 out: wknd 2 out)	2½	**5**	9/4 ^{1}	86	4
159^{8}	**Wamdha (IRE) (102)** (KAMorgan) **6-11-1** ASSmith (prom tl wknd appr 6th)	4	**6**	16/1	70	—
159^{*}	**Routing (112)** (NGAyliffe) **8-11-11** CMaude (bhd fr 6th)	1¼	**7**	7/2 ^{2}	79	—
159^{11}	**Shifting Moon (93)** (FJordan) **4-10-3b** PCarberry (w ldr to 5th: sn wknd: t.o whn p.u bef 3 out)		**P**	16/1	—	—
128^{6}	**Commanche Creek (87)** (MissJduPlessis) **6-9-9**$^{(5)}$ SophieMitchell (a bhd: t.o whn p.u bef 3 out)		**P**	11/1	—	—
				(SP 118.1%)	**9 Rn**	

3m 51.3 (4.30) CSF £65.94 CT £497.44 TOTE £12.20: £2.90 £1.40 £2.40 (£27.20) Trio £134.70 OWNER Mrs P. Joynes (ALCESTER) BRED M. H. D. Madden and Partners
LONG HANDICAP Commanche Creek 9-11
WEIGHT FOR AGE 4yo-3lb

Star Market, 6lb higher than when winning two outings ago, handles all types of ground and managed to pull out more when the runner-up looked dangerous at the final flight. (14/1)
12 Sarmatian (USA) seemed to be coming with a winning run, but Star Market would not be denied on the flat. (4/1)
Fieldridge had not shown much on the Flat recently, but this return to hurdles was a bit more encouraging. (9/1)
31* Rolfe (NZ) was 18lb higher than when winning a handicap in first-time blinkers here in May, and had won two novice races since. (9/4)

215 RICHARDSON DEVELOPMENTS OLDBURY STRATFORD SUMMER CUP H'CAP CHASE (0-125) (5-Y.O+) (Class D)

3-40 (3-41) **2m 4f (16 fncs)** £7,058.75 (£2,120.00: £1,022.50: £473.75) GOING minus 0.53 sec per fur (GF)

	Horse / details	Dist	Pos	SP	RR	SF
	Maple Dancer (89) (FJordan) **10-10-1** RGreene (a.p: led appr 3 out: lft clr last: drvn out)	—	**1**	14/1	100	32
180^{2}	**Andrelot (110)** (PBowen) **9-11-8b** RDunwoody (chsd ldr fr 4th: ev ch 4 out: outpcd appr 2 out: styd on flat)	3	**2**	4/1 ^{2}	119	51
68^{2}	**Henley Regatta (94)** (PRRodford) **8-10-6** SBurrough (hld up & bhd: hdwy 10th: ev ch appr 2 out: btn whn hmpd last)	4	**3**	12/1	99	31

				SP	RR	SF
94^{P}	**Magic Bloom (100)** (JMJefferson) **10-10-12** RichardGuest (hld up & bhd: hdwy 10th: one pce fr 3 out)	1¼	**4**	14/1	104	36
158^{6}	**Manamour (88)** (RLee) **9-10-0** CLlewellyn (led: mstke 9th: hdd appr 3 out: sn wknd)	6	**5**	9/1	88	20
9^{7}	**Wise Advice (IRE) (102)** (MDHammond) **6-11-0** RGarritty (bhd: sme hdwy appr 10th: nvr trbld ldrs)	¾	**6**	12/1	101	33
136*	**Nordic Sun (IRE) (116)** (LRLloyd-James) **8-12-0** MDwyer (prom: mstke 11th: wkng whn mstke 12th)	1½	**7**	5/1^{3}	114	46
104^{3}	**Flying Ziad (CAN) (88)** (HJManners) **13-9-7**(7) ADowling (a bhd: lost tch fr 10th)	6	**8**	20/1	81	13
104*	**Saskia's Hero (112)** (JFBottomley) **9-11-10** DerekByrne (hld up & bhd: hdwy 4 out: 2l 2nd whn fell last: unlucky)		**F**	2/1^{1}	—	—
	Poacher's Delight (94) (AGNewcombe) **10-10-6** BFenton (bhd: mstke 8th: sn t.o: p.u bef 11th)		**P**	16/1	—	—

(SP 119.4%) **10 Rn**

4m 50.3 (-5.70) CSF £66.29 CT £648.58 TOTE £16.80: £2.70 £2.20 £2.90 (£27.50) Trio £48.90 OWNER Dr Ian Shenkin (LEOMINSTER) BRED Hugh Gibney

LONG HANDICAP Flying Ziad (CAN) 8-12 Manamour 9-4

Maple Dancer had not scored for over three years and undoubtedly had his task made easier by the departure of the favourite at the final fence. (14/1: op 8/1)

180 Andrelot has dropped to a mark 9lb lower than when he last won a year ago. (4/1)

68 Henley Regatta, with a strike-rate of only one success in thirty-six attempts, is not one to row in with with any real confidence. (12/1: op 8/1)

9 Wise Advice (IRE) (12/1: op 8/1)

104* Saskia's Hero was reeling in the winner when finishing on the floor at the last. (2/1)

216 96.4 FM BRMB NOVICES' HURDLE (4-Y.O+) (Class E)

4-10 (4-11) **2m 6f 110y (12 hdls)** £2,192.00 (£612.00: £296.00) GOING minus 0.53 sec per fur (GF)

				SP	RR	SF
189^{6}	**Sigma Wireless (IRE)** (CaptTAForster) **7-11-5** SWynne (led to 2nd: led 6th: clr whn rdn appr 2 out: r.o wl)	—	**1**	Evens^{1}	79	—
100^{4}	**Dancing At Laharn (IRE) (85)** (MissSJWilton) **6-10-12** APMcCoy (hld up: reminder after 8th: hrd rdn & wnt 2nd after 3 out: no ch whn blnd last)	9	**2**	6/5^{2}	66	—
	Chaps (MissKMGeorge) **6-10-12** PMcLoughlin (led 2nd to 6th: jnd wnr 8th: rdn 9th: wknd 3 out)	2½	**3**	25/1	64	—
	Mister Generosity (IRE) (CWeedon) **5-10-12** MRichards (wl bhd fr 3rd: t.o)	dist	**4**	11/1^{3}	—	—

(SP 107.6%) **4 Rn**

5m 27.6 (11.60) CSF £2.44 TOTE £1.80 (£1.10) OWNER Mrs Richard Strachan & Mrs David Lewis (LUDLOW) BRED Killarkin Stud

189 Sigma Wireless (IRE), making a quick reappearance, did not beat much, but proved an appropriate winner of a race sponsored by a radio station. (Evens)

100 Dancing At Laharn (IRE) proved no match for the winner. (6/5)

Mister Generosity (IRE) (11/1: 7/1-12/1)

217 RICHARDSONS HAPPY FAMILY NOVICES' H'CAP HURDLE (0-100) (4-Y.O+) (Class E)

4-40 (4-41) **2m 110y (9 hdls)** £2,262.00 (£632.00: £306.00) GOING minus 0.53 sec per fur (GF)

				SP	RR	SF
183*	**Denomination (USA) (89)** (MCPipe) **4-11-4** CMaude (hld up: hdwy 5th: led after 3 out: lft clr 2 out: drvn out)	—	**1**	2/1^{1}	70	—
96*	**Zahid (USA) (96)** (KRBurke) **5-12-0** RJohnson (lw: hld up: hdwy appr 6th: led 3 out: sn hdd: ev ch whn slipped on landing 2 out: nt rcvr)	4	**2**	2/1^{1}	73	—
	Desert Challenger (IRE) (78) (JRJenkins) **6-10-10b** APMcCoy (led: sn clr: hdd 3 out: one pce)	4	**3**	9/1^{3}	51	—
105^{6}	**Little Rousillon (68)** (TRGreathead) **8-10-0** WHumphreys (hld up: hdwy 5th: wknd 3 out)	6	**4**	9/1^{3}	35	—
	Sweet Disorder (IRE) (83) (HJManners) **6-10-8**(7) ADowling (hld up: chsd ldr 5th tl appr 3 out: sn wknd)	4	**5**	11/2^{2}	47	—
	Prince of Spades (71) (FJordan) **4-9-11**(3) JCulloty (hld up: hdwy 5th: wknd appr 3 out)	2	**6**	9/1^{3}	33	—
128^{10}	**Countrywide Lad (68)** (MMadgwick) **7-10-0** BFenton (swtg: wl bhd fr 4th: t.o)	16	**7**	33/1	14	—
98^{P}	**Marketing Man (70)** (JWhite) **6-9-9**(7)ow2 DBohan (chsd ldr to 5th: sn wknd: bhd whn blnd & uns rdr last)		**U**	33/1	—	—

(SP 117.9%) **8 Rn**

3m 54.9 (7.90) CSF £6.46 CT £24.44 TOTE £2.90: £1.30 £1.30 £2.00 (£2.90) OWNER Martin Pipe Racing Club (WELLINGTON) BRED The Queen

LONG HANDICAP Little Rousillon 9-5 Prince of Spades 9-13 Countrywide Lad 9-11 Marketing Man 9-1

WEIGHT FOR AGE 4yo-3lb

183* Denomination (USA), raised 8lb for his win in a seller, found making the better jump at the second last settling the issue. (2/1)

96* Zahid (USA) still looked like making a real race of it when losing his hind legs on touching down over the penultimate hurdle. (2/1)

Desert Challenger (IRE) set the race up for the first two, but plugged on to finish third. (9/1: op 5/1)

Sweet Disorder (IRE) (11/2: 4/1-6/1)

T/Plpt: £190.80 (63.64 Tckts). T/Qdpt: £11.60 (54.4 Tckts). KH

0185-WORCESTER (L-H) (Good to firm)

Tuesday July 23rd

WEATHER: fine

218 LINCOMB MAIDEN HURDLE (4-Y.O+) (Class D)

2-00 (2-00) **2m 4f (10 hdls)** £2,973.00 (£828.00: £399.00) GOING minus 0.23 sec per fur (G)

				SP	RR	SF
22^{2}	**Born to Please (IRE)** (PJHobbs) **4-11-2** APMcCoy (hld up: j.slowly 7th: rdn to ld 2 out: wandered u.p flat: r.o wl)	—	**1**	11/8^{1}	69	3
156^{5}	**Ewar Imperial** (KOCunningham-Brown) **4-11-2** DGallagher (a.p: led 3 out to 2 out: one pce)	7	**2**	20/1	63	—
129^{3}	**Murberry (IRE)** (MrsIMcKie) **6-11-0** LHarvey (prom: led appr 5th: hdd 3 out: one pce)	2	**3**	13/2^{3}	57	—
60^{3}	**Big Treat (IRE) (82)** (PWHiatt) **4-10-13**(3) EHusband (led tl appr 5th: ev ch 3 out: hit 2 out: one pce)	nk	**4**	11/4^{2}	62	—
19^{P}	**Up the Tempo (IRE) (68)** (PaddyFarrell) **7-10-11**(3) JCulloty (hld up: hdwy 6th: rdn & outpcd whn stumbled appr 3 out: styd on flat)	1	**5**	16/1	56	—
	Sommersby (IRE) (78) (MrsNMacauley) **5-11-5** RDunwoody (lw: hld up: mstke 5th: hdwy 6th: rdn & wknd appr 3 out: t.o)	dist	**6**	16/1	—	—
133^{6}	**Carnival Clown** (KBishop) **4-11-2** RGreene (bhd fr 7th: t.o)	4	**7**	16/1	—	—
	Liberty James (MrsEMBrooks) **9-11-5** GUpton (a bhd: t.o whn mstke 5th: p.u bef 3 out)		**P**	33/1	—	—
	Its A Myth (AJChamberlain) **7-11-0** BPowell (bhd: mstke 4th: t.o whn p.u bef 7th)		**P**	66/1	—	—

Bowland Park (EJAlston) 5-11-0 PNiven (blnd & uns rdr 1st) ... U 20/1 — —
(SP 113.7%) 10 Rn

4m 50.1 (12.10) CSF £25.34 TOTE £2.20: £1.70 £4.00 £2.20 (£20.10) Trio £37.70 OWNER A B S Racing (MINEHEAD) BRED Mrs S. O'Riordan
WEIGHT FOR AGE 4yo-3lb
22 Born to Please (IRE) was again inclined to run about a bit, but stayed on well enough over this extra half-mile. (11/8)
Ewar Imperial got the trip better this time, but could not cope with the winner. (20/1)
129 Murberry (IRE) will need further if she is to win over timber. (13/2)
60 Big Treat (IRE) was dropping back in distance here. (11/4)
Up the Tempo (IRE) broke a blood-vessel when tried over three miles last time and does seem to need that sort of trip. (16/1)

219 HUDDINGTON NOVICES' HURDLE (4-Y.O+) (Class D)
2-30 (2-30) **2m (8 hdls)** £2,910.00 (£810.00: £390.00) GOING minus 0.23 sec per fur (G)

	Horse	Dist	Pos	SP	RR	SF
	Million Dancer (MCPipe) **4-10-9** DBridgwater (mde all: clr appr 3 out: eased flat)	—	1	3/1 2	78+	19
139[4]	**Supermodel (97)** (MrsNMacauley) **4-10-11v1** RDunwoody (chsd wnr to 5th: wnt 2nd appr 3 out: no ch whn j.rt last)	11	2	11/4 1	69	10
	Count of Flanders (IRE) (KAMorgan) **6-10-12** ASSmith (bit bkwd: hld up: chsd wnr fr 5th: outpcd appr 3 out: wknd appr 2 out)	17	3	7/2 3	50	—
183[10]	**Betabetcorbett (73)** (BPJBaugh) **5-10-12** TEley (prom: reminder after 3rd: wknd qckly 5th)	9	4	33/1	41	—
	At The Acorn (IRE) (100) (NoelChance) **5-10-12** RJohnson (bit bkwd: hld up: hrd rdn appr 5th: sn bhd)	12	5	9/2	29	—
	Wet Patch (IRE) (RHannon) **4-10-9** NWilliamson (hld up & bhd: mstke 5th: sn t.o)	24	6	7/2 3	5	—
	Maronetta (75) (MJRyan) **4-10-4** JRyan (a bhd: t.o whn p.u bef 3 out)		P	25/1	—	—

(SP 121.1%) 7 Rn

3m 44.3 (4.30) CSF £12.06 TOTE £4.80: £2.40 £1.60 (£4.90) OWNER Martin Pipe Racing Club (WELLINGTON) BRED Mrs M. A. Rae Smith
WEIGHT FOR AGE 4yo-3lb
Million Dancer has been gelded since finishing third in a mile and a half Newbury claimer over a year ago. (3/1)
139 Supermodel, tried in a visor, went in vain pursuit of the winner in the home straight. (11/4)
Count of Flanders (IRE) could not go with the winner on the home turn. (7/2)

220 RACING CHANNEL H'CAP CHASE (0-125) (5-Y.O+) (Class D)
3-00 (3-00) **2m 7f (18 fncs)** £4,185.00 (£1,160.00: £555.00) GOING minus 0.23 sec per fur (G)

	Horse	Dist	Pos	SP	RR	SF
158*	**Evangelica (USA) (110)** (MCPipe) **6-11-10** DBridgwater (chsd ldr: led appr 4 out: clr 2 out: eased flat)	—	1	8/11 1	112+	—
130*	**Waterford Castle (109)** (KCBailey) **9-11-6**(3) TJMurphy (hld up: hung lft & wnt 2nd appr 3 out: hrd rdn & btn whn mstkes 2 out & last)	5	2	9/4 2	108	—
64[5]	**Tour Leader (NZ) (87)** (RHBuckler) **7-10-1** BPowell (led tl appr 4 out: wknd 3 out)	21	3	4/1 3	71	—

(SP 108.7%) 3 Rn

6m 14.7 (36.70) CSF £2.52 TOTE £1.40: (£1.60) OWNER Martin Pipe Racing Club (WELLINGTON) BRED Helen C Alexander
158* Evangelica (USA) found no difficulty in defying a further 5lb rise in the Ratings in an uncompetitive race. (8/11)
130* Waterford Castle, up 6lb, did not help his rider when sent in pursuit of the winner. (9/4)
Tour Leader (NZ) set only a moderate pace. (4/1)

221 HAWKERS INVESTMENT CAPITOL LTD H'CAP HURDLE (0-125) (4-Y.O+) (Class D)
3-30 (3-30) **3m (12 hdls)** £2,726.00 (£818.00: £394.00: £182.00) GOING minus 0.23 sec per fur (G)

	Horse	Dist	Pos	SP	RR	SF
	Stormtracker (IRE) (105) (CWeedon) **7-10-10**(5) MichaelBrennan (chsd ldr fr 3rd: lft in ld appr 8th: sn clr: r.o wl)	—	1	11/4 2	86?	15
	The Black Monk (IRE) (95) (MCPipe) **8-10-5** DBridgwater (hld up in rr: hdwy appr 7th: chsd wnr appr 9th: wknd 2 out)	dist	2	5/2 1	—	—
103[7]	**Green Lane (USA) (112)** (JJoseph) **8-11-8** CLlewellyn (lw: hld up: wknd 8th)	20	3	12/1	—	—
	Jawani (IRE) (118) (DrJDScargill) **8-12-0** RDunwoody (lw: chsd ldr to 3rd: wknd 8th: t.o)	dist	4	11/4 2	—	—
	Same Difference (IRE) (103) (KRBurke) **8-10-13** ALarnach (t.o fr 3rd)	15	5	12/1	—	—
	Quiet Dawn (90) (JSKing) **10-10-0** APMcCoy (swtg: j.rt: led tl p.u lame appr 8th)		P	10/1 3	—	—
135[2]	**Daringly (90)** (RCurtis) **7-10-0** DMorris (hld up: hdwy 6th: wknd 8th: t.o whn p.u bef 3 out)		P	20/1	—	—

(SP 111.1%) 7 Rn

5m 46.1 (10.10) CSF £9.45 TOTE £3.80: £2.10 £1.50 (£5.20) OWNER Mr Tim Davis (CHIDDINGFOLD) BRED Mrs M. Brophy
LONG HANDICAP Quiet Dawn 9-4 Daringly 8-5
Stormtracker (IRE), raised 15lb for finishing second in his last two races, was no less than 25lb higher than when scoring over course and distance just over a year ago. (11/4)
The Black Monk (IRE) did not appear to see out the trip. (5/2)
Green Lane (USA) has already been dropped 7lb after a dismal comeback run last time. (12/1)

222 HEREFORD AND WORCESTER CHAMBER OF COMMERCE H'CAP CHASE (0-100) (5-Y.O+) (Class F)
4-00 (4-01) **2m (12 fncs)** £3,468.25 (£1,036.00: £495.50: £225.25) GOING minus 0.23 sec per fur (G)

	Horse	Dist	Pos	SP	RR	SF
207[3]	**Maggots Green (72)** (JMBradley) **9-10-0** APMcCoy (chsd ldr: led after 8th: clr 4 out: easily)	—	1	3/1 1	89+	10
187[8]	**Sydney Barry (NZ) (90)** (RHBuckler) **11-11-4** BPowell (prom: outpcd after 8th: styd on fr 2 out: no ch w wnr)	16	2	5/1	91	12
61[2]	**Micherado (FR) (92)** (SABrookshaw) **6-11-6** RJohnson (led tl after 8th: rdn & wknd 2 out)	5	3	7/2 2	88	9
	Cyrill Henry (IRE) (77) (SEarle) **7-10-5** CMaude (nvr nr ldrs)	6	4	4/1 3	67	—
	Astounded (76) (DJWintle) **9-10-4** WMarston (no ch fr 6th)	3½	5	10/1	63	—
66[17]	**Hugh Daniels (83)** (BPreece) **8-10-11** GaryLyons (a bhd: t.o fr 5th)	28	6	16/1	42	—
	Merlins Wish (USA) (100) (MCPipe) **7-12-0** DBridgwater (lw: reminders after 3rd: wl bhd fr 4th: t.o whn p.u bef 4 out)		P	5/1	—	—

(SP 115.5%) 7 Rn

3m 55.9 (4.90) CSF £17.34 TOTE £3.30: £1.60 £4.10 (£9.30) OWNER Mr E. A. Hayward (CHEPSTOW) BRED Swettenham Stud
LONG HANDICAP Maggots Green 9-12
207 Maggots Green banged a nerve when finishing lame at Southwell four days ago and had only to contend with being just wrong at the weights this time. (3/1)

Sydney Barry (NZ), tried in blinkers over timber last time, seems to need further when not making the running. (5/1)
61 Micherado (FR) did jump better here, but had no answer when taken on by the winner. (7/2)
Cyrill Henry (IRE) (4/1: 3/1-9/2)
Merlins Wish (USA) (5/1: 3/1-11/2)

223 CHAMPAGNE H'CAP HURDLE (0-105) (4-Y.O+) (Class F)

4-30 (4-31) **2m (8 hdls)** £2,267.50 (£630.00: £302.50) GOING minus 0.23 sec per fur (G)

				SP	RR	SF
159^{3}	**Out Ranking (FR) (100)** (MCPipe) **4-11-8** DBridgwater (mde all: j.rt 2 out & last: all out)	—	1	$4/1^{2}$	81	26
159^{2}	**El Grando (83)** (KOCunningham-Brown) **6-10-8** DGallagher (a.p: hrd rdn appr last: r.o flat)	nk	2	$4/1^{2}$	64	12
	Mr Snaggle (IRE) (95) (SEarle) **7-11-6** CMaude (hld up: hdwy 3 out: hrd rdn appr last: r.o wl flat)	s.h	3	14/1	76	24
159^{6}	**King's Shilling (USA) (95)** (HOliver) **9-11-1**(5) MichaelBrennan (hld up: rdn appr 3 out: no hdwy)	10	4	$9/2^{3}$	66	14
	Pair of Jacks (IRE) (83) (TJNaughton) **6-10-8** APMcCoy (prom tl wknd appr last)	s.h	5	$11/8^{1}$	54	2
71^{12}	**Batty's Island (103)** (BPreece) **7-11-7**(7) DFinnegan (chsd wnr tl rdn & wknd 4th: t.o)	30	6	11/1	44	—
				(SP 115.3%)		**6 Rn**

3m 45.6 (5.60) CSF £19.14 TOTE £4.50: £1.70 £2.80 (£7.00) OWNER Knight Hawks Partnership (WELLINGTON) BRED Jacques Beres
WEIGHT FOR AGE 4yo-3lb
159 Out Ranking (FR) needed Bridgwater at his strongest to hold on up the run-in. (4/1)
159 El Grando kept on in a driving finish. (4/1)
Mr Snaggle (IRE) needed soft ground to register his two wins in Ireland, but had also run well on a firm surface. He should not be inconvenienced by a longer trip. (14/1)
King's Shilling (USA) (9/2: op 3/1)
Pair of Jacks (IRE) had run pretty well when fourth on the Flat at the beginning of the month, so it was disappointing to see him go bust between the last two flights. (11/8)

T/Plpt: £37.80 (275.95 Tckts). T/Qdpt: £20.40 (34.21 Tckts). KH

224a-252a (Irish Racing) - See Computer Raceform

0212-STRATFORD-ON-AVON (L-H) (Good to firm, Good patches)

Saturday July 27th

Race 3: Approx dists - camera failure
WEATHER: fine

253 RICHARDSON OLDBURY KING GEORGE 'SURFERS PARADISE' NOVICES' HURDLE (4-Y.O+) (Class E)

2-25 (2-26) **2m 110y (9 hdls)** £2,276.00 (£636.00: £308.00) GOING: 0.16 sec per fur (G)

				SP	RR	SF
73*	**Coureur (99)** (MDHammond) **7-11-5** RGarritty (lw: hld up: stdy hdwy 5th: led after 2 out: hit last: r.o wl)	—	1	$6/5^{1}$	77	13
65*	**Karinska (96)** (MCChapman) **6-11-0** WWorthington (s.s: mstke 3rd: rdn 5th: hdwy appr 6th: outpcd appr 3 out: styd on wl flat)	2½	2	$5/1^{2}$	70	6
	I Have Him (95) (NoelChance) **9-10-12** BPowell (j.rt: led: mstke 4th: hdd after 2 out: one pce)	1½	3	$5/1^{2}$	66	2
	Fleet Cadet (MCPipe) **5-10-12** DBridgwater (bit bkwd: bhd tl hdwy 5th: one pce fr 3 out)	7	4	$5/1^{2}$	59	—
	Desert Calm (IRE) (MrsPNDutfield) **7-10-12b** PHolley (swtg: hld up: j.slowly 2nd: stdy hdwy 5th: rdn & wknd appr 2 out: blnd last)	9	5	$10/1^{3}$	51	—
	Mario's Dream (IRE) (MrsJGRetter) **8-10-12** DGallagher (swtg: bkwd: a bhd: t.o fr 5th)	dist	6	66/1	—	—
98P	**Dan de Lyon (68)** (BLlewellyn) **8-10-9**(3) JMagee (chsd ldr tl 3rd & rdn whn blnd & uns rdr 6th)		U	50/1	—	—
				(SP 108.0%)		**7 Rn**

4m 1.5 (14.50) CSF £6.89 TOTE £1.70: £1.20 £2.20 (£3.70) OWNER Mr Frank Hanson (MIDDLEHAM) BRED Gainsborough Stud Management Ltd
73* Coureur defied a penalty in a moderate race. (6/5)
65* Karinska needs a little further on a course as sharp as this. (5/1)
I Have Him is much better suited to a right-handed course. (5/1)

254 KING EDWARD 'GREAT BARRIER REEF' NOVICES' CHASE (5-Y.O+) (Class E)

3-00 (3-00) **2m 1f 110y (13 fncs)** £3,051.00 (£918.00: £444.00: £207.00) GOING minus 0.31 sec per fur (GF)

				SP	RR	SF
160*	**Stately Home (IRE) (98)** (PBowen) **5-11-2** RJohnson (j.w: led to 2nd: led 7th: clr appr 2 out: r.o wl)	—	1	$10/11^{1}$	88	25
	Distant Memory (PJHobbs) **7-10-12b** APMcCoy (a.p: rdn & ev ch whn j.slowly 3 out: no imp)	3½	2	$7/2^{2}$	78	18
132^{5}	**Telmar Systems (64)** (JWhite) **7-10-12** BFenton (lw: prom tl reminders after 6th: sn bhd)	14	3	20/1	65	—
188^{2}	**Bit of A Dream (IRE) (62)** (MrsSJSmith) **6-10-12** RichardGuest (swtg: hld up: mstke 8th: sn wl bhd)	1¼	4	13/2	64	—
	Pond House (IRE) (84) (MCPipe) **7-11-5** DBridgwater (nt j.w: bhd whn reminders after 5th: t.o whn p.u bef 9th)		P	$5/1^{3}$	—	—
213P	**Saxon Blade** (RMStronge) **8-10-12** WMcFarland (led 2nd tl hdd, blnd & uns rdr 7th)		U	33/1	—	—
				(SP 112.3%)		**6 Rn**

4m 12.9 (3.90) CSF £4.46 TOTE £1.90: £1.30 £1.70 (£4.30) OWNER Mr P. Bowen (HAVERFORDWEST) BRED Ash Hill Stud
WEIGHT FOR AGE 5yo-3lb
160* Stately Home (IRE) has taken to fences like a duck to water. (10/11: Evens-11/10)
Distant Memory, on his chasing debut, really needs further than this, and was fighting a losing battle after being comprehensively outjumped three out. (7/2)
Pond House (IRE) (5/1: op 3/1)

255 KING CHARLES WARRNAMBOOL TROPHY H'CAP HURDLE (0-120) (4-Y.O+) (Class D)

3-35 (3-35) **2m 110y (9 hdls)** £2,786.25 (£840.00: £407.50: £191.25) GOING: 0.16 sec per fur (G)

				SP	RR	SF
103*	**Ivy Edith (116)** (TGMills) **6-11-10** DBridgwater (mde all: hit 2 out: all out)	—	1	$4/1^{3}$	97	29
	Faustino (110) (PJHobbs) **4-11-1** APMcCoy (lw: s.s: hdwy 3rd: rdn 6th: ev ch whn hit last: r.o)	½	2	$5/4^{1}$	91	20
214*	**Star Market (120)** (JLSpearing) **6-12-0b** RDunwoody (lw: chsd ldr: rdn & ev ch whn hit 2 out: hit last: one pce)	2½	3	$11/4^{2}$	98	30

	Horse	Dist	Pos	SP	RR	SF
	Vain Prince (107) (NTinkler) **9-11-1b** MDwyer (prom tl wknd 5th)	20	**4**	10/1	66	—
159[F]	**Amazon Express (105)** (PBowen) **7-10-13** RJohnson (swtg: bhd: mstke 1st: rdn after 4th: t.o fr 3 out)	12	**5**	14/1	52	—
	Caxton (USA) (92) (JWhite) **9-10-0** BFenton (bit bkwd: a bhd: t.o fr 6th)	3	**6**	33/1	36	—
222[P]	**Merlins Wish (USA) (114)** (MCPipe) **7-11-1**(7) BMoore (reminders after 4th: sn bhd: t.o fr 6th)	2	**7**	20/1	56	—
				(SP 114.6%)		**7 Rn**

3m 58.8 (11.80) CSF £9.27 TOTE £4.80: £2.40 £1.40 (£4.90) OWNER Mr Glen Antill (EPSOM) BRED G. A. and Mrs Antill
LONG HANDICAP Caxton (USA) 9-6
WEIGHT FOR AGE 4yo-3lb
103* Ivy Edith, taken to post early, held on with not an ounce to spare after making the better jump at the last. (4/1)
Faustino was challenging strongly when losing valuable momentum at the last. (5/4)
214* Star Market could not overcome a 5lb rise in the weights for his recent course and distance win. (11/4)
Vain Prince (10/1: op 6/1)

256 GERARD MANN MERCEDES BENZ H'CAP CHASE (0-110) (5-Y.O+) (Class E)

4-10 (4-11) **3m (18 fncs)** £3,626.00 (£1,088.00: £524.00: £242.00) GOING minus 0.31 sec per fur (GF)

	Horse	Dist	Pos	SP	RR	SF
215*	**Maple Dancer (92)** (FJordan) **10-10-3**(7) MrGShenkin (a.p: led 15th: sn clr: drvn out)	—	**1**	9/1	106	31
215[4]	**Magic Bloom (98)** (JMJefferson) **10-11-2** RichardGuest (lw: hld up & bhd: hdwy 12th: styd on fr 2 out)	7	**2**	13/2[3]	107	32
136[2]	**Channel Pastime (93)** (DBurchell) **12-10-8**(3) GuyLewis (lw: a.p: chsd wnr fr 4 out: no imp)	2½	**3**	11/1	101	26
215[6]	**Wise Advice (IRE) (100)** (MDHammond) **6-11-4** RGarritty (lw: hld up & bhd: hdwy 7th: wknd appr 3 out)	20	**4**	10/1	94	19
158[7]	**Boxing Match (82)** (JMBradley) **9-10-0** APMcCoy (led tl after 2nd: led 10th to 15th: wknd 4 out)	8	**5**	14/1	71	—
23[6]	**Victory Anthem (82)** (PCClarke) **10-10-0** BFenton (bhd: sme hdwy whn mstke 12th: wknd 13th)	½	**6**	25/1	71	—
180*	**Nocatchim (95)** (KAMorgan) **7-10-13** ASSmith (prom: mstke & reminders 5th: mstke 15th: sn wknd)	5	**7**	8/1	80	5
158[P]	**Jimmy O'Dea (95)** (TTBill) **9-10-13v** JRailton (j.slowly 6th: sn bhd: t.o fr 10th)	1¼	**8**	20/1	80	5
	Harristown Lady (108) (MissVenetiaWilliams) **9-11-12v**[1] NWilliamson (hld up & bhd: gd hdwy 9th: wknd 12th: t.o)	14	**9**	9/2[2]	83	8
190[3]	**The Blue Boy (IRE) (102)** (PBowen) **8-11-6b** RJohnson (dropped rr 8th: t.o 10th: p.u bef 2 out)		**P**	4/1[1]	—	—
190[U]	**Morning Blush (IRE) (86)** (MCPipe) **6-10-4b** DBridgwater (rdn to ld after 2nd: hdd 10th: wknd qckly & p.u bef 12th)		**P**	8/1	—	—
190[7]	**Rusty Bridge (85)** (MrsSMJohnson) **9-10-3** WMarston (a bhd: t.o 10th: blnd & uns rdr 4 out)		**U**	16/1	—	—
				(SP 122.3%)		**12 Rn**

5m 53.8 (1.80) CSF £63.32 CT £606.75 TOTE £11.40: £3.40 £2.30 £2.40 (£49.10) Trio £203.10 OWNER Dr Ian Shenkin (LEOMINSTER) BRED Hugh Gibney
LONG HANDICAP Victory Anthem 9-12 Boxing Match 9-6
215* Maple Dancer, raised 3lb, is clearly in good heart and was certainly ridden as if the extra half-mile would not be a problem. (9/1: op 6/1)
94 Magic Bloom, 5lb better off with the winner than last Sunday, did seem suited to the longer trip, but only narrowed the margin of defeat by just over a length. (13/2)
136 Channel Pastime, stepping up to three miles, has dropped to a mark only 2lb higher than when he won at Ludlow in April. (11/1)
190 The Blue Boy (IRE) jumped off on level terms this time, but this was not one of his going days. (4/1)

257 KING HENRY 'WALKABOUT' H'CAP HURDLE (0-110) (4-Y.O+) (Class E)

4-45 (4-45) **3m 3f (14 hdls)** £2,262.00 (£632.00: £306.00) GOING: 0.16 sec per fur (G)

	Horse	Dist	Pos	SP	RR	SF
	Elite Reg (106) (MCPipe) **7-12-0v** DBridgwater (prom: mstke 5th: led after 9th: hrd rdn after 3 out: all out)	—	**1**	2/1[1]	84	23
131[3]	**Santella Boy (USA) (100)** (CJMann) **4-11-4** RDunwoody (hld up: hdwy 9th: hrd rdn appr 3 out: ev ch whn hit 2 out: rallied flat)	s.h	**2**	2/1[1]	78	13
131[4]	**Miss Pimpernel (78)** (ABarrow) **6-10-0** APMcCoy (hld up: 3rd whn blnd 8th: ev ch 3 out: sn wknd)	27	**3**	11/2[2]	40	—
184[2]	**Wordy's Wind (78)** (LWordingham) **7-9-7**(7) CRae (hld up: lost pl after 5th: hdwy 9th: wknd 10th: t.o)	23	**4**	8/1	26	—
184[6]	**Derring Bridge (90)** (MrsSMJohnson) **6-10-12** RJohnson (led to 8th: led 9th: sn hdd: wknd 10th: t.o)	17	**5**	13/2[3]	28	—
213[U]	**Storm Warrior (78)** (TWall) **11-9-11b**(3) RMassey (w ldr: led 8th to 9th: wknd 10th: t.o: fin lame)	dist	**6**	40/1	—	—
185[11]	**Gort (79)** (JHarriman) **8-9-8**(7)ow1 JPrior (nt j.w: bhd whn mstke & rdn 4th: t.o 7th: p.u bef 11th: lame)		**P**	25/1	—	—
135[F]	**Little Thyne (78)** (DrPPritchard) **11-10-0b** DrPPritchard (dropped rr 6th: sn t.o: p.u after 10th)		**P**	40/1	—	—
				(SP 115.2%)		**8 Rn**

6m 42.0 (23.00) CSF £6.27 CT £15.33 TOTE £2.90: £1.40 £1.10 £1.70 (£2.70) OWNER Martin Pipe Racing Club (WELLINGTON) BRED S. Wingfield Digby
LONG HANDICAP Wordy's Wind 9-6 Storm Warrior 9-4 Gort 8-8 Little Thyne 9-7
WEIGHT FOR AGE 4yo-4lb
Elite Reg is much better handicapped over hurdles than fences, but still had to work very hard to just hold on. (2/1)
131 Santella Boy (USA), not helped by an untidy jump at the penultimate flight, still appeared likely to pull it off halfway up the run-in, but the winner would not be denied. (2/1)
95 Miss Pimpernel, in the handicap this time, was consequently much better off with the runner-up than at Worcester, but did not seem to last home. (11/2)
184 Wordy's Wind (8/1: op 5/1)

258 RICHARDSONS KING ARTHUR 'FAIR DINKUM' NOVICES' H'CAP HURDLE (0-100) (4-Y.O+) (Class E)

5-20 (5-25) **2m 3f (10 hdls)** £2,178.00 (£608.00: £294.00) GOING: 0.16 sec per fur (G)

	Horse	Dist	Pos	SP	RR	SF
	Silver Sleeve (IRE) (77) (MDHammond) **4-10-8b** RDunwoody (hld up: hdwy to ld appr 3 out: drvn out)	—	**1**	5/1[3]	60	—
156*	**Sparts Fault (IRE) (78)** (PEccles) **6-10-12** RichardGuest (hld up: hdwy 7th: chsd wnr fr 3 out: one pce fr 2 out)	3	**2**	9/2[2]	59	—
156[2]	**Mutley (68)** (NJHawke) **6-10-2**ow2 CMaude (hld up in rr: r.o fr 2 out: n.d)	11	**3**	100/30[1]	39	—
	Idiom (66) (MrsJGRetter) **9-9-11**(3) JCulloty (bit bkwd: prom tl wknd appr 2 out)	nk	**4**	20/1	37	—
77[U]	**Spanish Blaze (IRE) (67)** (MrsMerritaJones) **8-10-1** APMcCoy (chsd ldr: led 6th tl appr 3 out: sn wknd)	9	**5**	100/30[1]	30	—
60[5]	**Pembridge Place (94)** (GFJohnsonHoughton) **5-12-0** AThornton (led to 6th: ev ch 3 out: 4th & rdn whn hmpd bnd appr 2 out: wknd qckly)	6	**6**	100/30[1]	52	—
				(SP 108.8%)		**6 Rn**

4m 38.4 (20.40) CSF £24.16 TOTE £4.30: £2.40 £2.70 (£17.10) OWNER The Outside Nine (MIDDLEHAM) BRED T. J. Rooney
LONG HANDICAP Idiom 9-8
WEIGHT FOR AGE 4yo-3lb

Silver Sleeve (IRE), fit from the Flat, was sharpened up by the refitting of blinkers. (5/1: 4/1-6/1)
156* Sparts Fault (IRE) pulled clear of the others in the home straight, but could not peg back the winner. (9/2)
156 Mutley was 9lb better off with the runner-up than when beaten only eight lengths at Worcester (100/30)
Spanish Blaze (IRE), dropping back in distance, has yet to make the first three after twelve starts. (100/30)
31 Pembridge Place, who probably failed to stay three miles last time, was just beginning to feel the pinch when chopped off on the inside on the home turn. (100/30: 2/1-7/2)

T/Plpt: £28.70 (333.21 Tckts). T/Qdpt: £7.50 (60.84 Tckts). KH

0253-STRATFORD-ON-AVON (L-H) (Good to firm, Good patches)
Wednesday July 31st
WEATHER: fine & sunny

259 A.H.P. TRAILERS WOMBOURNE CONDITIONAL (S) H'CAP HURDLE (0-90) (4-Y.O+) (Class G)
6-15 (6-16) **2m 110y (9 hdls)** £1,884.00 (£524.00: £252.00) GOING: 0.06 sec per fur (G)

				SP	RR	SF
183[P]	**Ragamuffin Romeo (66)** (HSawyer) **7-10-11** RMassey (swtg: hld up in rr: hdwy 3 out: rdn to ld nr fin)	—	1	14/1	48	—
	Indian Minor (60) (REPocock) **12-10-5** DJKavanagh (bit bkwd: a.p: led 3 out tl hrd rdn & ct cl home)	1	2	40/1	41	—
183[8]	**Heretical Miss (75)** (JFfitch-Heyes) **6-11-6** BFenton (hld up: hdwy 5th: hrd rdn 2 out: styd on)	2½	3	4/1[3]	54	3
212[3]	**King of Babylon (IRE) (72)** (FJordan) **4-11-0** LAspell (a.p. led appr 6th to 3 out: wkng whn mstke last)	3	4	7/2[2]	48	—
66[14]	**Doctor-J (IRE) (82)** (JWhite) **6-11-10**(3) DFinnegan (hld up: hdwy 4th: rdn & wknd appr 2 out)	½	5	11/2	57	6
183[7]	**Boost (65)** (MrsNMacauley) **4-10-7** EHusband (lw: trckd ldrs tl wknd appr 2 out)	1¾	6	13/2	39	—
212*	**Set-Em-Alight (69)** (BSmart) **6-10-7**(7) KHibbert (s.s: hld up in rr: effrt 6th: no imp fr next: fin lame)	8	7	11/4[1]	35	—
210[P]	**Kajostar (55)** (SWCampion) **6-10-0** OBurrows (a bhd: t.o fr 3 out)	dist	8	50/1	—	—
253[U]	**Dan de Lyon (67)** (BLlewellyn) **8-10-12b[1]** JMagee (led & sn clr: hit 3rd: hdd & wknd appr 6th: t.o: fell 2 out)		F	14/1	—	—
				(SP 115.3%)	**9 Rn**	

4m 1.8 (14.80) CSF £304.78 CT £2,400.74 TOTE £21.80: £3.10 £5.80 £1.30 (£315.20) Trio Not won; £110.42 to 2/8/96 OWNER Mrs D. Sawyer (ELY) BRED Stetchworth Park Stud Ltd
LONG HANDICAP Kajostar 9-12
WEIGHT FOR AGE 4yo-3lb
Bt in 3,200 gns
OFFICIAL EXPLANATION **Ragamuffin Romeo: regarding the improved form, connections reported that the gelding had made mistakes and returned with cuts at Southwell on his first run for two years.**
Ragamuffin Romeo, a tall individual with little or no form to his name, surprised even his connections with this much-improved effort. Every dog has his day. (14/1)
Indian Minor very nearly caused a major upset on this return to action after five years in the wilderness and, as there looks to be plenty of improvement to come, maybe there is a race in him. (40/1)
Heretical Miss did win a similar race almost twelve months ago and promised to get herself into the reckoning turning in. Over a trip possibly not testing enough, she lacked the speed to take a hand. (4/1)
212 King of Babylon (IRE) (7/2: 3/1-9/2)
Doctor-J (IRE) (11/2: 7/2-6/1)
212* Set-Em-Alight, content to bring up the rear, tried to close approaching the fourth last, but the effort was very short-lived, and it transpired that he was unsound on his return. (11/4)
Dan de Lyon (14/1: 10/1-16/1)

260 RICHARDSON NOVICES' HURDLE (4-Y.O+) (Class E)
6-45 (6-45) **2m 6f 110y (12 hdls)** £2,192.00 (£612.00: £296.00) GOING: 0.06 sec per fur (G)

				SP	RR	SF
181*	**Ordog Mor (IRE) (97)** (MGMeagher) **7-11-5** DerekByrne (led 2nd: clr 3 out: unchal)	—	1	2/5[1]	80	21
218[3]	**Murberry (IRE)** (MrsIMcKie) **6-10-7** LHarvey (lw: trckd ldrs: rdn & outpcd appr 3 out: styd on appr last)	20	2	5/1[2]	54	—
	Tug Your Forelock (GFJohnsonHoughton) **5-10-12** AThornton (a.p: wnt 2nd 8th: kpt on u.p flat)	9	3	20/1	52	—
258[2]	**Sparts Fault (IRE) (78)** (PEccles) **6-11-5** RichardGuest (lw: hld up & bhd: hdwy 9th: chsd wnr 3 out: wknd appr last)	nk	4	6/1[3]	59	—
189[8]	**Dickies Girl** (NMBabbage) **6-10-7** WMarston (led to 2nd: prom tl wknd appr 9th: t.o)	dist	5	20/1	—	—
	Flashing Sabre (HJManners) **4-10-9** MrACharles-Jones (bkwd: j.slowly 3rd & 5th: sn t.o: p.u after 7th)		P	100/1	—	—
				(SP 112.9%)	**6 Rn**	

5m 31.3 (15.30) CSF £3.04 TOTE £1.50: £1.10 £1.90 (£2.10) OWNER Mr M. R. Johnson (ORMSKIRK) BRED T. McKeever
WEIGHT FOR AGE 4yo-3lb
181* Ordog Mor (IRE), faced with little more than a good work-out, drew right away inside the last half-mile and cruised home at his leisure. (2/5)
218 Murberry (IRE) dropped away when the winner quickened things up approaching the third last and looked done for. She stayed on again though to secure the runner-up prize, and is at least earning something. (5/1: 3/1-11/1)
Tug Your Forelock moved into second place five out and promised to make a race of it, but he was in trouble two flights later and, as yet, seems to be of little account. (20/1)

261 BARRY ORDISH-PROPERTY H'CAP CHASE (0-120) (5-Y.O+) (Class D)
7-15 (7-15) **2m 1f 110y (13 fncs)** £3,847.00 (£1,156.00: £558.00: £259.00) GOING minus 0.57 sec per fur (F)

				SP	RR	SF
254*	**Stately Home (IRE) (105)** (PBowen) **5-10-10** 7x RJohnson (j.w: mde most: drvn clr appr last: easily)	—	1	11/8[2]	108+	24
207*	**Noblely (USA) (100)** (NJHWalker) **9-10-8** APMcCoy (lw: chsd wnr: drvn along 4 out: wknd appr last)	5	2	5/4[1]	98	17
215[8]	**Flying Ziad (CAN) (92)** (HJManners) **13-9-7**(7) ADowling (wl bhd tl hdwy 4 out: r.o wl flat)	¾	3	16/1	90	9
	Nuclear Express (92) (JMBradley) **9-10-0** BFenton (bkwd: lost pl 5th: t.o fr 8th)	10	4	50/1	81	—
	Snitton Lane (120) (CParker) **10-12-0** BStorey (bkwd: hdwy 4th: outpcd 8th: t.o fr 4 out)	dist	5	5/1[3]	—	—
				(SP 111.1%)	**5 Rn**	

4m 7.1 (-1.90) CSF £3.41 TOTE £2.20: £1.20 £1.40 (£1.50) OWNER Mr P. Bowen (HAVERFORDWEST) BRED Ash Hill Stud
LONG HANDICAP Flying Ziad (CAN) 8-8 Nuclear Express 8-8
WEIGHT FOR AGE 5yo-3lb

254* Stately Home (IRE), winning his third race within a month, showed what a progressive individual he is by shaking off the favourite readily between the last two and storming clear to win going away. (11/8)
207* Noblely (USA), a prolific winner, quite simply had no answer to his younger rival when the battle to the finish really got under way. (5/4)
104 Flying Ziad (CAN), dropped out at the start, always had far too much to do and, in the circumstances, did extremely well to go so close at the end. Ridden this way, he does need further. (16/1)
Snitton Lane (5/1: 7/2-11/2)

262 PROMOTA MAIDEN HURDLE (4-Y.O+) (Class E)

7-45 (7-46) **2m 110y (9 hdls)** £2,262.00 (£632.00: £306.00) GOING: 0.06 sec per fur (G)

	Horse	Dist	Pos	SP	RR	SF
186[3]	**Chancey Fella** (HEHaynes) **5-11-0** APMcCoy (lw: led: hrd drvn & hdd appr 2 out: rallied to ld flat: all out)	—	1	7/2[2]	70	14
	Samba Sharply (AHide) **5-11-0** PHide (lw: hld up: stdy hdwy 5th: j.slowly next: led on bit appr 2 out: hit last: sn hdd: rallied u.p)	½	2	7/4[1]	70	14
186[4]	**Sorisky** (BGubby) **4-10-11** RichardGuest (chsd wnr to 3 out: sn hrd rdn & outpcd)	13	3	11/2[3]	57	—
189[7]	**Miramare** (JWDufosee) **6-11-0** GUpton (bhd: hdwy u.p appr 3 out: nt rch ldrs)	2½	4	14/1	55	—
	Canary Falcon (HJCollingridge) **5-11-0** VSmith (hld up in rr: nvr plcd to chal)	2½	5	8/1	52	—
	Saint Amigo (CCowley) **4-10-11** JAMcCarthy (a bhd: t.o)	14	6	12/1	39	—
	Peutetre (65) (FJordan) **4-10-11b[1]** RGreene (trckd ldrs to 5th: sn wknd: t.o)	2½	7	20/1	36	—
	Canestrelli (USA) (51) (WGMann) **11-10-7**[(7)] MrAWintle (bkwd: trckd ldrs tl wknd appr 6th: t.o)	2	8	100/1	34	—
	Coralcious (IRE) (BLlewellyn) **5-10-11**[(3)] JMagee (bkwd: a bhd: t.o fr 5th)	dist	9	66/1	—	—
	Minidia (HJManners) **4-9-13**[(7)] ADowling (bit bkwd: s.s: t.o whn p.u after 5th)		P	50/1	—	—
	Colt D'Or (JWhite) **4-10-11** DGallagher (trckd ldrs tl broke down & p.u after 5th: dead)		P	20/1	—	—
				(SP 113.4%)	**11 Rn**	

3m 58.6 (11.60) CSF £9.16 TOTE £3.80: £1.50 £1.60 £1.30 (£4.60) Trio £6.00 OWNER Mrs H. E. Haynes (SWINDON) BRED R. R. Prettie
WEIGHT FOR AGE 4yo-3lb
186 Chancey Fella, settled down in the lead, looked a sitting duck when the favourite came on the scene, but the picture changed dramatically at the last and he produced the better battling qualities when they were most needed. (7/2)
Samba Sharply hurdled fluently on this debut and looked all set to win on the bridle when gaining a healthy lead into the penultimate flight, but he failed to go through with his effort after rapping the last. (7/4)
186 Sorisky had far more use made of him this time and was in trouble before reaching the home straight. (11/2)
Canary Falcon (8/1: op 5/1)

263 J. ROUND (MACHINERY) LTD., WEDNESBURY NOVICES' CHASE (5-Y.O+) (Class E)

8-15 (8-15) **2m 4f (15 fncs)** £3,051.00 (£918.00: £444.00: £207.00) GOING minus 0.57 sec per fur (F)

	Horse	Dist	Pos	SP	RR	SF
	Sonic Star (IRE) (DNicholson) **7-10-12** AMaguire (hld up: hdwy 8th: stumbled & rdr lost iron 10th: led after 3 out: drvn clr flat)	—	1	9/4[3]	91	31
182[3]	**Shikaree (IRE)** (MCPipe) **5-10-8** DBridgwater (hld up: hdwy 10th: ev ch whn blnd 4 out: rallied next: outpcd flat)	8	2	11/8[1]	85	21
	Sydmonton (NJHenderson) **10-10-12** RJohnson (bit bkwd: j.w: led tl after 3 out: ev ch next: rdn & wknd appr last)	5	3	20/1	81	21
	Forest Feather (IRE) (87) (CWeedon) **8-10-12b** MRichards (bit bkwd: hld up & bhd: hdwy 9th: ev ch 4 out: wknd after next)	4	4	2/1[2]	77	17
132[6]	**Jameswick (60)** (JWDufosee) **6-10-12** PHolley (swtg: trckd ldrs: ev ch 4 out: wknd qckly next: t.o)	16	5	33/1	65	5
160[5]	**Master Art** (JWDufosee) **6-10-12** GUpton (bit bkwd: prom: j.slowly 5th: wknd 9th: t.o whn p.u bef 3 out)		P	50/1	—	—
				(SP 115.9%)	**6 Rn**	

4m 52.7 (-3.30) CSF £5.84 TOTE £3.00: £1.40 £1.60 (£2.50) OWNER Mr R. F. Nutland (TEMPLE GUITING) BRED A.B. McDowell
WEIGHT FOR AGE 5yo-4lb
Sonic Star (IRE), at his best when fresh, was making stealthy progress when he pitched on his head at the penultimate open ditch, and his jockey all but went out of the side-door. Recovering to show ahead entering the straight, he was inclined to edge left, but had far too much pace for his pursuers. (9/4)
182 Shikaree (IRE) made his only serious jumping error when right in contention four out and, though he did rally, he had to admit the winner much too good for him. (11/8)
Sydmonton, who has been pointing with no success, ran a fine race on this debut over regulation fences and, with this run to put an edge on him, should have little trouble in making his mark at this game. (20/1)
Forest Feather (IRE) did not look fully wound up after ten weeks out of action, and was not really happy on this lively ground. He began a forward move inside the final mile and had reached a prominent position four out before lack of peak-fitness took its toll. (2/1)

264 RICHARDSON OLDBURY H'CAP HURDLE (0-110) (4-Y.O+) (Class E)

8-45 (8-45) **2m 3f (10 hdls)** £2,234.00 (£624.00: £302.00) GOING: 0.06 sec per fur (G)

	Horse	Dist	Pos	SP	RR	SF
	Jenzsoph (IRE) (100) (PJHobbs) **5-11-6**[(5)] DJKavanagh (lw: led & sn clr: hdd appr 3 out: rallied to ld last: sn clr)	—	1	11/4[1]	79	10
208[2]	**Strong John (IRE) (88)** (MESowersby) **8-10-10**[(3)] DParker (hld up & bhd: hdwy 6th: slt ld appr 3 out to last: sn outpcd)	2	2	4/1[2]	65	—
16[6]	**Circus Colours (96)** (JRJenkins) **6-11-7** SFox (s.v.s: hdwy ½-wy: disp ld appr 3 out: rdn & hdd last: one pce)	1¾	3	7/1	72	3
184[9]	**Milzig (USA) (75)** (JJoseph) **7-10-0** CLlewellyn (wl bhd tl styd on appr 2 out)	12	4	6/1	41	—
182[P]	**Hacketts Cross (IRE) (103)** (PEccles) **8-11-7**[(7)] MrRThornton (prom tl wknd appr 7th: t.o)	6	5	25/1	64	—
211[5]	**Ray River (91)** (KGWingrove) **4-10-13** JRyan (hdwy 4th: outpcd appr 7th: t.o)	1¾	6	7/1	50	—
71[9]	**Holy Joe (100)** (AJWilson) **14-11-11** DJBurchell (bit bkwd: lost pl 4th: sn t.o)	dist	7	20/1	—	—
	Lorcanjo (75) (DNCarey) **5-10-0** APMcCoy (trckd ldrs: rdn appr 6th: wknd & p.u after 3 out)		P	9/2[3]	—	—
				(SP 112.7%)	**8 Rn**	

4m 34.9 (16.90) CSF £13.22 CT £61.07 TOTE £3.40: £1.70 £1.80 £1.90 (£7.60) OWNER Superset Two (MINEHEAD) BRED A. T. Robinson
LONG HANDICAP Milzig (USA) 9-13 Lorcanjo 9-8
WEIGHT FOR AGE 4yo-3lb
STEWARDS' ENQUIRY Fox susp. 9&10/8/96 (improper use of the whip).
Jenzsoph (IRE) produced in top condition after a three month summer break, is a very fluent hurdler. Given a breather after setting the pace for two miles, she came back to take command at the last and ran on strongly for a comfortable success. (11/4)

208 Strong John (IRE) gained a slight lead approaching the third last, but needed to work hard to hold his advantage, and had little more to give when the winner renewed her challenge. (4/1)
Circus Colours gave away substantial ground at the start in an effort to get him to settle. Putting in his bid three out, he did a lot of tail-swishing when the pressure was on in the latter stages, and obviously has more ability than he cares to show. (7/1: op 9/2)

T/Plpt: £27.60 (333.22 Tckts). T/Qdpt: £1.50 (485.32 Tckts). IM

265a-281a (Irish Racing) - See Computer Raceform

BANGOR-ON-DEE (L-H) (Good to firm)
Friday August 2nd
WEATHER: overcast

282 M.F.M. AND MARCHER GOLD CLAIMING HURDLE (3-Y.O) (Class F)
3-10 (3-10) **2m 1f (9 hdls)** £2,234.00 (£624.00: £302.00) GOING minus 0.36 sec per fur (GF)

		Dist	Pos	SP	RR	SF
	Friendly Dreams (IRE) (PTDalton) **3-10-0b** TEley (led appr 2nd to 3 out: sn led again: clr next: unchal)	—	1	50/1	52	—
	Four Weddings (USA) (MCPipe) **3-11-12b** DBridgwater (nt j.w: a chsng ldrs: hrd rdn appr 2 out: no ch w wnr)	6	2	6/5[1]	72	—
	Balmoral Princess (JHPeacock) **3-10-6b** RBellamy (led: j.slowly 1st: sn hdd: led & blnd 3 out: sn hdd & nt rcvr)	3½	3	66/1	49+	—
	My Kind (NTinkler) **3-10-0** JOsborne (hld up: hdwy 6th: wknd appr 2 out: eased)	12	4	11/4[2]	32	—
	She's Simply Great (IRE) (JJO'Neill) **3-10-13**(5) RMcGrath (lw: stdd s: a in rr: t.o)	23	5	4/1[3]	28	—
	Inca Bird (TWall) **3-9-11**(3) RMassey (hld up in rr: lost tch 5th: t.o)	19	6	50/1	—	—
	All In Good Time (CWThornton) **3-11-0** MFoster (prom: hit 3rd: wknd 5th: t.o)	21	7	11/1	—	—
	Image Maker (IRE) (BPreece) **3-9-7**(7) DFinnegan (j.slowly 3rd: sn bhd: uns rdr next)		U	25/1	—	—
	Song For Jess (IRE) (FJordan) **3-10-9** RGreene (lw: uns rdr 1st)		U	25/1	—	—
				(SP 113.6%)		**9 Rn**

4m 8.6 (13.60) CSF £104.35 TOTE £65.40: £7.90 £1.10 £2.50 (£38.10) Trio £85.30 OWNER Mr J. W. Ellis (BURTON-ON-TRENT) BRED H. J. W. Steckmest
Friendly Dreams (IRE) clmd CBarnes £3,528
Friendly Dreams (IRE), a maiden on the Flat, turned good at the first time of asking over hurdles. The blinkers certainly had the desired effect. (50/1)
Four Weddings (USA) should have been a class apart on his Flat form but the name of this game is jumping and he made too many errors to keep himself in touch with the winner. (6/5: Evens-5/4)
Balmoral Princess would probably have won had she not made a mess of the third last and, with this experience under her belt, should be able to make her mark. (66/1)
My Kind barely stayed a mile on the Flat and, though patiently ridden here, found even this minimum trip beyond her. (11/4)
All In Good Time (11/1: 8/1-12/1)

283 CHRONICLE NEWSPAPERS NOVICES' CHASE (5-Y.O+) (Class D)
3-40 (3-40) **3m 110y (18 fncs)** £3,517.50 (£1,065.00: £520.00: £247.50) GOING minus 0.36 sec per fur (GF)

		Dist	Pos	SP	RR	SF
213*	**Sticky Money (97)** (MCPipe) **8-11-1** DBridgwater (led 3rd to 5th: led 10th: clr 4 out: eased flat)	—	1	8/13[1]	89+	8
190[2]	**Pharrago (IRE) (72)** (DBurchell) **7-11-0** DJBurchell (hld up: chsd wnr 12th: hit next: rdn 3 out: sn btn)	4	2	6/1[3]	85	4
184[3]	**Scrabo View (IRE)** (PBeaumont) **8-11-0** RSupple (hld up: reminders 9th: outpcd 4 out: sn bhd)	4	3	4/1[2]	83	2
135*	**Manor Rhyme (80)** (JCMcConnochie) **9-11-6** BPowell (lw: j.w: led to 3rd: led 5th to 10th: rdn & dropped rr 12th: t.o)	16	4	6/1[3]	78	—
				(SP 110.5%)		**4 Rn**

6m 12.7 (10.70) CSF £4.37 TOTE £1.30: (£2.60) OWNER Mrs D. Jenks (WELLINGTON) BRED Mrs D. Jenks
213* Sticky Money jumped much better than she did on her debut and the ease of this success can not be gauged by the official margin. (8/13)
190 Pharrago (IRE) closed on the winner out in the country, but he was in trouble before reaching the final ditch and is highly flattered to finish so close. (6/1: op 4/1)
184 Scrabo View (IRE) jumped adequately on this chasing debut and remained in touch until getting outpaced approaching the fourth last. The experience will not be lost. (4/1: 3/1-9/2)
135* Manor Rhyme (6/1: op 4/1)

284 NEW SEASON CONDITIONAL (S) H'CAP HURDLE (0-95) (4-Y.O+) (Class G)
4-15 (4-15) **2m 1f (9 hdls)** £1,952.00 (£547.00: £266.00) GOING minus 0.36 sec per fur (GF)

		Dist	Pos	SP	RR	SF
	Peter Monamy (92) (MCPipe) **4-11-8** DWalsh (hld up: shkn up after 3 out: jnd ldr next: led on bit last: comf)	—	1	4/5[1]	74+	12
	Green's Seago (USA) (67) (GRichards) **8-10-0** JCulloty (led after 4th: rdn & hit 2 out: hdd last: no ch w wnr)	2½	2	2/1[2]	47	—
188[6]	**Forgetful (95)** (DBurchell) **7-11-7**(7) JPrior (led & sn clr: j.bdly rt & hdd 4th: sn bhd: t.o)	dist	3	4/1[3]	—	—
	Our Mica (67) (LJBarratt) **6-9-11**(3) DJKavanagh (hld up in rr: rdn & outpcd 6th: sn t.o)	2½	4	12/1	—	—
137[P]	**Pimsboy (67)** (GROldroyd) **9-10-0v** GCahill (hld up: in rr whn slipped & fell bnd after 3rd)		S	33/1	—	—
				(SP 119.5%)		**5 Rn**

4m 2.1 (7.10) CSF £3.13 TOTE £1.60: £1.30 £1.30 (£2.20) OWNER Richard Green (Fine Paintings) (WELLINGTON) BRED R. Green
LONG HANDICAP Green's Seago (USA) 9-13 Our Mica 9-6 Pimsboy 9-0
WEIGHT FOR AGE 4yo-3lb
Bt in 6,250 gns; Green's Seago (USA) clmd SKavanagh £5,600
Peter Monamy won this on the bridle in the end, but he did need to be woken up entering the straight before he came back on the bit and sauntered home at his leisure. He proved plenty dear enough to retain. (4/5)
Green's Seago (USA), sure to strip fitter for this first run in ten weeks, proved a tough nut to wear down but, hard as he tried, he was a sitting duck from some way out. (2/1)
188 Forgetful, who has been trying her luck over fences, has only ever won on a right-handed track, and this sharp left-handed circuit had her trailing from halfway. (4/1)

285 WREXHAM LAGER H'CAP HURDLE (0-120) (4-Y.O+) (Class D)

4-45 (4-45) **2m 4f (11 hdls)** £2,723.00 (£824.00: £402.00: £191.00) GOING minus 0.36 sec per fur (GF)

				SP	RR	SF
	Diamond Cut (FR) (114) (MCPipe) **8-11-13** DBridgwater (mde all: sn clr: rdn out)	—	1	4/1 ^{2}	94	30
	Dancing Dove (IRE) (115) (GRichards) **8-12-0** ADobbin (bit bkwd: hld up: hdwy 7th: chsd wnr after 3 out: rdn appr last: one pce)	3	2	4/1 ^{2}	93	29
187^{4}	**First Crack (87)** (FJordan) **11-10-0** SWynne (hld up & bhd: hdwy 3 out: rdn & one pce appr last)	1¼	3	9/2 ^{3}	64	—
223^{4}	**King's Shilling (USA) (95)** (HOliver) **9-10-5**(3) JCulloty (hld up: hdwy 7th: rdn 3 out: wknd appr 2 out)	7	4	8/1	66	2
16^{3}	**Blue Raven (90)** (PJHobbs) **5-10-3** APMcCoy (bit bkwd: chsd wnr tl rdn 3 out: sn wknd)	9	5	2/1 ^{1}	54	—
97^{3}	**Playful Juliet (CAN) (88)** (ABailey) **8-10-1**ow1 TKent (bit bkwd: trckd ldrs tl wknd 6th: t.o)	13	6	14/1	41	—
223^{6}	**Batty's Island (99)** (BPreece) **7-10-5**(7) DFinnegan (a bhd: t.o fr 6th)	23	7	25/1	34	—
				(SP 113.1%)		**7 Rn**

4m 40.4 (4.40) CSF £18.95 TOTE £4.60: £2.10 £2.60 (£6.90) OWNER Martin Pipe Racing Club (WELLINGTON) BRED Jean, Andre and Eric Laborde and Claude Duval

LONG HANDICAP First Crack 9-11 Playful Juliet (CAN) 9-4

Diamond Cut (FR) only won once last season, but seemed more at home over this longer trip, and this is only the start for this term. (4/1: op 5/2)

Dancing Dove (IRE), carrying a bit of surplus flesh, ran as well as could be expected over a trip short of her best on such a fast track, and she will soon be paying her way again. (4/1)

First Crack, still looking like a mare in foal, was given plenty to do and, though she did stay on, she was never going well enough to get herself into contention. (9/2: 8/1-4/1)

16 Blue Raven did his level best to keep tabs on the winner, but the pace never dropped and he was under pressure and in deep trouble turning for home. (2/1)

286 ERBISTOCK NOVICES' H'CAP CHASE (0-100) (5-Y.O+) (Class E)

5-20 (5-20) **2m 4f 110y (15 fncs)** £2,996.00 (£908.00: £444.00: £212.00) GOING minus 0.36 sec per fur (GF)

				SP	RR	SF
254^{P}	**Pond House (IRE) (84)** (MCPipe) **7-10-12** DBridgwater (led: clr fr 9th: eased to walk flat)	—	1	13/2	90+	21
	Miners Rest (72) (PJHobbs) **8-10-0** APMcCoy (bit bkwd: a.p: chsd wnr fr 10th: nvr nr to chal)	3½	2	11/2 ^{3}	75	6
263^{4}	**Forest Feather (IRE) (87)** (CWeedon) **8-11-1b** MRichards (sn wl bhd: reminders 6th: hdwy whn blnd 4 out: no imp)	1¼	3	6/4 ^{1}	89	20
97^{P}	**Northern Nation (84)** (WClay) **8-10-12** RJohnson (bkwd: trckd ldrs tl wknd 9th: t.o)	dist	4	16/1	—	—
208^{4}	**Arctic Life (IRE) (100)** (JRJenkins) **7-12-0** JOsborne (bhd: reminders 7th: t.o whn p.u bef 2 out: lame)		P	11/4 ^{2}	—	—
188^{8}	**Warner Forpleasure (72)** (DMcCain) **10-10-0b** BHarding (bkwd: chsd wnr: reminders 9th: blnd next: t.o whn p.u bef 2 out)		P	50/1	—	—
188^{U}	**George Lane (73)** (FJordan) **8-10-1**ow1 RGreene (j.rt: a in rr: mstke 11th: blnd & uns rdr next)		U	10/1	—	—
				(SP 112.3%)		**7 Rn**

5m 3.9 (3.90) CSF £37.41 TOTE £5.90: £2.60 £2.10 (£10.20) OWNER Mr C. R. Fleet (WELLINGTON) BRED S. Banville

LONG HANDICAP Miners Rest 9-7 Warner Forpleasure 9-2 George Lane 9-10

OFFICIAL EXPLANATION **Pond House (IRE): regarding the improvement in form, connections reported that the gelding is a temperamental sort who does not always give his best.**

Pond House (IRE) completed a four-timer for Martin Pipe with a very smooth all-the-way success and, when he is allowed to dictate, he looks a useful chaser in the making. (13/2)

Miners Rest, placed between the Flags in the past season, could never get in a blow against the winner and would have been beaten ten lengths plus had that rival not been virtually pulled up nearing the finish. (11/2: 4/1-6/1)

263 Forest Feather (IRE), making a quick reappearance, just can not handle this lively ground. (6/4)

287 LLANGOLLEN NOVICES' HURDLE (4-Y.O+) (Class E)

5-50 (5-52) **2m 1f (9 hdls)** £2,626.00 (£736.00: £358.00) GOING minus 0.36 sec per fur (GF)

				SP	RR	SF
210^{3}	**Lancer (USA) (78)** (RTJuckes) **4-10-9** WMarston (chsd ldr fr 3rd: chal & lft in ld last: all out)	—	1	11/2 ^{2}	67	13
219*	**Million Dancer** (MCPipe) **4-11-2** DBridgwater (led: sn clr: mstke 3 out: rdn after next: blnd last: sn hdd: rallied cl home)	hd	2	2/7 ^{1}	74+	20
133^{10}	**Seven Wells** (JHPeacock) **4-10-9** RGreene (sn t.o: hdwy 5th: nvr nr ldrs)	dist	3	33/1	—	—
73^{P}	**Merely Mortal** (BPreece) **5-10-12** RJohnson (bkwd: lost tch 5th: t.o)	23	4	33/1	—	—
133^{8}	**Disco's Well** (ABailey) **5-10-12** TKent (pckd 3rd: a bhd: t.o)	8	5	20/1	—	—
133^{13}	**Tipsy Queen** (MissHCKnight) **5-10-4**(3) JCulloty (bit bkwd: prom: mstke 2nd: wknd 5th: t.o)	3	6	14/1 ^{3}	—	—
156^{8}	**Admiral's Guest (IRE)** (WClay) **4-10-9** TEley (sn pushed along: t.o fr 5th: p.u bef 2 out)		P	20/1	—	—
	Inteabadun (ABailey) **4-10-9** SWynne (ref to r: t.n.p)		R	50/1	—	—
				(SP 117.2%)		**8 Rn**

3m 59.0 (4.00) CSF £7.42 TOTE £3.90: £1.10 £1.10 £5.10 (£2.40) OWNER Mr A. C. W. Price (ABBERLEY) BRED Goodwood Thoroughbreds/Western Agency

WEIGHT FOR AGE 4yo-3lb

210 Lancer (USA), the only one able to stay in touch with the favourite, was putting in a determined challenge when left with the advantage at the last. This was just as well as he only got home by the skin of his teeth. (11/2)

219* Million Dancer always looked likely to keep the Pipe band-wagon rolling, but he was hard at work when missing out the final flight and, at the line, that meant the difference between winning and losing. (2/7: 1/5-30/100)

T/Plpt: £10.70 (637.9 Tckts). T/Qdpt: £9.70 (39.81 Tckts). IM

0134-MARKET RASEN (R-H) (Good to firm)

Saturday August 3rd

288 PREMIERE PLACEMENTS AMATEUR NOVICES' H'CAP HURDLE (0-100) (4-Y.O+) (Class F)

6-10 (6-11) **2m 1f 110y (8 hdls)** £2,110.00 (£585.00: £280.00) GOING minus 0.26 sec per fur (GF)

				SP	RR	SF
183^{3}	**Irie Mon (IRE) (79)** (MPBielby) **4-11-4**(7) MrAWintle (lw: hld up & bhd: hdwy whn hit 5th: led last: hung lft: styd on wl towards fin)	—	1	3/1 ^{2}	60	—

258* **Silver Sleeve (IRE) (82)** (MDHammond) **4-11-11b**(3) MrCBonner (sn chsng ldrs: led after 3 out to last: kpt on same pce) ....3 **2** 10/11[1] 60 —
139F **Poplin (76)** (JWharton) **5-11-4**(7) MrRThornton (mde most tl after 3 out: kpt on same pce appr last) ....nk **3** 6/1 54 —
Tony's Mist (74) (JMBradley) **6-11-2**(7) MrNHOliver (trckd ldrs: outpcd after 3 out: kpt on appr last) ....1½ **4** 5/1[3] 51 —
Noted Strain (IRE) (65) (DFBassett) **8-10-7**(7) MissKDiMarte (sn trckng ldrs: one pce fr 3 out) ....5 **5** 50/1 37 —
Avril Etoile (63) (CHJones) **6-10-5**(7) MissBSmall (chsd ldrs tl wknd appr 2 out) ....10 **6** 50/1 26 —
181P **Quixall Crossett (70)** (EMCaine) **11-11-0**(5) MrMHNaughton (sn bhd: pushed along 4th: t.o 2 out) ....19 **7** 66/1 16 —
183U **Arrogant Boy (64)** (SBClark) **7-10-8**(5)ow13 MrNWilson (hld up & plld hrd: bhd & pushed along 4th: sme hdwy appr 2 out: sn wknd: t.o) ....1¼ **8** 66/1 8 —
(SP 115.2%) **8 Rn**

4m 17.8 (14.80) CSF £5.95 CT £12.13 TOTE £4.10: £1.40 £1.10 £1.80 (£2.80) OWNER Sotby Farming Company Ltd (GRIMSBY) BRED Stan Policky
LONG HANDICAP Arrogant Boy 9-12
WEIGHT FOR AGE 4yo-3lb

183 Irie Mon (IRE) wore a tongue-strap and was dropped right out. After hitting the front, he then did his best to thrown it away, but his rider would have none of it. A bit of a character, he needs probably holding up until the last moment. (3/1)
258* Silver Sleeve (IRE), who had his tongue tied down, went for home, but found himself outpaced by the winner on the run-in. He probably needs two and a half miles. (10/11)
Poplin made the running and kept on in most determined fashion. This was easily her best race over hurdles so far. (6/1)
Tony's Mist, out of form of late on the Flat, stuck on after being outpaced. (5/1)

289 UNITED FRIENDLY (S) H'CAP HURDLE (0-95) (4-Y.O+) (Class G)

6-40 (6-40) **2m 5f 110y (10 hdls)** £1,576.00 (£436.00: £208.00) GOING minus 0.26 sec per fur (GF)

SP RR SF

134[9] **Joli's Great (66)** (MJRyan) **8-10-0b** JRyan (sn trckng ldrs: led 3 out: styd on wl flat) ....— **1** 14/1 44 —
188[7] **Lofty Deed (USA) (66)** (WJMusson) **6-10-0b** LHarvey (hld up: stdy hdwy 6th: ev ch 2 out: rdn & fnd nil flat) ....2 **2** 12/1 43 —
182[7] **George Ashford (IRE) (88)** (KAMorgan) **6-11-8v**[1] ASSmith (lw: led to 3 out: sn wl outpcd: hrd rdn & kpt on wl flat) ....2 **3** 7/2[2] 63 —
101[3] **Whistling Gipsy (67)** (HOliver) **11-10-1** JacquiOliver (s.s: bhd: hmpd 6th: sn chsng ldrs: kpt on one pce fr 3 out) ....5 **4** 5/1 38 —
185[2] **Yacht Club (77)** (JLEyre) **14-10-11** OPears (chsd ldrs: rdn & outpcd after 3 out: n.d after) ....hd **5** 3/1[1] 48 —
Rare Paddy (66) (BSRothwell) **7-10-0v**[1] RSupple (hld up: hdwy 7th: one pce appr 2 out) ....hd **6** 25/1 37 —
Mistroy (70) (MissMKMilligan) **6-10-1**(3) GCahill (hld up: effrt 7th: no imp: hit 2 out) ....2½ **7** 14/1 39 —
Lambson (69) (JPearce) **9-10-3** CLlewellyn (hld up & bhd: effrt 7th: rdn appr 2 out: nvr nr ldrs) ....1¼ **8** 13/2 37 —
Tharsis (76) (WJSmith) **11-10-5**(5) STaylor (lw: chsd ldrs tl wknd 7th: t.o 2 out) ....17 **9** 10/1 32 —
Catton Lady (66) (RCraggs) **6-9-11**(3) GLee (nt j.w: chsd ldrs tl lost pl 6th: t.o 2 out) ....13 **10** 50/1 12 —
Five From Home (IRE) (90) (MCPipe) **8-11-10** CMaude (chsd ldrs tl wknd qckly 6th: sn t.o: p.u bef 3 out) .... **P** 9/2[3] — —
(SP 131.3%) **11 Rn**

5m 21.2 (17.20) CSF £164.88 CT £672.75 TOTE £39.70: £5.30 £5.10 £2.00 (£77.70) Trio £102.00; £129.40 to Ripon 5/8/96 OWNER Enterprise Markets Ltd (NEWMARKET) BRED Mrs M. A. Ryan
LONG HANDICAP Lofty Deed (USA) 9-13 Joli's Great 9-12 Catton Lady 8-8 Rare Paddy 9-8
Bt in 2,500 gns

Joli's Great, who showed nothing first time, stayed on in determined fashion and clearly needs this sort of trip nowadays. (14/1)
Lofty Deed (USA) looked as though he could pick the winner up at any stage but, when it came to a struggle, he quickly called it a day. (12/1: op 8/1)
George Ashford (IRE), wearing a visor, made the running. Badly tapped for toe on the home turn, he was staying on when it was all over, and needs a stiffer test. (7/2)
101 Whistling Gipsy showed a poor action and his rider dismounted on pulling up. (5/1)
185 Yacht Club, now a true veteran, was tapped for foot starting the home turn. (3/1)

290 GRAHAME LILES NOVICES' CHASE (5-Y.O+) (Class D)

7-10 (7-10) **2m 4f (15 fncs)** £3,793.25 (£1,136.00: £545.50: £250.25) GOING minus 0.26 sec per fur (GF)

SP RR SF

213[2] **Hizal (72)** (HJManners) **7-11-0** MrACharles-Jones (trckd ldr: mstke 11th: rdn 3 out: lft in ld after 2 out: all out) ....— **1** 5/2[2] 72 —
206* **Sassiver (USA) (92)** (PAKelleway) **6-11-6b** RJohnson (j.slowly: led: sn drvn along: 3 lengths clr whn blnd 2 out: sn hdd: blnd last: hrd rdn & kpt on towards fin) ....2 **2** 4/7[1] 76 —
Ghedi (POL) (MPMuggeridge) **5-10-10** CLlewellyn (bit bkwd: plld hrd: trckd ldrs to 9th: sn wknd: t.o 3 out) ....dist **3** 7/1[3] — —
Mr Oriental (MrsVAAconley) **6-11-0** DerekByrne (bit bkwd: j.slowly: sn bhd: t.o 9th) ....dist **4** 20/1 — —
(SP 109.5%) **4 Rn**

5m 8.8 (17.80) CSF £4.28 TOTE £3.40 (£1.80) OWNER Mr H. J. Manners (SWINDON) BRED H. J. Manners
WEIGHT FOR AGE 5yo-4lb

213 Hizal, left with the prize at his mercy at the second last, had nothing at all to spare at the line. This was a poor event. (5/2)
206* Sassiver (USA), with the blinkers back on, would not have a cut at his fences. His rider was soon hard at work, but he still looked in command when he ploughed through the second last. Repeating the error at the final fence, even then his pilot did not call it a day. (4/7)
Ghedi (POL), a winner on the Flat in Poland, looked in need of the outing. Racing keenly, he kept tabs on the first two, but only for the first circuit. (7/1)
Mr Oriental looked fat and, dropped out at the start, he was schooled round. It is doubtful if he could have gone any quicker anyway. (20/1)

291 FASTNET FISH HURDLE (3-Y.O) (Class D)

7-40 (7-40) **2m 1f 110y (8 hdls)** £2,745.50 (£824.00: £397.00: £183.50) GOING minus 0.26 sec per fur (GF)

SP RR SF

Kernof (IRE) (MDHammond) **3-10-12** RGarritty (lw: trckd ldrs: led & hit 2 out: drvn clr flat) ....— **1** 5/4[1] 67 7
Home Cookin' (MCPipe) **3-10-7** CMaude (w ldr: led 5th: hdd & hit 2 out: ev ch whn mstke last: styd on) ....4 **2** 4/1[3] 58 —
Killmessan-Town (IRE) (JMCarr) **3-10-9**(3) FLeahy (mstke 2nd: drvn along: hdwy 5th: hrd rdn & one pce appr 2 out) ....14 **3** 5/1 51 —
Northern Falcon (MWEasterby) **3-10-7** MrNWilson (sn bhd: t.o & mstke 3 out: styd on appr next) ....1¼ **4** 20/1 44 —

			SP	RR	SF
	Another Quarter (IRE) (SPCWoods) **3-10-7** PHide (nt j.w: led: blnd 1st & 4th: hdd next: wknd appr 2 out) 1	5	7/2[2]	44	—
	Cowboy Dreams (IRE) (MHTompkins) **3-10-9b**[1](3) KGaule (chsd ldrs: drvn along 4th: wknd 3 out: eased) ...19	6	10/1	31	—
	Recall To Mind (MESowersby) **3-10-9**(3) DParker (a bhd) 1	7	25/1	30	—
	Limyski (MrsASwinbank) **3-10-9**(3) JSupple (bhd fr 5th) 2¼	8	50/1	28	—
			(SP 123.0%)	**8 Rn**	

4m 11.1 (8.10) CSF £7.29 TOTE £2.40: £1.50 £1.30 £1.60 (£4.70) OWNER Mr J. M. Gahan (MIDDLEHAM) BRED David Wallace

Kernof (IRE) looked to hold the upper hand when left two lengths clear at the last, and his rider left nothing to chance. His trainer reckons he can jump better than he did here. (5/4: 7/4-11/10)

Home Cookin', who is only small, was still right there when a second jumping error at the last sealed her fate. (4/1: op 5/2)

Killmessan-Town (IRE), an excitable sort, was a springer in the market. Hard at work to get onto the heels of the first two on the home turn, he was soon left trailing. (5/1: 12/1-4/1)

Northern Falcon stayed on late in the day and was probably flattered. (20/1)

Another Quarter (IRE), winner of a seller on the All-Weather a week earlier, was let down by her jumping. (7/2: 5/2-4/1)

292 LILES RACING H'CAP CHASE (0-115) (5-Y.O+) (Class E)

8-10 (8-11) **2m 4f (15 fncs)** £3,418.00 (£1,024.00: £492.00: £226.00) GOING minus 0.26 sec per fur (GF)

			SP	RR	SF
136[7]	**Drumstick (89)** (KCBailey) **10-11-5** JRailton (mde virtually all: rdn clr between last 2: eased towards fin) .....—	1	10/1	100	35
	Yaakum (92) (SEKettlewell) **7-11-8** RGarritty (hld up: stdy hdwy 6th: chal 3 out: sn rdn: fnd nil) 5	2	5/1[3]	99	34
222*	**Maggots Green (77)** (JMBradley) **9-10-7** RJohnson (chsd wnr: mstke 3rd: drvn along 9th: outpcd after 11th: 3rd & one pce whn mstke 2 out) 1¼	3	9/4[2]	83	18
207[4]	**Circulation (70)** (DMcCain) **10-10-0** BHarding (trckd ldrs: rdn 10th: wknd appr 3 out) 25	4	14/1	56	—
138*	**Rhossili Bay (98)** (MrsMReveley) **8-12-0** PNiven (lw: prom whn fell 2nd)	F	11/10[1]	—	—
	Wake Up Luv (90) (KGWingrove) **11-11-6** JRyan (hld up: wnt prom 6th: 3rd & ev ch whn fell 10th)	F	25/1	—	—
			(SP 114.7%)	**6 Rn**	

4m 54.5 (3.50) CSF £52.64 TOTE £10.60: £2.90 £2.30 (£19.60) OWNER Sarah Lady Allendale,E Hawkings,M Harris (UPPER LAMBOURN) BRED Mrs W. Hanson

LONG HANDICAP Circulation 9-11

Drumstick won his seventeenth race after a long spell in the wilderness, shooting clear between the last two and winning eased right up. (10/1)

Yaakum, fit from the Flat, moved up on the bridle and onto the heels of the winner on the home turn but, soon under pressure, he pulled out precious little. In the past, he has been known to break blood-vessels. (5/1: op 3/1)

222* Maggots Green was under pressure a long way from home, and it was only her rider's persistence that got her so close in the end. (9/4)

138* Rhossili Bay was out of it as early as the second fence. (11/10)

293 WEIGHTLIFTER MAIDEN HURDLE (4-Y.O+) (Class E)

8-40 (8-44) **2m 1f 110y (8 hdls)** £2,629.80 (£732.80: £353.40) GOING minus 0.26 sec per fur (GF)

			SP	RR	SF
	Field of Vision (IRE) (MrsASwinbank) **6-10-13**(3) JSupple (lw: chsd ldrs: mstke 1st: led 2 out: hld on towards fin) .....—	1	4/1[2]	76	20
	Silverdale Lad (KWHogg) **5-11-2** SWynne (swtg: hld up: hdwy 5th: ev ch 2 out: nt qckn towards fin) .....½	2	16/1	76	20
7[2]	**Forgotten Empress** (SEKettlewell) **4-10-8** RJohnson (lw: hld up & bhd: hdwy 4th: effrt appr 2 out: styd on wl towards fin) 2½	3	4/1[2]	68	9
	Ottavio Farnese (AHide) **4-10-13** PHide (trckd ldrs: led after 3 out: hdd next: ev ch last: kpt on same pce) ....½	4	10/1[3]	73	14
137[2]	**Sea God (90)** (MCChapman) **5-11-2** WWorthington (trckd ldrs: sddle slipped 3rd: wknd flat) 3½	5	9/4[1]	70	14
	Little Redwing (MDHammond) **4-10-8** RGarritty (stdy hdwy 4th: sn prom: wknd between last 2: eased) 9	6	12/1	56	—
253[4]	**Fleet Cadet** (MCPipe) **5-11-2b** CMaude (chsd ldrs: led 5th: hdd after next: sn wknd) 3½	7	4/1[2]	58	2
	Court Jester (MJRyan) **5-11-2** JRailton (bit bkwd: hdwy whn hit 3 out: sn drvn along: wknd next) 3½	8	10/1[3]	55	—
	Scallymill (KWHogg) **6-10-11** MFoster (plld hrd: trckd ldrs tl wknd 4th: t.o 3 out) .....dist	9	50/1	—	—
59[7]	**Ousefleet Boy** (MissMKMilligan) **4-10-13** AThornton (in tch to 4th: t.o 3 out) 8	10	50/1	—	—
	Hutcel Bell (RDEWoodhouse) **5-10-11** PNiven (chsd ldrs tl wknd 5th: sn t.o) 1¼	11	50/1	—	—
	Bargin Inn (JLHarris) **6-11-2** DGallagher (a bhd: t.o 5th) 14	12	50/1	—	—
137[F]	**Woodbine** (RDEWoodhouse) **6-11-2** DerekByrne (plld hrd: led to 5th: wknd qckly: t.o whn p.u bef 2 out)	P	50/1	—	—
			(SP 132.3%)	**13 Rn**	

4m 8.6 (5.60) CSF £63.57 TOTE £5.30: £2.40 £4.70 £2.00 (£34.80) Trio £114.50; £24.20 to Ripon 5/8/96 OWNER Mrs K. Morrell (RICHMOND) BRED Sean Collins

WEIGHT FOR AGE 4yo-3lb

Field of Vision (IRE) did just enough to take a modest event. (4/1)

Silverdale Lad, awash with sweat on his hurdling debut, proved most persistent and, in the end, was just held at bay. (16/1)

7 Forgotten Empress came again on the run-in and will be suited by a step up to two and a half miles. (4/1)

Ottavio Farnese, who lost his way on the Flat, made a satisfactory debut over hurdles. (10/1)

137 Sea God, whose saddle slipped from the third flight, gave his rider no option but to sit and suffer going to the last. (9/4)

Little Redwing was by no means knocked about, and might be good enough to win a seller or claimer. (12/1: op 8/1)

Fleet Cadet, with the blinkers on, took it up at the fifth but, when headed after the next, seemed very quick to call it a day. (4/1)

Court Jester (10/1: op 20/1)

T/Plpt: £591.00 (11.28 Tckts). T/Qdpt: £174.30 (1.84 Tckts). WG

NEWTON ABBOT (L-H) (Good to firm)

Saturday August 3rd

WEATHER: dry & sunny

294 THOROUGHBRED CLOTHING COMPANY PRESENTS SCUDAMORE HURDLE (3-Y.O) (Class D)

2-25 (2-25) **2m 1f (8 hdls)** £2,699.10 (£757.60: £369.30) GOING minus 0.40 sec per fur (GF)

		SP	RR	SF
Always Happy (MCPipe) **3-10-7** DBridgwater (lw: chsd ldr tl led after 6th: sn clr: eased flat) .....—	1	1/3[1]	64+	—
Bullpen Belle (PTWalwyn) **3-10-7** BPowell (led tl after 6th: sn outpcd: lft poor 2nd last) 10	2	5/1[2]	55	—
Ben Bowden (MBlanshard) **3-10-12** JOsborne (lw: hdwy to chse ldrs 5th: poor 2nd whn fell last: rmntd) .....dist	3	11/2[3]	—	—
Saucy Soul (WGMTurner) **3-10-5**(7) JPower (bkwd: a bhd: t.o fr 3rd: p.u bef 2 out)	P	20/1	—	—

Our Adventure (MPMuggeridge) **3-10-7** SCurran (bit bkwd: chsd ldrs: rdn 3rd: wknd after next: mstkes 5th & 6th: t.o whn p.u bef 2 out)........ **P** 25/1 — —
(SP 115.7%) **5 Rn**

4m 0.7 (7.70) CSF £2.86 TOTE £1.40: £1.30 £1.60 (£2.20) OWNER Knight Hawks Partnership (WELLINGTON) BRED Cheveley Park Stud Ltd
Always Happy, who was sticky at a couple of flights, won this poor event easily. (1/3)
Bullpen Belle set the pace until collared after the third last. (5/1: op 3/1)
Ben Bowden was in second place when coming to grief at the last. (11/2: op 7/2)

295 CLIVE MORGAN (S) HURDLE (4,5,6 & 7-Y.O) (Class G)
2-55 (2-56) **2m 1f (8 hdls)** £1,783.90 (£500.40: £243.70) GOING minus 0.40 sec per fur (GF)

SP RR SF

Indrapura (IRE) (MCPipe) **4-10-9** DBridgwater (hld up & bhd: hdwy to ld appr 2 out: wandered appr last: comf)........— **1** 5/1 59+ —
210* **Trade Wind (92)** (JGMO'Shea) **5-11-7v**(5) MichaelBrennan (bit bkwd: hdwy 6th: ev ch 2 out: hmpd, rdn & no ex flat)........½ **2** 9/2[3] 73 —
26[4] **Double Pendant (IRE)** (PJHobbs) **5-10-12** APMcCoy (led tl after 2nd: ev ch appr 2 out: outpcd appr last)......5 **3** 7/4[1] 54 —
212[4] **Clancy's Express (56)** (JCFox) **5-10-12** SFox (hdwy 6th: ev ch appr 2 out: rdn & wknd appr last)........5 **4** 16/1 49 —
Burnt Sienna (IRE) (JSMoore) **4-10-4** WMcFarland (led briefly after 2nd: led after 6th tl appr 2 out: wknd)........4 **5** 14/1 40 —
217[5] **Sweet Disorder (IRE) (80)** (HJManners) **6-10-0**(7) ADowling (bkwd: prom tl wknd fr 5th)........2 **6** 6/1 39 —
210[F] **Dr Dave (IRE)** (KMcAuliffe) **5-10-12** BPowell (bhd: rapid hdwy to ld appr 3rd: mstke next: hdd after 6th: wknd appr 2 out)........4 **7** 4/1[2] 40 —
(SP 118.0%) **7 Rn**

4m 6.6 (13.60) CSF £26.55 TOTE £4.80: £2.60 £2.50 (£5.10) OWNER Martin Pipe Racing Club (WELLINGTON) BRED John Burns
WEIGHT FOR AGE 4yo-3lb
Bt in 3,600 gns
STEWARDS' ENQUIRY Obj to Indrapura (IRE) by Brennan overruled.
Indrapura (IRE), who completed the Pipe double, ran about a bit over the last couple of flights. (5/1: op 5/2)
210* Trade Wind was given a bump by the winner before the last. (9/2)
26 Double Pendant (IRE) was also bumped by the winner and weakened soon after. (7/4)
Burnt Sienna (IRE) (14/1: op 8/1)
Sweet Disorder (IRE) (6/1: op 4/1)

296 FRANCIS KEARNS 70TH BIRTHDAY NOVICES' CHASE (5-Y.O+) (Class E)
3-30 (3-30) **2m 110y (13 fncs)** £2,845.50 (£861.00: £420.00: £199.50) GOING minus 0.40 sec per fur (GF)

SP RR SF

187[3] **Stapleford Lady (70)** (JSMoore) **8-10-7** WMcFarland (lw: a.p: chsd ldr 8th: led 10th: hld on wl u.p flat)........— **1** 4/1[3] 79 11
160[3] **Nordic Valley (IRE)** (MCPipe) **5-10-9** DBridgwater (mstke 3rd: chsd ldr next to 8th: rdn & disp ld 11th: hrd drvn flat: jst failed)........hd **2** 9/4[2] 84 13
188[5] **Duke of Dreams (69)** (RJBaker) **6-10-12** BPowell (bkwd: bhd: lost tch 8th: styd on fr 2 out)........12 **3** 11/1 72 4
Heresthedeal (IRE) (97) (GMMcCourt) **7-10-12** BClifford (lw: led to 10th: wknd next)........6 **4** 4/5[1] 66 —
Great Uncle (JWDufosee) **8-10-12** GUpton (bit bkwd: prom: mstke 4th: in tch to 8th: sn wknd: t.o)........dist **5** 25/1 — —
(SP 118.5%) **5 Rn**

4m 3.8 (3.80) CSF £13.49 TOTE £5.50: £1.80 £1.40 (£6.00) OWNER Mr C. Kyriakou (HUNGERFORD) BRED R. Searle
WEIGHT FOR AGE 5yo-3lb
OFFICIAL EXPLANATION **Heresthedeal (IRE): would not let himself down on the ground.**
187 Stapleford Lady, who loves it firm, is a really game mare who kept on under strong pressure. She will go for novice handicaps, and will win again. (4/1)
160 Nordic Valley (IRE) pressed the winner all the way to the line, but had met one a bit too tough. (9/4)
Heresthedeal (IRE), who jumped well in front, was struggling after being joined by the leading pair. (4/5: 10/11-Evens)

297 FORT GEORGE CONDITIONAL NOVICES' H'CAP HURDLE (0-100) (4-Y.O+) (Class F)
4-05 (4-05) **2m 6f (10 hdls)** £1,929.20 (£541.20: £263.60) GOING minus 0.40 sec per fur (GF)

SP RR SF

69[4] **Dream Here (95)** (JCFox) **8-12-0** BFenton (lw: hdwy 7th: led appr 2 out: styd on wl u.p flat)........— **1** 11/4[1] 73 22
258[4] **Idiom (67)** (MrsJGRetter) **9-10-0** JCulloty (hld up & bhd: hdwy 8th: rdn & ev ch last: no ex flat)........2 **2** 3/1[2] 44 —
Cashflow Crisis (IRE) (78) (JWMullins) **4-10-8** TJMurphy (hld up & bhd: hdwy 8th: ev ch 2 out: wknd appr last)........2½ **3** 7/2[3] 53 —
286[2] **Miners Rest (74)** (PJHobbs) **8-10-7** DJKavanagh (led to 3rd: led 4th tl appr 2 out: wknd qckly)........22 **4** 6/1 33 —
77[P] **Lac de Gras (IRE) (69)** (RCurtis) **5-10-2**ow2 DWalsh (in tch whn mstke 5th: chsd ldr after 6th tl wknd appr 2 out)........nk **5** 20/1 28 —
19[P] **Akiymann (USA) (87)** (MCPipe) **6-11-2**(4) BMoore (disp ld tl led 3rd: hdd next: wknd 6th: sn wl bhd)........dist **6** 4/1 — —
(SP 112.9%) **6 Rn**

5m 19.2 (7.20) CSF £10.91 TOTE £3.00: £1.70 £2.20 (£5.50) OWNER The Will To Win Partnership (MARLBOROUGH) BRED A. Gadd
LONG HANDICAP Idiom 9-11 Lac de Gras (IRE) 9-4
WEIGHT FOR AGE 4yo-3lb
69 Dream Here, a chaser in the making, did it well under topweight and can score again. (11/4)
Idiom had every chance at the last, but could not match the winner. (3/1)
Cashflow Crisis (IRE) could only stay on at one pace. (7/2)
286 Miners Rest (6/1: op 4/1)
Akiymann (USA) (4/1: op 9/4)

298 NEWTON ABBOT TOWN DAY H'CAP CHASE (0-120) (5-Y.O+) (Class D)
4-40 (4-40) **2m 5f 110y (16 fncs)** £3,458.00 (£1,046.00: £510.00: £242.00) GOING minus 0.40 sec per fur (GF)

SP RR SF

Sohail (USA) (99) (JSKing) **13-10-8** JCulloty (hld up: hdwy 13th: sn prom: ev ch 2 out: led last: qcknd flat)........— **1** 14/1 106 45
215[3] **Henley Regatta (97)** (PRRodford) **8-10-6**ow5 SBurrough (prom 8th: chsd ldr 13th: led next: hdd last: outpcd flat)........3½ **2** 11/2[3] 101 35

			SP	RR	SF
20[5]	**Muskora (IRE) (119)** (PJHobbs) **7-12-0b** APMcCoy (lw: led tl mstke & hdd 14th: ev ch 2 out: outpcd appr last) 3	**3**	7/4[1]	121	60
215[2]	**Andrelot (110)** (PBowen) **9-11-5b** MAFitzgerald (chsd ldr to 13th: grad wknd) 16	**4**	9/4[2]	100	39
190[4]	**Jim Valentine (91)** (DJWintle) **10-10-0b[1]** WMarston (mid div: mstkes 3rd & 6th: lost tch 12th) 13	**5**	13/2	72	11
158[12]	**The Lorryman (IRE) (92)** (NRMitchell) **8-10-1** SMcNeill (prom early: mstke 3rd: wknd 11th: t.o whn p.u bef 2 out)	**P**	9/1	—	—
			(SP 112.5%)	**6 Rn**	

5m 11.7 (-5.30) CSF £76.11 TOTE £15.60: £4.40 £2.90 (£42.10) OWNER Mrs Carrie Janaway (SWINDON) BRED W. R. O'Neill & W. H. Hodgkin in USA
LONG HANDICAP Jim Valentine 9-13
IN-FOCUS: This was Champion Amateur Jim Culloty's first win since turning professional.
Sohail (USA) tracked the leaders and, after leading at the last, quickly went clear. (14/1)
215 Henley Regatta, headed at the last, was soon outpaced. (11/2)
20 Muskora (IRE) made most of the running until headed after a mistake at the fourteenth. (7/4)
The Lorryman (IRE) (9/1: 12/1-8/1)

299 PHOENIX PRINT H'CAP HURDLE (0-110) (4-Y.O+) (Class E)
5-10 (5-10) **2m 1f (8 hdls)** £2,200.50 (£618.00: £301.50) GOING minus 0.40 sec per fur (GF)

			SP	RR	SF
	Country Star (IRE) (110) (CPEBrooks) **5-12-0** GBradley (lw: led & sn wl clr: breather appr 5th: qcknd appr 2 out: unchal) ....—	**1**	4/5[1]	99+	36
	Roca Murada (IRE) (100) (PJHobbs) **7-11-4** APMcCoy (hld up: hdwy to chse wnr 4th: outpcd appr 2 out) 11	**2**	3/1[2]	79	16
	Re Roi (IRE) (92) (JCFox) **4-10-4**(3) TJMurphy (hld up: hdwy 6th: outpcd appr 2 out) 1¾	**3**	20/1	69	3
	Pusey Street Boy (82) (JRBosley) **9-10-0** ILawrence (chsd ldrs tl wknd 6th) 3	**4**	14/1	56	—
214[P]	**Commanche Creek (82)** (MissJduPlessis) **6-9-9**(5) SophieMitchell (chsd wnr to 4th: bhd 6th) ....nk	**5**	7/1	56	—
	Cooley's Valve (IRE) (107) (MrsSDWilliams) **8-11-11** SMcNeill (chsd ldrs to 4th: wknd appr 2 out) 2	**6**	11/2[3]	79	16
			(SP 119.9%)	**6 Rn**	

3m 54.9 (1.90) CSF £4.03 TOTE £1.60: £1.30 £1.60 (£2.90) OWNER H R H Prince Fahd Salman (LAMBOURN) BRED M. L. Page
LONG HANDICAP Pusey Street Boy 9-12 Commanche Creek 9-13
WEIGHT FOR AGE 4yo-3lb
Country Star (IRE) landed this comfortably under topweight and is going to run at Auteuil in September, a course which apparently suits front-runners. (4/5)
Roca Murada (IRE), having his first outing for more than a year, weakened after the second last, and should come on for this. (3/1: op 2/1)
Re Roi (IRE), who is very free at home, needs settling to produce his best, and blew up in the closing stages. (20/1)

T/Plpt: £81.20 (63.9 Tckts). T/Qdpt: £51.60 (4.59 Tckts). T

0294-NEWTON ABBOT (L-H) (Good to firm)
Monday August 5th
WEATHER: overcast

300 HOLSWORTHY NOVICES' (S) HURDLE (4-Y.O+) (Class G)
2-15 (2-17) **2m 1f (8 hdls)** £1,893.10 (£531.60: £259.30) GOING minus 0.58 sec per fur (F)

			SP	RR	SF
295*	**Indrapura (IRE)** (MCPipe) **4-11-2** 7x DBridgwater (hld up & bhd: hdwy to chse ldrs after 6th: led appr last: comf) ....—	**1**	11/8[1]	71+	—
	Almapa (RJHodges) **4-10-6**(3) TDascombe (hdwy appr 5th: led next tl appr last: no ex) ....¾	**2**	10/1	63	—
210[2]	**Night Time (85)** (FJordan) **4-10-9**(7) MrGShenkin (lw: hld up & bhd: rdn & hdwy 6th: nt rch ldrs) 8	**3**	2/1[2]	63	—
212[2]	**Minnesota Fats (IRE) (66)** (MissMERowland) **4-10-9** GaryLyons (bhd: hdwy & in tch 6th: wknd appr 2 out)...nk	**4**	6/1[3]	56	—
	Galloping Guns (IRE) (BJLlewellyn) **4-10-6**(3) GuyLewis (chsd ldrs tl wknd 5th: t.o) ....dist	**5**	33/1	—	—
26[8]	**Kama Simba** (JWhite) **4-10-9b** APMcCoy (bit bkwd: mid div & rdn 4th: hdwy to chse ldr whn fell 5th)	**F**	7/1	—	—
212[F]	**On the Ledge (USA) (50)** (HJManners) **6-10-5**(7) ADowling (bkwd: led 1st: hdd 6th: sn wknd: p.u appr 2 out)....	**P**	100/1	—	—
253[6]	**Mario's Dream (IRE)** (MrsJGRetter) **8-10-12** DGallagher (bit bkwd: unruly & uns rdr bef s: led to 1st: 2nd whn rn out appr 5th)	**R**	40/1	—	—
			(SP 117.7%)	**8 Rn**	

3m 59.9 (6.90) CSF £15.00 TOTE £2.10: £1.10 £2.80 £1.10 (£13.90) OWNER Martin Pipe Racing Club (WELLINGTON) BRED John Burns
WEIGHT FOR AGE 4yo-3lb
Bt in 7,000 gns
295* Indrapura (IRE) followed up Saturday's course win with another comfortable success. (11/8: Evens-10/11)
Almapa, running for the first time over jumps, will come on for the experience, and will win in time. (10/1: 7/1-12/1)
210 Night Time could not live with the leading pair from the home turn. (2/1)

301 NEWTON ABBOT RACECOURSE CAR BOOT SALES H'CAP HURDLE (0-100) (4-Y.O+) (Class F)
2-45 (2-46) **2m 6f (10 hdls)** £1,958.60 (£549.60: £267.80) GOING minus 0.58 sec per fur (F)

			SP	RR	SF
	Springfield Dancer (91) (PJHobbs) **5-11-7** APMcCoy (lw: chsd ldr tl led 4th: clr fr 6th: unchal) ....—	**1**	9/2[3]	76	6
	Celestial Fire (80) (JWhite) **4-10-7** DGallagher (mid div: hdwy 6th: nt rch wnr) 18	**2**	11/1	52	—
187[6]	**Beam Me Up Scotty (IRE) (84)** (NJHawke) **7-11-0** CLlewellyn (bit bkwd: led to 4th: outpcd 6th: wknd after 8th) 1½	**3**	5/1	55	—
221[2]	**The Black Monk (IRE) (95)** (MCPipe) **8-11-11v** DBridgwater (lw: nvr gng wl: 4th whn sltly hmpd 5th: t.o 6th) ....dist	**4**	6/4[1]	—	—
185*	**Jennyellen (IRE) (98)** (PBowen) **7-12-0** RJohnson (lw: chsng ldrs whn fell 5th)	**F**	5/2[2]	—	—
185[12]	**Coeur Battant (FR) (70)** (RJBaker) **6-10-0** BPowell (bit bkwd: bhd: hdwy 8th: chal for poor 2nd whn fell last)....	**F**	40/1	—	—
			(SP 114.2%)	**6 Rn**	

5m 18.3 (6.30) CSF £41.10 TOTE £5.20: £2.90 £4.50 (£11.20) OWNER Mr & Mrs J A Northover (MINEHEAD) BRED J. L. Woolford
LONG HANDICAP Coeur Battant (FR) 9-4
WEIGHT FOR AGE 4yo-3lb
OFFICIAL EXPLANATION The Black Monk (IRE): was never travelling.

Springfield Dancer made this a good gallop and stayed on really well. (9/2)
Celestial Fire made headway from the sixth, but could never catch the winner. (11/1: 8/1-12/1)
Beam Me Up Scotty (IRE) (5/1: op 10/1)

302 MIDSUMMER NOVICES' CHASE (5-Y.O+) (Class E)

3-15 (3-15) **3m 2f 110y (20 fncs)** £3,051.30 (£856.80: £417.90) GOING minus 0.58 sec per fur (F)

	Runner	Dist	Pos	SP	RR	SF
213[3]	**Wakt (77)** (JWhite) **6-10-7** APMcCoy (j.w: mid div: shkn up to chse ldrs 14th: led 17th: sn clr: unchal)	—	1	11/4[2]	95	24
94*	**Southerly Gale (104)** (MCPipe) **9-11-12** DBridgwater (j.w: led 2nd: rdn 14th: hdd 17th: sn wknd)	11	2	Evens[1]	107	36
	Duke of Lancaster (IRE) (85) (MrsJPitman) **7-10-12v** RBellamy (led to 2nd: chsd ldrs tl rdn & wknd 15th: t.o)	dist	3	9/2[3]	—	—
218[P]	**Liberty James** (MrsEMBrooks) **9-10-12** GUpton (bkwd: a bhd: j.slowly 7th: lost tch 10th: t.o whn p.u bef 14th)		P	40/1	—	—
220[3]	**Tour Leader (NZ) (84)** (RHBuckler) **7-10-12** BPowell (4th & in tch whn blnd & uns rdr 10th)		U	6/1	—	—

(SP 111.6%) **5 Rn**

6m 30.3 (-3.70) CSF £5.84 TOTE £3.80: £1.30 £1.40 (£2.70) OWNER Mr John White (ASTON ROWANT) BRED Shadwell Estate Company Limited

213 Wakt, who just keeps galloping, broke her duck over fences and her trainer reckons she will probably stay four miles. (11/4)
94* Southerly Gale made most of the running but found her heavy weight just too much. (Evens)

303 LES FLETCHER MEMORIAL CHALLENGE TROPHY H'CAP HURDLE (0-100) (4-Y.O+) (Class F)

3-45 (3-45) **2m 1f (8 hdls)** £1,948.80 (£546.80: £266.40) GOING minus 0.58 sec per fur (F)

	Runner	Dist	Pos	SP	RR	SF
211[2]	**Verde Luna (82)** (DWPArbuthnot) **4-10-12** APMcCoy (lw: a.p: led appr 2 out: styd on wl u.p flat)	—	1	100/30[2]	68	8
	Missed the Boat (IRE) (79) (AGNewcombe) **6-10-12** AThornton (lw: hld up: hdwy appr 2 out: sn ev ch: sddle slipped appr last: kpt on)	¾	2	3/1[1]	64+	7
	Game Dilemma (75) (JWMullins) **5-10-8** RGreene (hdwy to chse wnr 2 out: ev ch tl outpcd appr last)	1½	3	8/1	59	2
	Sirtelimar (IRE) (92) (KCBailey) **7-11-8**(3) TJMurphy (bit bkwd: bhd: hdwy appr 6th: no ex fr 2 out)	1¾	4	9/1	74	17
223[3]	**Mr Snaggle (IRE) (95)** (SEarle) **7-12-0** CMaude (led to 2nd: chsd ldr tl led 5th: hdd appr 2 out: one pce)	1½	5	3/1[1]	76	19
211[3]	**Stay With Me (FR) (95)** (CREgerton) **6-12-0** JAMcCarthy (a in tch: chsd ldr 6th: led briefly appr 2 out: mstke 2 out: wknd qckly appr last)	16	6	6/1[3]	61	4
	Madraj (IRE) (77) (RJHodges) **8-10-10** WMcFarland (bkwd: a bhd: drvn along 4th: t.o)	dist	7	33/1	—	—
184[8]	**Gunmaker (80)** (BJLlewellyn) **7-10-13** MrJLLlewellyn (chsd ldr: led 2nd to 5th: sn rdn & wknd: t.o whn p.u bef 2 out)		P	12/1	—	—

(SP 119.1%) **8 Rn**

3m 55.0 (2.00) CSF £13.75 CT £68.24 TOTE £4.70: £1.70 £1.80 £2.10 (£5.80) OWNER Mr J. A. Leek (COMPTON) BRED A. Christodoulou
WEIGHT FOR AGE 4yo-3lb

211 Verde Luna jumped well and had the speed aswell and that won him the day. (100/30)
Missed the Boat (IRE) was an unlucky loser as his saddle slipped going to the last and the partnership did well to stay intact. (3/1: 7/4-100/30)
Game Dilemma, who had run previously in a seller, ran well until getting outpaced approaching the last. (8/1)
211 Stay With Me (FR) (6/1: op 4/1)

304 AUGUST NOVICES' H'CAP HURDLE (0-100) (4-Y.O+) (Class E)

4-15 (4-15) **2m 1f (8 hdls)** £2,190.00 (£615.00: £300.00) GOING minus 0.58 sec per fur (F)

	Runner	Dist	Pos	SP	RR	SF
137[7]	**Kindergarten Boy (IRE) (80)** (KCBailey) **5-11-0**(3) TJMurphy (mid div: hdwy to chse ldr 5th: led after next: clr 2 out: easily)	—	1	6/1	71+	—
	Southern Ridge (75) (RGFrost) **5-10-12** MrAHoldsworth (led & sn wl clr: hdd after 6th: outpcd appr 2 out)	8	2	25/1	59	—
258[3]	**Mutley (64)** (NJHawke) **6-10-1**ow1 CMaude (hld up: hdwy appr 6th: one pce appr 2 out)	1¾	3	11/2[3]	46	—
159[7]	**Courageous Knight (84)** (PHayward) **7-11-7** BFenton (bit bkwd: chsd ldrs tl wknd after 6th)	3½	4	11/4[2]	63	—
217*	**Denomination (USA) (94)** (MCPipe) **4-12-0** DBridgwater (bhd: in tch 5th: wknd appr next: t.o)	dist	5	11/10[1]	—	—
156[9]	**Don Tocino (69)** (JWhite) **6-10-6** SCurran (chsd ldr to 5th: wknd next: sn t.o)	2½	6	11/1	—	—

(SP 116.1%) **6 Rn**

3m 58.8 (5.80) CSF £83.81 TOTE £9.20: £3.00 £6.10 (£65.10) OWNER Mrs E. A. Lerpiniere (UPPER LAMBOURN) BRED Bernard Eivers
WEIGHT FOR AGE 4yo-3lb

Kindergarten Boy (IRE), who was not right last year, won this comfortably. (6/1)
Southern Ridge will win races if he can be taught to settle. (25/1)
217* Denomination (USA) ran a very poor race indeed. (11/10)
Don Tocino (11/1: 10/1-16/1)

305 NORTH BANK HIGHBURY H'CAP CHASE (0-110) (5-Y.O+) (Class E)

4-45 (4-45) **2m 110y (13 fncs)** £2,818.20 (£852.60: £415.80: £197.40) GOING minus 0.58 sec per fur (F)

	Runner	Dist	Pos	SP	RR	SF
215[5]	**Manamour (78)** (RLee) **9-10-6** CLlewellyn (lw: hld up: stdy hdwy 9th: chal 2 out: sn led & qcknd clr)	—	1	11/4[2]	89	23
261[2]	**Noblely (USA) (100)** (NJHWalker) **9-12-0** RFarrant (lw: chsd ldr tl led 9th: hdd appr last: outpcd)	3½	2	9/4[1]	108	42
261[3]	**Flying Ziad (CAN) (77)** (HJManners) **13-10-5**ow5 MrACharles-Jones (bit bkwd: hld up: hdwy 8th: chsd ldr next: wknd appr 2 out)	¾	3	5/1	84	13
	Gabish (72) (BScriven) **11-9-7**(7) MrRThornton (bit bkwd: bhd & outpcd tl sme hdwy 10th: n.d)	11	4	66/1	68	2
190[P]	**Tango's Delight (75)** (RJBaker) **8-10-3** BPowell (bkwd: a bhd: t.o)	16	5	16/1	56	—
	Prudent Peggy (76) (RGFrost) **9-10-4b**ow4 JFrost (a in rr: lost tch 7th: t.o)	2	6	20/1	55	—
15[5]	**Ramstar (99)** (PJHobbs) **8-11-13** APMcCoy (bit bkwd: led tl mstke 9th: wknd qckly next: t.o)	dist	7	100/30[3]	—	—

(SP 109.3%) **7 Rn**

3m 57.6 (-2.40) CSF £8.65 TOTE £3.40: £1.90 £1.50 (£4.60) OWNER Mr R. L. C. Hartley (PRESTEIGNE) BRED Mrs H. E. Bromhead
LONG HANDICAP Prudent Peggy 9-8 Gabish 8-13
OFFICIAL EXPLANATION Tango's Delight: hung to the right throughout the race.

Manamour dispelled rumours about his unwillingness and scored in decisive fashion. He has been schooled by Yogi Breisner after failing to jump left-handed. (11/4)
261 Noblely (USA), under his big weight, fought back well for second. (9/4)
261 Flying Ziad (CAN) was battled out of the runner-up spot by Noblely. (5/1: 7/2-11/2)

306 WHO'S WHO STANDARD N.H. FLAT RACE (4, 5 & 6-Y.O) (Class H)
5-15 (5-15) **2m 1f** £1,138.00 (£318.00: £154.00)

	Horse	Dist	Pos	SP	RR	SF
161*	**Kailash (USA)** (MCPipe) **5-12-4** DBridgwater (lw: hld up in tch: led 5f out: sn clr: easily)	—	1	2/7[1]	—	—
	Red Tel (IRE) (MCPipe) **4-11-1** CMaude (hld up & bhd: hdwy to chse wnr 2f out: no imp)	8	2	6/1[3]	—	—
161[14]	**Katharine's Song (IRE)** (DMHyde) **6-10-13** BPowell (bit bkwd: led to 5f out: wkng whn rn wd 2f out)	6	3	50/1	—	—
	Lucky Mo (BRMillman) **6-10-8**(5) DSalter (in tch tl grad wknd fnl 3f)	16	4	16/1	—	—
	Late Encounter (BJLlewellyn) **5-11-1**(3) GuyLewis (bkwd: chsd ldrs 3f: wknd 6f out)	6	5	50/1	—	—
133[4]	**Dragon Fly (IRE)** (CRBarwell) **5-11-4** BClifford (bit bkwd: hdwy to chse ldr after 3f: rn wd ent st: nt rcvr)	2½	6	11/2[2]	—	—
	Royal Salute (FJordan) **4-10-8**(7) MrGShenkin (chsd ldrs 10f)	2½	7	33/1	—	—
				(SP 120.2%)	**7 Rn**	

4m 1.2 (240.20) CSF £3.25 TOTE £1.60: £1.10 £2.50 (£2.70) OWNER Mr Mick Fletcher (WELLINGTON) BRED William C. Miller
WEIGHT FOR AGE 4yo-3lb
161* Kailash (USA), giving weight away all round, scored his fourth bumper success comfortably. (2/7)
Red Tel (IRE), a stablemate of the winner, ran well on this debut. (6/1: 4/1-13/2)
Katharine's Song (IRE), despite running wide two furlongs out, is improving. (50/1)

T/Plpt: £684.50 (14.41 Tckts). T/Qdpt: £67.90 (9.38 Tckts). T

307a-313a & 315a (Irish Racing) - See Computer Raceform

0310a-GALWAY (Ireland) (R-H) (Good)
Wednesday July 31st

314a DIGITAL GALWAY PLATE H'CAP CHASE (Gd 2) (4-Y.O+)
4-00 (4-02) **2m 6f (14 fncs)** £31,125.00 (£9,625.00: £4,625.00: £1,625.00)

Horse	Dist	Pos	SP	RR	SF
Life of a Lord (APO'Brien,Ireland) **10-12-0** CFSwan (cl up: 3rd & pushed along 8th: chsd ldr after 3 out: chal appr st: led jst ins fnl f: styd on)	—	1	9/2[2]	174	—
Bishops Hall (HdeBromhead,Ireland) **10-10-2**ow1 RDunwoody (hld up in tch: 4th 8th: wnt 2nd 4 out: led next: rdn early flat: hdd jst ins fnl f: styd on u.p)	1½	2	14/1	147	—
King Wah Glory (IRE) (PBurke,Ireland) **7-10-0**ow1 CO'Dwyer (hld up towards rr: hdwy 9th: 4th 2 out: 3rd u.p bef st: kpt on same pce)	8	3	9/4[1]	139	—
Second Schedual (MissAMMcMahon,Ireland) **11-10-6** MDwyer (hld up towards rr: hdwy 8th: closing 3rd 2 out: rdn & nt trble ldrs flat)	3	4	20/1	143	—
Tryfirion (IRE) (VBowens,Ireland) **7-9-7** BPowell (towards rr early: hdwy 8th: wnt mod 5th early flat: styd on)	3½	5	10/1	127	—
Swallows Nest (JWNicholson,Ireland) **9-9-7** WSlattery (in tch: mstke 5th: wnt 4th 4 out: hmpd 2 out: no imp u.p flat)	11	6	20/1	119	—
Kelly's Pearl (IRE) (APO'Brien,Ireland) **9-9-7** THorgan (mid div: hdwy 8th: mod 7th 4 out: no imp flat)	3	7	12/1	117	—
Another Grouse (EPMitchell,Ireland) **9-9-10**ow3 JPBroderick (towards rr 8th: t.o)	dist	8	50/1	—	—
Boro Vacation (IRE) (PMullins,Ireland) **7-9-10** PCarberry (led: hit 2nd & 9th: hdd bef 4 out: sn wknd: t.o)	9	9	8/1[3]	—	—
Loftus Lad (IRE) (EMO'Sullivan,Ireland) **8-9-10**ow3 MrJCulloty (towards rr: mstke 4 out: t.o)	20	10	66/1	—	—
Nobodys Son (DO'Connell,Ireland) **10-9-7** 3x TJMurphy (cl up: mstke 2nd: wkng whn mstke 4 out: dropped bhd: wl t.o)	7	11	66/1	—	—
Open Market (USA) (DKWeld,Ireland) **7-9-7** 4x NWilliamson (hld up: hdwy 8th: 5th 4 out: rdn & chsng ldrs whn fell 2 out)		F	9/1	—	—
Jassu (JEKiely,Ireland) **10-10-12**ow2 JFTitley (towards rr: mstke 5th: dropped bhd 10th: n.d whn p.u bef 3 out)		P	25/1	—	—
Anabatic (IRE) (MJPO'Brien,Ireland) **8-10-5** TPRudd (in tch tl lost pl & p.u bef 10th)		P	14/1	—	—
Minister for Fun (IRE) (EJO'Grady,Ireland) **8-9-8**ow1 FWoods (hld up mid div: mstke 4 out: n.d after next: p.u bef 2 out)		P	10/1	—	—
Ballybriken Castle (IRE) (DDuggan,Ireland) **9-9-7** PLMalone (sn bhd: mstke 4th: t.o bef 6th: p.u bef 8th)		P	200/1	—	—
An Maineach (IRE) (CaptDGSwan,Ireland) **7-9-4**(3) DJCasey (in tch: wnt 2nd 4th: slipped bef 9th: led 4 out: mstke & hdd next: lft 5th 2 out: j.slowly & uns rdr last)		U	20/1	—	—
			(SP 132.8%)	**17 Rn**	

5m 20.4 OWNER M. J. Clancy (PILTOWN) BRED John Costelloe
STEWARDS' ENQUIRY Slattery susp. 9-10/8/96 (excessive use of whip).
Life of a Lord won this for the second year running, despite his welter-burden. He looked very definitely second best for much of the final half-mile, but staying power swung it his way. (9/2)
Bishops Hall was travelling so well when he took over that it looked a question of how far, but this trip is a couple of furlongs beyond his optimum, and he was just outstayed. He could be in for a good season. (14/1)
King Wah Glory (IRE), well weighted on the pick of his novice form, never looked like winning. (9/4)
Kelly's Pearl (IRE) (12/1: op 7/1)

0312a-GALWAY (Ireland) (R-H) (Good)
Thursday August 1st

316a HARP LAGER NOVICES' HURDLE (4-Y.O+)
2-35 (2-37) **2m 4f (11 hdls)** £4,110.00 (£930.00: £390.00: £210.00)

Horse	Dist	Pos	SP	RR	SF
Clonagam (IRE) (APO'Brien,Ireland) **7-11-0** CFSwan (hld up towards rr: hdwy 7th: 3rd 2 out: led appr last: drew clr flat)	—	1	9/2[2]	85+	—
Tarthooth (IRE) (ALTMoore,Ireland) **5-11-0** FWoods (hld up towards rr: hdwy bef 7th: mstkes 4 out & 3 out: rdn & hdwy to ld bef 2 out: slt mstke 2 out: sn hdd: one pce)	2½	2	9/10[1]	83	—

Classic Silk (IRE) (MrsDJColeman,Ireland) **4-10-9** NWilliamson (hld up in tch: 4th & trckng ldrs 3 out: led 2 out tl appr last: one pce u.p flat) ....3 **3** 8/1 83 —

Well Armed (IRE) (DAKiely,Ireland) **5-11-0** PCarberry (in tch: chsng ldrs after 3 out: mod 5th 2 out: no imp appr last) ....9 **4** 16/1 73 —

218[5] **Up the Tempo (IRE)** (PaddyFarrell) **7-10-9** RDunwoody (towards rr: hdwy after 3 out: mod 6th bef st: styd on) ....½ **5** 25/1 68 —

Preceptor (IRE) (VBowens,Ireland) **7-11-11**(3) BBowens (led: hdd briefly 7th: hdd bef 2 out: 4th, rdn & nt qckn appr st) ....2 **6** 8/1 85 —

Celio Lucy (IRE) (WPMullins,Ireland) **6-10-6**(3) DJCasey (mid div: mstke 2nd: mod 9th & rdn 3 out: no imp).15 **7** 14/1 54 —

Middle Moggs (IRE) (DWachman,Ireland) **4-10-2** KFO'Brien (chsd ldr to 6th: 3rd 3 out: sn rdn & wknd: n.d next) ....7 **8** 20/1 49 —

Bulwark Hill (IRE) (PMullins,Ireland) **6-11-0** GBradley (cl up pllng hrd: led briefly 7th: 2nd whn mstkes 4 out & 3 out: sn rdn: btn appr 2 out) ....15 **9** 6/1[3] 42 —

Bracker (IRE) (MJCarroll,Ireland) **4-10-1**(7)ow1 MrCAMurphy (in tch: sn rdn: lost pl & n.d 4 out) ....2½ **10** 66/1 41 —

Deep Refrain (IRE) (DHassett,Ireland) **6-11-0** JFTitley (towards rr: n.d) ....4 **11** 25/1 37 —

Grove Victor (IRE) (PFGraffin,Ireland) **5-11-0b** CO'Dwyer (sn mid div: n.d fr 4 out) ....13 **12** 50/1 26 —

(SP 135.8%) **12 Rn**

4m 54.5 OWNER R. Galvin (PILTOWN)

317a ST JAMES'S GATE H'CAP HURDLE (0-123) (4-Y.O+)

3-10 (3-10) **3m** **(14 hdls)** £5,137.50 (£1,162.50: £487.50: £262.50)

SP RR SF

Cullenstown Lady (IRE) (PHughes,Ireland) **5-11-8** RDunwoody (chsd ldr: led after 9th: rdn after 2 out: styd on u.p whn chal) ....— **1** 7/2[2] 99 —

Glengarrif Girl (IRE) (MCPipe) **6-10-12b** DBridgwater (towards rr early: hdwy 9th: 4th 4 out: rdn & chsd wnr bef 2 out: chal u.p st: styd on nr fin) ....¾ **2** 7/4[1] 89 —

Buggsy Blade (IRE) (MrsDJColeman,Ireland) **10-10-0** MDuffy (hld up in tch: 2nd after 3 out: 3rd 2 out: no imp appr st) ....15 **3** 7/1[3] 67 —

Final Tub (VTO'Brien,Ireland) **13-10-1** THorgan (mid div: hdwy 4 out: chsng ldrs appr 2 out: no imp appr last) ....1½ **4** 16/1 67 —

Sudden Storm (IRE) (PMullins,Ireland) **5-9-11**(3) DJCasey (in tch early: mod 6th appr st: no imp) ....5½ **5** 12/1 62 —

Chuck (IRE) (MMcCullagh,Ireland) **6-9-11**(7) DMcCullagh (hld up mid div: chsng ldrs 4 out: mod 5th 2 out: rdn & no imp appr st) ....10 **6** 10/1 59 —

Marlast (IRE) (JGGroome,Ireland) **5-10-9** JShortt (mostly 3rd: mstke 3 out: rdn & wknd appr next) ....4 **7** 14/1 62 —

190[9] **Bravo Star (USA)** (PaddyFarrell) **11-9-7b** FWoods (led & clr tl mstke 4th: mstke & hdd 9th: sn wknd) ....10 **8** 25/1 39 —

Manetti (TStack,Ireland) **4-10-9** APMcCoy (n.d) ....8 **9** 12/1 58 —

Doneraile Park (IRE) (JJWalsh,Ireland) **9-10-11** NWilliamson (towards rr: rdn & no imp appr 2 out) ....8 **10** 20/1 46 —

Valamir (IRE) (PDelaney,Ireland) **6-9-7** BPowell (mid div: mstke 3rd: wknd 10th: n.d) ....12 **11** 66/1 20 —

Steel Dawn (RCurran,Ireland) **9-11-7**(7) MrRJCurran (in tch: mstke & lost pl 5 out: towards rr whn mstke 3 out: p.u) .... **P** 12/1 — —

Expedient Option (IRE) (APO'Brien,Ireland) **6-10-12** CFSwan (towards rr: rdn & bhd 5th: p.u bef next) .... **P** 10/1 — —

Derby Haven (IRE) (CaptSHWalford,Ireland) **9-10-6** SCLyons (hld up mid div: chsd ldrs 3 out: n.d appr next: p.u bef st) .... **P** 10/1 — —

(SP 144.1%) **14 Rn**

5m 45.9 OWNER P. Hughes (BAGENALSTOWN)

318a GUINNESS GALWAY H'CAP HURDLE (Gd 2) (4-Y.O+)

4-00 (4-00) **2m** **(9 hdls)** £27,750.00 (£8,700.00: £4,200.00: £1,500.00)

SP RR SF

Mystical City (IRE) (WPMullins,Ireland) **6-10-1**(3) DJCasey (hld up mid div: hdwy 6th: led bef st: rdn & styd on flat) ....— **1** 20/1 99 —

Space Trucker (IRE) (MrsJHarrington,Ireland) **5-10-11** NWilliamson (hld up towards rr: hdwy 5th: chal appr last: kpt on) ....2½ **2** 7/1[3] 104 —

Just Little (APO'Brien,Ireland) **4-10-3** CFSwan (hld up towards rr: hdwy 6th: 3rd, chal & edgd rt appr last: ev ch flat: kpt on) ....nk **3** 14/1 100 —

Khayrawani (IRE) (PBurke,Ireland) **4-10-6** 8x CO'Dwyer (prom: led 2nd: hdd bef st: cl 4th over last: no ex flat) ....3½ **4** 6/1[2] 100 —

Northern Fancy (IRE) (AJMartin,Ireland) **5-9-8**ow1 FWoods (hld up towards rr: hdwy appr 2 out: rdn & nt trble ldrs appr last: kpt on flat) ....3 **5** 25/1 80 —

Dreams End (PBowen) **8-11-3** RFarrant (in tch: chsng ldrs 2 out: kpt on same pce) ....hd **6** 20/1 103 —

Alasad (NMeade,Ireland) **6-10-11** PCarberry (prom early: hld up in tch: chsng ldrs 3 out: 2nd 2 out: 6th, u.p & one pce whn sltly hmpd bef st) ....7 **7** 7/1[3] 90 —

Dance Beat (IRE) (MrsJHarrington,Ireland) **5-11-7** JShortt (in tch: kpt on same pce fr 2 out) ....½ **8** 14/1 99 —

Phardy (IRE) (ALeahy,Ireland) **5-9-7** BPowell (hld up towards rr: hdwy 6th: kpt on) ....6 **9** 50/1 65 —

West On Bridge St (IRE) (VTO'Brien,Ireland) **6-10-0**ow2 DBridgwater (in tch: chsng ldrs 3 out: rdn & no imp appr last) ....s.h **10** 16/1 72 —

103[2] **Suivez** (MrsNMacauley) **6-10-11** JOsborne (towards rr: sltly hmpd bef 5th: n.d) ....3 **11** 20/1 80 —

Rupert Belle (IRE) (CPDonoghue,Ireland) **5-9-13**(3) 5x PHenley (towards rr: no imp appr 2 out: kpt on same pce) ....1 **12** 16/1 70 —

No Tag (IRE) (PatrickKelly,Ireland) **8-11-8** JFTitley (hld up: chsd ldr briefly: rdn 2 out: no imp appr st) ....4½ **13** 10/1 86 —

Talina's Law (IRE) (PMullins,Ireland) **4-10-12b** GBradley (cl up: rdn & chsd ldrs bef 3 out: wknd u.p after 3 out: n.d next) ....2 **14** 10/1 79 —

Treble Bob (IRE) (DKWeld,Ireland) **6-12-0** RDunwoody (towards rr: rdn ½-wy: kpt on: n.d) ....2½ **15** 20/1 87 —

Kawa-Kawa (PDelaney,Ireland) **9-9-12** SHO'Donovan (mid div: 11th at 5th: rdn & no imp after 3 out) ....8 **16** 50/1 49 —

Crossfarnogue (IRE) (APO'Brien,Ireland) **7-11-10** 7x THorgan (disp ld briefly: 10th at 5th: wknd: n.d fr 3 out) ....8 **17** 33/1 67 —

Ros Castle (AMullins,Ireland) **5-11-1b** APMcCoy (prom: chsd ldr 3rd tl after 3 out: sn rdn & wknd) ....2 **18** 14/1 56 —

Lady Arpel (IRE) (PO'Leary,Ireland) **4-10-12** KFO'Brien (nvr bttr than mid div) ....10 **19** 20/1 48 —

	Horse	Pos	SP	RR	SF
	State Princess (IRE) (GMLyons,Ireland) **6-10-9** AMaguire (towards rr: hdwy 6th: rdn & wknd after next) 5½	**20**	20/1	35	—
	Royal Albert (IRE) (PJFlynn,Ireland) **7-10-9** MDuffy (hld up mid div: slipped up bef 5th)	**S**	9/2 [1]	—	—
			(SP 146.7%)	**21 Rn**	

3m 39.2 OWNER Phantom Syndicate (MUINE BEAG)

319a ARTHUR GUINNESS N.H. FLAT RACE (5-Y.O+)
5-40 (5-43) **2m 2f** £4,110.00 (£930.00: £390.00: £210.00)

	Horse	Pos	SP	RR	SF
	Ask The Butler (IRE) (PBurke,Ireland) **5-11-9**(5) MrJarlathConnolly (plld hrd: hld up in tch: trckd ldrs 3f out: hdwy on outside to ld 1½f out: sn clr: easily) .....—	**1**	4/5 [1]	—	—
	Baby Jake (IRE) (DHassett,Ireland) **6-11-7**(7) MrBrianHassett (in tch: 4th ½-wy: disp ld 6f out: rdn & led under 3f out: hdd u.p & nt qckn 1½f out: kpt on same pce) 5½	**2**	7/1 [2]	—	—
	Written (IRE) (JGMurphy,Ireland) **6-12-0** MrPFenton (towards rr early: hdwy bef ½-wy: wnt 5th 6f out: 3rd & rdn over 3f out: 4th & nt trble ldrs 1½f out: kpt on) 3½	**3**	20/1	—	—
	Diamond Double (IRE) (APO'Brien,Ireland) **5-11-6**(3) MrBMCash (chsd ldr: disp ld 4f out: rdn & nt qckn fr 2f out) 1	**4**	8/1 [3]	—	—
	Glenreef Boy (IRE) (CPDonoghue,Ireland) **7-11-11**(3) PHenley (mid div: chsd ldrs 3f out: no imp 1½f out)...1½	**5**	16/1	—	—
	Barrigan's Hill (IRE) (MissURyan,Ireland) **6-11-7**(7) MrJohnMoloney (hld up mid div: rdn 3f out: no imp 1½f out) 3	**6**	14/1	—	—
	Dear Chris (IRE) (PatrickKelly,Ireland) **5-11-4**(5) MrRWalsh (in tch: nt trble ldrs 1½f out) .....nk	**7**	10/1	—	—
	Highest Call (IRE) (MHalford,Ireland) **5-12-0** MrMHalford (towards rr: hdwy over 6f out: mod 9th 1½f out: nvr nrr) 7	**8**	10/1	—	—
	Castleroyal (IRE) (IRFerguson,Ireland) **7-12-0** MrDMarnane (hld up in tch: chsd ldrs over 3f out: one pce 2f out) 3	**9**	12/1	—	—
	Marie's Pride (IRE) (MHourigan,Ireland) **5-11-2b**(7) MrDO'Meara (mid div: hdwy ½-wy: n.d 1½f out) 20	**10**	12/1	—	—
	Dawn Caller (IRE) (MrsJHarrington,Ireland) **5-11-7**(7) MrMWCarroll (rr of mid div: sme hdwy ½-wy: n.d fnl 4f) 5½	**11**	10/1	—	—
	Mc Clatchey (IRE) (PFGraffin,Ireland) **5-12-0** MrPFGraffin (clr to ½-wy: hdd 6f out: sn wknd) 2	**12**	20/1	—	—
	Eoins Lad (IRE) (MCunningham,Ireland) **5-12-0** MrAJMartin (mid div: no imp over 4f out) 2½	**13**	20/1	—	—
	Weaver Square (IRE) (VBowens,Ireland) **7-12-0** MrJANash (hld up towards rr: n.d) 2½	**14**	10/1	—	—
	Forgiveness (IRE) (JMonroe,Ireland) **6-11-7**(7) MrGMonroe (n.d) .....¾	**15**	50/1	—	—
	Corkers Flame (IRE) (TJO'Mara,Ireland) **5-11-11**(3) KWhelan (hld up in tch: rdn 6f out: n.d fnl 4f) 3	**16**	20/1	—	—
161[6]	**Moreceva (IRE)** (PaddyFarrell) **6-12-0** MrJPDempsey (mid div: towards rr & n.d 6f out: t.o) .....dist	**17**	14/1	—	—
	Howesshecutting (IRE) (TO'Neill,Ireland) **6-11-2**(7) MrGElliott (a towards rr: t.o) 1	**18**	25/1	—	—
	Carnmore Castle (IRE) (MMcDonagh,Ireland) **8-11-7b**(7) MrKNMcDonagh (in tch: rdn ½-wy: sn wknd: t.o) ..15	**19**	33/1	—	—
	The Breaser Fawl (IRE) (PatrickHassett,Ireland) **8-11-7**(7) MrDanielHassett (t.o) 3	**20**	20/1	—	—
	Mystical Rye (IRE) (MMcElhone,Ireland) **5-11-2**(7) MrADaly (dropped bhd ½-wy: wl t.o) 25	**21**	33/1	—	—
			(SP 185.6%)	**21 Rn**	

4m 11.4 OWNER Barry Lee McCoubrey (KILDARE)
STEWARDS' ENQUIRY Elliott susp. 10/8-6/9/96 (improper riding).

0315a-GALWAY (Ireland) (R-H) (Good to firm)
Friday August 2nd

321a TONY O'MALLEY MEMORIAL H'CAP CHASE (4-Y.O+)
5-50 (5-50) **2m 1f (12 fncs)** £5,780.00 (£1,240.00: £520.00: £280.00)

	Horse	Pos	SP	RR	SF
314a[5]	**Tryfirion (IRE)** (VBowens,Ireland) **7-11-10**(3) BBowens (hld up in tch: 4th whn mstke 7th: chsng ldrs whn mstkes 4 out & 2 out: styd on u.p to ld nr fin) .....—	**1**	9/4 [1]	122	—
	The Ridge Boreen (GFarrell,Ireland) **12-11-11** MDwyer (hld up: hdwy 3 out: wnt 3rd over next: 2nd early flat: sn chal: led over 1f out: rdn & kpt on: hdd nr fin) 1½	**2**	16/1	119	—
	Who's to Say (MissVenetiaWilliams) **10-11-13** NWilliamson (cl up: disp ld 8th: led bef 3 out tl over 1f out: rdn & one pce) 5½	**3**	13/2	115	—
	Nordic Thorn (IRE) (MBrassil,Ireland) **6-11-1** KFO'Brien (hld up: mstkes 4th & 6th: rdn & sme hdwy 4 out: hdwy & 5th appr 2 out: rdn & no imp early flat) 2½	**4**	9/2 [3]	101	—
	Synieyourmissed (IRE) (DHassett,Ireland) **7-9-9**ow1 THorgan (hld up & bhd: hdwy 4 out: mod 6th appr 2 out: styd on flat: nvr nrr) .....½	**5**	12/1	81	—
	Sandy Forest Lady (IRE) (DO'Connell,Ireland) **7-9-9**ow2 JPBroderick (cl up: disp ld 7th tl appr 3 out: cl 2nd 2 out: rdn & nt qckn early flat: 4th & no imp appr st) 13	**6**	6/1	68	—
	La Mode Lady (MrsFMO'Brien,Ireland) **11-9-7**(5) GCotter (led: jnd 7th: mstke & hdd next: 5th 4 out: wknd & no imp fr next) 7	**7**	8/1	65	—
	Shankorak (FBerry,Ireland) **9-10-13** CO'Dwyer (hld up in tch: rdn whn mstke 4 out: no imp after next) .....s.h	**8**	5/2 [2]	80	—
			(SP 129.8%)	**8 Rn**	

4m 21.7 OWNER Mrs M. T. Quinn (COLBINSTOWN)

0320a-GALWAY (Ireland) (R-H) (Good to firm)
Saturday August 3rd

323a LOW LOW GALWAY BLAZERS H'CAP CHASE (0-116) (4-Y.O+)
3-00 (3-02) **2m 6f** £4,110.00 (£930.00: £390.00: £210.00)

	Horse	Pos	SP	RR	SF
	Beet Statement (IRE) (WTMurphy,Ireland) **7-9-12** TJMitchell (towards rr: hdwy 9th: 6th 3 out: lft 2nd & hmpd 2 out: sn led: hld on flat) .....—	**1**	16/1	80	—
314a[8]	**Another Grouse** (EPMitchell,Ireland) **9-12-0** JPBroderick (in tch: 4th ½-wy: rdn & chsng ldrs 3 out: lft 3rd 2 out: sn chsng ldr: chsd wnr flat: styd on u.p) .....hd	**2**	10/1	110	—
	Castalino (StephenRyan,Ireland) **10-10-6** KFO'Brien (hld up: hdwy whn pckd 9th: rdn after 3 out: lft in ld, hmpd & hdd 2 out: ev ch flat: no ex) 1	**3**	10/1	87	—

				SP	RR	SF
	Balyara (IRE) (APO'Brien,Ireland) **6-11-10b** CFSwan (hld up towards rr: hdwy 3 out: lft 4th & hmpd 2 out: j.slowly last: no imp u.p flat)	2	**4**	15/2	104	—
	Fixed Assets (DCasey,Ireland) **9-9-6**(7) AO'Shea (mid div: rdn 3 out: hdwy between last 2: rdn & one pce flat)	5	**5**	20/1	75	—
	Springfort Lady (IRE) (JJWalsh,Ireland) **7-10-7** NWilliamson (cl up: disp ld briefly 11th: 3rd over next: 7th, rdn & one pce appr 2 out: no imp)	15	**6**	7/1[3]	72	—
317a[8]	**Bravo Star (USA)** (PaddyFarrell) **11-9-2**(5) TMartin (towards rr: n.d)	10	**7**	33/1	51	—
	Nebraska (MBrassil,Ireland) **10-11-1** RDunwoody (towards rr: 8th & hdwy whn bd mstke 4 out: no imp fr next)	12	**8**	10/1	64	—
	Kingston Way (MrsFMO'Brien,Ireland) **10-11-2**(5) GCotter (in tch: chsng ldrs 3 out: lft 4th & b.d next)		**B**	12/1	—	—
	Timely Affair (IRE) (ALTMoore,Ireland) **7-9-11b[1]** FWoods (in tch: wnt 2nd 9th: chsng ldrs whn slipped bdly 2 out: recovering whn b.d)		**B**	8/1	—	—
	Phairy Miracles (IRE) (PJHealy,Ireland) **7-10-7** PMVerling (disp ld fr 3rd: hdd briefly bef 9th: led 3 out: slipped & fell 2 out)		**F**	14/1	—	—
	Midnight Hour (IRE) (DTHughes,Ireland) **7-11-8** CO'Dwyer (cl up whn p.u after 7th: dead)		**P**	4/1[1]	—	—
9[4]	**Bald Joker** (DMcBratney,Ireland) **11-9-13** THorgan (led & disp ld to ½-wy: sn wknd: mstke 9th: p.u)		**P**	14/1	—	—
	Micks Delight (IRE) (RO'Leary,Ireland) **6-11-8b[1]** MDwyer (towards rr: mstke 5th: p.u bef 10th)		**P**	10/1	—	—
	Another Coq Hardi (IRE) (NMeade,Ireland) **8-10-8** PCarberry (bd mstke & lost pl 2nd: bhd 4th: p.u after next)		**P**	10/1	—	—
	Any Port (IRE) (AJMartin,Ireland) **6-10-9** PLMalone (blnd & uns rdr 1st)		**U**	6/1[2]	—	—
				(SP 149.7%)		**16 Rn**

5m 28.4 OWNER W. M. Sheehy (DUN LAOGHAIRE)

324a-325a, 320a & 322a (Irish Racing) - See Computer Raceform

LES LANDES (Jersey) (L-H) (Good to firm)

Sunday July 28th

326a B. J. O'CONNOR ANNIVERSARY H'CAP HURDLE (4-Y.O+)

3-00 (3-00) **2m** £720.00

				SP	RR	SF
	Clear Home (TBougourd,Guernsey) **10-10-0** AMcCabe	—	**1**		64	—
	Fools of Pride (IRE) (MissAVibert,Jersey) **4-10-5** BPowell	10	**2**		62	—
211[4]	**Northern Trial (USA)** (KRBurke) **8-12-0** ALarnach		**F**		—	—
						3 Rn

3m 51.0 Tote £5.40 (£10.40) OWNER T. Bougourd BRED Swettenham Stud

Northern Trial (USA) was travelling smoothly when falling fatally two out.

PLUMPTON (L-H) (Firm)

Friday August 9th

Race 6 abandoned - course unsafe

WEATHER: showers

327 HOVE NOVICES' HURDLE (4-Y.O+) (Class E)

2-30 (2-30) **2m 4f (12 hdls)** £2,343.00 (£648.00: £309.00) GOING minus 0.23 sec per fur (G)

				SP	RR	SF
100[5]	**Limosa (80)** (MrsLRichards) **5-10-7** MRichards (lw: hld up: lft 2nd appr 6th to 9th: led appr last: hrd rdn: r.o wl)	—	**1**	7/2[2]	64+	11
262[5]	**Canary Falcon** (HJCollingridge) **5-10-12** VSmith (lw: hdwy 7th: chsd ldr fr 9th: led 2 out tl appr last: unable qckn flat)	4	**2**	7/1	66	13
	Sir Galeforce (IRE) (RCurtis) **6-10-12** DMorris (chsd ldr: mstke 2nd: led after 5th: slipped bnd appr 6th: hdd 2 out: 3rd & btn whn j.slowly last)	8	**3**	13/2[3]	59	6
	Arctic Red River (IRE) (TPMcGovern) **7-10-12** AMaguire (lw: no hdwy fr 9th)	17	**4**	4/5[1]	46	—
	Fattash (USA) (PMooney) **4-10-4b**(5) SRyan (swtg: bhd fr 8th: t.o)	dist	**5**	33/1	—	—
	Brigadier Supreme (IRE) (PButler) **7-10-12** BFenton (bit bkwd: mstke 1st: bhd fr 6th: t.o whn p.u bef 9th)		**P**	33/1	—	—
	Shalik (IRE) (JRJenkins) **6-10-12** JRailton (led tl after 5th: 2nd whn s.u bnd appr 6th)		**S**	33/1	—	—
				(SP 112.4%)		**7 Rn**

4m 54.8 (7.80) CSF £24.79 TOTE £4.60: £2.10 £5.60 (£12.00) OWNER Mrs Lydia Richards (CHICHESTER) BRED Southcourt Stud

WEIGHT FOR AGE 4yo-3lb

OFFICIAL EXPLANATION **Arctic Red River (IRE): was never going on the firm ground.**

19 Limosa, who has failed to stay three miles in both her previous outings this season, was much happier over this shorter trip. Throwing down her challenge in the home straight, she poked a nostril in front approaching the final flight and, responding to pressure, proved too strong for her rivals to win a bad race. (7/2: 5/2-4/1)

Canary Falcon moved into second place entering the back straight for the final time. Gaining a narrow advantage two out, he was collared approaching the last and failed to quicken on the run-in. (7/1: 4/1-8/1)

Sir Galeforce (IRE), who won a maiden point-to-point at Wolverhampton before failing to complete in two subsequent runs between the Flags last season, went on soon after the fifth. Very lucky to remain on his feet as he slipped badly entering the home straight going to the next, he nevertheless remained in front but, collared two out, was soon in trouble. (13/2)

Arctic Red River (IRE), an ex-Irish gelding who won a bumper at Roscommon in June, was making no impression on the principals in the last mile. His jockey later reported that the gelding was never travelling well on the firm ground. He is worth another chance in a small race on better ground. (4/5)

328 STREAT CONDITIONAL (S) H'CAP CHASE (0-95) (5-Y.O+) (Class G)

3-00 (3-11) **2m (13 fncs)** £2,259.00 (£624.00: £297.00) GOING minus 0.74 sec per fur (F)

				SP	RR	SF
	Safety (USA) (81) (JWhite) **9-11-5b** TJMurphy (mde virtually all: easily)	—	**1**	3/1[1]	95+	4
	Afaltoun (70) (RLee) **11-10-8** PHenley (hld up: rdn 9th: chsd wnr fr 4 out: no imp)	4	**2**	13/2	80	—

	Horse / details		Pos	SP	RR	SF
261[4]	**Nuclear Express (72)** (JMBradley) **9-10-10** GuyLewis (lw: hld up: chsd wnr 8th to 4 out: one pce)	9	**3**	3/1 [1]	73	—
	Days of Thunder (90) (MrsSMOdell) **8-12-0** BFenton (lw: a bhd: t.o)	30	**4**	100/30 [2]	61	—
256[6]	**Victory Anthem (74)** (PCClarke) **10-10-12** MichaelBrennan (lw: chsd wnr 2nd to 8th: 4th whn blnd & uns rdr 4 out)		**U**	7/2 [3]	—	—
	Lavalight (70) (JWDufosee) **9-10-8** JCulloty (a bhd: 4th & no ch whn blnd & uns rdr last)		**U**	16/1	—	—
				(SP 114.5%)		**6 Rn**

3m 54.4 (2.40) CSF £20.22 TOTE £3.10: £2.00 £5.90 (£28.10) OWNER Mr Keith Sturgis (ASTON ROWANT)
No bid

Safety (USA), who loves to hear his feet rattle, dominated this bad field. Making all the running, he won with a ton in hand. He can win another small race. (3/1: op 2/1)

Afaltoun moved into second place four out, but had no hope with the winner. (13/2)

Nuclear Express moved into second place six out but, collared for that position two fences later, was made to look very pedestrian. (3/1)

329 BERWICK H'CAP HURDLE (0-110) (4-Y.O+) (Class E)

3-30 (3-35) **2m 1f (10 hdls)** £2,280.00 (£630.00: £300.00) GOING minus 0.23 sec per fur (G)

	Horse / details		Pos	SP	RR	SF
223[5]	**Pair of Jacks (IRE) (83)** (GLMoore) **6-10-3** CLlewellyn (lw: chsd ldr: led after 3 out: rdn out)	—	**1**	2/1 [2]	63	—
75[8]	**No Light (103)** (MrsIMcKie) **9-11-9** LHarvey (lw: hld up: rdn appr last: ev ch flat: r.o)	hd	**2**	5/1 [3]	83	—
	Zabargar (USA) (108) (TPMcGovern) **5-12-0** AMaguire (lw: hld up: rdn appr last: unable qckn)	2½	**3**	5/4 [1]	86	—
	Ikhtiraa (USA) (90) (RJO'Sullivan) **6-10-10b** DO'Sullivan (nt j.w: led: mstke 5th: hdd after 3 out: sn wknd)	19	**4**	6/1	50	—
				(SP 108.7%)		**4 Rn**

4m 14.1 (18.10) CSF £9.88 TOTE £2.30: (£4.20) OWNER Mr D. A. Wilson (EPSOM) BRED Loan and Development Corporation

223 Pair of Jacks (IRE) made the most of his light weight. Racing in second place, he gained command soon after the third last and, ridden along, kept on too gamely for the second and third on the run-in. (2/1)

62 No Light, settled in third place, mounted his challenge in the straight. Still in with every chance on the run-in, he found the winner too tough a nut to crack. (5/1: op 5/2)

Zabargar (USA), an ex-Irish gelding who won a maiden hurdle at Down Royal at the end of May, raced in fourth place. Throwing down his challenge in the straight, he was only about a length down going to the final flight, before topweight found him out. (5/4: op 2/1)

Ikhtiraa (USA) was not in one of his co-operative moods. Setting the pace, he jumped far from fluently and, once collared soon after the third last, he soon waved the flag. (6/1: 4/1-13/2)

330 CHAILEY NOVICES' H'CAP CHASE (0-100) (5-Y.O+) (Class E)

4-00 (4-00) **2m 5f (16 fncs)** £2,906.40 (£865.20: £411.60: £184.80) GOING minus 0.74 sec per fur (F)

	Horse / details		Pos	SP	RR	SF
286*	**Pond House (IRE) (91)** (MCPipe) **7-11-6** 7x DBridgwater (mde all: mstke 11th: clr appr 3 out: easily)	—	**1**	5/4 [1]	96+	35
72[2]	**Simply (IRE) (99)** (TPMcGovern) **7-12-0** AMaguire (chsd wnr to 4th: chsd wnr appr last: unable qckn)	8	**2**	11/8 [2]	98	37
102[P]	**Call Me Albi (IRE) (92)** (MrsLRichards) **5-11-3v** MRichards (lw: chsd wnr 4th tl appr last: sn wknd)	7	**3**	11/1 [3]	86	21
254[3]	**Telmar Systems (71)** (JWhite) **7-10-0b[1]** DGallagher (bhd fr 11th)	10	**4**	11/1 [3]	57	—
	Jimmy the Jackdaw (71) (PButler) **9-10-0** BFenton (bhd fr 7th)	17	**5**	25/1	44	—
	Cardan (71) (AGHobbs) **10-10-0** RGreene (bit bkwd: a bhd)	12	**6**	16/1	35	—
				(SP 112.9%)		**6 Rn**

5m 7.1 (-5.90) CSF £3.30 TOTE £2.40: £1.50 £2.00 (£2.20) OWNER Mr C. R. Fleet (WELLINGTON) BRED S. Banville
LONG HANDICAP Telmar Systems 9-7 Jimmy the Jackdaw 9-8 Cardan 9-5
WEIGHT FOR AGE 5yo-4lb

286* Pond House (IRE) had a nice stroll round. Making all the running, he forged clear turning out of the back straight to win as he pleased. (5/4: op Evens)

72 Simply (IRE), in second place early, regained that position approaching the last but, by that stage, the winner was home and dry. A small race is within his compass. (11/8)

13 Call Me Albi (IRE) moved into second place at the fourth, but he was out on his feet jumping the water, three out, and was collared for the runner-up berth approaching the final fence. (11/1: 6/1-12/1)

Telmar Systems (11/1: 6/1-12/1)

331 JEVINGTON HURDLE (3-Y.O) (Class E)

4-30 (4-32) **2m 1f (10 hdls)** £2,217.00 (£612.00: £291.00) GOING minus 0.23 sec per fur (G)

Horse / details		Pos	SP	RR	SF
Galway Blade (MissHCKnight) **3-10-7**(3) JCulloty (mde all: slipped bnd appr 2 out: drvn out)	—	**1**	2/1 [1]	57	—
Verulam (IRE) (JRJenkins) **3-10-10** GBradley (hdwy 4th: ev ch flat: r.o)	¾	**2**	11/4 [2]	56	—
Again Together (GLMoore) **3-10-5** DGallagher (chsd wnr: ev ch fr 3 out: unable qckn flat)	1¼	**3**	2/1 [1]	50	—
Amber Ring (MissKMGeorge) **3-10-5** DSkyrme (lw: hdwy 5th: one pce fr 3 out)	1½	**4**	33/1	49	—
Last But Not Least (MCPipe) **3-10-5** DBridgwater (lw: blnd 1st: a bhd: t.o whn p.u bef 4th)		**P**	8/1 [3]	—	—
Kings Nightclub (JWhite) **3-10-5** BFenton (lw: bhd fr 3 out: s.u bnd appr 2 out)		**S**	16/1	—	—
			(SP 113.3%)		**6 Rn**

4m 20.9 (24.90) CSF £7.71 TOTE £3.00: £1.80 £1.70 (£5.20) OWNER Mr T. Blade (WANTAGE) BRED J. and Mrs M. Beddis
OFFICIAL EXPLANATION **Last But Not Least: sustained a cut to a fore-leg.**

Galway Blade, with Alan Jarvis on the Flat, made virtually all the running. Despite slipping on the bend approaching the second last, he responded well to pressure and just proved too strong for the second and third. (2/1)

Verulam (IRE) looked fit considering he had not run since last October. Throwing down his challenge from the second last, he battled hard for the advantage on the run-in, but found the winner too good. (11/4)

Again Together, who finished second to Nikita's Star at Folkestone last month, raced in second place. Throwing down her challenge from the third last, she may well have got her head in front for a few strides, but failed to find another gear on the run-in. She can win a small race. (2/1)

Amber Ring moved up nicely with a circuit to go but, after travelling well in the back straight, failed to quicken from the third last. (33/1)

Last But Not Least (8/1: 4/1-8/1)

332 HICKSTEAD H'CAP HURDLE (0-120) (4-Y.O+) (Class D)

Abandoned - Course unsafe

T/Plpt: £55.90 (145.94 Tckts). T/Qdpt: £5.20 (113.17 Tckts). AK

0288-MARKET RASEN (R-H) (Good)

Saturday August 10th

WEATHER: fine

333 TOTE COMBINATION DUAL FORECAST NOVICES' CHASE (5-Y.O+) (Class D)

5-50 (5-51) **2m 4f (15 fncs)** £4,120.00 (£1,145.00: £550.00) GOING: 0.19 sec per fur (G)

	Runner	Dist	Pos	SP	RR	SF
131[2]	**Cats Run (IRE) (88)** (JohnUpson) **8-11-0** RSupple (lw: mde all: shkn up 3 out: clr last: eased flat)	—	1	7/4[2]	113+	21
296[2]	**Nordic Valley (IRE) (82)** (MCPipe) **5-10-10** DBridgwater (chsd ldrs: hit 7th: trckd wnr fr 9th: blnd 4 out: rdn & hit 2 out: sn btn)	20	2	10/11[1]	97	1
290[2]	**Sassiver (USA) (88)** (PAKelleway) **6-11-6** PNiven (cl up tl blnd bdly 9th: sn lost tch: t.o)	dist	3	4/1[3]	—	—
213[P]	**Signe de Mars (FR)** (MissZAGreen) **5-10-7**(3) DWalsh (sn wl bhd: t.o whn p.u bef 11th)		P	25/1	—	—
				(SP 112.6%)		**4 Rn**

5m 6.2 (15.20) CSF £3.78 TOTE £2.80: (£2.40) OWNER Mrs Ann Key (TOWCESTER) BRED John Brophy
WEIGHT FOR AGE 5yo-4lb

131 Cats Run (IRE), a faller on both his starts over fences last season, barely put a foot wrong here. Going clear from the second last, he was eased right down on the flat. He can win again. (7/4)

296 Nordic Valley (IRE), in with every chance rounding the home turn, was already sending out distress signals when clouting the second last. (10/11: Evens-11/10)

290 Sassiver (USA) was trotted up and down at the start beforehand as though something was thought to be amiss. He had no chance after ploughing through the ninth fence. (4/1)

Signe de Mars (FR), whose horsebox broke down en route, arrived with only minutes to spare which can hardly have helped his chances. (25/1)

334 SINGLETON/RICHARDSON H'CAP HURDLE (0-105) (4-Y.O+) (Class F)

6-20 (6-20) **2m 1f 110y (8 hdls)** £1,954.00 (£544.00: £262.00) GOING: 0.44 sec per fur (GS)

	Runner	Dist	Pos	SP	RR	SF
214[6]	**Wamdha (IRE) (100)** (KAMorgan) **6-11-11** ASSmith (mde all: set stdy pce: rdn & qcknd appr 2 out: r.o wl flat)	—	1	13/8[1]	76	39
	John Tufty (83) (JPearce) **5-10-8** MDwyer (lw: hld up: hdwy 3 out: trckd wnr appr next: rdn between last 2: kpt on flat)	1	2	7/2[2]	58	21
54[2]	**Elite Justice (85)** (SGollings) **4-10-7b** ADobbin (chsd ldrs: effrt & ev ch 3 out: btn whn blnd last)	11	3	13/8[1]	50	10
	Gavaskar (IRE) (75) (JCullinan) **7-10-0b[1]** BPowell (racd keenly: trckd wnr: rdn & hit 3 out: sn btn: t.o)	26	4	12/1[3]	16	—
				(SP 106.1%)		**4 Rn**

4m 18.5 (15.50) CSF £6.56 TOTE £2.30: (£4.30) OWNER Mr T. R. Pryke (MELTON MOWBRAY) BRED Sheikh Ahmed bin Rashid al Maktoum
WEIGHT FOR AGE 4yo-3lb

103 Wamdha (IRE) dictated a steady pace and, quickening the tempo going to the penultimate flight, was always finding enough to keep the runner-up at bay. (13/8)

John Tufty, held up at the rear of the field, moved through to track the winner rounding the home turn and kept on under pressure to the line, but was always just coming off second best in a race that developed into a four-furlong dash. (7/2)

54 Elite Justice chased the leaders, but came under pressure going to the second last and was already beaten when misjudging the final flight. (13/8)

Gavaskar (IRE) (12/1: op 7/1)

335 FRESHNEY PLACE H'CAP CHASE (0-115) (5-Y.O+) (Class E)

6-50 (6-50) **2m 6f 110y (15 fncs)** £3,851.75 (£1,154.00: £554.50: £254.75) GOING: 0.19 sec per fur (G)

	Runner	Dist	Pos	SP	RR	SF
256[2]	**Magic Bloom (99)** (JMJefferson) **10-11-8**(5) ECallaghan (lw: hld up in tch: j.rt 5th & 6th: chsd ldrs 9th: chal appr 2 out: led last: kpt on u.p)	—	1	11/8[1]	107	43
292*	**Drumstick (96)** (KCBailey) **10-11-10** AThornton (led tl blnd & hdd 11th: rallied to ld 3 out: sn strly chal: hdd last: kpt on)	1½	2	2/1[2]	103	39
292[F]	**Wake Up Luv (90)** (KGWingrove) **11-11-4** GBradley (trckd ldr: lft in ld 11th: rdn & hdd 3 out: sn btn)	23	3	9/2[3]	81	17
180[P]	**Truss (85)** (JohnUpson) **9-10-13** RSupple (in tch tl drvn along & outpcd 9th: sn bhd: t.o)	dist	4	13/2	—	—
190[14]	**Regardless (72)** (JPLeigh) **14-10-0** BPowell (sn wl bhd: t.o whn p.u bef 10th)		P	33/1	—	—
				(SP 109.9%)		**5 Rn**

5m 41.0 (14.00) CSF £4.34 TOTE £2.10: £1.50 £1.30 (£1.90) OWNER Mr Peter Nelson (MALTON) BRED J. C. Dimsdale
LONG HANDICAP Regardless 9-9

256 Magic Bloom won this through staying. Throwing down a strong challenge at the second last, she saw her race out in fine style. (11/8)

292* Drumstick did not help his chances by blundering badly at the eleventh fence, but came right back into it at the third last, only to find one too good in the winner when the chips were down. He has never won over this distance. (2/1)

Wake Up Luv, left in front when Drumstick ploughed through the eleventh, was headed at the third last and soon on the retreat. He can be made fitter yet. (9/2)

94 Truss lost touch from the ninth and was soon tailed off. (13/2)

336 SINGLETON BIRCH H'CAP CHASE (0-120) (5-Y.O+) (Class D)

7-20 (7-20) **2m 1f 110y (13 fncs)** £4,344.00 (£1,209.00: £582.00) GOING: 0.19 sec per fur (G)

	Runner	Dist	Pos	SP	RR	SF
292[2]	**Yaakum (91)** (SEKettlewell) **7-11-0** MAFitzgerald (lw: hld up: hdwy on bit 3 out: led between last 2: kpt on)	—	1	9/4[2]	99	23
296*	**Stapleford Lady (78)** (JSMoore) **8-10-1** WMcFarland (chsd ldrs: lft cl 2nd after 8th: rdn 3 out: kpt on fr 2 out)	2	2	7/4[1]	84	8
256[4]	**Wise Advice (IRE) (95)** (MDHammond) **6-11-4** RGarritty (chsd ldr: lft in ld after 8th: rdn 3 out: hit 2 out: sn hdd & no ex)	½	3	5/1	101	25
253[3]	**I Have Him (101)** (NoelChance) **9-11-10** BPowell (led & sn clr: j.b rt: rn out after 8th)		R	11/4[3]	—	—
				(SP 110.5%)		**4 Rn**

4m 27.9 (12.90) CSF £6.27 TOTE £3.30: (£2.70) OWNER Mr Ian Thompson (MIDDLEHAM) BRED Gainsborough Stud Management Ltd

292 Yaakum, much happier over this shorter trip, was given a peach of a ride and won cosily. (9/4)

296* Stapleford Lady ran right up to scratch, but was no match for the winner when the chips were down. (7/4)
9 Wise Advice (IRE) did not help his chances when hitting the penultimate fence and could find only one pace thereafter. (5/1)
253 I Have Him, a headstrong individual, was soon in a clear lead jumping badly to his right. After the eighth, he ran off the course, taking on a hurdle in the process. (11/4)

337 FRESHNEY PLACE NOVICES' HURDLE (4-Y.O+) (Class D)
7-50 (7-50) **2m 1f 110y (8 hdls)** £2,804.00 (£842.00: £406.00: £188.00) GOING: 0.44 sec per fur (GS)

				SP	RR	SF
186*	**Shahrani (105)** (MCPipe) **4-11-9** DBridgwater (led: clr whn reminders 2nd: drvn along after 3 out: nt fluent last 2: eased flat)	—	1	4/5[1]	74+	31
	China Mail (IRE) (KCBailey) **4-10-11** TJMurphy (bit bkwd: mstke 1st: chsd ldrs: hdwy 5th: kpt on one pce fr 2 out: no ch w wnr)	11	2	8/1	52	9
293[2]	**Silverdale Lad** (KWHogg) **5-11-0** MAFitzgerald (lw: hld up: hdwy 4th: 2nd & blnd next: lost pl: chsd wnr appr 2 out: sn btn)	2½	3	3/1[2]	50	10
	Marble Man (IRE) (91) (MDHammond) **6-11-0** RGarritty (in tch: hdwy 5th: chsng ldrs whn blnd bdly 3 out: nt rcvr)	dist	4	9/2[3]	—	—
293[9]	**Scallymill** (KWHogg) **6-10-9** MFoster (chsd wnr to 5th: sn lost pl & bhd: t.o)	8	5	40/1	—	—
293[11]	**Hutcel Bell** (RDEWoodhouse) **5-10-9** PNiven (sn t.o)	16	6	100/1	—	—
				(SP 113.3%)	**6 Rn**	

4m 19.9 (16.90) CSF £7.42 TOTE £1.80: £1.50 £2.20 (£6.70) OWNER Mr A S Helaissi and Mr S Helaissi (WELLINGTON) BRED R. V. Young
WEIGHT FOR AGE 4yo-3lb
186* Shahrani won well in the end, but needed plenty of rousting throughout to keep his mind on the job. (4/5)
China Mail (IRE), having his first outing since January, looked as though the run would do him good. (8/1)
293 Silverdale Lad blundered badly at the fifth, but rallied to chase the winner, only to stop dead in the home straight. (3/1)
Marble Man (IRE) had no chance after blundering very badly at the third last. (9/2)

338 INTERFLORA NOVICES' H'CAP HURDLE (0-95) (4-Y.O+) (Class F)
8-20 (8-21) **2m 5f 110y (10 hdls)** £1,954.00 (£544.00: £262.00) GOING: 0.44 sec per fur (GS)

				SP	RR	SF
65[3]	**Plinth (75)** (NAGraham) **5-11-0** GBradley (lw: cl up: mstkes 4th & 5th: rdn appr 2 out: hit last: r.o u.p to ld nr fin)	—	1	13/8[1]	54	—
157*	**Little Tincture (IRE) (68)** (MrsTJMcInnesSkinner) **6-10-2**(5) SophieMitchell (led: rdn 2 out: hdd & no ex towards fin)	½	2	9/2[3]	47	—
259*	**Ragamuffin Romeo (70)** (HSawyer) **7-10-9** NMann (mstke 1st: sn bhd: hit 4th: hdwy appr 2 out: styd on one pce)	5	3	9/2[3]	45	—
288[2]	**Silver Sleeve (IRE) (82)** (MDHammond) **4-11-4b** RGarritty (in tch: hdwy 6th: chsd ldrs & rdn 3 out: wknd fr 2 out)	11	4	7/2[2]	49	—
	River Challenge (IRE) (89) (JohnUpson) **5-12-0** RSupple (mstke 1st: chsd ldrs: drvn along & mstke 6th: lost tch & p.u lame after next)		P	5/1	—	—
				(SP 113.3%)	**5 Rn**	

5m 35.7 (31.70) CSF £8.73 TOTE £2.50: £1.60 £1.90 (£4.10) OWNER Mr T. H. Chadney (NEWMARKET) BRED Bloomsbury Stud
WEIGHT FOR AGE 4yo-3lb
65 Plinth gave a ragged display of jumping, but gamely forced his head in front in the dying strides. (13/8)
157* Little Tincture (IRE) made a bold attempt to lead from pillar-to-post, but was just denied near the finish. He is probably better over a little further. (9/2)
259* Ragamuffin Romeo, who ran in snatches after an early mistake, never threatened to trouble the first two. (9/2: 8/1-4/1)
288 Silver Sleeve (IRE), who came under pressure at the third last, was fighting a losing battle thereafter. (7/2)

T/Plpt: £39.60 (145.18 Tckts). T/Qdpt: £11.30 (28.86 Tckts). O'R

0218-WORCESTER (L-H) (Good becoming Good to soft)
Saturday August 10th
Race 4: one fence omitted
WEATHER: heavy showers

339 POLLY GARTER (S) H'CAP HURDLE (0-95) (4-Y.O+) (Class G)
6-00 (6-00) **2m (8 hdls)** £1,905.00 (£530.00: £255.00) GOING: 0.07 sec per fur (G)

				SP	RR	SF
288[4]	**Tony's Mist (73)** (JMBradley) **6-11-2** RJohnson (hld up: led 2 out: clr flat: r.o wl)	—	1	9/2[2]	68	26
219[4]	**Betabetcorbett (73)** (BPJBaugh) **5-11-2b**[1] TEley (lw: led to 2 out: one pce)	6	2	14/1	62	20
61[F]	**Colway Prince (IRE) (81)** (APJones) **8-11-10** SCurran (hld up: wl bhd 5th: rdn & hdwy 3 out: nvr nr ldrs)	10	3	8/1	60	18
185[3]	**Mylordmayor (59)** (PBowen) **9-10-2** RFarrant (chsd ldr to 3 out: sn wknd: 4th & no ch whn mstke last)	2½	4	8/1	36	—
289[2]	**Lofty Deed (USA) (66)** (WJMusson) **6-10-9b** LHarvey (hld up: hdwy 5th: rdn & wknd 3 out)	6	5	4/1[1]	37	—
	Al Skeet (USA) (57) (RJPrice) **10-10-0** NWilliamson (hld up: sme hdwy appr 3 out: sn wknd)	3	6	11/1	25	—
286[U]	**George Lane (73)** (FJordan) **8-10-11**(5) LAspell (lw: prom to 5th)	9	7	13/2[3]	32	—
	Tryph (83) (MDHammond) **4-11-9** AMaguire (hld up: hdwy 5th: wkng whn mstke 3 out)	5	8	13/2[3]	37	—
	Beaufan (78) (BRCambidge) **9-11-7** GaryLyons (dropped rr 4th: sn t.o)	30	9	33/1	2	—
299[4]	**Pusey Street Boy (80)** (JRBosley) **9-11-9** MBosley (hld up: fell 3rd)		F	9/1	—	—
				(SP 115.0%)	**10 Rn**	

3m 49.1 (9.10) CSF £56.44 CT £445.09 TOTE £4.00: £1.50 £2.40 £2.60 (£27.10) Trio £117.90 OWNER Mr Robert Bailey (CHEPSTOW) BRED Mrs Chris Harrington
WEIGHT FOR AGE 4yo-3lb
No bid
288 Tony's Mist finally broke his duck over hurdles at the twenty-third attempt. (9/2)
67 Betabetcorbett, sharpened up by the blinkers, was unable to cope with the winner. (14/1)
Colway Prince (IRE), reverting to hurdling after falling on his chasing debut, has not won for exactly three years. (8/1)
185 Mylordmayor would probably have been suited by further. (8/1)
Tryph (13/2: op 4/1)

340 EDGAR THOMPSON NOVICES' CHASE (5-Y.O+) (Class E)
6-30 (6-30) **2m (12 fncs)** £3,549.00 (£861.00) GOING: 0.07 sec per fur (G)

				SP	RR	SF
261*	**Stately Home (IRE) (108)** (PBowen) **5-12-2** RJohnson (mde all: clr 8th: hrd hld)	—	1	$5/4^{2}$	108++	23
284^{2}	**Green's Seago (USA)** (HMKavanagh) **8-10-9**(3) JCulloty (chsd wnr to 4th: lft 2nd 5th: no imp fr 8th)	18	2	$11/1^{3}$	69?	—
	Winter Belle (USA) (PJPrendergast,Ireland) **8-10-12v[1]** NWilliamson (hld up: wnt 2nd 4th: blnd & uns rdr 5th)		U	$8/11^{1}$	—	—
				(SP 110.7%)	**3 Rn**	

4m 4.2 (13.20) CSF £7.47 TOTE £2.30: (£2.30) OWNER Mr P. Bowen (HAVERFORDWEST) BRED Ash Hill Stud
WEIGHT FOR AGE 5yo-3lb
261* Stately Home (IRE) was left with a simple task once the favourite departed. (5/4)
284 Green's Seago (USA), nothing more than a selling hurdler, was making his chasing debut. (11/1: 8/1-12/1)
Winter Belle (USA), en route to the Doncaster Sales, put such a hole in the first ditch that it had to omitted in the other chase. (8/11: tchd Evens)

341 WEATHERBYS' SPONSORSHIP IN RACING H'CAP HURDLE (0-120) (4-Y.O+) (Class D)
7-00 (7-00) **2m (8 hdls)** £2,763.00 (£768.00: £369.00) GOING: 0.26 sec per fur (GS)

				SP	RR	SF
	Wadada (101) (DBurchell) **5-10-9** DJBurchell (a.p: led appr 5th: hdd last: led flat: drvn out)	—	1	5/1	79	—
	Samanid (IRE) (110) (TPMcGovern) **4-11-1** AMaguire (hld up: hdwy 5th: led last: hrd rdn & hdd flat: fnd nil)	3	2	$9/4^{1}$	85	—
255^{3}	**Star Market (120)** (JLSpearing) **6-12-0b** NWilliamson (led appr 3rd: hdd appr 5th: rdn & ev ch 3 out: wknd 2 out)	12	3	$3/1^{3}$	83	—
	Prerogative (105) (RSimpson) **6-10-13** DGallagher (lost pl 4th: no hdwy fr 3 out)	6	4	20/1	62	—
260^{5}	**Dickies Girl (92)** (NMBabbage) **6-10-0** WMarston (set slow pce: hdd appr 3rd: rdn & wknd 5th)	2	5	33/1	47	—
	Asterix (94) (JMBradley) **8-9-13**(3) GuyLewis (hld up: hdwy 5th: rdn & wknd appr 3 out)	4	6	7/1	45	—
255^{2}	**Faustino (112)** (PJHobbs) **4-10-12b**(5) DJKavanagh (hld up: mstke 3rd: rdn & wknd after 5th)	10	7	$11/4^{2}$	53	—
				(SP 119.3%)	**7 Rn**	

4m 7.3 (27.30) CSF £16.86 TOTE £5.80: £2.40 £2.60 (£27.90) OWNER Mrs Ruth Burchell (EBBW VALE) BRED A. Snipe
LONG HANDICAP Dickies Girl 8-1
WEIGHT FOR AGE 4yo-3lb
OFFICIAL EXPLANATION **Faustino: slipped approaching the first, was never going thereafter and could not handle the soft ground.**
Wadada, fit from the Flat, would have preferred further, especially with no pace early on, but at least the rain-softened ground put some emphasis on stamina. (5/1)
Samanid (IRE), the winner of a maiden hurdle at Naas in May, has had a couple of runs on the Flat at the Curragh during the summer. (9/4)
255 Star Market could not concede the weight in the rain-drenched ground. (3/1)
255 Faustino, blinkered for the first time, could not handle the rain-softened ground in a race where the jockeys were allowed to mount in the saddling boxes and go straight to the start. (11/4)

342 BACK UP STAFF 6TH ANNIVERSARY H'CAP CHASE (0-125) (5-Y.O+) (Class D)
7-30 (7-30) **2m 7f (16 fncs)** £3,591.75 (£1,074.00: £514.50: £234.75) GOING: 0.26 sec per fur (GS)

				SP	RR	SF
74^{2}	**Hillwalk (117)** (RCurtis) **10-12-0** DMorris (lost pl 9th: mstke 10th: rdn 4 out: styd on fr 2 out: led nr fin)	—	1	$7/1^{3}$	124	26
2^{2}	**The Yank (100)** (MDHammond) **10-10-11b** AMaguire (led: hrd rdn & hdd nr fin)	½	2	$11/2^{2}$	107	9
68*	**Comedy Road (97)** (RLee) **12-10-8** RJohnson (hld up: mstke 8th: hdwy 12th: ev ch 2 out: hrd rdn & one pce flat)	2	3	8/1	102	4
256^{3}	**Channel Pastime (93)** (DBurchell) **12-10-1**(3) GuyLewis (hdwy 8th: outpcd appr 4 out: rallied 2 out: one pce flat)	3½	4	8/1	96	—
220*	**Evangelica (USA) (115)** (MCPipe) **6-11-12** CMaude (wl bhd fr 5th)	26	5	$7/4^{1}$	100	2
158^{14}	**Gilston Lass (95)** (JSKing) **9-10-6** JRKavanagh (prom: mstkes 1st & 12th: wknd appr 4 out)	2½	6	25/1	78	—
	Celtic Laird (89) (MrsJPitman) **8-10-0** WMarston (prom to 10th: bhd fr 4 out)	9	7	10/1	66	—
190*	**Hurryup (93)** (RDickin) **9-10-1**(3) JCulloty (bhd: mstke 2nd: gd hdwy appr 9th: wknd 12th)	17	8	$7/1^{3}$	58	—
57^{P}	**Winnie Lorraine (99)** (RHAlner) **11-10-5**(5) PHenley (prom to 11th: bhd whn p.u bef 4 out)		P	20/1	—	—
				(SP 116.7%)	**9 Rn**	

6m (22.00) CSF £42.14 CT £289.01 TOTE £8.30: £2.70 £2.30 £2.20 (£21.40) Trio £36.30 OWNER Mr M. L. Shone (LAMBOURN) BRED Martin Ryan
LONG HANDICAP Celtic Laird 9-10
74 Hillwalk, three times a winner at Towcester, found stamina coming into play in the soggy ground. (7/1)
2 The Yank, 7lb better off with the winner than at Perth, again found Hillwalk his undoing, this time even closer to the finish. He deserves a change of fortune. (11/2: 4/1-6/1)
68* Comedy Road found this more competitive, but ran a good race off a 7lb higher mark. (8/1)
256 Channel Pastime found three miles in soft ground stretching his stamina reserves to the limit. (8/1)
220* Evangelica (USA), up a further 5lb, does have four wins to her credit on the soft, but was never going here. (7/4)

343 WELSH DRAGON NOVICES' H'CAP HURDLE (0-100) (4-Y.O+) (Class E)
8-00 (8-01) **2m 4f (10 hdls)** £2,320.00 (£645.00: £310.00) GOING: 0.26 sec per fur (GS)

				SP	RR	SF
65^{4}	**Bourdonner (84)** (MDHammond) **4-10-9** AMaguire (mde all: sn clr: mstkes 4th & 7th: rdn & r.o wl flat)	—	1	$11/4^{2}$	64	21
216*	**Sigma Wireless (IRE) (100)** (CaptTAForster) **7-12-0** SWynne (hld up: rdn & hdwy 7th: chsd wnr fr 3 out: ev ch flat: hrd rdn: unable qckn)	1¾	2	$3/1^{3}$	79	39
218*	**Born to Please (IRE) (92)** (PJHobbs) **4-11-3** RJohnson (prom: rdn 5th: wknd appr 2 out)	22	3	$7/4^{1}$	53	10
129^{6}	**Cheer's Baby (72)** (GraemeRoe) **6-10-0** NWilliamson (bhd: reminders after 5th: nvr nr ldrs)	1¾	4	20/1	32	—
293^{8}	**Court Jester (76)** (MJRyan) **5-10-4** DGallagher (chsd wnr: hit 2nd & 3rd: wknd after 3 out)	2½	5	8/1	34	—
	Mutual Memories (72) (NJHenderson) **8-10-0** JRKavanagh (bit bkwd: a bhd: t.o 7th: p.u bef 2 out)		P	14/1	—	—
				(SP 110.6%)	**6 Rn**	

4m 53.0 (15.00) CSF £10.64 TOTE £3.10: £1.90 £1.60 (£5.30) OWNER Mr Cornelius Lysaght (MIDDLEHAM) BRED The Overbury Stud
LONG HANDICAP Cheer's Baby 8-7 Mutual Memories 9-11
WEIGHT FOR AGE 4yo-3lb

65 Bourdonner managed to do the business in the rain-softened ground, despite serious reservations from his illustrious owner. (11/4)
216* Sigma Wireless (IRE), 15lb higher than when last seen in a handicap, was ironically outgunned by a horse owned by the radio's voice of racing. (3/1)
218* Born to Please (IRE) needs faster ground. (7/4)
Mutual Memories (14/1: 10/1-16/1)

344 CHELTENHAM AND THREE COUNTIES RACE CLUB NOVICES' HURDLE (4-Y.O+) (Class E)
8-30 (8-30) **2m (8 hdls)** £2,407.50 (£670.00: £322.50) GOING: 0.26 sec per fur (GS)

				SP	RR	SF
	Lord Tomanico (FR) (CJMann) **4-10-9** JRailton (mde all: clr 2 out: easily)	—	1	100/30 3	69+	2
287*	**Lancer (USA) (78)** (RTJuckes) **4-11-2** WMarston (chsd wnr: ev ch appr 3 out: sn rdn: no imp)	9	2	5/2 2	67	—
	Jebi (USA) (CMurray) **6-10-9**(3) KGaule (hld up: mstke 3rd: hdwy 5th: 3rd & no ch whn mstke last)	5	3	14/1	55	—
	Raven's Roost (IRE) (49) (GEJones) **5-10-12** PMcLoughlin (prom: ev ch appr 3 out: sn rdn & wknd)	15	4	16/1	40	—
	Belle Perk (IRE) (TPMcGovern) **5-10-7** AMaguire (hld up: hdwy whn mstke 5th: sn wknd: virtually p.u flat)	dist	5	7/4 1	—	—
	Martello Girl (IRE) (KSBridgwater) **4-10-4** TEley (a bhd: t.o whn p.u bef 2 out)		P	14/1	—	—
	Soccer Ball (TRWatson) **6-10-12** OPears (plld hrd: rdn appr 4th: wknd appr 3 out: t.o whn p.u bef 2 out)		P	33/1	—	—
				(SP 110.2%)	**7 Rn**	

3m 56.0 (16.00) CSF £11.22 TOTE £3.20: £2.30 £1.80 (£4.50) Trio £4.70 OWNER The Izz That Right Partnership (UPPER LAMBOURN) BRED Alain Brandebourger
WEIGHT FOR AGE 4yo-3lb
Lord Tomanico (FR) won on very soft ground over nine furlongs at Compiegne in July 1995, and the rain-lashed surface did not bother him. (100/30: op 2/1)
287* Lancer (USA) is only moderate and had a tough task, trying to concede weight to the winner. (5/2)
Jebi (USA), no great shakes on the Flat, has run up to ten furlongs, but has been sprinting recently. (14/1)
Belle Perk (IRE), a beaten favourite when third in a Roscommon bumper last month, probably needs fast ground. (7/4)

T/Plpt: £342.80 (20.22 Tckts). T/Qdpt: £52.60 (9.37 Tckts). KH

0339-WORCESTER (L-H) (Good, Good to soft & Soft patches)
Monday August 12th
Races 2 & 5 - one fence omitted
WEATHER: overcast

345 ENIGMA CONDITIONAL (S) H'CAP HURDLE (0-95) (4-Y.O+) (Class G)
2-15 (2-15) **3m (12 hdls)** £1,849.00 (£514.00: £247.00) GOING minus 0.02 sec per fur (G)

				SP	RR	SF
	Rampant Rosie (IRE) (70) (GRichards) **8-11-4v1** GCahill (hld up: wnt 2nd 9th: led 2 out: sn clr: easily)	—	1	2/1 2	58+	—
	Peniarth (58) (RJPrice) **10-10-6** BFenton (chsd ldr: led appr 9th to 2 out: one pce)	9	2	11/2	40	—
184 5	**Miss Souter (69)** (HSHowe) **7-11-3** GuyLewis (hld up: rdn after 8th: wknd appr 2 out)	6	3	13/8 1	47	—
101 5	**Cromaboo Crown (76)** (PJBevan) **5-11-10** TJMurphy (led tl appr 9th: sn wknd: t.o)	dist	4	4/1 3	—	—
				(SP 106.8%)	**4 Rn**	

5m 58.6 (22.60) CSF £10.24 TOTE £2.00 (£4.40) OWNER Mr George Kemp (PENRITH) BRED Kilshannig Stud
No bid
OFFICIAL EXPLANATION **Cromaboo Crown: finished distressed.**
Rampant Rosie (IRE), blinkered in her last three starts, was visored for the first time and took advantage of a rare opportunity to take a long-distance seller. (2/1)
Peniarth proved no match for the winner once headed. (11/2)
Miss Souter has yet to prove she stays this trip. (13/8)
Cromaboo Crown finished distressed. (4/1)

346 POMP AND CIRCUMSTANCE NOVICES' CHASE (5-Y.O+) (Class E)
2-45 (2-45) **2m 7f (16 fncs)** £3,101.00 (£861.00: £413.00) GOING minus 0.02 sec per fur (G)

				SP	RR	SF
283*	**Sticky Money (97)** (MCPipe) **8-11-7** DBridgwater (chsd ldr: led 6th: clr 4 out: hrd hld)	—	1	2/7 1	105++	—
283 2	**Pharrago (IRE) (72)** (DBurchell) **7-10-12** DJBurchell (hld up: chsd wnr 10th: no imp fr 4 out)	16	2	3/1 2	85	—
290 3	**Ghedi (POL)** (MPMuggeridge) **5-10-7** BPowell (led to 6th: mstke 11th: sn t.o)	dist	3	33/1 3	—	—
				(SP 105.7%)	**3 Rn**	

6m 11.1 (33.10) CSF £1.41 TOTE £1.50 (£1.50) OWNER Mrs D. Jenks (WELLINGTON) BRED Mrs D. Jenks
WEIGHT FOR AGE 5yo-4lb
283* Sticky Money found completing the hat-trick little more than a formality. (2/7)
283 Pharrago (IRE) was 8lb better off with the winner that at Bangor, but the margin of defeat was increased by twelve lengths. (3/1)

347 NIMROD H'CAP HURDLE (0-110) (4-Y.O+) (Class E)
3-15 (3-15) **2m 4f (10 hdls)** £2,267.50 (£630.00: £302.50) GOING minus 0.02 sec per fur (G)

				SP	RR	SF
139 2	**Clean Edge (USA) (97)** (JMackie) **4-11-2**(3) EHusband (lw: chsd ldr: led appr 7th: drvn out)	—	1	5/2 2	79	32
285 3	**First Crack (84)** (FJordan) **11-10-9** SWynne (lw: hld up: chsd wnr fr 2 out: one pce flat)	2	2	5/2 2	64	20
187*	**Coast Along (IRE) (94)** (PJBevan) **4-11-2** WWorthington (lw: hld up: wnt 2nd 7th tl wknd 2 out)	10	3	5/4 1	66	19
284 3	**Forgetful (92)** (DBurchell) **7-11-3** DJBurchell (lw: j.rt: led & sn clr: hdd appr 7th: sn wknd: t.o)	21	4	14/1 3	48	4
				(SP 108.3%)	**4 Rn**	

4m 46.9 (8.90) CSF £8.16 TOTE £3.80: £7.00 (£4.60) OWNER Mrs Sue Adams (CHURCH BROUGHTON) BRED Alice duPont Mills
WEIGHT FOR AGE 4yo-3lb
139 Clean Edge (USA) was 7lb higher than when winning a Uttoxeter seller in May. (5/2)
285 First Crack, in with a squeak at the last, would have preferred faster ground. (5/2)
187* Coast Along (IRE), up 5lb, has won on this sort of ground but not over this trip. (5/4)
284 Forgetful (14/1: 10/1-16/1)

348 PLUMB CENTER H'CAP HURDLE (0-130) (4-Y.O+) (Class C)

3-45 (3-46) **2m (8 hdls)** £3,468.25 (£1,036.00: £495.50: £225.25) GOING minus 0.02 sec per fur (G)

	Horse	Dist	Pos	SP	RR	SF
	Royal Thimble (IRE) (99) (NoelChance) **5-11-10** RJohnson (set v.slow pce tl appr 3rd: hrd rdn & qcknd to ld flat)	—	1	$5/2^{2}$	83	—
344^{2}	**Lancer (USA) (85)** (RTJuckes) **4-10-7** WMarston (hld up: led 2 out tl flat)	1½	2	$100/30^{3}$	68	—
300^{3}	**Night Time (85)** (FJordan) **4-10-0**(7) MrGShenkin (lw: led appr 3rd to 4th: hrd rdn appr last: one pce)	1½	3	$100/30^{3}$	66	—
264^{3}	**Circus Colours (97)** (JRJenkins) **6-11-8** AMaguire (plld hrd: led 4th to 2 out: hrd rdn: one pce)	s.h	4	$9/4^{1}$	78	—
				(SP 105.5%)		**4 Rn**

4m 20.0 (40.00) CSF £9.32 TOTE £3.00 (£5.80) OWNER Mrs M. Chance (LAMBOURN) BRED Somerville Stud
WEIGHT FOR AGE 4yo-3lb
Royal Thimble (IRE), fit from the Flat, managed to quicken again on the run-in in a race which developed into a sprint from the third last. (5/2)
344 Lancer (USA) found this race run in total contrast to the one he won at Bangor. (100/30)
300 Night Time lacked the required finishing speed in a race which was nothing more than a sprint from the half-mile pole. (100/30)
264 Circus Colours was hard to restrain, thanks to the funereal pace, and probably would have been better off getting on with it sooner. (9/4)

349 GERONTIUS NOVICES' H'CAP CHASE (0-100) (5-Y.O+) (Class E)

4-15 (4-15) **2m (11 fncs)** £2,877.00 (£861.00: £413.00: £189.00) GOING minus 0.02 sec per fur (G)

	Horse	Dist	Pos	SP	RR	SF
188*	**Willie Makeit (IRE) (78)** (RTPhillips) **6-11-3**(3) JCulloty (hld up: led 4 out: mstke 3 out: hrd rdn appr last: r.o)	—	1	$11/8^{1}$	92	23
	Scaraben (82) (SEKettlewell) **8-11-10** RJohnson (hld up: chsd wnr fr 3 out: hit last: hrd rdn: r.o)	1½	2	$13/8^{2}$	95	26
	Harrow Way (IRE) (69) (LWells) **6-10-11** SMcNeill (bkwd: chsd ldr: ev ch 4 out: one pce)	9	3	$10/1^{3}$	73	4
255^{6}	**Caxton (USA) (81)** (JWhite) **9-11-9** BFenton (hld up & bhd: no ch fr 4 out)	11	4	12/1	74	5
222^{5}	**Astounded (76)** (DJWintle) **9-11-1**(3) DWalsh (led to 4 out: sn wknd)	¾	5	12/1	68	—
				(SP 104.7%)		**5 Rn**

4m 0.7 (9.70) CSF £3.59 TOTE £1.80: £1.60 £1.10 (£2.00) OWNER Old Berks Three (LAMBOURN) BRED Mitchelstown Stud
188* Willie Makeit (IRE) defied a 7lb rise in the Ratings on this softer ground. (11/8)
Scaraben, a winner over a mile at Pontefract last month, stuck to his guns after clouting the final fence. (13/8)
Harrow Way (IRE) should at least strip fitter for the outing. (10/1: 7/1-11/1)
Astounded (12/1: 20/1-10/1)

350 CHANSON NOVICES' HURDLE (4-Y.O+ F & M) (Class E)

4-45 (4-45) **2m (8 hdls)** £2,390.00 (£665.00: £320.00) GOING minus 0.02 sec per fur (G)

	Horse	Dist	Pos	SP	RR	SF
293^{3}	**Forgotten Empress** (SEKettlewell) **4-10-7** RJohnson (lw: hld up: wnt 2nd appr 2 out: rdn to ld fnl 50y)	—	1	$2/1^{2}$	68	—
295^{5}	**Burnt Sienna (IRE)** (JSMoore) **4-10-7v** WMcFarland (lw: led & sn clr: hrd rdn & wnt lft flat: hdd last 50y)	1½	2	20/1	67?	—
191^{6}	**Regal Gem (IRE)** (CRBarwell) **5-10-10** BFenton (hld up: chsd clr ldr 5th tl appr 2 out: sn wknd)	16	3	$11/4^{3}$	51	—
	Sadler's Pearl (RTPhillips) **4-10-7** BPowell (no ch fr 5th)	6	4	16/1	45	—
	Last Laugh (IRE) (KCBailey) **4-10-7** TJMurphy (lw: chsd clr ldr: j.slowly 3rd: wknd appr 3 out)	dist	5	$6/4^{1}$	—	—
26^{P}	**Sister Jim** (RJPrice) **6-10-10** JRKavanagh (t.o fr 4th)	14	6	66/1	—	—
				(SP 112.1%)		**6 Rn**

3m 52.5 (12.50) CSF £28.41 TOTE £2.90: £1.80 £8.90 (£15.10) OWNER Mr R. Fenwick-Gibson (MIDDLEHAM) BRED Lord Bolton
WEIGHT FOR AGE 4yo-3lb
OFFICIAL EXPLANATION **Last Laugh (IRE): would not act on the ground and was not jumping with any confidence.**
293 Forgotten Empress kept straight on the run-in, which is more than can be said for the runner-up. (2/1)
Burnt Sienna (IRE), sharpened up by the visor, could not hold on after going left-handed under pressure on the run-in. (20/1)
191 Regal Gem (IRE), the winner of three bumpers here, was making her debut over timber. (11/4)
Last Laugh (IRE) was disappointing on her first run for her new stable. (6/4)

T/Plpt: £164.50 (42.77 Tckts). T/Qdpt: £25.50 (18.81 Tckts). KH

0206-SOUTHWELL (L-H) (Good)

Tuesday August 13th

WEATHER: overcast

351 CROMER NOVICES' H'CAP CHASE (0-100) (5-Y.O+) (Class E)

2-15 (2-15) **3m 110y (19 fncs)** £3,812.65 (£1,139.20: £545.10: £248.05) GOING: 0.50 sec per fur (GS)

	Horse	Dist	Pos	SP	RR	SF
289^{3}	**George Ashford (IRE) (82)** (KAMorgan) **6-12-0** ASSmith (a.p: reminders 12th: led appr 3 out: sn clr)	—	1	$4/1^{2}$	101	20
285^{5}	**Blue Raven (85)** (PJHobbs) **5-11-12** APMcCoy (mstkes: chsd ldrs: slt ld 14th to 4 out: wl outpcd fr 3 out)	20	2	$11/4^{1}$	91	5
288^{7}	**Quixall Crossett (61)** (EMCaine) **11-10-7** PMcLoughlin (reminders & lost tch 9th: n.d after)	13	3	20/1	58	—
	Abitmorfun (54) (JABennett) **10-10-0** LHarvey (led to 14th: led 4 out tl appr next: wknd qckly)	½	4	20/1	51	—
206^{3}	**Saint Bene't (IRE) (65)** (GProdromou) **8-10-11v** RFarrant (chsd ldr to 11th: sn lost pl & t.o)	6	5	$9/2^{3}$	58	—
258^{5}	**Spanish Blaze (IRE) (62)** (MrsMerritaJones) **8-10-8** JFTitley (lw: in tch tl fell 11th)		F	$9/2^{3}$	—	—
179^{P}	**The Gallopin'major (IRE) (75)** (MrsMReveley) **6-11-7** NSmith (bhd: hit 12th: p.u bef next)		P	5/1	—	—
				(SP 109.2%)		**7 Rn**

6m 38.7 (31.70) CSF £14.10 TOTE £3.90: £2.20 £2.00 (£5.40) OWNER Mr B. Leatherday (MELTON MOWBRAY) BRED Mrs Margaret Tully and R. Cutler
WEIGHT FOR AGE 5yo-5lb
289 George Ashford (IRE) stays forever and took these bigger obstacles really well. Although the opposition was very moderate, the style of victory suggests that further success is likely. (4/1: op 5/2)
285 Blue Raven spoiled his chances by backing off his fences and, continually having to struggle to regain ground, had spent all reserves by the third last. (11/4)
Quixall Crossett is very slow and had no chance from halfway. (20/1)
Abitmorfun ran out of fuel in a serious way in the home straight. (20/1)
258 Spanish Blaze (IRE) was the pick on looks and had not been asked a question when he fell with over a circuit to go. (9/2)

352 SKEGNESS H'CAP CHASE (0-110) (5-Y.O+) (Class E)

2-45 (2-45) **2m 4f 110y (16 fncs)** £3,882.50 (£1,160.00: £555.00: £252.50) GOING: 0.50 sec per fur (GS)

				SP	RR	SF
292[3]	**Maggots Green (75)** (JMBradley) **9-10-1** RJohnson (led to 9th: led 11th: styd on wl fr 3 out)	—	1	11/4[1]	88	21
305[2]	**Noblely (USA) (98)** (NJHWalker) **9-11-10** RFarrant (trckd ldrs: effrt 10th: chsd wnr fr 4 out: one pce fr 2 out)	4	2	11/4[1]	108	41
256[7]	**Nocatchim (92)** (KAMorgan) **7-11-4** ASSmith (cl up tl outpcd 9th: sn lost tch)	18	3	11/4[1]	88	21
	The Country Trader (102) (PJHobbs) **10-12-0b** APMcCoy (cl up: led 9th to 11th: wknd qckly)	dist	4	11/4[1]	—	—
				(SP 106.7%)		**4 Rn**

5m 22.6 (18.60) CSF £9.23 TOTE £4.50 (£4.20) OWNER Mr E. A. Hayward (CHEPSTOW) BRED Swettenham Stud

In Focus: All four runners were returned as joint-favourite, an extremely rare occurrence

292 Maggots Green is a tough sort who made full use of her light weight, and just kept galloping. (11/4)

305 Noblely (USA) looked to be travelling quite well when sat in behind but, asked for an effort in the straight, his stamina may have let him down. (11/4)

180* Nocatchim was never happy from halfway on this occasion and turned in a very disappointing effort. (11/4)

The Country Trader may well have needed this. (11/4)

353 YARMOUTH NOVICES' HURDLE (4-Y.O+) (Class E)

3-15 (3-15) **2m (9 hdls)** £2,448.00 (£678.00: £324.00) GOING: 0.71 sec per fur (S)

				SP	RR	SF
	Glenvally (BWMurray) **5-10-7** GBradley (lw: chsd ldr 3rd to 7th: styd on to ld between last 2: drvn clr)	—	1	5/2[2]	54	—
288*	**Irie Mon (IRE) (82)** (MPBielby) **4-10-9**(7) MrAWintle (lw: hld up: hdwy 5th: led appr 2 out tl between last 2: no ex)	6	2	8/15[1]	60	3
327[S]	**Shalik (IRE)** (JRJenkins) **6-10-12** JRailton (led & wl clr to 5th: hdd & wknd appr 2 out)	13	3	9/1[3]	40	—
	Chadleigh Walk (IRE) (SWCampion) **4-10-9** ASSmith (hld up: hit 4 out: n.d after)	2	4	12/1	38	—
				(SP 111.5%)		**4 Rn**

4m 5.3 (23.30) CSF £4.27 TOTE £3.50 (£1.70) OWNER Mrs M. Lingwood (MALTON) BRED Norton Grove Stud Ltd

WEIGHT FOR AGE 4yo-3lb

Glenvally took the eye in the paddock and proved to be a persistent customer in the race, responding to pressure to put it beyond doubt going to the last. (5/2)

288* Irie Mon (IRE) travelled quite well but, when the pressure was really on going to the last, his response was disappointing. (8/15: 4/11-4/7)

Shalik (IRE), a headstrong individual, went too fast for his own good and was out on his feet approaching the second last. (9/1)

Chadleigh Walk (IRE) just needs to improve his hurdling and there should be some improvement. (12/1)

354 SOUTHEND MAIDEN HURDLE (4-Y.O+) (Class E)

3-45 (3-45) **2m 4f 110y (11 hdls)** £2,259.00 (£624.00: £297.00) GOING: 0.71 sec per fur (S)

				SP	RR	SF
	Longcroft (SEKettlewell) **4-10-11** RJohnson (lw: effrt 6th: led 4 out: wl clr fr 2 out: wl eased flat)	—	1	Evens[1]	56+	—
217[3]	**Desert Challenger (IRE) (76)** (JRJenkins) **6-11-5b** APMcCoy (led tl hrd rdn & hdd appr 7th: no imp after)	12	2	5/4[2]	52	—
	Pertemps Flyer (53) (CJMann) **5-11-2**(3) JMagee (cl up fr 4th: led appr 7th to 4 out: wknd appr 2 out)	6	3	14/1[3]	47	—
	Skiplam Wood (54) (SGChadwick) **10-11-0** ADobbin (lost tch ½-wy: sme hdwy 4 out: n.d)	4	4	20/1	39	—
	Arrange A Game (MissJBower) **9-11-2**(3) TDascombe (mstkes: a wl bhd)	22	5	33/1	27	—
				(SP 108.8%)		**5 Rn**

5m 25.8 (39.80) CSF £2.48 TOTE £2.20: £1.10 £1.10 (£1.10) OWNER Mr J. S. Calvert (MIDDLEHAM) BRED Auldyn Stud Ltd

WEIGHT FOR AGE 4yo-3lb

Longcroft took to this game particularly well and won pulling up. She should have no problem in staying further. (Evens)

217 Desert Challenger (IRE) was given a ride and a half, but was never fully co-operating. (5/4: 4/5-11/8)

Pertemps Flyer showed something here until running out of steam going to the second last. (14/1: op 8/1)

355 BRIGHTON (S) H'CAP HURDLE (0-95) (4,5,6 & 7-Y.O) (Class G)

4-15 (4-15) **2m 4f 110y (11 hdls)** £1,859.00 (£514.00: £245.00) GOING: 0.71 sec per fur (S)

				SP	RR	SF
295[2]	**Trade Wind (92)** (JGMO'Shea) **5-11-9v**(5) MichaelBrennan (hld up: chal on bit whn blnd last: rdn to ld nr fin)	—	1	5/4[1]	71	14
	Antiguan Flyer (70) (GProdromou) **7-10-6** RFarrant (led: clr 6th to 3 out: kpt on u.p flat: jst ct)	nk	2	8/1	49?	—
212[5]	**Laser Light Lady (67)** (NPLittmoden) **4-10-0b[1]** BPowell (hld up: effrt 7th: rdn & btn appr 2 out)	26	3	25/1	26	—
264[6]	**Ray River (88)** (KGWingrove) **4-11-0**(7) MrAWintle (hld up: rdn 7th: sn btn)	s.h	4	11/4[2]	46	—
257[4]	**Wordy's Wind (70)** (LWordingham) **7-10-6** BFenton (chsd ldr tl outpcd appr 7th: last & rdn whn blnd & uns rdr 3 out)		U	3/1[3]	—	—
				(SP 111.1%)		**5 Rn**

5m 17.6 (31.60) CSF £9.92 TOTE £1.70: £1.10 £2.30 (£8.90) OWNER Mr Gary Roberts (WESTBURY-ON-SEVERN) BRED Mrs M. H. Hunter

LONG HANDICAP Laser Light Lady 9-3

WEIGHT FOR AGE 4yo-3lb

Bt in 5,000 gns

295 Trade Wind, ridden as though he does not want to hit the front too soon, almost blew it with a blunder at the last. (5/4: 4/5-11/8)

Antiguan Flyer put up a game attempt here after a long lay-off. (8/1)

Laser Light Lady, in blinkers for the first time, was asked for an effort on the final circuit, but never came up with anything. (25/1)

Ray River failed to fire at all here. (11/4)

356 BLACKPOOL H'CAP HURDLE (0-110) (4-Y.O+) (Class E)

4-45 (4-45) **2m (9 hdls)** £2,427.00 (£672.00: £321.00) GOING: 0.71 sec per fur (S)

				SP	RR	SF
	Rudi's Pride (IRE) (95) (SBBell) **5-11-4** NSmith (trckd ldrs: led 5th: hld on wl flat)	—	1	3/1[2]	77	—
303[3]	**Game Dilemma (77)** (JWMullins) **5-10-0** RGreene (hld up: hdwy to chal between last 2: kpt on towards fin)	nk	2	13/8[1]	59	—
255[4]	**Vain Prince (105)** (NTinkler) **9-12-0b** MDwyer (lw: trckd ldrs: effrt appr 2 out: ev ch appr last: one pce)	3	3	4/1[3]	84	—
32[8]	**Wordsmith (IRE) (88)** (JLHarris) **6-10-11** DGallagher (w ldr: led after 4th tl j.slowly & hdd 5th: ev ch tl rdn & btn appr last)	3	4	5/1	64	—
	Cheap Metal (79) (CSmith) **11-10-2b**ow2 MRanger (hld up: hdwy 4 out: effrt & hung bdly lft 2 out: sn btn)	12	5	25/1	43	—

	Horse		SP	RR	SF
	Tip it In (88) (ASmith) **7-10-11** MBrennan (slt ld tl after 4th: chsd ldrs tl rdn & wknd appr 2 out: t.o)...dist	6	11/1	—	—
			(SP 111.9%)		**6 Rn**

4m 13.6 (31.60) CSF £8.03 TOTE £4.20: £2.20 £1.30 (£3.30) OWNER Mrs Cheryl Owen (DRIFFIELD) BRED R. P. Ryan
LONG HANDICAP Game Dilemma 9-12 Cheap Metal 9-1
Rudi's Pride (IRE), in a messy race, proved to be a most determined sort and would not be denied once in front. (3/1)
303 Game Dilemma always looked to be going quite well here, but a rather big jump at the last cost her momentum and her chance. (13/8)
Vain Prince was not suited by the slow pace and perhaps more use should have been made of him. (4/1: op 5/2)
Wordsmith (IRE) had not been out for some time and ran accordingly. (5/1)
Cheap Metal, having his first run for almost two years, had his chances until hanging badly left in the closing stages. (25/1)

T/Plpt: £227.10 (43.38 Tckts). T/Qdpt: £31.40 (22.01 Tckts). AA

0300-NEWTON ABBOT (L-H) (Good to firm)
Thursday August 15th

357 JERZEES AMATEUR (S) H'CAP HURDLE (0-95) (4-Y.O+) (Class G)
5-50 (5-50) **2m 1f (8 hdls)** £1,838.50 (£516.00: £251.50) GOING minus 0.61 sec per fur (F)

	Horse		SP	RR	SF
	Nord Lys (IRE) (65) (BJLlewellyn) **5-10-2**(7) MissEJJones (hld up & bhd: hdwy to ld after 4th: sn clr: mstke 2 out: hld on wl u.p flat)...—	1	10/1	50	—
304[2]	**Southern Ridge (75)** (RGFrost) **5-10-12**(7) MrAHoldsworth (lw: plld hrd: led tl after 4th: outpcd & mstke next: styd on fr 2 out)...1½	2	6/5 [1]	59	—
	Air Command (BAR) (56) (CTNash) **6-9-7**(7) MrPPhillips (hld up: in tch 4th: outpcd after 6th: styd on strly fr 2 out)...hd	3	7/1	40	—
303[P]	**Gunmaker (80)** (BJLlewellyn) **7-11-5**(5) MrJLLlewellyn (hld up & bhd: hdwy & in tch 5th: chsd wnr next: wknd appr 2 out)...11	4	9/2 [3]	53	—
259[2]	**Indian Minor (63)** (REPocock) **12-10-0**(7) MrLJefford (in tch tl outpcd 5th)...3½	5	100/30 [2]	33	—
	Miss Norwait (64) (NBThomson) **6-10-1**(7)ow8 MrSDavis (bit bkwd: chsd ldr briefly after 2nd: bhd 4th: t.o next: blnd last)...dist	6	50/1	—	—
			(SP 110.3%)		**6 Rn**

3m 58.9 (5.90) CSF £21.58 TOTE £9.40: £3.40 £1.20 (£9.10) OWNER Mr N. Heath (BARGOED) BRED Lord Harrington
LONG HANDICAP Air Command (BAR) 9-10 Miss Norwait 9-9
No bid
STEWARDS' ENQUIRY Llewellyn susp. 24-27/8/96 (excessive use of whip).
Nord Lys (IRE) won what was a poor race, even by selling standards. Justifying the market support, he led at the fourth last and, soon going clear, held on well after a mistake two out. His yard has not had a winner since the spring, and they will now look for another small race for a follow-up success. (10/1)
304 Southern Ridge lost the lead down the back straight and was then given as easy a time as possible. He was running on towards the end, and should soon do a lot better. (6/5)
Gunmaker (9/2: op 9/4)

358 AUGUST EVENING HURDLE (3-Y.O) (Class E)
6-20 (6-20) **2m 1f (8 hdls)** £2,148.00 (£603.00: £294.00) GOING minus 0.61 sec per fur (F)

	Horse		SP	RR	SF
294[3]	**Ben Bowden** (MBlanshard) **3-10-10** DGallagher (lw: chsd ldr appr 5th: led appr 2 out: hld on wl u.s.p flat)...—	1	11/2 [2]	63	—
294*	**Always Happy** (MCPipe) **3-10-12** DBridgwater (lw: chsd ldrs: mstke 4th: led briefly after 6th: rdn 2 out: ev ch last: no ex flat)...¾	2	1/5 [1]	64	—
	Arch Enemy (IRE) (MissKMGeorge) **3-10-10** DSkyrme (bit bkwd: bhd: rapid hdwy to ld appr 4th: hdd & wknd after 6th: t.o)...dist	3	12/1 [3]	—	—
	Water Music Melody (TRGreathead) **3-10-5** WHumphreys (bit bkwd: led tl j.path appr 4th: wkng whn mstke next: t.o whn p.u bef last)...	P	25/1	—	—
			(SP 110.3%)		**4 Rn**

4m 1.3 (8.30) CSF £7.20 TOTE £5.10: (£1.20) OWNER The Lower Bowden Syndicate (UPPER LAMBOURN) BRED E. A. Badger
294 Ben Bowden is a half-brother to useful sprinter Bowden Rose. After making headway to chase the leaders at the fifth, he took the lead with two left to jump and came through to win under strong pressure from the long odds-on favourite. (11/2)
294* Always Happy, who beat the winner over course and distance last time, had every chance but could not confirm the form. (1/5)
Arch Enemy (IRE) led briefly at halfway, but soon dropped quickly away. (12/1)

359 MISSION IMPOSSIBLE NOVICES' CHASE (5-Y.O+) (Class E)
6-50 (6-50) **2m 5f 110y (16 fncs)** £2,818.20 (£852.60: £415.80: £197.40) GOING minus 0.61 sec per fur (F)

	Horse		SP	RR	SF
254[2]	**Distant Memory (98)** (PJHobbs) **7-10-12b** APMcCoy (lw: led to 4th: led 6th: clr 12th: slt mstke 14th: unchal)—	1	4/7 [1]	86	18
	Another Comedy (RLee) **6-10-12** RJohnson (hdwy to chse wnr & mstke 10th: outpcd fr 12th)...30	2	5/1 [3]	64	—
290*	**Hizal (72)** (HJManners) **7-11-5** MrACharles-Jones (chsd ldrs to 8th: wknd 11th: t.o)...6	3	7/2 [2]	66	—
	Saracen's Boy (IRE) (MRChurches) **8-10-12** MrLJefford (bit bkwd: led 4th to 6th: wknd 10th:t.o 12th)...8	4	40/1	53	—
296[5]	**Great Uncle** (JWDufosee) **8-10-7**(5) PHenley (bit bkwd: nt fluent & lost tch fr 5th: t.o)...10	5	33/1	46	—
			(SP 107.9%)		**5 Rn**

5m 16.6 (-0.40) CSF £3.63 TOTE £1.40: £1.20 £2.10 (£3.30) OWNER Mrs Ann Weston (MINEHEAD) BRED Gerald W. Leigh
254 Distant Memory, who only cost 800 guineas, was quickly sent to the front. Jumping well, this son of Don't Forget Me made a slight mistake on the final circuit, but it did not stop him winning as he pleased. (4/7)
Another Comedy should be able to find a weak novice chase. (5/1)

360 MIDSUMMER MAIDEN HURDLE (4-Y.O+) (Class E)
7-20 (7-20) **2m 6f (10 hdls)** £2,190.00 (£615.00: £300.00) GOING minus 0.61 sec per fur (F)

	Horse		SP	RR	SF
297[2]	**Idiom (67)** (MrsJGRetter) **9-11-2**(3) JCulloty (hld up & bhd: hdwy to ld appr 2 out: drvn out)...—	1	5/2 [1]	66	12
316a[5]	**Up the Tempo (IRE) (68)** (PaddyFarrell) **7-11-0** RGreene (hld up mid div: hdwy 8th: sn ev ch: rdn last: no ex flat)...2	2	3/1 [2]	60	6

				SP	RR	SF
31[8]	**Crown Ivory (NZ)** (PCRitchens) **8-11-5** SFox (lw: hld up in tch: hdwy 8th: one pce fr 2 out)	11	**3**	25/1	57	3
262[4]	**Miramare** (JWDufosee) **6-11-0**(5) PHenley (mid div tl wknd 7th)	2½	**4**	9/2[3]	55	1
19[6]	**Mr Poppleton (70)** (RBrotherton) **7-11-5** LHarvey (w ldrs tl outpcd 8th)	2	**5**	6/1	53	—
	Father Power (IRE) (85) (PBowen) **8-11-5** RJohnson (bit bkwd: led tl appr 2 out: wknd qckly)	1¼	**6**	6/1	52	—
	Kerrier (IRE) (HJManners) **4-11-2** MrACharles-Jones (bit bkwd: chsd ldr tl after 6th: wknd 8th: t.o whn p.u bef 2 out)		**P**	14/1	—	—
	Pollyanna (MPMuggeridge) **5-11-0** SCurran (w ldrs tl wknd 8th: t.o whn p.u bef 2 out)		**P**	20/1	—	—
				(SP 115.6%)		**8 Rn**

5m 15.2 (3.20) CSF £10.14 TOTE £3.40: £1.10 £1.10 £7.30 (£4.40) OWNER Mrs J. Carrington (EXETER) BRED Mrs G. R. Lewis
WEIGHT FOR AGE 4yo-3lb
297 Idiom provided another impressive win for Culloty. Making headway to lead two out, he was driven out on the flat and won easier than the margin suggests. Connections plan to give him a light campaign. (5/2)
218 Up the Tempo (IRE) was the only other serious contender, but could not cope with the winner. (3/1)

361 NIGHT IS YOUNG H'CAP CHASE (0-115) (5-Y.O+) (Class E)
7-50 (7-50) **2m 110y (13 fncs)** £2,859.15 (£865.20: £422.10: £200.55) GOING minus 0.61 sec per fur (F)

				SP	RR	SF
296[3]	**Duke of Dreams (76)** (RJBaker) **6-10-0** BPowell (hld up & bhd: rapid hdwy 11th: rdn & led appr 2 out: sn clr: unchal)	—	**1**	8/1[3]	84	16
305*	**Manamour (85)** (RLee) **9-10-9**[7x] CLlewellyn (chsd ldr tl lost pl 10th: r.o u.p appr last: no imp)	4	**2**	6/4[1]	89	21
	Toomuch Toosoon (IRE) (100) (MCPipe) **8-11-10** APMcCoy (led: mstkes 2nd & 9th: hdd appr 2 out: sn outpcd: wknd appr last)	8	**3**	6/4[1]	96	28
	Fenwick (88) (RJHodges) **9-10-9**(3) TDascombe (bit bkwd: chsd ldrs tl wknd appr 2 out)	3½	**4**	6/1[2]	81	13
305[4]	**Gabish (76)** (BScriven) **11-9-7**(7) MrRThornton (bkwd: in tch: mstke 3rd: wknd 8th: t.o 10th)	9	**5**	20/1	60	—
				(SP 110.2%)		**5 Rn**

3m 57.5 (-2.50) CSF £19.51 TOTE £7.50: £2.50 £1.10 (£4.30) OWNER Mrs V. W. Jones (TIVERTON) BRED H. D. and M. J. Gee
LONG HANDICAP Duke of Dreams 9-7 Gabish 8-9
Duke of Dreams, held up for most of the way, made rapid headway and took the lead with two to jump. Once in front, he soon went clear and proved impossible to catch. (8/1)
305* Manamour looked to be going best of all, but met with some unfortunate interference. (6/4)
Toomuch Toosoon (IRE) tried to make all, but a tendency to hang right, coupled with some below-par jumping, put his chance to rest early in the straight. (6/4: op 4/5)

362 BIRDIE H'CAP HURDLE (0-120) (4-Y.O+) (Class D)
8-20 (8-20) **2m 6f (10 hdls)** £2,699.10 (£757.60: £369.30) GOING minus 0.61 sec per fur (F)

				SP	RR	SF
214[3]	**Fieldridge (103)** (MPMuggeridge) **7-10-12** BPowell (mid div tl hdwy 8th: led appr 2 out: sn clr: unchal)	—	**1**	7/2[3]	86	31
264*	**Jenzsoph (IRE) (105)** (PJHobbs) **5-11-0** APMcCoy (lw: chsd ldr tl led 7th: mstke next: hdd appr 2 out: rdn & sn outpcd)	12	**2**	7/4[2]	79	24
285*	**Diamond Cut (FR) (119)** (MCPipe) **8-12-0** RJohnson (led to 7th: in tch tl wknd after next: sn outpcd)	4	**3**	6/4[1]	90	35
301[3]	**Beam Me Up Scotty (IRE) (91)** (NJHawke) **7-9-11**(3) JCulloty (mid div tl rdn & wknd 7th)	16	**4**	8/1	51	—
	Bit of A Touch (98) (RGFrost) **10-10-7** JFrost (bkwd: bhd 3rd: t.o fr 5th: p.u bef 2 out)		**P**	40/1	—	—
				(SP 112.1%)		**5 Rn**

5m 7.2 (-4.80) CSF £9.76 TOTE £4.80: £2.20 £1.40 (£5.30) OWNER The Charleston Partnership (LAMBOURN) BRED Mrs John Trotter
LONG HANDICAP Beam Me Up Scotty (IRE) 9-7
214 Fieldridge had a chance on his Flat form, and took advantage of the two market leaders battling it out in the early stages. With two left to jump, he took the lead and came home unchallenged. It is now possible that he might run on the Flat at Chester at the end of the month before he goes chasing. (7/2)
264* Jenzsoph (IRE) wore himself out in a battle for supremacy with the favourite. She finally took up the running after the seventh, but it was a short-lived effort as she was headed at the ninth. (7/4)
285* Diamond Cut (FR) set a fast pace, but it all proved too much when he was headed at the seventh, and he then gradually weakened. (6/4)

T/Plpt: £125.90 (69.45 Tckts). T/Qdpt: £4.40 (181.94 Tckts). T

363a-386a (Irish Racing) - See Computer Raceform

CLAIREFONTAINE (Deauville, France) (R-H) (Soft)
Friday August 9th

387a PRIX JACQUES PEILLON HURDLE (5-Y.O+)
5-09 (5-09) **2m 1f** £6,588.00

			SP	RR	SF
Profluent (USA) (JBertranDeBalanda,France) **5-10-6** DBressou	—	**1**		—	—
Raider (FR) (France) **7-10-6** LGerard	1½	**2**		—	—
C'Est Tres Bien (FR) (France) **6-10-12** TPoche	5	**3**		—	—
King Ubad (USA) (KOCunningham-Brown) **7-10-2** NMilliere (btn a dist)		**5**		—	—
					5 Rn

3m 53.82 P-M 2.20F: 1.60F 2.30F OWNER Mr P. A. Leonard BRED Juddmonte Farms
King Ubad (USA), returning to hurdles after four races on the Flat, raced in second place until halfway and then gradually weakened.

0282-BANGOR-ON-DEE (L-H) (Good to firm)
Saturday August 17th

388 EQE INTERNATIONAL HURDLE (3-Y.O) (Class E)
2-25 (2-25) **2m 1f (9 hdls)** £2,584.00 (£724.00: £352.00) GOING minus 0.44 sec per fur (GF)

				SP	RR	SF
282[3]	**Balmoral Princess** (JHPeacock) **3-10-5b** RBellamy (hld up: hdwy u.p 3 out: chal last: rdn to ld nr fin)	—	**1**	6/1	52	—

Still Here (IRE) (MJHeaton-Ellis) **3-10-10** NWilliamson (jnd ldr 5th: lft clr 3 out: rdn & mstke last: hdd nr fin) ....½ **2** 9/2[3] 57 —
291[7] **Recall To Mind** (MESowersby) **3-10-7b**(3) DParker (sn chsng ldrs: outpcd appr 3 out) ....20 **3** 50/1 38 —
291[3] **Killmessan-Town (IRE)** (JMCarr) **3-10-7**(3) FLeahy (prom: j.slowly & lost pl 5th: sn t.o) ....dist **4** 9/4[2] — —
282* **Friendly Dreams (IRE)** (MCPipe) **3-10-12b** DBridgwater (lost pl & rdn after 3rd: t.o fr 5th) ....29 **5** 2/1[1] — —
Skram (RDickin) **3-10-10** AMaguire (led tl fell 3 out) .... **F** 12/1 — —
Mill House Boy (IRE) (BSRothwell) **3-10-10** RSupple (bit bkwd: a bhd: t.o: fell last) .... **F** 50/1 — —
282[U] **Song For Jess (IRE)** (FJordan) **3-10-5** RGreene (lw: fell 1st) .... **F** 50/1 — —
(SP 110.1%) **8 Rn**

4m 6.9 (11.90) CSF £29.58 TOTE £8.40: £1.50 £1.60 £6.10 (£18.90) OWNER Mrs S. K. Maan (MUCH WENLOCK) BRED H. S. Maan
282 Balmoral Princess, ridden with more restraint then she was on her debut, hurdled the last more fluently than the runner-up and that enabled her to get off the mark. (6/1)
Still Here (IRE), an All-Weather winner on the Flat, was left with a ten length advantage three out, but his stride shortened dramatically at the last two, and an awkward jump at the last was the beginning of the end for him. (9/2)
291 Killmessan-Town (IRE) proved a big disappointment. (9/4: op 6/4)
282* Friendly Dreams (IRE) would not take hold of her bit and was already in trouble with a circuit to race. (2/1)

389 PRESTATYN NOVICES' H'CAP CHASE (0-100) (5-Y.O+) (Class E)
2-55 (2-57) **2m 1f 110y (12 fncs)** £3,018.00 (£848.00: £414.00) GOING minus 0.44 sec per fur (GF)

SP RR SF

340[2] **Green's Seago (USA) (68)** (HMKavanagh) **8-10-2**(5) PHenley (a.p: led 7th: clr appr 2 out: unchal) ....— **1** 7/2[3] 71 —
188[3] **Exclusion (80)** (JHetherton) **7-11-5** RMarley (stdd s: pckd 2nd: disp ld 7th to 3 out: wkng whn mstke next)..dist **2** 2/1[1] — —
61[P] **Sherwood Boy (85)** (KCBailey) **7-11-10** CLlewellyn (led: mstke 5th: hdd 7th: sn wknd: t.o) ....14 **3** 5/2[2] — —
286[4] **Northern Nation (77)** (WClay) **8-11-2** AMaguire (prom tl fell 4th) .... **F** 6/1 — —
304[6] **Don Tocino (64)** (JWhite) **6-10-3b** RBellamy (hdwy 3rd: wknd & rdn 7th: t.o whn fell last) .... **F** 12/1 — —
(SP 106.1%) **5 Rn**

4m 20.3 (10.30) CSF £9.91 TOTE £3.20: £1.70 £1.70 (£2.90) OWNER Mrs S. Kavanagh (BODENHAM) BRED Samuel D. Hinkle
340 Green's Seago (USA) won this with a superior display of jumping and made a quick contribution to his recent purchase price. (7/2)
188 Exclusion still does a lot of guessing and will find it hard to get off the mark over fences. (2/1)
Sherwood Boy, with a bit left to work on after a two month break, bowled along in front for over a mile but dropped away rather quickly after being headed and would seem to have some sort of problem. (5/2)

390 CONSTRUCTION SERVICES NOVICES' CHASE (5-Y.O+) (Class D)
3-25 (3-25) **2m 4f 110y (15 fncs)** £5,680.00 GOING minus 0.44 sec per fur (GF)

SP RR SF

Alqairawaan (110) (CJMann) **7-10-12** CLlewellyn (bit bkwd: lft alone 1st: hit 5th & 8th) ....— **1** 4/7[1] 118? 46
222[3] **Micherado (FR) (92)** (SABrookshaw) **6-11-5** TEley (lw: led & fell 1st) .... **F** 6/4[2] — —
(SP 103.6%) **2 Rn**

4m 54.9 (-5.10) TOTE £1.30 OWNER Mr Jack Joseph (UPPER LAMBOURN) BRED Snailwell Stud Co Ltd
Alqairawaan, careless on a couple of occasions on this debut over fences, had nothing more than a solo school round to land a considerable prize for his fortunate connections. (4/7)

391 ROYAL WELCH FUSILIERS TROPHY AMATEUR H'CAP HURDLE (0-120) (4-Y.O+) (Class E)
3-55 (3-55) **2m 4f (11 hdls)** £2,932.50 (£820.00: £397.50) GOING minus 0.44 sec per fur (GF)

SP RR SF

Royal Circus (90) (PWHiatt) **7-10-5**(7) MrPScott (swtg: led after 1st: styd on strly fr 2 out) ....— **1** 3/1[2] 69 —
343* **Bourdonner (87)** (MDHammond) **4-10-3**(3) MrCBonner (lw: nt j.w: led tl after 1st: rdn appr 2 out: btn whn hit last) ....3 **2** 8/11[1] 64 —
182[6] **Gone by (IRE) (102)** (JRJenkins) **8-11-3b**(7) MrRThornton (chsd ldng pair: lost tch 7th: t.o) ....13 **3** 4/1[3] 68 —
285[7] **Batty's Island (89)** (BPreece) **7-10-4b**[1](7) MissLBoswell (in rr tl blnd & uns rdr 6th) .... **U** 20/1 — —
(SP 107.7%) **4 Rn**

4m 49.2 (13.20) CSF £5.40 TOTE £3.70 (£1.90) OWNER Mr P. W. Hiatt (BANBURY) BRED Snailwell Stud Co Ltd
WEIGHT FOR AGE 4yo-3lb
Royal Circus was able to adopt his favoured front-running tactics and did not need to get serious to take the measure of the favourite. (3/1)
343* Bourdonner was let down by an inept display of hurdling, especially when the pressure was on, he was already beaten when untidy at the last. (8/11)

392 TELEGRAPH SERVICE STATIONS NOVICES' HURDLE (4-Y.O+) (Class E)
4-25 (4-25) **2m 4f (11 hdls)** £2,612.00 (£732.00: £356.00) GOING minus 0.44 sec per fur (GF)

SP RR SF

58[3] **Tukano (CAN) (98)** (JRJenkins) **5-11-5** GBradley (hld up: led 7th: clr appr last: easily) ....— **1** Evens[1] 66+ —
25[4] **Profit And Loss** (FMurphy) **5-10-7** AMaguire (bit bkwd: a.p: shkn up appr 2 out: sn outpcd) ....9 **2** 11/8[2] 47 —
First Bee (FJordan) **5-10-7** RSupple (bkwd: hld up & bhd: hdwy 8th: kpt on one pce appr 2 out) ....2½ **3** 33/1 45 —
Mellow Yellow (JMackie) **5-10-12** TEley (bit bkwd: plld hrd: hdwy 5th: rdn & wknd 8th: t.o) ....24 **4** 10/1[3] 31 —
287[P] **Admiral's Guest (IRE)** (WClay) **4-10-9v** NWilliamson (led: sn clr: hit 4th: reminders whn j.slowly & hdd 7th: wknd qckly: t.o) ....dist **5** 20/1 — —
(SP 108.9%) **5 Rn**

4m 51.0 (15.00) CSF £2.61 TOTE £1.90: £1.20 £1.10 (£1.50) OWNER Mrs T. McCoubrey (ROYSTON) BRED Windfields Farm
WEIGHT FOR AGE 4yo-3lb
58 Tukano (CAN) was a class apart on all known form, and he was able to pull clear on the bridle for an effortless success. (Evens)
25 Profit And Loss turned in a pleasing display on her hurdling debut, and she has certainly been taught her job. However, the only prize at stake in the final half mile was for runner-up. She will stay further and can be made fitter. (11/8)
First Bee looked very burly for this first run in sixteen months, but did not fare badly and there could be a small race for her. (33/1)

393 SHOWTIME NOVICES' H'CAP HURDLE (0-100) (4-Y.O+) (Class E)
5-00 (5-00) **2m 1f (9 hdls)** £2,584.00 (£724.00: £352.00) GOING minus 0.44 sec per fur (GF)

SP RR SF

344[4] **Raven's Roost (IRE) (54)** (GEJones) **5-10-0** PMcLoughlin (swtg: hld up: stdy hdwy 6th: led appr last: rdn out) ....— **1** 16/1 40 —

	Horse / details	Dist	Pos	SP	RR	SF
	Tawafij (USA) (75) (MDHammond) **7-11-7** RGarritty (swtg: lw: hld up & bhd: hdwy on bit appr 2 out: rdn & unable qckn flat)	1¾	2	$5/4^{1}$	59	—
219^{3}	**Count of Flanders (IRE) (78)** (KAMorgan) **6-11-10** ASSmith (bit bkwd: a.p: led appr 2 out tl appr last: sn rdn & wknd)	7	3	$3/1^{2}$	56	—
289^{6}	**Rare Paddy (60)** (BSRothwell) **7-10-6v** RSupple (led 3rd to 5th: led 6th tl appr 2 out: sn wknd)	8	4	8/1	30	—
217^{U}	**Marketing Man (55)** (JWhite) **6-10-1** RBellamy (bit bkwd: led to 3rd: led 5th to 6th: wkng whn hit 3 out)	20	5	33/1	6	—
348^{3}	**Night Time (85)** (FJordan) **4-11-7**$^{(7)}$ MrGShenkin (lw: hld up & bhd: lost pl 6th: t.o)	½	6	$7/2^{3}$	36	—

(SP 111.6%) **6 Rn**

4m 3.6 (8.60) CSF £35.36 TOTE £14.70: £3.60 £1.20 (£22.30) OWNER Mr Elwyn Jones (LAMPETER) BRED Mrs G. Lanzara
LONG HANDICAP Raven's Roost (IRE) 9-9
WEIGHT FOR AGE 4yo-3lb

Raven's Roost (IRE) caused a major upset with a well-deserved initial success, and there was no fluke about this. (16/1)
Tawafij (USA) had not run over hurdles for nearly two years, but was fit from the Flat. Turning in an impressive display of jumping, he was swinging off the bridle for most of the way and it looked a matter of how far when poised to challenge at the penultimate flight. Here his suspect stamina gave out and he could do little about it. (5/4)
219 Count of Flanders (IRE) still looked just short of peak fitness and after looking a live threat once in line for home, blew up at the last two. (3/1: op 9/2)
348 Night Time moved to post as if he was jarred up and struggled in the rear until becoming tailed off out in the country. (7/2)

T/Plpt: £129.30 (38.07 Tckts). T/Qdpt: £23.70 (8.3 Tckts) IM

0259-STRATFORD-ON-AVON (L-H) (Good to firm, Good patches)
Saturday August 17th
WEATHER: sunny

394 RICHARDSONS FORT RETAIL PARK CLAIMING HURDLE (4-Y.O+) (Class F)
2-20 (2-21) **2m 6f 110y (12 hdls)** £2,360.00 (£660.00: £320.00) GOING: 0.06 sec per fur (G)

	Horse / details	Dist	Pos	SP	RR	SF
	Viardot (IRE) (107) (MrsMReveley) **7-11-5** PNiven (hld up: chsd clr ldr 8th: hrd rdn 9th: lft in ld 2 out: r.o)	—	1	$9/4^{1}$	83+	23
	Acrow Line (DBurchell) **11-10-7** DJBurchell (bit bkwd: mstke 1st: hdwy to chse clr ldr 3rd to 6th: hrd rdn 9th: one pce)	6	2	6/1	67	7
184^{10}	**Riva's Book (USA) (79)** (MGMeagher) **5-10-13** APMcCoy (swtg: bhd: hrd rdn after 7th: no ch fr 8th)	21	3	14/1	58	—
264^{4}	**Milzig (USA) (73)** (JJoseph) **7-11-2** DSkyrme (t.o fr 4th)	dist	4	20/1	—	—
255^{7}	**Merlins Wish (USA) (107)** (MCPipe) **7-10-6**$^{(7)}$ GSupple (t.o fr 4th)	½	5	14/1	—	—
327^{5}	**Fattash (USA)** (PMooney) **4-10-0**$^{(5)}$ SRyan (nt j.w: t.o fr 8th)	8	6	100/1	—	—
362^{3}	**Diamond Cut (FR) (119)** (MCPipe) **8-11-1**$^{(7)}$ BMoore (lw: led: clr tl fell 2 out: dead)		F	$11/4^{2}$	—	—
301^{F}	**Jennyellen (IRE) (98)** (PBowen) **7-11-0** RJohnson (hld up: chsd clr ldr 6th: hit 7th: 4th & wkng whn fell 9th)		F	$7/2^{3}$	—	—
189^{10}	**Goodnight Vienna (IRE)** (MSheppard) **6-10-9**^{ow1} MrMMunrowd (chsd clr ldr to 3rd: wknd 5th: t.o whn p.u bef 3 out)		P	100/1	—	—

(SP 114.0%) **9 Rn**

5m 30.5 (14.50) CSF £15.03 TOTE £2.80: £1.20 £1.70 £2.80 (£9.70) Trio £41.20 OWNER The Mary Reveley Racing Club (SALTBURN) BRED Barronstown Stud
WEIGHT FOR AGE 4yo-3lb

Viardot (IRE) was only destined for second when the clear leader fell two out. (9/4)
Acrow Line, tailed off in a spin on the Flat a week ago, still looked short of peak fitness. (6/1)
Riva's Book (USA) (14/1: 10/1-16/1)
Merlins Wish (USA) (14/1: op 8/1)
362 Diamond Cut (FR), soon bowling along with a clear advantage, was still a dozen lengths to the good when taking a fatal fall at the penultimate hurdle. (11/4)

395 MONKS CROSS RICHARDSONS RETAIL DEVELOPMENT H'CAP CHASE (0-105) (5-Y.O+) (Class F)
2-50 (2-51) **3m (18 fncs)** £2,770.00 (£835.00: £405.00: £190.00) GOING minus 0.47 sec per fur (GF)

	Horse / details	Dist	Pos	SP	RR	SF
256*	**Maple Dancer (99)** (AGHobbs) **10-11-3**$^{(7)}$ MrGShenkin (a.p: chsd clr ldr 12th: led 2 out: sn rdn: r.o wl)	—	1	$7/4^{1}$	112	44
	Some Day Soon (100) (MBradstock) **11-11-11** PHolley (bit bkwd: led to 2 out: hrd rdn: one pce)	6	2	13/2	109	41
298*	**Sohail (USA) (103)** (JSKing) **13-12-0** RDunwoody (hdwy 12th: one pce fr 4 out)	9	3	$5/1^{2}$	106	38
256^{P}	**The Blue Boy (IRE) (102)** (PBowen) **8-11-13b** RJohnson (hdwy 10th: wknd 13th)	17	4	$6/1^{3}$	94	26
256^{5}	**Boxing Match (75)** (JMBradley) **9-10-0** BFenton (dropped rr 7th: hdwy 12th: wknd appr 14th)	11	5	8/1	59	—
	Paper Star (103) (MPMuggeridge) **9-12-0** BPowell (hdwy 10th: wknd 12th: t.o fr 13th)	22	6	10/1	73	5
342^{8}	**Hurryup (91)** (RDickin) **9-10-13**$^{(3)}$ JCulloty (prom tl blnd 12th: t.o whn p.u bef 3 out)		P	13/2	—	—
298^{P}	**The Lorryman (IRE) (85)** (NRMitchell) **8-10-10b**^{1} GUpton (nt j.w: bhd whn j.slowly 8th: sn t.o: p.u bef 12th)		P	20/1	—	—

(SP 118.9%) **8 Rn**

5m 49.7 (-2.30) CSF £13.45 CT £45.51 TOTE £3.10: £1.50 £1.70 £1.60 (£13.60) OWNER Dr Ian Shenkin (KINGSBRIDGE) BRED Hugh Gibney
LONG HANDICAP Boxing Match 9-13

256* Maple Dancer, raised a further 7lb, completed a Stratford hat trick and was his trainer's first winner. (7/4)
Some Day Soon adopted his favoured front-running tactics and this outing should have blown the cobwebs away. (13/2)
298* Sohail (USA) has never scored over three miles under Rules. (5/1)

396 STRATFORD-UPON-AVON FOODS MAIDEN HURDLE (I) (4-Y.O+) (Class E)
3-20 (3-20) **2m 110y (9 hdls)** £1,926.00 (£536.00: £258.00) GOING: 0.06 sec per fur (G)

	Horse / details	Dist	Pos	SP	RR	SF
186^{2}	**Zine Lane (96)** (MajorWRHern) **4-11-2** RFarrant (a.p: hit 6th: sn led: lft clr 3 out)	—	1	$4/9^{1}$	67	12
66^{12}	**Kutan (IRE) (64)** (MrsBarbaraWaring) **6-11-5** EByrne (hld up: wl bhd 4th: hdwy 3 out: lft poor 2nd 2 out)	19	2	33/1	49	—
	Dantean (RJO'Sullivan) **4-11-2** DO'Sullivan (hld up: hdwy appr 6th: lft poor 2nd 3 out: one pce)	1	3	$12/1^{3}$	48	—
	Tigh-Na-Mara (JMJefferson) **8-10-9**$^{(5)}$ ECallaghan (bit bkwd: prom: 3rd & wkng whn mstke 6th)	11	4	33/1	32	—
262^{6}	**Saint Amigo** (CCowley) **4-11-2** JAMcCarthy (prom to 5th: t.o)	dist	5	16/1	—	—

Athenian Alliance (JMBradley) 7-10-11(3) GuyLewis (prom to 5th: t.o) ....15 6 100/1 — —
300P On the Ledge (USA) (48) (HJManners) 6-10-12(7) ADowling (mskte 2nd: bhd whn rdn after 4th: sn t.o: p.u bef 2 out) .... P 200/1 — —
Lilac Rain (RMStronge) 4-10-11 WMcFarland (nt j.w: bhd fr 5th: t.o whn p.u bef 3 out) .... P 25/1 — —
262P Minidia (HJManners) 4-10-11 MrACharles-Jones (a bhd: t.o 4th: p.u after 5th) .... P 150/1 — —
Prince de Berry (83) (BJMeehan) 5-11-5 APMcCoy (led tl after 6th: 2 lengths 2nd whn blnd & uns rdr 3 out) .... U 11/4 2 — —
(SP 121.4%) 10 Rn

3m 59.3 (12.30) CSF £17.69 TOTE £1.50: £1.10 £3.30 £1.60 (£23.00) Trio £86.40 OWNER The Hopeful Partnership (LAMBOURN) BRED W. R. and S. J. Hern Partnership
WEIGHT FOR AGE 4yo-3lb
186 Zine Lane was in the process of taking command when left clear three from home. (4/9)
Kutan (IRE) won the separate race for the runner-up spot. (33/1)
Dantean, no great shakes on the Flat, is not guaranteed to really get the trip over hurdles. (12/1: op 8/1)
Prince de Berry, fit from the Flat, looked to be struggling to keep tabs on the winner when departing three out. (11/4)

397 STEVENAGE RICHARDSONS RETAIL NOVICES' HURDLE (4-Y.O+) (Class D)
3-50 (3-51) **2m 6f 110y (12 hdls)** £2,959.00 (£824.00: £397.00) GOING: 0.06 sec per fur (G)

SP RR SF
181 3 **Wynberg (95)** (CaptTAForster) **5-11-6** SWynne (chsd ldr: led appr 3rd: clr 3 out: eased flat) .... — 1 4/11 1 65+ —
Roskeen Bridge (IRE) (CWeedon) **5-11-0** MRichards (swtg: chsd wnr 4th: mstke 5th: hrd rdn & wknd appr 3 out) ....28 2 7/2 2 39 —
26 10 **Hatta River (USA)** (PTDalton) **6-11-0** RJohnson (hld up: mstke 8th: rdn & wknd 9th: t.o whn mstke 2 out) ..dist 3 11/1 3 — —
Crossing The Styx (KGWingrove) **10-11-0** MissAEmbiricos (led tl appr 3rd: reminder after 7th: sn t.o: p.u bef 3 out) .... P 14/1 — —
(SP 110.6%) 4 Rn

5m 41.5 (25.50) CSF £2.11 TOTE £1.40 (£1.50) OWNER Mrs D. Pridden (LUDLOW) BRED Cheveley Park Stud Ltd
181 Wynberg found no trouble winning a desperate contest. (4/11)
Roskeen Bridge (IRE) had been placed in three of his six starts in point-to-points in Ireland. (7/2)

398 PARKWAY RICHARDSONS WEDNESBURY H'CAP CHASE (0-120) (5-Y.O+) (Class D)
4-20 (4-21) **2m 1f 110y (13 fncs)** £3,978.00 (£1,108.00: £534.00) GOING minus 0.47 sec per fur (GF)

SP RR SF
340* **Stately Home (IRE) (108)** (PBowen) **5-12-0** RJohnson (j.rt: mde all: blnd 7th: drvn out) .... — 1 4/6 1 122 40
305 3 **Flying Ziad (CAN) (77)** (HJManners) **13-9-7**(7) ADowling (hld up: chsd wnr fr 4 out: one pce fr 2 out) 2 2 4/1 3 89 10
336 3 **Wise Advice (IRE) (95)** (MDHammond) **6-11-4** AThornton (chsd wnr tl hit 4 out: wknd appr 2 out) 14 3 5/2 2 94 15
(SP 108.6%) 3 Rn

4m 9.2 (0.20) CSF £3.15 TOTE £1.30 (£1.70) OWNER Mr P. Bowen (HAVERFORDWEST) BRED Ash Hill Stud
LONG HANDICAP Flying Ziad (CAN) 9-9
WEIGHT FOR AGE 5yo-3lb
340* Stately Home (IRE), who only won a seller over timber, took his earnings through the £20,000 barrier. He was far from impressive this time though and would probably have been beaten had there been something half decent in the race. (4/6)
305 Flying Ziad (CAN), much better off with the winner than when they last met, could not take advantage of his rival seemingly being below par. (4/1)

399 ATLANTIC WHARF RICHARDSONS CARDIFF CONDITIONAL H'CAP HURDLE (0-105) (4-Y.O+) (Class F)
4-55 (4-56) **2m 110y (9 hdls)** £2,192.00 (£612.00: £296.00) GOING: 0.06 sec per fur (G)

SP RR SF
284* **Peter Monamy (99)** (MCPipe) **4-12-0** DWalsh (lw: set slow pce: qcknd 3 out: drvn out) .... — 1 11/10 1 83 —
303 4 **Sirtelimar (IRE) (92)** (KCBailey) **7-11-10** TJMurphy (lw: trckd wnr fr 2nd: ev ch last: rdn & unable qckn) ....1¾ 2 5/4 2 74 —
341 6 **Asterix (92)** (JMBradley) **8-11-10** BFenton (hld up: rdn appr 2 out: no rspnse) ....6 3 9/2 3 69 —
(SP 110.2%) 3 Rn

4m 5.7 (18.70) CSF £2.74 TOTE £1.40 (£1.40) OWNER Richard Green (Fine Paintings) (WELLINGTON) BRED R. Green
WEIGHT FOR AGE 4yo-3lb
284* Peter Monamy got away quicker than the runner-up from the final flight and that proved decisive. (11/10: op 4/6)
Sirtelimar (IRE), ridden for speed, did not deliver the goods after being outjumped at the last. (5/4)
Asterix has been very busy on the Flat this year. (9/2)

400 STRATFORD-UPON-AVON FOODS MAIDEN HURDLE (II) (4-Y.O+) (Class E)
5-25 (5-28) **2m 110y (9 hdls)** £1,926.00 (£536.00: £258.00) GOING: 0.06 sec per fur (G)

SP RR SF
299 3 **Re Roi (IRE) (92)** (JCFox) **4-11-2** TJMurphy (hld up: hdwy 6th: styd on to ld last: drvn out) .... — 1 5/2 2 70 —
Anabranch (JMJefferson) **5-10-7**(7) MNewton (lw: chsd clr ldr 4th: led 3 out to 2 out: one pce flat) ....6 2 Evens 1 59 —
300 4 **Minnesota Fats (IRE) (66)** (MissMERowland) **4-11-2** GaryLyons (led: sn clr: hdd 3 out: led 2 out to last: wknd qckly) ....8 3 14/1 56 —
Risky Romeo (GCBravery) **4-11-2** RDunwoody (hld up: hdwy whn j.slowly 6th: hrd rdn appr 2 out: sn wknd) .4 4 4/1 3 53 —
Flair Lady (WGMTurner) **5-10-7**(7) JPower (chsd clr ldr to 4th: wknd appr 6th) ....18 5 33/1 30 —
Chief's Lady (JMBradley) **4-10-11** RJohnson (prom tl wknd 5th) ....12 6 50/1 19 —
300 5 **Galloping Guns (IRE)** (BJLlewellyn) **4-10-13**(3) GuyLewis (mstke 6th: a bhd) ....7 7 100/1 17 —
66 9 **Against The Clock (69)** (JWMullins) **4-11-2** SCurran (lw: a bhd: lost tch 5th: t.o) ....12 8 25/1 5 —
260P **Flashing Sabre** (HJManners) **4-10-9**(7) ADowling (t.o whn p.u bef 5th) .... P 200/1 — —
(SP 115.5%) 9 Rn

4m 2.2 (15.20) CSF £5.15 TOTE £4.50: £1.20 £1.40 £1.40 (£4.10) Trio £7.40 OWNER Mr J. C. Fox (MARLBOROUGH) BRED Mrs Larry Walsh
WEIGHT FOR AGE 4yo-3lb
299 Re Roi (IRE) owed this success to his ability to get the trip. (5/2)
Anabranch may have been just short of a gallop, but still looked set to score on the home turn. (Evens)
212 Minnesota Fats (IRE) has been running in sellers and did well to get back in front at the penultimate hurdle, but looked leg-weary on the run-in. (14/1)

T/Plpt: £5.10 (1,279.67 Tckts). T/Qdpt: £2.00 (100.75 Tckts) KH

0327-PLUMPTON (L-H) (Firm, Good to firm patches)
Monday August 19th
WEATHER: fine

401 PEACEHAVEN NOVICES' H'CAP HURDLE (0-100) (4-Y.O+ F & M) (Class E)
5-30 (5-33) **2m 1f (10 hdls)** £2,238.00 (£618.00: £294.00) GOING minus 0.43 sec per fur (GF)

	Horse	Dist	Pos	SP	RR	SF
77[2]	**Scamallach (IRE) (85)** (JRJenkins) **6-12-0b** GBradley (led after 1st: sn clr: r.o wl)	—	1	8/11[1]	64?	—
	Misty View (72) (JWhite) **7-11-1** APMcCoy (bit bkwd: chsd wnr 3rd to 5th: chsd wnr fr 3 out: rdn appr 2 out: unable qckn)	4	2	7/1[3]	47?	—
17[10]	**Siesta Time (USA) (57)** (CLPopham) **6-10-0** NWilliamson (lw: nt j.w: chsd wnr after 1st to 3rd: chsd wnr 5th to 3 out: wknd 2 out)	7	3	11/4[2]	26?	—
	Club Elite (73) (MFBarraclough) **4-10-13** AnnStokell (lw: plld hrd: led tl after 1st: wknd 6th)	8	4	12/1	34?	—
355[3]	**Laser Light Lady (60)** (NPLittmoden) **4-10-0b** BPowell (a bhd)	16	5	16/1	6?	—
				(SP 110.6%)		**5 Rn**

4m 20.4 (24.40) CSF £5.84 TOTE £1.40: £1.10 £2.10 (£3.40) OWNER Mrs Susan McCarthy (ROYSTON) BRED Kevin O'Donnell
LONG HANDICAP Laser Light Lady 9-10
WEIGHT FOR AGE 4yo-3lb

77 Scamallach (IRE) decided to move to the front after jumping only one hurdle. Strolling along in front, she proved far too strong for her rivals to win this appalling race. (8/11)
Misty View, out the back on the Flat at Windsor a week earlier, was having her first outing over hurdles since November 1993. Regaining second place three out, she was soon being bustled along but failed to get on terms with the winner. (7/1: 9/2-8/1)
Siesta Time (USA), who has been placed three times in sellers and claimers on the Flat this year, failed to have a cut at her hurdles and looked far from enthusiastic. In second place for much of the way, she looked very reluctant to put her best foot forward in the straight. (11/4)
Club Elite (12/1: 8/1-14/1)

402 LEICESTER DYERS AND RIP-OFF CLOTHING COMPANY HURDLE (3-Y.O) (Class E)
5-55 (5-57) **2m 1f (10 hdls)** £2,259.00 (£624.00: £297.00) GOING minus 0.43 sec per fur (GF)

	Horse	Dist	Pos	SP	RR	SF
331[2]	**Verulam (IRE)** (JRJenkins) **3-10-10** GBradley (hdwy 4th: led after 3 out: rdn out)	—	1	9/4[2]	56	—
	Bright Eclipse (USA) (JWHills) **3-10-10** CLlewellyn (lw: hdwy 7th: chsd wnr appr 3 out: 2nd & btn whn j.slowly last)	7	2	4/1[3]	49	—
291[2]	**Home Cookin'** (MCPipe) **3-10-5** DBridgwater (led: j.slowly 2nd & 3rd: hdd after 3 out: sn wknd: 3rd & no ch whn blnd last)	25	3	11/8[1]	21	—
331[3]	**Again Together** (GLMoore) **3-10-5** DGallagher (chsd ldr: mstke 5th: ev ch whn mstke 3 out: sn wknd)	½	4	9/2	20	—
	Governor's Bid (MrsLCJewell) **3-10-10** JRailton (swtg: a bhd: t.o fr 6th: p.u bef 3 out)		P	50/1	—	—
				(SP 113.0%)		**5 Rn**

4m 14.4 (18.40) CSF £10.75 TOTE £3.70: £1.50 £1.30 (£8.30) OWNER Mr R. M. Ellis (ROYSTON) BRED Etablissement Equine Investments
OFFICIAL EXPLANATION **Again Together: finished distressed.**

331 Verulam (IRE) moved up at the fourth. Sent to the front soon after the third last, he was ridden along to put the runner-up in his place. (9/4)
Bright Eclipse (USA), placed three times on the Flat this year, edged closer in the last mile appearing to be travelling well. Cruising into second place on the home turn, he was then asked for his effort but failed to find what was expected of him and a slow jump at the last sealed his fate. (4/1)
291 Home Cookin' streaked off in front but she looked rather reluctant at several hurdles most notably the second and third. Collared soon after the third last, she was quickly done with. She does not look one to place a great deal of faith in. (11/8)
331 Again Together, beaten only a length and a quarter by the winner here at the last meeting, raced in second place. With every chance when making a mistake three out, she then stopped as if shot. Her trainer reported that the filly finished distressed. (9/2)

403 DR. BERNARD ABEYSUNDERA H'CAP CHASE (0-110) (5-Y.O+) (Class E)
6-25 (6-25) **2m** £2,906.40 (£865.20: £411.60: £184.80) GOING minus 0.43 sec per fur (GF)

	Horse	Dist	Pos	SP	RR	SF
352[2]	**Noblely (USA) (98)** (NJHWalker) **9-11-10** RFarrant (led to 8th: led 4 out: clr appr 2 out: r.o wl)	—	1	5/4[2]	108	29
328*	**Safety (USA) (88)** (JWhite) **9-11-0b** TJMurphy (lw: chsd wnr fr 4th: led 8th to 4 out: wknd appr 2 out)	25	2	Evens[1]	73	—
328[U]	**Lavalight (76)** (JWDufosee) **9-9-11**(5)ow2 PHenley (mstke 2nd: bhd fr 3rd: t.o whn blnd 4 out)	14	3	33/1	47	—
328[U]	**Victory Anthem (74)** (PCClarke) **10-10-0** BFenton (lw: chsd ldr to 4th: wknd 7th: t.o fr 8th)	dist	4	10/1[3]	—	—
				(SP 106.5%)		**4 Rn**

3m 48.3 (-3.70) CSF £2.69 TOTE £1.70 (£1.10) OWNER Mr D. H. Cowgill (WANTAGE) BRED Societe Aland
LONG HANDICAP Lavalight 9-10

352 Noblely (USA), more at home over this trip, dictated matters from the front. Collared six out, he was back in front again two fences later and, forging clear entering the straight, bounded home to win in a time just over a second outside the course record. (5/4)
328* Safety (USA) likes to dictate but, on this occasion, he was unable to do so. Nevertheless, he got to the front six out but he was collared for that position two fences later and was a spent force turning into the straight. (Evens)

404 LONDON RACING CLUB H'CAP HURDLE (0-105) (4-Y.O+) (Class F)
6-55 (6-55) **2m 4f (12 hdls)** £2,029.20 (£561.20: £267.60) GOING minus 0.43 sec per fur (GF)

	Horse	Dist	Pos	SP	RR	SF
391[3]	**Gone by (IRE) (101)** (JRJenkins) **8-11-12v[1]** GBradley (lw: hdwy 9th: led 3 out: rdn out)	—	1	11/2	81	39
329[2]	**No Light (103)** (MrsIMcKie) **9-12-0** LHarvey (hld up: chsd wnr appr 2 out: ev ch 2 out: rdn appr last: unable qckn)	1¾	2	13/8[1]	82	40
16[7]	**Mr Geneaology (USA) (94)** (TPMcGovern) **6-11-5b** AMaguire (led: sn clr: hdd 3 out: sn wknd)	25	3	7/2[3]	53	11
301[2]	**Celestial Fire (80)** (JWhite) **4-10-2** APMcCoy (swtg: chsd ldr: ev ch 3 out: sn wknd)	5	4	9/4[2]	35	—
	Emallen (IRE) (75) (MrsLCJewell) **8-9-9b**(5) SophieMitchell (bit bkwd: swtg: bhd fr 9th)	2½	5	16/1	28	—
				(SP 112.4%)		**5 Rn**

4m 47.6 (0.60) CSF £14.44 TOTE £5.00: £1.90 £1.20 (£4.00) OWNER Mrs T. McCoubrey (ROYSTON) BRED James Robinson
LONG HANDICAP Emallen (IRE) 9-8
WEIGHT FOR AGE 4yo-3lb

64 Gone by (IRE), tailed off at Bangor on Saturday, looked in good shape in the paddock and bounced back here. Moving up early in the back straight, he went to the front three out and, ridden along, proved too good for the runner-up from the penultimate hurdle. (11/2: 4/1-6/1)
329 No Light eased his way into second place turning for home appearing to be travelling well. With every chance two out, he then found his welter burden anchoring him. (13/8)
Mr Geneaology (USA) was not going to hang around and, storming off in front, was soon clear. Collared three out, he stopped as if shot. (7/2)
301 Celestial Fire raced in second place. With every chance three from home, he then folded up. (9/4)
Emallen (IRE), looking in need of this first run since last October, disputed second place until tiring from the eighth. (16/1)

405 TRANS WORLD EXHIBITIONS NOVICES' H'CAP CHASE (0-100) (5-Y.O+) (Class E)

7-25 (7-25) **3m 1f 110y (20 fncs)** £3,486.00 (£840.00) GOING minus 0.43 sec per fur (GF)

				SP	RR	SF
302*	**Wakt (87)** (JWhite) **6-11-10** APMcCoy (lw: lft 2nd 3rd: led 6th to 7th: led 8th: hrd hld)	—	1	2/9 1	84++	15
330 5	**Jimmy the Jackdaw (63)** (PButler) **9-10-0b** BFenton (lw: led to 6th: led 7th to 8th: rdn appr 3 out: unable qckn)	5	2	5/1 2	57	—
213 F	**Priesthill (IRE) (65)** (DLWilliams) **7-10-2ow2** PHolley (2nd whn blnd 3rd: wknd 7th: t.o fr 10th: rel to r fr 12th: ref 4 out: continued: fell 4 out: rmntd: p.u bef 2 out)		P	10/1 3	—	—
				(SP 107.6%)		**3 Rn**

6m 29.8 (9.80) CSF £1.70 TOTE £1.10 (£1.20) OWNER Mr John White (ASTON ROWANT) BRED Shadwell Estate Company Limited
LONG HANDICAP Priesthill (IRE) 9-13
STEWARDS' ENQUIRY Holley susp. 28-30/8/96 (improper riding).
302* Wakt had no more than a stroll to beat two atrocious rivals. The winning distance is no reflection of her superiority, as her jockey was strangling her from the second last. (2/9)
Jimmy the Jackdaw, who made most to the eighth, was only on terms with the winner on sufferance turning out of the back straight and is greatly flattered to finish so close. He is still a maiden after thirty-three attempts. (5/1: 7/2-11/2)
Priesthill (IRE) (10/1: 8/1-12/1)

406 BUXTED NOVICES' HURDLE (4-Y.O+) (Class E)

7-55 (7-55) **2m 4f (12 hdls)** £2,343.00 (£648.00: £309.00) GOING minus 0.43 sec per fur (GF)

				SP	RR	SF
353 3	**Shalik (IRE)** (JRJenkins) **6-10-12** JRailton (lw: chsd ldr: led 2nd: mstke 7th: r.o wl)	—	1	2/1 2	40	—
297 5	**Lac de Gras (IRE) (59)** (RCurtis) **5-10-12** DMorris (chsd wnr fr 3rd: ev ch 2 out: unable qckn)	9	2	2/1 2	33	—
327 P	**Brigadier Supreme (IRE)** (PButler) **7-10-12b1** TJMurphy (led tl hdd & mstke 2nd: mstke 3rd: wknd 9th: t.o whn blnd 2 out)	dist	3	14/1 3	—	—
300 F	**Kama Simba** (JWhite) **4-10-9** APMcCoy (lw: nt j.w: hld up: mstkes 8th & 3 out: sn wknd: t.o whn p.u lame bef 2 out: dead)		P	13/8 1	—	—
				(SP 111.4%)		**4 Rn**

5m 1.8 (14.80) CSF £6.11 TOTE £3.40 (£3.00) OWNER Mr S. Curran (ROYSTON) BRED E. Roche
WEIGHT FOR AGE 4yo-3lb
353 Shalik (IRE) went to the front at the second. Asserting his authority from the second last, he romped home to complete a four-timer for Jenkins in an atrocious race. (2/1)
5 Lac de Gras (IRE) moved into second place at the third. On level terms with the winner two out, he was then tapped for toe. (2/1)
Brigadier Supreme (IRE) (14/1: 7/1-16/1)
Kama Simba had a real problem with his jumping and once again was far from fluent. His jockey tried to get him into the action in the back straight, but he stopped very quickly from the third last and was pulled up lame before the next. (13/8)

T/Plpt: £35.70 (159.01 Tckts). T/Qdpt: £12.10 (28.8 Tckts) AK

EXETER (R-H) (Firm)
Wednesday August 21st
WEATHER: sunny

407 BRAMBLE CONDITIONAL (S) H'CAP HURDLE (0-95) (4-Y.O+) (Class G)

2-25 (2-26) **2m 1f 110y (8 hdls)** £1,781.00 (£501.00: £245.00) GOING minus 0.75 sec per fur (F)

				SP	RR	SF
21 7	**Buglet (86)** (MCPipe) **6-11-6** DWalsh (lw: chsd ldr tl led 2 out: sn clr: comf)	—	1	5/1 3	68+	24
185 5	**Nordic Crown (IRE) (75)** (MCPipe) **5-10-9b** RMassey (a chsng ldrs: rdn 2 out: one pce appr last)	2½	2	3/1 1	55	11
304 5	**Denomination (USA) (93)** (MCPipe) **4-11-5(5)** GSupple (hld up & bhd: rdn & hdwy 6th: one pce 2 out)	3	3	4/1 2	70	23
301 F	**Coeur Battant (FR) (66)** (RJBaker) **6-10-0** TDascombe (led tl hdd 2 out: wknd appr last)	1¼	4	6/1	42	—
	Starshadow (66) (WGMTurner) **7-9-9(5)** JPower (bkwd: in tch to 4th: sn bhd)	dist	5	33/1	—	—
	Chelworth Wolf (70) (JLSpearing) **4-10-1** MichaelBrennan (bit bkwd: in tch to 4th: stdly wknd)	¾	6	12/1	—	—
362 4	**Beam Me Up Scotty (IRE) (81)** (NJHawke) **7-11-1v1** JCulloty (a bhd: wkng whn fell 6th)		F	3/1 1	—	—
				(SP 111.6%)		**7 Rn**

4m 1.1 (-2.90) CSF £18.96 TOTE £6.20: £3.10 £2.20 (£8.70) OWNER Mrs Helen Stoneman (WELLINGTON) BRED John Breslin
LONG HANDICAP Starshadow 9-0 Coeur Battant (FR) 9-13
WEIGHT FOR AGE 4yo-3lb
Bt in 3,600 gns
Buglet, running for only the second time in over two years, took this comfortably. (5/1: op 3/1)
134 Nordic Crown (IRE) had every chance but was never going to catch the winner. (3/1)
304 Denomination (USA) made headway from the sixth but was onepaced from two out. (4/1: 3/1-9/2)

408 INTERLINK EXPRESS DELIVERY MAIDEN HURDLE (4-Y.O+) (Class E)

2-55 (2-56) **2m 1f 110y (8 hdls)** £2,232.00 (£627.00: £306.00) GOING minus 0.75 sec per fur (F)

				SP	RR	SF
	Miss Foxy (RGFrost) **6-11-0** JFrost (bit bkwd: chsd ldr tl led appr 2 out: sn clr: easily)	—	1	33/1	59+	—
293 7	**Fleet Cadet** (MCPipe) **5-11-5b** DBridgwater (mid div tl rdn & hdwy 6th: in tch 2 out: one pce appr last)	6	2	2/1 2	59	—
300 2	**Almapa** (RJHodges) **4-10-13(3)** TDascombe (a same pl: rdn & no ex 2 out)	3½	3	6/4 1	55	—
350 3	**Regal Gem (IRE)** (CRBarwell) **5-11-0** BFenton (bhd 4th: stdly wknd)	¾	4	3/1 3	50	—

Falcons Dawn (61) (SGKnight) 9-11-5 MissLBlackford (bkwd: led tl hdd appr 2 out: sn wknd)....10 5 33/1 46 —
304[3] Mutley (63) (NJHawke) 6-11-2(3) JCulloty (a bhd: lost tch 5th)....11 6 5/1 35 —
Scottish Park (MCPipe) 7-11-0b APMcCoy (Withdrawn not under Starter's orders: hit head in preliminaries).... W 3/1[3] — —
(SP 145.9%) 6 Rn

4m 7.4 (3.40) CSF £99.24 TOTE £46.60: £7.40 £1.40 (£39.20) OWNER Mr P. A. Tylor (BUCKFASTLEIGH) BRED P. A. Tylor
WEIGHT FOR AGE 4yo-3lb
Miss Foxy caused an upset and won this poor event easily. (33/1)
293 Fleet Cadet, patiently ridden, was onepaced approaching the last. (2/1)
300 Almapa looked like he failed to get the trip. (6/4)
258 Mutley (5/1: 9/2-7/1)

409 CITY OF EXETER CHALLENGE BOWL H'CAP CHASE (0-120) (5-Y.O+) (Class D)
3-30 (3-30) **2m 3f (15 fncs)** £5,275.00 GOING minus 0.75 sec per fur (F)

				SP	RR	SF
298[2]	**Henley Regatta (94)** (PRRodford) **8-11-7** SBurrough (led 8th to 10th: led after next: sn clr: fin alone)	—	1	9/4[2]	101?	10
330*	**Pond House (IRE) (97)** (MCPipe) **7-11-10** DBridgwater (led to 8th: led 10th: hdd after next: wkng & mstkes 12th & 13th: p.u after 13th)		P	1/3[1]	—	—
				(SP 105.8%)		2 Rn

4m 41.8 (1.80) TOTE £3.00 OWNER Mr E. T. Wey (MARTOCK) BRED British Thoroughbred Racing and Breeding P L C
298 Henley Regatta won for only the second time in thirty-eight attempts and is going for the Norwegian Grand National. (9/4)
330* Pond House (IRE) was rather disappointing which was not surprising as this was his third run in nineteen days. (1/3)

410 INTERLINK EXPRESS PARCELS NOVICES' HURDLE (4-Y.O+) (Class D)
4-05 (4-05) **2m 3f (9 hdls)** £2,707.80 (£760.80: £371.40) GOING minus 0.75 sec per fur (F)

				SP	RR	SF
337*	**Shahrani (109)** (MCPipe) **4-12-1** DBridgwater (led 2nd: rdn & hdd briefly 2 out: led last: styd on u.p)	—	1	1/2[1]	82	38
343[3]	**Born to Please (IRE) (87)** (PJHobbs) **4-11-3** APMcCoy (led to 2nd: chsd wnr: in tch tl led 2 out: rdn, hung lft & hdd last: rdn & no ex flat)	1¼	2	7/4[2]	69	25
	On My Toes (RGFrost) **5-10-9** JFrost (bit bkwd: chsd ldrs tl lost tch 5th)	dist	3	12/1[3]	—	—
				(SP 110.7%)		3 Rn

4m 21.5 (-4.50) CSF £1.75 TOTE £1.10 (£1.10) OWNER Mr A S Helaissi and Mr S Helaissi (WELLINGTON) BRED R. V. Young
WEIGHT FOR AGE 4yo-3lb
337* Shahrani put in a game performance under his heavy weight and notched up his fourth win in a row. (1/2)
343 Born to Please (IRE) had a real battle with the winner in the final mile but found that rival just a bit too tough. (7/4)

411 INTERLINK EXPRESS DATA NOVICES' CHASE (5-Y.O+) (Class D)
4-35 (4-35) **2m 3f (15 fncs)** £3,550.00 (£1,075.00: £525.00: £250.00) GOING minus 0.75 sec per fur (F)

				SP	RR	SF
	Dubelle (JSKing) **6-10-4**(3) JCulloty (a.p: chsd ldr 10th: led next: clr 2 out: comf)	—	1	16/1	88	17
	Bishops Castle (IRE) (82) (RGFrost) **8-10-12** JFrost (chsd ldr early: lost pl: r.o 11th: chsd ldr next: ev ch 13th: hrd rdn & one pce)	5	2	12/1	89	18
359*	**Distant Memory (98)** (PJHobbs) **7-11-5b** APMcCoy (lw: led: mstke 10th: hdd next: wknd 12th)	23	3	Evens[1]	76	5
132[10]	**Our Nikki (58)** (PRRodford) **6-10-7** SBurrough (a bhd: styd on fr 13th)	12	4	25/1	54	—
	October Brew (USA) (MCPipe) **6-10-9b**(3) DWalsh (prom: chsd ldr: ev ch 7th: rdn & wknd fr 10th: t.o)	dist	5	6/1[3]	—	—
93[F]	**Robert's Toy (IRE) (116)** (MCPipe) **5-11-8b** DBridgwater (chsd ldrs tl wknd 9th: t.o)	3½	6	7/4[2]	—	—
305[5]	**Tango's Delight (75)** (RJBaker) **8-11-5** BPowell (mid div whn fell 6th)		F	25/1	—	—
302[P]	**Liberty James** (MrsEMBrooks) **9-10-12** GUpton (a bhd: t.o & p.u bef 12th)		P	66/1	—	—
				(SP 123.4%)		8 Rn

4m 36.1 (-3.90) CSF £167.28 TOTE £25.00: £3.70 £2.80 £1.00 (£30.10) OWNER Mr W. J. Lee (SWINDON)
WEIGHT FOR AGE 5yo-3lb
Dubelle, who had sore shins last season, jumped well on this chasing debut and won this comfortably. She should win again. (16/1)
Bishops Castle (IRE) should come on for this and can pick up a race. (12/1)
359* Distant Memory was headed after a mistake at the tenth and was going backwards thereafter. (Evens)

412 INTERLINK EXPRESS FREIGHT NOVICES' H'CAP HURDLE (0-100) (4-Y.O+) (Class E)
5-05 (5-06) **2m 6f (10 hdls)** £2,232.00 (£627.00: £306.00) GOING minus 0.75 sec per fur (F)

				SP	RR	SF
297[6]	**Akiymann (USA) (81)** (MCPipe) **6-11-10b** DBridgwater (chsd ldr tl led 6th: rdn & clr 2 out: unchal)	—	1	4/7[1]	67?	—
	Embley Buoy (60) (JWMullins) **8-10-3** SCurran (bit bkwd: led tl hdd 6th: rdn & outpcd appr 2 out)	16	2	9/4[2]	34	—
	Wissywis (IRE) (65) (FJYardley) **4-10-5** BFenton (a bhd: lost tch 5th: t.o)	dist	3	7/1[3]	—	—
				(SP 106.9%)		3 Rn

5m 19.1 (9.10) CSF £2.05 TOTE £1.20 (£1.50) OWNER Martin Pipe Racing Club (WELLINGTON) BRED H. H. Aga Khan
WEIGHT FOR AGE 4yo-3lb
Akiymann (USA), despite carrying his head high, won his first race after fourteen attempts (4/7: 2/5-8/13)
Embley Buoy was outpaced approaching two out. (9/4)

T/Plpt: £167.20 (24.92 Tckts). T/Qdpt: £18.80 (11.67 Tckts) T.

HEREFORD (R-H) (Firm)
Wednesday August 21st
WEATHER: fine but cloudy

413 MUCH MARCLE CONDITIONAL H'CAP HURDLE (0-100) (4-Y.O+) (Class F)
5-40 (5-41) **2m 3f 110y (11 hdls)** £2,570.00 (£720.00: £350.00) GOING minus 0.30 sec per fur (GF)

				SP	RR	SF
337[2]	**China Mail (IRE) (90)** (KCBailey) **4-11-8** TJMurphy (lw: hdwy 5th: hit 6th: rdn appr 3 out: led appr last: drvn out)	—	1	3/1[2]	71	—

	Horse / details	Dist	Pos	SP	RR	SF
	Slippery Max (72) (RTJuckes) **12-10-7** RMassey (bit bkwd: a.p: led after 3 out: hdd appr last: one pce flat)	5	**2**	20/1	49	—
344*	**Lord Tomanico (FR) (92)** (CJMann) **4-11-10** JMagee (lw: led to 3rd: led appr 7th: hdd after 3 out: sn rdn: wknd appr last)	10	**3**	1/2[1]	61	—
	Sukaab (80) (BJMRyall) **11-11-1** TDascombe (bkwd: reminder appr 3rd: hdwy 5th: wknd appr 7th)	10	**4**	9/1[3]	41	—
391U	**Batty's Island (89)** (BPreece) **7-11-7b**(3) DFinnegan (lw: led 3rd: rdn & hdd appr 7th: wknd 8th)	16	**5**	16/1	36	—

(SP 112.3%) **5 Rn**

4m 43.9 (12.90) CSF £34.22 TOTE £3.50: £1.40 £2.80 (£12.30) OWNER The Merlin Syndicate (UPPER LAMBOURN) BRED Airlie Stud and M. J. Ryan
WEIGHT FOR AGE 4yo-3lb
337 China Mail (IRE), fitter this time, forged clear on the short run-in to win an uncompetitive race. (3/1)
Slippery Max has not won over hurdles for five years, and this was presumably a pipe-opener for a return over fences. (20/1)
344* Lord Tomanico (FR), stepping up in distance, found the ground a lot faster than at Worcester. (1/2)

414 MALVERN LINK H'CAP CHASE (0-105) (5-Y.O+) (Class F)

6-10 (6-10) **2m 3f (14 fncs)** £3,186.00 (£896.00: £438.00) GOING minus 0.30 sec per fur (GF)

	Horse / details	Dist	Pos	SP	RR	SF
352*	**Maggots Green (82)** (JMBradley) **9-10-13** 7x RJohnson (lw: led to 2nd: led 10th: clr 3 out: mstke 2 out: eased flat)	—	**1**	9/4[3]	93+	—
335[2]	**Drumstick (96)** (KCBailey) **10-11-13** JRailton (led 2nd tl appr 4th: chsd wnr after 3 out: no imp)	5	**2**	7/4[2]	103	2
361[2]	**Manamour (82)** (RLee) **9-10-13** CLlewellyn (led appr 4th: hdd 10th: 2nd & btn whn mstke 3 out: eased whn no ch appr last)	30	**3**	6/4[1]	64	—

(SP 107.1%) **3 Rn**

4m 42.6 (12.60) CSF £5.59 TOTE £2.80 (£1.90) OWNER Mr E. A. Hayward (CHEPSTOW) BRED Swettenham Stud
352* Maggots Green, despite a penalty, was 2lb better off with Drumstick than when beaten nearly six lengths at Market Rasen. (9/4)
335 Drumstick could not confirm the form of his Market Rasen win over the winner here, on 2lb worse terms. (7/4)
361 Manamour disappointed off a mark 4lb higher than when winning at Newton Abbot. (6/4)

415 HENDRE H'CAP HURDLE (0-110) (4-Y.O+) (Class E)

6-40 (6-40) **3m 2f (13 hdls)** £2,822.00 (£792.00: £386.00) GOING minus 0.30 sec per fur (GF)

	Horse / details	Dist	Pos	SP	RR	SF
317a[2]	**Glengarrif Girl (IRE) (108)** (MCPipe) **6-12-0v** DBridgwater (lw: a.p: led after 3 out: hdd last: hrd rdn to ld nr fin)	—	**1**	4/6[1]	89	4
	Fox Chapel (87) (RTJuckes) **9-10-7** MAFitzgerald (lw: hld up: lft 2nd 2 out: led last: hrd rdn: edgd rt: hdd nr fin)	½	**2**	20/1	68	—
	Storm Drum (95) (KCBailey) **7-11-1b** TJMurphy (prom: rdn appr 3 out: wknd appr 2 out)	14	**3**	7/1[3]	67	—
397*	**Wynberg (102)** (CaptTAForster) **5-11-8** 7x SWynne (led tl after 3 out: w wnr whn fell 2 out)		**F**	15/8[2]	—	—

(SP 112.0%) **4 Rn**

6m 20.6 (17.60) CSF £8.99 TOTE £1.60 (£8.60) OWNER Mr David L'Estrange (WELLINGTON) BRED Nigel and Jean Longstaff
Glengarrif Girl (IRE), a good second at Galway, was 18lb higher than when winning on her final outing last season. Continually outjumped by Wynberg, she may have been a lucky winner. (4/6)
Fox Chapel seemed set to score at the last but did not look the most willing of battlers on the short tun-in. (20/1)
397* Wynberg jumped far better than the winner and it was ironic that he was the one who hit the deck. He might well have prevailed. (15/8)

416 WORMBRIDGE NOVICES' HURDLE (4-Y.O+) (Class E)

7-10 (7-11) **2m 1f (9 hdls)** £2,276.00 (£636.00: £308.00) GOING minus 0.30 sec per fur (GF)

	Horse / details	Dist	Pos	SP	RR	SF
262*	**Chancey Fella** (HEHaynes) **5-11-5** APMcCoy (mde all: sn clr: unchal)	—	**1**	2/11[1]	70?	20
400[7]	**Galloping Guns (IRE)** (BJLlewellyn) **4-10-9** BPowell (plld hrd: chsd wnr: no imp fr 3 out)	25	**2**	8/1[2]	40?	—
156[7]	**Pats Folly** (FJYardley) **5-10-7** PMcLoughlin (plld hrd: wnt 2nd briefly 6th: wknd 3 out)	19	**3**	10/1[3]	17?	—
99[14]	**Little Derring** (MrsSMJohnson) **5-10-7** RJohnson (nt j.w: t.o. fr 4th)	dist	**4**	16/1	—	—

(SP 110.7%) **4 Rn**

3m 58.3 (5.30) CSF £2.41 TOTE £2.20 (£2.00) OWNER Mrs H. E. Haynes (SWINDON) BRED R. R. Prettie
WEIGHT FOR AGE 4yo-3lb
262* Chancey Fella had a far more simple task than at Stratford. (2/11)
Galloping Guns (IRE) (8/1: op 12/1)
Pats Folly (10/1: op 6/1)

417 ACONBURY NOVICES' H'CAP CHASE (0-100) (5-Y.O+) (Class E)

7-40 (7-41) **3m 1f 110y (19 fncs)** £3,060.00 (£860.00: £420.00) GOING minus 0.30 sec per fur (GF)

	Horse / details	Dist	Pos	SP	RR	SF
179[2]	**Cuchullains Gold (IRE) (80)** (JWhite) **8-11-9** NWilliamson (hld up: led 4 out to 3 out: led after 2 out: j.lft & lft clr last)	—	**1**	6/4[1]	92	4
330[6]	**Cardan (62)** (AGHobbs) **10-10-5** BPowell (chsd ldr: led appr 3rd tl appr 8th: led 11th to 4 out: wknd qckly: lft poor 2nd last)	dist	**2**	12/1	—	—
302[3]	**Duke of Lancaster (IRE) (85)** (MrsJPitman) **7-12-0v** RBellamy (lw: led tl appr 3rd: led appr 8th: mstke 10th: hdd 11th: wknd 12th)	1¼	**3**	5/1	—	—
	Mutual Agreement (73) (PFNicholls) **9-11-2** APMcCoy (hld up: hdwy 4 out: led 3 out tl after 2 out: fell last)		**F**	5/2[2]	—	—
72[8]	**Miss Dotty (64)** (MCPipe) **6-10-7** DBridgwater (t.o fr 4th: p.u bef 10th)		**P**	9/2[3]	—	—

(SP 111.1%) **5 Rn**

6m 26.6 (16.60) CSF £14.78 TOTE £1.90: £1.10 £3.10 (£15.60) OWNER Mr M. A. McEvoy (ASTON ROWANT)
IN-FOCUS: Injury-hit Williamson rode his first winner since October 7th.
179 Cuchullains Gold (IRE) seemed to have matters in hand when left clear at the final fence. (6/4)
Cardan did not get the trip. (12/1)
Duke of Lancaster (IRE) (5/1: 3/1-11/2)
Mutual Agreement appeared to be getting the worst of the argument when barely picking up at the last. (5/2)
Miss Dotty (9/2: 3/1-5/1)

418 BORDER STANDARD N.H. FLAT RACE (4, 5 & 6-Y.O) (Class E)

8-10 (8-12) **2m 1f** £1,315.00 (£365.00: £175.00)

				SP	RR	SF
306[2]	**Red Tel (IRE)** (MCPipe) **4-11-1** DBridgwater (hld up: hdwy on ins after 6f: led over 3f out: hrd rdn & edgd lft over 1f out: all out)	—	1	2/1[1]	—	—
133[R]	**Rare Spread (IRE)** (MCPipe) **6-11-1**(3) DWalsh (lw: hld up: hdwy 7f out: hmpd 5f out: hrd rdn & ev ch whn carried lft over 1f out: r.o)	½	2	4/1	—	—
161[3]	**Powerful Spirit** (JGMO'Shea) **4-10-10**(5) MichaelBrennan (hld up & bhd: hdwy 6f out: rdn & r.o one pce fnl 2f)	2	3	5/2[2]	—	—
306[3]	**Katharine's Song (IRE)** (DMHyde) **6-10-13** BPowell (hld up: led 5f out tl over 3f out: wknd 2f out)	10	4	20/1	—	—
	Sierra Nevada (PFNicholls) **5-11-4** APMcCoy (bit bkwd: prom tl wknd over 2f out)	1½	5	6/1	—	—
319a[17]	**Moreceva (IRE)** (PaddyFarrell) **6-11-4** WMarston (prom 12f)	1½	6	25/1	—	—
191[10]	**Commando Dancer (IRE)** (GraemeRoe) **4-10-8**(7) ShaunGraham (nvr nr ldrs)	4	7	33/1	—	—
191[3]	**Pridewood Fuggle** (RJPrice) **6-11-4** AMaguire (prom 12f)	hd	8	7/2[3]	—	—
	Abbeydoran (MrsJEHawkins) **5-10-13** MBosley (hdwy 6f out: wknd over 4f out)	1½	9	33/1	—	—
306[5]	**Late Encounter** (BJLlewellyn) **5-11-4** RJohnson (bhd fnl 6: t.o)	18	10	50/1	—	—
	Tailormade Future (BPreece) **4-10-8**(7) DFinnegan (a bhd: t.o)	9	11	33/1	—	—
	Emma's Jewel (IRE) (HMKavanagh) **5-10-6**(7) TCMurphy (plld hrd: prom tl hung lft & wknd 5f out)	2½	12	25/1	—	—
	Frizzball (IRE) (CPEBrooks) **4-10-10** DGallagher (plld hrd: led 12f: wknd qckly: t.o)	5	13	12/1	—	—
161[15]	**Overseas Invader (IRE)** (PEccles) **4-11-1** NWilliamson (a bhd: t.o fnl 8f)	dist	14	25/1	—	—
				(SP 153.2%)	**14 Rn**	

3m 49.5 CSF £13.59 TOTE £4.30: £1.40 £2.20 £1.60 (£4.20) OWNER Mr Terry Neill (WELLINGTON) BRED Roseberry Ltd
WEIGHT FOR AGE 4yo-3lb

306 Red Tel (IRE) made hard work of this, and favourite backers were then made to sweat over the deliberations in the Stewards' Room. (2/1: 5/4-5/2)
133 Rare Spread (IRE) showed no signs of being wayward this time, and it must have been a fairly close decision as to whether he got the race in the Stewards' Room. (4/1: 5/2-9/2)
161 Powerful Spirit settled better than on his debut and seems to be going the right way. (5/2)
Frizzball (IRE) (12/1: 8/1-14/1)

T/Plpt: £72.30 (64.39 Tckts). T/Qdpt: £5.50 (84.22 Tckts) KH

CARTMEL (L-H) (Good to firm, Firm patches)

Thursday August 22nd

WEATHER: rain

419 BURLINGTON SLATE AMATEUR CLAIMING HURDLE (4-Y.O+) (Class F)

5-45 (5-45) **2m 1f 110y (8 hdls)** £1,892.50 (£530.00: £257.50) GOING minus 0.18 sec per fur (G)

				SP	RR	SF
62[10]	**Bures (IRE) (118)** (MHTompkins) **5-10-12v**(7) MrRWakley (mde all: styd on flat: unchal)	—	1	5/4[1]	83+	47
264[5]	**Hacketts Cross (IRE) (100)** (PEccles) **8-10-6**(7) MrRThornton (hld up: mstke 1st: hdwy 5th: wnt 2nd last: no ch w wnr)	8	2	5/1[3]	70+	34
339[2]	**Betabetcorbett (74)** (BPJBaugh) **5-10-6b**(7) MrAWintle (chsd wnr tl wknd last)	14	3	11/2	57	21
338[4]	**Silver Sleeve (IRE) (82)** (MDHammond) **4-11-0b**(3) MrCBonner (sn bhd: rdn 5th: n.d)	4	4	11/4[2]	60	21
138[P]	**Old Mortality** (RWThomson) **10-10-8**(5) MrRHale (sn bhd: t.o 2 out)	dist	5	33/1	—	—
	Toll Booth (JWHope) **7-9-9**(7) MissPRobson (wl bhd whn p.u after 2nd)		P	33/1	—	—
				(SP 109.0%)	**6 Rn**	

4m 2.3 (1.30) CSF £7.25 TOTE £2.10: £1.50 £1.50 (£4.70) OWNER Mr John Wimbs (NEWMARKET) BRED Oliver Murphy
WEIGHT FOR AGE 4yo-3lb

Bures (IRE) was found a simple task and, having shaken off the third horse between the last two, had only to be pushed out. (5/4: 4/5-11/8)
Hacketts Cross (IRE), who would have been meeting the winner on 12lb better terms in a handicap, probably ran up to his best. (5/1)
339 Betabetcorbett, unable to dominate, called it a day between the last two. (11/2)
338 Silver Sleeve (IRE) again wore a tongue-strap and ran a stale race. (11/4)

420 NIREX H'CAP CHASE (0-115) (5-Y.O+) (Class E)

6-15 (6-15) **2m 5f 110y (14 fncs)** £3,006.65 (£909.20: £443.10: £210.05) GOING minus 0.18 sec per fur (G)

				SP	RR	SF
	Earlymorning Light (IRE) (115) (GRichards) **7-12-0** ADobbin (trckd ldr: led 4 out: clr 2 out: eased towards fin)	—	1	10/11[1]	122+	30
9[3]	**Blazing Dawn (87)** (JSHubbuck) **9-10-0** BStorey (led to 4 out: rallied run-in: no ch w wnr)	2	2	4/1[3]	93	1
138[2]	**The Toaster (97)** (JJQuinn) **9-10-10** MDwyer (lw: trckd ldrs: effrt 4 out: wnt 2nd last: no imp)	1¼	3	7/4[2]	102	10
94[P]	**Miss Enrico (91)** (MissLucindaRussell) **10-10-4**ow2 AThornton (nt j.w: blnd 2nd: outpcd & pushed along 8th: t.o 4 out)	dist	4	25/1	—	—
				(SP 112.6%)	**4 Rn**	

5m 21.6 (9.60) CSF £4.72 TOTE £1.90 (£3.10) OWNER Mrs Ann Starkie (PENRITH) BRED Mrs D. A. Whitaker
LONG HANDICAP Blazing Dawn 9-11

Earlymorning Light (IRE), who had won three of his last five outings over fences, found this simple. Three miles will not be a problem. (10/11)
9 Blazing Dawn, 3lb out of the handicap, made the running and fought back to regain second spot near the line. (4/1)
138 The Toaster, stepping up half a mile, went in pursuit of the winner four out, but was not going to get near him. (7/4)
14 Miss Enrico seems to have lost her confidence at the moment. (25/1)

421 OXLEY DEVELOPMENTS NOVICES' CHASE (5-Y.O+) (Class E)

6-45 (6-45) **3m 2f (18 fncs)** £2,520.00 (£707.20: £344.60) GOING minus 0.02 sec per fur (G)

				SP	RR	SF
283[3]	**Scrabo View (IRE)** (PBeaumont) **8-10-12** RSupple (trckd ldr: mstke 13th: led next to 3 out: led 2 out: all out)	—	1	11/10[1]	90	15

Definite Maybe (IRE) (PFNicholls) **6-10-12b^{1}** APMcCoy (trckd ldrs: drvn along 8th: reminders 12th: led 3 out: hdd next: hrd rdn: edgd lft towards fin) ... 1 **2** 6/4^{2} 89 14
Donovans Reef (68) (MrsLMarshall) **10-11-2** AThornton (bit bkwd: led to 14th: sn wknd: t.o whn ref last: wnt on) ... dist **3** 28/1 — —
Sand King (NZ) (72) (MsLCPlater) **10-10-12b** DBentley (n j.w: t.o 8th: p.u bef 13th) ... **P** 13/2^{3} — —
213^{7} **Dustys Trail (IRE)** (PBowen) **7-10-12b^{1}** RJohnson (nt j.w: sn drvn along: t.o 8th: blnd 12th & 14th: p.u bef 4 out) ... **P** 12/1 — —
(SP 112.1%) **5 Rn**

6m 40.3 (16.30) CSF £3.12 TOTE £2.00: £1.30 £1.60 (£2.00) OWNER Mr Robin Mellish (BRANDSBY) BRED Mrs D. Minnis
283 Scrabo View (IRE), who made one serious jumping error, took a bad race with nothing at all to spare. (11/10)
Definite Maybe (IRE), a tall horse, won a maiden point in the spring. Never looking happy in his work, he was driven to the front three out, but was headed by the winner at the next. Given the full treatment on the run-in, in the end he ducked in behind the winner. (6/4)
Donovans Reef set the pace but stopped quickly four out, and was well in arrears when refusing at the last. (28/1)

422 COLONY CANDLE H'CAP HURDLE (0-120) (4-Y.O+) (Class D)
7-15 (7-16) **2m 6f (11 hdls)** £2,532.80 (£710.80: £346.40) GOING minus 0.02 sec per fur (G)

SP RR SF

255^{5} **Amazon Express (94)** (PBowen) **7-11-10** RJohnson (lw: chsd ldrs: outpcd & hit 4 out: styd on fr 2 out: hrd rdn to ld last 100y) ... — **1** 5/1^{3} 77 —
Take Two (92) (MissMKMilligan) **8-11-8** ADobbin (hld up: jnd ldr 8th: sn led: hrd rdn & hdd flat) ... 1 **2** 11/4^{2} 74 —
Valiant Dash (86) (JSGoldie) **10-10-13**(3) GCahill (led tl after 4 out: rallied & rn wd after last: styd on) ... 3 **3** 11/2 66 —
3^{3} **Master Ofthe House (90)** (MDHammond) **10-11-6** RGarritty (lw: trckd ldrs: chal 3 out: rdn appr last: wknd flat) ... 1½ **4** Evens^{1} 69 —
(SP 108.7%) **4 Rn**

5m 33.2 (22.20) CSF £16.35 TOTE £5.20 (£8.40) OWNER Mr T. M. Morris (HAVERFORDWEST) BRED Ewar Stud Farms
Amazon Express staged a revival after some inept efforts, but it took all his rider's strength and skill to get him in front on the run-in. (5/1)
Take Two, fit from the Flat, raced keenly. After seeing off the challenge of the fourth, he had to give best to the winner in the closing stages. This trip seems to stretch his stamina to the very limit. (11/4: op 9/2)
Valiant Dash, absent from hurdling for a year and a half, had had a run on the Flat two weeks earlier, and looked pretty straight. Forcing the pace, he was rallying when running wide on the final bend, but would have only have finished third. (11/2)
3 Master Ofthe House challenged on the bridle three from home, but his stamina seemed to give out after jumping the last. (Evens)

423 B.N.F.L. NOVICES' H'CAP CHASE (0-100) (5-Y.O+) (Class E)
7-45 (7-45) **2m 1f 110y (12 fncs)** £3,590.00 GOING minus 0.02 sec per fur (G)

SP RR SF

Seahawk Retriever (65) (PFNicholls) **7-10-9** APMcCoy (lw: trckd ldrs: hit 6th: lft wl clr next: blnd 4 out & last) ... — **1** 7/4^{2} 72? —
Another Nick (68) (JSHubbuck) **10-10-12** BStorey (sn t.o: fell 3rd) ... **F** 25/1 — —
389* **Green's Seago (USA) (75)** (HMKavanagh) **8-11-0**(5) 7x PHenley (lw: chsd ldrs tl fell 7th) ... **F** 5/4^{1} — —
389^{2} **Exclusion (80)** (JHetherton) **7-11-10** RMarley (led tl fell 7th) ... **F** 9/2^{3} — —
4^{P} **Boethius (USA) (80)** (MABarnes) **7-11-10** PWaggott (nt j.w: sn bhd: t.o 6th: poor 2nd whn ref last) ... **R** 12/1 — —
(SP 110.5%) **5 Rn**

4m 37.4 (26.40) CSF £2.50 TOTE £2.40: £2.30 (£1.40) OWNER Mrs Robert Blackburn (SHEPTON MALLET) BRED A. F. Budge (Equine) Ltd
Seahawk Retriever, who won two points in the spring but also failed to complete on four other occasions, was left out on his own at the seventh. (7/4)
389* Green's Seago (USA) was only a couple of lengths down on the leader when he fell at the seventh. (5/4)
389 Exclusion, who raced keenly, soon showed in a clear lead, but was only about a length up when he fell at the seventh. (9/2)

424 HOSPICE OF ST MARY OF FURNESS MAIDEN HURDLE (4-Y.O+) (Class E)
8-15 (8-15) **3m 2f (12 hdls)** £2,532.80 (£710.80: £346.40) GOING minus 0.02 sec per fur (G)

SP RR SF

Good Hand (USA) (SEKettlewell) **10-11-5** RJohnson (nt j.w: trckd ldrs: led between last 2: pushed clr flat: eased towards fin) ... — **1** 8/11^{1} 67+ —
351^{P} **The Gallopin'major (IRE)** (MrsMReveley) **6-11-5b^{1}** NSmith (trckd ldrs: led 4 out tl between last 2: no ch w wnr) ... 3 **2** 100/30^{3} 65 —
Megamunch (IRE) (58) (RTJuckes) **8-11-5** WMarston (chsd ldr: ev ch 3 out: one pce fr next) ... 2 **3** 16/1 64? —
186^{7} **Fenwick's Brother** (JLEyre) **6-11-5** OPears (led to 4 out: sn wl bhd: t.o) ... dist **4** 11/4^{2} — —
(SP 113.5%) **4 Rn**

6m 36.4 (29.40) CSF £3.60 TOTE £1.80 (£3.30) OWNER Uncle Jacks Pub (MIDDLEHAM) BRED Tauner Dunlap, Jr. and Brereton C. Jones
Good Hand (USA), making his hurdling debut at an advanced stage, did not jump fluently but, when put about his business after jumping the last, soon streaked clear. (8/11)
The Gallopin'major (IRE), in blinkers for the first time, failed to finish in five previous chases. Taking it up once the race began four out, he proved no match. (100/30)
Megamunch (IRE), an Irish point-to-point winner, is painfully slow. (16/1)
Fenwick's Brother, who ran badly last time, led on sufferance here. Once collared, he dropped away. (11/4)

T/Plpt: £115.40 (56.63 Tckts). T/Qdpt: £29.40 (15.89 Tckts). WG

425a-449a (Irish Racing) - See Computer Raceform

0419-CARTMEL (L-H) (Good to firm, Firm patches becoming Good to firm)
Saturday August 24th
WEATHER: heavy showers

450 BOOKMAKER & PUNTER NOVICES' HURDLE (4-Y.O+) (Class E)
2-25 (2-26) **2m 6f (13 hdls)** £2,232.50 (£620.00: £297.50) GOING: 0.08 sec per fur (G)

SP RR SF

Red Spectacle (IRE) (PCHaslam) **4-10-9** MFoster (lw: mde all: clr 2 out: drvn out) ... — **1** 3/1^{2} 58 10

				SP	RR	SF
	Commander Glen (IRE) (MDHammond) **4-10-9** RGarritty (hld up & bhd: stdy hdwy 5th: styd on fr 3 out: 4l 2nd & rdn whn blnd last)	8	**2**	11/1	52	4
	What's Secreto (USA) (HAlexander) **4-10-9** AMaguire (sn outpcd: rdn 5th: n.d)	dist	**3**	13/2[3]	—	—
218[U]	**Bowland Park** (EJAlston) **5-10-7** JCulloty (trckd ldrs tl wknd 6th: t.o 3 out)	2	**4**	25/1	—	—
354*	**Longcroft** (SEKettlewell) **4-10-11** RJohnson (trckd wnr: hit 6th: rdn 3 out: sn wknd: virtually p.u flat)	dist	**5**	8/11[1]	—	—
	Boyo (IRE) (TDEasterby) **5-10-12** LWyer (bit bkwd: nt j.w: sn bhd: pushed along 3rd: t.o 4 out: p.u bef 2 out)		**P**	9/1	—	—
				(SP 118.4%)		**6 Rn**

5m 26.9 (15.90) CSF £29.44 TOTE £4.70: £1.60 £3.90 (£25.80) OWNER Mr David Morgan (MIDDLEHAM) BRED J. Beckett
WEIGHT FOR AGE 4yo-3lb

Red Spectacle (IRE), who carried plenty of condition, set out to make his stamina tell, and he looked to be holding the upper hand when left clear at the final flight. (3/1)

Commander Glen (IRE), rather in and out on the Flat, won over seven furlongs at Carlisle this summer. Ridden to get the trip, he was staying on but flat out when he fell through the last. He would not have beaten the winner anyway. (11/1: op 7/1)

What's Secreto (USA), who looked as if the outing would do him good, was under pressure before halfway and soon lost touch. (13/2)

354* Longcroft, who won a poor race at Southwell, suddenly came under pressure three from home. Her stamina gave out completely and she was pulled up almost to a walk. (8/11: op 11/10)

451 LINDALE INN STEAKS CONDITIONAL (S) H'CAP HURDLE (0-90) (4-Y.O+) (Class G)

2-55 (2-55) **2m 6f (11 hdls)** £2,206.00 (£616.00: £298.00) GOING: 0.08 sec per fur (G)

				SP	RR	SF
	Huso (86) (PCHaslam) **8-11-7**(3) STaylor (bit bkwd: trckd ldrs: led 2 out: jst hld on)	—	**1**	2/1[2]	68	—
345*	**Rampant Rosie (IRE) (76)** (GRichards) **8-11-0v** GCahill (led to 6th: led 3 out to next: ev ch run in: hrd rdn & hung lft: jst failed)	s.h	**2**	10/11[1]	58	—
	Tony's Feelings (64) (MissLucindaRussell) **8-10-2** RMcGrath (plld hrd: trckd ldrs: led 6th to 3 out: wknd qckly next: t.o)	dist	**3**	6/1[3]	—	—
335[4]	**Truss (80)** (JohnUpson) **9-11-4b** DParker (plld hrd: trckd ldrs: rdn & lost pl after 4 out: sn bhd: t.o)	dist	**4**	8/1	—	—
				(SP 111.1%)		**4 Rn**

5m 39.7 (28.70) CSF £4.19 TOTE £3.20: (£1.90) OWNER Mrs C. Barclay (MIDDLEHAM) BRED Sheikh Mohammed bin Rashid al Maktoum
Bt in 4,200 gns

Huso, who has had a history of leg trouble and has been lightly-raced over the last three years, looked very much on the burly side. After a desperate battle, he just scraped home. (2/1)

345* Rampant Rosie (IRE), raised 6lb, hung into the winner on the run-in and, in the end, was just shaded. (10/11: 4/5-Evens)

Tony's Feelings, who wore a crossed-noseband, refused to settle and had run himself to a standstill by the penultimate flight. (6/1)

335 Truss (8/1: op 5/1)

452 CARLING PREMIER H'CAP CHASE (0-120) (5-Y.O+) (Class D)

3-30 (3-30) **3m 2f (18 fncs)** £3,457.00 (£1,036.00: £498.00: £229.00) GOING: 0.08 sec per fur (G)

				SP	RR	SF
14*	**Royal Vacation (100)** (GMMoore) **7-10-8** JCallaghan (lw: trckd ldrs: led 10th: hit 2 out: drew clr after last: eased towards fin)	—	**1**	5/4[1]	113+	47
395[4]	**The Blue Boy (IRE) (100)** (PBowen) **8-10-8b** RJohnson (racd wd: sn drvn along: rdn 12th: hdwy 5 out: chal 2 out: hit last: one pce)	15	**2**	13/2	104	38
342*	**Hillwalk (120)** (RCurtis) **10-12-0** DMorris (trckd ldrs: rdn & one pce fr 2 out)	6	**3**	5/2[2]	120	54
	Kushbaloo (115) (CParker) **11-11-9** BStorey (led 3rd to 7th: hit 8th & 9th: lost pl 11th: sme hdwy 2 out: n.d)	6	**4**	4/1[3]	111	45
94[3]	**Upwell (92)** (RJohnson) **12-10-0** KJohnson (led to 3rd: led 7th to 10th: rdn 12th: wknd 14th)	22	**5**	25/1	75	9
				(SP 110.2%)		**5 Rn**

6m 29.3 (5.30) CSF £8.58 TOTE £2.40: £1.20 £2.60 (£5.50) OWNER Mr G. P. Edwards (MIDDLEHAM) BRED Small Breeders' Group
LONG HANDICAP Upwell 8-6

OFFICIAL EXPLANATION **Kushbaloo: the rider reported that his orders were to lie handy and see how the race unfolded. He added that the gelding had not run for ten months, had had a shoulder injury in the past, and had got very tired on the final circuit.**

14* Royal Vacation, fit from the Flat, survived his one mistake two out. He needs fast ground and should win again. (5/4)

256 The Blue Boy (IRE), an enigma, was given a tremendous ride. Pulled wide and never on the bridle, his rider got him to challenge two out. A mistake at the last knocked him back to third, but he would not be denied and, with his jockey keeping right at him, he took second place in the closing stages. (13/2: op 4/1)

342* Hillwalk, raised 3lb, is probably in the grip of the Handicapper now. (5/2)

Kushbaloo looked pretty straight on his first outing for ten months. Unable to dominate, his jumping suffered. Dropping back to a mile from home, he ran on nicely over the last two and can be expected to do better next time. (4/1)

453 SUNLIGHT SERVICES H'CAP HURDLE (0-120) (4-Y.O+) (Class D)

4-05 (4-05) **2m 1f 110y (8 hdls)** £2,805.00 (£780.00: £375.00) GOING: 0.08 sec per fur (G)

				SP	RR	SF
21[P]	**Have a Nightcap (95)** (NPLittmoden) **7-10-9b** PNiven (w ldr: led 4th: styd on wl fr last)	—	**1**	5/1[3]	67	33
75[5]	**Ham N'Eggs (107)** (MDHammond) **5-11-7** RGarritty (lw: effrt 5th: chsd wnr between last 2: no imp)	1½	**2**	6/4[1]	78	44
	Zajira (IRE) (113) (PEccles) **6-11-13** AMaguire (led to 4th: rdn & lost pl 3 out)	20	**3**	5/2[2]	65	31
	Latin Leader (86) (CParker) **6-9-11b**(3) DParker (trckd ldrs: ev ch 3 out: wknd appr last)	7	**4**	11/2	32	—
211[7]	**Flintlock (IRE) (86)** (HAlexander) **6-9-9**(5) RMcGrath (mstke 2nd: sn rdn: bhd fr 5th)	15	**5**	10/1	18	—
	Tashreef (86) (JJBirkett) **6-10-0b** MMoloney (sn chsng ldrs: wknd 3 out)	3	**6**	20/1	16	—
				(SP 114.5%)		**6 Rn**

4m 7.9 (6.90) CSF £12.83 TOTE £5.70: £2.60 £1.30 (£4.60) OWNER Mrs G. A. Jennings (WOLVERHAMPTON) BRED Bruce Hobbs
LONG HANDICAP Flintlock (IRE) 9-9 Tashreef 9-8

Have a Nightcap, who has form on the Flat, over hurdles and over fences, is certainly versatile. A bit of a character, he seems to be at his best racing round the bends here. (5/1)

75 Ham N'Eggs was not as fluent as usual. Driven along in pursuit of the winner between the last two, he was never going to get in a blow. A more orthodox track should suit him better. (6/4)

Zajira (IRE), who looked very fit, is probably better on a right-handed track these days. (5/2: op 6/4)

Latin Leader, in blinkers for the first time, landed upsides three out, but called it a day going to the last. (11/2)

454 GRANT THORNTON NOVICES' CHASE (5-Y.O+) (Class E)
4-40 (4-41) **2m 1f 110y (12 fncs)** £3,437.00 (£833.00) GOING: 0.26 sec per fur (GS)

				SP	RR	SF
4[4]	**Reve de Valse (USA) (80)** (RJohnson) **9-10-12** KJohnson (led to last: styd on u.p to ld over 1f out: drew clr)	—	1	2/5 [1]	86	—
333[P]	**Signe de Mars (FR)** (MissZAGreen) **5-10-9** RFarrant (trckd wnr: led last: sn rdn & hdd: nt qckn)	11	2	8/1 [3]	76	—
423[F]	**Another Nick (68)** (JSHubbuck) **10-10-12** BStorey (blnd 4th: sn bhd: sme hdwy whn j.slowly 7th: t.o whn fell 4 out)		F	7/2 [2]	—	—
				(SP 104.8%)		**3 Rn**

4m 33.3 (22.30) CSF £3.00 TOTE £1.30 (£1.80) OWNER Mr Robert Johnson (NEWCASTLE-UPON-TYNE) BRED Delta Thoroughbreds, Inc.
WEIGHT FOR AGE 5yo-3lb
4 Reve de Valse (USA), who wore a tongue-strap, rallied under pressure and, in the end, won going right away. (2/5: op 1/4)
333 Signe de Mars (FR) ran easily his best race since coming here from France. (8/1)

455 RACING CHANNEL SATURDAY SERVICE NOVICES' HURDLE (4-Y.O+) (Class E)
5-10 (5-11) **2m 1f 110y (8 hdls)** £2,337.50 (£650.00: £312.50) GOING: 0.26 sec per fur (GS)

				SP	RR	SF
	Tempted (IRE) (JCHaynes) **8-10-4**(3) DParker (trckd ldr: led 4th: mstke last: styd on)	—	1	33/1	59	—
348[2]	**Lancer (USA) (85)** (RTJuckes) **4-11-2** MAFitzgerald (hld up: stdy hdwy 3 out: rdn & nt qckn flat)	3	2	7/2 [3]	68	1
293*	**Field of Vision (IRE)** (MrsASwinbank) **6-11-2**(3) JSupple (chsd ldrs: rdn 3 out: outpcd between last 2: kpt on)	¾	3	8/11 [1]	68	4
353*	**Glenvally** (BWMurray) **5-11-0** AMaguire (blnd 1st: chsd ldrs 4th tl wknd between last 2)	14	4	3/1 [2]	50	—
	Haughton Lad (IRE) (70) (FPMurtagh) **7-10-12** ADobbin (nt j.w: a in rr)	9	5	25/1	40	—
	Pattern Arms (DMoffatt) **4-10-9** DJMoffatt (hld up: hdwy to chse ldrs 5th: wknd between last 2)	5	6	16/1	35	—
	Jarvey (IRE) (70) (PEccles) **4-10-4**(5) DJKavanagh (led to 4th: wknd qckly next: t.o 3 out)	dist	7	33/1	—	—
				(SP 120.7%)		**7 Rn**

4m 19.8 (18.80) CSF £140.23 TOTE £22.10: £3.80 £2.00 (£61.80) OWNER Mr J. C. Haynes (LEVENS) BRED T. G. Curtin
WEIGHT FOR AGE 4yo-3lb
Tempted (IRE), who is not very big, overcame an absence of 1,379 days. A winner of a bumper and a maiden Flat race in Ireland, she raced keenly but her jumping was not 100%. Surviving a mistake at the last, she was never going to be overhauled. (33/1)
348 Lancer (USA) travelled smoothly as usual but, when the race began in earnest, he was half-hearted. (7/2)
293* Field of Vision (IRE), flat out three from home, struggled to keep up. Staying on at the finish, the rain-softened ground might have been against him. (8/11)
353* Glenvally, who almost went at the first, stopped in two strides between the last two. (3/1: 9/4-7/2)
Pattern Arms, bred for speed, looked very fit. He dropped right away between the last two and stamina could be a problem. (16/1)

T/Plpt: £340.10 (20.01 Tckts). T/Qdpt: £12.20 (21.23 Tckts). WG

0413-HEREFORD (R-H) (Good to firm, Good patches)
Saturday August 24th
WEATHER: overcast, showers

456 TARRINGTON AMATEUR H'CAP HURDLE (0-120) (4-Y.O+) (Class E)
5-30 (5-30) **2m 1f (9 hdls)** £2,206.00 (£616.00: £298.00) GOING minus 0.22 sec per fur (G)

				SP	RR	SF
348*	**Royal Thimble (IRE) (101)** (NoelChance) **5-10-12**(7) MrEJames (lw: trckd ldrs: chal & mstke 3 out: hit next: led appr last: drvn clr)	—	1	15/8 [1]	83	34
357[3]	**Air Command (BAR) (82)** (CTNash) **6-9-7**(7) MrPPhillips (led 3rd: mstke & hdd 6th: slt ld 3 out tl after next: rdn & one pce appr last)	3½	2	14/1	61	12
	Amlah (USA) (113) (PJHobbs) **4-11-7**(7) MrJCreighton (bit bkwd: a.p: jnd ldr 5th: led next to 3 out: led after 2 out tl appr last: one pce)	1	3	2/1 [2]	91	39
399[2]	**Sirtelimar (IRE) (92)** (KCBailey) **7-10-3**(7) MrRWakley (lw: hld up: hdwy 6th: rdn & wknd after 2 out)	16	4	9/4 [3]	55	6
339[6]	**Al Skeet (USA) (82)** (RJPrice) **10-9-7**(7) MissEJJones (bkwd: trckd ldrs tl wknd appr 6th: sn t.o)	9	5	33/1	36	—
	Pocono Knight (82) (CHJones) **6-9-7**(7) MissBSmall (bkwd: s.s: a bhd: t.o fr 6th)	8	6	33/1	29	—
	Final Ace (82) (MrsAPrice) **9-9-7**(7) MrRThornton (bkwd: led tl j.lft & hdd 3rd: sn wknd & t.o: p.u bef 2 out)		P	66/1	—	—
				(SP 112.9%)		**7 Rn**

3m 56.4 (3.40) CSF £23.27 CT £51.56 TOTE £3.60: £2.40 £2.10 (£14.40) OWNER Mrs M. Chance (LAMBOURN) BRED Somerville Stud
LONG HANDICAP Air Command (BAR) 8-0 Al Skeet (USA) 8-0 Pocono Knight 8-11 Final Ace 8-12
WEIGHT FOR AGE 4yo-3lb
348* Royal Thimble (IRE) did not hurdle fluently, but proved too smart for these rivals and won going away. (15/8)
Air Command (BAR) helped share the lead and remained in the thick of the action until getting outpaced on the run to the last. (14/1: 20/1-12/1)
Amlah (USA), just needing this first outing in two months, only got shaken up approaching the last and should not be long in making amends. (2/1)

457 WHITECROSS (S) H'CAP CHASE (0-95) (5-Y.O+) (Class G)
6-00 (6-00) **2m 3f (14 fncs)** £2,864.00 (£804.00: £392.00) GOING minus 0.22 sec per fur (G)

				SP	RR	SF
297[4]	**Miners Rest (66)** (PJHobbs) **8-10-0** APMcCoy (lw: led to 2nd: lft clr 7th: unchal)	—	1	11/4 [1]	76	—
361[4]	**Fenwick (88)** (RJHodges) **9-11-5**(3) TDascombe (hdwy 4th: lft 2nd 7th: no imp fr 3 out)	8	2	9/2 [2]	91	—
361[5]	**Gabish (66)** (BScriven) **11-9-7**(7) MrRThornton (in tch: hdwy 10th: rdn & wknd 3 out)	8	3	20/1	63	—
328[3]	**Nuclear Express (72)** (JMBradley) **9-10-6** BFenton (lw: hld up: hdwy 10th: nt rch ldrs)	3½	4	12/1	66	—
349[5]	**Astounded (73)** (DJWintle) **9-10-4**(3) DWalsh (lw: hdwy 4th: rdn & wknd 10th: no ch whn fell 3 out)		F	16/1	—	—
395[5]	**Boxing Match (73)** (JMBradley) **9-10-7** NWilliamson (led 3rd tl fell 7th)		F	9/2 [2]	—	—
328[2]	**Afaltoun (70)** (RLee) **11-9-13**(5) PHenley (bit bkwd: led 2nd to 3rd: wknd 8th: t.o: p.u bef 2 out)		P	5/1 [3]	—	—
335[3]	**Wake Up Luv (86)** (KGWingrove) **11-11-6** GBradley (mstke 1st: sn bhd: t.o whn p.u bef 2 out)		P	9/2 [2]	—	—

				SP	RR	SF
222^{2}	**Sydney Barry (NZ) (90)** (RHBuckler) **11-11-10** BPowell (lw: hld up & bhd: hit 10th: t.o whn p.u bef 2 out)		P	5/1^{3}	—	—
				(SP 132.9%)		**9 Rn**

4m 49.8 (19.80) CSF £17.35 CT £208.52 TOTE £3.00: £1.90 £1.90 £9.80 (£12.00) Trio £134.00; £86.85 to 26/8/96 OWNER Mr P. J. Hobbs (MINEHEAD) BRED B. B. Akerman
LONG HANDICAP Gabish 9-5 Miners Rest 9-13
No bid
286 Miners Rest only needed to put in a clear round to score here on this step down to selling company, and she would have trouble in finding another race as moderate as this. (11/4)
Fenwick still needed this run to put an edge on him and he was unable to get close enough to cause concern (9/2: op 3/1)

458 YARSOP HURDLE (3-Y.O) (Class E)
6-30 (6-30) **2m 1f (9 hdls)** £2,444.00 (£684.00: £332.00) GOING minus 0.22 sec per fur (G)

				SP	RR	SF
	Chief Mouse (MissHCKnight) **3-10-12** JFTitley (bit bkwd: led tl after 1st: led 6th: drvn clr appr last)	—	1	4/5^{1}	67	—
	Royal Rapport (JGMO'Shea) **3-10-7**(5) MichaelBrennan (hld up & bhd: hdwy 6th: one pce appr last)	3½	2	10/1^{3}	64	—
	Andsome Boy (CRBarwell) **3-10-12** BClifford (trckd ldrs: ev ch whn mstke 2 out: sn outpcd)	3½	3	10/1^{3}	60	—
388^{*}	**Balmoral Princess** (JHPeacock) **3-11-0b** RBellamy (led after 1st: j.slowly 4th: hdd 6th: ev ch whn hit 2 out: sn wknd: t.o)	11	4	9/4^{2}	52	—
	My Beautiful Dream (ADSmith) **3-10-9**ow2 FJousset (bkwd: prom tl j.slowly & lost tch 5th: sn wl bhd: t.o)	dist	5	20/1	—	—
	Copper Diamond (DBurchell) **3-10-7** DJBurchell (bkwd: sn wl bhd: t.o whn p.u bef 5th)		P	11/1	—	—
				(SP 117.6%)		**6 Rn**

4m 5.0 (12.00) CSF £9.25 TOTE £1.50: £1.70 £1.80 (£12.20) OWNER Lady Vestey (WANTAGE) BRED Lady Vestey
Chief Mouse, sure to strip fitter for this first run in over three months, certainly knew his job on this hurdling introduction, but he did not beat much and the form should not be overrated. (4/5)
Royal Rapport, a maiden sprinter on the Flat, ran promisingly on his first attempt at hurdling, and he should be able to improve with this experience under his belt. (10/1)
Andsome Boy showed more on his debut over hurdles than he had on the Flat and, had he not landed awkwardly when challenging for the lead at the penultimate flight, he may well have gained the runner-up prize. (10/1)
388* Balmoral Princess, the only one with previous experience, pressed the leaders and was still in with every chance when she got unsighted at the second last, and quickly lost her pitch. (9/4)

459 BBC HEREFORD & WORCESTER H'CAP HURDLE (0-125) (4-Y.O+) (Class D)
7-00 (7-00) **2m 3f 110y (11 hdls)** £2,864.00 (£804.00: £392.00) GOING minus 0.22 sec per fur (G)

				SP	RR	SF
341^{7}	**Faustino (111)** (PJHobbs) **4-12-0** APMcCoy (lw: chsd ldr: led on bit appr 2 out: v.easily)	—	1	11/10^{2}	94?	—
	La Menorquina (USA) (102) (DMarks) **6-11-8** JAMcCarthy (lw: led tl appr 2 out: sn rdn: no ch w wnr)	5	2	8/11^{1}	81	—
	Mabthul (USA) (80) (HJManners) **8-10-0** SCurran (bkwd: rel to r: tried to ref 1st: a t.o)	dist	3	20/1^{3}	—	—
				(SP 110.3%)		**3 Rn**

4m 49.1 (18.10) CSF £2.24 TOTE £1.90: (£1.10) OWNER The Bilbrook '4' (MINEHEAD) BRED D.J. and Mrs Deer
LONG HANDICAP Mabthul (USA) 8-8
WEIGHT FOR AGE 4yo-3lb
341 Faustino was always cantering and pulling double as long as he had a lead, but he did not find a lot when shown the front, and he had to be shaken up to make sure on the run-in. (11/10)
La Menorquina (USA), forced to make her own running, was always a sitting duck and the winner picked her off without much difficulty. (8/11)

460 HOLE IN THE WALL NOVICES' CHASE (5-Y.O+) (Class E)
7-30 (7-34) **3m 1f 110y (19 fncs)** £3,035.00 (£920.00: £450.00: £215.00) GOING minus 0.22 sec per fur (G)

				SP	RR	SF
405^{*}	**Wakt (87)** (JWhite) **6-11-7** APMcCoy (lw: led after 4th: sn clr: shkn up 3 out: styd on strly)	—	1	4/6^{1}	96	—
302^{U}	**Tour Leader (NZ) (84)** (RHBuckler) **7-10-12** BPowell (hld up: hdwy to chse wnr 8th: hrd rdn appr last: kpt on)	1½	2	5/2^{2}	86	—
359^{3}	**Hizal (72)** (HJManners) **7-11-5** MrACharles-Jones (hld up: lost tch 10th: wnt poor 3rd 3 out)	dist	3	7/1	—	—
257^{6}	**Storm Warrior (72)** (TWall) **11-10-9b**(3) RMassey (lw: chsd wnr 6th to 8th: poor 3rd fr 10th tl wknd 4 out)	dist	4	40/1	—	—
102^{P}	**Music Score (82)** (MrsLCTaylor) **10-10-12** AThornton (bit bkwd: led: iron broke 1st: hdd after 4th: t.o fr 10th: p.u bef 15th)		P	16/1	—	—
	Lord Antrim (IRE) (MBradstock) **7-10-12** PHolley (bkwd: unruly: rel to r: nt j.w: t.o whn p.u bef 9th)		P	4/1^{3}	—	—
				(SP 129.4%)		**6 Rn**

6m 33.3 (23.30) CSF £3.54 TOTE £1.50: £1.20 £1.30 (£3.80) OWNER Mr John White (ASTON ROWANT) BRED Shadwell Estate Company Limited
405* Wakt, winning for the second time this week, is on a roll at present, but she did have to work in the closing stages to complete her hat-trick. (4/6)
220 Tour Leader (NZ), given time to get his jumping together, delivered a determined challenge into the last, but the winner had kept a bit in reserve and was always holding him. (5/2)
290* Hizal (7/1: 5/1-8/1)
Music Score, whose jockey had the misfortune to break an iron when he landed in front over the first, had little option but to kick his other foot out. Remaining with the pace for almost a circuit, he then began to drop away, and was tailed off when pulled up in the country. (16/1)
Lord Antrim (IRE) (4/1: op 9/4)

461 ABERGAVENNY NOVICES' H'CAP HURDLE (0-95) (4-Y.O+) (Class F)
8-00 (8-02) **2m 1f (9 hdls)** £2,108.00 (£588.00: £284.00) GOING minus 0.22 sec per fur (G)

				SP	RR	SF
393^{*}	**Raven's Roost (IRE) (59)** (GEJones) **5-10-4** PMcLoughlin (lw: trckd ldrs: led appr 2 out: qcknd clr appr last)	—	1	3/1^{2}	50+	12
360^{5}	**Mr Poppleton (61)** (RBrotherton) **7-10-6** LHarvey (a.p: ev ch appr 2 out: sn outpcd)	10	2	9/2^{3}	43	5
259^{4}	**King of Babylon (IRE) (71)** (FJordan) **4-10-8**(5) LAspell (lw: hld up: hdwy 6th: kpt on u.p appr last)	5	3	8/1	48	7
339^{*}	**Tony's Mist (79)** (JMBradley) **6-11-10** RJohnson (trckd ldrs: hrd rdn & ev ch 2 out: sn outpcd)	4	4	9/4^{1}	52	14
341^{5}	**Dickies Girl (65)** (NMBabbage) **6-10-10** TJMurphy (led 2nd tl rdn & hdd appr 2 out: sn btn)	1½	5	10/1	37	—
343^{5}	**Court Jester (71)** (MJRyan) **5-11-2** DGallagher (led: pckd 1st: sn hdd & lost pl: rdn 3 out: n.d)	10	6	9/1	33	—
396^{6}	**Athenian Alliance (55)** (JMBradley) **7-9-11**(3) GuyLewis (bkwd: prom tl wknd 5th: t.o)	dist	7	33/1	—	—

				SP	RR	SF
	Paliapour (IRE) (62) (DJWintle) **5-10-7** WMarston (t: bkwd: in tch tl wknd appr 6th: t.o)	23	**8**	9/2[3]	—	—
				(SP 125.3%)		**8 Rn**

3m 58.4 (5.40) CSF £17.62 CT £94.48 TOTE £4.70: £1.40 £1.30 £1.70 OWNER Mr Elwyn Jones (LAMPETER) BRED Mrs G. Lanzara
WEIGHT FOR AGE 4yo-3lb

393* Raven's Roost (IRE) had less to beat than he did at Bangor, and he pulverised this opposition to win very easily indeed. (3/1: op 7/4)
Mr Poppleton, taking a big step down in distance, ran well all the way and there could be a small race to be won. (9/2)
212 King of Babylon (IRE) has only been competing in sellers, but he did not shape too badly here and seems to be getting the hang of the game. (8/1: 6/1-9/1)
339* Tony's Mist, forced to concede weight all round, had much more on his plate here, and he was at the end of his tether soon after negotiating the penultimate hurdle. (9/4)

T/Plpt: £52.20 (111.87 Tckts). T/Qdpt: £9.20 (46.94 Tckts). IM

0450-CARTMEL (L-H) (Good, Soft patches)
Monday August 26th
WEATHER: overcast

462 BBC RADIO CUMBRIA HURDLE (3-Y.O) (Class E)
2-00 (2-00) **2m 1f 110y (8 hdls)** £2,215.00 (£615.00: £295.00) GOING: 0.36 sec per fur (GS)

				SP	RR	SF
	Prelude To Fame (USA) (MissMKMilligan) **3-10-10** ADobbin (a.p: led after 5th: rdn clr flat)	—	**1**	7/1	71	20
	Go-Go-Power-Ranger (BEllison) **3-10-7**(3) GCahill (prom: chsd wnr fr 3 out: hrd rdn appr last: wknd flat)	8	**2**	9/4[2]	64	13
	Manoy (JHetherton) **3-10-10** RMarley (swtg: hld up: hdwy appr 5th: rdn 2 out: btn whn mstke last)	8	**3**	9/1	56	5
	Down The Yard (MCChapman) **3-10-5** WWorthington (hld up: hdwy 5th: nt fluent 6th: wknd appr 2 out)	6	**4**	6/1[3]	46	—
	Russian Rascal (IRE) (TDEasterby) **3-10-10** LWyer (hld up pllng hrd: hdwy appr 5th: sn pushed along: rdn and btn 2 out: t.o)	12	**5**	2/1[1]	40	—
388[3]	**Recall To Mind** (MESowersby) **3-10-7b**(3) DParker (led tl after 5th: sn wknd: t.o)	13	**6**	10/1	28	—
	Village Opera (GMMoore) **3-10-5** NBentley (chsd ldr to 3rd: dropped rr 5th: t.o)	17	**7**	25/1	8	—
				(SP 113.8%)		**7 Rn**

4m 16.1 (15.10) CSF £22.21 TOTE £9.80: £3.70 £2.00 (£19.80) OWNER Jumbo Racing Club (LEYBURN) BRED T. L. Folkerth

Prelude To Fame (USA) was off the mark at the first time of asking over hurdles and the way in which he saw this race out should stand him in good stead. (7/1)
Go-Go-Power-Ranger, a mile and half winner on the Flat, threw down his challenge at the second last, but found the winner too strong on this long run-in. (9/4)
Manoy, under pressure when close enough at the second last, had already been put in his place when making a hash of the final flight. (9/1)
Russian Rascal (IRE) refused to settle in the early stages and was a spent force some way out. (2/1)

463 HAMPSFELL (S) H'CAP HURDLE (0-90) (4-Y.O+) (Class G)
2-35 (2-35) **2m 1f 110y (8 hdls)** £2,278.20 (£635.20: £306.60) GOING: 0.36 sec per fur (GS)

				SP	RR	SF
	Steadfast Elite (IRE) (86) (JJO'Neill) **5-11-10** ARoche (hld up: stdy hdwy 5th: trckd ldrs gng wl: led last: r.o u.p)	—	**1**	4/1[3]	68	33
	Clover Girl (70) (BEllison) **5-10-5v**(3) GCahill (hld up: hdwy appr 6th: drvn 2 out: ev ch last: one pce flat)	6	**2**	9/4[1]	47	12
	Red March Hare (69) (DMoffatt) **5-10-7** DJMoffatt (bit bkwd: hld up: hdwy 4th: led appr 2 out: rdn & hdd last: wknd flat)	4	**3**	7/2[2]	42	7
5[P]	**On The Move (73)** (JJBirkett) **5-10-11** LO'Hara (prom tl outpcd fr 6th: t.o)	28	**4**	16/1	20	—
138[5]	**Ruppies (82)** (MCChapman) **9-11-6** WWorthington (bit bkwd: a bhd: t.o)	18	**5**	8/1	13	—
	Criminal Record (USA) (68) (PBradley) **6-10-6** RJohnson (w ldr tl led 4th: hdd appr 2 out: sn rdn & wknd: t.o)	7	**6**	10/1	—	—
419[5]	**Old Mortality (67)** (RWThomson) **10-10-5** BStorey (bit bkwd: led to 4th: rdn & wknd qckly fr next: t.o)	13	**7**	25/1	—	—
	See You Always (IRE) (69) (MABarnes) **6-10-7**ow7 PWaggott (bit bkwd: chsd ldrs: reminders 4th: sn btn: t.o)	8	**8**	12/1	—	—
354[4]	**Skiplam Wood (62)** (SGChadwick) **10-10-0** KJohnson (bit bkwd: bhd fr 4th: t.o)	12	**9**	25/1	—	—
				(SP 114.5%)		**9 Rn**

4m 16.2 (15.20) CSF £12.72 CT £29.88 TOTE £4.60: £1.70 £1.30 £1.20 (£4.60) OWNER Clayton Bigley Partnership Ltd (PENRITH) BRED Cecil Harris Bloodstock Ltd
LONG HANDICAP Skiplam Wood 9-5
No bid

Steadfast Elite (IRE), given a confident ride, was able to do everything as she wanted, and just had to be kept up to her work in the final 100 yards. (4/1)
Clover Girl looked really well in herself and it was only on the long run-in that she was shaken off. (9/4: op 9/2)
Red March Hare travelled well throughout the race, but lack of condition found her out in the closing stages. (7/2)

464 JOHN CALVERT DEB'S BALL H'CAP CHASE (0-130) (5-Y.O+) (Class C)
3-10 (3-11) **2m 1f 110y (12 fncs)** £4,419.00 (£1,332.00: £646.00: £303.00) GOING: 0.36 sec per fur (GS)

				SP	RR	SF
398*	**Stately Home (IRE) (113)** (PBowen) **5-10-13** RJohnson (lw: chsd ldr: mstke 2nd: led 4th: clr last: eased flat)	—	**1**	7/4[1]	123+	36
	Beaucadeau (105) (MABarnes) **10-10-8** PWaggott (bit bkwd: a.p: hit 5th: chsd wnr fr 7th: rdn & outpcd appr last)	8	**2**	4/1[2]	108	24
420[2]	**Blazing Dawn (97)** (JSHubbuck) **9-10-0** BStorey (led tl mstke & hdd 4th: wknd 8th)	1¼	**3**	9/2[3]	99	15
321a[3]	**Who's to Say (122)** (MissVenetiaWilliams) **10-11-11** NWilliamson (j.slowly 2nd: bhd tl hdwy 6th: mstke 7th: sn lost tch: t.o)	dist	**4**	7/4[1]	—	—
				(SP 110.9%)		**4 Rn**

4m 23.3 (12.30) CSF £7.93 TOTE £2.50 (£4.40) OWNER Mr P. Bowen (HAVERFORDWEST) BRED Ash Hill Stud
LONG HANDICAP Blazing Dawn 9-1
WEIGHT FOR AGE 5yo-3lb

398* Stately Home (IRE), notching his sixth win in just over six weeks, won this most emphatically. (7/4)
Beaucadeau found the progressive winner much too good on these terms. Sure to come on for the run, he is well handicapped at present. (4/1)
420 Blazing Dawn had a stiff task from 13lb out of the handicap. (9/2: 6/1-4/1)
Who's to Say had just tagged onto the others when he made a mess of the seventh, and that was the end of him. (7/4)

465 TOTE CREDIT H'CAP HURDLE (0-100) (4-Y.O+) (Class F)

3-45 (3-46) **3m 2f (12 hdls)** £2,238.00 (£618.00: £294.00) GOING: 0.36 sec per fur (GS)

				SP	RR	SF
422*	**Amazon Express (101)** (PBowen) **7-12-7** ^{7x} RJohnson (hld up: hdwy appr 9th: led appr 2 out: rdn clr flat: eased nr fin)	—	1	6/1	77	36
	Record Lover (IRE) (74) (MCChapman) **6-10-8** WWorthington (hld up & bhd: hdwy to chse ldrs fr 6th: rdn to chse wnr 3 out: one pce)	10	2	4/1^{3}	44	3
	Ballindoo (84) (RJArmson) **7-11-4** MrRArmson (lw: hld up: hdwy appr 9th: rdn & kpt on one pce fr 2 out)	13	3	14/1	46	5
27*	**Crazy Horse Dancer (USA) (84)** (FJordan) **8-11-4** MDwyer (bit bkwd: chsd ldr to 9th: sn rdn & wknd)	1½	4	3/1^{2}	45	4
451^{2}	**Rampant Rosie (IRE) (76)** (GRichards) **8-10-10v** ADobbin (led: blnd 3 out: hdd appr next: sn wknd)	¾	5	7/4^{1}	37	—
212^{6}	**Buyers Dream (IRE) (75)** (BEllison) **6-10-6**$^{(3)}$ GCahill (bhd: hit 7th: t.o)	27	6	5/1	19	—
185^{4}	**They All Forgot Me (66)** (AWCarroll) **9-10-0** MissCDyson (prom tl dropped rr 6th: t.o)	dist	7	25/1	—	—
				(SP 122.8%)		**7 Rn**

6m 32.4 (25.40) CSF £30.23 TOTE £7.10: £2.60 £2.50 (£38.00) OWNER Mr T. M. Morris (HAVERFORDWEST) BRED Ewar Stud Farms
LONG HANDICAP They All Forgot Me 9-12
422* Amazon Express landed his second course win in four days and defied a 7lb penalty in the process. This extended trip proved to be right up his street. (6/1)
Record Lover (IRE), having his first run over hurdles for two years but fit from the Flat, looked very one-paced in the closing stages. (4/1)
Ballindoo looked very well, but could never get in a real blow. His two wins to date have come in sellers and on faster ground than this. (14/1)
451 Rampant Rosie (IRE) tried to make all, but her blunder three from home stopped her in her tracks. (7/4: 9/4-6/4)

466 CROWTHER HOMES NOVICES' CHASE (5-Y.O+) (Class E)

4-20 (4-20) **2m 5f 110y (14 fncs)** £2,877.00 (£861.00: £413.00: £189.00) GOING: 0.36 sec per fur (GS)

				SP	RR	SF
421^{2}	**Definite Maybe (IRE)** (PFNicholls) **6-10-12b** RJohnson (lw: a.p: chsd ldr fr 5th: drvn 9th: hrd rdn to ld flat: sn clr)	—	1	5/4^{1}	89	4
454^{2}	**Signe de Mars (FR)** (MissZAGreen) **5-10-8** BStorey (led 4th: wandered appr 2 out: hdd & wknd flat)	22	2	5/1^{3}	73	—
8^{3}	**White Diamond (84)** (MissLucindaRussell) **8-10-12** MFoster (chsd ldrs: drvn & outpcd fr 10th)	18	3	6/4^{2}	59	—
421^{3}	**Donovans Reef (68)** (MrsLMarshall) **10-11-2** DBentley (bit bkwd: led to 4th: dropped rr 5th: t.o fr 9th)	dist	4	10/1	—	—
				(SP 110.2%)		**4 Rn**

5m 36.7 (24.70) CSF £6.76 TOTE £1.90 (£2.90) OWNER Mr B. C. Kilby (SHEPTON MALLET) BRED Miss Carrol Weld
WEIGHT FOR AGE 5yo-4lb
421 Definite Maybe (IRE) had to be rousted along to keep tabs on the leader setting out on the final circuit. He was then put under maximum pressure to get to the front but, once there, it was all over. (5/4)
454 Signe de Mars (FR) travelled well in the lead until wandering on the run to the second last. He surrendered quite tamely once headed and his pilot was very easy on him. (5/1)
8 White Diamond raced in a tongue-strap and was left well behind from five out. (6/4)

467 BET WITH THE TOTE MAIDEN HURDLE (4-Y.O+) (Class E)

4-55 (4-55) **2m 1f 110y (8 hdls)** £2,320.00 (£645.00: £310.00) GOING: 0.36 sec per fur (GS)

				SP	RR	SF
	Eternal City (GRichards) **5-11-5** ADobbin (bit bkwd: hld up & wl bhd: hdwy appr 2 out: sn rdn: styd on to ld nr fin)	—	1	11/4^{2}	75	4
293^{5}	**Sea God (90)** (MCChapman) **5-11-5** WWorthington (led & sn wl clr: rdn 2 out: hdd & no ex cl home)	2½	2	5/4^{1}	73	2
	Fatehalkhair (IRE) (BEllison) **4-10-13**$^{(3)}$ GCahill (lw: towards rr: hdwy to chse clr ldr appr 3 out: rdn to chal flat: kpt on one pce)	1¾	3	8/1	71	—
	Ingram Valley (DMoffatt) **6-11-0** DJMoffatt (bkwd: chsd clr ldr tl rdn & wknd appr 3 out: t.o)	23	4	12/1	45	—
	Shaa Spin (JBerry) **4-10-11** MMoloney (bkwd: bhd & drvn along ½-wy: t.o)	5	5	8/1	41	—
	Stone Cross (IRE) (MartinTodhunter) **4-11-2** MDwyer (lw: bhd: effrt 5th: sn btn: t.o)	dist	6	5/1^{3}	—	—
				(SP 117.7%)		**6 Rn**

4m 22.2 (21.20) CSF £6.82 TOTE £4.00: £1.90 £1.60 (£3.50) OWNER Mr R. Tyrer (PENRITH) BRED Mrs I. H. Lowe
WEIGHT FOR AGE 4yo-3lb
Eternal City, not fully wound up, made up an enormous amount of ground in the final half-mile and, with a nice run up the inside, got his head in front in the last 50 yards. He can go on from this. (11/4)
293 Sea God shot away from the outset and must have been over thirty lengths clear four from home. Once collared, he gamely fought off his first challenger, but had no answer when the winner caught him. He deserves compensation. (5/4)
Fatehalkhair (IRE), an impeccably-bred gelding, looked very fit and held every chance inside the final furlong, but could not find that bit extra required. (8/1)
Stone Cross (IRE) (5/1: op 5/2)

T/Plpt: £61.60 (69.92 Tckts). T/Qdpt: £43.40 (2.84 Tckts). J

FONTWELL (Fig. 8) (Good to firm)

Monday August 26th

WEATHER: overcast

468 CHICHESTER NOVICES' H'CAP HURDLE (0-100) (4-Y.O+) (Class E)

2-30 (2-30) **2m 6f 110y (11 hdls)** £2,237.80 (£620.80: £297.40) GOING: 0.00 sec per fur (G)

				SP	RR	SF
	Feeling Foolish (IRE) (63) (PJHobbs) **7-10-3**$^{(7)}$ MMoran (chsd ldr: rdn appr 2 out: led appr last: r.o)	—	1	12/1	48	—
338*	**Plinth (79)** (NAGraham) **5-11-12** AMaguire (lw: led: clr to 7th: rdn appr 2 out: hdd appr last: unable qckn)	3	2	5/6^{1}	62	—
327*	**Limosa (81)** (MrsLRichards) **5-12-0** MRichards (hld up: rdn & outpcd appr 3 out: kpt on one pce flat)	4	3	7/2^{3}	61	—

297³ **Cashflow Crisis (IRE) (78)** (JWMullins) **4-11-3**(5) SRyan (hld up: hrd rdn appr 2 out: grad wknd)....................9 **4** 11/4² 52 —
(SP 111.1%) **4 Rn**

5m 30.3 CSF £22.25 TOTE £9.30 (£22.25) OWNER Miss L. V. Bacon (MINEHEAD) BRED Mrs J. O'Halloran
WEIGHT FOR AGE 4yo-3lb

Feeling Foolish (IRE) put up a good performance to win here after 594 days off the course. He looked like winning comfortably when leading approaching the last but, in the end, had to be driven right out to do so. (12/1)
338* Plinth set a good pace and was well clear until collared by the winner between the last two. (5/6: 5/4-4/5)
327* Limosa never looked like taking a hand from the third last. (7/2: op 7/4)
297 Cashflow Crisis (IRE) was a beaten horse before the penultimate hurdle. (11/4)

469 BOW HILL (S) HURDLE (4-Y.O+) (Class G)

3-00 (3-00) **2m 2f 110y (9 hdls)** £1,825.40 (£504.40: £240.20) GOING: 0.00 sec per fur (G)

			SP	RR	SF
350²	**Burnt Sienna (IRE) (79)** (JSMoore) **4-10-4v** WMcFarland (lw: chsd ldr: led after 5th: clr next: rdn 2 out: hit last: all out)....—	**1**	13/8 ¹	44	—
404⁴	**Celestial Fire (80)** (JWhite) **4-11-2** AMaguire (hld up: hdwy to chse wnr appr 2 out: hrd rdn appr last: r.o)....2½	**2**	100/30 ³	54	—
	Lady Poly (54) (JRPoulton) **8-11-7b** LeesaLong (prom: chsd wnr 4 out tl appr 2 out: grad wknd)....19	**3**	40/1	39	—
	Scalp 'em (IRE) (DrPPritchard) **8-10-12** DrPPritchard (hld up in tch: rdn appr 3 out: sn wknd)....14	**4**	14/1	18	—
394⁶	**Fattash (USA)** (PMooney) **4-10-4b**(5) SRyan (hld up in tch: rdn appr 3 out: sn wknd)....12	**5**	40/1	8	—
400⁸	**Against The Clock (65)** (JWMullins) **4-10-9v** JRKavanagh (bhd fr 5th: t.o)....4	**6**	10/1	5	—
	Cast the Line (CREgerton) **6-11-5b** JAMcCarthy (t: bit bkwd: led to 5th: sn wknd: t.o whn p.u bef 3 out)....	**P**	2/1 ²	—	—
			(SP 115.1%)		**7 Rn**

4m 25.9 CSF £7.39 TOTE £2.80: £1.30 £2.10 (£2.60) OWNER B & E Bloodstock Ltd (HUNGERFORD) BRED Mrs Margaret Tully and R. Cutler
WEIGHT FOR AGE 4yo-3lb
No bid

OFFICIAL EXPLANATION **Cast the Line: the jockey pulled up because the gelding, who was recently tubed, was having breathing problems.**
350 Burnt Sienna (IRE) looked like winning easily when scooting into a clear lead after the fifth but, in the end, her rider had to get serious to withstand the runner-up's challenge. (13/8)
404 Celestial Fire made stealthy headway from the third last and momentarily looked dangerous approaching the last but, in the end, was well held. (100/30)
Lady Poly weakened quickly approaching the second last as lack of hard-condition told. (40/1)

470 NEWS H'CAP CHASE (0-115) (5-Y.O+) (Class E)

3-30 (3-32) **2m 3f (16 fncs)** £3,339.00 (£924.00: £441.00) GOING: 0.16 sec per fur (G)

			SP	RR	SF
	Henley Wood (92) (PJHobbs) **11-10-8**(3) GTormey (mde all: blnd 2 out: mstke last: r.o wl)....—	**1**	5/2 ³	102	27
403*	**Noblely (USA) (105)** (NJHWalker) **9-11-10** 7x RFarrant (chsd wnr to 5th: chsd wnr fr 9th: rdn appr 2 out: one pce)....10	**2**	11/8 ¹	107	32
	Armala (107) (JTGifford) **11-11-7**(5) LAspell (bit bkwd: prom tl wknd appr 3 out)....28	**3**	9/4 ²	85	10
403³	**Lavalight (81)** (JWDufosee) **9-10-0** JCulloty (mstkes 3rd & 4th: chsd wnr 5th to 9th: 3rd whn fell 11th)....	**F**	50/1	—	—
	Saffaah (USA) (109) (SGKnight) **9-12-0** MRichards (bit bkwd: bhd fr 7th: t.o fr next: p.u bef 3 out)....	**P**	14/1	—	—
			(SP 110.1%)		**5 Rn**

4m 50.5 (11.50) CSF £6.13 TOTE £3.50: £1.40 £1.40 (£3.40) OWNER Mr A. J. Scrimgeour (MINEHEAD) BRED Duke of Beaufort
LONG HANDICAP Lavalight 9-3

Henley Wood made all the running and won this comfortably, despite missing out the last two. (5/2)
403* Noblely (USA) has been in good form this season, and chased the winner from around halfway, but could make no impression over the final two fences. (11/8)
Armala looked and ran as though this was needed. (9/4: 7/4-11/4)
Saffaah (USA) (14/1: 10/1-16/1)

471 FISHBOURNE HURDLE (3-Y.O) (Class E)

4-00 (4-00) **2m 2f 110y (9 hdls)** £2,175.00 (£600.00: £285.00) GOING: 0.00 sec per fur (G)

			SP	RR	SF
388F	**Skram** (RDickin) **3-10-10** JCulloty (set stdy pce: qcknd appr 2 out: r.o wl)....—	**1**	2/1 ¹	58	—
331⁴	**Amber Ring** (MissKMGeorge) **3-10-5** JRKavanagh (lw: chsd wnr to 3 out: hrd rdn appr next: chsd wnr appr last: one pce)....5	**2**	2/1 ¹	49	—
	Yellow Dragon (IRE) (BAPearce) **3-10-10** LeesaLong (hld up: hdwy 3 out: n.m.r & lost pl appr next: rdn appr last: kpt on one pce flat)....¾	**3**	7/1 ³	53	—
331S	**Kings Nightclub** (JWhite) **3-10-5** AMaguire (hld up in tch: chsd wnr 3 out tl appr last: wknd flat)....6	**4**	11/4 ²	43	—
	Old Gold N Tan (JRPoulton) **3-10-5**(5) LAspell (plld hrd: prom tl wknd appr 2 out)....17	**5**	25/1	33	—
			(SP 109.7%)		**5 Rn**

4m 34.9 CSF £6.09 TOTE £2.90: £1.70 £1.50 (£3.50) OWNER Mr W. P. Evans (STRATFORD) BRED H. B. Ely

Skram set a very modest pace and was in the best position in front. He quickened after the second last and won quite comfortably. (2/1)
331 Amber Ring tried to get on terms with the winner over the final two, but made little impression. (2/1)
Yellow Dragon (IRE) went for an ambitious run up Kings Nightclub's inside approaching the second last. His rider had to rein back and lost valuable ground which probably cost him second place. (7/1)

472 STANE STREET NOVICES' CHASE (5-Y.O+) (Class E)

4-30 (4-30) **2m 2f (15 fncs)** £2,933.70 (£873.60: £415.80: £186.90) GOING: 0.16 sec per fur (G)

			SP	RR	SF
349³	**Harrow Way (IRE) (69)** (LWells) **6-10-12** AMaguire (j.w: mde all: clr appr last: comf)....—	**1**	3/1 ³	88+	—
330³	**Call Me Albi (IRE) (88)** (MrsLRichards) **5-10-9v** MRichards (a.p: chsd wnr fr 10th: hrd rdn appr 2 out: one pce)....2½	**2**	2/1 ²	86	—
336²	**Stapleford Lady (79)** (JSMoore) **8-11-0** WMcFarland (chsd wnr to 10th: hrd rdn 3 out: wknd fr next)....14	**3**	6/4 ¹	75	—
263⁵	**Jameswick (60)** (JWDufosee) **6-10-12** PHolley (hld up: blnd 9th: sn lost tch)....14	**4**	14/1	61	—
	Sandro (59) (MissLBower) **7-10-12b** LHarvey (a bhd: t.o fr 8th: p.u bef 3 out)....	**P**	20/1	—	—
			(SP 109.8%)		**5 Rn**

4m 49.5 (27.50) CSF £8.89 TOTE £3.10: £1.80 £1.50 (£4.00) OWNER Mrs Carrie Zetter-Wells (BILLINGSHURST) BRED Joseph Smiddy
WEIGHT FOR AGE 5yo-3lb

349 Harrow Way (IRE) won this with a bold display of jumping. His fencing should ensure further success. (3/1)
330 Call Me Albi (IRE) chased the winner from the tenth but, try as he might, he could make little impression. (2/1)
336 Stapleford Lady looked a tired horse over the final two fences. (6/4)

473 FONS H'CAP HURDLE (0-110) (4-Y.O+) (Class E)

5-00 (5-00) **2m 2f 110y (9 hdls)** £2,259.00 (£624.00: £297.00) GOING: 0.00 sec per fur (G)

				SP	RR	SF
348[4]	**Circus Colours (95)** (JRJenkins) **6-11-1** AMaguire (lw: hld up: gd hdwy appr last: led flat: r.o)	—	**1**	7/2[3]	78	—
329*	**Pair of Jacks (IRE) (84)** (GLMoore) **6-10-4** CLlewellyn (lw: a.p: led after 2 out: hdd flat: unable qckn)	½	**2**	6/4[1]	67	—
	Amaze (108) (LadyHerries) **7-11-7**(7) MrRThornton (swtg: a.p: led briefly 2 out: ev ch last: unable qckn)	1½	**3**	2/1[2]	89	—
303[6]	**Stay With Me (FR) (93)** (CREgerton) **6-10-13** JAMcCarthy (hld up: rdn appr 2 out: styd on one pce flat)	½	**4**	9/1	74	—
329[4]	**Ikhtiraa (USA) (84)** (RJO'Sullivan) **6-10-4** PHolley (led & sn clr: hdd 2 out: no ex flat)	1¼	**5**	12/1	64	—
				(SP 113.2%)		**5 Rn**

4m 23.7 CSF £9.08 TOTE £5.10: £2.00 £1.40 (£3.90) OWNER Mr S. Powell (ROYSTON) BRED Sir Robin McAlpine
348 Circus Colours is a tricky customer and was given a gem of a ride. Held up to the last possible moment, he hit the front late on without knowing he had had a race. (7/2: tchd 11/2)
329* Pair of Jacks (IRE) travelled like a winner throughout, and looked sure to win when leading approaching the last, but had no time to respond to the winner's late challenge. (6/4)
Amaze, never far away, had every chance at the final hurdle, but could not quicken. (2/1)
211 Stay With Me (FR) made headway over the final two without looking like getting on terms. (9/1: op 6/1)
329 Ikhtiraa (USA) (12/1: 8/1-14/1)

T/Plpt: £254.80 (10.75 Tckts). T/Qdpt: £5.90 (18.36 Tckts). SM

HUNTINGDON (R-H) (Good to firm)
Monday August 26th
WEATHER: overcast

474 MARCH CONDITIONAL (S) H'CAP HURDLE (0-90) (4-Y.O+) (Class G)

2-15 (2-19) **2m 4f 110y (10 hdls)** £1,849.00 (£514.00: £247.00) GOING minus 0.89 sec per fur (HD)

				SP	RR	SF
289*	**Joli's Great (70)** (MJRyan) **8-11-3b** BFenton (mde all: clr to 5th: clr appr 2 out: heavily eased flat)	—	**1**	Evens[1]	71?	—
17[F]	**Sakbah (USA) (60)** (JAPickering) **7-10-7** PHenley (bit bkwd: hld up: chsd wnr fr 6th: rdn & btn appr 2 out)	16	**2**	6/1	49	—
355[4]	**Ray River (84)** (KGWingrove) **4-11-11b**[1](3) DFinnegan (chsd clr ldr to 2nd & 4th to 6th: rdn & fnd nil after 7th)	28	**3**	7/2[3]	51	—
212[7]	**Swedish Invader (81)** (JWhite) **5-12-0** DJKavanagh (t: hld up: last & rdn appr 6th: t.o next: blnd last)	dist	**4**	3/1[2]	—	—
				(SP 111.5%)		**4 Rn**

4m 44.6 CSF £6.38 TOTE £2.00 (£4.20) OWNER Enterprise Markets Ltd (NEWMARKET) BRED Mrs M. A. Ryan
WEIGHT FOR AGE 4yo-3lb
Bt in 3,000 gns
289* Joli's Great turned this into a procession as soon as the very moderate pace lifted. (Evens)
Sakbah (USA) was burly after an absence and finished very leg-weary. (6/1)
355 Ray River declined to go with the others. (7/2)
Swedish Invader is not worth racing again on this showing. (3/1)

475 YELLING H'CAP CHASE (0-100) (5-Y.O+) (Class F)

2-45 (2-46) **2m 110y (12 fncs)** £3,873.00 (£942.00) GOING minus 0.89 sec per fur (HD)

				SP	RR	SF
	Far East (NZ) (70) (BdeHaan) **7-10-0** JOsborne (bit bkwd: j.w: led 4th: 10l clr 6th: jnd 2 out: styd on wl: lft clr last)	—	**1**	8/1	86	—
292[4]	**Circulation (70)** (DMcCain) **10-10-0** RSupple (bit bkwd: led to 4th: mstke 5th: chsd ldng pair fr 8th: one pce 2 out: lft 2nd last)	10	**2**	5/1[3]	76	—
328[4]	**Days of Thunder (90)** (MrsSMOdell) **8-11-6** BFenton (a bhd: hit 5th: mstke 6th & lost tch: t.o whn p.u bef 3 out)		**P**	7/2[2]	—	—
336*	**Yaakum (97)** (SEKettlewell) **7-11-13** MAFitzgerald (lw: hld up: wnt 2nd 8th: chal 2 out: drvn & fnd nil: 2nd & btn whn blnd & uns rdr last: rmntd)		**U**	8/13[1]	—	—
				(SP 111.9%)		**4 Rn**

4m 3.8 (1.80) CSF £35.31 TOTE £5.50 (£15.10) OWNER The Padrino Partnership (LAMBOURN) BRED C. P. Howells
LONG HANDICAP Circulation 9-9 Far East (NZ) 9-12
IN-FOCUS: **Yaakum was remounted to finish third, but the Judge had his back turned when the horse crossed the line, so the horse officially unseated.**
Far East (NZ) looked slightly in need of the run, but his jumping combined with the antics of his rivals enabled his trainer to get off the mark at long last. (8/1)
Circulation has not won for three years and is very much a plodder. (5/1)
336* Yaakum looked as if he could take the winner any time he wished, but he ducked the issue coming to the last, and was beaten when blundering his rider out of the saddle. (8/13)

476 OFFORD MAIDEN HURDLE (4-Y.O+) (Class E)

3-15 (3-16) **2m 110y (8 hdls)** £2,320.00 (£645.00: £310.00) GOING minus 0.89 sec per fur (HD)

				SP	RR	SF
	Wottashambles (LMontagueHall) **5-11-5** DMorris (hld up: hdwy 4th: led after 3 out: clr last: easily)	—	**1**	5/2[1]	80+	32
	Wanstead (IRE) (90) (JRJenkins) **4-11-2v** GBradley (lw: in tch: wnt 2nd after 5th: drvn & nt keen fr 2 out: no ch w wnr)	12	**2**	7/2[2]	68	17
	Witney-de-Bergerac (IRE) (JSMoore) **4-10-13**(3) JMagee (settled chsng ldrs: rdn & outpcd 5th: sme hdwy whn mstke 2 out: nvr able to chal)	nk	**3**	5/2[1]	68	17
461[6]	**Court Jester (71)** (MJRyan) **5-11-5b** BFenton (nt j.w: chsd ldr: led 5th tl after 3 out: wknd qckly: mstke last)	28	**4**	8/1	41	—
407[6]	**Chelworth Wolf (70)** (JLSpearing) **4-11-2** RSupple (chsd ldrs tl wknd 5th: t.o appr 2 out)	dist	**5**	33/1	—	—

Acquittal (IRE) (AStreeter) **4-11-2v** TEley (chsd ldrs tl wknd 5th: t.o whn p.u bef 2 out) .... **P** 6/1 3 — —
Baba Au Rhum (IRE) (IPWilliams) **4-11-2** JOsborne (lw: led tl hdd & mstke 5th: wknd qckly & eased: t.o whn p.u bef 2 out) .... **P** 6/1 3 — —
Kirkie Cross (KGWingrove) **4-10-4**(7) DFinnegan (last whn nearly ref 2nd: cont wl t.o: tried to ref 3rd & 4th: p.u bef 5th) .... **P** 33/1 — —
(SP 124.9%) **8 Rn**

3m 40.8 (-7.20) CSF £12.41 TOTE £3.50: £1.50 £1.30 £1.60 (£4.40) OWNER Dream On Racing Partnership (EPSOM) BRED Arthur Sims
WEIGHT FOR AGE 4yo-3lb
Wottashambles had plenty in hand and can probably win another moderate contest. (5/2)
Wanstead (IRE), placed over hurdles for the sixth time, is certainly not a willing battler. He did not appear to bleed here. (7/2)
Witney-de-Bergerac (IRE) could not keep up at halfway, but made some late progress, and may be seen to better advantage over further. (5/2)
Court Jester is deficient in stamina. (8/1)
Acquittal (IRE) (6/1: op 4/1)
Baba Au Rhum (IRE) (6/1: op 4/1)

477 BBC RADIO CAMBRIDGESHIRE NOVICES' CHASE (5-Y.O+) (Class D)
3-45 (3-46) **2m 4f 110y (16 fncs)** £3,745.50 (£1,038.00: £496.50) GOING minus 0.89 sec per fur (HD)

SP RR SF

263[3] **Sydmonton** (NJHenderson) **10-10-12** MAFitzgerald (disp ld to 2nd: stdd chsng ldr: pckd 12th: hdwy to disp ld after 3 out: led 2 out: styd on) .... — **1** 11/10 1 81 —
303[5] **Mr Snaggle (IRE) (89)** (SEarle) **7-10-12** CMaude (lw: hld up pllng hrd: stdy hdwy 12th: disp ld after 3 out tl blnd next: rallied, j.lft & mstke last: a hld after) .... 3½ **2** 2/1 2 78 —
330[4] **Telmar Systems (64)** (JWhite) **7-10-12b** BFenton (lw: nt j.w: led: wnt clr 9th to 13th: hdd u.p after 3 out: sn btn: t.o) .... dist **3** 8/1 — —
359[2] **Another Comedy** (RLee) **6-10-12** RichardGuest (j.b lft & mstkes: lost tch & blnd 9th: t.o whn p.u bef 12th) .... **P** 9/2 3 — —
(SP 110.2%) **4 Rn**

5m 2.6 (2.60) CSF £3.58 TOTE £2.00 (£2.30) OWNER Mr Peter Oldfield (LAMBOURN) BRED Dr John Wallace
263 Sydmonton jumped well on his return to the Henderson yard and that asset won the day here. He certainly does not have much finishing speed. (11/10)
223 Mr Snaggle (IRE) could probably have won this, but his jumping let him down in the closing stages. (2/1)
Telmar Systems was brakeing into the fences and downed tools as soon as he was headed. (8/1)

478 BANK HOLIDAY H'CAP HURDLE (0-110) (4-Y.O+) (Class E)
4-15 (4-17) **2m 110y (8 hdls)** £2,320.00 (£645.00: £310.00) GOING minus 0.89 sec per fur (HD)

SP RR SF

404* **Gone by (IRE) (108)** (JRJenkins) **8-12-0v** 7x GBradley (in tch: chal 3 out: led last: r.o) .... — **1** 11/4 3 91 32
334[2] **John Tufty (84)** (JPearce) **5-10-4** PHide (lw: hld up: hit 3rd: chal 3 out: ev ch last: drvn & no imp) 1¼ **2** 11/4 3 66 7
356[3] **Vain Prince (104)** (NTinkler) **9-11-10b** MAFitzgerald (lw: hld up: effrt & slt ld 3 out to last: eased whn btn flat) 3½ **3** 5/2 2 82 23
Layham Low (IRE) (100) (OSherwood) **5-11-6** JOsborne (bit bkwd: j.w: led to 3 out: eased whn btn) .... dist **4** 9/4 1 — —
(SP 112.7%) **4 Rn**

3m 42.8 (-5.20) CSF £9.74 TOTE £3.30 (£6.30) OWNER Mrs T. McCoubrey (ROYSTON) BRED James Robinson
404* Gone by (IRE) needs plenty of kidding and Bradley is just the man for the job. (11/4)
334 John Tufty had every chance at the last, but the winner was always finding enough. (11/4)
356 Vain Prince is used to long losing sequences and may be in the midst of another. (5/2)
Layham Low (IRE) looked a fortnight short of peak-fitness. He jumped well and will be an interesting proposition next time. (9/4)

479 ST NEOTS NOVICES' HURDLE (4-Y.O+) (Class E)
4-45 (4-48) **2m 4f 110y (10 hdls)** £2,192.00 (£612.00: £296.00) GOING minus 0.89 sec per fur (HD)

SP RR SF

257[2] **Santella Boy (USA) (103)** (CJMann) **4-11-2b** JRailton (trckd ldr hrd hld: led on bit last: qcknd clr) .... — **1** 8/13 1 68+ —
Kingsland Taverner (OSherwood) **5-10-12** JOsborne (unruly & uns rdr bef s: led tl rdn & hdd last: no ch w wnr) .... 4 **2** 11/8 2 58? —
Ballad Ruler (PAPritchard) **10-10-12** RSupple (chsd ldng pair: rdn 7th: lost tch appr 2 out: eased: t.o) .... dist **3** 12/1 3 — —
(SP 111.7%) **3 Rn**

4m 47.0 CSF £1.84 TOTE £1.40 (£1.10) OWNER The Link Leasing Partnership (UPPER LAMBOURN) BRED Galbreaph - Phillips Racing Partnership
WEIGHT FOR AGE 4yo-3lb
257 Santella Boy (USA) looked in tremendous shape and sprinted up the run-in for a facile success. (8/13)
Kingsland Taverner looks a bit of a comedian and was very awkward at the start. He was no match for the winner. (11/8)

T/Plpt: £616.40 (3.92 Tckts). T/Qdpt: £6.30 (15.49 Tckts). Mk

0357-NEWTON ABBOT (L-H) (Good, Good to firm patches)
Monday August 26th
WEATHER: sunny periods & showers

480 BANK HOLIDAY MONDAY (S) H'CAP HURDLE (0-95) (4-Y.O+) (Class G)
2-30 (2-30) **2m 6f (10 hdls)** £1,893.10 (£531.60: £259.30) GOING minus 0.51 sec per fur (GF)

SP RR SF

134[2] **North Bannister (73)** (TPMcGovern) **9-10-6** DGallagher (a.p: chsd ldr appr 7th: led next: clr 2 out: rdn out) .— **1** 15/8 1 55 —
323a[7] **Bravo Star (USA) (67)** (PaddyFarrell) **11-10-0** WMarston (led to 8th: ev ch tl no ex appr 2 out) .... 2 **2** 12/1 48 —
396[2] **Kutan (IRE) (67)** (MrsBarbaraWaring) **6-10-0** EByrne (hld up & bhd: styd on fr 8th: nt rch ldrs) .... 1 **3** 6/1 3 47 —
407[4] **Coeur Battant (FR) (67)** (RJBaker) **6-10-0** BPowell (hld up & bhd: hdwy 7th: sn prom: outpcd & wknd next) .14 **4** 8/1 37 —
Lawbuster (IRE) (71) (MrsRGHenderson) **4-9-10b**(5)ow1 DSalter (bit bkwd: in tch 6th: sme hdwy 8th: nvr nr ldrs) .... 21 **5** 40/1 25 —

				SP	RR	SF
	Auvillar (USA) (82) (JParfitt) **8-11-1b** TJMurphy (bit bkwd: chsd ldr tl appr 7th: wknd fr next)	12	6	10/1	28	—
301[4]	**The Black Monk (IRE) (94)** (MCPipe) **8-11-13** DBridgwater (nt fluent: rdn to stay in tch: wknd fr 7th)	3½	7	2/1[2]	37	—
	Rowhedge (71) (APJones) **10-10-4** SCurran (bkwd: chsd ldrs tl wknd appr 7th: t.o whn p.u bef 2 out)		P	12/1	—	—
				(SP 120.4%)	**8 Rn**	

5m 18.0 (6.00) CSF £23.10 CT £109.56 TOTE £2.70: £1.30 £2.50 £1.30 (£17.30) OWNER Mr T. P. McGovern (LEWES) BRED Lord Cadogan
LONG HANDICAP Coeur Battant (FR) 9-12 Lawbuster (IRE) 9-8 Bravo Star (USA) 9-10 Kutan (IRE) 9-12
WEIGHT FOR AGE 4yo-3lb
Bt in 3,100 gns
134 North Bannister enjoyed the easier ground and might go novice chasing given a bit more cut. (15/8)
Bravo Star (USA) set the pace, but could find no extra from the second last. He is better suited by faster ground (12/1)
396 Kutan (IRE) stayed on from the eighth, but was never going to catch the leaders. (6/1)

481 SANNACOTT NOVICES' HURDLE (4-Y.O+) (Class E)

3-00 (3-00) **2m 1f (8 hdls)** £2,211.00 (£621.00: £303.00) GOING minus 0.51 sec per fur (GF)

				SP	RR	SF
400*	**Re Roi (IRE) (92)** (JCFox) **4-11-2** TJMurphy (outpcd early: hdwy 6th: led after 2 out: mstke last: hld on wl)	—	1	2/1[2]	70	—
287[2]	**Million Dancer** (MCPipe) **4-11-2** DBridgwater (led & sn clr: mstke 4th: qcknd appr 5th: hdd after next: led 2 out: sn hdd: one pce)	1½	2	1/2[1]	69	—
408[3]	**Almapa** (RJHodges) **4-10-6**(3) TDascombe (gd hdwy to ld after 6th: hdd 2 out: ev ch tl wknd appr last)	1¼	3	11/1[3]	60	—
	Dry Sea (RGFrost) **5-10-12** JFrost (bit bkwd: chsd ldr to 6th: sn wknd)	14	4	11/1[3]	47	—
408[5]	**Falcons Dawn (61)** (SGKnight) **9-11-2**ow4 MissLBlackford (chsd ldrs tl rdn & wknd 5th)	16	5	50/1	36	—
				(SP 118.6%)	**5 Rn**	

3m 59.5 (6.50) CSF £3.60 TOTE £3.50: £1.30 £1.20 (£1.70) OWNER Mr J. C. Fox (MARLBOROUGH) BRED Mrs Larry Walsh
WEIGHT FOR AGE 4yo-3lb
400* Re Roi (IRE), patiently ridden, blundered at the last, but still held on well. (2/1)
287 Million Dancer needs a more galloping track. (1/2)
408 Almapa appeared not to last out. (11/1: op 5/1)
Dry Sea (11/1: 7/1-12/1)

482 CLOCK END NOVICES' CHASE (5-Y.O+) (Class E)

3-30 (3-30) **3m 2f 110y (20 fncs)** £2,859.15 (£865.20: £422.10: £200.55) GOING minus 0.51 sec per fur (GF)

				SP	RR	SF
	Clifton Set (CJMann) **5-10-7b** RDunwoody (led 9th: hdd 12th: led 14th: clr next: eased flat)	—	1	2/5[1]	91++	14
362[P]	**Bit of A Touch** (RGFrost) **10-10-12** JFrost (led to 9th: led 12th: pckd next: hdd 14th: outpcd next)	11	2	25/1	84	12
	Manor Bound (MrsSDWilliams) **6-10-7** SMcNeill (bit bkwd: chsd ldrs: mstke 10th: outpcd 14th: styd on fr 18th)	1½	3	8/1[3]	79	7
70[P]	**Brora Rose (IRE) (64)** (PRRodford) **8-10-7b** SBurrough (bkwd: bhd: mstke 1st: t.o fr 8th)	dist	4	20/1	—	—
417[P]	**Miss Dotty (64)** (MCPipe) **6-10-4b[1]**(3) DWalsh (nt j.w: mstke 1st: j.rt 5th & 12th: a bhd: t.o whn p.u bef 14th)		P	8/1[3]	—	—
	Master Kiwi (NZ) (FGHollis) **9-10-7**(5) DSalter (bit bkwd: in tch to 13th: grad wknd: t.o whn p.u bef 18th)		P	11/2[2]	—	—
				(SP 117.6%)	**6 Rn**	

6m 36.1 (2.10) CSF £10.87 TOTE £1.50: £1.20 £4.80 (£12.90) OWNER Mrs Christine Fennell (UPPER LAMBOURN) BRED Oping Enterprises
WEIGHT FOR AGE 5yo-5lb
Clifton Set did this well and his trainer is aiming him for a £19,000 novice chase at Worcester in early October. (2/5)
Bit of A Touch could not live with the winner when he went on six out. (25/1)
Miss Dotty (8/1: 6/1-10/1)

483 NEWTON ABBOT ANNUAL MEMBERS CLAIMING HURDLE (4-Y.O+) (Class G)

4-00 (4-00) **2m 1f (8 hdls)** £1,893.10 (£531.60: £259.30) GOING minus 0.51 sec per fur (GF)

				SP	RR	SF
399*	**Peter Monamy (101)** (MCPipe) **4-11-3b**(3) DWalsh (lw: chsd ldr tl led after 6th: clr appr last: comf)	—	1	7/4[1]	71+	—
356[2]	**Game Dilemma (79)** (JWMullins) **5-10-7**(7) OBurrows (mid div: hdwy & ev ch appr 2 out: styd on flat)	3	2	5/1	59	—
330[2]	**Simply (IRE) (108)** (TPMcGovern) **7-11-2** DGallagher (led tl after 6th: ev ch appr 2 out: one pce appr last)	2	3	9/4[2]	59	—
299[6]	**Cooley's Valve (IRE) (104)** (MrsSDWilliams) **8-11-5** SMcNeill (hdwy 6th: ev ch whn mstke 2 out: nt rcvr)	1¼	4	9/2[3]	61	—
65[6]	**Reefa's Mill (IRE) (81)** (JNeville) **4-11-0b** WMarston (hdwy to chse ldr 5th: rdn & wknd appr 2 out)	½	5	10/1	59	—
	Little Hooligan (86) (GFEdwards) **5-11-2b** BPowell (bit bkwd: hdwy to chse ldrs 5th: ev ch appr 2 out: sn wknd)	12	6	12/1	46	—
	Amber Lily (JMBradley) **4-10-0** TJMurphy (bkwd: hdwy 5th: ev ch after next: wknd appr 2 out)	8	7	50/1	26	—
93[4]	**Emerald Moon** (PRRodford) **9-10-10** SBurrough (bhd: hdwy & ev ch appr 2 out: sn wknd)	2½	8	25/1	31	—
394[5]	**Merlins Wish (USA) (91)** (MCPipe) **7-10-13** DBridgwater (a bhd: lost tch 4th: t.o)	dist	9	12/1	—	—
	Dazzle Me (ADSmith) **4-10-5**ow5 FJousset (bkwd: in tch tl wknd qckly after 4th: t.o whn p.u bef 6th)		P	50/1	—	—
				(SP 134.2%)	**10 Rn**	

4m 3.0 (10.00) CSF £12.71 TOTE £3.10: £1.40 £1.60 £1.30 (£6.10) OWNER Richard Green (Fine Paintings) (WELLINGTON) BRED R. Green
WEIGHT FOR AGE 4yo-3lb
399* Peter Monamy won this comfortably to make it three in a row (7/4)
356 Game Dilemma could not live with the winner when that one went by. (5/1)
Cooley's Valve (IRE) had every chance until making a mistake at the second last. (9/2)
Merlins Wish (USA) (12/1: 8/1-14/1)

484 SOUTH WEST RACING CLUB H'CAP CHASE (0-105) (5-Y.O+) (Class F)

4-30 (4-30) **2m 5f 110y (16 fncs)** £2,691.00 (£756.00: £369.00) GOING minus 0.51 sec per fur (GF)

				SP	RR	SF
414*	**Maggots Green (86)** (JMBradley) **9-11-0**7x TJMurphy (lw: led to 3rd: led 12th: clr appr 2 out: easily)	—	1	13/8[1]	98+	31
361*	**Duke of Dreams (79)** (RJBaker) **6-10-7** BPowell (hld up: hdwy 8th: chsd wnr 13th: rdn & wknd appr 2 out)	9	2	4/1[3]	84	17
	Wingspan (USA) (97) (AGNewcombe) **12-11-11** AThornton (bit bkwd: a.p: ev ch 13th: wknd fr next)	10	3	11/2	95	28
180[P]	**Seal King (90)** (MrsJGRetter) **11-11-4** DGallagher (hdwy 4th: in tch to 11th: grad wknd)	7	4	20/1	83	16
305[6]	**Prudent Peggy (75)** (RGFrost) **9-10-3b**ow3 JFrost (chsd wnr tl led 3rd: hdd 12th: wknd next)	6	5	14/1	63	—
361[3]	**Toomuch Toosoon (IRE) (100)** (MCPipe) **8-12-0** DBridgwater (a bhd: rdn & wknd 11th)	4	6	3/1[2]	85	18

Nick the Dreamer (100) (WGMTurner) 11-12-0 RDunwoody (bit bkwd: prom tl wknd 7th: sn t.o) ....dist 7 13/2 — —
(SP 123.2%) 7 Rn

5m 15.5 (-1.50) CSF £9.20 CT £28.35 TOTE £2.90: £1.70 £2.20 (£4.20) OWNER Mr E. A. Hayward (CHEPSTOW) BRED Swettenham Stud
LONG HANDICAP Prudent Peggy 9-8
414* Maggots Green, having her fourth outing this month, won this easily. (13/8)
361* Duke of Dreams was no match for the winner. (4/1: 3/1-9/2)
Wingspan (USA), running for the first time in nearly two years, showed some promise. (11/2: 10/1-5/1)

485 J C MILTON ELECTRICALS H'CAP HURDLE (0-115) (4-Y.O+) (Class E)

5-00 (5-00) **2m 6f (10 hdls)** £2,232.00 (£627.00: £306.00) GOING minus 0.51 sec per fur (GF)

	Horse		Pos	SP	RR	SF
	Blasket Hero (95) (MrsSDWilliams) **8-10-13b** SMcNeill (hld up & bhd: hdwy 8th: led 2 out: clr appr last: comf)	—	1	3/1 2	82	15
	The Minder (FR) (88) (GFEdwards) **9-10-1b**1(5) DSalter (bit bkwd: mid div: hdwy to ld appr 7th: clr next: hdd 2 out: wknd appr last)	13	2	7/1 3	66	—
342 5	**Evangelica (USA) (103)** (MCPipe) **6-11-7** DBridgwater (chsd ldrs tl rdn & wknd 8th)	20	3	13/8 1	66	—
	Fantastic Fleet (IRE) (101) (APJones) **4-11-2** SCurran (bit bkwd: chsd ldr to 7th: sn outpcd: wknd fr next)	4	4	13/8 1	61	—
	Passed Pawn (109) (MCPipe) **9-11-13** MissSVickery (led tl appr 7th: wknd qckly next)	5	5	12/1	66	—

(SP 121.4%) 5 Rn

5m 14.5 (2.50) CSF £20.96 TOTE £3.60: £1.60 £2.70 (£15.70) OWNER Miss H. J. Flower (SOUTH MOLTON) BRED M. Channon
WEIGHT FOR AGE 4yo-3lb
Blasket Hero won this comfortably. (3/1)
The Minder (FR) tried to slip his rivals when going clear at the eighth, but was caught two out. (7/1)
342 Evangelica (USA), having her first run over hurdles for some time, was a disappointment again. (13/8)

T/Plpt: £15.20 (245.74 Tckts). T/Qdpt: £7.80 (17.77 Tckts). T

0351-SOUTHWELL (L-H) (Good)
Monday August 26th

486 CANADA LIFE PROUD TO PROTECT NOVICES' H'CAP CHASE (0-105) (5-Y.O+) (Class D)

2-30 (2-30) **2m 4f 110y (16 fncs)** £4,150.00 (£1,150.00: £550.00) GOING: 0.57 sec per fur (S)

	Horse		Pos	SP	RR	SF
349*	**Willie Makeit (IRE) (85)** (RTPhillips) **6-11-10** JRailton (led 2nd to 10th: chsd ldr tl led appr 3 out: sn clr: drvn out)	—	1	5/6 1	92	19
423*	**Seahawk Retriever (72)** (PFNicholls) **7-10-11** 7x APMcCoy (hld up in rr: trckd wnr 9th: qcknd to ld next: rdn & hdd appr 3 out: kpt on one pce)	2	2	6/4 2	77	4
460 3	**Hizal (72)** (HJManners) **7-10-11** MrACharles-Jones (led to 2nd: trckd wnr: hit 9th: sn in rr: lost tch fr next: t.o)	dist	3	5/1 3	—	—

(SP 111.2%) 3 Rn

5m 31.2 (27.20) CSF £2.40 TOTE £1.80 (£1.40) OWNER Old Berks Three (LAMBOURN) BRED Mitchelstown Stud
349* Willie Makeit (IRE), running off a mark 7lb higher than his last win, completed a hat-trick in a weak race. (5/6)
423* Seahawk Retriever, jumping with a bit more fluency compared to his seasonal debut win at Cartmel, quickened to lead at the tenth off a funereal pace, but was collared going to the third last. (6/4)
290* Hizal, having finished tailed off two days earlier, was once again beaten out of sight. (5/1)

487 CANADA LIFE CHAMPION H'CAP CHASE (0-130) (5-Y.O+) (Class C)

3-00 (3-00) **3m 110y (19 fncs)** £5,287.50 (£1,575.00: £750.00: £337.50) GOING: 0.57 sec per fur (S)

	Horse		Pos	SP	RR	SF
298 4	**Andrelot (107)** (PBowen) **9-11-10b** APMcCoy (mde all: drew clr appr 13th: rdn 4 out: eased to walk cl home)	—	1	9/4 3	119	52
335*	**Magic Bloom (100)** (JMJefferson) **10-10-12**(5) ECallaghan (hld up: rdn 14th: chsd wnr 4 out: no imp)	4	2	7/4 2	109	42
351*	**George Ashford (IRE) (90)** (KAMorgan) **6-10-7v** ASSmith (in rr: reminders after 6th & 12th: sn struggling: kpt on u.p flat)	nk	3	13/8 1	99	32
	Spikey (NZ) (94) (JRJenkins) **10-10-4**(7) NTEgan (sn trckng wnr: reminder after 12th: lost pl 4 out: sn n.d)	12	4	16/1	95	28

(SP 111.1%) 4 Rn

6m 27.5 (20.50) CSF £6.32 TOTE £3.60 (£2.90) OWNER Mr H. Jones (HAVERFORDWEST) BRED Swettenham Stud
215 Andrelot ran out the easy winner and, in the process, was notching up his first triumph over three miles under rules. (9/4)
335* Magic Bloom was well and truly put in her place by the winner. (7/4)
351* George Ashford (IRE), refitted with a visor, failed to follow up his previous course and distance win. Off the bridle throughout the final circuit, he failed to land a serious blow. (13/8)

488 CANADA LIFE PENSION CLAIMING HURDLE (4-Y.O+) (Class F)

3-30 (3-30) **2m 4f 110y (11 hdls)** £2,047.40 (£566.40: £270.20) GOING: 0.78 sec per fur (S)

	Horse		Pos	SP	RR	SF
	Always Greener (IRE) (JWMullins) **5-10-3**(5) MichaelBrennan (bkwd: trckd ldrs: mstke 2nd: hdwy to ld appr 2 out: j.rt & mstke last: drvn out)	—	1	8/1	63	—
394 3	**Riva's Book (USA) (79)** (MGMeagher) **5-10-13** APMcCoy (in rr: rdn & hdwy 7th: led 3 out: sn drvn: hdd appr next: kpt on u.p)	1¼	2	9/4 1	67	—
389 F	**Northern Nation (84)** (WClay) **8-10-13** ASSmith (hld up in tch: mstke 4th: reminders after next: hdwy to chse ldr after 6th: wknd 3 out: t.o)	dist	3	5/1	—	—
355 2	**Antiguan Flyer (72)** (GProdromou) **7-10-6**(7) MrACoe (b: led: mstke 7th: hdd 3 out: wknd qckly: t.o)	5	4	5/2 2	—	—
413 2	**Slippery Max (72)** (RTJuckes) **12-10-7**(3) RMassey (hld up: struggling appr 4 out: sn lost tch: t.o whn p.u bef last)		P	4/1 3	—	—
	Smokey Track (60) (MrsJConway) **11-10-6**(5) STaylor (trckd ldr: rdn & wknd appr 7th: t.o whn p.u bef last)		P	40/1	—	—
	Anotherone to Note (NoTrainer,***) **5-10-0**(7) ADowling (tk keen hld: sn trckng ldrs: mstke 3rd: wknd qckly 5th: t.o whn p.u bef 7th)		P	50/1	—	—

(SP 111.5%) 7 Rn

5m 19.8 (33.80) CSF £24.77 TOTE £7.50: £2.40 £2.20 (£6.70) OWNER Mr Peter Houghton (AMESBURY) BRED Collinstown Stud Farm Ltd

Always Greener (IRE), a lightly-raced five-year-old, looked in need of the run, but overcame a last-hurdle mistake to lose her maiden tag. (8/1)
Riva's Book (USA) plugged on for the Champion Jockey's urging, but still failed to capitalise on the winner's last-flight blemish. (9/4: 6/4-5/2)
Northern Nation was reverting to the smaller obstacles, but failed to sparkle. He is one horse sorry to see the demise of All-Weather hurdling, as he was the winner of five races in that sphere. (5/1)

489 A-Z INSURANCE SERVICES NOVICES' HURDLE (4-Y.O+) (Class D)
4-00 (4-01) **3m 110y (13 hdls)** £2,794.00 (£832.00: £396.00: £178.00) GOING: 0.78 sec per fur (S)

Form	Horse	Dist	Pos	SP	RR	SF
260*	**Ordog Mor (IRE) (102)** (MGMeagher) **7-11-12** APMcCoy (mde all: qcknd & wl clr 9th: unchal)	—	1	1/6^{1}	80?	17
354^{5}	**Arrange A Game (46)** (MissJBower) **9-10-9b**$^{(5)}$ STaylor (bkwd: in rr: trckd wnr 3rd tl after 6th: reminders after 8th & lost tch: kpt on to take poor 2nd last)	dist	2	40/1	—	—
360^{3}	**Crown Ivory (NZ)** (PCRitchens) **8-11-0** SFox (trckd wnr to 3rd & again after 6th: blnd 8th: outpcd by wnr next: sn lost tch: lost 2nd last)	6	3	5/1^{2}	—	—
	Cruise Free (HJManners) **7-11-0** MrACharles-Jones (bkwd: nt fluent: trckd ldrs early: sn bhd: lost tch 6th: t.o)	dist	4	16/1^{3}	—	—
				(SP 110.7%)		**4 Rn**

6m 24.0 (38.00) CSF £6.12 TOTE £1.20 (£6.90) OWNER Mr M. R. Johnson (ORMSKIRK) BRED T. McKeever
260* Ordog Mor (IRE) completed a hat-trick of staying victories with the minimum of fuss. He can score again. (1/6: op 1/4)
Arrange A Game was clearly put in his place by the winner. (40/1)
Crown Ivory (NZ), having shown up early, began to struggle setting out on the final circuit, and was eventually beaten out of sight. (5/1)

490 ARTHUR ANDERSON (S) HURDLE (4,5,6 & 7-Y.O) (Class G)
4-30 (4-30) **2m (9 hdls)** £2,029.20 (£561.20: £267.60) GOING: 0.78 sec per fur (S)

Form	Horse	Dist	Pos	SP	RR	SF
	Simand (80) (GMMoore) **4-10-4** JCallaghan (hld up in tch: hdwy 5th: led next: clr appr 2 out: drvn & r.o flat)	—	1	4/1^{2}	55	6
400^{3}	**Minnesota Fats (IRE) (66)** (MissMERowland) **4-10-9** GaryLyons (hld up: hdwy 5th: drvn to chse wnr 2 out: one pce last)	3	2	5/1^{3}	57	8
	Summer Villa (JHetherton) **4-10-4** OPears (cl up: outpcd 3 out: mstke next: no imp)	14	3	6/1	38	—
	Trumble (MrsNMacauley) **4-10-9** APMcCoy (trckd ldrs: rdn 4 out: 3rd & drvn whn blnd 2 out: sn wknd)	18	4	3/1^{1}	25	—
	Rose Chime (IRE) (JLHarris) **4-10-4** PMcLoughlin (in tch: hdwy after 4th: sn trckng ldrs: blnd 3 out: drvn bef next: wknd)	½	5	12/1	20	—
353^{2}	**Irie Mon (IRE) (82)** (MPBielby) **4-10-13**$^{(3)}$ KGaule (swtg: hld up: effrt to chse ldrs 5th: wknd after 3 out)	13	6	3/1^{1}	19	—
259^{6}	**Boost (62)** (MrsNMacauley) **4-10-9** SWynne (b: led to 6th: wknd qckly after next)	8	7	12/1	4	—
353^{4}	**Chadleigh Walk (IRE)** (SWCampion) **4-10-9** ASSmith (prom tl wknd qckly 6th: t.o whn p.u bef 2 out)		P	20/1	—	—
400^{P}	**Flashing Sabre** (HJManners) **4-10-9** MrACharles-Jones (bkwd: plld hrd: sn in rr: lost tch 5th: t.o whn p.u bef 3 out)		P	33/1	—	—
				(SP 124.0%)		**9 Rn**

4m 4.6 (22.60) CSF £24.55 TOTE £5.70: £2.00 £2.10 £1.30 (£11.80) OWNER Ms Sigrid Walter (MIDDLEHAM) BRED R. V. Young
No bid
OFFICIAL EXPLANATION **Irie Mon (IRE): did not enjoy racing on the ground which, in the trainer's opinion, was loose on top.**
Simand, placed on the Flat recently, opened up her account over timber. She went clear before the penultimate flight and kept on well to score. (4/1)
400 Minnesota Fats (IRE), wearing a net-muzzle, was still in with a chance at the final flight, but could only go at the one pace on the run to the line. (5/1)
Summer Villa returned to hurdling, but was completely outpaced throughout the final half-mile. (6/1)
Trumble, a strong-puller on the level, was clearly going nowhere when blundering at the penultimate flight. (3/1)
Rose Chime (IRE), three times a winner on the Flat, was making her timber debut. Having made ground to track the leaders down the far side, she made a bad mistake at the third last and, from then on in, could not land a serious blow at the principals. (12/1: op 8/1)
Boost, having led early, went out like a light after the fifth. (12/1)

491 CANADA LIFE ASSURANCE H'CAP HURDLE (0-115) (4-Y.O+) (Class E)
5-00 (5-00) **2m 4f 110y (11 hdls)** £2,924.00 (£872.00: £416.00: £188.00) GOING: 0.78 sec per fur (S)

Form	Horse	Dist	Pos	SP	RR	SF
21^{F}	**Frontier Flight (USA) (87)** (MissLCSiddall) **6-11-2** SWynne (hld up: trckd ldrs 6th: led appr 2 out: clr bef last: eased cl home)	—	1	7/1	74+	4
	Tel E Thon (80) (MissCJECaroe) **9-10-9v** ILawrence (bkwd: prom: led 3rd tl appr 2 out: sn btn)	15	2	8/1	55	—
303*	**Verde Luna (86)** (DWPArbuthnot) **4-10-12** APMcCoy (hld up: trckd ldr 6th: drvn after 3 out: sn wknd)	22	3	7/4^{1}	44	—
391*	**Royal Circus (94)** (PWHiatt) **7-11-6**$^{(3)}$ EHusband (led to 3rd: prom tl lost pl 6th: rdn & lost tch next)	25	4	7/2^{3}	33	—
	Trumpet (95) (JGMO'Shea) **7-11-5**$^{(5)}$ MichaelBrennan (b: bkwd: bhd fr 4th: lost tch 7th: t.o)	29	5	5/2^{2}	11	—
				(SP 110.8%)		**5 Rn**

5m 18.8 (32.80) CSF £45.53 TOTE £8.70: £1.30 £3.30 (£52.00) OWNER Miss L. C. Siddall (TADCASTER) BRED Aaron U. Jones
WEIGHT FOR AGE 4yo-3lb
Frontier Flight (USA), on the deck in his previous two runs over hurdles, picked his feet up nicely to win easily. (7/1)
Tel E Thon, a front-runner, hit the buffers before the second from home. (8/1: op 5/1)
303* Verde Luna went out like a light just after jumping the third last. Although a winner over this trip in the past, he may appreciate a return to two miles after this poor effort. (7/4)
391* Royal Circus proved disappointing here. (7/2)

T/Plpt: £560.60 (4.09 Tckts). T/Qdpt: £89.80 (0.5 Tckts); £60.73 to Ripon 27/8/96. DO

0100-UTTOXETER (L-H) (Good to firm, Good patches)
Tuesday August 27th

492 HOUGHTON VAUGHAN 'N.H.' NOVICES' HURDLE (4-Y.O+) (Class D)
2-15 (2-16) **2m 4f 110y (10 hdls)** £2,731.00 (£766.00: £373.00) GOING minus 0.52 sec per fur (GF)

Form	Horse	Dist	Pos	SP	RR	SF
	Knucklebuster (IRE) (90) (PJHobbs) **6-10-10** APMcCoy (bit bkwd: a.p: led appr 6th: sn clr: unchal)	—	1	1/2^{1}	62+	2

	Horse			SP	RR	SF
408^{4}	**Regal Gem (IRE)** (CRBarwell) **5-10-5** BFenton (hld up & bhd: hdwy 7th: rdn 3 out: one pce)	8	2	11/2^{2}	51	—
287^{3}	**Seven Wells** (JHPeacock) **4-10-7** RBellamy (led tl appr 6th: sn rdn & outpcd)	9	3	50/1	49	—
260^{3}	**Tug Your Forelock (74)** (GFJohnsonHoughton) **5-10-10** AThornton (prom tl wknd 7th: t.o)	21	4	14/1	32	—
	Squirrellsdaughter (SABrookshaw) **9-9-12**(7) MissSBeddoes (bkwd: hld up: lost tch appr 7th: t.o)	18	5	20/1	13	—
	Lilly The Filly (MrsBarbaraWaring) **5-10-5** EByrne (s.s: hld up pllng hrd: lost tch appr 7th: t.o whn fell 3 out)		F	66/1	—	—
	Kingswell Boy (MCPipe) **10-10-10** DBridgwater (bit bkwd: ref to r: t.n.p)		R	8/1^{3}	—	—
				(SP 108.0%)	**7 Rn**	

4m 48.9 (4.90) CSF £3.46 TOTE £1.70: £1.30 £1.70 (£2.50) OWNER Mrs D. Poore (MINEHEAD) BRED T. J. Hodgins
WEIGHT FOR AGE 4yo-3lb

Knucklebuster (IRE), trained in the North last season, did not look fully wound up for this first outing since the spring but, in such a weak race, had a quiet school round and was never tested. (1/2)

350 Regal Gem (IRE), fitter than most and running over a more suitable trip, looked likely to prove a threat turning in, but she was soon flat to the boards and making no impression. (11/2)

24 Seven Wells gave the winner a lead until past halfway, but got left behind at the end of the back straight and his chance had gone. (50/1)

260 Tug Your Forelock (14/1: op 8/1)

Kingswell Boy (8/1: op 5/1)

493 CAFFREY'S H'CAP HURDLE (0-120) (4-Y.O+) (Class D)

2-45 (2-45) **2m 4f 110y (10 hdls)** £2,773.00 (£778.00: £379.00) GOING minus 0.52 sec per fur (GF)

	Horse			SP	RR	SF
341^{4}	**Prerogative (100)** (HSHowe) **6-10-11v** APMcCoy (bit bkwd: led 2nd: sn drvn clr: unchal)	—	1	14/1	88	28
347*	**Clean Edge (USA) (101)** (JMackie) **4-10-6**(3) EHusband (hld up: chsd wnr 5th: hit 7th: rdn 2 out: no imp)	7	2	6/5^{1}	84	21
419^{2}	**Hacketts Cross (IRE) (99)** (PEccles) **8-10-3**(7) MrRThornton (led: j.slowly & hdd 2nd: outpcd appr 3 out)	7	3	8/1^{3}	76	16
	Sheriff (117) (JWHills) **5-12-0** CLlewellyn (hld up in rr: pushed along 7th: no imp whn pckd 3 out)	dist	4	5/4^{2}	—	—
				(SP 107.7%)	**4 Rn**	

4m 41.9 (-2.10) CSF £29.15 TOTE £7.90: (£4.10) OWNER The Secret Partnership (TIVERTON) BRED The Queen
WEIGHT FOR AGE 4yo-3lb

Prerogative, well beaten on his only previous outing this term, looked the most backward of the field. With a forceful front-running ride, he was never seriously challenged and recorded his first success at the trip. (14/1)

347* Clean Edge (USA) looked to be waiting on the winner but, when the whips were cracking early in the straight, he soon decided the task was beyond him. (6/5: Evens-5/4)

419 Hacketts Cross (IRE), still to win in this country, kept tabs on the winner until feeling the strain and fading on the approach to the straight. (8/1)

Sheriff, hardly robust enough to carry topweight, and a very scratchy mover, was in trouble a mile out and was already trailing when landing on his head three out. (5/4)

494 WELLMAN PLC NOVICES' H'CAP CHASE (0-100) (5-Y.O+) (Class E)

3-15 (3-15) **3m 2f (20 fncs)** £2,814.00 (£852.00: £416.00: £198.00) GOING minus 0.52 sec per fur (GF)

	Horse			SP	RR	SF
	Warner's Sports (72) (PJHobbs) **7-10-11** APMcCoy (j.w: led 3rd to 5th: lft in ld next: clr fr ½-wy: unchal)	—	1	8/11^{1}	77	1
460^{P}	**Music Score (82)** (MrsLCTaylor) **10-11-7** AThornton (led to 3rd: lost tch 8th: styd on to go 2nd cl home)	13	2	8/1	79	3
417^{3}	**Duke of Lancaster (IRE) (85)** (MrsJPitman) **7-11-10v** WMarston (lw: led 5th: j.slowly & hdd next: chsd wnr: no ch whn blnd last)	nk	3	7/2^{2}	82	6
351^{5}	**Saint Bene't (IRE) (63)** (GProdromou) **8-10-2v** JCulloty (rdr lost iron 2nd: outpcd 8th: sn bhd)	2	4	7/1^{3}	59	—
351^{4}	**Abitmorfun (61)** (JABennett) **10-10-0** LHarvey (a bhd: t.o fr 16th)	dist	5	16/1	—	—
				(SP 109.6%)	**5 Rn**	

6m 35.7 (8.70) CSF £6.31 TOTE £1.50: £1.10 £11.90 (£11.40) OWNER Terry Warner Sports (MINEHEAD) BRED Peter Deal
LONG HANDICAP Abitmorfun 9-7

Warner's Sports turned in a bold display of jumping and, making virtually all, had nothing more than a solo school round for the final circuit. (8/11)

460 Music Score is not short on stamina and plugged on relentlessly to gain the runner-up prize in the dying strides. (8/1: 6/1-9/1)

Duke of Lancaster (IRE) appears to be a very slow learner as far as jumping fences is concerned, for he was assured of the runner-up spot when he took the last by the roots and, with the stuffing taken out of him, was out on his feet at the line. (7/2)

495 STREBEL BOILERS & RADIATORS H'CAP HURDLE (0-130) (4-Y.O+) (Class C)

3-45 (3-46) **3m 110y (12 hdls)** £3,667.50 (£1,030.00: £502.50) GOING minus 0.52 sec per fur (GF)

	Horse			SP	RR	SF
	Nirvana Prince (113) (BPreece) **7-11-10** AMaguire (nt j.w: hld up: hdwy to chse ldr appr 3 out: led & mstke last: r.o)	—	1	11/4^{2}	97	35
257*	**Elite Reg (110)** (MCPipe) **7-11-7v** DBridgwater (led: lft wl clr 4th: rdn appr 2 out: hdd last: eased whn btn)	4	2	11/8^{1}	91	29
187^{5}	**Ozzie Jones (89)** (NMBabbage) **5-10-0v** WMarston (lft poor 2nd 4th: wknd appr 3 out: t.o)	23	3	7/1^{3}	55	—
29^{4}	**Tallywagger (117)** (GMMoore) **9-11-7**(7) THogg (chsd ldr tl fell 4th)		F	11/4^{2}	—	—
				(SP 107.9%)	**4 Rn**	

5m 41.2 (-0.80) CSF £6.53 TOTE £4.10: (£2.40) OWNER Mr D. Portman (TELFORD) BRED Aldershawe Stud Farm
LONG HANDICAP Ozzie Jones 9-11

Nirvana Prince, a very welcome winner for his trainer, had an outing on the Flat three days ago, but he had almost forgotten how to jump hurdles. With the right man on top to pick him up time and time again, he won easily in the end, but he still looks a shadow of the useful individual he was a couple of seasons back. (11/4)

257* Elite Reg attempted to make all, but he had gone plenty fast enough in the early stages and had run himself into the ground approaching the second last. He also wore a tongue-strap this time. (11/8)

496 SQUARE AND COMPASS H'CAP CHASE (0-130) (5-Y.O+) (Class C)

4-15 (4-15) **2m 5f (16 fncs)** £5,361.00 (£1,314.00) GOING minus 0.52 sec per fur (GF)

	Horse			SP	RR	SF
390^{F}	**Micherado (FR) (94)** (SABrookshaw) **6-10-0** RJohnson (j.lft: mde all: hrd rdn flat: hld on gamely)	—	1	9/1^{3}	96	35
	Conti D'Estruval (FR) (122) (GBBalding) **6-12-0** APMcCoy (bit bkwd: hld up: rdr lost iron 7th: outpcd 10th: rallied appr 4 out: str chal flat: jst failed)	¾	2	Evens^{1}	123	62

298[3] **Muskora (IRE) (116)** (PJHobbs) **7-11-5b**(3) GTormey (lw: mstke 1st: chsd wnr: rdn to chal 11th: wknd next: wl bhd whn blnd & uns rdr 3 out)........ **U** 11/10[2] — —
(SP 107.6%) **3 Rn**

4m 58.1 (-6.90) CSF £16.36 TOTE £5.30: (£3.10) OWNER Mr Stanley Clarke (SHREWSBURY) BRED Ulrich Fricker
LONG HANDICAP Micherado (FR) 9-12
222 Micherado (FR) proved a very popular winner for the racecourse chairman after falling at the first on his previous outing. He had to work hard on the run-in to scrape home by the skin of his teeth. (9/1)
Conti D'Estruval (FR) usually needs a couple of runs to put an edge on him, but he ran up to his mark, trying to concede 28lb to the winner. With a trip to Ireland on the cards in the coming weeks, he is obviously not far off his best. (Evens)
298 Muskora (IRE) tried to pressurise the winner out in the country, but he was soon coming off second best and, giving up the chase at the end of the back straight, was destined for third prize when blundering away his jockey at the final ditch. (11/10: Evens-6/4)

497 CAFFREY'S CONDITIONAL NOVICES' HURDLE (4-Y.O+) (Class F)
4-45 (4-45) **2m (9 hdls)** £1,997.50 (£560.00: £272.50) GOING minus 0.52 sec per fur (GF)

	Horse / details	Dist	Pos	SP	RR	SF
481[2]	**Million Dancer** (MCPipe) **4-11-2** DWalsh (mde all: sn clr: rdn 6th: blnd last: hld on)	—	1	7/4[1]	78	15
	Kymin (IRE) (DJGMurraySmith) **4-10-4** RPainter (hld up & bhd: hdwy appr 2 out: drifted lft & r.o strly nr fin)	1½	2	3/1[2]	65	2
305[7]	**Ramstar** (PJHobbs) **8-10-12** GTormey (lw: chsd wnr: disp ld fr 6th: rdn 3 out: wknd fr next)	6	3	8/1	64	4
455[2]	**Lancer (USA) (85)** (RTJuckes) **4-11-2** RMassey (trckd ldrs: outpcd 6th: n.d after)	1¾	4	4/1[3]	69	6
284[S]	**Pimsboy (53)** (GROldroyd) **9-10-12v** PMidgley (mid div: no hdwy fr 6th)	20	5	40/1	42	—
397[3]	**Hatta River (USA)** (PTDalton) **6-10-12b** DParker (lw: nvr trbld ldrs)	s.h	6	20/1	42	—
392[4]	**Mellow Yellow** (JMackie) **5-10-12** EHusband (bit bkwd: a bhd & outpcd)	3	7	14/1	39	—
	Sharp Holly (IRE) (JABennett) **4-10-4** SophieMitchell (a bhd: t.o)	3	8	50/1	31	—
	Chesters Quest (RHollinshead) **4-10-9** JCulloty (mstke 1st: a bhd: t.o fr ½-wy)	1¾	9	33/1	34	—
	Good (IRE) (DTThom) **4-10-9** BFenton (swtg: bit bkwd: hld up: effrt & rdn appr 3 out: no imp: t.o)	9	10	50/1	25	—

(SP 113.2%) **10 Rn**

3m 43.1 (2.10) CSF £6.91 TOTE £3.30: £1.20 £1.20 £2.40 (£6.10) Trio £21.40 OWNER Martin Pipe Racing Club (WELLINGTON) BRED Mrs M. A. Rae Smith
WEIGHT FOR AGE 4yo-3lb
481 Million Dancer, a beaten odds-on favourite just over twenty-four hours earlier, moved to post as if he was feeling the ground. Setting a very strong pace, he needed to show all his battling qualities to shake off a persistent rival before galloping on relentlessly for a most deserved success. (7/4)
Kymin (IRE), a maiden stayer on the Flat, was taken off her legs somewhat on this initial outing over hurdles, but she did begin to stay on in the closing stages, and should be able to get off the mark at this game. (3/1)
15 Ramstar moved upside the winner on the bridle four out and looked set to score at will, but he could never quite poke his head in front and, made to work soon after entering the straight, faded out rather tamely. (8/1)

T/Plpt: £681.00 (14.91 Tckts). T/Qdpt: £106.30 (4.17 Tckts). IM

0345-WORCESTER (L-H) (Good to firm)
Wednesday August 28th
WEATHER: sun & showers

498 NEWLAND MAIDEN HURDLE (4-Y.O+) (Class F)
2-00 (2-00) **2m (8 hdls)** £2,213.00 (£618.00: £299.00) GOING minus 0.18 sec per fur (G)

	Horse / details	Dist	Pos	SP	RR	SF
	Alpine Mist (IRE) (JGMO'Shea) **4-10-11**(5) MichaelBrennan (bhd: hdwy 5th: rdn to disp ld 2 out: lft clr last)	—	1	3/1[1]	70?	12
	Lear Dancer (USA) (MissMERowland) **5-11-5** GaryLyons (a.p: slt ld fr 3 out: stumbled & almost fell last: nt rcvr)	11	2	3/1[1]	59+	4
	Pytchley Dawn (OO'Neill) **6-11-0** VSlattery (hld up: styd on fr 2 out: nvr nrr)	19	3	33/1	35	—
400[5]	**Flair Lady** (WGMTurner) **5-10-7**(7) JPower (trckd ldrs tl outpcd fr 5th)	6	4	25/1	29	—
	Triple Tie (USA) (MBlanshard) **5-11-0** DGallagher (led: clr whn hit 4th: hdd 3 out: wknd qckly: t.o)	7	5	7/2[2]	22	—
287[5]	**Disco's Well** (ABailey) **5-11-5b**[1] TKent (prom: rdn 5th: wknd appr 3 out: t.o)	dist	6	20/1	—	—
	Orinoco Venture (IRE) (DBurchell) **5-11-5** DJBurchell (bkwd: hld up in tch: wknd ½-wy: t.o whn p.u bef 3 out)		P	6/1[3]	—	—
	Masruf (IRE) (TThomsonJones) **4-11-2** MAFitzgerald (hld up in rr: t.o whn p.u bef 3 out)		P	8/1	—	—

(SP 109.2%) **8 Rn**

3m 48.1 (8.10)CSF £11.24 TOTE £3.40: £1.90 £1.30 £4.00 (£4.80)OWNER Mr Anthony Hughes (WESTBURY-ON-SEVERN) BRED J. G. O'Brien
WEIGHT FOR AGE 4yo-3lb
STEWARDS' ENQUIRY Burchell susp. 6 & 7/9/96 (careless riding).
Alpine Mist (IRE), a poor mover who has been placed over hurdles in Ireland, was not spared the whip and may well have had to settle for the runner-up prize had Lear Dancer not sprawled on landing at the last. (3/1: op 2/1)
Lear Dancer (USA), four times a winner on the Flat when the emphasis was on stamina, did not appear fully tuned up but he cruised to the front on the bridle early in the straight. He was beginning to feel the strain when he made a dreadful mistake at the last and his jockey did well to keep the partnership intact. (3/1)
Triple Tie (USA), soon bowling along in the lead jumping well, stopped to nothing after being headed and lack of fitness should not have been a problem. (7/2)
Masruf (IRE) (8/1: 4/1-9/1)

499 LEVY BOARD NOVICES' H'CAP HURDLE (0-100) (4-Y.O+) (Class E)
2-30 (2-30) **3m (12 hdls)** £2,234.00 (£624.00: £302.00) GOING minus 0.18 sec per fur (G)

	Horse / details	Dist	Pos	SP	RR	SF
413*	**China Mail (IRE) (90)** (KCBailey) **4-11-0** TJMurphy (lw: hld up & bhd: stdy hdwy 8th: ev ch whn lft clr 2 out: eased nr fin)	—	1	100/30[2]	76+	15
343[2]	**Sigma Wireless (IRE) (100)** (CaptTAForster) **7-12-0** SWynne (hld up: hdwy 9th: rdn appr 2 out: sn btn)	9	2	3/1[1]	80	23
338[2]	**Little Tincture (IRE) (72)** (MrsTJMcInnesSkinner) **6-9-9**(5) SophieMitchell (led to 9th: wknd 3 out)	11	3	9/2[3]	45	—

360[2] **Up the Tempo (IRE) (72)** (PaddyFarrell) **7-9-9**(5) MichaelBrennan (swtg: a bhd: t.o fr 8th) ....17 **4** 5/1 33 —
Written Agreement (73) (REPeacock) **8-9-10**(5)ow1 ChrisWebb (disp ld: led 9th tl fell 2 out) .... **F** 25/1 — —
St Kitts (78) (WGMTurner) **5-10-6** RDunwoody (bit bkwd: trckd ldrs to 8th: t.o whn p.u after next) .... **P** 3/1[1] — —
343[4] **Cheer's Baby (72)** (GraemeRoe) **6-10-0v[1]** RJohnson (lost pl 5th: t.o whn p.u after next: lame) .... **P** 40/1 — —
(SP 114.2%) **7 Rn**

5m 46.8 (10.80) CSF £13.21 TOTE £4.00: £2.40 £1.60 (£5.20) OWNER The Merlin Syndicate (UPPER LAMBOURN) BRED Airlie Stud and M. J. Ryan
LONG HANDICAP Up the Tempo (IRE) 9-5 Written Agreement 9-0 Little Tincture (IRE) 9-12 Cheer's Baby 8-11
WEIGHT FOR AGE 4yo-4lb
413* China Mail (IRE), patiently ridden over this extended trip, was poised to challenge and appeared to be travelling much the better when he was left clear at the penultimate flight. (100/30)
343 Sigma Wireless (IRE) found the concession of 14lb too much of a handicap from the turn into the straight and he is flattered to run the winner so close. (3/1)
Written Agreement, fit from the Flat, shared the lead well clear of the pursuing group and he had taken care of that rival but was feeling the strain and about to be challenged when crumpling up on landing at the second last. (25/1)
St Kitts, far from fully wound up, lost touch soon after halfway and was pulled up at the end of the back straight. (3/1)

500 STANFORD MARSH GROUP H'CAP CHASE (0-120) (5-Y.O+) (Class D)
3-00 (3-00) **2m 4f 110y (15 fncs)** £3,777.00 (£1,047.00: £501.00) GOING minus 0.18 sec per fur (G)

SP RR SF
342[3] **Comedy Road (98)** (RLee) **12-11-5** RJohnson (chsd ldr: led 11th: clr whn j.rt last: v.easily) ....— **1** 5/4[1] 102+ 42
Merlins Dream (IRE) (103) (OSherwood) **7-11-10** JOsborne (bit bkwd: hld up: hdwy 7th: led 9th to 11th: one pce fr 2 out) ....8 **2** 6/4[2] 101 41
342[7] **Celtic Laird (85)** (MrsJPitman) **8-10-6** WMarston (bkwd: j.rt: led to 9th: sn rdn: wknd 3 out: t.o) ....dist **3** 100/30[3] — —
(SP 107.5%) **3 Rn**

5m 4.2 (3.20) CSF £3.18 TOTE £2.10: (£1.50) OWNER Winsbury Livestock (PRESTEIGNE) BRED Miss G. Newall
342 Comedy Road had the edge in fitness and, though he did run across the final fence, had the prize in safekeeping by then. (5/4)
Merlins Dream (IRE) won first time out last term but he still has plenty left to work on and it was no surprise to see him fading after pressing the winner to the penultimate obstacle. (6/4)

501 BBC HEREFORD & WORCESTER HURDLE (3-Y.O) (Class E)
3-30 (3-32) **2m (8 hdls)** £2,302.50 (£640.00: £307.50) GOING minus 0.18 sec per fur (G)

SP RR SF
Sheath Kefaah (JRJenkins) **3-10-10** GBradley (hld up mid div: mstke 4th: hdwy to ld & j.lft last: drvn clr) ....— **1** 3/1[3] 59 —
358* **Ben Bowden** (MBlanshard) **3-11-3** DGallagher (a.p: slt ld appr 2 out: hdd & n.m.r last: rdn & unable qckn) ....3 **2** 5/2[1] 63 —
Lebedinski (IRE) (MrsPSly) **3-10-5** RMarley (bit bkwd: hld up & bhd: j.slowly 3rd: hdwy appr 3 out: ev ch next: one pce) ....4 **3** 9/1 47 —
Bath Knight (DJSffrenchDavis) **3-10-10** SMcNeill (led tl hdd & wknd appr 2 out) ....11 **4** 6/1 41 —
388[F] **Song For Jess (IRE)** (FJordan) **3-10-5** SWynne (a bhd: t.o fr 3 out) ....10 **5** 50/1 26 —
Remember Star (ADSmith) **3-10-5** FJousset (prom to 5th: sn rdn & wknd: t.o) ....dist **6** 20/1 — —
Indian Sunset (CREgerton) **3-10-10** JOsborne (bkwd: prom to 3 out: sn wknd: t.o) ....2 **7** 11/4[2] — —
Sans Pere (NMBabbage) **3-10-10** WMarston (a bhd: t.o fr 5th) ....1 **8** 20/1 — —
(SP 116.0%) **8 Rn**

3m 54.9 (14.90) CSF £10.67 TOTE £4.00: £1.20 £1.20 £2.10 (£3.60) Trio £19.40 OWNER Mr K. C. Payne (ROYSTON) BRED Ali K. Al Jafleh
Sheath Kefaah, a half-brother to two winners, did not impress to post but he warmed up once in action and, except for jumping badly right at the last, did nothing wrong and won more or less as he pleased. (3/1)
358* Ben Bowden had the benefit of previous experience over hurdles but he also had a penalty to contend with and the winner proved his match on the run in. (5/2)
Lebedinski (IRE), a disappointment on the Flat, shaped well on this hurdling debut and she should be able to make it pay at this game. (9/1)
Bath Knight (6/1: op 4/1)
Indian Sunset, unable to earn his corn in a limited number of appearances on the level, travelled comfortably in behind the leaders until dropping away rather quickly once in line for home. (11/4)

502 GRANDSTAND CONDITIONAL H'CAP HURDLE (0-110) (4-Y.O+) (Class E)
4-00 (4-00) **2m 4f (10 hdls)** £2,250.00 (£625.00: £300.00) GOING minus 0.18 sec per fur (G)

SP RR SF
347[2] **First Crack (84)** (FJordan) **11-10-7** LAspell (lw: hld up: lft in ld 3 out: sn clr: canter) ....— **1** 100/30[2] 69+ —
Tap On Tootsie (94) (TWall) **4-11-0** RMassey (bkwd: chsd ldr: hit 4th: rdn & wknd appr 2 out) ....15 **2** 7/2[3] 67 —
Script (80) (JRJenkins) **5-9-12**(5) NTEgan (bit bkwd: hld up: hdwy 5th: wknd appr 3 out: t.o) ....21 **3** 8/1 36 —
362[2] **Jenzsoph (IRE) (105)** (PJHobbs) **5-12-0** DJKavanagh (lw: led: rdn 6th: fell 3 out) .... **F** 15/8[1] — —
Clash of Cymbals (83) (JSMoore) **7-10-6** JMagee (bkwd: stdd s: in rr tl p.u after 4th: dismntd) .... **P** 9/2 — —
(SP 109.4%) **5 Rn**

4m 49.7 (11.70) CSF £13.69 TOTE £2.80: £1.30 £1.40 (£4.10) OWNER Mr D. Pugh (LEOMINSTER) BRED J. Wilding
WEIGHT FOR AGE 4yo-3lb
347 First Crack, always full of running waiting on the leaders, was just about to take over when left with the advantage three out. She did not need to come off the bridle to saunter home at her leisure. (100/30)
Tap On Tootsie looked burly after a three month break but put in a promising display until blowing up approaching the second last. (7/2)
362 Jenzsoph (IRE) set out to make it all and, though she had been given reminders, was still calling the tune when she fell three out. (15/8)

503 SONNY SOMERS NOVICES' H'CAP CHASE (0-100) (5-Y.O+) (Class E)
4-30 (4-30) **2m 7f (18 fncs)** £3,174.50 (£882.00: £423.50) GOING minus 0.18 sec per fur (G)

SP RR SF
Lucky Dollar (IRE) (95) (KCBailey) **8-11-13** AThornton (lw: mde all: clr whn mstke 3 out: unchal) ....— **1** 9/4[1] 106 —
351[2] **Blue Raven (85)** (PJHobbs) **5-10-13** APMcCoy (chsd wnr thrght: rdn & lost tch appr 4 out) ....23 **2** 11/4[2] 80 —
359[4] **Saracen's Boy (IRE) (68)** (MRChurches) **8-10-0b** MrLJefford (j.slowly 2nd & 5th: bhd whn mstke 10th: t.o whn blnd 14th) ....dist **3** 33/1 — —
Tipping Along (IRE) (74) (DRGandolfo) **7-10-6** RDunwoody (bkwd: trckd ldrs: mstke 3rd: reminders 9th: b.d 11th) .... **B** 11/4[2] — —

	Horse	Dist	Pos	SP	RR	SF
	Glenfinn Princess (96) (MrsMerritaJones) **8-12-0** JFTitley (bkwd: s.v.s: hdwy 10th: blnd & uns rdr next)		**U**	7/2 3	—	—
				(SP 109.3%)		**5 Rn**

5m 58.5 (20.50) CSF £8.18 TOTE £3.70: £1.50 £1.30 (£2.90) OWNER Mr G. P. D. Milne (UPPER LAMBOURN) BRED Edward Vaughan
LONG HANDICAP Saracen's Boy (IRE) 9-7
WEIGHT FOR AGE 5yo-4lb

Lucky Dollar (IRE), getting off the mark over fences, did it all from the front and did not need to get serious to run out a very comfortable winner. (9/4)

351 Blue Raven, much wiser than he was at Southwell, kept the winner company until getting left behind turning in. He should continue to progress. (11/4)

Tipping Along (IRE), with experience between the flags in Ireland two years ago, was not inconvenienced to be tackling regulation fences but he was carrying some surplus condition. Content to be given a lead, he still held every chance when brought down in a pile up at the open ditch a mile out. (11/4)

504 WICHENFORD INTERMEDIATE N.H. FLAT RACE (4, 5 & 6-Y.O F & M) (Class H)

5-00 (5-00) **2m** £1,196.00 (£331.00: £158.00)

	Horse	Dist	Pos	SP	RR	SF
	North End Lady (WSCunningham) **5-10-7**(7) MrRThornton (bit bkwd: hld up & bhd: hdwy 7f out: led over 1f out: r.o wl)	—	**1**	33/1	—	—
161 2	**Marlousion (IRE)** (CPEBrooks) **4-10-4**(7) MBerry (hld up: hdwy 3f out: hrd rdn over 1f out: edgd lft: r.o towards fin)	¾	**2**	4/7 1	—	—
	Gabrielle Gerard (MrsAMNaughton) **4-10-4**(7) RWilkinson (bit bkwd: hld up: hdwy ½-wy: led 3f out tl over 1f out: kpt on u.p)	1	**3**	33/1	—	—
418 4	**Katharine's Song (IRE)** (DMHyde) **6-11-0** JCulloty (led to 3f out: sn hrd rdn & wknd)	18	**4**	5/1 2	—	—
	Halam Bell (WGMTurner) **4-10-4**(7) JPower (trckd ldrs tl lost tch over 4f out: t.o)	18	**5**	9/1 3	—	—
418 9	**Abbeydoran** (MrsJEHawkins) **5-11-0** TJMurphy (prom: rdn & lost tch 6f out: t.o)	10	**6**	25/1	—	—
306 4	**Lucky Mo** (BRMillman) **6-10-9**(5) DSalter (hld up in rr: t.o fnl 6f)	16	**7**	5/1 2	—	—
24 14	**Derring Court** (EGBevan) **6-10-9**(5) PHenley (trckd ldrs over 10f: wknd qckly: t.o)	10	**8**	40/1	—	—
	Orchard Generation (BRMillman) **5-11-0** MrLJefford (bkwd: a bhd: t.o fr ½-wy)	dist	**9**	33/1	—	—
				(SP 122.1%)		**9 Rn**

3m 46.8 CSF £54.01 TOTE £21.20: £4.90 £1.10 £3.80 (£19.40) Trio £33.40 OWNER Mrs Vicky Cunningham (YARM) BRED Leslie R. Smith
WEIGHT FOR AGE 4yo-3lb

North End Lady, who comes from a winning family, made the long trip south pay off with a hard-earned success. Her action to post would suggest she will be much better when she can get her toe in. (33/1)

161 Marlousion (IRE) looks a bit of a nutcase judging by her antics in the paddock and on the course. Though she was pegging back the leaders at the finish, was never going to get there. (4/7: 4/9-4/6)

Gabrielle Gerard, sure to strip fitter with this run under her belt, was only tapped for speed on the run in and she looks a ready-made winner of a similar event. (33/1)

Halam Bell (9/1: op 6/1)
Lucky Mo (5/1: tchd 8/1)

T/Plpt: £23.90 (345.88 Tckts). T/Qdpt: £5.70 (73.33 Tckts). IM

SEDGEFIELD (L-H) (Good to firm)

Thursday August 29th

WEATHER: dry & windy

505 WELCOME TO A NEW SEASON CLAIMING HURDLE (4-Y.O+) (Class F)

2-10 (2-10) **2m 1f (8 hdls)** £2,059.00 (£574.00: £277.00) GOING minus 0.77 sec per fur (F)

	Horse	Dist	Pos	SP	RR	SF
	Brambles Way (MrsMReveley) **7-10-10b1** PNiven (hld up: hdwy 3 out: hung lft & led last: rdn out)	—	**1**	9/1 3	74?	27
419*	**Bures (IRE) (118)** (MHTompkins) **5-11-1v**(7) MrRWakley (trckd ldr: ducked lft 4th: sn led: clr 3 out: hdd last: nt qckn)	3	**2**	4/7 1	83	36
	Anorak (USA) (GMMoore) **6-10-13** JCallaghan (stdd s: nt j.w: mstke & lost pl 5th: styd on fr 2 out: n.d)	8	**3**	9/1 3	67	20
	Genesis Four (MrsLStubbs) **6-10-4**(3) GCahill (blnd 1st: hdwy to chse ldrs after 3 out: wknd next)	6	**4**	12/1	55	8
3 P	**Candid Lad (80)** (FSStorey) **9-10-7** BStorey (in tch tl wknd 3 out)	17	**5**	16/1	39	—
97 7	**Mcgillycuddy Reeks (IRE) (95)** (NTinkler) **5-10-5** JOsborne (lw: led tl after 4th: wknd qckly 3 out: sn t.o)	22	**6**	5/1 2	16	—
423 R	**Boethius (USA)** (MABarnes) **7-10-7** PWaggott (wl bhd fr 5th: t.o)	dist	**7**	33/1	—	—
	Red Trix (WRaw) **4-10-6** AThornton (bit bkwd: t.o 3rd: p.u bef 5th)		**P**	66/1	—	—
				(SP 118.3%)		**8 Rn**

3m 49.0 (-6.00) CSF £14.73 TOTE £5.70: £1.30 £1.10 £2.60 (£2.80) OWNER Mr Nigel Jones (SALTBURN) BRED W. P. S. Johnson
WEIGHT FOR AGE 4yo-3lb

Brambles Way, who was wearing blinkers for the first time and is a keen-going sort, hung left towards the leader between the last two. On the run-in, his Flat speed soon settled the issue. (9/1)

419* Bures (IRE), poking up on the inner, was left short of room at the fourth. Half a dozen lengths clear three out, he did not look to be enjoying himself and, on the run-in, and was outspeeded by the winner. (4/7)

Anorak (USA), dropped in at the start, lost ground with a mistake at the fifth. Staying on again at the finish, he is far from trustworthy these days. (9/1)

Genesis Four (12/1: 8/1-14/1)

506 LANDFORM NOVICES' HURDLE (4-Y.O+) (Class E)

2-40 (2-40) **2m 1f (8 hdls)** £2,318.00 (£648.00: £314.00) GOING minus 0.77 sec per fur (F)

	Horse	Dist	Pos	SP	RR	SF
73 2	**Brave Patriarch (IRE) (108)** (NJHenderson) **5-11-5** MAFitzgerald (lw: hld up: smooth hdwy to ld after 2 out: drvn out)	—	**1**	1/2 1	79	5
467 3	**Fatehalkhair (IRE)** (BEllison) **4-10-6**(3) GCahill (trckd ldrs: effrt 3 out: chal last: styd on towards fin)	¾	**2**	14/1	71	—
	Here Comes Herbie (84) (WStorey) **4-10-9** MMoloney (plld hrd: trckd ldrs: led 5th tl after 2 out: nt qckn run in)	2	**3**	9/1 3	69	—

				SP	RR	SF
	Robsera (IRE) (95) (JJQuinn) **5-10-12** LWyer (lw: hld up: hdwy to chse ldrs 3 out: rdn & one pce between last 2)	3½	4	7/1[2]	66	—
450[3]	**What's Secreto (USA) (78)** (HAlexander) **4-10-9b[1]** AMaguire (mde most to 5th: wknd appr 2 out)	7	5	20/1	60	—
189[5]	**Positivo (85)** (MissCJECaroe) **5-10-12** ILawrence (chsd ldrs: rdn after 3 out: sn wknd)	5	6	12/1	55	—
	Ihtimaam (FR) (MrsASwinbank) **4-10-9** JRailton (lw: prom: mstke 5th: lost pl after 3 out)	2	7	14/1	53	—
	The Cottonwool Kid (TKersey) **4-10-9** AThornton (led 4th: hdd next: sn rdn & lost pl: t.o 3 out)	dist	8	100/1	—	—
	Pallium (IRE) (MrsAMNaughton) **8-10-12** MFoster (hld up: nt j.w: lost tch 3 out: t.o whn p.u bef last)		P	25/1	—	—

(SP 119.8%) **9 Rn**

3m 56.1 (1.10) CSF £9.20 TOTE £1.40: £1.00 £2.10 £1.50 (£4.20) Trio £12.80 OWNER Mr Peter Winfield (LAMBOURN) BRED Peter Winfield in Ireland
WEIGHT FOR AGE 4yo-3lb
73 Brave Patriarch (IRE) looked to have been found a simple task but, in the end, had to struggle to get home. (1/2)
467 Fatehalkhair (IRE), who looked very fit, stuck on grimly up the hill and is sure to find an opening, especially on easier ground. (14/1)
Here Comes Herbie, runner-up in a claimer at Catterick in February, proved very keen. Pulling his way to the front at the fifth, he landed almost upsides at the last. Very willing, he should find an opening. (9/1)
Robsera (IRE), who looked fit despite a six-month absence, proved very keen. (7/1)

507 BARCLAYS BANK H'CAP CHASE (0-115) (5-Y.O+) (Class E)

3-10 (3-11) **2m 5f (16 fncs)** £3,049.25 (£914.00: £439.50: £202.25) GOING minus 0.77 sec per fur (F)

				SP	RR	SF
190[12]	**Turpin's Green (71)** (JSKing) **13-10-0** JCulloty (lw: chsd ldr: led 4 out: clr 2 out: drvn out)	—	1	4/1[2]	82	11
	Staigue Fort (IRE) (91) (DenysSmith) **8-11-6** PNiven (j.rt: led to 4 out: wknd appr 2 out)	14	2	7/2[1]	91	20
	Tresidder (99) (MWEasterby) **14-12-0** RGarritty (lw: hld up: hdwy 9th: wknd 4 out)	11	3	4/1[2]	91	20
	Mirage Dancer (71) (MissCJECaroe) **13-10-0** ILawrence (bit bkwd: hdwy to chse ldrs 9th: outpcd fr 12th)	hd	4	10/1	63	—
4[3]	**Boring (USA) (80)** (WStorey) **7-10-4(5)** RMcGrath (chsd ldrs fr 5th: wknd 4 out)	1¾	5	4/1[2]	71	—
420[4]	**Miss Enrico (89)** (MissLucindaRussell) **10-11-4** AThornton (sn bhd: blnd 11th: t.o 3 out)	dist	6	12/1	—	—
	More Joy (80) (MrsLMarshall) **8-10-9** DBentley (j.rt: rdn & lost pl 5th: t.o 9th: p.u bef 12th)		P	8/1[3]	—	—

(SP 110.1%) **7 Rn**

5m 6.3 (-4.70) CSF £16.77 TOTE £4.00: £1.50 £2.60 (£11.20) OWNER Mrs P. M. King (SWINDON) BRED Mrs A. W. Hughes
LONG HANDICAP Turpin's Green 9-10 Mirage Dancer 9-10
Turpin's Green, who is getting a bit long in the tooth, took this race, which was no better than a seller, in decisive fashion. (4/1: op 6/1)
Staigue Fort (IRE), who lost his way last season, continually lost ground jumping to the right and was tired two out. (7/2)
Tresidder looked fit, but this veteran is better served by the minimum trip. (4/1)
Mirage Dancer, 4lb out of the handicap, looked burly and was outpaced. (10/1)

508 SHARPS BEDROOM MAIDEN CHASE (5-Y.O+) (Class E)

3-40 (3-40) **2m 110y (13 fncs)** £2,905.00 (£805.00: £385.00) GOING minus 0.77 sec per fur (F)

				SP	RR	SF
	Prince Skyburd (MrsPMAAvison) **5-10-11(5)** ECallaghan (mde all: drew clr between last 2)	—	1	2/1[2]	78?	—
465[6]	**Buyers Dream (IRE)** (BEllison) **6-11-2v(3)** GCahill (chsd wnr fr 5th: pushed along 7th: rdn 3 out: wl btn whn blnd last)	17	2	4/5[1]	62?	—
351[3]	**Quixall Crossett (56)** (EMCaine) **11-11-5** PMcLoughlin (reminders 5th: lost tch 8th: t.o 4 out)	dist	3	4/1[3]	—	—

(SP 108.9%) **3 Rn**

4m 1.2 (3.20) CSF £3.81 TOTE £2.80: (£1.60) OWNER Mrs P. M. A. Avison (HELMSLEY) BRED Mrs P. M. A. Avison
WEIGHT FOR AGE 5yo-3lb
Prince Skyburd, who has time on his side, gave his two rivals a jumping lesson. (2/1)
Buyers Dream (IRE), ridden to keep up at halfway, was flat out three from home and was well beaten when ploughing through the last. (4/5)
351 Quixall Crossett, painfully slow, was struggling early on the final circuit and was miles behind from four out. (4/1)

509 DICKENS HOME IMPROVEMENTS H'CAP HURDLE (0-100) (4-Y.O+) (Class F)

4-10 (4-10) **2m 5f 110y (10 hdls)** £2,250.00 (£625.00: £300.00) GOING minus 0.77 sec per fur (F)

				SP	RR	SF
285[6]	**Playful Juliet (CAN) (77)** (ABailey) **8-10-10** SWynne (led to 3rd: led 3 out: 3l clr whn stumbled last: sn hdd: rallied gamely to ld cl home:)	—	1	7/1	58	17
451*	**Huso (86)** (PCHaslam) **8-11-5** MFoster (bit bkwd: trckd ldrs: ev ch fr 3 out: swtchd & styd on to ld sn after last: hdd cl home)	s.h	2	6/4[1]	67	26
134*	**Red Jam Jar (95)** (SBBell) **11-12-0** KJohnson (lw: led 3rd: hit 7th: hdd next: sn rdn & outpcd: kpt on between last 2)	7	3	5/2[2]	71	30
	Shelton Abbey (67) (JWade) **10-10-0b** AMaguire (pushed along 5th: lost tch after next: t.o 3 out)	dist	4	11/2[3]	—	—
	Copperhurst (IRE) (77) (WTKemp) **5-10-10** SMcDougall (prom to 6th: sn outpcd: mod 4th whn fell 3 out)		F	6/1	—	—
	What A Difference (IRE) (70) (WRaw) **7-10-3ow3** AThornton (bkwd: t.o 4th: p.u bef 6th)		P	100/1	—	—

(SP 111.7%) **6 Rn**

4m 55.3 (-4.70) CSF £17.32 TOTE £6.50: £3.40 £1.10 (£13.90) OWNER Mrs P. Hewitt (TARPORLEY) BRED Windfields Farm
LONG HANDICAP What A Difference (IRE) 9-0
97 Playful Juliet (CAN), a 100/1 winner of a novice chase in bad ground three years ago, has also been pointing. Three lengths to the good when slipping on landing at the last, in the end she scraped home by a whisker. (7/1)
451* Huso, running without a penalty for his Cartmel success, still looked to be carrying plenty of condition. In front soon after the last, in the end he was just shaded. (6/4)
134* Red Jam Jar, raised 10lb, was struggling after being headed three out but, to his credit, kept on again approaching the last. (5/2)
Shelton Abbey was in one of his unco-operative moods. (11/2)

510 MILTON KEYNES SURVEYS 'N.H.' NOVICES' HURDLE (4-Y.O+) (Class E)

4-40 (4-41) **2m 5f 110y (10 hdls)** £2,180.00 (£605.00: £290.00) GOING minus 0.77 sec per fur (F)

				SP	RR	SF
209[2]	**War Whoop** (CWThornton) **4-10-9** MFoster (lw: trckd ldrs: led appr 2 out: styd on u.p run in)	—	1	1/2[1]	66	—
424[2]	**The Gallopin'major (IRE)** (MrsMReveley) **6-10-12b** NSmith (led 6th tl appr 2 out: kpt on u.p run in)	2	2	7/2[2]	65	—
	Over Stated (IRE) (PCheesbrough) **6-10-12** RSupple (bit bkwd: in tch: outpcd 6th: lost pl after 3 out)	22	3	16/1	48	—
345[2]	**Peniarth (57)** (RJPrice) **10-10-7** AMaguire (chsd ldrs: pushed along 5th: sn wl outpcd & lost pl: sme hdwy fr 2 out)	nk	4	7/1[3]	43	—

450P **Boyo (IRE)** (TDEasterby) **5-10-12** LWyer (bit bkwd: chsd ldrs: outpcd & pushed along 6th: wknd appr 2 out) ....2½ **5** 20/1 46 —
Ahbejaybus (IRE) (TKersey) **7-10-12** AThornton (led to 6th: wknd after next: sn t.o) ....dist **6** 100/1 — —
(SP 113.0%) **6 Rn**

5m 6.6 (6.60) CSF £2.77 TOTE £1.40: £1.00 £2.30 (£1.80) OWNER Mr Guy Reed (MIDDLEHAM) BRED G. Reed
WEIGHT FOR AGE 4yo-3lb
209 War Whoop looked likely to win comfortably when taking it up but, in the end, had to be kept right up to his work. All he does is stay. (1/2)
424 The Gallopin'major (IRE) stuck to his guns and, in the end, made the winner struggle. (7/2)
Over Stated (IRE), who showed precious little last season, looked in need of the outing. (16/1)
345 Peniarth, who won a maiden point over a year ago, wore a tongue-strap. She was badly outpaced from halfway. (7/1)

T/Plpt: £30.50 (255.37 Tckts). T/Qdpt: £27.90 (11.25 Tckts) WG

511a-526a (Irish Racing) - See Computer Raceform

0387a-CLAIREFONTAINE (Deauville, France) (R-H) (Soft)
Friday August 23rd

527a PRIX DES TROENES HURDLE (5-Y.O+)
3-35 (3-36) **2m 1f** £6,588.00

				SP	RR	SF
299*	**Country Star (IRE)** (CPEBrooks) **5-10-6**ow2 GBradley	—	1		99+	—
	Leon Des Perrets (FR) (France) **5-10-2** LGerard	3	2		92?	—
	Darra (FR) (France) **5-9-11** FMenard	s.h	3		87?	—
						11 Rn

3m 57.5 P-M 2.20F: 1.80F 3.50F 1.80F (51.80F) OWNER Prince Fahd Salman (LAMBOURN) BRED M. L. Page
299* Country Star (IRE) made virtually all the running and, pushed out at the end, came home clear. He is due to return to France later this year for a hurdle event at Auteuil on September 18th.

0007-PERTH (R-H) (Good to firm)
Friday August 30th

528 ABTRUST INVERNESS NOVICES' HURDLE (4-Y.O+) (Class E)
2-20 (2-20) **2m 4f 110y (10 hdls)** £2,190.00 (£615.00: £300.00) GOING minus 0.37 sec per fur (GF)

				SP	RR	SF
	Anchorena (MissVenetiaWilliams) **4-10-4** RJohnson (hld up: effrt appr last: led flat: r.o)	—	1	7/2 2	59	10
410 2	**Born to Please (IRE) (87)** (PJHobbs) **4-11-2** APMcCoy (lw: chsd ldrs: rdn 4 out: chal 2 out: slt ld flat: sn hdd & nt qckn)	2	2	11/10 1	69	20
319a 9	**Castleroyal (IRE)** (IRFerguson,Ireland) **7-10-12** AMaguire (led 2nd tl flat: one pce)	½	3	4/1 3	62	16
293 6	**Little Redwing** (MDHammond) **4-10-6**ow2 RGarritty (lw: led to 2nd: cl up tl mstke & wknd 3 out)	25	4	4/1 3	40	—
				(SP 109.8%)		**4 Rn**

4m 52.2 (4.20) CSF £7.53 TOTE £5.70: (£3.90) OWNER A C & D S Partnership (HEREFORD) BRED Normanby Stud Ltd
WEIGHT FOR AGE 4yo-3lb
Anchorena, given a cracking ride, hardly knew she was in a race. Produced approaching the last, she showed by far the best turn of foot. (7/2: 5/2-4/1)
410 Born to Please (IRE) looked extremely well and ran his heart out, but he is short of a turn of speed. (11/10)
Castleroyal (IRE), having only his second run over hurdles, stays well. Maguire tried to make full use of this, but he was tapped for speed after the last. (4/1)
293 Little Redwing has the looks of a decent type, but her hurdling leaves a lot to be desired. This was a poor effort. (4/1)

529 ABTRUST FORT LAUDERDALE NOVICES' H'CAP CHASE (0-100) (5-Y.O+) (Class E)
2-55 (2-55) **2m 4f 110y (15 fncs)** £3,214.00 (£904.00: £442.00) GOING minus 0.37 sec per fur (GF)

				SP	RR	SF
457*	**Miners Rest (72)** (PJHobbs) **8-11-2** 7x APMcCoy (lw: j.lft: hit 2nd: led 3rd: hit 4 out: styd on u.p flat)	—	1	4/7 1	80	1
454*	**Reve de Valse (USA) (87)** (RJohnson) **9-12-3** 7x KJohnson (lw: hld up: chsd wnr fr 8th: rdn appr 4 out: ch last: no ex)	3	2	100/30 2	93	14
466 3	**White Diamond (84)** (MissLucindaRussell) **8-12-0** AThornton (led: j.lft 2nd: hdd 3rd: outpcd & lost tch fr 11th)	27	3	4/1 3	69	—
				(SP 106.7%)		**3 Rn**

5m 9.8 (10.80) CSF £2.50 TOTE £1.60: (£1.60) OWNER Mr P. J. Hobbs (MINEHEAD) BRED B. B. Akerman
457* Miners Rest, no great shakes, jumped left, and found enough when ridden to take a poor race. (4/7)
454* Reve de Valse (USA), in pursuit of the winner from halfway, kept responding to pressure from four out, but was never quite good enough. (100/30)
466 White Diamond is happy to follow anything round and never seems to want to go past. This was a poor effort though even by his standards. (4/1: 3/1-9/2)

530 ABERDEEN TRUST PLC H'CAP CHASE (0-115) (5-Y.O+) (Class E)
3-30 (3-30) **3m (18 fncs)** £4,115.00 (£1,010.00) GOING minus 0.37 sec per fur (GF)

				SP	RR	SF
342 2	**The Yank (102)** (MDHammond) **10-11-9b** RGarritty (lw: led 6th: clr 4 out: all out)	—	1	4/5 1	108	16
	Real Progress (IRE) (107) (PJHobbs) **8-12-0** APMcCoy (led to 6th: rdn along fr 10th: wl outpcd 14th: styd on fr 3 out: one pce flat)	6	2	6/4 2	109	17
	Kelpie the Celt (79) (MrsDThomson) **9-10-0** LO'Hara (lw: hld up: effrt 12th: outpcd next: sn wknd: p.u bef 3 out: lame)		P	8/1 3	—	—
				(SP 106.7%)		**3 Rn**

6m 7.9 (9.90) CSF £2.18 TOTE £1.70: (£1.40) OWNER Mrs A. Kane (MIDDLEHAM) BRED Tom Healy
LONG HANDICAP Kelpie the Celt 9-5

342 The Yank looked to have it sewn up when going clear four out, but he then came under pressure and had not an ounce to spare at the line. (4/5)
Real Progress (IRE), flat out to stay on terms with over a circuit left, stays all day and kept on really well. (6/4)
Kelpie the Celt was going well until suddenly running out of fuel six out. He was pulled up lame before three from home. (8/1: 6/1-12/1)

531 ABTRUST SINGAPORE (S) H'CAP HURDLE (0-90) (4-Y.O+) (Class G)

4-00 (4-01) **2m 110y (8 hdls)** £2,211.00 (£621.00: £303.00) GOING minus 0.37 sec per fur (GF)

				SP	RR	SF
	Vintage Red (62) (GRichards) **6-10-4** ADobbin (trckd ldrs: rdn to ld last: styd on)	—	**1**	6/1	43	7
463*	**Steadfast Elite (IRE) (93)** (JJO'Neill) **5-12-2**(5) 7x RMcGrath (trckd ldrs: styd on u.p flat: nt pce to chal)	2½	**2**	3/1[2]	72	36
419[4]	**Silver Sleeve (IRE) (82)** (MDHammond) **4-11-7v** RGarritty (trckd ldrs: led 3 out: hrd rdn & hdd last: no ex)	½	**3**	8/1	60	21
	Classy Kahyasi (IRE) (76) (IRFerguson,Ireland) **6-10-13**(5) MichaelBrennan (hld up: effrt 5th: hdwy u.s.p appr 2 out: sn btn)	5	**4**	4/1[3]	49	13
259[5]	**Doctor-J (IRE) (80)** (JWhite) **6-11-8b[1]** APMcCoy (lw: bhd: effrt 3 out: no imp)	10	**5**	9/4[1]	44	8
11[4]	**Cardenden (IRE) (73)** (JBarclay) **8-11-1** AThornton (led to 3 out: sn wknd)	22	**6**	20/1	15	—
				(SP 105.9%)		**6 Rn**

3m 49.8 (3.80) CSF £21.42 TOTE £6.80: £3.00 £1.60 (£10.50) OWNER Special Reserve Racing (PENRITH)
WEIGHT FOR AGE 4yo-3lb
No bid
OFFICIAL EXPLANATION **Doctor-J (IRE): ran too freely in the early stages in the first-time blinkers.**
Vintage Red, having his first run for his new stable, was given a fine ride and did it nicely, despite carrying his head at an angle. (6/1)
463* Steadfast Elite (IRE) always had the leaders within his sights, and stayed on under vigorous pressure after the last. (3/1: op 2/1)
419 Silver Sleeve (IRE), well handled, had his chances until finding it beyond him going to the last. (8/1: op 5/1)
Classy Kahyasi (IRE) used to tear off in front when previously in this country, but was ridden with restraint here, and it failed to work. (4/1)
Doctor-J (IRE) had blinkers on for the first time, but they did not work the oracle, as all he did was race far too freely early on. (9/4)

532 NORTH SOUND RADIO NOVICES' CHASE (5-Y.O+) (Class E)

4-30 (4-30) **2m (12 fncs)** £3,186.00 (£896.00: £438.00) GOING minus 0.37 sec per fur (GF)

				SP	RR	SF
17[6]	**Speaker's House (USA)** (MissLucindaRussell) **7-10-12** AThornton (hld up: smooth hdwy to ld 2 out: r.o)	—	**1**	3/1[3]	76+	—
349[4]	**Caxton (USA) (78)** (JWhite) **9-10-12** AMaguire (lw: trckd ldrs: chal 4 out: outpcd appr last: kpt on flat)	2	**2**	6/4[1]	74	—
	Richmond (IRE) (MissZAGreen) **8-10-12** BStorey (chsd ldrs: lft in ld appr 4 out: hdd & wknd 2 out)	20	**3**	8/1	54	—
	Islandreagh (IRE) (GRichards) **5-10-4** ADobbin (led tl sddle slipped & p.u appr 4 out)		**P**	11/4[2]	—	—
				(SP 102.8%)		**4 Rn**

4m 3.6 (12.60) CSF £7.01 TOTE £4.70: (£3.30) OWNER Mrs C. G. Greig (KINROSS) BRED Wakefield Farm
WEIGHT FOR AGE 5yo-3lb
Speaker's House (USA) took to this game particularly well and won in useful style. He looks likely to follow up. (3/1)
Caxton (USA), who looked well, had his chances. Despite keeping on after the last, he was always well second best. (6/4)
Richmond (IRE) has changed stables and was having his first attempt over fences. Once the heat was on, he was soon left behind. (8/1: op 4/1)
Islandreagh (IRE) looked quite a handful in the paddock, but did nothing wrong in the race until her saddle slipped and she was pulled up before four out. She would have taken all the beating. (11/4)

533 FAMOUS GROUSE H'CAP HURDLE (0-110) (4-Y.O+) (Class E)

5-05 (5-05) **3m 110y (12 hdls)** £3,048.00 (£924.00: £452.00: £216.00) GOING minus 0.37 sec per fur (GF)

				SP	RR	SF
391[2]	**Bourdonner (87)** (MDHammond) **4-10-6** RGarritty (lw: led to 3rd: led 6th: hit next: clr fr 3 out: styd on wl)	—	**1**	11/4[2]	70	2
422[3]	**Valiant Dash (86)** (JSGoldie) **10-10-6**(3) GCahill (lw: mstkes: led 3rd to 6th: outpcd 4 out: styd on appr last: no imp)	4	**2**	5/1[3]	66	2
10*	**Blooming Spring (IRE) (79)** (MrsDThomson) **7-10-2** LO'Hara (bhd: hdwy ½-wy: prom 4 out: rdn & no imp appr 2 out)	½	**3**	15/2	59	—
	Pride of May (IRE) (105) (CWFairhurst) **5-12-0** JCallaghan (bhd: effrt ½-wy: sn rdn & btn: t.o)	dist	**4**	13/2	—	—
6*	**Tough Test (IRE) (101)** (MrsJDGoodfellow) **6-11-10** BFenton (fell 1st)		**F**	13/8[1]	—	—
				(SP 106.5%)		**5 Rn**

5m 54.5 (8.50) CSF £13.97 TOTE £3.70: £1.10 £2.20 (£9.40) OWNER Mr Cornelius Lysaght (MIDDLEHAM) BRED The Overbury Stud
WEIGHT FOR AGE 4yo-4lb
391 Bourdonner jumped much better this time. After helping to set a cracking pace, he kept up the gallop in good style, although looking very tired from three out. (11/4)
422 Valiant Dash spoiled his chances by taking on the winner and making mistakes in the process. After looking well held, he did struggle on at the finish. (5/1: 7/2-11/2)
10* Blooming Spring (IRE) failed to go the early pace. She almost got into it three out, only then to look very one-paced. (15/2)

T/Plpt: £1,271.50 (7.67 Tckts). T/Qdpt: £99.20 (6.84 Tckts). AA

0528-PERTH (R-H) (Good to firm)

Saturday August 31st

WEATHER: fine

534 SCANIA 4-SERIES 'HORSEPOWER' HURDLE (3-Y.O) (Class E)

2-20 (2-23) **2m 110y (8 hdls)** £2,190.10 (£613.60: £298.30) GOING minus 0.41 sec per fur (GF)

				SP	RR	SF
	Rossel (USA) (PMonteith) **3-10-10** ADobbin (chsd ldrs: led 2 out: r.o u.p)	—	**1**	7/4[2]	66	—
	Ret Frem (IRE) (CParker) **3-10-10** BStorey (lw: chsd clr ldr: hdwy 5th: sn rdn: ev ch 2 out: nt qckn)	5	**2**	4/5[1]	61	—
	Phar Closer (WTKemp) **3-10-5b** SMcDougall (mstkes: led & sn wl clr: hdd 2 out: kpt on one pce)	1¼	**3**	25/1	55	—
	Skylight (MissMKMilligan) **3-10-7**(3) GCahill (bhd: rdn ½-wy: n.d)	13	**4**	25/1	47	—

282[4] **My Kind** (NTinkler) **3-10-5** JOsborne (bhd: effrt 5th: sn btn)....1¼ **5** 10/1 [3] 41 —
(SP 108.7%) **5 Rn**

3m 53.1 (7.10) CSF £3.36 TOTE £2.90: £1.40 £1.10 (£1.50) OWNER Underwoods (1996) Ltd (ROSEWELL) BRED Allen E. Paulson
OFFICIAL EXPLANATION **My Kind: the jockey reported that his instructions were to drop his mount in and make the best of his way home, but the filly was very keen early on, became outpaced and did not seem to stay.**
Rossel (USA) won really well at his first attempt at this game and the future looks quite bright. (7/4)
Ret Frem (IRE) had his chances throughout but, when the pressure was seriously on two from home, he failed to pull out any extra. Getting the trip could be the problem with him. (4/5)
Phar Closer had blinkers on at her first attempt at this game and went off like a scalded cat, but her jumping deteriorated as the race progressed and she was done with two out. (25/1)
282 My Kind failed to get into it, but was not knocked about. (10/1: 7/1-14/1)

535 JAMES HALSTEAD NOVICES' CHASE (5-Y.O+) (Class D)
2-50 (2-50) **3m (18 fncs)** £3,772.50 (£1,060.00: £517.50) GOING minus 0.41 sec per fur (GF)

				SP	RR	SF
411[3]	**Distant Memory (98)** (PJHobbs) **7-11-5b** APMcCoy (led to 2nd: chsd ldr: mstke 11th: sn rdn: led appr 2 out: all out)	—	**1**	Evens [1]	91	29
421*	**Scrabo View (IRE) (96)** (PBeaumont) **8-11-5** RSupple (lw: prom tl outpcd 10th: sn lost tch: styd on fr 4 out: ev ch 2 out: one pce flat)	2½	**2**	6/4 [2]	89	27
	National Choice (KCBailey) **10-10-12** AThornton (lw: j.lft: led fr 2nd: j.b lft 3 out: sn hdd: wl btn whn fell last: rmntd)	dist	**3**	5/1 [3]	—	—
				(SP 106.7%)	**3 Rn**	

6m 1.1 (3.10) CSF £2.62 TOTE £1.50: (£1.50) OWNER Mrs Ann Weston (MINEHEAD) BRED Gerald W. Leigh
411 Distant Memory took some riding but he kept responding. After being hampered by the leader three out, he soon led and then saw it out in determined style. (Evens)
421* Scrabo View (IRE) was feeling the pace with a circuit to go and looked very slow, but he did stay on from the fourth last and was close enough two out, but then lacked any change of gear. (6/4)
National Choice, despite jumping left, looked as though the race was his for much of the trip. Tired, he went violently left three out and, soon headed, was out on his feet when collapsing at the last. It would seem a left-handed track helps. (5/1)

536 SCANIA 1996 TRUCK OF THE YEAR NOVICES' HURDLE (4-Y.O+) (Class E)
3-20 (3-20) **3m 110y (12 hdls)** £2,178.20 (£610.20: £296.60) GOING minus 0.41 sec per fur (GF)

				SP	RR	SF
424*	**Good Hand (USA)** (SEKettlewell) **10-11-5** RJohnson (lw: a gng wl: hit 6th & 8th: led on bit 2 out: eased considerably towards fin)	—	**1**	4/7 [1]	69+	4
533[3]	**Blooming Spring (IRE) (79)** (MrsDThomson) **7-11-0** LO'Hara (led tl after 1st: chsd clr ldr: led 4 out to 2 out: kpt on towards fin: no imp)	½	**2**	7/4 [2]	64	—
	Kralingen (70) (NChamberlain) **4-9-10**(7) MissCMetcalfe (led after 1st & sn clr: hdd 4 out: wknd 2 out)	11	**3**	10/1 [3]	50	—
				(SP 109.1%)	**3 Rn**	

5m 57.3 (11.30) CSF £1.87 TOTE £1.40: (£1.10) OWNER Uncle Jacks Pub (MIDDLEHAM) BRED Tauner Dunlap, Jr. and Brereton C. Jones
WEIGHT FOR AGE 4yo-4lb
424* Good Hand (USA) made a couple of mistakes but, on the whole, his jumping was much better. Against this poor opposition, he looked a champion. (4/7)
533 Blooming Spring (IRE), having her second run in twenty-four hours, did all she could, but is very one-paced and was greatly flattered by her proximity to the winner. (7/4)
Kralingen gave the impression that she still needed this. Inclined to run down her hurdles, she set a good pace until running out of fuel two out. (10/1)

537 RELIABLE VEHICLES FOR SCANIA H'CAP CHASE (0-100) (5-Y.O+) (Class F)
3-55 (3-56) **2m (12 fncs)** £4,338.00 (£1,218.00: £594.00) GOING minus 0.41 sec per fur (GF)

				SP	RR	SF
76[3]	**Super Sharp (NZ) (79)** (HOliver) **8-10-7** JacquiOliver (lw: mde all: hit 4th: kpt on strly fr 4 out)	—	**1**	4/1 [2]	99	22
	Beldine (100) (PMonteith) **11-12-0** ADobbin (lw: hld up: effrt 4 out: sn rdn: hmpd next: no imp)	14	**2**	4/9 [1]	106	29
	Blazing Trail (IRE) (103) (MissLucindaRussell) **8-12-3** AThornton (chsd wnr: rdn fr 8th: blnd 3 out: sn btn)	11	**3**	9/2 [3]	98	21
				(SP 107.4%)	**3 Rn**	

3m 51.9 (0.90) CSF £6.00 TOTE £4.00: (£1.90) OWNER Mrs Sue Careless (CHELTENHAM) BRED Dr R. G. & Mrs L. A. Martin
76 Super Sharp (NZ) was very fit. Attacking his fences, he got his rivals off the bit by the fourth last and the race was always his. (4/1)
Beldine has won his share of races and loves this track, but he does like things to go his way and, once off the bit four out, he was never doing enough to make an impression. (4/9: op 4/6)
Blazing Trail (IRE), an Irish import, has always been happier with some give in the ground and was struggling in second place when a blunder three out finished him. (9/2: op 5/2)

538 HEATHER PRE-PACKS H'CAP HURDLE (0-120) (4-Y.O+) (Class D)
4-25 (4-25) **2m 110y (8 hdls)** £3,022.00 (£916.00: £448.00: £214.00) GOING minus 0.41 sec per fur (GF)

				SP	RR	SF
214[2]	**Sarmatian (USA) (95)** (MDHammond) **5-11-0** RGarritty (lw: hld up: hdwy on bit 3 out: led & mstke last: qcknd)	—	**1**	5/2 [1]	79	39
334*	**Wamdha (IRE) (102)** (KAMorgan) **6-11-7** ASSmith (a.p: led 2 out to last: no ex)	5	**2**	4/1 [2]	81	41
	Eden Dancer (108) (MrsMReveley) **4-11-10** PNiven (chsd ldr: led 5th to 2 out: sn btn)	12	**3**	5/2 [1]	76	33
347[4]	**Forgetful (85)** (DBurchell) **7-10-4** DJBurchell (led to 5th: wkng whn blnd 2 out)	5	**4**	8/1	48	8
478[3]	**Vain Prince (104)** (NTinkler) **9-11-9b** JOsborne (lw: chsd ldrs tl rdn & btn 3 out)	2½	**5**	8/1	64	24
	Hee's a Dancer (105) (MJCamacho) **4-11-2**(5) ECallaghan (hld up: effrt 5th: sn rdn & btn)	15	**6**	7/1 [3]	51	8
				(SP 111.9%)	**6 Rn**	

3m 44.2 (-1.80) CSF £11.98 TOTE £3.50: £1.20 £3.60 (£7.50) OWNER Mr S. T. Brankin (MIDDLEHAM) BRED David Allan
WEIGHT FOR AGE 4yo-3lb
214 Sarmatian (USA), who looked a picture, travelled on the bridle and won as he pleased, despite hitting the last. In this mood, he is certainly useful, but he is not one to trust entirely. (5/2)
334* Wamdha (IRE) was always thereabouts, but had no answer to the winner's turn of foot from the last. (4/1)

Eden Dancer had had a run on the Flat recently, but probably still needed this, and the Handicapper has also set him a stiffish task. (5/2)
284 Forgetful tried to gallop her rivals into the ground, but she was caught some way out and was done with when blundering two out. (8/1: 6/1-9/1)
Hee's a Dancer got very warm beforehand and ran most disappointingly, suggesting that this was too quick after his Flat outing only a week previously. (7/1: op 4/1)

539 SCANIA 4-SERIES 'KING OF THE ROAD' H'CAP HURDLE (0-110) (4-Y.O+) (Class E)

4-55 (4-55) **2m 4f 110y (10 hdls)** £2,710.00 (£820.00: £400.00: £190.00) GOING minus 0.41 sec per fur (GF)

	Horse	Dist	Pos	SP	RR	SF
528[2]	**Born to Please (IRE) (87)** (PJHobbs) **4-11-0** APMcCoy (lw: mde all: sn rdn clr: drvn fr ½-wy: styd on wl)	—	1	7/4[1]	69	14
453[6]	**Tashreef (77)** (JJBirkett) **6-10-7b** MMoloney (chsd wnr fr 4th tl wknd 3 out)	18	2	20/1	45	—
422[2]	**Take Two (94)** (MissMKMilligan) **8-11-10** ADobbin (lw: hld up: effrt ½-wy: hdwy u.p 4 out: nvr able to chal)	s.h	3	3/1[3]	62	10
	Souson (IRE) (89) (JWade) **8-11-5b** KJones (chsd wnr to 4th: rdn & wknd 4 out)	12	4	7/1	48	—
491*	**Frontier Flight (USA) (94)** (MissLCSiddall) **6-11-7**(3) 7x EHusband (lw: hld up: hdwy 4 out: sn chsng wnr: rdn & 10l 2nd whn fell 2 out)		F	2/1[2]	—	—

(SP 112.0%) **5 Rn**

4m 53.1 (5.10) CSF £22.05 TOTE £1.90: £1.20 £5.00 (£24.50) OWNER A B S Racing (MINEHEAD) BRED Mrs S. O'Riordan
WEIGHT FOR AGE 4yo-3lb
STEWARDS' ENQUIRY Dobbin susp. 11-14/9/96 (failure to ensure best possible placing).
528 Born to Please (IRE), given a superb ride, never looked happy, but his rider made his mind up for him and he kept answering the calls. (7/4)
Tashreef chased the winner from halfway, but looked very slow over the last three flights. (20/1)
422 Take Two began a run at halfway but, soon all out, he was never good enough, although he would have been second but for being eased in the closing stages. (3/1)
491* Frontier Flight (USA) went in pursuit of the winner after the fourth last, but was soon under pressure, and was a good ten lengths adrift and seemingly going nowhere when falling heavily two out. (2/1)

T/Plpt: £41.70 (226.29 Tckts). T/Qdpt: £17.00 (19.6 Tckts). AA

HEXHAM (L-H) (Firm)
Monday September 2nd
Meeting Abandoned after Race 1 - Course unsafe

540 BUCHANAN ORIGINAL HURDLE (3-Y.O) (Class E)

2-00 (2-00) **2m (8 hdls)** £2,658.00 (£642.00)

	Horse	Dist	Pos	SP	RR	SF
458[2]	**Royal Rapport** (JGMO'Shea) **3-10-5v**(5) MichaelBrennan (trckd ldr: hmpd 1st: led 3 out: slipped between last 2: hung bdly lft u.p & drew clr flat)	—	1	15/8[2]	65?	—
291*	**Kernof (IRE)** (MDHammond) **3-11-3** RGarritty (lw: j.slowly: led: j.rt 3rd: slipped next: hdd 3 out: ev ch & rdn last: nt qckn)	5	2	4/7[1]	67?	—
	Miss Impulse (MissJBower) **3-10-2**(3) TDascombe (bit bkwd: hld up: hit 5th: sn rdn & outpcd: prom whn s.u bnd appr 2 out)		S	10/1[3]	—	—

(SP 107.5%) **3 Rn**

4m 2.4 (14.40) CSF £3.20 TOTE £2.90: (£1.20) OWNER Mr Gary Roberts (WELFORD-ON-AVON) BRED P. Young
IN-FOCUS: **Overnight rain made the conditions treacherous and at various stages of the race all three runners lost their footing.**
458 Royal Rapport slipped and almost came down between the last two on what looked treacherous ground. Despite hanging badly left, he was driven clear on the run-in. (15/8)
291* Kernof (IRE) jumped hesitantly. Jumping badly right at the third, he slipped taking off at the next. Almost upsides at the last, he the found the winner much too good. His jumping will have to improve markedly if he is to progress. (4/7)
Miss Impulse, who wore a crossed-noseband, was still well in touch but struggling when she slipped and took a heavy fall on the flat after the third last. (10/1)

541 THELMA, MARJORIE, LYNDA AND JOYCE NOVICES' H'CAP HURDLE (0-100) (4-Y.O+) (Class E)
Abandoned - Course unsafe

542 LCL PILS LAGER (S) H'CAP CHASE (0-95) (5-Y.O+) (Class G)
Abandoned - Course unsafe

543 KEOGHAN'S ALE H'CAP HURDLE (0-105) (4-Y.O+) (Class F)
Abandoned - Course unsafe

544 JOHN HOGG HAULAGE H'CAP CHASE (0-110) (5-Y.O+) (Class E)
Abandoned - Course unsafe

545 FEDERATION BREWERY SPECIAL ALE STANDARD N.H. FLAT RACE (4, 5 & 6-Y.O) (Class H)
Abandoned - Course unsafe

T/Plpt: £2.60 (3,139.4 Tckts). WG

0480-NEWTON ABBOT (L-H) (Good)
Wednesday September 4th
WEATHER: sunny

546 MHV (S) HURDLE (4,5,6 & 7-Y.O) (Class G)

2-30 (2-30) **2m 6f (10 hdls)** £1,774.80 (£497.80: £242.40) GOING minus 0.58 sec per fur (F)

	Horse	Dist	Pos	SP	RR	SF
480[3]	**Kutan (IRE) (65)** (MrsBarbaraWaring) **6-10-12** EByrne (lw: hld up mid div: hdwy to chse ldr 6th: led appr 2 out: sn clr)	—	1	7/2[3]	47	6

Form	Horse / Trainer / Age-Weight / Jockey / Comment	Dist	Pos	SP	RR	SF
345^{3}	**Miss Souter (66)** (HSHowe) **7-11-7v** APMcCoy (led tl hdd & wknd appr 2 out)	13	**2**	5/1	47	6
412*	**Akiymann (USA) (82)** (MCPipe) **6-11-5b** DBridgwater (j.slowly: bhd 4th: rdn & wl bhd appr 7th: styd on fr next: nrst fin)	13	**3**	$3/1^{2}$	35	—
480^{4}	**Coeur Battant (FR) (63)** (RJBaker) **6-11-5** BPowell (bhd: styd on fr 8th: nvr nrr)	1¼	**4**	12/1	34	—
	Just-Mana-Mou (IRE) (88) (WGMTurner) **4-10-10** RDunwoody (lw: chsd ldr to 6th: rdn 8th: wknd)	2	**5**	$9/4^{1}$	26	—
408^{6}	**Mutley (61)** (NJHawke) **6-10-12** CMaude (a in rr: t.o whn p.u after 8th)		**P**	12/1	—	—
410^{3}	**On My Toes** (RGFrost) **5-10-7** JFrost (chsd ldrs tl rdn after 6th: grad wknd: p.u bef last)		**P**	16/1	—	—

(SP 115.9%) **7 Rn**

5m 16.6 (4.60) CSF £20.09 TOTE £5.10: £2.00 £2.90 (£17.50) OWNER Mr E. S. Chivers (CHIPPENHAM) BRED E. Moloney
WEIGHT FOR AGE 4yo-2lb
Bt in 3,700 gns
480 Kutan (IRE), in a very poor race, was never going to be caught after easing to the front. (7/2)
345 Miss Souter, trying to make her stamina tell over this slightly shorter trip, was done with once the winner went past. She might be worth a try over two and a half in similar grade. (5/1: 7/2-11/2)
412* Akiymann (USA) had one of his frequent off-days and only decided to stay on when it was all over. (3/1: 7/4-100/30)
Coeur Battant (FR) (12/1: op 8/1)
Just-Mana-Mou (IRE) was the one punters latched onto, with Dunwoody looking a significant booking, but he ran poorly. (9/4)

547 COOPER CALLAS KITCHEN AND BATHROOM DISTRIBUTORS NOVICES' CHASE (5-Y.O+) (Class E)

3-00 (3-00) **2m 110y (13 fncs)** £2,831.85 (£856.80: £417.90: £198.45) GOING minus 0.58 sec per fur (F)

Form	Horse / Trainer / Age-Weight / Jockey / Comment	Dist	Pos	SP	RR	SF
482^{2}	**Bit of A Touch** (RGFrost) **10-10-12** JFrost (lw: mde all: clr last: drvn out)	—	**1**	$4/1^{3}$	81	17
484^{2}	**Duke of Dreams (79)** (RJBaker) **6-11-5** BPowell (hld up mid div: hdwy to chse wnr 9th: ev ch 2 out: one pce appr last)	4	**2**	$7/4^{1}$	84	20
	Chickabiddy (GFEdwards) **8-10-7** MAFitzgerald (bit bkwd: bhd: hdwy to chse ldrs 7th: one pce fr 11th)	6	**3**	$9/4^{2}$	66	2
	Stormy Sunset (WWDennis) **9-10-5**(7)ow5 MrTDennis (bit bkwd: chsd ldrs: mstkes 3rd & 4th: wknd 8th: t.o)	dist	**4**	9/2	—	—
359^{5}	**Great Uncle** (JWDufosee) **8-10-7b**[1](5) PHenley (bhd 6th: rdn & sn wknd: t.o)	12	**5**	50/1	—	—
503^{3}	**Saracen's Boy (IRE) (61)** (MRChurches) **8-10-12** MrLJefford (chsd wnr tl mstke 8th: wkng whn mstke next: blnd & uns rdr 10th)		**U**	33/1	—	—

(SP 110.2%) **6 Rn**

4m 0.5 (0.50) CSF £10.83 TOTE £5.00: £1.70 £1.40 (£3.70) OWNER A E C Electric Fencing Ltd (Hotline) (BUCKFASTLEIGH) BRED Hesmonds Stud Ltd
482 Bit of A Touch, who had been catching cows on the gallops, was sent out in front over this shorter trip and never really looked like being overhauled. (4/1)
484 Duke of Dreams probably just found the penalty anchoring him having had every chance, but he remains in good form. (7/4)
Chickabiddy, a bit of an Exeter specialist, will have found this blowing away the cobwebs. (9/4)
Stormy Sunset (9/2: 3/1-5/1)

548 CHEF'S LARDER HURDLE (3-Y.O) (Class D)

3-30 (3-30) **2m 1f (8 hdls)** £2,725.70 (£765.20: £373.10) GOING minus 0.58 sec per fur (F)

Form	Horse / Trainer / Age-Weight / Jockey / Comment	Dist	Pos	SP	RR	SF
	Noble Lord (RHBuckler) **3-10-10** BPowell (hdwy to ld appr 5th: clr after next: unchal)	—	**1**	$9/2^{2}$	73+	—
	Tablets of Stone (IRE) (JRBosley) **3-10-10** MBosley (chsd ldr: outpcd whn mstke 6th: styd on appr 2 out: nvr nrr)	21	**2**	14/1	53	—
	Spring Campaign (IRE) (MCPipe) **3-10-10** DBridgwater (lw: a.p: chsd wnr 6th: ev ch tl wknd qckly appr 2 out)	14	**3**	$4/7^{1}$	40	—
	Premier Son (WGMTurner) **3-10-10** RDunwoody (chsd ldrs tl wknd appr 5th: t.o)	dist	**4**	$11/1^{3}$	—	—
282^{2}	**Four Weddings (USA)** (MCPipe) **3-10-10b** CMaude (led tl appr 5th: wknd qckly: t.o whn p.u bef 2 out)		**P**	$9/2^{2}$	—	—
	Taurean Fire (DFBassett) **3-10-5**(5) DJKavanagh (bhd: lost tch after 4th: p.u bef next: dismntd)		**P**	66/1	—	—

(SP 116.5%) **6 Rn**

4m 0.8 (7.80) CSF £48.19 TOTE £7.70: £2.40 £4.60 (£31.50) OWNER The Old Timers Partnership (BRIDPORT) BRED J. E. Swiers
Noble Lord, a maiden on the Flat at trips around ten furlongs, ran off 65 in his last race in that sphere. It will be interesting to see if he progresses over hurdles. (9/2)
Tablets of Stone (IRE) made a sound enough debut. Bred to be a sprinter, he ran as though he wants further than this. (14/1: 5/1-16/1)
Spring Campaign (IRE), clearly expected to make a winning bow, went backwards on the Flat last season and would not be one to take a short price about. (4/7: tchd 10/11)
Premier Son (11/1: 9/2-12/1)
282 Four Weddings (USA) (9/2: 11/4-5/1)

549 COOPER CALLAS KITCHEN AND BATHROOM DISTRIBUTORS NOVICES' HURDLE (4-Y.O+) (Class E)

4-00 (4-01) **2m 6f (10 hdls)** £2,200.50 (£618.00: £301.50) GOING minus 0.58 sec per fur (F)

Form	Horse / Trainer / Age-Weight / Jockey / Comment	Dist	Pos	SP	RR	SF
	Storm Run (IRE) (98) (PFNicholls) **6-10-12** APMcCoy (stdy hdwy to ld appr 7th: clr next: unchal)	—	**1**	$6/4^{1}$	65+	2
360*	**Idiom (70)** (MrsJGRetter) **9-11-5** JCulloty (lw: hld up mid div: hdwy to chse wnr 7th: outpcd next)	8	**2**	$100/30^{2}$	66	3
499*	**China Mail (IRE) (94)** (KCBailey) **4-11-3** TJMurphy (lw: hld up: hdwy 6th: chsd ldrs next: sn outpcd)	10	**3**	$6/4^{1}$	59	—
	The Last Mistress (JNeville) **9-10-7** RFarrant (chsd ldrs tl lost tch 6th: t.o)	dist	**4**	40/1	—	—
	Heaton (NZ) (HGRowsell) **9-10-12** BPowell (bit bkwd: led to 2nd: chsd ldr: in tch tl rdn & wknd 7th: t.o)	22	**5**	66/1	—	—
	Banks of The Bride (MrsBarbaraWaring) **6-10-12** EByrne (a bhd: lost tch 7th: t.o whn mstke last)	25	**6**	100/1	—	—
	Pioneer Princess (GFEdwards) **4-10-5** MAFitzgerald (a in rr: rdn & wknd 6th: t.o whn p.u bef 2 out)		**P**	$33/1^{3}$	—	—
	Tamars Cousin (MissJduPlessis) **6-10-12** GUpton (bit bkwd: led 2nd tl appr 7th: wknd qckly: t.o whn p.u bef 2 out)		**P**	100/1	—	—

(SP 111.9%) **8 Rn**

5m 16.9 (4.90) CSF £6.54 TOTE £2.50: £1.10 £1.10 £1.10 (£4.80) OWNER Mr J. W. Aplin (SHEPTON MALLET) BRED J. Browne
WEIGHT FOR AGE 4yo-2lb
Storm Run (IRE), a bumper winner, did not seem to possess the speed to win over the minimum trip over hurdles in four attempts last season, and made no mistake over this longer distance. He can win again. (6/4)
360* Idiom probably found his penalty anchoring him, having had every chance. (100/30: 5/2-4/1)
499* China Mail (IRE), weak in the market for this hat-trick bid, ran another sound race. (6/4)

550 BOOKER CASH & CARRY H'CAP CHASE (0-120) (5-Y.O+) (Class D)

4-30 (4-30) **3m 2f 110y (20 fncs)** £3,441.10 (£1,040.80: £507.40: £240.70) GOING minus 0.58 sec per fur (F)

				SP	RR	SF
	Rainbow Castle (95) (PFNicholls) **9-10-3** APMcCoy (hld up: hdwy 11th: chsd ldr 15th: rdn 2 out: led appr last: comf)	—	**1**	$2/1^{1}$	101+	31
342^{6}	**Gilston Lass (92)** (JSKing) **9-10-0** JCulloty (led: mstke 6th: rdn 2 out: hdd appr last: no ex)	4	**2**	10/1	96	26
452^{3}	**Hillwalk (120)** (RCurtis) **10-12-0** DMorris (hdwy & lft to chse ldr 10th: rdn & wknd 16th)	24	**3**	$4/1^{3}$	109	39
487*	**Andrelot (113)** (PBowen) **9-11-7b** 6x RDunwoody (in tch to 11th: wknd: sn t.o)	22	**4**	$9/4^{2}$	89	19
	Banntown Bill (IRE) (95) (MCPipe) **7-10-3v** DBridgwater (bhd 3rd: sn struggling: t.o whn p.u bef 12th)		**P**	9/1	—	—
342^{P}	**Winnie Lorraine (97)** (RHAlner) **11-10-5** CLlewellyn (bit bkwd: chsd ldr tl blnd & uns rdr 10th)		**U**	10/1	—	—

(SP 112.3%) **6 Rn**

6m 26.4 (-7.60) CSF £18.47 TOTE £3.20: £1.70 £3.70 (£11.60) OWNER Mr Jeffrey Hordle (SHEPTON MALLET) BRED Michael O'Connor
LONG HANDICAP Gilston Lass 9-11

Rainbow Castle, the second first-time-out winner to be sent out by Paul Nicholls at the meeting, took it comfortably. (2/1)
Gilston Lass had conditions to suit and showed a return to form. (10/1)
452 Hillwalk was racing off a 10lb higher mark than when successful on his seasonal comeback. (4/1)

551 ARMITAGE SHANKS BETTER BATHROOMS H'CAP HURDLE (0-110) (4-Y.O+) (Class E)

5-00 (5-00) **2m 1f (8 hdls)** £2,221.50 (£624.00: £304.50) GOING minus 0.58 sec per fur (F)

				SP	RR	SF
396*	**Zine Lane (98)** (MajorWRHern) **4-11-5** RFarrant (lw: chsng ldr whn hmpd & lft in ld 4th: hdd appr next: led after 6th: rdn & hld on u.p flat)	—	**1**	$2/1^{1}$	75	1
	Marchman (88) (JSKing) **11-10-11** JCulloty (bhd: stdy hdwy 6th: ev ch 2 out tl mstke last: nt rcvr)	2½	**2**	7/1	63+	—
456^{4}	**Sirtelimar (IRE) (88)** (KCBailey) **7-10-11** TJMurphy (hld up: hdwy 5th: ev ch 2 out: wknd appr last)	6	**3**	8/1	57	—
183^{2}	**Sian Wyn (83)** (KRBurke) **6-10-6** RDunwoody (prom: led appr 5th tl after next: wknd appr 2 out)	9	**4**	$6/1^{3}$	44	—
483^{6}	**Little Hooligan (86)** (GFEdwards) **5-10-9b** APMcCoy (bhd: hdwy 3rd: prom 6th tl rdn & wknd 2 out)	½	**5**	$6/1^{3}$	46	—
457^{3}	**Gabish (77)** (BScriven) **11-9-7**(7) MrRThornton (mid div tl wknd 5th: t.o)	dist	**6**	66/1	—	—
	Jewel Thief (87) (GBBalding) **6-10-10** BFenton (bit bkwd: a bhd: t.o 6th)	22	**7**	14/1	—	—
	Gold Medal (FR) (105) (MCPipe) **8-12-0** DBridgwater (led tl fell 4th)		**F**	12/1	—	—
223^{2}	**El Grando (83)** (KOCunningham-Brown) **6-10-6** AMaguire (lw: chsng ldrs whn hmpd 4th: p.u lame)		**P**	$3/1^{2}$	—	—

(SP 126.4%) **9 Rn**

3m 58.2 (5.20) CSF £17.28 CT £92.19 TOTE £2.40: £1.20 £3.00 £2.40 (£17.20) Trio £119.20 OWNER The Hopeful Partnership (LAMBOURN) BRED W. R. and S. J. Hern Partnership
LONG HANDICAP Gabish 8-2
WEIGHT FOR AGE 4yo-2lb

396* Zine Lane scrambled home after going on at the sixth. (2/1)
Marchman would have given the winner plenty to think about but for the blunder at the last. (7/1)
399 Sirtelimar (IRE) finished nicely clear of the rest. (8/1)
Jewel Thief (14/1: 8/1-16/1)
Gold Medal (FR) (12/1: op 6/1)

T/Plpt: £100.20 (90.88 Tckts). T/Qdpt: £82.40 (7.23 Tckts). T

0401-PLUMPTON (L-H) (Good to firm)

Thursday September 5th

WEATHER: sunny

552 PATCHAM CONDITIONAL H'CAP HURDLE (0-105) (4-Y.O+) (Class F)

2-30 (2-32) **2m 1f (10 hdls)** £2,138.40 (£592.40: £283.20) GOING minus 0.07 sec per fur (G)

				SP	RR	SF
491^{2}	**Tel E Thon (80)** (MissCJECaroe) **9-10-7v** DFortt (mde all: rdn appr last: r.o wl)	—	**1**	7/1	64	—
473^{2}	**Pair of Jacks (IRE) (84)** (GLMoore) **6-10-11** BFenton (lw: stdy hdwy 3 out: chsd wnr appr 2 out: ev ch last: unable qckn)	2½	**2**	$7/4^{1}$	66	—
403^{2}	**Safety (USA) (95)** (JWhite) **9-11-8b** TJMurphy (lw: chsd wnr tl appr 2 out: sn wknd)	20	**3**	$11/2^{3}$	58	—
502^{3}	**Script (79)** (JRJenkins) **5-10-1v**(5) NTEgan (lw: hdwy 3 out: wknd appr 2 out)	5	**4**	12/1	37	—
404^{5}	**Emallen (IRE) (73)** (MrsLCJewell) **8-10-0b** SophieMitchell (bhd fr 6th)	1½	**5**	25/1	30	—
	Antonio Mariano (SWE) (97) (JTGifford) **5-11-10** LAspell (bit bkwd: swtg: hld up: rdn 3 out: sn wknd: t.o)	26	**6**	$7/2^{2}$	29	—
	Aramon (77) (MJHaynes) **6-10-4b** MichaelBrennan (lw: 4th whn fell 7th)		**F**	10/1	—	—

(SP 107.1%) **7 Rn**

4m 8.6 (12.60) CSF £17.90 TOTE £8.70: £3.10 £1.20 (£7.40) OWNER Miss C. J. E. Caroe (THURLEIGH) BRED Mrs D. Manning
LONG HANDICAP Emallen (IRE) 9-10

491 Tel E Thon made every post a winning one and, rousted along approaching the final flight, proved too good for the runner-up on the flat. (7/1: 5/1-8/1)
473 Pair of Jacks (IRE) steadily crept into the action three from home and cruised up to throw down his challenge in the straight. Still in with every chance early on the run-in, he then failed to find what was required. (7/4)
403 Safety (USA) raced in second place and travelled well until collared for that position turning for home, from which point he fell in a heap. (11/2: 5/2-6/1)
Script made a brief effort three from home, but it came to little. (12/1: 10/1-16/1)
Antonio Mariano (SWE), a very nervy individual, got rather warm in the paddock, but settled a lot better in the race compared with last season. Travelling well entering the back straight for the final time, he was asked for his effort three from home, but found absolutely nothing. He will strip fitter for this. (7/2)

553 LINDFIELD (S) HURDLE (4-Y.O+) (Class G)

3-00 (3-00) **2m 4f (12 hdls)** £1,859.00 (£514.00: £245.00) GOING minus 0.07 sec per fur (G)

				SP	RR	SF
493^{3}	**Hacketts Cross (IRE) (99)** (PEccles) **8-11-5** AMaguire (hld up: chsd ldr after 3 out: shkn up to ld flat: r.o wl)	—	**1**	$13/8^{1}$	71	—

				SP	RR	SF
492[4]	**Tug Your Forelock (74)** (GFJohnsonHoughton) **5-10-12** AThornton (hdwy 4th: chsd ldr fr 5th: led 9th tl flat: r.o)	½	**2**	12/1[3]	64	—
492[R]	**Kingswell Boy** (MCPipe) **10-10-12** DBridgwater (lw: chsd ldr: lft in ld 4th: hdd 9th: ev ch 3 out: nt run on)	8	**3**	5/1[2]	57	—
	Roger's Pal (54) (AMoore) **9-11-5**(7) MBatchelor (bit bkwd: bhd fr 8th)	6	**4**	33/1	66	—
479[3]	**Ballad Ruler** (PAPritchard) **10-10-12** RSupple (lw: bhd fr 9th: t.o)	dist	**5**	33/1	—	—
	Dudwell Valley (IRE) (MrsLCJewell) **4-10-5** JRailton (bit bkwd: a bhd: t.o whn p.u bef 8th)		**P**	33/1	—	—
	Kesanta (WGMTurner) **6-10-7** APMcCoy (lw: led: clr whn blnd & uns rdr 4th)		**U**	13/8[1]	—	—
				(SP 109.4%)	**7 Rn**	

5m 5.0 (18.00) CSF £17.75 TOTE £2.70: £1.90 £3.50 (£4.20) OWNER Mr Brian Lewendon (LAMBOURN) BRED Lawrence Rowan
WEIGHT FOR AGE 4yo-2lb
No bid

493 Hacketts Cross (IRE) was given a good ride by Maguire. Moving into second place soon after the third last, Maguire was very keen to nurse the gelding home and, delivering a challenge in the straight, only shook his mount up to settle the issue on the run-in. (13/8)

260 Tug Your Forelock went on four from home. With the winner breathing down his neck in the straight, he was only there on sufferance and was worried out of it on the run-in. (12/1: op 8/1)

Kingswell Boy raced in second place until left in front at the fourth. He did not appear terribly enthusiastic about the prospect and was collared four out. Nevertheless, he still had every chance jumping the next but, with his jockey very keen not to get busy on him, the gelding simply would not have it. A pair of blinkers look essential. (5/1)

Kesanta, second in a seller at Beverley on the Flat twelve days earlier, was having her first run over hurdles for three years. Bowling along in front, she had established a clear advantage at the fourth, where she got rid of her rider. She is worth another chance in this company. (13/8)

554 DOUG WOOD NOVICES' H'CAP CHASE (0-100) (5-Y.O+) (Class E)

3-30 (3-30) **2m (13 fncs)** £2,933.70 (£873.60: £415.80: £186.90) GOING minus 0.61 sec per fur (F)

				SP	RR	SF
472*	**Harrow Way (IRE) (76)** (LWells) **6-10-7** [7x] AMaguire (lw: chsd ldr: led 4 out: comf)	—	**1**	4/7[1]	89+	—
296[4]	**Heresthedeal (IRE) (97)** (GMMcCourt) **7-12-0v**[1] BClifford (led to 4 out: unable qckn)	5	**2**	9/4[2]	105	14
	Seasamacamile (69) (RHBuckler) **9-10-0** BPowell (lw: pckd 6th: wl bhd to 2 out: nvr nrr)	8	**3**	8/1[3]	69	—
470[F]	**Lavalight (70)** (JWDufosee) **9-9-10**(5) PHenley (a wl bhd)	19	**4**	33/1	51	—
				(SP 108.5%)	**4 Rn**	

3m 55.4 (3.40) CSF £2.16 TOTE £1.30 (£1.50) OWNER Mrs Carrie Zetter-Wells (BILLINGSHURST) BRED Joseph Smiddy
LONG HANDICAP Seasamacamile 9-8

472* Harrow Way (IRE) raced in second place. Jumping into the lead four out, he comfortably had the measure of his only serious danger. (4/7)

296 Heresthedeal (IRE) was not going to hang around and set a brisk pace that only the winner could live with. Collared four out, he was soon put in his place. (9/4: 6/4-11/4)

555 HAYWARDS HEATH NOVICES' CLAIMING HURDLE (4-Y.O+) (Class F)

4-00 (4-01) **2m 1f (10 hdls)** £2,247.60 (£623.60: £298.80) GOING minus 0.07 sec per fur (G)

				SP	RR	SF
	Courbaril (SDow) **4-11-6** APMcCoy (lw: a.p: led appr 2 out: sn clr: easily)	—	**1**	3/1[1]	82+	10
469*	**Burnt Sienna (IRE) (79)** (JSMoore) **4-10-9v** WMcFarland (lw: a.p: led 6th tl appr 2 out: unable qckn)	10	**2**	5/1	62	—
407[3]	**Denomination (USA) (91)** (MCPipe) **4-11-3** DBridgwater (stdy hdwy fr 7th: rdn appr last: r.o one pce)	hd	**3**	9/2[3]	70	—
	Paper Cloud (RTPhillips) **4-10-3** JRailton (hdwy 5th: rdn appr 2 out: one pce)	2½	**4**	13/2	53	—
	Lucky Domino (MSheppard) **6-10-7** RJohnson (nvr nr to chal)	18	**5**	33/1	38	—
483[5]	**Reefa's Mill (IRE) (81)** (JNeville) **4-11-0b** WMarston (mid div whn blnd 6th: wknd 7th)	3½	**6**	12/1	44	—
	More Bills (IRE) (AMoore) **4-9-12**(7) MBatchelor (a bhd)	3	**7**	12/1	32	—
396[P]	**On the Ledge (USA) (48)** (HJManners) **6-10-0**(7) ADowling (a.p: led 5th to 6th: sn wknd)	16	**8**	100/1	17	—
	Gone For Lunch (89) (MissHCKnight) **5-10-13** JCulloty (bhd fr 7th)	1½	**9**	4/1[2]	22	—
	Radical Exception (IRE) (DLWilliams) **6-10-10** PHolley (s.s: mstke 2nd: a bhd: t.o whn p.u bef 7th)		**P**	50/1	—	—
	Solo Volumes (HGRowsell) **7-11-2** BPowell (led to 5th: wknd 6th: t.o whn p.u bef 3 out)		**P**	50/1	—	—
1917[7]	**Two Hearts** (JWDufosee) **4-9-12**(5) PHenley (lw: a bhd: t.o whn p.u bef 2 out)		**P**	33/1	—	—
	Woodlands Electric (PAPritchard) **6-10-7** RSupple (a bhd: t.o whn p.u bef 3 out)		**P**	100/1	—	—
				(SP 120.4%)	**13 Rn**	

4m 8.1 (12.10) CSF £17.60 TOTE £4.30: £1.70 £1.60 £1.80 (£12.30) Trio £10.60 OWNER Mr G. Steinberg (EPSOM) BRED George & Mrs Steinberg
WEIGHT FOR AGE 4yo-2lb
Courbaril clmd CBarnes £8,000; More Bills (IRE) clmd SHarrison £3,000

Courbaril, who refused to race once on the Flat this year but subsequently finished second in two sellers, seemed to enjoy himself on this hurdling debut. Always handy, he went to the front turning for home and forged clear to win with a ton in hand in this very poor race. (3/1)

469* Burnt Sienna (IRE) went to the front early on the final circuit. Collared turning for home, she found the winner far too good. (5/1)

407 Denomination (USA) steadily crept closer in the last half-mile and, with his jockey very keen to only give him the kid-glove treatment, the combination stayed on, only just failing to take second place. He looks the type who will resent stern pressure. (9/2: 3/1-5/1)

Paper Cloud took closer order setting out on the final circuit but, pushed along turning for home, failed to find that vital turn of foot. (13/2)

Gone For Lunch (4/1: 3/1-9/2)

556 GEORGE POOLE NOVICES' CHASE (5-Y.O+) (Class E)

4-30 (4-30) **2m 5f (16 fncs)** £2,976.00 (£888.00: £424.00: £192.00) GOING minus 0.61 sec per fur (F)

				SP	RR	SF
	Mill O'The Rags (IRE) (MrsDHaine) **7-10-12** JFTitley (mde all: comf)	—	**1**	6/4[1]	77+	10
411[4]	**Our Nikki (58)** (PRRodford) **6-10-7** SBurrough (mstke 2nd: hdwy 9th: chsd wnr fr 12th: mstke 2 out: unable qckn)	8	**2**	20/1	66	—
480*	**North Bannister (66)** (TPMcGovern) **9-10-12** GCrone (lft 2nd 4th tl mstke 12th: one pce)	6	**3**	11/4[2]	66	—
	Straight Laced (USA) (85) (PCClarke) **9-10-12** BFenton (a bhd: t.o fr 10th)	dist	**4**	33/1	—	—
360[4]	**Miramare** (JWDufosee) **6-10-7**(5) PHenley (bhd fr 6th: t.o fr 10th: p.u bef 3 out)		**P**	12/1	—	—
	Fort Gale (IRE) (CPEBrooks) **5-10-9** GBradley (bit bkwd: w ldr tl blnd & uns rdr 4th)		**U**	5/1[3]	—	—
486[3]	**Hizal (72)** (HJManners) **7-11-5** MrACharles-Jones (4th whn blnd & uns rdr 5th)		**U**	8/1	—	—
				(SP 109.8%)	**7 Rn**	

5m 15.5 (2.50) CSF £23.84 TOTE £1.80: £1.40 £2.70 (£11.10) OWNER Mr E. J. Fenaroli (NEWMARKET) BRED Noel Fenton
WEIGHT FOR AGE 5yo-3lb

Mill O'The Rags (IRE) made a winning debut over fences. Making it all, he comfortably had the measure of his only serious rival in the last half-mile. (6/4)
Our Nikki moved through to take second place five out. On the heels of the winner when making a mistake at the penultimate fence, she then failed to find the necessary turn of foot. (20/1)
480* North Bannister, left in second place at the fourth, was collared for that position when making a mistake five out. From that point, he could only plod on in his own time. (11/4)
Miramare (12/1: 7/1-14/1)
486 Hizal (8/1: op 7/2)

557 PEASE POTTAGE NOVICES' H'CAP HURDLE (0-100) (4-Y.O+) (Class E)
5-00 (5-00) **2m 4f (12 hdls)** £2,280.00 (£630.00: £300.00) GOING minus 0.07 sec per fur (G)

				SP	RR	SF
	Brassic Lint (73) (JNeville) **6-10-7** DBridgwater (mde all: sn clr: mstkes 7th & last: all out)	—	1	9/4[2]	61	13
327[2]	**Canary Falcon (82)** (HJCollingridge) **5-11-2** VSmith (lw: hdwy to chse wnr 9th: rdn appr 2 out: r.o)	3	2	7/2[3]	68	20
506[6]	**Positivo (85)** (MissCJECaroe) **5-11-5** ILawrence (chsd wnr to 7th: wknd 9th)	8	3	10/1	64	16
137*	**Efharisto (92)** (JWhite) **7-11-12b** AMaguire (lw: hld up: mstkes 3rd & 8th: hrd rdn: no rspnse: t.o fr 9th)	28	4	2/1[1]	49	1
71[4]	**First Class (94)** (GNAlford) **6-12-0** BFenton (lw: a.p: chsd wnr 7th to 9th: sn wknd: t.o whn p.u bef 2 out)		P	6/1	—	—
				(SP 109.7%)		**5 Rn**

4m 57.3 (10.30) CSF £9.56 TOTE £3.70: £2.10 £1.30 (£6.00) OWNER Mr K. M. Stanworth (NEWPORT, GWENT) BRED W. R. Jones
OFFICIAL EXPLANATION **Efharisto: was feeling the ground and made mistakes.**
Brassic Lint made a winning return to action. Storming off in front, he soon established a clear advantage, but he got very leg-weary in the last half-mile and, with the runner-up really closing the gap, he had not an ounce left to spare at the line. (9/4)
327 Canary Falcon moved into second place four out, but was some way behind the winner. However, with that rival stopping in the straight, he closed the gap and it looked as though he might succeed but, like his rival, he was also leg-weary, and failed to get on top. (7/2)
137 Positivo, in second place to the seventh, had burnt his boats entering the back straight for the final time. (10/1: 7/1-11/1)
137* Efharisto, held up towards the back, made a mistake setting out on the final circuit and, soon under pressure, found absolutely nothing and quickly dropped away. He does not look one to place a great deal of faith in. (2/1)

T/Plpt: £71.30 (126.12 Tckts). T/Qdpt: £35.30 (14.92 Tckts). AK

558a-578a (Irish Racing) - See Computer Raceform

WAREGEM (Brussels, Belgium) (R-H) (Firm)
Tuesday August 27th

579a PRIX FELIX DE RUYCK HURDLE (4-Y.O+)
2-45 (3-16) **2m 1f** £6,566.00

				SP	RR	SF
	Bagareur (BEL) (JMartens,Belgium) **7-10-9b[1]** FCheyer	—	1		100	—
	Celibate (IRE) (CJMann) **5-11-10** RDunwoody	6	2		109	—
	Le Mirabeau (FR) (JMartens,Belgium) **6-9-7** ESchepens	15	3		64	—
259[3]	**Heretical Miss** (JFfitch-Heyes) **6-10-11** PCarberry (btn over 26l)		5		—	—
	Do Be Ware (JFfitch-Heyes) **6-9-12** SCamabate (btn over 60l)		8		—	—
						9 Rn

No Time Taken TOTE 35BF: 17BF 22BF 18BF (78BF) OWNER M. Nuyttens BRED W. Buysse
Celibate (IRE) put up a grand performance considering he was giving weight to all his opponents. He adapted to the different style of hurdles very well and was always travelling well. He went to the front two flights from home despite making a slight mistake at that hurdle, and kept on well all the way to the line. This was a very good performance considering the different style of track.
259 Heretical Miss was prominent early on, but soon found the pace a bit too quick. She jumped very well though and gave a good account of herself.
Do Be Ware raced in mid-division for the early part of the race, but soon became well and truly tailed off.

580a GRAND STEEPLE CHASE DE FLANDRES (5-Y.O+)
3-15 (4-01) **2m 7f** £32,830.00

				SP	RR	SF
	Beau Noir (FR) (YFertillet,France) **6-10-6** HBlois	—	1		—	—
	Irish Stamp (IRE) (FMurphy) **7-11-7** PCarberry	3	2		—	—
	Line Lawyer (FR) (JOrtet,France) **5-10-8** PCorsi	3	3		—	—
						10 Rn

No Time Taken TOTE 102BF: 29BF 34BF 38BF (1044BF) OWNER L. Fertillet BRED P. Talvard & R. Alfandari
Irish Stamp (IRE) put in an excellent round of jumping and was ideally suited by these fences, but the only thing that may have been against him was the trip, which appeared on the short side. He made good headway to go third with five to jump and closed up to go second at the last, but found the winner's pace just too much. Giving weight to all his rivals, this was an excellent performance and he should have a great chance in the Velka Pardubicka.

0505-SEDGEFIELD (L-H) (Good to firm)
Friday September 6th

581 WINTER RAPE NOVICES' H'CAP CHASE (0-100) (5-Y.O+) (Class E)
2-25 (2-25) **3m 3f (21 fncs)** £2,914.50 (£876.00: £423.00: £196.50) GOING minus 0.90 sec per fur (HD)

				SP	RR	SF
510[2]	**The Gallopin'major (IRE) (75)** (MrsMReveley) **6-10-9b** NSmith (lw: trckd ldrs: hit 8th: led & lft clr 5 out: styd on wl fr 2 out: blnd last)	—	1	7/2[3]	87	—
487[3]	**George Ashford (IRE) (90)** (KAMorgan) **6-11-10v** ASSmith (led to 4th: outpcd & lost pl 14th: hdwy 4 out: ch 2 out: one pce)	4	2	9/4[2]	100	—
421[P]	**Dustys Trail (IRE) (67)** (PBowen) **7-10-1** RJohnson (pushed along most of wy: led 4th to 5th: outpcd 15th: hdwy 3 out: sn btn)	10	3	14/1	71	—

				SP	RR	SF
466^{4}	**Donovans Reef (68)** (MrsLMarshall) **10-10-2** DBentley (in tch tl outpcd fr 15th)	10	**4**	50/1	66	—
508^{3}	**Quixall Crossett (66)** (EMCaine) **11-10-0** KJohnson (prom tl outpcd 12th: sn bhd)	13	**5**	50/1	56	—
290^{4}	**Mr Oriental (66)** (MrsVAAconley) **6-10-0** JCulloty (a bhd: blnd 15th & p.u bef next)		**P**	50/1	—	—
417*	**Cuchullains Gold (IRE) (86)** (JWhite) **8-11-6b^{1}** NWilliamson (lw: hld up: led 5th tl hdd, blnd bdly & uns rdr 5 out)		**U**	5/4^{1}	—	—
				(SP 110.0%)		**7 Rn**

6m 50.0 (4.00) CSF £10.96 TOTE £4.60: £2.40 £1.40 (£4.80) OWNER Mr R. W. S. Jevon (SALTBURN) BRED Mrs A. Doyle
LONG HANDICAP Quixall Crossett 9-4 Mr Oriental 9-8
510 The Gallopin'major (IRE), an indifferent jumper, got it right at his ninth attempt over fences. He did it pretty well until really belting the last and is hopefully now on the right track. (7/2)
487 George Ashford (IRE) won two runs ago without the visor, but his performances with the headgear since have been disappointing. (9/4)
179 Dustys Trail (IRE), who did not want to know with the blinkers on last time, really took some riding here and was well short of speed over the last three fences. (14/1: 10/1-16/1)
417* Cuchullains Gold (IRE), very free in the blinkers first time, had just been headed when he made a diabolical blunder five out, eventually unshipping his rider. (5/4)

582 FEDERATION BREWERY H'CAP HURDLE (0-115) (4-Y.O+) (Class E)

2-55 (2-58) **2m 5f 110y (10 hdls)** £2,355.00 (£655.00: £315.00) GOING minus 0.90 sec per fur (HD)

				SP	RR	SF
16^{2}	**Red Valerian (114)** (GMMoore) **5-11-9v**(5) MichaelBrennan (lw: trckd ldrs: led on bit last: rdn & r.o)	—	**1**	2/1^{1}	90	41
533^{F}	**Tough Test (IRE) (101)** (MrsJDGoodfellow) **6-11-1** BFenton (chsd ldr: led 4 out tl hdd last: kpt on one pce)	4	**2**	7/2^{2}	74	25
264^{2}	**Strong John (IRE) (90)** (MESowersby) **8-10-1**(3) DParker (hld up: effrt 3 out: sn rdn & one pce)	11	**3**	11/2	55	6
465^{4}	**Crazy Horse Dancer (USA) (86)** (FJordan) **8-10-0** RJohnson (lw: chsd ldrs: outpcd appr 3 out: no imp after)	12	**4**	9/1	42	—
211^{P}	**Aide Memoire (IRE) (86)** (MrsBKBroad) **7-10-0** KJohnson (outpcd & lost tch fr 6th)	9	**5**	25/1	35	—
491^{4}	**Royal Circus (95)** (PWHiatt) **7-10-9** APMcCoy (led: drvn along fr 5th: hdd 4 out: wknd after 3 out)	9	**6**	5/1^{3}	38	—
356*	**Rudi's Pride (IRE) (97)** (SBBell) **5-10-11** NSmith (outpcd & bhd fr ½-wy: p.u after 3 out)		**P**	11/2	—	—
				(SP 116.8%)		**7 Rn**

4m 50.4 (-9.60) CSF £9.40 TOTE £2.30: £1.70 £2.00 (£7.40) OWNER Mrs Alurie O'Sullivan (MIDDLEHAM) BRED Mascalls Stud Farm
LONG HANDICAP Aide Memoire (IRE) 9-6 Crazy Horse Dancer (USA) 9-12
16 Red Valerian, fit from the Flat, really enjoyed this and, on the bridle throughout, settled it in good style after the last. (2/1)
6* Tough Test (IRE) ran a sound race after his heavy fall last time, and kept staying on, but he could not match the winner's turn of speed. (7/2)
264 Strong John (IRE) travelled well but, when asked to pick up, he proved to be well short of the necessary turn of foot. (11/2)
27* Crazy Horse Dancer (USA) found this company too hot once the pace was stepped up over the last four flights. (9/1)
491 Royal Circus is at his best when allowed to dominate. Taken on with a circuit to go, he had soon been seen off. (5/1)

583 RAISBY QUARRIES H'CAP CHASE (0-120) (5-Y.O+) (Class D)

3-25 (3-25) **2m 5f (16 fncs)** £3,457.00 (£1,036.00: £498.00: £229.00)

				SP	RR	SF
487^{2}	**Magic Bloom (100)** (JMJefferson) **10-11-0**(5) ECallaghan (a.p: blnd 8th: led 2 out: all out)	—	**1**	5/2^{1}	108	40
507^{2}	**Staigue Fort (IRE) (91)** (DenysSmith) **8-10-10** PNiven (chsd ldr: hit 8th: outpcd & hit 10th & 11th: styd on to chal 2 out: sn btn: fin 3rd, 10l: plcd 2nd)		**2**	5/1	91	23
	Crackling Frost (IRE) (81) (MrsDHaine) **8-10-0** NWilliamson (set str pce tl hdd & wknd 2 out: fin 4th, 7l: plcd 3rd)		**3**	4/1^{3}	76	8
464^{2}	**Beaucadeau (105)** (MABarnes) **10-11-10** PWaggott (mstke 4th: in tch to outpcd fr 4 out: fin 5th, 13l: plcd 4th)		**4**	3/1^{2}	90	22
	Clares Own (100) (JWade) **12-11-5** KJones (outpcd & bhd fr 7th: fin 6th, 7l: plcd 5th)		**5**	7/1	80	12
452^{2}	**The Blue Boy (IRE) (100)** (PBowen) **8-11-5b** RJohnson (pushed along thrght: lost tch 8th: hdwy 3 out: ev ch 2 out: sddle slipped & lost weight cloth: r.o towards fin: fin 2nd, s.h: disq)		**D**	7/1	108	40
				(SP 115.2%)		**6 Rn**

4m 59.8 (3.10 under best) (-11.20) CSF £18.16 TOTE £2.90: £2.00 £2.00 (£9.80) OWNER Mr Peter Nelson (MALTON) BRED J. C. Dimsdale
LONG HANDICAP Crackling Frost (IRE) 9-7
STEWARDS' ENQUIRY Callaghan susp. 16/9/96 & 1 day (excessive use of whip).
487 Magic Bloom, who made one poor jump halfway through the race, did it in determined style once in front from the second last. (5/2)
507 Staigue Fort (IRE) is at his best out in front and possibly over further, but he was taken on here and, after making mistakes on the final circuit, cried enough between the last two fences. (5/1)
Crackling Frost (IRE) went too fast for his own good after three months off and, once caught two out, soon gave up. (4/1)
464 Beaucadeau lost his way last season and has slipped down the handicap, but this was a moderate effort. (3/1)
452 The Blue Boy (IRE), never on the bridle, kept battling away and had every chance from the second last. After getting beaten by the minimum distance, he was disqualified as his saddle had slipped and he had lost his weight-cloth between the last two fences, hence his jockey failed to draw the correct weight in weighing in 11lb light. (7/1)

584 SAM BERRY NOVICES' CHASE (5-Y.O+) (Class E)

4-00 (4-00) **2m 5f (16 fncs)** £3,208.50 (£963.00: £464.00: £214.50) GOING minus 0.90 sec per fur (HD)

				SP	RR	SF
	Val de Rama (IRE) (DenysSmith) **7-10-12** PNiven (lw: trckd ldrs: blnd bdly 7th: led 11th: hit 12th & 4 out: styd on u.p flat)	—	**1**	10/11^{1}	84 t	17
508^{2}	**Buyers Dream (IRE) (70)** (BEllison) **6-10-9v**(3) GCahill (prom: outpcd whn blnd 9th: hdwy to chal 4 out: kpt on u.p flat)	nk	**2**	13/2^{2}	84 t	17
	Cardinal Sinner (IRE) (56) (JWade) **7-10-12** KJones (led to 9th: wknd 12th)	dist	**3**	20/1	—	—
451^{3}	**Tony's Feelings** (MissLucindaRussell) **8-10-12** AThornton (mstke 2nd: bhd: sme hdwy 3 out: n.d)	5	**4**	12/1	—	—
463^{8}	**See You Always (IRE)** (MABarnes) **6-10-12** PWaggott (in tch tl outpcd 10th: n.d after)	3	**5**	20/1	—	—
488^{P}	**Smokey Track** (MrsJConway) **11-10-2**(5) STaylor (effrt ½-wy: outpcd & lost tch fr 10th)	3	**6**	33/1	—	—
532^{3}	**Richmond (IRE)** (MissZAGreen) **8-10-12** BStorey (outpcd fr 9th: n.d after)	1	**7**	7/1^{3}	—	—
	Childsway (SJRobinson) **8-10-12** MAFitzgerald (chsd ldrs: led 9th to 11th: wknd 4 out)	8	**8**	11/1	—	—
	Durham Hornet (MissSHorner) **9-10-12** MFoster (bkwd: chsd ldrs tl outpcd fr 10th: no ch whn blnd & uns rdr 2 out)		**U**	20/1	—	—
				(SP 111.5%)		**9 Rn**

5m 5.1 (-5.90) CSF £6.87 TOTE £2.00: £1.10 £1.30 £6.20 (£4.70) Trio £78.40 OWNER Mr D. Morland (BISHOP AUCKLAND) BRED Mrs T. J. Riggs-Miller

Val de Rama (IRE) had nothing to beat here, but made hard work of it. After almost getting rid of his rider at the ditch with over a circuit to go, he had to really fight in the closing stages. He is the type to win his share of races on these tracks. (10/11: 4/7-Evens)
508 Buyers Dream (IRE), beaten in a three-horse race here last time, put up a better show on this occasion, and made the winner really fight. (13/2)
Cardinal Sinner (IRE) showed something, but he still has to improve a lot to have any real hopes. (20/1)
Childsway (11/1: 8/1-12/1)

585 STANLEY RACING NOVICES' HURDLE (4-Y.O+) (Class E)

4-30 (4-31) **2m 5f 110y (10 hdls)** £2,302.50 (£640.00: £307.50) GOING minus 0.90 sec per fur (HD)

				SP	RR	SF
60^{4}	**Sujud (IRE)** (MDHammond) **4-10-6**^{ow1} RGarritty (hld up: stdy hdwy appr 3 out: led 2 out: r.o)	—	1	5/2^{2}	66	1
506^{5}	**What's Secreto (USA) (78)** (HAlexander) **4-10-10b** PNiven (a chsng ldrs: ev ch 3 out: one pce fr 2 out)	7	2	9/1	65	1
350*	**Forgotten Empress** (SEKettlewell) **4-10-12** RJohnson (lw: hld up & bhd: effrt 4 out: sn rdn: nvr able rch ldrs)	7	3	13/8^{1}	62	—
	Young Steven (77) (WTKemp) **5-10-12b** SMcDougall (cl up: led 5th tl after 3 out: sn outpcd)	5	4	9/1	56	—
60^{9}	**Classic Crest (IRE) (85)** (GMMoore) **5-11-5v** NBentley (chsd ldrs tl outpcd fr 3 out)	12	5	8/1	54	—
497^{5}	**Pimsboy (53)** (GROldroyd) **9-10-9v**$^{(3)}$ PMidgley (lw: hit 4 out: sme hdwy next: rdn & no imp)	3½	6	20/1	44	—
528^{4}	**Little Redwing** (MDHammond) **4-10-2**$^{(3)}$ MrCBonner (effrt 4 out: rdn next: n.d)	2½	7	7/1^{3}	38	—
450^{4}	**Bowland Park** (EJAlston) **5-10-7** JCulloty (nt j.w: led to 5th: sn wknd: t.o whn p.u bef 2 out)		P	25/1	—	—
	Mount Keen (RDEWoodhouse) **4-10-10** MDwyer (in tch: reminders 4th & 5th: sn t.o: p.u bef 3 out)		P	16/1	—	—
	Whirlwind Romance (IRE) (59) (WTKemp) **5-10-8**^{ow1} KJones (bit bkwd: sn t.o: p.u bef 6th)		P	50/1	—	—
293^{10}	**Ousefleet Boy** (MissMKMilligan) **4-10-7**$^{(3)}$ GCahill (lost tch fr 4 out: t.o whn p.u bef 2 out)		P	50/1	—	—
396^{4}	**Tigh-Na-Mara** (JMJefferson) **8-10-3**$^{(5)ow1}$ ECallaghan (a.p: led after 3 out tl hdd & rn out 2 out)		R	12/1	—	—
				(SP 136.4%)	**12 Rn**	

4m 56.4 (-3.60) CSF £27.95 TOTE £4.10: £1.50 £2.20 £1.20 (£10.00) Trio £4.60 OWNER Mr D. J. Lever (MIDDLEHAM) BRED Shadwell Estate Company Limited
WEIGHT FOR AGE 4yo-2lb

60 Sujud (IRE) was always going best in this moderate event and won most convincingly. (5/2)
450 What's Secreto (USA) had his chances throughout, but looked very slow in the closing stages. (9/1)
350* Forgotten Empress sat out the back on the bridle but, when put into the race from three out, she was never doing enough. She was found to be lame on returning. (13/8)
Young Steven had his chances, but his limitations were well exposed over the last three hurdles. (9/1)
Tigh-Na-Mara was putting in by far her best performance to date when she suddenly decided to duck out at the second last, and crashed through the wing, injuring her rider. (12/1)

586 SEDGEFIELD MAIDEN HURDLE (4-Y.O+) (Class E)

5-05 (5-05) **2m 1f (8 hdls)** £2,495.00 (£695.00: £335.00) GOING minus 0.90 sec per fur (HD)

				SP	RR	SF
96^{3}	**Suas Leat (IRE)** (JMJefferson) **6-10-12**$^{(7)}$ MNewton (a.p: led 2 out: r.o)	—	1	13/2^{3}	63	11
393^{2}	**Tawafij (USA) (80)** (MDHammond) **7-11-5** RGarritty (lw: hld up & bhd: hdwy 3 out: chsd wnr fr 2 out: nt qckn towards fin)	1¾	2	6/4^{1}	61	9
505^{4}	**Genesis Four** (MrsLStubbs) **6-11-5** APMcCoy (lw: hld up: hdwy 5th: sn chsng ldrs: one pce fr 2 out)	7	3	14/1	55	3
	Funny Rose (70) (PMonteith) **6-10-11**$^{(3)}$ GCahill (lw: hld up & bhd: hdwy 5th: in tch appr 2 out: no imp after)	1½	4	14/1	48	—
	Trumped (IRE) (PMonteith) **4-10-12** ADobbin (led tl hdd 2 out: sn wknd)	3½	5	5/1^{2}	45	—
31^{6}	**Leap in the Dark (IRE) (71)** (MissLCSiddall) **7-11-5** AThornton (lw: chsd ldrs: effrt 3 out: grad wknd)	3	6	33/1	47	—
	Thaleros (78) (GMMoore) **6-11-5** JCallaghan (in tch tl outpcd fr 3 out)	¾	7	8/1	47	—
	Rule Out The Rest (MissSHorner) **5-11-5** MFoster (in tch to 5th: eased fr next)	4	8	14/1	43	—
455^{5}	**Haughton Lad (IRE) (68)** (FPMurtagh) **7-11-5** RSupple (prom to 5th: sn lost pl)	1¾	9	33/1	41	—
	Kanona (MrsASwinbank) **5-11-5** JSupple (mstkes: outpcd & bhd fr 4th)	19	10	33/1	23	—
	Golf Ball (TRWatson) **6-11-5** MAFitzgerald (prom to 4th: sn bhd)	6	11	16/1	18	—
	Dark Midnight (IRE) (60) (DALamb) **7-11-5** JBurke (effrt 4th: wknd appr 3 out: t.o)	25	12	33/1	—	—
455^{6}	**Pattern Arms** (DMoffatt) **4-11-3** DJMoffatt (rr div whn fell 5th)		F	25/1	—	—
	Tinklers Folly (DenysSmith) **4-11-3** PNiven (lw: prom to 5th: wknd qckly & p.u bef 2 out)		P	8/1	—	—
	Kashana (IRE) (WStorey) **4-10-12** MMoloney (rr div whn rn out 4th)		R	8/1	—	—
				(SP 144.8%)	**15 Rn**	

3m 52.3 (-2.70) CSF £18.70 TOTE £11.60: £2.50 £1.40 £3.90 (£8.40) Trio £15.10 OWNER Mrs J. M. Davenport (MALTON) BRED J. and Mrs Power
WEIGHT FOR AGE 4yo-2lb

96 Suas Leat (IRE) did the job required well, and looks likely to appreciate further in due course. (13/2)
393 Tawafij (USA), held up to get the trip, tried hard from the second last, but was always being held. He is obviously much better on the level. (6/4)
Genesis Four moved up nicely approaching three out but, soon under pressure, was then always finding the struggle too much. (14/1)
Funny Rose is a frustrating character who has more ability than she cares to show. (14/1)
Trumped (IRE), happy out in front, threw in the towel once caught two out. (5/1: op 3/1)
Kashana (IRE) (8/1: op 16/1)

T/Plpt: £11.90 (815.13 Tckts). T/Qdpt: £3.10 (178.43 Tckts). AA

0394-STRATFORD-ON-AVON (L-H) (Good, Good to firm patches)
Saturday September 7th

Race 5: One flight omitted
WEATHER: warm & sunny

587 RICHARDSONS BLACK PRINCE CONDITIONAL (S) H'CAP HURDLE (0-95) (4-Y.O+) (Class G)

2-20 (2-20) **2m 6f 110y (12 hdls)** £2,052.00 (£572.00: £276.00) GOING: 0.09 sec per fur (G)

				SP	RR	SF
264^{7}	**Holy Joe (93)** (DBurchell) **14-11-5**$^{(7)}$ JPrior (hdwy 5th: led 9th: rdn out)	—	1	25/1	73	32

				SP	RR	SF
461[3]	**King of Babylon (IRE) (70)** (FJordan) **4-10-1** LAspell (lw: stdd s: hdwy 6th: ev ch appr 2 out: wnt lft & hit last: no ex flat)	3	**2**	8/1	48	5
465[2]	**Record Lover (IRE) (75)** (MCChapman) **6-10-8** GHogan (lw: in tch: hdwy appr 9th: sn rdn: wknd 2 out)	6	**3**	100/30 [1]	49	8
474[2]	**Sakbah (USA) (67)** (JAPickering) **7-10-0** PHenley (hld up in rr: r.o fr 9th: nvr trbld ldrs)	4	**4**	25/1	38	—
134[7]	**Easy Over (USA) (69)** (MrsDThomas) **10-10-2** RMassey (swtg: prom to 9th)	½	**5**	20/1	39	—
480[2]	**Bravo Star (USA) (67)** (PaddyFarrell) **11-10-0** MichaelBrennan (nvr nr to chal)	nk	**6**	11/2 [3]	37	—
	To Be Fair (77) (PJHobbs) **9-10-10** GTormey (bkwd: led: hit 8th: mstke & hdd next: rdn & btn appr 2 out)	5	**7**	9/1	44	3
480[6]	**Auvillar (USA) (80)** (JParfitt) **8-10-13** TJMurphy (a bhd)	17	**8**	20/1	35	—
	Sir Pageant (82) (KSBridgwater) **7-11-1** JCulloty (bkwd: in tch to 7th)	½	**9**	12/1	36	—
	Canary Blue (IRE) (78) (PWHiatt) **5-10-11** EHusband (rdn & dropped rr 6th: sn bhd)	s.h	**10**	5/1 [2]	32	—
101[2]	**Erlemo (78)** (WClay) **7-10-11v** GuyLewis (prom: mstke 5th: rdn 8th: sn wknd)	5	**11**	11/2 [3]	29	—
510[4]	**Peniarth (67)** (RJPrice) **10-10-0** BFenton (lw: prom: blnd 2nd: wknd 5th: t.o whn p.u appr 2 out)		**P**	33/1	—	—
				(SP 119.5%)	**12 Rn**	

5m 30.7 (14.70) CSF £193.78 CT £778.51 TOTE £21.90: £3.10 £1.40 £1.90 (£123.70) Trio £68.70 OWNER Mr Simon Lewis (EBBW VALE) BRED Mrs Maureen F. Hogan

LONG HANDICAP Bravo Star (USA) 9-13 Sakbah (USA) 9-3 Peniarth 9-4

WEIGHT FOR AGE 4yo-2lb

No bid

IN-FOCUS: **This was a first winner for rider John Prior.**

Holy Joe, scoring for the first time since April last year, did not appear to be travelling best for most of the final mile, but he does stay and he stuck to his task most resolutely. (25/1)

461 King of Babylon (IRE), dropped in and given every chance to get this trip, looked to be cruising on the home turn, but found nothing once the chips were down. (8/1: 6/1-10/1)

465 Record Lover (IRE) was hard at work some way from home and had done his running by the straight. He has looked a stayer in the past and the tactics appeared the problem. (100/30)

474 Sakbah (USA), looking fitter and again stepped up in trip, only began to get into the race when it was all over. (25/1)

95 Easy Over (USA), outpaced four from home, just kept plugging on from that point. (20/1)

480 Bravo Star (USA) never got near the lead on this occasion and again found the ground against him. (11/2)

To Be Fair (9/1: 4/1-10/1)

101 Erlemo (11/2: 3/1-6/1)

588 CITY OF COVENTRY TROPHY H'CAP CHASE (0-120) (5-Y.O+) (Class D)

2-55 (2-55) **3m (18 fncs)** £3,899.00 (£1,172.00: £566.00: £263.00) GOING minus 0.52 sec per fur (GF)

				SP	RR	SF
484*	**Maggots Green (93)** (JMBradley) **9-10-1** RJohnson (w ldrs: led to 3rd: led 6th to next: led 9th tl after 10th: led 2 out to last: sn led again: drvn out)	—	**1**	9/1	100	31
452*	**Royal Vacation (107)** (GMMoore) **7-11-1** JCallaghan (hld up: led after 10th to 2 out: led & blnd last: sn hdd & nt qckn)	1¼	**2**	3/1 [2]	113	44
395*	**Maple Dancer (106)** (AGHobbs) **10-10-7**(7) MrGShenkin (hld up: hdwy 12th: rdn & no ex fr 2 out)	5	**3**	7/2 [3]	109	40
420*	**Earlymorning Light (IRE) (120)** (GRichards) **7-12-0** ADobbin (chsd ldrs: hit 13th: wknd 15th)	28	**4**	7/4 [1]	104	35
496[U]	**Muskora (IRE) (116)** (PJHobbs) **7-11-10b** RDunwoody (lw: led 3rd tl j.slowly & hdd 6th: led again next: blnd & hdd 9th: sn wknd: p.u bef 12th)		**P**	16/1	—	—
220[2]	**Waterford Castle (109)** (KCBailey) **9-11-3** TJMurphy (trckd ldrs to 13th: p.u bef 3 out)		**P**	8/1	—	—
				(SP 110.6%)	**6 Rn**	

5m 46.0 (-6.00) CSF £33.07 TOTE £7.70: £2.50 £2.30 (£21.80) OWNER Mr E. A. Hayward (CHEPSTOW) BRED Swettenham Stud

484* Maggots Green, given a marvellous ride, took the step up in trip and class in her stride, but gained the day principally thanks to her pilot sticking to the inside and keeping his cool. (9/1: 6/1-10/1)

452* Royal Vacation, restrained for a circuit, then pulled his way to the front. He looked to have got the better of a ding-dong battle with the winner between the last two, but met the final fence all wrong and lost his momentum and the race. (3/1: 2/1-7/2)

395* Maple Dancer, trying for a four-timer on the course this season, was going as well as any after the third last, but was showing signs of distress by the next. (7/2)

420* Earlymorning Light (IRE) was set a tough task by the Handicapper having been raised 5lb for a win in a muddling event. Stepping up in distance, he was beaten too far from home to blame the trip alone and would have preferred faster ground. (7/4)

220 Waterford Castle (8/1: 5/1-9/1)

589 PERTEMPS HURDLE (3-Y.O) (Class E)

3-25 (3-26) **2m 110y (9 hdls)** £2,458.00 (£688.00: £334.00) GOING: 0.09 sec per fur (G)

				SP	RR	SF
	Siberian Mystic (PGMurphy) **3-10-5** WMcFarland (chsd ldrs: led appr 2 out: clr whn hit last: drvn out)	—	**1**	7/1	49	—
501[5]	**Song For Jess (IRE)** (FJordan) **3-10-5** SWynne (hld up: hit 4th: hdwy 3 out: r.o flat)	1¾	**2**	100/1	47	—
462[4]	**Down The Yard** (MCChapman) **3-10-5** WWorthington (hdwy 6th: wnt 2nd & hit last: r.o)	½	**3**	20/1	47	—
471*	**Skram** (RDickin) **3-11-3** JCulloty (swtg: led tl 3 out: sn led again: hdd appr 2 out: sn btn)	1¼	**4**	9/1	58	—
	Uncle George (MHTompkins) **3-10-10v** AMaguire (plld hrd: w ldrs: ev ch whn blnd 2 out: nt rcvr)	3	**5**	4/1 [2]	48+	—
	Orange Order (IRE) (JWhite) **3-10-10** APMcCoy (lw: plld hrd: trckd ldrs: led & blnd 3 out: sn hdd & btn)	8	**6**	5/4 [1]	40	—
	Kentford Conquista (JWMullins) **3-10-5** SCurran (chsd ldrs to 6th)	11	**7**	50/1	24	—
	Little Kenny (TWall) **3-10-2**(3) RMassey (a bhd)	4	**8**	16/1	20	—
388[2]	**Still Here (IRE)** (MJHeaton-Ellis) **3-10-10** NWilliamson (lw: prom: mstke 3rd: sn wknd: blnd 6th)	16	**9**	13/2 [3]	10	—
458[P]	**Copper Diamond** (DBurchell) **3-9-13b**1(7)ow1 JPrior (mstkes: sn t.o)	dist	**10**	66/1	—	—
	Rapid Liner (HOliver) **3-10-10** JacquiOliver (bit bkwd: a bhd)	16	**11**	50/1	—	—
	Supermister (TDEasterby) **3-10-10** LWyer (a bhd: t.o whn p.u bef 2 out)		**P**	25/1	—	—
	Cashaplenty (NPLittmoden) **3-10-10** BPowell (in tch tl blnd & wknd 5th: p.u bef 3 out)		**P**	40/1	—	—
				(SP 123.6%)	**13 Rn**	

4m 4.2 (17.20) CSF £349.12 TOTE £12.60: £1.90 £12.40 £3.80 (£812.50) Trio Not won; £206.08 to 9/9/96 OWNER The Merry Men (BRISTOL) BRED Deerfield Farm

OFFICIAL EXPLANATION **Song For Jess (IRE): the rider reported that his instructions were to settle the filly and get her jumping as she had fallen twice. After a mistake, he could not improve his position until the straight. The trainer's representative added that the filly was still weak.**

Siberian Mystic, a recent Flat winner, is tall enough for this game and made a successful start to her hurdles career after taking over on the home turn. The mistake at the last seemed to knock the stuffing out of her and she barely got home. (7/1: 4/1-8/1)

Song For Jess (IRE) has twice failed to negotiate the first hurdle and was given time to get her act together, only to nearly come down at the fourth. In sixth place on the home turn, she found her rivals all stopping in front of her and, staying on, she finished best of all. (100/1)
Down The Yard looked likely to take a hand when beginning her move, but was leg-weary by the time she hit the final flight. (20/1)
471* Skram, a keen sort wearing a crossed-noseband, was led around by two handlers. He had given his all by the home turn. (9/1)
Uncle George, who has been called a name or two in the past, took a keen hold and was challenging for the lead when going down on his nose at the penultimate flight, thus forfeiting all chance. It remains to be seen whether his enthusiasm will last. (4/1: 3/1-9/2)
Orange Order (IRE), much the best of these on the level when winning a Kempton claimer for Guy Harwood, had just taken it up when meeting the third last completely wrong and losing all impetus. He is much better than his finishing position suggests. (5/4)

590 DICK FRANCIS 'TO THE HILT' NOVICES' CHASE (5-Y.O+) (Class D)

3-55 (3-56) **2m 5f 110y (17 fncs)** £4,430.00 (£1,230.00: £590.00) GOING minus 0.52 sec per fur (GF)

				SP	RR	SF
263*	**Sonic Star (IRE) (105)** (DNicholson) **7-11-6** AMaguire (lw: j.w: trckd ldrs: led after 4 out: lft clr next: wnt lft & hit 2 out: easily)	—	1	4/7^{1}	94+	33
486^{2}	**Seahawk Retriever (75)** (PFNicholls) **7-11-6** APMcCoy (led: hit 7th & 9th: hdd after 4 out: blnd next: no ch whn lft 2nd 2 out)	19	2	15/2^{3}	80	19
477^{2}	**Mr Snaggle (IRE) (91)** (SEarle) **7-11-0** CMaude (mstke 1st: nvr trbld ldrs: lft 3rd 2 out)	6	3	7/2^{2}	69	8
	Rapid Fire (IRE) (JMJefferson) **8-11-0** MDwyer (bit bkwd: prom: hit 7th: outpcd 10th: rallied 3 out: 2nd whn fell next)		F	20/1	—	—
360^{6}	**Father Power (IRE)** (PBowen) **8-11-0** RJohnson (prom to 9th: t.o whn p.u bef 2 out)		P	25/1	—	—
460^{P}	**Lord Antrim (IRE)** (MBradstock) **7-11-4b^{1ow4}** PHolley (w.r.s: t.o tl p.u bef 6th)		P	33/1	—	—
	Ennistymon (IRE) (78) (JWMullins) **5-10-6** SCurran (lw: a bhd: t.o whn p.u bef 12th)		P	50/1	—	—
				(SP 111.1%)	**7 Rn**	

5m 11.3 (-0.70) CSF £5.26 TOTE £1.40: £1.20 £2.10 (£2.70) OWNER Mr R. F. Nutland (TEMPLE GUITING) BRED A.B. McDowell
WEIGHT FOR AGE 5yo-3lb
263* Sonic Star (IRE) is really bold at his fences and put in a fine round, apart from running down two or three fences. Left clear for the last half-mile, he won easily enough, but gave the impression that this could be the limit of his stamina. (4/7)
486 Seahawk Retriever, allowed to force the pace this time, had just been headed by the winner when making a hash of the third last and stopping to little more than a walk. (15/2)
477 Mr Snaggle (IRE) was never going after an early mistake. (7/2)
Rapid Fire (IRE), who ran in Irish bumpers prior to winning on his debut between the Flags in March 1994, reportedly broke a blood-vessel that day and had not been seen since. Looking in need of the race, he shaped with some promise and was set to finish a clear second best without troubling the winner when hitting the deck. (20/1)

591 WILLIAM HILL H'CAP HURDLE (0-120) (4-Y.O+) (Class D)

4-25 (4-25) **2m 110y (8 hdls)** £2,901.50 (£872.00: £421.00: £195.50) GOING: 0.09 sec per fur (G)

				SP	RR	SF
	Fine Thyne (IRE) (108) (GHarwood) **7-11-2** MAFitzgerald (bit bkwd: a.p: led appr 3 out: clr 2 out: pushed out)	—	1	14/1	96+	17
483*	**Peter Monamy (101)** (MCPipe) **4-10-4b$^{(3)}$** DWalsh (chsd ldr: pushed along 6th: kpt on appr 2 out)	8	2	11/4^{1}	81	—
481*	**Re Roi (IRE) (97)** (JCFox) **4-10-3** TJMurphy (lw: hld up: hdwy appr 2 out: r.o flat)	4	3	3/1^{2}	73	—
456*	**Royal Thimble (IRE) (104)** (NoelChance) **5-10-12** RJohnson (lw: chsd ldrs: no hdwy fr 3 out)	¾	4	3/1^{2}	80	1
461*	**Raven's Roost (IRE) (92)** (GEJones) **5-10-0** PMcLoughlin (lw: hld up: hdwy 5th: rdn appr 2 out: 4th & btn whn blnd last)	2	5	16/1	66?	—
	Shoofk (120) (SDow) **5-12-0** RDunwoody (bit bkwd: j.rt: led: hdd appr 3 out: wkng whn hit 2 out)	10	6	13/2^{3}	84	5
	Windward Ariom (108) (PMitchell) **10-11-2** RSupple (hld up: blnd & uns rdr 2nd)		U	10/1	—	—
				(SP 111.6%)	**7 Rn**	

3m 58.9 (11.90) CSF £48.70 TOTE £15.00: £4.40 £1.70 (£20.40) OWNER Mr Peter Wiegand (PULBOROUGH) BRED Minch Bloodstock in Ireland
LONG HANDICAP Raven's Roost (IRE) 8-5
WEIGHT FOR AGE 4yo-2lb
Fine Thyne (IRE), running for only the second time since finishing down the field behind Danoli at the 1994 Cheltenham Festival, understandably looked short of peak-fitness but, given a chance by the Handicapper, was able to outclass this field, despite reaching for the final two hurdles as if coming to the end of his tether. (14/1: op 8/1)
483* Peter Monamy was never travelling particularly well, but stuck to the inside and kept plugging away. (11/4)
481* Re Roi (IRE) seems to be settling better now and might have benefited from being ridden closer to the pace on the final circuit, for he certainly began his move too late to trouble the winner. (3/1)
456* Royal Thimble (IRE) moved to post well and looked in great shape but, as the tempo rose in the last mile, she lacked the pace to complete her hat-trick. (3/1)
461* Raven's Roost (IRE) might have been suited by the muddling early pace, but still ran a marvellous race from so far out of the weights, and would have finished closer but for a bad mistake at the last. (16/1)
Shoofk, allowed to set his own pace, seemed to want to go right all the time and did not last long once headed. A right-handed track and more cut in the ground would be his favoured option. (13/2)

592 HARTSHORNE MOTOR SERVICES LTD (WALSALL) H'CAP CHASE (0-125) (5-Y.O+) (Class D)

4-55 (4-55) **2m 1f 110y (13 fncs)** £3,795.00 (£1,140.00: £550.00: £255.00) GOING minus 0.52 sec per fur (GF)

				SP	RR	SF
470^{2}	**Noblely (USA) (105)** (NJHWalker) **9-10-8** RFarrant (lw: prom: led 7th: rdn & hld on wl fr 2 out)	—	1	6/1^{3}	110	17
	Captain Khedive (125) (PFNicholls) **8-12-0** APMcCoy (hld up: hmpd after 6th: hdwy 9th: rdn 2 out: r.o flat)	nk	2	2/1^{1}	130	37
	Rex to the Rescue (IRE) (100) (RHAlner) **8-9-12$^{(5)}$** PHenley (sn chsng ldrs: hit 8th: kpt on fr 2 out)	2	3	8/1	103	10
464*	**Stately Home (IRE) (120)** (PBowen) **5-11-7** RJohnson (led tl hdd 7th: rdn 4 out: ev ch next: one pce)	1¼	4	9/4^{2}	122	27
484^{3}	**Wingspan (USA) (97)** (AGNewcombe) **12-10-0** JRKavanagh (mstke 4th: sn bhd)	dist	5	11/1	—	—
61^{4}	**Lowawatha (103)** (MrsEHHeath) **8-10-6** AThornton (lw: chsd ldrs: wkng whn mstke 9th)	1¼	6	16/1	—	—
138^{6}	**Shrewd John (100)** (RDEWoodhouse) **10-10-3^{ow3}** MDwyer (hld up: hdwy whn fell 10th)		F	14/1	—	—
				(SP 110.4%)	**7 Rn**	

4m 9.7 (0.70) CSF £17.22 TOTE £5.00: £2.00 £1.90 (£5.50) OWNER Mr D. H. Cowgill (WANTAGE) BRED Societe Aland
WEIGHT FOR AGE 5yo-2lb
470 Noblely (USA) could not get to the front for a circuit and his jumping was less than foot-perfect in the early stages as a result, but he proved a tough nut to crack once there. A fast-run race at around this trip suits him ideally, and he remains notably consistent. (6/1)

Captain Khedive, who is at his best in the first half of the season and has never won after the turn of the year, returned looking fit and well and soon recovered from landing steeply at the second, but was just worried out of it over the last two fences after travelling like a winner. (2/1)
Rex to the Rescue (IRE) often leads, but was unable to on this occasion, although he stuck on well in the straight. Led round by two handlers, he looked on great terms with himself but he failed to sparkle after a stunning debut last season, so he can not, therefore, be guaranteed to go on from here. (8/1: 6/1-9/1)
464* Stately Home (IRE) saw his winning streak ended. Losing his early lead soon after diving at the second fence, he nearly jumped back to the front with a superb leap at the third last and battled hard from that point, but he was not quite up to the task. (9/4)
484 Wingspan (USA) could never go the pace and is going to find it difficult in all bar the softest races. (11/1)
61 Lowawatha, none too fluent at the second, could never get to the front for more than a few strides and was shaken off soon after halfway. (16/1)
Shrewd John was moving forward threateningly when turning a terrifying-looking somersault four from home. (14/1: 10/1-16/1)

593 BIRD GROUPAGE SERVICES LTD (OLDBURY) 'N.H.' NOVICES' HURDLE (4-Y.O+) (Class E)
5-25 (5-26) **2m 110y (9 hdls)** £2,318.00 (£648.00: £314.00) GOING: 0.09 sec per fur (G)

	Horse / details	Dist	Pos	SP	RR	SF
400[2]	**Anabranch** (JMJefferson) **5-10-0**(7) MNewton (lw: chsd ldrs: led appr 6th: hit 2 out: blnd last: pushed out)	—	1	11/10[1]	71	3
	Dacelo (FR) (OSherwood) **5-10-12** JOsborne (lw: hld up: hdwy & hit 3 out: no ex fr next)	7	2	15/8[2]	69	1
	Smart Lord (JRBosley) **5-10-12** MBosley (hld up: hdwy 5th: ev ch next: wkng whn mstke 2 out)	28	3	40/1	42	—
401*	**Scamallach (IRE) (87)** (JRJenkins) **6-11-0b** GBradley (led tl appr 6th: sn wknd)	12	4	4/1[3]	32	—
	Millcroft Riviera (IRE) (RHAlner) **5-10-7**(5) PHenley (bit bkwd: chsd ldrs to 6th)	18	5	16/1	13	—
	Albert The Lion (IRE) (JNeville) **4-10-10** JCulloty (bit bkwd: in tch to 6th: sn wknd: p.u bef 2 out)		P	40/1	—	—
510[5]	**Boyo (IRE)** (TDEasterby) **5-10-12** LWyer (bhd: j.slowly & rn out 5th)		R	25/1	—	—

(SP 117.0%) **7 Rn**

4m 0.4 (13.40) CSF £3.66 TOTE £2.00: £1.60 £1.90 (£2.90) OWNER Mrs M. Barker (MALTON) BRED Mrs M. Barker
WEIGHT FOR AGE 4yo-2lb
400 Anabranch was in charge some way out, which was fortunate for she scrambled over the last couple of hurdles. (11/10)
Dacelo (FR) tried to get into the race in the latter stages, but looked decidedly short of speed as pressure was applied. (15/8)
Smart Lord was travelling very strongly when challenging at the fourth last, but stopped to nothing on the home turn. He may have needed this more than it appeared. (40/1)
401* Scamallach (IRE) tried to blaze the trail again, but stopped quickly once collared. (4/1)
Millcroft Riviera (IRE) needed this and was easily left behind in the final mile. (16/1)

T/Plpt: £872.50 (11.46 Tckts). T/Qdpt: £188.60 (2.7 Tckts). Dk

0407-EXETER (R-H) (Firm)
Wednesday September 11th
WEATHER: fine

594 DEVON COUNTY CARS MAIDEN HURDLE (4-Y.O+) (Class E)
2-20 (2-20) **2m 3f (9 hdls)** £2,347.50 (£660.00: £322.50) GOING minus 0.80 sec per fur (F)

	Horse / details	Dist	Pos	SP	RR	SF
	Killing Time (64) (DBurchell) **5-11-5** DJBurchell (hdwy 4th: sn lft in ld: clr 6th: drvn along appr 2 out: sn clr: easily)	—	1	12/1[3]	53+	4
418[2]	**Rare Spread (IRE)** (MCPipe) **6-11-5** DBridgwater (mstkes: hdwy to chse wnr 6th: in tch tl rdn & no imp 2 out)	29	2	1/2[1]	29	—
300[R]	**Mario's Dream (IRE)** (MrsJGRetter) **8-11-5** TJMurphy (plld hrd: in tch tl wknd 6th)	5	3	100/1	24	—
	My Harvinski (76) (IRJones) **6-10-12**(7) MissEJJones (bit bkwd: bhd: hdwy 5th: in tch tl outpcd appr 2 out: t.o)	11	4	12/1[3]	15	—
469[4]	**Scalp 'em (IRE) (67)** (DrPPritchard) **8-11-5** DrPPritchard (bit bkwd: chsd ldr to 6th: grad wknd: t.o)	½	5	33/1	15	—
	Crownhill Cross (BRMillman) **5-11-0**(5) DSalter (bit bkwd: bhd whn mstke 4th: wkng & mstke next: t.o)	3½	6	100/1	12	—
504[2]	**Marlousion (IRE)** (CPEBrooks) **4-10-12** GBradley (lw: led: hit 2nd: rn wd bnd & p.u after 4th)		P	5/2[2]	—	—

(SP 115.5%) **7 Rn**

4m 27.5 (1.50) CSF £18.61 TOTE £12.10: £3.20 £1.20 (£5.90) OWNER Mr Simon Lewis (EBBW VALE) BRED L. H. J. Ward
WEIGHT FOR AGE 4yo-2lb
OFFICIAL EXPLANATION **Marlousion (IRE): hung badly left-handed.**
Killing Time, having his first run for his new stable, took this easily. This looked a poor race. (12/1: op 6/1)
418 Rare Spread (IRE) did not jump fluently on this hurdling bow and was well outpointed by the winner. (1/2: op 4/5)
Mario's Dream (IRE) took a keen grip and may do better back over a shorter trip. (100/1)
My Harvinski (12/1: op 6/1)
504 Marlousion (IRE) (5/2: 7/4-11/4)

595 SCANIA 4-SERIES 'HORSEPOWER' NOVICES' CHASE (5-Y.O+) (Class E)
2-55 (2-55) **2m 1f 110y (12 fncs)** £2,827.00 (£856.00: £418.00: £199.00) GOING minus 0.59 sec per fur (F)

	Horse / details	Dist	Pos	SP	RR	SF
333[2]	**Nordic Valley (IRE) (82)** (MCPipe) **5-10-10** DBridgwater (chsd ldrs tl lost pl 10th: hrd rdn & led nr fin)	—	1	3/1[2]	89	30
411[2]	**Bishops Castle (IRE) (82)** (RGFrost) **8-10-12** JFrost (lw: led to 7th: lost pl 10th: rdn & str run appr last: led flat: hdd nr fin)	½	2	100/30[3]	89	32
411*	**Dubelle (82)** (JSKing) **6-11-0** JCulloty (lw: chsd ldr 3rd tl led 7th: rdn & hdd flat: no ex nr fin)	s.h	3	11/8[1]	91	34
556[U]	**Fort Gale (IRE)** (CPEBrooks) **5-10-10** GBradley (nt fluent: in tch tl wknd 9th)	12	4	10/1	78	19
556[U]	**Hizal (72)** (HJManners) **7-11-5** MrACharles-Jones (in tch tl j.slowly 8th: sn rdn & wknd: t.o)	29	5	40/1	58	1
554[3]	**Seasamacamile (63)** (RHBuckler) **9-10-7** BPowell (chsd ldr to 3rd: bhd whn mstke 5th: sn wknd: t.o)	14	6	14/1	33	—

(SP 108.4%) **6 Rn**

4m 12.8 (-3.20) CSF £12.11 TOTE £3.40: £1.90 £1.30 (£4.00) OWNER Pond House Racing (WELLINGTON) BRED David Shubotham
WEIGHT FOR AGE 5yo-2lb
333 Nordic Valley (IRE) gained a deserved, hard-fought success. He should continue to pick up prizemoney until the ground eases. (3/1)
411 Bishops Castle (IRE) ran just about to form with Dubelle and should soon get off the mark over fences. (100/30)

411* Dubelle found the penalty for her win last time making all the difference from the last. (11/8)
Fort Gale (IRE) (10/1: 6/1-12/1)

596 TWO RIVERS SECURITIES H'CAP HURDLE (0-105) (4-Y.O+) (Class F)
3-30 (3-31) **2m 1f 110y (8 hdls)** £2,027.20 (£569.20: £277.60) GOING minus 0.80 sec per fur (F)

		Dist	Pos	SP	RR	SF
223*	**Out Ranking (FR) (101)** (MCPipe) **4-11-10** DBridgwater (lw: mde all: clr appr 2 out: drvn out)	—	1	7/2^{2}	82	37
	Wollboll (79) (HJCollingridge) **6-10-4** VSmith (plld hrd: chsd wnr fr 4th: outpcd appr 2 out: rallied & ev ch last: no ex flat)	2	2	4/1^{3}	58	15
551^{5}	**Little Hooligan (83)** (GFEdwards) **5-10-8b** APMcCoy (a.p: ev ch 6th: outpcd appr 2 out)	5	3	8/1	58	15
551^{2}	**Marchman (88)** (JSKing) **11-10-13** JCulloty (hld up & bhd: mstke 3rd: hdwy & in tch 5th: wknd next: t.o)	29	4	15/8^{1}	36	—
393^{6}	**Night Time (80)** (FJordan) **4-9-10**(7) MrGShenkin (in tch tl wknd appr 6th: t.o)	21	5	16/1	9	—
473^{4}	**Stay With Me (FR) (92)** (CREgerton) **6-11-3** JOsborne (in tch whn mstke 4th: wknd fr next: t.o whn p.u bef 2 out)		P	4/1^{3}	—	—
555^{8}	**On the Ledge (USA) (75)** (HJManners) **6-9-7**(7) ADowling (bit bkwd: chsd ldr to 4th: sn lost pl: t.o whn p.u bef 2 out)		P	100/1	—	—

(SP 115.0%) **7 Rn**

3m 57.9 (-6.10) CSF £17.00 TOTE £4.70: £1.90 £2.90 (£11.40) OWNER Knight Hawks Partnership (WELLINGTON) BRED Jacques Beres
LONG HANDICAP On the Ledge (USA) 8-1
WEIGHT FOR AGE 4yo-2lb
223* Out Ranking (FR), off for six weeks, was off only a 1lb higher mark than when successful and again made it all. (7/2: 3/1-5/1)
Wollboll, lightly-raced over hurdles, could be off a very fair mark. (4/1: 5/1-11/4)
Little Hooligan showed a return to form. He won twice here last season and could well be capable of adding to his tally off his current mark. (8/1: 6/1-9/1)
551 Marchman had the winning of this on the book, but disappointed. There was no obvious excuse and he will not have the ground in his favour for much longer. (15/8)
473 Stay With Me (FR) (4/1: tchd 6/1)

597 SCANIA 1996 TRUCK OF THE YEAR H'CAP CHASE (0-100) (5-Y.O+) (Class F)
4-00 (4-01) **2m 6f 110y (17 fncs)** £3,344.30 (£1,012.40: £494.20: £235.10) GOING minus 0.59 sec per fur (F)

		Dist	Pos	SP	RR	SF
298^{5}	**Jim Valentine (84)** (DJWintle) **10-11-8** WMarston (bhd: hdwy 10th: led 15th: sn clr: eased flat)	—	1	7/1	100+	17
94^{7}	**Drumcullen (IRE) (84)** (KCBailey) **7-11-8** WMcFarland (led tl hdd briefly appr 14th: hdd next: sn outpcd)	6	2	6/1^{3}	96	13
457^{F}	**Boxing Match (73)** (JMBradley) **9-10-11** RJohnson (a.p: ev ch 13th tl rdn & wknd fr 2 out)	8	3	15/2	79	—
507*	**Turpin's Green (74)** (JSKing) **13-10-12** JCulloty (lw: chsd ldr 7th tl mstke 11th: led briefly appr 14th: rdn & ev ch tl wknd next)	25	4	7/1	62	—
529*	**Miners Rest (76)** (PJHobbs) **8-11-0** APMcCoy (lw: prom: chsd ldr: rdn 11th: ev ch next tl wknd appr 14th)	14	5	3/1^{1}	54	—
346^{3}	**Ghedi (POL) (65)** (MPMuggeridge) **5-10-0b** SCurran (a bhd: wkng whn fell 12th)		F	66/1	—	—
256^{P}	**Morning Blush (IRE) (86)** (MCPipe) **6-11-10v^{1}** DBridgwater (prom early: mstke 8th: sn bhd: t.o whn p.u bef 15th)		P	10/1	—	—
346^{2}	**Pharrago (IRE) (72)** (DBurchell) **7-10-10** DJBurchell (a bhd: mstke 10th: wknd fr next: t.o whn p.u bef 2 out)		P	5/1^{2}	—	—
460^{2}	**Tour Leader (NZ) (86)** (RHBuckler) **7-11-10** BPowell (a bhd: t.o 11th: mstke 15th: p.u lame)		P	15/2	—	—
551^{6}	**Gabish (62)** (BScriven) **11-9-7**(7) MrRThornton (prom tl rdn & wknd 13th: t.o whn p.u bef 2 out)		P	25/1	—	—

(SP 118.9%) **10 Rn**

5m 35.4 (4.40) CSF £45.81 CT £299.91 TOTE £10.70: £3.50 £2.70 £2.50 (£37.80) Trio £140.70; £158.55 to Doncaster 12/9/96 OWNER Mr R. H. L. Barnes (CHELTENHAM)
LONG HANDICAP Ghedi (POL) 9-9 Gabish 9-9
WEIGHT FOR AGE 5yo-3lb
190 Jim Valentine, without the blinkers and 7lb lower this time, won very easily. He could well defy a penalty. (7/1)
Drumcullen (IRE), an Irish point-to-point winner, was back in trip, but ran as though a step back up to three miles, and possibly more patient tactics, would suit. (6/1)
Boxing Match is slipping back down the weights. (15/2)
529* Miners Rest, bidding for a hat-trick, faded out of it disappointingly. (3/1)

598 WESTRUCKS FOR SCANIA H'CAP HURDLE (0-110) (4-Y.O+) (Class E)
4-30 (4-30) **2m 6f (10 hdls)** £2,611.50 (£734.00: £358.50) GOING minus 0.80 sec per fur (F)

		Dist	Pos	SP	RR	SF
479*	**Santella Boy (USA) (103)** (CJMann) **4-11-10b** JRailton (lw: hld up mid div: hdwy to chal last: sn led: comf)	—	1	11/10^{1}	78	—
407*	**Buglet (93)** (MCPipe) **6-10-13**(3) DWalsh (a.p: chsd ldr 7th: led appr 2 out: hdd flat: sn outpcd)	nk	2	2/1^{2}	68	—
465^{7}	**They All Forgot Me (77)** (AWCarroll) **9-10-0** MissCDyson (led tl appr 2 out: rdn & wknd appr last)	9	3	66/1	45	—
	Chucklestone (85) (JSKing) **13-10-8** JCulloty (chsd ldr: mstke 1st: mstke & lost pl 7th: chsd ldr 8th tl wknd 2 out)	s.h	4	3/1^{3}	53	—
546^{4}	**Coeur Battant (FR) (77)** (RJBaker) **6-10-0** BPowell (plld hrd: hld up & bhd: in tch tl bd mstke 5th: rallied appr 2 out: sn wknd)	5	5	25/1	42	—

(SP 111.3%) **5 Rn**

5m 22.4 (12.40) CSF £3.63 TOTE £1.80: £1.30 £1.30 (£2.40) OWNER The Link Leasing Partnership (UPPER LAMBOURN) BRED Galbreaph - Phillips Racing Partnership
LONG HANDICAP They All Forgot Me 8-10 Coeur Battant (FR) 9-0
WEIGHT FOR AGE 4yo-2lb
479* Santella Boy (USA), who stays further than this, was never going to be pegged back once sent to the front on the flat. (11/10)
407* Buglet seemed to stay this longer trip alright, but was never going to get back up against a proven stayer. (2/1)
They All Forgot Me, carrying 18lb more than his long-handicap weight, ran well in the circumstances. (66/1)

599 COX OF DEVON HURDLE (3-Y.O) (Class E)
5-00 (5-01) **2m 1f 110y (8 hdls)** £2,529.00 (£621.00) GOING minus 1.15 sec per fur (HD)

		Dist	Pos	SP	RR	SF
548*	**Noble Lord** (RHBuckler) **3-11-3** BPowell (lw: led & sn clr: eased 3rd: clr next: hit 2 out: unchal)	—	1	4/9^{1}	73?	—
388^{5}	**Friendly Dreams (IRE)** (MCPipe) **3-10-12v^{1}** DBridgwater (nt fluent: rdn & in tch 3rd: wknd appr next: t.o)	dist	2	13/2^{3}	—	—

			SP	RR	SF
501[2]	*Ben Bowden* (MBlanshard) **3-11-3** DGallagher (Withdrawn not under Starters' orders: faulty sddle)	**W**	11/4[2]	—	—
			(SP 109.2%)		**2 Rn**

4m 14.9 (10.90) TOTE £1.10 OWNER The Old Timers Partnership (BRIDPORT) BRED J. E. Swiers
548* Noble Lord followed up in what was effectively a no-race following the withdrawal of Ben Bowden. (4/9)
388 Friendly Dreams (IRE) was in trouble a long way out. (13/2: 6/1-14/1)

T/Plpt: £75.60 (104.76 Tckts). T/Qdpt: £15.90 (29.45 Tckts). T

0546-NEWTON ABBOT (L-H) (Good, Good to firm patches)
Thursday September 12th
WEATHER: sunny

600 COCA-COLA (S) HURDLE (4-Y.O+) (Class G)
2-20 (2-20) **2m 1f (8 hdls)** £1,965.90 (£552.40: £269.70) GOING: 0.03 sec per fur (G)

				SP	RR	SF
553*	**Hacketts Cross (IRE) (97)** (PEccles) **8-11-12** AMaguire (a.p: led 6th: drvn out: hld on wl)	—	**1**	5/2[1]	77	34
71[F]	**Twice the Groom (IRE) (89)** (RLee) **6-11-5b** RJohnson (hdwy 5th: sn prom: ev ch 2 out: no ex flat)	1¼	**2**	8/1	69	26
	Prestige Lady (BSmart) **5-10-7** CLlewellyn (hld up: str run 6th: ev ch 2 out: j.lft last 2: wknd flat)	3	**3**	10/1	54	11
456[6]	**Pocono Knight (65)** (CHJones) **6-10-5**(7) MKeighley (bit bkwd: hdwy 5th: ev ch 2 out: wknd appr last)	10	**4**	25/1	50	7
183[11]	**Java Shrine (USA) (75)** (JCTuck) **5-11-5** SMcNeill (bit bkwd: prom: led appr 5th to 6th: wknd 2 out)	7	**5**	14/1	50	7
555[2]	**Burnt Sienna (IRE) (79)** (JSMoore) **4-10-12v** WMcFarland (lw: dwlt: gd hdwy to ld after 4th: sn hdd & wknd)	20	**6**	11/4[2]	26	—
483[9]	**Merlins Wish (USA) (91)** (MCPipe) **7-11-12**(7) GSupple (n.d: t.o)	1¾	**7**	14/1	44	1
498[P]	**Orinoco Venture (IRE)** (DBurchell) **5-10-12** DJBurchell (hdwy 5th: chsng wnr whn mstke 6th: lost pl: ev ch 2 out: sn wknd: t.o)	5	**8**	14/1	18	—
483[7]	**Amber Lily** (JMBradley) **4-10-5** APMcCoy (in tch tl wknd appr 5th: t.o)	1	**9**	20/1	12	—
	Masimara Music (JMBradley) **5-10-7** BFenton (bit bkwd: n.d: t.o)	6	**10**	50/1	6	—
555[P]	**Solo Volumes** (HGRowsell) **7-10-12** BPowell (led tl after 4th: wknd appr next: t.o)	8	**11**	66/1	4	—
	Anna Bannanna (MCPipe) **4-9-12**(7) BMoore (bit bkwd: rel to r: drvn & in tch 3rd: wknd 5th: t.o whn p.u bef 2 out)		**P**	33/1	—	—
481[4]	**Dry Sea** (RGFrost) **5-10-12** JFrost (mid div whn p.u bef 4th: lame)		**P**	5/1[3]	—	—
497[8]	**Sharp Holly (IRE)** (JABennett) **4-10-5v** LHarvey (prom to 5th: grad wknd: t.o whn p.u bef 2 out)		**P**	50/1	—	—
288[6]	**Avril Etoile (60)** (CHJones) **6-10-7** GUpton (bit bkwd: nvr trbld ldrs: t.o whn p.u bef 2 out)		**P**	50/1	—	—
				(SP 131.0%)		**15 Rn**

4m 2.1 (9.10) CSF £23.78 TOTE £3.30: £1.40 £2.80 £4.90 (£23.70) Trio £103.60 OWNER Mr Brian Lewendon (LAMBOURN) BRED Lawrence Rowan
WEIGHT FOR AGE 4yo-2lb
Bt in 3,200 gns
OFFICIAL EXPLANATION **Burnt Sienna (IRE): was facing the wrong way when the tapes went up.**
553* Hacketts Cross (IRE) carries his head rather high. Connections believe that he has to be kept on the go while in form, and a handicap hurdle at Carlisle soon may be on the cards. (5/2)
Twice the Groom (IRE) was one of five in with a chance over the last two obstacles but, finding little on the run-in, could only finish best of the rest. (8/1)
Prestige Lady seemed to be travelling comfortably up with the pace and had every chance over the last two. She began jumping to the left on her last race last season and that came about here over the last two flights. Weakening on the flat, she was soon beaten. (10/1)
Pocono Knight weakened between the last two flights after having every chance. (25/1)
Java Shrine (USA) (14/1: op 6/1)
Merlins Wish (USA) (14/1: 12/1-20/1)

601 TETLEY BITTER CONDITIONAL H'CAP CHASE (0-100) (5-Y.O+) (Class F)
2-55 (2-57) **2m 110y (13 fncs)** £2,703.60 (£759.60: £370.80) GOING minus 0.59 sec per fur (F)

				SP	RR	SF
537*	**Super Sharp (NZ) (85)** (HOliver) **8-10-9**(5) GSupple (lw: chsd ldr tl led 4th: drvn out flat)	—	**1**	5/2[1]	93+	22
457[2]	**Fenwick (88)** (RJHodges) **9-11-3** TDascombe (hdwy 8th: sn prom: in tch 2 out: one pce appr last)	5	**2**	10/1	91	20
590[2]	**Seahawk Retriever (75)** (PFNicholls) **7-10-4** OBurrows (hld up & bhd: hdwy 9th: chsd wnr next: wknd 2 out)	5	**3**	6/1[3]	73	2
484[5]	**Prudent Peggy (71)** (RGFrost) **9-10-0b** TJMurphy (led to 4th: chsd wnr to 10th: sn wknd)	6	**4**	20/1	64	—
457[P]	**Afaltoun (71)** (RLee) **11-10-0** PHenley (prom tl rdn & wknd 8th: collapsed after r: dead)	3	**5**	33/1	61	—
486*	**Willie Makeit (IRE) (90)** (RTPhillips) **6-11-5** JCulloty (chsd ldrs to 7th: sn wknd)	5	**6**	5/2[1]	75	4
484[6]	**Toomuch Toosoon (IRE) (95)** (MCPipe) **8-11-10** DWalsh (hdwy 3rd: mstke next: in tch whn mstke 8th: rdn & wknd next)	½	**7**	11/2[2]	79	8
472[3]	**Stapleford Lady (79)** (JSMoore) **8-10-8** JMagee (mstke 2nd: a bhd: t.o 10th)	15	**8**	13/2	49	—
				(SP 116.9%)		**8 Rn**

3m 59.9 (-0.10) CSF £25.15 CT £125.58 TOTE £3.00: £1.30 £2.10 £1.80 (£11.60) OWNER Mrs Sue Careless (CHELTENHAM) BRED Dr R. G. & Mrs L. A. Martin
LONG HANDICAP Prudent Peggy 9-9 Afaltoun 9-13
STEWARDS' ENQUIRY Supple susp. 21 & 25-26/9/96 (excessive use of whip).
537* Super Sharp (NZ) won his second race since having a soft-palate operation in July. Taking it up from the fourth, the result was never in any doubt from then on. He is certainly in good heart at the moment and his trainer believes he could step up to two and a half miles. (5/2)
457 Fenwick was the only one in touch over the last two, but he could not sustain his challenge. (10/1)
590 Seahawk Retriever was slow into stride, but was well placed and seemed a major threat turning for home. The effort soon capitulated and he could not quicken in the straight. His best results have come over further. (6/1: op 4/1)

602 DRY BLACKTHORN NOVICES' CHASE (5-Y.O+) (Class E)
3-30 (3-30) **2m 5f 110y (16 fncs)** £2,913.75 (£882.00: £430.50: £204.75) GOING minus 0.59 sec per fur (F)

				SP	RR	SF
333*	**Cats Run (IRE) (96)** (JohnUpson) **8-11-5** RJohnson (lw: chsd ldr: led 5th to 7th: led 12th: clr appr last: rdn out)	—	**1**	Evens[1]	112	30

	Horse		Dist	Pos	SP	RR	SF
503*	**Lucky Dollar (IRE) (100)** (KCBailey) **8-11-5** AThornton (lw: led to 5th: led 7th to 12th: ev ch tl outpcd fr 2 out)		1½	2	11/8 2	111	29
503 2	**Blue Raven (83)** (PJHobbs) **5-10-9** APMcCoy (lw: in tch whn hit 4th: grad wknd fr 12th)		15	3	6/1 3	93	8
472 4	**Jameswick (60)** (JWDufosee) **6-10-12** PHolley (chsd ldrs tl mstke 9th: wknd next: t.o)		dist	4	50/1	—	—
	Bells Wood (AJKDunn) **7-10-12** CMaude (bit bkwd: bhd whn mstke 7th: wkng whn mstke next: t.o whn p.u bef 13th)			P	25/1	—	—

(SP 112.2%) **5 Rn**

5m 16.0 (-1.00) CSF £2.74 TOTE £1.90: £1.10 £1.50 (£1.70) OWNER Mrs Ann Key (TOWCESTER) BRED John Brophy
WEIGHT FOR AGE 5yo-3lb

333* Cats Run (IRE) is highly regarded by his trainer who believes his best trip is three miles plus. A run at either Kempton or Uttoxeter is on the cards for early October, and this will be followed by a Grade Two event at Towcester in November. He seems a very promising chaser. (Evens)
503* Lucky Dollar (IRE) set off in front but was outjumped over the last four fences. This was a decent effort nevertheless. (11/8)
503 Blue Raven put in a respectable effort and has time on his side to progress. (6/1: 5/1-8/1)

603 THURLESTONE HOTEL CENTENARY/100 YEARS CELEBRATIONS NOVICES' HURDLE (4-Y.O+) (Class E)

4-00 (4-00) **2m 1f (8 hdls)** £2,326.50 (£654.00: £319.50) GOING: 0.03 sec per fur (G)

	Horse	Dist	Pos	SP	RR	SF
357 2	**Southern Ridge (75)** (RGFrost) **5-10-12** MrAHoldsworth (lw: plld hrd: chsd ldr 4th tl led after 6th: clr 2 out: drvn out flat)	—	1	12/1	80	25
	Caddy's First (90) (SMellor) **4-10-10** NMann (bit bkwd: mid div: hdwy 5th: rdn to go 2nd appr last: no imp)	15	2	11/2 3	66	9
	Second Colours (USA) (MCPipe) **6-10-12** DBridgwater (hld up & bhd: hdwy 5th: sn prom: rdn to chse wnr appr 2 out: sn outpcd)	3	3	6/4 1	63	8
481 3	**Almapa** (RJHodges) **4-10-7**(3) TDascombe (a chsng ldrs: styd on fr 2 out: nvr nrr)	nk	4	7/2 2	63	6
497 3	**Ramstar** (PJHobbs) **8-10-9**(3) GTormey (lw: led tl after 6th: wknd appr 2 out)	12	5	11/1	52	—
	Colin's Pride (MrsSDWilliams) **5-10-7** SMcNeill (bkwd: a bhd: t.o 5th)	11	6	12/1	36	—
	Landlord (JARToller) **4-10-10b** JRailton (bit bkwd: chsd ldr to 4th: wknd appr 6th: t.o)	1½	7	14/1	40	—
400 6	**Chief's Lady** (JMBradley) **4-10-5** RJohnson (nvr trbld ldrs: t.o)	9	8	50/1	26	—
	Sharp Thrill (BSmart) **5-10-12** CLlewellyn (bit bkwd: a bhd: wknd 5th: t.o)	3	9	25/1	28	—
	Fair Attraction (JWDufosee) **4-10-5**(5) PHenley (bit bkwd: mid div tl wknd 5th: t.o)	28	10	50/1	2	—
	Bath Times (BRMillman) **4-10-0**(5) DSalter (bkwd: prom to 5th: sn wknd: t.o)	¾	11	50/1	—	—
498 5	**Triple Tie (USA)** (MBlanshard) **5-10-7** DGallagher (s.v.s: t.o thrght: p.u bef last)		P	20/1	—	—

(SP 122.5%) **12 Rn**

4m 1.2 (8.20) CSF £73.44 TOTE £11.10: £2.10 £1.80 £1.10 (£29.70) Trio £16.40 OWNER Mr R. G. Frost (BUCKFASTLEIGH) BRED A. Wilkinson and J. W. Brown
WEIGHT FOR AGE 4yo-2lb

357 Southern Ridge provided his jockey with his first win under Rules. Taking the initiative at the sixth, he soon went clear and, from then on, had only to defy the challenge of his closest rivals. Driven out on the flat, he won comfortably. (12/1)
Caddy's First took second over the last to win the battle for the runner-up prize. (11/2: 4/1-6/1)
Second Colours (USA) was tackling hurdles for the first time after a long career on the Flat. He would have appreciated the experience. (6/4)
481 Almapa is running consistently and deserves a change of fortune. (7/2)
Colin's Pride (12/1: 10/1-16/1)
Landlord (14/1: 9/1-20/1)

604 PURE GENIUS H'CAP CHASE (0-120) (5-Y.O+) (Class D)

4-30 (4-30) **2m 5f 110y (16 fncs)** £3,458.00 (£1,046.00: £510.00: £242.00) GOING minus 0.59 sec per fur (F)

	Horse	Dist	Pos	SP	RR	SF
	Herbert Buchanan (IRE) (93) (PFNicholls) **6-11-6** APMcCoy (hld up mid div: hdwy to chse ldr 12th: led 1 4th: hld on u.s.p flat)	—	1	15/8 1	103	36
	Time Enough (IRE) (97) (CPEBrooks) **7-11-10** GBradley (led & sn clr: hdd 14th: ev ch last: rdn & no ex nr fin)	1¼	2	11/2	106	39
	Clear Idea (IRE) (94) (RGFrost) **8-11-7** JFrost (chsd ldr to 12th: in tch last: rdn & styd on flat: nt rch ldrs)	½	3	13/2	103	36
409*	**Henley Regatta (94)** (PRRodford) **8-11-7** SBurrough (nt fluent early: hdwy 10th: in tch tl rdn & wknd fr 12th)	20	4	4/1 2	88	21
484 4	**Seal King (85)** (MrsJGRetter) **11-10-12** RJohnson (in tch whn mstke 10th: wknd 12th: t.o)	dist	5	5/1 3	—	—
	Fairy Park (96) (HOliver) **11-11-9** JacquiOliver (bkwd: a bhd: t.o whn mstke 13th: p.u bef next)		P	11/2	—	—

(SP 115.6%) **6 Rn**

5m 14.4 (-2.60) CSF £11.95 TOTE £2.40: £1.30 £3.60 (£8.70) OWNER Five For Fun (SHEPTON MALLET) BRED Lyle Buttimer

Herbert Buchanan (IRE), off a mark 5lb higher than when beaten by Maremma Gale in May, was produced to go clear off the final bend. He idles in front and had to be kept up to his work on the flat. (15/8)
Time Enough (IRE) turned in a decent effort and is sure to come on for the run. (11/2: 7/2-6/1)
Clear Idea (IRE), who has won all of his races on this track, put in a good show on his seasonal debut. (13/2)
Fairy Park (11/2: 3/1-6/1)

605 TEACHERS WHISKY CHALLENGE H'CAP HURDLE (0-120) (4-Y.O+) (Class D)

5-00 (5-00) **3m 3f (12 hdls)** £2,778.90 (£780.40: £380.70) GOING: 0.03 sec per fur (G)

	Horse	Dist	Pos	SP	RR	SF
394 2	**Acrow Line (108)** (DBurchell) **11-12-0** DJBurchell (hld up & bhd: hdwy 9th: led next: hrd rdn & hld on flat)	—	1	8/1	89	45
485*	**Blasket Hero (102)** (MrsSDWilliams) **8-11-8b** SMcNeill (lw: hld up & bhd: hdwy 9th: ev ch 2 out tl rdn & one pce flat)	1½	2	7/2 3	82	38
415*	**Glengarrif Girl (IRE) (108)** (MCPipe) **6-12-0v** DBridgwater (hdwy appr 9th: chsd wnr after next: rdn & ev ch 2 out: wknd appr last)	11	3	2/1 1	82	38
415 3	**Storm Drum (95)** (KCBailey) **7-11-1b** TJMurphy (chsd ldrs tl led 6th: hdd & mstke 10th: sn wknd)	12	4	16/1	61	17
	L'Uomo Piu (80) (ABarrow) **12-10-0** BPowell (bit bkwd: led to 4th: led 5th to next: wknd appr 9th: t.o)	dist	5	50/1	—	—
301*	**Springfield Dancer (99)** (PJHobbs) **5-11-5** APMcCoy (stdy hdwy 6th: chsd ldr 9th tl wknd after next: p.u bef 2 out)		P	4/1	—	—
465*	**Amazon Express (106)** (PBowen) **7-11-12** RJohnson (mid div: hdwy 9th: rdn next: wknd appr 2 out: p.u bef last: lame)		P	3/1 2	—	—

Anstey Gadabout (80) (DFBassett) **10-10-0** MrAHoldsworth (bit bkwd: chsd ldr tl led 4th: hdd next: mstke 7th: sn wknd: t.o whn p.u bef 9th) .... **P** 200/1 — —
(SP 120.0%) **8 Rn**

6m 34.9 (11.90) CSF £35.55 CT £72.45 TOTE £12.60: £2.60 £1.10 £1.50 (£23.50) OWNER Mr Rhys Thomas Williams (EBBW VALE) BRED W. A. de Vigier and J. Holmes
LONG HANDICAP Anstey Gadabout 8-8
394 Acrow Line put in a good round here and proved just too good. Hitting the front soon after turning for home, he held on well to the line. (8/1)
485* Blasket Hero put up a brave effort, but had met one too good in the winner. (7/2)
415* Glengarrif Girl (IRE) had conditions in her favour, but had given her all approaching the final obstacle. (2/1)
301* Springfield Dancer (4/1: 3/1-9/2)

T/Plpt: £20.20 (468.97 Tckts). T/Qdpt: £3.50 (182.55 Tckts). T

606a-629a (Irish Racing) - See Computer Raceform

0498-WORCESTER (L-H) (Chases Good to firm, Hdles Good to firm becoming Firm)
Friday September 13th
WEATHER: fine

630 NEW STREET NOVICES' HURDLE (4-Y.O+) (Class E)
2-20 (2-20) **2m 4f (10 hdls)** £2,547.50 (£710.00: £342.50) GOING minus 0.58 sec per fur (F)

	Horse / details	Dist	Pos	SP	RR	SF
476*	**Wottashambles (104)** (LMontagueHall) **5-11-5** DMorris (hld up: hdwy 6th: led 3 out: clr appr last: easily)	—	1	11/10 1	84+	36
	Basil Street (IRE) (100) (CJMann) **4-10-10** RDunwoody (hld up: gd hdwy after 7th: chsd wnr fr 3 out: rdn appr last: no imp)	3½	2	5/1 3	74	24
586 6	**Leap in the Dark (IRE) (71)** (MissLCSiddall) **7-10-12** AThornton (chsd ldr: led after 7th: hrd rdn & hdd 3 out: one pce)	3	3	50/1	72	24
594 P	**Marlousion (IRE)** (CPEBrooks) **4-10-5** DGallagher (plld hrd: lost pl 5th: mstke 7th: styd on flat)	10	4	16/1	59	9
498*	**Alpine Mist (IRE) (92)** (JGMO'Shea) **4-10-12**(5) MichaelBrennan (prom tl wknd appr 2 out)	4	5	5/1 3	68	18
	Jean de Florette (USA) (RCSpicer) **5-10-9**(3) EHusband (bhd fr 7th)	2½	6	66/1	59	11
	Dane Rose (MSheppard) **10-10-7** RJohnson (hld up & bhd: mstke 5th: sn lost tch)	1½	7	50/1	52	4
	Hydemilla (83) (MrsTDPilkington) **6-10-4**(3) GHogan (led tl after 7th: wknd qckly: t.o)	dist	8	16/1	—	—
392*	**Tukano (CAN) (101)** (JRJenkins) **5-11-12** GBradley (hld up & bhd: rdn & lost tch 6th: t.o whn p.u bef 2 out)		P	9/2 2	—	—

(SP 116.3%) **9 Rn**

4m 34.5 (-3.50) CSF £7.06 TOTE £2.00: £1.30 £1.90 £7.00 (£5.60) Trio £78.40 OWNER Dream On Racing Partnership (EPSOM) BRED Arthur Sims
WEIGHT FOR AGE 4yo-2lb
OFFICIAL EXPLANATION Tukano (CAN): the trainer reported that the gelding was never going on the ground.
476* Wottashambles stays well and likes fast ground. (11/10)
Basil Street (IRE) disappointed on his only start after breaking a blood-vessel at Haydock last December. (5/1)
Leap in the Dark (IRE) ran his best race for some time. (50/1)

631 BULL RING NOVICES' CHASE (5-Y.O+) (Class D)
2-55 (2-55) **2m 7f (18 fncs)** £3,591.75 (£1,074.00: £514.50: £234.75) GOING minus 0.58 sec per fur (F)

	Horse / details	Dist	Pos	SP	RR	SF
	Father Sky (OSherwood) **5-10-8** JOsborne (bit bkwd: j.w: led 2nd tl after 5th: led 14th: comf)	—	1	5/2 2	113+	—
482*	**Clifton Set** (CJMann) **5-11-1b** RDunwoody (prom: j.slowly 1st: led after 5th to 14th: rdn 3 out: j.rt last: hung lft: nt r.o)	7	2	4/6 1	115	—
503 U	**Glenfinn Princess (96)** (MrsMerritaJones) **8-10-7** MAFitzgerald (hld up in rr: hdwy 11th: nvr nr ldrs)	5	3	5/1 3	101	—
482 3	**Manor Bound** (MrsSDWilliams) **6-10-7** SMcNeill (sn bhd: t.o fr 10th)	dist	4	20/1	—	—
494 2	**Music Score (75)** (MrsLCTaylor) **10-10-12** AThornton (led tl mstke 2nd: bhd fr 10th: t.o whn p.u bef 14th)		P	50/1	—	—
	Giorgione (FR) (NJPomfret) **7-10-12** JCulloty (bkwd: prom to 9th: bhd whn p.u bef 13th)		P	66/1	—	—

(SP 113.5%) **6 Rn**

5m 44.7 (6.70) CSF £4.51 TOTE £3.40: £2.00 £1.40 (£2.10) OWNER Mr Kenneth Kornfeld (UPPER LAMBOURN) BRED Sheikh Mohammed
WEIGHT FOR AGE 5yo-3lb
Father Sky did not have to be 100% fit to dispose of the disappointing favourite. (5/2: op 5/4)
482* Clifton Set was already getting the worse of the argument when throwing in the towel on the flat. (4/6: Evens-11/10)
Glenfinn Princess al least got round in one piece. (5/1)

632 SELLY OAK NOVICES' H'CAP HURDLE (0-100) (4-Y.O+) (Class E)
3-25 (3-25) **3m (12 hdls)** £2,302.50 (£640.00: £307.50) GOING minus 0.58 sec per fur (F)

	Horse / details	Dist	Pos	SP	RR	SF
499 3	**Little Tincture (IRE) (73)** (MrsTJMcInnesSkinner) **6-10-4**ow3 GUpton (lw: hld up: hdwy to ld appr 7th to 3 out: led flat: all out)	—	1	9/1	53	1
	Hylters Chance (IRE) (69) (PJHobbs) **5-10-0** APMcCoy (lw: chsd ldr tl 6th: outpcd appr 3 out: swtchd rt last: rallied nr fin)	s.h	2	9/2 3	49	—
415 F	**Wynberg (97)** (CaptTAForster) **5-12-0** SWynne (hld up: wnt 2nd 9th: rdn to ld 3 out: edgd rt last: wnt lame & hdd flat)	3	3	15/8 1	75	26
546 3	**Akiymann (USA) (82)** (MCPipe) **6-10-13b** DBridgwater (lost pl 8th: styd on flat)	4	4	16/1	57	8
528*	**Anchorena (83)** (MissVenetiaWilliams) **4-10-11** NWilliamson (swtg: hld up in rr: mstke 6th: hdwy 7th: 4th whn p.u lame bef 8th)		P	9/4 2	—	—
406*	**Shalik (IRE) (72)** (JRJenkins) **6-10-3**ow3 JRailton (led & sn clr: hdd appr 7th: wknd qckly: t.o whn p.u bef 3 out)		P	16/1	—	—

(SP 105.5%) **6 Rn**

5m 38.9 (2.90) CSF £41.29 TOTE £13.00: £3.10 £1.90 (£23.50) OWNER Mrs T. J. McInnesSkinner (MELTON MOWBRAY)
LONG HANDICAP Hylters Chance (IRE) 9-13 Shalik (IRE) 9-13
WEIGHT FOR AGE 4yo-3lb
OFFICIAL EXPLANATION Anchorena: was lame on her near-fore.

338 Little Tincture (IRE) took advantage of the favourite breaking down on the run-in, but only just managed to hold on. (9/1)
Hylters Chance (IRE), with misfortune striking Wynberg, nearly pulled the race out of the fire. (9/2: op 3/1)
415 Wynberg would have prevailed had he stayed sound. (15/8)

633 SNOW HILL H'CAP CHASE (0-130) (5-Y.O+) (Class C)

3-55 (3-55) **2m (12 fncs)** £5,430.00 (£1,320.00) GOING minus 0.58 sec per fur (F)

				SP	RR	SF
592[2]	**Captain Khedive (125)** (PFNicholls) **8-12-0** APMcCoy (hld up: lft 2nd 7th: led 2 out: hrd hld)	—	1	4/7[1]	125+	41
	Houghton (113) (WJenks) **10-10-9**(7) MrRBurton (chsd ldr: led 4th to 2 out: no ch w wnr)	1¼	2	12/1[3]	96 t	28
592*	**Noblely (USA) (111)** (NJHWalker) **9-11-0** 6x RFarrant (led to 4th: 2nd whn blnd bdly & uns rdr 7th)		U	7/4[2]	—	—
				(SP 107.7%)		**3 Rn**

3m 49.2 (2.50 under best) (-1.80) CSF £4.62 TOTE £1.50: (£3.30) OWNER Khedive Partnership (SHEPTON MALLET) BRED Mrs Audrey Goodwin
592 Captain Khedive had his task made easier by the departure of Noblely. (4/7)
Houghton is flattered by his proximity to the winner. (12/1)
592* Noblely (USA) got rid of Farrant when trying to recover after finishing on his belly. (7/4)

634 MOOR STREET MAIDEN HURDLE (4-Y.O+) (Class F)

4-30 (4-31) **2m (8 hdls)** £2,353.00 (£658.00: £319.00) GOING minus 0.58 sec per fur (F)

				SP	RR	SF
	Blown Wind (IRE) (OSherwood) **5-11-5** JOsborne (bit bkwd: prom: lost pl 4th: rallied appr 5th: pckd 3 out: led 2 out: shkn up appr last: qcknd clr flat)	—	1	7/2[1]	76	31
396[3]	**Dantean** (RJO'Sullivan) **4-11-3** PHolley (hld up: hdwy 5th: ev ch 2 out: no imp)	8	2	20/1	68	21
350[5]	**Last Laugh (IRE)** (KCBailey) **4-10-12b**[1] TJMurphy (plld hrd: a.p: led 3 out to 2 out: one pce)	3	3	14/1	60	13
	Matamoros (GHarwood) **4-11-3** RDunwoody (a.p: one pce fr 3 out)	1½	4	4/1[2]	64	17
	Difficult Decision (IRE) (MrsMerritaJones) **5-11-5** MAFitzgerald (prom to 3 out)	3	5	16/1	61	16
490[5]	**Rose Chime (IRE)** (JLHarris) **4-10-12** PMcLoughlin (hdwy appr 2 out: nvr nrr)	1¼	6	50/1	54	7
	Camden's Ransom (USA) (HGRowsell) **9-11-5** BPowell (led to 3 out: eased whn btn appr last)	¾	7	66/1	59	14
	Spring Loaded (JGMO'Shea) **5-11-0**(5) MichaelBrennan (bhd tl r.o fr 3 out: nrst fin)	8	8	33/1	51	6
	Highly Charming (IRE) (91) (MissHCKnight) **4-11-3** JFTitley (lw: hdwy 5th: mstke 3 out: sn wknd)	3½	9	7/2[1]	47	—
	Northern Law (JohnBerry) **4-11-3** ILawrence (n.d)	2½	10	16/1	45	—
	Martha's Daughter (CaptTAForster) **7-11-0** AThornton (hdwy 3rd: wknd appr 3 out)	5	11	20/1	35	—
	Celestial Dollar (OO'Neill) **5-11-5** RJohnson (nvr nr ldrs)	3	12	20/1	37	—
476[2]	**Wanstead (IRE) (90)** (JRJenkins) **4-11-3v** GBradley (a bhd)	¾	13	8/1[3]	36	—
	Mister Gigi (IRE) (MissMERowland) **5-11-5** GaryLyons (prom to 5th)	5	14	14/1	31	—
	Punch (NTinkler) **4-11-0b**(3) EHusband (prom tl mstke 5th)	7	15	50/1	24	—
497[10]	**Good (IRE)** (DTThom) **4-11-3** BFenton (bhd fr 5th: t.o)	16	16	66/1	8	—
	Ragtime Song (JRJenkins) **7-10-12**(7) DYellowlees (bkwd: bhd tl fell last)		F	66/1	—	—
490[P]	**Flashing Sabre** (HJManners) **4-10-10**(7) ADowling (dropped rr 4th: t.o whn p.u bef 3 out)		P	100/1	—	—
				(SP 127.3%)		**18 Rn**

3m 38.2 (-1.80) CSF £67.44 TOTE £4.40: £2.00 £4.10 £2.80 (£88.30) Trio £208.70 OWNER Mr B. T. Stewart-Brown (UPPER LAMBOURN) BRED James O'Keeffe
WEIGHT FOR AGE 4yo-2lb
Blown Wind (IRE), supported in both runs in bumpers last season, appreciated this faster ground. He probably did not beat much, but this chasing type should come on for the outing. (7/2)
396 Dantean proved no match for the winner. (20/1)
350 Last Laugh (IRE) ran freely in the first-time blinkers. (14/1)
Mister Gigi (IRE) (14/1: op 7/1)

635 BIRMINGHAM H'CAP HURDLE (0-120) (4-Y.O+) (Class D)

5-00 (5-00) **2m (8 hdls)** £2,938.00 (£818.00: £394.00) GOING minus 0.58 sec per fur (F)

				SP	RR	SF
483[4]	**Cooley's Valve (IRE) (95)** (MrsSDWilliams) **8-10-8**(5) SophieMitchell (hld up: wnt 2nd 4th: led on bit appr last: shkn up flat: comf)	—	1	15/8[2]	81+	22
473[5]	**Ikhtiraa (USA) (82)** (RJO'Sullivan) **6-10-0** PHolley (led: hit 2 out: sn hdd: one pce)	4	2	11/4[3]	64	5
478*	**Gone by (IRE) (110)** (JRJenkins) **8-12-0v** GBradley (chsd ldr to 4th: rdn appr 3 out: one pce)	1½	3	6/5[1]	91	32
				(SP 106.9%)		**3 Rn**

3m 38.9 (-1.10) CSF £5.80 TOTE £2.60: (£2.20) OWNER Christopher Shirley Brasher (SOUTH MOLTON) BRED Airlie Stud
483 Cooley's Valve (IRE) took advantage of being dropped 5lb this season. (15/8)
329 Ikhtiraa (USA) found the winner galloping all over him from the penultimate hurdle. (11/4)
478* Gone by (IRE), raised 2lb, did win over two miles last time, but got tapped for speed here. (6/5)

T/Plpt: £335.50 (23.14 Tckts). T/Qdpt: £67.70 (6.84 Tckts). KH

0388-BANGOR-ON-DEE (L-H) (Good, Good to firm patches)

Saturday September 14th

WEATHER: fine

636 LONG SHOT 'N.H.' NOVICES' HURDLE (4-Y.O+) (Class E)

2-10 (2-10) **2m 1f (9 hdls)** £2,472.00 (£692.00: £336.00) GOING minus 0.30 sec per fur (GF)

				SP	RR	SF
	Danny Gale (IRE) (85) (GMMcCourt) **5-10-12** GBradley (lw: hld up in tch: wnt 2nd 5th: led appr 2 out: clr last)	—	1	7/2[2]	65	2
	Country Minstrel (IRE) (SADouch) **5-10-12** SMcNeill (bit bkwd: hld up: hdwy 6th: ev ch 2 out: sn rdn: one pce)	3½	2	40/1	62	—
	Follow de Call (DMcCain) **6-10-9**(3) DWalsh (swtg: bkwd: hld up & bhd: hdwy 6th: effrt appr 2 out: outpcd appr last)	6	3	100/1	56	—
	Ragosa (JWhite) **5-10-7** APMcCoy (bit bkwd: chsd ldr: led appr 5th: rdn & hdd appr 2 out: sn btn)	4	4	20/1[3]	47	—

467* **Eternal City (90)** (GRichards) **5-11-5** AMaguire (trckd ldrs to 4th: sn lost pl: n.d after)........8 **5** 8/11[1] 52 —
Shady Emma (FJordan) **4-10-5** SWynne (bkwd: a bhd)........2 **6** 66/1 38 —
Hymoss (WJenks) **5-10-7** TJenks (swtg: bkwd: led tl appr 5th: wknd after 3 out: t.o)........dist **7** 33/1 — —
418[3] **Powerful Spirit** (JGMO'Shea) **4-10-5**(5) MichaelBrennan (hld up: dropped rr 6th: btn whn hit 3 out: t.o)........5 **8** 7/2[2] — —
(SP 115.0%) **8 Rn**

4m 3.2 (8.20) CSF £83.26 TOTE £4.70: £1.20 £3.80 £6.20 (£71.50) OWNER Mr Robert Cox (WANTAGE) BRED Bryan Gerard Maguire
WEIGHT FOR AGE 4yo-2lb

Danny Gale (IRE), produced fit and well for this first outing since the spring, won this very much as he pleased and it would seem the hobday operation he has had since he last appeared has done the trick. (7/2)
Country Minstrel (IRE) did not look fit enough to do himself justice, but he turned in by far his best display yet. There could be a small race to be had. (40/1)
Follow de Call showed he is getting it together with a very promising display, and this was at least a step in the right direction. (100/1)
467* Eternal City came from behind when winning on his seasonal debut and, on this much faster ground, was in trouble soon after halfway. (8/11)

637 TOTE CREDIT CLUB NOVICES' CHASE (4-Y.O+) (Class D)
2-40 (2-40) **2m 4f 110y (15 fncs)** £3,517.50 (£1,065.00: £520.00: £247.50) GOING minus 0.30 sec per fur (GF)

SP RR SF

590* **Sonic Star (IRE) (108)** (DNicholson) **7-12-4** AMaguire (led 2nd to 4th: hit 10th: led 4 out: drew clr appr 2 out: unchal)........— **1** 4/9[1] 106+ 35
556* **Mill O'The Rags (IRE) (89)** (MrsDHaine) **7-11-12** JFTitley (swtg: led to 2nd: led 4th to 4 out: rdn & outpcd appr 2 out)........29 **2** 2/1[2] 77 6
Little By Little (BPreece) **6-11-6** AThornton (bkwd: dropped rr 9th: styd on to go 3rd towards fin: t.o)........dist **3** 33/1[3] — —
On the Tear (61) (FLloyd) **10-11-6** SMcNeill (bkwd: wnt poor 3rd 9th: rdn & no ex flat: t.o)........s.h **4** 33/1[3] — —
(SP 108.4%) **4 Rn**

5m 6.5 (6.50) CSF £1.65 TOTE £1.40: (£1.20) OWNER Mr R. F. Nutland (TEMPLE GUITING) BRED A.B. McDowell

590* Sonic Star (IRE) took more than the odd chance with his jumping, but such was his superiority that he was never off the bridle. He is getting experience all the time. (4/9)
556* Mill O'The Rags (IRE) could have found this race coming plenty soon enough, but he did make a race of it until having to admit the winner much too good for him. (2/1)

638 DICK FRANCIS H'CAP HURDLE (0-130) (4-Y.O+) (Class C)
3-10 (3-12) **2m 1f (9 hdls)** £3,371.25 (£1,020.00: £497.50: £236.25) GOING minus 0.30 sec per fur (GF)

SP RR SF

341[3] **Star Market (119)** (JLSpearing) **6-12-0b** APMcCoy (mde all: clr fr ½-wy: unchal)........— **1** 7/1 102 65
538* **Sarmatian (USA) (100)** (MDHammond) **5-10-9** RGarritty (lw: hld up in rr: stdy hdwy 5th: rdn appr 2 out: nt rch wnr)........8 **2** 9/4[1] 76 39
582* **Red Valerian (119)** (GMMoore) **5-12-0v** MAFitzgerald (hld up & bhd: effrt appr 3 out: nt rch ldrs)........6 **3** 5/2[2] 89 52
411[6] **Robert's Toy (IRE) (118)** (MCPipe) **5-11-13b** AMaguire (chsd wnr fr 4th tl wknd appr 2 out)........17 **4** 9/2[3] 72 35
Don du Cadran (FR) (106) (CaptTAForster) **7-11-1** AThornton (bit bkwd: prom tl wknd appr 5th: t.o)........15 **5** 14/1 46 9
453* **Have a Nightcap (100)** (NPLittmoden) **7-10-9b** MRichards (trckd ldrs to 5th: sn wknd: t.o)........9 **6** 10/1 31 —
591[U] **Windward Ariom (108)** (PMitchell) **10-11-3** ALarnach (pushed along fr 3rd: no ch whn fell 3 out)........ **F** 20/1 — —
(SP 110.5%) **7 Rn**

3m 52.1 (-2.90) CSF £21.56 TOTE £9.00: £4.10 £1.80 (£9.00) OWNER Mrs P. Joynes (ALCESTER) BRED M. H. D. Madden and Partners

341 Star Market took the bull by the horns in this mediocre contest and simply galloped his rivals into the ground. It is possible he could go chasing in the not-too-distant future. (7/1)
538* Sarmatian (USA) made steady progress in the final mile and stayed on willingly under pressure, but the winner was not stopping and he was unable to reach him. (9/4)
582* Red Valerian could not handle this step down in distance against stronger opposition than he had met so far this term, and his finishing position was as close as he was able to get. (5/2)
Don du Cadran (FR) (14/1: 8/1-16/1)
453* Have a Nightcap (10/1: op 6/1)

639 GREENALLS INNS NOVICES' H'CAP CHASE (0-100) (5-Y.O+) (Class E)
3-40 (3-40) **3m 110y (18 fncs)** £3,403.75 (£1,030.00: £502.50: £238.75) GOING minus 0.30 sec per fur (GF)

SP RR SF

494* **Warner's Sports (79)** (PJHobbs) **7-10-10** APMcCoy (disp ld fr 5th: led 9th: rdn 11th: clr 3 out: veered rt u.p flat: all out)........— **1** 4/6[1] 84 14
466* **Definite Maybe (IRE) (95)** (PFNicholls) **6-11-12b** MAFitzgerald (lw: chsd ldrs: reminders 8th: outpcd 12th: styd on u.p fr 2 out)........nk **2** 5/1[2] 100 30
Rent Day (69) (JWMullins) **7-10-0** SCurran (bit bkwd: lft 2nd 12th: rdn appr 2 out: wknd appr last)........10 **3** 40/1[3] 67 —
San Giorgio (90) (NATwiston-Davies) **7-11-7** CLlewellyn (bkwd: hld up: j.slowly 4th: rdn 10th: lost tch 13th: t.o)........dist **4** 5/1[2] — —
460* **Wakt (97)** (JWhite) **6-11-11**(3) GuyLewis (led to 9th: cl 2nd whn blnd & uns rdr 12th)........ **U** 5/1[2] — —
(SP 112.4%) **5 Rn**

6m 10.0 (8.00) CSF £4.44 TOTE £1.60: £1.30 £1.50 (£2.70) OWNER Terry Warner Sports (MINEHEAD) BRED Peter Deal
LONG HANDICAP Rent Day 9-9
STEWARDS' ENQUIRY McCoy susp. 25-26 & 28-29/9/96 (excessive use of whip).

494* Warner's Sports kept up his winning sequence and for most of the trip looked likely to win as he pleased, but he was getting leg-weary in the closing stages, and his jockey needed to be at his strongest to get him home. (4/6: op Evens)
466* Definite Maybe (IRE), a very hard ride, is not short of stamina and stayed on relentlessly inside the last half-mile to only just fail to concede 16lb to the winner. (5/1: op 3/1)
460* Wakt tried hard to extend her winning run and was still virtually upsides the winner when she met a ditch out in the country all wrong, and deposited her jockey. (5/1: 3/1-11/2)

640 GORDON MYTTON HOMES HURDLE (3-Y.O) (Class D)
4-10 (4-13) **2m 1f (9 hdls)** £2,827.00 (£856.00: £418.00: £199.00) GOING minus 0.30 sec per fur (GF)

SP RR SF

Silverdale Knight (KWHogg) **3-10-10** MFoster (trckd ldng pair: led appr 2 out: sn clr: easily)........— **1** 8/1 77+ 23

			SP	RR	SF
	Flying Green (FR) (NJHWalker) **3-10-7**$^{(3)}$ GuyLewis (chsd ldr: led after 6th: hdd & mstke 2 out: sn btn)........14	**2**	5/2^{2}	64	10
501^{4}	**Bath Knight** (DJSffrenchDavis) **3-10-10b**^{1} SMcNeill (plld hrd: led & sn clr: wknd & hdd after 6th)..................24	**3**	25/1	41	—
589^{2}	**Song For Jess (IRE)** (FJordan) **3-10-5** SWynne (lw: in tch: no hdwy fr 6th)...7	**4**	12/1	30	—
	Welcome Royale (IRE) (MHTompkins) **3-10-10** AMaguire (lw: hld up & bhd: sme hdwy fr 3 out: nvr nrr)......2½	**5**	5/1^{3}	32	—
458^{4}	**Balmoral Princess** (JHPeacock) **3-10-12b** RBellamy (a in rr)..1¼	**6**	16/1	33	—
501*	**Sheath Kefaah** (JRJenkins) **3-11-3** GBradley (lw: trckd ldrs tl wknd 5th: t.o)..9	**7**	2/1^{1}	30	—
	Flood's Fancy (LJBarratt) **3-10-5** CLlewellyn (a bhd: t.o)..dist	**8**	33/1	—	—
	Krasnik (IRE) (MrsDHaine) **3-10-10** JFTitley (bkwd: a bhd: t.o)..hd	**9**	14/1	—	—
	Tallulah Belle (NPLittmoden) **3-10-5** MRichards (hld up: sme hdwy whn fell 5th)	**F**	33/1	—	—
	Peyton Jones (ADSmith) **3-10-10** FJousset (bkwd: mid div: rdn 4th: t.o whn p.u bef 6th)	**P**	50/1	—	—
			(SP 121.6%)		**11 Rn**

3m 57.9 (2.90) CSF £27.81 TOTE £9.80: £2.20 £1.70 £5.10 (£27.70) Trio £111.80 OWNER Auldyn Stud Ltd (ISLE OF MAN) BRED Auldyn Stud Ltd

Silverdale Knight has not won beyond seven furlongs on the Flat, but he made quite an impressive start to his hurdling career and looks a natural for this game. (8/1: 6/1-10/1)

Flying Green (FR) has competed in better-class races on the Flat than the winner, and he was all the rage here, but his measure had already been taken when he made an untidy mistake at the penultimate flight. (5/2)

Bath Knight ran far too freely in his first-time blinkers and had run himself into the ground half a mile out. (25/1)

501* Sheath Kefaah found this opposition much stronger than he beat on his hurdling debut. (2/1)

641 DEAD CERT H'CAP HURDLE (0-105) (4-Y.O+) (Class F)

4-40 (4-43) **2m 4f (11 hdls)** £2,967.00 (£837.00: £411.00) GOING minus 0.30 sec per fur (GF)

			SP	RR	SF
	Bellroi (IRE) (92) (MHTompkins) **5-11-4** AMaguire (lw: chsd ldrs: led & j.slowly 7th: clr whn mstke last)........—	**1**	9/2^{3}	84	25
502*	**First Crack (87)** (FJordan) **11-10-13** SWynne (lw: hld up in tch: hdwy appr 3 out: rdn next: nt pce of wnr)........4	**2**	7/2^{1}	76	17
468^{2}	**Plinth (81)** (NAGraham) **5-10-7** MAFitzgerald (trckd ldrs: outpcd 7th: n.d after)...15	**3**	9/2^{3}	58	—
	Ilewin (98) (GMMcCourt) **9-11-10** GBradley (hld up in tch: hdwy 6th: rdn & wknd after 3 out)...............................2	**4**	4/1^{2}	73	14
	Prize Match (80) (JCTuck) **7-10-6** SMcNeill (bit bkwd: hld up in rr: hdwy 7th: nvr nrr)......................................¾	**5**	33/1	55	—
285^{4}	**King's Shilling (USA) (90)** (HOliver) **9-10-9**$^{(7)}$ GSupple (swtg: hld up in rr: effrt 8th: nt rch ldrs) 1½	**6**	9/1	63	4
	Severn Gale (86) (PFNicholls) **6-10-12** APMcCoy (hld up: hdwy 5th: jnd wnr 8th: wknd appr 2 out)..............3½	**7**	4/1^{2}	57	—
539^{2}	**Tashreef (75)** (JJBirkett) **6-10-1b** LO'Hara (trckd ldrs: rdn & outpcd after 3 out: sn bhd)....................................6	**8**	25/1	41	—
	Emperor Chang (USA) (76) (KOWarner) **9-10-2**^{ow1} TKent (bkwd: chsd ldr tl wknd 6th: t.o) 26	**9**	33/1	21	—
	Please Call (IRE) (77) (DPGeraghty) **7-10-3** JRKavanagh (bkwd: a bhd: t.o)..1	**10**	50/1	21	—
413^{5}	**Batty's Island (82)** (BPreece) **7-10-8** AThornton (lost tch 6th: t.o)...26	**11**	25/1	5	—
	Ibn Sina (USA) (74) (WClay) **9-10-0** SCurran (bkwd: a bhd: t.o)..2	**12**	50/1	—	—
	Buckley Boys (80) (MrsLWilliamson) **5-9-13**$^{(7)}$ MrRThornton (led to 7th: sn wknd: bhd whn p.u bef 2 out).........	**P**	33/1	—	—
	Lustreman (74) (JHPeacock) **9-10-0** RBellamy (bkwd: racd wd: in tch to ½-wy: t.o whn p.u bef 3 out)	**P**	40/1	—	—
			(SP 131.5%)		**14 Rn**

4m 41.1 (5.10) CSF £21.40 CT £73.24 TOTE £6.10: £3.80 £1.20 £1.70 (£14.60) Trio £12.50 OWNER Mrs G. A. E. Smith (NEWMARKET) BRED Mrs K. Twomey and Mrs S. O'Riordan

LONG HANDICAP Ibn Sina (USA) 9-10 Lustreman 9-5

Bellroi (IRE), a winner on the Flat last month, relished this extended trip and, except for a couple of minor mistakes, had the prize in safe-keeping from some way out. (9/2: 3/1-5/1)

502* First Crack, a consistent mare, had to admit her younger rival much too smart for her, though she never stopped trying. (7/2)

468 Plinth did keep staying on, but the battle was only for the minor prize. (9/2)

Ilewin was the subject of quite strong support but, when the principals stepped things up, he was left flat-footed. (4/1)

Severn Gale looked well tuned up for this return to action, and was travelling best when joining issue four out, but she failed to get the better of the winner and called enough turning in. (4/1)

T/Plpt: £230.90 (30.82 Tckts). T/Qdpt: £12.20 (36.4 Tckts). IM

0581-SEDGEFIELD (L-H) (Good to firm, Firm patches)
Saturday September 14th

642 JOHN WADE HIND TRUCK NOVICES' (S) H'CAP HURDLE (0-90) (4-Y.O+) (Class G)

1-50 (1-51) **2m 5f 110y (10 hdls)** £1,891.00 (£526.00: £253.00) GOING minus 1.05 sec per fur (HD)

			SP	RR	SF
585^{2}	**What's Secreto (USA) (80)** (HAlexander) **4-11-9b** PNiven (lw: chsd ldr: lft in ld 3rd: sn hdd: disp ld fr 4th: drvn along fr 4 out: led last: kpt on u.p)..............................—	**1**	11/10^{1}	65	—
586^{9}	**Haughton Lad (IRE) (68)** (FPMurtagh) **7-10-13** ARoche (in tch: hmpd 3rd: hdwy to chse ldrs 4 out: disp ld 3 out: no ex u.p flat)..............................4	**2**	16/1	50	—
587^{4}	**Sakbah (USA) (60)** (JAPickering) **7-10-5** NWilliamson (in tch: hdwy after 4 out: ev ch after 2 out: rdn & one pce flat)..............................1	**3**	5/1^{2}	41	—
585^{6}	**Pimsboy (62)** (GROldroyd) **9-10-4b**$^{(3)ow2}$ PMidgley (in tch: drvn along bef 3 out: one pce fr 2 out) 1¾	**4**	16/1	42	—
585^{P}	**Bowland Park (70)** (EJAlston) **5-11-1** TJMurphy (bhd: hdwy 5th: sn chsng ldrs: wknd bef 3 out) 18	**5**	40/1	37	—
586^{12}	**Dark Midnight (IRE) (60)** (DALamb) **7-10-5** JBurke (lw: prom: disp ld 4th tl rdn & wknd appr 2 out)..................4	**6**	40/1	24	—
489^{2}	**Arrange A Game (55)** (MissJBower) **9-9-9b**$^{(5)}$ STaylor (cl up: led after 3rd to next: nt fluent after: bhd fr 4 out)..............................9	**7**	50/1	12	—
	Anthony Bell (83) (TJCarr) **10-11-7**$^{(7)}$ TJComerford (bkwd: hld up & bhd: lost tch fr 4 out) 3½	**8**	12/1	37	—
	Top Fella (USA) (80) (PJDennis) **4-11-9b** DBentley (mstke 2nd: lost tch fr 6th: sn t.o)...................................dist	**9**	8/1^{3}	—	—
585^{5}	**Classic Crest (IRE) (80)** (GMMoore) **5-11-4v**$^{(7)}$ THogg (led tl fell 3rd)	**F**	5/1^{2}	—	—
			(SP 118.4%)		**10 Rn**

4m 58.1 (-1.90) CSF £18.54 CT £63.83 TOTE £2.10: £1.30 £2.60 £1.30 (£14.20) Trio £24.40 OWNER Mr A. Atkinson (LANCHESTER) BRED D J Stable & Phoenix Corp

LONG HANDICAP Arrange A Game 9-9

WEIGHT FOR AGE 4yo-2lb

Bt in 5,000 gns

585 What's Secreto (USA), entitled to win this, took plenty of hard driving from a long way out to see him home. (11/10)

Haughton Lad (IRE) turned in an improved display and had every chance until being outpaced by the winner on the flat. (16/1)
587 Sakbah (USA) looked dangerous between the final two flights, but failed to pull out as much as she had promised when the chips were down. (5/1)
Pimsboy was unable to match the pace of the principals in the closing stages. (16/1)
Classic Crest (IRE) took a crashing fall. (5/1)

643 SHOTTON NOVICES' HURDLE (4-Y.O+) (Class E)
2-20 (2-20) **2m 1f (8 hdls)** £2,477.50 (£690.00: £332.50) GOING minus 1.05 sec per fur (HD)

				SP	RR	SF
455[3]	**Field of Vision (IRE) (92)** (MrsASwinbank) **6-11-5** JSupple (lw: mde all: strly pressed fr 3 out: rdn & hit last: r.o wl flat)	—	1	7/2[3]	76	—
506[4]	**Robsera (IRE) (90)** (JJQuinn) **5-10-12** LWyer (trckd ldrs: effrt 3 out: ev ch between last 2: nt qckn flat)	3	2	100/30[2]	66	—
506[2]	**Fatehalkhair (IRE)** (BEllison) **4-10-7**(3) GCahill (chsd ldrs: effrt appr 2 out: ev ch & edgd lft between last 2: no ex flat)	nk	3	6/5[1]	66	—
586[5]	**Trumped (IRE)** (PMonteith) **4-10-5** BHarding (hld up & racd keenly: stdy hdwy to chse ldrs appr 3 out: rdn & wknd fr 2 out)	8	4	7/1	53	—
	Blanc Seing (FR) (JESwiers) **9-10-12** MrSSwiers (bkwd: hld up & bhd: grad lost tch fr 4 out: eased fr 3 out)	15	5	20/1	44	—
586[R]	**Kashana (IRE)** (WStorey) **4-10-5** MMoloney (in rr: hdwy 5th: rdn & btn appr 3 out)	3	6	9/1	36	—
	Quartz Hill (USA) (DALamb) **7-10-12** JBurke (trckd ldrs: chal appr 3 out: sn rdn: 4th & hld whn fell 2 out)		F	66/1	—	—
	Rhythmic Dancer (DANolan) **8-10-12** BStorey (hld up & plld v.hrd: lost tch fr 4 out: t.o whn p.u bef 2 out: b.b.v)		P	14/1	—	—
				(SP 126.2%)	**8 Rn**	

3m 53.1 (-1.90) CSF £16.51 TOTE £1.90: £1.30 £1.20 £1.10 (£6.60) OWNER Mrs K. Morrell (RICHMOND) BRED Sean Collins
WEIGHT FOR AGE 4yo-2lb
455 Field of Vision (IRE) turned in a good display and stayed on strongly when hard pressed form the top of the hill. (7/2: 5/2-4/1)
506 Robsera (IRE) turned the tables on Fatehalkhair on their previous meeting and looks capable of winning a race of this nature. (100/30)
506 Fatehalkhair (IRE) showed a tendency to edge left under pressure and it transpired that he had lost a shoe during the race. (6/5)
586 Trumped (IRE), who failed to settle, dropped away tamely from the second last. (7/1)
Blanc Seing (FR), who missed the whole of last season, looked very burly for his reappearance and had a quiet run round. He will have benefited from this run. (20/1)
Quartz Hill (USA) ran well until coming to the end of his tether at the top of the hill, and was clearly held when coming to grief two out. (66/1)

644 JOHNNY RIDLEY MEMORIAL H'CAP CHASE (0-120) (5-Y.O+) (Class D)
2-50 (2-50) **3m 3f (21 fncs)** £3,769.00 (£1,132.00: £546.00: £253.00) GOING minus 1.05 sec per fur (HD)

				SP	RR	SF
581*	**The Gallopin'major (IRE) (79)** (MrsMReveley) **6-10-2b** NSmith (hit 3rd: chsd ldrs: mstke 12th: hit 5 out: sn rdn: hdwy appr 2 out: styd on to ld last: r.o flat)	—	1	2/1[1]	88	21
583[2]	**Staigue Fort (IRE) (87)** (DenysSmith) **8-10-10** PNiven (lw: j.rt: led to 10th: led 13th to 4 out: sn drvn along: kpt on fr 2 out)	2½	2	5/1	95	28
583[D]	**The Blue Boy (IRE) (99)** (PBowen) **8-11-8b** NWilliamson (chsd ldr: hit 3rd: led 10th to 13th: led 4 out: clr 3 out: rdn next: hdd & no ex last)	3½	3	7/2[2]	104	37
581[2]	**George Ashford (IRE) (90)** (KAMorgan) **6-10-13v** ASSmith (in tch tl rdn & lost pl 16th: t.o)	dist	4	4/1[3]	—	—
	Go Silly (105) (BEllison) **10-11-11v**(3) GCahill (bkwd: mstkes: bhd: reminders 14th: sn t.o: p.u bef 17th)		P	6/1	—	—
				(SP 106.5%)	**5 Rn**	

6m 29.3 (-16.70) CSF £10.46 TOTE £2.30: £1.40 £2.10 (£7.00) OWNER Mr R. W. S. Jevon (SALTBURN) BRED Mrs A. Doyle
581* The Gallopin'major (IRE) looked in trouble after making a mistake five from home, but hit top gear on the run from the penultimate fence and won well in the end. (2/1)
583 Staigue Fort (IRE) again showed a tendency to jump out to his right, but ran up to scratch, and is nothing if not game. (5/1)
583 The Blue Boy (IRE) looked home and dry when going clear three out, but found next to nothing under pressure between the last two. (7/2)
Go Silly looked in need of the race and ran accordingly. (6/1)

645 RAMSIDE CATERING SERVICES H'CAP CHASE (0-115) (4-Y.O+) (Class E)
3-25 (3-25) **2m 5f (16 fncs)** £3,254.00 (£977.00: £471.00: £218.00) GOING minus 1.05 sec per fur (HD)

				SP	RR	SF
	McGregor The Third (112) (GRichards) **10-11-13** BHarding (bit bkwd: j.w: trckd ldrs: led on bit 10th: wnt clr fr 3 out: pushed out)	—	1	2/1[1]	126	37
	Rebel King (90) (MABarnes) **6-10-5** PWaggott (bit bkwd: chsd ldrs: w wnr fr 10th tl outpcd fr 3 out)	15	2	8/1	93	4
352[3]	**Nocatchim (90)** (KAMorgan) **7-10-5v** ASSmith (led to 4th: chsd ldrs: rdn 4 out: one pce fr 3 out)	6	3	7/1[3]	88	—
	Jendee (IRE) (86) (BEllison) **8-9-12**(3)ow1 GCahill (in rr: hdwy & in tch ½-wy: rdn along & lost tch 11th: poor 4th whn blnd bdly 2 out)	15	4	25/1	73	—
	Laurie-O (90) (DALamb) **12-10-5b**ow5 JBurke (bit bkwd: chsd ldrs: led 4th to 10th: wknd fr next)	15	5	33/1	65	—
584[6]	**Smokey Track (85)** (MrsJConway) **11-9-9**(5) STaylor (a bhd: t.o fr ½-wy)	4	6	50/1	57	—
398[3]	**Wise Advice (IRE) (95)** (MDHammond) **6-10-10** NWilliamson (in tch whn fell 2nd)		F	11/2[2]	—	—
583*	**Magic Bloom (100)** (JMJefferson) **10-11-1** RichardGuest (bdly hmpd 2nd: p.u bef next)		P	2/1[1]	—	—
				(SP 114.4%)	**8 Rn**	

5m (-11.00) CSF £16.93 CT £85.16 TOTE £2.60: £1.10 £2.00 £1.90 (£12.70) Trio £28.40; £32.46 to Nottingham 16/9/96 OWNER Mrs D. A. Whitaker (PENRITH) BRED Mrs D. A. Whitaker
LONG HANDICAP Smokey Track 7-13 Jendee (IRE) 9-11 Laurie-O 9-1
McGregor The Third, who looked beforehand as though the race was needed, bounced back to form here with a brilliant display of jumping. The cross-country chase at Cheltenham, a race which he won easily last year, looks to be next on the agenda. (2/1)
Rebel King, who looked in need of the race, ran really well until coming to the end of his tether at the third last. (8/1)
352 Nocatchim came under pressure at the fourth last and could then find only one pace. (7/1)
Laurie-O did a lot of the donkey work, but was in need of this first race of the season, and was out on his feet a mile from home. (33/1)
583* Magic Bloom, almost brought down by a faller at the second fence, was wisely pulled up before the next. (2/1)

646 PARTRIDGE HURDLE (3-Y.O) (Class E)
4-05 (4-06) **2m 1f (8 hdls)** £2,425.00 (£675.00: £325.00) GOING minus 1.05 sec per fur (HD)

				SP	RR	SF
462[2]	**Go-Go-Power-Ranger** (BEllison) **3-10-7**(3) GCahill (lw: chsd ldr: slt ld fr 5th: rdn 2 out: styd on wl flat)	—	1	4/1[2]	71	—

Cottage Prince (IRE) (JJQuinn) **3-10-10** LWyer (lw: hld up: hdwy 5th: prom next: ev ch between last 2: nt qckn flat)....5 **2** 15/2 66 —

462* **Prelude To Fame (USA)** (MissMKMilligan) **3-11-3** ASSmith (led to 5th: prom tl no ex 2 out)....2½ **3** 2/1[1] 71 —

291[4] **Northern Falcon** (MWEasterby) **3-10-5b** NWilliamson (a chsng ldrs: rdn & kpt on same pce fr 2 out)....1¼ **4** 12/1 58 —

Hobbs Choice (GMMoore) **3-10-5** NBentley (chsd ldrs: outpcd ½-wy: styd on fr 2 out)....3 **5** 12/1 55 —

Stoleamarch (MrsMReveley) **3-10-7**(3) GLee (racd keenly in tch: swvd rt 4th: outpcd appr 2 out)....nk **6** 25/1 60 —

No More Hassle (IRE) (MrsMReveley) **3-10-10** PNiven (hld up & plld hrd: stdy hdwy 2 out: nvr plcd to chal)....6 **7** 11/2[3] 54 —

Sleepy Boy (WStorey) **3-10-5**(5) RMcGrath (mstke 1st: hld up: nvr nr to chal)....5 **8** 50/1 49 —

The Black Dubh (IRE) (JJQuinn) **3-10-10** BStorey (hld up & plld hrd: in rr: n.d)....2½ **9** 20/1 47 —

Oxgang (IRE) (JGFitzGerald) **3-10-10** MDwyer (hit 1st: mid div tl wknd fr 3 out)....6 **10** 8/1 41 —

Hot Dogging (MrsPSly) **3-10-5** RMarley (bhd fr ½-wy)....7 **11** 14/1 30 —

540[S] **Miss Impulse** (MissJBower) **3-10-0**(5) STaylor (chsd ldrs tl rdn & btn 3 out)....10 **12** 20/1 20 —

Phantom Dancer (IRE) (MESowersby) **3-10-7**(3) DParker (bit bkwd: chsd ldrs to 5th: btn next)....6 **13** 25/1 20 —

Amylou (RAllan) **3-9-12**(7) SMelrose (bhd ½-wy: sn t.o: p.u bef 2 out).... **P** 40/1 — —

Fizzy Boy (IRE) (PMonteith) **3-10-10** BHarding (lost tch & bhd ½-wy: t.o whn p.u bef 2 out).... **P** 40/1 — —

(SP 137.7%) **15 Rn**

3m 52.4 (-2.60) CSF £36.57 TOTE £6.00: £2.00 £2.80 £1.70 (£24.80) Trio £25.50 OWNER Mr Kevin Brown (LANCHESTER) BRED Leslie R. Smith

OFFICIAL EXPLANATION **No More Hassle (IRE): the rider stated that his instructions had been to teach the gelding to settle as he had been inclined to run too freely in his Flat races. In the race the horse had pulled hard and not jumped the first two flights well, but going down the back straight improved his jumping and position to be on the heels of the leaders on the top bend, from which point he had no more to offer.**

462 Go-Go-Power-Ranger, given a positive ride, duelled for the lead from halfway and, taking a definite advantage at the last, stayed on well to the finish. (4/1)

Cottage Prince (IRE) made a promising hurdling debut and, after being in with every chance at the final flight, was unable to quicken on the flat. He should soon win a similar event. (15/2)

462* Prelude To Fame (USA), who had plenty of use made of him, could find nothing extra from the second last. (2/1)

291 Northern Falcon, always well to the fore, stayed on at the same pace in the closing stages. (12/1)

Hobbs Choice, a sprint winner on the Flat, lost her prominent pitch at halfway, but was noted staying on again in the closing stages. (12/1: op 8/1)

Stoleamarch, who took a keen hold, proved something of a handful, swerving to the outside at the fourth. Asked for an effort at the top of the hill, he was outpaced from two out. (25/1)

No More Hassle (IRE), who took a very keen hold early on, made steady headway in the closing stages under a very tender ride. The Stewards enquired into his running and riding, and accepted the explanations of connections that he needed to be settled in as he is a horse who does not respond to vigorous riding. (11/2: 4/1-6/1)

Sleepy Boy, who blundered at the first, was schooled round in midfield and showed a semblance of promise. (50/1)

647 ST LEGER CONDITIONAL H'CAP HURDLE (0-105) (4-Y.O+) (Class F)

4-35 (4-36) **2m 1f (8 hdls)** £2,407.50 (£670.00: £322.50) GOING minus 1.05 sec per fur (HD)

SP RR SF

582[3] **Strong John (IRE) (87)** (MESowersby) **8-10-13** DParker (hld up in tch gng wl: chal on bit 3 out: led 2 out: kpt on wl flat)....— **1** 4/1[2] 65 22

586* **Suas Leat (IRE) (87)** (JMJefferson) **6-10-10**(3) MNewton (hld up: stdy hdwy fr 4 out: ev ch appr last: r.o flat)....nk **2** 6/4[1] 65 22

Bolaney Girl (IRE) (80) (FPMurtagh) **7-10-6** ARoche (hld up & bhd: hdwy after 4 out: chsd ldrs fr 2 out: no ex appr last)....5 **3** 16/1 53 10

453[5] **Flintlock (IRE) (79)** (HAlexander) **6-10-5** RMcGrath (swtg: led to 3rd: chsd ldr: led 3 out to next: styd on one pce)....¾ **4** 12/1 51 8

463[2] **Clover Girl (74)** (BEllison) **5-10-0v** GCahill (in rr: hdwy 4 out: in tch & rdn appr 3 out: btn appr next)....26 **5** 6/1[3] 22 —

Wee Wizard (IRE) (90) (MABarnes) **7-11-2** STaylor (chsd ldrs tl rdn & btn after 4 out)....9 **6** 14/1 29 —

586[4] **Funny Rose (79)** (PMonteith) **6-10-0**(5)ow5 CMcCormack (a bhd: lost tch bef 3 out: t.o)....3 **7** 9/1 16 —

423[F] **Exclusion (85)** (JHetherton) **7-10-11** FLeahy (chsd ldr: led 3rd to 3 out: sn btn: t.o)....3½ **8** 6/1[3] 18 —

Fly to the End (USA) (77) (JJQuinn) **6-9-10**(7) SRudd (a in rr: t.o after 4 out)....¾ **9** 16/1 10 —

(SP 124.7%) **9 Rn**

3m 46.0 (-9.00) CSF £10.92 CT £84.21 TOTE £6.10: £2.20 £1.40 £2.40 (£3.90) Trio £8.40 OWNER Mr S. Birkinshaw BRED Joseph Smiddy

LONG HANDICAP Funny Rose 9-13 Clover Girl 9-11

STEWARDS' ENQUIRY McGrath susp. 25-26/9/96 (excessive use of whip).

582 Strong John (IRE) appreciated this drop in distance and, produced to lead on the bridle two out, had enough in reserve to keep the runner-up at bay on the run-in. (4/1)

586* Suas Leat (IRE), patiently ridden, was produced to have every chance approaching the final flight, but was just unable to peg back the winner. (6/4)

Bolaney Girl (IRE) made a promising return to action, but lacked the foot to trouble the first two in the closing stages. This run will not have been wasted on her. (16/1)

12 Flintlock (IRE) helped set a furious gallop, but was unable to pull out any extra in the final half-mile. His rider was later suspended for using his whip with undue force in the closing stages. (12/1)

463 Clover Girl made headway a mile from home but, soon driven along, was beaten before the penultimate flight. (6/1)

T/Plpt: £4.40 (1,534.3 Tckts). T/Qdpt: £3.80 (65.75 Tckts). O'R

0630-WORCESTER (L-H) (Good to firm)

Saturday September 14th

WEATHER: fine

648 POLLY HOWES CONDITIONAL (S) H'CAP HURDLE (0-95) (4-Y.O+) (Class G)

2-25 (2-32) **2m (8 hdls)** £2,129.00 (£594.00: £287.00) GOING minus 0.20 sec per fur (G)

SP RR SF

490[2] **Minnesota Fats (IRE) (70)** (MissMERowland) **4-10-1** GHogan (hld up: stdy hdwy 5th: led on bit appr last: drvn out)....— **1** 7/2[1] 57 —

				SP	RR	SF
	Corrin Hill (95) (RJHodges) **9-11-6**(8) JHarris (lw: hld up & bhd: hdwy appr 3 out: ev ch last: one pce)	3	**2**	7/1[3]	79	24
416[2]	**Galloping Guns (IRE) (69)** (BJLlewellyn) **4-10-0** ChrisWebb (lost pl 4th: gd hdwy after 5th: hit 3 out: ev ch 2 out: one pce)	3½	**3**	25/1	50	—
474[3]	**Ray River (76)** (KGWingrove) **4-10-7b** GTormey (hld up: rdn & hdwy 5th: ev ch last: wknd)	s.h	**4**	8/1	56	—
356[4]	**Wordsmith (IRE) (86)** (JLHarris) **6-11-5** JCulloty (a.p: ev ch 2 out: wknd last)	3½	**5**	7/2[1]	63	8
490*	**Simand (80)** (GMMoore) **4-10-11** DJKavanagh (lw: a.p: led 5th tl appr last: sn wknd)	2	**6**	5/1[2]	55	—
	Catwalker (IRE) (67) (HJMWebb) **5-10-0** SophieMitchell (sme hdwy whn mstke 2 out: n.d)	1¼	**7**	20/1	41	—
27[13]	**Lovelark (67)** (RLee) **7-10-0** BFenton (prom: led 3rd to 4th: wknd 5th)	4	**8**	40/1	37	—
488[P]	**Slippery Max (70)** (RTJuckes) **12-10-3v** RMassey (plld hrd: led 2nd to 3rd: wknd appr 2 out)	10	**9**	16/1	30	—
488[3]	**Northern Nation (75)** (WClay) **8-10-8v** PHenley (lw: prom: rdn appr 5th: wknd 3 out)	3	**10**	16/1	32	—
	Shedansar (IRE) (69) (RCSpicer) **4-10-0** EHusband (led: hit 1st: hdd 2nd: led 4th to 5th: wknd appr 3 out)	½	**11**	40/1	25	—
461[7]	***Athenian Alliance (69)*** (JMBradley) **7-9-11**(5)ow2 JPrior (Withdrawn not under Starter's orders: bolted bef s)		**W**	66/1	—	—
				(SP 111.5%)	**11 Rn**	

3m 47.6 (7.60) CSF £24.43 CT £439.50 TOTE £3.90: £1.40 £1.90 £3.70 (£24.20) Trio £53.60 OWNER Miss M. E. Rowland (LOWER BLIDWORTH) BRED Phylis Finegan
LONG HANDICAP Catwalker (IRE) 9-7 Lovelark 9-1 Galloping Guns (IRE) 9-10 Shedansar (IRE) 9-12 Athenian Alliance 8-9
WEIGHT FOR AGE 4yo-2lb
No bid

490 Minnesota Fats (IRE) has been improving and did this in pretty good style, despite being 4lb higher than when last in a handicap. (7/2)
Corrin Hill made a sound reappearance, especially when considering all five of his victories have come on right-handed courses. (7/1: op 4/1)
Galloping Guns (IRE), a moderate performer on the Flat for Dermot Weld, ran his best race since coming over to this country. (25/1)
474 Ray River could not take advantage of an 8lb lower mark. (8/1)
356 Wordsmith (IRE) may have found the ground a bit lively. (7/2)

649 QUEENSWAY MAIDEN HURDLE (4-Y.O+) (Class F)

2-55 (2-56) **3m (12 hdls)** £2,087.00 (£582.00: £281.00) GOING minus 0.20 sec per fur (G)

				SP	RR	SF
	Mister Blake (66) (RLee) **6-11-5** RJohnson (hld up & bhd: hdwy 9th: rdn 2 out: styd on to ld flat)	—	**1**	12/1	62	11
498[2]	**Lear Dancer (USA)** (MissMERowland) **5-11-5** GaryLyons (hld up: hdwy 5th: led appr 3 out: sn clr: rdn appr last: wknd & hdd flat)	4	**2**	6/4[1]	59	8
156[11]	**Saltis (IRE)** (ALForbes) **4-11-2** TEley (hdwy 7th: one pce fr 3 out)	2	**3**	40/1	58	4
	Flynn's Girl (IRE) (MrsJPitman) **7-11-0** WMarston (hld up & bhd: stdy hdwy 7th: wknd 2 out)	4	**4**	8/1	50	—
	Dragonmist (IRE) (51) (DBurchell) **6-10-7**(7) MissEJJones (a.p: led 9th tl appr 3 out: sn wknd)	1½	**5**	33/1	49	—
489[3]	**Crown Ivory (NZ)** (PCRitchens) **8-11-5** SFox (hdwy 6th: wknd appr 2 out)	1½	**6**	14/1	53	2
	Karen's Typhoon (IRE) (81) (PJHobbs) **5-11-5** JOsborne (w ldr: led after 6th to 9th: wknd 3 out: t.o)	dist	**7**	100/30[2]	—	—
549[5]	**Heaton (NZ)** (HGRowsell) **9-11-5** BPowell (led after 6th: wknd 8th: t.o)	2½	**8**	50/1	—	—
549[6]	**Banks of The Bride** (MrsBarbaraWaring) **6-11-5** EByrne (hld up & bhd: t.o 8th: blnd 3 out)	20	**9**	50/1	—	—
503[B]	**Tipping Along (IRE) (79)** (DRGandolfo) **7-11-5v**[1] RDunwoody (dropped rr 6th: t.o whn p.u bef 9th)		**P**	7/2[3]	—	—
	Padditate (IRE) (RJHodges) **7-11-2**(3) TDascombe (bkwd: prom to 7th: t.o whn p.u bef 3 out)		**P**	33/1	—	—
				(SP 123.0%)	**11 Rn**	

5m 49.3 (13.30) CSF £30.33 TOTE £10.20: £1.20 £1.10 £13.10 (£10.00) Trio £63.80; £55.74 to Nottingham 16/9/96 OWNER Mr W. D. Edwards (PRESTEIGNE) BRED Southcourt Stud
WEIGHT FOR AGE 4yo-3lb

Mister Blake, who has changed stables, was stepping up in trip and outstayed the flagging favourite. (12/1)
498 Lear Dancer (USA) was a bit too keen for his own good and failed to get home after looking all over the winner. (6/4: Evens-13/8)
Saltis (IRE) hurdled much better than on his debut. (40/1)
Flynn's Girl (IRE) was reverting to timber for her seasonal debut. (8/1)

650 DOWELANCO H'CAP CHASE (0-130) (5-Y.O+) (Class C)

3-30 (3-30) **2m 7f (18 fncs)** £4,467.50 (£1,340.00: £645.00: £297.50) GOING minus 0.20 sec per fur (G)

				SP	RR	SF
	Tartan Tradewinds (125) (GRichards) **9-12-0** RDunwoody (lw: hld up: wnt 2nd 3 out: led on bit after 2 out: qcknd clr flat: eased nr fin)	—	**1**	7/2[3]	130	20
588*	**Maggots Green (99)** (JMBradley) **9-10-2** RJohnson (led: hit 9th: rdn 3 out: hdd after 2 out: no ch w wnr)	6	**2**	9/4[2]	100	—
588[2]	**Royal Vacation (111)** (GMMoore) **7-11-0** JCallaghan (lw: chsd ldr: mstke & rdn 13th: mstke 3 out: sn wknd: blnd last)	7	**3**	11/8[1]	107	—
	Staunch Rival (USA) (120) (GThorner) **9-11-9** BPowell (lw: hld up: mstke 10th: sn lost pl: rallied appr 4 out: wknd 3 out: blnd 2 out)	24	**4**	11/2	99	—
				(SP 110.5%)	**4 Rn**	

5m 51.5 (13.50) CSF £10.71 TOTE £3.50: (£3.90) OWNER Mackinnon Mills (PENRITH) BRED E. J. O'Grady

Tartan Tradewinds looked a picture and Dunwoody was sitting pretty all the way up the home straight. (7/2)
588* Maggots Green, upped 6lb, confirmed the Stratford form with Royal Vacation on 2lb worse terms. (9/4)
588 Royal Vacation, upped 4lb, could not turn the tables on the runner-up on 2lb better terms than at Stratford last week. (11/8)
Staunch Rival (USA) (11/2: 4/1-6/1)

651 SOLIHULL H'CAP HURDLE (0-130) (4-Y.O+) (Class C)

4-00 (4-00) **2m 4f (10 hdls)** £4,116.50 (£1,144.00: £549.50) GOING minus 0.20 sec per fur (G)

				SP	RR	SF
362*	**Fieldridge (110)** (MPMuggeridge) **7-10-13** BPowell (lw: hld up: hdwy 5th: rdn to ld flat: r.o)	—	**1**	11/4[1]	92	48
341*	**Wadada (104)** (DBurchell) **5-10-7** DJBurchell (lw: hld up: hdwy 6th: led 7th: rdn 2 out: hdd flat)	2	**2**	11/4[1]	84	40
493*	**Prerogative (110)** (HSHowe) **6-10-13v** CMaude (led to 7th: wknd qckly: t.o: lft poor 3rd 3 out)	dist	**3**	15/2	—	—
485[4]	**Fantastic Fleet (IRE) (100)** (APJones) **4-10-1** RJohnson (lw: 4th & wkng whn b.d 3 out)		**B**	10/1	—	—
318a[11]	**Suivez (125)** (MrsNMacauley) **6-12-0** RDunwoody (prom: 3rd whn fell 3 out)		**F**	11/2[2]	—	—
502[F]	**Jenzsoph (IRE) (105)** (PJHobbs) **5-10-3**(5) DJKavanagh (hld up: fell 5th)		**F**	7/1[3]	—	—
478[4]	**Layham Low (IRE) (100)** (OSherwood) **5-10-3** JOsborne (lw: hld up: bdly hmpd 5th: p.u bef 6th)		**P**	7/1[3]	—	—
				(SP 114.6%)	**7 Rn**	

4m 37.3 (-0.70) CSF £10.43 CT £44.60 TOTE £4.00: £2.40 £1.50 (£4.80) Trio £33.50 OWNER The Charleston Partnership (LAMBOURN) BRED Mrs John Trotter
WEIGHT FOR AGE 4yo-2lb

362* Fieldridge, raised 7lb, beat a depleted field in an incident-packed race. (11/4)
341* Wadada, off a 3lb higher mark, should have appreciated this longer trip. (11/4)
493* Prerogative, upped 10lb, was not allowed anything like the same sort of leeway as at Uttoxeter. (15/2: 5/1-8/1)
103 Suivez (11/2: op 7/2)

652 CORPORATION STREET NOVICES' CHASE (5-Y.O+) (Class D)

4-35 (4-35) **2m (12 fncs)** £3,562.50 (£1,065.00: £510.00: £232.50) GOING minus 0.20 sec per fur (G)

				SP	RR	SF
579a[2]	**Celibate (IRE)** (CJMann) **5-10-10** RDunwoody (lw: a.p: bmpd 4 out: j.lft 3 out: led last: easily)	—	**1**	11/8[1]	110+	38
554[2]	**Heresthedeal (IRE) (97)** (GMMcCourt) **7-10-12v** BClifford (lw: led: rdn 2 out: hdd last: one pce)	2½	**2**	7/2[3]	108	38
	Mr Conductor (IRE) (RHAlner) **5-10-5**(5) PHenley (bit bkwd: hld up: hdwy after 8th: hmpd 4 out: sn wknd)	10	**3**	11/2	98	26
419[3]	**Betabetcorbett** (BPJBaugh) **5-10-10b** TEley (a.p: ev ch whn j.lft 4 out: sn wknd)	20	**4**	20/1	78	6
161[13]	**Wotanite** (OO'Neill) **6-10-12** VSlattery (bit bkwd: plld hrd in rr: hmpd 5th: sn t.o)	24	**5**	66/1	54	—
254[U]	**Saxon Blade** (RMStronge) **8-10-12** LHarvey (plld hrd: chsd ldr tl lost pl & bdly hmpd 5th: sn t.o)	1¼	**6**	50/1	52	—
	Holy Wanderer (USA) (TRGeorge) **7-10-9**(3) GHogan (lw: hld up & plld hrd: hdwy 4th: fell 5th)		**F**	3/1[2]	—	—

(SP 112.9%) **7 Rn**

3m 52.3 (1.30) CSF £6.41 TOTE £2.20: £1.50 £2.20 (£3.80) OWNER Stamford Bridge Partnership (UPPER LAMBOURN) BRED Miss Noirin Dunne
WEIGHT FOR AGE 5yo-2lb
579a Celibate (IRE) was reported to have schooled well and barely put a foot wrong. He can score again. (11/8)
554 Heresthedeal (IRE) had the advantage of previous experience over fences. (7/2)
Mr Conductor (IRE) should come on for this chasing debut. (11/2)
Holy Wanderer (USA) did not settle as well as his rider would have liked and was on the floor at the first ditch. (3/1)

653 EDGBASTON STANDARD OPEN N.H. FLAT RACE (4, 5 & 6-Y.O) (Class H)

5-05 (5-08) **2m** £1,385.00 (£385.00: £185.00)

				SP	RR	SF
	Never In Debt (AGHobbs) **4-10-9**(7) MrGShenkin (hld up: gd hdwy over 3f out: led ins fnl f: edgd lft: drvn out)	—	**1**	33/1	—	—
	Madhaze (IRE) (JSMoore) **5-11-4** WMcFarland (bkwd: gd hdwy 4f out: ev ch 1f out: unable qckn)	¾	**2**	33/1	—	—
	Solar Moon (RHBuckler) **5-10-13** BPowell (bkwd: gd hdwy 6f out: r.o one pce fnl f)	4	**3**	12/1	—	—
	Chief Gale (IRE) (JGMO'Shea) **4-10-11**(5) MichaelBrennan (chsd ldr: led over 6f out: clr over 3f out: rdn over 1f out: wknd & hdd ins fnl f)	2	**4**	7/2[1]	—	—
	Captain Felix (NZ) (AJKDunn) **6-11-4** CMaude (bit bkwd: prom tl wknd wl over 1f out)	5	**5**	16/1	—	—
	Celtic Firefly (RRowe) **4-10-11** RJohnson (bkwd: bhd tl r.o fnl 3f: nrst fin)	2	**6**	6/1	—	—
	Terrano Star (IRE) (DBurchell) **5-11-4** DJBurchell (plld hrd: led over 9f: wknd 4f out)	19	**7**	11/2[3]	—	—
	Lakeside Lad (DBurchell) **4-10-9**(7) JPrior (prom 12f)	¾	**8**	20/1	—	—
	Rosehall (MrsTDPilkington) **5-10-10**(3) GHogan (bit bkwd: bhd tl gd hdwy over 4f out: wknd 3f out)	4	**9**	25/1	—	—
	All Sewn Up (RJBaker) **4-11-2** LHarvey (bkwd: bhd fnl 8f)	6	**10**	16/1	—	—
	Klosters (RJHodges) **4-10-8**(3) TDascombe (bit bkwd: bhd fnl 3f)	2½	**11**	8/1	—	—
	Eye of The Storm (IRE) (JJQuinn) **5-11-4** RDunwoody (bkwd: prom over 12f: t.o)	12	**12**	9/2[2]	—	—
	Leopard Lady (WGMTurner) **4-10-4**(7) NWillmington (prom 8f: t.o)	10	**13**	20/1	—	—
	Pollifumas (JLHarris) **6-10-13** DGallagher (bkwd: sn t.o)	10	**14**	14/1	—	—
	Nanjizal (KSBridgwater) **4-11-2** TEley (bkwd: a bhd: t.o)	nk	**15**	33/1	—	—
	White Axle (IRE) (PEccles) **6-11-4** BFenton (a bhd: t.o)	16	**16**	25/1	—	—
418[11]	**Tailormade Future** (BPreece) **4-10-9**(7) DFinnegan (rdn 8f out: a bhd: t.o)	dist	**17**	25/1	—	—
	Miss Nonnie (MissLShally) **4-10-11** DLeahy (hdwy 10f out: wkng whn b.d 5f out)		**B**	16/1	—	—
	Teddy Edward (MrsAMNaughton) **6-10-11**(7) RWilkinson (prom: wkng whn s.u 5f out)		**S**	25/1	—	—

(SP 146.9%) **19 Rn**

3m 39.8 CSF £801.19 TOTE £36.00: £9.00 £13.30 £8.60 (£297.80) Trio Not won; £200.63 to Nottingham 16/9/96 OWNER Mr M. R. Clough (KINGSBRIDGE) BRED E. R. Clough
WEIGHT FOR AGE 4yo-2lb
STEWARDS' ENQUIRY Burchell susp. 25-26 & 28-29/9/96 (improper use of whip). Prior susp. 25-26 & 28-29/9/96 (improper & incorrect use of whip).
Never In Debt is a half-brother to winning hurdler Keep Out of Debt. (33/1)
Madhaze (IRE) ran a cracker, considering his burly appearance. (33/1)
Solar Moon is another who will strip fitter for the outing. (12/1: op 8/1)
Chief Gale (IRE) seemed to have this in the bag until his stride shortened inside the final quarter-mile. (7/2: 3/1-9/2)
Celtic Firefly (6/1: op 4/1)
Terrano Star (IRE) (11/2: op 7/2)

T/Plpt: £6,793.60 (1.15 Tckts). T/Qdpt: £290.20 (0.3 Tckts); £274.55 to Nottingham 16/9/96 KH

0468-FONTWELL (Fig. 8) (Good to firm, Firm patches)

Monday September 16th

No Standard Times Hdls crse due to crse alterations
WEATHER: hot

654 RANK CHALLENGE CUP HURDLE (3-Y.O) (Class E)

2-15 (2-15) **2m 2f 110y (9 hdls)** £2,406.00 (£666.00: £318.00) GOING: 0.00 sec per fur (G)

				SP	RR	SF
	The Legions Pride (JWHills) **3-10-10** JOsborne (led to 2nd: led 3rd tl flat: rdn to ld nr fin)	—	**1**	100/30[2]	65	—
	How Could-I (IRE) (MrsNMacauley) **3-10-5** AMaguire (hdwy 5th: lft 2nd 2 out: led flat: hrd rdn & hdd nr fin)	nk	**2**	5/1[3]	60	—
471[3]	**Yellow Dragon (IRE)** (BAPearce) **3-10-7**(3) KGaule (a.p: mstke 3rd: ev ch 3 out: rdn appr 2 out: 3rd whn blnd bdly 2 out: nt rcvr)	6	**3**	6/1	60	—
	Lord Ellangowan (IRE) (RIngram) **3-10-10** DGallagher (lw: hdwy 2 out: nvr nrr)	2½	**4**	20/1	57	—
589[4]	**Skram** (RDickin) **3-11-3** JCulloty (a.p: rdn 6th: sn wknd)	7	**5**	13/2	58	—
	Further Future (IRE) (JohnBerry) **3-10-10** ILawrence (a bhd)	8	**6**	12/1	44	—

	Horse	Details	Dist	Pos	SP	RR	SF
471^{4}	**Kings Nightclub**	(JWhite) **3-10-2b$^{1(3)}$** GuyLewis (hld up: mstke 6th: sn wknd)	15	7	25/1	26	—
471^{2}	**Amber Ring**	(MissKMGeorge) **3-10-5** JRKavanagh (lw: a.p: led 2nd to 3rd: 2nd whn fell 2 out)		F	12/1	—	—
402^{*}	**Verulam (IRE)**	(JRJenkins) **3-11-3** GBradley (bhd tl fell 5th)		F	$3/1^{1}$	—	—
	Scene Stealer	(ADSmith) **3-10-5** FJousset (a bhd: t.o whn p.u bef 6th)		P	50/1	—	—

(SP 118.3%) **10 Rn**

4m 28.3 CSF £19.55 TOTE £4.30: £1.30 £1.20 £2.20 (£12.40) Trio £42.90 OWNER Royal British Legion Racing Club (LAMBOURN) BRED Mrs R. D. Peacock

The Legions Pride, a maiden on the Flat, made the vast majority of the running until collared on the run-in. However, under a fine ride from Osborne, the colt showed tremendous battling qualities to get back up near the line. (100/30)

How Could-I (IRE), who won a selling handicap on the Flat at Nottingham in June, looked as if she was going to gain the day as she moved into the lead on the run-in. Nearly half a length up, she did little wrong, but found the tenacious winner getting back up near the line. (5/1)

471 Yellow Dragon (IRE), very well backed when finishing fourth in a seller on the Equitrack six days ago, poked a nostril in front three from home and was still only about a length down on the leader when an almighty mistake two from home cost him any chance he may still have had. (6/1)

Lord Ellangowan (IRE) was of little consequence on the Flat and, although he stayed on over the last two hurdles, one should not read much into that as this was a poor contest. (20/1)

471 Amber Ring was only about a length down on the leader when crashing to the deck at the penultimate flight. A maiden on the Flat, lack of pace is already proving a problem over hurdles. (12/1: op 8/1)

655 ARUNDEL (S) H'CAP HURDLE (0-95) (4-Y.O+) (Class G)

2-45 (2-46) **2m 2f 110y (9 hdls)** £1,943.00 (£538.00: £257.00) GOING: 0.00 sec per fur (G)

	Horse	Details	Dist	Pos	SP	RR	SF
	Nahrawali (IRE) (89)	(AMoore) **5-12-0** APMcCoy (swtg: a.p: led 5th: clr 6th: unchal)	—	1	$9/4^{1}$	90	—
	Credit Controller (IRE) (62)	(JFfitch-Heyes) **7-10-1** BFenton (hdwy 5th: chsd wnr appr 3 out: no imp)	13	2	11/1	52	—
556^{P}	**Miramare (63)**	(JWDufosee) **6-9-11**$^{(5)ow1}$ PHenley (lw: no hdwy fr 3 out)	7	3	$11/2^{3}$	47	—
488^{4}	**Antiguan Flyer (72)**	(GProdromou) **7-10-11** AMaguire (led to 5th: sn wknd)	9	4	$5/1^{2}$	48	—
596^{P}	**On the Ledge (USA) (61)**	(HJManners) **6-9-7**$^{(7)}$ ADowling (prom to 6th)	20	5	50/1	20	—
394^{4}	**Milzig (USA) (73)**	(JJoseph) **7-10-12** CLlewellyn (a bhd: t.o fr 2nd)	dist	6	7/1	—	—
406^{2}	**Lac de Gras (IRE) (63)**	(RCurtis) **5-10-2** DMorris (a bhd: t.o whn p.u bef 6th: b.b.v)		P	6/1	—	—
472^{P}	**Sandro (61)**	(MissLBower) **7-10-0b** LHarvey (prom to 3rd: t.o whn p.u bef last)		P	33/1	—	—
	What's the Joke (65)	(VGGreenway) **7-10-4** CMaude (lw: bhd fr 5th: t.o whn p.u bef last)		P	16/1	—	—
553^{4}	**Roger's Pal (61)**	(AMoore) **9-9-7**$^{(7)}$ MBatchelor (lw: uns rdr 1st)		U	9/1	—	—

(SP 118.7%) **10 Rn**

4m 24.6 CSF £25.54 CT £114.57 TOTE £3.20: £1.90 £3.20 £2.20 (£31.90) Trio £73.70 OWNER Mr C. F. Sparrowhawk (BRIGHTON) BRED His Highness the Aga Khans Studs S. C.

LONG HANDICAP Sandro 9-6 On the Ledge (USA) 9-1 Roger's Pal 9-7

No bid

Nahrawali (IRE), a Flat winner in France and Belgium, proved to be in a different class to these appalling rivals and came home at his leisure on the final circuit. (9/4: op 4/1)

Credit Controller (IRE), who showed nothing in two runs on the Flat this year, struggled into second place going to the third last but had absolutely no hope with the winner and is greatly flattered to finish so close. He has very limited ability. (11/1)

Miramare is a very poor individual and was making little impression over the last three hurdles. (11/2: 4/1-6/1)

101* Milzig (USA) (7/1: op 4/1)

406 Lac de Gras (IRE) (6/1: op 4/1)

Roger's Pal (9/1: 6/1-10/1)

656 ELTON VEHICLE CONTRACTS H'CAP CHASE (0-105) (5-Y.O+) (Class F)

3-15 (3-15) **2m 3f (16 fncs)** £3,070.40 (£741.60) GOING: 0.07 sec per fur (G)

	Horse	Details	Dist	Pos	SP	RR	SF
414^{3}	**Manamour (82)**	(RLee) **9-10-8** CLlewellyn (hdwy 6th: lft 2nd 12th: led & edgd lft appr last: j.rt last: r.o wl)	—	1	$7/2^{3}$	93	6
414^{2}	**Drumstick (96)**	(KCBailey) **10-11-8** JRailton (lw: led to 3rd: led 8th to 10th: lft in ld 12th: rdn appr 2 out: hdd appr last: blnd last: unable qckn)	10	2	$5/2^{2}$	99	12
	Top Miss (79)	(ASNeaves) **7-9-12**$^{(7)ow5}$ WGreatrex (bit bkwd: a bhd: t.o fr 9th: ref 3 out)		R	66/1	—	—
470^{*}	**Henley Wood (98)**	(PJHobbs) **11-11-7**$^{(3)}$ GTormey (w ldr: led 3rd: mstke 6th: hdd 8th: led 10th tl blnd & uns rdr 12th)		U	$8/11^{1}$	—	—

(SP 110.2%) **4 Rn**

4m 54.0 (15.00) CSF £11.29 TOTE £4.30: (£3.80) OWNER Mr R. L. C. Hartley (PRESTEIGNE) BRED Mrs H. E. Bromhead

LONG HANDICAP Top Miss 9-5

414 Manamour, beaten thirty lengths by Drumstick last time out, was meeting him on the same terms but managed to reverse the tables quite conclusively on this occasion. (7/2)

414 Drumstick, left in front again five out, was racing with his ears flat back in the straight and, collared approaching the last, was soon put in his place. Winner of seventeen races during his career, he appears to have lost his enthusiasm and has now won just once in nearly two years. (5/2)

470* Henley Wood, winner of this race last year, was still in front when a bad error got rid of his rider five out. Successful three times round here, he should soon make amends in a small handicap. (8/11)

657 STREBEL BOILERS AND RADIATORS SERIES H'CAP HURDLE (Qualifier) (0-110) (4-Y.O+) (Class E)

3-45 (3-45) **2m 6f 110y (11 hdls)** £2,385.00 (£660.00: £315.00) GOING: 0.00 sec per fur (G)

	Horse	Details	Dist	Pos	SP	RR	SF
	Kalasadi (USA) (98)	(VSoane) **5-11-6** JCulloty (chsd ldr fr 3rd: led 8th: clr appr 2 out: r.o wl)	—	1	$6/1^{3}$	82+	—
473^{*}	**Circus Colours (98)**	(JRJenkins) **6-11-6** AMaguire (lw: hdwy to chse wnr appr 2 out: no imp)	20	2	$5/2^{2}$	68	—
	Cabochon (102)	(JJoseph) **9-11-10** CLlewellyn (bit bkwd: bhd fr 8th: t.o)	dist	3	16/1	—	—
187^{2}	**Hostile Witness (IRE) (100)**	(DBurchell) **6-11-8** DJBurchell (3rd whn p.u bef 8th: lame)		P	$7/4^{1}$	—	—
582^{6}	**Royal Circus (93)**	(PWHiatt) **7-11-1** DBridgwater (lw: led to 8th: wknd appr 2 out: t.o whn p.u bef last)		P	7/1	—	—
257^{3}	**Miss Pimpernel (78)**	(ABarrow) **6-10-0v^{1}** APMcCoy (chsd ldr 1st to 3rd: wknd 4th: t.o fr 6th: p.u bef 8th)		P	7/1	—	—

(SP 110.1%) **6 Rn**

5m 27.0 CSF £19.82 TOTE £8.90: £3.30 £1.70 (£10.90) OWNER Mr G. A. Libson (ASTON ROWANT) BRED H H Aga Khans Stud S C

LONG HANDICAP Miss Pimpernel 9-10

Kalasadi (USA) made a winning debut for his new stable and, showing in front four out, forged clear from the next to win with plenty in hand. (6/1)
473* Circus Colours struggled into second place approaching the second last, but had no hope of reeling in the winner. He has never won over a trip this far before. (5/2)

658 FONTWELL H'CAP CHASE (0-120) (5-Y.O+) (Class D)

4-15 (4-15) **3m 2f 110y (22 fncs)** £3,460.00 (£1,030.00: £490.00: £220.00) GOING: 0.07 sec per fur (G)

	Horse	Dist	Pos	SP	RR	SF
	Frozen Drop (96) (PCRitchens) **9-11-11** SFox (lw: a.p: led 8th to 9th: led 11th: clr appr 3 out: eased flat)	—	1	9/4 2	99+	21
535*	**Distant Memory (99)** (PJHobbs) **7-12-0b** APMcCoy (mstke 5th: chsd ldr to 7th: mstke 12th: chsd wnr fr 14th: mstkes 4 out & 3 out: unable qckn)	5	2	11/8 1	99	21
605 5	**L'Uomo Piu (80)** (ABarrow) **12-10-9v1** BPowell (lw: led to 8th: led 9th to 11th: 3rd & no ch whn mstke 4 out)	7	3	10/1	76	—
595 5	**Hizal (77)** (HJManners) **7-10-6ow5** MrACharles-Jones (a bhd: t.o)	dist	4	14/1	—	—
494 3	**Duke of Lancaster (IRE) (77)** (MrsJPitman) **7-10-6v** WMarston (a bhd: t.o fr 6th: p.u bef 16th)		P	4/1 3	—	—
597 F	**Ghedi (POL) (75)** (MPMuggeridge) **5-10-0b** SCurran (4th whn blnd & uns rdr 13th)		U	50/1	—	—
				(SP 110.6%)		**6 Rn**

7m 1.5 (21.50) CSF £5.50 TOTE £3.70: £1.40 £1.70 (£3.80) OWNER Mr Jock Cullen (TIDWORTH) BRED R. R. Clarke
LONG HANDICAP Ghedi (POL) 8-13
WEIGHT FOR AGE 5yo-4lb
Frozen Drop looked a picture in the paddock for this first run of the season and, leading at the eleventh, had a useful advantage in the last half-mile. With the race safely in the bag, he was eased down in the closing stages and was value for far more than the winning distance. (9/4: 3/1-2/1)
535* Distant Memory had a real problem with the water jump and met it wrong on the three occasions he jumped it. Despite all McCoy's efforts, the gelding never looked like pegging back the winner in the last half-mile. (11/8: 4/5-13/8)
L'Uomo Piu was making a quick reappearance but, once collared at the eleventh, soon threw in the towel. He has not won for nearly two years and is not one to back with any confidence. (10/1)
486 Hizal (14/1: op 8/1)

659 COWFOLD SWIMMING POOL NOVICES' HURDLE (4-Y.O+) (Class E)

4-45 (4-45) **2m 6f 110y (11 hdls)** £2,364.00 (£654.00: £312.00) GOING: 0.00 sec per fur (G)

	Horse	Dist	Pos	SP	RR	SF
	Supreme Star (USA) (PRHedger) **5-10-12** MRichards (lw: nt j.w: a.p: chsd ldr appr 2 out: mstke 2 out: blnd last: swtchd rt flat: hrd rdn & led nr fin)	—	1	4/6 1	68	—
480 5	**Lawbuster (IRE) (64)** (MrsRGHenderson) **4-10-5b(5)** DSalter (chsd ldr: led 8th: hrd rdn flat: hdd nr fin)	1¼	2	50/1	67	—
593 4	**Scamallach (IRE) (87)** (JRJenkins) **6-11-0b** GBradley (hld up: rdn 3 out: one pce)	6	3	3/1 2	65	—
456 2	**Air Command (BAR) (68)** (CTNash) **6-10-5(7)** MrPPhillips (led to 8th: wknd appr 2 out: t.o)	dist	4	4/1 3	—	—
	Adilov (KOCunningham-Brown) **4-10-10** DGallagher (lw: mstkes: a bhd: t.o fr 7th)	dist	5	16/1	—	—
				(SP 112.8%)		**5 Rn**

5m 35.7 CSF £16.86 TOTE £1.70: £1.10 £5.90 (£21.50) OWNER Mr J. J. Whelan (CHICHESTER) BRED Peter M. Brant
WEIGHT FOR AGE 4yo-2lb
Supreme Star (USA) nearly threw this away with his jumping but a tremendous ride from Richards saw him snatch victory from the jaws of defeat close home. He will have to improve his jumping if he is to win again. (4/6)
Lawbuster (IRE) nearly caused a major upset and was only collared near the line. This performance could be misleading as the first half of the race was run at an absolute dawdle and the winner made errors at the last two hurdles, giving him far more of a chance. (50/1)
593 Scamallach (IRE) found it difficult under her penalty and was only plodding on at her own pace from the third last. (3/1)
456 Air Command (BAR) (4/1: 3/1-9/2)

T/Plpt: £397.20 (31.44 Tckts). T/Qdpt: £25.40 (32.88 Tckts). AK

660a-672a (Irish Racing) - See Computer Raceform

0474-HUNTINGDON (R-H) (Good to firm, Firm patches, Hdles becoming Firm) Friday September 20th

WEATHER: sunny

673 UPWOOD (S) H'CAP HURDLE (0-95) (4-Y.O+) (Class G)

2-20 (2-24) **3m 2f (12 hdls)** £1,905.00 (£530.00: £255.00) GOING minus 0.81 sec per fur (F)

	Horse	Dist	Pos	SP	RR	SF
642 7	**Arrange A Game (67)** (MissJBower) **9-9-9(5)** STaylor (a.p: led appr 3 out: pushed out)	—	1	33/1	48	—
404 3	**Mr Geneaology (USA) (88)** (TPMcGovern) **6-11-7b** APMcCoy (chsd ldrs: mstke 3rd: outpcd appr 9th: styd on fr 3 out: nt rch wnr)	1¼	2	9/2 2	68	—
587 3	**Record Lover (IRE) (75)** (MCChapman) **6-10-8** WWorthington (lw: chsd ldrs: one pce fr 3 out)	3½	3	7/2 1	53	—
642 3	**Sakbah (USA) (67)** (JAPickering) **7-10-0** NWilliamson (hld up: hdwy 8th: chsd wnr fr 3 out: rdn & hit last: sn btn)	1¼	4	7/1	44	—
289 5	**Yacht Club (75)** (JLEyre) **14-10-8** OPears (lw: prom: led after 7th tl appr 3 out: sn wknd)	7	5	5/1 3	48	—
587 2	**King of Babylon (IRE) (73)** (FJordan) **4-9-12(5)** LAspell (lw: v.rel to r: sn in tch: rdn 3 out: sn lost pl)	19	6	9/2 2	34	—
598 3	**They All Forgot Me (67)** (AWCarroll) **9-10-0** MissCDyson (led tl after 7th: sn wknd: btn whn mstke 3 out)	3½	7	25/1	26	—
553 2	**Tug Your Forelock (72)** (GFJohnsonHoughton) **5-10-5** AThornton (prom tl wknd appr 3 out)	3	8	8/1	29	—
587 9	**Sir Pageant (79)** (KSBridgwater) **7-10-12** DBridgwater (bit bkwd: hmpd 3rd: sn bhd: t.o whn p.u bef 2 out)		P	13/2	—	—
				(SP 119.0%)		**9 Rn**

6m 13.2 (7.20) CSF £165.27 CT £612.69 TOTE £89.80: £16.50 £2.30 £1.90 (£109.10) Trio £145.30 OWNER Mr A. M. McArdle (SOUTHWELL) BRED John P. Cahill
LONG HANDICAP Arrange A Game 8-11 They All Forgot Me 9-6 Sakbah (USA) 9-7
WEIGHT FOR AGE 4yo-3lb
No bid
489 Arrange A Game is now fully fit and put in a decent round of jumping, but must have benefited from the extended trip, for he was well beaten off a 12lb lower mark over half a mile less last time. (33/1)

404 Mr Geneaology (USA), stepping up in trip, lost his place as battle commenced, only to stay on rather too late. He could win a similar contest if the mood takes him. (9/2: 5/2-5/1)
587 Record Lover (IRE) stays this trip but looked short of any change of pace. (7/2)
642 Sakbah (USA) had beaten the winner on worse terms last time, but came off worse in their protracted battle from the third last. (7/1)
289 Yacht Club is better suited by less than three miles these days. (5/1: 4/1-6/1)
587 King of Babylon (IRE) confirmed the impression he left at Stratford that he is not in love with the game. (9/2)
553 Tug Your Forelock (8/1: 5/1-9/1)

674 OWL END NOVICES' CHASE (5-Y.O+) (Class E)

2-55 (2-57) **2m 110y (12 fncs)** £3,125.50 (£868.00: £416.50) GOING minus 0.81 sec per fur (F)

	Horse	Dist	Pos	SP	RR	SF
	Strong Promise (IRE) (GAHubbard) **5-10-7**(3) KGaule (hld up: led on bit after 2 out: hit last: easily)	—	1	2/5 1	99++	—
632P	**Shalik (IRE)** (JRJenkins) **6-10-5**(7) NTEgan (lw: led after 1st: hit 3rd & 5th: hdd 7th: lft in ld after 3 out: hdd after next: btn whn mstke last: fin 3rd, 17l: plcd 2nd)		2	25/1	77	—
	Ryton Run (MrsSMOdell) **11-11-2** BFenton (j.lft: sn bhd: fin 4th, 28l: plcd 3rd)		3	25/1	54	—
	Hang'em Out To Dry (IRE) (CPEBrooks) **5-10-10** GBradley (j.w: led tl after 1st: led 7th tl p.u after 3 out)		P	9/1 3	—	—
652F	**Holy Wanderer (USA)** (TRGeorge) **7-10-9**(3) GHogan (hld up: qcknd & ev ch whn hit last: r.o: fin 2nd, 6l: disq: plcd last)		D	100/30 2	93++	—

(SP 112.2%) **5 Rn**

4m 5.3 (3.30) CSF £9.02 TOTE £1.40: £1.10 £1.60 (£5.90) OWNER Mr G. A. Hubbard (WOODBRIDGE) BRED William McCarthy
WEIGHT FOR AGE 5yo-2lb
STEWARDS' ENQUIRY Hogan susp. 29/9 & 1-4/10/96 (failure to weigh in).
Strong Promise (IRE) has always looked a chaser in the making and won on his debut over fences with the minimum of effort. Jumping soundly, he was given a very confident ride and quickened well, despite brushing through the last. It will take a good one to beat him while the ground rides fast. (2/5: 8/13-1/3)
406* Shalik (IRE) looks headstrong and seemed beaten when presented with a clear lead at the third last. However, the writing was soon on the wall on the long run to the next. (25/1)
Ryton Run won two Hunter Chases in the space of three days in May 1995, but has run as if something is amiss since. (25/1)
Hang'em Out To Dry (IRE), a winner between the Flags, was making his chasing debut under Rules and jumped impeccably. He was still bowling along in front when pulling up suddenly a few strides after the third last. (9/1: 6/1-10/1)
652 Holy Wanderer (USA) was almost a match for the winner on some of his hurdle form and waited on that rival. Produced to challenge at the last, neither he nor Strong Promise jumped the obstacle well, but Holy Wanderer lost most impetus. He was disqualified after his rider failed to weigh in, but should soon be winning. (100/30)

675 DIDDINGTON NOVICES' HURDLE (4-Y.O+) (Class E)

3-25 (3-25) **2m 110y (8 hdls)** £2,722.50 (£760.00: £367.50) GOING minus 0.81 sec per fur (F)

	Horse	Dist	Pos	SP	RR	SF
	Mr Percy (IRE) (JTGifford) **5-10-12** PHide (lw: a.p: led 2 out: clr last: easily)	—	1	7/2 3	83+	52
555*	**Courbaril (103)** (MCPipe) **4-11-3** DBridgwater (lw: chsd ldrs: led 3 out: hdd next: eased whn btn flat)	8	2	9/4 1	82	49
	Nashaat (USA) (MCChapman) **8-10-12** WWorthington (lw: hdwy 4th: no imp fr 2 out)	14	3	10/1	62	31
593²	**Dacelo (FR)** (OSherwood) **5-10-12** JOsborne (chsd ldrs: one pce fr 3 out)	4	4	100/30 2	58	27
416*	**Chancey Fella (91)** (HEHaynes) **5-11-12** APMcCoy (led appr 5th tl hdd 3 out: sn wknd: fin lame)	3½	5	12/1	68	37
	Alcove (GFJohnsonHoughton) **5-10-12** AThornton (bit bkwd: in tch to 3 out)	9	6	10/1	46	15
	Shuttlecock (MrsNMacauley) **5-10-12** AMaguire (prom to 3 out)	1¼	7	20/1	45	14
	Spumante (88) (MPMuggeridge) **4-10-10** BPowell (nvr nrr)	3	8	20/1	42	9
603²	**Caddy's First (90)** (SMellor) **4-10-10** NMann (n.d)	½	9	12/1	41	8
	Mandys Royal Lad (JTGifford) **8-10-7**(5) LAspell (bit bkwd: nvr plcd to chal)	nk	10	20/1	41	10
	Ferens Hall (51) (MJRoberts) **9-10-12** PMcLoughlin (plld hrd: led tl appr 5th: sn wknd)	1¼	11	33/1	40	9
490P	**Chadleigh Walk (IRE)** (SWCampion) **4-10-7**(3) PMidgley (a bhd)	9	12	33/1	31	—
586³	**Genesis Four** (MrsLStubbs) **6-10-9**(3) GCahill (a bhd)	s.h	13	20/1	31	—
634F	**Ragtime Song** (JRJenkins) **7-10-5**(7) DYellowlees (lw: blnd 3rd: nvr trbld ldrs: t.o fr 3 out)	dist	14	33/1	—	—
	Clifton (RCurtis) **7-10-12** DMorris (prom to 3rd: t.o whn p.u bef 2 out: dead)		P	33/1	—	—
	Titanium Honda (IRE) (DCO'Brien) **5-10-12** DGallagher (mstke & dropped rr 4th: t.o whn p.u bef last)		P	33/1	—	—

(SP 143.4%) **16 Rn**

3m 36.4 (-11.60) CSF £13.05 TOTE £5.20: £2.50 £2.40 £5.30 (£17.00) Trio £142.70; £160.84 to Ayr 21/9/96 OWNER Felix Rosenstiel's Widow & Son (FINDON) BRED M. Fardy
WEIGHT FOR AGE 4yo-2lb
OFFICIAL EXPLANATION **Chancey Fella: the gelding stumbled having jumped the last, and completely lost his action on the run-in, having either broken down or rapped a joint.**
Mr Percy (IRE) looked well forward and sealed this with a good turn of foot. He suffered with sore shins last year, but will certainly win more races if the problem does not recur. (7/2)
555* Courbaril, having his first run for his new stable, lost little in defeat, considering he was conceding weight to a useful rival and had the rest well beaten. He was heavily eased on the run-in and those behind are flattered to have got this close to him. (9/4)
Nashaat (USA) does not get beyond seven furlongs on the level but, ridden to get the trip, showed enough to suggest a small race might be found while conditions remain undemanding. (10/1: op 5/1)
593 Dacelo (FR) again looked short of speed in the last half-mile. (100/30)
416* Chancey Fella took a while to get to the front as one rival all but bolted. Headed on the home turn, his action looked to have gone an he returned feelingly. (12/1)
Alcove had only run once in the last seventeen months and it showed. (10/1: 8/1-12/1)
603 Caddy's First (12/1: op 8/1)
Mandys Royal Lad, making a belated debut, was hunted round at the back to halfway but did show some promise, running on from that point. (20/1)

676 SINDALL CONSTRUCTION H'CAP CHASE (0-125) (5-Y.O+) (Class D)

3-55 (3-58) **2m 110y (12 fncs)** £4,323.00 (£1,047.00) GOING minus 0.81 sec per fur (F)

	Horse	Dist	Pos	SP	RR	SF
603⁵	**Ramstar (99)** (PJHobbs) **8-10-11** APMcCoy (chsd ldr: hit 6th & 8th: lft clr 3 out)	—	1	6/1 3	106?	8
601*	**Super Sharp (NZ) (88)** (HOliver) **8-10-0** JacquiOliver (lw: mstke 3rd: rdn & lost tch 8th: lft 2nd 3 out: t.o)	dist	2	Evens 1	—	—

				SP	RR	SF
592[4]	**Stately Home (IRE) (118)** (PBowen) **5-12-0** RJohnson (mstkes: led: blnd 6th: blnd & uns rdr 3 out)		U	6/4[2]	—	—

(SP 104.3%) **3 Rn**

4m 0.7 (-1.30) CSF £10.85 TOTE £5.40: (£2.50) OWNER Mr A. Loze (MINEHEAD) BRED Miss M. Benson
LONG HANDICAP Super Sharp (NZ) 9-11
WEIGHT FOR AGE 5yo-2lb

497 Ramstar, in a race where all three would have been happy to lead, could not get to the front until Stately Home departed. By that stage, the third of the trio was well beaten and he could come home at his leisure. (6/1: op 7/2)
601* Super Sharp (NZ), more used to leading than racing in last place, had had enough soon after halfway. (Evens)
592 Stately Home (IRE) was getting rather low at one or two fences whilst being harried for the lead and got the water all wrong. A second equally serious error three out was enough to lose his pilot. (6/4)

677 GOODLIFF H'CAP HURDLE (0-115) (4-Y.O+) (Class E)

4-25 (4-25) **2m 110y (8 hdls)** £2,442.50 (£680.00: £327.50) GOING minus 0.81 sec per fur (F)

				SP	RR	SF
	Prizefighter (97) (JLEyre) **5-11-1** OPears (lw: trckd ldrs: led on bit after 2 out: qcknd flat: easily)	—	1	13/8[1]	81+	37
75[6]	**Yubralee (USA) (109)** (MCPipe) **4-11-11** DBridgwater (led: hit 2nd: hdd after 2 out: no ch w wnr)	7	2	4/1[3]	86	40
551*	**Zine Lane (104)** (MajorWRHern) **4-11-6** RFarrant (prom: rdn 3 out: one pce)	1¾	3	100/30[2]	80	34
	King William (93) (NEBerry) **11-10-11** DGallagher (lw: bhd: kpt on fr 3 out: nvr trbld ldrs)	6	4	14/1	63	19
354[2]	**Desert Challenger (IRE) (82)** (JRJenkins) **6-10-0v** SFox (prom: rdn appr 3 out: btn whn blnd 2 out)	12	5	16/1	40	—
404[2]	**No Light (103)** (MrsIMcKie) **9-11-7** LHarvey (a bhd)	2½	6	4/1[3]	59	15

(SP 113.7%) **6 Rn**

3m 40.2 (-7.80) CSF £8.27 CT £16.84 TOTE £2.40: £2.10 £2.30 (£5.90) OWNER Diamond Racing Ltd (HAMBLETON) BRED J. K. Bloodstock Ltd
LONG HANDICAP Desert Challenger (IRE) 9-6
WEIGHT FOR AGE 4yo-2lb

Prizefighter looks as though he is going to be quite a handful in fast-ground two-mile hurdles for, in a race run to suit his speed, he fairly bolted in. (13/8)
Yubralee (USA) was allowed to dictate a steady early pace which he gradually wound up. Once the chips were down in the straight, he was on the wrong end of a one-sided argument. (4/1: 3/1-9/2)
551* Zine Lane ran well enough, but might have been suited by a stronger-run race to offset his lack of finishing pace. (100/30: 2/1-7/2)
King William, who won this race in 1992 and 1993, had a pipe-opener on the Flat but never offered his supporters much hope. (14/1: 10/1-16/1)
354 Desert Challenger (IRE) had soon had enough once the tempo quickened. (16/1)
404 No Light ran a rare bad race, never looking likely to get involved. (4/1: 5/2-9/2)

678 KNAPWELL AMATEUR H'CAP CHASE (0-110) (5-Y.O+) (Class E)

4-55 (4-56) **3m (19 fncs)** £3,840.00 (£1,065.00: £510.00) GOING minus 0.81 sec per fur (F)

				SP	RR	SF
597[2]	**Drumcullen (IRE) (84)** (KCBailey) **7-9-12**(7) MrRWakley (mde all: mstke & lft clr 2 out: comf)	—	1	5/2[2]	91+	—
604[P]	**Fairy Park (96)** (HOliver) **11-10-10**(7) MrNHOliver (hld up & bhd: hit 1st & 3rd: hdwy 2 out: hit last: too much to do)	3	2	9/1	101	—
530*	**The Yank (103)** (MDHammond) **10-11-7b**(3) MrCBonner (prom: rdn 11th: hit 14th & 16th: sn bhd)	dist	3	11/10[1]	—	—
	Finkle Street (IRE) (90) (GAHubbard) **8-10-6**(5) MrMRimell (lw: chsd wnr fr 9th: hit next: fell 2 out: dead)		F	7/2[3]	—	—

(SP 108.4%) **4 Rn**

6m 6.0 (9.00) CSF £16.15 TOTE £4.00: (£6.00) OWNER Mr Martyn Booth (UPPER LAMBOURN) BRED E. Burke

597 Drumcullen (IRE) does not seem to find a lot at the business end, but did not need to on this occasion. (5/2: 2/1-3/1)
Fairy Park, not travelling early on, was allowed to drop right out. On passing the favourite, he suddenly began to run, but had too big a task, despite staying on strongly. (9/1: 4/1-10/1)
530* The Yank rather lost interest after three good runs at the start of the 94-95 campaign and may be about to repeat the pattern. (11/10)

679 SEPTEMBER INTERMEDIATE OPEN N.H. FLAT RACE (4, 5 & 6-Y.O) (Class H)

5-25 (5-26) **2m 110y** £1,311.50 (£364.00: £174.50)

				SP	RR	SF
	Prototype (GFJohnsonHoughton) **5-11-4** AThornton (lw: hld up: hdwy 4f out: led over 1f out: comf)	—	1	10/1	—	—
	Ardenbar (JWPayne) **4-10-11** AMaguire (bit bkwd: prom: rdn & outpcd 3f out: rallied appr fnl f)	5	2	100/30[3]	—	—
191*	**Ultimate Smoothie** (MCPipe) **4-11-12** DBridgwater (trckd ldrs: led 5f out tl over 1f out: one pce)	4	3	7/4[1]	—	—
	Southerncrosspatch (JWhite) **5-11-4** SCurran (bit bkwd: bhd tl r.o fnl 4f)	8	4	33/1	—	—
	Lady Foley (IRE) (CJMann) **4-10-4**(7) DKiernan (bkwd: hdwy 7f out: wknd over 3f out)	5	5	5/2[2]	—	—
	Captain Navar (IRE) (JohnBerry) **6-11-4** VSmith (plld hrd: prom tl lost pl after 5f: kpt on fnl 4f)	7	6	12/1	—	—
	Paperwork Pete (IRE) (WStorey) **4-10-11**(5) RMcGrath (lw: chsd ldrs: ev ch 4f out: sn btn)	5	7	10/1	—	—
	Komaseph (KAMorgan) **4-11-2** ASSmith (lw: plld hrd: led after 5f to 9f out: sn wknd)	dist	8	10/1	—	—
	Havana Express (CADwyer) **4-11-2** ILawrence (bkwd: a bhd)	9	9	12/1	—	—
59[4]	**General Monty** (PatMitchell) **4-11-2** NWilliamson (lw: led 5f: led 9f out to 5f out: sn wknd)	1½	10	8/1	—	—
	Bertie (MrsJConway) **6-10-13**(5) STaylor (plld hrd: prom 8f: wknd qckly)	21	11	33/1	—	—
	Autumn Flame (IRE) (OBrennan) **5-10-6**(7) SPorritt (chsd ldrs 8f)	10	12	16/1	—	—

(SP 153.5%) **12 Rn**

3m 40.1 CSF £52.74 TOTE £26.20: £6.00 £1.80 £1.50 (£40.60) Trio £96.30 OWNER Mrs H. JohnsonHoughton (NEWMARKET) BRED Berkshire Equestrian Services Ltd
WEIGHT FOR AGE 4yo-2lb

Prototype, a fit, quite-attractive newcomer, was running away on the home turn and took this with something to spare. (10/1)
Ardenbar, a workmanlike daughter of Ardross, lost her good position on the home turn, only to stay on well in the last couple of furlongs. (100/30)
191* Ultimate Smoothie is on the small side and the double penalty found him out in the home straight. (7/4: 4/5-2/1)
Southerncrosspatch made late progress and ran much his best race to date. (33/1)
Lady Foley (IRE), a leggy filly, looked to need the race, but showed some promise. (5/2: op 6/1)
Captain Navar (IRE) took a keen hold early on, but was not a threat in the final mile. (12/1: 8/1-14/1)
Komaseph is arguably bred to be a sprinter and did not show anything like enough stamina. (10/1: 7/1-12/1)

T/Plpt: £185.50 (48.35 Tckts). T/Qdpt: £35.10 (12.95 Tckts). Dk

CARLISLE (R-H) (Firm)
Saturday September 21st
WEATHER: cloudy

680 ULLSWATER NOVICES' HURDLE (4-Y.O+) (Class E)
1-40 (1-42) **2m 4f 110y (11 hdls)** £1,660.00 (£460.00: £220.00) GOING minus 0.62 sec per fur (F)

	Horse			SP	RR	SF
585*	**Sujud (IRE) (87)** (MDHammond) **4-10-12** RGarritty (lw: hld up: hdwy 6th: led appr last: rdn clr flat)	—	1	Evens 1	77	34
586 7	**Thaleros (78)** (GMMoore) **6-10-12** JCallaghan (bit bkwd: hld up in tch: hdwy 6th: ev ch 2 out: one pce)	7	2	14/1	70	29
497*	**Million Dancer (96)** (MCPipe) **4-11-3b** DBridgwater (led: clr to 6th: hdd appr last: sn btn)	3½	3	9/4 2	74	31
	Pangeran (USA) (MrsASwinbank) **4-10-10** JSupple (chsd clr ldr fr 2nd tl rdn along bef 3 out: sn one pce)	1¼	4	16/1	66	23
510*	**War Whoop** (CWThornton) **4-11-3** MFoster (hld up: lost tch 4 out: t.o)	dist	5	7/2 3	—	—
337 5	**Scallymill** (KWHogg) **6-10-7** KWhelan (in tch: cl up 6th: wknd 4 out: t.o)	dist	6	50/1	—	—
	Polly Cinders (MrsJDGoodfellow) **5-10-7** BFenton (bkwd: chsd clr ldr to 2nd: lost pl bef 4th: sn bhd: t.o bef 6th)	dist	7	50/1	—	—
585 P	**Ousefleet Boy** (MissMKMilligan) **4-10-10** ADobbin (bkwd: bhd: reminders after 4th: j.slowly next: t.o whn p.u bef 6th)		P	50/1	—	—

(SP 121.4%) **8 Rn**

4m 45.4 (-5.60) CSF £15.61 TOTE £2.20: £1.10 £3.10 £1.50 (£13.30) OWNER Mr D. J. Lever (MIDDLEHAM) BRED Shadwell Estate Company Limited
WEIGHT FOR AGE 4yo-2lb
OFFICIAL EXPLANATION War Whoop: returned distressed.
585* Sujud (IRE), whose proven stamina came into play here, broke the course-record in the process. (Evens)
Thaleros could not live with the winner here and is still looking for that elusive first win over timber. (14/1: op 7/1)
497* Million Dancer, tackling the trip for the first time, found his stamina giving out around this testing circuit after setting the early pace. (9/4)
510* War Whoop (7/2: 5/2-4/1)

681 THIRLMERE NOVICES' CHASE (5-Y.O+) (Class E)
2-15 (2-15) **2m (12 fncs)** £2,099.00 (£632.00: £306.00: £143.00) GOING minus 0.62 sec per fur (F)

	Horse			SP	RR	SF
	To Be the Best (70) (DALamb) **6-10-12** JBurke (plld hrd: mde all: mstke 3rd: clr fr 3 out: eased flat)	—	1	6/1 3	79+	3
532 2	**Caxton (USA) (81)** (JWhite) **9-10-12** NWilliamson (hld up in rr: hdwy 5th: chsd wnr appr 4 out: drvn bef next: sn no imp: eased whn btn flat)	26	2	1/2 1	53	—
505 7	**Boethius (USA) (80)** (MABarnes) **7-10-12** PWaggott (bkwd: chsd wnr tl rdn appr 4 out: sn wknd)	16	3	12/1	37	—
584 7	**Richmond (IRE)** (MissZAGreen) **8-10-12** BStorey (b: chsd ldrs: outpcd & wl bhd after 5th: n.d)	nk	4	7/2 2	37	—

(SP 110.9%) **4 Rn**

3m 57.2 (3.20) CSF £9.57 TOTE £6.40: (£2.70) OWNER Exors of the late Mr R R Lamb (SEAHOUSES) BRED C. J. R. Trotter
To Be the Best, the youngest horse in the race, pulverised his elders to break his duck. (6/1: op 12/1)
532 Caxton (USA) disappointed, and his rider accepted the situation after the last. (1/2)
Boethius (USA) went out like a light four from home. This son of The Minstrel has never shown a glimmer of hope in twenty-one starts over obstacles. (12/1: op 7/1)

682 BROTHERSWATER H'CAP HURDLE (0-115) (4-Y.O+) (Class E)
2-50 (2-50) **2m 4f 110y (11 hdls)** £2,188.00 (£532.00) GOING minus 0.62 sec per fur (F)

	Horse			SP	RR	SF
410*	**Shahrani (109)** (MCPipe) **4-11-9** DBridgwater (mde all: rdn appr last: r.o)	—	1	4/6 1	94	11
635 3	**Gone by (IRE) (109)** (JRJenkins) **8-11-11v** GBradley (trckd wnr: chal 3 out: sn ev ch: drvn appr last: no ex)	4	2	5/4 2	91	10

(SP 104.4%) **2 Rn**

4m 55.0 (4.00) TOTE £1.40: OWNER Mr A S Helaissi and Mr S Helaissi (WELLINGTON) BRED R. V. Young
WEIGHT FOR AGE 4yo-2lb
410* Shahrani notched up his fifth victory on the bounce when running away from his solitary rival. His wins have been in weak contests and, in better-grade events, his jumping ability will be tested to the hilt as he is not the most fluent of leapers. (4/6)
635 Gone by (IRE) failed to pick up as well as the winner on the run to the last. (5/4)

683 'RED RUM' H'CAP CHASE (0-125) (5-Y.O+) (Class D)
3-25 (3-27) **3m (18 fncs)** £3,018.00 (£848.00: £414.00) GOING minus 0.62 sec per fur (F)

	Horse			SP	RR	SF
644 3	**The Blue Boy (IRE) (99)** (PBowen) **8-10-8b** NWilliamson (trckd ldr: drvn to chal 3 out: led jst after last: sn clr)	—	1	2/1 2	108	—
452 4	**Kushbaloo (115)** (CParker) **11-11-10** BStorey (lw: led: mstkes 10th & last: sn hdd & btn)	5	2	4/5 1	121	4
452 5	**Upwell (91)** (RJohnson) **12-10-0** KJohnson (chsd ldrs: lost tch ½-wy: t.o)	dist	3	33/1	—	—
550 P	**Banntown Bill (IRE) (95)** (MCPipe) **7-10-4v** DBridgwater (in tch: struggling 7th: bhd whn p.u bef 10th)		P	5/1 3	—	—
645 4	**Jendee (IRE) (92)** (BEllison) **8-9-12**(3)ow1 GCahill (b: bhd: t.o whn p.u bef 10th)		P	12/1	—	—

(SP 116.2%) **5 Rn**

5m 59.9 (5.20 under best) (7.90) CSF £4.15 TOTE £3.00: £1.10 £1.20 (£1.80) OWNER Mr T. M. Morris (HAVERFORDWEST) BRED B. R. and Mrs Firestone in Ireland
LONG HANDICAP Upwell 8-7 Jendee (IRE) 9-5
OFFICIAL EXPLANATION Banntown Bill (IRE): the rider reported that he had pulled up while still in contention because the horse was never striding out on the ground.
644 The Blue Boy (IRE), a dodgy character, was under pressure with three to jump and looked held going to the last. However, he made use of the runner-up's blemish at that obstacle and went on to break the course-record. (2/1)
452 Kushbaloo, stripping fitter here compared with his seasonal bow at Cartmel, looked set to land this race for the second consecutive year on the run to the last. However, he made a costly mistake there and lost all impetus. (4/5: op 5/4)
94 Upwell, for the second consecutive season, finished a remote third in this contest. He has not won since the spring of 1994. (33/1)
Banntown Bill (IRE) (5/1: 7/2-11/2)
Jendee (IRE) (12/1: op 8/1)

684 RYDAL WATER H'CAP HURDLE (0-100) (4-Y.O+) (Class F)

3-55 (3-57) **2m 1f (9 hdls)** £1,744.00 (£484.00: £232.00) GOING minus 0.62 sec per fur (F)

	Horse	Dist	Pos	SP	RR	SF
647[3]	**Bolaney Girl (IRE) (80)** (FPMurtagh) **7-10-8** ADobbin (hld up in rr: hdwy 4 out: led appr last: drew clr flat)	—	1	4/1[2]	60	4
	Stags Fell (72) (TAKCuthbert) **11-10-0** CarolCuthbert (bkwd: hld up in tch: hdwy 4 out: led appr 2 out: hdd appr last: no ex)	6	2	33/1	46	—
539[4]	**Souson (IRE) (86)** (JWade) **8-11-0b** KJones (prom: led after 4th: hdd 3 out: kpt on same pce)	s.h	3	10/1	60	4
12[5]	**Well Appointed (IRE) (96)** (BMactaggart) **7-11-10** BStorey (hld up in tch: hdwy 5th: led 3 out: hdd appr next: sn btn)	10	4	9/2[3]	61	5
	Sharp Sensation (100) (DWBarker) **6-12-0** PNiven (b: in tch: effrt 3 out: outpcd next)	3	5	11/2	62	6
539[3]	**Take Two (92)** (MissMKMilligan) **8-11-3**(3) GCahill (prom: ev ch 3 out: wknd next)	½	6	6/1	54	—
531[3]	**Silver Sleeve (IRE) (80)** (MDHammond) **4-10-6b** RGarritty (hld up: effrt 3 out: sn btn)	5	7	6/1	37	—
598[2]	**Buglet (93)** (MCPipe) **6-11-7** DBridgwater (led: hdd after 4th: wknd 4 out: t.o whn p.u bef next)		P	2/1[1]	—	—
				(SP 127.5%)	**8 Rn**	

4m 2.8 (1.80) CSF £90.15 CT £1,169.40 TOTE £5.00: £1.60 £6.60 £4.50 (£290.20) Trio £54.60; £70.00 to Musselburgh 23/9/96 OWNER Mr J. Proudfoot (CARLISLE) BRED David McNeilly

LONG HANDICAP Stags Fell 9-4

WEIGHT FOR AGE 4yo-2lb

OFFICIAL EXPLANATION **Buglet: lost her action on the firm ground.**

647 Bolaney Girl (IRE), who has a reputation for being a strong puller, settled off the pace before leading on the run to the last. She drew clear on the run-in to shave three seconds off the previous record for the course and distance. (4/1: op 6/1)

Stags Fell put in a fair effort, despite being 10lb out of the handicap and looking in need of the outing. He only gave best on the run to the last. (33/1)

Souson (IRE), a selling-class eight-year old, has never won over less than two and a half miles. (10/1: 6/1-12/1)

598 Buglet was a major flop, dropping out quickly four from home before being pulled up. According to her rider, she seemed to lose her action on the lightning-fast ground. (2/1)

685 BASSENTHWAITE LAKE NOVICES' CHASE (5-Y.O+) (Class E)

4-30 (4-30) **3m (18 fncs)** £2,060.00 (£620.00: £300.00: £140.00) GOING minus 0.62 sec per fur (F)

	Horse	Dist	Pos	SP	RR	SF
	German Legend (DALamb) **6-10-12** JBurke (bkwd: in tch: mstke 9th: disp ld 4 out: led flat: styd on gamely cl home)	—	1	9/1[3]	86	—
581[U]	**Cuchullains Gold (IRE) (86)** (JWhite) **8-11-5** NWilliamson (plld hrd: hld up in rr: hdwy 12th: led after next: jnd 4 out: hdd flat: no ex cl home)	2	2	10/11[1]	92	—
584[2]	**Buyers Dream (IRE) (71)** (BEllison) **6-10-9v**(3) GCahill (b: prom: led 11th: blnd 13th: sn hdd: one pce fr 3 out)	9	3	7/4[2]	79	—
507[P]	**More Joy (80)** (MrsLMarshall) **8-10-12b[1]** DBentley (led to 11th: wknd 14th: t.o)	dist	4	9/1[3]	—	—
421[P]	**Sand King (NZ) (72)** (MsLCPlater) **10-10-12v** ADobbin (b: bkwd: prom: mstke 1st & reminders: p.u bef 6th: lame)		P	10/1	—	—
				(SP 117.8%)	**5 Rn**	

6m 8.5 (16.50) CSF £18.46 TOTE £14.70: £3.70 £1.10 (£10.50) OWNER Mr D. G. Pryde (SEAHOUSES) BRED Miss P. Pacey

STEWARDS' ENQUIRY Burke susp. 1-3/10/96 (excessive use of whip).

German Legend, having fought a protracted duel with the runner-up over the last four obstacles, found a little more close home. A selling-class performer over timber, he still looked a bit burly in the paddock, but made a successful chasing debut here after suffering a virus last season. The downside of this victory was the suspension of his pilot for his overzealous use of the whip. (9/1)

581 Cuchullains Gold (IRE), running without blinkers this time, fought a sustained duel with the winner before giving best on the run-in. Once again he took a bit of a tug. (10/11)

584 Buyers Dream (IRE) made a mistake at the thirteenth and this did nothing for his cause. However, he was no match for the leading pair over the last three fences. (7/4)

686 DERWENT INTERMEDIATE OPEN N.H. FLAT RACE (4, 5 & 6-Y.O) (Class H)

5-05 (5-09) **2m 1f** £1,224.00 (£339.00: £162.00)

Horse	Dist	Pos	SP	RR	SF
Duraid (IRE) (DenysSmith) **4-11-9** RichardGuest (mid div: hdwy ½-wy: led over 3f out: pushed clr 2f out: easily)	—	1	1/2[1]	—	—
Sioux Warrior (CWThornton) **4-10-9**(7) NHorrocks (prom: effrt over 3f out: sn drvn: one pce)	6	2	6/1[2]	—	—
Henpecked (IRE) (MDHammond) **5-11-4** RGarritty (lw: hld up: hdwy ½-wy: chsd ldrs to 3f out: kpt on)	6	3	6/1[2]	—	—
Best Friend (GPKelly) **4-10-11** MrNWilson (led: hdd over 3f out: grad wknd)	1½	4	9/1	—	—
Four From Home (IRE) (JJO'Neill) **4-11-2** ARoche (b.hind: plld hrd: cl up: rdn over 3f out: sn outpcd)	16	5	8/1[3]	—	—
Grace And Favour (JWHope) **5-10-13** JBurke (in tch: effrt over 3f out: sn no imp)	3	6	20/1	—	—
The Knitter (JJBirkett) **4-11-2** MMoloney (in tch: lost pl 6f out: n.d after)	3½	7	20/1	—	—
Joe's Bit of Gold (TAKCuthbert) **4-10-11** PNiven (bkwd: hld up: hdwy 6f out: rdn 4f out: sn outpcd)	nk	8	14/1	—	—
Vale of Oak (JWHope) **5-10-13** BHarding (bkwd: mid div: effrt over 3f out: sn wknd)	5	9	25/1	—	—
In The Future (IRE) (BEllison) **5-10-10**(3) GCahill (b: bkwd: mid div: lost pl ½-wy: rdn & hdwy 5f out: wknd over 3f out)	1	10	16/1	—	—
Green An Castle (MissZAGreen) **6-10-13** MrTMorrison (b: bkwd: prom: wknd over 6f out: sn bhd)	20	11	25/1	—	—
Were's Me Money (FPMurtagh) **6-10-13** MissSueNichol (bkwd: a bhd: lost tch 4f out: t.o)	20	12	16/1	—	—
			(SP 152.0%)	**12 Rn**	

4m 3.3 CSF £6.92 TOTE £1.40: £1.40 £1.70 £1.70 (£5.60) Trio £5.10 OWNER Mr A. Suddes (BISHOP AUCKLAND) BRED Hussein Hurami

WEIGHT FOR AGE 4yo-2lb

Duraid (IRE) ran out an emphatic winner on this seasonal debut. This four-year old was bought privately out of Robert Armstrong's Newmarket stable for an undisclosed sum without ever gracing the racetrack, having previously cost 68,000 guineas as a yearling. He is very highly thought of by connections and is reputedly on course for a Flat campaign. (1/2: 4/5-Evens)

Sioux Warrior, a half-brother to a couple of winners, did not have the legs of the winner here. (6/1: 4/1-7/1)

Henpecked (IRE), a son of Henbit, ran a promising race without shaking up the leading pair. (6/1: op 5/2)

Best Friend (9/1: 5/1-10/1)

T/Plpt: £549.90 (7.47 Tckts). T/Qdpt: £21.80 (8.73 Tckts). DO

0333-MARKET RASEN (R-H) (Good to firm, Good patches)
Saturday September 21st

687 SCANIA 4-SERIES 'HORSEPOWER' NOVICES' H'CAP HURDLE (0-100) (4-Y.O+) (Class E)
2-10 (2-11) **2m 1f 110y (8 hdls)** £2,792.50 (£780.00: £377.50) GOING: 0.03 sec per fur (G)

				SP	RR	SF
300*	**Indrapura (IRE) (91)** (MCPipe) **4-11-10** CMaude (lw: hld up: hit 4th: hdwy appr 2 out: chal last: sn led: rdn out)	—	**1**	15/8[1]	73	23
338[3]	**Ragamuffin Romeo (70)** (HSawyer) **7-10-5** NMann (chsd ldr: led 2 out: hit last: sn hdd: r.o)	1¼	**2**	9/1	51	3
393[3]	**Count of Flanders (IRE) (75)** (KAMorgan) **6-10-10** ASSmith (lw: nt j.w: led to 2 out: ev ch last: one pce)	1¼	**3**	9/4[2]	55	7
467[2]	**Sea God (88)** (MCChapman) **5-11-9** WWorthington (hld up: hdwy appr 2 out: one pce appr last)	¾	**4**	4/1[3]	67	19
490[6]	**Irie Mon (IRE) (80)** (MPBielby) **4-10-13** RDunwoody (lw: hld up: hdwy appr 3 out: mstke 2 out: sn btn)	4	**5**	7/1	55	5
	Merryhill Gold (71) (JWCurtis) **5-10-6** LWyer (chsd ldrs to 3 out)	1¾	**6**	10/1	45	—
259[8]	**Kajostar (65)** (SWCampion) **6-9-7**(7) OBurrows (bit bkwd: prom to 3 out)	¾	**7**	50/1	38	—
497[6]	**Hatta River (USA) (66)** (PTDalton) **6-10-1b** AMaguire (lw: prom: mstkes 3rd & 5th: wknd qckly 3 out: t.o)	dist	**8**	20/1	—	—
				(SP 123.9%)		**8 Rn**

4m 14.9 (11.90) CSF £19.22 CT £39.04 TOTE £2.60: £1.50 £2.30 £1.30 (£16.50) OWNER Martin Pipe Racing Club (WELLINGTON) BRED John Burns
LONG HANDICAP Kajostar 8-12
WEIGHT FOR AGE 4yo-2lb
IN-FOCUS: **The last hurdle was resited much closer to the line than is normal, leaving a run in of about 150 yards.**
300* Indrapura (IRE) takes a good hold but was restrained until produced to win the race with the best jump at the last. (15/8: 6/4-5/2)
338 Ragamuffin Romeo looks capable of finding another race in this grade. A stayer on the Flat, he is well worth another try over further. (9/1)
393 Count of Flanders (IRE) once beat Karshi and Admiral's Well on the Flat but his jumping was slow and untidy, and he looks a shadow of that horse now. (9/4)
467 Sea God, restrained at the back in yet another change of tactics, is proving hard to win with, having just one All-Weather victory to his name in twenty-eight starts all told. (4/1)
353 Irie Mon (IRE) looked likely to take a hand when the mistake two out stopped him in his tracks. (7/1)

688 BBC RADIO LINCOLNSHIRE (S) HURDLE (3-Y.O) (Class G)
2-45 (2-45) **2m 1f 110y (8 hdls)** £2,136.00 (£596.00: £288.00) GOING: 0.00 sec per fur (G)

				SP	RR	SF
	In A Tizzy (PCHaslam) **3-10-5** APMcCoy (led after 1st: sn clr: pckd 2 out: pushed out)	—	**1**	13/2[3]	64	—
402[3]	**Home Cookin'** (MCPipe) **3-10-5** CMaude (prom: chsd wnr fr 4th: no imp appr 2 out)	7	**2**	5/2[1]	58	—
548[2]	**Tablets of Stone (IRE)** (JRBosley) **3-10-10** MBosley (hit 1st: hdwy 3 out: r.o wl flat)	¾	**3**	7/1	62	—
589[5]	**Uncle George** (MHTompkins) **3-10-10v** AMaguire (prom: rdn & no imp appr 2 out)	½	**4**	3/1[2]	62	—
	Hannahs Bay (MGMeagher) **3-10-2**(3) FLeahy (bhd: hdwy appr 3 out: nvr trbld ldrs)	1¼	**5**	25/1	55	—
462[6]	**Recall To Mind** (MESowersby) **3-10-7b**(3) DParker (led tl after 1st: 2nd whn blnd 4th: sn btn)	19	**6**	25/1	43	—
	Kai's Lady (IRE) (SWCampion) **3-9-12**(7) OBurrows (hdwy 5th: nvr rchd ldrs)	3½	**7**	40/1	35	—
	On The Home Run (JRJenkins) **3-9-12**(7) NTEgan (lw: nvr trbld ldrs)	6	**8**	25/1	29	—
	Early Warning (CREgerton) **3-10-5** JOsborne (lw: prom to 3rd)	1¾	**9**	13/2[3]	28	—
	Euro Express (TDEasterby) **3-10-10b** LWyer (lw: nvr plcd to chal)	1¾	**10**	14/1	31	—
	Sizzling Serenade (JAHarris) **3-10-5** PMcLoughlin (nt j.w: in tch to 4th)	8	**11**	25/1	19	—
	Seeking Destiny (IRE) (MCChapman) **3-10-10** WWorthington (in tch tl blnd 3rd)	10	**12**	20/1	15	—
	Fergal (USA) (MissJFCraze) **3-10-10** OPears (a bhd)	½	**13**	40/1	14	—
501[6]	**Remember Star** (ADSmith) **3-10-5** FJousset (prom to 5th)	2½	**14**	33/1	7	—
	Ghostly Apparition (JohnUpson) **3-10-10** RSupple (bit bkwd: mstkes 1st & 2nd: a bhd)	7	**15**	25/1	6	—
	Florrie'm (JLHarris) **3-10-5** DGallagher (a bhd)	19	**16**	40/1	—	—
	Eccentric Dancer (MPBielby) **3-10-5b** ASSmith (a bhd: t.o whn p.u bef 2 out)		**P**	14/1	—	—
				(SP 140.3%)		**17 Rn**

4m 16.6 (13.60) CSF £24.76 TOTE £6.50: £2.00 £1.70 £2.00 (£11.20) Trio £41.00 OWNER B & J Racing and Breeding Syndicate (MIDDLEHAM) BRED Mrs M. Watt
Bt in 6,000 gns
In A Tizzy established a clear lead early on and gave her rivals a jumping lesson. Very moderate on the level with a question mark against her temperament to boot, she promises to do a great deal better at this game, particularly on sharp tracks. (13/2)
402 Home Cookin' looked to do little wrong on this occasion but had run into one far too good. (5/2)
548 Tablets of Stone (IRE), knocked back into the midfield group by his mistake at the first, was again doing some sterling work in the closing stages. (7/1: op 3/1)
589 Uncle George ran moderately on the Flat four days earlier. (3/1: 7/4-7/2)
Hannahs Bay, very moderate on the level, did offer a little hope for the future when closing from the home turn. (25/1)

689 SCANIA 1996 TRUCK OF THE YEAR H'CAP CHASE (0-120) (5-Y.O+) (Class D)
3-15 (3-15) **2m 4f (15 fncs)** £4,497.00 (£1,356.00: £658.00: £309.00) GOING: 0.03 sec per fur (G)

				SP	RR	SF
550[4]	**Andrelot (113)** (PBowen) **9-11-12b** APMcCoy (lw: led 3rd: lft wl clr 2 out: blnd last: comf)	—	**1**	5/1[3]	121	54
500[2]	**Merlins Dream (IRE) (103)** (OSherwood) **7-11-2** JOsborne (bhd: hdwy 10th: r.o flat)	8	**2**	2/1[1]	105	38
650[2]	**Maggots Green (99)** (JMBradley) **9-10-12** RJohnson (lw: led to 2nd: rdn 11th: btn whn lft 2nd 2 out: mstke last)	1¼	**3**	5/2[2]	100	33
	Dark Oak (110) (JWCurtis) **10-11-9** LWyer (s.i.s: bhd: blnd 4 out: r.o fr next)	12	**4**	13/2	101	34
583[5]	**Clares Own (95)** (JWade) **12-10-8** AThornton (lw: led 2nd to 3rd: pushed along 7th: bhd fr 10th)	¾	**5**	25/1	85	18
633[2]	**Houghton (113)** (WJenks) **10-11-5**(7) MrRBurton (hit 6th: in tch to 11th)	20	**6**	8/1	87	20
645[F]	**Wise Advice (IRE) (95)** (MDHammond) **6-10-8** AMaguire (chsd wnr fr 6th tl fell 2 out)		**F**	8/1	—	—
				(SP 118.0%)		**7 Rn**

4m 57.0 (6.00) CSF £15.49 TOTE £8.40: £3.70 £1.60 (£9.20) OWNER Mr H. Jones (HAVERFORDWEST) BRED Swettenham Stud
487* Andrelot established a lead of some eight lengths in the first half-mile only to be joined by Wise Advice on the final circuit. Left clear by the departure of that rival, he gave his supporters palpitations by failing to lift a leg at the final fence. He does seem at his best when allowed to dominate. (5/1)
500 Merlins Dream (IRE) could not go at all for a circuit, but gradually warmed to the task and inherited second place on the run-in. (2/1)

650 Maggots Green, unable to lay up with the pace for more than half a mile, was well beaten and tired when left in second place at the penultimate fence. A blunder at the last stopped her in her tracks. (5/2)
Dark Oak won first time out two seasons back but never looked like repeating the feat. (13/2)
Clares Own briefly hit form after starting with a couple of below-par runs last year, but looks on the downgrade. (25/1)
633 Houghton has yet to beat a horse in two starts for his new stable. (8/1)

690 AUDREY BUTTERY REUNION H'CAP HURDLE (0-130) (4-Y.O+) (Class C)
3-45 (3-47) **3m (12 hdls)** £3,795.00 (£1,140.00: £550.00: £255.00) GOING: 0.03 sec per fur (G)

				SP	RR	SF
495F	**Tallywagger (116)** (GMMoore) **9-12-0** NBentley (chsd ldrs: led appr last: rdn out)	—	1	7/1	96	17
489*	**Ordog Mor (IRE) (102)** (MGMeagher) **7-11-0** APMcCoy (led tl appr last: unable qckn)	1	2	Evens 1	81	2
509³	**Red Jam Jar (93)** (SBBell) **11-10-5** NSmith (trckd ldrs: ev ch appr 2 out: no ex appr last)	2½	3	8/1	71	—
549³	**China Mail (IRE) (94)** (KCBailey) **4-10-3** TJMurphy (lw: hld up: hdwy 8th: rdn next: wknd appr 2 out)	27	4	9/2 3	54	—
539F	**Frontier Flight (USA) (95)** (MissLCSiddall) **6-10-4**(3) EHusband (lw: a bhd)	12	5	9/1	47	—
95P	**Moobakkr (USA) (92)** (KAMorgan) **5-10-4** ASSmith (disp ld to 4th: wknd 8th: p.u bef 2 out)		P	3/1 2	—	—
				(SP 126.8%)		6 Rn

5m 58.8 (19.80) CSF £16.07 TOTE £8.30: £3.60 £1.40 (£8.70) OWNER Mrs Susan Moore (MIDDLEHAM) BRED P. T. Flavin
WEIGHT FOR AGE 4yo-3lb
29 Tallywagger, a useful hurdler four seasons ago, is enjoying something of an Indian summer and is back to near his best. (7/1: op 9/2)
489* Ordog Mor (IRE) had to go a good clip for the final mile to shake off Moobakkr, but then steadied the pace. Quickening the pace with a circuit left, he was hard at work some time before he surrendered the lead, although he never gave up. (Evens)
509 Red Jam Jar, stepping up in trip, probably failed to last home as he was going as well as anything to the home turn. (8/1: 6/1-9/1)
549 China Mail (IRE) was finding this hard work some way out and could never get to grips with the leaders. (9/2)
539 Frontier Flight (USA) at least completed the course this time, but ran a lifeless race. (9/1: op 5/1)
Moobakkr (USA) resented not being allowed his own way in front. (3/1)

691 SCANLINK FOR SCANIA NOVICES' CHASE (5-Y.O+) (Class D)
4-20 (4-20) **3m 1f (19 fncs)** £4,174.00 (£1,164.00: £562.00) GOING: 0.03 sec per fur (G)

				SP	RR	SF
602*	**Cats Run (IRE) (103)** (JohnUpson) **8-11-12** RSupple (led tl appr 4th: led 11th tl appr 13th: led 3 out: clr next: easily)	—	1	1/4 1	117+	42
	Deise Marshall (IRE) (80) (JWade) **8-11-0** ASSmith (bit bkwd: led appr 4th to 11th: led appr 13th to 3 out: sn btn)	10	2	7/2 2	99	24
584U	**Durham Hornet** (MrsSarahHorner-Harker) **9-11-0** NSmith (bit bkwd: a bhd)	dist	3	14/1 3	—	—
				(SP 108.9%)		3 Rn

6m 22.6 (11.60) CSF £1.53 TOTE £1.20: (£1.20) OWNER Mrs Ann Key (TOWCESTER) BRED John Brophy
602* Cats Run (IRE), with the falling rain making the ground loose on top, looked as if he might have to struggle for much of the race, but class and fitness told in the straight. (1/4)
Deise Marshall (IRE) gave the winner a fright until lack of a recent run found him out. He should soon be winning. (7/2: 5/2-4/1)
Durham Hornet never threatened to make the slightest impression and is going to prove difficult to win with. (14/1)

692 SCANIA 4-SERIES 'KING OF THE ROAD' H'CAP HURDLE (0-120) (4-Y.O+) (Class D)
4-50 (4-51) **2m 3f 110y (10 hdls)** £3,103.00 (£934.00: £452.00: £211.00) GOING: 0.03 sec per fur (G)

				SP	RR	SF
641*	**Bellroi (IRE) (100)** (MHTompkins) **5-11-2** AMaguire (trckd ldr: blnd 5th: led appr 2 out: hit last: rdn out)	—	1	13/8 1	92	15
596²	**Wollboll (84)** (HJCollingridge) **6-10-0** VSmith (led tl appr 2 out: mstke last: no imp flat)	3½	2	7/1	73	—
	Scud Missile (IRE) (102) (GFJohnsonHoughton) **5-11-4** AThornton (prom tl outpcd appr 8th: kpt on appr last)	13	3	10/1	81	4
505²	**Bures (IRE) (112)** (MrsJBrown) **5-11-7**(7) BGrattan (hld up: r.o fr 3 out: nvr rchd ldrs)	1¼	4	20/1	89	12
538²	**Wamdha (IRE) (102)** (KAMorgan) **6-11-4** ASSmith (nvr trbld ldrs)	1¾	5	7/1	78	1
596P	**Stay With Me (FR) (92)** (CREgerton) **6-10-1**(7) MrRThornton (hdwy 3 out: wknd appr next)	8	6	14/1	61	—
591²	**Peter Monamy (103)** (MCPipe) **4-11-0b**(3) DWalsh (prom: mstke 2nd: wknd after 5th)	dist	7	5/1 3	—	—
651P	**Layham Low (IRE) (100)** (OSherwood) **5-11-2** JOsborne (prom tl rdn & wknd 7th: t.o whn p.u bef 2 out)		P	4/1 2	—	—
				(SP 120.3%)		8 Rn

4m 46.6 (13.60) CSF £13.53 CT £83.19 TOTE £2.50: £1.20 £1.80 £2.10 (£6.90) Trio £98.10 OWNER Mrs G. A. E. Smith (NEWMARKET) BRED Mrs K. Twomey and Mrs S. O'Riordan
LONG HANDICAP Wollboll 9-12
WEIGHT FOR AGE 4yo-2lb
641* Bellroi (IRE) is clearly useful on his day, but made his task harder by making a mess of the flight in front of the Stands on both circuits. He was dismounted after passing the post but any injury did not appear too serious. (13/8)
596 Wollboll has been making hay in Jersey for the last year and a half and looks well capable of winning here, as this developed into a two-horse race a long way from the finish. (7/1)
Scud Missile (IRE) looked fit but blew up in the back straight, only to stay on promisingly as he got his second wind. This should put him right. (10/1)
505 Bures (IRE), a former stablemate of the winner, seems to have gone the wrong way and is probably best watched for the moment. (20/1)
538 Wamdha (IRE) has yet to prove effective much beyond the minimum trip and a return to Huntingdon should be noted. (7/1)
473 Stay With Me (FR) crept forward at halfway, but made a concerted effort to close on the leaders on the home turn. He may have done too much too soon for the effort burst him. (14/1)

T/Plpt: £13.10 (568.21 Tckts). T/Qdpt: £3.40 (71.12 Tckts). Dk

0534-PERTH (R-H) (Good to firm)
Wednesday September 25th

693 BALLATHIE HOUSE HOTEL NOVICES' HURDLE (4-Y.O+) (Class D)
2-10 (2-11) **3m 110y (12 hdls)** £2,736.00 (£828.00: £404.00: £192.00) GOING: 0.21 sec per fur (G)

				SP	RR	SF
	Smart Approach (IRE) (80) (MrsMReveley) **6-10-9** PNiven (a.p: lft in ld appr 2 out: r.o)	—	1	4/1 2	66?	11

	Horse	Pos	SP	RR	SF
	Antarctic Wind (IRE) (MDHammond) **6-11-0** RGarritty (hld up: hdwy 4 out: chal next: outpcd fr 2 out)............6	**2**	20/1	67?	12
	Jubran (USA) (98) (JPDodds) **10-11-6** RichardGuest (hld up & bhd: hdwy 4 out: rdn & one pce fr 2 out) 3½	**3**	9/2 3	71	16
536 2	**Blooming Spring (IRE) (77)** (MrsDThomson) **7-11-1** LO'Hara (lw: in tch tl outpcd fr 3 out)...............................9	**4**	7/1	60	5
	Heddon Haugh (IRE) (74) (PCheesbrough) **8-11-0** RSupple (unruly s: led to 4 out: wknd qckly after next: p.u bef last)	**P**	66/1	—	—
642 F	**Classic Crest (IRE) (80)** (GMMoore) **5-11-6v** NBentley (cl up: rdn 8th: wknd qckly next: p.u bef 2 out)	**P**	33/1	—	—
	Rushen Raider (KWHogg) **4-10-11** MFoster (lw: trckd ldrs: led 4 out tl s.u bnd appr 2 out)	**S**	11/10 1	—	—
			(SP 107.5%)		**7 Rn**

6m 6.7 (20.70) CSF £55.03 TOTE £4.70: £2.00 £4.40 (£27.00) OWNER Mrs M. B. Thwaites (SALTBURN) BRED Thomas and John Lombard
WEIGHT FOR AGE 4yo-3lb

Smart Approach (IRE) was presented with this when the favourite slipped up, but she did it well, despite wandering about at her hurdles when in front. (4/1)
Antarctic Wind (IRE), a good-looking Irish import, probably just needed this and ran pretty well, suggesting that modest opportunities will be found. (20/1)
Jubran (USA) was held up to get the trip and failed to come up with the goods when asked for an effort approaching two out. (9/2)
536 Blooming Spring (IRE) (7/1: 4/1-8/1)
Rushen Raider looked be doing everything right and, although only just in front, he had not been asked the question when slipping on the bend approaching the second last. (11/10)

694 GREIG MIDDLETON NOVICES' CHASE (5-Y.O+) (Class E)

2-40 (2-40) **2m (12 fncs)** £3,046.25 (£920.00: £447.50: £211.25) GOING: 0.21 sec per fur (G)

	Horse	Pos	SP	RR	SF
	Blue Charm (IRE) (MrsSCBradburne) **6-10-12** AMaguire (trckd ldrs: led 3 out: r.o) ....—	**1**	4/1 3	91+	36
681*	**To Be the Best (70)** (DALamb) **6-11-5** JBurke (lw: led to 3 out: kpt on one pce)...............7	**2**	2/1 1	91	36
529 2	**Reve de Valse (USA) (88)** (RJohnson) **9-11-5** KJohnson (chsd ldrs: rdn 7th: one pce fr 3 out)..........4	**3**	5/1	87	32
647 6	**Wee Wizard (IRE)** (MABarnes) **7-10-12** PWaggott (outpcd & lost tch fr 5th: styd on u.p fr 3 out: n.d)..............4	**4**	14/1	76	21
532*	**Speaker's House (USA) (86)** (MissLucindaRussell) **7-11-5** AThornton (prom to 5th: sn rdn & btn: t.o whn p.u bef 3 out)	**P**	7/2 2	—	—
	Music Blitz (MrsDThomson) **5-10-10** BStorey (bhd: hdwy ½-wy: prom 4 out: 3rd & hrd rdn whn blnd & uns rdr 2 out)	**P**	8/1	—	—
	Strathtore Dream (IRE) (MissLAPerratt) **5-10-5** LO'Hara (mstkes: a bhd: p.u bef 4 out)	**P**	100/1	—	—
			(SP 111.0%)		**7 Rn**

3m 59.7 (8.70) CSF £11.70 TOTE £3.70: £1.90 £1.90 (£8.60) OWNER Mrs M. C. Lindsay (CUPAR) BRED Patrick Coghlan
WEIGHT FOR AGE 5yo-2lb

OFFICIAL EXPLANATION **Speaker's House (USA): the trainer reported that the going was not fast enough for the gelding.**
Blue Charm (IRE) was his usual excitable self in the preliminaries, but he did nothing wrong in the race and, jumping well, won decisively over a trip short of his best. (4/1)
681* To Be the Best showed his Carlisle win to be no fluke but, despite trying hard, he was outclassed from the second last. (2/1)
529 Reve de Valse (USA) ran well, being up with the pace throughout, but he proved well short of speed over the last three fences. (5/1)
Wee Wizard (IRE) did his usual and got well outpaced halfway through the race and, despite staying on, could never get into it. He probably needs further and softer ground. (14/1)
532* Speaker's House (USA) obviously has problems as he was under pressure by halfway and, stopping very quickly, was then pulled up. (7/2)
Music Blitz ran reasonably and, given softer conditions, better will be seen. (8/1)

695 MOULIN BREWERY AMATEUR H'CAP HURDLE (0-100) (4-Y.O+) (Class F)

3-10 (3-10) **2m 4f 110y (10 hdls)** £2,788.00 (£844.00: £412.00: £196.00) GOING: 0.21 sec per fur (G)

	Horse	Pos	SP	RR	SF
	Peggy Gordon (72) (MrsDThomson) **5-10-6** MrsAFarrell (hld up & bhd: gd hdwy 3 out: led appr 2 out: sn clr) ....—	**1**	12/1	62	20
95 6	**Able Player (USA) (86)** (KJDrewry) **9-10-13**(7) MrKDrewry (bhd: effrt 4 out: styd on u.p: nvr able to chal) 10	**2**	10/1	68	26
641 8	**Tashreef (72)** (JJBirkett) **6-10-1b**(5) MrMHNaughton (in tch: hdwy to chse ldrs 3 out: one pce fr next) ....½	**3**	14/1	54	12
647 4	**Flintlock (IRE) (78)** (HAlexander) **6-10-5**(7) MrRThornton (cl up: led 3rd to 5th: rdn to ld appr 3 out: hdd appr 2 out: sn btn).........16	**4**	7/2 2	47	5
533*	**Bourdonner (90)** (MDHammond) **4-11-5**(3) MrCBonner (lw: led tl j.slowly & blnd 3rd: led 5th: sn hdd: wknd fr 3 out).........3	**5**	6/5 1	57	13
6 2	**Nicholas Plant (94)** (JSGoldie) **7-11-7**(7) MrOMcPhail (chsd ldrs: led after 5th tl appr 3 out: btn whn blnd 2 out).........1½	**6**	6/1 3	60	18
	Good Team (80) (MDHammond) **11-10-7**(7) MissDVRussell (bit bkwd: prom tl rdn & wknd 4 out) 4	**7**	50/1	43	1
			(SP 107.4%)		**7 Rn**

5m 1.6 (13.60) CSF £97.80 CT £1,338.43 TOTE £16.90: £3.70 £3.10 (£45.00) OWNER Frank Flynn and Richard Madden (MILNATHORT) BRED Mrs M. D. Young
WEIGHT FOR AGE 4yo-2lb

OFFICIAL EXPLANATION **Bourdonner: the rider reported that the gelding was never travelling after blundering at the third.**
Peggy Gordon won early last season and, well suited by the strong gallop here, came from way behind to win with ease. (12/1)
95 Able Player (USA) certainly stays well and was keeping on when it was all too late. He is probably better suited by easier ground. (10/1: 6/1-12/1)
539 Tashreef looked dangerous three out but, once pressure was applied, he again looked slow. (14/1: 10/1-16/1)
647 Flintlock (IRE) failed to impress on looks and, after helping to set a very strong pace, had run himself into the ground two out. (7/2)
533* Bourdonner, taken on in the lead, did not seem to like it, and finally threw in the towel three out. He needs an aggressive ride and things to go his own way. (6/5)

696 ROYAL BANK OF SCOTLAND H'CAP CHASE (0-100) (5-Y.O+) (Class F)

3-40 (3-40) **3m (18 fncs)** £4,201.50 (£1,272.00: £621.00: £295.50) GOING: 0.21 sec per fur (G)

	Horse	Pos	SP	RR	SF
	Forward Glen (73) (PCheesbrough) **9-10-3b** RSupple (in tch: hdwy u.p 3 out: led appr last: styd on) ....—	**1**	20/1	81	18
	Solo Gent (92) (APJones) **7-11-8** SCurran (lw: a.p: led 14th tl appr last: kpt on one pce)...........6	**2**	100/30 2	96	33
190 8	**Bitacrack (79)** (JJBirkett) **9-10-9** LO'Hara (a.p: effrt & mstke 4 out: styd on fr 2 out: no imp)...........5	**3**	10/1	80	17
	Grand Scenery (IRE) (90) (HowardJohnson) **8-11-6** AMaguire (lw: mstkes: hld up & bhd: stdy hdwy ½-wy: blnd 14th: chal 4 out: hit 2 out: sn btn)...........s.h	**4**	4/1 3	91	28

Commandeer (IRE) (73) (MissMKMilligan) 6-10-3 ASSmith (mde most tl hdd 14th: outpcd fr 4 out) 8 5 20/1 68 5
645[2] **Rebel King (90)** (MABarnes) **6-11-6** PWaggott (prom: drvn along fr 12th: hit 13th: no imp after: fin lame) ....8 **6** 5/2[1] 80 17
2[P] **Off The Bru (94)** (MrsSCBradburne) **11-11-3**(7) MrMBradburne (cl up: disp ld 5th to 11th: chsd ldr tl mstke & wknd 4 out) 22 **7** 12/1 69 6
Bright Destiny (74) (JSGoldie) **5-9-11**(3) GLee (sn t.o) ....dist **8** 66/1 — —
Willie Sparkle (79) (MrsSCBradburne) **10-10-2**(7) AWatt (bit bkwd: chsd ldrs tl wknd fr 4 out: 5th & btn whn p.u bef last) .... **P** 15/2 — —
(SP 111.2%) **9 Rn**

6m 14.4 (16.40) CSF £77.61 CT £638.29 TOTE £16.30: £2.30 £1.90 £3.60 (£41.20) Trio £128.30 OWNER Mr P. Cheesbrough (BISHOP AUCKLAND) BRED N. Kennedy
LONG HANDICAP Bright Destiny 9-0
WEIGHT FOR AGE 5yo-4lb
Forward Glen, after seven races without the blinkers, this in-and-out performer had them back on. They probably made the difference in this moderate event. (20/1)
Solo Gent looked fit for his seasonal debut, and had his chances, but was short of toe from the last. (100/30)
136 Bitacrack is well enough handicapped and, after getting outpaced at a vital stage, did stay on, but never held any serious hopes. (10/1)
Grand Scenery (IRE), who jumped moderately early on, was then dropped right out. He spent much of the race on the bridle, but his jumping was always chancy when put into it, and he finally gave up two out. (4/1)
Commandeer (IRE) showed some ability here and gave the impression that he should be all the better for it. (20/1)
645 Rebel King has yet to show he stays anything like this trip and was struggling a long way out. (5/2)
Off The Bru (12/1: op 8/1)
Willie Sparkle needed this, but ran quite well. Tiring in the home straight, he was pulled up going to the last. (15/2)

697 ROYAL BANK OF SCOTLAND CLAIMING HURDLE (4-Y.O+) (Class F)

4-10 (4-11) **2m 110y (8 hdls)** £2,721.80 (£764.80: £373.40) GOING: 0.21 sec per fur (G)

SP RR SF
Brodessa (MrsMReveley) **10-10-13** PNiven (mde all: hit 5th: styd on wl fr 2 out) ....— **1** 11/10[1] 73 26
648[6] **Simand (77)** (GMMoore) **4-10-0** JCallaghan (trckd ldrs: effrt & ch 2 out: sn btn) ....7 **2** 10/1[3] 55 6
66[13] **Parish Walk (IRE) (84)** (KJDrewry) **5-10-13** MFoster (a chsng ldrs: outpcd 3 out: kpt on appr last) 1¼ **3** 20/1 65 18
600* **Hacketts Cross (IRE) (95)** (PEccles) **8-10-13** AMaguire (in tch: hdwy 3 out: sn ev ch: rdn & btn after 2 out) ....¾ **4** 9/4[2] 64 17
582[5] **Aide Memoire (IRE) (77)** (MrsBKBroad) **7-10-5** KJohnson (chsd ldrs tl lost pl 5th: n.d after) 8 **5** 50/1 49 2
648* **Minnesota Fats (IRE) (76)** (MissMERowland) **4-11-3** GaryLyons (hld up: hdwy 3 out: sn rdn & btn) 6 **6** 12/1 57 8
339[3] **Colway Prince (IRE) (80)** (APJones) **8-10-7** SCurran (bhd: effrt 5th: rdn & btn 3 out) ....23 **7** 14/1 22 —
Marco Magnifico (USA) (75) (MissLucindaRussell) **6-10-10** AThornton (t: outpcd & lost tch 4th: wl bhd after) ....¾ **8** 16/1 25 —
(SP 114.4%) **8 Rn**

3m 57.0 (11.00) CSF £11.94 TOTE £2.20: £1.20 £2.00 £5.20 (£5.60) OWNER Mr R. W. S. Jevon (SALTBURN) BRED B. Fairs
WEIGHT FOR AGE 4yo-2lb
Brodessa had a fairly simple task here, but did not particularly impress with his jumping, despite winning authoritatively. (11/10: 5/4-Evens)
490* Simand travelled quite well, but found the winner far too good when the pressure was applied. (10/1: op 6/1)
17 Parish Walk (IRE) ran as though longer trips might well suit. (20/1)
600* Hacketts Cross (IRE) looked dangerous when challenging after three out but, soon ridden, the effort was then always too much for his liking. (9/4)
Aide Memoire (IRE) is a law unto herself. (50/1)
648* Minnesota Fats (IRE) (12/1: op 8/1)
339 Colway Prince (IRE) (14/1: 10/1-16/1)

698 HIGHLAND SPRING NOVICES' HURDLE (4-Y.O+) (Class E)

4-40 (4-40) **2m 110y (8 hdls)** £2,780.00 (£780.00: £380.00) GOING: 0.21 sec per fur (G)

SP RR SF
Mithraic (IRE) (88) (WSCunningham) **4-10-5**(7) LMcGrath (lw: chsd ldrs: led 2 out: r.o) ....— **1** 5/1[3] 75 31
Supertop (95) (LLungo) **8-11-0** MFoster (lw: hld up: hdwy 5th: chsng ldrs 2 out: styd on: nt pce to chal) ....1½ **2** 13/8[1] 74 32
Dr Edgar (MDods) **4-10-12** RSupple (led to 2 out: 3rd & btn whn hit last) 10 **3** 14/1 64 20
586[2] **Tawafij (USA) (85)** (MDHammond) **7-11-0** RGarritty (chsd ldrs: effrt & mstke 3 out: one pce after) ....8 **4** 5/2[2] 56 14
I'm The Man (MrsESlack) **5-11-0** KJohnson (a bhd) ....16 **5** 20/1 41 —
Welburn Boy (RDEWoodhouse) **4-10-12** LWyer (nvr nr to chal) ....1½ **6** 20/1 39 —
Logani (60) (RMMcKellar) **6-10-6**(3) DParker (a bhd: t.o) ....dist **7** 100/1 — —
Flyaway Blues (MrsMReveley) **4-10-12** PNiven (lw: fell 1st) .... **F** 11/1 — —
643[P] **Rhythmic Dancer** (DANolan) **8-11-0** BStorey (swtg: plld hrd: a bhd: t.o whn p.u bef 3 out) .... **P** 40/1 — —
Court Joker (IRE) (90) (HAlexander) **4-10-5**(7) MrRThornton (swtg: w ldr: hit 4th: wknd next: t.o whn p.u bef 2 out) .... **P** 9/1 — —
(SP 121.3%) **10 Rn**

3m 55.7 (9.70) CSF £13.53 TOTE £10.20: £2.00 £1.70 £2.40 (£14.60) Trio £38.90 OWNER C P M Racing (YARM) BRED J. P. and Miss M. Mangan
WEIGHT FOR AGE 4yo-2lb
IN-FOCUS: **This was Laurie McGrath's first winner.**
Mithraic (IRE) has improved on the Flat and carried that on here, winning really well. (5/1)
Supertop is a funny customer, who often flatters only to deceive and, despite staying on here, was never doing enough. (13/8)
Dr Edgar proved disappointing on the Flat and probably has his own ideas about the game, but did show something here and may well pick up a race. (14/1)
586 Tawafij (USA) had his chances again, but failed to see it out. (5/2)
I'm The Man had a quiet run and looks likely to be all the better for it. (20/1)
Welburn Boy had an educational outing that should stand him in good stead. (20/1)
Flyaway Blues (11/1: op 6/1)

T/Plpt: £1,130.20 (9.5 Tckts). T/Qdpt: £179.20 (4.11 Tckts). AA

0693-PERTH (R-H) (Good, Good to firm patches)
Thursday September 26th
WEATHER: unsettled

699 MURRAYSHALL HOTEL HURDLE (3-Y.O) (Class D)
2-10 (2-10) **2m 110y (8 hdls)** £2,806.80 (£848.40: £413.20: £195.60) GOING: 0.49 sec per fur (GS)

				SP	RR	SF
	Tarry (AStreeter) **3-10-5** TEley (lw: a.p: slt ld last: styd on wl)	—	1	13/2[3]	58	23
	Globe Runner (JJO'Neill) **3-10-10** ARoche (bhd: hdwy & prom 5th: effrt appr 2 out: styd on one pce)	2	2	25/1	61	26
640*	**Silverdale Knight** (KWHogg) **3-11-3** MFoster (led: hit 3 out: hdd last: no ex)	½	3	4/5[1]	68	33
534*	**Rossel (USA)** (PMonteith) **3-11-3** ADobbin (lw: cl up tl wknd fr 2 out)	15	4	6/1[2]	53	18
	What Jim Wants (IRE) (JJO'Neill) **3-10-10** PNiven (lw: outpcd ½-wy: styd on fr 2 out: no imp)	2	5	33/1	44	9
534[2]	**Ret Frem (IRE)** (CParker) **3-10-10** BStorey (lw: prom tl outpcd 3 out: n.d after)	nk	6	9/1	44	9
	Thorntoun Estate (IRE) (MartinTodhunter) **3-10-10** MDwyer (chsd ldrs tl rdn & wknd 3 out)	19	7	16/1	25	—
654[2]	**How Could-I (IRE)** (MrsNMacauley) **3-10-5** AMaguire (in tch: mstke 4th: n.d after)	5	8	8/1	16	—
	Arrogant Heir (DHBrown) **3-10-10** LWyer (prom: blnd 4th: sn lost pl: t.o whn p.u bef 2 out)		P	33/1	—	—
	Mineral Water (MrsDThomson) **3-10-10** LO'Hara (mstkes: a bhd: t.o whn p.u bef 2 out)		P	66/1	—	—
				(SP 121.4%)		**10 Rn**

4m 0.7 (14.70) CSF £126.63 TOTE £10.90: £2.20 £6.30 £1.30 (£187.20) Trio £114.70 OWNER Mrs Chris Lester (HEDNESFORD) BRED Highclere Stud Ltd

Tarry, although only small, jumps well enough. She is determined and won in good style. (13/2)
Globe Runner, handily placed from halfway, kept responding to pressure over the last two flights and showed enough to suggest that a race can be found. (25/1)
640* Silverdale Knight, who has a moderate action, had to make his own running this time, and was done with when caught at the final flight. (4/5: Evens-11/8)
534* Rossel (USA) ran well until things proved too much from the penultimate flight. (6/1: 4/1-7/1)
What Jim Wants (IRE) gives the impression that, over further, better will be seen. (33/1)
534 Ret Frem (IRE) (9/1: 5/1-10/1)

700 TRAVAIL EMPLOYMENT GROUP MAIDEN HURDLE (4-Y.O+) (Class E)
2-40 (2-40) **2m 4f 110y (10 hdls)** £2,684.00 (£754.00: £368.00) GOING: 0.49 sec per fur (GS)

				SP	RR	SF
	Shonara's Way (91) (PMonteith) **5-11-0** ADobbin (chsd ldrs: chal 3 out: led next: styd on wl)	—	1	4/1[2]	66	28
	Jabaroot (IRE) (78) (RMMcKellar) **5-11-2**(3) GCahill (hld up: hdwy 6th: led 3 out to 2 out: one pce)	6	2	9/1	66	28
649[2]	**Lear Dancer (USA)** (MissMERowland) **5-11-5** GaryLyons (lw: hld up & bhd: gd hdwy 4 out: chsng ldrs & effrt next: hit 2 out: no imp)	9	3	11/4[1]	59	21
	Jonaem (IRE) (80) (MrsESlack) **6-11-5** KJohnson (bit bkwd: led to 3 out: sn outpcd)	1¾	4	10/1	58	20
450[2]	**Commander Glen (IRE)** (MDHammond) **4-11-0**(3) MrCBonner (lw: prom: hit 2nd: outpcd 6th: no imp after)	11	5	7/1	49	9
	Miss Lamplight (70) (FPMurtagh) **6-11-0** RSupple (bhd: effrt ½-wy: no imp)	6	6	16/1	40	2
	New Capricorn (USA) (CParker) **6-11-2**(3) DParker (bit bkwd: nvr nr to chal)	16	7	20/1	32	—
	Calder's Grove (MissLAPerratt) **6-11-5** LO'Hara (in tch to 4 out)	s.h	8	100/1	32	—
	Murphy's Run (IRE) (PEccles) **6-11-5** AMaguire (prom tl rdn & wknd 4 out: p.u bef 2 out)		P	11/2[3]	—	—
	Boston Man (RDEWoodhouse) **5-11-5** LWyer (chsd ldrs tl mstke & wknd 4 out: p.u bef last)		P	20/1	—	—
				(SP 110.0%)		**10 Rn**

5m 7.5 (19.50) CSF £34.09 TOTE £4.60: £1.80 £2.40 £1.40 (£22.90) Trio £21.80 OWNER Mr Alan Guthrie (ROSEWELL) BRED M. J. Simmonds
WEIGHT FOR AGE 4yo-2lb

Shonara's Way, after a very poor effort on the Flat last week, sprang a surprise and won this in determined fashion. It was a moderate event though. (4/1: op 5/2)
Jabaroot (IRE) is running quite well as present, but just failed to last out the trip. (9/1)
649 Lear Dancer (USA), dropped back in trip, travels well when on the bridle but is disappointing off it, and never got in a serious blow. (11/4)
Jonaem (IRE), in need of the run, went quite well until blowing up from the third last. (10/1: op 16/1)
450 Commander Glen (IRE) ran reasonably, but probably found this trip beyond him. (7/1: 5/1-8/1)

701 CLARENDON CARPETS H'CAP HURDLE (0-120) (4-Y.O+) (Class D)
3-10 (3-11) **2m 110y (8 hdls)** £3,371.25 (£1,020.00: £497.50: £236.25) GOING: 0.49 sec per fur (GS)

				SP	RR	SF
638[2]	**Sarmatian (USA) (100)** (MDHammond) **5-11-10** RGarritty (lw: trckd ldrs: effrt 2 out: disp ld last: hrd drvn & r.o)	—	1	6/4[1]	79	—
531*	**Vintage Red (76)** (GRichards) **6-10-0** ADobbin (set slow pce: qcknd after 5th: hdd flat: eased whn btn towards fin)	2	2	6/1	53	—
453[4]	**Latin Leader (85)** (CParker) **6-10-6b**(3) DParker (trckd ldrs: effrt 3 out: outpcd fr next)	6	3	12/1	56	—
643[2]	**Robsera (IRE) (90)** (JJQuinn) **5-11-0** LWyer (lw: hld up: effrt appr 2 out: sn outpcd)	8	4	4/1[3]	54	—
531[2]	**Steadfast Elite (IRE) (90)** (JJO'Neill) **5-11-0** ARoche (lw: hld up & bhd: outpcd 3 out: n.d)	3½	5	3/1[2]	50	—
				(SP 107.0%)		**5 Rn**

4m 22.8 (36.80) CSF £9.17 TOTE £2.30: £1.50 £1.40 (£4.90) OWNER Mr S. T. Brankin (MIDDLEHAM) BRED David Allan
LONG HANDICAP Vintage Red 9-5
OFFICIAL EXPLANATION Steadfast Elite (IRE): has to be held up and was not suited by the slow early pace.

638 Sarmatian (USA) was presented this thanks to the tactics of the other riders, who all held their mounts up, as he was always going to have the best turn of foot. (6/4)
531* Vintage Red is an edgy individual. He set a snail's pace and was outsprinted from the last. (6/1)
453 Latin Leader was held up in a very slowly-run event, which lost him all chances. (12/1: op 8/1)
643 Robsera (IRE) would have been better having more use made of him. (4/1)
531 Steadfast Elite (IRE) is not the easiest of rides and had no chance the way this was run. (3/1)

702 COOPERS & LYBRAND H'CAP CHASE (0-125) (4-Y.O+) (Class D)
3-40 (3-40) **2m (12 fncs)** £3,420.00 (£1,035.00: £505.00: £240.00) GOING: 0.49 sec per fur (GS)

				SP	RR	SF
583[4]	**Beaucadeau (100)** (MABarnes) **10-10-12** PWaggott (a.p: led 4 out: r.o wl fr next: collapsed after r: dead)	—	1	9/1	111	39

				SP	RR	SF
537[2]	**Beldine (100)** (PMonteith) **11-10-12** ADobbin (a.p: effrt 4 out: one pce fr next)	7	**2**	11/4[1]	104	32
	Newhall Prince (112) (AStreeter) **8-11-10** TEley (trckd ldrs: effrt 4 out: styd on one pce: hit last)	nk	**3**	11/4[1]	116	44
592[F]	**Shrewd John (97)** (RDEWoodhouse) **10-10-9** MDwyer (lw: hld up: effrt appr 3 out: nt pce to chal)	1¼	**4**	3/1[2]	99	27
464[3]	**Blazing Dawn (88)** (JSHubbuck) **9-10-0** BStorey (cl up: led 5th to 4 out: one pce)	hd	**5**	8/1[3]	90	18
	Sure Metal (111) (DMcCain) **13-11-9** DMcCain (led to 5th: wkng whn fell 8th)		**F**	50/1	—	—
538[5]	**Vain Prince (100)** (NTinkler) **9-10-12b** RGarritty (lw: sn t.o: p.u bef 6th)		**P**	8/1[3]	—	—
				(SP 112.5%)	**7 Rn**	

4m 3.5 (12.50) CSF £31.88 TOTE £8.90: £2.80 £2.20 (£6.40) OWNER Mr T. A. Barnes (PENRITH) BRED Lismacue Stud
LONG HANDICAP Blazing Dawn 9-10

583 Beaucadeau showed his old sparkle here and was given a fine ride, pinching it after showing the better turn of foot from the third last. On returning, he collapsed and died. (9/1: 5/1-10/1)

537 Beldine had plenty of chances but, when the pressure was on from four out, was never doing enough. (11/4: 2/1-3/1)

Newhall Prince, handily placed, was outsprinted over the last three and seemed to hang slightly. (11/4)

592 Shrewd John looked to be going quite well when held up but, when the pace suddenly increased from four out, he lacked the speed to make a real impression. (3/1)

464 Blazing Dawn, in a race that developed into a sprint up the straight, was tapped for toe. (8/1)

478 Vain Prince took no interest. (8/1)

703 HIGHLAND SPRING SCOTTISH CELEBRATION H'CAP HURDLE (0-115) (4-Y.O+) (Class E)

4-10 (4-10) **3m 110y (12 hdls)** £3,436.25 (£1,040.00: £507.50: £241.25) GOING: 0.49 sec per fur (GS)

				SP	RR	SF
533[2]	**Valiant Dash (85)** (JSGoldie) **10-10-4**(3) GLee (cl up: led 4 out: styd on gamely appr last)	—	**1**	5/1	68	26
	Twin Falls (IRE) (98) (GMMoore) **5-11-6** JCallaghan (hld up: effrt 8th: hdwy to chal 2 out: rdn & btn appr last)	8	**2**	4/1[3]	76	34
582[2]	**Tough Test (IRE) (101)** (MrsJDGoodfellow) **6-11-9** BFenton (prom: hit 2nd & 4th: slipped bnd appr 6th: rdn 4 out: sn lost tch)	12	**3**	6/4[1]	71	29
638[5]	**Don du Cadran (FR) (104)** (CaptTAForster) **7-11-12** AThornton (led to 4 out: wknd after next: t.o)	dist	**4**	5/2[2]	—	—
				(SP 105.2%)	**4 Rn**	

6m 7.6 (21.60) CSF £19.42 TOTE £4.90 (£8.30) OWNER Mr L. W. Dunbar (GLASGOW) BRED Greenland Park Stud

533 Valiant Dash stays forever and that was all that was required here. (5/1: op 3/1)

Twin Falls (IRE) has not won for almost two years and, after looking likely to rectify that three out, he came under pressure and found nothing over the next. (4/1)

582 Tough Test (IRE) was disappointing here and jumped sloppily. In a race where the strong pace should have suited him, he was the first beaten. (6/4)

Don du Cadran (FR), an edgy sort, made this a real test, but stopped as though shot once collared three out. (5/2)

704 PRESS & JOURNAL TAMEROSIA SERIES NOVICES' CHASE (Qualifier) (5-Y.O+) (Class D)

4-40 (4-40) **2m 4f 110y (15 fncs)** £3,436.25 (£1,040.00: £507.50: £241.25) GOING: 0.49 sec per fur (GS)

				SP	RR	SF
	Tighter Budget (USA) (MrsHDSayer) **9-11-0** MMoloney (led to 3rd: led 7th: drew clr fr 4 out)	—	**1**	13/8[2]	105?	38
	Bardaros (MissLucindaRussell) **7-11-0** AThornton (led 3rd to 7th: wknd fr 4 out)	dist	**2**	11/10[1]	—	—
	Kincardine Bridge (USA) (MrsSCBradburne) **7-10-7**(7) MrMBradburne (bhd: hdwy 9th: sn in tch: hit 4 out: sn btn: t.o)	21	**3**	9/1[3]	—	—
584[5]	**See You Always (IRE)** (MABarnes) **6-11-0** PWaggott (chsd ldrs tl outpcd 8th: sn hrd drvn & lost tch: t.o)	29	**4**	25/1	—	—
584[4]	**Tony's Feelings (60)** (MissLucindaRussell) **8-11-0** MFoster (bhd: sme hdwy whn fell 7th)		**F**	14/1	—	—
				(SP 106.2%)	**5 Rn**	

5m 15.9 (16.90) CSF £3.50 TOTE £2.30: £1.60 £1.20 (£2.20) OWNER Mrs Dianne Sayer (PENRITH) BRED Walter Haefner

Tighter Budget (USA) won a poor event in some style and looks likely to find further success. (13/8)

Bardaros, a winning pointer last year, found this a different proposition and failed to get home. (11/10)

Kincardine Bridge (USA) was just beginning to look dangerous when he suddenly tired, hit the fourth last and stopped as though shot. (9/1: 8/1-12/1)

See You Always (IRE) looked very moderate. (25/1)

705 E.B.F. HASTE YE BACK STANDARD N.H. FLAT RACE (4, 5 & 6-Y.O) (Class H)

5-10 (5-12) **2m 110y** £1,516.00 (£426.00: £208.00)

				SP	RR	SF
	Nishamira (IRE) (TDBarron) **4-10-8**(3) GTormey (hld up: hdwy to ld 3f out: rdn & r.o)	—	**1**	4/5[1]	—	—
	Golf Land (IRE) (LLungo) **4-10-11**(5) MrMHNaughton (hld up: hdwy 6f out: chal 2f out: kpt on one pce)	8	**2**	8/1	—	—
	Damien's Choice (IRE) (MissLAPerratt) **4-10-13**(3) FLeahy (unruly in paddock & bef s: hld up: hdwy & prom 7f out: ev ch 3f out: nt qckn appr fnl f)	5	**3**	9/1	—	—
	Water Font (IRE) (JJO'Neill) **4-11-2** ARoche (bhd: hdwy 7f out: styd on fnl 2f: no imp)	5	**4**	16/1	—	—
504*	**North End Lady** (WSCunningham) **5-10-13**(7) MrRThornton (lw: plld hrd: led after 6f to 3f out: sn btn)	nk	**5**	6/1[2]	—	—
	Monsieur Pink (AStreeter) **4-11-2** JCulloty (hld up: hdwy 6f out: nvr nr to chal)	12	**6**	7/1[3]	—	—
653[B]	**Miss Nonnie** (MissLShally) **4-10-8**(3) RMassey (nvr trbld ldrs)	9	**7**	20/1	—	—
653[S]	**Teddy Edward** (MrsAMNaughton) **6-11-4** JSupple (led 6f: chsd ldrs: outpcd whn stumbled bdly ent s: nt rcvr)	10	**8**	20/1	—	—
	Super Guy (JBarclay) **4-10-13**(3) GCahill (w.r.s: sn cl up: wknd 5f out)	½	**9**	25/1	—	—
	Smart In Socks (MissLucindaRussell) **5-11-4** BFenton (lost pl 7f out: wl bhd after)	4	**10**	16/1	—	—
	The Vale (IRE) (RMMcKellar) **4-10-13**(3) DParker (wl bhd fr ½-wy)	15	**11**	66/1	—	—
	Rinus Majestic (IRE) (DMcCain) **4-10-13**(3) DWalsh (bit bkwd: prom to ½-wy: lost tch 5f out)	8	**12**	50/1	—	—
				(SP 132.0%)	**12 Rn**	

4m 7.5 CSF £9.51 TOTE £2.00: £1.20 £3.00 £2.70 (£13.30) Trio £24.90 OWNER M P Burke Developments Ltd (THIRSK) BRED His Highness the Aga Khans Studs S. C.
WEIGHT FOR AGE 4yo-2lb

Nishamira (IRE), a sweaty customer, has some decent form, but did need keeping up to her work. (4/5)

Golf Land (IRE), looking likely to be all the better for this, ran a fine race. (8/1)

Damien's Choice (IRE) gave plenty of problems before the race, but he is a decent-looking sort and ran pretty well. If he can channel his energies, improvement is likely. (9/1)

Water Font (IRE) was staying on in a manner which suggested that some improvement is likely. (16/1)

504* North End Lady, in a race where there was no pace, pulled herself into the lead early on, and was later outsprinted in the last three furlongs. (6/1)

T/Plpt: £42.60 (250.55 Tckts). T/Qdpt: £16.90 (28.62 Tckts). AA

706a-716a (Irish Racing) - See Computer Raceform

0155a-AUTEUIL (Paris, France) (L-H) (Soft)
Wednesday September 18th

717a PRIX DE L'ORLEANAIS HURDLE (5-Y.O+)
4-25 (4-27) **2m 2f** £13,175.00

				SP	RR	SF
92a[2]	**Al Capone II (FR)** (BSecly,France) **8-10-1** JYBeaurain	—	**1**		104	—
527a*	**Country Star (IRE)** (CPEBrooks) **5-10-5** GBradley	10	**2**		99	—
527a[2]	**Leon Des Perrets (FR)** (France) **5-10-3** LGerard	6	**3**		92	—
						9 Rn

4m 21.0 P-M 2.30F: 1.10F 1.20F 2.00F (2.00F) OWNER Mr R. Fougedoire
527a* Country Star (IRE) used front-running tactics but he was outclassed when the winner came upsides to make a challenge. He ran his best race to date and his trainer hopes to get one more race into him before he goes to the sales.

0648-WORCESTER (L-H) (Good to firm)
Saturday September 28th
WEATHER: overcast

718 BOATHOUSE 'N.H' NOVICES' HURDLE (4-Y.O+) (Class E)
2-30 (2-31) **2m (8 hdls)** £2,460.00 (£685.00: £330.00)

				SP	RR	SF
	Come On Penny (88) (DRGandolfo) **5-10-7** MDwyer (hld up & bhd: stdy hdwy 5th: rdn to ld last: drvn out)	—	**1**	11/4[1]	66	8
19[P]	**Winter Rose (72)** (MSheppard) **5-10-12** BPowell (j.rt: led to 2nd: led appr 4th: hit 3 out: sn hdd: outpcd 2 out: styd on flat)	3½	**2**	14/1	68	10
634[5]	**Difficult Decision (IRE)** (MrsMerritaJones) **5-10-12** DerekByrne (hld up: hdwy 5th: rdn appr 3 out: ev ch last: wknd)	1¾	**3**	3/1[2]	66	8
	Faithful Hand (MrsSJSmith) **6-10-12** RichardGuest (hld up: stdy hdwy 3rd: led after 3 out: hdd last: wknd)	1¾	**4**	20/1	64	6
	Vallingale (IRE) (MissHCKnight) **5-10-7** JFTitley (bkwd: a.p: no hdwy fr 3 out)	3	**5**	11/2[3]	56	—
492[3]	**Seven Wells** (JHPeacock) **4-10-10** RBellamy (swtg: plld hrd: rdn appr 5th: n.d after)	¾	**6**	20/1	60	—
	Aydisun (RCurtis) **4-10-10** DMorris (bit bkwd: hld up & bhd: hdwy after 5th: 5th whn blnd 3 out: nt rcvr)	3½	**7**	33/1	57	—
	Ladymalord (JRBosley) **4-10-5** ILawrence (a bhd: t.o)	29	**8**	50/1	23	—
	Pacific Ridge (IRE) (MrsMerritaJones) **5-10-12** MAFitzgerald (bkwd: a bhd: t.o)	nk	**9**	12/1	27	—
	Caulkin (IRE) (ABarrow) **5-10-12** AThornton (prom tl wknd qckly 4th: t.o)	2½	**10**	33/1	25	—
	El Cordobes (IRE) (68) (WJenks) **5-10-12** TJenks (bit bkwd: swtg: plld hrd: led 2nd tl appr 4th: wknd qckly appr 3 out: t.o)	1¾	**11**	8/1	23	—
636[2]	**Country Minstrel (IRE)** (SADouch) **5-10-12** SMcNeill (hit 1st: bhd tl fell last)		**F**	10/1	—	—
	Insiouxbordinate (RTJuckes) **4-10-10** GaryLyons (a bhd: t.o 5th: p.u bef 3 out)		**P**	66/1	—	—
				(SP 120.5%)		**13 Rn**

3m 46.5 (6.50) CSF £38.07 TOTE £2.90: £1.50 £2.60 £1.90 (£17.40) Trio £18.30 OWNER Mr A. E. Frost (WANTAGE) BRED W. D. Hockenhull
WEIGHT FOR AGE 4yo-2lb
STEWARDS' ENQUIRY Jenks fined £80 (failure to ride past the Stands bef the start)
Come On Penny, the winner of a bumper on similar ground at Ludlow, proved best in a pretty moderate contest. (11/4)
Winter Rose did not seem suited to this return to two miles and may be better going right-handed. (14/1)
Difficult Decision (IRE), placed in Irish point-to-points, should do better when put over fences. (3/1)
Faithful Hand made a promising enough debut, but this race was not very good. (20/1)
Vallingale (IRE) should at least come on for the outing. (11/2)
Pacific Ridge (IRE) (12/1: tchd 8/1)

719 TOLLADINE H'CAP CHASE (0-130) (5-Y.O+) (Class C)
3-00 (3-00) **2m 7f (18 fncs)** £4,532.50 (£1,360.00: £655.00: £302.50) GOING minus 0.23 sec per fur (G)

				SP	RR	SF
	Iffeee (123) (PBowen) **9-11-7** AMaguire (j.rt: mde virtually all: rdn out)	—	**1**	10/1	130	28
	Have to Think (130) (PFNicholls) **8-12-0** MAFitzgerald (hld up: hdwy 10th: hit 14th: ev ch 3 out: one pce)	5	**2**	4/1[3]	134	32
28*	**Certain Angle (111)** (PJHobbs) **7-10-9** CMaude (prom: hit 11th: ev ch 3 out: hrd rdn 2 out: wknd flat)	½	**3**	6/4[1]	114	12
56[2]	**Wise Approach (130)** (KCBailey) **9-12-0** AThornton (w wnr to 13th: wknd appr 4 out)	6	**4**	3/1[2]	129	27
	Cokenny Boy (110) (MrsJPitman) **11-10-8** WMarston (hld up: hit 10th: sn wl bhd: t.o)	dist	**5**	4/1[3]	—	—
				(SP 114.1%)		**5 Rn**

5m 45.8 (7.80) CSF £43.57 TOTE £6.40: £2.10 £1.90 (£17.90) OWNER Mr T. M. Morris (HAVERFORDWEST) BRED Ronald Khoo
Iffeee, who won six times before losing his form at the end of a busy season last year, looked revitalised after a summer off. (10/1: op 6/1)
Have to Think was 11lb higher than when winning a Grade Two at the Punchestown Festival. This Irish import seems at his best with give in the ground. (4/1: 3/1-9/2)
28* Certain Angle, raised 6lb for his success at Uttoxeter in June, has never won off a mark as high as this. (6/4)
56 Wise Approach found disappointingly little when put to the test on the home turn. (3/1)

720 W & P FOOD SERVICE NOVICES' CHASE (5-Y.O+) (Class D)
3-35 (3-35) **2m 7f (18 fncs)** £3,884.25 (£1,164.00: £559.50: £257.25) GOING minus 0.23 sec per fur (G)

				SP	RR	SF
221*	**Stormtracker (IRE)** (CWeedon) **7-10-12** MRichards (lw: chsd ldr: led 5th: clr 2 out: rdn out)	—	**1**	3/1[2]	95	—

				SP	RR	SF
556[2]	**Our Nikki (65)** (PRRodford) **6-10-7** SBurrough (hld up & bhd: hdwy 11th: chsd wnr fr 4 out: styd on flat)	1	**2**	25/1	89	—
602[2]	**Lucky Dollar (IRE) (100)** (KCBailey) **8-11-5** AThornton (hld up & bhd: hdwy 12th: styd on fr 2 out)	5	**3**	15/8[1]	98	1
	Westerly Gale (IRE) (NJHenderson) **6-10-12** MAFitzgerald (bit bkwd: led to 5th: 2nd whn blnd 4 out: nt rcvr)	½	**4**	16/1	91	—
639[2]	**Definite Maybe (IRE) (95)** (PFNicholls) **6-11-5b** AMaguire (hld up mid div: reminders 8th: hdwy after 9th: wknd appr 4 out)	15	**5**	6/1[3]	87	—
499[2]	**Sigma Wireless (IRE)** (CaptTAForster) **7-10-12** SWynne (hld up: mstke 1st: hdwy 10th: wknd 14th)	8	**6**	6/1[3]	75	—
595[4]	**Fort Gale (IRE)** (CPEBrooks) **5-10-8** GBradley (hld up: blnd 11th: sn bhd: t.o)	23	**7**	14/1	58	—
	Dorans Way (IRE) (MissVenetiaWilliams) **5-10-3**(5) MichaelBrennan (prom: j.slowly 3rd: 4th whn fell 10th)		**F**	16/1	—	—
602[P]	**Bells Wood** (AJKDunn) **7-10-12** BPowell (prom tl wknd qckly 10th: t.o whn p.u bef 14th)		**P**	40/1	—	—
	War Flower (IRE) (AWCarroll) **8-10-7** WMarston (bkwd: blnd & uns rdr 1st)		**U**	66/1	—	—

(SP 114.6%) **10 Rn**

5m 53.3 (15.30) CSF £60.06 TOTE £4.00: £1.60 £3.70 £1.20 (£47.00) Trio £26.00 OWNER Mr Tim Davis (CHIDDINGFOLD) BRED Mrs M. Brophy

WEIGHT FOR AGE 5yo-3lb

221* Stormtracker (IRE), whose two wins over hurdles came over three miles here, never put a foot wrong on this chasing debut. He would have won by a wider margin but for idling in the closing stages. (3/1)
556 Our Nikki seemed suited to this longer trip. (25/1)
602 Lucky Dollar (IRE) never threatened to defy his penalty. (15/8)
Westerly Gale (IRE) was running a big race on this fencing debut until making a mess of the final ditch. Improvement can be expected. (16/1)
Fort Gale (IRE) (14/1: 10/1-16/1)

721 JOHN WHITT MEMORIAL H'CAP HURDLE (0-140) (4-Y.O+) (Class B)

4-10 (4-10) **2m 4f (10 hdls)** £4,922.50 (£1,480.00: £715.00: £332.50) GOING minus 0.23 sec per fur (G)

				SP	RR	SF
	Freddie Muck (105) (NATwiston-Davies) **6-10-3** CLlewellyn (w ldr: led 4th: qcknd clr 3 out: eased flat)	—	**1**	7/2[2]	87+	3
651*	**Fieldridge (115)** (MPMuggeridge) **7-10-13** BPowell (hld up: hdwy 6th: hrd rdn appr 2 out: r.o flat: no ch w wnr)	6	**2**	5/2[1]	92	8
587*	**Holy Joe (102)** (DBurchell) **14-10-0** AMaguire (set slow pce to 4th: hrd rdn & chsd wnr appr 2 out: no imp)	1½	**3**	12/1[3]	78	—
598*	**Santella Boy (USA) (106)** (CJMann) **4-10-2bow1** JRailton (hld up: hdwy 6th: 4th & btn whn hit last)	5	**4**	7/2[2]	78	—
630*	**Wottashambles (110)** (LMontagueHall) **5-10-8** DMorris (prom: wnt 2nd & mstke 5th: outpcd 3 out: wknd appr last)	9	**5**	5/2[1]	75	—
	Echo de Janser (FR) (130) (AGHobbs) **4-11-5**(7) MrGShenkin (bhd fr 7th: t.o)	dist	**6**	20/1	—	—

(SP 114.0%) **6 Rn**

4m 46.5 (8.50) CSF £12.29 TOTE £3.80: £2.10 £1.90 (£5.00) OWNER Mrs C. Twiston-Davies (CHELTENHAM) BRED N. A. Twiston-Davies

LONG HANDICAP Holy Joe 9-12

WEIGHT FOR AGE 4yo-2lb

Freddie Muck, not seen out since winning at Carlisle last November, defied a 5lb higher mark with the help of a positive ride. (7/2)
651* Fieldridge was up a further 5lb for beating a depleted field over course and distance last time. (5/2)
587* Holy Joe, 2lb wrong at the weights, was effectively 9lb higher than when winning a Stratford seller over further. (12/1)
598* Santella Boy (USA), raised 2lb, really needs a stronger-run race over this trip. (7/2)
630* Wottashambles was trying to make the transition to handicap company. (5/2)

722 EXCELNIR NOVICES' H'CAP CHASE (0-100) (5-Y.O+) (Class E)

4-45 (4-45) **2m (12 fncs)** £3,081.75 (£924.00: £444.50: £204.75) GOING minus 0.23 sec per fur (G)

				SP	RR	SF
508*	**Prince Skyburd (79)** (MrsPMAAvison) **5-10-12** DBridgwater (hld up: led 3 out: easily)	—	**1**	6/1	93+	32
	The Yokel (70) (BPJBaugh) **10-10-0**(5) PHenley (hld up: rdn & outpcd appr 4 out: styd on flat: no ch w wnr)	2½	**2**	20/1	82	23
601[3]	**Seahawk Retriever (72)** (PFNicholls) **7-10-7** MAFitzgerald (a.p: ev ch 3 out: rdn & wknd appr last: fin lame)	2	**3**	6/1	82	23
634[11]	**Martha's Daughter (88)** (CaptTAForster) **7-11-9** AThornton (hld up & bhd: r.o fr 2 out: nvr plcd to chal)	5	**4**	11/2[3]	93+	34
554*	**Harrow Way (IRE) (86)** (LWells) **6-11-7** AMaguire (led tl wknd 3 out)	2	**5**	5/2[1]	89	30
552[4]	**Script (68)** (JRJenkins) **5-10-1** WMarston (a bhd)	5	**6**	25/1	66	5
595[3]	**Dubelle (82)** (JSKing) **6-11-3** JCulloty (j.rt: chsd ldr to 3rd: wknd 6th: t.o fr 8th)	dist	**7**	11/4[2]	—	—
	Laura Lye (IRE) (67) (BdeHaan) **6-10-2** JRailton (bit bkwd: jnd ldr 3rd: wknd qckly appr 4 out: t.o whn p.u bef last)		**P**	20/1	—	—

(SP 112.6%) **8 Rn**

3m 53.5 (2.50) CSF £87.96 CT £677.21 TOTE £6.30: £1.70 £3.50 £1.40 (£45.30) Trio £41.10 OWNER Mrs P. M. A. Avison (HELMSLEY) BRED Mrs P. M. A. Avison

WEIGHT FOR AGE 5yo-2lb

508* Prince Skyburd may have won a bad race at Sedgefield, but is beginning to look a different animal over fences. (6/1)
The Yokel, runner-up in a Hunter Chase in May, found this trip on the short side. (20/1)
601 Seahawk Retriever, wearing a tongue strap, looked none too enthusiastic between the last two fences, but his rider dismounted after the finish as if he pulled up short. (6/1)
Martha's Daughter, following a couple of falls, reverted to hurdles for her comeback here a fortnight ago, and it appeared the brief was to get round in one piece. (11/2)
554* Harrow Way (IRE) could not defy a 10lb hike in the Ratings. (5/2)

723 LADBROKES H'CAP HURDLE (0-115) (4-Y.O+) (Class E)

5-15 (5-16) **2m (8 hdls)** £2,823.50 (£848.00: £409.00: £189.50) GOING minus 0.23 sec per fur (G)

				SP	RR	SF
473[3]	**Amaze (108)** (LadyHerries) **7-11-7**(7) MrRThornton (lw: chsd ldr: led after 3rd: drvn out)	—	**1**	2/1[1]	92	10
635*	**Cooley's Valve (IRE) (100)** (MrsSDWilliams) **8-11-1**(5) SophieMitchell (hdwy 4th: ev ch last: unable qckn)	1¾	**2**	4/1[3]	82	—
491[3]	**Verde Luna (86)** (DWPArbuthnot) **4-10-4** GBradley (hld up & bhd: hdwy appr 2 out: hrd rdn flat: one pce)	½	**3**	6/1	68	—
96[5]	**Hamadryad (IRE) (85)** (MrsVCWard) **8-10-5** DGallagher (hld up & bhd: mstke 3rd: hdwy 4th: r.o flat)	½	**4**	14/1	66	—
76[5]	**Fierce (90)** (JRJenkins) **8-10-3**(7) DYellowlees (bit bkwd: led: sn clr: hdd after 3rd: ev ch 2 out: wknd flat)	2½	**5**	14/1	69	—
	Wayfarers Way (USA) (89) (NJHenderson) **5-10-9** MAFitzgerald (plld hrd: a.p: ev ch appr 3 out: rdn appr last: eased whn btn flat)	4	**6**	100/30[2]	64	—

Swings'N'Things (USA) (93) (BPalling) 4-10-11 RFarrant (hdwy 4th: wknd appr 2 out) ....7 7 20/1 61 —
Tibbs Inn (83) (ABarrow) 7-10-3ow3 AThornton (a bhd) ....9 8 50/1 42 —
339[F] Pusey Street Boy (80) (JRBosley) 9-10-0 ILawrence (prom: hrd rdn & wknd after 5th: t.o fr 3 out) ....dist 9 14/1 — —
(SP 117.4%) 9 Rn

3m 50.4 (10.40) CSF £10.26 CT £37.34 TOTE £2.60: £1.60 £1.60 £1.30 (£4.60) Trio £14.10 OWNER Lady Katharine Phillips (LITTLEHAMPTON) BRED Lavinia Duchess of Norfolk
LONG HANDICAP Tibbs Inn 8-11
WEIGHT FOR AGE 4yo-2lb
473 Amaze stays well and had plenty of use made of him. (2/1: op 7/2)
635[*] Cooley's Valve (IRE) was raised 5lb for winning a weakly-contested event over course and distance. (4/1)
491 Verde Luna was 4lb higher than when winning at Newton Abbot. (6/1)
96 Hamadryad (IRE) only won a seller at Southwell in May, but showed improved form on this debut in handicap company. (14/1)

T/Plpt: £341.60 (32.64 Tckts). T/Qdpt: £15.00 (41.3 Tckts). KH

0600-NEWTON ABBOT (L-H) (Good to firm, Good patches becoming Good)
Sunday September 29th
WEATHER: drizzle

724 PAULINE TRUNDLE NOVICES' CHASE (5-Y.O+) (Class D)
2-30 (2-30) **2m 5f 110y (16 fncs)** £3,940.00 (£1,195.00: £585.00: £280.00) GOING minus 0.24 sec per fur (G)

SP RR SF

102[*] **Imperial Vintage (IRE) (93)** (MissVenetiaWilliams) **6-11-5** NWilliamson (lw: swtg: led 3rd: clr 6th: hit 11th: eased flat) ....— 1 7/2[3] 110+ 33
Lansdowne (PFNicholls) **8-10-12** MAFitzgerald (bit bkwd: mid div: hdwy to chse wnr 10th: wkng whn j.rt last 2) ....13 2 11/8[1] 93 16
He's a King (USA) (CLPopham) **6-10-9**(3) TDascombe (in tch tl wknd 10th) 8 3 6/1 87 10
River Gala (IRE) (68) (RJHodges) **6-10-12** RDunwoody (bit bkwd: led to 3rd: chsd wnr to 10th: grad wknd) 6 4 20/1 83 6
641[6] **King's Shilling (USA) (90)** (HOliver) **9-10-12** JacquiOliver (in tch tl wknd 9th: t.o) ....dist 5 14/1 — —
Pongo Waring (IRE) (MissHCKnight) **7-10-12** JFTitley (bkwd: bhd 5th: mstke & lost tch 7th: t.o whn p.u after next) .... P 100/30[2] — —
(SP 113.1%) 6 Rn

5m 22.1 (5.10) CSF £8.59 TOTE £4.20: £1.80 £1.90 (£3.40) OWNER Mr David Williams (HEREFORD) BRED W. J. Mernagh
OFFICIAL EXPLANATION **Pongo Waring (IRE): was scoped on returning and found to have blood in his lungs.**
102[*] Imperial Vintage (IRE), having his first run for his new stable, put in an almost perfect round of jumping from the front, and can surely follow up on this. (7/2: 2/1-4/1)
Lansdowne is taking time to get the hang of fencing and could never present a challenge to the easy winner. (11/8)
He's a King (USA) showed some encouragement for the future on this chasing debut. (6/1: 4/1-13/2)

725 PARTYFARE LTD (S) H'CAP HURDLE (0-95) (4-Y.O+) (Class G)
3-05 (3-05) **3m 3f (12 hdls)** £1,928.10 (£541.60: £264.30) GOING: 0.04 sec per fur (G)

SP RR SF

Better Bythe Glass (IRE) (95) (NATwiston-Davies) **7-11-11**(3) DWalsh (bit bkwd: a.p: led 9th: rdn & clr last: fin tired) ....— 1 13/8[1] 75 16
357[4] **Gunmaker (77)** (BJLlewellyn) **7-10-10** NWilliamson (lw: hdwy to chse wnr 10th: rdn & ev ch 2 out: no ex appr last) ....2½ 2 10/1 56 —
649[5] **Dragonmist (IRE) (67)** (DBurchell) **6-9-7**(7) MissEJJones (in tch to 10th: lost pl next: sn outpcd) ....8 3 10/1 41 —
605[4] **Storm Drum (91)** (KCBailey) **7-11-10b** TJMurphy (led to 2nd: rdn to ld 7th: hdd 9th: outpcd next) ....16 4 15/2 55 —
601[4] **Prudent Peggy (72)** (RGFrost) **9-10-5**ow4 JFrost (lw: led 2nd: hdd 7th: wknd 10th) ....12 5 7/1[3] 29 —
630[7] **Dane Rose (72)** (MSheppard) **10-10-5** AMaguire (bhd: hdwy fr 8th: chsd ldrs next: wknd 3 out) ....1½ 6 14/1 28 —
587[8] **Auvillar (USA) (78)** (JParfitt) **8-10-11v** CLlewellyn (prom to 7th: sn wknd: t.o) ....16 7 25/1 24 —
415[2] **Fox Chapel (87)** (RTJuckes) **9-11-6** MAFitzgerald (a bhd: wknd 7th: t.o whn p.u bef 2 out) .... P 9/2[2] — —
598[5] **Coeur Battant (FR) (67)** (RJBaker) **6-10-0** BPowell (a bhd: sn wl bhd: t.o whn p.u bef 2 out) .... P 16/1 — —
Merryhill Madam (67) (PBradley) **7-10-0** TEley (in tch to 7th: grad wknd: t.o whn p.u bef 2 out) .... P 20/1 — —
(SP 119.9%) 10 Rn

6m 45.9 (22.90) CSF £17.93 CT £119.52 TOTE £2.70: £1.30 £3.00 £3.70 (£19.00) Trio £153.20 OWNER Mr N. A. Twiston-Davies (CHELTENHAM) BRED Michael Barron
LONG HANDICAP Dragonmist (IRE) 8-12 Coeur Battant (FR) 9-7 Merryhill Madam 9-11
Bt in 3,400 gns
Better Bythe Glass (IRE) bounced back to his form of two seasons ago, despite topweight. His stamina carried the day, as he outstayed his only rival in the final mile, and he should be better for the outing. (13/8: 5/2-6/4)
Gunmaker, the only one to keep the winner company, had shot his bolt two from home. (10/1)
Dragonmist (IRE), 16lb out of the handicap, was never in contention for the main prize, but did well to stay on for the minor placing. (10/1)
415 Fox Chapel (9/2: op 3/1)

726 IN TOUCH RACING LTD H'CAP CHASE (0-100) (5-Y.O+) (Class F)
3-35 (3-36) **3m 2f 110y (20 fncs)** £2,775.00 (£840.00: £410.00: £195.00) GOING minus 0.24 sec per fur (G)

SP RR SF

550[*] **Rainbow Castle (100)** (PFNicholls) **9-12-0** PHide (a in tch: chsd ldr 14th: ev ch 2 out: led appr last: comf) ....— 1 2/1[1] 113+ 46
550[2] **Gilston Lass (89)** (JSKing) **9-11-3** JCulloty (led 2nd: clr 8th: rdn appr 2 out: hdd appr last: no ex) ....3 2 5/2[2] 100 33
631[4] **Manor Bound (76)** (MrsSDWilliams) **6-10-4** RFarrant (a bhd: t.o 8th) ....dist 3 16/1 — —
Its a Snip (91) (CJMann) **11-11-5b** RDunwoody (led to 2nd: chsd ldr tl wknd 14th: t.o) ....14 4 5/1[3] — —
Foxgrove (80) (RJPrice) **10-10-8** BFenton (bit bkwd: a bhd: sme hdwy 10th: sn t.o) ....11 5 10/1 — —
597[3] **Boxing Match (73)** (JMBradley) **9-10-1** NWilliamson (in tch to 14th: grad wknd: t.o) ....dist 6 12/1 — —
658[3] **L'Uomo Piu (77)** (ABarrow) **12-10-5v** BPowell (mid div: rdn 6th: grad wknd: t.o whn p.u after 13th) .... P 16/1 — —
683[P] **Banntown Bill (IRE) (95)** (MCPipe) **7-11-9** DBridgwater (bhd: sn t.o: p.u bef 9th) .... P 14/1 — —

				SP	RR	SF
639^{4}	**San Giorgio (90)** (NATwiston-Davies) **7-11-4b** CLlewellyn (3rd whn slt mstke 3rd: in tch tl wknd 9th: t.o whn p.u bef 16th)		P	7/1	—	—
				(SP 126.3%)	**9 Rn**	

6m 38.6 (4.60) CSF £8.06 CT £60.94 TOTE £2.90: £1.40 £1.50 £3.80 (£3.40) Trio £42.90 OWNER Mr Jeffrey Hordle (SHEPTON MALLET) BRED Michael O'Connor

550* Rainbow Castle repeated the result with the runner-up over course and distance of when they last met three weeks ago. Taking a lead from that rival until three from home, he eased upsides at the next and drew clear for a comfortable success. (2/1)

550 Gilston Lass could not take advantage of an 8lb pull with the winner and once more ran a sound race, but finished behind him yet again. She should find a small race soon. (5/2: op 4/1)

Its a Snip reportedly found the ground too fast here, but the outing served as a valuable prep-race for when he returns to the Czech Republic next month in a bid to win the Velka Pardubicka for the second year in succession. (5/1)

Foxgrove (10/1: 8/1-12/1)

727 LAVIS MEDICAL SYSTEMS NOVICES' HURDLE (4-Y.O+) (Class D)

4-10 (4-10) **2m 6f (10 hdls)** £2,814.00 (£852.00: £416.00: £198.00) GOING: 0.04 sec per fur (G)

				SP	RR	SF
	Hand Woven (118) (NATwiston-Davies) **4-10-10** CLlewellyn (a.p: led 7th: clr 2 out: easily)	—	1	$10/11^{1}$	90+	21
553^{U}	**Kesanta** (WGMTurner) **6-10-0**(7) JPower (bit bkwd: hld up & bhd: stdy hdwy 7th: chsng wnr appr last: no imp)	3½	2	16/1	73	16
	Garrynisk (IRE) (DRGandolfo) **6-10-9**(3) DFortt (bit bkwd: prom: led 4th: hdd 7th: ev ch tl one pce appr 2 out)	2	3	$6/1^{3}$	76	19
630^{2}	**Basil Street (IRE) (98)** (CJMann) **4-10-10** RDunwoody (hdwy & in tch 7th: wknd fr next)	9	4	$3/1^{2}$	70	11
	Kongies Melody (KBishop) **5-10-7** MAFitzgerald (bit bkwd: prom to 4th: wknd 7th: t.o)	dist	5	50/1	—	—
	Dtoto (75) (RJBaker) **4-10-10** BPowell (bit bkwd: mstke 3rd: in tch tl wknd 8th: 4th & btn whn fell last)		F	25/1	—	—
549^{2}	**Idiom (75)** (MrsJGRetter) **9-11-5** JCulloty (lw: in tch tl wknd 8th: t.o whn p.u bef 2 out)		P	$6/1^{3}$	—	—
	Flashmans Mistress (JMBradley) **9-10-7** BFenton (bkwd: led to 2nd: bhd 4th: p.u bef 2 out)		P	66/1	—	—
418^{10}	**Late Encounter** (BJLlewellyn) **5-10-9**(3) GuyLewis (in tch whn rn wd bnd after 2nd: bhd 5th: t.o whn p.u after next)		P	66/1	—	—
	Ballyhays (IRE) (NGAyliffe) **7-10-12** WMcFarland (bit bkwd: led 2nd to 4th: lost tch 6th: p.u bef 8th)		P	66/1	—	—
				(SP 122.1%)	**10 Rn**	

5m 24.1 (12.10) CSF £16.64 TOTE £1.60: £1.20 £2.50 £1.50 (£20.50) Trio £22.50 OWNER Mr Matt Archer & Miss Jean Broadhurst (CHELTENHAM) BRED Waverton Farm (Stow)

WEIGHT FOR AGE 4yo-2lb

Hand Woven completed a double for his stable. He will take a step back up in class next time, as his probable target is the Free Handicap Hurdle at Chepstow next weekend. This run should have blown away the cobwebs. (10/11: 4/6-Evens)

553 Kesanta, a consistent if moderate mare, should go one better before long in this class. (16/1)

Garrynisk (IRE) has won between the Flags in Ireland and is sure to improve for the experience. (6/1: 4/1-7/1)

728 J.C. MILTON ELECTRICALS H'CAP CHASE (0-110) (5-Y.O+) (Class E)

4-45 (4-45) **2m 5f 110y (16 fncs)** £5,451.25 (£1,660.00: £817.50: £396.25) GOING minus 0.24 sec per fur (G)

				SP	RR	SF
547*	**Bit of A Touch (82)** (RGFrost) **10-10-8** JFrost (led to 2nd: prom: led 9th: clr 2 out: comf)	—	1	$7/2^{2}$	93+	19
592^{5}	**Wingspan (USA) (94)** (AGNewcombe) **12-11-6** AThornton (mid div: hdwy 14th: rdn to chse wnr appr 2 out: no imp)	9	2	8/1	98	24
	Northern Optimist (82) (BJLlewellyn) **8-10-8** BPowell (a.p: disp ld 6th: ev ch 14th: rdn & wknd next)	10	3	12/1	79	5
601^{2}	**Fenwick (88)** (RJHodges) **9-10-11**(3) TDascombe (chsd ldrs tl wknd 11th)	20	4	$6/1^{3}$	70	—
597^{P}	**Gabish (74)** (BScriven) **11-9-7**(7) MrRThornton (a bhd: lost tch 10th: t.o)	16	5	40/1	44	—
	Crafty Chaplain (97) (DMcCain) **10-11-9** AMaguire (bkwd: a bhd: lost tch 8th: t.o)	17	6	7/1	54	—
23^{3}	**Charged (97)** (PJHobbs) **7-11-9** RDunwoody (in tch tl wknd 10th: t.o)	¾	7	$7/2^{2}$	54	—
604*	**Herbert Buchanan (IRE) (98)** (PFNicholls) **6-11-10** JCulloty (hld up: hdwy 10th: prom whn fell next)		F	$11/4^{1}$	—	—
604^{5}	**Seal King (83)** (MrsJGRetter) **11-10-9** TJMurphy (led 2nd to 9th: j.slowly 10th: fell next)		F	25/1	—	—
				(SP 123.0%)	**9 Rn**	

5m 23.2 (6.20) CSF £30.76 CT £285.78 TOTE £4.20: £1.60 £2.40 £2.50 (£21.60) Trio £47.80 OWNER A E C Electric Fencing Ltd (Hotline) (BUCKFASTLEIGH) BRED Hesmonds Stud Ltd

LONG HANDICAP Gabish 8-11

547* Bit of A Touch likes this track and followed up his win of three weeks ago over two and a half miles. His only potential rival Herbert Buchanan fell when looking dangerous. (7/2)

592 Wingspan (USA) put up a game display and, despite being rather long in the tooth, should be able to go one better in a similar event for his new stable. (8/1)

Northern Optimist (12/1: op 8/1)

604* Herbert Buchanan (IRE) looked all set to collect here as he had done a fortnight before, but came to grief at the fifth from home. (11/4: 2/1-3/1)

729 DEVON AND CORNWALL BOOKMAKERS H'CAP HURDLE (0-110) (4-Y.O+) (Class E)

5-15 (5-16) **2m 1f (8 hdls)** £2,801.00 (£848.00: £414.00: £197.00) GOING: 0.04 sec per fur (G)

				SP	RR	SF
551^{3}	**Sirtelimar (IRE) (88)** (KCBailey) **7-11-2** TJMurphy (hld up mid div: hdwy to chse ldrs 6th: led appr 2 out: comf)	—	1	$7/4^{1}$	68	—
	Zingibar (76) (JMBradley) **4-10-2** NWilliamson (chsng ldr whn hmpd 5th: lost pl: r.o & ev ch 2 out tl outpcd last)	1	2	9/1	55	—
648^{2}	**Corrin Hill (96)** (RJHodges) **9-11-7**(3) TDascombe (chsd ldrs tl wknd after 6th)	4	3	$3/1^{2}$	71	—
	Tordo (IRE) (94) (CJMann) **5-11-5b**(3) JMagee (bit bkwd: led tl appr 2 out: grad wknd)	2½	4	$3/1^{2}$	67	—
	Lucayan Gold (82) (KBishop) **12-10-10** RDunwoody (a bhd: wknd 5th: t.o)	dist	5	$4/1^{3}$	—	—
648^{W}	**Athenian Alliance (72)** (JMBradley) **7-10-0** BFenton (bit bkwd: a bhd: t.o 4th: p.u bef next)		P	66/1	—	—
				(SP 117.9%)	**6 Rn**	

4m 9.2 (16.20) CSF £16.15 TOTE £2.70: £1.30 £3.30 (£13.00) OWNER Quicksilver Racing Partnership (UPPER LAMBOURN) BRED Kilnamoragh Stud

LONG HANDICAP Athenian Alliance 8-4

WEIGHT FOR AGE 4yo-2lb

551 Sirtelimar (IRE) travelled well throughout the race, but he apparently only just gets home over the minimum trip, so he had to be given some encouragement when joined by the runner-up at the last flight. (7/4)
Zingibar would have presented more of a threat but for some interference four from home. (9/1: 5/1-10/1)
648 Corrin Hill had run his race by the penultimate hurdle. This was probably one of his off-days. (3/1: op 7/4)

T/Plpt: £175.40 (55.27 Tckts). T/Qdpt: £106.20 (4.06 Tckts). T

0642-SEDGEFIELD (L-H) (Good to firm)
Tuesday October 1st
WEATHER: fine

730 STANLEY RACING GOLDEN NUMBERS SERIES NOVICES' HURDLE (4-Y.O+) (Class E)
2-20 (2-20) **2m 5f 110y (10 hdls)** £2,232.50 (£620.00: £297.50) GOING minus 0.78 sec per fur (F)

				SP	RR	SF
586[8]	**Rule Out The Rest** (MrsSarahHorner-Harker) **5-10-12** AThornton (lft in ld appr 4th: hmpd by loose horse appr 2 out: styd on wl)	—	1	12/1[3]	45	6
585[R]	**Tigh-Na-Mara** (JMJefferson) **8-10-7** MDwyer (hld up: stdy hdwy 3 out: sn chsng wnr: rdn 2 out: no imp)	7	2	7/2[2]	35	—
586[10]	**Kanona** (MrsASwinbank) **5-10-12** JSupple (led: hmpd by loose horse & hdd appr 4th: drvn along 4 out: wknd fr next)	22	3	50/1	23	—
693[S]	**Rushen Raider** (KWHogg) **4-10-11** MFoster (j.b: plld hrd: trckd ldrs tl lost pl 6th: t.o 3 out: sn p.u: b.b.v)		P	2/7[1]	—	—
18[7]	**Papa's Boy (IRE) (86)** (HowardJohnson) **5-10-7(5)** STaylor (blnd & uns rdr 1st)		U	16/1	—	—
				(SP 115.5%)		**5 Rn**

4m 59.1 (-0.90) CSF £48.45 TOTE £11.20: £1.90 £1.20 (£16.80) OWNER Mrs Sarah Horner-Harker BRED Roy Edwards
WEIGHT FOR AGE 4yo-1lb
Rule Out The Rest showed the benefit of his initial outing. Making the best of his way home, he always looked in command in what was almost certainly a very poor race. (12/1)
585 Tigh-Na-Mara took a keen grip in last place. Sent in pursuit of the winner three out, she never looked like getting any closer. (7/2)
Kanona, who showed a very poor action going down, was legless three out. (50/1)
693 Rushen Raider, who looked very fit indeed, jumped with no confidence at all. Refusing to settle, he was in trouble a circuit from home. Tailed off three out, he was wisely pulled up. (2/7)

731 SATLEY PUNCH BOWL CLAIMING HURDLE (4-Y.O+) (Class F)
2-50 (2-50) **2m 1f** £2,442.50 (£680.00: £327.50) GOING minus 0.78 sec per fur (F)

				SP	RR	SF
675[7]	**Shuttlecock** (MrsNMacauley) **5-10-11** AMaguire (mde virtually all: styd on appr last: all out)	—	1	13/2	59	16
	Nonios (IRE) (96) (GMMoore) **5-11-12** JCallaghan (trckd ldrs: ev ch 2 out: kpt on same pce appr last)	2½	2	9/2[2]	72	29
463[3]	**Red March Hare (70)** (DMoffatt) **5-10-6** DJMoffatt (hld up: stdy hdwy 3 out: shkn up between last 2: kpt on same pce)	4	3	11/2[3]	48	5
647[5]	**Clover Girl (70)** (BEllison) **5-10-3v(3)** GCahill (effrt 4th: sn prom: one pce fr 2 out)	hd	4	9/1	48	5
684[2]	**Stags Fell (72)** (TAKCuthbert) **11-10-8** CarolCuthbert (sn w ldrs: bmpd 4th: wknd appr 2 out)	15	5	9/1	36	—
	Elltee-Ess (72) (RJWeaver) **11-10-4(7)** CRWeaver (bit bkwd: sn pushed along: bhd fr 4th)	13	6	50/1	26	—
652[2]	**Heresthedeal (IRE) (102)** (GMMcCourt) **7-10-7v(7)** RHobson (j.lft: w ldrs: bmpd 4th: lost pl 3 out)	4	7	5/4[1]	26	—
505[5]	**Candid Lad (78)** (FSStorey) **9-10-5** BStorey (effrt 4th: bhd fr 3 out)	6	8	8/1	11	—
				(SP 124.4%)		**8 Rn**

3m 51.6 (-3.40) CSF £36.05 TOTE £7.60: £2.20 £2.00 £2.00 (£18.70) OWNER Mrs N. Macauley (MELTON MOWBRAY) BRED A. B. Phipps
Shuttlecock, better known as an All-Weather Flat performer, was driven three lengths clear going to the last. That was sufficient to see him home up the hill. (13/2)
Nonios (IRE) moved upsides two out. Tending to hang under pressure, he had to give best going to the final flight. (9/2)
463 Red March Hare, second on the Flat a week ago, was restrained off the pace. Making ground in smooth style three out, she was under pressure between the last two and did no more than keep on at the same pace. (11/2)
647 Clover Girl showed a very poor action going down and was pushed along to improve at halfway. (9/1)
652 Heresthedeal (IRE) consistently lost ground jumping left and collided with Stags Fell at the fourth. Turning in a most disappointing effort, he dropped himself right out three from home. (5/4)

732 LAZENBY AND WILSON H'CAP CHASE (0-115) (5-Y.O+) (Class E)
3-25 (3-25) **2m 5f (16 fncs)** £3,418.00 (£1,024.00: £492.00: £226.00) GOING minus 0.78 sec per fur (F)

				SP	RR	SF
645[P]	**Magic Bloom (100)** (JMJefferson) **10-11-0** RichardGuest (hld up & bhd: hdwy 11th: styd on fr 3 out: led after last: drvn out)	—	1	3/1[2]	109	23
9[5]	**Charming Gale (90)** (MrsSCBradburne) **9-10-4v** AMaguire (j.boldly: led tl after last: no ex)	4	2	9/1	96	10
56[7]	**Cross Cannon (114)** (JWade) **10-12-0** TReed (hld up & bhd: hdwy & wnt prom 7th: hit 11th: sn lost pl: hit 3 out: rallied & prom next: wknd appr last)	13	3	11/2	110	24
683*	**The Blue Boy (IRE) (100)** (PBowen) **8-11-0b** APMcCoy (sn drvn along: chsd ldrs: hit 2nd & 10th: wknd appr 3 out)	10	4	7/2[3]	88	2
597[4]	**Turpin's Green (86)** (JSKing) **13-10-0** JCulloty (sn outpcd & bhd: t.o 9th)	dist	5	16/1	—	—
9*	**Unor (FR) (107)** (PMonteith) **10-11-7** ADobbin (trckd ldrs: wnt prom 8th: hit 4 out: rdn next: 2nd whn p.u lame bef 2 out)		P	9/4[1]	—	—
				(SP 109.3%)		**6 Rn**

5m 6.1 (-4.90) CSF £24.04 TOTE £3.30: £1.20 £4.00 (£19.20) OWNER Mr Peter Nelson (MALTON) BRED J. C. Dimsdale
LONG HANDICAP Turpin's Green 8-13
645 Magic Bloom, happy to sit off the pace in what was a strongly-run race, was brought with a well-timed challenge. (3/1)
9 Charming Gale, under a tremendous attacking ride from Maguire, set a strong pace and jumped boldly but, after getting the last slightly wrong, she then had no answer. (9/1)
Cross Cannon, having his first run for his new trainer, likes to come from off the pace in a strongly-run race. After a couple of errors, he was within reach of the first two two out, but lack of a recent outing then took its toll. (11/2)
683* The Blue Boy (IRE), soon flat out, was outjumped by Charming Gale and called it a day three out. (7/2)
507* Turpin's Green was soon being taken off his legs. (16/1)
9* Unor (FR) came under pressure three out and was second and making no impression when going lame. (9/4)

733 SPITFIRE NOVICES' CHASE (5-Y.O+) (Class E)
3-55 (3-55) **2m 5f (16 fncs)** £2,877.00 (£861.00: £413.00: £189.00) GOING minus 0.78 sec per fur (F)

				SP	RR	SF
179*	**Notable Exception (91)** (MrsMReveley) **7-11-5** PNiven (lw: wnt 2nd & hit 8th: led appr 2 out: drvn out)	—	**1**	11/10 1	99	25
584*	**Val de Rama (IRE)** (DenysSmith) **7-11-5** RichardGuest (a chsng ldrs: styd on one pce fr 2 out)	10	**2**	9/4 2	91	17
532^{P}	**Islandreagh (IRE)** (GRichards) **5-10-5** ADobbin (j.rt: led 3rd: blnd bdly 4 out: hdd appr 2 out: wknd & eased between last 2)	23	**3**	11/2 3	62	—
13^{6}	**Golden Savannah (75)** (MESowersby) **6-10-9**(3) DParker (hit 6th: mstke & reminders 8th: lost tch 11th)	8	**4**	16/1	61	—
584^{3}	**Cardinal Sinner (IRE) (56)** (JWade) **7-10-12** KJones (led to 3rd: blnd 7th: bhd fr 10th)	16	**5**	33/1	49	—
590^{F}	**Rapid Fire (IRE)** (JMJefferson) **8-10-12** MDwyer (hld up: sme hdwy 9th: wknd 11th: bhd whn p.u bef 2 out)		**P**	6/1	—	—

(SP 116.9%) **6 Rn**

5m 7.1 (-3.90) CSF £4.17 TOTE £2.00: £1.80 £2.00 (£2.40) OWNER Mr Roland Hope (SALTBURN) BRED Cliveden Stud
WEIGHT FOR AGE 5yo-2lb

179* Notable Exception, who reserves his best for hurdles round here, is not a natural jumper but he still took this in decisive fashion. (11/10)
584* Val de Rama (IRE) was on the heels of the winner two out, but was readily outpaced on the run-in. (9/4)
532 Islandreagh (IRE), pulled up first time when her saddle slipped, wore a crossed-noseband. Losing ground jumping to the right, she was firmly in command when she jumped badly right and fell through the fourth last. That knocked the stuffing out of her and, tired between the last two, she was then eased. She has time on her side. (11/2)
Golden Savannah was far from foot-perfect and was out of contention from early on the final circuit. (16/1)
584 Cardinal Sinner (IRE), who looked very fit, lost touch a circuit out. (33/1)

734 KIER NORTH EAST H'CAP HURDLE (0-120) (4-Y.O+) (Class D)
4-30 (4-30) **2m 5f 110y** £2,792.50 (£835.00: £400.00: £182.50) GOING minus 0.78 sec per fur (F)

				SP	RR	SF
638^{3}	**Red Valerian (119)** (GMMoore) **5-11-9v**(5) MichaelBrennan (sn trckng ldrs: led 3 out: hit next: pushed out flat)	—	**1**	10/11 1	101	23
	Scarba (95) (JMJefferson) **8-9-11**(7) MNewton (hld up: stdy hdwy 7th: chal 2 out: nt qckn appr last)	3½	**2**	8/1	74	—
182^{2}	**Superhoo (92)** (RCraggs) **5-10-1** BFenton (swtg: trckd ldrs: effrt 3 out: rdn & nt qckn appr last)	1¾	**3**	3/1 2	70	—
703^{3}	**Tough Test (IRE) (101)** (MrsJDGoodfellow) **6-10-7**(3) GCahill (w ldrs: rdn 3 out: one pce fr next)	3	**4**	11/2 3	77	—
695^{4}	**Flintlock (IRE) (91)** (HAlexander) **6-9-9**(5) RMcGrath (trckd ldrs: drvn 8th: kpt on fr 2 out: no imp)	4	**5**	25/1	64	—
690^{5}	**Frontier Flight (USA) (92)** (MissLCSiddall) **6-9-12**(3) EHusband (led to 3 out: wknd between last 2)	1½	**6**	9/1	64	—

(SP 117.7%) **6 Rn**

4m 58.2 (-1.80) CSF £8.71 TOTE £1.90: £1.60 £1.90 (£6.50) OWNER Mrs Alurie O'Sullivan (MIDDLEHAM) BRED Mascalls Stud Farm
LONG HANDICAP Flintlock (IRE) 9-1

638 Red Valerian, much happier back over this longer trip, travelled as sweet as a nut for the boy. Making a mistake two out, he had only to be pushed along to go clear on the run-in. (10/11)
Scarba, in a tongue-strap as usual, was almost upsides two out, but it was clear going to the last that he was second best. (8/1: 5/1-9/1)
182 Superhoo, warm beforehand, stuck on under pressure and seemed to stay the trip alright. (3/1)
703 Tough Test (IRE), 5lb better off with the winner for four lengths two outings ago, was made to look painfully one-paced on this ground. (11/2)
690 Frontier Flight (USA) (9/1: 6/1-10/1)

735 HURRICANE NOVICES' HURDLE (4-Y.O+) (Class E)
5-00 (5-00) **2m 1f** £2,302.50 (£640.00: £307.50) GOING minus 0.78 sec per fur (F)

				SP	RR	SF
647^{2}	**Suas Leat (IRE) (89)** (JMJefferson) **6-10-12**(7) MNewton (led 2nd to 4th: led 2 out: hung lft flat: styd on u.p)	—	**1**	9/4 2	63	9
	Canton Venture (SPCWoods) **4-10-11** PHide (led to 2nd: led 4th to 2 out: styd on same pce flat)	1¼	**2**	1/2 1	55	—
698^{P}	**Court Joker (IRE) (90)** (HAlexander) **4-10-11** PNiven (effrt 3 out: kpt on fr next: nvr nr ldrs)	12	**3**	16/1 3	44	—
634^{6}	**Rose Chime (IRE)** (JLHarris) **4-10-6** PMcLoughlin (chsd ldrs: drvn 5th: one pce fr 3 out)	3	**4**	16/1 3	36	—
	Top Skipper (IRE) (MartynWane) **4-10-11** ASSmith (bit bkwd: bhd fr 3 out)	16	**5**	50/1	26	—
	Salkeld King (IRE) (MABarnes) **4-10-11** PWaggott (chsd ldrs: drvn 3 out: sn lost pl)	3	**6**	50/1	23	—

(SP 113.1%) **6 Rn**

3m 55.0 (0.00) CSF £3.68 TOTE £3.10: £1.50 £1.10 (£1.40) OWNER Mrs J. M. Davenport (MALTON) BRED J. and Mrs Power
WEIGHT FOR AGE 4yo-1lb

647 Suas Leat (IRE) travelled strongly in a race run at a modest pace. On the run-in, with his rider using his whip in his right hand, he hung left but did just enough. He seems to need a left-handed track. (9/4)
Canton Venture, a winner seven times on the Flat this year, was hesitant at some of his hurdles. Within a length of the winner at the last, he could then make no inroads. A stayer on the level, he would have been better served forcing the pace. (1/2)
Court Joker (IRE), pulled up first time, could not live with the first two. (16/1)
490 Rose Chime (IRE), beaten in a seller first time, was flat out early on the final circuit. (16/1)

T/Plpt: £190.00 (65.7 Tckts). T/Qdpt: £7.20 (165.89 Tckts). WG

0594-EXETER (R-H) (Good, Good to firm patches)
Wednesday October 2nd
WEATHER: fine

736 SOUTH WEST RACING CLUB HURDLE (3-Y.O) (Class E)
2-15 (2-15) **2m 1f 110y (8 hdls)** £1,969.40 (£553.40: £270.20) GOING minus 0.40 sec per fur (GF)

				SP	RR	SF
	Doctor Green (FR) (MCPipe) **3-10-10v** APMcCoy (mde all: clr 6th: qcknd appr 2 out: hit last: unchal)	—	**1**	13/8 1	75	27
458*	**Chief Mouse** (MissHCKnight) **3-11-3** JFTitley (lw: hld up mid div: hdwy to chse wnr after 6th: sn hrd rdn: no imp)	12	**2**	13/8 1	71	23
458^{3}	**Andsome Boy** (CRBarwell) **3-10-10** BClifford (bit bkwd: chsd wnr tl mstke 4th: wknd next)	5	**3**	16/1 3	60	12
599^{W}	**Ben Bowden** (MBlanshard) **3-11-3** DGallagher (w ldrs tl wknd fr 5th)	4	**4**	10/1 2	63	15

688³ **Tablets of Stone (IRE)** (JRBosley) **3-10-10** MBosley (a bhd: mstke 3rd: t.o 6th)....dist **5** 10/1 ² — —
Seven Crowns (USA) (CLPopham) **3-10-10** NWilliamson (bit bkwd: a bhd: t.o 6th)....15 **6** 16/1 ³ — —
589⁹ **Still Here (IRE)** (MJHeaton-Ellis) **3-10-10v** AMaguire (hdwy to chse wnr 4th: lost pl after 6th: sn wknd: t.o)....26 **7** 16/1 ³ — —
640ᴾ **Peyton Jones** (ADSmith) **3-10-10** FJousset (bkwd: bhd 3rd: sn t.o)....dist **8** 80/1 — —
(SP 113.3%) **8 Rn**

4m 4.0 (0.00) CSF £4.45 TOTE £3.10: £1.30 £1.20 £1.50 (£2.60) OWNER Mr Jim Weeden (WELLINGTON) BRED The Queen
Doctor Green (FR) started the ball rolling for the Pipe five-timer in fine style, and had disposed of all rivals by the penultimate flight. Bought out of Lord Huntingdon's stable for 21,000 guineas, this Green Desert gelding looks a useful recruit to the team and should follow up on this encouraging debut. (13/8)
458* Chief Mouse, the only one to make a race of it with the winner, was done with by the second last and could find no more. (13/8)
458 Andsome Boy could not reverse the Hereford form with the second, even on 7lb better terms. (16/1)
501 Ben Bowden (10/1: op 5/1)

737 DOMINION OILS NOVICES' (S) HURDLE (4,5,6 & 7-Y.O) (Class G)
2-45 (2-47) **2m 3f (9 hdls)** £1,829.00 (£514.00: £251.00) GOING minus 0.40 sec per fur (GF)

				SP	RR	SF
680³	**Million Dancer (96)** (MCPipe) **4-11-1b**(3) DWalsh (lw: led: sn clr: hit 2 out & last: unchal)	—	1	1/2 ¹	66	28
468⁴	**Cashflow Crisis (IRE) (76)** (JWMullins) **4-11-4** SCurran (a chsng wnr: sme hdwy 6th: nvr able to get on terms)	16	2	11/2 ²	53	15
648⁸	**Lovelark (56)** (RLee) **7-10-7** AMaguire (bhd: mstke 6th: sme hdwy to chse ldrs 2 out: nvr nrr)	16	3	25/1	27	—
	Secret Serenade (RTJuckes) **5-10-12b¹** WMarston (bit bkwd: a mid div: wknd 6th)	3	4	10/1 ³	30	—
655ᴾ	**What's the Joke (60)** (VGGreenway) **7-10-7** CMaude (bit bkwd: a bhd: t.o 5th)	2½	5	33/1	22	—
396ᴾ	**Lilac Rain** (RMStronge) **4-10-6v¹** MAFitzgerald (prom tl wknd 5th: t.o next)	nk	6	50/1	22	—
653⁸	**Lakeside Lad** (DBurchell) **4-10-11** NWilliamson (bit bkwd: kicked at s: ref to r)		R	12/1	—	—
401³	**Siesta Time (USA) (53)** (DBurchell) **6-10-7** DJBurchell (kicked at s: t.n.p)		R	10/1 ³	—	—
504⁷	**Lucky Mo** (BRMillman) **6-10-2**(5) DSalter (unruly s: ref to r)		R	16/1	—	—

(SP 122.6%) **9 Rn**

4m 28.0 (2.00) CSF £4.47 TOTE £1.40: £1.80 £1.20 £2.60 (£2.90) Trio £34.80 OWNER Martin Pipe Racing Club (WELLINGTON) BRED Mrs M. A. Rae Smith
WEIGHT FOR AGE 4yo-1lb
Bt in 4,000 gns
680 Million Dancer, dropped down to selling company, had his task made even easier when three of the opposition decided not to take part. His hurdling was not foot-perfect, but he was still able to cruise home out in front. (1/2)
468 Cashflow Crisis (IRE) put up a fair effort after being dropped back down in distance again, but was never in contention for the main prize. (11/2)

738 DOMINION OILS NOVICES' CHASE (5-Y.O+) (Class E)
3-15 (3-15) **2m 3f (15 fncs)** £2,762.00 (£836.00: £408.00: £194.00) GOING minus 0.73 sec per fur (F)

				SP	RR	SF
724ᴾ	**Pongo Waring (IRE)** (MissHCKnight) **7-10-12** JFTitley (hld up: hdwy 10th: disp ld next: led 12th: hld on strly u.p)	—	1	12/1	84	16
	Hardy Weather (IRE) (DRGandolfo) **7-10-12** RDunwoody (led 6th: hdd briefly 9th: hdd 12th: hrd rdn & no ex fr 2 out)	4	2	4/1 ³	81	13
547³	**Chickabiddy** (GFEdwards) **8-10-7** MAFitzgerald (hld up: hdwy & mstke 9th: lost pl: rallied 13th: nvr nrr)	16	3	100/30 ²	62	—
263²	**Shikaree (IRE) (100)** (MCPipe) **5-10-10** APMcCoy (hld up: hdwy 11th: rdn next: sn outpcd)	12	4	4/5 ¹	56	—
	I Remember You (IRE) (67) (MrsRGHenderson) **6-10-12** JCulloty (led 2nd: hdd 4th: led briefly 9th: in tch tl wknd 11th)	25	5	20/1	36	—
	Coolteen Hero (IRE) (RHAlner) **6-10-12** WMcFarland (bit bkwd: prom & mstke 7th: ev ch tl wknd appr 11th)	¾	6	20/1	35	—
	Karlovac (RLee) **10-10-12** AMaguire (bit bkwd: led to 2nd: in tch to 4th: wknd 9th: t.o)	5	7	33/1	31	—
652⁶	**Saxon Blade** (RMStronge) **8-10-12** LHarvey (led 4th to 6th: wknd after next: t.o)	dist	8	66/1	—	—
	Chukkario (JRBosley) **10-10-12** MBosley (bhd & mstke 8th: sn t.o)	20	9	100/1	—	—
674³	**Ryton Run** (MrsSMOdell) **11-11-2** BFenton (a bhd: t.o 7th: p.u bef last)		P	50/1	—	—

(SP 123.2%) **10 Rn**

4m 38.5 (-1.50) CSF £58.83 TOTE £11.60: £2.20 £1.10 £1.20 (£11.80) Trio £17.80 OWNER Miss H. Knight (WANTAGE) BRED Joseph Smiddy
WEIGHT FOR AGE 5yo-1lb
OFFICIAL EXPLANATION **Pongo Waring (IRE): regarding the apparent improvement in form, the trainer stated that the gelding had been found to have broken a blood-vessel on returning home last time. The Vet suggested running him again quickly as the gelding had not previously bled. The trainer added that the gelding was more relaxed on this occasion, having been too excitable first time.**
Pongo Waring (IRE) broke a blood-vessel four days previously at Newton Abbot and pulled up. After showing little or nothing over fences, he opened his account here in pleasing fashion. (12/1: 8/1-14/1)
Hardy Weather (IRE) put up a game round, jumping well on this chase debut and taking on the winner at every opportunity, but was outstayed by that rival in the closing stages. He should open his account before long at this game. (4/1)
547 Chickabiddy has made a reasonable start to her chasing career, but was not in contention when losing her place after a bad blunder at the ninth. (100/30)
263 Shikaree (IRE) let the Pipe team down in their bid to go through the card with some inconsistent fencing. (4/5)

739 SCUDAMORE CLOTHING 0800 301 301 NOVICES' AMATEUR HURDLE (4-Y.O+) (Class F)
3-45 (3-45) **2m 1f 110y (8 hdls)** £2,051.30 (£576.80: £281.90) GOING minus 0.40 sec per fur (GF)

				SP	RR	SF
675²	**Courbaril (103)** (MCPipe) **4-11-7**(5) MrMRimell (mid div: mstke 5th: hdwy to chse ldr appr 2 out: led appr last: sn clr: easily)	—	1	11/8 ¹	82+	39
139³	**Political Panto (IRE) (105)** (MCPipe) **5-11-7**(5) MrAFarrant (led: sn wl clr: hdd 2 out: lost pl: rallied flat)	9	2	4/1	73	31
	Ritto (JNeville) **6-10-12**(7) MrRThornton (bit bkwd: hdwy to ld 2 out: hdd & wknd qckly)	7	3	7/2 ³	59	17
634⁹	**Highly Charming (IRE) (88)** (MissHCKnight) **4-10-12**(7) MrAWintle (chsd ldr tl wknd appr 2 out)	4	4	14/1	57	14
634³	**Last Laugh (IRE) (79)** (KCBailey) **4-10-7b**(7) MrRWakley (lw: mstkes: chsd ldrs tl bhd 4th)	26	5	100/30 ²	28	—
	Gaelic Million (IRE) (MissHCKnight) **5-10-7**(7) MrTPYoung (bit bkwd: a bhd: t.o 4th)	14	6	33/1	14	—

				SP	RR	SF
156^{P}	**Ardearned** (MrsJAYoung) **9-10-7**(7) MrACharles-Jones (a bhd: t.o 4th: fin lame)	18	**7**	100/1	—	—

(SP 118.0%) **7 Rn**

4m 4.9 (0.90) CSF £7.51 TOTE £2.30: £1.90 £2.40 (£3.20) OWNER Richard Green (Fine Paintings) (WELLINGTON) BRED George & Mrs Steinberg
WEIGHT FOR AGE 4yo-1lb
675 Courbaril followed up on his promising hurdles debut at Huntingdon and found his task an easy one. (11/8)
139 Political Panto (IRE) completed a Pipe one-two in this race, and after making nearly all, he was overtaken by his stable-mate when he lost interest on the home turn, only to rally when it was all too late. (4/1: 2/1-5/1)
Ritto made a useful hurdles debut. (7/2: 6/1-5/2)
Highly Charming (IRE) (14/1: 6/1-16/1)
634 Last Laugh (IRE) (100/30: 9/2-3/1)

740 DOMINION OILS H'CAP CHASE (0-115) (5-Y.O+) (Class E)

4-15 (4-15) **2m 1f 110y (12 fncs)** £2,736.00 (£828.00: £404.00: £192.00) GOING minus 0.73 sec per fur (F)

				SP	RR	SF
595*	**Nordic Valley (IRE) (83)** (MCPipe) **5-10-0** APMcCoy (chsd ldrs: ev ch 9th: chsd ldr 2 out: rdn to ld flat: r.o)	—	**1**	$7/2^{3}$	90	22
592^{3}	**Rex to the Rescue (IRE) (100)** (RHAlner) **8-10-13**(5) PHenley (led: clr tl chal 9th: hld on gamely tl hdd & unable qckn flat)	1¼	**2**	$100/30^{2}$	106	39
	Flapjack Lad (95) (NATwiston-Davies) **7-10-10**(3) DWalsh (lw: mstkes: chsd ldr: mstke 3rd: ev ch whn mstkes 9th & 10th: one pce appr last)	4	**3**	$2/1^{1}$	97	30
136^{P}	**Damas (FR) (110)** (MCPipe) **5-11-13** CMaude (chsd ldrs tl lost pl 5th: t.o 8th)	26	**4**	25/1	88	20
	Lake of Loughrea (IRE) (104) (KCBailey) **6-11-8** TJMurphy (lw: swtg: stdy hdwy 8th: 2nd & ev ch whn fell 10th)		**F**	$7/2^{3}$	—	—
	Dawn Chance (83) (RJHodges) **10-9-12**(3)ow1 TDascombe (fell 1st)		**F**	25/1	—	—
411^{F}	**Tango's Delight (82)** (RJBaker) **8-10-0** BPowell (bhd 3rd: t.o next: p.u bef 5th)		**P**	66/1	—	—

(SP 110.0%) **7 Rn**

4m 10.2 (-5.80) CSF £14.26 TOTE £4.20: £2.10 £2.00 (£8.60) OWNER Pond House Racing (WELLINGTON) BRED David Shubotham
LONG HANDICAP Dawn Chance 9-11 Tango's Delight 9-7
WEIGHT FOR AGE 5yo-1lb
595* Nordic Valley (IRE) had a fight on his hands here with the runner-up, but prevailed in a ding-dong battle to the line. He can complete the hat-trick. (7/2)
592 Rex to the Rescue (IRE) lost no caste in defeat, conceding 18lb to the eventual winner. Jumping boldly throughout, he was only worn down in the final 100 yards. (100/30)
Flapjack Lad has recently risen considerably in the weights and was let down here by some rather sketchy jumping. (2/1)
Lake of Loughrea (IRE) was going as well as any when coming to grief on the final circuit. (7/2)

741 DOMINION OILS H'CAP HURDLE (0-120) (4-Y.O+) (Class D)

4-45 (4-45) **2m 3f (9 hdls)** £2,792.20 (£784.20: £382.60) GOING minus 0.40 sec per fur (GF)

				SP	RR	SF
596*	**Out Ranking (FR) (109)** (MCPipe) **4-11-12** CMaude (lw: a.p: led 5th: styd on wl fr 2 out)	—	**1**	$6/1^{2}$	93	48
596^{3}	**Little Hooligan (82)** (GFEdwards) **5-10-0b** AMaguire (hld up & bhd: hdwy 5th: lost pl: rallied appr 2 out: nrst fin)	2	**2**	$7/1^{3}$	64	20
	Fleur de Tal (99) (WGMTurner) **5-10-10**(7) JPower (bit bkwd: a.p: chsd wnr 6th: in tch 2 out: wknd appr last)	1¾	**3**	20/1	80	36
	Morstock (110) (RJHodges) **6-12-0** MrMRimell (chsd ldrs tl one pce fr 7th)	15	**4**	12/1	78	34
651^{3}	**Prerogative (106)** (HSHowe) **6-11-10v** RDunwoody (led to 5th: wknd qckly 7th)	6	**5**	14/1	69	25
539*	**Born to Please (IRE) (90)** (PJHobbs) **4-10-7** APMcCoy (bhd: hdwy 5th: wknd 7th)	3	**6**	$6/1^{2}$	51	6
635^{2}	**Ikhtiraa (USA) (82)** (RJO'Sullivan) **6-10-0** PHolley (chsd ldr: ev ch appr 5th: wknd fr next)	8	**7**	14/1	36	—
	Lessons Lass (IRE) (102) (MissHCKnight) **4-11-5** JCulloty (bkwd: chsd ldrs tl rdn & wknd appr 2 out)	15	**8**	$5/2^{1}$	43	—
	Dominion's Dream (107) (MCPipe) **4-11-3v**(7) GSupple (a bhd: t.o 7th)	7	**9**	25/1	42	—
497^{4}	**Lancer (USA) (86)** (RTJuckes) **4-10-3** WMarston (a bhd: t.o 5th)	13	**10**	20/1	10	—
551^{F}	**Gold Medal (FR) (105)** (MCPipe) **8-11-2**(7) BMoore (bkwd: bhd fr 5th: sn t.o)	dist	**11**	14/1	—	—
684^{P}	**Buglet (92)** (MCPipe) **6-10-7**(3) DWalsh (nvr gng wl: rdn 2nd: bhd & p.u bef 4th)		**P**	16/1	—	—

(SP 116.6%) **12 Rn**

4m 24.7 (-1.30) CSF £43.36 CT £720.85 TOTE £6.10: £4.50 £2.20 £4.90 (£23.30) Trio £196.80; £166.39 to Newmarket 3/10/96 OWNER Knight Hawks Partnership (WELLINGTON) BRED Jacques Beres
WEIGHT FOR AGE 4yo-1lb
596* Out Ranking (FR) was 8lb higher than when winning here three weeks ago, but this did not deter her as she stayed on strongly over the last two, seeming to relish the extra couple of furlongs. (6/1: 4/1-7/1)
596 Little Hooligan again finished behind the winner but was making up ground nearing the line. He is slipping down the weights slowly and his turn cannot be far away. (7/1)
Fleur de Tal should be better for the run. (20/1)
Lessons Lass (IRE) was disappointing on this seasonal debut but should make amends soon. (5/2)
Gold Medal (FR) (14/1: op 8/1)

T/Plpt: £21.10 (483.3 Tckts). T/Qdpt: £12.00 (31.12 Tckts) T

0687-MARKET RASEN (R-H) (Good, Good to firm patches)

Thursday October 3rd

WEATHER: overcast WIND: strong

742 BURLEY FUEL EFFECT CONDITIONAL H'CAP CHASE (0-130) (5-Y.O+) (Class E)

2-10 (2-13) **2m 1f 110y (12 fncs)** £3,347.00 (£1,016.00: £498.00: £239.00) GOING minus 0.14 sec per fur (G)

				SP	RR	SF
633*	**Captain Khedive (130)** (PFNicholls) **8-12-0** GuyLewis (hld up: led 3 out: v.easily)	—	**1**	$2/5^{1}$	119+	30
722^{2}	**The Yokel (102)** (BPJBaugh) **10-10-0** PHenley (trckd ldrs: led 6th to 7th: 3rd & prom whn blnd 3 out: kpt on: no ch w wnr)	3½	**2**	$16/1^{3}$	88	—

				SP	RR	SF
475[2]	**Circulation (102)** (DMcCain) **10-10-0v[1]** DWalsh (mstkes: led & sn clr: stumbled & hdd 6th: led next: hit 8th & 9th: hdd 3 out: 3rd & wkng whn blnd 2 out)	13	**3**	25/1	76	—
56[5]	**Bally Parson (115)** (RDickin) **10-10-13** JCulloty (bit bkwd: mstkes: chsd ldrs: blnd 2nd: wknd 4 out)	18	**4**	9/4[2]	73	—
				(SP 111.9%)		**4 Rn**

4m 23.6 (8.60) CSF £5.98 TOTE £1.50 (£4.20) OWNER Khedive Partnership (SHEPTON MALLET) BRED Mrs Audrey Goodwin
LONG HANDICAP The Yokel 7-10 Circulation 7-5
633* Captain Khedive was one of only two carrying their correct weight and, with Bally Parson in need of the outing and running badly, he had only to turn in an exhibition round. (2/5: 1/3-1/2)
722 The Yokel, 32lb wrong at the weights, was in third and handy but under strong pressure when he blundered three out. (16/1)
475 Circulation, an incredible 37lb wrong at the weights, was also guilty of making serious jumping errors and was third and on the retreat when he fell through the second last. (25/1)
Bally Parson, absent for over three months, looked in need of the outing. He was badly let down by his jumping and lost touch four out. (9/4)

743 BURLEY BUTLER HEATED TROLLY NOVICES' HURDLE (4-Y.O+) (Class E)

2-45 (2-46) **2m 1f 110y (8 hdls)** £2,388.00 (£668.00: £324.00) GOING minus 0.14 sec per fur (G)

				SP	RR	SF
	Mister Rm (NATwiston-Davies) **4-10-11** CLlewellyn (nt j.w: mde all: sn clr: mstke 5th: unchal)	—	**1**	6/4[2]	75+	—
675[3]	**Nashaat (USA)** (MCChapman) **8-10-12** WWorthington (swtg: chsd ldrs: lft mod 2nd 2 out)	16	**2**	15/2[3]	60	—
	Java Red (IRE) (JGFitzGerald) **4-10-11** MDwyer (chsd ldrs tl wknd appr 2 out)	½	**3**	8/1	60	—
687[5]	**Irie Mon (IRE) (79)** (MPBielby) **4-10-11**(7) MrAWintle (hld up & bhd: sme hdwy appr 2 out: nvr nr ldrs)	8	**4**	20/1	60	—
497[7]	**Mellow Yellow** (JMackie) **5-10-9**(3) EHusband (chsd ldrs tl wknd after 3 out)	1¾	**5**	33/1	51	—
698[F]	**Flyaway Blues** (MrsMReveley) **4-10-11** PNiven (a bhd)	7	**6**	14/1	45	—
	Suvalu (USA) (MGMeagher) **4-10-11** LWyer (hld up & plld hrd: a bhd)	14	**7**	14/1	32	—
593*	**Anabranch (100)** (JMJefferson) **5-10-7**(7) MNewton (lw: hld up: hdwy 4th: 6l 2nd & rdn whn fell 2 out)		**F**	5/4[1]	—	—
	Fiery Footsteps (SWCampion) **4-10-6** JCulloty (sn bhd: t.o whn p.u bef 2 out)		**P**	50/1	—	—
687[7]	**Kajostar (52)** (SWCampion) **6-10-0**(7) OBurrows (bhd whn sddle slipped & p.u after 1st)		**P**	100/1	—	—
	Ballysokerry (IRE) (JParkes) **5-10-12** ADobbin (sn bhd: mstke 3rd: t.o whn rn out 5th)		**R**	66/1	—	—
				(SP 132.8%)		**11 Rn**

4m 15.6 (12.60) CSF £15.10 TOTE £2.70: £1.60 £1.70 £1.70 (£12.60) Trio £13.10 OWNER Mr F. J. Mills (CHELTENHAM) BRED Major and Mrs R. B. Kennard
WEIGHT FOR AGE 4yo-1lb
Mister Rm, a winner twice on the All-Weather at up to a mile this year, is not a natural jumper but his hurdling improved as the race progressed, and he was already well in command when left clear when the favourite fell at the penultimate flight. This will have set him off on the right road. (6/4)
675 Nashaat (USA), awash with sweat beforehand, was left in second place two out but, with his stamina giving out, only just held on for the runner-up spot. (15/2: 6/1-4/1)
Java Red (IRE) faded going to two out but, in the end, was only just denied second. (8/1)
687 Irie Mon (IRE) wore a tongue-strap as usual. After running badly on his last two starts, he was never a factor. (20/1)
593* Anabranch, given a patient ride, went in pursuit of the winner going to two out. She was under pressure and making no impression when she fell heavily at that flight. (5/4: Evens-6/4)

744 BURLEY VISIFLAME NOVICES' CHASE (5-Y.O+) (Class C)

3-15 (3-16) **2m 1f 110y (12 fncs)** £4,394.75 (£1,328.00: £646.50: £305.75) GOING minus 0.14 sec per fur (G)

				SP	RR	SF
	Jathib (CAN) (MrsMerritaJones) **5-10-11** DerekByrne (swtg: trckd ldr: led 9th: clr next: unchal)	—	**1**	5/2[2]	114	23
674*	**Strong Promise (IRE)** (GAHubbard) **5-10-13**(3) KGaule (lw: hld up: wnt mod 2nd 4 out: no imp)	27	**2**	4/9[1]	94	3
684[5]	**Sharp Sensation** (DWBarker) **6-10-12** PNiven (hld up: blnd 8th: styd on fr 3 out: n.d)	13	**3**	12/1[3]	77	—
673[3]	**Record Lover (IRE) (69)** (MCChapman) **6-10-12** WWorthington (bhd: wnt poor 3rd 3 out: one pce)	2½	**4**	33/1	75	—
531[5]	**Doctor-J (IRE)** (JWhite) **6-10-12** BFenton (bhd fr 6th: t.o 4 out)	18	**5**	50/1	59	—
674[2]	**Shalik (IRE)** (JRJenkins) **6-10-5**(7) NTEgan (plld hrd: mstkes: led: blnd 2nd & 8th: hdd 9th: wknd 4 out)	17	**6**	25/1	43	—
				(SP 114.2%)		**6 Rn**

4m 21.4 (6.40) CSF £3.97 TOTE £2.40: £1.80 £1.10 (£2.10) OWNER Crown Pkg & Mailing Svs Ltd (LAMBOURN) BRED Hill 'N Dale Farms
WEIGHT FOR AGE 5yo-1lb
OFFICIAL EXPLANATION **Strong Promise (IRE): the rider reported that the gelding did not move as well as he had on his previous run, felt wrong behind and gurgled in the later stages.**
Jathib (CAN), who showed useful and progressive form over long distances over hurdles last year, jumped quickly and boldly. Out on his own on the home turn, he was never in danger. This was a most encouraging start to his chasing career. (5/2)
674* Strong Promise (IRE), on his toes beforehand, was ridden with plenty of confidence but, over a trip short of his best, it proved misplaced. Moving up to show second four out, he was never going to get anywhere near the winner. He will need further than two miles. (4/9)
Sharp Sensation almost fell at the eighth. Given time to regain his confidence, connections will have taken encouragement from this debut over fences. (12/1)
674 Shalik (IRE) was very edgy in the paddock and, racing with his tongue tied down, set off like a five-furlong sprinter. Showing his fences no respect at all, he was out on his feet four from home. (25/1)

745 AIR PRODUCTS GASES H'CAP HURDLE (0-135) (4-Y.O+) (Class C)

3-50 (3-50) **2m 1f 110y (8 hdls)** £3,355.00 (£1,015.00: £495.00: £235.00) GOING minus 0.14 sec per fur (G)

				SP	RR	SF
62[4]	**Non Vintage (IRE) (130)** (MCChapman) **5-12-0** WWorthington (hdwy u.p 3 out: led last: drvn clr)	—	**1**	11/2	107	22
643*	**Field of Vision (IRE) (102)** (MrsASwinbank) **6-10-0** JSupple (lw: nt j.w: chsd ldrs: drvn 5th: led 2 out to last: nt qckn)	3	**2**	3/1[3]	76	—
538[3]	**Eden Dancer (108)** (MrsMReveley) **4-10-5** PNiven (lw: led to 2 out: rdn & one pce appr last)	3½	**3**	5/2[2]	79	—
	Distant Echo (IRE) (118) (RTPhillips) **6-11-2** RDunwoody (bit bkwd: drvn along & lost pl 5th: sn bhd)	18	**4**	7/4[1]	73	—
	Devilry (107) (RCraggs) **6-10-5b** BFenton (disp ld tl wknd after 3 out: sn bhd)	¾	**5**	12/1	61	—
				(SP 113.0%)		**5 Rn**

4m 12.9 (9.90) CSF £20.59 TOTE £5.60: £2.30 £2.30 (£5.50) OWNER Mr Alan Mann (MARKET RASEN) BRED Leon O'Coileain
LONG HANDICAP Field of Vision (IRE) 9-11
WEIGHT FOR AGE 4yo-1lb
OFFICIAL EXPLANATION **Distant Echo: lost both his front plates.**

62 Non Vintage (IRE), third in both the Tote Gold Trophy and County Hurdle last season, has been out of form of late on the Flat. Suited by the strong pace, he was persuaded to land in front at the last and soon had his race won. (11/2)
643* Field of Vision (IRE), stepping up from novice company and 3lb out of the handicap, did not jump well against these more experienced opponents. Under pressure some way from home, he showed in front two out, but had to admit best after making a slight error at the final flight. (3/1)
538 Eden Dancer, a free-running sort, did not find much under pressure. (5/2)
Distant Echo (IRE), having his first run for his new stable, started favourite, despite looking very burly. Under pressure soon after halfway, he seemed to take little interest. It transpired that he had lost both front shoes. (7/4)

746 BURLEY FORGE RANGE NOVICES' H'CAP CHASE (0-110) (5-Y.O+) (Class D)

4-25 (4-25) **3m 1f (19 fncs)** £3,779.00 (£1,142.00: £556.00: £263.00) GOING minus 0.14 sec per fur (G)

	Horse	Dist	Pos	SP	RR	SF
644*	**The Gallopin'major (IRE) (84)** (MrsMReveley) **6-11-10** NSmith (lw: hld up: hit 14th & 15th: chal 2 out: styd on u.p to ld flat)	—	**1**	13/8 1	87	41
	Mobile Messenger (NZ) (80) (TRGeorge) **8-11-6** MAFitzgerald (w ldrs: led 12th: rdn 4 out: hdd & nt qckn flat)	2	**2**	3/1 3	82	36
	Camp Bank (81) (NATwiston-Davies) **6-11-7** CLlewellyn (trckd ldrs: effrt 15th: styd on same pce fr 3 out)	3½	**3**	9/4 2	81?	35
	Final Beat (IRE) (82) (JWCurtis) **7-11-8** AThornton (mde most to 12th: rdn & outpcd whn mstke 3 out: kpt on)	2½	**4**	9/2	80?	34
	Auntie Lorna (60) (NJPomfret) **7-9-7**(7) MrRWakley (bit bkwd: swtg: plld hrd: w ldrs: mstke 11th: bhd fr 13th: t.o whn p.u bef 4 out)		**P**	33/1	—	—
				(SP 115.0%)		**5 Rn**

6m 18.0 (7.00) CSF £6.86 TOTE £2.60: £1.10 £1.80 (£5.10) OWNER Mr R. W. S. Jevon (SALTBURN) BRED Mrs A. Doyle
644* The Gallopin'major (IRE) is much improved of late. His rider sat tight when he made two jumping errors on the final circuit, and persuaded him to do enough to show ahead on the run-in. (13/8)
Mobile Messenger (NZ) was placed six times over fences last season, and his lack of a finishing kick was obvious here. (3/1)
Camp Bank, tailed off when he last ran over hurdles at Nottingham in January, jumped soundly on this chasing debut. Hard at work five out, he stayed on under pressure and can do better. (9/4)
Final Beat (IRE), placed four times over fences last season, looks painfully one-paced. (9/2: 3/1-5/1)

747 BURLEY ELECTRIC FIRE H'CAP HURDLE (0-130) (4-Y.O+) (Class C)

5-00 (5-00) **3m (12 hdls)** £3,371.25 (£1,020.00: £497.50: £236.25) GOING minus 0.14 sec per fur (G)

	Horse	Dist	Pos	SP	RR	SF
721*	**Freddie Muck (111)** (NATwiston-Davies) **6-11-2** 6x CLlewellyn (trckd ldrs: pushed along 4 out: n.m.r on ins appr 2 out: qcknd to ld 2 out: sn clr: eased flat)	—	**1**	10/11 1	98+	—
	Jalcanto (121) (MrsMReveley) **6-11-12** PNiven (mstkes: w ldrs: rdn & outpcd whn hit 2 out: kpt on appr last: no ch w wnr)	13	**2**	3/1 2	99?	—
690 2	**Ordog Mor (IRE) (105)** (MGMeagher) **7-10-10** DerekByrne (hld up: hdwy to ld after 7th: hdd 2 out: wknd appr last)	3½	**3**	3/1 2	81	—
	Master of the Rock (110) (JMackie) **7-10-12v**(3) EHusband (led tl after 7th: sn drvn along: wknd qckly 9th: sn t.o)	22	**4**	8/1 3	71	—
				(SP 113.5%)		**4 Rn**

6m 1.1 (22.10) CSF £4.02 TOTE £1.50 (£2.90) OWNER Mrs C. Twiston-Davies (CHELTENHAM) BRED N. A. Twiston-Davies
721* Freddie Muck, making a quick reappearance, had to be pushed along to go about his job halfway down the back straight. Squeezing through on the inner, he won in fine style in the end. He is due to go up significantly in the weights after his six-length win at Worcester. (10/11)
Jalcanto, winner of a seller on the Flat at Beverley in August, made numerous jumping errors. Struggling to keep up when hitting two out, he kept on going to the last, but had no chance with the winner. He does not seem to be as good as he was a juvenile. (3/1)
690 Ordog Mor (IRE), dropped out at the start, moved up sharply to lead going out onto the second circuit, but his stamina seemed to give out completely between the last two. (3/1)
Master of the Rock, who won his last four outings last season, was having his first run since January. Despite looking pretty straight, he dropped out early on the final circuit. (8/1: op 5/1)

T/Plpt: £28.00 (266.63 Tckts). T/Qdpt: £7.80 (50.43 Tckts). WG

TAUNTON (R-H) (Hard)

Thursday October 3rd

Race 3: One fence omitted. Race 4: One flight omitted.
WEATHER: unsettled

748 NORMAN READING MEMORIAL MAIDEN HURDLE (4-Y.O+) (Class E)

1-50 (1-50) **2m 3f 110y (10 hdls)** £2,295.00 (£645.00: £315.00) GOING minus 1.09 sec per fur (HD)

	Horse	Dist	Pos	SP	RR	SF
723 7	**Swings'N'Things (USA) (93)** (BPalling) **4-10-13** RFarrant (hld up: hdwy 3 out: led last: rdn out)	—	**1**	6/1 3	63	—
603 3	**Second Colours (USA)** (MCPipe) **6-11-5** APMcCoy (chsd ldr: mstke 3rd: hit 6th: sn rdn: led & hit 2 out: hdd last: unable qckn)	1½	**2**	7/2 2	67	—
	General Mouktar (MCPipe) **6-11-5b** CMaude (lw: led: wl clr 4th: hit 3 out: hdd 2 out: sn btn)	4	**3**	1/2 1	64	—
	Reine de La Chasse (FR) (83) (RJO'Sullivan) **4-10-13** AMcCabe (a bhd: t.o fr 3 out)	dist	**4**	14/1	—	—
				(SP 109.8%)		**4 Rn**

4m 27.8 (-3.20) CSF £22.20 TOTE £7.00 (£4.80) OWNER Mr D. Brennan (COWBRIDGE)
WEIGHT FOR AGE 4yo-1lb
Swings'N'Things (USA), a maiden on the Flat in Ireland for Dermot Weld, had finished third in a handicap hurdle at Tramore in August. This race was much weaker than the one she ran in at Worcester. (6/1: 9/2-8/1)
603 Second Colours (USA) was very novicey at his hurdles. (7/2: op 2/1)
General Mouktar, fit from the Flat, was blinkered for the first time over timber, and has never been one to find a lot under pressure. (1/2: 8/1-4/5)
Reine de La Chasse (FR) (14/1: op 8/1)

749 TAUNTON CASTLE (S) HURDLE (4-Y.O+) (Class G)

2-20 (2-20) **2m 1f (9 hdls)** £2,005.40 (£564.40: £276.20) GOING minus 1.09 sec per fur (HD)

Form	Horse	Dist	Pos	SP	RR	SF
603^{4}	**Almapa** (RJHodges) **4-10-11** PHolley (hld up: wnt 2nd 3 out: led last: drvn out)	—	**1**	4/1^{2}	63	23
408^{2}	**Fleet Cadet** (MCPipe) **5-10-12b** CMaude (hld up & bhd: hdwy 3 out: ev ch last: hrd rdn: one pce)	4	**2**	3/1^{1}	59	20
697^{4}	**Hacketts Cross (IRE) (95)** (PEccles) **8-11-12**(7) MrRThornton (hld up & bhd: hdwy 3 out: one pce fr 2 out)	1½	**3**	5/1	79	40
675^{11}	**Ferens Hall (53)** (MJRoberts) **9-10-12** PMcLoughlin (led 2nd: hdd & hmpd last: wknd)	3½	**4**	14/1	55	16
600^{3}	**Prestige Lady** (BSmart) **5-10-7** WMarston (nt j.w: hdwy appr 2 out: 5th & btn whn blnd last)	4	**5**	9/2^{3}	46	7
596^{5}	**Night Time (78)** (FJordan) **4-10-11**(7) MrGShenkin (nvr nr to chal)	5	**6**	14/1	53	13
600^{6}	**Burnt Sienna (IRE) (80)** (JSMoore) **4-10-13v** WMcFarland (led to 2nd: 2nd whn blnd 3 out: wknd 2 out)	hd	**7**	8/1	48	8
600^{5}	**Java Shrine (USA) (75)** (JCTuck) **5-11-5b** RBellamy (nvr nr ldrs)	1¾	**8**	20/1	51	12
655^{5}	**On the Ledge (USA) (50)** (HJManners) **6-10-5b^{1}**(7) ADowling (prom tl wknd 6th: t.o)	dist	**9**	66/1	—	—
	Old Master (IRE) (RJBaker) **5-10-12** BPowell (a bhd: t.o fr 6th)	10	**10**	50/1	—	—
634^{P}	**Flashing Sabre** (HJManners) **4-10-11** MrACharles-Jones (a bhd: t.o)	dist	**11**	100/1	—	—
357^{5}	**Indian Minor (60)** (REPocock) **12-10-12** NWilliamson (prom: mstkes 4th & 6th: wknd & p.u after 3 out: lame)		**P**	25/1	—	—

(SP 117.3%) **12 Rn**

3m 42.5 (-10.50) CSF £15.38 TOTE £4.50: £1.20 £1.70 £2.00 (£6.70) Trio £10.80 OWNER Mr P. Slade (SOMERTON) BRED Miss M. Carrington-Smith
WEIGHT FOR AGE 4yo-1lb
No bid

603 Almapa, dropped in class, had finished three and a half lengths behind the runner-up in August at Exeter on 5lb worse terms. (4/1)
408 Fleet Cadet could not confirm the Exeter form with the winner, despite being 5lb better off. (3/1)
697 Hacketts Cross (IRE) found the weight concession too much from the penultimate hurdle. (5/1)
Ferens Hall was nibbled at in the Ring and gave his supporters a decent run for their money. (14/1: op 25/1)

750 CURLAND H'CAP CHASE (0-125) (5-Y.O+) (Class D)

2-55 (2-55) **2m 3f (14 fncs)** £3,772.50 (£1,060.00: £517.50) GOING minus 1.09 sec per fur (HD)

Form	Horse	Dist	Pos	SP	RR	SF
676*	**Ramstar (103)** (PJHobbs) **8-11-10** APMcCoy (led 3rd tl mstke 6th: hit 9th: rdn 4 out: rallied to ld nr fin)	—	**1**	2/1^{2}	93	9
648^{9}	**Slippery Max (79)** (RTJuckes) **12-10-0** WMarston (led to 3rd: rdn 11th: outpcd appr 2 out: rallied flat)	hd	**2**	10/1	69	—
728^{5}	**Gabish (79)** (BScriven) **11-9-7**(7) MrRThornton (hld up: led 6th: hrd rdn & hdd nr fin)	1	**3**	20/1	68	—
	Powder Boy (97) (RJHodges) **11-11-4** BPowell (hld up: 3rd whn p.u lame bef 10th)		**P**	9/2^{3}	—	—
604^{3}	**Clear Idea (IRE) (94)** (RGFrost) **8-11-1** JFrost (hld up: blnd & uns rdr 5th: dead)		**U**	6/5^{1}	—	—

(SP 110.8%) **5 Rn**

4m 38.3 (-3.70) CSF £16.83 TOTE £2.00: £1.40 £3.40 (£8.60) OWNER Mr A. Loze (MINEHEAD) BRED Miss M. Benson
LONG HANDICAP Gabish 8-6 Slippery Max 9-11

676* Ramstar, upped 4lb, was all out to win another uncompetitive race. (2/1)
413 Slippery Max was 3lb out of the handicap for this return to fences, but probably would have pulled it out of the fire in another few yards. (10/1)
Gabish, despite his rider's allowance, was still carrying 15lb more than her long-handicap mark, but only got worn down in the shadow of the post. (20/1)
604 Clear Idea (IRE) was unfortunately fatally injured at the first fence in the home straight of the first circuit. (6/5)

751 SUMMERFIELD H'CAP HURDLE (0-115) (4-Y.O+) (Class E)

3-25 (3-26) **2m 1f (7 hdls)** £2,253.00 (£633.00: £309.00) GOING minus 1.09 sec per fur (HD)

Form	Horse	Dist	Pos	SP	RR	SF
	Indian Jockey (114) (MCPipe) **4-12-0** APMcCoy (lw: mde all: reminders appr 5th: clr appr 2 out: r.o wl)	—	**1**	7/4^{1}	99	52
552^{3}	**Safety (USA) (90)** (JWhite) **9-10-5b** AMaguire (chsd wnr: slipped bnd appr 4th: no imp appr 2 out)	2½	**2**	14/1	73	27
729^{3}	**Corrin Hill (96)** (RJHodges) **9-10-4**(7) JHarris (lw: hld up: mstke 4th: sn rdn: no hdwy fr 6th)	7	**3**	7/2^{2}	72	26
729*	**Sirtelimar (IRE) (95)** (KCBailey) **7-10-10** 7x TJMurphy (hld up: hdwy 5th: hrd rdn appr 2 out: 3rd & btn whn blnd last: eased)	8	**4**	4/1^{3}	64	18
	Harlequin Walk (IRE) (88) (RJO'Sullivan) **5-10-3b** PHolley (hld up: hmpd 2nd: wknd appr 2 out: mstke last)	9	**5**	5/1	48	2
638^{6}	**Have a Nightcap (99)** (NPLittmoden) **7-11-0v** BPowell (fell 2nd)		**F**	9/1	—	—

(SP 111.9%) **6 Rn**

3m 39.5 (-13.50) CSF £20.46 TOTE £2.20: £1.50 £2.10 (£7.70) OWNER Mr Stuart Mercer (WELLINGTON) BRED John Hayter
WEIGHT FOR AGE 4yo-1lb
STEWARDS' ENQUIRY Murphy susp. 12 & 14-16/10/96 (excessive use of whip).

Indian Jockey likes fast ground and made a successful transition to handicap company. (7/4)
552 Safety (USA) was unable to adopt his favoured front-running tactics. (14/1)
729 Corrin Hill was going right-handed this time, but was 4lb higher than the highest mark off which he has won. (7/2)
729* Sirtelimar (IRE) could not defy a penalty and his rider picked up a four-day whip-ban. (4/1)

752 THURLBEAR NOVICES' H'CAP CHASE (0-95) (5-Y.O+) (Class F)

4-00 (4-00) **2m 3f (15 fncs)** £3,049.20 (£748.80) GOING minus 1.09 sec per fur (HD)

Form	Horse	Dist	Pos	SP	RR	SF
602^{3}	**Blue Raven (83)** (DavidBrace) **5-11-10** AMaguire (led 3rd: j.slowly 10th: lft clr 3 out)	—	**1**	5/2^{2}	93	—
477^{3}	**Telmar Systems (64)** (JWhite) **7-10-6** SCurran (led: j.slowly 2nd: hdd 3rd: hit 6th: wknd 11th: lft poor 2nd 3 out)	14	**2**	9/1^{3}	62	—
597^{5}	**Miners Rest (76)** (PJHobbs) **8-11-4** APMcCoy (fell 2nd)		**F**	6/4^{1}	—	—
724^{4}	**River Gala (IRE) (68)** (RJHodges) **6-10-10** PHolley (hld up: wnt 2nd 8th: jnd wnr 10th: ev ch whn stumbled & uns rdr 3 out)		**U**	5/2^{2}	—	—

(SP 107.1%) **4 Rn**

4m 46.7 (4.70) CSF £16.02 TOTE £3.80 (£5.40) OWNER Mr David Brace BRED Mrs Pauline A. Hemmings
WEIGHT FOR AGE 5yo-1lb

602 Blue Raven had his task made easier by first the early departure of the favourite and then the demise of River Gala three out. He was dismounted after the finish after pulling up feelingly. (5/2)
477 Telmar Systems was fortunate to go home with second prize. (9/1)
597 Miners Rest got no further than the first ditch. (6/4)
River Gala (IRE) was making a good race of it when exiting three from home. (5/2)

753 WIVELISCOMBE HURDLE (3-Y.O) (Class E)

4-35 (4-35) **2m 1f (9 hdls)** £2,295.00 (£645.00: £315.00) GOING minus 1.09 sec per fur (HD)

	Horse	Dist	Pos	SP	RR	SF
	Cointosser (IRE) (MCPipe) **3-10-5** SWynne (hld up: hdwy appr 2 out: qcknd to ld flat: comf)	—	1	4/6[1]	64+	—
	Indira (PGMurphy) **3-10-5** WMcFarland (led tl flat)	2½	2	3/1[2]	62	—
688[15]	**Ghostly Apparition** (JohnUpson) **3-10-10** RSupple (chsd ldr tl appr 2 out: wknd appr last)	11	3	50/1	56	—
	Colebrook Willie (JRBosley) **3-10-10** MBosley (lw: prom: reminder appr 3 out: wknd appr 2 out: btn whn hit last)	5	4	50/1	52	—
	Trianna (RBrotherton) **3-10-5** LHarvey (lw: prom tl wknd qckly 3 out)	16	5	12/1	32	—
640[4]	**Song For Jess (IRE)** (FJordan) **3-10-0**(7)ow2 MrGShenkin (lw: nt j.w: plld hrd: bhd fr 5th: t.o whn p.u bef 2 out)		P	7/1[3]	—	—
458[5]	**My Beautiful Dream** (ADSmith) **3-10-5** FJousset (wl bhd fr 6th: p.u lame flat)		P	66/1	—	—
				(SP 110.6%)		**7 Rn**

3m 56.1 (3.10) CSF £2.95 TOTE £1.90: £1.40 £2.00 (£2.00) OWNER David Manning Associates (WELLINGTON) BRED Mellon Stud

Cointosser (IRE), four times a winner on the Flat this summer, was confidently ridden and came through to do the business in good style. (4/6)

Indira was claimed for £4,000 after winning over a mile and a half for Henry Candy at Chepstow in August. She must be capable of getting off the mark over timber before things get too competitive. (3/1)

Ghostly Apparition was only a sprinter on the Flat. (50/1)

Trianna (12/1: op 8/1)

T/Plpt: £221.50 (29.46 Tckts). T/Qdpt: £11.20 (36.32 Tckts). KH

754a-762a (Irish Racing) - See Computer Raceform

0758a-LISTOWEL (Ireland) (L-H) (Good to soft, Chase course Good)

Wednesday September 25th

763a GUINNESS KERRY NATIONAL H'CAP CHASE (Gd 2) (4-Y.O+)

3-50 (3-54) **3m (18 fncs)** £27,900.00 (£8,550.00: £4,050.00: £1,350.00)

	Horse	Dist	Pos	SP	RR	SF
314a[2]	**Bishops Hall** (HdeBromhead,Ireland) **10-9-12** FWoods (led 2nd to 5th: led 5 out: slt mstke & hdd 3 out: led bef 2 out: jnd appr last: rdn & styd on flat)	—	1	9/1	148+	—
314a[P]	**Anabatic (IRE)** (MJPO'Brien,Ireland) **8-9-10** TPRudd (hld up towards rr: hdwy after 12th: wnt 2nd 2 out: chal & ev ch last: kpt on)	1½	2	14/1	145	—
314a[4]	**Second Schedual** (MissAMMcMahon,Ireland) **11-10-1** MDwyer (hld up: chsng ldrs whn lft 4th 3 out: 3rd & chal whn mstke 2 out: nt qckn appr last)	5½	3	9/1	146	—
	Opera Hat (IRE) (JRHFowler,Ireland) **8-11-0** CO'Dwyer (hld up in tch: hdwy to ld 5th: hdd 5 out & lost pl: hdwy next: led briefly 3 out: sn jnd: hdd & nt qckn appr 2 out)	1½	4	12/1	158	—
314a[P]	**Jassu** (JEKiely,Ireland) **10-10-3**ow1 RDunwoody (in tch: lft 6th & sltly hmpd 3 out: sn n.d: t.o)	dist	5	8/1[3]	—	—
	Royal Mountbrowne (APO'Brien,Ireland) **8-10-4** AJO'Brien (mid div: mstke 2nd: towards rr fr 6th: lost tch 5 out: t.o)	14	6	20/1	—	—
	Beakstown (IRE) (PMullins,Ireland) **7-9-7** 7x TPTreacy (hld up in tch: chsng ldrs whn mstke 5 out: wknd appr next: t.o)	4½	7	8/1[3]	—	—
	Lord Singapore (IRE) (JJWalsh,Ireland) **8-9-7** NWilliamson (mstke 1st: hld up: 3rd whn slt mstke 4 out: cl 4th & chsng ldrs whn fell 3 out)		F	10/1	—	—
	Walkers Lady (IRE) (JohnO'Callaghan,Ireland) **8-9-0**(7) AO'Shea (towards rr whn fell 5th)		F	100/1	—	—
314a*	**Life of a Lord** (APO'Brien,Ireland) **10-12-3** CFSwan (led to 2nd: in tch 12th: sn lost pl & p.u: broke leg: dead) .		P	5/2[1]	—	—
314a[3]	**King Wah Glory (IRE)** (PBurke,Ireland) **7-9-8** THorgan (hld up: chsng ldrs 3 out: rdn, sddle slipped & uns rdr appr 2 out)		U	5/1[2]	—	—
				(SP 116.7%)		**11 Rn**

6m 7.8 OWNER T. J. Carroll (KNOCKEEN) BRED William O'Gorman

314a Bishops Hall, always in the front pair, went on five out. He blundered and was headed at the third last, but had gained the advantage again before the next. Joined again at the last, he showed real battling qualities. The Hennessy Cognac at Newbury is a target again, but he must have a sound surface. (9/1: op 6/1)

Anabatic (IRE), an improving fourth with four to jump, was second before the turn and gained a slight advantage early on the flat. He just could not quicken again and went under with some credit. He won a minor contest here later in the week and the Murphy's Chase is his pre-Christmas objective. (14/1)

Second Schedual still shows plenty of life. Left fourth three out, he was a challenging third when blundering at the next. (9/1)

Opera Hat (IRE) ran well on her first outing, leading from the fifth until headed five out. She got in front again briefly with three to jump, but was headed when making a mistake at the second last. She has to be in for another good season. (12/1: op 7/1)

Jassu is too slow for this company, even on soft ground. (8/1)

314a* Life of a Lord ended his career here when he shattered his off-fore after the twelfth. (5/2)

314a King Wah Glory (IRE), chasing the leaders, was certainly getting into it when the saddle slipped approaching two out, causing an involuntary bail-out. (5/1)

764a-780a (Irish Racing) - See Computer Raceform

0540-HEXHAM (L-H) (Firm)

Friday October 4th

WEATHER: squally showers WIND: str

781 FEDERATION BREWERY BUCHANAN ORIGINAL NOVICES' CONDITIONAL HURDLE (4-Y.O+) (Class F)

2-15 (2-15) **2m 4f 110y (10 hdls)** £1,992.80 (£550.80: £262.40) GOING: 0.09 sec per fur (G)

	Horse	Dist	Pos	SP	RR	SF
	Latvian (RAllan) **9-10-9v**(3) SMelrose (hld up: jnd ldr 7th: led 2 out: wandered & j.slowly last: nt keen: hld on towards fin)	—	1	11/4[3]	63	7

	Horse / details	Dist	Pos	SP	RR	SF
680^{4}	**Pangeran (USA)** (MrsASwinbank) **4-10-11** JSupple (j.slowly: led: blnd 6th: hdd 2 out: rallied & ev ch flat: nt qckn towards fin)	1½	2	$13/8^{1}$	62	5
642^{4}	**Pimsboy (60)** (GROldroyd) **9-10-12b** GCahill (sn pushed along: in tch: hit 5th: wnt prom 7th: wknd qckly appr 2 out)	27	3	14/1	41	—
630^{5}	**Alpine Mist (IRE) (92)** (JGMO'Shea) **4-11-4** MichaelBrennan (chsd ldrs: reminders 6th: 3rd & prom whn fell 3 out)		F	$7/4^{2}$	—	—
				(SP 107.8%)	**4 Rn**	

5m 4.7 (16.70) CSF £7.07 TOTE £3.30: (£4.10) OWNER Mr I. Bell (CORNHILL-ON-TWEED) BRED Fittocks Stud Ltd
WEIGHT FOR AGE 4yo-1lb

Latvian did everything he could to get out of it but even he, in such a poor contest, had to pass the post in front. (11/4)

Pangeran (USA) tended to run in snatches and did not jump fluently. With the winner putting on the brakes, he found himself almost upsides again on the run-in, but could not do quite enough. (13/8)

642 Pimsboy was already struggling when he hit the fifth. He looks a forlorn hope these days. (14/1)

498* Alpine Mist (IRE) was only a couple of lengths down when he slipped on landing and fell three out. Whether his stamina would have lasted out is open to doubt. (7/4)

782 PAT WAKELIN AND BRITISH RED CROSS NOVICES' HURDLE (4-Y.O+) (Class E)

2-45 (2-45) **3m (12 hdls)** £2,730.00 (£660.00) GOING: 0.09 sec per fur (G)

	Horse / details	Dist	Pos	SP	RR	SF
	Crofton Lake (JEDixon) **8-10-12** BStorey (bit bkwd: led to 2 out: led appr last: all out)	—	1	$5/4^{2}$	46	—
	Canonbiebothered (LLungo) **5-10-7** FPerratt (effrt appr 2 out: rdn to ld 2 out: hdd appr last: hung lft & styd on same pce towards fin)	¾	2	$8/13^{1}$	41?	—
				(SP 106.3%)	**2 Rn**	

6m 15.9 (35.90) TOTE £2.50: OWNER Mrs E. M. Dixon (CARLISLE) BRED Mrs E. M. Dixon

Crofton Lake set a modest pace. With the advantage of the inside, he regained the lead going to the last but, at the line, took a desperate contest with not an ounce to spare. (5/4: Evens-11/8)

Canonbiebothered, a leggy newcomer, moved up on the outside to lead two out. Never getting more than a length clear, she had to go the long way round on the uphill run to the last. Under severe pressure, she hung left on the run-in, but was held near the line. There can surely never have been a worse novice hurdle than this. (8/13)

783 JOHNNIE MARSHALL H'CAP CHASE (0-100) (5-Y.O+) (Class F)

3-15 (3-15) **2m 110y (12 fncs)** £2,981.16 (£727.20) GOING: 0.09 sec per fur (G)

	Horse / details	Dist	Pos	SP	RR	SF
641^{4}	**Ilewin (92)** (GMMcCourt) **9-11-10** GBradley (j.slowly: hit 7th: effrt 3 out: sn rdn & no imp: btn 9l: awrdd race)	---.	1	$4/9^{1}$	92	—
642^{8}	**Anthony Bell (89)** (TJCarr) **10-11-7** ADobbin (lw: mde all: clr 7th: pushed out: disq)	—	D	$7/4^{2}$	98	—
				(SP 105.6%)	**2 Rn**	

4m 16.6 (19.60) TOTE £2.60: OWNER Mr Peter Carr (STANGHOW) BRED Dr J. Mansergh-Wallace
STEWARDS ENQUIRY: 6/4/97 - Anthony Bell was disqualified after testing positive for a prohibited substance. Carr fined £350

Anthony Bell, tailed off over hurdles on his first outing for eleven months, was turned out here looking in tip-top trim. Allowed to set his own pace, he was clear and in no danger from halfway. (7/4)

641 Ilewin, 6lb lower than when he reappeared over hurdles, had his tongue tied down. He would not have a cut at his fences and, after hitting the seventh, took little interest. Bradley tried to get him on terms three out, but he did not want to know. (4/9)

784 LCL PILS LAGER (S) HURDLE (4-Y.O+) (Class G)

3-50 (3-50) **2m (8 hdls)** £2,067.00 (£572.00: £273.00) GOING: 0.09 sec per fur (G)

	Horse / details	Dist	Pos	SP	RR	SF
698^{2}	**Supertop (95)** (LLungo) **8-10-12** MDwyer (lw: hld up: stdy hdwy 5th: led on bit appr last: sn clr: easily)	—	1	$4/6^{1}$	63+	25
634^{8}	**Spring Loaded** (JGMO'Shea) **5-10-7(5)** MichaelBrennan (hdwy & prom 5th: kpt on appr last: no ch w wnr)	7	2	$9/2^{2}$	56	18
585^{7}	**Little Redwing (65)** (MDHammond) **4-10-7b1ow1** RGarritty (w ldr: reminders 4th: led next tl appr last: sn wknd)	5	3	8/1	47	7
735^{5}	**Top Skipper (IRE)** (MartynWane) **4-10-11** ASSmith (bit bkwd: chsd ldrs: effrt 3 out: one pce)	2	4	25/1	49	10
642^{9}	**Top Fella (USA) (75)** (PJDennis) **4-10-11b** DBentley (nt j.w: hit 1st: lost pl & reminders 4th: sn bhd)	15	5	14/1	34	—
642^{6}	**Dark Midnight (IRE) (56)** (DALamb) **7-10-12** JBurke (led to 5th: wknd qckly appr last)	hd	6	16/1	34	—
490^{4}	**Trumble (83)** (MrsNMacauley) **4-10-11** PHide (chsd ldrs tl wknd 3 out)	4	7	$7/1^{3}$	30	—
	Swank Gilbert (TAKCuthbert) **10-10-12** CarolCuthbert (bit bkwd: chsd ldrs: hit 4th: lost pl 3 out: t.o between last 2)	29	8	50/1	1	—
				(SP 120.1%)	**8 Rn**	

3m 57.1 (9.10) CSF £4.61 TOTE £1.60: £1.70 £1.10 £2.10 (£3.40) OWNER Mrs Barbara Lungo (CARRUTHERSTOWN) BRED Limestone Stud
WEIGHT FOR AGE 4yo-1lb
Bt in 2,800 gns

698 Supertop, who injured himself when falling on his third and final outing last season, found this simple and won very easily indeed. (4/6)

Spring Loaded, far from disgraced in non-selling company first time, stuck on to finish clear second best. (9/2)

528 Little Redwing, dropped in distance and tried in blinkers, faded going to the last. (8/1)

Top Skipper (IRE), having his second outing in three days, ran better. (25/1)

785 CONWAY ROBINSON H'CAP CHASE (0-100) (5-Y.O+) (Class F)

4-25 (4-25) **3m 1f (19 fncs)** £3,848.00 (£932.00) GOING: 0.09 sec per fur (G)

	Horse / details	Dist	Pos	SP	RR	SF
491^{5}	**Trumpet (96)** (JGMO'Shea) **7-11-5(5)** MichaelBrennan (led 3rd: drvn clr between last 2: eased towards fin)	—	1	$11/10^{1}$	103+	34
683^{3}	**Upwell (72)** (RJohnson) **12-10-0** KJohnson (led to 3rd: drvn along 13th: ch 4 out: wl outpcd between last 2)	7	2	$5/2^{2}$	75	6
645^{5}	**Laurie-O (77)** (DALamb) **12-10-5bow5** JBurke (w ldrs: blnd 8th: sn wknd: poor 3rd whn fell 15th)		F	$11/4^{3}$	—	—
645^{6}	**Smokey Track (72)** (MrsJConway) **11-9-9(5)** STaylor (j.slowly: sn bhd: last whn sltly hmpd & uns rdr 15th)		U	20/1	—	—
				(SP 107.6%)	**4 Rn**	

6m 26.3 (15.30) CSF £3.92 TOTE £1.70: (£2.20) OWNER Mr Costas Andreou (WELFORD-ON-AVON) BRED The Queen
LONG HANDICAP Upwell 9-12 Smokey Track 8-12

Trumpet, who came to grief on his only subsequent outing after taking this prize a year ago, found this a simple task and scored with the minimum of fuss. (11/10: 4/6-5/4)

683 Upwell, 2lb wrong at the weights, as usual proved woefully one-paced. (5/2)

645 Laurie-O took on the winner but was stopped in his tracks when he blundered at the eighth. He had lost touch when taking a heavy fall five out. It is a long time now since he last won. (11/4)

786 JOHN HOGG HAULAGE NOVICES' HURDLE (4-Y.O+) (Class E)

4-55 (4-55) **2m** **(8 hdls)** £2,364.00 (£654.00: £312.00) GOING: 0.09 sec per fur (G)

				SP	RR	SF
701[2]	**Vintage Red (67)** (GRichards) **6-11-5** ADobbin (hld up trckng ldrs: led after 2 out: pushed clr flat: eased towards fin)	—	**1**	15/8 [1]	76+	31
701[4]	**Robsera (IRE) (90)** (JJQuinn) **5-10-12** LWyer (lw: trckd ldrs: chal after 2 out: sn rdn: kpt on: no ch w wnr)	3½	**2**	15/8 [1]	66	21
680[2]	**Thaleros (84)** (GMMoore) **6-10-12** JCallaghan (hit 3rd: led next: hdd after 2 out: sn wl outpcd: kpt on)	2	**3**	9/4 [2]	64	19
	Amber Holly (70) (JEDixon) **7-10-7** BStorey (bkwd: led: hdd & blnd bdly 4th: continued t.o: p.u bef last)		**P**	10/1 [3]	—	—
				(SP 109.4%)		**4 Rn**

3m 57.3 (9.30) CSF £5.46 TOTE £3.00: (£2.40) OWNER Special Reserve Racing (PENRITH)

701 Vintage Red would incredibly have been meeting the runner-up on 25lb worse terms in a handicap. Travelling best throughout, he won with plenty to spare and connections would be wise to pull him out soon in a handicap under a penalty. (15/8)

701 Robsera (IRE), well beaten in handicap company last time, was always playing second fiddle. (15/8)

680 Thaleros made the best of his way home from the halfway mark, but was left for dead over the last two. (9/4)

787 HEXHAMSHIRE STANDARD N.H. FLAT RACE (4, 5 & 6-Y.O) (Class H)

5-25 (5-25) **2m** £1,306.00 (£361.00: £172.00)

				SP	RR	SF
686[2]	**Sioux Warrior** (CWThornton) **4-10-10**(7) NHorrocks (hld up: stdy hdwy 2f out: r.o wl to ld nr fin)	—	**1**	13/8 [2]	—	—
653[4]	**Chief Gale (IRE)** (JGMO'Shea) **4-10-12**(5) MichaelBrennan (lw: led after 3f to 3f out: shkn up to ld over 1f out: jst ct)	nk	**2**	6/4 [1]	—	—
	Lindajane (IRE) (MissZAGreen) **4-10-9**(3) GCahill (w ldrs: shkn up & led 3f out: hdd over 1f out: hrd rdn & kpt on same pce)	1¾	**3**	7/2 [3]	—	—
	Farmers Subsidy (MissMKMilligan) **4-11-3** DParker (led 3f: chsd ldrs: drvn & outpcd 4f out: wknd 2f out)	11	**4**	8/1	—	—
686[11]	**Green An Castle** (MissZAGreen) **6-10-13** MrTMorrison (bit bkwd: outpcd ½-wy: sn bhd: t.o fnl 4f)	dist	**5**	33/1	—	—
				(SP 114.4%)		**5 Rn**

3m 55.9 CSF £4.53 TOTE £1.90: £1.00 £20.20 (£1.30) OWNER Mr Guy Reed (MIDDLEHAM) BRED G. Reed

WEIGHT FOR AGE 4yo-1lb

686 Sioux Warrior was certainly given a cool ride. Saving ground sticking to the inner on the home turn, he showed a nice turn of foot to get up near the line. (13/8)

653 Chief Gale (IRE) regained the advantage turning for home. Despite a tendency to thrash his tail, he stuck on but was just outspeeded by the winner where it mattered most. (6/4)

Lindajane (IRE), a plain-looking filly, showed plenty of knee-action going down. Shaken up to make the best of her way home at the foot of the hill, she was collared turning in and could only stay on at the same pace under strong pressure. She had a tough introduction. (7/2)

Farmers Subsidy struggled to go the pace in the final half-mile. (8/1)

T/Plpt: £203.40 (36.32 Tckts). T/Qdpt: £21.00 (15.26 Tckts). WG

CHEPSTOW (L-H) (Good)

Saturday October 5th

WEATHER: fine but cloudy

788 STARTERS NOVICES' HURDLE (4-Y.O+) (Class C)

1-45 (1-45) **2m 110y (8 hdls)** £3,715.50 (£1,119.00: £542.00: £253.50) GOING minus 0.29 sec per fur (GF)

				SP	RR	SF
	Lake Kariba (119) (PFNicholls) **5-10-12** APMcCoy (hld up: mstke 3rd: hdwy 4th: led 4 out: comf)	—	**1**	4/6 [1]	75+	18
	Jalapeno (IRE) (NATwiston-Davies) **5-10-12** CLlewellyn (chsd ldr: led after 4th to 4 out: sn rdn: no imp)	5	**2**	15/2 [3]	70	13
21[8]	**Whistling Buck (IRE) (75)** (RRowe) **8-10-7**(5) LAspell (hld up: hdwy appr 4 out: r.o one pce fr 3 out)	1½	**3**	40/1	69	12
	Rangitikei (NZ) (CJMann) **5-10-12** RDunwoody (a.p: rdn appr 3 out: one pce)	2½	**4**	11/2 [2]	66	9
	Allow (IRE) (BLlewellyn) **5-10-12** MAFitzgerald (prom to 3 out)	8	**5**	33/1	59	2
	Lough Tully (IRE) (FJordan) **6-10-12** SWynne (bit bkwd: led tl after 4th: wknd appr 3 out)	12	**6**	16/1	47	—
	Saxon Mead (PJHobbs) **6-10-12** AMaguire (bkwd: hld up: hdwy 4th: wknd 4 out)	3½	**7**	8/1	44	—
	Irrepressible (IRE) (RJHodges) **5-10-12** ILawrence (hld up & bhd: hdwy after 4th: wknd 4 out)	½	**8**	50/1	43	—
594[4]	**My Harvinski (75)** (IRJones) **6-10-5**(7) MissEJJones (hld up: hdwy after 4th: wknd 4 out)	1	**9**	50/1	42	—
594[6]	**Crownhill Cross** (BRMillman) **5-10-7**(5) DSalter (bhd fr 4th: t.o)	dist	**10**	100/1	—	—
600[10]	**Masimara Music** (JMBradley) **5-10-7** BFenton (bhd fr 4th: t.o)	dist	**11**	100/1	—	—
	High Holme (RHBuckler) **5-10-12** BPowell (a bhd: t.o fr 4th)	10	**12**	50/1	—	—
498[3]	**Pytchley Dawn** (OO'Neill) **6-10-7** VSlattery (hmpd & fell 1st)		**F**	40/1	—	—
727[P]	**Late Encounter** (BJLlewellyn) **5-10-12** GBradley (j.slowly 1st: sn t.o: p.u bef 4 out)		**P**	66/1	—	—
				(SP 121.3%)		**14 Rn**

3m 53.5 (4.50) CSF £6.64 TOTE £1.80: £1.20 £1.70 £4.40 (£4.80) Trio £55.10 OWNER The Lake Kariba Partnership (SHEPTON MALLET) BRED Side Hill Stud and the Duke of Roxburgh's Stud

Lake Kariba had some useful form to his name last season and found this pretty straightforward. (4/6)

Jalapeno (IRE) showed promise in bumpers last season and will not always come up against one so smart. (15/2)

Whistling Buck (IRE) had finished third here in a Novices' Handicap back in May and seems to like this course. (40/1)

Rangitikei (NZ) ran well in each of his bumpers prior to winning one at Market Rasen and gave the impression another half-mile will not come amiss over hurdles. (11/2)

789 MERCEDES BENZ H'CAP CHASE (0-145) (5-Y.O+) (Class B)

2-15 (2-15) **3m (18 fncs)** £7,103.00 (£2,144.00: £1,042.00: £491.00) GOING minus 0.29 sec per fur (GF)

				SP	RR	SF
	General Crack (IRE) (120) (PFNicholls) **7-11-4** APMcCoy (hld up: wnt 2nd 12th: led appr 5 out: sn clr: easily)	—	**1**	9/4 [1]	136+	42
485[3]	**Evangelica (USA) (115)** (MCPipe) **6-10-13** CMaude (hld up: sltly hmpd 3rd: hdwy appr 8th: outpcd appr 5 out: styd on fr 2 out)	21	**2**	12/1	117	23

				SP	RR	SF
719*	**Iffeee (129)** (PBowen) **9-11-13** AMaguire (led after 2nd to 4th: led appr 8th tl appr 5 out: btn whn j.rt 4 out & 3 out)	2½	**3**	6/1[2]	129	35
	Grange Brake (125) (NATwiston-Davies) **10-11-6**(3) DWalsh (led tl after 2nd: led 4th tl appr 8th: rdn 11th: wknd after 12th)	1¾	**4**	10/1	124	30
650*	**Tartan Tradewinds (130)** (GRichards) **9-12-0** ADobbin (lw: hld up: hdwy appr 8th: wknd appr 5 out)	10	**5**	9/4[1]	123	29
719[3]	**Certain Angle (111)** (PJHobbs) **7-10-9** RDunwoody (3rd whn fell 3rd)		**F**	7/1[3]	—	—
	Florida Sky (109) (CPEBrooks) **9-10-7** GBradley (hld up: fell 6th)		**F**	10/1	—	—
	Good for a Laugh (110) (GAHam) **12-10-8** MAFitzgerald (bit bkwd: bhd fr 9th: t.o whn p.u bef 13th)		**P**	66/1	—	—
				(SP 115.7%)		**8 Rn**

5m 54.0 (1.00) CSF £25.92 CT £131.82 TOTE £3.30: £1.50 £2.90 £1.30 (£19.90) OWNER Mr J A Keighley and Mr Paul K Barber (SHEPTON MALLET) BRED Thomas Smyth

General Crack (IRE), 13lb higher than when successful at Stratford in May, still looked some way ahead of the handicapper here. (9/4)
485 Evangelica (USA), back over fences, went a poor second jumping the last. (12/1: op 8/1)
719* Iffeee, raised 6lb, found his tendency to jump out to the right surfacing once the winner swept past. (6/1)
Grange Brake, third in the Eider Chase, does seem to need marathon trips these days. (10/1)
650* Tartan Tradewinds, up 5lb, began to find the pace too hot entering the long home straight. (9/4)

790 FREE H'CAP HURDLE (4-Y.O) (Class B)

2-50 (2-50) **2m 110y (8 hdls)** £6,947.00 (£2,096.00: £1,018.00: £479.00) GOING minus 0.29 sec per fur (GF)

				SP	RR	SF
	Hamilton Silk (115) (MCPipe) **4-10-7** GBradley (hld up & bhd: stdy hdwy appr 4 out: led & hit last: r.o wl)	—	**1**	16/1	95	37
	Mim-Lou-and (110) (MissHCKnight) **4-10-2** JCulloty (s.i.s: sn prom: ev ch last: unable qckn)	2	**2**	8/1[3]	88	30
677[2]	**Yubralee (USA) (109)** (MCPipe) **4-10-1** CMaude (swtg: led to last: one pce)	½	**3**	14/1	87	29
727*	**Hand Woven (122)** (NATwiston-Davies) **4-11-0** 4x CLlewellyn (lw: chsd ldr to 4th: one pce fr 2 out)	1	**4**	11/2[2]	99	41
	Alltime Dancer (IRE) (125) (OSherwood) **4-11-3** JAMcCarthy (hld up: rdn appr 4 out: hdwy appr 3 out: one pce fr 2 out)	1½	**5**	8/1[3]	100	42
	Rising Dough (IRE) (108) (GLMoore) **4-10-0** LWyer (hld up & bhd: hdwy appr 4 out: one pce fr 3 out)	2	**6**	14/1	81	23
	Love The Blues (108) (DNicholson) **4-10-0** AMaguire (prom to 4 out)	3	**7**	9/2[1]	78	20
	Reaganesque (USA) (112) (PGMurphy) **4-10-4** RFarrant (hld up: hdwy 3rd: wknd 4 out: t.o)	20	**8**	8/1[3]	63	5
459*	**Faustino (114)** (PJHobbs) **4-10-6** 4x RDunwoody (hld up: rdn after 4th: bhd fr 4 out: t.o)	6	**9**	8/1[3]	59	1
	Iktasab (110) (PFNicholls) **4-10-2b1** APMcCoy (prom: 2nd whn fell 4 out)		**F**	9/2[1]	—	—
	Our Kris (132) (NJHenderson) **4-11-10b** MAFitzgerald (prom tl bdly hmpd 4 out: p.u bef 2 out)		**P**	8/1[3]	—	—
				(SP 126.5%)		**11 Rn**

3m 48.1 (-0.90) CSF £133.42 CT £1,707.25 TOTE £19.00: £3.80 £2.90 £2.40 (£70.90) Trio £226.80 OWNER Elite Racing Club (WELLINGTON) BRED Haydock Exhibitions Ltd

LONG HANDICAP Love The Blues 9-12 Rising Dough (IRE) 9-12

Hamilton Silk had only won a Bangor seller prior to this race but did have some fair form to his name before rather losing his way at the end of last season. (16/1)
Mim-Lou-and was 2lb higher than when runner-up on his only other outing in a handicap prior to winning on his last two runs. (8/1)
677 Yubralee (USA) had race-fitness on his side and did a fine job of pacemaking. (14/1)
727* Hand Woven was by no means disgraced and could well have found this return to two miles on the sharp side. (11/2)
Alltime Dancer (IRE) just lacked the acceleration to really make his presence felt. (8/1)
Rising Dough (IRE), fit from the Flat, looks well up to winning a run of the mill Novice hurdle. (14/1)
Love The Blues, who had a recent pipe-opener on the Flat, was 2lb out of the handicap and folded up early in the long home straight. (9/2)
Iktasab, described by his trainer as bone idle, had the blinkers to help him here and was running a big race when coming to grief. (9/2)

791 MARYLAND FARMHOUSE CHEDDAR NOVICES' CHASE (5-Y.O+) (Class B)

3-25 (3-28) **2m 3f 110y (16 fncs)** £8,756.00 (£2,144.00) GOING minus 0.29 sec per fur (GF)

				SP	RR	SF
	Call Equiname (PFNicholls) **6-11-0** RDunwoody (chsd ldr: led 7th: clr 3 out: pckd last: eased flat)	—	**1**	4/5[1]	113+	15
637*	**Sonic Star (IRE) (110)** (DNicholson) **7-11-8** AMaguire (s.s: hit 1st: gd hdwy after 12th: chsd wnr & hit 5 & 4 out: no imp)	18	**2**	11/8[2]	106+	8
738[4]	**Shikaree (IRE) (100)** (MCPipe) **5-10-12b** CMaude (hld up: hdwy 6th: chsd wnr fr 7th tl 3rd whn fell 5 out)		**F**	11/2[3]	—	—
	Priory Rose (GAHam) **9-10-9** RFarrant (bkwd: led to 7th: wknd qckly: t.o whn p.u bef 10th)		**P**	66/1	—	—
	Bill of Rights (MrsEBScott) **8-11-0** BPowell (Withdrawn not under Starter's orders: unruly at s)		**W**	100/1	—	—
				(SP 115.5%)		**4 Rn**

4m 56.6 (7.60) CSF £2.39 TOTE £1.80: £2.20 (£1.40) OWNER Mick Coburn, Barber, Lewis (SHEPTON MALLET) BRED Mrs L. Steele

WEIGHT FOR AGE 5yo-1lb

Call Equiname had to do little more than jump round and gave his supporters their only anxious moment at the last. (4/5)
637* Sonic Star (IRE) did not find these fences so easy to handle. (11/8)
738 Shikaree (IRE) was blinkered for the first time. (11/2)

792 SOUTH-WEST RACING CLUB NOVICES' H'CAP HURDLE (0-100) (4-Y.O+) (Class E)

4-00 (4-00) **2m 4f 110y (11 hdls)** £2,960.00 (£890.00: £430.00: £200.00) GOING minus 0.29 sec per fur (GF)

				SP	RR	SF
412[2]	**Embley Buoy (68)** (JWMullins) **8-10-0** SCurran (lw: a.p: led 6th: clr whn hit 2 out: drvn out)	—	**1**	50/1	49	31
502[2]	**Tap On Tootsie (91)** (TWall) **4-11-5**(3) RMassey (lw: prom: lost pl appr 4 out: styd on fr 2 out)	2½	**2**	9/2[2]	70	51
	Myblackthorn (IRE) (92) (PFNicholls) **6-11-3**(7) OBurrows (lw: hld up & bhd: gd hdwy appr 4 out: one pce fr 3 out)	4	**3**	14/1	68	50
	Crohane Quay (IRE) (91) (GBBalding) **7-11-2**(7)ow1 MrABalding (bit bkwd: hld up & bhd: hit 7th: hdwy & shkn up appr 3 out: nvr plcd to chal)	2	**4**	14/1	65+	46
649[7]	**Karen's Typhoon (IRE) (75)** (PJHobbs) **5-10-7** CMaude (prom: mstke 4th: lost pl appr 4 out: rdn & sme hdwy fr 2 out)	2½	**5**	12/1	47	29
632*	**Little Tincture (IRE) (73)** (MrsTJMcInnesSkinner) **6-10-5** GUpton (swtg: hld up: rdn & no hdwy fr 4 out)	6	**6**	10/1[3]	41	23
	Dajraan (IRE) (90) (NATwiston-Davies) **7-11-8** CLlewellyn (lw: hld up: hdwy appr 7th: wknd appr 3 out: fin lame)	1¾	**7**	5/4[1]	56	38
492[2]	**Regal Gem (IRE) (77)** (CRBarwell) **5-10-9** BFenton (a bhd)	4	**8**	14/1	40	22
	Pavlova (IRE) (85) (RRowe) **6-10-12**(5) LAspell (swtg: bit bkwd: prom: mstke 6th: rdn & wknd appr 4 out)	3½	**9**	12/1	46	28
	Queen's Award (IRE) (68) (RHBuckler) **7-10-0** BPowell (bkwd: hld up & bhd: hdwy 7th: wknd appr 4					

out) ...1½ 10 33/1 27 9
630[8] **Hydemilla (80)** (MrsTDPilkington) **6-10-9**(3) GHogan (swtg: led to 6th: wknd appr 4 out) ...½ **11** 25/1 39 21
Sands Point (90) (CLPopham) **6-11-8** MAFitzgerald (reminders appr 4th: bhd fr 5th: t.o whn p.u bef 4 out) .... **P** 12/1 — —
(SP 123.5%) **12 Rn**

4m 45.9 (-1.10) CSF £251.21 CT £3,101.71 TOTE £66.20: £12.20 £1.20 £2.90 (£185.80) Trio £224.40 OWNER Mrs Heather Bare (AMESBURY) BRED Mrs H. Bare
LONG HANDICAP Queen's Award (IRE) 9-5 Embley Buoy 8-12
WEIGHT FOR AGE 4yo-1lb
412 Embley Buoy has certainly had his problems over fences and caused a real upset from 16lb out of the handicap in this hurdle. (50/1)
502 Tap On Tootsie was 3lb lower than when runner-up on her reappearance. (9/2)
Myblackthorn (IRE), presumably having a pipe-opener before going back over fences, ran well for one who likes soft ground. (14/1: op 8/1)
Crohane Quay (IRE) had a quiet run and only appeared to come in for some cosmetic use of the whip. (14/1: op 8/1)
Karen's Typhoon (IRE) (12/1: op 8/1)
Dajraan (IRE) was reported to have finished lame behind. (5/4: 2/1-11/10)

793 VALETS H'CAP HURDLE (0-110) (4-Y.O+) (Class E)

4-35 (4-36) **2m 110y (8 hdls)** £2,940.50 (£884.00: £427.00: £198.50) GOING minus 0.29 sec per fur (GF)

SP RR SF
Mytton's Choice (IRE) (105) (DNicholson) **5-11-6**(7) MrRThornton (hld up: led 4 out: clr 3 out: r.o wl) ...— **1** 13/2[3] 96+ 51
552[2] **Pair of Jacks (IRE) (86)** (GLMoore) **6-10-8** RDunwoody (hld up & bhd: hdwy fr 3 out: no ch w wnr) ...11 **2** 11/4[1] 66 21
729[2] **Zingibar (79)** (JMBradley) **4-10-0** BFenton (bhd: rdn 4th: styd on fr 3 out: n.d) ...5 **3** 10/1 55 9
Ramsdens (IRE) (101) (NATwiston-Davies) **4-11-8** CLlewellyn (a.p: led appr 4 out: sn hdd: one pce) ...1½ **4** 9/2[2] 75 29
Knight in Side (83) (MCPipe) **10-10-5** CMaude (nvr nr to chal) ...hd **5** 13/2[3] 57 12
Zaitoon (IRE) (106) (DNicholson) **5-12-0** AMaguire (bkwd: led tl after 1st: wknd appr 4 out) ...½ **6** 10/1 79 34
601[7] **Toomuch Toosoon (IRE) (97)** (MCPipe) **8-11-5** BPowell (bhd fr 4th) ...16 **7** 20/1 55 10
Minster's Madam (85) (JNeville) **5-10-7v** JCulloty (bkwd: prom to 4 out) ...s.h **8** 10/1 43 —
Lime Street Blues (IRE) (82) (CPEBrooks) **5-10-4b** GBradley (bkwd: led after 1st tl appr 4 out: sn wknd: t.o) .8 **9** 10/1 32 —
21[P] **Will James (78)** (CJDrewe) **10-10-0b** SCurran (bkwd: prom to 4 out: t.o) ...12 **10** 33/1 17 —
Meanus Miller (IRE) (82) (RRowe) **8-10-4** DGallagher (hld up & bhd: 6th & no ch whn fell last: dead) ... **F** 16/1 — —
(SP 121.5%) **11 Rn**

3m 49.3 (0.30) CSF £24.24 CT £167.98 TOTE £9.30: £2.50 £1.30 £2.00 (£12.00) Trio £67.20 OWNER Mr Gordon Mytton (TEMPLE GUITING) BRED W. H. Elliott
LONG HANDICAP Will James 9-10 Zingibar 9-13
WEIGHT FOR AGE 4yo-1lb
Mytton's Choice (IRE), a springer in the market, was having his first run for David Nicholson having been off course for the best part of two years. A fine training performance. (13/2: 12/1-11/2)
552 Pair of Jacks (IRE), 3lb higher than when winning at Plumpton, found this a case of the winner having flown. (11/4)
729 Zingibar, as on his reappearance, had the visor left off. (10/1)
Ramsdens (IRE) needs further than this on decent ground. (9/2)

T/Plpt: £236.30 (67.67 Tckts). T/Qdpt: £83.10 (8 Tckts). KH

0492-UTTOXETER (L-H) (Good to firm becoming Good to firm, Firm patches)
Saturday October 5th
WEATHER: fine

794 NORTH STAFFORDSHIRE ADVERTISER NOVICES' HURDLE (4-Y.O+) (Class E)

2-30 (2-30) **2m (9 hdls)** £2,410.50 (£678.00: £331.50) GOING minus 0.45 sec per fur (GF)

SP RR SF
Nordic Breeze (IRE) (102) (MCPipe) **4-10-10** CO'Dwyer (hld up: hdwy 5th: led 2 out: pushed out) ...— **1** 11/10[1] 68+ —
Ela Man Howa (85) (ABailey) **5-10-11** TKent (prom: led after 4th: rdn & hdd 2 out: styd on same pce) ...3½ **2** 9/1 65 —
Culrain (51) (THCaldwell) **5-10-11** AThornton (hld up: styd on fr 2 out: nvr nrr) ...9 **3** 66/1 56 —
In Good Faith (106) (JJQuinn) **4-10-10** MDwyer (hld up: hdwy 6th: r.o one pce fr 2 out) ...hd **4** 9/4[2] 55 —
Dash To The Phone (USA) (74) (KAMorgan) **4-10-10** ASSmith (prom: rdn 3 out: no imp) ...2 **5** 8/1[3] 53 —
Eurolink Shadow (85) (DMcCain) **4-10-10** BHarding (bit bkwd: led 3rd: hdd after next: wkng whn mstke 2 out) ...¾ **6** 20/1 53 —
17[9] **Night Boat (73)** (WClay) **5-10-11** TEley (bit bkwd: hld up: hdwy 5th: wknd 3 out) ...2½ **7** 25/1 50 —
Timely Example (USA) (67) (BRCambidge) **5-10-11b** GaryLyons (nvr trbld ldrs) ...7 **8** 50/1 43 —
Pentland Squire (JMJefferson) **5-10-11** RichardGuest (hld up in tch: eased whn btn appr 3 out) ...3 **9** 16/1 40 —
Jaime's Joy (GraemeRoe) **6-9-13**(7) ShaunGraham (hld up: hit 2nd: a in rr) ...½ **10** 66/1 35 —
Nukud (USA) (GROldroyd) **4-10-7**(3) GCahill (s.s: hld up: a bhd) ...6 **11** 50/1 34 —
Chain Shot (JHPeacock) **11-10-11** RBellamy (bkwd: prom to 5th) ...2½ **12** 40/1 31 —
Christian Warrior (REPeacock) **7-10-6**(5) ChrisWebb (hld up: bhd fr 5th: t.o) ...dist **13** 66/1 — —
Fion Corn (MrsFMOwen) **9-10-11** JRKavanagh (bkwd: led to 3rd: p.u after next) ... **P** 25/1 — —
(SP 128.7%) **14 Rn**

3m 46.6 (5.60) CSF £12.75 TOTE £2.20: £1.40 £2.80 £15.10 (£14.00) Trio £234.10; £230.85 to Haydock 6/10/96 OWNER Mr Malcolm Jones (WELLINGTON) BRED P. F. N. Fanning
WEIGHT FOR AGE 4yo-1lb
Nordic Breeze (IRE), who had shown last term he had ability, had a nice confidence-booster. (11/10)
Ela Man Howa, representing the stable who had Nordic Breeze last season, was showing his first piece of form. (9/1)
Culrain came from out of the clouds to snatch the minor honours on the line. (66/1)
In Good Faith, yet again, flattered only to deceive. (9/4)

795 STAFFORDSHIRE YEOMANRY CHALLENGE CUP NOVICES' CHASE (5-Y.O+) (Class C)

3-00 (3-00) **3m (19 fncs)** £5,067.50 (£1,535.00: £750.00: £357.50) GOING minus 0.45 sec per fur (GF)

SP RR SF
631* **Father Sky** (OSherwood) **5-11-3** JOsborne (j.slowly 1st: blnd 2nd: chsd ldr 11th: chal 4 out: rdn & hld whn lft clr last) ...— **1** 4/11[1] 98 —

				SP	RR	SF
639[U]	**Wakt (97)** (JWhite) **6-11-10**(3) GuyLewis (hld up & in tch: rdn to chal 4 out: wknd next: lft poor 2nd last)	14	**2**	9/2[2]	96	—
	Phaedair (72) (PJHobbs) **6-11-0** JRKavanagh (hld up: t.o fr 7th)	dist	**3**	25/1	—	—
	Newtown Rosie (IRE) (MissAEEmbiricos) **7-10-9** JRyan (led tl after 2nd: led 5th tl fell last: rmntd)	¾	**4**	6/1[3]	—	—
720[U]	**War Flower (IRE)** (AWCarroll) **8-10-9** WMarston (bkwd: plld hrd: led after 2nd to 5th: wknd 11th: t.o)	24	**5**	50/1	—	—
				(SP 111.6%)	**5 Rn**	

6m 8.5 CSF £2.57 TOTE £1.40: £1.30 £1.90 (£1.60) OWNER Mr Kenneth Komfeld (UPPER LAMBOURN) BRED Sheikh Mohammed
WEIGHT FOR AGE 5yo-3lb
631* Father Sky did not impress with his fencing and was a very fortunate winner. (4/11)
639 Wakt, who rattled up an early season hat-trick against inferior opposition, found these a different kettle of fish. (9/2)
Newtown Rosie (IRE), a winning pointer, was desperately unlucky not to make a winning debut over regulation fences. (6/1)

796 SENTINEL H'CAP HURDLE (0-145) (4-Y.O+) (Class B)
3-30 (3-30) **2m 4f 110y (10 hdls)** £5,135.75 (£1,556.00: £760.50: £362.75) GOING minus 0.45 sec per fur (GF)

				SP	RR	SF
	Tullymurry Toff (IRE) (116) (JMJefferson) **5-10-9**(5) ECallaghan (hld up: hdwy to chse ldrs 8th: led 2 out: hit last: rdn out)	—	**1**	9/4[2]	96	28
	Call My Guest (IRE) (123) (REPeacock) **6-11-7** NWilliamson (bit bkwd: chsd ldrs: lft in ld 8th: hdd 2 out: styd on same pce)	6	**2**	6/1	98	30
	Sparkling Yasmin (120) (PJHobbs) **4-11-0**(3) GTormey (bit bkwd: trckd ldrs: outpcd 4 out: no imp after)	2½	**3**	7/2[3]	93	24
	Olympian (118) (JNeville) **9-11-2b** WMarston (bkwd: sn drvn along: hdwy to chse ldrs 6th: lost pl next: sn bhd)	7	**4**	10/1	86	18
638*	**Star Market (126)** (JLSpearing) **6-11-10b** DBridgwater (led: drvn along 7th: rn out next)		**R**	2/1[1]	—	—
				(SP 109.7%)	**5 Rn**	

4m 44.1 (0.10) CSF £13.48 TOTE £2.70: £1.40 £2.80 (£10.00) OWNER Mr John H Wilson and Mr J H Riley (MALTON) BRED Con Troy and David Fenton
WEIGHT FOR AGE 4yo-1lb
Tullymurry Toff (IRE), who finished last term in good style, continues to progress. (9/4)
Call My Guest (IRE), without success for nearly two seasons, is gradually coming down in the weights. (6/1)
Sparkling Yasmin, from a yard in good form, may well be better suited by some cut in the ground. (7/2)
Olympian remains a difficult ride. (10/1)

797 BRITANNIA BUILDING SOCIETY DUKE OF EDINBURGH'S AWARD H'CAP CHASE (0-120) (5-Y.O+) (Class D)
4-05 (4-06) **3m 2f (20 fncs)** £7,002.50 (£2,120.00: £1,035.00: £492.50) GOING minus 0.45 sec per fur (GF)

				SP	RR	SF
645*	**McGregor The Third (117)** (GRichards) **10-11-13** BHarding (a.p: led 4 out: sn clr)	—	**1**	7/4[1]	125	52
	Andros Prince (93) (MissAEEmbiricos) **11-10-3** JRKavanagh (sn wl bhd: styd on appr last: nvr nrr)	8	**2**	20/1	96	23
689*	**Andrelot (118)** (PBowen) **9-12-0b** NWilliamson (led 4th to 16th: rdn & wknd 2 out)	¾	**3**	10/1	121	48
691*	**Cats Run (IRE) (110)** (JohnUpson) **8-11-6** RSupple (bhd: rdn 7th: nvr able to chal)	1	**4**	11/2[3]	112	39
530[2]	**Real Progress (IRE) (105)** (PJHobbs) **8-10-12**(3) GTormey (trckd ldr tl wknd 16th)	14	**5**	10/1	98	25
678[2]	**Fairy Park (97)** (HOliver) **11-10-7** JacquiOliver (bhd & drvn along: hit 13th: sn t.o: p.u bef 2 out)		**P**	16/1	—	—
	Wrekengale (IRE) (110) (MrsJPitman) **6-11-6** WMarston (hld up in tch: lost pl qckly 15th: sn p.u: fin lame)		**P**	11/4[2]	—	—
	Childhay Chocolate (105) (PFNicholls) **8-11-1** PHide (led: mstke & hdd 4th: led 16th to 4 out: wknd qckly 3 out: wl bhd whn ref last)		**R**	8/1	—	—
				(SP 118.4%)	**8 Rn**	

6m 23.5 (0.70 under best) (-3.50) CSF £30.92 CT £261.05 TOTE £3.00: £1.50 £2.90 £3.00 (£30.90) OWNER Mrs D. A. Whitaker (PENRITH) BRED Mrs D. A. Whitaker
645* McGregor The Third, whose form tailed off after a bright start last term, could not have been more impressive. (7/4)
Andros Prince, as usual, does give himself an awful lot to do. (20/1)
689* Andrelot, although a winner over three miles, just seemed to struggle over this extra two furlongs. (10/1: op 6/1)

798 STAFFORDSHIRE REGIMENT CHALLENGE CUP H'CAP HURDLE (0-120) (4-Y.O+) (Class D)
4-40 (4-40) **2m (9 hdls)** £3,399.00 (£1,032.00: £506.00: £243.00) GOING minus 0.45 sec per fur (GF)

				SP	RR	SF
701[5]	**Steadfast Elite (IRE) (90)** (JJO'Neill) **5-9-9**(5) RMcGrath (trckd ldrs: led 2 out: sn clr)	—	**1**	6/4[1]	68	13
641[9]	**Emperor Chang (USA) (92)** (KOWarner) **9-10-2**ow2 TKent (bit bkwd: bhd tl styd on fr 2 out: n.d)	10	**2**	20/1	60	3
638[4]	**Robert's Toy (IRE) (116)** (MCPipe) **5-11-5**(7) GSupple (led to 2nd: hit 4th: led appr 3 out: hdd & wknd next)	8	**3**	7/4[2]	76	21
692[P]	**Layham Low (IRE) (95)** (OSherwood) **5-10-5b**[1] JOsborne (led 2nd tl appr 3 out: ev ch appr 2 out: sn wknd & eased)	19	**4**	5/2[3]	36	—
				(SP 109.7%)	**4 Rn**	

3m 41.3 (0.30) CSF £15.20 TOTE £2.30: (£20.10) OWNER Clayton Bigley Partnership Ltd (PENRITH) BRED Cecil Harris Bloodstock Ltd
LONG HANDICAP Emperor Chang (USA) 8-12
701 Steadfast Elite (IRE) had the race set up for him. With the front two taking each other on, they folded tamely two out and he was able to come through on the bridle and enjoy himself. (6/4)
Emperor Chang (USA) will be seen to better advantage over trips in excess of this when fit. (20/1)
93 Robert's Toy (IRE), without the headgear, does seem to need things to go his own way. (7/4)
478 Layham Low (IRE), wearing blinkers for the first time, folded very tamely when headed. (5/2)

799 QUEEN'S ROYAL LANCERS CHALLENGE CUP H'CAP CHASE (0-125) (5-Y.O+) (Class D)
5-10 (5-10) **2m 4f (15 fncs)** £4,201.50 (£1,272.00: £621.00: £295.50) GOING minus 0.45 sec per fur (GF)

				SP	RR	SF
	Bertone (IRE) (123) (KCBailey) **7-12-0** CO'Dwyer (a.p: chsd ldr 8th: led 2 out: styd on strly)	—	**1**	6/4[1]	132	—
496*	**Micherado (FR) (95)** (SABrookshaw) **6-10-0** JOsborne (j.lft: led to 2 out: no ex)	4	**2**	9/2[3]	101	—
131[9]	**East Houston (101)** (JJO'Neill) **7-10-6** ARoche (bit bkwd: bhd: hmpd 4th: hdwy 10th: wknd 3 out)	14	**3**	7/1	96	—
28[P]	**Mutual Trust (105)** (PBowen) **12-10-10** NWilliamson (chsd ldrs tl wknd 10th)	dist	**4**	20/1	—	—
500*	**Comedy Road (100)** (RLee) **12-10-0**(5) PHenley (prom tl fell 4th)		**F**	7/2[2]	—	—
	Corrarder (110) (JGSmyth-Osbourne) **12-11-1** JRailton (bit bkwd: a bhd: t.o fr 8th: p.u bef 2 out)		**P**	9/1	—	—
				(SP 107.7%)	**6 Rn**	

4m 42.6 (-20.40) CSF £7.77 TOTE £2.30: £1.70 £1.40 (£2.80) OWNER Mrs Harry Duffey (UPPER LAMBOURN) BRED Mrs Marie Behan
Bertone (IRE) was given a peach of a ride. Well suited to this fast ground, he just gradually crept there and barely broke sweat. (6/4)

496* Micherado (FR), if only he could get his jumping straightened out, could take advantage of being at the right end of the handicap. (9/2)
57* East Houston found these too sharp over this trip. (7/1)

800 GREEN'UN SPORTS FINAL 'N.H.' NOVICES' HURDLE (4-Y.O+) (Class C)

5-40 (5-40) **2m 6f 110y (12 hdls)** £4,151.25 (£1,260.00: £617.50: £296.25) GOING minus 0.45 sec per fur (GF)

				SP	RR	SF
	Samlee (IRE) (114) (PJHobbs) **7-10-11** DBridgwater (mde all: strly chal 3 out: r.o wl fr between last 2)	—	1	4/5[1]	71	27
181[P]	**Tipping The Line (103)** (MCPipe) **6-11-9** CO'Dwyer (a.p: ev ch & rdn 3 out: styd on one pce fr next)	4	2	9/4[2]	80	36
	Madge McSplash (JMJefferson) **4-10-5** MDwyer (in tch: effrt fnl circ: wknd qckly 2 out)	7	3	5/1[3]	58	13
	Riverbank Rose (70) (WClay) **5-10-6** TEley (bit bkwd: a.p: ev ch appr 3 out: rdn & nt qckn fr next)	20	4	14/1	44	—
	Musical Hit (PAPritchard) **5-10-11** RBellamy (bkwd: sn t.o: p.u after 4 out)		P	20/1	—	—

(SP 114.4%) **5 Rn**

5m 16.5 (-0.50) CSF £3.12 TOTE £1.60: £1.10 £1.60 (£1.50) Trio £2.10 OWNER White Lion Partnership (MINEHEAD) BRED Mrs. E. Moorhead
WEIGHT FOR AGE 4yo-1lb
Samlee (IRE), three times a winner over fences last term, had no difficulty landing the odds to get off the mark over hurdles. (4/5)
181 Tipping The Line, who found the ground not to his liking last time, would presumably have found this too firm as well. (9/4: op 6/4)

T/Plpt: £47.40 (187.22 Tckts). T/Qdpt: £26.40 (13.55 Tckts). CR

KELSO (L-H) (Firm)

Sunday October 6th

Race 5: One flight omitted
WEATHER: overcast

801 RADIO BORDERS NOVICES' HURDLE (4-Y.O+) (Class E)

2-30 (2-30) **2m 2f (10 hdls)** £1,884.00 (£524.00: £252.00) GOING minus 0.73 sec per fur (F)

				SP	RR	SF
700[5]	**Commander Glen (IRE)** (MDHammond) **4-10-11** RGarritty (lw: hld up: hdwy 4 out: led flat: rdn & r.o)	—	1	5/2[3]	73	—
643[3]	**Fatehalkhair (IRE) (90)** (BEllison) **4-10-8**(3) GCahill (chsd ldrs: led after 3 out tl flat: one pce)	8	2	9/4[2]	66	—
	Monaco Gold (IRE) (MrsMReveley) **4-10-11** PNiven (lw: hdwy & prom 4 out: outpcd next: styd on flat)	3	3	13/8[1]	63	—
698[5]	**I'm The Man** (MrsESlack) **5-10-12** KJohnson (led to 4th: chsd ldrs: disp ld after 3 out: r.o one pce)	s.h	4	7/1	63	—
	Granderise (IRE) (68) (DGSwindlehurst) **6-10-12** MrDSwindlehurst (plld hrd: led & hit 4th: mstke 3 out: sn hdd & one pce)	3½	5	66/1	60	—
	Walk In The Wild (DANolan) **4-10-6** BStorey (reminders 5th: outpcd & lost tch 4 out: t.o)	dist	6	100/1	—	—
698[7]	**Logani (60)** (RMMcKellar) **6-10-7** DParker (bit bkwd: prom to 5th: sn bhd: t.o)	s.h	7	150/1	—	—

(SP 113.1%) **7 Rn**

4m 17.2 (4.20) CSF £8.24 TOTE £4.00: £1.80 £1.50 (£4.00) OWNER Punters Haven Racing Club (MIDDLEHAM) BRED Des Vere Hunt Farming Co
WEIGHT FOR AGE 4yo-1lb
OFFICIAL EXPLANATION **Commander Glen (IRE): the trainer's representative reported that the gelding was better suited being settled over this slightly shorter trip and that a tongue-strap appeared to help.**
700 Commander Glen (IRE), dropped back in distance and wearing a tongue-strap for the first time, improved dramatically and won really well. (5/2)
643 Fatehalkhair (IRE) keeps running reasonably, but is short of a change of gear and is yet to win under any Rules. (9/4)
Monaco Gold (IRE) looked well enough but ran a bit flat and got outpaced at a vital stage. He may need a bit further. (13/8)
698 I'm The Man, put into the race this time, showed that, with experience, there is better to come. (7/1)
Granderise (IRE), looking likely to be all the better for this, pulled too hard for his own good, but still ran reasonably. (66/1)

802 HIGHLAND PARK 12 Y.O SINGLE MALT NOVICES' CHASE (5-Y.O+) (Class E)

3-00 (3-00) **3m 1f (19 fncs)** £2,125.00 (£640.00: £310.00: £145.00) GOING minus 0.73 sec per fur (F)

				SP	RR	SF
704*	**Tighter Budget (USA) (95)** (MrsHDSayer) **9-11-5** MMoloney (mde all: lft clr 4 out: v.easily)	—	1	4/6[1]	88++	—
581[5]	**Quixall Crossett (56)** (EMCaine) **11-10-5**(7) MrPMurray (a chsng ldrs: outpcd 12th: styd on fr 2 out: no ch w wnr)	12	2	150/1	73	—
685*	**German Legend (80)** (DALamb) **6-11-2**(3) GCahill (blnd bdly 2nd: bhd tl hdwy ½-wy: blnd 15th: wnt 2nd 3 out: one pce)	1¾	3	11/4[2]	79	—
696[8]	**Bright Destiny (60)** (JSGoldie) **5-10-9** DParker (in tch: effrt 14th: hmpd 4 out: n.d after)	½	4	66/1	72	—
	Royal Surprise (WGReed) **9-10-12** TReed (prom to 10th: sn outpcd)	3½	5	13/2[3]	70	—
704[F]	**Tony's Feelings (60)** (MissLucindaRussell) **8-10-12** MFoster (mstkes 8th & 9th: sn lost tch: n.d after)	1½	6	20/1	69	—
700[6]	**Miss Lamplight** (FPMurtagh) **6-10-7** ADobbin (a.p: wnt 2nd & blnd 11th: chal 15th: fell next)		F	9/1	—	—
	Jamarsam (IRE) (NWaggott) **8-10-12** KJohnson (prom to 6th: wl t.o whn p.u after 13th)		P	150/1	—	—

(SP 117.6%) **8 Rn**

6m 23.6 (13.60) CSF £45.73 TOTE £1.60: £1.10 £6.60 £1.30 (£48.60) OWNER Mrs Dianne Sayer (PENRITH) BRED Walter Haefner
WEIGHT FOR AGE 5yo-3lb
704* Tighter Budget (USA) jumped safely and well and, after his only serious rival fell four out, he won embarrassingly easily. (4/6)
508 Quixall Crossett is basically a plodder, but he does keep battling on. (150/1)
685* German Legend ran quite well considering he made two almighty blunders. (11/4)
Bright Destiny was just beginning to improve and looked a contender for second best when he was hampered four out, and was never happy thereafter. (66/1)
Miss Lamplight put in a useful first effort over fences, being the only one able to trouble the winner, but she was feeling the strain when she came to grief four out. (9/1)

803 MACALLAN 10 YEAR OLD SINGLE MALT HURDLE (3-Y.O) (Class E)

3-30 (3-30) **2m 110y (8 hdls)** £1,856.00 (£516.00: £248.00) GOING minus 0.73 sec per fur (F)

				SP	RR	SF
540[2]	**Kernof (IRE)** (MDHammond) **3-11-3b** RGarritty (mde most: clr fr 3 out)	—	1	6/1[3]	56+	13
282[5]	**She's Simply Great (IRE)** (JJO'Neill) **3-10-0**(5) RMcGrath (swtg: in tch: effrt 5th: styd on: no ch w wnr)	17	2	14/1	28	—
	Ballpoint (GMMoore) **3-10-10** JCallaghan (bhd: pushed along & hdwy 5th: slipped bnd appr next: blnd next: no imp)	10	3	5/6[1]	23	—

				SP	RR	SF
688[10]	**Euro Express** (TDEasterby) **3-10-10** LWyer (prom to 4th: sn outpcd & bhd: sme late hdwy)	nk	**4**	33/1	23	—
688*	**In A Tizzy** (PCHaslam) **3-10-12** MFoster (led to 1st: chsd wnr: rdn 3 out: sn btn)	8	**5**	7/4[2]	17	—
				(SP 114.8%)	**5 Rn**	

3m 45.3 (-0.70) CSF £54.05 TOTE £5.40: £2.20 £4.10 (£27.50) OWNER Mr J. M. Gahan (MIDDLEHAM) BRED David Wallace
OFFICIAL EXPLANATION **Ballpoint: slipped on the bend leaving the back straight and also pulled off a front shoe.**
540 Kernof (IRE), who had the blinkers on this time, was completely transformed and had galloped the opposition into the ground by the third last. (6/1)
She's Simply Great (IRE) has yet to win a race, but has shown ability on the Flat and this was a much-improved effort over hurdles. There could be a modest event to come her way. (14/1)
Ballpoint moved poorly to post on this very firm ground and, never happy, failed to get into it. (5/6)
Euro Express ran a shade better, but there is still some way to go. (33/1)
688* In A Tizzy could never dominate this time and ran badly, dropping out quickly and looking very tired from three out. (7/4)

804 FAMOUS GROUSE H'CAP CHASE (0-120) (5-Y.O+) (Class D)

4-00 (4-00) **3m 1f (19 fncs)** £3,403.75 (£1,030.00: £502.50: £238.75) GOING minus 0.73 sec per fur (F)

				SP	RR	SF
650[3]	**Royal Vacation (110)** (GMMoore) **7-11-10** JCallaghan (trckd ldrs: led 4 out: easily)	—	**1**	11/10[1]	113+	19
696[7]	**Off The Bru (95)** (MrsSCBradburne) **11-10-2**(7)ow3 MrMBradburne (mde most to 10th: chsd ldrs: outpcd whn hit 2 out: styd on: no imp)	6	**2**	3/1[3]	94	—
678[3]	**The Yank (103)** (MDHammond) **10-11-3b** RGarritty (cl up: disp ld 5th to 8th: led 10th to 4 out: wkng whn hit 2 out)	15	**3**	9/4[2]	93	—
785[2]	**Upwell (86)** (RJohnson) **12-10-0** KJohnson (wl bhd fr 4th: t.o)	dist	**4**	20/1	—	—
				(SP 108.2%)	**4 Rn**	

6m 10.3 (0.30) CSF £4.39 TOTE £1.80 (£2.80) OWNER Mr G. P. Edwards (MIDDLEHAM) BRED Small Breeders' Group
LONG HANDICAP Upwell 8-12
650 Royal Vacation found this easy meat and, always going well, led four out and bolted in. (11/10: Evens-5/4)
Off The Bru ran better this time, but found the winner in a different league. (3/1)
678 The Yank is showing little enthusiasm at the moment. (9/4)

805 COOPERS & LYBRAND AMATEUR H'CAP HURDLE (0-105) (4-Y.O+) (Class F)

4-30 (4-30) **2m 6f 110y (10 hdls)** £2,318.00 (£648.00: £314.00) GOING minus 0.73 sec per fur (F)

				SP	RR	SF
	Bridle Path (IRE) (80) (TDEasterby) **5-10-8**(3) KWhelan (a.p: led flat: r.o)	—	**1**	5/1	66	20
465[3]	**Ballindoo (84)** (RJArmson) **7-10-8**(7) MrRArmson (hld up: effrt 7th: ev ch last: swtchd flat & r.o one pce)	3½	**2**	8/1	68	22
	Tall Measure (87) (DGSwindlehurst) **10-10-11b**(7)ow8 MrDSwindlehurst (cl up: led after 5th tl flat: no ex)	nk	**3**	50/1	70	16
673[5]	**Yacht Club (71)** (JLEyre) **14-9-9**(7) MissAArmitage (led tl after 5th: cl up tl outpcd fr 2 out)	3½	**4**	9/1	52	6
700[2]	**Jabaroot (IRE) (83)** (RMMcKellar) **5-10-9**(5) MrRHale (bhd: effrt 7th: outpcd 4 out: sn wknd)	dist	**5**	5/2[1]	—	—
454[F]	**Another Nick (77)** (JSHubbuck) **10-10-1**(7) MissPRobson (sn outpcd & bhd)	5	**6**	50/1	—	—
703*	**Valiant Dash (88)** (JSGoldie) **10-10-12**(7) MrOMcPhail (outpcd ½-wy: 6th & rdn whn fell 4 out)		**F**	11/4[2]	—	—
690[3]	**Red Jam Jar (93)** (SBBell) **11-11-5**(5) MrNWilson (blnd & uns rdr 1st)		**U**	9/2[3]	—	—
				(SP 115.1%)	**8 Rn**	

5m 12.4 (-4.60) CSF £39.74 CT £1,600.60 TOTE £6.00: £1.60 £2.00 £3.60 (£16.50) Trio £12.50 OWNER Mr Fred Wilson (MALTON) BRED Wickfield Stud
Bridle Path (IRE), given a fine ride, won this well but is never one to rely on fully. (5/1)
465 Ballindoo had his chances here and kept staying on, but was short of a real turn of foot. Being hampered after the last made little difference. (8/1: op 5/1)
Tall Measure has not won for two years and had dropped way down the handicap, but did show he retains some ability. (50/1)
673 Yacht Club ran reasonably, but proved far too slow at the business end. (9/1)
700 Jabaroot (IRE) ran badly here and never looked happy. Something was obviously wrong with him. (5/2)
703* Valiant Dash seemed to be feeling his hard race of last time and was struggling in sixth when falling four out. (11/4)

806 BUNNAHABHAIN 12 YEAR OLD MALT H'CAP HURDLE (0-120) (4-Y.O+) (Class D)

5-00 (5-01) **2m 110y (8 hdls)** £2,248.00 (£628.00: £304.00) GOING minus 0.73 sec per fur (F)

				SP	RR	SF
677*	**Prizefighter (106)** (JLEyre) **5-11-10** OPears (lw: hld up: a gng wl: led flat: shkn up & r.o)	—	**1**	1/2[1]	98+	44
692[4]	**Bures (IRE) (110)** (MrsJBrown) **5-11-7**(7) BGrattan (cl up: led 5th: hit last: sn hdd & btn)	8	**2**	12/1	94	40
702[P]	**Vain Prince (100)** (NTinkler) **9-11-4b** RGarritty (lw: hld up: hdwy & prom ½-wy: shkn up 5th: one pce fr 3 out)	2½	**3**	8/1[3]	82	28
684[4]	**Well Appointed (IRE) (95)** (BMactaggart) **7-10-13** BStorey (lw: led to 5th: wl outpcd fr next)	5	**4**	3/1[2]	72	18
	Stylish Interval (91) (NWaggott) **4-10-8**ow1 RichardGuest (prom tl outpcd fr 5th)	7	**5**	33/1	61	5
681[4]	**Richmond (IRE) (84)** (MissZAGreen) **8-10-2** KWhelan (prom to 4th: sn rdn & wknd: t.o)	dist	**6**	33/1	—	—
				(SP 116.4%)	**6 Rn**	

3m 39.7 (-6.30) CSF £7.38 TOTE £1.50: £1.10 £3.00 (£6.30) OWNER Diamond Racing Ltd (HAMBLETON) BRED J. K. Bloodstock Ltd
WEIGHT FOR AGE 4yo-1lb
677* Prizefighter is in top form at the moment and had no difficulty in winning this. (1/2)
692 Bures (IRE) had been set a stiff task by the Handicapper, but ran well here, only to be well outclassed after the last. (12/1: op 8/1)
702 Vain Prince ran reasonably, but looked very slow when asked a question from four out. (8/1)
Well Appointed (IRE) is well enough handicapped but, as yet, has not found his form. (3/1)

T/Plpt: £193.30 (48.08 Tckts). T/Qdpt: £37.30 (10.94 Tckts). AA

KEMPTON (R-H) (Chases Good, Hdles Good to firm)
Sunday October 6th

807 CHILDREN'S CHOICE HURDLE (3-Y.O) (Class D)

2-10 (2-10) **2m (8 hdls)** £2,897.50 (£810.00: £392.50) GOING minus 0.27 sec per fur (GF)

SP RR SF

	Horse		Pos	SP	RR	SF
	Truancy (CJMann) **3-10-10** JRailton (lw: plld hrd: hld up: chsd ldr 3 out tl appr 2 out: led appr last: j.lft last: r.o wl)	—	1	8/1	75	8
640[F]	**Tallulah Belle** (NPLittmoden) **3-10-5** MRichards (lw: stdy hdwy fr 5th: 2nd whn mstke 2 out: unable qckn)	16	2	5/1[3]	54	—
699[8]	**How Could-I (IRE)** (MrsNMacauley) **3-10-5b** AMaguire (prom to 3 out: t.o)	dist	3	9/1	—	—
358[P]	**Water Music Melody** (TRGreathead) **3-10-5** WHumphreys (a bhd: t.o fr 4th)	4	4	50/1	—	—
	Soldier Blue (PJHobbs) **3-10-10** APMcCoy (bhd fr 3rd: t.o fr 4th)	14	5	8/1	—	—
	Kalao Tua (IRE) (JRFanshawe) **3-10-5** PHide (lft in ld 3rd: hdd appr last: 2nd & btn whn hmpd & fell last)		F	9/1	62?	—
589[6]	**Orange Order (IRE)** (JWhite) **3-10-10** NWilliamson (lw: led tl after 2nd: 4th & wkng whn p.u bef 5th)		P	7/2[2]	—	—
	Below The Red Line (MrsNMacauley) **3-10-10** MAFitzgerald (bit bkwd: bhd fr 3rd: t.o fr 4th: p.u bef 2 out)		P	33/1	—	—
	Canons Park (IABalding) **3-10-10** JOsborne (plld hrd: led after 2nd tl rn out 3rd)		R	5/2[1]	—	—

(SP 114.6%) **9 Rn**

3m 48.4 (6.40) CSF £43.85 TOTE £14.60: £2.70 £1.70 £2.00 (£19.20) Trio £141.20; £127.37 to Pontefract 7/10/96 OWNER Mr J. E. Funnell (UPPER LAMBOURN) BRED Mrs D. O. Joly

Truancy, whose best effort on the Flat this year was when finishing fourth in a handicap at Haydock back in June, was a different proposition on this hurdling debut and moved to the front approaching the last. However, he jumped badly left at that hurdle, causing Kalao Tua to come down, but he was definitely the best horse on the day. (8/1)

Tallulah Belle had finished second on the Flat at Brighton four days earlier. (5/1)

654 How Could-I (IRE) was close up until dropping away from the third last. (9/1)

Kalao Tua (IRE), who showed nothing in three outings on the Flat this year, was very unlucky not to have completed and showed definite signs of promise. She should be able to find a race. (9/1: 6/1-10/1)

Canons Park, who won a maiden on the Flat here as a two-year-old, had not seen a racecourse for thirteen months and, considering the length of the absence, looked pretty straight. (5/2)

808 STAINES NEWS & LEADER NOVICES' CHASE (4-Y.O+) (Class D)

2-40 (2-41) **2m** **(13 fncs)** £3,436.25 (£1,040.00: £507.50: £241.25) GOING minus 0.13 sec per fur (G)

	Horse		Pos	SP	RR	SF
652*	**Celibate (IRE)** (CJMann) **5-11-9** JRailton (lw: chsd ldr fr 2nd: led on bit appr last: easily)	—	1	11/8[2]	115+	11
	Greenback (BEL) (PJHobbs) **5-11-3** CLlewellyn (led: clr 3rd: j.slowly 8th: hdd appr last: unable qckn)	2½	2	5/4[1]	107+	3
674[D]	**Holy Wanderer (USA)** (TRGeorge) **7-11-1**(3) GHogan (lw: mstke 3rd: stdy hdwy fr 6th: rdn 3 out: sn wknd)	24	3	5/1[3]	83+	—
	Night in a Million (SWoodman) **5-11-3** JFTitley (bit bkwd: 2nd whn mstke 2nd: bhd fr 3rd: t.o fr 7th)	dist	4	33/1	—	—
681[2]	**Caxton (USA) (78)** (JWhite) **9-11-4** NWilliamson (bhd fr 6th: t.o whn p.u bef 8th)		P	20/1	—	—

(SP 110.9%) **5 Rn**

3m 54.9 (10.90) CSF £3.40 TOTE £2.10: £1.30 £1.60 (£2.00) OWNER Stamford Bridge Partnership (UPPER LAMBOURN) BRED Miss Noirin Dunne

WEIGHT FOR AGE 5yo-1lb

652* Celibate (IRE) put up a very impressive display and, with his jockey sitting very tightly on him, won with a ton in hand. The hat-trick looks on the cards. (11/8: Evens-6/4)

Greenback (BEL), winner of eight of his fifteen starts - the last coming in a handicap off 123 - slipped up at home and, as a result, missed the whole of last season. Reasonably straight for this reappearance, he made a highly-promising chasing debut and took the field along until eventually collared approaching the last. If given time to recover from this race, he should have no problems winning over fences. (5/4)

674 Holy Wanderer (USA) looked extremely well in the paddock, but was left for dead from the third last. (5/1: 7/2-11/2)

809 SUNDAY RACING H'CAP CHASE (0-135) (5-Y.O+) (Class C)

3-15 (3-16) **3m** **(19 fncs)** £4,788.00 (£1,449.00: £707.00: £336.00) GOING minus 0.13 sec per fur (G)

	Horse		Pos	SP	RR	SF
	Big Ben Dun (107) (CPEBrooks) **10-10-2** JOsborne (lw: chsd ldr: led appr last: rdn out)	—	1	7/2[3]	111	51
	Straight Talk (133) (PFNicholls) **9-12-0** APMcCoy (bit bkwd: led: clr 12th: rdn appr 3 out: hdd appr last: unable qckn flat)	2	2	5/2[1]	136	76
	Vicosa (IRE) (112) (RHAlner) **7-10-2**(5) PHenley (bit bkwd: hld up: rdn appr 2 out: wknd appr last)	25	3	11/2	98	38
	Bas de Laine (FR) (115) (MDHammond) **10-10-7**(3) MrCBonner (mstke 12th: bhd fr 13th: t.o fr 14th)	dist	4	4/1	—	—
30*	**Factor Ten (IRE) (118)** (MissHCKnight) **8-10-13** JFTitley (swtg: a bhd: blnd 5th: mstke 9th: t.o whn p.u after 12th)		P	3/1[2]	—	—

(SP 111.2%) **5 Rn**

5m 51.8 (-3.20) CSF £11.87 TOTE £4.40: £2.10 £1.80 (£3.90) OWNER Uplands Bloodstock (LAMBOURN) BRED F. Fennelly

Big Ben Dun looked very fit for this seasonal debut and made that tell against four rivals who had also been off for some time. (7/2)

Straight Talk, winner of three races last autumn, is now rated 18lb higher than at the beginning of last season. Sure to come on a lot for this, he goes particularly well when he can hear his feet rattle and has never won on ground worse than good. (5/2)

Vicosa (IRE) looked as though this reappearance was needed. (11/2)

Bas de Laine (FR), trained by Oliver Sherwood last season, usually goes well fresh. (4/1)

30* Factor Ten (IRE), winner of three novice chases, was put in against the big boys but he failed to jump well and, always at the back of the field, was pulled up after the twelfth. (3/1)

810 WWW.RACING.PRESS.NET H'CAP HURDLE (0-125) (4-Y.O+) (Class D)

3-50 (3-51) **2m 5f** **(10 hdls)** £3,598.75 (£1,090.00: £532.50: £253.75) GOING minus 0.27 sec per fur (GF)

	Horse		Pos	SP	RR	SF
605[2]	**Blasket Hero (105)** (MrsSDWilliams) **8-11-0b** NWilliamson (hdwy 7th: led appr last: drvn out)	—	1	7/2[3]	89	22
723*	**Amaze (111)** (LadyHerries) **7-10-13**(7) MrRThornton (swtg: hdwy 7th: rdn appr last: ev ch flat: unable qckn)	1½	2	5/2[1]	94	27
	Mr Copyforce (101) (MissBSanders) **6-10-10** MRichards (hdwy to chse ldr appr 7th: led appr 2 out tl appr last: ev ch flat: one pce)	¾	3	7/1	83	16
657[3]	**Cabochon (95)** (JJoseph) **9-10-4** CLlewellyn (w ldr: led 2nd to 5th: wknd 3 out)	17	4	20/1	64	—
	Cavina (108) (NAGraham) **6-11-3** GBradley (led: j.lft 1st: hdd 2nd: led 5th tl appr 2 out: sn wknd: t.o)	dist	5	3/1[2]	—	—
	Jimmy's Cross (IRE) (115) (GBBalding) **6-11-10** APMcCoy (a bhd: t.o whn p.u bef 2 out)		P	4/1	—	—

(SP 113.1%) **6 Rn**

4m 57.6 (5.60) CSF £12.17 TOTE £5.00: £1.90 £1.60 (£4.60) OWNER Miss H. J. Flower (SOUTH MOLTON) BRED M. Channon

605 Blasket Hero is steadily rising in the handicap - he was 10lb higher than when making a winning return to action in August - but that was not enough to stop him. (7/2)

723* Amaze saw out this longer trip well and was still battling hard for the advantage on the run-in before tapped for toe. (5/2)

Mr Copyforce, winner of two handicaps on the Flat this year, was only tapped for toe in the run-in. (7/1: 5/1-8/1)

Cabochon is at his best with some cut in the ground. (20/1)

Cavina looked pretty straight for this reappearance and made a lot of the running. (3/1: 5/2-4/1)
Jimmy's Cross (IRE) (4/1: 9/4-9/2)

811 KEMPTON PARK H'CAP CHASE (0-135) (5-Y.O+) (Class C)
4-20 (4-22) **2m 4f 110y (17 fncs)** £4,772.00 (£1,342.00: £656.00) GOING minus 0.13 sec per fur (G)

	Horse	Dist	Pos	SP	RR	SF
	Glemot (IRE) (134) (KCBailey) **8-11-13** JOsborne (led to 13th: led 4 out to 3 out: led 2 out to last: hrd rdn: led last strides)	—	**1**	3/1[2]	143	63
	Super Tactics (IRE) (116) (RHAlner) **8-10-4**(5) PHenley (swtg: hld up: rdn appr 2 out: led last: hrd rdn: hdd last strides)	nk	**2**	6/1[3]	125	45
496[2]	**Conti D'Estruval (FR) (122)** (GBBalding) **6-11-1** APMcCoy (swtg: chsd wnr: led 13th to 4 out: led 3 out to 2 out: wknd flat)	10	**3**	15/8[1]	123	43
742*	**Captain Khedive (130)** (PFNicholls) **8-11-9** PHide (lw: hld up: ev ch whn fell 13th)		**F**	15/8[1]	—	—
				(SP 108.9%)		**4 Rn**

5m 1.5 (0.50) CSF £15.51 TOTE £3.70: (£5.70) OWNER Mr Dennis Yardy (UPPER LAMBOURN) BRED A. Murphy
Glemot (IRE), off the course since breaking a blood-vessel at Stratford at the beginning of June, won first time out last season. (3/1)
Super Tactics (IRE), awash with sweat beforehand for this seasonal debut, looked sure to score as he jumped into the lead at the last. However, he had not bargained on the winner being quite so tenacious. This was a fine performance considering he has done all his winning with some cut in the ground, and he should not take long to find a race. (6/1)
496 Conti D'Estruval (FR) was collared by the winner two out and tied up from the last. (15/8)
742* Captain Khedive looked very well beforehand but we are none the wiser about whether he stays this longer trip as he was still travelling very well with every chance when falling five out. He should soon regain the winning thread. (15/8)

812 KIDS RACE FREE NOVICES' HURDLE (4-Y.O+) (Class D)
4-50 (4-52) **2m (8 hdls)** £2,840.00 (£860.00: £420.00: £200.00) GOING minus 0.27 sec per fur (GF)

	Horse	Dist	Pos	SP	RR	SF
	Mazzini (IRE) (RRowe) **5-10-7**(5) LAspell (bit bkwd: hdwy 4th: led last: drvn out)	—	**1**	20/1	75	18
634[13]	**Wanstead (IRE) (85)** (JRJenkins) **4-10-12b[1]** AMaguire (lw: a.p: led 2 out to last: hrd rdn: r.o)	¾	**2**	7/1[3]	75	17
	Ath Cheannaithe (FR) (95) (JNeville) **4-10-12** DBridgwater (lw: led to 2 out: ev ch last: unable qckn)	2	**3**	4/1[2]	73	15
	Samaka Hara (IRE) (86) (GraemeRoe) **4-10-12** NWilliamson (a.p: rdn appr 2 out: sn wknd)	10	**4**	8/1	63	5
	Jaazim (MMadgwick) **6-10-12** BFenton (nvr nr to chal)	2½	**5**	14/1	60	3
	Water Hazard (IRE) (SDow) **4-10-12** APMcCoy (bit bkwd: prom tl appr 2 out)	6	**6**	8/1	55	—
	Hunters Rock (IRE) (KCBailey) **7-10-12** AThornton (lw: hld up: j.slowly 5th: mstke 3 out: sn wknd)	2½	**7**	11/10[1]	51	—
603[6]	**Colin's Pride** (MrsSDWilliams) **5-10-7** RFarrant (bhd fr 3 out)	13	**8**	50/1	33	—
	Cultural Icon (USA) (PMitchell) **4-10-12** GBradley (a bhd)	10	**9**	33/1	29	—
	Mannagar (IRE) (JRPoulton) **4-10-5**(7) MrPO'Keeffe (a bhd)	21	**10**	50/1	8	—
	Millfield Miss (HEHaynes) **7-10-7** GUpton (bit bkwd: a wl bhd: t.o fr 4th: p.u bef last)		**P**	50/1	—	—
				(SP 122.6%)		**11 Rn**

3m 46.6 (4.60) CSF £145.02 TOTE £37.00: £3.90 £1.70 £2.00 (£82.40) Trio £264.60 OWNER Mr Nicholas Cooper (PULBOROUGH) BRED Mrs M. Little
WEIGHT FOR AGE 4yo-1lb
Mazzini (IRE) belied his paddock appearance, responding to pressure to win this poor event. (20/1)
476 Wanstead (IRE) ran much better with the first-time blinkers on. (7/1)
Ath Cheannaithe (FR), tailed off in a claimer at Windsor on the Flat back in May on his last outing, was a different kettle of fish here. (4/1)
Samaka Hara (IRE) had been off the track since running on the All-Weather at Lingfield back in February. (8/1)
Jaazim, who has run seventeen times on the Flat this year without winning, never posed a serious threat. (14/1)
Water Hazard (IRE) looked in need of this first run of the season. (8/1)
Hunters Rock (IRE), an ex-Irish gelding who won two fast ground bumpers there, was having his first run in just over a year. His jumping let him down here and he tamely dropped away from the third last. (11/10: 4/5-6/5)

T/Plpt: £460.20 (20.15 Tckts). T/Qdpt: £122.10 (4.97 Tckts). AK

0654-FONTWELL (Fig. 8) (Good to firm)
Monday October 7th

813 SUSAN CORK BIRTHDAY NOVICES' CLAIMING HURDLE (4-Y.O+) (Class F)
2-30 (2-30) **2m 6f 110y (11 hdls)** £2,138.40 (£592.40: £283.20) GOING: 0.00 sec per fur (G)

	Horse	Dist	Pos	SP	RR	SF
659[3]	**Scamallach (IRE) (85)** (JRJenkins) **6-11-4b** GBradley (hdwy 8th: chsd ldr fr 3 out: led appr last: comf)	—	**1**	11/2[2]	64+	—
749[4]	**Ferens Hall (53)** (MJRoberts) **9-10-8** PMcLoughlin (led: clr 2nd: hrd rdn appr 2 out: hdd appr last: wknd flat)	12	**2**	10/1[3]	46	—
156[6]	**Coolegale (55)** (LWells) **10-10-8** AMaguire (bit bkwd: a.p: chsd ldr 4th to 8th: wknd appr 2 out)	nk	**3**	20/1	45	—
690[4]	**China Mail (IRE) (93)** (KCBailey) **4-11-3b[1]** CO'Dwyer (reminders 5th: bhd fr 6th: t.o)	dist	**4**	13/8[1]	—	—
	Keep-On (JCPoulton) **8-10-0** TJMurphy (bhd fr 8th: t.o)	18	**5**	50/1	—	—
	Shalholme (JMBradley) **6-10-0** BFenton (bhd fr 8th: t.o)	23	**6**	40/1	—	—
	Churchtown Spirit (TPMcGovern) **5-10-12** GCrone (bit bkwd: a wl bhd: t.o fr 5th: p.u bef 8th)		**P**	33/1	—	—
	Greenside Chat (IRE) (88) (SDow) **6-11-3** APMcCoy (hdwy 6th: chsd ldr 8th to 3 out: 4th & wkng whn p.u bef 2 out)		**P**	13/8[1]	—	—
	Aerodynamic (MrsLCJewell) **10-10-0**(5) SophieMitchell (bit bkwd: chsd ldr 1st to 4th: wknd 5th: t.o whn p.u bef 8th)		**P**	20/1	—	—
				(SP 117.5%)		**9 Rn**

5m 34.9 CSF £53.10 TOTE £5.30: £1.20 £1.90 £3.30 (£21.30) Trio £82.10 OWNER Mrs Susan McCarthy (ROYSTON) BRED Kevin O'Donnell
WEIGHT FOR AGE 4yo-1lb
659 Scamallach (IRE) was given a nice ride by Bradley, who judged the race perfectly and was not bothered at all that the leader had established a thirty-length lead at one stage. She cruised into the lead approaching the last to win with plenty to spare. (11/2: 7/2-6/1)
749 Ferens Hall, making a quick reappearance, did not hang around and had established a lead of some thirty lengths at one stage, but he was gradually reeled in. This longer trip may have just found him out. (10/1: 8/1-12/1)
Coolegale looked in need of this first run in three months. (20/1)

690 China Mail (IRE), winner of two races in August, disappointed last time, and even the drop in class here and first-time blinkers was not enough to see him return to form. Punters knew their fate by halfway and he looks one to be wary of. (13/8: 5/4-15/8)
Greenside Chat (IRE) looked rough in the paddock for this reappearance. (13/8)

814 FRANK CUNDELL CHALLENGE TROPHY H'CAP CHASE (0-120) (5-Y.O+) (Class D)

3-00 (3-00) **2m 3f (16 fncs)** £3,720.00 (£1,110.00: £530.00: £240.00) GOING: 0.14 sec per fur (G)

				SP	RR	SF
	Aedean (93) (GPEnright) **7-10-1** AMaguire (lw: hld up: led 4 out to 3 out: led last: all out)	—	1	8/1	98	21
470[3]	**Armala (107)** (JTGifford) **11-10-10**(5) LAspell (lw: a.p: led 6th to 4 out: led 3 out to last: hrd rdn: r.o wl)	s.h	2	7/2[2]	112	35
656[U]	**Henley Wood (98)** (PJHobbs) **11-10-3**(3) GTormey (led 2nd to 3rd: lost pl 12th: rallied appr 3 out: r.o wl flat)	nk	3	3/1[1]	103	26
464[4]	**Who's to Say (120)** (MissVenetiaWilliams) **10-11-9**(5) MichaelBrennan (led to 2nd: led 3rd to 6th: rdn 4 out: 4th & btn whn mstke last)	5	4	10/1	121	44
20[6]	**Black Church (98)** (RRowe) **10-10-6** RDunwoody (lw: stdy hdwy 12th: rdn appr 2 out: sn wknd)	1¾	5	5/1[3]	97	20
	Kindle's Delight (105) (MissHCKnight) **8-10-13** JFTitley (bit bkwd: bhd fr 3 out)	12	6	11/2	94	17
728[2]	**Wingspan (USA) (94)** (AGNewcombe) **12-10-2** AThornton (mstkes 4th & 6th: a bhd: t.o)	dist	7	13/2	—	—
				(SP 112.8%)	**7 Rn**	

4m 49.4 (10.40) CSF £33.49 CT £93.60 TOTE £10.10: £3.50 £2.10 (£15.10) OWNER Mr M. B. Orpen-Palmer (LEWES) BRED Miss J. Chaplin
Aedean looked in really good shape for this seasonal bow and, jumping into the lead for the second time at the last, held on by the skin of his teeth. (8/1: 10/1-6/1)
470 Armala, a lot fitter for his recent run here, ran a fine race and battled his heart out to fail by only a whisker. A trip to the winner's enclosure looks imminent. (7/2)
656 Henley Wood, running on strongly, only just failed in a tight finish. (3/1: 2/1-100/30)
464 Who's to Say is often let down by his jumping. Apart from one victory over two and a quarter miles, all his winning has been done at two. (10/1: 6/1-12/1)
Black Church, 3lb higher than when last successful, was having his first run in four months but looked to be going really well as he eased his way into the action five out. However, when let down, he found lack of a recent run taking its toll. (5/1)

815 'SALMON SPRAY' CHALLENGE TROPHY H'CAP HURDLE (0-125) (4-Y.O+) (Class D)

3-30 (3-30) **2m 2f 110y (9 hdls)** £2,846.00 (£848.00: £404.00: £182.00) GOING: 0.00 sec per fur (G)

				SP	RR	SF
55[7]	**Chris's Glen (85)** (JMBradley) **7-10-0v** NWilliamson (chsd ldr: led 5th tl appr 2 out: hrd rdn & led flat: r.o wl)	—	1	10/1	67	—
591[3]	**Re Roi (IRE) (97)** (WGMTurner) **4-10-6**(5) PHenley (lw: hld up: chsd ldr fr 5th: led appr 2 out: hrd rdn & hdd flat: r.o)	½	2	7/4[1]	79	—
	Bon Voyage (USA) (102) (DMGrissell) **4-11-2** JRKavanagh (hld up: rdn appr 2 out: sn wknd)	8	3	9/4[2]	77	—
682[2]	**Gone by (IRE) (109)** (JRJenkins) **8-11-10v** GBradley (lw: a bhd)	4	4	4/1[3]	80	—
	Star of David (IRE) (103) (MissAEEmbiricos) **8-11-4** RDunwoody (led: clr 2nd: rel to r fr 3rd: hdd 5th: sn wknd: p.u bef 6th)		P	5/1	—	—
				(SP 112.9%)	**5 Rn**	

4m 37.0 CSF £26.89 TOTE £9.60: £2.20 £1.70 (£11.10) OWNER The Crown At Hambrook Racing Club (CHEPSTOW) BRED Mrs R. Bradley
LONG HANDICAP Chris's Glen 9-13
WEIGHT FOR AGE 4yo-1lb
OFFICIAL EXPLANATION **Star of David (IRE): was found to be suffering from a fibrillating heart after the race.**
Chris's Glen was given a fine ride by Williamson to win his first race over this slightly longer trip. (10/1: 6/1-11/1)
591 Re Roi (IRE), who has changed stables again since his last run, appeared to have made a winning move as he gained control approaching the second last, but his jockey got slightly unbalanced on the run-in and he was headed in the last 75 yards. (7/4)
Bon Voyage (USA) found lack of a recent run taking its toll over the last two hurdles. (9/4: op 6/4)
Star of David (IRE) (5/1: 4/1-6/1)

816 STREBEL BOILERS AND RADIATORS SERIES H'CAP HURDLE (Qualifier) (0-110) (4-Y.O+) (Class E)

4-00 (4-00) **2m 6f 110y (10 hdls)** £2,490.00 (£690.00: £330.00) GOING: 0.00 sec per fur (G)

				SP	RR	SF
	Victor Bravo (NZ) (103) (NAGaselee) **9-11-7b** CLlewellyn (hdwy 4th: led 2 out: j.lft last: comf)	—	1	16/1	89	—
	Sophie May (96) (GLMoore) **5-11-0** APMcCoy (hdwy appr 2 out: rdn appr last: unable qckn)	6	2	14/1	78	—
590[3]	**Mr Snaggle (IRE) (94)** (SEarle) **7-10-5**(7) BMcGann (hdwy 7th: led appr 2 out: sn hdd: one pce)	hd	3	6/1	76	—
655[U]	**Roger's Pal (82)** (AMoore) **9-9-7**(7) MBatchelor (lost pl 8th: r.o one pce fr 2 out)	5	4	66/1	60	—
	Karar (IRE) (109) (RRowe) **6-11-8**(5) LAspell (nvr nr to chal)	¾	5	6/1	87	—
	Captain Coe (87) (RCurtis) **6-10-5** DMorris (bit bkwd: led tl appr 2 out: sn wknd: lame)	6	6	3/1[1]	60	—
720[F]	**Dorans Way (IRE) (93)** (MissVenetiaWilliams) **5-10-6**(5) MichaelBrennan (hdwy 7th: ev ch appr 2 out: sn wknd)	18	7	25/1	54	—
	Punch's Hotel (110) (RRowe) **11-12-0b** NWilliamson (prom to 7th)	6	8	12/1	66	—
657[2]	**Circus Colours (98)** (JRJenkins) **6-11-2** AMaguire (lw: s.s: a bhd)	3	9	11/2[3]	52	—
692[3]	**Scud Missile (IRE) (102)** (GFJohnsonHoughton) **5-11-6** AThornton (lw: prom to 7th)	nk	10	9/2[2]	56	—
				(SP 112.7%)	**10 Rn**	

5m 31.8 CSF £182.31 CT £1,359.40 TOTE £20.30: £4.10 £4.10 £2.20 (£97.40) Trio £320.60 OWNER Mrs R. W. S. Baker (LAMBOURN) BRED A. W. Herbert
LONG HANDICAP Roger's Pal 8-0
Victor Bravo (NZ) eased his way to the front two out and, despite jumping left at the last, had things nicely under control to give his trainer a winner with his first runner in nearly five months. (16/1)
Sophie May, who looked rather rough in the paddock for this reappearance, never had a hope with the winner. (14/1: 8/1-16/1)
590 Mr Snaggle (IRE) is yet to win in this country. (6/1)
Roger's Pal, 28lb out of the handicap, did struggle on past beaten horses to finish a moderate fourth. He is no better than a poor plater. (66/1)
Karar (IRE) probably needs further than this as the one thing he does is stay. (6/1: 4/1-13/2)
Punch's Hotel (12/1: 9/2-14/1)

817 SINGLETON NOVICES' AMATEUR H'CAP CHASE (0-100) (5-Y.O+) (Class F)

4-30 (4-30) **3m 2f 110y (22 fncs)** £2,685.60 (£741.60: £352.80) GOING: 0.14 sec per fur (G)

				SP	RR	SF
595[6]	**Seasamacamile (71)** (RHBuckler) **9-9-7**(7) MrRThornton (lw: chsd ldr fr 4th: led 4 out: rdn out)	—	1	9/4[2]	72	—

				SP	RR	SF
658[2]	**Distant Memory (99)** (PJHobbs) **7-11-7b**(7) MrSMulcaire (led: pckd 18th: hdd 4 out: hrd rdn appr 2 out: unable qckn)	2½	2	4/5 1	99	—
213[6]	**Artful Arthur (75)** (LPGrassick) **10-9-11**(7)ow4 MrJGrassick (chsd ldr to 4th: wknd 15th: t.o)	dist	3	7/1 3	—	—
590[P]	**Ennistymon (IRE) (79)** (JWMullins) **5-9-12**(7)ow5 MrGWeatherley (lw: 4th whn mstke & uns rdr 4th)		U	8/1	—	—

(SP 109.9%) **4 Rn**

7m 14.5 (34.50) CSF £4.38 TOTE £3.40 (£1.90) OWNER Mr M. West (BRIDPORT) BRED Lt-Col J. A. and Mrs Dene
LONG HANDICAP Seasamacamile 9-6 Artful Arthur 9-11 Ennistymon (IRE) 9-4
WEIGHT FOR AGE 5yo-3lb
Seasamacamile is extremely moderate, but she had a talented rider aboard and, given a lovely ride, proved too good for the wayward runner-up. (9/4)
658 Distant Memory is not an easy ride. Though successful nine times, including twice this season, he is not one to be overly confident about. (4/5: 1/2-Evens)
Ennistymon (IRE) (8/1: 7/2-9/1)

818 LANGSTONE CONSERVATIVE CLUB NOVICES' HURDLE (4-Y.O+) (Class E)
5-00 (5-00) **2m 2f 110y (9 hdls)** £2,511.00 (£696.00: £333.00) GOING: 0.00 sec per fur (G)

				SP	RR	SF
	Mr Edgar (IRE) (JTGifford) **5-10-12** PHide (bit bkwd: hld up: lft in ld after 3 out: lft clr flat)	—	1	8/11 1	81	—
675[4]	**Dacelo (FR)** (OSherwood) **5-10-12** JOsborne (lw: led to 4th: led 6th tl tried to run out & hdd after 3 out: ev ch whn hung rt appr last: swvd rt & rdr lost irons flat: nt rcvr)	12	2	2/1 2	71+	—
675[9]	**Caddy's First (84)** (SMellor) **4-10-11** NMann (led 4th to 6th: wknd appr last)	5	3	9/1 3	66	—
	Zuno Flyer (USA) (AMoore) **4-10-11** APMcCoy (hld up: rdn 6th: 4th & btn whn mstke last)	1	4	14/1	65	—
	Allez Pablo (RRowe) **6-10-7**(5) LAspell (prom to 5th: t.o)	dist	5	50/1	—	—
	Ravus (KVincent) **6-10-12** ADicken (a bhd: t.o fr 5th)	8	6	66/1	—	—
	Hollow Wood (IRE) (DLWilliams) **5-10-12** BPowell (hdwy 4th: reminders 5th: sn wknd: t.o)	4	7	33/1	—	—

(SP 114.3%) **7 Rn**

4m 29.9 CSF £2.58 TOTE £1.60: £1.10 £1.60 (£1.90) OWNER Felix Rosenstiel's Widow & Son (FINDON) BRED M. J. Clancy and Miss Esther Feeney
WEIGHT FOR AGE 4yo-1lb
Mr Edgar (IRE) did not look fully fit but, with the wayward runner-up steering an erratic course, he was left clear on the run-in. (8/11: 1/2-Evens)
675 Dacelo (FR) thoroughly disgraced himself. In front early on the final circuit, he then tried to run out at just about every possible opportunity, ultimately causing Osborne to lose his irons on the flat. Dacelo has ability, but looks one to avoid. (2/1)
603 Caddy's First has had his chances but, after showing in front in the middle part of the race, had given his all from the second last. (9/1: 5/1-10/1)
Zuno Flyer (USA), fit from the Flat, was a spent force in the last half-mile. (14/1)

T/Plpt: £1,228.30 (12.03 Tckts). T/Qdpt: £126.10 (8.85 Tckts). AK

TOWCESTER (R-H) (Good to firm)
Wednesday October 9th
WEATHER: fine

819 ASCOTE (S) HURDLE (4, 5 & 6-Y.O) (Class G)
2-20 (2-23) **2m 5f (11 hdls)** £1,989.00 (£554.00: £267.00) GOING minus 0.11 sec per fur (G)

				SP	RR	SF
579a[8]	**Do Be Ware (61)** (JFfitch-Heyes) **6-11-5b** BFenton (chsd ldr: hit 1st: led appr last: sn rdn clr)	—	1	16/1	41?	—
697[3]	**Parish Walk (IRE) (80)** (KJDrewry) **5-10-12** AMaguire (lw: led: hit 3 out: wknd & hdd appr last: fin tired)	9	2	4/6 1	27	—
649[3]	**Saltis (IRE)** (ALForbes) **4-10-11** TEley (lw: chsd ldrs: lost pl 3 out: kpt on appr last)	nk	3	9/4 2	27	—
634[10]	**Northern Law** (JohnBerry) **4-10-11b**[1] ILawrence (bhd fr 4th: mstke & rdn next: t.o whn p.u bef 7th)		P	4/1 3	—	—

(SP 116.7%) **4 Rn**

5m 20.5 (18.50) CSF £28.42 TOTE £16.30 (£10.60) OWNER Mr John Ffitch-Heyes (LEWES) BRED R. and Mrs J. Digby-Ware
WEIGHT FOR AGE 4yo-1lb
No bid
579a Do Be Ware, who had previously seemed suited by a soft surface, handled this ground and won by stamina alone. (16/1)
697 Parish Walk (IRE), stepping up in trip, was made plenty of use of and paid the penalty in the last half-mile after looking all over the winner. (4/6)
649 Saltis (IRE), whose rider seemed to settle for third place some way out, found the first two going nowhere in the home straight. (9/4)
Northern Law, bandaged in front, moved poorly to post and was in trouble after the first mile. (4/1)

820 OLD STRATFORD NOVICES' HURDLE (4-Y.O+) (Class D)
2-50 (2-50) **2m (8 hdls)** £2,889.00 (£804.00: £387.00) GOING minus 0.11 sec per fur (G)

				SP	RR	SF
	Young Radical (IRE) (92) (JohnUpson) **4-10-11** RSupple (swtg: hld up: led on bit appr 2 out: rdn out)	—	1	4/6 1	63	1
	Tomal (RIngram) **4-10-11** APMcCoy (lw: a.p: mstke 5th: ev ch 2 out: hit last: edgd rt & no ex flat)	1¾	2	13/8 2	61	—
675[14]	**Ragtime Song** (JRJenkins) **7-10-12v** GBradley (lw: led: clr appr 3rd: rdn & hdd appr 2 out: one pce)	4	3	14/1 3	57	—
	Bite the Bullet (AJChamberlain) **5-10-12** BPowell (blnd 2nd: in tch tl appr 2 out)	13	4	33/1	44	—
	Prince Rico (WMBrisbourne) **5-10-12** SWynne (bkwd: bhd fr 3rd: t.o whn mstke next)	dist	5	33/1	—	—

(SP 110.6%) **5 Rn**

3m 57.2 (11.20) CSF £2.08 TOTE £1.50: £1.00 £3.30 (£1.10) OWNER Mr N. Jones (TOWCESTER) BRED Nicholas Power
WEIGHT FOR AGE 4yo-1lb
Young Radical (IRE) got warm beforehand and dived at the early hurdles, before cruising to the front on the home turn. Asked to go on and win his race from the last, he swished his tail but did just enough. (4/6: op 2/5)
Tomal, withdrawn lame at the start on the Flat less than a fortnight ago, was fit, but moved rather poorly. Low at a number of hurdles, he tended to hang in behind the winner in the straight and it was his pilot's efforts going to the last which gave him a clear view of the hurdle. (13/8)
Ragtime Song, who had worn a visor once on the Flat but never over hurdles, proved very keen but gave his hurdles plenty of air. Despite his early enthusiasm, he kept plugging away once headed and ought to stay further. (14/1)

Bite the Bullet is very moderate and the fact that he remained on the premises for so long suggests this was a very poor contest. (33/1)

821 BIDDLESDEN NOVICES' CHASE (5-Y.O+) (Class E)
3-20 (3-20) **2m 110y (12 fncs)** £3,101.00 (£861.00: £413.00) GOING minus 0.11 sec per fur (G)

				SP	RR	SF
637[2]	**Mill O'The Rags (IRE) (89)** (MrsDHaine) **7-11-5** JFTitley (led to 7th: led 4 out: lft clr next: rdn out)	—	**1**	Evens[1]	107?	27
722[4]	**Martha's Daughter (83)** (CaptTAForster) **7-10-7** AThornton (hld up: mstke 1st: lft 2nd 3 out: hdwy whn hit next: sn rdn & btn)	3	**2**	Evens[1]	92?	12
	Larks Tail (PRWebber) **8-10-7** RBellamy (lw: mstkes: a bhd)	22	**3**	33/1[3]	71?	—
	Royal Hand (MMadgwick) **6-10-12** BFenton (hit 1st: chsd ldr: led 7th tl hit 4 out: ev ch whn blnd & uns rdr next)		**U**	16/1[2]	—	—
				(SP 108.8%)		**4 Rn**

4m 9.3 (7.30) CSF £2.28 TOTE £1.90 (£1.30) OWNER Mr E. J. Fenaroli (NEWMARKET) BRED Noel Fenton

637 Mill O'The Rags (IRE) is taking to fences and likes this course. Jumping well for a novice, he needed to be shaken up from the last, but was probably just idling in front. (Evens)

722 Martha's Daughter was again dropped out, but does not jump like a natural. Close enough if good enough two out, she made a mistake which saw her off the bit in a couple of strides. (Evens)

Larks Tail looked fit, despite six months off, and did not jump well, notably at the fourth last. She has shown so little before that the fact that she was not completely tailed off behind two quite promising horses reflects either well on her or badly on them. (33/1)

Royal Hand has shown little over hurdles but attacked his fences and was with the winner when ploughing through the third last, severing the partnership. (16/1)

822 KPMG PASAS H'CAP HURDLE (0-100) (4-Y.O+) (Class F)
3-50 (3-50) **2m (8 hdls)** £2,285.00 (£635.00: £305.00) GOING minus 0.11 sec per fur (G)

				SP	RR	SF
	Snow Board (65) (MrsMerritaJones) **7-10-3**ow1 DerekByrne (bit bkwd: a.p: led 3 out: rdn & r.o wl flat)	—	**1**	9/2	49	20
687[2]	**Ragamuffin Romeo (72)** (HJCollingridge) **7-10-10** NMann (lw: prom: rdn appr 3 out: ev ch appr last: edgd lft & one pce)	2½	**2**	2/1[2]	54	26
692[2]	**Wollboll (86)** (HJCollingridge) **6-11-10** VSmith (lw: led to 4th: ev ch 3 out: one pce appr next)	¾	**3**	15/8[1]	67	39
647[8]	**Exclusion (80)** (JHetherton) **7-11-4** RMarley (plld hrd: led 4th to 3 out: sn wknd)	26	**4**	10/1	35	7
723[3]	**Verde Luna (87)** (DWPArbuthnot) **4-11-10** APMcCoy (lw: hld up: ev ch 3 out: btn whn fell next)		**F**	9/4[3]	—	—
				(SP 126.2%)		**5 Rn**

3m 51.0 (5.00) CSF £14.97 TOTE £5.30: £1.60 £1.60 (£8.10) OWNER Mr F. J. Sainsbury (LAMBOURN) BRED Juddmonte Farms
WEIGHT FOR AGE 4yo-1lb

Snow Board, having his first run for the stable, was racing over a distance some way short of his optimum, but looked thrown in if anywhere near his best. Not very fluent at the fourth last as the tempo quickened, he stayed on in tremendous style from the last and should win again. (9/2: 5/2-5/1)

687 Ragamuffin Romeo dropped back last briefly at the third from home, but his stamina came into play on the final climb. (2/1)

692 Wollboll ran another sound race but was not able to dictate the pace from halfway. (15/8)

423 Exclusion pulls hard when not at the head of affairs and is probably best left to bowl along. (10/1)

823 LILLINGSTONE LOVELL H'CAP CHASE (0-110) (5-Y.O+) (Class E)
4-20 (4-20) **3m 1f (18 fncs)** £3,197.00 (£956.00: £458.00: £209.00) GOING minus 0.11 sec per fur (G)

				SP	RR	SF
597*	**Jim Valentine (91)** (DJWintle) **10-11-0** WMarston (lw: plld hrd: a gng wl: led last: qcknd clr: easily)	—	**1**	2/1[1]	102+	39
658*	**Frozen Drop (102)** (PCRitchens) **9-11-11** SFox (lw: prom: led 9th tl hdd & hit last: unable qckn)	4	**2**	9/4[2]	110	47
57[7]	**K C'S Dancer (79)** (RDickin) **11-10-2** JCulloty (prom tl rdn 3 out: kpt on flat)	15	**3**	14/1	78	15
	Titus Andronicus (89) (NAGaselee) **9-10-12b** CLlewellyn (trckd ldrs: rdn appr 2 out: no imp)	2	**4**	4/1[3]	87	24
484[7]	**Nick the Dreamer (100)** (WGMTurner) **11-11-9** RDunwoody (lw: led to 9th: btn appr 3 out)	1½	**5**	10/1	97	34
	Woodlands Genhire (77) (PAPritchard) **11-10-0** AMaguire (prom to 10th: sn bhd)	dist	**6**	12/1	—	—
	Polar Region (105) (NJHenderson) **10-11-9**(5) MrCVigors (a bhd: hit 10th & 12th: t.o whn p.u bef 3 out)		**P**	7/1	—	—
				(SP 120.1%)		**7 Rn**

6m 20.2 (5.20) CSF £7.23 TOTE £2.20: £2.10 £2.40 (£2.50) OWNER Mr R. H. L. Barnes (CHELTENHAM)
LONG HANDICAP Woodlands Genhire 9-10

597* Jim Valentine was a revelation, for he beat an even stronger field than last time with even more contempt. (2/1)

658* Frozen Drop, raised a harsh-looking 6lb for his win in a virtual no-race last time, ran with credit, but his mistake at the last made no difference as the winner was laughing at him. (9/4)

K C'S Dancer won an amateurs' chase at Cheltenham last October and could be on for a repeat, for this was much his best run since. (14/1: 10/1-16/1)

Titus Andronicus often runs well fresh and looked a danger at the third last, but was struggling by the next as lack of a recent run told. (4/1: 5/2-9/2)

Nick the Dreamer is on the small side and tended to get too close to his fences, forfeiting ground. He is not the first to find jumping here a tricky business. (10/1: 7/1-11/1)

Polar Region (7/1: 4/1-8/1)

824 COSGROVE NOVICES' H'CAP HURDLE (0-100) (4-Y.O+) (Class E)
4-50 (4-50) **3m (12 hdls)** £2,262.00 (£632.00: £306.00) GOING minus 0.11 sec per fur (G)

				SP	RR	SF
632[2]	**Hylters Chance (IRE) (69)** (PJHobbs) **5-10-10** APMcCoy (mde all: drew clr fr 3 out: easily)	—	**1**	Evens[1]	59+	—
673*	**Arrange A Game (70)** (MissJBower) **9-10-6**(5) STaylor (prom: hit 7th & 8th: outpcd 3 out: kpt on flat)	20	**2**	100/30[2]	47	—
655[2]	**Credit Controller (IRE) (62)** (JFfitch-Heyes) **7-10-3** AMaguire (plld hrd: chsd wnr fr 8th: hit next: blnd & rdn 3 out: sn btn)	nk	**3**	7/2[3]	39	—
	Pennant Cottage (IRE) (60) (MissKWhitehouse) **8-9-10**(5)ow1 ChrisWebb (bit bkwd: chsd wnr to 8th)	13	**4**	16/1	28	—
	Young Tess (83) (IRBrown) **6-11-10** MrABrown (bit bkwd: blnd 7th: sn bhd)	7	**5**	7/1	46	—
				(SP 113.7%)		**5 Rn**

5m 58.7 (18.70) CSF £4.77 TOTE £1.60: £1.30 £1.80 (£4.40) OWNER Mrs Karola Vann (MINEHEAD) BRED Miss Judith Collins
LONG HANDICAP Pennant Cottage (IRE) 9-11

632 Hylters Chance (IRE) fairly bolted in for McCoy, who looks very much his favoured pilot. (Evens)

673* Arrange A Game did not help his cause with some sloppy jumping on the final circuit, but does seem to stay, as he snatched second place right on the line. (100/30)
655 Credit Controller (IRE) takes a good hold, but is an ungainly hurdler, often landing in a heap, normally without losing much ground. His mistake at the third last quickly left him chasing shadows and he tied up, losing second place right on the line. (7/2: 3/1-9/2)
Pennant Cottage (IRE) has yet to prove competitive under Rules. (16/1)
Young Tess (7/1: op 5/2)
T/Plpt: £420.80 (17.92 Tckts). T/Qdpt: £26.50 (20.73 Tckts). Dk

LUDLOW (R-H) (Firm)
Thursday October 10th
WEATHER: fine but cloudy

825 SCANIA 4-SERIES 'HORSEPOWER' (S) H'CAP HURDLE (0-90) (4-Y.O+) (Class G)
2-20 (2-21) **2m 5f 110y (11 hdls)** £1,968.00 (£548.00: £264.00) GOING minus 0.27 sec per fur (GF)

				SP	RR	SF
673[6]	**King of Babylon (IRE) (70)** (FJordan) **4-11-6**(3) LAspell (lw: chsd ldr: led 3 out: clr last)	—	1	9/4 1	57	6
655[P]	**Lac de Gras (IRE) (63)** (RCurtis) **5-11-3** DMorris (a.p: chal 3 out: rdn & one pce appr last)	3½	2	8/1	47	—
673[7]	**They All Forgot Me (59)** (AWCarroll) **9-10-13** MissCDyson (led to 3 out: sn hrd rdn: kpt on one pce)	2½	3	5/1 3	42	—
725[6]	**Dane Rose (70)** (MSheppard) **10-11-10** AMaguire (hld up in rr: hdwy 8th: rdn & outpcd appr 2 out)	1¼	4	5/2 2	52	2
	Awestruck (52) (BPreece) **6-10-3b**(3) GHogan (hld up in rr: effrt & rdn along appr 3 out: no imp: t.o)	16	5	10/1	22	—
737[R]	**Siesta Time (USA) (53)** (DBurchell) **6-10-7** DJBurchell (reluctant to r: ref 1st)		R	7/1	—	—
				(SP 108.7%)	**6 Rn**	

5m 14.2 (13.20) CSF £17.02 TOTE £2.90: £1.60 £2.40 (£7.60) OWNER Mr R. A. Hancocks (LEOMINSTER)
WEIGHT FOR AGE 4yo-1lb
673 King of Babylon (IRE) did not need to exert himself unduly to get off the mark in such a poor contest, and it is sure to get harder from now on. (9/4)
406 Lac de Gras (IRE), a parrot-mouthed gelding, put in a determined challenge three out, but the winner was galloping all over him and he had met his match between the last two. (8/1)
598 They All Forgot Me is not the force he once was and his front-running tactics soon came to an end entering the home straight. (5/1: op 3/1)
Awestruck (10/1: op 6/1)

826 KNIGHTON TRUCKS FOR SCANIA NOVICES' CHASE (4-Y.O+) (Class E)
2-50 (2-57) **2m (13 fncs)** £3,242.00 (£912.00: £446.00) GOING minus 0.27 sec per fur (GF)

				SP	RR	SF
	Tenayestelign (DMarks) **8-11-0** JAMcCarthy (bkwd: s.s: lft in ld appr 6th: hdd 9th: lft in ld appr 4 out: r.o wl)	—	1	4/1 2	61	—
738[P]	**Ryton Run** (MrsSMOdell) **11-11-9** BFenton (led to 2nd: slipped bnd after 5th: led 9th: slipped & hdd appr 4 out: mstke next: one pce)	3	2	20/1	67	—
808[3]	**Holy Wanderer (USA)** (TRGeorge) **7-11-2**(3) GHogan (led 2nd: sn wl clr: s.u bnd appr 6th: rmntd)	dist	3	4/7 1	—	—
722[P]	**Laura Lye (IRE) (62)** (BdeHaan) **6-11-0** JRailton (w.r.s. & uns rdr: t.n.p)		R	11/1	—	—
	Chapel of Barras (IRE) (BGee) **7-11-5** BPowell (Withdrawn not under Starter's orders: bolted bef s)		W	8/1 3	—	—
				(SP 107.8%)	**4 Rn**	

4m 9.6 (17.60) CSF £28.29 TOTE £4.30: £3.10 (£11.50) OWNER Mr G. J. King (UPPER LAMBOURN) BRED Snailwell Stud Co Ltd
Tenayestelign performs best when fresh but she did look very much in need of this seasonal debut. Taking over for a second time turning in, she stuck on really well and opened her account over fences. (4/1)
674 Ryton Run had trouble handling these tight bends and, losing his footing when in front approaching the fourth last, could never quite get back at the winner. With any luck at all he would have won this. (20/1)
808 Holy Wanderer (USA) took a fearsome hold in the early stages, and he had gone well clear when his feet went from under him turning into the back straight. He was remounted but had little chance of reaching the leading pair in a race he would probably have won unchallenged. (4/7)

827 RADIO SHROPSHIRE STAYERS' H'CAP HURDLE (0-120) (4-Y.O+) (Class D)
3-20 (3-20) **3m 2f 110y (13 hdls)** £2,787.00 (£782.00: £381.00) GOING minus 0.27 sec per fur (GF)

				SP	RR	SF
721[3]	**Holy Joe (99)** (DBurchell) **14-10-7** DJBurchell (j.w: led tl after 7th: rallied appr last: led flat: r.o wl)	—	1	3/1 2	80	—
	Nathan Blake (92) (WGMTurner) **11-9-7b**(7) JPower (bit bkwd: chsd wnr: led after 7th: qcknd clr 4 out: hdd & no ex flat)	2	2	25/1	72	—
703[4]	**Don du Cadran (FR) (99)** (CaptTAForster) **7-10-7b1** AThornton (chsd ldng pair fr 4th: rdn appr 3 out: r.o wl flat)	½	3	5/1 3	79	—
690*	**Tallywagger (120)** (GMMoore) **9-12-0** NBentley (racd wd: hld up: outpcd 4 out: sn btn)	9	4	5/4 1	94	—
725[4]	**Storm Drum (94)** (KCBailey) **7-9-9**(7)ow2 MrRWakley (hld up in rr: outpcd 8th: t.o fr 4 out)	5	5	10/1	65	—
644[4]	**George Ashford (IRE) (92)** (PRJohnson) **6-10-0** ASSmith (lost pl 4th: t.o fr 8th)	23	6	7/1	49	—
				(SP 111.5%)	**6 Rn**	

6m 20.9 (21.90) CSF £44.76 TOTE £4.40: £1.40 £4.40 (£64.40) OWNER Mr Simon Lewis (EBBW VALE) BRED Mrs Maureen F. Hogan
LONG HANDICAP Nathan Blake 9-10 Storm Drum 9-13 George Ashford (IRE) 9-9
721 Holy Joe jumps hurdles for fun even at his advanced stage and, in his element over this extended trip, shows that he still retains all his ability. (3/1)
Nathan Blake, successful three times at this track in the past, did not look fully wound up for this return to hurdles, but he quickened into a commanding lead on the long home turn and may well have stayed there had he not blown up. (25/1)
703 Don du Cadran (FR), fitted with blinkers for the first time, could never get himself into contention but he stayed on particularly well in the latter stages, and it could be that he needs a thorough test of stamina to bring out the best in him. (5/1)
690* Tallywagger usually finds such trips made to measure, but failed to hold his pitch when the leader quickened things up at the end of the back straight, and that was the end of him. (5/4)

828 SCANIA 1996 TRUCK OF THE YEAR TROPHY NOVICES' H'CAP CHASE (0-100) (5-Y.O+) (Class E)
3-50 (3-50) **2m 4f (17 fncs)** £3,648.00 (£1,028.00: £504.00) GOING minus 0.27 sec per fur (GF)

				SP	RR	SF
637[4]	**On the Tear (61)** (FLloyd) **10-10-4** CLlewellyn (bkwd: chsd ldr: led 12th: lft clr 4 out: all out)	—	1	6/1 3	68	—

				SP	RR	SF
637^{3}	**Little By Little (60)** (BPreece) **6-10-3** AThornton (bkwd: mstke 4th: hdwy 4 out: chal last: rdn & wnt lft flat: sn btn)	2	**2**	7/1	65	—
722^{6}	**Script (63)** (JRJenkins) **5-10-4** WMarston (hld up: j.slowly 10th: sn outpcd: rdn appr 4 out: styd on)	3	**3**	13/8^{2}	66	—
752*	**Blue Raven (90)** (DavidBrace) **5-12-3** ^{7x} AMaguire (led: j.b rt 7th: hdd 12th: disp ld whn fell 4 out)		**F**	11/8^{1}	—	—
				(SP 107.0%)		**4 Rn**

5m 14.1 (22.10) CSF £30.90 TOTE £7.90 (£7.90) OWNER Mr F. Lloyd (BANGOR-ON-DEE) BRED Martin McGrath
WEIGHT FOR AGE 5yo-2lb

On the Tear took the favourite on from the start, and still held a slight lead when left with a commanding advantage four out, but his stride began to shorten and he may well have emerged second best if the runner-up had steered a straight course from the last. (6/1)

Little By Little, a winner between the Flags, stayed on to challenge at the last but he hung badly left on this short run-in and gave away a winning opportunity. (7/1)

552 Script has not much confidence in his jumping as yet and he was always struggling with the pace, but he did stay on in the closing stages and time is on his side. (13/8)

752* Blue Raven had a battle on his hands but had rejoined the winner when he failed to take off at the fourth last and turned a somersault. He would have won. (11/8: op Evens)

829 SCANIA 4-SERIES INTERNATIONAL CHALLENGE NOVICES' HURDLE (4-Y.O+) (Class E)

4-20 (4-20) **2m (9 hdls)** £2,192.00 (£612.00: £296.00) GOING minus 0.27 sec per fur (GF)

				SP	RR	SF
	Sigma Run (IRE) (81) (JACEdwards) **7-10-12** THazlett (bit bkwd: mde all: sn clr: shkn up appr last: rdn out)	—	**1**	8/13^{1}	70	—
	Superensis (JohnBerry) **6-10-12** TWheeler (swtg: chsd wnr: outpcd appr 2 out: kpt on u.p flat)	2½	**2**	4/1^{3}	68	—
	Jon's Choice (BPreece) **8-10-12** CLlewellyn (hld up: stdy hdwy appr 3 out: chal 2 out: rdn & one pce flat)	hd	**3**	7/2^{2}	67	—
	Andy Coin (WMBrisbourne) **5-10-7** JFTitley (a bhd: effrt appr 3 out: no imp: t.o)	14	**4**	20/1	48	—
				(SP 108.9%)		**4 Rn**

3m 50.9 (13.90) CSF £3.30 TOTE £1.30 (£2.20) OWNER B G S Racing Partnership (ROSS-ON-WYE) BRED David Fenton

Sigma Run (IRE) has promised so much but achieved so little, but on occasions has looked to be a lost cause. He found the weakest contest to finally make his mark over hurdles and even then was all out to succeed. (8/13: 4/9-4/6)

Superensis jumped fluently on this hurdling debut and stayed on well in the closing stages after getting outpaced early in the straight. (4/1)

Jon's Choice, an All-Weather specialist on the Flat, has not yet won beyond seven furlongs and, though he delayed his challenge until as late as possible, failed to last home. Hee is going to find it increasingly difficulty to win at this game. (7/2)

830 KNIGHTON TRUCKS 'SCANIA KNOW-HOW' TROPHY H'CAP CHASE (0-100) (5-Y.O+) (Class F)

4-50 (4-52) **2m 4f (17 fncs)** £3,068.00 (£752.00) GOING minus 0.27 sec per fur (GF)

				SP	RR	SF
583^{3}	**Crackling Frost (IRE) (74)** (MrsDHaine) **8-10-2** JFTitley (j.w: plld hrd: led appr 4th: clr 8th: hit 4 out: unchal)	—	**1**	5/6^{1}	81	17
656^{2}	**Drumstick (96)** (KCBailey) **10-11-10** JRailton (lw: led tl appr 4th: rallied 13th: rdn 3 out: sn outpcd)	15	**2**	Evens^{2}	91	27
				(SP 104.5%)		**2 Rn**

4m 55.9 (3.90) TOTE £1.60 OWNER The Unlucky For Some Partnership (NEWMARKET) BRED James A. Slattery

583 Crackling Frost (IRE), a very bold jumper, took advantage of his lenient handicap mark, and ran out a most impressive winner in a good time. He looks set to climb the ladder of success. (5/6)

656 Drumstick tried hard to get back at the winner on the home turn and momentarily looked sure to do so, but he was being made to work early in the straight and found the concession of so much weight beyond him. (Evens)

831 SCANIA 4-SERIES 'KING OF THE ROAD' HURDLE (3-Y.O) (Class E)

5-20 (5-21) **2m (9 hdls)** £2,451.00 (£686.00: £333.00) GOING minus 0.27 sec per fur (GF)

				SP	RR	SF
	Hever Golf Diamond (TJNaughton) **3-10-12** NWilliamson (hld up & bhd: hdwy 5th: led appr 2 out: drvn clr flat)	—	**1**	11/4^{2}	63	13
753^{3}	**Ghostly Apparition** (JohnUpson) **3-10-12** RSupple (a.p: hrd rdn 2 out: nt pce of wnr)	7	**2**	4/1^{3}	56	6
589^{8}	**Little Kenny** (TWall) **3-10-4v**$^{(3)}$ RMassey (chsd ldr: led 5th: hit 3 out: sn hdd: one pce)	½	**3**	4/1^{3}	51	1
640^{3}	**Bath Knight** (DJSffrenchDavis) **3-10-12b** JFTitley (j.lft: led to 5th: hrd rdn appr 2 out: sn btn)	3	**4**	9/4^{1}	53	3
	Formentiere (JMBradley) **3-10-7** BFenton (bit bkwd: trckd ldrs tl rdn & outpcd appr 3 out)	4	**5**	33/1	44	—
753^{4}	**Colebrook Willie** (JRBosley) **3-10-12** MBosley (dropped rr 4th: t.o)	10	**6**	14/1	39	—
	Chillington (WMBrisbourne) **3-10-12** CLlewellyn (bkwd: hdwy 4th: wknd 4 out: t.o)	19	**7**	33/1	20	—
				(SP 110.0%)		**7 Rn**

3m 42.6 (5.60) CSF £12.89 TOTE £3.80: £3.20 £2.10 (£8.30) Trio £18.20 OWNER Hever Racing Club I (EPSOM) BRED Mrs L. Popely

Hever Golf Diamond, fit from the Flat, had little trouble in making a winning debut over hurdles and the ease of this success should do wonders for his confidence. (11/4)

753 Ghostly Apparition, never too far away, stayed on willingly under strong pressure in the latter stages, but had to admit the winner much too good. (4/1)

Little Kenny needed a visor on the Flat, and she performed much better than she did on her hurdling debut. She flattened the third last though when being challenged and did not remain in control for much longer. (4/1)

640 Bath Knight gave away valuable ground by jumping out to the left, but did help share the lead until feeling the strain approaching the penultimate flight. (9/4)

T/Plpt: £1,572.20 (4.26 Tckts). T/Qdpt: £80.70 (3.96 Tckts). IM

WINCANTON (R-H) (Firm)

Thursday October 10th

WEATHER: fine

832 HATHERLEIGH MAIDEN HURDLE (4-Y.O+ F & M) (Class E)

2-10 (2-13) **2m 6f (11 hdls)** £2,595.00 (£630.00) GOING minus 0.66 sec per fur (F)

				SP	RR	SF
497^{2}	**Kymin (IRE)** (DJGMurraySmith) **4-10-13** APMcCoy (chsd ldr to 5th: j.slowly 6th: jnd ldr 7th: led & lft clr 2 out: easily)	—	**1**	5/4^{1}	65	—

Galatasori Jane (IRE) (PFNicholls) **6-10-7**(7) OBurrows (hld up: wnt 2nd 5th to 7th: rdn & outpcd whn lft 2nd 2 out) ... 1¾ **2** 4/1[2] 64 —
727[2] **Kesanta** (WGMTurner) **6-11-0** RDunwoody (set slow pce: rdn & hdd whn fell 2 out) ... **F** 5/4[1] — —
(SP 108.9%) **3 Rn**

5m 36.2 (27.20) CSF £5.02 TOTE £2.10 (£3.00) OWNER Ms Diana Wilder (LAMBOURN) BRED Sheikh Mohammed bin Rashid al Maktoum
WEIGHT FOR AGE 4yo-1lb
IN-FOCUS: **It took 32 seconds to get to the first flight.**
497 Kymin (IRE) appeared to be going best when left clear at the penultimate hurdle and won hard held. (5/4: 11/10-6/4)
Galatasori Jane (IRE) won a point-to-point on fast ground and was also placed in bumpers in Ireland. She is flattered by her proximity to the winner. (4/1: 9/4-5/1)
727 Kesanta, very much the reluctant leader, looked to be getting the worst of the argument when departing. (5/4)

833 OAK CONDITIONAL H'CAP CHASE (0-105) (5-Y.O+) (Class F)
2-40 (2-44) **3m 1f 110y (21 fncs)** £2,804.00 (£842.00: £406.00: £188.00) GOING minus 0.66 sec per fur (F)

SP RR SF

678* **Drumcullen (IRE) (88)** (KCBailey) **7-11-0** TJMurphy (hld up: lft clr 16th: eased flat) ... — **1** 5/2[2] 99+ —
732[5] **Turpin's Green (74)** (JSKing) **13-10-0** JCulloty (hld up: sltly hmpd 16th: chsd wnr fr 3 out: no imp) ... 10 **2** 12/1 79 —
726[5] **Foxgrove (80)** (RJPrice) **10-10-6** DFortt (hld up: hdwy 15th: 3rd & no ch whn blnd last) ... 10 **3** 11/1[3] 79 —
726[P] **L'Uomo Piu (77)** (ABarrow) **12-10-3v** TDascombe (s.s: sn prom: lost pl 8th: blnd 10th: t.o fr 13th) ... dist **4** 20/1 — —
726[P] **Banntown Bill (IRE) (95)** (MCPipe) **7-11-7b** DWalsh (nvr gng wl: led to 6th: led 9th to 10th: wknd 12th: t.o fr 15th) ... dist **5** 25/1 — —
302[2] **Southerly Gale (100)** (MCPipe) **9-11-8**(4) GSupple (lw: hld up: led 10th tl fell 16th: dead) ... **F** 5/2[2] — —
Maremma Gale (IRE) (98) (NRMitchell) **8-11-10b** KGaule (chsd ldr: led 6th to 9th: lft 2nd & hmpd 16th: poor 4th & wkng whn p.u lame bef 3 out) ... **P** 9/4[1] — —
(SP 112.5%) **7 Rn**

6m 28.2 (9.20) CSF £26.81 TOTE £3.00: £2.10 £2.50 (£12.40) OWNER Mr Martyn Booth (UPPER LAMBOURN) BRED E. Burke
LONG HANDICAP Turpin's Green 9-11
STEWARDS' ENQUIRY Gaule susp. 19 & 22-24/10/96 (improper riding)
678* Drumcullen (IRE), up 4lb, found misfortune striking his two chief market rivals. (5/2)
732 Turpin's Green, 3lb out of the handicap, began to get the better of the separate battle for second three from home. (12/1: op 8/1)
Foxgrove was 7lb higher than when winning a Novice handicap at Plumpton in April. (11/1)
302 Southerly Gale unfortunately broke his off-hind leg. (5/2)
Maremma Gale (IRE) had been raised 17lb for winning on his two final outings last season. (9/4)

834 SOUTH-WEST RACING CLUB NOVICES' H'CAP HURDLE (0-100) (4-Y.O+) (Class E)
3-10 (3-15) **2m (8 hdls)** £2,302.50 (£640.00: £307.50) GOING minus 0.66 sec per fur (F)

SP RR SF

687* **Indrapura (IRE) (95)** (MCPipe) **4-11-13** CMaude (lw: hld up: wnt 2nd appr 2 out: hrd rdn appr last: led nr fin: all out) ... — **1** 8/11[1] 76 41
557[2] **Canary Falcon (82)** (RJO'Sullivan) **5-11-1** PHolley (lw: hld up: led 3 out: hrd rdn flat: hdd nr fin) ... ¾ **2** 3/1[2] 62 28
Sailep (FR) (86) (RJHodges) **4-11-1**(3) TDascombe (chsd ldr: lft in ld appr 4th: hdd 3 out: rdn & wknd appr 2 out) ... 27 **3** 5/1[3] 39 4
Indian Crown (67) (NBThomson) **6-10-0** JCulloty (led: clr whn hit 3rd: rn out bnd appr 4th) ... **R** 20/1 — —
723[8] **Tibbs Inn (67)** (ABarrow) **7-9-7**(7) MrRThornton (lw: hld up: 3rd whn s.u bnd appr 4th) ... **S** 14/1 — —
(SP 111.0%) **5 Rn**

3m 36.3 (-3.70) CSF £3.28 TOTE £1.40: £1.00 £2.20 (£1.70) OWNER Martin Pipe Racing Club (WELLINGTON) BRED John Burns
LONG HANDICAP Indian Crown 9-13 Tibbs Inn 9-10
WEIGHT FOR AGE 4yo-1lb
687* Indrapura (IRE) had to work hard to defy a 4lb hike in the ratings. (8/11)
557 Canary Falcon had previously been trained by Hugh Collingridge. (3/1)

835 POT BLACK H'CAP CHASE (0-120) (5-Y.O+) (Class D)
3-40 (3-42) **2m 5f (17 fncs)** £4,468.00 (£1,248.00: £604.00) GOING minus 0.66 sec per fur (F)

SP RR SF

728* **Bit of A Touch (89)** (RGFrost) **10-10-9** JFrost (swtg: chsd ldr: led 13th to 4 out: ev ch whn hmpd 3 out: rallied to ld flat) ... — **1** 2/1[3] 95 —
728[F] **Herbert Buchanan (IRE) (98)** (PFNicholls) **6-11-4** APMcCoy (hld up: j.slowly 10th: hdwy after 13th: lft clr 3 out: hdd flat) ... 1½ **2** 7/4[2] 103 —
750[3] **Gabish (80)** (BScriven) **11-9-7**(7) MrRThornton (led: rdn 12th: hdd 13th: wknd appr 3 out: t.o) ... dist **3** 25/1 — —
740[F] **Lake of Loughrea (IRE) (104)** (KCBailey) **6-11-10** CO'Dwyer (hld up: hdwy to ld 4 out: blnd & uns rdr 3 out) .... **U** 13/8[1] — —
(SP 111.6%) **4 Rn**

5m 16.6 (8.60) CSF £5.71 TOTE £3.60 (£2.50) OWNER A E C Electric Fencing Ltd (Hotline) (BUCKFASTLEIGH) BRED Hesmonds Stud Ltd
LONG HANDICAP Gabish 8-5
728* Bit of A Touch, up 7lb, fought back gamely to complete the hat-trick. (2/1)
728 Herbert Buchanan (IRE) found himself in front plenty soon enough. (7/4)
740 Lake of Loughrea (IRE) made the sort of error that O'Dwyer would have expected to have survived nine times out of ten. (13/8)

836 SHAFTESBURY CLAIMING HURDLE (3-Y.O) (Class F)
4-10 (4-12) **2m (8 hdls)** £2,320.00 (£645.00: £310.00) GOING minus 0.66 sec per fur (F)

SP RR SF

753* **Cointosser (IRE)** (MCPipe) **3-10-12** SWynne (hld up: hdwy appr 2 out: led last: rdn & r.o wl) ... — **1** 8/13[1] 74 12
736[4] **Ben Bowden** (MBlanshard) **3-10-13** JOsborne (w ldr: led 4th to 3 out: ev ch last: unable qckn) ... 5 **2** 7/1[3] 70 8
753[2] **Indira** (PGMurphy) **3-10-6** WMcFarland (led to 4th: led 3 out to last: one pce) ... 1¼ **3** 7/2[2] 62 —
Prove The Point (IRE) (MrsPNDutfield) **3-10-8** PHolley (hld up: j.slowly & reminders 4th: bhd fr 3 out) ... 23 **4** 20/1 41 —
654[3] **Yellow Dragon (IRE)** (BAPearce) **3-10-12**(3) KGaule (mstke 2nd: rdn appr 3 out: sn bhd) ... 3 **5** 8/1 45 —
688[14] **Remember Star** (ADSmith) **3-10-6** FJousset (bhd fr 5th: t.o) ... 26 **6** 100/1 10 —
(SP 113.5%) **6 Rn**

3m 39.7 (-0.30) CSF £5.49 TOTE £1.40: £1.10 £2.60 (£4.00) OWNER David Manning Associates (WELLINGTON) BRED Mellon Stud
753* Cointosser (IRE) had to work harder this time but forged clear in the final one hundred yards. (8/13)

501 Ben Bowden gave those who had laid the odds some anxious moments after the final flight. (7/1)
753 Indira was 6lb better off with the winner than at Taunton a week ago. (7/2)

837 WINCANTON NOVICES' HURDLE (4-Y.O+) (Class E)
4-40 (4-41) **2m 6f (11 hdls)** £2,232.50 (£620.00: £297.50) GOING minus 0.66 sec per fur (F)

	Horse	Dist	Pos	SP	RR	SF
739*	**Courbaril (103)** (MCPipe) **4-11-12** CMaude (lw: chsd ldr: led 6th: sn clr: hit 2 out: easily)	—	1	1/3 1	75+	28
655 3	**Miramare (62)** (CLPopham) **6-10-6**(3) TDascombe (hld up: chsd wnr fr 8th: rdn after 3 out: no imp)	21	2	12/1 3	42	—
	Ask Harry (IRE) (RHAlner) **5-10-4**(5) PHenley (bkwd: hld up: hdwy 8th: 3rd & no ch whn hit last)	2½	3	16/1	40	—
728 7	**Charged (96)** (PJHobbs) **7-10-9** APMcCoy (led to 6th: wknd 8th: t.o)	dist	4	4/1 2	—	—
	Lady Ness (JCTuck) **5-10-4** RBellamy (a bhd: t.o 7th: p.u bef last)		P	50/1	—	—
				(SP 110.5%)		**5 Rn**

5m 7.8 (-1.20) CSF £4.84 TOTE £1.40: £1.10 £2.80 (£4.90) OWNER Richard Green (Fine Paintings) (WELLINGTON) BRED George & Mrs Steinberg
WEIGHT FOR AGE 4yo-1lb
739* Courbaril took command at halfway. (1/3)
655 Miramare found the winner in a different league. (12/1)

T/Plpt: £37.10 (204.45 Tckts). T/Qdpt: £6.00 (74.64 Tckts). KH

838a-845a (Irish Racing) - See Computer Raceform

0515a-TIPPERARY (Ireland) (L-H) (Good to yielding, Chases Good)
Sunday October 6th

846a CROOM HOUSE STUD CHASE (4-Y.O+)
2-30 (2-31) **2m (11 fncs)** £4,110.00 (£930.00: £390.00: £210.00)

	Horse	Dist	Pos	SP	RR	SF
	Sound Man (IRE) (EJO'Grady,Ireland) **8-12-0** RDunwoody (chsd ldr tl led 4th: mstke next: clr bef 7th: v.easily)	—	1	1/4 1	145++	—
318a 9	**Phardy (IRE)** (ALeahy,Ireland) **5-11-0** THorgan (hld up: mod 3rd fr 2nd: wnt 2nd at 7th: no imp appr 2 out: eased flat)	20	2	12/1	115	—
763a 5	**Jassu** (JEKiely,Ireland) **10-11-11** CFSwan (4th & losing tch 4th: wl bhd 7th: n.d bef 2 out: styd on flat)	8	3	4/1 2	114	—
	Sandys Girl (IRE) (MMO'Sullivan,Ireland) **8-10-13** JPBroderick (n.d)	20	4	50/1	82	—
	What A Choice (IRE) (JFGleeson,Ireland) **6-10-8**(5) MJHolbrook (n.d)	7	5	66/1	75	—
	Savuti (IRE) (WJBurke,Ireland) **7-10-11**(7) MDMurphy (led to 4th: mstke 6th: dist 3rd 3 out: t.o)	9	6	8/1 3	71	—
				(SP 122.3%)		**6 Rn**

3m 53.6 OWNER David Lloyd (THURLES) BRED P. Scully in Ireland
Sound Man (IRE), carrying plenty of condition, led at the fourth and made a slight mistake at the next, but was clear before five out and won very easily. The Fortria Chase at Navan is his target for next month. (1/4)
Phardy (IRE) went second five furlongs out, but was making no impression before two furlongs out and was eased on the flat. (12/1: op 8/1)
763a Jassu began to lose touch from the fourth and was a remote third and no danger at all before the straight. (4/1: op 5/2)

847a-850a (Irish Racing) - See Computer Raceform

OVREVOLL (Oslo, Norway) (L-H) (Heavy)
Saturday October 5th

851a GLAVA NORSK GRAND NATIONAL CHASE (4-Y.O+)
2-50 **2m 5f** £8,410.00 (£4,203.00: £2,018.00: £1,346.00)

	Horse	Dist	Pos	SP	RR	SF
53a*	**Black Hero (FR)** (MrsRNilsen,Norway) **7-11-5** JTwomey	—	1		111	—
53a 2	**Serafin (POL)** (NPBogen,Norway) **12-11-5** RAKvisla	5½	2		107	—
604 4	**Henley Regatta** (PRRodford) **8-11-1** SBurrough	3½	3		100	—
	Thumbs Up (GMMcCourt) **10-10-10** BClifford	dist	4		—	—
						5 Rn

5m 53.4 TOTE 3.80KR: 1.00KR 1.00KR 1.00KR OWNER Stall Nor BRED F. Geffroy
409* Henley Regatta raced in third place and, after moving up to dispute second place with three left, could only keep on at the same pace.
Thumbs Up was always in the rear and lost touch with four left.

0680-CARLISLE (R-H) (Firm, Good to firm patches)
Friday October 11th
WEATHER: overcast WIND: str

852 SHAP HURDLE (3-Y.O) (Class E)
1-50 (1-50) **2m 1f (9 hdls)** £2,276.00 (£636.00: £308.00) GOING minus 0.61 sec per fur (F)

	Horse	Dist	Pos	SP	RR	SF
	Double Dash (IRE) (DMoffatt) **3-10-12** DJMoffatt (prom: mstke 4th: hdwy & mstke 3 out: blnd 2 out: styd on to ld fnl 100y)	—	1	7/4 2	64?	—
699 6	**Ret Frem (IRE)** (CParker) **3-10-12** BStorey (led to 5th: rdn after 3 out: lft in ld appr last: hdd & no ex flat)	3	2	6/4 1	61	—
	Lomond Lassie (USA) (MissJFCraze) **3-10-7** OPears (mstkes: t.o fr 4 out)	dist	3	20/1	—	—
688 5	**Hannahs Bay** (MGMeagher) **3-10-4**(3) FLeahy (cl up: led 5th tl p.u appr last: broke leg: dead)		P	2/1 3	—	—
				(SP 114.5%)		**4 Rn**

4m 17.2 (16.20) CSF £4.83 TOTE £3.00 (£3.20) OWNER The Sheroot Partnership (CARTMEL) BRED Minch Bloodstock
Double Dash (IRE) did not look too happy at his hurdles and was a lucky winner. This was a very poor event. (7/4)
534 Ret Frem (IRE) has looked a doubtful stayer, so this was not the track for him. (6/4: op 10/11)

688 Hannahs Bay had this sewn up when she broke her leg going to the last. (2/1)

853 DURDAR NOVICES' CHASE (5-Y.O+) (Class D)

2-20 (2-21) **2m 4f 110y (16 fncs)** £3,542.50 (£1,072.00: £523.00: £248.50) GOING minus 0.61 sec per fur (F)

				SP	RR	SF
	Show Your Hand (IRE) (LLungo) **8-10-12** MFoster (mde all: hit 4 out: r.o wl fr 2 out: eased towards fin)	—	1	$8/13^{1}$	62+	—
700^{8}	**Calder's Grove** (MissLAPerratt) **6-10-9**(3) GCahill (prom: effrt appr 9th: outpcd 3 out: styd on flat)	2½	2	$14/1^{3}$	60	—
	Kiltulla (IRE) (MrsSJSmith) **6-10-12** RichardGuest (plld hrd: a.p: ev ch 4 out: wknd flat)	1¼	3	$2/1^{2}$	59	—
	Bonny Johnny (DMoffatt) **6-10-12** DJMoffatt (bit bkwd: j.lft: chsd ldrs: lost pl 9th: mstke 4 out: sn btn)	4	4	20/1	56	—
				(SP 106.7%)		**4 Rn**

5m 16.9 (13.90) CSF £6.80 TOTE £1.60 (£8.10) OWNER Strathayr Publishers Ltd (CARRUTHERSTOWN) BRED B. Dunning

Show Your Hand (IRE) looked likely to be all the better for this after three years off, and jumped well out in front. Shaken up, he beat this moderate bunch in fair style. (8/13)

Calder's Grove had shown nothing previously, but he did stay on in the closing stages to show he is learning. Whether the form is worth anything, only time will tell. (14/1)

Kiltulla (IRE), warm beforehand, looks the type for this game. Once he learns to settle, there should be some improvement. (2/1)

Bonny Johnny needed this and did not help his cause by continually jumping left. (20/1)

854 HARRABY NOVICES' H'CAP HURDLE (0-100) (4-Y.O+) (Class E)

2-55 (2-56) **2m 4f 110y (11 hdls)** £2,332.00 (£652.00: £316.00) GOING minus 0.61 sec per fur (F)

				SP	RR	SF
700^{4}	**Jonaem (IRE) (80)** (MrsESlack) **6-11-10** KJohnson (hld up: hdwy to ld appr 4 out: hld on wl flat)	—	1	$3/1^{2}$	61	28
642^{2}	**Haughton Lad (IRE) (72)** (FPMurtagh) **7-11-2** ADobbin (a.p: hdwy to chal 2 out: hrd rdn & nt qckn flat)	1	2	9/2	52	19
687^{6}	**Merryhill Gold (70)** (JWCurtis) **5-11-0** LWyer (swtg: led to 3rd: a chsng ldrs: one pce fr 3 out)	12	3	$7/2^{3}$	41	8
786^{P}	**Amber Holly (70)** (JEDixon) **7-11-0** BStorey (hld up & bhd: hdwy to chal 4 out: wknd qckly after 3 out)	16	4	14/1	28	—
	Palace of Gold (73) (LLungo) **6-11-3** MFoster (w ldrs: led appr 7th tl appr 4 out: sn rdn & wknd)	13	5	$15/8^{1}$	21	—
	Cruising Kate (59) (SEKettlewell) **8-10-0**(3) GLee (bit bkwd: cl up: led 3rd tl appr 7th: sn wknd & t.o: p.u bef last)		P	14/1	—	—
				(SP 113.5%)		**6 Rn**

4m 50.6 (-0.40) CSF £15.60 TOTE £4.30: £1.80 £2.70 (£3.80) OWNER Mrs Evelyn Slack (HILTON)

OFFICIAL EXPLANATION **Palace of Gold: returned home jarred up.**

700 Jonaem (IRE) won a moderate race but had to really struggle to do so. He looks the type to improve with time though, and the bigger obstacles will be the game for him. (3/1)

642 Haughton Lad (IRE) is running well at the moment, but just lacks any change of speed to take command. (9/2)

Merryhill Gold, wearing his usual tongue-strap, got pretty warm beforehand and looked very slow. (7/2)

Amber Holly suddenly shot into contention four out, only to blow up after jumping the next. (14/1)

Palace of Gold has been running well this season, but mostly on ground a deal softer. (15/8)

855 CITY OF CARLISLE H'CAP CHASE (0-130) (5-Y.O+) (Class C)

3-30 (3-30) **2m (12 fncs)** £4,303.75 (£1,300.00: £632.50: £298.75) GOING minus 0.61 sec per fur (F)

				SP	RR	SF
732^{2}	**Charming Gale (94)** (MrsSCBradburne) **9-10-0v** LWyer (lw: j.w: mde all: r.o wl fr 4 out)	—	1	$11/4^{3}$	105	—
	Political Tower (122) (RNixon) **9-11-11**(3) GCahill (hld up: effrt appr 4 out: hdwy next: sn rdn & styd on: nvr able to chal)	7	2	$7/4^{1}$	126	17
702^{2}	**Beldine (100)** (PMonteith) **11-10-6** ADobbin (trckd ldrs: wnt 2nd 8th: rdn 3 out: one pce)	8	3	$2/1^{2}$	96	—
	Flash of Realm (FR) (97) (BMactaggart) **10-10-3** BStorey (chsd wnr tl rdn & btn appr 4 out)	16	4	6/1	77	—
				(SP 110.6%)		**4 Rn**

3m 56.3 (2.30) CSF £7.55 TOTE £4.20 (£5.00) OWNER Mrs John Etherton (CUPAR) BRED Eamonn McCarthy

LONG HANDICAP Charming Gale 9-10

732 Charming Gale looked particularly well and, although this trip was short of her best, she had too much courage for this bunch when it came down to a fight. (11/4)

Political Tower failed to impress on looks and, in the circumstances, ran pretty well. (7/4)

702 Beldine again had his chances but, when the pressure was on, again failed to come up with the goods. (2/1)

Flash of Realm (FR) would probably have needed this and was finally left struggling when the tap was turned on over the final four fences. (6/1)

856 ORTON CONDITIONAL H'CAP HURDLE (0-125) (4-Y.O+) (Class E)

4-00 (4-01) **2m 1f (9 hdls)** £2,220.00 (£620.00: £300.00) GOING minus 0.61 sec per fur (F)

				SP	RR	SF
806^{4}	**Well Appointed (IRE) (94)** (BMactaggart) **7-11-8** GLee (mde all: hld on wl flat)	—	1	$3/1^{3}$	77	—
731^{2}	**Nonios (IRE) (96)** (GMMoore) **5-11-10** ECallaghan (trckd wnr: shkn up after 3 out: disp ld appr last: rdn & nt qckn)	½	2	$11/4^{2}$	79	—
701^{3}	**Latin Leader (83)** (CParker) **6-10-11b** DParker (lw: trckd ldrs tl mstke & outpcd fr 3 out)	15	3	5/1	51	—
684*	**Bolaney Girl (IRE) (85)** (FPMurtagh) **7-10-13** ARoche (lw: unruly s: s.s: plld hrd: hdwy & prom 4 out: blnd next: sn rdn & btn)	1¾	4	$15/8^{1}$	52	—
781*	**Latvian (96)** (RAllan) **9-11-7v**(3) 7x SMelrose (prom: mstkes 4th & 5th: sn outpcd: n.d)	19	5	10/1	45	—
				(SP 112.2%)		**5 Rn**

4m 10.8 (9.80) CSF £10.99 TOTE £4.80: £1.80 £1.90 (£4.50) OWNER Drumlanrig Racing (HAWICK) BRED Oldtown Bloodstock Holdings Ltd

806 Well Appointed (IRE) proved most determined. After looking in trouble going to the last, he held on really well and looks likely to improve further. (3/1)

731 Nonios (IRE) had his chances but, when it came down to it, was just found wanting. (11/4)

701 Latin Leader, again held up, was left behind after a mistake three out. More forcing tactics might well help. (5/1)

684* Bolaney Girl (IRE) was up to her usual antics beforehand and pulled her rider's arms out for much of the trip. Asked for an effort three out, she made a mistake and immediately threw in the towel. (15/8)

781* Latvian was having none of it this time and gave up the ghost at halfway. (10/1)

857 BLACKWELL H'CAP CHASE (0-115) (5-Y.O+) (Class E)

4-35 (4-35) **3m (18 fncs)** £3,452.50 (£1,045.00: £510.00: £242.50) GOING minus 0.61 sec per fur (F)

				SP	RR	SF
683^{2}	**Kushbaloo (114)** (CParker) **11-12-0** BStorey (mstkes to ½-wy: mde all: kpt on gamely fr 3 out)	—	1	$6/4^{1}$	120	—

				SP	RR	SF
689^{4}	**Dark Oak (109)** (JWCurtis) **10-11-9** LWyer (lw: chsd wnr tl blnd 13th: hdwy to chal u.p 3 out: one pce fr next)	3	**2**	$5/1^{3}$	113	—
	Supposin (92) (MrsSJSmith) **8-10-6** RichardGuest (hld up: hdwy appr 4 out: rdn & ch appr last: nt qckn)	1½	**3**	10/1	95	—
732*	**Magic Bloom (107)** (JMJefferson) **10-11-2**(5) 7x ECallaghan (a.p: effrt 4 out: hrd drvn & ch appr last: no ex)	1¾	**4**	$7/4^{2}$	109	—
644^{P}	**Go Silly (105)** (BEllison) **10-11-2v**(3) GCahill (mstkes: lost tch fr 4 out: hit 2 out: p.u bef last)		**P**	8/1	—	—

(SP 113.2%) **5 Rn**

6m 13.8 (21.80) CSF £8.72 TOTE £2.10: £1.10 £3.60 (£4.30) OWNER Mr & Mrs Raymond Anderson Green (LOCKERBIE) BRED Andrew Murphy

683 Kushbaloo was not jumping with any confidence early on, but gradually got it together and showed fine courage to hold on. (6/4)
689 Dark Oak was snapping at the winner's heels throughout but, when it came down to a real struggle, it was always beyond him. (5/1: 7/2-6/1)
Supposin has had problems with broken blood-vessels in the past, but ran well here and should be all the better for it. (10/1: tchd 16/1)
732* Magic Bloom keeps running well, but was struggling from four out, and perhaps the Handicapper has just about got her measure. (7/4)
644 Go Silly failed to impress on looks and was never jumping all that well. (8/1: 9/2-10/1)

858 TARN CRAG STANDARD N.H. FLAT RACE (4, 5 & 6-Y.O) (Class H)

5-10 (5-13) **2m 1f** £1,646.00 (£456.00: £218.00)

				SP	RR	SF
	Northern Fusilier (JMJefferson) **4-11-3**(7) MNewton (hdwy ½-wy: led 7f out: easily)	—	**1**	$4/6^{1}$	—	—
	Look Sharpe (PBeaumont) **5-10-11**(7) BGrattan (a.p: chsd wnr fnl 3½f: no imp)	24	**2**	16/1	—	—
787^{3}	**Lindajane (IRE)** (MissZAGreen) **4-10-12** MrTMorrison (hld up: effrt 7f out: sn rdn & no imp)	30	**3**	$4/1^{2}$	—	—
686^{8}	**Joe's Bit of Gold** (TAKCuthbert) **4-10-9**(3) GCahill (in tch: outpcd 7f out: sn bhd)	6	**4**	25/1	—	—
686^{4}	**Best Friend** (JWCurtis) **4-10-7**(5) MichaelBrennan (led to 7f out: wknd 4f out)	22	**5**	$5/1^{3}$	—	—
686^{7}	**The Knitter** (JJBirkett) **4-10-10**(7) MrMDunne (prom to ½-wy: sn wknd: t.o)	dist	**6**	40/1	—	—
	Jed Abbey (RShiels) **4-10-5**(7) SMelrose (bit bkwd: unruly gng to s: ref to r: t.n.p)		**R**	14/1	—	—

(SP 115.5%) **7 Rn**

3m 59.8 CSF £11.45 TOTE £1.50: £1.10 £4.00 (£14.80) OWNER Mr Joe Donald (MALTON) BRED G. Revitt
WEIGHT FOR AGE 4yo-1lb

Northern Fusilier was different class to this lot and ran them ragged in the last half-mile. (4/6)
Look Sharpe put in a reasonable first effort, but could never get near the winner. He should be all the better for this. (16/1)
787 Lindajane (IRE) seemed to be feeling her Hexham race and never got into this. (4/1)
Jed Abbey (14/1: 10/1-16/1)

T/Plpt: £181.20 (35.16 Tckts). T/Qdpt: £37.60 (9.87 Tckts). AA

0673-HUNTINGDON (R-H) (Good to firm)
Friday October 11th

Race 6: one flight omitted
WEATHER: fine

859 EMERALD ISLE NOVICES' HURDLE (4-Y.O+) (Class E)

2-10 (2-11) **2m 4f 110y (10 hdls)** £2,320.00 (£645.00: £310.00) GOING minus 0.40 sec per fur (GF)

				SP	RR	SF
	Montel Express (IRE) (KCBailey) **4-10-11** CO'Dwyer (swtg: chsd ldrs: hmpd 5th: led appr 2 out: rdn out)	—	**1**	$5/2^{1}$	74+	—
	The Lad (LMontagueHall) **7-10-12** DMorris (chsd ldrs: ev ch fr 2 out: unable qckn nr fin)	nk	**2**	9/2	74	—
	Minor Key (IRE) (JRJenkins) **6-10-12** JOsborne (bkwd: led to 5th: one pce fr 2 out)	7	**3**	12/1	68	—
700^{3}	**Lear Dancer (USA)** (MissMERowland) **5-10-12b** APMcCoy (prom: led 5th: sn clr: wknd & hdd appr 2 out)	11	**4**	$11/4^{2}$	60	—
209*	**Pegasus Bay (85)** (DECantillon) **5-11-5** RDunwoody (lw: hdwy 5th: rdn & wknd appr 3 out: j.rt last)	18	**5**	9/1	53	—
	Ernest William (IRE) (GAHubbard) **4-10-8**(3) KGaule (bit bkwd: prom tl fell 5th)		**F**	40/1	—	—
	Master Goodenough (IRE) (AGFoster) **5-10-12** NWilliamson (bit bkwd: a bhd: t.o whn p.u bef 2 out)		**P**	14/1	—	—
636*	**Danny Gale (IRE) (92)** (GMMcCourt) **5-11-5** GBradley (lw: chsd ldrs: wkng whn hit 6th: t.o whn p.u bef 2 out)		**P**	$7/2^{3}$	—	—
	Jari (USA) (MJPolglase) **5-10-12** VSmith (rel to r: sn in tch: bhd fr 7th: t.o whn p.u bef 2 out)		**P**	50/1	—	—

(SP 124.4%) **9 Rn**

4m 47.8 CSF £14.75 TOTE £3.80: £1.50 £2.00 £4.60 (£12.50) Trio £33.60 OWNER Mrs Jacqueline Conroy (UPPER LAMBOURN)
WEIGHT FOR AGE 4yo-1lb
OFFICIAL EXPLANATION **Danny Gale (IRE): had made a noise.**

Montel Express (IRE), the winner of an Irish bumper, got warm beforehand and was led round by two handlers. He did nothing wrong though and held the runner-up a little more easily than the margin would suggest. (5/2: 2/1-3/1)
The Lad raced over hurdles in Ireland a couple of seasons back and was fit after a Flat campaign. Jumping well apart from the fourth last, he battled on well in the straight and ought to find a race. (9/2)
Minor Key (IRE), absent since one run in an Irish bumper in September '94, looked badly in need of the run, but did stick on after looking likely to fade on the final circuit. (12/1: op 6/1)
700 Lear Dancer (USA) is a bit of a monkey who needs holding up as long as possible, so these tactics were inexplicable. (11/4)
209* Pegasus Bay made ground towards the leaders travelling well enough on the final circuit, but did not appear to stay. (9/1: 6/1-10/1)
636* Danny Gale (IRE) moved well to post, but was easy to back and dropped away tamely on the final circuit. (7/2: 2/1-4/1)

860 JACK RAMPLY MEMORIAL NOVICES' CHASE (5-Y.O+) (Class D)

2-45 (2-46) **2m 4f 110y (16 fncs)** £3,562.50 (£1,065.00: £510.00: £232.50) GOING minus 0.40 sec per fur (GF)

				SP	RR	SF
744*	**Jathib (CAN)** (MrsMerritaJones) **5-11-3** DerekByrne (hld up: hit 9th: hdwy 11th: led appr 2 out: easily)	—	**1**	$1/4^{1}$	106+	44
	Icantelya (IRE) (90) (JWMullins) **7-10-12** PHide (prom: led 11th tl appr 2 out: one pce)	12	**2**	$10/1^{3}$	90	30
	Manor Mieo (GProdromou) **10-10-12**(7) MrACoe (bkwd: prom: led 10th to next: wknd 3 out)	dist	**3**	$6/1^{2}$	—	—
	Fabulous Francy (IRE) (MissAEEmbiricos) **8-10-12** JRyan (bit bkwd: prom: hit 9th: wkng whn mstke 12th)	12	**4**	20/1	—	—
	Sporting Fixture (IRE) (PEccles) **5-10-10** AThornton (bit bkwd: bhd fr 11th)	1¾	**5**	66/1	—	—
738^{8}	**Saxon Blade (62)** (RMStronge) **8-10-12** BPowell (led to 10th: sn wknd: j.lft last: t.o)	dist	**6**	100/1	—	—
	Ishma (IRE) (MrsLCJewell) **5-10-10** JRailton (bit bkwd: bhd tl p.u bef 9th)		**P**	100/1	—	—

	Horse	Dist	Pos	SP	RR	SF
	Clonattin Lady (IRE) (MrsLCJewell) **7-10-7** DLeahy (mstke 4th: rdn next: t.o whn p.u bef 10th)		**P**	100/1	—	—
				(SP 112.6%)		**8 Rn**

4m 57.8 (-2.20) CSF £3.73 TOTE £1.30: £1.10 £1.40 £1.10 (£2.90) OWNER Crown Pkg & Mailing Svs Ltd (LAMBOURN) BRED Hill 'N Dale Farms
WEIGHT FOR AGE 5yo-2lb
744* Jathib (CAN), ridden with plenty of confidence, won with a lot in hand and is going the right way. (1/4)
Icantelya (IRE), ex-Irish, looks up to finding a little race, for he jumped reasonably enough, and will not always run into a rival of this quality. (10/1: op 6/1)
Manor Mieo has a fantastic record between the Flags and it was a shame he turned up here in such a burly state, for he jumped like a stag and might have given the winner plenty to worry about at his best. (6/1: 7/2-7/1)
Fabulous Francy (IRE) became sketchier at his obstacles as the race progressed. (20/1)
Sporting Fixture (IRE) tried chasing on only his second start and did at least complete, though in his own time. (66/1)
Saxon Blade is headstrong and is yet to prove he stays even two miles. (100/1)

861 HUNTINGDON INTERNATIONAL CHALLENGE H'CAP HURDLE (0-110) (4-Y.O+) (Class E)
3-15 (3-18) **2m 5f 110y (10 hdls)** £2,215.00 (£615.00: £295.00) GOING minus 0.40 sec per fur (GF)

	Horse	Dist	Pos	SP	RR	SF
741[6]	**Born to Please (IRE) (90)** (PJHobbs) **4-10-8** AMaguire (mde most to 3 out: rdn to ld last: edgd lft flat)	—	**1**	Evens[1]	71	2
695[2]	**Able Player (USA) (86)** (KJDrewry) **9-10-5** WHarnett (lw: w ldr: led 3 out: mstke & rdr lost iron next: hdd last: n.m.r & no ex nr fin)	nk	**2**	2/1[2]	67	—
815[4]	**Gone by (IRE) (109)** (JRJenkins) **8-12-0v** GBradley (hld up: rdn & btn appr 3 out)	22	**3**	5/2[3]	73	5
				(SP 111.9%)		**3 Rn**

5m 7.4 (7.40) CSF £3.17 TOTE £2.00 (£1.90) OWNER A B S Racing (MINEHEAD) BRED Mrs S. O'Riordan
WEIGHT FOR AGE 4yo-1lb
539* Born to Please (IRE) justified favouritism but can hardly be said to have been impressive. He responded to a strong ride in the straight, but may have been slightly fortunate that no enquiry was called for, as he had leaned on his rival near the line. (Evens)
695 Able Player (USA) is a bit of a character but travelled sweetly, and looked sure to win when going clear on the home turn. Flattening the penultimate flight, he landed on all fours and was outbattled on the run-in. It should be said that his pilot had little room to use his whip in the finish. (2/1: 6/4-9/4)
682 Gone by (IRE) travelled well until being left struggling going to three out. He failed to win after August last season. (5/2)

862 HARTLEY'S JAM H'CAP CHASE (0-135) (5-Y.O+) (Class C)
3-50 (3-57) **2m 110y (12 fncs)** £4,337.50 (£1,300.00: £625.00: £287.50) GOING minus 0.40 sec per fur (GF)

	Horse	Dist	Pos	SP	RR	SF
	Fine Harvest (110) (JLSpearing) **10-11-9** DBridgwater (bit bkwd: mde all: rdn out)	—	**1**	7/2[2]	120	48
592[6]	**Lowawatha (100)** (MrsEHHeath) **8-10-13** AThornton (lw: chsd wnr: one pce appr last)	2½	**2**	7/2[2]	108	36
750*	**Ramstar (109)** (PJHobbs) **8-11-8** 6x APMcCoy (lw: trckd ldrs: effrt appr 2 out: rdn & btn appr last)	½	**3**	3/1[1]	116	44
723[5]	**Fierce (92)** (JRJenkins) **8-10-5v** JOsborne (hld up: rdn 7th: btn 3 out: t.o)	dist	**4**	3/1[1]	—	—
742[4]	**Bally Parson (115)** (RDickin) **10-12-0** JCulloty (nt j.w: dropped rr 6th: blnd & uns rdr 9th)		**U**	4/1[3]	—	—
				(SP 114.4%)		**5 Rn**

4m 0.6 (-1.40) CSF £14.98 TOTE £4.90: £2.30 £1.40 (£16.20) OWNER Miss A. Shirley-Priest (ALCESTER) BRED Mrs K. Cumiskey
Fine Harvest looked as though he would be just the better for the outing, although he looked like he had done plenty of work. Very keen at the start having been off for seventeen months, his attempts to get away were twice thwarted by the Starter but, once underway, he jumped round with style and would not be denied. He does seem to favour this course. (7/2)
592 Lowawatha is probably at his best when allowed to dominate, given his suspect stamina. He looked and ran well and should win when the opportunity to dominate arises. (7/2)
750* Ramstar, up 10lb for winning a couple of non-events, found this harder, but ran well. He remains in good heart. (3/1)
76 Fierce seemed rejuvenated by making the running over hurdles last time, but that option did not exist here and he had a non-going day. (3/1)

863 AUSTRALIA H'CAP HURDLE (0-130) (4-Y.O+) (Class C)
4-25 (4-25) **2m 110y (8 hdls)** £3,439.00 (£1,027.00: £491.00: £223.00) GOING minus 0.40 sec per fur (GF)

	Horse	Dist	Pos	SP	RR	SF
796[R]	**Star Market (126)** (JLSpearing) **6-12-0b** APMcCoy (lw: mde all: clr 4th: blnd 2 out: pushed out)	—	**1**	11/4[3]	113	56
692[5]	**Wamdha (IRE) (100)** (KAMorgan) **6-10-2** ASSmith (lw: chsd wnr fr 4th: no imp fr 2 out)	6	**2**	13/8[1]	81	24
723[2]	**Cooley's Valve (IRE) (101)** (MrsSDWilliams) **8-10-3** NWilliamson (lw: hld up: hdwy appr 3 out: mstke next: sn btn & eased)	4	**3**	5/2[2]	78	21
591[6]	**Shoofk (118)** (SDow) **5-11-6** RDunwoody (chsd wnr: hit 2nd & 5th: wkng whn mstke 3 out)	2½	**4**	7/2	93	36
				(SP 115.6%)		**4 Rn**

3m 45.5 (-2.50) CSF £7.61 TOTE £4.20 (£4.40) OWNER Mrs P. Joynes (ALCESTER) BRED M. H. D. Madden and Partners
638* Star Market did not hang about and gained due reward, as he had stretched these to breaking point by the home turn. (11/4)
692 Wamdha (IRE) had plenty to do to get near the leader by the time she took second place at halfway, and could do no more. (13/8)
723 Cooley's Valve (IRE) was given an odd ride. (5/2)
591 Shoofk has run poorly on the level since his last run over timber, and put in a sloppy round of jumping. (7/2)

864 GREAT BRITISH H'CAP CHASE (0-135) (5-Y.O+) (Class C)
4-55 (4-55) **3m (18 fncs)** £4,710.00 (£1,310.00: £630.00) GOING minus 0.40 sec per fur (GF)

	Horse	Dist	Pos	SP	RR	SF
719[4]	**Wise Approach (129)** (KCBailey) **9-12-0** CO'Dwyer (lw: j.w: mde all: rdn out)	—	**1**	5/2[1]	133	51
689[2]	**Merlins Dream (IRE) (103)** (OSherwood) **7-10-2** JOsborne (mstkes: chsd ldrs: rdn & ev ch whn blundered last: r.o wl nr fin)	nk	**2**	5/2[1]	107	25
74*	**Change the Reign (107)** (MissAEEmbiricos) **9-10-6** JRKavanagh (bit bkwd: mstkes 4th & 5th: prom tl rdn & wknd appr 2 out: t.o)	dist	**3**	3/1[2]	—	—
	Gilpa Valu (115) (MrsJPitman) **7-11-0** WMarston (bit bkwd: trckd wnr tl fell 8th)		**F**	5/2[1]	—	—
				(SP 110.7%)		**4 Rn**

5m 55.5 (0.90 under best) (-1.50) CSF £8.35 TOTE £3.90 (£2.30) OWNER Mrs S. Gee (UPPER LAMBOURN) BRED N.J.Connors
719 Wise Approach jumped for fun and just managed to last home. (5/2: 7/4-11/4)
689 Merlins Dream (IRE) did not look a safe conveyance, returning a string of minor jumping errors before making a hash of the last when upsides the winner. Hanging in behind that rival on the run to the line, he only got going again too late. It is becoming increasingly difficult to find excuses for him. (5/2: 2/1-3/1)

74* Change the Reign looked to need this and blew up approaching the second last. (3/1)
Gilpa Valu took a dreadful fall, which appeared to leave neither horse nor fence unscathed. (5/2)

865 HUNTINGDON INTERMEDIATE OPEN N.H. FLAT RACE (4, 5 & 6-Y.O) (Class H)

5-30 (5-31) **2m 110y** £1,763.00 (£493.00: £239.00)

	Horse	Dist	Pos	SP	RR	SF
	Scoundrel (KCBailey) **5-11-4** CO'Dwyer (bkwd: trckd ldrs: led on bit over 2f out: pushed out)	—	**1**	13/8[1]	—	—
	The Brewmaster (IRE) (IPWilliams) **4-11-3** JOsborne (a.p: rdn & ev ch 2f out: unable qckn)	1¾	**2**	8/1	—	—
	Bombadil (MartynMeade) **4-11-3** JRailton (bit bkwd: hdwy 5f out: rdn & one pce fnl 2f)	4	**3**	25/1	—	—
	El Crank Senor (RDEWoodhouse) **4-11-3** DerekByrne (plld hrd: prom: led 5f out tl over 2f out: sn btn)	s.h	**4**	12/1	—	—
	Arctic Flame (PTDalton) **5-10-13** APMcCoy (hld up: rdn & hdwy over 4f out: no imp fnl 2f)	2	**5**	10/1	—	—
679[2]	**Ardenbar** (JWPayne) **4-10-12** AMaguire (lw: led 7f: ev ch 4f: rdn & wknd 2f out)	7	**6**	4/1[2]	—	—
	Ermyns Pet (GLMoore) **5-10-11**(7) MAttwater (a.p: ev ch over 3f out: sn wknd)	2	**7**	5/1[3]	—	—
	Warrio (JRBosley) **6-11-4** MBosley (hld up & plld hrd: hdwy fnl 2f: nrst fin)	hd	**8**	33/1	—	—
	Gobalino Girl (IRE) (FGray) **4-10-12** RFarrant (in tch: rdn 3f out: no imp)	4	**9**	33/1	—	—
	Baba Sam (IRE) (PEccles) **5-11-4** AThornton (bkwd: effrt 8f out: btn 5f out)	1¼	**10**	33/1	—	—
	Denis Compton (JRinger) **5-11-4** BPowell (bit bkwd: hld up & bhd: sme hdwy fnl 3f)	hd	**11**	33/1	—	—
	A S Jim (OO'Neill) **5-11-4** VSlattery (lw: nvr trbld ldrs)	2½	**12**	33/1	—	—
679[4]	**Southerncrosspatch** (JWhite) **5-11-4** SCurran (lw: hdwy 7f out: sn rdn: wknd 4f out)	8	**13**	16/1	—	—
	Thermecon (IRE) (GAHubbard) **5-11-1**(3) KGaule (bkwd: plld hrd: w ldr: led 9f out to 5f out: sn wknd)	8	**14**	16/1	—	—
	Barton Blade (IRE) (MissHCKnight) **4-10-10**(7) MrAWintle (chsd ldrs 8f)	4	**15**	8/1	—	—
679[6]	**Captain Navar (IRE)** (JohnBerry) **6-11-4** ILawrence (bhd fnl 5f)	1¼	**16**	20/1	—	—
	Just Because (IRE) (TMJones) **4-11-3** CLlewellyn (lw: in tch 9f)	½	**17**	33/1	—	—
	Catch The Wind (KAMorgan) **6-10-13** ASSmith (plld hrd: hdwy 9f out: wknd 6f)	1½	**18**	14/1	—	—
	Toro Loco (IRE) (IPWilliams) **4-11-3** NWilliamson (hdwy 6f out: wknd qckly 4f out: t.o)	dist	**19**	20/1	—	—
306[7]	**Royal Salute** (FJordan) **4-11-3** SWynne (a bhd: t.o)	1½	**20**	33/1	—	—
	Sydillium (PJMakin) **4-11-3** MAFitzgerald (prom tl wknd 6f out: t.o)	11	**21**	12/1	—	—
	Pacifist (AGFoster) **5-10-6**(7) DCreech (bhd fnl 7f: p.u & dismntd 2f out)		**P**	33/1	—	—
				(SP 176.8%)	**22 Rn**	

3m 42.7 CSF £21.20 TOTE £2.50: £2.10 £1.50 £12.40 (£11.70) Trio £192.90; £62.51 to York 12/10/96 OWNER Mrs J. M. Corbett (UPPER LAMBOURN) BRED Mrs P. Nicholson

WEIGHT FOR AGE 4yo-1lb

Scoundrel must have been a lot fitter than he appeared and won this cosily. He should make a decent staying hurdler. (13/8: Evens-5/2)
The Brewmaster (IRE), keen on the way to post, took a bit of settling in the first couple of furlongs. He shaped with promise though and should not be hard to place. (8/1)
Bombadil made eyecatching ground leaving the back straight, but the effort rather petered out as the lack of a race found him out late in the day. (25/1)
El Crank Senor proved rather better than his name, being in the thick of things throughout. (12/1: op 33/1)
Arctic Flame ran respectably, although no match for the principals in the home straight. (10/1: 7/1-12/1)
679 Ardenbar, made plenty of use of, found the quickening pace beyond her in the last quarter-mile. (4/1: 3/1-5/1)
Ermyns Pet (5/1: op 6/4)
Warrio was noted staying on from the back when the race was over, and should come into his own when the ground eases. (33/1)
Denis Compton caught the eye when making a little late headway. (33/1)
Barton Blade (IRE) (8/1: 7/1-12/1)

T/Plpt: £341.00 (27.9 Tckts). T/Qdpt: £162.10 (2.43 Tckts). Dk

0636-BANGOR-ON-DEE (L-H) (Good to firm)

Saturday October 12th

WEATHER: overcast

866 BBC RADIO MERSEYSIDE NOVICES' HURDLE (4-Y.O+) (Class E)

2-05 (2-05) **2m 4f (11 hdls)** £2,710.00 (£760.00: £370.00) GOING minus 0.21 sec per fur (G)

	Horse	Dist	Pos	SP	RR	SF
	Ela Mata (MrsASwinbank) **4-10-11** JRailton (hld up in tch: qcknd to ld appr 3 out: sn clr: v.easily)	—	**1**	9/4[1]	64+	—
730[2]	**Tigh-Na-Mara (88)** (JMJefferson) **8-10-4**(5)ow2 ECallaghan (hld up in tch: hdwy to chse wnr 2 out: no imp)	5	**2**	11/2	57	—
718[5]	**Vallingale (IRE)** (MissHCKnight) **5-10-7** JFTitley (trckd ldrs: hrd rdn appr 2 out: one pce)	4	**3**	7/2[2]	52	—
	Jills Joy (IRE) (JNorton) **5-10-12** WFry (bit bkwd: chsd ldrs: rdn & outpcd appr 2 out: btn whn stumbled last)	4	**4**	40/1	54	—
	Le Baron (CREgerton) **5-10-12** JOsborne (hld up in tch: lost pl 7th: sn bhd: t.o)	17	**5**	4/1[3]	40	—
	Midnight Bob (JMackie) **5-10-12** RMarley (a in rr: t.o)	dist	**6**	25/1	—	—
	Sister Gale (MrsSJSmith) **4-10-6** RichardGuest (hld up in rr: effrt 6th: sn wknd: t.o)	16	**7**	25/1	—	—
	Fashion Leader (IRE) (CWeedon) **5-10-12** MRichards (bkwd: sn drvn along: bhd tl p.u bef 3 out)		**P**	12/1	—	—
	Boxit Again (JMackie) **6-10-12** TEley (plld hrd: led after 1st to 7th: sn wknd: t.o whn p.u bef 2 out)		**P**	33/1	—	—
	Just Like Dad (MartinTodhunter) **4-10-11** MDwyer (led to 1st: chsd ldr: led 7th:hdd & wknd appr 3 out: wnt lame & p.u bef 2 out)		**P**	9/1	—	—
				(SP 119.1%)	**10 Rn**	

4m 48.8 (12.80) CSF £14.74 TOTE £3.60: £1.40 £1.50 £1.90 (£12.30) Trio £12.80 OWNER Mr F. J. Sainsbury (RICHMOND) BRED Darley Stud Management Co Ltd

WEIGHT FOR AGE 4yo-1lb

Ela Mata was not 100% for this first outing since the spring but, given a very confident ride, stole the race by quickening clear approaching the third last. (9/4)
730 Tigh-Na-Mara had the edge in fitness, but her pilot allowed the winner to take first run, and she always had too much to do. (11/2)
718 Vallingale (IRE) still has a bit left to work on and, attempting a longer trip, stayed on at her own pace inside the last half-mile. (7/2)
Le Baron had his tongue tied down on this hurdling debut, but needed this run badly and was never able to get himself into the action. (4/1: op 5/2)

867 STADCO H'CAP CHASE (0-115) (5-Y.O+) (Class E)

2-35 (2-35) **2m 1f 110y (12 fncs)** £3,818.00 (£1,154.00: £562.00: £266.00) GOING minus 0.21 sec per fur (G)

	Horse	Dist	Pos	SP	RR	SF
722*	**Prince Skyburd (86)** (MrsPMAAvison) **5-10-0** AMaguire (a.p: led 3 out: rdn out)	—	**1**	8/11[1]	95	7
728[6]	**Crafty Chaplain (97)** (DMcCain) **10-10-9**(3) DWalsh (j.w: a.p: led appr 6th to 3 out: kpt on u.p)	2	**2**	14/1	104	17
	Regal Romper (IRE) (108) (MrsSJSmith) **8-11-9** RichardGuest (bkwd: hld up in rr: sme hdwy whn blnd 4 out: nt rcvr)	23	**3**	5/1[2]	94	7
689[6]	**Houghton (109)** (WJenks) **10-11-3**(7) MrRBurton (led tl appr 6th: lost pl & rdn next: sn bhd)	2½	**4**	11/1[3]	93	6
	Uncle Bert (IRE) (94) (GMMcCourt) **6-10-9** BClifford (bkwd: sn chsng ldrs: wknd after 4 out: t.o)	3½	**5**	5/1[2]	75	—
				(SP 106.2%)		**5 Rn**

4m 16.2 (6.20) CSF £8.72 TOTE £1.40: £1.10 £3.60 (£14.80) OWNER Mrs P. M. A. Avison (HELMSLEY) BRED Mrs P. M. A. Avison
WEIGHT FOR AGE 5yo-1lb

722* Prince Skyburd completed his hat-trick with ease and has certainly found his mark since being put over fences. (8/11: 4/5-Evens)
Crafty Chaplain invariably runs well because he is such a fluent jumper. He stuck on well when the task had looked hopeless to make sure the winner knew he had been in a race. (14/1)
Regal Romper (IRE) ran up a sequence of wins at the start of last season, but looked a bit ring-rusty here, and a bad mistake at the final ditch, four out, left him in no-man's land. (5/1: 7/2-11/2)
689 Houghton (11/1: 7/1-12/1)

868 NUMARK H'CAP HURDLE (0-110) (4-Y.O+) (Class E)

3-05 (3-05) **2m 1f (9 hdls)** £3,176.25 (£960.00: £467.50: £221.25) GOING minus 0.21 sec per fur (G)

	Horse	Dist	Pos	SP	RR	SF
692[6]	**Stay With Me (FR) (88)** (CREgerton) **6-11-4** JOsborne (swtg: a.p: led on bit appr 2 out: sn clr: v.easily)	—	**1**	5/1	73+	26
	Pharare (IRE) (92) (RDEWoodhouse) **6-11-8** MDwyer (trckd ldrs: rdn 3 out: kpt on: no ch w wnr)	5	**2**	4/1[3]	72	25
641[11]	**Batty's Island (77)** (BPreece) **7-10-4**(3) GHogan (bhd: lost tch 6th: styd on fr 3 out: nvr nrr)	6	**3**	20/1	52	5
657[P]	**Royal Circus (90)** (PWHiatt) **7-11-3**(3) EHusband (led to 4th: led 5th tl appr 2 out: sn outpcd)	2	**4**	8/1	63	16
729[4]	**Tordo (IRE) (94)** (CJMann) **5-11-7b**(3) JMagee (bit bkwd: chsd ldrs: led 4th to 5th: wknd 3 out: t.o)	13	**5**	100/30[1]	55	8
718[2]	**Winter Rose (86)** (MSheppard) **5-11-2** BPowell (prom tl wknd qckly 5th: t.o)	½	**6**	7/2[2]	46	—
	Saymore (90) (WClay) **10-11-6** TEley (bkwd: a in rr: t.o fr 3 out)	3	**7**	20/1	47	—
	River Wye (IRE) (90) (GHYardley) **4-11-5** BFenton (hld up & bhd: lost tch appr 6th: t.o)	21	**8**	8/1	28	—
641[P]	**Lustreman (70)** (JHPeacock) **9-10-0** RBellamy (bit bkwd: a bhd: t.o ½-wy: p.u bef 2 out)		**P**	50/1	—	—
				(SP 115.7%)		**9 Rn**

4m 0.4 (5.40) CSF £23.86 CT £334.69 TOTE £3.90: £1.90 £1.70 £5.40 (£9.90) Trio £30.90 OWNER Mrs Sandra Roe (CHADDLEWORTH)
BRED Mr and Mrs Henri Rossi and Gerard Desnoues
LONG HANDICAP Lustreman 9-7
WEIGHT FOR AGE 4yo-1lb
OFFICIAL EXPLANATION **Winter Rose: hung right throughout the race.**

692 Stay With Me (FR) cruised through on the bridle to take command early in the straight and did not need to be asked a question to storm clear. (5/1)
Pharare (IRE) was certainly not helped by this step back to the minimum trip on this fast track, but he did his best to make a race of it and will benefit from the run. (4/1)
Batty's Island, showing his first glimpse of form for some time, stayed on well in the last half-mile and a longer trip would be in his favour. (20/1)
582 Royal Circus has hardly got the speed to win over this trip nowadays, and was struggling to hold on from the turn into the straight. (8/1)
Tordo (IRE), still looking big and well, remained in the firing-line until the pace picked up and left him struggling before reaching the home straight. (100/30)

869 WILLIS CORROON H'CAP CHASE (0-120) (5-Y.O+) (Class D)

3-40 (3-40) **3m 110y (18 fncs)** £4,507.00 (£1,366.00: £668.00: £319.00) GOING minus 0.21 sec per fur (G)

	Horse	Dist	Pos	SP	RR	SF
809[P]	**Factor Ten (IRE) (118)** (MissHCKnight) **8-12-0** JFTitley (j.w: chsd ldr: lft in ld 4 out: sn clr: easily)	—	**1**	3/1[2]	130+	42
	Ali's Alibi (117) (MrsMReveley) **9-11-13** PNiven (bkwd: hld up in rr: effrt appr 3 out: chsd wnr appr last: no imp)	4	**2**	5/6[1]	126	38
725[7]	**Auvillar (USA) (93)** (JParfitt) **8-10-3v** CLlewellyn (led: reminders 12th: mstke & hdd 4 out: sn btn)	19	**3**	25/1[3]	90	2
	Millies Own (94) (PJHobbs) **9-10-1**(3)ow1 GTormey (bit bkwd: trckd ldng pair: wkng whn blnd 3 out: sn t.o)	29	**4**	3/1[2]	72	—
				(SP 108.4%)		**4 Rn**

6m 8.2 (6.20) CSF £5.73 TOTE £3.50 (£1.60) OWNER Premier Crops Ltd (WANTAGE) BRED Mrs F. J. Maxwell
OFFICIAL EXPLANATION **Ali's Alibi: the jockey reported that he had intended to drop his mount in, and make his effort from there, but the gelding was careful at the fences, gurgled on the last circuit and would not have responded to more vigorous riding.**

809 Factor Ten (IRE), well suited by this strongly-run race, turned in a bold display of jumping and sauntered home as he pleased. (3/1)
Ali's Alibi did not win a race last term and has never won on ground as lively as this, but punters plunged on him as if defeat was out of the question. (5/6)
Auvillar (USA), responding to a strong ride, will have trouble staying this trip if ridden without restraint, and it came as no surprise to see him flagging inside the last half-mile. (25/1)

870 THELWALL MEMORIAL TROPHY NOVICES' CHASE (5-Y.O+) (Class D)

4-20 (4-20) **2m 4f 110y (15 fncs)** £3,663.75 (£1,110.00: £542.50: £258.75) GOING minus 0.21 sec per fur (G)

	Horse	Dist	Pos	SP	RR	SF
	The Last Fling (IRE) (MrsSJSmith) **6-10-12** RichardGuest (chsd ldr: chal & mstke 2 out: led last: r.o wl)	—	**1**	10/11[1]	113+	33
652[3]	**Mr Conductor (IRE)** (RHAlner) **5-10-10** MAFitzgerald (j.w: led tl bdly hmpd by loose horses & hdd last: sn btn)	6	**2**	11/4[2]	108	26
	Bridepark Rose (IRE) (89) (GMMcCourt) **8-10-7** BClifford (bkwd: chsd ldng pair fr 8th tl lost pl 4 out)	22	**3**	7/1[3]	86	6
738[7]	**Karlovac (60)** (RLee) **10-10-12b** AMaguire (bhd & outpcd tl sme late hdwy)	18	**4**	33/1	77	—
289[7]	**Mistroy** (MissMKMilligan) **6-10-7** ASSmith (a bhd: t.o fr ½-wy)	11	**5**	33/1	64	—
641[12]	**Ibn Sina (USA)** (WClay) **9-10-12** TEley (chsd ldrs: hmpd by loose horses & lost pl 8th: sn t.o)	19	**6**	50/1	54	—
	Highland Way (IRE) (MartinTodhunter) **8-10-12** MDwyer (swtg: bit bkwd: fell 1st)		**F**	8/1	—	—

	Glamanglitz (PTDalton) **6-10-12** CLlewellyn (hld up in rr: fell 4th)		**F**	12/1	—	—
				(SP 118.2%)	**8 Rn**	

5m 3.4 (3.40) CSF £4.00 TOTE £2.00: £1.20 £1.10 £2.70 (£2.60) OWNER Michael Jackson Bloodstock Ltd (BINGLEY) BRED G. Stewart
WEIGHT FOR AGE 5yo-2lb

The Last Fling (IRE) has plenty of ability and, though he may have been a shade lucky to make a winning debut over fences, can only get better with this behind him. (10/11)
652 Mr Conductor (IRE) had to contend with loose horses from an early stage, but did not let them distract him until they forced him to take avoiding action into the last, where he propped on landing after being headed and had little chance of getting back. (11/4)
Glamanglitz (12/1: op 20/1)

871 COCK BANK NOVICES' HURDLE (4-Y.O+) (Class E)

4-50 (4-51) **2m 1f (9 hdls)** £2,878.00 (£808.00: £394.00) GOING minus 0.21 sec per fur (G)

				SP	RR	SF
	Contrafire (IRE) (MrsASwinbank) **4-10-11** JSupple (lw: chsd ldrs: led after 6th: sn clr: comf)	—	**1**	3/1[2]	70+	26
	Inn At the Top (JNorton) **4-10-11** WFry (a.p: chsd wnr fr 2 out: styd on)	3	**2**	16/1	67	23
743[F]	**Anabranch (100)** (JMJefferson) **5-10-9**(5) ECallaghan (lw: trckd ldrs: hrd rdn & wknd appr 2 out)	12	**3**	4/1[3]	58	15
794[2]	**Ela Man Howa (85)** (ABailey) **5-10-12** TKent (led tl after 6th: wknd qckly appr 2 out)	18	**4**	6/4[1]	39	—
	Studio Thirty (CASmith) **4-10-11** PNiven (hld up: effrt appr 3 out: nvr nrr)	5	**5**	25/1	34	—
	Beau Matelot (90) (MissMKMilligan) **4-10-11** ASSmith (bit bkwd: mid div tl wknd 5th: t.o)	24	**6**	9/1	12	—
	Naked Feelings (MartinTodhunter) **4-10-11** MDwyer (nvr nr ldrs: t.o fr 3 out)	2	**7**	33/1	10	—
	Biya (IRE) (DMcCain) **4-10-8**(3) DWalsh (bkwd: trckd ldrs tl lost tch 6th: t.o)	8	**8**	25/1	2	—
	Young Benson (TWall) **4-10-8**(3) RMassey (a bhd: t.o)	3	**9**	16/1	—	—
	Beths Wish (GMPrice) **7-10-7** BFenton (bkwd: mstke 1st: a bhd: t.o)	27	**10**	50/1	—	—
	Nunson (RDickin) **7-10-12** RBellamy (bkwd: chsd ldrs to 5th: sn wknd: t.o)	18	**11**	50/1	—	—
	Caherass Court (IRE) (BPreece) **5-10-4**(3) GHogan (a bhd: t.o whn fell 6th)		**F**	50/1	—	—
	Galafron (WClay) **4-10-11** TEley (bkwd: a bhd: t.o whn p.u bef 3 out)		**P**	50/1	—	—
				(SP 125.2%)	**13 Rn**	

3m 58.9 (3.90) CSF £47.25 TOTE £3.50: £1.60 £2.60 £1.60 (£24.70) Trio £56.10 OWNER G B Turnbull Ltd (RICHMOND) BRED Thoroughbred Trust in Ireland
WEIGHT FOR AGE 4yo-1lb

Contrafire (IRE), a useful winner on the Flat, did not impress to post on this hurdling debut, but he knew his job once in action, and brushed aside this opposition without much trouble. (3/1)
Inn At the Top, unable to trouble the Judge on the Flat, showed plenty of promise on this hurdles debut and, given another half-mile, should be able to open his account. (16/1)
743 Anabranch, far more experienced than most, could not get in a blow against the principals, but the fact that she got round safely will be a big confidence-booster. (4/1)
794 Ela Man Howa may well need further at this game and, though he helped force the pace, he looked very one-paced from the turn into the straight. (6/4: 2/1-5/4)

872 BANGOR STANDARD OPEN N.H. FLAT RACE (4, 5 & 6-Y.O F & M) (Class H)

5-20 (5-21) **2m 1f** £1,679.00 (£469.00: £227.00)

				SP	RR	SF
	Lady Rebecca (MissVenetiaWilliams) **4-11-3** AMaguire (hld up in tch: shkn up, swvd lft & led wl over 1f out: rdn out)	—	**1**	7/2[2]	—	—
705*	**Nishamira (IRE)** (TDBarron) **4-11-10** MDwyer (hld up gng wl: ev ch whn bdly hmpd wl over 1f out: rallied gamely fnl f: jst failed)	nk	**2**	2/1[1]	—	—
	Hutcel Loch (RDEWoodhouse) **5-11-4** ASSmith (mde most tl hdd & outpcd wl over 1f out)	15	**3**	33/1	—	—
	Night Escapade (IRE) (CWeedon) **4-11-3** MRichards (hld up: hdwy 5f out: ev ch 2f out: sn rdn & outpcd)	2	**4**	20/1	—	—
	Lippy Louise (MrsMReveley) **4-11-3** PNiven (hld up in rr: stdy hdwy fnl 4f: nt rch ldrs)	5	**5**	15/2	—	—
99[3]	**Nenagh Gunner** (JJQuinn) **6-11-4** LWyer (hld up in tch: effrt & rdn 3f out: sn outpcd)	1	**6**	12/1	—	—
679[5]	**Lady Foley (IRE)** (CJMann) **4-10-10**(7) DKiernan (hld up: hdwy 4f out: rdn & wknd over 2f out)	3	**7**	16/1	—	—
	Distant Hills (JPDodds) **4-11-3** RichardGuest (trckd ldrs tl wknd over 3f out)	15	**8**	12/1	—	—
504[5]	**Halam Bell** (WGMTurner) **4-11-3** PHolley (hld up: hdwy 6f out: wknd over 3f out)	15	**9**	25/1	—	—
	Carlingford Gale (IRE) (TRGeorge) **5-11-4** MAFitzgerald (hld up in tch: rdn & wknd 4f out)	½	**10**	5/1[3]	—	—
	Grey Dante (IRE) (SABrookshaw) **5-10-11**(7) MissSBeddoes (mid div tl wknd 5f out)	2	**11**	33/1	—	—
	Briden (JMJefferson) **4-10-12**(5) ECallaghan (trckd ldrs 12f: sn hrd rdn: grad wknd)	1	**12**	20/1	—	—
504[3]	**Gabrielle Gerard** (MrsAMNaughton) **4-10-10**(7) RWilkinson (racd wd: a bhd)	¾	**13**	16/1	—	—
705[7]	**Miss Nonnie** (MissLShally) **4-11-3** DLeahy (w ldr tl rdn & wknd over 5f out)	hd	**14**	33/1	—	—
	Barlot (JMackie) **4-11-3** TEley (bkwd: a bhd: t.o)	1¼	**15**	25/1	—	—
	Baronburn (SABrookshaw) **6-10-11**(7) MrRBurton (bkwd: unruly bef s: bhd fr ½-wy: t.o)	dist	**16**	33/1	—	—
	African Bride (IRE) (DBrace) **6-11-4** MissPJones (bkwd: prom tl wknd wl over 4f out: t.o)	19	**17**	14/1	—	—
	Caspian Dawn (MrsSJSmith) **6-10-11**(7) MrPMurray (racd wd: trckd ldrs 10f: sn wknd: t.o)	26	**18**	33/1	—	—
				(SP 149.7%)	**18 Rn**	

3m 58.1 CSF £12.42 TOTE £3.80: £1.60 £1.50 £18.20 (£3.90) Trio £137.80; £157.28 to 14/10/96 OWNER Kinnersley Optimists (HEREFORD) BRED Needwood Stud
WEIGHT FOR AGE 4yo-1lb

Lady Rebecca, who has changed stables since last season, and made a bee-line for the inside rail when delivering her challenge under a right-handed drive just inside the final quarter-mile pole, causing considerable trouble in doing so. Surprisingly no objection was called. (7/2)
705* Nishamira (IRE) was always travelling smoothly just in behind the leaders and was full of running when forced to check as the winner dived across her a furlong out. She put in a renewed, strong, late challenge and only just failed. (2/1)
Hutcel Loch did a good job of pacemaking until finding the quickening tempo more than she could cope with from the turn into the straight. (33/1)
Night Escapade (IRE) ran extremely well on this racecourse debut and will be all the better for it. (20/1)
Lippy Louise failed to get close enough to cause concern, but does appear to have ability. (15/2: 5/1-8/1)
Distant Hills (12/1: op 8/1)
Carlingford Gale (IRE) (5/1: 14/1-25/1)

T/Plpt: £59.20 (120.41 Tckts). T/Qdpt: £20.80 (10.81 Tckts). IM

0781-HEXHAM (L-H) (Good to firm, Firm patches)
Saturday October 12th
WEATHER: overcast

873 CAPITAL SHOPPING CENTRES NOVICES' H'CAP CHASE (0-95) (5-Y.O+) (Class F)
2-20 (2-20) **2m 110y (12 fncs)** £2,491.20 (£741.60: £352.80: £158.40) GOING minus 0.38 sec per fur (GF)

	Horse	Dist	Pos	SP	RR	SF
784[2]	**Spring Loaded (70)** (JGMO'Shea) **5-10-3**(5) MichaelBrennan (hld up: wnt prom 4th: led 3 out: rdn out flat)	—	1	9/4[2]	81	11
	Mr Reiner (IRE) (76) (JWade) **8-11-1** KJones (chsd ldrs: drvn along 3 out: styd on u.p flat)	1¼	2	5/1[3]	86	17
694[3]	**Reve de Valse (USA) (87)** (RJohnson) **9-11-12** KJohnson (lw: led to 3 out: one pce appr last)	4	3	2/1[1]	93	24
	Hazel Crest (72) (MESowersby) **9-10-11** DParker (bit bkwd: trckd ldrs tl wknd after 2 out)	12	4	12/1	66	—
206[5]	**Dear Emily (74)** (JESwiers) **8-10-13** MrSSwiers (outpcd & bhd fr 4th)	dist	5	7/1	—	—
681[3]	**Boethius (USA) (75)** (MABarnes) **7-11-0b[1]** PWaggott (chsd ldrs: drvn along 6th: hit 4 out: sn lost pl)	2	6	20/1	—	—
				(SP 105.7%)		**6 Rn**

4m 1.2 (4.20) CSF £11.87 TOTE £2.20: £1.60 £4.70 (£7.60) OWNER Panther Racing Ltd (WELFORD-ON-AVON)
WEIGHT FOR AGE 5yo-1lb

784 Spring Loaded, who looked to have been given a good chance at the weights on this chasing bow, took it up travelling strongly but, in the end, had to be kept up to it. (9/4)

Mr Reiner (IRE) looked as if the outing would do him good and stuck on grimly all the way to the line. (5/1)

694 Reve de Valse (USA), wearing a tongue-strap as usual, jumped soundly in front but, under his big weight, could do no more going to the last. (2/1)

Hazel Crest (12/1: op 7/1)

874 METRO CENTRE HURDLE (3-Y.O) (Class E)
2-50 (2-50) **2m (8 hdls)** £2,217.00 (£612.00: £291.00) GOING minus 0.38 sec per fur (GF)

	Horse	Dist	Pos	SP	RR	SF
646[5]	**Hobbs Choice** (GMMoore) **3-10-5** NBentley (sn trckng ldr: led appr last: hit last: hung lft u.p: jst hld on)	—	1	10/11[1]	55	—
	Silent Guest (IRE) (MDHammond) **3-10-10** RGarritty (led 1st tl appr last: hrd rdn & rallied flat: nt qckn nr fin)	nk	2	3/1[2]	60	4
688[7]	**Kai's Lady (IRE)** (SWCampion) **3-10-0**(5) MichaelBrennan (chsd ldrs: pushed along 4th: rdn 3 out: sn wknd)	30	3	20/1	25	—
	Most Wanted (IRE) (JJO'Neill) **3-10-0**(5) RMcGrath (outpcd & pushed along 4th: lost tch 3 out)	26	4	9/2[3]	—	—
688[6]	**Recall To Mind** (MESowersby) **3-10-10b** DParker (led: j.slowly & hdd 1st: mstke 3rd: wl bhd fr 5th)	nk	5	14/1	3	—
	Vales Ales (RMMcKellar) **3-10-7**(3) GCahill (sn pushed along: lost tch 4th: t.o whn p.u bef next)		P	20/1	—	—
				(SP 111.8%)		**6 Rn**

3m 54.1 (6.10) CSF £3.98 TOTE £1.80: £1.30 £1.60 (£3.10) OWNER Miss Liz Hobbs (MIDDLEHAM) BRED F. Hines

646 Hobbs Choice looked in control when she fell through the final flight. Hanging left under pressure, in the end it was a desperate thing. (10/11)

Silent Guest (IRE), who showed very little on the level, rallied under a strong ride, but could not find quite sufficient to worry the winner out of it. (3/1)

Kai's Lady (IRE) wore a tongue-strap and was pushed along to keep up at halfway. She lost touch with the first two after three out. (20/1)

Recall To Mind (14/1: op 8/1)

875 REGIONAL RAILWAYS NOVICES' CHASE (5-Y.O+) (Class E)
3-20 (3-20) **3m 1f (19 fncs)** £2,961.00 (£882.00: £420.00: £189.00) GOING minus 0.38 sec per fur (GF)

	Horse	Dist	Pos	SP	RR	SF
535[2]	**Scrabo View (IRE) (96)** (PBeaumont) **8-11-5** RSupple (lw: chsd ldrs: drvn along 13th: hrd rdn flat: led last 75y: all out)	—	1	2/1[1]	86	—
802[5]	**Royal Surprise** (WGReed) **9-10-12** TReed (w ldrs: led & rdn along 15th: hdd & nt qckn towards fin)	nk	2	7/1	79	—
704[2]	**Bardaros** (MissLucindaRussell) **7-10-12** AThornton (lw: chsd ldrs: outpcd 4 out: ev ch last: one pce)	2½	3	11/4[2]	77	—
685[4]	**More Joy (70)** (MrsLMarshall) **8-10-12** DBentley (j.rt: mde most to 15th: ev ch last: one pce)	½	4	11/1	77	—
733[4]	**Golden Savannah (75)** (MESowersby) **6-10-12** DParker (chsd ldrs: drvn along & outpcd 12th: wknd 14th)	16	5	16/1	67	—
802[3]	**German Legend (80)** (DALamb) **6-11-5** JBurke (in tch: blnd 14th: wknd 4 out)	8	6	7/2[3]	69	—
785[U]	**Smokey Track (56)** (MrsJConway) **11-10-2**(5) STaylor (nt j.w: sn outpcd: hdwy u.p 10th: wknd 12th: sn bhd: t.o)	dist	7	33/1	—	—
	Clonroche Lucky (IRE) (JWade) **6-10-12** KJones (bit bkwd: w ldrs tl wknd 15th: bhd whn p.u bef 3 out)		P	20/1	—	—
				(SP 116.6%)		**8 Rn**

6m 25.7 (14.70) CSF £15.65 TOTE £2.40: £1.10 £1.80 £1.40 (£8.40) OWNER Mr Robin Mellish (BRANDSBY) BRED Mrs D. Minnis

535 Scrabo View (IRE), fresh and well after a six-week break, made really hard work of this, and only his rider's endeavours forced his head in front in the closing stages. (2/1)

Royal Surprise showed the benefit of his Hexham outing. Driven along and making the best of his way home five out, he was only edged out near the line. He looks a stayer through and through. (7/1)

704 Bardaros, struggling to keep up four out, landed almost level at the last but, tending to hang right, could only keep on at the one pace. (11/4)

More Joy, with the blinkers left off, ran much better, making the running, despite jumping right. He had no more to offer on the run-in after landing almost upsides at the last. (11/1)

876 HENNESSY COGNAC SPECIAL NOVICES' HURDLE (4-Y.O+) (Class B)
3-50 (3-50) **2m (8 hdls)** £6,192.00 (£1,712.00: £816.00) GOING minus 0.38 sec per fur (GF)

	Horse	Dist	Pos	SP	RR	SF
784*	**Supertop (95)** (LLungo) **8-10-12** MFoster (lw: hld up: stdy hdwy 4th: effrt & hit last: styd on to ld flat)	—	1	9/2[3]	79	31
735*	**Suas Leat (IRE) (96)** (JMJefferson) **6-10-12** MNewton (lw: trckd ldrs: led 2 out: blnd last: hdd & nt qckn flat)	2	2	9/2[3]	77	29
735[2]	**Canton Venture** (SPCWoods) **4-10-11** PHide (j.slowly: led to 2 out: ev ch last: styd on same pce)	1	3	2/1[1]	76	27
	King Rat (IRE) (JGMO'Shea) **5-10-12** MichaelBrennan (chsd ldrs: kpt on one pce fr 2 out)	10	4	15/2	66	18
735[3]	**Court Joker (IRE) (82)** (HAlexander) **4-10-11** BStorey (hld up & bhd: hdwy 2 out: nvr nr ldrs)	6	5	16/1	60	11
643[5]	**Blanc Seing (FR)** (JESwiers) **9-10-12** MrSSwiers (bit bkwd: chsd ldrs tl lost pl 4th: sn bhd: sme hdwy 2 out: n.d)	5	6	33/1	55	7
253*	**Coureur (104)** (MDHammond) **7-10-12** RGarritty (lw: hld up: stdy hdwy 4th: effrt 2 out: wknd appr last: virtually p.u: lame)	6	7	9/4[2]	49	1

			Pos	SP	RR	SF
	General Muck (IRE) (HowardJohnson) **7-10-12** STaylor (chsd ldrs: drvn along 3 out: sn lost pl)	12	**8**	33/1	37	—
585P	**Whirlwind Romance (IRE) (59)** (WTKemp) **5-10-7** SMcDougall (sn bhd: j.b rt 3rd: sn p.u)		**P**	66/1	—	—

(SP 125.5%) **9 Rn**

3m 48.3 (0.30) CSF £25.66 TOTE £6.50: £2.10 £1.30 £1.10 (£14.80) Trio £7.40 OWNER Mrs Barbara Lungo (CARRUTHERSTOWN) BRED Limestone Stud

WEIGHT FOR AGE 4yo-1lb

784* Supertop obviously gained confidence from his effortless victory in a seller here eight days ago. After falling through the last, he did more than enough on the run-in. (9/2)
735* Suas Leat (IRE) made the best of his way home, but was under pressure when he fell through the last. It would have been a close thing had he avoided the error. (9/2)
735 Canton Venture, whose jockey set off with the intention of making this a true test, slowed up at the first and ran about at the second. Back upsides at the last, he could do no more. (2/1)
King Rat (IRE) was left behind over the last two. An easier finish would put less strain on his stamina. (15/2)
735 Court Joker (IRE), a headstrong sort, was dropped right out. Picking up ground nicely at the finish, this will have put him on the right road. (16/1)
643 Blanc Seing (FR) is not without hope, but looked very burly. (33/1)
253* Coureur took a keen grip. Trying to close two out, he dropped right away going to the last and was virtually pulled up when he was found to be lame. (9/4)

877 METRO CENTRE 10TH BIRTHDAY H'CAP CHASE (0-110) (5-Y.O+) (Class E)

4-25 (4-25) **2m 4f 110y (15 fncs)** £3,586.80 (£865.20) GOING minus 0.38 sec per fur (GF)

			Pos	SP	RR	SF
689F	**Wise Advice (IRE) (95)** (MDHammond) **6-11-2** RGarritty (mde virtually all: drvn clr after 3 out)	—	**1**	5/6[1]	101	1
696P	**Willie Sparkle (79)** (MrsSCBradburne) **10-10-0** ADobbin (jnd wnr 3rd: hit 11th: sn rdn & no imp)	8	**2**	10/11[2]	79	—

(SP 106.9%) **2 Rn**

5m 7.5 (10.50) TOTE £1.50 OWNER Mr A. G. Chappell (MIDDLEHAM)

336 Wise Advice (IRE) had come to grief on his two previous outings and was not surprisingly hesitant. In the end, he scored decisively. (5/6)
696 Willie Sparkle was pulled up first time. He was upsides here when he hit the eleventh and, soon driven along, proved no match. (10/11)

878 IN SITU H'CAP HURDLE (0-100) (4-Y.O+) (Class F)

4-55 (4-55) **3m (12 hdls)** £2,108.40 (£582.40: £277.20) GOING minus 0.38 sec per fur (GF)

			Pos	SP	RR	SF
5094	**Shelton Abbey (63)** (JWade) **10-10-3b** KJones (lw: trckd ldrs gng wl: led on bit appr last: hit last: sn hdd: hrd rdn to ld towards fin)	—	**1**	13/2	49	5
782*	**Crofton Lake (62)** (JEDixon) **8-10-2** BStorey (bit bkwd: chsd ldrs: effrt 3 out: ev ch flat: nt qckn)	2½	**2**	7/1	46	2
8052	**Ballindoo (84)** (RJArmson) **7-11-10** MrRArmson (w ldrs: led 7th tl appr last: led flat: hdd & no ex fnl 75y)	nk	**3**	2/1[1]	68	24
7863	**Thaleros (83)** (GMMoore) **6-11-9** JCallaghan (trckd ldrs: ev ch tl wknd appr last)	4	**4**	3/1[3]	65	21
509F	**Copperhurst (IRE) (73)** (WTKemp) **5-10-13** SMcDougall (led to 7th: drvn along & lost pl 9th: t.o whn p.u bef last)		**P**	11/4[2]	—	—

(SP 110.8%) **5 Rn**

5m 46.4 (6.40) CSF £39.39 TOTE £8.50: £2.20 £3.90 (£13.70) OWNER Mr John Wade (MORDON) BRED Mrs A. T. Grantham

509 Shelton Abbey, who looked in tremendous nick beforehand, travelled strongly on the bridle and, for once, never looked like dropping himself out. Simply running away when taking it up going to the last, he fell through the final flight and then tried to down tools, but his rider would not allow it and, under a forceful ride, he was persuaded to regain the advantage in the closing stages. (13/2)
782* Crofton Lake still looked as if the outing would do him good and stepped up considerably on his win in a two-horse race here eight days earlier. He looks a potential chaser. (7/1)
805 Ballindoo appreciated the step up in distance. (2/1)
786 Thaleros looked half-hearted. (3/1)

T/Plpt: £41.50 (134.39 Tckts). T/Qdpt: £13.40 (22.96 Tckts). WG

0718-WORCESTER (L-H) (Good to firm)
Saturday October 12th

879 DUNCAN FEARNLEY AMATEUR (S) H'CAP HURDLE (0-95) (4-Y.O+) (Class G)

2-25 (2-25) **2m (8 hdls)** £2,087.00 (£582.00: £281.00) GOING minus 0.04 sec per fur (G)

			Pos	SP	RR	SF
7234	**Hamadryad (IRE) (85)** (MrsVCWard) **8-10-13**(7) MrRThornton (hld up: stdy hdwy 4th: led on bit 2 out: rdn out)	—	**1**	100/30[1]	73+	25
7497	**Burnt Sienna (IRE) (79)** (JSMoore) **4-10-6v**(7) MrEJames (led to 2 out: one pce)	6	**2**	11/1	61	12
5553	**Denomination (USA) (90)** (MCPipe) **4-11-5**(5) MrAFarrant (hld up & bhd: hdwy 5th: r.o one pce fr 2 out)	2½	**3**	13/2[2]	70	21
	Glowing Path (77) (RJHodges) **6-10-9**(3) MrCBonner (hld up: hdwy appr 3 out: 4th & btn whn mstke 2 out)	¾	**4**	8/1	56	8
	Forcing Two (USA) (70) (NATwiston-Davies) **5-9-12b**(7) MrJGoldstein (prom tl j.slowly 3rd: styd on flat)	3½	**5**	7/1[3]	45	—
6483	**Galloping Guns (IRE) (69)** (BJLlewellyn) **4-9-10**(7) MissEJJones (prom: ev ch 3 out: wknd 2 out)	s.h	**6**	12/1	44	—
7498	**Java Shrine (USA) (74)** (JCTuck) **5-10-2**(7)ow2 MrAWintle (j.slowly 3rd & 4th: no hdwy fr 3 out)	1	**7**	12/1	48	—
6487	**Catwalker (IRE) (65)** (HJMWebb) **5-9-7**(7) MrOMcPhail (nvr nr to chal)	6	**8**	25/1	33	—
5945	**Scalp 'em (IRE) (68)** (DrPPritchard) **8-9-10**(7)ow3 DrPPritchard (chsd ldr to 4th: rdn & wknd appr 3 out)	7	**9**	33/1	29	—
5556	**Reefa's Mill (IRE) (78)** (JNeville) **4-10-9**(3) MrMRimell (bhd fr 5th)	6	**10**	11/1	33	—
6004	**Pocono Knight (68)** (CHJones) **6-9-10**(7) MissBSmall (a bhd)	1	**11**	16/1	22	—
7496	**Night Time (75)** (FJordan) **4-10-2**(7) MrGShenkin (a bhd)	½	**12**	12/1	29	—
834S	**Tibbs Inn (68)** (ABarrow) **7-9-10**(7)ow3 MrRWidger (s.s: bhd most of wy: t.o)	20	**13**	20/1	2	—
	Doc's Coat (71) (CPWildman) **11-9-13**(7) MrEBabington (bkwd: wl bhd fr 3rd: t.o)	9	**14**	33/1	—	—

(SP 120.1%) **14 Rn**

3m 48.4 (8.40) CSF £36.89 CT £208.46 TOTE £4.20: £1.40 £3.60 £2.00 (£27.60) Trio £8.80 OWNER Mrs R F Key & Mrs V C Ward (GRANTHAM) BRED P. Myerscough

LONG HANDICAP Scalp 'em (IRE) 9-9 Tibbs Inn 9-10 Catwalker (IRE) 9-11

WEIGHT FOR AGE 4yo-1lb

No bid

723 Hamadryad (IRE), reverting to selling company, proved much too sharp for these platers. (100/30)
555 Burnt Sienna (IRE) found the winner galloping all over her in the home straight. (11/1: op 7/1)
555 Denomination (USA) was only 1lb higher than when he won a seller at Southwell in July. (13/2)
Glowing Path has obviously had his training problems, but was a springer in the market, despite a lengthy absence. (8/1: op 12/1)
Forcing Two (USA) finished second over three and a quarter miles at Hereford last season, and probably found this trip inadequate. (7/1: op 9/2)
Java Shrine (USA) (12/1: op 8/1)

880 MEB POWERLINE NOVICES' CHASE (5-Y.O+) (Class E)

2-55 (2-55) **2m 7f (18 fncs)** £3,174.50 (£882.00: £423.50) GOING minus 0.04 sec per fur (G)

Form	Horse	Dist	Pos	SP	RR	SF
631[3]	**Glenfinn Princess (96)** (MrsMerritaJones) **8-10-7** DerekByrne (hld up: mstke 11th: hdwy & j.lft 12th: led 4 out: clr whn hit 3 out: easily)	—	1	7/4[2]	101+	9
724*	**Imperial Vintage (IRE) (100)** (MissVenetiaWilliams) **6-11-12** APMcCoy (led: mstke 11th: blnd 14th: hdd 4 out: sn btn)	14	2	13/8[1]	110	18
791[F]	**Shikaree (IRE) (95)** (MCPipe) **5-10-9b** CMaude (nt j.w: chsd ldr to 5th: wnt 2nd 8th tl wknd appr 4 out: virtually p.u flat)	dist	3	11/4[3]	—	—
	Capo Castanum (80) (MissHCKnight) **7-10-12** GBradley (chsd ldr 5th to 8th: 3rd whn hmpd & uns rdr 12th)		U	11/1	—	—
				(SP 109.5%)	**4 Rn**	

5m 52.3 (14.30) CSF £4.77 TOTE £2.70 (£2.30) OWNER Mr Patrick McGinty (LAMBOURN) BRED H. C. and K. A. James
WEIGHT FOR AGE 5yo-2lb
631 Glenfinn Princess took advantage of a nice pull in the weights in an uncompetitive race. (7/4)
724* Imperial Vintage (IRE) nearly unshipped his rider five from home, and found the weight concession far too great from the next. (13/8)
Capo Castanum (11/1: 7/1-12/1)

881 PERTEMPS HURDLE (3-Y.O) (Class E)

3-25 (3-25) **2m (8 hdls)** £2,360.00 (£660.00: £320.00) GOING minus 0.04 sec per fur (G)

Form	Horse	Dist	Pos	SP	RR	SF
	Agdistis (HThomsonJones) **3-10-7** LHarvey (plld hrd: led on bit appr 3 out: sn clr: v.easily)	—	1	5/4[1]	64+	4
640[8]	**Flood's Fancy** (LJBarratt) **3-10-7** DerekByrne (dropped rr 4th: hdwy appr 3 out: chsd wnr fr 2 out: no imp)	7	2	40/1	57	—
654[F]	**Amber Ring** (MissKMGeorge) **3-10-7** JRKavanagh (led to 3rd: chsd wnr 3 out to 2 out: wknd appr last)	8	3	6/1	49	—
	Chipalata (TWDonnelly) **3-10-12** PMcLoughlin (bit bkwd: bhd tl r.o fr 2 out: n.d)	21	4	50/1	33	—
	Indian Wolf (BJLlewellyn) **3-10-12** ILawrence (prom: mstke 4th: wknd appr 3 out)	25	5	33/1	8	—
589[10]	**Copper Diamond** (DBurchell) **3-10-0b**(7) JPrior (sn prom: wknd 5th)	3½	6	50/1	—	—
753[P]	**Song For Jess (IRE)** (FJordan) **3-10-7** SWynne (a bhd)	7	7	12/1	—	—
654[F]	**Verulam (IRE)** (JRJenkins) **3-11-5** GBradley (hld up mid div: eased whn btn 3 out)	6	8	5/1[3]	—	—
807[4]	**Water Music Melody** (TRGreathead) **3-10-7** GaryLyons (stdd s: a bhd: t.o)	dist	9	50/1	—	—
	Royal Then (FR) (JNeville) **3-10-12** DBridgwater (bkwd: prom: led appr 5th tl appr 3 out: 4th & wkng whn fell 2 out)		F	100/30[2]	—	—
294[P]	**Our Adventure** (MPMuggeridge) **3-10-7** SCurran (bit bkwd: w ldr: led 3rd tl appr 5th: wknd qckly: t.o whn p.u bef 3 out)		P	50/1	—	—
	Desert Scout (KMcAuliffe) **3-10-12** WMarston (dropped rr 4th: t.o whn p.u bef 5th)		P	25/1	—	—
				(SP 123.2%)	**12 Rn**	

3m 50.3 (10.30) CSF £44.11 TOTE £1.90: £1.10 £4.30 £2.80 (£23.40) Trio £87.80; £86.59 to 14/10/96 OWNER Whitting Commodities Ltd (NEWMARKET) BRED Whitting Commodities Ltd
Agdistis, twice a runner-up in ten-furlong maidens, was a rare runner over timber for her stable these days. Eventually settling down after being too keen early on, she looks the type to run up a sequence. (5/4: 4/5-11/8)
Flood's Fancy stepped up considerably on his debut, but had no chance with the winner. (40/1)
654 Amber Ring could not go with the easy winner in the home straight. (6/1)
589 Song For Jess (IRE) (12/1: 8/1-14/1)
402* Verulam (IRE) (5/1: 7/2-11/2)

882 DOMESTIC APPLIANCES DISTRIBUTORS' H'CAP CHASE (0-140) (5-Y.O+) (Class B)

3-55 (3-55) **2m 4f 110y (15 fncs)** £4,922.50 (£1,480.00: £715.00: £332.50) GOING minus 0.04 sec per fur (G)

Form	Horse	Dist	Pos	SP	RR	SF
	Philip's Woody (115) (NJHenderson) **8-10-10** JRKavanagh (hld up & plld hrd: hdwy appr 7th: hrd rdn appr 2 out: led flat: all out)	—	1	2/1[2]	119	37
864*	**Wise Approach (135)** (KCBailey) **9-11-9**(7) 6x MrRWakley (led: hit 7th: rdn & hdd flat)	1¼	2	9/4[3]	138	56
740[2]	**Rex to the Rescue (IRE) (105)** (RHAlner) **8-9-9**(5) PHenley (chsd ldr: ev ch appr 4 out: sn rdn & wknd: no ch whn blnd last)	dist	3	7/4[1]	—	—
342[4]	**Channel Pastime (106)** (DBurchell) **12-10-1**ow1 DJBurchell (t.o fr 6th)	11	4	9/1	—	—
				(SP 110.5%)	**4 Rn**	

5m 6.2 (5.20) CSF £6.44 TOTE £2.50 (£2.40) OWNER Mr K. G. Knox (LAMBOURN) BRED Conkwell Grange Stud Ltd
LONG HANDICAP Rex to the Rescue (IRE) 9-9 Channel Pastime 9-2
Philip's Woody found strength from the saddle tipping the scales in his favour in the closing stages. (2/1)
864* Wise Approach found the combination of a penalty for his exertions yesterday and the fact his rider was up against a professional telling towards the finish. (9/4: 6/4-5/2)
740 Rex to the Rescue (IRE) is probably more effective over two miles. (7/4)

883 APOLLO 2000 H'CAP CHASE (0-100) (5-Y.O+) (Class F)

4-30 (4-33) **2m (12 fncs)** £2,805.00 (£780.00: £375.00) GOING minus 0.04 sec per fur (G)

Form	Horse	Dist	Pos	SP	RR	SF
728[3]	**Northern Optimist (82)** (BJLlewellyn) **8-11-4** APMcCoy (wnt 2nd 4th: led appr 2 out: r.o wl)	—	1	5/2[2]	99	31
742[2]	**The Yokel (72)** (BPJBaugh) **10-10-3**(5) PHenley (chsd ldr to 4th: rdn appr 4 out: rallied appr last: no imp)	7	2	7/4[1]	82	14
676[2]	**Super Sharp (NZ) (88)** (HOliver) **8-11-10** JacquiOliver (led: pckd 7th: rdn 4 out: hdd appr 2 out: wknd last)	11	3	11/2	87	19
740[F]	**Dawn Chance (79)** (RJHodges) **10-10-12**(3) TDascombe (bhd fr 8th: poor 4th whn mstke 3 out: b.b.v)	dist	4	10/1	—	—
	Lodestone Lad (IRE) (85) (RDickin) **6-11-7** DerekByrne (bkwd: t.o 4th: p.u & dismntd bef 7th)		P	9/2[3]	—	—

Red Match (68) (RJHodges) 11-10-4 NMann (bkwd: t.o 4th: p.u bef 2 out) P 16/1 — —
(SP 113.5%) 6 Rn

3m 57.9 (6.90) CSF £7.18 TOTE £3.20: £1.90 £1.10 (£4.80) OWNER Mackworth Snooker Club PT (BARGOED) BRED A. D. Bottomley
Northern Optimist seemed better suited to this shorter trip. (5/2)
742 The Yokel does appear to get tapped for toe at the minimum trip. (7/4)
676 Super Sharp (NZ) has gone up 9lb for his two victories this season. (11/2: op 5/2)
Dawn Chance (10/1: 7/1-11/1)

884 ASKO APPLIANCES H'CAP HURDLE (0-130) (4-Y.O+) (Class C)
5-00 (5-00) **2m 4f (10 hdls)** £3,673.00 (£1,099.00: £527.00: £241.00) GOING minus 0.04 sec per fur (G)

	Horse	Dist	Pos	SP	RR	SF
721[5]	**Wottashambles (108)** (LMontagueHall) **5-11-5** DMorris (mde all: clr 2 out: easily)	—	1	3/1[2]	92+	26
741[3]	**Fleur de Tal (100)** (WGMTurner) **5-10-4**(7) JPower (chsd wnr fr 3rd: rdn appr 2 out: btn whn hit last)	5	2	3/1[2]	80	14
459[2]	**La Menorquina (USA) (100)** (DMarks) **6-10-11** JAMcCarthy (chsd wnr to 3rd: rdn 3 out: one pce)	1½	3	5/2[1]	79	13
605*	**Acrow Line (117)** (DBurchell) **11-12-0** DJBurchell (hld up: reminders appr 6th: sn bhd)	13	4	10/1[3]	85	19
	Tim (IRE) (111) (JRJenkins) **6-11-8** GBradley (hld up: rdn appr 7th: sn bhd: t.o)	17	5	3/1[2]	66	—

(SP 112.7%) 5 Rn

4m 48.1 (10.10) CSF £11.64 TOTE £3.70: £3.20 £1.60 (£10.90) OWNER Dream On Racing Partnership (EPSOM) BRED Arthur Sims
721 Wottashambles only arrived just before the race, having been stuck in a hold up on the M40 when disappointing here last time. (3/1)
741 Fleur de Tal seemed to be travelling strongly until finding disappointingly little when put to the test. (3/1)
459 La Menorquina (USA), down 2lb, lacked the required turn of foot. (5/2)
605* Acrow Line (10/1: op 6/1)

T/Plpt: £134.60 (53.61 Tckts). T/Qdpt: £23.40 (11.01 Tckts). KH

0724-NEWTON ABBOT (L-H) (Good, Good to soft patches becoming Good to soft)
Monday October 14th
WEATHER: rain

885 SIMPKINS EDWARDS ACCOUNTANTS MAIDEN HURDLE (I) (4-Y.O+) (Class E)
2-15 (2-17) **2m 1f (8 hdls)** £1,955.50 (£548.00: £266.50) GOING: 0.42 sec per fur (GS)

	Horse	Dist	Pos	SP	RR	SF
306*	**Kailash (USA)** (MCPipe) **5-11-5** APMcCoy (lw: a in tch: stdy hdwy to ld after 6th: sn clr: easily)	—	1	2/5[1]	77++	2
	Blaze of Oak (USA) (96) (JMBradley) **5-11-5** BFenton (bit bkwd: hdwy to ld 5th: hdd next: outpcd appr 2 out)	7	2	5/1[2]	70	—
	Quaker Waltz (JCTuck) **6-11-0** RBellamy (bit bkwd: a.p: led 6th: sn hdd: rdn & outpcd appr 2 out)	1½	3	50/1	64	—
	Southsea Scandals (IRE) (KBishop) **5-11-5** MAFitzgerald (bit bkwd: mid div: rdn & r.o fr 6th: nt rch ldrs)	5	4	11/1	64	—
	Smart In Velvet (PRHedger) **6-11-0** ILawrence (in tch tl wknd after 6th)	3½	5	40/1	56	—
649[P]	**Padditate (IRE)** (RJHodges) **7-11-2**(3) TDascombe (bit bkwd: chsng ldr whn mstke 1st: t.o whn fell 6th)		F	100/1	—	—
	Polo Kit (IRE) (RJO'Sullivan) **5-11-5** PHolley (bkwd: in tch: led briefly appr 5th: 2nd whn blnd next: sn wknd: p.u bef 2 out)		P	7/1[3]	—	—
	Parade Racer (PGMurphy) **5-11-5** WMcFarland (bkwd: a bhd: lost tch after 4th: t.o whn p.u bef 2 out)		P	14/1	—	—
	Baxworthy Lord (CLPopham) **5-11-5** JOsborne (lw: chsd ldrs tl lft in ld 4th: hdd appr next: sn wknd: t.o whn p.u bef 2 out)		P	50/1	—	—
	Decor (IRE) (RGFrost) **6-11-5** JFrost (bit bkwd: mid div tl wknd fr 5th: t.o whn p.u bef 2 out)		P	16/1	—	—
	Dante's Rubicon (IRE) (60) (NGAyliffe) **5-11-5** CMaude (bit bkwd: nvr trbld ldrs: t.o whn p.u bef 2 out)		P	66/1	—	—
	Minneola (ABarrow) **4-10-6**(7) MrRThornton (bit bkwd: a bhd: t.o whn p.u bef 6th)		P	100/1	—	—
737[R]	**Lucky Mo** (BRMillman) **6-10-9**(5) DSalter (led & wl clr tl rn out 4th)		R	66/1	—	—

(SP 132.8%) 13 Rn

4m 14.8 (21.80) CSF £4.02 TOTE £1.60: £1.40 £1.20 £5.90 (£2.90) Trio £55.70 OWNER Mr Mick Fletcher (WELLINGTON) BRED William C. Miller
WEIGHT FOR AGE 4yo-1lb
306* Kailash (USA) made an impressive start to his hurdling career with a convincing win, and landed the first leg of a treble for his pilot. (2/5)
Blaze of Oak (USA), a consistent type who should pick up a similar event this winter, raced up with the winner until unable to match that rival for toe from the home turn. (5/1)
Quaker Waltz showed her first glimpse of form and put up a good effort after an absence of well over two years. (50/1)
Polo Kit (IRE) (7/1: op 4/1)
Parade Racer (14/1: 8/1-16/1)
Lucky Mo, a temperamental sort, was bowling along in front when he suddenly crashed through the outside wing of the fourth. He would be worth following if he ever starts to co-operate. (66/1)

886 BOWRING MARSH AND MCLENNAN LTD H'CAP CHASE (0-125) (5-Y.O+) (Class D)
2-45 (2-46) **2m 110y (13 fncs)** £3,508.70 (£1,061.60: £517.80: £245.90) GOING: 0.22 sec per fur (G)

	Horse	Dist	Pos	SP	RR	SF
	Merry Panto (IRE) (92) (CPEBrooks) **7-10-3** JOsborne (hld up mid div: stdy hdwy 10th: led appr last: rdn out)	—	1	5/1[3]	99	31
676[U]	**Stately Home (IRE) (118)** (PBowen) **5-12-0** AMaguire (led to 8th: led 11th tl appr last: one pce)	1¾	2	4/1[2]	123	54
789[P]	**Good for a Laugh (110)** (GAHam) **12-11-7** SBurrough (bit bkwd: chsd ldrs tl wknd 10th)	13	3	33/1	103	35
728[4]	**Fenwick (90)** (RJHodges) **9-9-12b**(1)(3)ow1 TDascombe (chsd ldr to 5th: in tch tl mstke 10th: sn wknd)	1½	4	7/1	81	12
	James the First (115) (PFNicholls) **8-11-12** APMcCoy (bit bkwd: j.slowly 1st & 2nd: chsd ldr 5th: led 8th to 11th: rdn & wknd appr last)	3	5	6/5[1]	103	35
547[2]	**Duke of Dreams (89)** (RJBaker) **6-10-0** BPowell (a bhd: sn lost tch: t.o 8th: p.u bef 10th)		P	5/1[3]	—	—

(SP 114.2%) 6 Rn

4m 8.2 (8.20) CSF £23.40 TOTE £4.70: £2.00 £2.50 (£13.10) OWNER Uplands Bloodstock (LAMBOURN) BRED Michael Fleming
LONG HANDICAP Fenwick 9-10 Duke of Dreams 9-7
WEIGHT FOR AGE 5yo-1lb

Merry Panto (IRE), produced fit and well after a break of almost a year and a half, made a successful return to chasing. Travelling strongly and jumping boldly throughout, he made steady progress to wear down the tiring leaders over the final two obstacles. (5/1)
676 Stately Home (IRE) put up a good effort under topweight and was only outbattled on the run-in. (4/1)
601 Fenwick (7/1: op 9/2)
James the First, back on his favourite track after a break, was disappointing. (6/5)

887 SPA-TRANS LTD NOVICES' CHASE (5-Y.O+) (Class E)

3-15 (3-16) **2m 5f 110y (16 fncs)** £2,995.65 (£907.20: £443.10: £211.05) GOING: 0.22 sec per fur (G)

				SP	RR	SF
	Strong Tarquin (IRE) (PFNicholls) **6-10-12** APMcCoy (a.p: disp ld 14th: led appr last: lft clr last)	—	1	5/1[3]	107	39
	Keep it Zipped (IRE) (OSherwood) **6-10-12** JOsborne (bit bkwd: mid div: hdwy 10th: styd on fr 2 out: no imp)	29	2	5/4[1]	85	17
	Wilkins (RJO'Sullivan) **7-10-12** PHolley (chsd ldr tl led 4th: hdd whn mstke 14th: sn wknd)	1¼	3	20/1	85	17
547[4]	**Stormy Sunset** (WWDennis) **9-10-3**(7)ow3 MrTDennis (bhd: styd on fr 13th: nvr nrr)	5	4	16/1	79	8
	Duke of Aprolon (JTGifford) **9-10-12** PHide (bit bkwd: led to 4th: in tch tl wknd 13th: t.o)	6	5	12/1	76	8
	Call Me River (IRE) (64) (PRHedger) **8-10-12** ILawrence (lw: in tch to 9th: wknd 11th: t.o)	4	6	25/1	73	5
	La Mezeray (MrsJEHawkins) **8-10-7** MBosley (bit bkwd: bhd tl hdwy 10th: wknd 14th: t.o)	7	7	50/1	63	—
	Swing Quartet (IRE) (NATwiston-Davies) **6-10-7** CLlewellyn (lw: a.p: chsd ldr 12th: led 14th: hdd & ev ch whn fell last)		F	3/1[2]	—	—
	Vareck II (FR) (MCPipe) **9-10-12** CMaude (bit bkwd: a bhd: wknd 10th: t.o whn p.u bef 13th)		P	20/1	—	—
472[2]	**Call Me Albi (IRE) (83)** (MrsLRichards) **5-10-10v** MRichards (mid div tl wknd 10th: t.o whn p.u bef 13th)		P	20/1	—	—
	Kindly Lady (MrsSDWilliams) **8-10-7** MAFitzgerald (bkwd: a bhd: wkng whn mstke 10th: t.o whn p.u bef 2 out)		P	12/1	—	—
				(SP 127.5%)	**11 Rn**	

5m 28.1 (11.10) CSF £12.14 TOTE £7.20: £1.10 £1.50 £4.50 (£8.40) Trio £66.30 OWNER Mr Paul K Barber and Mr J A Keighley (SHEPTON MALLET) BRED Maurice Fenton
WEIGHT FOR AGE 5yo-2lb
Strong Tarquin (IRE) stepped up on his successful point-to-point form and scored on this chasing bow. His jumping has been a little sketchy in the past, but he showed conviction here going into his fences. Both the experience and the outing should bring him on. (5/1: op 3/1)
Keep it Zipped (IRE) did not show the same flair he displayed over hurdles on this chase debut, and his attitude could be a bit questionable. (5/4)
Wilkins would have finished closer but for hitting four from home. (20/1)
Duke of Aprolon (12/1: 7/1-14/1)
Swing Quartet (IRE) was booked for the runner-up spot when departing at the last. (3/1)

888 CO-OPERATIVE BANK PLC CONDITIONAL H'CAP HURDLE (0-100) (4-Y.O+ F & M) (Class F)

3-45 (3-45) **2m 1f (8 hdls)** £1,919.40 (£538.40: £262.20) GOING: 0.42 sec per fur (GS)

				SP	RR	SF
	Hullo Mary Doll (73) (AJChamberlain) **7-10-12** ChrisWebb (chsd ldr 3rd: led 5th: clr appr 2 out: unchal)	—	1	8/1	66	—
407[2]	**Nordic Crown (IRE) (75)** (MCPipe) **5-10-11b**(3) BMoore (lw: led to 5th: outpcd fr next)	14	2	4/1[3]	55	—
641[7]	**Severn Gale (85)** (PFNicholls) **6-11-10** OBurrows (bhd: hdwy & mstke 5th: hit next: wknd appr 2 out)	2½	3	5/2[2]	63	—
793[8]	**Minster's Madam (84)** (JNeville) **5-11-9v** DWalsh (chsd ldr: led briefly appr 3rd: in tch appr 6th: sn wknd: t.o)	dist	4	2/1[1]	—	—
	Fame And Fantasy (IRE) (84) (NoelChance) **5-11-9** PHenley (bkwd: lost tch & rdn 4th: t.o whn p.u after 6th)		P	9/2	—	—
	Safe Secret (67) (RBrotherton) **5-10-6** TDascombe (bkwd: bhd 4th: rdn & lost tch next: p.u bef 2 out)		P	16/1	—	—
				(SP 117.1%)	**6 Rn**	

4m 18.8 (25.80) CSF £37.44 TOTE £6.30: £2.80 £2.10 (£5.30) OWNER Plough Twenty (Ashto Keynes) (SWINDON) BRED A. B. Barraclough
Hullo Mary Doll, on this first run for her new stable, appears to have got the hang of this game and, drawing clear after three from home, won as she pleased. (8/1: 6/1-9/1)
407 Nordic Crown (IRE) seems in the Handicapper's grip. (4/1)
641 Severn Gale should have found this relatively easy, but hardly got into it. (5/2)

889 BEVAN ASHFORD SOLICITORS NOVICES' CHASE (5-Y.O+) (Class E)

4-15 (4-16) **2m 110y (13 fncs)** £2,859.15 (£865.20: £422.10: £200.55) GOING: 0.22 sec per fur (G)

				SP	RR	SF
	Ambassador Royale (IRE) (MissAEBroyd) **8-10-12** MAFitzgerald (a.p: chsd ldr 8th: led appr 2 out: sn clr: easily)	—	1	14/1	85+	5
	The Lancer (IRE) (77) (DRGandolfo) **7-10-9**(3) DFortt (bit bkwd: mid div: outpcd 10th: styd on strly fr 2 out)	2½	2	12/1	83	3
	Lord Nitrogen (USA) (85) (BJLlewellyn) **6-10-12** BPowell (bit bkwd: led 3rd tl appr 2 out: sn outpcd)	1¼	3	20/1	81	1
	Mr Playfull (86) (RGFrost) **6-10-12** JFrost (bit bkwd: mid div: lost pl 10th: styd on appr 2 out)	½	4	2/1[1]	81	1
160[4]	**Legal Artist (IRE) (82)** (MissCJohnsey) **6-10-12** LHarvey (chsd ldrs tl wknd 10th)	2½	5	12/1	79	—
	King's Gold (MrsLRichards) **6-10-12** MRichards (bit bkwd: a bhd: lost tch 10th: t.o whn p.u bef 2 out)		P	10/1	—	—
731[7]	**Heresthedeal (IRE) (97)** (GMMcCourt) **7-10-12v** BClifford (led: j.slowly 2nd: hdd next: ev ch whn mstke 7th: p.u after 8th: broke leg: dead)		P	3/1[2]	—	—
724[3]	**He's a King (USA)** (CLPopham) **6-10-9**(3) TDascombe (lw: chsd ldrs tl wknd 7th: t.o whn p.u bef 2 out: lame)		P	7/2[3]	—	—
791[P]	**Priory Rose** (GAHam) **9-10-7** SBurrough (bkwd: a bhd: t.o 8th: p.u bef 2 out)		P	33/1	—	—
				(SP 119.4%)	**9 Rn**	

4m 16.5 (16.50) CSF £148.21 TOTE £17.20: £2.20 £3.40 £4.90 (£80.50) Trio £243.20; £58.25 to Leicester 15/10/96 OWNER Miss Alison Broyd (CRICKHOWELL) BRED S. Stanhope and Sheikh M. Alamuddin
Ambassador Royale (IRE) opened his account on this rain-softened ground. (14/1)
The Lancer (IRE), after six months off, stayed on well in the closing stages, and will improve further for the outing and the experience. (12/1)
Lord Nitrogen (USA) has shown very moderate form to date, but gave connections more hope here. (20/1)
72 Legal Artist (IRE) (12/1: op 6/1)

890 SIMPKINS EDWARDS ACCOUNTANTS MAIDEN HURDLE (4-Y.O+) (Class E)

4-45 (4-45) **2m 1f (8 hdls)** £1,945.00 (£545.00: £265.00) GOING: 0.42 sec per fur (GS)

				SP	RR	SF
739[3]	**Ritto** (JNeville) **6-11-5** APMcCoy (a.p: led & hung sltly lft 2 out: hld on u.p flat)	—	1	100/30[2]	78	26

	Horse	Dist	Pos	SP	RR	SF
	Devon Peasant (LGCottrell) **4-10-13** MrLJefford (lw: hld up mid div: rdn & gd hdwy appr 2 out: sltly hmpd & ev ch last: no ex flat)	½	**2**	14/1	73	20
	Shift Again (IRE) (OSherwood) **4-10-13** JOsborne (lw: chsng ldrs: lft 2nd 3rd: led next to 2 out: wknd appr last)	3	**3**	5/1	70	17
	Lord Rooble (IRE) (JTGifford) **5-11-5** PHide (bit bkwd: hdwy to chse ldr 4th: ev ch tl wknd appr 2 out)	28	**4**	9/2[3]	48	—
	The Proms (IRE) (NATwiston-Davies) **5-11-5** CLlewellyn (chsng ldr whn lft in ld 3rd: hdd next: wknd fr 5th)	20	**5**	5/2[1]	30	—
	Arthur's Special (MCPipe) **6-10-7**(7) GSupple (bit bkwd: a bhd: t.o 5th)	12	**6**	40/1	13	—
737[7]	**Seven Brooks (74)** (JCFox) **6-11-5** SFox (bit bkwd: mid div tl wknd fr 6th: t.o)	nk	**7**	50/1	18	—
	The Cheese Baron (SMellor) **5-11-0**(5) ChrisWebb (bit bkwd: bhd: hdwy 5th: lost tch next: t.o)	dist	**8**	50/1	—	—
	George Bull (MajorWRHern) **4-11-4** RFarrant (led 1st: sn clr: fell 3rd)		**F**	11/2	—	—
	War Requiem (IRE) (RJO'Sullivan) **6-11-5** PHolley (bit bkwd: prom whn sltly hmpd 3rd: rdn & wknd 5th: t.o whn p.u bef 2 out)		**P**	10/1	—	—
	Topanga (90) (JABennett) **4-11-4** LHarvey (bit bkwd: led to 1st: bhd & rdn 4th: t.o whn p.u bef 2 out)		**P**	20/1	—	—
718[8]	**Ladymalord** (JRBosley) **4-10-13** MBosley (a bhd: t.o 5th: p.u bef 2 out)		**P**	100/1	—	—

(SP 129.8%) **12 Rn**

4m 9.3 (16.30) CSF £49.06 TOTE £7.00: £2.20 £2.20 £2.40 (£84.20) Trio £111.10 OWNER Park Industrial Supplies (Wales) Ltd (NEWPORT, GWENT) BRED Highclere Stud Ltd
WEIGHT FOR AGE 4yo-1lb

739 Ritto, after a successful campaign on the Flat for Barry Hills, a useful handicapper on the Flat for Barry Hills, outstayed these. Stamina is his forte and he should have a bright future ahead of him at this game. (100/30)
Devon Peasant, after an absence of over four months, made a very encouraging comeback. She looks one to keep an eye on. (14/1: op 8/1)
Shift Again (IRE) looked to hold all the aces when taking it up at the fourth but, once headed, her interest seemed to wain and she faded. She might have more ability than she cares to show. (5/1: 5/2-11/2)
George Bull, a rare runner here for the Hern stable, was making his hurdling debut. He departed very early here, but should still be watched. (11/2: 4/1-6/1)

891 TRU-MARK FINANCIAL SERVICES LTD. NOVICES' H'CAP HURDLE (0-100) (4-Y.O+) (Class E)
5-15 (5-16) **2m 6f (10 hdls)** £2,242.50 (£630.00: £307.50) GOING: 0.42 sec per fur (GS)

	Horse	Dist	Pos	SP	RR	SF
	Rosie-B (71) (NMBabbage) **6-9-7**(7) MrRThornton (chsd ldrs: wnt 2nd 7th: led 2 out: clr appr last: easily)	—	**1**	11/2	61	22
	Luke Warm (71) (DRGandolfo) **6-10-0** AMaguire (hdwy appr 5th: chsd ldr next: led 8th tl rdn & hdd 2 out: wknd appr last)	10	**2**	9/2[2]	54	15
649[P]	**Tipping Along (IRE) (79)** (DRGandolfo) **7-10-3**(5) SophieMitchell (bhd: styd on fr 8th: nvr nrr)	21	**3**	16/1	47	8
	Mu-Tadil (72) (RJBaker) **4-10-0** BPowell (prom early: lost pl 5th: styd on appr 2 out: nvr nrr)	3½	**4**	16/1	37	—
488*	**Always Greener (IRE) (82)** (JWMullins) **5-10-6**(5) MichaelBrennan (hdwy appr 7th: wknd fr next: t.o)	25	**5**	8/1	29	—
737*	**Million Dancer (96)** (MCPipe) **4-11-10b** CMaude (led & wl clr tl hdd 8th: sn wknd: p.u bef last)		**P**	5/1[3]	—	—
824*	**Hylters Chance (IRE) (76)** (PJHobbs) **5-10-5** 7x APMcCoy (chsd ldr tl after 6th: rdn & wknd next: t.o whn p.u bef 2 out)		**P**	4/5[1]	—	—
737[5]	**What's the Joke (74)** (VGGreenway) **7-10-3**ow3 JRailton (chsd ldrs early: bhd 5th: t.o whn p.u bef 2 out)		**P**	33/1	—	—

(SP 131.6%) **8 Rn**

5m 29.1 (17.10) CSF £32.52 CT £363.16 TOTE £6.20: £2.00 £1.50 £3.10 (£10.80) OWNER Internet Racing (CHELTENHAM) BRED J. A. D. Engineering Ltd
LONG HANDICAP Mu-Tadil 9-12 Rosie-B 9-8 Luke Warm 9-11 What's the Joke 8-11
WEIGHT FOR AGE 4yo-1lb
OFFICIAL EXPLANATION **Hylters Chance (IRE): did not act on the soft ground.**

Rosie-B made a successful comeback for her new in-form stable. She should be followed. (11/2: 3/1-6/1)
Luke Warm ran a sound race, but was no match for the easy winner. He may benefit from a bit further again. (9/2)
488* Always Greener (IRE) (8/1: op 5/1)
737* Million Dancer found topweight in this, his first handicap, anchoring him down. (5/1: op 11/4)

T/Plpt: £910.30 (16.27 Tckts). T/Qdpt: £154.80 (6.01 Tckts). T

0730-SEDGEFIELD (L-H) (Good to firm)
Tuesday October 15th

Race 6: One fence omitted
WEATHER: cloudy

892 JOHN WADE HAULAGE CONDITIONAL (S) H'CAP HURDLE (0-95) (4-Y.O+) (Class G)
2-15 (2-15) **2m 5f 110y (10 hdls)** £1,835.00 (£510.00: £245.00) GOING minus 0.27 sec per fur (GF)

	Horse	Dist	Pos	SP	RR	SF
805[U]	**Red Jam Jar (92)** (SBBell) **11-12-0** GCahill (mde all: styd on wl fr 3 out)	—	**1**	7/2[2]	72	26
693[P]	**Classic Crest (IRE) (75)** (GMMoore) **5-10-11v** MichaelBrennan (hld up: hdwy 4 out: hrd rdn & ev ch appr 2 out: kpt on one pce)	2	**2**	10/1	54	8
878*	**Shelton Abbey (70)** (JWade) **10-10-6b** 7x GHogan (hld up: effrt appr 4 out: hdwy 3 out: rdn & nt r.o fr 2 out)	5	**3**	9/2[3]	45	—
684[3]	**Souson (IRE) (86)** (JWade) **8-11-1b**(7) MarkBrown (chsd ldrs tl outpcd 4 out: rdn & no imp after)	3½	**4**	11/4[1]	58	12
183[5]	**High Flown (USA) (76)** (RonaldThompson) **4-10-11** GLee (a.p: chal 3 out: rdn & btn appr next)	7	**5**	14/1	43	—
734[5]	**Flintlock (IRE) (77)** (HAlexander) **6-10-13** RMcGrath (hld up: hdwy & prom 4 out: wknd fr next)	19	**6**	6/1	30	—
730[U]	**Papa's Boy (IRE) (85)** (HowardJohnson) **5-11-7** STaylor (in tch tl fell 5th)		**F**	12/1	—	—
	Heavens Above (68) (MrsJBrown) **4-10-3**ow3 ECallaghan (bit bkwd: hld up: effrt ½-wy: outpcd 6th: t.o whn p.u after 3 out)		**P**	33/1	—	—
675[12]	**Chadleigh Walk (IRE) (65)** (SWCampion) **4-10-0** OBurrows (outpcd & bhd whn bdly hmpd 5th: t.o tl p.u after 3 out)		**P**	50/1	—	—

(SP 109.7%) **9 Rn**

5m 8.5 (8.50) CSF £32.41 CT £132.63 TOTE £3.90: £1.70 £2.10 £1.50 (£27.90) Trio £25.10 OWNER Mr C. H. P. Bell (DRIFFIELD) BRED Majors Racing International Ltd
LONG HANDICAP Heavens Above 9-9 Chadleigh Walk (IRE) 9-7
WEIGHT FOR AGE 4yo-1lb
No bid

690 Red Jam Jar seems at his best when giving weight in this type of company and he was always too tough for this lot. (7/2: op 9/4)
642 Classic Crest (IRE) looked well and has obviously got his confidence back but he needed some strong driving to challenge approaching two out and then found the winner too determined. (10/1)
878* Shelton Abbey seems to have taken on a new lease of life this season but he decided he had had enough here two from home. (9/2: 11/4-5/1)
684 Souson (IRE) failed to impress on looks and, struggling four out, then failed to offer a threat. (11/4)
High Flown (USA), who has not been out for over two months, had his chances until stopping going to the penultimate flight. (14/1)
695 Flintlock (IRE) has not fired as yet this season. (6/1)

893 SIX & OUT H'CAP HURDLE (0-95) (4-Y.O+) (Class F)

2-45 (2-45) **2m 1f (8 hdls)** £2,101.00 (£586.00: £283.00) GOING minus 0.27 sec per fur (GF)

				SP	RR	SF
731^{4}	**Clover Girl (70)** (BEllison) **5-10-6v**(3) GCahill (hld up: hdwy 5th: led 2 out: styd on u.p)	—	**1**	5/1^{3}	50	1
	Fen Terrier (90) (FPMurtagh) **4-12-0** ADobbin (chsd ldrs tl outpcd appr 2 out: styd on wl towards fin)	1½	**2**	11/2	69	19
	Marsden Rock (85) (NBMason) **9-11-3**(7) SHaworth (trckd ldrs: led 3 out to 2 out: no ex flat)	nk	**3**	7/2^{2}	63	14
697^{2}	**Simand (78)** (GMMoore) **4-11-2** JCallaghan (lw: hld up: hdwy 5th: sn chsng ldrs: one pce fr 2 out)	3	**4**	5/2^{1}	54	4
647^{9}	**Fly to the End (USA) (73)** (JJQuinn) **6-10-12v** DerekByrne (led to 3 out: wknd next)	1¾	**5**	16/1	47	—
697^{8}	**Marco Magnifico (USA) (74)** (MissLucindaRussell) **6-10-13v**^{1} AThornton (t: bhd: lost tch 5th: n.d after)	11	**6**	9/1	38	—
784^{6}	**Dark Midnight (IRE) (63)** (DALamb) **7-9-13**(3)ow2 DWalsh (in tch tl wknd appr 3 out)	25	**7**	20/1	3	—
735^{6}	**Salkeld King (IRE) (75)** (MABarnes) **4-10-13** PWaggott (bhd: hmpd bnd after 3rd: hdwy 5th: sn rdn & btn)	8	**8**	25/1	7	—
805^{6}	**Another Nick (70)** (JSHubbuck) **10-10-9** BStorey (chsd ldrs to 4th: sn rdn & wknd: p.u bef last)		**P**	50/1	—	—
697^{5}	**Aide Memoire (IRE) (77)** (MrsBKBroad) **7-11-2** KJohnson (chsd ldrs: outpcd whn n.m.r & s.u after 3 out)		**S**	11/1	—	—
				(SP 117.6%)	**10 Rn**	

4m 3.3 (8.30) CSF £30.70 CT £99.69 TOTE £5.10: £1.40 £3.00 £2.00 (£22.00) Trio £46.50 OWNER Mr Kevin Brown (LANCHESTER) BRED Mrs Kathrine Rea
LONG HANDICAP Dark Midnight (IRE) 9-9
WEIGHT FOR AGE 4yo-1lb
731 Clover Girl, given a good ride, was produced two out and always had the edge from then on. (5/1)
Fen Terrier has changed stables and showed a good attitude this time. Judging by the way she finished, she should be all the better for this. (11/2: 3/1-6/1)
Marsden Rock travelled well, looking the winner for much of the trip, but failed to see it out. She is not one who finds a lot off the bridle but is likely to be all the better for this. (7/2)
697 Simand had his chances but the effort required was always beyond him from the second last. (5/2)
Fly to the End (USA), tried in a visor here, attempted to gallop his rivals into the ground but was collared three out and had little more to give. (16/1)
Marco Magnifico (USA) was sent out with more spare parts than a garage and they failed to have the desired effect. (9/1)
697 Aide Memoire (IRE) (11/1: 8/1-12/1)

894 RED ONION H'CAP HURDLE (0-125) (4-Y.O+) (Class D)

3-15 (3-15) **2m 5f 110y (10 hdls)** £2,745.50 (£824.00: £397.00: £183.50) GOING minus 0.27 sec per fur (GF)

				SP	RR	SF
493^{2}	**Clean Edge (USA) (102)** (JMackie) **4-10-1**(3) EHusband (lw: prom tl outpcd 4 out: hdwy to ld 2 out: r.o)	—	**1**	15/2	89	16
733*	**Notable Exception (107)** (MrsMReveley) **7-10-10** PNiven (lw: trckd ldrs: disp ld 3 out tl hdd next: hrd rdn & one pce)	9	**2**	2/1^{1}	87	15
734^{2}	**Scarba (97)** (JMJefferson) **8-9-7**(7) MNewton (lw: hld up: effrt 4 out: sn rdn: hdwy appr 2 out: sn btn)	5	**3**	5/1^{3}	74	2
	Down the Fell (118) (HowardJohnson) **7-11-7** NWilliamson (led to 3 out: sn btn)	30	**4**	8/1	72	—
	Exemplar (IRE) (100) (MrsSJSmith) **8-9-10**(7)ow3 MrPMurray (cl up & mstke 2nd: sn bhd)	28	**5**	20/1	33	—
	Urban Dancing (USA) (112) (BEllison) **7-10-12**(3) GCahill (hld up & bhd: p.u bef last)		**P**	11/1	—	—
734*	**Red Valerian (125)** (GMMoore) **5-11-9v**(5) MichaelBrennan (lw: trckd ldrs: disp ld 3 out to 2 out: broke down & p.u bef last)		**P**	5/2^{2}	—	—
				(SP 114.5%)	**7 Rn**	

5m 4.8 (4.80) CSF £22.22 TOTE £8.50: £1.70 £1.70 (£8.80) OWNER Mrs Sue Adams (CHURCH BROUGHTON) BRED Alice duPont Mills
LONG HANDICAP Exemplar (IRE) 9-8
WEIGHT FOR AGE 4yo-1lb
493 Clean Edge (USA) came back here after seven weeks off looking magnificent and appreciated this longer trip. The further they went the better he got. (15/2)
733* Notable Exception looked well handicapped on his return to hurdling but, despite trying hard, found the winner far too strong. (2/1)
734 Scarba, held up as usual, came off the bit some way out this time and, although having a slight chance approaching two out, he was never doing enough. A couple of seasons ago, he liked the ground to be at its softest. (5/1)
Down the Fell, who likes to dominate, won second time out last year and this should have put him straight. (8/1)
Exemplar (IRE) put in a very awkward jump at only the second flight and was never going thereafter. (20/1)
734* Red Valerian raced with every chance but looked beaten when breaking down badly after the second last. (5/2)

895 CHILTON CLUB H'CAP CHASE (0-115) (5-Y.O+) (Class E)

3-45 (3-45) **2m 110y (13 fncs)** £2,990.75 (£896.00: £430.50: £197.75) GOING minus 0.27 sec per fur (GF)

				SP	RR	SF
742^{3}	**Circulation (78)** (DMcCain) **10-9-13v**(3)ow2 DWalsh (led tl blnd & hdd 5th: chsd ldr: styd on to ld cl home)	—	**1**	12/1	88	—
	Thunderstruck (82) (HowardJohnson) **10-10-6** NWilliamson (cl up: led 5th: blnd bdly 8th: rdn appr last: hdd & no ex towards fin)	1½	**2**	11/2^{3}	91	—
855^{3}	**Beldine (100)** (PMonteith) **11-11-10** ADobbin (chsd clr ldrs: effrt & mstke 7th: no imp)	19	**3**	7/4^{1}	90	—
507^{3}	**Tresidder (99)** (MWEasterby) **14-11-9** RGarritty (chsd ldrs: effrt 7th: n.d)	15	**4**	100/30^{2}	75	—
783*	**Anthony Bell (90)** (TJCarr) **10-11-0** RichardGuest (chsd clr ldrs tl wknd fr 7th: p.u bef 3 out)		**P**	100/30^{2}	—	—
				(SP 105.6%)	**5 Rn**	

4m 7.3 (9.30) CSF £59.00 TOTE £12.30: £2.00 £3.60 (£17.10) OWNER Mr John Singleton (CHOLMONDELEY) BRED G. L. Barker
LONG HANDICAP Circulation 9-3
742 Circulation, 11lb out of the handicap, put up another 2lb overweight but his young rider was certainly worth it and, after surviving a bad blunder early on, he galvanised his mount into action after the last to take a very narrow gap and get up late on. (12/1)
Thunderstruck helped set a tremendous pace and did remarkably well to remain upright after a blunder and a half six from home but that obviously sapped reserves and, very tired, he was picked off near the line. (11/2)

855 Beldine refuses to have a cut at his fences at the moment and was never giving enough effort to have a chance in this. (7/4)
507 Tresidder found all this happening far too quickly and was wisely not knocked about. (100/30)
783* Anthony Bell was found out here, looking in trouble from halfway, and was finally pulled up. (100/30)

896 SCOTMAIL H'CAP CHASE (0-100) (5-Y.O+) (Class F)

4-15 (4-15) **3m 3f (13 fncs)** £2,823.50 (£848.00: £409.00: £189.50) GOING minus 0.27 sec per fur (GF)

				SP	RR	SF
683P	**Jendee (IRE) (82)** (BEllison) **8-10-7**(3) GCahill (a in tch: led 14th to last: styd on to ld cl home)	—	1	16/1	96	28
746*	**The Gallopin'major (IRE) (87)** (MrsMReveley) **6-11-1b** NSmith (trckd ldrs gng wl: led last: rdn & fnd nil flat: ct cl home)	nk	2	13/8[1]	101	33
696[4]	**Grand Scenery (IRE) (90)** (HowardJohnson) **8-11-4** NWilliamson (lw: hld up & bhd: hdwy 15th: rdn & no imp fr 3 out)	21	3	7/2[2]	91	23
785*	**Trumpet (100)** (JGMO'Shea) **7-11-9**(5) MichaelBrennan (mde most fr 3rd tl hdd 14th: cl up tl mstke & wknd 3 out)	1¼	4	6/1[3]	101	33
696*	**Forward Glen (79)** (PCheesbrough) **9-10-7b** RSupple (lw: trckd ldrs: effrt 4 out: sn rdn & btn)	6	5	6/1[3]	76	8
804[4]	**Upwell (72)** (RJohnson) **12-10-0** KJohnson (led to 3rd: cl up tl lost pl 10th: sn wl bhd)	28	6	20/1	52	—
702[5]	**Blazing Dawn (84)** (JSHubbuck) **9-10-12** BStorey (trckd ldrs: chal 13th: wknd qckly 15th: p.u bef 3 out)		P	6/1[3]	—	—
				(SP 113.8%)	**7 Rn**	

6m 50.3 (4.30) CSF £41.03 CT £106.31 TOTE £19.90: £6.10 £2.20 (£20.70) OWNER Ferrograph Ltd (LANCHESTER) BRED Miss Audrey F. Thompson
LONG HANDICAP Upwell 9-12
Jendee (IRE) has changed stables this season and, after two moderate runs, won his fourth race over this course and distance here. There was certainly no fluke about it. (16/1)
746* The Gallopin'major (IRE) looked likely to make it four in a row, but when sent on at the last, he found nothing under pressure and was worried out of it. Judging by the way he travels, he will win more races. (13/8)
696 Grand Scenery (IRE) is a funny customer who needs things to go just right, and he came off the bit too far from home on this occasion. (7/2)
785* Trumpet looked to have plenty on his plate here, and after forcing the pace, looked in trouble when a mistake three out finished his hopes. (6/1)
696* Forward Glen looked well enough but was not in a going mood this time. (6/1)

897 LBW NOVICES' CHASE (4-Y.O+) (Class E)

4-45 (4-45) **2m 5f (21 fncs)** £3,036.25 (£910.00: £437.50: £201.25) GOING minus 0.27 sec per fur (GF)

				SP	RR	SF
4P	**Le Denstan (70)** (MrsDThomson) **9-11-5** TReed (hld up & bhd: hdwy whn blnd 5 out: gd hdwy appr last: r.o wl to ld cl home)	—	1	20/1	91	21
694*	**Blue Charm (IRE) (93)** (MrsSCBradburne) **6-11-12** AMaguire (led 2nd: rdn appr last: hdd & nt qckn towards fin)	1¾	2	5/6[1]	97	27
733[2]	**Val de Rama (IRE) (93)** (DenysSmith) **7-11-12** RichardGuest (in tch: hit 5 out & outpcd: hdwy to chal last: sn btn)	8	3	7/2[2]	91	21
685[3]	**Buyers Dream (IRE) (71)** (BEllison) **6-11-2v**(3) GCahill (led to 2nd: cl up: ev ch whn blnd 2 out: nt rcvr)	1	4	8/1[3]	83	13
	Up For Ransome (IRE) (HowardJohnson) **7-11-5** NWilliamson (in tch: hdwy 10th: mstke next: sn btn)	20	5	14/1	68	—
694[4]	**Wee Wizard (IRE) (80)** (MABarnes) **7-11-5** PWaggott (nt j.w: sn drvn along: nvr trbld ldrs)	30	6	8/1[3]	45	—
733P	**Rapid Fire (IRE)** (JMJefferson) **8-11-0**(5) ECallaghan (b.d 1st)		B	14/1	—	—
	Forever Shy (IRE) (MrsKMLamb) **8-10-12**(7) MissSLamb (fell 1st)		F	50/1	—	—
802[6]	**Tony's Feelings (60)** (MissLucindaRussell) **8-11-5** AThornton (a bhd: t.o whn p.u bef 2 out)		P	33/1	—	—
	Karenastino (MrsSJSmith) **5-10-10**(7) MrPMurray (cl up tl blnd & uns rdr 8th)		U	50/1	—	—
				(SP 123.9%)	**10 Rn**	

5m 18.9 (7.90) CSF £38.09 TOTE £17.80: £4.60 £1.10 £1.90 (£28.80) Trio £19.50 OWNER Mr L. Wright (MILNATHORT) BRED S. Powell
WEIGHT FOR AGE 5yo-2lb
4 Le Denstan is a most frustrating character, and looked to have blown it when blundering five out, but he suddenly found an overdrive going to the last and swooped to conquer late on. (20/1)
694* Blue Charm (IRE), taking a strong hold, was soon in front but, just when he had seen off virtually all the opposition, the winner came out of the clouds to catch him. (5/6)
733 Val de Rama (IRE) loves this track and looked a big danger when rallying under pressure going to the last, but he was then found wanting for stamina. (7/2)
685 Buyers Dream (IRE) ran well, holding every chance, but a bad blunder two out put paid to his hopes. (8/1)
Up For Ransome (IRE), an Irish import, from a stable that is not quite firing as yet, made a mistake at the tenth, which stopped him in his tracks. (14/1: 8/1-16/1)
694 Wee Wizard (IRE) looked to be hating this and was never going or jumping at any stage. (8/1)

898 100 NOT OUT INTERMEDIATE OPEN N.H. FLAT RACE (4, 5 & 6-Y.O) (Class H)

5-15 (5-15) **2m 1f (16 fncs)** £1,259.00 (£349.00: £167.00)

				SP	RR	SF
686*	**Duraid (IRE)** (DenysSmith) **4-11-13** RichardGuest (lw: trckd ldrs: led 5f out: pushed out fnl f)	—	1	4/7[1]	—	—
	Big Perks (IRE) (RAFahey) **4-11-3** RMarley (hld up: hdwy to chal 5f out: outpcd over 2f out: kpt on wl towards fin)	2½	2	9/1	—	—
	Gazanali (IRE) (GMMoore) **5-11-4** NBentley (a chsng ldrs: rdn over 2f out: kpt on same pce)	½	3	12/1	—	—
	Mr Hatchet (IRE) (HowardJohnson) **5-10-13**(5) GFRyan (led & sn clr: hdd 5f out: sn btn)	dist	4	16/1	—	—
	Silver Minx (MrsMReveley) **4-11-3** PNiven (nvr nr to chal)	6	5	7/1[3]	—	—
	Wild Cat Bay (JNorton) **4-10-12**(5) ECallaghan (prom tl outpcd fnl 5f)	5	6	33/1	—	—
	Toshiba House (IRE) (BEllison) **5-10-10**(3) GCahill (drvn along after 4f: sn t.o)	13	7	33/1	—	—
	Air Bridge (RMWhitaker) **4-11-3** NWilliamson (lost tch fr ½-wy: t.o)	1¼	8	10/1	—	—
705[4]	**Water Font (IRE)** (JJO'Neill) **4-11-3** ARoche (lw: in tch 5f out: 4th & btn whn p.u wl over 1f out)		P	5/1[2]	—	—
				(SP 131.4%)	**9 Rn**	

3m 56.9 CSF £8.33 TOTE £1.60: £1.00 £3.80 £3.70 (£19.30) Trio £10.20 OWNER Mr A. Suddes (BISHOP AUCKLAND) BRED Hussein Hurami
WEIGHT FOR AGE 4yo-1lb
686* Duraid (IRE) certainly travels well and won nicely again, under a double penalty. (4/7)
Big Perks (IRE) is a massive individual who should improve as he strengthens. (9/1: 4/1-10/1)

Gazanali (IRE) ran a decent race and kept plugging away, but was short of a real turn of speed to do anything serious about it. (12/1: op 6/1)
Mr Hatchet (IRE), a lean sort, went bolting out in front and needs to settle to do better. (16/1)
Silver Minx (7/1: 5/1-8/1)

T/Plpt: £142.00 (109.37 Tckts). T/Qdpt: £24.10 (50.5 Tckts). AA

0736-EXETER (R-H) (Good to firm)
Wednesday October 16th
WEATHER: sunny & showers

899 DEAN & DYBALL CONDITIONAL (S) H'CAP HURDLE (0-90) (4-Y.O+) (Class G)
2-10 (2-11) **2m 3f (9 hdls)** £1,829.00 (£514.00: £251.00) GOING minus 0.21 sec per fur (G)

				SP	RR	SF
737^{2}	**Cashflow Crisis (IRE) (76)** (JWMullins) **4-10-10**(3) SRyan (lw: hld up: hdwy 4th: chsd ldr 6th: led after next: sn clr: eased flat)	—	**1**	11/4 1	63+	23
	Fawley Flyer (74) (WGMTurner) **7-10-7**(5) JPower (bit bkwd: a.p: wnt 2nd appr 2 out: str run flat: nt rch wnr)	¾	**2**	10/1	60	21
879^{8}	**Catwalker (IRE) (62)** (HJMWebb) **5-10-0b** SophieMitchell (hdwy 6th: r.o appr 2 out: nvr nrr)	16	**3**	9/1	35	—
869^{3}	**Auvillar (USA) (70)** (JParfitt) **8-10-8v** MichaelBrennan (chsd ldr tl led appr 6th: hdd appr 2 out: rdn & sn wknd)	10	**4**	10/1	35	—
594^{3}	**Mario's Dream (IRE) (65)** (MrsJGRetter) **8-10-3** GHogan (swvd s & bhd: wl bhd 4th: r.o: nvr nrr)	25	**5**	12/1	8	—
741^{P}	**Buglet (90)** (MCPipe) **6-12-0v1** DWalsh (led tl appr 6th: rdn & wknd qckly: t.o)	7	**6**	15/2 3	28	—
66^{15}	**Celcius (71)** (MCPipe) **12-10-4**(5) GSupple (chsd ldrs to 5th: sn wknd: t.o)	9	**7**	11/1	1	—
469^{6}	**Against The Clock (63)** (CLPopham) **4-9-7**(7) TO'Connor (bhd fr 5th: t.o 7th)	15	**8**	20/1	—	—
825*	**King of Babylon (IRE) (77)** (FJordan) **4-11-0** 7x LAspell (a bhd: t.o whn fell bnd after 4th)		**F**	4/1 2	—	—
	Colour Scheme (77) (HSHowe) **9-10-8**(7) BMcGann (bit bkwd: a bhd: t.o whn p.u bef last)		**P**	20/1	—	—
				(SP 112.2%)		**10 Rn**

4m 31.7 (5.70) CSF £26.62 CT £194.55 TOTE £2.00: £1.40 £3.70 £2.70 (£17.00) Trio £61.60 OWNER Mr C. D. Tilly (AMESBURY) BRED Rosemount House Stud
LONG HANDICAP Against The Clock 9-12
WEIGHT FOR AGE 4yo-1lb
No bid
737 Cashflow Crisis (IRE) is in good form at present. In a strongly-run event, he had enough in hand over his rivals to be eased considerably near the line, and future plans are to have a few more outings over hurdles and then go chasing in the spring. (11/4)
Fawley Flyer finished a creditable second, considering he had not been out since falling over fences nearly eighteen months ago. (10/1)
Catwalker (IRE) has been slightly out of sorts of late, but appreciated this surface. (9/1)
684 Buglet (15/2: 9/2-8/1)

900 DEAN & DYBALL NOVICES' HURDLE (4-Y.O+) (Class E)
2-40 (2-41) **2m 3f (9 hdls)** £2,305.50 (£648.00: £316.50) GOING minus 0.21 sec per fur (G)

				SP	RR	SF
837*	**Courbaril (110)** (MCPipe) **4-11-11**(7) GSupple (hdwy & disp ld 6th: led next: sn clr: easily)	—	**1**	5/4 1	93+	38
	Rum Customer (CRBarwell) **5-10-12** BFenton (bit bkwd: bhd: hdwy 5th: r.o fr 2 out: lft poor 2nd last)	10	**2**	12/1	64	10
649^{6}	**Crown Ivory (NZ)** (PCRitchens) **8-10-12** SFox (in tch 5th: lost pl: styd on 2 out: lft poor 3rd last)	8	**3**	33/1	57	3
	Castleconner (IRE) (80) (RGFrost) **5-10-12** JFrost (bit bkwd: bhd: styd on fr 2 out)	4	**4**	25/1	54	—
829*	**Sigma Run (IRE) (81)** (JACEdwards) **7-11-5** MAFitzgerald (chsd ldr tl led 4th: hdd & wknd appr 6th)	2½	**5**	12/1	58	4
675^{8}	**Spumante (85)** (MPMuggeridge) **4-10-11** BPowell (chsd ldr tl after 3rd: wknd 5th)	5	**6**	8/1	47	—
820^{4}	**Bite the Bullet (55)** (AJChamberlain) **5-10-12** LHarvey (bit bkwd: prom to 5th: wknd next)	¾	**7**	100/1	47	—
788^{10}	**Crownhill Cross** (BRMillman) **5-10-7**(5) DSalter (bit bkwd: nvr trbld ldrs: rdn & wknd 6th: t.o)	dist	**8**	100/1	—	—
	Connaught's Pride (PJHobbs) **5-10-7** APMcCoy (bit bkwd: chsd ldrs 5th: wkng whn mstke 7th: sn t.o)	½	**9**	9/4 2	—	—
	Frome Lad (WGMTurner) **4-10-4**(7) JPower (bit bkwd: in tch to 6th: grad wknd: t.o)	dist	**10**	14/1	—	—
	Trail Boss (IRE) (98) (MissHCKnight) **5-10-12** JFTitley (led to 4th: led appr 6th: hdd next: 2nd & in tch whn fell last)		**F**	6/1 3	—	—
	Bickleigh Belle (SGKnight) **6-10-4**(3) TDascombe (bkwd: s.s: a bhd: t.o whn p.u bef 2 out)		**P**	100/1	—	—
	Kirby Moorside (DJMinty) **5-10-12** JRailton (bkwd: a bhd: t.o 7th: p.u bef last)		**P**	100/1	—	—
				(SP 133.4%)		**13 Rn**

4m 32.3 (6.30) CSF £19.03 TOTE £2.00: £1.20 £4.30 £7.70 (£20.30) Trio £36.20 OWNER Richard Green (Fine Paintings) (WELLINGTON) BRED George & Mrs Steinberg
WEIGHT FOR AGE 4yo-1lb
837* Courbaril defied his welter burden easily, but did not beat much. (5/4: op Evens)
Rum Customer, making his hurdling debut, put in a respectable performance against more experienced rivals. (12/1: op 8/1)
489 Crown Ivory (NZ) made up a lot of ground in the closing stages and may appreciate further. (33/1)
Trail Boss (IRE) looked booked for second when falling at the last. (6/1: op 3/1)

901 DEAN & DYBALL CHALLENGE TROPHY NOVICES' CHASE (5-Y.O+) (Class D)
3-10 (3-10) **2m 6f 110y (17 fncs)** £3,758.60 (£1,137.80: £555.40: £264.20) GOING minus 0.51 sec per fur (GF)

				SP	RR	SF
738*	**Pongo Waring (IRE) (95)** (MissHCKnight) **7-11-6** JFTitley (lw: a in tch: chsd ldr 11th: led 14th: rdn appr last: clr flat)	—	**1**	13/8 1	95	—
	Frazer Island (IRE) (RRowe) **7-10-11**(3) LAspell (bit bkwd: bhd: hdwy 10th: chsd wnr & ev ch 15th: rdn appr last: wknd flat)	8	**2**	7/1	83	—
722^{7}	**Dubelle (82)** (JSKing) **6-11-1** APMcCoy (a.p: led 11th: hdd & mstke 14th: wknd next)	13	**3**	15/2	75	—
720^{2}	**Our Nikki (72)** (PRRodford) **6-10-9** SBurrough (bhd: mstke 2nd: sme hdwy 12th: nvr nrr)	6	**4**	8/1	65	—
720^{4}	**Westerly Gale (IRE)** (NJHenderson) **6-11-0** MAFitzgerald (led to 11th: sn wknd)	5	**5**	7/2 2	66	—
	Emerald Knight (IRE) (RHAlner) **6-10-9**(5) PHenley (bkwd: a bhd: wknd 11th: t.o)	dist	**6**	5/1 3	—	—
549^{4}	**The Last Mistress (73)** (JNeville) **9-10-9** WMarston (chsd ldr to 10th: wknd qckly next: t.o)	4	**7**	40/1	—	—
				(SP 114.8%)		**7 Rn**

5m 45.7 (14.70) CSF £12.65 TOTE £2.10: £2.10 £3.40 (£21.20) OWNER Miss H. Knight (WANTAGE) BRED Joseph Smiddy

738* Pongo Waring (IRE) won for the fourth time in four starts here. He apparently does not appreciate soft ground so, when the going eases, he may be given a rest. (13/8)
Frazer Island (IRE) won a couple of point-to-points in Ireland last season, but showed little form under Rules. He jumped well here and connections feel he will be better over three miles. (7/1: 5/1-8/1)
595 Dubelle won on her chasing debut, but has shown disappointingly little since. (15/2)
Emerald Knight (IRE) (5/1: op 3/1)

902 WILLIAM HILL 'GOLDEN OLDIES' N.H. FLAT RACE (4-Y.O+) (Class H)

3-40 (3-40) **1m 5f** £1,502.00 (£422.00: £206.00)

				SP	RR	SF
682*	**Shahrani** (MCPipe) **4-12-0** PScudamore (led & sn clr: unchal)	—	1	2/7[1]	—	—
	Bright Sapphire (DBurchell) **10-12-0** MCaswell (chsd wnr after 2f to 8f out: chsd wnr over 2f out: no imp)	11	2	14/1	—	—
	Saafi (IRE) (RJBaker) **5-12-0** CBrown (s.s: hdwy ½-wy: chsd ldrs 6f out: one pce fnl 2½f)	8	3	25/1	—	—
	Trauma (IRE) (WGMTurner) **4-11-9** GHolmes (bit bkwd: hdwy to chse wnr 5f out: rdn & wknd fnl 2½f)	hd	4	33/1	—	—
788[9]	**My Harvinski** (IRJones) **6-12-0** SEarle (lw: bhd: rdn & styd on fnl 3f: nvr nrr)	6	5	33/1	—	—
	Calogan (BSmart) **9-12-0** BSmart (bit bkwd: chsd wnr 2f: wknd 6f out)	19	6	20/1	—	—
408[W]	**Scottish Park** (MCPipe) **7-12-2** MGallemore (bit bkwd: a bhd: t.o 6f out)	2	7	10/1[3]	—	—
	Risky Rose (RHollinshead) **4-11-13** PSmith (bkwd: s.s: mid div 5f: wknd 6f out: t.o)	19	8	5/1[2]	—	—
727[P]	**Ballyhays (IRE)** (NGAyliffe) **7-12-4** CBroad (s.s: a bhd: t.o 6f out)	20	9	50/1	—	—
				(SP 126.7%)	**9 Rn**	

3m 12.1 CSF £7.32 TOTE £1.40: £1.10 £1.70 £4.80 (£8.70) Trio £34.50 OWNER Mr A S Helaissi and Mr S Helaissi (WELLINGTON) BRED R. V. Young
682* Shahrani, who has won his last five races over hurdles, quickly put this beyond doubt. (2/7)
Bright Sapphire was racing on the Flat for the first time in nearly three years. (14/1)
Saafi (IRE) is a poor individual, both over obstacles and on the Flat, so connections must have been happy to finish in the minor berth here. (25/1)
Risky Rose (5/1: 7/2-11/2)

903 DEAN & DYBALL NOVICES' H'CAP CHASE (0-100) (5-Y.O+) (Class E)

4-10 (4-10) **2m 1f 110y (12 fncs)** £3,235.10 (£978.80: £477.40: £226.70) GOING minus 0.51 sec per fur (GF)

				SP	RR	SF
595[2]	**Bishops Castle (IRE) (82)** (RGFrost) **8-11-10** JFrost (lw: led 2nd to 5th: led next: clr 2 out: easily)	—	1	11/4[2]	82+	15
738[3]	**Chickabiddy (78)** (GFEdwards) **8-11-6** MAFitzgerald (lw: in tch tl lost pl 5th: hdwy appr 9th: chsd wnr 2 out: no imp)	1¾	2	5/2[1]	76	9
738[5]	**I Remember You (IRE) (67)** (MrsRGHenderson) **6-10-4**(5) DSalter (lw: 2nd whn sltly hmpd 2nd & lost pl: stdy hdwy 7th: chsd wnr next: ev ch tl wknd 2 out)	13	3	7/1	54	—
	Speedy Snapsgem (IRE) (70) (PJHobbs) **6-10-12** APMcCoy (bit bkwd: led to 2nd: led briefly 5th: rdn next: wknd fr 8th: t.o)	dist	4	7/2[3]	—	—
740[P]	**Tango's Delight (75)** (RJBaker) **8-11-3** BPowell (bhd fr 3rd: t.o 8th)	9	5	25/1	—	—
727[P]	**Idiom (70)** (MrsJGRetter) **9-10-12** JRKavanagh (chsd ldrs: 4th & in tch whn fell 8th)		F	6/1	—	—
826[R]	**Laura Lye (IRE) (62)** (BdeHaan) **6-10-4** JRailton (s.s: bhd whn fell 4th)		F	20/1	—	—
				(SP 112.9%)	**7 Rn**	

4m 21.7 (5.70) CSF £9.62 TOTE £2.80: £2.30 £2.00 (£2.30) OWNER A E C Electric Fencing Ltd (Hotline) (BUCKFASTLEIGH) BRED Mrs Dolors Dinneen
595 Bishops Castle (IRE), although carrying topweight, ran out a comfortable winner. (11/4)
738 Chickabiddy simply met one too good in the winner. (5/2)
I Remember You (IRE), making his second appearance over fences, can go on from here. (7/1)
Speedy Snapsgem (IRE), who showed very little over hurdles, is bred for chasing, but may require a stiffer test of stamina. (7/2)

904 DEAN & DYBALL H'CAP HURDLE (0-130) (4-Y.O+) (Class C)

4-40 (4-41) **2m 1f 110y (8 hdls)** £2,717.00 (£762.00: £371.00) GOING minus 0.21 sec per fur (G)

				SP	RR	SF
	Crack On (115) (PJHobbs) **6-12-0** APMcCoy (bit bkwd: hld up & bhd: stdy hdwy to ld appr 2 out: sn clr: easily)	—	1	7/4[1]	101+	42
741*	**Out Ranking (FR) (115)** (MCPipe) **4-11-13** CMaude (lw: led tl appr 2 out: rdn & sn outpcd)	9	2	7/4[1]	93	33
741[2]	**Little Hooligan (87)** (GFEdwards) **5-9-7b**(7) MrRThornton (lw: chsd ldr to 6th: ev ch tl rdn & wknd appr 2 out)	20	3	9/4[2]	47	—
721[6]	**Echo de Janser (FR) (115)** (AGHobbs) **4-11-6**(7) MrGShenkin (chsd ldrs tl rdn & wknd qckly 5th: t.o)	dist	4	12/1[3]	—	—
				(SP 111.2%)	**4 Rn**	

4m 8.0 (4.00) CSF £5.05 TOTE £2.50 (£2.70) OWNER Mr D. R. Peppiatt (MINEHEAD) BRED Mrs Audrey Goodwin
LONG HANDICAP Little Hooligan 9-12
WEIGHT FOR AGE 4yo-1lb
Crack On, making his seasonal appearance against race-fit rivals, looked a progressive individual last season. The plan is apparently to go chasing at some point this season, and he looks the type to make the grade over fences. (7/4)
741* Out Ranking (FR) is in good heart at present and, with conditions to suit, confirmed the form with Little Hooligan, despite the suggestion before the race that she was in season. She should soon recapture winning ways. (7/4)

905 DEAN & DYBALL NOVICES' H'CAP HURDLE (0-100) (4-Y.O+ F & M) (Class E)

5-10 (5-11) **2m 1f 110y (8 hdls)** £2,169.00 (£609.00: £297.00) GOING minus 0.21 sec per fur (G)

				SP	RR	SF
739[5]	**Last Laugh (IRE) (79)** (KCBailey) **4-11-7b** APMcCoy (hld up in tch: led appr 2 out: clr appr last: drvn out)	—	1	4/1[3]	58	9
725[3]	**Dragonmist (IRE) (63)** (DBurchell) **6-10-6** DJBurchell (gd hdwy to ld 4th: rdn appr 2 out: sn hdd: rallied u.s.p flat: jst failed)	s.h	2	4/1[3]	42	—
792[11]	**Hydemilla (75)** (MrsTDPilkington) **6-11-1**(3) GHogan (chsd ldr to 4th: wknd fr 6th)	12	3	5/1	43	—
879[2]	**Burnt Sienna (IRE) (79)** (JSMoore) **4-11-7v** WMcFarland (led to 4th: ev ch tl rdn & wknd appr 2 out)	6	4	7/2[2]	42	—
832[F]	**Kesanta (85)** (WGMTurner) **6-11-7**(7) JPower (chsd ldrs tl wknd fr 5th)	5	5	3/1[1]	43	—
	Worth the Wait (57) (FJordan) **5-10-0** SWynne (bit bkwd: a bhd: t.o fr 4th: fin lame)	dist	6	33/1	—	—
	Welton Rambler (58) (TNeedham) **9-9-12**(3)ow1 TDascombe (bkwd: a bhd: t.o 4th)	11	7	66/1	—	—

834R **Indian Crown (66)** (NBThomson) **6-10-2**(7) JHarris (bit bkwd: in tch whn rn out 3rd) .... **R** 10/1 — —
(SP 117.4%) **8 Rn**

4m 14.9 (10.90) CSF £19.70 CT £74.65 TOTE £4.80: £2.00 £1.70 £2.30 (£5.30) OWNER Charles Eden Ltd (UPPER LAMBOURN) BRED Brigitte Wolff in Ireland
LONG HANDICAP Worth the Wait 9-12 Welton Rambler 9-7
WEIGHT FOR AGE 4yo-1lb
634 Last Laugh (IRE) was booked for an easy win when going into the lead at the second last but, once in front, did very little and held on by a only whisker at the finish. She does not seem one to rely on. (4/1)
725 Dragonmist (IRE) ideally needs further but still put in a decent effort. (4/1)
Hydemilla is possibly only selling class, but ran well enough here to fill the minor berth. (5/1: 4/1-6/1)
879 Burnt Sienna (IRE) is much better than this. She needs things to go all her own way but, when they do, she will be the one to be on. (7/2)

T/Plpt: £18.70 (564.57 Tckts). T/Qdpt: £11.00 (64.05 Tckts). T

WETHERBY (L-H) (Good to firm)
Wednesday October 16th
WEATHER: overcast

906 GOLDSBOROUGH HURDLE (3-Y.O) (Class D)
2-20 (2-21) **2m (9 hdls)** £3,055.00 (£855.00: £415.00) GOING minus 0.33 sec per fur (GF)

	Horse	Dist	Pos	SP	RR	SF
	Lagan (KAMorgan) **3-10-12** ASSmith (mde all: mstke 4th: kpt on strly fr 3 out)	—	1	20/1	76	29
	Falcon's Flame (USA) (MrsJRRamsden) **3-10-12** RGarritty (lw: hld up & bhd: hdwy 4 out: sn chsng ldrs: kpt on one pce fr 2 out)	5	2	8/1	71	24
	Phantom Haze (MissSEHall) **3-10-12** NBentley (trckd ldrs: stdy hdwy to chse wnr 3 out: sn rdn & one pce)	6	3	9/2 2	65	18
699²	**Globe Runner** (JJO'Neill) **3-10-12** ARoche (bhd: hdwy u.p 4 out: one pce fr 2 out)	4	4	4/1 1	61	14
	Jackson Park (TDEasterby) **3-10-12** LWyer (lw: trckd ldrs: blnd 4 out: btn next)	6	5	9/2 2	55	8
	Eric's Bett (FMurphy) **3-10-12** KWhelan (mstkes: in tch: effrt appr 3 out: sn btn)	2	6	7/1 3	53	6
646¹³	**Phantom Dancer (IRE)** (MESowersby) **3-10-12** DParker (chsd ldrs tl outpcd fr 3 out)	9	7	40/1	44	—
699P	**Arrogant Heir** (DHBrown) **3-11-1**ow3 MrARebori (in tch: hit 5th: no imp fr 4 out)	1¾	8	66/1	45	—
	Lucky Bea (MWEasterby) **3-10-12** NWilliamson (bhd: sme hdwy 4 out: nvr nr to chal)	nk	9	10/1	42	—
589P	**Cashaplenty** (NPLittmoden) **3-10-12** MrDVerco (w wnr tl rdn & btn appr 3 out)	1¼	10	66/1	41	—
	Son of Anshan (MrsASwinbank) **3-10-12** JSupple (mstkes: nvr nr to chal)	½	11	33/1	40	—
	Alzotic (IRE) (JNorton) **3-10-12** WFry (a rr div)	23	12	25/1	17	—
	Most Respectful (DenysSmith) **3-10-12** PNiven (in tch tl wknd fr 3 out)	2	13	14/1	15	—
	Gilling Dancer (IRE) (PCalver) **3-10-12** BStorey (a bhd)	7	14	12/1	8	—
	Propolis Power (IRE) (MWEasterby) **3-10-12** AThornton (a rr div)	16	15	50/1	—	—
	Bridlington Bay (JLEyre) **3-10-12** OPears (rr div whn fell 4th)		F	25/1	—	—
	Countess of Cadiz (USA) (MissJFCraze) **3-10-7** ADobbin (a bhd: t.o whn p.u bef 3 out)		P	66/1	—	—
	Autofyr (JSWainwright) **3-10-6**(3)ow2 PMidgley (sn bhd: t.o whn p.u bef 3 out)		P	66/1	—	—
807²	**Tallulah Belle** (NPLittmoden) **3-10-7** MRichards (blnd & uns rdr 3rd)		U	10/1	—	—

(SP 138.3%) **19 Rn**

3m 43.2 (1.20) CSF £173.33 TOTE £49.40: £7.20 £3.30 £1.60 (£148.40) Trio £163.00; £160.73 to Redcar 17/10/96 OWNER Wild Racing (MELTON MOWBRAY) BRED Saeed Manana
Lagan stays well and made full use of his stamina here. Stepping on the gas three out, he soon had all his rivals in trouble and just needed pushing along to make sure of it. (20/1)
Falcon's Flame (USA), purposely taken to post last, produced a run from behind to chase the winner from the second last but, despite a valiant attempt, was not making any progress from then on. (8/1)
Phantom Haze, who had not been out for over two months, appeared to be going really well approaching the third last but, soon asked for an effort, failed to pick up. He is still a maiden on the Flat, but ought to be able rectify that at this game. (9/2)
699 Globe Runner, always having to work hard to improve, had given his best by the second last and failed to get in a real blow. (4/1)
Jackson Park ran quite well, but a bad blunder four out steadied him somewhat. The experience should see improvement. (9/2)
Eric's Bett spoilt his chances with some indifferent hurdling and would perhaps be better suited by easier ground. (7/1)
Arrogant Heir seems to be gradually improving, but still made the odd mistake. (66/1)
Lucky Bea ran as though this experience was needed. (10/1)

907 BOBBY RENTON NOVICES' H'CAP CHASE (0-105) (5-Y.O+) (Class D)
2-50 (2-51) **3m 1f (18 fncs)** £3,636.00 (£1,098.00: £534.00: £252.00) GOING minus 0.64 sec per fur (F)

	Horse	Dist	Pos	SP	RR	SF
	Mony-Skip (IRE) (85) (MrsSJSmith) **7-11-9** RichardGuest (a.p: led 3 out: sn clr: hit last)	—	1	5/2 2	99	—
696⁵	**Commandeer (IRE) (73)** (MissMKMilligan) **6-10-11** ASSmith (lw: led to 3 out: one pce)	11	2	10/1	80	—
691²	**Deise Marshall (IRE) (80)** (JWade) **8-11-4** AMaguire (cl up tl wknd fr 4 out)	7	3	11/8 1	83	—
802²	**Quixall Crossett (63)** (EMCaine) **11-9-8**(7)ow1 MrPMurray (prom tl outpcd fr 10th: styd on again fr 3 out)	1½	4	25/1	65	—
	Cool Weather (IRE) (86) (PCheesbrough) **8-11-10** RSupple (mstkes 1st & 10th: outpcd & bhd fr 12th)	7	5	13/2 3	83	—
	Carson City (82) (MJWilkinson) **9-11-6** PNiven (hld up: hit 9th: sn chsng ldrs: wknd 4 out)	14	6	9/1	70	—

(SP 106.9%) **6 Rn**

6m 16.7 CSF £21.42 TOTE £3.00: £1.70 £3.30 (£17.10) OWNER Mr Trevor Hemmings (BINGLEY) BRED Michael Moakley
LONG HANDICAP Quixall Crossett 9-8
Mony-Skip (IRE) took a long time to get it together last season, but has obviously continued that improvement and won this moderate event in really good style. (5/2)
696 Commandeer (IRE) took the eye in the paddock and ran a sound race out in front, but found the winner far too good over the last three fences. (10/1)
691 Deise Marshall (IRE) has yet to win a race, but he has ability, and a modest event should come his way in due course. (11/8)
802 Quixall Crossett stays well, but is slow and would seem to need extreme distances. (25/1)
Cool Weather (IRE), who put in a couple of poor jumps, was completely outpaced after halfway and basically ran moderately. (13/2: 4/1-7/1)
Carson City had his chances from halfway, but stopped very quickly from four out as though something is wrong with him. (9/1)

908 YORKSHIRE-TYNE TEES TELEVISION H'CAP HURDLE (0-135) (4-Y.O+) (Class C)

3-20 (3-21) **2m (9 hdls)** £3,574.00 (£1,072.00: £516.00: £238.00) GOING minus 0.33 sec per fur (GF)

				SP	RR	SF
	Desert Fighter (105) (MrsMReveley) **5-10-11** PNiven (lw: a cl up: led 3 out: rdn & r.o wl flat)	—	**1**	4/1^{2}	88	22
701*	**Sarmatian (USA) (104)** (MDHammond) **5-10-10** RGarritty (hld up: hdwy 4 out: ev ch appr last: r.o)	¾	**2**	5/1^{3}	86	20
806*	**Prizefighter (114)** (JLEyre) **5-11-6** OPears (lw: prom: outpcd 3 out: kpt on wl towards fin)	6	**3**	6/4^{1}	90	24
	Direct Route (IRE) (122) (HowardJohnson) **5-12-0** NWilliamson (trckd ldrs: hdwy to chal whn mstke 3 out: nt qckn fr next)	½	**4**	11/2	98	32
	Done Well (USA) (118) (PMonteith) **4-11-9** ADobbin (hld up: styd on fr 2 out: nvr nr to chal)	1	**5**	8/1	93	26
	Shining Edge (110) (TDEasterby) **4-11-1** LWyer (cl up: led 4th to 3 out: wknd)	½	**6**	9/1	84	17
	Roi du Nord (FR) (96) (SWCampion) **4-10-1** AMaguire (plld hrd: led to 4th: wknd qckly appr 3 out)	dist	**7**	20/1	—	—
356^{6}	**Tip it In (94)** (ASmith) **7-10-0** MBrennan (cl up: mstke 5th: sn t.o)	dist	**8**	100/1	—	—
				(SP 118.9%)	**8 Rn**	

3m 44.7 (2.70) CSF £23.50 CT £39.26 TOTE £5.20: £1.60 £1.90 £1.50 (£16.10) OWNER Mr A. Frame (SALTBURN) BRED P. D. and Mrs Player
LONG HANDICAP Tip it In 9-5
WEIGHT FOR AGE 4yo-1lb

Desert Fighter, who won at this meeting last year, is in top form at present and won well again. (4/1)
701* Sarmatian (USA), suited by the steady pace, was produced in the home straight, only to find the winner had got first run. (5/1)
806* Prizefighter was not as his best here and got outpaced when the tempo increased three out, but he was keeping on well at the finish. A stronger gallop would probably have been in his favour. (6/4)
Direct Route (IRE), from a yard that is yet to hit to form, ran well, but was not helped by a mistake three out. He will do better before long. (11/2)
Done Well (USA), given a pipe-opener on the Flat recently, put in a useful first effort of the season and should soon show improvement. (8/1)
Shining Edge ran reasonably and had his chances until it turned into a sprint over the last three flights. (9/1)

909 GORDON FOSTER H'CAP CHASE (0-135) (5-Y.O+) (Class C)

3-50 (3-50) **2m 4f 110y (15 fncs)** £4,497.00 (£1,356.00: £658.00: £309.00) GOING minus 0.64 sec per fur (F)

				SP	RR	SF
	General Command (IRE) (114) (GRichards) **8-10-7** RDunwoody (mde most: hld on wl flat)	—	**1**	10/11^{1}	124	57
811*	**Glemot (IRE) (135)** (KCBailey) **8-12-0** JOsborne (lw: a.p: hdwy to chal 3 out: nt qckn flat)	3	**2**	5/2^{2}	143	76
	De Jordaan (115) (WSCunningham) **9-10-8** NWilliamson (hld up: hdwy & ev ch 4 out: sn rdn & one pce)	16	**3**	20/1	110	43
732^{3}	**Cross Cannon (114)** (JWade) **10-10-7** AMaguire (disp ld 3rd to 11th: wknd 4 out)	29	**4**	8/1	87	20
11^{3}	**Lochnagrain (IRE) (111)** (MrsMReveley) **8-10-4**ow1 PNiven (blnd 1st & 3rd: sn t.o: p.u bef 2 out)		**P**	11/2^{3}	—	—
				(SP 112.2%)	**5 Rn**	

4m 53.6 (-13.40) CSF £3.58 TOTE £1.80: £1.30 £1.50 (£2.40) OWNER Mr Robert Ogden (PENRITH) BRED Miss M. Fenton

General Command (IRE) was a bit edgy and warm in the preliminaries, but he did the job required well and picked up nicely when strongly challenged in the home straight. (10/11: tchd Evens)
811* Glemot (IRE), the pick on looks, moved up to challenge three out but, when it came down to a battle, he was just found wanting. (5/2)
De Jordaan, who likes this fast ground, ran a useful race and ought to be able to find a suitable event before long. (20/1)
732 Cross Cannon likes things to go all his own way and was probably made too much use of here. (8/1)
11 Lochnagrain (IRE) hated this and, after two terrible jumps early on, managed to struggle round tailed off until his rider decided enough was enough two out. (11/2)

910 HALLFIELD NOVICES' HURDLE (4-Y.O+) (Class D)

4-20 (4-23) **2m 4f 110y (10 hdls)** £3,107.50 (£870.00: £422.50) GOING minus 0.33 sec per fur (GF)

				SP	RR	SF
	Share Options (IRE) (TDEasterby) **5-10-12** LWyer (chsd ldrs: slt ld 2 out: all out)	—	**1**	8/1	72	23
693^{2}	**Antarctic Wind (IRE)** (MDHammond) **6-10-12** RGarritty (lw: chsd ldrs: chal 3 out: kpt on u.p flat)	¾	**2**	9/2^{2}	71	22
	Highbeath (94) (MrsMReveley) **5-11-5** PNiven (chsd ldrs: rdn 4 out: kpt on: nt pce to chal)	7	**3**	3/1^{1}	73	24
	Parklife (IRE) (PCHaslam) **4-10-11** MFoster (led to 2nd: led 6th to 2 out: cl 3rd & hrd rdn whn blnd last)	2	**4**	9/2^{2}	64	14
730*	**Rule Out The Rest** (MrsSarahHorner-Harker) **5-11-5** AThornton (led 2nd: blnd 4th: hdd 6th: wknd appr 3 out)	4	**5**	10/1	68	19
781^{2}	**Pangeran (USA)** (MrsASwinbank) **4-10-11** JSupple (hdwy & in tch 4 out: sn rdn & no imp)	12	**6**	12/1	52	2
694^{P}	**Music Blitz (86)** (MrsDThomson) **5-10-12** TReed (hld up & bhd: effrt appr 3 out: rdn & nvr able to chal)	11	**7**	6/1^{3}	43	—
	Euro Thyne (IRE) (TDEasterby) **6-10-12** RDunwoody (bhd: shkn up ½-wy: nvr rchd ldrs)	14	**8**	20/1	32	—
	Lifebuoy (IRE) (JRTurner) **5-10-12** WFry (chsd ldrs: hit 5th: outpcd fr 4 out)	1¼	**9**	33/1	31	—
630^{6}	**Jean de Florette (USA)** (RCSpicer) **5-10-9**(3) EHusband (in tch to 6th)	½	**10**	33/1	31	—
784^{4}	**Top Skipper (IRE)** (MartynWane) **4-10-11** ADobbin (prom to ½-wy)	nk	**11**	16/1	31	—
	Evezio Rufo (NPLittmoden) **4-10-11** MrDVerco (a rr div)	2½	**12**	20/1	29	—
99^{4}	**Millennium Man** (EWeymes) **5-10-12** JCallaghan (in tch to 6th)	2½	**13**	14/1	27	—
	Nelson Must (WABethell) **6-10-12** ASSmith (bit bkwd: a wl bhd)	9	**14**	50/1	20	—
	Baraqueta (JLEyre) **4-10-11** OPears (lost tch fr 6th)	7	**15**	20/1	14	—
	Willie Wannabe (IRE) (MrsDThomson) **6-10-12** LO'Hara (bhd & mstke 4 out: n.d)	3	**16**	50/1	12	—
				(SP 140.2%)	**16 Rn**	

4m 50.7 (3.70) CSF £47.08 TOTE £9.40: £2.50 £1.60 £2.10 (£16.90) Trio £21.20 OWNER Mr Steve Hammond (MALTON) BRED John Walsh
WEIGHT FOR AGE 4yo-1lb

Share Options (IRE), who looks the type to do well at this game as he strengthens and gains experience, showed fine courage to win this. (8/1: 6/1-9/1)
693 Antarctic Wind (IRE) put in a useful performance and should not be long in finding a race. (9/2)
Highbeath ran reasonably, but looked short of speed even at this trip. He either needs further yet or easier ground. (3/1)
Parklife (IRE) showed improved form when stepping up in trip on the Flat recently and put in a promising effort. But for a blunder at the last, he would have been third. (9/2)
730* Rule Out The Rest found this a lot more competitive, but still ran quite well until things really hotted up over the last three flights. (10/1: op 6/1)
781 Pangeran (USA), a very lean individual, failed to make any impression here. (12/1)
694 Music Blitz, given plenty to do, only stayed on when it was too late. (6/1: op 10/1)
Euro Thyne (IRE) never showed much here, but he does look the type for this game given time. (20/1)

911 ASKHAM RICHARD NOVICES' H'CAP HURDLE (0-105) (4-Y.O+) (Class D)

4-50 (4-53) **3m 1f (12 hdls)** £3,226.50 (£972.00: £471.00: £220.50) GOING minus 0.33 sec per fur (GF)

				SP	RR	SF
	Pebble Beach (IRE) (79) (GMMoore) **6-11-0** JCallaghan (a.p: led appr 3 out: drvn out)	—	1	5/1[3]	63	18
693*	**Smart Approach (IRE) (90)** (MrsMReveley) **6-11-11** PNiven (lw: hld up: hdwy ½-wy: chsng ldrs & rdn appr 3 out: styd on one pce)	7	2	Evens[1]	70	25
792[6]	**Little Tincture (IRE) (71)** (MrsTJMcInnesSkinner) **6-10-6** GUpton (cl up: led 4th tl appr 3 out: sn outpcd)	18	3	7/2[2]	39	—
	Garbo's Boy (78) (JRTurner) **6-10-13** WFry (led 1st to 4th: wknd 4 out)	3	4	6/1	44	—
	Cool Steel (IRE) (77) (MrsJBrown) **4-10-5**(5) ECallaghan (bit bkwd: lost tch fr 8th: t.o)	dist	5	20/1	—	—
693P	**Heddon Haugh (IRE) (70)** (PCheesbrough) **8-10-5** RSupple (hld up: effrt ½-wy: sn rdn & btn: t.o)	dist	6	16/1	—	—
	Ole Ole (79) (MrsEMoscrop) **10-11-0** TReed (led to 1st: cl up tl rdn & wknd 6th: t.o whn p.u bef last)		P	33/1	—	—

(SP 116.8%) **7 Rn**

6m 0.1 (7.10) CSF £10.50 CT £18.07 TOTE £5.70: £2.30 £1.50 (£3.20) OWNER The Pebble Beach Partnership (MIDDLEHAM)
WEIGHT FOR AGE 4yo-2lb

Pebble Beach (IRE), wearing a tongue-strap, looked fit and did the business in good style, with his rider leaving nothing to chance and driving him out to the line. (5/1)

693* Smart Approach (IRE) had her chances from halfway but, when the tap was really turned on from three out, her limitations were well exposed. (Evens)

632* Little Tincture (IRE) tried to warm the pace up from halfway but, once collared approaching three out, looked very slow. (7/2)

Garbo's Boy raced with the leaders, but found things happening too quickly for his liking over the last four flights. (6/1)

Cool Steel (IRE) needed this and was left some way behind soon after hallway. (20/1)

T/Plpt: £50.50 (220.95 Tckts). T/Qdpt: £2.80 (443.62 Tckts). AA

0748-TAUNTON (R-H) (Good to firm)
Thursday October 17th

WEATHER: fine

912 WATCHET CLAIMING HURDLE (3-Y.O) (Class G)

1-50 (1-51) **2m 1f (9 hdls)** £1,836.50 (£514.00: £249.50) GOING minus 1.11 sec per fur (HD)

				SP	RR	SF
836*	**Cointosser (IRE)** (RGFrost) **3-11-4** SWynne (lw: hld up & bhd: gd hdwy fr 3 out: led flat: wandered: r.o wl)	—	1	11/10[1]	74	18
836[2]	**Ben Bowden** (MBlanshard) **3-11-3** JOsborne (lw: chsd ldr: ev ch last: unable qckn)	3	2	9/1	70	14
836[3]	**Indira** (PGMurphy) **3-10-0** WMcFarland (prom: mstke 2nd: led appr 2 out tl flat)	¾	3	3/1[2]	53	—
831*	**Hever Golf Diamond** (TJNaughton) **3-11-9** NWilliamson (lw: hld up: hdwy 6th: ev ch 2 out: one pce flat)	¾	4	15/2[3]	75	19
736[3]	**Andsome Boy** (CRBarwell) **3-11-0** BClifford (led tl appr 2 out: wknd appr last)	13	5	10/1	54	—
654[7]	**Kings Nightclub** (JWhite) **3-10-0**(3) GuyLewis (hld up: hdwy 4th: wknd qckly 3 out: t.o)	dist	6	50/1	—	—
	Lunar Gris (RMStronge) **3-10-0** BPowell (a bhd: t.o)	2½	7	100/1	—	—
	Red Time (MSSaunders) **3-11-3** PHolley (lw: a bhd: t.o)	3½	8	20/1	—	—
	Lady Magnum (IRE) (JNeville) **3-10-9** DBridgwater (lw: a bhd: t.o)	8	9	40/1	—	—
	Brin-Lodge (IRE) (KSBridgwater) **3-10-0** VSlattery (blnd 1st: a bhd: t.o)	dist	10	100/1	—	—
736[8]	**Peyton Jones** (ADSmith) **3-10-5b**[1] FJousset (prom: hmpd 2nd: wknd 5th: t.o)	5	11	100/1	—	—

(SP 115.6%) **11 Rn**

3m 44.9 (-8.10) CSF £11.08 TOTE £1.90: £1.10 £2.10 £1.30 (£8.10) Trio £7.80 OWNER Mr M. C. Pipe (BUCKFASTLEIGH) BRED Mellon Stud
Indira clmd MrsSPopham £3,000

836* Cointosser (IRE), despite being 2lb worse off with the runner-up and 12lb worse off with the third than at Wincanton last week, came from off a fast pace to complete the hat-trick. (11/10: 6/4-Evens)

836 Ben Bowden narrowed the margin of defeat by two lengths. (9/1)

836 Indira could not turn the tables on the first two, despite being 12lb and 13lb better off at the weights than at Wincanton. (3/1)

831* Hever Golf Diamond, although this was only a claimer, was trying to concede weight to better rivals than the ones he had met at Ludlow. (15/2: 5/1-8/1)

913 DONYATT (S) H'CAP HURDLE (0-90) (4-Y.O+) (Class G)

2-25 (2-25) **2m 1f (9 hdls)** £1,920.50 (£538.00: £261.50) GOING minus 1.11 sec per fur (HD)

				SP	RR	SF
	Mutawali (IRE) (68) (RJBaker) **6-10-11** DLeahy (hld up & bhd: hdwy 6th: led flat: r.o wl)	—	1	12/1	50	16
339[4]	**Mylordmayor (57)** (PBowen) **9-10-0b**[1] RFarrant (a.p: led appr 2 out to last: one pce)	3½	2	11/1	36	2
749*	**Almapa (80)** (RJHodges) **4-11-5**(3) TDascombe (lw: hld up: hdwy 6th: led last: sn hdd: one pce)	s.h	3	3/1[1]	59	24
749[2]	**Fleet Cadet (76)** (MCPipe) **5-11-5b** CMaude (hld up & bhd: hdwy 5th: hrd rdn & r.o one pce fr 2 out)	2½	4	7/2[2]	52	18
603[9]	**Sharp Thrill (67)** (BSmart) **5-10-10** CLlewellyn (a.p: ev ch whn hit 2 out: one pce)	s.h	5	14/1	43	9
879[9]	**Scalp 'em (IRE) (60)** (DrPPritchard) **8-10-3** DrPPritchard (hld up: hdwy 6th: one pce fr 3 out)	4	6	66/1	33	—
600[7]	**Merlins Wish (USA) (81)** (MCPipe) **7-11-10b**[1] APMcCoy (led 2nd: rdn 5th: hdd appr 2 out: sn wknd)	6	7	8/1[3]	48	14
812[8]	**Colin's Pride (60)** (MrsSDWilliams) **5-9-12b**[1](5)ow3 PHenley (rdn appr 5th: a bhd)	7	8	11/1	20	—
837[2]	**Miramare (62)** (CLPopham) **6-10-5** MAFitzgerald (lw: led to 2nd: wknd 5th)	4	9	9/1	19	—
879[10]	**Reefa's Mill (IRE) (78)** (JNeville) **4-11-6b** DBridgwater (lw: prom to 6th: t.o)	12	10	20/1	23	—
813[6]	**Shalholme (57)** (JMBradley) **6-10-0** NWilliamson (a bhd: t.o fr 3 out)	2½	11	40/1	—	—
555[5]	**Lucky Domino (61)** (MSheppard) **6-10-4** AMaguire (a bhd: t.o)	4	12	14/1	—	—

(SP 114.7%) **12 Rn**

3m 43.9 (-9.10) CSF £119.18 CT £454.92 TOTE £12.10: £3.90 £3.40 £1.60 (£57.10) Trio £70.10 OWNER Mr John Warren (TIVERTON) BRED Cyclades Farming Co
LONG HANDICAP Colin's Pride 9-13 Shalholme 9-12
WEIGHT FOR AGE 4yo-1lb
No bid

Mutawali (IRE), let down by some poor jumping in several races in this grade last season, never put a foot wrong here. (12/1: op 8/1)

339 Mylordmayor seemed to be sharpened up by the first-time blinkers. (11/1: 8/1-12/1)

749* Almapa found this more competitive than the very weak contest she won here a week ago. (3/1)

749 Fleet Cadet again found the lack of a turn of foot a problem. (7/2)
Sharp Thrill, dropped into a seller, was backed at long odds and gave his supporters a real run for their money. (14/1: 12/1-20/1)
Colin's Pride (11/1: 7/1-12/1)

914 LANSDOWNE CHEMICAL H'CAP CHASE (0-120) (5-Y.O+) (Class D)

3-00 (3-00) **3m (19 fncs)** £3,533.75 (£1,070.00: £522.50: £248.75) GOING minus 1.11 sec per fur (HD)

Form	Horse	Dist	Pos	SP	RR	SF
732^{4}	**The Blue Boy (IRE) (99)** (PBowen) **8-11-8b** NWilliamson (hmpd 2nd: hdwy to ld 6th: hrd rdn appr 3 out: hdd 2 out: led last: r.o wl)	—	**1**	$11/2^{3}$	106	32
833^{*}	**Drumcullen (IRE) (88)** (KCBailey) **7-10-11** WMcFarland (hit 2nd: chsd ldr 13th: hit 3 out: slt ld 2 out: hdd last: unable qckn)	2	**2**	$10/11^{1}$	94	20
814^{3}	**Henley Wood (98)** (PJHobbs) **11-11-4**(3) GTormey (chsd ldr to 13th: hit 15th: sn rdn: ev ch fr 3 out: unable qckn flat)	nk	**3**	$4/1^{2}$	104	30
750^{2}	**Slippery Max (77)** (RTJuckes) **12-10-0** WMarston (led: hit 1st: hdd 6th: wknd 14th: t.o)	dist	**4**	20/1	—	—
823^{5}	**Nick the Dreamer (100)** (WGMTurner) **11-11-9** AThornton (fell 2nd)		**F**	11/1	—	—
740^{4}	**Damas (FR) (107)** (MCPipe) **5-11-13b** APMcCoy (bdly hmpd & uns rdr 2nd)		**U**	15/2	—	—
				(SP 112.6%)		**6 Rn**

5m 43.2 (1.10 under best) (-13.80) CSF £10.80 TOTE £6.80: £1.90 £1.20 (£5.30) OWNER Mr T. M. Morris (HAVERFORDWEST) BRED B. R. and Mrs Firestone in Ireland
LONG HANDICAP Slippery Max 9-13
WEIGHT FOR AGE 5yo-3lb
732 The Blue Boy (IRE), on the same mark as when winning at Carlisle, this enigmatic character was given a fine ride by Williamson. (11/2)
833* Drumcullen (IRE), off the same mark as Wincanton last week, was due to go up a further 7lb after winning a couple of soft races. (10/11)
814 Henley Wood, 6lb higher than when successful at Fontwell, seems to stay well enough but has yet to score beyond nineteen furlongs under Rules. (4/1: op 5/2)

915 TIVERTON NOVICES' HURDLE (4-Y.O+) (Class E)

3-35 (3-37) **2m 1f (9 hdls)** £2,389.50 (£672.00: £328.50) GOING minus 1.11 sec per fur (HD)

Form	Horse	Dist	Pos	SP	RR	SF
812^{3}	**Ath Cheannaithe (FR) (92)** (JNeville) **4-10-11** DBridgwater (mde all: reminders after 5th: r.o wl)	—	**1**	$6/4^{1}$	74+	16
	Lonicera (RHAlner) **6-10-2**(5) PHenley (bit bkwd: a.p: chsd wnr 5th: hit 3 out: r.o flat: nt trble wnr)	1¾	**2**	33/1	67+	10
748^{2}	**Second Colours (USA)** (MCPipe) **6-10-12** APMcCoy (lw: prom: blnd 2nd: chsd wnr 4th: mstke 5th: wknd 3 out)	7	**3**	$5/1^{3}$	66	9
603^{*}	**Southern Ridge (85)** (RGFrost) **5-11-5** MrAHoldsworth (hld up: hdwy after 4th: 4th whn blnd 3 out: nt rcvr)	14	**4**	$4/1^{2}$	60	3
253^{5}	**Desert Calm (IRE) (93)** (MrsPNDutfield) **7-10-12** PHolley (nvr trbld ldrs)	2	**5**	12/1	51	—
653^{10}	**All Sewn Up** (RJBaker) **4-10-11** BPowell (chsd wnr: mstke 2nd: wkng whn blnd 5th)	16	**6**	66/1	36	—
749^{10}	**Old Master (IRE)** (RJBaker) **5-10-12** DLeahy (a bhd)	5	**7**	100/1	31	—
	Russells Runner (NJHawke) **5-10-12** SBurrough (bhd fr 5th: t.o)	10	**8**	100/1	22	—
	Mystic Legend (IRE) (JJSheehan) **4-10-11** PHide (bhd fr 5th: t.o)	1	**9**	25/1	21	—
	Mr Cube (IRE) (JMBradley) **6-10-12** NWilliamson (bhd fr 5th: t.o)	11	**10**	11/1	10	—
	Mr Jasper (NBThomson) **4-10-11** DMorris (a bhd: t.o)	15	**11**	100/1	—	—
	Another Hubblick (PFNicholls) **5-10-5**(7) OBurrows (fell 2nd)		**F**	33/1	—	—
820^{2}	***Tomal*** (RIngram) **4-10-11** AMaguire (Withdrawn not under Starter's orders: lame at s)		**W**	7/1	—	—
				(SP 119.4%)		**12 Rn**

3m 43.8 (-9.20) CSF £35.88 TOTE £2.50: £1.10 £6.00 £1.60 (£41.70) Trio £63.50 OWNER Mr J. Neville (NEWPORT, GWENT) BRED Russlson and Campbell Stud
WEIGHT FOR AGE 4yo-1lb
812 Ath Cheannaithe (FR), without the headgear this time, again made the running and his rider was able to take things easy close home. (6/4)
Lonicera, although a shade flattered by his proximity to the winner, should come on for the outing and seems capable of taking a similar event. (33/1)
748 Second Colours (USA) looked tremendously well, but has yet to get the hang of hurdling. (5/1: 11/4-11/2)
603* Southern Ridge was just beginning to feel the pace when a bad error put all doubts to rest. (4/1)

916 CAVENDISH TECHNOLOGY H'CAP HURDLE (0-110) (4-Y.O+) (Class E)

4-05 (4-05) **2m 3f 110y (10 hdls)** £2,736.00 (£828.00: £404.00: £192.00) GOING minus 1.11 sec per fur (HD)

Form	Horse	Dist	Pos	SP	RR	SF
692^{7}	**Peter Monamy (101)** (MCPipe) **4-11-10b** APMcCoy (hld up: reminder after 5th: hdwy appr 2 out: hrd rdn & str run to ld last strides)	—	**1**	$4/1^{3}$	83	20
793^{3}	**Zingibar (78)** (JMBradley) **4-10-1** NWilliamson (lw: a.p: led on bit after 3 out: hrd rdn flat: hdd last strides)	s.h	**2**	$3/1^{2}$	60	—
	Mutazz (USA) (105) (MajorWRHern) **4-12-0** RFarrant (lw: a.p: led 3 out: sn hdd: wknd 2 out)	6	**3**	$7/4^{1}$	82	19
	Take a Flyer (IRE) (85) (RJHodges) **6-10-6b**(3) TDascombe (led to 3 out: sn wknd)	5	**4**	9/2	58	—
798^{2}	**Emperor Chang (USA) (84)** (KOWarner) **9-10-8** TKent (hld up: bhd fr 3 out: virtually p.u flat)	dist	**5**	8/1	—	—
				(SP 110.7%)		**5 Rn**

4m 22.8 (-8.20) CSF £14.94 TOTE £4.50: £2.50 £1.30 (£6.30) OWNER Richard Green (Fine Paintings) (WELLINGTON) BRED R. Green
WEIGHT FOR AGE 4yo-1lb
OFFICIAL EXPLANATION **Peter Monamy: had made mistakes and shown no enthusiasm at Market Rasen.**
591 Peter Monamy, woken up with a circuit to go, would probably have been happy to throw in the towel, but McCoy was in no mood to concede defeat. (4/1: op 5/2)
793 Zingibar was galloping all over his rivals when taking it up leaving the back straight, but this extended trip may just have caught him out. He will have to come down a few pounds on this evidence. (3/1)
Mutazz (USA) was 9lb higher than when winning a seller over course and distance in April. (7/4)

917 ISEFLO IODINE CHALLENGE CUP NOVICES' CHASE (5-Y.O+) (Class E)

4-35 (4-35) **2m 110y (13 fncs)** £3,536.00 (£844.00) GOING minus 1.11 sec per fur (HD)

Form	Horse	Dist	Pos	SP	RR	SF
738^{6}	**Coolteen Hero (IRE)** (RHAlner) **6-10-12** WMcFarland (mde all: clr 7th: mstke 4 out: lft wl clr 3 out)	—	**1**	$9/4^{3}$	85?	—
821^{U}	**Royal Hand (67)** (MMadgwick) **6-10-12** BFenton (chsd wnr to 4 out: lft poor 2nd 3 out)	dist	**2**	$2/1^{2}$	—	—
821^{3}	**Larks Tail** (PRWebber) **8-10-7** RBellamy (hld up: lost pl 7th: hdwy to chse wnr 4 out: btn whn fell 3 out)		**F**	16/1	—	—

				SP	RR	SF
826*	**Tenayestelign (85)** (DMarks) **8-11-0** JAMcCarthy (hld up: hdwy to disp 2nd whn blnd & uns rdr 8th)		U	13/8 1	—	—
				(SP 108.1%)		**4 Rn**

3m 59.7 (-0.30) CSF £6.56 TOTE £2.60 (£2.70) OWNER J P M & J W Cook (BLANDFORD) BRED T. Simmons
Coolteen Hero (IRE) was quite happy to force the pace over this sharp two miles. (9/4)
821 Royal Hand finished runner-up by default. (2/1)
826* Tenayestelign got caught out by the first ditch. (13/8)

918 OCTOBER STANDARD OPEN N.H. FLAT RACE (4, 5 & 6-Y.O) (Class H)

5-10 (5-11) **2m 1f** £1,194.00 (£334.00: £162.00)

				SP	RR	SF
	Mrs Em (PFNicholls) **4-10-12** APMcCoy (hld up: stdy hdwy 6f out: led wl over 1f out: r.o wl)	—	1	7/1	—	—
	Woodstock Wanderer (IRE) (PBowen) **4-11-3** AMaguire (hld up & bhd: gd hdwy 5f out: chsd wnr over 1f out: no imp)	5	2	4/1 2	—	—
	Moonlight Escapade (IRE) (RJHodges) **5-11-8**(3) TDascombe (a.p: led 8f out tl wl over 1f out: one pce)	4	3	11/2 3	—	—
191 5	**Summerway Legend** (DWPArbuthnot) **4-10-12** GBradley (lw: hld up: hdwy 7f out: wknd 2f out)	4	4	4/1 2	—	—
418*	**Red Tel (IRE)** (MCPipe) **4-11-10** CMaude (hld up & plld hrd: rdn over 3f out: sn wknd)	9	5	9/4 1	—	—
653 13	**Leopard Lady** (NJHawke) **4-10-12** MAFitzgerald (prom tl wknd 3f out)	¾	6	66/1	—	—
	Weather Wise (WGMTurner) **4-10-10**(7) NWillmington (bit bkwd: mde most to 8f out: wknd 3f out)	5	7	20/1	—	—
	Don't Argue (SGKnight) **5-11-4** MissLBlackford (bkwd: a bhd)	1	8	66/1	—	—
	Hidden Valley (RGFrost) **4-11-3** JFrost (bkwd: bhd fnl 6f)	3½	9	33/1	—	—
	Little Embers (JMBradley) **4-10-12** NWilliamson (bkwd: a bhd)	12	10	25/1	—	—
	Josephine Grey (SNCole) **5-10-13** AThornton (a bhd)	nk	11	66/1	—	—
653 15	**Nanjizal** (KSBridgwater) **4-11-3** VSlattery (prom 10f)	8	12	33/1	—	—
	Rowbet Jack (KOCunningham-Brown) **4-11-3** BFenton (bkwd: a bhd: t.o 7f out: p.u ins fnl f)		P	20/1	—	—
				(SP 122.4%)		**13 Rn**

3m 41.4 CSF £33.81 TOTE £7.20: £2.00 £1.80 £2.10 (£16.70) Trio £28.60 OWNER Mr G. Z. Mizel (SHEPTON MALLET) BRED Guest Leasing and Bloodstock Co
WEIGHT FOR AGE 4yo-1lb
Mrs Em is a half-sister to winning hurdler With Impunity. (7/1: op 3/1)
Woodstock Wanderer (IRE) showed promise for the future, but had to be content with playing second fiddle. (4/1: 3/1-9/2)
Moonlight Escapade (IRE), bought for 24,000 guineas at Doncaster August Sale, won a bumper in Ireland in July, but disappointed under a penalty next time. (11/2: op 3/1)
Summerway Legend looked in fine fettle, but failed to deliver the goods when the chips were down. (4/1)
418* Red Tel (IRE) had his limitations exposed in no uncertain manner. (9/4)

T/Plpt: £49.40 (199.13 Tckts). T/Qdpt: £10.40 (41.76 Tckts). KH

919a-929a (Irish Racing) - See Computer Raceform

0154a-PARDUBICE (Czech Republic) (Good)
Sunday October 13th

930a VELKA PARDUBICKA CESKE POJISTOVNY CHASE (6-Y.O+)

2-45 **4m 2f 110y (31 fncs)** £24,155.00 (£13,889.00: £10,266.00)

				SP	RR	SF
	Cipisek (CZE) (JVana,CzechRepublic) **8-10-0** VSnitkovskij	—	1		115?	—
580a 2	**Irish Stamp (IRE)** (FMurphy) **7-10-7** NWilliamson	4½	2		119	—
726 4	**Its a Snip** (CJMann) **11-10-7b** RDunwoody	dist	3		—	—
						21 Rn

9m 35.1 OWNER Staj Luka BRED St Cesky Brod
580a Irish Stamp (IRE), in touch, made headway to go third from four out. From then on he chased the winner, but could make no impression.
726 Its a Snip led the field until five out and then kept on at the one pace.

0456-HEREFORD (R-H) (Good to firm)
Friday October 18th

931 E.B.F. 'N.H.' NOVICES' HURDLE (Qualifier) (4, 5 & 6-Y.O) (Class E)

1-50 (1-50) **2m 1f (9 hdls)** £2,276.00 (£636.00: £308.00) GOING minus 0.09 sec per fur (G)

				SP	RR	SF
	Sounds Like Fun (MissHCKnight) **5-11-0** JFTitley (chsd ldr: led after 4th: shkn up flat: cleverly)	—	1	1/2 1	58+	24
718 6	**Seven Wells** (JHPeacock) **4-10-13** RBellamy (hld up: jnd wnr 5th: ev ch 2 out: rallied flat)	2½	2	8/1 3	56	21
787 2	**Chief Gale (IRE)** (JGMO'Shea) **4-10-8**(5) MichaelBrennan (hld up: ev ch whn hit 2 out: rn wd bnd appr last: one pce)	2½	3	5/2 2	53	18
	Cruisinforabruisin (RJPrice) **6-11-0** MrMJackson (plld hrd: led & sn clr: hdd after 4th: wknd 5th: t.o)	dist	4	20/1	—	—
				(SP 111.1%)		**4 Rn**

4m (7.00) CSF £4.55 TOTE £1.40 (£3.50) OWNER Mrs H. Brown (WANTAGE) BRED B. King
WEIGHT FOR AGE 4yo-1lb
Sounds Like Fun, the winner of a Ludlow bumper last January, found a soft race to start his hurdling career. (1/2)
492 Seven Wells tried to mount a renewed effort, but the winner was merely toying with him. (8/1)
787 Chief Gale (IRE) became unbalanced on the home turn after missing out the penultimate flight. (5/2)

932 OVREVOLL H'CAP CHASE (0-120) (5-Y.O+) (Class D)

2-20 (2-20) **3m 1f 110y (19 fncs)** £3,533.75 (£1,070.00: £522.50: £248.75) GOING minus 0.09 sec per fur (G)

				SP	RR	SF
395 2	**Some Day Soon (100)** (MBradstock) **11-11-5** PHolley (j.w: mde all: clr 4th: wl clr 15th: unchal)	—	1	11/8 1	111	40
395 6	**Paper Star (103)** (MPMuggeridge) **9-11-8** BPowell (chsd wnr tl lost pl 13th: rallied & wnt 2nd 3 out: no ch w wnr)	20	2	7/1 3	102	31

		Dist	Pos	SP	RR	SF
833[3]	**Foxgrove (81)** (RJPrice) **10-9-7**(7) MissEJJones (hld up: hdwy 7th: hit 9th: reminders after 11th: lost pl 14th: rallied appr 3 out: 3rd & btn whn mstke 2 out)	11	**3**	11/1	73	2
835[U]	**Lake of Loughrea (IRE) (104)** (KCBailey) **6-11-9** CO'Dwyer (hld up: blnd 3rd: hdwy 10th: chsd wnr 13th: outpcd 15th: wknd appr 2 out)	14	**4**	13/8[2]	87	16
823[P]	**Polar Region (105)** (NJHenderson) **10-11-5**(5) MrCVigors (hld up: mstke 6th: t.o fr 9th)	22	**5**	7/1[3]	74	3
				(SP 113.5%)		**5 Rn**

6m 16.9 (6.90) CSF £10.11 TOTE £2.30: £1.10 £3.10 (£4.50) OWNER Mr C. Elgram (WANTAGE) BRED Thomas Kinsella
LONG HANDICAP Foxgrove 9-13
395 Some Day Soon was on the same mark as when second at Stratford two months ago. (11/8)
Paper Star has registered all four of her wins at Plumpton. (7/1: op 9/2)
833 Foxgrove, 1lb out of the handicap, was due to go down a further 3lb. (11/1)
835 Lake of Loughrea (IRE) made a mess of the first ditch and it could of been a lack of stamina which took him out of contention for the minor places. (13/8)

933 SCUDAMORE CLOTHING 0800 301301 NOVICES' CHASE (5-Y.O+) (Class E)

2-55 (2-55) **2m (12 fncs)** £3,305.40 (£929.40: £454.20) GOING minus 0.09 sec per fur (G)

		Dist	Pos	SP	RR	SF
	Sublime Fellow (IRE) (122) (NJHenderson) **6-10-12** MAFitzgerald (j.lft: led to 3rd: led 7th: clr appr 3 out: easily)	—	**1**	2/5[1]	102?	24
	Mead Court (IRE) (NoelChance) **6-10-12** RJohnson (led 3rd to 7th: hit 4 out: sn btn: fin distressed)	dist	**2**	9/4[2]	—	—
791[W]	**Bill of Rights** (MrsEBScott) **8-10-12** BPowell (nt j.w: lft poor 3rd 2nd: a t.o)	dist	**3**	50/1	—	—
636[3]	**Follow de Call** (DMcCain) **6-10-9**(3) DWalsh (3rd whn fell 2nd)		**F**	16/1[3]	—	—
				(SP 110.0%)		**4 Rn**

3m 57.6 (6.60) CSF £1.69 TOTE £1.50 (£1.50) OWNER Lady Annabel Goldsmith (LAMBOURN) BRED John Kent
OFFICIAL EXPLANATION **Mead Court (IRE): finished distressed.**
Sublime Fellow (IRE) had a simple task here, especially with his market rival finishing distressed. (2/5)
Mead Court (IRE) was reported by his trainer to have finished distressed. (9/4)

934 SANKEY VENDING NOVICES' HURDLE (4-Y.O+) (Class E)

3-25 (3-26) **3m 2f (13 hdls)** £2,276.00 (£636.00: £308.00) GOING minus 0.09 sec per fur (G)

		Dist	Pos	SP	RR	SF
812[7]	**Hunters Rock (IRE) (105)** (KCBailey) **7-10-12** CO'Dwyer (hld up: hdwy appr 9th: led last: pushed out)	—	**1**	7/4[1]	64+	4
	Copper Coil (77) (WGMTurner) **6-10-5**(7) JPower (bit bkwd: chsd ldr: led appr 2 out: hdd last: one pce)	2½	**2**	11/2	63	3
649*	**Mister Blake (75)** (RLee) **6-11-5** RJohnson (hld up: hdwy appr 9th: wknd appr 2 out)	11	**3**	5/1[3]	63	3
	Summer Haven (66) (NMLampard) **7-10-2**(5) ChrisWebb (led tl appr 2 out: wknd appr last)	1½	**4**	20/1	50	—
	Mayb-Mayb (68) (JNeville) **6-10-12** NWilliamson (hdwy appr 9th: mstke 10th: wknd 3 out)	15	**5**	9/2[2]	46	—
	Slight Panic (NMBabbage) **8-10-7** VSlattery (tk keen hold: bhd fr 10th)	9	**6**	12/1	35	—
	Milly le Moss (IRE) (RJEckley) **7-10-2**(5) MichaelBrennan (swtg: bit bkwd: tk keen hold: bhd whn mstke 10th: t.o)	dist	**7**	12/1	—	—
837[3]	**Ask Harry (IRE)** (RHAlner) **5-10-7**(5) PHenley (plld hrd: prom: rdn appr 3 out: 5th & btn whn fell 2 out)		**F**	14/1	—	—
				(SP 113.4%)		**8 Rn**

6m 20.4 (17.40) CSF £11.13 TOTE £2.50: £1.10 £1.10 £1.50 (£7.30) OWNER Mrs Harry Duffey (UPPER LAMBOURN) BRED M. V. Hough
812 Hunters Rock (IRE) found this a totally different ball game to Kempton's sharp two miles. (7/4)
Copper Coil ought to be able to win a similar event before things get too competitive. (11/2)
649* Mister Blake had to shoulder a penalty for beating the subsequently disappointing Lear Dancer at Worcester. (5/1)
Mayb-Mayb (9/2: 5/1-8/1)

935 FRIENDS OF ARTHUR ELLIOTT MEMORIAL NOVICES' H'CAP CHASE (0-100) (5-Y.O+) (Class E)

4-00 (4-00) **2m 3f (14 fncs)** £2,845.50 (£861.00: £420.00: £199.50) GOING minus 0.09 sec per fur (G)

		Dist	Pos	SP	RR	SF
870[4]	**Karlovac (65)** (RLee) **10-10-0** AMaguire (hld up: outpcd 9th: rallied to ld after 2 out: rdn & hung bdly lft flat: r.o)	—	**1**	7/2[2]	77	—
724[5]	**King's Shilling (USA) (84)** (HOliver) **9-11-5** JacquiOliver (hld up: hdwy 5th: led 8th: clr appr 3 out: blnd 2 out: sn hdd: nt rcvr)	7	**2**	4/1[3]	90	4
826[2]	**Ryton Run (89)** (MrsSMOdell) **11-11-10** BFenton (led to 2nd: led 3rd to 8th: rdn & wknd appr 3 out)	16	**3**	6/1	82	—
821[2]	**Martha's Daughter (83)** (CaptTAForster) **7-11-4** AThornton (hld up: hdwy 10th: rdn & wknd appr 3 out)	hd	**4**	10/11[1]	76	—
	Sungia (IRE) (65) (GraemeRoe) **7-10-0v**[1] WMarston (led 2nd to 3rd: 4th whn fell 9th)		**F**	50/1	—	—
				(SP 110.8%)		**5 Rn**

4m 43.7 (13.70) CSF £15.77 TOTE £4.80: £3.70 £2.90 (£11.40) OWNER Mr Richard Lee (PRESTEIGNE)
LONG HANDICAP Karlovac 9-9 Sungia (IRE) 9-9
Karlovac, 5lb out of the handicap, was supported in the Ring and the way he performed on the run-in suggests he would not have caught King's Shilling but for that rival's bad error two out. (7/2)
King's Shilling (USA) seemed in control when making a hash of the tricky second last. (4/1)
826 Ryton Run did not find forcing tactics paying dividends. (6/1: op 4/1)
821 Martha's Daughter was a very uneasy favourite in the face of the support for the winner. (10/11: 4/7-Evens)

936 FOWNHOPE H'CAP HURDLE (0-120) (4-Y.O+) (Class D)

4-35 (4-35) **2m 3f 110y (11 hdls)** £2,717.00 (£762.00: £371.00) GOING minus 0.09 sec per fur (G)

		Dist	Pos	SP	RR	SF
861*	**Born to Please (IRE) (95)** (PJHobbs) **4-10-11** 7x APMcCoy (w ldr: led appr 7th: clr appr 3 out: r.o wl)	—	**1**	3/1[2]	85	16
751[3]	**Corrin Hill (94)** (RJHodges) **9-10-8**(3) TDascombe (hld up: chsd wnr appr 3 out: no imp appr last)	8	**2**	3/1[2]	77	9
815*	**Chris's Glen (91)** (JMBradley) **7-10-8v** 7x NWilliamson (hld up: chsd wnr 7th tl wknd appr 3 out)	29	**3**	4/1[3]	51	—
	Lackendara (107) (MissHCKnight) **9-11-3**(7) MrAWintle (bit bkwd: plld hrd: led tl appr 7th: sn wknd: t.o)	21	**4**	5/1	49	—
815[2]	**Re Roi (IRE) (97)** (WGMTurner) **4-10-8**(5) PHenley (hld up: lost tch 7th: t.o whn p.u bef 3 out: b.b.v)		**P**	5/2[1]	—	—
				(SP 115.2%)		**5 Rn**

4m 40.6 (9.60) CSF £11.91 TOTE £3.80: £2.20 £1.10 (£5.30) OWNER A B S Racing (MINEHEAD) BRED Mrs S. O'Riordan
WEIGHT FOR AGE 4yo-1lb
861* Born to Please (IRE) had only been put up 2lb for his win a week ago, so that was 5lb more than the Handicapper would have given him. (3/1)

751 Corrin Hill, dropped 2lb, was not closing the gap going to the final flight. (3/1)
815* Chris's Glen, forced to carry a 7lb penalty, had only been raised 4lb for his Fontwell win by the Handicapper. (4/1)
Lackendara (5/1: op 5/2)
815 Re Roi (IRE) was reported by his trainer to have bled from the nose. (5/2)

T/Plpt: £58.10 (129.53 Tckts). T/Qdpt: £16.20 (22.4 Tckts). KH

0801-**KELSO (L-H) (Firm, Good to firm patches)**
Saturday October 19th
WEATHER: fine WIND: str

937 EDINBURGH CITY FOOTBALL CLUB NOVICES' AMATEUR HURDLE (4-Y.O+) (Class E)
2-00 (2-00) **2m 6f 110y (11 hdls)** £2,178.00 (£608.00: £294.00) GOING minus 0.49 sec per fur (GF)

				SP	RR	SF
	Ilengar (IRE) (MrsJDGoodfellow) **7-11-2**(5) MrRHale (led 2nd: cl up: styd on to ld after last)	—	1	100/30 2	57	13
	Teacher (IRE) (RAllan) **6-11-0**(7) MrARobson (plld hrd: trckd ldrs: led 8th: hit 2 out: hdd after last: one pce)	3½	2	6/1	55	11
	Side of Hill (BMactaggart) **11-11-0**(7) MissPRobson (led 2nd to 8th: one pce fr 3 out)	18	3	7/4 1	42	—
	Wee Tam (LLungo) **7-11-2**(5) MrMHNaughton (w ldrs: hit 2nd: ev ch appr 3 out: hit next: wandered & wknd between last 2)	3½	4	9/2 3	39	—
801 6	**Walk In The Wild** (DANolan) **4-11-5**(7)ow12 MissSCassels (lw: s.s: a bhd: t.o)	24	5	66/1	28	—
	Overwhelm (IRE) (VThompson) **8-11-4b1**(3) MrMThompson (in tch: reminders 5th: bhd fr 7th)	dist	6	33/1	—	—
686 6	**Grace And Favour** (MrsNHope) **5-10-11**(7)ow2 MrAParker (lost pl 4th: bhd fr ½-wy: t.o whn p.u bef 3 out)		P	12/1	—	—
				(SP 104.0%)		**7 Rn**

5m 23.0 (6.00) CSF £19.49 TOTE £4.90: £2.30 £2.00 (£21.10) OWNER Mr J. D. Goodfellow (EARLSTON) BRED John F. Carmody
WEIGHT FOR AGE 4yo-1lb
Ilengar (IRE), a winning ex-Irish pointer, made this first appearance in this country a successful one. His stamina came into play on this occasion, and his future looks to be over fences. (100/30)
Teacher (IRE) drifted dramatically in the Ring but he actually defied those signals when looking all over the winner until getting outstayed on the run-in. (6/1: op 7/4)
Side of Hill has never won over hurdles, but this pipe-opener will have put him spot on for another campaign over fences. (7/4)

938 RANK HOVIS MILLERS ROTHBURY HOME BAKERY NOVICES' CHASE (5-Y.O+) (Class E)
2-30 (2-30) **3m 1f (19 fncs)** £2,762.00 (£836.00: £408.00: £194.00) GOING minus 0.49 sec per fur (GF)

				SP	RR	SF
802*	**Tighter Budget (USA) (100)** (MrsHDSayer) **9-11-13** MMoloney (lw: mde all: clr 3 out: comf)	—	1	4/7 1	107+	35
	Woodford Gale (IRE) (103) (MissLucindaRussell) **6-10-13** AThornton (chsd wnr thrght: rdn & one pce fr 3 out)	18	2	4/1 2	82	10
529 3	**White Diamond (79)** (MissLucindaRussell) **8-10-13v** MFoster (chsd ldng pair: rdn 4 out: sn outpcd)	2½	3	6/1 3	80	8
802 4	**Bright Destiny (60)** (JSGoldie) **5-10-10** DParker (bhd fr 12th)	17	4	16/1	69	—
853 2	**Calder's Grove** (MissLAPerratt) **6-10-10**(3) GCahill (n.d)	s.h	5	10/1	69	—
704 3	**Kincardine Bridge (USA)** (MrsSCBradburne) **7-10-6**(7) MrMBradburne (bhd fr 12th: t.o whn fell 4 out)		F	50/1	—	—
				(SP 114.9%)		**6 Rn**

6m 11.7 (1.70) CSF £3.51 TOTE £1.70: £1.10 £2.30 (£3.90) OWNER Mrs Dianne Sayer (PENRITH) BRED Walter Haefner
WEIGHT FOR AGE 5yo-3lb
802* Tighter Budget (USA) completed his early season hat-trick with consummate ease, by an aggregate of over sixty lengths. The last time he went chasing a couple of years ago he failed to get round in three attempts, but he is in fine fettle at the minute, and may now have a short break before coming back here in mid-November. (4/7)
Woodford Gale (IRE) had some fair form in the early part of last season and looks as though a race can be found soon, especially with a bit more ease in the ground. (4/1)
529 White Diamond, who ran in a tongue-strap, looks to have a questionable temperament and his stablemate Woodford Gale looks to be the better future prospect. (6/1)

939 WEATHERBYS INFORMATION TECHNOLOGY NOVICES' HURDLE (4-Y.O+) (Class E)
3-05 (3-06) **2m 110y (8 hdls)** £2,402.00 (£672.00: £326.00) GOING minus 0.49 sec per fur (GF)

				SP	RR	SF
337 4	**Marble Man (IRE) (91)** (MDHammond) **6-10-12** DBentley (lw: a.p: hit 5th: led flat: rdn & styd on wl)	—	1	2/1 1	73	—
	Adamatic (IRE) (95) (RAllan) **5-10-12**(7) SMelrose (hld up: hdwy 5th: led appr last: rdr lost whip & hdd flat: kpt on)	¾	2	11/4 2	79	4
854 4	**Amber Holly (65)** (JEDixon) **7-10-7** FPerratt (chsd ldrs: rdn & hit last: kpt on)	2½	3	14/1	65	—
743 6	**Flyaway Blues** (MrsMReveley) **4-10-11** PNiven (hld up: hdwy 3 out: r.o one pce fr last)	½	4	5/1 3	69	—
643 4	**Trumped (IRE)** (PMonteith) **4-10-6** ADobbin (hdwy 5th: rdn 2 out: no ex)	¾	5	7/1	64	—
	Victor Laszlo (RAllan) **4-10-11** BStorey (hdwy appr 3 out: sn rdn & no imp)	7	6	20/1	62	—
801 4	**I'm The Man** (MrsESlack) **5-10-12** KJohnson (prom: rdn 3 out: sn btn)	2	7	8/1	60	—
	Forbes (IRE) (HowardJohnson) **5-10-12** NWilliamson (bhd: hdwy 3 out: sn rdn & wknd)	hd	8	20/1	60	—
	Persuasive Talent (IRE) (DALamb) **5-10-12** JBurke (led 1st: rdn 3 out: hdd appr last: sn wknd)	10	9	100/1	50	—
	Lumback Lady (BMactaggart) **6-10-4**(3) GLee (w ldrs tl wknd 3 out)	6	10	50/1	39	—
	Backhander (IRE) (MartynWane) **4-10-8**(3) GCahill (a bhd)	½	11	33/1	44	—
	Crockalawn (IRE) (VThompson) **8-10-12** MrMThompson (chsd ldrs: rdn & wknd qckly appr 2 out)	17	12	200/1	27	—
705 9	**Super Guy** (JBarclay) **4-10-11** AThomton (blnd 1st: prom tl wknd 5th: t.o)	9	13	33/1	19	—
858 6	**The Knitter** (JJBirkett) **4-10-11** MMoloney (a rr: t.o)	2	14	200/1	17	—
				(SP 126.3%)		**14 Rn**

3m 51.6 (5.60) CSF £8.08 TOTE £3.00: £1.80 £1.60 £7.10 (£3.40) Trio £27.70 OWNER Mr D. J. Lever (MIDDLEHAM) BRED E. Farrell
WEIGHT FOR AGE 4yo-1lb
337 Marble Man (IRE) travelled well throughout and got the upper hand on the run-in. He looks a chaser in the making. (2/1)
Adamatic (IRE) tracked the leaders going well and jumped ahead coming into the last. It would have been a lot closer had his young rider not dropped his stick halfway up the run-in. (11/4)
854 Amber Holly was never far away and kicked on in the style that suggests he could be picking up a similar event in the not-too-distant future. (14/1)

Flyaway Blues again ran an encouraging race. Having come from out the back, he too should be kept in mind for the future. (5/1)
643 Trumped (IRE) is not quite producing the goods after a successful campaign on the Flat. It may pay to watch him until he shows better. (7/1)
Victor Laszlo came up into the proceedings from three out, and this first outing over hurdles will have done him the world of good. (20/1)
Forbes (IRE) looks one for the future. He came to the end of his tether at the last, but the way he was tenderly handled up until then suggests he should be kept in mind for later on. (20/1)

940 GREENMANTLE ALE ANTHONY & JOHNNIE MARSHALL TROPHY H'CAP CHASE (0-125) (5-Y.O+) (Class D)
3-40 (3-40) **3m 1f (19 fncs)** £4,255.00 (£1,045.00) GOING minus 0.49 sec per fur (GF)

				SP	RR	SF
809^{4}	**Bas de Laine (FR) (111)** (MDHammond) **10-11-2b** PNiven (mde all: lft clr 4 out: hit next: comf)	—	1	$7/2^{3}$	120	52
2^{4}	**Rocket Run (IRE) (107)** (MissLucindaRussell) **8-10-12** AThornton (chsd wnr tl hit 10th: lft 2nd 4 out: no imp on wnr)	dist	2	$6/4^{1}$	—	—
	Over the Deel (119) (HowardJohnson) **10-11-10** NWilliamson (hld up: hdwy to chse wnr fr 10th: 4l 2nd whn fell 4 out)		F	$3/1^{2}$	—	—
804^{2}	**Off The Bru (95)** (MrsSCBradburne) **11-10-0** BStorey (prom whn blnd & uns rdr 13th)		U	$7/2^{3}$	—	—
				(SP 109.4%)		**4 Rn**

6m 2.0 (3.30 under best) (-8.00) CSF £8.65 TOTE £3.90 (£2.80) OWNER R K Bids Ltd (MIDDLEHAM) BRED Pascal Couturier
LONG HANDICAP Off The Bru 9-6
809 Bas de Laine (FR) has clearly had training problems through the years and struck here on just his second outing for his new trainer. The change of scenery has obviously rekindled his enthusiasm. (7/2)
2 Rocket Run (IRE), most disappointing on his seasonal reappearance back in June, again failed to sparkle here. However, many of his trainer's horses have needed an outing or two to bring them to the fore, and he should not be discarded just yet. (6/4)
Over the Deel, who has completed the course over the big Aintree fences successfully four times, was four lengths behind the winner and still to be asked a serious question when he crashed out of contention. (3/1)

941 EXTRORDINAIR H'CAP HURDLE (0-115) (4-Y.O+) (Class E)
4-10 (4-11) **2m 110y (8 hdls)** £2,206.00 (£616.00: £298.00) GOING minus 0.49 sec per fur (GF)

				SP	RR	SF
	Tom Brodie (111) (HowardJohnson) **6-12-0** NWilliamson (hld up gng wl: smooth hdwy 3 out: led last: drvn out)	—	1	$9/2^{3}$	94	46
856^{2}	**Nonios (IRE) (97)** (GMMoore) **5-11-0v** NBentley (cl up: chal 2 out: kpt on u.p flat)	1½	2	$3/1^{2}$	79	31
745^{3}	**Eden Dancer (106)** (MrsMReveley) **4-11-8** PNiven (lw: mde most: rn wd paddock bnd appr 4th: hdd last: rallied flat: styd on)	2½	3	$3/1^{2}$	85	36
806^{3}	**Vain Prince (99)** (NTinkler) **9-11-2b** AThornton (chsd ldrs: rdn & one pce fr 2 out)	nk	4	11/2	78	30
745^{2}	**Field of Vision (IRE) (100)** (MrsASwinbank) **6-11-3b** JSupple (cl up: lft in ld briefly appr 4th: tried to ref 4th: sn bhd)	½	5	$5/2^{1}$	78	30
				(SP 112.1%)		**5 Rn**

3m 44.1 (-1.90) CSF £16.91 TOTE £6.00: £2.60 £1.40 (£6.90) OWNER Mrs M. W. Bird (CROOK) BRED E.S Knape
WEIGHT FOR AGE 4yo-1lb
OFFICIAL EXPLANATION **Field of Vision (IRE): would not face the first-time blinkers.**
Tom Brodie, looking as though the race would put an edge on him, travelled supremely well throughout but, in the end, had to be driven out to make sure of it. Some improvement can be expected from this. (9/2)
856 Nonios (IRE), equipped with the visor for the first time, had every chance on the run-in, but just failed to put his best foot forward when it mattered. (3/1)
745 Eden Dancer cut out the donkey-work and, although rallying in the closing stages, was always destined for minor honours. (3/1)
745 Field of Vision (IRE), an obvious contender on form, was a major disappointment. His trainer later informed the Stewards that the gelding would not face the blinds which where on for the first time. (5/2)

942 W & T HARKIN H'CAP HURDLE (0-120) (4-Y.O+) (Class D)
4-40 (4-40) **2m 6f 110y (11 hdls)** £2,528.00 (£708.00: £344.00) GOING minus 0.49 sec per fur (GF)

				SP	RR	SF
695^{6}	**Nicholas Plant (92)** (JSGoldie) **7-11-7**(3) GLee (chsd ldr: led 4 out: rdn & styd on wl fr 2 out: eased nr fin)	—	1	$7/2^{2}$	83	40
854*	**Jonaem (IRE) (83)** (MrsESlack) **6-11-1** KJohnson (lw: trckd ldrs: reminders & hit 4 out: ev ch next: one pce u.p)	5	2	$13/8^{1}$	70	27
878^{2}	**Crofton Lake (68)** (JEDixon) **8-10-0** BStorey (in tch: mstke & outpcd 7th: n.d after)	13	3	11/2	46	3
734^{6}	**Frontier Flight (USA) (89)** (MissLCSiddall) **6-11-7** ADobbin (hld up: hdwy 6th: rdn & one pce fr 2 out)	1¼	4	5/1	66	23
868^{4}	**Royal Circus (89)** (PWHiatt) **7-11-4**(3) EHusband (led: rdn 7th: hdd next: sn wknd)	20	5	$4/1^{3}$	52	9
				(SP 112.4%)		**5 Rn**

5m 15.3 (-1.70) CSF £9.40 TOTE £4.70: £1.80 £1.30 (£4.00) OWNER Mrs M. F. Paterson (GLASGOW) BRED Mrs J. A. Armstrong
LONG HANDICAP Crofton Lake 9-9
6 Nicholas Plant gets every yard of this trip and, in the end, it was his stamina that saw him pull well clear from the second last. (7/2: op 9/4)
854* Jonaem (IRE), turned out looking well after his recent success, was under pressure at halfway and did not get the trip as well as the winner. (13/8: op 5/2)
878 Crofton Lake looks a chaser in the making and was doing all his best work at the finish, but lacked toe. (11/2)
690 Frontier Flight (USA) (5/1: op 3/1)
868 Royal Circus was again a disappointment for his supporters, and seems to be a little below-par at the moment and can be discounted until he shows some signs of a form revival. (4/1)

T/Plpt: £120.20 (44.81 Tckts). T/Qdpt: £206.50 (6.32 Tckts). GB

0807-KEMPTON (R-H) (Chases Good, Good to firm patches, Hdles Good to firm)
Saturday October 19th

943 FERRY BOAT H'CAP CHASE (0-145) (5-Y.O+) (Class B)
2-15 (2-15) **2m (13 fncs)** £4,351.00 (£1,318.00: £644.00: £307.00) GOING minus 0.09 sec per fur (G)

				SP	RR	SF
811^{2}	**Super Tactics (IRE) (117)** (RHAlner) **8-9-9**(5) PHenley (swtg: hld up: chsd ldr fr 7th: led 2 out: comf)	—	1	$4/1^{3}$	127+	20

	Horse	Dist	Pos	SP	RR	SF
	Clay County (145) (MDHammond) **11-12-0** RGarritty (lw: led to 2 out: unable qckn)	10	**2**	13/8 [2]	145	38
811[F]	**Captain Khedive (130)** (PFNicholls) **8-10-13** APMcCoy (lw: mstke & lost pl 4th: rdn fr 6th: rallied 9th: wknd appr 3 out)	22	**3**	6/5 [1]	108	1
	Lasata (117) (RMCarson) **11-10-0** DMorris (bit bkwd: plld hrd: blundered 1st: chsd ldr 3rd to 7th: sn wknd: wl bhd whn mstke 9th: t.o)	dist	**4**	25/1	—	—
				(SP 107.4%)	**4 Rn**	

3m 48.7 (0.60 under best) (4.70) CSF £10.01 TOTE £3.50 (£3.60) OWNER Mr H. V. Perry (BLANDFORD) BRED James Robinson
LONG HANDICAP Super Tactics (IRE) 9-13 Lasata 9-4
811 Super Tactics (IRE), 7lb higher than he has ever won off, smashed the two-year-old course-record by just over half a second. (4/1: op 5/2)
Clay County looked in good shape for this first run of the season and bowled along in front until put in his place by the winner form the second last. A grand servant over the years, this two-mile specialist should soon open his account for the campaign. (13/8)
811 Captain Khedive looked extremely well beforehand, but was slightly messed about by another rival on the stable bend setting out on the final circuit and, from that point, was never travelling or co-operating, despite McCoy's efforts. This was a blot on his copybook. (6/5: 4/5-5/4)

944 RIVERDALE HURDLE (3-Y.O) (Class D)

2-50 (2-51) **2m** **(8 hdls)** £2,915.00 (£815.00: £395.00) GOING minus 0.09 sec per fur (G)

	Horse	Dist	Pos	SP	RR	SF
	Classic Defence (IRE) (JWHills) **3-10-12** JOsborne (lw: led to 5th: led 3 out: clr appr 2 out: mstke last: comf)	—	**1**	3/1 [1]	72+	10
	A Chef Too Far (RRowe) **3-10-9**(3) LAspell (hdwy to chse wnr appr 2 out: no imp)	6	**2**	9/2 [3]	66	4
	Squire's Occasion (CAN) (RAkehurst) **3-10-12** APMcCoy (hld up: rdn appr 2 out: one pce)	5	**3**	7/2 [2]	61	—
	Typhoon Lad (SDow) **3-10-12** ADicken (lw: plld hrd: rdn flat: nvr plcd to chal)	s.h	**4**	12/1	61+	—
	Sunley Secure (NoelChance) **3-10-12** RJohnson (hld up: rdn 5th: wknd flat)	2½	**5**	7/1	58	—
699*	**Tarry** (AStreeter) **3-10-12** GBradley (a.p: led 5th to 3 out: rdn appr 2 out: sn wknd)	s.h	**6**	6/1	58	—
807[5]	**Soldier Blue** (PJHobbs) **3-10-7**(5) DJKavanagh (lw: chsd wnr to 5th: wknd 3 out)	21	**7**	40/1	37	—
	Premier Generation (IRE) (DWPArbuthnot) **3-10-12** RDunwoody (hdwy 4th: wknd appr 2 out)	1¼	**8**	7/1	36	—
				(SP 114.8%)	**8 Rn**	

3m 51.4 (9.40) CSF £15.98 TOTE £3.90: £1.40 £1.80 £1.70 (£8.00) Trio £7.60 OWNER Mr J. W. Robb (LAMBOURN) BRED James Hennessy
OFFICIAL EXPLANATION **Typhoon Lad: pulls hard and has to be settled, and was only able to run on past beaten horses.**
Classic Defence (IRE), winner of two races on the Flat this year, made a highly-pleasing debut over timber and won doing handsprings. He can go in again. (3/1)
A Chef Too Far, winner of a maiden on the Flat in the mud at Newbury back in May, raced with his tongue tied down. With some easing in the ground, he should find a race. (9/2)
Squire's Occasion (CAN), an ex-Irish gelding, comes from a stable that excels with this type of horse. (7/2: 9/4-4/1)
Typhoon Lad caught the eye on this hurdling debut. Taking a very keen hold in the early part of the race, he was in behind the leaders turning for home, but his jockey still sat very quietly and only rousted him along from the last, just failing to take third prize. Once he learns to settle, considerable improvement can be expected. (12/1: op 8/1)
Sunley Secure won two of his thirteen races on the Flat for Mick Channon this year. (7/1: 4/1-15/2)
699* Tarry is extremely small for this game and had given her all two from home. (6/1)
Premier Generation (IRE) (7/1: op 7/2)

945 CAPTAIN QUIST HURDLE (4-Y.O+) (Class B)

3-20 (3-20) **2m** **(8 hdls)** £4,765.25 (£1,442.00: £703.50: £334.25) GOING minus 0.09 sec per fur (G)

	Horse	Dist	Pos	SP	RR	SF
	Chief's Song (138) (SDow) **6-11-8** RDunwoody (mde all: drvn out)	—	**1**	7/2 [3]	120	56
	Warm Spell (135) (GLMoore) **6-11-8** APMcCoy (lw: hld up: rdn 3 out: r.o one pce fr 2 out)	1	**2**	3/1 [1]	119	55
	Home Counties (IRE) (147) (DMoffatt) **7-11-8** DJMoffatt (hdwy appr 2 out: hrd rdn appr last: r.o one pce)	nk	**3**	3/1 [1]	119	55
790[P]	**Our Kris (132)** (NJHenderson) **4-10-13v** MAFitzgerald (chsd wnr: ev ch 2 out: wknd appr last)	14	**4**	100/30 [2]	97	32
	Cumbrian Challenge (IRE) (139) (TDEasterby) **7-11-5** RGarritty (bit bkwd: hld up: rdn appr 2 out: wknd)	22	**5**	5/1	80	16
				(SP 112.0%)	**5 Rn**	

3m 43.3 (1.30) CSF £13.34 TOTE £3.20: £1.60 £1.60 (£3.90) OWNER Mrs Anne Devine (EPSOM) BRED Chrishall Grange Stud Co Ltd
WEIGHT FOR AGE 4yo-1lb
Chief's Song, who lost his way in the second half of last season, was tailed off on the Flat in August, but his trainer reported him in good order and said he would be very disappointed if the gelding did not finish in the first two. He was not let down, and this can only have done Chief's Song the world of good. (7/2: 5/2-4/1)
Warm Spell, officially worst in, hinted at a return to form when fourth in an amateur riders' event on the Flat at Ascot last week, but he does not do things very fast. At his best at this time of the year with some cut in the ground, he can find a race if the rain comes. (3/1: op 2/1)
Home Counties (IRE) was fit from the Flat and stayed on in the straight, only just losing out for second prize. (3/1)
Our Kris raced in second and looked a real danger to the winner two out. However, he stopped as if shot going to the final flight. (100/30)
Cumbrian Challenge (IRE), who went novice chasing last season with plenty of success, was reverting to the minor obstacles for this return but did not look fully fit. (5/1)

946 CHARISMA GOLD CUP H'CAP CHASE (0-150) (5-Y.O+) (Class B)

3-55 (3-55) **3m** **(19 fncs)** £10,260.00 (£3,105.00: £1,515.00: £720.00) GOING minus 0.09 sec per fur (G)

	Horse	Dist	Pos	SP	RR	SF
789*	**General Crack (IRE) (128)** (PFNicholls) **7-11-2** APMcCoy (j.lft: hld up: chsd ldr fr 10th: led 13th to last: led flat: drvn out)	—	**1**	8/11 [1]	135	68
799*	**Bertone (IRE) (130)** (KCBailey) **7-11-4** CO'Dwyer (stdy hdwy 13th: led last tl flat: unable qckn)	1¾	**2**	7/2 [2]	136	69
390*	**Alqairawaan (112)** (CJMann) **7-10-0** CLlewellyn (led: mstke 12th: hdd 13th: mstke 4 out: ev ch appr last: r.o flat)	nk	**3**	8/1 [3]	118	51
	Bavard Dieu (IRE) (140) (NAGaselee) **8-12-0** RDunwoody (bhd fr 14th: t.o)	dist	**4**	8/1 [3]	—	—
	Nevada Gold (112) (FJYardley) **10-10-0** PMcLoughlin (lw: bhd fr 9th: t.o fr 12th)	9	**5**	33/1	—	—
	Sir Peter Lely (130) (MDHammond) **9-11-1b**(3) MrCBonner (bit bkwd: chsd ldr to 10th: wknd 12th: t.o)	6	**6**	16/1	—	—
804*	**Royal Vacation (112)** (GMMoore) **7-10-0** JCallaghan (lw: a bhd: mstke 11th: t.o fr 12th: p.u bef 4 out)		**P**	12/1	—	—
				(SP 118.9%)	**7 Rn**	

5m 51.6 (-3.40) CSF £4.06 TOTE £1.60: £1.50 £2.50 (£3.00) OWNER Mr J A Keighley and Mr Paul K Barber (SHEPTON MALLET) BRED Thomas Smyth
LONG HANDICAP Nevada Gold 9-2 Alqairawaan 9-12 Royal Vacation 9-13

789* General Crack (IRE), who suffers from stringhalt in his near-hind leg, was not at all suited by this sharp right-handed track, and his trainer confessed afterwards that he had been worried all week long. Jumping left at several of his fences, most notably the third last, he just got back up in a driving finish. He will be much happier back on a galloping left-handed track, and can extend his winning sequence, despite a rise of 27lb since his first handicap chase success back at Wincanton in May. (8/11)
799* Bertone (IRE) was facing much stiffer opposition, but lost absolutely nothing in defeat. A return to winning ways can be expected in the near future. (7/2)
390* Alqairawaan, winner of four of his six races over hurdles two seasons ago, may have been having only his second ever run over fences, but he ran an absolute blinder against experienced rivals, despite hurdling some of the obstacles. He looks set for a successful campaign over fences and can certainly land his share of novice events. (8/1)
Bavard Dieu (IRE) is high in the handicap after two wins in the spring. (8/1: 5/1-9/1)
804* Royal Vacation (12/1: 6/1-14/1)

947 THAMES NOVICES' CHASE (5-Y.O+) (Class D)

4-30 (4-30) **2m (13 fncs)** £3,685.00 (£1,035.00: £505.00) GOING minus 0.09 sec per fur (G)

				SP	RR	SF
	Land Afar (PRWebber) **9-11-0** MDwyer (hld up: led 3 out: shkn up appr last: easily)	—	1	13/8^{1}	117+	15
	Amancio (USA) (GHarwood) **5-10-13** RDunwoody (bkwd: chsd ldr: ev ch 3 out: unable qckn fr 2 out)	5	2	11/4^{3}	112	9
808^{2}	**Greenback (BEL)** (PJHobbs) **5-10-13** CLlewellyn (led tl hdd & mstke 3 out: sn wknd)	12	3	5/2^{2}	100	—
	Wilde Music (IRE) (CPEBrooks) **6-11-0** GBradley (bit bkwd: nvr plcd to chal)	1¼	4	11/1	99	—
	Ice Magic (69) (FJYardley) **9-11-0v** PMcLoughlin (bit bkwd: 4th whn mstke 8th: sn wknd)	12	5	50/1	87	—
	Nordansk (MMadgwick) **7-11-0** BFenton (lw: 4th whn blnd bdly 9th: nt rcvr)	8	6	11/1	79	—
				(SP 112.0%)		**6 Rn**

3m 52.8 (8.80) CSF £6.29 TOTE £2.30: £1.70 £1.70 (£4.40) OWNER Mr T. J. Ford (BANBURY) BRED Grange Stud (UK)
WEIGHT FOR AGE 5yo-1lb
Land Afar, a smart hurdler who did not win as often as one would have thought for a horse of his ability, was let down by his jumping on several occasions, most notably in two Champion Hurdles, but he made the perfect start to his chasing career, on this seasonal debut and did not put a foot wrong. This will of done his confidence no end of good and he can now go on from here. (13/8)
Amancio (USA), winner of last season's Imperial Cup at Sandown, looked far from fit but still gave a really good account of himself on this chasing debut, despite rather ballooning some of his fences. He should not be difficult to win with. (11/4)
808 Greenback (BEL) did not jump as fluently as he did here two weeks ago, but took them along until calling it a day from the third last. (5/2)
Wilde Music (IRE) was given a nice educational ride on this chasing debut, with his jockey doing little more than nursing him around. Sure to strip a lot fitter for this, no doubt the kindness will be repaid in due course. (11/1: 6/1-12/1)
Nordansk, first past the post on two occasions on the Flat this year, looked in good shape and had just moved up a couple of places when all but falling five out. (11/1: 6/1-12/1)

948 PARK H'CAP HURDLE (0-150) (4-Y.O+) (Class B)

5-00 (5-00) **2m 5f (10 hdls)** £4,697.00 (£1,421.00: £693.00: £329.00) GOING minus 0.09 sec per fur (G)

				SP	RR	SF
	Fired Earth (IRE) (123) (JRFanshawe) **8-10-11** JOsborne (bit bkwd: chsd ldr to 2nd: lost pl 4th: rallied 7th: chsd ldr fr 3 out: led on bit appr last: r.o wl)	—	1	6/1	106+	25
796^{2}	**Call My Guest (IRE) (123)** (REPeacock) **6-10-11** APMcCoy (chsd ldr 2nd to 4th: led 7th tl appr last: unable qckn)	10	2	15/8^{1}	98	17
	Givus a Call (IRE) (113) (JTGifford) **6-9-12**(3)ow1 LAspell (hld up: hmpd 3 out: sn wknd)	8	3	12/1	82	—
	Barna Boy (IRE) (137) (NJHenderson) **8-11-11** MAFitzgerald (plld hrd: chsd ldrs fr 4th: led 5th to 7th: sn wknd: t.o)	dist	4	9/4^{2}	—	—
	Hops and Pops (140) (RHAlner) **9-11-9**(5) PHenley (swtg: bit bkwd: led to 5th: 3rd & btn whn fell 3 out)		F	3/1^{3}	—	—
				(SP 112.5%)		**5 Rn**

4m 59.5 (7.50) CSF £16.99 TOTE £6.10: £1.70 £1.30 (£6.80) OWNER Mrs J. Fanshawe (NEWMARKET) BRED J. Mamakos in Ireland
LONG HANDICAP Givus a Call (IRE) 9-5
Fired Earth (IRE) may not have looked fully wound up for this reappearance, but that did not stop him toying with the opposition. Absolutely swinging off the bridle in the last half-mile, he was only allowed to go on approaching the last and quickly had the race sewn up on the run-in. (6/1: op 4/1)
796 Call My Guest (IRE) has been steadily coming down the handicap but was easily brushed aside on the run-in. (15/8)
Givus a Call (IRE), who failed to complete in four outings last season, got round on this reappearance but was left for dead from the third last, having been slightly hampered by the faller. (12/1: 8/1-14/1)
Barna Boy (IRE) pulled far too hard for his own good and, after showing in front in the middle part of the race, was a spent force early in the back straight. (9/4)
Hops and Pops, with something left to work on, bowled along in front to halfway, but appeared held in third place, although her jockey had not got serious on her, when falling three out. (3/1: 2/1-100/30)
T/Plpt: £71.70 (150.33 Tckts). T/Qdpt: £10.40 (54.03 Tckts). AK

0587-STRATFORD-ON-AVON (L-H) (Good, Good to firm patches)
Saturday October 19th

WEATHER: overcast, drizzle race 4 onwards

949 SHOTTERY MEADOW LADIES' H'CAP HURDLE (0-100) (4-Y.O+) (Class F)

2-25 (2-25) **2m 110y (9 hdls)** £2,444.00 (£684.00: £332.00) GOING minus 0.11 sec per fur (G)

				SP	RR	SF
	Simone's Son (IRE) (80) (GBarnett) **8-10-8b** JacquiOliver (bit bkwd: chsd ldrs: led appr 3 out: sn qcknd clr: r.o flat)	—	1	10/1	60	6
793^{2}	**Pair of Jacks (IRE) (87)** (GLMoore) **6-10-10**(5) MissPJones (hld up: hdwy appr 3 out: r.o wl appr last: nt rch wnr)	1¼	2	13/8^{1}	66	12
916^{2}	**Zingibar (78)** (JMBradley) **4-9-12**(7) MissPGundry (prom tl lost pl 5th: r.o again fr 3 out)	1¾	3	7/2^{2}	55	—
	Weeheby (USA) (96) (MFBarraclough) **7-11-10** AnnStokell (chsd ldrs: ev ch appr 3 out: sn outpcd)	11	4	11/2	62	8
862^{4}	**Fierce (89)** (JRJenkins) **8-11-3** LeesaLong (prom: led 5th tl appr 3 out: sn wknd)	½	5	12/1	55	1
	San Diego Charger (IRE) (84) (ABarrow) **5-10-12** SophieMitchell (lw: hld up: slipped after 4th: effrt 3 out: nvr trbld ldrs)	s.h	6	4/1^{3}	50	—

				SP	RR	SF
93[P]	**Quick Decision (IRE) (72)** (JKCresswell) **5-9-7**(7) MissEJJones (led: hit 2nd & 4th: hdd next: wkng whn blnd 3 out)	29	**7**	50/1	10	—
				(SP 114.4%)	**7 Rn**	

3m 56.3 (9.30) CSF £26.01 CT £63.96 TOTE £11.70: £2.50 £1.60 (£9.50) OWNER Mr George Barnett (STOKE-ON-TRENT) BRED B. J. Kruger
LONG HANDICAP Quick Decision (IRE) 8-10
WEIGHT FOR AGE 4yo-1lb
Simone's Son (IRE), brought back out of retirement by connections because he looked well in himself, did look less than fully race-fit. Given a terrific chance by some lenient handicapping, he was travelling much the best some way from home, although he did tie up near the end. He can win again. (10/1)
793 Pair of Jacks (IRE) seemed to be set plenty to do and was in no position to respond when the winner kicked for home. (13/8)
916 Zingibar appeared to lose his action turning into the back straight for the final time, losing plenty of ground. It was something of a surprise therefore to see him stay on so well in the straight. (7/2)
Weeheby (USA) had the benefit of a prep-run on the level, but was easily brushed aside in the last half-mile. (11/2)
San Diego Charger (IRE) slipped going out on the final circuit and was never travelling thereafter. He looked reasonably fit here, but normally takes a couple of runs to come to hand. (4/1)

950 RICHARDSONS (S) HURDLE (4,5,6 & 7-Y.O) (Class G)
2-55 (2-59) **2m 110y (9 hdls)** £2,556.00 (£716.00: £348.00) GOING minus 0.11 sec per fur (G)

				SP	RR	SF
156[3]	**Pickens (USA) (89)** (NTinkler) **4-10-11** LWyer (blnd 1st: chsd ldrs: lft clr 2 out: rdn out)	—	**1**	3/1[1]	69	11
731*	**Shuttlecock** (MrsNMacauley) **5-11-5** AMaguire (led tl appr 3 out: lft 2nd 2 out: one pce)	7	**2**	3/1[1]	69	12
	Ranger Sloane (AStreeter) **4-10-11** RFarrant (hdwy 6th: hit last: r.o)	1¼	**3**	20/1	61	3
	Griffin's Girl (PMooney) **4-10-1**(5) SRyan (hdwy 6th: one pce appr last)	2½	**4**	50/1	54	—
600[2]	**Twice the Groom (IRE) (87)** (RLee) **6-11-5b** LHarvey (hdwy 5th: wknd appr 2 out)	2½	**5**	9/2[2]	63	6
401[2]	**Misty View (70)** (JWhite) **7-10-7** JRKavanagh (hld up: hdwy 4th: no imp fr 3 out)	5	**6**	10/1	46	—
794[8]	**Timely Example (USA) (67)** (BRCambidge) **5-10-12b** GaryLyons (in tch: r.o strly appr last: nvr plcd to chal)	3½	**7**	10/1	48	—
	Dashing Dancer (IRE) (ALForbes) **5-10-12** TEley (w ldr tl wknd appr 3 out)	3½	**8**	20/1	45	—
825[5]	**Awestruck (46)** (BPreece) **6-10-9b**(3) GHogan (nvr nr to chal)	10	**9**	50/1	35	—
788[F]	**Pytchley Dawn** (OO'Neill) **6-10-7** VSlattery (nt j.w: nvr nr to chal)	6	**10**	20/1	24	—
	Theydon Pride (66) (KFClutterbuck) **7-10-9**(3) DWalsh (prom to 5th)	¾	**11**	33/1	28	—
744[6]	**Shalik (IRE) (65)** (JRJenkins) **6-10-12**(7) NTEgan (prom tl wknd after 5th)	7	**12**	20/1	29	—
655[P]	**Sandro (51)** (MissLBower) **7-11-12b**(7) MClinton (bhd fr 6th)	13	**13**	50/1	30	—
	Monkey's Wedding (HMKavanagh) **5-10-12** SFox (hld up: blnd 4th: a bhd)	19	**14**	66/1	—	—
687[8]	**Hatta River (USA) (61)** (PTDalton) **6-10-12** WMarston (lw: prom to 5th: sn rdn & bhd)	¾	**15**	33/1	—	—
826[W]	**Chapel of Barras (IRE)** (BGee) **7-11-12** MrPGee (bit bkwd: hit 3rd: fell next)		**F**	20/1	—	—
262[3]	**Sorisky** (BGubby) **4-10-11** RichardGuest (swtg: hdwy 5th: led appr 3 out: clr whn fell 2 out)		**F**	15/2[3]	70+	—
	Rub Al Khali (AStreeter) **5-10-12** TJMurphy (bit bkwd: in tch tl fell 6th)		**F**	33/1	—	—
				(SP 138.1%)	**18 Rn**	

3m 55.8 (8.80) CSF £13.28 TOTE £4.70: £1.90 £2.20 £10.50 (£7.20) Trio £140.10 OWNER Mr Philip Grundy (MALTON) BRED Allen E. Paulson
WEIGHT FOR AGE 4yo-1lb
Bt in 4,000 gns
156 Pickens (USA) ended his stable's losing spell in the most fortunate of circumstances, for he looked held when presented with a clear lead at the second last. (3/1)
731* Shuttlecock, beaten on the Flat four days ago, looked beaten when Sorisky kicked clear, but kept on to the line. (3/1)
Ranger Sloane showed improved form and, but for his error at the last, would have finished a couple of lengths closer. (20/1)
Griffin's Girl, on her toes beforehand, was very untidy at the second, but she jumped better thereafter and showed enough stamina to win a similar race. (50/1)
600 Twice the Groom (IRE) again finished weakly after looking sure to take a hand. (9/2)
401 Misty View, who carries condition, took a bit of settling on the way to post. (10/1)
Timely Example (USA) caught the eye, but is probably a bit of a monkey, for he did all his running when the race was over. (10/1: 12/1-8/1)
262 Sorisky, in a muck-sweat but dropping in class, had matters well in hand when capsizing at the second last. He can find a similar race. (15/2)

951 CORSTORPHINE & WRIGHT H'CAP CHASE (0-120) (5-Y.O+) (Class D)
3-25 (3-29) **2m 1f 110y (13 fncs)** £3,684.50 (£1,106.00: £533.00: £246.50) GOING minus 0.11 sec per fur (G)

				SP	RR	SF
	Eastern Magic (89) (GBarnett) **8-10-0** RFarrant (lw: hdwy 7th: led appr last: hdd flat: v.hrd drvn & rallied to ld post)	—	**1**	20/1	98	31
886[2]	**Stately Home (IRE) (118)** (PBowen) **5-12-0** AMaguire (led to 2nd: w ldr tl led 4 out: hdd next: drvn & r.o gamely to ld flat: ct post)	s.h	**2**	7/2[3]	127	59
883*	**Northern Optimist (89)** (BJLlewellyn) **8-10-0** BPowell (chsd ldrs: led 3 out: blnd next: sn hdd & btn)	2	**3**	6/1	96	29
	Newlands-General (115) (PFNicholls) **10-11-12** PHide (lw: led 2nd tl hdd & hit 4 out: sn wknd)	15	**4**	11/4[1]	108	41
702[4]	**Shrewd John (95)** (RDEWoodhouse) **10-10-6** LWyer (hld up & bhd: nvr nr to chal)	14	**5**	6/1	76	9
862[3]	**Ramstar (108)** (PJHobbs) **8-11-2**(3) GTormey (w ldrs tl 2nd: j.slowly next: t.o fr 7th)	dist	**6**	12/1	—	—
702[3]	**Newhall Prince (112)** (AStreeter) **8-11-9** TEley (lw: hit 1st: bhd fr 7th: p.u bef 3 out)		**P**	3/1[2]	—	—
				(SP 114.9%)	**7 Rn**	

4m 11.3 (2.30) CSF £82.89 TOTE £22.00: £6.10 £1.90 (£41.00) OWNER Mrs Christine Smith (STOKE-ON-TRENT) BRED C. Wiggins
LONG HANDICAP Northern Optimist 9-12 Eastern Magic 9-8
WEIGHT FOR AGE 5yo-1lb
STEWARDS' ENQUIRY Farrant susp. 29-31/10 & 1-2 & 4-5/11/96 (excessive use of whip).
OFFICIAL EXPLANATION Newhall Prince: ran very flat.
Eastern Magic looked fully fit, despite a five-month lay-off, but his win owed much to the front-runners doing much to cut each other's throat. Headed on the run-in, he responded gamely to an extremely strong ride, which he is unlikely to forget in a hurry. (20/1)
886 Stately Home (IRE) is very honest and put up a tremendous display for a five-year-old with top weight. Going hammer and tongs with Newlands-General, he got up at the fourth last, but was quickly headed. He looked sure to fold, but rallied as the leaders found the going tough in the straight. (7/2)
883* Northern Optimist waited on the front-runners and looked to have just taken command when ploughing through the second last, changing the picture completely. (6/1)

Newlands-General looked fit but could never shake off Stately Home, and his challenge quickly faded after a mistake four out cost him the lead. (11/4)
702 Shrewd John, settled off the pace, soon found himself detached as the leaders set a terrific pace. Those up front finished so tired that his jockey might not have persevered long enough. (6/1)
862 Ramstar tried to go with the leaders, but his game plan was in ruins as early as the third. This should be ignored. (12/1)

952 WILLIAM HILL H'CAP HURDLE (0-135) (4-Y.O+) (Class C)

4-00 (4-00) **2m 3f (10 hdls)** £3,652.00 (£1,096.00: £528.00: £244.00) GOING minus 0.11 sec per fur (G)

	Horse	Dist	Pos	SP	RR	SF
	Make a Stand (114) (MCPipe) **5-11-10** CMaude (led after 1st: clr appr 2 out: hit last: rdn out)	—	1	5/4^{1}	99	46
	Barford Sovereign (104) (JRFanshawe) **4-10-13** PHide (swtg: prom: hit 6th: chsd wnr appr 3 out: rdn after next: r.o)	3½	2	5/1^{3}	86	32
790^{8}	**Reaganesque (USA) (110)** (PGMurphy) **4-11-5** RFarrant (led tl after 1st: w wnr tl rdn & btn appr 3 out)	22	3	7/1	74	20
	Dally Boy (106) (TDEasterby) **4-11-1** LWyer (hld up: effrt 7th: nvr nr ldrs)	8	4	9/2^{2}	63	9
	Stoney Valley (113) (JRJenkins) **6-11-9** AMaguire (hld up & bhd: nvr plcd to chal)	29	5	10/1	45	—
868^{7}	**Saymore (90)** (WClay) **10-10-0** SWynne (bhd fr 5th)	1	6	50/1	22	—
	Rafters (100) (JMBradley) **7-10-10** TJMurphy (bit bkwd: prom to 6th: bhd whn p.u bef 2 out)		P	12/1	—	—

(SP 110.5%) **7 Rn**

4m 22.0 (4.00) CSF £7.41 TOTE £2.10: £1.70 £2.10 (£4.50) OWNER Mr P. A. Deal (WELLINGTON) BRED R. M. West
LONG HANDICAP Saymore 9-12
WEIGHT FOR AGE 4yo-1lb
Make a Stand began this campaign as he left off last, making most of the running for a facile success. Jumping fast and accurately apart from the final flight, where he got too close, he looks a tough nut to crack. (5/4: op Evens)
Barford Sovereign got warm but ran a fine race, chasing the winner hard over the final two flights. (5/1)
Reaganesque (USA) ran better than at Chepstow, but was still in trouble some way from home. (7/1)
Dally Boy, off since April, looked ring-rusty in the last mile and was not knocked about. (9/2)
Stoney Valley, returning after thirteen months off, may have needed the race more than it appeared, but was soon some way adrift and was never put into the race. (10/1)

953 A.H.P. TRAILERS WOMBOURNE H'CAP CHASE (0-135) (5-Y.O+) (Class C)

4-35 (4-36) **2m 5f 110y (16 fncs)** £4,987.50 (£1,500.00: £725.00: £337.50) GOING minus 0.11 sec per fur (G)

	Horse	Dist	Pos	SP	RR	SF
	Larry's Lord (IRE) (117) (PFNicholls) **7-10-11** PHide (j.w: led to 3rd: led 6th: comf)	—	1	11/4^{2}	125+	58
	Garrylough (IRE) (113) (DRGandolfo) **7-10-4**(3) DFortt (hdwy 10th: mstke 12th: chsd wnr appr 2 out: no imp)	5	2	9/4^{1}	117	50
789^{F}	**Certain Angle (111)** (PJHobbs) **7-10-5** DBridgwater (prom: chsd wnr 10th: sn rdn: wknd appr 2 out)	17	3	5/1^{3}	103	36
799^{F}	**Comedy Road (106)** (RLee) **12-10-0** RJohnson (hld up: effrt 9th: wknd appr 2 out)	5	4	12/1	94	27
789^{3}	**Iffeee (128)** (PBowen) **9-11-8** AMaguire (w ldr: led 3rd to 6th: rdn 9th: sn wknd: t.o)	dist	5	11/2	—	—
	Master Boston (IRE) (130) (RDEWoodhouse) **8-11-10** LWyer (prom: mstke & lost pl 11th: blnd 4 out: p.u bef next)		P	10/1	—	—

(SP 106.3%) **6 Rn**

5m 9.8 (-2.20) CSF £8.44 TOTE £3.30: £2.10 £1.20 (£3.60) OWNER John Blackwell, Terr Nichols (SHEPTON MALLET) BRED Lawrence Doyle
LONG HANDICAP Comedy Road 9-8
Larry's Lord (IRE) returned fit and looked the same horse as last season between the fences, but his jumping is much-improved on this evidence. If he keeps this up, he is set for a successful season. (11/4)
Garrylough (IRE) appeared ready and looks a well-handicapped young mare, but had no answer to the winner in the straight. She will not always find things so tough and should find more races. (9/4)
719 Certain Angle looks just about in the Handicapper's grip at present, and will always be vulnerable to the sort of well-handicapped horses that beat him here. (5/1)
500* Comedy Road found the step up in class too much to handle. (12/1)
789 Iffeee does not like being taken on at the best of times and the winner was continually outjumping him, and had him on the retreat by halfway. He needs things his own way. (11/2)

954 BARNSLEY ASSOCIATES 'N.H.' NOVICES' HURDLE (4-Y.O+) (Class D)

5-05 (5-06) **2m 6f 110y (12 hdls)** £3,155.00 (£950.00: £460.00: £215.00) GOING minus 0.11 sec per fur (G)

	Horse	Dist	Pos	SP	RR	SF
	Tarrs Bridge (IRE) (CJMann) **5-11-0** JRailton (lw: trckd ldrs: led appr 2 out: comf)	—	1	12/1	68+	24
	Inner Temple (CaptTAForster) **6-11-0** SWynne (bit bkwd: hit 3rd: hdwy 8th: chsng wnr whn hit 2 out: mstke last: no imp)	7	2	14/1	63	19
	Mr Strong Gale (IRE) (PFNicholls) **5-11-0** PHide (chsd ldrs: rdn & btn whn blnd 2 out)	15	3	9/2^{3}	52	8
	Jhal Frezi (ABarrow) **8-10-7**(7) MrRThornton (plld hrd: prom tl lost pl after 4 out: r.o again appr last)	2½	4	25/1	51	7
	Cosa Fuair (IRE) (85) (KCBailey) **6-11-0** WMcFarland (prom: led after 8th: hdd appr 3 out: sn wknd)	5	5	9/1	47	3
	Up The Creek (IRE) (MissMERowland) **4-10-7** GaryLyons (bit bkwd: hld up: hdwy 6th: led appr 3 out tl appr next: sn wknd)	9	6	66/1	35	—
739^{6}	**Gaelic Million (IRE)** (MissHCKnight) **5-10-9** JFTitley (bhd tl r.o fr 3 out)	14	7	12/1	26	—
397^{2}	**Roskeen Bridge (IRE)** (CWeedon) **5-11-0** MRichards (hit 1st: bhd tl sme late hdwy)	12	8	20/1	22	—
	Carey's Cottage (IRE) (MrsPTownsley) **6-11-0** LHarvey (nvr nr to chal)	s.h	9	50/1	22	—
718^{3}	**Difficult Decision (IRE)** (MrsMerritaJones) **5-11-0** DerekByrne (lw: bhd fr 7th)	1½	10	5/1	21	—
794^{10}	**Jaime's Joy** (GraemeRoe) **6-10-2**(7) ShaunGraham (a bhd)	nk	11	66/1	16	—
	Linford (IRE) (CaptTAForster) **6-11-0** MrRBevis (in tch tl hit 8th)	16	12	25/1	9	—
492^{F}	**Lilly The Filly** (MrsBarbaraWaring) **5-10-9** EByrne (hit 4th: a bhd)	20	13	66/1	—	—
	Bitofamixup (IRE) (MJRoberts) **5-11-0** BPowell (prom: hit 5th: wknd 8th)	6	14	4/1^{2}	—	—
859^{3}	**Minor Key (IRE)** (JRJenkins) **6-11-0** AMaguire (led tl after 8th: ev ch whn fell next)		F	3/1^{1}	—	—
	B Fifty Two (IRE) (LWells) **5-10-7**(7) DSlattery (bkwd: prom to 7th: t.o whn p.u bef 3 out)		P	66/1	—	—

(SP 132.3%) **16 Rn**

5m 24.9 (8.90) CSF £162.89 TOTE £20.10: £4.60 £4.40 £2.60 (£131.80) Trio £168.90; £142.78 to Pontefract 21/10/96 OWNER The Tuesday Syndicate (UPPER LAMBOURN) BRED David McGrath
WEIGHT FOR AGE 4yo-1lb
OFFICIAL EXPLANATION **Difficult Decision (IRE): is still weak and backward, wants softer ground and was never travelling well.**

Tarrs Bridge (IRE), an Irish import, looked on fine terms with himself and won what was probably an ordinary race in good style. (12/1: 6/1-14/1)
Inner Temple failed to complete in two points in May, and still showed signs of inexperience when ballooning the final two flights. A good-looking gelding who moves well, he should improve in time. (14/1)
Mr Strong Gale (IRE), a powerfully-built gelding making his hurdles debut, shaped well until lack of as run told in the final half-mile. (9/2: 3/1-5/1)
Jhal Frezi, done no favours by the faller four out, should have finished rather closer. (25/1)
Cosa Fuair (IRE), stepping up in trip, took a keen hold and was running on empty in the last half-mile. (9/1)
Up The Creek (IRE), making her debut, really caught the eye when rushing through to lead going to three out. The effort could not be sustained, but there is definitely some ability there. (66/1)
718 Difficult Decision (IRE) (5/1: 3/1-6/1)
Bitofamixup (IRE) (4/1: 3/1-9/2)

955 JONES LANG WOOTTON MAIDEN HURDLE (4-Y.O+) (Class E)

5-40 (5-41) **2m 110y (9 hdls)** £2,757.50 (£770.00: £372.50) GOING minus 0.11 sec per fur (G)

				SP	RR	SF
	Iron N Gold (TCasey) **4-11-4** DBridgwater (lw: hld up: hdwy 3 out: led last: rdn out)	—	**1**	11/2^{3}	72	—
262^{2}	**Samba Sharply** (AHide) **5-11-5** PHide (swtg: in tch: hdwy appr 3 out: ev ch 2 out: unable qckn flat)	nk	**2**	5/2^{1}	72	—
	Flying Fiddler (IRE) (MJRoberts) **5-11-5** BPowell (a.p: led 6th to last: r.o)	s.h	**3**	12/1	72	—
	Silly Money (87) (TDEasterby) **5-11-5** LWyer (bit bkwd: bhd tl r.o fr 3 out: nrst fin)	6	**4**	14/1	66	—
	Swan Street (NZ) (CJMann) **5-11-5** JRailton (in tch: mstke 5th: hdwy appr 3 out: wknd appr last)	6	**5**	10/1	60	—
885^{2}	**Blaze of Oak (USA) (96)** (JMBradley) **5-11-5** RJohnson (plld hrd: prom to 3 out)	3½	**6**	5/1^{2}	57	—
593^{3}	**Smart Lord** (JRBosley) **5-11-5** MBosley (nvr nrr)	1¼	**7**	33/1	55	—
812^{4}	**Samaka Hara (IRE) (86)** (GraemeRoe) **4-11-4** RichardGuest (prom tl appr 2 out)	nk	**8**	10/1	55	—
	Total Asset (ALForbes) **6-11-5** TEley (bkwd: prom: wkng whn hmpd appr 2 out)	5	**9**	50/1	50	—
	Sloe Brandy (MrsHLWalton) **6-11-0** MrAWalton (a bhd)	2	**10**	33/1	43	—
653^{9}	**Rosehall** (MrsTDPilkington) **5-10-11**(3) GHogan (bit bkwd: prom: hit 3rd & next: sn bhd)	22	**11**	33/1	22	—
	Racing Telegraph (CNAllen) **6-11-5** JFTitley (led to 6th: wkng whn hit next)	10	**12**	16/1	17	—
	Braydon Forest (CJDrewe) **4-11-4** WMarston (fell 2nd)		**F**	12/1	—	—
	Nagara Sound (87) (BPreece) **5-11-5** AMaguire (hld up: hdwy appr 3 out: rdn next: 4th & btn whn fell last)		**F**	8/1	—	—
	Rizal (USA) (RJEckley) **4-11-1**(3) DWalsh (bit bkwd: rel to r: sn in tch: wknd 6th: fell 2 out)		**F**	50/1	—	—
				(SP 130.6%)	**15 Rn**	

4m 1.6 (14.60) CSF £19.96 TOTE £5.80: £2.40 £2.00 £3.90 (£12.70) Trio £22.80 OWNER A Family Affair Partnership (DORKING) BRED M. F. Kentish
WEIGHT FOR AGE 4yo-1lb
Iron N Gold did this well and is bound to improve once set a stiffer test of stamina. (11/2)
262 Samba Sharply again looked the likely winner when produced at the second last, but did not find as much as might have been expected. (5/2)
Flying Fiddler (IRE) made more than a satisfactory seasonal debut, stretching the field from the fourth last and keeping on well once headed. (12/1)
Silly Money made a lot of late ground and looks worth another try over further. (14/1)
Swan Street (NZ) shows knee-action and would probably benefit from softer ground. He did well to get back into the action after a mistake at a vital stage, and looks the sort to progress. (10/1)
885 Blaze of Oak (USA), still a maiden despite a lot of chances on the level, is going to need to settle to do better at the winter game. (5/1)
812 Samaka Hara (IRE) (10/1: 8/1-12/1)

T/Plpt: £176.50 (60.36 Tckts). T/Qdpt: £55.60 (8.41 Tckts). Dk

0552-PLUMPTON (L-H) (Good to firm)
Tuesday October 22nd

WEATHER: sunny

956 JOE & CO MAIDEN HURDLE (4-Y.O+) (Class E)

2-20 (2-20) **2m 1f (10 hdls)** £2,700.00 (£750.00: £360.00) GOING: 0.33 sec per fur (GS)

				SP	RR	SF
	Regal Pursuit (IRE) (NJHenderson) **5-11-0** MAFitzgerald (hld up: led appr 3 out: clr appr 2 out: r.o wl)	—	**1**	7/2^{2}	63	7
	Wakeel (USA) (SDow) **4-11-4** RDunwoody (swtg: stdy hdwy 7th: chsd wnr appr 3 out: 2nd & no ch whn pckd last)	10	**2**	5/6^{1}	59	2
	Docklands Courier (BJMcMath) **4-11-4** CLlewellyn (hld up: mstke 3rd: rdn 7th: sn wknd)	17	**3**	14/1	43	—
	Greenwich Again (TGMills) **4-11-4** DBridgwater (w ldr: led 6th tl appr 3 out: sn wknd)	1¾	**4**	5/1^{3}	41	—
818^{3}	**Caddy's First (84)** (SMellor) **4-11-4** NMann (bhd fr 7th: t.o)	dist	**5**	14/1	—	—
	Zamalek (USA) (GLMoore) **4-11-4** AMaguire (led to 6th: wknd 7th: t.o)	7	**6**	33/1	—	—
	Zadok (JFfitch-Heyes) **4-11-4** BFenton (a bhd: t.o)	2½	**7**	50/1	—	—
820^{3}	**Ragtime Song (52)** (JRJenkins) **7-10-12v**(7) NTEgan (a bhd: t.o)	7	**8**	25/1	—	—
	Hardy Breeze (IRE) (DMGrissell) **5-11-5** JRKavanagh (bkwd: a bhd: t.o whn p.u bef 3 out)		**P**	40/1	—	—
818^{5}	**Allez Pablo** (RRowe) **6-11-2**(3) LAspell (w.r.s: a t.o: p.u bef 7th)		**P**	100/1	—	—
	Barbrallen (MrsLCJewell) **4-10-13** DLeahy (lw: a bhd: mstke 2nd: t.o whn p.u bef 7th)		**P**	100/1	—	—
				(SP 119.9%)	**11 Rn**	

4m 14.5 (18.50) CSF £6.59 TOTE £3.90: £1.20 £1.70 £3.80 (£2.80) Trio £38.00 OWNER Mr Larry Tracey (LAMBOURN) BRED A. Tarry
WEIGHT FOR AGE 4yo-1lb
Regal Pursuit (IRE) may not have been as good as the runner-up on the Flat, but a few hurdles can be a great leveller and he took this in clear-cut fashion, despite an absence of eight months. (7/2: op 2/1)
Wakeel (USA), who finished third to Yeast in a Class B race at Ascot in the summer, was reported to have schooled well, but was well held when pecking badly at the final flight. His trainer reported afterwards that this was very much an experimental run and that the gelding will now be put away for the winter after a long season on the Flat. (5/6)
Docklands Courier, a moderate maiden on the Flat, is going to have problems over hurdles if this is the best he can do. (14/1: 10/1-16/1)
Greenwich Again, winner of two small races on the Flat this year, disputed the lead at a suicidal pace and it came as no surprise that he quickly tired once collared approaching the third last. Once he learns to settle, improvement can be expected. (5/1)
818 Caddy's First (14/1: 8/1-16/1)

957 JOE & CO (S) H'CAP CHASE (0-90) (5-Y.O+) (Class G)

2-50 (2-50) **3m 1f 110y (20 fncs)** £2,595.00 (£720.00: £345.00) GOING minus 0.39 sec per fur (GF)

Form	Horse	Dist	Pos	SP	RR	SF
880^U	**Capo Castanum (80)** (MissHCKnight) **7-11-4** TJMurphy (t: swtg: stdy hdwy 12th: led 16th: blnd 2 out: drvn out)	—	1	4/1^1	89	21
53a^6	**Raglan Road (84)** (MissAEEmbiricos) **12-11-8** JRyan (a.p: rdn appr last: r.o)	3½	2	8/1^3	91	23
70^P	**Brindley House (82)** (RCurtis) **9-11-6** DMorris (bit bkwd: a.p: led 14th tl blnd & hdd 16th: mstke 4 out: unable qckn)	5	3	14/1	86	18
726^3	**Manor Bound (72)** (MrsSDWilliams) **6-10-10** NWilliamson (lw: hdwy 14th: sn wknd)	20	4	12/1	63	—
	Opal's Tenspot (72) (JMBradley) **9-10-10** RJohnson (swtg: bit bkwd: hdwy 12th: wknd 14th)	½	5	12/1	63	—
	Fighting Days (USA) (89) (AMoore) **10-11-13** BPowell (hdwy 13th: wknd 14th: t.o)	20	6	14/1	67	—
823^6	**Woodlands Genhire (71)** (PAPritchard) **11-10-9v** AMaguire (lw: chsd ldr to 8th: wknd 11th: t.o)	4	7	8/1^3	47	—
494^4	**Saint Bene't (IRE) (63)** (GProdromou) **8-9-10**(5)ow1 MichaelBrennan (a bhd: t.o fr 7th)	1¼	8	16/1	38	—
179^3	**The West's Asleep (67)** (JFfitch-Heyes) **11-10-5** BFenton (bit bkwd: bhd fr 14th: t.o)	dist	9	9/2^2	—	—
833^4	**L'Uomo Piu (71)** (ABarrow) **12-10-6**(3) TDascombe (led to 14th: sn wknd: t.o whn p.u bef 2 out)		P	20/1	—	—
	Mr Clancy (IRE) (81) (JGO'Neill) **8-11-5** SCurran (bit bkwd: chsd ldr 8th to 11th: sn wknd: t.o whn p.u bef 14th)		P	8/1^3	—	—
	Telf (62) (PCClarke) **16-9-9**(5) DJKavanagh (a bhd: tried to ref & uns rdr 7th)		U	50/1	—	—

(SP 112.8%) **12 Rn**

6m 27.1 (7.10) CSF £31.67 CT £365.49 TOTE £4.90: £1.90 £2.60 £8.30 (£29.00) Trio £188.00 OWNER Mr D. C. G. Gyle-Thompson (WANTAGE) BRED D. Gyle-Thompson
LONG HANDICAP Saint Bene't (IRE) 9-7 Telf 9-4
Bt in 5,600 gns

Capo Castanum found the drop in class enabling him to get off the mark, but had to be kept up to his work on the run-in to win an appalling race. (4/1)
53a Raglan Road, who finished sixth in the Swedish Grand National four months ago, got his second wind from two out and ran on to take second prize. A poor performer these days, he has not won for four years. (8/1)
Brindley House, carrying condition for this first run in four months, has yet to win in this country and, after several poor efforts, was taking a drop in class. (14/1)
Opal's Tenspot (12/1: op 7/1)
Fighting Days (USA) (14/1: 8/1-16/1)
Mr Clancy (IRE) (8/1: op 12/1)

958 KNIGHT FRANK CENTENARY H'CAP HURDLE (0-105) (4-Y.O+) (Class F)

3-20 (3-20) **2m 4f (12 hdls)** £2,047.40 (£566.40: £270.20) GOING: 0.33 sec per fur (GS)

Form	Horse	Dist	Pos	SP	RR	SF
899^2	**Fawley Flyer (74)** (WGMTurner) **7-10-13** RDunwoody (lw: w ldr: led 4th: clr appr 2 out: eased flat)	—	1	9/4^2	61+	18
824^3	**Credit Controller (IRE) (61)** (JFfitch-Heyes) **7-10-0** BFenton (t.o 9th to 2 out: hdwy appr last: r.o)	11	2	9/1	39	—
879^13	**Tibbs Inn (61)** (ABarrow) **7-9-7**(7) MrRThornton (hdwy 9th: r.o one pce fr 3 out)	nk	3	33/1	39	—
788^3	**Whistling Buck (IRE) (84)** (RRowe) **8-11-6**(3) LAspell (lw: hdwy 2nd: chsd wnr fr 9th: rdn appr 2 out: 2nd & no ch whn blnd last)	½	4	2/1^1	62	19
	Durshan (USA) (80) (JRJenkins) **7-11-5v** NWilliamson (hld up: rdn 9th: sn wknd: t.o)	25	5	11/2	38	—
29^7	**Macedonas (77)** (GThorner) **8-11-2** BPowell (lw: reminder 5th: hdwy 6th: wknd 8th: t.o)	10	6	20/1	27	—
	Madame President (IRE) (88) (CPMorlock) **5-11-10**(3) GHogan (led to 4th: wknd 9th: t.o whn p.u bef 2 out)		P	5/1^3	—	—

(SP 113.9%) **7 Rn**

5m 5.9 (18.90) CSF £20.12 CT £470.19 TOTE £2.80: £1.60 £2.10 (£7.70) Trio £109.90; £17.03 to Newcastle 23/10/96 OWNER Mr David Chown (SHERBORNE) BRED Shepherds Farm Ltd
LONG HANDICAP Credit Controller (IRE) 9-13 Tibbs Inn 9-9

899 Fawley Flyer looked in good trim in the paddock and confirmed the promise shown at Exeter last week. The winning margin was no true reflection of his superiority in this dreadful race. (9/4)
824 Credit Controller (IRE) ran an extraordinary race, for he was being bustled along early on the final circuit and was tailed off in the back straight. Running on from the penultimate hurdle, he stayed on to snatch second prize in the last couple of strides. (9/1: 6/1-10/1)
Tibbs Inn has no ability and the fact that he managed to get placed for the first time shows what a dreadful race this was. (33/1)
Durshan (USA) (11/2: 4/1-6/1)

959 HIGHWAY MOTOR POLICIES AT LLOYDS H'CAP CHASE (0-120) (5-Y.O+) (Class D)

3-50 (3-50) **2m 5f (16 fncs)** £3,562.35 (£1,060.80: £504.90: £226.95) GOING minus 0.39 sec per fur (GF)

Form	Horse	Dist	Pos	SP	RR	SF
	Zambezi Spirit (IRE) (88) (MrsMerritaJones) **7-10-0** DerekByrne (chsd ldr fr 5th: led 11th: clr 4 out: easily)	—	1	11/4^1	105+	24
	Mine's an Ace (NZ) (95) (MissVenetiaWilliams) **9-10-7** NWilliamson (hld up: chsd wnr fr 11th: rdn 12th: no imp)	11	2	4/1^3	104	23
814^5	**Black Church (98)** (RRowe) **10-10-10** RDunwoody (lw: hrd rdn & no hdwy fr 12th)	4	3	11/4^1	104	23
830^2	**Drumstick (94)** (KCBailey) **10-10-6b^1** JRailton (lw: led & sn clr: hdd 11th: sn wknd)	13	4	15/2	90	9
932^2	**Paper Star (103)** (MPMuggeridge) **9-11-1** BPowell (chsd ldr to 5th: wknd 6th: t.o whn p.u bef 12th)		P	3/1^2	—	—
	Be Surprised (88) (AMoore) **10-10-0** JRKavanagh (a bhd: t.o fr 4th: p.u bef 10th)		P	50/1	—	—

(SP 112.1%) **6 Rn**

5m 12.7 (-0.30) CSF £13.10 TOTE £4.50: £2.10 £2.10 (£8.20) OWNER Mr P. C. Townsend (LAMBOURN) BRED Patrick Day
LONG HANDICAP Zambezi Spirit (IRE) 9-9 Be Surprised 9-1

Zambezi Spirit (IRE) may have been having his first run in six months and carrying 16lb more than when he last won, but he is not the type that takes much getting fit. Well supported in the Offices in the morning, he absolutely scooted up and can win again. (11/4)
Mine's an Ace (NZ), having his first run in nearly five months, was in vain pursuit of the winner from the sixth last. (4/1)
814 Black Church was left for dead by the front two over the last five. (11/4)
830 Drumstick found the application of blinkers not having the desired effect. (15/2: 5/1-8/1)

960 A. R. DENNIS NOVICES' HURDLE (4-Y.O+) (Class E)

4-20 (4-20) **2m 4f (12 hdls)** £2,385.00 (£660.00: £315.00) GOING: 0.33 sec per fur (GS)

Form	Horse	Dist	Pos	SP	RR	SF
	Sleeptite (FR) (WGMTurner) **6-10-12** RDunwoody (chsd ldr to 4th: led appr 3 out: hrd rdn appr last: r.o wl)	—	1	7/1^3	62	14

				SP	RR	SF
659*	**Supreme Star (USA)** (PRHedger) **5-11-5** MRichards (hdwy 3 out: chsd wnr appr 2 out: r.o one pce)	3	**2**	9/4^{1}	67	19
812^{2}	**Wanstead (IRE) (93)** (JRJenkins) **4-10-11b** AMaguire (hdwy 8th: mstke 9th: one pce)	11	**3**	9/4^{1}	51	2
818^{4}	**Zuno Flyer (USA)** (AMoore) **4-10-11** NWilliamson (hld up: rdn 9th: lost pl 3 out: r.o one pce fr 2 out)	5	**4**	20/1	47	—
885^{P}	**Polo Kit (IRE)** (RJO'Sullivan) **5-10-12** PHolley (chsd ldr fr 4th: led 8th tl appr 3 out: wknd appr 2 out)	nk	**5**	11/4^{2}	47	—
185^{10}	**Slightly Special (IRE) (63)** (BAPearce) **4-10-11** CLlewellyn (led to 8th: sn wknd: t.o)	dist	**6**	50/1	—	—
813^{3}	**Coolegale (67)** (LWells) **10-10-9b^{1}**(3) GHogan (hdwy 3rd: wknd 8th: t.o)	7	**7**	33/1	—	—
	Night Thyne (IRE) (MJRoberts) **4-10-11** BPowell (bit bkwd: hdwy 3 out: 4th & no ch whn p.u bef 2 out: dismntd)		**P**	16/1	—	—
				(SP 116.3%)	**8 Rn**	

5m 6.8 (19.80) CSF £22.49 TOTE £7.30: £1.70 £1.10 £1.40 (£17.30) OWNER Mr David Chown (SHERBORNE) BRED Ronald Reeves in France
WEIGHT FOR AGE 4yo-1lb

Sleeptite (FR), who had broken down thirteen months ago at Wolverhampton on the Flat, swept into the lead approaching the third last and, given a few reminders going to the final flight, never looked like being caught. (7/1)
659* Supreme Star (USA) jumped better than at Fontwell, although still not very fluently. (9/4)
812 Wanstead (IRE) was made to look very pedestrian from the fourth last. (9/4)

961 JOE & CO NOVICES' H'CAP HURDLE (0-100) (4-Y.O+) (Class E)

4-50 (4-52) **2m 1f (10 hdls)** £2,448.00 (£678.00: £324.00) GOING: 0.33 sec per fur (GS)

				SP	RR	SF
834^{2}	**Canary Falcon (82)** (RJO'Sullivan) **5-11-1** PHolley (lw: hld up: led appr 2 out: rdn out)	—	**1**	15/8^{1}	67	—
812*	**Mazzini (IRE) (95)** (RRowe) **5-11-11**(3) LAspell (swtg: hdwy 7th: chsd wnr appr 2 out: unable qckn)	5	**2**	4/1^{3}	75	—
	Blurred Image (IRE) (67) (JCPoulton) **5-10-0** TJMurphy (hdwy 3 out: rdn appr 2 out: one pce)	3	**3**	33/1	45	—
	First Instance (IRE) (76) (DMGrissell) **6-10-9** BFenton (hdwy 3 out: r.o one pce)	3	**4**	12/1	51	—
812^{6}	**Water Hazard (IRE) (82)** (SDow) **4-11-0** RDunwoody (hdwy 7th: led appr 3 out tl appr 2 out: sn wknd)	5	**5**	3/1^{2}	52	—
	Deptford Belle (70) (RCurtis) **6-10-3** DMorris (nvr nr to chal)	15	**6**	33/1	26	—
	Bowles Patrol (IRE) (68) (JohnUpson) **4-10-0** RSupple (bit bkwd: swtg: a.p: led 7th tl appr 3 out: sn wknd)	2½	**7**	14/1	22	—
	Full of Tricks (67) (JJBridger) **8-10-0** LHarvey (led to 6th: sn wknd: t.o)	dist	**8**	50/1	—	—
	Jacksons Bay (70) (TCasey) **6-10-3** EMurphy (bit bkwd: w ldr: led 6th to 7th: sn wknd: t.o)	5	**9**	33/1	—	—
	Farmer's Tern (IRE) (84) (PButler) **4-10-9**(7) MrRThornton (bhd fr 6th: t.o)	1¼	**10**	9/1	—	—
	Just a Beau (67) (MrsLCJewell) **5-9-9**(5) SophieMitchell (prom to 6th: t.o)	18	**11**	66/1	—	—
				(SP 116.4%)	**11 Rn**	

4m 18.8 (22.80) CSF £9.36 CT £165.03 TOTE £2.20: £1.10 £1.60 £13.50 (£4.50) Trio £75.40 OWNER Mr L. Pipe (WHITCOMBE) BRED Gainsborough Stud Management Ltd
LONG HANDICAP Full of Tricks 9-11 Bowles Patrol (IRE) 9-13 Just a Beau 9-2
WEIGHT FOR AGE 4yo-1lb

834 Canary Falcon gained a richly-deserved victory after several near-misses. (15/8)
812* Mazzini (IRE) had a ding-dong battle for second place in the straight and, although winning that battle, never looked like winning the war. He needs to come down in the handicap. (4/1: 5/2-9/2)
Blurred Image (IRE), without a run in five months, had a good battle for second prize in the straight but lost out. (33/1)
First Instance (IRE), having his first run in six months, stayed on from the third last without ever posing a threat. (12/1)
812 Water Hazard (IRE) went on approaching the third last, but he was collared soon after and dropped away. (3/1)
Farmer's Tern (IRE) (9/1: 6/1-10/1)

T/Plpt: £74.50 (175.69 Tckts). T/Qdpt: £7.60 (109.14 Tckts). AK

WARWICK (L-H) (Firm, Good to firm patches)
Tuesday October 22nd
WEATHER: unsettled

962 RAGLEY HALL HURDLE (3-Y.O) (Class D)

2-10 (2-10) **2m (8 hdls)** £3,109.00 (£874.00: £427.00) GOING minus 0.69 sec per fur (F)

				SP	RR	SF
736*	**Doctor Green (FR)** (MCPipe) **3-11-4v** APMcCoy (mde all: clr 3 out: eased flat)	—	**1**	4/6^{1}	82+	37
807^{F}	**Kalao Tua (IRE)** (JRFanshawe) **3-10-7** PHide (prom: mstke 4th: chsd wnr 3 out: blnd next: no imp)	9	**2**	7/1^{3}	62	17
	Hal Hoo Yaroom (MajorWRHern) **3-10-12** RFarrant (nt j.w: chsd wnr to 5th: sn btn)	3½	**3**	5/2^{2}	64	19
	Topaglow (IRE) (PTDalton) **3-10-12** TEley (prom to 5th)	2½	**4**	33/1	61	16
881^{2}	**Flood's Fancy** (LJBarratt) **3-10-7** RichardGuest (mid div: hdwy after 3rd: outpcd 5th: no ch whn mstke last)	2½	**5**	25/1	54	9
807^{3}	**How Could-I (IRE)** (MrsNMacauley) **3-10-7b** AThornton (hld up: nvr trbld ldrs)	2	**6**	25/1	52	7
	Colour Counsellor (RMFlower) **3-10-12b** JOsborne (mid div: hdwy after 3rd: wknd 5th)	24	**7**	20/1	33	—
	The Grey Weaver (RMFlower) **3-10-5**(7) JKMcCarthy (hld up: a in rr)	5	**8**	66/1	28	—
	I Say Dancer (IRE) (LJBarratt) **3-10-7** SWynne (hld up: plld hrd: a in rr: t.o)	29	**9**	66/1	—	—
881^{5}	**Indian Wolf** (BJLlewellyn) **3-10-12** ILawrence (hld up: fell 5th)		**F**	66/1	—	—
	Embroidered (RMFlower) **3-10-4**(3) GTormey (hld up: blnd & uns rdr 3rd)		**U**	66/1	—	—
				(SP 122.4%)	**11 Rn**	

3m 36.9 (-5.10) CSF £6.51 TOTE £1.70: £1.10 £3.30 £1.10 (£5.90) Trio £6.20 OWNER Mr Jim Weeden (WELLINGTON) BRED The Queen
736* Doctor Green (FR) supplemented his Exeter win in good style. He is sure to take plenty of beating in the near future. (4/6: op Evens)
807 Kalao Tua (IRE) should not be too hard to place. (7/1)
Hal Hoo Yaroom, superior to the winner on the level, ran about approaching the hurdles and will need to brush up his jumping. (5/2)

963 COUGHTON COURT CLAIMING HURDLE (4-Y.O+) (Class G)

2-40 (2-40) **2m (8 hdls)** £1,920.50 (£538.00: £261.50) GOING minus 0.69 sec per fur (F)

				SP	RR	SF
751*	**Indian Jockey (119)** (MCPipe) **4-11-12** APMcCoy (mde all: hrd rdn flat: all out)	—	**1**	1/7^{1}	98	52
739^{4}	**Highly Charming (IRE) (88)** (MissHCKnight) **4-10-7**(7) MrAWintle (chsd wnr: chal 3 out: rdn appr last: r.o)	s.h	**2**	6/1^{2}	86?	40
	The Deaconess (MrsALMKing) **5-10-3** GaryLyons (swtg: hld up: hdwy 4th: nvr nr ldrs)	19	**3**	50/1	55	10
24^{5}	**Roc Age** (GWDavies) **5-11-7** MrJNolan (bit bkwd: hld up in tch: rdn appr 4th: sn bhd)	6	**4**	33/1^{3}	67	22
262^{8}	**Canestrelli (USA) (51)** (WGMann) **11-10-8** MrPScott (bkwd: hld up: a bhd: t.o)	20	**5**	50/1	34	—

	Horse				SP	RR	SF
	Commanche Storm (IRE) (WGMann) **4-10-2**$^{(7)ow4}$ MrPO'Keeffe (bkwd: hld up: bhd fr 4th: sn t.o)	dist	6		100/1	—	—

(SP 109.6%) **6 Rn**

3m 35.2 (-6.80) CSF £1.60 TOTE £1.10: £1.00 £2.30 (£1.70) OWNER Mr Stuart Mercer (WELLINGTON) BRED John Hayter
WEIGHT FOR AGE 4yo-1lb
Highly Charming (IRE) clmd MBarraclough £6,000
751* Indian Jockey needed all of McCoy's strength to get him home. (1/7)
Highly Charming (IRE), who can only improve physically, made the winner pull out all the stops. (6/1)
The Deaconess may well need another outing. (50/1)

964 HATTON COUNTRY WORLD NOVICES' CHASE (5-Y.O+) (Class D)

3-10 (3-10) **2m 4f 110y (17 fncs)** £3,458.00 (£1,046.00: £510.00: £242.00) GOING minus 0.69 sec per fur (F)

Form	Horse	Dist	Pos	SP	RR	SF
741^{5}	**Prerogative** (HSHowe) **6-11-0v** APMcCoy (mde all: lft clr 11th: pushed out)	—	1	$15/8^{2}$	93	3
	Elite Governor (IRE) (NMLampard) **7-11-0** JOsborne (prom: mstke & lost pl 4th: hdwy to chse wnr 11th: no imp fr 2 out)	12	2	$4/1^{3}$	84	—
917^{F}	**Larks Tail** (PRWebber) **8-10-9** RBellamy (hld up: hdwy 8th: wkng whn hit 3 out)	27	3	20/1	58	—
860^{2}	**Icantelya (IRE) (90)** (JWMullins) **7-11-0** PHide (prom: blnd & lost pl 2nd: rdn 6th: hdwy 8th: wknd 11th)	18	4	$7/4^{1}$	49	—
746^{P}	**Auntie Lorna (60)** (NJPomfret) **7-10-2**$^{(7)}$ MrRWakley (swtg: s.i.s: a in rr: fell 4 out)		F	50/1	—	—
870^{F}	**Glamanglitz** (PTDalton) **6-11-0** TEley (chsd wnr 2nd tl stumbled & uns rdr 11th)		U	11/2	—	—

(SP 113.3%) **6 Rn**

5m 8.3 (4.30) CSF £9.35 TOTE £2.20: £1.20 £2.30 (£4.60) OWNER The Secret Partnership (TIVERTON) BRED The Queen
651 Prerogative, a moody but useful hurdler, outclassed some moderate rivals to get off the mark over fences. (15/8)
Elite Governor (IRE), a winning pointer, finds these regulation fences need a little more jumping. (4/1)
860 Icantelya (IRE), lucky to stay on his feet at the second, was never really travelling after. (7/4)

965 CARLISLE & GOUGH NOVICES' HURDLE (4-Y.O+) (Class D)

3-40 (3-40) **2m 3f (9 hdls)** £2,773.00 (£778.00: £379.00) GOING minus 0.69 sec per fur (F)

Form	Horse	Dist	Pos	SP	RR	SF
794^{3}	**Culrain (65)** (THCaldwell) **5-11-0** AThornton (hld up: hdwy 5th: led after 3 out: sn clr)	—	1	$9/4^{2}$	56	—
735^{4}	**Rose Chime (IRE) (66)** (JLHarris) **4-10-8** PMcLoughlin (prom: hit 3rd: rdn 3 out: styd on same pce)	8	2	$15/8^{1}$	44	—
	Kirov Royale (MarkCampion) **5-10-9** JOsborne (trckd ldrs: lost pl & blnd 5th: n.d after)	8	3	$3/1^{3}$	38	—
	Calleva Star (IRE) (RHAlner) **5-11-0** WMcFarland (bkwd: led: mstke 4th: hdd & wknd after 3 out)	1¼	4	4/1	42	—
737^{6}	**Lilac Rain** (RMStronge) **4-10-5v**$^{(3)}$ DWalsh (chsd ldr tl rdn & wknd appr 3 out)	16	5	20/1	23	—

(SP 115.3%) **5 Rn**

4m 21.8 (1.80) CSF £6.95 TOTE £3.40: £1.40 £1.20 (£2.40) OWNER Mr A. J. McDonald (WARRINGTON) BRED Stetchworth Park Stud Ltd
WEIGHT FOR AGE 4yo-1lb
794 Culrain could not have found a worse event in which to get off the mark. He will find things tougher from now on. (9/4)
735 Rose Chime (IRE) will have a job to find another race as poor as this. (15/8)
Calleva Star (IRE) was too fat to do herself justice. (4/1)

966 WARWICK CASTLE H'CAP CHASE (0-115) (5-Y.O+) (Class E)

4-10 (4-10) **3m 2f (20 fncs)** £3,282.50 (£920.00: £447.50) GOING minus 0.69 sec per fur (F)

Form	Horse	Dist	Pos	SP	RR	SF
789^{2}	**Evangelica (USA) (115)** (MCPipe) **6-12-0** APMcCoy (hld up: hit 10th: outpcd 13th: rallied next: rdn to ld flat: styd on)	—	1	$13/8^{1}$	105	38
604^{2}	**Time Enough (IRE) (98)** (CPEBrooks) **7-10-11** GBradley (chsd ldr: led 4th to 12th: led 2 out: hit last: hdd & unable qckn flat)	1	2	$9/4^{3}$	87	20
	Celtic Silver (89) (MrsSJSmith) **8-10-2** RichardGuest (bit bkwd: led to 4th: led 12th: hdd 2 out: sn btn)	4	3	$7/4^{2}$	76	9

(SP 105.2%) **3 Rn**

6m 21.3 (-3.70) CSF £4.63 TOTE £2.00 (£2.30) OWNER Martin Pipe Racing Club (WELLINGTON) BRED Helen C Alexander
789 Evangelica (USA), who races with her tongue tied down, found this company more to her liking. (13/8)
604 Time Enough (IRE), trying this extended trip, races keenly, but does not get very high at some of his fences. (9/4: op 6/4)
Celtic Silver, whose bold jumping will stand him in good stead, will strip fitter for the outing. (7/4)

967 LORD LEICESTER HOSPITAL H'CAP HURDLE (0-125) (4-Y.O+) (Class D)

4-40 (4-41) **2m (8 hdls)** £3,124.00 (£766.00) GOING minus 0.69 sec per fur (F)

Form	Horse	Dist	Pos	SP	RR	SF
790*	**Hamilton Silk (120)** (MCPipe) **4-12-0** JOsborne (hld up in tch: led on bit & hit last: hrd hld)	—	1	$5/6^{1}$	106+	32
159^{4}	**Kalzari (USA) (91)** (AWCarroll) **11-10-0** APMcCoy (swtg: trckd ldr: plld hrd: led 3 out: rdn & hdd last: no ch w wnr)	6	2	$3/1^{3}$	71	—
	Daytona Beach (IRE) (103) (DJSffrenchDavis) **6-10-12** GBradley (bkwd: led: hdd 3 out: p.u bef next: lame)		P	$2/1^{2}$	—	—

(SP 112.9%) **3 Rn**

3m 40.2 (-1.80) CSF £3.38 TOTE £1.70 (£2.60) OWNER Elite Racing Club (WELLINGTON) BRED Haydock Exhibitions Ltd
LONG HANDICAP Kalzari (USA) 9-13
WEIGHT FOR AGE 4yo-1lb
790* Hamilton Silk made light of carrying topweight and had no more than a decent school round. (5/6)
103 Kalzari (USA), who tends to race freely, found the winner in a different class, despite receiving 24lb. (3/1)

T/Plpt: £9.30 (679.36 Tckts). T/Qdpt: £8.30 (35.78 Tckts). CR

0899-EXETER (R-H) (Good to firm, Good patches)
Wednesday October 23rd

968 KRAFT JACOB SUCHARD NOVICES' HURDLE (4-Y.O+) (Class E)

1-50 (1-51) **2m 1f 110y (8 hdls)** £2,326.50 (£654.00: £319.50) GOING minus 0.11 sec per fur (G)

Form	Horse	Dist	Pos	SP	RR	SF
	Edgemoor Prince (PJHobbs) **5-10-12** RDunwoody (lw: chsd ldr tl led appr 4th: rdn appr last: styd on u.p flat)	—	1	$4/1^{2}$	79	—

Form	Horse	Dist	Pos	SP	RR	SF
790[F]	**Iktasab (110)** (PFNicholls) **4-11-4b** APMcCoy (mid div: hdwy to chse ldr after 6th: rdn & ev ch 2 out: hrd rdn & wknd flat)	5	**2**	2/7[1]	81	—
	Steer Point (RGFrost) **5-10-12** MrAHoldsworth (bit bkwd: hld up: hdwy 5th: r.o 2 out: nt rch ldrs)	21	**3**	33/1	55	—
885[P]	**Decor (IRE)** (RGFrost) **6-10-12** JFrost (bit bkwd: led tl appr 4th: wknd fr next)	4	**4**	20/1[3]	52	—
	Aradia's Diamond (TKeddy) **5-10-7** NWilliamson (bit bkwd: a bhd: lost tch 6th)	s.h	**5**	33/1	47	—
954[13]	**Lilly The Filly** (MrsBarbaraWaring) **5-10-7** EByrne (mid div: hdwy to chse wnr 5th: mstke next: sn wknd)	28	**6**	100/1	21	—
915[11]	**Mr Jasper** (NBThomson) **4-10-11** DMorris (plld hrd: in tch tl rdn & wknd 5th: t.o)	dist	**7**	150/1	—	—

(SP 110.1%) **7 Rn**

4m 18.0 (14.00) CSF £5.19 TOTE £4.80: £1.30 £1.10 (£1.60) OWNER The Racing Hares (MINEHEAD) BRED Mrs A. C. Wakeham
WEIGHT FOR AGE 4yo-1lb
Edgemoor Prince, making his hurdling debut, caused an upset and will come on for this. (4/1)
790 Iktasab, a bit of a character, could never get near the winner in the straight. (2/7)
Steer Point made headway from the fifth, but was never going to reach the front two. (33/1)

969 KITSONS (S) H'CAP HURDLE (0-95) (4-Y.O+) (Class G)

2-20 (2-21) **2m 1f 110y (8 hdls)** £1,887.80 (£530.80: £259.40) GOING minus 0.11 sec per fur (G)

Form	Horse	Dist	Pos	SP	RR	SF
	Aslar (IRE) (59) (JSMoore) **7-10-3** WMcFarland (mid div: hdwy 6th: led appr 2 out: clr last: comf)	—	**1**	8/1[3]	43	—
879[4]	**Glowing Path (76)** (RJHodges) **6-11-3**(3) TDascombe (a.p: chsd wnr appr last: no imp)	4	**2**	8/1[3]	56	—
888[2]	**Nordic Crown (IRE) (75)** (MCPipe) **5-11-5b** CMaude (led to 3rd: led 5th: rdn & hdd appr 2 out: one pce)	4	**3**	7/1[2]	52	—
899[3]	**Catwalker (IRE) (62)** (HJMWebb) **5-10-6b** RDunwoody (lw: bhd: r.o appr 2 out: nrst fin)	1¾	**4**	14/1	37	—
587[7]	**To Be Fair (77)** (PJHobbs) **9-11-0**(7) MrSDurack (prom: chsd ldr after 6th tl mstke 2 out: wknd)	1¾	**5**	14/1	51	—
900[7]	**Bite the Bullet (56)** (AJChamberlain) **5-10-0** BPowell (led 3rd to 5th: in tch tl rdn & wknd appr 2 out)	7	**6**	20/1	23	—
879[6]	**Galloping Guns (IRE) (67)** (BJLlewellyn) **4-10-7**(3) GuyLewis (hdwy to chse ldrs 5th: wknd appr 2 out)	18	**7**	20/1	18	—
749[5]	**Prestige Lady (68)** (BSmart) **5-10-12** CLlewellyn (bhd: lost tch after 2nd: sme hdwy next: sn bhd)	6	**8**	12/1	13	—
905[7]	**Welton Rambler (56)** (TNeedham) **9-10-0** PHolley (bit bkwd: chsd ldrs tl wknd 6th)	6	**9**	100/1	—	—
899[5]	**Mario's Dream (IRE) (65)** (MrsJGRetter) **8-10-9** MAFitzgerald (chsng ldrs whn fell 5th)		**F**	33/1	—	—
185[7]	**Sovereign Niche (IRE) (80)** (MCPipe) **8-11-10b** APMcCoy (ref to r: t.n.p)		**R**	11/1	—	—
899*	**Cashflow Crisis (IRE) (76)** (JWMullins) **4-11-0**(5) SRyan (lw: in tch whn uns rdr 6th)		**U**	5/4[1]	—	—

(SP 122.0%) **12 Rn**

4m 15.3 (11.30) CSF £66.52 CT £437.41 TOTE £9.80: £2.20 £2.50 £2.10 (£62.70) Trio £118.90 OWNER Mrs P. M. Ratcliffe (HUNGERFORD)
LONG HANDICAP Bite the Bullet 9-8 Welton Rambler 9-8
WEIGHT FOR AGE 4yo-1lb
No bid
Aslar (IRE), who has not run for almost two years, won this comfortably. He has got a pin in his off-fore knee and, as long as his legs hold out, he will win again. (8/1: 6/1-9/1)
879 Glowing Path chased the winner, but was never going to reach the winner. (8/1)
888 Nordic Crown (IRE), headed approaching two out, was one-paced over the last. (7/1)
To Be Fair (14/1: op 8/1)
600 Prestige Lady (12/1: op 8/1)
134 Sovereign Niche (IRE) planted himself at the start and refused to race. (11/1: op 6/1)

970 BOOKER FOODSERVICE FIRST FOR SERVICE DUCHY OF CORNWALL CUP NOVICES' CHASE (5-Y.O+) (Class D)

2-50 (2-50) **2m 6f 110y (17 fncs)** £4,140.00 (£1,260.00: £620.00: £300.00) GOING minus 0.11 sec per fur (G)

Form	Horse	Dist	Pos	SP	RR	SF
889[4]	**Mr Playfull (86)** (RGFrost) **6-11-0** JFrost (lw: chsd ldrs tl led 5th: hdd briefly 12th: hdd 2 out: drvn to ld flat)	—	**1**	5/2[2]	96	—
	Goldenswift (IRE) (GBBalding) **6-10-9** APMcCoy (prom: ev ch 13th: led 2 out: rdn & hdd flat: no ex)	5	**2**	5/6[1]	87	—
	Mingus (USA) (83) (RHBuckler) **9-11-0** BPowell (bit bkwd: hld up: hdwy 12th: in tch tl wknd appr 2 out)	10	**3**	10/1	85	—
901[4]	**Our Nikki (72)** (PRRodford) **6-10-9** SBurrough (in tch tl stumbled after 10th: nt rcvr: t.o)	27	**4**	9/1[3]	61	—
	Yes We Are (ABarrow) **10-10-9** MAFitzgerald (bit bkwd: led to 1st: lost pl after 6th: sn bhd: t.o whn p.u bef 15th)		**P**	33/1	—	—
887[P]	**Vareck II (FR)** (MCPipe) **9-10-7**(7) BMoore (led to 5th: prom: led briefly 12th: wknd qckly after next: p.u bef 15th)		**P**	40/1	—	—
639[3]	**Rent Day (64)** (JWMullins) **7-10-9** SCurran (mid div: hdwy after 9th: sn in tch: mstke 12th: chsd wnr appr 14th: 3rd & btn whn blnd & uns rdr 15th)		**U**	16/1	—	—

(SP 113.5%) **7 Rn**

5m 53.3 (22.30) CSF £4.82 TOTE £2.90: £2.20 £1.10 (£2.50) OWNER Mr P. A. Tylor (BUCKFASTLEIGH) BRED P. A. Tylor
Mr Playfull, suited by the step up in trip, stayed on well. (5/2)
Goldenswift (IRE), making his chasing debut, jumped well, but could not live with the winner. He should soon be winning. (5/6)
Mingus (USA), who had not run for well over a year, ran a decent comeback race and should soon open his account. (10/1)

971 KITSONS H'CAP HURDLE (0-105) (4-Y.O+) (Class F)

3-20 (3-20) **2m 3f (9 hdls)** £2,706.70 (£761.20: £372.10) GOING minus 0.11 sec per fur (G)

Form	Horse	Dist	Pos	SP	RR	SF
822*	**Snow Board (77)** (MrsMerritaJones) **7-10-2**ow2 DerekByrne (in tch to 4th: rdn 7th: hrd rdn & hdwy appr 2 out: r.o u.p to ld flat)	—	**1**	7/4[1]	57	15
	Relative Chance (75) (JSKing) **7-10-0** NWilliamson (bhd: hdwy 6th: led appr 2 out to 2 out: led appr last: rdn & hdd flat: no ex)	1¾	**2**	12/1	54	14
	Handson (88) (BRMillman) **4-10-7**(5) DSalter (bit bkwd: hld up & bhd: gd hdwy 6th: sn prom: led & hit 2 out: hdd & wknd appr last)	12	**3**	14/1	56	15
904[3]	**Little Hooligan (85)** (GFEdwards) **5-10-10b** APMcCoy (bhd: hdwy 5th: chsd ldrs next: rdn & wknd 2 out)	19	**4**	100/30[2]	37	—
902[2]	**Bright Sapphire (79)** (DBurchell) **10-10-4** DJBurchell (led 2nd to 4th: led briefly appr 2 out: sn wknd)	3	**5**	8/1	29	—
	Mr Flutts (78) (JCTuck) **10-10-3** RBellamy (bkwd: chsd ldr tl wknd 7th)	1¼	**6**	16/1	27	—
884[2]	**Fleur de Tal (99)** (WGMTurner) **5-11-3**(7) JPower (led to 2nd: prom: led 5th tl hdd & wknd appr 2 out)	hd	**7**	13/2[3]	48	8
741[9]	**Dominion's Dream (104)** (MCPipe) **4-11-7v**(7) GSupple (bhd fr 4th: t.o 6th)	2½	**8**	25/1	51	10
868[6]	**Winter Rose (82)** (MSheppard) **5-10-7** BPowell (chsd ldr tl led 4th: hdd & wknd next: t.o)	6	**9**	16/1	24	—
916[4]	**Take a Flyer (IRE) (85)** (RJHodges) **6-10-7b**(3) TDascombe (mid div tl wknd 6th: t.o whn p.u bef 2 out)		**P**	12/1	—	—

Allahrakha (75) (MHill) **5-10-0** SFox (bkwd: prom to ½-wy: wknd 6th: t.o whn p.u bef last)........ P 20/1 — —
(SP 126.3%) **11 Rn**

4m 33.1 (7.10) CSF £23.71 CT £226.08 TOTE £2.90: £1.30 £6.20 £3.70 (£14.50) Trio £206.50; £87.29 to Newbury 24/10/96 OWNER Mr F. J. Sainsbury (LAMBOURN) BRED Juddmonte Farms
LONG HANDICAP Allahrakha 9-11 Snow Board 9-11
WEIGHT FOR AGE 4yo-1lb
822* Snow Board stayed on well after looking beaten three out. He has had back problems. (7/4)
Relative Chance ran well and should pick up a race. (12/1: op 8/1)
Handson had every chance until hitting two out. (14/1)

972 BOOKER FOODSERVICE FIRST FOR SERVICE NOVICES' H'CAP CHASE (0-100) (5-Y.O+) (Class E)
3-50 (3-50) **2m 1f 110y (8 fncs)** £2,971.55 (£898.40: £437.70: £207.35) GOING minus 0.11 sec per fur (G)

	Horse	Dist	Pos	SP	RR	SF
	Playing Truant (81) (DRGandolfo) **8-11-10** RDunwoody (chsd ldrs: mstke 6th: ev ch last: rdn & styd on to ld flat)	—	1	4/1 3	90	18
903²	**Chickabiddy (78)** (GFEdwards) **8-11-7** MAFitzgerald (bkwd: chsd ldr tl led 2 out: rdn, hdd & no ex flat)	1	2	11/8 1	86	14
551⁷	**Jewel Thief (78)** (GBBalding) **6-11-7v** APMcCoy (chsd ldrs: reminders 4th & 5th: lost tch 7th: t.o)	dist	3	9/2	—	—
889³	**Lord Nitrogen (USA) (85)** (BJLlewellyn) **6-12-0** BPowell (led to 2 out: ev ch whn fell last: rmntd)	6	4	5/2 2	—	—
738⁹	**Chukkario (57)** (JRBosley) **10-10-0** ILawrence (mstke 1st: a bhd: t.o whn p.u after 5th)		P	100/1	—	—

(SP 109.8%) **5 Rn**

4m 27.7 (11.70) CSF £9.54 TOTE £5.60: £3.20 £1.20 (£4.90) OWNER Mr David Moon (WANTAGE) BRED The Queen
Playing Truant, who had not won for four years, did it well after a good battle with Chickabiddy from the last. (4/1)
903 Chickabiddy led two out but was headed after the last and had no more to give. (11/8)
Jewel Thief never looked happy and did not jump well either. (9/2: op 3/1)

973 BOOKER FOODSERVICE FIRST FOR SERVICE NOVICES' HURDLE (4-Y.O+) (Class E)
4-20 (4-20) **2m 6f (11 hdls)** £2,305.50 (£648.00: £316.50) GOING minus 0.11 sec per fur (G)

	Horse	Dist	Pos	SP	RR	SF
800*	**Samlee (IRE) (114)** (PJHobbs) **7-11-5** APMcCoy (lw: mde all: mstke 9th: hld on u.p flat)	—	1	1/2 1	86	—
	Kendal Cavalier (96) (GBBalding) **6-10-12** BFenton (bit bkwd: bhd 4th: t.o 6th: stdy hdwy 9th: styd on flat: nt rch wnr)	1¼	2	7/2 2	78	—
748³	**General Mouktar** (MCPipe) **6-10-12v** CMaude (lw: hdwy to chse wnr 7th: ev ch 2 out tl wknd flat)	7	3	7/1 3	73	—
	Glistening Dawn (90) (TKeddy) **6-11-0b** RJohnson (hdwy appr 7th: ev ch tl wknd appr 2 out)	22	4	20/1	59	—
	Gerry's Pride (IRE) (79) (JWMullins) **5-10-12** SCurran (bit bkwd: chsd ldrs tl wknd appr 2 out)	4	5	25/1	54	—
	Profession (FGray) **5-10-12** RFarrant (bkwd: a bhd: wknd 7th: t.o whn p.u bef next)		P	100/1	—	—
913⁸	**Colin's Pride (56)** (MrsSDWilliams) **5-10-2b**(5) SophieMitchell (chsd wnr tl wknd qckly 7th: t.o whn p.u bef next)		P	100/1	—	—

(SP 112.0%) **7 Rn**

5m 32.2 (22.20) CSF £2.67 TOTE £1.40: £1.10 £1.60 (£2.20) OWNER White Lion Partnership (MINEHEAD) BRED Mrs. E. Moorhead
800* Samlee (IRE) made hard work of this and will now go chasing. (1/2: op 4/5)
Kendal Cavalier stayed on after the last and will come on for this. (7/2: 5/2-4/1)
748 General Mouktar had every chance two out until he cried enough after the last. (7/1: op 3/1)

T/Plpt: £18.30 (441.49 Tckts). T/Qdpt: £3.80 (150.63 Tckts). T

0825-LUDLOW (R-H) (Firm, Good to firm patches)
Thursday October 24th
Race 4: one fence omitted
WEATHER: fine

974 HALFORD NOVICES' HURDLE (4-Y.O+) (Class E)
2-20 (2-20) **2m (9 hdls)** £2,388.00 (£668.00: £324.00) GOING minus 0.79 sec per fur (F)

	Horse	Dist	Pos	SP	RR	SF
859⁵	**Pegasus Bay (85)** (DECantillon) **5-11-5** JOsborne (lw: stdd s: hdwy 6th: led 2 out: clr last: easily)	—	1	20/1	75+	8
	Todd (USA) (PMitchell) **5-10-12** GBradley (sn chsng ldr: led & hit 3 out: hdd next: one pce)	4	2	12/1	64	—
	Drakestone (92) (RLBrown) **5-10-12** RJohnson (bkwd: hld up: hdwy appr 3 out: rdn & r.o flat)	2½	3	11/1	62	—
915*	**Ath Cheannaithe (FR) (92)** (JNeville) **4-11-4** DBridgwater (mde most tl hdd appr 3 out: sn wknd & eased)	5	4	6/4 1	64	—
876⁴	**King Rat (IRE)** (JGMO'Shea) **5-10-7**(5) MichaelBrennan (in tch: j.slowly & lost pl 4th: kpt on again fr 2 out)	4	5	11/4 2	53	—
829²	**Superensis** (JohnBerry) **6-10-12** ILawrence (s.s: a in rr)	12	6	25/1	41	—
871⁹	**Young Benson** (TWall) **4-10-8**(3) RMassey (lw: racd keenly: trckd ldrs tl wknd qckly appr 3 out: t.o)	18	7	33/1	23	—
900⁶	**Spumante (85)** (MPMuggeridge) **4-10-11b**[1] BPowell (a bhd: t.o fr 5th)	10	8	16/1	13	—
905*	**Last Laugh (IRE) (79)** (KCBailey) **4-10-13b** APMcCoy (swtg: a bhd: t.o fr 6th)	1½	9	6/1 3	13	—
	Bargash (PDEvans) **4-10-11** GaryLyons (chsd ldrs tl wknd appr 3 out: t.o)	5	10	25/1	6	—
865¹⁵	**Barton Blade (IRE)** (MissHCKnight) **4-10-11** JFTitley (prom: mstke 2nd: bhd fr ½-wy: t.o)	7	11	25/1	—	—

(SP 122.1%) **11 Rn**

3m 36.9 (-0.10) CSF £216.35 TOTE £27.00: £3.60 £3.30 £3.40 (£50.70) Trio Not won; £233.39 to Doncaster 25/10/96 OWNER Mr Don Cantillon (NEWMARKET) BRED R. P. Dineen
WEIGHT FOR AGE 4yo-1lb
859 Pegasus Bay, much happier back over the minimum trip, left these rivals standing between the last two. (20/1)
Todd (USA), a winner on the All-Weather on the Flat, showed plenty of promise on this hurdling debut, and should not have much trouble in going one better. (12/1)
Drakestone looked very burly for this seasonal bow, but was putting in some serious work in the latter stages. There is certainly a race in him. (11/1: 8/1-12/1)
915* Ath Cheannaithe (FR) could never get away from the runner-up and, at the end of the day, that was probably the main reason that they had nothing left in the tank after taking one another on from the start. (6/4: op 9/4)
876 King Rat (IRE), not at all happy on such fast ground, lost touch with the leaders before halfway and, though he did make some late progress, he was never a factor. (11/4)
905* Last Laugh (IRE) (6/1: 4/1-13/2)

975 CASTLE (S) H'CAP CHASE (0-90) (5-Y.O+) (Class G)

2-50 (2-50) **2m (13 fncs)** £2,668.00 (£748.00: £364.00) GOING minus 0.44 sec per fur (GF)

				SP	RR	SF
886[4]	**Fenwick (85)** (RJHodges) **9-11-8**(3) TDascombe (trckd ldrs: led 4 out: clr fr 2 out: comf)	—	1	3/1[2]	94	27
531[6]	**Cardenden (IRE) (73)** (JBarclay) **8-10-13** AThornton (w ldr: led appr 6th to 4 out: wknd 2 out)	11	2	14/1	71	4
751[2]	**Safety (USA) (88)** (JWhite) **9-12-0b** AMaguire (led tl appr 6th: styd on one pce fr 2 out)	4	3	5/2[1]	82	15
15[P]	**Master Salesman (73)** (MrsVCWard) **13-10-13** JRKavanagh (bkwd: hld up & bhd: hdwy 6th: chal 4 out: wknd qckly appr 2 out)	1¼	4	20/1	66	—
835[3]	**Gabish (60)** (BScriven) **11-9-7**(7) MrRThornton (trckd ldrs tl outpcd 8th)	8	5	15/2[3]	45	—
222[6]	**Hugh Daniels (72)** (BPreece) **8-10-9**(3) GHogan (bkwd: lost pl 5th: sn t.o)	28	6	20/1	29	—
68[P]	**Salcombe Harbour (NZ) (63)** (DrPPritchard) **12-10-3** DrPPritchard (bkwd: a bhd: t.o)	2½	7	33/1	17	—
883[P]	**Red Match (68)** (RJHodges) **11-10-8** BPowell (bkwd: chsd ldng pair to 6th: wl bhd whn p.u bef 9th)		P	25/1	—	—
873*	**Spring Loaded (78)** (JGMO'Shea) **5-10-12**(5) MichaelBrennan (hld up: hdwy 9th: rdn & hld whn blnd & uns rdr 2 out)		U	5/2[1]	—	—

(SP 116.9%) **9 Rn**

3m 55.5 (3.50) CSF £38.89 CT £109.49 TOTE £3.90: £1.30 £2.40 £1.60 (£25.70) Trio £22.40 OWNER Major A. W. C. Pearn (SOMERTON) BRED A. E. Bishop

LONG HANDICAP Gabish 9-11

WEIGHT FOR AGE 5yo-1lb

Bt in 4,800 gns

601 Fenwick took advantage of this step down to selling company with a runaway success, and this versatile individual who can win at all trips can score again now that he has returned to form. (3/1)

11 Cardenden (IRE) tried hard to make a race of it, but the winner took his measure early in the straight and he was soon fighting a lost cause. (14/1: 10/1-16/1)

751 Safety (USA), taken on from the break, was forced to give best out in the country and, though he did stay on, he had to admit the leading pair too good for him at the weights. (5/2)

Master Salesman has not won a race for a few years and he is now a bit long in the tooth. He did not fare badly in this company, and there could be a race in him still at this level. (20/1)

873* Spring Loaded (5/2: op 6/4)

976 FARMERS STORES H'CAP HURDLE (0-120) (4-Y.O+) (Class D)

3-20 (3-20) **2m (9 hdls)** £2,684.00 (£812.00: £396.00: £188.00) GOING minus 0.79 sec per fur (F)

				SP	RR	SF
790[3]	**Yubralee (USA) (111)** (MCPipe) **4-11-10** APMcCoy (mde all: sn clr: eased flat)	—	1	11/8[1]	97+	14
	Cyrus the Great (IRE) (105) (KCBailey) **4-11-4** GBradley (bkwd: chsd wnr fr 3rd: rdn appr 3 out: no imp)	6	2	9/4[2]	85	2
868*	**Stay With Me (FR) (95)** (CREgerton) **6-10-9** JOsborne (chsd wnr to 3rd: sn lost tch: rallied appr 3 out: wknd appr last)	8	3	9/4[2]	67	—
	Cabin Hill (100) (MrsAPrice) **10-11-0** MrMJackson (bkwd: outpcd: a t.o)	28	4	20/1	44	—
	Petitjean (IRE) (98) (PWegmann) **5-10-12** TEley (bkwd: bhd & outpcd whn fell 4th)		F	14/1[3]	—	—

(SP 115.1%) **5 Rn**

3m 36.6 (-0.40) CSF £4.97 TOTE £2.10: £1.10 £1.50 (£2.70) OWNER Mr D. A. Johnson (WELLINGTON) BRED Gainsborough Farm Inc

WEIGHT FOR AGE 4yo-1lb

790 Yubralee (USA), one of only two who were race-fit, was always going a gear faster than his rivals, and recorded his first success on such lively ground. (11/8)

Cyrus the Great (IRE) usually needs a race or two to put an edge on him, and his brave attempt to threaten the winner had come to an end before reaching the home straight. (9/4)

868* Stay With Me (FR) could not compete with the strong pace set by the winner, even though he was receiving 15lb, but it must be said that this was something of a disappointing effort. (9/4)

Petitjean (IRE) (14/1: 10/1-16/1)

977 LUDLOW MOTORS NOVICES' CHASE (5-Y.O+) (Class E)

3-50 (3-50) **2m 4f (16 fncs)** £3,035.00 (£920.00: £450.00: £215.00) GOING minus 0.44 sec per fur (GF)

				SP	RR	SF
880[2]	**Imperial Vintage (IRE) (104)** (MissVenetiaWilliams) **6-11-12** APMcCoy (mde all: mstke 3 out: clr whn blnd last: unchal)	—	1	1/2[1]	102	31
216[2]	**Dancing At Laharn (IRE)** (MissSJWilton) **6-10-12** GaryLyons (chsd wnr: rdn & pckd 3 out: sn outpcd)	14	2	9/2[2]	77	6
828[2]	**Little By Little (60)** (BPreece) **6-10-12** AThornton (lost tch ½-wy: t.o)	dist	3	10/1	—	—
	Native Rambler (IRE) (54) (MrsAPrice) **6-10-12** MrMJackson (bkwd: a bhd: t.o fr 7th)	20	4	50/1	—	—
653[7]	**Terrano Star (IRE)** (DBurchell) **5-10-7**(3) GuyLewis (bit bkwd: 3rd whn fell 7th)		F	8/1[3]	—	—
889[P]	**Priory Rose** (GAHam) **9-10-7** SBurrough (swtg: bkwd: trckng ldrs whn fell 4th)		F	66/1	—	—

(SP 108.5%) **6 Rn**

4m 55.3 (3.30) CSF £3.04 TOTE £1.40: £1.10 £2.20 (£2.30) OWNER Mr David Williams (HEREFORD) BRED W. J. Mernagh

WEIGHT FOR AGE 5yo-2lb

880 Imperial Vintage (IRE) only had to get a clear round to win this poor event, but he does take chances and it was probably as well these fences were not too solid. (1/2)

216 Dancing At Laharn (IRE) could need a stiff test of stamina over fences, for he is a winner between the Flags, and he was only shaken off after landing awkwardly at the third last. (9/2)

Terrano Star (IRE) (8/1: 7/2-9/1)

978 HAZLIN DOORS NOVICES' H'CAP HURDLE (0-100) (4-Y.O+) (Class E)

4-20 (4-20) **2m 5f 110y (11 hdls)** £2,276.00 (£636.00: £308.00) GOING minus 0.79 sec per fur (F)

				SP	RR	SF
900[3]	**Crown Ivory (NZ) (66)** (PCRitchens) **8-10-9** SFox (hld up in rr: hdwy 8th: rdn appr 2 out: styd on to ld flat)	—	1	100/30[3]	49	6
819[3]	**Saltis (IRE) (76)** (ALForbes) **4-11-4** GaryLyons (hld up: hdwy 5th: led after 8th: clr whn hit 3 out: rdn appr last: hdd & no ex flat)	1¾	2	9/1	58	14
77[4]	**One More Dime (IRE) (72)** (JLNeedham) **6-10-8**(7) MrRThornton (bkwd: lost pl 5th: t.o)	dist	3	8/1	—	—
792[5]	**Karen's Typhoon (IRE) (74)** (PJHobbs) **5-11-3b**[1] APMcCoy (led tl wknd & hdd after 8th: sn t.o)	4	4	13/8[1]	—	—

			SP	RR	SF
	Curragh Peter (81) (MrsPBickerton) **9-11-7**(3) GuyLewis (bkwd: chsd ldr tl appr 6th: wknd qckly: t.o) ....dist	**5**	25/1	—	—
913[2]	**Mylordmayor (57)** (PBowen) **9-10-0b** RFarrant (chsd ldrs: 2nd whn mstke 7th: p.u & dismntd bef next)	**P**	9/4[2]	—	—
			(SP 116.9%)		**6 Rn**

4m 59.3 (-1.70) CSF £28.14 TOTE £5.00: £2.40 £3.20 (£12.20) OWNER Mrs B. D. Adams (TIDWORTH) BRED R. J. & W. P. McKinnon
WEIGHT FOR AGE 4yo-1lb
900 Crown Ivory (NZ) needed to work hard to open his account and it was his undoubted stamina that proved the deciding factor. (100/30)
819 Saltis (IRE) finished ahead of the winner last month, but he was meeting him on 12lb worse terms this time and, though he looked to have the prize sewn up turning in, had probably kicked for home too soon. (9/1: op 7/2)
One More Dime (IRE) (8/1: 5/1-9/1)
Karen's Typhoon (IRE) raced much too freely in his first-time blinkers, and he had run himself to a standstill at the end of the back straight.(13/8)
913 Mylordmayor (9/4: 3/1-2/1)

979 COURT OF HILL AMATEUR H'CAP CHASE (0-110) (5-Y.O+) (Class E)

4-50 (4-50) **2m 4f (17 fncs)** £3,110.10 (£873.60: £426.30) GOING minus 0.44 sec per fur (GF)

			SP	RR	SF
	Coolree (IRE) (105) (PFNicholls) **8-11-11**(7) MrJTizzard (bit bkwd: a.p: led 12th: blnd 3 out: clr last).............—	**1**	2/1[2]	113	38
63[6]	**Oscail An Doras (IRE) (108)** (FMurphy) **7-12-4**(3) KWhelan (hld up & bhd: hdwy 10th: chsd wnr fr 13th: one pce fr 3 out) 5	**2**	6/4[1]	112	37
867[4]	**Houghton (105)** (WJenks) **10-11-11**(7) MrRBurton (chsd ldr: blnd 10th: sn lost tch: t.o) ....dist	**3**	5/1	—	—
	Mr Primetime (IRE) (90) (CPEBrooks) **6-10-10**(7) MrEJames (bkwd: led: clr 6th: hdd 12th: 3rd & wkng whn fell 4 out)	**F**	100/30[3]	—	—
825[3]	**They All Forgot Me (80)** (AWCarroll) **9-10-0**(7) MissCDyson (outpcd & bhd: t.o whn uns rdr 4 out)....................	**U**	25/1	—	—
			(SP 116.9%)		**5 Rn**

4m 54.9 (2.90) CSF £5.62 TOTE £3.20: £1.60 £1.60 (£3.50) OWNER Mr B. T. R. Weston (SHEPTON MALLET) BRED Joe Logan
LONG HANDICAP They All Forgot Me 9-3
Coolree (IRE) invariably performs well when fresh, but he did not look right in his coat and the fact that he could win easily in such condition, would suggest there is plenty more improvement to follow. (2/1)
63 Oscail An Doras (IRE) looked well-tuned up for this first outing since the summer and he looked to be travelling best entering the straight, but when the button was pressed, the response was nil. (6/4)
Mr Primetime (IRE) really attacked his fences in the early stages and soon raced clear, but lack of peak fitness caught up with him down the back straight, and he was legless when he came to grief. (100/30: 9/4-7/2)

980 CLUN INTERMEDIATE N.H. FLAT RACE (4, 5 & 6-Y.O) (Class H)

5-20 (5-20) **2m** £1,316.80 (£364.80: £174.40)

			SP	RR	SF
865*	**Scoundrel** (KCBailey) **5-11-4**(7) MrRWakley (a.p: led on bit 3f out: sn clr: canter) ....—	**1**	4/9[1]	—	—
	Gunner Sid (BPreece) **5-10-11**(7) MissLBoswell (bkwd: hld up: hdwy ½-wy: chsd wnr fnl 2f: no imp).............14	**2**	14/1	—	—
	Tafzal (PWegmann) **5-10-11**(7) SFowler (bkwd: hld up & bhd: hdwy 6f out: one pce fnl 3f).............................nk	**3**	33/1	—	—
	Strike A Light (IRE) (MissHCKnight) **4-10-10**(7) MrAWintle (hld up & bhd: hdwy 4f out: nvr nrr)........................6	**4**	9/2[2]	—	—
	Gergaash (GThorner) **4-10-10**(7) ClareThorner (bkwd: hld up: hdwy 5f out: nt rch ldrs)...............................1¼	**5**	16/1	—	—
	Milling Brook (JMBradley) **4-10-10**(7) JPower (hld up: hdwy 5f out: nvr nrr)..3½	**6**	50/1	—	—
918[7]	**Weather Wise** (WGMTurner) **4-10-10**(7) NWillmington (prom tl wknd over 4f out)..2½	**7**	50/1	—	—
	Mr C-I-P (IRE) (KSBridgwater) **5-10-13**(5) MichaelBrennan (bkwd: hdwy 10f out: led 7f out to 3f out: sn wknd) 3	**8**	66/1	—	—
918[6]	**Leopard Lady** (NJHawke) **4-10-5**(7) MrRThornton (trckd ldrs over 10f: sn lost tch) 6	**9**	50/1	—	—
	Barnetts Boy (JMBradley) **4-11-0**(3) DWalsh (bit bkwd: unruly s: bhd fr ½-wy: t.o).......................................4	**10**	20/1	—	—
	Derring Knight (NJPomfret) **6-11-4v**[1] MrASansome (bkwd: a bhd: t.o)..7	**11**	100/1	—	—
	Syban (BPreece) **5-11-1**(3) GHogan (prom tl wknd 6f out: t.o)...4	**12**	66/1	—	—
	Deference Due (IRE) (RJPrice) **5-11-4** MrMJackson (bkwd: prom: led after 6f to 7f out: wknd qckly over 3f out: t.o)..........................24	**13**	33/1	—	—
918[10]	**Little Embers** (JMBradley) **4-10-9**(3) RMassey (a bhd: t.o) 15	**14**	50/1	—	—
	Teeton Two (RHBuckler) **5-10-11b**[1](7) MrBDixon (plld hrd: led 6f: wknd qckly: t.o).......................................dist	**15**	12/1[3]	—	—
			(SP 130.1%)		**15 Rn**

3m 30.9 CSF £9.75 TOTE £1.50: £1.10 £2.50 £12.30 (£6.00) Trio £120.50 OWNER Mrs J. M. Corbett (UPPER LAMBOURN) BRED Mrs P. Nicholson
WEIGHT FOR AGE 4yo-1lb
865* Scoundrel carries a lot of condition but he is in a class of his own in these contests, and he does look to be a real racehorse. (4/9)
Gunner Sid did well to win a separate race for the runner-up spot and, if he can steer clear of anything as good as the winner, he must have a chance of going one better. (14/1: op 7/1)
Tafzal stayed on well in this racecourse debut, and with this run to sharpen him up, should be able to show further improvement. (33/1)
Strike A Light (IRE) was unable to get himself into contention but he is short of experience as yet. (9/2: 5/2-5/1)
Teeton Two (12/1: 20/1-33/1)

T/Plpt: £93.30 (104.76 Tckts). T/Qdpt: £6.00 (135.9 Tckts). IM

0981a - 1002a : (Irish Racing) - See Computer Raceform

0140a-LIMERICK (Ireland) (R-H) (Yielding)
Sunday October 20th

1003a MURPHY IRISH STOUT MUNSTER NATIONAL (LISTED) H'CAP CHASE (5-Y.O+)
4-15 (4-23) **3m (16 fncs)** IR £12,900.00 (IR £3,700.00: IR £1,700.00: IR £500.00)

	Horse	Dist	Pos	SP	RR	SF
	Three Brownies (MFMorris,Ireland) **9-10-1b** CO'Dwyer (chd ldr tl led 13th: jnd briefly bef 2 out: rdn & styd on whn chal)	—	1	16/1	117	—
763a[F]	**Lord Singapore (IRE)** (JJWalsh,Ireland) **8-10-13** NWilliamson (hld up: hdwy 10th: 3rd & rdn 4 out: wnt 2nd & slt mstke 2 out: chal u.p & ev ch nr last: no ex)	3	2	11/4[1]	127	—
	Twin Rainbow (IRE) (PDOsborne,Ireland) **9-10-1** LPCusack (in tch: rdn & chsng ldrs 4 out: cl 4th whn mstke 2 out: one pce u.p appr last: lft 3rd: kpt on same pce)	10	3	6/1[3]	108	—
763a[3]	**Second Schedual** (MissAMMcMahon,Ireland) **11-11-12** RDunwoody (hld up: chsd ldrs fr 12th: 6th 3 out: rdn & no imp after 2 out: kpt on)	2	4	5/1[2]	132	—
	Minella Lad (JohnNallen,Ireland) **10-11-3** THorgan (hld up: mstke 7th: mod 7th 3 out: no imp next)	20	5	16/1	110	—
	Beat The Second (IRE) (VTO'Brien,Ireland) **8-10-0** FWoods (in tch early: mostly mid div: n.d)	20	6	16/1	79	—
	Love the Lord (IRE) (DO'Connell,Ireland) **6-11-0** TPTreacy (in tch: mstke 1st: lost pl bef 11th: n.d fr 4 out)	12	7	8/1	85	—
	Heist (NMeade,Ireland) **7-10-8** MDwyer (hld up in tch: j.slowly 4th: 5th at 12th: rdn & hdwy after 2 out: wnt mod 3rd st: btn whn fell last)		F	10/1	—	—
	Lisselan Prince (IRE) (FSutherland,Ireland) **8-10-10** JFTitley (led: slipped & j.slowly 3rd: j.slowly 7th: mstke & jnd 12th: hdd 4 out: disp ld again appr 2 out: 3rd & slt mstke 2 out: wkng whn fell last)		F	10/1	—	—
763a[6]	**Royal Mountbrowne** (APO'Brien,Ireland) **8-12-0** CFSwan (hld up towards rr: hdwy 4th: 7th at 10th: towards rr whn mstke next: dropped bhd: p.u bef 3 out)		P	12/1	—	—
	Ballyboden (IRE) (MHourigan,Ireland) **9-10-0** MPHourigan (in tch: n.d 4 out: p.u bef 2 out)		P	20/1	—	—
	Albert's Fancy (IRE) (PJPDoyle,Ireland) **10-10-0** FrancisFlood (a towards rr: mstkes: lost tch 8th: n.d whn p.u bef 4 out)		P	50/1	—	—

(SP 119.0%) **12 Rn**

5m 58.7 OWNER Mrs A. M. Daly (FETHARD)

Three Brownies, making his first appearance since Aintree, belied the doubts about his fitness. Always in the first pair, he went on after the second last and stayed on strongly when challenged. Liverpool again in December and then another tilt at the National is the plan. (16/1)
Lord Singapore (IRE) went second when blundering two out, but still had every chance approaching the last. He could not quicken on the flat and softer ground will be in his favour. (11/4)
Twin Rainbow (IRE), having his first outing since finishing second to Billygoat Gruff at Punchestown, made a pleasing reappearance. Fourth when making a mistake two out, he was not finding much under pressure coming to the last and, after being left third, could only keep on at the one pace. (6/1)
763a Second Schedual, in sixth three out, could only stay on steadily from the next. (5/1)
Heist, successful in a minor event at Navan five days previously, was a moderate third and represented no threat when falling at the last. (10/1)

NR

1004a - 1006a : (Irish Racing) - See Computer Raceform

FAKENHAM (L-H) (Good, Good to firm patches)
Friday October 25th
Race 5: one flight omitted
WEATHER: unsettled

1007 WALSINGHAM (S) H'CAP HURDLE (0-95) (4-Y.O+) (Class G)
2-20 (2-20) **2m (9 hdls)** £2,713.50 (£828.00: £409.00: £199.50) GOING: 0.38 sec per fur (GS)

	Horse	Dist	Pos	SP	RR	SF
879*	**Hamadryad (IRE) (89)** (MrsVCWard) **8-11-5**(7) MrRThornton (lw: hld up: hit 4th: ev ch whn hit 2 out: sn led: clr whn blnd last)	—	1	15/8[2]	73	20
955[9]	**Total Asset (65)** (ALForbes) **6-10-2** GaryLyons (bit bkwd: prom: led 3rd to next: led 6th: sn hdd: r.o flat)	5	2	12/1	44	—
	Alosaili (78) (JCullinan) **9-11-1** VSlattery (a.p: led appr 3 out tl appr last: sn btn)	¾	3	20/1	56	3
822[2]	**Ragamuffin Romeo (72)** (HJCollingridge) **7-10-9** RichardGuest (prom: outpcd 3 out: no ch after)	7	4	11/8[1]	43	—
	Tondres (USA) (84) (JNorton) **5-11-7** WFry (bit bkwd: hld up & bhd: r.o fr 2 out: nvr nrr)	15	5	33/1	40	—
723[9]	**Pusey Street Boy (74)** (JRBosley) **9-10-11** MBosley (t: lw: lost pl 3rd: bhd fr 5th)	15	6	10/1	15	—
	Ben Connan (IRE) (67) (JohnWhyte) **6-9-11**(7)ow4 MrRWakley (bit bkwd: bhd fr 5th)	5	7	100/1	3	—
	Lock Tight (USA) (63) (MissCJECaroe) **6-10-0** DLeahy (swtg: bkwd: t.o fr 5th)	dist	8	100/1	—	—
949[5]	**Fierce (89)** (JRJenkins) **8-11-12b[1]** GBradley (led to 3rd: led 4th tl hdd & blnd 6th: p.u bef next)		P	7/1[3]	—	—

(SP 115.9%) **9 Rn**

4m 1.5 (17.50) CSF £22.44 CT £313.45 TOTE £2.60: £1.50 £2.70 £3.00 (£17.20) Trio £109.70 OWNER Mrs R F Key & Mrs V C Ward (GRANTHAM) BRED P. Myerscough
LONG HANDICAP Ben Connan (IRE) 9-0 Lock Tight (USA) 9-0
No bid

879* Hamadryad (IRE) did not jump fluently, but was always travelling well and had the race won when flattening the last. He is above plating-class in this mood. (15/8: 5/4-2/1)
Total Asset, who will probably be better again for the race, found this course a little too tight, but still ran well. (12/1: 6/1-14/1)
Alosaili, off since May 1995, returned looking pretty fit and only ran out of gas going to the last. He has proved hard to win with in the past, but does look on a winning mark at present. (20/1)
822 Ragamuffin Romeo looked to be wasting his time over two miles on such a sharp track. (11/8)
Tondres (USA) had a nightmare over hurdles when tried a couple of seasons back, but did better this time, although he will probably need further. (33/1)
Pusey Street Boy ran no sort of race. (10/1)
862 Fierce (7/1: op 4/1)

1008 WEATHERBYS STUD BOOK CONDITIONAL H'CAP CHASE (0-110) (5-Y.O+) (Class E)

2-50 (2-51) **3m 110y (18 fncs)** £3,308.20 (£1,009.60: £498.80: £243.40) GOING: 0.21 sec per fur (G)

	Horse	Dist	Pos	SP	RR	SF
	Sprowston Boy (81) (MCChapman) **13-10-4**(5) RossBerry (bit bkwd: bhd: hdwy appr 2 out: rdn to ld flat)	—	1	$7/2^{2}$	91	4
720^{3}	**Lucky Dollar (IRE) (100)** (KCBailey) **8-12-0** GHogan (led to 6th: hit 14th: led appr 2 out tl flat: no ex)	2½	2	$5/4^{1}$	108	21
	Joker Jack (72) (RDean) **11-10-0** TDascombe (j.w: led 6th tl appr 2 out: kpt on)	2	3	40/1	79	—
896^{4}	**Trumpet (100)** (JGMO'Shea) **7-12-0** MichaelBrennan (prom: 3rd & rdn whn pckd 4 out: wknd appr 2 out)	dist	4	$4/1^{3}$	—	—
	Soloman Springs (USA) (84) (MrsVCWard) **6-10-12v** DParker (hmpd & j.slowly 1st: sn t.o: p.u bef 7th)		P	9/2	—	—

(SP 107.3%) **5 Rn**

6m 27.1 (24.10) CSF £7.80 TOTE £3.30: £1.70 £1.10 (£3.30) OWNER Mr Geoff Whiting (MARKET RASEN) BRED Mrs R. Newton
LONG HANDICAP Joker Jack 9-4

Sprowston Boy enjoys his outings here and proved as game as ever when the chips were down. (7/2)
720 Lucky Dollar (IRE), fluent in the early stages, did not look too happy once he surrendered the lead. (5/4: op evens)
Joker Jack jumped well for one who does most of his racing over timber. (40/1)
896 Trumpet needs to hear his hooves rattle and did not run to his best. (4/1: op 2/1)

1009 WIMPEY HOMES NOVICES' CHASE (5-Y.O+) (Class E)

3-20 (3-20) **2m 110y (12 fncs)** £3,321.50 (£1,013.00: £500.00: £243.50) GOING: 0.21 sec per fur (G)

	Horse	Dist	Pos	SP	RR	SF
745^{5}	**Devilry (100)** (RCraggs) **6-10-12** RJohnson (hld up & bhd: blnd 3rd: hdwy 8th: led flat: rdn out)	—	1	$3/1^{2}$	86	13
950^{12}	**Shalik (IRE)** (JRJenkins) **6-10-5**(7) NTEgan (led after 1st: clr 3 out: hdd flat: unable qckn)	4	2	25/1	82	9
947^{4}	**Wilde Music (IRE)** (CPEBrooks) **6-10-12** GBradley (lw: hld up & bhd: hdwy whn blnd & lost tch 8th: hdwy appr 2 out: eased appr last)	1	3	$4/7^{1}$	81	8
975^{U}	**Spring Loaded (78)** (JGMO'Shea) **5-10-13**(5) MichaelBrennan (chsd ldr: hit 4 out: wknd after next)	11	4	$9/2^{3}$	78	4
744^{5}	**Doctor-J (IRE)** (JWhite) **6-10-12** BFenton (lw: led tl after 1st: bhd fr 7th)	26	5	33/1	45	—
677^{5}	**Desert Challenger (IRE)** (JRJenkins) **6-10-12b** SFox (prom: 3rd whn fell 9th)		F	10/1	—	—
972^{P}	**Chukkario (57)** (JRBosley) **10-10-12** MBosley (j.b: bhd tl p.u bef 5th)		P	66/1	—	—
860^{P}	**Ishma (IRE)** (MrsLCJewell) **5-10-11b** TJMurphy (j.b: prom to 5th: t.o whn p.u bef 9th)		P	66/1	—	—

(SP 125.7%) **8 Rn**

4m 14.5 (14.50) CSF £59.53 TOTE £4.50: £1.30 £3.90 £1.10 (£49.80) OWNER A T McAllister & S Wilson (SEDGEFIELD) BRED Tarworth Bloodstock Investments Ltd
WEIGHT FOR AGE 5yo-1lb

Devilry, whose pilot did well to sit tight after an early mistake, was set an awful lot to do and only began to get going in the last half-mile. This tight track was probably against him and he is better than this. (3/1)
744 Shalik (IRE) tried to slip the field and, with the two favourites sat so far out of their ground, is probably flattered by the result. (25/1)
947 Wilde Music (IRE), reappearing just six days after his seasonal debut, probably found this coming too soon, but tended to hang right and did not handle the track. He still looked as though he might take a hand after the second last, but his pilot had accepted defeat by the last. (4/7)
873* Spring Loaded, having his second run in twenty-four hours, hit four out and was soon in trouble. (9/2)
531 Doctor-J (IRE), only a plater over hurdles, was soon in trouble. (33/1)

1010 MICHAEL SCOTNEY TURF ACCOUNTANT H'CAP HURDLE (0-105) (4-Y.O+) (Class F)

3-50 (3-50) **2m (9 hdls)** £3,355.00 (£1,024.00: £506.00: £247.00) GOING: 0.38 sec per fur (GS)

	Horse	Dist	Pos	SP	RR	SF
949^{2}	**Pair of Jacks (IRE) (87)** (GLMoore) **6-10-8**(3) DFortt (trckd ldrs: led 2 out: hit last: rdn out)	—	1	$2/1^{1}$	73	10
908^{7}	**Roi du Nord (FR) (96)** (SWCampion) **4-11-2**(3) PMidgley (lw: hdwy 6th: ev ch 2 out: rdn whn blnd last)	2	2	5/1	80	16
65^{P}	**Red Light (82)** (JRJenkins) **4-9-12v**(7) NTEgan (lw: hld up: hit 3rd: hdwy 3 out: r.o flat)	6	3	14/1	60	—
786^{2}	**Robsera (IRE) (85)** (JJQuinn) **5-10-9** LWyer (lw: hld up: rdn & hit 3 out: nvr able to chal)	1½	4	$9/4^{2}$	62	—
	Viaggio (84) (ALForbes) **8-10-8v** GaryLyons (bit bkwd: led to 2 out: sn btn)	½	5	25/1	60	—
	Watch My Lips (102) (MHTompkins) **4-11-8**(3) KGaule (bit bkwd: hld up: effrt 6th: nvr trbld ldrs)	¾	6	$9/2^{3}$	77	13
	Salisong (85) (JohnWhyte) **7-10-2**(7) MrRWakley (chsd ldr: hit 5th: dropped rr next)	hd	7	9/1	60	—

(SP 119.5%) **7 Rn**

4m 0.7 (16.70) CSF £12.47 TOTE £2.50: £1.30 £3.00 (£10.10) OWNER Mr D. A. Wilson (BRIGHTON) BRED Loan and Development Corporation
WEIGHT FOR AGE 4yo-1lb

949 Pair of Jacks (IRE), on this fast track and with no early pace, found his stamina not an issue and won well. (2/1)
Roi du Nord (FR) moved upsides the winner four from home but, although the two had it between them, was getting the worse of the argument when landing in a heap at the last. (5/1)
Red Light looked ready, despite being absent since June, but could do little to close the gap on the first two from the penultimate flight. (14/1: 10/1-16/1)
Viaggio set a steady pace for a circuit before picking up the tempo. Headed jumping the second last, he was soon outpaced. (25/1)
Watch My Lips looks to have strengthened during the summer and seemed very well in himself. The way the race was run probably did not suit his waiting tactics and he is worth keeping in mind. (9/2: op 2/1)
Salisong (9/1: op 6/1)

1011 LITTLE SNORING HURDLE (3-Y.O) (Class D)

4-20 (4-20) **2m (8 hdls)** £2,733.00 (£834.00: £412.00: £201.00) GOING: 0.38 sec per fur (GS)

	Horse	Dist	Pos	SP	RR	SF
646^{2}	**Cottage Prince (IRE)** (JJQuinn) **3-10-9** LWyer (a.p: led 3 out: rdn out)	—	1	$2/1^{1}$	66	—
944^{5}	**Sunley Secure** (NoelChance) **3-10-12** RJohnson (a.p: ev ch appr 2 out: btn whn hit last)	3	2	$3/1^{2}$	66	—
646^{6}	**Stoleamarch** (ALForbes) **3-10-9** GaryLyons (in tch: 4th & rdn whn hit 3 out: kpt on)	1¾	3	16/1	61	—
	The Great Flood (CADwyer) **3-10-9** RichardGuest (r.o fr 2 out: nvr able to chal)	7	4	10/1	54	—
	Eurobox Boy (APJarvis) **3-10-12** DerekByrne (hld up: rdn appr 2 out: nvr able to chal)	nk	5	$9/2^{3}$	57	—
402^{4}	**Again Together** (GLMoore) **3-10-4** BFenton (lw: led to 3 out: sn wknd)	2½	6	10/1	46	—
881^{8}	**Verulam (IRE)** (JRJenkins) **3-11-2** GBradley (lw: hmpd 2nd: a bhd)	9	7	13/2	49	—
	Nordic Hero (IRE) (APJarvis) **3-10-9** ALarnach (b.d 2nd)		B	12/1	—	—

	Horse	Dist	Pos	SP	RR	SF
	It's Dawan (PMitchell) **3-10-6**(3) LAspell (b.d 2nd)		B	14/1	—	—
	Kulshi Momken (JNorton) **3-10-9** WFry (j.rt & fell 2nd)		F	25/1	—	—
				(SP 132.1%)		**10 Rn**

4m 2.8 (18.80) CSF £9.56 TOTE £2.80: £1.30 £1.20 £5.20 (£4.30) Trio £32.60 OWNER Mrs Kay Thomas (MALTON) BRED Owen Bourke

646 Cottage Prince (IRE) lacked a turn of foot on the level and was wisely made plenty of use of and, although not fluent at the last, still jumped it better than his challenger. (2/1)

944 Sunley Secure, just six days after his hurdling debut, ran a sound race, but already appeared held when untidy at the last. (3/1)

646 Stoleamarch has changed stables since his hurdles debut and stayed on under a strong ride. (16/1)

The Great Flood, a disappointing horse on the level, had just one behind him going to two out before staying on quite well. (10/1)

Eurobox Boy, just about the pick of these on the Flat, took a good hold going down and is not a guaranteed stayer. Held up, he found little off the bridle in the last half-mile. (9/2: 2/1-5/1)

402 Again Together clipped the top of the fifth and set a decent pace, which she increased on the final circuit. Once headed, she dropped away quickly. (10/1)

Nordic Hero (IRE) (12/1: op 8/1)

It's Dawan (14/1: 12/1-20/1)

1012 DEREHAM H'CAP CHASE (0-100) (5-Y.O+) (Class F)

4-50 (4-53) **2m 5f 110y (16 fncs)** £4,342.50 (£1,230.00: £607.50) GOING: 0.21 sec per fur (G)

	Horse	Dist	Pos	SP	RR	SF
867[2]	**Crafty Chaplain (97)** (DMcCain) **10-11-8**(3) DWalsh (lw: trckd ldr: led after 10th: hit 2 out: rdn out)	—	1	2/1[2]	105	38
830*	**Crackling Frost (IRE) (79)** (MrsDHaine) **8-10-7** GBradley (lw: led tl after 10th: mstke 3 out: sn rdn: no imp appr last)	8	2	4/7[1]	81	14
860[4]	**Fabulous Francy (IRE) (72)** (MissAEEmbiricos) **8-10-0** JRyan (mstkes 4th & 5th: sn t.o)	dist	3	8/1[3]	—	—
507[4]	**Mirage Dancer (72)** (MissCJECaroe) **13-10-0** ILawrence (bkwd: bhd tl fell 3rd)		F	16/1	—	—
				(SP 114.0%)		**4 Rn**

5m 29.9 (14.90) CSF £3.65 TOTE £2.70 (£1.50) OWNER Mr D. McCain (CHOLMONDELEY) BRED M. A. Doyle

LONG HANDICAP Mirage Dancer 9-9

OFFICIAL EXPLANATION **Fabulous Francy (IRE): finished distressed.**

867 Crafty Chaplain has suffered from seconditis throughout his career and it is easy to see why, for he looks anything but an easy ride once in front. (2/1)

830* Crackling Frost (IRE) looked a good horse while he was getting his own way, but not nearly as good when asked to play someone else's tune. (4/7)

860 Fabulous Francy (IRE) made two horrendous early blunders and was then hunted round for the place money. (8/1: 6/1-9/1)

1013 WEATHERBYS 'STARS OF TOMORROW' STANDARD OPEN N.H. FLAT RACE (4, 5 & 6-Y.O) (Class H)

5-20 (5-21) **2m** £1,196.00 (£331.00: £158.00)

	Horse	Dist	Pos	SP	RR	SF
	Boots Madden (IRE) (MissVenetiaWilliams) **6-11-4** RJohnson (lw: prom: led over 3f out: rdn out)	—	1	4/1[2]	—	—
	First Light (JJQuinn) **4-11-3** LWyer (lw: s.s: hdwy 6f out: chsd wnr fnl 2f: no imp)	6	2	9/2[3]	—	—
	Big Stan's Boy (CPEBrooks) **5-11-4** GBradley (bit bkwd: hld up: hdwy 8f out: btn over 2f out)	14	3	7/4[1]	—	—
865[6]	**Ardenbar** (JWPayne) **4-10-12** RichardGuest (chsd ldr tl led 6f out: hdd over 3f out: sn btn)	1¼	4	4/1[2]	—	—
	Cranbrook Lad (RCurtis) **4-11-3** DMorris (bit bkwd: hdwy 7f out: rdn 3f out: eased whn btn fnl f)	21	5	25/1	—	—
865[8]	**Warrio** (JRBosley) **6-11-4** MBosley (bit bkwd: chsd ldrs 11f)	s.h	6	20/1	—	—
	Barrie Stir (JWhite) **4-11-0**(3) GuyLewis (prom 10f)	2	7	13/2	—	—
	Counter Attack (IRE) (MissAEEmbiricos) **5-10-13** JRyan (in tch: rdn & hmpd 7f out: sn bhd)	3	8	16/1	—	—
	Holkham Bay (LWordingham) **4-10-12**(5) MichaelBrennan (prom tl wknd 5f out)	5	9	8/1	—	—
679[9]	**Havana Express** (CADwyer) **4-11-3** ILawrence (a bhd)	17	10	20/1	—	—
705[12]	**Rinus Majestic (IRE)** (DMcCain) **4-11-0**(3) DWalsh (led 10f: wknd qckly: t.o)	dist	11	25/1	—	—
				(SP 142.1%)		**11 Rn**

3m 53.8 CSF £25.93 TOTE £6.40: £2.10 £2.30 £1.50 (£28.90) Trio £20.10 OWNER Mr L. J. A. Phipps (HEREFORD) BRED Michael Hickey

WEIGHT FOR AGE 4yo-1lb

Boots Madden (IRE) cost 20,000 guineas at the Doncaster Sales, but is a really attractive chasing type. Looking fit and well, he would hardly be suited to such a tight track, but ran out an impressive winner in a fast time, and his future looks bright. (4/1: op 7/4)

First Light, a tall, rangy newcomer, looked fit, but caught a real tartar, despite running well. He lost as much ground at the start as he was beaten by. (9/2: 8/1-4/1)

Big Stan's Boy, a lengthy newcomer, showed knee-action and did not look fully wound up. Making his move on the outside of the field with a circuit left, he was easily left behind once the chips were down. (7/4)

865 Ardenbar was made to look pedestrian by the first two as the race developed. (4/1: op 5/2)

Cranbrook Lad got on the back of the leading group going out on the final circuit but, easily left behind, the situation was accepted and he was eased to almost a walk near the finish. (25/1)

865 Warrio could not go the pace from halfway on this tight track. (20/1)

T/Plpt: £37.90 (228.86 Tckts). T/Qdpt: £9.90 (61.81 Tckts). Dk

NEWBURY (L-H) (Chases Good to firm, Hdles Good)

Friday October 25th

WEATHER: fine

1014 CRUX EASTON HURDLE (3-Y.O) (Class C)

2-10 (2-13) **2m 110y (8 hdls)** £3,730.00 (£1,120.00: £540.00: £250.00) GOING minus 0.32 sec per fur (GF)

	Horse	Dist	Pos	SP	RR	SF
	Kerawi (NATwiston-Davies) **3-11-0** CLlewellyn (w ldr fr after 1st: led flat: rdn out)	—	1	9/2[3]	80	42
	Le Teteu (FR) (BobJones) **3-11-0** DBridgwater (gd hdwy 5th: ev ch flat: unable qckn)	1½	2	7/1	79	41
	Serenus (USA) (NJHenderson) **3-11-0** MAFitzgerald (led after 1st: rdn appr last: hdd flat: one pce)	1¼	3	4/1[2]	77	39
	Circus Star (DNicholson) **3-11-0** AMaguire (plld hrd: led tl after 1st: ev ch fr 3 out: one pce flat)	2	4	6/4[1]	75	37
	Laughing Buccaneer (DNCarey) **3-11-0** BPowell (nvr nrr: t.o)	dist	5	25/1	—	—
	Rivercare (IRE) (MJPolglase) **3-11-0** VSmith (prom to 2nd: t.o)	17	6	20/1	—	—
736[6]	**Seven Crowns (USA)** (CLPopham) **3-11-0** NWilliamson (prom to 2nd: t.o)	3½	7	33/1	—	—

	Horse	Pos	SP	RR	SF
	Classical Joker (RHAlner) **3-10-9** WMcFarland (hdwy 2nd: wknd 5th: t.o) 9	**8**	25/1	—	—
	Petros Gem (MJBolton) **3-10-9** PHide (hdwy 2nd: wknd 4th: t.o) 1	**9**	50/1	—	—
	Gold Lance (USA) (RJO'Sullivan) **3-11-0** PHolley (bit bkwd: bhd fr 5th: t.o) 1	**10**	16/1	—	—
	Dish The Dosh (DBurchell) **3-10-9** DJBurchell (a bhd: t.o) ....dist	**11**	33/1	—	—
	Locket (JABennett) **3-10-9** LHarvey (mstke 4th: bhd fr 5th: t.o whn p.u bef 2 out)	**P**	33/1	—	—
	Cast A Fly (IRE) (MSalaman) **3-10-9** BClifford (rel to r: t.o tl p.u bef 2nd)	**P**	50/1	—	—

(SP 121.8%) **13 Rn**

3m 49.1 (-0.90) CSF £34.28 TOTE £6.10: £1.70 £1.70 £1.80 (£14.10) Trio £16.20 OWNER Mr Matt Archer & Miss Jean Broadhurst (CHELTENHAM) BRED Juddmonte Farms

IN-FOCUS: **The first four pulled well clear and could all pay their way.**

Kerawi may not have seen a racecourse before, but he comes from a stable that knows how to get them spot on at the first time of asking. (9/2)

Le Teteu (FR) won a handicap on the Flat at Haydock in June. Swinging off the bridle in the straight, he may well have got his head in front for a few strides on the run-in before the winner found a bit extra. He should soon go one better. (7/1)

Serenus (USA) made the frame in each of his four runs on the Flat, but he lacked pace and that may well be the case over hurdles. (4/1: op 5/2)

Circus Star, who won a maiden on the Flat this year for Sir Mark Prescott, pulled far too hard for his own good in the early stages, but nevertheless was on level terms in the straight until tapped for toe from the final flight. Once he learns to settle, he can open his account. (6/4)

1015 FLEETLEASE ANNIVERSARY H'CAP HURDLE (0-145) (5-Y.O+) (Class B)

2-40 (2-41) **2m 110y (8 hdls)** £5,059.00 (£1,424.00: £697.00) GOING minus 0.32 sec per fur (GF)

	Horse	Pos	SP	RR	SF
717a[2]	**Country Star (IRE) (122)** (CPEBrooks) **5-10-8** JOsborne (mde all: pushed out) ....—	**1**	2/1[2]	102	42
793*	**Mytton's Choice (IRE) (117)** (DNicholson) **5-10-3** AMaguire (chsd wnr: blnd 3rd: ev ch appr last: mstke last: unable qckn) 1½	**2**	Evens[1]	96	36
	Oh So Risky (142) (DRCElsworth) **9-12-0** PHolley (a in rr) 15	**3**	100/30[3]	106	46

(SP 106.4%) **3 Rn**

3m 47.8 (-2.20) CSF £4.02 TOTE £2.50 (£1.30) OWNER H R H Prince Fahd Salman (LAMBOURN) BRED M. L. Page

717a Country Star (IRE) has been raised 12lb since his Newton Abbot victory at the beginning of August but has since run two good races in France. Racing with his tongue tied down, he adopted his front-running role and needed only to be nudged along to have the measure of the runner up. He now goes to the sales. (2/1)

793* Mytton's Choice (IRE) who has risen 12lb since his recent success, raced in second place but nearly got rid of Maguire at the third. Nevertheless, he was still in with every chance going to the final flight but an error at that hurdle did him no favours and he failed to find another gear. (Evens)

Oh So Risky, who failed by a short head to give Large Action 24lb here in the 1994 Tote Gold Trophy, is a shadow of his former self and has won just once since 1991. He had a disastrous campaign last season and after travelling well in the race, tamely dropped away two out. It is very sad to see a horse of his calibre run like this and he should be retired. (100/30)

1016 KONE LIFTS H'CAP CHASE (5-Y.O+) (Class B)

3-10 (3-10) **2m 4f (16 fncs)** £7,469.00 (£2,084.00: £1,007.00) GOING minus 0.32 sec per fur (GF)

	Horse	Pos	SP	RR	SF
	Strong Medicine (126) (KCBailey) **9-10-4** CO'Dwyer (hld up: lft 2nd appr 4 out: led appr 2 out: rdn out) ....—	**1**	11/4[2]	133	22
	Easthorpe (141) (MissHCKnight) **8-11-5** JFTitley (bit bkwd: led 2nd to 3rd: led 5th to 9th: led 11th tl appr 2 out: hrd rdn flat: r.o) 1½	**2**	5/2[1]	147	36
	Commercial Artist (150) (NAGaselee) **10-12-0** CLlewellyn (hld up: 3rd whn blnd bdly 4 out: sn wknd) 20	**3**	12/1	140	29
	Egypt Mill Prince (149) (MrsJPitman) **10-11-13** WMarston (bit bkwd: led 3rd to 5th: led 9th to 11th: 2nd whn p.u bef 4 out: lame)	**P**	7/2[3]	—	—
314a[9]	**Boro Vacation (IRE) (130)** (PFNicholls) **7-10-8** APMcCoy (led: mstke 1st: mstke & hdd 2nd: mskte 8th: bhd fr 9th: blnd & uns rdr 11th)	**U**	7/2[3]	—	—

(SP 107.4%) **5 Rn**

4m 57.3 (2.30) CSF £9.12 TOTE £3.70: £1.60 £1.70 (£3.90) OWNER Dr D. B. A. Silk (UPPER LAMBOURN) BRED E. O'Neill

Strong Medicine, having his first run in six months, now goes straight for the Hennessy, which does seem an extremely ambitious move. (11/4)

Easthorpe takes a bit of getting fit according to his trainer, but ran a big race, making sure the winner did not have things all his own way and sticking to his task commendably well to the end. A prolific two-mile winner, this was his first venture over this trip but he definitely saw it out, and he will now head for the Murphys - formerly the Mackeson. (5/2)

Commercial Artist, who has had a soft-palate operation, is more at home over three miles with some cut in the ground. A bad mistake four out when about two lengths down sealed his fate. (12/1)

Egypt Mill Prince, looking as though the run would do him good, disputed the lead and was still travelling well in second when breaking down approaching the fourth last. (7/2)

Boro Vacation (IRE), an ex-Irish gelding who won four on the trot in the spring, was making his debut for his new stable, but he seems to have a problem with his jumping if this run is anything to go by, and gave McCoy no chance of staying in the saddle at the sixth last. (7/2)

1017 NEWBURY AUTUMN HURDLE (4-Y.O) (Class B)

3-40 (3-40) **2m 110y (8 hdls)** £4,796.00 (£1,448.00: £704.00: £332.00) GOING minus 0.32 sec per fur (GF)

	Horse	Pos	SP	RR	SF
	Mistinguett (IRE) (132) (NATwiston-Davies) **4-10-12** CLlewellyn (led after 1st: comf) ....—	**1**	3/1[2]	101	51
	Hatta Breeze (129) (DNicholson) **4-10-12** AMaguire (hld up: chsd wnr fr 2 out: unable qckn) 7	**2**	13/2	94	44
	Paddy's Return (IRE) (141) (FMurphy) **4-11-7** RDunwoody (led tl after 1st: hrd rdn & ev ch 3 out: wknd appr last) 10	**3**	10/11[1]	94	44
790[5]	**Alltime Dancer (IRE) (125)** (OSherwood) **4-11-3** JOsborne (lw: prom to 5th: t.o) ....dist	**4**	4/1[3]	—	—

(SP 110.7%) **4 Rn**

3m 46.6 (-3.40) CSF £16.36 TOTE £4.50 (£10.80) OWNER Mr John Duggan (CHELTENHAM) BRED Michael Quirke

Mistinguett (IRE), an unfurnished filly who was beaten fair and square by Paddy's Return on two occasions last season, gained her revenge here and, soon at the head of affairs, comfortably had the measure of her rivals at the second last. (3/1)

Hatta Breeze, off the track since running a moody sort of race at Punchestown back in April, struggled into second place two out but never threatened to reel in the winner. (13/2: 3/1-7/1)

Paddy's Return (IRE) did not really have conditions in his favour and, although in with every chance three from home, Dunwoody was hard at work and punters knew their fate from the penultimate hurdle. He will come into his own over two and a half miles in a strongly-run race with blinkers back on. (10/11: 5/4-4/5)
790 Alltime Dancer (IRE) goes well on a sound surface, which made this performance even more disappointing as he looked in trouble from the cross hurdle. (4/1)

1018 PENWOOD NOVICES' CHASE (5-Y.O+) (Class D)

4-10 (4-10) **2m 1f (13 fncs)** £4,062.00 (£1,132.00: £546.00) GOING minus 0.32 sec per fur (GF)

				SP	RR	SF
	Plunder Bay (USA) (118) (NJHenderson) **5-11-6** MAFitzgerald (lw: mstke 2nd: chsd ldr to 7th: chsd ldr appr 4 out: hrd rdn appr last: led flat: all out)	—	**1**	4/6^{1}	100+	49
	Clifton Game (MRChannon) **6-11-2** AThornton (chsd ldr fr 7th: led 8th: pckd 9th: hdd flat: r.o wl)	nk	**2**	9/2^{3}	95	45
889*	**Ambassador Royale (IRE) (91)** (MissAEBroyd) **8-11-7** AMaguire (led tl blnd & hdd 8th: mstke 9th: wknd appr 3 out: t.o)	dist	**3**	9/4^{2}	—	—
				(SP 109.0%)		**3 Rn**

4m 2.9 (-1.10) CSF £3.35 TOTE £1.60 (£2.70) OWNER W V & Mrs E S Robins (LAMBOURN) BRED Marion G. Montanari
WEIGHT FOR AGE 5yo-1lb
Plunder Bay (USA), the only runner without a recent run under his belt, had a real fight on his hands and full marks must go to Fitzgerald who beavered away and eventually managed to get the gelding narrowly in front on the run-in. (4/6)
Clifton Game, winner of a maiden handicap on the Flat at Yarmouth in August, gave the winner some serious problems. Sent on six out, he looked to be travelling far better than the winner between the last two fences and, although collared on the run-in, refused to give way and only just went down. He jumped well in the main on this chasing debut and, with this experience under his belt, should be able to pick up a similar event before long. (9/2: tchd 3/1)
889* Ambassador Royale (IRE) took the field along, but a bad error six out lost him the advantage. Punters knew their fate early in the straight. (9/4)

1019 OCTOBER H'CAP HURDLE (0-145) (4-Y.O+) (Class B)

4-40 (4-40) **3m 110y (12 hdls)** £4,919.00 (£1,472.00: £706.00: £323.00) GOING minus 0.32 sec per fur (GF)

				SP	RR	SF
724^{2}	**Lansdowne (118)** (PFNicholls) **8-10-9** APMcCoy (hld up: rdn appr last: led flat: r.o wl)	—	**1**	7/2^{2}	98	2
	Jack Button (IRE) (136) (BobJones) **7-11-13** DBridgwater (bit bkwd: stdy hdwy 3 out: led 2 out tl flat: unable qckn)	1½	**2**	5/1	115	19
	Yes Man (IRE) (112) (MissHCKnight) **7-10-3** JFTitley (bit bkwd: led to 2 out: one pce)	4	**3**	7/4^{1}	88	—
	Newton Point (137) (DNicholson) **7-12-0** AMaguire (chsd ldr: rdn 8th: ev ch 2 out: one pce)	s.h	**4**	9/2^{3}	113	17
884^{4}	**Acrow Line (114)** (DBurchell) **11-10-5** DJBurchell (prom to 3 out)	18	**5**	14/1	79	—
	Mr Kermit (129) (AJWilson) **5-11-6** LHarvey (prom to 3 out)	5	**6**	14/1	90	—
721^{2}	**Fieldridge (118)** (MPMuggeridge) **7-10-9** BPowell (hdwy 8th: wknd 3 out)	4	**7**	9/1	77	—
				(SP 116.8%)		**7 Rn**

5m 45.4 (9.10 under best) (-0.60) CSF £20.24 TOTE £4.00: £1.90 £2.50 (£11.30) OWNER Mr R. F. Denmead (SHEPTON MALLET) BRED J. A. C. Drake
724 Lansdowne made the transition back to hurdles a winning one. Shaken up going to the last, he gained control on the run-in and proved too strong for the runner-up. (7/2: op 6/1)
Jack Button (IRE), who damaged a tendon in the 1995 Chester Cup, had been off the course since, but ran an absolute blinder on this return. He appeared to be travelling best of all going to the final flight, but lack of a recent run took its toll on the run-in and he was passed. Given time to recover from this, he should be winning before long, especially if the ground is soft. (5/1: 7/2-11/2)
Yes Man (IRE), looking as if the run would do him good, took the field along to the second last before failing to quicken. (7/4)
Newton Point was in tremendous form last season and, as a result, climbed in the handicap. A stuffy individual who needs a lot of coaxing, he will come on for this and should soon return to the winner's enclosure. (9/2)
605* Acrow Line, who found this company too hot, was in trouble going to the third last. (14/1)
Mr Kermit (14/1: op 8/1)

T/Plpt: £158.30 (109.23 Tckts). T/Qdpt: £42.80 (21.59 Tckts). AK

0852-CARLISLE (R-H) (Good, Chases Good to firm patches)
Saturday October 26th

WEATHER: showery

1020 GREAT GABLE NOVICES' HURDLE (4-Y.O+) (Class E)

1-55 (1-55) **2m 1f (9 hdls)** £2,486.00 (£696.00: £338.00) GOING minus 0.13 sec per fur (G)

				SP	RR	SF
871*	**Contrafire (IRE)** (MrsASwinbank) **4-11-4** JSupple (lw: trckd ldrs: led 5th: hit last: pushed clr: comf)	—	**1**	4/11^{1}	75+	—
801^{3}	**Monaco Gold (IRE)** (MrsMReveley) **4-10-8**(3) GCahill (lw: trckd ldr: effrt & hit 3 out: nt qckn appr last)	5	**2**	6/1^{2}	63	—
794^{9}	**Pentland Squire** (JMJefferson) **5-10-12** RichardGuest (hld up: wnt prom 5th: outpcd fr 3 out)	20	**3**	16/1	45	—
939^{3}	**Amber Holly (65)** (JEDixon) **7-10-7** BStorey (wnt prom 5th: rdn & wknd 3 out)	12	**4**	8/1^{3}	28	—
586^{F}	**Pattern Arms** (DMoffatt) **4-10-11** DJMoffatt (chsd ldrs: effrt 6th: wknd after next)	16	**5**	33/1	18	—
	Homecrest (BEllison) **4-10-11** ADobbin (hld up: nt j.w: sme hdwy 5th: wknd after next)	17	**6**	25/1	2	—
	Stinging Bee (WGReed) **5-10-12** TReed (bit bkwd: outpcd & bhd fr 6th)	11	**7**	100/1	—	—
	Regal Domain (IRE) (MrsLMarshall) **5-10-12** DBentley (bit bkwd: rdn & lost pl 5th: t.o 3 out)	21	**8**	33/1	—	—
	Le Amber (IRE) (ACWhillans) **7-10-7** BHarding (plld hrd: led & sn clr: hdd 5th: t.o 3 out)	8	**9**	100/1	—	—
				(SP 116.3%)		**9 Rn**

4m 16.2 (15.20) CSF £3.40 TOTE £1.30: £1.00 £1.70 £2.60 (£2.10) Trio £9.80 OWNER G B Turnbull Ltd (RICHMOND) BRED Thoroughbred Trust in Ireland
WEIGHT FOR AGE 4yo-1lb
871* Contrafire (IRE) took this modest event with something in hand. (4/11: 4/7-1/3)
801 Monaco Gold (IRE) ran much better than first time, but proved no match for the winner. (6/1: op 7/2)
Pentland Squire, a chasing type, took a keen hold and, asked to do just enough to secure third spot, was by no means knocked about. (16/1)
939 Amber Holly, who made no appeal whatsoever in the paddock, did not run up to her Kelso form. (8/1: op 5/1)

1021 SADDLEBACK NOVICES' HURDLE (4-Y.O+) (Class E)

2-25 (2-28) **2m 4f 110y (11 hdls)** £2,556.00 (£716.00: £348.00) GOING minus 0.13 sec per fur (G)

				SP	RR	SF
	Shanavogh (90) (GMMoore) **5-10-12** JCallaghan (wnt prom 4th: led 3 out: hit last: styd on strly)	—	**1**	3/1[2]	72	33
866*	**Ela Mata** (MrsASwinbank) **4-11-4** JSupple (lw: trckd ldrs: chal 3 out: rdn & nt qckn between last 2)	5	**2**	6/4[1]	75	35
910[5]	**Rule Out The Rest** (MrsSarahHorner-Harker) **5-11-5** MFoster (lw: chsd ldrs: led 6th to 3 out: sn outpcd: rallied between last 2)	3	**3**	8/1[3]	73	34
866[7]	**Sister Gale** (MrsSJSmith) **4-10-6** RichardGuest (bhd: hdwy 8th: outpcd fr 3 out)	24	**4**	50/1	42	2
910[9]	**Lifebuoy (IRE)** (JRTurner) **5-10-12** TReed (sn bhd: hdwy 3 out: styd on flat)	nk	**5**	33/1	47	8
	Trap Dancer (PMonteith) **8-10-12** ADobbin (bkwd: hld up: stdy hdwy 7th: prom 3 out: grad wknd)	1½	**6**	33/1	46	7
	Emilymoore (82) (PBeaumont) **5-10-7** RSupple (s.s: bhd: hdwy u.p 7th: rdn & wknd 3 out)	nk	**7**	16/1	40	1
	Signor Nortone (DWWhillans) **4-10-11** BHarding (hld up: t.o 3 out)	dist	**8**	20/1	—	—
3[4]	**Dalusman (IRE) (76)** (IRFerguson,Ireland) **8-10-12** RDunwoody (bhd fr 6th: t.o)	nk	**9**	10/1	—	—
7[3]	**Mullins (IRE)** (DMoffatt) **5-10-12** DJMoffatt (hld up: hdwy 8th: wknd qckly next: t.o)	1	**10**	20/1	—	—
878[4]	**Thaleros (81)** (GMMoore) **6-10-12** NBentley (w ldrs: led 4th to 6th: hrd rdn & blnd 8th: sn wknd: t.o)	4	**11**	14/1	—	—
785[F]	**Laurie-O (66)** (DALamb) **12-10-12b** JBurke (chsd ldrs tl lost pl 5th: t.o 3 out)	17	**12**	100/1	—	—
	To Say The Least (MrsNHope) **6-10-5**(7) SHaworth (bkwd: nt j.w: sn bhd: wl t.o 5th)	dist	**13**	100/1	—	—
	Kirchwyn Lad (RShiels) **8-10-12** BStorey (led to 4th: wknd 6th: t.o 3 out: p.u bef last)		**P**	9/1	—	—
	Clairabell (IRE) (JIACharlton) **5-10-7** KJohnson (chsd ldrs to 5th: sn lost pl: wl t.o whn p.u bef last)		**P**	25/1	—	—
787[4]	**Farmers Subsidy** (MissMKMilligan) **4-10-11** DParker (prom to 5th: t.o 7th: p.u bef 3 out)		**P**	50/1	—	—
				(SP 132.9%)	**16 Rn**	

4m 55.7 (4.70) CSF £8.18 TOTE £5.40: £2.00 £1.60 £5.00 (£8.10) Trio £15.80 OWNER Mr Sean Graham (MIDDLEHAM) BRED Brick Kiln Stud Farm

WEIGHT FOR AGE 4yo-1lb

Shanavogh, well supported in the market, stayed on really well to win going away. (3/1: op 6/1)
866* Ela Mata, a weak-looking type, found the winner much too strong from the last. (6/4)
910 Rule Out The Rest, who helped set the pace, was tapped for foot at the bottom of the hill, but was staying on nicely at the finish and will be suited by three miles. (8/1)
Sister Gale, a weak-looking type, ran much better than she had first time. (50/1)
Lifebuoy (IRE), an excitable type, will be suited by three miles. (33/1)
Trap Dancer, a point-to-point winner, faded up the hill and will presumably soon switch to fences. (33/1)
878 Thaleros (14/1: op 8/1)

1022 HELVELLYN NOVICES' CHASE (4-Y.O+) (Class D)

2-55 (2-59) **2m 4f 110y (16 fncs)** £3,829.80 (£1,160.40: £567.20: £270.60) GOING minus 0.13 sec per fur (G)

				SP	RR	SF
	Solomon's Dancer (USA) (GRichards) **6-11-5** ADobbin (lw: trckd ldrs: stumbled bnd bef 10th: led 4 out: shkn up between last 2: styd on strly)	—	**1**	10/11[1]	114	43
528[3]	**Castleroyal (IRE)** (IRFerguson,Ireland) **7-11-11** RDunwoody (led 3rd to 4th: led 12th to next: kpt on u.p flat: no imp)	2½	**2**	4/1[2]	118	47
	Shawwell (81) (JIACharlton) **9-11-5** BStorey (hld up: stdy hdwy 10th: sn prom: wknd 3 out)	26	**3**	25/1	92	21
	Bold Account (IRE) (99) (GMMoore) **6-11-5** NBentley (hld up: stdy hdwy 10th: shkn up & wknd 4 out)	1½	**4**	8/1	91	20
	Dawn Lad (IRE) (MrsASwinbank) **7-11-5** JSupple (prom whn mstke 7th: bhd fr 10th)	16	**5**	20/1	78	7
102[5]	**Movac (IRE) (96)** (MissLucindaRussell) **7-11-11** MFoster (sn prom: wknd 11th)	4	**6**	6/1[3]	81	10
	Kenmore-Speed (MrsSJSmith) **9-11-5** RichardGuest (trckd ldrs: led 4th to 12th: wknd 4 out: eased)	13	**7**	16/1	65	—
873[2]	**Mr Reiner (IRE) (80)** (JWade) **8-11-5** KJones (bhd & outpcd 8th: p.u after 10th)		**P**	20/1	—	—
	Garcall (DWWhillans) **10-11-5** DBentley (bkwd: led to 3rd: lost pl 7th: t.o whn p.u bef 10th)		**P**	33/1	—	—
	Alicharger (70) (PMonteith) **6-11-2**(3) GCahill (sn bhd: t.o whn p.u bef 11th)		**P**	33/1	—	—
	Fox on the Run (GRichards) **9-11-5** BHarding (hld up: stdy hdwy 7th: p.u lame after 10th)		**P**	50/1	—	—
802[P]	**Jamarsam (IRE)** (NWaggott) **8-11-5** KJohnson (sn bhd: t.o whn p.u bef 11th)		**P**	200/1	—	—
	The Energiser (67) (DALamb) **10-11-5** JBurke (s.s: t.o whn p.u bef 10th)		**P**	200/1	—	—
				(SP 125.9%)	**13 Rn**	

5m 7.2 (4.20) CSF £5.47 TOTE £1.80: £1.50 £1.20 £4.00 (£4.00) Trio £29.40 OWNER Mr J. Hales (PENRITH) BRED David Hart

Solomon's Dancer (USA) never put a foot wrong and looks a very useful recruit. (10/11)
528 Castleroyal (IRE) ran really well and time will show that he faced a stiff task in trying to give 6lb to the winner. (4/1)
Shawwell tired up the hill as if just in need of the outing. (25/1)
Bold Account (IRE) ran with some promise and will be suited by a step up to three miles. (8/1)
4 Movac (IRE) (6/1: 9/2-7/1)
Kenmore-Speed, an excitable type, missed all last season. He showed that he retains much of his old ability, running really well until becoming leg-weary four from home. Allowed to come up the hill in his own time, he will soon step up considerably on this. (16/1)

1023 LADBROKES LUCKY CHOICE H'CAP HURDLE (0-115) (5-Y.O+) (Class E)

3-25 (3-29) **3m 110y (12 hdls)** £2,290.00 (£640.00: £310.00) GOING minus 0.13 sec per fur (G)

				SP	RR	SF
	Jocks Cross (IRE) (107) (GRichards) **5-12-0** ADobbin (lw: trckd ldrs: outpcd & rdn 8th: hdwy to ld appr 2 out: styd on wl u.p)	—	**1**	7/4[1]	91	—
	Grate Deel (IRE) (87) (PBeaumont) **6-10-8** RSupple (led to 5th: led 3 out tl appr next: nt qckn flat)	4	**2**	4/1	68	—
894[5]	**Exemplar (IRE) (91)** (MrsSJSmith) **8-10-12** RichardGuest (chsd ldrs: outpcd 8th: hdwy & ev ch 3 out: one pce fr next)	2½	**3**	100/30[2]	71	—
916[5]	**Emperor Chang (USA) (81)** (KOWarner) **9-9-13**(3)ow2 GCahill (chsd ldrs: outpcd 8th: ev ch & rdn 3 out: wknd appr last)	8	**4**	16/1	56	—
	The Stitcher (IRE) (103) (WGReed) **6-11-10** TReed (racd keenly: trckd ldr: led 5th to 3 out: wknd qckly & eased)	dist	**5**	7/2[3]	—	—
				(SP 107.5%)	**5 Rn**	

6m 13.1 (29.10) CSF £8.11 TOTE £1.90: £1.50 £2.10 (£4.00) OWNER Mrs Gill Harrison (PENRITH) BRED David McGrath

LONG HANDICAP Emperor Chang (USA) 9-13

Jocks Cross (IRE), who is not very big, proved well suited by the step up to three miles. After getting outpaced when the tempo increased a mile from home, in the end he won going away. He will be even better suited by carrying less weight in a better-class handicap. (7/4)

Grate Deel (IRE), who looks a chaser, could not match the winner for foot on the run-in. (4/1)
894 Exemplar (IRE) ran much better than he had done first time. (100/30)
798 Emperor Chang (USA), out of the handicap and carrying overweight, was not disgraced. (16/1)
The Stitcher (IRE), a keen-going type, stopped in two strides three out, his stamina having run right out. (7/2)

1024 SCAFELL H'CAP CHASE (0-125) (5-Y.O+) (Class D)
3-55 (3-59) **3m (18 fncs)** £3,576.30 (£1,082.40: £528.20: £251.10) GOING minus 0.13 sec per fur (G)

				SP	RR	SF
909*	**General Command (IRE) (118)** (GRichards) **8-11-10** RDunwoody (lw: trckd ldrs: shkn up to ld after 3 out: pushed clr flat: easily)	—	**1**	$8/11^{1}$	126+	6
857^{3}	**Supposin (96)** (MrsSJSmith) **8-10-2**^{ow2} RichardGuest (hdwy 12th: styd on u.p fr 4 out: nt qckn appr last)	7	**2**	$7/1^{3}$	99	—
57^{8}	**Gale Ahead (IRE) (100)** (GMMoore) **6-10-6** NBentley (trckd ldrs: rdn & outpcd 3 out: kpt on appr last)	4	**3**	10/1	101	—
857*	**Kushbaloo (117)** (CParker) **11-11-9** BStorey (lw: led tl after 3 out: wknd between last 2)	13	**4**	$3/1^{2}$	109	—
857^{P}	**Go Silly (103)** (BEllison) **10-10-6v**(3) GCahill (outpcd & bhd fr 12th)	20	**5**	20/1	82	—
	Greenhill Raffles (122) (MissLucindaRussell) **10-12-0** MFoster (hld up: hdwy & prom 12th: sn lost pl)	14	**6**	20/1	91	—
				(SP 114.0%)		**6 Rn**

6m 11.4 (19.40) CSF £6.31 TOTE £1.50: £1.40 £2.90 (£3.00) OWNER Mr Robert Ogden (PENRITH) BRED Miss M. Fenton
LONG HANDICAP Supposin 9-12
909* General Command (IRE) proved well suited by the step up in distance. He scored with plenty in hand and is a good deal better than his current handicap mark. (8/11)
857 Supposin, who has a history of breaking blood-vessels, finished an honourable second. (7/1)
57 Gale Ahead (IRE) ran well and this outing will have put an edge on him. (10/1)
857* Kushbaloo found this company too strong. (3/1)
857 Go Silly, pulled up on his first two outings, jumped better and is suited by extreme distances. (20/1)
Greenhill Raffles was struggling badly fully a mile from home. (20/1)

1025 OLD MAN OF CONISTON H'CAP HURDLE (0-110) (4-Y.O+) (Class E)
4-30 (4-31) **2m 1f (9 hdls)** £2,360.00 (£660.00: £320.00) GOING minus 0.13 sec per fur (G)

				SP	RR	SF
941^{5}	**Field of Vision (IRE) (100)** (MrsASwinbank) **6-11-10** JSupple (lw: trckd ldrs: drvn along 6th: sn outpcd: hrd rdn & styd on fr 3 out: led last 50y)	—	**1**	$7/2^{2}$	82	—
876*	**Supertop (98)** (LLungo) **8-11-8** MFoster (lw: hld up: wnt prom 6th: rdn to ld between last 2: hit last: hdd & no ex towards fin)	1¼	**2**	$2/1^{1}$	79	—
856^{3}	**Latin Leader (81)** (CParker) **6-10-5b** DParker (trckd ldrs: rdn & outpcd after 6th: styd on fr 2 out)	1¾	**3**	14/1	60	—
893^{2}	**Fen Terrier (92)** (FPMurtagh) **4-11-1** ADobbin (lw: led to 2nd: w ldrs: one pce appr last)	½	**4**	$7/2^{2}$	71	—
856*	**Well Appointed (IRE) (97)** (BMactaggart) **7-11-4**(3) GLee (lw: racd keenly: led 2nd tl appr last: wknd towards fin)	¾	**5**	$4/1^{3}$	75	—
	Jumbo Star (84) (JEDixon) **6-10-8** BStorey (bkwd: prom tl outpcd & lost pl 4th: sn bhd: t.o fr 3 out)	dist	**6**	33/1	—	—
	Environmental Law (78) (WMcKeown) **5-9-13**(3) GCahill (bit bkwd: outpcd & bhd fr 4th: t.o 3 out)	s.h	**7**	20/1	—	—
				(SP 112.1%)		**7 Rn**

4m 17.8 (16.80) CSF £10.41 TOTE £4.90: £3.00 £1.90 (£7.60) OWNER Panther Racing Ltd (RICHMOND) BRED Sean Collins
WEIGHT FOR AGE 4yo-1lb
941 Field of Vision (IRE), with the blinkers left off, responded to strong pressure to get up near the line. (7/2)
876* Supertop looked sure to succeed when going on travelling strongly between the last two but, after hitting the final flight, he was soon struggling and was edged out near the line. He does not look the bravest of battlers. (2/1)
856 Latin Leader, closely matched with Well Appointed on course and distance running, rallied under pressure. (14/1)
893 Fen Terrier had her measure taken going to the last. (7/2)
856* Well Appointed (IRE) would not settle and his stamina seemed to give out on the run-in. (4/1)

1026 GREAT DODD STANDARD N.H. FLAT RACE (4, 5 & 6-Y.O) (Class H)
5-00 (5-00) **2m 1f** £1,070.00 (£295.00: £140.00)

				SP	RR	SF
858*	**Northern Fusilier** (JMJefferson) **4-11-6**(7) MNewton (lw: hld up: stdy hdwy 9f out: led over 4f out: pushed clr over 1f out)	—	**1**	$8/13^{1}$	—	—
	Natural Talent (CParker) **4-11-3** DParker (led 3f: chal over 4f out: styd on one pce)	9	**2**	14/1	—	—
	Chill Factor (MrsMReveley) **6-10-11**(7) CMcCormack (a chsng ldrs: drvn along & outpcd over 2f out: kpt on fnl f)	5	**3**	14/1	—	—
	Old Cavalier (JJO'Neill) **5-11-4** ARoche (hld up: effrt 6f out: sn drvn along: one pce fnl 3f)	4	**4**	$8/1^{3}$	—	—
	Qattara (IRE) (WMcKeown) **6-11-8**(3) GCahill (bit bkwd: in tch: drvn 6f out: outpcd fnl 2f)	15	**5**	$4/1^{2}$	—	—
	Faster Ron (IRE) (RAllan) **5-10-11**(7) SMelrose (bit bkwd: chsd ldrs tl lost pl 4f out)	6	**6**	50/1	—	—
858^{2}	**Look Sharpe** (PBeaumont) **5-10-11**(7) BGrattan (led after 3f tl over 4f out: wknd 3f out)	4	**7**	16/1	—	—
858^{R}	**Jed Abbey** (RShiels) **4-10-5**(7) SHaworth (bit bkwd: prom tl lost pl 6f out: t.o whn m wd 3f out)	dist	**8**	33/1	—	—
	Monicas Buzz (ACWhillans) **6-10-6**(7) MDunne (in tch: drvn along 6f out: sn lost pl: t.o 3f out)	7	**9**	50/1	—	—
	Bloom'in Junes (IRE) (MrsLWilliamson) **4-10-12** MrRHale (bkwd: lost pl 7f out: sn wl t.o)	dist	**10**	50/1	—	—
				(SP 121.1%)		**10 Rn**

4m 11.1 CSF £10.91 TOTE £1.60: £1.10 £2.60 £1.30 (£6.30) Trio £52.50 OWNER Mr Joe Donald (MALTON) BRED G. Revitt
WEIGHT FOR AGE 4yo-1lb
858* Northern Fusilier, who has plenty of size and scope, had to be kept right up to his work and will be suited by two and a half miles over hurdles. (8/13)
Natural Talent, a typical offspring of Kris, showed plenty of knee-action going down. (14/1)
Chill Factor struggled to keep up and will need three miles over hurdles. (14/1)
Old Cavalier, an Irish point-to-point winner, was being driven along and only stayed on at the one pace soon after halfway. He looks a chaser. (8/1: op 5/1)
Qattara (IRE), in need of the outing, tired in the closing stages. (4/1)

T/Plpt: £5.20 (1,259.04 Tckts). T/Qdpt: £18.80 (80.51 Tckts). WG

0742-MARKET RASEN (R-H) (Good)

Saturday October 26th

WEATHER: fine

1027 ASSOCIATED BRITISH PORTS (S) H'CAP HURDLE (0-95) (4, 5 & 6-Y.O) (Class G)

2-15 (2-23) **2m 1f 110y (8 hdls)** £1,982.00 (£552.00: £266.00) GOING: 0.17 sec per fur (G)

Form	Horse	Dist	Pos	SP	RR	SF
687^{3}	**Count of Flanders (IRE) (76)** (KAMorgan) **6-11-2** ASSmith (mde all: unchal)	—	1	$11/4^{1}$	56	28
455^{4}	**Glenvally (81)** (BWMurray) **5-11-2**(5) ECallaghan (hld up: mstke 2nd: hdwy appr 2 out: rdn flat: no imp)	3½	2	12/1	58	30
892^{6}	**Flintlock (IRE) (71)** (HAlexander) **6-10-11** PNiven (prom: chsd wnr 4th to next: lost pl appr 3 out: lft poor 3rd last)	13	3	$7/1^{3}$	36	8
687^{4}	**Sea God (88)** (MCChapman) **5-12-0** WWorthington (swtg: hld up: hdwy 5th: wknd appr 2 out)	4	4	15/2	49	21
784^{3}	**Little Redwing (69)** (MDHammond) **4-10-8b** RGarritty (hld up: nvr trbld ldrs)	½	5	8/1	30	1
950^{3}	**Ranger Sloane (83)** (AStreeter) **4-11-8** GaryLyons (hld up: hdwy 5th: wknd appr 2 out)	3½	6	15/2	41	12
910^{11}	**Top Skipper (IRE) (68)** (MartynWane) **4-10-7** NSmith (bhd fr 5th)	4	7	12/1	22	—
893^{5}	**Fly to the End (USA) (72)** (JJQuinn) **6-10-12v** DerekByrne (prom to 5th)	4	8	14/1	22	—
648^{5}	**Wordsmith (IRE) (85)** (JLHarris) **6-11-11** PMcLoughlin (hld up: bhd fr 5th)	6	9	10/1	30	2
743^{P}	**Kajostar (66)** (SWCampion) **6-10-3**(3)ow6 DWalsh (s.s: hdwy 3rd: wkng whn mstke next: t.o)	19	10	40/1	—	—
416^{3}	**Pats Folly (62)** (FJYardley) **5-10-2**ow2 WMcFarland (a bhd: t.o)	hd	11	33/1	—	—
337^{6}	**Hutcel Bell (60)** (RDEWoodhouse) **5-10-0** LWyer (chsd wnr to 4th: wknd 3 out: p.u bef next)		P	50/1	—	—
	Fenian Court (IRE) (82) (HowardJohnson) **5-11-8** NWilliamson (prom: plld hrd: chsd wnr 5th: 3rd & wkng whn blnd & uns rdr last)		U	$6/1^{2}$	—	—

(SP 126.6%) **13 Rn**

4m 14.4 (11.40) CSF £35.39 CT £203.91 TOTE £3.90: £1.60 £4.90 £2.10 (£37.50) Trio £97.60 OWNER Mr K. A. Morgan (MELTON MOWBRAY) BRED London Thoroughbred Services Ltd

LONG HANDICAP Pats Folly 9-8 Hutcel Bell 9-0 Kajostar 9-7

WEIGHT FOR AGE 4yo-1lb

Bt in 3,000 gns

687 Count of Flanders (IRE) made the most of a drop in class. (11/4: op 6/1)

455 Glenvally, winner of a poor race at Southwell, seems to have found his level. (12/1)

892 Flintlock (IRE), dropping back in trip, was easily left behind over the final three flights. (7/1)

687 Sea God, who was just behind the winner last time, was more comprehensively beaten here. (15/2)

784 Little Redwing (8/1: 6/1-9/1)

950 Ranger Sloane (15/2: 5/1-8/1)

784 Top Skipper (IRE) (12/1: op 8/1)

Fenian Court (IRE), who races keenly, would have been third, albeit a poor third, but for capsizing at the final flight. (6/1)

1028 LINCOLNSHIRE BEEF DAY NOVICES' CHASE (5-Y.O+) (Class D)

2-45 (2-54) **2m 4f (15 fncs)** £3,968.75 (£1,190.00: £572.50: £263.75) GOING: 0.17 sec per fur (G)

Form	Horse	Dist	Pos	SP	RR	SF
	Simply Dashing (IRE) (TDEasterby) **5-10-12** LWyer (chsd ldr: led 7th to 8th: led 4 out: clr next: nearly carried out last)	—	1	$8/13^{1}$	92+	25
744^{4}	**Record Lover (IRE) (69)** (MCChapman) **6-11-0** WWorthington (prom: led 9th to 4 out: no ch w wnr)	21	2	$12/1^{3}$	75	10
	Cader Idris (MrsMReveley) **7-11-0** PNiven (prom: hmpd 4th: led 8th: hdd & hit 9th: sn lost pl)	11	3	$12/1^{3}$	66	1
	Gems Lad (MrsSJSmith) **9-10-7**(7) RWilkinson (bkwd: hld up: rdn 9th: sn bhd)	1½	4	66/1	65	—
870^{5}	**Mistroy** (MissMKMilligan) **6-10-9** ASSmith (hld up in tch: lft in ld 4th: hdd 7th: wknd 9th)	dist	5	50/1	—	—
	Uncle Keeny (IRE) (JJO'Neill) **6-11-0** MDwyer (led tl blnd & uns rdr 4th)		U	$5/2^{2}$	—	—

(SP 109.3%) **6 Rn**

5m 4.2 (13.20) CSF £7.66 TOTE £1.60: £1.10 £3.00 (£5.10) OWNER Mr Steve Hammond (MALTON) BRED Eastward Bloodstock Holdings Ltd

WEIGHT FOR AGE 5yo-2lb

Simply Dashing (IRE) was just that. Apart from one slight error two out, he jumped very well and, despite the efforts of a loose Uncle Keeny who bumped into him and nearly carried him out at the last, he ran out, as expected, a very easy winner. A progressive hurdler last term, he looks to have a bright future over fences. (8/13)

673 Record Lover (IRE) ran as well as could be expected and was simply outclassed. (12/1)

Cader Idris, a winning pointer, found these too sharp and probably needs a stiffer test. (12/1)

Uncle Keeny (IRE), who took the first three fences well, got it hopelessly wrong at the fourth and paid the penalty. (5/2)

1029 HOWARD SMITH TOWAGE AND SALVAGE H'CAP CHASE (0-130) (5-Y.O+) (Class C)

3-15 (3-25) **3m 1f (19 fncs)** £4,560.25 (£1,372.00: £663.50: £309.25) GOING: 0.17 sec per fur (G)

Form	Horse	Dist	Pos	SP	RR	SF
857^{2}	**Dark Oak (110)** (JWCurtis) **10-11-0** LWyer (led to 4th: led appr last: edgd rt flat: rdn out)	—	1	$9/2^{3}$	116	31
	Deep Decision (100) (PCheesbrough) **10-10-4** ASSmith (prom: lost pl 5th: hdwy 12th: led 4 out: hdd appr last: r.o)	nk	2	10/1	106	21
857^{4}	**Magic Bloom (105)** (JMJefferson) **10-10-4**(5) ECallaghan (hld up: hdwy 15th: hit 3 out: r.o flat)	2½	3	13/2	109	24
799^{3}	**East Houston (101)** (JJO'Neill) **7-10-5** NWilliamson (hld up: hit 14th: hdwy 4 out: rdn 2 out: styd on same pce)	3½	4	$7/2^{2}$	103	18
880*	**Glenfinn Princess (99)** (MrsMerritaJones) **8-10-3** DerekByrne (prom: led 4th to 4 out: sn wknd)	15	5	$7/4^{1}$	91	6
550^{3}	**Hillwalk (120)** (RCurtis) **10-11-7**(3) DWalsh (chsd ldrs: mstkes 9th & 11th: outpcd 14th: n.d after)	4	6	12/1	110	25
	Son of Iris (103) (MrsMReveley) **8-10-7** PNiven (bkwd: prom: j.slowly 5th & 6th: sn bhd: t.o whn p.u bef 9th)		P	6/1	—	—

(SP 121.2%) **7 Rn**

6m 26.1 (15.10) CSF £43.09 TOTE £5.60: £2.40 £2.60 (£28.20) OWNER Mrs M. E. Curtis (DRIFFIELD) BRED Mrs Hazel O'Haire

857 Dark Oak, who seems to reserve his best for here, was winning over his furthest trip to date. (9/2)

Deep Decision, who won over this trip as a novice, made the winner pull out all the stops and should soon go one better. (10/1)

857 Magic Bloom seemed to take an age to get going. (13/2)

799 East Houston travelled well, but found little when coming off the bridle. (7/2)

880* Glenfinn Princess, although jumping boldly in front, may be better suited coming from off the pace. (7/4)

1030 GLOBAL SHIPPING SERVICES MAIDEN HURDLE (4-Y.O+) (Class D)

3-45 (3-56) **2m 1f 110y (8 hdls)** £3,291.50 (£992.00: £481.00: £225.50) GOING: 0.17 sec per fur (G)

	Horse	Dist	Pos	SP	RR	SF
788[4]	**Rangitikei (NZ)** (CJMann) **5-11-5** JRailton (chsd ldrs: led appr 2 out: sn hdd: rdn whn lft clr last)	—	1	4/1[1]	75	25
	Pip's Dream (MJRyan) **5-11-0** JRyan (bit bkwd: led: hdd appr 2 out: sn btn: lft 2nd last)	8	2	11/1	63	13
743[2]	**Nashaat (USA) (89)** (MCChapman) **8-11-5** WWorthington (swtg: chsd ldrs: wknd appr 2 out: lft poor 3rd last)	nk	3	9/1	67	17
	Early Peace (IRE) (MJPolglase) **4-11-5** VSmith (mid div: hdwy appr 2 out: r.o)	3	4	33/1	66	15
	Kilnamartyra Girl (JParkes) **6-10-11**(3) PMidgley (prom: drvn along 3 out: styd on same pce)	5	5	12/1	55	5
871[4]	**Ela Man Howa (85)** (ABailey) **5-11-5** TKent (nvr trbld ldrs)	2	6	9/1	58	8
	Shared Risk (JNorton) **4-11-0**(5) ECallaghan (hld up: styd on fr 2 out: nrst fin)	2½	7	33/1	57	6
	Segala (IRE) (JJO'Neill) **5-11-5** MDwyer (hld up: effrt 5th: n.d)	5	8	20/1	51	1
	Reflex Hammer (JohnUpson) **5-11-5** KFO'Brien (bit bkwd: hld up: nvr trbld ldrs)	¾	9	5/1[2]	51	1
698[3]	**Dr Edgar** (MDods) **4-11-5** PNiven (lw: prom tl wknd qckly appr 2 out)	10	10	8/1	43	—
	Lady Swift (KWHogg) **5-11-0** RGarritty (a in rr)	6	11	33/1	31	—
	Past Master (USA) (SGollings) **8-11-5** ASSmith (bkwd: prom to 5th)	¾	12	13/2	35	—
	Otter Prince (TRGeorge) **7-10-12**(7) CBHynes (bkwd: blnd 1st: a wl bhd)	8	13	50/1	28	—
871[7]	**Naked Feelings** (MartinTodhunter) **4-11-5** MMoloney (swtg: hld up: a in rr)	4	14	50/1	25	—
866[6]	**Midnight Bob** (JMackie) **5-11-5** RMarley (prom: blnd bdly & lost pl 5th: sn bhd & t.o)	29	15	50/1	—	—
	Durano (TDEasterby) **5-11-5** LWyer (lw: trckd ldrs: led & hit 2 out: fell last)		F	11/2[3]	76?	—
700[P]	**Boston Man** (RDEWoodhouse) **5-11-0**(5) DJKavanagh (hld up: a bhd: t.o whn p.u bef 3 out)		P	50/1	—	—

(SP 133.9%) **17 Rn**

4m 15.6 (12.60) CSF £48.06 TOTE £4.00: £2.20 £2.60 £2.80 (£26.20) Trio £82.70 OWNER Mrs J. M. Mayo (UPPER LAMBOURN) BRED D. P. and Mrs S. G. Price

WEIGHT FOR AGE 4yo-1lb

788 Rangitikei (NZ), winner of a bumper here, looked booked for the runner-up spot when presented with the race at the last. (4/1: 3/1-9/2)
Pip's Dream, a winner on the level, will be sharper with this outing under her belt. (11/1)
743 Nashaat (USA), a winner up to a mile on the Flat, seems to have trouble lasting home over hurdles. (9/1)
Early Peace (IRE), fit from the Flat, will have learnt from this. (33/1)
Durano, who looked straight enough beforehand, was unlucky not to get off the mark. (11/2)

1031 UNITED EUROPEAN CAR CARRIERS H'CAP HURDLE (0-125) (4-Y.O+) (Class D)

4-20 (4-27) **3m (12 hdls)** £2,921.00 (£878.00: £424.00: £197.00) GOING: 0.17 sec per fur (G)

	Horse	Dist	Pos	SP	RR	SF
796[4]	**Olympian (114)** (JNeville) **9-11-11b** NWilliamson (s.i.s: led 2nd to 9th: led & hit 2 out: styd on wl)	—	1	11/1	92	14
726[P]	**San Giorgio (96)** (NATwiston-Davies) **7-10-7** TJenks (chsd ldr: led 9th: hdd 2 out: mstke last: r.o one pce)	3	2	6/1	72	—
	Elburg (IRE) (95) (TRGeorge) **6-10-6** DerekByme (s.s: hdwy 8th: wknd 3 out)	15	3	10/1	61	—
181[2]	**River Room (107)** (KCBailey) **6-11-4** JRailton (led to 2nd: wknd 3 out)	7	4	11/4[1]	68	—
894*	**Clean Edge (USA) (108)** (JMackie) **4-11-0**(3) EHusband (hld up: bhd fr 7th)	6	5	3/1[2]	65	—
	Nick the Beak (IRE) (103) (JohnUpson) **7-11-0** KFO'Brien (prom tl wknd after 3 out)	1½	6	8/1	59	—
	Just Supposen (IRE) (97) (BSRothwell) **5-10-8** MDwyer (hld up: t.o whn p.u bef 3 out)		P	20/1	—	—
	Dockmaster (99) (MissMKMilligan) **5-10-10** ASSmith (hld up: lost tch 8th: t.o whn p.u bef 2 out)		P	11/2[3]	—	—

(SP 114.6%) **8 Rn**

6m 2.1 (23.10) CSF £68.01 CT £624.09 TOTE £11.90: £2.40 £1.50 £1.80 (£27.30) OWNER Mr J. Neville (NEWPORT, GWENT) BRED Seend Stud

WEIGHT FOR AGE 4yo-2lb

OFFICIAL EXPLANATION **Clean Edge (USA): was difficult at the start.**

796 Olympian, better for his outing at Uttoxeter, was on one of his going days. (11/1)
San Giorgio was returning to hurdles after a few outings over fences. (6/1)
Elburg (IRE), who has shown signs of temperament before, was again very reluctant to line up. (10/1: op 16/1)
181 River Room, a winner here twice, found these handicappers too good. (11/4)
894* Clean Edge (USA) (3/1: op 2/1)

1032 COBELFRET/EXXTOR NOVICES' CHASE (4-Y.O+) (Class E)

4-55 (4-56) **2m 1f 110y (12 fncs)** £3,496.00 (£1,048.00: £504.00: £232.00) GOING: 0.17 sec per fur (G)

	Horse	Dist	Pos	SP	RR	SF
894[4]	**Down the Fell** (HowardJohnson) **7-11-4** NWilliamson (led to 2nd: lft in ld 8th: sn clr)	—	1	2/1[2]	105?	32
870[F]	**Highland Way (IRE)** (MartinTodhunter) **8-11-4** MDwyer (hld up & bhd: hdwy to chse wnr 4 out: no imp fr next)	20	2	7/1	87?	14
	Stormhill Pilgrim (MJRoberts) **7-11-4** PMcLoughlin (led 2nd to 5th: hit 9th: grad wknd)	dist	3	20/1	—	—
897[U]	**Karenastino** (MrsSJSmith) **5-10-10**(7) RWilkinson (bhd fr 5th)	9	4	50/1	—	—
	Thornton Gate (TDEasterby) **7-11-4** LWyer (chsd ldr: led 5th tl fell 8th)		F	6/5[1]	—	—
	Wren Warbler (MrsPRobeson) **6-10-13** ASSmith (fell 2nd)		F	5/1[3]	—	—

(SP 114.7%) **6 Rn**

4m 26.1 (11.10) CSF £14.82 TOTE £2.70: £1.40 £2.30 (£6.50) OWNER Mr Howard Johnson (CROOK) BRED J. R. Raine

WEIGHT FOR AGE 5yo-1lb

894 Down the Fell, as last year, won second time out, his run at Sedgefield having put an edge on him. (2/1)
Highland Way (IRE), who only got as far as the first on his chasing debut, had a nice school round. (7/1)
Thornton Gate, a useful hurdler, had travelled and jumped well until departing six out. (6/5: 8/11-5/4)

1033 PARK SOCIAL/TRIMESH GUARDIANS MAIDEN OPEN N.H. FLAT RACE (4, 5 & 6-Y.O) (Class H)

5-25 (5-25) **1m 5f 110y** £1,238.00 (£343.00: £164.00)

	Horse	Dist	Pos	SP	RR	SF
898[5]	**Silver Minx** (MrsMReveley) **4-11-5** PNiven (led tl over 2f out: rallied to ld over 1f out: rdn out)	—	1	8/1	—	—
	Nifaaf (USA) (KAMorgan) **4-11-0** ASSmith (lw: a.p: chsd wnr 4f out: rdn to ld over 2f out: hdd over 1f out: unable qckn)	¾	2	3/1[2]	—	—
	Lepton (IRE) (JWCurtis) **5-11-5** LWyer (bit bkwd: chsd ldrs: rdn & ev ch over 2f out: r.o one pce)	5	3	14/1	—	—
	Primitive Heart (HowardJohnson) **4-11-5** ALarnach (chsd ldrs tl rdn & wknd 2f out)	4	4	6/1[3]	—	—
	Phar Enough (IRE) (JGFitzGerald) **4-11-5** WDwan (bit bkwd: prom: rdn 3f out: sn btn)	4	5	6/1[3]	—	—

	Horse / details	Dist	Pos	SP	RR	SF
	Marnies Wolf (RTate) **5-11-5** MrsFNeedham (hld up: plld hrd: hdwy 5f out: rdn & wknd over 2f out)	nk	6	20/1	—	—
	Jackho (MissJBower) **4-11-0**(5) STaylor (bkwd: mid div: rdn ½-wy: wknd over 3f out)	8	7	33/1	—	—
	Welsh Spinner (IRE) (MrsIMcKie) **5-11-5** WMcFarland (bit bkwd: hld up: wknd over 3f out)	½	8	33/1	—	—
865[10]	**Baba Sam (IRE)** (PEccles) **5-11-5** NWilliamson (hld up: hdwy ½-wy: wknd 4f out)	7	9	14/1	—	—
	Lord of The Loch (IRE) (LLungo) **5-11-5** MDwyer (uns rdr s)		U	2/1[1]	—	—
				(SP 122.0%)	**10 Rn**	

3m 17.5 CSF £31.98 TOTE £8.20: £2.00 £1.70 £3.00 (£12.40) Trio £22.20 OWNER Mrs E. A. Kettlewell (SALTBURN) BRED T. E. Phillips

Silver Minx put his experience to good use and proved very game. (8/1)

Nifaaf (USA), one of the fittest in the paddock, was only just run out of it. (3/1: 5/2-100/3)

Lepton (IRE), a winning point-to-pointer, needs a stiffer test of stamina. (14/1: op 8/1)

Primitive Heart, who showed a little ability last term, should do better when put over hurdles. (6/1)

Phar Enough (IRE), who was in need of the outing, was easily left behind once in line for home. (6/1: 3/1-7/1)

Lord of The Loch (IRE) succeeded where most had failed, first going one way and then the other, and depositing Mark Dwyer on his backside at the start. (2/1: 3/1-7/4)

T/Plpt: £569.60 (13.59 Tckts). T/Qdpt: £169.20 (2.52 Tckts). CR

0879-WORCESTER (L-H) (Good)

Saturday October 26th

WEATHER: overcast

1034 CITY AND COUNTY CONDITIONAL H'CAP HURDLE (0-105) (4-Y.O+) (Class F)

2-05 (2-05) **2m (8 hdls)** £2,087.00 (£582.00: £281.00) GOING: 0.24 sec per fur (G)

	Horse / details	Dist	Pos	SP	RR	SF
798*	**Steadfast Elite (IRE) (95)** (JJO'Neill) **5-11-10** RMcGrath (hld up: stdy hdwy 3rd: chsd clr ldr appr 3 out: r.o wl flat: led last strides)	—	1	4/1[2]	77	12
781F	**Alpine Mist (IRE) (90)** (JGMO'Shea) **4-11-4v[1]** MichaelBrennan (hld up: hdwy 3rd: led appr 5th: sn clr: wknd flat: ct last strides)	hd	2	6/1	72	6
949[3]	**Zingibar (79)** (JMBradley) **4-10-2**(5) JPower (led tl appr 5th: sn lost pl: rallied 3 out: styd on flat)	1¼	3	100/30[1]	60	—
	Scottish Wedding (77) (TWall) **6-10-6** RMassey (bit bkwd: prom: rdn & lost pl 5th: rallied appr 3 out: one pce fr 2 out)	3	4	11/1	55	—
	Slipmatic (85) (AndrewTurnell) **7-10-11**(3) CRae (bkwd: plld hrd: prom to 4th)	10	5	11/2[3]	53	—
	Thuhool (87) (RRowe) **8-10-9**(7) AGarrity (bit bkwd: nvr nr ldrs)	s.h	6	9/1	55	—
	Anlace (84) (SMellor) **7-10-13** ChrisWebb (lw: a bhd)	2½	7	6/1	49	—
793[10]	**Will James (72)** (CJDrewe) **10-10-1b** GuyLewis (prom tl rdn & j.slowly 5th: t.o)	9	8	33/1	28	—
	Bill and Win (85) (TWall) **5-11-0** GHogan (bit bkwd: bhd: mstke 3rd: t.o whn p.u bef 2 out)		P	33/1	—	—
				(SP 111.2%)	**9 Rn**	

3m 56.5 (16.50) CSF £25.10 CT £76.73 TOTE £4.70: £1.80 £2.00 £1.30 (£11.90) Trio £6.10 OWNER Clayton Bigley Partnership Ltd (PENRITH) BRED Cecil Harris Bloodstock Ltd

WEIGHT FOR AGE 4yo-1lb

798* Steadfast Elite (IRE), up 5lb, had to dig deep to win another weak race. (4/1)

781 Alpine Mist (IRE), tried in a visor for this return to two miles, just failed to last home. (6/1: 9/2-7/1)

949 Zingibar ran a similar race to his effort at Stratford a week ago, and may need a bit more cut in the ground. (100/30)

Scottish Wedding should come on for the outing. (11/1)

Slipmatic, no less than 24lb lower than when last seen in a handicap, will strip fitter next time. (11/2)

Thuhool (9/1: op 4/1)

Anlace (6/1: 4/1-13/2)

1035 JOHN BURKE MEMORIAL H'CAP CHASE (0-125) (5-Y.O+) (Class D)

2-35 (2-35) **2m (12 fncs)** £3,562.50 (£1,065.00: £510.00: £232.50) GOING: 0.24 sec per fur (G)

	Horse / details	Dist	Pos	SP	RR	SF
	Zeredar (NZ) (95) (KCBailey) **6-10-4** CO'Dwyer (hld up & bhd: pckd 3rd: hdwy 6th: wnt 2nd 4 out: chal whn hit 3 out: hrd rdn to ld flat)	—	1	11/4[1]	106	38
951[4]	**Newlands-General (115)** (PFNicholls) **10-11-10** APMcCoy (lft in ld 1st: hrd rdn & hdd flat)	¾	2	7/2[2]	125	57
	Seod Rioga (IRE) (114) (SMellor) **7-11-9** NMann (lw: lost pl 4th: bhd whn blnd 8th: n.d after)	24	3	10/1	100	32
207[2]	**Full O'Praise (NZ) (105)** (PCalver) **9-11-0** MAFitzgerald (prom tl wknd 3 out)	¾	4	9/1	91	23
	Man Mood (FR) (112) (CPEBrooks) **5-11-6** GBradley (chsd ldr tl appr 4 out: sn wknd)	3	5	14/1	95	26
	The Caumrue (IRE) (105) (GBBalding) **8-11-0** BClifford (a bhd)	7	6	10/1	81	13
886[3]	**Good for a Laugh (102)** (GAHam) **12-10-4**(7) MrGShenkin (a bhd)	nk	7	12/1	77	9
862*	**Fine Harvest (115)** (JLSpearing) **10-11-10** DBridgwater (led tl fell 1st)		F	5/1[3]	—	—
	Miami Splash (97) (SEarle) **9-10-6** CMaude (bhd fr 4th: blnd bdly 6th: p.u bef 7th)		P	10/1	—	—
				(SP 117.2%)	**9 Rn**	

3m 57.9 (6.90) CSF £12.45 CT £76.03 TOTE £4.10: £1.70 £1.20 £2.50 (£9.20) Trio £78.10; £55.07 to Wetherby 27/10/96 OWNER I M S Racing (UPPER LAMBOURN) BRED Miss E. S. Parton

WEIGHT FOR AGE 5yo-1lb

Zeredar (NZ), a winner over both hurdles and fences in New Zealand, was rather novicey at some of his obstacles before taking advantage of the pull in the weights on the run-in. (11/4)

951 Newlands-General, possibly not helped by a loose horse two out, ran a fine race trying to concede the weight, and should soon go one better. (7/2: 5/2-4/1)

Seod Rioga (IRE) managed to win over the sharp two miles at Fakenham, but basically needs further. (10/1: op 6/1)

207 Full O'Praise (NZ) was 3lb lower than the mark off which he registered his two handicap wins. (9/1)

Man Mood (FR) was still 20lb higher than when taking advantage of a lenient mark on his British debut at Hereford last November. (14/1: 6/1-16/1)

Good for a Laugh (12/1: 16/1-10/1)

1036 JOHN MURPHY 75TH BIRTHDAY E.B.F. 'N.H.' QUALIFIER NOVICES' HURDLE (4, 5 & 6-Y.O) (Class E)

3-05 (3-06) **2m 2f (9 hdls)** £2,477.50 (£690.00: £332.50) GOING: 0.24 sec per fur (G)

	Horse / details	Dist	Pos	SP	RR	SF
	Bietschhorn Bard (82) (DRGandolfo) **6-10-11**(3) DFortt (lw: hld up & bhd: gd hdwy appr 3 out: led appr last: r.o wl)	—	**1**	14/1	63	35
	Mythical Approach (IRE) (DNicholson) **6-11-0** AMaguire (trckd ldrs: led appr 2 out: hdd appr last: unable qckn)	2	**2**	11/4[1]	61	33
	Dontleavethenest (IRE) (RCurtis) **6-11-10** DMorris (hld up: hdwy 6th: ev ch 3 out: wknd appr last)	8	**3**	16/1	64	36
	Rhythm And Blues (RHBuckler) **6-11-0** BPowell (a.p: 4th & btn whn hit last)	4	**4**	20/1	51	23
	Pentlands Flyer (IRE) (NATwiston-Davies) **5-11-0** CLlewellyn (plld hrd: prom: wknd appr 2 out: hit last)	2	**5**	6/1	49	21
	Mesp (IRE) (JGMO'Shea) **5-10-9** RJohnson (hdwy 5th: wkng whn blnd 3 out)	12	**6**	50/1	33	5
	Sylvester (IRE) (MissAEBroyd) **6-11-0** MAFitzgerald (led tl wknd appr 2 out)	5	**7**	50/1	34	6
	Bound For Gold (MissHCKnight) **5-11-0** JFTitley (bkwd: prom: eased whn btn appr 3 out)	9	**8**	16/1	26	—
	Sir Dante (IRE) (RRowe) **5-11-0** PHide (bit bkwd: prom to 6th)	5	**9**	11/2[3]	21	—
915[F]	**Another Hubblick** (PFNicholls) **5-10-7**(7) OBurrows (a bhd)	2½	**10**	66/1	19	—
	Bel-de-Moor (MPMuggeridge) **4-10-8** WMarston (a bhd)	1	**11**	50/1	13	—
418[5]	**Sierra Nevada** (PFNicholls) **5-11-0** APMcCoy (a bhd)	2	**12**	16/1	16	—
	Storm Tiger (IRE) (SMellor) **5-11-0** NMann (bkwd: bhd fr 5th: t.o)	24	**13**	33/1	—	—
504[4]	**Katharine's Song (IRE)** (DMHyde) **6-10-9** GBradley (a bhd: t.o whn p.u bef 3 out)		**P**	50/1	—	—
	Southern Nights (KCBailey) **6-11-0** CO'Dwyer (lw: hld up & plld hrd: hdwy 5th: prom whn p.u lame bef 3 out)		**P**	4/1[2]	—	—
636[8]	**Powerful Spirit** (JGMO'Shea) **4-10-8**(5) MichaelBrennan (chsd ldr tl j.slowly 4th: wknd 6th: t.o whn p.u bef 3 out)		**P**	33/1	—	—
	Olden Days (GThorner) **4-10-13** TJMurphy (bkwd: bhd fr 5th: t.o whn p.u bef 3 out)		**P**	50/1	—	—
	Ceannaire (IRE) (PWinkworth) **6-11-0** JOsborne (bkwd: prom: mstke 1st: wknd qckly 6th: t.o whn p.u bef 3 out)		**P**	14/1	—	—
	Hold The Fort (AJKDunn) **5-11-0** LHarvey (bkwd: a bhd: t.o whn p.u bef 3 out)		**P**	100/1	—	—

(SP 130.2%) **19 Rn**

4m 20.7 (10.70) CSF £50.92 TOTE £17.00: £5.60 £2.60 £4.70 (£38.20) Trio £53.40 OWNER Mr A. W. F. Clapperton (WANTAGE) BRED A. W. F. Clapperton

WEIGHT FOR AGE 4yo-1lb

Bietschhorn Bard adopted different tactics and came with a well-timed run. (14/1: 10/1-16/1)

Mythical Approach (IRE), an Irish point-to-point winner, is out of a half-sister to Ballyhane and will not have to improve much to get off the mark. (11/4)

Dontleavethenest (IRE) won a maiden hurdle at Roscommon in June and was not disgraced under his penalty. (16/1)

Rhythm And Blues had finished third on heavy ground in a bumper at Towcester. (20/1)

Pentlands Flyer (IRE), a disappointing favourite in his second bumper at Catterick, was a bit keen early on, but will be better for the experience. (6/1)

Sir Dante (IRE) (11/2: 11/4-6/1)

Southern Nights was bang in contention when going lame on the home turn. (4/1)

1037 FRED RIMELL MEMORIAL NOVICES' CHASE (5-Y.O+) (Class D)

3-35 (3-37) **2m 4f 110y (15 fncs)** £4,337.50 (£1,300.00: £625.00: £287.50) GOING: 0.24 sec per fur (G)

	Horse / details	Dist	Pos	SP	RR	SF
791*	**Call Equiname** (PFNicholls) **6-11-6** APMcCoy (chsd ldr: led after 6th: rdn & r.o wl flat)	—	**1**	8/13[1]	124	39
591*	**Fine Thyne (IRE)** (GHarwood) **7-11-0** MAFitzgerald (hld up: mstke 5th: lft 2nd 10th: ev ch last: unable qckn)	1½	**2**	5/1[3]	117	32
	Coverdale Lane (MrsSJSmith) **9-10-13** MrPMurray (bhd fr 7th: t.o)	dist	**3**	66/1	—	—
887[F]	**Swing Quartet (IRE)** (NATwiston-Davies) **6-10-9** CLlewellyn (mstke 6th: bhd fr 9th: t.o)	dist	**4**	9/2[2]	—	—
952[P]	**Rafters** (JMBradley) **7-11-0** RJohnson (prom: 2nd whn fell 10th)		**F**	33/1	—	—
	Millfrone (IRE) (RRowe) **6-11-0** PHide (led & sn clr: hdd after 6th: wknd qckly: t.o whn p.u bef 10th)		**P**	33/1	—	—
	Eventsinternashnal (MSheppard) **7-11-0** BPowell (s.s: t.o tl p.u bef 3rd)		**P**	100/1	—	—
741[4]	**Morstock** (RJHodges) **6-11-0** JFrost (pckd 1st: blnd & uns rdr 3rd)		**U**	12/1	—	—

(SP 112.8%) **8 Rn**

5m 14.2 (13.20) CSF £4.15 TOTE £1.60: £1.20 £1.40 £5.80 (£3.20) OWNER Mick Coburn, Barber, Lewis (SHEPTON MALLET) BRED Mrs L. Steele

791* Call Equiname, taken out at Newbury the day before because of the firmish ground, managed to find a bit more when challenged at the final fence. (8/13)

591* Fine Thyne (IRE) made a promising start to his chasing career and briefly seemed capable of causing an upset jumping the final fence. He will not always meet one so smart. (5/1)

Coverdale Lane went a poor third on the home turn. (66/1)

887 Swing Quartet (IRE) ran as if something was amiss, but she was rather inconsistent over hurdles. (9/2)

1038 DURR 25TH ANNIVERSARY CELEBRATION NOVICES' H'CAP CHASE (0-100) (5-Y.O+) (Class E)

4-10 (4-10) **2m 7f (18 fncs)** £3,363.00 (£1,014.00: £492.00: £231.00) GOING: 0.24 sec per fur (G)

	Horse / details	Dist	Pos	SP	RR	SF
	Express Travel (IRE) (72) (RCurtis) **8-10-0** DMorris (hld up: gd hdwy fr 14th: led 4 out: r.o wl)	—	**1**	20/1	85	—
	Ivy House (IRE) (88) (JJO'Neill) **8-11-2** AMaguire (blnd 2nd: hdwy appr 4 out: ev ch 2 out: one pce)	2½	**2**	11/2[2]	99	—
	Now We Know (IRE) (83) (MSheppard) **8-10-11** BPowell (bit bkwd: hdwy 9th: lost pl 4 out: styd on flat)	1½	**3**	14/1	93	—
887*	**Strong Tarquin (IRE) (100)** (PFNicholls) **6-12-0** APMcCoy (hld up & plld hrd: hdwy 7th: led 12th tl after 14th: one pce)	¾	**4**	11/4[1]	110	6
64[P]	**Its Grand (72)** (JMBradley) **7-10-0** TJMurphy (bit bkwd: prom: led after 14th: hdd 4 out: wknd appr 2 out)	1½	**5**	40/1	81	—
936[3]	**Chris's Glen (83)** (JMBradley) **7-10-11v** RJohnson (hdwy 9th: hit 11th: ev ch 4 out: wknd appr 2 out)	13	**6**	16/1	83	—
817*	**Seasamacamile (72)** (RHBuckler) **9-9-7**(7) MrRThornton (hit 7th: t.o fr 10th)	dist	**7**	16/1	—	—
	Seymour Spy (85) (MrsARHewitt) **7-10-13** SWynne (bkwd: bhd fr 12th: t.o)	8	**8**	10/1	—	—
	Dominie (IRE) (95) (KCBailey) **8-11-9b** CO'Dwyer (bit bkwd: chsd ldrs: wkng whn mstke 14th: t.o whn p.u bef 2 out)		**P**	9/1	—	—
	Flaming Miracle (IRE) (72) (GBarnett) **6-10-0b** RFarrant (plld hrd: hdwy to ld after 5th: hdd 12th: wknd qckly: t.o whn p.u bef 4 out)		**P**	20/1	—	—

				SP	RR	SF
	Scrabble (72) (MrsSJSmith) **7-10-0** MrPMurray (bit bkwd: blnd bdly 9th: sn bhd: t.o 12th: p.u bef 4 out)		**P**	40/1	—	—
	The Go Ahead (IRE) (92) (CaptTAForster) **6-11-6** AThornton (lft in ld 1st: hdd 5th: wknd 12th: t.o whn p.u bef 4 out)		**P**	14/1	—	—
	Spearhead Again (IRE) (89) (KSBridgwater) **7-11-3** MAFitzgerald (bit bkwd: prom: led 5th: sn hdd: mstke 10th: wknd 12th: t.o whn p.u bef 4 out)		**P**	6/1[3]	—	—
970[P]	**Yes We Are (73)** (ABarrow) **10-10-1**[ow1] PHolley (bhd: blnd 6th & 7th: t.o whn p.u bef 10th)		**P**	100/1	—	—
	Gallic Girl (IRE) (72) (CLPopham) **6-9-11**(3) TDascombe (bkwd: blnd & uns rdr 1st)		**U**	40/1	—	—
	Country Keeper (75) (BJMRyall) **8-10-3**[ow3] GUpton (blnd & uns rdr 1st)		**U**	50/1	—	—
	Cardinal Rule (IRE) (72) (MissVenetiaWilliams) **7-10-0** WMarston (led tl hmpd & uns rdr 1st)		**U**	12/1	—	—
				(SP 128.0%)	**17 Rn**	

6m 6.2 (28.20) CSF £121.52 CT £1,498.98 TOTE £21.70: £3.80 £1.60 £3.10 £1.70 (£91.90) Trio Not won; £264.27 to Wetherby 27/10/96
OWNER Mr Michael Low (LAMBOURN) BRED Winston Honner
LONG HANDICAP Its Grand 9-9 Flaming Miracle (IRE) 9-5 Seasamacamile 9-11 Gallic Girl (IRE) 9-11 Country Keeper 9-7 Cardinal Rule (IRE) 9-12

Express Travel (IRE), a winner between the Flags, had got in on a useful mark on this first run over fences. (20/1)
Ivy House (IRE) was reverting to fences after three disappointing runs over hurdles last season and his prospects did not seem bright when he made a hash of the first ditch. (11/2)
Now We Know (IRE), a remote fifth in the four-miler at the Festival in March, found his second wind in the closing stages and will come on for the run. Softer ground should help. (14/1: op 8/1)
887* Strong Tarquin (IRE) kept plugging away under his big weight. (11/4)
Its Grand, 5lb out of the handicap, probably found the ground too fast when pulled up on his fencing debut in June. (40/1)
936 Chris's Glen found this trip beyond him on his first run over the major obstacles. (16/1)
Dominie (IRE) (9/1: 6/1-10/1)

1039 LADBROKES H'CAP HURDLE (0-135) (4-Y.O+) (Class C)
4-40 (4-42) **2m 4f (10 hdls)** £3,731.50 (£1,117.00: £536.00: £245.50) GOING: 0.24 sec per fur (G)

				SP	RR	SF
	Teen Jay (117) (BJLlewellyn) **6-11-7** VSlattery (hld up: stdy hdwy 5th: led 2 out: drvn out)	—	**1**	15/2	100	25
	Nahri (USA) (110) (JMackie) **5-11-0** APMcCoy (hld up: hdwy appr 3 out: ev ch 2 out: r.o one pce flat)	1½	**2**	9/1	92	17
	Balanak (USA) (120) (DRGandolfo) **5-11-10** AMaguire (hld up & bhd: hdwy 6th: ev ch last: unable qckn)	nk	**3**	8/1	102	27
	Go Ballistic (124) (JGMO'Shea) **7-12-0** MAFitzgerald (hld up: hdwy appr 3 out: one pce fr 2 out)	3½	**4**	11/2[3]	103	28
884*	**Wottashambles (113)** (LMontagueHall) **5-11-3** DMorris (hld up: hdwy appr 5th: led appr 3 out: hdd 2 out: sn wknd)	2½	**5**	5/1[2]	90	15
884[3]	**La Menorquina (USA) (98)** (DMarks) **6-10-2** JAMcCarthy (led after 1st: hdd 7th: wknd 3 out)	nk	**6**	7/1	75	—
	Celtino (99) (CaptTAForster) **8-10-3** SWynne (nvr nr to chal)	1	**7**	14/1	75	—
	Spring to Glory (104) (PHayward) **9-10-8** BFenton (hld up & plld hrd: bhd fr 5th)	2	**8**	25/1	78	3
	Needwood Muppet (112) (AJWilson) **9-11-2** LHarvey (led tl after 1st: led 7th: sn hdd: wknd 3 out)	8	**9**	16/1	80	5
	Arithmetic (113) (MrsJPitman) **6-11-3** WMarston (prom tl wknd appr 3 out)	12	**10**	4/1[1]	71	—
	Danzig Island (IRE) (103) (WJenks) **5-10-7** CLlewellyn (bkwd: prom tl blnd 6th: t.o)	dist	**11**	16/1	—	—
	Hello Me Man (IRE) (103) (BJLlewellyn) **8-10-7** MrJLLlewellyn (bkwd: bhd fr 5th: t.o whn p.u bef 3 out)		**P**	40/1	—	—
	Just for a Reason (97) (RTJuckes) **4-10-0** RJohnson (bkwd: a bhd: t.o whn p.u bef 2 out)		**P**	40/1	—	—
				(SP 124.6%)	**13 Rn**	

4m 54.3 (16.30) CSF £69.97 CT £515.69 TOTE £9.90: £2.80 £3.30 £3.90 (£21.80) Trio £95.60 OWNER Gemini Associates (BARGOED) BRED Sheikh Mohammed bin Rashid al Maktoum
LONG HANDICAP Just for a Reason 9-7
WEIGHT FOR AGE 4yo-1lb

Teen Jay, 7lb higher than when scoring at Aintree in May, won at Redcar last week and showed no ill-effects of a busy campaign on the Flat. (15/2: 7/2-8/1)
Nahri (USA), 4lb higher than the second of his two wins last year, does seem best when fresh. (9/1: op 6/1)
Balanak (USA) ran a fine race for one who really needs it soft. (8/1)
Go Ballistic graduated to fences last season and this should serve as a useful pipe-opener. (11/2)
884* Wottashambles, raised 5lb, found this a bit more competitive. (5/1)
884 La Menorquina (USA) was 7lb better off with Wottashambles for a six and a half-length beating here last time. (7/1: op 12/1)
Arithmetic folded up tamely on the home turn and seems to need more give underfoot. (4/1)

T/Plpt: £39.60 (251.67 Tckts). T/Qdpt: £15.50 (25.81 Tckts). KH

0859-HUNTINGDON (R-H) (Good)
Sunday October 27th
WEATHER: unsettled

1040 HENKEL CONDITIONAL (S) H'CAP HURDLE (0-95) (4-Y.O+) (Class G)
2-00 (2-01) **3m 2f (12 hdls)** £1,919.00 (£534.00: £257.00) GOING: 0.19 sec per fur (G)

				SP	RR	SF
	Tiger Claw (USA) (81) (AGHobbs) **10-11-2**(3) OBurrows (bit bkwd: trckd ldrs: led after 3 out: hit next: rdn out)	—	**1**	10/1	62	2
641[10]	**Please Call (IRE) (72)** (DPGeraghty) **7-10-5**(5) THagger (lw: in tch: hit 7th: hdwy next: led 3 out: sn hdd & kpt on)	1¼	**2**	33/1	52	—
950[9]	**Awestruck (62)** (BPreece) **6-10-0b** GHogan (hdwy 8th: kpt on fr 2 out)	3	**3**	16/1	40	—
891[3]	**Tipping Along (IRE) (78)** (DRGandolfo) **7-11-2** SophieMitchell (chsd ldrs: no imp appr 2 out)	½	**4**	9/2[2]	56	—
827[5]	**Storm Drum (90)** (KCBailey) **7-11-9b**(5) WWalsh (trckd ldrs: hit 4th: rdn 3 out: wknd appr last)	4	**5**	13/2[3]	66	6
	Snowy Lane (IRE) (67) (JNeville) **8-10-5b** TDascombe (prom to 9th)	dist	**6**	7/1	—	—
960[6]	**Slightly Special (IRE) (64)** (BAPearce) **4-10-0** KGaule (led: hit 5th: blnd 9th: hdd next: sn wknd)	20	**7**	33/1	—	—
828[3]	**Script (73)** (JRJenkins) **5-10-4**(7) DYellowlees (a bhd)	6	**8**	15/2	—	—
819*	**Do Be Ware (74)** (JFfitch-Heyes) **6-10-12** DJKavanagh (prom: rdn 7th: sn wknd: t.o whn p.u bef 2 out)		**P**	13/2[3]	—	—
731[6]	**Elltee-Ess (65)** (RJWeaver) **11-9-10**(7) CRWeaver (lw: a bhd: t.o whn p.u bef 2 out)		**P**	33/1	—	—
474*	**Joli's Great (75)** (MJRyan) **8-10-13b** MichaelBrennan (w ldr 3rd tl wknd 8th: t.o whn p.u bef 2 out)		**P**	11/4[1]	—	—

				SP	RR	SF
	Christian Soldier (62) (PButler) **9-10-0v[1]** DWalsh (bkwd: t.o whn p.u bef 8th)		P	33/1	—	—
				(SP 122.5%)		**12 Rn**

6m 34.0 (28.00) CSF £245.36 CT £4,643.50 TOTE £12.00: £2.90 £8.50 £3.20 (£565.20) Trio Not won; £207.32 to Leicester 28/10/96 OWNER Unity Farm Holiday Centre Ltd (KINGSBRIDGE) BRED Ian A. Balding
LONG HANDICAP Slightly Special (IRE) 9-13 Awestruck 9-0 Christian Soldier 9-3
WEIGHT FOR AGE 4yo-2lb
No bid
Tiger Claw (USA), off for over a year, looked to have been let in very lightly as a result. Well in his coat but looking in need of the race, he was cruising until hitting the front, but landed flat-footed at the second last and was all out to keep going into the strong head-wind. (10/1: op 6/1)
Please Call (IRE), having only his second run since coming over from Ireland, looked much fitter this time and ran accordingly. (33/1)
Awestruck benefited from the step up in trip, but took his losing run under both codes to twenty-two. (16/1)
503 Tipping Along (IRE) began to struggle with half a mile left to run and may not quite have got the trip. (9/2: 3/1-5/1)
Storm Drum is not the horse he was. (13/2: op 4/1)
474* Joli's Great (11/4: 7/4-3/1)

1041 JAGUAR NOVICES' H'CAP CHASE (0-95) (5-Y.O+) (Class F)
2-30 (2-36) **2m 4f 110y (16 fncs)** £2,940.50 (£884.00: £427.00: £198.50) GOING: 0.19 sec per fur (G)

				SP	RR	SF
821*	**Mill O'The Rags (IRE) (95)** (MrsDHaine) **7-12-0** JFTitley (lw: a.p: rdn 4 out: led appr 2 out: clr last: fin tired).	—	1	3/1[2]	112	44
	Dalametre (67) (JGSmyth-Osbourne) **9-10-0** WMarston (mde most to 4 out: lft in ld next: hdd appr 2 out: btn whn hit last)	7	2	11/1	79	11
601[6]	**Willie Makeit (IRE) (87)** (RTPhillips) **6-11-6** JRailton (j.w: a.p: wkng whn hit last)	10	3	6/1	91	23
	Castle Chief (IRE) (90) (JTGifford) **7-11-9** PHide (bkwd: bhd fr 11th)	10	4	5/2[1]	86	18
935[2]	**King's Shilling (USA) (84)** (HOliver) **9-11-3** JacquiOliver (mstkes 1st & 9th: bhd fr 11th)	1¼	5	11/2	79	11
935[F]	**Sungia (IRE) (70)** (GraemeRoe) **7-10-3v**ow3 TJenks (mstkes: bhd tl p.u bef 8th)		P	50/1	—	—
828*	**On the Tear (67)** (FLloyd) **10-10-0** CLlewellyn (lw: a bhd: t.o whn p.u bef 4 out)		P	11/1	—	—
901[5]	**Westerly Gale (IRE) (76)** (NJHenderson) **6-10-9** MAFitzgerald (lw: w ldr tl led 4 out: blnd & uns rdr next)		U	9/2[3]	—	—
				(SP 120.1%)		**8 Rn**

5m 12.6 (12.60) CSF £32.68 CT £174.75 TOTE £3.60: £1.30 £2.70 £2.20 (£30.30) Trio £90.10 OWNER Mr E. J. Fenaroli (NEWMARKET) BRED Noel Fenton
LONG HANDICAP Sungia (IRE) 9-7 On the Tear 9-10 Dalametre 9-12
821* Mill O'The Rags (IRE) took charge on the home turn, but found the wet and windy conditions stretching his stamina to the limit, as he prefers firmer ground. (3/1: op 7/4)
Dalametre looked pretty fit, despite nearly eighteen months off, and broke the tape when the Starter tried to hold the field. Setting the pace, he jumped right on occasions, and only found lack of peak-fitness beating him over the last two fences. (11/1)
486* Willie Makeit (IRE) produced some fine leaps to stay in contention, making his only real mistake when out on his feet at the last. (6/1: 7/2-13/2)
Castle Chief (IRE), off for over a year and a half, was making his chasing debut and looks the type, although easily left behind on this occasion. (5/2)
935 King's Shilling (USA) made mistakes as he tried to stay in touch. (11/2)
828* On the Tear (11/1: 6/1-12/1)
720 Westerly Gale (IRE) had just taken up the running and was going best when pitching on landing at the third last, unseating his rider. (9/2)

1042 PEUGEOT NOVICES' HURDLE (4-Y.O+) (Class E)
3-00 (3-09) **2m 4f 110y (10 hdls)** £2,617.50 (£730.00: £352.50) GOING: 0.19 sec per fur (G)

				SP	RR	SF
871[2]	**Inn At the Top** (JNorton) **4-10-11** DerekByrne (lw: trckd ldrs: led 3 out: tried to run out & rdn next: mstke last: eased nr fin)	—	1	11/8[1]	67	—
	Salmon Breeze (IRE) (NJHenderson) **5-10-12** MAFitzgerald (bit bkwd: w ldrs: hit 7th: sn rdn: kpt on fr next)	14	2	100/30[3]	56	—
890[4]	**Lord Rooble (IRE)** (JTGifford) **5-10-12** PHide (led to 3 out: sn rdn & btn)	7	3	3/1[2]	51	—
955[8]	**Samaka Hara (IRE) (86)** (GraemeRoe) **4-10-11** TJenks (in tch tl appr 3 out)	dist	4	20/1	—	—
631[P]	**Giorgione (FR)** (NJPomfret) **7-10-5**(7) MrRWakley (bit bkwd: prom tl wknd after 5th: t.o whn p.u bef 2 out)		P	50/1	—	—
	Gunner John (TCasey) **5-10-12** DBridgwater (bit bkwd: bhd fr 5th: t.o whn p.u bef 3 out)		P	16/1	—	—
25[10]	**Rosslayne Serenade** (RJWeaver) **5-10-0**(7) CRWeaver (bit bkwd: hdwy 4th: wknd 7th: t.o whn p.u bef 2 out)		P	50/1	—	—
	Goatsfut (IRE) (BPreece) **6-10-9**(3) GHogan (tried to ref & uns rdr 1st)		U	14/1	—	—
				(SP 111.4%)		**8 Rn**

4m 54.9 CSF £6.00 TOTE £1.80: £1.10 £1.30 £1.50 (£3.70) Trio £3.20 OWNER Mrs Sylvia Blakeley (BARNSLEY) BRED Crest Stud Ltd
WEIGHT FOR AGE 4yo-1lb
STEWARDS' ENQUIRY Byrne susp. 5-8/11/96 (excessive use of whip).
871 Inn At the Top travelled well, but looked a tricky ride once in front and threatened to crash through the wing at the penultimate flight, before his pilot took remedial action. Byrne got a ban, but his actions appeared motivated by self-preservation. (11/8)
Salmon Breeze (IRE) shaped quite well, staying on, despite looking short of full fitness. (100/30: 6/4-7/2)
Lord Rooble (IRE) faded once headed on the home turn and does appear one-paced. (3/1: op 2/1)
812 Samaka Hara (IRE) is rather small for this game and did nothing to suggest he gets beyond two miles. (20/1)
Goatsfut (IRE) (14/1: 8/1-16/1)

1043 HENKEL TEROSON AUTOMOTIVE H'CAP CHASE (0-120) (5-Y.O+) (Class D)
3-30 (3-36) **3m (18 fncs)** £3,915.00 (£1,170.00: £560.00: £255.00) GOING: 0.19 sec per fur (G)

				SP	RR	SF
864[2]	**Merlins Dream (IRE) (103)** (OSherwood) **7-10-11** JAMcCarthy (led 2nd to next: w ldr whn blnd 14th: j.lft & mstke 2 out: sn led: pushed out)	—	1	2/1[2]	107	30
	Romany Creek (IRE) (120) (JPearce) **7-12-0v** DBridgwater (bit bkwd: led 3rd: mstkes 10th & 13th: hit 2 out: sn hdd & btn)	18	2	6/1	112	35
809[3]	**Vicosa (IRE) (112)** (RHAlner) **7-10-13**(7) MrRThornton (mstkes: nvr gng wl: bhd fr 15th)	8	3	13/8[1]	99	22
	Sorbiere (100) (NJHenderson) **9-10-8** MAFitzgerald (led to 2nd: sn dropped rr: hdwy 10th: btn & eased 3 out)	nk	4	3/1[3]	87	10
				(SP 110.7%)		**4 Rn**

6m 11.3 (14.30) CSF £11.09 TOTE £2.50 (£6.10) OWNER Mr W. S. Watt (UPPER LAMBOURN) BRED Neville Bourke

864 Merlins Dream (IRE) did not jump too well in the last mile, doing the splits at the water, but he found a soft race and did the job well. (2/1)
Romany Creek (IRE) looked some way short of full fitness on his first outing for the stable, but took lengths out of his rivals at some of the fences. The mistake two out stopped him in his tracks. (6/1: 4/1-7/1)
809 Vicosa (IRE) did not go a yard, possibly on account of the rain-softened ground. (13/8)
Sorbiere, given an odd ride, lost his place rapidly on the run to the second last as he was eased down, but his pilot did then ride him along after the last, just failing to take third prize. (3/1)

1044 FORD E.B.F. 'N.H.' QUALIFIER NOVICES' HURDLE (4, 5 & 6-Y.O) (Class E)

4-00 (4-03) **2m 110y (8 hdls)** £2,390.00 (£665.00: £320.00) GOING: 0.19 sec per fur (G)

				SP	RR	SF
	Beacon Flight (IRE) (BdeHaan) **5-11-0** CLlewellyn (set slow pce: qcknd appr 2 out: rdn out)	—	1	7/2[3]	64	—
	Peace Lord (IRE) (MrsDHaine) **6-11-0** GBradley (plld hrd: trckd ldrs: ev ch last: unable qckn)	1½	2	2/1[2]	63	—
	Darakshan (IRE) (MissHCKnight) **4-10-13** JFTitley (trckd wnr: ev ch 2 out: one pce)	½	3	11/8[1]	62	—
	Cyphratis (IRE) (MrsJPitman) **5-11-0** WMarston (trckd ldrs tl outpcd appr 2 out)	5	4	6/1	57	—
	Quare Dream's (IRE) (TCasey) **5-10-9** DBridgwater (bit bkwd: hld up: blnd 2nd: no ch fr 2 out)	14	5	25/1	39	—
59[6]	**Saboteuse** (JCPoulton) **4-10-8** TJMurphy (hld up & plld hrd: hdwy 3 out: btn appr next)	4	6	50/1	35	—
				(SP 117.8%)		**6 Rn**

4m 10.0 (22.00) CSF £11.10 TOTE £5.40: £2.40 £1.70 (£5.40) OWNER The Heyfleet Partnership (LAMBOURN) BRED Gerard Burke
WEIGHT FOR AGE 4yo-1lb
Beacon Flight (IRE) was allowed to set his own pace and only kicked on on the home turn, having too much speed for his rivals. He has the potential to progress further. (7/2)
Peace Lord (IRE) found the sedate pace all against him, but still ran on really well in the straight. He should find a race. (2/1)
Darakshan (IRE) looked well in his coat and this race, which developed into a three-furlong sprint, should put him right. (11/8)
Cyphratis (IRE), a quite attractive newcomer, is impossible to assess on this as he was outpaced in the straight, but appeared to finish with plenty of petrol still in the tank. (6/1: op 4/1)
Quare Dream's (IRE), a big, tall mare, looked clumsy at her hurdles, and was comprehensively outpaced once the sprint began. (25/1)
Saboteuse, bred for speed not stamina, ought to have been suited by such a false run race but was not. (50/1)

1045 ROVER H'CAP HURDLE (0-115) (4-Y.O+) (Class E)

4-30 (4-31) **2m 110y (8 hdls)** £2,267.50 (£630.00: £302.50) GOING: 0.19 sec per fur (G)

				SP	RR	SF
	Menelave (IRE) (99) (OSherwood) **6-10-13** JAMcCarthy (lw: hld up: hdwy 5th: led appr 3 out: j.lft & sddle slipped 2 out: rdn out)	—	1	11/2	81	25
	Youbetterbelieveit (IRE) (110) (CPEBrooks) **7-11-10** GBradley (bit bkwd: chsd ldrs: ev ch appr last: unable qckn)	2½	2	15/8[1]	90	34
863[2]	**Wamdha (IRE) (100)** (KAMorgan) **6-11-0** ASSmith (prom: lost pl 5th: n.d after)	21	3	11/4[2]	59	3
815[3]	**Bon Voyage (USA) (100)** (DMGrissell) **4-10-13** JRKavanagh (led tl after 3rd: wknd 5th)	14	4	100/30[3]	46	—
	Porphyrios (106) (KCBailey) **5-11-6** CLlewellyn (prom: led after 3rd tl appr 3 out: sn wknd)	18	5	10/1	34	—
	Captain Tandy (IRE) (90) (CSmith) **7-10-4** MRanger (bhd fr 4th: t.o whn p.u bef 3 out)		P	50/1	—	—
				(SP 111.0%)		**6 Rn**

3m 59.0 (11.00) CSF £15.44 TOTE £7.00: £2.40 £1.90 (£8.60) OWNER Mr R. B. Holt (UPPER LAMBOURN) BRED J. O'Keeffe
WEIGHT FOR AGE 4yo-1lb
Menelave (IRE), always travelling well, soon had matters in hand once let down, but her saddle slipped when she jumped crookedly at the second last. She is progressing well and can win again. (11/2: op 7/2)
Youbetterbelieveit (IRE), not quite as fit as the winner, will stay further and showed plenty of ability on only his third start over hurdles. (15/8)
863 Wamdha (IRE) is some way below her best at present, and lost her pitch completely when the tempo quickened, only to stay on from a long way back. (11/4: 2/1-3/1)
815 Bon Voyage (USA) did not run well over what is likely to prove an inadequate trip. (100/30)
Porphyrios ran badly here on his only previous visit. (10/1: op 4/1)

T/Plpt: £1,264.30 (8.22 Tckts). T/Qdpt: £16.30 (37.37 Tckts). Dk

0906-WETHERBY (L-H) (Good)

Sunday October 27th

Race 2: one flight omitted
WEATHER: fine but windy WIND: str bhd

1046 YORKSHIRE RACING CLUB NOVICES' HURDLE (4-Y.O+) (Class C)

1-20 (1-20) **2m 7f (12 hdls)** £3,860.00 (£1,160.00: £560.00: £260.00) GOING minus 0.07 sec per fur (G)

				SP	RR	SF
910[3]	**Highbeath (94)** (MrsMReveley) **5-11-6** PNiven (a.p. disp ld 7th tl led 3 out: rdn whn lft clr last)	—	1	8/11[1]	73?	—
	Movie Man (JRTurner) **4-10-12** ADobbin (in tch: effrt 4 out: ch appr next: sn rdn & btn)	16	2	33/1	55	—
897[B]	**Rapid Fire (IRE)** (JMJefferson) **8-10-7**(7) MNewton (led to 4th: prom tl outpcd fr 4 out: sme hdwy 3 out: no imp)	6	3	33/1	52	—
	Hotspur Street (MWEasterby) **4-10-12** NWilliamson (hld up & bhd: hdwy 7th: rdn & btn appr 3 out)	4	4	7/1[3]	48	—
60[7]	**Young Kenny (94)** (PBeaumont) **5-11-6** RSupple (mde most fr 4th to 3 out: cl 2nd & btn whn fell last)		F	15/2	—	—
	Elliott's Wish (IRE) (HowardJohnson) **5-11-0** AMaguire (lost tch 4 out: t.o whn p.u bef 2 out)		P	14/1	—	—
866[2]	**Tigh-Na-Mara (86)** (JMJefferson) **8-10-4**(5) ECallaghan (lw: blnd & uns rdr 2nd)		U	7/2[2]	—	—
				(SP 116.9%)		**7 Rn**

5m 45.0 (123.00) CSF £20.37 TOTE £1.80: £1.50 £5.90 (£49.30) OWNER Mr A. Sharratt (SALTBURN) BRED Huttons Ambo Stud
WEIGHT FOR AGE 4yo-1lb
910 Highbeath won a moderate event here and struggled to do so, but he certainly showed he stays. (8/11: op 5/4)
Movie Man was always close enough if good enough, but he proved far too slow when the pressure was on. (33/1)
590 Rapid Fire (IRE) failed completely over the bigger obstacles this year, but this should have helped boost his confidence. (33/1)
Hotspur Street always gives the impression that softer ground would suit him better, and he was struggling some way out here. (7/1)
Young Kenny made a race of it with the winner, but he looked held when falling heavily at the last. (15/2)

1047 MICKY HAMMOND OWNERS (S) H'CAP HURDLE (0-95) (4-Y.O+) (Class G)

1-50 (1-51) **2m 4f 110y (10 hdls)** £2,460.00 (£685.00: £330.00) GOING minus 0.07 sec per fur (G)

				SP	RR	SF
	Belle Rose (IRE) (67) (GRichards) **6-10-0** ADobbin (chsd ldrs: effrt & hmpd 2 out: led flat: styd on wl)	—	**1**	10/1	57	10
	Furietto (IRE) (95) (MDHammond) **6-12-0** RGarritty (cl up: led 4 out tl flat: one pce)	4	**2**	7/1 2	82	35
	Highland Park (82) (RCraggs) **10-11-1** AMaguire (bhd: hdwy ½-wy: styd on u.p fr 3 out: no imp)	10	**3**	4/1 1	61	14
892*	**Red Jam Jar (94)** (SBBell) **11-11-10**(3) GCahill (led to 4 out: sn outpcd)	1½	**4**	4/1 1	72	25
893 6	**Marco Magnifico (USA) (72)** (MissLucindaRussell) **6-10-5v** AThornton (t: in tch: outpcd 4 out: styd on again u.p fr 2 out)	3½	**5**	16/1	47	—
	Dancing Dancer (73) (DPGeraghty) **7-10-6** RSupple (chsd ldrs tl wknd appr 3 out)	2½	**6**	9/1	46	—
505 3	**Anorak (USA) (93)** (GMMoore) **6-11-12** JCallaghan (effrt 5th: rdn & no imp fr 4 out)	5	**7**	8/1	62	15
587 10	**Canary Blue (IRE) (76)** (PWHiatt) **5-10-6**(3) EHusband (outpcd & bhd fr 5th: n.d after)	1¼	**8**	10/1	44	—
876 P	**Whirlwind Romance (IRE) (67)** (WTKemp) **5-10-0** SMcDougall (hld up: rr div whn blnd 2 out: n.d)	2	**9**	50/1	34	—
897 6	**Wee Wizard (IRE) (87)** (MABarnes) **7-11-6** NWilliamson (hdwy 5th: prom whn blnd 4 out: wknd next)	1	**10**	16/1	53	6
	Joyrider (91) (MissMKMilligan) **5-11-10** ASSmith (in tch tl wknd fr 4 out)	5	**11**	14/1	53	6
	Seconds Away (67) (JSGoldie) **5-9-11**(3) GLee (a bhd)	18	**12**	50/1	15	—
781 3	**Pimsboy (70)** (GROldroyd) **9-10-3v**ow3 RichardGuest (mstkes: t.o whn p.u bef 2 out)		**P**	25/1	—	—
805 4	**Yacht Club (67)** (JLEyre) **14-10-0** OPears (lw: prom whn blnd & uns rdr 2nd)		**U**	15/2 3	—	—

(SP 129.8%) **14 Rn**

4m 56.2 (9.20) CSF £77.84 CT £308.63 TOTE £13.50: £2.90 £2.50 £2.10 (£50.20) Trio £200.90 OWNER The Belles (PENRITH) BRED Con Ryan

LONG HANDICAP Whirlwind Romance (IRE) 9-6 Belle Rose (IRE) 9-13 Seconds Away 9-0 Pimsboy 9-7

No bid

Belle Rose (IRE) showed she has progressed from last year. But for being almost knocked over two out, she would have won more convincingly. (10/1)

Furietto (IRE), in the thick of things throughout, almost put the winner out of the race two out when jumping across her, and that would have been his best chance. (7/1)

Highland Park, trying to win this for the second race running, was very much on his toes but, off the bit some way out, was never anything like good enough. (4/1)

892* Red Jam Jar did his usual and went off in front, but he had his limitations exposed in the home straight in this much more competitive event. (4/1)

893 Marco Magnifico (USA), whose rider even had spurs on this time, only ran on when the wind was behind him and not blowing into his tube. (16/1)

Dancing Dancer ran as though this was just needed. (9/1)

1048 J. E. HARTLEY MEMORIAL H'CAP CHASE (0-140) (5-Y.O+) (Class B)

2-20 (2-21) **3m 1f (18 fncs)** £4,471.00 (£1,348.00: £654.00: £307.00) GOING: 0.00 sec per fur (G)

				SP	RR	SF
	Sounds Strong (IRE) (114) (DNicholson) **7-10-8** AMaguire (lw: hld up: blnd 10th: stdy hdwy 12th: led & j.lft 3 out: blnd 2 out: rdn & r.o)	—	**1**	11/4 2	128	—
797*	**McGregor The Third (124)** (GRichards) **10-11-4** BHarding (cl up: chal 12th: ev ch & hmpd 3 out: nt qckn after)	6	**2**	5/4 1	134	—
	Silver Stick (125) (MWEasterby) **9-11-5v** NWilliamson (led 2nd to 3 out: sn outpcd)	4	**3**	14/1	133	—
	Fiveleigh Builds (130) (MissLucindaRussell) **9-11-10** AThornton (lw: led to 2nd: cl up: outpcd 12th: wknd fr 14th)	22	**4**	9/1	124	—
180 3	**Pims Gunner (IRE) (110)** (MDHammond) **8-10-4** ADobbin (prom tl outpcd appr 4 out)	3½	**5**	11/1	101	—
	Toogood to Be True (134) (TDEasterby) **8-12-0** LWyer (bit bkwd: trckd ldrs tl blnd 14th: sn btn: eased fr last)	dist	**6**	5/1 3	—	—

(SP 112.8%) **6 Rn**

6m 16.0 CSF £6.48 TOTE £3.70: £2.00 £1.30 (£3.10) OWNER Mrs David Thompson (TEMPLE GUITING) BRED S. Banville

Sounds Strong (IRE) did well against these more experienced rivals, but almost threw it away with a terrible blunder two out. He does look well handicapped at the moment. (11/4)

797* McGregor The Third put in his usual good jumping round, but he took a hefty knock from the winner three out, and was already struggling with the pace and was well second best from there on. (5/4: 11/1-11/8)

Silver Stick ran a useful first race of the season, but is much better over marathon distances. (14/1)

Fiveleigh Builds is probably high enough in the weights after a super season last year, and his stable is not as yet in top form. He might need a bit more time to come right. (9/1)

180 Pims Gunner (IRE) ran quite well and left the impression that he should be all the better for this, his first effort for three and a half months.(11/1)

Toogood to Be True has done well physically and looked likely to benefit from this. A mistake five out soon steadied him. (5/1)

1049 SANDERSON BRAMALL MOTOR GROUP NOVICES' H'CAP HURDLE (0-105) (4-Y.O+) (Class D)

2-50 (2-51) **2m (9 hdls)** £3,036.00 (£846.00: £408.00) GOING minus 0.07 sec per fur (G)

				SP	RR	SF
876 2	**Suas Leat (IRE) (96)** (JMJefferson) **6-11-2**(7) MNewton (bhd: hdwy ½-wy: chal 3 out: styd on u.p to ld post)	—	**1**	9/2 2	77	28
698*	**Mithraic (IRE) (97)** (WSCunningham) **4-11-2**(7) LMcGrath (t: a cl up: led 3 out: hrd rdn flat: jst ct)	s.h	**2**	6/1	78	28
5 2	**Teejay'n'aitch (IRE) (77)** (JSGoldie) **4-10-0**(3) GLee (in tch: effrt appr 3 out: styd on: nvr able to chal)	8	**3**	11/1	50	—
955 4	**Silly Money (90)** (TDEasterby) **5-11-3** LWyer (lw: hld up: hdwy 4 out: prom & rdn next: nt pce to chal)	2	**4**	9/2 2	61	12
	Monyman (IRE) (97) (MDHammond) **6-11-10** RGarritty (hld up: hdwy 4 out: ev ch 3 out: wknd next)	2	**5**	5/1 3	66	17
794 5	**Dash To The Phone (USA) (74)** (KAMorgan) **4-9-11**(3) RMassey (led tl hdd 3 out: sn btn)	2	**6**	12/1	41	—
	Mr Christie (78) (MissLCSiddall) **4-10-4** AThornton (prom tl lost pl 4 out: styd on again fr 2 out)	4	**7**	20/1	41	—
	Storming Lorna (IRE) (74) (WMcKeown) **6-9-12**(3)ow1 GCahill (nvr nr to chal)	6	**8**	33/1	31	—
	Rambollina (85) (MWEasterby) **5-10-12** NWilliamson (hld up & bhd: n.d)	½	**9**	20/1	41	—
786*	**Vintage Red (89)** (GRichards) **6-11-2** ADobbin (lw: chsd ldrs tl lost pl appr 3 out)	4	**10**	3/1 1	41	—
806 5	**Stylish Interval (89)** (NWaggott) **4-11-1** RichardGuest (chsd ldrs tl wknd 4 out)	6	**11**	20/1	35	—
	Sayraf Dancer (IRE) (79) (MrsAMNaughton) **7-10-6** MFoster (in tch: blnd 3rd: hit 4 out: sn lost pl)	1	**12**	20/1	24	—

(SP 130.3%) **12 Rn**

3m 49.9 (7.90) CSF £32.77 CT £271.28 TOTE £5.50: £1.70 £3.10 £2.40 (£17.40) Trio £30.00 OWNER Mrs J. M. Davenport (MALTON) BRED J. and Mrs Power
LONG HANDICAP Storming Lorna (IRE) 9-8
WEIGHT FOR AGE 4yo-1lb
876 Suas Leat (IRE) is a really tough sort who stays particularly well, and that won him the day. (9/2)
698* Mithraic (IRE), although tubed on this very windy day, did have the wind behind him in the straight and tried his heart out, but his rider got rather carried away on the run-in and was just touched off. (6/1)
5 Teejay'n'aitch (IRE) ran another fair race, but was never doing enough to seriously get into it. (11/1: 8/1-12/1)
955 Silly Money looked dangerous when improving approaching three out, but then proved short of speed, and may need a bit further. (9/2)
Monyman (IRE) came there looking very dangerous three out, but then the lack of a recent run told. He may also need longer distances. (5/1)
Dash To The Phone (USA) had a visor on for the first time when putting in his best effort last season. If fitted with the headgear again, he might be worth keeping in mind. (12/1: op 8/1)
Mr Christie gives the impression that he has more ability, but is still a maiden under both Rules. (20/1)
Rambollina, after missing all last season, just had a pipe-opener here and should be all the better for it. (20/1)

1050 BRITISH FIELD SPORTS SOCIETY MAIDEN AMATEUR HURDLE (4-Y.O+) (Class E)
3-20 (3-20) **2m 4f 110y (10 hdls)** £2,075.00 (£575.00: £275.00) GOING minus 0.07 sec per fur (G)

				SP	RR	SF
	Keen To The Last (FR) (103) (MDHammond) **4-11-6**(3) MrCBonner (a.p: slt ld 3 out: kpt on wl)	—	**1**	9/4[2]	78	16
	Baher (USA) (69) (MrsASwinbank) **7-11-3**(7) MrChrisWilson (mde most to 3 out: rallied flat)	1¼	**2**	33/1	77	16
	Beggars Banquet (IRE) (PBeaumont) **6-11-10** MrsAFarrell (lw: sn chsng ldrs: outpcd appr 3 out: rdn 2 out: kpt on one pce)	8	**3**	10/11[1]	71	10
	Our Rainbow (MrsPSly) **4-10-11**(7) MissLAllan (bit bkwd: a in tch: kpt on u.p fr 3 out: nt pce to chal)	3	**4**	20/1	63	1
218[4]	**Big Treat (IRE) (78)** (PWHiatt) **4-11-2**(7) MrPScott (cl up tl wknd 4 out)	20	**5**	14/1	53	—
	Tartan Mix (IRE) (JAMoore) **5-11-5**(5) MrNWilson (bit bkwd: hld up & wl bhd: sme late hdwy)	½	**6**	66/1	52	—
	L'Eglise Belle (JJO'Neill) **4-10-11**(7) MrLCorcoran (hld up: hdwy 5th: wknd appr 3 out: dead)	13	**7**	8/1[3]	37	—
	Polo Pony (IRE) (JohnUpson) **4-11-2**(7) MissPRobson (t.o fr 5th)	6	**8**	33/1	38	—
	Barnstormer (65) (EAElliott) **10-11-5**(5) MrRHale (bit bkwd: t.o fr 5th)	6	**9**	33/1	33	—
	Last Try (IRE) (BSRothwell) **5-11-10** MrSSwiers (in tch tl wknd 4 out)	6	**10**	20/1	28	—
	Allexton Lad (MissJBower) **5-11-3**(7) MrJApiafi (chsd ldrs to 6th: sn wl bhd)	7	**11**	66/1	23	—
				(SP 122.3%)	**11 Rn**	

5m 0.7 (13.70) CSF £62.51 TOTE £2.70: £1.10 £6.50 £1.20 (£129.50) Trio £30.40 OWNER Mr D E Allen & Mr S Balmer (MIDDLEHAM) BRED Lawn Stud
WEIGHT FOR AGE 4yo-1lb
Keen To The Last (FR), fit from the Flat, made that tell and was always doing just enough. (9/4)
Baher (USA), from a yard in top form, looked likely to benefit from this and ran a fine race, fighting back when looking beaten. (33/1)
Beggars Banquet (IRE), whose yard is not yet firing, ran quite well, but was always short of toe in the home straight. (10/11: 8/11-evens)
Our Rainbow looks slow, but did keep battling on when all looked lost, and is likely to be all the better for it. (20/1)
218 Big Treat (IRE) is a lean individual who basically looks short of toe. (14/1)
Tartan Mix (IRE) looked burly and had what can only be described as an educational. He could be interesting in modest company. (66/1)

1051 ROBERT BOWETT SAAB LTD NOVICES' H'CAP CHASE (0-105) (5-Y.O+) (Class D)
3-50 (3-50) **2m (12 fncs)** £3,561.00 (£1,068.00: £514.00: £237.00) GOING minus 0.07 sec per fur (G)

				SP	RR	SF
70[9]	**Ballyline (IRE) (79)** (WTKemp) **5-11-1** TReed (bit bkwd: led 4th: qcknd flat: comf)	—	**1**	100/30[2]	86+	13
873[4]	**Hazel Crest (72)** (MESowersby) **9-10-9** DParker (lw: hld up: effrt 8th: chal 2 out: nt qckn flat)	4	**2**	14/1	75	3
	Chorus Line (IRE) (79) (PBeaumont) **7-11-2** RSupple (bit bkwd: lft in ld 1st: hdd 4th: lost pl 4 out: styd on & ch last: sn btn)	2½	**3**	7/2[3]	80	8
873[3]	**Reve de Valse (USA) (87)** (RJohnson) **9-11-10** KJohnson (lw: chsd ldrs: effrt 4 out: outpcd whn mstke 2 out: no imp after)	8	**4**	4/1	80	8
704[4]	**See You Always (IRE) (63)** (MABarnes) **6-10-0** NWilliamson (a.p: shkn up appr 4 out: sn ev ch: outpcd whn hrd rdn & blnd 2 out: p.u bef last)		**P**	25/1	—	—
853*	**Show Your Hand (IRE) (80)** (LLungo) **8-11-3** MFoster (led tl stumbled bdly & uns rdr 1st)		**U**	15/8[1]	—	—
				(SP 110.6%)	**6 Rn**	

4m 2.1 (10.10) CSF £35.41 TOTE £4.90: £2.30 £2.70 (£31.80) OWNER The 49 Partnership (DUNS) BRED James O'Keeffe
LONG HANDICAP See You Always (IRE) 9-10
WEIGHT FOR AGE 5yo-1lb
70 Ballyline (IRE), although looking a shade burly, jumped round in good style and won really well. He ought to find further success. (100/30)
Hazel Crest has come on for his first run of the season and a modest race can be found. (14/1: 10/1-16/1)
Chorus Line (IRE) looked likely to be all the better for this and ran well enough to suggest that her luck should change this year. (7/2)
873 Reve de Valse (USA) was always close enough, but proved well short of speed when it mattered. (4/1)
704 See You Always (IRE) had his chances, but seemed to lose his action at times. After a bad blunder two out, he was then pulled up and dismounted. (25/1)
853* Show Your Hand (IRE) jumped the first alright but stumbled a stride after, giving his rider no chance of staying aboard. (15/8)

1052 ROBERT CLARK & SONS STEEPLEJACKS AND ENGINEERING LTD INTERMEDIATE OPEN N.H. FLAT RACE (4, 5 & 6-Y.O) (Class H)
4-20 (4-20) **2m** £1,406.00 (£391.00: £188.00)

				SP	RR	SF
898*	**Duraid (IRE)** (DenysSmith) **4-12-3** RichardGuest (lw: hld up: qcknd to ld 1f out: r.o wl)	—	**1**	7/4[1]	—	—
	Good Vibes (TDEasterby) **4-11-3** LWyer (hld up: stdy hdwy ½-wy: ev ch 3f out: styd on wl)	1½	**2**	11/2[3]	—	—
	Little Crumplin (MWEasterby) **4-11-3** NWilliamson (cl up: led over 4f out: qcknd: hdd 1f out: kpt on)	2	**3**	20/1	—	—
	Rothari (BSRothwell) **4-11-3** RSupple (hdwy 5f out: styd on wl: nvr able to chal)	2	**4**	20/1	—	—
	Strong Mint (IRE) (MrsMReveley) **5-11-4** PNiven (bit bkwd: bhd: rn green 6f out: styd on strly fnl 2f)	5	**5**	9/1	—	—
	Gale Force (IRE) (PBeaumont) **5-10-11**(7) BGrattan (bit bkwd: trckd ldrs: effrt 4f out: r.o one pce)	nk	**6**	7/2[2]	—	—
	Desert Devil (GRichards) **4-11-3** ADobbin (lw: hld up: effrt 4f out: no imp)	10	**7**	8/1	—	—
705[8]	**Teddy Edward** (MrsAMNaughton) **6-11-4** JSupple (in tch tl outpcd fnl 4f)	2	**8**	33/1	—	—

686[3]	**Henpecked (IRE)** (MDHammond) **5-11-4** RGarritty (lw: led tl over 4f out: sn wknd) 3½	**9**	15/2	—	—
898[7]	**Toshiba House (IRE)** (BEllison) **5-10-10**(3) GCahill (cl up tl wknd fnl 4f) 1	**10**	50/1	—	—
	Selectric (IRE) (JWade) **5-11-4** KJones (a bhd) 16	**11**	50/1	—	—
	Ragdon (MrsARHewitt) **5-11-4** SWynne (prom tl wknd 4f out) 8	**12**	50/1	—	—
705[5]	**North End Lady** (WSCunningham) **5-10-13**(7) LMcGrath (s.s: sddle slipped: a t.o) 27	**13**	20/1	—	—
59[2]	**Supreme Comfort (IRE)** (EMCaine) **4-10-12** MrPMurray (lost tch 6f out: p.u 3f out)	**P**	20/1	—	—
			(SP 134.7%)	**14 Rn**	

3m 48.6 CSF £13.30 TOTE £3.10: £1.90 £2.30 £5.00 (£12.60) Trio £151.70 OWNER Mr A. Suddes (BISHOP AUCKLAND) BRED Hussein Hurami
WEIGHT FOR AGE 4yo-1lb

898* Duraid (IRE) won his fourth bumper in some style against what looked like useful opposition. (7/4)
Good Vibes put up a very promising effort, and looks the type to improve with experience. (11/2: 3/1-6/1)
Little Crumplin ran a super first race and looks a fair recruit to this game. (20/1)
Rothari has changed stables this year and seems to have improved, running really well in what appeared to be a decent bumper. (20/1)
Strong Mint (IRE) was the pick as far as the future goes. He was very much in need of this and ran green but, gradually realising what was required, finished well. Much more will be heard of him. (9/1)
Gale Force (IRE) came here with a big reputation, but did look likely to benefit from this. He is a real chaser for the future and anything he does in the meantime will be a bonus. (7/2)
Desert Devil looks a useful type, but may be a bit of a character. No doubt this will have done him good. (8/1)

T/Jkpt: £40,724.00 (1.18 Tckts). T/Plpt: £163.30 (80.3 Tckts). T/Qdpt: £15.70 (37.13 Tckts). AA

0832-WINCANTON (R-H) (Good to firm)
Sunday October 27th
WEATHER: unsettled

1053 WITCHAMPTON NOVICES' HURDLE (4-Y.O+) (Class E)
2-10 (2-11) **2m (8 hdls)** £2,635.00 (£735.00: £355.00) GOING minus 0.11 sec per fur (G)

			SP	RR	SF
	Rosencrantz (IRE) (98) (MissVenetiaWilliams) **4-11-4** RJohnson (hld up: hdwy appr 2 out: hrd rdn to ld last stride) ......—	**1**	5/1	81	53
	El Don (100) (MJRyan) **4-11-4** JRyan (hld up: hdwy 3 out: led flat: hdd last stride) ......s.h	**2**	8/1	81	53
794*	**Nordic Breeze (IRE) (102)** (MCPipe) **4-11-4** APMcCoy (a.p: led appr 2 out: hdd flat: unable qckn) 2	**3**	11/4 1	79	51
	Kilmington (IRE) (JTGifford) **7-10-9**(3) LAspell (hld up: stdy hdwy after 3 out: nvr nr to chal) 18	**4**	20/1	54	27
	Policemans Pride (FR) (MMadgwick) **7-10-12** GUpton (hld up: led after 3 out: hdd appr 2 out: sn wknd) 9	**5**	66/1	45	18
890[3]	**Shift Again (IRE) (91)** (OSherwood) **4-10-6b** JOsborne (hld up: j.slowly 4th: no hdwy fr 3 out) 1¼	**6**	4/1 3	39	11
812[5]	**Jaazim** (MMadgwick) **6-10-12** BFenton (hld up: hdwy 5th: wknd appr 2 out) 3	**7**	25/1	41	14
600[11]	**Solo Volumes** (HGRowsell) **7-10-12** BPowell (a bhd: t.o fr 3 out) 26	**8**	150/1	15	—
890[6]	**Arthur's Special** (MCPipe) **6-10-0**(7) GSupple (prom: mstke 1st: wknd 4th: t.o) ......½	**9**	50/1	9	—
	Mapengo (JCullinan) **5-10-12** VSlattery (led tl after 3 out: wknd qckly appr 2 out: t.o) 5	**10**	100/1	9	—
	Trouble At Mill (JLBrown) **6-10-12** MrJLLlewellyn (bkwd: prom to 4th: t.o) 1	**11**	66/1	8	—
	Shrimp (RHAlner) **5-10-7** WMcFarland (bkwd: bhd: mstke 2nd: t.o fr 3 out) 4	**12**	50/1	—	—
	Wise 'n' Shine (NMLampard) **5-10-2**(5) ChrisWebb (bkwd: a bhd: t.o fr 5th) 4	**13**	100/1	—	—
890*	**Ritto (98)** (JNeville) **6-11-5** RDunwoody (hld up: hdwy 5th: ev ch 2 out: sn rdn & wknd qckly: mstke last: p.u flat)	**P**	7/2 2	—	—
			(SP 114.8%)	**14 Rn**	

3m 40.8 (0.80) CSF £39.47 TOTE £5.90: £2.00 £1.80 £1.70 (£21.50) Trio £35.60 OWNER Mr L. J. Fulford (HEREFORD) BRED Sheikh Mohammed bin Rashid al Maktoum
WEIGHT FOR AGE 4yo-1lb

Rosencrantz (IRE), the easy winner of a maiden hurdle at Chepstow in May, had apparently been working well at home but needed Johnson at his strongest to snatch it. (5/1)
El Don, with the benefit of a recent pipe-opener on the Flat, battled hard on the run-in, only to be pipped on the post. (8/1)
794* Nordic Breeze (IRE) found the race turning out to be a good deal more competitive than Uttoxeter. (11/4)
Kilmington (IRE) would have gone close to winning a point-to-point when falling at Badbury Rings in March, and one was left with the impression this was a warm-up prior to going novice chasing. (20/1)
Policemans Pride (FR) will presumably now return to novice chasing. (66/1)
890 Shift Again (IRE) did not find the blinkers working the oracle. (4/1)

1054 NETHER WALLOP NOVICES' CHASE (5-Y.O+) (Class D)
2-40 (2-42) **3m 1f 110y (21 fncs)** £3,943.00 (£1,098.00: £529.00) GOING minus 0.11 sec per fur (G)

			SP	RR	SF
	Hanakham (IRE) (RJHodges) **7-11-0** RDunwoody (j.w: w ldr: led 16th: clr 2 out: easily) ......—	**1**	9/4 2	113+	11
720*	**Stormtracker (IRE)** (CWeedon) **7-11-6** CO'Dwyer (mde most to 16th: rdn appr 3 out: wknd 2 out) 17	**2**	9/4 2	108	6
795*	**Father Sky** (OSherwood) **5-11-9** JOsborne (hld up: hdwy appr 10th: lost pl appr 12th: rallied 15th: rdn & wknd 17th: t.o) ......dist	**3**	7/4 1	—	—
720[5]	**Definite Maybe (IRE) (93)** (PFNicholls) **6-11-6b** APMcCoy (nvr gng wl: slipped bnd appr 4th: reminders appr 5th: sn lost tch: t.o whn p.u bef 12th)	**P**	10/1 3	—	—
			(SP 107.0%)	**4 Rn**	

6m 34.8 (15.80) CSF £6.91 TOTE £3.20 (£4.50) OWNER Mr M. Brereton (SOMERTON) BRED Eamonn McCarthy
WEIGHT FOR AGE 5yo-3lb

Hanakham (IRE) beat the enigmatic but useful Harwell Lad twenty lengths, despite conceding 7lb, when last seen between the Flags in March 1995. Well backed, he did not let his supporters down and looks decidedly useful. (9/4)
720* Stormtracker (IRE), probably not helped by the incessant rain, was trying to concede weight to a potentially smart recruit. (9/4: op 6/4)
795* Father Sky was never really relishing the task in hand and it would come as no surprise to see him tried in headgear. (7/4)
639 Definite Maybe (IRE) (10/1: 6/1-11/1)

1055 DESERT ORCHID SOUTH WESTERN PATTERN H'CAP CHASE (Gd 2) (5-Y.O+) (Class A)

3-10 (3-11) **2m 5f (17 fncs)** £18,660.00 (£7,060.50: £3,455.25: £1,574.25) GOING minus 0.11 sec per fur (G)

				SP	RR	SF
	Coulton (168) (OSherwood) **9-11-10** JOsborne (mde all: shkn up appr last: r.o wl)	—	**1**	2/1[2]	170	47
	Gales Cavalier (IRE) (160) (DRGandolfo) **8-11-2** RDunwoody (bit bkwd: chsd wnr: rdn appr 2 out: no imp)	3	**2**	11/10[1]	160	37
	Martomick (147) (KCBailey) **9-10-3** CO'Dwyer (hld up: hit 7th: hdwy 13th: wnt 2nd briefly & hit 4 out: sn wknd)	29	**3**	5/2[3]	125	2
951[2]	**Stately Home (IRE) (149)** (PBowen) **5-10-3** RJohnson (bhd fr 12th: t.o)	26	**4**	25/1	107	—
				(SP 113.4%)		**4 Rn**

5m 12.8 (4.80) CSF £4.66 TOTE £2.40 (£2.00) OWNER Mr M. G. St Quinton (UPPER LAMBOURN) BRED Walter Mariti
LONG HANDICAP Martomick 10-1 Stately Home (IRE) 8-0
WEIGHT FOR AGE 5yo-2lb

Coulton disappointed after last year's win in this event and seems the type who is best when fresh. (2/1)
Gales Cavalier (IRE) was blowing hard after the race and it looked beforehand as if he might be just short of peak-fitness. (11/10)
Martomick missed last season with a leg injury and had just begun to look dangerous when missing out at the cross fence, four from home. (5/2)

1056 PORTMAN NOVICES' HURDLE (4-Y.O+) (Class E)

3-40 (3-45) **2m 6f (11 hdls)** £2,512.50 (£700.00: £337.50) GOING minus 0.11 sec per fur (G)

				SP	RR	SF
	Jolis Absent (80) (MJRyan) **6-10-7b** JRyan (hld up: lost pl 7th: rallied appr 2 out: led flat: styd on)	—	**1**	12/1	75	—
739[2]	**Political Panto (IRE) (105)** (MCPipe) **5-11-5** APMcCoy (led & sn wl clr: hit 3 out: wknd & hdd flat)	6	**2**	2/1[1]	83	2
859[2]	**The Lad** (LMontagueHall) **7-10-12** JOsborne (chsd clr ldr tl appr 2 out: wknd appr last)	26	**3**	9/4[2]	57	—
	Imperial Honors (IRE) (NMLampard) **5-10-7**(5) ChrisWebb (a wl bhd)	4	**4**	100/1	54	—
918[3]	**Moonlight Escapade (IRE)** (RJHodges) **5-10-12** RDunwoody (nt j.w: hld up: bhd fr 8th: t.o)	dist	**5**	4/1[3]	—	—
968[7]	**Mr Jasper** (NBThomson) **4-10-10** SBurrough (s.s: a wl bhd: t.o)	13	**6**	150/1	—	—
918[8]	**Don't Argue** (SGKnight) **5-11-0**ow2 MissLBlackford (wl bhd: pckd 1st: blnd 3rd: t.o whn p.u after 3 out)		**P**	100/1	—	—
900[P]	**Bickleigh Belle** (SGKnight) **6-10-7** LHarvey (a wl bhd: t.o whn p.u bef 8th)		**P**	150/1	—	—
900[2]	***Rum Customer*** (CRBarwell) **5-10-12** BFenton (Withdrawn not under Starter's orders: veterinary advice)		**W**	9/2	—	—
				(SP 113.3%)		**8 Rn**

5m 25.4 (16.40) CSF £25.11 TOTE £14.20: £1.60 £1.10 £1.10 (£9.20) Trio £6.20 OWNER Mrs Karola Vann (NEWMARKET) BRED Mrs M. A. Ryan
WEIGHT FOR AGE 4yo-1lb

Jolis Absent found the combination of first-time blinkers and her ability to really get the trip doing the trick. (12/1)
739 Political Panto (IRE) seems at his best when trying to run the opposition ragged, but got outstayed by the winner on this occasion. (2/1)
859 The Lad, stepping up in trip, eventually got found out by the runner-up's tearaway tactics. (9/4)
Imperial Honors (IRE) showed nothing in three bumpers last season. (100/1)

1057 BLACKDOWN H'CAP CHASE (0-110) (5-Y.O+) (Class E)

4-10 (4-14) **3m 1f 110y (21 fncs)** £4,224.00 (£1,272.00: £616.00: £288.00) GOING minus 0.11 sec per fur (G)

				SP	RR	SF
	Special Account (94) (CRBarwell) **10-11-1** BFenton (bkwd: hld up: rdn after 13th: hdwy 15th: led 2 out: drvn out)	—	**1**	14/1	102	—
823[2]	**Frozen Drop (102)** (PCRitchens) **9-11-9** SFox (chsd ldr: mstke 11th: led 15th to 2 out: r.o one pce flat)	¾	**2**	9/2[2]	110	—
726*	**Rainbow Castle (107)** (PFNicholls) **9-12-0** APMcCoy (hld up: hdwy 16th: ev ch 4 out: rdn & sltly outpcd 3 out: rallying whn pckd last: one pce)	1¼	**3**	10/11[1]	114	—
817[2]	**Distant Memory (99)** (PJHobbs) **7-11-6b** JOsborne (hit 6th & 7th: lost pl 8th: hit 14th: bhd fr 17th: t.o)	dist	**4**	7/1[3]	—	—
799[4]	**Mutual Trust (100)** (PBowen) **12-11-7** RJohnson (led to 15th: rdn 16th: wknd appr 3 out: fell last)		**F**	20/1	—	—
914[F]	**Nick the Dreamer (94)** (WGMTurner) **11-11-1** RDunwoody (3rd whn fell 9th)		**F**	12/1	—	—
	Tearful Prince (79) (CWMitchell) **12-10-0** BPowell (hdwy 8th: bdly hmpd & uns rdr 9th)		**U**	9/1	—	—
				(SP 112.2%)		**7 Rn**

6m 44.6 (25.60) CSF £68.04 TOTE £19.60: £7.10 £2.70 (£34.40) OWNER Mr Tony Fiorillo (TIVERTON) BRED J. P. N. Parker
LONG HANDICAP Tearful Prince 9-9

Special Account, who successfully reverted to hurdles last season, has obviously had his interest in fences rekindled and belied his burly paddock appearance. (14/1: 10/1-16/1)
823 Frozen Drop continues in good form and came up against a horse at the top of his game in Jim Valentine last time. (9/2)
726* Rainbow Castle, raised a stone for his two victories this season, needed a big one at the final fence but just nodded a little on landing. (10/11)
817 Distant Memory was not helped by the rain, which must have slightly eased the going. (7/1)

1058 BLANDFORD H'CAP HURDLE (0-120) (4-Y.O+) (Class D)

4-40 (4-41) **2m (8 hdls)** £3,006.50 (£834.00: £399.50) GOING minus 0.11 sec per fur (G)

				SP	RR	SF
	Dark Nightingale (92) (OSherwood) **6-10-12** JOsborne (mde all: v.easily)	—	**1**	6/5[1]	79+	16
916*	**Peter Monamy (103)** (MCPipe) **4-11-8b** APMcCoy (chsd wnr: hit 3rd: rdn 3 out: btn whn hit last)	3	**2**	13/8[2]	87	23
915[5]	**Desert Calm (IRE) (90)** (MrsPNDutfield) **7-10-10** PHolley (hld up: rdn after 3 out: wknd flat)	5	**3**	9/1	69	6
	Top Wave (104) (MissAEEmbiricos) **8-11-10** JRyan (bhd fr 3 out: t.o)	dist	**4**	5/1[3]	—	—
				(SP 110.2%)		**4 Rn**

3m 47.7 (7.70) CSF £3.45 TOTE £2.00 (£1.60) OWNER Miss Liz Clark (UPPER LAMBOURN) BRED R.W.Fidler
WEIGHT FOR AGE 4yo-1lb

Dark Nightingale never broke sweat to make a successful return. She may be at her best caught fresh. (6/5)
916* Peter Monamy did try his best, but could not force the winner to break sweat. (13/8)
Desert Calm (IRE) won four times on the Flat at up to ten furlongs in Ireland, but has proved disappointing over hurdles so far. (9/1: op 5/1)
Top Wave (5/1: 4/1-6/1)

T/Plpt: £509.30 (21.52 Tckts). T/Qdpt: £36.90 (15.93 Tckts). KH

CHELTENHAM (L-H) (Good to firm, Firm patches)
Tuesday October 29th
WEATHER: fine

1059 CHELTENHAM AND THREE COUNTIES RACE CLUB MAIDEN HURDLE (4-Y.O+) (Class D)
1-40 (1-41) **2m 110y (Old) (8 hdls)** £2,801.00 (£848.00: £414.00: £197.00) GOING: 0.03 sec per fur (G)

	Horse		Pos	SP	RR	SF
	Herbert Lodge (IRE) (KCBailey) **7-11-6** CO'Dwyer (lw: plld hrd: led after 1st: shkn up appr last: comf)	—	1	11/8[1]	81+	10
	Charlie Parrot (IRE) (MCPipe) **6-11-6** APMcCoy (bit bkwd: hld up & bhd: hdwy 5th: chsd wnr appr last: unable qckn flat)	1½	2	10/1	80	9
955[2]	**Samba Sharply** (AHide) **5-11-6** PHide (chsd wnr fr 3rd tl rdn appr last: wknd flat)	8	3	11/2[3]	72	1
	Mr Gordon Bennett (RDickin) **5-10-13**(7) XAizpuru (plld hrd: bhd fr 3rd: t.o)	dist	4	100/1	—	—
939[14]	**The Knitter** (JJBirkett) **4-11-5** PMcLoughlin (led tl after 1st: sn wl bhd: t.o whn fell 2 out)		F	100/1	—	—
871[5]	**Studio Thirty** (CASmith) **4-11-5** PNiven (chsd wnr to 3rd: cl 4th whn fell 3 out)		F	25/1	—	—
	Set the Fashion (DLWilliams) **7-11-6v** RDunwoody (fell 1st)		F	8/1	—	—
955[F]	**Rizal (USA)** (RJEckley) **4-11-2**(3) DWalsh (ref to r: t.n.p)		R	100/1	—	—
	Marching Marquis (IRE) (NoelChance) **5-11-6** RJohnson (bdly hmpd & uns rdr 1st)		U	7/4[2]	—	—

(SP 120.9%) **9 Rn**

4m 4.8 (13.80) CSF £15.66 TOTE £2.80: £1.40 £1.60 £1.40 (£13.80) Trio £12.90 OWNER Mrs David Thompson (UPPER LAMBOURN) BRED Mrs Bernadette Hayden
WEIGHT FOR AGE 4yo-1lb
Herbert Lodge (IRE) has had more than his fair share of problems since finishing second to Berude Not To on his hurdling debut here nearly two years ago. His trainer is hoping he will turn out to be good enough for the Supreme Novices' at the Festival. (11/8: 4/6-6/4)
Charlie Parrot (IRE), despite not looking fully tuned up, made a highly-promising debut over timber and should have little difficulty opening his account. (10/1)
955 Samba Sharply found this company a bit hotter than when runner-up in a couple of weak affairs at Stratford. (11/2)
Set the Fashion (8/1: 4/1-9/1)

1060 FRENCHIE NICHOLSON CONDITIONAL H'CAP HURDLE (0-135) (4-Y.O+) (Class E)
2-15 (2-15) **2m 110y (Old) (8 hdls)** £2,220.00 (£620.00: £300.00) GOING: 0.03 sec per fur (G)

	Horse		Pos	SP	RR	SF
743*	**Mister Rm (106)** (NATwiston-Davies) **4-11-13** DWalsh (mde all: drvn out)	—	1	Evens[1]	91	46
942[4]	**Frontier Flight (USA) (85)** (MissLCSiddall) **6-10-7** EHusband (hld up: stdy hdwy appr 3 out: chsd wnr appr last: no imp)	4	2	7/1[3]	66	22
967[2]	**Kalzari (USA) (90)** (AWCarroll) **11-10-12** MichaelBrennan (lw: hld up & bhd: hdwy 3 out: one pce fr 2 out)	3	3	7/1[3]	68	24
862[U]	**Bally Parson (86)** (RDickin) **10-10-1**(7) XAizpuru (chsd wnr tl wknd appr 3 out: mstke 2 out)	6	4	14/1	58	14
820*	**Young Radical (IRE) (92)** (JohnUpson) **4-10-13** DParker (lw: hld up: wnt 2nd & pckd 3 out: sn wknd)	26	5	5/2[2]	39	—

(SP 110.2%) **5 Rn**

3m 57.5 (6.50) CSF £7.50 TOTE £1.90: £1.10 £2.50 (£4.40) OWNER Mr F J Mills & Mr W Mills (CHELTENHAM) BRED Major and Mrs R. B. Kennard
WEIGHT FOR AGE 4yo-1lb
743* Mister Rm seemed more polished at his hurdles this time. (Evens)
690 Frontier Flight (USA), dropped 4lb, would probably have preferred further. (7/1)
967 Kalzari (USA) moved up menacingly, but not could match his younger rivals. (7/1: 5/1-8/1)
742 Bally Parson had a confidence-restorer over hurdles. (14/1)
820* Young Radical (IRE) found this a good deal more competitive than Towcester. (5/2)

1061 BUSINESS TO BUSINESS DIRECT NOVICES' H'CAP CHASE (0-110) (5-Y.O+) (Class D)
2-50 (2-50) **2m 4f 110y (Old) (15 fncs)** £4,562.00 (£1,118.00) GOING: 0.03 sec per fur (G)

	Horse		Pos	SP	RR	SF
744[2]	**Strong Promise (IRE) (106)** (GAHubbard) **5-11-11**(3) KGaule (lw: hld up: qcknd to ld 2 out: pushed clr flat)	—	1	4/6[1]	106+	23
901*	**Pongo Waring (IRE) (103)** (MissHCKnight) **7-11-13** JFTitley (lw: led to 5th: led 12th to 2 out: one pce)	11	2	11/8[2]	94	13
	Ashmead Rambler (IRE) (77) (PJHobbs) **6-10-1**ow1 CMaude (w ldr: led 5th to 12th: cl 3rd whn fell 2 out)		F	11/1[3]	—	—

(SP 110.4%) **3 Rn**

5m 18.3 (16.30) CSF £1.92 TOTE £1.70 (£1.10) OWNER Mr G. A. Hubbard (WOODBRIDGE) BRED William McCarthy
LONG HANDICAP Ashmead Rambler (IRE) 9-5
WEIGHT FOR AGE 5yo-2lb
744 Strong Promise (IRE) got back on the right track and may reappear at Ascot on Saturday before a tilt at the Murphy's Gold Cup. (4/6)
901* Pongo Waring (IRE) found the winner too much of a handful. (11/8)
Ashmead Rambler (IRE), 9lb out of the handicap, was in the process of giving more than a reasonable account of himself when departing. (11/1: 8/1-14/1)

1062 BUSINESS MARKET ANALYSIS NOVICES' HURDLE (4-Y.O+) (Class C)
3-25 (3-26) **3m 2f (Old) (13 hdls)** £3,755.00 (£1,055.00: £515.00) GOING: 0.03 sec per fur (G)

	Horse		Pos	SP	RR	SF
934*	**Hunters Rock (IRE) (105)** (KCBailey) **7-11-5** CO'Dwyer (lw: hld up: hdwy 9th: led on bit after 2 out: v.easily)	—	1	10/11[1]	95+	15
800[2]	**Tipping The Line (108)** (MCPipe) **6-11-10** APMcCoy (w ldr: reminders after 8th: led appr 10th: hdd after 2 out: no ch w wnr)	10	2	11/8[2]	94	14
813*	**Scamallach (IRE) (89)** (JRJenkins) **6-11-5b** GBradley (hdwy 6th: wknd 10th: t.o)	dist	3	8/1[3]	—	—
	Win a Hand (76) (BJMRyall) **6-10-9** GUpton (bkwd: led tl wknd qckly appr 10th: t.o whn p.u bef 3 out)		P	14/1	—	—
968[6]	**Lilly The Filly** (MrsBarbaraWaring) **5-10-9** EByrne (plld hrd early: a bhd: t.o 8th: p.u bef 3 out)		P	100/1	—	—

(SP 113.3%) **5 Rn**

6m 37.4 (20.40) CSF £2.57 TOTE £1.90: £1.30 £1.30 (£1.60) OWNER Mrs Harry Duffey (UPPER LAMBOURN) BRED M. V. Hough
934* Hunters Rock (IRE) was not fluent at some of his hurdles, but the manner in which he disposed of the runner-up could not be faulted. (10/11: 8/11-evens)
800 Tipping The Line proved no match for the winner at these weights. (11/8)
813* Scamallach (IRE) had more on her plate here, and did not appear to stay the trip. (8/1: 5/1-9/1)

1063 ENIGMA NIGHTCLUB AMATEUR H'CAP CHASE (0-125) (5-Y.O+) (Class E)

4-00 (4-00) **3m 1f (Old) (19 fncs)** £3,493.00 (£1,054.00: £512.00: £241.00) GOING: 0.03 sec per fur (G)

				SP	RR	SF
	Coome Hill (IRE) (124) (WWDennis) **7-12-0**(7) MrTDennis (w ldr: led 6th tl appr 8th: led 14th: clr 2 out: easily)	—	**1**	11/8[1]	131+	44
797[3]	**Andrelot (118)** (PBowen) **9-11-8b**(7) MrRThornton (a.p: led appr 8th: hdd 14th: hrd rdn appr 3 out: no imp)	7	**2**	9/4[2]	121	34
797[R]	**Childhay Chocolate (105)** (PFNicholls) **8-10-9**(7) MrJTizzard (plld hrd: led to 6th: outpcd 13th: 3rd & btn whn hit 3 out & 2 out)	15	**3**	3/1[3]	98	11
932[3]	**Foxgrove (96)** (RJPrice) **10-10-0**(7) MrPScott (bhd fr 7th)	9	**4**	20/1	83	—
823[3]	**K C'S Dancer (96)** (RDickin) **11-10-0**(7) MrRWakley (lost pl 7th: mstke 10th: hit 12th: sn wl bhd)	8	**5**	10/1	78	—
817[3]	**Artful Arthur (103)** (LPGrassick) **10-10-7v**1(7)ow7 MrAWintle (t.o fr 3rd: tried to ref & blnd 14th: p.u bef 15th)		**P**	66/1	—	—
				(SP 113.2%)		**6 Rn**

6m 23.5 (14.50) CSF £4.83 TOTE £2.30: £1.30 £1.40 (£3.00) OWNER Mrs Jill Dennis (BUDE) BRED Mrs S. O'Connell
LONG HANDICAP Foxgrove 9-2 K C'S Dancer 8-12 Artful Arthur 8-4
Coome Hill (IRE), scoring first time out for the fourth successive season, made a successful transition to handicap company. (11/8: evens-6/4)
797 Andrelot seemed to stay the trip well enough, but simply met one too good in the progressive winner. (9/4)
Childhay Chocolate was 7lb higher than when winning at Southwell in May. (3/1)
823 K C'S Dancer (10/1: 8/1-14/1)

1064 ROSEHILL HURDLE (3-Y.O) (Class C)

4-30 (4-32) **2m 110y (Old) (8 hdls)** £3,468.75 (£1,050.00: £512.50: £243.75) GOING: 0.03 sec per fur (G)

				SP	RR	SF
962*	**Doctor Green (FR)** (MCPipe) **3-11-8v** APMcCoy (lw: mde all: clr 4th: rdn appr last: r.o wl)	—	**1**	2/5[1]	86	33
912[2]	**Ben Bowden** (MBlanshard) **3-11-3** JOsborne (lw: a.p: chsd wnr fr 3 out: no imp)	11	**2**	8/1[3]	70	17
	Yezza (IRE) (APJarvis) **3-10-7** AMaguire (hld up: hdwy 5th: wknd appr 2 out)	15	**3**	7/1[2]	46	—
589*	**Siberian Mystic** (PGMurphy) **3-10-12** WMcFarland (lw: chsd wnr: 2nd & btn whn mstke 3 out: sn wknd)	8	**4**	7/1[2]	43	—
	Quiet Moments (IRE) (PGMurphy) **3-10-12** WMarston (bkwd: plld hrd: bhd fr 5th)	13	**5**	50/1	30	—
944[7]	**Soldier Blue** (PJHobbs) **3-10-12** RDunwoody (prom to 5th: t.o)	dist	**6**	40/1	—	—
	Startingo (RLBrown) **3-10-12** TJMurphy (stdd s: hdwy & mstke 2nd: sn lost pl: t.o whn p.u bef 5th)		**P**	66/1	—	—
906[8]	**Arrogant Heir** (DHBrown) **3-10-13**ow1 MrARebori (bhd tl m out & uns rdr after 4th)		**R**	66/1	—	—
				(SP 114.9%)		**8 Rn**

3m 59.6 (8.60) CSF £4.53 TOTE £1.50: £1.30 £1.20 £1.10 (£3.60) OWNER Mr Jim Weeden (WELLINGTON) BRED The Queen
962* Doctor Green (FR) completed the hat-trick. (2/5)
912 Ben Bowden was 12lb better off than when beaten about twenty lengths by the winner at Exeter. (8/1: 5/1-10/1)
Yezza (IRE) might struggle to get two miles over timber on this evidence. (7/1)
589* Siberian Mystic got found out by this stiff course. (7/1: 5/1-8/1)

T/Plpt: £5.40 (2,050.37 Tckts). T/Qdpt: £2.80 (246.78 Tckts). KH

1059-CHELTENHAM (L-H) (Firm, Good to firm patches)
Wednesday October 30th

WEATHER: overcast

1065 CHELTENHAM SPONSORSHIP CLUB 'N.H.' NOVICES' HURDLE (4-Y.O+) (Class D)

1-10 (1-11) **2m 110y (Old) (8 hdls)** £2,787.00 (£782.00: £381.00) GOING: 0.32 sec per fur (GS)

				SP	RR	SF
885*	**Kailash (USA)** (MCPipe) **5-11-6** APMcCoy (hld up & bhd: hdwy 4th: led 2 out: canter)	—	**1**	1/8[1]	80++	38
	Shannon Lad (IRE) (77) (AWCarroll) **6-11-0** TJMurphy (bkwd: chsd ldrs: wnt 2nd appr last: no imp)	9	**2**	8/1[2]	65	23
915[6]	**All Sewn Up** (RJBaker) **4-10-13** LHarvey (bit bkwd: led after 1st: sn clr: wkng whn blnd 3 out: hdd next: fin tired)	11	**3**	50/1	55	12
974[11]	**Barton Blade (IRE)** (MissHCKnight) **4-10-13** JFTitley (led tl after 1st: j.slowly 3rd: rdn 5th: wknd qckly appr 2 out: t.o)	18	**4**	16/1[3]	37	—
	Chan The Man (NJHWalker) **5-10-11**(3) GuyLewis (a bhd: lost tch 5th: t.o)	dist	**5**	50/1	—	—
				(SP 109.8%)		**5 Rn**

4m 2.8 (11.80) CSF £1.92 TOTE £1.10: £1.10 £1.50 (£1.60) OWNER Mr Mick Fletcher (WELLINGTON) BRED William C. Miller
WEIGHT FOR AGE 4yo-1lb
885* Kailash (USA) kept up his winning sequence with another facile success and probably thinks this game is easy. (1/8)
Shannon Lad (IRE) was too backward to do himself justice here, but he showed the right commitment and could be finding his way. (8/1)

1066 LLOYDS BOWMAKER NOVICES' CHASE (5-Y.O+) (Class D)

1-40 (1-40) **2m (Old) (12 fncs)** £3,701.00 (£1,118.00: £544.00: £257.00) GOING minus 0.04 sec per fur (G)

				SP	RR	SF
808*	**Celibate (IRE)** (CJMann) **5-11-11** APMcCoy (lw: hld up: led after 4 out: mstke 2 out: drvn out flat)	—	**1**	Evens[1]	116+	43
860*	**Jathib (CAN)** (MrsMerritaJones) **5-11-11** DerekByrne (lw: j.rt: a.p: ev ch whn j.slowly last: swtchd lft & no ex flat)	2½	**2**	Evens[1]	114	41
	Cheeka (81) (CSmith) **7-11-0** MRanger (bkwd: a bhd: lost tch appr 3 out)	18	**3**	80/1[3]	84	12
862[2]	**Lowawatha (99)** (MrsEHHeath) **8-11-6** AThornton (set str pce: clr 6th: hdd & wknd after 4 out: t.o)	dist	**4**	16/1[2]	—	—
				(SP 107.1%)		**4 Rn**

3m 58.9 (5.90) CSF £2.22 TOTE £1.90 (£1.20) OWNER Stamford Bridge Partnership (UPPER LAMBOURN) BRED Miss Noirin Dunne
WEIGHT FOR AGE 5yo-1lb
808* Celibate (IRE) has really taken to fences and, with only the runner-up to beat inside the last half-mile, proved too strong up the hill. (Evens)
860* Jathib (CAN) has won both his races over fences going right-handed and was not so happy going the other way. That, plus a slow jump when in contention at the last, cost him his unbeaten record. (Evens)

1067 TIM EMANUEL H'CAP HURDLE (0-145) (4-Y.O+) (Class B)

2-15 (2-15) **2m 5f (Old) (10 hdls)** £4,833.50 (£1,463.00: £714.00: £339.50) GOING: 0.32 sec per fur (GS)

				SP	RR	SF
900*	**Courbaril (115)** (MCPipe) **4-11-2** APMcCoy (mde all: clr 2 out: hld on nr fin)	—	**1**	2/1[2]	95	65

	Horse	Dist	Pos	SP	RR	SF
747*	**Freddie Muck (119)** (NATwiston-Davies) **6-11-4**(3) DWalsh (lw: chsd wnr: rdn after 7th: styd on wl towards fin)	1¼	2	15/8[1]	98	69
	Blaze Away (USA) (122) (IABalding) **5-11-10** GBradley (lw: hld up: outpcd appr 3 out: sn rdn: btn whn blnd last)	4	3	2/1[2]	98	69
	Peatswood (120) (MRChannon) **8-11-8** AThornton (bkwd: trckd ldrs tl wknd appr 2 out)	3	4	20/1[3]	94	65
	Tug of Peace (120) (GBBalding) **9-11-8** BClifford (bkwd: a bhd: outpcd 6th: sn t.o)	29	5	25/1	72	43
				(SP 110.1%)		**5 Rn**

5m 1.2 (3.20) CSF £5.89 TOTE £2.90: £1.50 £1.40 (£2.50) OWNER Richard Green (Fine Paintings) (WELLINGTON) BRED George & Mrs Steinberg

WEIGHT FOR AGE 4yo-1lb

900* Courbaril has won his races coming from off the pace, but forceful tactics paid off this time and he is proving a good money-spinner.(2/1)

747* Freddie Muck looked to be in trouble when bustled along four out, but he stayed on really well on the run-in. Stamina would appear his strong suit. (15/8)

Blaze Away (USA), fit from the Flat, was content to wait on the leaders. Getting tapped for toe running downhill to the third last, he was being made to work when he landed on his head at the final flight and that put paid to what slight chance remained. (2/1)

Peatswood travelled well in pursuit of the leaders until blowing up on the approach to the penultimate flight. (20/1)

1068 JEWSON NOVICES' CHASE (5-Y.O+) (Class D)

2-50 (2-54) **3m 1f (Old) (19 fncs)** £3,759.50 (£1,136.00: £553.00: £261.50) GOING minus 0.04 sec per fur (G)

	Horse	Dist	Pos	SP	RR	SF
907*	**Mony-Skip (IRE) (92)** (MrsSJSmith) **7-11-12** RichardGuest (hld up: chsd ldrs 10th: blnd 4 out: led after 2 out: drvn out)	—	1	4/7[1]	98	31
957*	**Capo Castanum (80)** (MissHCKnight) **7-11-6** TJMurphy (t: hld up: stdy hdwy 15th: chsd wnr appr last)	4	2	5/2[2]	89	22
887[7]	**La Mezeray** (MrsJEHawkins) **8-10-6**(3) DWalsh (chsd ldr: led 14th: sn clr: wkng whn mstke 2 out: sn hdd & btn)	10	3	20/1[3]	72	5
	Inch Emperor (IRE) (AWCarroll) **6-11-0** WMarston (bit bkwd: racd keenly: led & sn clr: hdd 14th: grad wknd: t.o)	14	4	20/1[3]	68	1
887[P]	**Kindly Lady** (MrsSDWilliams) **8-10-9** GUpton (bit bkwd: a bhd: t.o appr 3 out)	8	5	20/1[3]	58	—
970[P]	**Vareck II (FR)** (MCPipe) **9-10-7**(7) BMoore (dropped rr 7th: t.o whn p.u bef 4 out)		P	20/1[3]	—	—
				(SP 111.3%)		**6 Rn**

6m 23.7 (14.70) CSF £2.19 TOTE £1.50: £1.10 £1.30 (£1.60) OWNER Mr Trevor Hemmings (BINGLEY) BRED Michael Moakley

907* Mony-Skip (IRE) looked to have blown it when blundering his way through the final ditch, four out, but his jockey sat tight and, taking over on the long run between the last two, was driven out firmly to the line. (4/7)

957* Capo Castanum, who has been tubed, showed he is better class than a selling plater, but he was up against a proven stayer here and was fighting a losing battle from the second last. (5/2)

La Mezeray, a winner six times between the Flags, showed her first glimpse of form under Rules and, had she not taken the penultimate fence by the roots, she would have finished much closer. (20/1)

1069 NEVILLE RUSSELL NOVICES' HURDLE (4-Y.O+) (Class D)

3-25 (3-26) **2m 5f (Old) (10 hdls)** £3,532.00 (£868.00) GOING: 0.32 sec per fur (GS)

	Horse	Dist	Pos	SP	RR	SF
876[3]	**Canton Venture** (SPCWoods) **4-10-13** AMaguire (led 2nd: lft clr 2 out: unchal)	—	1	1/6[1]	76?	—
	Peatsville (IRE) (MRChannon) **4-10-13** AThornton (hld up: wnt 2nd 3 out: blnd next: btn whn hit last)	dist	2	5/1[2]	—	—
964[F]	**Auntie Lorna** (NJPomfret) **7-11-0**ow5 MrASansome (lw: led to 2nd: jnd wnr 6th: wknd & p.u appr 2 out: lame)		P	20/1[3]	—	—
				(SP 107.1%)		**3 Rn**

5m 28.1 (30.10) CSF £1.42 TOTE £1.20 (£1.30) OWNER Dr Frank Chao (NEWMARKET) BRED High Point B/stock Ltd & Chao Racing & B/stock Ltd

WEIGHT FOR AGE 4yo-1lb

876 Canton Venture, sure to be much happier over this longer trip, had little more than a school round and will not always find it so easy. (1/6)

Peatsville (IRE) did promise to make a race of it three out, but he was lucky to remain on his feet after a mistake at the next and that sealed his fate. (5/1)

1070 STUDD CHALLENGE CUP H'CAP CHASE (0-135) (5-Y.O+) (Class C)

4-00 (4-00) **2m 4f 110y (Old) (15 fncs)** £4,394.75 (£1,328.00: £646.50: £305.75) GOING minus 0.04 sec per fur (G)

	Horse	Dist	Pos	SP	RR	SF
882[2]	**Wise Approach (130)** (KCBailey) **9-12-0** CO'Dwyer (lw: led tl after 4 out: led 2 out tl appr last: rallied to ld flat: r.o wl)	—	1	7/4[1]	136	56
882*	**Philip's Woody (115)** (NJHenderson) **8-10-13** JRKavanagh (lw: hld up & bhd: hdwy 4 out: chal 2 out: sn led: hdd & no ex flat)	1½	2	9/4[2]	120	40
814[4]	**Who's to Say (118)** (MissVenetiaWilliams) **10-10-11**(5) MichaelBrennan (a.p: led after 4 out to 2 out: ev ch whn blnd last: nt rcvr)	11	3	7/1	114	34
882[4]	**Channel Pastime (102)** (DBurchell) **12-9-11**(3) GuyLewis (lw: chsd ldr tl rdn & wknd after 11th: t.o)	27	4	25/1	77	—
909[3]	**De Jordaan (115)** (WSCunningham) **9-10-13** AMaguire (hld up: outpcd 8th: hdwy 4 out: rdn & hld whn fell last)		F	3/1[3]	—	—
				(SP 108.5%)		**5 Rn**

5m 6.7 (4.70) CSF £5.70 TOTE £2.50: £1.60 £1.60 (£2.00) OWNER Mrs S. Gee (UPPER LAMBOURN) BRED N.J.Connors

LONG HANDICAP Channel Pastime 9-5

882 Wise Approach gained his revenge on the runner-up, despite meeting him on 2lb worse terms, by staying on strongest up the final climb.(7/4)

882* Philip's Woody, produced to win his race approaching the last, did not find the expected response when challenged on the flat and this stiffer track proved just too much. (9/4)

814 Who's to Say, in the action all the way, was hard at work but in with every chance when a bad mistake at the last all but severed the partnership. He has not yet won at this trip, but would seem to be recovering his useful Irish form. (7/1)

909 De Jordaan finds this trip beyond him, especially on such a stiff track, and he was in fourth place but making no impression when turning a somersault at the last. (3/1)

1071 WEATHERBYS 'STARS OF TOMORROW' STANDARD N.H. FLAT RACE (4, 5 & 6-Y.O) (Class H)

4-30 (4-32) **2m 110y (Old)** £1,604.00 (£444.00: £212.00)

	Horse	Dist	Pos	SP	RR	SF
	Tidal Force (IRE) (PJHobbs) **5-10-13**(5) DJKavanagh (a.p: led 3f out: pushed clr fnl f)	—	1	6/4[1]	—	—

	Horse	Dist	Pos	SP		
	Countryman (IRE) (JACEdwards) **5-10-11**(7) MrBPotts (lost tch after 6f: hdwy 4f out: ev ch over 2f out: one pce)	5	**2**	9/4 ^{2}	—	—
872^{7}	**Lady Foley (IRE)** (CJMann) **4-10-9b^{1}**(3) JMagee (lw: hld up: hdwy 5f out: ev ch 2f out: one pce)	1¼	**3**	7/1	—	—
	Willows Roulette (AGHobbs) **4-10-10**(7) OBurrows (hld up: hdwy over 4f out: kpt on one pce fnl 2f)	¾	**4**	7/1	—	—
980^{11}	**Derring Knight** (NJPomfret) **6-11-4v** MrASansome (bkwd: racd wd: prom tl wknd 3f out)	13	**5**	50/1	—	—
	Burfords For Scrap (RDickin) **4-10-10**(7) XAizpuru (a bhd: t.o)	12	**6**	20/1	—	—
	Stickwiththehand (MrsJSidebottom) **5-11-4** MrJJukes (bkwd: led tl hdd & wknd 3f out: t.o)	20	**7**	20/1	—	—
	Lumo (IRE) (KSBridgwater) **5-11-1**(3) RMassey (bkwd: prom tl rn out & uns rdr over 8f out)		**U**	5/1 ^{3}	—	—
				(SP 123.9%)	**8 Rn**	

4m 1.9 CSF £5.76 TOTE £2.10: £1.10 £1.60 £1.70 (£2.40) OWNER Mr Ian Steers (MINEHEAD) BRED J. F. and P. A. Lavery
WEIGHT FOR AGE 4yo-1lb
STEWARDS' ENQUIRY Magee susp. 8-9/11/96 (excessive use of whip).

Tidal Force (IRE) did not look fully wound up for this racecourse debut, but he turned in a workmanlike performance to succeed. He can only improve. (6/4)

Countryman (IRE), a big, strong, chasing type who can be made much fitter, posed a threat two furlongs out but, once off the bridle, could only stay on at the one pace. He should not be long in making his mark. (9/4: 2/1-100/30)

679 Lady Foley (IRE) did have the edge in fitness and was tried in blinkers for the first time but, when a question was asked below the distance, she had to admit the leading pair just too strong for her. (7/1)

Willows Roulette, sure to strip fitter for the run, did keep staying on in the closing stages and will be all the wiser for the experience. (7/1: 5/1-8/1)

T/Plpt: £3.20 (2,771.58 Tckts). T/Qdpt: £1.90 (315.37 Tckts). IM

0813-**FONTWELL** (Fig. 8) (Good, Good to firm patches)
Wednesday October 30th

WEATHER: unsettled

1072 FONTWELL PARK ANNUAL MEMBERS (S) H'CAP HURDLE (0-95) (4-Y.O+) (Class G)

1-30 (1-31) **2m 2f 110y (9 hdls)** £2,010.20 (£557.20: £266.60) GOING: 0.35 sec per fur (GS)

	Horse	Dist	Pos	SP	RR	SF
	Burlington Sam (NZ) (70) (AGHobbs) **8-10-6**(7) MrGShenkin (hld up: hdwy appr 3rd: mstke & reminder 3 out: led appr 2 out: hrd rdn appr last: drvn out)	—	**1**	12/1 ^{3}	63	—
913^{5}	**Sharp Thrill (67)** (BSmart) **5-10-10** JOsborne (hld up: hdwy 6th: ev ch 2 out: wknd flat: fin tired)	8	**2**	5/2 ^{1}	53	—
958^{2}	**Credit Controller (IRE) (60)** (JFfitch-Heyes) **7-10-3** BFenton (hld up: pckd 2nd: styd on fr 2 out: nvr nrr)	5	**3**	9/2 ^{2}	42	—
960*	**Sleeptite (FR) (88)** (WGMTurner) **6-11-10**(7) 7x JPower (prom: led 5th tl appr 2 out: sn wknd)	6	**4**	5/2 ^{1}	65	—
159^{9}	**Cavo Greco (USA) (73)** (JJoseph) **7-11-2** DSkyrme (bit bkwd: hld up & bhd: hdwy appr 6th: nvr nr ldrs)	10	**5**	25/1	41	—
	Ruth's Gamble (63) (MrsLCJewell) **8-10-1v**(5) SophieMitchell (bit bkwd: hdwy 3rd: wknd 5th)	hd	**6**	25/1	31	—
655^{4}	**Antiguan Flyer (71)** (GProdromou) **7-11-0** RJohnson (bit bkwd: led to 2nd: led 3rd to 5th: wknd qckly after 3 out)	2½	**7**	14/1	37	—
	Damcada (IRE) (67) (AWCarroll) **8-10-10** BPowell (bkwd: bhd fr 3rd: t.o)	16	**8**	14/1	19	—
956^{8}	**Ragtime Song (58)** (JRJenkins) **7-9-8b^{1}**(7)ow1 NTEgan (plld hrd: led 2nd to 3rd: rdn & wknd qckly appr 5th: t.o)	15	**9**	12/1 ^{3}	—	—
879^{14}	**Doc's Coat (65)** (CPWildman) **11-10-8** MAFitzgerald (bkwd: a bhd: t.o fr 6th)	27	**10**	33/1	—	—
655^{6}	**Milzig (USA) (69)** (JJoseph) **7-10-12** CLlewellyn (sn t.o: p.u bef 4th)		**P**	25/1	—	—
				(SP 118.5%)	**11 Rn**	

4m 33.3 (15.30) CSF £40.28 CT £147.72 TOTE £19.60: £5.00 £1.40 £1.50 (£50.00) Trio £78.40 OWNER Mrs Jackie Reip (KINGSBRIDGE)
BRED G. H. L. Broughton
LONG HANDICAP Ragtime Song 9-9
No bid

Burlington Sam (NZ), dropped into a seller, looked well tuned up and seemed to appreciate this better ground. (12/1)
913 Sharp Thrill did not appear suited to this extended trip. (5/2)
958 Credit Controller (IRE) needs to revert to a longer distance. (9/2)
960* Sleeptite (FR) found the weight concession too great. (5/2)
820 Ragtime Song (12/1: 8/1-14/1)

1073 DEREK WIGAN MEMORIAL NOVICES' H'CAP CHASE (0-100) (5-Y.O+) (Class E)

2-05 (2-05) **2m 2f (15 fncs)** £3,036.25 (£910.00: £437.50: £201.25) GOING: 0.50 sec per fur (GS)

	Horse	Dist	Pos	SP	RR	SF
887^{3}	**Wilkins (75)** (RJO'Sullivan) **7-11-5** PHolley (led after 1st to 3rd: led appr 6th to 7th: led 8th: hrd rdn appr last: r.o wl)	—	**1**	5/2 ^{1}	86	12
	Sugar Hill (IRE) (83) (JTGifford) **6-11-13** PHide (bit bkwd: led tl after 1st: led 3rd tl appr 6th: led 7th tl mstke 8th: hrd rdn appr last: no imp)	2½	**2**	9/2 ^{3}	92	18
889^{2}	**The Lancer (IRE) (82)** (DRGandolfo) **7-11-9**(3) DFortt (hld up & bhd: hdwy 9th: one pce fr 3 out)	11	**3**	3/1 ^{2}	81	7
	Master Pangloss (IRE) (62) (AndrewTurnell) **6-9-13**(7) CRae (bkwd: plld hrd: mstkes: a.p: 4th & btn whn blnd 2 out & last)	9	**4**	25/1	53	—
808^{4}	**Night in a Million (67)** (SWoodman) **5-10-10** RJohnson (prom: mstke 7th: wknd appr 3 out)	12	**5**	12/1	47	—
961^{9}	**Jacksons Bay (65)** (TCasey) **6-10-6**(3) GHogan (hld up & bhd: mstke 6th: hdwy 9th: wknd appr 3 out)	hd	**6**	33/1	45	—
935^{3}	**Ryton Run (84)** (MrsSMOdell) **11-12-0** BFenton (mstke 2nd: sn bhd: t.o fr 11th)	21	**7**	14/1	46	—
	Precious Wonder (57) (PButler) **7-9-8**(7) MrRThornton (lw: prom whn mstke 2nd: bhd whn blnd 9th: fell 3 out)		**F**	20/1	—	—
656^{R}	**Top Miss (65)** (ASNeaves) **7-10-2**(7) WGreatrex (blnd 1st: a bhd: t.o whn p.u bef 4 out)		**P**	66/1	—	—
	Lets Go Now (IRE) (60) (MrsLCJewell) **6-10-4** DLeahy (chsd ldrs to 8th: t.o whn p.u bef 4 out)		**P**	33/1	—	—
889^{P}	**King's Gold (78)** (MrsLRichards) **6-11-8** MRichards (a bhd: t.o whn p.u bef 3 out)		**P**	11/1	—	—
	Kentavrus Way (IRE) (57) (AMoore) **5-10-0** BPowell (bit bkwd: bhd whn blnd & uns rdr 6th)		**U**	12/1	—	—
				(SP 118.1%)	**12 Rn**	

4m 45.4 (23.40) CSF £13.48 CT £32.09 TOTE £3.60: £1.20 £1.60 £1.70 (£7.10) Trio £6.50 OWNER Mr Fred Honour (WHITCOMBE) BRED Major J. S. R. Edmunds and J. S. Delahooke
WEIGHT FOR AGE 5yo-1lb

887 Wilkins found this a much easier race than the one in which he reappeared at Newton Abbot. (5/2: 2/1-3/1)
Sugar Hill (IRE) may well have preferred a longer trip, and it still looked as of his trainer had left something to work on. (9/2: 4/1-6/1)

889 The Lancer (IRE) could never get to grips with the two principals and might benefit from a stiffer test of stamina. (3/1: op 2/1)
Master Pangloss (IRE) should come on for the outing, but his fencing was no better than last season. (25/1)
935 Ryton Run (14/1: 7/1-16/1)

1074 STREBEL BOILERS AND RADIATORS SERIES FINAL H'CAP HURDLE (4-Y.O+) (Class B)

2-40 (2-40) **2m 6f 110y (11 hdls)** £6,775.00 (£2,050.00: £1,000.00: £475.00) GOING: 0.35 sec per fur (GS)

				SP	RR	SF
816*	**Victor Bravo (NZ) (109)** (NAGaselee) **9-12-0b** CLlewellyn (a.p: reminders 8th: hrd rdn to ld appr last: edgd lft flat: all out)	—	1	4/1[2]	97	—
657*	**Kalasadi (USA) (106)** (VSoane) **5-11-11** MRichards (bhd: pushed along after 7th: hdwy appr 2 out: styd on flat)	2½	2	11/4[1]	92	—
816[4]	**Roger's Pal (81)** (AMoore) **9-9-7**(7) MBatchelor (hld up: hdwy 7th: rdn 8th: ev ch 2 out: one pce)	1¾	3	33/1	66	—
816[5]	**Karar (IRE) (109)** (RRowe) **6-11-11**(3) LAspell (swtg: led tl appr last: sn wknd)	3	4	8/1[3]	92	—
	Old Archives (IRE) (92) (LWells) **7-10-11** PHide (bit bkwd: hld up: stdy hdwy after 3 out: one pce fr 2 out)	3	5	20/1	73	—
816[10]	**Scud Missile (IRE) (100)** (GFJohnsonHoughton) **5-11-5** ILawrence (hld up & bhd: hdwy 6th: ev ch 2 out: sn wknd)	½	6	16/1	80	—
816[3]	**Mr Snaggle (IRE) (94)** (SEarle) **7-10-13** CMaude (hld up: hdwy appr 2 out: wknd appr last)	2½	7	8/1[3]	73	—
816[2]	**Sophie May (96)** (GLMoore) **5-11-1** JOsborne (bhd fr 8th: b.b.v)	4	8	11/4[1]	72	—
	Muntafi (102) (GHarwood) **5-11-7** MAFitzgerald (bit bkwd: prom tl wknd qckly appr 2 out: t.o)	dist	9	9/1	—	—
				(SP 119.1%)	**9 Rn**	

5m 39.7 (23.70) CSF £15.24 CT £293.33 TOTE £4.20: £1.70 £1.40 £6.30 (£7.10) Trio £105.00 OWNER Mrs R. W. S. Baker (LAMBOURN) BRED A. W. Herbert
LONG HANDICAP Roger's Pal 9-1

816* Victor Bravo (NZ), raised 6lb, had a hard race and an enquiry was held after the Vet considered the gelding had been injured through whip use. The Stewards were satisfied though that the trainer and jockey were unaware of the hypersensitivity of the horse's skin and took no action. (4/1: op 2/1)
657* Kalasadi (USA) had been upped 8lb for winning something of a non-event over course and distance last month. (11/4: 4/1-5/2)
816 Roger's Pal was only rated 13lb out of the handicap this time and kept plugging away for his young rider. (33/1)
816 Karar (IRE) tried to bring his stamina into play by forcing the pace. (8/1)
Old Archives (IRE), dropped 10lb, travelled ominously well through the race until lack of a recent run found him out in the home straight. (20/1)
692 Scud Missile (IRE) has yet to prove he gets this trip. (16/1)
816 Mr Snaggle (IRE) really needs softer ground than this. (8/1: op 5/1)
816 Sophie May was reported by her trainer to have bled from the nose. (11/4)
Muntafi (9/1: 6/1-10/1)

1075 ACTION RESEARCH FOR THE CRIPPLED CHILD NOVICES' CHASE (5-Y.O+) (Class E)

3-15 (3-15) **3m 2f 110y (22 fncs)** £2,688.00 (£798.00: £378.00: £168.00) GOING: 0.50 sec per fur (GS)

				SP	RR	SF
887[2]	**Keep it Zipped (IRE)** (OSherwood) **6-10-12b** JOsborne (hld up: j.slowly & lost pl 10th: hdwy 18th: led 3 out: r.o wl)	—	1	7/4[1]	94	29
	Grey Gorden (IRE) (RCurtis) **8-10-12** DMorris (prom: led 6th: clr 16th: hdd 3 out: one pce)	6	2	11/2	90	25
1038[7]	**Seasamacamile (69)** (RHBuckler) **9-10-7**(7) MrRThornton (led tl after 1st: lost pl 7th: sme hdwy fr 3 out)	18	3	20/1	82	17
1008[3]	**Joker Jack (62)** (RDean) **11-10-9**(3) TDascombe (hld up: hdwy & mstke 14th: wknd appr 3 out)	1	4	20/1	79	14
860[3]	**Manor Mieo** (GProdromou) **10-11-5** RJohnson (bit bkwd: led after 1st to 6th: hit 7th: outpcd 16th: rallied & ev ch appr 3 out: sn wknd)	26	5	4/1[3]	70	5
746[2]	**Mobile Messenger (NZ) (80)** (TRGeorge) **8-10-12** MAFitzgerald (t.o 3rd: p.u bef 3 out)		P	11/4[2]	—	—
	Pinoccio (DCO'Brien) **9-10-12** BFenton (rel to r: t.o tl p.u bef 14th)		P	50/1	—	—
860[P]	**Clonattin Lady (IRE)** (MrsLCJewell) **7-10-7b[1]** DLeahy (bkwd: t.o 3rd: p.u bef 13th)		P	100/1	—	—
	Herbidacious (IRE) (MJRoberts) **6-10-7** BPowell (bkwd: nt j.w: t.o whn p.u bef 4th)		P	100/1	—	—
				(SP 111.9%)	**9 Rn**	

7m 6.0 (26.00) CSF £10.87 TOTE £2.30: £1.50 £2.30 £3.80 (£8.20) Trio £48.60 OWNER Mrs Luisa Stewart-Brown (UPPER LAMBOURN) BRED J. Fogarty

887 Keep it Zipped (IRE) had worn blinkers on his final outing over hurdles and found the leaders coming back to him over this longer trip. (7/4)
Grey Gorden (IRE), five times a winner between the Flags, would not have been inconvenienced by softer ground, and made sure this was a true test of stamina. (11/2)
817* Seasamacamile is always going to struggle to defy a penalty and is better off in novice handicaps. (20/1)
1008 Joker Jack is another who would have been better off in a handicap. (20/1)
860 Manor Mieo still looked short of a gallop. (4/1)

1076 FORD AMATEUR H'CAP CHASE (0-105) (5-Y.O+) (Class F)

3-50 (3-50) **2m 3f (16 fncs)** £2,786.40 (£770.40: £367.20) GOING: 0.50 sec per fur (GS)

				SP	RR	SF
835[2]	**Herbert Buchanan (IRE) (98)** (PFNicholls) **6-11-2**(7) MrJTizzard (hld up: stdy hdwy 9th: led flat: drvn out)	—	1	10/11[1]	105	17
	Master Comedy (77) (MissLBower) **12-9-9b**(7)ow2 MrRWakley (led tl blnd 3 out: led last: sn hdd: r.o)	¾	2	16/1	83	—
951[6]	**Ramstar (103)** (PJHobbs) **8-11-7**(7) MrSMulcaire (chsd ldr fr 6th: hit 9th: led 3 out to last: wknd)	7	3	7/2[2]	104	16
	Fichu (USA) (75) (MrsLRichards) **8-9-7**(7) MrRThornton (hld up & bhd: hdwy appr 10th: wknd appr 3 out)	11	4	7/1	66	—
817[U]	**Ennistymon (IRE) (76)** (JWMullins) **5-9-7**(7) MrGWeatherley (bhd fr 9th)	1¼	5	40/1	66	—
	Durrington (85) (MJBolton) **10-10-7**(3)ow8 MrMRimell (bkwd: chsd ldr to 6th: wkng whn hit 11th: bhd whn fell 12th)		F	5/1[3]	—	—
				(SP 112.1%)	**6 Rn**	

5m 3.5 (24.50) CSF £13.19 TOTE £2.00: £1.50 £3.00 (£8.90) OWNER Five For Fun (SHEPTON MALLET) BRED Lyle Buttimer
LONG HANDICAP Fichu (USA) 9-11 Ennistymon (IRE) 9-2
WEIGHT FOR AGE 5yo-1lb

835 Herbert Buchanan (IRE) looked the likely winner some way out but, as usual, did not find much when striking the front. (10/11:4/6-Evens)
Master Comedy has registered all three of his wins here, and had dropped to a mark 2lb lower than when last winning in April 1994. (16/1)
951 Ramstar had been dropped back to the same rating as the second of his two victories last season. (7/2: op 9/4)
Fichu (USA), 3lb out of the handicap, was a springer in the market. (7/1)

1077 MIDDLETON MAIDEN HURDLE (4-Y.O+) (Class E)

4-20 (4-20) **2m 6f 110y (11 hdls)** £2,595.00 (£720.00: £345.00) GOING: 0.35 sec per fur (GS)

				SP	RR	SF
	Spring Gale (IRE) (OSherwood) **5-11-6** JOsborne (hld up: stdy hdwy appr 4th: led 2 out: rdn & r.o wl flat)	—	1	2/1[1]	74+	—
	Dream Leader (IRE) (MJRoberts) **6-11-6** JRailton (hdwy 3rd: rdn & ev ch 2 out: one pce)	11	2	6/1	66	—
934[2]	**Copper Coil (85)** (WGMTurner) **6-10-13**(7) JPower (led after 1st: hdd 3 out: one pce fr 2 out)	¾	3	4/1[2]	66	—
	Core Business (LadyHerries) **5-11-6** EMurphy (lw: s.s: hdwy 5th: one pce fr 2 out)	3	4	6/1	64	—
659[2]	**Lawbuster (IRE) (75)** (MrsRGHenderson) **4-11-0b**(5) DSalter (a.p: led 3 out to 2 out: sn wknd)	12	5	11/1	55	—
	Snowy Petrel (IRE) (94) (KCBailey) **4-11-5** CLlewellyn (prom tl wknd appr 2 out)	2½	6	9/2[3]	53	—
	Noddadante (IRE) (NRMitchell) **6-11-7**[ow1] MrNRMitchell (bkwd: s.s: hdwy whn mstke 8th: wknd 3 out)	6	7	50/1	49	—
956[P]	**Allez Pablo** (RRowe) **6-11-3**(3) LAspell (bhd fr 8th)	3	8	100/1	47	—
960[7]	**Coolegale (67)** (LWells) **10-10-13**(7) DSlattery (a bhd)	10	9	66/1	40	—
	Solar Warrior (JFfitch-Heyes) **6-11-6b[1]** BFenton (bkwd: a bhd)	½	10	100/1	39	—
	One More Man (IRE) (JTGifford) **5-11-6** PHide (bkwd: led tl after 1st: wknd appr 3 out: t.o)	12	11	20/1	31	—
	Tracey Trooper (AGHobbs) **5-11-1** BPowell (hdwy 3rd: wknd 6th: t.o)	1¾	12	50/1	25	—
866[P]	**Fashion Leader (IRE)** (CWeedon) **5-11-6** MRichards (prom to 7th: t.o whn p.u bef 2 out)		P	50/1	—	—
	Humminbirdprincess (JJSheehan) **5-11-1** ADicken (bit bkwd: s.s: plld hrd: p.u & dismntd bef 6th)		P	50/1	—	—
818[6]	**Ravus** (KVincent) **6-11-6** GCrone (a bhd: t.o whn p.u after 7th)		P	100/1	—	—

(SP 125.5%) **15 Rn**

5m 43.5 (27.50) CSF £14.52 TOTE £3.50: £2.60 £3.50 £3.20 (£32.70) Trio £54.80 OWNER Crabb, Ead, Moore (UPPER LAMBOURN) BRED T. J. Hurley

WEIGHT FOR AGE 4yo-1lb

Spring Gale (IRE) finished a good third in a bumper last season and stayed on strongly when asked to assert after the final flight. e can score again. (2/1)

Dream Leader (IRE) did his best and may well have been stretching his stamina to the limit. (6/1)

934 Copper Coil forced the pace, but was really not suited by this shorter trip. All he does is stay. (4/1: 5/2-9/2)

Core Business finished behind the winner at Huntingdon last season and ought to be capable of stepping up on this hurdling debut. (6/1)

659 Lawbuster (IRE) found himself handcuffed going to the final flight. (11/1: 7/1-12/1)

Snowy Petrel (IRE), tried in blinkers on his final outing last season, could well have found this trip beyond him. (9/2: op 3/1)

T/Plpt: £14.50 (891 Tckts). T/Qdpt: £4.90 (163.65 Tckts). KH

0892-SEDGEFIELD (L-H) (Good to firm)

Thursday October 31st

WEATHER: overcast

1078 STONEGRAVE AGGREGATES (S) H'CAP HURDLE (0-90) (3-Y.O+) (Class G)

1-10 (1-10) **2m 1f (8 hdls)** £1,877.00 (£522.00: £251.00) GOING minus 0.29 sec per fur (GF)

				SP	RR	SF
1027[8]	**Fly to the End (USA) (72)** (JJQuinn) **6-11-4** LWyer (hld up: hdwy ½-wy: led 3 out: styd on wl)	—	1	10/1	51	—
893*	**Clover Girl (74)** (BEllison) **5-11-3v**(3) GCahill (lw: hld up: hdwy 5th: ev ch 2 out: nt qckn)	3	2	5/4[1]	50	—
289[10]	**Catton Lady (54)** (RCraggs) **6-9-11**(3) GLee (chsd ldrs: outpcd appr 2 out: styd on fr last)	1¾	3	33/1	29	—
1027[7]	**Top Skipper (IRE) (68)** (MartynWane) **4-10-13** ASSmith (led after 1st to 5th: rdn & one pce)	5	4	10/1	38	—
1027[U]	**Fenian Court (IRE) (82)** (HowardJohnson) **5-11-9**(5) STaylor (lw: led tl after 1st: chsd ldrs: rdn appr 3 out: sn outpcd)	8	5	7/2[2]	44	—
1047[5]	**Marco Magnifico (USA) (72)** (MissLucindaRussell) **6-11-4v** AThornton (t: cl up: reminders appr 4th: lost pl after next)	5	6	11/1	30	—
463[4]	**On The Move (70)** (JJBirkett) **5-11-2** LO'Hara (nvr nr ldrs)	9	7	16/1	19	—
694[P]	**Strathtore Dream (IRE) (54)** (MissLAPerratt) **5-9-7**(7) MDunne (plld hrd: cl up: led 5th to 3 out: wknd qckly)	15	8	50/1	—	—
	Nick the Bill (56) (JWade) **5-10-2** ADobbin (swtg: a bhd)	½	9	9/1[3]	—	—
	Shut Up (58) (MrsEMoscrop) **7-10-4** KJohnson (prom tl outpcd 4th: hit next & sn wl bhd)	½	10	50/1	—	—

(SP 115.9%) **10 Rn**

4m 5.5 (10.50) CSF £21.86 CT £373.22 TOTE £11.10: £2.00 £1.20 £5.20 (£7.00) Trio £75.50; £95.71 to Newmarket 1/11/96 OWNER Mr Ian Muir (MALTON) BRED Eaglestone Farm Inc

LONG HANDICAP Strathtore Dream (IRE) 9-9 Catton Lady 9-6

WEIGHT FOR AGE 4yo-1lb

No bid

OFFICIAL EXPLANATION Clover Girl: was lame in front.

893 Fly to the End (USA), after two races wearing a visor, had it removed this time and it seemed to work the oracle. (10/1)

893* Clover Girl ran a sound race, but just found the rejuvenated winner too strong this time and, on finishing, was found to be lame. (5/4)

Catton Lady, from 8lb out of the handicap, showed her first signs of form here and, judging by the way she struggled on, she should get further. (33/1)

784 Top Skipper (IRE) had his chances, but looked very slow when the pressure was on. (10/1)

1027 Fenian Court (IRE) showed up well, but found little when ridden. (7/2)

1047 Marco Magnifico (USA) showed little enthusiasm when pressure was applied at halfway. (11/1)

Nick the Bill, more than a handful in the paddock, showed nothing in the race. (9/1)

1079 E.B.F 'N.H.' NOVICES' HURDLE (4, 5 & 6-Y.O) (Class D)

1-40 (1-40) **2m 1f (8 hdls)** £2,889.00 (£804.00: £387.00) GOING minus 0.29 sec per fur (GF)

				SP	RR	SF
	Flaming Hope (IRE) (MrsNHope) **6-10-9** JBurke (lw: mde most: hld on wl flat)	—	1	33/1	64	—
939[2]	**Adamatic (IRE) (92)** (RAllan) **5-11-3**(7) SMelrose (hld up: stdy hdwy 5th: rdn appr 2 out: ev ch appr last: nt qckn towards fin)	½	2	11/8[1]	79	—
705[2]	**Golf Land (IRE)** (LLungo) **4-10-13** MDwyer (lw: hld up: hdwy 5th: chal 2 out: rdn & mstke last: wknd)	2	3	3/1[2]	67	—
718[4]	**Faithful Hand** (MrsSJSmith) **6-11-0** RichardGuest (cl up: disp ld 3 out to next: wknd appr last)	5	4	100/30[3]	62	—
	One More Bill (JWade) **6-11-0** ADobbin (prom tl rdn & wknd 3 out)	22	5	25/1	41	—
	Rysanshyn (RJohnson) **4-10-8** KJohnson (bkwd: outpcd & lost tch 4th: n.d after)	7	6	25/1	30	—

				SP	RR	SF
	Joe Luke (IRE) (GMMoore) **4-10-13** JCallaghan (mstkes: a wl bhd)	4	**7**	16/1	31	—
	Whitemoss Leader (IRE) (JBarclay) **6-10-9** AThornton (chsd ldrs tl lost pl appr 2 out: p.u appr last)		**P**	14/1	—	—
	Polly Star (LLungo) **6-10-9** MFoster (p.u lame appr 3rd)		**P**	50/1	—	—
				(SP 115.3%)		**9 Rn**

4m 11.3 (16.30) CSF £75.53 TOTE £262.30: £12.70 £1.00 £1.50 (£39.10) Trio £57.40 OWNER Exors of the late Mr J W Hope BRED R. C. A. Latta

WEIGHT FOR AGE 4yo-1lb

STEWARDS' ENQUIRY Burke susp. 9-11/11/96 (excessive use of whip).

Flaming Hope (IRE) had shown nothing in three runs last season, but this performance was no fluke. (33/1)

939 Adamatic (IRE) does not really look the type for this sharp and undulating track, but he did keep battling on when all looked lost. (11/8)

705 Golf Land (IRE) needed some firm handling to get him going after three out and then looked the likely winning jumping the next but, after an awkward landing at the last, he threw in the towel. (3/1)

718 Faithful Hand seems to be having trouble in seeing the trip out as he again ran out of steam going to the last. (100/30)

One More Bill, having only his second race over hurdles, showed ability until dropping away three out. (25/1)

Whitemoss Leader (IRE), who failed to impress on looks, nevertheless ran quite well until something went amiss two out, and she was pulled up. (14/1)

1080 MITSUBISHI TV, VIDEO AND HIFI H'CAP HURDLE (0-100) (4-Y.O+) (Class F)

2-10 (2-10) **3m 3f 110y (13 hdls)** £2,267.50 (£630.00: £302.50) GOING minus 0.29 sec per fur (GF)

				SP	RR	SF
	Troodos (89) (MrsASwinbank) **10-11-10** JSupple (lw: hld up: smooth hdwy to ld 2 out: pushed clr appr last)	—	**1**	9/4[2]	76	—
878[3]	**Ballindoo (84)** (RJArmson) **7-11-5** MrRArmson (set slow pce to 3rd: cl up: led 4 out to 2 out: one pce)	5	**2**	2/1[1]	68	—
	Hudson Bay Trader (USA) (80) (PBeaumont) **9-11-1** RSupple (swtg: bit bkwd: w ldrs tl rdn & outpcd fr 3 out)	15	**3**	11/1[3]	55	—
942[3]	**Crofton Lake (65)** (JEDixon) **8-10-0** BStorey (led 3rd to 4 out: sn rdn & btn)	25	**4**	2/1[1]	25	—
	Swiss Gold (70) (MissMKMilligan) **6-10-5** ASSmith (hld up: hit 4 out: sn rdn & btn)	s.h	**5**	12/1	30	—
				(SP 113.5%)		**5 Rn**

7m 6.1 (31.10) CSF £7.07 TOTE £3.20: £1.60 £1.10 (£3.40) OWNER Scotnorth Racing Ltd (RICHMOND) BRED A. G. Forty

LONG HANDICAP Crofton Lake 9-12

Troodos, from a yard bang in form, was turned out looking superb after a long lay off and, always going best, was allowed to take things easy after the last. (9/4: op 7/2)

878 Ballindoo helped set a snail's pace and was then well outpointed in the closing stages. (2/1)

Hudson Bay Trader (USA) needed this and, in a messy race, ran reasonably. (11/1)

942 Crofton Lake brings a new dimension to one-paced, and had no chance with the way this race was run. (2/1: 6/4-9/4)

Swiss Gold has yet to show any signs of ability. (12/1)

1081 ROWENA COLEMAN H'CAP HURDLE (0-110) (4-Y.O+) (Class E)

2-40 (2-40) **2m 5f 110y (10 hdls)** £2,860.75 (£856.00: £410.50: £187.75) GOING minus 0.29 sec per fur (GF)

				SP	RR	SF
	Tribune (84) (CWThornton) **5-10-12** MFoster (cl up: led 4th: hit 2 out: styd on u.p)	—	**1**	20/1	66	4
703[2]	**Twin Falls (IRE) (98)** (GMMoore) **5-11-12** JCallaghan (hld up: hdwy to chse ldrs 3 out: outpcd next: styd on & hung lft flat)	4	**2**	7/2[1]	77	15
801*	**Commander Glen (IRE) (94)** (MDHammond) **4-11-7** RGarritty (hld up: hdwy 4 out: ev ch fr next tl wknd appr last)	nk	**3**	7/2[1]	73	10
1021[3]	**Rule Out The Rest (92)** (MrsSarahHorner-Harker) **5-11-6** AThornton (chsd ldrs tl outpcd fr 3 out)	7	**4**	4/1[2]	66	4
	Manettia (IRE) (86) (MrsMReveley) **7-10-11**(3) GLee (prom tl lost pl appr 4 out: nvr plcd to chal after)	15	**5**	10/1	48	—
942[2]	**Jonaem (IRE) (83)** (MrsESlack) **6-10-11** KJohnson (led to 4th: chsd ldrs tl outpcd appr 3 out: n.d after)	1¾	**6**	5/1[3]	44	—
695*	**Peggy Gordon (80)** (MrsDThomson) **5-10-8** LO'Hara (hld up: effrt 3 out: no imp)	2	**7**	4/1[2]	40	—
				(SP 115.0%)		**7 Rn**

5m 10.2 (10.20) CSF £82.92 TOTE £25.90: £6.40 £2.20 (£32.30) OWNER Hexagon Racing (MIDDLEHAM) BRED R. G. Bonson

WEIGHT FOR AGE 4yo-1lb

OFFICIAL EXPLANATION **Manettia (IRE): was found to be lame after the race.**

Tribune, having his first run for almost twenty months, did it well, despite making the odd mistake when obviously tiring. Given time to recover from this, he should continue to improve. (20/1)

703 Twin Falls (IRE) has plenty of ability but, when it comes down to a fight, he seems to lack the heart for it. (7/2)

801* Commander Glen (IRE) looked threatening four out, only to cry enough going to the last, suggesting that this trip is probably just too far. (7/2)

1021 Rule Out The Rest had his chances, but looked very slow from the third last. (4/1)

Manettia (IRE) ran well after a lengthy absence and was certainly not knocked about, but was later reported lame. (10/1)

942 Jonaem (IRE) ran poorly here, dropping tamely away when the pressure was applied three out. (5/1)

695* Peggy Gordon won first time out last season and then did little afterwards, but she was not suited by this race and needs a flat-out gallop. (4/1)

1082 ALDERCLAD H'CAP CHASE (0-110) (5-Y.O+) (Class E)

3-10 (3-10) **3m 3f (21 fncs)** £2,976.00 (£888.00: £424.00: £192.00) GOING minus 0.29 sec per fur (GF)

				SP	RR	SF
896[P]	**Blazing Dawn (81)** (JSHubbuck) **9-10-3** BStorey (cl up: led 7th: all out)	—	**1**	9/2[3]	91	—
911[P]	**Ole Ole (82)** (MrsEMoscrop) **10-10-4** LWyer (lft in ld 6th: hdd next: cl up: rdn 4 out: outpcd 2 out: styd on flat)	nk	**2**	20/1	92	—
896*	**Jendee (IRE) (88)** (BEllison) **8-10-7**(3) GCahill (lw: mstkes: prom: outpcd 4 out: hdwy u.p appr last: nvr able to chal)	3½	**3**	5/4[1]	96	4
689[5]	**Clares Own (90)** (JWade) **12-10-12** KJones (prom tl oupcd fr 15th)	dist	**4**	12/1	—	—
8*	**Temple Garth (102)** (PBeaumont) **7-11-10** RSupple (led tl fell 6th)		**F**	7/4[2]	—	—
				(SP 111.4%)		**5 Rn**

6m 58.9 (12.90) CSF £48.25 TOTE £4.30: £3.50 £5.00 (£15.80) OWNER Mr J. S. Hubbuck (HEXHAM) BRED Mrs J. Wilkinson

OFFICIAL EXPLANATION **Jendee (IRE): was not suited by the ground.**

702 Blazing Dawn, a funny customer, was presented with this and just managed to last home. (9/2)

Ole Ole, who won here a couple of seasons ago, would have done so again in another couple of strides. No doubt moderate events on this track will see him with further chances. (20/1)

896* Jendee (IRE) showed just what an exasperating character he is, and never really jumped with any fluency from start to finish. (5/4: op evens)
689 Clares Own has lost his way these days. (12/1)
8* Temple Garth only needed to stand up to win this, but did not manage it. (7/4)

1083 JAYNE THOMPSON MEMORIAL NOVICES' CHASE (5-Y.O+) (Class E)
3-40 (3-41) **2m 5f (16 fncs)** £3,150.00 (£945.00: £455.00: £210.00) GOING minus 0.29 sec per fur (GF)

			SP	RR	SF
894^{2}	**Notable Exception (98)** (MrsMReveley) **7-11-12** PNiven (hld up: hdwy ½-wy: led 3 out: kpt on wl flat).........—	1	6/5^{1}	99	28
897*	**Le Denstan (77)** (MrsDThomson) **9-11-5** TReed (hld up & bhd: rapid hdwy 3 out: disp ld 2 out: blnd last: rdn & no ex).........1½	2	4/1^{2}	91	20
	Kenmare River (IRE) (RCollins) **6-10-12** AThornton (swtg: chsd ldrs: led 10th to 3 out: wknd next).........18	3	16/1	70	—
897^{5}	**Up For Ransome (IRE)** (HowardJohnson) **7-10-7b^{1}**(5) GFRyan (lw: mstke 5th: sn prom: rdn & one pce fr 12th).........14	4	16/1	60	—
	Osgathorpe (79) (RTate) **9-10-12** MrsFNeedham (bit bkwd: plld hrd: cl up tl lost pl 8th: hdwy 10th: sn wknd) 17	5	25/1	47	—
1022^{P}	**The Energiser (67)** (DALamb) **10-10-12** JBurke (w ldr: blnd 8th: wknd 10th).........1	6	100/1	46	—
	Desert Brave (IRE) (MrsSJSmith) **6-10-12** RichardGuest (prom tl rdn & wknd 9th).........6	7	9/1	41	—
733^{5}	**Cardinal Sinner (IRE) (56)** (JWade) **7-10-12** KJones (led: blnd 8th: hdd 10th: sn wknd: p.u bef 3 out).........	P	50/1	—	—
897^{3}	**Val de Rama (IRE) (89)** (DenysSmith) **7-11-5** RGarritty (blnd & uns rdr 2nd).........	U	11/2^{3}	—	—
854^{3}	**Merryhill Gold** (JWCurtis) **5-10-5**(5) DJKavanagh (in tch whn blnd & uns rdr 6th).........	U	20/1	—	—
			(SP 114.2%)	**10 Rn**	

5m 18.4 (7.40) CSF £6.15 TOTE £1.40: £1.10 £1.40 £3.40 (£4.20) Trio £40.80 OWNER Mr Roland Hope (SALTBURN) BRED Cliveden Stud
WEIGHT FOR AGE 5yo-2lb

894 Notable Exception, who has got his jumping together these days, certainly stays and had too much courage for the runner-up. (6/5)
897* Le Denstan has an unbelievable turn of foot for a chaser but, if anything, he saw the front too soon and failed to prolong the effort. (4/1)
Kenmare River (IRE) sweated up badly as he has done before, but ran reasonably, and has the ability to pick up a small race. (16/1)
897 Up For Ransome (IRE), in blinkers for the first time, was never happy. (16/1)
Osgathorpe needed this and ran too freely until blowing up six out. (25/1)
Desert Brave (IRE) needed the experience, but did drop out a long way from home. (9/1)

1084 QUARRINGTON STANDARD N.H. FLAT RACE (4, 5 & 6-Y.O) (Class H)
4-10 (4-12) **2m 1f** £1,070.00 (£295.00: £140.00)

			SP	RR	SF
	Brighter Shade (IRE) (MrsMReveley) **6-10-11**(7) CMcCormack (bit bkwd: trckd ldrs: led 2f out: r.o wl).........—	1	7/2^{3}	—	—
	Blood Brother (JBarclay) **4-10-10**(7) NHorrocks (led to 2f out: kpt on one pce).........7	2	3/1^{2}	—	—
898^{3}	**Gazanali (IRE)** (GMMoore) **5-10-13**(5) MichaelBrennan (swtg: a.p: ev ch over 2f out: hrd rdn & sn btn).........2½	3	10/11^{1}	—	—
	Farriers Fantasy (MrsNHope) **4-10-5**(7) SHaworth (prom: outpcd 5f out: sn btn).........30	4	25/1	—	—
	Safety Tip (WStorey) **4-10-9**(3) GCahill (prom tl wknd over 4f out).........dist	5	10/1	—	—
	Not So Prim (GPKelly) **4-10-12** MrCMulhall (bkwd: wl t.o fnl 7f).........dist	6	50/1	—	—
			(SP 114.5%)	**6 Rn**	

4m 1.0 CSF £13.87 TOTE £3.30: £2.80 £1.80 (£4.30) OWNER Mr D. S. Hall (SALTBURN) BRED N. J. Connors
WEIGHT FOR AGE 4yo-1lb

Brighter Shade (IRE), a really nice type, looked in need of this if anything, but it turned out to be a moderate event and he won anyway. Chasing will be his game. (7/2: 5/2-4/1)
Blood Brother looked lean and fit and ran pretty well, but was short of a turn of foot in the closing stages. (3/1: 2/1-7/2)
898 Gazanali (IRE) was very edgy and sweated in the preliminaries and, once off the bit in the race, found little. He seems to be going the wrong way for the time being. (10/11: 5/4-8/11)
Safety Tip (10/1: 8/1-12/1)

T/Plpt: £238.30 (32.01 Tckts). T/Qdpt: £52.60 (10.85 Tckts). AA

0949-STRATFORD-ON-AVON (L-H) (Good)
Thursday October 31st
WEATHER: overcast

1085 RICHARDSON'S PARKWAY MAIDEN HURDLE (I) (4-Y.O+) (Class E)
1-20 (1-20) **2m 6f 110y (12 hdls)** £2,040.00 (£565.00: £270.00) GOING: 0.42 sec per fur (GS)

			SP	RR	SF
	Carole's Crusader (91) (DRGandolfo) **5-10-11**(3) DFortt (led tl flat: led last strides: all out).........—	1	5/1^{2}	78	35
	Flying Gunner (112) (DNicholson) **5-11-5** AMaguire (hld up: hdwy 9th: led flat: hrd rdn & hdd last strides) ...s.h	2	8/13^{1}	83	40
973^{3}	**General Mouktar** (MCPipe) **6-11-5v** APMcCoy (hld up: hdwy 9th: 3rd & btn whn blnd 2 out).........16	3	13/2^{3}	72	29
	Little Notice (IRE) (CaptTAForster) **5-11-5** SWynne (hdwy 6th: wknd 3 out).........18	4	12/1	59	16
	Javelin Cool (IRE) (GAHubbard) **5-11-2**(3) KGaule (bkwd: prom tl wknd 8th: t.o).........dist	5	66/1	—	—
800^{P}	**Musical Hit** (PAPritchard) **5-11-5** RBellamy (plld hrd: mstkes: bhd fr 7th: t.o).........15	6	66/1	—	—
	Gan Awry (PRWebber) **9-11-0** MrPScott (bit bkwd: plld hrd: prom tl wknd 9th: t.o).........5	7	50/1	—	—
	Delire d'Estruval (FR) (IPWilliams) **5-11-5b^{1}** JOsborne (bkwd: prom tl wknd rapidly & p.u bef 9th).........	P	14/1	—	—
	La Bella Villa (KSBridgwater) **6-11-0** DBridgwater (bkwd: bhd: t.o whn mstke 8th: p.u bef 3 out).........	P	50/1	—	—
900^{P}	**Kirby Moorside** (DJMinty) **5-11-5** BPowell (bhd: reminders after 7th: t.o whn p.u bef 8th).........	P	100/1	—	—
	Super Brush (IRE) (PRJohnson) **4-10-13** MSharratt (bkwd: a bhd: t.o whn p.u bef 2 out).........	P	100/1	—	—
			(SP 115.2%)	**11 Rn**	

5m 33.4 (17.40) CSF £7.84 TOTE £7.50: £1.10 £1.20 £1.20 (£2.80) Trio £5.10 OWNER Mrs C. Skipworth (WANTAGE) BRED D. J. and Mrs Deer
WEIGHT FOR AGE 4yo-1lb

Carole's Crusader, having her first outing for David Gandolfo, showed fine battling qualities in the closing stages and will go chasing in the near future. (5/1)
Flying Gunner stays well, but lacked the acceleration to shake off the winner on the run-in. (8/13)
973 General Mouktar was already well held when making a hash of the penultimate hurdle. (13/2)
Little Notice (IRE) narrowly won his only point-to-point at Bitterley in April and his future will lie over fences. (12/1: 6/1-14/1)
Delire d'Estruval (FR) (14/1: 6/1-16/1)

1086 RICHARDSON DEVELOPMENTS LTD (S) HURDLE (4,5,6 & 7-Y.O) (Class G)
1-50 (1-51) **2m 110y (9 hdls)** £1,940.00 (£540.00: £260.00) GOING: 0.42 sec per fur (GS)

				SP	RR	SF
888[3]	**Severn Gale (84)** (PFNicholls) **6-11-0** APMcCoy (mde all: clr 5th: r.o wl)	—	1	9/4[1]	75	11
950[4]	**Griffin's Girl** (PMooney) **4-10-1**(5) SRyan (hld up: hdwy to chse wnr fr 6th: no imp)	15	2	9/1	54	—
902[5]	**My Harvinski (75)** (IRJones) **6-10-5**(7) MissEJJones (chsd wnr to 6th: btn whn mstke 3 out)	6	3	20/1	53	—
950*	**Pickens (USA) (90)** (NTinkler) **4-11-4** JOsborne (prom tl lost pl after 4th: n.d after)	10	4	100/30[2]	50	—
950[10]	**Pytchley Dawn** (OO'Neill) **6-10-7** VSlattery (bit bkwd: prom to 5th)	½	5	33/1	38	—
950[F]	**Chapel of Barras (IRE) (92)** (BGee) **7-11-12** MrPGee (hld up & plld hrd: hdwy 3rd: wknd qckly appr 6th:t.o)	dist	6	20/1	—	—
903[F]	**Laura Lye (IRE) (70)** (BdeHaan) **6-10-7** JRailton (nt j.w: sn bhd: t.o whn p.u bef 3 out)		P	12/1	—	—
	Oozlem (IRE) (74) (LMontagueHall) **7-10-9**(3) KGaule (prom: rdn appr 5th: wknd rapidly & p.u bef 6th)		P	5/1[3]	—	—
67[7]	**Woodlands Energy (55)** (PAPritchard) **5-10-7** RBellamy (a bhd: t.o 5th: p.u bef 3 out)		P	33/1	—	—
	Komiamaite (DBurchell) **4-10-11** DJBurchell (a bhd: t.o whn p.u bef 6th)		P	8/1	—	—
	Hard To Break (RTJuckes) **5-10-12** GaryLyons (bhd: hit 4th: t.o whn p.u bef 6th)		P	50/1	—	—
				(SP 116.7%)		**11 Rn**

4m 5.2 (18.20) CSF £21.25 TOTE £2.00: £1.60 £1.70 £4.30 (£8.90) Trio £34.40 OWNER Mr R. M. Phillips (SHEPTON MALLET) BRED Broomhill Stud
WEIGHT FOR AGE 4yo-1lb
Sold J Allen 7,000 gns
888 Severn Gale, dropped into a seller, adopted totally different tactics and ran her field ragged. (9/4)
950 Griffin's Girl had to be content to play second fiddle. (9/1)
My Harvinski finished second when last seen in this grade. (20/1)
950* Pickens (USA) lost his pitch with a circuit to go. (100/30)
Komiamaite (8/1: op 5/1)

1087 PSM COMPUTERS H'CAP CHASE (0-135) (5-Y.O+) (Class C)
2-20 (2-20) **2m 1f 110y (13 fncs)** £4,815.00 (£1,340.00: £645.00) GOING: 0.08 sec per fur (G)

				SP	RR	SF
	Callisoe Bay (IRE) (135) (OSherwood) **7-12-0** JOsborne (w ldr tl hit 3rd: nt fluent 9th: led 3 out to 2 out: led last: rdn & r.o wl)	—	1	4/7[1]	139	72
	Southampton (120) (GBBalding) **6-10-13** APMcCoy (hld up: hdwy 4 out: rdn to ld 2 out: hdd last: unable qckn)	2	2	2/1[2]	122	55
851a[4]	**Thumbs Up (130)** (GMMcCourt) **10-11-9** BClifford (led to 3 out: wknd appr 2 out)	26	3	6/1[3]	108	41
				(SP 111.3%)		**3 Rn**

4m 11.2 (2.20) CSF £2.07 TOTE £2.00 (£1.50) OWNER Mr R. Waters (UPPER LAMBOURN) BRED Hugh Suffern Bloodstock Ltd
Callisoe Bay (IRE) ran here instead of in a much better race at Ascot on Saturday. Still not the polished article over fences, he prevailed after briefly looking in trouble two out. (4/7)
Southampton, without his usual visor, did look to be gaining the upper hand at the penultimate fence, but found the favourite too strong from the last. (2/1)
851a Thumbs Up, dropped nearly a stone, did not cut much ice on his seasonal reappearance in Norway. (6/1: 4/1-13/2)

1088 ARCHIE SCOTT BENEVOLENT FUND CUP H'CAP HURDLE (0-115) (4-Y.O+) (Class E)
2-50 (2-50) **2m 6f 110y (12 hdls)** £2,442.50 (£680.00: £327.50) GOING: 0.42 sec per fur (GS)

				SP	RR	SF
954*	**Tarrs Bridge (IRE) (92)** (CJMann) **5-10-7** JRailton (a.p: led 3 out: sn rdn clr: all out)	—	1	9/4[1]	76	28
	Fortunes Course (IRE) (107) (JSKing) **7-11-1**(7) MrAWintle (chsd ldr: led appr 4th: blnd 9th: hdd 3 out: rallied flat)	½	2	7/1[3]	91	43
	Silver Standard (100) (CaptTAForster) **6-11-1** SWynne (hld up: hdwy appr 9th: one pce fr 3 out)	16	3	6/1[2]	72	24
	Northern Village (108) (SDow) **9-11-9** ADicken (bit bkwd: bhd tl styd on fr 3 out: n.d)	1	4	14/1	80	32
952[2]	**Barford Sovereign (106)** (JRFanshawe) **4-11-6** PHide (hld up: hdwy 8th: wknd appr 3 out)	½	5	9/4[1]	77	28
	Pettaugh (IRE) (93) (GAHubbard) **8-10-5**(3) KGaule (bkwd: prom: rdn after 8th: wknd appr 3 out)	½	6	12/1	64	16
	John Naman (IRE) (87) (DPGeraghty) **7-9-9**(7) GSupple (bkwd: hld up: hdwy 6th: wknd appr 9th: t.o)	dist	7	20/1	—	—
880[3]	**Shikaree (IRE) (112)** (MCPipe) **5-11-13b** APMcCoy (hld up: hdwy 8th: 5th whn mstke 9th: sn wknd: t.o)	1¼	8	10/1	—	—
673[P]	**Sir Pageant (85)** (KSBridgwater) **7-10-0** VSlattery (a bhd: t.o fr 9th)	dist	9	66/1	—	—
905[3]	**Hydemilla (86)** (MrsTDPilkington) **6-9-12**(3)ow1 GHogan (led tl appr 4th: wknd after 5th: t.o whn p.u bef 3 out)		P	33/1	—	—
				(SP 121.0%)		**10 Rn**

5m 33.6 (17.60) CSF £18.18 CT £79.30 TOTE £4.00: £1.30 £2.30 £2.10 (£16.10) Trio £30.30 OWNER The Tuesday Syndicate (UPPER LAMBOURN) BRED David McGrath
LONG HANDICAP Sir Pageant 8-13 Hydemilla 9-3
WEIGHT FOR AGE 4yo-1lb
954* Tarrs Bridge (IRE), the winner of a maiden point in Ireland, went for home from the third last and, in the end, the post came only just in time. (9/4)
Fortunes Course (IRE) stayed on again from the last and a bad error four from home may have cost her the race. (7/1)
Silver Standard, raised 9lb for his victory in blinkers at the end of last season, was 6lb higher than when winning this race last year. (6/1)
Northern Village, never in the race with a chance, should at least find this putting an edge on him. (14/1: 8/1-16/1)
952 Barford Sovereign, up 2lb, found this event a good bit more competitive. (9/4)
Pettaugh (IRE) prefers softer ground and will strip fitter next time. (12/1)

1089 REG LOMAS FAREWELL H'CAP CHASE (0-120) (5-Y.O+) (Class D)
3-20 (3-22) **3m 4f (21 fncs)** £3,684.50 (£1,106.00: £533.00: £246.50) GOING: 0.08 sec per fur (G)

				SP	RR	SF
	Church Law (97) (MrsLCTaylor) **9-10-6** AMaguire (hld up & bhd: hdwy appr 17th: led 2 out: r.o wl)	—	1	7/2[2]	104	30
	Court Melody (IRE) (115) (PFNicholls) **8-11-10b** APMcCoy (hld up: hdwy 8th: outpcd 3 out: styd on flat)	2½	2	4/1[3]	121	47
809*	**Big Ben Dun (112)** (CPEBrooks) **10-11-7** GBradley (hld up: hdwy 8th: jnd ldrs 16th: led 3 out to 2 out: 2nd & btn whn mstke last)	5	3	6/4[1]	115	41
864[3]	**Change the Reign (107)** (MissAEEmbiricos) **9-11-2** JRyan (led tl after 5th: led 9th to 3 out: sn wknd)	4	4	7/1	107	33
	Tipp Mariner (98) (OSherwood) **11-10-7** JOsborne (led tl after 5th: led 7th to 9th: outpcd 17th: hit 4 out: t.o whn p.u bef 2 out)		P	5/1	—	—

Form	Horse	Dist	Pos	SP	RR	SF
795[5]	**War Flower (IRE) (91)** (AWCarroll) **8-10-0** TJMurphy (Withdrawn not under Starter's orders: lame)		**W**	66/1	—	—
				(SP 112.9%)		**5 Rn**

7m 12.0 (12.00) CSF £15.85 TOTE £4.30: £2.10 £2.20 (£10.30) OWNER Mrs L. C. Taylor (CHIPPING WARDEN) BRED Col Sir John Thomson
LONG HANDICAP War Flower (IRE) 7-13
Church Law, who was entered in Saturday's Charlie Hall when it was re-opened, landed a bit of a touch here under a confident ride. (7/2)
Court Melody (IRE) got caught a shade flat-footed when the chips were down, but stamina was certainly not a problem. (4/1: op 9/4)
809* Big Ben Dun, raised 4lb for his Kempton win, did not have the fitness edge over his main rivals this time. (6/4)
864 Change the Reign was 4lb higher than when winning over three and a quarter here in the summer. (7/1)

1090 RICHARDSON'S PARKWAY MAIDEN HURDLE (II) (4-Y.O+) (Class E)
3-50 (3-52) **2m 6f 110y (12 hdls)** £2,022.50 (£560.00: £267.50) GOING: 0.42 sec per fur (GS)

Form	Horse	Dist	Pos	SP	RR	SF
	Jack Tanner (IRE) (DNicholson) **7-11-5** AMaguire (hld up: stdy hdwy 7th: led appr 2 out: v.easily)	—	**1**	1/5 [1]	61++	1
	Lord Khalice (IRE) (GAHubbard) **5-10-12**(7) NRossiter (chsd ldr: led 4th tl appr 2 out: no ch w wnr)	11	**2**	33/1	53	—
	Madam's Walk (NATwiston-Davies) **6-11-0** CLlewellyn (nt j.w: rn in snatches: gd hdwy appr 9th: wknd appr 2 out)	6	**3**	11/1 [3]	44	—
788[6]	**Lough Tully (IRE)** (FJordan) **6-11-5** SWynne (no hdwy fr 3 out)	3	**4**	20/1	47	—
954[12]	**Linford (IRE)** (CaptTAForster) **6-11-5** MrRBevis (hld up: hdwy 7th: 4th whn mstke 9th: wknd qckly: t.o)	dist	**5**	50/1	—	—
871[10]	**Beths Wish** (GMPrice) **7-11-0** BFenton (a bhd: t.o)	16	**6**	100/1	—	—
636[4]	**Ragosa** (JWhite) **5-11-0** JRKavanagh (a bhd: t.o whn p.u bef 3 out)		**P**	40/1	—	—
	Gutteridge (IRE) (TKeddy) **6-11-5** RJohnson (hld up: hdwy 7th: wknd appr 2 out: p.u bef last)		**P**	10/1 [2]	—	—
	Lady Noso (MrsJPitman) **5-11-0** WMarston (bkwd: prom tl wknd after 8th: t.o whn p.u bef 3 out)		**P**	10/1 [2]	—	—
	Smart Act (IRBrown) **7-11-5** MrABrown (bkwd: plld hrd: prom tl mstke 7th: p.u bef 8th)		**P**	100/1	—	—
	Flinters (63) (MrsLWilliamson) **9-10-12b**(7) MrRThornton (led to 4th: wknd after 7th: t.o whn p.u bef 3 out)		**P**	50/1	—	—
				(SP 125.9%)		**11 Rn**

5m 45.7 (29.70) CSF £12.53 TOTE £1.30: £1.10 £6.10 £1.40 (£20.20) Trio £133.80 OWNER Lady Harris (TEMPLE GUITING) BRED G. Quirk
Jack Tanner (IRE), not seen out since finishing fourth in the Sun Alliance, made light work of this simple task. (1/5)
Lord Khalice (IRE), a half-brother to a bumper winner and a winning hurdler, found the hot-pot favourite in a different class. (33/1)
Madam's Walk looked very novicey on this debut over timber. (11/1)
Lough Tully (IRE) was trying a longer trip. (20/1)
Gutteridge (IRE) (10/1: op 20/1)

1091 RICHARDSON'S THE FORUM STEVENAGE NOVICES' H'CAP HURDLE (0-100) (4-Y.O+) (Class E)
4-20 (4-21) **2m 110y (9 hdls)** £2,355.00 (£655.00: £315.00) GOING: 0.42 sec per fur (GS)

Form	Horse	Dist	Pos	SP	RR	SF
1007[4]	**Ragamuffin Romeo (72)** (HJCollingridge) **7-10-11** APMcCoy (a.p: led appr 6th: clr whn hit 2 out: drvn out)	—	**1**	9/2 [3]	54	—
	Lets Be Frank (80) (NoelChance) **5-11-5** RJohnson (hld up: hdwy 5th: chsd wnr fr 6th: rdn 3 out: one pce)	3	**2**	7/2 [1]	59	—
913[3]	**Almapa (82)** (RJHodges) **4-11-3**(3) TDascombe (hld up: hdwy 5th: wknd 6th)	dist	**3**	8/1	—	—
723[6]	**Wayfarers Way (USA) (88)** (NJHenderson) **5-11-13** MAFitzgerald (hld up: hdwy after 5th: mstke 6th: wknd 3 out)	2½	**4**	7/2 [1]	—	—
	Glendoe (IRE) (75) (AndrewTurnell) **5-10-7**(7) CRae (hld up: hdwy whn mstke 5th: sn bhd)	1½	**5**	12/1	—	—
793[9]	**Lime Street Blues (IRE) (82)** (CPEBrooks) **5-11-7b** GBradley (led to 2nd: hit 6th: 3rd & wkng whn hit 2 out)	½	**6**	5/1	—	—
950[F]	**Sorisky (87)** (BGubby) **4-11-11** AMaguire (s.s: a bhd: t.o)	dist	**7**	4/1 [2]	—	—
	Pharly Reef (75) (DBurchell) **4-10-13** DJBurchell (plld hrd: led 2nd tl appr 6th: sn wknd: t.o)	6	**8**	10/1	—	—
	Woodlands Lad Too (70) (PAPritchard) **4-10-8** RBellamy (s.s: t.o 5th: p.u bef 6th)		**P**	33/1	—	—
				(SP 130.1%)		**9 Rn**

4m 10.1 (23.10) CSF £22.20 CT £120.17 TOTE £5.50: £1.70 £1.40 £2.10 (£19.20) Trio £64.50 OWNER Mrs D. Sawyer (NEWMARKET) BRED Stetchworth Park Stud Ltd
WEIGHT FOR AGE 4yo-1lb
1007 Ragamuffin Romeo, disappointing for his new trainer in a seller last week, threw down the gauntlet starting down the back straight for the final time. (9/2: 6/1-4/1)
Lets Be Frank, dropped 5lb, was having his first run for Noel Chance. Try as he might, he could not peg back the winner. (7/2)
913 Almapa had been raised 2lb for his third in a Taunton seller. (8/1)
Wayfarers Way (USA) looks weighted up to the hilt on this evidence. (7/2)

T/Plpt: £34.00 (272.15 Tckts). T/Qdpt: £16.20 (33.15 Tckts). KH

1092a - 1117a : (Irish Racing) - See Computer Raceform

0866-BANGOR-ON-DEE (L-H) (Good to soft)
Friday November 1st
WEATHER: fine & sunny

1118 HALLIWELL LANDAU NOVICES' CLAIMING HURDLE (4-Y.O+) (Class F)
1-10 (1-10) **2m 1f (9 hdls)** £2,850.00 (£800.00: £390.00) GOING: 0.97 sec per fur (S)

Form	Horse	Dist	Pos	SP	RR	SF
834*	**Indrapura (IRE) (96)** (MCPipe) **4-11-12** APMcCoy (hld up gng wl: led on bit appr last: canter)	—	**1**	1/2 [1]	81+	30
794[7]	**Night Boat (73)** (WClay) **5-10-8** TEley (hdwy 5th: led appr 2 out tl appr last: rdn & no ex flat)	1¼	**2**	11/1 [3]	62	11
980[6]	**Milling Brook** (JMBradley) **4-11-6** RJohnson (hld up: hdwy 6th: chsd ldng pair appr 2 out: no imp)	21	**3**	50/1	54	3
1[2]	**Birequest (78)** (DMoffatt) **5-10-11** DJMoffatt (bkwd: chsd ldrs: led appr 4th tl after 3 out: wknd qckly)	12	**4**	9/2 [2]	34	—
974[7]	**Young Benson** (TWall) **4-11-0**(3) RMassey (chsd ldrs: led after 3 out: sn hdd & wknd)	4	**5**	33/1	36	—
	The Fence Shrinker (DMcCain) **5-10-11**(3) DWalsh (bkwd: prom: disp ld fr 5th tl wknd appr 2 out: t.o)	20	**6**	50/1	14	—
	Blue Lugana (NBycroft) **4-10-8** DBentley (bit bkwd: a bhd: t.o)	15	**7**	50/1	—	—
980[14]	**Little Embers** (JMBradley) **4-10-0b**[1] BFenton (a bhd: t.o)	6	**8**	66/1	—	—
	Irish Perry (TMorton) **9-11-7** CLlewellyn (bkwd: a bhd: t.o)	6	**9**	16/1	—	—
866[P]	**Boxit Again** (JMackie) **6-10-5** WMarston (led tl hdd & wknd appr 4th: t.o whn p.u bef next)		**P**	40/1	—	—

			Pos	SP	RR	SF
	Haido'hart (BSRothwell) **4-10-8** MAFitzgerald (chsd ldrs to 6th: sn lost tch: t.o whn p.u bef 2 out)		P	20/1	—	—
653^{17}	**Tailormade Future** (BPreece) **4-10-5** GaryLyons (mstke 3rd: a bhd: t.o whn p.u bef 5th)		P	66/1	—	—
				(SP 118.1%)	**12 Rn**	

4m 21.2 (26.20) CSF £7.16 TOTE £1.40: £1.10 £2.00 £4.50 (£5.50) Trio £51.30 OWNER Martin Pipe Racing Club (WELLINGTON) BRED John Burns

STEWARDS' ENQUIRY Massey susp. 11-13/11/96 (excessive use of whip).

834* Indrapura (IRE) showed he can handle softer ground with one of his easiest wins yet and did it all on the bridle. (1/2)

Night Boat performed much better this time and finished clear of the remainder, but the winner was in a class of his own. (11/1)

1 Birequest had a run on the Flat nine days ago, but he was still as fat as a pig here and was down to a walk on entering the straight. (9/2)

1119 CORBETT BOOKMAKERS H'CAP CHASE (0-125) (5-Y.O+) (Class D)

1-40 (1-40) **2m 4f 110y (15 fncs)** £4,667.75 (£1,412.00: £688.50: £326.75) GOING: 0.65 sec per fur (S)

			Pos	SP	RR	SF
	Major Bell (123) (ACWhillans) **8-12-0** BHarding (chsd ldrs: led appr 2 out: r.o wl)	—	1	$9/2^{3}$	130	55
740^{3}	**Flapjack Lad (96)** (NATwiston-Davies) **7-9-12**(3)ow1 DWalsh (lw: led: hit 3rd: rdn & hdd appr 2 out: kpt on u.p)	2½	2	7/1	101	25
	Rustic Air (105) (JGFitzGerald) **9-10-10** MDwyer (bkwd: hld up in tch: stdy hdwy 10th: drvn along whn mstke 2 out: nt rcvr)	1¼	3	12/1	109	34
	Sailor Jim (110) (PTDalton) **9-11-1** CMaude (bit bkwd: hld up: styd on fr 3 out: nvr nrr)	2	4	14/1	113	38
	Too Plush (103) (AndrewTurnell) **7-10-8** LHarvey (bit bkwd: hld up: j.slowly 10th: rdn 4 out: sn btn)	10	5	$4/1^{2}$	98	23
953^{2}	**Garrylough (IRE) (113)** (DRGandolfo) **7-11-4** RDunwoody (prom: reminders 10th: wknd 4 out: t.o)	8	6	$2/1^{1}$	102	27
	Real Glee (IRE) (105) (JJQuinn) **7-10-10** MAFitzgerald (bkwd: bhd: mstke 7th: btn whn blnd 2 out: t.o)	20	7	16/1	78	3
814*	**Aedean (95)** (GPEnright) **7-10-0** JRKavanagh (lw: hld up in rr: reminders 9th: t.o whn blnd 4 out: p.u bef 2 out)		P	8/1	—	—
				(SP 115.4%)	**8 Rn**	

5m 18.9 (18.90) CSF £32.66 CT £321.43 TOTE £5.20: £1.40 £1.40 £2.80 (£22.40) OWNER Mr Ian Middlemiss (HAWICK) BRED Major Peter Bell

Major Bell showed last season what a useful individual he was and this performance, giving weight to race-fit rivals, only goes to prove he is still on the upgrade. (9/2)

740 Flapjack Lad made an early mistake, but his jumping was good for most of the way and he stuck on willingly after being headed to go down fighting. (7/1)

Rustic Air did not look fully tuned up, but he ran extremely well and must have gone close to winning had he not nearly bit the dust at the second last. He should soon make amends. (12/1: 8/1-14/1)

Sailor Jim usually needs a run to put an edge on him and this quiet school round will have done him the power of good. (14/1)

Too Plush, successful in this event last year, did give the impression the run was needed and he will be much sharper next time he appears. (4/1)

953 Garrylough (IRE) sat on the heels of the leader going well, but her jockey became anxious out in the country and, with no response forthcoming to a couple of reminders, she was not persevered with when all chance had gone. (2/1)

1120 JONES PECKOVER NOVICES' CHASE (5-Y.O+) (Class D)

2-10 (2-10) **2m 1f 110y (12 fncs)** £4,032.50 (£1,220.00: £595.00: £282.50) GOING: 0.65 sec per fur (S)

			Pos	SP	RR	SF
	Around The Gale (IRE) (DRGandolfo) **5-10-12** RDunwoody (j.w: led 2nd to 3rd: led 6th to 7th: led 8th: drew clr fr 2 out)	—	1	$4/5^{1}$	115	36
1037^{F}	**Rafters** (JMBradley) **7-10-12** RJohnson (chsd ldrs: hrd rdn appr 2 out: one pce)	12	2	25/1	104	25
	Monymoss (IRE) (MrsSJSmith) **7-10-5**(7) RWilkinson (trckd ldrs: outpcd 8th: styd on fr 2 out)	1¼	3	33/1	103	24
32^{4}	**Naiysari (IRE)** (PMRich) **8-10-12** WMarston (bit bkwd: hld up: hdwy 7th: nt rch ldrs)	10	4	$10/1^{3}$	94	15
933*	**Sublime Fellow (IRE) (122)** (NJHenderson) **6-11-5** MAFitzgerald (led to 2nd: led 7th to 8th: hrd rdn appr 2 out: sn btn)	8	5	$2/1^{2}$	93	14
	Heathyards Boy (DMcCain) **6-10-9**(3) DWalsh (bkwd: prom to 7th: sn lost tch: t.o)	15	6	66/1	73	—
652^{4}	**Betabetcorbett** (BPJBaugh) **5-10-12b** TJMurphy (led 3rd tl hdd & blnd 6th: wknd 8th: t.o whn mstke 3 out)	1¼	7	100/1	72	—
	Captain Stockford (PWegmann) **9-10-12** TEley (bkwd: a bhd: t.o whn p.u bef 3 out)		P	100/1	—	—
	Jymjam Johnny (IRE) (JJO'Neill) **7-10-12** MDwyer (bkwd: hld up in rr: p.u after 3 out)		P	12/1	—	—
975^{6}	**Hugh Daniels (72)** (BPreece) **8-10-12** VSlattery (a bhd: t.o whn p.u bef 8th)		P	200/1	—	—
	Twice Shy (IRE) (MSheppard) **5-10-12** BPowell (bkwd: sn t.o: p.u bef 7th)		P	200/1	—	—
				(SP 116.9%)	**11 Rn**	

4m 27.1 (17.10) CSF £20.43 TOTE £1.90: £1.10 £1.90 £3.60 (£18.20) Trio £93.40 OWNER Mr T. J. Whitley (WANTAGE) BRED Mrs M. O'Driscoll

OFFICIAL EXPLANATION **Jymjam Johnny (IRE): was found to be lame as a result of gravel in his foot.**

Around The Gale (IRE) did not look quite as forward as some of his rivals, but he turned in a classy performance on this debut over fences and does look set to go places. (4/5: 11/10-8/11)

Rafters got his jumping together this time and ran extremely well. He should not have much trouble in winning races. (25/1)

Monymoss (IRE) needs a much longer trip than he had here and was only getting into top gear when the race was over. (33/1)

Naiysari (IRE), given time to get him jumping together on his fencing debut, was never put into the race at any stage, but the experience will stand him in good stead. (10/1)

933* Sublime Fellow (IRE) helped share the pace, but he was in serious trouble half a mile out and could do little more than gallop on the spot. (2/1)

1121 NEILSON COBBOLD CONDITIONAL H'CAP HURDLE (0-110) (4-Y.O+) (Class E)

2-45 (2-45) **2m 4f (11 hdls)** £2,927.00 (£822.00: £401.00) GOING: 0.97 sec per fur (S)

			Pos	SP	RR	SF
	Cassio's Boy (80) (RJEckley) **5-10-6** DJKavanagh (hld up in tch: hdwy 3 out: rdn appr last: r.o to ld nr fin)	—	1	10/1	63	15
1034^{3}	**Zingibar (79)** (JMBradley) **4-10-0**(5) JPower (led 3rd: hrd rdn & ct last strides)	hd	2	$6/1^{3}$	62	14
868^{3}	**Batty's Island (82)** (BPreece) **7-10-1**(7)ow6 WGreatrex (chsd ldrs: styd on one pce fr 2 out)	16	3	25/1	52	—
533^{4}	**Pride of May (IRE) (96)** (CWFairhurst) **5-11-3v**(5) NHorrocks (bit bkwd: led to 3rd: wknd 8th)	5	4	20/1	62	14
952^{6}	**Saymore (85)** (WClay) **10-10-11** RMassey (hld up & bhd: hdwy 8th: nt rch ldrs)	1½	5	33/1	50	2
893^{3}	**Marsden Rock (86)** (NBMason) **9-10-9**(3) SHaworth (hld up & bhd: reminders 6th: no imp: t.o)	dist	6	8/1	—	—
	Brancher (91) (JNorton) **5-11-3** ECallaghan (hld up: hdwy 8th: rdn & ev ch whn fell last)		F	11/1	—	—
793^{4}	**Ramsdens (IRE) (101)** (NATwiston-Davies) **4-11-13** DWalsh (bit bkwd: prom tl wknd qckly 8th: t.o whn p.u 3 out)		P	$9/4^{1}$	—	—

				SP	RR	SF
641[2]	**First Crack (90)** (FJordan) **11-11-2** LAspell (lw: trckd ldrs tl wknd appr 3 out: p.u bef next)		P	6/1[3]	—	—
888*	**Hullo Mary Doll (82)** (AJChamberlain) **7-10-8** ChrisWebb (hld up in rr: effrt 7th: wknd next: t.o whn p.u bef last)		P	9/2[2]	—	—

(SP 117.6%) **10 Rn**

5m 5.9 (29.90) CSF £63.88 CT £1,337.92 TOTE £14.20: £3.90 £2.10 £4.70 (£44.80) Trio £85.50 OWNER Lyonshall Racing (KINGTON) BRED Mrs E. C. Carberry

Cassio's Boy did well to succeed on his seasonal debut, but he had to pull out all the stops to force his head in front right on the line. (10/1)

1034 Zingibar is consistent and never stops trying, but fortune has gone against him so far this season and he hardly deserved to be touched off this time. (6/1)

868 Batty's Island performs best when not so much use is made of him and he had been hung out to dry from the turn into the straight. (25/1)

Brancher made smooth progress inside the final mile and was challenging strongly but hard at work when he departed at the final flight. He should be given the chance to make amends. (11/1: op 5/1)

793 Ramsdens (IRE) still looked to be carrying condition and the way he stopped to nothing inside the last mile would only go to confirm that judgement. (9/4)

1122 TARPORLEY HUNT H'CAP CHASE (0-100) (5-Y.O+) (Class F)

3-20 (3-20) **3m 110y (18 fncs)** £3,582.50 (£1,085.00: £530.00: £252.50) GOING: 0.65 sec per fur (S)

				SP	RR	SF
	Basilicus (FR) (100) (MrsSJSmith) **7-11-7**(7) RWilkinson (hld up in tch: hdwy 12th: led 3 out: lft clr last)	—	1	20/1	113	45
	Bally Clover (100) (MissVenetiaWilliams) **9-12-0** APMcCoy (bit bkwd: a.p: mstkes 10th & 11th: led 4 out to 3 out: sn btn)	13	2	11/2[3]	105	37
	Leinthall Princess (80) (JLNeedham) **10-10-8** BFenton (bit bkwd: mstke 1st: rdn 9th: styd on fr 4 out: nvr nrr)	¾	3	25/1	84	16
	Ardcroney Chief (90) (DRGandolfo) **10-11-4** MAFitzgerald (bkwd: prom: hrd rdn 3 out: sn btn)	1½	4	11/1	93	25
899[4]	**Auvillar (USA) (86)** (JParfitt) **8-11-0v** CLlewellyn (bhd: hrd rdn 14th: nt rch ldrs: t.o)	dist	5	40/1	—	—
957[5]	**Opal's Tenspot (72)** (JMBradley) **9-10-0** RJohnson (a bhd: t.o)	9	6	25/1	—	—
797[2]	**Andros Prince (94)** (MissAEEmbiricos) **11-11-8** JRyan (a wl bhd: t.o)	½	7	5/1[2]	—	—
	Absolatum (72) (JParfitt) **9-10-0** WMarston (bkwd: a t.o)	dist	8	50/1	—	—
797P	**Fairy Park (96)** (HOliver) **11-11-10** JacquiOliver (a bhd: t.o fr 12th: blnd 4 out: p.u bef next)		P	33/1	—	—
339[9]	**Beaufan (85)** (BRCambidge) **9-10-13** GaryLyons (bit bkwd: prom: pckd & lost pl 9th: t.o whn p.u after 12th)		P	50/1	—	—
957[3]	**Brindley House (82)** (RCurtis) **9-10-10** DMorris (chsd ldrs to 12th: sn lost tch: t.o whn p.u bef 3 out)		P	10/1	—	—
	Bendor Mark (90) (MJWilkinson) **7-11-4** JFTitley (bkwd: hld up: hdwy 9th: wknd 14th: p.u bef 3 out)		P	10/1	—	—
	Flimsy Truth (83) (MHWeston) **10-10-11** MrJJukes (j.w: led to 4 out: wknd & p.u bef 2 out)		P	14/1	—	—
1038[2]	**Ivy House (IRE) (88)** (JJO'Neill) **8-11-2** MDwyer (hld up: stdy hdwy 14th: slt ld & rdn whn blnd & uns rdr last)		U	6/4[1]	—	—

(SP 127.0%) **14 Rn**

6m 28.1 (26.10) CSF £123.00 CT £2,568.84 TOTE £29.80: £5.00 £2.30 £3.90 (£112.60) Trio £450.70; £457.13 to Newmarket 2/11/96 OWNER Mrs S. Smith (BINGLEY) BRED Francois Rolland

LONG HANDICAP Absolatum 9-4

Basilicus (FR) only had a single outing last term, but he was produced fit and well for this seasonal reappearance and, though his task was made easier at the last, there was nothing to say that he would not have won in any case. (20/1)

Bally Clover made more than the odd mistake, but he remained in the firing-line until lack of a previous outing began to take its toll inside the last half-mile. (11/2)

Leinthall Princess, winner of her only previous race here two years ago, could never get herself into contention, but she did stay on in the latter stages to make the prizes. (25/1)

Ardcroney Chief gave chase to the leaders until feeling the strain and dropping away before reaching the home straight. (11/1: 6/1-12/1)

797 Andros Prince (5/1: 7/2-11/2)

957 Brindley House (10/1: op 6/1)

Flimsy Truth gave a grand display of jumping and made the running to the fourth last before blowing up. He is a winner between the Flags and ought to be able to find an opening under Rules. (14/1)

1038 Ivy House (IRE), making a quick reappearance, travelled well throughout and had just taken a slight lead when his legs gave way landing over the last and his pilot had no chance of remaining in the saddle. He did look to have the edge, but he had been given a couple of reminders and the winner was certainly not stopping. (6/4)

1123 STANLEY LEISURE H'CAP HURDLE (0-110) (4-Y.O+) (Class E)

3-55 (3-56) **2m 1f (9 hdls)** £3,176.25 (£960.00: £467.50: £221.25) GOING: 0.97 sec per fur (S)

				SP	RR	SF
	Centaur Express (106) (AStreeter) **4-11-10** TEley (mde all: clr 5th: unchal)	—	1	100/30[1]	92+	50
	Tanseeq (88) (MGMeagher) **5-10-6** BHarding (hld up: hdwy 6th: kpt on appr last: no ch w wnr)	7	2	11/2[3]	67	25
863[3]	**Cooley's Valve (IRE) (101)** (MrsSDWilliams) **8-11-0**(5) SophieMitchell (lw: hld up & bhd: styd on fr 3 out: nvr nrr)	9	3	6/1	72+	30
	United Front (98) (JNeville) **4-11-2** DBridgwater (bit bkwd: prom: outpcd 4th: effrt & rdn appr 2 out: no imp)	½	4	8/1	69	27
893S	**Aide Memoire (IRE) (82)** (MrsBKBroad) **7-10-0** KJohnson (chsd ldrs to ½-wy: sn wknd)	6	5	20/1	47	5
	Dahlia's Best (USA) (100) (MissMERowland) **6-11-4** GaryLyons (bkwd: chsd ldrs to 5th: sn rdn & wknd)	6	6	25/1	59	17
	Pridewood Picker (90) (RJPrice) **9-10-8** APMcCoy (bit bkwd: hld up: hdwy 5th: rdn & wknd appr 2 out: t.o)	7	7	4/1[2]	43	1
749[3]	**Hacketts Cross (IRE) (95)** (PEccles) **8-10-13** RJohnson (bkwd: a bhd: t.o)	5	8	13/2	43	1
214P	**Shifting Moon (89)** (FJordan) **4-10-7b** SWynne (chsd wnr: blnd 6th: sn lost pl: bhd whn p.u bef 2 out)		P	14/1	—	—
	Muizenberg (83) (EHOwenjun) **9-10-1**ow1 AThornton (bkwd: trckd ldrs to 6th: wknd qckly: p.u bef 2 out)		P	33/1	—	—

(SP 115.4%) **10 Rn**

4m 16.3 (21.30) CSF £20.46 CT £95.67 TOTE £4.40: £2.00 £2.30 £2.60 (£15.30) Trio £41.70 OWNER Centaur Racing (HEDNESFORD) BRED John Burt and Peter Gordon Partnership

LONG HANDICAP Aide Memoire (IRE) 9-7 Muizenberg 9-10

OFFICIAL EXPLANATION Cooley's Valve (IRE): the gelding was unable to improve his position on the good to soft ground, and only ran on through beaten horses in the latter stages.

Centaur Express enjoyed himself blazing a trail and nothing was ever going well enough to get in a blow. (100/30)

Tanseeq came from off the pace and stayed on pleasingly in the closing stages, but the winner was being eased down by then and he is flattered to finish in the same parish. (11/2: 7/2-6/1)

863 Cooley's Valve (IRE) may not have relished this softer ground, but he was never put into the race at any stage and it came as no surprise when the Stewards enquired into his running. (6/1)

United Front, who will strip fitter with this run under his belt, came to the end of his tether approaching the penultimate flight and finished very leg-weary. (8/1)
Shifting Moon (14/1: 10/1-16/1)

1124 BANGOR INTERMEDIATE OPEN N.H. FLAT RACE (4, 5 & 6-Y.O) (Class H)
4-30 (4-30) **2m 1f** £1,721.00 (£481.00: £233.00)

	Horse / details	Dist	Pos	SP	RR	SF
	Johnny-K (IRE) (DNicholson) **5-11-8**(3) RMassey (hld up: hdwy 6f out: led over 2f out: sn clr: v.easily)	—	1	13/8[1]	—	—
	Welsh Silk (DRGandolfo) **4-10-13**(5) SophieMitchell (bkwd: mid div: hdwy to ld over 4f out: hdd over 2f out: one pce)	9	2	12/1	—	—
	Zander (NATwiston-Davies) **4-10-11**(7) LSuthern (bit bkwd: hld up: hdwy ½-wy: ev ch over 2f out: sn rdn & outpcd)	4	3	6/1[3]	—	—
	Callindoe (IRE) (JLNeedham) **6-10-13** BFenton (s.s: hdwy 6f out: nvr nr to chal)	1¾	4	50/1	—	—
	The Croppy Boy (JNeville) **4-11-4** DBridgwater (hld up & bhd: hdwy over 3f out: nvr nrr)	3½	5	20/1	—	—
	My Shenandoah (IRE) (HOliver) **5-11-4** JacquiOliver (bkwd: chsd ldr: led ½-wy tl hdd over 4f out: grad wknd)	4	6	10/1	—	—
	Soundpost (DMoffatt) **4-11-4** DJMoffatt (in tch: hdwy 5f out: rdn & wknd over 3f out)	13	7	12/1	—	—
918[5]	**Red Tel (IRE)** (MCPipe) **4-11-11** APMcCoy (hld up in rr: nvr plcd to chal)	¾	8	9/1	—	—
	Larkshill (IRE) (JGFitzGerald) **5-11-4** MDwyer (bkwd: trckd ldrs tl rdn & wknd 4f out)	½	9	9/2[2]	—	—
	High Handed (IRE) (THCaldwell) **5-11-4** AThornton (a in rr: t.o)	23	10	33/1	—	—
	Jemaro (IRE) (WJenks) **5-11-4** TJenks (chsd ldrs over 10f: t.o)	10	11	50/1	—	—
	The Secret Grey (DMcCain) **5-11-1**(3) DWalsh (prom over 6f: sn wknd: t.o)	4	12	50/1	—	—
653[14]	**Pollifumas** (JLHarris) **6-10-6**(7) RWilkinson (bkwd: a bhd: t.o)	2½	13	50/1	—	—
	Glendronach (BRCambidge) **4-10-13** GaryLyons (a bhd: t.o)	5	14	50/1	—	—
980[10]	**Barnetts Boy** (JMBradley) **4-11-4** TJMurphy (led to ½-wy: wknd qckly: t.o)	dist	15	50/1	—	—
	Scholar Green (GHYardley) **4-11-4** RJohnson (trckd ldrs over 10f: sn wknd: t.o)	6	16	33/1	—	—
	Kyle David (IRE) (FJordan) **4-11-4** SWynne (bkwd: a in rr: t.o)	8	17	25/1	—	—
872[15]	**Barlot** (JMackie) **4-10-13** TEley (bkwd: a bhd: t.o)	dist	18	50/1	—	—
				(SP 133.3%)	**18 Rn**	

4m 13.4 CSF £22.15 TOTE £2.70: £2.20 £3.30 £2.20 (£24.50) Trio £42.40 OWNER Norwood Partners (TEMPLE GUITING) BRED Denis Howard
Johnny-K (IRE), who got a bit edgy in the paddock, won this pulling the proverbial bus and it will be interesting when his attentions are switched to hurdles. (13/8)
Welsh Silk gave a good account of himself on this racecourse debut and will be more the finished article next time. (12/1: 6/1-14/1)
Zander was quietly fancied to make a winning debut, but he had run his race soon after entering the straight and the position had to be accepted. He should soon be making his mark. (6/1)
Callindoe (IRE), last to leave the start, made relentless progress in the final mile and does look to have ability. (50/1)
The Croppy Boy, fitter than many, ran a sound race without ever looking to be a serious challenger. He is sure to be all the wiser for the experience. (20/1)
My Shenandoah (IRE), a big, scopey individual with a bit still left to work on, showed he does possess ability and, the sooner his attentions are switched to jumping, the better. (10/1)
Soundpost (12/1: tchd 20/1)
918 Red Tel (IRE) (9/1: 4/1-10/1)

T/Plpt: £324.80 (38.75 Tckts). T/Qdpt: £201.10 (4.68 Tckts). IM

1046-WETHERBY (L-H) (Good)
Friday November 1st
Race 2: flag start
WEATHER: fine

1125 LINTON H'CAP HURDLE (0-145) (4-Y.O) (Class B)
1-30 (1-30) **2m (9 hdls)** £4,825.00 (£1,450.00: £700.00: £325.00) GOING: 0.11 sec per fur (G)

	Horse / details	Dist	Pos	SP	RR	SF
1053[2]	**El Don (101)** (MJRyan) **4-9-11**(3) KGaule (trckd ldrs: led appr last: drvn out)	—	1	11/4[2]	81	13
	Highbank (103) (MrsMReveley) **4-9-13**(3) GLee (a.p: slt ld 3 out: hdd appr last: kpt on wl)	¾	2	9/1	82	14
	Elpidos (119) (MDHammond) **4-11-4** RGarritty (hld up: hdwy & ev ch 2 out: styd on u.p flat)	¾	3	4/1[3]	98	30
790[2]	**Mim-Lou-and (113)** (MissHCKnight) **4-10-12** PNiven (lw: trckd ldrs: effrt 3 out: kpt on: nt pce to chal)	1¼	4	5/2[1]	90	22
1017[4]	**Alltime Dancer (IRE) (125)** (OSherwood) **4-11-10** JOsborne (lw: led to 3 out: outpcd fr next)	7	5	10/1	95	27
	Holders Hill (IRE) (114) (MGMeagher) **4-10-13** AMaguire (hld up: effrt 3 out: ch next: sn btn)	5	6	16/1	79	11
	Dawn Mission (106) (TDEasterby) **4-10-5** LWyer (bit bkwd: mstke 1st: w ldr: disp ld 3 out: wknd & eased fr next)	6	7	10/1	65	—
				(SP 109.3%)	**7 Rn**	

3m 51.4 (9.40) CSF £23.10 TOTE £4.60: £1.10 £3.90 (£19.90) OWNER Mr Don Morris (NEWMARKET) BRED Ian Hunter
LONG HANDICAP El Don 9-13
1053 El Don, given a confident ride, travelled really well and, although not finding much when in front, he always had the edge. (11/4)
Highbank, who seems to act on any ground, certainly stays well and has improved physically. He should go on from here. (9/1)
Elpidos let connections down when punted on the Flat recently, but this was a much better effort and, although always looking held, he did respond to pressure in the closing stages. (4/1)
790 Mim-Lou-and got outpaced and short of room at a vital stage, but was noted keeping on well at the end. Either a flat-out gallop or a bit further would probably help. (5/2)
1017 Alltime Dancer (IRE) is not quite firing at the moment and put up little fight when tackled. (10/1)
Holders Hill (IRE), having his first run for some time, shaped as though it were needed. (16/1)
Dawn Mission looked burly and, once beaten from the second last, was wisely given an easy time. (10/1: 8/1-12/1)

1126 WETHERBY NOVICES' CHASE (5-Y.O+) (Class D)
2-00 (2-01) **2m (12 fncs)** £4,062.00 (£1,132.00: £546.00) GOING: 0.11 sec per fur (G)

	Horse / details	Dist	Pos	SP	RR	SF
	Golden Hello (TDEasterby) **5-11-0** LWyer (a.p: led appr 4 out: blnd 2 out: rdn whn lft clr last)	—	1	8/13[1]	96	32

1051[3] **Chorus Line (IRE) (79)** (PBeaumont) **7-10-9** RSupple (swtg: led tl appr 4 out: sn outpcd) ....16 **2** 4/1[2] 75 11
853[3] **Kiltulla (IRE)** (MrsSJSmith) **6-11-0** RichardGuest (cl up: outpcd whn blnd 3 out: nt rcvr) ....21 **3** 7/1[3] 59 —
Flat Top (95) (MWEasterby) **5-11-0** AMaguire (lw: hld up: hdwy appr 4 out: disp ld 3 out: chal & rdn whn fell last) .... **F** 7/1[3] — —
(SP 106.9%) **4 Rn**

4m 0.4 (8.40) CSF £3.19 TOTE £1.50: (£2.80) OWNER Mr G. E. Shouler (MALTON) BRED Bearstone Stud
Golden Hello has always looked to have more ability than he really cares to show and this game could be the making of him. He was fortunate when a serious rival fell at the last and presented him with the race. (8/13: 4/9-4/6)
1051 Chorus Line (IRE) ran well against this hot company and run-of-the-mill events should come her way. (4/1)
853 Kiltulla (IRE) found this company a bit too warm, but still ran a super race and was allowed to come home in his own time after a blunder three out. (7/1)
Flat Top jumped the ditches particularly well, but was inclined to fiddle the rest. He still ran a super race and may well have beaten the winner but for clipping the top of the last and failing to regain his legs. (7/1)

1127 GREEN HAMMERTON H'CAP HURDLE (0-135) (4-Y.O+) (Class C)

2-35 (2-35) **2m 4f 110y (10 hdls)** £2,792.50 (£835.00: £400.00: £182.50) GOING: 0.11 sec per fur (G)

SP RR SF

Burnt Imp (USA) (115) (GMMoore) **6-11-9** JCallaghan (bit bkwd: cl up: led fr 6th: all out) ....— **1** 5/1 97 33
Tara Rambler (IRE) (116) (MissSEHall) **7-11-10** NBentley (bit bkwd: trckd ldrs: hdwy to chal 3 out: outpcd appr last: styd on towards fin) ....hd **2** 13/2 98 34
952[4] **Dally Boy (106)** (TDEasterby) **4-11-0** LWyer (lw: led to 6th: outpcd appr 3 out: hit 2 out: styd on towards fin) ..2 **3** 4/1[3] 86 22
Master Hyde (USA) (113) (WStorey) **7-11-2**(5) RMcGrath (hld up: effrt appr 3 out: rdn & nt r.o) ....10 **4** 3/1[2] 86 22
Admirals Seat (98) (MWEasterby) **8-10-6** AMaguire (lw: hld up: effrt 4 out: rdn & btn appr next: p.u bef 2 out: dismntd) .... **P** 15/8[1] — —
(SP 109.8%) **5 Rn**

4m 59.6 (12.60) CSF £29.32 TOTE £6.00: £2.60 £1.80 (£13.40) OWNER N B Mason (Farms) Ltd (MIDDLEHAM) BRED Rodney P. Carothers & Brereton C. Jones in USA
Burnt Imp (USA), who looked in need of this, beat another unfit rival. His best may well come over the bigger obstacles. (5/1)
Tara Rambler (IRE) looked burly, but ran a cracker and, provided this has not taken too much out of him, he should really come into his own this season. (13/2)
952 Dally Boy disappointed last time, but showed something here, staying on at the end after looking well beaten. (4/1: op 5/2)
Master Hyde (USA) looked to be going well until being asked a question turning for home, from which point he quickly cried enough. (3/1)
Admirals Seat looked the part, but ran most disappointingly, dropping away tamely from the fourth last and being pulled up. His rider thought he was lame, but that did not seem to be the case. However, something was obviously wrong. (15/8)

1128 HARRY WHARTON MEMORIAL H'CAP CHASE (0-135) (5-Y.O+) (Class C)

3-10 (3-10) **2m (12 fncs)** £4,744.00 (£1,432.00: £696.00: £328.00) GOING: 0.11 sec per fur (G)

SP RR SF

867[3] **Regal Romper (IRE) (108)** (MrsSJSmith) **8-10-2** RichardGuest (mde all: hld on wl fr 4 out) ....— **1** 6/1[3] 118 45
Aljadeer (USA) (110) (MWEasterby) **7-10-4b** AMaguire (hld up: mstkes 2nd & 5th: hdwy to chse ldrs 3 out: hrd rdn & kpt on towards fin) ....½ **2** 3/1[2] 120 47
855[2] **Political Tower (122)** (RNixon) **9-11-2** ADobbin (lw: cl up: mstke 2nd & 4th: rdn 3 out: nt qckn fr next) ....2½ **3** 5/4[1] 129 56
Konvekta King (IRE) (130) (OSherwood) **8-11-10** JOsborne (swtg: hld up: effrt 8th: wknd after 4 out) ....30 **4** 3/1[2] 107 34
(SP 108.7%) **4 Rn**

3m 55.0 (3.00) CSF £20.32 TOTE £5.30: (£6.10) OWNER Mrs S. Smith (BINGLEY) BRED E. Walshe
867 Regal Romper (IRE) failed to impress on looks, but his performance did the talking and, really attacking his fences, he deservedly held on. (6/1: op 7/2)
Aljadeer (USA) is the sort who looks after himself, but was given some serious help from the saddle here and was eating up the ground at the finish. (3/1: op 2/1)
855 Political Tower ran another fair race but, after early mistakes, was then outbattled in the closing stages. (5/4)
Konvekta King (IRE) sweated up and dragged his lad round the paddock, wasting valuable energy and, after racing freely, not surprisingly ran out of fuel early in the home straight. (3/1)

1129 TOCKWITH NOVICES' CHASE (5-Y.O+) (Class C)

3-45 (3-45) **3m 1f (18 fncs)** £4,523.00 (£1,364.00: £662.00: £311.00) GOING: 0.00 sec per fur (G)

SP RR SF

870* **The Last Fling (IRE)** (MrsSJSmith) **6-11-5** RichardGuest (lw: hld up: stdy hdwy 4 out: led 2 out: r.o wl) ....— **1** 5/6[1] 109 —
Chopwell Curtains (TDEasterby) **6-11-0** LWyer (chsd ldr fr 5th: mstke 13th: ev ch 2 out: r.o wl) ....3 **2** 11/4[2] 102 —
Young Dubliner (IRE) (EBolger,Ireland) **7-11-5** AMaguire (led 3rd to 2 out: sn outpcd) ....14 **3** 3/1[3] 98 —
907[2] **Commandeer (IRE) (69)** (MissMKMilligan) **6-11-0** ASSmith (mstkes early: led to 3rd: outpcd & lost tch ½-wy: sn t.o) ....dist **4** 25/1 — —
(SP 110.1%) **4 Rn**

6m 20.4 CSF £3.40 TOTE £2.00 (£2.60) OWNER Michael Jackson Bloodstock Ltd (BINGLEY) BRED G. Stewart
870* The Last Fling (IRE), who sat off the pace, picked up immediately when asked and won really well. He looks a very useful recruit to this game. (5/6: evens-4/5)
Chopwell Curtains stays forever and, the further they went, the better he got. Plenty of opportunities will be found. (11/4)
Young Dubliner (IRE) wears a tongue-strap and has changed his ways these days, but this company proved beyond him when the heat was really turned on in the home straight. (3/1)
907 Commandeer (IRE) was completely outclassed here. (25/1)

1130 HORNSHAW NOVICES' CONDITIONAL H'CAP HURDLE (0-105) (5-Y.O+) (Class F)

4-20 (4-21) **3m 1f (12 hdls)** £2,092.50 (£580.00: £277.50) GOING: 0.11 sec per fur (G)

SP RR SF

792[10] **Queen's Award (IRE) (66)** (RHBuckler) **7-9-9**(5) MGriffiths (hld up: hdwy ½-wy: led 4 out: styd on strly) ....— **1** 20/1 55 12
934[3] **Mister Blake (84)** (RLee) **6-11-4** GHogan (in tch: outpcd 8th: styd on fr 2 out: no imp) ....15 **2** 9/1[3] 63 20
911* **Pebble Beach (IRE) (87)** (GMMoore) **6-11-7** MichaelBrennan (lw: chsd ldr: effrt 4 out: sn hrd rdn: btn next) ....2 **3** 2/1[1] 65 22

				SP	RR	SF
911[2]	**Smart Approach (IRE) (92)** (MrsMReveley) **6-11-5**(7) TJComerford (lw: prom tl lost pl 7th: sme hdwy 3 out: hit next: sn wknd)	12	**4**	2/1[1]	62	19
1056*	**Jolis Absent (87)** (MJRyan) **6-11-7b** 7x KGaule (mstkes: led to 4 out: hrd rdn & sn wknd)	19	**5**	9/4[2]	45	2
907[4]	**Quixall Crossett (66)** (EMCaine) **11-9-7b**(7) TristanDavidson (outpcd & lost tch ½-wy: sn t.o)	dist	**6**	50/1	—	—
				(SP 114.2%)	**6 Rn**	

6m 8.4 (15.40) CSF £146.59 TOTE £26.80: £6.20 £2.20 (£49.40) OWNER Mr R. H. Buckler (BRIDPORT) BRED M. Lynch
LONG HANDICAP Queen's Award (IRE) 9-7 Quixall Crossett 9-6
Queen's Award (IRE) won this in particularly good style and had obviously improved no end for his new stable. His young rider impressed no end. (20/1)
934 Mister Blake stays well but in his own time, and he was struggling a long way from home on this occasion. (9/1)
911* Pebble Beach (IRE) was obviously feeling his hard race of last time and, coupled with his 8lb rise in the weights, he was anchored come the third last. (2/1)
911 Smart Approach (IRE) was never really happy here and a mistake two out finally put paid to any hopes of a place. (2/1)
1056* Jolis Absent, who came from behind last time, did just the opposite here and was never happy or jumping well. She gave up the ghost before the home turn. (9/4)

T/Plpt: £8,366.70 (1.03 Tckts). T/Qdpt: £1,003.10 (0.73 Tckts); £366.02 to Newmarket 2/11/96. AA

ASCOT (R-H) (Good to firm, Firm patches)
Saturday November 2nd
WEATHER: overcast

1131 BINFIELD HURDLE (3-Y.O) (Class C)
12-50 (12-50) **2m 110y (9 hdls)** £4,175.00 (£1,025.00) GOING: 0.18 sec per fur (G)

				SP	RR	SF
944[3]	**Squire's Occasion (CAN)** (RAkehurst) **3-11-0** APMcCoy (chsd ldr: led appr 3 out: clr appr 2 out: easily)	—	**1**	2/7[1]	66?	—
881[3]	**Amber Ring** (MissKMGeorge) **3-10-9** JRKavanagh (lw: led: mstkes 3rd & 5th: hdd appr 3 out: wknd appr 2 out)	12	**2**	11/4[2]	49	—
				(SP 104.4%)	**2 Rn**	

4m 12.3 (22.30) TOTE £1.20: OWNER Chelgate Public Relations Ltd (EPSOM) BRED Spring Farm & Associates
944 Squire's Occasion (CAN) had no more than a stroll round to beat his very poor rival and pick up some decent prizemoney. (2/7)
881 Amber Ring set a very sedate pace, but he jumped to his left at several hurdles and made notable mistakes at the third and fifth. Headed approaching the third last, he was easily brushed aside turning for home. He is a very poor individual who lacks any sort of pace. (11/4)

1132 UNITED HOUSE DEVELOPMENT NOVICES' HURDLE (4-Y.O+) (Class C)
1-20 (1-21) **2m 110y (9 hdls)** £3,468.75 (£1,050.00: £512.50: £243.75) GOING: 0.18 sec per fur (G)

				SP	RR	SF
	Cipriani Queen (IRE) (JTGifford) **6-10-9** PHide (chsd ldr: rdn appr 2 out: led appr last: r.o wl)	—	**1**	3/1[2]	56	13
	Riding Crop (IRE) (NJHenderson) **6-11-0** MAFitzgerald (a.p: rdn 6th: r.o wl flat)	¾	**2**	Evens[1]	60	17
	Sahel (IRE) (JWMullins) **8-11-0** SCurran (plld hrd: led: clr appr 2 out: wknd & hdd appr last)	5	**3**	9/2[3]	55	12
859F	**Ernest William (IRE)** (GAHubbard) **4-10-11**(3) KGaule (hld up: rdn 3 out: wknd appr 2 out)	24	**4**	12/1	32	—
	Al Helal (JRJenkins) **4-11-0** APMcCoy (hld up: mstke 3rd: j.slowly 4th: rdn 6th: wknd 3 out)	21	**5**	15/2	12	—
	Lizium (JCFox) **4-10-9** SFox (swtg: in rr whn blnd bdly & uns rdr 2nd)		**U**	33/1	—	—
				(SP 115.6%)	**6 Rn**	

4m 2.9 (12.90) CSF £6.49 TOTE £3.80: £2.10 £1.40 (£2.90) OWNER Tor Royal Racing Club (FINDON) BRED Swettenham Stud
IN-FOCUS: **This was a dreadful Novice event by Ascot standards.**
Cipriani Queen (IRE), without a run since January, looked pretty straight for this return and leading approaching the last, was not going to be caught by the runner-up in time. (3/1)
Riding Crop (IRE) was making his hurdling and seasonal debut, but he got rather tapped for toe as the pace increased four out, but he stayed on nicely from the second last and was cutting back the lee-way all the way to the line. A nice chasing type, he needs a much stronger pace or further to be seen to best effect. (Evens)
Sahel (IRE), who won over a mile for John Gosden in 1992, has been in Dubai since and was having his first run in twenty months on this return. Looking reasonably straight, he took a keen hold and set the pace. Forging clear from the third last, he appeared to be travelling well, but tied up badly in the straight and was out on his feet when collared approaching the last. He needs time to recover from this and an easy two miles. (9/2: op 8/1)
Ernest William (IRE) (12/1: 7/1-14/1)
Al Helal (15/2: 5/1-8/1)

1133 BAGSHOT H'CAP CHASE (5-Y.O+) (Class B)
1-55 (1-55) **3m 110y (20 fncs)** £8,013.00 (£2,424.00: £1,182.00: £561.00) GOING: 0.18 sec per fur (G)

				SP	RR	SF
1039[4]	**Go Ballistic (121)** (JGMO'Shea) **7-10-4**ow1 MAFitzgerald (mstke 12th: hdwy 14th: chsd ldr fr 15th: led on bit appr last: easily)	—	**1**	2/1[2]	129	55
809[2]	**Straight Talk (133)** (PFNicholls) **9-11-2** APMcCoy (lw: led to 12th: led 14th: rdn 4 out: hdd appr last: unable qckn)	8	**2**	6/4[1]	136	63
	Arthur's Minstrel (128) (DNicholson) **9-10-11** RJohnson (chsd ldr 6th to 9th: 3rd whn blnd 13th: rdn 15th: one pce)	5	**3**	6/1	128	55
1016[3]	**Commercial Artist (145)** (NAGaselee) **10-12-0** WMarston (chsd ldr 2nd to 6th: chsd ldr fr 9th: led 12th to 14th: rdn 15th: sn wknd)	20	**4**	16/1	131	58
	Senor El Betrutti (IRE) (138) (MrsSusanNock) **7-11-7** GBradley (bkwd: 4th whn blnd 3rd: bhd fr 11th)	24	**5**	11/2[3]	109	36
				(SP 108.9%)	**5 Rn**	

6m 8.5 (3.50) CSF £5.14 TOTE £2.80: £1.30 £1.40 (£2.20) OWNER Mrs B. J. Lockhart (WESTBURY-ON-SEVERN) BRED J. Bowen
1039 Go Ballistic, winner of a valuable novice chase here in April, was all the better for a recent pipe-opener over hurdles and absolutely scooted up, travelling supremely well and cruising into the lead on the bridle approaching the last to win doing handsprings. (2/1)
809 Straight Talk was being bustled along from four out with the winner sitting on his heels travelling supremely well. It was only a matter of time before he was headed and, once that happened approaching the last, he was firmly put in his place. He should soon go one better. (6/4)

Arthur's Minstrel, third in last season's Scottish National, looked in good shape for this reappearance, but never looked like quickening up over the last six fences. At his best with some cut in the ground, his long-term objective is the Grand National. (6/1)
1016 Commercial Artist was racing over a far more suitable trip on this occasion, but the ground was far too lively for him and he had given his all from the sixth last. (16/1)
Senor El Betrutti (IRE) looked anything but fit and, over a trip too far for him, never threatened. A very useful novice over two and a half miles last season, he needs a right-handed track and to be able to dominate, and ran badly on several occasions when unable to do so. (11/2: 7/2-6/1)

1134 UNITED HOUSE CONSTRUCTION H'CAP CHASE (5-Y.O+) (Class B)

2-30 (2-30) **2m (12 fncs)** £16,693.75 (£5,050.00: £2,462.50: £1,168.75) GOING: 0.18 sec per fur (G)

				SP	RR	SF
	Storm Alert (142) (DNicholson) **10-11-9** RJohnson (lw: led to 2nd: led 3 out: rdn 2 out: blnd last: all out)	—	1	Evens[1]	148	80
	Big Matt (IRE) (144) (NJHenderson) **8-11-11** MAFitzgerald (lw: hld up: rdn to chse wnr appr 2 out: r.o wl flat)	nk	2	2/1[2]	150	82
1087[3]	**Thumbs Up (130)** (GMMcCourt) **10-10-11** BClifford (led 2nd to 3 out: wknd appr 2 out)	15	3	14/1	121	53
	Uncle Ernie (147) (JGFitzGerald) **11-12-0** APMcCoy (bit bkwd: hld up: rdn 4 out: sn wknd)	16	4	100/30[3]	122	54
				(SP 113.1%)		**4 Rn**

3m 51.8 (0.80) CSF £3.43 TOTE £1.90: (£1.80) OWNER Mrs Dawn Perrett (TEMPLE GUITING) BRED John Hennessy
Storm Alert has made this race his own, winning it in 1993 and 1994 and finishing third last year. He failed to win last season and, although a very useful two-mile specialist who ran some good races, he is certainly one to bet against as he has won just twice in the last three years. (Evens)
Big Matt (IRE), who clashed with the winner on several occasions last season, most noticeably when beating him a neck in this race last year, was meeting him on 18lb worse terms but looked in tremendous shape. Although awkward at the final fence, he ran on really strongly and would surely have prevailed with a little further to go. He should soon open his account. (2/1)
1087 Thumbs Up, last of three at Stratford on Thursday, made the vast majority of the running but, collared three from home, was soon put to bed. (14/1)
Uncle Ernie, with something left to work on, has never won on ground better than good and is now rated 15lb higher than at the end of last season. (100/30)

1135 VALLEY GARDENS NOVICES' H'CAP HURDLE (0-105) (4-Y.O+) (Class D)

3-05 (3-05) **2m 4f (11 hdls)** £3,842.50 (£1,080.00: £527.50) GOING: 0.18 sec per fur (G)

				SP	RR	SF
	Clod Hopper (IRE) (67) (WRMuir) **6-10-0** MRichards (chsd ldr: led 4th: lft clr appr 2 out: r.o)	—	1	11/2	63	—
792[2]	**Tap On Tootsie (91)** (TWall) **4-11-10** APMcCoy (lw: led tl mstke & hdd 4th: 3rd whn mstke, hmpd & lost pl 5th: rallied 7th: chsd wnr 8th to 3 out: lft 2nd appr 2 out: no imp)	21	2	7/4[1]	70	—
557[3]	**Positivo (80)** (MissCJECaroe) **5-10-13** DLeahy (hld up: lft 2nd 5th: wknd 7th)	13	3	9/1	49	—
792*	**Embley Buoy (73)** (JWMullins) **8-10-6** SCurran (4th whn b.d 5th)		B	5/1[3]	—	—
	Lyphard's Fable (USA) (74) (TRGeorge) **5-10-7** RJohnson (bit bkwd: 2nd whn fell 5th)		F	12/1	—	—
969*	**Aslar (IRE) (69)** (JSMoore) **7-10-2** WMcFarland (b: lw: hld up: mstke 5th: 3rd whn mstke 8th: mstke & chsd wnr 3 out: 2nd whn p.u appr 2 out: lame)		P	100/30[2]	—	—
				(SP 109.2%)		**6 Rn**

5m 2.1 (20.10) CSF £14.59 TOTE £6.30: £1.80 £1.50 (£4.60) OWNER Mr T. J. Parrott (LAMBOURN) BRED P. and D. James
LONG HANDICAP Clod Hopper (IRE) 9-13
IN-FOCUS: **This was an appalling, uncompetitive event.**
Clod Hopper (IRE), placed in a couple of sellers for Hilary Parrott last season, was having his first run in eleven months, but was virtually handed this race on a plate, beating two very moderate rivals. (11/2: 8/1-5/1)
792 Tap On Tootsie, left second going to the penultimate hurdle, can consider herself fortunate to pick up the prizemoney. (7/4)
792* Embley Buoy (5/1: 7/2-11/2)
Lyphard's Fable (USA) (12/1: op 6/1)
969* Aslar (IRE), heavily bandaged in front, was still travelling well in second when pulled up lame approaching the second last. (100/30: 5/2-4/1)

1136 STANLAKE NOVICES' CHASE (5-Y.O+) (Class D)

3-40 (3-40) **2m 3f 110y (16 fncs)** £4,986.00 (£1,224.00) GOING: 0.18 sec per fur (G)

				SP	RR	SF
1061*	**Strong Promise (IRE) (106)** (GAHubbard) **5-11-5**(3) 4x KGaule (mde all: shkn up appr last: easily)	—	1	1/8[1]	104++	10
954[F]	**Minor Key (IRE)** (JRJenkins) **6-11-1** GBradley (chsd wnr: mstkes 8th & 11th: rdn appr 2 out: btn whn mstke last: eased flat)	27	2	6/1[2]	75?	—
				(SP 103.2%)		**2 Rn**

5m 7.2 (20.20) TOTE £1.10: OWNER Mr G. A. Hubbard (WOODBRIDGE) BRED William McCarthy
1061* Strong Promise (IRE) has probably had more exercise at home than he had here, but he will have gained some valuable experience and picked up some decent money to boot. (1/8)
859 Minor Key (IRE), winner of two Irish point-to-points earlier in the year, was making his chasing debut under Rules, but he was not in the same league as the winner. (6/1)

1137 COPPER HORSE H'CAP HURDLE (4-Y.O+) (Class B)

4-10 (4-11) **2m 110y (9 hdls)** £4,992.75 (£1,512.00: £738.50: £351.75) GOING: 0.18 sec per fur (G)

				SP	RR	SF
	Silver Groom (IRE) (132) (RAkehurst) **6-11-4**(5) SRyan (lw: stdy hdwy fr 6th: led appr 2 out: rdn appr last: eased flat)	—	1	5/2[2]	117	54
863[4]	**Shoofk (115)** (SDow) **5-10-6** APMcCoy (led & sn clr: hdd appr 2 out: 2nd & btn whn mstke last)	8	2	4/1[3]	92	29
948[4]	**Barna Boy (IRE) (133)** (NJHenderson) **8-11-10** MAFitzgerald (lw: stdy hdwy fr 6th: wknd appr 2 out)	1¼	3	8/1	109	46
	Charming Girl (USA) (127) (OSherwood) **5-11-4** JOsborne (chsd ldr tl appr 2 out: sn wknd)	nk	4	Evens[1]	103	40
952[5]	**Stoney Valley (110)** (JRJenkins) **6-9-8**(7) NTEgan (a bhd: t.o fr 6th)	dist	5	14/1	—	—
				(SP 116.3%)		**5 Rn**

3m 56.6 (6.60) CSF £12.19 TOTE £3.10: £1.30 £1.70 (£6.50) OWNER The Silver Darling Partnership (EPSOM) BRED Holborn Trust Co
Silver Groom (IRE), fit from the Flat, went on approaching the second last and was eased considerably on the run-in. The winning distance is no true reflection of his superiority. (5/2: op 6/4)
863 Shoofk tore off like a scolded cat and it was no surprise that the others eventually reeled him in. (4/1)

948 Barna Boy (IRE) steadily crept closer from the fourth last, but was left for dead turning for home. This trip is well short of his best. (8/1: 7/1-11/1)
Charming Girl (USA), all the rage in the market, was the only runner who attempted to keep tabs on the tearaway leader, but she was collared for that position approaching the second last and Osborne held her together from that point. (Evens)
952 Stoney Valley (14/1: op 7/1)

T/Plpt: £5.10 (1,625.54 Tckts). T/Qdpt: £4.40 (127.95 Tckts). AK

0937-KELSO (L-H) (Good, Good to firm patches)
Saturday November 2nd
WEATHER: overcast WIND: str

1138 ISLE OF SKYE BLENDED SCOTCH WHISKY NOVICES' H'CAP CHASE (0-100) (5-Y.O+) (Class E)
1-00 (1-00) **3m 1f (19 fncs)** £2,944.00 (£892.00: £436.00: £208.00) GOING minus 0.34 sec per fur (GF)

				SP	RR	SF
	Seeking Gold (IRE) (72) (JBarclay) **7-10-4** BStorey (a.p: led 15th: lft clr 3 out: comf)	—	1	7/1^{3}	84	7
1022^{P}	**Mr Reiner (IRE) (80)** (JWade) **8-10-12** KJones (bhd: hdwy ½-wy: styd on one pce fr 3 out)	9	2	7/1^{3}	86	9
581^{4}	**Donovans Reef (68)** (MrsLMarshall) **10-10-0** KJohnson (chsd ldrs to 10th: hdwy again 4 out: sn btn)	dist	3	20/1	—	—
938^{3}	**White Diamond (79)** (MissLucindaRussell) **8-10-11v** PNiven (prom tl rdn & lost tch ½-wy: n.d after)	13	4	4/1^{2}	—	—
1022^{P}	**Alicharger (70)** (PMonteith) **6-10-2** ADobbin (chsd ldrs: blnd 6th: reminder 13th: wknd next)	14	5	20/1	—	—
938^{4}	**Bright Destiny (70)** (JSGoldie) **5-10-0** DParker (prom to 8th: outpcd & wl bhd fr 13th)	16	6	25/1	—	—
	Mister Trick (IRE) (68) (LLungo) **6-10-0** MFoster (prom: blnd 9th: sn rcvrd: disp 2nd whn fell 4 out)		F	3/1^{1}	—	—
1022^{6}	**Movac (IRE) (90)** (MissLucindaRussell) **7-11-8** MMoloney (led: shkn up 13th: hdd 15th: 5l 2nd & rdn whn blnd & uns rdr 3 out)		U	3/1^{1}	—	—
				(SP 108.4%)	**8 Rn**	

6m 18.0 (8.00) CSF £46.81 CT £751.50 TOTE £9.20: £1.60 £3.00 £4.70 (£32.90) Trio £57.70; £40.67 to Southwell 4/11/96 OWNER Gilry (LESLIE) BRED John Bourke
LONG HANDICAP Bright Destiny 9-4 Mister Trick (IRE) 9-9 Donovans Reef 9-7
WEIGHT FOR AGE 5yo-2lb
Seeking Gold (IRE) looked fit and, although only slow, does stay. She kept her feet as her main rivals fell by the wayside. (7/1)
873 Mr Reiner (IRE), from a yard not really firing, could never seriously get into it, but did show something. (7/1)
421 Donovans Reef has been disappointing since winning a hunter chase here two seasons ago, and there was no encouragement here.(20/1)
938 White Diamond proved as unreliable as ever. (4/1)
Mister Trick (IRE) was close enough when falling four out. (3/1: op 2/1)
4 Movac (IRE) is from a yard that can do little right this season. and he looked in trouble when blundering his rider out of the saddle three out. (3/1: 2/1-100/30)

1139 ROSALIND BIRTHDAY 'N.H.' NOVICES' HURDLE (4-Y.O+) (Class D)
1-30 (1-30) **2m 6f 110y (11 hdls)** £2,762.00 (£836.00: £408.00: £194.00) GOING minus 0.34 sec per fur (GF)

				SP	RR	SF
910^{2}	**Antarctic Wind (IRE)** (MDHammond) **6-10-12** RGarritty (lw: trckd ldrs: led 6th: clr 3 out: drvn out)	—	1	1/2^{1}	70	14
1021^{6}	**Trap Dancer** (PMonteith) **8-10-12** ADobbin (wnt prom ½-wy: styd on u.p fr 2 out: nvr able to chal)	7	2	7/1^{3}	65	9
939^{7}	**I'm The Man** (MrsESlack) **5-10-12** KJohnson (chsd ldrs: chal 7th: hrd rdn next: one pce fr 3 out)	2½	3	8/1	63	7
1047^{9}	**Whirlwind Romance (IRE) (59)** (WTKemp) **5-10-7** SMcDougall (prom tl rdn & lost pl ½-wy: styd on again fr 4 out: no imp)	3	4	66/1	56	—
392^{2}	**Profit And Loss** (FMurphy) **5-10-7** KWhelan (hdwy & prom ½-wy: sn rdn: one pce fr 4 out)	6	5	5/1^{2}	52	—
	Ethical Note (IRE) (MrsSJSmith) **5-10-12** RichardGuest (led to 2nd: cl up tl outpcd fr 7th)	11	6	20/1	49	—
1050^{9}	**Barnstormer (65)** (EAElliott) **10-10-12** DParker (prom tl wknd qckly 7th)	2½	7	50/1	47	—
1026^{6}	**Faster Ron (IRE)** (RAllan) **5-10-5**(7) SMelrose (bhd: sme hdwy 3 out: hit 2 out: sn wknd)	3½	8	66/1	45	—
	Seldom But Severe (IRE) (EAElliott) **6-10-12** KJones (a bhd)	16	9	33/1	33	—
910^{13}	**Millennium Man** (EWeymes) **5-10-12** JCallaghan (led 2nd to 6th: wknd next)	2½	10	33/1	32	—
				(SP 122.5%)	**10 Rn**	

5m 23.4 (6.40) CSF £5.38 TOTE £1.50: £1.10 £1.80 £2.20 (£5.40) Trio £8.20 OWNER Mr Gordon Brown (MIDDLEHAM) BRED James A. Slattery
910 Antarctic Wind (IRE) looked magnificent and stamped his authority on this some way out, but he needed all his rider's attentions to keep him going at the last. (1/2)
1021 Trap Dancer looks to be improving all the time and should pick up a race in due course. (7/1)
801 I'm The Man ran better over this longer trip and seems to be going the right way. (8/1)
Whirlwind Romance (IRE) is a very lean individual but he does stay and, when stamina is at a premium, there might be a modest event to be found. (66/1)
392 Profit And Loss looked pretty slow here and may well need plenty of give in the ground to come into her own. (5/1: 7/2-6/1)
Ethical Note (IRE), from a yard in form, ran as though this was needed. (20/1)

1140 NEWTON INVESTMENT MANAGEMENT H'CAP CHASE (0-120) (5-Y.O+) (Class D)
2-00 (2-00) **2m 1f (12 fncs)** £4,006.50 (£1,212.00: £591.00: £280.50) GOING minus 0.34 sec per fur (GF)

				SP	RR	SF
	Briar's Delight (90) (RAllan) **8-10-10v** BHarding (trckd ldrs: led flat: styd on u.p)	—	1	7/4^{2}	99	9
	Weaver George (IRE) (100) (WStorey) **6-11-6** MMoloney (led tl hung lft & hdd after 6th: led 8th tl hdd flat: kpt on)	3	2	4/1^{3}	106	16
867*	**Prince Skyburd (93)** (MrsPMAAvison) **5-10-8**(5) ECallaghan (lw: hld up & bhd: effrt & mstke 3 out: hdwy next & sn chsng ldrs: one pce flat)	4	3	6/4^{1}	95	5
855^{4}	**Flash of Realm (FR) (97)** (BMactaggart) **10-11-3v** BStorey (cl up tl wknd last)	6	4	8/1	94	4
				(SP 107.5%)	**4 Rn**	

4m 13.1 (6.10) CSF £7.67 TOTE £3.20 (£10.60) OWNER Mr A. Clark (CORNHILL-ON-TWEED) BRED R. G. Starbuck
OFFICIAL EXPLANATION **Prince Skyburd: began to gurgle, and though asked a question there was little response. He then made a bad mistake at the third last which may have affected his subsequent placing.**
Briar's Delight loves this track and always looked to be going best, but he did need riding out to make sure of it. (7/4: op 3/1)

Weaver George (IRE) has only ever run over hurdles on this track and his rider had quite a job persuading him to take the longer chase course at one stage, and that could well have made the difference. (4/1)
867* Prince Skyburd sat off the pace, but his jumping was occasionally indifferent and, when a real effort was required, his response was not what it should have been. (6/4: 4/5-13/8)
855 Flash of Realm (FR), a keen sort, travels well but, when it comes down to a struggle, there is little response. Perhaps a drop in class is what he needs. (8/1)

1141 HARROW HOTEL DALKEITH NOVICES' (S) HURDLE (4, 5 & 6-Y.O) (Class G)

2-30 (2-31) **2m 110y (8 hdls)** £2,316.00 (£651.00: £318.00) GOING minus 0.34 sec per fur (GF)

				SP	RR	SF
1049[11]	**Stylish Interval (89)** (NWaggott) **4-10-12** ADobbin (unruly s: a.p: led 3 out: hrd rdn flat: jst hld on)	—	1	4/1[2]	69	20
939[4]	**Flyaway Blues** (MrsMReveley) **4-10-12** PNiven (prom tl outpcd & mstke 4th: hdwy 3 out: ev ch flat: hrd rdn: nt resolute: jst failed)	s.h	2	4/5[1]	69	20
643[6]	**Kashana (IRE)** (WStorey) **4-10-7v** MMoloney (lw: reminders after 3rd: sn prom: hrd rdn 3 out: styd on one pce)	11	3	11/1	53	4
1027[5]	**Little Redwing (64)** (MDHammond) **4-10-7b** RGarritty (mde most to 3 out: 4th & btn whn blnd 2 out)	8	4	13/2[3]	46	—
1047[12]	**Seconds Away (53)** (JSGoldie) **5-10-9**(3) GLee (in tch: outpcd 5th: no imp after)	5	5	33/1	46	—
	Moofaji (FWatson) **5-10-12** JCallaghan (outpcd & bhd tl sme late hdwy)	1¼	6	14/1	45	—
	Barik (IRE) (BMactaggart) **6-10-12** BStorey (plld hrd: wnt prom 4th: 2nd & struggling whn hit 2 out: sn wknd)	7	7	33/1	38	—
	Mary's Case (IRE) (MrsJDGoodfellow) **6-10-12** TReed (hit 3rd: a bhd)	1	8	11/1	37	—
937[5]	**Walk In The Wild** (DANolan) **4-10-7** SMcDougall (disp ld to 3rd: rdn & wknd 5th)	dist	9	100/1	—	—

(SP 119.1%) **9 Rn**

3m 49.2 (3.20) CSF £7.55 TOTE £5.70: £1.80 £1.00 £3.80 (£3.20) Trio £11.30 OWNER Mrs J. Waggott (SPENNYMOOR) BRED R. J. Turner
No bid
STEWARDS' ENQUIRY Dobbin susp. 11-13/11/96 (excessive use of whip).
Stylish Interval, very awkward at the start, had more courage than the runner-up when the chips were down and had plenty of help from the saddle. (4/1)
939 Flyaway Blues has the ability to win races such as this with ease but, as ever, he showed he has his own ideas about the game. (4/5: tchd evens)
Kashana (IRE), in a visor for the first time over hurdles, was continually off the bit and may well need further. (11/1: op 7/1)
784 Little Redwing is both slow and clumsy. (13/2)
Seconds Away is only small for this game, but jumped well enough, only to find the effort beyond him from four out. (33/1)
Moofaji ran as though longer trips are needed. (14/1: 10/1-16/1)

1142 SALVESEN FOOD SERVICES H'CAP CHASE (0-120) (5-Y.O+) (Class D)

3-00 (3-06) **2m 6f 110y (17 fncs)** £5,182.80 (£1,568.40: £765.20: £363.60) GOING minus 0.34 sec per fur (GF)

				SP	RR	SF
946[P]	**Royal Vacation (110)** (GMMoore) **7-11-7** JCallaghan (hld up: effrt 4 out: led flat: drvn out)	—	1	6/1	116	47
966[3]	**Celtic Silver (92)** (MrsSJSmith) **8-10-3**ow3 RichardGuest (hld up: effrt 4 out: blnd next: gd hdwy appr last & sn chsng ldrs: kpt on towards fin)	½	2	4/1[3]	98	26
940*	**Bas de Laine (FR) (115)** (MDHammond) **10-11-12b** RGarritty (led: mstke 6th & 13th: hdd flat: kpt on)	½	3	100/30[1]	120	51
	Stop the Waller (IRE) (114) (FMurphy) **7-11-11** KWhelan (bit bkwd: a chsng ldrs: drvn along 3 out: one pce appr last)	6	4	12/1	115	46
323a[4]	**Balyara (IRE) (105)** (MrsMReveley) **6-11-2** PNiven (mstkes & bhd: styd on fr 3 out: nrst fin)	1¼	5	8/1	105	36
	Golden Fiddle (IRE) (101) (JKMOliver) **8-10-12** BStorey (bit bkwd: in tch: outpcd 12th: styd on fr last)	¾	6	14/1	101	32
	Gala Water (89) (TDCDun) **10-10-0** RSupple (chsd ldrs tl blnd & wknd 4 out)	5	7	66/1	85	16
938*	**Tighter Budget (USA) (104)** (MrsHDSayer) **9-11-1** MMoloney (chsd ldrs: blnd 11th: ev ch 2 out: wknd last)	4	8	7/2[2]	97	28
909[4]	**Cross Cannon (111)** (JWade) **10-11-8** KJones (hld up & bhd whn fell 4th)		F	16/1	—	—

(SP 112.4%) **9 Rn**

5m 31.2 (-0.80) CSF £27.60 CT £83.72 TOTE £7.80: £1.50 £1.50 £1.90 (£26.00) Trio £39.30 OWNER Mr G. P. Edwards (MIDDLEHAM) BRED Small Breeders' Group
LONG HANDICAP Gala Water 9-11 Celtic Silver 9-13
OFFICIAL EXPLANATION Royal Vacation: explaining the winner's improvement, the trainer reported that on his previous run the gelding was unable to get back into the race after two mistakes and that he was outclassed.
804* Royal Vacation, happier in this company, was off a generous mark and, getting first run on the runner-up, made it tell. (6/1)
966 Celtic Silver, patiently ridden this time, put up a gallant effort from the second last, but was never quite doing things quickly enough. His turn will surely come. (4/1)
940* Bas de Laine (FR) stays well, but just got tapped for toe. He is one to watch for in marathon events. (100/30)
Stop the Waller (IRE), likely to be all the better for this, ran well and ought to improve next time. (12/1)
Balyara (IRE) is not the best if jumpers, but he does stay and was getting the hang of things as the race progressed. (8/1: 6/1-10/1)
Golden Fiddle (IRE) ran really well here when looking burly and will surely come into his own this season. (14/1: op 8/1)
938* Tighter Budget (USA), never able to dominate in this company, made one particularly bad jumping error and, when beaten at the last, was eased. (7/2)

1143 OOH AAH DAILY STAR H'CAP HURDLE (0-125) (4-Y.O+) (Class D)

3-30 (3-34) **2m 6f 110y (11 hdls)** £3,387.50 (£1,025.00: £500.00: £237.50) GOING minus 0.34 sec per fur (GF)

				SP	RR	SF
1023[3]	**Exemplar (IRE) (93)** (MrsSJSmith) **8-10-3**ow3 RichardGuest (hld up: stdy hdwy fr 7th: mstke last: led flat: r.o)	—	1	100/30[3]	81	18
827[4]	**Tallywagger (118)** (GMMoore) **9-11-7**(7) THogg (hld up: hdwy to jn ldrs 6th: lost pl next: styd on fr 2 out)	1¾	2	9/1	105	45
942*	**Nicholas Plant (96)** (JSGoldie) **7-10-3**(3) GLee (mde most: hit 5th: hdd & no ex fnl 150y)	s.h	3	5/2[1]	83	23
	Ralitsa (IRE) (102) (MDHammond) **4-10-12** RGarritty (trckd ldrs: chal 3 out: rdn appr last: r.o one pce)	1¼	4	3/1[2]	88	28
	D'Arblay Street (IRE) (90) (WTKemp) **7-10-0** SMcDougall (chsd ldrs tl outpcd 4 out: kpt on flat)	1¾	5	14/1	75	15
	Marlingford (90) (MrsJJordan) **9-9-9**(5) STaylor (disp ld to 3rd: cl up tl rdn & wknd 4 out)	dist	6	66/1	—	—
	Bark'n'bite (95) (MrsMReveley) **4-10-5** PNiven (bhd: mstke 7th: t.o)	dist	7	6/1	—	—

(SP 109.1%) **7 Rn**

5m 19.5 (2.50) CSF £27.53 CT £70.06 TOTE £4.20: £1.70 £2.90 (£9.20) OWNER Mrs S. Smith (BINGLEY) BRED Mrs R. Stewart
LONG HANDICAP D'Arblay Street (IRE) 9-10 Marlingford 9-1
1023 Exemplar (IRE), ridden with patience, let the others fight it out and then picked them off after the last. (100/30)

827 Tallywagger ran in snatches and may have found this a bit too short. (9/1: op 6/1)
942* Nicholas Plant did his usual and forced the pace, but was flat out a long way from home and was done for toe at the last. (5/2)
Ralitsa (IRE) had his chances but, when it came down to a struggle, he was never doing enough. He has the ability when things go his way. (3/1)
D'Arblay Street (IRE), who won with blinkers on last season, found this trip too sharp. (14/1)
Bark'n'bite (6/1: op 7/2)

1144 LEVY BOARD CONDITIONAL H'CAP HURDLE (0-115) (4-Y.O+) (Class E)
4-00 (4-04) **2m 110y (8 hdls)** £2,220.00 (£620.00: £300.00) GOING minus 0.34 sec per fur (GF)

				SP	RR	SF
1025[4]	**Fen Terrier (92)** (FPMurtagh) **4-10-10** ECallaghan (in tch: hdwy u.p 3 out: led last: all out)	—	1	4/1[3]	71	33
	Kemo Sabo (82) (CParker) **4-10-0** DParker (chsd ldrs: outpcd 3 out: styd on flat: wandered u.p: jst failed)	hd	2	33/1	61	23
1049[3]	**Teejay'n'aitch (IRE) (82)** (JSGoldie) **4-10-0** GLee (in tch: hdwy & ev ch flat: nt qckn)	3	3	5/1	58	20
941[2]	**Nonios (IRE) (98)** (GMMoore) **5-10-11v**(5) THogg (in tch: effrt 3 out: ch flat: hung lft & no ex)	4	4	100/30[2]	70	32
1025[5]	**Well Appointed (IRE) (97)** (BMactaggart) **7-10-12**(3) SMelrose (lw: chsd ldrs: chal 4th: one pce fr 2 out)	¾	5	11/2	68	30
	Nooran (82) (ACWhillans) **5-10-0** STaylor (prom: effrt 5th: rdn to ld appr 2 out: hdd & wknd last)	11	6	14/1	43	5
941[3]	**Eden Dancer (106)** (MrsMReveley) **4-11-5**(5) CMcCormack (lw: led tl hdd appr 2 out: sn wknd)	2½	7	5/2[1]	64	26
894[P]	**Urban Dancing (USA) (110)** (BEllison) **7-12-0** DJKavanagh (a bhd)	10	8	16/1	59	21
				(SP 119.2%)	**8 Rn**	

3m 45.7 (-0.30) CSF £86.22 CT £622.07 TOTE £6.10: £1.90 £4.10 £1.60 (£99.60) Trio £90.80; £93.45 to Southwell 4/11/96 OWNER Mr K. G. Fairbairn (CARLISLE) BRED Racing Thoroughbreds P L C
LONG HANDICAP Kemo Sabo 9-12 Teejay'n'aitch (IRE) 9-9
STEWARDS' ENQUIRY Callaghan susp. 11-12/11/96 (excessive use of whip).
1025 Fen Terrier seemed well suited by the strong pace and just found enough under pressure. (4/1)
Kemo Sabo, disappointing last year, put up a decent effort this time and, had he really concentrated and run straight after the last, would probably have won. (33/1)
1049 Teejay'n'aitch (IRE) has been promising to win a race under both codes for some time and ran another good race here, but just failed to go through with it. (5/1)
941 Nonios (IRE) had his chances, but hung left when ridden and failed to produce the goods. (100/30)
1025 Well Appointed (IRE) beat himself by taking on Eden Dancer. (11/2: 7/2-6/1)
Nooran ran pretty well after almost two months off and should be all the better for it. (14/1: 10/1-25/1)
941 Eden Dancer is much better going right-handed. (5/2)

T/Plpt: £381.30 (20.38 Tckts). T/Qdpt: £43.60 (13.67 Tckts). AA

0962-WARWICK (L-H) (Good to firm)
Saturday November 2nd
WEATHER: rain

1145 JAMES HIGGINS CONDITIONAL H'CAP HURDLE (0-100) (4-Y.O+) (Class F)
12-40 (12-40) **2m (8 hdls)** £2,174.80 (£602.80: £288.40) GOING minus 0.83 sec per fur (F)

				SP	RR	SF
969[2]	**Glowing Path (76)** (RJHodges) **6-10-2**(8) JHarris (tk keen hold: a.p: led appr last: r.o wl)	—	1	8/1	66	9
	Supermick (80) (WRMuir) **5-11-0** ABates (hld up: hdwy 4th: chsd wnr appr last: no imp)	4	2	11/2[2]	66	9
951[P]	**Newhall Prince (87)** (AStreeter) **8-11-7b** LAspell (lw: led: clr 4th: hdd appr last: sn btn)	2½	3	8/1	71	14
976[3]	**Stay With Me (FR) (94)** (CREgerton) **6-12-0** MichaelBrennan (a.p: one pce fr 3 out)	½	4	7/1	77	20
1010*	**Pair of Jacks (IRE) (92)** (GLMoore) **6-11-4**(8) MAttwater (hld up & bhd: hdwy 5th: nt rch ldrs)	4	5	6/1[3]	71	14
483[2]	**Game Dilemma (80)** (JWMullins) **5-10-11**(3) OBurrows (nvr nr to chal)	1¼	6	10/1	58	1
974*	**Pegasus Bay (94)** (DECantillon) **5-12-0** GHogan (lw: plld hrd mid div: no hdwy fr 3 out)	2½	7	9/2[1]	69	12
971[3]	**Handson (88)** (BRMillman) **4-11-5**(3) DSalter (nvr nr ldrs)	3	8	11/2[2]	60	3
	Out of The Blue (66) (MWEckley) **4-9-9**(5) JMogford (prom: j.slowly 5th: sn rdn & wknd)	7	9	25/1	31	—
648[4]	**Ray River (76)** (KGWingrove) **4-10-10b** RMassey (a bhd)	2½	10	16/1	39	—
949[6]	**San Diego Charger (IRE) (84)** (ABarrow) **5-11-4** SophieMitchell (plld hrd mid div: dropped rr & mstke 4th: t.o)	16	11	12/1	31	—
961[5]	**Water Hazard (IRE) (79)** (SDow) **4-10-3**(10) RElkins (plld hrd: bhd tl fell 2 out)		F	11/1	—	—
				(SP 132.8%)	**12 Rn**	

3m 39.3 (-2.70) CSF £53.79 CT £350.79 TOTE £21.10: £5.40 £2.10 £1.40 (£64.80) Trio £133.40; £50.74 to Southwell 4/11/96 OWNER Mr P. Slade (SOMERTON) BRED M. B. O'Gorman
LONG HANDICAP Out of The Blue 9-13
969 Glowing Path, who missed most of last season with leg trouble, had put in a couple of sound efforts in selling company. (8/1)
Supermick scored twice on the Flat this season, but one of those was over fourteen furlongs, so this sharp two miles was not in his favour. (11/2: 4/1-6/1)
702 Newhall Prince, with the blinkers refitted for this return to hurdles, was 25lb lower than his chase rating. (8/1)
976 Stay With Me (FR) was 6lb higher than when winning at Bangor two outings ago. (7/1)
1010* Pair of Jacks (IRE) was raised 5lb for his Fakenham win last time. (6/1)
483 Game Dilemma may just have needed this. (10/1: op 5/1)
974* Pegasus Bay did not help his chance by proving difficult to settle. (9/2)
971 Handson (11/2: 4/1-6/1)
949 San Diego Charger (IRE) (12/1: 8/1-14/1)
961 Water Hazard (IRE) (11/1: 6/1-12/1)

1146 ARNOLD LODGE SCHOOL H'CAP CHASE (0-110) (5-Y.O+) (Class E)
1-10 (1-10) **2m (12 fncs)** £3,286.00 (£914.00: £439.50) GOING minus 0.83 sec per fur (F)

				SP	RR	SF
883[3]	**Super Sharp (NZ) (86)** (HOliver) **8-11-0** JacquiOliver (mde all: r.o wl fr 2 out)	—	1	6/1[3]	101	25
895*	**Circulation (75)** (DMcCain) **10-10-0v**(3)ow3 DWalsh (chsd wnr: rdn 9th: mstke 3 out: no imp fr 2 out)	7	2	6/1[3]	83	4
951[3]	**Northern Optimist (87)** (BJLlewellyn) **8-11-1** MrJLLlewellyn (hld up: hit 5th: n.d after)	1¾	3	3/1[2]	93	17
1035*	**Zeredar (NZ) (100)** (KCBailey) **6-12-0** JOsborne (j.rt: bhd whn j.slowly 5th: t.o whn p.u bef 3 out)		P	10/11[1]	—	—
				(SP 106.0%)	**4 Rn**	

3m 49.1 (0.50 under best) (-4.90) CSF £28.50 TOTE £6.30 (£9.70) OWNER Mrs Sue Careless (CHELTENHAM) BRED Dr R. G. & Mrs L. A. Martin
LONG HANDICAP Circulation 9-12
OFFICIAL EXPLANATION **Zeredar (NZ): the jockey reported that the horse had initially run keenly but had soon come off the bridle, started to jump right and was never travelling thereafter.**
883 Super Sharp (NZ), dropped 2lb, had been freshened up by a three-week break. (6/1)
895* Circulation was only 2lb out of the handicap this time. (6/1)
951 Northern Optimist was never a threat after clouting the first ditch. (3/1)
1035* Zeredar (NZ), very disappointing, was the subject of an enquiry. (10/11)

1147 BSPH H'CAP CHASE (0-130) (5-Y.O+) (Class C)
1-40 (1-40) **3m 2f (20 fncs)** £4,692.00 (£1,416.00: £688.00: £324.00) GOING minus 0.83 sec per fur (F)

				SP	RR	SF
966[2]	**Time Enough (IRE) (98)** (CPEBrooks) **7-10-3** JFTitley (w ldr tl hit 3rd: led appr 14th: r.o wl fr 2 out)	—	1	4/5[1]	106	—
	Copper Mine (123) (OSherwood) **10-12-0** JOsborne (bit bkwd: hld up: rdn & outpcd appr 14th: chsd wnr fr 15th: eased whn btn flat)	18	2	9/4[2]	120	12
	Cropredy Lad (97) (PRWebber) **9-10-2**ow1 AThornton (led tl appr 14th: wknd 16th)	30	3	7/2[3]	76	—
1040[P]	**Elltee-Ess (97)** (RJWeaver) **11-9-9v**(7)ow2 CRWeaver (nt j.w: sn t.o)	dist	4	66/1	—	—
				(SP 110.0%)	**4 Rn**	

6m 23.7 (-1.30) CSF £2.92 TOTE £1.80: (£1.80) OWNER The Lewis Partnership (LAMBOURN) BRED T. O'Brien
LONG HANDICAP Elltee-Ess 8-5
966 Time Enough (IRE) had things pretty much his own way here, so his jumping problems never surfaced. (4/5: op evens)
Copper Mine did not look fully wound up. (9/4: op 6/4)
Cropredy Lad had run his race five out. (7/2)

1148 TENSATOR H'CAP HURDLE (0-130) (4-Y.O+) (Class C)
2-15 (2-15) **2m 3f (9 hdls)** £3,600.00 (£1,080.00: £520.00: £240.00) GOING minus 0.83 sec per fur (F)

				SP	RR	SF
	Runaway Pete (USA) (119) (MCPipe) **6-11-7**(3) DWalsh (lw: mde all: rdn 6th: r.o wl fr 2 out)	—	1	11/8[1]	103	—
1037[U]	**Morstock (110)** (RJHodges) **6-10-12**(3) TDascombe (plld hrd early: chsd wnr fr 5th: one pce fr 2 out)	4	2	11/4[2]	91	—
103[F]	**Djais (FR) (119)** (JRJenkins) **7-11-10** JFTitley (hld up: wknd appr 2 out: eased whn btn appr last)	17	3	9/2[3]	85	—
1072[4]	**Sleeptite (FR) (97)** (WGMTurner) **6-9-9**(7)ow2 JPower (chsd ldr: mstke 2nd: wknd 5th: t.o)	18	4	12/1	48	—
	Grand Applause (IRE) (103) (MSalaman) **6-10-8** DBridgwater (bkwd: s.s: reminders after 1st: j.rt 4th: t.o whn p.u bef 5th)		P	6/1	—	—
				(SP 108.9%)	**5 Rn**	

4m 14.9 (-5.10) CSF £5.22 TOTE £2.00: £1.20 £1.60 (£2.70) OWNER Mr J. D. Smeaden (WELLINGTON) BRED Allen Gardner
LONG HANDICAP Sleeptite (FR) 9-4
Runaway Pete (USA), who had a pipe-opener in the Cesarewitch, is not the most fluent of hurdlers and required plenty of rousting along. (11/8)
Morstock had got no further than the third on his fencing bow a week ago. (11/4: 3/1-9/2)
Djais (FR) needs a stiffer test of stamina. (9/2: 2/1-5/1)
1072 Sleeptite (FR) (12/1: op 8/1)

1149 ST MARY'S (S) HURDLE (3-Y.O) (Class G)
2-45 (2-45) **2m (8 hdls)** £1,691.00 (£466.00: £221.00) GOING minus 0.83 sec per fur (F)

				SP	RR	SF
912[3]	**Indira** (CLPopham) **3-10-4**(3) TDascombe (mde all: rdn whn lft clr 2 out: r.o wl)	—	1	7/4[1]	57	2
912[9]	**Lady Magnum (IRE)** (JNeville) **3-10-7** DBridgwater (hld up & bhd: hdwy whn mstke 3 out: hmpd 2 out: hrd rdn & r.o wl flat)	3	2	10/1	54	—
962[6]	**How Could-I (IRE)** (MrsNMacauley) **3-10-7b** AThornton (a.p: lft 2nd & hmpd 2 out: one pce)	1¾	3	11/2[3]	52	—
	Bluntswood Hall (RHollinshead) **3-10-12** GaryLyons (a.p: one pce fr 3 out)	4	4	66/1	53	—
	Fijon (IRE) (JPearce) **3-10-7** VSmith (hdwy appr 4th: btn whn hmpd 2 out)	8	5	9/1	40	—
	In Cahoots (ADSmith) **3-10-12** FJousset (hld up: hdwy 5th: btn whn hmpd 2 out)	5	6	7/1	40	—
501[3]	**Lebedinski (IRE)** (MrsPSly) **3-10-7** RMarley (hld up & bhd: hdwy 4th: rdn & outpcd 5th: btn whn hmpd 2 out)	7	7	5/1[2]	28	—
	Shanoora (IRE) (MrsNMacauley) **3-10-4**(3) EHusband (plld hrd: prom tl wknd 4th)	2	8	25/1	26	—
962[8]	**The Grey Weaver** (RMFlower) **3-10-5**(7) JKMcCarthy (bhd fr 4th)	5	9	66/1	26	—
	Storm Wind (IRE) (KRBurke) **3-10-12** ALarnach (plld hrd: prom tl wknd 4th)	2½	10	20/1	24	—
	Bites (TTBill) **3-10-7** JRailton (mstke 3rd: a bhd)	5	11	33/1	14	—
874[3]	**Kai's Lady (IRE)** (SWCampion) **3-10-6**(3)ow2 PMidgley (bhd fr 4th)	½	12	25/1	15	—
831[7]	**Chillington** (WMBrisbourne) **3-10-12b** SWynne (plld hrd: w ldr tl wknd appr 5th)	2½	13	50/1	16	—
962[7]	**Colour Counsellor** (RMFlower) **3-10-9**(3) DFortt (hld up: hdwy appr 4th: w wnr whn fell 2 out)		F	12/1	—	—
912[10]	**Brin-Lodge (IRE)** (KSBridgwater) **3-10-7** VSlattery (plld hrd: mstke 2nd: bhd whn blnd 4th: sn t.o: p.u bef last)		P	66/1	—	—
				(SP 129.5%)	**15 Rn**	

3m 40.4 (-1.60) CSF £20.67 TOTE £2.60: £1.70 £3.20 £2.30 (£29.40) Trio £141.90 OWNER Mr M. A. Long (TAUNTON) BRED Wheelersland Stud
No bid
912 Indira jumps pretty well, but was probably a shade fortunate to score. (7/4)
Lady Magnum (IRE) seems to be going the right way and finished in a style which suggests she can take a similar event. (10/1)
807 How Could-I (IRE) did not seem to be going as well as the unlucky Colour Counsellor at the second last. (11/2: 4/1-6/1)
Bluntswood Hall had shown nothing in All-Weather maidens on the Flat. (66/1)
Fijon (IRE) (9/1: 6/1-10/1)
In Cahoots (7/1: 5/1-8/1)
Colour Counsellor seemed to be travelling better than the winner when departing at the penultimate hurdle. (12/1: op 8/1)

1150 OFFCHURCH NOVICES' CHASE (5-Y.O+) (Class D)
3-20 (3-20) **2m 4f 110y (17 fncs)** £4,090.00 (£1,140.00: £550.00) GOING minus 0.83 sec per fur (F)

				SP	RR	SF
870[2]	**Mr Conductor (IRE)** (RHAlner) **5-10-13** AThornton (lft in ld 2nd: wl clr fr 10th: eased considerably flat)	—	1	4/7[1]	109++	—
	Hawaiian Sam (IRE) (98) (AndrewTurnell) **6-11-0** GCrone (bkwd: bhd fr 8th: wnt poor 2nd appr last)	12	2	11/4[2]	100	—

				SP	RR	SF
964[2]	**Elite Governor (IRE)** (NMLampard) **7-10-9**(5) ChrisWebb (chsd wnr fr 2nd: hit 8th & 9th: blnd 10th: sn no ch)	2½	3	9/2[3]	98	—
860[5]	**Sporting Fixture (IRE)** (PEccles) **5-10-13** JAMcCarthy (fell 1st)		F	66/1	—	—
	Lucknam Dreamer (61) (MrsBarbaraWaring) **8-11-0** EByrne (led tl blnd bdly 2nd: sn bhd: p.u & dismntd bef 7th)		P	40/1	—	—
				(SP 112.4%)	**5 Rn**	

5m 6.1 (2.10) CSF £2.62 TOTE £1.50: £1.00 £2.50 (£1.60) OWNER Mr P M De Wilde (BLANDFORD) BRED Miss Laura Devitt
WEIGHT FOR AGE 5yo-1lb
870 Mr Conductor (IRE), who spent last season acclimatising over hurdles having arrived from Ireland, was a distance clear from halfway until eased to a walk on the run-in. (4/7)
Hawaiian Sam (IRE), carrying condition, was inclined to balloon some of his fences. (11/4: 7/4-3/1)
964 Elite Governor (IRE) could never recover from making a hash of the second ditch. (9/2: 6/1-4/1)

1151 WEATHERBYS 'STARS OF TOMORROW' N.H. FLAT RACE (4, 5 & 6-Y.O) (Class H)
3-55 (3-55) **2m** £1,364.00 (£379.00: £182.00)

				SP	RR	SF
	Danzante (IRE) (RMStronge) **4-11-1**(3) DWalsh (hld up: lft in ld over 2f out: drvn out)	—	1	11/4[2]	—	—
	Ditopero (WGMTurner) **4-10-11**(7) NWillmington (bit bkwd: a.p: led 8f out tl rn wd bnd 2f out: unable qckn fnl f)	1¾	2	7/4[1]	—	—
	Becky's Lad (MrsDThomas) **6-11-1**(3) GuyLewis (swtg: bit bkwd: a.p: ev ch 2f out: wknd over 1f out)	5	3	40/1	—	—
	Laird O'Rhynie (KGWingrove) **4-10-11**(7) MrAWintle (bkwd: hdwy 7f out: wknd 3f out)	5	4	8/1	—	—
	Abyss (NPLittmoden) **4-11-4** MrDVerco (bkwd: bhd fnl 5f: t.o)	dist	5	8/1	—	—
918[12]	**Nanjizal** (KSBridgwater) **4-10-13**(5) MichaelBrennan (led 6f: wknd 6f out: t.o)	2	6	33/1	—	—
	Honest George (KSBridgwater) **5-11-1**(3) RMassey (bkwd: plld hrd: led after 6f to 8f out: sn wknd: t.o)	dist	7	7/2[3]	—	—
				(SP 112.9%)	**7 Rn**	

4m 0.5 CSF £7.69 TOTE £4.60: £2.30 £1.60 (£4.20) OWNER Mr David Hallums (NEWBURY) BRED Kilnamoragh Stud
STEWARDS' ENQUIRY Wilmington susp: 11-12/11/96 (excessive use of the whip)
Danzante (IRE), a half-brother to this season's seven-furlong juvenile winner Test The Water, won a weak contest. (11/4: 2/1-3/1)
Ditopero did not handle the home turn at all well and his rider picked up a two-day whip-ban. (7/4)
Becky's Lad was rather warm beforehand. (40/1)
Laird O'Rhynie (8/1: op 5/1)
Abyss (8/1: op 5/1)

T/Plpt: £196.00 (26.65 Tckts). T/Qdpt: £3.90 (101.78 Tckts). KH

1125-WETHERBY (L-H) (Good)
Saturday November 2nd
WEATHER: overcast WIND: str

1152 BOLTON PERCY NOVICES' HURDLE (4-Y.O+) (Class C)
12-50 (12-50) **2m (9 hdls)** £4,159.00 (£1,252.00: £606.00: £283.00) GOING minus 0.27 sec per fur (GF)

				SP	RR	SF
	Queen of Spades (IRE) (NATwiston-Davies) **6-10-9** CLlewellyn (lw: mde all: qcknd 6th: clr next: unchal)	—	1	Evens[1]	94+	24
	Endowment (MrsMReveley) **4-10-11**(3) GCahill (lw: outpcd & drvn along 5th: styd on fr next: chsd wnr fr 3 out: no imp)	18	2	20/1	81	11
1049[2]	**Mithraic (IRE) (97)** (WSCunningham) **4-10-11**(7) LMcGrath (t: a in tch: styd on one pce fr 3 out)	5	3	8/1[3]	80	10
1030[F]	**Durano** (TDEasterby) **5-11-0** LWyer (lw: sn prom: wnt 2nd after 6th: wknd appr next)	1¼	4	6/1[2]	75	5
341[2]	**Samanid (IRE) (112)** (MissLCSiddall) **4-11-4** CMaude (chsd ldrs tl wknd fr 3 out)	1¼	5	9/1	78	8
1050[10]	**Last Try (IRE)** (BSRothwell) **5-11-0** BPowell (racd wd: jnd ldrs 5th: wknd appr 3 out)	7	6	50/1	67	—
	L'Equipe (IRE) (CJMann) **6-11-0** RDunwoody (hld up: stdy hdwy 5th: drvn along next: sn lost pl)	7	7	11/1	60	—
	Penrose Lad (NZ) (DNicholson) **6-11-0** AMaguire (a in rr)	½	8	8/1[3]	59	—
876[6]	**Blanc Seing (FR)** (JESwiers) **9-11-0b** MrSSwiers (bit bkwd: lost pl 4th: sn drvn along: wl bhd fr 3 out)	9	9	50/1	50	—
	Clever Boy (IRE) (JWCurtis) **5-10-11**(3) FLeahy (bit bkwd: chsd ldrs tl wknd qckly after 6th: sn bhd)	13	10	50/1	37	—
	Hopeful Lord (IRE) (PCheesbrough) **4-10-7**(7) MrSPHennessy (bit bkwd: fell 1st)		F	50/1	—	—
	Dont Forget Curtis (IRE) (GMMoore) **4-11-0** NBentley (bhd fr 5th: 6th & styd on whn fell 3 out)		F	50/1	—	—
	B The One (JJQuinn) **5-11-0** DerekByrne (hmpd 1st: bhd whn p.u after 3rd)		P	14/1	—	—
				(SP 126.1%)	**13 Rn**	

3m 44.8 (2.80) CSF £21.81 TOTE £2.00: £1.30 £4.10 £1.90 (£22.30) Trio £96.10 OWNER Mrs R. Vaughan (CHELTENHAM) BRED William McCarthy
OFFICIAL EXPLANATION **B The One: had lost his action.**
Queen of Spades (IRE), a winner of two bumpers, is a grand type of mare. Making her own running and jumping particularly well, she had her race won some way from home. She scored in a time almost four seconds faster than Direct Route in the handicap later in the day and it is no wonder her trainer regards her as something special. (Evens)
Endowment struggled to keep up at halfway. Keeping on over the last three to finish clear second best, he will be suited by two and a half miles. (20/1)
1049 Mithraic (IRE), who has been tubed, ran as well as could be expected under his penalty. (8/1)
1030 Durano had his limitations exposed in this much stronger company. (6/1: op 3/1)
341 Samanid (IRE) (9/1: 11/2-10/1)
L'Equipe (IRE) (11/1: 8/1-12/1)

1153 ARTHUR STEPHENSON NOVICES' H'CAP CHASE (5-Y.O+) (Class C)
1-20 (1-20) **2m 4f 110y (15 fncs)** £4,589.50 (£1,381.00: £668.00: £311.50) GOING minus 0.27 sec per fur (GF)

				SP	RR	SF
	Potter's Bay (IRE) (105) (DNicholson) **7-11-10** AMaguire (stdd s: hld up & bhd: stdy hdwy 11th: led 2 out: pushed out flat)	—	1	2/1[1]	112+	55
	Random Harvest (IRE) (92) (MrsMReveley) **7-10-11** RDunwoody (prom: blnd 5th: led appr 3 out to 2 out: no ch w wnr)	2	2	3/1[2]	97	40
	Rye Crossing (IRE) (96) (TDEasterby) **6-11-1** LWyer (bit bkwd: prom early: sn bhd: styd on u.p fr 3 out)	16	3	9/2[3]	89	32

	Horse	Dist	Pos	SP	RR	SF
	Tico Gold (82) (PCheesbrough) **8-9-12**(3)ow1 GCahill (outpcd 6th: hdwy 3 out: styd on one pce)	hd	**4**	16/1	75	17
907^{5}	**Cool Weather (IRE) (86)** (PCheesbrough) **8-10-5** ASSmith (jnd ldr 6th: outpcd fr 3 out)	1¾	**5**	20/1	78	21
	Grundon (IRE) (84) (MrsLCTaylor) **7-10-3b**ow1 GUpton (led & mstke 2nd: hdd appr 3 out: sn wknd)	11	**6**	20/1	67	9
746^{3}	**Camp Bank (81)** (NATwiston-Davies) **6-10-0** CLlewellyn (w ldrs: hit 4th: drvn along 8th: wknd after 11th)	1¼	**7**	11/2	63	6
746^{4}	**Final Beat (IRE) (82)** (JWCurtis) **7-10-1** CO'Dwyer (chsd ldrs tl lost pl after 11th)	10	**8**	10/1	56	—
950^{11}	**Theydon Pride (81)** (KFClutterbuck) **7-10-0** TJMurphy (w ldrs tl wknd 11th: bhd whn blnd next)	2½	**9**	100/1	53	—
				(SP 117.4%)		**9 Rn**

5m 6.2 (-0.80) CSF £8.32 CT £21.63 TOTE £2.80: £1.50 £1.50 £1.90 (£5.90) Trio £10.70 OWNER Mrs J. E. Potter (TEMPLE GUITING) BRED Colman O'Flynn

LONG HANDICAP Tico Gold 9-10 Theydon Pride 8-10

Potter's Bay (IRE), a winner twice over hurdles last season, was most impressive on this chasing debut. Dropped in at the start and given a patient ride, he jumped soundly. Travelling best some way from home, he had only to be pushed out even under topweight. Connections will have been delighted by this. (2/1)

Random Harvest (IRE) survived one bad mistake. Sticking on under pressure, he was the only one to make a race of it with the winner and is sure to win races, especially over three miles. (3/1)

Rye Crossing (IRE) seemed to drop himself right out. With only one behind him three out, he finished to some purpose and, provided he takes to this game, he is sure to make his mark. (9/2)

Tico Gold, out of the handicap and carrying overweight, is no lost cause. All he does is stay. (16/1)

907 Cool Weather (IRE) is still a maiden over fences after seventeen attempts. (20/1)

1154 STANLEY RACING H'CAP HURDLE (0-135) (4-Y.O+) (Class C)

1-50 (1-51) **2m (9 hdls)** £3,710.50 (£1,114.00: £537.00: £248.50) GOING minus 0.27 sec per fur (GF)

	Horse	Dist	Pos	SP	RR	SF
908^{4}	**Direct Route (IRE) (122)** (HowardJohnson) **5-11-2** AMaguire (hld up: stdy hdwy 6th: led 2 out: pushed clr: eased towards fin)	—	**1**	11/8 1	106+	13
	Fourth in Line (IRE) (129) (MJWilkinson) **8-11-9** RDunwoody (led to 3 out: no ch w wnr)	5	**2**	6/1 3	108	15
	Kaitak (IRE) (121) (JMCarr) **5-10-12**(3) FLeahy (chsd ldrs: kpt on one pce fr 3 out)	4	**3**	6/1 3	96	3
908*	**Desert Fighter (111)** (MrsMReveley) **5-10-2**(3) GCahill (lw: chsd ldr: pushed along 5th: wknd 3 out: wl btn whn blnd next)	4	**4**	9/4 2	82	—
945^{5}	**Cumbrian Challenge (IRE) (134)** (TDEasterby) **7-12-0** LWyer (bhd: stdy hdwy 6th: wknd next)	¾	**5**	13/2	104	11
				(SP 114.8%)		**5 Rn**

3m 48.7 (6.70) CSF £9.27 TOTE £2.20: £1.50 £2.30 (£7.80) OWNER Mr Chris Heron (CROOK) BRED Mrs Noeleen Roche

908 Direct Route (IRE) showed the benefit of his initial outing and won this easing down, having been travelling best some way from home. (11/8)

Fourth in Line (IRE) was having his first outing for Mark Wilkinson after changing hands for 25,000 guineas. He looked just in need of the outing and is better suited by more give underfoot. (6/1)

Kaitak (IRE) looked and ran as if possibly just in need of the outing. (6/1)

908* Desert Fighter, turned out in tip-top trim, showed that he has two ways of running, never looking happy. (9/4)

945 Cumbrian Challenge (IRE) is not very big to be shouldering twelve stone and will no doubt soon revert to fences. (13/2)

1155 PETERHOUSE GROUP H'CAP CHASE (0-145) (5-Y.O+) (Class B)

2-20 (2-20) **2m 4f 110y (15 fncs)** £7,230.00 (£2,030.00: £990.00) GOING minus 0.27 sec per fur (GF)

	Horse	Dist	Pos	SP	RR	SF
1055^{4}	**Stately Home (IRE) (118)** (PBowen) **5-10-6** RDunwoody (mde all: lft clr 8th: blnd 2 out: unchal)	—	**1**	7/1 3	122	29
	Joe White (119) (HowardJohnson) **10-10-8** ASSmith (in tch: lft 2nd 8th: one pce fr 4 out)	10	**2**	14/1	115	23
946^{2}	**Bertone (IRE) (135)** (KCBailey) **7-11-10** CO'Dwyer (blnd 4th: hmpd 8th: wnt mod 2nd 11th: wknd & eased last)	14	**3**	11/8 2	120	28
	Hill of Tullow (IRE) (139) (DNicholson) **7-12-0** AMaguire (lw: trckd wnr tl fell 8th)		**F**	6/5 1	—	—
				(SP 106.7%)		**4 Rn**

5m 5.3 (-1.70) CSF £47.44 TOTE £6.10: (£13.70) OWNER Mr P. Bowen (HAVERFORDWEST) BRED Ash Hill Stud

WEIGHT FOR AGE 5yo-1lb

951 Stately Home (IRE) thrives on his racing and is still only five. After the melee at the eighth, he virtually only had to put in a clear round. (7/1: 5/1-8/1)

Joe White jumped soundly and will be suited by the big fences when he returns to Aintree, the scene of his John Hughes Memorial success. (14/1: 10/1-16/1)

946 Bertone (IRE) had already made one bad mistake when almost brought down by Hill of Tullow, and was fighting a losing battle from there on. (11/8)

Hill of Tullow (IRE) took a crashing fall at the eighth, but hopefully will be none the worse for it. (6/5: evens-5/4)

1156 TOTE WEST YORKSHIRE HURDLE (Gd 2) (4-Y.O+) (Class A)

2-50 (2-50) **3m 1f (12 hdls)** £12,500.00 (£4,730.00: £2,315.00: £1,055.00) GOING minus 0.27 sec per fur (GF)

	Horse	Dist	Pos	SP	RR	SF
	Trainglot (145) (JGFitzGerald) **9-11-0** RDunwoody (trckd ldrs: shkn up to ld 2 out: qcknd clr flat)	—	**1**	7/4 1	132+	27
	What a Question (IRE) (MFMorris,Ireland) **8-10-9** CO'Dwyer (trckd ldrs: led 9th to 2 out: no ch w wnr)	8	**2**	2/1 2	122	17
	Difficult Times (IRE) (GMLyons,Ireland) **4-10-13** LWyer (lw: led to 2nd: led 8th to next: sn wl outpcd)	14	**3**	5/1 3	118	12
745*	**Non Vintage (IRE) (132)** (MCChapman) **5-11-0** WWorthington (outpcd & drvn along 6th: kpt on fr 3 out: n.d)	20	**4**	16/1	105	—
	Treasure Again (IRE) (140) (MrsMerritaJones) **7-11-4** DerekByrne (nt j.w: led 2nd to 8th: wknd after next)	12	**5**	11/2	101	—
945^{4}	**Our Kris (130)** (MESowersby) **4-10-13** ASSmith (lw: bhd fr 7th: t.o)	dist	**6**	25/1	—	—
1030^{12}	**Past Master (USA) (92)** (SGollings) **8-11-0** AMaguire (bhd fr 6th: t.o 8th: p.u bef 3 out)		**P**	100/1	—	—
				(SP 112.5%)		**7 Rn**

5m 58.1 (2.00 under best) (5.10) CSF £5.45 TOTE £2.40: £1.80 £1.70 (£3.00) OWNER Marquesa de Moratalla (MALTON) BRED Marquesa de Moratalla

WEIGHT FOR AGE 4yo-1lb

Trainglot, fit from the Flat, had to put about his job but, in the end, did it in good style. He lacks the size and substance to carry big weights in handicaps. (7/4)

What a Question (IRE) made the best of her way home, but it was obvious some way out that the winner would have too much foot for her. (2/1)

Difficult Times (IRE) lacks size and, once the race began in earnest, was easily swept aside. (5/1)

745* Non Vintage (IRE) ran as well as could be expected, considering he would have been receiving almost a stone from Trainglot in a handicap. (16/1)

Treasure Again (IRE) looked to have a stiff task under his penalty. Despite looking fit, he was let down by his jumping and dropped right away on the home turn. (11/2)

1157 CHARLIE HALL CHASE (Gd 2) (5-Y.O+) (Class A)

3-25 (3-25) **3m 1f (18 fncs)** £18,300.00 (£6,922.50: £3,386.25: £1,541.25) GOING minus 0.27 sec per fur (GF)

				SP	RR	SF
	One Man (IRE) (175) (GRichards) **8-11-10** RDunwoody (hld up: smooth hdwy to ld 4 out: pushed clr flat)	—	**1**	8/11[1]	170	—
	Barton Bank (157) (DNicholson) **10-11-10** AMaguire (lw: led: hit 9th: hdd 4 out: styd on: no ch w wnr)	7	**2**	6/1	166	—
	Young Hustler (155) (NATwiston-Davies) **9-11-2** CMaude (chsd ldrs: pushed along 14th: wl outpcd appr next)	6	**3**	11/2[3]	154	—
	Scotton Banks (IRE) (163) (TDEasterby) **7-11-10** LWyer (lw: chsd ldrs: shkn up 9th: lost pl 11th: hdwy u.p & prom 14th: wknd appr next)	14	**4**	5/1[2]	153	—
				(SP 104.2%)		**4 Rn**

6m 11.4 CSF £4.51 TOTE £1.60: (£3.10) OWNER Mr J. Hales (PENRITH) BRED Hugh J. Holohan

One Man (IRE) looked on good terms with himself and if anything on the big side. Jumping really well and racing keenly, he looked like winning by a wide margin up the home straight but, after hitting the front, tended to idle and, pushed out, there did not seem to a lot in hand at the line. After one or two more outings, he will attempt to repeat his win in the King George Chase on Boxing Day. Whether he finds sufficient at the end of his races to come up the hill at Cheltenham, only time will tell. (8/11)

Barton Bank, attempting to win this race for the third time in five years, set a strong pace and jumped better than on many occasions in the past but, even so, the winner still proved much too good. (6/1)

Young Hustler, a reliable sort, is not quite as good as he once was and has now only won once in his last seventeen starts. (11/2)

Scotton Banks (IRE) seemed to run in snatches. He looked fit beforehand but hopefully this outing will have blown away the cobwebs because he is certainly very useful on his day. (5/1)

1158 WENSEYDALE HURDLE (Gd 2) (3-Y.O) (Class A)

4-00 (4-00) **2m (9 hdls)** £9,690.00 (£3,668.25: £1,796.63: £820.12) GOING minus 0.27 sec per fur (GF)

				SP	RR	SF
	Bellator (GBBalding) **3-10-12** BFenton (hld up: stdy hdwy 5th: led 3 out: readily)	—	**1**	4/1[3]	86+	15
906[5]	**Jackson Park** (TDEasterby) **3-10-12** LWyer (w ldr: led 4th: hdd & hit 3 out: kpt on: no ch w wnr)	8	**2**	16/1	78	7
912[4]	**Hever Golf Diamond** (TJNaughton) **3-10-12** RDunwoody (hld up: stdy hdwy 5th: kpt on same pce fr 3 out)	3	**3**	16/1	75	4
1014*	**Kerawi** (NATwiston-Davies) **3-11-2** CLlewellyn (w ldrs: rdn & lost pl 5th: sme hdwy appr 3 out: sn no ch)	12	**4**	6/5[1]	67	—
906*	**Lagan** (KAMorgan) **3-11-2** ASSmith (trckd ldrs: ev ch 3 out: wknd appr next)	¾	**5**	7/2[2]	66	—
646[3]	**Prelude To Fame (USA)** (MissMKMilligan) **3-10-12** AMaguire (in tch: lost pl after 5th)	1¾	**6**	14/1	61	—
	Six Clerks (IRE) (JGFitzGerald) **3-10-12** FLeahy (bit bkwd: in tch: hmpd 4th: hdwy u.p 6th: sn wknd)	7	**7**	25/1	54	—
874*	**Hobbs Choice** (GMMoore) **3-10-7** NBentley (bhd: hdwy 5th: rdn & wknd appr 3 out)	nk	**8**	33/1	48	—
	Sizzling Symphony (RAFahey) **3-10-12** DerekByrne (hld up: a bhd: t.o)	dist	**9**	66/1	—	—
	Gulf of Siam (MissSEHall) **3-10-12** DBentley (prom whn blnd 4th: sn bhd: t.o whn p.u bef 2 out)		**P**	25/1	—	—
803*	**Kernof (IRE)** (MDHammond) **3-11-2b** CO'Dwyer (mde most tl mstke & hdd 4th: wknd qckly after 6th: bhd whn p.u bef 2 out)		**P**	14/1	—	—
906[7]	**Phantom Dancer (IRE)** (MESowersby) **3-10-12** GCahill (bhd: t.o whn p.u bef 3 out)		**P**	50/1	—	—
				(SP 126.9%)		**12 Rn**

3m 47.3 (5.30) CSF £62.98 TOTE £5.20: £1.90 £3.60 £3.90 (£56.60) Trio £373.90 OWNER Mr P. Richardson (ANDOVER) BRED Theakston Stud

Bellator looked a useful recruit and took this in fine style. The Levy Board must have plenty of money because this race carried £15,000 added. The same field would have lined up for a third as much. (4/1)

906 Jackson Park ran and jumped much better than on his debut, but the winner still proved much too good. (16/1)

912 Hever Golf Diamond was only fourth in a claimer last time and this emphasised the modest form of this race which carried an inflated prize. (16/1)

1014* Kerawi, a Flat type, showed a good action going down, but was struggling badly to get into the contest after losing ground at the fifth. (6/5: evens-10/11)

906* Lagan had his limitations exposed under his penalty. (7/2)

803* Kernof (IRE) (14/1: op 8/1)

T/Plpt: £123.40 (106.47 Tckts). T/Qdpt: £25.90 (23.36 Tckts). WG

NEWCASTLE (L-H) (Good to firm, Good patches)

Monday November 4th

WEATHER: fine WIND: STR

1159 'BARBOUR' NORTHUMBRIA HURDLE (3-Y.O) (Class E)

1-25 (1-26) **2m (8 hdls)** £2,274.00 (£639.00: £312.00) GOING minus 0.42 sec per fur (GF)

				SP	RR	SF
874[2]	**Silent Guest (IRE)** (MDHammond) **3-10-12** RGarritty (led: hit 3 out: mstke 2 out: sn hdd: lft in ld last: all out)	—	**1**	3/1[2]	60	26
	The Boozing Brief (USA) (CParker) **3-10-12** DParker (lw: chsd wnr fr 3rd: chal 5th: rdn & outpcd after 4 out: lft 2nd last: hrd rdn & no ex)	2	**2**	6/4[1]	58	24
852*	**Double Dash (IRE)** (DMoffatt) **3-11-5** DJMoffatt (lw: mstkes: lost tch fr 4th)	11	**3**	7/1	54	20
	Rattle (JJO'Neill) **3-10-12** ARoche (chsd ldrs tl outpcd fr 3 out)	7	**4**	20/1	40	6
906[9]	**Lucky Bea** (MWEasterby) **3-10-9(3)** PMidgley (lw: a.p: led after 2 out tl fell last)		**F**	4/1[3]	59?	—
	Duntalkin (JMJefferson) **3-10-9ow2** RichardGuest (bit bkwd: t.o fr 3rd: p.u bef last)		**P**	12/1	—	—
				(SP 110.0%)		**6 Rn**

3m 52.8 (0.80) CSF £7.52 TOTE £3.10: £1.90 £1.10 (£2.80) OWNER Mrs Patricia Wilson (MIDDLEHAM) BRED Eamon and Mary Salmon

874 Silent Guest (IRE) made this a real test of stamina and that won him the day. He might well still have won had Lucky Bea not fallen at the last. (3/1)

The Boozing Brief (USA) was a shade disappointing. Off the bit some way out, he struggled on, but was never good enough. Perhaps experience will improve him. (6/4)

852* Double Dash (IRE) was clumsy and was soon left behind. Although making a little late progress when the leaders tired, he never had a hope. (7/1)

Rattle has not been out for over three months and ran out of fuel approaching the third last. He has yet to win a race of any kind. (20/1)

906 Lucky Bea had just taken it up, but was so tired that he collapsed on landing at the last. It was doubtful whether he would have lasted home had he remained upright. (4/1)

1160 'BARBOUR' BEDALE NOVICES' CHASE (5-Y.O+) (Class E)

1-55 (1-55) **3m (19 fncs)** £2,918.00 (£884.00: £432.00: £206.00) GOING minus 0.07 sec per fur (G)

	Horse		SP	RR	SF
	Billsbrook (RBrewis) **6-10-12** KJohnson (w ldr: led & blnd 12th: hdd 4 out: led 3 out: styd on wl) .....—	1	14/1	96	—
1022[4]	**Bold Account (IRE) (99)** (GMMoore) **6-10-12** NBentley (led 4th tl blnd & hdd 12th: led 4 out: hdd & mstke next: sn rdn & no ex) 8	2	11/8[2]	91	—
	Trickle Lad (IRE) (FMurphy) **7-10-9**(3) KGaule (hld up: hdwy whn hit 15th: mstke next: sn rdn & no imp) 2	3	5/4[1]	89	—
	Broomhill Duker (IRE) (HowardJohnson) **6-10-12** NWilliamson (led to 4th: chsd ldrs tl blnd bdly 13th: hdwy 4 out: one pce fr 2 out) 3	4	66/1	87	—
1130[6]	**Quixall Crossett (56)** (EMCaine) **11-10-12** MrPMurray (outpcd & bhd fr 14th) 21	5	66/1	73	—
875[3]	**Bardaros** (MissLucindaRussell) **7-10-12** AThornton (mstkes: in tch tl wknd 15th: p.u bef 2 out)	P	6/1[3]	—	—
			(SP 110.5%)		**6 Rn**

6m 17.1 (25.10) CSF £32.24 TOTE £15.40: £2.00 £1.30 (£14.30) OWNER Mr R. Brewis (BELFORD) BRED Mrs R. Brewis

Billsbrook, after over a year off, looked likely to be all the better for this, but he did the job well and hopefully this is only the start of things for him. (14/1)

1022 Bold Account (IRE) took the winner on, but was getting the worst of the exchanges when a mistake three out finished him. The experience should stand him in good stead. (11/8)

Trickle Lad (IRE), from a yard not firing as yet, probably needed this and should benefit from it. (5/4: op 4/6)

Broomhill Duker (IRE) virtually put himself out of it with a terrible blunder at the thirteenth and did well to almost get back into it. Provided he has not done himself any damage, he should certainly pick up a race or two. (66/1)

907 Quixall Crossett again had his lack of pace exposed. (66/1)

875 Bardaros, whose jumping went to pieces, was wisely pulled up. (6/1: 5/1-8/1)

1161 'BARBOUR' BURGHLEY NOVICES' HURDLE (4-Y.O+) (Class E)

2-25 (2-27) **2m 4f (10 hdls)** £2,274.00 (£639.00: £312.00) GOING minus 0.07 sec per fur (G)

	Horse		SP	RR	SF
	Stan's Your Man (MrsJDGoodfellow) **6-10-9**(3) GCahill (mde all: hung lft appr 2 out: styd on strly) .....—	1	7/1[2]	74+	17
1021*	**Shanavogh (98)** (GMMoore) **5-11-5** JCallaghan (lw: trckd ldrs: wnt 2nd & mstke 3 out: sn hrd drvn: hit last: nt qckn) 3½	2	4/9[1]	78	21
630[3]	**Leap in the Dark (IRE) (78)** (MissLCSiddall) **7-10-12** AThornton (a cl up: rdn appr 3 out: r.o one pce) 4	3	14/1	68	11
1046[4]	**Hotspur Street** (MWEasterby) **4-10-12** LWyer (lw: in tch: hdwy 4 out: blnd 2 out: no imp) 5	4	9/1[3]	64	7
	Fingerhill (IRE) (VThompson) **7-10-12** MrMThompson (cl up: one pce fr 4 out) 13	5	100/1	54	—
	Joe Jagger (IRE) (MDHammond) **5-10-12** RGarritty (prom tl wknd appr 3 out) 1½	6	20/1	52	—
	Noble Monarch (IRE) (HowardJohnson) **7-10-12** NWilliamson (hld up: stdd after 5th: hit 7th: hdwy 4 out: sn rdn & btn) .....s.h	7	50/1	52	—
	Castle Red (IRE) (JWade) **5-10-12** KJones (chsd ldrs tl rdn & wknd fr 4 out) 4	8	9/1[3]	49	—
	Tibbi Blues (WStorey) **9-10-7** MMoloney (blnd 1st: a bhd: p.u bef 3 out)	P	14/1	—	—
			(SP 122.8%)		**9 Rn**

4m 58.7 (10.70) CSF £10.84 TOTE £6.70: £1.70 £1.40 £1.70 (£4.10) Trio £24.60 OWNER Mrs J. D. Goodfellow (EARLSTON) BRED Mrs J. D. Goodfellow

Stan's Your Man, a big, plain sort, just jumps and gallops and, despite running green early in the straight, kept on strongly. Plenty more will be seen of him, especially when he goes chasing. (7/1)

1021* Shanavogh had his chances, but made a mistake when trying to match the winner three out and was fighting a lost cause from then on.(4/9)

630 Leap in the Dark (IRE), whose Flat form was disappointing last season, is certainly showing more enthusiasm for this game at present. (14/1)

1046 Hotspur Street is proving a shade disappointing and a blunder two out cost him any faint hopes of a place. (9/1: op 6/1)

Fingerhill (IRE) ran reasonably, racing up with the pace until blowing up in the home straight. (100/1)

Joe Jagger (IRE) had the benefit of a run on the Flat recently, but still seemed to need this and stopped in the home straight. (20/1)

Castle Red (IRE) (9/1: op 6/1)

1162 'BARBOUR' DURHAM H'CAP CHASE (0-125) (5-Y.O+) (Class D)

2-55 (2-56) **3m (19 fncs)** £3,501.25 (£1,060.00: £517.50: £246.25) GOING minus 0.07 sec per fur (G)

	Horse		SP	RR	SF
	Aly Daley (IRE) (97) (HowardJohnson) **8-10-0** NWilliamson (mde virtually all: hit 1st & 10th: rdn along fr 12th: styd on gamely fr 4 out) .....—	1	6/1	108	32
2[P]	**Ceilidh Boy (120)** (MrsJDGoodfellow) **10-11-9** ASSmith (a.p: ev ch fr 12th: mstke 4 out: hit 2 out: kpt on towards fin) .....¾	2	14/1	131	55
	Strong Deel (IRE) (119) (FMurphy) **8-11-8** MFoster (bit bkwd: trckd ldrs: hit 12th: chal & hit 16th: 3rd & hrd rdn whn blnd last) 12	3	4/1[3]	122	46
869[2]	**Ali's Alibi (117)** (MrsMReveley) **9-11-6** PNiven (bhd: effrt 15th: sn prom & hrd drvn: no imp fr 4 out) 3½	4	9/4[1]	117	41
	High Padre (125) (JGFitzGerald) **10-11-11**(3) FLeahy (lw: chsd ldrs: reminders 9th: hdwy to disp ld next: mstke 12th & sn lost pl) 2	5	4/1[3]	124	48
1024[6]	**Greenhill Raffles (122)** (MissLucindaRussell) **10-11-11** AThornton (chsd ldrs tl blnd bdly & wknd 15th) 26	6	100/1	104	28
1024[3]	**Gale Ahead (IRE) (100)** (GMMoore) **6-10-3**ow2 NBentley (blnd & uns rdr 1st)	U	7/2[2]	—	—
			(SP 114.9%)		**7 Rn**

5m 56.0 (4.00) CSF £67.11 TOTE £5.90: £2.70 £4.80 (£38.50) OWNER Mr Michael Tobitt (CROOK) BRED Pat Holohan

Aly Daley (IRE) was given a brilliant ride and, although off the bit some way out and making some mistakes, he kept going in game fashion to hold on really well. (6/1)

2 Ceilidh Boy has had problems with his jumping, but was much improved and a repeat of this will surely see him back on the winning trail. (14/1)

Strong Deel (IRE) got it all wrong last season and has now changed stables. It looked as though he might well be coming back to form with this promising effort. (4/1)

869 Ali's Alibi is a funny customer who is never one to rely on, but he has plenty of ability when in the mood and that was not the case here. (9/4)

High Padre looked well enough, but ran in snatches. This was not his true form. (4/1)

1024 Greenhill Raffles has lost his way at the moment. (100/1)

1163 'BARBOUR' BILLY BOW H'CAP HURDLE (0-125) (4-Y.O+) (Class D)

3-25 (3-25) **2m (8 hdls)** £2,752.20 (£769.20: £372.60) GOING minus 0.42 sec per fur (GF)

				SP	RR	SF
941*	**Tom Brodie (115)** (HowardJohnson) **6-11-11** NWilliamson (a gng wl: stdy hdwy to ld 2 out: shkn up & r.o flat)	—	1	7/4[1]	95	49
908[5]	**Done Well (USA) (118)** (PMonteith) **4-12-0** ADobbin (hld up & bhd: hdwy 3 out: ev ch last: kpt on u.p)	1¼	2	3/1[3]	97	51
806[2]	**Bures (IRE) (110)** (MrsJBrown) **5-10-13**(7) BGrattan (led to 2 out: kpt on)	¾	3	8/1	88	42
908[6]	**Shining Edge (110)** (TDEasterby) **4-11-6** LWyer (trckd ldrs: ev ch appr 3 out: rdn & fnd nil 2 out)	4	4	7/1	84	38
	Once More for Luck (IRE) (113) (MrsMReveley) **5-11-9** PNiven (lw: trckd ldrs tl j.slowly & outpcd 4 out: btn whn blnd 2 out)	21	5	5/2[2]	66	20
				(SP 113.5%)		**5 Rn**

3m 50.3 (-1.70) CSF £7.21 TOTE £2.20: £2.50 £1.10 (£4.20) OWNER Mrs M. W. Bird (CROOK) BRED E.S Knape

941* Tom Brodie travelled on the bridle and, always having the edge, found plenty when ridden. (7/4)

908 Done Well (USA) likes to come from behind, but was having to struggle to get there in the straight, and the winner had the edge on him throughout. (3/1)

806 Bures (IRE) is running consistently well, although he is continually tapped for toe in the closing stages. (8/1: 6/1-9/1)

908 Shining Edge looked to be going well until an effort was required over the last three flights, from which point he soon cried enough. (7/1)

Once More for Luck (IRE) has bags of ability, but took a dislike to things on this occasion and would have none of it when asked a question. (5/2)

1164 W.K. BACKHOUSE AMATEUR H'CAP CHASE (0-115) (5-Y.O+) (Class E)

3-55 (3-55) **2m 110y (13 fncs)** £2,801.00 (£848.00: £414.00: £197.00) GOING minus 0.07 sec per fur (G)

				SP	RR	SF
1082*	**Blazing Dawn (88)** (JSHubbuck) **9-10-10**(7) 7x MissPRobson (a.p: rdn to ld last: styd on wl)	—	1	4/1[3]	101	33
895[2]	**Thunderstruck (82)** (HowardJohnson) **10-10-4**(7) MrRThornton (led: hit 2 out: hdd last: no ex)	4	2	5/2[2]	91	23
	Vicaridge (95) (RBrewis) **9-11-3**(7) MrARobson (bit bkwd: chsd ldrs: hit 10th: one pce fr 4 out)	7	3	9/4[1]	97	29
	Auburn Boy (91) (MWEasterby) **9-11-3**(3) MrCBonner (lw: nt j.w: bhd: effrt 6th: sn outpcd)	14	4	5/2[2]	80	12
	Monaughty Man (85) (EMCaine) **10-10-7**(7) MrPMurray (in tch: outpcd whn hit 6th: sn bhd: t.o whn blnd & uns rdr 4 out)		U	40/1	—	—
				(SP 110.4%)		**5 Rn**

4m 4.0 (6.00) CSF £13.35 TOTE £4.30: £2.30 £1.20 (£3.70) OWNER Mr J. S. Hubbuck (HEXHAM) BRED Mrs J. Wilkinson

1082* Blazing Dawn has come good of late but, although this trip was a bit on the short side, he was suited by the strong pace to be well on top by the finish. (4/1)

895 Thunderstruck, a strong-pulling front-runner, again failed to last home. (5/2)

Vicaridge looked likely to benefit from this and found this trip too sharp. He should be kept in mind for a return to form. (9/4)

Auburn Boy looked really well, but would not have a cut at his fences and was soon out of it. (5/2: op 6/4)

T/Plpt: £49.60 (196.28 Tckts). T/Qdpt: £17.80 (61.15 Tckts). AA

0956-PLUMPTON (L-H) (Soft, Heavy home st)
Monday November 4th

WEATHER: unsettled & heavy rain

1165 STANMER MAIDEN HURDLE (4-Y.O+) (Class F)

1-35 (1-35) **2m 4f (12 hdls)** £2,156.60 (£597.60: £285.80) GOING: 1.55 sec per fur (HY)

				SP	RR	SF
	Bayerd (IRE) (CREgerton) **5-11-5** JOsborne (a.p: led 2 out: all out)	—	1	11/2[3]	73	27
955[3]	**Flying Fiddler (IRE) (97)** (MJRoberts) **5-11-5** BPowell (lw: hdwy appr 3 out: rdn appr 2 out: chsd wnr appr last: unable qckn)	1¾	2	2/1[2]	72	26
	Second Step (IRE) (DRGandolfo) **5-11-5** RDunwoody (bit bkwd: hdwy appr 3 out: rdn appr 2 out: wknd appr last)	12	3	6/1	62	16
	Bella Sedona (LadyHerries) **4-11-0** EMurphy (hld up: chsd ldr fr 8th: led appr 3 out to 2 out: wknd appr last)	2½	4	6/4[1]	55	9
968[4]	**Decor (IRE)** (RJHodges) **6-11-2**(3) TDascombe (led tl appr 3 out: sn wknd)	17	5	10/1	46	—
718[10]	**Caulkin (IRE)** (ABarrow) **5-11-5** DBridgwater (a bhd)	½	6	40/1	46	—
	Upham Rascal (60) (DRGandolfo) **5-11-5** DLeahy (lw: chsd ldr to 8th: wknd 9th)	1	7	33/1	45	—
				(SP 117.5%)		**7 Rn**

5m 28.7 (41.70) CSF £16.89 TOTE £9.10: £4.10 £2.00 (£14.90) Trio £6.20 OWNER Mr J. J. King (CHADDLEWORTH) BRED Cornelius Nyhan

IN-FOCUS: With an inch and a quarter the night before, the ground was extremely testing and this was borne out by the times, the first race was nearly 50 seconds outside the course record.

Bayerd (IRE), off the track for six months, made a winning debut over hurdles, despite finishing very tired indeed. (11/2: 4/1-6/1)

955 Flying Fiddler (IRE) struggled into second approaching the last, but was very leg weary and unable to peg back the winner. (2/1: 5/4-5/2)

Second Step (IRE) did not looking fully wound up for this first run in over thirteen months. (6/1: 3/1-13/2)

Bella Sedona, fit from the Flat, appeared to be travelling sweetly as she cruised into the lead approaching the third last, but stopped quickly when collared. (6/4)

1166 BALCOMBE CONDITIONAL (S) H'CAP HURDLE (0-95) (4-Y.O+) (Class G)

2-05 (2-05) **2m 1f (10 hdls)** £1,859.00 (£514.00: £245.00) GOING: 1.55 sec per fur (HY)

				SP	RR	SF
888[4]	**Minster's Madam (81)** (JNeville) **5-11-9v** TDascombe (w ldr: led 3rd: clr 7th: unchal)	—	1	9/4[1]	75?	14
	Rachael's Owen (85) (CWeedon) **6-11-13** GHogan (hdwy to chse wnr fr 7th: no imp)	dist	2	5/2[2]	—	—
	Bresil (USA) (58) (KRBurke) **7-9-7**(7) MarkBrown (lw: hdwy 6th: wknd 7th: t.o)	30	3	14/1	—	—
899[8]	**Against The Clock (58)** (CLPopham) **4-9-7b**[1](7) TO'Connor (prom to 6th)	5	4	20/1	—	—
1007[3]	**Alosaili (78)** (JCullinan) **9-11-6** DFortt (lw: a bhd: t.o)	1¾	5	3/1[3]	—	—
950[5]	**Twice the Groom (IRE) (86)** (RLee) **6-11-9b**(5) MGriffiths (bhd fr 6th: t.o)	5	6	5/1	—	—

Form	Horse	Dist	Pos	SP	RR	SF
975^{P}	**Red Match (61)** (RJHodges) **11-9-12**(5) JHarris (led to 3rd: wknd 6th: in rr whn blnd 7th: t.o)	dist	7	33/1	—	—

(SP 115.4%) **7 Rn**

4m 35.3 (39.30) CSF £8.20 TOTE £2.80: £2.20 £2.70 (£5.00) OWNER Mr J. Neville (NEWPORT, GWENT) BRED Heathfields Farm
LONG HANDICAP Against The Clock 9-11
No bid
Minster's Madam, whose three previous wins all came in the mud, revelled in the conditions and was given a lovely ride. (9/4)
Rachael's Owen, who has changed stables since last season, struggled into a remote second early in the back straight. (5/2: op 5/4)
Bresil (USA) (14/1: op 6/1)
950 Twice the Groom (IRE) (5/1: 4/1-6/1)

1167 JOLLY TANNERS AT STAPLEFIELD H'CAP CHASE (0-120) (5-Y.O+) (Class D)
2-35 (2-36) **2m 5f (16 fncs)** £3,947.40 (£1,091.40: £520.20) GOING: 1.11 sec per fur (HY)

Form	Horse	Dist	Pos	SP	RR	SF
	Beau Babillard (110) (PFNicholls) **9-11-6b** APMcCoy (a.p: led 12th: drvn out)	—	1	4/1^{3}	121	54
959*	**Zambezi Spirit (IRE) (95)** (MrsMerritaJones) **7-10-5** DerekByrne (hdwy & pckd 6th: led 9th: mstke 11th: hdd 12th: rdn appr 2 out: unable qckn)	2	2	15/8^{1}	105	38
	Mr Matt (IRE) (105) (DMGrissell) **8-11-1** BFenton (pckd 1st: hdwy 10th: wknd 12th: t.o)	dist	3	16/1	—	—
	Really a Rascal (105) (DRGandolfo) **9-11-1** RDunwoody (hdwy 10th: wknd 12th: t.o whn p.u bef 2 out)		P	5/2^{2}	—	—
1063^{2}	**Andrelot (118)** (PBowen) **9-12-0** AMaguire (led to 9th: wknd 10th: t.o whn p.u bef 12th)		P	6/1	—	—
	Whippers Delight (IRE) (93) (GFHCharles-Jones) **8-10-3** DBridgwater (bit bkwd: chsd ldr to 9th: wknd 10th: t.o whn p.u bef 11th)		P	9/2	—	—

(SP 121.7%) **6 Rn**

5m 40.4 (27.40) CSF £12.55 CT £102.15 TOTE £4.10: £3.00 £1.60 (£8.90) OWNER Mrs C. I. A. Paterson (SHEPTON MALLET) BRED C. P. Millikin
IN-FOCUS: **A fifteen minute downpour before this race made conditions even more testing.**
Beau Babillard had been off the course for six months, but revelled in the mud. (4/1)
959* Zambezi Spirit (IRE) was facing completely different conditions to those at the last meeting here when he scooted in. (15/8: 5/4-2/1)
1063 Andrelot (6/1: op 4/1)

1168 CUCKFIELD NOVICES' HURDLE (4-Y.O+) (Class E)
3-05 (3-06) **2m 1f (10 hdls)** £2,574.00 (£714.00: £342.00) GOING: 1.55 sec per fur (HY)

Form	Horse	Dist	Pos	SP	RR	SF
834^{3}	**Sailep (FR) (80)** (RJHodges) **4-10-9**(3) TDascombe (chsd ldr: led appr 2 out: all out)	—	1	7/2^{3}	77	—
1053^{6}	**Shift Again (IRE) (88)** (OSherwood) **4-10-7b** JOsborne (led tl appr 2 out: unable qckn)	2	2	9/4^{1}	70	—
	Zacaroon (JFfitch-Heyes) **5-10-7** APMcCoy (a.p: rdn 3 out: sn wknd: t.o)	dist	3	20/1	—	—
961^{3}	**Blurred Image (IRE) (67)** (JCPoulton) **5-10-12** TJMurphy (lw: a bhd: t.o)	24	4	14/1	—	—
	Not To Panic (IRE) (KRBurke) **6-10-7** RJohnson (bit bkwd: bhd fr 7th: t.o)	21	5	7/1	—	—
	Spitfire Bridge (IRE) (GMMcCourt) **4-10-12** BClifford (a bhd: t.o whn p.u bef 3 out)		P	12/1	—	—
974^{4}	**Ath Cheannaithe (FR) (92)** (JNeville) **4-11-5b** DBridgwater (lw: a bhd: t.o whn p.u bef 7th)		P	11/4^{2}	—	—
	Bold Charlie (SMellor) **4-10-12** NMann (bhd fr 5th: t.o whn p.u bef 3 out)		P	33/1	—	—

(SP 114.2%) **8 Rn**

4m 41.0 (45.00) CSF £11.32 TOTE £3.40: £1.10 £1.50 £2.30 (£5.20) Trio £33.70 OWNER Mr P. Slade (SOMERTON) BRED L. Henry, L. Rouillere-Henry & Pierric Rouxel
Sailep (FR), who finished third to Darter and Bolivar in the mud at Windsor in January, was much happier back on this surface. (7/2)
1053 Shift Again (IRE) had shaken off all bar the winner in the last half-mile. (9/4: 6/4-5/2)
Zacaroon, fit from the Flat, was left for dead in the last half-mile. (20/1)
Spitfire Bridge (IRE) (12/1: 6/1-14/1)
974 Ath Cheannaithe (FR) (11/4: 2/1-7/2)

1169 CHAILEY H'CAP CHASE (0-115) (5-Y.O+) (Class E)
3-35 (3-37) **2m (13 fncs)** £2,906.40 (£865.20: £411.60: £184.80) GOING: 1.11 sec per fur (HY)

Form	Horse	Dist	Pos	SP	RR	SF
867^{5}	**Uncle Bert (IRE) (94)** (GMMcCourt) **6-10-4**(3) DFortt (lost pl 9th: rallied appr last: led flat: r.o wl)	—	1	5/2^{2}	99	26
917*	**Coolteen Hero (IRE) (88)** (RHAlner) **6-10-1**ow1 WMcFarland (led tl appr 2 out: unable qckn flat)	5	2	4/1^{3}	88	14
886^{5}	**James the First (115)** (PFNicholls) **8-12-0** APMcCoy (lw: chsd ldr: mstke 2nd: hrd rdn 7th: led appr 2 out: wknd & hdd flat)	s.h	3	4/5^{1}	115	42
1075^{4}	**Joker Jack (89)** (RDean) **11-9-13**(3)ow2 TDascombe (lw: a in rr: t.o fr 6th)	dist	4	14/1	—	—

(SP 110.8%) **4 Rn**

4m 16.2 (24.20) CSF £10.80 TOTE £4.00 (£11.50) OWNER Mr Alec Tuckerman (WANTAGE) BRED Daniel O'Riordan
LONG HANDICAP Coolteen Hero (IRE) 9-10 Joker Jack 8-8
Uncle Bert (IRE), with the front two fading in the straight, it did not need much of an effort to sweep into the lead on the run-in. (5/2: 7/4-11/4)
917* Coolteen Hero (IRE) was collared approaching the second last. Very tired indeed, he almost got back on level terms on the run-in before the winner swept by. (4/1: 9/4-9/2)
886 James the First seems far from happy when not in front, and McCoy was rousting the gelding along before eventually getting to the front approaching the second last, but he looked far from enthusiastic and the winner swept by. (4/5: tchd evens)
1075 Joker Jack (14/1: 10/1-16/1)

1170 PLUMPTON AUTUMN H'CAP HURDLE (0-100) (4-Y.O+) (Class F)
4-05 (4-05) **2m 4f (12 hdls)** £2,083.80 (£576.80: £275.40) GOING: 1.55 sec per fur (HY)

Form	Horse	Dist	Pos	SP	RR	SF
958*	**Fawley Flyer (81)** (WGMTurner) **7-10-11** RDunwoody (lw: a.p: mstke 2nd: chsd ldr fr 6th: rdn 3 out: led 2 out: hrd rdn flat: r.o)	—	1	2/1^{1}	65	—
	Titan Empress (72) (SMellor) **7-10-2v** NMann (led 2nd: mstke 7th: hdd 2 out: unable qckn)	8	2	11/4^{2}	50	—
	Country Store (95) (APJones) **7-11-11** SCurran (led to 2nd: rdn 9th: sn wknd: t.o)	dist	3	3/1^{3}	—	—
	Daring King (92) (MJBolton) **6-11-8** PHide (bit bkwd: a bhd: t.o fr 9th)	3	4	13/2	—	—
	Soleil Dancer (IRE) (83) (DMGrissell) **8-10-13** BFenton (bit bkwd: a bhd: t.o fr 9th)	30	5	14/1	—	—
890^{P}	**Topanga (90)** (JABennett) **4-11-6** LHarvey (bit bkwd: bhd fr 8th: t.o fr 9th)	7	6	10/1	—	—

(SP 114.1%) **6 Rn**

5m 37.3 (50.30) CSF £7.78 CT £13.74 TOTE £2.70: £1.70 £2.10 (£3.90) OWNER Mr David Chown (SHERBORNE) BRED Shepherds Farm Ltd

958* Fawley Flyer, who hacked up on a fast surface at the last meeting here, coped well enough with the mud. (2/1: 5/4-9/4)
Titan Empress, reverting to hurdles for this seasonal debut, appeared to be travelling better than the winner turning for home but, collared two out, she was soon put in her place. (11/4)
Country Store, whose only previous success came in the mud, looked reasonably straight for this seasonal debut. (3/1)
Daring King (13/2: 4/1-7/1)
Soleil Dancer (IRE) (14/1: op 8/1)
Topanga (10/1: 6/1-12/1)

T/Plpt: £68.10 (163.27 Tckts). T/Qdpt: £19.10 (60.39 Tckts). AK

0968-**EXETER** (R-H) (Good to soft, Good patches)
Tuesday November 5th
WEATHER: overcast

1171 WILLIAM HILL CREDIT NOVICES' HURDLE (4-Y.O+) (Class E)
1-15 (1-17) **2m 1f 110y (8 hdls)** £2,826.00 (£786.00: £378.00) GOING: 0.27 sec per fur (GS)

				SP	RR	SF
	It's A Gem (JTGifford) **7-10-9**(3) LAspell (mid div: hdwy appr 2 out: rdn to ld flat: styd on wl)	—	1	50/1	78	37
890[2]	**Devon Peasant** (LGCottrell) **4-10-7** MrLJefford (a.p: led appr 2 out tl appr last: lft in ld & hmpd last: sn hdd & no ex)	½	2	9/1	73	32
788*	**Lake Kariba (119)** (PFNicholls) **5-11-5** APMcCoy (lw: a in tch: one pce appr last)	4	3	2/1[1]	81	40
	Ross Dancer (IRE) (JSMoore) **4-10-9**(3) JMagee (bit bkwd: bhd tl styd on appr 2 out)	22	4	100/1	54	13
1060*	**Mister Rm (106)** (NATwiston-Davies) **4-11-5** CLlewellyn (led tl appr 2 out: sn wknd)	5	5	3/1[3]	56	15
	Gentle Breeze (IRE) (JTGifford) **4-10-7** PHide (chsd ldrs tl wknd 6th)	1½	6	25/1	43	2
1036[4]	**Rhythm And Blues** (RHBuckler) **6-10-12** BPowell (mid div tl wknd appr 6th)	3	7	16/1	45	4
788[7]	**Saxon Mead** (PJHobbs) **6-10-12** AMaguire (bit bkwd: prom tl wknd fr 5th)	¾	8	16/1	44	3
902[3]	**Saafi (IRE)** (RJBaker) **5-10-12** DLeahy (hdwy 4th: rdn & wknd 6th: t.o)	dist	9	100/1	—	—
	Ecu de France (IRE) (PCRitchens) **6-10-12** SFox (bit bkwd: a bhd: t.o 6th)	hd	10	100/1	—	—
1053[8]	**Solo Volumes** (HGRowsell) **7-10-12** MBrennan (a bhd: mstke 3rd: sn t.o)	dist	11	200/1	—	—
	Filch (PGMurphy) **5-10-7** BFenton (bkwd: a bhd: t.o 6th)	hd	12	100/1	—	—
	Credo Boy (KBishop) **7-10-12** SBurrough (bit bkwd: fell 1st)		F	33/1	—	—
885[P]	**Parade Racer** (PGMurphy) **5-10-12** WMcFarland (bit bkwd: chsd ldr tl wknd qckly fr 4th: t.o whn p.u)		P	100/1	—	—
1036[P]	**Hold The Fort** (AJKDunn) **5-10-7**(5) DJKavanagh (bkwd: a bhd: t.o 6th: p.u bef 2 out)		P	200/1	—	—
1059[U]	**Marching Marquis (IRE)** (NoelChance) **5-10-12** MAFitzgerald (a.p: chsd ldr 4th: led appr last: clr whn blnd & uns rdr last)		U	5/2[2]	79?	—
				(SP 123.4%)	**16 Rn**	

4m 14.1 (10.10) CSF £410.19 TOTE £108.60: £15.60 £2.20 £1.40 (£499.70) Trio £256.60; £253.02 to Newton Abbot 6/11/96 OWNER Capt F. Tyrwhitt-Drake (FINDON) BRED F. Tyrwhitt-Drake

It's A Gem belied his odds and, travelling strongly, was produced with a challenge two from home, but perhaps can be considered a fortunate winner as his main rival departed at the final obstacle. He should come into his own over further and will probably go chasing this season. (50/1)
890 Devon Peasant featured prominently throughout the race, but was eventually worn down by the lucky winner. She should be capable of picking up a similar event. (9/1: 4/1-10/1)
788* Lake Kariba should be suited by further. (2/1)
Marching Marquis (IRE) had it sewn up until blundering and unshipping Fitzgerald at the final flight. (5/2)

1172 WILLIAM HILL LUCKY CHOICE (S) HURDLE (3-Y.O) (Class G)
1-45 (1-47) **2m 1f 110y (8 hdls)** £1,859.00 (£514.00: £245.00) GOING: 0.27 sec per fur (GS)

				SP	RR	SF
	Stone Island (PJHobbs) **3-10-12** RDunwoody (in tch: chsd ldr 6th: sn led: mstke last: hld on gamely)	—	1	11/2[2]	59?	—
	Bryanston Square (IRE) (CREgerton) **3-10-12b[1]** JOsborne (prom: chsd ldr 5th: ev ch 2 out tl rdn & no ex flat)	½	2	9/1	59?	—
	Flash In The Pan (IRE) (JSMoore) **3-10-7** WMcFarland (mid div: stdy hdwy 5th: ev ch 2 out tl rdn & no ex last)	1	3	10/1	53?	—
688[2]	**Home Cookin'** (MCPipe) **3-10-7** APMcCoy (led to 3rd: led 4th: hdd after 6th: rdn & wknd appr 2 out: t.o)	dist	4	6/4[1]	—	—
	Blossom Dearie (RGFrost) **3-10-7** JFrost (bit bkwd: bhd: sme hdwy 6th: t.o)	4	5	14/1	—	—
	Dramatic Act (CRBarwell) **3-10-7** BFenton (plld hrd: chsd ldr tl led 3rd: hdd next: wknd appr 6th: p.u bef 2 out)		P	6/1[3]	—	—
	Bus Way Girl (JParfitt) **3-10-7** CLlewellyn (bkwd: a bhd: p.u after 5th)		P	25/1	—	—
	Paulton (KBishop) **3-10-12** MAFitzgerald (mstke 1st: a bhd: t.o whn p.u bef 6th)		P	20/1	—	—
1014[11]	**Dish The Dosh** (DBurchell) **3-10-7** DJBurchell (chsd ldrs tl lost tch 5th: ref next)		R	11/1	—	—
				(SP 112.4%)	**9 Rn**	

4m 28.0 (24.00) CSF £46.94 TOTE £7.70: £2.10 £3.60 £1.50 (£9.40) Trio £46.50 OWNER Mr P. J. Hobbs (MINEHEAD) BRED C. A. and R. M. Cyzer
No bid

Stone Island, a half-brother to several winners on the Flat but rather disappointing for Charles Cyzer, looks a useful recruit to this game. (11/2)
Bryanston Square (IRE) followed the winner through until two from home when he could dig no deeper. A race of this type should be within his ability. (9/1: 5/1-10/1)
Flash In The Pan (IRE) (10/1: 6/1-11/1)
688 Home Cookin' made a lot of the early running but faded from the third from home, despite her rider's urgings. (6/4)
Dramatic Act (6/1: 4/1-7/1)
Dish The Dosh (11/1: 16/1-10/1)

1173 WILLIAM HILL HALDON GOLD CHALLENGE CUP H'CAP CHASE (Gd 2) (5-Y.O+) (Class A)
2-15 (2-16) **2m 1f 110y (12 fncs)** £17,985.80 (£6,805.14: £3,330.07: £1,516.99) GOING: 0.27 sec per fur (GS)

				SP	RR	SF
	Absalom's Lady (152) (MissGayKelleway) **8-10-7** DBridgwater (hld up & bhd: hdwy 6th: led 8th: rdn next: mstkes 10th & 2 out: hld on gamely)	—	1	8/1	140	59

			SP	RR	SF
1055*	**Coulton (169)** (OSherwood) **9-11-10** JOsborne (lw: led tl appr 8th: lost pl: rallied to chse wnr last: no imp)...2½	**2**	13/8 [1]	155	74
	Pimberley Place (IRE) (152) (NATwiston-Davies) **8-10-7** CLlewellyn (plld hrd: prom to 8th: rdn & styd on fr 10th)...1¼	**3**	66/1	137	56
	Travado (159) (NJHenderson) **10-11-0** MAFitzgerald (chsd ldr 5th to 8th: ev ch next tl wknd last) ...s.h	**4**	15/8 [2]	144	63
	Nakir (FR) (152) (DNicholson) **8-10-7** AMaguire (lw: in tch to 7th: grad wknd)...11	**5**	4/1 [3]	127	46
	Terao (152) (MCPipe) **10-10-7** APMcCoy (bit bkwd: chsd ldr to 5th: wknd next: t.o 9th)...dist	**6**	16/1	—	—
			(SP 111.4%)	**6 Rn**	

4m 19.8 (3.80) CSF £20.55 TOTE £6.60: £2.10 £1.10 (£5.50) OWNER Whitcombe Manor Racing Stables Ltd (WHITCOMBE) BRED Casterbridge Stud

LONG HANDICAP Pimberley Place (IRE) 7-7 Absalom's Lady 9-4 Nakir (FR) 9-9 Terao 9-1

Absalom's Lady, backed from 16/1, this was obviously no shock to her shrewd connections, although she was running from 17lb out of the handicap. Getting off to a hesitant start, she was then held up well off the pace and her pilot sat quietly for the time being. Asked for an effort at the sixth, she began her smooth progress through the field. Given a few reminders to take up the running four from home, she pecked very badly on landing after three out and the combination were fortunate to stay intact. Despite looking tired at her final few fences, she held on gamely for her new stable's first National Hunt success this season. She heads now for the King George. (8/1: 10/1-16/1)

1055* Coulton dictated the pace and looked set to follow up on his Wincanton victory of nine days previously. Unable to retaliate, when taken on and headed by the eventual winner, he came back with a last fence challenge but to no avail. (13/8)

Pimberley Place (IRE), sometimes unreliable and racing here from three stone out of the handicap, put up an encouraging effort and stayed on well for third place. (66/1)

Travado apparently got very tired in the ground. (15/8: 5/4-2/1)

Nakir (FR) was disappointing considering the encouraging reports of connections. (4/1)

1174 WILLIAM HILL DEBIT CARD NOVICES' H'CAP HURDLE (0-100) (4-Y.O+) (Class E)

2-45 (2-47) **2m 3f (9 hdls)** £2,547.20 (£709.20: £341.60) GOING: 0.27 sec per fur (GS)

			SP	RR	SF
788 [5]	**Allow (IRE) (78)** (BLlewellyn) **5-10-11** MAFitzgerald (hdwy to chse ldr 5th to 7th: rallied to chse ldr 2 out: rdn to ld after last: r.o strly)...—	**1**	9/2 [2]	67	25
891 [P]	**Million Dancer (95)** (MCPipe) **4-12-0b** APMcCoy (lw: led tl after last: wknd qckly) ...7	**2**	10/1	78	36
	Cracking Prospect (85) (BRMillman) **5-10-13**(5) DSalter (bit bkwd: mid div: hdwy 7th: rdn & in tch 2 out: wknd appr last)...6	**3**	20/1	63	21
891 [2]	**Luke Warm (72)** (DRGandolfo) **6-10-5**ow1 RDunwoody (mid div: hdwy to chse ldr 7th to 2 out: rdn & sn wknd)10	**4**	7/2 [1]	42	—
	Coole Hill (IRE) (87) (DNicholson) **5-11-6** AMaguire (bit bkwd: bhd: hdwy 7th: nvr able to chal) ...9	**5**	11/2 [3]	49	7
1038 [P]	**Spearhead Again (IRE) (80)** (KSBridgwater) **7-10-13** DBridgwater (a bhd)...9	**6**	16/1	35	—
968 [3]	**Steer Point (74)** (RGFrost) **5-10-7** JFrost (a bhd)...7	**7**	16/1	23	—
	French Buck (IRE) (92) (NATwiston-Davies) **6-11-11** CLlewellyn (chsd ldr tl after 4th: wknd fr 7th)...2	**8**	11/2 [3]	39	—
915 [7]	**Old Master (IRE) (67)** (RJBaker) **5-10-0** BPowell (bhd: hdwy 4th: wknd 7th)...10	**9**	100/1	6	—
641 [3]	**Plinth (80)** (NAGraham) **5-10-13** JOsborne (in tch to 5th: grad wknd: t.o) ...22	**10**	8/1	—	—
1053 [5]	**Policemans Pride (FR) (80)** (MMadgwick) **7-10-13** GUpton (chsd ldrs to 5th: grad wknd: t.o whn p.u bef last) ..	**P**	20/1	—	—
792 [P]	**Sands Point (86)** (CLPopham) **6-11-2**(3) TDascombe (bit bkwd: chsd ldrs to 4th: wknd 7th: p.u & dsmntd bef last: lame)...	**P**	16/1	—	—
	Freeline Lustre (IRE) (68) (PGMurphy) **6-10-1** WMcFarland (bit bkwd: a bhd: t.o 5th: p.u after next) ...	**P**	50/1	—	—
			(SP 121.5%)	**13 Rn**	

4m 39.9 (13.90) CSF £45.86 CT £759.60 TOTE £5.60: £1.70 £3.10 £5.80 (£27.70) Trio £202.90; £60.03 to Newton Abbot 6/11/96 OWNER Mrs M. Llewellyn (SWANSEA) BRED M. Kura

LONG HANDICAP Old Master (IRE) 9-12

Allow (IRE) was produced with a perfectly-timed run to snatch the spoils after the last. (9/2)

891 Million Dancer put up a gallant effort and went clear to lead until after the last, when top weight got the better of him, and he was passed by the winner. (10/1: 8/1-12/1)

Cracking Prospect looked on the verge of mounting a challenge after the third flight from home, only to fade from then on. He was done no favours by this step up in trip. (20/1)

891 Luke Warm was a shade disappointing here and could do no more in the closing stages. (7/2)

Coole Hill (IRE) will do better in time. (11/2: 4/1-6/1)

French Buck (IRE) (11/2: 4/1-6/1)

1175 WILLIAM HILL DEVON & EXETER H'CAP CHASE (0-135) (5-Y.O+) (Class C)

3-15 (3-15) **2m 6f 110y (17 fncs)** £4,856.25 (£1,470.00: £717.50: £341.25) GOING: 0.27 sec per fur (GS)

			SP	RR	SF
	Fools Errand (IRE) (105) (GBBalding) **6-10-5** APMcCoy (a.p: mstke 10th: led appr 14th: sn clr: easily) ...—	**1**	5/1 [3]	109+	1
	Class of Ninetytwo (IRE) (122) (CaptTAForster) **7-11-8** RDunwoody (chsd ldr tl led 10th: hdd appr 14th: outpcd fr next) ...7	**2**	7/2 [2]	121	13
	Dom Samourai (FR) (117) (MCPipe) **5-11-2b** JFrost (bhd: hdwy 15th: r.o strly appr last: nt rch ldrs)...2½	**3**	11/1	114	5
	Oatis Regrets (128) (MissHCKnight) **8-12-0** JOsborne (led tl mstke 10th: mstke next: wknd 14th) ...1	**4**	9/4 [1]	125	17
	Spuffington (120) (JTGifford) **8-11-6** PHide (bit bkwd: bhd: hdwy appr 14th: one pce fr 2 out)...4	**5**	13/2	114	6
650 [4]	**Staunch Rival (USA) (120)** (GThorner) **9-11-6** MAFitzgerald (a bhd: t.o fr 6th) ...dist	**6**	14/1	—	—
	Harwell Lad (IRE) (120) (RHAlner) **7-11-6** MrRNuttall (chsd ldrs to 7th: wknd qckly 9th: p.u bef 10th) ...	**P**	6/1	—	—
			(SP 112.3%)	**7 Rn**	

5m 54.2 (23.20) CSF £21.19 TOTE £4.60: £1.70 £2.40 (£5.40) OWNER Mrs David Russell (ANDOVER) BRED K. E. and Mrs Moeran in Ireland

WEIGHT FOR AGE 5yo-1lb

Fools Errand (IRE), best when fresh and well-handicapped on this step up from novice company, won this with considerable ease. (5/1)

Class of Ninetytwo (IRE) will benefit from this outing when he tackles further on his next outing. (7/2)

Dom Samourai (FR) made eye-catching late headway going to the last but could get no nearer to the first two. (11/1: 7/1-12/1)

Oatis Regrets ran as though he needed the race. (9/4)

Staunch Rival (USA) (14/1: 8/1-16/1)

1176 WILLIAM HILL INDEX H'CAP HURDLE (0-120) (4-Y.O+ F & M) (Class D)

3-45 (3-45) **2m 3f (9 hdls)** £2,898.00 (£864.00: £412.00: £186.00) GOING: 0.27 sec per fur (GS)

			SP	RR	SF
	Sail by the Stars (99) (CaptTAForster) **7-10-12** RDunwoody (chsd ldrs: led appr 2 out: styd on strly flat)...—	**1**	6/1 [3]	83	32

	Horse	Dist	Pos	SP	RR	SF
1058*	**Dark Nightingale (99)** (OSherwood) **6-10-12** JOsborne (hld up & bhd: hdwy 6th: ev ch 2 out tl rdn & outpcd flat)	5	**2**	13/8 1	79	28
	Mariners Mirror (104) (NATwiston-Davies) **9-11-3** MrMRimell (bit bkwd: hdwy to chse ldr 4th: ev ch tl wknd appr last)	11	**3**	7/1	75	24
904²	**Out Ranking (FR) (114)** (MCPipe) **4-11-13** APMcCoy (lw: led tl appr 2 out: rdn & sn wknd)	7	**4**	3/1 2	79	28
	Stac-Pollaidh (89) (KCBailey) **6-10-2** JRailton (nt fluent: mstkes 1st & 3rd: chsd ldr to 4th: wknd qckly 6th)	3½	**5**	8/1	51	—
	Koo's Promise (87) (CLPopham) **5-9-11**(3) TDascombe (bit bkwd: in tch to 4th: rdn next: bhd 7th: t.o)	27	**6**	25/1	26	—
1039⁶	**La Menorquina (USA) (97)** (DMarks) **6-10-5**(5) SophieMitchell (bhd: hdwy 6th: 5th & styng on u.p whn fell 2 out)		**F**	10/1	—	—
				(SP 113.9%)		**7 Rn**

4m 38.1 (12.10) CSF £15.73 TOTE £6.40: £4.30 £2.10 (£8.90) OWNER Mr T. F. F. Nixon (LUDLOW) BRED T. F. F. Nixon
LONG HANDICAP Koo's Promise 9-4
Sail by the Stars ran out a convincing winner in a moderate event. She will benefit from further. (6/1)
1058* Dark Nightingale continually dogged by wind problems, looked dangerous when produced two out, but on reaching the flat was outpaced by the winner. (13/8)
Mariners Mirror (7/1: 5/1-15/2)
Stac-Pollaidh (8/1: 6/1-9/1)
1039 La Menorquina (USA) (10/1: 6/1-11/1)

1177 EXETER LEVY BOARD STANDARD OPEN N.H. FLAT RACE (4, 5 & 6-Y.O F & M) (Class H)

4-15 (4-17) **2m 1f 110y** £1,259.00 (£349.00: £167.00)

	Horse	Dist	Pos	SP	RR	SF
	Curraduff Moll (IRE) (NATwiston-Davies) **5-10-11**(7) LSuthern (a.p: chsd ldr after 4f tl led 4f out: rdn & styd on wl)	—	**1**	14/1	—	—
	Potter's Gale (IRE) (DNicholson) **5-11-11** AMaguire (lw: hld up mid div: hdwy ½-wy: chsd wnr 3f out: one pce ins fnl f)	1½	**2**	Evens 1	—	—
	Just Jasmine (KBishop) **4-11-4** JOsborne (a.p: rdn & one pce fr 3f out)	3½	**3**	20/1	—	—
	Kosheen (IRE) (MissHCKnight) **5-10-11**(7) MrAWintle (bit bkwd: mid div: hdwy 6f out: wknd 2f out)	12	**4**	12/1	—	—
	Jaydeebee (MMadgwick) **5-11-4** GUpton (bit bkwd: chsd ldrs: one pce fr 5f out)	4	**5**	33/1	—	—
653³	**Solar Moon** (RHBuckler) **5-11-4** BPowell (bit bkwd: hld up: hdwy 6f out: wknd 4f out)	9	**6**	11/1	—	—
	Dolce Notte (IRE) (MCPipe) **6-11-4** APMcCoy (lw: led to 4f out: sn wknd)	15	**7**	7/2 2	—	—
	Lotschberg Express (DRGandolfo) **4-11-4** RDunwoody (bhd: hdwy ½-wy: wknd 6f out: t.o)	19	**8**	10/1 3	—	—
	Miss Night Owl (RGFrost) **5-11-4** JFrost (bit bkwd: a bhd: t.o 6f out)	hd	**9**	33/1	—	—
	Miss Starteam (RGFrost) **6-11-4** MrAHoldsworth (bkwd: a bhd: t.o 6f out)	1¼	**10**	66/1	—	—
	Pharmorefun (IRE) (GBBalding) **4-11-4** BFenton (bkwd: bhd: sme hdwy 6f out: wknd qckly: t.o)	3	**11**	14/1	—	—
	Alice Shorelark (SGKnight) **5-11-4** MrTGreed (bkwd: prom to ½-wy: wknd qckly 7f out: t.o)	dist	**12**	100/1	—	—
872⁹	**Halam Bell** (WGMTurner) **4-11-4** PHolley (bkwd: bhd fr 7f out: t.o)	10	**13**	50/1	—	—
	Let You Know (IRE) (TRGeorge) **6-11-4** MAFitzgerald (bkwd: a bhd: t.o)	18	**14**	50/1	—	—
				(SP 127.7%)		**14 Rn**

4m 12.8 CSF £28.48 TOTE £15.50: £3.20 £1.10 £5.70 (£11.10) Trio £137.50 OWNER Mr John Duggan (CHELTENHAM) BRED Peter Breen
Curraduff Moll (IRE) travelled sweetly to cruise into the lead half a mile from home, from which point she stayed on gamely when looking tired. (14/1: op 6/1)
Potter's Gale (IRE) made good headway to move up the field before halfway showing a useful turn of foot. Finishing strongly, she could not get quite there in time. An event of this kind is well within her grasp. (Evens)
Just Jasmine was always up in the leading group but could not muster a change of gear in the final half mile. (20/1)
Kosheen (IRE) will progress for this introduction. (12/1: 7/1-14/1)
653 Solar Moon (11/1: 8/1-12/1)
Dolce Notte (IRE) set the pace and ran well for a time, but had run her race four furlongs from home and was a spent force. (7/2)
Lotschberg Express (10/1: 6/1-11/1)
Pharmorefun (IRE) (14/1: 6/1-16/1)
T/Plpt: £319.60 (33.93 Tckts). T/Qdpt: £38.20 (19.64 Tckts). T

1145-WARWICK (L-H) (Good to firm)
Tuesday November 5th
WEATHER: fine

1178 JOHN PYM NOVICES' HURDLE (4-Y.O+) (Class E)

1-25 (1-38) **2m (8 hdls)** £2,477.50 (£690.00: £332.50) GOING minus 0.62 sec per fur (F)

	Horse	Dist	Pos	SP	RR	SF
	Chickawicka (IRE) (BPalling) **5-10-12** GBradley (mde all: tried to rn out 2nd: clr 5th: tried to run out 2 out: eased flat)	—	**1**	7/4 1	68+	27
	Above the Cut (USA) (CPMorlock) **4-10-12** CMaude (hld up: stdy hdwy appr 4th: lft 2nd 3 out: no imp)	7	**2**	33/1	61	20
955⁷	**Smart Lord** (JRBosley) **5-10-12** MBosley (plld hrd: mid div: r.o fr 3 out: n.d)	6	**3**	25/1	55	14
963²	**Highly Charming (IRE) (91)** (MFBarraclough) **4-10-12** RJohnson (prom to 5th)	15	**4**	11/4 2	40	—
963³	**The Deaconess** (MrsALMKing) **5-10-7** GaryLyons (prom tl mstke 5th)	2	**5**	33/1	33	—
73⁵	**Irish Wildcard (NZ) (67)** (HOliver) **8-10-12** JacquiOliver (s.s: nvr trbld ldrs)	11	**6**	50/1	27	—
963⁴	**Roc Age** (GWDavies) **5-10-0**(7) MrJNolan (prom to 4th)	1	**7**	50/1	21	—
	Schwartzndigger (IRE) (TWDonnelly) **6-10-12** TEley (bkwd: mstke 3rd: a bhd)	5	**8**	50/1	21	—
1036ᴾ	**Katharine's Song (IRE)** (DMHyde) **6-10-7** NWilliamson (prom tl wknd 4th)	¾	**9**	66/1	15	—
	The Brewer (JCTuck) **4-10-12** RBellamy (bkwd: w.r.s: a bhd)	3	**10**	25/1	17	—
	Laburnum Gold (IRE) (MrsJPitman) **5-10-12** WMarston (bkwd: prom: 2nd whn fell 3 out)		**F**	4/1 3	—	—
	Tungsten (IRE) (NJHenderson) **5-10-12** JRKavanagh (bhd: reminders appr 4th: t.o whn p.u bef 2 out)		**P**	14/1	—	—
1059ᴿ	**Rizal (USA)** (RJEckley) **4-10-9b**1(3) DWalsh (reluctant to r: t.o tl p.u bef 5th)		**P**	66/1	—	—
	Web of Steel (CJHemsley) **6-10-12** BClifford (s.s: t.o whn p.u bef 4th)		**P**	100/1	—	—
	Design (IRE) (JGMO'Shea) **6-10-2**(5) MichaelBrennan (prom: 5th & wkng whn hmpd & uns rdr 3 out)		**U**	7/1	—	—
				(SP 125.6%)		**15 Rn**

3m 39.0 (-3.00) CSF £54.98 TOTE £2.80: £1.80 £6.10 £2.00 (£59.60) Trio £186.20; £209.86 to Newton Abbot 6/11/96 OWNER Merthyr Motor Auctions (COWBRIDGE) BRED Charlton Down Stud

Chickawicka (IRE), successful over seven at Epsom in July, found fast ground helping him to get the trip. Adopting his favourite front-running tactics, he gave his rider a couple of anxious moments. (7/4: 5/4-2/1)
Above the Cut (USA) had some useful form to his name when registering wins at Kempton and Newbury as a juvenile. Tried in blinkers in his last three runs after being disappointing this season, it seems as if hurdling may have rekindled his interest. (33/1)
593 Smart Lord proved a handful to settle. (25/1)
963 Highly Charming (IRE) was in trouble once the winner went for home in this stronger company. (11/4)
963 The Deaconess finished a lot nearer to Highly Charming this time, but it did not do her much good. (33/1)
Laburnum Gold (IRE) was struggling to go with the winner when misjudging the third last, but will at least strip fitter for the run. (4/1)
Tungsten (IRE) (14/1: op 6/1)
Design (IRE) (7/1: 5/1-8/1)

1179 THOMAS FAIRFAX NOVICES' CHASE (5-Y.O+) (Class D)

1-55 (2-01) **2m (12 fncs)** £3,639.00 (£1,092.00: £526.00: £243.00) GOING minus 0.62 sec per fur (F)

	Horse	Dist	Pos	SP	RR	SF
	Brazil Or Bust (IRE) (PRWebber) **5-11-0** MDwyer (hld up & bhd: hdwy 4 out: led last: rdn out)	—	1	5/2^{2}	100	20
	Slingsby (IRE) (NAGaselee) **6-11-0** AThornton (chsd ldr: led 7th to last: r.o)	nk	2	9/4^{1}	100	20
900^{5}	**Sigma Run (IRE)** (JACEdwards) **7-11-0** RJohnson (led to 7th: 3rd & wkng whn mstke 3 out)	19	3	5/1	81	1
	Kino's Cross (AJWilson) **7-11-0** LHarvey (hld up: hdwy appr 6th: wkng whn hmpd 3 out)	19	4	11/4^{3}	62	—
	Copper Cable (70) (CSmith) **9-11-0** MRanger (prom to 6th)	2½	5	33/1	59	—
964^{3}	**Larks Tail** (PRWebber) **8-10-9** RBellamy (hld up & plld hrd: bhd whn mstke 6th: sn t.o: blnd 3 out)	dist	6	20/1	—	—
947^{5}	**Ice Magic (69)** (FJYardley) **9-11-0v** PMcLoughlin (prom: 4th & wkng whn fell 3 out)		F	10/1	—	—
	Strange Ways (HJManners) **8-11-0** MrACharles-Jones (bhd tl blnd & uns rdr 5th)		U	25/1	—	—
				(SP 123.3%)	**8 Rn**	

3m 53.6 (-0.40) CSF £9.04 TOTE £4.40: £1.40 £1.20 £1.70 (£7.80) Trio £29.10 OWNER Mrs C. A. Waters (BANBURY) BRED Thomas McCreery
Brazil Or Bust (IRE), patiently ridden, justified stable-confidence with this successful debut over fences. (5/2)
Slingsby (IRE), who has changed stables, stuck to his guns when headed on this first outing over the larger obstacles, and can win a similar event on this evidence. (9/4)
829* Sigma Run (IRE), graduating to fences, did well to find a suitable opportunity over hurdles and is not going to find things any easier in this sphere by the look of it. (5/1)
Kino's Cross needed softer ground over timber than he encountered here. (11/4: 2/1-3/1)

1180 EARL OF STRAFFORD NOVICES' HURDLE (4-Y.O+) (Class E)

2-25 (2-29) **2m 3f (9 hdls)** £2,302.50 (£640.00: £307.50) GOING minus 0.62 sec per fur (F)

	Horse	Dist	Pos	SP	RR	SF
955^{11}	**Rosehall** (MrsTDPilkington) **5-10-4**$^{(3)}$ GHogan (prom: lost pl 6th: hmpd 2 out: rallied to ld flat)	—	1	33/1	46	—
960^{3}	**Wanstead (IRE) (89)** (JRJenkins) **4-10-12b** GBradley (bit bkwd: prom: lost pl 6th: rallied appr last: styd on flat)	nk	2	4/1	51	—
965*	**Culrain (78)** (THCaldwell) **5-11-5** AThornton (hld up: hdwy appr 5th: rdn 3 out: led & pckd last: hdd flat)	2	3	7/2^{3}	56	—
1053^{13}	**Wise 'n' Shine** (NMLampard) **5-10-2**$^{(5)}$ ChrisWebb (a.p: r.o one pce fr 2 out)	hd	4	66/1	44	—
	Club Caribbean (PJHobbs) **4-10-7** NWilliamson (hld up & plld hrd: hdwy 5th: lft in ld 2 out: hdd last: fin tired)	3	5	3/1^{2}	42	—
	Brown And Mild (JohnBerry) **5-10-9**$^{(3)}$ DFortt (bit bkwd: led to 6th: sn wknd)	8	6	33/1	40	—
	Operetto (IRE) (MrsSusanNock) **6-10-12** MrEJames (plld hrd: prom: lft in ld after 3 out: fell 2 out)		F	12/1	—	—
	Ali's Delight (MDMcMillan) **5-10-12** LWyer (bit bkwd: bhd fr 5th: t.o whn p.u bef 3 out)		P	33/1	—	—
818^{2}	**Dacelo (FR) (95)** (OSherwood) **5-10-12** JAMcCarthy (hld up: hdwy 4th: led 6th: clr whn rn out bnd after 3 out)		R	7/4^{1}	—	—
				(SP 121.6%)	**9 Rn**	

4m 32.1 (12.10) CSF £155.18 TOTE £87.50: £21.40 £1.90 £1.50 (£174.70) Trio £77.90 OWNER Mrs T. D. Pilkington (STOW-ON-THE-WOLD) BRED Mrs T. D. Pilkington
Rosehall came through to win a poor event, which would be a natural for 'What Happened Next' on A Question Of Sport. (33/1)
960 Wanstead (IRE) could not peg back the winner in a race where the form seems likely to amount to little. (4/1: 5/2-5/1)
965* Culrain, penalised for his course and distance win, is basically only a selling plater. (7/2)
Wise 'n' Shine will do well to find another novice hurdle as bad as this. (66/1)
Club Caribbean was well beaten in a point-to-point in Ireland and one can not help thinking that she missed out on a golden opportunity. (3/1)
Operetto (IRE) (12/1: op 8/1)
818 Dacelo (FR) started a short price here because this was such a poor event, but his temperament reappeared on the home turn. (7/4: 5/4-15/8)

1181 EARL OF WARWICK H'CAP HURDLE (0-105) (4-Y.O+) (Class F)

2-55 (2-56) **2m 3f (9 hdls)** £2,011.00 (£556.00: £265.00) GOING minus 0.62 sec per fur (F)

	Horse	Dist	Pos	SP	RR	SF
	Desert Force (IRE) (83) (AStreeter) **7-11-8** GBradley (hld up: hdwy 4th: led 3 out: r.o wl)	—	1	11/4^{1}	59+	—
954^{5}	**Cosa Fuair (IRE) (85)** (KCBailey) **6-11-10** CO'Dwyer (hld up: chsd wnr fr 2 out: hrd rdn: no imp)	6	2	9/2^{2}	56	—
1121^{P}	**Hullo Mary Doll (82)** (AJChamberlain) **7-11-2**$^{(5)}$ MichaelBrennan (hld up: lost pl 5th: hdwy appr 2 out: btn whn hit last)	3	3	9/2^{2}	50	—
1034^{8}	**Will James (67)** (CJDrewe) **10-10-3b**$^{(3)}$ GuyLewis (hld up: hdwy & ev ch 3 out: sn rdn: wknd appr last)	4	4	14/1^{3}	32	—
971^{4}	**Little Hooligan (82)** (GFEdwards) **5-11-7b** RJohnson (prom: ev ch 3 out: sn wknd)	7	5	9/2^{2}	41	—
942^{5}	**Royal Circus (84)** (PWHiatt) **7-11-6**$^{(3)}$ EHusband (led: hit 4th: rdn 5th: hdd 3 out: sn wknd)	1¾	6	9/2^{2}	42	—
1034^{7}	**Anlace (82)** (SMellor) **7-11-2**$^{(5)}$ ChrisWebb (hld up: s.u after 4th)		S	9/2^{2}	—	—
				(SP 124.2%)	**7 Rn**	

4m 20.9 (0.90) CSF £16.09 TOTE £3.90: £2.00 £3.10 (£12.00) OWNER Mr G. Fierro (HEDNESFORD) BRED Stephen Stanhope
Desert Force (IRE), having his first run for Andy Streeter, was dropped 8lb and made a winning debut for the second successive season. Well suited by fast ground, he unfortunately has fragile legs. (11/4)
954 Cosa Fuair (IRE), settled going well, did not find much when put to the test on the home turn and may be better suited to a more galloping course. (9/2)
888* Hullo Mary Doll had presumably found the ground too soft when pulled up at Bangor last week. (9/2)
Will James came through to match strides with the winner at the third last, but soon came off the bit. (14/1)
741 Little Hooligan was back to the same mark as when runner-up to Out Ranking at Exeter. (9/2)
942 Royal Circus had dropped to a mark 6lb lower than when winning on his seasonal reappearance. (9/2)

1182 OLIVER CROMWELL H'CAP CHASE (0-125) (5-Y.O+) (Class D)
3-25 (3-25) **2m 4f 110y (17 fncs)** £5,740.00 GOING minus 0.62 sec per fur (F)

				SP	RR	SF
959[4]	**Drumstick (92)** (KCBailey) **10-10-9** CO'Dwyer (chsd ldr: blnd 2nd: led appr 11th: lft alone appr 12th)	—	1	5/4[2]	103?	—
1035[5]	**Man Mood (FR) (112)** (CPEBrooks) **5-12-0** GBradley (led tl appr 11th: p.u bef 12th)		P	4/7[1]	—	—
				(SP 108.1%)		**2 Rn**

5m 16.4 (12.40) TOTE £1.90 OWNER Sarah Lady Allendale (UPPER LAMBOURN) BRED Mrs W. Hanson
WEIGHT FOR AGE 5yo-1lb
959 Drumstick, not the force of old, has been retired on a winning note, having won eighteen races and over £80,000 in prizemoney.(5/4)
1035 Man Mood (FR) apparently found his breathing problems resurfacing and will be tried next with his tongue tied. (4/7)

1183 EARL OF ESSEX NOVICES' H'CAP HURDLE (0-100) (4-Y.O+) (Class E)
3-55 (3-55) **2m (8 hdls)** £2,302.50 (£640.00: £307.50) GOING minus 0.62 sec per fur (F)

				SP	RR	SF
	Portscatho (IRE) (85) (APJones) **4-11-4** SCurran (bit bkwd: chsd ldr: led 4th: all out)	—	1	100/30[2]	71	19
1010[3]	**Red Light (82)** (JRJenkins) **4-10-8v**(7) NTEgan (hld up: hdwy 4th: ev ch 2 out: sn rdn & hung lft: rallied nr fin)	nk	2	5/1	68	16
461[2]	**Mr Poppleton (67)** (RBrotherton) **7-10-0** LHarvey (led to 4th: wknd after 3 out)	11	3	4/1[3]	42	—
1060[4]	**Bally Parson (86)** (RDickin) **10-10-12**(7) XAizpuru (hld up: outpcd fr 3 out)	3	4	10/1	58	6
1034[2]	**Alpine Mist (IRE) (92)** (JGMO'Shea) **4-11-6v**(5) MichaelBrennan (prom tl mstke 3 out)	12	5	9/4[1]	52	—
1027[6]	**Ranger Sloane (78)** (AStreeter) **4-10-11** GBradley (bhd fr 4th)	7	6	9/2	31	—
				(SP 117.8%)		**6 Rn**

3m 42.1 (0.10) CSF £19.18 TOTE £4.20: £3.10 £2.10 (£13.60) OWNER Miss Jacqueline Doyle (EASTBURY) BRED The Duke of Marlborough
LONG HANDICAP Mr Poppleton 9-11
Portscatho (IRE) got struck into when second in first-time blinkers at Wincanton last March and was not considered quite right on his final two outings last term. (100/30)
1010 Red Light hung into the winner from the penultimate hurdle and his young rider seemed unable to pull his whip through to the correct hand. (5/1)
461 Mr Poppleton, 3lb out of the handicap, got burnt off rounding the home turn. (4/1: 3/1-9/2)
1060 Bally Parson continues to try in vain to break his duck over timber. (10/1: 7/1-11/1)
1034 Alpine Mist (IRE) has been raised 2lb for being pipped near the post in the first-time visor at Worcester. (9/4)
950 Ranger Sloane (9/2: 3/1-5/1)

T/Plpt: £386.00 (20.54 Tckts). T/Qdpt: £67.80 (7.7 Tckts). KH/IM

HAYDOCK (L-H) (Good)
Wednesday November 6th
WEATHER: sunny & heavy showers

1184 BIRCHFIELD HURDLE (3-Y.O) (Class D)
1-15 (1-15) **2m (8 hdls)** £3,067.00 (£862.00: £421.00) GOING: 0.45 sec per fur (GS)

				SP	RR	SF
358[2]	**Always Happy** (MCPipe) **3-11-1** CMaude (lw: hld up in rr: stdy hdwy 3 out: led last: all out)	—	1	Evens[1]	63	40
906[4]	**Globe Runner** (JJO'Neill) **3-11-0** ARoche (hld up in tch: hdwy appr 2 out: rdn & r.o wl flat)	1¼	2	4/1[2]	61	38
906[11]	**Son of Anshan** (MrsASwinbank) **3-11-0** JSupple (a.p: ev ch fr 2 out: kpt on u.p flat)	hd	3	33/1	61	38
	Kingfisher Brave (MGMeagher) **3-11-0** LWyer (led to last: hrd rdn & wknd flat)	3½	4	14/1	57	34
	Whothehellisharry (JBerry) **3-11-0** MMoloney (hld up in tch: hdwy appr 3 out: ev ch next: wknd flat)	1¼	5	25/1	56	33
881[F]	**Royal Then (FR)** (JNeville) **3-11-0** NWilliamson (bkwd: hld up: styd on u.p flat: nvr nrr)	4	6	9/1	52	29
	Star Blakeney (GBarnett) **3-11-0** RFarrant (hld up: hdwy 3 out: rdn & edgd lft appr last: no imp)	s.h	7	50/1	52	29
	Meltemison (MDHammond) **3-10-11**(3) MrCBonner (lw: nvr nr to chal)	hd	8	15/2	52	29
	Sousse (MrsMReveley) **3-10-9** PNiven (bit bkwd: hld up: effrt appr 3 out: wknd next)	1½	9	7/1[3]	45	22
	Radmore Brandy (PDEvans) **3-10-9** GaryLyons (prom: ev ch 2 out: rdn & wknd last)	1½	10	14/1	44	21
	Snow Domino (IRE) (JMJefferson) **3-11-0** MDwyer (a in rr)	4	11	14/1	45	22
	Grasshopper (JLSpearing) **3-10-9**(5) MichaelBrennan (trckd ldrs tl wknd appr 3 out: t.o)	29	12	16/1	16	—
	John-T (JBerry) **3-11-0** LO'Hara (a bhd: t.o)	8	13	20/1	8	—
	Ballykissangel (NBycroft) **3-11-0** DBentley (prom tl wknd 5th: sn t.o)	15	14	50/1	—	—
836[4]	**Prove The Point (IRE)** (MrsPNDutfield) **3-10-9** MrLJefford (in tch tl wknd appr 3 out: t.o)	3	15	25/1	—	—
	Appeal Again (IRE) (DBurchell) **3-11-0** DJBurchell (bkwd: a bhd: t.o)	dist	16	25/1	—	—
1011[3]	**Stoleamarch** (ALForbes) **3-11-0** TEley (hdwy 4th: wkng whn wnt lame & p.u appr last)		P	10/1	—	—
				(SP 162.4%)		**17 Rn**

3m 53.9 (11.90) CSF £8.24 TOTE £2.00: £1.60 £1.90 £17.80 (£4.60) Trio £60.90 OWNER Knight Hawks Partnership (WELLINGTON) BRED Cheveley Park Stud Ltd
358 Always Happy, at her best when fresh, benefited from a very confident ride and won readily, despite getting a bit leg-weary due to the gale-force head-wind on this long run-in. (Evens)
906 Globe Runner, rather small for jumping, stayed on strongly in the closing stages and should be able to pick up a race. (4/1)
Son of Anshan, still not looking quite cherry-ripe, nevertheless ran a fine race and, if there is any more improvement to come, he looks a ready-made winner. (33/1)
Kingfisher Brave set out to make every post a winning one on this hurdling debut, but he was deep in trouble after being collared at the last and gradually faded on the flat. These tactics could pay off for him round one of the sharper tracks. (14/1)
Whothehellisharry looked the likely winner when joining issue at the penultimate flight, but he was very leg-weary on reaching the flat and was brushed aside with ease. He should be able to improve with this experience under his belt. (25/1)
Meltemison (15/2: 4/1-8/1)
Sousse, a big, strong, attractive filly not fully wound up for this racecourse debut, never really got into contention, but she is sure to be much wiser for the experience and is worth bearing in mind. (7/1)

1185 PRESTON AMATEUR H'CAP HURDLE (0-125) (4-Y.O+) (Class E)
1-45 (1-45) **2m 4f (10 hdls)** £2,759.00 (£774.00: £377.00) GOING: 0.45 sec per fur (GS)

			SP	RR	SF
	Palosanto (IRE) (118) (MCPipe) **6-11-5**(5) MrAFarrant (mde virtually all: clr whn hit 3 out & 2 out: unchal) ....—	1	2/5[1]	103+	34
355*	**Trade Wind (96)** (DFBassett) **5-9-9**(7) MissKDiMarte (hld up & wl bhd: wnt 2nd last: too much to do) 10	2	3/1[2]	73	4
	Zip Your Lip (94) (MrsPTownsley) **6-9-7**(7) MissCTownsley (bkwd: plld hrd: w wnr early: lost tch 7th: t.o) 23	3	15/2[3]	53	—
			(SP 108.2%)		**3 Rn**

4m 56.0 (19.00) CSF £1.88 TOTE £1.40 (£1.20) OWNER **Mr B. A. Kilpatrick (WELLINGTON)** BRED W. R. Jackson
LONG HANDICAP Zip Your Lip 9-9

Palosanto (IRE), faced with a simple task, did not hurdle fluently, but he had a virtual solo school round and won easing down by a very long-looking ten lengths. (2/5)

355* Trade Wind, operating from a different stable and having his first outing in almost three months, is probably not an ideal ride for a female and he just went round in his own time. (3/1: op 2/1)

1186 RADIO CITY H'CAP CHASE (0-130) (5-Y.O+) (Class C)
2-15 (2-15) **2m (12 fncs)** £5,784.00 (£1,624.00: £792.00) GOING: 0.45 sec per fur (GS)

			SP	RR	SF
951*	**Eastern Magic (99)** (GBarnett) **8-10-0** RFarrant (lw: hld up: j.slowly 4th: chsd ldr fr 4 out: rdn to ld flat: r.o wl) ....—	1	4/1[3]	107	14
1155*	**Stately Home (IRE) (123)** (PBowen) **5-11-3**(7) 5x MrRThornton (j.w: led tl hdd & no ex flat) 4	2	6/4[1]	127	34
	Pats Minstrel (113) (RChampion) **11-11-0b** ADobbin (bkwd: chsd ldr: rdn & wknd 4 out: t.o) ....dist	3	7/1	—	—
	No Pain No Gain (IRE) (123) (JTGifford) **8-11-10** BStorey (bkwd: hld up in rr: mstke 2nd: fell 7th)	F	13/8[2]	—	—
			(SP 110.6%)		**4 Rn**

4m 10.1 (15.10) CSF £9.90 TOTE £5.50 (£3.70) OWNER Mrs Christine Smith (STOKE-ON-TRENT) BRED C. Wiggins
LONG HANDICAP Eastern Magic 9-5

951* Eastern Magic confirmed his superiority over the favourite on 11lb worse terms and has certainly found his form this year. (4/1)

1155* Stately Home (IRE) gave an exhibition of jumping from the front, but he has been kept very busy in the past month and was tapped for finished speed on this return to the minimum trip. (6/4)

No Pain No Gain (IRE) is not always the safest of conveyances, especially over the minimum trip and he had already taken more than the odd chance before he went a pearler down the back straight. (13/8)

1187 WARRINGTON NOVICES' HURDLE (4-Y.O+) (Class D)
2-45 (2-45) **2m (8 hdls)** £3,011.00 (£846.00: £413.00) GOING: 0.45 sec per fur (GS)

			SP	RR	SF
	Advance East (MDods) **4-10-12** RSupple (lw: hld up & bhd: hdwy 3 out: led flat: comf)..............—	1	14/1	75	42
1053[3]	**Nordic Breeze (IRE) (102)** (MCPipe) **4-11-4** NWilliamson (led tl flat: rallied u.p nr fin)..............1¾	2	6/4[1]	79	46
	Grandinare (USA) (JJO'Neill) **4-10-7**(5) RMcGrath (bit bkwd: a.p: ev ch 2 out: styd on u.p towards fin)..........nk	3	14/1	73	40
	Galen (IRE) (MrsMReveley) **5-10-12** PNiven (hld up & bhd: styd on fr 2 out: nvr nrr) 19	4	12/1	54	21
	Three Wild Days (99) (TPTate) **4-10-12** RGarritty (chsd ldrs tl outpcd appr 2 out)..............8	5	5/1[3]	46	13
	Star Selection (JMackie) **5-10-9**(3) EHusband (plld hrd: chsd ldr: blnd 5th: sn lost pl)..............2	6	9/2[2]	44	11
	Heighth of Fame (DBurchell) **5-10-12** DJBurchell (prom: chsd ldr fr 5th: rdn & btn between last 2)..............hd	7	16/1	44	11
1036[5]	**Pentlands Flyer (IRE)** (NATwiston-Davies) **5-10-12** CMaude (bit bkwd: prom tl wknd 5th)..............1	8	6/1	43	10
	Rood Music (MGMeagher) **5-10-12** LWyer (bhd: rdn 5th: no imp)..............nk	9	16/1	43	10
1030[8]	**Segala (IRE)** (JJO'Neill) **5-10-12** ARoche (bit bkwd: hld up in tch: hdwy appr 3 out: wknd qckly after next)...1¾	10	20/1	41	8
	Cliburnel News (IRE) (ALForbes) **6-10-7** TEley (a bhd: t.o) 7	11	16/1	29	—
	Royrace (WMBrisbourne) **4-10-12** SWynne (a bhd: t.o) ....dist	12	50/1	—	—
	Intendant (JGFitzGerald) **4-10-12** MDwyer (bkwd: hld up & bhd: t.o whn p.u bef last)	P	14/1	—	—
	Scott's Risk (LJBarratt) **6-10-12** RichardGuest (bkwd: t.o fr ½-wy: p.u bef 3 out)	P	50/1	—	—
			(SP 143.2%)		**14 Rn**

3m 52.9 (10.90) CSF £39.63 TOTE £29.60: £4.70 £1.50 £6.90 (£32.20) Trio £306.90 OWNER Mr A. F. Monk (DARLINGTON) BRED Chippenham Lodge Stud

Advance East, a maiden on the Flat who had promised so much, came good at the first time of asking at this game and this could be the making of him. (14/1)

1053 Nordic Breeze (IRE), probably more effective when ridden from off the pace, did the donkey-work here until the final 200 yards and his determined late rally was always being comfortably held. (6/4)

Grandinare (USA), on the sidelines for almost twelve months and looking to be carrying surplus condition, turned in an extremely promising performance and, with further improvement to come, should have little trouble in paying his way, (14/1: op 8/1)

Galen (IRE), bred to stay extreme distances, had a quiet school round in the rear until passing beaten rivals to reach his finishing position. (12/1)

Three Wild Days did look as though he had done plenty of work, but there is nothing like a race to blow away the cobwebs, and he can soon leave this run behind. (5/1)

Star Selection finished a creditable ninth in the 1994 Derby and has not been disgraced in hot company on the Flat this term. He looked something to be on on this debut over hurdles, but he was inclined to run a bit free and was on the heels of the leader when he clouted the fourth last hard. Losing his pitch, he had little hope of getting back into it. (9/2)

1188 RADIO CITY H'CAP HURDLE (0-120) (5-Y.O+) (Class D)
3-15 (3-15) **2m (8 hdls)** £2,745.00 (£770.00: £375.00) GOING: 0.45 sec per fur (GS)

		SP	RR	SF
Chai-Yo (104) (JABOld) **6-11-3** GUpton (hld up in rr: hdwy to ld on bit last: pushed out nr fin)..............—	1	5/2[1]	89	—
Saint Ciel (USA) (104) (FJordan) **8-11-3** SWynne (bit bkwd: a.p: outpcd appr last: rdn & kpt on flat)..............2	2	7/1	87	—
Lord Mcmurrough (IRE) (110) (JNeville) **6-11-9** RFarrant (bit bkwd: hld up: chsd ldr fr 4th: ev ch last: one pce)..............3	3	5/1	90	—
Thursday Night (IRE) (108) (JGFitzGerald) **5-11-7** LWyer (bit bkwd: set slow pce: hdd last: sn drvn along & outpcd)..............1¾	4	7/1	86	—
Seasonal Splendour (IRE) (115) (MCPipe) **6-12-0** CMaude (hld up in tch: outpcd 3 out: sn rdn & btn) 4	5	7/2[2]	89	—
Cool Luke (IRE) (106) (FMurphy) **7-11-5** NWilliamson (bkwd: chsd ldrs to 3 out: sn rdn & wknd)..............4	6	9/2[3]	76	—
		(SP 110.6%)		**6 Rn**

4m 7.1 (25.10) CSF £17.40 TOTE £3.00: £2.20 £2.90 (£9.00) OWNER Mr Nick Viney (WROUGHTON) BRED Mrs Audrey Goodwin

Chai-Yo, sharpened up by a recent outing on the Flat, made this transition into handicap company lc easy with a very comfortable success, and he is a the right end of the handicap to take advantage. (5/2)
Saint Ciel (USA), sure to strip fitter next time, battled on to gain the runner-up prize without giving the winner much cause for concern. (7/1)
Lord Mcmurrough (IRE) needs a stiffer test of stamina than he had here, but he performed with credit and his on good terms with himself. (5/1)
Thursday Night (IRE) does not usually set the pace but, with nobody else prepared to do so, had little option, seeing that he does need a true test of stamina at this trip. Outpaced when the sprint to the post developed on the run-in, he will be all the better for therun. (7/1)
Seasonal Splendour (IRE) did win first time out last season, but she had a four-month break to overcome this time and was struggling from the turn into the straight. (7/2)
Cool Luke (IRE), looking very burly for this return to action, was finding the quickening tempo too great for him early in the straight and was forced to accept that this was not going to be his day. (9/2)

1189 GLENGOYNE SINGLE HIGHLAND MALT & TAMEROSIA SERIES (QUAL) NOVICES' CHASE (5-Y.O+)(Class D)
3-45 (3-45) **3m (18 fncs)** £4,030.00 (£1,130.00: £550.00) GOING: 0.45 sec per fur (GS)

				SP	RR	SF
977*	**Imperial Vintage (IRE) (104)** (MissVenetiaWilliams) **6-11-12** NWilliamson (mde all: mstke 4 out: j.lft last: rdn out)	—	1	100/30 2	114	26
1120 3	**Monymoss (IRE)** (MrsSJSmith) **7-10-9**(7) RWilkinson (lft 2nd 13th: rdn appr last: kpt on towards fin)	1¾	2	5/1 3	103	15
	Royal Paris (IRE) (MrsSJSmith) **8-11-2** RichardGuest (bkwd: chsng wnr whn blnd 6th: sn lost tch: t.o fr 10th)	dist	3	12/1	—	—
	Cherry Orchid (JLNeedham) **9-11-2** RSupple (bkwd: dropped rr 5th: sn t.o: p.u bef 14th)		P	50/1	—	—
	Wisley Wonder (IRE) (NATwiston-Davies) **6-11-2** CMaude (bkwd: chsd wnr: pushed along 12th: blnd & uns rdr next)		U	8/13 1	—	—

(SP 111.3%) **5 Rn**

6m 25.1 (27.10) CSF £17.39 TOTE £2.90: £2.40 £3.00 (£7.20) OWNER Mr David Williams (HEREFORD) BRED W. J. Mernagh
977* Imperial Vintage (IRE), despite conceding weight all round, only needed to put in a clear round to succeed here. He managed to do that with the exception of a couple of minor errors, but he had to be kept up to his work right to the end. (100/30: op 7/4)
1120 Monymoss (IRE) might have found this race coming much too soon, but he was back over a more suitable trip and he made the winner fight hard to hold him at bay. (5/1)
Wisley Wonder (IRE), a well-made individual on short legs, jumped these big fences well and gave chase to the winner until his legs buckled underneath him six out and he dislodged his jockey. He did appear to be holding his own at the time, but the pressure had not been on and paddock inspection suggested this run was needed. (8/13)

1190 WEATHERBYS 'STARS OF TOMORROW' N.H. FLAT RACE (4, 5 & 6-Y.O F & M) (Class H)
4-15 (4-16) **2m** £1,208.00 (£338.00: £164.00)

				SP	RR	SF
	Marello (MrsMReveley) **5-11-7**(3) GCahill (hld up: hdwy 3f out: led appr fnl f: comf)	—	1	4/11 1	—	—
	Country Orchid (MrsMReveley) **5-11-0** PNiven (hld up: hdwy over 3f out: kpt on one pce fnl f)	1¼	2	8/1 2	—	—
	Hurst Flyer (FPMurtagh) **4-11-0** ADobbin (hld up: hdwy over 2f out: styd on wl towards fin)	s.h	3	16/1	—	—
	Bridled Tern (JMJefferson) **5-10-9**(5) ECallaghan (bkwd: slt ld after 4f to 7f out: led 4f out: sn clr: hdd appr fnl f: one pce)	1	4	8/1 2	—	—
	Lovely Rascal (JJO'Neill) **4-10-9**(5) RMcGrath (bkwd: hld up in tch: effrt 3f out: nt trble ldrs)	1	5	9/1 3	—	—
872 5	**Lippy Louise** (MrsMReveley) **4-11-0** RHodge (set slow pce 4f: prom tl wknd over 2f out)	2½	6	10/1	—	—
	Herballistic (JGMO'Shea) **4-10-9**(5) MichaelBrennan (chsd ldrs over 12f: sn wknd)	½	7	33/1	—	—
	Lady Rosebury (RJPrice) **6-11-0** NWilliamson (bkwd: prom: led 7f out to 4f out: sn wknd: t.o)	16	8	25/1	—	—

(SP 127.3%) **8 Rn**

4m 5.7 CSF £5.37 TOTE £1.40: £1.10 £1.90 £2.30 (£3.30) Trio £28.60 OWNER Mrs M. Williams (SALTBURN) BRED R. Chugg
Marello kept up her unbeaten record with a cleverly-gained success. She has been reported to have schooled well over hurdles and she could make up into a useful stayer when her attention is switched to jumping. (4/11)
Country Orchid, an unraced stablemate to the winner, looks made for the jumping game, but she turned in a pleasing display on this debut and she could be the one with the more scope for improvement. (8/1)
Hurst Flyer did not cut much ice on her debut in the spring, but she showed much-improved form here and is certainly heading in the right direction. (16/1)
Bridled Tern, a tall, somewhat unfurnished mare very much in need of this first outing in over eighteen months, must have pleased her connections with this promising effort, and she can only improve on this. (8/1: op 5/1)
Lovely Rascal, a sister to prolific winner Scally Owen, almost defied her burly looks on this racecourse debut and it would seem she does not intend to let the family name down. (9/1: 5/1-10/1)
872 Lippy Louise helped share the pace, but found the quickening tempo too much for her inside the final quarter-mile. (10/1)

T/Plpt: £106.90 (81.41 Tckts). T/Qdpt: £50.60 (11.76 Tckts). IM

0943-KEMPTON (R-H) (Good)
Wednesday November 6th
WEATHER: overcast WIND: blustery

1191 USM BOWL NOVICES' HURDLE (4-Y.O+) (Class E)
1-35 (1-37) **2m 5f (10 hdls)** £2,360.00 (£660.00: £320.00) GOING: 0.32 sec per fur (GS)

				SP	RR	SF
	Millersford (NAGaselee) **5-10-10** JRKavanagh (lw: stdy hdwy 7th: led 2 out: pushed out)	—	1	11/2 3	76	28
	Quaff (IRE) (JTGifford) **6-10-10** PHide (stdy hdwy 7th: rdn appr 2 out: unable qckn)	3	2	7/2 2	74	26
	Mountain Path (NJHenderson) **6-10-10** MAFitzgerald (hld up: ev ch 2 out: rdn appr last: one pce)	2½	3	11/2 3	72	24
	Spring Double (IRE) (NATwiston-Davies) **5-10-10** CLlewellyn (led to 2 out: sn wknd)	15	4	2/1 1	60	12
	Winnow (AndrewTurnell) **6-9-12**(7) CRae (swtg: stdy hdwy 7th: wknd appr 2 out)	2	5	66/1	54	6
	Dominos Ring (IRE) (105) (MrsHLWalton) **7-10-10** MrAWalton (bit bkwd: prom tl appr 2 out)	16	6	7/1	47	—
	Kraton Garden (USA) (81) (TCasey) **4-10-10** EMurphy (prom to 3 out)	14	7	20/1	36	—
	Checks And Stripes (IRE) (CWeedon) **5-10-10** MRichards (prom to 6th: t.o)	dist	8	33/1	—	—
960 4	**Zuno Flyer (USA)** (AMoore) **4-10-10** BPowell (swtg: a bhd: blnd 3rd: t.o fr 6th)	1½	9	33/1	—	—
1044 5	**Quare Dream's (IRE)** (TCasey) **5-10-5** CO'Dwyer (bit bkwd: plld hrd: chsd ldr 2nd to 3 out: sn wknd: t.o whn p.u bef 2 out)		P	25/1	—	—

Fast Forward Fred (LMontagueHall) **5-10-10** DMorris (bit bkwd: a bhd: t.o whn p.u bef 7th)............................ **P** 14/1 — —
(SP 121.5%) **11 Rn**

5m 7.2 (15.20) CSF £24.53 TOTE £7.70: £2.50 £1.50 £2.60 (£14.00) Trio £34.30 OWNER Mrs Derek Fletcher (LAMBOURN) BRED Mrs F. A. H. Murray

Millersford was the paddock pick and put up a performance to match, leading at the second last and needing only to be nudged along to dispose of his rivals on the run-in. His trainer is half-tempted to send him straight over fences. (11/2: 4/1-6/1)

Quaff (IRE), without a run since January, won the battle for second on the run-in, but failed to get the better of Millersford. (7/2)

Mountain Path, who cost 20,000 guineas, was making his racecourse debut rather late in life, but definitely has ability. He looks the type to do well at this game and should not be difficult to win with. (11/2: 4/1-6/1)

Spring Double (IRE) looked straight for this reappearance. (2/1)

Dominos Ring (IRE) (7/1: 9/2-8/1)

Fast Forward Fred (14/1: 6/1-16/1)

1192 JOHNSONS INTERNATIONAL NOVICES' CHASE (5-Y.O+) (Class D)

2-05 (2-06) **3m (19 fncs)** £3,517.50 (£1,065.00: £520.00: £247.50) GOING minus 0.06 sec per fur (G)

	Horse / Trainer / Weight / Jockey / Comment	Dist	Pos	SP	RR	SF
	Baronet (IRE) (110) (DNicholson) **6-11-0** AMaguire (lw: led 4th to 5th: led 14th: mstke 4 out: r.o wl)	—	1	8/13 1	91	23
1041 4	**Castle Chief (IRE) (90)** (JTGifford) **7-11-0** PHide (led 5th to 8th: ev ch 2 out: unable qckn)	7	2	4/1 2	86	18
	Ourownfellow (IRE) (RCurtis) **7-11-0** DMorris (lw: hld up: led 8th: j.lft 12th: hdd 14th: ev ch 3 out:sn wknd)	8	3	5/1 3	81	13
	Parliamentarian (IRE) (85) (TCasey) **7-11-0** CO'Dwyer (bit bkwd: led to 4th: wknd 13th: t.o fr 15th)	dist	4	16/1	—	—
	Glentower (IRE) (CLPopham) **8-11-0** MAFitzgerald (bhd fr 14th: blnd 3 out: 4th & no ch whn fell 2 out)		F	12/1	—	—

(SP 112.1%) **5 Rn**

6m 6.7 (11.70) CSF £3.55 TOTE £1.70: £1.20 £1.60 (£2.30) OWNER Mrs David Thompson (TEMPLE GUITING) BRED Mrs N. Flynn

Baronet (IRE) did not set the world alight on this seasonal and chasing debut, but he did the job well enough. In front six out, he rather fiddled the fourth last and lost the lead momentarily, but he was in command in the straight and managed to brush his two main rivals aside from the penultimate fence. He will have learnt a lot from this. (8/13)

1041 Castle Chief (IRE) ran much better here and was only put in his place from the penultimate fence. He should soon be winning.(4/1)

Ourownfellow (IRE) may have been off the track since May 1994, but he looked very fit for this reappearance and ran a fine race, holding every chance early in the straight before tiring. Considering how fit he was, there must be a question mark about how much he can improve. (5/1)

1193 MIRROR SELECT CONDITIONAL CLAIMING HURDLE (4, 5 & 6-Y.O) (Class F)

2-35 (2-35) **2m (8 hdls)** £2,234.00 (£624.00: £302.00) GOING: 0.32 sec per fur (GS)

	Horse / Trainer / Weight / Jockey / Comment	Dist	Pos	SP	RR	SF
1145 5	**Pair of Jacks (IRE) (92)** (GLMoore) **6-11-7** DFortt (lw: chsd ldr: hrd rdn appr last: led nr fin)	—	1	3/1 2	71	31
659 5	**Adilov** (JJBridger) **4-10-7** SophieMitchell (lw: hld up: rdn appr last: ev ch flat: r.o wl)	nk	2	33/1	57	17
963*	**Indian Jockey (117)** (MCPipe) **4-11-13** DWalsh (led & sn clr: mstke 3 out: hrd rdn: hdd nr fin)	½	3	8/11 1	76	36
974 9	**Last Laugh (IRE) (83)** (KCBailey) **4-9-13**(5) WWalsh (hld up: rdn 2 out: sn wknd)	13	4	4/1 3	40	—
1073 5	**Night in a Million (71)** (SWoodman) **5-11-1** KGaule (hld up: rdn 4th: wknd appr 2 out)	14	5	16/1	37	—

(SP 111.7%) **5 Rn**

3m 55.1 (13.10) CSF £41.41 TOTE £3.90: £1.40 £5.80 (£78.70) OWNER Mr D. A. Wilson (BRIGHTON) BRED Loan and Development Corporation

1145 Pair of Jacks (IRE) was meeting the favourite on much worse terms than in a handicap, but still managed to gain the day. Travelling nicely entering the straight, he got up near the line. (3/1)

Adilov was a complete revelation. Still travelling well in behind the leader entering the straight, he was one of three battling for honours on the run-in and only just lost out. (33/1)

963* Indian Jockey, racing with his tongue tied down, may have won both his races this season, but he is no easy ride. Adopting his usual front-running tactics, he soon established a clear advantage, but gave the distinct impression he had had enough in the back straight and quickly came back to his field. With his jockey having to work exceptionally hard after the gelding made a mistake three out, he maintained the lead and still looked as if he was going to win jumping the last. However, he was worried out of it in the closing stages. (8/11: 1/2-4/5)

1194 SPORTING LIFE TROPHY H'CAP CHASE (0-120) (5-Y.O+) (Class D)

3-05 (3-05) **3m (19 fncs)** £3,501.25 (£1,060.00: £517.50: £246.25) GOING minus 0.06 sec per fur (G)

	Horse / Trainer / Weight / Jockey / Comment	Dist	Pos	SP	RR	SF
914 2	**Drumcullen (IRE) (96)** (KCBailey) **7-11-0** CO'Dwyer (led 2nd tl mstke & hdd 12th: led 14th tl appr 2 out: lft in clr ld appr last: r.o)	—	1	4/1 3	104	21
959 P	**Paper Star (103)** (MPMuggeridge) **9-11-7** BPowell (led to 2nd: wknd 10th)	8	2	33/1	106	23
158 8	**Funcheon Gale (92)** (RCurtis) **9-10-10** DMorris (nt j.w: nvr nr to chal)	3	3	9/2	93	10
953 3	**Certain Angle (106)** (PJHobbs) **7-11-10** AMaguire (hld up: led 12th to 14th: ev ch whn blnd 4 out: sn wknd)	1¾	4	7/2 2	106	23
946 5	**Nevada Gold (100)** (FJYardley) **10-11-4** PMcLoughlin (lw: prom to 9th)	nk	5	7/1	99	16
1043 4	**Sorbiere (100)** (NJHenderson) **9-11-4b** MAFitzgerald (lw: bhd tl fell 13th)		F	9/1	—	—
	Master Orchestra (IRE) (103) (MissHCKnight) **7-11-7** JFTitley (lw: hld up: w ldr fr 15th: led appr 2 out tl p.u appr last: lame)		P	9/4 1	—	—

(SP 116.6%) **7 Rn**

6m 7.7 (12.70) CSF £76.90 TOTE £4.20: £1.80 £5.30 (£84.40) OWNER Mr Martyn Booth (UPPER LAMBOURN) BRED E. Burke

914 Drumcullen (IRE) found Lady Luck smiling on him. He was definitely held in second place and about a length down when Master Orchestra pulled up lame going to the final fence, leaving him in splendid isolation. (4/1)

932 Paper Star was in trouble early on the final circuit but, with Master Orchestra pulling up and Certain Angle making a bad mistake, he found himself coming through for a very moderate second place on the run-in. All four of her victories to date have come on firm ground at Plumpton. (33/1)

158 Funcheon Gale, returning after a four-month break, jumped far from fluently and was out the back until struggling on to finish a very flattering third. Some easing in the ground would be in his favour. (9/2)

953 Certain Angle is prone to making errors and that was again the case here. (7/2)

Nevada Gold may be falling sharply in the handicap, but his performances do not seem to be getting any better. (7/1)

1043 Sorbiere (9/1: 6/1-10/1)

Master Orchestra (IRE), who looked in good heart for this reappearance, was set for victory when going lame approaching the final fence. (9/4)

1195 ACE CUP NOVICES' CHASE (5-Y.O+) (Class D)

3-35 (3-38) **2m 4f 110y (17 fncs)** £3,825.00 (£1,075.00: £525.00) GOING minus 0.06 sec per fur (G)

				SP	RR	SF
1037[2]	**Fine Thyne (IRE)** (GHarwood) **7-11-0** MAFitzgerald (a.p: chsd ldr 10th to 4 out: led 2 out: lft clr last)	—	1	6/5[1]	117	21
	Mystic Isle (IRE) (NAGaselee) **6-11-0** CLlewellyn (bit bkwd: hld up: mstke 7th: 4th whn mstke 3 out: sn wknd: lft poor 2nd last)	dist	2	9/1	—	—
	Sunset and Vine (TCasey) **9-11-0** CO'Dwyer (bit bkwd: bhd fr 6th: t.o fr 13th)	dist	3	20/1	—	—
	Key To Moyade (IRE) (MJWilkinson) **6-11-0** ILawrence (bit bkwd: 5th whn carried out bef 9th)		C	33/1	—	—
947[6]	**Nordansk** (MMadgwick) **7-11-0** DMorris (lw: hdwy 10th: ev ch 3 out: blnd 2 out: 3rd & btn whn fell last)		F	9/1	—	—
947[3]	**Greenback (BEL)** (PJHobbs) **5-10-13** AMaguire (hdwy 11th: led 4 out to 2 out: 2nd & btn whn fell last)		F	9/2[3]	—	—
	Wixoe Wonder (IRE) (MBradstock) **6-11-0** PHolley (led & sn clr: hdd & fell 4 out)		F	66/1	—	—
	Mr Jervis (IRE) (JTGifford) **7-11-0** PHide (bit bkwd: chsd ldr to 8th: 3rd whn p.u bef 9th: lame)		P	4/1[2]	—	—

(SP 112.8%) **8 Rn**

5m 11.6 (10.60) CSF £11.60 TOTE £2.30: £1.40 £2.10 £3.00 (£10.50) Trio £60.60 OWNER Mr Peter Wiegand (PULBOROUGH) BRED Minch Bloodstock in Ireland

WEIGHT FOR AGE 5yo-1lb

1037 Fine Thyne (IRE) put up a polished display. Travelling well, he cruised into the lead at the second last and had the race in the bag when his two main rivals fell independently at the final fence. He can win again. (6/5: evens-5/4)

Mystic Isle (IRE), not looking fully wound up for this seasonal debut, had given his all early in the straight but, with Greenback and Nordansk both falling at the final fence, he found himself handed second prize. He would prefer a bit further and some cut in the ground. (9/1: 6/1-10/1)

947 Nordansk, who made an horrendous mistake on his chasing debut at the last meeting here, was again let down by his jumping at a critical stage. A couple of lengths down and held when falling at the final fence, he can pick up a race, maybe back over two miles, once he masters the art of jumping fences. (9/1)

947 Greenback (BEL), held up to get this much longer trip, was about a couple of lengths down and held when falling at the final fence. He does stay this trip and should soon find a suitable opportunity. (9/2)

1196 FIESTA MAGAZINE H'CAP HURDLE (0-135) (4-Y.O+) (Class C)

4-05 (4-06) **3m 110y (12 hdls)** £3,436.25 (£1,040.00: £507.50: £241.25) GOING: 0.32 sec per fur (GS)

				SP	RR	SF
	Ocean Hawk (USA) (128) (NATwiston-Davies) **4-11-11** CLlewellyn (hld up: led 9th: sn clr: easily)	—	1	9/4[1]	114+	56
1019[7]	**Fieldridge (115)** (MPMuggeridge) **7-10-13** BPowell (hdwy 9th: chsd wnr appr 2 out: no imp)	13	2	14/1	93	36
1031*	**Olympian (118)** (JNeville) **9-11-2b** MrMPFitzgerald (chsd ldr 2nd to 3 out: one pce)	6	3	7/1	92	35
948[3]	**Givus a Call (IRE) (109)** (JTGifford) **6-10-7** PHide (nvr nr to chal)	3	4	8/1	81	24
	Harding (102) (SMellor) **5-10-0** NMann (chsd ldr to 2nd: chsd wnr 3 out tl appr 2 out: wknd appr last)	7	5	3/1[2]	69	12
	Dark Honey (130) (SDow) **11-12-0** ADicken (bit bkwd: a bhd: t.o fr 8th)	dist	6	20/1	—	—
	Jadidh (107) (ABarrow) **8-10-5** PHolley (bit bkwd: a bhd: t.o fr 8th)	1¼	7	14/1	—	—
902*	**Shahrani (113)** (MCPipe) **4-10-7**(3) DWalsh (swtg: led & sn clr: hdd 9th: wknd qckly: t.o whn p.u bef 2 out)		P	6/1[3]	—	—
1039[5]	**Wottashambles (111)** (LMontagueHall) **5-10-9** DMorris (bhd fr 8th: t.o fr 9th: p.u bef 2 out)		P	6/1[3]	—	—

(SP 126.0%) **9 Rn**

5m 59.2 (13.20) CSF £32.59 CT £188.44 TOTE £3.50: £1.70 £3.60 £2.30 (£69.70) Trio £63.10 OWNER Mr Matt Archer & Miss Jean Broadhurst (CHELTENHAM) BRED Brereton C. Jones

WEIGHT FOR AGE 4yo-1lb

Ocean Hawk (USA) had no problems with this much longer trip and did not even break sweat to win, cruising into the lead four out and pulling clear to win with any amount in hand. The winning distance is no true reflection of his superiority and he could have won by twice that. (9/4)

721 Fieldridge has never won off a mark as high as this before, but did struggle into second place approaching the second last if having no hope of reeling in the clear winner. (14/1)

1031* Olympian was 4lb higher for his recent success. (7/1: 5/1-15/2)

948 Givus a Call (IRE) never threatened. (8/1)

Harding would find a bit of cut in the ground in his favour. (3/1)

902* Shahrani, unbeaten over hurdles, mainly in weak events, gave himself no chance of staying this longer trip as he tore off in front. A return to a shorter distance and lower grade is required. (6/1: 4/1-13/2)

T/Plpt: £228.80 (48.96 Tckts). T/Qdpt: £81.50 (11.81 Tckts). AK

0885-NEWTON ABBOT (L-H) (Heavy)

Wednesday November 6th

WEATHER: sunny & showers WIND: v.str

1197 ANFIELD NOVICES' HURDLE (4-Y.O+) (Class E)

1-25 (1-25) **3m 3f (12 hdls)** £2,284.50 (£642.00: £313.50) GOING: 1.15 sec per fur (HY)

				SP	RR	SF
973[2]	**Kendal Cavalier (100)** (GBBalding) **6-10-10** BFenton (lw: led 3rd tl after 10th: rallied to ld last: all out)	—	1	15/8[1]	78	35
	Denise's Profiles (NATwiston-Davies) **6-10-10** DBridgwater (hld up & bhd: hdwy 7th: led after 10th to last: kpt on wl u.p)	hd	2	9/4[2]	78	35
	Bramblehill Buck (IRE) (PFNicholls) **7-10-10** APMcCoy (a.p: chsd wnr 9th tl wknd after next)	25	3	6/1[3]	63	20
1077[3]	**Copper Coil (85)** (WGMTurner) **6-10-3**(7) JPower (led to 3rd: ev ch tl wknd 9th)	25	4	12/1	48	5
900[4]	**Castleconner (IRE) (80)** (RGFrost) **5-10-10** JFrost (chsd ldrs tl wknd 9th)	15	5	20/1	39	—
824[4]	**Pennant Cottage (IRE) (55)** (MissKWhitehouse) **8-10-0**(5) ChrisWebb (prom to 7th: sn t.o)	dist	6	50/1	—	—
	Karicleigh Man (PJHobbs) **6-10-10** RDunwoody (bit bkwd: hdwy 5th: in tch 8th: wknd fr next: t.o whn p.u bef last)		P	6/1[3]	—	—
	Hopperdante (IRE) (TRGeorge) **6-10-5** RJohnson (bit bkwd: j.slowly 1st & 2nd: in tch 5th: no hdwy 9th: t.o whn p.u bef last)		P	20/1	—	—
499[4]	**Up the Tempo (IRE) (63)** (PaddyFarrell) **7-10-5** WMarston (a bhd: lost tch 6th: t.o whn p.u after 8th)		P	25/1	—	—
891[4]	**Mu-Tadil (70)** (RJBaker) **4-10-10** DLeahy (bhd 4th: t.o 7th: p.u bef 2 out)		P	33/1	—	—

Form	Horse (Trainer) Age-Wt Jockey (comment)	Dist	Pos	SP	RR	SF
594^{2}	**Rare Spread (IRE)** (MCPipe) **6-10-10** GBradley (bhd: hdwy 7th: wknd 9th: t.o whn p.u bef last)		**P**	14/1	—	—

(SP 126.8%) **11 Rn**

7m 2.3 (39.30) CSF £6.93 TOTE £2.50: £1.10 £1.60 £2.20 (£4.40) Trio £7.00 OWNER Mr Michael WingfieldDigby (ANDOVER) BRED A. L. Holland

WEIGHT FOR AGE 4yo-1lb

OFFICIAL EXPLANATION **Rare Spread (IRE): the jockey reported that the gelding, who has a tendency to do this on a left-handed track, was hanging badly to the right throughout the race and had no more to give so he pulled him up.**

973 Kendal Cavalier appreciated the underfoot conditions here and battled on well to the line. He may now go for a long-distance hurdle at Cheltenham later this month. (15/8)

Denise's Profiles, like the winner, had conditions to suit as his two bumper wins had come on soft and heavy ground. This was a brave performance and he will not always meet one so good. (9/4)

Bramblehill Buck (IRE), a half-brother to the winner, has won three times here, but over the larger obstacles. (6/1: op 4/1)

1077 Copper Coil once again lacked pace at the business end. (12/1)

594 Rare Spread (IRE) (14/1: op 6/1)

1198 OLD TRAFFORD (S) H'CAP HURDLE (0-95) (4-Y.O+) (Class G)

1-55 (1-55) **2m 1f (8 hdls)** £1,865.80 (£523.80: £255.40) GOING: 1.15 sec per fur (HY)

Form	Horse (Trainer) Age-Wt Jockey (comment)	Dist	Pos	SP	RR	SF
	Royal Standard (70) (PMRich) **9-9-13v**(7) DFinnegan (mde all: clr after 6th)	—	1	15/2	56?	22
	Alice's Mirror (73) (KBishop) **7-10-9** RJohnson (chsd ldrs: lost pl 5th: styd on appr 2 out: nvr nrr)	26	2	7/1 3	35	1
1145*	**Glowing Path (76)** (RJHodges) **6-10-5**(7) JHarris (prom: chsd wnr appr 2 out: no imp)	½	3	7/4 1	37	3
913^{6}	**Scalp 'em (IRE) (64)** (DrPPritchard) **8-10-0** DrPPritchard (hdwy 4th: rdn & wknd appr 6th)	9	4	33/1	17	—
	Al Haal (USA) (71) (RJO'Sullivan) **7-10-7** AMcCabe (bit bkwd: chsd ldrs: ev ch 6th: grad wknd)	6	5	14/1	18	—
913*	**Mutawali (IRE) (75)** (RJBaker) **6-10-11** DLeahy (a bhd: t.o 5th)	26	6	4/1 2	—	—
749^{P}	**Indian Minor (64)** (REPocock) **12-9-9b**(5) DJKavanagh (chsd ldrs tl wknd appr 5th: t.o)	dist	7	20/1	—	—
	Touch Silver (92) (HJManners) **6-11-7**(7) ADowling (bkwd: a bhd: t.o 4th)	6	8	15/2	—	—
	Nita's Choice (66) (AGNewcombe) **6-10-2**ow2 AThornton (j.slowly 2nd: a bhd: t.o 4th: p.u bef last)		P	20/1	—	—
969^{R}	**Sovereign Niche (IRE) (80)** (MCPipe) **8-11-2** APMcCoy (ref to r: t.n.p)		R	10/1	—	—
899^{P}	**Colour Scheme (68)** (HSHowe) **9-9-11v**1(7) BMcGann (rn out bnd after 2nd)		R	20/1	—	—

(SP 125.4%) **11 Rn**

4m 19.8 (26.80) CSF £57.95 CT £124.30 TOTE £14.60: £2.70 £2.20 £1.10 (£38.50) Trio £47.00 OWNER Mr P. M. Rich (USK) BRED Swettenham Stud

LONG HANDICAP Scalp 'em (IRE) 9-8 Nita's Choice 9-0 Indian Minor 9-10

No bid

Royal Standard, belatedly opening his account over hurdles, could not have won this any easier. (15/2: 5/1-9/1)

Alice's Mirror appreciates soft ground and won the battle for the only prize left on offer. (7/1)

1145* Glowing Path was disappointing here after previous decent efforts in similar contests. (7/4)

Al Haal (USA) (14/1: 10/1-16/1)

913* Mutawali (IRE), racing off a mark 7lb higher than when winning last time, would not have appreciated the testing conditions and will do better on a faster surface. (4/1)

1199 RODGERS OF BRIXTON NOVICES' CHASE (5-Y.O+) (Class E)

2-25 (2-25) **2m 5f 110y (16 fncs)** £3,077.55 (£932.40: £455.70: £217.35) GOING: 1.15 sec per fur (HY)

Form	Horse (Trainer) Age-Wt Jockey (comment)	Dist	Pos	SP	RR	SF
	Punters Overhead (IRE) (124) (PFNicholls) **8-10-12** APMcCoy (chsd ldr tl led 10th: rdn & styd on flat)	—	1	2/1 1	105	35
	Super Coin (120) (RLee) **8-10-12** RJohnson (bhd: hdwy 8th: chsd wnr 12th: ev ch 2 out: one pce)	2	2	100/30 2	104	34
	Amber Spark (IRE) (88) (DRGandolfo) **7-10-12** RDunwoody (bhd: mstke 4th: hdwy 12th: wkng & mstke 2 out)	3½	3	7/1	101	31
970*	**Mr Playfull (91)** (RGFrost) **6-11-5** JFrost (led to 10th: wknd fr 12th)	25	4	4/1 3	89	19
	Purbeck Cavalier (RHAlner) **7-10-12** WMcFarland (bkwd: chsd ldrs tl wknd 12th)	14	5	12/1	72	2
	Bold Acre (JMBradley) **6-10-12** TJMurphy (bit bkwd: in tch to 12th: grad wknd)	19	6	12/1	58	—
887^{4}	**Stormy Sunset** (WWDennis) **9-10-2**(7)ow2 MrTDennis (lw: mid div: wknd 12th: fell next)		F	14/1	—	—
	Vosne Romanee II (FR) (MCPipe) **9-10-5**(7) GSupple (a bhd: wkng whn fell 13th)		F	25/1	—	—
1038^{U}	**Country Keeper (65)** (BJMRyall) **8-10-9**(3) TDascombe (bit bkwd: fell 2nd)		F	33/1	—	—
720^{P}	**Bells Wood** (AJKDunn) **7-10-12** LHarvey (bit bkwd: prom: disp ld 5th: wknd 10th: mstke next: bhd whn fell 13th)		F	50/1	—	—
	Paddy Burke (IRE) (AGNewcombe) **6-10-12** AThornton (in tch to 7th: bhd 9th: t.o whn p.u bef 2 out)		P	33/1	—	—
	Lower Bitham (REPocock) **9-10-2**(5) DJKavanagh (bhd 7th: t.o whn p.u after 13th)		P	50/1	—	—
	Colette's Choice (IRE) (82) (GAHam) **7-10-7** SBurrough (bit bkwd: mid div whn blnd & uns rdr 6th)		U	33/1	—	—

(SP 127.6%) **13 Rn**

5m 49.3 (32.30) CSF £9.53 TOTE £2.70: £2.00 £1.10 £2.10 (£4.60) Trio £25.70 OWNER Mrs Elaine Hutchinson (SHEPTON MALLET) BRED Martin Kenirons in Ireland

Punters Overhead (IRE), who ran in some decent novice chases last season, jumped well and showed to be a class above these. (2/1: 6/4-9/4)

Super Coin, another with creditable form to his name, has generally raced at shorter distances and, although doing well, was slightly one-paced. He should not be long in going one better. (100/30)

Amber Spark (IRE), an ex-Irish gelding, would have finished a little closer but for a mistake at the penultimate fence. Nevertheless, he ran well behind decent opposition and could well go on from this. (7/1)

970* Mr Playfull, carrying a penalty for a win at Exeter, was struggling at these weights. (4/1)

Bold Acre (12/1: 8/1-14/1)

1200 BARCLAYS BANK 'N.H.' NOVICES' HURDLE (4-Y.O+) (Class E)

2-55 (2-57) **2m 6f (10 hdls)** £2,400.00 (£675.00: £330.00) GOING: 1.15 sec per fur (HY)

Form	Horse (Trainer) Age-Wt Jockey (comment)	Dist	Pos	SP	RR	SF
	Seymourswift (DRGandolfo) **6-10-5** RDunwoody (hld up in tch: disp ld 2 out: rdn & rallied to ld nr fin)	—	1	11/1	70	29
	Mr Cotton Socks (104) (RGFrost) **8-10-10** JFrost (led 3rd tl rdn & hdd nr fin)	s.h	2	11/4 2	75	34
	One For Navigation (IRE) (PFNicholls) **4-10-10** APMcCoy (in tch 3rd: lost pl 6th: rdn, in tch & mstke 7th: wknd next)	dist	3	8/11 1	—	—
1030^{13}	**Otter Prince** (TRGeorge) **7-10-10** RJohnson (hdwy to chse ldr 6th: rdn & wknd appr 2 out)	1¾	4	66/1	—	—
	Miss Secret (CWMitchell) **6-10-5** DBridgwater (bkwd: a bhd: t.o)	dist	5	66/1	—	—
954^{4}	**Jhal Frezi** (ABarrow) **8-10-10** AProcter (bit bkwd: prom to 7th: sn t.o)	8	6	12/1	—	—

	Horse	Dist	Pos	SP	RR	SF
	Alone Home (IRE) (CJMann) **5-10-10** JRailton (bit bkwd: prom to 7th: t.o whn p.u bef 2 out)		P	8/1[3]	—	—
	Tolcarne Lady (KBishop) **7-10-5** LHarvey (bkwd: a bhd: wknd 6th: t.o whn p.u bef 8th)		P	50/1	—	—
	Rainbow Fountain (NMLampard) **9-10-0**(5) ChrisWebb (led to 3rd: rdn & wknd 6th: p.u bef next)		P	20/1	—	—
418[6]	**Moreceva (IRE)** (PaddyFarrell) **6-10-10** WMarston (a bhd: t.o whn p.u after 6th)		P	50/1	—	—
913[9]	**Miramare (60)** (CLPopham) **6-10-7**(3) TDascombe (a bhd: t.o whn p.u bef last)		P	50/1	—	—
	Ashley House (BRMillman) **7-10-5**(5) DSalter (bit bkwd: hdwy 5th: wknd 7th: p.u bef 2 out)		P	50/1	—	—
	Blakeway (GAHam) **9-10-5** SBurrough (in tch to 5th: t.o whn p.u bef 2 out)		P	66/1	—	—
	Bid For Tools (IRE) (AGNewcombe) **4-10-10** AThornton (bkwd: a bhd: t.o 4th: p.u after 6th)		P	66/1	—	—

(SP 130.3%) **14 Rn**

5m 44.6 (32.60) CSF £42.15 TOTE £12.90: £2.50 £1.30 £1.30 (£16.20) Trio £10.00 OWNER Starlight Racing (WANTAGE) BRED G. Edwards
Seymourswift has been out for some time with sore shins and, in a terrific battle to the line, got up to take the honours close home. (11/1)
Mr Cotton Socks, a half-brother to Mr Flanagan, did nothing wrong, but could not sustain his lead in the closing stages. He had been out for some time and would have appreciated the run. (11/4: 2/1-3/1)
One For Navigation (IRE), a decent point-to-pointer in Ireland, came here with a big reputation. However, he soon weakened after a mistake and was never going to get any nearer than a minor place. (8/11)

1201 WILLIAM HILL TRIAL H'CAP HURDLE (0-130) (4-Y.O+) (Class C)
3-25 (3-26) **2m 1f (8 hdls)** £3,420.00 (£1,035.00: £505.00: £240.00) GOING: 1.15 sec per fur (HY)

	Horse	Dist	Pos	SP	RR	SF
	Mouse Bird (IRE) (114) (DRGandolfo) **6-10-12** RDunwoody (rdn & hdwy after 6th: led appr last: sn clr: eased flat)	—	1	7/2[2]	103+	17
1148[2]	**Morstock (110)** (RJHodges) **6-10-5**(3) TDascombe (chsd ldr: ev ch 6th: wknd appr 2 out)	7	2	4/1[3]	92	6
	Cadougold (FR) (123) (MCPipe) **5-11-7** APMcCoy (hdwy 4th: led 6th: hdd 2 out: wknd appr last)	s.h	3	3/1[1]	105	19
	Holdimclose (110) (RGFrost) **6-10-8** JFrost (bit bkwd: led to 6th: wknd qckly appr 2 out)	15	4	5/1	78	—
	Frogmarch (USA) (130) (RTPhillips) **6-12-0** JRailton (a bhd: lost tch 5th)	6	5	7/2[2]	93	7
	World Express (IRE) (104) (BRMillman) **6-9-11**(5)ow2 DSalter (bit bkwd: bhd fr 6th: sn wknd)	8	6	15/2	59	—

(SP 117.9%) **6 Rn**

4m 22.2 (29.20) CSF £17.28 TOTE £3.00: £2.10 £1.70 (£6.50) OWNER Mr Osbert Pierce (WANTAGE) BRED Airlie Stud
LONG HANDICAP World Express (IRE) 9-12
Mouse Bird (IRE) has only one success to his name and that came over course and distance on soft ground last year. Although a handful to ride, he won this with more in hand than the winning margin suggests. (7/2)
1148 Morstock had the advantage of a few runs already this season, but was never going to trouble the winner. (4/1: 3/1-9/2)
Cadougold (FR) held a slight advantage at the sixth, but it did not last and he was soon beaten. (3/1)

1202 STAMFORD BRIDGE H'CAP CHASE (0-110) (5-Y.O+) (Class E)
3-55 (3-55) **3m 2f 110y (20 fncs)** £2,900.10 (£877.80: £428.40: £203.70) GOING: 1.15 sec per fur (HY)

Horse	Dist	Pos	SP	RR	SF
Bond Jnr (IRE) (110) (PFNicholls) **7-12-0** APMcCoy (lw: led 1st: clr 15th: fin tired)	—	1	5/6[1]	125	26
Rocky Park (92) (GBBalding) **10-10-10** BFenton (bhd 6th: hdwy & mstke 10th: chsd wnr 16th: no imp)	6	2	6/1[3]	103	4
Shamarphil (93) (RHAlner) **10-10-11** MissSBarraclough (bit bkwd: chsng ldrs tl mstke 9th & lost pl: styd on fr 16th)	2½	3	8/1	103	4
Steeple Jack (85) (KBishop) **9-10-3** SBurrough (bit bkwd: prom tl wknd 12th: mstkes 14th & 15th)	3½	4	5/1[2]	93	—
Scotoni (95) (RJO'Sullivan) **10-10-13** SCurran (bit bkwd: led to 1st: chsd wnr to 16th: grad wknd)	21	5	16/1	90	—
Tapageur (95) (MCPipe) **11-10-6**(7) GSupple (a bhd: mstke 3rd: t.o whn p.u bef 17th)		P	6/1[3]	—	—

(SP 116.8%) **6 Rn**

7m 23.1 (49.10) CSF £6.52 TOTE £1.60: £1.40 £2.60 (£5.50) OWNER Mr Paul Barber (SHEPTON MALLET)
Bond Jnr (IRE) goes well fresh and ran out an easy winner, although looking very tired at the finish. (5/6: 4/6-11/10)
Rocky Park had been off for some time and put in a decent effort here. He will be better for this run. (6/1: op 7/2)
Shamarphil, who won a novice handicap in heavy ground here in 1994, has shown little since. (8/1)
Tapageur (6/1: 4/1-7/1)

1203 HIGHBURY STANDARD N.H. FLAT RACE (4, 5 & 6-Y.O) (Class H)
4-25 (4-25) **2m 1f** £1,236.00 (£346.00: £168.00)

	Horse	Dist	Pos	SP	RR	SF
679[3]	**Ultimate Smoothie** (MCPipe) **4-12-0** GBradley (lw: hld up & bhd: hdwy 6f out: led ins fnl f: comf)	—	1	7/1	—	—
	Lord Foley (NZ) (CJMann) **4-11-1**(3) JMagee (bit bkwd: hdwy 7f out: led 2f out: rdn & hdd ins fnl f)	1¼	2	9/1	—	—
	Ivory Coaster (NZ) (BdeHaan) **5-11-4** JOsborne (lw: racd wd: in tch: led 3f out to 2f out: styd on)	1¼	3	9/4[1]	—	—
25[9]	**Arctic Chanter** (BRMillman) **4-10-13**(5) DSalter (bit bkwd: chsd ldrs tl led 5f out: hdd 3f out: sn wknd)	12	4	33/1	—	—
	Defendtherealm (RGFrost) **5-11-4** MrAHoldsworth (bit bkwd: in tch to 3f out: sn wknd)	¾	5	50/1	—	—
	Tain Ton (NATwiston-Davies) **4-10-11**(7) MKeighley (a mid div: wknd 5f out)	¾	6	14/1	—	—
	Lucky Call (NZ) (AGHobbs) **5-10-11**(7) MrGShenkin (bkwd: bhd: hdwy 7f out: no imp)	8	7	11/2[2]	—	—
	Dukes Castle (IRE) (RGFrost) **5-11-4** JFrost (bkwd: prom to 5f out: sn wknd)	¾	8	11/2[2]	—	—
653[5]	**Captain Felix (NZ)** (AJKDunn) **6-10-13**(5) DJKavanagh (bkwd: prom tl wknd 5f out)	2½	9	14/1	—	—
	Frankie Muck (NATwiston-Davies) **4-10-11**(7) LSuthern (bit bkwd: a bhd)	5	10	6/1[3]	—	—
	Zaggy Lane (MrsRGHenderson) **4-11-4** BFenton (bkwd: mid div to ½-wy: sn wknd)	5	11	50/1	—	—
	Kind Cleric (PJHobbs) **5-11-4** APMcCoy (in tch to ½-wy: sn t.o)	12	12	14/1	—	—
	Murray's Million (JSSmith) **4-11-4** TJMurphy (bkwd: a bhd: t.o)	15	13	50/1	—	—
	Mingay (GrahamRichards) **5-10-11**(7) MissEJJones (bit bkwd: led & sn clr: hdd 5f out: wknd qckly: t.o)	19	14	66/1	—	—

(SP 128.6%) **14 Rn**

4m 20.3 (259.30) CSF £67.35 TOTE £4.00: £2.40 £3.50 £1.90 (£128.10) Trio £106.90 OWNER Isca Bloodstock (WELLINGTON) BRED Fares Stables Ltd
679 Ultimate Smoothie defied a 10lb penalty to prove his worth and won this comfortably. (7/1: 4/1-8/1)
Lord Foley (NZ), from a stable in form, proved the best of the debutants and could go on from here. (9/1: 4/1-10/1)
Ivory Coaster (NZ), the subject of support on his Newbury debut, stayed on well at the end. He was expected to do better here. (9/4: 4/1-2/1)
Dukes Castle (IRE) (11/2: 4/1-6/1)
Frankie Muck (6/1: op 4/1)
Kind Cleric (14/1: 8/1-16/1)

T/Jkpt: £29,554.50 (1.1 Tckts). T/Plpt: £6.80 (2,361.45 Tckts). T/Qdpt: £4.50 (188.01 Tckts). T

1027-MARKET RASEN (R-H) (Good, Good to soft home st)
Thursday November 7th
WEATHER: raining

1204 'STUDENTS IN FREE TODAY' CONDITIONAL H'CAP HURDLE (0-110) (4-Y.O+) (Class E)
1-20 (1-22) **2m 1f 110y (8 hdls)** £2,250.00 (£625.00: £300.00) GOING: 0.80 sec per fur (S)

				SP	RR	SF
908[8]	**Tip it In (80)** (ASmith) **7-9-12**(5) NHorrocks (sn chsng ldrs: styd on appr 2 out: led flat: rdn out)	—	**1**	9/1	54	19
871[3]	**Anabranch (98)** (JMJefferson) **5-11-4**(3) MNewton (hld up: jnd ldr 5th: led appr 2 out tl flat: nt qckn)	1½	**2**	7/2[2]	71	36
1145[3]	**Newhall Prince (87)** (AStreeter) **8-10-10b** LAspell (led 4th tl appr 2 out: wknd between last 2)	11	**3**	9/4[1]	50	15
1030[3]	**Nashaat (USA) (89)** (MCChapman) **8-10-7**(5) RossBerry (plld hrd: sn trckng ldrs: outpcd 5th: n.d after)	7	**4**	4/1[3]	45	10
	Monday Club (102) (JCTuck) **12-11-11** DWalsh (pushed along 3rd: sn lost tch: t.o whn p.u bef 3 out)		**P**	14/1	—	—
	Mill Thyme (95) (MrsMReveley) **4-11-4** GLee (unruly s: led: drvn along & hdd 4th: nt r.o: sn bhd: t.o whn p.u bef 2 out)		**P**	7/2[2]	—	—
				(SP 111.9%)	**6 Rn**	

4m 24.5 (21.50) CSF £36.91 TOTE £7.30: £2.80 £2.00 (£21.40) OWNER Mrs M. Dunning (BEVERLEY) BRED Miss C. L. Armstrong

OFFICIAL EXPLANATION **Tip it In: regarding the apparent improvement in form, the trainer reported that the gelding had had a soft-palate operation before his last run, jumped poorly and that the yard was suffering from a virus.**

Tip it In staged a revival and was backed at long odds to do so. (9/1: 20/1-8/1)

871 Anabranch made the best of her way home, but her stamina seems strictly limited. (7/2)

1145 Newhall Prince, with the blinkers back on, took it up early on the second circuit, but called it a day between the last two. (9/4)

1030 Nashaat (USA), awash with sweat beforehand, would not settle. (4/1)

Mill Thyme, who gave problem at the start, downed tools in a couple of strides after being headed. (7/2)

1205 DANIEL CRANE EXHIBITION HURDLE (3-Y.O) (Class D)
1-50 (1-53) **2m 1f 110y (8 hdls)** £3,148.00 (£878.00: £424.00) GOING: 0.80 sec per fur (S)

				SP	RR	SF
736[2]	**Chief Mouse** (MissHCKnight) **3-11-5** JFTitley (mde virtually all: qcknd clr between last 2: hit last)	—	**1**	11/4[1]	71	5
	Crabbie's Pride (MGMeagher) **3-10-12** AMaguire (a chsng ldrs: kpt on fr 2 out: no ch w wnr)	5	**2**	12/1	59	—
	Mock Trial (IRE) (MrsJRRamsden) **3-10-12** RGarritty (hld up: stdy hdwy 3 out: rdn between last 2: nt qckn)	nk	**3**	5/1[2]	59	—
	The Butterwick Kid (RAFahey) **3-10-12** PNiven (hld up: hdwy on outside to jn ldrs 3 out: wknd next)	4	**4**	7/1	56	—
1011*	**Cottage Prince (IRE)** (JJQuinn) **3-11-5** LWyer (chsd ldrs tl rdn & wknd after 2 out)	5	**5**	11/2[3]	58	—
	Baasm (JNorton) **3-10-7**(5) ECallaghan (hdwy to chse ldrs 5th: 6th whn blnd 2 out: kpt on)	3	**6**	10/1	48	—
	Boy Blakeney (MrsSJSmith) **3-10-12** RichardGuest (prom: hmpd 3 out: sn wl outpcd)	1¾	**7**	20/1	47	—
	Alwarqa (MDHammond) **3-10-7** DBentley (hld up & bhd: stdy hdwy appr 2 out: nvr plcd to chal)	¾	**8**	10/1	41+	—
291[5]	**Another Quarter (IRE)** (MCChapman) **3-10-7** WWorthington (hld up: stdy hdwy 5th: wknd appr 2 out)	7	**9**	16/1	35	—
	Craigmore Magic (USA) (MissMKMilligan) **3-10-12** ASSmith (w ldrs: wkng whn hmpd & mstke 3 out)	6	**10**	25/1	34	—
	Fiasco (MJCamacho) **3-10-7** JOsborne (jnd ldrs 5th: ev ch tl wknd appr 2 out)	s.h	**11**	16/1	29	—
	Landfall (JGFitzGerald) **3-10-9**(3) FLeahy (hit 2nd: bhd & drvn along 4th: t.o whn p.u between last 2)		**P**	14/1	—	—
	Extremely Friendly (BobJones) **3-10-12** DBridgwater (chsd ldrs tl lost pl after 4th: t.o whn p.u bef ast)		**P**	5/1[2]	—	—
	Rozel Bay (DJWintle) **3-10-7** WMarston (bhd & drvn along 5th: t.o whn p.u bef last)		**P**	25/1	—	—
				(SP 144.6%)	**14 Rn**	

4m 31.6 (28.60) CSF £40.90 TOTE £3.10: £1.30 £3.70 £2.20 (£48.20) Trio £24.20 OWNER Lady Vestey (WANTAGE) BRED Lady Vestey

736 Chief Mouse paid a compliment to Doctor Green, quickening clear between the last two. He was in no danger when he hit the last. (11/4)

Crabbie's Pride, who has been running badly of late on the Flat, shaped by no means badly. (12/1)

Mock Trial (IRE), given a patient ride, moved up after three out, looking likely to make a race of it with the winner, but he could only keep on at the same pace under pressure. (5/1: 3/1-11/2)

The Butterwick Kid moved up on the outside to join issue three out, but his stamina seemed to give out between the last two. (7/1)

1011* Cottage Prince (IRE) (11/2: 4/1-6/1)

Baasm (10/1: op 16/1)

Alwarqa, a winner over an extended two miles at Pontefract, had an educational here. Dropped out at the rear, she showed definite promise, keeping on nicely over the last two. She is capable of a lot better. (10/1: op 6/1)

Landfall (14/1: 10/1-16/1)

1206 JOLLY FISHERMAN NOVICES' CHASE (4-Y.O+) (Class D)
2-20 (2-21) **2m 4f (15 fncs)** £3,977.00 (£1,196.00: £578.00: £269.00) GOING: 0.80 sec per fur (S)

				SP	RR	SF
1028*	**Simply Dashing (IRE)** (TDEasterby) **5-11-10** LWyer (trckd ldr: blnd 4 out: sn led: clr 2 out: easily)	—	**1**	8/13[1]	130+	53
	Mr Pickpocket (IRE) (106) (MissHCKnight) **8-11-5** JFTitley (led tl after 4 out: eased whn no ch w wnr appr 2 out)	dist	**2**	15/8[2]	—	—
1022[7]	**Kenmore-Speed** (MrsSJSmith) **9-11-5** RichardGuest (chsd ldrs: outpcd whn hit 11th: styd on wl flat)	6	**3**	10/1[3]	—	—
1028[2]	**Record Lover (IRE) (69)** (MCChapman) **6-11-5** WWorthington (sn chsng ldrs: drvn along 8th: lost tch 4 out)	21	**4**	20/1	—	—
	Fair Ally (MESowersby) **6-11-5** DParker (hld up: sme hdwy 8th: no ch whn blnd 2 out)	20	**5**	50/1	—	—
1083[U]	**Merryhill Gold** (JWCurtis) **5-10-13**(5) DJKavanagh (j.lft: lost pl 4th: t.o 11th)	10	**6**	40/1	—	—
	Monymax (IRE) (MrsSJSmith) **7-10-12**(7) RWilkinson (mstkes: sn bhd: t.o 11th)	10	**7**	50/1	—	—
	Jac Del Prince (PFNicholls) **6-11-5** PHide (hit 2nd: in tch tl lost pl 7th: wl bhd whn p.u bef last)		**P**	20/1	—	—
				(SP 121.7%)	**8 Rn**	

5m 12.0 (21.00) CSF £2.39 TOTE £1.60: £1.20 £1.10 £2.10 (£1.90) OWNER Mr Steve Hammond (MALTON) BRED Eastward Bloodstock Holdings Ltd

WEIGHT FOR AGE 5yo-1lb

1028* Simply Dashing (IRE) survived a bad blunder four out, but it cost him no ground at all and he took this in easy fashion. He looks as though he can improve further yet. (8/13)

Mr Pickpocket (IRE) jumped boldly in front but, once the winner stepped up a gear, it was all over in a matter of strides, and his rider sensibly accepted. (15/8)

1022 Kenmore-Speed still does not look 100%. Left behind by the first two down the back on the final circuit, he stayed on in spirited fashion on the run-in and will be an interesting prospect in a novices' handicap. (10/1)

1207 ROBERT PEAK BOOKMAKER H'CAP HURDLE (0-115) (4-Y.O+) (Class E)

2-50 (2-50) **2m 5f 110y (10 hdls)** £2,310.60 (£641.60: £307.80) GOING: 0.80 sec per fur (S)

				SP	RR	SF
909[P]	**Lochnagrain (IRE) (108)** (MrsMReveley) **8-11-10** PNiven (led 2nd: drvn clr between last 2: eased towards fin)	—	**1**	9/2[3]	97+	—
	Singlesole (90) (MrsPSly) **11-10-6** RMarley (led to 2nd: w wnr: rdn & hit 2 out: sn wl outpcd)	12	**2**	9/2[3]	70	—
1050*	**Keen To The Last (FR) (102)** (MDHammond) **4-11-4** RGarritty (a chsng ldrs: rdn 3 out: one pce appr next)	8	**3**	9/4[1]	76	—
	Gymcrak Tiger (IRE) (91) (GHolmes) **6-10-7** AMaguire (hld up: hdwy on outside appr 3 out: sn rdn: nvr nr to chal)	1½	**4**	4/1[2]	64	—
1074[6]	**Scud Missile (IRE) (99)** (GFJohnsonHoughton) **5-11-1** ILawrence (chsd ldrs: pushed along 7th: sn wl outpcd)	4	**5**	11/2	69	—
	Cuillin Caper (84) (TRWatson) **4-10-0** DBridgwater (effrt 6th: wknd after next: sn bhd: t.o)	dist	**6**	10/1	—	—
1086[6]	**Chapel of Barras (IRE) (92)** (BGee) **7-10-8** MrPGee (hld up & plld hrd: bhd fr 6th: wl t.o)	dist	**7**	33/1	—	—
				(SP 114.5%)	**7 Rn**	

5m 43.7 (39.70) CSF £23.31 CT £51.36 TOTE £6.10: £2.70 £2.60 (£15.90) OWNER Lightbody of Hamilton Ltd (SALTBURN) BRED Michael Cuddy

LONG HANDICAP Cuillin Caper 9-12

909 Lochnagrain (IRE) has not really taken to fences, despite two wins in novice chases, and was much happier over the minor obstacles. Stepping up the gallop once in line for home, he was able to ease up towards the finish. (9/2)

Singlesole usually runs well on his first two or three outings. After matching strides with the winner, he was getting the worse of the argument when he fell through the second last. (9/2: 6/1-4/1)

1050* Keen To The Last (FR), done no favours by the Handicapper, was flat out and getting nowhere three from home. (9/4)

Gymcrak Tiger (IRE) won this race last year off a 3lb lower mark and was given plenty to do here. Making ground on the outside going to three out, he was soon flat out and making no impression. (4/1)

1208 JACKSONS NOVICES' HURDLE (4-Y.O+) (Class D)

3-20 (3-20) **2m 1f 110y (8 hdls)** £3,232.00 (£902.00: £436.00) GOING: 0.80 sec per fur (S)

				SP	RR	SF
	Alabang (MJCamacho) **5-10-12** JOsborne (stdd s: hld up & plld hrd: jnd ldrs 4th: led after 3 out: hit next: sn clr: easily)	—	**1**	6/4[1]	65+	8
1030[7]	**Shared Risk** (JNorton) **4-10-7**(5) ECallaghan (hdwy 5th: wnt 2nd appr 2 out: no ch w wnr)	9	**2**	12/1	57	—
	North Bear (MrsSJSmith) **4-10-12** RichardGuest (led tl after 3 out: one pce appr next)	1¼	**3**	9/1	56	—
	Efaad (IRE) (JNorton) **5-10-9**(3) GLee (outpcd 4th: hdwy u.p 3 out: 4th whn blnd bdly last)	10	**4**	25/1	47	—
	Murphy's Gold (IRE) (RAFahey) **5-10-12** LWyer (plld hrd: sn trckng ldrs: lost pl appr 2 out)	13	**5**	7/1[3]	35	—
	Menaldi (IRE) (PCheesbrough) **6-10-12** RSupple (sn bhd: hdwy 5th: nvr nr to chal)	1	**6**	12/1	34	—
872[6]	**Nenagh Gunner** (JJQuinn) **6-10-7** BFenton (sn bhd: sme hdwy 3 out: n.d)	4	**7**	16/1	25	—
	Ferrers (MrsPSly) **5-10-12** RMarley (chsd ldrs: hit 3rd: drvn along 5th: lost pl appr 2 out)	1½	**8**	6/1[2]	29	—
1059[F]	**Studio Thirty** (CASmith) **4-10-12** WMarston (w ldrs: rdn & wknd 5th)	15	**9**	15/2	15	—
	Corbleu (IRE) (SBBell) **6-10-12** KJohnson (trckd ldrs: lost pl bef 4th: t.o 2 out)	15	**10**	12/1	1	—
858[5]	**Best Friend** (JWCurtis) **4-10-4**(3) FLeahy (chsd ldrs tl rdn & wknd 5th: t.o 2 out)	7	**11**	25/1	—	—
	Mubariz (IRE) (CSmith) **4-10-12** MRanger (sn bhd: t.o 4th: p.u after next)		**P**	14/1	—	—
				(SP 131.9%)	**12 Rn**	

4m 29.3 (26.30) CSF £21.96 TOTE £2.20: £1.50 £3.30 £2.10 (£14.40) Trio £54.00 OWNER Elite Racing Club (MALTON) BRED Mrs S. Camacho

Alabang, a winner three times on the Flat this year, was turned out in particularly good trim. Dropped in at the start, he took a keen grip and pulled his way to the front after three out and, after hitting the next, he soon sprinted clear. He does not lack ability, but would not want the ground any softer and does not find as much as would seem likely when he comes off the bridle. (6/4)

Shared Risk kept on to finish second best, but the winner was in a different league. (12/1)

North Bear made all the running to win a mile and a half seller on the Flat. He led on sufferance here, but was left for dead by the winner going to two out. (9/1)

Efaad (IRE), a poor stayer on the Flat, was disputing third place when he blundered very badly at the final flight. (25/1)

Murphy's Gold (IRE), a come-from-behind miler on the Flat, took a keen grip and her stamina seemed to give out going to two out. (7/1: op 9/2)

Corbleu (IRE) (12/1: op 8/1)

1209 MARKET RASEN CHAMBER OF TRADE AND COMMERCE H'CAP CHASE (0-105) (5-Y.O+) (Class F)

3-50 (3-51) **3m 1f (19 fncs)** £2,951.75 (£884.00: £424.50: £194.75) GOING: 0.80 sec per fur (S)

				SP	RR	SF
	Griffins Bar (79) (MrsPSly) **8-10-4** RMarley (led 2nd to 6th: led after 4 out: styd on wl flat)	—	**1**	12/1	91	8
	Westwell Boy (100) (PBeaumont) **10-11-11** RSupple (led to 2nd: led 6th tl after 4 out: kpt on same pce fr 2 out)	3½	**2**	5/1[3]	110	27
823*	**Jim Valentine (98)** (DJWintle) **10-11-9** WMarston (hld up: effrt & hit 11th: wnt prom 14th: outpcd 3 out: kpt on appr last)	3	**3**	2/1[1]	106	23
	Sparrow Hall (92) (JGFitzGerald) **9-11-3** WDwan (chsd ldrs: blnd 15th: kpt on fr 3 out)	1¼	**4**	20/1	99	16
	Juke Box Billy (IRE) (86) (MrsJBrown) **8-10-11** ADobbin (sn trckng ldrs: effrt 3 out: 4th & wkng whn mstke last)	13	**5**	9/1	85	2
1029[P]	**Son of Iris (103)** (MrsMReveley) **8-12-0** PNiven (sme hdwy 12th: wknd 14th)	dist	**6**	10/1	—	—
1029[2]	**Deep Decision (101)** (PCheesbrough) **10-11-12** ASSmith (chsd ldrs: outpcd 15th: sn wknd)	nk	**7**	9/2[2]	—	—
	Bosworth Field (IRE) (75) (MrsSarahHorner-Harker) **8-10-0** BFenton (sn bhd: blnd 13th: sn t.o)	26	**8**	33/1	—	—
1024[2]	**Supposin (92)** (MrsSJSmith) **8-11-3** RichardGuest (bhd: effrt & hit 13th: sn lost tch: t.o 3 out)	7	**9**	9/2[2]	—	—
	Hurricane Andrew (IRE) (88) (JAMoore) **8-10-13** MrNWilson (sn bhd: t.o 9th: p.u bef 13th)		**P**	16/1	—	—
				(SP 126.7%)	**10 Rn**	

6m 46.9 (35.90) CSF £71.22 CT £161.47 TOTE £20.70: £4.80 £2.00 £1.30 (£44.10) Trio £77.00 OWNER Mr M. S. Smith (PETERBOROUGH) BRED Mrs P. Sly

LONG HANDICAP Bosworth Field (IRE) 9-10

Griffins Bar, despite having his first outing for over a year and a half, was well supported at long odds. Looking fit, he helped force the pace and had his race won jumping the last. (12/1)

Westwell Boy, who won his final two outings last term when his jumping was much improved, helped force the pace, but could only keep on at the same pace from two out. The outing looked as if it was needed and he prefers faster ground. (5/1)

823* Jim Valentine, from a 7lb higher mark, was struggling after hitting the eleventh. Struggling to keep up three out, he stayed on again going to the last. (2/1)

Sparrow Hall has broken blood-vessels in the past, and had the stuffing knocked out of him after a blunder at the fifteenth. To his credit, he kept on again over the last three. (20/1)
Juke Box Billy (IRE), having his first outing since changing stables, shaped nicely, but this trip may be beyond him. (9/1)
Son of Iris still looked in need of the outing. (10/1: op 6/1)
1029 Deep Decision (9/2: 3/1-5/1)

T/Plpt: £119.90 (95.64 Tckts). T/Qdpt: £14.10 (73.21 Tckts). WG

1210a - 1215a : (Irish Racing) - See Computer Raceform

1105a-LEOPARDSTOWN (Dublin, Ireland) (L-H) (Soft)
Monday October 28th

1216a IDEAL MINIMISER HIGH EFFICIENT BOILER CHASE (5-Y.O+)
2-45 (2-49) **2m 5f (13 fncs)** IR £4,795.00 (IR £1,085.00: IR £455.00: IR £245.00) GOING: 0.37 sec per fur (GS)

				SP	RR	SF
1003a[P]	**Royal Mountbrowne** (APO'Brien,Ireland) **8-12-0** THorgan (mde all: mstkes 4 out & 3 out: kpt on u.p flat: hld on)	—	1	9/2 [2]	139	—
	Feathered Gale (ALTMoore,Ireland) **9-12-0** CO'Brien (hld up: mod 3rd 4 out: hdwy next: 2nd, rdn & effrt appr last: styd on u.p flat: jst failed)	s.h	2	5/1 [3]	139	—
763a[4]	**Opera Hat (IRE)** (JRHFowler,Ireland) **8-11-9** CO'Dwyer (chsd wnr: lost pl briefly after 5th: chsd wnr 4 out: rdn after 2 out: 3rd & no imp appr last: one pce)	9	3	4/7 [1]	127	—
763a[7]	**Beakstown (IRE)** (PMullins,Ireland) **7-12-0** TPTreacy (hld up: last fr 6th: hdwy bef 2 out: rdn & no imp after 2 out)	15	4	8/1	121	—
				(SP 109.6%)		**4 Rn**

5m 39.4 (2.40) OWNER Mrs J. O'Kane (PILTOWN) BRED Sidney J. Smith
Royal Mountbrowne improved considerably on his Limerick effort last time, making virtually all the running. He battled on well on the flat and, although appearing to be high enough in the Ratings, could still have a good season. (9/2: op 3/1)
Feathered Gale looked burlier than the winner, but stayed on strongly in the straight and had every chance from the last, before not being abused. Newbury's Hennessy Cognac Gold Cup is a possibility. (5/1: op 5/2)
763a Opera Hat (IRE) appeared to have plenty in hand at these weights, but hung to the left all the way down the back straight and her jockey said that she had run flat. She should not be written off. (4/7)
Beakstown (IRE) found this ground too holding and the company too hot. (8/1)

1217a - 1230a : (Irish Racing) - See Computer Raceform

0985a-NAVAN (Ireland) (L-H) (Soft)
Saturday November 2nd

1231a FORTRIA E.B.F. H'CAP CHASE (Gd 3) (4-Y.O+)
1-45 (1-48) **2m 1f (10 fncs)** IR £6,850.00 (IR £1,550.00: IR £650.00: IR £350.00)

				SP	RR	SF
763a[2]	**Anabatic (IRE)** (MJPO'Brien,Ireland) **8-10-1**ow1 TPRudd (hld up: hdwy bef 3 out: disp ld 2 out: led & drew clr bef last: eased fnl 100y)	—	1	100/30 [2]	137+	—
846a*	**Sound Man (IRE)** (EJO'Grady,Ireland) **8-12-0** NWilliamson (led & sn clr: jnd bef 2 out: rdn, hdd & wknd wl bef last: eased whn btn)	20	2	1/4 [1]	145	—
	Corston Dancer (IRE) (JABerry,Ireland) **8-10-0b** THorgan (wl t.o fr 3rd)	dist	3	50/1 [3]	—	—
				(SP 105.0%)		**3 Rn**

4m 14.0 (-10.00) OWNER William Phelan (NAAS)
763a Anabatic (IRE) seems to have put his jumping problems well behind him. Closing from the third last, he took over between the last two and was a dozen lengths to the good jumping the last. The Murphy's Gold Cup at Cheltenham is his objective. (100/30)
846a* Sound Man (IRE), soon clear, was not jumping with his usual sparkle and was slow over a couple. He appeared to be in trouble at the third last and threw in the towel quite tamely when headed between the last two, being eased down before the last. He can be made fitter, but the fact remains he was trying to win this from a mark 20lb higher than last year. (1/4)
Corston Dancer (IRE) was always tailed off. (50/1)

1233a 'FOR AUCTION' NOVICES' HURDLE (Gd 3) (4-Y.O+)
2-45 (2-45) **2m (10 hdls)** IR £3,082.50 (IR £697.50: IR £292.50: IR £157.50)

				SP	RR	SF
	Radanpour (IRE) (WPMullins,Ireland) **4-11-3** DCasey (hld up: mstkes 3rd & 5th: rdn after 3 out: slt mstke & lft 2nd next: chal u.p whn lft in ld & mstke last: styd on: eased nr fin)	—	1	7/4 [2]	82+	—
	Caitriona's Choice (IRE) (MCunningham,Ireland) **5-11-8** NWilliamson (hld up: slt mstke 5th: sn trckng ldrs: lft 3rd 2 out: sn rdn: lft 2nd & sltly hmpd last: one pce u.p)	2½	2	12/1	80	—
	Knockaulin (IRE) (FFlood,Ireland) **5-11-4** FrancisFlood (mstke 4th: sn t.o)	dist	3	33/1	—	—
	Zimulante (IRE) (CaptDGSwan,Ireland) **5-11-4** CFSwan (led: bd mstke 2nd: hdd bef 3 out: lft in ld next: sn u.p: broke leg jst bef last: dead)		F	4/1 [3]	—	—
	Liss De Paor (IRE) (APO'Brien,Ireland) **5-11-6** THorgan (hld up chsng ldr: led bef 3 out: gng clr whn fell 2 out)		F	Evens [1]	—	—
				(SP 117.0%)		**5 Rn**

3m 58.6 (1.60) OWNER P. P. T. Bridson (MUINE BEAG)
Radanpour (IRE), waited with, made mistakes and was being ridden along early in the straight. Left second two out, he was under pressure and not making much progress when left in front at the last, and just kept on at one pace. He was a fortunate winner and has to improve on this. (7/4)
Caitriona's Choice (IRE) had little chance of being involved when left second at the last. He just kept on at the one pace. (12/1)
Zimulante (IRE) ran in front, but was picked off easily before the third last. Left in front again after the next, he was under pressure but still holding an advantage when breaking a fore-leg on the approach to the next. (4/1)

Liss De Paor (IRE) ran second under restraint until leading three out. Three lengths clear and going on, she fell at the second last with victory assured. (Evens)

1234a LISMULLEN HURDLE (Gd 3) (4-Y.O+)
3-15 (3-18) **2m 4f (11 hdls)** IR £6,850.00 (IR £1,550.00: IR £650.00: IR £350.00)

Horse	Dist	Pos	SP	RR	SF
Urubande (IRE) (APO'Brien,Ireland) **6-12-0** CFSwan (mde all: hit 3 out: rdn after last: wknd fnl 100y: jst hld on)	—	1	9/4[1]	128+	—
New Co (IRE) (MFMorris,Ireland) **8-11-8**(3) DJCasey (hld up: hdwy after 4 out: 4th & swtchd rt appr last: styd on wl flat: jst failed)	s.h	2	7/1	125	—
Notcomplainingbut (IRE) (PMullins,Ireland) **5-11-4**(5) GCotter (hld up in rr: hdwy bef 4 out: wnt 2nd bef next: sn ev ch: rdn & no ex between last 2: styd on towards fin)	nk	3	7/2[3]	123	—
Cockney Lad (IRE) (NMeade,Ireland) **7-12-0** MrGJHarford (hld up in tch: clsng 3rd bef 2 out: sn ev ch: chsng wnr last: kpt on)	½	4	9/2	127	—
Ultra Flutter (MHourigan,Ireland) **9-11-11** NWilliamson (chsd wnr 7th tl lost pl after 4 out: sn bhd: t.o)	dist	5	16/1	—	—
Gentle Buck (IRE) (MJByrne,Ireland) **7-11-11** KFO'Brien (chsd wnr: nt fluent: 3rd whn mstke 7th: wknd qckly 3 out: sn bhd: t.o)	5½	6	3/1[2]	—	—

(SP 114.6%) **6 Rn**

4m 54.4 (1.40) OWNER M. G. St Quinton (PILTOWN) BRED George J. King

Urubande (IRE) looking big and hairy and will have benefited greatly from this. Light in the market, he made all the running and his jumping, apart from a mistake three out, was much more fluent than last season. He blew up between the last two and, ridden after the last, just managed to hold on without having a hard race. The Champion Hurdle is still in his sights, but everything would point towards the Stayers' Hurdle being a more realistic target. (9/4: op 6/4)

New Co (IRE) was only a moderate fourth when switched to the outer before the last. He staged a powerful run up the hill that only just failed. (7/1)

Notcomplainingbut (IRE), waited with at the back of the field, made good headway before four out to land second over the next. She had every chance before the last, but just could not quicken. (7/2)

Cockney Lad (IRE) made headway on the outer to go third three out and, holding every chance when second over the last, just could not quicken. (9/2: op 9/4)

Ultra Flutter dropped right out before the straight and finished tailed off. (16/1)

Gentle Buck (IRE) was far from fluent in second place when quickly weakening in the straight and finishing tailed off. He will now go novice chasing. (3/1: op 2/1)

NR

1235a - 1239a : (Irish Racing) - See Computer Raceform

1095a-PUNCHESTOWN (Naas, Ireland) (R-H) (Soft)
Sunday November 3rd

1240a IRISH FIELD NOVICES' CHASE (Gd 3) (5-Y.O+)
2-45 (2-47) **2m 4f (14 fncs)** IR £6,910.00 (IR £1,550.00: IR £650.00: IR £350.00)

Horse	Dist	Pos	SP	RR	SF
Dorans Pride (IRE) (MHourigan,Ireland) **7-11-6** JPBroderick (sn chsng ldr: led after 10th: clr bef 2 out: easily)	—	1	1/2[1]	102+	—
The Subbie (IRE) (TFoley,Ireland) **7-11-6** CO'Dwyer (hld up: mstkes 9th & 10th: 3rd bef 3 out: 2nd, rdn & chsd wnr appr 2 out: no imp between last 2: kpt on same pce)	11	2	3/1[2]	93	—
Crehelp Express (IRE) (VBowens,Ireland) **6-10-11** NWilliamson (hld up: mstkes 6th & 10th: 2nd & chsd wnr 3 out: 3rd & btn appr next)	15	3	7/1[3]	72	—
Vulpin de Laugere (FR) (MrsSABramall,Ireland) **9-10-13**(3) KWhelan (led tl after 10th: rdn & chsd wnr tl appr 3 out: n.d appr 2 out)	7	4	25/1	72	—
Friday Thirteenth (IRE) (DPugh,Ireland) **7-11-6** APowell (cl 2nd whn fell 1st: rmntd: wl t.o)	dist	5	33/1	—	—

(SP 111.0%) **5 Rn**

5m 20.2 (7.20) OWNER T. J. Doran (PATRICKSWELL) BRED Hugh Suffern Bloodstock Ltd

Dorans Pride (IRE) ran second and did not appear able to gain the upper hand at his fences until being sent on before four out. Clear over the last two, he won without being asked any serious questions and this was just another step in his chasing education. (1/2)

The Subbie (IRE) settled just off the pace and jumped well, despite a mistake five out. He was sent after the winner before two out, but it was an impossible task. (3/1)

Crehelp Express (IRE) took a strong pull early on, but soon settled. Making a mistake five out, he soon began to struggle after the next and was beaten three out. (7/1)

Vulpin de Laugere (FR) made the running and outjumped the winner until weakening four out. (25/1)

1241a - 1243a : (Irish Racing) - See Computer Raceform

0873-HEXHAM (L-H) (Good to firm)
Friday November 8th
WEATHER: heavy rain WIND: str

1244 SERVICE WELDING GROUP CONDITIONAL H'CAP CHASE (0-105) (5-Y.O+) (Class F)
1-20 (1-20) **2m 4f 110y (15 fncs)** £2,846.00 (£848.00: £404.00: £182.00) GOING minus 0.13 sec per fur (G)

	Horse	Dist	Pos	SP	RR	SF
897[4]	**Buyers Dream (IRE) (76)** (BEllison) **6-10-0v** GCahill (outpcd 9th: hdwy to jn ldrs 3 out: led appr last: drvn out)	—	1	9/2[2]	84	4
1012*	**Crafty Chaplain (100)** (DMcCain) **10-11-10** DWalsh (lw: j.rt: led 7th: hit 10th: hdd & hit last: no ex)	4	2	3/1[1]	105	25
896[5]	**Forward Glen (76)** (PCheesbrough) **9-10-0b** GLee (chsd ldrs: pushed along 9th: one pce fr 3 out)	1¾	3	5/1[3]	80	—
	Lie Detector (104) (CParker) **8-11-11**(3) DParker (trckd ldrs tl lost pl 3 out: styd on flat)	6	4	13/2	103	23
1008[4]	**Trumpet (96)** (JGMO'Shea) **7-11-3v**(3) MichaelBrennan (led to 7th: drvn along 11th: ev ch tl wknd appr last)	2	5	11/2	93	13

	Horse	Details	Dist	Pos	SP	RR	SF
877[2]	**Willie Sparkle (76)**	(MrsSCBradburne) **10-9-9**(5) AWatt (last whn blnd & uns rdr 3rd)		U	3/1[1]	—	—

(SP 113.6%) **6 Rn**

5m 7.2 (10.20) CSF £17.43 TOTE £8.40: £2.40 £1.60 (£6.00) OWNER Mr Brian Chicken (LANCHESTER) BRED H and Y Bloodstock Co
LONG HANDICAP Buyers Dream (IRE) 9-9

897 Buyers Dream (IRE), 5lb out of the handicap, made no mistake, despite not looking 100% in love with the game. His young rider should go far. (9/2)

1012* Crafty Chaplain, 3lb higher, tended to lose ground jumping right and his measure had been taken when he clouted the last. (3/1)

896 Forward Glen, a moody individual, took little interest when the race began in earnest, but was staying on again at the finish. (5/1)

Lie Detector, running over a trip short of his best, dropped out three from home, but stayed on in promising fashion from the last. (13/2)

1008 Trumpet, rather taken off his legs over this inadequate trip, dropped out quickly going to the last after having every chance. (11/2)

877 Willie Sparkle, attempting to repeat last year's win in this event, was whipping them in when he parted company with his rider at only the third fence. (3/1)

1245 KARNHEATH NOVICES' HURDLE (4-Y.O+) (Class E)

1-50 (1-50) **2m 4f 110y (10 hdls)** £2,532.00 (£702.00: £336.00) GOING minus 0.13 sec per fur (G)

	Horse	Details	Dist	Pos	SP	RR	SF
1050[3]	**Beggars Banquet (IRE)**	(PBeaumont) **6-10-5**(7) BGrattan (j.lft: trckd ldr: led 5th: swvd lft last: hung lft flat: styd on)	—	1	10/11[1]	73	16
	Paperising	(GRichards) **4-10-12** ADobbin (lw: trckd ldrs: effrt 2 out: ev ch whn n.m.r last: nt qckn)	1¼	2	6/4[2]	72	15
	The Next Waltz (IRE)	(LLungo) **5-10-12** MFoster (hld up: stdy hdwy 3 out: nvr nr to chal)	20	3	9/1[3]	56+	—
782[2]	**Canonbiebothered**	(LLungo) **5-10-7** FPerratt (chsd ldrs: ev ch tl wknd appr 2 out)	13	4	25/1	41	—
1079[5]	**One More Bill**	(JWade) **6-10-12** KJones (chsd ldrs: drvn along 6th: wknd after next)	dist	5	25/1	—	—
	Promise To Try (IRE)	(MABarnes) **4-10-2**(5) STaylor (chsd ldrs to wknd 3 out)	nk	6	50/1	—	—
	Leighten Lass (IRE)	(JIACharlton) **5-10-7** KJohnson (s.s: nt j.w: a bhd: t.o 7th)	1¼	7	25/1	—	—
	Royal Palm	(VThompson) **4-10-12** MrMThompson (chsd ldrs: drvn along 6th: wknd 3 out: t.o)	dist	8	33/1	—	—
	Shildon (IRE)	(GPKelly) **8-10-12** MrCMulhall (led to 5th: wknd qckly next: sn t.o: p.u bef 2 out)		P	50/1	—	—

(SP 120.8%) **9 Rn**

4m 57.6 (9.60) CSF £2.76 TOTE £1.80: £1.00 £2.00 £3.40 (£1.70) Trio £8.30 OWNER Mr E. H. Ruddock (BRANDSBY) BRED T A O'Donnell

1050 Beggars Banquet (IRE), who did not take the eye in the paddock, tended to jump left, but he let the runner-up up his inner on the final turn. Ducking left at the last, his rider then persisted in using his whip in his right hand and he went across the runner-up on the run-in, but he was just over a length clear. (10/11: 4/6-Evens)

Paperising, a bumper winner, was having his first outing since switching stables. Looking particularly well, he was driven up on the inside of the winner between the last two. Almost upsides when left short of room on the inner at the last, he was then beaten on merit. (6/4)

The Next Waltz (IRE) looked pretty straight. Patiently ridden from off the pace, he stayed on in promising fashion over the last three without ever being asked to do enough to get near the first two. He is sure to improve. (9/1: 6/1-10/1)

782 Canonbiebothered got tired going to two out. (25/1)

1246 ROBSON BROWN COMMUNICO MAIDEN CHASE (5-Y.O+) (Class F)

2-20 (2-20) **3m 1f (19 fncs)** £2,935.80 (£878.40: £421.20: £192.60) GOING minus 0.13 sec per fur (G)

	Horse	Details	Dist	Pos	SP	RR	SF
1028[4]	**Gems Lad**	(MrsSJSmith) **9-11-5** RichardGuest (w ldrs: mstkes 2nd & 9th: led 10th: hit 2 out: styd on wl)	—	1	7/1	91	6
1129[4]	**Commandeer (IRE) (69)**	(MissMKMilligan) **6-11-5** ADobbin (led: hit 1st: hdd 10th: sn outpcd: rallied 14th: styd on flat)	9	2	5/1	85	—
	Pantara Prince (IRE)	(JIACharlton) **7-11-5** NWilliamson (hld up: hit 4th: wnt prom 11th: rdn 2 out: wknd appr last)	3½	3	5/2[1]	83	—
875[2]	**Royal Surprise (76)**	(WGReed) **9-11-5** TReed (lw: chsd ldrs: j.slowly & lost pl 10th: mstke 13th: sn bhd: styd on appr last)	2½	4	9/2[3]	81	—
875[4]	**More Joy (74)**	(BEllison) **8-11-2**(3) GCahill (prom: blnd 12th: rdn & hit 3 out: sn wknd)	10	5	5/1	75	—
907[3]	**Deise Marshall (IRE) (76)**	(JWade) **8-11-5** KJones (chsd ldrs: blnd 13th: wknd 15th)	7	6	4/1[2]	71	—
	Aylesbury Lad (IRE) (72)	(DALamb) **7-11-5** JBurke (w ldrs tl wknd 12th: sn bhd: t.o)	24	7	33/1	55	—
	Small N Smart	(DSAlder) **6-11-5** KJohnson (bit bkwd: nt j.w: bhd: sme hdwy whn fell 9th)		F	33/1	—	—

(SP 118.5%) **8 Rn**

6m 29.7 (18.70) CSF £39.81 TOTE £8.90: £1.60 £2.40 £1.50 (£14.30) Trio £30.40 OWNER Miss J. Wood (BINGLEY) BRED Miss J. U. Wood

Gems Lad, who certainly does not lack size, survived three jumping errors to pull clear on the uphill run to the last. All he does is stay. (7/1: 5/1-8/1)

1129 Commandeer (IRE), whose jumping was not without blemishes, dropped himself out setting off on the final circuit, but decided to stay on again up the hill on the run to the last. (5/1)

Pantara Prince (IRE), who won a point-to-point in Ireland and was placed between the Flags over here, travelled strongly and looked as though he could take the winner at any time but, coming under pressure two out, he was legless going to the last. The outing was presumably needed. (5/2)

875 Royal Surprise, a moody individual, dropped himself right out when jumping slowly a circuit from home. Well in arrears after a mistake at the thirteenth, he decided to stay on again going to the last. (9/2)

875 More Joy had every chance, but a mistake three out was the final straw. (5/1)

907 Deise Marshall (IRE) (4/1: 3/1-9/2)

1247 BUILDING MAINTENANCE COMPANY (S) H'CAP HURDLE (0-90) (4-Y.O+) (Class G)

2-50 (2-51) **2m 4f 110y (10 hdls)** £1,725.00 (£475.00: £225.00) GOING minus 0.13 sec per fur (G)

	Horse	Details	Dist	Pos	SP	RR	SF
1047*	**Belle Rose (IRE) (74)**	(GRichards) **6-11-1** ADobbin (trckd ldrs: rdn to ld last: styd on)	—	1	Evens[1]	63	17
	Kings Minstral (IRE) (63)	(DALamb) **6-10-4**ow3 JBurke (led 3rd: hdd last: nt qckn)	3	2	33/1	50	1
27[5]	**Antartictern (USA) (77)**	(GROldroyd) **6-11-1**(3) GCahill (in tch: drvn along 7th: one pce fr 2 out)	10	3	5/1[2]	56	10
	Chummy's Saga (69)	(LLungo) **6-10-10** MFoster (plld hrd: sn trckng ldrs: ev ch tl wknd appr 2 out)	7	4	12/1	42	—
1078[3]	**Catton Lady (59)**	(RCraggs) **6-9-11**(3) GLee (trckd ldrs tl wknd 2 out)	12	5	14/1	23	—
	Helens Bay (IRE) (81)	(VThompson) **6-11-8** MrMThompson (drvn along 6th: lost tch next)	10	6	20/1	37	—
1027[10]	**Kajostar (59)**	(SWCampion) **6-9-7**(7) OBurrows (bhd: drvn along 6th: n.d)	4	7	33/1	12	—
	Meadowleck (59)	(WGYoung) **7-10-0** BStorey (led to 3rd: outpcd after 6th: wknd next)	hd	8	33/1	12	—
1078[9]	**Nick the Bill (63)**	(JWade) **5-10-4**ow4 KJones (plld hrd: chsd ldrs: drvn along 7th: lost pl next)	2½	9	20/1	14	—
1021[8]	**Signor Nortone (74)**	(DWWhillans) **4-11-1** BHarding (chsd ldrs: drvn along 6th: lost pl after next)	9	10	10/1[3]	18	—
	Circle Boy (68)	(WStorey) **9-10-4**(5) RMcGrath (fell 2nd)		F	5/1[2]	—	—

				SP	RR	SF
892[F]	**Papa's Boy (IRE) (83)** (HowardJohnson) **5-11-5**(5) GFRyan (plld hrd: trckd ldrs: ev ch 2 out: 5th & wl btn whn fell last: dead)		F	14/1	—	—

(SP 131.8%) **12 Rn**

4m 58.1 (10.10) CSF £36.28 CT £129.68 TOTE £1.90: £1.60 £13.40 £1.20 (£60.20) Trio £118.60 OWNER The Belles (PENRITH) BRED Con Ryan
LONG HANDICAP Nick the Bill 9-11 Kajostar 9-8 Meadowleck 9-7 Catton Lady 9-1
Bt in 3,200 gns
1047* Belle Rose (IRE), from a 7lb higher mark, was always travelling best and had taken the measure of her only serious rival at the last. (Evens)
Kings Minstral (IRE) ran easily his best race so far, travelling strongly in front, but he was booked for second spot when he put in a clumsy jump at the last. (33/1)
Antartictern (USA) stayed on in half-hearted fashion as usual. (5/1)
Chummy's Saga, who took a fierce grip, had no more to give between the last two. (12/1)
Signor Nortone (10/1: op 6/1)

1248 JOHN EUSTACE SMITH TROPHY NOVICES' H'CAP CHASE (0-95) (4-Y.O+) (Class F)
3-20 (3-20) **2m 110y (12 fncs)** £2,655.00 (£792.00: £378.00: £171.00) GOING minus 0.13 sec per fur (G)

				SP	RR	SF
	Abbeylands (IRE) (81) (HowardJohnson) **8-11-5** NWilliamson (mde all: clr fr 8th: rdn out flat: unchal)	—	1	7/2[1]	91	30
1051*	**Ballyline (IRE) (86)** (WTKemp) **5-11-10** TReed (lw: hld up & bhd: hdwy 9th: effrt between last 2: styd on: no imp)	3½	2	7/2[1]	93	32
1126[3]	**Kiltulla (IRE) (65)** (MrsSJSmith) **6-10-3**ow3 RichardGuest (chsd ldrs: wnt 2nd 3 out: wknd appr last)	8	3	5/1[3]	64	—
1051[U]	**Show Your Hand (IRE) (80)** (LLungo) **8-11-4** MFoster (chsd wnr tl wknd 3 out)	16	4	7/2[1]	63	2
1051[2]	**Hazel Crest (72)** (MESowersby) **9-10-10** DParker (lost pl 6th: n.d)	10	5	12/1	46	—
733[3]	**Islandreagh (IRE) (80)** (GRichards) **5-11-4** ADobbin (mstkes: chsd ldrs: blnd 6th: wknd 9th)	2½	6	9/2[2]	51	—
	Nijway (78) (MABarnes) **6-11-2** MMoloney (bit bkwd: s.s: mstkes: a bhd: t.o fr 8th)	dist	7	14/1	—	—
	Mountain Fox (IRE) (72) (VThompson) **6-10-10**ow9 MrMThompson (chsd ldrs: blnd 6th: bhd whn blnd 8th: t.o)	hd	8	50/1	—	—
1066[3]	**Cheeka (81)** (CSmith) **7-11-5** MRanger (wnt prom 7th: hit next: sn lost pl: p.u bef 3 out)		P	12/1	—	—
466[2]	**Signe de Mars (FR) (81)** (MissZAGreen) **5-11-5** BStorey (bhd tl p.u bef 5th)		P	16/1	—	—
	Fine Tune (IRE) (62) (MrsSCBradburne) **6-10-0** BHarding (bit bkwd: prom whn blnd & uns rdr 4th)		U	16/1	—	—

(SP 137.3%) **11 Rn**

4m 3.1 (6.10) CSF £18.32 CT £62.65 TOTE £4.20: £2.60 £1.00 £3.20 (£4.80) Trio £19.60 OWNER Mr Chris Heron (CROOK) BRED Mrs Mave Egan
LONG HANDICAP Fine Tune (IRE) 9-12
OFFICIAL EXPLANATION **Ballyline (IRE): the rider reported that due to the very strong pace, the gelding found nothing when let down.**
Abbeylands (IRE), who looked to have been given a good chance at the weights, was out on his own from halfway. (7/2)
1051* Ballyline (IRE), raised 7lb, seemed to be given an injudicious ride. Sitting out of his ground, he only made his effort between the last two on the uphill run but, after getting within four lengths of the winner halfway up the run-in, his exertions took their toll and he could make no further impression. With a better ride, he must have seriously troubled the winner. (7/2)
1126 Kiltulla (IRE) ran his best race over fences so far. (5/1)
1051 Show Your Hand (IRE) travelled nicely, but got tired three from home. (7/2)

1249 MUSE AND COMPANY H'CAP HURDLE (0-100) (4-Y.O+) (Class F)
3-50 (3-50) **2m (8 hdls)** £2,174.80 (£602.80: £288.40) GOING minus 0.13 sec per fur (G)

				SP	RR	SF
	Apollo's Daughter (65) (JLGoulding) **8-10-0** ADobbin (hld up: hdwy to trck ldrs 3 out: styd on to ld flat: r.o)	—	1	6/1	47	—
910[6]	**Pangeran (USA) (82)** (MrsASwinbank) **4-11-3** JSupple (chsd ldr: led after 5th tl flat: kpt on)	2½	2	2/1[1]	62	—
	Tiotao (IRE) (70) (CParker) **6-10-5** DParker (trckd ldrs: effrt 2 out: nt qckn appr last)	3	3	6/1	47	—
695[3]	**Tashreef (72)** (JJBirkett) **6-10-7b** MMoloney (hit 1st: chsd ldrs: one pce appr last)	2	4	3/1[2]	47	—
1047[7]	**Anorak (USA) (91)** (GMMoore) **6-11-12v** JCallaghan (chsd ldrs: drvn along 5th: lost pl bef 3 out)	9	5	3/1[2]	57	—
32[7]	**Marsh's Law (86)** (GPKelly) **9-11-7** MrCMulhall (sn bhd: t.o 5th)	21	6	11/2[3]	31	—
	Gone Ashore (IRE) (65) (MABarnes) **5-10-0** NWilliamson (led tl after 5th: wknd qckly: t.o 2 out)	dist	7	16/1	—	—

(SP 133.2%) **7 Rn**

4m 2.8 (14.80) CSF £20.87 TOTE £13.00: £3.90 £3.10 (£26.60) OWNER Mrs M. Goulding
LONG HANDICAP Gone Ashore (IRE) 9-9
Apollo's Daughter, given a patient ride in a race run in appalling conditions, got right on top on the run-in. (6/1)
910 Pangeran (USA), who looked very fit indeed, made the best of his way home and struck on under pressure, but the winner proved much too good in the final 100 yards. (2/1)
Tiotao (IRE), who showed precious little last season, travelled strongly but, under pressure, did not find an awful lot, though he did keep on to the end. (6/1)
695 Tashreef has two ways of running and is basically half-hearted. (3/1)
Marsh's Law (11/2: 4/1-6/1)

T/Plpt: £18.20 (473.79 Tckts). T/Qdpt: £8.90 (115.73 Tckts). WG

0794-UTTOXETER (L-H) (Good)
Friday November 8th
WEATHER: fine

1250 HOUGHTON VAUGHAN MAIDEN HURDLE (4-Y.O+) (Class E)
1-10 (1-10) **2m 6f 110y (12 hdls)** £2,484.00 (£699.00: £342.00) GOING: 0.13 sec per fur (G)

				SP	RR	SF
1085[3]	**General Mouktar** (MCPipe) **6-11-5** APMcCoy (hld up & bhd: stdy hdwy 8th: led after 3 out: sn clr)	—	1	4/1[2]	72	19
	Victoria Day (BAMcMahon) **4-11-0** RDunwoody (hdwy 5th: led 9th to 4 out: sn rdn: no ch w wnr)	7	2	16/1	62	9
	Pru's Profiles (IRE) (NATwiston-Davies) **5-11-5** DBridgwater (hld up & bhd: hdwy 9th: styd on u.p fr 2 out)	½	3	12/1	67	14
1050[4]	**Our Rainbow** (MrsPSly) **4-11-0** RMarley (w ldr: led 7th to 9th: lft in ld & bdly hmpd 3 out: sn hdd & nt cvr)	1¼	4	10/1	61	8
	Barton Ward (SABrookshaw) **5-11-5** RJohnson (bit bkwd: hld up in tch: hdwy 8th: ev ch whn bdly hmpd 3 out: nt rcvr)	½	5	6/1	65	12
1036[6]	**Mesp (IRE)** (JGMO'Shea) **5-11-0** MAFitzgerald (bhd tl sme late hdwy)	8	6	33/1	55	2

	Fancy Nancy (IRE) (MissCJohnsey) **5-11-0** LHarvey (bkwd: hld up in rr: styd on fr 3 out: nvr nrr)	2½	**7**	100/1	53	—
	Supremo (IRE) (MJWilkinson) **7-11-5** CLlewellyn (bkwd: mid div: no hdwy fr 3 out)	¾	**8**	12/1	57	4
	Burntwood Melody (PTDalton) **5-11-5** WMarston (bkwd: nvr nr to chal)	3	**9**	50/1	55	2
	Zamorston (NTinkler) **7-11-2**$^{(3)}$ EHusband (bkwd: chsd ldrs to 9th: sn wknd)	¾	**10**	16/1	55	2
955^{6}	**Blaze of Oak (USA) (89)** (JMBradley) **5-11-5** TJMurphy (chsd ldrs to 8th: sn rdn & wknd: t.o)	12	**11**	16/1	46	—
	Seven Potato More (IRE) (SirJohnBarlowBt) **6-11-5** ASSmith (bkwd: mid div tl wknd 8th: t.o)	2½	**12**	40/1	44	—
	Sovereign Grit (IRE) (KCBailey) **6-11-5** CO'Dwyer (swtg: bit bkwd: hdwy 4th: mstke 6th: pushed along whn sltly hmpd 3 out: t.o)	¾	**13**	$9/4^{1}$	44	—
	Lastoftheidiots (TWall) **7-11-2**$^{(3)}$ RMassey (led to 7th: wknd next: t.o)	14	**14**	100/1	34	—
	Gales of Laughter (CaptTAForster) **7-11-5** AThornton (bit bkwd: hld up in tch: hdwy to ld 4 out: fell 3 out)		**F**	$9/2^{3}$	—	—
636^{6}	**Shady Emma** (FJordan) **4-11-0** SWynne (lost pl 6th: t.o whn p.u bef 3 out)		**P**	50/1	—	—
				(SP 136.6%)		**16 Rn**

5m 34.6 (17.60) CSF £68.15 TOTE £4.10: £1.50 £4.50 £4.10 (£40.50) Trio £86.20 OWNER Mr A. S. Helaissi (WELLINGTON) BRED Stetchworth Park Stud Ltd

1085 General Mouktar has taken time to open his account at this game, but he succeeded here with the minimum of fuss, and this easy day's work could well go a long way to changing his attitude to the game. (4/1)

Victoria Day, fit from the Flat, gave of her best, but she caught the winner on one of his going days. (16/1)

Pru's Profiles (IRE) never really got in to the race, but this was his first attempt at the trip, and he did stay on to show a glimpse of promise for the future. (12/1)

1050 Our Rainbow, from a stable just striking form, turned in a pleasing display and may well have chased the winner home had she not been stopped in her tracks by the faller three out. (10/1)

Barton Ward looks to be a bit of a handful, but he settled once in action. Fortunate not to be brought down when holding every chance three out, he should have little trouble in making the grade. (6/1)

Sovereign Grit (IRE), who was never going particularly well after a mistake at the sixth, was ridden and had little chance when slightly hampered by the faller three out. (9/4)

Gales of Laughter, runner-up on his only outing last season, looked very much in need of this, but he had just struck the front when he fell heavily at the third last. He will be on a recovery mission in the near future. (9/2)

1251 HOLSTEN PILS NOVICES' (S) HURDLE (4-Y.O+) (Class G)

1-40 (1-43) **2m 4f 110y (10 hdls)** £1,931.00 (£541.00: £263.00) GOING: 0.13 sec per fur (G)

				SP	RR	SF
891^{5}	**Always Greener (IRE) (76)** (JWMullins) **5-11-0** SCurran (chsd ldrs: led appr 3 out: hrd rdn & edgd lft flat: hld on)	—	**1**	$11/2^{3}$	57	1
905^{2}	**Dragonmist (IRE) (66)** (DBurchell) **6-10-7** DJBurchell (hld up in tch: hdwy 3 out: hrd rdn appr next: styng on whn n.m.r towards fin)	nk	**2**	$9/4^{1}$	50	—
866^{5}	**Le Baron** (CREgerton) **5-10-12** JOsborne (a.p: outpcd appr 2 out: rallied u.p flat)	1½	**3**	$3/1^{2}$	54	—
58^{6}	**Oakbury (IRE) (61)** (MissLCSiddall) **4-10-12** AThornton (hld up: hdwy 6th: rdn 3 out: nvr able to chal)	4	**4**	6/1	51	—
1040^{3}	**Awestruck (62)** (BPreece) **6-10-12b** RJohnson (hld up: hdwy 5th: outpcd appr 3 out: n.d after)	4	**5**	9/1	47	—
392^{5}	**Admiral's Guest (IRE)** (WClay) **4-10-12** TEley (hdwy 6th: wknd appr 3 out: t.o)	17	**6**	20/1	34	—
1053^{9}	**Arthur's Special** (MCPipe) **6-10-7** APMcCoy (prom: led 6th tl appr 3 out: wknd qckly: t.o)	6	**7**	12/1	24	—
1090^{6}	**Beths Wish** (GMPrice) **7-10-7** BFenton (a bhd: t.o)	12	**8**	25/1	15	—
737^{4}	**Secret Serenade** (RTJuckes) **5-10-12** WMarston (prom bef p.u bef 4th: lame)		**P**	14/1	—	—
	Cool Mandy (RJPrice) **5-10-7** JRKavanagh (bkwd: wl bhd tl p.u bef 6th)		**P**	50/1	—	—
963^{6}	**Commanche Storm (IRE)** (WGMann) **4-10-12b**^{1} MrPScott (plld hrd: led to 6th: wknd qckly: t.o whn p.u bef 2 out)		**P**	50/1	—	—
1090^{P}	**Smart Act** (IRBrown) **7-10-12** MrABrown (bkwd: mstke 1st: hdwy 4th: wknd 6th: t.o whn p.u bef 2)		**P**	50/1	—	—
958^{3}	**Tibbs Inn (58)** (ABarrow) **7-10-5**$^{(7)}$ MrRThornton (ref to r: t.n.p)		**R**	14/1	—	—
				(SP 131.0%)		**13 Rn**

5m 3.5 (19.50) CSF £19.05 TOTE £8.10: £2.30 £1.30 £1.90 (£13.20) Trio £10.10 OWNER Mr Peter Houghton (AMESBURY) BRED Collinstown Stud Farm Ltd

No bid

488* Always Greener (IRE) made it two for the season on this step down in class, but she needed to pull out all the stops to hold on nearing the finish. (11/2)

905 Dragonmist (IRE) is not enjoying the best of fortune, and she was being tightened up when rallying strongly on the flat. With no objection or Stewards' enquiry being called for, it may not have been as tight as it looked. (9/4)

866 Le Baron, still looking on the burly side, looked done for approaching the penultimate flight, but he renewed his effort on the run-in and he should be able to find a race at this level. (3/1: 2/1-100/30)

Oakbury (IRE) does not seem to be in love with this game and, though he did stay on under strong pressure, he lacked the pace to go through with his effort. (6/1)

1040 Awestruck failed to hold his pitch entering the straight. (9/1)

Arthur's Special (12/1: 16/1-10/1)

1252 JOHN PARTRIDGE NOVICES' H'CAP CHASE (0-100) (5-Y.O+) (Class E)

2-10 (2-10) **2m 5f (16 fncs)** £3,113.00 (£944.00: £462.00: £221.00) GOING minus 0.15 sec per fur (G)

				SP	RR	SF
799^{2}	**Micherado (FR) (96)** (SABrookshaw) **6-11-12** RJohnson (lw: mde all: j.lft: mstke 8th: blnd bdly last: all out)	—	**1**	$4/1^{2}$	108	41
	Bironi (95) (CaptTAForster) **7-11-11** SWynne (bit bkwd: hdwy 12th: chsd wnr fr 3 out: styd on u.p flat)	4	**2**	$3/1^{1}$	104	37
1083^{7}	**Desert Brave (IRE) (77)** (MrsSJSmith) **6-10-0**$^{(7)}$ RWilkinson (chsd ldrs: wnt 2nd 9th: kpt on one pce fr 3 out)	4	**3**	16/1	83	16
	Golden Drum (IRE) (74) (JACEdwards) **6-10-4**^{ow4} MAFitzgerald (bit bkwd: mstke 2nd: chsd wnr to 9th: grad wknd: t.o)	15	**4**	20/1	69	—
1038^{6}	**Chris's Glen (83)** (JMBradley) **7-10-13v** TJMurphy (chsd ldrs to 12th: sn wknd: t.o)	9	**5**	8/1	71	4
1038^{P}	**Dominie (IRE) (95)** (KCBailey) **8-11-11b** CO'Dwyer (a in rr: t.o)	21	**6**	10/1	67	—
	Sense of Value (90) (JSSmith) **7-11-6** WMarston (bkwd: chsd ldrs to ½-wy: sn wknd: t.o)	dist	**7**	20/1	—	—
	Prussian Storm (IRE) (70) (MBradstock) **7-10-0** PHolley (s.s: in rr tl fell 4 out)		**F**	40/1	—	—
935^{*}	**Karlovac (70)** (RLee) **10-10-0** AMaguire (a bhd: t.o 11th: p.u bef 4 out)		**P**	$5/1^{3}$	—	—
870^{3}	**Bridepark Rose (IRE) (89)** (GMMcCourt) **8-11-5** BClifford (mid div whn blnd & uns rdr 6th)		**U**	$5/1^{3}$	—	—
				(SP 116.4%)		**10 Rn**

5m 11.3 (6.30) CSF £15.59 CT £157.07 TOTE £3.90: £1.40 £2.00 £3.40 (£5.90) Trio £95.70 OWNER Mr Stanley Clarke (SHREWSBURY) BRED Ulrich Fricker

LONG HANDICAP Prussian Storm (IRE) 9-4

799 Micherado (FR) takes so many chances with his jumping that he needs to be kept at these easier tracks. This success has got to go down to his jockey who performed wonders to keep the partnership together. (4/1)

Bironi, ridden with restraint on this seasonal debut, did well to run the race-fit winner so close, and he will be much sharper next time. (3/1)

1083 Desert Brave (IRE) lacks experience over fences and, in such a fast-run race, did more than his share of guessing, but it is to his credit that he performed so well and his turn will come. (16/1)

Golden Drum (IRE) survived an early mistake on this chasing debut, and chased the winner at a respectable distance before blowing up and dropping away inside the last mile. (20/1)

1038 Chris's Glen (8/1: op 5/1)

1253 FLINT BISHOP & BARNETT NOVICES' H'CAP HURDLE (0-100) (3-Y.O+) (Class E)

2-40 (2-40) **2m (9 hdls)** £2,347.50 (£660.00: £322.50) GOING: 0.13 sec per fur (G)

	Horse			SP	RR	SF
	Bassenhally (83) (MrsPSly) **6-10-12** RMarley (bit bkwd: a.p: led appr 3 out to last: rallied u.p to ld flat)	—	1	13/2	63	15
1091*	**Ragamuffin Romeo (79)** (HJCollingridge) **7-10-8** 8x APMcCoy (a.p: chal 2 out: slt ld last: hdd & no ex flat)	1¼	2	9/4 1	58	10
189*	**Prussia (99)** (WClay) **5-12-0** RJohnson (bkwd: chsd ldrs: hrd drvn & outpcd appr 3 out: styd on appr last)	7	3	8/1	71	23
944^{6}	**Tarry (90)** (AStreeter) **3-10-3** TEley (mid div: kpt on appr last: nvr nrr)	4	4	7/2 2	58	—
654^{5}	**Skram (87)** (RDickin) **3-10-0** AMaguire (chsd ldr: mstke 3rd: led after 6th: sn hdd: wknd 2 out)	4	5	10/1	51	—
	Time Leader (71) (RDickin) **4-10-0** BPowell (a in rr)	1¾	6	20/1	33	—
931^{4}	**Cruisinforabruisin (71)** (RJPrice) **6-10-0** JRKavanagh (bit bkwd: a bhd)	1½	7	25/1	32	—
969^{7}	**Galloping Guns (IRE) (71)** (BJLlewellyn) **4-10-0** SCurran (a bhd: t.o fr 6th)	16	8	20/1	16	—
1049^{6}	**Dash To The Phone (USA) (72)** (KAMorgan) **4-10-1v** ASSmith (lw: led tl after 6th: sn rdn & wknd: t.o)	4	9	5/1 3	13	—

(SP 116.6%) **9 Rn**

3m 52.8 (11.80) CSF £20.75 CT £109.86 TOTE £7.00: £2.00 £1.10 £2.40 (£15.80) Trio £23.70 OWNER Thorney Racing Club (PETERBOROUGH) BRED Mrs P. Sly

LONG HANDICAP Skram 9-12 Cruisinforabruisin 9-8 Galloping Guns (IRE) 9-6 Time Leader 9-13

WEIGHT FOR AGE 3yo-16lb

Bassenhally had to work hard to get off the mark, but he showed the right attitude and will strip fitter with this outing under his belt. (13/2)

1091* Ragamuffin Romeo, twice a winner already this season, did look to be in control when jumping the final flight in front, but the winner proved just the stronger in an all-out duel to the finish. (9/4)

189* Prussia finds this minimum trip not quite far enough, but he was carrying surplus condition for this return to action, and he will find his way again when stepped up to two and a half miles. (8/1: op 9/2)

944 Tarry could never go the pace and was some way adrift until beginning to stay on when it was all but over. (7/2)

589 Skram took the leader on and did eventually show ahead, but he had probably done too much too soon, for he was legless halfway up the straight. (10/1: op 6/1)

1254 UNDERGEAR 'TERRA TIRE' NOVICES' CHASE (5-Y.O+) (Class D)

3-10 (3-10) **2m (12 fncs)** £3,826.25 (£1,160.00: £567.50: £271.25) GOING minus 0.15 sec per fur (G)

	Horse			SP	RR	SF
	Mulligan (IRE) (DNicholson) **6-10-12** AMaguire (j.w: mde all: comf)	—	1	4/9 1	99+	39
1038^{P}	**Flaming Miracle (IRE) (63)** (GBarnett) **6-10-12b** RFarrant (a.p: chsd wnr fr 8th: no imp fr 3 out)	6	2	33/1	93	33
	Scottish Bambi (PRWebber) **8-10-12** JOsborne (bkwd: hld up: hit 5th: hdwy 8th: one pce fr 3 out)	3½	3	10/1 3	90	30
1007^{2}	**Total Asset** (ALForbes) **6-10-12** GaryLyons (in rr whn blnd 4th: nvr nr ldrs)	10	4	33/1	80	20
889^{5}	**Legal Artist (IRE) (82)** (MissCJohnsey) **6-10-12** LHarvey (lw: a in rr: lost tch 8th: t.o)	19	5	12/1	61	1
1120^{7}	**Betabetcorbett** (BPJBaugh) **5-10-12v** TEley (chsd ldrs tl lost pl & rdn 6th: t.o whn p.u bef 4 out)		P	33/1	—	—
972^{4}	**Lord Nitrogen (USA) (81)** (BJLlewellyn) **6-10-12** APMcCoy (chsd wnr to 8th: wkng whn blnd & uns rdr 4 out)		U	9/2 2	—	—

(SP 113.0%) **7 Rn**

3m 52.1 (2.10) CSF £13.96 TOTE £1.50: £1.50 £3.60 (£12.50) OWNER Lady Harris (TEMPLE GUITING) BRED Sandford Bloodstock Ltd

Mulligan (IRE), who changed hands for 100,000 guineas in May, did everything asked of him on this chasing debut, and outclassed the opposition to win as he pleased. A compact, strongly-made sort, he did not look fully wound up and such an easy introduction was tailor-made. (4/9)

Flaming Miracle (IRE), much wiser for the experience gained on his debut last month, did his best to make a race of it, but he was always fighting a lost cause, and will do well to steer clear of one as useful as the winner. (33/1)

Scottish Bambi was far from foot-perfect at this first attempt at the bigger obstacles, but he should have learnt plenty and the outing will have helped put an edge on him. (10/1)

72 Legal Artist (IRE) (12/1: op 8/1)

1255 STREBEL BOILERS AND RADIATORS H'CAP HURDLE (0-120) (4-Y.O+) (Class D)

3-40 (3-40) **2m 4f 110y (10 hdls)** £2,814.00 (£852.00: £416.00: £198.00) GOING: 0.13 sec per fur (G)

	Horse			SP	RR	SF
	Deymiar (IRE) (114) (DRGandolfo) **4-11-10** RDunwoody (hld up: stdy hdwy 3 out: led last: hld on wl nr fin)	—	1	3/1 2	94	27
	High Grade (110) (MissSJWilton) **8-11-6** APMcCoy (bit bkwd: a.p: led appr 6th to 3 out: rallied u.p flat)	nk	2	10/1	90	23
868^{2}	**Pharare (IRE) (92)** (RDEWoodhouse) **6-10-2** LWyer (lw: plld hrd: lft in ld after 5th: sn hdd: led 3 out to last: hrd rdn & one pce flat)	4	3	15/8 1	69	2
	Tight Fist (IRE) (113) (MissHCKnight) **6-11-9** JFTitley (bkwd: hld up: effrt & drvn along appr 3 out: sn no imp: t.o)	21	4	5/1	73	6
916^{3}	**Mutazz (USA) (105)** (MajorWRHern) **4-11-1** RFarrant (hld up: outpcd appr 3 out: sn t.o)	12	5	100/30 3	56	—
131^{8}	**Laughing Gas (IRE) (97)** (MrsNMacauley) **7-10-7** PHide (led tl wnt lame & p.u after 5th)		P	25/1	—	—

(SP 112.5%) **6 Rn**

4m 58.8 (14.80) CSF £26.47 TOTE £3.40: £1.50 £3.90 (£15.90) OWNER Mr T. J. Whitley (WANTAGE) BRED His Highness the Aga Khans Studs S. C.

Deymiar (IRE) did not have so much use made of him on this occasion, but that was probably just as well, for he was coming to the end of his tether on the run to the line. (3/1)

High Grade gave his local supporters something to shout about, especially in the closing stages, but he has not won a race since the 1993/94 season, and has just lost the habit of winning. (10/1)

868 Pharare (IRE), in and out of the lead from the start, had no answer to the winner's superior pace from the last. (15/8)

916 Mutazz (USA), held up to get the trip, was beginning to labour on the home turn, and may do better returning to two miles. (100/30)

1256 HOLSTEN PILS H'CAP HURDLE (0-100) (4-Y.O+) (Class F)

4-10 (4-10) **3m 110y (12 hdls)** £2,379.00 (£669.00: £327.00) GOING: 0.13 sec per fur (G)

				SP	RR	SF
1031[3]	**Elburg (IRE) (93)** (TRGeorge) **6-11-10** MAFitzgerald (hld up: hdwy 7th: led 3 out: sn clr: v.easily)	—	1	14/1	83+	34
1080[2]	**Ballindoo (84)** (RJArmson) **7-11-1** MrRArmson (hld up: hdwy 7th: one pce fr 3 out)	10	2	4/1[2]	68	19
971[6]	**Mr Flutts (77)** (JCTuck) **10-10-8** SMcNeill (hld up: hdwy 9th: nvr nrr)	6	3	12/1	57	8
800[4]	**Riverbank Rose (70)** (WClay) **5-10-1** TEley (w ldr: led 7th to 3 out: sn rdn & wknd)	1	4	16/1	49	—
	Apachee Flower (77) (HSHowe) **6-10-8** APMcCoy (bit bkwd: hld up: reminders after 7th: sme hdwy fr 3 out: nvr nrr)	5	5	9/4[1]	53	4
1121[3]	**Batty's Island (75)** (BPreece) **7-10-6** AMaguire (prom: mstke 5th: wknd 9th)	13	6	15/2	42	—
971[5]	**Bright Sapphire (75)** (DBurchell) **10-10-6** DJBurchell (trckd ldrs tl outpcd appr 3 out: sn t.o)	15	7	9/1	32	—
978[2]	**Saltis (IRE) (77)** (ALForbes) **4-10-7** GaryLyons (hld up: hdwy ½-wy: wknd appr 3 out: t.o)	7	8	7/1[3]	30	—
	Provence (80) (AWCarroll) **9-10-11** WMarston (bkwd: prom tl wknd qckly 9th: t.o)	dist	9	25/1	—	—
	Kayfaat (USA) (85) (MCPipe) **8-10-9**(7) BMoore (led tl after 2nd: wknd 8th: t.o)	13	10	10/1	—	—
978[5]	**Curragh Peter (72)** (MrsPBickerton) **9-10-0**(3) GuyLewis (plld hrd: led after 2nd to 7th: wknd qckly: t.o whn p.u bef 3 out)		P	33/1	—	—
	Astral Invasion (USA) (86) (GMMcCourt) **5-11-3** BClifford (bkwd: bhd & rdn 6th: t.o whn p.u bef 8th)		P	16/1	—	—
				(SP 127.0%)	**12 Rn**	

5m 57.2 (15.20) CSF £69.37 CT £661.98 TOTE £10.60: £2.70 £2.00 £5.00 (£25.40) Trio £262.00 OWNER Mrs Alison Gamble (ROSS-ON-WYE) BRED Sheikh Mohammed bin Rashid al Maktoum

WEIGHT FOR AGE 4yo-1lb

1031 Elburg (IRE) went the wrong way last year and looked a shadow of his former self, but a change of stables has rekindled him, and this runaway success would suggest he is back to something like his best. (14/1)

1080 Ballindoo took closer order going out into the country for the second time but, like the rest of his rivals, was caught flat-footed when the winner quickened things up. (4/1)

Mr Flutts began to stay on inside the last half-mile but, by then, the winner had set sail for home. (12/1)

Riverbank Rose may fare better if not so much use is made of her, for once again she was left struggling when the race began in earnest. (16/1)

Apachee Flower, off the racecourse for seven months, looked to have something left to work on and, given reminders at halfway, was never a factor at any stage. (9/4: op 4/1)

1121 Batty's Island, with the pace for two and a half miles, ran as if he failed to last the trip. More patient tactics are needed at such an extended trip. (15/2)

Kayfaat (USA) (10/1: 6/1-11/1)

T/Plpt: £28.70 (435.14 Tckts). T/Qdpt: £7.80 (131.34 Tckts). IM

0788-CHEPSTOW (L-H) (Good to soft, Hdles Soft patches)

Saturday November 9th

WEATHER: sunny

1257 OSMINGTON MILLS HOLIDAYS AND PERMIT TRAINERS ASSOCIATION H'CAP CHASE (0-130) (5-Y.O+) (Class C)

1-15 (1-15) **2m 110y (12 fncs)** £6,905.00 (£2,090.00: £1,020.00: £485.00) GOING: 0.53 sec per fur (GS)

				SP	RR	SF
	Benjamin Lancaster (98) (MAGriffin) **12-9-7**(7) MGriffiths (chsd ldr: led 3 out: rdn out)	—	1	16/1	101	41
1035[2]	**Newlands-General (115)** (PFNicholls) **10-11-3** APMcCoy (set str pce: hit 3rd: hdd 3 out: one pce)	2½	2	11/10[1]	116	56
1120[4]	**Naiysari (IRE) (108)** (PMRich) **8-10-10** WMarston (bhd & outpcd: tk poor 3rd pl 8th: no imp)	14	3	10/1	95	35
	Northern Saddler (122) (RJHodges) **9-11-10** RDunwoody (bit bkwd: chsd clr ldng pair to 8th: wknd 3 out: t.o)	17	4	2/1[2]	93	33
	Olliver Duckett (100) (MrsJSidebottom) **7-10-2**ow2 MSharratt (bkwd: a bhd: t.o fr 7th)	3	5	50/1	68	6
1146[3]	**Northern Optimist (98)** (BJLlewellyn) **8-10-0** RJohnson (a outpcd: t.o fr ½-wy)	9	6	8/1[3]	57	—
				(SP 109.0%)	**6 Rn**	

4m 8.4 (10.40) CSF £32.48 TOTE £14.50: £3.10 £1.20 (£9.40) OWNER Mr M. Griffin (LISKEARD) BRED M. A. Griffin

LONG HANDICAP Benjamin Lancaster 9-13 Olliver Duckett 8-6 Northern Optimist 9-3

Benjamin Lancaster failed to win a race last year, but showed that he still retains ability with a convincing success in this truly-run contest. (16/1)

1035 Newlands-General is a bit headstrong and, when he does stop pulling, there is not a lot left in the tank. With the winner keeping tabs on him, he easily got brushed aside in the latter stages. (11/10)

1120 Naiysari (IRE), taken off his legs in this slightly better-class race, was never within striking range of the principals. (10/1:op 6/1)

Northern Saddler can win first time up, but he was at full stretch from the word go, and lack of peak-fitness began to take its toll early in the straight. (2/1)

1146 Northern Optimist (8/1: 5/1-9/1)

1258 TOTE SILVER TROPHY H'CAP HURDLE (4-Y.O+) (Class B)

1-45 (1-46) **2m 4f 110y (11 hdls)** £16,217.00 (£4,886.00: £2,368.00: £1,109.00) GOING: 0.53 sec per fur (GS)

				SP	RR	SF
	Castle Sweep (IRE) (135) (DNicholson) **5-10-10** RJohnson (mstkes: hld up gng wl: led & hit 2 out: sn clr: v.impressive)	—	1	9/4[1]	126+	58
1015[2]	**Mytton's Choice (IRE) (125)** (DNicholson) **5-9-7**(7) MrRThornton (hld up: hdwy 6th: led 4 out to 2 out: sn outpcd)	10	2	14/1	108	40
	Silver Shred (130) (MCPipe) **5-10-5** RDunwoody (hld up & bhd: hdwy appr 4 out: sn rdn: styd on one pce)	6	3	9/2[3]	109	41
790[4]	**Hand Woven (125)** (NATwiston-Davies) **4-10-0** CLlewellyn (bhd: reminders 6th: hdwy next: outpcd fr 3 out)	6	4	9/1	99	31
	Muse (149) (DRCElsworth) **9-11-10** AProcter (swtg: bit bkwd: led & sn clr: wknd & hdd appr 4 out: sn btn)	10	5	25/1	115	47
1148*	**Runaway Pete (USA) (125)** (MCPipe) **6-10-0** 3x SWynne (chsd ldrs: rdn & lost tch 6th: rallied appr 4 out: outpcd fr next)	2½	6	20/1	89	21
	Dr Leunt (IRE) (136) (PJHobbs) **5-10-11** APMcCoy (bit bkwd: nt j.w: chsd ldr tl led appr 4 out: sn hdd, rdn & btn)	5	7	11/2	96	28

	Horse	Dist	Pos	SP	RR	SF
1039*	**Teen Jay (125)** (BJLlewellyn) **6-10-0** 3x VSlattery (lw: hld up & bhd: t.o fr 7th)	30	**8**	14/1	62	—
	Jet Rules (IRE) (127) (MrsJPitman) **6-10-2** WMarston (bit bkwd: chsd ldrs tl wknd appr 4 out: t.o)	1¼	**9**	4/1 [2]	63	—
	Meditator (125) (APJones) **12-10-0** BFenton (bkwd: lost pl 4th: sn t.o)	11	**10**	50/1	52	—
				(SP 118.2%)	**10 Rn**	

4m 57.9 (10.90) CSF £30.81 CT £123.30 TOTE £3.70: £1.70 £3.30 £1.60 (£28.60) Trio £61.30 OWNER Lord Vestey (TEMPLE GUITING) BRED Patrick Cody

LONG HANDICAP Runaway Pete (USA) 9-8 Mytton's Choice (IRE) 9-6 Teen Jay 9-6 Hand Woven 9-11 Meditator 9-10

Castle Sweep (IRE) began the season in the best possible fashion with a most impressive display. If he can brush up his hurdling, he will definitely go to the top this term. (9/4)

1015 Mytton's Choice (IRE), receiving a lot of weight from his stablemate, still gave a good account of himself in this company, and his future looks bright. (14/1)

Silver Shred looked well tuned up for this initial outing of the season and did try to make her presence felt soon after entering the straight, but the leading pair quickened the tempo and she was left in their wake. (9/2)

790 Hand Woven is hardly up to this class and was struggling to stay in touch from the turn for home. (9/1)

Muse had a run on the Flat last month, but he still looked far from the finished article. After setting a telling gallop for two miles, he found the concession of so much weight beyond him. (25/1)

1148* Runaway Pete (USA) had to admitt himself outclassed, and was never going well enough to give supporters any encouragement. (20/1)

Dr Leunt (IRE), an ex-Irish gelding who was reported to have been trained with this race in mind, could not overcome an absence of over 600 days. After making more than his fair share of mistakes, he called enough before he reached the third last. (11/2)

1259 RISING STARS NOVICES' CHASE (Gd 2) (5-Y.O+) (Class A)

2-15 (2-20) **2m 3f 110y (16 fncs)** £13,786.00 (£4,776.00: £2,338.00) GOING: 0.53 sec per fur (GS)

Horse	Dist	Pos	SP	RR	SF
See More Business (IRE) (PFNicholls) **6-11-0** APMcCoy (hld up: mstke 4th: led 4 out: sn clr: easily)	—	**1**	8/13 [1]	120+	51
Wee Windy (IRE) (JTGifford) **7-11-0** RDunwoody (bit bkwd: j.w: led to 4 out: sn rdn: r.o one pce)	8	**2**	5/1 [3]	113	44
Buckhouse Boy (NATwiston-Davies) **6-11-0** TJenks (lw: chsd ldr to 4 out: wkng whn blnd 2 out)	11	**3**	2/1 [2]	104	35
			(SP 111.9%)	**3 Rn**	

5m 2.2 (13.20) CSF £3.46 TOTE £1.50 (£1.90) OWNER Mr Paul K Barber and Mr J A Keighley (SHEPTON MALLET) BRED Ian Bryant

See More Business (IRE), a winner between the Flags as a five-year-old, took to these regulation fences like a duck to water and, apart from a minor error, could hardly have been more impressive. (8/13)

Wee Windy (IRE), having his first taste of fences, gave a bold display of jumping from the front, but he was more in need of the run than the winner, and his measure had been taken from some way out. (5/1)

Buckhouse Boy attempted to match strides with the leader, but he was always coming off second best, and had already accepted the position when an untidy effort at the penultimate fence took the stuffing out of him. (2/1)

1260 REMEMBRANCE 'N.H.' NOVICES' HURDLE (4-Y.O+) (Class D)

2-50 (2-51) **2m 4f 110y (11 hdls)** £3,233.00 (£974.00: £472.00: £221.00) GOING: 0.53 sec per fur (GS)

	Horse	Dist	Pos	SP	RR	SF
	Minella Derby (IRE) (PFNicholls) **6-10-12** RJohnson (hdwy 5th: hit 3 out & 2 out: led & mstke last: hld on)	—	**1**	4/1 [3]	74	19
	Hurdante (IRE) (GBBalding) **6-10-12** BFenton (lw: plld hrd: mstke 3rd: mde most to last: rallied u.p cl home)	.1	**2**	9/1	73	18
	The Reverend Bert (IRE) (106) (GBBalding) **8-10-12** APMcCoy (hld up: hdwy 7th: ev ch 3 out: wknd next)	8	**3**	5/2 [1]	67	12
	Stormy Passage (IRE) (PJHobbs) **6-10-5**(7) MrRThornton (bit bkwd: chsd ldrs to 3 out: wknd qckly)	3½	**4**	8/1	64	9
	Arturo (CaptTAForster) **5-10-12** SWynne (bkwd: trckd ldrs to 4 out: sn rdn & wknd)	10	**5**	20/1	56	1
	Logical Step (IRE) (104) (DRGandolfo) **6-10-12** RDunwoody (hld up: effrt appr 4 out: sn rdn & no imp: t.o)	16	**6**	3/1 [2]	44	—
	King's Courtier (IRE) (77) (SMellor) **7-10-12** NMann (bit bkwd: lost tch 5th: sn t.o)	18	**7**	25/1	30	—
	Supreme Kellycarra (IRE) (MissHCKnight) **5-10-0**(7) MrAWintle (hld up: hdwy 7th: wknd appr 3 out: t.o)	1	**8**	12/1	24	—
	Kedge Anchor Man (AGFoster) **5-10-12** WMarston (bit bkwd: chsd ldrs to 4 out: 5th & btn whn fell last)		**F**	14/1	—	—
	Dunnicks Country (70) (FGTucker) **6-10-0**(7) MGriffiths (bkwd: chsd ldrs to 6th: wl bhd whn p.u bef 4 out)		**P**	25/1	—	—
890[8]	**The Cheese Baron** (SMellor) **5-10-7**(5) ChrisWebb (a bhd: t.o whn p.u bef 4 out)		**P**	33/1	—	—
	Queen Of The Suir (IRE) (NRMitchell) **7-10-7** VSlattery (bkwd: mstkes: sn t.o: p.u bef 4 out)		**P**	50/1	—	—
				(SP 126.4%)	**12 Rn**	

5m 9.1 (22.10) CSF £39.40 TOTE £4.70: £2.20 £2.30 £1.30 (£16.80) Trio £12.90 OWNER Mr B. C. Kilby (SHEPTON MALLET) BRED Countess Doenhoff

Minella Derby (IRE), a 45,000 guinea buy after winning a bumper in Ireland, still has plenty to learn about the art of hurdling, but he did the business on this debut, and an even longer trip will suit him better. (4/1: op 5/4)

Hurdante (IRE) ended his time in Ireland with a runaway success in a bumper, but he ran much too freely on this hurdling debut. He still made the winner know he had been in a race and should have little trouble in going one better. (9/1)

The Reverend Bert (IRE) had plenty of hurdling experience last season, and did look to have done a lot of work in preparation for this. After moving through to give himself every chance three out, he was getting the worst of the argument at the next. (5/2)

Stormy Passage (IRE) shaped promisingly on this hurdling debut, being in the action until lack of peak-condition told on the run to the second last. (8/1)

Arturo is slowly coming to hand and will be all the better for this much-needed pipe-opener. (20/1)

Logical Step (IRE), too backward to do himself justice on this occasion, was never able to prove a threat. (3/1)

Kedge Anchor Man (14/1: op 50/1)

1261 STAYERS NOVICES' HURDLE (4-Y.O+) (Class D)

3-25 (3-26) **3m (12 hdls)** £2,823.50 (£848.00: £409.00: £189.50) GOING: 0.53 sec per fur (GS)

	Horse	Dist	Pos	SP	RR	SF
1085[2]	**Flying Gunner (112)** (DNicholson) **5-11-0** RJohnson (lw: chsd ldrs: led 4 out: mstke next: clr appr last)	—	**1**	4/7 [1]	80	—
	Jet Boys (IRE) (98) (MrsJPitman) **6-11-0** WMarston (lw: hld up: hdwy 6th: outpcd 8th: styd on again fr 2 out)	.8	**2**	9/2 [2]	75	—
	Mendip Prince (IRE) (PJHobbs) **6-11-0** RDunwoody (bit bkwd: led to 2nd: led 5th to 4 out: wknd 2 out)	¾	**3**	5/1 [3]	74	—
	Country Blue (PFNicholls) **5-11-0** APMcCoy (bkwd: hld up in tch: ev ch 4 out: wknd next: t.o)	dist	**4**	10/1	—	—
	La Chance (MrsHLWalton) **6-11-0** MrAWalton (bkwd: drvn along ½-wy: sn t.o)	dist	**5**	50/1	—	—
748[4]	**Reine de La Chasse (FR) (78)** (RJO'Sullivan) **4-10-8** AMcCabe (hld up: hdwy 6th: wknd qckly: p.u bef 4 out)		**P**	25/1	—	—
1037[P]	**Eventsinternashnal** (MSheppard) **7-11-4b** 1ow4 MrJMPritchard (bkwd: led 2nd to 5th: wknd qckly next: t.o whn p.u after 8th)		**P**	100/1	—	—
954[11]	**Jaime's Joy** (GraemeRoe) **6-10-9** TJenks (sn t.o: p.u after 8th)		**P**	200/1	—	—
				(SP 114.9%)	**8 Rn**	

6m 30.6 (50.60) CSF £3.74 TOTE £1.70: £1.10 £1.30 £1.10 (£2.70) OWNER Mr Maryan Green (TEMPLE GUITING) BRED Mrs E. A. Prowting

WEIGHT FOR AGE 4yo-1lb
1085 Flying Gunner kept up his stable's impressive start to the season with an effortless success and, though he may not have beaten much, he could hardly have won any easier. (4/7: 4/5-evens)
Jet Boys (IRE), like most from his yard, is sure to strip fitter next time. Though he was inclined to run in snatches, he was staying on well at the finish. (9/2: op 2/1)
Mendip Prince (IRE) only had a single outing last term and finished tailed off on that occasion. Understandably looking burly, he did make the majority of the running to the fourth last before gradually fading, and was only denied the runner-up prize nearing the line. (5/1)
Country Blue (10/1: 7/1-12/1)

1262 NIMBLE H'CAP HURDLE (0-120) (4-Y.O+) (Class D)
3-55 (3-59) **2m 110y (8 hdls)** £2,784.50 (£836.00: £403.00: £186.50) GOING: 0.53 sec per fur (GS)

	Horse / details		Pos	SP	RR	SF
	Potentate (USA) (117) (MCPipe) **5-12-0** APMcCoy (mde all: clr 3rd: mstke 2 out: sn rdn: r.o wl)	—	1	4/5 1	106	12
	Phar From Funny (105) (GBBalding) **5-11-2** BFenton (bit bkwd: stdd s: hdwy to chse wnr 5th: rdn & one pce appr last)	6	2	9/2 2	88	—
	Nothingtodowithme (92) (CaptTAForster) **6-10-3** SWynne (chsd wnr to 5th: wknd 3 out)	6	3	6/1	69	—
	Moment of Glory (IRE) (114) (DRGandolfo) **5-11-11b1** RDunwoody (bkwd: a in rr)	4	4	8/1	88	—
1145 11	**San Diego Charger (IRE) (89)** (ABarrow) **5-9-7(7)** MrRThornton (rdn & dropped rr ½-wy: sn t.o)	11	5	33/1	52	—
	Monicasman (IRE) (116) (APJarvis) **6-11-13** WMarston (hld up in tch: lost pl appr 4 out: t.o)	29	6	11/2 3	51	—

(SP 117.5%) **6 Rn**

4m 11.9 (22.90) CSF £5.18 TOTE £1.80: £1.10 £2.00 (£2.90) OWNER Mr Jim Weeden (WELLINGTON) BRED Stelcar Stables Incorporated
LONG HANDICAP San Diego Charger (IRE) 9-7
Potentate (USA), successful three times over course and distance last season, continued where he left off, but he did have to work in the closing stages before running out a comfortable winner. (4/5: op 5/4)
Phar From Funny would have made a race of it had he been as straight in condition as the winner, but he still ran a race full of promise, and should soon go one better. (9/2: op 3/1)
Nothingtodowithme, in pursuit of the winner, did not hurdle as fluently as that rival and, though he did look well wound up, he was treading ground from the third last. (6/1)
Moment of Glory (IRE) (8/1: op 4/1)
Monicasman (IRE) has won first time out for the past couple of years and did look fit enough this time, but he was in deep trouble soon after turning in and was extremely leg-weary at the finish. (11/2: 3/1-6/1)

T/Plpt: £4.60 (2,794.96 Tckts). T/Qdpt: £2.30 (258.55 Tckts). IM

1159-NEWCASTLE (L-H) (Good, Good to firm patches)
Saturday November 9th
One fence omitted
WEATHER: fine

1263 E.B.F. 'N.H.' NOVICES' HURDLE (4, 5 & 6-Y.O) (Class E)
1-00 (1-01) **2m (9 hdls)** £2,295.00 (£645.00: £315.00) GOING minus 0.51 sec per fur (GF)

	Horse / details		Pos	SP	RR	SF
1152P	**B The One** (JJQuinn) **5-11-0** RGarritty (hld up: stdy hdwy 5th: hrd rdn flat: led towards fin)	—	1	6/1	63	25
1079 4	**Faithful Hand** (MrsSJSmith) **6-10-7(7)** RWilkinson (mde most tl hdd nr fin)	1¼	2	4/1 2	62	24
	Nick Ross (RBrewis) **5-11-0** ADobbin (bit bkwd: hdwy & prom 3 out: rdn & nt qckn fr next)	5	3	11/2 3	57	19
	King Pin (PBeaumont) **4-11-0** RSupple (bit bkwd: hld up: stdy hdwy 5th: rdn 3 out: hung lft & hit next:sn btn)	5	4	9/4 1	52	14
	Scotton Green (TDEasterby) **5-11-0** LWyer (lw: chsd ldrs: rdn 3 out: wknd appr next)	5	5	8/1	47	9
1033 4	**Primitive Heart** (HowardJohnson) **4-11-0** ALarnach (chsd ldrs: rdn 6th: sn wl outpcd)	2½	6	9/1	44	6
939 9	**Persuasive Talent (IRE)** (DALamb) **5-11-0** BHarding (plld hrd: trckd ldrs: rdn 6th: wknd & eased after next)	18	7	66/1	26	—
1052 8	**Teddy Edward** (MrsAMNaughton) **6-11-0** JSupple (plld hrd: w ldrs: hit 2nd: lost pl after 5th: sn bhd)	10	8	50/1	16	—
	Ar Aghaidh Abhaile (IRE) (MissMKMilligan) **5-11-0** ASSmith (bkwd: bhd fr 5th)	15	9	14/1	1	—
	Un Poco Loco (MrsJBrown) **4-11-0** PNiven (bit bkwd: blnd 4th: sn wl bhd)	13	10	20/1	—	—

(SP 116.4%) **10 Rn**

3m 52.1 (0.10) CSF £28.42 TOTE £10.00: £3.30 £1.50 £1.10 (£15.60) Trio £30.80 OWNER Mr Andrew Page and Mr John Pollard (MALTON) BRED Mrs P. Nicholson
B The One, a bumper winner, had to be pulled up after being hampered at Wetherby a week earlier. Responding to strong pressure, he got up near the line. (6/1)
1079 Faithful Hand seemed to be travelling comfortably in front. His rider never picked up his whip on the run-in and, in the end, the winning combination proved just too strong. (4/1)
Nick Ross, having his first outing for almost a year, looked in need of it. Sticking on under pressure, he should improve, and will be suited by an extra half-mile. (11/2)
King Pin, who showed plenty of foot when winning two bumpers at Market Rasen last season, looked as if the outing would do him the power of good. Making ground on the bridle soon after halfway, he came under pressure three out. Hanging left, he hit the next and could then make no impression. The outing will surely bring him on, but it was still rather disappointing. (9/4)
1033 Primitive Heart (9/1: op 5/1)

1264 TOP OF THE NORTH NOVICES' CHASE (4-Y.O+) (Class E)
1-30 (1-30) **2m 110y (12 fncs)** £2,853.00 (£864.00: £422.00: £201.00) GOING minus 0.16 sec per fur (G)

	Horse / details		Pos	SP	RR	SF
1022*	**Solomon's Dancer (USA)** (GRichards) **6-11-9** ADobbin (lw: trckd ldrs: slt ld 3 out: styd on u.p flat: all out)	—	1	5/6 1	106	39
1032*	**Down the Fell** (HowardJohnson) **7-11-9** NWilliamson (led to 3 out: ev ch flat: r.o u.p)	¾	2	3/1 2	105	38
897 2	**Blue Charm (IRE) (93)** (MrsSCBradburne) **6-11-9** RGarritty (w ldrs: rdn & outpcd appr 2 out: styd on wl flat)	1¾	3	16/1 3	104	37
1022 3	**Shawwell (81)** (JIACharlton) **9-11-3** BStorey (outpcd & pushed along 5th: hdwy & in tch 9th: wkng whn hit next)	25	4	50/1	73	6
1126*	**Golden Hello** (TDEasterby) **5-11-9** LWyer (lw: j.rt: hit 7th: prom whn fell next)		F	3/1 2	—	—

(SP 112.4%) **5 Rn**

4m 2.5 (4.50) CSF £3.76 TOTE £1.70: £1.10 £1.90 (£2.30) OWNER Mr J. Hales (PENRITH) BRED David Hart

1022* Solomon's Dancer (USA) was not as fluent this time, but was clever to get himself out of trouble. Over a trip that will prove short of his best, he showed the right sort of spirit to gain the upper hand near the line. He will stay three miles in time. (5/6)
1032* Down the Fell gave a sound exhibition of jumping and, sticking to his task when headed, gave the winner a rare old tussle. (3/1)
897 Blue Charm (IRE), tapped for foot going to two out, stuck on strongly on the run-in. A winner twice over hurdles at Musselburgh last season, he will be suited by a step up in distance. (16/1)
1126* Golden Hello continually lost ground jumping to his right. After hitting the seventh, he fell at the next, but had never looked happy up to that point. (3/1)

1265 JACKDAW H'CAP HURDLE (0-135) (4-Y.O+) (Class C)

2-05 (2-05) **3m (13 hdls)** £3,355.00 (£1,015.00: £495.00: £235.00) GOING minus 0.16 sec per fur (G)

				SP	RR	SF
1023*	**Jocks Cross (IRE) (112)** (GRichards) **5-11-7** ADobbin (mde virtually all: styd on wl u.p fr 3 out)	—	1	11/8[1]	97	47
1143[2]	**Tallywagger (118)** (GMMoore) **9-11-13** JCallaghan (chsd wnr: pushed along 9th: one pce fr 2 out)	5	2	5/2[2]	100	50
1083*	**Notable Exception (107)** (MrsMReveley) **7-11-2** PNiven (lw: trckd ldrs: pushed along 8th: rdn & ev ch 3 out: one pce)	3	3	3/1[3]	87	37
	Attadale (119) (LLungo) **8-12-0** MFoster (bit bkwd: trckd ldrs: pushed along 7th: wknd qckly 4 out: t.o)	dist	4	9/1	—	—
				(SP 105.7%)		**4 Rn**

5m 45.0 (3.00) CSF £4.64 TOTE £2.00 (£2.50) OWNER Mrs Gill Harrison (PENRITH) BRED David McGrath
1023* Jocks Cross (IRE) ensured there was no hanging about and, sticking on under pressure from three out, always looked in command. (11/8)
1143 Tallywagger matched strides with the winner, but was pushed along three-quarters of a mile from home, and could not match his younger rival over the last two. (5/2)
1083* Notable Exception, equally effective over fences, was pushed along some way from home. Almost upsides three out, he could then do more than stick on at the one pace. (3/1)
Attadale, out of sorts last term, slipped right down the Ratings. Carrying plenty of belly, he weakened quickly four out, and the jury is out as to how much of the old ability remains. (9/1: op 9/2)

1266 PEATY SANDY H'CAP CHASE (0-135) (5-Y.O+) (Class C)

2-40 (2-40) **3m 6f (22 fncs)** £4,463.40 (£1,351.20: £659.60: £313.80) GOING minus 0.16 sec per fur (G)

				SP	RR	SF
	Into the Red (120) (MrsMReveley) **12-11-3** PNiven (wnt prom 10th: led 5 out to 2 out: styd on wl u.p to ld flat)	—	1	14/1	126	36
1142*	**Royal Vacation (112)** (GMMoore) **7-10-9** JCallaghan (hld up: hit 6th: wnt prom 12th: chal 4 out: led 2 out tl flat: nt qckn)	1¾	2	7/2[2]	117	27
	Kilcolgan (104) (MrsJDGoodfellow) **9-9-12**(3)ow1 GCahill (lost pl 9th: wnt prom 12th: sn drvn along: ev ch whn blnd 4 out: styd on u.p fr 2 out: nt qckn flat)	nk	3	9/2[3]	109	18
1155[2]	**Joe White (119)** (HowardJohnson) **10-11-2** NWilliamson (wnt prom 12th: chal 6 out: wknd 2 out)	25	4	3/1[1]	109	19
789[4]	**Grange Brake (124)** (NATwiston-Davies) **10-11-4**(3) DWalsh (nt j.w: led: blnd & hdd 5 out: wknd appr 3 out)	5	5	7/2[2]	111	21
937[3]	**Side of Hill (103)** (BMactaggart) **11-9-11**(3) GLee (w ldrs tl lost pl 12th: sn bhd)	½	6	50/1	90	—
1142[6]	**Golden Fiddle (IRE) (103)** (JKMOliver) **8-10-0** BStorey (chsd ldrs: ev ch whn blnd 5 out: wknd 3 out)	¾	7	6/1	89	—
940[U]	**Off The Bru (111)** (MrsSCBradburne) **11-10-1**(7)ow8 MrMBradburne (w ldr: hit 17th: sn bhd)	2½	8	25/1	96	—
				(SP 114.4%)		**8 Rn**

7m 37.4 (7.40) CSF £58.44 CT £237.59 TOTE £12.30: £2.60 £1.80 £1.90 (£21.10) OWNER Mr J. Huckle (SALTBURN) BRED M. W. Hickey
LONG HANDICAP Side of Hill 9-2 Golden Fiddle (IRE) 9-12 Off The Bru 8-12
STEWARDS' ENQUIRY Cahill susp. 18-20/11/96 (excessive use of whip)
Into the Red, having his first outing for Mary Reveley, looked in particularly good shape. Out of sorts last season, apparently due to a lung infection, he showed plenty of enthusiasm and his bottomless stamina came into play on the run-in. He has already shown he can jump the Grand National fences, and is on course for a repeat bid here in the Eider, a race he won in 1993. (14/1)
1142* Royal Vacation, who loves this fast ground, came there cruising on the home turn but, after hitting the front, was outstayed by the winner on the run-in. (7/2)
Kilcolgan, a bit of a character, looked as if the outing would do him good. Tending to run in snatches, he kept on strongly under pressure from two out, but could not find that extra spurt on the run-in. (9/2)
1155 Joe White moved up smoothly to challenge six out, but his stamina seemed to give out at the second last. (3/1)
789 Grange Brake, who was very hesitant in his jumping, made the running, but was being challenged when he blundered five out. (7/2)

1267 EKBALCO H'CAP HURDLE (0-145) (4-Y.O+) (Class B)

3-10 (3-12) **2m (9 hdls)** £4,824.40 (£1,460.20: £712.60: £338.80) GOING minus 0.51 sec per fur (GF)

				SP	RR	SF
1154*	**Direct Route (IRE) (128)** (HowardJohnson) **5-10-11** NWilliamson (hld up: stdy hdwy 4th: led 2 out: drvn out flat)	—	1	11/8[1]	105	51
1144[8]	**Urban Dancing (USA) (117)** (BEllison) **7-9-11**(3) GCahill (chsd ldrs: ev ch 2 out: kpt on wl u.p flat)	¾	2	100/1	93?	39
	Marchant Ming (IRE) (130) (MDHammond) **4-10-13** RGarritty (w ldrs: led 3rd to 4th: led 3 out to 2 out: nt qckn flat)	1	3	11/1	105	51
1032[F]	**Thornton Gate (127)** (TDEasterby) **7-10-10** LWyer (hld up: hdwy & prom 6th: rdn 3 out: wknd appr next)	7	4	9/2[3]	95	41
1163[2]	**Done Well (USA) (118)** (PMonteith) **4-10-1** ADobbin (hld up: wnt prom 4th: sddle slipped next: grad lost pl fr 3 out)	10	5	7/2[2]	76	22
1156[6]	**Our Kris (125)** (MESowersby) **4-10-8b** DParker (chsd ldrs: led & hit 4th: hdd 3 out: sn wknd)	½	6	25/1	83	29
	Jazilah (FR) (140) (RAllan) **8-11-2**(7) SMelrose (led: hdd & hit 3rd: drvn along & lost pl 5th: t.o next)	dist	7	25/1	—	—
945[3]	**Home Counties (IRE) (145)** (DMoffatt) **7-12-0** DJMoffatt (fell 1st)		F	7/2[2]	—	—
	Rarfy's Dream (117) (DMcCune) **8-10-0** BStorey (bhd fr 4th: fell next)		F	200/1	—	—
				(SP 122.2%)		**9 Rn**

3m 45.5 (-6.50) CSF £71.52 CT £1,107.05 TOTE £2.20: £1.10 £5.00 £2.10 (£125.70) Trio Not won; £129.52 to Folkestone 11/11/96 OWNER Mr Chris Heron (CROOK) BRED Mrs Noeleen Roche
LONG HANDICAP Urban Dancing (USA) 9-5 Rarfy's Dream 9-7
OFFICIAL EXPLANATION Done Well (USA): his saddle slipped.
1154* Direct Route (IRE), from a 6lb higher mark, took it up travelling smoothly but, tending to idle in front, had to be driven right out. (11/8)
Urban Dancing (USA), 9lb out of the handicap and having shown nothing on his two previous outings this season, belied his long odds and, in the end, made the winner pull out almost all the stops. (100/1)
Marchant Ming (IRE), a soft-ground specialist, was out of sorts on the Flat this back-end, but ran really well. When the ground eases, he will no doubt soon make his mark. (11/1)

1032 Thornton Gate, given a confidence-booster over hurdles after his fall on his chasing debut, was dropped in at the start. Moving up travelling as well as the winner at halfway, he tired going to two out. This should have done his confidence no harm at all. (9/2)
1163 Done Well (USA) took a keen grip and, after his saddle slipped at the fifth, all his rider could do was to sit still and complete the course. (7/2)
945 Home Counties (IRE) (7/2: 5/2-4/1)

1268 SWIFT H'CAP CHASE (0-125) (5-Y.O+) (Class D)

3-45 (3-45) **2m 4f (15 fncs)** £3,702.50 (£1,040.00: £507.50) GOING minus 0.16 sec per fur (G)

				SP	RR	SF
	Easby Joker (117) (SEKettlewell) **8-12-0** PNiven (t: mstke 3rd: jnd ldr 9th: led 11th: shkn up & styd on wl flat)	—	1	11/8 2	127	8
855*	**Charming Gale (95)** (MrsSCBradburne) **9-10-6v** LWyer (led to 11th: sn rdn: ev ch 2 out: kpt on same pce flat)	5	2	Evens 1	101	—
1142F	**Cross Cannon (111)** (JWade) **10-11-8** TReed (hld up: jnd ldrs 11th: chal 2 out: sn rdn: nt qckn flat)	½	3	5/1 3	117	—

(SP 108.8%) **3 Rn**

5m 9.0 (16.00) CSF £2.97 TOTE £2.00 (£2.00) OWNER Mr G. R. Orchard (MIDDLEHAM) BRED C. S. Wates
Easby Joker, who looked on good terms with himself in the paddock, took time to settle after a mistake at the third. When shaken up after the last, he found easily the best turn of foot. (11/8: op 4/5)
855* Charming Gale jumps for fun, but lacks foot at the business end. The first to come under pressure, she kept on all the way to the line, but could not match the winner for toe. (Evens)
909 Cross Cannon, who likes to come from off the pace in a fast-run race, moved up travelling easily to challenge two out but, once off the bridle, he could only keep on at the same pace. (5/1: op 3/1)

T/Plpt: £81.30 (68.53 Tckts). T/Qdpt: £18.30 (25.49 Tckts). WG

SANDOWN (R-H) (Good, Good to firm patches)
Saturday November 9th
WEATHER: fine

1269 COUNTY SOUND RADIO HURDLE (3-Y.O) (Class D)

12-55 (12-56) **2m 110y (8 hdls)** £2,801.00 (£848.00: £414.00: £197.00) GOING: 0.06 sec per fur (G)

				SP	RR	SF
	Shooting Light (IRE) (PGMurphy) **3-11-3** CO'Dwyer (lw: a.p: led appr 2 out: clr appr last: pushed out)	—	1	12/1	91	10
	Pleasureland (IRE) (RCurtis) **3-11-3** DMorris (lw: hdwy appr 2 out: chsd wnr appr last: no imp)	5	2	50/1	86?	5
1131*	**Squire's Occasion (CAN)** (RAkehurst) **3-11-5(5)** SRyan (a.p: rdn & n.m r appr 2 out: r.o one pce)	7	3	8/1 3	86	5
1064*	**Doctor Green (FR)** (MCPipe) **3-11-10v** CMaude (led tl appr 2 out: hrd rdn appr last: one pce)	¾	4	13/8 1	86	5
1014 3	**Serenus (USA)** (NJHenderson) **3-11-3** MAFitzgerald (chsd ldr tl appr 2 out: one pce)	¾	5	7/4 2	78	—
	Hanbitooh (USA) (GHarwood) **3-11-3** GBradley (bit bkwd: hld up: rdn appr 2 out: sn wknd: t.o)	dist	6	10/1	—	—
	Deux Carr (USA) (BobJones) **3-11-0** JFTitley (bit bkwd: bhd fr 3rd: t.o fr 5th)	26	7	14/1	—	—
	Sterling Fellow (DLWilliams) **3-11-0b(3)** KGaule (a bhd: t.o fr 3 out)	9	8	14/1	—	—

(SP 117.6%) **8 Rn**

4m 4.2 (13.20) CSF £272.79 TOTE £16.00: £2.40 £6.30 £1.90 (£474.90) OWNER Mr J. M. Brown (BRISTOL) BRED The Earl of Harrington
STEWARDS' ENQUIRY Ryan susp. 18-19/11/96 (excessive use of whip).
Shooting Light (IRE), the winner of a maiden on soft ground at Hamilton in May for Michael Jarvis, changed hands in the summer for 21,000 guineas. Looking in tremendous shape for this hurdling debut, he put up a very polished display, leading approaching the penultimate hurdle and forging clear to win with the minimum of fuss. Further success awaits him. (12/1: op 8/1)
Pleasureland (IRE), a staying maiden on the Flat for Peter Makin, was sold for just 3,000 guineas but looked in great heart for this hurdling debut and showed promise. (50/1)
1131* Squire's Occasion (CAN) did struggle on again up the hill to finish third. He may be worth trying over further. (8/1)
1064* Doctor Green (FR), a typical early-season Pipe juvenile, once again adopted front-running tactics but, collared approaching the second last, his unbeaten record was soon in shreds as he plodded on at the one pace. (13/8)
1014 Serenus (USA) once again had his lack of pace exposed. (7/4)
Hanbitooh (USA), a maiden on the Flat, was sold out of Ed Dunlop's stable for 22,000 guineas but did not look fully tuned up for this hurdling debut, his first run in over five months, and so it proved. (10/1: 7/1-12/1)
Deux Carr (USA) (14/1: 6/1-16/1)

1270 ALDANITI NOVICES' CHASE (5-Y.O+) (Class D)

1-25 (1-27) **2m (13 fncs)** £3,737.50 (£1,050.00: £512.50) GOING: 0.06 sec per fur (G)

				SP	RR	SF
	Aardwolf (CPEBrooks) **5-11-0** GBradley (bit bkwd: led tl hdd & pckd 8th: led 4 out: clr appr last: easily)	—	1	8/1	114+	44
947 2	**Amancio (USA)** (GHarwood) **5-11-0** CMaude (lw: 3rd whn mstke 3rd: chsd wnr fr 5th: led 8th to 4 out: ev ch whn blnd 3 out: rdn 2 out: fnd nil)	19	2	5/4 1	95	25
961 8	**Full of Tricks (69)** (JJBridger) **8-11-0** DMorris (lw: bhd fr 4th: t.o fr 6th)	dist	3	150/1	—	—
1018*	**Plunder Bay (USA) (118)** (NJHenderson) **5-11-7** MAFitzgerald (lw: chsd wnr to 5th: 3rd whn fell 6th)		F	7/2 3	—	—
	Grooving (IRE) (JTGifford) **7-11-0** PHide (bkwd: swtg: fell 1st)		F	9/4 2	—	—

(SP 109.2%) **5 Rn**

3m 55.8 (4.80) CSF £17.67 TOTE £6.10: £2.40 £1.70 (£8.00) OWNER Lady Camilla Dempster (LAMBOURN) BRED Sheikh Mohammed bin Rashid al Maktoum
Aardwolf, pulled up in three handicap hurdles last season, did not look fully wound up for this seasonal debut, but chasing is obviously going to be his game. Jumping these tricky fences well in the main, he is sure to be a lot fitter for this, and can win again.(8/1: 11/2-9/1)
947 Amancio (USA) was something of a disappointment considering how well he travelled during the race. After making a bad error at the Pond Fence, his pilot was still sitting nicely on him but, when shaking him up two out, the gelding found nothing. There must be a doubt about him for the time being. (5/4: 4/5-11/8)
1018* Plunder Bay (USA) (7/2: 9/4-4/1)

1271 LONDON RACING CLUB H'CAP HURDLE (0-145) (4-Y.O+) (Class B)
1-55 (1-55) **2m 110y (8 hdls)** £4,879.00 (£1,477.00: £721.00: £343.00) GOING: 0.06 sec per fur (G)

	Horse	Dist	Pos	SP	RR	SF
904*	**Crack On (123)** (PJHobbs) **6-10-12** MAFitzgerald (a gng wl: hld up: lft 3rd at 3rd: led on bit last: shkn up: comf)	—	**1**	Evens[1]	107+	41
	Lightening Lad (125) (JSKing) **8-11-0** CMaude (led tl mstke & hdd 3 out: led appr 2 out to last: unable qckn)	2½	**2**	5/1[3]	107	41
967*	**Hamilton Silk (128)** (MCPipe) **4-11-3** GBradley (lw: hdwy appr 2 out: rdn appr last: one pce)	4	**3**	9/2[2]	106	40
1156[4]	**Non Vintage (IRE) (132)** (MCChapman) **5-11-7** WWorthington (lw: hdwy appr 2 out: rdn appr last: sn wknd)	4	**4**	11/2	106	40
	Lonesome Train (USA) (134) (CWeedon) **7-11-9** MRichards (bit bkwd: chsd ldr: led 3 out tl appr 2 out: sn wknd: t.o)	30	**5**	11/1	79	13
	Maneree (111) (NACallaghan) **9-10-0** JFTitley (a bhd: t.o fr 4th)	dist	**6**	25/1	—	—
	Kingsfold Pet (135) (MJHaynes) **7-11-10** DSkyrme (3rd whn fell 3rd)		**F**	12/1	—	—

(SP 120.1%) **7 Rn**

3m 56.2 (5.20) CSF £6.94 TOTE £2.20: £1.50 £2.60 (£5.40) OWNER Mr D. R. Peppiatt (MINEHEAD) BRED Mrs Audrey Goodwin
LONG HANDICAP Maneree 9-13

904* Crack On has risen 8lb for his bloodless Exeter victory, but that was not going to stop him from treating this much more competitive field with contempt. Always travelling supremely well, he cruised into the lead on the bridle at the final flight. He looks one to follow this season and it would be no surprise to see his attentions switched to the major obstacles before the season's end. (Evens)
Lightening Lad, winner of both his starts last season, was upped in class for this reappearance, but ran really well. He should not take long to open his account for the season. (5/1)
967* Hamilton Silk has already shot up 13lb since his Free Handicap win at Chepstow last month. The Handicapper has his measure for the time being. (9/2)
1156 Non Vintage (IRE), back over a more suitable trip, had given his all soon after jumping that flight. (11/2)
Lonesome Train (USA), off the course since finishing fifth in the William Hill Handicap Hurdle here last December, did not look fully wound up, but still ran well. (11/1: 7/1-12/1)
Kingsfold Pet (12/1: op 7/1)

1272 SOUTH EAST RACECOURSE OF THE YEAR H'CAP CHASE (0-130) (5-Y.O+) (Class C)
2-30 (2-30) **2m 4f 110y (17 fncs)** £4,810.75 (£1,456.00: £710.50: £337.75) GOING: 0.06 sec per fur (G)

	Horse	Dist	Pos	SP	RR	SF
1016*	**Strong Medicine (129)** (KCBailey) **9-12-0** CO'Dwyer (lw: hld up: chsd ldr 10th to 12th: chsd ldr appr 2 out: led last: pushed out)	—	**1**	6/4[1]	136	30
	Golden Spinner (122) (NJHenderson) **9-11-7** MAFitzgerald (lw: led: mstke 1st: hdd last: unable qckn)	1¼	**2**	9/4[2]	128	22
56[P]	**Shaarid (USA) (112)** (IABalding) **8-10-11** GBradley (chsd ldr 6th to 10th: chsd ldr fr 12th: rdn & ev ch 3 out: wknd appr last)	12	**3**	8/1	109	3
	King Credo (120) (SWoodman) **11-11-5** JFTitley (chsd ldr to 6th: wknd 7th: t.o)	dist	**4**	14/1	—	—
811[3]	**Conti D'Estruval (FR) (122)** (GBBalding) **6-11-7** PHide (hld up: 3rd whn blnd & uns rdr 13th)		**U**	9/2[3]	—	—

(SP 106.7%) **5 Rn**

5m 13.3 (14.30) CSF £4.84 TOTE £2.40: £1.40 £1.20 (£2.90) OWNER Dr D. B. A. Silk (UPPER LAMBOURN) BRED E. O'Neill

1016* Strong Medicine, whose connections wisely decided not to enter him for the Hennessy, followed up his recent Newbury win under a very confident ride. He has never won on ground worse than good. (6/4)
Golden Spinner looked in good shape for this first run of the season, and showed plenty of promise. An early success looks on the cards. (9/4)
Shaarid (USA), pretty straight for this first run in five months, is a top-of-the-ground performer. (8/1)
King Credo is not a natural chaser and so it was no surprise to see him run so badly on this return. He surely deserves retirement. (14/1: 8/1-16/1)
811 Conti D'Estruval (FR) (9/2: op 5/2)

1273 GUNPOWDER PLOT H'CAP CHASE (5-Y.O+) (Class B)
3-00 (3-02) **3m 110y (22 fncs)** £6,742.50 (£2,040.00: £995.00: £472.50) GOING: 0.06 sec per fur (G)

	Horse	Dist	Pos	SP	RR	SF
	Inchcailloch (IRE) (118) (JSKing) **7-10-1** CMaude (hld up: chsd ldr appr 3 out: rdn to ld nr fin)	—	**1**	2/1[1]	130	13
	Grey Smoke (124) (MissHCKnight) **6-10-7** JFTitley (chsd ldr: led 4th to 5th: led 4 out: rdn appr last: hdd nr fin)	½	**2**	9/4[2]	136	19
	Betty's Boy (IRE) (127) (KCBailey) **7-10-10** CO'Dwyer (hld up: shkn up appr 2 out: sn wknd)	14	**3**	11/4[3]	130	13
	Cool Dawn (IRE) (137) (RHAlner) **8-11-6** MissDHarding (bit bkwd: led 5th to 4 out: wknd appr 3 out)	1½	**4**	11/2	139	22
	Willsford (145) (MrsJPitman) **13-11-11**(3) GHogan (bit bkwd: led to 4th: wknd 15th: t.o)	dist	**5**	16/1	—	—

(SP 112.0%) **5 Rn**

6m 16.2 (14.20) CSF £6.70 TOTE £2.70: £1.70 £1.40 (£3.30) OWNER Mr F. J. Carter (SWINDON) BRED Hascombe and Valiant Studs

Inchcailloch (IRE), a versatile performer who recently won the Cesarewitch, had no problems with this longer trip, and was always going to get there up the hill. (2/1)
Grey Smoke, impressive winner of three novice chases last season, made a fine reappearance. He should soon be winning. (9/4)
Betty's Boy (IRE) was given a very considerate ride on this reappearance. Gradually easing his way into the action in the back straight for the final time, he appeared to be travelling well turning for home but, with his jockey doing little on him, he faded going to two out. He is sure to come on in leaps and bounds for this and the kindness will no doubt be repaid in due course. (11/4)
Cool Dawn (IRE), who looked as though the run would do him good, decided to get to the front and there was little his jockey could do about it but, once headed, he soon tired. A very talented hunter chaser who finished third in last year's Irish National, he can win his share of races this term but, if he is going to remain outside the hunter chase sphere, he really must have a professional on board. (11/2: 7/2-6/1)

1274 SURREY RACING NOVICES' H'CAP HURDLE (0-105) (4-Y.O+) (Class D)
3-30 (3-35) **2m 6f (11 hdls)** £2,840.00 (£860.00: £420.00: £200.00) GOING: 0.06 sec per fur (G)

	Horse	Dist	Pos	SP	RR	SF
1031[4]	**River Room (104)** (KCBailey) **6-11-7**(7) WWalsh (lw: a.p: chsd ldr appr 2 out: rdn appr last: led nr fin)	—	**1**	11/1	87	44
891[P]	**Hylters Chance (IRE) (76)** (PJHobbs) **5-10-0** LHarvey (lw: led: clr appr 2 out: wknd & hdd nr fin)	nk	**2**	9/2[3]	59	16
	El Freddie (93) (JABOld) **6-11-3** GUpton (bit bkwd: mstke 3rd: rdn 8th: hdwy appr last: r.o one pce)	9	**3**	7/2[2]	69	26
1135[B]	**Embley Buoy (76)** (JWMullins) **8-10-0** SCurran (lw: chsd ldr tl after 3rd: chsd ldr 6th tl appr 2 out: one pce)	nk	**4**	15/2	52	9
1135[3]	**Positivo (77)** (MissCJECaroe) **5-10-1** DLeahy (nvr nr to chal)	3	**5**	16/1	51	8
	Rovestar (85) (JSKing) **5-10-9** CMaude (hld up: hrd rdn appr 2 out: sn wknd)	6	**6**	9/1	55	12

				SP	RR	SF
954^{9}	**Carey's Cottage (IRE) (76)** (MrsPTownsley) **6-10-0** MRichards (s.s: a bhd)	9	**7**	66/1	39	—
859*	**Montel Express (IRE) (100)** (KCBailey) **4-11-10** CO'Dwyer (sme hdwy & mstke 3 out: sn wknd)	2½	**8**	$5/2^{1}$	61	18
900^{F}	**Trail Boss (IRE) (98)** (MissHCKnight) **5-11-8** JFTitley (a.p: chsd ldr after 3rd to 6th: 4th whn mstke 8th: wknd 2 out)	10	**9**	13/2	52	9

(SP 119.8%) **9 Rn**

5m 23.6 (10.60) CSF £57.60 CT £195.65 TOTE £11.40: £2.40 £1.60 £1.20 (£24.40) Trio £27.20 OWNER Mr Douglas Allum (UPPER LAMBOURN) BRED E. Stuart Knape

LONG HANDICAP Carey's Cottage (IRE) 9-2 Hylters Chance (IRE) 9-13 Embley Buoy 9-11

1031 River Room eventually managed to struggle into the lead near the line. (11/1: op 6/1)

824* Hylters Chance (IRE), back on his favoured fast ground, was given an enterprising ride and nearly succeeded. (9/2)

El Freddie, yet to open his account over hurdles, is now 8lb higher than at the end of last season and did not look fully wound up for this reappearance. (7/2)

792* Embley Buoy was collared for second approaching two out and could only go up and down in the same place. (15/2)

557 Positivo is a poor performer who has had plenty of chances. (16/1)

900 Trail Boss (IRE) (13/2: 4/1-7/1)

1275 WEATHERBYS 'STARS OF TOMORROW' STANDARD OPEN N.H. FLAT RACE (4, 5 & 6-Y.O) (Class H)

4-00 (4-08) **2m 110y** £1,997.50 (£560.00: £272.50)

				SP	RR	SF
	Mr Markham (IRE) (JTGifford) **4-11-4** PHide (hdwy over 2f out: led ins fnl f: rdn out)	—	**1**	8/1	—	—
	Wade Road (IRE) (MissHCKnight) **5-11-11** JFTitley (lw: hld up: led over 2f out tl ins fnl f: unable qckn)	1	**2**	$Evens^{1}$	—	—
679*	**Prototype** (GFJohnsonHoughton) **5-11-11** MAFitzgerald (rdn & hdwy over 2f out: one pce)	11	**3**	$6/1^{3}$	—	—
	Forest Musk (IRE) (PJHobbs) **5-10-13**(5) DJKavanagh (chsd ldr: led over 3f out tl over 2f out: sn wknd)	¾	**4**	16/1	—	—
	Aztec Warrior (KCBailey) **5-10-11**(7) MrRWakley (lw: a.p: rdn over 2f out: sn wknd)	6	**5**	33/1	—	—
	Saucy Nun (IRE) (IPWilliams) **4-10-13** CMaude (lw: hdwy over 3f out: wknd 2f out)	½	**6**	50/1	—	—
865^{2}	**The Brewmaster (IRE)** (IPWilliams) **4-11-4** GBradley (hdwy 7f out: wknd over 2f out)	8	**7**	$11/2^{2}$	—	—
	Diamond Lady (MissBSanders) **4-10-13** MRichards (nvr nr to chal)	½	**8**	33/1	—	—
	Knight's Crest (IRE) (RDickin) **6-11-4** DerekByrne (nvr nrr)	5	**9**	33/1	—	—
	Stencil (PMooney) **4-10-13**(5) SRyan (bit bkwd: hld up: rdn over 4f out: wknd over 3f out)	6	**10**	33/1	—	—
	Freno (IRE) (KCBailey) **5-11-4** CO'Dwyer (hdwy over 4f out: wknd over 3f out)	6	**11**	8/1	—	—
	Bellidium (AEJessop) **4-10-10**(3) RMassey (bit bkwd: led & sn clr: hdd over 3f out: wkng whn hung bdly lft over 2f out)	8	**12**	50/1	—	—
	Miss Bartholomew (MrsJPitman) **6-10-10**(3) GHogan (bkwd: prom 12f)	22	**13**	33/1	—	—
	Thunder Road (IRE) (RDickin) **5-11-4** RBellamy (prom over 10f)	10	**14**	33/1	—	—

(SP 129.3%) **14 Rn**

3m 52.2 CSF £16.64 TOTE £8.50: £1.90 £1.40 £2.60 (£8.60) Trio £15.30 OWNER Felix Rosenstiel's Widow & Son (FINDON) BRED M. Ryan

Mr Markham (IRE) made a very encouraging debut. He got the better of the well-regarded runner-up inside the final furlong, with the pair finishing well clear of the remainder. (8/1: 6/1-10/1)

Wade Road (IRE), highly impressive when winning at Ascot in April, is well-regarded at home and looked set for another smooth victory as he cruised into the lead over a quarter of a mile out, but the winner soon came on the scene and he had to settle for second best. Eight flights of hurdles should bring out the best in him and he could be an exciting recruit. (Evens)

679* Prototype, with a 7lb penalty for his smooth Huntingdon victory seven weeks ago, could do little to prevent the front two from pulling right away. (6/1: 3/1-13/2)

Forest Musk (IRE) was placed in several points before being sold for 17,000 Irish Guineas. A few obstacles and a longer trip will probably be in his favour. (16/1)

Aztec Warrior looked in good shape for this debut, but had given his all over quarter of a mile from home. (33/1)

Saucy Nun (IRE) looked pretty straight for this debut but, after making an effort early in the straight, had shot her bolt over a quarter of a mile out. (50/1)

865 The Brewmaster (IRE) (11/2: 4/1-6/1)

T/Plpt: £279.30 (35.01 Tckts). T/Qdpt: £9.60 (68.49 Tckts). AK

1250-UTTOXETER (L-H) (Good to firm, Good patches)

Saturday November 9th

WEATHER: fine

1276 PRD FASTENERS MAIDEN HURDLE (I) (4-Y.O+) (Class E)

12-40 (12-40) **2m (9 hdls)** £1,987.00 (£557.00: £271.00) GOING: 0.25 sec per fur (GS)

				SP	RR	SF
	Green Green Desert (FR) (OSherwood) **5-11-5** DBridgwater (lw: hld up: gd hdwy to ld after 6th: mstke & j.lft 3 out: comf)	—	**1**	$8/13^{1}$	73+	2
955^{5}	**Swan Street (NZ)** (CJMann) **5-11-5** JRailton (hld up: hdwy 6th: ev ch after 2 out: sn rdn: one pce flat)	3½	**2**	$7/2^{2}$	70	—
65^{7}	**Cavil (70)** (WClay) **4-11-5** AThornton (a.p: rdn 3 out: kpt on one pce)	8	**3**	20/1	62	—
	Barton Scamp (SABrookshaw) **4-11-5** TEley (hld up: hdwy 6th: rdn appr 2 out: wknd appr last)	1¼	**4**	$10/1^{3}$	60	—
	Fastini Gold (MDIUsher) **4-11-2**(3) FLeahy (bhd: styd on fr 3 out: nvr nrr)	8	**5**	25/1	52	—
1118^{7}	**Blue Lugana** (NBycroft) **4-11-5** DBentley (in tch tl wknd 6th)	1½	**6**	50/1	51	—
950^{8}	**Dashing Dancer (IRE)** (ALForbes) **5-11-5** GaryLyons (hld up: kpt on fr 3 out: n.d)	2½	**7**	50/1	48	—
396^{5}	**Saint Amigo** (RMWhitaker) **4-11-5v** DerekByrne (led to 4th: led after 5th: hdd after next: rdn & wknd 3 out)	2	**8**	50/1	46	—
	Dictation (USA) (JJO'Neill) **4-11-5** ARoche (nvr nr ldrs)	4	**9**	16/1	42	—
	Monty (GHYardley) **4-11-0**(5) MichaelBrennan (bit bkwd: mid div: mstke 2nd: lost tch 5th: t.o)	14	**10**	50/1	28	—
	Knave of Diamonds (RHAlner) **4-11-5** WMcFarland (chsd ldrs: rdn 6th: wknd appr 3 out: t.o)	dist	**11**	25/1	—	—
1132^{5}	**Al Helal** (JRJenkins) **4-10-12v^{1}**(7) NTEgan (fell 1st)		**F**	25/1	—	—
	My Handsome Prince (PJBevan) **4-11-5v** RBellamy (bit bkwd: prom to 5th: t.o whn p.u bef 3 out)		**P**	50/1	—	—
	Scboo (REPeacock) **7-11-2**(3) DFortt (bit bkwd: led 4th: hdd & wknd qckly after 5th: t.o whn p.u bef 2 out)		**P**	100/1	—	—

(SP 126.2%) **14 Rn**

3m 59.1 (18.10) CSF £3.62 TOTE £1.70: £1.30 £1.50 £3.10 (£2.50) Trio £7.10 OWNER Mr Darren Mercer (UPPER LAMBOURN) BRED Gainsborough Stud Management

Green Green Desert (FR) gave the supporters who laid the odds on him only one serious fright when diving left and making a mess of the third last. This frustrating character has the ability to go a long way at this game, but whether he will produce it is another matter. (8/13)
955 Swan Street (NZ), unfortunate to come up against such a classy Flat horse in this modest contest, should have little trouble in finding a similar race. (7/2)
Cavil was never far off the front, but lacked the turn of foot required at the business end of the race. (20/1)
Barton Scamp made up a lot of ground to get onto the heels of the leaders turning for home, but had come to the end of his tether before getting too close to the last. He should come on for the run and a longer trip and softer ground may be in his favour. (10/1)
Fastini Gold, a one-paced maiden on the Flat, kept on through beaten horses in the closing stages. (25/1)
Blue Lugana may have difficulty in even getting the minimum trip over hurdles. (50/1)

1277 DERBY EVENING TELEGRAPH H'CAP CHASE (0-145) (5-Y.O+) (Class B)

1-10 (1-10) **2m 5f (16 fncs)** £7,346.00 (£2,066.00: £1,008.00) GOING minus 0.03 sec per fur (G)

				SP	RR	SF
	Call it a Day (IRE) (135) (DNicholson) **6-11-9** AMaguire (chsd ldr: led 5th to 8th: slt ld fr 12th: rdn 2 out: drvn out)	—	1	8/11[1]	141	32
	Lord Gyllene (NZ) (119) (SABrookshaw) **8-10-7** TEley (chsd ldrs: led 11th: hdd 12th: rdn 3 out: ev ch whn mstke last: no ex)	2½	2	9/4[2]	123	14
946[4]	**Bavard Dieu (IRE) (140)** (NAGaselee) **8-12-0** AThornton (led to 5th: led 8th to 11th: rdn & outpcd 12th: kpt on appr last)	5	3	5/1[3]	140	31
				(SP 105.3%)	**3 Rn**	

5m 15.7 (10.70) CSF £2.40 TOTE £1.50 (£1.40) OWNER Mrs Jane Lane (TEMPLE GUITING) BRED Mrs Kathleen Banville
Call it a Day (IRE), a very genuine, consistent gelding, battled on well to get the better of the runner-up in a lengthy duel. This should have put him spot on, and he looks set for another good season. (8/11)
Lord Gyllene (NZ) had a ding-dong battle with the winner from a long way out, but seemed to be just coming off second best when a mistake at the last sealed his fate. This was a fine effort as he looked just in need of the run. (9/4)
946 Bavard Dieu (IRE), ridden a long way out and on the retreat before four from home, looked sure to finish tailed off but, getting his second wind, was closing all the way to the line. (5/1)

1278 PRD FASTENERS MAIDEN HURDLE (II) (4-Y.O+) (Class E)

1-40 (1-40) **2m (9 hdls)** £1,976.50 (£554.00: £269.50) GOING: 0.25 sec per fur (GS)

				SP	RR	SF
	Mywend's (IRE) (CPEBrooks) **6-11-5** DGallagher (hld up in tch: led 3 out: comf)	—	1	4/1[3]	79+	38
1036[P]	**Southern Nights** (KCBailey) **6-11-5** AThornton (hld up: hdwy 6th: rdn appr 3 out: styd on u.p flat)	5	2	2/1[1]	74	33
	Smolensk (IRE) (JBerry) **4-11-5** MMoloney (in tch: hdwy 6th: ev ch 3 out: sn rdn & one pce)	nk	3	16/1	74	33
	Cypress Avenue (IRE) (MrsVCWard) **4-11-0**(5) MichaelBrennan (mid div: hdwy 6th: rdn 3 out: kpt on same pce)	s.h	4	9/1	74	33
	Vendoon (IRE) (MJHeaton-Ellis) **6-11-5** DBridgwater (led to 3rd: chsd ldr tl wknd after 3 out)	11	5	12/1	63	22
1010[4]	**Robsera (IRE) (84)** (JJQuinn) **5-11-2v**[1](3) FLeahy (led 3rd to 3 out: wknd qckly)	3	6	7/2[2]	60	19
	Daring Ryde (JPSmith) **5-11-5** TEley (wl bhd fr 4th: t.o)	25	7	50/1	35	—
	Chantro Bay (JPearce) **8-11-5** MDwyer (hld up: hdwy appr 3 out: sn btn)	nk	8	33/1	34	—
794[11]	**Nukud (USA)** (GROldroyd) **4-10-12v**[1](7) CMcCormack (bkwd: bhd fr 5th: t.o)	21	9	50/1	13	—
1085[P]	**Super Brush (IRE)** (PRJohnson) **4-10-9**(5) GESmith (bkwd: a bhd: t.o)	26	10	66/1	—	—
1059[4]	**Mr Gordon Bennett** (RDickin) **5-10-12**(7) XAizpuru (prom to 4th: t.o)	10	11	50/1	—	—
	That Old Feeling (IRE) (JWhite) **4-11-5** AMaguire (a bhd: t.o whn fell last)		F	14/1	—	—
				(SP 116.1%)	**12 Rn**	

3m 51.1 (10.10) CSF £11.50 TOTE £4.70: £1.30 £1.80 £3.40 (£10.90) Trio £92.90 OWNER Uplands Bloodstock (LAMBOURN) BRED B. J. Ryan
STEWARDS' ENQUIRY Leahy susp. 18 & 23/11/96 (careless riding & improper use of whip).
Mywend's (IRE) won this with the minimum of fuss. He carries a lot of condition and is likely to improve further. (4/1: 3/1-9/2)
1036 Southern Nights made hard work of trying to join the leaders turning for home and, for a long time, was getting nowhere. However, he stuck on well on the run-in to snatch second close home. (2/1)
Smolensk (IRE), flat to the boards when upsides the winner three out, tried hard but could do nothing about it. This will have sharpened him up. (16/1)
Cypress Avenue (IRE) made a satisfactory debut over hurdles. He has some decent Flat form, but rather lost his way this season although, if his interest can be rekindled in a new yard, he may come good at this game. (9/1)

1279 MASON RICHARDS H'CAP CHASE (0-125) (5-Y.O+) (Class D)

2-10 (2-11) **3m 2f (20 fncs)** £3,858.75 (£1,170.00: £572.50: £273.75) GOING minus 0.03 sec per fur (G)

				SP	RR	SF
	Idiot's Lady (120) (MrsJPitman) **7-11-9** MDwyer (hld up in tch: led 3 out: clr next: mstke last: easily)	—	1	4/1[3]	131+	35
	Rectory Garden (IRE) (113) (CaptTAForster) **7-11-2** AThornton (w ldr: led 10th to 3 out: sn rdn & outpcd)	5	2	11/4[1]	121	25
	Musthaveaswig (125) (DNicholson) **10-12-0** AMaguire (a.p: ev ch 16th: mstke 4 out: sn rdn & wknd)	8	3	7/2[2]	128	32
1043[2]	**Romany Creek (IRE) (120)** (JPearce) **7-11-9v** DBridgwater (chsd ldrs tl wknd 4 out)	18	4	5/1	112	16
789[F]	**Florida Sky (109)** (CPEBrooks) **9-10-12** DGallagher (mde most to 10th: chsd ldr tl mstke 15th: sn wknd:t.o)	dist	5	12/1	—	—
1119[4]	**Sailor Jim (110)** (PTDalton) **9-10-13** JRailton (hld up in tch: fell 13th)		F	11/2	—	—
				(SP 108.6%)	**6 Rn**	

6m 39.3 (12.30) CSF £14.06 TOTE £4.30: £2.10 £1.70 (£6.30) OWNER Mrs J. Ollivant (UPPER LAMBOURN) BRED Mrs J. Ollivant
Idiot's Lady, always where she wanted to be, came through to take the lead three out, and had the race won in next to no time. Making her only mistake at the last, she was still able to saunter home. (4/1: 3/1-9/2)
Rectory Garden (IRE), never out of the first two, looked sure to take a hand, but was left flat-footed once the winner swept by. (11/4)
Musthaveaswig made this a good effort on this first run for fifteen months. He was close enough until clouting four from home, and that ended his challenge. (7/2)
1043 Romany Creek (IRE) ran well until dropping away over half a mile from home. He does seem to be plenty high enough in the weights at the moment. (5/1)
Florida Sky (12/1: 8/1-14/1)

1280 STAINLESS THREADED FASTENERS 10TH ANNIVERSARY CLASSIC NOVICES' HURDLE (Gd 2) (4-Y.O+) (Class A)

2-45 (2-45) **2m 4f 110y (10 hdls)** £10,486.87 (£3,633.75: £1,779.38) GOING: 0.25 sec per fur (GS)

	Horse	Dist	Pos	SP	RR	SF
1090*	**Jack Tanner (IRE)** (DNicholson) **7-11-0** AMaguire (lw: trckd ldr: led 3 out: sn clr: eased flat)	—	**1**	30/100[1]	96++	22
952*	**Make a Stand (123)** (MCPipe) **5-11-4** MDwyer (led to 3 out: sn outpcd)	dist	**2**	3/1[2]	—	—
	Manasis (NZ) (SABrookshaw) **5-11-0** TEley (bkwd: chsd ldr: pushed along 6th: sn wknd: t.o)	dist	**3**	20/1[3]	—	—
				(SP 106.7%)		**3 Rn**

5m 0.1 (16.10) CSF £1.49 TOTE £1.30 (£1.10) OWNER Lady Harris (TEMPLE GUITING) BRED G. Quirk

1090* Jack Tanner (IRE) won this in effortless fashion, and his ability to stay further and act on softer ground should stand him in good stead in the coming months. (30/100)

952* Make a Stand made the running, jumping well, but found the winner cantering all over him. His jockey was not hard on him when the outcome became obvious. (3/1)

Manasis (NZ), a real strong, chasing type, was well outpointed here. (20/1)

1281 EUROFAST PETROCHEMICAL SUPPLIES NOVICES' CHASE (5-Y.O+) (Class D)

3-20 (3-20) **3m (19 fncs)** £3,858.75 (£1,170.00: £572.50: £273.75) GOING minus 0.03 sec per fur (G)

	Horse	Dist	Pos	SP	RR	SF
827[3]	**Don du Cadran (FR)** (CaptTAForster) **7-11-0** AThornton (chsd ldr: led 15th: lft clr 2 out: comf)	—	**1**	9/2[2]	103+	—
	Loch Garman Hotel (IRE) (PTDalton) **7-11-0** TEley (led to 15th: rdn & wknd appr 3 out: lft 2nd 2 out)	24	**2**	7/1[3]	87	—
	Pharanear (IRE) (DNicholson) **6-11-0** AMaguire (j.slowly 1st: mstke 2nd: bhd tl hdwy 12th: chsd wnr appr 4 out: rdn & hld whn fell 2 out: rmntd)	dist	**3**	4/11[1]	—	—
	Ainsi Soit Il (FR) (GMMcCourt) **5-10-9**(3) DFortt (bit bkwd: bhd fr 6th: lost tch 11th: poor 3rd whn ref last: cont)	20	**4**	33/1	—	—
				(SP 107.0%)		**4 Rn**

6m 16.2 CSF £23.76 TOTE £4.60 (£6.30) OWNER Lord Cadogan (LUDLOW) BRED Mme Pierre Grolleau

WEIGHT FOR AGE 5yo-2lb

827 Don du Cadran (FR) made a promising chasing debut. He was getting the better of the duel with the favourite when that one came to grief two from home. (9/2)

Loch Garman Hotel (IRE), a winning Irish point-to-pointer, probably found this ground a bit lively. With this run under his belt and softer ground, he should improve. (7/1)

Pharanear (IRE), making his chasing debut, was given time to get his jumping together after looking hesitant at the first two fences. He got upsides the eventual winner three out, but was a length or more behind when coming to grief at the next. (4/11)

1282 DERBY EXPRESS CONDITIONAL H'CAP HURDLE (0-120) (4-Y.O+) (Class E)

3-50 (3-50) **2m (9 hdls)** £2,920.00 (£820.00: £400.00) GOING: 0.25 sec per fur (GS)

	Horse	Dist	Pos	SP	RR	SF
976*	**Yubralee (USA) (115)** (MCPipe) **4-12-0** EHusband (mde all: clr 2nd: unchal: eased flat)	—	**1**	5/4[1]	95+	27
	Doolar (USA) (87) (PTDalton) **9-10-0** MichaelBrennan (bit bkwd: a chsng wnr: cl up 6th: mstke 3 out: sn wknd)	5	**2**	25/1	62?	—
794[6]	**Eurolink Shadow (89)** (DMcCain) **4-10-2**ow2 DFortt (lost tch 5th: t.o)	dist	**3**	14/1	—	—
1034*	**Steadfast Elite (IRE) (98)** (JJO'Neill) **5-10-11** RMcGrath (fell 1st)		**F**	9/4[2]	—	—
	Jemima Puddleduck (94) (AStreeter) **5-10-0**(7)ow1 WGreatrex (chsd ldrs tl blnd & uns rdr 4th)		**U**	7/2[3]	—	—
				(SP 107.9%)		**5 Rn**

3m 55.3 (14.30) CSF £18.42 TOTE £2.50: £1.30 £3.90 (£21.40) OWNER Mr D. A. Johnson (WELLINGTON) BRED Gainsborough Farm Inc

LONG HANDICAP Eurolink Shadow 9-12 Doolar (USA) 9-8

976* Yubralee (USA) made light work of this simple task after the early departure of his market rival. (5/4)

Doolar (USA), in need of this after an eighteen-month absence, put up a game performance, although he was flattered by his proximity to the winner. (25/1)

Eurolink Shadow never threatened to take a hand and was trailing from halfway. (14/1: op 8/1)

T/Plpt: £78.70 (82.3 Tckts). T/Qdpt: £77.50 (3.53 Tckts). J

1053-WINCANTON (R-H) (Good, Good to firm patches)

Saturday November 9th

WEATHER: fine

1283 E.B.F. 'N.H.' QUALIFIER NOVICES' HURDLE (4, 5 & 6-Y.O) (Class E)

1-05 (1-06) **2m (8 hdls)** £2,600.00 (£725.00: £350.00) GOING minus 0.12 sec per fur (G)

	Horse	Dist	Pos	SP	RR	SF
961[2]	**Mazzini (IRE) (95)** (RRowe) **5-11-3**(7) MrPO'Keeffe (lw: mde all: rdn 2 out: r.o wl)	—	**1**	10/1	75	32
	Neat Feat (IRE) (DRCElsworth) **5-11-0** PHolley (hld up: hdwy 5th: r.o flat: nt trble wnr)	5	**2**	5/2[2]	60	17
1059[2]	**Charlie Parrot (IRE)** (MCPipe) **6-11-0** JOsborne (hld up & bhd: hdwy 3rd: chsd wnr after 3 out: hung rt fr 2 out: wknd flat)	7	**3**	5/2[2]	53	10
	Silver Thyne (IRE) (MrsJPitman) **4-11-0** RFarrant (bkwd: bhd: j.lft 3rd: reminders after 3 out: no rspnse)	11	**4**	9/4[1]	42	—
	West Bay Breeze (RHBuckler) **4-10-9** BPowell (bkwd: prom: j.slowly 4th: wknd 3 out)	10	**5**	9/1[3]	27	—
	Gale Spring (IRE) (RJHodges) **4-10-6**(3) TDascombe (prom: chsd wnr 3rd: mstke 3 out: wknd appr 2 out)	5	**6**	50/1	22	—
	Admiral Bruny (IRE) (NAGaselee) **5-11-0** JRKavanagh (bit bkwd: plld hrd: a bhd: t.o)	dist	**7**	14/1	—	—
	Paramount Leader (DMarks) **4-11-0** JAMcCarthy (bit bkwd: sn bhd: t.o whn p.u bef 3 out)		**P**	100/1	—	—
				(SP 116.6%)		**8 Rn**

3m 46.4 (6.40) CSF £34.18 TOTE £10.20: £2.00 £1.60 £1.20 (£13.70) OWNER Mr Nicholas Cooper (PULBOROUGH) BRED Mrs M. Little

961 Mazzini (IRE) stays pretty well and had a fitness advantage over the majority of his rivals. (10/1: 7/1-11/1)

Neat Feat (IRE) did well in bumpers early last season prior to an outing over hurdles a year ago. He gave the impression a longer trip should help. (5/2)

1059 Charlie Parrot (IRE) did not prove very co-operative in the home straight and this was most disappointing after his promising run last time. (5/2)

Silver Thyne (IRE) finished over thirty-five lengths in front of Charlie Parrot when winning a bumper at Newton Abbot in May. However, like most of his stable so far this season, he needed the outing. (9/4)
Admiral Bruny (IRE) (14/1: op 7/1)

1284 SILVER BUCK H'CAP CHASE (0-115) (5-Y.O+) (Class E)

1-35 (1-35) **2m 5f (17 fncs)** £4,328.00 (£1,304.00: £632.00: £296.00) GOING minus 0.12 sec per fur (G)

			SP	RR	SF
20^{4}	**Monks Jay (IRE) (88)** (GThorner) **7-10-4** ILawrence (hld up: led last: drvn out) ....—	1	10/1	91	1
1070^{4}	**Channel Pastime (93)** (DBurchell) **12-10-6**(3) GuyLewis (a.p: lft in ld 3 out: hdd last: unable qckn) 2½	2	16/1	94	4
1035^{6}	**The Caumrue (IRE) (105)** (GBBalding) **8-11-7** BClifford (hld up: hdwy 12th: rdn after 13th: one pce fr 3 out) ...5	3	5/1^{3}	102	12
953^{4}	**Comedy Road (100)** (RLee) **12-11-2** PMcLoughlin (hdwy 12th: sn rdn: one pce fr 3 out) ....nk	4	9/1	97	7
959^{3}	**Black Church (96)** (RRowe) **10-10-12** DO'Sullivan (s.s: mstke 8th: hdwy 12th: wknd 3 out: mstke last) 11	5	9/1	85	—
	Maxxum Express (IRE) (87) (GBBalding) **8-10-3**ow2 RichardGuest (bit bkwd: s.s: t.o fr 5th) ....dist	6	20/1	—	—
	Duhallow Lodge (110) (CRBarwell) **9-11-12** JRKavanagh (bit bkwd: led to 2nd: wkng whn fell 4 out)	F	12/1	—	—
	Miss Marigold (96) (RJHodges) **7-10-9b**(3) TDascombe (bkwd: plld hrd: led 4th: clr 6th: blnd 12th: hdd appr 4 out: wknd appr 3 out: t.o whn fell 2 out)	F	4/1^{2}	—	—
	Beatson (IRE) (95) (RHBuckler) **7-10-11** BPowell (bit bkwd: prom: chsd ldr 9th: led appr 4 out tl fell 3 out)........	F	9/1	—	—
	Jumbeau (100) (PRChamings) **11-11-2** SMcNeill (led 2nd to 4th: pckd 8th: sn bhd: t.o fr 12th: p.u bef 2 ut).......	P	12/1	—	—
1076*	**Herbert Buchanan (IRE) (101)** (PFNicholls) **6-10-10**(7) MrJTizzard (blnd & uns rdr 3rd)......................................	U	9/4^{1}	—	—
932^{4}	**Lake of Loughrea (IRE) (104)** (KCBailey) **6-11-6** JOsborne (Withdrawn not under Starter's orders: lame in paddock)	W	5/1^{3}	—	—
			(SP 149.2%)	**11 Rn**	

5m 20.9 (12.90) CSF £150.44 CT £839.65 TOTE £13.70: £3.30 £3.70 £2.20 (£112.20) Trio £60.00; £9.30 to Folkestone 11/11/96 OWNER Mr J. A. Cover (WANTAGE) BRED Jeremy Hill
20 Monks Jay (IRE) found this longer trip no problem off a mark 3lb lower than when fourth at Worcester on Derby Day. (10/1)
342 Channel Pastime, out of the handicap on his last two outings, could not hold the winner from the final fence. (16/1)
The Caumrue (IRE) had his jumping problems last season, but lack of acceleration on ground plenty lively enough for him was the problem here. (5/1)
953 Comedy Road was 2lb higher than when making his fitness advantage pay off in a three-runner affair at Worcester in August. (9/1)
959 Black Church has slipped to a mark only 1lb higher than when successful at Chepstow on Easter Monday. (9/1)
Beatson (IRE) was possibly just short of peak-fitness, but would have gone close had he stood up. (9/1)
1076* Herbert Buchanan (IRE) is inclined to have the odd jumping lapse, and gave his rider little chance of staying aboard. (9/4)

1285 K. J. PIKE & SONS NOVICES' H'CAP CHASE (0-100) (5-Y.O+) (Class E)

2-05 (2-06) **3m 1f 110y (21 fncs)** £3,834.00 (£1,152.00: £556.00: £258.00) GOING minus 0.12 sec per fur (G)

			SP	RR	SF
	God Speed You (IRE) (82) (CPMorlock) **7-11-9b** JRKavanagh (led 5th tl appr 14th: led 4 out: clr 3 out: r.o wl) ....—	1	7/1^{3}	106	18
887^{6}	**Call Me River (IRE) (64)** (PRHedger) **8-10-5** ILawrence (hld up: hdwy 11th: chsd wnr appr 3 out: no imp) 10	2	20/1	82	—
1032^{3}	**Stormhill Pilgrim (70)** (MJRoberts) **7-10-11** PMcLoughlin (led 2nd to 5th: led appr 14th to 4 out: sn wknd) 8	3	14/1	83	—
1038^{5}	**Its Grand (69)** (JMBradley) **7-10-10** TJMurphy (led to 2nd: rdn 17th: wknd 18th)...1½	4	13/2^{2}	81	—
	Ceridwen (74) (TRGreathead) **6-11-1** PHolley (bkwd: hld up: mstke 10th: lost pl 13th: n.d after) 14	5	16/1	77	—
970^{4}	**Our Nikki (72)** (PRRodford) **6-10-13** SBurrough (a bhd: t.o) 17	6	16/1	64	—
1057^{U}	**Tearful Prince (74)** (CWMitchell) **12-11-1** SMcNeill (a bhd: t.o whn p.u bef 16th)	P	7/1^{3}	—	—
970^{3}	**Mingus (USA) (83)** (RHBuckler) **9-11-10** BPowell (bhd: blnd 9th: t.o whn p.u & dismntd bef 15th)........................	P	8/1	—	—
1040*	**Tiger Claw (USA) (83)** (AGHobbs) **10-11-3**(7) OBurrows (a bhd: t.o 7th: p.u bef 15th)..	P	12/1	—	—
1038^{U}	**Cardinal Rule (IRE) (70)** (MissVenetiaWilliams) **7-10-11** RFarrant (nt j.w: rdn after 12th: sn bhd: t.o whn p.u bef 4 out: b.b.v)	P	8/1	—	—
	Market Gossip (63) (RHAlner) **6-10-1**(3) PHenley (bkwd: prom tl mstke 12th: bhd whn blnd 14th: t.o whn p.u bef 15th)	P	3/1^{1}	—	—
1068^{P}	**Vareck II (FR) (60)** (MCPipe) **9-9-8**(7) BMoore (bhd fr 10th: t.o whn p.u bef 14th)..	P	33/1	—	—
			(SP 119.4%)	**12 Rn**	

6m 35.1 (16.10) CSF £118.60 CT £1,740.20 TOTE £6.20: £2.10 £3.70 £4.70 (£53.60) Trio Not won; £156.20 to Folkestone 11/11/96 OWNER Wallop (WANTAGE) BRED Mrs Vincent O'Brien
OFFICIAL EXPLANATION **Cardinal Rule (IRE): had bled from the nose.**
God Speed You (IRE) was inclined to make mistakes last season, but never put a foot wrong here and provided his trainer with his first winner. (7/1)
Call Me River (IRE) had probably found the ground too soft on his reappearance at Newton Abbot. (20/1)
Stormhill Pilgrim may need more patient tactics over this sort of trip. (14/1)
1038 Its Grand found this ground too lively. (13/2)
Market Gossip won two of his three points last season, but looked as though this was needed, and his jumping did not come up to scratch. (3/1)

1286 WEST COUNTRY H'CAP HURDLE (0-130) (4-Y.O+) (Class C)

2-35 (2-35) **2m 6f (11 hdls)** £5,540.00 (£1,670.00: £810.00: £380.00) GOING minus 0.12 sec per fur (G)

			SP	RR	SF
	Gysart (IRE) (113) (MCPipe) **7-11-3b** JOsborne (mde all: sn clr: rdn appr 2 out: r.o) ....—	1	13/8^{1}	90	48
1019*	**Lansdowne (124)** (PFNicholls) **8-11-7**(7) OBurrows (hld up: hdwy appr 8th: chsd wnr appr 2 out: one pce flat) 4	2	3/1^{2}	98	56
810*	**Blasket Hero (107)** (MrsSDWilliams) **8-10-11b** SMcNeill (bhd tl styd on appr 2 out: n.d)...................................12	3	7/2^{3}	72	30
1196^{7}	**Jadidh (107)** (ABarrow) **8-10-6**(5) DSalter (a bhd: t.o)..dist	4	16/1	—	—
952^{3}	**Reaganesque (USA) (108)** (PGMurphy) **4-10-12** RFarrant (chsd wnr tl appr 2 out: sn btn & eased: t.o) 9	5	6/1	—	—
	Prince Teeton (108) (RHBuckler) **7-10-5**(7)ow3 MrJTizzard (3rd whn fell 3rd)	F	14/1	—	—
			(SP 112.2%)	**6 Rn**	

5m 11.2 (2.20) CSF £6.67 CT £12.42 TOTE £2.40: £1.50 £1.90 (£4.10) OWNER The Hon Mrs R Cobbold (WELLINGTON) BRED J. Ward
Gysart (IRE) improved considerably when tried in blinkers last spring, and defied a 19lb rise in the weights for his two previous handicap wins. (13/8)
1019* Lansdowne, raised 6lb for his Newbury win, really needs more give in the ground than he encountered here. (3/1)
810* Blasket Hero, up a further 2lb, looks in the Handicapper's grip in this sort of company. (7/2)
952 Reaganesque (USA) won three handicaps on the Flat in the summer, but is not transferring that improvement to hurdles. (6/1)

1287 BADGER BEER H'CAP CHASE (0-145) (5-Y.O+) (Class B)

3-10 (3-10) **3m 1f 110y (21 fncs)** £13,888.00 (£4,204.00: £2,052.00: £976.00) GOING minus 0.03 sec per fur (G)

				SP	RR	SF
1063*	**Coome Hill (IRE) (130)** (WWDennis) **7-11-7** JFrost (hld up: hdwy 12th: led 2 out: r.o wl)	—	1	2/1[1]	142	32
909[2]	**Glemot (IRE) (135)** (KCBailey) **8-11-12** JOsborne (lw: led to 6th: led 7th: j.lft 13th: hdd 2 out: btn whn blnd last)	10	2	10/1	141	31
973*	**Samlee (IRE) (110)** (PJHobbs) **7-10-1** JRKavanagh (prom: reminders after 6th: rdn appr 14th: wknd appr 3 out)	10	3	9/2[2]	110	—
	Run Up the Flag (122) (JTGifford) **9-10-10**(3) LAspell (hld up: hdwy 17th: wknd 2 out: eased whn btn flat)	hd	4	5/1[3]	121	11
1133[2]	**Straight Talk (133)** (PFNicholls) **9-11-3**(7) MrJTizzard (chsd ldr: led 6th to 7th: rdn & wknd 15th)	1¾	5	13/2	131	21
	Well Briefed (122) (RHBuckler) **9-10-13** BPowell (bhd: mstke 11th: t.o whn blnd 15th: p.u bef 3 out)		P	20/1	—	—
1067[5]	**Tug of Peace (113)** (GBBalding) **9-10-4** BClifford (bhd fr 15th: p.u bef 17th)		P	14/1	—	—
	Garrison Savannah (130) (MrsJPitman) **13-11-7** RFarrant (bkwd: dropped rr 11th: t.o whn p.u bef 3 out)		P	20/1	—	—
1089[3]	**Big Ben Dun (112)** (CPEBrooks) **10-10-3b[1]** RichardGuest (plld hrd: prom: mstke 12th: wknd appr 3 out: 6th whn blnd & uns rdr 2 out)		U	12/1	—	—
				(SP 114.5%)	**9 Rn**	

6m 29.1 (10.10) CSF £20.30 CT £72.05 TOTE £3.20: £1.40 £3.00 £1.70 (£19.20) Trio £15.20 OWNER Mrs Jill Dennis (BUDE) BRED Mrs S. O'Connell

STEWARDS' ENQUIRY Aspell susp. 18-21/11/96 (failure to ensure best possible placing).

IN-FOCUS: 1991 Gold Cup winner and Grand National runner-up Garrison Savannah was retired after this event.

1063* Coome Hill (IRE), professionally handled for the first time, defied a 6lb rise in the weights. He could be a lively outsider in the Hennessy with his penalty putting him only 3lb out of the handicap. (2/1)

909 Glemot (IRE) has never won over three miles, and came up against a progressive and possibly well-handicapped rival. (10/1)

973* Samlee (IRE) was pretty highly tried on this return to fences, and only finished third because Run Up the Flag's rider was caught napping. (9/2)

Run Up the Flag should have finished third and his rider picked up a four-day ban. (5/1)

1133 Straight Talk is racing off a mark 5lb higher than the highest off which he has won. (13/2: op 4/1)

Tug of Peace (14/1: 10/1-16/1)

1089 Big Ben Dun ran far too freely in the first-time headgear. (12/1: op 8/1)

1288 TANGLEFOOT ELITE HURDLE (Gd 2) (4-Y.O+) (Class A)

3-45 (3-46) **2m (8 hdls)** £12,860.00 (£4,868.00: £2,384.00: £1,088.00) GOING minus 0.12 sec per fur (G)

				SP	RR	SF
318a[6]	**Dreams End (131)** (PBowen) **8-10-12** RFarrant (a.p: wnt 2nd appr 5th: led & mstke last: drvn out)	—	1	7/2[3]	113	74
318a[2]	**Space Trucker (IRE)** (MrsJHarrington,Ireland) **5-10-12** JOsborne (hld up: hmpd 5th: hdwy 3 out: slt ld 2 out tl rdn last: unable qckn)	2½	2	9/2	111	72
	Ground Nut (IRE) (125) (RHBuckler) **6-10-12** BPowell (led & sn clr: hdd 2 out: sn wknd)	8	3	20/1	103	64
1017*	**Mistinguett (IRE) (136)** (NATwiston-Davies) **4-10-7** CLlewellyn (nvr nr to chal)	6	4	2/1[1]	92	53
	Eskimo Nel (IRE) (137) (JLSpearing) **5-10-7** RichardGuest (hld up: hmpd 5th: hdwy 3 out: wknd appr 2 out)	2½	5	9/4[2]	89	50
948[F]	**Hops and Pops (139)** (RHAlner) **9-10-11** PHenley (chsd ldr tl after 4th: j.slowly 5th: sn bhd)	22	6	9/1	71	32
	Arabian Bold (IRE) (RTJuckes) **8-10-12** PHolley (bkwd: bhd fr 4th: t.o fr 3 out)	dist	7	50/1	—	—
	Hard to Figure (RJHodges) **10-10-12** TDascombe (hld up: mstke 4th: sn bhd: t.o whn p.u bef 2 out)		P	33/1	—	—
				(SP 124.2%)	**8 Rn**	

3m 35.2 (-4.80) CSF £20.11 TOTE £4.50: £1.20 £1.50 £3.00 (£10.70) OWNER Mr T. G. Price (HAVERFORDWEST) BRED Hascombe and Valiant Studs

Dreams End has been in good form on the Flat this autumn, and came here instead of running in the November Handicap because the ground at Doncaster was considered too soft. (7/2)

Space Trucker (IRE) had finished seven lengths in front of the winner in the Galway Hurdle on 6lb better terms. (9/2)

Ground Nut (IRE) adopted his usual front-running tactics, but is more effective with give in the ground. (20/1)

1017* Mistinguett (IRE) could never get into the race and possibly found this ground on the fast side. (2/1)

Eskimo Nel (IRE) is another better with more give in the ground. (9/4)

948 Hops and Pops could never get to her favourite position at the head of affairs. (9/1: 6/1-10/1)

1289 WEATHERBYS 'STARS OF TOMORROW' INTERMEDIATE OPEN N.H. FLAT RACE (4, 5 & 6-Y.O) (Class H)

4-15 (4-17) **2m** £1,458.50 (£406.00: £195.50)

				SP	RR	SF
872*	**Lady Rebecca** (MissVenetiaWilliams) **4-11-6** RFarrant (swtg: a.p: led over 2f out: rdn out)	—	1	100/30[1]	—	—
	Quini Eagle (FR) (MCPipe) **4-11-4** CLlewellyn (bit bkwd: led tl over 2f out: one pce)	6	2	6/1[3]	—	—
	Pot Black Uk (PJHobbs) **5-10-11**(7) MMoran (hdwy 8f out: one pce fnl 2f)	2½	3	10/1	—	—
	Wentworth (USA) (GThorner) **4-10-11**(7) ClareThorner (plld hrd: hdwy after 6f: wknd 4f out)	13	4	13/2	—	—
	Kylami (NZ) (AGHobbs) **4-10-11**(7) MrGShenkin (styd on fnl 3f: nt rch ldrs)	3	5	20/1	—	—
	Nigel's Boy (DMLloyd) **4-10-11**(7) OBurrows (plld hrd: prom 12f)	1	6	50/1	—	—
	Endeavour (FR) (MJRoberts) **4-11-4** BPowell (bkwd: nvr nr to chal)	1	7	50/1	—	—
	Bavardier (IRE) (GBBalding) **5-11-4** BClifford (bkwd: wnt lft s: nvr nrr)	nk	8	14/1	—	—
	Dark Challenger (IRE) (MrsJPitman) **4-11-4** ILawrence (bit bkwd: hdwy 8f out: wknd 5f out)	s.h	9	13/2	—	—
	Borodino (IRE) (RRowe) **4-11-4** DO'Sullivan (bkwd: nvr nr ldrs)	¾	10	14/1	—	—
	Stellar Force (IRE) (OSherwood) **5-11-4** JOsborne (bit bkwd: prom 10f: eased whn btn over 2f out)	5	11	7/2[2]	—	—
	Mo's Boy (SEarle) **5-11-4** SMcNeill (bkwd: a bhd)	5	12	20/1	—	—
	Missed The Match (REPocock) **6-11-4** PMcLoughlin (bit bkwd: prom 8f)	10	13	66/1	—	—
	Fair Haul (RGFrost) **5-11-4** JFrost (bkwd: bhd fnl 6f: t.o)	18	14	50/1	—	—
	Sophies Dream (JMBradley) **5-11-4** TJMurphy (bit bkwd: prom 10f: t.o)	11	15	50/1	—	—
	Special Topic (APJones) **6-10-13** RichardGuest (bit bkwd: bhd fnl 7f: t.o)	2	16	50/1	—	—
	Beweldered (RGFrost) **4-11-4** MrAHoldsworth (bit bkwd: a bhd: t.o)		17	50/1	—	—
				(SP 131.5%)	**17 Rn**	

3m 35.8 CSF £24.03 TOTE £3.60: £1.60 £2.80 £2.70 (£17.30) Trio £58.50 OWNER Kinnersley Optimists (HEREFORD) BRED Needwood Stud

872* Lady Rebecca, unimpressive in the paddock, was ridden clear through the final furlong. (100/30)

Quini Eagle (FR) took the field along at a good clip and did not cave in when taken on by the winner. Like most of his stable, he should certainly help to pay his way. (6/1: 4/1-7/1)
Pot Black Uk, out of a winning hurdler, made a respectable start to his career. (10/1)
Wentworth (USA) did not help his rider by refusing to settle. (13/2)
Kylami (NZ) was one of the fittest newcomers in the field. (20/1)
Nigel's Boy did his best to pull his rider's arms out. (50/1)
Bavardier (IRE) (14/1: 10/1-16/1)
Stellar Force (IRE), out of a mare who won an Irish bumper, was not knocked about and this kindness should be repaid in due course. (7/2)

T/Plpt: £195.60 (60.64 Tckts). T/Qdpt: £22.20 (36.78 Tckts). KH

1020-CARLISLE (R-H) (Good, Good to soft patches)
Monday November 11th

One flight omitted
WEATHER: fine

1290 'ANZIO' NOVICES' HURDLE (4-Y.O+) (Class E)
1-00 (1-01) **3m 110y (10 hdls)** £2,262.00 (£632.00: £306.00) GOING minus 0.02 sec per fur (G)

				SP	RR	SF
	Military Academy (GRichards) **7-10-12** RDunwoody (lft in ld after 5th: styd on strly fr 3 out)	—	**1**	7/2 ^{3}	70+	—
	Ben Cruachan (IRE) (JMJefferson) **6-10-12** MDwyer (hld up: hdwy & prom 6th: wnt 2nd 2 out: eased whn btn flat)	10	**2**	3/1 ^{2}	64+	—
1130^{3}	**Pebble Beach (IRE) (87)** (GMMoore) **6-11-5** JCallaghan (a.p: chal 4 out: mstke 3 out: sn btn)	9	**3**	10/1	65	—
1026^{3}	**Chill Factor** (MrsMReveley) **6-10-12** PNiven (in tch tl outpcd fr 4 out)	10	**4**	8/1	51	—
135^{P}	**Ruber** (RWThomson) **9-10-12** BStorey (led to 1st: cl up tl outpcd fr 3 out)	6	**5**	200/1	47	—
	South Coast Star (IRE) (HowardJohnson) **6-10-12** AMaguire (bit bkwd: hld up & bhd: sme hdwy 3 out: nvr nr to chal)	4	**6**	33/1	45	—
	Kirtle Monstar (LLungo) **5-10-12** FPerratt (led 1st tl rn wd & hdd after 5th: sn t.o: p.u bef last)		**P**	66/1	—	—
	Swanbister (IRE) (92) (LLungo) **6-11-5** MFoster (hld up: hmpd 5th: sddle slipped & uns rdr 200y after)		**U**	11/4 ^{1}	—	—
1046^{F}	**Young Kenny (94)** (PBeaumont) **5-11-5** RSupple (swtg: cl up tl blnd & uns rdr 5th)		**U**	5/1	—	—
				(SP 115.7%)	**9 Rn**	

6m 10.0 (26.00) CSF £13.79 TOTE £4.20: £2.00 £1.10 £1.30 (£7.80) Trio £31.10 OWNER Mr Robert Ogden (PENRITH) BRED P. M. Prior-Wandesforde

Military Academy appreciated this trip and won in useful style. This particularly attractive sort will be one to follow over the bigger obstacles. (7/2)
Ben Cruachan (IRE), a big, strong, chasing type, ran well here and was wisely not knocked about when beaten. (3/1)
1130 Pebble Beach (IRE) looked in good trim and had his chances, but was feeling the pace when a mistake three out finished any hopes. (10/1)
1026 Chill Factor, slow but sure, was left wanting for pace over the last four flights. (8/1)
Ruber has won hunter chases in the past, but it is a long time since he showed anything positive. (200/1)
South Coast Star (IRE), having his first run for over two years, needed it and gave the impression that some good should come from it. (33/1)

1291 E.B.F. TATTERSALLS IRELAND NOVICES' CHASE (5-Y.O+ Mares Only) (Class E)
1-30 (1-31) **2m 4f 110y (16 fncs)** £3,403.75 (£1,030.00: £502.50: £238.75) GOING minus 0.02 sec per fur (G)

				SP	RR	SF
1176^{3}	**Mariners Mirror** (NATwiston-Davies) **9-10-12** MrMRimell (j.w: led 4th: lft wl clr appr 4 out)	—	**1**	2/1 ^{2}	94?	42
1037^{3}	**Coverdale Lane** (MrsSJSmith) **9-11-2** MrPMurray (led 2nd to 4th: outpcd fr ½-wy: sn lost tch)	dist	**2**	15/2	—	—
	Miss Colette (MrsDThomson) **8-10-12** LO'Hara (prom tl outpcd fr 9th: 3rd & no ch whn fell 2 out: rmntd)	dist	**3**	25/1	—	—
	Miss Tino (JPDodds) **8-10-12** AThornton (lost tch 8th: sn t.o & j.b lft: poor 3rd whn hmpd & ref last: cont)	2½	**4**	100/1	—	—
	Owens Quest (IRE) (TJEtherington) **6-10-12** RRourke (lw: mstkes: hdwy ½-wy: 10l 3rd whn fell 12th)		**F**	16/1	—	—
8^{2}	**Cabbery Rose (IRE)** (PFGraffin,Ireland) **8-11-5** RDunwoody (fell 1st)		**F**	4/1 ^{3}	—	—
	Rich Desire (FMurphy) **7-10-12** AMaguire (led to 2nd: chsd ldrs: ev ch tl p.u lame appr 4 out)		**P**	13/8 ^{1}	—	—
				(SP 113.9%)	**7 Rn**	

5m 7.6 (4.60) CSF £15.85 TOTE £2.60: £1.10 £3.30 (£9.00) OWNER Mr F. J. Mills (CHELTENHAM) BRED E. J. Praill, Mrs M. Scudamore and M. J. Scudamore

Mariners Mirror, typically for this stable, was turned out looking ultra-fit. Jumping well, she made it a real test of stamina and was presented with the prize when her only serious rival broke down approaching four out. (2/1)
1037 Coverdale Lane is slow but does struggle on. Feeling the pace by halfway, she soon found this well beyond her. (15/2)
Miss Colette has not been out for some time and was struggling a long way out before falling two from home. (25/1)
Miss Tino would have been a very remote third of three had there been any justice, but the loose Miss Colette caused her to refuse at the last and then beat her when remounted. (100/1)
Owens Quest (IRE) was very iffy with her jumping in the early stages, but had just made some ground when falling five out. She stayed down for quite a while. (16/1)
Rich Desire kept tabs on the winner and the issue was still in doubt until she broke down going to the fourth last. (13/8)

1292 BROWN COW AT COCKERMOUTH NOVICES' H'CAP HURDLE (0-100) (4-Y.O+) (Class E)
2-00 (2-00) **2m 4f 110y (10 hdls)** £2,360.00 (£660.00: £320.00) GOING minus 0.02 sec per fur (G)

				SP	RR	SF
1021^{5}	**Lifebuoy (IRE) (77)** (JRTurner) **5-10-12**ow2 TReed (lw: a.p: led after 3 out: r.o wl)	—	**1**	8/1	64	21
1050^{2}	**Baher (USA) (88)** (MrsASwinbank) **7-11-9** JSupple (led to 3 out: hit next & one pce)	9	**2**	7/2 ^{1}	68	27
1161^{3}	**Leap in the Dark (IRE) (78)** (MissLCSiddall) **7-10-13** AThornton (lw: a cl up: led 3 out: sn hdd: wknd fr next)	3½	**3**	4/1 ^{2}	55	14
854^{2}	**Haughton Lad (IRE) (72)** (FPMurtagh) **7-10-7** ARoche (chsd ldrs: outpcd appr 3 out: no imp after)	2½	**4**	5/1 ^{3}	47	6
	Menshaar (USA) (86) (LLungo) **4-11-7** MDwyer (in tch: one pce fr 4 out)	¾	**5**	10/1	61	20
1025^{7}	**Environmental Law (73)** (WMcKeown) **5-10-5**(3) GCahill (chsd ldrs tl outpcd 6th: styd on fr 3 out: n.d)	nk	**6**	16/1	48	7
	Fenloe Rambler (IRE) (89) (RJohnson) **5-11-10** MrPJohnson (bkwd: t.o fr 4th)	dist	**7**	16/1	—	—
	Corston Joker (87) (LLungo) **6-11-8** MFoster (prom: effrt 6th: wknd qckly fr 3 out: fell last)		**F**	8/1	—	—
876^{5}	**Court Joker (IRE) (82)** (HAlexander) **4-11-3** PNiven (a rr div: p.u bef 2 out)		**P**	15/2	—	—

				SP	RR	SF
1046^{3}	**Rapid Fire (IRE) (65)** (JMJefferson) **8-9-7**(7) MNewton (lost tch fr 6th: p.u bef 2 out)		**P**	7/1	—	—

(SP 126.2%) **10 Rn**

5m 1.4 (10.40) CSF £36.94 CT £123.62 TOTE £10.30: £2.00 £1.80 £1.70 (£37.60) Trio £167.00; £30.59 to Lingfield 12/11/96 OWNER Miss S. J. Turner (HELPERBY) BRED Michael J. Byrne

1021 Lifebuoy (IRE) looked particularly fit and won this modest contest in good style. (8/1)
1050 Baher (USA) had shot 19lb up the weights since his last run and was made to look very one-paced. (7/2)
1161 Leap in the Dark (IRE) had his chances, but found the struggle too much once serious pressure was applied. (4/1)
854 Haughton Lad (IRE) was short of that vital turn of foot at any stage. (5/1)
Menshaar (USA) looked likely to be all the better for this and showed a little, but proved very slow over the last four flights. (10/1: 7/1-14/1)
Environmental Law ran better, but is sadly lacking in speed. (16/1)

1293 SCOTS GUARDS 'LUCIUS' CHALLENGE CUP H'CAP CHASE (0-125) (5-Y.O+) (Class D)

2-30 (2-30) **3m (18 fncs)** £4,535.20 (£1,372.60: £669.80: £318.40) GOING minus 0.02 sec per fur (G)

				SP	RR	SF
	Parsons Boy (114) (GRichards) **7-11-6** BHarding (hld up: hdwy ½-wy: rdn to chal whn mstke last: led 100y out: styd on wl)	—	**1**	5/1^{3}	122	13
	Ubu Val (FR) (118) (WABethell) **10-11-10** ASSmith (lw: chsd ldrs: led 14th tl flat: kpt on wl)	nk	**2**	16/1	126	17
	Holy Sting (IRE) (94) (NATwiston-Davies) **7-10-0b** CLlewellyn (chsd ldrs tl lost pl 9th: hdwy to ld 12th: hdd 14th: one pce fr 3 out)	4	**3**	7/1	99	—
	Pennine Pride (94) (MDHammond) **9-10-0** AMaguire (led to 10th: lost tch next: styd on again fr 3 out)	13	**4**	14/1	91	—
	Seven Towers (IRE) (115) (MrsMReveley) **7-11-7** PNiven (prom tl outpcd 11th: no imp after)	2½	**5**	4/1^{2}	110	1
1142^{4}	**Stop the Waller (IRE) (114)** (FMurphy) **7-11-6** KWhelan (cl up: led 10th to 12th: wknd 4 out)	1½	**6**	7/2^{1}	108	—
1162^{U}	**Gale Ahead (IRE) (98)** (GMMoore) **6-10-4** NBentley (lw: chsd ldrs tl lost pl 10th: hdwy & rdn 12th: wknd 4 out)	14	**7**	14/1	83	—
1029^{4}	**East Houston (100)** (JJO'Neill) **7-10-6** ARoche (lw: hld up & bhd: effrt whn hit 14th: sn btn)	2	**8**	16/1	83	—
1122*	**Basilicus (FR) (107)** (MrsSJSmith) **7-10-13** RichardGuest (mstkes early: reminders 7th: outpcd fr 12th: wknd appr 4 out)	19	**9**	5/1^{3}	78	—
	Howcleuch (103) (JKMOliver) **9-10-9** BStorey (bit bkwd: hdwy & prom 10th: wknd next)	5	**10**	16/1	70	—

(SP 119.0%) **10 Rn**

6m 10.1 (18.10) CSF £71.17 CT £516.39 TOTE £5.30: £1.70 £3.50 £2.40 (£32.90) Trio £150.20 OWNER Mr B. Ridge (PENRITH) BRED Bretton Bloodstock Plc

LONG HANDICAP Holy Sting (IRE) 9-13 Pennine Pride 9-13

Parsons Boy, from a stable that can do little wrong, continued his improvement and took this step up to handicap company in game style. (5/1)
Ubu Val (FR), who looked in particularly good form, stays really well and kept fighting back when looking held. (16/1)
Holy Sting (IRE) has done his winning on much more testing ground and that is obviously what he needs to be at his best. (7/1)
Pennine Pride just stays and, after getting well outpaced halfway through this, was finishing well, albeit too late. (14/1: op 8/1)
Seven Towers (IRE) was taken off his legs when the pace increased a mile from home and, although struggling on, was no further danger. It seems extreme distances will suit him. (4/1)
1142 Stop the Waller (IRE) ran well until suddenly running out of fuel four out. It seems that his stable can do little right at present. (7/2)

1294 HYNDBURN BRIDGE AT CLAYTON-LE-MOORS H'CAP HURDLE (0-110) (4-Y.O+) (Class E)

3-00 (3-00) **3m 110y (10 hdls)** £2,318.00 (£648.00: £314.00) GOING minus 0.02 sec per fur (G)

				SP	RR	SF
	Haile Derring (101) (NATwiston-Davies) **6-11-5** CLlewellyn (mde most: pushed clr fr 6th: eased flat)	—	**1**	11/10^{1}	88+	18
1080*	**Troodos (95)** (MrsASwinbank) **10-10-13** JSupple (lw: hld up & bhd: wnt 2nd 4 out: no ch w wnr)	9	**2**	4/1^{2}	76+	6
	Stormy Coral (IRE) (92) (CParker) **6-10-10** BStorey (bit bkwd: hld up: stdy hdwy 3 out: nvr rchd ldrs)	10	**3**	7/1^{3}	67	—
	Plumbob (IRE) (91) (LLungo) **7-10-9** MFoster (a.p: one pce fr 4 out)	7	**4**	20/1	61	—
	Persian House (110) (JMJefferson) **9-12-0** MDwyer (outpcd ½-wy: nvr nr to chal: dead)	14	**5**	16/1	71	1
	Quiet Mistress (82) (WABethell) **6-10-0** ASSmith (lw: w wnr: hit 6th & sn outpcd: hrd rdn & wknd 3 out)	1	**6**	14/1	42	—
	Shallow River (IRE) (95) (RCollins) **5-10-13** AThornton (hld up & bhd: n.d)	1½	**7**	14/1	54	—
1121^{4}	**Pride of May (IRE) (93)** (CWFairhurst) **5-10-11v** JCallaghan (prom tl wknd 4 out)	¾	**8**	8/1	52	—
1031^{P}	**Dockmaster (94)** (MissMKMilligan) **5-10-12** LWyer (prom tl wknd 4 out)	10	**9**	14/1	46	—
	Maybe O'Grady (IRE) (94) (WSCunningham) **7-10-5**(7) LMcGrath (bit bkwd: a bhd)	5	**10**	14/1	43	—

(SP 128.5%) **10 Rn**

5m 59.7 (15.70) CSF £6.85 CT £22.81 TOTE £2.00: £1.70 £1.60 £1.10 (£2.30) Trio £6.80 OWNER Mrs V. Stockdale (CHELTENHAM) BRED Mrs V. Stockdale

Haile Derring left nothing to chance here and made this a real test. He had galloped all rivals into the ground before the third last and won easing down. (11/10: 6/4-evens)
1080* Troodos, given plenty to do, went in pursuit of the winner four out, but was never good enough to make any impression. He is nevertheless much improved this season. (4/1: op 5/2)
Stormy Coral (IRE), needing this, ran well and will do better in due course, probably over fences. (7/1: 9/2-8/1)
Plumbob (IRE) ran a fine race and this should have helped put him straight. (20/1)
Persian House ran reasonably, but then collapsed and died after the race. (16/1)
Quiet Mistress tried to take the winner on, but that proved to be her undoing. (14/1)

1295 GREYHOUND AT HALTON H'CAP CHASE (0-125) (5-Y.O+) (Class D)

3-30 (3-30) **2m (12 fncs)** £3,458.00 (£1,046.00: £510.00: £242.00) GOING minus 0.02 sec per fur (G)

				SP	RR	SF
1128*	**Regal Romper (IRE) (110)** (MrsSJSmith) **8-11-10** RichardGuest (a.p: led after 4 out: r.o wl flat)	—	**1**	6/4^{1}	119	14
	Pagliaccio (99) (MDHammond) **8-10-13** RGarritty (led 3rd to 5th: a.p: chal 2 out: hit last: rallied)	½	**2**	9/2	108	3
	Solba (USA) (110) (CParker) **7-11-10** BStorey (a in tch: kpt on fr 4 out: nt pce to chal)	9	**3**	12/1	110	5
1140^{2}	**Weaver George (IRE) (100)** (WStorey) **6-11-0** MMoloney (w ldrs: led 6th: hit next: hdd 4 out: sn outpcd)	6	**4**	7/2^{2}	94	—
	Super Sandy (89) (FTWalton) **9-10-3** DParker (led to 3rd: led 5th to 6th: cl up tl wknd 2 out)	3	**5**	20/1	80	—
	Potato Man (100) (BEllison) **10-10-11**(3) GCahill (bhd: effrt appr 4 out: sn rdn & btn)	4	**6**	4/1^{3}	87	—

(SP 112.9%) **6 Rn**

4m 6.7 (12.70) CSF £8.28 TOTE £2.50: £2.80 £1.40 (£7.90) OWNER Mrs S. Smith (BINGLEY) BRED E. Walshe

1128* Regal Romper (IRE), a tough sort, just kept battling away when challenged. (6/4)
Pagliaccio tended to go to his right in the early stages, but then settled down quite well, only to blot his copy-book with a mistake at the last and, despite rallying, was always fighting a lost cause. (9/2)

Solba (USA), over a trip which appears too sharp, ran pretty well and is likely to be all the better for it. (12/1: op 7/1)
1140 Weaver George (IRE) struggled to gain command and found this too competitive over the last four fences. (7/2)
Super Sandy showed plenty until blowing up two out. (20/1)
Potato Man left the impression that the run should bring him on. (4/1)

1296 'TUMBLEDOWN' STANDARD OPEN N.H. FLAT RACE (4, 5 & 6-Y.O) (Class H)
4-00 (4-00) **2m 1f** £1,070.00 (£295.00: £140.00)

				SP	RR	SF
	Colour Code (MrsASwinbank) **4-11-4** JSupple (a.p: led wl over 1f out: styd on strly)	—	**1**	13/2[3]	—	—
1052[2]	**Good Vibes** (TDEasterby) **4-11-4** LWyer (trckd ldrs: led 4f out tl wl over 1f out: kpt on)	5	**2**	4/1[2]	—	—
	Ardrina (FMurphy) **5-10-13** AMaguire (chsd ldrs: chal 4f out: one pce fnl 3f)	2	**3**	16/1	—	—
	The Crooked Oak (NATwiston-Davies) **4-10-11**(7) MKeighley (cl up: led 6f out to 4f out: sn rdn & btn)	10	**4**	2/1[1]	—	—
	Cheater (IRE) (HowardJohnson) **5-11-4** NWilliamson (led to 6f out: one pce fnl 4f)	1¾	**5**	14/1	—	—
1084*	**Brighter Shade (IRE)** (MrsMReveley) **6-11-4**(7) CMcCormack (lw: hld up: hdwy 7f out: chsng ldrs 4f out: sn rdn & btn)	nk	**6**	10/1	—	—
	Bold Statement (GMMoore) **4-11-4** NBentley (hld up: hdwy 6f out: swvd rt 3f out & styd on one pce)	1¼	**7**	16/1	—	—
1124[9]	**Larkshill (IRE)** (JGFitzGerald) **5-11-4** MDwyer (n.d)	½	**8**	25/1	—	—
	Magpie Melody (IRE) (LLungo) **5-11-4** MFoster (n.d)	14	**9**	16/1	—	—
1026[2]	**Natural Talent** (CParker) **4-11-4** DParker (chsd ldrs tl outpcd fnl 5f)	1¾	**10**	16/1	—	—
	Jessica One (IRE) (MrsMReveley) **5-10-13** PNiven (hld up: hdwy & in tch ½-wy: grad wknd fnl 4f)	¾	**11**	10/1	—	—
	Jervaulx (IRE) (GRichards) **5-11-4** RDunwoody (hdwy & prom 10f out: wknd 4f out)	2	**12**	2/1[1]	—	—
	General Parker (MissMKMilligan) **5-11-4** ASSmith (n.d)	2	**13**	100/1	—	—
	Jessolle (GRichards) **4-10-13** BHarding (a rr div)	7	**14**	20/1	—	—
	Jennie's Prospect (JJO'Neill) **5-10-13**(5) RMcGrath (prom tl wknd 6f out)	4	**15**	16/1	—	—
	Nautilus The Third (IRE) (MDHammond) **5-11-4** RGarritty (n.d)	¼	**16**	20/1	—	—
	Brook House (BBousfield) **5-10-10**(3) GLee (a rr div)	6	**17**	200/1	—	—
	Karena's Prince (MrsSJSmith) **4-11-4** RichardGuest (t.o)	dist	**18**	20/1	—	—
	Boyzontoowa (IRE) (RCollins) **4-11-4** AThornton (t.o)	12	**19**	50/1	—	—
	Samite (IRE) (SJLeadbetter) **5-11-4** NLeach (bkwd: a bhd: wl t.o)	dist	**20**	200/1	—	—

(SP 176.3%) **20 Rn**

4m 4.1 CSF £42.97 TOTE £32.10: £8.60 £1.60 £5.00 (£17.00) Trio Not won; £193.61 to Lingfield 12/11/96 OWNER Mr G. A. Swinbank (RICHMOND) BRED Meon Valley Stud
Colour Code, a well-bred, well-supported newcomer, won this useful bumper in most determined style. (13/2: op 14/1)
1052 Good Vibes has come across two very useful opponents so far and, though he is inclined to take quite a hold in the early stages, he did little wrong, and should find an opening soon. (4/1)
Ardrina had chances throughout, but was just short of toe in the last half-mile. She gives the impression she will need extreme distances over hurdles. (16/1)
The Crooked Oak was fit and fancied here and had shown fair ability last season, but found this too hot. (2/1)
Cheater (IRE) ran a fair race and is likely to be all the better for it. (14/1)
1084* Brighter Shade (IRE) was without doubt the pick of the paddock, but was put in his place. Chasing will be the game for him. (10/1)
Jessica One (IRE) (10/1: op 5/1)
Jervaulx (IRE) came here with a reputation that should have terrified the opposition, but he found it all too much and was wisely not knocked about when not up to the task. (2/1: 6/4-5/2)

T/Plpt: £51.40 (185.39 Tckts). T/Qdpt: £9.50 (134.3 Tckts). AA

0974-LUDLOW (R-H) (Good to firm)
Tuesday November 12th
WEATHER: overcast & cold

1297 NORTON MAIDEN HURDLE (4-Y.O+) (Class E)
1-10 (1-10) **2m 5f 110y (11 hdls)** £2,332.00 (£652.00: £316.00) GOING minus 0.17 sec per fur (G)

				SP	RR	SF
	Medford (WGMTurner) **6-10-12**(7) JPower (bit bkwd: hld up in tch: hdwy to ld 2 out: pckd last: drvn out)	—	**1**	4/1[3]	74	24
1180[R]	**Dacelo (FR) (95)** (OSherwood) **5-11-5** JOsborne (hld up & bhd: hdwy appr 6th: chsd ldr 8th: swtchd lft appr last: unable qckn)	4	**2**	5/6[1]	71	21
978[3]	**One More Dime (IRE) (70)** (JLNeedham) **6-11-0** BFenton (led: clr 7th: hdd 2 out: one pce)	¾	**3**	12/1	66	16
1052[12]	**Ragdon** (MrsARHewitt) **5-11-5** SWynne (bit bkwd: chsd ldr to 8th: wknd qckly: t.o)	dist	**4**	20/1	—	—
829[3]	**Jon's Choice** (BPreece) **8-11-5** VSlattery (a bhd: pushed along ½-wy: sn t.o)	17	**5**	12/1	—	—
1059[F]	**Set the Fashion** (DLWilliams) **7-11-5v** PHolley (hld up & bhd: lost tch 7th: t.o whn p.u bef 3 out)		**P**	3/1[2]	—	—

(SP 119.7%) **6 Rn**

5m 9.8 (8.80) CSF £8.18 TOTE £5.50: £2.60 £1.00 (£5.10) OWNER Mr P. F. Coombes (SHERBORNE) BRED Miss C. Leigh
Medford has shown some signs of ability in the past, despite being very lightly-raced and, though he was carrying surplus condition here, he was always going too well for the temperamental favourite, and won with quite a bit in hand. (4/1)
1180 Dacelo (FR), patiently ridden, tried to do it all on the bridle but, when switched towards the stands' rail between the last two, he may have seen too much daylight and failed to go through with his effort. (5/6: 4/5-evens)
One More Dime (IRE) enjoys bowling along in front and did not go down without a fight. These forceful tactics will pay off one of these days. (12/1: op 7/1)
829 Jon's Choice (12/1: op 8/1)

1298 HUGH SUMNER H'CAP CHASE (0-105) (5-Y.O+) (Class F)
1-40 (1-40) **2m (13 fncs)** £3,048.00 (£924.00: £452.00: £216.00) GOING minus 0.17 sec per fur (G)

				SP	RR	SF
1076[4]	**Fichu (USA) (72)** (MrsLRichards) **8-10-0** MRichards (bit bkwd: hld up: hdwy 7th: lft clr 3 out: v.easily)	—	**1**	6/1	86+	—
975*	**Fenwick (88)** (RJHodges) **9-10-13**(3) TDascombe (trckd ldrs tl rdn & outpcd 9th: styd on u.p fr 2 out)	11	**2**	2/1[1]	91	—
1041[3]	**Willie Makeit (IRE) (86)** (RTPhillips) **6-11-0** AMaguire (chsd ldrs: rdn & outpcd appr 3 out: sn btn)	2	**3**	11/2	87	—
	Spinning Steel (99) (PRRodford) **9-11-13** SBurrough (bkwd: chsd ldr: blnd 7th: sn lost tch)	2	**4**	4/1[3]	98	6
794[12]	**Chain Shot (77)** (JHPeacock) **11-10-5b** RBellamy (bkwd: a bhd: t.o fr ½-wy)	25	**5**	25/1	51	—

				SP	RR	SF
	Lobster Cottage (88) (KCBailey) **8-11-2** AThornton (bkwd: led & sn clr: mstke 4 out: fell next)		**F**	$9/4^{2}$	—	—

(SP 117.6%) **6 Rn**

4m 1.8 (9.80) CSF £18.50 TOTE £7.40: £2.40 £1.50 (£8.00) OWNER Mr B. Seal (CHICHESTER) BRED Thomas P. Whitney
1076 Fichu (USA), much more effective over this minimum trip, was poised to challenge when left with a clear advantage three out. He was travelling best at the time, so it is doubtful if the result was affected. (6/1)
975* Fenwick dropped out of contention at the end of the back straight and appeared to have run his race, but he stayed on again in the closing stages without being able to get anywhere near the winner. (2/1)
1041 Willie Makeit (IRE) waited on the leaders, but could not respond when the tempo picked up early in the straight. He finds this trip on such a tight track just that bit too sharp for him. (11/2)
Spinning Steel, very keen to get on with it on this seasonal debut, failed to recover from a bad mistake down the back straight. He will be all the better for this spin and should be able to return to winning ways. (4/1: 3/1-9/2)
Lobster Cottage took time to get his jumping right last season and a mistake four out obviously took its toll, for he barely took off at the next and finished in a heap. This run was needed and he deserves a chance to make amends. (9/4)

1299 BLANDFORD BETTING CONDITIONAL (S) H'CAP HURDLE (0-95) (4-Y.O+) (Class G)
2-10 (2-10) **2m (9 hdls)** £2,010.00 (£560.00: £270.00) GOING minus 0.17 sec per fur (G)

				SP	RR	SF
1072*	**Burlington Sam (NZ) (77)** (AGHobbs) **8-10-9**(3) OBurrows (chsd ldr: led after 6th: drvn clr flat)	—	**1**	$7/2^{2}$	62	9
1123^{8}	**Hacketts Cross (IRE) (93)** (PEccles) **8-12-0** PHenley (hld up in rr: hdwy appr 3 out: styd on u.p flat)	3½	**2**	7/1	75	22
1166^{6}	**Twice the Groom (IRE) (86)** (RLee) **6-11-7** GHogan (led to 6th: rdn & ev ch 2 out: one pce)	1¼	**3**	12/1	66	13
949^{7}	**Quick Decision (IRE) (65)** (JKCresswell) **5-9-9**(5) NTEgan (bit bkwd: hld up: hdwy 6th: rdn appr 3 out: one pce)	2½	**4**	50/1	43	—
1174^{9}	**Old Master (IRE) (65)** (RJBaker) **5-10-0** GFRyan (hld up in tch: effrt 6th: rdn 3 out: one pce)	1¼	**5**	33/1	42	—
1088^{9}	**Sir Pageant (70)** (KSBridgwater) **7-10-2b**(3) MGriffiths (chsd ldrs: rdn & wkng whn mstke 2 out)	2½	**6**	33/1	44	—
1166^{3}	**Bresil (USA) (65)** (KRBurke) **7-9-7**(7) MarkBrown (hld up: effrt appr 3 out: nt rch ldrs)	3	**7**	20/1	36	—
879^{7}	**Java Shrine (USA) (69)** (JCTuck) **5-10-4** DFortt (prom: hrd drvn 6th: grad wknd)	½	**8**	5/1	40	—
1086^{5}	**Pytchley Dawn (68)** (OO'Neill) **6-10-3** DJKavanagh (hld up: effrt 6th: sn pushed along: nt rch ldrs)	½	**9**	25/1	38	—
1121^{5}	**Saymore (81)** (WClay) **10-11-2** EHusband (hld up: a in rr)	nk	**10**	$9/2^{3}$	51	—
1253^{8}	**Galloping Guns (IRE) (65)** (BJLlewellyn) **4-10-0** GuyLewis (prom tl wknd after 6th: t.o)	11	**11**	20/1	24	—
868^{P}	**Lustreman (65)** (JHPeacock) **9-10-0** TDascombe (prom: slt ld 6th: sn hdd & wknd: t.o)	dist	**12**	50/1	—	—
1034^{P}	**Bill and Win (78)** (TWall) **5-10-13** GESmith (bkwd: prom to 6th: sn lost pl: t.o)	12	**13**	25/1	—	—
	Tadellal (IRE) (90) (WGMTurner) **5-11-6**(5) JPower (s.s: in rr whn p.u bef 4 out: lame)		**P**	$100/30^{1}$	—	—

(SP 127.4%) **14 Rn**

3m 45.01 (8.01) CSF £28.24 CT £253.09 TOTE £4.10: £1.50 £3.70 £2.90 (£10.50) Trio £39.70 OWNER Mrs Jackie Reip (KINGSBRIDGE) BRED G. H. L. Broughton
LONG HANDICAP Galloping Guns (IRE) 9-12 Lustreman 9-9 Quick Decision (IRE) 9-3 Bresil (USA) 9-7
No bid
OFFICIAL EXPLANATION **Tadellal (IRE): was lame.**
1072* Burlington Sam (NZ) travelled well all the way and had the prize sewn up from some way out. This is certainly his class. (7/2: op 2/1)
749 Hacketts Cross (IRE) would need a stiffer test of stamina on such a fast track, and he was only finding top gear when the race was all but over. (7/1: 5/1-8/1)
950 Twice the Groom (IRE) adopted forceful tactics on this occasion and ran a race full of promise. He could be on the way back. (12/1: op 8/1)
Quick Decision (IRE) did not shape badly from 11lb out of the handicap, but still lacked the pace to get himself into the action. (50/1)
Old Master (IRE) is of little account on what he has shown so far, though this was at least a step in the right direction. (33/1)
Sir Pageant, having a rare outing at the minimum trip, was driven to hold on when a mistake at the penultimate flight stopped him in his tracks. (33/1)
Saymore (9/2: op 10/1)

1300 BATES & HUNT GROUP NOVICES' CHASE (5-Y.O+) (Class D)
2-40 (2-41) **2m 4f (17 fncs)** £3,776.00 (£1,148.00: £564.00: £272.00) GOING minus 0.17 sec per fur (G)

				SP	RR	SF
1254^{5}	**Legal Artist (IRE) (82)** (MissCJohnsey) **6-10-12** LHarvey (hld up in tch: led 12th: clr 3 out: unchal)	—	**1**	5/1	79	4
1041^{P}	**On the Tear (63)** (FLloyd) **10-11-4** SMcNeill (hdwy 5th: ev ch 4 out: one pce fr next)	14	**2**	16/1	74	—
13^{8}	**Dormston Boyo (72)** (TWall) **6-10-5**(7) MrRThornton (led to 2nd: led appr 10th to 12th: ev ch 4 out: wknd next)	1½	**3**	25/1	67	—
887^{P}	**Call Me Albi (IRE) (83)** (MrsLRichards) **5-10-12v** MRichards (hld up & bhd: effrt & rdn appr 4 out: nvr nr ldrs)	1¾	**4**	$7/2^{3}$	66	—
1199^{6}	**Bold Acre** (JMBradley) **6-10-12** RJohnson (bit bkwd: prom tl wknd appr 4 out)	¾	**5**	$5/2^{2}$	65	—
	Seachest (MissVAStephens) **7-10-7** MissVStephens (bkwd: j.w: led 2nd tl appr 10th: sn wknd: t.o)	dist	**6**	20/1	—	—
1039^{11}	**Danzig Island (IRE)** (WJenks) **5-10-12b** TJenks (hld up & bhd: hdwy whn fell 10th)		**F**	$15/8^{1}$	—	—

(SP 116.7%) **7 Rn**

5m 4.7 (12.70) CSF £62.53 TOTE £5.00: £2.40 £4.20 (£36.60) OWNER Mr T. A. Johnsey (CHEPSTOW) BRED D. and P. Magnier in Ireland
WEIGHT FOR AGE 5yo-1lb
72 Legal Artist (IRE), winning his first race since the 1993/94 season, did not need to extend himself unduly to beat these second-raters. (5/1)
828* On the Tear was on the heels of the leaders four out but, once the pace lifted, he was left in no man's land. (16/1)
Dormston Boyo, sharpened up by an outing on the Flat last week, helped share the pacemaking until outpaced over the last three.(25/1)
472 Call Me Albi (IRE), given a very patient ride, could not respond when popped the question on the home turn, but he did stay on to secure the minor prize right on the line. (7/2)
Danzig Island (IRE), given time to adapt on this chasing debut, had just got himself into the action when turning a somersault starting the final circuit. (15/8)

1301 E.B.F. 'N.H.' QUALIFIER NOVICES' HURDLE (4, 5 & 6-Y.O) (Class E)
3-10 (3-10) **2m (9 hdls)** £2,262.00 (£632.00: £306.00) GOING minus 0.17 sec per fur (G)

				SP	RR	SF
	Lady Peta (IRE) (103) (NJHenderson) **6-11-0** MAFitzgerald (lw: hld up: stdy hdwy 4th: led on bit appr last: rdn out)	—	**1**	$4/5^{1}$	74	29
1044^{3}	**Darakshan (IRE)** (MissHCKnight) **4-11-0** JFTitley (led: clr 4th: hdd appr last: rallied u.p nr fin)	nk	**2**	$5/4^{2}$	74	29
	Welsh Loot (IRE) (OSherwood) **5-11-0** JOsborne (bit bkwd: chsd ldr: hit 4th: lost tch appr 3 out)	17	**3**	$11/1^{3}$	57	12
	Optimistic Affair (AStreeter) **5-11-0** TEley (bkwd: prom tl outpcd appr 3 out)	½	**4**	50/1	56	11

980[13] **Deference Due (IRE)** (RJPrice) **5-11-0** AThornton (a bhd: t.o fr 6th)....dist **5** 100/1 — —
(SP 111.3%) **5 Rn**

3m 41.2 (4.20) CSF £2.12 TOTE £1.60: £1.00 £3.30 (£1.50) OWNER Mr B. M. Collins (LAMBOURN) BRED Mrs M. Farrell
Lady Peta (IRE) did not have a great deal to beat and he looked as though he would win on the bridle, but he was beginning to tie up on reaching the flat and was all on to hold on at the finish. (4/5)
1044 Darakshan (IRE) has got plenty of speed, which is surprising for one who won a two-mile bumper, and an attempt to gallop the opposition into the ground almost succeeded. He should not have much trouble in winning at this game. (5/4)
Welsh Loot (IRE) (11/1: 6/1-12/1)

1302 TOTE CREDIT H'CAP CHASE (0-115) (5-Y.O+) (Class E)

3-40 (3-40) **3m (19 fncs)** £3,501.25 (£1,060.00: £517.50: £246.25) GOING minus 0.17 sec per fur (G)

			SP	RR	SF
	Lord of the West (IRE) (90) (JJO'Neill) **7-10-8** AMaguire (bit bkwd: j.w: hld up & bhd: stdy hdy fr ½-wy: led 2 out: sn clr: impressive)....—	**1**	5/2[2]	105+	45
1054[3]	**Father Sky (110)** (OSherwood) **5-11-12b[1]** JOsborne (a.p: rdn 14th: styd on fr 2 out)....8	**2**	9/2[3]	120	58
1057[3]	**Rainbow Castle (107)** (PFNicholls) **9-11-11** APMcCoy (j.w: led: pushed along appr 4 out: hdd 2 out: sn btn)..4	**3**	5/6[1]	114	54
799[P]	**Corrarder (110)** (JGSmyth-Osbourne) **12-12-0** WMarston (bkwd: chsd ldr fr 4th to 8th: wknd 14th: t.o)....dist	**4**	12/1	—	—
1057[F]	**Mutual Trust (95)** (PBowen) **12-10-13** RJohnson (chsd ldrs tl blnd & lost pl 7th: bhd whn p.u bef 10th)....	**P**	12/1	—	—

(SP 116.7%) **5 Rn**

5m 59.6 (-0.40) CSF £13.15 TOTE £4.00: £1.50 £2.00 (£6.50) OWNER Anne Duchess of Westminster (PENRITH) BRED Christy Fitzgerald
WEIGHT FOR AGE 5yo-2lb
Lord of the West (IRE) put his point-to-point experience to good use to open his account over regulation fences under a very good ride. As he will be much sharper with this run under his belt, he ought to be able to go on from here. (5/2)
1054 Father Sky was unable to concede so much weight to the winner, even with the added bonus of blinkers for the first time, but he did nothing wrong, and there could be another race to be won. (9/2: op 11/4)
1057 Rainbow Castle runs best when produced from off the pace and his attempt to make all had come to an end at the penultimate obstacle. (5/6)
Corrarder (12/1: 7/1-14/1)

1303 SHOBDON INTERMEDIATE CLAIMING N.H. FLAT RACE (4, 5 & 6-Y.O) (Class H)

4-10 (4-10) **2m** £1,305.60 (£361.60: £172.80)

			SP	RR	SF
	Poppy's Dream (JWharton) **6-10-1**(7) MrRThornton (bit bkwd: hld up: hdwy 6f out: led over 3f out: clr appr fnl f)....—	**1**	5/1[2]	—	—
865[12]	**A S Jim** (OO'Neill) **5-10-4**(5) DJKavanagh (hld up: hdwy 4f out: rdn & veered bdly lft over 1f out: no imp)......20	**2**	6/1[3]	—	—
	Forofivetwohundred (IRE) (MCPipe) **6-10-12**(7) GSupple (bkwd: led after 2f: clr after 6f: rdn 7f out: hdd over 3f out: sn btn)....6	**3**	6/1[3]	—	—
	Daydream Believer (MSalaman) **4-10-3**(7) NTEgan (hld up: hdwy ½-wy: wnt 2nd briefly 5f out: sn drvn along & wknd)....18	**4**	12/1	—	—
980[12]	**Syban** (BPreece) **5-9-12**(7) MissLBoswell (bit bkwd: a bhd: t.o fr ½-wy)....10	**5**	50/1	—	—
1151[2]	**Ditopero** (WGMTurner) **4-10-2**(7) JPower (led 2f: chsd ldr tl wknd 5f out: sn t.o)....22	**6**	8/13[1]	—	—

(SP 116.8%) **6 Rn**

3m 39.1 CSF £31.27 TOTE £6.90: £3.30 £8.50 (£10.90) OWNER Mr John Wharton (MELTON MOWBRAY) BRED Mrs M. Mann
Poppy's Dream looked as though the run was needed on this debut, but she outclassed the opposition without too much trouble and won this poor contest with the minimum of fuss. (5/1)
A S Jim, staying on but making very little impression when almost going through the stands' rail below the distance, may well improve in time. (6/1)
Forofivetwohundred (IRE), a big, backward, cumbersome gelding who should make a chaser in time, did not have an easy introduction to racing and almost certainly set too fast a pace, which in the end proved his undoing. (6/1: op 5/2)
Daydream Believer (12/1: op 6/1)
1151 Ditopero took the leader on and the pair of them were soon twenty lengths clear, but the plan backfired and they only succeeded in beating themselves. (8/13)

T/Plpt: £37.90 (229.3 Tckts). T/Qdpt: £24.00 (34.61 Tckts). IM

1078-SEDGEFIELD (L-H) (Good, Good to firm patches)

Tuesday November 12th

WEATHER: fine but cloudy

1304 JOHN WADE HAULAGE (S) H'CAP HURDLE (0-95) (4-Y.O+) (Class G)

12-50 (12-50) **3m 3f 110y (13 hdls)** £1,877.00 (£522.00: £251.00) GOING: 0.08 sec per fur (G)

			SP	RR	SF
1078[4]	**Top Skipper (IRE) (63)** (MartynWane) **4-10-0** ASSmith (in tch: chsd ldrs fr 8th: led 2 out: hung rt: rdn out) ...—	**1**	10/1	47	14
1040[6]	**Snowy Lane (IRE) (64)** (JNeville) **8-10-2hb** NWilliamson (led 2nd to 2 out: n.m.r & swtchd appr last: mstke last: styd on towards fin)....½	**2**	7/1[3]	48	16
1152[9]	**Blanc Seing (FR) (74)** (JESwiers) **9-10-12b** MrSSwiers (hdwy & prom 8th: ev ch appr 2 out: rdn & nt qckn)....5	**3**	9/1	55	23
1143[5]	**D'Arblay Street (IRE) (86)** (WTKemp) **7-11-10b** SMcDougall (chsd ldrs: chal 6th tl rdn & btn appr 2 out)........8	**4**	11/8[1]	62	30
1139[7]	**Barnstormer (63)** (EAElliott) **10-10-1** DParker (hdwy & prom 8th: outpcd & wknd fr 4 out)....dist	**5**	14/1	—	—
289[9]	**Tharsis (72)** (WJSmith) **11-10-5**(5) STaylor (bhd: rdn 8th: sn t.o)....7	**6**	10/1	—	—
937[6]	**Overwhelm (IRE) (72)** (VThompson) **8-10-10b**ow3 MrMThompson (prom tl drvn along & wknd 7th: sn t.o) ...dist	**7**	50/1	—	—
1082[3]	**Jendee (IRE) (83)** (BEllison) **8-11-4**(3) GCahill (prom: blnd 5th: sn lost pl: p.u bef 9th)....	**P**	5/2[2]	—	—
893[7]	**Dark Midnight (IRE) (62)** (DALamb) **7-10-0** BHarding (rdn 8th: sn wknd: wl t.o whn p.u bef 3 out)....	**P**	20/1	—	—
	Arthur Bee (62) (BBousfield) **9-9-11**(3) GLee (led to 2nd: lost tch 8th: wl t.o whn p.u bef 3 out)....	**P**	33/1	—	—

(SP 127.7%) **10 Rn**

6m 50.3 (15.30) CSF £77.58 CT £616.01 TOTE £13.40: £2.20 £1.70 £1.80 (£15.90) Trio £66.60 OWNER Mrs H. H. Wane (RICHMOND) BRED G. J. Cullinan
LONG HANDICAP Dark Midnight (IRE) 9-8 Arthur Bee 9-13
WEIGHT FOR AGE 4yo-1lb
Bt in 3,000 gns

STEWARDS' ENQUIRY Obj. to Top Skipper by Williamson overruled.
OFFICIAL EXPLANATION Jendee (IRE): was later found to be suffering from back problems.
1078 Top Skipper (IRE) appreciated this big step up in trip and, despite hanging right in the closing stages, was always doing just enough. (10/1)
Snowy Lane (IRE) stays forever but is slow. After being intimidated by the winner, he was switched going to the last and a poor jump probably made all the difference. (7/1)
876 Blanc Seing (FR), trying a much longer trip, had his chances until running out of stamina from the second last. (9/1)
1143 D'Arblay Street (IRE) would have picked this lot up and carried them at his best, but he was not quite up to it. (11/8: evens-6/4)
Barnstormer has lost his form altogether for the time being. (14/1)
1082 Jendee (IRE), switched back to hurdling presumably to regain his confidence, again wanted nothing to do with it. (5/2)

1305 HENNESSY COGNAC SPECIAL SERIES NOVICES' HURDLE (4-Y.O+) (Class B)

1-20 (1-20) **2m 1f (8 hdls)** £5,654.00 (£1,712.00: £836.00: £398.00) GOING: 0.08 sec per fur (G)

				SP	RR	SF
505*	**Brambles Way (103)** (MrsMReveley) **7-11-0b** PNiven (in tch: smooth hdwy to ld between last 2: shkn up & qcknd flat)	—	**1**	8/1	79+	28
1020*	**Contrafire (IRE) (108)** (MrsASwinbank) **4-11-0** JSupple (lw: led: clr fr 2nd: hit 5th: hdd between last 2: one pce)	4	**2**	4/5^{1}	75	24
1049*	**Suas Leat (IRE) (102)** (JMJefferson) **6-11-4** MNewton (a.p: effrt 3 out: one pce fr next)	10	**3**	9/2^{2}	70	19
	Bollin Frank (TDEasterby) **4-11-0** LWyer (plld hrd: chsd ldr: ev ch 3 out: wknd appr next)	8	**4**	11/2^{3}	58	7
	Fassan (IRE) (105) (MDHammond) **4-11-0** RGarritty (bit bkwd: in tch: effrt 5th: wknd fr next)	7	**5**	9/2^{2}	52	1
	Oneoftheoldones (JNorton) **4-11-0** DerekByrne (plld hrd: bhd & wkng whn fell 3 out)		**F**	33/1	—	—
1020^{6}	**Homecrest** (BEllison) **4-11-0** GCahill (lost tch fr 5th: p.u bef 2 out)		**P**	33/1	—	—
1141^{7}	**Barik (IRE)** (BMactaggart) **6-11-0** BStorey (lw: lost tch fr 5th: p.u bef 2 out)		**P**	33/1	—	—
1052^{11}	**Selectric (IRE)** (JWade) **5-11-0** KJones (t.o fr 3rd: p.u bef 2 out)		**P**	50/1	—	—
				(SP 129.2%)	**9 Rn**	

4m 4.0 (9.00) CSF £16.11 TOTE £6.00: £1.50 £1.10 £1.70 (£7.90) Trio £5.50 OWNER Mr Nigel Jones (SALTBURN) BRED W. P. S. Johnson
505* Brambles Way was suited by the strong pace and, although always tending to hang left, he had a bit more up his sleeve. (8/1)
1020* Contrafire (IRE) tried to gallop the opposition into the ground, but his hurdling was never that fluent and he was comfortably picked off going to the last. (4/5: evens-5/4)
1049* Suas Leat (IRE) is a game and consistent sort, but he was always finding this company just too good. (9/2)
Bollin Frank raced a bit too freely early on and, after chasing the winner, failed to see out the trip. (11/2)
Fassan (IRE), looking likely to be all the better for this, had been found out by the third last. (9/2)

1306 RACING CHANNEL H'CAP CHASE (0-110) (5-Y.O+) (Class E)

1-50 (1-50) **2m 110y (13 fncs)** £2,922.50 (£875.00: £420.00: £192.50) GOING: 0.08 sec per fur (G)

				SP	RR	SF
1035^{4}	**Full O'Praise (NZ) (100)** (PCalver) **9-12-0** LWyer (a cl up: led 9th: all out)	—	**1**	11/2^{3}	109	15
1083^{U}	**Val de Rama (IRE) (89)** (DenysSmith) **7-11-3** PNiven (lw: bhd: mstke 8th: hdwy appr 2 out: r.o: too much to do)	1½	**2**	5/1^{2}	97	3
1164^{2}	**Thunderstruck (82)** (HowardJohnson) **10-10-10** NWilliamson (led to 2nd: cl up: hmpd 5th: one pce fr 4 out)	16	**3**	5/2^{1}	74	—
975^{4}	**Master Salesman (72)** (MrsVCWard) **13-10-0** DParker (bhd: sme hdwy fr 4 out: n.d)	11	**4**	25/1	53	—
1140^{4}	**Flash of Realm (FR) (96)** (BMactaggart) **10-11-10v** BStorey (nvr wnt pce)	¾	**5**	8/1	77	—
	Port in a Storm (88) (MDHammond) **7-10-13**$^{(3)}$ MrCBonner (nvr trbld ldrs)	9	**6**	12/1	60	—
	Parson's Lodge (IRE) (79) (LLungo) **8-10-7** MFoster (bit bkwd: cl up: blnd 4th: fell next)		**F**	12/1	—	—
1146^{2}	**Circulation (72)** (DMcCain) **10-9-11v**$^{(3)}$ DWalsh (lw: led 2nd: blnd 8th: hdd next: 6l 2nd & wkng whn fell 2 out)		**F**	5/1^{2}	—	—
951^{5}	**Shrewd John (92)** (RDEWoodhouse) **10-11-6b^{1}** MDwyer (a bhd: p.u bef 3 out)		**P**	7/1	—	—
				(SP 120.1%)	**9 Rn**	

4m 13.2 (15.20) CSF £32.08 CT £79.39 TOTE £8.20: £2.60 £1.30 £1.40 (£15.30) Trio £13.20 OWNER Lord Zetland (RIPON) BRED Cranbrook Stables Ltd
LONG HANDICAP Circulation 9-12 Master Salesman 9-8
1035 Full O'Praise (NZ), well suited by the frenetic pace, had stolen just enough of an advantage by the second last to last home. (11/2)
897 Val de Rama (IRE) found it happening far too quickly for his liking and made the odd mistake but, as the leaders tired late on, he picked up well. (5/1)
1164 Thunderstruck, up with the strong pace as normal, was struggling by the fourth last and treading water thereafter. (5/2)
975 Master Salesman found the pace too fast for his liking, but did make a little late progress. (25/1)
1140 Flash of Realm (FR) found the pace far too strong. (8/1)
1146 Circulation set his usual break-neck pace until a blunder steadied him at the eighth, and he was out on his feet, although still in second, when failing to take off at the penultimate fence. (5/1)

1307 DICK BREWITT MEMORIAL H'CAP CHASE (0-100) (5-Y.O+) (Class F)

2-20 (2-20) **3m 3f (21 fncs)** £2,838.00 (£849.00: £407.00: £186.00) GOING: 0.08 sec per fur (G)

				SP	RR	SF
1122^{U}	**Ivy House (IRE) (92)** (JJO'Neill) **8-11-9** MDwyer (hld up: smooth hdwy fr 15th: led 2 out: sn clr: easily)	—	**1**	2/1^{1}	103	27
1162*	**Aly Daley (IRE) (104)** (HowardJohnson) **8-12-7** ^{7x} NWilliamson (lw: led to 14th: sn drvn along: kpt on fr 3 out: no ch w wnr)	3½	**2**	4/1^{2}	113	37
1082^{2}	**Ole Ole (84)** (MrsEMoscrop) **10-11-1** LWyer (prom: mstke 8th & sn bhd: styd on fr 4 out: no imp)	½	**3**	13/2	93	17
	Call the Shots (IRE) (90) (JWade) **7-11-7** KJones (w ldr: blnd 13th: led next to 4 out: one pce)	1	**4**	7/1	98	22
875*	**Scrabo View (IRE) (96)** (PBeaumont) **8-11-13b** RSupple (chsd ldrs tl outpcd fr 16th)	8	**5**	7/1	99	23
1164*	**Blazing Dawn (91)** (JSHubbuck) **9-11-8** ^{7x} BStorey (in tch: hdwy on bit to ld 4 out: hdd & wknd qckly 2 out)	2	**6**	11/2^{3}	93	17
1142^{7}	**Gala Water (86)** (TDCDun) **10-11-3** TReed (mstkes: prom: ev ch 16th tl mstke & rdr lost irons 4 out: p.u bef last)		**P**	9/1	—	—
1063^{4}	**Foxgrove (77)** (RJPrice) **10-10-8** RichardGuest (bhd: effrt 13th: sn rdn & wknd: p.u bef 2 out)		**P**	14/1	—	—
				(SP 123.7%)	**8 Rn**	

7m 5.5 (19.50) CSF £11.05 CT £42.54 TOTE £2.70: £1.10 £1.80 £1.80 (£5.90) OWNER Mrs L. R. Joughin (PENRITH) BRED Miss Penny Downes
1122 Ivy House (IRE) is good when he gets it right. He did it on the bridle here. (2/1)
1162* Aly Daley (IRE) had a hard race last time and, despite battling gamely, was made to look very ordinary by the winner. (4/1)
1082 Ole Ole lost his place after a mistake early on and also lost a shoe. He then confirmed his promise of last time by eating up ground late on. (13/2)

Call the Shots (IRE), from a yard right out of form, ran well, but had given his best by the fourth last. (7/1)
875* Scrabo View (IRE) had his chances, but did not look happy from a long way out, and finally cried enough five from home. (7/1)
1164* Blazing Dawn was back to his old tricks, sailing through on the bridle, only to stop as though shot two out. He obviously has some sort of problem. (11/2)
Gala Water found this track too sharp and made mistakes. After a particularly bad one four out, an iron broke and she was eventually pulled up. (9/1)

1308 JOHN HELLENS NOVICES' CHASE (4-Y.O+) (Class E)

2-50 (2-50) **2m 5f (16 fncs)** £2,945.25 (£882.00: £423.50: £194.25) GOING: 0.08 sec per fur (G)

				SP	RR	SF
1028^{3}	**Cader Idris** (MrsMReveley) **7-11-4** PNiven (lw: led tl mstke & hdd 9th: lft in ld 3 out: hit last: styd on)	—	**1**	6/1^{2}	83	7
1153^{8}	**Final Beat (IRE) (82)** (JWCurtis) **7-11-4b^{1}** LWyer (chsd ldrs tl outpcd 10th: styd on fr 2 out: nvr able to chal)	4	**2**	6/1^{2}	80	4
1161^{5}	**Fingerhill (IRE)** (VThompson) **7-11-4** MrMThompson (a.p: effrt: hmpd & mstke 4 out: rdn & btn 2 out)	19	**3**	33/1	66	—
1083^{6}	**The Energiser (67)** (DALamb) **10-11-4** JBurke (chsd ldrs tl wknd fr 11th)	26	**4**	50/1	46	—
1028^{U}	**Uncle Keeny (IRE)** (JJO'Neill) **6-11-4** MDwyer (lw: cl up: blnd 7th: p.u lame bef 10th)		**P**	4/7^{1}	—	—
	Dear Jean (MESowersby) **6-10-13** DParker (mstke 6th: sn outpcd & t.o: p.u bef 11th)		**P**	20/1^{3}	—	—
1022^{5}	**Dawn Lad (IRE)** (MrsASwinbank) **7-11-4** JSupple (lw: hdwy & prom whn blnd & uns rdr 11th)		**U**	6/1^{2}	—	—
1124^{10}	**High Handed (IRE)** (THCaldwell) **5-10-12**(5) STaylor (bhd: hit 4th: shkn up & gd hdwy to ld 9th: 3l clr whn blnd & uns rdr 3 out)		**U**	50/1	—	—
				(SP 118.1%)		**8 Rn**

5m 30.4 (19.40) CSF £39.15 TOTE £4.10: £1.40 £1.70 £1.60 (£7.90) OWNER Mr D. R. Wellicome (SALTBURN) BRED D. R. Wellicome
WEIGHT FOR AGE 5yo-1lb
1028 Cader Idris appeared lucky, but this game is all about getting round in one piece, and that is all that was needed for him. (6/1)
746 Final Beat (IRE) gave the impression that longer trips might be the answer. (6/1)
1161 Fingerhill (IRE), although very tired at the finish, did show something and may well pick up a race in due course. (33/1)
The Energiser has very little to recommend him. (50/1)
1028 Uncle Keeny (IRE), despite one bad mistake, was on the bridle when going lame entering the back straight. (4/7)
Dawn Lad (IRE) was responding well to driving and bang in contention when getting it all wrong at the sixth last. (6/1)
High Handed (IRE) is a most ungainly-looking sort, but he suddenly picked up after a couple of reminders with a circuit to go and was some three lengths clear and galloping on strongly when he stepped at the third last, giving his rider no chance of staying aboard. (50/1)

1309 STANLEY RACING NOVICES' HURDLE (4-Y.O+) (Class E)

3-20 (3-20) **2m 5f 110y (10 hdls)** £2,285.00 (£635.00: £305.00) GOING: 0.08 sec per fur (G)

				SP	RR	SF
1021^{2}	**Ela Mata (98)** (MrsASwinbank) **4-11-5** JRailton (lw: hdwy ½-wy: led 6th & qcknd: hit 3 out: styd on u.p appr last)	—	**1**	3/1^{2}	75	22
1052*	**Duraid (IRE)** (DenysSmith) **4-10-12** RichardGuest (lw: hld up: gd hdwy 4 out: chal on bit next: rdn appr last: fnd nil)	7	**2**	4/6^{1}	63+	10
866^{4}	**Jills Joy (IRE)** (JNorton) **5-10-9**(3) GLee (prom: outpcd 4 out: kpt on fr 2 out: no imp)	2½	**3**	25/1	61	8
1049^{4}	**Silly Money (90)** (TDEasterby) **5-10-12** LWyer (cl up: led 3rd to 6th: rdn & wknd after 3 out)	10	**4**	4/1^{3}	54	1
1180^{3}	**Culrain (78)** (THCaldwell) **5-11-0**(5) STaylor (prom tl outpcd appr 4 out: sn bhd: t.o)	dist	**5**	12/1	—	—
	Alicat (IRE) (JWCurtis) **5-10-12** RGarritty (led to 1st: chsd ldrs tl wknd qckly 5th: t.o whn p.u bef 2 out)		**P**	50/1	—	—
	Rustic Warrior (JWade) **6-10-12** KJones (plld hrd: led 1st to 3rd: t.o fr 6th: p.u bef 3 out)		**P**	100/1	—	—
				(SP 119.5%)		**7 Rn**

5m 14.5 (14.50) CSF £5.57 TOTE £4.70: £2.00 £1.10 (£2.20) OWNER Mr F. J. Sainsbury (RICHMOND) BRED Darley Stud Management Co Ltd
1021 Ela Mata, well suited by this type of track, really stepped on the pace in the back straight, and plain and simply outstayed the favourite. (3/1: op 2/1)
1052* Duraid (IRE) hurdled brilliantly and, after improving four out, it looked a question of when and how far. His stamina suddenly gave out though going to the last, and it was also later reported that he had lost a shoe during the race. (4/6)
Jills Joy (IRE) looked one-paced, but he does stay well. (25/1)
1049 Silly Money, trying a longer trip, proved disappointing and failed to get home. (4/1)
1180 Culrain, as his form suggested, was not up to this. (12/1: op 8/1)

1310 LEVY BOARD H'CAP HURDLE (0-105) (4-Y.O+ F & M) (Class F)

3-50 (3-50) **2m 5f 110y (10 hdls)** £1,987.50 (£550.00: £262.50) GOING: 0.08 sec per fur (G)

				SP	RR	SF
1046^{U}	**Tigh-Na-Mara (86)** (JMJefferson) **8-10-7**(7) MNewton (lw: hld up: gd hdwy 4 out: led appr 2 out: styd on)	—	**1**	5/2^{2}	71	10
1121^{6}	**Marsden Rock (82)** (NBMason) **9-10-3**(7) SHaworth (trckd ldrs: chal 3 out: rdn & nt qckn fr next)	6	**2**	7/1	63	2
1130^{4}	**Smart Approach (IRE) (90)** (MrsMReveley) **6-11-4** PNiven (lw: w ldrs: led 4 out tl appr 2 out: 3rd & btn whn blnd last)	2	**3**	13/8^{1}	69	8
	Chadwick's Ginger (100) (WHTinning) **8-11-7**(7) BGrattan (lw: chsd ldrs: led 5th to 4 out: sn outpcd: kpt on towards fin)	4	**4**	9/2^{3}	76	15
	Millies Image (72) (FPMurtagh) **5-10-0** RSupple (led to 5th: outpcd next: n.d after)	dist	**5**	8/1	—	—
1247^{6}	**Helens Bay (IRE) (81)** (VThompson) **6-10-9** MrMThompson (chsd ldrs tl outpcd fr 6th)	2½	**6**	20/1	—	—
1049^{8}	**Storming Lorna (IRE) (72)** (WMcKeown) **6-9-11**(3) GCahill (bhd: effrt 4 out: sn btn: p.u bef 2 out)		**P**	25/1	—	—
				(SP 117.1%)		**7 Rn**

5m 16.9 (16.90) CSF £19.00 TOTE £4.10: £1.40 £3.30 (£10.90) OWNER Mr Bryan Gordon (MALTON) BRED Bryan Gordon
LONG HANDICAP Millies Image 9-7 Storming Lorna (IRE) 9-9
866 Tigh-Na-Mara both looked and travelled well, and was always on top from the second last. (5/2)
893 Marsden Rock raced with every chance but, when it came down to a fight, she was found wanting. (7/1)
1130 Smart Approach (IRE) helped force the pace, but was struggling some way out and a blunder at the last made no difference. (13/8)
Chadwick's Ginger seems to have lost her dash these days at this game and may do better if returning to the bigger obstacles. (9/2)
Millies Image (8/1: op 12/1)

T/Plpt: £43.10 (212.01 Tckts). T/Qdpt: £5.50 (194.97 Tckts). AA

1138-KELSO (L-H) (Good)
Wednesday November 13th

Race 5 - two fences omitted
WEATHER: fine

1311 SCOTTISH SPORTS AID FOUNDATION NOVICES' H'CAP CHASE (0-100) (5-Y.O+) (Class E)

1-10 (1-10) **2m 1f (12 fncs)** £3,048.00 (£924.00: £452.00: £216.00) GOING minus 0.29 sec per fur (GF)

				SP	RR	SF
1049[5]	**Monyman (IRE) (92)** (MDHammond) **6-11-13** RGarritty (lw: j.w: hld up: hdwy 7th: led flat: rdn & r.o)	—	1	13/8[1]	103	24
1248[2]	**Ballyline (IRE) (86)** (WTKemp) **5-11-7** MDwyer (led 2nd tl flat: kpt on wl)	1½	2	15/8[2]	96	17
1083[2]	**Le Denstan (84)** (MrsDThomson) **9-11-5** TReed (hld up: smooth hdwy 8th: ev ch last: rdn & nt qckn)	2½	3	7/2[3]	91	12
1160[5]	**Quixall Crossett (65)** (EMCaine) **11-9-9**(5) STaylor (outpcd 7th: styd on fr 2 out: no imp)	14	4	100/1	59	—
1081[2]	**Twin Falls (IRE) (93)** (GMMoore) **5-12-0** JCallaghan (hld up & bhd: pushed along 4 out: n.d)	5	5	9/1	82	3
1138[5]	**Alicharger (65)** (PMonteith) **6-9-11**(3) GCahill (led to 2nd: cl up: hit 5th: rdn appr 7th: sn outpcd)	2	6	33/1	53	—
1164[U]	**Monaughty Man (85)** (EMCaine) **10-11-6** MrPMurray (chsd ldrs tl outpcd 3 out: wknd fr next)	2½	7	66/1	70	—
				(SP 110.5%)		**7 Rn**

4m 14.5 (7.50) CSF £4.77 TOTE £2.50: £2.30 £1.30 (£2.60) OWNER Mr Trevor Hemmings (MIDDLEHAM) BRED Lady Naylor Leyland
LONG HANDICAP Alicharger 9-12 Quixall Crossett 9-5
1049 Monyman (IRE) is a natural at this game and better looks likely as he tries further. (13/8)
1248 Ballyline (IRE), ridden from the front this time, did little wrong other than meet a very useful opponent. (15/8)
1083 Le Denstan, dropped back in trip, went really well throughout the race, but just saw too much daylight too soon. (7/2)
1160 Quixall Crossett is a good, honest sort, but he was far too slow for this trip. (100/1)
1081 Twin Falls (IRE), at his first attempt over fences, had an educational, but there is still something to learn. This trip was also on the short side. (9/1: 4/1-12/1)

1312 SCOTDISC LINE DANCER NOVICES' HURDLE (4-Y.O+) (Class E)

1-40 (1-40) **2m 110y (8 hdls)** £2,388.00 (£668.00: £324.00) GOING minus 0.07 sec per fur (G)

				SP	RR	SF
	Del Piero (IRE) (MDHammond) **5-10-12** RGarritty (lw: hld up: hdwy 3 out: styd on to ld fnl 100y)	—	1	6/1	66	10
1030[5]	**Kilnamartyra Girl (87)** (JParkes) **6-10-7** PNiven (trckd ldrs: led after 2 out & qcknd: hung lft flat: hdd fnl 100y)	nk	2	7/1	61	5
1152[3]	**Mithraic (IRE) (102)** (WSCunningham) **4-10-12**(7) LMcGrath (t: lw: plld hrd: trckd ldrs: outpcd & nt clr run 3 out: swtchd wd & styd on: nt pce to chal)	6	3	2/1[1]	67	11
939[10]	**Lumback Lady** (BMactaggart) **6-10-4**(3) GLee (in tch: hdwy & ch 2 out: nt qckn flat)	½	4	100/1	54	—
937[2]	**Teacher (IRE)** (RAllan) **6-10-12** BHarding (led after 3rd tl after 2 out: sn outpcd)	3	5	4/1[3]	57	1
	Callernish Dan (IRE) (MartinTodhunter) **6-10-12** MDwyer (lw: trckd ldrs: mstke & outpcd 3 out: no imp after)	11	6	7/2[2]	46	—
1161[7]	**Noble Monarch (IRE)** (HowardJohnson) **7-10-12** NWilliamson (stdd s: bhd tl effrt 3 out: btn appr last)	2	7	16/1	44	—
1033[3]	**Lepton (IRE)** (JWCurtis) **5-10-12** LWyer (led 2nd tl after 3rd: w ldrs tl wknd 2 out)	2½	8	10/1	42	—
	My Missile (RGCockburn) **6-10-7** LO'Hara (led to 2nd: lost tch 5th: sn t.o)	dist	9	100/1	—	—
1020[8]	**Regal Domain (IRE)** (MrsLMarshall) **5-10-12** DBentley (wl bhd fr 4th: t.o)	dist	10	66/1	—	—
				(SP 120.8%)		**10 Rn**

3m 55.9 (9.90) CSF £45.24 TOTE £7.60: £1.90 £2.40 £1.50 (£17.40) Trio £18.50 OWNER Mr Frank Hanson (MIDDLEHAM) BRED Mrs M. Dunny
STEWARDS' ENQUIRY Todhunter fined £85 under Rule 150(i) (horse late into paddock).
Del Piero (IRE) has run in bumpers in Ireland and acquitted himself well at his first attempt over hurdles here. He ran as though he should get further. (6/1)
Kilnamartyra Girl, yet to win a race over hurdles, certainly has the ability, but threw this away by hanging left after the last. (7/1)
1152 Mithraic (IRE), in a messy race, got messed about when making his effort and was then tapped for toe in the final sprint. (2/1)
Lumback Lady improved considerably on her previous run and ought to be able to win a race. (100/1)
937 Teacher (IRE), not really suited by this slow early pace, pulled his way to the front and could well also need further. (4/1)
Callernish Dan (IRE) looked in good trim, but ran most disappointingly, finding little when the pace hotted up. (7/2)
Noble Monarch (IRE) is showing signs of improvement. (16/1)

1313 ASHLEYBANK INVESTMENTS REG TWEEDIE NOVICES' CHASE (5-Y.O+) (Class D)

2-10 (2-10) **3m 1f (19 fncs)** £4,182.00 (£1,266.00: £618.00: £294.00) GOING minus 0.29 sec per fur (GF)

				SP	RR	SF
1160[3]	**Trickle Lad (IRE)** (FMurphy) **7-11-0** NWilliamson (lw: hld up & bhd: effrt 14th: hdwy 4 out: led flat: r.o u.p)	—	1	5/2[1]	90	23
1142[8]	**Tighter Budget (USA) (103)** (MrsDianneSayer) **9-12-4** MMoloney (lw: j.rt: led: blnd 3 out: hdd flat: kpt on u.p)	1½	2	7/2[2]	107	40
734[4]	**Tough Test (IRE)** (MrsJDGoodfellow) **6-10-11**(3) GCahill (chsd ldrs: blnd 15th: chal 2 out: outpcd appr last: kpt on flat)	s.h	3	7/2[2]	89	22
1138*	**Seeking Gold (IRE) (79)** (JBarclay) **7-11-1** BStorey (chsd ldrs tl outpcd fr 3 out)	8	4	5/1[3]	85	18
1153[5]	**Cool Weather (IRE) (86)** (PCheesbrough) **8-11-0** RSupple (chsd ldrs: hit 5th: effrt 4 out: wknd appr last)	2	5	11/2	83	16
	Strongalong (IRE) (PCheesbrough) **6-11-0** TReed (mstke 7th: sn wl bhd)	30	6	50/1	63	—
				(SP 107.0%)		**6 Rn**

6m 17.3 (7.30) CSF £10.39 TOTE £2.60: £1.40 £1.60 (£3.60) OWNER Mrs H. F. Prendergast (MIDDLEHAM) BRED J. K. Magee
1160 Trickle Lad (IRE) did the business this time, but it was never easy. He gave the impression that he should come on further with the run. (5/2: op 6/4)
1142 Tighter Budget (USA) gave a lot of ground away by continually jumping right. A right-handed track should help solve that. (7/2)
734 Tough Test (IRE) put in a decent first effort over fences here and kept galloping in when looking in trouble. (7/2)
1138* Seeking Gold (IRE) is honest but slow, and was always tapped for speed here. (5/1)
1153 Cool Weather (IRE) has been trying to win a chase for two years and has the ability but never fully comes up with the goods. (11/2)

1314 GLENMUIR SPORTSWEAR H'CAP HURDLE (0-125) (4-Y.O+) (Class D)

2-40 (2-41) **2m 2f (10 hdls)** £2,736.00 (£828.00: £404.00: £192.00) GOING minus 0.07 sec per fur (G)

				SP	RR	SF
1079[2]	**Adamatic (IRE) (96)** (RAllan) **5-10-0** LWyer (lw: trckd ldr: hit 6th: led flat: hung lft: all out)	—	1	5/2[1]	79	—

Stash the Cash (IRE) (98) (MDHammond) **5-10-2** DBentley (hld up: stdy hdwy 3 out: ev ch flat: styd on towards fin) ... ½ **2** 3/1 [2] 81 —

1025* **Field of Vision (IRE) (104)** (MrsASwinbank) **6-10-8** JSupple (lw: trckd ldrs: outpcd appr 4 out: rdn to chal 2 out: nt qckn flat) ... 2½ **3** 5/2 [1] 84 —

1144[5] **Well Appointed (IRE) (97)** (BMactaggart) **7-9-12**(3) GLee (lw: led: qcknd appr 6th: hdd flat: no ex) ... ½ **4** 9/1 77 —

Common Sound (IRE) (120) (JBarclay) **5-11-10** MDwyer (lw: hld up: effrt 3 out: sn btn: hit last) ... 27 **5** 9/2 [3] 76 —

(SP 110.3%) **5 Rn**

4m 30.8 (17.80) CSF £9.62 TOTE £3.40: £1.70 £1.60 (£4.00) OWNER Mr Geoff Adam (CORNHILL-ON-TWEED) BRED R. P. Adam Ltd
LONG HANDICAP Adamatic (IRE) 9-10

1079 Adamatic (IRE), although 4lb out of the handicap, still looked well treated and, heavily supported, managed to scramble home. He gives the impression that he does not want to be in front too long. (5/2: op 4/1)
Stash the Cash (IRE), having his first run for his new stable, put up a useful performance and improvement looks likely. (3/1)
1025* Field of Vision (IRE) gets outpaced at various stages of the race, but he does keep struggling on, although he is basically short of speed. (5/2)
1144 Well Appointed (IRE) really hotted the pace up at halfway, but he was picked off in the closing stages, and is short of finishing speed. (9/1)
Common Sound (IRE), an Irish import, looked fairly straight, but failed to make any impression and tired considerably in the closing stages. (9/2)

1315 TAVERN MIDDLEMAS H'CAP CHASE (0-135) (5-Y.O+) (Class C)

3-10 (3-12) **2m 6f 110y (14 fncs)** £5,158.10 (£1,560.80: £761.40: £361.70) GOING minus 0.29 sec per fur (GF)

SP RR SF

1142[3] **Bas de Laine (FR) (115)** (MDHammond) **10-10-13** RGarritty (lw: mde all: r.o strly fr 9th: rdn out) ... — **1** 3/1 [3] 122 49

1048[4] **Fiveleigh Builds (128)** (MissLucindaRussell) **9-11-9**(3) GCahill (lw: chsd ldrs: hit 5th: ev ch whn blnd 2 out: one pce after) ... 8 **2** 7/1 129 56

1029* **Dark Oak (113)** (JWCurtis) **10-10-11** LWyer (lw: outpcd 9th: hdwy 4 out: sn chsng ldrs: one pce fr 2 out) ... 3 **3** 5/1 112 39

588[4] **Earlymorning Light (IRE) (119)** (GRichards) **7-11-3** BHarding (lw: chsd ldrs: mstke & outpcd 3 out: eased whn btn flat) ... dist **4** 2/1 [1] — —

1162[3] **Strong Deel (IRE) (119)** (FMurphy) **8-11-3** NWilliamson (lw: hld up: outpcd whn blnd & uns rdr 10th) ... **U** 11/4 [2] — —

(SP 114.2%) **5 Rn**

5m 29.5 (-2.50) CSF £19.89 TOTE £3.80: £1.30 £5.00 (£12.00) OWNER R K Bids Ltd (MIDDLEHAM) BRED Pascal Couturier

1142 Bas de Laine (FR), who jumps and stays, was given a superb ride and galloped his rivals into the ground before the final fence. (3/1)
1048 Fiveleigh Builds put up a useful effort and, but for a bad mistake two out, might well have given the winner problems. (7/1)
1029* Dark Oak was tapped for speed when things really hotted up on the final circuit, but he does stay and kept galloping on, albeit in vain. (5/1)
588 Earlymorning Light (IRE) looks good on his day but, returning here after two months off, ran out of fuel three out. He was then eased a good deal when beaten. (2/1)
1162 Strong Deel (IRE) was getting momentarily left behind when he made an awful blunder at the tenth, giving his rider no chance. (11/4)

1316 LANGHOLM DYEING COMPANY NOVICES' H'CAP HURDLE (0-100) (4-Y.O+) (Class E)

3-40 (3-41) **2m 6f 110y (11 hdls)** £2,584.00 (£724.00: £352.00) GOING minus 0.07 sec per fur (G)

SP RR SF

1152[10] **Clever Boy (IRE) (64)** (JWCurtis) **5-10-0** LWyer (bhd: gd hdwy 3 out: styd on u.p flat to ld cl home) ... — **1** 10/1 54 12

Kasirama (IRE) (73) (MDHammond) **5-10-9** RGarritty (hld up: gd hdwy 3 out: disp ld & stumbled last: ev ch flat: nt qckn towards fin) ... ¾ **2** 11/2 [3] 63 21

Cash Box (IRE) (76) (TJCarr) **8-10-12** NSmith (hld up: hdwy ½-wy: led 2 out: hung lft flat: hdd & no ex towards fin) ... hd **3** 12/1 65 23

1046[2] **Movie Man (75)** (JRTurner) **4-10-11** TReed (a.p: led 4 out tl mstke & hdd 2 out: wknd flat) ... 14 **4** 7/1 54 12

1050[6] **Tartan Mix (IRE) (71)** (JAMoore) **5-10-7** JSupple (mde most to 4 out: wknd appr 2 out) ... 4 **5** 6/1 48 6

1046[P] **Elliott's Wish (IRE) (64)** (HowardJohnson) **5-10-0** NWilliamson (cl up: disp ld 7th to 3 out: rdn & wknd 2 out) .3 **6** 16/1 39 —

1139[4] **Whirlwind Romance (IRE) (64)** (WTKemp) **5-10-0b**[1] SMcDougall (chsd ldrs tl wknd fr 4 out) ... 11 **7** 8/1 31 —

Tweedswood (IRE) (92) (PBeaumont) **6-11-7**(7) BGrattan (lw: trckd ldrs tl lost pl ½-wy: n.d after) ... nk **8** 5/2 [1] 58 16

1144[6] **Nooran (78)** (ACWhillans) **5-11-0** BHarding (trckd ldrs: rdn 4 out: btn & eased fr 2 out: t.o) ... dist **9** 7/2 [2] — —

(SP 126.7%) **9 Rn**

5m 27.0 (10.00) CSF £64.19 CT £631.47 TOTE £14.60: £2.20 £2.20 £1.70 (£118.00) Trio £217.60; £131.82 to Taunton 14/11/96 OWNER Mrs M. E. Curtis (DRIFFIELD) BRED William Drew
LONG HANDICAP Clever Boy (IRE) 9-7 Whirlwind Romance (IRE) 9-10 Elliott's Wish (IRE) 9-8
OFFICIAL EXPLANATION **Tweedswood (IRE): was not suited by the track and had gurgled.**

Clever Boy (IRE), appreciating this step up in trip, needed every yard of it and also looked as though there is a bit more to work on. (10/1: op 16/1)
Kasirama (IRE) seems to be going the right way this year and this run should help bring him on. (11/2)
Cash Box (IRE) failed to impress on looks, but ran well only to throw it away by hanging on the run-in. (12/1)
1046 Movie Man ran pretty well until a mistake steadied him two out, and should find a race in due course. (7/1)
1050 Tartan Mix (IRE), given no chance last time, made it on this occasion, only to run out of petrol two out. Nevertheless, this should have taught him something. (6/1)
Elliott's Wish (IRE) has the looks of a decent type and at last showed something this time, but there is still more needed. (16/1)
1144 Nooran looked ultra-fit but ran disappointingly and, stopping quickly, was eased a good deal in the closing stages. (7/2)

T/Plpt: £129.00 (68.35 Tckts). T/Qdpt: £31.20 (17.8 Tckts). AA

1014-NEWBURY (L-H) (Good)
Wednesday November 13th

Race 2 - one fence omitted fnl circ
WEATHER: fine

1317 E.B.F. 'N.H.' QUALIFIER NOVICES' HURDLE (4, 5 & 6-Y.O) (Class D)

1-20 (1-27) **2m 110y (8 hdls)** £3,135.50 (£944.00: £457.00: £213.50) GOING: 0.06 sec per fur (G)

SP RR SF

Aerion (OSherwood) **5-11-0** JOsborne (lw: a gng wl: hdwy 2 out: led last: qcknd: comf) ... — **1** 8/11 [1] 82+ 25

Tower Street (JTGifford) **5-10-11**(3) LAspell (hdwy appr 2 out: ev ch last: unable qckn) ... 3½ **2** 20/1 79 22

Ever Blessed (IRE) (MrsJPitman) **4-11-0** WMarston (bit bkwd: 9th whn blnd 2 out: hdwy & mstke last: r.o wl) ... nk **3** 13/2 [2] 78+ 21

The Captain's Wish (103) (DNicholson) 5-11-3(7) MrRThornton (hdwy 2nd: ev ch last: one pce)....s.h 4 10/1 3 88 31
Tompetoo (IRE) (NATwiston-Davies) 5-10-11(3) DWalsh (lw: a.p: led 2 out to last: one pce)....s.h 5 10/1 3 78 21
Maid For Adventure (IRE) (MissHCKnight) 5-10-9 BFenton (nvr nr to chal)....3½ 6 33/1 70 13
Safeglide (IRE) (JTGifford) 6-11-0 PHide (bit bkwd: led to 2 out: sn wknd)....3½ 7 20/1 71 14
Strathminster (KCBailey) 5-11-0 CO'Dwyer (bit bkwd: stdy hdwy appr 2 out: one pce)....nk 8 14/1 71 14
Kentford Tina (JWMullins) 5-10-9 SCurran (bit bkwd: nvr nrr)....2 9 25/1 64 7
Snowshill Harvest (IRE) (AndrewTurnell) 5-11-0 MAFitzgerald (bit bkwd: stdy hdwy appr 2 out: wknd appr last)....1½ 10 25/1 68 11
China Gem (IRE) (CPEBrooks) 5-11-0 GBradley (bit bkwd: a bhd)....14 11 33/1 54 —
1036 13 Storm Tiger (IRE) (SMellor) 5-11-0 NMann (bit bkwd: prom to 5th)....3½ 12 50/1 51 —
Rathkeal (IRE) (MJHeaton-Ellis) 5-11-0 DGallagher (prom to 3 out)....9 13 33/1 42 —
Mr Goonhilly (RHAlner) 6-11-0 AThornton (prom to 3 out)....4 14 50/1 38 —
Millcroft Regatta (IRE) (RHAlner) 4-10-11(3) PHenley (bit bkwd: hdwy 3rd: wknd 4th)....11 15 33/1 28 —
865 7 Ermyns Pet (GLMoore) 5-11-0 DO'Sullivan (hdwy 3rd: wknd 4th)....17 16 33/1 11 —
Classicaction (IRE) (MissCJohnsey) 5-11-0 LHarvey (bit bkwd: a bhd: t.o whn p.u bef 2 out: dismntd).... P 50/1 — —
Our Pete (JRBosley) 5-11-0 MBosley (Withdrawn not under Starter's orders: bolted bef s).... W 50/1 — —
(SP 135.8%) **17 Rn**

3m 59.1 (9.10) CSF £19.45 TOTE £1.70: £1.30 £4.50 £1.80 (£33.70) Trio £70.60 OWNER P Chamberlain, D Addiscott Partnership (UPPER LAMBOURN) BRED Mrs David Page

Aerion, who has shown plenty of promise at home, was all the rage in the market for this hurdling debut and did not let his supporters down under an extremely confident ride from Jamie Osborne. Showing a lovely turn of foot to quicken right away, further success awaits. (8/11)

Tower Street made a very encouraging racecourse debut. Sure to be fitter and wiser for this, he should not take long to find a suitable opportunity. (20/1)

Ever Blessed (IRE) made a very encouraging hurdling debut. Making a very bad mistake two out, he nevertheless picked up ground, with his jockey not being unduly hard on him and, although making another error at the final flight, he ran on in eyecatching style, only just failing to take second prize. Sure to strip a lot fitter for this, he should have no problems opening his account. (13/2)

The Captain's Wish, with a 10lb penalty for his win at Bangor in May, still had every chance at the final flight before tapped for toe. He should soon be winning. (10/1: op 4/1)

Tompetoo (IRE), who ran well in the mud on his hurdling debut at Chepstow at February, moved to the front at the second last but, collared at the final flight, failed to find another gear. Connections should soon find a race for him. (10/1: op 5/1)

Maid For Adventure (IRE), racing in midfield, never threatened to get in a blow at the leaders. (33/1)

Strathminster (14/1: op 5/1)

1318 LIONEL VICK MEMORIAL NOVICES' H'CAP CHASE (0-110) (5-Y.O+) (Class D)

1-50 (1-58) **3m (17 fncs)** £3,519.00 (£1,062.00: £516.00: £243.00) GOING minus 0.10 sec per fur (G)

SP RR SF

970 2 Goldenswift (IRE) (86) (GBBalding) 6-11-1 BFenton (lw: hdwy 13th: led 3 out: comf)....— 1 2/1 1 97+ 21
Lottery Ticket (IRE) (99) (JACEdwards) 7-12-0 JOsborne (led 2nd: pckd 3rd: hdd 6th: led 12th to 4 out: rdn appr 2 out: 2nd & btn whn mstke last)....2½ 2 7/1 108 32
1008 2 Lucky Dollar (IRE) (99) (KCBailey) 8-12-0 CO'Dwyer (hdwy 4 out: rdn appr 2 out: one pce)....3 3 13/2 106 30
1038 P The Go Ahead (IRE) (92) (CaptTAForster) 6-11-7 AThornton (led to 2nd: led 6th to 12th: led 4 out to 3 out: wknd flat)....4 4 12/1 97 21
1073 2 Sugar Hill (IRE) (87) (JTGifford) 6-11-2 PHide (hdwy 12th: wknd 4 out)....nk 5 4/1 2 92 16
Ballyedward (IRE) (88) (RHBuckler) 6-11-3 BPowell (bit bkwd: 4th whn blnd bdly 2nd: nt rcvr: t.o fr 4th: p.u bef 7th).... P 12/1 — —
1041 U Westerly Gale (IRE) (76) (NJHenderson) 6-10-5 MAFitzgerald (4th whn blnd & uns rdr 3rd).... U 9/2 3 — —
(SP 112.7%) **7 Rn**

6m 2.4 (12.40) CSF £14.88 CT £68.45 TOTE £2.60: £1.60 £3.30 (£11.50) OWNER Mrs S. Watts (ANDOVER) BRED Ted O'Rourke

970 Goldenswift (IRE) put up a very polished performance, giving a good display of jumping. She won without turning a hair and can follow up. (2/1)

Lottery Ticket (IRE), having to shoulder topweight for this chasing and seasonal debut, should soon open his account over the major obstacles. (7/1: 4/1-8/1)

1008 Lucky Dollar (IRE) is pretty exposed and, under topweight, never threatened to be a major force. (13/2: 9/2-7/1)

The Go Ahead (IRE) ran much better than at Worcester. (12/1: op 5/1)

1073 Sugar Hill (IRE) was taking a step up in distance. (4/1)

Ballyedward (IRE) (12/1: op 5/1)

1041 Westerly Gale (IRE) (9/2: op 5/2)

1319 TOM MASSON TROPHY HURDLE (4-Y.O+) (Class B)

2-20 (2-28) **2m 5f (11 hdls)** £5,218.00 (£1,448.00: £694.00) GOING: 0.06 sec per fur (G)

SP RR SF

Mandys Mantino (132) (JTGifford) 6-11-8 PHide (chsd ldr: lft in ld bnd after 4th: rdn out)....— 1 Evens 1 97 —
Little Buck (IRE) (125) (LWells) 8-11-4 CO'Dwyer (bit bkwd: hld up: ev ch 2 out: swtchd lft appr last: unable qckn flat)....4 2 12/1 90 —
1148 3 Djais (FR) (119) (JRJenkins) 7-11-4 GBradley (hld up: mstke 3 out: ev ch 2 out: wknd last)....5 3 10/1 3 86 —
Danjing (IRE) (131) (MCPipe) 4-10-9 JOsborne (led tl rn out bnd after 4th).... R 6/4 2 — —
Karshi (139) (MissHCKnight) 6-10-9 NoJockey (Withdrawn not under Starter's orders: no rdr available).... W — —
(SP 106.8%) **4 Rn**

5m 20.1 (26.10) CSF £8.87 TOTE £1.70: £1.90 (£3.90) OWNER Mr John Plackett (FINDON) BRED Miss J. U. Wood

IN-FOCUS: **With no-one wanting to lead, it was eleven seconds after the tape had gone back before they even broke into a canter.**

Mandys Mantino, a useful prospect who was unbeaten in four runs last season, did not have the race run to suit him. He wanted to be held up, but the race was run at a crawl and he found himself in front with a circuit to go. Looking in serious danger in the straight, he kept plugging away and managed to break the runner-up on the flat. A big, strapping individual who has chaser written all over him, he will come on for the run and will be far better suited by a stronger-run race. He will have one more outing over hurdles before connections decide whether to switch him to the major obstacles. (Evens)

Little Buck (IRE), an ex-Irish gelding who won twice in the mud last season, looked as though this first run for his new stable would do him good. Nevertheless, he appeared to be cruising in the straight and looked sure to pick off the winner at any time, but that rival kept on finding more. When the ground gets really soft, he will come into his own. (12/1: 5/1-14/1)

1148 Djais (FR) needs a test and that is not what he got here. Nevertheless, he had every chance at the penultimate hurdle before the front two quickened away. (10/1: 6/1-12/1)
Danjing (IRE), sold out of Simon Sherwood's stable for 28,000 guineas at then end of last season, was fit from the Flat, but thoroughly disgraced himself here. Forced to make the running, he decided he had done enough and ducked out to the stable's entrance setting out on the final circuit. (6/4)

1320 HALLOWE'EN NOVICES' CHASE (5-Y.O+) (Class D)
2-50 (2-56) **2m 4f (16 fncs)** £3,899.00 (£1,172.00: £566.00: £263.00) GOING minus 0.10 sec per fur (G)

				SP	RR	SF
	Redeemyourself (IRE) (JTGifford) **7-11-3** PHide (chsd ldr fr 6th: blnd 8th: led 3 out: easily)	—	1	6/4^{1}	111+	—
	Madison County (IRE) (PJHobbs) **6-11-3** CO'Dwyer (hld up: led 4 out tl blnd bdly & hdd 3 out: wknd appr last)	12	2	9/4^{2}	101	—
	Court Master (IRE) (RHBuckler) **8-11-3** BPowell (led tl hdd & lft in ld 12th: hdd 4 out: wknd 2 out)	10	3	12/1	93	—
	Felloo (IRE) (91) (TRGeorge) **7-11-3** WMarston (bit bkwd: chsd ldr to 6th: wknd 11th: t.o)	20	4	25/1	77	—
1062^{3}	**Scamallach (IRE) (82)** (JRJenkins) **6-10-12b** GBradley (hdwy 10th: wknd 12th: 4th & no ch whn fell last)		F	20/1	—	—
	Scorpion Bay (DJSffrenchDavis) **8-11-3** PHolley (bhd fr 11th: t.o whn fell 3 out)		F	66/1	—	—
	Macgeorge (IRE) (RLee) **6-11-3** PMcLoughlin (bit bkwd: hdwy 3rd: mstke 8th: 3rd whn blnd & rdr lost irons 9th: led & uns rdr 12th)		U	9/2^{3}	—	—
				(SP 106.7%)		**7 Rn**

5m 13.5 (18.50) CSF £4.72 TOTE £2.00: £1.10 £2.00 (£2.10) OWNER Mrs T. Brown (FINDON) BRED P. Hogan
Redeemyourself (IRE), who had a slight leg problem after winning over hurdles at Sandown last December, made the perfect start to his chasing career and, cruising to the front three out, won in tremendous style. He looks the type to do really well at this game and further success awaits him. (6/4)
Madison County (IRE), sold out of Dermot Weld's stable for 50,000 guineas, looked straight for this seasonal and chasing debut and had a nostril in front when making an horrendous mistake at the third last. Not surprisingly he could never really recover from this, and he tired going to the final fence. He looks certain to win a similar event in the near future, especially if there is some cut in the ground. (9/4)
Court Master (IRE), without a run since April 1995, made the vast majority of the running. (12/1: 7/1-14/1)
Macgeorge (IRE) (9/2: op 7/1)

1321 JOHN HUGO GWYNNE 50TH BUSINESS YEAR CONDITIONAL H'CAP CHASE (0-125) (5-Y.O+) (Class E)
3-20 (3-21) **2m 1f (13 fncs)** £3,629.00 (£1,024.00: £497.00) GOING minus 0.10 sec per fur (G)

				SP	RR	SF
943*	**Super Tactics (IRE) (122)** (RHAlner) **8-12-0** PHenley (hld up: led appr last: r.o wl)	—	1	2/1^{2}	129+	49
886*	**Merry Panto (IRE) (98)** (CPEBrooks) **7-10-1**(3) MBerry (hld up: chsd ldr fr 7th: ev ch appr last: unable qckn)	1¾	2	6/4^{1}	103	23
1257^{4}	**Northern Saddler (122)** (RJHodges) **9-12-0** TDascombe (w ldr: led 6th tl appr last: sn wknd)	15	3	4/1^{3}	113	33
	High Alltitude (IRE) (105) (MJHeaton-Ellis) **8-10-11** DFortt (hld up: ev ch whn fell 4 out)		F	9/1	—	—
1167^{P}	**Whippers Delight (IRE) (94)** (GFHCharles-Jones) **8-10-0** DWalsh (led to 6th: wknd 8th: t.o whn p.u bef 3 out)		P	12/1	—	—
				(SP 111.0%)		**5 Rn**

4m 8.4 (4.40) CSF £5.27 TOTE £2.80: £1.80 £1.30 (£1.90) OWNER Mr H. V. Perry (BLANDFORD) BRED James Robinson
LONG HANDICAP Whippers Delight (IRE) 9-13
943* Super Tactics (IRE) put up a very polished display. Covered up, he was produced in the straight to lead approaching the last and soon asserted. He is better on a right-handed track. (2/1: 6/4-9/4)
886* Merry Panto (IRE), who has risen 6lb for his recent success, was still on terms approaching the last before the winner asserted. (6/4)
1257 Northern Saddler is at his best when allowed to dominate and ran much better than at Chepstow on Saturday, only tiring approaching the last. A bit of cut in the ground would not go amiss. (4/1)
High Alltitude (IRE), 10lb lower than when finishing third to Northern Saddler at Newton Abbot a year ago, his only run last season, was bang on terms when taking a crashing fall at the fourth last. As long as that has not knocked his confidence too much, he should soon pick up a race. (9/1)

1322 COLD ASH NOVICES' H'CAP HURDLE (0-110) (4-Y.O+) (Class D)
3-50 (3-53) **3m 110y (12 hdls)** £2,765.00 (£830.00: £400.00: £185.00) GOING: 0.06 sec per fur (G)

				SP	RR	SF
1130*	**Queen's Award (IRE) (77)** (RHBuckler) **7-9-7**(7) MGriffiths (lw: hdwy 5th: led 8th: clr appr 2 out: eased nr fin)	—	1	9/4^{1}	56+	—
	Spaceage Gold (99) (JABOld) **7-11-8** GUpton (hrd rdn & hdwy appr 2 out: r.o one pce)	4	2	6/1	75	—
	Percy Thrower (105) (NATwiston-Davies) **9-11-11**(3) DWalsh (led to 6th: rdn 3 out: one pce)	hd	3	5/1^{3}	81	—
969^{6}	**Bite the Bullet (77)** (AJChamberlain) **5-9-7**(7) OBurrows (hld up: rdn 3 out: wknd appr last)	23	4	100/1	38	—
1274*	**River Room (110)** (KCBailey) **6-11-12**(7) 6x WWalsh (a.p: led 6th tl pckd & hdd 8th: wknd 9th)	20	5	11/2	58	—
813^{4}	**China Mail (IRE) (90)** (JABennett) **4-10-12** LHarvey (lw: a bhd: t.o fr 9th)	dist	6	20/1	—	—
1135*	**Clod Hopper (IRE) (77)** (WRMuir) **6-10-0** BPowell (prom to 9th: t.o)	2½	7	6/1	—	—
1077^{9}	**Coolegale (88)** (LWells) **10-10-4b**(7)ow11 DSlattery (prom to 7th: t.o fr 9th)	3	8	66/1	—	—
1069*	**Canton Venture (98)** (SPCWoods) **4-11-6** PHide (stdy hdwy 8th: 2nd whn blnd bdly 3 out: nt rcvr: 3rd & no ch whn fell last)		F	4/1^{2}	—	—
				(SP 118.6%)		**9 Rn**

5m 58.2 (12.20) CSF £15.78 CT £57.05 TOTE £3.40: £1.20 £1.70 £2.00 (£14.10) Trio £18.00 OWNER Mr R. H. Buckler (BRIDPORT) BRED M. Lynch
LONG HANDICAP Queen's Award (IRE) 9-12 Clod Hopper (IRE) 9-12 Coolegale 9-4 Bite the Bullet 8-2
WEIGHT FOR AGE 4yo-1lb
1130* Queen's Award (IRE) may have been 11lb higher than when slamming the opposition at Wetherby earlier in the month, but that was not going to stop him treating this field with contempt. Leading at the eighth, he was rousted along to forge clear from the third last and, with the race well and truly in the bag, was eased considerably in the closing stages. The winning distance is certainly no true reflection of his superiority. (9/4: op 7/2)
Spaceage Gold, at the back of the field for much of the trip, struggled on past beaten rivals in the straight to take second prize, but is greatly flattered to finish so close as the winner was eased right down. (6/1: op 4/1)
Percy Thrower, 17lb higher than when winning a handicap hurdle at Uttoxeter in May, took the field along to halfway, but was made to look very pedestrian in the straight. (5/1)
820 Bite the Bullet, still carrying 19lb more than his long-handicap weight, despite his rider's 7lb allowance, chased the leaders, but he was only fighting for place money in the straight and tired going to the final flight. (100/1)

1069* Canton Venture showed his inexperience. Appearing to be travelling really well, he was disputing second place when all but falling three out. Not surprisingly, he could never recover and was well held in third place when eventually crashing to the deck at the final flight. (4/1)

T/Plpt: £5.40 (2,162.1 Tckts). T/Qdpt: £4.10 (209.86 Tckts). AK

1034-WORCESTER (L-H) (Good)
Wednesday November 13th
WEATHER: fine

1323 ASTLEY NOVICES' HURDLE (4-Y.O+) (Class E)
1-00 (1-04) **2m 4f (10 hdls)** £2,722.50 (£760.00: £367.50) GOING: 0.36 sec per fur (GS)

				SP	RR	SF
	Mighty Moss (IRE) (DNicholson) **5-10-5**$^{(7)}$ MrFHutsby (hld up: hdwy 5th: led 7th: clr appr last: pushed out)	—	1	13/8^{1}	82+	27
	Denham Hill (IRE) (CJMann) **5-10-12** JRailton (hld up & plld hrd: hdwy 4th: ev ch 3 out: rdn 2 out: no imp)	11	2	50/1	73?	18
1088^{P}	**Hydemilla (74)** (MrsTDPilkington) **6-10-4**$^{(3)}$ GHogan (plld hrd: led after 1st: hdd 7th: wknd appr 3 out)	20	3	50/1	52	—
1036*	**Bietschhorn Bard (92)** (DRGandolfo) **6-11-5** RDunwoody (hld up & bhd: hdwy 6th: wknd appr 3 out)	2	4	11/2^{3}	63	8
	Warner For Players (IRE) (PJHobbs) **5-10-12** APMcCoy (hld up: hdwy 5th: rdn & wknd appr 3 out)	1¾	5	2/1^{2}	54	—
	Sammorello (IRE) (NATwiston-Davies) **5-10-12** CLlewellyn (prom tl wknd 6th: t.o)	29	6	20/1	31	—
1085^{5}	**Javelin Cool (IRE)** (GAHubbard) **5-10-9**$^{(3)}$ KGaule (plld hrd: chsd ldr tl rdn & wknd 6th: t.o)	16	7	100/1	18	—
1180^{4}	**Wise 'n' Shine** (NMLampard) **5-10-2**$^{(5)}$ ChrisWebb (prom to 6th: t.o)	17	8	50/1	—	—
974^{3}	**Drakestone (90)** (RLBrown) **5-10-12** RJohnson (bhd fr 6th: t.o)		9	12/1	—	—
	Mr Motivator (TKeddy) **6-10-12** SMcNeill (bkwd: bhd fr 5th: sn t.o)		10	100/1	—	—
	Kaladross (WJenks) **5-10-12** TJenks (bkwd: a bhd: t.o whn fell 3 out)		F	20/1	—	—
1171^{F}	**Credo Boy** (KBishop) **7-10-12** RGreene (bit bkwd: a bhd: t.o whn p.u bef 3 out)		P	50/1	—	—
	Sula's Dream (GAHam) **7-10-7** SBurrough (bkwd: bhd: mstkes 1st & 4th: t.o 5th: p.u bef 3 out)		P	100/1	—	—
	Dextra (IRE) (SEarle) **6-10-12** CMaude (bkwd: led tl after 1st: wknd appr 7th: t.o whn p.u bef 3 out)		P	33/1	—	—
				(SP 117.8%)	**14 Rn**	

4m 53.9 (15.90) CSF £66.14 TOTE £2.20: £1.50 £9.10 £7.90 (£60.90) Trio Not won; £274.70 to Taunton 14/11/96 OWNER Mr K. Hutsby (TEMPLE GUITING) BRED Lady Melissa Brooke

Mighty Moss (IRE), very useful in bumpers last season, made an impressive start to his hurdling career and connections hope he will develop into a Sun Alliance candidate. (13/8)

Denham Hill (IRE), a half-brother to Cogent, stepped up on his efforts in bumpers last season and would not have to improve much to get off the mark. (50/1)

905 Hydemilla soon pulled her way to the front, but had run her race shortly after being passed four out. (50/1)

1036* Bietschhorn Bard, hobdayed since last season, never really looked like supplementing last month's course win. (11/2: op 11/4)

Warner For Players (IRE) had the ground on the soft side on each of his three runs in bumpers. (2/1: op 3/1)

1324 DUNLEY LIMITED H'CAP CHASE (0-135) (5-Y.O+) (Class C)
1-30 (1-30) **2m 7f 110y (18 fncs)** £5,025.00 (£1,400.00: £675.00) GOING: 0.36 sec per fur (GS)

			SP	RR	SF
Cherrynut (125) (PFNicholls) **7-10-13** APMcCoy (bit bkwd: hld up: mstke 3rd: j.slowly 12th: hdwy & hit 14th: led appr 2 out: edgd lft flat: rdn out)	—	1	3/1^{2}	123	—
Billygoat Gruff (133) (DNicholson) **7-11-7** AMaguire (led to 4th: led 6th tl appr 2 out: rdn & r.o one pce flat)	2½	2	8/11^{1}	129	—
King Lucifer (IRE) (130) (DNicholson) **7-11-4** RJohnson (bit bkwd: led 4th to 6th: rdn appr 3 out: wknd appr last)	4	3	3/1^{2}	124	—
			(SP 107.9%)	**3 Rn**	

6m 8.6 CSF £5.27 TOTE £3.20 (£1.90) OWNER Hunt & Co (Bournemouth) Ltd (SHEPTON MALLET) BRED R. Burton

Cherrynut, making his debut in handicap company, again showed a dislike for water jumps. He had to be kept up to his work after going to the far rail on the run-in. (3/1)

Billygoat Gruff looked the fittest of the three and may have been better off setting a stronger pace. He is still on course for a tilt at the Hennessy and softer ground will help his cause. (8/11)

King Lucifer (IRE) made a respectable seasonal debut and will come on for the outing. (3/1: op 2/1)

1325 PLUMB CENTER H'CAP HURDLE (0-130) (4-Y.O+) (Class C)
2-00 (2-00) **2m (8 hdls)** £3,556.00 (£1,063.00: £509.00: £232.00) GOING: 0.36 sec per fur (GS)

				SP	RR	SF
	Teinein (FR) (121) (CaptTAForster) **5-11-7** APMcCoy (hld up: hdwy 5th: mstke 3 out: sn led: easily)	—	1	4/1^{2}	108+	28
1201*	**Mouse Bird (IRE) (119)** (DRGandolfo) **6-11-5b**^{1} ^{5x} RDunwoody (hld up & bhd: hdwy 5th: hrd rdn & chsd wnr appr 2 out: no imp)	3	2	5/2^{1}	103	23
	Chicodari (128) (DNicholson) **4-12-0** AMaguire (hld up: hdwy 5th: one pce fr 2 out)	1	3	9/2^{3}	111	31
	Khalidi (IRE) (115) (DRGandolfo) **7-10-10**$^{(5)}$ SophieMitchell (plld hrd: w ldr: led appr 5th tl after 3 out: sn wknd)	10	4	11/1	88	8
1123^{7}	**Pridewood Picker (100)** (RJPrice) **9-9-9**$^{(5)}$ DJKavanagh (hld up: hdwy 4th: wknd appr 3 out)	4	5	25/1	69	—
	Inculcate (IRE) (108) (CWeedon) **5-10-8** MRichards (hld up: j.slowly & lost pl 4th: rdn & rallied appr 3 out: sn wknd)	13	6	11/1	64	—
1123^{4}	**United Front (100)** (JNeville) **4-10-0** RJohnson (led tl appr 5th: rdn & wknd appr 3 out: t.o)	dist	7	16/1	—	—
	Society Guest (118) (AndrewTurnell) **10-10-11**$^{(7)}$ CRae (3rd whn blnd & uns rdr 3rd)		U	6/1	—	—
				(SP 107.4%)	**8 Rn**	

3m 54.2 (14.20) CSF £12.86 CT £34.47 TOTE £5.30: £1.90 £1.10 £2.30 (£6.30) OWNER Mr Simon Sainsbury (LUDLOW) BRED Tomohiro Wada

LONG HANDICAP United Front 9-12 Pridewood Picker 9-3

Teinein (FR) won so easily that it would come as no surprise to see his imminent transition to fences put on hold. (4/1)

1201* Mouse Bird (IRE), blinkered for the first time, despite being successful at Newton Abbot, had to contend with a penalty and, more importantly, faster ground. (5/2)

Chicodari, looking big and well, had plenty of weight for a four-year-old. It will be interesting to see if the blinkers are re-fitted next time. (9/2)

Khalidi (IRE) took a keen hold and found lack of a previous outing his undoing when the chips were down. (11/1: 8/1-12/1)

Pridewood Picker ran a reasonable race from out of the handicap. (25/1)
Inculcate (IRE) needs the blinkers refitted and plenty of give in the ground, but will at least strip fitter for the run. (11/1)

1326 WORCESTER NOVICES' CHASE (Gd 2) (5-Y.O+) (Class A)

2-30 (2-30) **2m 7f 110y (18 fncs)** £12,386.00 (£4,695.55: £2,305.28: £1,058.17) GOING: 0.36 sec per fur (GS)

				SP	RR	SF
	Pleasure Shared (IRE) (PJHobbs) **8-11-1** CMaude (mstke 1st: hdwy 10th: pckd 3 out: rdn to sn ld: all out)	—	**1**	9/2[2]	137	—
1120*	**Around The Gale (IRE)** (DRGandolfo) **5-10-13** RDunwoody (a.p: ev ch appr 2 out: rallied flat)	nk	**2**	11/4[1]	136	—
1068*	**Mony-Skip (IRE) (99)** (MrsSJSmith) **7-11-1** RichardGuest (bkwd: prom: blnd 2nd: led 9th tl after 3 out: wknd flat)	8	**3**	16/1	131	—
1189[U]	**Wisley Wonder (IRE)** (NATwiston-Davies) **6-11-1** CLlewellyn (prom tl wknd 4 out)	7	**4**	13/2	127?	—
	Cool Runner (MrsSusanNock) **6-11-1** RBellamy (bkwd: bhd tl fell 12th)		**F**	50/1	—	—
	Castlekellyleader (IRE) (PFNicholls) **7-11-1** APMcCoy (hld up: fell 9th)		**F**	5/1[3]	—	—
	Buttercup Joe (DNicholson) **6-11-1** AMaguire (bit bkwd: prom tl p.u lame after 14th)		**P**	9/2[2]	—	—
	Seachange (MJWilkinson) **7-11-1** ILawrence (bhd tl hdwy 9th: mstke 12th: p.u bef 13th: dead)		**P**	40/1	—	—
	Tennessee Twist (IRE) (MrsJPitman) **6-11-1** RFarrant (bhd: hmpd 9th: t.o whn p.u bef 14th)		**P**	12/1	—	—
1068[4]	**Inch Emperor (IRE)** (AWCarroll) **6-11-1** TJMurphy (bit bkwd: led to 9th: sn wknd: t.o whn p.u bef 14th)		**P**	200/1	—	—
				(SP 111.5%)	**10 Rn**	

6m 6.5 CSF £15.66 TOTE £5.50: £1.90 £1.40 £2.40 (£8.40) Trio £32.60 OWNER Mr Tony Eaves (MINEHEAD) BRED N.J Tector
WEIGHT FOR AGE 5yo-1lb

Pleasure Shared (IRE), who progressed into one of the best novice hurdlers last season, made a successful start to his chasing career in the best novice chase run so far this term. He got a bit tired in the closing stages and had to pull out all the stops, but looks an exciting prospect. (9/2: 3/1-5/1)
1120* Around The Gale (IRE) has never won on ground better than good to soft and, losing nothing in defeat, can soon regain winning ways. (11/4)
1068* Mony-Skip (IRE) gave a good account of himself against a couple of useful rivals. (16/1)
1189 Wisley Wonder (IRE) may find two and a half miles far enough over fences for the time being. (13/2)
Castlekellyleader (IRE) developed into a smart novice hurdler last season. (5/1)
Tennessee Twist (IRE) (12/1: op 8/1)

1327 LEVY BOARD NOVICES' H'CAP HURDLE (0-105) (4-Y.O) (Class D)

3-00 (3-02) **2m (8 hdls)** £2,847.00 (£792.00: £381.00) GOING: 0.36 sec per fur (GS)

				SP	RR	SF
1118*	**Indrapura (IRE) (100)** (MCPipe) **4-12-0** APMcCoy (rdn & hdwy appr 5th: led last: rdn out)	—	**1**	9/4[1]	81	36
1091[2]	**Lets Be Frank (82)** (NoelChance) **5-10-10** RJohnson (a.p: led 5th to last: unable qckn)	1¼	**2**	11/2	62	17
1253[6]	**Time Leader (72)** (RDickin) **4-10-0** RBellamy (bit bkwd: wl bhd tl gd hdwy 5th: hrd rdn appr last: one pce)	8	**3**	25/1	44	—
	Blazing Miracle (74) (MrsRGHenderson) **4-9-11**(5)ow2 DSalter (nvr nr to chal)	8	**4**	33/1	38	—
	Fairies Farewell (83) (OSherwood) **6-10-11** JAMcCarthy (bkwd: hld up: hdwy appr 5th: hrd rdn appr 3 out: wknd 2 out)	3½	**5**	7/2[2]	43	—
	Colwall (74) (MissPMWhittle) **5-10-2** CLlewellyn (bkwd: hld up: hdwy 5th: wknd appr 3 out)	12	**6**	16/1	22	—
1027*	**Count of Flanders (IRE) (82)** (KAMorgan) **6-10-10** ASSmith (chsd ldr tl wknd 3 out)	8	**7**	9/2[3]	22	—
	Sweet Trentino (IRE) (83) (MTate) **5-10-11** AMaguire (a bhd: t.o whn p.u bef 3 out)		**P**	14/1	—	—
	Kings Vision (72) (WJenks) **4-10-0** SWynne (bkwd: a bhd: t.o whn p.u bef 3 out)		**P**	33/1	—	—
1036[7]	**Sylvester (IRE) (75)** (MissAEBroyd) **6-10-3** DBridgwater (plld hrd: led to 5th: wknd 3 out: p.u bef 2 out)		**P**	20/1	—	—
	Young Tycoon (NZ) (83) (AJWilson) **5-10-11** RGreene (bit bkwd: bhd fr 4th: t.o whn p.u bef 3 out)		**P**	33/1	—	—
				(SP 116.5%)	**11 Rn**	

3m 54.0 (14.00) CSF £14.22 CT £212.97 TOTE £3.30: £1.50 £1.50 £5.30 (£6.90) Trio £136.20 OWNER Martin Pipe Racing Club (WELLINGTON) BRED John Burns
LONG HANDICAP Kings Vision 9-13 Blazing Miracle 9-7 Time Leader 9-12

1118* Indrapura (IRE), now unbeaten in six races over timber, has progressed from winning a couple of sellers in typical Martin Pipe style. (9/4)
1091 Lets Be Frank had been raised 2lb for finishing second at Stratford. (11/2)
Time Leader, coming from a long way back, was only stoked up when the first two had flown and might be worth keeping an eye on next time. (25/1)
Blazing Miracle could well do better when reverting to a longer trip. (33/1)
Fairies Farewell, supported in the market, found disappointingly little in the final half-mile. (7/2)
1027* Count of Flanders (IRE) (9/2: op 7/1)
Sweet Trentino (IRE) (14/1: op 8/1)

1328 TALFAB TROPY H'CAP CHASE (0-100) (5-Y.O+) (Class F)

3-30 (3-30) **2m (12 fncs)** £3,731.50 (£1,117.00: £536.00: £245.50) GOING: 0.36 sec per fur (GS)

				SP	RR	SF
1045[5]	**Porphyrios (98)** (KCBailey) **5-11-12** CLlewellyn (bkwd: j.slowly 1st: sn wl bhd: rapid hdwy after 8th: rdr lost iron last: led nr fin)	—	**1**	8/1[2]	105	28
	Reeshloch (88) (AndrewTurnell) **7-10-9b**(7) CRae (lw: hdwy 6th: led 4 out: clr 2 out: hdd nr fin)	1¼	**2**	9/1[3]	94	17
	Thats the Life (77) (TRGeorge) **11-10-5** RJohnson (t: bkwd: led to 3rd: led 6th to 8th: one pce fr 3 out)	10	**3**	25/1	73	—
	Brown Robber (72) (MrsRGHenderson) **8-10-0** RFarrant (hld up: hdwy 8th: one pce fr 4 out)	1¾	**4**	20/1	66	—
	Dress Dance (IRE) (85) (NRMitchell) **6-10-8**(5) SophieMitchell (lw: a wl bhd)	15	**5**	16/1	64	—
	Who Am I (IRE) (84) (RHAlner) **6-10-12** APMcCoy (bkwd: prom: j.slowly 4th: mstke 5th: led 8th to 4 out: sn wknd)	nk	**6**	11/2[1]	63	—
1035[7]	**Good for a Laugh (95)** (GAHam) **12-11-2**(7) MrGShenkin (bkwd: mstke 4th: bhd fr 7th: t.o)	18	**7**	11/2[1]	56	—
972[3]	**Jewel Thief (74)** (GBBalding) **6-10-2v** BClifford (sn wl bhd: t.o fr 5th)	dist	**8**	12/1	—	—
	High Low (USA) (100) (WJenks) **8-12-0** TJenks (led 3rd to 6th: wknd 8th: t.o whn p.u bef 4 out)		**P**	9/1[3]	—	—
	The Minister (IRE) (82) (RChampion) **7-10-10** AMaguire (bkwd: prom to 8th: bhd whn blnd 4 out: p.u bef 3 out)		**P**	11/2[1]	—	—
1010[5]	**Viaggio (75)** (ALForbes) **8-10-3v** RBellamy (bhd fr 7th: t.o whn p.u bef 4 out)		**P**	20/1	—	—
1018[3]	**Ambassador Royale (IRE) (91)** (MissAEBroyd) **8-11-5** DBridgwater (bit bkwd:prom tl wnt lame & p.u after 6th)		**P**	11/2[1]	—	—
				(SP 119.6%)	**12 Rn**	

4m 7.0 (16.00) CSF £71.71 CT £1,577.55 TOTE £9.40: £2.10 £3.90 £8.90 (£28.30) Trio £277.00; £351.14 to Taunton 13/11/96 OWNER Mr Ian Bullerwell (UPPER LAMBOURN) BRED A. Christodoulou

LONG HANDICAP Brown Robber 9-4
1045 Porphyrios, on his debut over fences, landing running, despite diving at the last and causing his rider to lose an iron. He should stay further. (8/1: op 5/1)
Reeshloch showed none of his old jumping problems and it was probably just lack of condition that proved his undoing. (9/1)
Thats the Life, having his first outing since June 1995, ran a sound enough race. (25/1)
Brown Robber, 10lb out of the handicap, was carrying condition, but did enough to suggest he is no lost cause. (20/1)
Who Am I (IRE) needs to polish up his jumping, but got better as the race progressed. (11/2)
Good for a Laugh was struggling after an error at the fourth. (11/2)
High Low (USA) (9/1: 6/1-10/1)
The Minister (IRE) was already out with the washing when making a hash of the last ditch. (11/2: 4/1-6/1)
1018 Ambassador Royale (IRE) unfortunately seemed to have broken down quite badly. (11/2)

1329 WYCHBOLD STANDARD OPEN N.H. FLAT RACE (4, 5 & 6-Y.O) (Class H)
4-00 (4-03) **2m** £1,427.00 (£397.00: £191.00)

				SP	RR	SF
1013*	**Boots Madden (IRE)** (MissVenetiaWilliams) **6-11-11** RJohnson (lw: hld up: hdwy 5f out: hrd rdn over 2f out: led wl ins fnl f: r.o)	—	**1**	7/2[1]	—	—
	Another Cockpit (PJHobbs) **4-10-13**(5) DJKavanagh (mde most: rdn over 2f out: hdd wl ins fnl f)	1¼	**2**	12/1	—	—
	Rachel Louise (TKeddy) **4-10-13** DBridgwater (bit bkwd: hld up: gd hdwy over 4f out: ev ch 2f out: one pce fnl f)	3	**3**	12/1	—	—
	Super Rapier (IRE) (GAHubbard) **4-11-4** RichardGuest (hld up & bhd: gd hdwy fnl 2f: fin wl)	9	**4**	25/1	—	—
	Symphony's Son (IRE) (DNicholson) **5-11-4** AMaguire (bit bkwd: hld up & bhd: gd hdwy over 4f out: wknd over 1f out)	¾	**5**	6/1[2]	—	—
	Domindross (PFNicholls) **4-11-4** APMcCoy (bkwd: nvr nr to chal)	1	**6**	8/1[3]	—	—
	Eurofast Pet (IRE) (SABrookshaw) **6-11-4** CMaude (bit bkwd: nvr nr to chal)	2	**7**	14/1	—	—
	New Leaf (IRE) (DRGandolfo) **4-10-13**(5) SophieMitchell (bkwd: nvr trbld ldrs)	hd	**8**	20/1	—	—
	Shariakandi (FR) (JSKing) **4-11-4** CLlewellyn (prom 11f)	nk	**9**	25/1	—	—
	Loch Na Keal (CPMorlock) **4-10-13** JRKavanagh (hrd rdn & hdwy 4f out: wknd over 2f out)	1½	**10**	12/1	—	—
	Hills Gamble (PJBevan) **6-11-4** WWorthington (bkwd: plld hrd: prom tl wknd 3f out)	1½	**11**	33/1	—	—
	Firecrown (MrsPRobeson) **6-11-4** MRichards (bit bkwd: bhd fnl 5f)	16	**12**	33/1	—	—
	Look In The Mirror (NATwiston-Davies) **5-10-11**(7) LSuthern (prom tl rdn & wknd over 3f out)	1¼	**13**	9/1	—	—
	Small Flame (IRE) (OBrennan) **5-10-13** MBrennan (bkwd: a bhd)	s.h	**14**	33/1	—	—
	Arctic Fusilier (MissHCKnight) **5-10-11**(7) MrAWintle (prom tl wknd over 3f out)	2½	**15**	9/1	—	—
1071[3]	**Lady Foley (IRE)** (CJMann) **4-10-13b** RDunwoody (lw: trckd ldrs: rdn & wknd over 3f out: t.o)	21	**16**	12/1	—	—
1151[3]	**Becky's Lad** (MrsDThomas) **6-11-1**(3) GuyLewis (swtg: prom 10f: t.o)	9	**17**	66/1	—	—
	Above Suspicion (IRE) (CJames) **4-11-4** SMcNeill (plld hrd mid div: hdwy 6f out: wknd over 4f out: t.o)	6	**18**	33/1	—	—
	High Statesman (TTBill) **4-11-4** JRailton (bkwd: bhd fnl 6f: t.o)	5	**19**	66/1	—	—
	Sabrecool (IRE) (GAHubbard) **5-11-1**(3) KGaule (stumbled after 5f: a bhd: t.o)	17	**20**	50/1	—	—
	Arklow King (IRE) (PWegmann) **4-10-11**(7) SFowler (bkwd: prom 9f: t.o)	27	**21**	66/1	—	—
				(SP 135.7%)	**21 Rn**	

3m 56.7 CSF £45.66 TOTE £3.60: £1.70 £7.10 £2.90 (£40.20) Trio £183.30; £80.05 to Taunton 14/11/96 OWNER Mr L. J. A. Phipps (HEREFORD) BRED Michael Hickey
1013* Boots Madden (IRE), a winner between the Flags in Ireland, defied a penalty and got the better of a good tussle in the final quarter-mile. (7/2)
Another Cockpit proved a tough nut to crack at the head of affairs and this was an improvement on his efforts in the spring. (12/1: op 6/1)
Rachel Louise was supported in the market and rewarded any each-way money. (12/1: op 33/1)
Super Rapier (IRE), out of a winning pointer, was noted putting in some good work in the later stages. (25/1)
Symphony's Son (IRE) showed ability in these events last season and this will have put an edge on him. (6/1)
Domindross will do better in due course. (8/1: op 3/1)
Eurofast Pet (IRE) will come on for the outing. (14/1: 10/1-16/1)
Look In The Mirror (9/1: 6/1-10/1)
Arctic Fusilier (9/1: 6/1-10/1)

T/Jkpt: £13,240.70 (1.18 Tckts). T/Plpt: £352.80 (33.2 Tckts). T/Qdpt: £36.40 (29.2 Tckts). KH

0912-TAUNTON (R-H) (Good to firm)
Thursday November 14th
WEATHER: overcast

1330 SOUTH-WEST AMATEUR H'CAP HURDLE (0-110) (4-Y.O+) (Class G)
1-00 (1-00) **2m 3f 110y (10 hdls)** £1,941.50 (£544.00: £264.50) GOING minus 0.90 sec per fur (HD)

				SP	RR	SF
	Nova Run (100) (NJHenderson) **7-11-0**(5) MrCVigors (swtg: bit bkwd: a.p: lft 2nd 7th: led 2 out: j.rt last: rdn & r.o wl)	—	**1**	4/1[2]	90	35
1086*	**Severn Gale (90)** (JSAllen) **6-10-2**(7) MrNBradley (led after 1st: hdd 2 out: one pce)	6	**2**	17/2	75	20
1121[2]	**Zingibar (81)** (JMBradley) **4-9-7**(7) MrRThornton (hld up: hdwy appr 7th: wknd appr 2 out)	14	**3**	15/8[1]	55	—
1262[5]	**San Diego Charger (IRE) (82)** (ABarrow) **5-9-8**(7) MrOMcPhail (hld up: rdn & hdwy appr 2 out: nt rch ldrs)	hd	**4**	16/1	56	1
915[4]	**Southern Ridge (85)** (RGFrost) **5-9-11**(7) MrAHoldsworth (prom tl stdd & lost pl 3rd: hdwy 7th: wknd appr last)	2	**5**	7/1[3]	57	2
	Glen Mirage (84) (MJCoombe) **11-9-10**(7) MissMCoombe (bkwd: wl bhd fr 2nd)	8	**6**	14/1	49	—
1185[3]	**Zip Your Lip (89)** (MrsPTownsley) **6-10-1**(7) MissCTownsley (hld up: sme hdwy 7th: wknd after 3 out)	2	**7**	20/1	53	—
	Albeit (83) (REvans) **6-9-9**(7)ow2 MissCEvans (a bhd: t.o)	26	**8**	50/1	25	—
	Always Remember (100) (PJHobbs) **9-10-12**(7) MrRWidger (bkwd: led tl after 1st: wknd appr 6th: t.o)	dist	**9**	16/1	—	—
971[7]	**Fleur de Tal (97)** (WGMTurner) **5-10-9**(7) MrGShenkin (prom: 2nd whn fell 7th)		**F**	9/1	—	—
	Fearless Wonder (109) (DFBassett) **5-11-7b**(7) MissKDiMarte (bkwd: sn t.o: p.u bef 3 out)		**P**	25/1	—	—
				(SP 116.8%)	**11 Rn**	

4m 21.7 (-9.30) CSF £34.68 CT £76.06 TOTE £5.90: £1.90 £3.20 £1.10 (£18.40) Trio £17.40 OWNER Mr S. Keeling (LAMBOURN) BRED Catfoss Farming and Developments Ltd

LONG HANDICAP Albeit 8-7
Nova Run, who won first time out last season, did not impress in the paddock, but proved too good for this sort of company. He could well go novice chasing shortly. (4/1)
1086* Severn Gale had been raised 5lb for winning a non-handicap seller at Stratford. (17/2: 5/1-9/1)
1121 Zingibar was disappointing, and may have found this ground a bit lively. (15/8: op 3/1)
949 San Diego Charger (IRE) was still 5lb higher than when scoring at Stratford in April. (16/1)
915 Southern Ridge seemed set to finish a well-beaten third until running out of stamina. (7/1)
884 Fleur de Tal (9/1: op 6/1)

1331 WSM MERCEDES BENZ 'ACTROS' NOVICES' H'CAP CHASE (0-100) (5-Y.O+) (Class E)
1-30 (1-30) **2m 3f (15 fncs)** £3,144.00 (£884.00: £432.00) GOING minus 0.90 sec per fur (HD)

				SP	RR	SF
972[2]	**Chickabiddy (78)** (GFEdwards) **8-11-0** RJohnson (chsd ldr: led after 4 out: lft clr 3 out)	—	1	5/2[2]	92	—
1061[F]	**Ashmead Rambler (IRE) (67)** (PJHobbs) **6-10-3** CMaude (tk keen hold: led 11th tl after 4 out: cl 4th whn lft 2nd & hmpd 3 out)	23	2	4/1[3]	62	—
1254[U]	**Lord Nitrogen (USA) (81)** (BJLlewellyn) **6-11-3** MrJLLlewellyn (led: hit 5th: reminders appr 7th: hdd & hit 9th: wknd 10th: t.o fr 4 out)	15	3	7/1	63	—
740*	**Nordic Valley (IRE) (88)** (MCPipe) **5-11-10** APMcCoy (nt fluent: hld up: cl 3rd & rdn whn fell 2 out)		F	6/4[1]	—	—
	Oxford Quill (72) (RCurtis) **9-10-8** DMorris (bkwd: hld up & plld hrd: led 9th to 11th:2nd & ev ch whn fell 3 out)		F	12/1	—	—
				(SP 108.8%)	**5 Rn**	

4m 43.6 (1.60) CSF £11.35 TOTE £3.00: £1.10 £3.50 (£9.20) OWNER Mr G. F. Edwards (MINEHEAD) BRED G. Reed
972 Chickabiddy, not very big but a good jumper, was being pressed on all sides when left with the race on a plate at the tricky third last. (5/2)
1061 Ashmead Rambler (IRE) was giving the impression he was just about to find disappointingly little when the whole complexion of the race changed three out. (4/1)
889 Lord Nitrogen (USA) (7/1: 9/2-15/2)
740* Nordic Valley (IRE), raised 5lb, was being ridden along when departing, but had found plenty under pressure in his last two wins. (6/4)
Oxford Quill, off course for over a year, was running a surprisingly big race for one carrying plenty of condition when coming togrief. (12/1)

1332 ORCHARD PORTMAN (S) H'CAP HURDLE (0-90) (3-Y.O+) (Class G)
2-00 (2-01) **2m 1f (9 hdls)** £2,004.50 (£562.00: £273.50) GOING minus 0.90 sec per fur (HD)

				SP	RR	SF
1181[5]	**Little Hooligan (82)** (GFEdwards) **5-11-10** RJohnson (hld up: lost pl appr 5th: rdn appr 6th: rallied after 3 out: led flat: drvn out)	—	1	6/1[3]	64	8
1168[4]	**Blurred Image (IRE) (67)** (JCPoulton) **5-10-9** TJMurphy (hld up: stdy hdwy 6th: led, j.lft & hit 2 out: hdd flat)	2	2	8/1	47	—
1198[6]	**Mutawali (IRE) (75)** (RJBaker) **6-11-3** DLeahy (hld up: mstke 5th: hdwy 3 out: hrd rdn & r.o one pce flat)	1½	3	4/1[2]	54	—
1251[R]	**Tibbs Inn (58)** (ABarrow) **7-9-7**(7) MrRThornton (unruly & led into s: hdwy 4th: mstkes 5th & 6th: led appr 2 out: sn hdd: one pce)	3½	4	16/1	33	—
969[5]	**To Be Fair (76)** (PJHobbs) **9-10-11**(7) MrSDurack (chsd ldr tl after 3 out: wknd 2 out)	3½	5	9/1	48	—
1166[5]	**Alosaili (78)** (JCullinan) **9-11-6** VSlattery (nvr nr to chal)	4	6	9/1	46	—
836[6]	**Remember Star (74)** (ADSmith) **3-10-0** FJousset (a bhd)	2	7	66/1	41	—
1198[R]	**Colour Scheme (65)** (HSHowe) **9-10-7v** BPowell (a bhd)	3	8	50/1	29	—
1064[6]	**Soldier Blue (75)** (PJHobbs) **3-10-1b[1]** APMcCoy (led tl appr 2 out: sn wknd)	3	9	7/1	36	—
1149*	**Indira (84)** (CLPopham) **3-10-7**(3) TDascombe (3rd whn blnd & uns rdr 2nd)		U	11/4[1]	—	—
				(SP 113.9%)	**10 Rn**	

3m 52.0 (-1.00) CSF £47.37 CT £194.65 TOTE £4.50: £1.60 £2.60 £2.00 (£17.90) Trio £46.70 OWNER Mr G. F. Edwards (MINEHEAD) BRED E. Kendrick
LONG HANDICAP Remember Star 8-9
WEIGHT FOR AGE 3yo-16lb
Sold AFear 3,200 gns
1181 Little Hooligan was 6lb higher than when first past the post in this event last year, when five of the first six home were disqualified for by-passing the last hurdle on the wrong side. (6/1)
961 Blurred Image (IRE) had been all at sea in the testing conditions at Plumpton last time. (8/1)
1198 Mutawali (IRE), who failed to handle heavy ground last time, had been raised 7lb for his win in a similar event here, but was already due to drop 2lb in future handicaps. (4/1)
958 Tibbs Inn refused to take part at Uttoxeter last week and again played up at the start. (16/1)
To Be Fair has come back this season after a four-year lay-off. (9/1)
1007 Alosaili was due to drop 6lb in the Ratings at the weekend. (9/1)
1149* Indira had been described by her trainer as a good jumper when winning at Warwick, but it can be a dangerous thing to tempt providence. (11/4)

1333 WEATHERBYS STATISTICAL RECORD NOVICES' HURDLE (4-Y.O+) (Class E)
2-30 (2-31) **2m 1f (9 hdls)** £2,358.00 (£663.00: £324.00) GOING minus 0.90 sec per fur (HD)

				SP	RR	SF
1053*	**Rosencrantz (IRE) (104)** (MissVenetiaWilliams) **4-11-12** NWilliamson (hld up: hdwy appr 6th: led & hit last: lft clr)	—	1	Evens[1]	88	29
1183*	**Portscatho (IRE) (85)** (APJones) **4-11-5b** SMcNeill (prom: outpcd 3 out: r.o flat: no ch w wnr)	11	2	10/1[3]	71	12
	Magic Wizard (80) (NJHawke) **5-10-12** CMaude (a.p: one pce fr 3 out)	3½	3	66/1	60	1
	Adonisis (DRCElsworth) **4-10-12** AProcter (hdwy after 3 out: one pce fr 2 out)	hd	4	25/1	60	1
	Questan (MCPipe) **4-10-12b[1]** APMcCoy (hld up: hdwy appr 6th: 2nd whn blnd 3 out: sn wknd)	14	5	2/1[2]	47	—
1168[P]	**Ath Cheannaithe (FR) (92)** (JNeville) **4-11-5** RJohnson (led tl appr 5th: wknd 3 out)	3½	6	12/1	51	—
902[4]	**Trauma (IRE)** (WGMTurner) **4-10-0**(7) NWillmington (plld hrd: sn prom: wknd 5th: bhd whn mstke 6th: t.o)	dist	7	66/1	—	—
653[11]	**Klosters** (RJHodges) **4-10-4**(3) TDascombe (a bhd: t.o)	3	8	66/1	—	—
1065[3]	**All Sewn Up** (RJBaker) **4-10-12** BPowell (a bhd: t.o fr 4th)	7	9	66/1	—	—
	Out on a Promise (IRE) (NJHWalker) **4-10-5**(7) DFinnegan (plld hrd: prom: led appr 5th: clr 3 out: hdd & fell last)		F	10/1[3]	66?	—
885[P]	**Minneola** (ABarrow) **4-10-0**(7) MrRThornton (a bhd: t.o 4th: p.u bef 3 out)		P	66/1	—	—
1044[6]	**Saboteuse** (JCPoulton) **4-10-7** TJMurphy (a bhd: t.o whn p.u bef 6th)		P	66/1	—	—

	Horse	Dist	Pos	SP	RR	SF
	Nigels Choice (ADSmith) **4-10-12** FJousset (bkwd: bhd whn rn v.wd bnd appr 3rd: t.o whn rn wd & p.u bef 5th)		**P**	66/1	—	—

(SP 123.5%) **13 Rn**

3m 47.5 (-5.50) CSF £11.66 TOTE £2.40: £1.80 £2.20 £11.40 (£7.90) Trio £110.50 OWNER Mr L. J. Fulford (HEREFORD) BRED Sheikh Mohammed bin Rashid al Maktoum

1053* Rosencrantz (IRE) seemed beforehand to have less to do than when scraping home at Wincanton. Patiently ridden, he was galloping all over Out on a Promise when that rival came to grief at the last. (Evens)
1183* Portscatho (IRE) had the blinkers refitted after winning a poor race at Warwick. (10/1)
Magic Wizard, although beaten a fair way, ran his best race over timber to date. (66/1)
Adonisis had been given a pipe-opener on the Flat at the end of last month. (25/1)
Questan, who managed to win at Saint-Cloud on the Flat, probably needs softer ground. (2/1)
974 Ath Cheannaithe (FR) (12/1: op 7/1)
Out on a Promise (IRE) (10/1: 7/1-14/1)

1334 WSM MERCEDES BENZ 'VITO' NOVICES' HURDLE (4-Y.O+) (Class D)
3-00 (3-00) **3m 110y (12 hdls)** £2,801.00 (£848.00: £414.00: £197.00) GOING minus 0.90 sec per fur (HD)

	Horse	Dist	Pos	SP	RR	SF
	Honey Mount (NJHWalker) **5-10-12** NWilliamson (hld up: stdy hdwy appr 9th: led last: drvn out)	—	**1**	$9/4^{1}$	67	31
1197^{4}	**Copper Coil (85)** (WGMTurner) **6-10-5**(7) JPower (led to 2nd: led 3 out to last: unable qckn)	2	**2**	$9/2^{3}$	66	30
1251^{2}	**Dragonmist (IRE) (66)** (DBurchell) **6-10-7h** DJBurchell (hld up: hdwy 8th: one pce fr 2 out)	6	**3**	6/1	57	21
832^{2}	**Galatasori Jane (IRE)** (PFNicholls) **6-10-7** APMcCoy (led 2nd tl appr 4th: led 8th to 3 out: one pce)	3	**4**	$7/2^{2}$	55	19
	Frank Naylar (RHBuckler) **5-10-5**(7) MGriffiths (bit bkwd: prom to 7th)	18	**5**	8/1	48	12
1197^{P}	**Mu-Tadil (70)** (RJBaker) **4-10-11** BPowell (nvr gng wl: w ldr: led appr 4th to 8th: wknd 9th)	¾	**6**	40/1	48	11
1178^{9}	**Katharine's Song (IRE)** (DMHyde) **6-10-7** BFenton (a bhd: t.o fr 8th)	20	**7**	40/1	30	—
1086^{P}	**Laura Lye (IRE) (66)** (BdeHaan) **6-10-7** JRailton (prom: ev ch 3 out: wknd appr 2 out: t.o)	10	**8**	50/1	23	—
1203^{8}	**Dukes Castle (IRE)** (RGFrost) **5-10-12** JFrost (bit bkwd: hld up: mstke 1st: bhd whn fell 3 out)		**F**	8/1	—	—

(SP 114.5%) **9 Rn**

5m 39.6 (-12.40) CSF £12.11 TOTE £3.30: £1.50 £1.20 £1.70 (£5.70) Trio £11.00 OWNER Mr Paul Green (WANTAGE) BRED Cliveden Stud
WEIGHT FOR AGE 4yo-1lb

Honey Mount, a well-backed favourite, had pulled too hard on his two outings over timber last season, but was brought with a nicely-timed run here. (9/4)
1197 Copper Coil appreciated this firmer surface but, once again, lack of finishing pace proved his undoing. (9/2)
1251 Dragonmist (IRE) is basically only a staying selling plater. (6/1: 7/2-13/2)
832 Galatasori Jane (IRE) should do better once put over fences. (7/2)
Frank Naylar (8/1: op 4/1)

1335 WSM MERCEDES BENZ 'SPRINTER' H'CAP CHASE (0-105) (5-Y.O+) (Class F)
3-30 (3-30) **3m (19 fncs)** £2,801.00 (£848.00: £414.00: £197.00) GOING minus 0.90 sec per fur (HD)

	Horse	Dist	Pos	SP	RR	SF
1068^{3}	**La Mezeray (78)** (MrsJEHawkins) **8-10-0**(3)ow3 DWalsh (hld up: mstke & rdn 14th: styd on to ld last 50y: all out)	—	**1**	5/1	84	—
914^{3}	**Henley Wood (98)** (PJHobbs) **11-11-9** LHarvey (led to 4 out: led 2 out to last 50y)	1	**2**	$7/2^{3}$	103	5
1038^{U}	**Gallic Girl (IRE) (76)** (CLPopham) **6-9-12**(3)ow1 TDascombe (hld up: led 4 out to 2 out: wknd flat)	6	**3**	33/1	77	—
1284^{U}	**Herbert Buchanan (IRE) (101)** (PFNicholls) **6-11-12** APMcCoy (hld up: hit 6th: blnd bdly 7th: sn wl bhd: hdwy 14th: hit 3 out: sn wknd)	11	**4**	$7/4^{1}$	95	—
914*	**The Blue Boy (IRE) (103)** (PBowen) **8-12-0b** NWilliamson (chsd ldr to 13th: 3rd whn fell 14th)		**F**	$9/4^{2}$	—	—
	Rhoman Fun (IRE) (75) (RHBuckler) **7-10-0** BPowell (hld up: 3rd whn blnd bdly 11th: bhd whn p.u after 12th)		**P**	11/1	—	—

(SP 117.3%) **6 Rn**

5m 59.9 (2.90) CSF £21.99 TOTE £7.10: £3.20 £2.00 (£16.90) OWNER Mrs J. E. Hawkins (NEWPORT, GWENT)
LONG HANDICAP Gallic Girl (IRE) 9-8 La Mezeray 9-10 Rhoman Fun (IRE) 9-5
STEWARDS' ENQUIRY Walsh susp. 23 & 25/11/96 + 1 day (excessive use of whip).

1068 La Mezeray, 4lb out of the handicap, had to dig deep to land the spoils. (5/1)
914 Henley Wood confirmed the impression he stays, but could not hold the winner towards the finish. (7/2)
Gallic Girl (IRE), an Irish import, should fare better in novice handicaps on this evidence. (33/1)
1284 Herbert Buchanan (IRE) has failed to stay this trip in the past, but did well to get back into contention after a terrible blunder at the seventh. (7/4)
914* The Blue Boy (IRE) took what turned out to be a fatal fall at the penultimate ditch. (9/4)
Rhoman Fun (IRE) (11/1: 7/1-12/1)

1336 WEATHERBYS 'STARS OF TOMORROW' STANDARD OPEN N.H. FLAT RACE (4, 5 & 6-Y.O) (Class H)
4-00 (4-01) **2m 1f** £1,215.00 (£340.00: £165.00)

	Horse	Dist	Pos	SP	RR	SF
	Midas (KRBurke) **5-11-4** APMcCoy (hld up & plld hrd: hdwy 7f out: ev ch over 2f out: unable qckn fnl f: fin 2nd, 1½l: awrdd r)	—	**1**	$3/1^{2}$	—	—
	Little Jake (IRE) (NoelChance) **6-11-4** RJohnson (a.p: ev ch 3f out: one pce fnl 2f: fin 3rd, 3½l: plcd 2nd)		**2**	$7/4^{1}$	—	—
	King of The Blues (JSKing) **4-11-4** TJMurphy (bit bkwd: plld hrd: prom tl wknd 2f out: fin 4th, 5l: plcd 3rd)		**3**	$11/2^{3}$	—	—
1177^{13}	**Halam Bell** (WGMTurner) **4-10-13** PHolley (lw: chsd ldr 11f: wknd over 2f out: fin 5th, 7l: plcd 4th)		**4**	33/1	—	—
	Dunnicks Town (FGTucker) **4-11-4** GUpton (bkwd: nvr trbld ldrs: fin 6th, 5l: plcd 5th)		**5**	20/1	—	—
	Boozys Dream (NBThomson) **5-11-4** SBurrough (hld up & plld hrd: rdn 8f out: sn bhd: t.o)	27	**7**	16/1	—	—
	Countess Millie (MissKWhitehouse) **4-10-8**(5) ChrisWebb (bkwd: led 11f: sn wknd: t.o)	6	**8**	33/1	—	—
	Aqua Amber (JMBradley) **4-11-4** BFenton (bkwd: a bhd: t.o fnl 6f)	1½	**9**	50/1	—	—
1177^{9}	**Miss Night Owl** (RGFrost) **5-10-13** JFrost (pld hrd: prom: hmpd 6f out: wknd & eased 3f out)	13	**10**	16/1	—	—
	Scoring Pedigree (IRE) (JWMullins) **4-11-4** SCurran (bit bkwd: hld up & bhd: gd hdwy on ins to ld 6f out: rdn 2f out: r.o wl: fin 1st: disq: plcd last)		**D**	$3/1^{2}$	—	—

(SP 126.1%) **10 Rn**

3m 51.0 CSF £9.12 TOTE £4.50: £1.10 £2.90 £1.60 (£7.00) Trio £4.90 OWNER D G & D J Robinson (WANTAGE) BRED D. Robinson
STEWARDS' ENQUIRY Curran susp. 23 & 25-27/11/96 (irresponsible riding).

Midas got the race in the Stewards' Room, despite not being involved in the key incident in the back straight. (3/1)
Little Jake (IRE) was one of the fittest of the newcomers. (7/4: 5/4-2/1)

King of The Blues proved a handful to settle and will be sharper for the outing. (11/2: op 5/2)
Halam Bell had finished in the next parish in a previous outing. (33/1)
Miss Night Owl, the sufferer in the incident, was given an easy time when her chance had gone in the home straight. (16/1)
Scoring Pedigree (IRE) was supported in the Ring. His rider seemed to have a blood-rush in the back straight and barged Miss Night Owl when shooting up the inside to lead. It came as no surprise to find Curran finding himself in hot water. (3/1: 4/1-5/2)

T/Plpt: £23.00 (455.6 Tckts). T/Qdpt: £10.30 (81.29 Tckts). KH

0819-TOWCESTER (R-H) (Good)
Thursday November 14th
WEATHER: fine

1337 FLURRY KNOX (S) HURDLE (4,5,6 & 7-Y.O) (Class G)
1-20 (1-21) **2m (8 hdls)** £2,115.00 (£590.00: £285.00) GOING: 0.12 sec per fur (G)

				SP	RR	SF
	Willy Star (BEL) (MrsSJSmith) **6-10-12** RichardGuest (trckd ldrs: led 2 out: clr whn hit last: rdn out)	—	**1**	4/1[3]	62	25
	Tamandu (CJames) **6-11-0** MrEJames (led: rdn 3 out: hdd & hit next: one pce)	6	**2**	11/4[2]	58	21
	Cross Talk (IRE) (NTinkler) **4-10-12** JOsborne (nt j.w: hdwy whn blnd 5th: ev ch appr 2 out: one pce)	½	**3**	6/5[1]	56	19
1086[3]	**My Harvinski (76)** (IRJones) **6-10-5**(7) MissEJJones (chsd ldrs to 3 out)	14	**4**	10/1	42	5
1039[P]	**Just for a Reason (89)** (RTJuckes) **4-10-12** WMarston (bit bkwd: prom tl rdn & btn appr 2 out)	3½	**5**	15/2	38	1
	Brown Eyed Girl (BJMcMath) **4-10-7** CLlewellyn (prom tl rdn & wknd appr 2 out)	5	**6**	20/1	28	—
679[12]	**Autumn Flame (IRE)** (OBrennan) **5-10-7** MBrennan (lw: hld up & plld hrd: nvr nr ldrs)	2	**7**	16/1	26	—
25[8]	**Derrybelle** (DLWilliams) **5-10-7** MClarke (w ldr tl wknd qckly appr 3 out)	dist	**8**	14/1	—	—
	Master Upex (ASNeaves) **4-10-6**(7)ow1 WGreatrex (bkwd: nt j.w: a bhd)	11	**9**	25/1	—	—
1036[P]	**Olden Days** (GThorner) **4-10-12** ILawrence (bit bkwd: s.i.s: rdn 4th: a bhd: t.o whn p.u bef 2 out)		**P**	20/1	—	—
915[W]	***Tomal*** (RIngram) **4-10-12** AMaguire (Withdrawn not under Starter's orders: by permission of the Stewards)		**W**		—	—
				(SP 138.9%)		**10 Rn**

3m 55.5 (9.50) CSF £17.85 TOTE £5.10: £1.80 £1.60 £1.10 (£16.60) Trio £6.70 OWNER Mrs S. Smith (BINGLEY) BRED Madame W. Verwey
No bid
Willy Star (BEL) had no problem staying the trip, despite taking a good hold, and was well in control in the straight. (4/1)
Tamandu had a pipe-opener on the Flat recently and dictated the pace. Flat-footed at the last two hurdles, he was no match for the winner. (11/4: 7/4-3/1)
Cross Talk (IRE), making his hurdles debut, won recently on the Flat, but was having his nineteenth race of the year. Far from fluent at his hurdles, he looked in charge between the flights, but his moderate jumping eventually took its toll. (6/5: evens-5/4)
1086 My Harvinski was easily outpaced from the third last, but has yet to prove that a step up in trip would be beneficial. (10/1: 8/1-12/1)
Just for a Reason still looked as if the race would do him good, but has failed to shine since changing stables. (15/2)
Brown Eyed Girl, given a break after an unsuccessful Flat campaign, jumped adequately and stamina may have been a problem on such a stiff track. (20/1)
Derrybelle (14/1: 7/1-16/1)

1338 TIFFIELD H'CAP CHASE (0-125) (5-Y.O+) (Class D)
1-50 (1-50) **3m 1f (18 fncs)** £3,738.00 (£1,119.00: £537.00: £246.00) GOING minus 0.05 sec per fur (G)

				SP	RR	SF
	Ballyea Boy (IRE) (101) (DNicholson) **6-11-6** AMaguire (j.w: led 10th: rdn & wandered appr last: sn hdd: led again nr fin)	—	**1**	3/1[2]	107	40
1122[4]	**Ardcroney Chief (90)** (DRGandolfo) **10-10-9** RDunwoody (w ldrs: rdn & led last: ct nr fin)	nk	**2**	5/1	96	29
1142[2]	**Celtic Silver (93)** (MrsSJSmith) **8-10-12** RichardGuest (hld up: hit 8th: hdwy 11th: rdn appr 2 out: nt clr run & swtchd appr last: one pce)	4	**3**	7/4[1]	96	29
1194*	**Drumcullen (IRE) (102)** (KCBailey) **7-11-0**(7) 6x MrRWakley (led: hit 6th: hdd 10th: mstke 12th: sn no ch)	dist	**4**	4/1[3]	—	—
	Nicklup (105) (CaptTAForster) **9-11-10** AThornton (lw: fell 2nd)		**F**	9/2	—	—
				(SP 116.2%)		**5 Rn**

6m 23.7 (8.70) CSF £16.46 TOTE £3.50: £1.80 £3.00 (£12.60) OWNER Mr Denis Barry (TEMPLE GUITING) BRED Ted O'Rourke
Ballyea Boy (IRE), still a maiden over hurdles, wore a crossed-noseband and looked very well handicapped for his chasing debut on the best of his form. Wandering and pricking his ears approaching the last, he did not exactly battle his heart out in a tight finish before getting up. Whether it was just inexperience or an attitude problem - he had finished second five times in the last two seasons - only time will tell, but there is a chance blinkers might help. (3/1: op 2/1)
1122 Ardcroney Chief, without a win since the end of 1994 and over nearly half a mile further than his longest ever winning trip, was in the van throughout, travelling well, but found his stamina stretched by the stiff uphill finish. (5/1)
1142 Celtic Silver, whose previous record on stiff tracks is not good, looked to be struggling until coming into the picture turning for home. But for having to switch he might have gone close but, although he was hampered by the winner, both of the first two were coming off a true line, and going for such a narrow gap between them was bound to be risky. (7/4)
1194* Drumcullen (IRE) was the reverse of the old adage, a winner without a penalty, as he inherited his win last time when looking held. He found things far too tough on the final circuit, but was no more than ten lengths behind jumping the second last. (4/1: 3/1-9/2)

1339 KEYLINE BUILDERS' MERCHANTS NOVICES' H'CAP HURDLE (0-100) (4-Y.O+) (Class E)
2-20 (2-20) **2m (8 hdls)** £2,302.50 (£640.00: £307.50) GOING: 0.12 sec per fur (G)

				SP	RR	SF
1030*	**Rangitikei (NZ) (97)** (CJMann) **5-12-0** RDunwoody (lw: trckd ldr: led after 3 out: clr whn blnd next: hit last: easily)	—	**1**	13/8[1]	84+	38
1183[3]	**Mr Poppleton (69)** (RBrotherton) **7-10-0** JOsborne (led tl after 3 out: kpt on same pce)	6	**2**	5/1[3]	50	4
476[3]	**Witney-de-Bergerac (IRE) (90)** (JSMoore) **4-11-7** WMcFarland (trckd ldrs: one pce appr 2 out)	3½	**3**	5/2[2]	68	22
31[9]	**Shers Delight (IRE) (88)** (OBrennan) **6-11-5** MBrennan (prom tl wknd appr 2 out)	13	**4**	5/1[3]	53	7
1132[4]	**Ernest William (IRE) (75)** (GAHubbard) **4-10-3**(3) KGaule (chsd ldrs tl blnd & lost pl 4th: n.d after)	22	**5**	11/2	18	—
	Swing Lucky (70) (AGBlackmore) **11-10-1**ow1 DSkyrme (bit bkwd: hld up & bhd: n.d)	1½	**6**	16/1	11	—
1168[P]	**Bold Charlie (69)** (SMellor) **4-10-0** NMann (plld hrd: prom tl appr 4th)	6	**7**	25/1	4	—
				(SP 125.1%)		**7 Rn**

3m 56.0 (10.00) CSF £11.01 CT £19.62 TOTE £2.70: £2.00 £3.10 (£6.60) OWNER Mrs J. M. Mayo (UPPER LAMBOURN) BRED D. P. and Mrs S. G. Price

LONG HANDICAP Mr Poppleton 9-9 Swing Lucky 9-11
1030* Rangitikei (NZ) looked the part and did not need luck this time for, although he flattened the last two flights, he proved a league too good for these. (13/8)
1183 Mr Poppleton, still a maiden over hurdles, stuck to his task once headed, but was made to look pedestrian. (5/1: op 5/2)
476 Witney-de-Bergerac (IRE) was travelling as well as any at the third last, but could not pick up to mount a challenge. He stays two miles on the level and might be a very different proposition when stepped up in trip. (5/2)
Shers Delight (IRE), without the visor that transformed him last May and having his first run for five months, was shaken off come the home turn, but is better than this. (5/1)
Ernest William (IRE) did the splits at the fourth, losing many lengths, and was not punished with all hope gone. (11/2)
Swing Lucky gave the impression that he will improve for this, but is not likely to win more than the poorest selling race these days. (16/1)

1340 IRISH R M NOVICES' CHASE (4-Y.O+) (Class E)
2-50 (2-50) **2m 110y (12 fncs)** £3,104.50 (£931.00: £448.00: £206.50) GOING minus 0.05 sec per fur (G)

				SP	RR	SF
	Second Call (CaptTAForster) **7-10-12** RDunwoody (led to 6th: mstke next: outpcd appr 3 out: styd on wl to ld 2 out: sn clr: easily)	—	**1**	15/8[1]	85+	18
1195[C]	**Key To Moyade (IRE) (98)** (MJWilkinson) **6-11-3** ILawrence (prom: led 9th to 2 out: sn btn)	14	**2**	8/1[3]	76	9
	Thinking Twice (USA) (NJHenderson) **7-11-3** JRKavanagh (hld up & plld hrd: effrt 3 out: no ch whn j.rt next)	13	**3**	15/8[1]	64	—
1179[5]	**Copper Cable (70)** (CSmith) **9-11-3** MRanger (lw: w ldrs: mstke 5th: led 6th to 8th: sn bhd)	5	**4**	50/1	59	—
1165[7]	**Upham Rascal** (DRGandolfo) **5-11-3** SWynne (lw: fell 1st)		**F**	50/1	—	—
214[5]	**Rolfe (NZ)** (DNicholson) **6-11-3b** AMaguire (hld up: blnd 5th: hdwy to ld 8th: hdd next: ev ch 3 out: wknd qckly & p.u bef next: b.b.v)		**P**	2/1[2]	—	—
				(SP 117.9%)	**6 Rn**	

4m 11.0 (9.00) CSF £15.83 TOTE £3.00: £1.30 £3.10 (£7.90) OWNER Mr J. H. Day (LUDLOW) BRED C. J. R. Trotter
OFFICIAL EXPLANATION **Rolfe (NZ): bled from the nose.**
Second Call finally got her act together over fences at the seventh attempt. She is not very tall, but is strong and should find another small race. (15/8)
Key To Moyade (IRE), a very good mover who looked well in his coat, briefly established a clear lead after the third last, but was hard at work up the hill to the next and was soon collared. (8/1)
Thinking Twice (USA), who normally needs his first run back after a break, jumped rather deliberately as he got tired in the last half-mile. (15/8: 5/4-2/1)
Copper Cable certainly has the size to make a chaser, but was hesitant at the downhill fence and looked ponderous once the serious business began. (50/1)
214 Rolfe (NZ) overjumped at the downhill fence and slid along on landing, his pilot doing well to stay aboard. This did not cost him much ground, but he stopped in a stride after the third last and was pulled up before the next with a broken blood-vessel. He has looked a tricky ride in the past. (2/1: 5/4-9/4)

1341 MOONLIGHTER 'N.H.' NOVICES' HURDLE (4-Y.O+ F & M) (Class E)
3-20 (3-21) **2m (8 hdls)** £2,407.50 (£670.00: £322.50) GOING: 0.12 sec per fur (G)

				SP	RR	SF
1177[2]	**Potter's Gale (IRE)** (DNicholson) **5-10-7** AMaguire (lw: hld up & plld hrd: hdwy appr 3 out: led 2 out: sn clr: comf)	—	**1**	4/6[1]	60+	2
630[4]	**Marlousion (IRE)** (CPEBrooks) **4-10-7** DGallagher (led to 2nd: ev ch 3 out: led appr next: sn hdd & one pce)	5	**2**	9/1	55	—
	Lady High Sheriff (IRE) (CaptTAForster) **6-10-7** SWynne (led 2nd to next: ev ch 3 out: kpt on same pce)	1½	**3**	16/1	54	—
	Bridge Delight (MJWilkinson) **7-10-0**(7) DCO'Connor (bit bkwd: plld hrd: trckd ldrs: ev ch appr 2 out: sn rdn & one pce)	¾	**4**	40/1	53	—
	Moor Hall Lady (NMBabbage) **5-10-7** WMarston (a.p: led 3 out: sn hdd & btn)	2	**5**	12/1	51	—
	Dark Phoenix (IRE) (OBrennan) **6-10-7** MBrennan (bit bkwd: w ldr: led 3rd to 3 out: sn btn)	hd	**6**	16/1	51	—
	River Bay (IRE) (MissHCKnight) **5-10-7** JOsborne (mstke 1st: trckd ldrs: wkng whn mstke 2 out)	2½	**7**	9/2[2]	48	—
	Maylin Magic (TCasey) **5-10-7** RDunwoody (trckd ldrs: rdn appr 2 out: sn btn)	hd	**8**	5/1[3]	48	—
1036[11]	**Bel-de-Moor** (MPMuggeridge) **4-10-7** CLlewellyn (swtg: a bhd)	8	**9**	50/1	40	—
	Miss Mylette (IRE) (DJWintle) **5-10-7** RBellamy (swtg: sn bhd)	14	**10**	50/1	26	—
	September Breeze (IRE) (TPTate) **5-10-7** RGarritty (bit bkwd: prom: 6th & btn whn fell last)		**F**	25/1	—	—
				(SP 134.5%)	**11 Rn**	

3m 59.8 (13.80) CSF £9.55 TOTE £1.60: £1.10 £2.40 £4.80 (£7.50) Trio £50.90 OWNER Mr J. E. Potter (TEMPLE GUITING) BRED Colman O'Flynn
OFFICIAL EXPLANATION **Dark Phoenix (IRE): blew up after being slightly hampered on the home turn.**
1177 Potter's Gale (IRE) took this hurdles debut in good style eventually, having looked a class apart in the paddock, but not before giving trouble at the start and jumping off a couple of lengths behind the others. (4/6)
504 Marlousion (IRE) had more hurdling experience than most of these and made it count, although she could not change gear once in line for home. (9/1: 6/1-10/1)
Lady High Sheriff (IRE) had an unfortunate start over hurdles last season, but looks to be learning. (16/1)
Bridge Delight took a strong hold early on and was already held when meeting the last flight awkwardly. (40/1)
Moor Hall Lady, having her first run since May, made a respectable hurdles debut, jumping soundly in the main. (12/1)
Dark Phoenix (IRE) has a good, raking stride and was just behind the leaders when short of room momentarily on the home turn. The situation was quickly accepted and she is on the way back. (16/1)
River Bay (IRE) (9/2: 3/1-5/1)
Maylin Magic (5/1: 3/1-11/2)

1342 WICKEN H'CAP HURDLE (0-120) (4-Y.O+) (Class D)
3-50 (3-51) **2m 5f (11 hdls)** £2,951.75 (£884.00: £424.50: £194.75) GOING: 0.12 sec per fur (G)

				SP	RR	SF
	Euphonic (92) (IABalding) **6-10-1** JOsborne (lw: plld hrd: hdwy 7th: led appr 2 out: hit last: rdn out)	—	**1**	11/4[1]	75	9
1088[3]	**Silver Standard (100)** (CaptTAForster) **6-10-9b** SWynne (chsd ldrs: rdn 3 out: kpt on wl appr last)	2	**2**	3/1[2]	82	16
1088[2]	**Fortunes Course (IRE) (111)** (JSKing) **7-10-13**(7) MrAWintle (w ldrs: lft in ld appr 3 out:hdd appr next: kpt on)	2	**3**	3/1[2]	91	25
1123[6]	**Dahlia's Best (USA) (97)** (MissMERowland) **6-10-6** GaryLyons (hdwy 8th: rdn appr 2 out: sn btn)	3	**4**	33/1	75	9
1176[F]	**La Menorquina (USA) (97)** (DMarks) **6-10-6** JAMcCarthy (hld up: hdwy 7th: ev ch appr 2 out: btn appr last)	2	**5**	8/1	73	7
	Braes of Mar (119) (NJHenderson) **6-11-7**(7) TCMurphy (chsd ldrs to 7th)	11	**6**	9/1	87	21

				SP	RR	SF
	Merilena (IRE) (97) (GAHubbard) **6-9-13**(7)ow6 NRossiter (bkwd: led to 3rd: wknd appr 3 out)	29	7	11/1	43	—
1031[5]	**Clean Edge (USA) (105)** (JMackie) **4-10-11**(3) EHusband (s.s: bhd tl p.u lame after 7th: dead)		P	6/1[3]	—	—
	Pyramis Prince (IRE) (103) (JohnWhyte) **6-10-12** AMaguire (bit bkwd: w ldr: led 3rd tl p.u lame appr 3 out)		P	16/1	—	—
				(SP 129.2%)	**9 Rn**	

5m 16.5 (14.50) CSF £12.52 CT £26.00 TOTE £3.60: £2.00 £1.60 £1.30 (£6.40) Trio £8.10 OWNER Mr Paul Stamp (KINGSCLERE) BRED Kingsbrooke Stud

LONG HANDICAP Merilena (IRE) 9-10

Euphonic, in good order on the Flat in late summer, looked well and never seriously looked like being beaten. Although he was bustled along in the closing stages, he gave the impression that he was idling in front, and there was more to come if needed. (11/4: 2/1-7/2)

1088 Silver Standard looked to enjoy the finishing hill, reversing Stratford form with Fortunes Course, but the Handicapper may have his measure at present. (3/1)

1088 Fortunes Course (IRE) was not made as much use of as usual and only got to the front when Pyramis Prince broke down at the bottom of the hill. Her five wins have all come on tight tracks. (3/1)

Dahlia's Best (USA) ran much better on this second start in this country and is worth keeping an eye on. (33/1)

1039 La Menorquina (USA) moved up menacingly on the home turn, but her effort petered out by the last. She does not look to quite get this trip. (8/1)

Braes of Mar, more of a chaser these days, looks pretty harshly treated over hurdles at the moment. (9/1: op 5/1)

Merilena (IRE) (11/1: 10/1-16/1)

T/Jkpt: £4,765.10 (1.49 Tckts). T/Plpt: £26.40 (455.79 Tckts). T/Qdpt: £7.50 (127.02 Tckts). Dk

AYR (L-H) (Good)
Friday November 15th

WEATHER: overcast

1343 GALLOWAY HILLS MAIDEN HURDLE (I) (4-Y.O+) (Class E)

12-25 (12-27) **2m (9 hdls)** £1,996.00 (£556.00: £268.00) GOING: 0.39 sec per fur (GS)

				SP	RR	SF
1152[2]	**Endowment** (MrsMReveley) **4-11-5b** PNiven (lw: mde all: sn clr: hit 3 out & 2 out: styd on u.p flat)	—	1	5/4[1]	76	44
1187[3]	**Grandinare (USA)** (JJO'Neill) **4-11-5b[1]** MDwyer (a chsng wnr: ev ch last: no ex)	3	2	6/4[2]	73	41
	Bill's Pride (PMonteith) **5-11-0** ADobbin (bhd: hdwy 5th: nvr trbld ldrs)	27	3	50/1	41	9
	Bowcliffe (83) (MrsAMNaughton) **5-11-5** JSupple (a chsng ldrs: no imp fr 5th)	3½	4	20/1	43	11
	Public Way (IRE) (NChamberlain) **6-10-12**(7) MissCMetcalfe (lost pl ½-wy: sme late hdwy)	9	5	100/1	34	2
	Percy Parrot (ACWhillans) **4-11-5** BHarding (bhd: hdwy 5th: sn rdn & n.d)	2½	6	20/1	31	—
	Loveyoumillions (IRE) (NTinkler) **4-11-5** LWyer (hit 2nd: bhd: hdwy 4th: sn wknd)	27	7	10/1	4	—
7[6]	**Grinnell (65)** (DMcCune) **6-11-5v** KJohnson (prom to 3rd: t.o fr 5th)	dist	8	200/1	—	—
705[10]	**Smart In Socks** (MissLucindaRussell) **5-11-5** AThornton (prom tl lost pl 4th: sn t.o)	1	9	50/1	—	—
	Fils de Cresson (IRE) (JRAdam) **6-11-5** JRailton (hdwy 4th: 3rd whn fell next)		F	8/1[3]	—	—
	Gallant Major (MABarnes) **4-11-5** JBurke (blnd 1st: prom to 4th: sn t.o: p.u bef 3 out)		P	100/1	—	—
				(SP 120.6%)	**11 Rn**	

3m 47.9 (10.90) CSF £3.49 TOTE £1.50: £1.00 £1.90 £3.70 (£1.90) Trio £13.20 OWNER Mr R. Hilley (SALTBURN) BRED Bloomsbury Stud

IN-FOCUS: **This looked a desperate race if paddock appearance is anything to go by.**

1152 Endowment had the blinkers on and left nothing to chance. He was tired over the last three and had nothing to spare. (5/4: 10/11-6/4)

1187 Grandinare (USA), like the winner with blinkers on for the first time, was the only one to keep tabs on him. When he had a chance, he failed to come up with the goods, and may need further. (6/4: op 9/4)

Bill's Pride, whose action suggests that soft ground would help, showed a little, but there is still some way to go. (50/1)

Bowcliffe managed to win a race on the Flat this season, but was beaten a long way out. (20/1)

Public Way (IRE) last ran over hurdles almost three years ago and, in the circumstances, this was not too bad an effort. (100/1)

Percy Parrot looked fit, but never gave any hopes. (20/1)

Loveyoumillions (IRE) (10/1: op 5/1)

1344 MOSSBLOWN CONDITIONAL (S) H'CAP HURDLE (0-95) (4-Y.O+) (Class G)

12-55 (12-56) **2m 4f (11 hdls)** £1,982.00 (£552.00: £266.00) GOING: 0.39 sec per fur (GS)

				SP	RR	SF
1025[3]	**Latin Leader (81)** (CParker) **6-11-5b** DParker (hld up: stdy hdwy 4 out: chal 3 out: slt ld 2 out: styd on appr last)	—	1	4/1[2]	69	27
805[3]	**Tall Measure (85)** (DGSwindlehurst) **10-11-9b** GCahill (mde most tl hdd 2 out: kpt on one pce)	4	2	5/1	70	28
1047[3]	**Highland Park (82)** (RCraggs) **10-11-1**(5) CMcCormack (lw: a.p: pushed along appr 4 out: styd on: nvr able to chal)	1	3	9/2[3]	66	24
	Skane River (IRE) (71) (GRichards) **5-10-6**(3) MDunne (trckd ldr: hit 7th: ev ch & rdn 3 out: btn whn hit last)	2	4	7/2[1]	53	11
	Nawtinookey (62) (MartinTodhunter) **6-10-0** GLee (bit bkwd: chsd ldrs: hit 4th: rdn appr 3 out: one pce)	3½	5	33/1	42	—
1247[4]	**Chummy's Saga (69)** (LLungo) **6-10-0**(7) IJardine (hld up: gd hdwy 6th: rdn & btn appr 3 out)	hd	6	12/1	49	7
	We're in the Money (62) (MissJBower) **12-9-7**(7) ClaudineFroggitt (a bhd)	18	7	33/1	27	—
	Troy's Dream (76) (MDHammond) **5-10-9**(5) RBurns (in tch: hit 6th: wknd appr 3 out)	6	8	8/1	36	—
1049[12]	**Sayraf Dancer (IRE) (76)** (MrsAMNaughton) **7-11-0** JSupple (plld hrd: jnd ldrs 5th: wknd after next)	6	9	14/1	32	—
1247[F]	**Circle Boy (68)** (WStorey) **9-10-6** RMcGrath (bit bkwd: bhd: sme hdwy 6th: wknd 4 out)	¾	10	13/2	23	—
856[5]	**Latvian (86)** (RAllan) **9-11-7v**(3) SMelrose (lost tch fr 6th)	15	11	25/1	29	—
				(SP 125.6%)	**11 Rn**	

4m 59.6 (18.60) CSF £24.61 CT £88.07 TOTE £5.10: £1.90 £1.80 £2.10 (£29.50) Trio £31.60 OWNER Mr & Mrs Raymond Anderson Green (LOCKERBIE) BRED Cheveley Park Stud Ltd

LONG HANDICAP Nawtinookey 9-6

No bid

1025 Latin Leader always looked to be going best, but it took some strong assistance to persuade him to take command going to the second last. (4/1)

805 Tall Measure is a game front-runner who deserves to pick up a race. (5/1)

1047 Highland Park is running consistently well, but is just short of that vital turn of foot to take the opportunity. (9/2)

Skane River (IRE) was really put into the race this time, only to find things too tough late on. This run should improve him. (7/2)

Nawtinookey showed some reasonable form two years ago on this track and gave signs of coming back here for his new stable. (33/1)

1247 Chummy's Saga does not seem to get home these days. (12/1)
Circle Boy (13/2: 4/1-7/1)

1345 GALLOWAY HILLS MAIDEN HURDLE (II) (4-Y.O+) (Class E)

1-30 (1-31) **2m (9 hdls)** £1,982.00 (£552.00: £266.00) GOING: 0.39 sec per fur (GS)

				SP	RR	SF
	Clare Maid (IRE) (GRichards) **7-11-0** ADobbin (trckd ldrs: led 3 out: r.o)	—	**1**	3/1^{2}	63+	10
	Jaunty General (CParker) **5-11-5** BStorey (lw: lft in ld 1st: hdd 3 out: kpt on same pce)	4	**2**	7/1^{3}	64	11
1078^{5}	**Fenian Court (IRE) (77)** (MissJBower) **5-11-0** ASSmith (hld up: stdy hdwy appr 3 out: styd on: nt pce tochal)	2½	**3**	16/1	57	4
1021^{10}	**Mullins (IRE)** (DMoffatt) **5-11-5** DJMoffatt (trckd ldrs: effrt appr 3 out: sn outpcd)	5	**4**	25/1	57	4
	Sunny Leith (PMonteith) **5-11-2**(3) GCahill (bit bkwd: prom tl outpcd 4 out: styd on towards fin)	7	**5**	50/1	50	—
1079^{3}	**Golf Land (IRE)** (LLungo) **4-11-5** MDwyer (mstkes: trckd ldrs: effrt whn hit 3 out: sn btn)	6	**6**	9/4^{1}	44	—
	Akito Racing (IRE) (MartinTodhunter) **5-11-0** PNiven (bit bkwd: in tch tl outpcd appr 3 out)	8	**7**	50/1	31	—
	Dara Knight (IRE) (RBSmyth,Ireland) **7-10-12**(7) GMartin (swtg: plld hrd: prom tl blnd 4 out: sn t.o)	dist	**8**	50/1	—	—
	Jarrow (MrsAMNaughton) **5-11-5** JSupple (bit bkwd: hld up: fell 4th)		**F**	20/1	—	—
	Judicious Norman (IRE) (JRAdam) **5-11-5** JRailton (led tl j.b lft & uns rdr 1st)		**U**	3/1^{2}	—	—
				(SP 113.6%)	**10 Rn**	

3m 54.2 (17.20) CSF £22.02 TOTE £3.00: £1.40 £2.40 £3.60 (£8.40) Trio £24.80 OWNER Mr Leslie Lowry (PENRITH) BRED L. Lowry
Clare Maid (IRE), an Irish import, won this really well, but the opposition were not up to much. (3/1)
Jaunty General ran quite well, but was easily tapped for toe late on. (7/1)
1078 Fenian Court (IRE), patiently ridden this time, ran much better. This should have boosted his confidence. (16/1)
7 Mullins (IRE) had his chances, but was firmly put in his place when the pressure was on over the last three flights. (25/1)
Sunny Leith, who needed the experience and the run for fitness, shaped as though stiffer tests would suit. (50/1)
1079 Golf Land (IRE), a sloppy jumper, was most disappointing when pressure was applied. (9/4)

1346 GLENGOYNE SINGLE HIGHLAND MALT TAMEROSIA SERIES (QUALIFIER) NOVICES' CHASE (5-Y.O+) (Class D)

2-05 (2-05) **2m (12 fncs)** £3,675.00 (£1,110.00: £540.00: £255.00) GOING: 0.39 sec per fur (GS)

				SP	RR	SF
	Sparky Gayle (IRE) (CParker) **6-11-0** BStorey (lw: hld up: gd hdwy 8th: led 2 out: r.o strly)	—	**1**	2/1^{1}	110++	43
	Bold Boss (GMMoore) **7-11-0** NBentley (hld up: hdwy to ld 6th: mstke 4 out: hdd 2 out: sn btn)	12	**2**	11/2^{2}	98+	31
	Jack Doyle (IRE) (JJO'Neill) **5-11-0** MDwyer (bit bkwd: hld up: smooth hdwy 8th: 4th whn blnd 3 out: styd on: no imp)	4	**3**	8/1^{3}	94+	27
910^{7}	**Music Blitz** (MrsDThomson) **5-11-0** TReed (a chsng ldrs: one pce fr 4 out)	1¾	**4**	33/1	92	25
1022^{2}	**Castleroyal (IRE)** (IRFerguson,Ireland) **7-11-6** LWyer (chsd ldrs tl outpcd 4 out: fin lame)	7	**5**	2/1^{1}	91	24
1248^{7}	**Nijway (78)** (MABarnes) **6-11-0** JBurke (led: hit 5th: hdd next: nt j.w after: no imp fr 4 out)	1	**6**	100/1	84	17
856^{4}	**Bolaney Girl (IRE)** (FPMurtagh) **7-10-9** RSupple (hld up: hdwy & in tch 7th: grad wknd appr 4 out)	nk	**7**	33/1	79	12
	Uk Hygiene (IRE) (MDHammond) **6-11-0** RGarritty (bit bkwd: nvr nr to chal)	3	**8**	20/1	81	14
	Crosshot (RMcDonald) **9-11-0** KJones (prom to 8th)	3	**9**	50/1	78	11
	Singing Sand (PMonteith) **6-11-0** ADobbin (a bhd: blnd 7th)	1½	**10**	33/1	76	9
	Grand as Owt (65) (DMcCune) **6-11-0** KJohnson (a bhd)	16	**11**	200/1	60	—
1009*	**Devilry (100)** (RCraggs) **6-11-6** ASSmith (bhd: blnd 4th: n.d)	¾	**12**	14/1	66	—
1248^{U}	**Fine Tune (IRE) (60)** (MrsSCBradburne) **6-11-0** AThornton (chsd ldrs: hdwy whn hit 8th: sn wknd)	7	**13**	200/1	53	—
	Paint Your Wagon (NChamberlain) **6-11-0** DJMoffatt (mstkes: bhd whn blnd & uns rdr 3rd)		**U**	200/1	—	—
				(SP 117.9%)	**14 Rn**	

3m 55.3 (10.30) CSF £12.58 TOTE £3.00: £1.30 £2.40 £4.50 (£13.00) Trio £24.40 OWNER Mr & Mrs Raymond Anderson Green (LOCKERBIE) BRED Thomas Walsh
Sparky Gayle (IRE), despite the trip being on the short side, won in really good style. Plenty more opportunities should be found. (2/1: 6/4-5/2)
Bold Boss put up a good show at his first attempt at chasing and will not always meet one so useful. (11/2)
Jack Doyle (IRE), looking likely to benefit from this, showed fair ability. Once he gets his jumping fully together, his turn will come. (8/1: 4/1-9/1)
910 Music Blitz showed enough here to suggest that there is a race or two in him. (33/1)
1022 Castleroyal (IRE) never seemed happy at his fences and was found to be lame on pulling up. (2/1)
Nijway hit more fences than he jumped cleanly. There is more improvement to come if he ever gets the hang of things. (100/1)
856 Bolaney Girl (IRE) has her own ideas about the game, but she does have ability and did jump reasonably. (33/1)
Uk Hygiene (IRE) needed this and should improve as a result. (20/1)

1347 FIVEWAYS H'CAP HURDLE (0-130) (4-Y.O+) (Class C)

2-40 (2-41) **3m 110y (12 hdls)** £3,415.00 (£1,030.00: £500.00: £235.00) GOING: 0.39 sec per fur (GS)

				SP	RR	SF
1207*	**Lochnagrain (IRE) (113)** (MrsMReveley) **8-11-2** 5x PNiven (lw: trckd ldrs: disp ld appr 3 out: outpcd 2 out: rallied to disp ld last: led post)	—	**1**	4/6^{1}	94	40
509^{2}	**Huso (97)** (PCHaslam) **8-9-9**(5) STaylor (hld up: hdwy 7th: disp ld appr 3 out: led 2 out: hdd & no ex towards fin)	s.h	**2**	7/1^{3}	78?	24
1255^{3}	**Pharare (IRE) (97)** (RDEWoodhouse) **6-10-0** LWyer (lw: led tl appr 3 out: one pce)	14	**3**	3/1^{2}	69	15
	Palacegate King (125) (ACWhillans) **7-11-9**(5) ECallaghan (hld up: hdwy 4 out: wknd after next)	5	**4**	11/1	94	40
	Dig Deeper (104) (RAllan) **9-10-7** ADobbin (w ldr tl rdn & wknd 4 out)	19	**5**	20/1	60	6
	Marchwood (98) (NChamberlain) **9-9-8**(7)ow1 MissCMetcalfe (mstkes: wnt prom ½-wy: wknd 7th)	5	**6**	25/1	51	—
				(SP 114.4%)	**6 Rn**	

6m 3.5 (17.50) CSF £5.93 TOTE £1.60: £1.40 £2.40 (£3.90) OWNER Lightbody of Hamilton Ltd (SALTBURN) BRED Michael Cuddy
LONG HANDICAP Pharare (IRE) 9-9 Huso 9-5 Marchwood 9-7
1207* Lochnagrain (IRE) was inclined to hang when put under maximum pressure, but he was well handled and, in a desperate finish, just got there. (4/6)
509 Huso put in a terrific effort from 9lb of the handicap. (7/1)
1255 Pharare (IRE) likes to make it, but was continually pestered by Dig Deeper. Once he had shaken him off, he was picked off by the front pair. (3/1)
Palacegate King, from a stable that is not really firing, ran reasonably and should be all the better for it, especially when he gets his desired soft ground. (11/1: 5/1-12/1)
Dig Deeper stopped quickly on the home turn. (20/1)

1348 JOAN MACKAY NOVICES' H'CAP CHASE (0-105) (5-Y.O+) (Class D)

3-15 (3-16) **2m 4f (17 fncs)** £3,616.50 (£1,092.00: £531.00: £250.50) GOING: 0.39 sec per fur (GS)

	Horse / Details	Dist	Pos	SP	RR	SF
	Monnaie Forte (IRE) (90) (JRAdam) **6-11-0** JRailton (bit bkwd: chsd ldrs: outpcd 4 out: 8l 3rd whn lft clr last)	—	1	12/1	98	14
	Bells Hill Lad (83) (JBarclay) **9-10-7** ADobbin (chsd ldr: blnd 12th: rdn to chal 4 out: sn outpcd)	10	2	14/1	83	—
	Diamond Sprite (USA) (79) (RBSmyth,Ireland) **9-9-10**(7) GMartin (swtg: bhd: lost tch fr 9th)	dist	3	25/1	—	—
1120P	**Jymjam Johnny (IRE) (100)** (JJO'Neill) **7-11-10** MDwyer (plld hrd: hdwy 11th: rdn 3 out: chal whn fell last: rmntd)	dist	4	2/1 2	—	—
1264³	**Blue Charm (IRE) (93)** (MrsSCBradburne) **6-11-3** RGarritty (trckd ldrs tl fell 5th)		F	10/11 1	—	—
1248⁴	**Show Your Hand (IRE) (80)** (LLungo) **8-10-4** MFoster (led: mstke 2nd: rdn & slt ld whn fell last)		F	10/1 3	—	—
1051P	**See You Always (IRE) (76)** (MABarnes) **6-10-0** BStorey (hmpd & uns rdr 5th)		U	33/1	—	—

(SP 116.0%) **7 Rn**

5m 16.4 (21.40) CSF £128.44 CT £3,699.20 TOTE £10.90: £2.50 £4.80 (£78.10) Trio £54.50 OWNER Mr James Adam (GORDON) BRED E. Stuart Knape

LONG HANDICAP See You Always (IRE) 8-11

Monnaie Forte (IRE), after a long absence, was running a nice race and not being knocked about when he was presented with this. (12/1: op 8/1)

Bells Hill Lad, after a year off, ran really well and made only one serious mistake. He is much better suited by soft ground. (14/1)

Diamond Sprite (USA), who sweated up, never gave any signs of hope. (25/1)

Jymjam Johnny (IRE) spent much of the race pulling for his head. He did respond to pressure in the straight and was challenging strongly, but looking just second best, when falling at the last. (2/1)

1264 Blue Charm (IRE) (10/11: evens-11/10)

1248 Show Your Hand (IRE) put up a brave attempt to make all and was hanging on by the skin of his teeth when falling at the last. (10/1: 8/1-12/1)

1349 LAGG 'N.H.' NOVICES' HURDLE (4-Y.O+) (Class E)

3-45 (3-47) **3m 110y (17 hdls)** £2,402.00 (£672.00: £326.00) GOING: 0.39 sec per fur (GS)

	Horse / Details	Dist	Pos	SP	RR	SF
1139²	**Trap Dancer** (PMonteith) **8-10-12** ADobbin (a.p: led 4 out: styd on wl)	—	1	3/1 2	67	8
	Bold Fountain (IRE) (GMMoore) **5-10-12** NBentley (hld up: mstkes: hdwy ½-wy: ev ch 3 out: hrd rdn & one pce)	7	2	Evens 1	62	3
	Phar Echo (IRE) (LLungo) **5-10-12** MFoster (bhd: hdwy to jn ldrs 7th: outpcd appr 3 out)	10	3	10/1	56	—
	Pocaire Gaoithe (IRE) (WStorey) **6-10-12** MMoloney (bit bkwd: prom: outpcd & mstke 8th: styd on fr 3 out)	s.h	4	25/1	56	—
	Alnbrook (ACWhillans) **5-10-12** KJohnson (chsd ldrs tl wknd appr 3 out)	3	5	25/1	54	—
1139⁶	**Ethical Note (IRE)** (MrsSJSmith) **5-10-5**(7) RWilkinson (mde most to 4 out: sn rdn & btn)	14	6	25/1	45	—
910¹⁶	**Willie Wannabe (IRE)** (MrsDThomson) **6-10-12** TReed (rdn 8th: nvr trbld ldrs)	3½	7	100/1	43	—
	Jigginstown (JJO'Neill) **9-10-12** ARoche (bhd: sme hdwy 8th: sn btn)	12	8	15/2 3	35	—
1247⁸	**Meadowleck (52)** (WGYoung) **7-10-7** BStorey (cl up: disp ld 6th to 8th: sn wknd)	11	9	100/1	23	—
	Smart In Satin (MissLucindaRussell) **6-10-12** AThornton (mstkes: hdwy ½-wy: sn wknd: p.u bef 4 out)		P	33/1	—	—
1139⁵	**Profit And Loss** (FMurphy) **5-10-7** MDwyer (outpcd fr 7th: sn bhd: p.u bef 3 out)		P	12/1	—	—

(SP 120.0%) **11 Rn**

6m 13.0 (27.00) CSF £6.21 TOTE £3.30: £1.50 £1.00 £2.40 (£3.10) Trio £15.10 OWNER Mr A. Dawson (ROSEWELL) BRED Littleton Stud

1139 Trap Dancer, who stays particularly well and is game, was well on top from the second last. (3/1)

Bold Fountain (IRE), after almost a year off, ran really well, but his hurdling left something to be desired. Once it improves, better will be seen. (Evens)

Phar Echo (IRE), put in the race at halfway, found lack of experience against him in the home straight. This should help bring him on. (10/1:op 6/1)

Pocaire Gaoithe (IRE), needing this, looked a real stayer. (25/1)

Alnbrook ran reasonably for his new stable and there looks more to come. (25/1)

1139 Profit And Loss ran poorly on ground faster than she prefers. (12/1: op 7/1)

T/Jkpt: Not won; £2,784.36 to Windsor 16/11/96. T/Plpt: £751.80 (14.16 Tckts). T/Qdpt: £92.20 (12.27 Tckts). AA

1065-CHELTENHAM (L-H) (Good to firm)

Friday November 15th

WEATHER: overcast

1350 COLN VALLEY FISH AND GAME COMPANY AMATEUR H'CAP CHASE (0-130) (5-Y.O+) (Class E)

1-15 (1-15) **2m 4f 110y (Old) (15 fncs)** £3,160.00 (£955.00: £465.00: £220.00) GOING: 0.18 sec per fur (G)

	Horse / Details	Dist	Pos	SP	RR	SF
	Dancing Vision (IRE) (111) (EMcNamara,Ireland) **6-10-1**(7)ow1 MrJTMcNamara (hld up in rr: hdwy whn hmpd 3 out: led on bit last: r.o wl)	—	1	4/1 3	112	44
979*	**Coolree (IRE) (114)** (PFNicholls) **8-10-4**(7) MrJTizzard (nt j.w: hld up: stdy hdwy 6th: j.rt & hit 3 out: led appr last: sn hdd: hung lft flat: nt qckn)	1¾	2	9/4 1	114	47
1182P	**Man Mood (FR) (117)** (CPEBrooks) **5-10-6**(7) MrEJames (hld up: hdwy 8th: led after 2 out: hdd appr last: wknd flat)	8	3	16/1	110	42
1147³	**Cropredy Lad (106)** (PRWebber) **9-9-10**(7)ow3 MrPScott (led to 5th: led 11th tl after 2 out: wknd)	6	4	11/1	95	25
979²	**Oscail An Doras (IRE) (113)** (FMurphy) **7-10-5**(5) MrRThornton (prom: lost pl 8th: rallied 10th: rdn appr 3 out: wknd appr 2 out)	10	5	11/4 2	94	27
	Spanish Light (IRE) (132) (SirJohnBarlowBt) **7-11-8**(7)ow5 MrDBarlow (bkwd: plld hrd: chsd ldr: led 5th to 11th: wknd qckly after 4 out: t.o whn p.u bef last)		P	4/1 3	—	—

(SP 111.7%) **6 Rn**

5m 9.1 (7.10) CSF £12.77 TOTE £4.00: £1.90 £1.80 (£5.00) OWNER Mr James Carey (RATHKEALE) BRED A. Tarry

LONG HANDICAP Spanish Light (IRE) 11-5 Man Mood (FR) 10-8 Coolree (IRE) 10-6 Oscail An Doras (IRE) 10-5 Dancing Vision (IRE) 10-2 Cropredy Lad 9-7

WEIGHT FOR AGE 5yo-1lb

Dancing Vision (IRE) had to overcome his rider nearly being unseated when Coolree jumped across him three out, but he still came there galloping all over the favourite going to the last. (4/1)

979* Coolree (IRE) gave young Tizzard a horrible ride over these fences, which culminated in him ducking in behind the winner on the run-in. (9/4: op 6/4)
1182 Man Mood (FR) ran much better with his tongue tied down. (16/1)
1147 Cropredy Lad was dropped in distance. (11/1)
979 Oscail An Doras (IRE) had only been beaten five lengths by the runner-up at Ludlow and was 4lb better off. (11/4: 2/1-3/1)

1351 SCUDAMORE CLOTHING 0800 301 301 NOVICES' HURDLE (4-Y.O+) (Class C)

1-50 (1-50) **2m 5f (Old) (10 hdls)** £3,680.00 (£1,115.00: £545.00: £260.00) GOING: 0.18 sec per fur (G)

				SP	RR	SF
	Hunting Lore (IRE) (117) (NJHenderson) **5-11-8** MAFitzgerald (bkwd: nt j.w: rdn & hdwy appr 3 out: outpcd appr 2 out: rallied to ld flat: all out)	—	**1**	9/4^{2}	79	25
219^{2}	**Supermodel (90)** (MrsNMacauley) **4-10-8**$^{(5)}$ MrRThornton (hld up: hdwy 4th: rdn appr 3 out: led 2 out: sn clr: wknd last: hdd flat)	1¼	**2**	20/1	69	15
1292^{3}	**Leap in the Dark (IRE) (78)** (MissLCSiddall) **7-11-0** AMaguire (hdwy 6th: outpcd 7th: lft 3rd last)	9	**3**	66/1	63	9
1180^{F}	**Operetto (IRE)** (MrsSusanNock) **6-11-0** MrEJames (wl bhd 3rd: nvr nr ldrs)	1¾	**4**	66/1	62	8
	Blaaziing Joe (IRE) (DLWilliams) **5-11-0** PHolley (bit bkwd: bhd: mstke 4th: lost tch fr 6th: t.o)	dist	**5**	66/1	—	—
1067*	**Courbaril (120)** (MCPipe) **4-11-8** APMcCoy (led & sn clr: hit 3 out, slipped & fell)		**F**	8/11^{1}	—	—
968*	**Edgemoor Prince** (PJHobbs) **5-11-4** RDunwoody (chsd ldr: lft in ld 3 out: hdd 2 out: cl 3rd & rallying whn slipped bdly last: sn p.u)		**P**	7/1^{3}	74?	—
				(SP 110.4%)		**7 Rn**

5m 14.5 (16.50) CSF £33.83 TOTE £3.00: £1.70 £3.90 (£17.40) OWNER Mr Milton Ritzenberg (LAMBOURN) BRED Miss Anne Casey
Hunting Lore (IRE), far from fluent at his hurdles, blew up coming down the hill but, with Coubaril unluckily capsizing, he found his second wind to collar a rival who tired going to the final flight. (9/4: op 5/4)
219 Supermodel has been racing on the Flat since finishing second in a visor in July at Worcester. She seemed to have it in the bag rounding the elbow, but the stiff climb to the finish found her out. (20/1)
1292 Leap in the Dark (IRE) got left for dead at the top of the hill. (66/1)
1067* Courbaril had a commanding advantage when he unluckily clipped the top of the downhill flight, three out, and could not recover on the greasy surface. (8/11: op 5/4)
968* Edgemoor Prince was staying on again in third place when he unluckily slipped and did the splits at the final flight. (7/1)

1352 MITSUBISHI SHOGUN H'CAP CHASE (0-145) (5-Y.O+) (Class B)

2-25 (2-28) **2m (Old) (12 fncs)** £6,827.00 (£2,066.00: £1,008.00: £479.00) GOING: 0.18 sec per fur (G)

				SP	RR	SF
1128^{4}	**Konvekta King (IRE) (125)** (OSherwood) **8-11-2** JOsborne (led to 3rd: chsd ldr tl blnd 4 out: sn lost pl: rdn & rallied to ld last: r.o wl)	—	**1**	10/1	129	53
1087^{2}	**Southampton (120)** (GBBalding) **6-10-11v** APMcCoy (hld up: lft 2nd 4 out: ev ch whn pckd 2 out: one pce)	2½	**2**	11/8^{1}	122	46
	Lord Dorcet (IRE) (133) (JIACharlton) **6-11-10** RDunwoody (bit bkwd: led 3rd to last: wknd)	4	**3**	6/4^{2}	131+	55
943^{3}	**Captain Khedive (130)** (PFNicholls) **8-11-7** AMaguire (hld up in rr: mstkes 2nd & 7th: sn wl bhd: t.o)	29	**4**	9/2^{3}	99	23
				(SP 109.4%)		**4 Rn**

3m 58.3 (5.30) CSF £22.61 TOTE £10.80 (£6.20) OWNER Konvekta Ltd (UPPER LAMBOURN) BRED Peter Kehoe in Ireland
1128 Konvekta King (IRE), dropped 5lb, was in trouble after belting the ditch at the top of the hill. Really responding to pressure on the home turn, the fact that Lord Dorcet appeared to blow up helped him greatly. (10/1)
1087 Southampton, with his visor refitted, lost valuable momentum when on his nose at the penultimate fence. (11/8: op evens)
Lord Dorcet (IRE) developed into a useful novice last season, and looks set for another successful campaign as it was only lack of a recent outing that beat him here. (6/4)
943 Captain Khedive again found a Grade One course exposing his jumping deficiencies. (9/2)

1353 MURPHY'S 'IN A BOTTLE' HURDLE (4-Y.O) (Class B)

3-00 (3-01) **2m 110y (Old) (8 hdls)** £5,896.00 (£1,656.00: £808.00) GOING: 0.18 sec per fur (G)

				SP	RR	SF
318a^{3}	**Just Little** (APO'Brien,Ireland) **4-10-12** CFSwan (hld up: stdy hdwy to ld on bit last: v.easily)	—	**1**	8/13^{1}	95+	37
1125^{4}	**Mim-Lou-and (115)** (MissHCKnight) **4-11-0** JOsborne (chsd ldrs: chal whn j.slowly 3 out: rdn to ld after 2 out: hdd last: no ch w wnr)	7	**2**	9/2^{3}	90	32
1152^{5}	**Samanid (IRE) (110)** (MissLCSiddall) **4-11-3** AMaguire (led tl after 2 out: sn wknd)	21	**3**	25/1	73	15
1319^{R}	**Danjing (IRE) (131)** (MCPipe) **4-11-3b** APMcCoy (ref to r: t.n.p)		**R**	3/1^{2}	—	—
				(SP 108.9%)		**4 Rn**

3m 58.9 (7.90) CSF £3.56 TOTE £1.60 (£2.00) OWNER Mr S. O'Farrell (PILTOWN) BRED Moyglare Stud Farm Ltd
Just Little was third in the Galway Hurdle when ridden with supreme confidence, and it turned out to be totally justified. She will reappear here tomorrow before being put away for the spring. (8/13)
1125 Mim-Lou-and found the winner laughing at him. (9/2)
341 Samanid (IRE), up in class, was possibly a bit too keen for his own good. (25/1)
1319 Danjing (IRE), who changed hands for 28,000 guineas at Ascot June Sales, had the blinkers refitted and is looking an expensive buy. (3/1: op 6/4)

1354 STEEL PLATE AND SECTIONS NOVICES' CHASE (5-Y.O+) (Class B)

3-35 (3-35) **3m 1f (Old) (19 fncs)** £8,430.00 (£2,070.00) GOING: 0.18 sec per fur (G)

				SP	RR	SF
1054^{2}	**Stormtracker (IRE) (107)** (CWeedon) **7-11-5** MRichards (lw: chsd ldr to 4th: led after 15th: mstke 4 out: wl clr fr 3 out)	—	**1**	8/1^{3}	86	9
869*	**Factor Ten (IRE) (123)** (MissHCKnight) **8-11-8** AMaguire (led: mstke 15th: sn hdd: wknd 3 out: b.b.v)	dist	**2**	15/8^{2}	—	—
1136^{2}	**Minor Key (IRE)** (JRJenkins) **6-11-0** JOsborne (chsd ldr 4th tl fell 9th)		**F**	25/1	—	—
1129*	**The Last Fling (IRE) (118)** (MrsSJSmith) **6-11-5** RichardGuest (hld up: hdwy 7th: hit 8th: lft 2nd 9th: 3rd whn blnd & uns rdr 14th)		**U**	8/13^{1}	—	—
				(SP 111.6%)		**4 Rn**

6m 34.4 (25.40) CSF £21.48 TOTE £7.80 (£4.80) OWNER Mr Tim Davis (CHIDDINGFOLD) BRED Mrs M. Brophy
OFFICIAL EXPLANATION **Factor Ten (IRE): bled from the nose.**
1054 Stormtracker (IRE) survived an anxious moment at the final ditch, but was safe - the only other finisher bled. This was a non-event. (8/1: 6/1-9/1)
869* Factor Ten (IRE) lost the advantage after missing out at the fifth from home and was subsequently found to have bled. (15/8)

1129* The Last Fling (IRE) shot his rider over his head at the penultimate ditch. (8/13)

1355 EUROBALE CONDITIONAL H'CAP HURDLE (0-130) (4-Y.O+) (Class E)
4-05 (4-05) **2m 5f (Old) (10 hdls)** £3,046.00 (£856.00: £418.00) GOING: 0.18 sec per fur (G)

				SP	RR	SF
1201^{6}	**World Express (IRE) (100)** (BRMillman) **6-10-6b** DSalter (chsd ldr: led & hit 3 out: clr last: r.o wl)	—	1	5/2^{2}	86	8
1121^{P}	**Ramsdens (IRE) (100)** (NATwiston-Davies) **4-10-6b^{1}** DWalsh (led to 3 out: hrd rdn after 2 out: one pce)	7	2	10/11^{1}	81	3
1175^{6}	**Staunch Rival (USA) (118)** (GThorner) **9-11-5$^{(5)}$** ClareThorner (hld up: wl bhd fr 7th: t.o whn hit rail bnd after 2 out)	12	3	7/1	90	12
1137^{5}	**Stoney Valley (105)** (JRJenkins) **6-10-6$^{(5)}$** NTEgan (hld up & plld hrd: hit 3rd: hdwy appr 3 out: 3rd & btn whn fell last)		F	5/1^{3}	—	—
				(SP 110.1%)		**4 Rn**

5m 15.2 (17.20) CSF £5.09 TOTE £3.70 (£2.30) OWNER Mr M. Dragisic (CULLOMPTON) BRED D. Twomey
World Express (IRE), with the blinkers refitted, really needs it much softer than this, but still proved good enough in an uncompetitive race. (5/2)
1121 Ramsdens (IRE) should have been up to beating the winner on ground that did not suit his rival. (10/11: 4/5-evens)
Staunch Rival (USA) showed no sparkle back over hurdles. (7/1)
952 Stoney Valley, dropped 8lb this season, is struggling to recapture his form of last year. (5/1)

T/Plpt: £8,426.30 (2 Tckts). T/Qdpt: £721.00 (1.92 Tckts). KH

1343-AYR (L-H) (Good)
Saturday November 16th
WEATHER: overcast

1356 SEAN GRAHAM HURDLE (3-Y.O) (Class E)
12-35 (12-35) **2m (8 hdls)** £2,346.00 (£656.00: £318.00) GOING: 0.42 sec per fur (GS)

				SP	RR	SF
699^{4}	**Rossel (USA)** (PMonteith) **3-11-4** ADobbin (lw: a cl up: led appr 3 out: sn clr)	—	1	8/1	67	32
1159^{2}	**The Boozing Brief (USA)** (CParker) **3-10-12b** DParker (led tl appr 3 out: one pce)	13	2	7/2^{3}	48	13
	Swynford Supreme (JFBottomley) **3-10-12** DerekByrne (chsd ldrs: kpt on fr 3 out: no imp)	2½	3	25/1	46	11
699^{7}	**Thorntoun Estate (IRE)** (MartinTodhunter) **3-10-12** MDwyer (bhd: hdwy 4 out: blnd next: styd on)	5	4	50/1	41	6
1159^{4}	**Rattle** (JJO'Neill) **3-10-7$^{(5)}$** RMcGrath (in tch: outpcd 5th: styd on fr 2 out)	nk	5	66/1	40	5
	Mapleton (MrsSJSmith) **3-10-5$^{(7)}$** RWilkinson (hit 3rd: sn chsng ldrs: outpcd fr 4 out)	3	6	14/1	37	2
	Sounds Devious (CParker) **3-10-7** BStorey (bit bkwd: bhd: hdwy 4 out: sn btn)	12	7	33/1	20	—
	Cry Baby (ACWhillans) **3-10-12** MFoster (chsd ldrs tl rdn & wknd after 4 out)	5	8	14/1	20	—
	Precious Girl (DMoffatt) **3-10-7** DJMoffatt (hld up & bhd: n.d)	15	9	15/2	—	—
1184^{2}	**Globe Runner** (JJO'Neill) **3-10-12** ARoche (lw: pushed along & hdwy 4th: chsng ldrs whn hit 4 out: sn hrd drvn: p.u bef next)		P	3/1^{2}	—	—
	Northern Motto (JSGoldie) **3-10-9$^{(3)}$** GLee (blnd & uns rdr 1st)		U	11/4^{1}	—	—
				(SP 120.3%)		**11 Rn**

3m 50.7 (13.70) CSF £34.89 TOTE £10.20: £1.80 £1.80 £2.70 (£9.80) Trio £141.00; £113.21 to Fontwell 17/11/96 OWNER Mr Allan Melville (ROSEWELL) BRED Allen E. Paulson
OFFICIAL EXPLANATION **Globe Runner: appeared to be lame behind.**
699 Rossel (USA), after two months off, was really good here and is obviously on the upgrade. (8/1)
1159 The Boozing Brief (USA) had blinkers on this time and showed a bit more, but was well outpointed by the winner over the last three. (7/2)
Swynford Supreme showed next to nothing in six outings on the Flat, but there was a little encouragement here. (25/1)
Thorntoun Estate (IRE) did better this time and there is probably more to come once his hurdling improves. (50/1)
1159 Rattle failed to impress on looks and never looked likely to take a hand in things. (66/1)
Mapleton (14/1: 10/1-16/1)
1184 Globe Runner seems to have a problem as he was never happy here. Something looked to have gone amiss when he pulled up. (3/1)

1357 SEAN GRAHAM NOVICES' CHASE (5-Y.O+) (Class D)
1-05 (1-07) **3m 1f (19 fncs)** £3,714.00 (£1,122.00: £546.00: £258.00) GOING: 0.42 sec per fur (GS)

				SP	RR	SF
	Naughty Future (JJO'Neill) **7-11-0** ARoche (mstkes: hld up: stdy hdwy 11th: led 4 out: styd on)	—	1	11/2^{3}	87	10
1246^{3}	**Pantara Prince (IRE)** (JIACharlton) **7-11-0** ADobbin (a.p: rdn appr 4 out: one pce)	7	2	20/1	83	6
	Kings Sermon (IRE) (PBeaumont) **7-11-0** RSupple (lw: led: blnd 3rd & 4th: hdd 11th: blnd 12th: one pce fr 4 out)	3	3	33/1	81	4
1160^{2}	**Bold Account (IRE)** (GMMoore) **6-11-0** NBentley (mstkes: chsd ldrs tl wknd appr 4 out)	23	4	13/2	66	—
824^{2}	**Arrange A Game** (MissJBower) **9-10-9$^{(5)}$** STaylor (sn outpcd & bhd: rdn 10th: sn t.o)	2	5	100/1	65	—
1189^{3}	**Royal Paris (IRE)** (MrsSJSmith) **8-11-0** TReed (chsd ldrs: led 11th tl hdd & fell 4 out)		F	16/1	—	—
	Crown Equerry (IRE) (GRichards) **6-11-0** NWilliamson (lw: blnd bdly 1st: p.u sn after)		P	5/4^{1}	—	—
	The Bird O'Donnell (FMurphy) **10-10-7$^{(7)}$** MrTJBarry (lw: in tch tl rdn & wknd fr 11th: p.u bef 3 out)		P	4/1^{2}	—	—
				(SP 107.7%)		**8 Rn**

6m 36.1 (29.10) CSF £78.46 TOTE £6.10: £1.80 £1.70 £6.00 (£39.70) OWNER Mr A. K. Collins (PENRITH) BRED Roy Edwards
Naughty Future has only ever won here and this was his first attempt at these bigger obstacles. Although he did it well, his jumping leaves plenty to be desired. (11/2)
1246 Pantara Prince (IRE) stays well, but is short of speed. His jumping should find him a race in due course. (20/1)
Kings Sermon (IRE), a particularly attractive sort, should step up on this no end once his jumping improves. (33/1)
1160 Bold Account (IRE) spoilt his chances by some sloppy jumping. (13/2)
824 Arrange A Game was completely outclassed here. (100/1)
Royal Paris (IRE) ran a fine race and appeared a shade unlucky to fall. Time should see him win races. (16/1)
Crown Equerry (IRE) (5/4: op evens)
The Bird O'Donnell looked fit enough but proved disappointing. To give him the benefit, his stable has yet to really strike form.(4/1)

1358 SEAN GRAHAM BOOKMAKERS H'CAP HURDLE (0-110) (4-Y.O+) (Class E)

1-35 (1-39) **2m (8 hdls)** £2,668.00 (£748.00: £364.00) GOING: 0.42 sec per fur (GS)

				SP	RR	SF
908[2]	**Sarmatian (USA) (108)** (MDHammond) **5-11-12** RGarritty (lw: hld up: hdwy 4 out: led last: all out)	—	**1**	4/1[3]	87	41
1125[2]	**Highbank (103)** (MrsMReveley) **4-11-4**(3) GLee (lw: trckd ldrs: led 3 out to last: rallied)	½	**2**	7/4[1]	82	36
	Miss Greenyards (84) (ACWhillans) **5-10-2** DParker (a chsng ldrs: effrt & ch 3 out: nt qckn)	10	**3**	7/2[2]	53	7
	Cittadino (102) (CWThornton) **6-11-6** MFoster (hld up: hdwy to ld after 4 out: hdd & blnd 3 out: sn btn)	6	**4**	4/1[3]	65	19
5[4]	**Triennium (USA) (82)** (PMonteith) **7-10-0** ADobbin (hld up: hdwy 4 out: rdn & btn after next)	2½	**5**	17/2	42	—
1123[5]	**Aide Memoire (IRE) (82)** (MrsBKBroad) **7-9-11**(3) GCahill (lost tch 4th: sme late hdwy)	hd	**6**	50/1	42	—
1143[6]	**Marlingford (82)** (MrsJJordan) **9-9-9**(5) STaylor (led to 4th: cl up tl wknd 4 out)	½	**7**	100/1	41	—
	Familiar Art (89) (DMoffatt) **5-10-7** DJMoffatt (cl up: led 4th tl after 4 out: sn wknd)	23	**8**	50/1	25	—
1267[F]	**Rarfy's Dream (110)** (DMcCune) **8-12-0** KJohnson (lw: prom tl wknd qckly 5th: p.u bef 3 out)		**P**	100/1	—	—
				(SP 115.0%)		**9 Rn**

3m 50.4 (13.40) CSF £10.91 CT £23.48 TOTE £3.70: £1.10 £1.60 £1.40 (£3.00) Trio £8.90 OWNER Mr S. T. Brankin (MIDDLEHAM) BRED David Allan

LONG HANDICAP Marlingford 9-9 Aide Memoire (IRE) 9-7

908 Sarmatian (USA) found things going all his way and, given a really good ride, pinched it at the final flight before just lasting home. (4/1)

1125 Highbank always looked as though he was going to win this, but he just got tapped for toe approaching the last, and his chance had then gone. (7/4)

Miss Greenyards, from a yard just coming to hand, showed enough to suggest that she will improve in due course. (7/2)

Cittadino showed enough to suggest that a bit of cut in the ground or even a bit further might well help. (4/1)

5 Triennium (USA) travels well, but does not seem to want to really struggle, and may have a problem. There is more ability there. (17/2)

697 Aide Memoire (IRE) runs when she is in the mood, which is not very often. (50/1)

1359 SEAN GRAHAM LIMITED H'CAP CHASE (5-Y.O+) (Class B)

2-10 (2-10) **3m 1f (19 fncs)** £10,065.00 (£3,045.00: £1,485.00: £705.00) GOING: 0.42 sec per fur (GS)

				SP	RR	SF
	The Grey Monk (IRE) (144) (GRichards) **8-10-5** ADobbin (lw: trckd ldr: led appr 4 out: rdn clr appr last: eased flat)	—	**1**	4/5[1]	145	35
	Jodami (165) (PBeaumont) **11-11-12** MDwyer (lw: trckd ldrs tl outpcd 15th: styd on wl fr 2 out: no ch w wnr)	5	**2**	11/2[3]	163	53
	Morceli (IRE) (153) (HowardJohnson) **8-11-0** NWilliamson (mde most tl hdd appr 4 out: styd on u.p: btn appr last)	nk	**3**	3/1[2]	151	41
	Morgans Harbour (144) (MrsMReveley) **10-10-5** PNiven (outpcd & lost tch 11th: styd on fr 4 out)	7	**4**	25/1	137	27
	Better Times Ahead (144) (GRichards) **10-10-5** LO'Hara (bit bkwd: hld up: outpcd & lost tch 11th: styd on fr 4 out)	1¼	**5**	11/1	136	26
				(SP 108.1%)		**5 Rn**

6m 24.0 (17.00) CSF £5.13 TOTE £1.70: £1.30 £2.40 (£3.20) OWNER Mr Alistair Duff (PENRITH) BRED James Doran

LONG HANDICAP The Grey Monk (IRE) 9-10 Morgans Harbour 9-10 Better Times Ahead 10-1

The Grey Monk (IRE), who has done really well physically, now looks the finished article and his jumping has come on no end. This should have put him straight for the Hennessy and the future looks very bright indeed. (4/5)

Jodami may have lost some of his speed, but this was a super performance and his long term objective - the Grand National - seems a mouth-watering prospect. (11/2)

Morceli (IRE) looked very lean here, but ran a smashing race, putting in some incredible leaps, only to find stamina the problem. Plenty of top-class opportunities could be found him. (3/1)

Morgans Harbour was not really suited when this turned out to be a sprint on the final circuit. He ran well enough to suggest that more will be seen of him before long. (25/1)

Better Times Ahead, in need of this, was not knocked about and should improve a fair deal for the outing. (11/1: 8/1-12/1)

1360 SEAN GRAHAM H'CAP HURDLE (0-120) (4-Y.O+) (Class D)

2-40 (2-44) **2m 4f (11 hdls)** £3,629.50 (£1,096.00: £533.00: £251.50) GOING: 0.42 sec per fur (GS)

				SP	RR	SF
1127*	**Burnt Imp (USA) (120)** (GMMoore) **6-12-0** JCallaghan (a chsng ldrs: hdwy 3 out: led flat: styd on u.p)	—	**1**	7/2[1]	101	50
	Crystal Gift (100) (ACWhillans) **4-10-5**(3) GCahill (led to 1st: chsd ldr: disp ld 3 out: led last: sn hdd & nt qckn)	2½	**2**	10/1	79	28
1143[3]	**Nicholas Plant (96)** (JSGoldie) **7-10-1**(3) GLee (lw: mstkes: led 1st tl hdd last: kpt on)	1	**3**	4/1[2]	74	23
	Mr Knitwit (114) (PMonteith) **9-11-8** ADobbin (bit bkwd: hld up & bhd: smooth hdwy 4 out: sn chsng ldrs: rdn & btn after 3 out)	7	**4**	33/1	87	36
1081[3]	**Commander Glen (IRE) (94)** (MDHammond) **4-9-13**(3) MrCBonner (hld up: rdn 6th: nvr nr to chal)	1¾	**5**	15/2[3]	65	14
1188[6]	**Cool Luke (IRE) (104)** (FMurphy) **7-10-12** NWilliamson (hld up & bhd: hdwy ½-wy: chsng ldrs appr 3 out: sn rdn & fnd nil)	3½	**6**	4/1[2]	72	21
585[4]	**Young Steven (92)** (MrsSCBradburne) **5-10-0** MFoster (chsd ldrs: hit 6th: sn rdn: wknd qckly fr 4 out)	¾	**7**	100/1	60	9
	Grandman (IRE) (94) (DMoffatt) **5-10-2** DJMoffatt (in tch to ½-wy: sn wknd)	5	**8**	14/1	58	7
	Royal Citizen (IRE) (98) (JFBottomley) **7-10-6** DerekByrne (lost tch fr ½-wy: hit 7th & 4 out: p.u bef 3 out)		**P**	14/1	—	—
	Bend Sable (IRE) (114) (FSStorey) **6-11-8** BStorey (bit bkwd: hld up: lost tch fr 6th: p.u bef 2 out)		**P**	16/1	—	—
				(SP 106.2%)		**10 Rn**

4m 56.0 (15.00) CSF £31.44 CT £107.12 TOTE £3.60: £1.40 £2.00 £1.70 (£12.10) Trio £46.60 OWNER N B Mason (Farms) Ltd (MIDDLEHAM) BRED Rodney P. Carothers & Brereton C. Jones in USA

LONG HANDICAP Young Steven 8-13

1127* Burnt Imp (USA) seems to do things the hard way, but he does respond to pressure and settled it at the last. He looks as though there is still more to come. (7/2)

Crystal Gift is game and consistent, but lack of a run probably made the difference. (10/1)

1143 Nicholas Plant set a really strong pace, but his hurdling was moderate to say the least. In the circumstances, this was not a bad effort. (4/1)

Mr Knitwit was a useful performer two seasons ago and has changed stables. He looked likely to be all the better for this and should now improve. (33/1)

1081 Commander Glen (IRE) never looked happy and failed to get in a blow. (15/2)

1188 Cool Luke (IRE) had his chances but, once off the bit, it was the same disappointing answer. (4/1: 3/1-9/2)

1361 SEAN GRAHAM BOOKMAKERS H'CAP CHASE (0-135) (5-Y.O+) (Class C)

3-10 (3-12) **2m (12 fncs)** £4,744.00 (£1,432.00: £696.00: £328.00) GOING: 0.42 sec per fur (GS)

				SP	RR	SF
1128[3]	**Political Tower (122)** (RNixon) **9-11-2** ADobbin (chsd ldrs: hit 5th: led 4 out: hrd rdn fr 2 out: hld on wl)	—	1	9/4[1]	130	30
321a[4]	**Nordic Thorn (IRE) (117)** (MBrassil,Ireland) **6-10-11** NWilliamson (chsd ldrs tl blnd & outpcd 8th: hdwy u.p 3 out: ev ch last: nt qckn)	2½	2	9/4[1]	123	23
1295*	**Regal Romper (IRE) (115)** (MrsSJSmith) **8-10-2**(7) 5x RWilkinson (led tl blnd 2nd: cl up: led 7th to 4 out: rallied u.p & ev ch last: no ex)	s.h	3	5/2[2]	120	20
	Montrave (106) (PMonteith) **7-9-11**(3) GCahill (in tch: hdwy 8th: one pce fr next)	8	4	14/1	103	3
	All the Aces (134) (JJO'Neill) **9-12-0** MDwyer (bit bkwd: lost tch fr 4th)	22	5	16/1	109	9
	One for the Pot (110) (MrsAMNaughton) **11-10-4** MFoster (bit bkwd: led 2nd to 7th: wknd appr 4 out: eased whn btn)	s.h	6	12/1[3]	85	—
				(SP 110.4%)	**6 Rn**	

3m 59.0 (14.00) CSF £7.32 TOTE £2.80: £1.10 £1.20 (£4.50) OWNER Mr G. R. S. Nixon (SELKIRK) BRED R. Nixon
LONG HANDICAP Montrave 9-7

1128 Political Tower was given plenty of help from the saddle and, in the end, battled on well. (9/4)
Nordic Thorn (IRE) was never happy, but his rider refused to accept things, and his persistence got him into contention, only to cry enough at the last. (9/4)
1295* Regal Romper (IRE) would win no prizes on looks, but he has plenty of courage. (5/2)
Montrave put in a decent first effort of the season and is going to be in the reckoning from now on. He does not win very often though. (14/1)
All the Aces, an Irish import, was obviously having a pipe-opener and, never getting into it, will probably need further in time. (16/1)
One for the Pot ran well and loves this track. He blew up on the home turn. (12/1)

1362 SEAN GRAHAM STANDARD OPEN N.H. FLAT RACE (4, 5 & 6-Y.O) (Class H)

3-40 (3-41) **2m** £1,070.00 (£295.00: £140.00)

				SP	RR	SF
	Ardarroch Prince (MrsMReveley) **5-11-4** PNiven (lw: hld up: hdwy ½-wy: rdn to ld ins fnl f: r.o)	—	1	9/4[1]	—	—
1033[U]	**Lord of The Loch (IRE)** (LLungo) **5-11-4** MFoster (lw: trckd ldrs: slt ld 3f out: rdn over 1f out: hdd ins fnl f: kpt on)	1¼	2	10/1	—	—
	Ardronan (IRE) (JJO'Neill) **6-11-6**(5) RMcGrath (lw: hld up: hdwy 7f out: drvn along & chsng ldrs 3f out: kpt on)	3½	3	6/1[2]	—	—
1052[5]	**Strong Mint (IRE)** (MrsMReveley) **5-11-1**(3) GLee (bhd: hdwy 3f out: styd on strly towards fin)	6	4	7/1	—	—
1084[2]	**Blood Brother** (JBarclay) **4-10-11**(7) NHorrocks (led to 3f out: ev ch tl wknd over 1f out)	½	5	25/1	—	—
898[8]	**Air Bridge** (RMWhitaker) **4-11-4** DerekByrne (a chsng ldrs: effrt 3f out: r.o one pce)	½	6	100/1	—	—
	Skiddaw Knight (IRE) (MrsMReveley) **5-11-1**(3) GCahill (bhd: hdwy 6f out: sn prom: one pce fnl 3f)	6	7	33/1	—	—
	The Stuffed Puffin (IRE) (LLungo) **4-11-4** MDwyer (mid div: effrt 5f out: no imp)	3	8	10/1	—	—
	Harfdecent (MrsMReveley) **5-10-11**(7) TJComerford (bit bkwd: hdwy on outside 6f out: nvr trbld ldrs)	nk	9	33/1	—	—
	Teelin Bay (IRE) (CParker) **4-11-4** DParker (mid div: hdwy 7f out: wknd 4f out)	nk	10	16/1	—	—
	Chinook's Daughter (IRE) (GRichards) **4-10-13** ADobbin (bit bkwd: hld up: hdwy ½-wy: wknd fnl 4f)	2½	11	8/1	—	—
	Political Millstar (RNixon) **4-11-4** NBentley (bit bkwd: bhd: rdn ½-wy: sme late hdwy)	1¼	12	100/1	—	—
1124[7]	**Soundpost** (DMoffatt) **4-11-4** DJMoffatt (chsd ldrs tl wknd fnl 4f)	1½	13	20/1	—	—
1033[7]	**Jackho** (MissJBower) **4-11-4** JCallaghan (prom tl wknd fnl 5f)	8	14	50/1	—	—
1052[6]	**Gale Force (IRE)** (PBeaumont) **5-10-11**(7) BGrattan (w ldrs tl wknd over 3f out)	2½	15	13/2[3]	—	—
	Carnanee (IRE) (IRFerguson,Ireland) **6-11-4** MrBRHamilton (nvr bttr than mid div)	9	16	100/1	—	—
	Tadpole (IRE) (BEllison) **4-11-4** DBentley (effrt 6f out: n.d)	1½	17	33/1	—	—
	Roadway Joker (MABarnes) **5-11-4** JBurke (lost tch fr ½-wy: t.o)	dist	18	100/1	—	—
	Movisa (WJSmith) **6-10-8**(5) STaylor (sn bhd: t.o fr ½-wy)	5	19	100/1	—	—
	Young Endeavour (JJO'Neill) **4-11-4** ARoche (p.u 10f out)		P	10/1	—	—
				(SP 139.5%)	**20 Rn**	

3m 51.0 CSF £27.16 TOTE £3.50: £2.40 £2.50 £2.40 (£23.60) Trio £21.20 OWNER Mr W. G. McHarg (SALTBURN) BRED W. G. McHarg

Ardarroch Prince, a shade disappointing last year, got it right this time and looks the type to do well in staying events over hurdles. (9/4: 2/1-3/1)
1033 Lord of The Loch (IRE) looked to be going best of all for much of the trip, but was just outbattled late on. His turn will come. (10/1: 5/1-12/1)
Ardronan (IRE) kept on really well in the last half-mile and will need a stiffer test of stamina. (6/1)
1052 Strong Mint (IRE), a stable-companion of the winner, is gradually getting the hang of things and again finished strongly. He is beginning to look a useful prospect. (7/1: 4/1-8/1)
1084 Blood Brother keeps getting tapped for toe at the business end, but will no doubt find his mark over hurdles. (25/1)
Air Bridge, despite taking a strong hold, improved no end on his initial outing, and is obviously learning fast. (100/1)
The Stuffed Puffin (IRE) (10/1: 6/1-12/1)
Chinook's Daughter (IRE) looks a real National Hunt prospect and needed this, but still showed plenty of ability. In time she will be one to watch. (8/1)
1052 Gale Force (IRE) (13/2: 7/2-7/1)
Young Endeavour (10/1: 4/1-12/1)

T/Plpt: £59.30 (189.49 Tckts). T/Qdpt: £3.50 (203.9 Tckts). AA

1350-CHELTENHAM (L-H) (Good to firm)

Saturday November 16th

Race 5 - no time taken. Vis: poor races 5 & 6
WEATHER: fog & drizzle

1363 FUGGLES IMPERIAL H'CAP HURDLE (4-Y.O+) (Class B)

1-10 (1-11) **3m 2f (Old) (13 hdls)** £6,645.00 (£2,010.00: £980.00: £465.00) GOING: 0.20 sec per fur (G)

				SP	RR	SF
1074*	**Victor Bravo (NZ) (113)** (NAGaselee) **9-10-5b** CLlewellyn (lw: hld up in rr: stdy hdwy 9th: led appr 2 out: styd on strly)	—	1	15/8[2]	95	13
605[3]	**Glengarrif Girl (IRE) (108)** (MCPipe) **6-10-0v** APMcCoy (a.p: lft in ld 3 out: sn hdd: hrd rdn & one pce appr last)	2½	2	13/8[1]	89	7

1031[2] **San Giorgio (109)** (NATwiston-Davies) **7-10-1**ow1 TJenks (led tl after 4th: led after 7th tl slipped & almost fell 3 out: nt rcvr) ....dist **3** 5/1[3] — —

1288[6] **Hops and Pops (136)** (RHAlner) **9-12-0** RDunwoody (led after 4th: clr 6th: hdd after next: sn wknd: t.o) ......dist **4** 5/1[3] — —

(SP 106.2%) **4 Rn**

6m 37.0 (20.00) CSF £4.89 TOTE £2.70 (£2.20) OWNER Mrs R. W. S. Baker (LAMBOURN) BRED A. W. Herbert
LONG HANDICAP Glengarrif Girl (IRE) 9-11 San Giorgio 9-5

1074* Victor Bravo (NZ) kept up his impressive start to the season with another clear-cut success. Though he adopted more patient tactics here, the outcome was just the same. (15/8)

605 Glengarrif Girl (IRE) may well have needed this after two months out of action, and she was presented with a golden opportunity three out, had she been able to take it. (13/8)

1031 San Giorgio, bowling along in the lead when he all but slipped up three out, had to settle for the minor prize. (5/1)

1288 Hops and Pops is not getting it together this term and may benefit from a complete break. (5/1)

1364 WADWORTH 6X NOVICES' CHASE (5-Y.O+) (Class C)

1-45 (1-46) **2m 4f 110y (Old) (15 fncs)** £5,134.50 (£1,442.00: £703.50) GOING: 0.20 sec per fur (G)

SP RR SF

1153* **Potter's Bay (IRE) (113)** (DNicholson) **7-11-5** AMaguire (lw: hld up: mstke 4th: swtchd rt & qcknd to ld appr last: comf) ....— **1** 2/7[1] 95+ 29

1122P **Flimsy Truth (83)** (MHWeston) **10-11-6**ow6 MrMHarris (swtg: j.w: led & sn clr: hdd appr last: one pce)....3½ **2** 10/1[3] 93 21

General Pongo (97) (TRGeorge) **7-11-0** RDunwoody (bkwd: chsd ldr tl wknd appr last: eased whn btn)........13 **3** 9/2[2] 77 11

(SP 105.1%) **3 Rn**

5m 16.9 (14.90) CSF £2.76 TOTE £1.30 (£2.00) OWNER Mrs J. E. Potter (TEMPLE GUITING) BRED Colman O'Flynn

1153* Potter's Bay (IRE) was not quite so foot-perfect with his jumping of these stiffer fences, but the dawdling pace was not in his favour and, in the end, he accomplished what he had set out to do. (2/7)

1122 Flimsy Truth gave a good account of himself and impressed with his jumping, but he had to admit the winner a class apart. (10/1)

General Pongo, waiting on the leader, was beginning to feel the strain when the winner nudged him aside approaching the last. He was allowed to complete in his own time. (9/2)

1365 MURPHY'S DRAUGHTFLOW H'CAP HURDLE (4-Y.O+) (Class B)

2-20 (2-23) **2m 110y (Old) (8 hdls)** £27,126.00 (£8,208.00: £4,004.00: £1,902.00) GOING: 0.20 sec per fur (G)

SP RR SF

1288[2] **Space Trucker (IRE) (136)** (MrsJHarrington,Ireland) **5-11-11** JOsborne (lw: hld up in rr: hdwy 2 out: led on bit last: sn clr) ....— **1** 7/1[3] 119+ 73

318a* **Mystical City (IRE) (135)** (WPMullins,Ireland) **6-11-7**(3) DJCasey (hld up & bhd: hdwy 5th: rdn & j.rt last: kpt on u.p) 3½ **2** 9/1 115 69

1137[3] **Barna Boy (IRE) (130)** (NJHenderson) **8-11-5** MAFitzgerald (lw: hld up: hdwy appr 2 out: rdn & r.o flat) ....½ **3** 25/1 109 63

1015* **Country Star (IRE) (128)** (CPEBrooks) **5-11-3** GBradley (lw: swtg: chsd ldr: led between last 2: hdd last: one pce) ....1¼ **4** 9/2[2] 106 60

1280[2] **Make a Stand (123)** (MCPipe) **5-10-12** AMaguire (set str pce: hdd after 2 out: rdn & one pce flat) 1 **5** 10/1 100 54

945* **Chief's Song (139)** (SDow) **6-12-0** RDunwoody (lw: chsd clr ldng pair: hit 3 out: sn rdn & wknd)....7 **6** 7/1[3] 109 63

1271* **Crack On (130)** (PJHobbs) **6-11-5** APMcCoy (lw: mstke 1st: rr whn hit 5th: t.o) ....17 **7** 3/1[1] 84 38

1288* **Dreams End (137)** (PBowen) **8-11-12** RFarrant (lw: hld up mid div: outpcd appr 2 out: sn btn: t.o) 13 **8** 15/2 78 32

1353* **Just Little (131)** (APO'Brien,Ireland) **4-11-6** 6x CO'Dwyer (hld up in rr: stdy hdwy whn hit 3 out: ev ch whn fell next) .... **F** 7/1[3] — —

(SP 115.4%) **9 Rn**

3m 54.1 (3.10) CSF £60.53 CT £1,349.66 TOTE £8.50: £2.20 £2.30 £3.50 (£35.90) Trio £327.50 OWNER Mrs E. Queally (IRELAND) BRED John Harrington

OFFICIAL EXPLANATION **Crack On: was never travelling or jumping, and according to his pilot the race may have come too soon, after his run seven days ago. His trainer later reported the gelding was distressed after the race.**

1288 Space Trucker (IRE) must have had an off-day when beaten last week at Wincanton, for he won this with great ease. (7/1)

Mystical City (IRE), possibly better when she can get her toe in, nevertheless ran up to her mark and could be well worth a try over further. (9/1)

1137 Barna Boy (IRE) looks to be on the way back and should find his way when stepped up another half-mile. (25/1)

1015* Country Star (IRE) likes to make the running, but was denied that role. (9/2)

1280 Make a Stand, facing his stiffest task to date, made sure the pace was strong and his measure was only taken on the run to the last. He should be winning again before long. (10/1)

945* Chief's Song did his level best to keep tabs on the tearaway pacemakers, but he was at full stretch when he met the third last all wrong, and that was the end of him. (7/1)

1271* Crack On had more on his plate and his jumping was not up to scratch. (3/1)

1353* Just Little, carrying a 6lb penalty for winning here yesterday, was making stealthy progress when she got too close to the third last. Recovering her momentum quickly, she was poised to challenge and going extremely well when she met the penultimate flight all wrong and paid the penalty. (7/1)

1366 MURPHY'S GOLD CUP H'CAP CHASE (Gd 3) (5-Y.O+) (Class A)

2-55 (3-01) **2m 4f 110y (Old) (15 fncs)** £38,270.00 (£14,330.00: £7,015.00: £3,025.00: £1,362.50: £697.50) GOING: 0.20 sec per fur (G)

SP RR SF

Challenger du Luc (FR) (142) (MCPipe) **6-10-2b** RDunwoody (hld up & bhd: stdy hdwy fr 4 out: led last: all out) ....— **1** 7/1[3] 150 73

1136* **Strong Promise (IRE) (141)** (GAHubbard) **5-9-11**(3) KGaule (lw: j.w: a.p: lft in ld after 4 out: hdd last: rallied gamely cl home) ....hd **2** 14/1 149 71

Addington Boy (IRE) (150) (GRichards) **8-10-10** BHarding (lw: hld up mid div: hdwy 11th: sltly hmpd after 4 out: one pce flat) ....3½ **3** 5/1[2] 155 78

1231a* **Anabatic (IRE) (146)** (MJPO'Brien,Ireland) **8-10-6** TPRudd (hld up: hdwy 10th: ev ch 2 out: rdn & one pce appr last) 5 **4** 11/1 147 70

1157[2] **Barton Bank (159)** (DNicholson) **10-11-5** AMaguire (chsd ldr: ev ch 2 out: nt clr run appr last: sn btn) 5 **5** 12/1 156 79

1134[2] **Big Matt (IRE) (144)** (NJHenderson) **8-10-4** MAFitzgerald (lw: hld up in tch: lost pl ½-wy: effrt u.p appr 2 out: no imp) ....11 **6** 9/2[1] 133 56

1272* **Strong Medicine (140)** (KCBailey) **9-10-0** 3x CO'Dwyer (swtg: hld up in rr: effrt appr 3 out: sn rdn & wknd: t.o) 14 **7** 20/1 118 41

Form	Horse / Connections	Dist	Pos	SP	RR	SF
1277[3]	**Bavard Dieu (IRE) (140)** (NAGaselee) **8-10-0** CLlewellyn (bhd: rdn 7th: sn t.o)	¾	**8**	40/1	117	40
1016[2]	**Easthorpe (141)** (MissHCKnight) **8-10-1** JOsborne (lw: chsd ldrs tl wknd appr 2 out: t.o)	½	**9**	10/1	118	41
	Kibreet (146) (PJHobbs) **9-10-6** APMcCoy (bkwd: in tch tl wknd 4 out: t.o)	4	**10**	8/1	120	43
1173*	**Absalom's Lady (141)** (MissGayKelleway) **8-10-1** 6x DBridgwater (lw: a bhd: t.o whn p.u bef 3 out: lame)		**P**	11/1	—	—
	Dublin Flyer (168) (CaptTAForster) **10-12-0** BPowell (lw: j.w: led tl s.u after 4 out)		**S**	7/1[3]	—	—

(SP 118.3%) **12 Rn**

4m 59.9 (-2.10) CSF £89.03 CT £489.91 TOTE £7.40: £3.00 £2.80 £2.50 (£75.40) Trio £101.70 OWNER Mr D. A. Johnson (WELLINGTON)
BRED Mme Jeanne-Marie Bizard
LONG HANDICAP Strong Medicine 9-3 Strong Promise (IRE) 8-9
WEIGHT FOR AGE 5yo-1lb
STEWARDS' ENQUIRY Gaule susp. 25-28/11/96 (excessive use of whip).

Challenger du Luc (FR) benefited from a brilliant ride and was still on the bridle when leading at the last. He hung on for dear life close home, despite lack of a recent race showing its effects. (7/1)

1136* Strong Promise (IRE) is being asked to conquer mountains at a very early stage of his career and has done little wrong. This narrow defeat from 19lb out of the handicap is sure to be penalised and, unless he is as tough as old boots, the stuffing could be taken out of him. (14/1)

Addington Boy (IRE) ran a tremendous race on this seasonal debut and was fortunate not to be brought down five furlongs out when Dublin Flyer's jockey rolled right in front of him. Trying hard to deliver his challenge, he did not fail for the want of commitment and looks set to enjoy another rewarding year. (5/1)

1231a* Anabatic (IRE), a very much-improved Irish raider, could have found this trip on such a testing track too much, for he was in with a live chance until the hill took its toll. (11/1)

1157 Barton Bank, in the firing-line from the start, looked to be finding the quickening tempo a problem when he was tightened up on the inside rail approaching the last. Three miles plus looks more suitable. (12/1)

1134 Big Matt (IRE) ran a bit flat and never threatened to get back into the action after losing his pitch going out into the country. (9/2)

1173* Absalom's Lady is likely to be out of action for some time. (11/1)

Dublin Flyer looked well tuned up and was forcing the pace and showing no sign of stopping when his feet went from under him on the downhill run to the third last. (7/1)

1367 FLOWERS ORIGINAL H'CAP CHASE (5-Y.O+) (Class B)

3-30 (3-33) **3m 3f 110y (Old) (21 fncs)** £10,834.50 (£3,042.00: £1,483.50) GOING: 0.20 sec per fur (G)

Form	Horse / Connections	Dist	Pos	SP	RR	SF
966*	**Evangelica (USA) (121)** (MCPipe) **6-10-0** APMcCoy (lw: hld up: led 3 out: clr last: drvn out)	—	**1**	13/8[1]	127+	—
1147[2]	**Copper Mine (123)** (OSherwood) **10-10-2** JOsborne (led: clr 5th: j.slowly 7th to 10th: hdd 3 out: rallied & wnt lft flat: no imp)	5	**2**	3/1[3]	126	—
1055[3]	**Martomick (145)** (KCBailey) **9-11-10** CO'Dwyer (lw: nt j.w: a in rr: t.o fr 2 out)	17	**3**	2/1[2]	138	—
1273[5]	**Willsford (135)** (MrsJPitman) **13-11-0** RFarrant (chsd ldr tl p.u after 16th: collapsed: dead)		**P**	15/2	—	—

(SP 108.2%) **4 Rn**

0m CSF £6.15 TOTE £2.60 (£3.10) OWNER Martin Pipe Racing Club (WELLINGTON) BRED Helen C Alexander
LONG HANDICAP Evangelica (USA) 9-10

966* Evangelica (USA) made it win number four with a very comfortably-gained success from 4lb out of the handicap. (13/8)

1147 Copper Mine enjoys a stiff test of stamina and does like to dictate, which he succeeded in doing, until the winner took his measure and left him struggling on the uphill run to the last. (3/1)

1055 Martomick, jumping poorly, she struggled to lay up with the principals from going out into the country. Something must have been amiss. (2/1)

Willsford came to the end of a very successful career when he suffered a heart attack a mile from home. This was to have been his last race before retirement, and he will be missed by many. (15/2)

1368 MACKESON NOVICES' HURDLE (Gd 2) (4-Y.O+) (Class A)

4-05 (4-09) **2m 110y (Old) (8 hdls)** £8,792.00 (£3,327.10: £1,628.55: £742.35) GOING: 0.20 sec per fur (G)

Form	Horse / Connections	Dist	Pos	SP	RR	SF
1065*	**Kailash (USA)** (MCPipe) **5-10-12** APMcCoy (lw: mde all: sn clr: mstke 2 out: easily)	—	**1**	3/1[3]	94+	5
1059*	**Herbert Lodge (IRE)** (KCBailey) **7-10-12** CO'Dwyer (hld up: hdwy to chse wnr 3 out: hrd rdn next: no imp)	7	**2**	2/1[2]	87	—
1276*	**Green Green Desert (FR)** (OSherwood) **5-10-12** DBridgwater (lw: chsd wnr fr 3rd tl appr 3 out: sn lost tch)	15	**3**	11/8[1]	73	—
	Foxies Lad (NMBabbage) **5-10-12** VSlattery (bkwd: a bhd: mstke 5th: sn t.o)	3	**4**	20/1	70	—
	Soviet Bride (IRE) (SDow) **4-10-7** RDunwoody (chsd wnr: j.b rt 3rd & 4th: sn lost tch: t.o)	8	**5**	10/1	57	—

(SP 114.3%) **5 Rn**

4m 6.8 (15.80) CSF £9.29 TOTE £3.20: £1.80 £1.60 (£3.40) OWNER Mr Mick Fletcher (WELLINGTON) BRED William C. Miller

1065* Kailash (USA) goes from strength to strength and completed a treble for his stable, which could have been a real money-spinner for his bookmaker owner. (3/1: op 7/4)

1059* Herbert Lodge (IRE) has only been tried at this minimum trip since his attention was switched to hurdles, but his future would seem to be over extended trips. (2/1)

1276* Green Green Desert (FR) may have trouble staying this trip on this track, but had thrown in the towel a long way out, and may need more time between races. (11/8)

Soviet Bride (IRE) lost ground by jumping out to the right at an early stage. From halfway, she was well out of contention. (10/1: op 6/1)

T/Plpt: £211.30 (171.22 Tckts). T/Qdpt: £46.90 (50.7 Tckts). IM

1040-HUNTINGDON (R-H) (Good)
Saturday November 16th

WEATHER: overcast

1369 KIMBOLTON NOVICES' HURDLE (4-Y.O+) (Class E)

1-00 (1-01) **2m 110y (8 hdls)** £2,722.50 (£760.00: £367.50) GOING minus 0.23 sec per fur (G)

Form	Horse / Connections	Dist	Pos	SP	RR	SF
675*	**Mr Percy (IRE) (110)** (JTGifford) **5-11-5** PHide (lw: a.p: led after 4th: pushed out)	—	**1**	4/9[1]	85	47
	Mentmore Towers (IRE) (MrsJPitman) **4-10-12** WMarston (bit bkwd: w ldrs: led appr 4th: sn hdd: ev ch last: rdn & unable qckn)	1	**2**	5/1[2]	77	39
1044[2]	**Peace Lord (IRE)** (MrsDHaine) **6-10-9**(3) GHogan (a.p: one pce fr 2 out)	9	**3**	7/1[3]	68	30

				SP	RR	SF
293^{4}	**Ottavio Farnese** (AHide) **4-10-9**(3) LAspell (plld hrd: hdwy & hit 3 out: no imp appr next: hit last)	7	**4**	25/1	62	24
	Lookingforarainbow (IRE) (BobJones) **8-10-12** VSmith (hld up & plld hrd: hdwy 5th: nvr able to chal)	9	**5**	10/1	53	15
476^{P}	**Baba Au Rhum (IRE)** (IPWilliams) **4-10-12** DGallagher (bhd: hdwy 5th: wknd appr 2 out)	1	**6**	50/1	52	14
1204^{4}	**Nashaat (USA) (86)** (MCChapman) **8-10-12** WWorthington (swtg: plld hrd: chsd ldrs to 5th)	3	**7**	33/1	49	11
1187^{9}	**Rood Music** (MGMeagher) **5-10-12** LWyer (led tl appr 4th: wknd appr 3 out)	hd	**8**	50/1	49	11
	Mudlark (JNorton) **4-10-12** WFry (in tch tl hit 5th)	½	**9**	33/1	48	10
885^{3}	**Quaker Waltz** (JCTuck) **6-10-7** SMcNeill (chsd ldrs to 5th)	7	**10**	50/1	37	—
1208^{5}	**Murphy's Gold (IRE)** (RAFahey) **5-10-12** RMarley (hld up: a bhd: t.o)	dist	**11**	25/1	—	—
	Rossell Island (IRE) (MrsJPitman) **5-10-12** RJohnson (trckd ldrs tl b.d 3rd)		**B**	20/1	—	—
1042^{P}	**Rosslayne Serenade** (RJWeaver) **5-10-0**(7) CRWeaver (prom tl fell 3rd)		**F**	50/1	—	—
1278^{8}	**Chantro Bay** (JPearce) **8-10-12** NMann (prom tl kicked, broke leg & p.u after 3rd: dead)		**P**	33/1	—	—
1278^{7}	**Daring Ryde** (JPSmith) **5-10-12v**[1] ASSmith (plld hrd: prom to 4th: t.o whn p.u bef 2 out)		**P**	50/1	—	—
1178^{8}	**Schwartzndigger (IRE)** (TWDonnelly) **6-10-12** JRKavanagh (mstke 2nd: a bhd: t.o whn p.u bef 2 out)		**P**	50/1	—	—
				(SP 140.5%)	**16 Rn**	

3m 48.5 (0.50) CSF £4.45 TOTE £1.50: £1.10 £2.00 £1.70 (£4.00) Trio £10.60 OWNER Felix Rosenstiel's Widow & Son (FINDON) BRED M. Fardy

675* Mr Percy (IRE) was challenged in the home straight, but always had matters well in hand. (4/9: op 4/6)
Mentmore Towers (IRE), a newcomer to hurdles, has the scope to grow into a useful horse and, despite looking likely to be better for the race, showed plenty by racing up with the pace throughout. He failed to quicken much when put to work, but this was a promising debut, and another half-mile looks within his grasp. (5/1: 4/1-7/1)
1044 Peace Lord (IRE) ran well in this much faster-run race, but proved short of speed in the straight. (7/1)
293 Ottavio Farnese is not yet a fluent jumper of hurdles and his action suggests soft ground may help. (25/1)
Lookingforarainbow (IRE) finds it difficult to win on the level and was having his first run in four years over hurdles. If he settles, he can win a race. (10/1)
Baba Au Rhum (IRE), much improved on the Flat since his last run over hurdles, at least managed to complete this time as even the minimum trip stretches his stamina. (50/1)

1370 SOUTHOE HURDLE (3-Y.O) (Class E)

1-30 (1-32) **2m 110y (8 hdls)** £2,547.50 (£710.00: £342.50) GOING minus 0.23 sec per fur (G)

				SP	RR	SF
1149^{5}	**Fijon (IRE)** (JPearce) **3-10-5** NMann (blnd 2nd: hdwy 4th: led last: rdn out)	—	**1**	33/1	63	11
	Belmarita (IRE) (GAHubbard) **3-10-5** RJohnson (prom: led appr 2 out to last: unable qckn)	2	**2**	4/1 2	61	9
	Soldier Mak (AHide) **3-10-10** PHide (trckd ldrs: ev ch 2 out: rdn & one pce flat)	2	**3**	12/1	64	12
1158^{7}	**Six Clerks (IRE)** (JGFitzGerald) **3-10-7**(3) FLeahy (a.p: led 5th tl appr 2 out: one pce)	1¼	**4**	8/1 3	63	11
	Precious Island (PTDalton) **3-10-5** JSupple (led tl after 1st: one pce appr 3 out)	5	**5**	50/1	53	1
1184^{4}	**Kingfisher Brave** (MGMeagher) **3-10-10** LWyer (led after 1st to 5th: sn wknd)	6	**6**	4/1 2	52	—
1205^{9}	**Another Quarter (IRE)** (MCChapman) **3-10-5** WWorthington (lw: hdwy 3 out: nvr trbld ldrs)	3½	**7**	33/1	44	—
1149^{7}	**Lebedinski (IRE)** (MrsPSly) **3-10-5** RMarley (hdwy appr 3 out: nvr rchd ldrs)	3½	**8**	50/1	41	—
	Alarico (FR) (IPWilliams) **3-10-10** DGallagher (plld hrd: hdwy 4th: nvr nr ldrs)	1¼	**9**	50/1	44	—
	Pontevedra (IRE) (KAMorgan) **3-10-5** ASSmith (plld hrd: chsd ldrs tl appr 5th)	3½	**10**	20/1	36	—
	Flint And Steel (BobJones) **3-10-10** VSmith (bit bkwd: a bhd)	1¾	**11**	14/1	39	—
640^{2}	**Flying Green (FR)** (NJHWalker) **3-10-10** JAMcCarthy (hld up: hdwy appr 4th: wknd 3 out)	5	**12**	3/1 1	34	—
1011^{5}	**Eurobox Boy** (APJarvis) **3-10-10** WMarston (lw: prom tl wknd 5th)	9	**13**	14/1	26	—
	Classic Daisy (RCSpicer) **3-10-2**(3) EHusband (bhd: hmpd 4th: b.d by loose horse appr next)		**B**	50/1	—	—
1184^{6}	**Royal Then (FR)** (JNeville) **3-10-10** JRKavanagh (lw: prom to 5th: t.o whn p.u bef 2 out)		**P**	10/1	—	—
1011^{F}	**Kulshi Momken** (JNorton) **3-10-10** WFry (bhd tl blnd & uns rdr 4th)		**U**	50/1	—	—
				(SP 126.7%)	**16 Rn**	

3m 53.6 (5.60) CSF £153.97 TOTE £26.10: £6.40 £2.30 £3.20 (£71.20) Trio £268.90; £340.98 to Fontwell 17/11/96 OWNER The Fijon Partnership (NEWMARKET) BRED Gay O'Callaghan

Fijon (IRE), stepping up from selling company, caused an upset, but was almost out of the race at the second. She has not always impressed with her attitude, but she did absolutely nothing wrong here, as she was not going best on the home turn. (33/1)
Belmarita (IRE) is not very tall but is a stocky mare and took to this game well. She stayed very well on the Flat and will relish the step up to two and a half. (4/1)
Soldier Mak was cantering on the heels of the leaders turning for home, but did not find much in the way of speed once let down. Softer ground will help. (12/1)
Six Clerks (IRE), dropped in class from his debut, did his best to force the issue, but lack of gears was his downfall. (8/1: 4/1-10/1)
Precious Island has been gradually improving in four appearances on the Flat, and this hurdles debut was not without promise. (50/1)
1184 Kingfisher Brave did not stay in front as long as he did at Haydock, and was gradually left behind in the closing stages. (4/1:op 5/2)
1011 Eurobox Boy again looked to find staying the trip a problem. (14/1: op 5/1)

1371 TOSELAND NOVICES' CHASE (5-Y.O+) (Class D)

2-00 (2-01) **2m 4f 110y (16 fncs)** £3,825.75 (£1,146.00: £550.50: £252.75) GOING minus 0.23 sec per fur (G)

				SP	RR	SF
	Lively Knight (IRE) (105) (JTGifford) **7-10-12** PHide (a.p: outpcd after 3 out: led last: drvn out)	—	**1**	5/2 2	113	50
62*	**Mister Drum (IRE)** (MJWilkinson) **7-10-12** WMarston (led: hit 4th: rdn clr appr 2 out: hdd last: rallied nr fin)	½	**2**	7/2 3	113+	50
	Wild West Wind (IRE) (MissHCKnight) **6-10-12** RJohnson (lw: w ldrs: hit 7th: pckd 11th: wknd 3 out)	29	**3**	6/5 1	90	27
333^{3}	**Sassiver (USA) (87)** (PAKelleway) **6-11-2**(3) GHogan (chsd ldrs: pckd 12th: sn btn)	17	**4**	25/1	84	21
	Master Hope (IRE) (DNicholson) **7-10-12** RBellamy (lw: hmpd 1st: hdwy whn mstke 7th: btn whn blnd 12th)	7	**5**	16/1	71	8
1206^{4}	**Record Lover (IRE) (69)** (MCChapman) **6-10-12** WWorthington (chsd ldrs to 10th)	16	**6**	25/1	59	—
70^{P}	**Arr Eff Bee** (JPSmith) **9-10-12b** ASSmith (a bhd)	14	**7**	66/1	48	—
	Strong Stuff (IRE) (KCBailey) **6-10-12** SMcNeill (bkwd: fell 1st)		**F**	8/1	—	—
1073^{P}	**Lets Go Now (IRE) (60)** (MrsLCJewell) **6-10-12** MBrennan (rdn 6th: sn wl bhd: p.u bef 13th)		**P**	66/1	—	—
950^{15}	**Hatta River (USA)** (PTDalton) **6-10-12b** JSupple (nt j.w: hmpd 1st: sn t.o: p.u bef 13th)		**P**	66/1	—	—
				(SP 125.4%)	**10 Rn**	

4m 58.0 (-2.00) CSF £12.25 TOTE £3.70: £1.40 £1.50 £1.50 (£5.50) Trio £3.60 OWNER Mr A. D. Weller (FINDON) BRED Jack Forristal

Lively Knight (IRE) had the benefit of a previous run over fences, having not gone on after a debut success over timber last winter. Outpaced on the home turn, he was tired but stuck to his guns to jump to the front at the last. He jumped well and, if this hard race does not leave its mark, more success should come his way. (5/2: 7/4-11/4)

62* Mister Drum (IRE), much the best of these over hurdles, had not run for five months. Jumping well in the main, he was made plenty of use of. Lack of a recent race then told and he blew up, but he will certainly win over fences on this evidence. (7/2)
Wild West Wind (IRE) was never able to get to the front and stopped to nothing on the home turn. This was a disappointing debut. (6/5)
333 Sassiver (USA) found the leading group always going too fast for him. (25/1)
Master Hope (IRE) has been hard to train, this being only his second run since April 1994. Brought to a standstill at the first, he showed enough, despite some sloppy jumping, and may find a race if he stays sound. (16/1)
1028 Record Lover (IRE) will struggle outside selling class. (25/1)
Strong Stuff (IRE) (8/1: 6/1-10/1)

1372 BUSINESS CLUB H'CAP HURDLE (0-125) (4-Y.O+) (Class D)

2-30 (2-31) **3m 2f (12 hdls)** £2,931.00 (£816.00: £393.00) GOING minus 0.23 sec per fur (G)

			SP	RR	SF
1256*	**Elburg (IRE) (102)** (TRGeorge) **6-10-10** RJohnson (lw: hld up: hdwy 8th: led next: clr 2 out: hit last: easily) ..—	1	7/4^{1}	85+	—
1039^{10}	**Arithmetic (113)** (MrsJPitman) **6-11-7** WMarston (trckd ldrs: ev ch whn hit 3 out: no imp appr next)................6	2	5/2^{2}	92	—
	Uluru (IRE) (117) (CPMorlock) **8-11-11** JRKavanagh (lw: w ldrs: led & qcknd after 7th: hdd 9th: sn outpcd)...17	3	3/1^{3}	86	—
	Rubins Boy (92) (NJHWalker) **10-10-0** ASSmith (bkwd: hld up & plld hrd: hdwy 9th: nvr able to chal)...........2½	4	20/1	59	—
1256^{9}	**Provence (95)** (AWCarroll) **9-10-0**(3)ow3 GHogan (w ldrs: j.slowly 5th: lost pl & rdn 8th)..................................nk	5	50/1	62	—
1207^{2}	**Singlesole (92)** (MrsPSly) **11-10-0** RMarley (led tl after 7th: wknd appr 3 out: eased fr next)........................dist	6	11/2	—	—
			(SP 112.0%)		**6 Rn**

6m 24.7 (18.70) CSF £6.32 TOTE £2.40: £1.30 £1.60 (£3.00) OWNER Mrs Alison Gamble (ROSS-ON-WYE) BRED Sheikh Mohammed bin Rashid al Maktoum
LONG HANDICAP Provence 8-9 Singlesole 9-12
1256* Elburg (IRE) does have a kink at the start, but got off on terms and fairly bolted in. He looks on good terms with himself and is in his best form for years. (7/4)
1039 Arithmetic is sure to go novice chasing before long as he really looks the part, but he did not jump well in the closing stages here, hitting three out and already being held when not fluent at the last. (5/2)
Uluru (IRE) goes exceptionally well fresh, but needs a truly-run race and did not get one here. Forced to quicken the pace on the final circuit, he was easily brushed aside when the principals kicked for home. (3/1)
Rubins Boy, off since breaking down eighteen months ago, is better known as a chaser. He was very keen to get on with things in the early stages, but did not stay on at the end. (20/1)
Provence did not look a threat once the pace lifted. (50/1)
1207 Singlesole was in trouble once the tempo quickened. (11/2: 7/2-6/1)

1373 MACER GIFFORD H'CAP CHASE (0-130) (5-Y.O+) (Class C)

3-00 (3-00) **2m 4f 110y (16 fncs)** £4,597.50 (£1,380.00: £665.00: £307.50) GOING minus 0.23 sec per fur (G)

			SP	RR	SF
	Shining Light (IRE) (100) (DNicholson) **7-10-2** RJohnson (chsd ldrs: led 2 out: wandered flat: rdn out) ....—	1	5/1	114	39
	Mr President (IRE) (98) (CPEBrooks) **7-10-0** DGallagher (bit bkwd: hld up: hdwy 8th: hit 2 out: ev ch flat: r.o)..........1¼	2	4/1^{2}	111	36
	Act of Parliament (IRE) (105) (KCBailey) **8-10-7b** SMcNeill (w ldr: led 11th to 2 out: sn btn)..........................11	3	7/2^{1}	109	34
1119^{3}	**Rustic Air (106)** (JGFitzGerald) **9-10-8** WDwan (trckd ldrs: hit 13th: rdn & btn appr 2 out) 6	4	4/1^{2}	106	31
	Puritan (CAN) (115) (NTinkler) **7-11-3b** MissPJones (bit bkwd: mstke 7th: bhd fr 11th)..................................16	5	14/1	102	27
	Denver Bay (120) (JTGifford) **9-11-5**(3) LAspell (led to 11th: rdn & wknd 3 out)..5	6	9/2^{3}	103	28
1272^{U}	**Conti D'Estruval (FR) (122)** (GBBalding) **6-11-10** BClifford (nt j.w: in tch to 12th: t.o whn p.u bef 2 ut)	P	5/1	—	—
			(SP 120.4%)		**7 Rn**

4m 58.6 (-1.40) CSF £24.94 TOTE £6.50: £2.10 £1.40 (£11.30) OWNER The Deeley Partnership (TEMPLE GUITING) BRED Mrs A. Furlong
LONG HANDICAP Mr President (IRE) 9-13
Shining Light (IRE) won first time out two seasons ago and is capable of going well fresh. He could have won more easily but for giving his rider problems on the run-in. (5/1)
Mr President (IRE) looked to be cruising on the home turn, but a mistake at the second last changed the picture, and he was getting the worst of things when not entirely fluent at the last. He will come on for the race. (4/1)
Act of Parliament (IRE) seems to need to be kept fresh, but could never establish a clear lead and was a sitting duck on the home turn. (7/2: 3/1-9/2)
Puritan (CAN) has yet to rediscover his form since his crashing fall at Cheltenham. (14/1)
Denver Bay has gone up a lot in the handicap. (9/2)

1374 WILLINGHAM H'CAP HURDLE (0-120) (4-Y.O+) (Class D)

3-35 (3-36) **2m 110y (8 hdls)** £2,868.00 (£798.00: £384.00) GOING minus 0.23 sec per fur (G)

			SP	RR	SF
	Henrietta Howard (IRE) (102) (MrsDHaine) **6-10-12**(3) GHogan (trckd ldrs: led appr 2 out: clr last: eased nr fin) ....—	1	16/1	88+	28
1188^{3}	**Lord Mcmurrough (IRE) (110)** (JNeville) **6-11-9** WMarston (lw: led tl appr 2 out: kpt on)...............................6	2	9/2^{3}	90	30
884^{5}	**Tim (IRE) (104)** (JRJenkins) **6-10-10**(7) DYellowlees (in tch: dropped rr 4th: r.o wl fr 3 out)................................7	3	8/1	77	17
	Tejano Gold (USA) (113) (PBradley) **6-11-12** RJohnson (bit bkwd: w ldrs tl wknd appr 3 out)..............................5	4	8/1	82	22
1123^{2}	**Tanseeq (88)** (MGMeagher) **5-10-1** LWyer (lw: s.i.s: bhd: hit 3rd: effrt appr 3 out: nvr nr ldrs)..........................7	5	11/2	50	—
1045*	**Menelave (IRE) (108)** (OSherwood) **6-11-7** JAMcCarthy (in tch tl rdn & btn appr 3 out)....................................2	6	9/4^{1}	68	8
1145^{7}	**Pegasus Bay (93)** (DECantillon) **5-10-6** SMcNeill (lw: stdd s: hdwy 5th: wknd appr 2 out)................................7	7	12/1	46	—
	Lucy Tufty (87) (JPearce) **5-10-0** VSmith (lw: in tch: hdwy 5th: rdn & wknd appr 2 out)....................................4	8	4/1^{2}	36	—
	Nagobelia (97) (JPearce) **8-10-10** NMann (bit bkwd: bhd fr 5th)..2	9	20/1	44	—
			(SP 124.9%)		**9 Rn**

3m 51.9 (3.90) CSF £86.00 CT £587.40 TOTE £23.20: £4.60 £2.00 £1.90 (£54.20) Trio £176.00; £89.27 to Fontwell 17/11/96 OWNER Mrs Solna ThomsonJones (NEWMARKET) BRED Mrs N. Johnston
LONG HANDICAP Lucy Tufty 9-12
Henrietta Howard (IRE), who looked very fit, runs well fresh and won a strange race in which most of the horses never got near enough to land a blow. After being ridden clear, she was eased near the finish and the winning distance could have been two or three lengths more. (16/1)
1188 Lord Mcmurrough (IRE) held a long-time lead over all the field except the winner. He needs further to be seen at his best. (9/2: 7/1-4/1)
Tim (IRE) has won over much further. (8/1: 7/1-12/1)
Tejano Gold (USA) has run well fresh in the past, but was feeling the pinch starting the home turn as lack of full fitness found him out. (8/1: tchd 12/1)

1123 Tanseeq had always given the leaders too much start. (11/2: op 7/2)
1045* Menelave (IRE) ran a stinker and was one of the first beaten. (9/4)
Lucy Tufty, in the form of her life on the Flat, had had a hard race on soft ground just five days earlier, and this may have come too soon. (4/1)

T/Plpt: £137.80 (74.79 Tckts). T/Qdpt: £21.70 (26.42 Tckts). Dk

WINDSOR (Fig. 8) (Chases Good to firm, Hdles Good)
Saturday November 16th
WEATHER: sunny

1375 SCANIA 4-SERIES NOVICES' HURDLE (I) (4-Y.O+) (Class E)
12-40 (12-41) **2m (8 hdls)** £2,110.00 (£585.00: £280.00) GOING minus 0.43 sec per fur (GF)

	Horse	Dist	Pos	SP	RR	SF
	Secret Spring (FR) (PRHedger) **4-10-12** MRichards (stdy hdwy appr 3 out: led 2 out: rdn out)	—	**1**	11/4[2]	79	5
	Danegold (IRE) (MRChannon) **4-10-12** AThornton (a.p: ev ch 2 out: unable qckn)	3½	**2**	7/1	76	2
	No Pattern (GLMoore) **4-10-12** JRailton (lw: stdy hdwy appr 3 out: ev ch 2 out: one pce)	3½	**3**	9/4[1]	72	—
1178[F]	**Laburnum Gold (IRE)** (MrsJPitman) **5-10-12** ILawrence (lw: plld hrd: chsd ldr: led 5th to 2 out: 4th & btn whn mstke last)	5	**4**	7/1	67	—
1178[2]	**Above the Cut (USA)** (CPMorlock) **4-10-12** CMaude (led to 5th: wknd appr last)	10	**5**	10/1	57	—
	Museum (IRE) (PWinkworth) **5-10-12** DLeahy (nvr plcd to chal)	hd	**6**	33/1	57	—
1152[7]	**L'Equipe (IRE)** (CJMann) **6-10-9**(3) JMagee (a mid div)	9	**7**	12/1	48	—
	Kumari King (IRE) (74) (AWCarroll) **6-10-12** DMorris (a bhd)	4	**8**	33/1	44	—
1132[3]	**Sahel (IRE)** (JWMullins) **8-10-12** SCurran (mstke 4th: stdy hdwy appr 3 out: wknd appr 2 out)	8	**9**	4/1[3]	36	—
	Seminole Wind (CRBarwell) **5-10-12** BFenton (bit bkwd: bhd fr 4th)	12	**10**	33/1	24	—
	Aganerot (IRE) (AGHobbs) **6-10-12** RGreene (bhd fr 3 out)	2½	**11**	25/1	21	—
	Northern Spruce (IRE) (AGFoster) **4-10-12** WMcFarland (7th whn mstke 5th: sn wknd)	22	**12**	33/1	—	—
				(SP 134.8%)	**12 Rn**	

3m 53.3 (5.30) CSF £24.06 TOTE £5.00: £1.90 £2.90 £1.50 (£25.10) Trio £30.40 OWNER Mr M. K. George (CHICHESTER) BRED Timothy D. Rootes

Secret Spring (FR), winner of two races on the Equitrack in February, put up a useful display, leading two out and needing only to be ridden along to assert. (11/4)
Danegold (IRE) was generally disappointing on the Flat this year, but showed much more sparkle with hurdles in front of him, holding every chance at the second last before the winner asserted. A small race can be found for him. (7/1)
No Pattern showed a lot of promise in two runs over hurdles last season, but failed to win on the Flat this year. Cruising into the action going to the third last, he was one of several with every chance before tapped foe toe, but should soon be winning. (9/4)
1178 Laburnum Gold (IRE) took a very keen hold and had got to the front by the fourth last. Collared two hurdles later, he was soon sending out distress signals and a mistake at the last made no difference to his chances. (7/1: op 4/1)
1178 Above the Cut (USA) set little more than a crawl in the early stages and was back-pedalling in the latter stages. (10/1)
Museum (IRE) caught the eye on his first outing for his new stable. He looks one to watch. (33/1)
L'Equipe (IRE) (12/1: 6/1-14/1)
1132 Sahel (IRE) was put to sleep at the back of the field in an attempt to get this easy two miles. After taking closer order going to the third last, he tired going to the next and does not get this trip. (4/1)

1376 SCANIA VEHICLE MANAGEMENT NOVICES' CHASE (5-Y.O+) (Class E)
1-10 (1-11) **3m (18 fncs)** £3,965.50 (£1,189.00: £572.00: £263.50) GOING minus 0.43 sec per fur (GF)

	Horse	Dist	Pos	SP	RR	SF
1286[3]	**Blasket Hero** (MrsSDWilliams) **8-10-12b** BFenton (nt j.w: hdwy 10th: led 12th: lft clr 4 out: j.lft last 3: rdn out)	—	**1**	11/10[1]	74?	—
1072[8]	**Damcada (IRE) (67)** (AWCarroll) **8-10-12** TJMurphy (bit bkwd: chsd ldrs to 5th: mstke 14th: lft 2nd 4 out: no imp)	7	**2**	25/1	69	—
	The Herbivore (IRE) (MJRoberts) **7-10-12** JRailton (bit bkwd: chsd ldr fr 5th: led 8th to 10th: wknd 4 out)	12	**3**	33/1	61	—
818[7]	**Hollow Wood (IRE)** (DLWilliams) **5-10-10** AThornton (bhd fr 10th: t.o fr 13th)	dist	**4**	11/1[3]	—	—
1075[2]	**Grey Gorden (IRE)** (RCurtis) **8-10-12** DMorris (led to 8th: led 10th to 12th: 2nd & ev ch whn fell 4 out)		**F**	5/4[2]	—	—
				(SP 107.2%)	**5 Rn**	

6m 9.6 (14.60) CSF £16.66 TOTE £1.90: £1.10 £5.50 (£8.30) OWNER Miss H. J. Flower (SOUTH MOLTON) BRED M. Channon
WEIGHT FOR AGE 5yo-2lb

1286 Blasket Hero made several errors in the first half of this chasing debut, but still managed to get to the front at the twelfth. Left clear after his only serious rival fell four out, he jumped badly to his left over the last three, but was still too good for the rest. (11/10: 4/6-5/4)
Damcada (IRE), winner of two sellers over hurdles, still did not look fully fit, despite a recent run. (25/1)
1075 Grey Gorden (IRE) was still on terms with the winner when crashing to the deck at the fourth last. He should soon find a race and would be helped by some rain. (5/4)

1377 SCANIA 4-SERIES 'HORSEPOWER' HURDLE (3-Y.O) (Class E)
1-40 (1-47) **2m (8 hdls)** £2,687.50 (£750.00: £362.50) GOING minus 0.43 sec per fur (GF)

	Horse	Dist	Pos	SP	RR	SF
	Far Dawn (USA) (MrsAJPerrett) **3-10-12** CMaude (lw: led to 4th: led 3 out: clr appr last: comf)	—	**1**	6/4[1]	74+	—
1269[8]	**Sterling Fellow** (DLWilliams) **3-10-12v**[1] MClarke (hdwy appr 2 out: rdn appr last: r.o one pce flat)	4	**2**	16/1	70	—
	Samara Song (WGMTurner) **3-10-5**(7) JPower (lw: stdy hdwy appr 3 out: hrd rdn appr last: one pce)	3	**3**	25/1	67	—
1149[F]	**Colour Counsellor** (RMFlower) **3-10-12** DO'Sullivan (lw: hdwy 5th: rdn appr last: one pce)	s.h	**4**	5/1[2]	67	—
	Stonecutter (MRChannon) **3-10-12** PHolley (lw: no hdwy fr 3 out)	5	**5**	6/1[3]	62	—
1149[6]	**In Cahoots** (ADSmith) **3-10-12** FJousset (nvr nr to chal)	2	**6**	12/1	60	—
	Young Mazaad (IRE) (DCO'Brien) **3-10-12** TJMurphy (prom tl appr 2 out)	2	**7**	8/1	58	—
	Hawanafa (JSMoore) **3-10-7** WMcFarland (a.p: led 4th tl j.slowly & hdd 5th: led appr 3 out: sn hdd: wknd)	nk	**8**	20/1	53	—
	Illegally Yours (LMontagueHall) **3-10-7** RGreene (hld up: rdn 3 out: sn wknd)	1¾	**9**	10/1	51	—
1011[B]	**It's Dawan** (PMitchell) **3-10-12** LHarvey (mstke 3rd: mid div whn mstke 3 out: sn wknd)	¾	**10**	25/1	55	—
	Impending Danger (KSBridgwater) **3-10-12** VSlattery (hmpd 1st: mstke 2nd: a bhd)	1¼	**11**	40/1	54	—

				SP	RR	SF
831^{6}	**Colebrook Willie** (JRBosley) **3-10-12** MBosley (a.p: led 5th tl appr 3 out: sn wknd)	1½	**12**	20/1	52	—
962^{U}	**Embroidered** (RMFlower) **3-10-0**(7) JKMcCarthy (a bhd)	3	**13**	40/1	44	—
	Half An Inch (IRE) (TMJones) **3-10-12** DLeahy (bit bkwd: bhd fr 5th)	18	**14**	25/1	31	—
1149^{9}	**The Grey Weaver** (RMFlower) **3-10-9**(3) TDascombe (prom to 3 out)	16	**15**	40/1	15	—
	Duralock Fencer (PGMurphy) **3-10-12** JRailton (fell 1st)		**F**	33/1	—	—
	Moylough Rebel (JELong) **3-10-12** BFenton (lw: mid div whn s.u bnd appr 3 out)		**S**	40/1	—	—
	General Henry (AMoore) **3-10-5**(7) MBatchelor (bhd whn blnd & uns rdr 3rd)		**U**	40/1	—	—
	Aavasaksa (FR) (AGNewcombe) **3-10-12** AThornton (bkwd: bhd whn blnd & uns rdr 3 out)		**U**	33/1	—	—
				(SP 143.9%)	**19 Rn**	

3m 55.6 (7.60) CSF £29.65 TOTE £2.70: £1.80 £6.80 £8.70 (£38.10) Trio £129.50 OWNER Mr Peter Wiegand (PULBOROUGH) BRED Galbreath/Phillips Racing Partnership

STEWARDS' ENQUIRY Bosley susp. 25-27/11/96 (excessive use of the whip).

Far Dawn (USA), winner of a maiden on the Flat this year, looks the part for this game and put up a very polished display, leading at the third last and forging clear from the next to win with plenty in hand. He can win again. (6/4)

Sterling Fellow, a real stayer on the Flat, found this too sharp, but did stay on to win the battle for second. (16/1)

Samara Song, a plater on the Flat, was only scrapping for minor honours over the last two. (25/1)

1149 Colour Counsellor moved up soon after halfway, but was only battling for minor honours in the straight. (5/1)

1378 SCANIA NATIONAL ACCOUNTS H'CAP HURDLE (0-100) (4-Y.O+) (Class E)

2-15 (2-16) **2m 4f (10 hdls)** £2,798.00 (£778.00: £374.00) GOING minus 0.43 sec per fur (GF)

				SP	RR	SF
1077^{2}	**Dream Leader (IRE) (85)** (MJRoberts) **6-11-7** JRailton (led tl after 1st: led 2 out: wandered appr last: hrd rdn: hdd nr fin: led last stride)	—	**1**	5/2^{1}	69	31
1034^{5}	**Slipmatic (85)** (AndrewTurnell) **7-11-0**(7) CRae (led after 1st: hdd 2 out: hung lft appr last: hrd rdn: led nr fin: hdd last stride)	s.h	**2**	7/1	69	31
1274^{5}	**Positivo (76)** (MissCJECaroe) **5-10-12** DLeahy (lost pl appr 3 out: rallied appr last: r.o one pce)	4	**3**	10/1	57	19
	Bossymoss (IRE) (75) (AStreeter) **7-10-11** TEley (a.p: rdn 3 out: one pce)	½	**4**	6/1^{3}	55	17
960^{2}	**Supreme Star (USA) (89)** (PRHedger) **5-11-11** AThornton (hdwy & mstke 7th: rdn appr 2 out: wknd appr last)	3	**5**	7/2^{2}	67	29
969^{4}	**Catwalker (IRE) (64)** (HJMWebb) **5-9-9b**(5) SophieMitchell (a bhd)	3	**6**	14/1	40	2
961^{4}	**First Instance (IRE) (76)** (DMGrissell) **6-10-12** BFenton (hld up: rdn appr 3 out: sn wknd)	1½	**7**	7/1	50	12
973^{5}	**Gerry's Pride (IRE) (79)** (JWMullins) **5-11-1** SCurran (a.p: ev ch 3 out: wknd appr 2 out)	19	**8**	6/1^{3}	38	—
				(SP 120.1%)	**8 Rn**	

4m 47.7 (1.70) CSF £19.80 CT £140.50 TOTE £2.10: £1.10 £3.00 £2.60 (£15.40) Trio £91.60 OWNER Mr Mike Roberts (HAILSHAM) BRED Frank Barry

LONG HANDICAP Catwalker (IRE) 9-11

STEWARDS' ENQUIRY Rae susp. 25-30/11/96 (excessive use of whip).

1077 Dream Leader (IRE) did not appreciate being in front and wandered about going to the final flight. Looking just as unenthusiastic as the runner-up, he managed to have a whisker in front on the line. (5/2)

1034 Slipmatic ran much better here but, after being headed two out, she ducked to her left and, along with the winner, was not over-keen about the job in hand. Leading briefly, she was then headed on the line. (7/1)

1274 Positivo has had plenty of chances. (10/1)

Bossymoss (IRE), on his seasonal debut, is 7lb higher than when winning his only race to date at Warwick in May. (6/1)

960 Supreme Star (USA) still does not jump convincingly. (7/2)

961 First Instance (IRE) (7/1: 10/1-6/1)

1379 SCANIA 1996 TRUCK OF THE YEAR H'CAP CHASE (0-120) (5-Y.O+) (Class D)

2-50 (2-50) **2m 5f (15 fncs)** £4,352.25 (£1,308.00: £631.50: £293.25) GOING minus 0.43 sec per fur (GF)

				SP	RR	SF
1119^{5}	**Too Plush (103)** (AndrewTurnell) **7-10-13** LHarvey (mde all: rdn out)	—	**1**	7/2^{2}	108	8
1284^{W}	**Lake of Loughrea (IRE) (104)** (KCBailey) **6-11-0** AThornton (hdwy 11th: chsd wnr fr 4 out: unable qckn)	5	**2**	4/1^{3}	105	5
1284^{F}	**Duhallow Lodge (110)** (CRBarwell) **9-11-6** BFenton (hld up: pckd 11th: one pce fr 4 out)	3½	**3**	10/1	109	9
814^{6}	**Kindle's Delight (103)** (MissHCKnight) **8-10-13** TJMurphy (mstke 3rd: rdn 8th: bhd fr 11th)	4	**4**	9/2	99	—
1284*	**Monks Jay (IRE) (93)** (GThorner) **7-10-3** ILawrence (hdwy 7th: rdn 4 out: sn wknd)	5	**5**	5/2^{1}	85	—
1070^{3}	**Who's to Say (118)** (MissVenetiaWilliams) **10-11-9**(5) MrRThornton (a.p: 3rd whn mstke 3 out: sn wknd)	8	**6**	5/1	104	4
				(SP 114.7%)	**6 Rn**	

5m 15.8 (6.80) CSF £16.81 TOTE £4.60: £2.00 £2.80 (£8.70) OWNER Mrs C. C. Williams (WANTAGE) BRED Miss B. Sykes

1119 Too Plush was allowed to stride along in front on this occasion and was not going to be denied. (7/2)

932 Lake of Loughrea (IRE) failed to stay three and a quarter last time and was happier at this trip. (4/1)

Duhallow Lodge was made to look very pedestrian over the last four. (10/1: 8/1-12/1)

1284* Monks Jay (IRE), 5lb higher for his Wincanton victory last week, was in trouble early in the straight. (5/2: 7/4-11/4)

1070 Who's to Say has yet to win beyond two and a quarter miles. (5/1: 7/2-11/2)

1380 SCANIA 4-SERIES NOVICES' HURDLE (II) (4-Y.O+) (Class E)

3-25 (3-26) **2m (8 hdls)** £2,092.50 (£580.00: £277.50) GOING minus 0.43 sec per fur (GF)

				SP	RR	SF
655*	**Nahrawali (IRE) (101)** (AMoore) **5-10-12**(7) MBatchelor (a.p: mstkes 1st & 2nd: chsd ldr fr 5th: led & mstke 3 out: clr appr last: r.o wl)	—	**1**	7/4^{2}	87?	36
	Battleship Bruce (97) (TCasey) **4-10-7**(5) SRyan (lw: stdy hdwy 5th: chsd wnr fr 3 out: ev ch appr 2 out: 2nd & btn whn mstke last)	12	**2**	13/8^{1}	68	17
	Hazaaf (USA) (ADSmith) **7-10-12** FJousset (bit bkwd: swtg: hdwy 3 out: 3rd & no ch whn mstke last)	5	**3**	14/1	63	12
	Little Shefford (MPMuggeridge) **4-10-12** SCurran (led to 3 out: sn wknd)	14	**4**	25/1	49	—
	Trehane (NAGraham) **4-10-7** JRailton (lw: chsd ldr to 5th: wknd appr 3 out)	7	**5**	9/1	37	—
	Queen of Shannon (IRE) (AWCarroll) **8-10-7** TJMurphy (a bhd: t.o whn p.u bef 2 out)		**P**	10/1	—	—
	Lanesra Breeze (TJNaughton) **4-10-12** AThornton (a bhd: t.o whn p.u bef 2 out)		**P**	20/1	—	—
	Miss The Beat (SMellor) **4-10-2**(5) ChrisWebb (a bhd: t.o whn p.u bef 2 out)		**P**	25/1	—	—
955^{F}	**Braydon Forest** (CJDrewe) **4-10-9**(3) GuyLewis (mstke 2nd: a bhd: t.o whn p.u bef 2 out)		**P**	7/1^{3}	—	—

				SP	RR	SF
1178P	**Web of Steel** (CJHemsley) **6-10-12** MBosley (bhd fr 5th: t.o whn p.u bef 2 out)		**P**	25/1	—	—
				(SP 129.0%)		**10 Rn**

3m 47.8 (-0.20) CSF £5.50 TOTE £2.60: £1.40 £1.10 £4.50 (£2.60) Trio £10.20 OWNER Mr C. F. Sparrowhawk (BRIGHTON) BRED His Highness the Aga Khans Studs S. C.

IN-FOCUS: **This seemed the weaker of the two divisions of this event but this was by far the fastest time of the four races run over two miles on the day.**

655* Nahrawali (IRE), who made a couple of awkward jumps early on, forged clear going to the final flight for a decisive victory. This was his rider's first winner. (7/4: 5/4-9/4)

Battleship Bruce failed to win on the Flat this year, but looked in good shape for his new stable. He should soon find a race. (13/8)

Hazaaf (USA) has been racing in France, but did not look fully wound up, and was held in third when flattening the final flight. (14/1)

Little Shefford, on his first run for his new stable, set the pace but, collared three out, found lack of a previous run taking its toll. (25/1)

Trehane (9/1: 6/1-10/1)

Queen of Shannon (IRE) (10/1: 8/1-12/1)

1381 SCANIA 4-SERIES 'KING OF THE ROAD' H'CAP HURDLE (0-110) (4-Y.O+) (Class E)

4-00 (4-00) **2m (8 hdls)** £2,997.25 (£898.00: £431.50: £198.25) GOING minus 0.43 sec per fur (GF)

				SP	RR	SF
1145²	**Supermick (83)** (WRMuir) **5-11-1** MRichards (led 3rd to 3 out: rdn appr 2 out: led last strides)	—	1	6/4 1	64	17
	Dontdressfordinner (81) (RJHodges) **6-10-10**(3) TDascombe (lw: hld up: led 3 out: rdn appr 2 out: hdd last strides)	hd	2	8/1	62	15
	Kelly Mac (88) (DCO'Brien) **6-11-6** TJMurphy (led to 3rd: lost pl 3 out: rallied flat: r.o wl)	nk	3	7/1	69	22
1193*	**Pair of Jacks (IRE) (92)** (GLMoore) **6-11-5**(5) MrRThornton (lw: a.p: ev ch 3 out: unable qckn flat)	2	4	100/30 2	71	24
	Muhtashim (IRE) (89) (JFfitch-Heyes) **6-11-7** BFenton (nvr nr to chal)	4	5	14/1	64	17
1181S	**Anlace (82)** (SMellor) **7-10-9**(5) ChrisWebb (lw: bhd fr 5th)	7	6	9/2 3	50	3
1181⁴	**Will James (68)** (CJDrewe) **10-9-11b**(3) GuyLewis (lw: hld up: rdn 3 out: sn wknd)	2½	7	12/1	33	—
	Added Dimension (IRE) (91) (PWinkworth) **5-11-9** DLeahy (bit bkwd: hdwy 5th: sn wknd)	23	8	14/1	33	—
				(SP 125.9%)		**8 Rn**

3m 51.3 (3.30) CSF £14.83 CT £66.37 TOTE £2.50: £1.40 £2.40 £2.40 (£11.80) OWNER Mrs J. M. Muir (LAMBOURN) BRED James Thom and Sons

LONG HANDICAP Will James 9-11

1145 Supermick, whose only previous win came in a seller, showed real battling qualities. Headed three from home, he refused to give way and got back in front with a few yards to spare. (6/4: 5/2-11/8)

Dontdressfordinner looked very straight for this seasonal debut and only just failed to make a winning start for his new connections. (8/1)

Kelly Mac, off the track since May, probably found the ground a bit too lively for him. (7/1: 4/1-8/1)

1193* Pair of Jacks (IRE) is in good heart this season and threw down his challenge in the straight. On the dash from the final flight, he was tapped for toe. (100/30)

Muhtashim (IRE) (14/1: 8/1-16/1)

Added Dimension (IRE) (14/1: 10/1-16/1)

T/Jkpt: £1,955.90 (3.63 Tckts). T/Plpt: £47.90 (197.7 Tckts). T/Qdpt: £13.10 (37.66 Tckts). AK

1363-CHELTENHAM (L-H) (Good, Good to firm patches)

Sunday November 17th

WEATHER: overcast

1382 CARLTON REFRIGERATION FRASER DIGBY CONDITIONAL H'CAP HURDLE (0-115) (4-Y.O+) (Class E)

1-05 (1-05) **2m 110y (Old) (8 hdls)** £2,316.00 (£651.00: £318.00) GOING: 0.52 sec per fur (GS)

				SP	RR	SF
1145⁸	**Handson (87)** (BRMillman) **4-10-0** DSalter (hld up in rr: pckd 1st: mstke 5th: outpcd appr 2 out: rdn appr last: str run to ld last strides)	—	1	7/2 2	63	26
798³	**Robert's Toy (IRE) (113)** (MCPipe) **5-11-7**(5) BMoore (lw: plld hrd: w ldr: led appr last: rdn flat: ct last strides)	nk	2	7/1	89	52
	Hay Dance (95) (PJHobbs) **5-10-8** DJKavanagh (hld up: hdwy 5th: led 2 out: rdn & hdd appr last: one pce)	1¼	3	7/2 2	70	33
1171⁵	**Mister Rm (111)** (NATwiston-Davies) **4-11-10** DWalsh (led to 2 out: sn rdn & wknd)	11	4	5/2 1	75	38
1181³	**Hullo Mary Doll (87)** (AJChamberlain) **7-10-0** ChrisWebb (prom: rdn appr 3 out: wknd appr 2 out)	1½	5	12/1	49	12
1060³	**Kalzari (USA) (87)** (AWCarroll) **11-9-9**(5) LSuthern (hld up & plld hrd: bhd fr 5th: sn t.o)	dist	6	6/1 3	—	—
				(SP 107.5%)		**6 Rn**

4m 4.5 (13.50) CSF £23.03 TOTE £4.50: £1.80 £2.40 (£14.80) OWNER Burrow Racing (CULLOMPTON) BRED Mrs A. Dale

LONG HANDICAP Hullo Mary Doll 9-6 Kalzari (USA) 9-13

971 Handson really appreciated this stiff uphill finish and came from nowhere for an unlikely win. (7/2)

798 Robert's Toy (IRE), dropped 3lb, got the better of the battle with Hay Dance, only to have victory snatched away at the death. (7/1: 4/1-8/1)

Hay Dance won a Ballinrobe maiden hurdle in July and then finished fourth in better company at the Galway Festival. (7/2)

1060* Mister Rm was 5lb higher than when scoring over course and distance at the end of last month. (5/2)

1181 Hullo Mary Doll, 8lb out of the handicap, was effectively a stone higher than when winning on her seasonal reappearance. (12/1)

1383 FOOD BROKERS-GLOYSTARNE H'CAP CHASE (0-135) (5-Y.O+) (Class C)

1-40 (1-42) **3m 1f (Old) (19 fncs)** £4,856.25 (£1,470.00: £717.50: £341.25) GOING: 0.52 sec per fur (GS)

				SP	RR	SF
1147*	**Time Enough (IRE) (105)** (CPEBrooks) **7-10-0** JOsborne (lw: j.w: mde all: clr 3 out: easily)	—	1	9/4 1	116+	12
1070²	**Philip's Woody (115)** (NJHenderson) **8-10-10** JRKavanagh (hld up & bhd: hdwy 4 out: chsd wnr appr 3 out: sn rdn: no imp)	9	2	3/1 3	120	16
1057²	**Frozen Drop (105)** (PCRitchens) **9-10-0** SFox (chsd wnr 3rd tl appr 10th: mstke 4 out: bhd whn blnd 3 out)	14	3	11/4 2	101	—
1043³	**Vicosa (IRE) (112)** (RHAlner) **7-10-4**(3) PHenley (nt j.w: hld up & bhd: mstke 11th: rdn & hdwy after 4 out: wknd 3 out)	16	4	9/2	98	—
1194²	**Paper Star (105)** (MPMuggeridge) **9-10-0** BPowell (chsd wnr to 3rd: wnt 2nd appr 10th tl rdn appr 3 out: 4th & wkng whn mstke 2 out)	10	5	20/1	85	—
				(SP 105.4%)		**5 Rn**

6m 34.9 (25.90) CSF £8.28 TOTE £2.70: £1.60 £1.50 (£2.70) OWNER The Lewis Partnership (LAMBOURN) BRED T. O'Brien

LONG HANDICAP Frozen Drop 9-12 Time Enough (IRE) 9-12 Paper Star 9-12
1147* Time Enough (IRE), whose jumping has benefited from the tuition of Yogi Breisner, was just out of the handicap and so effectively 7lb higher than when winning at Warwick. (9/4)
1070 Philip's Woody has yet to win beyond two and a half miles, but simply met one too good on this occasion. (3/1: 2/1-100/30)
1057 Frozen Drop, struggling when making a hash of the third last, has always stayed well and plugged on to secure the minor berth. (11/4)
1043 Vicosa (IRE) had better ground this time, but his jumping again left a lot to be desired. (9/2)

1384 MURPHY'S NOVICES' H'CAP HURDLE (4-Y.O+) (Class C)
2-15 (2-17) **3m 2f (Old) (13 hdls)** £4,856.25 (£1,470.00: £717.50: £341.25) GOING: 0.52 sec per fur (GS)

				SP	RR	SF
1130^{2}	**Mister Blake (84)** (RLee) **6-10-0** RJohnson (hld up: hdwy 9th: nt clr run & swtchd rt after 3 out: led 2 out: sn hdd: led flat: r.o wl)	—	**1**	9/1	63	—
1322*	**Queen's Award (IRE) (84)** (RHBuckler) **7-9-7**(7) 6x MGriffiths (hld up: hdwy 9th: led after 2 out: rdn & hdd flat: one pce)	3½	**2**	2/1 1	62	—
1174^{5}	**Coole Hill (IRE) (87)** (DNicholson) **5-10-3** AMaguire (hld up: stdy hdwy appr 3 out: lft 3rd last: one pce)	2	**3**	9/1	64	—
1074^{5}	**Old Archives (IRE) (89)** (LWells) **7-10-5** JOsborne (prom: ev ch 3 out: wknd 2 out)	20	**4**	7/1 3	53	—
1274^{2}	**Hylters Chance (IRE) (84)** (PJHobbs) **5-10-0** LHarvey (led to 2 out: eased whn btn appr last)	18	**5**	8/1	37	—
1062^{2}	**Tipping The Line (108)** (MCPipe) **6-11-10** RDunwoody (lw: chsd ldr to 9th: rdn & wknd 10th)	2	**6**	7/1 3	60	—
	Fort Deely (IRE) (93) (EMcNamara,Ireland) **5-10-9** NWilliamson (hld up & plld hrd: hdwy 8th: rdn 10th: ev ch whn n.m.r on ins 3 out: 3rd & btn whn slipped & fell last)		**F**	3/1 2	—	—
				(SP 114.4%)	**7 Rn**	

6m 55.9 (38.90) CSF £26.51 TOTE £10.30: £2.60 £1.70 (£13.70) OWNER Mr W. D. Edwards (PRESTEIGNE) BRED Southcourt Stud
LONG HANDICAP Queen's Award (IRE) 9-5 Hylters Chance (IRE) 9-11
1130 Mister Blake had been beaten fifteen lengths by Queen's Award at Wetherby, but turned the tables on 18lb better terms. (9/1: 5/1-10/1)
1322* Queen's Award (IRE) had given the winner a fifteen-length drubbing at Wetherby, but could not confirm the form on 18lb worse terms. (2/1)
1174 Coole Hill (IRE) was back to a more suitable trip, but could never get to grips with the first two. (9/1: op 6/1)
1074 Old Archives (IRE) did not appear to get the trip. (7/1)
1274 Hylters Chance (IRE) only succeeded in setting the race up for others. (8/1: 9/2-9/1)
1062 Tipping The Line was 8lb higher than when winning a handicap at Worcester in June. (7/1: 4/1-8/1)

1385 SPORTING INDEX CROSS COUNTRY CHASE (5-Y.O+) (Class B)
2-50 (2-52) **3m 7f (Cross Country) (30 fncs)** £8,488.75 (£2,560.00: £1,242.50: £583.75) GOING: 0.52 sec per fur (GS)

				SP	RR	SF
1048^{2}	**McGregor The Third (125)** (GRichards) **10-11-2** BHarding (chsd ldr: led 12th to 15th: led 19th: clr appr last: easily)	—	**1**	5/6 1	120	—
$930a^{2}$	**Irish Stamp (IRE) (119)** (FMurphy) **7-11-5** NWilliamson (hld up: stdy hdwy 12th: lft 2nd 25th: ev ch 3 out: hrd rdn after 2 out: sn btn)	18	**2**	11/4 2	112	—
1075^{3}	**Seasamacamile (69)** (RHBuckler) **9-10-5** AMaguire (hld up: hdwy 12th: lost pl 16th: rallied 22nd: one pce fr 25th)	19	**3**	33/1	87	—
190^{10}	**Cool Character (IRE) (69)** (RHBuckler) **8-10-7** BPowell (bhd tl hdwy 23rd: one pce fr 25th)	1½	**4**	33/1	88	—
1202^{3}	**Shamarphil (93)** (RHAlner) **10-10-5** MissSBarraclough (wl bhd fr 19th)	7	**5**	11/1	82	—
	Marketplace (IRE) (PavelSlozil,CzechRepublic) **5-10-13** PavelSlozil (lw: prom tl wknd 17th)	3	**6**	33/1	90	—
$930a^{3}$	**Its a Snip (91)** (CJMann) **11-11-5b** RDunwoody (led: slipped 3rd: hdd 6th: 2nd whn p.u lame bef 25th)		**P**	7/1 3	—	—
	Furtado (FR) (JVana,CzechRepublic) **7-10-10** JosefVana (lw: plld hrd: prom: mstke 2nd: led 6th to 12th: led 15th to 19th: wknd 21st: t.o whn p.u bef 26th)		**P**	33/1	—	—
				(SP 113.8%)	**8 Rn**	

8m 27.1 CSF £3.38 TOTE £2.00: £1.70 £1.10 £2.80 (£2.50) OWNER Mrs D. A. Whitaker (PENRITH) BRED Mrs D. A. Whitaker
WEIGHT FOR AGE 5yo-2lb
1048 McGregor The Third again put his eventing experience to good use and the fact that the distance of this race had been increased by nearly a mile did not bother him. He is quoted at 33/1 for the Grand National. (5/6)
930a Irish Stamp (IRE) would have been 9lb better off with the winner had this been a handicap. (11/4)
1075 Seasamacamile had an impossible task at the weights with the two principals. (33/1)
Cool Character (IRE), coming back after a wind operation, is another who had no chance at these weights. (33/1)
1202 Shamarphil (11/1: 10/1-16/1)

1386 STAKIS CASINOS NOVEMBER NOVICES' CHASE (Gd 2) (5-Y.O+) (Class A)
3-25 (3-28) **2m (Old) (12 fncs)** £11,780.00 (£4,454.00: £2,177.00: £989.00) GOING: 0.52 sec per fur (GS)

				SP	RR	SF
1066*	**Celibate (IRE) (122)** (CJMann) **5-11-0** RDunwoody (chsd ldr: lft in ld 6th: mstke 7th: rdn out)	—	**1**	6/4 2	125	16
947*	**Land Afar** (PRWebber) **9-11-0** MDwyer (hld up gng wl: nt fluent 2 out: chsd wnr appr last: sn rdn: no imp)	6	**2**	5/6 1	119	10
	Hedgehopper (IRE) (109) (CWeedon) **8-11-0** MRichards (led tl mstke 6th: wknd appr last)	10	**3**	9/1 3	109	—
1018^{2}	**Clifton Game** (MRChannon) **6-11-0** AThornton (hld up: hdwy after 4 out: disp cl 3rd whn fell 2 out: rmntd)	dist	**4**	16/1	—	—
				(SP 110.4%)	**4 Rn**	

4m 11.7 (18.70) CSF £3.10 TOTE £2.30 (£1.40) OWNER Stamford Bridge Partnership (UPPER LAMBOURN) BRED Miss Noirin Dunne
1066* Celibate (IRE) continues from strength to strength and sealed victory with a spectacular leap at the final fence. (6/4)
947* Land Afar found surprisingly little after not handling the penultimate fence particularly well. (5/6)
Hedgehopper (IRE) lost the lead when landing in a heap at the water, but was only shaken off once in line for home. It should be remembered that he was rated far inferior to the runner-up over hurdles. (9/1: 5/1-10/1)
1018 Clifton Game, dropped back to two miles, was probably just beginning to feel the pinch when coming to grief at the second last. (16/1)

1387 TONY WRIGHT BENEFIT HURDLE (3-Y.O) (Class D)
4-00 (4-00) **2m 110y (Old) (8 hdls)** £2,829.00 (£794.00: £387.00) GOING: 0.52 sec per fur (GS)

				SP	RR	SF
599*	**Noble Lord** (RHBuckler) **3-11-12** BPowell (mde all: clr appr 3 out: easily)	—	**1**	6/1	92+	43
1184*	**Always Happy** (MCPipe) **3-11-7** CMaude (lw: hld up & bhd: hdwy 2 out: hrd rdn appr last: no ch w wnr)	15	**2**	7/2 3	73	24
1064^{2}	**Ben Bowden** (SWoodman) **3-11-6** AMaguire (chsd wnr to 3 out: wnt 2nd again after 2 out: no imp)	1¼	**3**	9/1	70	21
962^{4}	**Topaglow (IRE)** (PTDalton) **3-11-0** TEley (hld up: hdwy appr 3 out: sn rdn & wknd)	7	**4**	25/1	58	9
	Brandon Magic (IABalding) **3-11-0** RDunwoody (nt j.w: hld up: wknd 3 out: bhd whn mskte 2 out: t.o)	30	**5**	2/1 1	28	—

Seattle Alley (USA) (PRWebber) **3-11-0** JOsborne (hld up: chsd wnr 3 out tl wknd after 2 out: virtually p.u flat: t.o)....dist **6** 5/2[2] — —
753[5] **Trianna** (RBrotherton) **3-10-9** LHarvey (a bhd: t.o whn p.u bef 3 out: sdlle slipped) .... **P** 50/1 — —
(SP 114.2%) **7 Rn**

4m 6.1 (15.10) CSF £25.68 TOTE £6.70: £2.00 £1.90 (£7.30) OWNER The Old Timers Partnership (BRIDPORT) BRED J. E. Swiers
OFFICIAL EXPLANATION Trianna: her saddle slipped.
599* Noble Lord was a real drifter in the market, but found no difficulty in defying his double penalty. (6/1: op 4/1)
1184* Always Happy stayed on under pressure to win the separate race for second. (7/2)
1064 Ben Bowden could not live with the winner from the top of the hill. (9/1)
Topaglow (IRE) could only manage a short-lived effort coming down the hill. (25/1)
Brandon Magic has plenty to learn about the art of hurdling. (2/1)

T/Plpt: £59.10 (429.3 Tckts). T/Qdpt: £12.50 (176.11 Tckts) KH

1072-FONTWELL (Fig. 8) (Good becoming Good to soft)
Sunday November 17th
WEATHER: rain

1388 RICHMOND PARK CONSERVATIVE CLUB MAIDEN HURDLE (I) (4-Y.O+) (Class E)
12-20 (12-21) **2m 2f 110y (9 hdls)** £2,490.00 (£690.00: £330.00) GOING: 1.17 sec per fur (HY)

SP RR SF
Gloriana (LadyHerries) **4-11-0** MAFitzgerald (led to 2nd: led 5th: drvn out)....— **1** 11/4[1] 65+ —
Nordic Spree (IRE) (AMoore) **4-11-5** PHolley (stdy hdwy 3 out: lost pl appr 2 out: rallied appr last: r.o one pce)....2½ **2** 10/1 68 —
Jakes Justice (IRE) (JTGifford) **5-11-5** PHide (stdy hdwy 3 out: rdn appr 2 out: 2nd & btn whn mstke last)..s.h **3** 100/30[3] 68 —
1170[6] **Topanga (84)** (JABennett) **4-11-5b[1]** DBridgwater (a.p: 2nd whn mstke 2 out: one pce)....5 **4** 14/1 64 —
Sails Legend (102) (JELong) **5-11-5** DGallagher (bit bkwd: hdwy & ev ch 3 out: hrd rdn appr 2 out: sn wknd) .6 **5** 5/1 58 —
954[3] **Mr Strong Gale (IRE)** (PFNicholls) **5-11-5** APMcCoy (lw: led 3rd to 5th: ev ch 3 out: wknd appr 2 out: t.o) ..dist **6** 3/1[2] — —
Kaifoon (USA) (PCRitchens) **7-11-5** BFenton (bit bkwd: a bhd: t.o fr 6th)....dist **7** 14/1 — —
Little Luke (IRE) (PButler) **5-11-5** TJMurphy (lw: a bhd: t.o fr 6th)....8 **8** 40/1 — —
Quisti (PRHedger) **6-11-5** DO'Sullivan (s.s: a t.o)....14 **9** 33/1 — —
905[R] **Indian Crown (66)** (NBThomson) **6-11-0b[1]** SBurrough (plld hrd: led 2nd to 3rd: wknd 5th: t.o fr 6th)....8 **10** 50/1 — —
1118[8] **Little Embers** (JMBradley) **4-10-7v[1](7)** JPower (lw: mstke 4th: bhd whn blnd & uns rdr 5th).... **U** 50/1 — —
(SP 123.1%) **11 Rn**

4m 49.4 (31.40) CSF £29.61 TOTE £3.30: £1.10 £3.80 £1.90 (£59.70) Trio £78.80 OWNER Mr D. S. W. Blacker (LITTLEHAMPTON) BRED D. Blacker
Gloriana, winner of a mile handicap on the Flat at Haydock back in August, knew what was required of her on this hurdling debut. She travelled well and will win again as long as she is not raised too much in class. (11/4: 7/4-3/1)
Nordic Spree (IRE), a half-brother to Moonax, had a recent spin on the Flat and ran his best race to date. (10/1: 16/1-8/1)
Jakes Justice (IRE) was not subjected to a hard time on this hurdling debut and showed promise. Sure to have learnt a lot from this, he should soon find a novice event. (100/30: 2/1-7/2)
Topanga, fitted with blinkers for the first time, ran his best race of the season. (14/1)
Sails Legend looked in need of this reappearance. (5/1)
954 Mr Strong Gale (IRE) flopped in the mud last season, so may need a sound surface. (3/1)

1389 WALBERTON NOVICES' CHASE (5-Y.O+) (Class E)
12-50 (12-51) **2m 3f (16 fncs)** £3,474.00 (£964.00: £462.00) GOING: 1.17 sec per fur (HY)

SP RR SF
Oban (MissHCKnight) **6-10-12** GBradley (lw: hld up: rdn appr 3 out: led flat: drvn out)....— **1** 5/1[3] 113 46
Headwind (IRE) (JTGifford) **5-10-11** PHide (hdwy to chse ldr after 6th: led 2 out: mstke last: hdd flat:r.o wl) s.h **2** Evens[1] 112 45
1150* **Mr Conductor (IRE) (108)** (RHAlner) **5-11-4** AThornton (led to 2 out: wknd appr last)....13 **3** 15/8[2] 108 41
1037[P] **Millfrone (IRE)** (RRowe) **6-10-12** DO'Sullivan (chsd ldr tl after 6th: sn wknd: t.o fr 10th: p.u bef 3 out).... **P** 33/1 — —
Victory Gate (USA) (71) (MrsLCJewell) **11-10-12** JRailton (bhd fr 5th: t.o whn p.u bef 10th).... **P** 40/1 — —
1270[3] **Full of Tricks (69)** (JJBridger) **8-10-12** DBridgwater (lw: bhd fr 4th: t.o whn p.u bef 7th).... **P** 50/1 — —
1285[6] **Our Nikki (72)** (PRRodford) **6-10-7** SBurrough (bhd whn mstke & uns rdr 3rd).... **U** 33/1 — —
(SP 111.7%) **7 Rn**

5m 5.0 (26.00) CSF £10.01 TOTE £5.20: £1.40 £1.10 (£3.70) OWNER Lord Hartington (WANTAGE) BRED Willingham House Stud
Oban looked in tremendous shape for this seasonal reappearance and, under a lovely ride from Bradley, made a winning debut over fences. (5/1: 7/2-11/2)
Headwind (IRE) should have made a winning debut over fences. With his pilot oozing confidence entering the straight, he showed narrowly in front two out but had not banked on such a tenacious winner. Compensation awaits. (Evens)
1150* Mr Conductor (IRE) did a fine job of pacemaking but, collared two out, was soon left behind. (15/8)

1390 FORD (S) H'CAP HURDLE (0-90) (4-Y.O+) (Class G)
1-25 (1-26) **2m 2f 110y (9 hdls)** £2,075.00 (£575.00: £275.00) GOING: 1.17 sec per fur (HY)

SP RR SF
Sprintfayre (61) (JELong) **8-10-0** DGallagher (racd wd: led to 3rd: led 5th: all out)....— **1** 12/1 37 —
Kashan (IRE) (61) (PHayward) **8-10-0** BFenton (lost pl 6th: rallied to chse wnr appr 2 out: unable qckn)....1 **2** 33/1 36 —
1072[2] **Sharp Thrill (68)** (BSmart) **5-10-7** CLlewellyn (a.p: chsd wnr after 3 out tl appr 2 out: sn wknd)....17 **3** 13/2[3] 28 —
1074[3] **Roger's Pal (79)** (AMoore) **9-10-11(7)** MBatchelor (lost pl 4th: r.o one pce fr 2 out)....16 **4** 6/1[2] 26 —
1145[6] **Game Dilemma (80)** (JWMullins) **5-10-12(7)** OBurrows (hdwy fr 3 out: nvr nrr)....2½ **5** 7/1 24 —
Jonjas Chudleigh (81) (RGFrost) **9-11-6** JFrost (lw: nvr nr to chal)....26 **6** 16/1 3 —
1091[8] **Pharly Reef (72)** (DBurchell) **4-10-11** DJBurchell (hdwy 5th: wknd 6th)....1¾ **7** 14/1 — —
1072[6] **Ruth's Gamble (61)** (MrsLCJewell) **8-10-0v** DLeahy (a.p: led 3rd to 5th: ev ch 3 out: sn wknd)....s.h **8** 16/1 — —
1145[F] **Water Hazard (IRE) (78)** (SDow) **4-11-3** ADicken (a bhd: t.o)....dist **9** 12/1 — —
National Flag (FR) (73) (KRBurke) **6-10-12v[1]** APMcCoy (bit bkwd: hld up: rdn 5th: sn wknd: t.o)....26 **10** 7/2[1] — —
1073[F] **Precious Wonder (68)** (PButler) **7-10-2(5)** MrRThornton (hdwy 5th: sn wknd: t.o)....s.h **11** 16/1 — —
634[4] **Matamoros (88)** (MrsAJPerrett) **4-11-13** MAFitzgerald (bhd fr 4th: t.o whn p.u bef 6th).... **P** 13/2[3] — —

				SP	RR	SF
934^{F}	**Ask Harry (IRE) (61)** (RHAlner) **5-10-0** DBridgwater (prom to 3rd: t.o whn p.u bef 6th)		P	16/1	—	—
961^{11}	**Just a Beau (61)** (MrsLCJewell) **5-9-9**(5) SophieMitchell (prom to 3rd: t.o whn p.u bef 6th)		P	33/1	—	—
1077^{8}	**Allez Pablo (62)** (RRowe) **6-9-12**(3)ow1 LAspell (hdwy 5th: sn wknd: t.o whn p.u bef 3 out)		P	14/1	—	—
				(SP 133.8%)	**15 Rn**	

4m 47.9 (29.90) CSF £316.00 CT £2,569.25 TOTE £21.40: £4.30 £27.90 £2.30 (£714.40) Trio £1,295.40; £1,131.23 to Leicester 18/11/96
OWNER Mrs O. C. Foster (PLUMPTON) BRED Mrs E. M. Gauvain
LONG HANDICAP Kashan (IRE) 9-7 Ruth's Gamble 9-13 Ask Harry (IRE) 9-6 Sprintfayre 9-13 Just a Beau 9-8 Allez Pablo 9-9
No bid

Sprintfayre, without a run in six months, raced wide in search of the better ground and made the vast majority of the running, but he was very leg weary in the straight in the rain-softened ground. (12/1)
Kashan (IRE), 7lb out of the handicap and without a run in eight months, made a pleasing reappearance. Moving into second approaching the second last, he grimly tried to get on terms with the winner, but was just tapped for toe. (33/1)
1072 Sharp Thrill appeared to be going well as he moved into second soon after the third last but, collared for that position going to the next, soon capitulated. He did not stay, especially in this ground. (13/2)
1074 Roger's Pal, whose two wins to date have both come in this grade, struggled on past beaten horses tol finish a very moderate fourth. (6/1)
1145 Game Dilemma did little more than plod on past very tired rivals. (7/1)
Jonjas Chudleigh has been off the course for a year and, given sympathetic handling, lobbed around without ever looking likely to get into it.(16/1)
961 Water Hazard (IRE) (12/1: 7/1-14/1)

1391 TOTE BOOKMAKERS H'CAP CHASE (0-120) (5-Y.O+) (Class D)
2-00 (2-00) **3m 2f 110y (22 fncs)** £5,260.00 (£1,290.00) GOING: 1.17 sec per fur (HY)

				SP	RR	SF
1122^{2}	**Bally Clover (100)** (MissVenetiaWilliams) **9-11-5** RFarrant (led 2nd to 5th: led & lft clr 2 out: eased flat)	—	1	5/4^{1}	105	1
1194^{F}	**Sorbiere (100)** (NJHenderson) **9-11-5b** MAFitzgerald (lw: hld up: mstke 4th: rdn 17th: sn wknd: t.o whn lft 2nd 2 out)	dist	2	7/2^{3}	—	—
1063^{3}	**Childhay Chocolate (105)** (PFNicholls) **8-11-10** APMcCoy (led to 2nd: led 5th: blnd 17th: rdn 4 out: hdd & fell 2 out)		F	2/1^{2}	—	—
	The Widget Man (105) (MissLBower) **10-11-10** PHide (mstke 15th: bhd whn blnd 16th: blnd bdly & p.u 18th)		P	9/1	—	—
				(SP 110.0%)	**4 Rn**	

7m 36.7 (56.70) CSF £5.48 TOTE £2.40 (£3.70) OWNER Mr James Williams (HEREFORD) BRED Peter Magnier
1122 Bally Clover was handed this race on a plate. Travelling well, he had just poked a nostril in front when his only serious rival capsized at the penultimate fence. He would have won anyway. (5/4)
1043 Sorbiere was in trouble six out and was tailed off when presented with the runner-up prize two out. (7/2)
1063 Childhay Chocolate made the vast majority of the running, but had just been marginally headed when falling at the second last. (2/1)

1392 BET WITH THE TOTE H'CAP HURDLE (0-115) (4-Y.O+) (Class E)
2-35 (2-35) **2m 6f 110y (11 hdls)** £3,782.00 (£1,136.00: £548.00: £254.00) GOING: 1.17 sec per fur (HY)

				SP	RR	SF
1262^{4}	**Moment of Glory (IRE) (112)** (DRGandolfo) **5-11-13** GBradley (hld up & bhd: racd wd: stdy hdwy 3 out: led last: drvn out)	—	1	9/1	93	—
1121*	**Cassio's Boy (85)** (RJEckley) **5-10-0** DGallagher (hld up: chsd ldr fr 8th: led 3 out to last: r.o)	nk	2	4/1^{3}	66	—
	Eulogy (IRE) (113) (RRowe) **6-12-0** DO'Sullivan (lw: led to 3 out: 3rd whn mstke 2 out: sn wknd)	19	3	5/2^{1}	80	—
	Smuggler's Point (USA) (110) (JJBridger) **6-11-11** DBridgwater (chsd ldr after 1st to 8th: wknd appr 2 out)	17	4	10/1	65	—
557^{P}	**First Class (90)** (GNAlford) **6-10-5** RGreene (bhd fr 4th: t.o)	dist	5	25/1	—	—
692*	**Bellroi (IRE) (105)** (MHTompkins) **5-11-6** APMcCoy (a bhd: t.o)	dist	6	7/2^{2}	—	—
1074^{2}	**Kalasadi (USA) (106)** (VSoane) **5-11-7** MAFitzgerald (chsd ldr tl after 1st: wknd 5th: t.o whn p.u bef 2 ut)		P	4/1^{3}	—	—
				(SP 113.7%)	**7 Rn**	

5m 59.1 (43.10) CSF £41.44 TOTE £11.00: £4.00 £1.70 (£21.00) OWNER Mrs David Moon (WANTAGE) BRED H and Y Bloodstock Co in Ireland
LONG HANDICAP Cassio's Boy 9-13
Moment of Glory (IRE) was given a tremendous ride by Bradley, who took an extremely wide course in search of better ground, and only shook up the gelding at the third last. Poking a whisker in front at the final flight, he held on in a tight finish. (9/1)
1121* Cassio's Boy went for home three out and, although collared at the final flight, stuck to his guns really well to the bitter end. (4/1)
Eulogy (IRE) was beginning to tire when making a mistake at the penultimate hurdle. He should soon pick up a race. (5/2)
Smuggler's Point (USA) has had a recent spin on the Flat, but finally called it a day approaching the second last. (10/1: 7/1-12/1)
1074 Kalasadi (USA) (4/1: op 5/2)

1393 WEATHERBYS 1997 DIARY H'CAP CHASE (0-125) (5-Y.O+) (Class D)
3-10 (3-10) **2m 2f (15 fncs)** £4,430.00 (£1,230.00: £590.00) GOING: 1.17 sec per fur (HY)

				SP	RR	SF
1257^{2}	**Newlands-General (115)** (PFNicholls) **10-12-0** APMcCoy (mde all: mstke 8th: lft clr 4 out: unchal)	—	1	5/4^{1}	126	23
	Dear Do (104) (NJHenderson) **9-11-3** MAFitzgerald (hld up: chsd wnr after 4 out: no imp)	22	2	9/4^{2}	95	—
	The Carrot Man (107) (PWinkworth) **8-11-6** PHide (lw: chsd wnr: blnd 2nd: blnd bdly 4 out: nt rcvr: t.o)	dist	3	4/1^{3}	—	—
	Kytton Castle (99) (RDickin) **9-10-12** RBellamy (lw: 3rd whn fell 11th)		F	6/1	—	—
				(SP 109.5%)	**4 Rn**	

4m 56.3 (34.30) CSF £4.22 TOTE £1.90 (£1.80) OWNER Mr C. Murphy (SHEPTON MALLET) BRED J. M. Castle
1257 Newlands-General set a brisk pace with topweight in rain-softened ground and, with his main rival making an horrendous mistake at the water, four out, he was allowed to come home at his leisure. (5/4)
Dear Do moved into second soon after the fourth last, but never looked like reeling in the winner. He will come on for this seasonal debut. (9/4)
The Carrot Man, winner of this race last year, looked in good shape for this seasonal debut and was still travelling well in second when going for a swim in the water jump, four out. (4/1)
Kytton Castle looked in good shape, considering she had not had a run in fourteen months, and was still travelling well in third when falling five out. (6/1)

1394 RICHMOND PARK CONSERVATIVE CLUB MAIDEN HURDLE (II) (4-Y.O+) (Class E)
3-45 (3-45) **2m 2f 110y (9 hdls)** £2,469.00 (£684.00: £327.00) GOING: 1.17 sec per fur (HY)

				SP	RR	SF
	Claireswan (IRE) (97) (MHTompkins) **4-11-2**(3) KGaule (lw: a.p: led 6th: rdn out)	—	1	5/1^{2}	73	—
	Dancetillyoudrop (IRE) (PFNicholls) **5-11-5** APMcCoy (lw: hdwy & mstke 6th: ev ch: mstke 2 out: unable qckn)	9	2	5/4^{1}	65	—

				SP	RR	SF
1193[2]	**Adilov** (JJBridger) **4-11-0**(5) SophieMitchell (hdwy 6th: rdn appr 2 out: one pce)	2½	**3**	20/1	63	—
1165[2]	**Flying Fiddler (IRE) (97)** (MJRoberts) **5-11-5** MAFitzgerald (lw: chsd ldr to 5th: ev ch 3 out: wknd appr 2 out)	13	**4**	11/2[3]	52	—
1171[4]	**Ross Dancer (IRE)** (JSMoore) **4-11-2**(3) JMagee (lw: hld up: rdn 6th: sn wknd)	18	**5**	7/1	36	—
1276[2]	**Swan Street (NZ)** (CJMann) **5-11-5** JRailton (rdn & hdwy 3 out: wknd appr 2 out)	2½	**6**	7/1	34	—
	I Recall (IRE) (PHayward) **5-11-5** BFenton (led to 6th: wknd after 3 out)	16	**7**	50/1	20	—
	Charter Lane (IRE) (MrsLCJewell) **6-11-5** DLeahy (lw: bhd fr 2nd: t.o)	13	**8**	66/1	9	—
	Sharp Elver (IRE) (PRHedger) **4-11-0** PHide (hdwy 3rd: mstke 2nd: wknd 3 out: t.o whn p.u bef last)		**P**	40/1	—	—
700[P]	**Murphy's Run (IRE)** (PEccles) **6-11-0**(5) MrRThornton (prom to 5th: t.o whn p.u bef last)		**P**	50/1	—	—
1250[11]	**Blaze of Oak (USA) (79)** (JMBradley) **5-10-12b**(7) JPower (lw: plld hrd: prom to 6th: t.o whn p.u bef last)		**P**	16/1	—	—

(SP 120.0%) **11 Rn**

4m 49.1 (31.10) CSF £11.35 TOTE £5.40: £1.30 £1.70 £3.40 (£5.40) Trio £27.30 OWNER Claire and Beryl (NEWMARKET) BRED Thomas Bean

Claireswan (IRE), fit from the Flat, went on four out and, with only two rivals to worry about in the straight, was ridden along to assert. (5/1: op 5/2)

Dancetillyoudrop (IRE), an ex-Irish gelding who won a bumper at Naas in June, was sold for 35,000 guineas at Doncaster in August. Making his hurdling debut, he did not show much respect for the obstacles and was clumsy at a number of them. Nevertheless, he was still in contention at the second last before the winner began to assert. (5/4)

1193 Adilov showed his Kempton run to be no flash in the pan and was one of only three in contention entering the straight before tapped for toe from the penultimate hurdle. (20/1)

1165 Flying Fiddler (IRE), with every chance soon after the third last, had given his all entering the straight. (11/2)

T/Jkpt: Not won; £2,549.83 to Leicester 18/11/96. T/Plpt: £383.90 (27.18 Tckts). T/Qdpt: £119.50 (8.56 Tckts) AK

1395a - 1396a : (Irish Racing) - See Computer Raceform

1225a-CLONMEL (Ireland) (R-H) (Yielding to soft)
Thursday November 7th

1397a MORRIS OIL CHASE (Gd 2) (5-Y.O+)
2-00 (2-01) **2m 4f (14 fncs)** IR £12,900.00 (IR £3,700.00: IR £1,700.00: IR £500.00)

				SP	RR	SF
1216a*	**Royal Mountbrowne** (APO'Brien,Ireland) **8-11-7** CFSwan (mde all: mstke 10th: rdn appr last: styd on)	—	**1**	6/1[3]	139+	—
	Belvederian (MFMorris,Ireland) **9-11-7** CO'Dwyer (hld up in tch: effrt appr 2 out: rdn appr last: kpt on)	4	**2**	6/1[3]	136	—
1003a[7]	**Love the Lord (IRE)** (DO'Connell,Ireland) **6-11-9** TPTreacy (mostly 2nd: disp ld briefly 4 out: rdn & effrt 2 out: kpt on)	½	**3**	12/1	137	—
	Merry Gale (IRE) (JTRDreaper,Ireland) **8-12-0** MDwyer (hld up in tch: pushed along bef st: 4th & no imp between last 2)	11	**4**	6/4[1]	134	—
	Antonin (FR) (MrsSABramall,Ireland) **8-12-0** KWhelan (mstke 5th: reminders whn mstke 7th: rdn & lost tch after next: dist 7th & n.d bef 2 out: styd on)	10	**5**	5/2[2]	126	—
	King of the Gales (ALTMoore,Ireland) **9-12-0** FWoods (hld up: no imp whn mstke 3 out)	3½	**6**	8/1	123	—
	Love and Porter (IRE) (JJO'Connor,Ireland) **8-11-2** DHO'Connor (hld up towards rr: mod 5th & no imp bef 2 out)	s.h	**7**	12/1	111	—
	Nuaffe (PAFahy,Ireland) **11-12-0** TJMitchell (a towards rr: n.d)	7	**8**	20/1	117	—

(SP 128.4%) **8 Rn**

5m 16.0 OWNER Mrs J. O'Kane (PILTOWN) BRED Sidney J. Smith

1216a* Royal Mountbrowne, boasting a fitness advantage over most of his rivals, made all the running and stayed on strongly. (6/1: op 4/1)

Belvederian, in third place from halfway, made an effort early inside the straight when second approaching the last, but could not quicken on the flat. (6/1: op 4/1)

Love the Lord (IRE) improved to dispute briefly four out, but was done with between the last two. She is going the right way. (12/1)

Merry Gale (IRE) looked well and had no difficulty going the pace. Tracking the leaders three out, he looked a possibility down the hill but appeared to blow up in a matter of strides before the straight, and was a beaten fourth before the last two. (6/4)

Antonin (FR), who had made all the running when winning at Wexford previously, was never travelling here and was subsequently found to be 'clinically abnormal'. (5/2)

1398a - 1404a : (Irish Racing) - See Computer Raceform

0928a-NAAS (Ireland) (L-H) (Yielding to soft)
Saturday November 9th

1405a QUINNS OF NAAS NOVICES' CHASE (5-Y.O+)
2-30 (2-31) **2m 40y (10 fncs)** IR £4,795.00 (IR £1,085.00: IR £455.00: IR £245.00)

				SP	RR	SF
	Danoli (IRE) (TFoley,Ireland) **8-11-7** TPTreacy (hld up: hdwy 5th: 4th whn slt mstke next: 3rd & pushed along after 3 out: hung lft fr 2 out: led after last: rdn out)	—	**1**	2/7[1]	96	—
318a[17]	**Crossfarnogue (IRE)** (APO'Brien,Ireland) **7-10-9**(5) JButler (led: hit 2 out: hdd early flat: kpt on samepce)	2½	**2**	10/1	87	—
	What It Is (IRE) (JHScott,Ireland) **7-10-9** PatrickMcWilliams (in tch: chsd ldr bef 3 out: effrt whn mstke 2 out: slt mstke last: one pce)	11	**3**	20/1	71	—
	Headbanger (MMLynch,Ireland) **9-11-0** DHO'Connor (hld up: 5th 3 out: no imp next)	8	**4**	14/1	68	—
1240a[3]	**Crehelp Express (IRE)** (VBowens,Ireland) **6-10-6**(3) BBowens (cl up early: lost tch 3 out)	25	**5**	7/1[3]	38	—
	Amble Speedy (IRE) (ALTMoore,Ireland) **6-11-0** FWoods (towards rr: mstke 4th: n.d)	1½	**6**	14/1	42	—
	Punting Pete (IRE) (WPMullins,Ireland) **6-10-11**(3) DJCasey (cl up: 2nd whn hit 2nd: 3rd 3 out: wknd & no imp appr next)	3½	**7**	6/1[2]	38	—
	Persian Power (IRE) (NMeade,Ireland) **8-11-0** CFSwan (towards rr: mstke 5th: n.d)	6	**8**	10/1	32	—
	Time And Charges (IRE) (FBerry,Ireland) **6-10-7**(7) RPHogan (plld hrd: cl up: 6th at 6th: fell next)		**F**	25/1	—	—

(SP 144.7%) **9 Rn**

4m 14.9 (6.90) OWNER D. J. O'Neill (BAGENALSTOWN) BRED W. Austin in Ireland

Danoli (IRE) showing none of his usual exuberance, settled well at the rear and it wasn't until approaching the fifth last that he began to pick off the field. He landed fourth there after jumping sluggishly and was being ridden along with three to jump. In third place and hanging left before two out, it looked as if defeat was a possibility as he continued to lean out going to the last. Landing in second place, he was in front in a couple of strides and stayed on up the hill. This was not as visually impressive over fences as his debut at Clonmel, but the educational value of the exercise might yet be proved worth it. (2/7)
Crossfarnogue (IRE) made the running and stretched away just before the straight, but had no answer to the winner's class from the last. (10/1)
What It Is (IRE), second from three out, was not in contention when clouting the last. (20/1)
Persian Power (IRE) (10/1: op 6/1)

1406a - 1409a : (Irish Racing) - See Computer Raceform

1216a-LEOPARDSTOWN (Dublin, Ireland) (L-H) (Yielding)
Sunday November 10th

1410a COMMOLOGY H'CAP CHASE (5-Y.O+)
3-30 (3-30) **2m 1f (11 fncs)** IR £4,410.00 (IR £930.00: IR £390.00)

	Horse	Dist	Pos	SP	RR	SF
	Fiftysevenchannels (IRE) (EBolger,Ireland) **7-10-7** CFSwan (mde all: qcknd early st: jnd last: rdn & styd on wl flat)	—	**1**	14/1[3]	122	—
	Klairon Davis (FR) (ALTMoore,Ireland) **7-12-0** FWoods (plld hrd: hld up in rr: hdwy after 2 out: chal last: ev ch flat: rdn & styd on)	½	**2**	1/3[1]	143	—
	Brockley Court (MrsJHarrington,Ireland) **9-10-7** CO'Dwyer (disp ld: j.slowly 4th: cl 2nd st: 3rd & nt qckn appr last: sn no imp)	20	**3**	5/2[2]	103	—
				(SP 110.2%)		**3 Rn**

4m 17.8 (-5.20) OWNER J. A. Cooper (BRUREE) BRED P. Neary in Ireland
Fiftysevenchannels (IRE), a full 28lb out of the handicap, made all the running, and his superior fitness, allied to the good tactical ride, made the difference on the flat. (14/1)
Klairon Davis (FR), in last place of the three, made unhurried progress from the second last to get on terms before the final fence. There was little response when asked for an extra effort on the flat and the situation was accepted late on the run-in. He will be tighter tuned for the Tingle Creek Chase at Sandown in December, and the faster pace will suit. (1/3)
Brockley Court dropped right away in the straight. (5/2)
NR

1411a - (Irish Racing) - See Computer Raceform

LEICESTER (R-H) (Chases Good to firm, Hdles Good to soft)
Monday November 18th
Race 1 - One hurdle omitted 2nd circuit
WEATHER: fine

1412 STOUGHTON NOVICES' HURDLE (4-Y.O+) (Class E)
12-55 (12-56) **2m (8 hdls)** £2,924.80 (£812.80: £390.40) GOING minus 0.22 sec per fur (G)

	Horse	Dist	Pos	SP	RR	SF
	Daraydan (IRE) (MCPipe) **4-10-12** APMcCoy (j.w: mde all: lft clr 4th: unchal)	—	**1**	4/9[1]	80+	37
	Dana Point (IRE) (MrsSJSmith) **4-10-5**(7) RWilkinson (chsd wnr tl blnd & lost pl 4th: rallied to go 2nd 3 out: mstke next: no imp)	16	**2**	16/1	64?	21
	Ely's Harbour (IRE) (OSherwood) **5-10-12** JOsborne (bkwd: wl bhd tl styd on fr 2 out)	20	**3**	10/1[3]	44	1
1013[6]	**Warrio** (JRBosley) **6-10-12** MBosley (bhd: rdn 3 out: no imp)	2½	**4**	66/1	42	—
	Seymour's Double (MrsARHewitt) **5-10-12** SWynne (lw: lft 2nd 4th: wknd appr 3 out)	8	**5**	66/1	34	—
	Upper Club (IRE) (PRWebber) **4-10-7** RBellamy (hdwy 4th: chsd wnr fr next: wknd 3 out: t.o)	14	**6**	66/1	15	—
	Smart Casanova (MJWilkinson) **7-10-12** CLlewellyn (bkwd: trckd ldrs to 5th: sn wknd: t.o)	½	**7**	66/1	19	—
1026*	**Northern Fusilier** (JMJefferson) **4-10-12** MDwyer (lw: fell 2nd: dead)		**F**	3/1[2]	—	—
	Riverbank Red (WClay) **5-10-7** TEley (a bhd: t.o whn p.u bef 4 out)		**P**	33/1	—	—
				(SP 118.1%)		**9 Rn**

3m 46.4 (1.40) CSF £8.92 TOTE £1.30: £1.00 £4.60 £3.30 (£11.90) Trio £9.50 OWNER Mr D. A. Johnson (WELLINGTON) BRED His Highness the Aga Khans Studs S. C.
Daraydan (IRE), a useful stayer on the Flat, had a fairly easy introduction to his hurdling career. Although he is sure to benefit from further, he made sure there was no hanging about and won in quite a respectable time. (4/9)
Dana Point (IRE), a twelve-furlong winner on the Flat last month, may well have given the winner a run for his money had he hurdled more fluently. Losses are only lent. (16/1)
Ely's Harbour (IRE), making a belated racecourse debut, was given plenty of time to grasp what was needed and his final placing was as close as he got. (10/1: op 5/1)
1026* Northern Fusilier (3/1: 2/1-100/30)

1413 JUNIOR (S) HURDLE (3 & 4-Y.O) (Class G)
1-25 (1-26) **2m (9 hdls)** £2,952.00 (£822.00: £396.00) GOING minus 0.22 sec per fur (G)

	Horse	Dist	Pos	SP	RR	SF
1058[2]	**Peter Monamy (103)** (MCPipe) **4-12-0b** APMcCoy (a.p: rdn appr 5th: led 3 out: drvn out)	—	**1**	11/8[1]	67	13
1149[4]	**Bluntswood Hall** (RHollinshead) **3-10-5** GaryLyons (trckd ldrs: ev ch fr 3 out: rdn & no ex flat)	2	**2**	12/1	58	—
	Dark Truffle (MrsJCecil) **3-10-1**ow1 TKent (hld up in rr: hdwy 5th: styd on flat: nvr nrr)	7	**3**	9/1[3]	47	—
1205[7]	**Boy Blakeney** (MrsSJSmith) **3-9-12**(7) RWilkinson (hld up: hdwy u.p 3 out: styd on appr last)	2	**4**	20/1	49+	—
1184[15]	**Prove The Point (IRE)** (MrsPNDutfield) **3-10-0** PHolley (hld up: hdwy 6th: rdn next: nt rch ldrs)	3½	**5**	50/1	41	—
640[9]	**Krasnik (IRE)** (MrsDHaine) **3-10-2b**1(3) GHogan (led 2nd: sn clr: hdd 3 out: wknd next)	8	**6**	50/1	38	—
1149[8]	**Shanoora (IRE)** (MrsNMacauley) **3-9-11**(3) EHusband (hld up & bhd: hdwy appr 3 out: nvr nrr)	¾	**7**	50/1	32	—
1251[6]	**Admiral's Guest (IRE)** (WClay) **4-11-7** TEley (nvr nrr)	1	**8**	50/1	36	—
	Tee Tee Too (IRE) (AWCarroll) **4-11-7** CLlewellyn (nvr trbld ldrs)	3	**9**	33/1	33	—

				SP	RR	SF
1086[2]	**Griffin's Girl** (PMooney) **4-11-2** NWilliamson (a in rr)	4	**10**	11/1	24	—
	Duet (JSKing) **3-10-0** TJMurphy (prom tl rdn & wknd 3 out)	2½	**11**	33/1	21	—
1276[8]	**Saint Amigo** (RMWhitaker) **4-11-7** DerekByrne (nvr nr to chal)	¾	**12**	20/1	26	—
	Open Affair (APJarvis) **3-9-7**(7) CDavies (lw: a bhd: t.o)	21	**13**	20/1	—	—
	Norfolk Glory (DJGMurraySmith) **4-11-7** DGallagher (bit bkwd: hld up: hdwy 5th: rdn & btn whn fell last)		**F**	33/1	—	—
	Air Wing (MHTompkins) **3-10-5** AMaguire (lw: led to 2nd: wkng whn fell 6th)		**F**	10/1	—	—
1276[F]	**Al Helal** (JRJenkins) **4-11-0v**(7) NTEgan (chsd ldrs tl fell 5th)		**F**	50/1	—	—
1184[11]	**Snow Domino (IRE)** (JMJefferson) **3-10-5** MDwyer (lw: in rr whn p.u bef 3 out)		**P**	8/1 [2]	—	—
548[P]	**Four Weddings (USA)** (MCPipe) **3-10-5b** CMaude (a in rr: t.o whn p.u bef 6th)		**P**	14/1	—	—
1011[B]	**Nordic Hero (IRE)** (APJarvis) **3-10-5** RJohnson (lw: a bhd: t.o whn p.u bef 2 out)		**P**	20/1	—	—
1278[9]	**Nukud (USA)** (GROldroyd) **4-11-0v**(7) CMcCormack (a bhd: t.o whn p.u bef 2 out)		**P**	50/1	—	—
	Arch Angel (IRE) (GFHCharles-Jones) **3-10-0** DBridgwater (blnd & uns rdr 1st)		**U**	33/1	—	—
				(SP 137.6%)	**21 Rn**	

3m 55.1 (10.10) CSF £19.93 TOTE £1.80: £2.10 £2.40 £1.50 (£17.50) Trio £89.80 OWNER Richard Green (Fine Paintings) (WELLINGTON) BRED R. Green
WEIGHT FOR AGE 3yo-16lb
No bid
OFFICIAL EXPLANATION **Boy Blakeney: the jockey reported that the horse was outpaced early, lost his tongue-strap turning into the back straight and gurgled thereafter. He also hung in the back straight and had to be held together to stay balanced. The trainer's representative added that the gelding is small and moderate, and that he was pleased with his performance today.**
1058 Peter Monamy had to work hard to record win number five for his season, but he was conceding weight all round and this success was thoroughly deserved. (11/8: op evens)
1149 Bluntswood Hall turned in an improved performance and is definitely going the right way. (12/1: op 8/1)
Dark Truffle, a maiden on the Flat, was never put into the race on this hurdling debut, but she did stay on and a slightly stiffer test of stamina would not go amiss. (9/1: 6/1-10/1)
Boy Blakeney wears a tongue strap and was ridden with more restraint this time. His relentless late progress caught the eyes of the Stewards. (20/1)
Prove The Point (IRE), hard at work early in the straight, failed to summon up the speed to make her presence felt. (50/1)
Krasnik (IRE), soon bowling along in a clear lead in his first-time blinkers, came back to his field entering the straight and he had run his race before the last. (50/1)
1086 Griffin's Girl (11/1: 8/1-12/1)
Norfolk Glory still looked in need of this, but did not shape badly until he bit the dust at the last. (33/1)
Snow Domino (IRE) (8/1: op 5/1)
282 Four Weddings (USA) (14/1: 8/1-16/1)

1414 LEICESTER NOVICES' CHASE (5-Y.O+) (Class E)
1-55 (1-55) **2m 1f (12 fncs)** £3,451.50 (£954.00: £454.50) GOING minus 0.22 sec per fur (G)

				SP	RR	SF
1179[3]	**Sigma Run (IRE)** (JACEdwards) **7-10-12** RJohnson (lw: mstke 1st: chsd ldr: j.slowly 4 out: led on bit 2 out: canter)	—	**1**	7/4 [2]	79+	13
1120[P]	**Captain Stockford** (PWegmann) **9-10-12** JRKavanagh (bit bkwd: led: mstke 4th: hdd 2 out: sn btn)	11	**2**	25/1	69	3
1179[6]	**Larks Tail** (PRWebber) **8-10-7** RBellamy (hld up in rr: hdwy 8th: rdn & wknd 3 out)	6	**3**	14/1	58	—
	Lothian Jem (JWharton) **7-10-2**(5) MrRThornton (bkwd: chsd ldng pair tl fell 6th)		**F**	9/2 [3]	—	—
1169[2]	**Coolteen Hero (IRE) (88)** (RHAlner) **6-11-5** WMcFarland (w.r.s & uns rdr)		**U**	5/4 [1]	—	—
				(SP 109.5%)	**5 Rn**	

4m 17.6 (7.60) CSF £24.02 TOTE £2.50: £1.10 £13.50 (£15.40) OWNER B G S Racing Partnership (ROSS-ON-WYE) BRED David Fenton
IN-FOCUS: **This turned out to be trainer John Edwards' last winner.**
1179 Sigma Run (IRE) did not fulfil the promise expected of him over hurdles, but he won this mediocre contest without coming off the bridle. It is to be hoped this boosts his confidence. (7/4)
Captain Stockford has had plenty of experience over fences and gave it his best shot here, only to find the winner a class apart. He will strip fitter next time. (25/1)
Lothian Jem (9/2: op 10/1)
1169 Coolteen Hero (IRE) (5/4: 4/5-11/8)

1415 MIDLAND H'CAP CHASE (0-110) (5-Y.O+) (Class E)
2-25 (2-25) **3m (18 fncs)** £3,655.00 (£1,090.00: £520.00: £235.00) GOING minus 0.22 sec per fur (G)

				SP	RR	SF
1189*	**Imperial Vintage (IRE) (110)** (MissVenetiaWilliams) **6-12-0** NWilliamson (lw: j.w: mde all: clr last: eased flat)	—	**1**	5/4 [1]	115	3
	Celtic Town (108) (OSherwood) **8-11-12** JAMcCarthy (bkwd: chsd wnr: j.slowly 10th: reminders 14th: one pce fr 2 out)	3	**2**	11/4 [3]	111	—
	Far Senior (109) (PWegmann) **10-11-13** JRKavanagh (bkwd: a.p: shkn up 3 out: sn btn)	2½	**3**	20/1	110	—
1029[3]	**Magic Bloom (105)** (JMJefferson) **10-11-4**(5) ECallaghan (hld up in rr: mstke 14th: outpcd 2 out)	1¼	**4**	2/1 [2]	106	—
				(SP 109.2%)	**4 Rn**	

6m 13.7 (19.70) CSF £4.71 TOTE £2.10 (£2.80) OWNER Mr David Williams (HEREFORD) BRED W. J. Mernagh
1189* Imperial Vintage (IRE) had the edge in fitness and, turning in a polished display of jumping, galloped his rivals into submission. Had he not been eased right down on the flat, he would have won by ten to fifteen lengths at least. (5/4: op evens)
Celtic Town runs best fresh, but he looked burly for this seasonal debut and, in the circumstances, ran as well as could be expected. (11/4: 2/1-3/1)
Far Senior usually needs a run to put an edge on him and will be much sharper next time he appears. (20/1)
1029 Magic Bloom did have the tongue-strap back on, but it made little or no difference, for she was always bringing up the rear. (2/1)

1416 LADBROKES STEVE WALSH TESTIMONIAL H'CAP HURDLE (0-130) (4-Y.O+) (Class C)
2-55 (2-55) **2m (9 hdls)** £5,692.00 (£1,696.00: £808.00: £364.00) GOING minus 0.22 sec per fur (G)

				SP	RR	SF
1039[2]	**Nahri (USA) (112)** (JMackie) **5-10-11** TEley (hld up: hdwy 3 out: chal & mstke last: led flat: sn clr)	—	**1**	7/2 [2]	92	35
	Kingdom of Shades (USA) (121) (AndrewTurnell) **6-11-6** NWilliamson (bkwd: chsd ldr fr 3rd: rdn to ld appr 2 out: hdd & one pce flat)	3	**2**	4/1 [3]	98	41
	Mizyan (IRE) (126) (JEBanks) **8-11-11** MrJGTownson (lost pl 4th: styd on again fr 2 out: nvr nrr)	7	**3**	16/1	96	39
1282*	**Yubralee (USA) (115)** (MCPipe) **4-11-0** APMcCoy (set str pce: sn wl clr: wknd & hdd appr 2 out: sn btn)	2	**4**	7/4 [1]	83	26

	Horse	Dist	Pos	SP	RR	SF
1154[2]	**Fourth in Line (IRE) (129)** (MJWilkinson) **8-12-0** CLlewellyn (bit bkwd: prom tl wknd appr 6th: t.o)	18	**5**	6/1	79	22
1262[6]	**Monicasman (IRE) (115)** (APJarvis) **6-11-0** RJohnson (sn bhd & pushed along: n.d: t.o)	2½	**6**	12/1	63	6

(SP 106.4%) **6 Rn**

3m 46.6 (1.60) CSF £15.54 TOTE £4.50: £2.10 £2.50 (£13.60) OWNER Mrs Sue Adams (CHURCH BROUGHTON) BRED Shadwell Farm Inc

1039 Nahri (USA) followed up his success in this event last year with another easy success, but almost threw it away when diving at the last and landing in a heap. (7/2)

Kingdom of Shades (USA), a big, strong individual who has chaser written all over him, almost belied his burly appearance with a very promising seasonal debut in this first handicap. He could prove top class when he is switched to fences. (4/1: op 5/2)

Mizyan (IRE) dropped to the rear at halfway, but was staying on again in the latter stages. He finds this trip much too sharp. (16/1)

1282* Yubralee (USA) could not maintain his winning sequence in this higher-grade event, but he did set a scorching pace until this more yielding ground took the sting out of him. (7/4)

1262 Monicasman (IRE) (12/1: 7/1-141/)

1417 DESBOROUGH NOVICES' H'CAP HURDLE (0-100) (4-Y.O+ F & M) (Class E)

3-25 (3-25) **2m 4f 110y (11 hdls)** £2,427.00 (£672.00: £321.00) GOING minus 0.22 sec per fur (G)

	Horse	Dist	Pos	SP	RR	SF
973[4]	**Glistening Dawn (90)** (TKeddy) **6-11-13b** SMcNeill (mstke 1st: chsd ldrs: slt ld 3 out: drvn out flat)	—	**1**	10/1	73	33
1130[5]	**Jolis Absent (91)** (MJRyan) **6-12-0b** APMcCoy (hld up in rr: hdwy 8th: rdn appr last: r.o)	1½	**2**	4/1[2]	73	33
1256[4]	**Riverbank Rose (68)** (WClay) **5-10-5** TEley (led to 3 out: rdn & rallied last: styd on)	1¼	**3**	6/1[3]	49	9
	Quinag (89) (KCBailey) **5-11-12** JAMcCarthy (bit bkwd: trckd ldrs: ev ch 8th: rdn appr 2 out: sn btn)	6	**4**	8/1	65	25
1310*	**Tigh-Na-Mara (93)** (JMJefferson) **8-11-9**(7) 7x MNewton (hld up & bhd: mstke 6th: styd on fr 3 out: nvr nrr)	s.h	**5**	7/2[1]	69	29
	Children's Choice (IRE) (73) (CNAllen) **5-10-10** CLlewellyn (hld up: hdwy 7th: wknd 3 out: t.o)	25	**6**	7/2[1]	30	—
	Fortunes Rose (IRE) (65) (JSKing) **4-10-2** TJMurphy (bit bkwd: prom: chsd ldr fr 5th tl wknd 3 out: t.o)	2	**7**	20/1	20	—
673[4]	**Sakbah (USA) (63)** (JAPickering) **7-10-0** NWilliamson (hld up: hdwy appr 7th: wknd 3 out: t.o)	7	**8**	14/1	13	—
1207[6]	**Cuillin Caper (79)** (TRWatson) **4-11-2** RJohnson (prom tl lost pl appr 7th: sn t.o)	dist	**9**	12/1	—	—
	Sharmoor (83) (MissLCSiddall) **4-11-6** AThornton (bkwd: trckd ldrs tl wknd 3 out: t.o)	8	**10**	14/1	—	—

(SP 124.7%) **10 Rn**

4m 55.9 (6.90) CSF £49.89 CT £248.77 TOTE £10.90: £3.40 £1.30 £1.60 (£22.70) Trio £21.40 OWNER Mr David Milburn (HANLEY SWAN) BRED David Milburn

Glistening Dawn got the better of the long-time leader three out, but did not find as much as expected when let down, although it must be said she always appeared well in control. (10/1)

1130 Jolis Absent, twice a winner on the Flat, ran much better with less use made of her, but her determined late flourish was being matched stride for stride nearing the line. (4/1)

1256 Riverbank Rose, stepping down in distance, ran her best race for quite some time and is ready to strike again. (6/1)

Quinag ran better than her final placing would suggest on this seasonal debut and, with this badly-needed outing under her belt, she should soon improve. (8/1)

1310* Tigh-Na-Mara never fully recovered from a careless mistake down the back straight over a trip shorter than her ideal, and she completed a very miserable day for her stable. (7/2: 5/2-4/1)

Children's Choice (IRE) pays her way on the Flat, but struggles at this game and has not mastered it yet. (7/2)

1418 LEVY BOARD H'CAP HURDLE (0-120) (4-Y.O+) (Class D)

3-55 (4-01) **2m 4f 110y (11 hdls)** £3,054.00 (£912.00: £436.00: £198.00) GOING minus 0.22 sec per fur (G)

	Horse	Dist	Pos	SP	RR	SF
	Barryben (92) (WMBrisbourne) **7-10-0**(3) RMassey (bit bkwd: led to 4th: led 3 out: clr last: r.o)	—	**1**	11/1	72+	24
	General Tonic (102) (DRGandolfo) **9-10-8**(5) SophieMitchell (hld up & bhd: stdy hdwy 8th: styd on flat: nt rch wnr)	3	**2**	4/1[3]	80	32
	Ehtefaal (USA) (89) (JSKing) **5-10-0** TJMurphy (bkwd: hld up: hdwy appr 7th: styd on one pce fr 2 out)	8	**3**	6/1	60	12
1088[5]	**Barford Sovereign (106)** (JRFanshawe) **4-11-3** JOsborne (trckd ldng pair: effrt & rdn appr 3 out: no imp)	6	**4**	5/2[1]	73	25
	Super Ritchart (93) (BPalling) **8-10-4** RFarrant (bkwd: trckd ldrs to 3 out: sn rdn & btn)	¾	**5**	20/1	59	11
1196[P]	**Shahrani (113)** (MCPipe) **4-11-10** APMcCoy (led 4th to 3 out: sn rdn & wknd)	6	**6**	100/30[2]	75	27
747[4]	**Master of the Rock (108)** (JMackie) **7-11-2v**(3) EHusband (bit bkwd: hld up in rr: hit 5th: t.o fr 8th)	15	**7**	9/2	58	10

(SP 117.2%) **7 Rn**

4m 52.1 (3.10) CSF £51.72 TOTE £12.70: £2.10 £2.30 (£21.00) OWNER Mrs Mary Brisbourne (NESSCLIFFE) BRED A. H. Brisbourne

LONG HANDICAP Ehtefaal (USA) 9-12

Barryben has only won a seller in the past but, with his stable on a roll, added to the score with a fairly comfortable success. He would seem to be getting better with age. (11/1)

General Tonic looked to have plenty left to work on, and this promising effort should go a long way towards putting an edge on him. (4/1)

Ehtefaal (USA) had a very light campaign last term and was not fully wound up for this return to action, but he performed with credit and can only get better. (6/1)

1088 Barford Sovereign failed to pick up when given the office early in the straight and proved most disappointing. She has only won races at nearby Huntingdon and it could be that she does not travel well. (5/2)

Super Ritchart is something of a standing dish round here, but he has been off the track for twenty months and lack of peak fitness was taking its toll in the last half-mile. (20/1)

1196 Shahrani likes to bounce off the ground, but the recent rains had put paid to that, and his forceful tactics had come to an end once he was collared. (100/30)

747 Master of the Rock still has plenty of room for improvement and, over a trip well short of his best, always found the tempo too hot. (9/2)

T/Jkpt: £3,242.00 (2.19 Tckts). T/Plpt: £99.00 (93.19 Tckts). T/Qdpt: £39.60 (13.6 Tckts). IM

1165-PLUMPTON (L-H) (Good to soft, Soft patches)

Monday November 18th

WEATHER: fine & sunny

1419 RINGMER CONDITIONAL (S) H'CAP HURDLE (0-95) (4-Y.O+) (Class G)

1-05 (1-05) **2m 4f (12 hdls)** £1,909.40 (£528.40: £252.20) GOING: 0.71 sec per fur (S)

	Horse	Dist	Pos	SP	RR	SF
958[4]	**Whistling Buck (IRE) (82)** (RRowe) **8-11-1**(7) AGarrity (lw: hdwy 7th: chsd ldr fr 9th: led 3 out: r.o wl)	—	**1**	5/1[3]	63	20

			Pos	SP	RR	SF
1170*	**Fawley Flyer (85)** (WGMTurner) **7-11-6**(5) JPower (lw: chsd ldr tl mstke 5th: lost pl 7th: rallied 8th: chsd wnr after 3 out: ev ch 2 out: unable qckn flat)	1	**2**	7/4[1]	65	22
1200[P]	**Miramare (60)** (CLPopham) **6-10-0** TDascombe (hdwy to ld 8th: hdd 3 out: sn wknd)	17	**3**	16/1	27	—
1040[P]	**Do Be Ware (70)** (JFfitch-Heyes) **6-10-10b** DWalsh (lw: led to 8th: sn wknd)	16	**4**	11/1	24	—
1191[9]	**Zuno Flyer (USA) (71)** (AMoore) **4-10-4**(7) MBatchelor (hdwy 6th: wknd 9th)	3½	**5**	9/1	22	—
1072[3]	**Credit Controller (IRE) (60)** (JFfitch-Heyes) **7-10-0** PHenley (lw: hld up: rdn 8th: sn wknd)	18	**6**	4/1[2]	—	—
	Kalakate (84) (JJBridger) **11-11-10** GuyLewis (bit bkwd: hld up: rdn 8th: sn wknd)	4	**7**	9/1	17	—
				(SP 107.2%)		**7 Rn**

5m 14.9 (27.90) CSF £12.90 TOTE £6.50: £1.70 £2.30 (£4.90) OWNER Mr M. P. Sampson (PULBOROUGH) BRED Thomas Coffey
LONG HANDICAP Miramare 9-13
No bid
IN-FOCUS: This was a first winner, on only his second ride, for Andrew Garrity.
788 Whistling Buck (IRE) reversed last month's form with the runner-up. His trainer admitted afterwards that the gelding is an in-and-out performer and a difficult ride. (5/1)
1170* Fawley Flyer, a winner twice over this course and distance this season, has risen 11lb since the first of them. He was rather sticky at some of his hurdles. (7/4: op evens)
837 Miramare has yet to win a race at this game and the fact that he changed hands recently for just 1,900 guineas says it all. (16/1)
819* Do Be Ware (11/1: 8/1-12/1)
Kalakate (9/1: 6/1-10/1)

1420 SIR EMILE LITTLER CHALLENGE CUP H'CAP CHASE (0-115) (5-Y.O+) (Class E)

1-35 (1-35) **2m 5f** **(16 fncs)** £3,097.50 (£924.00: £441.00: £199.50) GOING: 0.71 sec per fur (S)

			Pos	SP	RR	SF
	Woodlands Boy (IRE) (96) (RCurtis) **8-10-8**(3) DWalsh (rdn 9th: hdwy appr 3 out: led flat: r.o wl)	—	**1**	12/1	103	30
1167[3]	**Mr Matt (IRE) (105)** (DMGrissell) **8-11-6** BFenton (hdwy 11th: led appr 3 out: hrd rdn appr last: hdd flat: unable qckn)	1½	**2**	10/1	111	38
	Credon (103) (SWoodman) **8-11-4** RDunwoody (bit bkwd: hld up: hrd rdn appr 3 out: r.o flat)	1	**3**	13/2[2]	108	35
887[5]	**Duke of Aprolon (87)** (JTGifford) **9-10-2**ow2 PHide (led tl blnd & hdd 6th: led 10th tl hdd & lft in ld 12th: hdd appr 3 out: hrd rdn appr last: one pce)	3½	**4**	7/1[3]	89	14
1170[2]	**Titan Empress (85)** (SMellor) **7-10-0v** NMann (a.p: led 6th to 10th: wknd appr 3 out)	6	**5**	6/1[1]	83	10
	Jurassic Classic (109) (MrsLRichards) **9-11-10** MRichards (bkwd: a bhd: t.o)	dist	**6**	7/1[3]	—	—
	Knockaverry (IRE) (102) (MJWilkinson) **8-11-3** ILawrence (bit bkwd: bhd fr 4th: t.o)	¾	**7**	6/1[1]	—	—
	Mighty Frolic (105) (MissSEdwards) **9-11-6** MrTHills (prom to 12th: 6th & no ch whn blnd bdly 3 out: t.o whn p.u bef 2 out)		**P**	12/1	—	—
	The Motcombe Oak (95) (MMadgwick) **10-10-10** GUpton (bit bkwd: bhd fr 4th: t.o whn p.u bef 12th)		**P**	50/1	—	—
1321[P]	**Whippers Delight (IRE) (93)** (GFHCharles-Jones) **8-10-8** MAFitzgerald (lw: j.lft 1st: bhd fr 2nd: t.o whn j.slowly 4th: p.u bef 5th)		**P**	20/1	—	—
1284[5]	**Black Church (92)** (RRowe) **10-10-7** DO'Sullivan (lw: hld up: led, lft stirrup broke & hdd 12th: 4th whn blnd & uns rdr 4 out)		**U**	6/1[1]	—	—
				(SP 112.4%)		**11 Rn**

5m 36.7 (23.70) CSF £108.38 CT £770.71 TOTE £12.30: £3.30 £3.20 £2.10 (£101.80) Trio £150.10 OWNER Mr Stan Moore (LAMBOURN) BRED W. J. Vance
LONG HANDICAP Duke of Aprolon 9-4 Titan Empress 9-13
Woodlands Boy (IRE) never does things in a hurry and that was well demonstrated here. He is an out-and-out stayer who revels in the mud.(12/1)
Mr Matt (IRE) has not won for two years and, having fallen in the weights as a result, ran better here. Four of his five wins to date have come with plenty of cut in the ground. (10/1: op 20/1)
Credon, looking big and well for this reappearance, stayed on nicely from the second last. He has always looked a chaser and, with cut in the ground, should find a small handicap before long. (13/2)
Duke of Aprolon, carrying 12lb more than his long-handicap weight, made the vast majority of the running until approaching the third last. (7/1)
1170 Titan Empress, reverting to fences, showed in front briefly in the middle part of the race, but was at the end of her tether going to the water, three out. (6/1)
Knockaverry (IRE) (6/1: op 4/1)
1284 Black Church looked in fine shape in the paddock, but did not have luck on his side. He had just moved smoothly to the front and taken a lovely leap at the fifth last when his jockey's left stirrup broke. O'Sullivan did well to stay in the saddle, but he had no control of the gelding and it was no surprise that he was unseated at the next. He has slipped nicely in the weights and should now be ready to strike. (6/1)

1421 GEORGE RIPLEY MEMORIAL CHALLENGE TROPHY H'CAP CHASE (0-105) (5-Y.O+) (Class F)

2-05 (2-05) **2m** **(13 fncs)** £2,786.40 (£770.40: £367.20) GOING: 0.71 sec per fur (S)

			Pos	SP	RR	SF
883[4]	**Dawn Chance (77)** (RJHodges) **10-11-10** RDunwoody (led tl mstke & hdd 4 out: 2nd & rdn whn lft in clr ld 2 out)	—	**1**	5/4[2]	85?	—
1169[4]	**Joker Jack (67)** (RDean) **11-10-11**(3) TDascombe (mstke 4th: chsd wnr to 6th: wknd 7th: t.o fr 8th: lft 2nd 2 out)	dist	**2**	6/1[3]	—	—
1335[3]	**Gallic Girl (IRE) (69)** (CLPopham) **6-11-2** MAFitzgerald (chsd ldr fr 6th: mstke & led 4 out: fell 2 out: rmntd: t.o)	dist	**3**	11/10[1]	—	—
				(SP 106.3%)		**3 Rn**

4m 25.0 (33.00) CSF £5.85 TOTE £1.80 (£3.20) OWNER Mr G. Small (SOMERTON) BRED Mesdames H. E. and G. E. Small
Dawn Chance had luck on his side for, after setting the pace to the fourth last, he was held when presented the race as the leader fell two out.(5/4)
1075 Joker Jack is extremely slow and so it is very surprising that this poor performer has been competing at two miles recently. (6/1)
1335 Gallic Girl (IRE), who failed to stay three miles last week, was taking a big drop in class, but looked set for her first victory in this absolutely desperate race when falling two out. (11/10)

1422 KNIGHT INTERNATIONAL 'N.H.' NOVICES' HURDLE (4-Y.O+) (Class E)

2-35 (2-35) **2m 4f** **(12 hdls)** £2,616.00 (£726.00: £348.00) GOING: 0.71 sec per fur (S)

			Pos	SP	RR	SF
	Scotby (BEL) (RHBuckler) **6-10-12** BPowell (mde virtually all: rdn out)	—	**1**	20/1	78	25
	Dantes Cavalier (IRE) (DRGandolfo) **6-10-12** RDunwoody (stdy hdwy 8th: chsd wnr fr 3 out: rdn appr 2 out: unable qckn)	1¾	**2**	7/4[1]	77+	24

			SP	RR	SF
1042^{3}	**Lord Rooble (IRE)** (JTGifford) **5-10-12** PHide (hld up: shkn up appr last: one pce) 2	**3**	$15/2^{3}$	75	22
	Chilled (IRE) (MrsJPitman) **4-10-12** WMarston (a.p: chsd wnr 8th to 3 out: wknd appr 2 out) 16	**4**	12/1	62	9
	Dukes Meadow (IRE) (KCBailey) **6-10-12** CO'Dwyer (hld up: mstke & rdn 8th: sn wknd) 22	**5**	$11/4^{2}$	45	—
	Dictum (IRE) (MissHCKnight) **5-10-12** GBradley (bkwd: hdwy 6th: wknd 3 out) 10	**6**	$15/2^{3}$	37	—
	Brackenheath (IRE) (DMGrissell) **5-10-12** BFenton (bit bkwd: a bhd) ....¾	**7**	16/1	36	—
	Little Earn (MissHCKnight) **6-10-5**(7) MrAWintle (bkwd: a bhd) 13	**8**	66/1	26	—
885^{5}	**Smart In Velvet** (PRHedger) **6-10-7** ILawrence (bhd fr 6th: t.o whn p.u bef 2 out)	**P**	20/1	—	—
813^{P}	**Churchtown Spirit** (TPMcGovern) **5-10-7** GCrone (chsd ldr to 6th: sn wknd: t.o whn p.u bef 9th)	**P**	66/1	—	—
	Flaming Rose (IRE) (RRowe) **6-10-7** DO'Sullivan (a bhd: t.o whn p.u bef 3 out)	**P**	66/1	—	—
	White In Front (JCPoulton) **5-10-9**(3) DWalsh (bit bkwd: bhd fr 8th: t.o whn p.u bef 2 out)	**P**	100/1	—	—
			(SP 115.1%)		**12 Rn**

5m 10.7 (23.70) CSF £50.95 TOTE £25.20: £6.50 £2.20 £2.20 (£21.80) Trio £31.40 OWNER Mrs E. B. Gardiner (BRIDPORT) BRED P. Madelein

Scotby (BEL), who has changed stables since his last run a year ago, made virtually all and, ridden along, kept the runner-up at bay. His trainer considers him a Cheltenham Festival candidate given the soft ground that he likes and believes he will stay three miles. (20/1)
Dantes Cavalier (IRE), winner of the 1995 Aintree bumper, has been off the course since. This race should have put him straight and he should be a different prospect next time out. (7/4)
1042 Lord Rooble (IRE) was hardly given an industrious ride. Held up on this occasion, he had several lengths to make up on the front two entering the straight and, with his jockey doing little more than shake him up, the gelding could never get on terms. (15/2)
Chilled (IRE), making his hurdling debut, tired as lack of a recent run took its toll. (12/1)
Dictum (IRE) (15/2: 4/1-8/1)

1423 TRANS WORLD EXHIBITIONS MAIDEN CHASE (4-Y.O+) (Class F)

3-05 (3-07) **2m 5f (16 fncs)** £2,865.60 (£856.80: £410.40: £187.20) GOING: 0.71 sec per fur (S)

			SP	RR	SF
	Mammy's Choice (IRE) (RHAlner) **6-10-12**(3) PHenley (chsd ldr fr 5th: pckd 9th: led 12th: all out) ....—	**1**	12/1	97	35
1199^{3}	**Amber Spark (IRE) (100)** (DRGandolfo) **7-11-6** RDunwoody (lw: hmpd 1st: stdy hdwy 11th: chsd wnr fr 12th: ev ch fr 2 out: unable qckn flat) ....¾	**2**	$6/4^{1}$	101	39
	Ramstown Lad (IRE) (KCBailey) **7-11-6** CO'Dwyer (hdwy 12th: 3rd whn blnd bdly 2 out: nt rcvr) 20	**3**	10/1	86	24
	Tellicherry (MissHCKnight) **7-11-1** GBradley (hld up: hmpd 1st: ev ch 12th: wknd 4 out) ....½	**4**	$5/2^{2}$	81	19
1075^{P}	**Pinoccio** (DCO'Brien) **9-11-6** PHide (chsd ldr to 5th: wknd 11th) 4	**5**	66/1	83	21
1085^{P}	**Delire d'Estruval (FR)** (IPWilliams) **5-11-5b** BPowell (lw: led: mstke 4th: hdd 12th: sn wknd) 9	**6**	20/1	76	13
	The Wayward Bishop (IRE) (MrsLCTaylor) **7-11-6** GUpton (a bhd: t.o fr 10th) ....dist	**7**	66/1	—	—
	Just 'n Ace (IRE) (MissSEdwards) **5-11-5** MrTHills (fell 1st)	**F**	$11/2^{3}$	—	—
1012^{3}	**Fabulous Francy (IRE) (70)** (MissAEEmbiricos) **8-11-6** JRyan (lw: hld up: blnd 1st: rdn 11th: sn wknd: t.o whn p.u bef 2 out)	**P**	33/1	—	—
	Cruise Control (RRowe) **10-11-6** DO'Sullivan (bkwd: bmpd 1st: bhd fr 9th: t.o whn p.u bef 4 out)	**P**	16/1	—	—
	The Weatherman (AEJessop) **8-11-6** NMann (bit bkwd: blnd, hmpd & uns rdr 1st)	**U**	66/1	—	—
			(SP 118.8%)		**11 Rn**

5m 36.1 (23.10) CSF £29.28 TOTE £15.70: £3.50 £1.10 £2.40 (£25.10) Trio £47.10 OWNER Mr David Young (BLANDFORD) BRED J. P. N. Parker

WEIGHT FOR AGE 5yo-1lb

Mammy's Choice (IRE), winner of a point-to-point last season, gained control five out and, in a tremendous struggle with the runner-up, held on with little left in the tank. Connections reported afterwards that she must have soft ground. (12/1)
1199 Amber Spark (IRE), done no favours in the first-fence melee, was given plenty of time to recover. Battling hard for the advantage, he just failed to find that necessary turn of foot on the run-in. He should soon be winning. (6/4: tchd 9/4)
Ramstown Lad (IRE), without a run since January, appeared to be travelling well turning for home, but he was just being pushed along when a very bad error at the second last stopped him in his tracks. Connections should find a race before long. (10/1: 6/1-12/1)
Tellicherry was one of several in line five out before tiring as lack of a recent run took its toll. (5/2)

1424 PEASE POTTAGE NOVICES' HURDLE (4-Y.O+) (Class E)

3-35 (3-39) **2m 1f (10 hdls)** £2,364.00 (£654.00: £312.00) GOING: 0.71 sec per fur (S)

			SP	RR	SF
1053^{P}	**Ritto (95)** (JNeville) **6-11-5** MAFitzgerald (mde all: rdn out) ....—	**1**	$9/4^{2}$	78	—
956^{3}	**Docklands Courier** (BJMcMath) **4-10-12** JRyan (lw: lost pl 6th: rallied appr 2 out: chsd wnr last: r.o) 2½	**2**	6/1	69	—
	Mullintor (IRE) (RRowe) **5-10-12** DO'Sullivan (hdwy & mstke 7th: ev ch whn j.bdly rt 3 out: j.rt last 2: r.o one pce) 3½	**3**	$11/2^{3}$	65	—
	Memory's Music (MMadgwick) **4-10-12** BFenton (lw: plld hrd: mstke & lost pl 7th: rallied appr 2 out: no ex) 1½	**4**	20/1	64	—
1168^{3}	**Zacaroon** (JFfitch-Heyes) **5-10-7** GBradley (hdwy 7th: chsd wnr 3 out to last: sn wknd) ....½	**5**	33/1	59	—
1165^{3}	**Second Step (IRE)** (DRGandolfo) **5-10-12** RDunwoody (hdwy 7th: wknd appr 2 out: t.o) ....dist	**6**	$2/1^{1}$	—	—
	Galway Boss (IRE) (IPWilliams) **4-10-12** BPowell (lw: prom to 7th: t.o) 14	**7**	10/1	—	—
	Franks Jester (MrsJPitman) **5-10-12** WMarston (chsd wnr to 7th: sn wknd: t.o whn p.u bef 2 out)....	**P**	25/1	—	—
			(SP 114.4%)		**8 Rn**

4m 40.1 (44.10) CSF £15.12 TOTE £2.90: £1.10 £2.00 £1.70 (£14.10) OWNER Park Industrial Supplies (Wales) Ltd (NEWPORT, GWENT) BRED Highclere Stud Ltd

OFFICIAL EXPLANATION Ritto: made a noise.

890* Ritto was much happier being allowed to dominate on soft ground and, setting a sedate pace in the early stages, was ridden along in the straight to win this bad race. (9/4: 6/4-3/1)
956 Docklands Courier ran better in this bad race and, after losing his pitch early on the final circuit, came through to take second place at the last. (6/1: 7/2-7/1)
Mullintor (IRE) could well have been involved in the finish but for some very erratic jumping in the second half of the race. If his hurdling problems can be ironed out, there is a small novice event waiting for him. (11/2)
Memory's Music was fit from the Flat. (20/1)
1168 Zacaroon moved into second place three out, but she was collared for that position at the last and had little more to offer. (33/1)
1165 Second Step (IRE) stopped as if shot turning for home. (2/1)
Galway Boss (IRE) (10/1: op 5/1)

T/Plpt: £103.50 (87.7 Tckts). T/Qdpt: £10.10 (74.12 Tckts). AK

1197-NEWTON ABBOT (L-H) (Heavy)

Tuesday November 19th

One fence omitted
WEATHER: heavy showers

1425 PHILIP BOWEN 50TH BIRTHDAY (S) HURDLE (4,5,6 & 7-Y.O) (Class G)

1-00 (1-00) **2m 1f (8 hdls)** £1,783.90 (£500.40: £243.70) GOING: 1.40 sec per fur (HY)

	Horse	Dist	Pos	SP	RR	SF
	Urban Lily (73) (RJHodges) **6-10-7b**(7) JHarris (mde all: rdn appr last: hld on u.p flat)	—	1	3/1[2]	48	—
	Yet Again (MissGayKelleway) **4-10-12** DBridgwater (bit bkwd: hld up & bhd: rapid hdwy after 6th: ev ch 2 out: disp ld last: drvn & no ex nr fin)	½	2	13/2	46	—
1276[5]	**Fastini Gold** (MDIUsher) **4-10-12** WMcFarland (chsd ldrs: ev ch 6th: wknd appr 2 out)	10	3	4/1[3]	36	—
727[5]	**Kongies Melody** (KBishop) **5-10-7** RGreene (in tch tl wknd 5th)	23	4	11/1	10	—
879[3]	**Denomination (USA) (89)** (MCPipe) **4-11-12** APMcCoy (chsd wnr tl wknd qckly after 6th)	22	5	9/4[1]	8	—
1069[2]	**Peatsville (IRE)** (MRChannon) **4-10-12** AThornton (hdwy after 4th: in tch tl wknd qckly after 6th: p.u bef 2 out)		P	9/2	—	—

(SP 115.6%) **6 Rn**

4m 43.3 (50.30) CSF £20.41 TOTE £4.10: £1.70 £3.20 (£7.80) OWNER Mrs C. J. Cole (SOMERTON) BRED Mrs C. J. Cole
No bid
OFFICIAL EXPLANATION **Denomination (USA): the jockey reported that the gelding pulled hard in the early stages, began to gurgle after the second hurdle in the back straight and thereafter he did not persevere.**
Urban Lily battled on gamely through the mud to hold off the challenge of the runner-up. (3/1)
Yet Again, a moderate plater on the Flat, was making his hurdles debut. He came with a threatening challenge at the last, but could not peg back the winner. (13/2: 3/1-7/1)
879 Denomination (USA) put up an extremely poor display but, on returning, his jockey said the horse had gurgled. (9/4)

1426 SOUTH WEST RACING CLUB NOVICES' H'CAP CHASE (0-100) (4-Y.O+) (Class E)

1-30 (1-30) **2m 5f 110y (13 fncs)** £2,982.00 (£903.00: £441.00: £210.00) GOING: 1.40 sec per fur (HY)

	Horse	Dist	Pos	SP	RR	SF
	Orswell Lad (99) (PJHobbs) **7-11-13** RDunwoody (prom: led 6th to next: led 8th to 10th: led last: rdn out)	—	1	11/4[2]	111	23
	Foxtrot Romeo (100) (CPEBrooks) **6-12-0** DGallagher (a.p: led 7th to 8th: led 10th: hdd last: rdn & rallied flat: jst failed)	s.h	2	9/2	112	24
1199[F]	**Country Keeper (75)** (BJMRyall) **8-10-3**[ow3] GUpton (bhd: hdwy 8th: chsd ldrs 11th: one pce appr 2 out)	15	3	33/1	76	—
1285[4]	**Its Grand (72)** (JMBradley) **7-10-0** TJMurphy (led 1st to 3rd: prom to 9th: grad wknd)	s.h	4	4/1[3]	73	—
1199[U]	**Colette's Choice (IRE) (82)** (GAHam) **7-10-10** AThornton (led 3rd to 5th: prom tl wknd 8th: t.o)	dist	5	14/1	—	—
1038[4]	**Strong Tarquin (IRE) (100)** (PFNicholls) **6-12-0** APMcCoy (in tch tl wknd 8th: t.o)	dist	6	9/4[1]	—	—
1285[P]	**Vareck II (FR) (72)** (MCPipe) **9-9-7**(7) BMoore (in tch tl mstke 8th: grad wknd: t.o)	12	7	33/1	—	—
1197[5]	**Castleconner (IRE) (78)** (RGFrost) **5-10-5**[ow3] JFrost (lw: led to 1st: in tch whn mstke 8th: sn wknd: p.u bef 11th)		P	16/1	—	—

(SP 114.0%) **8 Rn**

6m 2.6 (45.60) CSF £14.61 CT £291.21 TOTE £4.00: £1.60 £2.30 £3.30 (£10.10) Trio Not won; £64.64 to Hereford 20/11/96 OWNER Mr R. M. E. Wright (MINEHEAD) BRED G. Amey
LONG HANDICAP Its Grand 9-9 Vareck II (FR) 9-2 Country Keeper 9-7
WEIGHT FOR AGE 5yo-1lb
Orswell Lad came back from an enforced absence of nearly two years due to leg problems and made a successful chasing debut. He can follow up on this ground. (11/4)
Foxtrot Romeo, making his seasonal debut, made a race of it with the winner, and looked like he had it in the bag until that one came with a strong last-furlong challenge. (9/2: 5/2-5/1)
Country Keeper ran into the prizes and put in a clear round, but was never a threat to the first two. (33/1)
Colette's Choice (IRE) (14/1: 10/1-16/1)
1038 Strong Tarquin (IRE) looks to have lost his enthusiasm for the present. (9/4)

1427 FAUCETS SIRRUS SHOWER VALVES AND FITTINGS NOVICES' HURDLE (4-Y.O+) (Class D)

2-00 (2-01) **2m 1f (8 hdls)** £2,845.40 (£799.40: £390.20) GOING: 1.40 sec per fur (HY)

	Horse	Dist	Pos	SP	RR	SF
1171[3]	**Lake Kariba (119)** (PFNicholls) **5-11-6** APMcCoy (lw: led 2nd: clr appr 2 out: unchal)	—	1	2/1[1]	92	17
1171[2]	**Devon Peasant** (LGCottrell) **4-10-9** MrLJefford (a w ldrs: gd hdwy to chse wnr 5th: outpcd appr 2 out)	15	2	9/4[2]	67	—
	Nordance Prince (IRE) (MissGayKelleway) **5-11-0** DBridgwater (bit bkwd: bhd: hdwy 5th: chsd ldrs next: wknd appr 2 out)	18	3	9/4[2]	55+	—
1171[P]	**Parade Racer** (PGMurphy) **5-11-0** WMcFarland (led to 2nd: chsd wnr to 5th: grad wknd)	nk	4	25/1	55	—
1039[P]	**Hello Me Man (IRE) (98)** (BJLlewellyn) **8-11-0** MrJLLlewellyn (bit bkwd: bhd: styd on fr 6th: nvr nrr)	1½	5	25/1	53	—
	Cool Gunner (JSKing) **6-11-0** CMaude (bkwd: sme hdwy 5th: wknd next)	9	6	20/1	45	—
	Walter's Destiny (CWMitchell) **4-11-0** SMcNeill (bit bkwd: chsd ldrs tl wknd 5th)	1½	7	25/1	43	—
	Palladium Boy (MrsJGRetter) **6-11-0** RDunwoody (bit bkwd: mid div tl wknd appr 2 out)	1	8	14/1[3]	42	—
	Imalight (82) (RGFrost) **7-10-9** JFrost (mid div whn fell 4th)		F	16/1	—	—
1171[8]	**Saxon Mead** (PJHobbs) **6-11-0** MAFitzgerald (in tch tl rdn 5th: wknd next: t.o whn p.u bef 2f out)		P	16/1	—	—
	Bryan Robson (USA) (JWMullins) **5-11-0** SCurran (bkwd: a rr: t.o whn p.u bef 2 out)		P	66/1	—	—
1171[9]	**Saafi (IRE)** (RJBaker) **5-11-0** BPowell (a rr div: t.o 6th: blnd & uns rdr last)		U	66/1	—	—

(SP 132.6%) **12 Rn**

4m 28.3 (35.30) CSF £7.67 TOTE £2.90: £1.50 £1.60 £1.90 (£2.50) Trio £1.60 OWNER The Lake Kariba Partnership (SHEPTON MALLET) BRED Side Hill Stud and the Duke of Roxburgh's Stud
1171 Lake Kariba reversed Exeter form with the runner-up and seemed quite happy in this testing ground. He is improving and will go chasing next season. (2/1)
1171 Devon Peasant could not confirm the Exeter form with the winner, just finding the struggle too much after the penultimate obstacle. (9/4: 6/4-5/2)
Nordance Prince (IRE) put up a fair performance to run into the prizes on this surface after a break of almost two years. (9/4)

1428 CLAUDE WHITLEY MEMORIAL CHALLENGE CUP H'CAP CHASE (0-120) (5-Y.O+) (Class D)

2-30 (2-30) **3m 2f 110y (17 fncs)** £3,559.40 (£1,077.20: £525.60: £249.80) GOING: 1.40 sec per fur (HY)

				SP	RR	SF
	Flow (92) (RHBuckler) **7-10-5** BPowell (a.p: chsd ldr 13th: led 15th: clr appr 2 out: eased flat)	—	1	7/1[3]	101+	—
1197[3]	**Bramblehill Buck (IRE) (102)** (PFNicholls) **7-11-1** APMcCoy (lw: led to 2nd: led 3rd to 5th: led 7th to 13th: wknd fr next)	8	2	7/2[2]	106	1
1175[3]	**Dom Samourai (FR) (117)** (MCPipe) **5-12-0b** CMaude (prom: led 5th: hdd & mstke 7th: led 13th to 15th: sn outpcd)	nk	3	8/1	121	14
1202[2]	**Rocky Park (92)** (GBBalding) **10-10-5** BFenton (mstke 4th: hdwy 8th: chsd ldrs tl wknd 11th)	22	4	100/30[1]	83	—
	Sorrel Hill (100) (PJHobbs) **9-10-13** MAFitzgerald (bit bkwd: chsd ldrs tl wknd 11th)	½	5	10/1	90	—
1089*	**Church Law (102)** (MrsLCTaylor) **9-11-1** DBridgwater (a rr div: lost tch 9th: t.o whn p.u after 11th)		P	100/30[1]	—	—
	Desperate (100) (AGFoster) **8-10-6**(7) DCreech (bkwd: bhd 3rd: t.o whn p.u bef 12th)		P	20/1	—	—
	Fast Thoughts (114) (DRGandolfo) **9-11-13** RDunwoody (led 2nd: j.slowly next: in tch tl blnd bdly 6th: nt rcvr: t.o whn p.u after 11th)		P	9/1	—	—
				(SP 115.8%)	**8 Rn**	

7m 33.5 (59.50) CSF £30.17 CT £184.05 TOTE £8.20: £2.00 £2.00 £2.10 (£39.60) Trio £27.00 OWNER Mrs C. J. Dunn (BRIDPORT) BRED C. J. and Mrs Dunn

WEIGHT FOR AGE 5yo-2lb

OFFICIAL EXPLANATION **Church Law: was unsuited by the heavy ground.**

Flow, on her chasing and seasonal debut, hails from a stable in form and did everything asked of her. (7/1)

1197 Bramblehill Buck (IRE), despite putting up a good effort and featuring prominently, found the step up in trip a bit too much on this ground and finished legless. (7/2)

1175 Dom Samourai (FR), suited to front-running, lost the lead six from home and could do no more. (8/1: op 5/1)

Fast Thoughts was running a useful-looking race until a blunder at the sixth fence stopped him in his tracks. (9/1: 11/2-10/1)

1429 WILLIAM HILL H'CAP HURDLE (0-135) (4-Y.O+) (Class C)

3-00 (3-00) **2m 6f (10 hdls)** £3,485.00 (£1,055.00: £515.00: £245.00) GOING: 1.40 sec per fur (HY)

				SP	RR	SF
796[3]	**Sparkling Yasmin (119)** (PJHobbs) **4-11-8** BPowell (lw: chsd ldrs tl led 5th: hdd next: led 7th to 8th: chsd ldr: rdn to ld last strides)	—	1	6/1[3]	96	53
1201[4]	**Holdimclose (110)** (RGFrost) **6-10-13** JFrost (lw: hld up & bhd: gd hdwy 7th: led next: rdn & hdd last strides)	s.h	2	10/1	87	44
	Oatis Rose (97) (MSheppard) **6-10-0** CO'Dwyer (bit bkwd: a.p: disp ld 8th to 2 out: sn wknd)	18	3	10/1	61	18
1174*	**Allow (IRE) (97)** (BLlewellyn) **5-9-9**(5) MrRThornton (in tch to 7th: grad wknd)	15	4	7/1	50	7
1039[3]	**Balanak (USA) (121)** (DRGandolfo) **5-11-10v** RDunwoody (in tch tl rdn & wknd fr 8th)	22	5	9/4[1]	58	15
725*	**Better Bythe Glass (IRE) (100)** (NATwiston-Davies) **7-10-3** CLlewellyn (led to 5th: led 6th: hdd next: wknd 8th: t.o)	dist	6	10/1	—	—
1260[3]	**The Reverend Bert (IRE) (106)** (GBBalding) **8-10-9** APMcCoy (hdwy 5th: in tch tl wknd appr 8th: t.o)	12	7	4/1[2]	—	—
1286[4]	**Jadidh (99)** (ABarrow) **8-9-11**(5) DSalter (bhd 3rd & fell 6th)		F	14/1	—	—
1039[9]	**Needwood Muppet (110)** (AJWilson) **9-10-13** LHarvey (bit bkwd: bhd 4th: rdn & wknd 6th: t.o whn p.u bef 2 out)		P	16/1	—	—
				(SP 117.4%)	**9 Rn**	

5m 47.5 (35.50) CSF £57.56 CT £540.77 TOTE £5.90: £1.70 £3.90 £1.70 (£51.10) Trio £162.40 OWNER Mr Victor Palmer (MINEHEAD) BRED A. B. Barraclough

LONG HANDICAP Oatis Rose 9-12 Allow (IRE) 9-3

796 Sparkling Yasmin, the only four-year-old in the field, is an out-and-out stayer and has a bright future ahead of her over the longer trips. (6/1)

Holdimclose can surely go one better soon, especially with a bit less cut in the ground. (10/1: 8/1-12/1)

Oatis Rose, after an absence of seven months and looking in need of the run, will improve for this and could be one to follow in these conditions, possibly over further. (10/1)

1039 Balanak (USA), with the headgear back on, was very disappointing. (9/4)

1430 FAUCETS A & J GUMMERS H'CAP CHASE (0-115) (5-Y.O+) (Class E)

3-30 (3-30) **2m 110y (11 fncs)** £2,831.85 (£856.80: £417.90: £198.45) GOING: 1.40 sec per fur (HY)

				SP	RR	SF
	Well Timed (92) (RGFrost) **6-10-5**ow5 JFrost (hdwy to chse ldr 10th: outpcd, rdn & rallied last: led last strides)	—	1	7/2[3]	93	—
1169[3]	**James the First (115)** (PFNicholls) **8-12-0** APMcCoy (led 2nd: clr 10th: rdn & no ex whn chal flat: hdd last strides)	s.h	2	6/4[1]	116	28
882[3]	**Rex to the Rescue (IRE) (100)** (RHAlner) **8-10-10**(3) PHenley (led to 2nd: chsd ldrs tl mstke 9th & wknd)	7	3	3/1[2]	94	6
1298[2]	**Fenwick (88)** (RJHodges) **9-9-12**(3) TDascombe (in tch: chsd ldr 9th tl wknd next)	20	4	3/1[2]	63	—
				(SP 112.2%)	**4 Rn**	

4m 35.6 (35.60) CSF £8.87 TOTE £4.10 (£3.50) OWNER Mrs G. A. Robarts (BUCKFASTLEIGH) BRED Mrs G. A. Roberts

STEWARDS' ENQUIRY McCoy susp. 28-20/11/96 (excessive use of whip).

Well Timed lived up to his name here and, after showing decent hurdles form for this stable, had things in his favour here on this debut over fences under Rules. Suited by the testing ground, he can surely take advantage of his low mark again in the near future. (7/2)

1169 James the First put up a game effort, but was fully exposed here. (6/4)

882 Rex to the Rescue (IRE) (3/1: 2/1-100/30)

1298 Fenwick (3/1: 2/1-100/30)

1431 BOUNDERIES INTERMEDIATE OPEN N.H. FLAT RACE (4, 5 & 6-Y.O) (Class H)

4-00 (4-01) **2m 1f** £1,201.00 (£336.00: £163.00)

				SP	RR	SF
	Iranos (FR) (MCPipe) **4-11-4** APMcCoy (lw: led 2f: disp ld tl led 7f out: sn clr: unchal)	—	1	9/4[1]	50 f	—
653*	**Never In Debt** (AGHobbs) **4-11-4**(7) MrGShenkin (lw: hld up: hdwy 5f out: chsd wnr 2f out: no imp)	11	2	10/1	47 f	—
	April Seventh (IRE) (JNeville) **5-11-4** WMarston (bit bkwd: a.p: chsd wnr 4f out to 3f out: outpcd)	2	3	16/1	38 f	—
	Country Tarquin (RJHodges) **4-11-4** RDunwoody (hdwy ½-wy: in tch 5f out: chsd wnr 3f out to 2f out: outpcd)	s.h	4	7/2[2]	38 f	—

	Horse		Pos	SP	RR	SF
	Dom Beltrano (FR) (NATwiston-Davies) **4-10-11**(7) LSuthern (bit bkwd: bhd: hdwy ½-wy: sn prom: chsd wnr 5f out to 4f out: wknd 2f out)	¾	**5**	11/2	37 f	—
	Greenfield George (IRE) (PJHobbs) **5-11-4** LHarvey (bit bkwd: hdwy ½-wy: in tch 7f out: wknd 5f out: t.o)	25	**6**	15/2	14 f	—
	Sprig Muslin (DRGandolfo) **4-11-1**(5) SophieMitchell (a bhd: t.o 7f out)	¾	**7**	9/2 3	15 f	—
	Mr Agriwise (RGFrost) **5-11-4** JFrost (bkwd: a rr div: t.o 7f out)	11	**8**	20/1	2 f	—
1203 11	**Zaggy Lane** (MrsRGHenderson) **4-10-13**(5) DSalter (bit bkwd: chsd wnr tl led after 2f: hdd 7f out: sn wknd: t.o)	24	**9**	66/1	—	—
1203 5	**Defendthereealm** (RGFrost) **5-11-4** MrAHoldsworth (bkwd: prom to ½-wy: sn t.o)	10	**10**	14/1	—	—
	She's The Governor (NGAyliffe) **5-10-13** BPowell (bkwd: a bhd: lost tch ½-wy: t.o whn p.u over 2f out)		**P**	66/1	—	—

(SP 127.7%) **11 Rn**

4m 24.9 (263.90) CSF £25.79 TOTE £4.20: £1.10 £2.50 £3.60 (£15.10) Trio £73.10 OWNER Mr B. A. Kilpatrick (WELLINGTON) BRED Patrick Champion

Iranos (FR) made a most encouraging debut and will surely be capable of following up in these events, and then over hurdles. (9/4: 2/1-3/1)
653* Never In Debt, from a stable in form, just met one far too good. (10/1: op 5/1)
April Seventh (IRE) never presented a threat to the first two, and will be more of a proposition when put over hurdles. (16/1)
Country Tarquin will be an interesting hurdles debutant. (7/2)
Dom Beltrano (FR) (11/2: 4/1-6/1)
Greenfield George (IRE) (15/2: 9/2-8/1)
Defendthereealm (14/1: 16/1-25/1)

T/Plpt: £411.60 (24.64 Tckts). T/Qdpt: £61.90 (24.84 Tckts) T

1152-WETHERBY (L-H) - Tuesday November 19th
1432 Abandoned-Snow

1184-HAYDOCK (L-H) (Good)
Wednesday November 20th
WEATHER: overcast & sunny spells

1438 NEWTON-LE-WILLOWS POLICE NOVICES' HURDLE (4-Y.O+ F & M) (Class D)
1-10 (1-10) **2m (8 hdls)** £2,885.00 (£810.00: £395.00) GOING: 0.25 sec per fur (GS)

	Horse		Pos	SP	RR	SF
1190*	**Marello** (MrsMReveley) **5-10-7** PNiven (hld up & bhd: hdwy 5th: chal & hit 2 out: led appr last: comf)	—	**1**	2/1 2	89++	46
1152*	**Queen of Spades (IRE)** (NATwiston-Davies) **6-11-0** CLlewellyn (lw: led tl appr last: rdn & styd on: no ch w wnr)	2½	**2**	1/2 1	94	51
	Anglesey Sea View (ABailey) **7-10-7** TKent (chsd ldr fr 3rd to 3 out: sn outpcd)	28	**3**	20/1 3	59	16
1187 11	**Cliburnel News (IRE)** (ALForbes) **6-10-7** TEley (trckd ldrs: lost tch appr 3 out)	16	**4**	33/1	43	—
	Scally Hicks (BPJBaugh) **5-10-7** GaryLyons (bkwd: a in rr: t.o)	28	**5**	66/1	15	—
	Miss Mont (FPMurtagh) **7-10-7** RHodge (bkwd: a in rr: t.o)	6	**6**	66/1	9	—
	Prussian Eagle (IRE) (MBradstock) **4-10-7** RDunwoody (bit bkwd: a bhd: t.o fr ½-wy)	17	**7**	25/1	—	—
	Meesonette (BEllison) **4-10-7** BHarding (bkwd: prom to 4th: sn wknd: t.o)	1¼	**8**	66/1	—	—
1245 6	**Promise To Try (IRE)** (MABarnes) **4-10-2**(5) STaylor (bit bkwd: chsd ldrs to 4th: sn lost tch: t.o)	14	**9**	66/1	—	—
1190 4	**Bridled Tern** (JMJefferson) **5-10-7** MDwyer (bit bkwd: hld up in rr: fell 3rd)		**F**	20/1 3	—	—
955 10	**Sloe Brandy** (MrsHLWalton) **6-10-7** MrAWalton (chsd ldrs to 5th: 5th & btn whn fell 2 out)		**F**	66/1	—	—

(SP 123.8%) **11 Rn**

3m 48.1 (6.10) CSF £3.37 TOTE £2.80: £1.30 £1.10 £1.90 (£1.30) Trio £2.50 OWNER Mrs M. Williams (SALTBURN) BRED R. Chugg

1190* Marello had the ability to win at this minimum trip on her hurdling debut and, as she is sure to be suited to a test of stamina, she must be followed until beaten. (2/1)
1152* Queen of Spades (IRE) earned rave reports when successful on her seasonal reappearance and attempted to do a repeat demolition job here, but she would have needed to have been extra special to give weight away to the useful winner. (1/2)
Anglesey Sea View, fit from the Flat for this hurdling debut, is sure to need a stiffer test of stamina and, in the circumstances, showed plenty of promise. (20/1)

1439 LIVERPOOL H'CAP HURDLE (0-120) (4-Y.O+) (Class D)
1-40 (1-40) **2m (8 hdls)** £2,759.00 (£774.00: £377.00) GOING: 0.25 sec per fur (GS)

	Horse		Pos	SP	RR	SF
1188 2	**Saint Ciel (USA) (105)** (FJordan) **8-11-6** RSupple (hld up: hdwy after 5th: slt ld last: r.o wl)	—	**1**	11/8 1	87	38
	Circus Line (95) (MWEasterby) **5-10-10** MDwyer (bit bkwd: plld hrd: a.p: disp ld last: kpt on towards fin)	1¾	**2**	7/2 2	75	26
1154 4	**Desert Fighter (111)** (MrsMReveley) **5-11-12** PNiven (trckd ldrs: ev ch last: unable qckn flat)	2	**3**	5/1 3	89	40
	Nashville Star (USA) (100) (RMathew) **5-11-1v** RBellamy (bkwd: led to last: one pce flat)	2½	**4**	25/1	76	27
	Eurotwist (112) (SEKettlewell) **7-11-10**(3) GLee (hld up in rr: nvr plcd to chal)	1¼	**5**	10/1	87	38
	Innocent George (94) (MissLCSiddall) **7-10-9** RDunwoody (bkwd: chsd ldr to appr 3 out: wknd appr last)	nk	**6**	14/1	68	19
1125 6	**Holders Hill (IRE) (113)** (MGMeagher) **4-12-0** LWyer (bit bkwd: hld up in rr: no ch whn fell last)		**F**	9/1	—	—

(SP 110.6%) **7 Rn**

3m 52.7 (10.70) CSF £6.22 TOTE £1.90: £1.20 £2.10 (£2.90) OWNER Tam Racing (LEOMINSTER) BRED Delsol Farm

1188 Saint Ciel (USA) reserves his best for this track and, in making it win number four over course and distance, won with more in hand than the margin suggests. (11/8)
Circus Line needed the run after being out of action for eight months, but he turned in a fine performance and should not be long in going one better. (7/2)
1154 Desert Fighter has done all his winning on a sound surface and, with the ground riding dead after yesterday's downpour, was tapped for toe on the run-in. (5/1)
Nashville Star (USA) looked burly on this first outing in a year, but he did a grand job of pacemaking until blowing up approaching the last. He obviously retains plenty of ability and can soon improve on this. (25/1)
Eurotwist needs to come from behind, but was never put into the race on this occasion and is surely capable of better. (10/1)
Innocent George, at his best in the early part of last season, did look tubby for this belated return to action and was treading water from the turn into the straight. (14/1)

1440 EDWARD HANMER MEMORIAL LIMITED H'CAP CHASE (5-Y.O+) (Class B)

2-10 (2-10) **3m (18 fncs)** £10,035.75 (£3,036.00: £1,480.50: £702.75) GOING minus 0.25 sec per fur (GF)

			SP	RR	SF
	Unguided Missile (IRE) (148) (GRichards) **8-11-0** RDunwoody (bit bkwd: j.w: chsd ldr: led 9th: clr appr last: eased nr fin)—	1	10/11[1]	156+	32
	Couldnt Be Better (160) (CPEBrooks) **9-11-12** GBradley (bkwd: j.w: hld up: disp ld 4 out: wknd appr last)4	2	11/4[3]	165+	41
1055[2]	**Gales Cavalier (IRE) (160)** (DRGandolfo) **8-11-12** MDwyer (led to 9th: chsd wnr appr last: wknd flat)20	3	5/2[2]	152	28
1311[4]	**Quixall Crossett (139)** (EMCaine) **11-10-0**(5) STaylor (j.w: a t.o)dist	4	500/1	—	—
			(SP 107.8%)		**4 Rn**

6m 15.6 (17.60) CSF £3.53 TOTE £1.70 (£2.30) OWNER Mr D. E. Harrison (PENRITH) BRED Samac Ltd and Potomac Ltd
LONG HANDICAP Quixall Crossett 4-6
Unguided Missile (IRE) can be made fitter, but he did everything asked of him here and won in a canter. Still rather lightly-raced, he should enjoy another good season. (10/11: 5/3-4/5)
Couldnt Be Better has won first time out for the past couple of seasons including this event twelve months ago, but there were cobwebs to be blown away this time and he was at the end of his tether between the last two. Connections were delighted with this run and he now goes for a repeat in the Hennessy in ten days' time. (11/4)
1055 Gales Cavalier (IRE) failed to see out this extended trip, but he ran well until getting very leg-weary on the run-in. (5/2)

1441 HINDLEY GREEN H'CAP HURDLE (0-135) (4-Y.O+) (Class C)

2-40 (2-41) **2m 4f (10 hdls)** £3,468.75 (£1,050.00: £512.50: £243.75) GOING: 0.25 sec per fur (GS)

			SP	RR	SF
796*	**Tullymurry Toff (IRE) (120)** (JMJefferson) **5-11-0**(5) ECallaghan (chsd ldrs: led 2 out: sn clr: easily)—	1	3/1[3]	105+	8
1258[2]	**Mytton's Choice (IRE) (126)** (DNicholson) **5-11-6**(5) MrRThornton (bit bkwd: sn chsng ldr: led 5th to 2 out: outpcd appr last)3½	2	3/1[3]	108	11
	Turnpole (IRE) (128) (MrsMReveley) **5-11-13** PNiven (hld up: hit 4th: effrt appr 3 out: nvr able to chal)3	3	5/2[1]	108	11
	Mr Bureaucrat (NZ) (119) (SABrookshaw) **7-11-4** ADobbin (hld up & bhd: hdwy 7th: wknd appr 2 out: t.o)16	4	11/1	86	—
1185*	**Palosanto (IRE) (122)** (MCPipe) **6-11-7** CLlewellyn (bit bkwd: led & sn clr: hdd 5th: rdn & wknd next: t.o)12	5	11/4[2]	79	—
	Little Gunner (118) (RJPrice) **6-11-3** RDunwoody (Withdrawn not under Starter's orders: veterinary advice)	W	10/1	—	—
			(SP 122.7%)		**5 Rn**

4m 58.8 (21.80) CSF £11.29 TOTE £3.30: £1.40 £1.80 (£5.00) OWNER Mr John H Wilson and Mr J H Riley (MALTON) BRED Con Troy and David Fenton
796* Tullymurry Toff (IRE), a very progressive individual, is getting better with every outing. A trip to the Festival for the Coral Cup has been pencilled in after this runaway success. (3/1)
1258 Mytton's Choice (IRE) is still to prove he really stays this trip, but he continues to run well and there is no doubt he has commitment. (3/1)
Turnpole (IRE), thought by his trainer to be in the grip of the Handicapper over hurdles, will soon switch his attentions to fences, and there seems no reason why he can not make the grade. (5/2)
1185* Palosanto (IRE) was unable to cope with the step up in class, and was throwing out distress signals on the home turn. (11/4)

1442 WARGRAVE H'CAP CHASE (0-130) (5-Y.O+) (Class C)

3-10 (3-10) **2m (12 fncs)** £4,349.25 (£1,314.00: £639.50: £302.25) GOING minus 0.25 sec per fur (GF)

			SP	RR	SF
1134[3]	**Thumbs Up (125)** (GMMcCourt) **10-12-0** RDunwoody (lw: j.w: led 4th tl appr 2 out: led last: rdn out)—	1	13/8[1]	130	47
1350[P]	**Spanish Light (IRE) (122)** (SirJohnBarlowBt) **7-11-11** ADobbin (bkwd: j.w: led to 4th: led appr 2 out to last: wknd flat)7	2	11/4[3]	120	37
696[6]	**Rebel King (97)** (MABarnes) **6-9-9**(5) STaylor (lw: sn chsng ldrs: rdn 6th: wknd whn hit 4 out)11	3	13/2	84	1
1295[6]	**Potato Man (100)** (BEllison) **10-10-3** BHarding (lw: trckd ldrs tl lost pl 8th: sn t.o)dist	4	9/4[2]	—	—
1311[7]	**Monaughty Man (97)** (EMCaine) **10-10-0** MrPMurray (bkwd: bhd whn rn out & crashed thro rails after 4th)	R	25/1	—	—
			(SP 112.7%)		**5 Rn**

4m 5.9 (10.90) CSF £6.33 TOTE £2.50: £1.20 £2.30 (£3.40) OWNER Mrs B. Taylor (WANTAGE) BRED Peader McCoy
LONG HANDICAP Rebel King 9-7 Monaughty Man 9-2
STEWARDS' ENQUIRY Taylor susp. 29-30/11/96 (improper use of whip).
1134 Thumbs Up has taken a long time to regain winning ways, but he found a suitable opening and, though he did make hard work of it, he was well on top at the end. (13/8)
Spanish Light (IRE) has changed stables since last season and was making a quick return to action. Racing over an inadequate trip and still looking fat, he performed with credit and should have little trouble recapturing his true form. (11/4: 2/1-3/1)

1443 EARLESTOWN H'CAP HURDLE (0-120) (4-Y.O+) (Class D)

3-40 (3-40) **2m 7f 110y (12 hdls)** £2,815.00 (£790.00: £385.00) GOING: 0.25 sec per fur (GS)

			SP	RR	SF
1294*	**Haile Derring (107)** (NATwiston-Davies) **6-12-2** 6x CLlewellyn (disp ld: led appr 2 out: styd on strly flat)—	1	8/13[1]	90+	19
1181*	**Desert Force (IRE) (90)** (AStreeter) **7-10-13** GBradley (lw: hld up: hdwy 9th: jnd wnr 2 out: rdn & one pceflat) 4	2	4/1[2]	70	—
1170[3]	**Country Store (91)** (APJones) **7-11-0** SCurran (bit bkwd: disp ld: hdd & hit 2 out: wknd qckly)20	3	16/1[3]	58	—
1126[F]	**Flat Top (99)** (MWEasterby) **5-11-8** MDwyer (hld up: hit 8th: rdn & outpcd appr 3 out: sn t.o)9	4	4/1[2]	60	—
			(SP 107.8%)		**4 Rn**

5m 57.8 (25.80) CSF £3.24 TOTE £1.60 (£2.00) OWNER Mrs V. Stockdale (CHELTENHAM) BRED Mrs V. Stockdale
1294* Haile Derring had a 6lb penalty to overcome, but he was meeting inferior rivals and brushed them aside with ease. (8/13)
1181* Desert Force (IRE) is useful in his own class but, even with such a pull in the weights, had to admit the winner too good for him on the run-in. (4/1)
1170 Country Store helped force the pace, but she could never get away from the winner and had shot her bolt after clouting the penultimate hurdle. (16/1)
1126 Flat Top, very unlucky on his chasing debut at the beginning of the month, dropped out of contention on the home turn and was soon tailed off. He invariably needs a race. (4/1)

T/Plpt: £9.20 (1,264.01 Tckts). T/Qdpt: £9.50 (68.82 Tckts). IM

0931-HEREFORD (R-H) (Good to soft)
Wednesday November 20th
WEATHER: fine but cold

1444 MARDEN HURDLE (3-Y.O) (Class E)
1-00 (1-02) **2m 1f (9 hdls)** £2,486.00 (£696.00: £338.00) GOING: 0.15 sec per fur (G)

	Horse	Dist	Pos	SP	RR	SF
	Crown And Cushion (TRGreathead) **3-10-12** PHolley (bhd tl hdwy appr 5th: lft 2nd 3 out: lft in ld appr 2 out: r.o)	—	1	100/1	56	—
1064[4]	**Siberian Mystic** (PGMurphy) **3-11-0** WMcFarland (lw: hld up: hdwy 5th: ev ch appr 2 out: btn whn mstke last)	10	2	10/1[3]	49	—
	Warning Reef (CLPopham) **3-10-12** RJohnson (hdwy 4th: mstke 5th: 3rd whn blnd 3 out: no ch whn blnd 2 out)	dist	3	5/1[2]	—	—
1172[P]	**Paulton** (KBishop) **3-10-12** RGreene (nvr nr ldrs)	3	4	100/1	—	—
1149[2]	**Lady Magnum (IRE)** (JNeville) **3-10-7** NMann (lw: hld up & bhd: nvr nr ldrs)	25	5	10/1[3]	—	—
	Worth The Bill (FJordan) **3-10-12** SWynne (a bhd)	14	6	50/1	—	—
	Irish Kinsman (GHYardley) **3-10-12** JRKavanagh (a bhd)	nk	7	33/1	—	—
1184[12]	**Grasshopper** (JLSpearing) **3-10-9**(3) DWalsh (a bhd: t.o)	dist	8	33/1	—	—
	Noble Colours (SGGriffiths) **3-10-12** MrJJukes (trckd ldrs: b.d 3rd)		B	100/1	—	—
1269[7]	**Deux Carr (USA)** (BobJones) **3-10-12** VSmith (prom: lft 2nd 3rd: blnd 4th: 2nd whn fell 3 out)		F	40/1	—	—
	Come On In (RDickin) **3-10-5**(7) XAizpuru (prom: 2nd whn fell 3rd)		F	66/1	—	—
	Fursan (USA) (NATwiston-Davies) **3-10-12** DBridgwater (led: clr 4th: rdn & wknd appr 3 out: p.u bef 2 out)		P	8/11[1]	—	—
1064[5]	**Quiet Moments (IRE)** (PGMurphy) **3-10-12** RFarrant (prom tl wknd 5th: bhd whn p.u bef 3 out)		P	50/1	—	—
	Secret Gift (MrsJPitman) **3-10-4**(3) GHogan (a bhd: t.o whn p.u bef 2 out)		P	10/1[3]	—	—
831[3]	**Little Kenny** (TWall) **3-10-7v** BPowell (p.u bef 3rd)		P	16/1	—	—
831[5]	**Formentiere** (JMBradley) **3-10-0**(7) MrAWintle (a bhd: t.o whn p.u bef 3 out)		P	25/1	—	—

(SP 128.3%) **16 Rn**

4m 10.5 (17.50) CSF £824.25 TOTE £138.40: £16.20 £2.60 £1.70 (£355.40) Trio £121.80; £137.34 to Wincanton 21/11/96 OWNER Mrs S. Greathead (CHIPPING NORTON) BRED S. Scarsbrook

Crown And Cushion had shown nothing in four outings in lowly company on the Flat for Ken Bridgwater, but the form of this race will probably not amount to much. (100/1)

1064 Siberian Mystic found this company and course easier than at Cheltenham last time, but the extended two miles did not help. (10/1: op 6/1)

Warning Reef, although a maiden of the Flat, was rated higher than the horse who started odds-on for this event, but his jumping was appalling in the second half of the race. (5/1: op 5/2)

Paulton had been pulled up in a seller on his debut. (100/1)

1149 Lady Magnum (IRE) never seemed to be given a chance to get into the race and can do much better than this when reverting to selling company. (10/1)

Deux Carr (USA), bought for 8,000 guineas as a three-year-old, ran better in this company, but his jumping obviously needs to improve. (40/1)

Fursan (USA) was bought for 24,000 guineas out of Neil Graham's stable at Newmarket July Sales after finishing second in a staying handicap at Newbury. Beginning to flounder on the climb to three out, connections could not offer an explanation as to why he suddenly hit the wall. (8/11: op 11/10)

Secret Gift (10/1: 7/1-12/1)

1445 BACTON AMATEUR H'CAP CHASE (0-100) (5-Y.O+) (Class F)
1-30 (1-31) **2m 3f (14 fncs)** £2,878.00 (£808.00: £394.00) GOING: 0.15 sec per fur (G)

	Horse	Dist	Pos	SP	RR	SF
	Poppets Pet (86) (JWMullins) **9-11-3**(7) MrABalding (led to 3rd: lft in ld appr last: r.o wl)	—	1	11/1	95	3
725[5]	**Prudent Peggy (69)** (RGFrost) **9-10-0**(7) MrAHoldsworth (hld up: hdwy 10th: r.o one pce fr 2 out)	1¾	2	10/1	77	—
	Wayuphill (87) (JJO'Neill) **9-11-4**(7) MrLCorcoran (lw: hld up: hdwy 9th: one pce fr 3 out)	7	3	4/1[1]	89	—
	Where's Willie (FR) (97) (NATwiston-Davies) **7-12-4**(3) MrMRimell (led 3rd: clr appr 3 out: rdn after 2 out: wnt lame & hdd appr last)	1¾	4	4/1[1]	97	5
1122[6]	**Opal's Tenspot (69)** (JMBradley) **9-10-0**(7) MissVRoberts (nvr nr to chal)	16	5	20/1	56	—
1257[6]	**Northern Optimist (87)** (BJLlewellyn) **8-11-6**(5) MrJLLlewellyn (prom to 4 out)	2	6	4/1[1]	72	—
1335[P]	**Rhoman Fun (IRE) (69)** (RHBuckler) **7-10-0**(7) MrPScott (a bhd)	6	7	6/1[3]	49	—
1122[5]	**Auvillar (USA) (79)** (JParfitt) **8-10-10v**(7) MrAWintle (mstke 5th: bhd fr 8th: t.o)	20	8	20/1	42	—
1076[5]	**Ennistymon (IRE) (69)** (JWMullins) **5-10-0**(7) MrGWeatherley (hdwy 9th: mstke 10th: wknd 3 out: no ch whn fell last)		F	33/1	—	—
869[4]	**Millies Own (93)** (PJHobbs) **9-11-10**(7) MrRWidger (a bhd: t.o whn p.u bef 3 out)		P	5/1[2]	—	—
1307[P]	**Foxgrove (77)** (RJPrice) **10-10-8**(7) MissEJJones (prom to 7th: t.o whn p.u bef 3 out)		P	20/1	—	—
1179[U]	**Strange Ways (74)** (HJManners) **8-10-5**(7)ow5 MrACharles-Jones (bhd: mstke 5th: t.o 7th: p.u bef 3 out)		P	40/1	—	—
975[7]	**Salcombe Harbour (NZ) (69)** (DrPPritchard) **12-10-0**(7) DrPPritchard (bhd fr 4 out: t.o whn p.u bef 2 out)		P	50/1	—	—

(SP 130.0%) **13 Rn**

4m 51.4 (21.40) CSF £113.99 CT £485.56 TOTE £18.00: £5.50 £2.40 £1.70 (£55.60) Trio £128.50; £92.36 to Wincanton 21/11/96 OWNER Pipers Partnership (AMESBURY) BRED Mrs O. M. Lusty

LONG HANDICAP Prudent Peggy 10-4 Ennistymon (IRE) 10-2 Rhoman Fun (IRE) 10-4 Opal's Tenspot 10-4 Strange Ways 9-12 Salcombe Harbour (NZ) 9-8

Poppets Pet, three times a runner-up in small handicap chases in the early part of last season, was helped by Where's Willie going wrong nearing the final fence. (11/1: op 6/1)

Prudent Peggy, who has slipped to a mark which meant she was out of the handicap here, showed improved form on ground which was still not really soft enough for her. (10/1)

Wayuphill won her novice chase at Fairyhouse on ground much softer than this and is now being given a chance by the Handicapper. (4/1)

Where's Willie (FR), 5lb higher than when second in a novice handicap at Doncaster in February, appeared to have matters under control when misfortune struck nearing the final fence. (4/1: 3/1-9/2)

Opal's Tenspot needs further than this nowadays. (20/1)

1146 Northern Optimist wants faster ground, especially over an extended trip like this. (4/1)

Millies Own (5/1: op 3/1)

1446 BRIDSTOW (S) H'CAP HURDLE (0-90) (4-Y.O+) (Class G)

2-00 (2-00) **2m 1f (9 hdls)** £1,940.00 (£540.00: £260.00) GOING: 0.15 sec per fur (G)

				SP	RR	SF
1198[3]	**Glowing Path (82)** (RJHodges) **6-11-2**(7) JHarris (a gng wl: led on bit 3 out: rdn out)	—	**1**	3/1[2]	74	31
128[8]	**Lawnswood Junior (87)** (JLSpearing) **9-12-0** DBridgwater (hld up & bhd: hdwy 5th: chsd wnr appr 2 out: no imp)	13	**2**	7/2[3]	67	24
1198[4]	**Scalp 'em (IRE) (59)** (DrPPritchard) **8-10-0** DrPPritchard (chsd ldr tl appr 4th: sn lost pl: styd on fr 3 out)	1½	**3**	14/1	37	—
1337[4]	**My Harvinski (76)** (IRJones) **6-10-10**(7) MissEJJones (led tl appr 4th: led 5th to 3 out: sn wknd)	9	**4**	12/1	46	3
1198[2]	**Alice's Mirror (73)** (KBishop) **7-11-0** RJohnson (prom to 4th: n.d after)	8	**5**	6/4[1]	35	—
1299[7]	**Bresil (USA) (59)** (KRBurke) **7-9-7**(7) MarkBrown (chsd ldrs tl wknd 4th)	9	**6**	8/1	13	—
	Them Times (IRE) (66) (FJordan) **7-10-7** SWynne (hld up & bhd: mstke 5th: sn t.o)	23	**7**	20/1	—	—
1166[4]	**Against The Clock (59)** (CLPopham) **4-9-7b**(7) TO'Connor (prom: led appr 4th: hdd 5th: mstke 6th: sn wknd)	2	**8**	25/1	—	—
				(SP 121.3%)	**8 Rn**	

4m 4.2 (11.20) CSF £14.18 CT £119.07 TOTE £3.40: £1.60 £1.10 £2.50 (£17.00) OWNER Mr P. Slade (SOMERTON) BRED M. B. O'Gorman
LONG HANDICAP Scalp 'em (IRE) 9-13 Bresil (USA) 9-8 Against The Clock 9-7
No bid

1198 Glowing Path could well have found the ground too testing at Newton Abbot last time and had no problem with a 6lb higher mark. (3/1: 7/4-100/30)
Lawnswood Junior was always playing second fiddle. (7/2)
Scalp 'em (IRE) was running off a mark 4lb lower than when finishing nine lengths behind the winner in the heavy ground last time. (14/1: op 8/1)
1337 My Harvinski, already due to go down 2lb, found the winner galloping all over him three from home. (12/1: op 8/1)
1198 Alice's Mirror finished just in front of the winner on 6lb worse terms at Newton Abbot, but the ground was much more testing there. (6/4)

1447 BOGMARSH NOVICES' CHASE (5-Y.O+) (Class E)

2-30 (2-30) **3m 1f 110y (19 fncs)** £3,009.30 (£911.40: £445.20: £212.10) GOING: 0.15 sec per fur (G)

				SP	RR	SF
1281*	**Don du Cadran (FR) (99)** (CaptTAForster) **7-11-5** AThornton (hld up: hdwy 12th: rdn & chal whn lft clr 2 out)	—	**1**	6/1[3]	110	19
	Mount Serrath (IRE) (100) (CREgerton) **8-10-12** JAMcCarthy (lw: hld up: hdwy to ld 11th: hdd 15th: btn whn lft 2nd 2 out)	7	**2**	8/1	99	8
1285[P]	**Cardinal Rule (IRE) (70)** (MissVenetiaWilliams) **7-10-12** RFarrant (prom: mstke 14th: blnd 4 out: wknd qckly: no ch whn j.b lft last)	25	**3**	25/1	83	—
795[4]	**Newtown Rosie (IRE)** (MissAEEmbiricos) **7-10-7** JRyan (led 3rd to 11th: wknd qckly after 4 out)	3½	**4**	6/1[3]	76	—
	Snowdon Lily (PRWebber) **5-10-2**(3) EHusband (in rr tl b.d 7th)		**B**	33/1	—	—
	Bonnifer (IRE) (MJWilkinson) **7-10-12** ILawrence (bkwd: bhd tl fell 7th)		**F**	50/1	—	—
	What's Your Story (IRE) (DNicholson) **7-10-12** RJohnson (hld up: mstke 10th: hdwy 12th: led after 4 out tl fell 2 out)		**F**	7/4[1]	—	—
	Picketstone (PRWebber) **9-10-12** MrPScott (bit bkwd: prom tl wknd 13th: t.o whn p.u bef 15th)		**P**	50/1	—	—
1285[P]	**Mingus (USA) (83)** (RHBuckler) **9-10-12** BPowell (lost tch 12th: t.o whn p.u bef 15th)		**P**	20/1	—	—
1037[4]	**Swing Quartet (IRE) (94)** (NATwiston-Davies) **6-10-7** TJenks (lw: led to 3rd: wknd qckly after 11th: sn t.o: p.u bef 15th)		**P**	7/1	—	—
	Jultara (IRE) (100) (JACEdwards) **7-10-12** JRKavanagh (hld up: hdwy 12th: led 15th tl after 4 out: 3rd & wkng whn blnd bdly & uns rdr 3 out)		**U**	7/2[2]	—	—
				(SP 126.2%)	**11 Rn**	

6m 31.6 (21.60) CSF £52.44 TOTE £7.70: £1.80 £2.90 £8.90 (£57.60) Trio £110.20; £141.31 to Wincanton 21/11/96 OWNER Lord Cadogan (LUDLOW) BRED Mme Pierre Grolleau
WEIGHT FOR AGE 5yo-2lb

1281* Don du Cadran (FR) was again helped by the departure of a rival at the penultimate fence, but did not appear to be travelling best on this occasion. (6/1)
Mount Serrath (IRE) can win a race on this evidence given that his jumping problems are behind him. (8/1: 13/2-10/1)
Cardinal Rule (IRE) stopped to nothing after making a nonsense of the final ditch. (25/1)
795 Newtown Rosie (IRE) had no hard-luck story this time and it should be remembered that Father Sky has probably been over-rated. (6/1)
What's Your Story (IRE) seemed to have the edge on the winner when departing at the difficult penultimate fence. (7/4)
Jultara (IRE), his trainer's final runner, had just begun to struggle when giving his pilot no chance of staying aboard. (7/2)

1448 BISHOPS FROME NOVICES' H'CAP HURDLE (0-100) (4-Y.O+) (Class E)

3-00 (3-01) **2m 3f 110y (11 hdls)** £2,388.00 (£668.00: £324.00) GOING: 0.15 sec per fur (G)

				SP	RR	SF
1327[2]	**Lets Be Frank (84)** (NoelChance) **5-11-10** RJohnson (a.p: led appr 3 out: rdn out)	—	**1**	2/1[1]	79	3
591[5]	**Raven's Roost (IRE) (76)** (GEJones) **5-11-2** PMcLoughlin (hld up: gd hdwy after 6th: ev ch 3 out: one pce fr 2 out)	9	**2**	7/1[3]	64	—
1322[7]	**Clod Hopper (IRE) (75)** (WRMuir) **6-10-10**(5) ABates (a.p: led 6th tl appr 3 out: sn btn)	2	**3**	10/1	61	—
	Arioso (62) (JLNeedham) **8-9-13**(3) GHogan (hdwy appr 7th: wknd appr 3 out)	10	**4**	33/1	40	—
594*	**Killing Time (78)** (DBurchell) **5-11-4** DJBurchell (nvr nr to chal)	1¼	**5**	7/1[3]	55	—
	Steel Gem (IRE) (76) (PMRich) **7-10-9**(7) MGriffiths (lw: nvr nr ldrs)	3½	**6**	8/1	50	—
1145[9]	**Out of The Blue (63)** (MWEckley) **4-9-10v**(7) JMogford (lw: prom tl wknd appr 7th)	2½	**7**	16/1	35	—
1200[4]	**Otter Prince (60)** (TRGeorge) **7-10-0** RFarrant (prom tl mstke 7th: t.o)	22	**8**	6/1[2]	14	—
	Parisian (65) (JABennett) **11-10-5** LHarvey (hdwy 7th: wknd after 8th: t.o)	¾	**9**	20/1	18	—
824[5]	**Young Tess (76)** (IRBrown) **6-11-2** MrABrown (a bhd: t.o)	¾	**10**	12/1	29	—
	Indian Temple (75) (KBishop) **5-11-1** RGreene (bit bkwd: a bhd: t.o)	29	**11**	20/1	4	—
718[F]	**Country Minstrel (IRE) (84)** (SADouch) **5-11-7**(3) DWalsh (prom to 7th: bhd whn p.u bef 3 out)		**P**	12/1	—	—
	Nuns Lucy (65) (FJordan) **5-10-5** SWynne (lost tch 5th: t.o whn p.u bef 7th)		**P**	25/1	—	—
	Forburies (IRE) (62) (APJames) **7-10-2** BPowell (bkwd: a bhd: t.o whn p.u bef 3 out)		**P**	50/1	—	—
	Althrey Aristocrat (IRE) (65) (FLloyd) **6-10-5** SMcNeill (led to 6th: sn wknd: t.o whn p.u bef 2 out)		**P**	50/1	—	—
				(SP 134.3%)	**15 Rn**	

4m 52.5 (21.50) CSF £17.98 CT £117.44 TOTE £2.60: £1.10 £2.40 £2.60 (£10.40) Trio £28.50 OWNER Mrs M. M. Stobart (LAMBOURN) BRED Malcolm Armitage Penney

1327 Lets Be Frank, again raised 2lb, was already due to go up a further 1lb and seems suited to this longer trip. (2/1)

591 Raven's Roost (IRE) shot himself in the foot by running a big race from way out of the handicap last time and was running off a mark 17lb higher than the second of his two victories. (7/1: op 9/2)
1135* Clod Hopper (IRE), penalised 10lb for winning a soft race at Ascot, was 2lb lower after flopping over three miles next time. He was already due to go down another couple of pounds. (10/1)
Arioso fell at the first when tried over fences at the end of last season. (33/1)
594* Killing Time may not have been suited by the give underfoot. (7/1: op 4/1)
Young Tess (12/1: op 8/1)
636 Country Minstrel (IRE) (12/1: op 7/1)

1449 BRIDGE SOLLARS NOVICES' H'CAP CHASE (0-95) (4-Y.O+) (Class F)
3-30 (3-34) **2m (12 fncs)** £2,814.00 (£852.00: £416.00: £198.00) GOING: 0.15 sec per fur (G)

				SP	RR	SF
1254^{3}	**Scottish Bambi (78)** (PRWebber) **8-10-11** AThornton (hld up: hdwy 7th: led appr 3 out: sn clr: easily)	—	1	7/4^{1}	98+	22
	Poucher (IRE) (95) (CaptTAForster) **6-12-0** SWynne (hld up: hdwy 8th: wnt 2nd appr last: no ch w wnr)	10	2	5/1^{3}	105	29
	Northern Singer (71) (RJHodges) **6-10-4** PHolley (bkwd: w ldr: led 4th: j.slowly 5th: hit 7th: hdd appr 3 out: sn btn)	12	3	9/1	69	—
1041^{5}	**King's Shilling (USA) (82)** (HOliver) **9-11-1** JacquiOliver (prom to 9th: no ch whn blnd 2 out)	8	4	10/1	72	—
917^{U}	**Tenayestelign (85)** (DMarks) **8-11-4** JAMcCarthy (nt j.w: hld up & bhd: no ch whn blnd 2 out)	9	5	10/1	66	—
	Knowing (76) (PGWatkins) **9-10-2**(7) MrAWintle (bkwd: a bhd)	11	6	33/1	46	—
1189^{P}	**Cherry Orchid (69)** (JLNeedham) **9-9-13**(3)ow2 GHogan (bit bkwd: mstke 8th: a bhd: t.o)	16	7	33/1	23	—
1118^{6}	**The Fence Shrinker (70)** (DMcCain) **5-10-0**(3)ow3 DWalsh (bkwd: hld up: hdwy 5th: wknd 8th: t.o)	18	8	33/1	6	—
1331^{2}	**Ashmead Rambler (IRE) (68)** (PJHobbs) **6-10-1**ow1 CMaude (prom: 2nd whn carried out by loose horse appr 4 out)		C	7/1	—	—
	Wot No Gin (67) (AJWilson) **7-10-0** RJohnson (bhd: mstke 6th: hdwy 7th: in tch whn fell 4 out)		F	20/1	—	—
885^{P}	**Baxworthy Lord (68)** (CLPopham) **5-9-8**(7)ow1 TO'Connor (prom: hit 1st: blnd & uns rdr 2nd)		U	33/1	—	—
903*	**Bishops Castle (IRE) (87)** (RGFrost) **8-11-6** JFrost (led to 4th: 2nd whn blnd & uns rdr 5th)		U	11/4^{2}	—	—

(SP 136.9%) **12 Rn**

4m 1.8 (10.80) CSF £12.61 CT £62.99 TOTE £2.70: £1.50 £1.40 £4.30 (£9.40) Trio £52.90 OWNER Mr William Kelly (BANBURY) BRED Cheveley Park Stud Ltd
LONG HANDICAP Cherry Orchid 9-7 The Fence Shrinker 9-7 Wot No Gin 9-12 Baxworthy Lord 9-7
1254 Scottish Bambi, a well-backed favourite, never put a foot wrong on this occasion and should continue to progress. (7/4: 5/2-13/8)
Poucher (IRE) settled much better and his jumping benefited greatly as a result. He looks one to keep on the right side. (5/1: 5/2-11/2)
Northern Singer, on his chasing bow, had a long look at the first ditch, and should come on for the run. (9/1: 6/1-10/1)
1041 King's Shilling (USA) did win over hurdles on the soft, but really needs a faster surface. (10/1: op 6/1)
917 Tenayestelign looks harshly treated for winning a non-event at Ludlow and the change of ground was also not in her favour. (10/1: op 5/1)
1331 Ashmead Rambler (IRE) was unluckily forced around the wings of the last ditch. (7/1: op 9/2)
Wot No Gin, on his fencing debut, was just getting into the picture when possibly distracted by the incident with the loose horses at the final ditch. A longer trip will help. (20/1)
903* Bishops Castle (IRE) (11/4: 2/1-3/1)

1450 WEATHERBYS 'STARS OF TOMORROW' STANDARD N.H. FLAT RACE (4, 5 & 6-Y.O F & M) (Class H)
4-00 (4-05) **2m 1f** £1,395.20 (£387.20: £185.60)

				SP	RR	SF
	Melstock Meggie (MrsJPitman) **6-10-11**(3) GHogan (bit bkwd: a gng wl: led on bit over 2f out: comf)	—	1	8/1	56 f	—
1190^{5}	**Lovely Rascal** (JJO'Neill) **4-10-9**(5) RMcGrath (hld up: gd hdwy fnl 3f: nt trble wnr)	2	2	9/4^{1}	54 f	—
1177^{4}	**Kosheen (IRE)** (MissHCKnight) **5-10-7**(7) MrAWintle (hld up: stdy hdwy 9f out: sltly outpcd 5f out: styd on one pce fnl 3f)	1¼	3	9/2^{3}	53 f	—
	Where's Miranda (GMMcCourt) **4-10-7**(7) RHobson (bit bkwd: bhd tl gd hdwy fnl 3f: nvr nrr)	nk	4	20/1	53 f	—
1177^{3}	**Just Jasmine** (KBishop) **4-10-7**(7) GSupple (prom: led 7f out tl over 2f out: wknd fnl f)	7	5	5/2^{2}	46 f	—
	Winnetka Gal (IRE) (NATwiston-Davies) **4-10-7**(7) LSuthern (bit bkwd: hdwy on ins 10f out: wknd 2f out)	2	6	13/2	44 f	—
	Fun While It Lasts (CaptTAForster) **5-10-9**(5) ABates (bkwd: a bhd)	20	7	11/1	25 f	—
1190^{8}	**Lady Rosebury** (RJPrice) **6-10-7**(7) MGriffiths (hld up: hrd rdn 7f out: bhd fnl 5f: t.o)	16	8	50/1	10 f	—
	Tomorrows Harvest (RJHodges) **4-10-7**(7) JHarris (bhd fnl 5f: t.o)	15	9	20/1	—	—
	Tinker's Cuss (APJones) **5-10-11**(3) DWalsh (bit bkwd: a bhd: t.o fnl 6f)	9	10	33/1	—	—
	Pollerton's Dream (MrsDThomas) **6-10-11**(3) GuyLewis (bkwd: prom 11f: t.o)	1¼	11	50/1	—	—
	Silver Quill (GBBalding) **5-10-13**(7)ow6 MrABalding (bkwd: dropped rr 8f out: sn t.o)	9	12	12/1	—	—
1177^{14}	**Let You Know (IRE)** (TRGeorge) **6-10-7**(7) CBHynes (led 10f: wknd qckly 5f out: t.o)	1¼	13	50/1	—	—

(SP 136.3%) **13 Rn**

4m 1.0 CSF £28.49 TOTE £7.40: £2.00 £1.20 £2.70 (£12.60) Trio £33.80 OWNER Mrs Kay Birchenhough (UPPER LAMBOURN) BRED Mrs Kay Birchenhough
Melstock Meggie fulfilled the promise shown at Uttoxeter over eighteen months ago and has obviously had her problems since. (8/1: op 7/2)
1190 Lovely Rascal clearly stays well, but was never going to bother the winner. (9/4: 3/1-2/1)
1177 Kosheen (IRE), out of a useful Irish hurdler, kept staying on and should get further when put over hurdles. (9/2: op 3/1)
Where's Miranda, whose dam won over hurdles and stayed two and a half miles, did all her best work in the latter stages. (20/1)
1177 Just Jasmine had finished twelve lengths ahead of the third at Exeter. (5/2)
Winnetka Gal (IRE) found lack of peak-fitness taking its toll on the home turn. (13/2: 11/4-7/1)
Fun While It Lasts (11/1: 7/1-12/1)
Silver Quill (12/1: 5/1-14/1)

T/Jkpt: Not won; £2,287.75 to Warwick 21/11/96. T/Plpt: £467.70 (23.52 Tckts). T/Qdpt: £26.80 (43.35 Tckts). KH

1191-KEMPTON (R-H) (Good to soft)
Wednesday November 20th

Race 4 - one fence omitted
WEATHER: overcast

1451 UXBRIDGE NOVICES' CONDITIONAL H'CAP HURDLE (0-100) (4-Y.O+) (Class F)
12-50 (12-50) **2m (8 hdls)** £1,960.30 (£550.80: £268.90) GOING minus 0.10 sec per fur (G)

				SP	RR	SF
961*	**Canary Falcon (87)** (RJO'Sullivan) **5-10-12**(7) NWillmington (hld up in tch: led appr 2 out: drvn out)	—	1	13/2^{3}	68	—
1168*	**Sailep (FR) (88)** (RJHodges) **4-11-6** TDascombe (hld up: hdwy to chse ldr 3 out: hrd rdn appr 2 out: one pce)	2	2	7/1	67	—
1253^{2}	**Ragamuffin Romeo (82)** (HSawyer) **7-11-0** DJKavanagh (hld up: hdwy 5th: hrd rdn 6th: one pce)	3½	3	6/1^{2}	58	—
	Prime of Life (IRE) (90) (JMPEustace) **6-11-5**(3) CRae (bit bkwd: in rr: sme hdwy appr 2 out: hrd rdn appr last: styd on flat)	½	4	11/1	65	—
1168^{2}	**Shift Again (IRE) (83)** (OSherwood) **4-10-12b**(3) DThomas (led to 2nd: led again 4th: hdd appr 2 out: wknd appr last)	2	5	13/2^{3}	56	—
1165^{4}	**Bella Sedona (96)** (LadyHerries) **4-11-9**(5) JPower (bhd fr 5th)	25	6	8/1	44	—
	Nothing Doing (IRE) (68) (WJMusson) **7-10-0** KGaule (nt j.w: prom: lft in ld 3rd: hdd next: wknd 5th)	9	7	4/1^{1}	7	—
1183^{2}	**Red Light (85)** (JRJenkins) **4-10-12v**(5) NTEgan (a bhd)	10	8	9/1	14	—
	All Over Red Rover (70) (AWCarroll) **4-10-2** ChrisWebb (bkwd: led 2nd tl blnd & uns rdr 3rd)		U	14/1	—	—
				(SP 109.6%)	**9 Rn**	

4m 1.0 (19.00) CSF £44.31 CT £239.94 TOTE £9.50: £2.20 £2.20 £1.40 (£16.50) Trio £31.80 OWNER Mr L. Pipe (WHITCOMBE) BRED Gainsborough Stud Management Ltd

OFFICIAL EXPLANATION **Nothing Doing (IRE): hung right-handed throughout the race.**

IN-FOCUS: **Nathan Willmington was riding his first winner.**

961* Canary Falcon travelled like a winner throughout. He took it up approaching the penultimate hurdle and, although very tired, saw it out well. (13/2)

1168* Sailep (FR) moved up at halfway. He had every chance over the final three flights but, although keeping on, never looked like getting to the winner. (7/1)

1253 Ragamuffin Romeo ran rather in snatches and only had the one pace to offer over the final two flights. (6/1)

Prime of Life (IRE) looked in need of this, but made some headway up the straight to show promise for the future. (11/1)

1168 Shift Again (IRE) cut out the early running, but was beaten before the second last. (13/2)

1165 Bella Sedona never gave her supporters any hope. (8/1: op 5/1)

Nothing Doing (IRE) jumped poorly and never looked like being involved in the finish. (4/1: 3/1-9/2)

1183 Red Light (9/1: op 6/1)

All Over Red Rover (14/1: op 25/1)

1452 STAINES NOVICES' CHASE (5-Y.O+) (Class D)
1-20 (1-21) **2m (13 fncs)** £3,566.25 (£1,080.00: £527.50: £251.25) GOING: 0.81 sec per fur (S)

				SP	RR	SF
1254*	**Mulligan (IRE)** (DNicholson) **6-11-6** AMaguire (lw: j.w: led to 4th: w ldr 8th: led next: clr 3 out: easily)	—	1	4/6^{1}	136++	39
1009^{3}	**Wilde Music (IRE)** (CPEBrooks) **6-11-0** DGallagher (racd in mod 3rd pl: hdwy fr 2 out: wnt 2nd last: kpt on)	11	2	12/1^{3}	119	22
	Feel the Power (IRE) (128) (KCBailey) **8-11-0** CO'Dwyer (w ldr to 3rd: led 4th: hdd 9th: wknd 2 out)	6	3	6/4^{2}	113	16
	Marksman Sparks (DrDChesney) **6-11-0** SBurrough (mstke 1st: a bhd)	16	4	50/1	97	—
				(SP 109.7%)	**4 Rn**	

4m 2.9 (18.90) CSF £6.86 TOTE £1.40 (£2.80) OWNER Lady Harris (TEMPLE GUITING) BRED Sandford Bloodstock Ltd

1254* Mulligan (IRE) put up a superb round of jumping and is a high-class novice. (4/6)

1009 Wilde Music (IRE) appeared unable to go the early pace, but kept on for a distant second. (12/1: 8/1-14/1)

Feel the Power (IRE) did not jump particularly fluently and was a tired horse up the straight. (6/4)

1453 E.B.F. 'N.H.' (QUALIFIER) NOVICES' HURDLE (4, 5 & 6-Y.O) (Class D)
1-50 (1-51) **2m (8 hdls)** £2,969.00 (£834.00: £407.00) GOING minus 0.10 sec per fur (G)

				SP	RR	SF
	Not For Turning (IRE) (OSherwood) **5-11-0** JOsborne (led to 2nd: remained prom: rdn appr 2 out: hit 2 out: led flat: drvn out)	—	1	3/1^{1}	73	—
	Royal Event (DRGandolfo) **5-11-0** AMaguire (led 5th: hdd flat: r.o)	hd	2	7/1	73	—
	Halona (100) (CPEBrooks) **6-10-9** DGallagher (s.s: took keen hold: hld up in rr: hdwy appr 2 out: styd on strly flat)	3	3	11/2^{2}	65	—
	Far Springs (IRE) (KCBailey) **5-11-0** CO'Dwyer (hld up: hdwy 3 out: ev ch 2 out: rdn appr last: one pce)	¾	4	12/1	69	—
	Bay Fair (JRBosley) **4-10-9** MRichards (hld up: hdwy appr 2 out: shkn up appr last: styd on flat)	3½	5	33/1	61	—
	Strong Paladin (IRE) (JTGifford) **5-11-0** PHide (hld up in tch: rdn appr 2 out: one pce)	½	6	6/1^{3}	65	—
	Tremplin (IRE) (NJHenderson) **5-10-9** MAFitzgerald (chsd ldrs: ev ch 2 out: wknd appr last)	3	7	12/1	57	—
1036^{9}	**Sir Dante (IRE)** (RRowe) **5-11-0** DO'Sullivan (prom tl wknd appr 2 out)	2½	8	10/1	60	—
	Line of Conquest (RJHodges) **6-11-0** NWilliamson (bit bkwd: led 2nd to 5th: wkng whn blnd last)	7	9	8/1	53	—
	Mr Hemp (AGFoster) **4-11-0** DerekByrne (bit bkwd: a bhd)	8	10	66/1	45	—
	Physical Fun (AGBlackmore) **5-11-0** DSkyrme (bit bkwd: bhd fr 5th)	1¼	11	66/1	43	—
1065^{2}	**Shannon Lad (IRE) (77)** (AWCarroll) **6-11-0** DMorris (mid div tl rdn & wknd appr 2 out)	5	12	16/1	38	—
1124^{8}	**Red Tel (IRE)** (MCPipe) **4-11-0** APMcCoy (in tch to 6th)	13	13	14/1	25	—
1124^{6}	**My Shenandoah (IRE)** (HOliver) **5-11-0** VSlattery (s.s: a bhd)	nk	14	20/1	25	—
	Derring Jack (AWCarroll) **5-11-0** TJMurphy (in tch to 6th: bhd whn fell last)		F	66/1	—	—
	Teluk (IRE) (MrsJPitman) **5-11-0** WMarston (bit bkwd: a bhd: t.o whn p.u bef 2 out)		P	33/1	—	—
				(SP 130.4%)	**16 Rn**	

3m 57.4 (15.40) CSF £24.77 TOTE £4.70: £2.40 £2.80 £2.30 (£25.70) Trio £37.90 OWNER Mr Charles Engel (UPPER LAMBOURN) BRED Ronald O'Neill

Not For Turning (IRE), favourite for his bumper last year and again today, fulfilled that with a game display. (3/1)

Royal Event was always travelling well and, early in the straight, looked the most likely winner. Headed on the run-in by the favourite, he kept on gamely and can find a similar event. (7/1: 5/1-8/1)

Halona ran an eyecatching race. Taking a keen grip, her rider was at pains to settle her and she had a lot to do turning for home. Although she stayed on well, she could never reach the first two in time, but there is definitely a race in her. (11/2: 7/2-6/1)

Far Springs (IRE) moved through promisingly turning for home, but found a quickening burst beyond him. (12/1: op 7/1)
Bay Fair ran a promising race, making good headway all the way up the straight, and is one to watch out for in a similar event. (33/1)
Strong Paladin (IRE) had his chance approaching two out, but could not find a change of gear. (6/1)
Sir Dante (IRE) (10/1: 8/1-12/1)

1454 LIMBER HILL LIMITED H'CAP CHASE (0-145) (5-Y.O+) (Class B)

2-20 (2-25) **2m 4f 110y (16 fncs)** £4,715.20 (£1,426.60: £695.80: £330.40) GOING: 0.81 sec per fur (S)

				SP	RR	SF
	Trying Again (140) (DRGandolfo) **8-11-3** JOsborne (a.p: chsd ldr 10th: led 6 out: rdn appr last: r.o)	—	1	$15/8^1$	133	65
	Old Bridge (IRE) (132) (AndrewTurnell) **8-10-9** NWilliamson (hld up: hdwy 6 out: chsd wnr appr 2 out: one pce)	7	2	$7/2^2$	120	52
936^4	**Lackendara (130)** (MissHCKnight) **9-10-7** BFenton (led: hdd 6 out: rdn appr 3 out: one pce)	4	3	50/1	114	46
1321*	**Super Tactics (IRE) (130)** (RHAlner) **8-10-4**(3) PHenley (hld up: mstke 7th: wknd appr 3 out: bhd whn blnd 2 out)	22	4	$9/2^3$	97	29
	Suny Bay (IRE) (144) (CPEBrooks) **7-11-7** DGallagher (bit bkwd: chsd ldr 6th to 10th: wknd appr 3 out:b.b.v)	5	5	$9/2^3$	107	39
1070*	**Wise Approach (132)** (KCBailey) **9-10-9** CO'Dwyer (lw: fell 1st: dead)		F	7/1	—	—
	Bo Knows Best (IRE) (130) (GLMoore) **7-10-7** APMcCoy (bit bkwd: chsd ldr tl fell 5th)		F	20/1	—	—
				(SP 112.6%)		**7 Rn**

5m 15.4 (14.40) CSF £8.45 TOTE £2.70: £1.30 £2.40 (£5.50) OWNER Mr W. H. Dore (WANTAGE) BRED R. D. M. Sharp
LONG HANDICAP Super Tactics (IRE) 9-13 Lackendara 9-9 Bo Knows Best (IRE) 9-12
OFFICIAL EXPLANATION **Old Bridge (IRE): gurgled during the race.**
Suny Bay (IRE): bled from the nose.
Trying Again, a very useful hurdler two seasons ago, is beginning to look as if he will be just as good over fences. His jumping got better through the race and he is starting to look a more than useful chaser. (15/8)
Old Bridge (IRE) ran well on his seasonal debut here and moved through threateningly early in the straight, but found the winner holding too many guns. (7/2)
Lackendara ran well on his return to chasing, cutting out much of the running and keeping on nicely once headed. (50/1)
1321* Super Tactics (IRE) did not jump as well as usual and was a spent force from the fourth from home. (9/2)
Suny Bay (IRE) ran disappointingly, getting badly outpaced over the final four fences. It later transpired he had broken a blood-vessel. (9/2: op 9/4)

1455 HANWORTH H'CAP HURDLE (0-130) (4-Y.O+) (Class C)

2-50 (2-55) **2m 5f (10 hdls)** £3,501.25 (£1,060.00: £517.50: £246.25) GOING minus 0.10 sec per fur (G)

				SP	RR	SF
1374^3	**Tim (IRE) (104)** (JRJenkins) **6-10-6** JOsborne (hld up: hdwy to chse ldr 3 out: led gng wl 2 out: clr last: pushed out)	—	1	$15/2^3$	85	48
1255^2	**High Grade (113)** (MissSJWilton) **8-11-1** NWilliamson (lw: a.p: rdn appr 2 out: r.o one pce flat)	5	2	8/1	90	53
	The Toiseach (IRE) (112) (JRFanshawe) **5-11-0** PHide (chsd ldr to 3 out: rdn appr 2 out: one pce)	2	3	$3/1^2$	88	51
	Chaprassi (IRE) (122) (MCPipe) **7-11-10** APMcCoy (lw: led: sn clr: rdn 3 out: hdd & blnd 2 out: wknd appr last)	9	4	$8/11^1$	91	54
	Welshman (111) (MBlanshard) **10-10-13** DGallagher (sn bhd: t.o fr 5th)	dist	5	20/1	—	—
				(SP 110.5%)		**5 Rn**

5m 12.3 (20.30) CSF £48.49 TOTE £8.50: £2.00 £3.90 (£12.70) OWNER Mr P. W. Piper (ROYSTON) BRED C. Farrell
1374 Tim (IRE), although held up, looked the winner a long way out. He moved through smoothly to lead at the penultimate hurdle and had no trouble drawing clear. (15/2: 5/1-8/1)
1255 High Grade ran a sound race. Never far away, he could not match the winner's burst of speed. (8/1: 6/1-9/1)
The Toiseach (IRE) ran a sound race on this seasonal debut, and can find a small handicap. (3/1: op 2/1)
Chaprassi (IRE) appeared to go too fast for his own good and was a spent force when blundering at the second last. (8/11: evens-4/6)
Welshman could never go the pace. (20/1)

1456 HALLIFORD NOVICES' CHASE (5-Y.O+) (Class D)

3-20 (3-22) **3m (19 fncs)** £2,323.30 (£2,323.30: £527.50: £251.25) GOING: 0.81 sec per fur (S)

				SP	RR	SF
1195*	**Fine Thyne (IRE)** (MrsAJPerrett) **7-11-6** MAFitzgerald (hld up: chsd ldr 3 out: led last: hrd rdn flat: jnd line)	—	1	$6/4^1$	123	55
	Berude Not to (IRE) (OSherwood) **7-11-0** JOsborne (chsd ldr: led 15th: hdd last: hrd rdn flat: r.o to jn wnr line)	—	1	$7/4^2$	117+	49
	Apple John (RHAlner) **7-10-11**(3) PHenley (swtg: j.lft: led: clr 3rd to 10th: hdd 15th: wknd appr 2 out)	dist	3	$4/1^3$	—	—
1192^3	**Ourownfellow (IRE)** (RCurtis) **7-11-0** DMorris (in tch: blnd 13th: sn wknd: t.o)	dist	4	6/1	—	—
				(SP 110.6%)		**4 Rn**

6m 18.9 (23.90) CSF £2.19 £2.32 TOTE £1.20 £1.10: (£1.70) OWNER Mr Peter Wiegand (PULBUROUGH)/Mr G. Addiscott (UPPER LAMBOURN) BRED Minch Bloodstock in Ireland/Ronald O'Neill in Ireland
1195* Fine Thyne (IRE), held up under a confident ride, looked like winning cosily when leading at the last, but found Berude Not to rallying strongly and only held on to share the spoils. (6/4)
Berude Not to (IRE) ran a fine race here. jumping safely and well, he took it up down the far side, but looked beaten when headed by the favourite at the last. To his credit, he rallied gamely and would have won solely in another stride. (7/4: evens-15/8)
Apple John jumped left throughout and needs to improve his jumping if he is to fulfil his potential. (4/1)
1192 Ourownfellow (IRE) was soon well behind. (6/1)

1457 FRENCH STREET STANDARD OPEN N.H. FLAT RACE (4, 5 & 6-Y.O) (Class H)

3-50 (3-54) **2m** £1,416.50 (£394.00: £189.50)

				SP	RR	SF
1289^2	**Quini Eagle (FR)** (MCPipe) **4-11-4** APMcCoy (mde all: rdn over 1f out: r.o)	—	1	$11/4^1$	64 f	—
	Jack Gallagher (MissBSanders) **5-11-4** MRichards (a.p: chsd wnr 5f out: rdn 2f out: r.o)	1¾	2	12/1	62 f	—
	Shekels (IRE) (CPEBrooks) **5-10-11**(7) MBerry (in rr: hdwy over 3f out: kpt on one pce ins fnl f)	6	3	16/1	56 f	—
	Military Law (MissHCKnight) **5-11-4** TJMurphy (bit bkwd: a.p: rdn over 2f out: one pce)	½	4	16/1	56 f	—
	Stanmore (IRE) (CPEBrooks) **4-11-4** DGallagher (hdwy ½-wy: rdn over 2f out: one pce)	2	5	14/1	54 f	—
	Stormyfairweather (IRE) (NJHenderson) **4-11-4** MAFitzgerald (hld up: hdwy 6f out: one pce fnl 3f)	4	6	$7/2^2$	50 f	—
	Charlie Banker (IRE) (KRBurke) **4-11-4** ALarnach (bit bkwd: in rr: hdwy 3f out: one pce)	4	7	25/1	46 f	—
	Quick Bowler (IRE) (DNicholson) **4-11-1**(3) RMassey (bit bkwd: nvr nrr)	3	8	6/1	43 f	—
	Sidanora (IRE) (KCBailey) **6-11-4** CO'Dwyer (bit bkwd: mid div: effrt 6f out: wknd 2f out)	6	9	7/1	37 f	—

Mike's Music (IRE) (DMGrissell) **5-11-4** BFenton (nvr nrr) ....5 **10** 33/1 32 f —
Lively Encounter (IRE) (MrsMerritaJones) **5-11-4** DerekByrne (mid div: sme hdwy whn bdly hmpd over 3f out: nt rcvr) ....1¼ **11** 5/1 3 31 f —
Normandy Duke (NZ) (CJMann) **4-11-1**(3) JMagee (w'like, q lt made: in rr: bhd whn rn wd 4f out: nvr nrr)....1¼ **12** 20/1 29 f —
Feebee Five (SPCWoods) **4-10-13** PHide (neat, unf: hld up: hdwy & n.m.r on ins over 3f out: no hdwy fnl 2f) ....3 **13** 12/1 21 f —
1362[14] **Jackho** (MissJBower) **4-11-1**(3) TDascombe (chsd ldrs: wkng whn hmpd over 3f out)....hd **14** 33/1 26 f —
Fiddler's Leap (IRE) (MissHCKnight) **4-11-4** JOsborne (unf: str, deep g: bit bkwd: bhd fnl 4f) ....hd **15** 6/1 26 f —
Derrys Prerogative (AWCarroll) **6-11-4** JRailton (chsd ldrs: wkng whn hmpd over 3f out)....10 **16** 33/1 16 f —
Spring Blade (SDow) **4-11-4** ADicken (bhd fnl 5f: t.o)....25 **17** 33/1 — —
Persian Sunset (IRE) (MissJBower) **4-10-10**(3) KGaule (bit bkwd: chsd wnr 11f: sn wknd: t.o) ....dist **18** 33/1 — —
Sou Sou Westerly (IRE) (CWeedon) **5-11-4** NWilliamson (bit bkwd: a bhd: t.o)....dist **19** 16/1 — —
Private Memories (AWCarroll) **6-11-4** WMarston (bhd fnl 5f: t.o)....dist **20** 33/1 — —
(SP 172.6%) **20 Rn**

3m 52.7 CSF £46.47 TOTE £4.10: £2.00 £5.90 £24.00 (£40.40) Trio Not won; £346.26 to Wincanton 21/11/96 OWNER Mr B. A. Kilpatrick (WELLINGTON) BRED Michel le Baron
1289 Quini Eagle (FR) made all the running and never saw another horse. (11/4)
Jack Gallagher was never far away and kept on gamely in the final two furlongs. A similar event can be found for this big, chasing type. (12/1)
Shekels (IRE), settled in the rear, made steady headway in the final three furlongs and can improve. (16/1)
Military Law looked just in need of the race beforehand and ran well until lack of condition told over the final two flights. (16/1)
Stanmore (IRE) ran with some promise and was not punished when beaten. (14/1: 10/1-16/1)
Stormyfairweather (IRE) made good headway approaching the straight and was not knocked about once his chances had gone. (7/2)
Feebee Five (12/1: op 8/1)

T/Plpt: £61.20 (153.76 Tckts). T/Qdpt: £21.90 (31.3 Tckts). SM

1304-SEDGEFIELD (L-H) - Thursday November 21st
1458 Abandoned-Snow

1178-WARWICK (L-H) (Good)
Thursday November 21st
WEATHER: sunny but cold

1465 ETHELFLEDA'S MOUNT CONDITIONAL H'CAP CHASE (0-115) (5-Y.O+) (Class E)
1-20 (1-20) **2m 4f 110y (17 fncs)** £3,393.00 (£948.00: £459.00) GOING minus 0.22 sec per fur (G)

SP RR SF

1119[2] **Flapjack Lad (98)** (NATwiston-Davies) **7-11-10** DWalsh (a.p: led 10th to 11th: hrd rdn appr 2 out: btn whn mstke last: 2nd btn 13l: awrdd race) ....— **1** 5/2 2 101 33
1284[2] **Channel Pastime (93)** (DBurchell) **12-11-5** GuyLewis (hld up: reminders 10th: chsd ldng pair fr 12th: no imp: 3rd btn 13l & 7l: plcd 2nd) **2** 6/1 90 22
River Red (79) (KFrost) **10-10-5** KGaule (bkwd: hld up in rr: effrt & mstke 12th: sn t.o: fin 4th btn 13l, 7l & dist: plcd 3rd) .... **3** 33/1 — —
1335[2] **Henley Wood (98)** (PJHobbs) **11-11-10** DJKavanagh (led to 3rd: lost pl 8th: t.o whn p.u bef 11th) .... **P** 5/1 — —
1012[2] **Crackling Frost (IRE) (77)** (MrsDHaine) **8-10-3** GHogan (j.w: led 3rd to 10th: wknd 12th: t.o whn p.u after 3 out) .... **P** 7/2 3 — —
Eastern River (74) (CaptTAForster) **10-10-0** ABates (bit bkwd: hld up: hdwy 8th: led 11th: drew clr fr 2 out: disq plcd last:) .... **D** 9/4 1 87 19
(SP 115.5%) **6 Rn**

5m 8.0 (4.00) CSF £8.26 TOTE £3.00: £2.00 £2.50 (£5.30) OWNER Mr T. H. Ounsley (CHELTENHAM) BRED Cobhall Court Stud
STEWARDS' ENQUIRY Eastern River disqualified and placed last; prohibited substance (procaine), in urine. Trainer fined £500
1119 Flapjack Lad, always where he wanted to be, found the weight concession taking its toll on the home turn and was easily brushed aside. (5/2: op 6/4)
1284 Channel Pastime did look set to get into the action when closing up a mile out but, with the principals keeping up the gallop, he could not summon the pace to do so. (6/1: 7/2-13/2)
Eastern River will strip fitter with this run under his belt but, off bottom weight, won this weak event with the minimum of fuss.(9/4)

1466 HARBURY (S) H'CAP HURDLE (0-100) (4-Y.O+) (Class G)
1-50 (1-52) **2m 3f (9 hdls)** £1,691.00 (£466.00: £221.00) GOING minus 0.22 sec per fur (G)

SP RR SF

1299[6] **Sir Pageant (71)** (KSBridgwater) **7-10-0b** DBridgwater (plld hrd: a.p: chal 2 out: led last: rdn out)....— **1** 10/1 52 —
1256[7] **Bright Sapphire (71)** (DBurchell) **10-10-0** DJBurchell (hdwy 4th: led next to last: rdn & no ex flat) ....2 **2** 10/1 50 —
Katballou (71) (KGWingrove) **7-9-7**(7) MrOMcPhail (bit bkwd: trckd ldrs: rdn 3 out: styd on fr next)....5 **3** 40/1 46 —
1337[2] **Tamandu (78)** (CJames) **6-10-7** MrEJames (hld up: hdwy 5th: one pce fr 2 out)....hd **4** 5/1 2 53 —
1299[2] **Hacketts Cross (IRE) (93)** (PEccles) **8-11-8** APMcCoy (hld up: hdwy 5th: rdn appr 2 out: nt rch ldrs) ....10 **5** 7/2 1 60 —
1145[10] **Ray River (74)** (KGWingrove) **4-10-3b** JRyan (hld up in rr: hdwy fr 3 out: nvr nrr)....2 **6** 11/1 39 —
725[2] **Gunmaker (79)** (BJLlewellyn) **7-10-8** MrJLLlewellyn (chsd ldrs to 6th: sn rdn & outpcd) ....nk **7** 9/1 44 —
1088[7] **John Naman (IRE) (84)** (DPGeraghty) **7-10-6**(7) GSupple (lost pl ½-wy: sn bhd: t.o) ....19 **8** 14/1 33 —
899[F] **King of Babylon (IRE) (74)** (FJordan) **4-10-3** RSupple (a bhd: t.o) ....5 **9** 14/1 19 —
950[2] **Shuttlecock (89)** (MrsNMacauley) **5-11-4** AMaguire (led to 5th: wkng whn mstke next: sn t.o) ....21 **10** 5/1 2 16 —
Coxwell Steptoe (95) (MissHCKnight) **6-11-3**(7) MrAWintle (bkwd: prom to 5th: bhd whn fell 2 out).... **F** 6/1 3 — —
1332[8] **Colour Scheme (71)** (HSHowe) **9-10-0v** BPowell (chsd ldrs to 5th: sn wknd: t.o whn p.u bef 2 out) .... **P** 40/1 — —
(SP 124.6%) **12 Rn**

4m 24.3 (4.30) CSF £100.20 CT £3,487.23 TOTE £11.20: £2.60 £3.00 £17.70 (£41.80) Trio £262.20; £295.54 to Ascot 22/11/96 OWNER The Dirty Dozen (LAPWORTH) BRED Stud-On-The-Chart
LONG HANDICAP Bright Sapphire 9-13 Katballou 9-3 Sir Pageant 9-13 Colour Scheme 9-8
No bid
1299 Sir Pageant, much happier back over this more suitable trip, pinched the spoils with a bold leap at the last. (10/1)

902 Bright Sapphire proved a tough nut to crack on this step down in class and a race of this description could get him back to winning ways. (10/1)
Katballou ran well after over fourteen months out of action without giving the leading pair much cause for concern. (40/1)
1337 Tamandu, patiently ridden, moved onto the heels of the leaders inside the final mile, but he was struggling to hold his pitch turning in and was never a serious factor. (5/1)
1299 Hacketts Cross (IRE) should have been in his element on this return to a longer trip, but he failed to pick up when sent about his business and proved something of a damp squib. (7/2)
648 Ray River, doing all his best work inside the last half-mile, had been set an impossible task and was just not up to it. (11/1: 8/1-12/1)

1467 SCOTTISH EQUITABLE/JOCKEYS ASSOCIATION SERIES (QUALIFIER) H'CAP HURDLE (0-125) (4-Y.O+) (Class D)

2-20 (2-23) **2m 3f (9 hdls)** £2,908.50 (£806.00: £385.50) GOING minus 0.22 sec per fur (G)

				SP	RR	SF
	Domappel (105) (MrsJCecil) **4-10-11** TKent (hld up: chsd ldr fr 5th: chal 2 out: sn led: comf)	—	1	7/2^{2}	93+	—
1258^{6}	**Runaway Pete (USA) (122)** (MCPipe) **6-12-0** APMcCoy (lw: led: sn rdn along: hdd after 2 out: sn btn)	9	2	7/4^{1}	102	—
	Grouseman (114) (MissHCKnight) **10-10-13b**(7) MrAWintle (bkwd: w ldr to 5th: lost pl next: sn t.o)	21	3	6/1	77	—
	Winsford Hill (94) (PJHobbs) **5-10-0** AMaguire (bit bkwd: chsd ldrs tl wknd appr 6th: sn wl bhd: t.o)	7	4	5/1	51	—
1180*	**Rosehall (95)** (MrsTDPilkington) **5-9-12**(3)ow1 GHogan (a bhd: outpcd 5th: t.o)	11	5	50/1	43	—
1258^{8}	**Teen Jay (122)** (BJLlewellyn) **6-12-0** VSlattery (hld up & bhd: lost tch 5th: t.o whn fell 3 out: dead)		F	4/1^{3}	—	—
				(SP 111.5%)		**6 Rn**

4m 22.6 (2.60) CSF £9.66 TOTE £4.50: £2.10 £1.80 (£5.10) OWNER Mr M. C. Banks (NEWMARKET) BRED Bolton Grange
LONG HANDICAP Rosehall 8-7
Domappel, fit from the Flat, was travelling best from some way out and it was only a matter of when his pilot pressed the button. (7/2)
1258 Runaway Pete (USA), off the bridle from the start, did hold on to his lead, but the writing was on the wall long before he reached the straight. (7/4)
Grouseman blew up halfway down the back straight and, though he did stay on to make the prizes, he had to admit this pipe-opener was badly needed. (6/1)
1039* Teen Jay (4/1: 3/1-9/2)

1468 SHIRLEY MAIDEN CHASE (5-Y.O+) (Class D)

2-50 (2-50) **3m 2f (20 fncs)** £3,691.00 (£1,108.00: £534.00: £247.00) GOING minus 0.22 sec per fur (G)

				SP	RR	SF
	Dromhana (IRE) (PFNicholls) **6-11-5** APMcCoy (bit bkwd: sn chsng ldrs: lft in ld 3 out: rdn next: fin tired)	—	1	13/8^{1}	91	20
	The Shy Padre (IRE) (93) (MrsJPitman) **7-11-5** WMarston (bit bkwd: mstke 2nd: hdwy 8th: led after 10th: pckd & hdd 3 out: one pce)	2	2	5/1^{3}	90	19
	Anythingyoulike (CASmith) **7-11-5** MRichards (bkwd: hdwy 7th: mstke 15th: sn lost tch: styd on fr 2 out)	7	3	25/1	86	15
	Peptic Lady (IRE) (MCPipe) **6-11-0** CMaude (mstkes: prom tl lost pl 8th: styd on again fr 3 out)	½	4	16/1	80	9
	Arctic Madam (PFNicholls) **7-10-7**(7) OBurrows (bkwd: in tch tl wknd 14th)	9	5	14/1	75	4
	Coney Road (75) (CPEBrooks) **7-11-5** GBradley (bit bkwd: hld up & bhd: hdwy 13th: 3rd & rdn whn blnd bdly 3 out: nt rcvr)	dist	6	3/1^{2}	—	—
1192^{4}	**Parliamentarian (IRE) (85)** (TCasey) **7-11-5** DBridgwater (hld up in rr: effrt 14th: no imp: t.o)	5	7	9/1	—	—
1326^{P}	**Inch Emperor (IRE)** (AWCarroll) **6-11-5** TJMurphy (mde most tl after 10th: wknd & p.u bef 15th)		P	33/1	—	—
	The Brud (80) (OSherwood) **8-11-5** JOsborne (bkwd: disp ld to 3rd: blnd & uns rdr 6th)		U	10/1	—	—
				(SP 118.2%)		**9 Rn**

6m 36.6 (11.60) CSF £10.17 TOTE £2.70: £1.20 £1.80 £6.10 (£5.10) Trio £50.00 OWNER Mr John Blackwell (SHEPTON MALLET) BRED Lawson Burriss
Dromhana (IRE), a smart performer between the Flags in Ireland, found a very simple event to start his career under Rules, but he did finish very leg-weary and will be all the sharper next time. (13/8: 11/10-7/4)
The Shy Padre (IRE) has not yet quite mastered the art of jumping fences but, if he had not landed on his head three out, he could well have taken the measure of the favourite. (5/1)
Anythingyoulike, a winning point-to-pointer on much softer ground than he had here, was close enough to cause concern when he ran into the bottom of a fence down the back straight. Losing his momentum, he had little chance of getting back into it. (25/1)
Peptic Lady (IRE) did well to complete the course on this debut under Rules, for she made so many jumping errors that most jockeys would have called it a day. (16/1)
Arctic Madam (14/1: 6/1-16/1)
Coney Road made relentless progress in the final mile, but still had plenty on his plate when he landed on his knees three out and, with his chance gone, he was allowed to school over the last two. (3/1)
Parliamentarian (IRE) (9/1: op 6/1)
The Brud (10/1: 6/1-12/1)

1469 SHIPSTON H'CAP CHASE (0-145) (5-Y.O+) (Class B)

3-20 (3-22) **3m 2f (20 fncs)** £8,302.00 (£2,038.00) GOING minus 0.22 sec per fur (G)

				SP	RR	SF
1175^{2}	**Class of Ninetytwo (IRE) (122)** (CaptTAForster) **7-11-5** APMcCoy (lw: mde all: clr 13th: styd on strly)	—	1	2/1^{2}	127	36
1279*	**Idiot's Lady (127)** (MrsJPitman) **7-11-10** WMarston (lw: j.rt: chsd wnr thrght: effrt & rdn appr 2 out: nt pce to chal)	2	2	5/2^{3}	131	40
1048*	**Sounds Strong (IRE) (121)** (DNicholson) **7-11-4** AMaguire (hld up & bhd: chal 2nd whn fell 14th)		F	Evens^{1}	—	—
				(SP 111.9%)		**3 Rn**

6m 30.5 (5.50) CSF £6.11 TOTE £2.80: (£3.00) OWNER Lord Cadogan (LUDLOW) BRED Mrs Patricia Mackean
IN-FOCUS: **This win enabled Tony McCoy to break Peter Scudamore's record for the fastest 100 winners.**
1175 Class of Ninetytwo (IRE) is clever enough to put in a short one on the odd occasion he meets a fence wrong and a clear round won this for him. (2/1)
1279* Idiot's Lady continually jumped out to the right, something she had not done before and, with the winner gaining ground at most obstacles, she was always at full stretch in an effort to get to terms. (5/2: 11/8-11/4)
1048* Sounds Strong (IRE) appeared to do everything right as long as he was on the bridle, but he had just been asked for an effort when his legs buckled on landing at the start of the back straight. He was travelling well within himself at the time and he would have taken all the beating. (Evens)

1470 ASHORNE NOVICES' HURDLE (4-Y.O+) (Class E)

3-50 (3-51) **2m (8 hdls)** £2,721.00 (£756.00: £363.00) GOING minus 0.22 sec per fur (G)

	Horse	Dist	Pos	SP	RR	SF
	Hurricane Lamp (DNicholson) **5-10-12** AMaguire (plld hrd: trckd ldrs: led 2 out: sn clr: impressive)	—	**1**	9/4[1]	79+	41
1278[3]	**Smolensk (IRE)** (JBerry) **4-10-12** MMoloney (chsd ldrs: rdn 3 out: styd on appr last: no ch w wnr)	5	**2**	16/1	74	36
1178*	**Chickawicka (IRE)** (BPalling) **5-11-5** RFarrant (led to 2 out: sn rdn & outpcd)	½	**3**	9/4[1]	81	43
	Kilcarne Bay (IRE) (OSherwood) **6-10-12** GBradley (bit bkwd: hld up: stdy hdwy fr 3 out: nvr nrr)	4	**4**	11/2[3]	70	32
910[12]	**Evezio Rufo** (NPLittmoden) **4-10-12v** JRKavanagh (hdwy 3rd: wknd appr 2 out)	4	**5**	66/1	66	28
1375[5]	**Above the Cut (USA)** (CPMorlock) **4-10-12** CMaude (trckd ldrs to 5th: wknd qckly)	7	**6**	33/1	59	21
	Mr Darcy (PRWebber) **4-10-12** RBellamy (bkwd: nvr bttr than mid div)	1¾	**7**	100/1	57	19
	Break the Rules (MCPipe) **4-10-12** APMcCoy (prom: disp ld 4th & 5th: wknd after 3 out)	1¾	**8**	9/2[2]	55	17
1178[5]	**The Deaconess** (MrsALMKing) **5-10-7** GaryLyons (a in rr: t.o)	8	**9**	150/1	42	4
1337[W]	**Tomal** (RIngram) **4-10-12** DGallagher (lost pl 3rd: sn bhd: t.o)	7	**10**	25/1	40	2
	Don't Mind If I Do (IRE) (PRWebber) **5-10-12** MrPScott (bkwd: mstkes: a in rr: t.o)	14	**11**	66/1	26	—
	White Claret (RAkehurst) **4-10-12** DBridgwater (lw: trckd ldrs to 4th: sn lost tch: t.o)	½	**12**	15/2	26	—
	Becky's Girl (RBrotherton) **6-10-7** PHolley (a bhd: t.o)	15	**13**	150/1	6	—
	Mr Rough (DMorris) **5-10-12** MRichards (a bhd: t.o whn p.u bef last)		**P**	25/1	—	—
	Persian Butterfly (RMStronge) **4-10-7** BPowell (sddle slipped & p.u bef 3rd)		**P**	150/1	—	—
				(SP 129.3%)	**15 Rn**	

3m 42.5 (0.50) CSF £38.46 TOTE £4.00: £2.30 £2.60 £1.70 (£45.10) Trio £24.80 OWNER Mr & Mrs F C Welch and Mr R A Barrs (TEMPLE GUITING) BRED Mrs S. C. Welch

OFFICIAL EXPLANATION **Mr Rough: finished distressed.**

Persian Butterfly: saddle slipped.

Hurricane Lamp missed a day's work when he spent Tuesday in the horsebox on an aborted trip to Wetherby but, such is his class, he made a very impressive hurdling debut. It will come as a big surprise if he fails to reach the top. (9/4: 6/4-5/2)

1278 Smolensk (IRE) kept battling away to gain the runner-up prize on the flat and will do well to steer clear of anything as useful as the winner. (16/1)

1178* Chickawicka (IRE) tried to put his previous experience to good use by making all, but the winner was taking one stride to his two turning out of the back straight and it was obvious he was only there on sufferance. (9/4: 2/1-3/1)

Kilcarne Bay (IRE), given a very kind introduction to hurdles, will probably need a stiffer test of stamina, but this experience will stand him in good stead when he reappears. (11/2: 5/2-6/1)

Evezio Rufo ran better than he did on his hurdling debut and this shorter trip probably suited him, but he does appear to need softer ground. (66/1)

Break the Rules, a middle-distance winner on the Flat, looked the one to beat when joining issue at halfway, but he went out like a light on the home turn and there appeared no obvious excuse. (9/2: 5/2-5/1)

T/Jkpt: £7,100.00 (0.3 Tckts); £4,510.23 to Ascot 22/11/96. T/Plpt: £365.70 (39.63 Tckts). T/Qdpt: £11.70 (129.8 Tckts) IM

1283-WINCANTON (R-H) (Good)

Thursday November 21st

WEATHER: fine

1471 U.W.E.S.U. STILL STANDING NOVICES' H'CAP HURDLE (0-100) (4-Y.O+) (Class E)

1-30 (1-34) **2m (8 hdls)** £2,267.50 (£630.00: £302.50) GOING minus 0.09 sec per fur (G)

	Horse	Dist	Pos	SP	RR	SF
1091[4]	**Wayfarers Way (USA) (87)** (NJHenderson) **5-11-10** MAFitzgerald (hld up: hdwy appr 2 out: led last: rdn out)	—	**1**	4/1[2]	69	37
	Calvaro (IRE) (69) (APJarvis) **5-10-6** RJohnson (plld hrd early: a.p: led appr last: sn hdd: r.o one pce)	1¾	**2**	25/1	49	17
	Ashby Hill (IRE) (81) (RRowe) **5-11-4** DO'Sullivan (nt fluent: hld up & plld hrd: hdwy & ev ch whn mstke 2 out: one pce)	1¾	**3**	4/6[1]	60	28
21[6]	**Eleanora Muse (70)** (PaddyFarrell) **6-10-7** RDunwoody (led tl appr last: wknd flat)	9	**4**	4/1[2]	40	8
1042[4]	**Samaka Hara (IRE) (79)** (GraemeRoe) **4-11-2** TJenks (chsd ldr: mstke 3 out: hrd rdn & wknd qckly appr 2 out: b.b.v)	dist	**5**	11/1[3]	—	—
				(SP 112.2%)	**5 Rn**	

3m 45.7 (5.70) CSF £47.79 TOTE £5.00: £1.20 £9.20 (£23.70) OWNER Lady Tennant (LAMBOURN) BRED Wooden Horse Investments

OFFICIAL EXPLANATION **Samaka Hara (IRE): bled from the nose.**

IN-FOCUS: **Trainers were allowed to withdraw horses without penalty at the meeting because of the fast ground.**

1091 Wayfarers Way (USA) got off the mark in an uncompetitive handicap by Wincanton standards. (4/1: 3/1-9/2)

Calvaro (IRE) ran easily his best race to date. (25/1)

Ashby Hill (IRE) has gone up two stone in the Flat Ratings having won five times since she last ran over hurdles. However, she still remains a doubtful stayer and the combination of some indifferent jumping and refusing to settle did not help her cause. (4/6)

21 Eleanora Muse was possibly just in need of this. (4/1: 3/1-9/2)

1042 Samaka Hara (IRE) (11/1: 8/1-12/1)

1472 TOTE BOOKMAKERS NOVICES' H'CAP CHASE (0-105) (5-Y.O+) (Class D)

2-00 (2-03) **2m 5f (17 fncs)** £4,048.50 (£1,218.00: £589.00: £274.50) GOING minus 0.09 sec per fur (G)

	Horse	Dist	Pos	SP	RR	SF
	Highland Jack (85) (AndrewTurnell) **6-10-10** RDunwoody (s.s: gd hdwy 10th: wnt 2nd 4 out: rdn appr 3 out: rallied to ld fnl 50y)	—	**1**	6/1[3]	93	—
1252[2]	**Bironi (97)** (CaptTAForster) **7-11-8** SWynne (j.rt: chsd ldr: led 11th: 3l clr whn blnd last: hdd last 50y)	2	**2**	9/4[1]	104	8
	At The Grove (IRE) (100) (KCBailey) **6-11-11** CO'Dwyer (hld up & bhd: hdwy 11th: wknd after 4 out)	12	**3**	10/1	97	1
1300*	**Legal Artist (IRE) (83)** (MissCJohnsey) **6-10-8** 6x LHarvey (prom: blnd 5th: lost pl 9th: rdn & rallied 4 out: wknd appr 3 out)	9	**4**	10/1	74	—
1285[3]	**Stormhill Pilgrim (75)** (MJRoberts) **7-10-0b[1]** PMcLoughlin (led: hit 1st: mstke & hdd 11th: mstke 13th: wknd 4 out)	3	**5**	14/1	63	—
	Purbeck Rambler (76) (GBBalding) **5-10-0** BClifford (bit bkwd: a bhd: t.o)	dist	**6**	25/1	—	—
	Sweet Buck (75) (RCPugh) **7-10-0** MSharratt (t.o fr 7th)	dist	**7**	66/1	—	—
	Ferny Ball (IRE) (78) (CaptTAForster) **8-10-3**ow3 AThornton (fell 2nd)		**F**	33/1	—	—
793[6]	**Zaitoon (IRE) (101)** (DNicholson) **5-11-11** RJohnson (hmpd & uns rdr 2nd)		**U**	11/2[2]	—	—

1174³ **Cracking Prospect (80)** (BRMillman) **5-9-13**(5) DSalter (lw: plld hrd: lft 3rd 8th: lost pl 9th: bhd whn blnd & uns rdr 13th) ... **U** 10/1 — —
Whirly (IRE) (90) (RHAlner) **7-11-1** SMcNeill (bit bkwd: prom: mstke 1st: 3rd whn blnd bdly & uns rdr 8th) ... **U** 13/2 — —
1073⁴ **Master Pangloss (IRE) (75)** (AndrewTurnell) **6-9-7**(7) CRae (hit 1st: blnd & uns rdr 4th) ... **U** 25/1 — —
(SP 119.8%) **12 Rn**

5m 24.7 (16.70) CSF £19.06 CT £125.11 TOTE £6.90: £1.90 £1.30 £3.00 (£6.90) Trio £64.10 OWNER Karen Gibbons & Breda Cardiff (WANTAGE) BRED J. J. Smith
LONG HANDICAP Stormhill Pilgrim 9-9 Sweet Buck 8-13 Ferny Ball (IRE) 9-1 Master Pangloss (IRE) 9-1
WEIGHT FOR AGE 5yo-1lb
Highland Jack responded to pressure to take advantage of the favourite's blunder at the final fence. He may run in headgear in the future to help his concentration during a race. (6/1)
1252 Bironi, inclined to dive to the right at his fences, would still have prevailed had he not made his only real error at the last. (9/4)
At The Grove (IRE), placed in novice chases in Ireland, was bought for 14,000 guineas at Doncaster May Sales. He may have needed this more than was apparent beforehand for, just as he began to look dangerous, he was on the retreat. (10/1)
1300* Legal Artist (IRE) found this a different kettle of fish and was hardly helped by making a hash of the downhill cross fence on the first circuit. (10/1)
1285 Stormhill Pilgrim, dropping back in distance, again forced the pace, but his jumping seemed to suffer in the first-time blinkers. (14/1: op 8/1)
Zaitoon (IRE) (11/2: 4/1-6/1)

1473 HAMILTON LITESTAT H'CAP CHASE (0-130) (5-Y.O+) (Class C)
2-30 (2-33) **3m 1f 110y (21 fncs)** £6,775.00 (£2,050.00: £1,000.00: £475.00) GOING minus 0.09 sec per fur (G)

SP RR SF

Andre Laval (IRE) (110) (KCBailey) **7-10-11** CO'Dwyer (bit bkwd: hld up: hdwy 13th: led 16th to 2 out: led last: rdn out) ... — **1** 9/4² 115 —
Beaurepaire (IRE) (108) (RHAlner) **8-10-9** SMcNeill (bit bkwd: led to 14th: lost pl 17th: rallied 4 out: led 2 out to last: unable qckn) ... 1¼ **2** 11/2 112 —
1302³ **Rainbow Castle (107)** (PFNicholls) **9-10-8** PHide (trckd ldr: led 14th to 16th: one pce fr 3 out) ... 4 **3** 100/30³ 109 —
Le Meille (IRE) (113) (APJarvis) **7-11-0** RJohnson (hld up & plld hrd: blnd 2nd: mstke 10th: hdwy 13th: mstke 16th: wknd 4 out: t.o) ... dist **4** 6/4¹ — —
(SP 109.2%) **4 Rn**

6m 39.4 (20.40) CSF £11.56 TOTE £2.90: £3.10 (£9.20) OWNER Mrs Christopher Wright (UPPER LAMBOURN) BRED Ronald Scanlon
Andre Laval (IRE) made a successful transition to handicap company having missed an engagement at Newton Abbot two days ago, because of the heavy ground. (9/4)
Beaurepaire (IRE) lost nothing in defeat and should come on a bit for the outing. (11/2)
1302 Rainbow Castle, again 7lb higher than for the second of his wins, was already due to drop 2lb. (100/30)
Le Meille (IRE) found the combination of refusing to settle and a couple of poor jumps eventually catching up with him. (6/4)

1474 TOTE BETTING SHOP H'CAP HURDLE (0-135) (4-Y.O+) (Class C)
3-00 (3-03) **2m (8 hdls)** £3,470.00 (£1,040.00: £500.00: £230.00) GOING minus 0.09 sec per fur (G)

SP RR SF

1201² **Morstock (110)** (RJHodges) **6-10-7**(3) TDascombe (mde all: sn clr: hit 2nd & 2 out: drvn out) ... — **1** 3/1² 92 46
1262² **Phar From Funny (106)** (GBBalding) **5-10-6** BFenton (hld up: rdn & chsd wnr appr 2 out: r.o one pce flat) ... 2 **2** 4/5¹ 86 40
1271³ **Hamilton Silk (128)** (MCPipe) **4-12-0** RDunwoody (chsd wnr fr 3rd tl rdn & wknd appr 2 out: t.o) ... dist **3** 7/2³ — —
Vision of Freedom (IRE) (105) (SNCole) **8-10-5** AThornton (mstke 3rd: sn t.o: b.b.v) ... dist **4** 9/1 — —
(SP 112.8%) **4 Rn**

3m 41.1 (1.10) CSF £5.89 TOTE £4.20: (£3.20) OWNER Mrs M. Fairbairn (SOMERTON) BRED Mrs M. Fairbairn and M. R. Pascall
OFFICIAL EXPLANATION **Vision of Freedom (IRE): bled from the nose.**
1201 Morstock caught the other three napping at the start and stole enough of an advantage that the favourite could not get to him. (3/1)
1262 Phar From Funny allowed the winner to get a flyer at the start. Despite gradually reducing the deficit from the final flight, he lived up to his name as far as those who laid the odds were concerned. (4/5: 10/11-evens)
1271 Hamilton Silk could possibly have been accused of baulking the favourite and Vision of Freedom at the start, but they all really fell foul of the winner's tactics. (7/2)
Vision of Freedom (IRE), having allowed the winner plenty of rope at the start, lost interest after an error at the hurdle going away from the Stands. (9/1)

1475 E.B.F. TATTERSALLS (IRELAND) (QUALIFIER) NOVICES' CHASE (5-Y.O+ Mares Only) (Class D)
3-30 (3-31) **2m (13 fncs)** £3,457.00 (£1,036.00: £498.00: £229.00) GOING minus 0.09 sec per fur (G)

SP RR SF

1176⁶ **Koo's Promise** (CLPopham) **5-10-9**(3) TDascombe (lw: hld up: outpcd 9th: styd on fr 2 out: led nr fin) ... — **1** 8/1³ 86 10
1252ᵁ **Bridepark Rose (IRE) (89)** (PCRitchens) **8-10-12** SFox (led appr 2nd: clr 6th: hdd appr 3 out: wkng whn mstke 2 out: lft in ld last: hdd nr fin) ... nk **2** 11/4² 86 10
1197ᴾ **Up the Tempo (IRE)** (PaddyFarrell) **7-10-12** AThornton (bhd: mstke 9th: sn t.o) ... dist **3** 16/1 — —
1340* **Second Call** (CaptTAForster) **7-11-4** RDunwoody (led tl appr 2nd: led appr 3 out: 20l clr whn fell last: rmntd) ... dist **4** 4/9¹ — —
(SP 112.9%) **4 Rn**

4m 2.8 (9.80) CSF £26.26 TOTE £5.10 (£8.50) OWNER G A Warren Ltd (TAUNTON)
Koo's Promise looked destined to finish a poor third on her debut over fences turning for home. However, with the favourite well clear when coming to grief at the last, she collared the tired runner-up at the death. (8/1)
Bridepark Rose (IRE), who has changed stables, was so leg-weary when the leader fell at the final fence that she always appeared likely to be collared by the winner. (11/4)
1340* Second Call made her only error with the race at her mercy. (4/9)

1476 GREAT WESTERN NOVICES' HURDLE (4-Y.O+) (Class C)
4-00 (4-03) **2m 6f (11 hdls)** £3,834.00 (£1,152.00: £556.00: £258.00) GOING minus 0.09 sec per fur (G)

SP RR SF

1053⁴ **Kilmington (IRE)** (JTGifford) **7-11-0** PHide (a.p: led 8th: hrd rdn appr last: r.o wl) ... — **1** 11/2³ 66 25
Captain Jack (MCPipe) **6-11-0** RDunwoody (bit bkwd: led to 2nd: led 5th to 8th: ev ch 2 out: one pce) ... 3 **2** 9/4² 64 23
Atavistic (IRE) (CLPopham) **4-11-0** MAFitzgerald (bit bkwd: hld up & bhd: hdwy 6th: hit last: r.o one pce) ... s.h **3** 10/1 64 23

				SP	RR	SF
	Menesonic (IRE) (RHAlner) **6-10-11**(3) PHenley (bkwd: a.p: rdn 3 out: no hdwy)	6	**4**	12/1	59	18
1062*	**Hunters Rock (IRE) (115)** (KCBailey) **7-11-10** CO'Dwyer (hld up & bhd: stdy hdwy fr 8th: rdn & wknd appr last)	1¼	**5**	6/5[1]	69	28
1200[5]	**Miss Secret** (CWMitchell) **6-10-9** AThornton (hdwy 6th: rdn 3 out: wknd appr 2 out)	25	**6**	66/1	35	—
1327[P]	**Young Tycoon (NZ) (83)** (AJWilson) **5-11-0** LHarvey (bhd fr 7th)	1½	**7**	66/1	39	—
	Red Bronze (IRE) (CRBarwell) **5-11-0** BFenton (a bhd)	2½	**8**	20/1	37	—
1178[10]	**The Brewer** (JCTuck) **4-11-0** SMcNeill (swtg: a bhd: t.o)	dist	**9**	33/1	—	—
	Black Statement (IRE) (APJarvis) **6-11-0** RJohnson (lw: prom to 8th: t.o whn p.u bef 2 out)		**P**	25/1	—	—
1056[6]	**Mr Jasper** (NBThomson) **4-11-0b**[1] SBurrough (plld hrd: led 2nd to 5th: wknd 6th: t.o whn p.u bef 8th)		**P**	100/1	—	—
				(SP 123.9%)	**11 Rn**	

5m 17.8 (8.80) CSF £18.39 TOTE £5.20: £1.30 £1.70 £2.20 (£9.70) Trio £39.50 OWNER Mr H. T. Pelham (FINDON)

1053 Kilmington (IRE), remaining over hurdles but upped in trip, had a far more aggressive ride this time. (11/2: 4/1-6/1)

Captain Jack, a smart staying handicapper in 1994, was bought out of Luca Cumani's yard for 100,000 guineas and wore blinkers when racing too freely on his hurdling debut at Ascot the best part of two years ago. He can be made fitter and should soon start making a contribution to his large purchase price. (9/4: 2/1-3/1)

Atavistic (IRE), the winner of an Ayr bumper for Roger Fisher, will find this putting an edge on him, and he should not be hard to place. (10/1)

Menesonic (IRE), an Irish import, ran a sound race for one apparently carrying plenty of condition. (12/1)

1062* Hunters Rock (IRE) found these rivals a fair bit stronger than those he had disposed of in collecting a double-penalty. (6/5: 4/5-5/4)

T/Plpt: £12,540.10 (0.74 Tckts); £4,406.01 to Ascot 22/11/96. T/Qdpt: £1,444.20 (0.75 Tckts); £487.93 to Ascot 22/11/96 KH

1477a - 1484a : (Irish Racing) - See Computer Raceform

1237a-PUNCHESTOWN (Naas, Ireland) (R-H) (Soft)

Saturday November 16th

1485a LOCKS RESTAURANT NOVICES' HURDLE (4-Y.O+)

1-15 (1-15) **2m (9 hdls)** IR £3,767.50 (IR £852.50: IR £357.50: IR £192.50)

				SP	RR	SF
	Noble Thyne (IRE) (PMullins,Ireland) **6-11-0** TPTreacy (led: clr after 3rd tl appr 2 out: mstke 2 out: hdd appr last: led early flat: rdn & styd on)	—	**1**	4/5[1]	105	—
	Istabraq (IRE) (APO'Brien,Ireland) **4-10-9** CFSwan (hld up: wnt mod 2nd at 4th: hdwy after 3 out: mstke next: led appr last: mstke & hdd last: rdn & rallied nr fin)	hd	**2**	6/4[2]	105	—
	Saving Bond (IRE) (NMeade,Ireland) **4-10-9** RHughes (hld up towards rr early: wnt mod 3rd after 3 out: no imp appr last)	20	**3**	8/1[3]	85	—
	Tullabawn (IRE) (MrsJHarrington,Ireland) **4-10-9** TJMitchell (in tch: mstke 3rd: mod 3rd bef 3 out: 4th & no imp after 2 out)	11	**4**	25/1	74	—
	Hollybank Buck (IRE) (AJMartin,Ireland) **6-11-7** APowell (in tch: mod 6th & no imp bef 2 out: kpt on)	2½	**5**	12/1	78	—
1233a[3]	**Knockaulin (IRE)** (FFlood,Ireland) **5-11-0** FrancisFlood (hld up towards rr: styd on after 2 out: nvr nrr)	5½	**6**	25/1	66	—
	Shannon Gale (IRE) (PBurke,Ireland) **4-10-9** LPCusack (chsd ldr to 4th: 3rd whn mstke next: mod 5th after 3 out: no imp between last 2)	3½	**7**	25/1	62	—
	Barley Meadow (IRE) (TGMcCourt,Ireland) **4-10-9** HRogers (in tch early: lost tch after 5th: n.d 3 out)	8	**8**	66/1	54	—
	Cristys Picnic (IRE) (MFMorris,Ireland) **6-11-0** FWoods (towards rr: n.d fr 3 out)	1½	**9**	20/1	53	—
	Cahonis (IRE) (MHourigan,Ireland) **4-10-9** MPHourigan (towards rr: mstke 2nd: t.o)	20	**10**	33/1	33	—
				(SP 135.1%)	**10 Rn**	

3m 57.2 OWNER C. Maye (GORESBRIDGE)

Noble Thyne (IRE) had experience on his side and made virtually all. He made a mistake two out and briefly lost the initiative approaching the last, but was able to assert himself again on the run-in. With improvement certain to be forthcoming, he looks a serious Sun Alliance candidate. (4/5)

Istabraq (IRE), an ex-John Gosden-trained half-brother to Secreto, put up a good display on his first outing over hurdles. In second place from four out, he was getting on terms when blundering two out and loomed up on the outer to head the eventual winner before the last, but a mistake there cost him the initiative. Although he battled on well on the flat, he just had to give best. He looks sure to go on from this. (6/4)

1486a CRADDOCKSTOWN NOVICES' CHASE (Gd 3) (4-Y.O+)

1-45 (1-45) **2m (11 fncs)** IR £6,850.00 (IR £1,550.00: IR £650.00: IR £350.00)

				SP	RR	SF
	Jeffell (ALTMoore,Ireland) **6-11-7** FWoods (mde all: lft clr between last 2: eased flat)	—	**1**	4/1[2]	92+	—
	Bobbyjo (IRE) (TCarberry,Ireland) **6-11-4**(3) KWhelan (in tch: mstke 2nd: chsng ldrs 3 out: lft mod 3rd between last 2: nt trble wnr)	8	**2**	20/1	84	—
	The Outback Way (IRE) (JJO'Connor,Ireland) **6-12-3b** DHO'Connor (mostly 2nd: mod 3rd 2 out: no imp whn lft mod 2nd between last 2: slt mstke last: one pce)	5½	**3**	4/1[2]	89	—
1216a[4]	**Beakstown (IRE)** (PMullins,Ireland) **7-12-3** TPTreacy (hld up: towards rr whn mstke 6th: hdwy after next: 3rd whn mstke 4 out: sn lost tch: 5th & no imp 2 out)	1½	**4**	5/1[3]	87	—
	Roche Mentor (IRE) (TCarberry,Ireland) **6-11-7** JPBroderick (towards rr: mstkes: fell 7th)		**F**	100/1	—	—
318a[8]	**Dance Beat (IRE)** (MrsJHarrington,Ireland) **5-11-6** CFSwan (hld up: mstke 5th: chsd wnr fr 4 out: chal 2 out: no ex u.p whn wknd qckly & p.u between last 2: broke leg: dead)		**P**	11/10[1]	—	—
				(SP 110.0%)	**6 Rn**	

4m 21.0 (12.00) OWNER Thomas Bailey (NAAS)

Jeffell, with some confidence behind him in the market, made all the running. This would seem to be his ideal trip and the demise of Dance Beat made no difference to the result. (4/1: op 6/1)

Bobbyjo (IRE) can certainly be followed in lesser company on this showing. (20/1)

The Outback Way (IRE) is really only a handicapper and had a stiff task in trying to concede 10lb to the winner. (4/1: op 5/2)

Dance Beat (IRE) chased the winner from four out, but was not making any impression when breaking a leg between the last two fences. (11/10: op 4/7)

1487a MORGIANA HURDLE (Gd 2) (4-Y.O+)
2-15 (2-15) **2m (9 hdls)** IR £9,675.00 (IR £2,775.00: IR £1,275.00: IR £375.00)

	Horse	Dist	Pos	SP	RR	SF
1234a[4]	**Cockney Lad (IRE)** (NMeade,Ireland) **7-12-0** CFSwan (hld up in tch: trckng ldrs 2 out: led last: qcknd clr flat: easily)	—	1	5/4[1]	115+	—
	Hill Society (IRE) (NMeade,Ireland) **4-11-2** RHughes (hld up: 2nd after 2 out: chal early st: led briefly nr last: slt mstke last: rdn & nt qckn)	1½	2	6/1	107	—
318a[19]	**Lady Arpel (IRE)** (PO'Leary,Ireland) **4-10-8** KFO'Brien (sn led: wnt clr appr 3 out: hit next: jnd early st: rdn & hdd nr last: slt mstke last: one pce flat)	1½	3	10/1	97	—
	Mayasta (IRE) (FBerry,Ireland) **6-10-13** FWoods (hld up towards rr: n.d)	25	4	5/1[3]	72	—
	Padashpan (USA) (WPMullins,Ireland) **7-10-11**(7) PMorris (chsd ldr to 3rd: 4th whn slt mstke 5th: lost tch bef next: n.d)	4	5	10/1	73	—
	Derrymoyle (IRE) (MCunningham,Ireland) **7-12-0** JPBroderick (hld up: rdn & chsd ldrs 3 out: btn bef next)	4½	6	7/2[2]	79	—

(SP 115.8%) **6 Rn**

3m 53.2 OWNER D. Daly (NAVAN)

1234a Cockney Lad (IRE), travelling well, was not finding a lot of room until squeezing through on the inner to lead at the last, and he settled things in a matter of strides. He worked his way out of handicap class and a tilt at the Hattons Grace at Fairyhouse would be worthwhile. (5/4)

Hill Society (IRE), a stable-companion of the winner, was close up from two out and had every chance at the last, but could not match the winner's turn of foot. (6/1)

Lady Arpel (IRE), clear until after three out, was still in contention at the last. (10/1)

Derrymoyle (IRE), friendless in the betting, dropped right away before two out. All is obviously not well with him. (7/2: op 2/1)

NR

1488a - 1491a : (Irish Racing) - See Computer Raceform

1230a-NAVAN (Ireland) (L-H) (Chases Good to yielding, Hdles Yielding)
Sunday November 17th

1492a 'MONKSFIELD' NOVICES' HURDLE (Gd 3) (4-Y.O+)
1-15 (1-19) **2m 4f (11 hdls)** IR £6,850.00 (IR £1,550.00: IR £650.00: IR £350.00)

	Horse	Dist	Pos	SP	RR	SF
316a[2]	**Tarthooth (IRE)** (ALTMoore,Ireland) **5-11-7** FWoods (mde all: styd on wl)	—	1	5/2[2]	89+	—
1233a*	**Radanpour (IRE)** (WPMullins,Ireland) **4-11-2**(3) DJCasey (hld up in tch: mstke 5th: lost pl briefly appr next: chsd wnr 3 out: lft mod 2nd next: no imp u.p appr last)	5½	2	5/1[3]	88	—
	Gallopen Garry (IRE) (SOO'Brien,Ireland) **6-11-10** JRBarry (rdn & hdwy 7th: wnt 2nd bef next: rdn bef 3 out: mstke & lft mod 4th 2 out: no imp)	11	3	10/1	79	—
	Mullover (MrsJHarrington,Ireland) **5-11-7** TJMitchell (chsd ldr bef 4th tl appr 4 out: rdn bef 3 out: no imp whn lft mod 3rd 2 out)	4	4	14/1	73	—
	Adaramann (IRE) (TMWalsh,Ireland) **4-10-13**(3) MrRWalsh (towards rr: rdn after 7th: n.d 3 out: kpt on)	15	5	25/1	61	—
	Ballinaboola Grove (IRE) (DKinsella,Ireland) **9-10-11**(7) JMMaguire (rn 5th: rdn & hdwy 7th: lost tch u.p after 4 out: n.d)	15	6	50/1	46	—
	Who Is Ed (IRE) (AJMartin,Ireland) **5-11-4** JPBroderick (hld up towards rr: sme hdwy 7th: n.d after next: dropped bhd: t.o)	dist	7	150/1	—	—
1233a[F]	**Liss De Paor (IRE)** (APO'Brien,Ireland) **5-11-5** CFSwan (chsd ldr early: hld up in tch: mstke 7th: chsd wnr 3 out: rdn & no imp whn fell 2 out)		F	8/13[1]	—	—
	Monsieur Dupont (IRE) (LComer,Ireland) **6-11-4** JKKinane (towards rr: dropped bhd & p.u after 4th)		P	200/1	—	—

(SP 129.9%) **9 Rn**

4m 55.3 (2.30) OWNER Mrs H de Burgh (NAAS) BRED Glen Barrow Farm

Tarthooth (IRE), always travelling strongly in front, was left clear two out and survived a last-flight blunder to win virtually unchallenged. (5/2)

1233a* Radanpour (IRE), held up in touch, was going really well four out. Left second two out, he found disappointingly little and was well held before the last. (5/1)

Gallopen Garry (IRE) had an impossible task at these weights, but kept on from two out. (10/1)

1233a Liss De Paor (IRE) again found the second last her undoing. She had made smooth enough headway to go second and was poised to challenge when coming down. (8/13)

1495a TROYTOWN H'CAP CHASE (Gd 2) (4-Y.O+)
2-45 (2-48) **3m (13 fncs)** IR £9,675.00 (IR £2,775.00: IR £1,275.00: IR £375.00)

	Horse	Dist	Pos	SP	RR	SF
1003a[2]	**Lord Singapore (IRE)** (JJWalsh,Ireland) **8-10-8**(3) DJCasey (hld up in tch: wnt 2nd 3 out: disp ld 2 out: sn hdd: rallied u.p to ld last: rdn clr flat)	—	1	5/1[2]	129	—
1003a[F]	**Heist** (NMeade,Ireland) **7-10-4** KFO'Brien (hld up towards rr: hdwy 7th: wnt 3rd 3 out: disp ld next: sn led: rdn appr last: hdd last: nt qckn u.p early flat)	3½	2	12/1	120	—
	Johnny Setaside (IRE) (NMeade,Ireland) **7-11-8** CFSwan (cl up: led briefly 8th: led 4 out to 2 out: 3rd u.p & nt qckn appr last)	14	3	11/8[1]	128	—
1003a[4]	**Second Schedual** (MissAMMcMahon,Ireland) **11-11-4** JPBroderick (mid div: rdn 9th: mod 6th 3 out: 4th & no imp 2 out: kpt on same pce)	11	4	10/1	117	—
1397a[3]	**Love the Lord (IRE)** (DO'Connell,Ireland) **6-11-2** TPTreacy (in tch: 2nd & chsng ldr whn hit 3 out: sn rdn & wknd)	9	5	13/2[3]	109	—
	Fissure Seal (ALTMoore,Ireland) **10-11-6** FWoods (mstke 1st: towards rr: losing tch 7th: n.d whn mstke 2 out: styd on)	¾	6	14/1	113	—
1397a*	**Royal Mountbrowne** (APO'Brien,Ireland) **8-11-9**(5) JButler (hit 1st: sn led: mstkes: mstke & hdd briefly 8th: mstke & hdd 4 out: 3rd whn hit next: sn wknd: n.d)	20	7	8/1	107	—
	Spankers Hill (IRE) (SJTreacy,Ireland) **7-10-5**(5) GCotter (in tch: lost tch bef 8th: n.d)	13	8	12/1	81	—
1397a[7]	**Love and Porter (IRE)** (JJO'Connor,Ireland) **8-10-10** DHO'Connor (in ld whn hit 1st: sn hdd: wknd 9th: p.u bef 3 out)		P	14/1	—	—

				SP		
1003a^{3}	**Twin Rainbow (IRE)** (PDOsborne,Ireland) **9-10-0** LPCusack (towards rr: j.slowly 1st & 2nd: reminders sn after: dropped bhd after 6th: p.u bef next)		P	15/2	—	—
1397a^{8}	**Nuaffe** (PAFahy,Ireland) **11-11-8** TJMitchell (in tch: reminders next: lost tch 9th: dropped bhd: p.u bef 3 out)		P	33/1	—	—
				(SP 135.7%)		**11 Rn**

6m 5.3 (0.30) OWNER Mrs E. Farrelly

1003a Lord Singapore (IRE), queueing up for his chance in a decent race like this, began to get on top from the second last and, appreciating the uphill climb, was in control all the way from the last. It is difficult to imagine him as anything more than a handicapper. (5/1: op 3/1)

1003a Heist came through to have every chance two out, but was doing a fair bit of wandering before the last, and just did not have the determination of the winner on the flat. (12/1: op 8/1)

Johnny Setaside (IRE), always in touch, led after four out but, headed before two out, capitulated rather quickly on the run down to the next. The ground was not as soft as he prefers it, but this was a disappointing effort and this hardly augurs well for his Hennessy chance. (11/8)

1003a Second Schedual just plugged on at one pace. (10/1)

1397a Love the Lord (IRE), in contention when clouting the third last, was soon beaten. (13/2)

1397a* Royal Mountbrowne put in a round of uncharacteristic blunders and was done with four from home. (8/1: op 4/1)

NR

1496a - 1497a : (Irish Racing) - See Computer Raceform

0717a-AUTEUIL (Paris, France) (L-H) (Very Soft)
Sunday November 10th

1498a PRIX LA HAYE JOUSSELIN CHASE (5-Y.O+)
2-35 (2-35) **3m 3f 110y** £105,402.00

				SP	RR	SF
717a*	**Al Capone II (FR)** (BSecly,France) **8-10-4** JYBeaurain	—	1		156?	—
	Baccarat Collonges (FR) (France) **7-10-4** PChevalier	15	2		147?	—
	Val D'Alene (FR) (FDoumen,France) **9-10-4** AKondrat	1½	3		146?	—
	Algan (FR) (FDoumen,France) **8-10-4** LMetais	3	4		144?	—
						8 Rn

7m 25.0 P-M 1.40F: 1.10F 1.50F 1.70F (4.20F) OWNER Mr R. Fougedoire

Val D'Alene (FR) stayed on well at the end after being mid-division for most of the way, but was never going well enough to challenge.

Algan (FR) went clear with the winner on the second circuit, but was beaten with three left to jump and finished very tired.

AINTREE (L-H) (Good, Good to firm patches becoming Good)
Friday November 22nd
WEATHER: unsettled

1499 SOUTHPORT NOVICES' HURDLE (4-Y.O+) (Class D)
1-10 (1-11) **2m 110y (9 hdls)** £3,009.00 (£912.00: £446.00: £213.00) GOING: 0.63 sec per fur (S)

				SP	RR	SF
	Tremendisto (96) (CaptJWilson) **6-10-12** ADobbin (led & sn clr: hdd & hit 3 out: rallied to ld appr last: drew clr)	—	1	4/1^{2}	70	31
1187^{5}	**Three Wild Days (99)** (TPTate) **4-10-12** RGarritty (chsd ldr: led 3 out tl appr last: hrd rdn: one pce)	6	2	3/1^{1}	64	25
1152^{8}	**Penrose Lad (NZ)** (DNicholson) **6-10-12** RJohnson (chsd ldrs: blnd 3rd: drvn along appr 3 out: sn btn)	1¼	3	3/1^{1}	63	24
1049^{7}	**Mr Christie (75)** (MissLCSiddall) **4-10-12** AThornton (bit bkwd: trckd ldrs: pushed along ½-wy: hrd rdn appr 3 out: kpt on)	1¼	4	14/1	62	23
1187^{10}	**Segala (IRE)** (JJO'Neill) **5-10-12** NWilliamson (hld up & bhd: hdwy appr 3 out: rdn & wknd appr last)	2½	5	16/1	59	20
	Star Master (LLungo) **5-10-12** MDwyer (bit bkwd: hld up: a in rr: t.o fr 3 out)	dist	6	7/1^{3}	—	—
1118^{5}	**Young Benson** (TWall) **4-10-9**(3) RMassey (prom tl wknd after 6th: t.o)	dist	7	50/1	—	—
1276^{9}	**Dictation (USA)** (JJO'Neill) **4-10-12** ARoche (lw: plld hrd: hld up: hit 5th: wknd & p.u bef 3 out)		P	20/1	—	—
	Bold Street (IRE) (ABailey) **6-10-12** TKent (hld up: hdwy 6th: reminder 3 out: sn wknd: p.u bef last)		P	20/1	—	—
	Kings Cay (IRE) (THCaldwell) **5-10-12** LWyer (bkwd: a bhd: t.o fr 6th: p.u bef 2 out)		P	8/1	—	—
				(SP 117.6%)		**10 Rn**

4m 10.9 (16.90) CSF £15.79 TOTE £3.90: £1.40 £1.40 £1.80 (£5.60) Trio £4.30 OWNER Mr Doug Marshall (PRESTON) BRED Mrs C. R. Philipson

Tremendisto, fit from the Flat, relished this return to hurdles and at long last got off the mark. He eventually won going away and this success was not coming out of turn. (4/1)

1187 Three Wild Days had a running battle with the winner from the break and looked to have the edge when gaining command early in the straight but, when the chips were down, he was forced to give best. (3/1)

Penrose Lad (NZ), still not fully wound up, stuck on bravely from the turn into the straight, but the leading pair were always going too well for him. (3/1)

1049 Mr Christie looks to be a hard ride, but he does keep plugging away, and there looks to be a race or two in him. (14/1)

Segala (IRE) made ground from the rear on the home turn, but was unable to get close enough to cause concern and was at the end of his tether between the last two. (16/1)

Star Master (7/1: 10/1-6/1)

1500 LYDIATE NOVICES' CONDITIONAL H'CAP HURDLE (0-110) (4-Y.O+) (Class E)
1-45 (1-45) **2m 4f (11 hdls)** £2,626.00 (£736.00: £358.00) GOING: 0.63 sec per fur (S)

				SP	RR	SF
1025^{2}	**Supertop (100)** (LLungo) **8-11-7**(7) IJardine (stdd s: hld up in rr: smooth hdwy appr 7th: led on bit appr last: sn clr)	—	1	5/2^{1}	91+	8
	Killbally Boy (IRE) (86) (HowardJohnson) **6-11-0** GFRyan (bit bkwd: chsd ldr: mstke 4th: led 7th: hrd rdn & hdd appr last: sn btn)	13	2	11/4^{2}	67	—
	Auntie Alice (80) (JGFitzGerald) **6-10-8** GLee (bkwd: trckd ldng pair: drvn along appr 3 out: sn btn)	6	3	7/2^{3}	56	—
1256^{P}	**Curragh Peter (72)** (MrsPBickerton) **9-10-0** GuyLewis (led to 7th: mstke next: wknd appr 2 out: t.o)	15	4	33/1	36	—
1030^{6}	**Ela Man Howa (84)** (ABailey) **5-10-9**(3) DJKavanagh (hld up & bhd: effrt appr 3 out: sn no imp: t.o)	9	5	9/2	41	—

1077[5] **Lawbuster (IRE) (78)** (MrsRGHenderson) **4-10-6b** PHenley (hld up: drvn along ½-wy: t.o whn p.u after 8th)..... **P** 10/1 — —
(SP 107.7%) **6 Rn**

5m 13.1 (31.10) CSF £8.91 TOTE £2.40: £1.50 £2.00 (£2.60) OWNER Mrs Barbara Lungo (CARRUTHERSTOWN) BRED Limestone Stud
LONG HANDICAP Curragh Peter 9-8
IN-FOCUS: **This was a first winner under Rules for Ian Jardine.**
1025 Supertop defied topweight under a very confident ride and, in this kind of form, has not stopped winning yet. (5/2)
Killbally Boy (IRE), like the winner attempting the trip for the first time, tried hard to make this a true test of stamina, but he was at a disadvantage regarding peak-fitness, and he had shot his bolt on reaching the flat. Losses will be recovered with interest. (11/4)
Auntie Alice, sure to strip fitter for the run, was in with every chance until tying up between the last two. (7/2)

1501 JOHN PARRETT MEMORIAL H'CAP CHASE (0-135) (5-Y.O+) (Class C)
2-20 (2-20) **3m 1f (Mildmay) (19 fncs)** £8,310.00 (£2,040.00) GOING: 0.63 sec per fur (S)

	Horse / details	Dist	Pos	SP	RR	SF
1315*	**Bas de Laine (FR) (120)** (MDHammond) **10-11-4** 5x RGarritty (j.rt: led after 3rd: j.slowly & hdd 4th: led 11th: drew clr fr 4 out)	—	1	9/4 1	130	23
1315[2]	**Fiveleigh Builds (128)** (MissLucindaRussell) **9-11-12** AThornton (lw: hmpd & mstke 3rd: lft in ld 4th: mstke & hdd 11th: blnd next: wknd 4 out)	dist	2	4/1 3	—	—
1279[3]	**Musthaveaswig (125)** (DNicholson) **10-11-9** RJohnson (j.bdly: drvn along ½-wy: t.o fr 12th: j.v.slowly 2 out: p.u bef last)		P	9/4 1	—	—
	Whaat Fettle (130) (GRichards) **11-12-0** ADobbin (bkwd: led tl after 3rd: dropped rr 8th: sn t.o: p.u bef 12th)		P	3/1 2	—	—

(SP 106.5%) **4 Rn**

6m 48.4 (31.40) CSF £9.48 TOTE £3.00 (£5.20) OWNER R K Bids Ltd (MIDDLEHAM) BRED Pascal Couturier
OFFICIAL EXPLANATION **Musthaveaswig: slipped on the bend early on as well as on going into his fences. As a result, he soon lost interest.**
1315* Bas de Laine (FR) showed that he does not need to make all, but he did show a tendency to jump to the right, though he had the prize in the safe-keeping before reaching the home straight. (9/4)
1315 Fiveleigh Builds is a far-from-fluent jumper and his attempt to keep tabs on the winner was doomed to failure from some way out. (4/1)
1279 Musthaveaswig just could not master these fences and, bustled along going out in the country for the final time, failed to pick up at all. After virtually stopping to negotiate the second last, he was wisely pulled up. (9/4)
Whaat Fettle has, for the past few seasons, turned in a very lack-lustre performance on his initial outing. Whatever the cause, he has soon recaptured his form, so as yet we will just have to wait and see. (3/1)

1502 CROSTON LANGENBERGER H'CAP HURDLE (0-120) (4-Y.O+) (Class D)
2-50 (2-51) **2m 110y (9 hdls)** £4,162.50 (£1,260.00: £615.00: £292.50) GOING: 0.63 sec per fur (S)

	Horse / details	Dist	Pos	SP	RR	SF
1188*	**Chai-Yo (110)** (JABOld) **6-11-5** GUpton (lw: hld up & bhd: stdy hdwy appr 3 out: led on bit last: pushed clr)	—	1	13/8 1	97+	15
	King Athelstan (USA) (108) (BAMcMahon) **8-11-3** DerekByrne (chsd ldr: led 4th: clr 3 out: hdd last: sn outpcd)	7	2	9/1	88	6
1358*	**Sarmatian (USA) (114)** (MDHammond) **5-11-9** 6x RGarritty (hld up: plld wd & hdwy 3 out: btn appr last)	13	3	4/1 2	82	—
	Hawwam (91) (EJAlston) **10-10-0** LWyer (trckd ldrs: rdn 3 out: sn btn)	11	4	16/1	48	—
1325[5]	**Pridewood Picker (91)** (RJPrice) **9-9-9**(5) DJKavanagh (lw: hld up: hdwy appr 3 out: sn rdn & wknd)	5	5	12/1	43	—
1267[5]	**Done Well (USA) (119)** (PMonteith) **4-12-0** ADobbin (hld up & bhd: effrt & rdn appr 3 out: no imp: t.o)	dist	6	4/1 2	—	—
1193[3]	**Indian Jockey (112)** (MCPipe) **4-11-4**(3) DWalsh (led & sn clr: rel to r & hdd 4th: mstke next: wknd appr 3 out: t.o)	17	7	7/1 3	—	—

(SP 114.2%) **7 Rn**

4m 16.1 (22.10) CSF £15.14 TOTE £3.00: £1.70 £4.40 (£14.80) OWNER Mr Nick Viney (WROUGHTON) BRED Mrs Audrey Goodwin
LONG HANDICAP Pridewood Picker 9-12 Hawwam 9-13
1188* Chai-Yo had the race set up for him with a confirmed front-runner in the field and, cruising through to lead on the bit at the last, had no trouble storming clear. (13/8)
King Athelstan (USA) held a useful lead turning in, but the winner soon began to make progress and, though he gave of his all, he was leaden-footed on the run-in. There was no disgrace in this defeat and he can soon make amends. (9/1)
1358* Sarmatian (USA) failed to overcome a 6lb penalty and could not muster the pace to give himself a live chance. (4/1)
1267 Done Well (USA) ran no race at all and may have found the rain-softened ground too testing with all his weight. (4/1)

1503 LIVERPOOL NOVICES' CHASE (5-Y.O+) (Class D)
3-20 (3-20) **3m 1f (Mildmay) (19 fncs)** £4,464.00 (£1,254.00: £612.00) GOING: 0.63 sec per fur (S)

	Horse / details	Dist	Pos	SP	RR	SF
1192*	**Baronet (IRE) (115)** (DNicholson) **6-11-5** RJohnson (led: mstke 9th: blnd & hdd 12th: led 15th to 4 out: sn lost pl: rallied u.p appr last: led flat: r.o)	—	1	2/5 1	110	18
1206[3]	**Kenmore-Speed** (MrsSJSmith) **9-11-0** NWilliamson (hld up in rr: mstke 12th: led 4 out tl flat: no ex u.p)	2	2	9/2 2	104	12
	Slotamatique (IRE) (GRichards) **7-11-0** ADobbin (bit bkwd: j.w: w wnr: led 12th to 15th: rallied u.p appr last: eased whn btn nr fin)	3½	3	9/2 2	102?	10

(SP 107.8%) **3 Rn**

6m 50.6 (33.60) CSF £2.33 TOTE £1.10: (£1.80) OWNER Mrs David Thompson (TEMPLE GUITING) BRED Mrs N. Flynn
1192* Baronet (IRE) is nothing to look at and may not have the scope to handle the hustle and bustle of this game, but he has won both of his starts over fences as yet, and looks are only skin-deep. (2/5)
1206 Kenmore-Speed could be coming to himself now and, though he may not quite have lasted home on this first attempt at this extended trip, he made the hot-pot work hard to reel him in. (9/2)
Slotamatique (IRE) ran extremely well after fourteen months out of action and his jumping alone will ensure he wins his share of races. He will be a lot sharper for the run. (9/2)

1504 WEATHERBYS 'STARS OF TOMORROW' INTERMEDIATE N.H. FLAT RACE (4, 5 & 6-Y.O) (Class H)
3-50 (3-51) **2m 110y** £1,934.50 (£542.00: £263.50)

	Horse / details	Dist	Pos	SP	RR	SF
1296[2]	**Good Vibes** (TDEasterby) **4-11-4** LWyer (mde virtually all: rn wd & hdd briefly 5f out: qcknd clr 3f out: drifted rt fnl f: easily)	—	1	9/4 1	53 f	—
1013[2]	**First Light** (JJQuinn) **4-11-4** RJohnson (hld up & bhd: hdwy 4f out: styd on appr fnl f: no ch w wnr)	4	2	3/1 2	49 f	—
	Meadow Hymn (IRE) (JGFitzGerald) **5-11-4** WDwan (hld up: hdwy 6f out: one pce fnl 2f)	4	3	20/1	45 f	—
	Whip Hand (IRE) (JGFitzGerald) **5-11-11** MDwyer (bkwd: hld up: hdwy ½-wy: wknd 2f out)	1	4	100/30 3	51 f	—

Mac's Supreme (IRE) (FMurphy) **4-11-4** NWilliamson (hld up & bhd: sme hdwy 3f out: nvr nrr)....................21 **5** 12/1 24 f —
Dashanti (DNicholson) **5-11-1**(3) RMassey (bkwd: chsd ldrs tl wknd 3f out)....................9 **6** 10/1 15 f —
686^{5} **Four From Home (IRE)** (JJO'Neill) **4-11-4** ARoche (trckd ldrs tl wknd ent st)....................8 **7** 20/1 7 f —
872^{4} **Night Escapade (IRE)** (CWeedon) **4-10-13** MRichards (prom: slt ld 5f out: sn hdd & wknd over 3f out)........1¾ **8** 10/1 1 f —
1329^{13} **Look In The Mirror** (NATwiston-Davies) **5-10-11**(7) LSuthern (prom over 10f: t.o)....................24 **9** 12/1 — —
Cashel Quay (IRE) (MrsPBickerton) **6-11-1**(3) GuyLewis (bkwd: trckd ldrs: rdn 5f out: sn wknd: t.o)....................2 **10** 33/1 — —
Dantes Amour (IRE) (MDHammond) **5-11-4** RGarritty (a bhd: t.o fnl 3f)....................dist **11** 10/1 — —
(SP 134.0%) **11 Rn**

4m 11.4 CSF £10.67 TOTE £3.10: £1.90 £1.50 £8.50 (£3.40) Trio £52.60 OWNER Mr G. E. Shouler (MALTON) BRED Mrs Trisha Dunbar
1296 Good Vibes decided to force the pace this time and, though he gave away a lot of ground by running wide leaving the back straight, he quickened things up once in line for home and soon had his challengers in trouble. (9/4)
1013 First Light ran another promising race, staying on best of all in the latter stages. His turn is merely delayed. (3/1: 2/1-100/30)
Meadow Hymn (IRE) finished ahead of his better-fancied stablemate and will be all the wiser for the experience. (20/1)
Whip Hand (IRE) had a 7lb penalty for winning on his only previous outing twenty months ago, but he looked far from fully wound up and should improve considerably with this run under his belt. (100/30)
Mac's Supreme (IRE) stayed on past beaten rivals to reach his finishing position, but was not knocked about and the kindness will be repaid. (12/1: op 8/1)
Dashanti was behind the leaders travelling strongly until lack of a recent outing began to take its toll early in the straight. He should be worth keeping in mind. (10/1: op 6/1)

T/Plpt: £14.60 (812.2 Tckts). T/Qdpt: £9.70 (110.8 Tckts). IM

1131-ASCOT (R-H) (Good to firm)
Friday November 22nd
WEATHER: overcast

1505 TRAVELLING THE TURF RACECOURSE OF THE YEAR NOVICES' CONDITIONAL HURDLE (4-Y.O+) (Class C)
1-00 (1-01) **2m 4f (11 hdls)** £3,517.50 (£1,065.00: £520.00: £247.50) GOING: 0.50 sec per fur (GS)

SP RR SF
Royal Raven (IRE) (JTGifford) **5-11-4** LAspell (bit bkwd: a.p: led 8th: r.o wl)....................— **1** 100/30 2 74 14
956* **Regal Pursuit (IRE) (103)** (NJHenderson) **5-10-10**(7) THagger (a.p: chsd ldr fr 5th: ev ch whn mstke 8th: unable qckn)....................4 **2** 5/6 1 70 10
1394^{3} **Adilov** (JJBridger) **4-11-4** SophieMitchell (lw: hld up: rdn appr 2 out: one pce)....................s.h **3** 9/1 71 11
Satcotino (IRE) (MHTompkins) **5-10-13** KGaule (a bhd)....................24 **4** 14/1 47 —
1077^{11} **One More Man (IRE)** (JTGifford) **5-10-8**(10) WGreatrex (chsd ldr to 5th: wknd 8th)....................8 **5** 20/1 45 —
931^{3} **Chief Gale (IRE)** (JGMO'Shea) **4-11-4** GHogan (lw: led to 8th: wknd 3 out)....................15 **6** 8/1 3 33 —
(SP 110.2%) **6 Rn**

5m 6.2 (24.20) CSF £6.25 TOTE £3.50: £1.50 £1.40 (£2.70) OWNER Mr A. D. Weller (FINDON) BRED Pat Hickey
Royal Raven (IRE), who showed promise in two bumpers last season, belied his paddock appearance on this hurdling and seasonal debut. Appreciating the longer trip, he moved to the front four out and had the measure of his two main rivals in the straight. (100/30: 2/1-7/2)
956* Regal Pursuit (IRE) was on level terms with the winner when hitting the fourth last. In the straight, she was only battling for second prize. (5/6: evens-11/10)
1394 Adilov continues to show promise over hurdles and goes very well for Sophie Mitchell. Easing his way into the action in the last mile, he was only scrapping for the runner-up spot in the straight. There is a small race waiting for him. (9/1)
Satcotino (IRE) (14/1: op 6/1)
931 Chief Gale (IRE) failed to see out this longer trip. (8/1: 4/1-9/1)

1506 CHARLES DAVIS NOVICES' H'CAP CHASE (5-Y.O+) (Class C)
1-35 (1-36) **3m 110y (20 fncs)** £6,970.00 (£2,110.00: £1,030.00: £490.00) GOING: 0.50 sec per fur (GS)

SP RR SF
1326^{3} **Mony-Skip (IRE) (99)** (MrsSJSmith) **7-10-5** RichardGuest (chsd ldr: mstke 12th: led 15th: lft clr last)....................— **1** 11/8 1 113 38
1318^{3} **Lucky Dollar (IRE) (99)** (KCBailey) **8-10-5** CO'Dwyer (lw: j.slowly 1st: mstke 11th: j.lft 12th: rdn 4 out: hdwy appr 2 out: lft mod 2nd last)....................7 **2** 11/2 2 108 33
1354^{F} **Minor Key (IRE) (94)** (JRJenkins) **6-10-0** JOsborne (led: mstkes 1st & 11th: hdd 15th: wknd 16th: t.o)........dist **3** 14/1 3 — —
1153^{2} **Random Harvest (IRE) (94)** (MrsMReveley) **7-10-0** DGallagher (lw: hld up: chsd wnr fr 16th: mstke 3 out: rdn appr 2 out: 2nd whn fell last: rmntd: t.o)....................dist **4** 11/8 1 — —
(SP 106.3%) **4 Rn**

6m 22.5 (17.50) CSF £7.41 TOTE £2.00 (£3.60) OWNER Mr Trevor Hemmings (BINGLEY) BRED Michael Moakley
LONG HANDICAP Minor Key (IRE) 9-7 Random Harvest (IRE) 9-13
1326 Mony-Skip (IRE) regained the winning thread. Leading five out, he had about a length to spare over Random Harvest, and appeared to be in command, when that rival fell at the last. (11/8)
1318 Lucky Dollar (IRE) has had plenty of chances, but still does not look convincing over the major obstacles. Connections can consider themselves extremely fortunate to collect a useful second prize. (11/2: op 3/1)
1136 Minor Key (IRE), 7lb out of the handicap, took the field along to the sixth last. (14/1: 10/1-16/1)
1153 Random Harvest (IRE), much happier over this longer trip, is prone to making mistakes and that proved his downfall here. He was about a length down and looking held when falling at the last, before remounted for fourth prize. There are races waiting to be won with him. (11/8)

1507 SCUDAMORE CLOTHING 0800 301 301 'N.H.' NOVICES' HURDLE (4-Y.O+) (Class C)
2-10 (2-11) **3m (13 hdls)** £3,631.25 (£1,100.00: £537.50: £256.25) GOING: 0.50 sec per fur (GS)

SP RR SF
1085* **Carole's Crusader (107)** (DRGandolfo) **5-10-12** RDunwoody (lw: mde all: clr appr 2 out: easily)....................— **1** 100/30 2 84+ 25
1261* **Flying Gunner (112)** (DNicholson) **5-11-3** AMaguire (a.p: chsd wnr fr 5th: hrd rdn appr 2 out: mstke 2 out: sn wknd)....................9 **2** 6/4 1 83 24
1297^{2} **Dacelo (FR) (95)** (OSherwood) **5-10-12** JOsborne (hdwy appr 2 out: one pce)....................9 **3** 20/1 72 13
Supreme Charm (IRE) (KCBailey) **4-10-11** CO'Dwyer (hld up: rdn 3 out: wknd appr 2 out)....................4 **4** 8/1 69 9
1283^{3} **Charlie Parrot (IRE)** (MCPipe) **6-10-12** APMcCoy (nvr nr to chal)....................11 **5** 16/1 62 3
Coole Cherry (CRBarwell) **6-10-12** BFenton (lw: prom to 7th: t.o)....................27 **6** 33/1 44 —

1250[3] **Pru's Profiles (IRE)** (NATwiston-Davies) **5-10-12** DBridgwater (chsd wnr to 5th: wknd 10th: t.o whn p.u after 3 out) .... P 12/1 — —
1278* **Mywend's (IRE)** (CPEBrooks) **6-11-3** GBradley (mstke 1st: hdwy 6th: 4th & wkng whn p.u after 3 out: lame) ... P 4/1[3] — —
1200P **Ashley House** (BRMillman) **7-10-7**(5) DSalter (swtg: bhd fr 6th: t.o fr 8th: p.u bef 10th) .... P 100/1 — —
(SP 116.5%) **9 Rn**

6m 2.5 (23.50) CSF £8.49 TOTE £3.20: £1.40 £1.40 £3.20 (£2.70) Trio £17.60 OWNER Mrs C. Skipworth (WANTAGE) BRED D. J. and Mrs Deer

WEIGHT FOR AGE 4yo-1lb

1085* Carole's Crusader, who beat the runner-up a whisker at Stratford first time out, put up a very polished display and, making all the running, surged clear turning for home to win with a ton in hand. Further success awaits her. (100/30)
1261* Flying Gunner moved into second place with just over a circuit to race but, try as he might, he failed to contain the winner from the third last. (6/4)
1297 Dacelo (FR) has proved himself to be very temperamental this season, but at least he behaved himself this time. (20/1)
Supreme Charm (IRE), an ex-Irish gelding who won two bumpers in the summer, was making his hurdling debut after an absence of nearly five months. (8/1: 5/1-9/1)
1250 Pru's Profiles (IRE) (12/1: 7/1-20/1)

1508 COOPERS & LYBRAND ASCOT HURDLE (Gd 2) (4-Y.O+) (Class A)

2-40 (2-43) **2m 4f** **(11 hdls)** £16,986.87 (£5,883.75: £2,879.38) GOING: 0.50 sec per fur (GS)

SP RR SF
1258[5] **Muse (145)** (DRCElsworth) **9-11-0** PHolley (mde virtually all: clr 2 out: r.o wl) .... — 1 13/8[2] 114? 38
1288[4] **Mistinguett (IRE) (134)** (NATwiston-Davies) **4-10-9** CLlewellyn (nt j.w: chsd wnr to 6th: chsd wnr fr 7th: ev ch appr 2 out: sn wknd) .... 10 2 8/11[1] 101 25
1196[2] **Fieldridge (115)** (MPMuggeridge) **7-11-0** BPowell (hld up: chsd wnr 6th to 7th: rdn appr 2 out: sn wknd) .... 6 3 15/2[3] 101 25
(SP 107.8%) **3 Rn**

4m 58.5 (16.50) CSF £3.04 TOTE £2.30 (£1.30) OWNER White Horse Racing Ltd (WHITCOMBE) BRED Lord Rotherwick
IN-FOCUS: **After the withdrawal of the two favourites, Castle Sweep and Large Action, on account of the ground, it left a quite pathetic turnout of just three for this valuable £25,000 added event, and yet owners are still moaning about lack of prizemoney!**
1258 Muse did not have much to beat to land this valuable prize and gained his first success since February 1994. (13/8)
1288 Mistinguett (IRE) failed to jump with any fluency and continually got underneath her hurdles. The fast ground may have been against her. (8/11)
1196 Fieldridge, way inferior to his two rivals, was left behind turning for home. (15/2: 6/1-10/1)

1509 GERRARD AND NATIONAL H'CAP CHASE (4-Y.O+) (Class B)

3-10 (3-12) **2m** **(12 fncs)** £10,092.60 (£2,833.60: £1,381.80) GOING: 0.50 sec per fur (GS)

SP RR SF
1134* **Storm Alert (145)** (DNicholson) **10-11-12** AMaguire (led tl after 2nd: led 4 out: rdn flat: r.o wl) .... — 1 6/5[1] 151 83
1087* **Callisoe Bay (IRE) (137)** (OSherwood) **7-11-4** JOsborne (nt j.w: led after 2nd: ev ch 2 out to 4 out: unable qckn) .... 3½ 2 11/8[2] 140 72
Dancing Paddy (147) (KOCunningham-Brown) **8-12-0** RichardGuest (mstke 3rd: blnd 4th: mstke 7th: hdwy appr 2 out: rdn appr last: wknd flat) .... 4 3 5/1[3] 146 78
1298[4] **Spinning Steel (120)** (PRRodford) **9-10-1**ow1 SBurrough (lw: chsd wnr to 2nd: 3rd whn fell 4th) .... F 50/1 — —
(SP 106.2%) **4 Rn**

3m 56.9 (5.90) CSF £3.00 TOTE £1.70: £1.70 (£1.80) OWNER Mrs Dawn Perrett (TEMPLE GUITING) BRED John Hennessy
LONG HANDICAP Spinning Steel 8-8
1134* Storm Alert managed to follow up his recent success here, but that was surely due to his rivals' inability to jump. Although he has now won both his starts this season, he still looks one to bet against. (6/5)
1087* Callisoe Bay (IRE) did not look a natural jumper in the first half of last season and, although he improved by the end of the campaign, he now appears to have slipped back again, continually making errors. (11/8)
Dancing Paddy, racing with his tongue tied down, suffered from jumping problems last season and they reared their ugly head again on this seasonal debut. (5/1)

1510 LADBROKE TRIAL H'CAP HURDLE (0-145) (4-Y.O+) (Class B)

3-40 (3-46) **2m 110y** **(9 hdls)** £6,589.10 (£2,019.80: £1,004.40: £496.70) GOING: 0.50 sec per fur (GS)

SP RR SF
Executive Design (128) (MrsMReveley) **4-11-3** PNiven (stdy hdwy 6th: led 2 out: rdn out) .... — 1 3/1[1] 111+ 60
1137[4] **Charming Girl (USA) (127)** (OSherwood) **5-11-2** JOsborne (stdy hdwy 6th: ev ch last: unable qckn) .... 3 2 9/2[2] 107 56
1137[2] **Shoofk (114)** (SDow) **5-10-3** RDunwoody (chsd ldr: led 4th to 2 out: r.o flat) .... hd 3 7/1 94 43
1154[3] **Kaitak (IRE) (120)** (JMCarr) **5-10-9** AMaguire (a.p: chsd ldr fr 5th: ev ch 3 out: hrd rdn appr 2 out: one pce) .1½ 4 6/1[3] 99 48
1288[3] **Ground Nut (IRE) (125)** (RHBuckler) **6-11-0** BPowell (led to 4th: lost pl 6th: rallied flat: r.o one pce) .... 1¾ 5 9/2[2] 102 51
1347[4] **Palacegate King (125)** (ACWhillans) **7-11-0** BHarding (bhd fr 6th) 20 6 16/1 82 31
Sovereigns Parade (113) (NJHenderson) **4-10-2** MAFitzgerald (bit bkwd: hdwy 3 out: wknd appr 2 out) 1¾ 7 9/1 69 18
1271[4] **Non Vintage (IRE) (131)** (MCChapman) **5-11-6** WWorthington (lw: bhd whn fell 2nd) .... F 10/1 — —
(SP 113.1%) **8 Rn**

3m 59.2 (9.20) CSF £15.71 CT £77.12 TOTE £3.60: £1.70 £1.70 £1.70 (£6.00) Trio £15.40 OWNER Mr L. T. Foster (SALTBURN) BRED L. T. and M. Foster
Executive Design, who had had a recent run on the Flat, cruised into the lead two out and, ridden along, disposed of the runner-up from the last. Connections will now consider the Ladbroke Hurdle at Leopardstown in January. (3/1: tchd 9/2)
1137 Charming Girl (USA) settled better on this occasion and was put to sleep at the back of the field. Creeping into the action in Swinley Bottom, she appeared to be travelling well in the straight and still had every chance at the final flight before tapped for toe. (9/2: op 3/1)
1137 Shoofk was collared two out and tapped for toe, although to his credit he stayed on nicely on the flat, only just failing to regain second prize. (7/1)
1154 Kaitak (IRE) had every chance at the third last, but the whip was shown turning for home and he could only go up and down in the same place. (6/1: op 4/1)
1288 Ground Nut (IRE) found this two miles on fast ground too sharp and, having lost his pitch four out, stayed on nicely again from the last. (9/2)
Sovereigns Parade (9/1: 6/1-10/1)
T/Jkpt: £9,679.60 (0.69 Tckts); £4,226.31 to Ascot 23/11/96. T/Plpt: £206.30 (144.33 Tckts). T/Qdpt: £22.40 (146.32 Tckts). AK

1499-AINTREE (L-H) (Good, Mildmay & Hdles Good to soft patches)
Saturday November 23rd
WEATHER: unsettled

1511 TOTE BOOKMAKERS NOVICES' CHASE (5-Y.O+) (Class C)
1-05 (1-05) **2m 4f (Mildmay) (16 fncs)** £5,658.00 (£1,588.00: £774.00: £367.00) GOING: 0.46 sec per fur (GS)

				SP	RR	SF
1264[2]	**Down the Fell** (HowardJohnson) **7-11-8** NWilliamson (j.w: mde all: rdn clr appr last: unchal)	—	1	5/1[2]	110	47
1311*	**Monyman (IRE) (97)** (MDHammond) **6-11-8** RGarritty (hld up: lft 2nd & hmpd 12th: ev ch 3 out: sn rdn: btn whn j.v.slowly last)	15	2	6/1[3]	98	35
	Ah Shush (IRE) (NoelChance) **8-11-3** APMcCoy (bit bkwd: dropped rr & j.slowly 8th: mstke 10th: sn wl bhd)	3½	3	14/1	90	27
1206*	**Simply Dashing (IRE)** (TDEasterby) **5-11-11** LWyer (j.slowly 3rd: chsd wnr fr 6th: ev ch whn fell 12th)		F	2/5[1]	—	—
				(SP 109.0%)	**4 Rn**	

5m 13.4 (15.40) CSF £24.57 TOTE £5.60 (£11.50) OWNER The Sun Punters Club (CROOK) BRED J. R. Raine
WEIGHT FOR AGE 5yo-1lb
1264 Down the Fell stays this trip well and, giving another exhibition of jumping, gradually forged clear for a very comfortable success. (5/1)
1311* Monyman (IRE) lacks the experience of the winner, but he almost got on terms three out before getting leg-weary in this rain-softened ground. (6/1)
Ah Shush (IRE), a winner between the Flags in Ireland in the spring of last year, looked as though he had done plenty of work for this debut under Rules, but he dropped to the rear at halfway, and does look to need a much stiffer test of stamina. (14/1: op 8/1)
1206* Simply Dashing (IRE), settled on the heels of the winner, had not been asked a question when he ran into the bottom of the fifth last and turned a somersault. (2/5)

1512 STANLEY LEISURE CHILDREN IN NEED H'CAP HURDLE (0-140) (4-Y.O+) (Class B)
1-35 (1-35) **2m 110y (9 hdls)** £10,377.00 (£3,141.00: £1,533.00: £729.00) GOING: 0.46 sec per fur (GS)

				SP	RR	SF
1163*	**Tom Brodie (120)** (HowardJohnson) **6-11-0** NWilliamson (hld up: hdwy appr 3 out: hrd drvn appr last: styd on to ld cl home)	—	1	7/2[2]	99	15
	Master Beveled (129) (PDEvans) **6-11-9** APMcCoy (a.p: led 2 out: hrd rdn & ct nr fin)	¾	2	11/4[1]	107	23
	Forestal (108) (SGGriffiths) **4-10-2** ADobbin (bit bkwd: led & sn clr: wknd & hdd 2 out: sn btn)	9	3	12/1	78	—
	Surrey Dancer (130) (MrsMReveley) **8-11-7**(3) GLee (bit bkwd: hld up in rr: t.o fr 3 out)	19	4	8/1	81	—
1125[3]	**Elpidos (119)** (MDHammond) **4-10-13** RGarritty (lw: nt j.w: bhd whn slightly hmpd 5th: t.o whn blnd 2 out)	dist	5	11/4[1]	—	—
1267[4]	**Thornton Gate (127)** (TDEasterby) **7-11-7** LWyer (chsd ldr fr 4th: fell next)		F	7/1[3]	—	—
				(SP 106.9%)	**6 Rn**	

4m 12.3 (18.30) CSF £12.16 TOTE £3.60: £2.00 £2.40 (£6.70) OWNER Mrs M. W. Bird (CROOK) BRED E.S Knape
OFFICIAL EXPLANATION **Elpidos: was unsuited by the dead ground.**
1163* Tom Brodie has done all his winning on a sounder surface, but he continued his winning sequence for this term with a dogged display that enabled him to take charge nearing the finish. (7/2)
Master Beveled kicked on from the penultimate flight and looked to be well in control, but his stride shortened on the flat and he was run out of it inside the last 50 yards. (11/4)
Forestal acts well when he can get his toe in, but he looked just short of a gallop and so this promising effort suggests that he will soon be carrying on from where he left off last season. (12/1)
1125 Elpidos turned in a very inept display of hurdling and was always behind and outpaced. His jockey reported that he could not handle this dead ground. (11/4)

1513 CROWTHER HOMES BECHER H'CAP CHASE (6-Y.O+) (Class B)
2-10 (2-10) **3m 3f (National) (22 fncs)** £25,666.40 (£8,978.40: £4,389.20: £1,886.00) GOING: 0.46 sec per fur (GS)

				SP	RR	SF
1266*	**Into the Red (131)** (MrsMReveley) **12-10-0** ADobbin (hld up: hdwy 15th: led 2 out: rdn & r.o wl)	—	1	9/2[3]	137	4
1157[3]	**Young Hustler (155)** (NATwiston-Davies) **9-11-10** CMaude (lw: j.rt: led to 2 out: rallied flat: no ex fnl 100y)	3½	2	13/8[1]	159	26
1287[2]	**Glemot (IRE) (135)** (KCBailey) **8-10-4** CO'Dwyer (lw: j.w: ev ch last: rdn & wknd flat)	8	3	7/1	134	1
1157[4]	**Scotton Banks (IRE) (159)** (TDEasterby) **7-12-0** RGarritty (blnd 2nd: sn rcvrd to chse ldrs: wknd 4 out: t.o)	30	4	4/1[2]	140	7
1162[6]	**Greenhill Raffles (132)** (MissLucindaRussell) **10-9-12**(3)ow1 PHenley (rdr lost irons 2nd: mstke 5th: bhd whn fell 14th)		F	66/1	—	—
1266[4]	**Joe White (131)** (HowardJohnson) **10-10-0** NWilliamson (mstke 2nd: in rr whn fell 13th)		F	12/1	—	—
1287[5]	**Straight Talk (131)** (PFNicholls) **9-10-0** APMcCoy (chsd ldrs: reminders 5th: btn whn blnd & uns rdr 4 out)		U	11/2	—	—
1122[7]	**Andros Prince (131)** (MissAEEmbiricos) **11-10-0** JRyan (a bhd: t.o whn blnd & uns rdr last)		U	100/1	—	—
				(SP 114.3%)	**8 Rn**	

7m 15.7 (30.70) CSF £11.79 CT £44.88 TOTE £4.60: £1.40 £1.50 £1.70 (£4.50) OWNER Mr J. Huckle (SALTBURN) BRED M. W. Hickey
LONG HANDICAP Into the Red 9-7 Greenhill Raffles 9-0 Joe White 9-2 Straight Talk 9-13 Andros Prince 7-4
1266* Into the Red, winner of this race two years ago and a faller when in contention twelve months ago, gained his revenge over the favourite and once again showed these fences hold no terrors for him. (9/2)
1157 Young Hustler attempted to repeat last year's all-the-way success and may well have done so had the stormy weather kept away, but he was the winner on merit, trying to concede so much weight. He still looks as good as ever. (13/8)
1287 Glemot (IRE) produced a very promising performance on this first appearance over these big fences and only failed as lack of stamina appeared to take its toll on the long run-in. His jumping was a joy to watch and he has still got a whole future in front of him. (7/1)
1157 Scotton Banks (IRE) all but departed at the second and, though he recovered to press the leaders, he was feeling the strain inside the final mile. From then on, the main thing in mind must have been to complete the course. (4/1)

1514 TOTE CREDIT HURDLE (3-Y.O) (Class B)
2-45 (2-46) **2m 110y (9 hdls)** £5,151.75 (£1,554.00: £754.50: £354.75) GOING: 0.46 sec per fur (GS)

				SP	RR	SF
1158*	**Bellator** (GBBalding) **3-11-5** APMcCoy (chsd ldr: led 6th: sn clr: hit last: canter)	—	1	5/6[1]	102+	12
1387*	**Noble Lord** (RHBuckler) **3-11-0** BPowell (led & sn clr: hdd 6th: outpcd appr 3 out)	15	2	7/4[2]	83	—
	Onyourown (IRE) (HowardJohnson) **3-11-0** NWilliamson (lw: nt j.w: hrd drvn 6th: wknd appr 3 out: t.o)	dist	3	5/1[3]	—	—
	Stretching (IRE) (ABailey) **3-11-0** JMcLaughlin (a bhd: t.o fr ½-wy)	dist	4	66/1	—	—
				(SP 109.1%)	**4 Rn**	

4m 13.9 (19.90) CSF £2.58 TOTE £1.80 (£1.40) OWNER Mr P. Richardson (ANDOVER) BRED Theakston Stud
1158* Bellator won more readily than he did on his debut and, of the juveniles seen out so far this term, he must rank right near the top. That may well still be the case at the end of the term. (5/6)
1387* Noble Lord lost his unbeaten run over hurdles and was thrashed in the process, but he has done all his winning on much faster ground than he had here. (7/4)
Onyourown (IRE), an attractive ex-Irish youngster who is closely related to several winners, did not hurdle fluently on this debut and was tenderly handled when all chance had gone. He has won on yielding ground on the Flat and will soon leave this form behind once he gets his act together. (5/1)

1515 TOWN GREEN H'CAP CHASE (0-135) (5-Y.O+) (Class C)
3-15 (3-16) **2m 4f (Mildmay) (16 fncs)** £6,344.00 (£1,556.00) GOING: 0.46 sec per fur (GS)

				SP	RR	SF
1284³	**The Caumrue (IRE) (105)** (GBBalding) **8-10-11** APMcCoy (lw: plld hrd: j.w: led 9th: j.bdly lft 3 out: rdn out)	—	1	8/15 1	108	8
1272³	**Shaarid (USA) (112)** (IABalding) **8-11-1**(3) MrCBonner (lw: led to 9th: ev ch whn mstke 2 out: rdn & one pce flat)	2½	2	6/4 2	113	13
				(SP 105.2%)		**2 Rn**

5m 22.0 (24.00) TOTE £1.50 OWNER The On The Run Partnership (ANDOVER) BRED Mrs Hazel O'Haire
1284 The Caumrue (IRE) had everything in his favour this time and, except for running across the third last, he jumped impeccably and stayed on strongly to the line. (8/15)
1272 Shaarid (USA) is a fast-ground specialist, so the wet spell over the last couple of days did his cause no good at all, but he gave it his best shot. (6/4)

1516 E.B.F. 'N.H.' (QUALIFIER) NOVICES' HURDLE (4, 5 & 6-Y.O) (Class C)
3-50 (3-52) **2m 110y (9 hdls)** £3,936.00 (£1,096.00: £528.00) GOING: 0.46 sec per fur (GS)

				SP	RR	SF
	Lucia Forte (KCBailey) **5-10-9** CO'Dwyer (bit bkwd: hld up in rr: hdwy to ld appr last: sn clr: v.easily)	—	1	11/8 1	61+	—
1044*	**Beacon Flight (IRE)** (BdeHaan) **5-11-5** NWilliamson (set slow pce: qcknd 3 out: hdd appr last: nt pce of wnr)	7	2	7/4 2	64	—
	Hydro (IRE) (MDHammond) **5-11-0** RGarritty (bkwd: chsd ldr tl wknd appr 2 out)	6	3	5/2 3	53	—
				(SP 107.0%)		**3 Rn**

4m 20.1 (26.10) CSF £3.67 TOTE £2.30 (£1.40) OWNER Mrs Lucia Farmer (UPPER LAMBOURN) BRED Mrs K. I. Hayward
Lucia Forte looked the most backward of the trio, but she is a strongly-made mare and will probably always carry condition. Given time to adapt to hurdles, due to the sedate pace, she quickened up impressively to show in front at the last, and she can only get better with this experience behind her. (11/8)
1044* Beacon Flight (IRE) won from the front on his previous outing and he dictated at his own pace this time but, when it developed into a sprint to the line, he was found wanting. (7/4)
Hydro (IRE) will need a stiffer test of stamina to show his true worth, but he hurdled well enough and will be more the finished article next time he appears. (5/2)

T/Plpt: £112.40 (149.3 Tckts). T/Qdpt: £5.70 (194.36 Tckts) IM

1505-ASCOT (R-H) (Good to firm)
Saturday November 23rd
WEATHER: sunny

1517 HOLLOWAYS GATE NOVICES' HURDLE (4-Y.O+) (Class C)
12-45 (12-46) **2m 110y (9 hdls)** £3,517.50 (£1,065.00: £520.00: £247.50) GOING: 0.20 sec per fur (G)

				SP	RR	SF
	Resist the Force (USA) (JTGifford) **6-11-5** PHide (a gng wl: hld up: led on bit appr last: v.easily)	—	1	5/1 3	82++	12
	Carlito Brigante (PRWebber) **4-11-5** JOsborne (a.p: ev ch appr last: unable qckn)	7	2	9/4 1	75+	5
	Take Cover (IRE) (MHTompkins) **5-11-5** AMaguire (led tl appr last: wknd flat)	6	3	6/1	69	—
	The Stager (IRE) (JRJenkins) **4-11-5** GBradley (bit bkwd: plld hrd: mstke 1st: hdwy 6th: ev ch appr 2 out: sn wknd)	8	4	9/1	62	—
	Blue And Royal (IRE) (VSoane) **4-11-5** CLlewellyn (chsd ldr to 6th: wknd appr 2 out)	4	5	40/1	58?	—
1333⁴	**Adonisis** (DRCElsworth) **4-11-5** AProcter (plld hrd: bhd fr 3 out)	8	6	12/1	50	—
	Seventeens Lucky (BobJones) **4-11-5** VSmith (hld up: rdn 3 out: wknd appr 2 out: b.b.v)	8	7	9/2 2	42	—
	River Monarch (JTGifford) **5-10-12**(7) MrPO'Keeffe (mstke 5th: a bhd: t.o)	21	8	20/1	22	—
	Night Flare (FR) (SWoodman) **4-11-5** RDunwoody (bit bkwd: mstke 5th: prom to 6th: t.o whn p.u bef 2 out)		P	6/1	—	—
				(SP 119.1%)		**9 Rn**

4m 5.6 (15.60) CSF £16.47 TOTE £5.80: £1.90 £1.30 £1.70 (£9.80) Trio £12.20 OWNER Mrs Barbara Hogan (FINDON)
Resist the Force (USA), a maiden on the Flat for Charles Cyzer, changed hands for a mere 1,400 guineas and has not run since September 1993. However, despite the long absence, he could hardly have been more impressive, travelling really well throughout and leading on the bridle going to the last before scooting clear on the run-in to win with a ton in hand. He looks potentially very useful if this run is anything to go by. (5/1)
Carlito Brigante, winner of a Pontefract handicap and fourth in the Magnet Cup at York for Lynda Ramsden on the Flat this year, made a promising debut. He should soon pick up a race. (9/4)
Take Cover (IRE) did a fine job of pacemaking, but was soon brushed aside. (6/1: op 4/1)
The Stager (IRE), winner of a seven-furlong event at Newmarket in May, did not look fully tuned up for this hurdling debut, his first run in five months, but did well before lack of a recent run took its toll. (9/1: 5/1-10/1)
Blue And Royal (IRE), who had a couple of runs on the Flat recently, failed to complete in two novice hurdles last season, but did get round on this occasion. (40/1)
Seventeens Lucky (9/2: 3/1-5/1)
Night Flare (FR) (6/1: 7/2-7/1)

1518 GARDNER MERCHANT H'CAP CHASE (5-Y.O+) (Class B)
1-20 (1-21) **3m 110y (20 fncs)** £10,761.00 (£3,021.00: £1,473.00) GOING: 0.20 sec per fur (G)

				SP	RR	SF
1273*	**Inchcailloch (IRE) (124)** (JSKing) **7-11-4** RDunwoody (chsd ldr: mstke 11th: led 15th r.o wl)	—	1	Evens 1	132	58

	Horse	Details	Dist	Pos	SP	RR	SF
1133*	**Go Ballistic (129)**	(JGMO'Shea) **7-11-9** MAFitzgerald (hld up: chsd wnr fr 16th: ev ch whn mstke 2 out: unable qckn)	3½	**2**	Evens[1]	135	61
1383[5]	**Paper Star (106)**	(MPMuggeridge) **9-10-0** CLlewellyn (led to 15th: 2nd & btn whn blnd 16th: t.o)	dist	**3**	22/1[2]	—	—
					(SP 104.3%)	**3 Rn**	

6m 12.4 (7.40) CSF £2.14 TOTE £1.90 (£1.10) OWNER Mr F. J. Carter (SWINDON) BRED Hascombe and Valiant Studs
LONG HANDICAP Paper Star 9-9
1273* Inchcailloch (IRE) was not going to let a 6lb rise stop him in this valuable race which was effectively a match. (Evens)
1133* Go Ballistic, 7lb higher for his facile win here three weeks ago, had every chance when rather awkward at the penultimate fence and then found the winner too strong. (Evens)
1194 Paper Star was totally out of her class - all four of her victories have come at Plumpton - but got round for a decent third prize. (22/1)

1519 AURELIUS HURDLE (3-Y.O) (Class B)

1-55 (1-55) **2m 110y (9 hdls)** £4,879.00 (£1,477.00: £721.00: £343.00) GOING: 0.20 sec per fur (G)

	Horse	Details	Dist	Pos	SP	RR	SF
	Lear Jet (USA)	(BobJones) **3-11-3** RDunwoody (hld up: chsd ldr fr 6th: rdn appr 2 out: led last: r.o wl)	—	**1**	9/1	87	16
	Blurred (IRE)	(MHTompkins) **3-11-3** AMaguire (lw: stdy hdwy 6th: led on bit appr 2 out: mstke & hdd last: unable qckn)	2	**2**	5/4[1]	85+	14
1269[4]	**Doctor Green (FR)**	(MCPipe) **3-11-7v** CLlewellyn (led: sn clr: mstke 6th: hdd appr 2 out: wknd appr last)	14	**3**	4/1[2]	85	14
1269[3]	**Squire's Occasion (CAN)**	(RAkehurst) **3-11-7** MAFitzgerald (chsd ldr to 6th: wknd appr 2 out)	5	**4**	13/2	80	9
1158[3]	**Hever Golf Diamond**	(TJNaughton) **3-11-7** JOsborne (wl bhd fr 3rd)	6	**5**	12/1	75	4
	Sam Rockett	(PMooney) **3-11-3** KGaule (a bhd: t.o fr 6th)	dist	**6**	50/1	—	—
	Mr Wild (USA)	(RAkehurst) **3-11-3** SRyan (mstke & uns rdr 2nd)		**U**	9/2[3]	—	—
					(SP 115.6%)	**7 Rn**	

4m 4.1 (14.10) CSF £20.55 TOTE £8.90: £2.20 £1.40 (£7.50) OWNER Godorphal Racing Partnership (NEWMARKET) BRED Newgate Stud Farm Inc.
Lear Jet (USA), winner of a Bath maiden on the Flat for Paul Cole in April, ran disappointingly in claimers on his last two starts and was sold out of that stable for 9,000 guineas, but he made a very pleasing hurdling debut. Victory did not look on the cards entering the straight, but he proved too strong for Blurred on the run-in. It will be interesting to see how he goes on from here. (9/1: 6/1-10/1)
Blurred (IRE), winner of a Doncaster handicap and disqualified after winning a similar event on the Flat at Redcar recently, looked very well beforehand and appeared set to make a winning debut over hurdles as he cruised into the lead approaching the second last but, untidy at the last, he failed to find what was required. Compensation awaits. (5/4)
1269 Doctor Green (FR) is finding life tougher in these better-class juvenile races. (4/1: 5/2-9/2)
1269 Squire's Occasion (CAN) was left for dead turning for home. He is worth a try over further in a bid to offset his lack of acceleration. (13/2: 3/1-7/1)
Mr Wild (USA) (9/2: 6/1-9/1)

1520 FIRST NATIONAL BANK GOLD CUP H'CAP CHASE (Gd 2) (5-Y.O+) (Class A)

2-30 (2-30) **2m 3f 110y (16 fncs)** £25,984.00 (£9,837.20: £4,818.60: £2,200.20) GOING: 0.20 sec per fur (G)

	Horse	Details	Dist	Pos	SP	RR	SF
1366[2]	**Strong Promise (IRE) (122)**	(GAHubbard) **5-10-5**(3) KGaule (lw: a.p: led 7th: shkn up flat: r.o wl)	—	**1**	11/8[1]	133	54
1119*	**Major Bell (129)**	(ACWhillans) **8-11-1** BHarding (chsd wnr fr 7th: ev ch 3 out: hrd rdn appr last: unable qckn)	4	**2**	9/2[2]	137	58
1352[2]	**Southampton (120)**	(GBBalding) **6-10-6v** BFenton (stdy hdwy 11th: rdn appr 2 out: one pce)	5	**3**	13/2[3]	124	45
1155[3]	**Bertone (IRE) (135)**	(KCBailey) **7-11-7** JOsborne (stdy hdwy 11th: ev ch 3 out: wknd appr 2 out)	12	**4**	10/1	129	50
1270[F]	**Plunder Bay (USA) (118)**	(NJHenderson) **5-10-4** MAFitzgerald (lw: stdy hdwy 11th: wknd appr 2 out)	9	**5**	16/1	104	25
1173[3]	**Pimberley Place (IRE) (125)**	(NATwiston-Davies) **8-10-11** CLlewellyn (lw: a bhd: blnd 6th: t.o fr 10th)	dist	**6**	20/1	—	—
1154[5]	**Cumbrian Challenge (IRE) (129)**	(TDEasterby) **7-11-1** AMaguire (led to 7th: 5th & wkng whn mstke 3 out: t.o)	13	**7**	9/1	—	—
1133[5]	**Senor El Betrutti (IRE) (138)**	(MrsSusanNock) **7-11-10** GBradley (bit bkwd: prom to 6th: t.o whn p.u bef 10th)		**P**	9/1	—	—
					(SP 113.4%)	**8 Rn**	

4m 51.5 (4.50) CSF £7.69 CT £26.23 TOTE £2.30: £1.50 £2.10 £1.30 (£5.60) Trio £6.70 OWNER Mr G. A. Hubbard (WOODBRIDGE) BRED William McCarthy
OFFICIAL EXPLANATION **Senor El Betrutti (IRE): his rider reported the gelding was never going and hung badly throughout.**
1366 Strong Promise (IRE) had a very hard race at Cheltenham last Saturday, but this exciting novice showed no ill-effects and, jumping like an old hand, proved the handicap snip - he is set to rise a massive 22lb in future handicaps - many thought he would. He is an extremely talented individual who loves to hear his feet rattle and to be kept on the go - the only problem for connections is trying to place him as he is sure to be murdered by the Handicapper. (11/8: evens-6/4)
1119* Major Bell was facing his stiffest assignment to date and went down with all guns blazing. Despite a steady rise in the weights, he should soon return to the winner's enclosure. (9/2)
1352 Southampton seems better suited to two and a half miles these days. (13/2)
1155 Bertone (IRE) was 5lb higher than when running a cracking race in the Charisma Gold Cup at Kempton. (10/1: 7/1-11/1)
1018* Plunder Bay (USA) had shot his bolt turning for home. (16/1)
1173 Pimberley Place (IRE) showed his Exeter run to be a flash in the pan and was always at the back of the field. He is still not one to trust. (20/1)
1154 Cumbrian Challenge (IRE), reverting to fences, adopted different tactics on this occasion but that could not help him bounce back to form. He is yet to recover the sparkle that helped him win four times last season. (9/1)
1133 Senor El Betrutti (IRE), still not looking fully fit, was back over his optimum trip, but was unable to dominate and ran another dreadful race. He has plenty of ability as he showed last year, but looks one to avoid. (9/1)

1521 HURST PARK NOVICES' CHASE (5-Y.O+) (Class B)

3-05 (3-05) **2m (12 fncs)** £7,300.00 (£2,050.00: £1,000.00) GOING: 0.20 sec per fur (G)

	Horse	Details	Dist	Pos	SP	RR	SF
1015[3]	**Oh So Risky**	(DRCElsworth) **9-11-3** PHolley (chsd ldr fr 3rd: led 7th: shkn up flat: r.o wl)	—	**1**	9/4[2]	115?	48
	Dream Ride (IRE)	(DNicholson) **6-11-3** AMaguire (blnd bdly 1st: chsd ldr to 3rd: lft 2nd 3 out: hrd rdn appr last: unable qckn)	7	**2**	11/8[1]	108?	41
1319[3]	**Djais (FR)**	(JRJenkins) **7-11-3** RDunwoody (a bhd: t.o fr 4 out)	22	**3**	9/2	86?	19
1140[3]	**Prince Skyburd (93)**	(MrsPMAAvison) **5-11-3** MAFitzgerald (lw: led to 7th: 2nd whn fell 3 out)		**F**	4/1[3]	—	—
					(SP 111.1%)	**4 Rn**	

3m 57.9 (6.90) CSF £5.60 TOTE £3.30 (£2.90) OWNER Mr M. Tabor (WHITCOMBE) BRED Barrettstown Stud Farms Ltd

1015 Oh So Risky, a one-time top-class hurdler, was coming to fences very late in life, but connections had little alternative - he had gone well off the boil over hurdles. Putting in a good display of jumping, connections must have been delighted to see the old boy bounce back and win his first race since November 1994, but the jury remains out on how he will cope with better opposition. (9/4)
Dream Ride (IRE) looked straight for this chasing debut, but he almost got rid of his rider at the very first fence and was not fluent at several fences after that. He should soon find a race, but needs to polish up his jumping. (11/8)
1319 Djais (FR) cut little ice on this chasing debut, but found this trip far too sharp. (9/2)
1140 Prince Skyburd, a complete revelation over fences this season, set the pace to the sixth last and was still close up in second when departing at the third last. (4/1)

1522 LION GATE H'CAP HURDLE (4-Y.O+) (Class B)

3-40 (3-41) **3m (13 hdls)** £5,414.80 (£1,638.40: £799.20: £379.60) GOING: 0.20 sec per fur (G)

				SP	RR	SF
1196[3]	**Olympian (118)** (JNeville) **9-10-7b** MAFitzgerald (chsd ldr: rdn appr 2 out: led nr fin)	—	1	14/1	98	1
1196*	**Ocean Hawk (USA) (140)** (NATwiston-Davies) **4-12-0** CLlewellyn (lw: rdn & hdwy appr 2 out: led flat: hdd nr fin)	nk	2	8/11[1]	120	22
1286*	**Gysart (IRE) (120)** (MCPipe) **7-10-9b** AMaguire (led: sn clr: mstke 7th: rdn appr 2 out: hdd flat: r.o)	hd	3	2/1[2]	100	3
1392*	**Moment of Glory (IRE) (115)** (DRGandolfo) **5-10-4** RDunwoody (hld up: mstke 3 out: rdn appr 2 out: unable qckn flat)	2	4	11/2	93	—
*948**	***Fired Earth (IRE) (129)*** (JRFanshawe) **8-11-4** JOsborne (Withdrawn not under Starter's orders: Veterinary advice)		W	5/1[3]	—	—
				(SP 129.9%)	**4 Rn**	

6m 1.8 (22.80) CSF £25.04 TOTE £12.30: £6.60 (£7.10) OWNER Mr J. Neville (NEWPORT, GWENT) BRED Seend Stud
WEIGHT FOR AGE 4yo-1lb
1196 Olympian, beaten nineteen lengths by the runner-up at Kempton earlier in the month, just managed to turn the tables on 12lb better terms. (14/1)
1196* Ocean Hawk (USA), who has been raised 12lb for his demolition job at Kempton earlier in the month, was just worried out of it near the line. (8/11: evens-6/4)
1286* Gysart (IRE), 7lb higher for his Wincanton success, was given an enterprising ride and quickly poached about ten lengths on his rivals at the start. Although reeled in turning for home, he still kept his head in front until worried out of it on the run-in. (2/1)
1392* Moment of Glory (IRE) failed to find the necessary turn of turn of foot on the run-in. (11/2: 4/1-6/1)

T/Jkpt: £10,283.50 (0.09 Tckts); £13,180.29 to Catterick 25/11/96. T/Plpt: £923.50 (26.95 Tckts). T/Qdpt: £350.00 (4.13 Tckts). AK

CATTERICK (L-H) (Good to firm)
Saturday November 23rd

One fence omitted
WEATHER: fine

1523 GOATHLAND MAIDEN HURDLE (4-Y.O+ F & M) (Class F)

1-10 (1-10) **2m 3f (10 hdls)** £1,793.00 (£498.00: £239.00) GOING minus 0.34 sec per fur (GF)

				SP	RR	SF
1438[3]	**Anglesey Sea View** (ABailey) **7-11-0** TKent (lw: j.lft: mstkes: chsd ldrs: led after 3 out: clr whn hit 2 out)	—	1	1/4[1]	56	—
968[5]	**Aradia's Diamond** (TKeddy) **5-11-0** SMcNeill (a chsng ldrs: one pce fr 3 out)	11	2	8/1[3]	47	—
	Appearance Money (IRE) (80) (FMurphy) **5-10-7**(7) MissElizabethDoyle (hdwy to ld 5th: hdd after 3 out: 2nd & wl btn whn blnd last)	3	3	33/1	44	—
	Philbecky (JMJefferson) **5-10-11**(3) ECallaghan (outpcd ½-wy: rdn 3 out)	9	4	33/1	37	—
1208[11]	**Best Friend** (JWCurtis) **4-11-0** JCallaghan (lw: effrt 6th: in tch 3 out: sn rdn & btn)	2½	5	25/1	35	—
	About Midnight (FPMurtagh) **7-11-0** ARoche (led to 5th: wkng whn blnd 3 out)	30	6	66/1	9	—
	Ringrone (IRE) (VThompson) **7-11-0** MrMThompson (in tch to 5th: sn wl bhd)	1½	7	66/1	8	—
	Restate (IRE) (FMurphy) **5-10-7**(7) MrTJBarry (sn bhd: t.o)	dist	8	50/1	—	—
1344[5]	**Nawtinookey (60)** (MartinTodhunter) **6-11-0** BStorey (lw: hld up: fell 6th)		F	6/1[2]	—	—
1345[7]	**Akito Racing (IRE)** (MartinTodhunter) **5-11-0** MMoloney (bhd: bdly hmpd 6th: p.u bef 2 out)		P	14/1	—	—
				(SP 126.7%)	**10 Rn**	

4m 45.5 (20.50) CSF £4.23 TOTE £1.50: £1.10 £1.90 £4.20 (£4.40) Trio £21.70 OWNER Mrs P. Hewitt (TARPORLEY) BRED J. A. Hewitt
OFFICIAL EXPLANATION **Akito Racing (IRE): was struck in the face by a faller, causing her to bleed.**
1438 Anglesey Sea View had a simple task, but her hurdling still left a lot to be desired. (1/4)
Aradia's Diamond is slow but sure. (8/1)
Appearance Money (IRE) showed a little but, apart from the winner, it looked a very poor event. (33/1)
Philbecky, a reasonable-looking sort who needed this experience, will probably want longer trips. (33/1)
Best Friend looked fit, but proved to be rather moderate. (25/1)
1344 Nawtinookey (6/1: 10/1-5/1)

1524 DARLINGTON AND STOCKTON TIMES NOVICES' H'CAP HURDLE (0-100) (4-Y.O+) (Class E)

1-40 (1-40) **2m (8 hdls)** £1,830.20 (£507.20: £242.60) GOING minus 0.34 sec per fur (GF)

				SP	RR	SF
1152[6]	**Last Try (IRE) (86)** (BSRothwell) **5-11-4**(3) GCahill (cl up: led after 3 out: clr next: styd on wl)	—	1	4/1[3]	71	15
1263[5]	**Scotton Green (74)** (TDEasterby) **5-10-9** JCallaghan (chsd ldrs: outpcd appr 2 out: styd on flat)	5	2	6/1	54	—
1343[4]	**Bowcliffe (81)** (MrsAMNaughton) **5-11-2** JSupple (in tch: hdwy 3 out: wnt 2nd next: no imp)	¾	3	12/1	60	4
1161[6]	**Joe Jagger (IRE) (74)** (MDHammond) **5-10-9** DBentley (prom: outpcd whn mstke 2 out: no imp)	1	4	6/1	52	—
1345[4]	**Mullins (IRE) (80)** (DMoffatt) **5-11-1** DJMoffatt (bhd: hdwy & in tch 3 out: sn btn)	10	5	10/1	48	—
1312[2]	**Kilnamartyra Girl (89)** (JParkes) **6-11-7**(3) PMidgley (prom: hit 5th: sn rdn & lost tch)	2	6	7/2[2]	55	—
1079*	**Flaming Hope (IRE) (79)** (MrsNHope) **6-11-0**ow1 JBurke (lw: led: blnd 4th: blnd 3 out: sn hdd & btn)	9	7	11/4[1]	36	—
5[8]	**Coquet Gold (65)** (FTWalton) **5-10-0** BStorey (a bhd)	13	8	33/1	9	—
				(SP 117.2%)	**8 Rn**	

3m 49.1 (6.10) CSF £26.48 CT £242.67 TOTE £10.20: £3.60 £2.00 £1.50 (£16.10) OWNER Mr H. J. Harenberg (MALTON) BRED H. J. Harenberg
LONG HANDICAP Coquet Gold 9-13
OFFICIAL EXPLANATION **Flaming Hope (IRE): was found to have pulled muscles on the inside of her off-hind leg on returning to the yard.**

Last Try (IRE), wearing a tongue-strap, won a poor race well. (4/1)
Scotton Green, a chasing type, gave the impression that further should suit. (6/1: op 4/1)
1343 Bowcliffe ran better this time and could well pick up a moderate event. (12/1)
1161 Joe Jagger (IRE) looked pretty slow when the pace was on over the last three flights. (6/1)
1345 Mullins (IRE) still has plenty of improving to do to have a chance. (10/1)
1312 Kilnamartyra Girl ran as though something was wrong and was never happy from halfway. (7/2)
1079* Flaming Hope (IRE) looked particularly well, but spoiled all chances with some very poor hurdling. (11/4)

1525 NORTHERN ECHO 'RACING NORTH' NOVICES' CHASE (4-Y.O+) (Class E)

2-10 (2-10) **2m (11 fncs)** £2,816.20 (£850.60: £413.80: £195.40) GOING minus 0.34 sec per fur (GF)

				SP	RR	SF
1311[5]	**Twin Falls (IRE) (88)** (GMMoore) **5-11-3** JCallaghan (chsd ldr: lft in ld appr 5th: qcknd clr 3 out: eased flat)	—	**1**	10/1	103	16
939*	**Marble Man (IRE)** (MDHammond) **6-11-3** DBentley (a.p: chsd wnr fr 6th: outpcd whn hit 3 out: no imp after)	13	**2**	11/4[2]	90	3
1306[2]	**Val de Rama (IRE) (93)** (DenysSmith) **7-11-7**(3) GCahill (bhd: hit 4th: hdwy 7th: disp 2nd whn hit 3 out: no imp)	8	**3**	5/1[3]	89	2
1308[3]	**Fingerhill (IRE)** (VThompson) **7-11-3** MrMThompson (chsd ldrs: blnd 6th: outpcd & hit 8th: n.d after)	20	**4**	25/1	62	—
1346[3]	**Jack Doyle (IRE)** (JJO'Neill) **5-11-3** ARoche (lw: stdd s: smooth hdwy & 3rd whn fell 8th)		**F**	Evens[1]	—	—
853[4]	**Bonny Johnny** (DMoffatt) **6-11-3** DJMoffatt (last whn fell 8th)		**F**	100/1	—	—
1083[P]	**Cardinal Sinner (IRE) (56)** (JWade) **7-11-3** KJones (led: 5l clr whn took wrong crse appr 5th)		**R**	100/1	—	—

(SP 108.3%) **7 Rn**

3m 57.6 (5.60) CSF £34.03 TOTE £11.20: £3.10 £1.90 (£16.00) Trio £5.70 OWNER Mrs Susan Moore (MIDDLEHAM) BRED Newgate Stud Co
STEWARDS' ENQUIRY Jones susp. 2-4/12/96 (failure to acquaint himself w crse).
1311 Twin Falls (IRE), given an aggressive ride this time, obviously learnt plenty from his previous outing and won most emphatically. (10/1: 6/1-12/1)
939* Marble Man (IRE) ran reasonably at this first attempt over fences, but was no match for the winner when the heat was on. (11/4: op 7/4)
1306 Val de Rama (IRE) has had some hard races already this season and was let down by lack of pace and mistakes at vital stages.(5/1: 7/2-6/1)
1308 Fingerhill (IRE) will need to improve his jumping a good deal. (25/1)
1346 Jack Doyle (IRE) was swinging off the bit and had just moved into third when falling four from home. (Evens)

1526 CALDERPRINT CLAIMING HURDLE (3-Y.O) (Class G)

2-40 (2-47) **2m (8 hdls)** £1,849.00 (£514.00: £247.00) GOING minus 0.34 sec per fur (GF)

				SP	RR	SF
1011[4]	**The Great Flood** (CADwyer) **3-10-11** ILawrence (chsd ldrs: led after 3 out: kpt on wl flat)	—	**1**	4/1[2]	55	12
1205[8]	**Alwarqa** (MDHammond) **3-10-9** DBentley (hld up: smooth hdwy fr 4th: disp ld 2 out: sn hrd drvn: one pce flat)	2½	**2**	15/8[1]	51	8
462[5]	**Russian Rascal (IRE)** (TDEasterby) **3-11-12** SMcNeill (hdwy 4th: chsng ldrs fr 3 out: kpt on flat)	2	**3**	14/1	66	23
1356[4]	**Thorntoun Estate (IRE)** (MartinTodhunter) **3-10-5b**(3) ECallaghan (unruly leaving paddock: bhd: hdwy & prom 3 out: one pce fr next)	7	**4**	8/1	41	—
906[15]	**Propolis Power (IRE)** (MWEasterby) **3-10-11**(3) PMidgley (a.p: nt qckn fr 3 out)	11	**5**	50/1	36	—
1377[3]	**Samara Song** (WGMTurner) **3-10-10**(7) NWillmington (chsd ldrs: effrt 3 out: btn appr next)	6	**6**	9/2[3]	33	—
	Brogans Brush (JSHaldane) **3-9-12**(7) NHorrocks (wl bhd tl sme hdwy fr 3 out)	13	**7**	200/1	8	—
1205[11]	**Fiasco** (MJCamacho) **3-10-2**(7) MNewton (chsd ldrs tl rdn & wknd fr 3 out)	12	**8**	20/1	—	—
803[5]	**In A Tizzy** (PCHaslam) **3-10-12** MFoster (lw: led & sn clr: hit 4th: hdd & wknd after 3 out)	1	**9**	9/1	2	—
	Winn Caley (CWFairhurst) **3-10-9** JCallaghan (nt j.w: a bhd)	5	**10**	33/1	—	—
906[F]	**Bridlington Bay** (JLEyre) **3-10-11** NSmith (bhd fr ½-wy)	8	**11**	50/1	—	—
1158[P]	**Phantom Dancer (IRE)** (MESowersby) **3-11-0** BStorey (chsd ldrs to ½-wy: sn lost pl)	8	**12**	25/1	—	—
1332[U]	**Indira (84)** (CLPopham) **3-10-3**(3) TDascombe (lost tch fr 5th)	14	**13**	11/2	—	—
1205[10]	**Craigmore Magic (USA)** (MissMKMilligan) **3-10-5b** ASSmith (mstkes: wl bhd whn p.u bef 2 out)		**P**	25/1	—	—
1184[14]	**Ballykissangel** (NBycroft) **3-11-6** MMoloney (lost tch fr 4th: p.u bef 2 out)		**P**	100/1	—	—
	Noir Esprit (JMCarr) **3-10-10**(7) CMcCormack (in tch whn rn out 3 out)		**R**	33/1	—	—

(SP 139.9%) **16 Rn**

3m 47.8 (4.80) CSF £12.99 TOTE £5.70: £1.60 £1.90 £3.70 (£13.40) Trio £32.00 OWNER Richard Flood Bloodstock Ltd (NEWMARKET) BRED Roldvale Ltd
1011 The Great Flood proved very determined and that was the deciding factor. (4/1: op 5/2)
1205 Alwarqa, an out and out stayer on the Flat, looked sure to win this two out, only to get outbattled. Longer trips will suit at this game. (15/8: op 9/2)
462 Russian Rascal (IRE) has always been a free-running sort, but this was a much-improved effort. He seems to be learning. (14/1)
1356 Thorntoun Estate (IRE), in blinkers for the first time, gave plenty of problems on the way to the start and then showed he has ability when he decides to fully use it. (8/1)
Propolis Power (IRE) had shown next to nothing previously under both Rules, but there was certainly a hint of something here. (50/1)
1377 Samara Song had his chances, but failed to see it out. (9/2)
803 In A Tizzy, who went freely to post, raced in the same manner and had not surprisingly shot her bolt turning for home. (9/1)

1527 DICK BREWITT MEMORIAL CHALLENGE CUP H'CAP CHASE (0-115) (5-Y.O+) (Class E)

3-10 (3-18) **2m 3f (13 fncs)** £2,851.25 (£860.00: £417.50: £196.25) GOING minus 0.34 sec per fur (GF)

				SP	RR	SF
1119[7]	**Real Glee (IRE) (105)** (JJQuinn) **7-11-4** TReed (led fr 5th: mstke 7th: blnd & hdd 9th: rallied to ld & hit last: sn hdd: led post)	—	**1**	4/1[3]	109	—
1140*	**Briar's Delight (95)** (RAllan) **8-10-8v** BStorey (trckd ldrs: led 9th to last: sn led again: jst ct)	hd	**2**	15/8[1]	99	—
1306[6]	**Port in a Storm (88)** (MDHammond) **7-10-1** DBentley (led to 5th: grad lost pl: stdy hdwy appr last: nvr plcd to chal)	4	**3**	10/1	89	—
1204[3]	**Newhall Prince (112)** (AStreeter) **8-11-11v[1]** TEley (chsd ldrs: hit 10th: hdwy u.p 3 out: ev ch & hit last: sn btn)	hd	**4**	4/1[3]	113	—
1293[8]	**East Houston (97)** (JJO'Neill) **7-10-10** JCallaghan (hld up: effrt whn fell 10th)		**F**	3/1[2]	—	—

(SP 108.9%) **5 Rn**

4m 52.0 (13.00) CSF £11.15 TOTE £6.90: £2.30 £1.50 (£4.90) OWNER Mr John Stone (MALTON) BRED S. Cotter
Real Glee (IRE) has an engine, but his jumping was still clumsy and it was only his courage that got him home in front. (4/1)
1140* Briar's Delight jumped the rest out of sight, but he perhaps saw the front too soon in the circumstances, and was just worried out of it.(15/8)

Port in a Storm seemed to catch connections by surprise and was given a very tender ride but, as he has shown in the past, he is not one to rely on. (10/1: op 6/1)
1204 Newhall Prince was tried in a visor for the first time and was back on the track he loves, but his dash of last season was never really there. (4/1)
1029 East Houston, held up as usual, was still last but not that far away when falling four out. (3/1)

1528 WOOD HOUSE H'CAP HURDLE (0-115) (4-Y.O+) (Class E)
3-40 (3-41) **3m 1f 110y (12 hdls)** £2,247.40 (£626.40: £302.20) GOING minus 0.34 sec per fur (GF)

				SP	RR	SF
1127[3]	**Dally Boy (106)** (TDEasterby) **4-11-7**(3) ECallaghan (mde all: clr whn blnd 2 out: styd on)	—	**1**	5/2[2]	89	11
1294[4]	**Plumbob (IRE) (90)** (LLungo) **7-10-9** MFoster (chsd ldrs: rdn 4 out: styd on nvr able to chal)	3½	**2**	7/2[3]	71	—
1256[2]	**Ballindoo (88)** (RJArmson) **7-10-7**ow5 MrRArmson (hld up: effrt 3 out: sn rdn & no imp)	1¼	**3**	6/1	68	—
1057[F]	**Nick the Dreamer (97)** (WGMTurner) **11-10-9**(7) NWillmington (j.slowly: lost tch 4 out)	dist	**4**	8/1	—	—
1294[2]	**Troodos (95)** (MrsASwinbank) **10-11-0** JSupple (w wnr fr 4th tl fell 7th)		**F**	6/4[1]	—	—
				(SP 116.2%)		**5 Rn**

6m 20.0 (13.00) CSF £11.20 TOTE £3.00: £1.10 £2.20 (£6.70) OWNER Mr T. H. Bennett (MALTON) BRED Mrs L. Popely
WEIGHT FOR AGE 4yo-1lb
1127 Dally Boy had no fears about the trip and saw it out most determinedly. (5/2)
1294 Plumbob (IRE) was always close enough if good enough, but proved too slow. (7/2)
1256 Ballindoo carried 5lb overweight, which certainly did not help his cause. (6/1)
823 Nick the Dreamer, who almost refused at one hurdle, jumped several others very slowly and looked none too keen. (8/1)
1294 Troodos was upsides the winner when taking a heavy fall with a circuit to go. (6/4)

T/Plpt: £265.30 (30.52 Tckts). T/Qdpt: £54.30 (10.3 Tckts). AA

1204-MARKET RASEN (R-H) - Saturday November 23rd
1529 Abandoned-Frost

1337-TOWCESTER (R-H) (Good)
Saturday November 23rd
WEATHER: fine

1536 THOMAS COOK MAIDEN HURDLE (I) (4-Y.O+) (Class F)
12-30 (12-33) **2m 5f (11 hdls)** £1,849.00 (£514.00: £247.00) GOING: 0.37 sec per fur (GS)

				SP	RR	SF
	Forest Ivory (NZ) (DNicholson) **5-11-5** RJohnson (trckd ldrs: hmpd appr 3 out: led appr last: sn rdn clr)	—	**1**	8/11[1]	77+	19
	Fine Sir (TThomsonJones) **6-11-5** DGallagher (prom: mstke 6th: led appr 3 out tl appr last: one pce)	6	**2**	11/2[3]	72	14
1274[3]	**El Freddie (93)** (JABOld) **6-11-5** GUpton (a.p: led 7th tl appr 3 out: sn btn)	11	**3**	3/1[2]	64	6
980[7]	**Weather Wise** (WGMTurner) **4-11-5** AThornton (chsd ldrs: no imp fr 3 out)	14	**4**	50/1	53	—
1250[9]	**Burntwood Melody** (PTDalton) **5-11-5** WMarston (hld up: hdwy 6th: nvr rchd ldrs)	11	**5**	33/1	45	—
	Gemma's Wager (IRE) (62) (MarkCampion) **6-11-0** LHarvey (bit bkwd: prom: led 5th to 7th: wknd appr 3 out)	1½	**6**	50/1	39	—
	High Mood (TRGeorge) **6-10-12**(7) CHynes (bkwd: in tch to 6th)	6	**7**	100/1	39	—
	Lothian Commander (DMcCain) **4-11-5** TJenks (chsd ldrs to 8th)	5	**8**	50/1	36	—
1050[8]	**Polo Pony (IRE)** (JohnUpson) **4-11-5** RSupple (led to 5th: wknd 7th)	4	**9**	50/1	32	—
	Hit The Bid (IRE) (IPWilliams) **5-11-5** JRKavanagh (a bhd)	2	**10**	66/1	31	—
1341[6]	**Dark Phoenix (IRE)** (OBrennan) **6-11-0** MBrennan (hld up: hdwy 7th: wknd qckly appr 2 out)	dist	**11**	6/1	—	—
	Camino (RJSmith) **9-11-5** DBridgwater (bkwd: a bhd: p.u bef 2 out)		**P**	33/1	—	—
	Honeybed Wood (70) (IRBrown) **8-11-0** MrABrown (bkwd: chsd ldrs: ev ch whn blnd 8th: sn wknd: p.u bef 2 out)		**P**	66/1	—	—
	Nero's Gem (CFCJackson) **5-11-0** WMcFarland (j.bdly: a bhd: t.o whn p.u bef 2 out)		**P**	50/1	—	—
				(SP 132.2%)		**14 Rn**

5m 23.8 (21.80) CSF £6.38 TOTE £1.60: £1.20 £2.00 £1.40 (£3.80) Trio £3.20 OWNER The Old Foresters Partnership (TEMPLE GUITING) BRED P. S. and Mrs C. Nelson
Forest Ivory (NZ), making his hurdles debut on ground faster than he raced on last season, lost his pitch when sandwiched between horses going to three out, but was not put off and recovered the ground quickly. Coming away once in front, this was a very promising start. (8/11)
Fine Sir, a tall, lean gelding, wore bandages but moved well to post. He looked fit enough but, after racing up with the pace, was getting tired in the closing stages. He is lightly-raced but should find an opening if he can stay sound. (11/2: 7/2-6/1)
1274 El Freddie, a second-season novice, was still travelling well at the bottom of the hill, but the stiff finish caught him out as it does so many. (3/1)
Weather Wise, a small newcomer to hurdles, ran respectably, but was quickly left behind once the race properly began. (50/1)
Burntwood Melody made some ground in the last half-mile, but from a long way back. His best hope looks to be selling company. (33/1)
Gemma's Wager (IRE) has been campaigned at two miles five furlongs and beyond over hurdles and has yet to show she stays. (50/1)
1341 Dark Phoenix (IRE), stepping up in trip, certainly did not stay, but she stopped so quickly turning for home that the problem may be more serious. (6/1)

1537 AKELEY NOVICES' (S) HURDLE (4-Y.O+) (Class G)
1-00 (1-01) **2m (8 hdls)** £2,185.00 (£610.00: £295.00) GOING: 0.37 sec per fur (GS)

				SP	RR	SF
	Harry (66) (DBurchell) **6-10-12** DJBurchell (hld up: hdwy 5th: led 2 out: sn clr: pushed out)	—	**1**	7/1	63	33
1337*	**Willy Star (BEL)** (MrsSJSmith) **6-10-12**(7) RWilkinson (a.p: rdn 2 out: kpt on: nt trble wnr)	8	**2**	11/8[1]	62	32
1390*	**Sprintfayre (60)** (JELong) **8-11-5** DGallagher (led tl after 2nd: led appr 2 out: sn hdd & no ex)	5	**3**	8/1	57	27
209[4]	**Saracen Prince (USA) (81)** (CLPopham) **4-10-12** RJohnson (bhd: r.o fr 3 out: nvr trbld ldrs)	2½	**4**	13/2[3]	48	18
1413[F]	**Al Helal** (JRJenkins) **4-10-12v** WMarston (led after 2nd: hdd appr 2 out: wkng whn blnd last)	15	**5**	33/1	33	3
	Nautical Jewel (MDIUsher) **4-10-12** WMcFarland (hdwy 3rd: wknd appr 3 out)	1½	**6**	6/1[2]	31	1
1148[4]	**Sleeptite (FR) (86)** (WGMTurner) **6-11-5** AThornton (in tch to 5th)	3	**7**	6/1[2]	35	5
1171[10]	**Ecu de France (IRE)** (PCRitchens) **6-10-12** SFox (chsd ldrs to 5th)	19	**8**	50/1	9	—
933[F]	**Follow de Call** (DMcCain) **6-10-12** TJenks (swtg: bit bkwd: a bhd)	2½	**9**	16/1	7	—

				SP	RR	SF
1329^{14}	**Small Flame (IRE)** (OBrennan) **5-10-7** MBrennan (rdn 3rd: a bhd)	dist	**10**	25/1	—	—
	Polli Pui (WMBrisbourne) **4-10-4**(3) RMassey (bhd whn fell 4th)		**F**	20/1	—	—
1339^{6}	**Swing Lucky (66)** (AGBlackmore) **11-11-5** DSkyrme (prom to 4th: t.o whn p.u bef 3 out)		**P**	11/1	—	—
1445^{P}	**Strange Ways** (HJManners) **8-10-5**(7) ADowling (bit bkwd: a bhd: t.o whn p.u bef 2 out)		**P**	50/1	—	—
				(SP 137.3%)	**13 Rn**	

3m 57.7 (11.70) CSF £18.63 TOTE £10.70: £2.20 £1.40 £3.00 (£17.00) Trio £76.00 OWNER Mr Simon Lewis (EBBW VALE) BRED Jephanil Bt in 3,000 gns

Harry had the benefit of a pipe-opener on the Flat twelve days ago and was a decisive winner once sent for home in the straight. (7/1)
1337* Willy Star (BEL), a similar horse to the winner on the level, found the penalty too much. Although he did stay on in the straight, he could never find the speed to mount a challenge. (11/8)
1390* Sprintfayre looked very much on his toes in the paddock, but did well considering that it was just six days since his comeback win. (8/1)
7 Saracen Prince (USA), a good mover, stayed the trip on this stiff course surprisingly well without landing a blow. How much further he might stay is open to question given his history. (13/2: op 4/1)
Al Helal took a strong hold as usual, but did manage to stay upright this time, although not getting home on this stiff track. Letting him bowl along on an easy track may see improvement. (33/1)
Nautical Jewel, who certainly flew too high on his only previous hurdles start, had beaten the winner on the Flat recently, but did not handle this stiff course nearly as well. (6/1)

1538 ALDERTON NOVICES' CHASE (5-Y.O+) (Class D)

1-30 (1-30) **3m 1f (18 fncs)** £3,942.75 (£1,182.00: £568.50: £261.75) GOING: 0.13 sec per fur (G)

				SP	RR	SF
	Bankhead (IRE) (110) (JLSpearing) **7-11-0** DBridgwater (nt j.w: hdwy 6th: led appr 2 out: rdn out)	—	**1**	3/1^{2}	109	41
	Little Martina (IRE) (97) (DMGrissell) **8-10-13** JRKavanagh (chsd ldrs: ev ch whn hit 3 out: rdn next: r.o)	3	**2**	3/1^{2}	106	38
1150^{2}	**Hawaiian Sam (IRE) (98)** (AndrewTurnell) **6-11-0** GCrone (chsd ldr tl lft in ld 9th: hdd appr 2 out: kpt on)	1¾	**3**	11/1	106	38
	Robsand (IRE) (GBBalding) **7-11-0** BClifford (in tch: hdwy 4 out: hit 2 out: no imp)	15	**4**	16/1	96	28
	Majors Legacy (IRE) (CaptTAForster) **7-11-0** AThornton (trckd ldrs: ev ch 11th: no imp fr 13th)	7	**5**	14/1	92	24
1206^{2}	**Mr Pickpocket (IRE) (106)** (MissHCKnight) **8-11-0** RJohnson (led 2nd tl blnd bdly & lost pl 9th: mstke next: no ch after)	5	**6**	7/4^{1}	89	21
1200^{P}	**Rainbow Fountain** (NMLampard) **9-10-4**(5) ChrisWebb (sn bhd: p.u bef last)		**P**	50/1	—	—
1281^{2}	**Loch Garman Hotel (IRE)** (PTDalton) **7-11-0** WMarston (lw: uns rdr 1st)		**U**	6/1^{3}	—	—
1423^{6}	**Delire d'Estruval (FR)** (IPWilliams) **5-10-12b** LHarvey (lw: led to 2nd: ev ch whn pckd 13th: rdn next: wkng whn blnd & uns rdr 3 out)		**U**	50/1	—	—
				(SP 125.5%)	**9 Rn**	

6m 25.8 (10.80) CSF £13.11 TOTE £4.30: £1.50 £1.20 £2.30 (£10.20) Trio £18.90 OWNER Mrs Liz Brazier (ALCESTER) BRED Ronald O'Neill
WEIGHT FOR AGE 5yo-2lb

Bankhead (IRE), a neatly-made, formerly-useful hurdler who did well between the Flags in the spring, did not jump very quickly and was losing ground at the fences without making mistakes. His superiority on the flat can not be denied, but how high he can go in this sphere will depend on his jumping. (3/1)
Little Martina (IRE), a winner of an Ascot Hunter Chase earlier in the year, looked as though she would come on for the outing, despite looking on good terms with herself. She proved brave in the straight and should soon be winning. (3/1)
1150 Hawaiian Sam (IRE) took the step up in trip in his stride and, having jumped soundly, ought to find a race before long. (11/1: 6/1-12/1)
Robsand (IRE), very lightly-raced in the last couple of years, was making hard work of closing on the leaders when the mistake halted his progress. He should come on for the run. (16/1)
Majors Legacy (IRE), a tall, good mover, dropped away as soon as the tempo picked up. (14/1: op 8/1)
1206 Mr Pickpocket (IRE) stepped into the fence passing the Stands with a circuit left and dropped from first to nearly last in the process. A hesitant jump at the next saw him lose further ground and this is best forgotten. (7/4)
1281 Loch Garman Hotel (IRE) (6/1: tchd 10/1)

1539 THOMAS COOK MAIDEN HURDLE (II) (4-Y.O+) (Class F)

2-05 (2-08) **2m 5f (11 hdls)** £1,835.00 (£510.00: £245.00) GOING: 0.37 sec per fur (GS)

				SP	RR	SF
1042^{2}	**Salmon Breeze (IRE)** (NJHenderson) **5-11-5** JRKavanagh (lw: chsd ldrs: lost pl & rdn appr 3 out: styd on wl to ld appr last: rdn out)	—	**1**	11/4^{1}	65	3
1309^{3}	**Jills Joy (IRE)** (JNorton) **5-11-0**(5) DJKavanagh (a.p: led appr 3 out: wknd & hdd appr last)	4	**2**	6/1^{3}	62	—
	Fashion Maker (IRE) (MrsIMcKie) **6-11-5** LHarvey (bkwd: in tch: lost pl & rdn 6th: r.o wl appr last)	4	**3**	50/1	59	—
1378^{3}	**Positivo (76)** (MissCJECaroe) **5-11-5** DLeahy (chsd ldrs: lost pl 6th: rallied appr 3 out: no imp fr next)	2½	**4**	8/1	57	—
1090^{4}	**Lough Tully (IRE)** (FJordan) **6-11-5** RSupple (bhd: hdwy 6th: wknd appr 2 out)	4	**5**	8/1	54	—
1191^{5}	**Winnow (82)** (AndrewTurnell) **6-10-7**(7) CRae (hld up & plld hrd: hdwy appr 6th: ev ch 3 out: rdn & wknd appr next)	1	**6**	8/1	48	—
1085^{4}	**Little Notice (IRE)** (CaptTAForster) **5-11-5** SWynne (chsd ldrs tl appr 2 out)	1	**7**	3/1^{2}	52	—
1174^{6}	**Spearhead Again (IRE) (78)** (KSBridgwater) **7-11-5** DBridgwater (led tl appr 3 out: wknd appr next)	20	**8**	8/1	37	—
	Barristers Boy (JABOld) **6-11-5** GUpton (a bhd)	hd	**9**	14/1	37	—
	Surprise Guest (IRE) (TTClement) **5-11-5** RJohnson (prom to 8th: fin lame)	16	**10**	33/1	25	—
1261^{5}	**La Chance** (MrsHLWalton) **6-11-5** MrAWalton (bkwd: a bhd)	13	**11**	50/1	15	—
1077^{7}	**Noddadante (IRE)** (NRMitchell) **6-11-5** MrNRMitchell (a bhd)	7	**12**	25/1	10	—
	Joy For Life (IRE) (61) (RMStronge) **5-11-0** VSlattery (a bhd: t.o whn p.u bef 2 out)		**P**	16/1	—	—
				(SP 133.7%)	**13 Rn**	

5m 28.5 (26.50) CSF £21.25 TOTE £2.40: £1.50 £2.00 £9.50 (£10.90) Trio £296.10; £291.99 to Catterick25/11/96 OWNER The Salmon Racing Partnership (LAMBOURN) BRED William Kavanagh

1042 Salmon Breeze (IRE) looks to have rather more stamina than speed, for he was taken off his feet when the leaders picked up the tempo inside the final mile. They probably did too much too soon, for the leader was stopping going to the last and the winner was still running on strongly. (11/4: 13/8-3/1)
1309 Jills Joy (IRE) was probably made too much use of, for he looked the winner coming up the hill, but was getting very tired in the closing stages. With a little more patience, a race should come his way. (6/1)
Fashion Maker (IRE) looked to need the race and seemed likely to finish nearer last than first for much of the final circuit but, as the leaders tied up, he came home really well to show his first signs of ability. (50/1)
1378 Positivo again ran rather in snatches. (8/1)
1090 Lough Tully (IRE) was not knocked about once his measure had been taken and gives the impression he may do better in time. (8/1)

Winnow took a fierce grip and delayed the start with her tactics. Going best of all approaching the third last, she had faded dramatically inside a furlong, but left the impression that there is a race in her when things go right. (8/1: 5/1-10/1)
Barristers Boy (14/1: 7/1-16/1)

1540 NATIONAL LETTERBOX MARKETING H'CAP CHASE (0-120) (5-Y.O+) (Class D)
2-35 (2-35) **2m 6f (16 fncs)** £3,591.75 (£1,074.00: £514.50: £234.75) GOING: 0.13 sec per fur (G)

Form	Horse	Dist	Pos	SP	RR	SF
1175*	**Fools Errand (IRE) (112)** (GBBalding) **6-11-6** BClifford (lw: trckd ldrs: led 2 out: sn rdn: edgd rt & hld on wl flat)	—	1	9/4[1]	117	50
1338F	**Nicklup (105)** (CaptTAForster) **9-10-13** AThornton (mde most to 11th: led 3 out to next: rdn & ev ch last: unable qckn)	hd	2	6/1	110	43
1167P	**Really a Rascal (105)** (DRGandolfo) **9-10-13** RJohnson (hld up: hdwy 4 out: one pce flat)	2½	3	12/1	108	41
1175[5]	**Spuffington (120)** (JTGifford) **8-11-11**(3) LAspell (lw: w ldrs: led 11th to 3 out: wknd appr next)	17	4	9/2[3]	111	44
	Three Saints (IRE) (96) (CaptTAForster) **7-10-4** SWynne (bit bkwd: mstkes: nvr nr to chal)	10	5	7/2[2]	80	13
	Makes Me Goosey (IRE) (98) (MrsIMcKie) **8-10-6** LHarvey (hdwy 7th: wknd 12th)	¾	6	9/2[3]	81	14
	Call Home (IRE) (120) (MissSEdwards) **8-12-0** MrTHills (bhd fr 12th)	dist	7	8/1	—	—
				(SP 122.4%)	**7 Rn**	

5m 37.4 (8.40) CSF £16.25 CT £127.29 TOTE £3.60: £1.60 £3.20 (£8.30) OWNER Mrs David Russell (ANDOVER) BRED K. E. and Mrs Moeran in Ireland
STEWARDS' ENQUIRY Thornton susp. 2-3/12/96 (excessive use of the whip).
1175* Fools Errand (IRE), who would have liked the ground softer, still managed a hard-fought win after travelling best for most of the trip, and has not stopped winning yet. (9/4)
Nicklup jumped well and put in another sound effort, rallying strongly in the straight. Unfortunately, her pilot continued to ride her out after the line. (6/1)
Really a Rascal ran his best race for some time and looked a possible winner approaching the last before his exertions took their toll. (12/1)
Spuffington may well find this a touch too far, for the stiff climb to two out was the undoing of him. (9/2)
Three Saints (IRE) did not look fully wound up, jumped disappointingly and never looked like taking a hand. (7/2)
Makes Me Goosey (IRE) found race-fit rivals had his measure in the final half-mile. (9/2)

1541 WOODEND 'N.H.' NOVICES' HURDLE (4-Y.O+) (Class D)
3-10 (3-10) **3m (12 hdls)** £3,351.00 (£936.00: £453.00) GOING: 0.37 sec per fur (GS)

Form	Horse	Dist	Pos	SP	RR	SF
1278[2]	**Southern Nights** (KCBailey) **6-11-0** AThornton (hdwy 7th: led 9th: clr whn hit last: sddle slipped & ducked lft flat)	—	1	8/1	69	5
1317[11]	**China Gem (IRE)** (CPEBrooks) **5-11-0** DGallagher (hld up: hdwy 7th: chsd wnr appr 2 out: no imp)	5	2	33/1	66	2
1290U	**Young Kenny (94)** (PBeaumont) **5-11-6** RSupple (hld up: hdwy 8th: one pce fr 2 out)	1¼	3	20/1	71	7
1322[2]	**Spaceage Gold (99)** (JABOld) **7-11-0** GUpton (prom tl rdn & wknd appr 2 out)	5	4	5/2[2]	62	—
1261[2]	**Jet Boys (IRE) (98)** (MrsJPitman) **6-11-0** WMarston (chsd ldrs: rdn 7th: sn no imp)	8	5	11/8[1]	56	—
1260[5]	**Arturo** (CaptTAForster) **5-11-0** SWynne (hld up: hdwy 9th: wknd appr 2 out)	nk	6	12/1	56	—
1297*	**Medford (95)** (WGMTurner) **6-10-13**(7) JPower (hdwy 7th: rdn & wknd 3 out)	25	7	12/1	45	—
	Luker Boy (IRE) (DNicholson) **6-11-0** RJohnson (lw: hld up: rdn & hdwy 8th: sn btn: p.u bef 2 out)		P	16/1	—	—
885[4]	**Southsea Scandals (IRE)** (KBishop) **5-11-0** RGreene (a bhd: t.o whn p.u bef 3 out)		P	20/1	—	—
	Bayline Star (IRE) (MissHCKnight) **6-11-0** JRKavanagh (bit bkwd: a bhd: t.o whn p.u bef last)		P	4/1[3]	—	—
1200P	**Alone Home (IRE)** (CJMann) **5-11-0b1** JRailton (led 2nd to 9th: sn wknd: t.o whn p.u bef 2 out)		P	33/1	—	—
	Moonlighter (CFCJackson) **6-10-9** WMcFarland (chsd ldrs to 9th: sn wknd: p.u bef 2 out)		P	50/1	—	—
1085[6]	**Musical Hit** (PAPritchard) **5-11-0** LHarvey (hit 5th: sn t.o: p.u bef 9th)		P	66/1	—	—
954[8]	**Roskeen Bridge (IRE)** (CWeedon) **5-11-0** MRichards (led to 2nd: wknd 7th: t.o whn p.u bef last)		P	66/1	—	—
1165[6]	**Caulkin (IRE)** (ABarrow) **5-10-9**(5) MrRThornton (w ldr to 7th: t.o whn p.u bef 2 out)		P	66/1	—	—
				(SP 144.9%)	**15 Rn**	

6m 7.8 (27.80) CSF £235.43 TOTE £11.20: £2.80 £9.30 £3.80 (£707.80) Trio £448.50; £448.59 to Catterick 25/11/96 OWNER Mr J. Perriss (UPPER LAMBOURN) BRED Mrs Patricia Morgan
OFFICIAL EXPLANATION **Bayline Star (IRE): gurgled during the race.**
1278 Southern Nights, stepping up considerably in trip, saw it out well and had the race won when a slipping saddle all but cost him victory. But for the mishap, he would have been an impressive winner, and he is value for a lot more than the winning margin. (8/1: 5/1-9/1)
China Gem (IRE), settled in the rear for the first circuit, then began to make progress but, by the time he went second, the winner was long gone. (33/1)
1046 Young Kenny did not noticeably put a foot wrong this time, but could do little more than plug on in the last half-mile. (20/1)
1322 Spaceage Gold found the stiff climb into the home straight bringing his effort to an end. (5/2: op 4/1)
1261 Jet Boys (IRE) seems to need plenty of riding to keep him going and is probably no better than this. (11/8)
1260 Arturo, a neat gelding who looks sure to handle softer ground, did not quite last home on his first try at the trip. (12/1: 8/1-14/1)
Bayline Star (IRE) (4/1: 5/2-9/2)

1542 PLUMPTON END H'CAP HURDLE (0-120) (4-Y.O+) (Class D)
3-45 (3-45) **2m (8 hdls)** £2,910.00 (£810.00: £390.00) GOING: 0.37 sec per fur (GS)

Form	Horse	Dist	Pos	SP	RR	SF
	Jefferies (91) (JABOld) **7-10-10** GUpton (mde virtually all: drew clr & hit last: easily)	—	1	5/2[2]	66	4
1191[6]	**Dominos Ring (IRE) (105)** (MrsHLWalton) **7-11-5**(5) MrRThornton (lw: in tch: jnd ldrs & hit 5th: rdn & lost pl next: styd on fr 2 out)	2½	2	10/1	78	16
1339[4]	**Shers Delight (IRE) (87)** (OBrennan) **6-10-6** MBrennan (hld up: rdn & hdwy 5th: ev ch next: wknd appr last)	3½	3	9/2[3]	56	—
	Too Sharp (100) (MissHCKnight) **8-11-5** RJohnson (prom tl wknd appr 2 out)	14	4	10/1	55	—
1262[3]	**Nothingtodowithme (92)** (CaptTAForster) **6-10-11** SWynne (lw: trckd ldrs tl rdn & btn appr 3 out: eased)	15	5	11/8[1]	32	—
1256P	**Astral Invasion (USA) (81)** (GMMcCourt) **5-10-0b** BClifford (w wnr to 5th: sn wknd)	dist	6	8/1	—	—
				(SP 118.2%)	**6 Rn**	

4m 3.8 (17.80) CSF £23.58 TOTE £4.60: £2.70 £2.90 (£15.80) OWNER Miss S. Blumberg (WROUGHTON) BRED R. D. & Mrs J. S. Chugg
OFFICIAL EXPLANATION **Nothingtodowithme: finished with his tongue over the bit.**
Jefferies looked really well in his coat and does seem to run well fresh. Making all at a good pace on the slowest ground of the afternoon, he made his stamina tell. (5/2: op 5/1)
Dominos Ring (IRE) looked well beaten at the third last, but kept battling away, despite holding his head high as usual. (10/1)

1339 Shers Delight (IRE), again without the visor, had to be ridden to squeeze through on the inside when beginning his move, and was at the end of his tether by the home turn. (9/2)
Too Sharp broke a blood-vessel last time out and returned from his break over hurdles over an inadequate trip. In the circumstances, she shaped well enough. (10/1: op 6/1)
1262 Nothingtodowithme seemed to be travelling well enough to halfway, but then lost his way completely and was allowed to coast in. He apparently got his tongue over his bit and this is best forgotten. (11/8)
Astral Invasion (USA) probably found the fact that the ground had become sticky right against him. (8/1: op 5/1)

T/Plpt: £131.00 (84.24 Tckts). T/Qdpt: £89.60 (6.15 Tckts). Dk

1523-CATTERICK (L-H) - Monday November 25th
1543 Abandoned-Snow

FOLKESTONE (R-H) (Chases Good, Good to soft patches, Hdles Good to soft)
Monday November 25th
WEATHER: fine

1550 BREDE NOVICES' CONDITIONAL HURDLE (4-Y.O+) (Class F)
1-00 (1-00) **2m 6f 110y (11 hdls)** £2,138.40 (£592.40: £283.20) GOING: 0.47 sec per fur (GS)

				SP	RR	SF
	Emerald Statement (IRE) (DMGrissell) **6-10-12** GHogan (a.p: led 8th: clr appr last: v.easily)	—	**1**	$5/1^{3}$	77+	13
1275^{4}	**Forest Musk (IRE)** (PJHobbs) **5-10-12** DJKavanagh (hdwy 6th: ev ch 2 out: unable qckn)	24	**2**	$6/4^{1}$	60	—
1394^{5}	**Ross Dancer (IRE)** (JSMoore) **4-10-12** JMagee (a.p: chsd ldr fr 5th: led 7th to 8th: rdn & ev ch 2 out: one pce)	8	**3**	10/1	54	—
1090^{2}	**Lord Khalice (IRE)** (GAHubbard) **5-10-6**(6) NRossiter (hld up: rdn & mstke 8th: sn wknd)	27	**4**	$4/1^{2}$	35	—
1328^{6}	**Who Am I (IRE) (89)** (RHAlner) **6-10-12** PHenley (lw: mstke 2nd: hdwy 6th: wknd 8th)	14	**5**	13/2	25	—
1077^{6}	**Snowy Petrel (IRE) (90)** (KCBailey) **4-10-9b**(3) WWalsh (led: clr 2nd: hdd 7th: wknd 8th)	18	**6**	7/1	12	—
973^{P}	**Profession** (FGray) **5-10-6v**1(6) JKMcCarthy (bhd fr 7th: t.o fr 8th)	dist	**7**	50/1	—	—
1150^{F}	**Sporting Fixture (IRE)** (PEccles) **5-10-12** GESmith (hrd rdn 3rd: a bhd: t.o fr 7th)	1½	**8**	50/1	—	—
	Madam Rose (IRE) (JWMullins) **6-10-1**(6) DavidTurner (a bhd: t.o whn tried to run out bnd appr 7th)	dist	**9**	33/1	—	—
1337^{9}	**Master Upex** (ASNeaves) **4-10-6**(6) WGreatrex (chsd ldr to 5th: sn wknd: t.o whn p.u bef 6th)		**P**	66/1	—	—
				(SP 119.9%)	**10 Rn**	

5m 42.3 (25.30) CSF £12.75 TOTE £5.40: £2.50 £1.30 £4.00 (£10.60) Trio £42.50 OWNER The Hon Mrs C Yeates (ROBERTSBRIDGE) BRED Mrs Mary Doyle
Emerald Statement (IRE), winner of an Irish maiden point-to-point in the spring by fifteen lengths, made a highly impressive debut over hurdles. Leading at the fourth last, he surged clear without turning a hair on the long run to the final flight to win with his head in his chest. Further success awaits him. (5/1)
1275 Forest Musk (IRE) appreciated the longer trip for this hurdling debut and was one of three in line two out before left standing by the winner. (6/4)
Ross Dancer (IRE) played an active role from the start and was still close enough if good enough at the second last before tapped for toe. (10/1)
1090 Lord Khalice (IRE) was uneasy in the market and did not take the eye in the paddock. Punters knew their fate fully four hurdles from the finish. (4/1: op 5/2)
1328 Who Am I (IRE) took closer order with a circuit to race but had been hung out to dry four from home. (13/2)
1077 Snowy Petrel (IRE) once again probably found the trip beyond him although he was in trouble fully a mile out having set the pace. (7/1: op 9/2)

1551 E.B.F. 'N.H.' (QUALIFIER) NOVICES' HURDLE (4, 5 & 6-Y.O) (Class E)
1-30 (1-30) **2m 1f 110y (8 hdls)** £2,385.00 (£660.00: £315.00) GOING: 0.47 sec per fur (GS)

				SP	RR	SF
	Boardroom Shuffle (IRE) (JTGifford) **5-11-0** PHide (a.gng wl: hdwy 3rd: led on bit appr last: v.easily)	—	**1**	$8/11^{1}$	80++	34
	Splendid Thyne (TCasey) **4-11-0** MAFitzgerald (bit bkwd: chsd ldr fr 2nd: led 2 out tl appr last: unable qckn)	10	**2**	$5/1^{3}$	71?	25
	Fantasy Line (PRWebber) **5-10-9** JOsborne (hdwy 3rd: ev ch appr last: one pce)	1¾	**3**	8/1	64?	18
	Charlie's Folly (BdeHaan) **5-11-0** CLlewellyn (mstke 1st: chsd ldr to 2nd: dropped rr 5th: rallied appr last: sn wknd)	10	**4**	20/1	60?	14
	Arctic Triumph (MBradstock) **5-11-0** PHolley (j.lft: led to 2 out: wknd appr last)	22	**5**	8/1	40?	—
1329^{4}	**Super Rapier (IRE)** (GAHubbard) **4-11-0** APMcCoy (hdwy 3rd: rdn 2 out: wknd appr last)	3½	**6**	$9/2^{2}$	37?	—
1013^{5}	**Cranbrook Lad** (RCurtis) **4-11-0** DMorris (bhd fr 5th: t.o whn p.u bef last)		**P**	50/1	—	—
				(SP 121.7%)	**7 Rn**	

4m 20.8 (14.80) CSF £5.50 TOTE £1.50: £1.40 £1.60 (£3.00) OWNER Mr A. D. Weller (FINDON) BRED Stonethorn Stud Farms Ltd
Boardroom Shuffle (IRE) put up a highly impressive display under a very confident ride despite some sloppy jumping in places. Leading on the bridle going to the final flight, his jockey had to do absolutely nothing on him for the gelding to surge clear to win in tremendous style. A nice big stamp of a horse who has the word chaser written all over him, he looks an exciting prospect. (8/11)
Splendid Thyne, not looking fully wound up for his first run of the season and hurdling debut, nevertheless moved to the front two out but was firmly put in his place by the winner once collared approaching the final flight. (5/1)
Fantasy Line made an encouraging debut and had every chance going to the final flight before easily brushed aside by the winner.(8/1: 4/1-10/1)
Charlie's Folly, whose dam comes from the same family as Dramatist, dropped to last place a mile from home but he almost got back into it going on the long downhill run before tiring early in the straight. (20/1)
Arctic Triumph continually jumped to his left but nevertheless set the pace to the second last before calling it a day. (8/1: 5/1-9/1)
1329 Super Rapier (IRE), who caught the eye in a bumper last time out, was being bustled along two from home and soon called it aday. (9/2)

1552 DAILY MAIL NOVICES' H'CAP CHASE (0-100) (5-Y.O+) (Class E)
2-00 (2-02) **2m (12 fncs)** £3,436.25 (£1,040.00: £507.50: £241.25) GOING: 0.47 sec per fur (GS)

				SP	RR	SF
	Scoresheet (IRE) (86) (JTGifford) **6-11-0** PHide (a.p: led 2 out: shkn up & hung lft flat: r.o wl)	—	**1**	$4/1^{3}$	100	33
1328^{2}	**Reeshloch (93)** (AndrewTurnell) **7-11-7** MAFitzgerald (reminder & hdwy 6th: rdn appr 2 out: unable qckn)	13	**2**	$100/30^{2}$	94	27
1390^{10}	**National Flag (FR) (77)** (KRBurke) **6-10-5**ow5 ALarnach (a.p: led 4 out to 2 out: wknd appr last)	1½	**3**	25/1	77	5

			SP	RR	SF
1074[8]	**Sophie May (91)** (GLMoore) **5-11-5** APMcCoy (lw: hld up: rdn 4 out: wknd 3 out) 7	**4**	7/1	84	17
1414[U]	**Coolteen Hero (IRE) (88)** (RHAlner) **6-11-2** WMcFarland (mstkes: led to 4 out: wknd appr 2 out) ....nk	**5**	7/1	80	13
1381[6]	**Anlace (75)** (SMellor) **7-9-12**(5) ChrisWebb (bhd fr 3rd) 5	**6**	10/1	62	—
1371[P]	**Lets Go Now (IRE) (72)** (MrsLCJewell) **6-10-0** DLeahy (a bhd: mstke 2nd: hmpd 5th: t.o fr 6th) ....dist	**7**	66/1	—	—
1073[6]	**Jacksons Bay (73)** (TCasey) **6-9-12**(3)ow1 GHogan (lw: prom to 5th: 6th & btn whn fell 3 out)	**F**	33/1	—	—
1179*	**Brazil Or Bust (IRE) (100)** (PRWebber) **5-12-0** JOsborne (lw: bhd tl fell 5th)	**F**	2/1[1]	—	—

(SP 118.8%) **9 Rn**

4m 6.2 (14.20) CSF £17.38 CT £271.42 TOTE £5.60: £2.30 £1.10 £5.40 (£9.00) Trio £133.40 OWNER Pell-Mell Partners (FINDON) BRED Capt. D. Foster and B. Corscadden

LONG HANDICAP Lets Go Now (IRE) 9-2 Jacksons Bay 9-5 National Flag (FR) 9-7

Scoresheet (IRE), looking pretty straight for his first run in thirteen months, led at the second last and, although hanging badly left on the run in, still kept on well for a cosy success. (4/1)

1328 Reeshloch took closer order early on the final circuit, and plodded on to take second prize on the run-in, although having no hope with the winner. (100/30: 6/4-7/2)

National Flag (FR), carrying 12lb more than his long handicap weight, went on four from home but, collared at the second last, was soon in trouble. (25/1)

1074 Sophie May probably found this trip too sharp on this chasing debut and was getting left behind from the third last. (7/1)

Anlace (10/1: 6/1-12/1)

1553 DAVID CAMERON MEMORIAL H'CAP HURDLE (0-105) (4-Y.O+) (Class F)

2-30 (2-30) **2m 6f 110y (11 hdls)** £3,028.00 (£904.00: £432.00: £196.00) GOING: 0.47 sec per fur (GS)

			SP	RR	SF
1031[6]	**Nick the Beak (IRE) (100)** (JohnUpson) **7-11-3**(7) GSupple (hdwy 8th: led after 2 out: rdn out) ....—	**1**	6/1[3]	85	1
1330[6]	**Glen Mirage (82)** (MJCoombe) **11-10-6** MissMCoombe (gd hdwy appr last: chsd wnr fr last: r.o) 3½	**2**	20/1	65	—
1330[F]	**Fleur de Tal (95)** (WGMTurner) **5-10-12**(7) JPower (hdwy 3 out: rdn 2 out: unable qckn) 9	**3**	14/1	71	—
1088[6]	**Pettaugh (IRE) (93)** (GAHubbard) **8-10-10**(7) NRossiter (bit bkwd: lost pl 6th: r.o one pce fr 2 out) 1	**4**	9/2[2]	68	—
	Paddysway (91) (RHBuckler) **9-11-1** BPowell (hld up: rdn 3 out: sn wknd) 1	**5**	6/1[3]	66	—
1384[4]	**Old Archives (IRE) (86)** (LWells) **7-10-10b**[1] PHide (led tl after 2 out: sn wknd) ....¾	**6**	9/1	60	—
	Whitebonnet (IRE) (84) (CREgerton) **6-10-8** JOsborne (a.p: rdn 2 out: wknd qckly: t.o) ....dist	**7**	10/1	—	—
1256[5]	**Apachee Flower (76)** (HSHowe) **6-10-0v**[1] APMcCoy (hld up: rdn 3 out: sn wknd: t.o) 20	**8**	9/2[2]	—	—
1058[4]	**Top Wave (99)** (MissAEEmbiricos) **8-11-9** JRyan (prom to 8th: t.o) ....dist	**9**	16/1	—	—
1419*	**Whistling Buck (IRE) (82)** (RRowe) **8-10-6** DO'Sullivan (lw: hdwy 8th: wknd appr 2 out: t.o whn p.u bef last)	**P**	7/2[1]	—	—

(SP 123.6%) **10 Rn**

5m 50.3 (33.30) CSF £102.32 CT £1,488.98 TOTE £8.10: £2.00 £5.60 £5.40 (£123.40) Trio £212.20; £32.88 to Huntingdon 26/11/96 OWNER Sir Nicholas Wilson (TOWCESTER) BRED Mrs R. Fitzgerald

LONG HANDICAP Apachee Flower 9-13

OFFICIAL EXPLANATION **Whistling Buck (IRE): was not suited by the softer ground.**

Nick the Beak (IRE), out of form last season, went on soon after the penultimate hurdle and, rousted along, kept on well to win his first race in nearly two years. (6/1)

Glen Mirage ran much better here. Still out with the washing in the back straight for the final time, he made tremendous strides from the second last and, taking second place at the final flight, kept on well if never looking likely to get to the winner in time. (20/1)

884 Fleur de Tal took closer order three from home but failed to find another gear on the long run from the second last. (14/1: 10/1-16/1)

1088 Pettaugh (IRE), still not looking fully wound up, lost his pitch with a circuit to go but did plod on again on the long run to the final flight. Stamina rather than speed is his forte. (9/2)

1554 DAILY MAIL H'CAP CHASE (0-100) (5-Y.O+) (Class F)

3-00 (3-00) **3m 2f (19 fncs)** £4,302.00 (£1,296.00: £628.00: £294.00) GOING: 0.47 sec per fur (GS)

			SP	RR	SF
1194[3]	**Funcheon Gale (92)** (RCurtis) **9-11-6** DMorris (lw: hdwy 11th: led appr 2 out: wandered appr last: j.lft last: wandered flat: rdn out) ....—	**1**	6/4[1]	97	10
1445[7]	**Rhoman Fun (IRE) (72)** (RHBuckler) **7-9-9**(5) MrRThornton (hld up: chsd wnr fr 2 out: unable qckn flat) 1¾	**2**	6/1	76	—
1421[2]	**Joker Jack (73)** (RDean) **11-9-12**(3)ow1 TDascombe (chsd ldr: led 5th tl appr 2 out: one pce) 3½	**3**	20/1	75	—
1076[2]	**Master Comedy (75)** (MissLBower) **12-9-10b**(7) MrRWakley (a bhd) 20	**4**	5/1[3]	65	—
1284[P]	**Jumbeau (100)** (PRChamings) **11-11-11**(3) MrCBonner (lw: prom to 7th: t.o whn p.u bef 13th)	**P**	8/1	—	—
1089[P]	**Tipp Mariner (98)** (OSherwood) **11-11-12b** JOsborne (led: blnd 2nd: mstke & hdd 5th: mstkes 10th & 11th: wknd 13th: t.o whn p.u bef 2 out)	**P**	3/1[2]	—	—
	Deependable (90) (MrsLRichards) **9-11-4b** MRichards (bit bkwd: hdwy 11th: wknd 3 out: t.o whn p.u bef last) ..	**P**	12/1	—	—

(SP 119.5%) **7 Rn**

6m 54.3 (34.30) CSF £11.08 TOTE £2.70: £1.60 £3.20 (£19.80) OWNER Kings Of The Road Partnership (LAMBOURN) BRED Patrick Moakley

LONG HANDICAP Rhoman Fun (IRE) 9-8 Joker Jack 9-9

1194 Funcheon Gale is not the best of jumpers but he moved to the front approaching the second last and, although wandering about, still plodded better than this rivals to win this appalling race. (6/4)

Rhoman Fun (IRE) moved into second place and was only about a length down jumping the final fence before failing to find another gear. (6/1: 9/2-7/1)

1421 Joker Jack was racing over a far more suitable trip on this occasion and consequently ran better, leading from the fifth until collared two from home. (20/1)

Jumbeau (8/1: op 5/1)

Deependable (12/1: 7/1-14/1)

1555 BIGGIN HILL INTERMEDIATE OPEN N.H. FLAT RACE (4, 5 & 6-Y.O F & M) (Class H)

3-30 (3-31) **2m 1f 110y** £1,301.00 (£361.00: £173.00)

			SP	RR	SF
	Bula Vogue (IRE) (RRowe) **6-11-0** DO'Sullivan (led 12f: lost pl over 4f out: rallied over 2f out: led 1f out: drvn out) ....—	**1**	11/1	28 f	—
	Supreme Troglodyte (IRE) (CPMorlock) **4-11-0** JRKavanagh (bit bkwd: hmpd over 6f out: hdwy over 5f out: led wl over 1f out to 1f out: r.o) ....¾	**2**	25/1	27 f	—
	Plaid Maid (IRE) (MBradstock) **4-11-0** PHolley (hdwy over 6f out: rdn & ev ch wl over 1f out: unable qckn)..2½	**3**	12/1	25 f	—
	Royal Ruler (IRE) (JTGifford) **5-11-0** PHide (bit bkwd: hld up: led over 5f out tl wl over 1f out: sn wknd) 6	**4**	2/1[1]	20 f	—

	Horse	Dist	Pos	SP	RR	SF
	Good Thyne Girl (MissHCKnight) **4-11-0** JOsborne (hdwy over 4f out: wknd over 2f out)	4	**5**	3/1 2	16 f	—
1177⁶	**Solar Moon** (RHBuckler) **5-11-0** BPowell (hdwy over 5f out: wknd 3f out)	hd	**6**	11/1	16 f	—
	Yarsley Jester (DMGrissell) **4-11-0** BFenton (bkwd: lost pl 11f out: rallied 9f out: wknd 5f out)	7	**7**	14/1	9 f	—
	Tawny Warbler (MrsPRobeson) **4-11-0** MRichards (prom over 10f)	11	**8**	25/1	—	—
	Castle Lynch (IRE) (RHAlner) **4-10-11**(3) PHenley (lw: a bhd)	13	**9**	9/1	—	—
	Aintgotwon (AHide) **5-10-11**(3) LAspell (hdwy over 8f out: bdly hmpd over 6f out: wknd 5f out)	15	**10**	16/1	—	—
	Blameless (MrsDHaine) **4-10-11**(3) GHogan (fair sort: bit bkwd: chsd wnr 11f: wknd over 3f out)	hd	**11**	11/2 3	—	—
	Ballyquintet (IRE) (HBHodge) **5-11-0** SMcNeill (a bhd: t.o)	dist	**12**	33/1	—	—
	Real Lucille (MDMcMillan) **4-11-0** MAFitzgerald (bit bkwd: prom over 9f: t.o)	dist	**13**	20/1	—	—
	Tabbitts Hill (PRWebber) **4-11-0** MrPScott (lengthy, unf: bkwd: hmpd over 6f out: bhd fnl 6f: t.o)	6	**14**	10/1	—	—
				(SP 145.1%)	**14 Rn**	

4m 25.6 CSF £252.95 TOTE £16.10: £3.50 £5.80 £5.90 (£712.10; £822.44 to Huntingdon 26/11/96) Trio £171.20 OWNER The In Vogue Partnership (PULBOROUGH) BRED Daniel J. O'Keeffe

Bula Vogue (IRE), winner of an Irish mares' maiden point-to-point in the spring, set the pace but, once collared over five furlongs from home, that looked to be the end of her part in the race. However, she had other ideas and, getting back into the action entering the straight, regained the advantage a furlong out and held on well in a driving finish. (11/1)

Supreme Troglodyte (IRE), sold this year for 3,600 guineas, did not look fully wound up but nevertheless came through to lead early in the short straight. Collared a furlong from home, she kept on well to the line. (25/1)

Plaid Maid (IRE) was battling for the advantage early in the straight before tapped for toe. (12/1: 8/1-14/1)

Royal Ruler (IRE), not looking fully fit for this reappearance, went on at the top of the hill but, collared early in the straight, found lack of race-fitness taking its toll. (2/1)

Good Thyne Girl, who changed hands for just 2,000 guineas as a four-year-old, took closer order running down the hill but had been hung out to dry entering the short home straight. (3/1)

653 Solar Moon (11/1: 8/1-12/1)

Blameless (11/2: 4/1-6/1)

Tabbitts Hill (10/1: 6/1-14/1)

T/Plpt: £2,991.40 (4.4 Tckts). T/Qdpt: £323.90 (4.44 Tckts). AK

1382-CHELTENHAM (L-H) (Good to firm, Good patches)

Tuesday November 26th

WEATHER: fine

1556 CHELTENHAM RACECOURSE OF THE YEAR H'CAP HURDLE (0-135) (4-Y.O+) (Class C)

1-00 (1-00) **2m 5f (Old) (10 hdls)** £3,468.75 (£1,050.00: £512.50: £243.75) GOING: 0.25 sec per fur (GS)

	Horse	Dist	Pos	SP	RR	SF
1067³	**Blaze Away (USA) (122)** (IABalding) **5-11-8** JOsborne (chsd ldr fr 5th: led flat: rdn out)	—	**1**	13/8 2	98	26
1351F	**Courbaril (120)** (MCPipe) **4-11-6** APMcCoy (led: reminders after 5th: sn clr: hung rt: swished tail & hdd flat)	3	**2**	Evens 1	94	22
1392⁶	**Bellroi (IRE) (103)** (MHTompkins) **5-10-3** AMaguire (lw: chsd ldr to 4th: wknd 7th)	13	**3**	4/1 3	67	—
	Blazer Moriniere (FR) (128) (PCRitchens) **7-12-0** SFox (t.k.h: wl bhd fr 5th: t.o)	dist	**4**	66/1	—	—
				(SP 109.6%)	**4 Rn**	

5m 15.7 (17.70) CSF £3.55 TOTE £2.40 (£2.30) OWNER Mr Paul Mellon (KINGSCLERE) BRED Paul Mellon

1067 Blaze Away (USA), 6lb better off than when beaten over five lengths by the second here last month, was undoubtedly aided by the runner-up's antics. (13/8)

1351 Courbaril had beaten the winner just over five lengths on 6lb better terms over course and distance last month. With a useful lead when his stride shortened nearing the last, he gave the distinct impression he was heading for the paddock. (Evens)

692* Bellroi (IRE) should have preferred this faster ground but was beaten at the top of the hill. (4/1)

1557 LANSDOWN NOVICES' H'CAP CHASE (0-110) (5-Y.O+) (Class D)

1-35 (1-35) **2m 4f 110y (Old) (15 fncs)** £3,720.50 (£1,124.00: £547.00: £258.50) GOING: 0.25 sec per fur (GS)

	Horse	Dist	Pos	SP	RR	SF
1061²	**Pongo Waring (IRE) (103)** (MissHCKnight) **7-12-0** JOsborne (j.w: chsd ldr: led 3 out: rdn appr last: r.o)	—	**1**	11/4 1	112	52
1364²	**Flimsy Truth (91)** (MHWeston) **10-11-2** AMaguire (led to 3 out: rallied appr last: hrd rdn & edgd lft flat: r.o)	1	**2**	8/1	99	39
	Glenalla Star (IRE) (100) (CPEBrooks) **7-11-11** GBradley (bit bkwd: hit 2nd: hdwy 5th: ev ch whn j.slowly 3 out: wknd flat: fin tired)	8	**3**	3/1 2	102	42
	Pearl's Choice (IRE) (88) (JCMcConnochie) **8-10-13** RFarrant (no hdwy fr 4 out)	2	**4**	25/1	88	28
1041*	**Mill O'The Rags (IRE) (100)** (MrsDHaine) **7-11-11** NWilliamson (lw: hld up: rdn after 11th: sn bhd: t.o)	dist	**5**	9/2 3	—	—
1311²	**Ballyline (IRE) (88)** (WTKemp) **5-10-12** MDwyer (prom tl lost pl 4 out: 4th whn fell 3 out)		**F**	3/1 2	—	—
				(SP 109.8%)	**6 Rn**	

5m 13.8 (11.80) CSF £20.62 TOTE £3.20: £2.10 £2.60 (£9.20) OWNER Miss H. Knight (WANTAGE) BRED Joseph Smiddy

WEIGHT FOR AGE 5yo-1lb

1061 Pongo Waring (IRE) had been faced with what subsequently turned out to be an impossible task, in trying to concede weight to Strong Promise over course and distance last month. (11/4: 2/1-3/1)

1364 Flimsy Truth deserves full marks for the way he fought back up the hill, and again came up against a useful sort. (8/1: 6/1-9/1)

Glenalla Star (IRE) was just about to lead when outjumped by the winner three out. He seemed to blow up in the closing stages on ground lively enough for him. (3/1)

Pearl's Choice (IRE) ran her best race since coming over from Ireland. (25/1)

1041* Mill O'The Rags (IRE), up 5lb, was making heavy weather of it at the top of the hill. (9/2)

1311 Ballyline (IRE), trying a longer trip, seemed held when coming to grief. (3/1)

1558 VFB HOLIDAYS H'CAP CHASE (0-145) (5-Y.O+) (Class B)

2-10 (2-10) **3m 1f (Old) (19 fncs)** £6,762.00 (£2,046.00: £998.00: £474.00) GOING: 0.25 sec per fur (GS)

	Horse	Dist	Pos	SP	RR	SF
	Yorkshire Gale (130) (JTGifford) **10-11-10** NWilliamson (lw: hld up: led on bit 3 out: rdn & qcknd clr after 2 out: drvn out)	—	**1**	4/1 3	142	54
1273³	**Betty's Boy (IRE) (127)** (KCBailey) **7-11-7** CO'Dwyer (hld up: blnd 7th: hdwy 12th: led 15th to 3 out: outpcd after 2 out)	21	**2**	11/4 2	126	38
1367²	**Copper Mine (123)** (OSherwood) **10-11-3** JOsborne (lw: led to 13th: wknd 14th)	15	**3**	8/1	112	24

				SP	RR	SF
1273[2]	**Grey Smoke (129)** (MissHCKnight) **6-11-9** GBradley (chsd ldr: reminder after 10th: led 13th to 15th: wknd 4 out)	8	**4**	11/10[1]	113	25
				(SP 105.4%)		**4 Rn**

6m 21.2 (12.20) CSF £12.91 TOTE £3.70 (£5.10) OWNER Mr Bill Naylor (FINDON) BRED Miss Y. McClintock and Mrs D. P. O'Brien
OFFICIAL EXPLANATION Grey Smoke: finished distressed.
Yorkshire Gale looked particularly well and completed a hat-trick of seasonal reappearance wins in impressive style. Connections are thinking in terms of the National at the moment. (4/1)
1273 Betty's Boy (IRE) landed on top of the second ditch and proved no match for the winner, and needs to come down in the weights. (11/4)
1367 Copper Mine got left for dead once things began to hot up. (8/1: op 5/1)
1273 Grey Smoke, raised 5lb for his narrow defeat by Inchcailloch, may be better suited to forcing the pace. (11/10)

1559 NEWENT HURDLE (4-Y.O+) (Class B)
2-45 (2-46) **2m 110y (Old) (8 hdls)** £7,335.00 (£2,060.00: £1,005.00) GOING: 0.25 sec per fur (GS)

				SP	RR	SF
1319*	**Mandys Mantino (132)** (JTGifford) **6-11-4** PHide (mde all: clr 3rd: hit 3 out: hrd rdn after 2 out: all out)	—	**1**	11/8[1]	102	48
	Serenity Prayer (USA) (BruceMiller,USA) **6-11-7** ChipMiller (chsd wnr tl mstke 3 out: rallied flat: r.o)	½	**2**	11/4[3]	105	51
1325[3]	**Chicodari (128)** (DNicholson) **4-10-9** AMaguire (hld up: chsd wnr fr 3 out: ev ch appr last: hrd rdn: eased whn btn nr fin)	7	**3**	7/4[2]	86	32
				(SP 105.1%)		**3 Rn**

3m 59.0 (8.00) CSF £4.41 TOTE £2.10 (£1.90) OWNER Mr John Plackett (FINDON) BRED Miss J. U. Wood
1319* Mandys Mantino sensibly insured this would be a reasonable stamina test, over a trip which might be on the short side for him nowadays. (11/8: op evens)
Serenity Prayer (USA), a winner of six of his last seven hurdle races in the States, may well have prevailed here, had he not missed out at the third last. (11/4)
1325 Chicodari, only declared when the race was re-opened, again had the blinkers left off. (7/4)

1560 EVERYMAN THEATRE ROBIN HOOD NOVICES' CHASE (5-Y.O+) (Class C)
3-20 (3-20) **3m 1f (Old) (19 fncs)** £7,245.00 GOING: 0.25 sec per fur (GS)

				SP	RR	SF
1415*	**Imperial Vintage (IRE) (110)** (MissVenetiaWilliams) **6-11-6** NWilliamson (hld up: ev ch whn lft alone 4 out)	—	**1**	11/8[2]	115	—
1054*	**Hanakham (IRE) (118)** (RJHodges) **7-11-6** JOsborne (led tl blnd & uns rdr 4 out)		**U**	8/13[1]	—	—
				(SP 104.0%)		**2 Rn**

6m 56.5 (47.50) TOTE £1.70 OWNER Mr David Williams (HEREFORD) BRED W. J. Mernagh
1415* Imperial Vintage (IRE) had just closed on his solitary opponent, and seemed to be going best, when left alone at the final ditch. (11/8)
1054* Hanakham (IRE) did not seem to be travelling as well as the winner, when departing at the ditch at the top of the hill. (8/13)

1561 GO RACING IN IRELAND 'N.H.' NOVICES' HURDLE (4-Y.O+) (Class C)
3-55 (3-55) **3m 2f (Old) (13 hdls)** £3,501.25 (£1,060.00: £517.50: £246.25) GOING: 0.25 sec per fur (GS)

				SP	RR	SF
1541[4]	**Spaceage Gold (99)** (JABOld) **7-11-2** GUpton (lw: led tl appr last: rallied to ld nr fin: all out)	—	**1**	5/4[1]	75	—
1088*	**Tarrs Bridge (IRE) (100)** (CJMann) **5-11-10** JRailton (hld up: hdwy 8th: squeezed thro on ins & bmpd after 2 out: led appr last: rdn & hdd nr fin)	1	**2**	11/8[2]	82	—
1197[P]	**Rare Spread (IRE)** (MCPipe) **6-11-2** CMaude (hld up in rr: lost tch appr 8th: gd hdwy 10th: hung rt fr 3 out: btn whn rn wd bnd appr last)	27	**3**	11/2[3]	58	—
	News From Afar (MrsSDWilliams) **5-11-2** AMaguire (w ldr: hit 1st: rdn after 6th: wknd appr 3 out: t.o)	dist	**4**	14/1	—	—
				(SP 108.6%)		**4 Rn**

6m 54.6 (37.60) CSF £3.21 TOTE £2.20 (£1.60) OWNER Spaceage Plastics Ltd (WROUGHTON) BRED S. Hadley
1541 Spaceage Gold was short of pace when trying to close the door, as the runner-up went up the inside after the penultimate hurdle. However he fought back in the closing stages in the style of a dour stayer. (5/4)
1088* Tarrs Bridge (IRE) looked sure to score when slipping up the inside of the winner going to the elbow, but got outstayed under his double penalty towards the finish. (11/8: 10/11-6/4)
594 Rare Spread (IRE) had run out at halfway when in the lead on his bumper debut, and his temperament was again very much in evidence here. (11/2: 8/1-5/1)

T/Plpt: £466.70 (25.37 Tckts). T/Qdpt: £46.80 (22.99 Tckts). KH

1369-HUNTINGDON (R-H) (Good to soft)
Tuesday November 26th
Race 2 - one fence omitted final circuit
WEATHER: fine

1562 HOUGHTON (S) H'CAP HURDLE (0-95) (4-Y.O+) (Class G)
12-40 (12-40) **3m 2f (12 hdls)** £2,031.00 (£566.00: £273.00) GOING: 0.45 sec per fur (GS)

				SP	RR	SF
1256[3]	**Mr Flutts (75)** (JCTuck) **10-10-10** SMcNeill (hit 7th: hdwy next: led appr last: rdn out)	—	**1**	4/1[1]	57	11
1294[6]	**Quiet Mistress (80)** (WABethell) **6-11-1b[1]** ASSmith (mde most tl wnt clr after 9th: hdd appr last: rdn & kpt on)	1¼	**2**	13/2[2]	61	15
1466[3]	**Katballou (65)** (KGWingrove) **7-9-7(7)** MrOMcPhail (a.p: one pce fr 3 out)	11	**3**	8/1	40	—
1285[P]	**Tiger Claw (USA) (88)** (AGHobbs) **10-11-2(7)** OBurrows (trckd ldrs to 9th)	dist	**4**	7/1[3]	—	—
	Mardood (80) (SBClark) **11-10-8(7)** MissRClark (bit bkwd: w ldr to 8th: wknd next)	5	**5**	14/1	—	—
1372[5]	**Provence (73)** (AWCarroll) **9-10-5(3)** GHogan (prom to 8th)	1¼	**6**	9/1	—	—
1357[5]	**Arrange A Game (69)** (MissJBower) **9-10-1(3)** TDascombe (sn pushed along: in tch to 8th)	18	**7**	10/1	—	—
934[7]	**Milly le Moss (IRE) (65)** (RJEckley) **7-10-0** RJohnson (chsd ldrs to 7th)	nk	**8**	8/1	—	—
1304[6]	**Tharsis (72)** (WJSmith) **11-10-2(5)** STaylor (lw: hit 3rd: rdn 6th: bhd fr 8th)	13	**9**	25/1	—	—
1374[9]	**Nagobelia (93)** (JPearce) **8-12-0** NMann (a bhd: t.o fr 8th)	dist	**10**	14/1	—	—
1250[4]	**Our Rainbow (85)** (MrsPSly) **4-11-5** RMarley (lw: in tch to 7th: t.o whn p.u bef 9th)		**P**	4/1[1]	—	—
	Fast Run (IRE) (76) (JWMullins) **8-10-11** BFenton (bit bkwd: a bhd: t.o whn p.u bef last)		**P**	12/1	—	—
1448[9]	**Parisian (65)** (JABennett) **11-10-0** LHarvey (t.o whn p.u bef 2 out)		**P**	25/1	—	—

				SP	RR	SF
1007^{8}	**Lock Tight (USA) (65)** (MissCJECaroe) **6-10-0** DLeahy (dropped rr 6th: blnd next: t.o whn p.u bef 8th)............		**P**	50/1	—	—
				(SP 137.8%)	**14 Rn**	

6m 34.5 (28.50) CSF £32.79 CT £198.85 TOTE £5.60: £2.10 £2.20 £2.60 (£23.00) Trio £87.00 OWNER Mr J. C. Tuck (DIDMARTON) BRED G. S. Tuck
LONG HANDICAP Katballou 9-9 Milly le Moss (IRE) 9-7 Lock Tight (USA) 8-8
WEIGHT FOR AGE 4yo-1lb
No bid
OFFICIAL EXPLANATION Milly Le Moss (IRE): was later found to have sore shins.
1256 Mr Flutts, scoring for the first time in over five years, was dropping in grade and travelled quite well on the final circuit, although he did not find a lot once in front. (4/1: op 5/2)
1294 Quiet Mistress looked to be hating the first time blinkers in the paddock, walking round with her ears back, but her performance was transformed and she ran to something like her form of eighteen months ago. (13/2)
1466 Katballou, making a very quick reappearance after his seasonal debut, was always in the firing line but got very tired over a trip which may be beyond his best. (8/1: 5/1-10/1)
1040* Tiger Claw (USA) could not repeat his recent course and distance win off a 7lb higher mark. (7/1)
Mardood is a light of former days but still tries hard in this type of race. (14/1: 10/1-16/1)
1372 Provence was again in trouble after the first couple of miles. (9/1)
Nagobelia (14/1: 10/1-16/1)

1563 HEALTH-SPA WATER NOVICES' CHASE (4-Y.O+) (Class E)
1-15 (1-17) **2m 4f 110y (15 fncs)** £3,994.75 (£1,198.00: £576.50: £265.75) GOING: 0.45 sec per fur (GS)

				SP	RR	SF
1371^{2}	**Mister Drum (IRE)** (MJWilkinson) **7-11-5** WMarston (j.rt: mde virtually all: hit 5th & 12th: comf)	—	**1**	$11/4^{2}$	116+	57
1259^{2}	**Wee Windy (IRE)** (JTGifford) **7-11-5** RDunwoody (trckd wnr: hit 3rd: ev ch whn mstke 3 out: rdn appr next: kpt on flat)	3½	**2**	$4/5^{1}$	113	54
1179^{2}	**Slingsby (IRE) (99)** (NAGaselee) **6-11-5** AThornton (prom: pckd 1st: mstke 11th: rdn & one pce whn hit last)	hd	**3**	$8/1^{3}$	113	54
	Haunting Music (IRE) (MrsAJPerrett) **8-11-5** MAFitzgerald (lw: chsd ldrs tl lost pl 10th: rdn & hdwy appr 2 out: wknd appr last)	4	**4**	12/1	110	51
	Pearl Epee (90) (DNicholson) **7-11-0** RBellamy (lw: in tch tl hit 12th)	29	**5**	16/1	82	23
	Another Venture (IRE) (92) (FMurphy) **6-11-5** BFenton (nvr nr to chal)	16	**6**	20/1	75	16
1253*	**Bassenhally (83)** (MrsPSly) **6-11-5** RMarley (lw: in tch: hit 7th: wkng whn blnd 12th)	¾	**7**	16/1	74	15
	My Warrior (MarkCampion) **8-11-5** MSharratt (bit bkwd: j.b: a bhd)	10	**8**	100/1	67?	8
	Rathfardon (IRE) (FMurphy) **8-10-12**(7) MrTJBarry (bkwd: a bhd)	nk	**9**	100/1	66?	7
1374^{7}	**Pegasus Bay** (DECantillon) **5-11-4** SMcNeill (lw: in tch: effrt 10th: 5th whn fell 3 out)		**F**	33/1	—	—
	Hancock (JHetherton) **4-10-6** DerekByrne (j.b: fell 4th)		**F**	50/1	—	—
1340^{F}	**Upham Rascal (60)** (DRGandolfo) **5-11-4** DLeahy (t.o whn tried to ref 3rd: p.u bef next)		**P**	50/1	—	—
	Old Redwood (MrsLWilliamson) **9-11-5** LO'Hara (bit bkwd: prom: j.slowly 10th: sn wknd: bhd whn blnd 3 out: p.u bef next)		**P**	100/1	—	—
1320^{F}	**Scorpion Bay** (DJSffrenchDavis) **8-11-5** PHolley (bhd whn blnd & uns rdr 8th)		**U**	50/1	—	—
				(SP 129.3%)	**14 Rn**	

5m 11.9 (11.90) CSF £5.41 TOTE £3.80: £1.40 £1.30 £1.50 (£2.40) Trio £3.60 OWNER Mr Malcolm Batchelor (BANBURY) BRED David Mooney
WEIGHT FOR AGE 4yo-13lb, 5yo-1lb
1371 Mister Drum (IRE) was happy forcing the pace and won well, but drifted down one or two of his fences, in a manner which suggests he may struggle to be so effective on left-handed courses. (11/4)
1259 Wee Windy (IRE) jumped adequately on the whole but his mistake three out came as the tempo quickened and he quickly lost second place, only to regain it on the flat. On such a sharp course this is an inadequate trip and he really needs three miles. (4/5)
1179 Slingsby (IRE), wearing a cross noseband and stepping up in trip, was still just second when hitting the last. This trip may be stretching his stamina. (8/1: 6/1-9/1)
Haunting Music (IRE) looked fit but ran like a horse who had been absent for seven months, dropping back at halfway only to get a second wind. He looks the type to do well at this game. (12/1: op 8/1)
Pearl Epee is tall but lacks gears and does look to need further. (16/1)

1564 WEATHERBYS VAT SERVICE H'CAP CHASE (0-110) (5-Y.O+) (Class E)
1-50 (1-50) **3m (18 fncs)** £3,036.25 (£910.00: £437.50: £201.25) GOING: 0.45 sec per fur (GS)

				SP	RR	SF
696^{2}	**Solo Gent (92)** (APJones) **7-11-6** SMcNeill (lw: trckd ldrs: led appr last: sn pushed clr)	—	**1**	$7/2^{3}$	105	28
1318^{5}	**Sugar Hill (IRE) (84)** (JTGifford) **6-10-9**(3) LAspell (trckd ldr: led 15th tl blnd & hdd next: led 2 out: sn hdd & one pce)	9	**2**	$3/1^{2}$	91	14
	Distinctive (IRE) (96) (MJWilkinson) **7-11-10** RDunwoody (bit bkwd: led to 15th: led next to 2 out: btn whn hit last)	1½	**3**	$5/2^{1}$	102	25
1244^{5}	**Trumpet (96)** (JGMO'Shea) **7-11-10v** RJohnson (chsd ldrs: hit 9th: wknd 14th)	27	**4**	12/1	84	7
1284^{6}	**Maxxum Express (IRE) (85)** (GBBalding) **8-10-13** RichardGuest (bhd: hdwy 11th: rdn 13th: sn wknd)	8	**5**	15/2	68	—
	Carlingford Lakes (IRE) (87) (TThomsonJones) **8-11-1** MAFitzgerald (mstkes: bhd fr 12th: p.u bef 15th)		**P**	4/1	—	—
	Tim Soldier (FR) (79) (MFBarraclough) **9-10-7** JRKavanagh (bit bkwd: mstkes 3rd & 12th: sn bhd: p.u bef 15th)		**P**	20/1	—	—
				(SP 120.0%)	**7 Rn**	

6m 21.3 (24.30) CSF £14.61 TOTE £3.80: £2.20 £1.80 (£6.10) OWNER Mr A. A. King (EASTBURY) BRED H. G. Llewellyn
696 Solo Gent does tend to jump right and this course, which is on the turn most of the way, suits him ideally. He now has three wins and two places to his credit from five outings. (7/2)
1318 Sugar Hill (IRE) might well have won this with a trouble-free round, and it is only a matter of time before he gets off the mark. (3/1)
Distinctive (IRE) handed out a jumping lesson from the front until lack of a run caught him out. This was a rather weak contest but he will win his share of handicaps this season. (5/2: op 6/4)
1244 Trumpet found the sticky ground right against him. (12/1: 8/1-14/1)
Maxxum Express (IRE) is gradually returning to form after a long lay-off. (15/2)

1565 HOECHST ROUSSEL PANACUR E.B.F 'N.H.' QUALIFIER NOVICES' HURDLE (4-Y.O+ F & M) (Class E)

2-25 (2-25) **2m 5f 110y (10 hdls)** £2,460.00 (£685.00: £330.00) GOING: 0.45 sec per fur (GS)

	Horse	Dist		SP	RR	SF
	Gaye Fame (KCBailey) **5-10-12** SMcNeill (lw: a.p: led 6th: mstke next: rdn out)	—	**1**	$9/4^{2}$	65+	21
1341^{2}	**Marlousion (IRE)** (CPEBrooks) **4-10-12** DGallagher (chsd ldrs: ev ch last: unable qckn)	1¼	**2**	$6/1^{3}$	64	20
1341^{3}	**Lady High Sheriff (IRE) (70)** (CaptTAForster) **6-10-12** SWynne (chsd ldrs to 7th: btn whn lft 3rd & hmpd 2 out)	13	**3**	9/1	54	10
1197^{P}	**Hopperdante (IRE)** (TRGeorge) **6-10-12** RJohnson (prom to 6th)	dist	**4**	33/1	—	—
1200^{*}	**Seymourswift (100)** (DRGandolfo) **6-11-5** RDunwoody (lw: prom: 3rd & rdn whn fell 2 out)		**F**	$6/4^{1}$	—	—
	Primitive Penny (MrsDHaine) **5-10-9**(3) GHogan (led to 6th: wknd next: t.o whn p.u bef 2 out)		**P**	14/1	—	—
	Briery Gale (CaptTAForster) **6-10-12** AThornton (hdwy 5th: wknd qckly 3 out: p.u bef next)		**P**	16/1	—	—
1250^{6}	**Mesp (IRE)** (JGMO'Shea) **5-10-12** MAFitzgerald (lw: in tch to 4th: t.o whn p.u bef 6th)		**P**	20/1	—	—
	Off Piste Sally (FMurphy) **4-10-12** BFenton (bkwd: blnd 3rd: sn wl bhd: t.o whn p.u bef 6th)		**P**	33/1	—	—
1171^{6}	**Gentle Breeze (IRE)** (JTGifford) **4-10-9**(3) LAspell (in tch to 7th: bhd whn p.u bef 2 out)		**P**	10/1	—	—

(SP 127.3%) **10 Rn**

5m 21.0 (21.00) CSF £17.11 TOTE £3.50: £1.70 £1.60 £2.50 (£12.40) Trio £19.80 OWNER Mr Noel Cronin (UPPER LAMBOURN) BRED Mrs Mercy Rimell

Gaye Fame, out of a winning sister to Black Humour, is certainly bred to do well and although rather neat, is well made and looks in fine shape. She won in only workmanlike style but will be a tough nut to crack in mares' races. (9/4)

1341 Marlousion (IRE) got very stirred up beforehand, but did better over this longer trip, having a ding-dong battle in the straight. (6/1)

1341 Lady High Sheriff (IRE) shows plenty of knee action but was already struggling when forced to swerve violently, to avoid being brought down at the second last. (9/1: 6/1-10/1)

Hopperdante (IRE), an Irish Point winner, dropping in trip from her debut, at least got round but more in her own time. (33/1)

1200* Seymourswift, a big danger on the home turn, was losing touch with the first two when taking a crashing fall at the second last. (6/4)

1566 PETERBOROUGH CHASE (Gd 2) (5-Y.O+) (Class A)

3-00 (3-00) **2m 4f 110y (16 fncs)** £18,125.00 (£6,858.50: £3,356.75: £1,529.75) GOING: 0.45 sec per fur (GS)

	Horse	Dist		SP	RR	SF
1366^{S}	**Dublin Flyer (168)** (CaptTAForster) **10-11-1** BPowell (lw: trckd ldr: led after 3 out: rdn & blnd last: easily)	—	**1**	$4/9^{1}$	157+	53
1440^{3}	**Gales Cavalier (IRE) (159)** (DRGandolfo) **8-11-10** RDunwoody (led tl after 3 out: hit next: sn btn: eased flat)	18	**2**	$7/2^{2}$	152+	48
	Kadi (GER) (140) (DNicholson) **7-11-1** RJohnson (bit bkwd: chsd ldrs: hit 10th: no imp)	9	**3**	$5/1^{3}$	136	32
1440^{4}	**Quixall Crossett (56)** (EMCaine) **11-11-1** STaylor (lw: wl bhd: hit 2nd: blnd bdly 10th: hdwy 3 out: r.o)	dist	**4**	250/1	—	—
	Stage Player (82) (MissCJECaroe) **10-11-1** ILawrence (wl bhd: hdwy 5th: wkng whn hit 10th)	10	**5**	100/1	—	—
1442^{R}	**Monaughty Man (76)** (EMCaine) **10-11-1** MrPMurray (a bhd)	3½	**6**	200/1	—	—

(SP 110.0%) **6 Rn**

5m 11.9 (11.90) CSF £2.37 TOTE £1.30: £1.10 £2.20 (£1.60) OWNER Mr J. B. Sumner (LUDLOW) BRED Marston Stud

1366 Dublin Flyer is ideally suited going left-handed, but at these weights it made little difference, and his last-fence blunder was due to lack of concentration more than anything else. (4/9)

1440 Gales Cavalier (IRE) was attempting the impossible in trying to give the winner 9lb, as he would be receiving 9lb from that rival in a handicap. In the circumstances he ran as well as could be hoped. (7/2)

Kadi (GER), off since April last year, looked terrifically well in his coat but just in need of this and was soon taken off his feet. He is very flattered by the final distances as both of the leading pair were eased considerably. (5/1)

1311 Quixall Crossett, owed much to his pilot who did a magnificent job in keeping the partnership together setting out on the final circuit, and they got their just reward by staying on from a long way behind to earn fourth prize. (250/1)

Stage Player is not as good as he once was. (100/1)

Monaughty Man chased shadows for two miles before giving up. (200/1)

1567 TOTE H'CAP HURDLE (0-130) (4-Y.O+) (Class C)

3-35 (3-35) **2m 110y (8 hdls)** £5,177.50 (£1,555.00: £750.00: £347.50) GOING: 0.45 sec per fur (GS)

	Horse	Dist		SP	RR	SF
1325^{*}	**Teinein (FR) (128)** (CaptTAForster) **5-12-0** APMcCoy (hld up: led 2 out: canter)	—	**1**	$8/13^{1}$	108+	64
	Marius (IRE) (112) (JTGifford) **6-10-9**(3) LAspell (plld hrd: w ldr: led 5th: hdd 2 out: no ch w wnr)	3½	**2**	$100/30^{2}$	89	45
	Chef Comedien (IRE) (120) (MJWilkinson) **6-11-6** RDunwoody (bit bkwd: chsd ldrs tl rdn & btn appr 2 out)	17	**3**	$15/2^{3}$	80	36
	Cawarra Boy (107) (CJames) **8-10-7** MrEJames (hld up: hdwy 5th: rdn & btn next)	1¾	**4**	14/1	65	21
	Albemine (USA) (121) (MrsJCecil) **7-11-7** TKent (lw: led to 5th: wknd appr 2 out)	6	**5**	10/1	74	30
1271^{6}	**Maneree (106)** (NACallaghan) **9-10-6** DGallagher (a bhd)	18	**6**	20/1	41	—
677^{3}	**Zine Lane (103)** (JGMO'Shea) **4-10-3**ow1 MAFitzgerald (prom to 4th)	28	**7**	10/1	11	—

(SP 126.4%) **7 Rn**

3m 57.7 (9.70) CSF £3.86 TOTE £1.60: £1.40 £1.40 (£3.40) OWNER Mr Simon Sainsbury (LUDLOW) BRED Tomohiro Wada

1325* Teinein (FR) cruised to the front jumping the penultimate flight, to win with embarrassing ease. This race did not take much winning as most of his rivals were out of form or unsuited by the ground, but he could not have been more impressive. (8/13)

Marius (IRE) looked well in his coat but just in need of the run, and belied that by running a fine race and will not always meet one so well handicapped. (100/30: 4/1-6/1)

Chef Comedien (IRE), an ex-Irish hurdler who was returning after eighteen months off, ran really well until fading on the home turn and is well worth keeping an eye on. He looks well handicapped on some of his old form. (15/2)

Cawarra Boy looked fit enough but is higher in the handicap than when scoring his wins last season, and was in trouble by the third last. (14/1: 6/1-16/1)

Albemine (USA) looked in great condition but needs faster ground to be seen at his best. (10/1: op 5/1)

Maneree could not stay in touch over this trip and was not duly punished. Her chances will come over further, probably over further. (20/1)

677 Zine Lane (10/1: 7/1-12/1)

T/Jkpt: £1,209.90 (13.4 Tckts). T/Plpt: £12.00 (1,324.35 Tckts). T/Qdpt: £4.90 (273.19 Tckts). Dk

1257-CHEPSTOW (L-H) (Ch Good to soft, Hdles Soft)
Wednesday November 27th
WEATHER: overcast

1568 GALWAY NOVICES' HURDLE (4-Y.O+) (Class C)
1-25 (1-28) **2m 4f 110y (11 hdls)** £3,965.75 (£1,196.00: £580.50: £272.75) GOING: 0.66 sec per fur (S)

	Horse	Details	Dist	Pos	SP	RR	SF
1323*	**Mighty Moss (IRE)**	(DNicholson) **5-10-12**(7) MrFHutsby (a.p: led appr 5th: hit 4 out: clr 2 out: easily)	—	1	Evens[1]	87+	38
	Glitter Isle (IRE) (101)	(JTGifford) **6-10-11**(3) LAspell (a.p: ev ch 4 out: no imp)	6	2	12/1[3]	77	28
1203[12]	**Kind Cleric**	(PJHobbs) **5-11-0** RDunwoody (hld up: stdy hdwy appr 7th: styd on fr 2 out)	3	3	66/1	75	26
1422*	**Scotby (BEL)**	(RHBuckler) **6-11-5** BPowell (lw: prom: wknd appr 4 out: btn whn mstke 3 out)	4	4	12/1[3]	77	28
	Kings Cherry (IRE)	(JABOld) **8-10-7**(7) MrGBaines (bkwd: s.s: nvr nrr)	15	5	100/1	60	11
1412*	**Daraydan (IRE)**	(MCPipe) **4-11-5** APMcCoy (a.p: ev ch appr 4 out: sn rdn & wknd)	3½	6	5/4[2]	62	13
1327[4]	**Blazing Miracle (65)**	(MrsRGHenderson) **4-10-4**(5) DSalter (bit bkwd: prom to 7th)	4	7	100/1	49	—
1323[9]	**Drakestone (81)**	(RLBrown) **5-11-0** RJohnson (led tl appr 5th: hit 6th: wknd appr 4 out)	1¼	8	66/1	53	4
	Red Branch (IRE)	(JSKing) **7-11-0** TJMurphy (bkwd: hld up: sme hdwy 6th: wknd appr 4 out)	9	9	100/1	46	—
1453[14]	**My Shenandoah (IRE)**	(HOliver) **5-11-0** VSlattery (s.s: a bhd)	5	10	66/1	42	—
	Harry the Horse (95)	(JABOld) **8-11-0** GUpton (bkwd: bhd fr 7th: t.o)	3	11	25/1	40	—
1203[7]	**Lucky Call (NZ)**	(AGHobbs) **5-11-0** RGreene (bkwd: prom tl wknd appr 4 out: t.o)	dist	12	100/1	—	—
1118[9]	**Irish Perry**	(TMorton) **9-10-9** MSharratt (bkwd: rel to r: a wl bhd: t.o)	dist	13	100/1	—	—
	Happy Jack	(PJJones) **5-11-0** DLeahy (bkwd: bhd: mstke 6th: sn t.o: p.u bef 4 out)		P	100/1	—	—
1171[12]	**Filch**	(PGMurphy) **5-10-9** JRKavanagh (bkwd: hld up & plld hrd: j.slowly 4th: t.o 7th: p.u bef 4 out)		P	100/1	—	—

(SP 125.1%) **15 Rn**

5m 8.2 (21.20) CSF £14.18 TOTE £2.00: £1.50 £3.10 £5.60 (£13.80) Trio £164.40 OWNER Mr K. Hutsby (TEMPLE GUITING) BRED Lady Melissa Brooke

1323* Mighty Moss (IRE) continues to progress along the right lines and this was an even more polished performance than at Worcester. It is going to take a useful sort to lower his colours. (Evens)

Glitter Isle (IRE) was the only one to really make a race of it in the long home straight but the winner proved much too smart. This potential chaser deserved to get off the mark over hurdles on this evidence. (12/1)

Kind Cleric, a half-brother to Joliver, is out of a half-sister to Eider Chase winner David's Duky and Rolls Rambler. Staying on in eye-catching style on this hurdling debut, he is one to note. (66/1)

1422* Scotby (BEL) may have found this coming too soon but in any case this race was a fair bit hotter than the event he won at Plumpton. (12/1: op 5/1)

1412* Daraydan (IRE), runner-up in the Chester Cup and fourth in the Goodwood Cup, should not have been inconvenienced by this longer trip so perhaps it was the ground that found him out. (5/4: evens-6/4)

1569 SLIGO (S) HURDLE (4,5,6 & 7-Y.O) (Class G)
1-55 (2-00) **2m 4f 110y (11 hdls)** £1,940.00 (£540.00: £260.00) GOING: 0.66 sec per fur (S)

	Horse	Details	Dist	Pos	SP	RR	SF
1334[3]	**Dragonmist (IRE) (67)**	(DBurchell) **6-10-7h** DJBurchell (hld up: hdwy 5th: rdn appr 4 out: led 2 out: styd on)	—	1	8/1[3]	57	—
1427[4]	**Parade Racer**	(PGMurphy) **5-10-12** GUpton (led to 3rd: led 6th: lft clr 7th: j.rt 3 out: hdd & hit 2 out: one pce)	6	2	5/2[2]	57	—
1426[P]	**Castleconner (IRE) (80)**	(RGFrost) **5-10-12b**[1] RDunwoody (a.p: one pce fr 4 out)	9	3	16/1	50	—
1417[7]	**Fortunes Rose (IRE) (65)**	(JSKing) **4-10-7** TJMurphy (hld up & bhd: hdwy 7th: rdn 4 out: one pce)	20	4	33/1	30	—
1053[11]	**Trouble At Mill**	(JLBrown) **6-10-12** PMcLoughlin (bhd tl hdwy 7th: wknd 4 out: t.o)	19	5	33/1	20	—
1380[P]	**Lanesra Breeze**	(TJNaughton) **4-10-12** CMaude (a bhd: t.o)	17	6	50/1	7	—
1322[6]	**China Mail (IRE) (86)**	(JABennett) **4-11-5** RJohnson (a bhd: t.o)	6	7	20/1	9	—
	Strike-a-Pose	(BJLlewellyn) **6-11-0** MrJLLlewellyn (bkwd: a bhd: t.o)	5	8	16/1	—	—
	Kadiri (IRE)	(JRBosley) **5-10-12** WMcFarland (hld up: hdwy whn mstke 6th: wknd after 7th: t.o)	15	9	20/1	—	—
1303[3]	**Forofivetwohundred (IRE)**	(MCPipe) **6-10-12** APMcCoy (prom: hit 5th: rdn whn lft 2nd & bdly hmpd 7th: nt rcvr: t.o)	dist	10	12/1	—	—
1047[2]	**Furietto (IRE) (98)**	(MDHammond) **6-11-5** AMaguire (lw: led 3rd to 4th: 2nd whn fell 7th)		F	5/4[1]	—	—
1299[8]	**Java Shrine (USA) (62)**	(JCTuck) **5-11-5** SMcNeill (hld up: hdwy 5th: wknd appr 4 out: t.o whn p.u bef 2 out)		P	25/1	—	—
1413[F]	**Norfolk Glory**	(DFBassett) **4-10-5**(7) MrRWakley (swtg: led 4th tl wknd qckly 6th: t.o whn p.u bef 4 out)		P	33/1	—	—
1450[11]	**Pollerton's Dream**	(MrsDThomas) **6-10-4**(3) GuyLewis (bit bkwd: prom: rdn appr 5th: wknd 6th: t.o whn p.u bef 4 out)		P	66/1	—	—

(SP 129.2%) **14 Rn**

5m 16.1 (29.10) CSF £28.64 TOTE £8.40: £1.30 £1.10 £4.00 (£24.30) Trio £249.80; £70.38 to Carlisle 28/11/96 OWNER Mr D. Roderick (EBBW VALE) BRED W. J. O'Regan

No bid

1334 Dragonmist (IRE), hardly winning out of turn, owes this success to her abundant reserves of stamina. (8/1)

Parade Racer, upped in trip and dropped in class, was always keen to force the pace but eventually got outstayed by the winner. (5/2: op 5/1)

Castleconner (IRE) had been pulled up when tried over fences last time. (16/1)

Fortunes Rose (IRE) tried to work her way into the picture on the long run to the fourth last but soon came under pressure. (33/1)

1303 Forofivetwohundred (IRE) (12/1: op 6/1)

1047 Furietto (IRE) looked something of a good thing against this bunch but the bookmakers were rescued yet again. (5/4: op evens)

1570 DONEGAL H'CAP CHASE (0-120) (5-Y.O+) (Class D)
2-25 (2-28) **2m 3f 110y (16 fncs)** £3,755.50 (£1,048.00: £506.50) GOING: 0.66 sec per fur (S)

	Horse	Details	Dist	Pos	SP	RR	SF
	Bells Life (IRE) (120)	(PJHobbs) **7-11-11**(3) GTormey (lw: hld up: j.slowly 6th: led & lft clr 2 out: eased flat)	—	1	2/1[1]	131+	50
1167*	**Beau Babillard (115)**	(PFNicholls) **9-11-9b** APMcCoy (hld up: hit 11th: hdwy appr 5 out: wknd 4 out)	16	2	11/4[2]	113	32
1257*	**Benjamin Lancaster (100)**	(MAGriffin) **12-10-1**(7) MGriffiths (led: reminder after 11th: hdd 5 out: wknd 3 out: lft 2nd 2 out)	2½	3	3/1[3]	96	15
814[2]	**Armala (108)**	(JTGifford) **11-10-13**(3) LAspell (lw: t.k.h: chsd ldr: led 5 out: hdd & fell 2 out)		F	11/4[2]	—	—

(SP 111.7%) **4 Rn**

5m 8.7 (19.70) CSF £7.27 TOTE £2.90 (£3.50) OWNER Mr R. Gibbs (MINEHEAD) BRED Dr Welby Henry

Bells Life (IRE) likes soft ground and made it three wins from three appearances at Chepstow. He was just in the process of mastering Armala when handed the race on a plate. (2/1: 11/8-9/4)

1167* Beau Babillard had struggled at Plumpton to beat a horse who did not revel in the mud and was 5lb higher here. (11/4)
1257* Benjamin Lancaster found this race a bit more competitive off a 2lb higher mark. (3/1)
814 Armala gave the impression he wanted to go a stride quicker and may have been better off making the running. He appeared to be just getting the worst of the argument when coming to grief. (11/4)

1571 INDEPENDENT INSURANCE H'CAP HURDLE (0-130) (4-Y.O+) (Class C)

2-55 (2-58) **3m (12 hdls)** £3,715.50 (£1,119.00: £542.00: £253.50) GOING: 0.66 sec per fur (S)

				SP	RR	SF
1418^{2}	**General Tonic (102)** (DRGandolfo) **9-10-0**$^{(5)}$ SophieMitchell (hld up: gd hdwy after 8th: led 3 out: r.o wl)	—	**1**	11/1	85	—
1074^{4}	**Karar (IRE) (107)** (RRowe) **6-10-10** DO'Sullivan (hld up: hdwy 6th: edgd lft & styd on flat)	1¾	**2**	13/2^{2}	89	—
	Miss Diskin (IRE) (110) (RHBuckler) **7-10-13** AMaguire (hdwy 7th: ev ch 3 out: one pce)	3½	**3**	14/1	90	—
1286^{2}	**Lansdowne (125)** (PFNicholls) **8-11-7**$^{(7)}$ OBurrows (hld up: hdwy 7th: wknd 3 out: pckd 2 out)	7	**4**	10/1	100	—
1342^{3}	**Fortunes Course (IRE) (111)** (JSKing) **7-10-7**$^{(7)}$ MrAWintle (led to 4th: wknd 3 out: pckd 2 out)	2½	**5**	8/1	84	—
	Top Javalin (NZ) (99) (NJHawke) **9-9-9**$^{(7)}$ MGriffiths (bkwd: led 4th to 3 out: sn wknd)	2½	**6**	25/1	71	—
1019^{5}	**Acrow Line (110)** (DBurchell) **11-10-13** DJBurchell (a bhd: t.o)	22	**7**	16/1	67	—
	St Ville (99) (RHBuckler) **10-10-2**^{ow1} SMcNeill (bkwd: prom to 8th: t.o)	2½	**8**	20/1	54	—
	Royal Piper (NZ) (102) (AJWilson) **9-10-5** RGreene (bkwd: a bhd: t.o)	dist	**9**	14/1	—	—
1019^{3}	**Yes Man (IRE) (112)** (MissHCKnight) **7-11-1** RDunwoody (prom to 7th: t.o)	¾	**10**	3/1^{1}	—	—
1363^{2}	**Glengarrif Girl (IRE) (108)** (MCPipe) **6-10-11v** APMcCoy (hld up mid div: b.d bnd after 5th)		**B**	9/1	—	—
1441^{W}	**Little Gunner (118)** (RJPrice) **6-11-7** RBellamy (bkwd: hld up & plld hrd: b.d bnd after 5th)		**B**	20/1	—	—
1429^{3}	**Oatis Rose (97)** (MSheppard) **6-10-0** RJohnson (mid div whn hit rails & fell bnd after 5th)		**F**	15/2^{3}	—	—
	Lucky Lane (113) (SEarle) **12-11-2b** CMaude (bkwd: prom to 5th: bhd whn hrd rdn after 6th: t.o whn p.u bef last)		**P**	33/1	—	—
	Spring Hebe (100) (BJMRyall) **6-10-3**^{ow3} GUpton (bkwd: hld up & bhd: bdly hmpd bnd after 5th: t.o whn p.u bef 2 out)		**P**	25/1	—	—

(SP 128.0%) **15 Rn**

6m 25.7 (45.70) CSF £78.85 CT £949.16 TOTE £11.30: £2.90 £2.60 £6.10 (£30.60) Trio £198.20 OWNER Starlight Racing (WANTAGE) BRED Michael O'Connor

LONG HANDICAP Oatis Rose 9-12 Spring Hebe 9-7

OFFICIAL EXPLANATION Yes Man (IRE): gurgled during the race.

1418 General Tonic, already due to go up 2lb following his reappearance last week, appreciated this stiffer test of stamina. (11/1)
1074 Karar (IRE), 3lb lower than when winning this race last season, threw away whatever chance he had by coming off a true line on the run-in. (13/2)
Miss Diskin (IRE) made a satisfactory reappearance off a mark 11lb higher than when she scored at Newton Abbot in April. (14/1: op 8/1)
1286 Lansdowne has gone up a further 1lb and looks in the Handicapper's grip now. (10/1)
1342 Fortunes Course (IRE) had been raised 4lb for a narrow defeat at Stratford two outings ago. (8/1)
Top Javalin (NZ), dropped nearly a stone, ran a fine race until blowing up and, and this soft ground specialist is now 20lb lower than when last visiting the winner's enclosure back in March 1993. (25/1)
1019 Yes Man (IRE) has never won on ground worse than good to soft but this was still bitterly disappointing. (3/1)

1572 TIPPERARY NOVICES' CHASE (5-Y.O+) (Class E)

3-25 (3-33) **2m 110y (12 fncs)** £3,070.50 (£924.00: £447.00: £208.50) GOING: 0.66 sec per fur (S)

				SP	RR	SF
	Or Royal (FR) (MCPipe) **5-11-5** APMcCoy (a.p: led 3 out: drvn out)	—	**1**	10/11^{1}	105++	44
1199^{2}	**Super Coin (120)** (RLee) **8-10-12** AMaguire (plld hrd: led 3rd: hit 5 out: pckd 4 out: hdd 3 out: ev ch whn pckd last: swtchd rt: hrd rdn: r.o)	1	**2**	11/4^{2}	97+	36
	Gordon (PRWebber) **5-10-12** CMaude (bkwd: mstke 1st: hdwy 8th: nt rch ldrs)	18	**3**	40/1	80	19
1328^{5}	**Dress Dance (IRE) (85)** (NRMitchell) **6-10-7**$^{(5)}$ SophieMitchell (chsd ldr to 7th: wknd appr 5 out)	1¼	**4**	66/1	78	17
1091^{5}	**Glendoe (IRE)** (AndrewTurnell) **5-10-12** GUpton (bit bkwd: hld up: hdwy 5th: wknd appr 5 out: lft 3rd & blnd 3 out)	s.h	**5**	40/1	78	17
	Mystic Court (IRE) (AndrewTurnell) **5-10-12** SMcNeill (bhd fr 7th: t.o)	30	**6**	20/1	49	—
	Bankonit (IRE) (DJDavies) **8-10-12b** TJMurphy (bkwd: j.b: a in rr: t.o)	dist	**7**	66/1	—	—
1325^{2}	**Mouse Bird (IRE)** (DRGandolfo) **6-10-12** RDunwoody (hld up: hdwy 6th: 3rd whn fell 3 out)		**F**	7/2^{3}	—	—
1423^{7}	**The Wayward Bishop (IRE)** (MrsLCTaylor) **7-10-12** JRKavanagh (bit bkwd: led to 3rd: hit 6th: 3rd whn blnd & uns rdr 8th)		**U**	100/1	—	—

(SP 114.9%) **9 Rn**

4m 13.9 (15.90) CSF £3.75 TOTE £2.10: £1.50 £1.20 £6.80 (£3.30) Trio £53.00 OWNER Mr D. A. Johnson (WELLINGTON) BRED Haras du Mezeray S. A.

Or Royal (FR) was purchased for around £80,000 after winning on the Flat in France in 1994 and twice over hurdles and a Novice Chase at Auteuil last season. With a real battle on his hands up the long home straight, sounder jumping tipped the scales in his favour. (10/11: tchd evens)
1199 Super Coin, reverting to two miles, would probably have prevailed had he not been let down by some novicey fencing over the last five obstacles. (11/4: 2/1-3/1)
Gordon, who lost his way over hurdles last season, had a nice introduction to chasing and improvement can be expected. (40/1)
Dress Dance (IRE), although again well beaten, fared better than on his debut over fences a fortnight ago. (66/1)
Glendoe (IRE), a half-brother to Sounds Strong has accomplished little in four runs over timber. (40/1)
1325 Mouse Bird (IRE) had the blinkers left off for this transition to the major obstacles and looked booked to finish a fair third when departing. (7/2: 4/1-9/1)

1573 WEATHERBYS 'STARS OF TOMORROW' STANDARD OPEN N.H. FLAT RACE (4, 5 & 6-Y.O) (Class H)

3-55 (4-05) **2m 110y** £1,744.00 (£484.00: £232.00)

				SP	RR	SF
1289*	**Lady Rebecca** (MissVenetiaWilliams) **4-11-9** AMaguire (a gng wl: led on bit 4f out: cleverly)	—	**1**	5/2^{2}	65 f	—
	Shore Party (IRE) (NATwiston-Davies) **4-10-11**$^{(7)}$ LSuthern (small, unf: chsd ldr 10f: hrd rdn & ev ch 2f out: edgd lft fnl f: no ch w wnr)	2½	**2**	7/4^{1}	58 f	—
	Strong Tel (IRE) (MCPipe) **6-11-4** RHughes (bit bkwd: hld up: gd hdwy over 6f out: led 5f out to 4f out: hrd rdn & wknd wl over 1f out)	12	**3**	20/1	46 f	—
	Repeat Offer (PDCundell) **4-11-4** CMaude (bit bkwd: hdwy over 6f out: wknd 3f out)	2	**4**	33/1	44 f	—
	Fine Spirit (NMLampard) **4-10-8**$^{(5)}$ ChrisWebb (prom tl wknd 3f out)	12	**5**	66/1	27 f	—

	Horse (Trainer) Age-Wt Jockey (comment)	Dist	Pos	SP	RR	SF
	Mister Chips (JSKing) **5-11-4** RDunwoody (bit bkwd: hld up & bhd: hdwy 5f out: nvr nr to chal)	6	**6**	11/1	27 f	—
	St Mellion Leisure (IRE) (MCPipe) **4-11-4** APMcCoy (bkwd: led 2f: led 9f out: hung rt & hdd 5f out: wknd 4f out.)	½	**7**	100/30[3]	26 f	—
1071[4]	**Willows Roulette** (AGHobbs) **4-10-11**(7) OBurrows (plld hrd: chsd ldrs 10f)	1¼	**8**	12/1	25 f	—
	Vansell (RHBuckler) **5-10-13** SMcNeill (bkwd: prom 10f)	10	**9**	20/1	10 f	—
	Country Kris (BJMRyall) **4-11-4** GUpton (bhd most of wy)	1	**10**	66/1	14 f	—
	Baby Lancaster (MAGriffin) **5-10-11**(7) MGriffiths (bkwd: a bhd)	½	**11**	66/1	14 f	—
	Saucy's Wolf (NJHawke) **6-10-11**(7) MrJTizzard (bkwd: prom 9f: t.o)	25	**12**	200/1	—	—
1289[13]	**Missed The Match** (REPocock) **6-11-4** PMcLoughlin (bkwd: a bhd: t.o)	2	**13**	100/1	—	—
	Fortunes Gleam (IRE) (JSKing) **5-10-13** TJMurphy (bit bkwd: a bhd: t.o)	dist	**14**	20/1	—	—
1203[14]	**Mingay** (GrahamRichards) **5-11-4** MrsSBosley (bit bkwd: sddle slipped: led after 2f out to 9f out: wknd qckly: t.o)	2	**15**	100/1	—	—

(SP 128.2%) **15 Rn**

4m 16.0 CSF £7.35 TOTE £3.40: £1.40 £1.50 £4.50 (£6.50) Trio £58.30 OWNER Kinnersley Optimists (HEREFORD) BRED Needwood Stud

1289* Lady Rebecca continues from strength to strength and, with Maguire at his most cheeky in the final half-mile, this soft ground held no terrors for her. (5/2: op 6/4)

Shore Party (IRE), a 25,000 guineas brother to Valerios King, is also related to Dakyns Boy. Try as he might, he could not get the winner to break sweat when no-one else could even make a race of it. (7/4)

Strong Tel (IRE), out of a sister to Ten Plus, did not look fully tuned up and did much better than his two bumper efforts last term. (20/1)

Repeat Offer, out of a six furlong winner, only cost 675 guineas as a yearling. (33/1)

Fine Spirit is out of an unraced half-sister to Captain Christy. (66/1)

Mister Chips, a half-brother to Mister Feathers, had an educational outing and was one of the few to show real promise for the future. (11/1)

T/Jkpt: £7,100.00 (0.59 Tckts); £1,582.38 to Uttoxeter 28/11/96. T/Plpt: £186.90 (77.15 Tckts). T/Qdpt: £26.90 (40.29 Tckts). KH

1244-HEXHAM (L-H) (Good, Good to firm patches)
Wednesday November 27th

one fence and one flight omitted

WEATHER: fine & sunny

1574 FEDERATION BREWERY LCL PILS NOVICES' CHASE (5-Y.O+) (Class E)

1-05 (1-05) **3m 1f (17 fncs)** £3,479.70 (£1,041.60: £499.80: £228.90) GOING: 0.13 sec per fur (G)

	Horse (Trainer) Age-Wt Jockey (comment)	Dist	Pos	SP	RR	SF
1129[2]	**Chopwell Curtains** (TDEasterby) **6-10-12** PNiven (lw: sn chsng ldrs: led after 3 out: styd on u.p flat)	—	**1**	1/2[1]	89	37
	Mamica (MDods) **6-10-12** NSmith (hdwy to jn ldrs 12th: chal last: nt qckn)	1	**2**	20/1	88	36
1153[4]	**Tico Gold (77)** (PCheesbrough) **8-10-9**(3) GCahill (mstkes: chsd ldrs: rdn & ev ch whn blnd 2 out: btn whn blnd last)	11	**3**	10/1[3]	81	29
1308[U]	**Dawn Lad (IRE)** (MrsASwinbank) **7-10-12** JSupple (lw: mstkes: wnt prom 9th: sn drvn along: hit 3 out: wknd appr last)	6	**4**	9/1[2]	78	26
1246[7]	**Aylesbury Lad (IRE) (72)** (DALamb) **7-10-12** JBurke (w ldrs: led 8th tl after 3 out: wknd between last 2)	1¼	**5**	50/1	77	25
	Senora d'Or (BMactaggart) **6-10-7** BStorey (mstkes: hdwy to jn ldrs 12th: wknd between last 2)	9	**6**	14/1	66	14
1246[4]	**Royal Surprise (76)** (WGReed) **9-10-12** TReed (chsd ldrs: rdn & outpcd 10th: sn bhd)	27	**7**	12/1	54	2
1308[P]	**Dear Jean** (MESowersby) **6-10-7** DParker (mstkes: sn bhd)	9	**8**	33/1	43	—
1206[7]	**Monymax (IRE)** (MrsSJSmith) **7-10-12** RichardGuest (bit bkwd: mde most to 8th: wknd 4 out)	11	**9**	50/1	41	—
1246[F]	**Small N Smart** (DSAlder) **6-10-12** KJohnson (hit 4th: a wl bhd)	4	**10**	50/1	38	—
	Monksaan (IRE) (MDHammond) **7-10-12** RGarritty (fell 3rd)		**F**	10/1[3]	—	—
1346[6]	**Nijway (73)** (MABarnes) **6-10-7**(5) STaylor (mstkes: prom tl blnd & lost pl 12th: blnd & uns rdr 4 out)		**U**	20/1	—	—

(SP 127.6%) **12 Rn**

6m 22.5 (11.50) CSF £14.05 TOTE £1.20: £1.20 £6.20 £1.30 (£38.40) Trio £105.10 OWNER Durham Drapes Ltd (MALTON) BRED Mrs A. C. Wakeham

1129 Chopwell Curtains is never one to do anything in impressive fashion. Though he looked to make hard work of it, he was always just doing enough and will be better suited by a more galloping track. (1/2)

Mamica ran really well and, after throwing down a strong challenge at the last, found the winner too determined. He jumped soundly throughout and will find a race. (20/1)

1153 Tico Gold did not jump well as usual. Upsides when falling through the second last, he was beaten when he hit the last. All he does is stay. (10/1)

1308 Dawn Lad (IRE) needs to brush up on his jumping but is not without some ability. (9/1)

Aylesbury Lad (IRE) ran perhaps his best race over fences, jumping much better than on some occasions in the past. (50/1)

Senora d'Or, a winner of two points, had trouble adapting to the regulation fences but showed some promise until tiring as if in need of the outing between the last two. (14/1)

Monksaan (IRE) (10/1: op 6/1)

1575 FEDERATION BREWERY SPECIAL ALE NOVICES' H'CAP HURDLE (0-100) (3-Y.O+) (Class E)

1-35 (1-36) **2m 4f 110y (8 hdls)** £2,595.00 (£720.00: £345.00) GOING: 0.13 sec per fur (G)

	Horse (Trainer) Age-Wt Jockey (comment)	Dist	Pos	SP	RR	SF
1247[2]	**Kings Minstral (IRE) (66)** (DALamb) **6-10-5** JBurke (led after 3rd: wnt clr appr last: hit last: styd on wl)	—	**1**	11/1[3]	51	7
	Dashmar (63) (MsLCPlater) **9-10-2** DBentley (prom tl rdn along & outpcd after 5th: hdwy 2 out: styd on flat)	6	**2**	20/1	43	—
1316*	**Clever Boy (IRE) (67)** (JWCurtis) **5-10-6** NWilliamson (lw: hld up: hdwy 5th: shkn up between last 2: kpt on one pce)	nk	**3**	5/2[2]	47	3
1292*	**Lifebuoy (IRE) (84)** (JRTurner) **5-11-9** TReed (hld up: hdwy 5th: ev ch 2 out: sn rdn: one pce appr last)	1¾	**4**	2/1[1]	63	19
1292[6]	**Environmental Law (72)**(WMcKeown) **5-10-8**(3) GCahill (chsd ldrs: drvn along 5th:wknd qckly between last 2)	28	**5**	11/1[3]	29	—
1158[5]	**Lagan (100)** (KAMorgan) **3-11-8** ASSmith (lw: led tl after 3rd: drvn along 5th: wknd after 2 out)	18	**6**	5/2[2]	43	—
1438[6]	**Miss Mont (61)** (FPMurtagh) **7-10-0** RHodge (plld hrd: sn trckng ldrs: lost pl appr 6th: sn bhd: t.o whn p.u bef last)		**P**	33/1	—	—

(SP 114.8%) **7 Rn**

5m 3.7 (15.70) CSF £144.97 CT £657.76 TOTE £25.30: £7.60 £10.50 (£38.40) OWNER Exors of the late Mr R R Lamb (SEAHOUSES)

LONG HANDICAP Miss Mont 9-11

WEIGHT FOR AGE 3yo-17lb

1247 Kings Minstral (IRE) showed that his much improved effort here last time was no fluke, and had already quickened clear when he hit the final flight hard. (11/1)

Dashmar, who showed next to nothing last season and has since changed hands cheaply, came with a renewed effort on the run-in. (20/1)

1316* Clever Boy (IRE), 3lb higher, moved up travelling nicely at the fifth. Short of room on the inside and looking unsuited by the turn, he seemed to lose his back legs on the home turn - slippery due to the overnight frost. Keeping on at the finish, he is worth another try on a more orthodox track. (5/2)

1292* Lifebuoy (IRE), 7lb higher, moved up traveling strongly, but under pressure between the last two, he did not find a lot. He possibly needed this after the recent bad weather. (2/1)

1292 Environmental Law stopped as if shot on the long run to the final flight. He probably needs much more give. (11/1: 7/1-12/1)

1158 Lagan was most disappointing, being under pressure some way out and dropping right out after the second last. (5/2: op 5/4)

1576 KEOGHANS NOVICES' CHASE (5-Y.O+) (Class E)

2-05 (2-06) **2m 110y (10 fncs)** £3,206.70 (£957.60: £457.80: £207.90) GOING: 0.13 sec per fur (G)

				SP	RR	SF
1316^{6}	**Elliott's Wish (IRE)** (HowardJohnson) **5-10-12** NWilliamson (hit 4th: hdwy to chse ldr 6th: lft in ld last: all out)	—	1	16/1	81	17
1346^{8}	**Uk Hygiene (IRE) (80)** (MDHammond) **6-10-12** RGarritty (led to 4th: styd on u.p flat)	½	2	4/1^{2}	81	17
939^{12}	**Crockalawn (IRE)** (VThompson) **8-10-12** MrMThompson (bit bkwd: led 4th tl appr last: one pce)	2½	3	50/1	78	14
1525^{F}	**Bonny Johnny** (DMoffatt) **6-10-12** DJMoffatt (mstkes: sn bhd: styd on wl fr 2 out: nt rch ldrs)	1	4	50/1	77	13
	Dark Buoy (67) (BMactaggart) **7-10-12** BStorey (sn outpcd & bhd: styd on between last 2)	4	5	33/1	73	9
1047^{10}	**Wee Wizard (IRE) (77)** (MABarnes) **7-10-7$^{(5)}$** STaylor (hit 4th: sn bhd: styd on fr 2 out)	1½	6	25/1	72	8
1346^{13}	**Fine Tune (IRE) (60)** (MrsSCBradburne) **6-10-12** AThornton (lw: in tch: hit 5th: sn chsng ldrs: wknd 2 out)	nk	7	33/1	72	8
8^{4}	**Mister Casual (72)** (WGReed) **7-10-12** TReed (sn bhd: sme hdwy 2 out: n.d)	4	8	25/1	68	4
1032^{2}	**Highland Way (IRE)** (MartinTodhunter) **8-10-12** MDwyer (lw: chsd ldrs: ev ch whn fell 7th)		F	4/1^{2}	—	—
424^{4}	**Fenwick's Brother** (MrsSJSmith) **6-10-12** MrPMurray (w ldrs whn slipped & fell 2nd)		F	33/1	—	—
1206^{5}	**Fair Ally** (MESowersby) **6-10-12** DParker (chsd ldrs: ev ch whn slipped & fell 2 out)		F	33/1	—	—
1349^{6}	**Ethical Note (IRE)** (MrsSJSmith) **5-10-12** RichardGuest (chsd ldrs: ev ch whn fell 7th)		F	20/1	—	—
1346^{7}	**Bolaney Girl (IRE) (75)** (FPMurtagh) **7-10-7** BHarding (lw: hld up: hdwy & prom 3 out: styng on whn s.u between last 2)		S	8/1^{3}	—	—
1264^{F}	**Golden Hello** (TDEasterby) **5-11-5** PNiven (hld up: gd hdwy 3 out: led appr last: 4l clr whn j.slowly, swvd rt, blnd & uns rdr last)		U	7/4^{1}	—	—

(SP 121.5%) **14 Rn**

4m 8.9 (11.90) CSF £74.49 TOTE £11.00: £2.00 £1.60 £13.50 (£23.30) Trio £100.20; £70.61 to Carlisle 28/11/96 OWNER Mr David Fulton (CROOK) BRED Michael Higgins

1316 Elliott's Wish (IRE), a keen-going sort, had been a major disappointment up to now. He had luck on his side and after being left clear at the last, he seemed to put the brakes on up the run-in and in the end, just scraped home. This was probably a poor race. (16/1)

1346 Uk Hygiene (IRE), after making the running, stuck on strongly under pressure at the last but could not quite close the gap. (4/1: 6/1-7/2)

Crockalawn (IRE) looked burly but ran easily his best race so far, helping force the pace. (50/1)

853 Bonny Johnny, an erratic pointer, hardly jumped a fence properly. Soon out with the washing, he made up a good deal of ground from two out. (50/1)

Dark Buoy showed precious little over hurdles but was far from disgraced on this fencing debut. It is hard to know what to make of this race, as those out with the washing closed on the first three from the last. (33/1)

897 Wee Wizard (IRE), who seems to have lost his way, ran his best race for some time. (25/1)

Fair Ally was still bang in the firing line when he slipped on landing and fell two out. (33/1)

1139 Ethical Note (IRE) was on the heels of the leaders and traveling strongly when falling. (20/1)

1346 Bolaney Girl (IRE), a frustrating sort over hurdles, was on the heels of the first four and staying on, when she slipped up at the foot of the hill between the last two fences. (8/1)

1264 Golden Hello was four lengths clear with his race won when he slowed up at the last, swerved right on landing and parted company with his rider. He certainly does not lack ability, but there is definitely a question mark over his attitude. (7/4: 11/10-2/1)

1577 FEDERATION BREWERY H'CAP HURDLE (0-105) (4-Y.O+) (Class F)

2-35 (2-35) **2m (6 hdls)** £2,156.60 (£597.60: £285.80) GOING: 0.13 sec per fur (G)

				SP	RR	SF
1204^{2}	**Anabranch (98)** (JMJefferson) **5-11-2$^{(7)}$** MNewton (trckd ldrs gng wl: led 2 out: qcknd clr appr last: easily)	—	1	9/2^{1}	94+	30
1204*	**Tip it In (85)** (ASmith) **7-10-3$^{(7)}$** NHorrocks (hld up: lost pl 4th: styd on appr last: r.o towards fin)	12	2	5/1^{2}	69	5
1292^{P}	**Court Joker (IRE) (77)** (HAlexander) **4-10-2** BStorey (led to 3rd: styd on same pce appr last)	1½	3	12/1	60	—
1144^{4}	**Nonios (IRE) (97)** (GMMoore) **5-11-8v** NBentley (w ldr: led 3rd to 2 out: one pce: eased nr fin)	hd	4	11/2^{3}	79	15
1164^{4}	**Auburn Boy (103)** (MWEasterby) **9-12-0** RGarritty (hld up: hdwy 4th: chsd wnr between last 2: wknd towards fin)	4	5	13/2	81	17
	In a Moment (USA) (75) (CGrant) **5-10-0** JCallaghan (lw: drvn along 4th: sn bhd: kpt on flat)	¾	6	10/1	53	—
1047^{11}	**Joyrider (91)** (MissMKMilligan) **5-11-2** ASSmith (in tch: outpcd & drvn along 4th: styd on flat)	¾	7	10/1	68	4
1314^{4}	**Well Appointed (IRE) (95)** (BMactaggart) **7-11-3$^{(3)}$** GLee (trckd ldrs: effrt after 2 out: one pce)	3½	8	11/2^{3}	68	4
1078*	**Fly to the End (USA) (75)** (JJQuinn) **6-10-0** NWilliamson (hld up: drvn along 4th: wknd 2 out: sn bhd)	30	9	6/1	18	—

(SP 119.1%) **9 Rn**

3m 59.0 (11.00) CSF £26.28 CT £233.79 TOTE £4.30: £2.60 £2.80 £2.40 (£12.20) Trio £31.80 OWNER Mrs M. Barker (MALTON) BRED Mrs M. Barker

LONG HANDICAP In a Moment (USA) 9-12

STEWARDS' ENQUIRY Bentley susp. 6-7 & 9/12/96 (failure to ensure best possible placing)

1204 Anabranch was going best throughout. Quickening clear going to the last, she won with plenty in hand. (9/2)

1204* Tip it In seemed to lose his action slightly coming down the hill and was out of contention between the last two. Picking up ground on the uphill run to the last, he was staying on in good style at the finish. (5/1)

876 Court Joker (IRE) settled well in front. (12/1)

1144 Nonios (IRE) ran his usual sound race but seems to be in the grip of the Handicapper. He would have finished third but for being eased near the line. (11/2)

1164 Auburn Boy, reverting to hurdles, went second between the last two, but then showed a very poor action and weakened towards the finish. (13/2)

In a Moment (USA), Chris Grant's first runner as a trainer, looked in good shape. He struggled to go the pace soon after halfway, but kept on towards the finish. He has been an unreliable character in the past. (10/1)

1578 FEDERATION BREWERY BUCHANAN H'CAP CHASE (0-95) (4-Y.O+) (Class F)

3-05 (3-05) **2m 4f 110y (13 fncs)** £2,962.80 (£820.80: £392.40) GOING: 0.13 sec per fur (G)

	Horse	Dist	Pos	SP	RR	SF
1244*	**Buyers Dream (IRE) (81)** (BEllison) **6-10-11v(3)** GCahill (hdwy 8th: styd on u.p fr 2 out: led last: hld on towards fin)	—	1	7/1[3]	91	17
1244[U]	**Willie Sparkle (76)** (MrsSCBradburne) **10-10-9** MFoster (outpcd ½-wy: hdwy u.p 2 out: ev ch flat: styd on towards fin)	nk	2	14/1	86	12
896[3]	**Grand Scenery (IRE) (90)** (HowardJohnson) **8-11-9** NWilliamson (hld up & plld hrd: gd hdwy 9th: styd on u.p fr 2 out)	2½	3	13/2[2]	98	24
1209[5]	**Juke Box Billy (IRE) (86)** (MrsJBrown) **8-11-5** ADobbin (hld up: wnt prom 7th: led appr last: sn hdd & no ex)	2	4	6/1[1]	92	18
1445[3]	**Wayuphill (87)** (JJO'Neill) **9-11-1(5)** RMcGrath (lw: trckd ldrs: hit 3rd: led 10th tl appr last: wknd flat)	2½	5	7/1[3]	91	17
1209[P]	**Hurricane Andrew (IRE) (88)** (JAMoore) **8-11-7** MrNWilson (sn bhd: styd on fr 2 out: nt rch ldrs)	4	6	25/1	89	15
1307[P]	**Gala Water (86)** (TDCDun) **10-11-5** TReed (lw: in tch to 5th: hit 8th: sn outpcd & bhd: styd on appr last)	2½	7	16/1	85	11
1308*	**Cader Idris (86)** (MrsMReveley) **7-11-5** PNiven (lw: hit 1st: lost pl 7th: sme hdwy 2 out: n.d)	nk	8	6/1[1]	85	11
1138[U]	**Movac (IRE) (90)** (MissLucindaRussell) **7-11-9** AThornton (w ldrs: led 7th to 10th: wknd appr last)	½	9	13/2[2]	89	15
1244[3]	**Forward Glen (76)** (PCheesbrough) **9-10-9b** ASSmith (hit 1st: sn bhd: sme hdwy whn hit 2 out: n.d)	5	10	11/1	71	—
1295[5]	**Super Sandy (88)** (FTWalton) **9-11-7** KJohnson (chsd ldrs tl lost pl 10th)	13	11	16/1	73	—
1266[6]	**Side of Hill (91)** (BMactaggart) **11-11-7(3)** GLee (j.rt: led to 7th: wkng whn blnd 3 out)	8	12	14/1	69	—
1348[U]	**See You Always (IRE) (67)** (MABarnes) **6-9-9(5)** STaylor (chsd ldrs tl wknd 8th)	1¼	13	50/1	44	—
1209[9]	**Supposin (92)** (MrsSJSmith) **8-11-11** RichardGuest (a in rr)	10	14	8/1	62	—

(SP 130.6%) **14 Rn**

5m 12.5 (15.50) CSF £98.02 CT £629.76 TOTE £10.20: £3.60 £5.10 £1.80 (£105.40) Trio £137.20; £154.69 to Carlisle 28/11/96 OWNER Mr Brian Chicken (LANCHESTER) BRED H and Y Bloodstock Co

LONG HANDICAP See You Always (IRE) 9-6

1244* Buyers Dream (IRE), who took twenty attempts to break his duck, made it two out of two. Hanging fire on the run-in, he did just enough in the end. (7/1)

1244 Willie Sparkle staged something of a revival and made the winner pull out all the stops at the end. (14/1)

896 Grand Scenery (IRE), who took a keen grip in the early stages, stuck on under pressure and will be suited by a step back up to three. (13/2)

1209 Juke Box Billy (IRE), whose jumping stood up well, looked a real danger until he ran out of gas after showing in front going to the last. (6/1)

1445 Wayuphill jumped boldly on the whole. After setting sail for home, he ran out of steam after the final fence. (7/1: 5/1-8/1)

Hurricane Andrew (IRE), having his first outing for his new stable, was soon struggling badly. Picking up ground over the last two, he will be suited by a step up to three miles. (25/1)

1138 Movac (IRE) (13/2: op 4/1)

1579 FEDERATION BREWERY MEDALLION LAGER INTERMEDIATE OPEN N.H. FLAT RACE (4, 5 & 6-Y.O) (Class H)

3-35 (3-36) **2m** £1,343.00 (£373.00: £179.00)

	Horse	Dist	Pos	SP	RR	SF
1296[7]	**Bold Statement** (GMMoore) **4-11-4** NBentley (lw: mde all: shkn up & styd on strly appr fnl f)	—	1	5/1[3]	55 f	—
	For Cathal (IRE) (MrsMReveley) **5-11-4** PNiven (hld up: stdy hdwy & prom 6f out: kpt on wl appr fnl f: no ch w wnr)	4	2	4/1[2]	51 f	—
	Bobby Grant (CGrant) **5-11-4** NWilliamson (a chsng ldrs: kpt on wl fnl 2f)	1¼	3	20/1	50 f	—
1362[2]	**Lord of The Loch (IRE)** (LLungo) **5-11-4** MFoster (lw: hld up: stdy hdwy ½-wy: shkn up 2f out: grad wknd)	3	4	11/8[1]	47 f	—
1296[16]	**Nautilus The Third (IRE)** (MDHammond) **5-11-4** RGarritty (chsd wnr tl wknd over 2f out)	8	5	16/1	39 f	—
	Run For The Mill (JMJefferson) **4-10-11(7)** MNewton (w'like, unf: bit bkwd: chsd ldrs tl wknd 3f out)	5	6	7/1	34 f	—
	Tartan Joy (IRE) (JAMoore) **5-11-4** NSmith (sn bhd: styd on fnl 3f)	nk	7	25/1	33 f	—
	Boris Brook (RAllan) **5-10-11(7)** SMelrose (bit bkwd: sn bhd: drvn along ½-wy: styd on fnl 2f: n.d)	4	8	50/1	29 f	—
	Queens Brigade (FTWalton) **4-11-4** BStorey (sn bhd: sme hdwy 2f out: n.d)	¾	9	50/1	29 f	—
	Guile Point (DALamb) **5-10-13** JBurke (in tch tl wknd 5f out)	4	10	50/1	20 f	—
1362[11]	**Chinook's Daughter (IRE)** (GRichards) **4-10-13** ADobbin (hld up: sme hdwy ½-wy: wknd 4f out)	4	11	10/1	16 f	—
	Only A Sioux (JRTurner) **4-11-4** WFry (wl bhd fr ½-wy)	14	12	50/1	7 f	—
1084[5]	**Safety Tip** (WStorey) **4-10-13** MMoloney (in tch lost pl ½-wy: sn btn: t.o)	dist	13	50/1	—	—
	Magslass (JJO'Neill) **4-10-8(5)** RMcGrath (a bhd: t.o)	3½	14	20/1	—	—

(SP 129.4%) **14 Rn**

3m 57.6 CSF £25.54 TOTE £7.70: £1.20 £1.30 £7.60 (£15.30) Trio £103.40; £91.80 to Carlisle 28/11/96 OWNER Mr R. I. Graham (MIDDLE-HAM) BRED Juddmonte Farms

Bold Statement ensured there was no hanging about. Quickening clear on the home turn, he will need at least two and half miles over hurdles. (5/1)

For Cathal (IRE) certainly took the eye in the paddock, and has already won a point-to-point in Ireland. By no means knocked about, he should be an interesting type when he steps up to hurdling company. (4/1: 2/1-9/2)

Bobby Grant, a rangy type, ran really well and should be capable of better. (20/1)

1362 Lord of The Loch (IRE) looked very lean and pulled out little under pressure. (11/8)

Nautilus The Third (IRE) had his tongue tied down and faded badly at the start of the uphill climb to the final furlong. (16/1)

Run For The Mill, a strong sort, ran well until fading in the final three furlongs. He ought to be capable of better. (7/1: 8/1-14/1)

1362 Chinook's Daughter (IRE) (10/1: 8/1-12/1)

T/Plpt: £5,145.30 (1.85 Tckts). T/Qdpt: £97.70 (8.63 Tckts). WG

1375-WINDSOR (Fig. 8) (Good)

Wednesday November 27th

WEATHER: fine

1580 RIVER THAMES 'N.H' NOVICES' HURDLE (I) (4-Y.O+) (Class D)

12-45 (12-46) **2m 4f (10 hdls)** £2,602.00 (£722.00: £346.00) GOING minus 0.19 sec per fur (G)

	Horse	Dist	Pos	SP	RR	SF
1301*	**Lady Peta (IRE) (103)** (NJHenderson) **6-11-4** MAFitzgerald (hdwy 7th: led on bit appr last: all out)	—	1	Evens[1]	74	24

				SP	RR	SF
1341[7]	**River Bay (IRE)** (MissHCKnight) **5-10-7** BFenton (a.p: led 7th: mstke 2 out: hdd appr last: pecked last: hrd rdn: r.o wl flat)	hd	**2**	9/2 [3]	63	13
1289[9]	**Dark Challenger (IRE)** (MrsJPitman) **4-10-12** WMarston (hdwy 5th: wknd 3 out)	9	**3**	10/1	61	11
871[11]	**Nunson** (RDickin) **7-10-12** CLlewellyn (hdwy 3rd: wknd 5th)	14	**4**	33/1	50	—
	Grosvenor (IRE) (FMurphy) **5-10-12** JOsborne (bit bkwd: a.p: rdn 3 out: sn wknd)	2	**5**	2/1 [2]	48	—
	The Millmaster (IRE) (JohnUpson) **5-10-12b[1]** RSupple (mstke 2nd: prom to 7th)	19	**6**	40/1	33	—
1451[U]	**All Over Red Rover (70)** (AWCarroll) **4-10-12** PHide (n.j.w: led to 7th: sn wknd)	19	**7**	20/1	18	—
				(SP 120.7%)	**7 Rn**	

4m 53.7 (7.70) CSF £6.47 TOTE £1.90: £1.30 £2.10 (£3.30) Trio £3.20 OWNER Mr B. M. Collins (LAMBOURN) BRED Mrs M. Farrell

1301* Lady Peta (IRE) once again demonstrated he does not like to be in front too early. Absolutely swinging off the bridle as he eased his way into the lead approaching the final flight, he then thought he had done enough on the run-in and, with the runner-up rallying in tremendous style, he found the line only just saving him. He really must be held up until the very last possible minute. (Evens)

River Bay (IRE) ran much better here and was sent on four out. Untidy at the penultimate hurdle, he was soon headed by the winner and pecked badly on landing at the final flight. Despite going a couple of lengths down on her rival, she rallied in tremendous style and would surely have prevailed in a few more strides. (9/2: op 3/1)

Dark Challenger (IRE) took closer order early on the final circuit but was in trouble three from home. (10/1: 6/1-12/1)

1581 RIVER THAMES 'N.H.' NOVICES' HURDLE (II) (4-Y.O+) (Class D)

1-15 (1-15) **2m 4f (10 hdls)** £2,581.00 (£716.00: £343.00) GOING minus 0.19 sec per fur (G)

				SP	RR	SF
	Sparkling Spring (IRE) (KCBailey) **5-10-12** CO'Dwyer (hdwy 3 out: rdn & wandered appr last: led last: r.o wl)	—	**1**	11/1	76	28
	Best of Friends (IRE) (MissHCKnight) **6-10-12** BFenton (lw: lost pl 7th: rallied appr 2 out: ev ch last: r.o wl)	½	**2**	4/1 [3]	76	28
	None Stirred (IRE) (JTGifford) **6-10-12** PHide (hdwy to ld after 7th: hdd 2 out: ev ch flat: r.o wl)	s.h	**3**	5/2 [2]	76	28
1191*	**Millersford** (NAGaselee) **5-11-4** CLlewellyn (lw: a.p: rdn & ev ch appr 2 out: unable qckn flat)	2	**4**	2/1 [1]	80	32
1378*	**Dream Leader (IRE) (90)** (MJRoberts) **6-11-4** JRailton (lw: led: mstke 3rd: hdd after 7th: led 2 out to last: one pce)	2	**5**	9/1	78	30
1351[4]	**Operetto (IRE)** (MrsSusanNock) **6-10-12** DBridgwater (prom to 3 out)	13	**6**	25/1	62	14
1203[3]	**Ivory Coaster (NZ)** (BdeHaan) **5-10-12** JOsborne (prom tl appr 2 out)	20	**7**	15/2	46	—
1013[7]	**Barrie Stir** (JWhite) **4-10-12** DGallagher (a bhd: t.o whn p.u bef 3 out)		**P**	25/1	—	—
1180[P]	**Ali's Delight** (MDMcMillan) **5-10-12** MAFitzgerald (hdwy 5th: wknd 6th: t.o whn p.u bef 3 out)		**P**	100/1	—	—
				(SP 120.7%)	**9 Rn**	

4m 51.0 (5.00) CSF £53.27 TOTE £12.10: £4.00 £1.30 £1.30 (£48.20) Trio £40.70 OWNER Mr E. Benfield (UPPER LAMBOURN) BRED Mrs H. McCormick

Sparkling Spring (IRE) made the perfect start to his racing career. One of a host of horses throwing down a challenge in the straight, he poked a nostril in front at the final flight and held on well. (11/1: 5/1-12/1)

Best of Friends (IRE) looked in good shape for this seasonal debut. Outpaced on the long loop from the fourth last, he managed to get back into it going to the penultimate hurdle and was soon throwing down a determined challenge. He stuck to his task really well to the bitter end and only just lost out. A big, imposing individual who has chaser written all over him, he should not be difficult to win with. (4/1)

None Stirred (IRE), without a run in nearly a year, went on soon after the fourth last. Collared two from home, he refused to give way and battled his heart out to the bitter end. He should soon be winning. (5/2)

1191* Millersford, one of several with every chance approaching the second last, was only about a length down jumping the final flight before tapped for toe. Staying is his game and his future undoubtedly lies over fences. (2/1)

1378* Dream Leader (IRE), who set the pace until after the fourth last, was back in front again two out but, once collared at the final flight, could only go up and down in the same place. (9/1: 6/1-10/1)

1582 WINDSOR NOVICES' H'CAP CHASE (0-100) (5-Y.O+) (Class E)

1-45 (1-47) **3m (18 fncs)** £3,241.00 (£973.00: £469.00: £217.00) GOING minus 0.19 sec per fur (G)

				SP	RR	SF
1285[2]	**Call Me River (IRE) (64)** (PRHedger) **8-10-1** ILawrence (lw: a.p: chsd ldr fr 9th: led 4 out: clr appr 2 out: r.o wl)	—	**1**	6/1 [1]	82	20
1206[P]	**Jac Del Prince (64)** (PFNicholls) **6-10-1**ow1 PHide (led to 4 out: unable qckn)	11	**2**	33/1	75	12
1447[3]	**Cardinal Rule (IRE) (70)** (MissVenetiaWilliams) **7-10-7** RFarrant (lw: a.p: rdn 4 out: 3rd & btn whn j.lft 2 out)	20	**3**	14/1	67	5
1447[P]	**Mingus (USA) (83)** (RHBuckler) **9-10-13**(7) MrBDixon (mid div whn mstkes 3rd & 7th: hdwy 4 out: wknd 3 out)	2½	**4**	25/1	79	17
1468[U]	**The Brud (80)** (OSherwood) **8-11-3** JAMcCarthy (lw: nvr plcd to chal)	hd	**5**	14/1	76	14
1331[F]	**Oxford Quill (72)** (RCurtis) **9-10-9** DMorris (nvr nr to chal)	6	**6**	9/1 [2]	64	2
1335*	**La Mezeray (76)** (MrsJEHawkins) **8-10-10**(3) DWalsh (prom to 14th)	7	**7**	6/1 [1]	63	1
1426[4]	**Its Grand (67)** (JMBradley) **7-10-1b[1]**(3) TDascombe (prom to 7th: t.o whn hmpd 4 out)	25	**8**	10/1 [3]	37	—
	Bournel (83) (CRBarwell) **8-11-6** BFenton (a bhd: t.o)	6	**9**	33/1	49	—
1472[U]	**Master Pangloss (IRE) (63)** (AndrewTurnell) **6-10-0** LHarvey (mid div whn blnd 7th: bhd whn fell 4 out)		**F**	16/1	—	—
1318[U]	**Westerly Gale (IRE) (76)** (NJHenderson) **6-10-13** MAFitzgerald (a.p: 5th whn fell 4 out)		**F**	6/1 [1]	—	—
1376[2]	**Damcada (IRE) (67)** (AWCarroll) **8-10-4** WMarston (bhd fr 6th: t.o whn p.u after 14th)		**P**	12/1	—	—
1371[4]	**Sassiver (USA) (87)** (PAKelleway) **6-11-7**(3) GHogan (mid div whn mstke 3rd: bhd fr 5th: t.o whn p.u after 14th)		**P**	16/1	—	—
1281[4]	**Ainsi Soit Il (FR) (80)** (GMMcCourt) **5-11-1b** BClifford (a bhd: t.o whn blnd & uns rdr 4 out)		**U**	33/1	—	—
	Romany Blues (63) (CPEBrooks) **7-10-0** DGallagher (prom to 12th: mstke 13th: 4th & no ch whn blnd & uns rdr last)		**U**	9/1 [2]	—	—
	The Whole Hog (IRE) (78) (KCBailey) **7-11-1** CO'Dwyer (mid div whn blnd 14th: t.o whn blnd & uns rdr 4 out)		**U**	16/1	—	—
				(SP 123.3%)	**16 Rn**	

6m 0.4 (5.40) CSF £161.14 CT £2,404.66 TOTE £6.10: £1.80 £5.50 £3.70 £10.10 (£112.90) Trio £140.90 OWNER The Larkin Around Partnership (CHICHESTER) BRED S. Banville

LONG HANDICAP Jac Del Prince 9-11 Romany Blues 9-13 Master Pangloss (IRE) 9-13

WEIGHT FOR AGE 5yo-2lb

1285 Call Me River (IRE) gained control four out and surged clear from the next for a decisive victory. (6/1)

Jac Del Prince attempted to make all the running. Collared four out, he failed to contain the winner from the next. (33/1)

1447 Cardinal Rule (IRE) was never far away but the writing was on the wall in the straight, and he was held in third place when jumping violently to his left at the penultimate fence. (14/1)

970 Mingus (USA) got round on this occasion but was in trouble three from home. (25/1)

The Brud appeared to have little more than a schooling session, connections no doubt very keen to get him round in one piece as he unseated his rider early on on his reappearance. Hopefully this will have done his confidence some good and it would be no surprise to see him pop up in a little race. (14/1)
1331 Oxford Quill (9/1: op 6/1)
1376 Damcada (IRE) (12/1: op 8/1)

1583 E.B.F. SUNNINGHILL 'N.H.' QUALIFIER NOVICES' HURDLE (4, 5 & 6-Y.O) (Class D)

2-15 (2-18) **2m (8 hdls)** £3,078.00 (£858.00: £414.00) GOING minus 0.19 sec per fur (G)

				SP	RR	SF
	Ready Money Creek (IRE) (OSherwood) **5-11-0** JOsborne (lost pl appr 3 out: rallied to chse ldr 2 out: hrd rdn: led flat: r.o wl)	—	**1**	10/11[1]	76	27
1301[2]	**Darakshan (IRE)** (MissHCKnight) **4-11-0** JRailton (led: rdn appr last: hdd flat: unable qckn)	2	**2**	7/2[3]	74	25
	Henrys Port (MartynMeade) **6-11-0** MRichards (lost pl 3rd: rallied appr last: r.o)	2	**3**	66/1	72	23
1283[2]	**Neat Feat (IRE)** (DRCElsworth) **5-11-0** AProcter (hdwy 4th: chsd ldr 3 out to 2 out: one pce)	2½	**4**	3/1[2]	70	21
	Tree Creeper (IRE) (AndrewTurnell) **4-11-0** LHarvey (nvr nr to chal)	1¾	**5**	25/1	68	19
26[5]	**Ilewin Janine (IRE)** (PCRitchens) **5-10-9** SFox (plld hrd: chsd ldr to 3 out: sn wknd)	12	**6**	33/1	51	2
	O My Love (MissHCKnight) **5-10-9** BFenton (hld up: rdn appr 3 out: sn wknd)	9	**7**	50/1	42	—
1275[11]	**Freno (IRE)** (KCBailey) **5-11-0** CO'Dwyer (a bhd)	7	**8**	20/1	40	—
	Nishaman (NJHenderson) **5-11-0** MAFitzgerald (a bhd)	7	**9**	25/1	33	—
	Reach The Clouds (IRE) (JohnUpson) **4-11-0** RSupple (prom to 7th)	17	**10**	14/1	16	—
1317[14]	**Mr Goonhilly** (RHAlner) **6-11-0** ILawrence (hdwy 4th: wknd 5th: t.o whn p.u bef 2 out)		**P**	66/1	—	—
				(SP 126.6%)	**11 Rn**	

3m 52.6 (4.60) CSF £5.12 TOTE £2.10: £1.10 £1.20 £9.00 (£4.10) Trio £174.80 OWNER Roach Foods Ltd (UPPER LAMBOURN) BRED P. Budds
OFFICIAL EXPLANATION **Freno (IRE): the rider reported that he was unable to ride the gelding effectively, due to an ankle injury sustained in the previous race.**
Ready Money Creek (IRE), well regarded at home, gave supporters some anxious moments on this hurdling debut as he got outpaced on the long loop from the fourth last. However, he managed to get back into the action in the straight and, with his jockey bustling him along, the combination managed to get in front on the run-in. Once there they had the situation nicely in hand. He might appreciate a bit further. (10/11: 4/7-11/10)
1301 Darakshan (IRE) made a bold bid from the front and looked likely to succeed early in the straight. However, collared on the run-in, he found the winner too good. (7/2)
Henrys Port, making his seasonal debut, stayed on from the second last for third prize. (66/1)
1283 Neat Feat (IRE) was slightly disappointing and, having moved into second place three out, was collared for that position at the next and could only keep on at one pace. A bit further would probably be in his favour. (3/1)
Reach The Clouds (IRE) (14/1: 20/1-12/1)

1584 DATCHET H'CAP CHASE (0-110) (4-Y.O+) (Class E)

2-45 (2-46) **2m (12 fncs)** £3,104.50 (£931.00: £448.00: £206.50) GOING minus 0.19 sec per fur (G)

				SP	RR	SF
1146[P]	**Zeredar (NZ) (100)** (KCBailey) **6-11-4b[1]** CLlewellyn (a.p: led appr 2 out: comf)	—	**1**	100/30[1]	103+	—
943[4]	**Lasata (107)** (RMCarson) **11-11-11** DMorris (hdwy 7th: led 4 out tl appr 2 out: unable qckn)	4	**2**	20/1	106	3
1298*	**Fichu (USA) (82)** (MrsLRichards) **8-10-0** MRichards (hdwy appr 3 out: r.o one pce)	3	**3**	6/1[3]	78	—
	Red Bean (100) (KVincent) **8-11-4** ADicken (lost pl appr 4 out: rallied appr last: r.o one pce)	hd	**4**	8/1	96	—
1306[F]	**Circulation (85)** (DMcCain) **10-10-0v(3)ow3** DWalsh (led to 4 out: wknd appr last)	½	**5**	10/1	80	—
	Sister Rosza (IRE) (96) (MrsSLamyman) **8-11-0** RFarrant (bhd fr 8th)	8	**6**	20/1	83	—
	Pegmarine (USA) (83) (MrsAMWoodrow) **13-9-12(3)ow1** GHogan (prom to 5th)	¾	**7**	16/1	70	—
1284[F]	**Miss Marigold (96)** (RJHodges) **7-10-11b(3)** TDascombe (hdwy 8th: wknd 3 out: bhd whn blnd 2 out)	2	**8**	6/1[3]	81	—
	The Flying Footman (97) (RDickin) **10-11-1** JOsborne (bhd fr 6th)	2	**9**	16/1	80	—
	Early Drinker (100) (OSherwood) **8-11-4** JAMcCarthy (a bhd: t.o)	dist	**10**	7/2[2]	—	—
				(SP 115.4%)	**10 Rn**	

4m 1.9 (11.90) CSF £56.37 CT £345.38 TOTE £3.10: £1.70 £5.90 £1.80 (£27.40) Trio £158.70 OWNER I M S Racing (UPPER LAMBOURN) BRED Miss E. S. Parton
LONG HANDICAP Pegmarine (USA) 9-11 Fichu (USA) 9-10 Circulation 9-2
1146 Zeredar (NZ) found the application of blinkers a real help and, leading approaching the second last, scooted away for a decisive victory. (100/30)
Lasata went on four from home but, collared approaching the second last, found the winner too strong. (20/1)
1298* Fichu (USA) struggled on over the last four fences for third prize without posing a real threat. (6/1: op 4/1)
Red Bean, who has not seen a racecourse since April 1995, has since changed stables and, after getting outpaced on the long loop to the fourth last, stayed on again from the penultimate fence, only just failing to take third prize. (8/1: op 14/1)
1306 Circulation, carrying 12lb more that his long handicap weight, took the field along to the fourth last. (10/1)

1585 WHITE HART CONDITIONAL H'CAP HURDLE (0-120) (4-Y.O+) (Class E)

3-15 (3-16) **2m (8 hdls)** £2,320.00 (£645.00: £310.00) GOING minus 0.19 sec per fur (G)

				SP	RR	SF
1381[2]	**Dontdressfordinner (87)** (RJHodges) **6-10-0** TDascombe (a.p: chsd ldr appr 5th: led appr 2 out: r.o wl)	—	**1**	3/1[1]	70	17
1381[4]	**Pair of Jacks (IRE) (92)** (GLMoore) **6-10-5** DFortt (hld up: chsd wnr appr 2 out: unable qckn)	4	**2**	9/2[3]	71	18
	August Twelfth (87) (DCO'Brien) **8-10-0** DWalsh (stdy hdwy fr 2 out: r.o wl flat: nvr plcd to chal)	nk	**3**	20/1	66+	13
1416[4]	**Yubralee (USA) (115)** (MCPipe) **4-12-0** EHusband (led 2nd tl appr 2 out: sn wknd)	2	**4**	4/1[2]	92	39
	Tickerty's Gift (112) (GLMoore) **6-11-6(5)** MAttwater (hld up: one pce fr 3 out)	6	**5**	9/1	83	30
	Somerset Dancer (USA) (87) (JJBridger) **9-9-11(3)** DJKavanagh (a bhd: t.o)	dist	**6**	33/1	—	—
1389[P]	**Full of Tricks (87)** (JJBridger) **8-9-9(5)** JPower (chsd ldr 2nd tl appr 5th: sn wknd: t.o)	22	**7**	66/1	—	—
1382[6]	**Kalzari (USA) (87)** (AWCarroll) **11-10-0** PHenley (bhd fr 4th: t.o whn p.u bef 2 out)		**P**	10/1	—	—
1325[6]	**Inculcate (IRE) (105)** (CWeedon) **5-11-4b** GHogan (led to 2nd: wknd 4th: t.o whn p.u bef 5th: lame)		**P**	5/1	—	—
				(SP 108.1%)	**9 Rn**	

3m 51.8 (3.80) CSF £14.81 CT £174.63 TOTE £3.40: £1.10 £1.80 £3.70 (£4.20) Trio £106.50 OWNER A G Fear And Dontdressfordinner Partners (SOMERTON) BRED D. R. Tucker
LONG HANDICAP Dontdressfordinner 9-10 Full of Tricks 8-1 Kalzari (USA) 9-9 Somerset Dancer (USA) 9-7
STEWARDS' ENQUIRY O'Brien fined £400 & Walsh susp. 6-7 & 9/12/96 (schooling in public).

1381 Dontdressfordinner, 4lb out of the handicap, was sent to the front approaching the second last and managed to shake off the runner-up. (3/1)
1381 Pair of Jacks (IRE) continues to run well. Moving into second place approaching the penultimate hurdle, he failed to cope with the winner. (9/2)
August Twelfth, whose problems last season included leg trouble and an abscess on his neck which needed to be operated on, was given such a quiet ride punters would have been forgiven for thinking his jockey had fallen asleep. Receiving no assistance, the gelding crept closer over the last two hurdles and, running on really strongly on the run-in, only just failed to take second prize. At his best in the mud, he looks one to note with interest. (20/1)
1416 Yubralee (USA), soon at the head of affairs, made this a searching gallop but, collared approaching the second last, was soon done with. (4/1)
Tickerty's Gift was making little impression over the last three hurdles. Some mud and two and a half miles are required. (9/1: 6/1-10/1)

1586 CRANBOURNE H'CAP HURDLE (0-125) (4-Y.O+) (Class D)
3-45 (3-45) **2m 6f 110y (11 hdls)** £2,952.00 (£822.00: £396.00) GOING minus 0.19 sec per fur (G)

				SP	RR	SF
	Copper Boy (107) (RHBuckler) **7-11-9** BPowell (mde virtually all: comf)	—	**1**	7/2^{2}	94+	39
1392^{P}	**Kalasadi (USA) (104)** (VSoane) **5-11-6b** MRichards (a.p: rdn 3 out: r.o one pce)	6	**2**	10/1	87	32
741^{8}	**Lessons Lass (IRE) (102)** (MissHCKnight) **4-11-4** JOsborne (chsd wnr: ev ch 3 out: wknd last)	7	**3**	10/1	80	25
958^{P}	**Madame President (IRE) (84)** (CPMorlock) **5-9-11**$^{(3)}$ GHogan (lost pl 8th: r.o one pce fr 2 out)	nk	**4**	16/1	62	7
1394*	**Claireswan (IRE) (99)** (MHTompkins) **4-11-1** DGallagher (lw: lost pl 6th: rallied 8th: sn wknd)	¾	**5**	9/4^{1}	76	21
	Jackson Flint (95) (TThomsonJones) **8-10-11** MAFitzgerald (no hdwy fr 3 out)	9	**6**	33/1	66	11
	Raqib (109) (PCRitchens) **5-11-11** SFox (nvr nr to chal)	¾	**7**	9/1	79	24
	Spinnaker (105) (NAGaselee) **6-11-7** CLlewellyn (bit bkwd: mstke 5th: a bhd)	2½	**8**	12/1	73	18
1429^{F}	**Jadidh (91)** (ABarrow) **8-10-2**$^{(5)}$ DSalter (bhd fr 8th)	10	**9**	25/1	52	—
	Strokesaver (IRE) (94) (CPEBrooks) **6-10-10** GBradley (bit bkwd: hdwy 5th: wknd appr 3 out)	1½	**10**	8/1^{3}	54	—
	Dont Tell the Wife (112) (CREgerton) **10-11-9**$^{(5)}$ MrRThornton (a bhd)	3	**11**	20/1	70	15
1170^{4}	**Daring King (88)** (MJBolton) **6-10-4** PHide (prom to 7th: t.o whn p.u bef 2 out)		**P**	12/1	—	—
				(SP 125.1%)	**12 Rn**	

5m 28.4 (5.40) CSF £37.53 CT £305.05 TOTE £4.90: £1.60 £3.00 £3.50 (£35.90) Trio £160.80 OWNER Mr C. Raymond (BRIDPORT) BRED C. H. Raymond
LONG HANDICAP Madame President (IRE) 9-13
Copper Boy has had a leg problem and as a result has been off the track since March 1995. Making virtually all the running, he surged clear from the second last for a very decisive victory. His trainer describes him as the most exciting horse he has got. (7/2)
1074 Kalasadi (USA), never far away, struggled on to take second prize on the run-in without posing a threat to the winner. (10/1:7/1-12/1)
741 Lessons Lass (IRE) raced in second place. The main danger to the winner three from home, she was soon brushed aside. This trip may have been a little beyond her. (10/1: 7/1-12/1)
Madame President (IRE), who got rather outpaced four from home, struggled on over the last two hurdles, only just failing to take fourth prize. (16/1)
Spinnaker (12/1: 7/1-14/1)
Strokesaver (IRE) (8/1: op 5/1)
Daring King (12/1: op 8/1)

T/Plpt: £20.60 (540.29 Tckts). T/Qdpt: £8.90 (93.67 Tckts). AK

1290-CARLISLE (R-H) - Thursday November 28th
1587 Abandoned-Frost

1330-TAUNTON (R-H) (Good to firm)
Thursday November 28th
WEATHER: fine but cloudy

1594 BEECH NOVICES' HURDLE (4-Y.O+) (Class C)
1-25 (1-26) **2m 1f (9 hdls)** £3,566.25 (£1,080.00: £527.50: £251.25) GOING minus 0.31 sec per fur (GF)

				SP	RR	SF
1425^{2}	**Yet Again** (MissGayKelleway) **4-11-0** DBridgwater (hld up: hdwy appr 6th: hrd rdn to ld nr fin)	—	**1**	16/1	74	34
1375*	**Secret Spring (FR)** (PRHedger) **4-11-6** MRichards (hld up: hdwy 5th: led 2 out: rdn & hdd nr fin)	1¼	**2**	8/13^{1}	79	39
1333^{F}	**Out on a Promise (IRE)** (NJHWalker) **4-11-0** RHughes (led to 3rd: ev ch 2 out: sn wknd)	10	**3**	4/1^{2}	63	23
	Roderick Hudson (JARToller) **4-11-0** NWilliamson (chsd ldr: led 3rd: j.slowly 5th: hdd & mstke 2 out: sn wknd)	1¾	**4**	16/1	62	22
	Sparkling Buck (OSherwood) **4-10-9** JAMcCarthy (hdwy after 4th: ev ch 3 out: wknd appr 2 out)	26	**5**	7/1^{3}	32	—
	Office Hours (WGMTurner) **4-11-0** WMcFarland (wl bhd fr 6th)	6	**6**	40/1	32	—
1178^{7}	**Roc Age** (GWDavies) **5-10-2**$^{(7)}$ JTNolan (prom to 5th)	1	**7**	50/1	26	—
	Antigua's Treasure (IRE) (ABarrow) **7-10-9**$^{(5)}$ MrRThornton (j.slowly 1st: sn bhd: t.o fr 6th)	7	**8**	100/1	24	—
1431^{4}	**Country Tarquin** (RJHodges) **4-10-7**$^{(7)}$ JHarris (lw: mstke 1st: a bhd: t.o fr 6th)	1½	**9**	16/1	23	—
603^{7}	**Landlord** (MrsJEHawkins) **4-10-11**$^{(3)}$ DWalsh (bit bkwd: a bhd: t.o fr 6th)	10	**10**	66/1	13	—
1394^{P}	**Sharp Elver (IRE)** (PRHedger) **4-10-9** PHide (hdwy after 4th: wknd qckly 3 out: t.o)	2½	**11**	33/1	6	—
1289^{14}	**Fair Haul** (RGFrost) **5-11-0** BPowell (a bhd: t.o 5th: p.u bef 2 out)		**P**	100/1	—	—
	Racing Hawk (USA) (MSSaunders) **4-11-0v^{1}** PHolley (blnd & uns rdr 2nd)		**U**	40/1	—	—
				(SP 125.3%)	**13 Rn**	

3m 53.8 (0.80) CSF £26.21 TOTE £9.90: £1.40 £1.10 £1.80 (£8.70) Trio £8.20 OWNER Mr A. P. Griffin (WHITCOMBE) BRED Aston Park Stud
1425 Yet Again, a runner-up in a seller on his debut at Newton Abbot, appreciated this much sounder surface, and Bridgwater had told connections that the gelding was much better than a selling plater. (16/1)
1375* Secret Spring (FR), not really suited by this extended two miles, seemed to get outstayed by the winner in the closing stages. (8/13)
Out on a Promise (IRE) did settle better this time and might benefit from more patient tactics. (4/1)
Roderick Hudson did manage to win over seven on the Flat. Although he is bred to stay further, his stamina was never put to the test. (16/1)
Sparkling Buck made a satisfactory debut over hurdles for one who needed the run and may require further. (7/1: 5/1-8/1)

1595 MAPLE (S) HURDLE (3-Y.O) (Class G)
1-55 (1-55) **2m 1f (9 hdls)** £1,994.00 (£559.00: £272.00) GOING minus 0.31 sec per fur (GF)

				SP	RR	SF
	Theme Arena (MCPipe) **3-10-5** RHughes (led to 2nd: led 5th: pckd 3 out: clr 2 out: easily)	—	1	$7/1^{3}$	55+	15
	Jammy Jenny (NATwiston-Davies) **3-10-5** TJenks (a.p: chsd wnr appr 6th: ev ch appr 2 out: no imp)	7	2	12/1	48	8
1413^{3}	**Dark Truffle** (MrsJCecil) **3-10-5** JAMcCarthy (hld up: hdwy 5th: 3rd & btn whn hit 2 out)	1¼	3	$7/4^{1}$	47	7
	Hayling-Billy (PRHedger) **3-10-3**(7) MClinton (nvr nr to chal)	3½	4	25/1	49	9
1172*	**Stone Island** (PJHobbs) **3-11-3** NWilliamson (hld up & plld hrd: mstke 5th: hdwy appr 6th:rdn & wknd 3out)	15	5	$11/2^{2}$	42	2
1377^{12}	**Colebrook Willie** (JRBosley) **3-10-10** MBosley (nvr nr ldrs)	7	6	25/1	28	—
1377^{6}	**In Cahoots** (ADSmith) **3-10-10** FJousset (lw: plld hrd: prom to 6th)	1¾	7	10/1	27	—
912^{8}	**Red Time** (MSSaunders) **3-10-10** PHolley (led 2nd: hdd & blnd 5th: sn wknd)	3	8	25/1	24	—
1526^{6}	**Samara Song** (WGMTurner) **3-10-3**(7) NWillmington (chsd ldrs tl wknd qckly 3 out)	5	9	$7/1^{3}$	19	—
	Nantgarw (DRCElsworth) **3-10-5** AProcter (a bhd: t.o)	dist	10	12/1	—	—
1184^{16}	**Appeal Again (IRE)** (DBurchell) **3-10-10** DJBurchell (bhd tl fell 3 out)		F	20/1	—	—
1387^{P}	**Trianna** (RBrotherton) **3-10-5** LHarvey (a bhd: t.o whn p.u after 5th)		P	50/1	—	—
1172^{5}	**Blossom Dearie** (RGFrost) **3-10-5b**[1] BPowell (a bhd: t.o 6th: p.u bef 2 out)		P	33/1	—	—
	Ewar Bold (KOCunningham-Brown) **3-10-10** BFenton (lw: blnd & uns rdr 3rd)		U	14/1	—	—
				(SP 129.1%)	**14 Rn**	

3m 56.4 (3.40) CSF £85.53 TOTE £9.40: £2.00 £2.60 £1.30 (£81.20) Trio £79.00 OWNER Mr Antony Sofroniou (WELLINGTON) BRED Halevale Ltd

Bt in 2,500 gns

Dark Truffle clmd DGamble £5,000

Theme Arena, who had shown nothing in three appearances on the Flat for Stan Mellor, was nibbled at in the market and gave Hughes his first win over hurdles in this country. (7/1)

Jammy Jenny was breathing down the neck of the winner on the home turn and was only put under pressure when the winner had flown. (12/1: op 7/1)

1413 Dark Truffle could not go with the front two from the third last, and may well have been unsuited by this sharp course. (7/4)

Hayling-Billy had a couple of outings on the Flat last month and will be better for the experience. (25/1)

1172* Stone Island did not settle as well as Williamson would have liked. (11/2: 4/1-6/1)

In Cahoots (10/1: op 6/1)

1596 MENDIP PLYWOOD NOVICES' CHASE (5-Y.O+) (Class C)
2-25 (2-25) **2m 3f (15 fncs)** £4,531.25 (£1,370.00: £667.50: £316.25) GOING minus 0.31 sec per fur (GF)

				SP	RR	SF
1195^{F}	**Greenback (BEL)** (PJHobbs) **5-10-13** NWilliamson (led to 2nd: led 4th: j.lft last 3: r.o wl)	—	1	Evens[1]	99	18
	Jovial Man (IRE) (RJO'Sullivan) **7-11-0** DBridgwater (lw: hld up: hdwy appr 9th: ev ch 3 out: wknd 2 out)	11	2	$7/2^{2}$	91	10
	Ramallah (90) (MissHCKnight) **7-11-0** BFenton (bit bkwd: hdwy appr 9th: rdn & r.o one pce fr 3 out)	4	3	$7/2^{2}$	87	6
965^{4}	**Calleva Star (IRE)** (RHAlner) **5-10-10**(3) PHenley (hld up: outpcd 9th: 5th & no ch whn blnd 3 out)	½	4	20/1	86	5
1195^{F}	**Wixoe Wonder (IRE)** (MBradstock) **6-11-0** PHolley (led 2nd tl overjumped 4th: wknd 11th)	4	5	$10/1^{3}$	84	3
1199^{P}	**Paddy Burke (IRE)** (AGNewcombe) **6-10-11**(3) GHogan (lw: a bhd: t.o 9th: p.u bef 3 out)		P	33/1	—	—
1449^{U}	**Baxworthy Lord (60)** (CLPopham) **5-10-10**(3) TDascombe (a bhd: t.o 9th: p.u bef 3 out)		P	50/1	—	—
				(SP 113.2%)	**7 Rn**	

4m 47.9 (5.90) CSF £4.86 TOTE £2.00: £1.40 £2.40 (£3.20) OWNER Mr Jack Joseph (MINEHEAD) BRED Patrick Madelein

1195 Greenback (BEL) was inclined to jump a shade left-handed over the last three, but that did not stop him pulling clear. (Evens)

Jovial Man (IRE), making his chasing debut, could not go with the winner from the third last. He should have little trouble in going one better, and a longer trip or softer ground will help. (7/2: 5/2-4/1)

Ramallah, trained by John White last season, kept plugging away on his fencing debut on ground on the lively side for him. He should come on for the outing. (7/2)

965 Calleva Star (IRE), graduating to the major obstacles, did well to contest the minor honours after being virtually on the floor three out. (20/1)

Wixoe Wonder (IRE) was in the air for a long way at the second ditch. (10/1)

1597 OAK NOVICES' H'CAP HURDLE (4-Y.O+) (Class C)
2-55 (2-56) **2m 1f (9 hdls)** £3,533.75 (£1,070.00: £522.50: £248.75) GOING minus 0.31 sec per fur (GF)

				SP	RR	SF
1382^{3}	**Hay Dance (95)** (PJHobbs) **5-10-3**(3) GTormey (hld up: hdwy appr 2 out: led & j.rt last: edgd rt flat: drvn out)	—	1	$11/4^{2}$	77	5
1333*	**Rosencrantz (IRE) (108)** (MissVenetiaWilliams) **4-11-5** NWilliamson (hld up: led 2 out: rdn: hdd & n.m.r last: unable qckn)	2	2	$2/5^{1}$	88	16
593^{5}	**Millcroft Riviera (IRE) (89)** (RHAlner) **5-9-11**(3) PHenley (led to 2 out: hmpd last: one pce)	1¼	3	25/1	68?	—
396^{U}	**Prince de Berry (91)** (GAHam) **5-10-2**ow2 PHolley (chsd ldr to 3 out: wknd 2 out)	10	4	$14/1^{3}$	61?	—
1208^{9}	**Studio Thirty (89)** (CASmith) **4-10-0** DBridgwater (nt j.w: bhd tl p.u bnd appr 5th)		P	20/1	—	—
				(SP 113.4%)	**5 Rn**	

3m 58.9 (5.90) CSF £4.29 TOTE £3.20: £2.40 £1.00 (£1.10) OWNER Wessex Go Racing Partnership (MINEHEAD) BRED Limestone Stud

LONG HANDICAP Millcroft Riviera (IRE) 9-1 Prince de Berry 9-8 Studio Thirty 9-1

1382 Hay Dance was rightly allowed to keep the race after interfering with the third at the final flight. (11/4)

1333* Rosencrantz (IRE) was trying a longer trip on this debut in handicap company. (2/5)

593 Millcroft Riviera (IRE), 13lb out of the handicap, ran easily his best race since finishing third on his debut at Wincanton in March. (25/1)

396 Prince de Berry had been bought out of Brian Meehan's yard for 4,800 guineas. (14/1)

1598 MENDIP PLYWOOD H'CAP CHASE (0-125) (5-Y.O+) (Class D)
3-25 (3-25) **3m (19 fncs)** £4,810.75 (£1,456.00: £710.50: £337.75) GOING minus 0.31 sec per fur (GF)

				SP	RR	SF
1379^{3}	**Duhallow Lodge (109)** (CRBarwell) **9-11-10** BFenton (hld up: hdwy 12th: led last: drvn out)	—	1	$7/2^{3}$	113	24
1202^{5}	**Scotoni (95)** (RJO'Sullivan) **10-10-10** BPowell (chsd ldr: led 12th to last: hrd rdn: r.o)	½	2	6/1	99	10
1391*	**Bally Clover (107)** (MissVenetiaWilliams) **9-11-8** NWilliamson (led 6th to 8th: led 9th to 12th: ev ch whn mstke 3 out: nt rcvr)	9	3	$100/30^{2}$	105	16
1335^{4}	**Herbert Buchanan (IRE) (101)** (PFNicholls) **6-11-2** PHide (hld up: blnd bdly 12th (water): nt rcvr)	dist	4	4/1	—	—

Form	Runner	Dist	Pos	SP	RR	SF
1194^{4}	**Certain Angle (106)** (PJHobbs) **7-11-7** DBridgwater (led: slipped bnd appr 5th: hdd 6th: led 8th to 9th: wknd qckly 13th: p.u bef 14th)		P	9/4^{1}	—	—
				(SP 110.4%)		**5 Rn**

6m 5.8 (8.80) CSF £20.20 TOTE £4.90: £1.90 £2.70 (£13.20) OWNER Mr Robin Barwell (TIVERTON)
1379 Duhallow Lodge had to work hard to repeat last season's win in this event off a 9lb lower mark. (7/2)
Scotoni, supported in the morning exchanges, at least put any doubts to rest that he did not stay three miles. (6/1)
1391* Bally Clover, raised 7lb, also had to contend with faster ground, and belting the tricky fence three from home could not have come at a worse time. (100/30)
1335 Herbert Buchanan (IRE) does seem to have the odd lapse of concentration, and this time left his hind legs in the water with a circuit to go. (4/1)
1194 Certain Angle had an anxious moment on the bend into the back straight on the first circuit, and stopped as if something was amiss, before being pulled up going to the penultimate ditch. (9/4)

1599 WALNUT H'CAP HURDLE (0-120) (4-Y.O+) (Class D)

3-55 (3-55) **2m 3f 110y (10 hdls)** £2,762.00 (£836.00: £408.00: £194.00) GOING minus 0.31 sec per fur (GF)

Form	Runner	Dist	Pos	SP	RR	SF
	Road to Au Bon (USA) (78) (RJBaker) **8-10-2** BPowell (led to 3 out: led flat: all out)	—	1	14/1	59	—
	Beyond Our Reach (100) (RJHodges) **8-11-7**(3) TDascombe (a.p: rdn & sltly outpcd appr 2 out: rallied & ev ch flat: r.o)	nk	2	8/1	81	14
1553^{3}	**Fleur de Tal (95)** (WGMTurner) **5-10-12**(7) JPower (a.p: led 3 out: mstke last: hdd flat: r.o)	½	3	13/2	75	8
1332*	**Little Hooligan (85)** (RJHodges) **5-10-2**(7) JHarris (hld up: rdn & hdwy appr 2 out: styd on flat)	2½	4	8/1	63	—
1392^{5}	**First Class (83)** (GNAlford) **6-10-7** RGreene (plld hrd: prom: outpcd 3 out: styd on flat)	1	5	5/1^{3}	61	—
1330^{4}	**San Diego Charger (IRE) (80)** (ABarrow) **5-9-13**(5) MrRThornton (hld up: rdn appr 6th: no hdwy fr 2 out)	½	6	11/1	57	—
1381*	**Supermick (86)** (WRMuir) **5-10-10** MRichards (lw: hld up: rdn 3 out: wknd flat)	5	7	13/8^{1}	59	—
1378^{5}	**Supreme Star (USA) (88)** (PRHedger) **5-10-12b** DBridgwater (hld up: sme hdwy 6th: wknd 7th: eased whn btn appr 2 out)	25	8	4/1^{2}	40	—
				(SP 125.3%)		**8 Rn**

4m 40.7 (9.70) CSF £113.43 CT £745.72 TOTE £23.40: £4.80 £2.10 £1.60 (£34.20) Trio £49.50 OWNER Mr M. H. Holland (TIVERTON) BRED Samuel D. Hinkle
IN-FOCUS: **This race was run at a muddling pace until the tempo quickened going to the fourth last.**
Road to Au Bon (USA) eventually stepped up the tempo going to the fourth last, and stayed on dourly in the closing stages. Off the course since August '94, this was a fine piece of training. (14/1: 8/1-16/1)
Beyond Our Reach fought back gamely from the final flight, but the weight concession proved too much. (8/1)
1553 Fleur de Tal found her occasional jumping problems rearing their ugly head when strongly pressed at the final flight. (13/2)
1332* Little Hooligan was 3lb higher for winning a seller here a fortnight ago. (8/1: 5/1-9/1)
First Class, dropped 9lb, took a strong hold and would have preferred a more truly-run race. (5/1)
1330 San Diego Charger (IRE) is now only 3lb higher than the mark off which he won in April. (11/1: 8/1-12/1)
1378 Supreme Star (USA) (4/1: 3/1-5/1)

T/Plpt: £96.60 (213.37 Tckts). T/Qdpt: £30.80 (82.86 Tckts). KH

1276-UTTOXETER (L-H) - Thursday November 28th

1600 Abandoned-Frost

1607a - 1627a : (Irish Racing) - See Computer Raceform

1118-BANGOR-ON-DEE (L-H) (Chases Good to soft becoming Soft, Hdles Good becoming Good to soft) Friday November 29th

Race 2: one fence omitted
WEATHER: heavy showers

1628 CLASSIC RACING BOOKS (S) HURDLE (4,5,6 & 7-Y.O) (Class G)

1-20 (1-21) **2m 1f (9 hdls)** £2,036.00 (£571.00: £278.00) GOING: 0.96 sec per fur (S)

Form	Runner	Dist	Pos	SP	RR	SF
1537^{2}	**Willy Star (BEL)** (MrsSJSmith) **6-11-5** RichardGuest (a.p: led appr 6th: clr last: comf)	—	1	11/4^{1}	71+	38
1500^{5}	**Ela Man Howa (84)** (ABailey) **5-10-12** NWilliamson (hld up in rr: hdwy 5th: one pce fr 2 out)	3	2	6/1^{3}	61	28
1278^{6}	**Robsera (IRE) (84)** (JJQuinn) **5-10-12** MDwyer (hld up: hdwy 4th: chal & hit 2 out: kpt on u.p)	1	3	8/1	60	27
1417^{10}	**Sharmoor (83)** (MissLCSiddall) **4-10-7** AThornton (chsd ldrs: rdn appr 2 out: sn btn)	9	4	12/1	47	14
	The Final Spark (GRichards) **5-10-7** BHarding (bkwd: hld up: sme hdwy fr 3 out: nvr nrr)	3½	5	12/1	44	11
1390^{7}	**Pharly Reef (68)** (DBurchell) **4-10-12** DJBurchell (styd on fr 3 out: nvr nrr)	2	6	14/1	47	14
	Tirmizi (USA) (97) (MrsASwinbank) **5-11-5** JSupple (bkwd: prom to 4th: sn lost pl)	3½	7	5/1^{2}	50	17
1425^{5}	**Denomination (USA) (89)** (MCPipe) **4-11-5**(7) BMoore (a in rr: t.o)	14	8	12/1	44	11
871^{8}	**Biya (IRE) (75)** (DMcCain) **4-10-9**(3) DWalsh (bit bkwd: chsd ldrs to 6th: grad wknd: t.o)	nk	9	33/1	30	—
1247^{3}	**Antartictern (USA) (76)** (GROldroyd) **6-10-12** ADobbin (prom tl wknd qckly appr 3 out: t.o)	13	10	10/1	18	—
1276^{7}	**Dashing Dancer (IRE)** (ALForbes) **5-10-12** GaryLyons (a bhd: t.o)	nk	11	33/1	17	—
893^{4}	**Simand (78)** (GMMoore) **4-11-0** JCallaghan (hld up in rr: lost tch 6th: sn t.o)	3½	12	12/1	16	—
1412^{P}	**Riverbank Red** (WClay) **5-10-7** TEley (led tl hdd & wknd appr 6th: t.o)	2	13	20/1	7	—
1446^{4}	**My Harvinski (74)** (IRJones) **6-10-5v**^{1}(7) MissEJJones (a rr div: t.o)	8	14	20/1	5	—
1251^{4}	**Oakbury (IRE) (64)** (MissLCSiddall) **4-10-12** MRichards (chsd ldrs tl wknd qckly 5th: sn t.o)	13	15	14/1	—	—
	Gallardini (IRE) (94) (BSRothwell) **7-11-9**(3) GCahill (bkwd: lost tch 5th: t.o whn p.u bef last)		P	12/1	—	—
				(SP 145.0%)		**16 Rn**

4m 17.8 (22.80) CSF £22.76 TOTE £3.60: £1.80 £2.00 £3.40 (£17.20) Trio £30.40 OWNER Mrs S. Smith (BINGLEY) BRED Madame W. Verwey
No bid
1537 Willy Star (BEL) seems to be much happier over this shorter trip and, always travelling comfortably, won with the minimum of fuss. (11/4)
871 Ela Man Howa ran much better on this step down in class and there could be a race in him at this level. (6/1)

786 Robsera (IRE) is not the most fluent of hurdlers but, if he had not clouted the penultimate flight and landed flat-footed at the last, he would have made a race of it. (8/1)
Sharmoor is pretty moderate and was struggling to hang on from the run into the straight. (12/1)
The Final Spark, very much in need of the run on her hurdling debut, stayed on steadily inside the last half-mile. She will be much the wiser next time. (12/1: 8/1-14/1)
Pharly Reef did make some late progress, but was never able to get within striking range of the principals. (14/1)
Tirmizi (USA), subject of some inspired wagers early on, was too backward to do himself justice and was in trouble out in the country. (5/1: op 3/1)
1425 Denomination (USA) (12/1: 8/1-14/1)
893 Simand (12/1: 6/1-14/1)
1251 Oakbury (IRE) (14/1: op 8/1)
Gallardini (IRE) (12/1: 8/1-16/1)

1629 JPCS NOVICES' H'CAP CHASE (0-100) (4-Y.O+) (Class E)

1-50 (1-55) **2m 4f 110y (14 fncs)** £3,290.00 (£995.00: £485.00: £230.00) GOING: 0.96 sec per fur (S)

				SP	RR	SF
1364^{3}	**General Pongo (90)** (TRGeorge) **7-11-4** MDwyer (chsd ldrs: led 7th to 4 out: chal last: rdn to ld flat)	—	1	10/1	109	17
1472^{U}	**Whirly (IRE) (90)** (RHAlner) **7-11-4** AThornton (a.p: led 4 out tl flat: unable qckn)	1½	2	7/1^{3}	108	16
1083^{3}	**Kenmare River (IRE) (72)** (RCollins) **6-9-9**$^{(5)}$ MrRThornton (hdwy 9th: wknd 4 out)	28	3	20/1	68	—
1189^{2}	**Monymoss (IRE) (98)** (MrsSJSmith) **7-11-12** RichardGuest (led to 4th: lost pl ½-wy: n.d after)	3½	4	9/2^{2}	91	—
972*	**Playing Truant (82)** (DRGandolfo) **8-10-7**$^{(3)}$ DFortt (hld up: hdwy 9th: nt rch ldrs)	3½	5	4/1^{1}	73	—
1348*	**Monnaie Forte (IRE) (90)** (JRAdam) **6-11-4** JRailton (lw: chsd ldrs to 9th: wkng whn p.u bef next)		P	7/1^{3}	—	—
1300^{3}	**Dormston Boyo (72)** (TWall) **6-10-0** DBridgwater (swtg: sn t.o: p.u bef 7th)		P	25/1	—	—
1060^{2}	**Frontier Flight (USA) (80)** (MissLCSiddall) **6-10-5**$^{(3)}$ EHusband (blnd 3rd: bhd fr 8th: t.o whn p.u bef 3 out)		P	16/1	—	—
1120^{6}	**Heathyards Boy (74)** (DMcCain) **6-9-13**$^{(3)ow2}$ DWalsh (bit bkwd: led 4th to 7th: sn lost pl: t.o whn p.u bef 3 out)		P	33/1	—	—
1032^{4}	**Karenastino (73)** (MrsSJSmith) **5-10-0** MrPMurray (lost pl 6th: t.o whn p.u bef last)		P	50/1	—	—
1300^{2}	**On the Tear (72)** (FLloyd) **10-10-0** SWynne (a bhd: t.o whn p.u bef 3 out)		P	25/1	—	—
	Choisty (IRE) (92) (MrsASwinbank) **6-11-6** JSupple (bit bkwd: blnd & uns rdr 1st)		U	4/1^{1}	—	—
1252^{5}	***Chris's Glen (80)*** *(JMBradley)* ***7-10-8v*** *NWilliamson (Withdrawn not under Starter's orders: veterinary advice)*		W	16/1	—	—
				(SP 121.4%)	**12 Rn**	

5m 33.9 (33.90) CSF £70.31 CT £1,252.01 TOTE £11.10: £3.40 £1.90 £4.40 (£46.30) Trio £171.70; £198.38 to Newcastle 30/11/96 OWNER Mrs J. K. Powell (ROSS-ON-WYE) BRED R. R. Evans Bloodstock Ltd
LONG HANDICAP On the Tear 9-5 Heathyards Boy 9-10 Karenastino 9-1
WEIGHT FOR AGE 5yo-1lb

1364 General Pongo had less on his plate this time and, under an inspired ride, at long last found an opening. (10/1)
Whirly (IRE) turned in a much-improved display of jumping and only found lack of peak-fitness catching him out in the duel to the line. (7/1)
1083 Kenmare River (IRE), waiting on the leaders, closed up a mile out, but he got very leg-weary in the latter stages and the leading pair had got away. (20/1)
1189 Monymoss (IRE) needs a longer trip to bring out the best in him, but he also performs better on a sounder surface and he was making hard work of it from a long way out. (9/2: op 3/1)
972* Playing Truant could not handle this stamina-sapping ground, but he did get round in one piece and there will be other days. (4/1)

1630 RUABON H'CAP HURDLE (0-110) (4-Y.O+) (Class E)

2-20 (2-23) **2m 1f (9 hdls)** £2,814.00 (£852.00: £416.00: £198.00) GOING: 0.96 sec per fur (S)

				SP	RR	SF
1374^{5}	**Tanseeq (86)** (MGMeagher) **5-10-7** DerekByrne (hld up: hdwy appr 3 out: led last: comf)	—	1	9/2^{1}	70+	14
1145^{4}	**Stay With Me (FR) (94)** (CREgerton) **6-10-10**$^{(5)}$ MrRThornton (chsd ldrs: led 6th to last: rdn & no ex flat)	1½	2	6/1^{2}	77	21
	Kintavi (82) (TWDonnelly) **6-10-3** TEley (bit bkwd: hld up & bhd: hdwy appr 3 out: wknd 2 out)	9	3	25/1	56	—
	Colorful Ambition (106) (MrsASwinbank) **6-11-13** JRailton (lw: hld up & bhd: stdy hdwy appr 6th: wknd appr last)	nk	4	7/1	80	24
1330^{3}	**Zingibar (79)** (JMBradley) **4-10-0** TJMurphy (chsd ldr: lft in ld 4th: hdd 6th: wknd appr 2 out)	nk	5	6/1^{2}	53	—
1256^{10}	**Kayfaat (USA) (81)** (MCPipe) **8-9-9v**$^{1(7)}$ BMoore (chsd ldrs tl wknd appr 3 out)	2½	6	16/1	52	—
1360^{8}	**Grandman (IRE) (90)** (DMoffatt) **5-10-11** DJMoffatt (prom tl wknd appr 3 out)	nk	7	13/2^{3}	61	5
1034^{4}	**Scottish Wedding (79)** (TWall) **6-10-0** DBridgwater (bhd: drvn along ½-wy: effrt 6th: wknd appr 2 out)	5	8	8/1	—	—
1325^{7}	**United Front (95)** (JNeville) **4-11-2** NWilliamson (led tl fell 4th)		F	8/1	—	—
	Daily Sport Girl (92) (BJLlewellyn) **7-10-13** MrJLLlewellyn (bkwd: hld up: hdwy 4th: ev ch appr 3 out: wknd qckly: p.u bef next)		P	9/1	—	—
				(SP 114.5%)	**10 Rn**	

4m 20.7 (25.70) CSF £28.88 CT £547.79 TOTE £5.30: £2.10 £2.30 £4.20 (£24.80) Trio £237.80 OWNER Miss N. C. Taylor (ORMSKIRK) BRED Shadwell Estate Company Limited
LONG HANDICAP Scottish Wedding 9-12
STEWARDS' ENQUIRY B Llewellyn fined £400 & J Llewellyn susp. 9-11/12/96 (schooling in public).

1374 Tanseeq has been knocking at the door and, given a very competent ride, won with far more in hand than the official margin suggests. (9/2)
1145 Stay With Me (FR) has done all his winning when he can hear his feet rattle, but he did nothing wrong here and will be back. (6/1)
Kintavi ran extremely well for one who has been off the track for over twenty-one months, and he will be much fitter with this outing under his belt. (25/1)
Colorful Ambition moved up smoothly inside the final mile, but the weight on ground far too testing for him took its toll, and he could only plug on at the one pace from the penultimate flight. (7/1)
1330 Zingibar failed to make the frame for the first time this term, but he gave his best, which was not good enough on the day. (6/1)
Kayfaat (USA), brought back to the minimum trip, held his pitch in the chasing group until feeling the strain before reaching the straight. (16/1)
Daily Sport Girl, having her first outing in five months, was on the heels of the leaders approaching the third last, but she weakened and was pulled up before the next. Her rider was suspended after the Stewards decided all was not what it should have been. (9/1: 5/1-10/1)

1631 MAELOR H'CAP CHASE (0-130) (4-Y.O+) (Class C)

2-50 (2-51) **2m 4f 110y (15 fncs)** £4,409.50 (£1,336.00: £653.00: £311.50) GOING: 0.96 sec per fur (S)

				SP	RR	SF
	River Mandate (120) (CaptTAForster) **9-11-12** AThornton (bit bkwd: chsd ldr: rdn 3 out: styd on gamely to ld nr fin)	—	1	15/8^{1}	131	27

	Horse	Dist	Pos	SP	RR	SF
	Even Blue (IRE) (115) (DMcCain) **8-11-4**(3) DWalsh (bkwd: j.w: led tl hrd rdn & hdd cl home)	½	**2**	2/1[2]	126	22
1167[P]	**Andrelot (118)** (PBowen) **9-11-10b** NWilliamson (hld up: reminders 7th: j.slowly 10th & next: sn t.o)	dist	**3**	10/1[3]	—	—
1442[2]	**Spanish Light (IRE) (122)** (SirJohnBarlowBt) **7-12-0** ADobbin (hld up: hdwy 9th: wknd qckly appr 4 out: sn t.o)	24	**4**	2/1[2]	—	—
				(SP 110.5%)		**4 Rn**

5m 32.9 (32.90) CSF £5.71 TOTE £2.80: (£4.00) OWNER Anne Duchess of Westminster (LUDLOW) BRED J. P. N. Parker
STEWARDS' ENQUIRY Walsh susp. 6&8-9/12/96 (excessive use of whip).

River Mandate can handle testing ground, but he was returning after almost two years out of action and defied his burly looks with an ultra-game performance to keep up his impressive winning sequence. (15/8)

Even Blue (IRE) won over course and distance on his debut last year and tried hard to repeat the feat, but the useful winner does not know the meaning of defeat. (2/1)

1063 Andrelot (10/1: 7/1-11/1)

1442 Spanish Light (IRE) has won on soft ground, but this was something else and, after travelling best for almost two miles, he stopped to a walk after jumping the final ditch four out. (2/1)

1632 MALISE NICOLSON MEMORIAL NOVICES' CHASE (5-Y.O+) (Class D)

3-20 (3-20) **3m 110y (18 fncs)** £3,745.00 (£1,135.00: £555.00: £265.00) GOING: 0.96 sec per fur (S)

	Horse	Dist	Pos	SP	RR	SF
1538*	**Bankhead (IRE) (110)** (JLSpearing) **7-11-5** DBridgwater (plld hrd: hld up & bhd: hdwy 12th: chal & lft in ld 2 out: styd on strly)	—	**1**	100/30[2]	109	—
	Lansborough (GRichards) **6-10-12** BHarding (bit bkwd: hld up gng wl: led appr 3 out: stumbled & hdd next: rdn & no ex flat)	3	**2**	10/11[1]	100+	—
1294[7]	**Shallow River (IRE)** (RCollins) **5-10-10** AThornton (j.w: led to 4th: led 11th to 12th: lft in ld 14th: hdd & wknd 3 out)	dist	**3**	33/1	—	—
	Gold Pigeon (IRE) (72) (BSRothwell) **7-10-4**(3) GCahill (bit bkwd: prom to 12th: sn wknd: t.o)	26	**4**	33/1	—	—
	Island Jewel (JRBosley) **8-10-12** MBosley (prom: mstke 8th: wknd 12th: p.u bef 14th)		**P**	9/1	—	—
	Over The Wrekin (72) (JLNeedham) **9-10-12** RichardGuest (bkwd: hld up: hdwy 9th: wknd 11th: t.o whn p.u bef 4 out)		**P**	50/1	—	—
	Benbulbin (IRE) (JWMullins) **6-10-12** SCurran (bkwd: led 4th to 11th: sn lost tch: t.o whn p.u bef 2 out)		**P**	40/1	—	—
1357*	**Naughty Future** (JJO'Neill) **7-11-5** MDwyer (hld up: hdwy 8th: led 12th tl blnd & uns rdr 14th)		**U**	9/2[3]	—	—
				(SP 113.9%)		**8 Rn**

6m 55.3 (53.30) CSF £6.49 TOTE £4.00: £1.50 £1.20 £3.60 (£3.30) OWNER Mrs Liz Brazier (ALCESTER) BRED Ronald O'Neill
WEIGHT FOR AGE 5yo-2lb

1538* Bankhead (IRE) had time to measure his fences in this slowly-run event and, presented with the advantage two out, completed a quick follow-up to his initial success over fences under Rules. (100/30)

Lansborough jumped from fence to fence on this chasing debut and looked all over the winner when leading into the straight, but he knuckled on landing at the penultimate obstacle and was unable to recover. Unproven at the trip, he may have been getting leg-weary, but he does look a very promising recruit. (10/11: evens-11/10)

Shallow River (IRE) turned in a pleasing display on this first look at fences and should not have much difficulty making the grade. (33/1)

Island Jewel (9/1: 5/1-10/1)

1357* Naughty Future jumped to the front soon after going out into the country for the final time and would have been the one to beat had he not run into the bottom of the fifth last and dislodged his pilot. (9/2: op 3/1)

1633 HANMER 'N.H.' NOVICES' HURDLE (4-Y.O+) (Class D)

3-50 (3-54) **2m 1f (9 hdls)** £3,081.00 (£866.00: £423.00) GOING: 0.96 sec per fur (S)

	Horse	Dist	Pos	SP	RR	SF
	Crimson King (IRE) (CaptTAForster) **5-10-12** AThornton (chsd ldrs: mstke 3rd: led appr 3 out: clr last: unchal)	—	**1**	7/2[2]	80+	23
	Market Mayhem (JLSpearing) **6-10-12** RichardGuest (bit bkwd: a.p: styd on fr 2 out: no ch w wnr)	11	**2**	50/1	70	13
1084[3]	**Gazanali (IRE)** (GMMoore) **5-10-12** NBentley (hld up: hdwy 5th: rdn & r.o one pce fr 3 out)	2½	**3**	33/1	67	10
1203*	**Ultimate Smoothie** (MCPipe) **4-10-12** CMaude (hld up & bhd: gd hdwy appr 3 out: nt rch ldrs)	3	**4**	9/2[3]	65	8
1124*	**Johnny-K (IRE)** (DNicholson) **5-10-12** NWilliamson (hld up in tch: hdwy 5th: chal & stumbled 2 out: btn whn blnd last: eased)	1	**5**	Evens[1]	64+	7
1030[9]	**Reflex Hammer** (JohnUpson) **5-10-12** RSupple (chsd ldrs: rdn appr 3 out: sn btn)	8	**6**	20/1	56	—
1118[3]	**Milling Brook** (JMBradley) **4-10-5**(7) JPower (trckd ldrs tl wknd appr 3 out)	7	**7**	50/1	49	—
	Kentucky Gold (IRE) (MrsLWilliamson) **7-10-12** LO'Hara (bkwd: nvr nr ldrs)	3½	**8**	100/1	46	—
1079[7]	**Joe Luke (IRE)** (GMMoore) **4-10-12** JCallaghan (nvr plcd to chal)	1	**9**	50/1	45	—
	Lucky Tanner (MissHCKnight) **5-10-12** TJMurphy (bit bkwd: prom to 3 out: wknd qckly: t.o)	23	**10**	33/1	24	—
1345[U]	**Judicious Norman (IRE)** (JRAdam) **5-10-12** JRailton (lw: led tl hdd & wknd appr 3 out: t.o)	3	**11**	10/1	21	—
1124[12]	**The Secret Grey** (DMcCain) **5-10-9**(3) DWalsh (bit bkwd: prom to 5th: sn lost pl: t.o)	dist	**12**	100/1	—	—
1013[11]	**Rinus Majestic (IRE)** (DMcCain) **4-10-12** BHarding (bhd whn p.u bef 2 out)		**P**	100/1	—	—
1289[15]	**Sophies Dream** (JMBradley) **5-10-7**(5) MrRThornton (a bhd: t.o whn p.u bef 2 out)		**P**	100/1	—	—
	Manvulane (IRE) (92) (MrsCJBlack) **6-10-12** DBridgwater (bkwd: a in rr: t.o whn p.u bef 2 out)		**P**	20/1	—	—
				(SP 124.7%)		**15 Rn**

4m 19.6 (24.60) CSF £133.50 TOTE £5.00: £1.40 £27.70 £5.00 (£246.20) Trio £440.90; £496.87 to Newcastle 30/11/96 OWNER Mr Simon Sainsbury (LUDLOW) BRED John Harrington

OFFICIAL EXPLANATION Johnny-K (IRE): finished distressed.

Crimson King (IRE), very short on experience, kept up his stable's good recent run with a very easy success, and he can still improve on this. (7/2: 4/1-5/2)

Market Mayhem showed he is going the right way with his best performance yet and there would seem much better to follow. (50/1)

1084 Gazanali (IRE) found things happening too quickly on this hurdling debut, but he did keep plugging away and will come into his own when tackling a longer trip. (33/1)

1203* Ultimate Smoothie could make a name for himself when he is tried over a more suitable trip, for he did little wrong here except that he lacked the speed to deliver a challenge. (9/2: 5/2-5/1)

1124* Johnny-K (IRE), landing in a heap when challenging for the lead at the penultimate hurdle, was out on his feet when bungling the last, and his jockey kept hold of his head and allowed him to complete in his own time. He did look to be going every bit as well as the winner when he made the first of his errors and, except that the trip could have been inadequate, it is difficult to find a reason for such a poor performance. (Evens)

T/Plpt: £506.60 (23.98 Tckts). T/Qdpt: £77.00 (16.55 Tckts). IM

1317-NEWBURY (L-H) (Good)
Friday November 29th
WEATHER: fine

1634 FRESHMAN'S HURDLE (3-Y.O) (Class C)
1-00 (1-00) **2m 110y (8 hdls)** £3,938.00 (£1,184.00: £572.00: £266.00) GOING: 0.43 sec per fur (GS)

	Horse	Dist	Pos	SP	RR	SF
	White Sea (IRE) (MCPipe) **3-10-7** CFSwan (a.p: led after 4th: comf)	—	**1**	7/1	92+	47
1269*	**Shooting Light (IRE)** (PGMurphy) **3-11-3** GBradley (lw: hdwy 3rd: chsd wnr appr 2 out: mstke last: unable qckn)	5	**2**	5/1 2	97	52
	Summer Spell (USA) (NJHenderson) **3-10-12** MAFitzgerald (stdy hdwy 3 out: rdn appr 2 out: one pce)	15	**3**	2/1 1	78+	33
	Samakaan (IRE) (DNicholson) **3-10-12** AMaguire (a.p: rdn appr last: one pce)	¾	**4**	5/1 2	77+	32
1014 2	**Le Teteu (FR)** (BobJones) **3-10-12** RDunwoody (hld up: rdn appr 2 out: one pce)	3	**5**	13/2 3	74	29
1269 2	**Pleasureland (IRE)** (RCurtis) **3-10-12** DMorris (lw: nvr nr to chal)	19	**6**	20/1	56	11
1377 2	**Sterling Fellow** (DLWilliams) **3-10-12b** MClarke (nvr nrr)	18	**7**	33/1	38	—
	Red Raja (PMitchell) **3-10-12** DGallagher (a mid div)	7	**8**	66/1	31	—
	Apache Park (USA) (MSheppard) **3-10-12** CLlewellyn (nvr nrr)	1¼	**9**	50/1	30	—
1205*	**Chief Mouse** (MissHCKnight) **3-11-8** JOsborne (led tl after 1st: wknd 4th)	2½	**10**	16/1	38	—
1444 3	**Warning Reef** (CLPopham) **3-10-12** SMcNeill (prom to 5th)	3½	**11**	50/1	24	—
1014 5	**Laughing Buccaneer** (DNCarey) **3-10-12** BPowell (lw: nvr nrr)	1¼	**12**	66/1	23	—
	Claire's Dancer (IRE) (AndrewTurnell) **3-10-12** LHarvey (prom to 3rd)	½	**13**	33/1	23	—
1011 2	**Sunley Secure** (NoelChance) **3-10-12** WMarston (prom to 4th)	4	**14**	33/1	19	—
	Northern Clan (AJChamberlain) **3-10-5(7)** OBurrows (a bhd)	1½	**15**	66/1	17	—
1370 12	**Flying Green (FR)** (NJHWalker) **3-10-12b1** RFarrant (led after 1st tl after 4th: sn wknd)	½	**16**	33/1	17	—
1377 8	**Hawanafa** (JSMoore) **3-10-7** WMcFarland (bhd fr 5th)	26	**17**	66/1	—	—
944 2	**A Chef Too Far** (RRowe) **3-10-12** DO'Sullivan (hdwy 4th: wknd 5th)	3	**18**	16/1	—	—
944 8	**Premier Generation (IRE)** (DWPArbuthnot) **3-10-12** ILawrence (mstke 3rd: hdwy 4th: wknd 5th)	nk	**19**	66/1	—	—
	Petros Pride (MJBolton) **3-10-7** PHide (bhd whn blnd 2nd: t.o whn p.u bef 5th)		**P**	66/1	—	—
402 2	**Bright Eclipse (USA)** (MissKWhitehouse) **3-10-7(5)** ChrisWebb (bhd fr 4th: t.o whn p.u bef 3 out)		**P**	66/1	—	—

(SP 135.2%) **21 Rn**

3m 58.8 (8.80) CSF £41.75 TOTE £11.10: £2.30 £2.30 £1.60 (£22.70) Trio £26.80 OWNER Mr T. M. Hely-Hutchinson (WELLINGTON) BRED Rathbarry Stud

White Sea (IRE), winner of a mile and a half handicap on the Flat this year for Paul Cole, made a very pleasing debut over hurdles. In front soon after halfway, she had no problems asserting her authority from the second last for a very decisive victory. The Finale Hurdle at Chepstow is now a possibility. (7/1)

1269* Shooting Light (IRE) once again looked in very good shape but was unable to reel in the winner. He too may go for the Finale Hurdle at Chepstow. (5/1)

Summer Spell (USA), who finished third in a listed race at Goodwood for Roger Charlton on the Flat, was certainly the best of these on Flat form. Despite being only lightly-made for this game, he should soon pick up a race, especially if it is soft - his only victory on the Flat came with some cut. (2/1: 6/4-5/2)

Samakaan (IRE), an ex-Irish colt who won twice for John Oxx, made a pleasing debut, racing in the front rank before tapped for toe from the second last. He should soon find a race. (5/1: 5/2-6/1)

1014 Le Teteu (FR) chased the leaders, but never looked like quickening up over the last three hurdles. (13/2)

1269 Pleasureland (IRE) was being pushed along in the back straight, but never looked like getting into the action. He may be worth trying over further. (20/1)

1635 OXFORDSHIRE NOVICES' CHASE (5-Y.O+) (Class C)
1-30 (1-31) **3m (18 fncs)** £4,627.00 (£1,396.00: £678.00: £319.00) GOING: 0.43 sec per fur (GS)

	Horse	Dist	Pos	SP	RR	SF
	Hatcham Boy (IRE) (DNicholson) **6-11-3** AMaguire (hdwy 10th: led 3 out tl j.lft & hdd last: hrd rdn: led flat: r.o wl)	—	**1**	8/1	112	31
	Welcome Call (IRE) (OSherwood) **6-11-3** JOsborne (j.rt: chsd ldr fr 4th: led 10th to 3 out: led last tl flat: unable qckn)	1½	**2**	10/11 1	111	30
1326 4	**Wisley Wonder (IRE) (122)** (NATwiston-Davies) **6-11-3** CLlewellyn (lw: led tl j.slowly & hdd 10th: hrd rdn appr 2 out: r.o one pce)	1	**3**	7/1 3	110	29
	Act of Faith (NAGaselee) **6-11-3** WMarston (blnd 1st: hdwy 12th: rdn appr 2 out: one pce)	2	**4**	8/1	109	28
1320 2	**Madison County (IRE)** (PJHobbs) **6-11-3** RDunwoody (hdwy 12th: hrd rdn appr 2 out: wknd appr last)	14	**5**	5/1 2	100	19
1376*	**Blasket Hero (100)** (MrsSDWilliams) **8-11-7b** BFenton (a bhd: mstke 3rd: t.o whn p.u bef 3 out)		**P**	20/1	—	—
1447 4	**Newtown Rosie (IRE)** (MissAEEmbiricos) **7-10-12** JRyan (prom to 4th: t.o whn p.u bef 9th: b.b.v)		**P**	33/1	—	—
	Claymore Lad (JSKing) **6-11-3** PHide (bit bkwd: chsd ldr to 4th: wknd 14th: t.o whn p.u bef 3 out)		**P**	100/1	—	—

(SP 112.5%) **8 Rn**

6m 11.6 (21.60) CSF £14.99 TOTE £10.40: £2.00 £1.20 £1.60 (£9.20) OWNER Mr Robert Benton (TEMPLE GUITING) BRED Aiden Murphy

OFFICIAL EXPLANATION **Newtown Rosie (IRE): bled from the nose.**

Hatcham Boy (IRE) moved into a narrow lead three out, but he jumped out to his left at the final fence, giving away the advantage. It looked as though he had thrown the race away, but Maguire got down to work on the gelding and the combination managed to get back up. (8/1)

Welcome Call (IRE) is extremely well regarded and this chasing debut was eagerly awaited. Jumping more and more out to his right in the second half of the race, he nevertheless led at the tenth but, once again jumping right out to the right, lost the advantage at the third last. Nevertheless, he was back in front again at the final fence before worried out of it on the flat. His trainer reported afterwards that the gelding finished distressed. A big, powerful individual who has chaser written all over him, he still looks a very exciting prospect and should soon bounce back from this defeat. (10/11: 5/4-4/5)

1326 Wisley Wonder (IRE) took the field along, but almost came to a grinding halt at the tenth and, jumping really slowly, only just got over the fence. Not surprisingly, he lost the advantage and considerable ground, but he steadily worked his way back into the action and stayed on well for third prize. (7/1)

Act of Faith, making his chasing debut, took closer order at the twelfth, but failed to quicken over the last three fences. (8/1: 6/1-9/1)

1320 Madison County (IRE) showed promise here recently which makes this performance rather disappointing. Maybe this trip is beyond him. (5/1)

1636 BRIMPTON H'CAP HURDLE (0-140) (4-Y.O+) (Class B)

2-00 (2-03) **2m 110y (8 hdls)** £4,900.00 (£1,480.00: £720.00: £340.00) GOING: 0.43 sec per fur (GS)

				SP	RR	SF
	Mister Morose (IRE) (128) (NATwiston-Davies) **6-11-4** CLlewellyn (chsd ldr: led 2 out: r.o wl)	—	**1**	14/1	123+	39
1502*	**Chai-Yo (115)** (JABOld) **6-10-5**[5x] GUpton (stdy hdwy appr 2 out: r.o flat)	8	**2**	5/2[1]	102	18
	Intermagic (110) (JCFox) **6-10-0** SFox (bit bkwd: led: clr 2nd: hdd 2 out: unable qckn)	1¾	**3**	25/1	96	12
1201[3]	**Cadougold (FR) (123)** (MCPipe) **5-10-13** CFSwan (rdn appr 2 out: hdwy appr last: one pce)	3½	**4**	10/1	105	21
	Bolivar (IRE) (114) (RAkehurst) **4-9-13**(5) SRyan (prom tl appr 2 out)	18	**5**	8/1[3]	79	—
	Abbey Street (IRE) (122) (OSherwood) **4-10-12** JOsborne (hld up: rdn 3 out: sn wknd)	6	**6**	15/2[2]	81	—
1271[F]	**Kingsfold Pet (135)** (MJHaynes) **7-11-11** DSkyrme (bhd fr 3 out)	16	**7**	12/1	78	—
	Master Tribe (IRE) (120) (MrsJPitman) **6-10-10** WMarston (bit bkwd: bhd fr 3 out)	21	**8**	12/1	43	—
1340[3]	**Thinking Twice (USA) (138)** (NJHenderson) **7-12-0** MAFitzgerald (bhd fr 4th: t.o)	dist	**9**	25/1	—	—
	Edelweis du Moulin (FR) (127) (FMurphy) **4-11-3** RDunwoody (lw: 6th whn fell 3 out)		**F**	5/2[1]	—	—
				(SP 118.9%)	**10 Rn**	

4m 3.0 (13.00) CSF £47.49 CT £808.88 TOTE £19.00: £3.40 £1.70 £4.40 (£35.10) Trio £185.80 OWNER Mrs J. Mould (CHELTENHAM) BRED Mrs S. Brennan

LONG HANDICAP Intermagic 9-10

Mister Morose (IRE) made the perfect return to action, leading at the second last and forging clear for a very decisive victory. (14/1: 10/1-16/1)

1502* Chai-Yo, winner of both his starts this season, is set to rise another 5lb in future handicaps. Given a quiet ride, he gradually crept closer in the straight and ran on nicely to secure second prize. (5/2)

Intermagic, not looking fully wound up for this reappearance, attempted to run his field ragged and soon had a clear advantage. Collared two out, he was soon put in his place, but did manage to hold on for third prize. (25/1)

1201 Cadougold (FR), bustled along in the straight, stayed on for fourth without posing a threat. (10/1)

Bolivar (IRE) (8/1: 6/1-9/1)

Master Tribe (IRE) (12/1: 8/1-14/1)

Edelweis du Moulin (FR), considered a Champion Hurdle outsider, only got round twice last season from four starts and did not have much luck on this return. (5/2: 7/4-11/4)

1637 JACKY UPTON H'CAP CHASE (0-145) (5-Y.O+) (Class B)

2-30 (2-31) **2m 4f (16 fncs)** £7,488.20 (£2,110.40: £1,025.20) GOING: 0.43 sec per fur (GS)

				SP	RR	SF
1272[2]	**Golden Spinner (125)** (NJHenderson) **9-11-0** MAFitzgerald (lw: mstke 1st: chsd ldr fr 8th: led 12th: comf)	—	**1**	4/1[2]	132+	31
	Around the Horn (135) (JTGifford) **9-11-10** SMcNeill (hld up: chsd wnr appr 3 out: no imp)	9	**2**	10/1	135	34
1287[P]	**Well Briefed (122)** (RHBuckler) **9-10-11** BPowell (led to 12th: 2nd whn mstke 4 out: wknd 3 out)	8	**3**	25/1	115	14
	River Bounty (126) (CPEBrooks) **10-11-1** GBradley (hld up: blnd 10th: 5th & btn whn b.d 4 out)		**B**	7/1	—	—
1366[7]	**Strong Medicine (134)** (KCBailey) **9-11-9** JAMcCarthy (mstke 2nd: hdwy 12th: 4th whn fell 4 out)		**F**	6/1[3]	—	—
	Go Universal (IRE) (134) (CPEBrooks) **8-11-9** DGallagher (chsd ldr to 8th: wknd 10th: 6th & no ch whn fell 4 out)		**F**	15/2	—	—
	Major Summit (IRE) (134) (JTGifford) **7-11-9** PHide (a.p: 3rd whn blnd & uns rdr 12th)		**U**	10/11[1]	—	—
				(SP 123.9%)	**7 Rn**	

5m 12.3 (17.30) CSF £39.47 CT £831.45 TOTE £4.60: £1.90 £3.90 (£17.40) Trio £46.60 OWNER Mrs Hugh Maitland-Jones (LAMBOURN) BRED Mrs C. I. Henty

1272 Golden Spinner jumped into the lead at the Cross Fence, five out, and comfortably had the measure of his two remaining rivals in the straight. (4/1: 3/1-9/2)

Around the Horn moved into second place approaching the third last, but could not master the winner. (10/1: op 6/1)

Well Briefed, in front to the fifth last, had been hung out to dry three from home. (25/1)

1272* Strong Medicine took closer order at the Cross Fence, five out, and was in fourth place when coming to grief at the next. (6/1: op 4/1)

Go Universal (IRE) (15/2: 5/1-8/1)

Major Summit (IRE), looking in good shape for his reappearance, was travelling really well in third place when blundering away his rider at the Cross Fence, five out. Compensation awaits. (10/11: evens-5/4)

1638 NEWBURY SHOPPING ARCADE NOVICES' CONDITIONAL H'CAP HURDLE (0-110) (4-Y.O+) (Class E)

3-00 (3-01) **2m 5f (11 hdls)** £2,880.00 (£805.00: £390.00) GOING: 0.43 sec per fur (GS)

				SP	RR	SF
1429[4]	**Allow (IRE) (86)** (BLlewellyn) **5-10-10** DJKavanagh (lw: hdwy 3 out: hrd rdn appr last: led flat: r.o wl)	—	**1**	6/1	74	10
1317[4]	**The Captain's Wish (102)** (DNicholson) **5-11-9**(3) RMassey (hld up: led appr 3 out tl flat: unable qckn)	3	**2**	3/1[1]	88	24
	Wreckless Man (84) (JABOld) **9-10-0**(8) EGreehy (bit bkwd: hdwy 3 out: wknd appr last)	nk	**3**	20/1	70	6
1327[3]	**Time Leader (76)** (RDickin) **4-9-4**(10) XAizpuru (hdwy 8th: ev ch 3 out: wknd appr last)	9	**4**	16/1	55	—
1334*	**Honey Mount (90)** (NJHWalker) **5-11-0** GuyLewis (hld up: ev ch 2 out: wknd appr last)	6	**5**	4/1[2]	64	—
978*	**Crown Ivory (NZ) (76)** (PCRitchens) **8-10-0** TDascombe (hdwy 7th: wknd 3 out)	nk	**6**	12/1	50	—
1165*	**Bayerd (IRE) (100)** (CREgerton) **5-11-10** LAspell (hld up: rdn 3 out: sn wknd)	10	**7**	8/1	66	2
1323[3]	**Hydemilla (78)** (MrsTDPilkington) **6-10-2** GHogan (led tl appr 3 out: sn wknd)	14	**8**	12/1	34	—
1278[5]	**Vendoon (IRE) (76)** (MJHeaton-Ellis) **6-10-0** KGaule (chsd ldr: ev ch 3 out: sn wknd)	23	**9**	9/2[3]	14	—
1135[F]	**Lyphard's Fable (USA) (76)** (TRGeorge) **5-9-4**(10) CHynes (bit bkwd: mstke 5th: a bhd: t.o)	30	**10**	25/1	—	—
1322[4]	**Bite the Bullet (76)** (AJChamberlain) **5-10-0** OBurrows (prom to 7th: t.o)		**11**	25/1	—	—
	Dissolve (77) (NMLampard) **4-10-1** ChrisWebb (bkwd: prom to 5th: t.o)		**12**	50/1	—	—
	Smart Rebal (IRE) (79) (JAkehurst) **8-10-0**(3)ow3 MBerry (p.u bef 5th: dead)		**P**	66/1	—	—
				(SP 125.8%)	**13 Rn**	

5m 16.7 (22.70) CSF £24.23 CT £325.65 TOTE £8.10: £2.10 £1.80 £3.70 (£17.10) Trio £93.30 OWNER Mrs M. Llewellyn (SWANSEA) BRED M. Kura

LONG HANDICAP Time Leader 9-8 Crown Ivory (NZ) 9-9 Lyphard's Fable (USA) 9-12 Bite the Bullet 8-8 Smart Rebal (IRE) 9-1

1174* Allow (IRE) stays well and, gradually reeling in the leaders, managed to get on top on the run-in. (6/1)

1317 The Captain's Wish appreciated this longer trip and moved to the front approaching the third last. He appeared to be travelling much better than the winner, but that rival eventually managed to wear him down on the run-in. (3/1)

Wreckless Man, looking as though this reappearance would do him good, stylishly moved into the action three from home, but had come to the end of his tether going to the final flight. (20/1)

1327 Time Leader, one of several with every chance early in the straight, had shot his bolt approaching the last. (16/1)

1334* Honey Mount threw down his challenge in the straight, but had come to the end of his tether approaching the final flight. (4/1)

1165* Bayerd (IRE) (8/1: 11/2-9/1)

1639 SONNING NOVICES' HURDLE (4-Y.O+) (Class C)
3-30 (3-33) **3m 110y (12 hdls)** £3,727.00 (£1,126.00: £548.00: £259.00) GOING: 0.43 sec per fur (GS)

				SP	RR	SF
	Yahmi (IRE) (116) (JABOld) **6-11-0** JOsborne (a.gng wl: hld up: led appr last: easily)	—	**1**	5/2 2	92+	20
1476 4	**Menesonic (IRE)** (RHAlner) **6-10-11**(3) PHenley (lw: a.p: led appr 3 out tl appr last: unable qckn)	11	**2**	20/1	85	13
1368 2	**Herbert Lodge (IRE) (110)** (KCBailey) **7-11-5** GBradley (stdy hdwy 9th: ev ch appr last: one pce)	4	**3**	9/4 1	87	15
	Jobsagoodun (NJHenderson) **5-11-0** JRKavanagh (bit bkwd: hdwy 9th: ev ch appr 2 out: one pce)	1¾	**4**	50/1	81	9
1132 2	**Riding Crop (IRE)** (NJHenderson) **6-11-0** MAFitzgerald (prom tl appr 2 out)	4	**5**	12/1	78	6
	I'm A Chippy (IRE) (GBBalding) **6-11-0** BFenton (nvr nr to chal)	8	**6**	16/1	73	1
	Deel Quay (IRE) (KCBailey) **5-11-0** JAMcCarthy (bit bkwd: a mid div)	3	**7**	50/1	71	—
1322 3	**Percy Thrower (105)** (NATwiston-Davies) **9-11-10** CLlewellyn (led to 6th: cl up tl wknd 3 out)	3	**8**	10/1	79	7
	Maurachas (IRE) (MrsJPitman) **6-11-0** WMarston (s.s: a t.o)	dist	**9**	20/1	—	—
1322 F	**Canton Venture (98)** (SPCWoods) **4-11-5** AMaguire (hdwy 8th: wknd 9th: t.o)	10	**10**	12/1	—	—
1323 P	**Dextra (IRE)** (SEarle) **6-11-0** ILawrence (lw: bhd fr 6th: t.o)	12	**11**	66/1	—	—
	Chatergold (IRE) (APJarvis) **4-11-0** CFSwan (a bhd: t.o)	nk	**12**	33/1	—	—
1191 2	**Quaff (IRE)** (JTGifford) **6-11-0** PHide (bhd fr 3 out: p.u bef last)		**P**	11/2 3	—	—
1369 5	**Lookingforarainbow (IRE)** (BobJones) **8-11-0** VSmith (a.p: led 6th tl appr 3 out: sn wknd: t.o whn p.u bef 2 out)		**P**	25/1	—	—
	Butchers Minstrel (JSMoore) **4-11-0** WMcFarland (a bhd: t.o whn p.u bef 9th)		**P**	66/1	—	—
	Drum Battle (95) (WGMTurner) **4-11-0** GUpton (bit bkwd: chsd ldr to 6th: wknd 8th: t.o whn p.u bef 3 out)		**P**	25/1	—	—
				(SP 132.1%)	**16 Rn**	

6m 10.3 (24.30) CSF £52.17 TOTE £3.60: £1.40 £6.10 £2.10 (£59.30) Trio £93.80 OWNER Mr W. E. Sturt (WROUGHTON) BRED Barronstown Stud

WEIGHT FOR AGE 4yo-1lb

Yahmi (IRE) made a very pleasing reappearance. Always travelling supremely well, he cruised into the lead approaching the final flight and sprinted away on the run-in to win with a ton in hand. Further success awaits him. (5/2)

1476 Menesonic (IRE) moved to the front approaching the third last but, collared by the winner going to the final flight, was well and truly put in his place. (20/1)

1368 Herbert Lodge (IRE) seemed very much at home over this much longer trip and cruised into the action turning out of the back straight. With every chance going to the final flight, he then failed to find another gear. (9/4)

Jobsagoodun, who looked as though the run would do him good, was close enough if good enough going to the penultimate hurdle before tapped for toe. (50/1)

1132 Riding Crop (IRE) played an active role until coming to the end of his tether approaching the second last. (12/1: op 8/1)

1322 Canton Venture (12/1: 8/1-14/1)

T/Jkpt: Not won; £5,744.69 to Newbury 30/11/96. T/Plpt: £112.90 (192.47 Tckts). T/Qdpt: £36.80 (46.56 Tckts). AK

1438-HAYDOCK (L-H) (Good)
Saturday November 30th
WEATHER: fine & sunny

1640 WHITE LODGE 'N.H.' NOVICES' HURDLE (4-Y.O+) (Class C)
1-10 (1-10) **2m 4f (10 hdls)** £3,875.00 (£1,175.00: £575.00: £275.00) GOING: 0.53 sec per fur (GS)

				SP	RR	SF
1161 2	**Shanavogh (101)** (GMMoore) **5-11-3** JCallaghan (trckd ldrs: led 2 out: hrd rdn & edgd lft flat: hld on)	—	**1**	9/1	78	31
1290 U	**Swanbister (IRE) (92)** (LLungo) **6-11-3** RFarrant (a.p: led 3 out to 2 out: rallied u.p flat)	½	**2**	10/1	78	31
1339*	**Rangitikei (NZ) (103)** (CJMann) **5-11-8** JRailton (lw: hld up in tch: ev ch 3 out: rdn appr next: one pce)	8	**3**	11/2 3	76	29
1245 2	**Paperising** (GRichards) **4-10-12** BHarding (hld up: hit 5th: hdwy 7th: nt rch ldrs)	2½	**4**	9/2 2	64	17
1052 4	**Rothari** (BSRothwell) **4-10-12** DGallagher (prom: j.rt 7th: wknd 3 out)	13	**5**	20/1	54	7
	Glenbower (MDHammond) **4-10-9**(3) MrCBonner (bkwd: hld up: sme hdwy fr 3 out: hit next: nvr nrr)	3	**6**	33/1	51	4
1260 2	**Hurdante (IRE)** (GBBalding) **6-10-12** BFenton (lw: led to 3 out: sn rdn & wknd)	7	**7**	11/8 1	46	—
	Grand Cru (MrsMReveley) **5-10-9**(3) GCahill (bit bkwd: nvr nr ldrs)	9	**8**	16/1	39	—
1368 4	**Foxies Lad** (NMBabbage) **5-10-12** VSlattery (a in rr)	6	**9**	9/1	34	—
	Adib (USA) (GMMoore) **6-10-12** NBentley (bit bkwd: mid div tl wknd appr 3 out: t.o)	5	**10**	33/1	30	—
	Reluckino (JGMO'Shea) **6-10-5**(7) JTNolan (bkwd: a bhd: t.o)	¾	**11**	25/1	29	—
1250 12	**Seven Potato More (IRE)** (SirJohnBarlowBt) **6-10-12** JBurke (bkwd: chsd ldrs to 6th: sn wknd: t.o)	13	**12**	33/1	19	—
	The Other Man (IRE) (MissLCSiddall) **6-10-12** AThornton (bkwd: a bhd: t.o)	4	**13**	33/1	16	—
1536 8	**Lothian Commander** (DMcCain) **4-10-12** DBridgwater (bkwd: trckd ldrs to 7th: sn wknd: t.o)	½	**14**	25/1	15	—
	Noquita (NZ) (JCMcConnochie) **9-10-12** MSharratt (bkwd: a bhd: t.o)	dist	**15**	33/1	—	—
	Silver Grove (JJO'Neill) **6-10-7**(5) RMcGrath (bkwd: a in rr: t.o whn blnd & uns rdr last)		**U**	25/1	—	—
				(SP 141.7%)	**16 Rn**	

4m 56.6 (19.60) CSF £98.61 TOTE £15.20: £3.00 £2.50 £2.00 (£67.60) Trio £38.20 OWNER Mr Sean Graham (MIDDLEHAM) BRED Brick Kiln Stud Farm

1161 Shanavogh had to fight hard to hold on nearing the finish after looking well in control at the last, but he did veer over towards the far rail and no doubt forfeited ground by doing so. (9/1)

Swanbister (IRE), well suited by a true test of stamina, was fairly eating up ground on this long run-in, but the post was always going to arrive too soon. Losses are merely lent. (10/1)

1339* Rangitikei (NZ) did not quite last home over this longer trip after travelling really well at the penultimate flight. He can soon return to winning ways. (11/2: 4/1-6/1)

1245 Paperising, attempting to come from off the pace inside the final mile, could not muster the speed to get to terms. (9/2: 3/1-5/1)

1052 Rothari showed plenty of promise on this hurdling debut and, with this experience sharpening him up, will soon be improving on this. (20/1)

Glenbower, making a belated racecourse debut, was beginning to realise what was required in the latter stages and should be able to go on from here. (33/1)

1260 Hurdante (IRE) again did too much too soon and had kept nothing in reserve for a final battle. Experience will settle him. (11/8)

1641 RAINFORD H'CAP CHASE (0-115) (5-Y.O+) (Class E)

1-40 (1-40) **2m 4f (15 fncs)** £3,176.25 (£960.00: £467.50: £221.25) GOING: 0.53 sec per fur (GS)

				SP	RR	SF
1578^{5}	**Wayuphill (87)** (JJO'Neill) **9-9-10**$^{(5)}$ RMcGrath (j.w: hld up: hdwy to ld 2 out: sn clr: impressive)	—	1	9/1^{3}	101+	14
1373^{2}	**Mr President (IRE) (102)** (CPEBrooks) **7-11-2** DGallagher (w.r.s: wl bhd tl hdwy 7th: wnt 2nd 4 out: wknd appr 2 out)	16	2	Evens^{1}	103	16
1279^{F}	**Sailor Jim (110)** (PTDalton) **9-11-10** BHarding (lw: j.w: led to 2 out: sn rdn & btn)	½	3	4/1^{2}	111	24
1244^{2}	**Crafty Chaplain (100)** (DMcCain) **10-11-0** DBridgwater (j.w: plld hrd: prom tl outpcd appr 2 out)	4	4	4/1^{2}	98	11
	Nickle Joe (105) (MTate) **10-11-5** WMarston (bkwd: prom: pushed along ½-wy: wknd 10th: t.o)	dist	5	14/1	—	—
				(SP 106.7%)		**5 Rn**

5m 17.8 (20.80) CSF £17.47 TOTE £9.50: £2.30 £1.10 (£4.90) OWNER Mr D. Phelan (PENRITH)

1578 Wayuphill appreciated this easier track and more patient tactics and, taking advantage of her lenient handicap mark, had no trouble brushing aside these rivals. (9/1)

1373 Mr President (IRE) was in no hurry to take up a prominent position at the start, but he whipped round as the tape was released and must have lost all of fifteen to twenty lengths. (Evens)

1119 Sailor Jim jumped these big fences as well as ever, but the winner had taken his measure at the second last and the weight concession soon told. (4/1)

1244 Crafty Chaplain, restrained under a strong hold, found the quickening tempo more than he could cope with on the run to the penultimate fence. (4/1)

1642 PETER RICHARDSON HALF CENTURY CLAIMING HURDLE (4-Y.O+) (Class F)

2-10 (2-10) **2m 4f (10 hdls)** £2,193.50 (£616.00: £300.50) GOING: 0.53 sec per fur (GS)

				SP	RR	SF
1176^{4}	**Out Ranking (FR) (112)** (MCPipe) **4-11-0**$^{(7)}$ BMoore (j.rt: mde all: clr whn hit last)	—	1	9/4^{2}	93	30
	Roberty Lea (127) (MrsMReveley) **8-11-9**$^{(3)}$ GCahill (bkwd: chsd wnr fr 3rd: drvn along appr 3 out: no imp)	8	2	7/4^{1}	92	29
1439^{5}	**Eurotwist (112)** (SEKettlewell) **7-10-11**$^{(3)}$ GLee (hld up in tch: effrt 3 out: no imp)	5	3	4/1^{3}	76	13
971^{8}	**Dominion's Dream (98)** (MCPipe) **4-10-5v**$^{(7)}$ GSupple (hld up in rr: styd on fr 2 out: nvr nrr)	2½	4	12/1	72	9
	Ifallelsefails (94) (LLungo) **8-10-10**$^{(7)}$ IJardine (bkwd: bhd: pushed along 4th: hdwy 7th: wknd fr 3 out)	14	5	16/1	65	2
	Kadari (97) (WClay) **7-10-6v** AThornton (bit bkwd: prom tl wknd 3 out: t.o)	dist	6	15/2	—	—
1327^{P}	**Sweet Trentino (IRE) (83)** (MTate) **5-10-11** WMarston (bkwd: hld up: hit 7th: sn lost tch: t.o)	dist	7	16/1	—	—
				(SP 118.4%)		**7 Rn**

4m 57.9 (20.90) CSF £6.77 TOTE £3.40: £2.10 £1.40 (£3.70) OWNER Knight Hawks Partnership (WELLINGTON) BRED Jacques Beres

904 Out Ranking (FR) made her first attempt at the trip a winning one with a smooth all-the-way success, but she did enjoy the edge in fitness and not too much should be made of the way in which she achieved it. (9/4)

Roberty Lea has not won a race for two years and he did look very much in need of this pipe-opener. He performed with promise and the ability is still there. (7/4: 11/10-2/1)

1439 Eurotwist, always finding the pace too hot, did not fire at all and possibly needs more cut than he had here. (4/1)

Dominion's Dream never got into the race at all, but she did stay on, and is capable of better. (12/1)

1643 TIM MOLONY MEMORIAL H'CAP CHASE (0-140) (5-Y.O+) (Class B)

2-40 (2-40) **3m 4f 110y (22 fncs)** £6,729.50 (£2,036.00: £993.00: £471.50) GOING: 0.53 sec per fur (GS)

				SP	RR	SF
1293*	**Parsons Boy (120)** (GRichards) **7-10-8** BHarding (lw: hld up: drvn to chal 3 out: led after next: drew clr flat)	—	1	13/8^{2}	127	17
1469*	**Class of Ninetytwo (IRE) (125)** (CaptTAForster) **7-10-13** AThornton (lw: led: hit 2 out: sn hdd & btn)	9	2	11/8^{1}	127	17
1162^{5}	**High Padre (125)** (JGFitzGerald) **10-10-10**$^{(3)}$ FLeahy (bit bkwd: prom: hit 10th: outpcd 16th: styd on again fr 2 out)	1½	3	7/1	126	16
	Diamond Fort (112) (JCMcConnochie) **11-10-0** RFarrant (bkwd: dropped rr 9th: t.o fr 17th)	dist	4	16/1	—	—
	Killeshin (133) (HJManners) **10-11-7** SCurran (bkwd: hld up & bhd: j.slowly 4th & 14th: sn rdn: t.o fr 17th)	16	5	11/2^{3}	—	—
				(SP 114.0%)		**5 Rn**

7m 36.2 (31.20) CSF £4.31 TOTE £2.30: £1.60 £1.10 (£2.00) OWNER Mr B. Ridge (PENRITH) BRED Bretton Bloodstock Plc

LONG HANDICAP Diamond Fort 9-11

1293* Parsons Boy, a very progressive chaser still ahead of the Handicapper, stayed extremely well and showed these big fences hold no fears for him. At this stage of his career, the sky is the limit. (13/8)

1469* Class of Ninetytwo (IRE) tried hard to burn off his rivals by setting a strong gallop, and the winner was the only one able to stay with him, but he began to tire once in line for home and had shot his bolt when untidy at the second last. (11/8)

1162 High Padre found his form in the early part of last season, but still looked to need this run to put an edge on him. Losing touch with the principals down the back straight, he stayed on strongly once he had got his second wind and will be the one to beat from now on. (7/1)

1644 MAKERFIELD NOVICES' CHASE (5-Y.O+) (Class D)

3-10 (3-12) **2m (12 fncs)** £3,740.00 (£1,130.00: £550.00: £260.00) GOING: 0.53 sec per fur (GS)

				SP	RR	SF
	Oat Couture (LLungo) **8-11-0** AThornton (bit bkwd: a.p: led & hit 2 out: drifted lft flat: all out)	—	1	10/1	100	45
1257^{3}	**Naiysari (IRE) (105)** (PMRich) **8-11-0** WMarston (j.w: led: rdn 3 out: hdd next: rallied u.p flat)	1½	2	6/1	99	44
	Garolo (FR) (CPEBrooks) **6-11-0** DGallagher (racd wd: a chsng ldrs: ev ch 2 out: sn rdn: one pce)	1½	3	100/30^{3}	97	42
	Speedwell Prince (IRE) (NATwiston-Davies) **6-11-0** DBridgwater (bkwd: swvd lft s: nt j.w: chsd ldrs fr 5th tl wknd 4 out: t.o)	dist	4	9/4^{2}	—	—
1346^{2}	**Bold Boss** (GMMoore) **7-11-0** NBentley (hld up: mstke 4th: sn wl bhd: hmpd 7th: nt rcvr: t.o)	dist	5	15/8^{1}	—	—
1449^{8}	**The Fence Shrinker (60)** (DMcCain) **5-11-0** BHarding (hld up: mstke 5th: fell 7th)		F	33/1	—	—
				(SP 114.9%)		**6 Rn**

4m 7.3 (12.30) CSF £59.37 TOTE £10.00: £2.70 £2.70 (£16.00) OWNER Mackinnon Mills (CARRUTHERSTOWN) BRED Springhill Bloodstock Ltd

Oat Couture, produced fit enough to win after 579 days out of action, was certainly a feather in the cap of his trainer. Full of running when nosing ahead at the penultimate fence, he had to display his true courage to hang on as he was nearing the end of his tether close home. (10/1)

1257 Naiysari (IRE) adopted more forceful tactics and turned in a bold display of jumping from the front. Rallying under strong pressure on the flat, he went down fighting and that initial success over fences is near at hand. (6/1)

Garolo (FR) usually comes to hand early and he lost no caste in defeat on this chasing debut. He does look to be a ready-made winner. (100/30)

Speedwell Prince (IRE) was not geared up to tackling these big fences on his debut and, with lack of peak-fitness also taking its toll, he was trailing from the turn out of the back straight. (9/4)
1346 Bold Boss, settled in the rear, misjudged the water, due to the sun directly in his face, and lost quite a lot of ground. Trying to recover, he was stopped in his stride when a rival fell in front of him towards the end of the back straight and was unable to recover. This run can safely be forgotten. (15/8)

1645 HAYDOCK GOLD CARD (QUALIFIER) H'CAP HURDLE (4-Y.O+) (Class B)
3-40 (3-42) **2m 6f (12 hdls)** £4,992.75 (£1,512.00: £738.50: £351.75) GOING: 0.53 sec per fur (GS)

				SP	RR	SF
	Anzum (130) (DNicholson) **5-11-6** WMarston (prom: blnd 6th: styd on u.p to ld cl home)	—	1	13/2 2	109	44
1360*	**Burnt Imp (USA) (125)** (GMMoore) **6-11-1** JCallaghan (lw: hld up in tch: hdwy 3 out: rdn & styd on strly nr fin)	hd	2	5/1 1	104	39
1528*	**Dally Boy (110)** (TDEasterby) **4-9-11**(3) FLeahy (a.p: led 9th: clr appr last: drifted rt & hdd fnl strides)	hd	3	5/1 1	89	24
	Outset (IRE) (125) (MDHammond) **6-10-12**(3) MrCBonner (hld up gng wl: hdwy 9th: ev ch 2 out: wknd flat)	10	4	8/1 3	97	32
	Izza (110) (WStorey) **5-9-9**(5) RMcGrath (stdd s: smooth hdwy 9th: wknd appr 2 out)	17	5	8/1 3	69	4
	Allegation (137) (MCPipe) **6-11-6v**(7) BMoore (bkwd: trckd ldrs: led 7th tl hdd 9th: sn wknd: t.o)	20	6	20/1	82	17
	Beachy Head (126) (JJO'Neill) **8-11-2** AThornton (bkwd: hld up: a bhd: t.o)	5	7	16/1	67	2
1441 5	**Palosanto (IRE) (119)** (MCPipe) **6-10-9** RFarrant (lw: chsd ldrs tl wknd appr 3 out: t.o)	8	8	9/1	54	—
	Give Best (110) (JJO'Neill) **5-10-0** BHarding (hld up: hdwy appr 9th: wknd 3 out: t.o)	1¾	9	16/1	44	—
	Village Reindeer (NZ) (121) (PCalver) **9-10-11** GaryLyons (bit bkwd: a bhd: t.o: p.u bef 9th)		P	11/1	—	—
	Superior Risk (IRE) (138) (NATwiston-Davies) **7-12-0** DBridgwater (bkwd: set str pce to 5th: wknd 8th: t.o: p.u bef 3 out)		P	13/2 2	—	—
	Arabian Sultan (112) (MCPipe) **9-9-9**(7) GSupple (bkwd: plld hrd: sn chsng ldr: led 5th to 7th: wknd qckly: t.o: p.u bef 3 out)		P	16/1	—	—
				(SP 123.0%)	**12 Rn**	

5m 28.7 (18.70) CSF £37.89 CT £165.50 TOTE £5.30: £2.30 £1.80 £2.00 (£19.20) Trio £23.90 OWNER The Old Foresters Partnership (TEMPLE GUITING) BRED Cobhall Court Stud
LONG HANDICAP Give Best 9-4 Izza 9-6
Anzum has done the majority of his winning when there has been plenty of cut in the ground, but he won this due to his undoubted stamina coming into play. Marston did extremely well to keep the partnership intact when the gelding was on his knees at the sixth. (13/2: op 4/1)
1360* Burnt Imp (USA) only just failed in his attempt to complete his hat-trick, but it was a very close-run affair and he is holding his form well.(5/1)
1528* Dally Boy looked to hold all the aces when landing over the last with a healthy lead, but he tended to drift over towards the stands' rail on the flat and was worn down in the shadow of the post. (5/1)
Outset (IRE) travelled strongly just behind the leaders for most of the way and still had a live chance at the last, but he tied up rather quickly on the flat. Had he not already won at the trip, lack of stamina would have been an obvious excuse. (8/1)
Izza, fit from the Flat, closed up smoothly turning in and looked sure to take a hand in proceedings, but she was galloping on the spot between the last two and failed to go through with her effort. (8/1)
1441 Palosanto (IRE) (9/1: op 6/1)
Superior Risk (IRE) (13/2: 9/2-7/1)

T/Plpt: £72.40 (176.04 Tckts). T/Qdpt: £17.90 (46.77 Tckts). IM

1634-NEWBURY (L-H) (Good)
Saturday November 30th
WEATHER: fine

1646 FULKE WALWYN CHASE (5-Y.O+) (Class C)
12-45 (12-45) **2m 4f (16 fncs)** £5,920.00 (£1,780.00: £860.00: £400.00) GOING: 0.37 sec per fur (GS)

				SP	RR	SF
1259 3	**Buckhouse Boy (122)** (NATwiston-Davies) **6-11-0** CMaude (bdly hmpd 1st: sn chsng clr ldr: lft clr 9th: mstke 11th: unchal)	—	1	5/2 1	120+	49
	Foodbroker Star (IRE) (JTGifford) **6-11-0** PHide (bit bkwd: hld up: styd on to go 2nd last: no ch w wnr)	25	2	20/1	100+	29
	Take the Buckskin (TThomsonJones) **9-11-0** NWilliamson (bit bkwd: blnd 3rd: no hdwy fr 4 out)	3	3	9/2 2	98+	27
1320 3	**Court Master (IRE)** (RHBuckler) **8-11-0** BPowell (lw: hld up: chsd wnr fr 9th: no imp: wkng whn mstke last)	6	4	10/1	93	22
	Garnwin (IRE) (NJHenderson) **6-11-0** MAFitzgerald (bkwd: b.d 1st)		B	12/1	—	—
	Two John's (IRE) (PFNicholls) **7-11-0** CFSwan (bit bkwd: led tl fell 1st)		F	6/1	—	—
	Art Prince (IRE) (CPEBrooks) **6-11-0** GBradley (lft in ld 1st: clr tl fell 9th)		F	12/1	—	—
	Proud Toby (IRE) (GBBalding) **6-11-0** BClifford (bkwd: bhd: blnd 9th: t.o whn p.u bef 12th)		P	16/1	—	—
	Colonel In Chief (IRE) (FMurphy) **6-11-0** JOsborne (bit bkwd: hld up: hit 2nd: poor 4th whn blnd 12th: p.u bef 4 out)		P	11/2 3	—	—
1328 4	**Brown Robber (71)** (MrsRGHenderson) **8-11-0** GUpton (bhd: mstkes 5th & 7th: t.o whn p.u bef 12th)		P	66/1	—	—
				(SP 113.0%)	**10 Rn**	

5m 6.0 (11.00) CSF £42.58 TOTE £2.80: £1.60 £4.50 £1.60 (£36.20) Trio £37.40 OWNER The Bawtry Boys (CHELTENHAM) BRED J. A. Taylor
1259 Buckhouse Boy has been waiting for some give in the ground. After nearly being brought down at the first, he had things all his own way once left clear. (5/2)
Foodbroker Star (IRE) made a reasonable-enough start to his chasing career and a longer trip should help. (20/1)
Take the Buckskin, graduating to fences, made a mess of the first ditch and was a bit awkward at the water. He should be better for the experience, but will need three miles. (9/2)
1320 Court Master (IRE), continuing on the comeback trail following a problem with a fetlock joint, has won between the flags in Ireland. (10/1)
Garnwin (IRE) (12/1: 8/1-14/1)
Art Prince (IRE), placed in Irish bumpers, had won two Irish point-to-points from nine attempts, but was only ridden by Bradley after his stable-companion came out. (12/1)
Colonel In Chief (IRE) (11/2: 4/1-6/1)

1647 EQUI LIFE WORK FORMULA LONG DISTANCE HURDLE (Gd 2) (4-Y.O+) (Class A)

1-15 (1-17) **3m 110y (12 hdls)** £12,380.00 (£4,684.00: £2,292.00: £1,044.00) GOING: 0.37 sec per fur (GS)

	Horse	Dist	Pos	SP	RR	SF
1156^{2}	**What a Question (IRE)** (MFMorris,Ireland) **8-10-9** GBradley (lw: hld up: stdy hdwy 7th: led appr 2 out: drvn out)	—	1	4/1^{2}	131	31
	Antapoura (IRE) (APO'Brien,Ireland) **4-10-8** CFSwan (lw: hld up: hdwy appr 9th: rdn 2 out: ev ch last: r.o)	1¾	2	10/1	130	29
1156*	**Trainglot (151)** (JGFitzGerald) **9-11-7** NWilliamson (hld up: hdwy appr 9th: hit 3 out: sn rdn & ev ch: edgd rt appr last: one pce)	6	3	11/8^{1}	138	38
	Minella Man (JohnNallen,Ireland) **9-11-0** FWoods (a.p: led appr 3 out: sn hdd: wkng whn nt clr run appr last)	7	4	10/1	126	26
1319^{2}	**Little Buck (IRE) (125)** (LWells) **8-11-0** SMcNeill (hld up: hdwy appr 3 out: ev ch 2 out: wknd appr last)	nk	5	25/1	126?	26
70^{P}	**Top Spin (136)** (JRJenkins) **7-11-0** BPowell (hld up: gd hdwy appr 9th: ev ch 3 out: sn wknd)	22	6	40/1	112	12
	Ruling (USA) (KRBurke) **10-11-0** ALarnach (hld up: bhd fr 9th)	7	7	40/1	107	7
1019^{2}	**Jack Button (IRE) (140)** (BobJones) **7-11-0** JOsborne (lw: led tl appr 3 out: wknd appr last: eased whn btn)	½	8	9/2^{3}	107	7
	Hebridean (150) (PRWebber) **9-11-0** MAFitzgerald (lw: chsd ldr to 8th: rallied 3 out: sn wknd)	6	9	33/1	103	3
1359^{5}	**Better Times Ahead (152)** (GRichards) **10-11-7** ADobbin (prom: rdn after 8th: sn wknd)	4	10	10/1	107	7
1196^{6}	**Dark Honey (125)** (SDow) **11-11-0** ADicken (bit bkwd: prom tl wknd 6th: t.o fr 8th)	dist	11	66/1	—	—
				(SP 120.7%)	**11 Rn**	

6m 3.4 (17.40) CSF £40.93 TOTE £5.80: £1.50 £2.40 £1.30 (£29.50) Trio £14.70 OWNER Mrs Miles Valentine (FETHARD) BRED R. A. and Mrs St George

WEIGHT FOR AGE 4yo-1lb

1156 What a Question (IRE), 7lb better off with Trainglot for an eight-length defeat at Wetherby, was able to pull out a bit more on the flat to keep the persistent runner-up at bay. (4/1: 3/1-9/2)

Antapoura (IRE), taking a big step up in class, ran a marvellous for one so young against these seasoned campaigners. Only forced to give best close home, a lot more will be heard of her. (10/1)

1156* Trainglot could not confirm an eight-length beating of the winner at Wetherby on 7lb worse terms. A tired horse on his return to the unsaddling enclosure, the feeling was he may have been dehydrated. (11/8: 2/1-5/4)

Minella Man was by no means disgraced on ground which was not really soft enough for him. (10/1: op 6/1)

1319 Little Buck (IRE) is another who really wants the ground more testing, but it should be remembered he has yet to win beyond two and a half miles. (25/1)

13 Top Spin looked much more at home back over hurdles. (40/1)

1359 Better Times Ahead (10/1: op 6/1)

1648 BONUSPRINT GERRY FEILDEN HURDLE (Gd 2) (4-Y.O+) (Class A)

1-50 (1-50) **2m 110y (8 hdls)** £13,131.00 (£4,546.00: £2,223.00) GOING: 0.37 sec per fur (GS)

	Horse	Dist	Pos	SP	RR	SF
	Zabadi (IRE) (138) (DNicholson) **4-11-6** NWilliamson (lw: hld up: wnt 2nd 5th: hrd rdn appr last: styd on to ld nr fin)	—	1	11/4^{2}	130?	34
1234a*	**Urubande (IRE)** (APO'Brien,Ireland) **6-11-6** CFSwan (led tl after 1st: led after 4th: hrd rdn flat: hdd nr fin)	½	2	4/6^{1}	130	34
1405a^{7}	**Punting Pete (IRE)** (WPMullins,Ireland) **6-11-0** GBradley (led after 1st: mstke 4th: sn hdd: wknd & eased appr 3 out)	dist	3	12/1	—	—
1369*	**Mr Percy (IRE) (118)** (JTGifford) **5-11-0** PHide (lw: hld up: 3rd whn fell 3rd)		F	11/2^{3}	—	—
				(SP 109.7%)	**4 Rn**	

4m 3.4 (13.40) CSF £4.93 TOTE £3.00 (£1.80) OWNER Lady Harris (TEMPLE GUITING) BRED The Aga Khans Studs S.C.

Zabadi (IRE), one of last season's leading juveniles, knuckled down gamely under pressure in the closing stages to really pull this one out of the fire. He is likely to have one more run before the Christmas Hurdle at Kempton. (11/4)

1234a* Urubande (IRE), dropping back to two miles, seemed to have matters well under control until possibly idling on the run-in. His trainer thinks he would have preferred a more truly-run race and will continue to campaign his charge over this trip until a decision about the gelding's Cheltenham target is made. (4/6)

Punting Pete (IRE) was reverting to hurdles after a couple of unsuccessful outings over fences in Ireland. (12/1: op 6/1)

1369* Mr Percy (IRE) (11/2: op 10/1)

1649 HENNESSY COGNAC GOLD CUP H'CAP CHASE (Gd 3) (5-Y.O+) (Class A)

2-25 (2-30) **3m 2f 110y (21 fncs)** £48,283.20 (£18,249.56: £8,914.78: £4,044.46) GOING: 0.37 sec per fur (GS)

	Horse	Dist	Pos	SP	RR	SF
1287*	**Coome Hill (IRE) (136)** (WWDennis) **7-10-0** 4x JOsborne (lw: led to 6th: led after 11th to 13th: led after 2 out: r.o wl)	—	1	11/2^{2}	153+	60
1359*	**The Grey Monk (IRE) (139)** (GRichards) **8-10-3** 4x ADobbin (lw: prom: mstke 5th: led 13th: rdn & hdd after 2 out: one pce)	4	2	13/8^{1}	154	61
	Lo Stregone (150) (TPTate) **10-11-0b** CFSwan (sn chsng ldr: led 6th to 7th: hrd rdn appr 4 out: wknd 2 out: lft 3rd last)	12	3	10/1	157	64
	Midnight Caller (137) (NoelChance) **10-10-1**ow1 MAFitzgerald (lw: mstkes: hld up: hdwy 13th: wknd 4 out)	17	4	20/1	134	40
	Dextra Dove (137) (SEarle) **9-10-1** CMaude (bit bkwd: hld up: hdwy appr 4 out: wknd appr 2 out: 4th & no ch whn blnd last)	½	5	12/1	134	41
1216a^{2}	**Feathered Gale (147)** (ALTMoore,Ireland) **9-10-11** FWoods (hld up: hit 17th: bhd whn mstke 4 out)	18	6	14/1	133	40
1454^{2}	**Old Bridge (IRE) (136)** (AndrewTurnell) **8-10-0** SMcNeill (hld up: hdwy 11th: wknd 4 out: virtually p.u flat: b.b.v)	24	7	25/1	107	14
1440^{2}	**Couldnt Be Better (160)** (CPEBrooks) **9-11-10** GBradley (bit bkwd: hld up: rdn appr 4 out: sn bhd: virtually p.u flat)	½	8	16/1	131	38
1366*	**Challenger du Luc (FR) (146)** (MCPipe) **6-10-10b** 4x NWilliamson (lw: hld up: last whn fell 14th)		F	11/2^{2}	—	—
946*	**General Crack (IRE) (136)** (PFNicholls) **7-10-0** PHide (prom tl wknd 4 out: bhd whn p.u bef 2 out)		P	7/1^{3}	—	—
1266^{5}	**Grange Brake (137)** (NATwiston-Davies) **10-9-12b**(3)ow1 DWalsh (prom: led 7th tl after 11th: ev ch 3 out: 3rd & wkng whn blnd & uns rdr last)		U	100/1	—	—
				(SP 120.3%)	**11 Rn**	

6m 40.6 (5.60) CSF £14.49 CT £82.71 TOTE £6.20: £1.80 £1.70 £2.10 (£8.40) Trio £20.00 OWNER Mrs Jill Dennis (BUDE) BRED Mrs S. O'Connell

LONG HANDICAP Coome Hill (IRE) 9-8 Old Bridge (IRE) 9-10 Midnight Caller 9-13 General Crack (IRE) 9-13 Grange Brake 9-2

OFFICIAL EXPLANATION Old Bridge (IRE): bled from the nose.

1287* Coome Hill (IRE), trained on a dairy farm, like Gold Cup winner Norton's Coin, again showed the attraction of National Hunt racing, in that the little man can occasionally compete at the highest level. With the favourite already cooked, he sealed victory with a big leap at the final fence and both trainer and jockey were subsequently talking in terms of the Grand National. (11/2)
1359* The Grey Monk (IRE) would have been set to carry 10lb more had the weights not been published early. Well placed to be unbeaten in seven races over fences, this version of the Great White Hope from Greystoke had to admit he had met one too good on the day. (13/8)
Lo Stregone ran a fine race on his seasonal reappearance and connections will no doubt again be aiming him at the Grand National, which he missed last year because of a temperature. (10/1)
Midnight Caller, lightly-raced in recent years, was let down by some of his old jumping problems. (20/1)
Dextra Dove, who ended last season with foot problems, gave a really good account of himself until tiring when lack of peak-fitness began to tell. (12/1)
1216a Feathered Gale was a stone higher than when a distance second in last season's Midlands Grand National. (14/1)
1454 Old Bridge (IRE) has yet to win beyond two and a half miles. (25/1)
1440 Couldnt Be Better, still not fully wound up, was trying to repeat last year's Hennessy win off a 13lb higher mark. (16/1)
1366* Challenger du Luc (FR), switched off in last place, had yet to make a move when coming to grief. (11/2)
1266 Grange Brake, 12lb out of the handicap, was battling it out for third and fourth when depositing his rider at the final fence. (100/1)

1650 NORTH STREET H'CAP CHASE (0-145) (5-Y.O+) (Class B)

2-55 (3-03) **2m 1f (13 fncs)** £6,845.60 (£2,064.80: £1,002.40: £471.20) GOING: 0.37 sec per fur (GS)

				SP	RR	SF
	Ask Tom (IRE) (140) (TPTate) **7-11-9** RGarritty (chsd ldr: led 4 out: clr 2 out: r.o wl)	—	**1**	7/4[1]	148+	81
1173[5]	**Nakir (FR) (140)** (DNicholson) **8-11-9** ADobbin (lw: hld up: sme hdwy appr 9th: styd on fr 2 out:no ch w wnr)	27	**2**	5/1[3]	123	56
1134[4]	**Uncle Ernie (145)** (JGFitzGerald) **11-12-0** CFSwan (hld up & bhd: chsd wnr fr 2 out: no imp)	nk	**3**	5/1[3]	127	60
	Sound Reveille (145) (CPEBrooks) **8-12-0** GBradley (led to 4 out: wknd appr 2 out: p.u bef last: continued)	dist	**4**	9/1	—	—
	Front Street (135) (OSherwood) **9-11-4** JOsborne (hld up: sme hdwy appr 9th: sn wknd: bhd whn p.u bef 2 out)		**P**	3/1[2]	—	—
1454[F]	**Bo Knows Best (IRE) (121)** (GLMoore) **7-10-4** MAFitzgerald (t.o 5th: p.u bef 9th)		**P**	12/1	—	—
				(SP 112.4%)	**6 Rn**	

4m 8.0 (4.00) CSF £10.17 TOTE £2.30: £1.60 £2.50 (£5.30) OWNER Mr B. T. Stewart-Brown (TADCASTER) BRED Capt S. H. Walford
Ask Tom (IRE), a useful novice last season, had a facile win on this transition to handicap company. Quite lightly-raced, there seems no reason why he should not continue to progress. (7/4)
1173 Nakir (FR) got up for second place near the finish and is likely to be dropped further by the Handicapper. (5/1)
1134 Uncle Ernie, dropped 2lb, looked like an old gunslinger up against a young gun at these weights. (5/1)
Sound Reveille, who has had more than his fair share of problems, could never shake off the winner and Bradley seemed keen not to unnecessarily abuse his mount. (9/1: 6/1-10/1)
Front Street has had a wind operation, but unfortunately it may not have worked. (3/1)

1651 SPEEN NOVICES' HURDLE (4-Y.O+) (Class C)

3-25 (3-33) **2m 110y (8 hdls)** £4,370.00 (£1,310.00: £630.00: £290.00) GOING: 0.37 sec per fur (GS)

				SP	RR	SF
	Hoh Warrior (IRE) (CPEBrooks) **5-11-0** GBradley (bit bkwd: hld up: hdwy appr 3 out: led flat: r.o wl)	—	**1**	50/1	92	38
1438[2]	**Queen of Spades (IRE)** (NATwiston-Davies) **6-11-5** CMaude (led to 2 out: rdn & n.m.r flat: r.o one pce)	3	**2**	9/4[1]	94	40
1427[3]	**Nordance Prince (IRE)** (MissGayKelleway) **5-10-9**(5) ABates (lw: hld up: hdwy 5th: led 2 out: sn hrd rdn: hdd flat: edgd lft: r.o one pce)	s.h	**3**	20/1	89	35
	Nasone (IRE) (JTGifford) **5-11-0** PHide (lw: hld up: hdwy appr 3 out: one pce fr 2 out)	4	**4**	7/1[2]	85	31
	Donnington (IRE) (OSherwood) **6-11-0** JOsborne (lw: hld up: sme hdwy on ins 4th: nvr nr to chal)	14	**5**	9/4[1]	72	18
	Murphy's Malt (IRE) (APO'Brien,Ireland) **4-11-10** CFSwan (hld up: hdwy 4th: ev ch 3 out: mstke 2 out: sn wknd)	5	**6**	7/1[2]	77	23
	Fairy Knight (RHannon) **4-11-0** SMcNeill (hld up: hdwy 5th: wknd 2 out)	1¾	**7**	10/1[3]	65	11
	John Drumm (PRWebber) **5-11-0** RGarritty (bit bkwd: hdwy 2nd: ev ch 3 out: wknd 2 out)	2	**8**	20/1	63	9
1394[7]	**I Recall (IRE)** (PHayward) **5-11-0** ADobbin (lw: nvr trbld ldrs)	10	**9**	66/1	53	—
	Hi Marble (IRE) (MrsMerritaJones) **5-10-9** DerekByrne (bkwd: n.d)	3½	**10**	33/1	45	—
1517[6]	**Adonisis** (DRCElsworth) **4-11-0** AProcter (lw: prom: rdn after 4th: wknd appr 3 out: t.o)	17	**11**	66/1	34	—
	English Invader (RAkehurst) **5-11-0** BPowell (hdwy 4th: wknd 3 out: t.o)	¾	**12**	25/1	33	—
1132[U]	**Lizium** (JCFox) **4-10-6**(3) DWalsh (bit bkwd: bhd fr 5th: t.o)	13	**13**	66/1	15	—
	Grand Crack (IRE) (JCFox) **4-11-0** PMcLoughlin (bit bkwd: a bhd: t.o)	1½	**14**	50/1	19	—
1427[P]	**Bryan Robson (USA)** (JWMullins) **5-11-0b[1]** BClifford (prom to 4th: t.o)	dist	**15**	66/1	—	—
	Calon Lan (IRE) (NJHenderson) **5-11-0** MAFitzgerald (bkwd: prom tl fell 3rd)		**F**	12/1	—	—
	Multan (GLMoore) **4-10-7**(7) MAttwater (plld hrd: a bhd: t.o whn p.u bef last)		**P**	50/1	—	—
	Croagh Patrick (JCFox) **4-11-0** SFox (lw: a bhd: t.o whn p.u bef last)		**P**	50/1	—	—
	Bowcliffe Court (IRE) (RAkehurst) **4-10-9**(5) SRyan (prom: p.u bef 2nd: sddle slipped)		**P**	7/1[2]	—	—
				(SP 145.9%)	**19 Rn**	

4m 1.3 (11.30) CSF £173.45 TOTE £120.90: £15.80 £1.60 £3.90 (£216.60) Trio £1,152.40; £1,460.91 to 2/12/96 OWNER Mr D. F. Allport (LAMBOURN) BRED T. Horgan
Hoh Warrior (IRE), pulled up on soft ground at Newton Abbot in May, came with a well-timed run to send the Bookmakers home happy. (50/1)
1438 Queen of Spades (IRE), adopting her usual front-running tactics, would have been awarded second place had the photo not gone her way, but the winner beat her fair and square. (9/4)
1427 Nordance Prince (IRE), who caused the second to be squeezed up against the stands' rail, can win a run-of-the-mill novice hurdle on this evidence. (20/1)
Nasone (IRE) won here in March before finishing tenth in the Festival Bumper. Never quite able to get to grips with the principals, an extra half-mile might help. (7/1)
Donnington (IRE), who won an uncompetitive bumper on firm ground at Ascot in April 1995, had a minor leg problem last season. Apparently well fancied, this has to be considered a disappointing run. (9/4: 7/2-2/1)
Murphy's Malt (IRE) had a 10lb penalty for beating a big field at Naas three weeks ago. (7/1)
Fairy Knight, fit from the Flat, made a reasonable start to his hurdling career, assuming this mile and a half winner got the trip. (10/1)
John Drumm, a dual bumper winner, will find this putting an edge on him and should last longer next time. (20/1)
Bowcliffe Court (IRE) (7/1: 5/1-8/1)

T/Jkpt: Not won; £15,713.38 to Worcester 2/12/96. T/Plpt: £30.40 (1,107.82 Tckts). T/Qdpt: £26.80 (54.96 Tckts). KH

1263-NEWCASTLE (L-H) (Good)
Saturday November 30th

One fence omitted. Hdles course altered - Hdles on Flat crse in home st
WEATHER: overcast

1652 NEWCASTLE BUILDING SOCIETY HURDLE (3-Y.O) (Class D)
12-10 (12-11) **2m (9 hdls)** £3,072.10 (£865.60: £424.30) GOING: 0.30 sec per fur (GS)

				SP	RR	SF
1158^{2}	**Jackson Park** (TDEasterby) **3-10-12** RDunwoody (lw: cl up: led 4th tl blnd & hdd 4 out: disp ld next: r.o u.p flat)	—	**1**	2/1^{1}	78	35
1184^{3}	**Son of Anshan** (MrsASwinbank) **3-10-12** MrCWilson (lw: a.p: hdwy 4 out: ev ch last: r.o)	nk	**2**	12/1	78	35
1356*	**Rossel (USA)** (PMonteith) **3-11-8** AMaguire (lw: a cl up: disp ld 4 out: no ex flat)	1	**3**	11/2^{2}	87	44
1184^{8}	**Meltemison** (MDHammond) **3-10-5**(7) RBurns (hld up: hdwy on bit 3 out: fin strly: nvr plcd to chal)	5	**4**	33/1	72+	29
	Bold Classic (IRE) (CGrant) **3-10-13**ow1 TReed (prom: kpt on one pce fr 3 out)	10	**5**	14/1	63	19
1205^{3}	**Mock Trial (IRE)** (MrsJRRamsden) **3-10-12** MrSSwiers (lw: chsd ldrs: effrt 4 out: no imp after)	s.h	**6**	11/2^{2}	62	19
646^{4}	**Northern Falcon** (MWEasterby) **3-10-7b** CLlewellyn (led to 4th: led 4 out: hdd & wknd next: blnd last)	¾	**7**	33/1	56	13
1205^{5}	**Cottage Prince (IRE)** (JJQuinn) **3-11-3** JShortt (lw: in tch: nt qckn fr 4 out)	1¼	**8**	33/1	65	22
699^{5}	**What Jim Wants (IRE)** (JJO'Neill) **3-10-12** BStorey (in tch: styd on fr 3 out)	s.h	**9**	50/1	60	17
	Nexsis Star (MrsSJSmith) **3-10-12** RichardGuest (dwlt: hdwy 4 out: nvr nr to chal)	nk	**10**	50/1	59	16
1159^{F}	**Lucky Bea** (MWEasterby) **3-10-9**(3) PMidgley (hld up & bhd: hdwy 4 out: nvr nr to chal)	nk	**11**	20/1	59	16
	Mua-Tab (MDHammond) **3-10-7** DBentley (nvr nr ldrs: dead)	¾	**12**	33/1	53	10
1514^{3}	**Onyourown (IRE)** (HowardJohnson) **3-10-7**(5) GFRyan (nvr bttr than mid div)	12	**13**	12/1	46	3
1356^{5}	**Rattle** (JJO'Neill) **3-10-5**(7) DJewett (nvr trbld ldrs)	nk	**14**	100/1	46	3
	Joe Shaw (MrsMReveley) **3-10-12** PNiven (bhd: stdy hdwy fr 4th: nvr nr to chal)	nk	**15**	33/1	46	3
1184^{5}	**Whothehellisharry** (JBerry) **3-10-12** MMoloney (lw: chsd ldrs tl outpcd fr 4 out)	½	**16**	20/1	45	2
	Bank On Inland (JRTurner) **3-10-7** WFry (a bhd)	8	**17**	100/1	32	—
906^{6}	**Eric's Bett** (FMurphy) **3-10-12** MFoster (chsd ldrs tl rdn & wknd 4 out)	nk	**18**	33/1	37	—
1158^{6}	**Prelude To Fame (USA)** (MissMKMilligan) **3-11-3** ASSmith (blnd 3rd: a bhd)	½	**19**	33/1	41	—
1158^{8}	**Hobbs Choice** (GMMoore) **3-10-9**(3) ECallaghan (bhd fr ½-wy)	2	**20**	33/1	34	—
1413^{4}	**Boy Blakeney** (MrsSJSmith) **3-10-12** MrPMurray (dwlt: a bhd)	nk	**21**	50/1	34	—
	Oversman (JGFitzGerald) **3-10-12** MDwyer (hdwy ½-wy: wknd & eased fr 4 out)	6	**22**	11/1^{3}	28	—
	Just Rory (MissZAGreen) **3-10-12** KJohnson (sn wl bhd: t.o whn p.u bef 3 out)		**P**	100/1	—	—
1356^{2}	**The Boozing Brief (USA)** (CParker) **3-10-12b** DParker (chsd ldrs tl blnd & uns rdr 4 out)		**U**	20/1	—	—
				(SP 141.2%)	**24 Rn**	

3m 53.6 (1.60) CSF £28.43 TOTE £2.30: £1.40 £6.00 £2.00 (£28.10) Trio £51.10 OWNER Mr C. H. Stevens (MALTON) BRED M. H. Easterby
STEWARDS' ENQUIRY Hammond fined £1,000, Burns susp. 9-14 & 16/12/96 & Meltemison susp. 3/12/96-1/1/97 under Rule 151 (ii) (schooling in public).

1158 Jackson Park put up a thrilling performance, especially after making a bad blunder four out, and there would seem to be better to come.(2/1)
1184 Son of Anshan ran a very good race and should soon go one better. (12/1)
1356* Rossel (USA) put up a super performance under a double penalty. (11/2)
Meltemison got a bit warm beforehand. He looked as though he would have been in the shake up with a try and the Stewards noticed this. (33/1)
Bold Classic (IRE) ran well and will probably do better over further. (14/1)
1205 Mock Trial (IRE) had his chances, but just found this company too hot in the home straight. (11/2)
646 Northern Falcon, after over two months off, did her utmost, but her measure had been taken when she really belted the last. (33/1)
699 What Jim Wants (IRE) left the impression that, over further, he should improve. (50/1)
Nexsis Star was a very moderate performer on the level, but he showed something here and is worth bearing in mind. (50/1)
Joe Shaw will improve once he gets his hurdling together. (33/1)

1653 TOMMY MCNICHOLAS NOVICES' CHASE (4-Y.O+) (Class C)
12-40 (12-44) **2m 4f (15 fncs)** £5,340.50 (£1,619.00: £792.00: £378.50) GOING: 0.30 sec per fur (GS)

				SP	RR	SF
1346*	**Sparky Gayle (IRE)** (CParker) **6-11-9** BStorey (lw: hld up: smooth hdwy ½-wy: led 11th: rdn & r.o wl flat)	—	**1**	4/6^{1}	108+	42
1264*	**Solomon's Dancer (USA)** (GRichards) **6-11-13** RDunwoody (lw: a.p: chsd ldrs fr 8th: effrt 3 out: kpt on towards fin)	2½	**2**	9/4^{2}	110	44
1348^{F}	**Blue Charm (IRE) (100)** (MrsSCBradburne) **6-11-9** AMaguire (cl up: led fr 4th: hit 7th: hdd 11th: ev ch & hit last: no ex)	2½	**3**	8/1^{3}	104	38
	Chipped Out (MartinTodhunter) **6-11-4** MDwyer (nt j.w: bhd tl hdwy 8th: nvr trbld ldrs)	20	**4**	16/1	83	17
1311^{3}	**Le Denstan (84)** (MrsDThomson) **9-11-9** TReed (mstkes 8th & 2 out: nvr trbld ldrs)	12	**5**	20/1	78	12
911^{4}	**Garbo's Boy** (JRTurner) **6-11-4** WFry (bit bkwd: mstkes: a bhd)	12	**6**	200/1	64	—
1358^{7}	**Marlingford** (MrsJJordan) **9-10-11**(7) LMcGrath (hit 1st: led 2nd to 4th: chsd ldrs tl wknd 10th)	2½	**7**	200/1	62	—
1139^{9}	**Seldom But Severe (IRE)** (EAElliott) **6-11-4** KJohnson (mstkes: a bhd)	3	**8**	200/1	59	—
1246^{5}	**More Joy (72)** (BEllison) **8-11-4** ASSmith (hit 8th: a bhd)	2½	**9**	200/1	57	—
1525^{4}	**Fingerhill (IRE)** (VThompson) **7-11-4** MrMThompson (led to 2nd: cl up tl mstke & uns rdr 10th)		**U**	100/1	—	—
				(SP 115.5%)	**10 Rn**	

5m 7.0 (14.00) CSF £2.51 TOTE £1.70: £1.00 £1.20 £2.10 (£1.50) Trio £2.90 OWNER Mr & Mrs Raymond Anderson Green (LOCKERBIE) BRED Thomas Walsh

1346* Sparky Gayle (IRE) impressed with his jumping again and did the business in good style, always having the edge from three out, but he did just leave the impression that he does not want to be in front too long. (4/6)
1264* Solomon's Dancer (USA) always looked held here but, to his credit, he kept on particularly well in the closing stages and looks likely to appreciate further. (9/4)
1264 Blue Charm (IRE) keeps running consistently well and really attacks his fences, but was always well held in the closing stages. (8/1)
Chipped Out worked a miracle in getting round in one piece as his jumping was sketchy throughout, and that needs to improve. (16/1)
1311 Le Denstan was always finding this company too hot and made mistakes. (20/1)
1525 Fingerhill (IRE) ran quite well until unshipping his rider six out. (100/1)

1654 BRULINES NOVICES' HURDLE (4-Y.O+) (Class E)

1-10 (1-15) **3m (13 hdls)** £2,536.50 (£714.00: £349.50) GOING: 0.30 sec per fur (GS)

				SP	RR	SF
	Agistment (JGFitzGerald) **5-10-12** MDwyer (lw: trckd ldrs: smooth hdwy to chal 3 out: led last: shkn up & qcknd)	—	**1**	100/30[2]	84+	41
1258[4]	**Hand Woven (123)** (NATwiston-Davies) **4-11-4** CLlewellyn (lw: led tl hdd last: kpt on)	4	**2**	2/1[1]	88	44
1290*	**Military Academy** (GRichards) **7-11-5** RDunwoody (lw: a cl up: chal 3 out: kpt on)	1¼	**3**	4/1[3]	88	45
1384[3]	**Coole Hill (IRE) (86)** (DNicholson) **5-10-7** AMaguire (lw: hdwy & prom 7th: chal appr 3 out: rdn & one pce)	11	**4**	12/1	68	25
1343[2]	**Grandinare (USA)** (JJO'Neill) **4-10-11** RichardGuest (hld up: hdwy 8th: mstke 3 out: styd on)	nk	**5**	11/1	73	29
1360[2]	**Crystal Gift (102)** (ACWhillans) **4-11-1**(3) ECallaghan (a chsng ldrs: rdn 4 out: wknd next)	14	**6**	10/1	71	27
1349[3]	**Phar Echo (IRE)** (LLungo) **5-10-12** MFoster (in tch: no real hdwy fr 4 out)	5	**7**	50/1	60	17
1290[4]	**Chill Factor** (MrsMReveley) **6-10-12** PNiven (bhd: hdwy 4 out: nvr nr to chal)	¾	**8**	66/1	60	17
1208[6]	**Menaldi (IRE)** (PCheesbrough) **6-10-12** ASSmith (bit bkwd: hdwy & prom 7th: wknd after 4 out)	3	**9**	50/1	58	15
1349[8]	**Jigginstown** (JJO'Neill) **9-10-5**(7) LCooper (wl bhd tl styd on fr 4 out)	½	**10**	200/1	58	15
911[5]	**Cool Steel (IRE) (72)** (MrsJBrown) **4-10-11** MrSSwiers (hdwy 4 out: nvr trbld ldrs)	nk	**11**	200/1	57	13
	Clongour (IRE) (FMurphy) **6-10-5**(7) MissElizabethDoyle (plld hrd: bhd tl sme late hdwy)	3	**12**	33/1	55	12
	See More Ghosts (IRE) (MrsASwinbank) **5-10-12** MrCWilson (bhd tl sme hdwy fr 4 out)	s.h	**13**	100/1	55	12
	Element of Risk (IRE) (WSCunningham) **6-10-5**(7) LMcGrath (a rr div)	1¼	**14**	25/1	54	11
1190[6]	**Lippy Louise** (MrsMReveley) **4-10-6** NSmith (nt j.w: a rr div)	14	**15**	100/1	40	—
1349[4]	**Pocaire Gaoithe (IRE)** (WStorey) **6-10-12** MMoloney (chsd ldrs tl wknd fr 8th)	1½	**16**	50/1	44	1
1290[5]	**Ruber** (RWThomson) **9-10-12** BStorey (cl up tl wknd fr 8th)	½	**17**	200/1	44	1
1292[7]	**Fenloe Rambler (IRE) (85)** (RJohnson) **5-10-12** KJohnson (sn wl bhd)	2	**18**	100/1	42	—
1290[6]	**South Coast Star (IRE)** (HowardJohnson) **6-10-7**(5) GFRyan (a bhd)	2½	**19**	100/1	41	—
1349[7]	**Willie Wannabe (IRE)** (MrsDThomson) **6-10-12** MissPRobson (hdwy 7th: wknd 9th)	½	**20**	200/1	40	—
	Knockbride (IRE) (FMurphy) **7-10-5**(7) MrTJBarry (t.o whn p.u bef 3 out)		**P**	100/1	—	—
	Cragnabuoy (IRE) (100) (WGReed) **6-10-5**(7) BGrattan (t.o whn p.u bef last)		**P**	25/1	—	—
	Blond Moss (SEKettlewell) **6-10-12** DBentley (bit bkwd: a bhd: t.o whn p.u bef 3 out)		**P**	300/1	—	—
1021[13]	**To Say The Least** (WTKemp) **6-10-5**(7) AKSmith (bit bkwd: chsd ldrs tl wknd 9th: p.u: broke down)		**P**	300/1	—	—
	Triona's Hope (IRE) (EMCaine) **7-10-12** MrPMurray (mstkes: t.o whn p.u bef 3 out)		**P**	300/1	—	—
				(SP 127.5%)	**25 Rn**	

5m 55.2 (13.20) CSF £9.46 TOTE £4.60: £2.30 £1.70 £1.80 (£6.80) Trio £17.70 OWNER Marquesa de Moratalla (MALTON) BRED Dunchurch Lodge Stud Co

WEIGHT FOR AGE 4yo-1lb

Agistment did it well on this first attempt over hurdles and is a really useful stayer in the making. (100/30)
1258 Hand Woven was obviously not worried about the trip as he attempted to make all, but found the winner too good late on. (2/1)
1290* Military Academy ran well but was always short of toe over the last three. He will come into his own over fences. (4/1)
1384 Coole Hill (IRE) had her chances but failed to see it out from the third last. (12/1)
1343 Grandinare (USA) stayed the trip well enough, but he gives the impression that he might just have his own ideas about the game. (11/1: op 6/1)
1360 Crystal Gift, trying his longest trip to date, did not appear to get it on this occasion. (10/1)
1349 Phar Echo (IRE) is still learning and will do better in due course. (50/1)
1290 Chill Factor just stays and proved too slow to get into this. (66/1)
Menaldi (IRE) needed this but ran quite well. (50/1)
Jigginstown had a quiet run and this out and out stayer will be interesting once put back over fences, now he has regained his confidence. (200/1)

1655 MD FOODS H'CAP CHASE (0-130) (5-Y.O+) (Class C)

1-45 (1-49) **3m (18 fncs)** £7,100.00 (£2,150.00: £1,050.00: £500.00) GOING: 0.30 sec per fur (GS)

				SP	RR	SF
	Turning Trix (123) (DNicholson) **9-11-13** AMaguire (lw: trckd ldrs: led 2 out: hit last: shkn up & r.o flat)	—	**1**	7/4[1]	131	61
	Road by the River (IRE) (97) (PCheesbrough) **8-10-1** BStorey (trckd ldrs: led 11th tl hdd & blnd 2 out: kpt on flat)	8	**2**	33/1	100	30
1162[4]	**Ali's Alibi (115)** (MrsMReveley) **9-11-5** PNiven (in tch: hdwy 11th: chal 3 out tl wknd flat)	2	**3**	9/2[2]	116	46
	Front Line (113) (JJO'Neill) **9-11-3** MMoloney (in tch tl outpcd 10th: sme hdwy 4 out: n.d)	16	**4**	25/1	104	34
1315[U]	**Strong Deel (IRE) (119)** (FMurphy) **8-11-9** CLlewellyn (hld up & bhd: effrt & mstkes fr ½-wy: n.d)	16	**5**	13/2	99	29
1162[2]	**Ceilidh Boy (124)** (MrsJDGoodfellow) **10-12-0** ASSmith (lw: drvn along fr 10th: no imp)	nk	**6**	6/1[3]	104	34
1244[4]	**Lie Detector (104)** (CParker) **8-10-8** MDwyer (led to 4th: sn bhd)	15	**7**	6/1[3]	74	4
	Merry Master (123) (GMMoore) **12-11-13** MrMArmytage (j.rt: led fr 7th: hit 9th: hdd 11th: wkng whn fell 14th)		**F**	20/1	—	—
1315[4]	**Earlymorning Light (IRE) (119)** (GRichards) **7-11-9** RDunwoody (led 4th to 7th: chsd ldrs: hit 12th & 13th: ev ch tl wknd qckly appr 3 out: p.u bef 2 out)		**P**	10/1	—	—
				(SP 117.1%)	**9 Rn**	

6m 3.5 (11.50) CSF £45.09 CT £214.18 TOTE £2.40: £1.10 £9.60 £1.60 (£117.20) Trio £107.40 OWNER Mr Mel Davies (TEMPLE GUITING) BRED Robert McCarthy

Turning Trix won this particularly well despite showing a tendency to hang left at the last, and he does seem to be at his best when fresh. (7/4)
Road by the River (IRE) ran a smashing race after 18 months off and hopefully he is now back on the right tracks. (33/1)
1162 Ali's Alibi had his chances here but then stopped as if something was wrong after the last. (9/2)
Front Line ran reasonably here and, after disappointing all of last season, his jumping was certainly more encouraging this time. (25/1)
1315 Strong Deel (IRE) seems to have lost his confidence and never got into this. (13/2)
1162 Ceilidh Boy was never going or jumping at any stage and would seem to have a problem. (6/1)
1244 Lie Detector looked to have lost things after six fences and was never happy thereafter. (6/1: op 7/2)
1315 Earlymorning Light (IRE) (10/1: op 5/1)

1656 NEWCASTLE BUILDING SOCIETY 'FIGHTING FIFTH' (LIMITED) H'CAP HURDLE (Gd 2) (4-Y.O+) (Class A)

2-15 (2-19) **2m (9 hdls)** £22,022.00 (£8,333.85: £4,079.43: £1,859.72) GOING minus 0.25 sec per fur (GF)

				SP	RR	SF
1365*	**Space Trucker (IRE) (144)** (MrsJHarrington,Ireland) **5-10-4** JShortt (lw: hld up: hdwy ½-wy: led 2 out: blnd last: r.o wl u.p)	—	**1**	5/2[2]	143	61

1258* **Castle Sweep (IRE) (144)** (DNicholson) **5-10-4** AMaguire (lw: chsd ldr: led 5th: hit next & 3 out: hdd 2 out: ev ch flat: kpt on)....1 **2** 11/8[1] 142 60

Dato Star (IRE) (144) (JMJefferson) **5-10-4** MDwyer (lw: hld up: hdwy ½-wy: ev ch 4 out: outpcd next: styd on wl appr last)....s.h **3** 5/2[2] 142 60

1267[F] **Home Counties (IRE) (145)** (DMoffatt) **7-10-5**[ow1] DJMoffatt (chsd ldrs tl outpcd fr 4 out)....17 **4** 8/1[3] 126 43

1267[3] **Marchant Ming (IRE) (144)** (MDHammond) **4-10-4** DBentley (set str pce & sn clr: hit 2nd: hdd 5th: wknd after 4 out)....21 **5** 25/1 104 22

1267[7] **Jazilah (FR) (144)** (RAllan) **8-10-4** ASSmith (a wl bhd)....dist **6** 100/1 — —

Granville Again (144) (MrsAMNaughton) **10-10-4** MFoster (bit bkwd: outpcd fr 3rd: t.o whn p.u bef 4 out).... **P** 100/1 — —

1510[F] **Non Vintage (IRE) (144)** (MCChapman) **5-10-4** WWorthington (outpcd & bhd fr 3rd: rn out appr 3 out).... **R** 20/1 — —

(SP 120.9%) **8 Rn**

3m 46.2 (-5.80) CSF £6.56 CT £8.29 TOTE £3.30: £1.20 £1.10 £1.50 (£3.20) Trio £2.00 OWNER Mrs E. Queally (IRELAND) BRED John Harrington

LONG HANDICAP Castle Sweep (IRE) 10-7 Dato Star (IRE) 9-9 Home Counties (IRE) 10-5 Marchant Ming (IRE) 9-4 Jazilah (FR) 9-9 Granville Again 10-0 Non Vintage (IRE) 9-5

OFFICIAL EXPLANATION **Granville Again: was found to have an irregular heartbeat and is to be retired.**

IN-FOCUS: **All of the runners were out of the handicap owing to the overnight declaration of Alderbrook, who was withdrawn on the day due to the ground.**

1365* Space Trucker (IRE) wears a pricker on his off-side and needs a strong gallop which he got here, but he was in front long enough and almost threw it away at the last. (5/2)

1258* Castle Sweep (IRE) has the engine but as yet his jumping leaves plenty to be desired, and he will never be top-class until that is rectified. (11/8)

Dato Star (IRE) ran well on ground plenty fast enough and his rider reported that the gelding choked during the race. If his problems can be sorted out then there is plenty more to come. (5/2)

945 Home Counties (IRE) found himself completely outclassed when the pressure was on from the fourth last. (8/1: 6/1-9/1)

1267 Marchant Ming (IRE), on ground faster than he really prefers and from two stone out of the handicap, went off like a sprinter and not surprisingly was done with approaching three out. (25/1)

1657 DOUGLAS SMITH MEMORIAL H'CAP CHASE (0-125) (5-Y.O+) (Class D)

2-45 (2-47) **2m 4f** **(15 fncs)** £3,810.00 (£1,155.00: £565.00: £270.00) GOING: 0.30 sec per fur (GS)

SP RR SF

1268* **Easby Joker (123)** (SEKettlewell) **8-12-0** PNiven (t: lw: hld up: hdwy ½-wy: led on bit appr last: rdn & r.o flat)....— **1** 4/1[2] 135 37

1209[7] **Deep Decision (100)** (PCheesbrough) **10-10-5** ASSmith (a chsng ldrs: kpt on wl towards fin)....1½ **2** 10/1 111 13

1128[2] **Aljadeer (USA) (110)** (MWEasterby) **7-11-1b** RDunwoody (lw: mstke 4th: hdwy 8th: sn chsng ldrs: kpt on fr 3 out: nvr able to chal)....4 **3** 5/2[1] 118 20

1295[2] **Pagliaccio (99)** (MDHammond) **8-10-4** AMaguire (lw: mstkes: bhd: hdwy 10th: styd on u.p fr 3 out: nvr able to chal)....3 **4** 4/1[2] 104 6

1373[5] **Puritan (CAN) (112)** (NTinkler) **7-11-3b** MissPJones (trckd ldrs: effrt 3 out: r.o one pce)....¾ **5** 16/1 117 19

1164[3] **Vicaridge (95)** (RBrewis) **9-10-0** KJohnson (lw: led tl after 5th: led fr 7th: hit 8th: hdd & wknd appr last)....1 **6** 11/2[3] 99 1

1527[F] **East Houston (97)** (JJO'Neill) **7-10-2** MMoloney (mstkes: hld up & bhd: effrt 8th: no imp)....12 **7** 12/1 91 —

1373[4] **Rustic Air (105)** (JGFitzGerald) **9-10-10** MDwyer (mstkes: chsd ldrs: blnd 9th: wknd 3 out)....15 **8** 7/1 87 —

1307[6] **Blazing Dawn (95)** (JSHubbuck) **9-10-0** MissPRobson (cl up: led after 5th to 7th: wknd 9th: b.b.v)....9 **9** 20/1 70 —

1566[6] **Monaughty Man (95)** (EMCaine) **10-10-0** MrPMurray (nt j.w: wl bhd fr ½-wy)....nk **10** 100/1 70 —

(SP 124.9%) **10 Rn**

5m 9.7 (16.70) CSF £42.25 CT £112.80 TOTE £3.70: £1.40 £2.70 £1.20 (£21.70) Trio £15.90 OWNER Mr G. R. Orchard (MIDDLEHAM) BRED C. S. Wates

LONG HANDICAP Blazing Dawn 9-10 Monaughty Man 8-9

OFFICIAL EXPLANATION **Blazing Dawn: bled from the nose.**

1268* Easby Joker travelled and jumped well this time and, although he needed keeping up to his work after the last, there were never any doubts about the result. (4/1)

1029 Deep Decision ran a useful race and after looking beaten finished particularly well. (10/1)

1128 Aljadeer (USA) ran a fair race but was never doing enough to take a serious hand in things. (5/2)

1295 Pagliaccio has the ability but it is his jumping that lets him down mostly. (4/1)

1373 Puritan (CAN) is off a high enough mark at present but did run quite well here and seems to be striking form. (16/1)

1164 Vicaridge would probably have preferred a stronger gallop and got outpaced in the closing stages. (11/2)

1527 East Houston spoiled his chances with some poor jumping. (12/1)

1119 Rustic Air ran as though something was wrong. (7/1)

1658 CHISHOLM BOOKMAKERS H'CAP HURDLE (0-125) (4-Y.O+) (Class D)

3-15 (3-16) **2m** **(9 hdls)** £3,452.50 (£1,045.00: £510.00: £242.50) GOING minus 0.25 sec per fur (GF)

SP RR SF

1439[2] **Circus Line (97)** (MWEasterby) **5-10-5** MDwyer (lw: mstkes: mde all: styd on wl fr 2 out)....— **1** 2/1[1] 79 24

1502[6] **Done Well (USA) (118)** (PMonteith) **4-11-12** RichardGuest (trckd ldrs: effrt appr 3 out: kpt on)....3½ **2** 11/2[3] 97 42

1163[4] **Shining Edge (108)** (TDEasterby) **4-11-2** ASSmith (chsd ldrs: ev ch appr 3 out: nt qckn appr last)....1 **3** 11/1 86 31

1143[4] **Ralitsa (IRE) (102)** (MDHammond) **4-10-3**(7) RBurns (hld up: hdwy 3 out: styd on towards fin)....1¼ **4** 10/1 78 23

1144* **Fen Terrier (95)** (FPMurtagh) **4-10-0**(3) ECallaghan (chsd ldrs: effrt 4 out: one pce fr next)....¾ **5** 14/1 71 16

1358[4] **Cittadino (100)** (CWThornton) **6-10-8** MFoster (mstkes: outpcd & bhd tl sme late hdwy)....16 **6** 11/2[3] 60 5

1439[3] **Desert Fighter (111)** (MrsMReveley) **5-11-5** PNiven (in tch: hdwy 4 out: wknd & eased appr last)....1 **7** 5/1[2] 70 15

1360[6] **Cool Luke (IRE) (102)** (FMurphy) **7-10-7**(3) LAspell (chsd ldrs: ev ch 4 out: sn rdn & wknd)....8 **8** 10/1 53 —

1127[4] **Master Hyde (USA) (112)** (WStorey) **7-11-6** MMoloney (in tch tl rdn & wknd 4 out)....6 **9** 11/1 57 2

Dual Image (108) (JGFitzGerald) **9-11-2** WDwan (bkwd: wl bhd fr 3rd)....12 **10** 25/1 41 —

(SP 126.1%) **10 Rn**

3m 54.5 (2.50) CSF £14.23 CT £96.12 TOTE £2.60: £1.20 £2.10 £3.50 (£11.30) Trio £43.40 OWNER Mrs P. A. H. Hartley (SHERIFF HUTTON) BRED Havenwood Construction Ltd

OFFICIAL EXPLANATION **Cittadino: was found to be suffering from a lung infection on return.**

1439 Circus Line, in a race full of iffy characters, galloped them into the ground and, had he jumped at all well, would have won easily. (2/1)

1502 Done Well (USA) ran much better this time and was keeping on most determinedly. (11/2)

1163 Shining Edge had his chances but again found the struggle too much. (11/1)

1143 Ralitsa (IRE) showed enough to suggest that when in the mood there is a race to be picked up. (10/1)
1144* Fen Terrier had his limitations exposed here. (14/1)
1358 Cittadino ran as though something was wrong and was never jumping or going well. (11/2)

T/Plpt: £2.70 (6,785.82 Tckts). T/Qdpt: £1.90 (646.36 Tckts). AA

1465-**WARWICK** (L-H) (Good)
Saturday November 30th
WEATHER: overcast WIND: str

1659 NORTH LEAMINGTON SCHOOL NOVICES' HURDLE (4-Y.O+) (Class C)
12-30 (12-31) **2m (8 hdls)** £4,302.00 (£1,296.00: £628.00: £294.00) GOING minus 0.14 sec per fur (G)

				SP	RR	SF
	Ionio (USA) (MrsVCWard) **5-11-0** JRKavanagh (plld hrd early: a.p: rdn 3 out: pckd 2 out: led flat: r.o wl)	—	**1**	10/1	79	29
1453[2]	**Royal Event** (DRGandolfo) **5-10-11**(3) DFortt (a.p: led appr 2 out tl flat: unable qckn)	1¾	**2**	7/4[1]	77	27
1187[6]	**Star Selection** (JMackie) **5-10-11**(3) EHusband (plld hrd: led 2nd tl appr 2 out: sn btn)	6	**3**	14/1	71	21
1470[5]	**Evezio Rufo** (NPLittmoden) **4-11-0v** LHarvey (prom tl wknd 2 out)	5	**4**	14/1	66	16
	Mazirah (RCurtis) **5-11-0** DMorris (hdwy 4th: wknd appr 2 out)	6	**5**	66/1	60	10
1275[7]	**The Brewmaster (IRE)** (IPWilliams) **4-10-11**(3) GHogan (lw: led to 2nd: wkng whn hit 2 out)	5	**6**	25/1	55	5
	Sun of Spring (JWhite) **6-11-0** TJMurphy (bit bkwd: in tch: no imp appr 3 out)	2	**7**	25/1	53	3
1303[2]	**A S Jim** (OO'Neill) **5-10-8**(7)ow1 MrAMitchell (bhd: hdwy appr 4th: wknd 5th)	14	**8**	66/1	40	—
1305[F]	**Oneoftheoldones** (JNorton) **4-11-0** DerekByrne (bit bkwd: a bhd)	5	**9**	100/1	34	—
	Gale Wargame (IRE) (OSherwood) **5-11-0** JAMcCarthy (bkwd: in tch to 5th: wkng whn blnd next)	13	**10**	11/4[2]	21	—
	Talk Back (IRE) (MissHCKnight) **4-11-0** MRichards (bit bkwd: hdwy 4th: wknd appr 3 out: p.u bef 2 out)		**P**	7/2[3]	—	—
	Our Tom (JWharton) **4-10-9**(5) MrRThornton (lw: j.b: t.o fr 5th: p.u bef 3 out)		**P**	40/1	—	—
1380[P]	**Web of Steel** (CJHemsley) **6-11-0** MBosley (rdn 3rd: bhd fr 5th: t.o whn p.u bef last)		**P**	100/1	—	—
	Penny's Wishing (CSmith) **4-10-9** MRanger (t.o fr 3rd: p.u bef 2 out)		**P**	100/1	—	—
1336[8]	**Countess Millie** (MissKWhitehouse) **4-10-4**(5) ChrisWebb (blnd & uns rdr 1st)		**U**	100/1	—	—
				(SP 124.8%)	**15 Rn**	

3m 46.8 (4.80) CSF £26.98 TOTE £13.60: £2.80 £1.20 £4.10 (£19.20) Trio £31.40 OWNER Mrs R F Key & Mrs V C Ward (GRANTHAM) BRED Flaxman Holdings Ltd
OFFICIAL EXPLANATION **Talk Back (IRE): had choked.**
Ionio (USA), fifth in the 1994 St Leger, lost his form on the level during 1995 and has become disappointing. Hurdles seemed to rejuvenate him for he battled his way to the front in good style despite being none too fluent at either of the last two hurdles. (10/1)
1453 Royal Event, a good mover, ran another promising race although the winner found too much speed for him, and he looks likely to stay further. (7/4)
1187 Star Selection, still rather keen, was able to make much of the running on this occasion and ran better as a result. (14/1: 10/1-16/1)
1470 Evezio Rufo ran a similar race to last time but was easily left behind from the home turn. He tried long trips on the level but won at nine furlongs. (14/1)
Mazirah, a long way below his best on the Flat this year, ran a bit better with eight flights of hurdles in front of him but this could well be as good as he is. (66/1)
865 The Brewmaster (IRE), a nice, chasing type, made a satisfactory hurdles debut and will do better in time. (25/1)
Gale Wargame (IRE) was well backed despite looking anything but fully wound up and was losing ground when the mistake three out finished him completely. (11/4: 4/1-9/4)
Talk Back (IRE) moved up promisingly at halfway but pulled up on the home turn having choked. (7/2: 7/4-4/1)

1660 TILTYARD BRIDGE H'CAP CHASE (0-125) (5-Y.O+) (Class D)
1-00 (1-01) **2m (12 fncs)** £3,577.50 (£1,080.00: £525.00: £247.50) GOING minus 0.14 sec per fur (G)

				SP	RR	SF
1035[F]	**Fine Harvest (115)** (JLSpearing) **10-11-10** TJMurphy (mde all: j.rt 4th & 6th: slipped after 5th & appr 2 out: hit 2 out: comf)	—	**1**	11/4[2]	119+	50
1183[4]	**Bally Parson (112)** (RDickin) **10-11-7** DerekByrne (hld up: blnd 5th: pckd next: hit 3 out: styd on appr next)	4	**2**	6/1	112	43
1350[3]	**Man Mood (FR) (112)** (CPEBrooks) **5-11-7** MrEJames (hdwy 5th: chsd wnr 9th: sn rdn & no imp)	2	**3**	9/2[3]	110	41
1379[2]	**Lake of Loughrea (IRE) (105)** (KCBailey) **6-11-0b**[1] JAMcCarthy (in tch: rdn & hit 3 out: sn btn)	7	**4**	5/2[1]	96	27
1204[P]	**Monday Club (112)** (JCTuck) **12-11-7** RBellamy (plld hrd: chsd wnr to 9th: wkng whn mstke last)	9	**5**	20/1	94	25
1186[3]	**Pats Minstrel (110)** (RChampion) **11-11-5b** MRichards (chsd ldrs: mstkes 4th & 7th: sn rdn & wknd)	28	**6**	8/1	64	—
	Count Barachois (USA) (96) (MrsEHHeath) **8-10-5** RSupple (bkwd: prom tl mstke 4th: t.o fr 6th)	26	**7**	16/1	24	—
				(SP 109.5%)	**7 Rn**	

3m 56.4 (2.40) CSF £17.20 TOTE £2.80: £1.50 £2.90 (£11.50) OWNER Miss A. Shirley-Priest (ALCESTER) BRED Mrs K. Cumiskey
862* Fine Harvest is proving hard to peg back and, despite the odd fencing lapse, never looked being beaten. He did drift right at the odd fence and would prefer to go right-handed. (11/4)
1183 Bally Parson returned to something like his best after two confidence boosters over hurdles. (6/1)
1350 Man Mood (FR), again with his tongue tied down, went a clear second on the home turn but could never got to the winner and could not sustain the effort. (9/2: 3/1-5/1)
1379 Lake of Loughrea (IRE), dropped back in trip, could never go the pace of the winner and does need further. (5/2)
Monday Club looked full of beans going to post and ran his best race for a long time. He is not the horse he was but is capable of finding another race. (20/1)
Pats Minstrel was not able to dominate and lost interest soon after halfway. (8/1)

1661 WARWICKSHIRE COLLEGE OF AGRICULTURE H'CAP HURDLE (0-145) (4-Y.O+) (Class B)
1-35 (1-35) **2m 3f (9 hdls)** £5,052.50 (£1,520.00: £735.00: £342.50) GOING minus 0.14 sec per fur (G)

				SP	RR	SF
1429[5]	**Balanak (USA) (120)** (DRGandolfo) **5-10-1**(5) SophieMitchell (hld up: hdwy appr 2 out: str run to ld flat)	—	**1**	14/1	104	26
1319[W]	**Karshi (139)** (MissHCKnight) **6-11-11** MRichards (led to 5th: led appr last: hdd & unable qckn flat)	1¼	**2**	13/2[3]	122	44
1441[2]	**Mytton's Choice (IRE) (126)** (DNicholson) **5-10-7**(5) MrRThornton (nt j.w: chsd ldr tl led & hit 5th: hdd appr last: one pce)	1	**3**	9/4[1]	108	30
	Hooded Hawk (IRE) (114) (NJHenderson) **5-10-0** JRKavanagh (lw: trckd ldrs: lost pl after 5th: styd on fr 3 out)	5	**4**	16/1	92	14

				SP	RR	SF
1467*	**Domappel (114)** (MrsJCecil) **4-10-0** TKent (hld up: hit 2nd: hdwy & hit 6th: sn rdn & no imp)	8	**5**	9/4[1]	85	7
	Sun Surfer (FR) (136) (CaptTAForster) **8-11-8** SWynne (bit bkwd: blnd 2 out: nvr nr ldrs)	1½	**6**	6/1[2]	106	28
	Castle Courageous (133) (LadyHerries) **9-11-5** EMurphy (bkwd: prom to 5th: eased whn hit 3 out)	1½	**7**	14/1	102	24
1125[5]	**Alltime Dancer (IRE) (124)** (OSherwood) **4-10-10** JAMcCarthy (hld up: nvr trbld ldrs)	2½	**8**	12/1	91	13
	Indian Quest (116) (NAGaselee) **7-9-13**(3)ow2 GHogan (bkwd: prom tl wknd 3 out)	1½	**9**	25/1	81	1
				(SP 119.9%)	**9 Rn**	

4m 24.3 (4.30) CSF £95.30 CT £261.55 TOTE £17.20: £3.40 £2.40 £1.10 (£52.60) Trio £111.80 OWNER Mr W. H. Dore (WANTAGE) BRED H. H. Aga Khan's Studs Societe Civile in USA

LONG HANDICAP Hooded Hawk (IRE) 9-9 Domappel 9-13 Indian Quest 9-10

1429 Balanak (USA) won in the most extraordinary manner. Out the back and apparently not travelling for most of the race, he suddenly found his feet turning for home and, with the two clear leaders out on their feet going to the last, found a great turn of foot to gain an unlikely victory. Generally out of form since the efforts that saw him go off favourite for last year's Triumph Hurdle, he can hardly be guaranteed to reproduce this. (14/1)

Karshi, third to Urubande at the Festival last year, had a running battle with Mytton's Choice for the lead which he eventually won only for the winner to pounce late. He really looks the part now and should find further success. (13/2)

1441 Mytton's Choice (IRE) took Karshi on but made a string of mistakes and the one when in front at the second last finally beat him. (9/4)

Hooded Hawk (IRE) looked fit but ran as if he needs a bit further. He has the make and shape of a chaser and it can only be a matter of time before he takes on bigger obstacles. (16/1)

1467* Domappel looked rather hairy but still ran better than his finishing position as his second mistake curtailed a promising move. (9/4)

Sun Surfer (FR), over a trip now short of his best, could never get into the race but should at least strip sharper for this next time. (6/1)

Castle Courageous (14/1: 7/1-16/1)

1125 Alltime Dancer (IRE) (12/1: 8/1-14/1)

1662 STAMINA TEST H'CAP CHASE (0-125) (5-Y.O+) (Class D)

2-05 (2-05) **3m 2f (20 fncs)** £5,264.00 (£1,592.00: £776.00: £368.00) GOING minus 0.14 sec per fur (G)

				SP	RR	SF
	Christmas Gorse (113) (NAGaselee) **10-11-6**(3) GHogan (hld up: hdwy 11th: led appr 2 out: rdn out)	—	**1**	10/1	125	13
1428[P]	**Church Law (102)** (MrsLCTaylor) **9-10-12** RSupple (hld up: hdwy 13th: hit 3 out: styd on fr next: nt rch wnr)	1	**2**	9/2[3]	113	1
1293[6]	**Stop the Waller (IRE) (114)** (FMurphy) **7-11-5**(5) MrRThornton (led 4th tl appr 2 out: one pce)	4	**3**	5/1	123	11
1428[P]	**Desperate (100)** (AGFoster) **8-10-10** MRichards (bit bkwd: lft 2nd 6th: rdn 3 out: wkng whn mstke next)	30	**4**	20/1	91	—
1473[2]	**Beaurepaire (IRE) (108)** (RHAlner) **8-11-1**(3) PHenley (lw: prom tl mstke & lost pl 12th: sn rdn: t.o whn p.u bef 4 out)		**P**	2/1[1]	—	—
1415[3]	**Far Senior (108)** (PWegmann) **10-11-4** JRKavanagh (led to 3rd: dropped rr 6th: t.o whn p.u bef 15th)		**P**	14/1	—	—
1287[3]	**Samlee (IRE) (110)** (PJHobbs) **7-11-3**(3) GTormey (lw: led 3rd to 4th: j.slowly 5th: uns rdr next)		**U**	100/30[2]	—	—
				(SP 111.8%)	**7 Rn**	

6m 42.7 (17.70) CSF £48.97 CT £227.87 TOTE £13.50: £3.80 £2.80 (£36.80) OWNER Mr D. R. Stoddart (LAMBOURN) BRED D. R. Stoddart

OFFICIAL EXPLANATION **Beaurepaire (IRE): was hanging badly and never travelling.**

Christmas Gorse, winner of the National Hunt Chase at the 1994 Cheltenham Festival, had run just three times since and has obviously been difficult to train. Bandaged in front but looking just about fit enough to do himself justice, he took advantage of a lenient handicap mark to gain a hard-fought win. He had a pretty hard race in the end and will probably take some time to recover given the length of his lay-off. (10/1)

1089* Church Law really does stay and bore down relentlessly on the leaders in the final mile, just failing to get up in time. His one appearance at three and a half miles brought about a victory and he will be interesting when asked to tackle further still. (9/2: 3/1-5/1)

1293 Stop the Waller (IRE) is certainly on his way back and must have run somewhere near his best here, making much of the running for the first time since he scored at Sedgefield in February. (5/1)

Desperate would have coped with softer ground and did look to need the run but ran well to the home run before being dropped. (20/1)

1473 Beaurepaire (IRE) was a big disappointment and the mistake nine from home only speeded up the inevitable. (2/1)

1663 EMMA BRAZENDALE NOVICES' H'CAP HURDLE (0-100) (3-Y.O+) (Class E)

2-35 (2-38) **2m (8 hdls)** £2,692.80 (£750.80: £362.40) GOING minus 0.14 sec per fur (G)

				SP	RR	SF
1274[6]	**Rovestar (83)** (JSKing) **5-11-4** TJMurphy (lw: hdwy 5th: lft in ld last: rdn out)	—	**1**	5/1[1]	72	25
1253[5]	**Skram (84)** (RDickin) **3-9-10**(7) XAizpuru (w ldr: led 4th tl appr 2 out: ev ch flat: r.o)	2	**2**	14/1	71	8
1339[2]	**Mr Poppleton (67)** (RBrotherton) **7-10-2** LHarvey (led to 3rd: one pce appr 2 out)	4	**3**	7/1[3]	50	3
1377[4]	**Colour Counsellor (81)** (RMFlower) **3-10-0** RSupple (prom: led appr 2 out: mstke: sn hdd: eased nr fin)	2½	**4**	6/1[2]	62	—
1178[3]	**Smart Lord (87)** (JRBosley) **5-11-8** MBosley (lw: s.i.s: bhd tl r.o fr 3 out)	hd	**5**	12/1	67	20
1375[6]	**Museum (IRE) (80)** (PWinkworth) **5-11-1** DLeahy (chsd ldrs to 3 out)	6	**6**	7/1[3]	54	7
	Schnozzle (IRE) (90) (KSBridgwater) **5-11-8**(3) RMassey (nvr nr to chal)	18	**7**	12/1	46	—
1278[F]	**That Old Feeling (IRE) (75)** (JWhite) **4-10-7**(3) GuyLewis (bhd fr 5th)	13	**8**	16/1	18	—
1339[7]	**Bold Charlie (65)** (SMellor) **4-10-0** NMann (prom to 4th)	1	**9**	50/1	7	—
	Dodgy Dancer (74) (MrsLWilliamson) **6-10-9** LO'Hara (bkwd: in tch tl hmpd 4th)	¾	**10**	16/1	16	—
	Alpha Leather (65) (LPGrassick) **5-10-0** MrJGrassick (bkwd: b.d 3rd)		**B**	66/1	—	—
1339[3]	**Witney-de-Bergerac (IRE) (89)** (JSMoore) **4-11-10v** WMcFarland (fell 3rd)		**F**	10/1	—	—
859[P]	**Master Goodenough (IRE) (73)** (AGFoster) **5-10-1**(7)ow8 DCreech (led 3rd: hdd & fell next)		**F**	50/1	—	—
	Ethbaat (USA) (93) (MJHeaton-Ellis) **5-12-0** MRichards (lw: hld up & plld hrd: hdwy after 3rd: wknd 5th: p.u bef last)		**P**	17/2	—	—
129[11]	**Daring Hen (IRE) (85)** (RTJuckes) **6-11-6** PHolley (bkwd: bhd fr 4th: t.o whn p.u bef last)		**P**	25/1	—	—
718[7]	**Aydisun (66)** (RCurtis) **4-10-1** DMorris (bit bkwd: hdwy whn ran out 4th)		**R**	6/1[2]	—	—
1470[10]	**Tomal (70)** (RIngram) **4-10-5** JRKavanagh (chsd ldrs: led after 2 out: stumbled & uns rdr last)		**U**	14/1	59?	—
				(SP 139.6%)	**17 Rn**	

3m 48.4 (6.40) CSF £76.08 CT £479.22 TOTE £8.80: £2.50 £3.90 £1.90 £2.10 (£133.30) Trio Not won; £140.12 to 2/12/96 OWNER Mr G. Burr (SWINDON) BRED G. Burr

LONG HANDICAP Bold Charlie 9-9 Alpha Leather 9-11

WEIGHT FOR AGE 3yo-16lb

Rovestar, taken down quietly, found this shorter trip the answer although he was a slightly fortunate winner. (5/1: op 8/1)

1253 Skram did well for a juvenile, racing keenly with the pace all the way, and would appear to be improving. (14/1)

1339 Mr Poppleton wore a cross noseband but did look rather onepaced on such a sharp track and ought to stay a little further. (7/1)

1377 Colour Counsellor, in good form on the Flat during the summer, moved moderately to post but ran well until having no more to give going to the last. He wore headgear on most occasions on the Flat and it will be interesting to see if they bring about an improvement when fitted over timber. (6/1: 4/1-13/2)
1178 Smart Lord, side on when the tapes went up, probably did well to get so close. (12/1: op 8/1)
1375 Museum (IRE) again ran prominently until fading in the last half-mile and does seem a slow learner. (7/1)
1339 Witney-de-Bergerac (IRE) (10/1: 7/1-11/1)
820 Tomal looked just in charge when he stumbled over the final flight, shooting his rider out of the side door. (14/1: op 8/1)

1664 SARAH DEALTRY NOVICES' CHASE (4-Y.O+) (Class D)

3-05 (3-07) **2m (12 fncs)** £3,951.00 (£1,188.00: £574.00: £267.00) GOING minus 0.14 sec per fur (G)

Form	Horse	Dist	Pos	SP	RR	SF
	Flight Lieutenant (USA) (109) (TCasey) **7-11-5** JAMcCarthy (hdwy 6th: lft in ld 4 out: clr whn hit 2 out: pushed out)	—	**1**	6/1	109	39
1449*	**Scottish Bambi (88)** (PRWebber) **8-11-11** RBellamy (hdwy 4th: mstke 7th: lft 2nd & hmpd 2 out)	17	**2**	5/2[2]	98	28
913[10]	**Reefa's Mill (IRE)** (JNeville) **4-10-7** PHolley (in tch to 7th: styd on fr 2 out)	13	**3**	50/1	79	—
	Nautical George (IRE) (JohnUpson) **6-11-5** RSupple (bit bkwd: plld hrd: prom to 5th: lost pl & blnd 8th: n.d after)	3	**4**	20/1	76	6
1254[P]	**Betabetcorbett** (BPJBaugh) **5-11-5** TEley (mstke 4 out: a bhd)	14	**5**	50/1	62	—
	Odell (IRE) (KCBailey) **6-11-5** WMcFarland (bkwd: j.rt: led tl appr 6th: wkng whn hit 9th)	1½	**6**	7/1	61	—
	Exterior Profiles (IRE) (NATwiston-Davies) **6-11-5** MrMRimell (trckd ldrs: hit 3rd & 4th: led appr 6th: pckd 8th: clr whn fell next)		**F**	2/1[1]	—	—
1414[2]	**Captain Stockford (60)** (PWegmann) **9-11-5** JRKavanagh (swtg: plld hrd: chsd ldr tl blnd 4th: sn lost pl: t.o whn p.u bef 2 out)		**P**	50/1	—	—
1414[F]	**Lothian Jem** (JWharton) **7-10-9**(5) MrRThornton (j.b: sn t.o: p.u bef 5th)		**P**	40/1	—	—
1255[4]	**Tight Fist (IRE)** (MissHCKnight) **6-11-5** MRichards (bit bkwd: hdwy 7th: chsng wnr whn blnd & uns rdr 2 out)		**U**	4/1[3]	—	—
				(SP 121.8%)	**10 Rn**	

3m 57.8 (3.80) CSF £21.32 TOTE £7.70: £1.60 £1.70 £9.00 (£12.80) Trio £140.20; £144.16 to 2/12/96 OWNER Mrs Laura Pegg (DORKING) BRED Dale Barlage
WEIGHT FOR AGE 4yo-12lb
Flight Lieutenant (USA) has always had more in the way of ability than application but did seem to be enjoying himself and he has the size and scope to prove quite useful. (6/1: 4/1-13/2)
1449* Scottish Bambi, impressive off a plater's mark in a novice handicap last time, looked to have it all to do here under a penalty but ran really well although he was not making any impression on the winner when left second. (5/2)
Reefa's Mill (IRE) dropped out starting down the back but finished to some purpose. This was a satisfactory chasing debut. (50/1)
Nautical George (IRE) proved hard to settle both on the way to post and in the early stages. He paid the penalty as the race developed. (20/1)
419 Betabetcorbett never got into this but would surely find life a lot easier in novice handicaps. (50/1)
Odell (IRE) looked badly in need of the race but showed some promise although his jumping was rather slipshod on occasions. (7/1)
Exterior Profiles (IRE) paid the penalty for enthusiasm, for he was fairly running away starting down the back, jumping fast and low at the first three fences before coming to grief at the fourth. (2/1)

1665 NORTON LINDSEY STANDARD N.H. FLAT RACE (4, 5 & 6-Y.O) (Class H)

3-35 (3-36) **2m** £1,374.50 (£382.00: £183.50)

Form	Horse	Dist	Pos	SP	RR	SF
1203[2]	**Lord Foley (NZ)** (CJMann) **4-11-1**(3) JMagee (hdwy 9f out: led on bit over 1f out: sn rdn clr: easily)	—	**1**	3/1[2]	69 f	—
1124[3]	**Zander** (NATwiston-Davies) **4-10-11**(7) LSuthern (lw: led 7f: led 8f out tl over 3f out: led over 2f out tl appr fnl f: unable qckn)	5	**2**	5/1[3]	64 f	—
	Tristram's Image (NZ) (NJHenderson) **5-10-13**(5) MrCVigors (lw: a.p: led over 3f out tl over 2f out: one pce)	7	**3**	6/4[1]	57 f	—
1124[5]	**The Croppy Boy** (JNeville) **4-11-1**(3) TDascombe (in tch: jnd ldrs 8f out: one pce fnl 2f)	2	**4**	11/1	55 f	—
	Oxbridge Lady (NATwiston-Davies) **5-10-6**(7) MKeighley (hdwy 9f out: rdn: wknd & edgd lft over 2f out)	¾	**5**	12/1	49 f	—
1275[12]	**Bellidium** (AEJessop) **4-10-10**(3) GTormey (plld hrd: hdwy 7f out: wkng whn hung lft over 1f out)	1	**6**	66/1	48 f	—
1124[16]	**Scholar Green** (GHYardley) **4-11-1**(3) PHenley (r.o fnl 3f: nrst fin)	4	**7**	66/1	49 f	—
	Mistress Tudor (SMellor) **5-10-10**(3) EHusband (bkwd: nvr nrr)	9	**8**	33/1	35 f	—
	Gaf (BRCambidge) **4-11-1**(3) RMassey (bkwd: prom 8f)	6	**9**	66/1	34 f	—
	Master Harry (IRE) (MrsJPitman) **4-11-1**(3) GHogan (bit bkwd: hld up & bhd: sme hdwy 5f out: nvr plcd to chal)	16	**10**	6/1	18 f	—
	Moor Dance Man (NPLittmoden) **6-11-4** MrDVerco (prom 10f)	1¼	**11**	66/1	17 f	—
	Byhookorbycrook (IRE) (JCullinan) **4-10-8**(5) DJKavanagh (bhd fnl 8f)	16	**12**	50/1	—	—
	Tatibag (MissKWhitehouse) **4-10-13**(5) SophieMitchell (bit bkwd: a bhd)	¾	**13**	50/1	—	—
865[19]	**Toro Loco (IRE)** (IPWilliams) **4-10-13**(5) MrRThornton (prom: led 9f out to 8f out: sn wknd)	8	**14**	50/1	—	—
	Toddys Lass (JAPickering) **4-10-10**(3) DFortt (unf: bit bkwd: w ldr 7f)	dist	**15**	50/1	—	—
24[12]	**Aber Glen** (NASmith) **6-10-6**(7) MrAWintle (bit bkwd: chsd ldrs 8f: wkng whn p.u 4f out)		**P**	66/1	—	—
				(SP 130.2%)	**16 Rn**	

3m 48.4 CSF £18.74 TOTE £4.00: £2.00 £1.70 £2.10 (£10.00) Trio £5.60 OWNER Foley Steelstock (UPPER LAMBOURN) BRED J. D. Corcoran
1203 Lord Foley (NZ), despite looking a little green on the home turn, won in impressive style once brought to the stands' rail and is clearly quite useful. (3/1: 2/1-7/2)
1124 Zander, made more use of this time, found the winner laughing at him approaching the final furlong. (5/1: 5/2-11/2)
Tristram's Image (NZ), off for eighteen months since his debut, returned looking fit and well. This was a solid effort from this rangy gelding who ought to win races. (6/4: op 7/2)
1124 The Croppy Boy again ran well but again finished behind Zander. (11/1: 8/1-12/1)
Oxbridge Lady, a rather lengthy mare, is a good walker and was running a big race until proving green as pressure was applied. (12/1:9/2-14/1)
Bellidium proved difficult to settle and again her steering gave problems in the straight. (66/1)
Scholar Green was noted doing some good late running and may improve given time. (66/1)
Master Harry (IRE), a tall, attractive newcomer from the family of Danny Harrold and Golden Freeze, looked to need the race but was given a pretty gentle introduction and should come good in time. (6/1: op 7/2)

T/Plpt: £238.10 (36.85 Tckts). T/Qdpt: £133.20 (5.26 Tckts). Dk

1311-KELSO (L-H) (Good, Good to firm patches)

Monday December 2nd

Races 3 & 5: two fences omitted
WEATHER: fine WIND: str

1666 JOHN HOGG NOVICES' HURDLE (I) (4-Y.O+) (Class D)

12-30 (12-33) **2m 110y (8 hdls)** £2,502.00 (£756.00: £368.00: £174.00) GOING minus 0.13 sec per fur (G)

				SP	RR	SF
	Mister Ross (IRE) (HowardJohnson) **6-10-12** ASSmith (a chsng ldrs: led appr 2 out: r.o wl)	—	**1**	25/1	72+	3
	Shinerolla (CParker) **4-10-12** DParker (lw: trckd ldrs: chsd wnr fr 2 out: one pce)	7	**2**	$6/1^{3}$	65	—
1263^{4}	**King Pin** (PBeaumont) **4-10-12** RSupple (hld up: stdy hdwy appr 2 out: shkn up flat: styd on towards fin)	3	**3**	13/2	62+	—
1309^{2}	**Duraid (IRE)** (DenysSmith) **4-10-12** RichardGuest (lw: prom: effrt appr 2 out: no ex)	6	**4**	$11/10^{1}$	57	—
1343^{3}	**Bill's Pride (79)** (PMonteith) **5-10-7** ADobbin (in tch: rdn 3 out: btn next)	11	**5**	20/1	41	—
	Calder King (JLEyre) **5-10-12** BStorey (nvr bttr than mid div)	4	**6**	12/1	42	—
	Greek Gold (IRE) (DWBarker) **7-10-12** PNiven (nvr trbld ldrs)	13	**7**	200/1	29	—
	Jalmaid (HAlexander) **4-10-2**(5) RMcGrath (a rr div)	nk	**8**	100/1	24	—
	Nizaal (USA) (RAllan) **5-10-12** BHarding (hld up: a bhd)	16	**9**	20/1	14	—
	Political Bill (JIACharlton) **5-10-12** KJohnson (nvr rchd ldrs)	1¾	**10**	100/1	12	—
1305^{P}	**Barik (IRE) (70)** (BMactaggart) **6-10-9**(3) GLee (led tl hdd & wknd appr 2 out)	nk	**11**	500/1	12	—
	Obvious Risk (EMCaine) **5-10-12** MrPMurray (prom to ½-wy: sn bhd)	¾	**12**	100/1	11	—
	Kierchem (IRE) (CGrant) **5-10-12** JCallaghan (chsd ldrs to 5th: sn lost pl & bhd)	dist	**13**	25/1	—	—
794^{4}	**In Good Faith (100)** (JJQuinn) **4-10-12** MDwyer (in tch whn fell 4th)		**F**	$3/1^{2}$	—	—
1245^{8}	**Royal Palm** (VThompson) **4-10-12** MrMThompson (wl bhd whn blnd & uns rdr 5th)		**U**	200/1	—	—

(SP 129.3%) **15 Rn**

3m 56.5 (10.50) CSF £164.77 TOTE £26.70: £4.20 £2.60 £1.50 (£102.80) Trio £113.20 OWNER Mr Gordon Brown (CROOK) BRED Mrs Kathleen Creedon and Con O'Leary

Mister Ross (IRE), the winner of a maiden point in Ireland, changed hands for 18,000 guineas at Doncaster Sales. Always travelling well, he had the race in safe-keeping jumping the last and stayed on particularly well. He can only go on to better things. (25/1)
Shinerolla, a decent handicapper on the Flat, jumped well in the main on this hurdling debut and looks the type to go one better. (6/1)
1263 King Pin caught the eye. Held up travelling well, he came through approaching the last and finished full of running. (13/2)
1309 Duraid (IRE) is proving expensive to follow since turning his attention to hurdling. There were no excuses here because he was back in trip having failed to stay last time. (11/10)
1343 Bill's Pride, under pressure from three out, just appeared to be outdone on this occasion. A drop in grade would be appreciated.(20/1)
Calder King, an effective handicapper on the Flat, looks the sort that could well take to this game with a run or two under his belt. (12/1)

1667 JOHN HOGG NOVICES' HURDLE (II) (4-Y.O+) (Class D)

1-00 (1-02) **2m 110y (8 hdls)** £2,489.00 (£752.00: £366.00: £173.00) GOING minus 0.13 sec per fur (G)

				SP	RR	SF
1412^{2}	**Dana Point (IRE)** (MrsSJSmith) **4-10-12** RichardGuest (lw: a.p: slt ld last: r.o wl flat)	—	**1**	$5/2^{1}$	74	1
	Malta Man (IRE) (PCheesbrough) **6-10-12** ASSmith (hld up: hdwy 3 out: disp ld last: styd on same pce flat)	4	**2**	16/1	70	—
1263^{3}	**Nick Ross** (RBrewis) **5-10-12** KJohnson (lw: in tch: slt ld 2 out: hdd last: no ex)	10	**3**	$9/2^{3}$	60	—
	Doubling Dice (69) (RAllan) **5-10-5**(7) SMelrose (wl bhd: stdy hdwy 2 out: rdn & one pce flat)	2½	**4**	100/1	58	—
7^{P}	**Drakewrath (IRE)** (RABartlett) **6-10-12** DParker (chsd ldrs: rdn & outpcd fr 3 out)	½	**5**	33/1	58	—
1312*	**Del Piero (IRE) (96)** (MDHammond) **5-11-5** RGarritty (trckd ldrs: rdn appr last: sn btn)	7	**6**	$3/1^{2}$	58	—
1345^{5}	**Sunny Leith** (PMonteith) **5-10-9**(3) GCahill (in tch: ev ch 3 out: grad wknd)	½	**7**	25/1	50	—
1030^{10}	**Dr Edgar** (MDods) **4-10-12** RSupple (led tl hdd 2 out: sn btn)	hd	**8**	20/1	50	—
1524^{6}	**Kilnamartyra Girl (87)** (JParkes) **6-10-7** PNiven (mid div tl wknd 3 out)	20	**9**	5/1	26	—
1345^{F}	**Jarrow** (MrsAMNaughton) **5-10-12** MFoster (mid div: wknd appr 3 out)	2½	**10**	50/1	28	—
939^{13}	**Super Guy** (JBarclay) **4-10-12** BStorey (a bhd)	15	**11**	100/1	14	—
1343^{6}	**Percy Parrot** (ACWhillans) **4-10-12** BHarding (in tch to ½-wy)	2	**12**	40/1	12	—
1052^{7}	**Desert Devil** (GRichards) **4-10-12** ADobbin (wl bhd fr ½-wy)	1	**13**	12/1	11	—
	Glint of Ayr (72) (RobertGoldie) **6-10-7** JCallaghan (fell 2nd)		**F**	100/1	—	—
1312^{10}	**Regal Domain (IRE)** (MrsLMarshall) **5-10-12** DBentley (cl up: wknd qckly 4th: t.o whn p.u bef 2 out)		**P**	100/1	—	—

(SP 121.9%) **15 Rn**

3m 57.0 (11.00) CSF £39.22 TOTE £4.20: £1.30 £5.80 £1.60 (£26.60) Trio £76.30 OWNER Mrs S. Smith (BINGLEY) BRED T. N. Leonard

1412 Dana Point (IRE), taking the shortest way round, stayed on well up the run-in and was head and shoulders above the rest. (5/2)
Malta Man (IRE), looking as if the race would do him good, made steady ground all the way up the straight and was in with a live chance at the last, before lack of fitness told. He will strip a lot fitter for this. (16/1)
1263 Nick Ross, another who looked as if the race would just put an edge on him, had little left in reserve once headed by the winner. (9/2)
Doubling Dice, just looking in need of this, was adrift until making stealthy ground at the second last. There are better things to come. (100/1)
Drakewrath (IRE) was well placed until getting outpaced three out. He should be straighter for this. (33/1)
1312* Del Piero (IRE), a course and distance winner last time, was never going well enough to follow that up. (3/1)
1052 Desert Devil (12/1: 8/1-14/1)

1668 JACK BRITTON MEMORIAL NOVICES' CHASE (5-Y.O+) (Class C)

1-30 (1-32) **3m 1f (15 fncs)** £4,642.45 (£1,405.60: £686.30: £326.65) GOING minus 0.13 sec per fur (G)

				SP	RR	SF
1313^{4}	**Seeking Gold (IRE) (79)** (JBarclay) **7-11-0** BStorey (lw: a.p: ev ch whn lft in ld last: styd on wl)	—	**1**	10/1	97	37
340^{U}	**Winter Belle (USA)** (HowardJohnson) **8-11-0** ADobbin (bhd: in tch ½-wy: ev ch last: styd on one pce)	6	**2**	$7/2^{3}$	93	33
1313^{2}	**Tighter Budget (USA) (104)** (MrsDianneSayer) **9-12-1** MMoloney (led to 11th: ev ch tl wknd appr last)	21	**3**	$5/2^{2}$	95	35
1574^{F}	**Monksaan (IRE)** (MDHammond) **7-10-11**(3) MrCBonner (in tch & rdn ½-wy: sn bhd: t.o)	30	**4**	7/1	61	1
1313^{3}	**Tough Test (IRE)** (MrsJDGoodfellow) **6-10-11**(3) GCahill (lw: chsd ldr: slt ld 11th: u.p whn fell last)		**F**	$9/4^{1}$	—	—
	Aristodemus (MrsLMarshall) **7-11-0** DBentley (bhd whn fell 12th)		**F**	14/1	—	—
1313^{6}	**Strongalong (IRE) (64)** (PCheesbrough) **6-11-0** ASSmith (in tch & rdn whn fell 12th)		**F**	50/1	—	—
1209^{8}	**Bosworth Field (IRE) (71)** (MrsSarahHorner-Harker) **8-11-0** RichardGuest (a bhd: t.o whn p.u bef 3 out)		**P**	50/1	—	—

(SP 113.7%) **8 Rn**

6m 15.5 (5.50) CSF £41.89 TOTE £8.90: £2.60 £2.80 £1.30 (£21.70) Trio £24.70 OWNER Gilry (LESLIE) BRED John Bourke
STEWARDS' ENQUIRY Horner-Harker fined £85 under Rule 149 (iii) (failing to present number-cloth)

1313 Seeking Gold (IRE), in a race which turned into a real test of stamina, found this right up her street. (10/1)
340 Winter Belle (USA) held every chance at the last, but was outstayed by the winner from that point. (7/2: op 9/4)
1313 Tighter Budget (USA) has been on the go for a long time and could be feeling the effects of that, and also the three penalties that he had to shoulder. (5/2)
Monksaan (IRE) is reasonably thought of at home, but failed to get round on his debut last time, and was hunted round at the back this time to complete. He could well continue to progress. (7/1)
1313 Tough Test (IRE), a reasonable third on his chase debut last time, was under pressure but still in front when capsizing at the last. It is open to question as to whether he would have held on up the run-in. (9/4)

1669 J. RUTHERFORD (EARLSTON) LTD. H'CAP HURDLE (0-125) (4-Y.O+) (Class D)

2-00 (2-01) **2m 2f (10 hdls)** £3,271.90 (£918.40: £447.70) GOING minus 0.13 sec per fur (G)

				SP	RR	SF
1314²	**Stash the Cash (IRE) (99)** (MDHammond) **5-10-6** RGarritty (lw: trckd ldrs: led appr last: drvn along flat: all out)	—	1	8/11 1	81	6
1360⁴	**Mr Knitwit (113)** (PMonteith) **9-11-6** ADobbin (trckd ldr: disp ld appr last: r.o u.p flat)	hd	2	11/4 2	95	20
	Coqui Lane (121) (JMDun) **9-12-0** TReed (led: rdn & hdd between last 2: sn wknd)	24	3	7/2 3	82	7
				(SP 106.8%)		3 Rn

4m 22.5 (9.50) CSF £2.72 TOTE £1.50 (£1.10) OWNER Mr G. Shiel (MIDDLEHAM) BRED Airlie Stud in Ireland
1314 Stash the Cash (IRE) travelled strongly throughout but, in the end, was flat to the boards to hold on. (8/11)
1360 Mr Knitwit, straighter than on his seasonal reappearance, made the winner pull out all the stops and, on softer ground and over further, is well capable of winning a race. (11/4)
Coqui Lane made the running until totally outpaced and is set to strip a lot fitter. (7/2)

1670 JOHN HINCHCLIFFE MEMORIAL CHAMPION H'CAP CHASE (5-Y.O+) (Class B)

2-30 (2-30) **3m 4f (17 fncs)** £10,172.25 (£3,078.00: £1,501.50: £713.25) GOING minus 0.13 sec per fur (G)

				SP	RR	SF
1293⁵	**Seven Towers (IRE) (115)** (MrsMReveley) **7-10-6** PNiven (lw: pushed along thrght: outpcd 5 out: hdwy u.p whn sltly hmpd last: styd on wl to ld cl home)	—	1	11/4 1	121	29
1506*	**Mony-Skip (IRE) (114)** (MrsSJSmith) **7-10-5** RichardGuest (lw: hld up & bhd: gd hdwy 3 out: led flat tl ct towards fin)	hd	2	3/1 2	120	28
1209²	**Westwell Boy (109)** (PBeaumont) **10-10-0** RSupple (j.w: led 7th tl hdd flat: kpt on)	4	3	11/2	113	21
1048⁵	**Pims Gunner (IRE) (109)** (MDHammond) **8-10-0** BHarding (in tch: ev ch appr last: one pce)	1½	4	5/1	112	20
1307²	**Aly Daley (IRE) (109)** (HowardJohnson) **8-10-0** ADobbin (mde most to 7th: cl up tl wknd qckly 4 out)	21	5	8/1	99	7
1578⁷	**Gala Water (109)** (TDCDun) **10-10-0** BStorey (prom tl wknd 3 out)	7	6	50/1	95	3
1266³	**Kilcolgan (109)** (MrsJDGoodfellow) **9-10-0** ASSmith (lw: chsd ldrs: 4th & styng on u.p whn fell last)		F	9/2 3	—	—
				(SP 115.0%)		7 Rn

7m 2.3 (0.60 under best) (6.30) CSF £11.11 CT £37.52 TOTE £3.10: £2.80 £1.60 (£6.10) OWNER Mrs E. A. Murray (SALTBURN) BRED J. Mernagh
LONG HANDICAP Westwell Boy 9-8 Pims Gunner (IRE) 9-12 Aly Daley (IRE) 9-8 Gala Water 8-5 Kilcolgan 9-9
1293 Seven Towers (IRE) was never on the bridle at all and made his pilot earn his fee. Described by his trainer as bone idle, he could well be the type to go on now he has hit winning form. He stays forever, and softer ground would be even more to his liking. (11/4)
1506* Mony-Skip (IRE) travelled best of all throughout and must have had his supporters ready to collect halfway up the run-in. When he was caught, it came as as much of a surprise to his pilot as to anyone else. (3/1)
1209 Westwell Boy put in a sound jumping display and still looked to be in the driving seat clearing the last, but he ran out of steam slightly on the run-in. He deserves to win a useful staying contest. (11/2)
1048 Pims Gunner (IRE) is again just looking a shade off his best form. (5/1)
1266 Kilcolgan was in fourth place when crashing out at the last. He is the type that would have relished the battle up the hill, and a staying race is well within his capabilities. (9/2)

1671 E. SCARTH & SON H'CAP HURDLE (0-130) (4-Y.O+) (Class C)

3-00 (3-00) **2m 6f 110y (11 hdls)** £3,820.00 (£1,156.00: £564.00: £268.00) GOING minus 0.13 sec per fur (G)

				SP	RR	SF
1347*	**Lochnagrain (IRE) (116)** (MrsMReveley) **8-11-9** PNiven (lw: hld up: hdwy 3 out: shkn up to ld flat: r.o wl)	—	1	5/2 1	96	25
1349*	**Trap Dancer (93)** (PMonteith) **8-10-0** ADobbin (lw: chsd ldrs: ev ch flat: nt pce of wnr)	8	2	11/4 2	67	—
	Trump (113) (CParker) **7-11-6** DParker (lw: trckd ldrs: led appr 2 out: hdd & one pce flat)	1¼	3	14/1	86	15
1347⁵	**Dig Deeper (98)** (RAllan) **9-10-5** BHarding (led tl hdd appr 2 out: sn btn)	11	4	14/1	64	—
1360³	**Nicholas Plant (96)** (JSGoldie) **7-10-0(3)** GLee (chsd clr ldr tl wknd 3 out)	5	5	100/30 3	58	—
1265²	**Tallywagger (117)** (GMMoore) **9-11-10** JCallaghan (hld up & bhd: reminders 7th: sn btn)	1¼	6	6/1	78	7
1304⁴	**D'Arblay Street (IRE) (93)** (WTKemp) **7-10-0b** SMcDougall (a bhd)	½	7	16/1	54	—
				(SP 111.8%)		7 Rn

5m 28.0 (11.00) CSF £9.27 TOTE £2.50: £1.10 £1.70 (£4.00) OWNER Lightbody of Hamilton Ltd (SALTBURN) BRED Michael Cuddy
LONG HANDICAP Trap Dancer 9-12 D'Arblay Street (IRE) 9-7
1347* Lochnagrain (IRE) continues to show his old sparkle and duly completed his hat-trick here. Cruising past the second and third on the run-in, he was laughing at them on the way to the line and is clearly in good heart at the moment. He could still go back over fences later in the season. (5/2)
1349* Trap Dancer had all bar the winner cooked as he attempted to follow up his recent win in good style at Ayr. (11/4)
Trump looked fairly straight for this seasonal debut and ran his heart out. He is now set to go chasing. (14/1: 8/1-16/1)
1360 Nicholas Plant missed out the odd hurdle here, but otherwise ran as well as could be expected. (100/30)
1265 Tallywagger, who is right off the boil at present, was sending out distress signals halfway down the far side on the final circuit. (6/1)

1672 OSWALD HUGHES MAIDEN AMATEUR HURDLE (4-Y.O+) (Class E)

3-30 (3-30) **2m 6f 110y (11 hdls)** £2,346.00 (£656.00: £318.00) GOING minus 0.13 sec per fur (G)

				SP	RR	SF
	Pharmistice (IRE) (MrsASwinbank) **5-11-3(7)** MrChrisWilson (in tch: hit 3rd: styd on to ld flat)	—	1	25/1	66	3
1316³	**Cash Box (IRE) (77)** (TJCarr) **8-11-3(7)** MrCMulhall (lw: in tch: hdwy 3 out: led last: hdd flat: kpt on)	1¼	2	11/2	65	2
	Black Ice (IRE) (TPTate) **5-11-3(7)** MrWBurnell (mde most fr 4th: hdd last: one pce)	6	3	5/1 3	61	—
	More Champagne (MrsDThomson) **6-11-0(5)** MissPRobson (prom: one pce fr 2 out)	1	4	66/1	55	—
1296⁵	**Cheater (IRE)** (HowardJohnson) **5-11-5(5)** MissPJones (lw: chsd ldrs: rdn & no ex fr 2 out)	hd	5	7/2 2	60	—
1245³	**The Next Waltz (IRE) (85)** (LLungo) **5-11-5(5)** MrMHNaughton (hld up: hdwy 8th: sn rdn & no imp)	6	6	7/1	56	—

Form	Horse	Dist	Pos	SP	RR	SF
	Crashballoo (IRE) (PCheesbrough) **5-11-3**(7) MrAParker (n.d)	12	**7**	8/1	47	—
1208[7]	**Nenagh Gunner** (JJQuinn) **6-11-5** MrSSwiers (bhd fr ½-wy)	2½	**8**	10/1	41	—
	Woodstock Lodge (USA) (VThompson) **8-11-7**(3) MrMThompson (prom to ½-wy: sn bhd: t.o)	dist	**9**	66/1	—	—
	La Riviera (IRE) (JIACharlton) **4-11-5**(5) MrNWilson (a bhd: t.o)	24	**10**	33/1	—	—
1316[2]	**Kasirama (IRE) (75)** (MDHammond) **5-11-7**(3) MrCBonner (mid div tl wknd 8th: p.u bef 2 out)		**P**	5/2[1]	—	—
1311[6]	**Alicharger** (PMonteith) **6-11-5**(5) MrRHale (led to 4th: wknd qckly after 7th: t.o whn p.u bef 3 out)		**P**	50/1	—	—
	Lyford Cay (IRE) (JRBewley) **6-11-3**(7) MrDSwindlehurst (sn bhd: t.o whn p.u after 6th)		**P**	40/1	—	—
	Marks Refrain (EMCaine) **12-11-3**(7) MrPMurray (sn bhd: t.o whn p.u after 6th)		**P**	100/1	—	—

(SP 130.7%) **14 Rn**

5m 35.2 (18.20) CSF £156.53 TOTE £30.90: £6.10 £2.90 £1.40 (£138.60) Trio £241.80 OWNER Mr John Halliday (RICHMOND) BRED J. Mernagh

OFFICIAL EXPLANATION **Kasirama (IRE): gurgled on the home turn.**

Pharmistice (IRE) showed no signs of form last season, and even his trainer had to talk his owner into keeping him in training. This came as a pleasant surprise. (25/1)

1316 Cash Box (IRE) struck the front at the last and seems to be gradually getting the hang of things. He is worth another try. (11/2)

Black Ice (IRE) was the subject of encouraging reports. He is a great big sort and a chaser in the making. (5/1)

1296 Cheater (IRE) jumped adequately on this hurdling debut and looks set to be a stayer once he gains experience. (7/2)

1245 The Next Waltz (IRE), probably still on the weak side, made steady ground on the final circuit, but was making little impression towards the end. He needs more time. (7/1)

Crashballoo (IRE) (8/1: 5/1-10/1)

99 Nenagh Gunner (10/1: 7/1-11/1)

T/Plpt: £192.20 (45.76 Tckts). T/Qdpt: £13.50 (70.69 Tckts). GB

1471-**WINCANTON** (R-H) (Good to firm)
Monday December 2nd

WEATHER: fine WIND: str

1673 CERNE ABBAS 'N.H.' NOVICES' HURDLE (4-Y.O+) (Class E)

1-20 (1-20) **2m 6f (11 hdls)** £2,670.00 (£745.00: £360.00) GOING minus 0.13 sec per fur (G)

Form	Horse	Dist	Pos	SP	RR	SF
1334[4]	**Galatasori Jane (IRE)** (PFNicholls) **6-10-0**(7) LCummins (lw: a.p: rdn to ld appr 2 out: styd on wl flat)	—	**1**	14/1	73	7
1378[2]	**Slipmatic (89)** (AndrewTurnell) **7-10-0**(7) CRae (hld up: hdwy 7th: ev ch whn hit last: one pce)	5	**2**	3/1[2]	69	3
1329[2]	**Another Cockpit** (PJHobbs) **4-10-12** APMcCoy (trckd ldrs: rdn & outpcd appr 2 out: styd on flat)	4	**3**	4/1[3]	72	6
1417[4]	**Quinag (89)** (KCBailey) **5-10-7** JAMcCarthy (lw: prom: led 5th to 3 out: wknd 2 out)	1½	**4**	9/1	65	—
1334[2]	**Copper Coil (85)** (WGMTurner) **6-10-5**(7) JPower (a.p: no hdwy fr 3 out)	6	**5**	11/1	66	—
1476*	**Kilmington (IRE) (110)** (JTGifford) **7-11-5** PHide (led to 5th: led 3 out tl appr 2 out: sn wknd)	1¼	**6**	7/4[1]	72	6
1476[7]	**Young Tycoon (NZ) (78)** (AJWilson) **5-10-12** LHarvey (mid div: wknd after 3 out: eased whn no ch 2 out)	dist	**7**	66/1	—	—
1412[4]	**Warrio** (JRBosley) **6-10-12** MBosley (a bhd: t.o)	17	**8**	50/1	—	—
1438[7]	**Prussian Eagle (IRE)** (MBradstock) **4-10-7** PHolley (s.s: a bhd: t.o 8th: p.u bef 2 out)		**P**	33/1	—	—
1388[6]	**Mr Strong Gale (IRE)** (PFNicholls) **5-10-5**(7) OBurrows (lw: hld up: hdwy 7th: in tch whn stumbled & rdr lost irons after 3 out: p.u bef 2 out)		**P**	14/1	—	—
1536[P]	**Camino** (RJSmith) **9-10-12b[1]** CMaude (plld hrd: jnd ldrs 3rd: wknd qckly 7th: t.o whn p.u bef 2 out)		**P**	33/1	—	—
	Rambling On (CJDrewe) **6-10-9**(3) PHenley (bkwd: a bhd: t.o whn p.u bef 2 out)		**P**	50/1	—	—
1388[9]	**Quisti** (PRHedger) **6-10-12** MRichards (a bhd: t.o whn p.u after 3 out)		**P**	33/1	—	—
	Stormhill Harpie (JCABatchelor) **5-10-7** SBurrough (bit bkwd: plld hrd: prom to 6th: t.o 8th: p.u bef 2 out)		**P**	66/1	—	—

(SP 128.8%) **14 Rn**

5m 20.6 (11.60) CSF £56.00 TOTE £23.10: £3.30 £1.80 £1.60 (£247.40) Trio £32.40 OWNER Mr B. L. Blinman (SHEPTON MALLET)

STEWARDS' ENQUIRY Rae susp. 11-14 & 16-18/12/96 (excessive use of whip)

1334 Galatasori Jane (IRE) showed improved form and seemed to relish the battle more than the runner-up. (14/1)

1378 Slipmatic looked none too enthusiastic and her rider again incurred the wrath of the Stewards, picking up another whip-ban. (3/1)

1329 Another Cockpit, graduating to hurdles, is out of a mare who won over three miles plus, and gave the impression that he requires further. (4/1: op 5/2)

1417 Quinag may have found this trip beyond her best. (9/1)

1334 Copper Coil would have been better off trying to draw the sting out of the others by forcing the pace. (11/1)

1476* Kilmington (IRE) had plenty of use made of him and found disappointingly little in the home straight. (7/4)

1388 Mr Strong Gale (IRE) looked to be travelling well when appearing to clip the heels of a rival at the end of the back straight. (14/1: 8/1-16/1)

1674 SOMERSET CONDITIONAL H'CAP CHASE (0-120) (5-Y.O+) (Class E)

1-50 (1-50) **3m 1f 110y (21 fncs)** £3,570.00 (£870.00) GOING minus 0.13 sec per fur (G)

Form	Horse	Dist	Pos	SP	RR	SF
	Badastan (IRE) (110) (PJHobbs) **7-11-11b** GTormey (mde all: rdn appr 3 out: r.o wl)	—	**1**	2/1[1]	117	—
	Price's Hill (107) (KCBailey) **9-11-3**(5) WWalsh (hit 2nd: wnt 2nd 5th: ev ch whn mstke 3 out: hit 2 out: r.o one pce flat)	2	**2**	4/1	113	—
1473[3]	**Rainbow Castle (105)** (PFNicholls) **9-11-3**(3) OBurrows (fell 2nd)		**F**	5/2[2]	—	—
1420[3]	**Credon (103)** (SWoodman) **8-11-4** PHenley (chsd wnr to 5th: rdn after 17th: sn lost tch: t.o whn p.u bef last)		**P**	100/30[3]	—	—

(SP 105.0%) **4 Rn**

6m 42.5 (23.50) CSF £8.41 TOTE £2.40 (£4.30) OWNER In Touch Racing Club (MINEHEAD) BRED H. H. Aga Khan

Badastan (IRE), not inconvenienced by the fast ground, made a successful comeback off a mark 4lb higher than when narrowly beaten by General Rusty at Uttoxeter fourteen months ago. (2/1)

Price's Hill would have preferred softer ground, but his old jumping problems were again to the fore. (4/1: 5/2-9/2)

1675 CHARD CLAIMING HURDLE (3-Y.O) (Class F)

2-20 (2-22) **2m (8 hdls)** £2,372.50 (£660.00: £317.50) GOING minus 0.13 sec per fur (G)

Form	Horse	Dist	Pos	SP	RR	SF
1444[5]	**Lady Magnum (IRE)** (JNeville) **3-10-9** PHide (a.p: led 4th: rdn out)	—	**1**	16/1	65	31
1387[2]	**Always Happy** (MCPipe) **3-11-7** APMcCoy (hld up: hdwy appr 2 out: chsd wnr appr last: no imp)	4	**2**	8/11[1]	73	39
1377[5]	**Stonecutter** (MRChannon) **3-11-6v[1]** RHughes (hld up: hdwy 4th: outpcd appr 2 out: styd on flat)	7	**3**	6/1[2]	65	31

			SP	RR	SF
1444[2]	**Siberian Mystic** (PGMurphy) **3-10-12** WMcFarland (hld up: hdwy 4th: rdn & ev ch appr 2 out: sn wknd).......nk	**4**	13/2[3]	57	23
1526[13]	**Indira (82)** (CLPopham) **3-9-11**(3) TDascombe (a.p: ev ch whn hit 2 out: sn wknd)........2	**5**	7/1	43	9
1595[5]	**Stone Island** (PJHobbs) **3-10-8b**(3) GTormey (hld up: hdwy 4th: rdn & wknd appr 2 out)........3	**6**	14/1	51	17
1413[P]	**Four Weddings (USA)** (MCPipe) **3-10-5v** CMaude (led: reminder after 1st: hdd 4th: ev ch appr 2 out: sn wknd)........17	**7**	20/1	28	—
	Miss Pravda (BJLlewellyn) **3-10-12** MrJLLlewellyn (a bhd: t.o fr 5th)........dist	**8**	25/1	—	—
1413[5]	**Prove The Point (IRE)** (MrsPNDutfield) **3-10-3** PHolley (prom: rdn after 3rd: sn wknd: t.o whn p.u bef 2 out)....	**P**	33/1	—	—
			(SP 122.1%)	**9 Rn**	

3m 43.5 (3.50) CSF £28.86 TOTE £15.50: £6.10 £1.50 £1.90 (£14.80) Trio £36.30 OWNER Magnum Construction Ltd (NEWPORT, GWENT) BRED M. B. O'Toole

OFFICIAL EXPLANATION **Lady Magnum (IRE): accounting for the filly's apparent improvement, her trainer reported she was better suited by the good to firm ground, and also by the fact that she was able to get away with the field at the start.**

1444 Lady Magnum (IRE) was far more positively ridden than at Hereford. The Stewards enquired into the improved form and were told that the mare had got away on level terms this time, and liked the faster ground. (16/1)

1387 Always Happy had no excuses and simply met one too good at the weights. (8/11)

Stonecutter, tried in a visor, stayed on again in the closing stages to snatch the minor berth after looking well held. (6/1)

1444 Siberian Mystic was forced to check for a stride or two on the inside entering the home straight, but should by no means be considered unlucky. (13/2)

1332 Indira had beaten the winner three lengths on 9lb better terms at Warwick when Lady Magnum probably did not have the run of the race. (7/1: op 7/2)

1595 Stone Island, making a quick reappearance, rather surprisingly seemed to settle better in the headgear, but the end result was just the same. (14/1: 7/1-16/1)

1676 NIGHTINGALE SINGS H'CAP CHASE (0-120) (5-Y.O+) (Class D)

2-50 (2-50) **2m 5f (17 fncs)** £4,524.00 (£1,264.00: £612.00) GOING minus 0.13 sec per fur (G)

			SP	RR	SF
1379*	**Too Plush (109)** (AndrewTurnell) **7-11-7** LHarvey (prom: hit 6th: j.slowly 10th: rdn after 13th: poor 3rd whn lft clr 2 out)........—	**1**	5/2[2]	108	—
	Five to Seven (USA) (112) (PFNicholls) **7-11-10** APMcCoy (led to 8th: led 12th: 6l clr whn bdly hmpd by loose horse & ref 2 out: continued)........dist	**2**	2/1[1]	—	—
	The Mine Captain (98) (OSherwood) **9-10-10** JAMcCarthy (a.p: led 8th to 12th: 2nd & btn whn lft in ld, bdly hmpd by loose horse, ref & uns rdr 2 out: cont)........3	**3**	5/2[2]	—	—
1515*	**The Caumrue (IRE) (108)** (GBBalding) **8-11-6** BClifford (hld up: fell 7th)........	**F**	4/1[3]	—	—
			(SP 110.5%)	**4 Rn**	

5m 31.5 (23.50) CSF £7.40 TOTE £2.70 (£5.70) OWNER Mrs C. C. Williams (WANTAGE) BRED Miss B. Sykes

1379* Too Plush, raised 6lb, was only destined to finish a remote last of three until the mini Foinavon-style pile-up happened at the second last. (5/2)

Five to Seven (USA) was bought for 20,000 guineas out of Chris Thornton's stable at Doncaster September Sales. Having burnt off The Mine Captain early in the home straight, he was robbed of victory in the melee at the second last. (2/1)

The Mine Captain briefly looked to be having his lucky day when misfortune struck Five to Seven, but the loose horse came back across the fence and stopped him too. (5/2)

1677 ORCHARD FM NOVICES' CHASE (5-Y.O+ Mares Only) (Class E)

3-20 (3-21) **2m (13 fncs)** £2,856.00 (£858.00: £414.00: £192.00) GOING minus 0.13 sec per fur (G)

			SP	RR	SF
1475[4]	**Second Call (104)** (CaptTAForster) **7-11-7** APMcCoy (a.p: led after 9th: lft clr 4 out: easily)........—	**1**	1/2[1]	93+	2
	Josifina (AGFoster) **5-11-0** CMaude (hld up: hdwy 6th: outpcd 9th: lft 2nd 4 out: no ch w wnr)........5	**2**	9/2[2]	81	—
1475*	**Koo's Promise (83)** (CLPopham) **5-11-4**(3) TDascombe (led to 3rd: pckd 4th: outpcd 9th: hmpd 4 out: r.o one pce fr 3 out)........2	**3**	12/1[3]	86	—
	Mistress Rosie (72) (MHill) **9-11-0** SFox (bhd fr 7th: j.rt 8th: sn t.o)........dist	**4**	16/1	—	—
	Relkowen (AndrewTurnell) **6-11-0** MRichards (w ldr: led 3rd tl after 9th: cl 2nd whn fell 4 out)........	**F**	9/2[2]	—	—
1475[3]	**Up the Tempo (IRE)** (PaddyFarrell) **7-11-0** JRKavanagh (t.o 4th: p.u bef 4 out)........	**P**	33/1	—	—
			(SP 119.5%)	**6 Rn**	

4m 6.1 (13.10) CSF £3.75 TOTE £1.50: £1.40 £2.00 (£3.20) OWNER Mr J. H. Day (LUDLOW) BRED C. J. R. Trotter

1475 Second Call made amends for her unlucky defeat here last time. (1/2)

Josifina proved no match for the winner on her fencing bow. (9/2)

1475* Koo's Promise was penalised for her most fortunate victory over the winner here last time. (12/1: 8/1-14/1)

Relkowen was giving a good account of herself in her first race over the major obstacles when departing at the downhill cross fence. (9/2)

1678 MANSTON H'CAP HURDLE (0-115) (4-Y.O+) (Class E)

3-50 (3-50) **2m 6f (11 hdls)** £2,427.00 (£672.00: £321.00) GOING minus 0.13 sec per fur (G)

			SP	RR	SF
1250*	**General Mouktar (96)** (MCPipe) **6-11-0** APMcCoy (hld up: hdwy after 3 out: led flat: cleverly)........—	**1**	7/4[1]	79+	14
1474*	**Morstock (110)** (RJHodges) **6-11-11**(3) TDascombe (hld up: hdwy after 3 out: ev ch last: hrd rdn: unable qckn)........1¼	**2**	6/1	92	27
1342[2]	**Silver Standard (102)** (CaptTAForster) **6-11-6b** CMaude (a.p: led after 3 out tl flat: hrd rdn: unable qckn)......½	**3**	2/1[2]	84	19
810[5]	**Cavina (108)** (NAGraham) **6-11-12** PHide (chsd ldr: lft in ld 3 out: sn hdd: wknd appr 2 out)........dist	**4**	7/2[3]	—	—
1334[6]	**Mu-Tadil (82)** (RJBaker) **4-9-7**(7) NTEgan (nt j.w: t.o fr 6th)........dist	**5**	50/1	—	—
1455[5]	**Welshman (104)** (MBlanshard) **10-11-8** JRKavanagh (led tl stumbled bdly & hdd 3 out: nt rcvr: p.u bef 2 out)...	**P**	16/1	—	—
			(SP 114.0%)	**6 Rn**	

5m 20.5 (11.50) CSF £11.76 TOTE £2.50: £1.70 £1.90 (£4.60) OWNER Mr A. S. Helaissi (WELLINGTON) BRED Stetchworth Park Stud Ltd

LONG HANDICAP Mu-Tadil 8-11

1250* General Mouktar, given a peach of a ride, scored without knowing he had been in a race. (7/4)

1474* Morstock did not try to steal it at the start this time. (6/1: 4/1-7/1)

1342 Silver Standard, up 2lb, was off a mark 8lb above the highest off which he had won. (2/1)

810 Cavina, not given a hard time once her chance had gone, does not appear very well handicapped. (7/2)

1455 Welshman was still in front when stumbling and, assuming he did not do himself a mischief, this form can be safely ignored. (16/1)

T/Plpt: £127.30 (74.83 Tckts). T/Qdpt: £16.10 (75.83 Tckts). KH

1323-WORCESTER (L-H) (Good to soft)

Monday December 2nd

Race 2: one fence omitted
WEATHER: fine & sunny

1679 RUSHOCK NOVICES' HURDLE (4-Y.O+ F & M) (Class E)

12-40 (12-42) **2m (8 hdls)** £2,407.50 (£670.00: £322.50) GOING: 0.86 sec per fur (S)

				SP	RR	SF
1450*	**Melstock Meggie** (MrsJPitman) **6-10-12** WMarston (lw: a.p: led after 5th: mstke last: rdn & edgd rt flat: r.o)	—	**1**	3/1^{3}	58	6
1341^{5}	**Moor Hall Lady** (NMBabbage) **5-10-12** AMaguire (mid div: pckd 1st: hdwy 4th: ev ch whn blnd 2 out: one pce flat)	3	**2**	6/1	55	3
	Slippery Fin (WGMTurner) **4-10-5**(7) NWillmington (bkwd: hld up in tch: effrt appr 5th: one pce fr 2 out)	3	**3**	25/1	52	—
	Fairelaine (KCBailey) **4-10-5**(7) MrRWakley (bit bkwd: hld up & bhd: j.slowly 1st: hdwy 3 out: styd on)	2½	**4**	16/1	50	—
1369^{10}	**Quaker Waltz** (JCTuck) **6-10-12** SMcNeill (hld up: hdwy to chse ldrs 5th: no imp fr next)	5	**5**	20/1	45	—
1388*	**Gloriana** (LadyHerries) **4-11-5** MAFitzgerald (led: mstke 2nd: hdd after 5th: wknd next: sn eased: t.o)	13	**6**	9/4^{1}	39	—
1470^{P}	**Persian Butterfly** (RMStronge) **4-10-9**(3) DWalsh (bit bkwd: j.rt: chsd ldr to 5th: drvn & wknd appr next: t.o)	10	**7**	66/1	22	—
1337^{8}	**Derrybelle** (DLWilliams) **5-10-12** MClarke (bhd fr 3rd: t.o)	17	**8**	50/1	5	—
1470^{13}	**Becky's Girl** (RBrotherton) **6-10-12** NMann (bit bkwd: a bhd: t.o fr 5th)	dist	**9**	66/1	—	—
	Konvekta Queen (IRE) (OSherwood) **5-10-12** JOsborne (bit bkwd: cl up: pckd 3rd: wkng whn mstke next: t.o whn p.u bef 5th)		**P**	5/2^{2}	—	—
1457^{18}	**Persian Sunset (IRE)** (MissJBower) **4-10-12** DBridgwater (bit bkwd: a bhd: t.o whn p.u bef 3 out)		**P**	66/1	—	—
	Cupronickel (IRE) (DBurchell) **4-10-12** DJBurchell (bkwd: a bhd: t.o 5th: p.u bef next)		**P**	100/1	—	—
1448^{P}	**Forburies (IRE) (55)** (APJames) **7-10-12b**^{1} BPowell (chsd ldrs: j.slowly 3rd: lost pl qckly: t.o whn p.u bef 5th)		**P**	100/1	—	—

(SP 121.5%) **13 Rn**

4m 5.3 (25.30) CSF £20.61 TOTE £4.20: £1.50 £1.80 £3.20 (£13.20) Trio £72.20 OWNER Mrs Kay Birchenhough (UPPER LAMBOURN) BRED Mrs Kay Birchenhough

OFFICIAL EXPLANATION **Konvekta Queen (IRE): the rider reported that the mare lost her action in the back straight and began to jump poorly. Fearing something was amiss, he pulled her up, although she appeared fine soon afterwards.**

1450* Melstock Meggie was able to make a winning debut over hurdles, but won with very little to spare and is sure to be more impressive over further. (3/1)

1341 Moor Hall Lady improved on her initial outing over hurdles and may have got closer to winning had her jumping been as fluent as the winners. (6/1)

Slippery Fin, very lightly-raced, was making her hurdling debut. She moved through to pose a threat running in, but found lack of peak-fitness taking its toll when the race began in earnest. (25/1)

Fairelaine, a mediocre performer on the Flat, ran respectably on this hurdling debut and should have no trouble improving on this. (16/1)

885 Quaker Waltz edged closer on the home turn and briefly threatened danger before her one pace proved inadequate. (20/1)

1388* Gloriana dropped away rather quickly after being headed at the end of the back straight and, though she was eased when beaten, this was a very much below-par performance. (9/4: op 6/4)

1680 BET WITH THE TOTE QUALIFIER NOVICES' CHASE (5-Y.O+) (Class E)

1-10 (1-12) **2m 4f 110y (14 fncs)** £3,605.00 (£1,085.00: £525.00: £245.00) GOING: 0.86 sec per fur (S)

				SP	RR	SF
1281^{3}	**Pharanear (IRE)** (DNicholson) **6-10-12** AMaguire (chsd ldrs: mstke 7th: rdn 11th: led last: sn hdd: rallied u.p to ld nr fin)	—	**1**	5/1^{3}	119	55
1156^{5}	**Treasure Again (IRE)** (MrsMerritaJones) **7-10-12** DerekByrne (hld up: hdwy 7th: jnd ldr 3 out: led briefly flat: r.o)	nk	**2**	11/4^{1}	119	55
	Three Philosophers (IRE) (CaptTAForster) **7-10-12** SWynne (led 3rd to last: one pce)	5	**3**	6/1	115	51
	Stay Lucky (NZ) (NJHenderson) **7-11-5** MAFitzgerald (a chsng ldrs: rdn & hit 2 out: kpt on one pce)	hd	**4**	8/1	122	58
1320^{U}	**Macgeorge (IRE)** (RLee) **6-10-12** CLlewellyn (bhd: mstke 3rd: lost tch 6th: stdy hdwy 10th: no imp fr 3 out: t.o)	dist	**5**	9/2^{2}	—	—
1340^{2}	**Key To Moyade (IRE) (98)** (MJWilkinson) **6-10-12** ILawrence (mid div tl lost tch 11th: t.o)	17	**6**	16/1	—	—
	Domaine de Pron (FR) (MrsLCTaylor) **5-10-12** MSharratt (bkwd: mid div: mstke 2nd: wknd 9th: t.o)	5	**7**	50/1	—	—
1447^{F}	**Bonnifer (IRE)** (MJWilkinson) **7-10-12** WMarston (bkwd: in tch tl mstke 9th: t.o)	dist	**8**	66/1	—	—
	The Booley House (IRE) (97) (VSoane) **6-10-12** BPowell (bkwd: led to 2nd: fell 5th)		**F**	14/1	—	—
1646^{F}	**Two John's (IRE)** (PFNicholls) **7-10-12** GBradley (prom: mstke 7th: drvn in 4th whn p.u bef last: lame)		**P**	9/1	—	—
1260^{P}	**Dunnicks Country** (FGTucker) **6-10-7** GUpton (mstke 3rd: lost tch 6th: t.o whn p.u bef 8th)		**P**	66/1	—	—
	Caracol (JNeville) **7-10-12** DBridgwater (bkwd: led 2nd to 3rd: wknd 8th: t.o whn p.u bef 3 out)		**P**	50/1	—	—
	Be Brave (TJEtherington) **6-10-12** NMann (bkwd: a bhd: lost tch 6th: t.o whn p.u bef 3 out)		**P**	50/1	—	—
	Il Bambino (HJManners) **8-10-5**(7) ADowling (bit bkwd: a bhd: lost tch 6th: j.slowly 8th: t.o whn p.u bef 10th)		**P**	50/1	—	—
1332^{4}	**Tibbs Inn** (ABarrow) **7-10-7**(5) MrRThornton (reluctant to r: ref 1st)		**R**	66/1	—	—
	Easy Breezy (CJMann) **6-10-12** JRailton (b.d 5th)		**U**	25/1	—	—
1429^{7}	**The Reverend Bert (IRE)** (GBBalding) **8-10-12** BFenton (hmpd & uns rdr 5th)		**U**	14/1	—	—

(SP 132.3%) **17 Rn**

5m 20.0 (19.00) CSF £19.36 TOTE £5.20: £1.30 £2.40 £2.10 (£7.50) Trio £18.40 OWNER Stainless Threaded Fasteners Ltd (TEMPLE GUITING) BRED Seamus Kennedy

STEWARDS' ENQUIRY Byrne susp. 11-13/12/96 (excessive use of whip).

1281 Pharanear (IRE), stepping back to two and a half miles, makes hard work of fencing, but had the right man on top to get the best out of him, and this success is down to Maguire. (5/1: op 3/1)

1156 Treasure Again (IRE) turned in a bold display of jumping and was always travelling like the winner but, when it developed into a sprint to the line, strength from the saddle proved the deciding factor. (11/4)

Three Philosophers (IRE) jumped much better than he did on many occasions last season, and made the leading pair pull out all the stops to get the better of him. (6/1: op 4/1)

Stay Lucky (NZ), a winner on the Flat as well as over fences in New Zealand, needed the run after a break of over three months, and he pressed the leaders until an untidy effort at what was now the penultimate obstacle took the stuffing out of him. (8/1)

Macgeorge (IRE) (9/2: 4/1-6/1)

Two John's (IRE) survived the odd mistake and remained in the action, but was fourth and in trouble when he was pulled up and dismounted approaching the last. (9/1: 6/1-10/1)

1681 RIVER SEVERN H'CAP HURDLE (0-125) (4-Y.O+) (Class D)
1-40 (1-40) **2m 4f (10 hdls)** £3,120.00 (£870.00: £420.00) GOING: 0.86 sec per fur (S)

	Horse	Dist	Pos	SP	RR	SF
	Big Strand (IRE) (107) (MCPipe) **7-11-5**(3) DWalsh (hld up: stdy hdwy 5th: mstke 3 out: slt ld last: hrd rdn & r.o flat)	—	1	5/1^{2}	85	38
1286^{5}	**Reaganesque (USA) (105)** (PGMurphy) **4-11-6** RFarrant (chsd ldr: led appr 5th: rdn 2 out: hdd last: ev ch flat: no ex fnl 100y)	4	2	6/1	80	33
1074^{7}	**Mr Snaggle (IRE) (91)** (SEarle) **7-10-6** AMaguire (hld up: hdwy 7th: sn chsng ldrs: wknd 2 out)	18	3	5/1^{2}	51	4
1428^{P}	**Fast Thoughts (109)** (DRGandolfo) **9-11-5**(5) SophieMitchell (led: sn clr: hdd appr 5th: wknd next: sn lost tch: t.o)	17	4	16/1	56	9
1417*	**Glistening Dawn (97)** (TKeddy) **6-10-12b** SMcNeill (hld up: hdwy 5th: wknd 7th: t.o)	dist	5	4/1^{1}	—	—
	Major Nova (100) (NASmith) **7-11-1** JRyan (bkwd: sn wl bhd: t.o whn p.u bef 3 out)		P	20/1	—	—
	Nuns Cone (93) (REPeacock) **8-10-5**(3) GHogan (bkwd: prom tl lost pl qckly appr 5th: t.o whn p.u bef 7th)		P	16/1	—	—
	Trecento (92) (JMackie) **5-10-7** WMarston (hld up: hdwy 3rd: wknd 7th: t.o whn p.u bef next)		P	5/1^{2}	—	—
	Manolete (103) (MrsMerritaJones) **5-11-4** DerekByrne (bit bkwd: chsd ldrs tl wknd 7th: t.o whn p.u bef 2 ut)		P	11/2^{3}	—	—
				(SP 116.2%)	**9 Rn**	

5m 3.4 (25.40) CSF £32.50 CT £144.03 TOTE £6.60: £3.00 £2.00 £1.20 (£21.90) Trio £87.20; £3.69 to Newcastle 3/12/96 OWNER Mr E. C. Jones (WELLINGTON) BRED M. Parkhill

Big Strand (IRE) had to dig deep on this long run-in, but he always appeared to have the measure of his nearest challenger. (5/1: op 5/2)

1286 Reaganesque (USA) is finding it hard to get back to winning ways, but he gave it his best shot here, and fortune will favour him before long. (6/1)

1074 Mr Snaggle (IRE) has not won since he came over from Ireland, and the way he was left behind from the penultimate flight would suggest he either needs more testing ground or a longer trip. (5/1)

1417* Glistening Dawn, reluctant to leave the paddock, seemed to do nothing wrong once in action, though she did lose her place passing the stables at the end of the back straight. In this mood, she is not worth bothering with. (4/1: op 5/2)

Manolete (11/2: op 3/1)

1682 KEMPSEY H'CAP CHASE (0-135) (4-Y.O+) (Class C)
2-10 (2-11) **2m (12 fncs)** £4,467.50 (£1,340.00: £645.00: £297.50) GOING: 0.86 sec per fur (S)

	Horse	Dist	Pos	SP	RR	SF
	Mister Oddy (123) (JSKing) **10-11-7** MAFitzgerald (in tch: hdwy 6th: led 4 out: clr 2 out: eased flat)	—	1	7/1	134	40
1442*	**Thumbs Up (130)** (GMMcCourt) **10-11-11**(3) DFortt (a.p: rdn to chse wnr appr 3 out: no imp)	6	2	6/1	135	41
	Random Assault (NZ) (130) (DNicholson) **7-12-0** AMaguire (bit bkwd: plld hrd: led: sn clr: hit 4th: hdd 8th: sn led again: hdd 4 out: grad wknd)	6	3	4/1^{3}	129	35
1393*	**Newlands-General (118)** (PFNicholls) **10-11-2** GBradley (sn chsng ldr: led & hit 8th: sn hdd: wkng whn blnd 4 out)	1¼	4	9/4^{1}	116	22
	Seek The Faith (USA) (107) (MSheppard) **7-10-5** BPowell (bkwd: in rr: effrt & hdwy appr 4 out: wknd bef next)	8	5	9/4^{1}	97	3
1393^{F}	**Kytton Castle (102)** (RDickin) **9-10-0** RBellamy (bit bkwd: a bhd: lost tch 8th: t.o whn p.u bef 4 out)		P	7/1	—	—
*1352**	***Konvekta King (IRE) (128)*** (OSherwood) **8-11-12** JOsborne (Withdrawn not under Starter's orders: veterinary advice)		W	3/1^{2}	—	—
				(SP 145.8%)	**6 Rn**	

4m 10.9 (19.90) CSF £44.13 TOTE £10.50: £3.70 £2.70 (£20.70) OWNER Mrs R. M. Hill (SWINDON) BRED V. N. F. Tjolle

LONG HANDICAP Random Assault (NZ) 74-1 Kytton Castle 9-11

Mister Oddy hardly knows how to run a bad race and, though he is reaching the veteran stage, he still retains the ability to show the young pretenders a thing or two. (7/1)

1442* Thumbs Up would have brushed the winner aside in his heyday, but time is catching up with him and he had no option but to settle for the runner-up prize. (6/1: 7/2-7/1)

Random Assault (NZ), a very versatile performer in his native New Zealand, ran much too freely in his first outing in this country. Surviving an early mistake, he made his share of the running until calling enough once straightened up for home. He will win once he gets acclimatised. (4/1)

1393* Newlands-General had just struck the front when he misjudged the fifth last, and was struggling to hang on when another poor effort at the final ditch, four out, all but severed the partnership. (9/4)

Seek The Faith (USA) made a winning start last season and is thought to be best when fresh, but he looked far from the finished article here and ran accordingly. (9/4)

1393 Kytton Castle (7/1: 12/1-8/1)

1683 SPETCHLEY 'N.H.' NOVICES' HURDLE (4-Y.O+) (Class E)
2-40 (2-43) **2m 4f (10 hdls)** £2,915.00 (£815.00: £395.00) GOING: 0.86 sec per fur (S)

	Horse	Dist	Pos	SP	RR	SF
1536*	**Forest Ivory (NZ)** (DNicholson) **5-11-3** AMaguire (hld up in tch: led appr 3 out: clr next: pushed out flat)	—	1	Evens^{1}	87+	41
1422^{2}	**Dantes Cavalier (IRE)** (DRGandolfo) **6-10-7**(3) DFortt (hld up: hdwy 6th: chsd wnr appr last: r.o)	2½	2	3/1^{2}	78	32
	Aut Even (IRE) (CaptTAForster) **6-10-10** SWynne (bit bkwd: mid div: hdwy appr 7th: chsd wnr 2 out: wknd flat)	10	3	16/1	70	24
1323^{2}	**Denham Hill (IRE)** (CJMann) **5-10-10** JRailton (trckd ldrs: chal whn stumbled 3 out: sn rdn: grad wknd)	1½	4	7/1^{3}	69	23
1394^{2}	**Dancetillyoudrop (IRE)** (PFNicholls) **5-10-10** MAFitzgerald (hld up in tch: hdwy 7th: ev ch 3 out:wknd next)	10	5	10/1	61	15
1317^{13}	**Rathkeal (IRE)** (MJHeaton-Ellis) **5-10-10** DGallagher (nt trble ldrs)	10	6	50/1	53	7
	Loughdoo (IRE) (RLee) **8-10-7**(3) GHogan (bkwd: hld up: sme late hdwy: nvr nrr)	½	7	66/1	52	6
	Cast of Thousands (CREgerton) **5-10-10** JOsborne (bkwd: hld up: hdwy to chse ldrs 3 out: wknd appr next)	11	8	20/1	44	—
1470^{11}	**Don't Mind If I Do (IRE)** (PRWebber) **5-10-10** MrPScott (bit bkwd: sn chsng ldrs: wknd appr 7th: t.o)	1½	9	100/1	42	—
	Careysville (IRE) (TRGeorge) **5-10-5**(5) MrRThornton (bkwd: cl up: rdn 3 out: wkng whn mstke next: t.o)	1½	10	66/1	41	—
1283^{5}	**West Bay Breeze** (RHBuckler) **4-10-5** BPowell (hld up: hdwy appr 5th: wkng whn mstke 3 out: t.o)	2	11	50/1	35	—
1191^{4}	**Spring Double (IRE)** (NATwiston-Davies) **5-10-10** CLlewellyn (led to 4th: regained ld 7th: hdd appr next: sn wknd: t.o)	15	12	9/1	28	—
1431^{6}	**Greenfield George (IRE)** (PJHobbs) **5-10-5**(5) DJKavanagh (bkwd: chsd ldrs: led 5th to 7th: wknd appr 3 out: t.o)	18	13	40/1	13	—

				SP	RR	SF
1457[16]	**Derrys Prerogative** (AWCarroll) **6-10-10** DBridgwater (bit bkwd: a bhd: t.o)	18	**14**	100/1	—	—
1422[8]	**Little Earn** (MissHCKnight) **6-10-3**(7) MrAWintle (a bhd: t.o)	14	**15**	100/1	—	—
1297[4]	**Ragdon** (MrsARHewitt) **5-10-10** GUpton (a bhd: t.o whn p.u bef 3 out)		**P**	66/1	—	—
1090[P]	**Gutteridge (IRE)** (TKeddy) **6-10-10** SMcNeill (chsd ldrs to 6th: sn wknd: t.o whn p.u flat)		**P**	20/1	—	—
1448[P]	**Althrey Aristocrat (IRE) (60)** (FLloyd) **6-10-7**(3) DWalsh (bit bkwd: prom: led 4th to 5th: sn wknd: t.o whn p.u bef 7th)		**P**	100/1	—	—
1197[P]	**Karicleigh Man** (PJHobbs) **6-10-10** GBradley (hld up: hdwy appr 5th: wknd appr 7th: t.o whn p.u bef 3 ut)		**P**	25/1	—	—
1341[10]	**Miss Mylette (IRE)** (DJWintle) **5-10-5** TJenks (prom: mstke 5th: wknd 7th: t.o whn p.u bef 2 out)		**P**	100/1	—	—
	Hanaford Point (IRE) (MrsJPitman) **7-10-5** WMarston (bkwd: nt j.w: chsd ldrs: bhd fr 5th: t.o whn p.u bef 7th)		**P**	33/1	—	—
1453[F]	**Derring Jack** (AWCarroll) **5-10-10** TJMurphy (a bhd: blnd & uns rdr 2 out)		**U**	100/1	—	—

(SP 145.6%) **22 Rn**

5m 1.4 (23.40) CSF £5.42 TOTE £2.00: £1.50 £1.10 £5.60 (£4.70) Trio £56.40 OWNER The Old Foresters Partnership (TEMPLE GUITING) BRED P. S. and Mrs C. Nelson

1536* Forest Ivory (NZ), supported to the exclusion of the rest, duly obliged with the minimum of fuss and is beginning to look more than a bit useful. (Evens)

1422 Dantes Cavalier (IRE) ran another promising race and, though he was unable to trouble the winner, he finished ten lengths clear of the rest. Another half-mile would be in his favour. (3/1)

Aut Even (IRE), winner of a bumper in Ireland, is not just getting it together over here, but there was plenty to like about this performance, and he could be a different proposition once his attentions are turned to fences. (16/1)

1323 Denham Hill (IRE), poised to challenge when losing his footing three out, was soon being bustled along and, with the pace not dropping, was unable to hold his pitch. (7/1: 5/1-8/1)

1394 Dancetillyoudrop (IRE) did pose a serious threat three out, but he had been made to work to get there, and had shot his bolt before reaching the next. He will be more at home over three miles. (10/1: op 6/1)

Cast of Thousands, carrying far too much condition for this hurdling debut, will be winning once tuned up. (20/1)

1191 Spring Double (IRE) (9/1: 6/1-10/1)

1684 MALVERN H'CAP CHASE (0-100) (4-Y.O+) (Class F)

3-10 (3-11) **2m 7f 110y (18 fncs)** £2,910.00 (£810.00: £390.00) GOING: 0.86 sec per fur (S)

				SP	RR	SF
1302*	**Lord of the West (IRE) (98)** (JJO'Neill) **7-12-0** AMaguire (lw: hld up & bhd: hdwy appr 10th: mstke 12th: rdn appr last: led flat: all out)	—	**1**	5/2[2]	108	35
1465*	**Eastern River (80)** (CaptTAForster) **10-10-10** SWynne (hld up: hdwy 9th: led & blnd 4 out: sn hdd: regained ld 2 out: hrd rdn & hdd flat: no ex)	1	**2**	7/4[1]	89	16
	Hangover (75) (RLee) **10-10-2**(3) GHogan (bit bkwd: a.p: lft in ld 4 out: hdd 2 out: wknd last)	11	**3**	20/1	77	4
1029[5]	**Glenfinn Princess (96)** (MrsMerritaJones) **8-11-12** DerekByrne (sn wl bhd: stdy hdwy 14th: nt rch ldrs)	3	**4**	5/1[3]	96	23
1122[3]	**Leinthall Princess (80)** (JLNeedham) **10-10-10** BFenton (chsd ldrs tl wknd 12th)	12	**5**	12/1	72	—
1420[5]	**Titan Empress (80)** (SMellor) **7-10-10v** NMann (led 3rd: hit & hdd 4 out: sn wknd)	3	**6**	9/1	70	—
1391[2]	**Sorbiere (98)** (NJHenderson) **9-12-0b** MAFitzgerald (lw: chsd ldrs tl wknd 14th: t.o whn p.u bef last)		**P**	14/1	—	—
1122[P]	**Beaufan (79)** (BRCambidge) **9-10-9** GaryLyons (bkwd: bhd: reminders 9th: t.o whn p.u bef 13th)		**P**	50/1	—	—
	Coasting (87) (GBBalding) **10-11-3** JRailton (bkwd: led to 3rd: wknd 10th: mstke 12th: t.o whn p.u bef next)		**P**	14/1	—	—

(SP 119.4%) **9 Rn**

6m 18.5 CSF £7.31 CT £63.77 TOTE £3.80: £1.50 £1.30 £3.60 (£2.80) Trio £96.20 OWNER Anne Duchess of Westminster (PENRITH) BRED Christy Fitzgerald

1302* Lord of the West (IRE) had to show his true grit to succeed on this occasion but, once Maguire gets a taste of victory, he is a tough man to beat, and that was the case here. (5/2)

1465* Eastern River, fortunate to remain on his feet after walking through the last ditch, four out, fought back to show in front again, but he hung off a true line on the flat under strong pressure and was forced to give best. (7/4)

Hangover has not won for a long time, and he only appeared a couple of times last season, but performed with credit on this initial outing, and can only improve on this. (20/1)

1029 Glenfinn Princess, given plenty to do, stayed on steadily inside the last mile without threatening to take a hand in proceedings. (5/1)

1122 Leinthall Princess (12/1: 8/1-14/1)

1420 Titan Empress (9/1: 11/2-10/1)

1685 WEATHERBYS 'STARS OF TOMORROW' MAIDEN N.H. FLAT RACE (4, 5 & 6-Y.O) (Class H)

3-40 (3-42) **2m** £1,448.00 (£403.00: £194.00)

				SP	RR	SF
	Billingsgate (DrDChesney) **4-10-12**(7) NWillmington (lengthy, unf: hld up: hdwy 10f out: led 4f out: edgd lft fnl f: r.o)	—	**1**	50/1	74 f	—
	Dark Orchard (IRE) (WRMuir) **5-11-0**(5) ABates (chsd ldrs: chal 2f out: rdn & edgd lft: rdr lost whip: no ex ins fnl f)	4	**2**	33/1	70 f	—
1296[3]	**Ardrina** (FMurphy) **5-10-9**(5) MrRThornton (a chsng ldrs: outpcd fnl 3f)	12	**3**	3/1[1]	53 f	—
	Landa's Counsel (DRGandolfo) **5-10-9**(5) SophieMitchell (bit bkwd: hld up: hdwy 5f out: nt rch ldrs)	4	**4**	7/2[2]	49 f	—
1203[6]	**Tain Ton** (NATwiston-Davies) **4-10-12**(7) MKeighley (hld up: hdwy over 3f out: nt rch ldrs)	¾	**5**	16/1	53 f	—
1335[5]	**Irish Delight** (RCurtis) **4-11-2**(3) DWalsh (prom: rdn 6f out: wknd over 2f out)	1½	**6**	12/1	52 f	—
1303[4]	**Daydream Believer** (MSalaman) **4-10-11**(3) RMassey (nvr plcd to chal)	20	**7**	100/1	27 f	—
1450[3]	**Kosheen (IRE)** (MissHCKnight) **5-10-7**(7) MrAWintle (prom: slt ld over 4f out: sn hdd: grad wknd)	1	**8**	11/2	26 f	—
	Classic Chat (JLSpearing) **4-10-12**(7) MissCSpearing (bkwd: led over 11f: grad wknd)	¾	**9**	16/1	30 f	—
	Otago Heights (NZ) (MrsJPitman) **4-11-2**(3) GHogan (bkwd: trckd ldrs tl wknd over 3f out)	¾	**10**	5/1[3]	29 f	—
	Nicanjon (JSAllen) **5-10-12**(7) XAizpuru (a in rr)	10	**11**	20/1	19 f	—
	Social Insecurity (IRE) (SGollings) **5-11-0**(5) DJKavanagh (dipped, unf: a in rr: t.o)	3½	**12**	50/1	16 f	—
1450[6]	**Winnetka Gal (IRE)** (NATwiston-Davies) **4-10-7**(7) LSuthern (prom tl wknd 6f out: t.o)	1½	**13**	10/1	9 f	—
1071[6]	**Burfords For Scrap** (RDickin) **4-10-12**(7) MrFHutsby (chsd ldrs over 10f: sn lost tch: t.o)	2	**14**	66/1	12 f	—
1450[12]	**Silver Quill** (GBBalding) **5-11-0** RArnold (bkwd: a bhd: t.o)	¾	**15**	20/1	7 f	—
	Spirit of Success (NMLampard) **6-11-5** MrAKinane (bkwd: s.s: bhd fr ½-wy: t.o)	22	**16**	100/1	—	—
1457[20]	**Private Memories** (AWCarroll) **6-11-5** MissCDyson (a bhd: t.o)	1½	**17**	100/1	—	—
	Bit 'o' Sunshine (CASmith) **5-10-7**(7) BClarke (bkwd: chsd ldrs 10f: sn wknd: t.o)	dist	**18**	50/1	—	—
	Alright Guvnor (NASmith) **6-10-9**(5) GESmith (a in rr: t.o: p.u ins fnl f)		**P**	100/1	—	—

				SP	RR	SF
	Supreme Crusader (IRE) (WGMcKenzie-Coles) **5-11-2**(3) DFortt (bkwd: chsd ldrs 10f: sn wknd: t.o whn p.u ins fnl f)		**P**	100/1	—	—
				(SP 132.6%)		**20 Rn**

3m 56.6 CSF £1,023.06 TOTE £31.30: £9.70 £11.40 £1.70 (£420.90) Trio Not won; £242.59 to Newcastle 3/12/96 OWNER Dr D. Chesney (DORCHESTER) BRED Mrs Marie Lee

Billingsgate did look as if he could be made fitter, but kicked on entering the straight and, despite running green, stayed on strongly to the finish. (50/1)

Dark Orchard (IRE), having his first outing for his new stable, ran by far his best race yet and, had his rider not dropped his whip inside the last quarter-mile, he may well have won. (33/1)

1296 Ardrina held her pitch in the chasing group but, once the tempo lifted early in the straight, she was caught flat-footed. (3/1)

Landa's Counsel, off the track for over nine months, looked and ran as though the outing was badly needed. (7/2: op 9/4)

Tain Ton never got within striking range of the principals, but he did stay on, and would seem to be open to improvement. (16/1)

Irish Delight pushed the pace and held on until feeling the strain over a quarter of a mile out. He will be better for this outing. (12/1: 8/1-14/1)

1450 Kosheen (IRE) (11/2: 3/1-6/1)

Otago Heights (NZ) (5/1: 4/1-6/1)

1450 Winnetka Gal (IRE) (10/1: op 5/1)

T/Jkpt: £15,666.30 (0.1 Tckts); £19,858.73 to Newcastle 3/12/96. T/Plpt: £125.00 (91.63 Tckts). T/Qdpt: £20.80 (41.37 Tckts). IM

1652-NEWCASTLE (L-H) (Good, Good to firm patches becoming Good to soft)
Tuesday December 3rd

two fences omitted

WEATHER: raining

1686 LEVY BOARD CONDITIONAL H'CAP HURDLE (0-110) (4-Y.O+) (Class E)
12-30 (12-31) **2m (8 hdls)** £2,284.50 (£642.00: £313.50) GOING: 0.05 sec per fur (G)

				SP	RR	SF
1144[2]	**Kemo Sabo (84)** (CParker) **4-10-5** DParker (mde all: clr appr 3 out: styd on wl)	—	**1**	7/2[2]	71	—
1577[5]	**Auburn Boy (103)** (MWEasterby) **9-11-10** PMidgley (hld up: effrt 5th: outpcd next: styd on fr 2 out: no ch w wnr)	8	**2**	13/2	82	4
	Barton Heights (90) (MrsMReveley) **4-10-6**(5) MHerrington (a chsng ldrs: one pce fr 4 out)	2	**3**	4/1[3]	67	—
1358[5]	**Triennium (USA) (79)** (PMonteith) **7-10-0** GCahill (in tch: wnt 2nd 3 out: hit next: sn btn)	1¼	**4**	7/1	55	—
	Skiddaw Samba (84) (MrsMReveley) **7-10-0**(5) CMcCormack (in tch: outpcd 4 out: nvr nr to chal after)	2	**5**	20/1	58	—
1358[3]	**Miss Greenyards (84)** (ACWhillans) **5-10-5** STaylor (chsd ldrs tl wknd fr 4 out)	22	**6**	7/4[1]	36	—
1523[3]	**Appearance Money (IRE) (88)** (FMurphy) **5-10-2**(7)ow8 FBogle (bhd: sme hdwy 5th: sn wknd)	8	**7**	20/1	32	—
	Doon Ridge (80) (MissLCSiddall) **5-9-12**(3) MNewton (prom tl mstke & wknd qckly 5th: p.u bef 4 out)		**P**	33/1	—	—
				(SP 116.9%)		**8 Rn**

4m 6.6 (14.60) CSF £24.75 CT £86.51 TOTE £3.10: £1.10 £1.80 £4.10 (£26.00) OWNER Mr R. Nichol (LOCKERBIE) BRED Stud-On-The-Chart

1144 Kemo Sabo gained his first win over hurdles here and did it particularly well. (7/2)

1577 Auburn Boy has plenty of ability if caught in the right mood and decided to put his best foot forward over the final two flights when it was all too late to have a chance. (13/2)

Barton Heights ran well over a trip short of his best. (4/1)

1358 Triennium (USA) had his chances but, when really asked to struggle, he soon showed his true colours. (7/1)

Skiddaw Samba, off the track for well over two and a half years, put up a decent show and will no doubt be all the better for it. (20/1)

1358 Miss Greenyards was most disappointing, dropping tamely away over the last four flights as though something was wrong. (7/4)

1687 POLYFLOR AND NEWCASTLE FLOORING NOVICES' HURDLE (4-Y.O+) (Class E)
1-00 (1-00) **2m (8 hdls)** £2,536.50 (£714.00: £349.50) GOING: 0.05 sec per fur (G)

				SP	RR	SF
1208*	**Alabang** (MJCamacho) **5-11-5** PNiven (hld up: led on bit 2 out: hit last: easily)	—	**1**	10/11[1]	75+	26
1020[3]	**Pentland Squire** (JMJefferson) **5-10-12** RichardGuest (trckd ldrs: led after 4 out to 3 out: 3rd & btn whn blnd last)	6	**2**	14/1	62	13
1026[5]	**Qattara (IRE)** (WMcKeown) **6-10-9**(3) GCahill (chsd ldrs: led 3 out to 2 out: wknd flat)	2	**3**	20/1	60	11
	Pappa Charlie (USA) (CParker) **5-10-12** BStorey (a in tch: one pce fr 4 out)	10	**4**	10/1	50	1
1499[4]	**Mr Christie (78)** (MissLCSiddall) **4-10-12** RSupple (chsd ldrs: hit 5th: rdn & no imp after)	5	**5**	8/1[3]	45	—
	Prince of Saints (IRE) (MDHammond) **5-10-12** RGarritty (hld up: stdy hdwy ½-wy: prom 4 out: nt qckn fr next)	3	**6**	20/1	42	—
	Kildrummy Castle (JGFitzGerald) **4-10-12** WDwan (plld hrd: nvr bttr than mid div)	24	**7**	7/1[2]	18	—
	Laughing Fontaine (IRE) (FMurphy) **6-10-12** KWhelan (hld up & bhd: sme hdwy 5th: n.d)	3	**8**	8/1[3]	15	—
1312[7]	**Noble Monarch (IRE)** (HowardJohnson) **7-10-12** NWilliamson (cl up: led 4 out: sn hdd & wknd)	¾	**9**	20/1	14	—
	Edstone (IRE) (JWCurtis) **4-10-12** JCallaghan (mstkes: hdwy & prom after 3rd: wknd fr 5th)	9	**10**	33/1	5	—
1346[U]	**Paint Your Wagon** (NChamberlain) **6-10-13**ow1 TReed (led to 4 out: wknd)	¾	**11**	50/1	6	—
	Hawk Hill Boy (FPMurtagh) **5-10-12** ASSmith (hld up & bhd: n.d)	7	**12**	50/1	—	—
	Parry (SBBell) **4-10-7** KJohnson (bhd fr ½-wy)	1½	**13**	100/1	—	—
1438[8]	**Meesonette** (BEllison) **4-10-7** BHarding (chsd ldrs to 5th)	26	**14**	100/1	—	—
	Rubislaw (MrsKMLamb) **4-10-5**(7) MissSLamb (wl bhd fr 3rd)	3	**15**	100/1	—	—
1579[13]	**Safety Tip** (WStorey) **4-10-7** MMoloney (wl bhd fr 3rd)	14	**16**	100/1	—	—
				(SP 128.0%)		**16 Rn**

4m 1.9 (9.90) CSF £15.67 TOTE £1.50: £1.60 £2.10 £4.50 (£12.00) Trio £43.00 OWNER Elite Racing Club (MALTON) BRED Mrs S. Camacho

1208* Alabang had been sweating beforehand. He did it without coming off the bridle and, while things go his way, he looks extremely useful.(10/11)

1020 Pentland Squire ran well but seems short of a change of gear, and may need further. (14/1)

1026 Qattara (IRE) ran well on his hurdles debut here, but he was well short of speed in the closing stages. (20/1)

Pappa Charlie (USA) looks every inch a chaser and this was not a bad effort on his first attempt over obstacles. (10/1)

1499 Mr Christie was off the bridle a long way out and never fully co-operated thereafter. (8/1)

Prince of Saints (IRE) put up a reasonable first effort over hurdles and probably blew up in the closing stages. (20/1)

1688 RAMSIDE EVENT CATERING H'CAP CHASE (0-135) (5-Y.O+) (Class C)

1-30 (1-30) **2m 110y (10 fncs)** £4,468.00 (£1,354.00: £662.00: £316.00) GOING: 0.60 sec per fur (S)

				SP	RR	SF
1361*	**Political Tower (125)** (RNixon) **9-11-10** ADobbin (lw: trckd ldrs: hit 4 out: disp ld 2 out: led & blnd last: hld on wl)	—	1	6/4^{1}	131	30
	Timbucktoo (115) (JKMOliver) **9-11-0** BStorey (hld up: hit 4 out: hdwy 2 out: styd on wl towards fin)	nk	2	4/1^{3}	121	20
1361^{3}	**Regal Romper (IRE) (115)** (MrsSJSmith) **8-11-0** RichardGuest (led tl hdd & mstke last: sn btn)	7	3	2/1^{2}	114	13
1361^{6}	**One for the Pot (110)** (MrsAMNaughton) **11-10-9** MFoster (wnt prom 4th: ev ch 3 out: nt qckn)	½	4	5/1	108	7
	Nobodys Flame (IRE) (103) (SIPittendrigh) **8-9-13**(3)ow2 GCahill (prom: mstke 5th: sn wknd: p.u bef 2 out)		P	100/1	—	—
				(SP 111.0%)		**5 Rn**

4m 17.4 (19.40) CSF £7.35 TOTE £2.10: £3.10 £2.70 (£4.90) OWNER Mr G. R. S. Nixon (SELKIRK) BRED R. Nixon
LONG HANDICAP Nobodys Flame (IRE) 8-11
1361* Political Tower looked a picture and, but for a bad mistake at the last, would have been more convincing. (6/4)
Timbucktoo, an Irish import, was given a kind introduction here and certainly finished well, but always just too late. He ought to progress and should go in the mud. (4/1)
1361 Regal Romper (IRE) ran his usual game race, but this ever-softening ground found him out. (2/1)
1361 One for the Pot is improving with every run and should find his mark in due course. (5/1)

1689 NEWCASTLE FLOORING AND HALSTEAD'S NOVICES' HURDLE (4-Y.O+) (Class E)

2-00 (2-01) **2m 4f (10 hdls)** £2,589.00 (£729.00: £357.00) GOING: 0.60 sec per fur (S)

				SP	RR	SF
1245*	**Beggars Banquet (IRE) (105)** (PBeaumont) **6-10-12**(7) BGrattan (lw: trckd ldrs: led 3 out: pushed out)	—	1	9/2^{3}	92	46
1042*	**Inn At the Top** (JNorton) **4-11-5** WFry (sn trckng ldrs: led 4 out to 3 out: outpcd appr last: styd on wl towards fin)	½	2	9/2^{3}	92	46
1139*	**Antarctic Wind (IRE) (99)** (MDHammond) **6-11-5** RGarritty (a.p: effrt 4 out: one pce)	26	3	9/1	71	25
1161*	**Stan's Your Man (99)** (MrsJDGoodfellow) **6-11-2**(3) GCahill (chsd ldrs: one pce fr 4 out)	11	4	4/1^{2}	62	16
1278^{4}	**Cypress Avenue (IRE)** (MrsVCWard) **4-10-12** DParker (in tch: mstke 7th & sn outpcd: styd on fr 3 out)	½	5	7/1	55	9
1499*	**Tremendisto (98)** (CaptJWilson) **6-11-5** ADobbin (cl up: led 5th to 4 out: grad wknd)	3½	6	12/1	59	13
	Lostris (IRE) (MDods) **5-10-7** NSmith (nvr nr to chal)	nk	7	100/1	47	1
1345^{2}	**Jaunty General** (CParker) **5-10-12** BStorey (in tch: blnd 3rd: hdwy 6th: wknd after 4 out)	7	8	20/1	46	—
1030^{P}	**Boston Man** (RDEWoodhouse) **5-10-12** JCallaghan (mstke 5th: hdwy next & sn prom: wknd 4 out)	10	9	150/1	38	—
1362^{15}	**Gale Force (IRE)** (PBeaumont) **5-10-12** RSupple (hld up & bhd: hdwy ½-wy: mstke 3 out & wknd)	½	10	50/1	38	—
1654^{16}	**Pocaire Gaoithe (IRE)** (WStorey) **6-10-12** MMoloney (rdn & lost pl 4th: n.d after)	10	11	100/1	30	—
875^{P}	**Clonroche Lucky (IRE)** (JWade) **6-10-12** FPerratt (a bhd)	12	12	100/1	20	—
1312^{8}	**Lepton (IRE)** (JWCurtis) **5-10-12** PNiven (lost tch fr 5th: t.o whn p.u bef 3 out)		P	25/1	—	—
	Clavering (IRE) (HowardJohnson) **6-10-12** NWilliamson (mstkes: chsd ldr tl wknd 6th: t.o whn p.u bef 3 out)		P	7/2^{1}	—	—
	Magic Times (CGrant) **5-10-12** JRailton (led to 5th: sn wknd: t.o whn p.u bef 3 out)		P	100/1	—	—
1296^{13}	**General Parker** (MissMKMilligan) **5-10-12** ASSmith (prom to 5th: t.o whn p.u bef 3 out)		P	100/1	—	—
1245^{7}	**Leighten Lass (IRE)** (JIACharlton) **5-10-7** KJohnson (sn t.o: p.u bef 3 out)		P	100/1	—	—
	Bold'n (70) (NBMason) **9-10-5**(7) SHaworth (sn bhd: t.o whn p.u bef 3 out)		P	200/1	—	—
	Moon Castle (IRE) (VThompson) **8-10-13**ow1 MrMThompson (a bhd: t.o whn p.u bef 3 out)		P	500/1	—	—
				(SP 126.6%)		**19 Rn**

5m 5.5 (17.50) CSF £23.80 TOTE £5.20: £3.00 £2.30 £3.90 (£13.70) Trio £18.70 OWNER Mr E. H. Ruddock (BRANDSBY) BRED T A O'Donnell
OFFICIAL EXPLANATION **Clavering (IRE): the Vet reported that the gelding showed a slight nasal discharge.**
1245* Beggars Banquet (IRE) has done all his winning on faster ground previously, but he took well to these conditions and would have won more easily but for idling. (9/2)
1042* Inn At the Top did not really impress on looks, but his performance could not be faulted this time, and he kept fighting back when looking well held. (9/2: 3/1-5/1)
1139* Antarctic Wind (IRE) had his chances, but the conditions seemed to find him out in the home straight. (9/1: op 5/1)
1161* Stan's Your Man, probably happier on faster ground, was left struggling when the pressure was on over the last four. (4/1)
1278 Cypress Avenue (IRE) ran as though there is better to come should he really take to this game. (7/1)
1499* Tremendisto, stepping up in trip and on much more testing ground, was found wanting when pressure was applied. (12/1)
Lostris (IRE) has yet to win a race of any sort and just stays. (100/1)

1690 GOSFORTH PARK H'CAP HURDLE (0-135) (4-Y.O+) (Class C)

2-30 (2-30) **3m (12 hdls)** £3,517.50 (£1,065.00: £520.00: £247.50) GOING: 0.60 sec per fur (S)

				SP	RR	SF
	Sedvicta (103) (MrsMReveley) **4-10-0**(3) GCahill (a cl up: led 3 out: drvn out)	—	1	6/5^{1}	—	—
	Leading Prospect (100) (MrsJDGoodfellow) **9-10-0** ASSmith (led to 3 out: kpt on wl)	1¾	2	25/1	—	—
	Act the Wag (IRE) (104) (MartinTodhunter) **7-10-4** BHarding (trckd ldrs: outpcd 4 out: hdwy next: rdn & styd on one pce)	9	3	100/30^{3}	—	—
1294^{10}	**Maybe O'Grady (IRE) (100)** (WSCunningham) **7-9-7**(7) LMcGrath (hld up: hdwy on bit to chal 4 out: outpcd appr next: n.d after)	2	4	16/1	—	—
	Uncle Doug (128) (MrsMReveley) **5-12-0** PNiven (trckd ldrs tl grad wknd fr 4 out)	8	5	9/4^{2}	—	—
				(SP 109.0%)		**5 Rn**

6m 27.2 (45.20) CSF £18.02 TOTE £2.00: £1.90 £17.00 (£15.30) OWNER The Mary Reveley Racing Club (SALTBURN) BRED H. Young
LONG HANDICAP Maybe O'Grady (IRE) 9-4 Leading Prospect 9-10
Sedvicta got the ground he likes and, although never really that convincing, he did the job required. The Handicapper surely can not overpunish him. (6/5)
Leading Prospect set a steady pace and gradually warmed it up in the final mile but, despite a valiant effort, was always second best. He might be slightly flattered by the way the race was run. (25/1)
Act the Wag (IRE) had a nice pipe-opener and should be straight now for a return to chasing. (100/30)
Maybe O'Grady (IRE) goes well on the bridle and, after appearing to blow up, got his second wind at the finish. He looks likely to improve. (16/1)
Uncle Doug ran reasonably and was not overpunished when beaten. (9/4)

1691 NORTHERN RACING NOVICES' CHASE (5-Y.O+) (Class D)

3-00 (3-00) **3m (15 fncs)** £3,663.75 (£1,110.00: £542.50: £258.75) GOING: 0.60 sec per fur (S)

		Dist		SP	RR	SF
	Majority Major (IRE) (PCheesbrough) **7-10-12** ASSmith (hld up: stdy hdwy fr 10th: led flat: rdn & r.o)	—	**1**	14/1	93	14
1264[4]	**Shawwell (81)** (JIACharlton) **9-10-12** BStorey (cl up: led 6th to 8th: chal whn hit 3 out: led 2 out: hdd flat: kpt on wl)	1½	**2**	9/2[3]	92	13
1574[7]	**Royal Surprise (76)** (WGReed) **9-10-12b[1]** TReed (mstke 1st: lft in ld 3rd: hdd 6th: led 8th to 2 out: outpcd flat)	14	**3**	14/1	83	4
	Corporal Kirkwood (IRE) (MartinTodhunter) **6-10-12** ADobbin (in tch: hdwy 10th: one pce fr 3 out)	3	**4**	20/1	81	2
1574[9]	**Monymax (IRE)** (MrsSJSmith) **7-10-12** RichardGuest (chsd ldrs: hmpd & wknd 12th)	30	**5**	33/1	61	—
1308[4]	**The Energiser (67)** (DALamb) **10-10-12** JBurke (bhd: effrt 10th: no imp)	1½	**6**	66/1	60	—
	Distillery Hill (IRE) (74) (VThompson) **8-10-12** MrMThompson (chsd ldrs tl blnd & lost pl 8th: bdly hmpd 12th: n.d after)	22	**7**	20/1	45	—
1574[3]	**Tico Gold (77)** (PCheesbrough) **8-10-9**(3) GCahill (chsd ldrs tl fell 10th)		**F**	3/1[2]	—	—
1308[2]	**Final Beat (IRE) (82)** (JWCurtis) **7-10-12** PNiven (in tch: chsd ldrs 9th tl fell 12th)		**F**	8/1	—	—
	Niki Dee (IRE) (PBeaumont) **6-10-12** RSupple (led tl fell 3rd)		**F**	5/2[1]	—	—
1160[4]	**Broomhill Duker (IRE) (80)** (HowardJohnson) **6-10-12** NWilliamson (mstkes: hdwy to chse ldrs whn hit 4 out: 5th & btn whn blnd & uns rdr 2 out)		**U**	7/1	—	—

(SP 122.7%) **11 Rn**

6m 22.0 (30.00) CSF £73.74 TOTE £29.40: £2.90 £2.10 £3.80 (£60.90) Trio £43.80 OWNER Mr John Jones (BISHOP AUCKLAND) BRED M. O'Brien

Majority Major (IRE), from a yard coming to form, was turned out in good trim and, given a patient ride, won nicely. (14/1)
1022 Shawwell, an unpredictable customer but quite useful on his day, should find his first win over fences coming before long. (9/2)
1246 Royal Surprise is slow but sure and the headgear helped, but he was well tapped for toe late on. (14/1)
Corporal Kirkwood (IRE) has not been out for over eighteen months and there is something to work on. (20/1)
Monymax (IRE) has the appearance of a plodder and ran similarly. (33/1)
1574 Tico Gold was beginning to finally make his presence felt when he came to grief. (3/1)
1308 Final Beat (IRE) was bang in contention when falling heavily five out. (8/1)
Niki Dee (IRE) refused to settle and, meeting the third fence all wrong, had no chance of remaining upright. (5/2: 6/4-11/4)
1160 Broomhill Duker (IRE) did his best to get rid of his rider throughout the race, but he was amazingly still there with a chance at the fourth last, but was then beaten when finally parting company two out. (7/1)

1692 ST. MODWEN STANDARD OPEN N.H. FLAT RACE (4, 5 & 6-Y.O) (Class H)

3-30 (3-33) **2m** £1,469.00 (£409.00: £197.00)

		Dist		SP	RR	SF
191[2]	**Mr Lurpak** (MrsMReveley) **4-11-4** PNiven (hld up & bhd: hdwy ½-wy: led 2f out: r.o wl)	—	**1**	5/2[1]	66 f	—
	Cherry Dee (PBeaumont) **5-10-6**(7) BGrattan (cl up: effrt 4f out: one pce fnl 2f)	8	**2**	10/1	53 f	—
	Billy Buckskin (JNorton) **4-11-4** WFry (hld up: hdwy ½-wy: rdn to chse ldrs 4f out: kpt on wl)	½	**3**	16/1	58 f	—
	Nutty Solera (CParker) **6-11-11** BStorey (hld up: hdwy ½-wy: led 4f out to 2f out: one pce)	3	**4**	8/1[3]	62 f	—
	Southern Cross (MWEasterby) **4-11-8**(3) PMidgley (chsd ldrs: outpcd 4f out: kpt on u.p fnl 2f)	1	**5**	9/1	61 f	—
	Revolt (TDEasterby) **4-11-4** RichardGuest (styd on fnl 3f: nrst fin)	3½	**6**	12/1	50 f	—
1504[3]	**Meadow Hymn (IRE)** (JGFitzGerald) **5-11-4** WDwan (styd on fnl 3f: nvr trbld ldrs)	6	**7**	9/2[2]	44 f	—
	Deerhunter (DWBarker) **5-11-4** RMarley (cl up tl outpcd fnl 3½f)	2	**8**	100/1	42 f	—
	Eirespray (IRE) (MDHammond) **5-11-4** RGarritty (mid div: outpcd 4f out: kpt on towards fin)	1¾	**9**	20/1	40 f	—
	Alan's Pride (IRE) (WMcKeown) **5-10-10**(3) GCahill (lw: led tl hdd & wknd 4f out)	hd	**10**	12/1	35 f	—
	Santa Barbara (IRE) (CGrant) **5-10-13** RSupple (nvr nr ldrs)	4	**11**	20/1	31 f	—
	Smiddy Lad (RShiels) **5-11-4** DBentley (prom tl grad wknd fnl 5f)	2	**12**	16/1	34 f	—
	Top Ace (GFWhite) **4-11-4** BHarding (bhd: hdwy ½-wy: n.d)	2	**13**	16/1	32 f	—
	Milenberg Joys (PCalver) **4-11-4** DParker (chsd ldrs tl rdn & wknd 4f out)	6	**14**	100/1	26 f	—
1362[12]	**Political Millstar** (RNixon) **4-11-4** NBentley (chsd ldrs tl wknd fnl 5f)	2	**15**	16/1	24 f	—
	Sam Champagne (IRE) (TDEasterby) **4-11-4** KWhelan (drvn along ½-wy: n.d)	2½	**16**	14/1	22 f	—
	Salem Beach (MartinTodhunter) **4-10-10**(3) GLee (prom 10f)	4	**17**	16/1	13 f	—
	Ottadini (IRE) (WGReed) **4-10-13** TReed (n.d)	16	**18**	100/1	—	—
	Moubeed (USA) (HowardJohnson) **6-11-4** NWilliamson (prom: rdn 6f out: wknd 4f out)	nk	**19**	10/1	1 f	—
	Whatyeronabout (IRE) (GMMoore) **4-10-13** JCallaghan (nvr bttr than mid div)	11	**20**	14/1	—	—
	Fly Executive (SIPittendrigh) **5-10-13**(5) MrMHNaughton (bit bkwd: a bhd)	2	**21**	100/1	—	—
	Tidal Race (IRE) (JSHaldane) **4-11-4** ADobbin (t.o)	dist	**22**	33/1	—	—
	Miss Fortina (JWCurtis) **4-10-10**(3) FLeahy (lost tch fr ½-wy: t.o)	10	**23**	100/1	—	—
1296[20]	**Samite (IRE)** (SJLeadbetter) **5-11-4** NLeach (a bhd: t.o)	2	**24**	100/1	—	—

(SP 162.6%) **24 Rn**

3m 59.7 CSF £34.48 TOTE £4.30: £3.00 £3.00 £9.60 (£28.40) Trio £259.30; £146.09 to Catterick 4/12/96 OWNER MD Foods Plc (SALTBURN) BRED Exors of the late Countess of Durham

191 Mr Lurpak, who looks a Flat-race type, won this in really useful style and obviously appreciated the easier ground. (5/2)
Cherry Dee, a real National Hunt type, had every chance but was short of toe when it mattered. Staying will be her game. (10/1)
Billy Buckskin had to work to get into contention and kept struggling on, but was always too slow to do anything about it. (16/1)
Nutty Solera, a winner of an Irish point and bumper, showed ability here, but was too slow in the last half-mile. (8/1)
Southern Cross had been sweating beforehand and ran as though this was just needed. (9/1)
Revolt was just getting the hang of things as the race progressed and will appreciate a test of stamina. (12/1: 10/1-16/1)
1504 Meadow Hymn (IRE) was staying on well and is obviously still learning. (9/2: op 3/1)

T/Jkpt: £24,090.90 (0.6 Tckts); £13,572.38 to Catterick 4/12/96. T/Plpt: £104.90 (102.56 Tckts). T/Qdpt: £27.00 (29.95 Tckts). AA

1425-NEWTON ABBOT (L-H) (Heavy)

Tuesday December 3rd

One fence omitted
WEATHER: changeable

1693 KERRY NOVICES' LADIES' H'CAP HURDLE (0-100) (4-Y.O+) (Class E)

12-50 (12-51) **2m 1f (8 hdls)** £2,190.00 (£615.00: £300.00) GOING: 1.86 sec per fur (HY)

	Horse / details	Dist	Pos	SP	RR	SF
1451[5]	**Shift Again (IRE) (82)** (OSherwood) **4-11-2b**(5) SophieMitchell (chsd ldrs 3rd: led appr 2 out: rdn & styd on flat)	—	**1**	2/1[2]	65	28
	Tap Shoes (IRE) (67) (RJBaker) **6-10-6** MissMCoombe (bit bkwd: chsd ldrs: hdwy 5th: disp ld 2 out: no ex fr last)	1¼	**2**	9/2[3]	49	12
1198*	**Royal Standard (84)** (PMRich) **9-11-9v** AnnStokell (lw: led tl hdd & wknd appr 2 out)	10	**3**	6/5[1]	56	19
	Celtic Emerald (61) (RJEckley) **8-10-0** MissCThomas (bit bkwd: chsd ldr to 3rd: wknd appr 5th: t.o next)	dist	**4**	33/1	—	—
1628[8]	**Denomination (USA) (89)** (MCPipe) **4-12-0** MissSVickery (racd wd: chsd ldrs tl wknd 5th: 4th & t.o whn fell 2 out)		**F**	10/1	—	—
1448[P]	**Nuns Lucy (61)** (FJordan) **5-10-0b[1]** JacquiOliver (bit bkwd: mstke 1st: a bhd: rdn & t.o after 4th: p.u after 6th)		**P**	25/1	—	—

(SP 112.8%) **6 Rn**

4m 33.7 (40.70) CSF £10.70 TOTE £2.70: £2.50 £4.20 (£6.70) OWNER Mr R. J. Bassett (UPPER LAMBOURN) BRED Buckram Thoroughbred Enterprises Inc
LONG HANDICAP Celtic Emerald 9-11 Nuns Lucy 9-11

1451 Shift Again (IRE) scored her first success over hurdles here a shade comfortably. After jumping slightly left at the final flight, she was kept up to her work and the heavy ground did not prove a problem. (2/1)
Tap Shoes (IRE) would have appreciated the ground and has shown ability in the past. He could find little more when the winner went on and may well have needed this run. (9/2)
1198* Royal Standard won over course and distance on similar ground last month but, after trying to repeat that all-the-way success, was beaten from the second last. (6/5: 4/5-11/8)
1425 Denomination (USA) (10/1: 5/1-11/1)

1694 DUBLIN NOVICES' H'CAP CHASE (0-100) (5-Y.O+) (Class E)

1-20 (1-20) **2m 5f 110y (13 fncs)** £2,913.75 (£882.00: £430.50: £204.75) GOING: 1.86 sec per fur (HY)

	Horse / details	Dist	Pos	SP	RR	SF
1449[2]	**Poucher (IRE) (95)** (CaptTAForster) **6-11-9** SWynne (hdwy 8th: sn prom: led 12th: clr 2 out: eased flat)	—	**1**	7/2[2]	106	26
1430*	**Well Timed (93)** (RGFrost) **6-11-7** BPowell (chsd ldrs tl led 3rd: hdd next: led 9th: hdd 12th: one pce appr 2 out)	13	**2**	9/2[3]	94	14
1426[5]	**Colette's Choice (IRE) (79)** (GAHam) **7-10-2**(5) MrRThornton (bhd: lost tch 7th: styd on fr 2 out)	14	**3**	25/1	70	—
1428[5]	**Sorrel Hill (100)** (PJHobbs) **9-12-0b[1]** APMcCoy (led to 3rd: led 4th to 9th: wknd 11th)	3½	**4**	5/1	88	8
1472[6]	**Purbeck Rambler (72)** (GBBalding) **5-10-0** BFenton (rdn & hdwy 8th: ev ch next tl mstke 11th: nt rcvr: t.o)	25	**5**	20/1	42	—
964[4]	**Icantelya (IRE) (88)** (JWMullins) **7-11-2** PHide (mstke 1st: chsd ldrs tl wknd 9th: t.o)	13	**6**	10/1	48	—
1423[2]	**Amber Spark (IRE) (94)** (DRGandolfo) **7-11-5**(3) DFortt (fell 5th)		**F**	11/8[1]	—	—

(SP 116.9%) **7 Rn**

6m 10.5 (53.50) CSF £18.80 TOTE £4.40: £2.10 £2.70 (£7.20) OWNER Mrs A. L. Wood (LUDLOW) BRED John Ryan
LONG HANDICAP Purbeck Rambler 9-13

1449 Poucher (IRE) stayed extremely well and, with a liking for the ground, finished clear of the rest. He is going the right way. (7/2: 2/1-4/1)
1430* Well Timed, in and out of the lead, was finally disposed of when the winner went clear with two to jump. He did, however, finish clear of the remainder of the field and will not always meet one so good. (9/2)
Colette's Choice (IRE) seemed as though she was going to be tailed off at halfway, but stayed on in the last half-mile. (25/1)

1695 WEXFORD 'N.H.' NOVICES' HURDLE (4-Y.O+) (Class E)

1-50 (1-50) **2m 1f (8 hdls)** £2,221.50 (£624.00: £304.50) GOING: 1.86 sec per fur (HY)

	Horse / details	Dist	Pos	SP	RR	SF
1260[4]	**Stormy Passage (IRE)** (PJHobbs) **6-10-12** AMaguire (lw: chsd ldr tl led after 4th: clr appr 2 out: unchal)	—	**1**	11/10[1]	69+	33
1427[5]	**Hello Me Man (IRE) (88)** (BJLlewellyn) **8-10-12** MrJLLlewellyn (gd hdwy after 4th: disp ld next: rdn & outpcd appr 2 out)	17	**2**	4/1[3]	53	17
1431[10]	**Defendtherealm** (RGFrost) **5-10-12** MrAHoldsworth (chsd ldrs tl after 5th: styd on wl u.p fr 2 out)	5	**3**	33/1	48	12
	Shanagore Warrior (IRE) (SMellor) **4-10-12** NMann (bit bkwd: sme hdwy after 4th: wknd appr 6th)	11	**4**	9/1	38	2
1056[5]	**Moonlight Escapade (IRE)** (RJHodges) **5-10-9**(3) TDascombe (lw: prom & ev ch 6th: wknd appr 2 out)	4	**5**	8/1	34	—
1203[9]	**Captain Felix (NZ)** (AJKDunn) **6-10-12** SMcNeill (a bhd: lost tch 5th: t.o whn p.u bef 2 out)		**P**	20/1	—	—
1333[9]	**All Sewn Up** (RJBaker) **4-10-12** CMaude (led tl after 4th: wknd qckly appr next: t.o whn p.u bef 2 out)		**P**	25/1	—	—
1177[7]	**Dolce Notte (IRE)** (MCPipe) **6-10-7** APMcCoy (in tch tl appr 5th: sn wknd: t.o whn p.u bef 2 out)		**P**	3/1[2]	—	—
	Zen Or (JWMullins) **5-10-7** SCurran (bkwd: prom & mstke 2nd: bhd 4th: t.o whn p.u bef 2 out)		**P**	50/1	—	—

(SP 127.2%) **9 Rn**

4m 30.5 (37.50) CSF £6.82 TOTE £1.70: £1.10 £1.90 £7.70 (£3.70) Trio £23.80 OWNER Mr Peter Luff (MINEHEAD) BRED Denis J. Murphy

1260 Stormy Passage (IRE) took the lead at halfway and had burnt off his rivals with two to jump. He seems a decent prospect and his trainer believes he will go on to better things. (11/10: evens-5/4)
Hello Me Man (IRE) put up a decent effort and was the only one able to put in a reasonable challenge to the winner, but his chance had gone two from home. (4/1: 5/2-9/2)
Defendtherealm, whose two previous runs had come in bumpers, is gradually progressing. (33/1)
Shanagore Warrior (IRE) made a reasonable start to his jumping career. (9/1: op 5/1)
918 Moonlight Escapade (IRE) (8/1: 6/1-9/1)
1177 Dolce Notte (IRE) (3/1: 9/4-7/2)

1696 CORK H'CAP CHASE (0-100) (5-Y.O+) (Class F)

2-20 (2-20) **2m 110y (12 fncs)** £2,628.00 (£738.00: £360.00) GOING: 1.86 sec per fur (HY)

	Horse / details	Dist	Pos	SP	RR	SF
1073[3]	**The Lancer (IRE) (82)** (DRGandolfo) **7-10-7**(3) DFortt (lw: chsd ldr tl led after 5th: clr 10th: unchal)	—	**1**	5/1[2]	99	22
	Hawaiian Youth (IRE) (99) (GMMcCourt) **8-11-13** AMaguire (bit bkwd: hdwy to chse wnr 6th: outpcd fr 9th)	19	**2**	5/2[1]	98	21
1430[4]	**Fenwick (87)** (RJHodges) **9-10-12**(3) TDascombe (hdwy 7th: ev ch 9th: outpcd & wknd next)	3½	**3**	14/1	82	5

	Horse / details	Dist	Pos	SP	RR	SF
1570[3]	**Benjamin Lancaster (100)** (MAGriffin) **12-11-7**(7) MGriffiths (lw: prom to 7th: wknd 9th)	4	**4**	13/2	91	14
1331[F]	**Nordic Valley (IRE) (88)** (MCPipe) **5-11-2** APMcCoy (bhd: sme hdwy 7th: wknd 9th)	2	**5**	11/2[3]	77	—
1445[2]	**Prudent Peggy (72)** (RGFrost) **9-10-0** MrAHoldsworth (a bhd: rdn appr 6th: sn t.o)	18	**6**	11/2[3]	44	—
1328[3]	**Thats the Life (77)** (TRGeorge) **11-10-5** MAFitzgerald (in tch to 8th: grad wknd: t.o whn p.u bef last)		**P**	9/1	—	—
1298[5]	**Chain Shot (72)** (JHPeacock) **11-10-0** RBellamy (led tl hdd & wknd after 5th: t.o whn p.u bef last)		**P**	50/1	—	—

(SP 108.0%) **8 Rn**

4m 38.9 (38.90) CSF £16.06 CT £126.12 TOTE £5.00: £1.90 £1.20 £2.60 (£12.20) OWNER Mr A. E. Frost (WANTAGE) BRED J. O'Keeffe
LONG HANDICAP Prudent Peggy 9-11

1073 The Lancer (IRE), who finished second to Ambassador Royale over course and distance on his seasonal debut, found the opposition easier on this occasion. (5/1: op 3/1)

Hawaiian Youth (IRE), who had not been seen out for over a year, was unable to go with the winner when that rival kicked for home. He would have appreciated this run after such an absence. (5/2)

1298 Fenwick was beaten some way out. (14/1: op 8/1)

1328 Thats the Life (9/1: op 6/1)

1697 LIMERICK H'CAP CHASE (0-110) (5-Y.O+) (Class E)

2-50 (2-50) **3m 2f 110y (17 fncs)** £2,954.70 (£894.60: £436.80: £207.90) GOING: 1.86 sec per fur (HY)

	Horse / details	Dist	Pos	SP	RR	SF
1428[2]	**Bramblehill Buck (IRE) (102)** (PFNicholls) **7-11-6b** APMcCoy (lw: chsd ldrs to 5th: lost pl 8th: rallied to ld 12th: clr 2 out: fin tired)	—	**1**	3/1[2]	119	15
1540[5]	**Three Saints (IRE) (96)** (CaptTAForster) **7-11-0** SWynne (lw: hdwy 6th: in tch 11th: ev ch whn hit 15th: sn outpcd)	16	**2**	4/1[3]	103	—
	A N C Express (110) (JSKing) **8-12-0** CMaude (bit bkwd: prom & ev ch 12th: wknd 14th)	8	**3**	5/2[1]	113	9
	Jailbreaker (93) (BRMillman) **9-10-6**(5) DSalter (bit bkwd: chsd ldrs to 11th: lost pl: rallied to chse wnr 12th tl wknd appr 2 out)	5	**4**	10/1	93	—
1202[4]	**Steeple Jack (85)** (KBishop) **9-10-3** RGreene (a bhd: lost tch 11th: t.o)	7	**5**	9/1	80	—
1385[5]	**Shamarphil (93)** (RHAlner) **10-10-11** MissSBarraclough (in rr whn mstke 6th: t.o fr 12th)	18	**6**	10/1	77	—
	Golden Opal (90) (RHBuckler) **11-10-1**(7) MGriffiths (in tch tl wknd 6th: t.o whn p.u bef 2 out)		**P**	14/1	—	—
1279[5]	**Florida Sky (105)** (CPEBrooks) **9-11-2**(7) MBerry (lw: led tl hdd & wknd 12th: p.u bef 14th)		**P**	14/1	—	—
1426[3]	**Country Keeper (85)** (BJMRyall) **8-10-3**ow3 GUpton (bhd: hdwy 8th: in tch tl wknd appr 12th: t.o whn p.u bef 14th)		**P**	25/1	—	—

(SP 118.9%) **9 Rn**

7m 43.3 (69.30) CSF £15.16 CT £31.27 TOTE £3.60: £1.50 £1.60 £1.20 (£7.30) Trio £8.60 OWNER T and J A Curry (SHEPTON MALLET)
BRED E. A. Bourke
LONG HANDICAP Country Keeper 8-11

1428 Bramblehill Buck (IRE) has secured all four of his career wins here and has never finished out of the first three. Although finishing clear, he was kept up to his work to the line. (3/1)

1540 Three Saints (IRE) lost all hope of any chance he may have had, when blundering at the fifteenth, but would have found it difficult to stay with the winner in any case. He travels well, but has to brush up his jumping. (4/1: 11/4-9/2)

A N C Express had not been seen out for over a year and a half and, with the burden of topweight, was always up against it. He should come on greatly for the run. (5/2)

1202 Shamarphil (10/1: op 6/1)

1698 SLIGO H'CAP HURDLE (0-125) (4-Y.O+) (Class D)

3-20 (3-20) **2m 6f (10 hdls)** £2,805.50 (£788.00: £384.50) GOING: 1.86 sec per fur (HY)

	Horse / details	Dist	Pos	SP	RR	SF
1176*	**Sail by the Stars (105)** (CaptTAForster) **7-10-11** DGallagher (lw: led briefly 4th: chsd ldr tl led 7th: sn clr: unchal)	—	**1**	4/5[1]	86+	47
1467[2]	**Runaway Pete (USA) (122)** (MCPipe) **6-12-0** APMcCoy (led: hdd briefly 4th: hdd 7th: wknd after next)	dist	**2**	8/1[3]	—	—
	Ambleside (IRE) (112) (MrsSDWilliams) **5-11-4** SMcNeill (bit bkwd: chsd ldr to 3rd: lost pl: hdwy & ev ch 8th: sn wknd)	20	**3**	5/2[2]	—	—
	Kilcoran Bay (104) (JWMullins) **4-10-10** RGreene (bit bkwd: bhd: hdwy & in tch 8th: sn wknd: t.o whn ref 2 out)		**R**	11/1	—	—
1176[5]	**Stac-Pollaidh (94)** (KCBailey) **6-9-7**(7) WWalsh (prom to 7th: wkng whn blnd & uns rdr 8th)		**U**	12/1	—	—

(SP 111.3%) **5 Rn**

5m 56.3 (44.30) CSF £6.96 TOTE £1.70: £1.30 £4.10 (£3.80) OWNER Mr T. F. F. Nixon (LUDLOW) BRED T. F. F. Nixon
LONG HANDICAP Stac-Pollaidh 9-7

1176* Sail by the Stars, a lightly-raced daughter of Celtic Cone, justified favouritism to take this for her in-form trainer. (4/5: evens-6/5)

1467 Runaway Pete (USA) held an early lead but, with topweight in this heavy ground, he was always up against it. (8/1: op 5/1)

Ambleside (IRE) seemed slightly backward on this seasonal appearance. (5/2)

Kilcoran Bay (11/1: 6/1-12/1)

T/Plpt: £25.40 (445.07 Tckts). T/Qdpt: £4.50 (268.75 Tckts). T

1543-CATTERICK (L-H) (Good)
Wednesday December 4th

WEATHER: overcast WIND: str

1699 ELLERTON HURDLE (I) (3-Y.O) (Class E)

12-20 (12-20) **2m (8 hdls)** £2,364.00 (£654.00: £312.00) GOING: 0.15 sec per fur (G)

	Horse / details	Dist	Pos	SP	RR	SF
	Priddy Fair (DWBarker) **3-10-7** RichardGuest (hld up: smooth hdwy appr 2 out: led between last 2: pushed out)	—	**1**	16/1	61	—
	Fro (HAlexander) **3-10-7** BStorey (led 3rd tl after 2 out: kpt on)	1½	**2**	9/2[3]	60	—
1387[4]	**Topaglow (IRE)** (PTDalton) **3-10-12** NWilliamson (led to 3rd: w ldr tl outpcd fr 2 out)	4	**3**	7/2[2]	61	—
1253[4]	**Tarry (88)** (AStreeter) **3-11-0v** TEley (chsd ldrs: outpcd whn hit 2 out: n.d after)	2½	**4**	5/2[1]	60	—
1356[3]	**Swynford Supreme** (JFBottomley) **3-10-9**(3) ECallaghan (lw: cl up: mstke 3rd: rdn & btn appr 2 out)	7	**5**	7/2[2]	51	—
1184[10]	**Radmore Brandy** (GRichards) **3-10-7** ADobbin (trckd ldrs tl wknd appr 2 out)	5	**6**	5/1	41	—

	Horse	Dist	Pos	SP	RR	SF
	Needle Match (JJO'Neill) **3-10-7**(5) RMcGrath (trckd ldrs tl wknd appr 2 out)	3	**7**	20/1	43	—
	Gautby Henpecked (GMMoore) **3-10-7** JCallaghan (mstkes: a bhd)	4	**8**	8/1	34	—
852[3]	**Lomond Lassie (USA)** (TKersey) **3-10-7** OPears (outpcd & bhd fr 4th)	19	**9**	100/1	15	—
1159[P]	**Duntalkin** (JMJefferson) **3-10-0**(7) MNewton (mstkes: a bhd)	4	**10**	50/1	11	—

(SP 132.6%) **10 Rn**

3m 58.8 (15.80) CSF £90.64 TOTE £111.90: £4.70 £2.40 £1.80 (£193.50) Trio Not won; £69.95 to Leicester 5/12/96 OWNER The Ebor Partnership (RICHMOND) BRED Stetchworth Park Stud Ltd

Priddy Fair showed next to nothing on the Flat over trips at up to ten furlongs, but took to this game well and won in a most authoritative manner. (16/1)
Fro, a real stayer on the level, tried hard, but was done for toe and will probably need further. (9/2)
1387 Topaglow (IRE), well beaten in two previous efforts, was dropped in class here, but was still never good enough when the pressure was applied. (7/2)
1253 Tarry had the visor on but to little effect, and she was done with two out. (5/2)
1356 Swynford Supreme raced too freely for his own good and had run himself out going to the second last. (7/2)
Radmore Brandy had recently changed stables, but unfortunately not engines. (5/1)
Needle Match has the looks for this game, but probably raced a bit freely and blew up. (20/1)
Gautby Henpecked (8/1: op 5/1)

1700 ELLERTON HURDLE (II) (3-Y.O) (Class E)

12-50 (12-51) **2m (8 hdls)** £2,343.00 (£648.00: £309.00) GOING: 0.15 sec per fur (G)

	Horse	Dist	Pos	SP	RR	SF
1526[3]	**Russian Rascal (IRE)** (TDEasterby) **3-10-12** RGarritty (trckd ldrs: led appr 2 out: r.o)	—	**1**	6/4[1]	66	11
1652[18]	**Eric's Bett** (FMurphy) **3-10-12** KWhelan (in tch: effrt 3 out: chsd wnr fr next: one pce flat)	3	**2**	20/1	63	8
1526[R]	**Noir Esprit** (JMCarr) **3-10-9**(3) FLeahy (cl up: led after 3 out tl appr 2 out: sn outpcd)	9	**3**	12/1	54	—
1526[2]	**Alwarqa** (MDHammond) **3-10-7** DBentley (lw: mstkes: cl up tl outpcd appr 2 out)	2½	**4**	7/1[3]	47	—
1652[13]	**Onyourown (IRE)** (HowardJohnson) **3-10-12** NWilliamson (hld up: effrt appr 2 out: rdn & nvr able to chal)	7	**5**	10/1	45	—
1159[3]	**Double Dash (IRE)** (DMoffatt) **3-11-5** DJMoffatt (prom tl lost pl 5th: styd on again fr 2 out)	½	**6**	20/1	51	—
1205[2]	**Crabbie's Pride** (MGMeagher) **3-10-12** ADobbin (led tl after 3 out: sn wknd)	1¼	**7**	3/1[2]	43	—
	Perpetual Light (JJQuinn) **3-10-7** BHarding (hld up: hdwy 3 out: sn wknd)	¾	**8**	20/1	37	—
	Diamond Beach (GMMoore) **3-10-12** NBentley (mstke 4th: wknd next)	17	**9**	12/1	25	—
	Recruitment (JRTurner) **3-10-12** TReed (hld up: lost tch fr 3 out)	2½	**10**	20/1	23	—
	Northern Diamond (IRE) (MissMERowland) **3-10-12** GaryLyons (in tch: hdwy 5th: wknd appr 2 out)	¾	**11**	100/1	22	—

(SP 122.0%) **11 Rn**

3m 56.0 (13.00) CSF £30.17 TOTE £2.30: £1.20 £4.40 £3.40 (£28.40) Trio £137.30; £58.05 to Leicester 5/12/96 OWNER Mr C. H. Stevens (MALTON) BRED R. M. Fox

OFFICIAL EXPLANATION Onyourown (IRE): finished distressed.

1526 Russian Rascal (IRE), given a fine ride, got things right, despite pulling quite hard, and was always doing enough when in front. (6/4)
906 Eric's Bett needed plenty of help from the saddle to get into contention but, despite struggling on, was never good enough to peg back the winner. (20/1)
Noir Esprit, after running out last time, did nothing wrong here until weakening at the second last. (12/1)
1526 Alwarqa spoiled all chances with some very deliberate jumping, and will need to improve considerably on that score. (7/1)
1514 Onyourown (IRE), dropped out the back, responded to pressure late on, but never had a hope and was later said to be distressed. (10/1)
1159 Double Dash (IRE) was certainly not suited by this trip on this track, and was only running on when it was too late. (20/1)

1701 BROMPTON CONDITIONAL H'CAP HURDLE (0-110) (4-Y.O+) (Class E)

1-20 (1-21) **2m 3f (10 hdls)** £2,427.00 (£672.00: £321.00) GOING: 0.15 sec per fur (G)

	Horse	Dist	Pos	SP	RR	SF
1577[2]	**Tip it In (85)** (ASmith) **7-10-2**(5) NHorrocks (led to 4th: led after 3 out: hld on wl)	—	**1**	5/1[3]	71	—
1658[4]	**Ralitsa (IRE) (102)** (MDHammond) **4-11-5**(5) RBurns (lw: hld up: stdy hdwy to chal 2 out: hrd rdn & nt qckn flat)	½	**2**	11/4[2]	88	—
	Sudden Spin (98) (JNorton) **6-11-3**(3) BGrattan (cl up: mstke 2 out: styd on u.p towards fin)	1	**3**	7/1	83	—
1249[5]	**Anorak (USA) (88)** (GMMoore) **6-10-3**(7) NHannity (hdwy to ld 4th: hdd after 3 out: sn outpcd: styd on towards fin)	1	**4**	33/1	72	—
1500*	**Supertop (106)** (LLungo) **8-11-9**(5) IJardine (hld up & bhd: hdwy ½-wy: ev ch 3 out: hrd rdn & one pce appr next)	3½	**5**	9/4[1]	87	—
	Fryup Satellite (80) (MrsJBrown) **5-10-2** GCahill (lw: plld hrd early: lost pl ½-wy: hdwy u.p appr 2 out: nvr able to chal)	s.h	**6**	25/1	61	—
1282[2]	**Doolar (USA) (81)** (PTDalton) **9-10-0**(3) MNewton (outpcd fr ½-wy)	15	**7**	7/1	49	—
	Danbys Gorse (89) (JMJefferson) **4-10-11** ECallaghan (cl up tl wknd appr 2 out)	6	**8**	16/1	52	—
	Friendly Knight (83) (JSHaldane) **6-10-5** FLeahy (plld hrd: chsd ldrs tl wknd 3 out)	16	**9**	33/1	33	—
1204[P]	**Mill Thyme (95)** (MrsMReveley) **4-11-3** GLee (a wl bhd: t.o)	dist	**10**	14/1	—	—
	Red Beacon (86) (JLGoulding) **9-10-8** JSupple (cl up tl mstke & wknd qckly 7th: t.o)	2	**11**	14/1	—	—

(SP 128.0%) **11 Rn**

4m 50.1 (25.10) CSF £19.94 CT £92.77 TOTE £7.60: £2.50 £1.80 £3.50 (£12.00) Trio £39.60 OWNER Mrs M. Dunning (BEVERLEY) BRED Miss C. L. Armstrong

1577 Tip it In is a determined sort and, once in front on the turn, he would not be denied. (5/1)
1658 Ralitsa (IRE) travelled well and looked to have things in hand on the home turn but, when an effort was required, he was never doing enough. (11/4)
Sudden Spin, in a messy race, got outpaced at a vital stage and, judging by the way he finished, another 50 yards might well have seen him winning. (7/1)
505 Anorak (USA) runs when in the mood and this was not a bad effort. He was staying on again at the end. (33/1)
1500* Supertop gave a few problems at the start and then came there cruising three out, only to come under pressure and find little soon after. (9/4)
Fryup Satellite looked in tremendous shape and ran a fair first race of the season. He should be better for it. (25/1)
1204 Mill Thyme (14/1: 7/1-16/1)

1702 BOBBY FAULKNER MEMORIAL CHALLENGE TROPHY H'CAP CHASE (0-105) (4-Y.O+) (Class F)

1-50 (1-50) **2m (12 fncs)** £2,976.00 (£888.00: £424.00: £192.00) GOING: 0.15 sec per fur (G)

				SP	RR	SF
1051[4]	**Reve de Valse (USA) (85)** (RJohnson) **9-10-8** KJohnson (led to 2nd: chsd ldrs tl mstke & outpcd 8th: styd on fr 3 out: led last: drvn out)	—	1	7/1	96	19
1169*	**Uncle Bert (IRE) (99)** (MissLucindaRussell) **6-11-8** AThornton (cl up fr 5th: led & hmpd 3 out: hdd last: no ex)	7	2	9/2[3]	103	26
1306*	**Full O'Praise (NZ) (105)** (PCalver) **9-12-0** TReed (trckd ldrs: ev ch 3 out: one pce fr next)	12	3	3/1[1]	97	20
2[7]	**Positive Action (90)** (MABarnes) **10-10-8**(5) STaylor (prom tl outpcd fr 7th)	29	4	14/1	53	—
1252[3]	**Desert Brave (IRE) (81)** (MrsSJSmith) **6-10-4**ow4 RichardGuest (led 2nd: jnd & fell 3 out)		F	4/1[2]	—	—
1306[3]	**Thunderstruck (82)** (HowardJohnson) **10-10-5** NWilliamson (nt j.w: last whn p.u bef 7th)		P	7/1	—	—
1576[S]	**Bolaney Girl (IRE) (77)** (FPMurtagh) **7-10-0** ADobbin (ref to s: t.n.p)		R	9/2[3]	—	—
				(SP 113.0%)		**7 Rn**

4m 2.6 (10.60) CSF £35.08 CT £103.75 TOTE £9.40: £3.30 £1.90 (£12.10) OWNER Mr Robert Johnson (NEWCASTLE-UPON-TYNE) BRED Delta Thoroughbreds, Inc.

LONG HANDICAP Bolaney Girl (IRE) 9-12

1051 Reve de Valse (USA) looked out of things after a mistake five out and was then left struggling but, as the others fell by the wayside, he stayed on to take it up from the last. (7/1)

1169* Uncle Bert (IRE), having his first run since changing stables, had his chances, but just failed to see it out on this occasion. (9/2: op 3/1)

1306* Full O'Praise (NZ) was always there with every chance, but that final dash was never forthcoming. (3/1)

Positive Action failed to give any signs of hope. (14/1: 10/1-16/1)

1252 Desert Brave (IRE), over a trip a bit on the sharp side, tried to force it, but had just been joined in the lead and was struggling when departing three out. It would have been interesting had he stood up. (4/1)

1306 Thunderstruck, from a yard that has had horses running badly in the last few days, ran a stinker, ploughing through fences until wisely pulling up. (7/1: 5/1-8/1)

1576 Bolaney Girl (IRE) was up to her old tricks here and refused point-blank to jump off. (9/2)

1703 CALDERPRINT (S) H'CAP HURDLE (0-95) (4-Y.O+) (Class G)

2-20 (2-20) **2m (8 hdls)** £2,285.00 (£635.00: £305.00) GOING: 0.15 sec per fur (G)

				SP	RR	SF
1141[2]	**Flyaway Blues (84)** (MrsMReveley) **4-11-10** PNiven (lw: hld up: hdwy on bit 3 out: led appr last: blnd last & sn hdd: led fnl 50y)	—	1	3/1[1]	69	32
1344[6]	**Chummy's Saga (67)** (LLungo) **6-10-7** MFoster (hld up: stdy hdwy fr 4th: led after 3 out to last: led flat: hdd & no ex towards fin)	nk	2	10/1[3]	52	15
1141[4]	**Little Redwing (65)** (MDHammond) **4-10-5v**[1]ow1 RGarritty (a in tch: effrt 3 out: styd on one pce fr next)	7	3	12/1	43	5
1358[6]	**Aide Memoire (IRE) (75)** (RJohnson) **7-11-1** KJohnson (hld up: hdwy 3 out: sn chsng ldrs: one pce fr next)	¾	4	20/1	52	15
1304[P]	**Arthur Bee (61)** (BBousfield) **9-9-12**(3)ow1 FLeahy (rr div tl styd on u.p fr 2 out)	½	5	33/1	37	—
892[P]	**Heavens Above (60)** (FMurphy) **4-10-0** KWhelan (lw: hld up: hdwy 5th: one pce fr 2 out)	4	6	20/1	32	—
1358[8]	**Familiar Art (80)** (DMoffatt) **5-11-6** DJMoffatt (bhd & pushed along tl styd on fr 2 out)	13	7	16/1	39	2
334[3]	**Elite Justice (83)** (SGollings) **4-11-9b** ADobbin (lw: led 2nd: hit 3rd: sn clr: hdd & wknd after 3 out)	2½	8	10/1[3]	40	3
	My Handy Man (64) (DWBarker) **5-10-4**ow2 RichardGuest (hld up: smooth hdwy & prom 3 out: wknd next)	s.h	9	8/1[2]	21	—
1141[5]	**Seconds Away (60)** (JSGoldie) **5-9-11**(3) GLee (hld up: hdwy 5th: wknd 2 out)	3½	10	14/1	13	—
510[3]	**Over Stated (IRE) (63)** (PCheesbrough) **6-10-3** RSupple (chsd ldrs tl rdn & wknd 3 out)	1	11	16/1	15	—
1247[5]	**Catton Lady (60)** (RCraggs) **6-10-0** PMcLoughlin (lw: n.d)	1	12	50/1	11	—
1304[P]	**Dark Midnight (IRE) (64)** (DALamb) **7-10-4b**[1]ow4 JBurke (prom tl wknd 3 out)	3½	13	100/1	12	—
	Ragazzo (IRE) (68) (JSWainwright) **6-10-5**(3)ow8 PMidgley (n.d)	3	14	10/1[3]	13	—
1305[P]	**Homecrest (62)** (BEllison) **4-9-13v**(3)ow2 GCahill (n.d)	1¼	15	100/1	6	—
1577[9]	**Fly to the End (USA) (75)** (JJQuinn) **6-11-1** BHarding (chsd ldrs tl wknd after 3 out)	4	16	8/1[2]	15	—
1078[10]	**Shut Up (60)** (MrsEMoscrop) **7-9-7**(7) CMcCormack (prom to 3 out)	4	17	50/1	—	—
731[8]	**Candid Lad (73)** (FSStorey) **9-10-13** BStorey (bhd fr ½-wy)	4	18	14/1	5	—
	Vintage Taittinger (IRE) (68) (MissLucindaRussell) **4-10-3**(5) RMcGrath (n.d)	s.h	19	25/1	—	—
	Battuta (77) (MissJFCraze) **7-11-3** NWilliamson (led to 2nd: cl up to 4th: sn wknd: t.o)	dist	20	16/1	—	—
5[3]	**Charlistiona (65)** (JPDodds) **5-10-5** AThornton (prom tl lost pl 3 out: p.u bef next)		P	10/1[3]	—	—
	Lady Khadija (60) (NTinkler) **10-9-11**(3) EHusband (sn t.o: p.u bef 4th)		P	100/1	—	—
				(SP 145.5%)		**22 Rn**

3m 53.7 (10.70) CSF £36.31 CT £327.10 TOTE £4.20: £2.30 £2.90 £2.60 £3.20 (£37.90) Trio £111.80 OWNER Carnoustie Racing Club Ltd (SALTBURN) BRED Miss K. Rausing

LONG HANDICAP Heavens Above 9-13 Catton Lady 9-7 Arthur Bee 9-11 Shut Up 9-5 Dark Midnight (IRE) 9-10 Homecrest 9-4 Seconds Away 9-7 Lady Khadija 9-4

Bt in 3,400 gns

1141 Flyaway Blues was always going much the best here, but he still did his best to throw it away and only just got home. (3/1: op 5/1)

1344 Chummy's Saga travelled well but, when it came down to a struggle, he was tapped for toe. (10/1)

1141 Little Redwing had her chances, but again proved short of pace. (12/1)

1358 Aide Memoire (IRE) has changed stables and produced a better effort here, but was still never doing enough. (20/1)

Arthur Bee is unpredictable and only decided to run when it was too late. (33/1)

Heavens Above, who looked in good shape, showed a little and may at last be learning. (20/1)

1704 CHARLES VICKERY MEMORIAL CUP H'CAP CHASE (0-110) (5-Y.O+) (Class E)

2-50 (2-52) **3m 1f 110y (19 fncs)** £3,261.30 (£974.40: £466.20: £212.10) GOING: 0.15 sec per fur (G)

				SP	RR	SF
1503[2]	**Kenmore-Speed (95)** (MrsSJSmith) **9-11-3** RichardGuest (trckd ldrs: hit 6th: led 10th tl blnd & hdd 15th: styd on to ld last)	—	1	6/4[1]	104	14
1293[7]	**Gale Ahead (IRE) (97)** (GMMoore) **6-11-5** NBentley (a.p: led 15th tl hdd last: kpt on)	2	2	8/1	105	15
1266[8]	**Off The Bru (87)** (MrsSCBradburne) **11-10-2**(7) MrMBradburne (chsd ldrs: outpcd 12th: hdwy 4 out: no imp)	11	3	9/1	88	—
1578[10]	**Forward Glen (80)** (PCheesbrough) **9-9-13b**(3)ow2 GCahill (bhd: hdwy 11th: hit 14th: no imp after)	26	4	9/1	65	—
1284[4]	**Comedy Road (100)** (RLee) **12-11-8** NWilliamson (bhd: hdwy 11th: 3rd whn hit 14th & 15th: sn btn)	30	5	6/1[2]	66	—
1347[6]	**Marchwood (105)** (NChamberlain) **9-11-13** TReed (bhd tl fell 12th)		F	50/1	—	—
	Mullingar (IRE) (93) (JIACharlton) **7-11-1** ADobbin (a bhd: t.o whn p.u bef 15th)		P	20/1	—	—
	Snook Point (82) (DALamb) **9-10-4**ow4 JBurke (led to 7th: wknd 10th: p.u bef 12th)		P	25/1	—	—

			Pos	SP	RR	SF
1527[3]	**Port in a Storm (88)** (MDHammond) **7-10-7**(3) MrCBonner (lw: cl up: led 7th to 10th: wknd 12th: p.u bef 2 out)		P	7/1[3]	—	—
	Twin States (98) (JRTurner) **7-11-6** AThornton (prom whn blnd & uns rdr 7th)		U	10/1	—	—

(SP 117.6%) **10 Rn**

6m 40.3 (22.30) CSF £13.58 CT £76.33 TOTE £2.10: £1.40 £1.70 £3.00 (£13.50) Trio £46.20 OWNER Mr K. M. Dacker (BINGLEY) BRED Mrs Davina Whiteman

LONG HANDICAP Snook Point 9-11 Forward Glen 9-12

1503 Kenmore-Speed did well for a novice in handicap company and proved he really stays. (6/4)

1024 Gale Ahead (IRE) put in his best performance for some time, only to find the winner too determined. (8/1)

804 Off The Bru ran one of his better races, but was still never doing enough over the last four fences. (9/1)

1244 Forward Glen, from a yard going well at the moment, soon decided it was not for him after a mistake six out. (9/1)

1284 Comedy Road is happier over shorter trips and, after a mistake late on, then tired. (6/1)

1527 Port in a Storm was tried at too long a trip here and was made too much use of. (7/1: op 4/1)

1705 STREETLAM 'N.H.' NOVICES' HURDLE (4-Y.O+) (Class E)

3-20 (3-21) **2m 3f (10 hdls)** £2,595.00 (£720.00: £345.00) GOING: 0.15 sec per fur (G)

			Pos	SP	RR	SF
	Lagen Bridge (IRE) (DMoffatt) **7-10-10** DJMoffatt (lw: trckd ldrs: chal 7th: led after 3 out: hung bdly lft: pushed out)	—	1	25/1	63	—
1263*	**B The One** (JJQuinn) **5-11-3** RGarritty (trckd ldrs: effrt & ev ch 2 out: kpt on one pce)	1	2	7/4[1]	69	—
1263[2]	**Faithful Hand** (MrsSJSmith) **6-10-10** RichardGuest (trckd ldrs tl lost pl after 3 out: no imp after)	24	3	9/4[2]	42	—
	Robert The Brave (JMJefferson) **4-10-7**(3) ECallaghan (hdwy ½-wy: styd on: n.d)	14	4	50/1	30	—
1033*	**Silver Minx** (MrsMReveley) **4-10-10** PNiven (mstkes: led tl hdd & wknd after 3 out)	10	5	9/4[2]	22	—
	Hadaway Lad (HowardJohnson) **4-10-10** NWilliamson (lost tch fr ½-wy)	4	6	14/1[3]	18	—
1504[7]	**Four From Home (IRE)** (JJO'Neill) **4-10-5**(5) RMcGrath (bhd: effrt ½-wy: n.d)	12	7	25/1	8	—
	Rasin Luck (RCraggs) **6-10-5** BStorey (chsd ldrs tl wknd fr 6th)	15	8	25/1	—	—
1263[6]	**Primitive Heart** (HowardJohnson) **4-10-10** ALarnach (a bhd)	12	9	16/1	—	—
1349[P]	**Smart In Satin** (MissLucindaRussell) **6-10-10** AThornton (nt j.w: a bhd)	15	10	100/1	—	—
	Make A Buck (LLungo) **6-10-10** MFoster (t.o fr ½-wy)	20	11	33/1	—	—
1052[9]	**Henpecked (IRE)** (MDHammond) **5-10-7**(3) MrCBonner (in tch tl wknd 7th: bhd whn fell last)		F	16/1	—	—

(SP 133.8%) **12 Rn**

4m 44.6 (19.60) CSF £73.42 TOTE £12.30: £2.90 £2.40 £1.00 (£15.80) Trio £21.30 OWNER Mrs Eileen Milligan (CARTMEL) BRED James Flahavan

Lagen Bridge (IRE) looked and travelled well, but he did his best to throw it away when in front by hanging left, and his saddle was also said to have slipped. (25/1)

1263* B The One stays and is honest, but is certainly short of a turn of foot on tracks such as this. (7/4)

1263 Faithful Hand had his chances, and was certainly not knocked about when the leaders turned it on from the third last. (9/4)

Robert The Brave was staying on as though a real test of stamina should suit. (50/1)

1033* Silver Minx was taken to post early then went tearing off in front and had not surprisingly run himself out by the home turn. He obviously has his problems. (9/4)

Hadaway Lad (14/1: 20/1-33/1)

T/Jkpt: Not won; £16,876.16 to Leicester 5/12/96. T/Plpt: £364.30 (24.55 Tckts). T/Qdpt: £17.50 (62.64 Tckts). AA

1388-FONTWELL (Fig. 8) (Good, Good to soft patches)

Wednesday December 4th

Race 1 - last flight omitted fnl circ

WEATHER: fine

1706 EARTHAM HURDLE (I) (3-Y.O) (Class E)

12-40 (12-41) **2m 2f 110y (8 hdls)** £2,364.00 (£654.00: £312.00) GOING: 0.39 sec per fur (GS)

			Pos	SP	RR	SF
1269[5]	**Serenus (USA)** (NJHenderson) **3-10-12** JRKavanagh (a.p: led 4th: easily)	—	1	3/1[2]	81+	—
	Academy House (IRE) (RAkehurst) **3-10-12** APMcCoy (hld up: rdn 3 out: chsd wnr fr last: no imp)	14	2	4/5[1]	69	—
1387[3]	**Ben Bowden** (SWoodman) **3-11-5** JOsborne (led after 1st to 4th: ev ch 2 out: unable qckn)	7	3	8/1[3]	70	—
1269[6]	**Hanbitooh (USA)** (MrsAJPerrett) **3-10-12** CMaude (lw: led tl after 1st: rdn 3 out: one pce)	1½	4	16/1	62	—
1444[P]	**Quiet Moments (IRE)** (PGMurphy) **3-10-12** WMarston (lw: prom to 5th)	18	5	50/1	46	—
	Princely Affair (JMBradley) **3-10-12** TJMurphy (rdn & hdwy 3 out: wknd 2 out)	3½	6	25/1	43	—
	Tathmin (JRBosley) **3-10-12** MBosley (blnd 5th: a bhd)	1	7	66/1	42	—
1377[9]	**Illegally Yours** (LMontagueHall) **3-10-7** DMorris (prom to 5th)	6	8	33/1	32	—
	Private Percival (JRPoulton) **3-10-12** ADicken (a bhd: t.o)	dist	9	66/1	—	—
	Bold Start Lady (EAWheeler) **3-10-0**(7) MGriffiths (a bhd: mstke 4th: fell 5th)		F	66/1	—	—
1014[10]	**Gold Lance (USA)** (RJO'Sullivan) **3-10-12b**[1] DO'Sullivan (lw: prom to 5th: t.o whn p.u bef last)		P	14/1	—	—

(SP 117.4%) **11 Rn**

4m 36.3 (18.30) CSF £5.45 TOTE £3.90: £1.40 £1.10 £1.40 (£2.40) Trio £2.50 OWNER W V & Mrs E S Robins (LAMBOURN) BRED Foxfield

1269 Serenus (USA) has looked paceless on several occasions on the Flat and over jumps. In this low-grade race, he had no problems and surged clear from the second last to win with his head in his chest. (3/1)

Academy House (IRE), an ex-Irish colt who was bought out of Aidan O'Brien's yard for 20,000 guineas, failed to reel in the winner. He may need further as he has won over two miles on the Flat. (4/5: 1/2-5/6)

1387 Ben Bowden has been running consistently this season and ran another sound race under a 7lb penalty. (8/1: 6/1-9/1)

1269 Hanbitooh (USA) ran better in this lower-grade event, but was made to look very pedestrian. (16/1)

1707 SELSEY (S) HURDLE (4,5,6 & 7-Y.O) (Class G)

1-10 (1-11) **2m 2f 110y (9 hdls)** £2,010.20 (£557.20: £266.60) GOING: 0.39 sec per fur (GS)

			Pos	SP	RR	SF
	Zesti (TTClement) **4-10-12** NMann (lw: stdy hdwy 6th: led appr 2 out: clr appr last: easily)	—	1	5/1[2]	63+	—
1569[6]	**Lanesra Breeze** (TJNaughton) **4-10-12** CMaude (hld up: rdn 6th: chsd wnr fr last: no imp)	8	2	33/1	56	—
1390[9]	**Water Hazard (IRE) (73)** (SDow) **4-10-12** ADicken (a.p: led 6th tl appr 2 out: one pce)	1¼	3	7/1	55	—
1419[6]	**Credit Controller (IRE) (57)** (JFfitch-Heyes) **7-10-12b** JRKavanagh (hdwy appr 2 out: one pce)	3	4	11/1	52	—

				SP	RR	SF
1422^{P}	**Churchtown Spirit** (TPMcGovern) **5-10-7** GCrone (bhd fr 6th: t.o)	dist	**5**	33/1	—	—
	Mini Fete (FR) (KRBurke) **7-10-7** DBridgwater (bit bkwd: bhd fr 5th: t.o)	hd	**6**	9/1	—	—
1413^{10}	**Griffin's Girl** (PMooney) **4-10-2**$^{(5)}$ SRyan (lw: a.p: ev ch 3 out: 4th & btn whn mstke 2 out: t.o)	8	**7**	6/1^{3}	—	—
1422^{P}	**Flaming Rose (IRE)** (RRowe) **6-10-7** DO'Sullivan (lw: prom to 4th: t.o)	22	**8**	50/1	—	—
1388^{8}	**Little Luke (IRE)** (PButler) **5-10-12** TJMurphy (led to 6th: sn wknd: t.o)	1½	**9**	33/1	—	—
1424^{4}	**Memory's Music** (MMadgwick) **4-10-12** BFenton (stdy hdwy 6th: rdn appr 2 out: 5th & no ch whn fell last)		**F**	5/2^{1}	—	—
	Gemini Mist (MrsPNDutfield) **5-10-7** PHolley (a.p: rdn 6th: wknd 3 out: bhd whn p.u bef last)		**P**	12/1	—	—
				(SP 108.8%)	**11 Rn**	

4m 41.1 (23.10) CSF £114.15 TOTE £4.50: £1.40 £12.40 £2.20 (£70.20) Trio £209.80; £268.94 to Leicester 5/12/96 OWNER Miss R. J. Bryant (NEWMARKET) BRED Biddestone Stud

No bid

Zesti, with a recent run on the Flat under his belt, trotted up on this hurdling debut in a dreadful race. This was Terry Clement's first winner over jumps. (5/1)

Lanesra Breeze ran his best race to date in this appalling race. (33/1)

961 Water Hazard (IRE), collared approaching the second last, was then only treading water. (7/1: 9/2-8/1)

1072 Credit Controller (IRE), very exposed, only plodded on past tired rivals in the last half-mile. (11/1: 6/1-12/1)

1086 Griffin's Girl (6/1: op 3/1)

1424 Memory's Music, taking a drop in class, appeared to be travelling well as he crept closer in the back straight but, when his jockey asked him for an effort turning for home, he found disappointingly little, and was well beaten when falling at the final flight. (5/2)

1708 NORFOLK CHALLENGE CUP NOVICES' H'CAP CHASE (0-100) (4-Y.O+) (Class E)

1-40 (1-41) **2m 2f (15 fncs)** £3,124.80 (£932.40: £445.20: £201.60) GOING: 0.39 sec per fur (GS)

				SP	RR	SF
1420^{4}	**Duke of Aprolon (82)** (JTGifford) **9-11-7** PHide (led to 3rd: led appr 3 out: clr appr 2 out: easily)	—	**1**	5/2^{1}	94+	26
1298^{3}	**Willie Makeit (IRE) (85)** (RTPhillips) **6-11-10** JRailton (stdy hdwy 9th: chsd wnr appr 2 out: no imp)	16	**2**	5/1	83	15
1552^{F}	**Jacksons Bay (63)** (TCasey) **6-10-2** DBridgwater (hdwy appr 3 out: rdn appr last: one pce)	¾	**3**	12/1	60	—
	Albury Grey (61) (TPMcGovern) **9-10-0** GCrone (nvr nr to chal)	8	**4**	50/1	51	—
1300^{5}	**Bold Acre (84)** (JMBradley) **6-11-9** TJMurphy (lw: stdy hdwy 9th: 3rd whn mstke 10th: hrd rdn appr 2 out: wknd appr last)	1½	**5**	7/2^{2}	73	5
1572^{4}	**Dress Dance (IRE) (85)** (NRMitchell) **6-11-5**$^{(5)}$ SophieMitchell (rdn 8th: sme hdwy 10th: 5th whn mstke 4 out: sn wknd)	½	**6**	9/2^{3}	73	5
1585^{7}	**Full of Tricks (69)** (JJBridger) **8-10-8** DMorris (w wnr: led 3rd tl appr 3 out: sn wknd)	16	**7**	33/1	43	—
	Hidden Pleasure (79) (TMJones) **10-11-4** DLeahy (bkwd: fell 3rd)		**F**	14/1	—	—
1073^{U}	**Kentavrus Way (IRE) (61)** (AMoore) **5-10-0** BPowell (bit bkwd: a bhd: blnd bdly 4th: t.o whn p.u bef 3 out)		**P**	20/1	—	—
1423^{5}	**Pinoccio (80)** (DCO'Brien) **9-11-2**$^{(3)}$ DWalsh (prom to 8th: t.o whn p.u bef 3 out)		**P**	20/1	—	—
				(SP 114.4%)	**10 Rn**	

4m 39.6 (17.60) CSF £14.35 CT £112.66 TOTE £2.60: £1.10 £2.40 £2.70 (£7.10) Trio £28.80 OWNER The First Eleven Partnership (FINDON) BRED Jeremiah McCarthy

LONG HANDICAP Kentavrus Way (IRE) 9-10 Albury Grey 9-13

1420 Duke of Aprolon, taking a drop in distance, set off at a good pace along with Full of Tricks. Showing in front approaching the third last, he soon surged clear to win this bad race in fine style - gaining his first success in over three and a half years. (5/2)

1298 Willie Makeit (IRE) found the winner not for the catching. (5/1)

Jacksons Bay could only struggle on at one pace over the last three. (12/1)

Albury Grey, who has been at stud and produced foals in '94 and '95, looked pretty straight for this first run in over three and a half years, and stayed on past tiring rivals to pick up some prizemoney. (50/1)

Bold Acre crept into contention on the final circuit and was vying for the runner-up spot in the straight until tiring from the second last. (7/2)

1572 Dress Dance (IRE) never looked like getting into it. (9/2: op 5/2)

1709 A & D LANDSCAPES H'CAP HURDLE (0-125) (4-Y.O+) (Class D)

2-10 (2-10) **2m 2f 110y (9 hdls)** £3,054.20 (£846.20: £404.60) GOING: 0.39 sec per fur (GS)

				SP	RR	SF
	Supreme Lady (IRE) (110) (MissHCKnight) **5-11-8** JOsborne (hdwy 6th: led appr 2 out: clr appr last: r.o wl)	—	**1**	9/4^{1}	94	—
955*	**Iron N Gold (97)** (TCasey) **4-10-9** DBridgwater (hdwy 3 out: ev ch appr 2 out: unable qckn)	11	**2**	7/2^{2}	72	—
1392^{4}	**Smuggler's Point (USA) (109)** (JJBridger) **6-11-7** DMorris (a.p: rdn 3 out: one pce)	1	**3**	10/1	83	—
1585^{5}	**Tickerty's Gift (112)** (GLMoore) **6-11-3**$^{(7)}$ MAttwater (lw: led tl appr 2 out: one pce)	nk	**4**	9/1	85	—
1045^{4}	**Bon Voyage (USA) (97)** (DMGrissell) **4-10-9b**^{1} JRKavanagh (hld up: rdn 3 out: one pce)	3	**5**	9/1	68	—
	Lucky Eddie (IRE) (105) (PJHobbs) **5-11-3** CMaude (prom to 3 out)	12	**6**	9/2^{3}	65	—
1381^{5}	**Muhtashim (IRE) (89)** (JFfitch-Heyes) **6-10-1** BFenton (lw: blnd 3rd: a bhd)	14	**7**	9/1	37	—
	Raahin (USA) (88) (SWoodman) **11-10-0** MRichards (lw: bhd whn blnd 4th: t.o whn p.u bef 6th)		**P**	50/1	—	—
				(SP 112.2%)	**8 Rn**	

4m 37.7 (19.70) CSF £9.89 CT £56.08 TOTE £2.60: £1.70 £1.10 £2.80 (£4.40) OWNER The Supreme Lady Partnership (WANTAGE) BRED Mrs Anne Kerr

LONG HANDICAP Raahin (USA) 9-2

Supreme Lady (IRE) made a fine return to action. Sent on approaching the second last, she soon forged clear for a decisive victory. (9/4)

955* Iron N Gold had every chance turning for home before left for dead by the winner. (7/2)

1392 Smuggler's Point (USA) was made to look very one-paced from the third last. (10/1: 8/1-12/1)

1585 Tickerty's Gift is at his best in the mud, but nevertheless took the field along until collared approaching the second last. (9/1)

Muhtashim (IRE) (9/1: 6/1-10/1)

1710 SIDLESHAM CONDITIONAL H'CAP HURDLE (0-110) (4-Y.O+) (Class E)

2-40 (2-40) **2m 6f 110y (11 hdls)** £2,280.00 (£630.00: £300.00) GOING: 0.39 sec per fur (GS)

				SP	RR	SF
	Mirador (88) (RCurtis) **5-11-6** DWalsh (lw: hdwy 8th: chsd ldr appr 2 out: led appr last: easily)	—	**1**	13/8^{1}	80+	—
1586^{P}	**Daring King (88)** (MJBolton) **6-11-6** LAspell (a.p: chsd wnr fr 5th: led 8th tl appr last: unable qckn)	8	**2**	10/1	74	—
792^{9}	**Pavlova (IRE) (82)** (RRowe) **6-10-9**$^{(5)}$ AGarrity (lw: hdwy appr 2 out: r.o one pce)	3½	**3**	10/1	66	—
1394^{4}	**Flying Fiddler (IRE) (92)** (MJRoberts) **5-11-10b**^{1} PHenley (lw: hld up: rdn appr 2 out: sn wknd)	5	**4**	7/1^{3}	72	—
1390^{4}	**Roger's Pal (77)** (AMoore) **9-10-4**$^{(5)}$ MBatchelor (lw: chsd ldr 2nd to 5th: rdn 6th: wknd appr 2 out)	6	**5**	10/1	53	—
1392^{2}	**Cassio's Boy (86)** (RJEckley) **5-11-4** DJKavanagh (lw: rdn & hdwy 3 out: wknd appr 2 out)	18	**6**	2/1^{2}	49	—
1585^{6}	**Somerset Dancer (USA) (80)** (JJBridger) **9-10-12** KGaule (a bhd: t.o whn p.u bef 6th)		**P**	33/1	—	—

				SP	RR	SF
1550[7]	**Profession (70)** (FGray) **5-9-9v**(7)ow2 JKMcCarthy (led to 8th: sn wknd: t.o whn p.u bef 2 out)		**P**	50/1	—	—

(SP 116.1%) **8 Rn**

5m 50.0 (34.00) CSF £17.02 CT £115.23 TOTE £1.90: £1.10 £2.30 £2.50 (£18.30) OWNER Mrs J Whitehead,J McGivern & Two Kates (LAMBOURN) BRED Miss T. P. Pile
LONG HANDICAP Profession 8-13
OFFICIAL EXPLANATION **Cassio's Boy: was found to be lame the following morning with a knee injury.**
Mirador, second in the Ascot Stakes at the Royal Meeting, found this a simple task in comparison, and treated her rivals with contempt, cruising into the lead approaching the last and winning without turning a hair. She can follow up. (13/8)
Daring King was firmly put in his place by the winner. (10/1)
Pavlova (IRE) struggled on in the last half-mile to snatch third. (10/1)
1394 Flying Fiddler (IRE) chased the leaders, but the distress signals were there for all to see turning for home and he soon capitulated. (7/1: 9/2-8/1)
1390 Roger's Pal is no better than a plater. (10/1: 8/1-12/1)
1392 Cassio's Boy was very disappointing and a brief effort three from home came to little. His jockey later reported the horse never felt right. (2/1: 5/4-9/4)

1711 MUNDHAM NOVICES' CHASE (5-Y.O+) (Class E)

3-10 (3-10) **3m 2f 110y (22 fncs)** £3,080.00 (£920.00: £440.00: £200.00) GOING: 0.39 sec per fur (GS)

				SP	RR	SF
	Flaked Oats (PFNicholls) **7-10-10** APMcCoy (lw: hdwy 3rd: led 4 out: r.o wl)	—	**1**	11/8[1]	97+	26
	Parahandy (IRE) (GBBalding) **6-10-10** BFenton (a.p: chsd wnr appr 3 out: unable qckn)	4	**2**	13/2	95	24
1376[F]	**Grey Gorden (IRE)** (RCurtis) **8-10-10** DMorris (led to 4 out: sn wknd)	14	**3**	6/1[3]	86	15
1075*	**Keep it Zipped (IRE) (99)** (OSherwood) **6-11-7** JOsborne (chsd ldr tl mstke 4th: lost pl & nvr gng wl fr 7th: no hdwy fr 16th)	6	**4**	4/1[2]	94	23
	Langton Parmill (WGMTurner) **11-10-3**(7) NWillmington (hdwy 6th: mstke 13th: wknd 16th: fell 18th)		**F**	40/1	—	—
	Apatura Hati (RHAlner) **7-10-2**(3) PHenley (lw: a bhd: t.o whn p.u bef last)		**P**	9/1	—	—
	Rolled Gold (MissVenetiaWilliams) **7-10-10** DBridgwater (a bhd: mstke 1st: t.o whn p.u bef 9th)		**P**	16/1	—	—
	Little Rowley (MrsLRichards) **7-10-10** MRichards (blnd 2nd: bhd fr 11th: t.o whn p.u bef 3 out)		**P**	66/1	—	—

(SP 109.5%) **8 Rn**

7m 2.6 (22.60) CSF £9.70 TOTE £1.90: £1.40 £1.20 £1.70 (£7.00) OWNER Mr E. B. Swaffield (SHEPTON MALLET) BRED E. B. Swaffield
Flaked Oats, a very useful pointer who won six under that code, had things nicely under control in the straight. He can win again. (11/8)
Parahandy (IRE), successful in a couple of points, moved into second place approaching the third last but, try as he might, failed to get to terms with the winner. (13/2: 5/1-8/1)
1376 Grey Gorden (IRE) did a fine job of pacemaking but, collared at the water, was soon hung out to dry. (6/1)
1075* Keep it Zipped (IRE) was not in a co-operative mood this time and, losing his pitch from the seventh, was never travelling from that point. He has ability, but is not one to place a great deal of faith in. (4/1)
Apatura Hati (9/1: 6/1-12/1)

1712 EARTHAM HURDLE (II) (3-Y.O) (Class E)

3-40 (3-42) **2m 2f 110y (9 hdls)** £2,343.00 (£648.00: £309.00) GOING: 0.39 sec per fur (GS)

				SP	RR	SF
	Jelali (IRE) (DJGMurraySmith) **3-10-12** DGallagher (hdwy 5th: led appr 2 out: rdn & r.o)	—	**1**	11/4[2]	65	—
	Siberian Henry (BSmart) **3-10-12** CLlewellyn (chsd ldr: led 6th tl appr 2 out: unable qckn)	4	**2**	9/1	62	—
	Province (CJMann) **3-10-12** JRailton (lw: a.p: ev ch appr 2 out: one pce)	3½	**3**	5/4[1]	59	—
	Veronica Franco (BAPearce) **3-10-4**(3) KGaule (nvr nr to chal)	8	**4**	33/1	47	—
	Classy Chief (JWhite) **3-10-12** TJMurphy (lw: hdwy 6th: wknd appr 2 out)	1¼	**5**	7/1[3]	51	—
	Ember (RTPhillips) **3-10-7** DBridgwater (lw: hdwy 3 out: rdn appr 2 out: wknd appr last)	1½	**6**	20/1	44	—
1377[13]	**Embroidered** (RMFlower) **3-10-0**(7) JKMcCarthy (hdwy 6th: ev ch 3 out: wknd appr 2 out)	24	**7**	33/1	24	—
	Reem Fever (IRE) (DWPArbuthnot) **3-10-7** APMcCoy (bhd fr 6th: t.o)	dist	**8**	12/1	—	—
	Red Rusty (USA) (PRHedger) **3-10-12** MRichards (mstke 3rd: bhd whn p.u bef 5th: b.b.v)		**P**	16/1	—	—
1014[9]	**Petros Gem** (MJBolton) **3-10-7** PHide (led to 6th: sn wknd: t.o whn p.u bef last)		**P**	33/1	—	—

(SP 120.8%) **10 Rn**

4m 48.2 (30.20) CSF £26.61 TOTE £3.30: £1.20 £1.90 £1.40 (£14.90) Trio £10.00 OWNER The Fort Partnership (LAMBOURN) BRED Knocktoran Stud
OFFICIAL EXPLANATION **Red Rusty (USA): bled from the nose.**
Jelali (IRE) made a winning start to his hurdling career. He would really like it softer according to his trainer. (11/4)
Siberian Henry, collared approaching the second last, found the winner too good. (9/1: op 20/1)
Province won a maiden on the Flat at Newmarket for Geoff Lewis this year, but was not very convincing over hurdles and was a bit keen early on. (5/4: op 1/2)
Veronica Franco struggled on past beaten horses to be nearest at the line. (33/1)
Classy Chief, fit from the Flat, took closer order early on the final circuit, but had been hung out to dry approaching the second last. (7/1)
Reem Fever (IRE) (12/1: 8/1-14/1)

T/Plpt: £120.30 (93.46 Tckts). T/Qdpt: £11.70 (84.25 Tckts). AK

0486-SOUTHWELL (L-H) (Good)

Wednesday December 4th

WEATHER: fine & sunny

1713 E.B.F. CHASING IN MIND 'N.H.' QUALIFIER NOVICES' HURDLE (4, 5 & 6-Y.O) (Class E)

1-00 (1-01) **2m 4f 110y (11 hdls)** £2,301.00 (£636.00: £303.00) GOING: 0.29 sec per fur (GS)

				SP	RR	SF
	Lance Armstrong (IRE) (GMMcCourt) **6-11-0** AMaguire (trckd ldrs: led 5th: clr 2 out: easily)	—	**1**	4/6[1]	54+	—
	Dry Hill Lad (JNorton) **5-11-0** WFry (chsd ldrs: rdn & one pce fr 3 out)	5	**2**	12/1	50	—
1453[13]	**Red Tel (IRE)** (MCPipe) **4-11-0** MAFitzgerald (lw: hld up: effrt & pushed along 6th: sn outpcd: hrd rdn & styd on between last 2)	1	**3**	4/1[2]	49	—
	Carly-J (FSJackson) **5-10-9** MrNKent (trckd ldrs: effrt appr 2 out: sn rdn: one pce)	nk	**4**	25/1	44	—
1301[4]	**Optimistic Affair** (AStreeter) **5-11-0** ALarnach (lw: in tch: hit 6th: sn bhd: t.o 8th)	dist	**5**	6/1[3]	—	—

1021P	**Farmers Subsidy** (GMMoore) **4-10-7**(7) THogg (w ldrs: outpcd & drvn along 6th: sn bhd)......9	6	33/1	—	—
1263[9]	**Ar Aghaidh Abhaile (IRE)** (MissMKMilligan) **5-11-0** ASSmith (mde most to 5th: wknd 8th: t.o 2 out)......dist	7	20/1	—	—
960P	**Night Thyne (IRE)** (MJRoberts) **4-10-11**(3) GHogan (hld up: wnt prom 6th: rdn 3 out: 5th & wl btn whn fell last)	F	14/1	—	—
1336[4]	**Halam Bell** (WGMTurner) **4-10-9** RGreene (j.b 1st & 2nd: bhd whn tried to ref & uns rdr 3rd)......	U	33/1	—	—

(SP 123.1%) **9 Rn**

5m 12.0 (26.00) CSF £10.49 TOTE £1.60: £1.10 £2.60 £1.10 (£6.60) Trio £19.10 OWNER Mr G. L. Porter (WANTAGE) BRED Tom Curran

IN-FOCUS: **The prominent showing of the fourth shows what a poor event this was.**

Lance Armstrong (IRE), a winner twice over fences last season, took this very weak contest without coming out of second gear. (4/6: 1/2-4/5)

Dry Hill Lad, who had shown ability in points, was very much on his toes beforehand. (12/1)

918 Red Tel (IRE) walked very stiffly behind in the paddock. Outpaced setting out on to the final circuit, he stuck on under strong pressure between the last two. (4/1)

Carly-J, who has shown only poor form in selling company, was far from disgraced. (25/1)

1714 WELLAND NOVICES' CHASE (5-Y.O+) (Class E)

1-30 (1-31) **2m (13 fncs)** £3,206.70 (£957.60: £457.80: £207.90) GOING: 0.29 sec per fur (GS)

			SP	RR	SF
1120[5]	**Sublime Fellow (IRE) (118)** (NJHenderson) **6-11-5** MAFitzgerald (lw: trckd ldr: led 7th: clr 4 out)......—	1	9/4 1	118	59
	Formal Invitation (IRE) (DNicholson) **7-10-12** AMaguire (hld up: hdwy 7th: styd on fr 3 out: no imp)......8	2	9/4 1	103	44
1298F	**Lobster Cottage (88)** (KCBailey) **8-11-5** CO'Dwyer (hld up & bhd: gd hdwy 7th: sn chsng wnr: wknd 3 out)..23	3	9/2 3	87	28
1009[2]	**Shalik (IRE) (81)** (JRJenkins) **6-10-5**(7) NTEgan (led to 7th: blnd 9th: sn lost pl)......10	4	20/1	70	11
1248P	**Cheeka (76)** (CSmith) **7-10-12** MRanger (outpcd & bhd fr 7th)......3	5	33/1	67	8
1576F	**Ethical Note (IRE)** (MrsSJSmith) **5-10-5**(7) RWilkinson (chsd ldrs: drvn along 6th: sn bhd: t.o 4 out)......24	6	33/1	43	—
1166*	**Minster's Madam** (JNeville) **5-10-4v**(3) TDascombe (chsd ldrs: blnd 3rd: 3rd whn fell 7th)......	F	16/1	—	—
1254[2]	**Flaming Miracle (IRE) (72)** (GBarnett) **6-10-12b** RFarrant (mstkes: wnt prom 6th: lost pl 8th: t.o whn p.u after 4 out)......	P	4/1 2	—	—
949[4]	**Weeheby (USA)** (MFBarraclough) **7-10-12** SMcNeill (blnd & uns rdr 3rd)......	U	10/1	—	—

(SP 125.3%) **9 Rn**

3m 59.2 (6.20) CSF £8.27 TOTE £3.60: £3.80 £1.00 £3.10 (£6.90) Trio £16.60 OWNER Lady Annabel Goldsmith (LAMBOURN) BRED John Kent

1120 Sublime Fellow (IRE) had things all his own way here, and this will have done his confidence no harm at all. (9/4)

Formal Invitation (IRE) was having his first outing for almost four years, but looked in good trim beforehand. Given time to get his eye in, he went second three out and, though keeping on, was never going to bother the winner. The outing will surely have done him good. (9/4)

1298 Lobster Cottage, a free-going sort, is anything but a fluent jumper. After moving into second place at the eighth, he tired badly over the last three. (9/2)

1009 Shalik (IRE) was again far from foot-perfect. (20/1)

949 Weeheby (USA) (10/1: 8/1-12/1)

1715 SAIL INN H'CAP HURDLE (0-120) (4-Y.O+) (Class D)

2-00 (2-06) **2m (9 hdls)** £2,888.00 (£798.00: £380.00) GOING: 0.29 sec per fur (GS)

			SP	RR	SF
1630[2]	**Stay With Me (FR) (94)** (CREgerton) **6-10-4**(5) MrRThornton (lw: trckd ldrs: led 5th: clr 2 out: drvn out)......—	1	5/2 2	77	24
1123P	**Shifting Moon (85)** (FJordan) **4-10-0b** SWynne (trckd ldrs: led 4th to next: rdn 3 out: no ch w wnr whn hit last)......10	2	14/1	58	5
1413*	**Peter Monamy (103)** (MCPipe) **4-11-4b** MAFitzgerald (chsd ldrs: outpcd & drvn along 4th: one pce)......4	3	7/2 3	72	19
1333[6]	**Ath Cheannaithe (FR) (87)** (JNeville) **4-10-2hb** AMaguire (led: blnd 2nd: hdd 4th: sn lost pl & bhd:t.o 3 out)dist	4	10/1	—	—
	Isaiah (113) (MrsJCecil) **7-12-0** TKent (bit bkwd: mstkes: bhd whn blnd 5th: p.u bef 2 out)......	P	7/1	—	—
1502[2]	**King Athelstan (USA) (108)** (BAMcMahon) **8-11-9** DerekByrne (nvr gng wl: bhd: effrt & drvn along 5th: no rspnse: p.u bef 2 out: fin lame)......	P	2/1 1	—	—

(SP 112.4%) **6 Rn**

3m 53.6 (11.60) CSF £27.86 TOTE £3.20: £1.80 £4.80 (£14.60) OWNER Mrs Sandra Roe (CHADDLEWORTH) BRED Mr and Mrs Henri Rossi and Gerard Desnoues

LONG HANDICAP Shifting Moon 9-13

OFFICIAL EXPLANATION **King Athelstan (USA): was lame.**

1630 Stay With Me (FR), a keen-going sort, had this won some way out. (5/2)

Shifting Moon, pulled up on his two latest outings, wore a tongue-strap and was lightly-backed at long odds but, in the end, proved no match whatsoever. (14/1: op 33/1)

1413* Peter Monamy, back in handicap company, was under pressure with a circuit to go. (7/2)

974 Ath Cheannaithe (FR) seems to have lost his way altogether. (10/1)

Isaiah looked very burly. He never took to these obstacles and, after making several mistakes, was leg weary when pulled up. (7/1: 4/1-8/1)

1502 King Athelstan (USA) had to be re-plated beforehand. He ran a stinker and was never going, but was later found to be lame, probably due to spreading a plate before the race and pricking his foot. (2/1)

1716 GRENVILLE CHADWICK RETIREMENT NOVICES' H'CAP CHASE (0-100) (5-Y.O+) (Class E)

2-30 (2-32) **3m 110y (19 fncs)** £3,479.70 (£1,041.60: £499.80: £228.90) GOING: 0.29 sec per fur (GS)

			SP	RR	SF
	Ocean Leader (89) (MrsDHaine) **9-11-3** AMaguire (lw: hld up & bhd: stdy hdwy 13th: led 3 out: shkn up & drew clr flat: eased towards fin)......—	1	7/4 1	100	25
1371[6]	**Record Lover (IRE) (72)** (MCChapman) **6-10-0** WWorthington (drvn along & in tch 9th: outpcd 4 out: styd on u.p fr next: no ch w wnr)......3	2	16/1	81	6
1506[2]	**Lucky Dollar (IRE) (99)** (KCBailey) **8-11-13** CO'Dwyer (lw: trckd ldrs: rdn appr 3 out: 3rd & one pce whn blnd last)......½	3	3/1 3	108	33
	Tactix (72) (MissMKMilligan) **6-10-0** ASSmith (bit bkwd: mstkes: hld up: hdwy 13th: kpt on fr 3 out: nvr nr to chal)......4	4	50/1	78	3
	Ring Corbitts (84) (MJRoberts) **8-10-9**(3) GHogan (trckd ldr: led 12th to 14th: sn lost pl)......10	5	20/1	84	9
	Dunlir (75) (PRRodford) **6-10-3**ow3 SBurrough (trckd ldrs: blnd 15th: sn wl bhd: t.o 3 out)......dist	6	20/1	—	—
1246*	**Gems Lad (86)** (MrsSJSmith) **9-11-0** MAFitzgerald (led: blnd & hdd 12th: led 14th: mstke & hdd 3 out: 3rd & outpcd whn fell 2 out)......	F	5/2 2	—	—

1075[5] **Manor Mieo (90)** (GProdromou) **10-10-11**(7) MrACoe (trckd ldrs: drvn along whn blnd & uns rdr 4 out).............. **U** 6/1 — —
(SP 121.6%) **8 Rn**

6m 28.1 (21.10) CSF £27.18 CT £77.82 TOTE £2.90: £2.20 £2.00 £1.00 (£14.80) Trio £16.30 OWNER Sir Peter Gibbings (NEWMARKET) BRED W. Lombard

LONG HANDICAP Tactix 9-7 Dunlir 9-11 Record Lover (IRE) 9-11

Ocean Leader, a grand, chasing type, was turned out in particularly good trim. Given a patient ride, he moved up on the bridle and took this with plenty to spare. Still a novice over fences, he looks to have plenty of improvement in him, even at nine and, in this sort of company, he is well worth keeping on the right side. (7/4)

1371 Record Lover (IRE), who has not won for three years, tended to run in snatches. Keeping on under pressure, he is flattered by the winning margin. (16/1)

1506 Lucky Dollar (IRE) as usual travelled strongly but did not find much under pressure, and was held in third when he ploughed through the last. (3/1)

Tactix, who looked burly on this chasing debut, made mistakes. Given a patient ride, she showed some ability, staying on over the last three.(50/1)

1246* Gems Lad, a big sort, made the running but was not fluent at these obstacles, and was in third and struggling when he came to grief two out. (5/2)

1075 Manor Mieo, who looks more a hunter than a chaser, took a keen grip, but he was just starting to be tapped for toe when he blundered and gave his rider no chance four out. (6/1)

1717 THAMES H'CAP CHASE (0-115) (5-Y.O+) (Class E)

3-00 (3-01) **2m 4f 110y (16 fncs)** £4,560.00 (£1,260.00: £600.00) GOING: 0.29 sec per fur (GS)

	Horse / details	Btn	Pos	SP	RR	SF
	Netherby Said (91) (MissMKMilligan) **6-11-1** ASSmith (lw: plld hrd: mde all: j.rt: lft wl clr 4 out)	—	1	7/2[3]	109+	13
1340[4]	**Copper Cable (76)** (CSmith) **9-10-0** MRanger (trckd ldrs: lft mod 2nd 4 out: v.tired whn blnd last)	dist	2	25/1	—	—
979[3]	**Houghton (100)** (WJenks) **10-11-3**(7) MrRBurton (hit 2nd: drvn along 7th: t.o fr 10th)	3½	3	12/1	—	—
1039[7]	**Celtino (97)** (CaptTAForster) **8-11-7** SWynne (hld up: wnt 2nd 12th: 8l bhd & closing whn fell next)		F	7/4[2]	—	—
1167[2]	**Zambezi Spirit (IRE) (98)** (MrsMerritaJones) **7-11-8** DerekByrne (hit 1st: wnt 2nd 4th: drvn along 12th: 3rd & btn whn sltly hmpd next: wknd qckly & sn p.u: b.b.v)		P	Evens[1]	—	—

(SP 120.1%) **5 Rn**

5m 24.7 (20.70) CSF £44.08 TOTE £5.40: £4.40 £6.80 (£30.70) OWNER Mrs S. Sunter (LEYBURN) BRED J. Sunter

LONG HANDICAP Copper Cable 9-8

OFFICIAL EXPLANATION Zambezi Spirit (IRE): bled from the nose.

Netherby Said looked very fit on this reappearance and first run for his new trainer. Taking a keen grip but tending to jump out to his right, he had an advantage of about eight lengths when left out on his own four out. A promising sort, he starts the season well handicapped and is worth following. (7/2)

1340 Copper Cable, left a moderate second four out, was so tired he could do no more than scramble over the last. (25/1)

689 Houghton has lost his way and was under pressure and losing touch a circuit from home. (12/1)

Celtino had just moved into second spot and looked full of running, if still with work to do, when he fell four out. (7/4)

1167 Zambezi Spirit (IRE) looked a shade on the light side and suddenly came under pressure five out. Third and beaten when slightly hampered by a faller at the next, he stopped in two strides and was pulled up. He had broken a blood-vessel, not for the first time. (Evens)

1718 NENE CONDITIONAL H'CAP HURDLE (0-110) (4-Y.O+) (Class E)

3-30 (3-31) **2m 4f 110y (11 hdls)** £2,406.00 (£666.00: £318.00) GOING: 0.29 sec per fur (GS)

	Horse / details	Btn	Pos	SP	RR	SF
1419[2]	**Fawley Flyer (86)** (WGMTurner) **7-11-1**(5) JPower (sn trckng ldr: led 5th: rdn & hung lft between last 2: styd on)	—	1	7/2[2]	67	24
1443[2]	**Desert Force (IRE) (90)** (AStreeter) **7-11-10** GHogan (lw: hld up: pushed along & chsd ldrs 6th: rdn 3 out: swtchd rt appr last: styd on towards fin)	1	2	7/4[1]	70	27
1344[7]	**We're in the Money (66)** (MissJBower) **12-9-7**(7) ClaudineFroggitt (in tch to 6th: sn wl bhd: sme hdwy 2 out: n.d)	dist	3	33/1	—	—
1121[P]	**First Crack (87)** (FJordan) **11-11-7** GTormey (hld up: effrt & pushed along 6th: wkng whn hit 3 out)	5	4	7/1[3]	—	—
	Target Line (73) (MrsSJSmith) **6-10-4**(3) RWilkinson (led to 5th: wknd 4 out)	2	5	8/1	—	—
	Precipice Run (86) (JJBirkett) **11-11-6** RMassey (j.rt: sme hdwy 7th: wknd next)	s.h	6	16/1	—	—
1008[P]	**Soloman Springs (USA) (78)** (MrsVCWard) **6-10-12v** DFortt (outpcd & drvn along 6th: sn bhd)	6	7	12/1	—	—
	Rain-N-Sun (84) (JLHarris) **10-11-4** TDascombe (chsd ldrs tl lost pl 6th: sn bhd)	19	8	10/1	—	—
1249[4]	**Tashreef (72)** (JJBirkett) **6-10-3b**(3) SMelrose (reluctant to r: ref 1st)		R	11/1	—	—

(SP 116.1%) **9 Rn**

5m 3.9 (17.90) CSF £9.71 CT £153.36 TOTE £4.60: £1.30 £1.40 £11.50 (£2.20) Trio £79.90 OWNER Mr David Chown (SHERBORNE) BRED Shepherds Farm Ltd

LONG HANDICAP We're in the Money 9-3

STEWARDS' ENQUIRY Obj. to Fawley Flyer by Hogan overruled.

1419 Fawley Flyer always looked to just have the edge on the favourite. Hanging left under pressure between the last two, he forced the second to switch but, staying on, won on merit. (7/2: 2/1-4/1)

1443 Desert Force (IRE), under pressure to close the gap three out, was a length and a half down when forced to switch right approaching the last. Reeling in the winner at the line, it would be wrong to say he was unlucky. (7/4)

We're in the Money, getting long in the tooth and lightly-raced, dropped right out on the final circuit. Keeping up the gallop over the last two, she snatched third spot near the line, but was a parish behind the first two. (33/1)

641 First Crack, who had her tongue tied down, was losing touch when she crashed through the third last. (7/1)

Target Line was legless four out. (8/1)

Precipice Run has lost his way. (16/1)

1249 Tashreef (11/1: 8/1-12/1)

T/Plpt: £75.50 (116.61 Tckts). T/Qdpt: £53.20 (13.44 Tckts). WG

1412-LEICESTER (R-H) - Thursday December 5th

1719 Abandoned-Fog

1580-WINDSOR (Fig. 8) (Chase Good, Good to firm patches, Hdles Good)
Thursday December 5th
WEATHER: sunny

1726 SPITAL NOVICES' HURDLE (I) (4-Y.O+) (Class E)
12-30 (12-31) **2m (8 hdls)** £2,075.00 (£575.00: £275.00) GOING minus 0.19 sec per fur (G)

				SP	RR	SF
1375^{2}	**Danegold (IRE)** (MRChannon) **4-10-12** RHughes (hdwy appr 3 out: led appr last: rdn out)	—	**1**	$3/1^{1}$	77	37
1451^{2}	**Sailep (FR) (91)** (RJHodges) **4-11-2**(3) TDascombe (lw: hdwy to chse ldr 4th: led 3 out tl appr last: unable qckn)	7	**2**	10/1	77	37
1651^{7}	**Fairy Knight** (RHannon) **4-10-12** NWilliamson (hdwy 5th: ev ch 2 out: one pce flat)	hd	**3**	$7/2^{3}$	70	30
	Night City (LadyHerries) **5-10-12** JOsborne (hdwy appr 3 out: ev ch 2 out: wknd last)	6	**4**	$100/30^{2}$	64	24
	Ilandra (IRE) (RAkehurst) **4-10-7** APMcCoy (hdwy 5th: mstke 3 out: sn wknd)	4	**5**	14/1	55	15
	Music Please (KCBailey) **4-10-12** CO'Dwyer (bit bkwd: hdwy 5th: ev ch 2 out: wknd appr last)	4	**6**	25/1	56	16
	Jovie King (IRE) (KMcAuliffe) **4-10-12** BPowell (hdwy 5th: sn wknd)	10	**7**	25/1	46	6
1424^{6}	**Second Step (IRE) (89)** (DRGandolfo) **5-10-9**(3) DFortt (nvr nr to chal)	4	**8**	14/1	42	2
1453^{10}	**Mr Hemp** (AGFoster) **4-10-12** DerekByrne (nvr nrr)	nk	**9**	50/1	42	2
1380^{3}	**Hazaaf (USA)** (ADSmith) **7-10-12** FJousset (bit bkwd: prom to 4th)	½	**10**	14/1	41	1
	Mansur (IRE) (NJHenderson) **4-10-12** MAFitzgerald (led to 3 out: wknd qckly appr 2 out)	3	**11**	5/1	38	—
1168^{5}	**Not To Panic (IRE)** (KRBurke) **6-10-7** ALarnach (a bhd)	6	**12**	50/1	27	—
1517^{P}	**Night Flare (FR)** (SWoodman) **4-10-12** MRichards (chsd ldr 2nd to 4th: wknd appr 3 out)	5	**13**	33/1	27	—
1394^{P}	**Murphy's Run (IRE)** (PEccles) **6-10-7b**[1](5) MrRThornton (prom to 4th)	8	**14**	50/1	19	—
99^{7}	**Crustygun** (OO'Neill) **6-10-9**(3) GHogan (bit bkwd: a bhd)	14	**15**	33/1	5	—
				(SP 135.5%)		**15 Rn**

3m 49.9 (1.90) CSF £35.15 TOTE £4.50: £2.20 £3.40 £1.10 (£16.10) Trio £32.30 OWNER Circular Distributors Ltd (UPPER LAMBOURN) BRED Barronstown Stud and Ron Con Ltd

1375 Danegold (IRE) confirmed the promise shown here three weeks ago and was ridden along to pull clear on the run-in. (3/1)
1451 Sailep (FR), with a 7lb penalty to contend with, showed in front strides after the third last, but found the winner far too strong on the run-in. (10/1: 7/1-12/1)
1651 Fairy Knight, making a quick reappearance, ran much better here and was only tapped for toe from the last. (7/2)
Night City, a winner of a nine-furlong handicap at Newbury on the Flat in the mud this year, moved up to throw down his challenge in the straight, only to tire at the final flight. Some rain would help him. (100/30: 6/4-7/2)
Ilandra (IRE), fit from the Flat, found a mistake three sealing her fate. (14/1: 10/1-16/1)
Music Please had not been seen on a racecourse since his two-year-old days, but has developed into a big, strapping individual who looks every inch a chaser. He had every chance two out before lack of a recent run took its toll going to the last. Improvement can be expected. (25/1)
1424 Second Step (IRE) (14/1: 10/1-20/1)
1380 Hazaaf (USA) (14/1: 8/1-16/1)
Mansur (IRE) (5/1: tchd 8/1)

1727 PALEY STREET H'CAP HURDLE (0-120) (4-Y.O+ F & M) (Class D)
1-00 (1-00) **2m (8 hdls)** £2,747.00 (£821.00: £393.00: £179.00) GOING minus 0.19 sec per fur (G)

				SP	RR	SF
1330^{2}	**Severn Gale (92)** (JSAllen) **6-9-13**(7) XAizpuru (mde virtually all: drvn out)	—	**1**	$7/1^{3}$	75	28
1188^{5}	**Seasonal Splendour (IRE) (114)** (MCPipe) **6-12-0** APMcCoy (hld up: hrd rdn appr 2 out: ev ch flat: unable qckn)	1½	**2**	$9/2^{2}$	96	49
	Pedaltothemetal (IRE) (90) (PMitchell) **4-10-1**(3) GTormey (a.p: ev ch 3 out: rdn appr 2 out: one pce flat)	1¾	**3**	14/1	70	23
1374*	**Henrietta Howard (IRE) (109)** (MrsDHaine) **6-11-6**(3) GHogan (lw: hld up: rdn appr 2 out: eased whn btn flat)	20	**4**	$15/8^{1}$	69	22
1630^{P}	**Daily Sport Girl (92)** (BJLlewellyn) **7-9-13**(7) MissEJJones (hdwy 5th: sn wknd)	13	**5**	12/1	39	—
	Cosmic Star (86) (PWinkworth) **6-10-0** BFenton (bit bkwd: a bhd)	1½	**6**	100/1	31	—
1176^{2}	**Dark Nightingale (100)** (OSherwood) **6-11-0** JOsborne (chsd wnr to 5th: wknd qckly: t.o)	dist	**7**	$15/8^{1}$	—	—
				(SP 115.6%)		**7 Rn**

3m 50.7 (2.70) CSF £35.84 TOTE £12.10: £2.50 £2.40 (£21.40) OWNER Mrs Carol Allen (ALCESTER) BRED Broomhill Stud
LONG HANDICAP Cosmic Star 7-10
OFFICIAL EXPLANATION **Dark Nightingale: finished distressed.**
IN-FOCUS: **This was Aizpuru's first career win.**

1330 Severn Gale put up a really gutsy display. Making virtually all the running, she was given no peace by the second and third in the straight, but battled her heart out. (7/1: 6/1-9/1)
1188 Seasonal Splendour (IRE) bounced back to form after a rather disappointing reappearance, if unable to get the better of the winner. (9/2: op 3/1)
Pedaltothemetal (IRE) battled hard in the straight for the lead, only to be done for toe on the run-in. (14/1: 10/1-16/1)
1374* Henrietta Howard (IRE) has been raised 7lb for her recent success, and her jockey eased her right down on the run-in when all hope of success had gone. (15/8)
1176 Dark Nightingale is off a mark 8lb higher than she has ever won off and, after racing in second to the fourth last, then stopped as if shot. Osborne later reported she was in a distressed state. (15/8)

1728 WOODSIDE NOVICES' CHASE (5-Y.O+) (Class E)
1-30 (1-32) **3m (18 fncs)** £3,104.50 (£931.00: £448.00: £206.50) GOING minus 0.19 sec per fur (G)

				SP	RR	SF
1428*	**Flow (100)** (RHBuckler) **7-11-0** BPowell (hld up: led 14th: drvn out)	—	**1**	$2/1^{1}$	101	22
	Secret Bid (IRE) (91) (RHAlner) **6-10-9**(3) PHenley (hdwy 14th: 3rd whn pckd 4 out: chsd wnr fr 2 out: ev ch flat: unable qckn nr fin)	1½	**2**	10/1	98	19
	Garethson (IRE) (MissHCKnight) **5-10-11** DBridgwater (bit bkwd: hld up: rdn 14th: ev ch appr 2 out: wknd appr last)	25	**3**	$4/1^{2}$	81	1
1318^{P}	**Ballyedward (IRE) (88)** (RHBuckler) **6-10-12** PHolley (lw: hld up: hrd rdn 12th: wknd 13th)	hd	**4**	14/1	81	2

1472*	**Highland Jack (88)** (AndrewTurnell) **6-11-5b**[1] NWilliamson (lw: hld up: mstkes 3rd & 9th: wknd appr 3 out: t.o) 30	**5**	9/2[3]	68	—
1422[5]	**Dukes Meadow (IRE)** (KCBailey) **6-10-12b**[1] CO'Dwyer (led to 4th: 7th & wkng whn fell 10th)	**F**	6/1	—	—
	Sheriffmuir (100) (MrsLWadham) **7-10-9**(3) GHogan (hdwy 8th: wknd 9th: hmpd 10th: mstke 11th: t.o whn p.u bef 4 out)	**P**	12/1	—	—
1376[3]	**The Herbivore (IRE)** (MJRoberts) **7-10-12** JRailton (a.p: led 4th to 14th: sn wknd: t.o whn p.u bef 3 out)	**P**	33/1	—	—
590[P]	**Lord Antrim (IRE)** (RMStronge) **7-10-9**(3) DWalsh (t: prom to 11th: t.o whn p.u after 14th)	**P**	40/1	—	—
			(SP 114.6%)	**9 Rn**	

6m 4.2 (9.20) CSF £20.33 TOTE £3.10: £1.10 £4.70 £1.50 (£21.90) Trio £34.60 OWNER Mrs C. J. Dunn (BRIDPORT) BRED C. J. and Mrs Dunn
WEIGHT FOR AGE 5yo-1lb

1428* Flow is an out-and-out stayer who is well suited by some cut. Despite not having it on this occasion, she managed to keep the very determined runner-up at bay on the run-in. (2/1)
Secret Bid (IRE) may have been off the track for over a year, but he gave the winner a real fright on this chasing debut. (10/1: tchd 16/1)
Garethson (IRE), winner of two Irish points this year, was sold for 30,000 guineas at Doncaster May Sales and showed plenty of promise on this first run for his new connections. Looking as though the run would do him good, he was bustled up to the leaders turning for home and was soon throwing down a determined challenge, before tiring at the second last as lack of a recent run took its toll. He should soon find a novice event. (4/1)
Ballyedward (IRE) (14/1: 10/1-20/1)
Dukes Meadow (IRE) (6/1: 7/2-13/2)
Sheriffmuir (12/1: op 7/1)

1729 SPITAL NOVICES' HURDLE (II) (4-Y.O+) (Class E)
2-00 (2-04) **2m (8 hdls)** £2,057.50 (£570.00: £272.50) GOING minus 0.19 sec per fur (G)

			SP	RR	SF
	Proton (RAkehurst) **6-10-12** APMcCoy (lw: a.p: led appr 3 out: hrd rdn appr last: r.o wl) ....—	**1**	7/1[3]	95	28
	Desert Green (FR) (RHannon) **7-10-12** NWilliamson (lw: hdwy appr 3 out: chsd wnr appr 2 out: ev ch last: wknd flat) 9	**2**	15/8[1]	86	19
1380[2]	**Battleship Bruce (95)** (TCasey) **4-10-12** DBridgwater (hdwy appr 2 out: sn wknd) 18	**3**	7/2[2]	68	1
956[7]	**Zadok** (JFfitch-Heyes) **4-10-9**(3) PHenley (lw: hdwy 4th: wknd appr 3 out) 8	**4**	66/1	60	—
73[4]	**I'm a Dreamer (IRE) (103)** (MissMERowland) **6-11-5** GaryLyons (lost pl 4th: r.o one pce fr 2 out) 4	**5**	12/1	63	—
1369[4]	**Ottavio Farnese** (AHide) **4-10-9**(3) LAspell (prom tl appr 2 out) 4	**6**	7/1[3]	52	—
	Reverse Thrust (PRHedger) **5-10-5**(7) MClinton (prom to 5th) 13	**7**	33/1	39	—
1663[F]	**Master Goodenough (IRE) (65)** (AGFoster) **5-10-5**(7) DCreech (led: clr whn mstke 3rd: hdd appr 3 out: sn wknd) 5	**8**	66/1	34	—
1380[P]	**Braydon Forest** (CJDrewe) **4-10-12** JRailton (uns rdr & bolted bef s: bhd fr 4th) 26	**9**	50/1	8	—
	Ilsley Star (RMStronge) **6-10-12** MrJRees (a bhd) 10	**10**	66/1	—	—
	Ki Chi Saga (USA) (MMadgwick) **4-10-12** DMorris (lw: prom to 5th) 1½	**11**	20/1	—	—
1375[10]	**Seminole Wind** (CRBarwell) **5-10-12** BFenton (bhd fr 3rd: t.o) ....dist	**12**	66/1	—	—
	Callonescy (IRE) (DCO'Brien) **4-10-9**(3) DWalsh (mid div whn mstke 2nd: t.o whn p.u bef 3 out)	**P**	66/1	—	—
	Zajko (USA) (LadyHerries) **6-10-12** MAFitzgerald (mid div whn blnd 5th: sn wknd: t.o whn p.u bef last)	**P**	7/1[3]	—	—
			(SP 119.3%)	**14 Rn**	

3m 51.9 (3.90) CSF £19.21 TOTE £7.80: £1.40 £1.30 £1.60 (£6.00) Trio £8.70 OWNER Persian War Racing (EPSOM) BRED Lord Halifax

Proton was disappointing on the Flat this year, but hurdling has revitalised him, and he showed good battling qualities before sprinting away on the run-in. (7/1)
Desert Green (FR), winner of the Jubilee Handicap at Kempton in May, looked in tremendous shape in the paddock for this hurdling debut. Moving nicely into second at the second last, he was off the bridle at the next and left standing on the run-in. The jury is out over whether he gets the trip. (15/8)
1380 Battleship Bruce made a brief effort approaching the second last. (7/2)
Zadok had shot his bolt approaching the third last. (66/1)
I'm a Dreamer (IRE) (12/1: 7/1-14/1)
1369 Ottavio Farnese (7/1: 5/1-8/1)
Zajko (USA) (7/1: 4/1-8/1)

1730 WRAYSBURY H'CAP CHASE (0-125) (5-Y.O+) (Class D)
2-30 (2-30) **2m (12 fncs)** £3,871.50 (£1,074.00: £514.50) GOING minus 0.19 sec per fur (G)

			SP	RR	SF
1584*	**Zeredar (NZ) (107)** (KCBailey) **6-11-2b** 7x CO'Dwyer (lw: led 3rd: blnd 3 out: easily) ....—	**1**	4/5[1]	122+	7
1393[2]	**Dear Do (104)** (NJHenderson) **9-10-13** MAFitzgerald (hld up: chsd wnr appr 4 out: rdn appr 3 out: unable qckn) 8	**2**	9/4[2]	111	—
1379[6]	**Who's to Say (115)** (MissVenetiaWilliams) **10-11-10v**[1] NWilliamson (chsd ldr to 3rd: chsd wnr 4th tl appr 4 out: hrd rdn appr 3 out: 3rd & no ch whn blnd 2 out) 12	**3**	9/2[3]	110	—
1272[4]	**King Credo (119)** (SWoodman) **11-12-0v**[1] JOsborne (led to 3rd: mstke 4th: 3rd whn blnd bdly 6th: nt rcvr: t.o whn p.u bef 8th)	**P**	10/1	—	—
			(SP 113.6%)	**4 Rn**	

3m 59.7 (9.70) CSF £3.08 TOTE £1.80 (£1.50) OWNER I M S Racing (UPPER LAMBOURN) BRED Miss E. S. Parton

1584* Zeredar (NZ) could hardly have won more easily. In front from the third, even a bad error at the third last could not stop him winning very easily. (4/5)
1393 Dear Do, winner of this race last year, had no chance with the winner. (9/4)
1379 Who's to Say was back over a more suitable trip but, having lost second place going to the fourth last, was soon in trouble. (9/2)
1272 King Credo must now surely be retired. (10/1: op 6/1)

1731 DORNEY AMATEUR H'CAP CHASE (0-115) (4-Y.O+) (Class E)
3-00 (3-00) **2m 5f (15 fncs)** £3,059.00 (£917.00: £441.00: £203.00) GOING minus 0.19 sec per fur (G)

			SP	RR	SF
1373[3]	**Act of Parliament (IRE) (105)** (KCBailey) **8-11-7b**(7) MrRWakley (rdn & hdwy appr 2 out: led flat: r.o wl) ....—	**1**	100/30[2]	114	37
1430[3]	**Rex to the Rescue (IRE) (100)** (RHAlner) **8-11-4**(5) MrRThornton (lw: led to 7th: led 8th: hrd rdn appr last: hdd flat: unable qckn) 2	**2**	6/1	108	31
1350[2]	**Coolree (IRE) (112)** (PFNicholls) **8-12-0**(7) MrJTizzard (rdn & hdwy appr 3 out: one pce) 6	**3**	4/1[3]	115	38
1073*	**Wilkins (84)** (RJO'Sullivan) **7-10-0**(7) MrPO'Keeffe (a.p: mstke 4th: led 7th to 8th: ev ch 4 out: wknd appr last)7	**4**	11/4[1]	82	5

				SP	RR	SF
1420P	**Whippers Delight (IRE) (89)** (GFHCharles-Jones) **8-10-5**(7) MrACharles-Jones (lw: chsd ldr to 6th: wknd 8th)	19	**5**	33/1	72	—
1321[2]	**Merry Panto (IRE) (102)** (CPEBrooks) **7-11-4**(7) MrEJames (bhd tl fell last)		**F**	100/30[2]	—	—
	Call Me Early (92) (RMStronge) **11-10-8**(7) MrJRees (lw: mstke 5th: bhd fr 6th: blnd 9th: t.o whn p.u bef last)		**P**	25/1	—	—
				(SP 113.9%)	**7 Rn**	

5m 16.3 (7.30) CSF £21.48 TOTE £3.20: £2.00 £1.60 (£9.00) OWNER Mr J. Perriss (UPPER LAMBOURN) BRED Mrs Susan Bury
LONG HANDICAP Wilkins 10-5

1373 Act of Parliament (IRE), off a better mark than last season, bounced back to form. Picking up ground approaching the second last, he came with a nice run to lay down the law on the run-in. (100/30)

882 Rex to the Rescue (IRE) made the vast majority of the running and, responding to pressure, looked as if he would hold on, only to be worried out of it in the last 50 yards. (6/1)

1350 Coolree (IRE) had plenty of weight to shoulder and, after taking closer order approaching the third last, then found his welter burden taking its toll. (4/1)

1073* Wilkins, 9lb higher than when winning at Fontwell last time out, had every chance four from home, but was soon being bustled along and finally tired soon after the second last. (11/4)

1321 Merry Panto (IRE) ran disappointingly and never gave his supporters much to cheer about. (100/30: 9/4-7/2)

1732 PANGBOURNE H'CAP HURDLE (0-105) (4-Y.O+) (Class F)

3-30 (3-31) **2m 4f (10 hdls)** £2,101.00 (£586.00: £283.00) GOING minus 0.19 sec per fur (G)

				SP	RR	SF
1448*	**Lets Be Frank (90)** (NoelChance) **5-11-5** MAFitzgerald (lw: hdwy 7th: led appr last: r.o wl)	—	**1**	5/2[1]	78	31
1166[2]	**Rachael's Owen (84)** (CWeedon) **6-10-13** MRichards (hdwy 6th: led 7th tl appr last: unable qckn)	2½	**2**	12/1	70	23
971[2]	**Relative Chance (77)** (JSKing) **7-10-6** NWilliamson (hdwy 7th: hrd rdn appr 2 out: one pce)	11	**3**	7/2[2]	54	7
1585[3]	**August Twelfth (87)** (DCO'Brien) **8-10-13**(3) DWalsh (lw: hdwy appr 3 out: hrd rdn appr 2 out: one pce)	3½	**4**	7/2[2]	61	14
1174P	**Policemans Pride (FR) (75)** (MMadgwick) **7-10-4** BFenton (led to 7th: wknd appr 3 out)	2	**5**	50/1	48	1
958[5]	**Durshan (USA) (76)** (JRJenkins) **7-10-5** JOsborne (lw: hdwy 4th: wknd appr 2 out)	9	**6**	16/1	42	—
1418[5]	**Super Ritchart (90)** (BPalling) **8-11-5** RFarrant (bit bkwd: prom tl appr 3 out)	9	**7**	20/1	48	1
	Cambo (USA) (95) (MCBanks) **10-11-10** DBridgwater (bit bkwd: prom to 5th)	6	**8**	14/1	49	2
641[5]	**Prize Match (80)** (JCTuck) **7-10-9** RBellamy (lw: bhd fr 7th)	1¼	**9**	25/1	33	—
1585*	**Dontdressfordinner (83)** (RJHodges) **6-10-9**(3) TDascombe (bhd fr 3 out)	7	**10**	5/1[3]	30	—
1342[4]	**Dahlia's Best (USA) (95)** (MissMERowland) **6-11-10** GaryLyons (lost pl 4th: rallied 6th: wknd 7th)	14	**11**	16/1	31	—
	Pyrrhic Dance (79) (MJHaynes) **6-10-8** DSkyrme (prom to 7th)	11	**12**	50/1	6	—
1381[7]	**Will James (72)** (CJDrewe) **10-9-12b**(3)ow1 GuyLewis (a bhd)	3½	**13**	50/1	—	—
				(SP 130.3%)	**13 Rn**	

4m 51.8 (5.80) CSF £33.57 CT £102.78 TOTE £4.60: £1.40 £4.40 £1.30 (£32.60) Trio £31.30 OWNER Mrs M. M. Stobart (LAMBOURN) BRED Malcolm Armitage Penney
LONG HANDICAP Will James 9-5

1448* Lets Be Frank looked in good shape beforehand and defied a 6lb rise in the weights, leading approaching the last and soon asserting. (5/2)

1166 Rachael's Owen ran much better here. In front four out, he was collared approaching the last and put in his place by the winner.(12/1)

971 Relative Chance was only battling for minor honours over the last two. (7/2)

1585 August Twelfth was certainly not given the kid-glove treatment on this occasion, but was still only battling for minor honours over the last two, and prefers the mud. (7/2)

1053 Policemans Pride (FR), in front to the fourth last, soon had bellows to mend. (50/1)

Cambo (USA) (14/1: op 8/1)

T/Plpt: £110.80 (99.21 Tckts). T/Qdpt: £14.50 (145.84 Tckts) AK

1733a - 1736a : (Irish Racing) - See Computer Raceform

1395a-CLONMEL (Ireland) (R-H) (Heavy)
Sunday November 24th

1737a TIPPERARY RACECOURSE CHASE (Gd 3) (5-Y.O+)

2-15 (2-17) **2m** IR £6,850.00 (IR £1,550.00: IR £650.00: IR £350.00)

				SP	RR	SF
1231a[2]	**Sound Man (IRE)** (EJO'Grady,Ireland) **8-12-0** RDunwoody (hld up: trckd ldrs fr 3 out: chal whn slt mstke 2 out: shkn up & swtchd rt appr last: rdn to ld flat: r.o wl)	—	**1**	4/7[1]	147	—
1495a[7]	**Royal Mountbrowne** (APO'Brien,Ireland) **8-11-7** CFSwan (led: j.slowly & lft 6th & hdd: j.lft 7th: disp ld after 3 out: hdd u.p flat: kpt on same pce)	1	**2**	5/1[2]	139	—
1397a[2]	**Belvederian** (MFMorris,Ireland) **9-11-7** CO'Dwyer (cl up: disp ld 5th: led next: jnd after 3 out: hdd appr next: cl 3rd whn bd mstke 2 out: no imp appr last)	8	**3**	11/2[3]	131	—
	Arctic Weather (IRE) (MJPO'Brien,Ireland) **7-11-7** TPRudd (hld up towards rr: sltly hmpd 3rd: lost tch 8th)	10	**4**	10/1	121	—
1495a[5]	**Love the Lord (IRE)** (DO'Connell,Ireland) **6-11-9** JPBroderick (cl up: disp ld briefly 3rd: lost tch after 6th: n.d fr 3 out)	5	**5**	10/1	118	—
	Hannies Girl (IRE) (FFlood,Ireland) **7-10-9**(7) LJFleming (rdr lost irons 1st: p.u bef next)		**P**	50/1	—	—
				(SP 115.8%)	**6 Rn**	

4m 4.4 OWNER David Lloyd (THURLES) BRED P. Scully in Ireland

1231a Sound Man (IRE) might not have appreciated the very heavy ground, but this was not one of his better performances. He challenged on the outside going to the second last, but was forced into an error when the leader jumped across him. Switched to the inner, he showed a turn of foot from the last and was a snug enough winner, but it is difficult to translate this rather ponderous success into a live chance in the Tingle Creek. (4/7)

1495a Royal Mountbrowne certainly seems to benefit from Charlie Swan's presence in the saddle. Beaten almost sixty lengths in a handicap last time after numerous mistakes, he had the advantage in the straight and his deviation from a straight line at the second last possibly cost him more than he was beaten by. Having said that, he had nothing to match the winner's turn of foot. (5/1)

1397a Belvederian, over a trip far too sharp, was left behind over the last two. (11/2)

1495a Love the Lord (IRE) (10/1: op 6/1)

1738a - 1746a : (Irish Racing) - See Computer Raceform

1607a-FAIRYHOUSE (Dublin, Ireland) (R-H) (Yielding)
Saturday November 30th

1747a JUVENILE HURDLE (Gd 3) (3-Y.O)
12-30 (12-31) **2m (9 hdls)** IR £6,850.00 (IR £1,550.00: IR £650.00: IR £350.00)

Horse / details	Dist	Pos	SP	RR	SF
Spirit Dancer (IRE) (GMLyons,Ireland) **3-10-9** SCLyons (led: rdn after 3 out: hdd briefly bef next: jnd appr last: styd on u.p flat)	—	1	12/1	89	—
Highly Motivated (APO'Brien,Ireland) **3-10-2**(5) JButler (prom early: mid div fr 2nd: hdwy 4 out: led briefly appr 2 out: ducked lft & hdd: disp ld & edgd rt u.p wl bef last: unable qckn flat)	1½	2	4/1 2	86	—
Greenhue (IRE) (MJPO'Brien,Ireland) **3-10-12** TPRudd (hld up: hdwy 4th: effrt whn hmpd between last 2: wnt 2nd after last: kpt on)	hd	3	7/1	90	—
Miss Pennyhill (IRE) (ASadik,Ireland) **3-9-13**(5) TMartin (chsd ldr: lost pl after 3rd: mid div 4 out: styd on wl flat)	3	4	20/1	79	—
Evriza (IRE) (APO'Brien,Ireland) **3-10-10** PMcWilliams (in tch: lost pl after 4 out: hdwy after next: 4th & no imp appr last: kpt on)	s.h	5	6/1	85	—
Corn Abbey (IRE) (CCollins,Ireland) **3-10-2**(7) APSweeney (hld up: nt fluent: mstke 5th: mid div whn mstke 2 out: r.o wl fr last)	4	6	14/1	80	—
Narrow Focus (USA) (MTorrens,Ireland) **3-10-9** APowell (hld up: hdwy 4th: wnt 3rd briefly bef 4 out: lost pl bef next: kpt on fr 2 out)	nk	7	20/1	80	—
Tax Reform (USA) (DGMcArdle,Ireland) **3-10-9** HRogers (hld up: hdwy after 5th: led briefly wl bef 2 out: 5th & btn whn mstke last)	3	8	20/1	77	—
Autobabble (IRE) (SAKirk,Ireland) **3-10-9** TJMitchell (bhd: kpt on fr 3 out: nvr nrr)	9	9	25/1	68	—
Broken Rites (IRE) (WMRoper,Ireland) **3-10-9**(3) GCotter (mstke 2nd: n.d)	hd	10	8/1	71	—
Choosey's Treasure (IRE) (APO'Brien,Ireland) **3-10-7**(3) RPO'Brien (n.d)	1½	11	5/1 3	67	—
Dr Bones (IRE) (TBergin,Ireland) **3-10-6**(3) KWhelan (prom early: mid div 5th: n.d fr 4 out)	1½	12	20/1	65	—
Iacchus (IRE) (APO'Brien,Ireland) **3-10-7b1**(5) MJHolbrook (s.s: cl up fr 2nd: wnt 2nd after next: reminders bef 4 out: wknd u.p bef next)	10	13	16/1	58	—
River Rock (IRE) (VBowens,Ireland) **3-10-6**(3) BBowens (a bhd)	3	14	20/1	52	—
Grimes (CRoche,Ireland) **3-10-9** CO'Dwyer (cl up fr 2nd: 3rd whn mstke 5th: sn lost pl: sme hdwy bef 3 out: sn wknd: eased whn btn)	½	15	2/1 1	51	—
Blue Bit (IRE) (NMeade,Ireland) **3-10-9** RHughes (n.d fr 4th: t.o whn p.u after 3 out)		P	8/1	—	—

(SP 166.9%) **16 Rn**

3m 55.0 (10.00) OWNER Edward Campbell (KILTALE)
STEWARDS' ENQUIRY Butler susp. 9-12/12/96 (excessive use of whip). Collins fined £300, Sweeney susp. 9-18/12/96 & Corn Abbey (IRE) susp. 21 days (schooling in public)

Spirit Dancer (IRE) showed much improved form here, making most of the running. Headed briefly two out, he quickly regained the initiative and stayed on best of all under pressure at the last. (12/1)
Highly Motivated certainly missed the presence of Charlie Swan. She led early in the straight, but wandered around before the last two flights and, although staying on again well near the finish, she was always lacking assistance. (4/1)
Greenhue (IRE), third from three out, did not get a clear run between the last two flights, but kept on well from the last. (7/1: op 4/1)
Miss Pennyhill (IRE) stayed on well from the last without ever posing a threat. (20/1)
Evriza (IRE) was prominent until dropping away four out. She came back in the straight, landing fourth over the last, but only found the one pace on the flat. (6/1: op 4/1)
Corn Abbey (IRE) finished well to earn a twenty-day suspension for himself and a ten-day holiday for his rider. (14/1)
Broken Rites (IRE) (8/1: op 5/1)
Choosey's Treasure (IRE) never showed with a chance at any stage. (5/1)
Grimes (2/1: op Evens)
Blue Bit (IRE) (8/1: op 5/1)

1748a - 1749a : (Irish Racing) - See Computer Raceform

1750a PIERSE PORTERSTOWN H'CAP CHASE (Gd 3) (5-Y.O+)
2-00 (2-05) **3m 1f (19 fncs)** IR £9,675.00 (IR £2,775.00: IR £1,275.00: IR £375.00)

Prev	Horse / details	Dist	Pos	SP	RR	SF
1495a3	**Johnny Setaside (IRE)** (NMeade,Ireland) **7-11-5** MrGJHarford (cl up: wnt 2nd over 13th: mstke & lft in ld next: slt mstke 3 out: clr bef next: styd on wl)	—	1	7/4 1	143	—
	Son Of War (PMcCreery,Ireland) **9-11-11**(3) USmyth (hld up: mstke & lost pl 5th: rdn 5 out: wnt 2nd after 3 out: kpt on same pce)	10	2	10/1 3	146	—
846a3	**Jassu** (JEKiely,Ireland) **10-11-3** APowell (in tch to 12th: wnt mod 4th between last 2: rdn & styd on flat)	5	3	8/1 2	125	—
	Topical Tip (IRE) (JEMulhern,Ireland) **7-10-4**(3) GCotter (cl up: wnt 2nd bef 9th: lost pl 13th: 3rd & no imp after 3 out: one pce)	4	4	16/1	113	—
	Carrigeen Kerria (IRE) (RHLalor,Ireland) **8-10-7** DJCasey (bhd: hdwy 5th: n.d fr 5 out: mod 5th 2 out: t.o)	dist	5	16/1	—	—
	Ballyhire Lad (IRE) (APO'Brien,Ireland) **7-10-8** LPCusack (bhd: mstke 2nd: n.d: t.o)	5½	6	10/1 3	—	—
1495a8	**Spankers Hill (IRE)** (SJTreacy,Ireland) **7-10-7** DHO'Connor (led appr 3rd tl mstke & hdd 7th: lost pl 9th: rallied & wnt 2nd 5 out: chsd ldr tl wknd appr 3 out: sn bhd: t.o)	20	7	10/1 3	—	—
1003a*	**Three Brownies** (MFMorris,Ireland) **9-10-7b** CO'Dwyer (led tl appr 3rd: led 7th tl fell 14th: dead)		F	7/4 1	—	—

(SP 122.9%) **8 Rn**

6m 33.9 (2.90) OWNER John O'Meara (NAVAN) BRED Sean Kinsella

1495a Johnny Setaside (IRE) had his task greatly simplified when the leader fell six from home. Going clear after a mistake three out, he won unchallenged. (7/4)
Son Of War, twice the winner of this race, made a pleasing reappearance. After a mistake at the fifth, he was chasing the winner from three out without ever getting on terms. (10/1)
846a Jassu never held out any chance, going a moderate fourth before the last two and just plugging on. (8/1)
Topical Tip (IRE), 8lb out of the handicap, kept in touch to three out before fading. (16/1)
Ballyhire Lad (IRE) (10/1: op 6/1)

1751a SILLOGUE NOVICES' HURDLE (Gd 3) (5-Y.O+)
2-30 (2-47) **3m (14 hdls)** IR £6,850.00 (IR £1,550.00: IR £650.00: IR £350.00)

	Horse	Dist	Pos	SP	RR	SF
1492a*	**Tarthooth (IRE)** (ALTMoore,Ireland) **5-11-10** CO'Brien (disp ld tl led 4 out: rdn appr last: styd on flat)	—	**1**	1/3[1]	99	—
	Flamingo Flower (IRE) (PCasey,Ireland) **8-10-13**(3) MrPJCasey (hld up in rr: stdy hdwy fr 4 out: 2nd after 2 out: rdn appr last: kpt on: nt trble wnr)	3	**2**	14/1	89	—
	Allatrim (IRE) (EJO'Grady,Ireland) **6-11-2** RHughes (hld up in tch: wnt 2nd after 4 out: slt mstke 2 out: rdn & btn appr last)	5½	**3**	14/1	85	—
1492a[4]	**Mullover** (MrsJHarrington,Ireland) **5-11-7** TJMitchell (in tch: 3rd & rdn after 3 out: no imp fr 2 out)	6	**4**	12/1[3]	86	—
	Leamhog (IRE) (APO'Brien,Ireland) **6-11-4** CO'Dwyer (led to 4 out: wknd qckly bef next: t.o)	dist	**5**	16/1	—	—
	Ballinlammy Rose (IRE) (APO'Brien,Ireland) **6-11-5**(5) JButler (a bhd: t.o)	15	**6**	4/1[2]	—	—

(SP 121.9%) **6 Rn**

6m 3.6 (15.60) OWNER Mrs H de Burgh (NAAS) BRED Glen Barrow Farm
1492a* Tarthooth (IRE) disputed until going on four out. He had to be stirred up approaching the last, but was much too good for these. (1/3: op 1/2)
Flamingo Flower (IRE) ran above herself, going second after two out and putting in an unavailling challenge from the last. (14/1: op 8/1)
Allatrim (IRE), chasing the winner from four out, blundered two out and just kept on at the one pace. (14/1: op 7/1)
Mullover (12/1: op 7/1)
Ballinlammy Rose (IRE), with his tongue tied down, was never in the race and finished tailed off. (4/1: op 9/4)

1752a NEW STAND H'CAP HURDLE (Gd 3) (4-Y.O+)
3-00 (3-15) **2m (9 hdls)** IR £6,850.00 (IR £1,550.00: IR £650.00: IR £350.00)

	Horse	Dist	Pos	SP	RR	SF
	Dardjini (USA) (NMeade,Ireland) **6-11-13**ow-1 RHughes (hld up: trckd ldrs fr 5th: wnt 2nd 2 out: effrt on bridle appr last: rdn to ld flat: r.o u.p)	—	**1**	5/1[2]	115	—
	Family Way (ALTMoore,Ireland) **9-10-11**(7) DWO'Sullivan (cl up: led appr 2 out: hdd flat: rdn & styd on: jst failed)	s.h	**2**	12/1	106	—
1233a[2]	**Caitriona's Choice (IRE)** (MCunningham,Ireland) **5-10-6** LPCusack (hld up in rr: hmpd 5th: hdwy 3 out: kpt on flat)	3	**3**	10/1	91	—
	Bolino Star (IRE) (SJTreacy,Ireland) **5-11-8**(3) GCotter (hld up in rr whn sltly hmpd 5th: in tch 3 out: r.o u.p flat)	2	**4**	7/1	108	—
	Metastasio (DGMcArdle,Ireland) **4-11-3** HRogers (prom: bdly hmpd 5th: sn bhd: rdn & hdwy after 3 out: styd on nr fin)	2	**5**	11/2[3]	103	—
	Major Jamie (IRE) (ALTMoore,Ireland) **5-10-6** DJCasey (prom: mstke 3rd: lft in ld 5th: slt mstke 4 out: sn hdd: rallied & 3rd whn mstke last: no imp flat)	s.h	**6**	9/2[1]	87	—
	Tidjani (IRE) (FBerry,Ireland) **4-10-4** TJMitchell (hld up: hdwy 4 out: lost pl after next: styd on fr last)	3	**7**	12/1	87	—
318a[14]	**Talina's Law (IRE)** (PMullins,Ireland) **4-10-10b**(7) AO'Shea (in tch: rdn & no imp after 3 out: kpt on)	¾	**8**	7/1	99	—
321a*	**Tryfirion (IRE)** (VBowens,Ireland) **7-11-8**(3) BBowens (cl up: led appr 3 out to 2 out: 5th & btn appr last)	nk	**9**	9/1	102	—
1487a[3]	**Lady Arpel (IRE)** (PO'Leary,Ireland) **4-11-3** CO'Dwyer (hld up: hdwy whn hmpd 5th: trckng ldrs bef 3 out: 4th 2 out: sn wknd)	6	**10**	11/2[3]	93	—
	Dashing Dollar (IRE) (APO'Brien,Ireland) **5-10-5**(5) JButler (mstke 2nd: in tch tl wknd 3 out)	10	**11**	9/1	71	—
	Jo Jo Boy (IRE) (FFlood,Ireland) **7-10-7** MrFJFlood (led tl fell 5th)		**F**	10/1	—	—

(SP 144.2%) **12 Rn**

3m 57.2 (12.20) OWNER The High Street Racing Synd (NAVAN)
Dardjini (USA), making his first appearance in a handicap and having his first run since October 1994, was cruising on the outside between the last two flights and it looked a question of just how far he was going to win by. In the end, he just scraped home by a short head without being asked an over-serious question. An idea of what he had in hand might be guessed from the fact that he has been upped 5lb. Even with re-assessment, he could be a serious Ladbroke candidate. (5/1)
Family Way, making his reappearance and the apparent less-fancied of the stable's two runners, went on before two out. He looked likely to be swallowed up by the winner after the last, but battled on with real determination. (12/1: op 8/1)
1233a Caitriona's Choice (IRE), hampered by a faller at the fifth, was getting into it again two out. He landed third over the last, but the first two had gone. (10/1: op 6/1)
Bolino Star (IRE) ran well on her first handicap outing. Hampered at the fifth, she was in touch three out and stayed on well on the run-in. (7/1: op 4/1)
Metastasio, another hampered at the fifth flight, was staying on again from three out to be nearest at the finish. (11/2)
Major Jamie (IRE), a course winner here last time out, made plenty of jumping mistakes, but was still there when blundering at the last. (9/2: op 3/1)
Tidjani (IRE) (12/1: op 8/1)
Dashing Dollar (IRE) (9/1: op 6/1)
NR

1753a - 1756a : (Irish Racing) - See Computer Raceform

1747a-FAIRYHOUSE (Dublin, Ireland) (R-H) (Yielding)
Sunday December 1st

1757a AVONMORE ROYAL BOND NOVICES' HURDLE (Gd 1) (4-Y.O+)
1-40 (1-47) **2m (9 hdls)** IR £16,250.00 (IR £4,750.00: IR £2,250.00: IR £750.00)

	Horse	Dist	Pos	SP	RR	SF
1485a[2]	**Istabraq (IRE)** (APO'Brien,Ireland) **4-11-9** CFSwan (led early: led 3 out: clr 2 out: mstke last: easily)	—	**1**	11/8[1]	121+	—
	Palette (IRE) (WPMullins,Ireland) **4-11-4** DJCasey (hld up: wnt mod 2nd bef 2 out: rdn & styd on: no ch w wnr)	4½	**2**	14/1	112	—
1485a*	**Noble Thyne (IRE)** (PMullins,Ireland) **6-12-0** TPTreacy (led 2nd: jnd 5th: hdd 3 out: rdn bef st: 3rd & btn appr 2 out: one pce)	15	**3**	13/8[2]	102	—
	Charlie Foxtrot (IRE) (NMeade,Ireland) **4-11-9** RHughes (hld up in tch: 4th & trckng ldrs whn slt mstke 3 out: 4th & rdn bef st: no imp appr 2 out)	11	**4**	11/2[3]	91	—
	Three Scholars (WPMullins,Ireland) **5-12-0** RDunwoody (towards rr: mod 6th & reminders 5th: n.d)	s.h	**5**	14/1	90	—

	Horse	Dist	Pos	SP	RR	SF
1427*	**Lake Kariba** (PFNicholls) **5-12-0** APMcCoy (s.s: sn in tch: rdn 5th: mod 5th next: n.d 3 out: kpt on flat)	½	6	7/1	90	—
	Doone Braes (IRE) (WAMurphy,Ireland) **6-12-0** USmyth (a bhd: t.o)	dist	7	200/1	—	—

(SP 121.9%) **7 Rn**

3m 47.8 (2.80) OWNER John McManus (PILTOWN) BRED Shadwell Estate Company Limited

1485a Istabraq (IRE) shared the lead until going on after three out. Clear into the straight, a mistake at the last did not interfere with his supremacy and he won virtually unchallenged. (11/8)

Palette (IRE), going second before the straight, stayed on without making any real impression on the winner. (14/1: op 7/1)

1485a* Noble Thyne (IRE) had the winner a short-head behind him at Punchestown, but was totally unable to confirm the form here. He led and disputed until weakening after three out, and was a beaten third before the straight. (13/8)

Charlie Foxtrot (IRE), fourth and ridden before three out, was never able to demonstrate the ability he showed at Naas. (11/2)

Three Scholars (14/1: op 8/1)

1427* Lake Kariba lost some lengths when the tape went up and was being ridden along to keep in touch after halfway. A mistake four out saw him unable to threaten afterwards. (7/1: op 4/1)

1758a CHIQUITA DRINMORE NOVICES' CHASE (Gd 1) (5-Y.O+)

2-10 (2-19) **2m 4f (15 fncs)** IR £22,750.00 (IR £6,650.00: IR £3,150.00: IR £1,050.00)

	Horse	Dist	Pos	SP	RR	SF
1240a*	**Dorans Pride (IRE)** (MHourigan,Ireland) **7-11-10** RDunwoody (prom: disp ld 7th: led bef next to 10th: disp ld bef 3 out: led appr last: rdn & styd on wl flat)	—	1	5/4 1	130+	—
1259*	**See More Business (IRE)** (PFNicholls) **6-11-10** APMcCoy (led bef 2nd: jnd 7th: hdd bef next: led again whn mstke 10th: mstke 4 out: jnd bef next: led 2 out: hdd nr last: styd on u.p flat)	1	2	5/2 2	129	—
	Executive Options (IRE) (PMcCreery,Ireland) **7-11-5** CLlewellyn (5th whn bd mstke 4th: lost tch after next: n.d 4 out: t.o)	dist	3	14/1	—	—
	Another Point (IRE) (MHourigan,Ireland) **8-11-5** MPHourigan (in tch: towards rr fr 9th: n.d 4 out: t.o)	nk	4	66/1	—	—
1405a*	**Danoli (IRE)** (TFoley,Ireland) **8-11-10** TPTreacy (cl up whn fell 3rd)		F	100/30 3	—	—
	Dramatic Venture (IRE) (WPMullins,Ireland) **7-11-5** DJCasey (towards rr: 5th whn fell 6th)		F	20/1	—	—
1486a3	**The Outback Way (IRE)** (JJO'Connor,Ireland) **6-11-10b** DHO'Connor (hld up towards rr: mstke & sltly hmpd 6th: wnt 4th at 8th: mod 3rd 4 out: no imp next: n.d whn ref last)		R	20/1	—	—
	Macallister (IRE) (VBowens,Ireland) **6-11-5** CO'Dwyer (led early: rdn & lost tch bef 4 out: n.d appr 2 out: hmpd & uns rdr last)		U	25/1	—	—

(SP 117.6%) **8 Rn**

5m 11.8 (10.80) OWNER T. J. Doran (PATRICKSWELL) BRED Hugh Suffern Bloodstock Ltd

1240a* Dorans Pride (IRE) made his only real mistake early on when slow over the fourth. He was a clear second from six out and appeared to be travelling better turning in, but was not asked to go on until approaching the last. He did not have an easy race and his jumping, while careful rather than cautious, might still leave cause for concern in better company. Connections are rather ruling out the Sun Alliance, and talk of a Gold Cup tilt after this performance is premature. (5/4)

1259* See More Business (IRE) made a mistake at the third and was soon sent on. Tracked by the winner on the inside, he made mistakes six out and four out and, headed approaching the last, kept on well on the flat. He would be no forlorn hope to turn this form around with the winner in the future, and the Feltham at Kempton on Boxing Day looks an ideal sort of race for him. (5/2)

Executive Options (IRE) made an early mistake at the fourth and was never a contender, being left a remote third at the last. (14/1)

1405a* Danoli (IRE) hit the top of the third and came down. He schooled over the course after racing and his jumping was adequate, although he still has a tendency to jump left. (100/30)

1759a AVONMORE HATTON'S GRACE HURDLE (Gd 1) (4-Y.O+)

2-40 (2-49) **2m 4f (11 hdls)** IR £26,000.00 (IR £7,600.00: IR £3,600.00: IR £1,200.00)

	Horse	Dist	Pos	SP	RR	SF
	Large Action (IRE) (OSherwood) **8-12-0** JOsborne (wnt 2nd after 7th: led bef 3 out: clr between last 2: rdn & styd on)	—	1	9/4 2	137	—
1487a*	**Cockney Lad (IRE)** (NMeade,Ireland) **7-11-9** RHughes (hld up: wnt mod 3rd & rdn after 3 out: no imp appr last: kpt on same pce)	6	2	8/1	127	—
	Theatreworld (IRE) (APO'Brien,Ireland) **4-11-4** CFSwan (hld up: cl 2nd after 3 out: rdn & chsd wnr appr next: no imp between last 2: kpt on same pce)	1	3	6/4 1	126	—
1326F	**Castlekellyleader (IRE)** (PFNicholls) **7-11-9** APMcCoy (led: mstkes: clr bef 6th to 8th: hdd bef 3 out: mstke 3 out: sn wknd: lft mod 4th & n.d 2 out)	25	4	6/1 3	106	—
1487a5	**Padashpan (USA)** (WPMullins,Ireland) **7-11-9** TPTreacy (n.d)	4	5	25/1	103	—
13652	**Mystical City (IRE)** (WPMullins,Ireland) **6-11-4** DJCasey (a towards rr)	2	6	9/1	97	—
1492a2	**Radanpour (IRE)** (WPMullins,Ireland) **4-11-4** RDunwoody (chsd ldr: mstke 6th: wknd bef 3 out: lft dist 5th 2 out: n.d whn fell last)		F	14/1	—	—
1234a2	**New Co (IRE)** (MFMorris,Ireland) **8-11-9** CO'Dwyer (hld up: 5th 3 out: mod 4th & n.d whn fell 2 out)		F	8/1	—	—

(SP 127.8%) **8 Rn**

4m 49.8 (-0.20) OWNER B. T. Stewart-Brown (UPPER LAMBOURN) BRED Mrs J. A. Harold-Barry in Ireland

Large Action (IRE), looking as though the race would do him good, went second five out. He led before three out and made a procession of things up the straight, winning very easily indeed. (9/4)

1487a* Cockney Lad (IRE) improved to go fourth with three to jump, but was a beaten third turning into the straight. He stayed on to go second approaching the last, without threatening. (8/1)

Theatreworld (IRE), a surprise favourite, went second after three out. He was never able to take advantage of the doubt regarding Large Action's fitness and had cried enough between the last two. (6/4)

1326 Castlekellyleader (IRE) set off in front and was clear before the fourth. He weakened quickly after four out and was well beaten before the straight. (6/1: op 4/1)

NR

1760a - 1761a : (Irish Racing) - See Computer Raceform

1171-EXETER (R-H) (Good)
Friday December 6th
WEATHER: misty

1762 TRIPLEPRINT NOVICES' CONDITIONAL H'CAP HURDLE (0-105) (4-Y.O+) (Class F)
12-50 (12-51) **2m 2f (8 hdls)** £2,156.60 (£597.60: £285.80) GOING: 0.46 sec per fur (GS)

Form	Horse	Dist	Pos	SP	RR	SF
1299*	**Burlington Sam (NZ) (83)** (AGHobbs) **8-11-9** OBurrows (lw: chsd ldr tl led appr 2 out: drvn out)	—	1	11/4 ^{2}	65	—
1638^{4}	**Time Leader (70)** (RDickin) **4-10-1**(9) XAizpuru (hld up & bhd: hdwy 6th: ev ch 2 out: drvn & no ex flat)	1½	2	7/4 ^{1}	51	—
978^{4}	**Karen's Typhoon (IRE) (72)** (PJHobbs) **5-10-9**(3) GTormey (hmpd s: bhd: styd on fr 2 out)	3½	3	8/1	50	—
1471^{4}	**Eleanora Muse (66)** (PaddyFarrell) **6-10-6** GuyLewis (led 2nd to 3rd: led 4th tl rdn & hdd appr 2 out: sn wknd)	3½	4	9/2 ^{3}	40	—
1550^{9}	**Madam Rose (IRE) (60)** (JWMullins) **6-9-5**(9) DavidTurner (bit bkwd: led to 2nd: led 3rd: hdd & mstke next: wknd 6th: t.o)	dist	5	20/1	—	—
1425*	**Urban Lily (84)** (RJHodges) **6-11-4b**(6) JHarris (lw: hmpd & uns rdr s)		U	6/1	—	—
1563^{P}	**Upham Rascal (66)** (DRGandolfo) **5-10-3**(3)ow6 DFortt (unruly s, shied at tape & uns rdr)		U	20/1	—	—

(SP 116.1%) **7 Rn**

4m 37.8 (27.80) CSF £7.96 TOTE £3.10: £1.50 £1.40 (£2.70) OWNER Mrs Jackie Reip (KINGSBRIDGE) BRED G. H. L. Broughton

1299* Burlington Sam (NZ), stepping up from recent wins in selling company, made it three out of three for the season. His next target could be a small novice hurdle over Christmas. (11/4)

1638 Time Leader, 6lb out of the handicap at Newbury last time out, was dropping in class here. Never able to get on terms with the winner, he is due to go up 6lb after this race and may find it difficult to find another opportunity like this. (7/4)

978 Karen's Typhoon (IRE) has disappointed so far this season in events further than this and, although hampered at the start, was staying on reasonably well at the end. (8/1: 5/1-9/1)

1425* Urban Lily was unfortunate to unseat her rider in a melee at the start. She will be out for revenge given another chance. (6/1: 4/1-13/2)

1763 BONUSPRINT (S) H'CAP CHASE (0-95) (5-Y.O+) (Class G)
1-20 (1-21) **2m 2f (12 fncs)** £2,469.00 (£684.00: £327.00) GOING: 0.29 sec per fur (GS)

Form	Horse	Dist	Pos	SP	RR	SF
1569^{3}	**Castleconner (IRE) (75)** (RGFrost) **5-10-8b** MrAHoldsworth (lw: a.p: led 9th: clr last: drvn out)	—	1	12/1	82	19
1582^{U}	**The Whole Hog (IRE) (78)** (KCBailey) **7-10-4**(7) MrRWakley (mid div: styd on 9th: chsd wnr last: no imp)	10	2	14/1	76	13
1696^{3}	**Fenwick (87)** (RJHodges) **9-11-3**(3) TDascombe (hld up & bhd: hdwy 4th: ev ch 9th: wknd 2 out)	3	3	9/2 ^{3}	82	19
1192^{F}	**Glentower (IRE) (90)** (CLPopham) **8-11-9** AMaguire (bit bkwd: bhd: styd on fr 9th: nvr nrr)	½	4	6/1	85	22
1200^{6}	**Jhal Frezi (69)** (ABarrow) **8-10-2** AProcter (hdwy 4th: sn in tch: wknd appr 9th)	¾	5	5/2 ^{1}	63	—
411^{5}	**October Brew (USA) (86)** (MCPipe) **6-11-5b** APMcCoy (led to 3rd: led 4th to 9th: rdn & wknd next: t.o)	dist	6	7/2 ^{2}	—	—
632^{4}	**Akiymann (USA) (71)** (MCPipe) **6-9-11b**(7) GSupple (a bhd: mstke 2nd: t.o 8th)	dist	7	16/1	—	—
1328^{8}	**Jewel Thief (70)** (GBBalding) **6-10-3v** RGreene (a bhd: t.o 3rd)	20	8	14/1	—	—
1202^{P}	**Tapageur (95)** (MCPipe) **11-11-7**(7) BMoore (bit bkwd: bhd: wknd 4th: t.o whn p.u bef 7th)		P	20/1	—	—
1677^{P}	**Up the Tempo (IRE) (68)** (PaddyFarrell) **7-9-12**(3)ow1 GuyLewis (a bhd: t.o whn p.u bef 10th)		P	33/1	—	—
1664^{P}	**Captain Stockford (67)** (PWegmann) **9-10-0** WMarston (chsd ldr tl led 3rd: hdd next: chsd ldr to 8th: wknd qckly next: p.u bef 2 out)		P	33/1	—	—

(SP 120.8%) **11 Rn**

4m 35.5 (14.50) CSF £149.41 CT £798.15 TOTE £14.40: £2.10 £7.50 £1.70 (£72.70) Trio £98.40; £98.49 to Sandown 7/12/96 OWNER Mrs G. A. Robarts (BUCKFASTLEIGH) BRED Niall Langan

LONG HANDICAP Up the Tempo (IRE) 9-9 Captain Stockford 9-7

No bid

1569 Castleconner (IRE) scored convincingly, but in a very weak contest. (12/1: 8/1-14/1)

The Whole Hog (IRE), dropped in class, stayed on towards the end and, never making any impression on the winner, may be better suited by further. (14/1: op 7/1)

1696 Fenwick is nothing but consistent in these low-grade events. (9/2: op 3/1)

954 Jhal Frezi is still a maiden after seventeen attempts and should improve on this. (5/2)

1764 TRIPLEPRINT NOVICES' CHASE (5-Y.O+) (Class C)
1-50 (1-51) **2m 2f (12 fncs)** £5,047.25 (£1,508.00: £721.50: £328.25) GOING: 0.29 sec per fur (GS)

Form	Horse	Dist	Pos	SP	RR	SF
	Guinda (IRE) (NATwiston-Davies) **6-10-9** CLlewellyn (hld up mid div: rdn 10th: lft 2nd 2 out: r.o to ld flat)	—	1	11/1	103	35
1371*	**Lively Knight (IRE) (115)** (JTGifford) **7-11-6** PHide (lw: led 2nd to 9th: wkng whn lft in clr ld 2 out: rdn & hdd flat)	1	2	7/2 ^{2}	113	45
1371^{3}	**Wild West Wind (IRE)** (MissHCKnight) **6-11-0** JOsborne (lw: led to 2nd: rdn 6th: lft 3rd 2 out: one pce)	10	3	9/1	98	30
	Flippance (NAGaselee) **6-11-0** WMarston (bit bkwd: prom: chsd ldr briefly 5th: wknd fr 8th)	nk	4	50/1	98	30
1474^{2}	**Phar From Funny** (GBBalding) **5-11-0** APMcCoy (lw: hld up: stdy hdwy to chse ldr 8th: led next: clr whn stumbled bdly 2 out: nt rcvr)	5	5	8/1 ^{3}	94++	26
1199^{5}	**Purbeck Cavalier** (RHAlner) **7-11-0** GUpton (bit bkwd: a bhd: t.o 5th)	dist	6	66/1	—	—
	Squire Silk (AndrewTurnell) **7-11-0** RDunwoody (lw: mstke 1st: hld up & bhd: hdwy 8th: ev ch whn bdly hmpd after 2 out & uns rdr: rmntd)	dist	7	4/5 ^{1}	—	—
	Robins Pride (IRE) (CLPopham) **6-10-11**(3) TDascombe (bit bkwd: mstke 2nd: hdwy to chse ldr 6th to 8th: wknd appr next: t.o whn p.u bef last)		P	33/1	—	—
1179^{4}	**Kino's Cross (98)** (AJWilson) **7-11-0** AMaguire (bhd fr 5th: t.o whn p.u bef 10th)		P	20/1	—	—

(SP 118.4%) **9 Rn**

4m 31.7 (10.70) CSF £47.54 TOTE £18.40: £3.30 £1.50 £1.30 (£18.40) Trio £35.00 OWNER Mrs J. K. Powell (CHELTENHAM) BRED Mrs J. F. Stothers

Guinda (IRE) was fortunate here on this fencing debut. Looking set for third place, the leader stumbled two from home and in the melee hampered the odds-on favourite, who unseated his rider as a result. Left in second place, she ran on well, but this form should not be taken at face value. (11/1: 6/1-12/1)

1371* Lively Knight (IRE) was left clear by the fiasco at the second last, but was swallowed up by the winner on the flat. He jumped well and can soon return to winning ways. (7/2)

1371 Wild West Wind (IRE) finished closer to Lively Knight than he had done last time out. (9/1: 6/1-10/1)

1474 Phar From Funny was in the process of making an impressive debut over fences and was going clear when stumbling on landing at the second last. When he managed to get to his feet, he was then hit by the favourite. McCoy performed wonders to stay in the saddle and, on this evidence, there is a decent novice chase to be won. (8/1: 6/1-9/1)
Squire Silk would surely have been in contention at the finish, but was hampered two from home. After being unseated, his jockey remounted to see the race through, albeit in an unfortunate last place. (4/5)

1765 BONUSPRINT H'CAP CHASE (0-120) (5-Y.O+) (Class D)

2-20 (2-21) **2m 7f 110y (17 fncs)** £4,192.20 (£1,254.60: £601.80: £275.40) GOING: 0.29 sec per fur (GS)

				SP	RR	SF
1338*	**Ballyea Boy (IRE) (106)** (DNicholson) **6-11-3** AMaguire (lw: a.p: led 14th: hld on u.p flat)	—	1	5/2[1]	117	20
1428[4]	**Rocky Park (92)** (GBBalding) **10-10-3** BFenton (a.p: lost pl 15th: mstke last: rallied flat)	¾	2	14/1	103	6
	Red Parade (NZ) (95) (NJHawke) **8-10-6** RGreene (bit bkwd: hld up: hdwy 11th: ev ch 15th: one pce)	3	3	9/1	103	6
1426*	**Orswell Lad (105)** (PJHobbs) **7-10-13**(3) GTormey (hdwy & mstke 14th: one pce)	4	4	13/2	111	14
1540[4]	**Spuffington (114)** (JTGifford) **8-11-11** PHide (lw: led to 14th: ev ch 2 out: wknd qckly appr last)	1½	5	10/1	119	22
1473*	**Andre Laval (IRE) (113)** (KCBailey) **7-11-3**(7) MrRWakley (bhd: hdwy 12th: nvr nrr)	¾	6	5/1[2]	117	20
1119[6]	**Garrylough (IRE) (113)** (DRGandolfo) **7-11-10** RDunwoody (bhd: hdwy 12th: nvr nrr)	½	7	6/1[3]	117	20
1057*	**Special Account (97)** (CRBarwell) **10-10-8** APMcCoy (lw: chsd ldrs tl wknd 13th)	nk	8	8/1	101	4
	Ghia Gneuiagh (113) (NATwiston-Davies) **10-11-10** CLlewellyn (bit bkwd: a bhd: t.o)	dist	9	20/1	—	—
	Mr Invader (102) (NAGaselee) **9-10-13** WMarston (bit bkwd: a bhd: t.o)	2½	10	16/1	—	—
1379[4]	**Kindle's Delight (101)** (MissHCKnight) **8-10-12** JOsborne (prom to 13th: grad wknd: t.o whn p.u bef last)		P	20/1	—	—
				(SP 125.1%)		**11 Rn**

6m 8.7 (21.70) CSF £36.32 CT £257.41 TOTE £3.90: £1.90 £5.50 £1.80 (£114.30) Trio £105.60 OWNER Mr Denis Barry (TEMPLE GUITING) BRED Ted O'Rourke
1338* Ballyea Boy (IRE) seemed to be idling when leading on the run-in and had to be rousted along to the line. He had more in hand than the winning margin suggests. (5/2)
1202 Rocky Park would certainly benefit from a clear round of jumping once in a while, but he nevertheless showed improved form here. (14/1)
Red Parade (NZ), on his first outing for over a year, was seen to have a chance with three to jump. One-paced in the final stages, he can come on for this run. (9/1)

1766 E.B.F. TRIPLEPRINT 'N.H.' NOVICES' HURDLE (QUALIFIER) (4, 5 & 6-Y.O) (Class D)

2-50 (2-51) **2m 2f (8 hdls)** £4,020.40 (£1,205.20: £579.60: £266.80) GOING: 0.46 sec per fur (GS)

				SP	RR	SF
1275[2]	**Wade Road (IRE)** (MissHCKnight) **5-11-0** RDunwoody (lw: a.p: chsd ldr 4th: led appr 2 out: qcknd clr: easily)	—	1	5/4[1]	84+	37
	The Land Agent (JWMullins) **5-11-0** SCurran (prom: led 5th tl appr 2 out: sn outpcd)	23	2	5/2[3]	64	17
1453[8]	**Sir Dante (IRE)** (RRowe) **5-11-0** DO'Sullivan (lw: mstke 1st: chsd ldrs: styd on fr 2 out)	4	3	12/1	60	13
	Leap Frog (NAGaselee) **5-11-0** WMarston (bit bkwd: hld up & bhd: hdwy 5th: nt rch ldrs)	2	4	25/1	58	11
1457*	**Quini Eagle (FR)** (MCPipe) **4-11-0** APMcCoy (lw: led: hdd & j.slowly 5th: wknd appr 2 out)	3	5	9/4[2]	56	9
	Flaxley Wood (RHBuckler) **5-11-0** BFenton (bkwd: a bhd)	4	6	66/1	52	5
	Master Bomber (IRE) (RHAlner) **5-11-0** JOsborne (bkwd: bhd fr 5th)	dist	7	66/1	—	—
1053[12]	**Shrimp** (RHAlner) **5-10-9** CLlewellyn (bit bkwd: a bhd)	¾	8	66/1	—	—
	Mylink (IRE) (DNicholson) **6-11-0** AMaguire (bit bkwd: hdwy 3rd: wknd 6th: t.o)	6	9	10/1	—	—
1427[8]	**Palladium Boy** (MrsJGRetter) **6-11-0** GUpton (bit bkwd: prom to 3rd: sn wknd: t.o whn p.u bef 2 out)		P	50/1	—	—
1594[P]	**Fair Haul** (RGFrost) **5-11-0** MrAHoldsworth (bit bkwd: chsd ldr to 4th: wknd 6th: p.u bef 2 out)		P	200/1	—	—
1062[P]	**Lilly The Filly** (MrsBarbaraWaring) **5-10-9** PHide (a bhd: t.o whn p.u bef 2 out)		P	200/1	—	—
				(SP 131.8%)		**12 Rn**

4m 24.1 (14.10) CSF £5.46 TOTE £2.20: £1.50 £1.10 £2.30 (£8.10) Trio £25.80 OWNER Lord Chelsea (WANTAGE) BRED John O'Connor
1275 Wade Road (IRE), a half-brother to Three Philosophers, justified favouritism by winning this very impressively indeed. His trainer will be patient with this useful novice as he is considered mentally immature. (5/4)
The Land Agent, like the winner, has shown useful form in bumpers and, although beaten by a considerable distance in second place, will certainly come on for the run. (5/2)
Sir Dante (IRE) improved here on his two recent runs and will do better with time. (12/1: 8/1-14/1)
1457* Quini Eagle (FR) proved disappointing. (9/4: 6/4-5/2)
Mylink (IRE) (10/1: 5/1-12/1)

1767 BONUSPRINT H'CAP HURDLE (0-105) (4-Y.O+) (Class F)

3-20 (3-21) **2m 2f (8 hdls)** £2,174.80 (£602.80: £288.40) GOING: 0.46 sec per fur (GS)

				SP	RR	SF
1642[4]	**Dominion's Dream (98)** (MCPipe) **4-11-0v**(7) GSupple (lw: led to 3rd: chsd ldrs tl led appr last: styd on flat)	—	1	14/1	80	30
1542*	**Jefferies (98)** (JABOld) **7-11-7** GUpton (bit bkwd: hdwy 3rd: in tch: one pce appr last)	2	2	6/5[1]	78	28
1274[4]	**Embley Buoy (77)** (JWMullins) **8-10-0** SCurran (lw: chsd ldr tl led 3rd: hdd & wknd appr last)	2	3	14/1	55	5
1382*	**Handson (90)** (BRMillman) **4-10-8**(5) DSalter (lw: hdwy 4th: in tch tl wknd appr 2 out)	3	4	4/1[2]	66	16
1599[2]	**Beyond Our Reach (100)** (RJHodges) **8-11-6**(3) TDascombe (a bhd)	2½	5	7/1	74	24
1418*	**Barryben (99)** (WMBrisbourne) **7-11-5**(3) RMassey (no hdwy 5th)	11	6	6/1[3]	63	13
	Fontainerouge (IRE) (85) (GBBalding) **6-10-8** APMcCoy (bkwd: mstke 1st: a bhd)	4	7	7/1	45	—
1448[11]	**Indian Temple (77)** (KBishop) **5-10-0** RGreene (bkwd: a bhd)	hd	8	50/1	37	—
	First Century (IRE) (102) (BPalling) **7-11-11** RDunwoody (bit bkwd: hdwy 4th: wknd 6th: t.o)	dist	9	20/1	—	—
	Classic Pal (USA) (79) (NRMitchell) **5-10-2**ow1 DSkyrme (a bhd: p.u bef 2 out)		P	25/1	—	—
				(SP 128.6%)		**10 Rn**

4m 27.4 (17.40) CSF £33.09 CT £253.81 TOTE £14.90: £2.60 £1.20 £3.40 (£20.10) Trio £146.70; £90.94 to Sandown 7/12/96 OWNER Martin Pipe Racing Club (WELLINGTON) BRED Aston Park Stud
LONG HANDICAP Indian Temple 9-7 Embley Buoy 9-13
STEWARDS' ENQUIRY Supple fined £125 (disregarding orders of the starter).
1642 Dominion's Dream stepped up from her Haydock run last week. Prominent throughout, she took the lead at the last and stayed on well on the run-in. Consistent in sellers and claimers last season, she will do well to repeat that form in handicap company. (14/1: 10/1-16/1)
1542* Jefferies, 7lb higher than when winning at Towcester last month, was slightly one-paced in the closing stages. (6/5)
1274 Embley Buoy was a shock 50/1 winner at Chepstow in October when 16lb out of the handicap, and has since proved that the effort was no fluke. (14/1)
1382* Handson (4/1: 3/1-9/2)
1418* Barryben (6/1: 4/1-7/1)

Fontainerouge (IRE) (7/1: op 4/1)

T/Plpt: £79.40 (146.42 Tckts). T/Qdpt: £22.10 (53.13 Tckts). T

1444-HEREFORD (R-H) (Good to soft, Good patches)
Friday December 6th
WEATHER: cloudy

1768 WIDEMARSH NOVICES' HURDLE (4-Y.O+) (Class E)
12-40 (12-41) **2m 3f 110y (11 hdls)** £2,542.00 (£712.00: £346.00) GOING: 0.24 sec per fur (G)

Form	Horse / details	Dist	Pos	SP	RR	SF
1329*	**Boots Madden (IRE)** (MissVenetiaWilliams) **6-10-12** NWilliamson (hld up: rdn & hdwy appr 7th: led after 8th: rdn & hdd 3 out: led 2 out: rdn out)	—	1	2/1[1]	73+	14
	Supreme Flyer (IRE) (KCBailey) **6-10-12** CO'Dwyer (bit bkwd: hld up: hdwy 7th: led 3 out to 2 out: sn rdn: ev ch last: one pce)	2½	2	10/1[3]	71	12
	Balleswhidden (BSmart) **4-10-12** ILawrence (bkwd: hld up: hdwy 6th: ev ch 3 out: wknd 2 out)	17	3	9/1[2]	57	—
1323[5]	**Warner For Players (IRE)** (PJHobbs) **5-10-12** BPowell (prom: mstke 1st: hrd rdn after 6th: lost pl 7th: n.d after)	6	4	2/1[1]	52	—
1536[5]	**Burntwood Melody** (PTDalton) **5-10-12** JSupple (bhd whn rdn appr 6th: nvr nr ldrs)	3	5	33/1	50	—
1568[10]	**My Shenandoah (IRE)** (HOliver) **5-10-12** VSlattery (hld up & bhd: sme hdwy fr 2 out: n.d)	½	6	50/1	49	—
1026[4]	**Old Cavalier** (JJO'Neill) **5-10-12** MAFitzgerald (hld up: hdwy after 6th: led after 8th: hdd 3 out: sn wknd)	nk	7	9/1[2]	49	—
1541[7]	**Medford (97)** (WGMTurner) **6-10-12**(7) JPower (prom: led appr 7th tl after 8th: sn wknd)	13	8	20/1	45	—
1476[9]	**The Brewer** (JCTuck) **4-10-12** SMcNeill (bhd fr 7th)	3½	9	50/1	35	—
	Madam Muck (NATwiston-Davies) **5-10-7** TJenks (bkwd: bhd fr 7th)	5	10	10/1[3]	26	—
1580[4]	**Nunson** (RDickin) **7-10-9**(3) MrCBonner (lw: a bhd: t.o)	26	11	50/1	10	—
	Achill Prince (IRE) (NGAyliffe) **5-10-12** WMcFarland (bkwd: led & sn clr: j.lft 5th: hdd appr 7th: bhd whn blnd 8th: t.o)	12	12	50/1	—	—
	Chili Heights (KBishop) **6-10-12** DBridgwater (a bhd: t.o whn p.u bef 3 out)		P	25/1	—	—
1568[P]	**Filch** (PGMurphy) **5-10-7b[1]** RFarrant (lw: chsd ldr to 5th: sn rdn: wknd qckly: t.o whn p.u bef 3 out)		P	66/1	—	—
1323[10]	**Mr Motivator** (TKeddy) **6-10-12** DLeahy (bit bkwd: a bhd: t.o whn p.u bef 3 out)		P	100/1	—	—
	Althrey Gale (IRE) (FLloyd) **5-10-12** SWynne (bit bkwd: nt j.w: a bhd: t.o whn p.u bef 3 out)		P	100/1	—	—

(SP 127.7%) **16 Rn**

4m 47.7 (16.70) CSF £22.67 TOTE £3.30: £1.40 £3.40 £3.00 (£23.60) Trio £29.30 OWNER Mr L. J. A. Phipps (HEREFORD) BRED Michael Hickey

1329* Boots Madden (IRE) completed a hat-trick on this first run over hurdles, and needed every yard of the trip to outbattle a somewhat reluctant runner-up. (2/1: 11/10-9/4)
Supreme Flyer (IRE) had been blinkered on his last run at Thurles in April and, looking at his head-carriage from the second last, one could see why. (10/1)
Balleswhidden looked in need of this and it was probably lack of fitness rather than the longer trip that found him out. (9/1: 12/1-8/1)
1323 Warner For Players (IRE) is not fulfilling the promise he showed in bumpers last season. (2/1)
1026 Old Cavalier (9/1: 5/1-10/1)

1769 SIDNEY PHILLIPS FOR PUBS H'CAP CHASE (0-110) (5-Y.O+) (Class E)
1-10 (1-10) **2m 3f (14 fncs)** £3,087.00 (£936.00: £458.00: £219.00) GOING: 0.24 sec per fur (G)

Form	Horse / details	Dist	Pos	SP	RR	SF
1584[6]	**Sister Rosza (IRE) (96)** (MrsSLamyman) **8-11-3** RFarrant (hld up & plld hrd: hdwy 8th: rdn appr last: r.o wl to ld flat)	—	1	33/1	102	—
1584[3]	**Fichu (USA) (79)** (MrsLRichards) **8-10-0** MRichards (j.w: a.p: led appr 9th: clr appr last: rdn & hdd flat)	1	2	4/1[2]	84	—
1584[2]	**Lasata (107)** (RMCarson) **11-12-0** DMorris (lw: hld up: hdwy 9th: ev ch whn blnd 3 out: hit 2 out: sn wknd)	14	3	3/1[1]	100	—
1379[5]	**Monks Jay (IRE) (91)** (GThorner) **7-10-12** ILawrence (hld up: hdwy appr 9th: wknd appr 4 out: t.o)	18	4	3/1[1]	69	—
	Star of Italy (86) (CPMorlock) **9-10-7** LHarvey (bkwd: chsd ldr to 8th: wknd appr 10th: t.o whn p.u bef 3 out)		P	10/1	—	—
	Over the Pole (107) (PRChamings) **9-11-11**(3) MrCBonner (bkwd: j.lft: led: clr 3rd: hdd appr 9th: wkng whn blnd 10th: t.o whn p.u bef 3 out)		P	9/1	—	—
	Winspit (IRE) (86) (RHAlner) **6-10-4**(3) PHenley (hld up & plld hrd: mstke 7th: hdwy & pckd 9th: cl 4th whn blnd & uns rdr 4 out)		U	9/2[3]	—	—

(SP 110.2%) **7 Rn**

4m 51.8 (21.80) CSF £141.70 TOTE £34.50: £5.10 £3.20 (£58.70) OWNER Mr P. Lamyman (LINCOLN) BRED James W. Curtin
LONG HANDICAP Fichu (USA) 9-13

Sister Rosza (IRE) won a two-mile chase on heavy ground at Punchestown in January. Due to drop 3lb after a run at Windsor last week, she appreciated this extended trip and ended a three-year barren spell for her trainer. (33/1)
1584 Fichu (USA) had finished nine lengths in front of Sister Rosza on 3lb better terms at Windsor last week, but did not seem quite so suited to this longer distance as the winner. (4/1: op 5/2)
1584 Lasata had the first two behind him at Windsor last week, but a bad error three from home did not help him get this extra three furlongs. (3/1: op 2/1)
1379 Monks Jay (IRE) had been dropped 2lb and it is beginning to look as if his Wincanton victory was something of a fluke. (3/1)
Winspit (IRE) looked reasonably treated on this handicap debut and, after taking a strong hold, was well there when getting rid of his rider at the final ditch. (9/2: op 3/1)

1770 PENCOED (S) HURDLE (4,5,6 & 7-Y.O) (Class G)
1-40 (1-44) **2m 1f (9 hdls)** £2,108.00 (£588.00: £284.00) GOING: 0.24 sec per fur (G)

Form	Horse / details	Dist	Pos	SP	RR	SF
1537*	**Harry (84)** (DBurchell) **6-11-5** DJBurchell (hld up & plld hrd: hdwy 4th: led after 3 out: clr after 2 out: easily)	—	1	11/10[1]	80+	8
1091[6]	**Lime Street Blues (IRE) (80)** (CPEBrooks) **5-10-12b** GBradley (led after 1st to 4th:chsd wnr fr 2 out: no imp)	6	2	13/2[2]	67	—
	Proud Image (GMMcCourt) **4-10-12** BClifford (a.p: one pce fr 3 out)	5	3	10/1	63	—
	Comeonup (JMBradley) **5-10-12** NWilliamson (hld up & bhd: hdwy appr 5th: wknd 2 out)	11	4	25/1	52	—
1569[8]	**Strike-a-Pose** (BJLlewellyn) **6-11-0** MrJLLlewellyn (a.p: led 4th tl after 3 out: wknd 2 out)	2½	5	14/1	52	—
1369[P]	**Daring Ryde** (JPSmith) **5-10-12** AThornton (bit bkwd: hld up: hdwy whn hmpd 5th: rdn & wknd appr 2 out)	1¼	6	50/1	49	—
1299[4]	**Quick Decision (IRE) (59)** (JKCresswell) **5-10-5**(7) NTEgan (rdn & hdwy appr 5th: wknd appr 3 out)	4	7	33/1	45	—

				SP	RR	SF
	Smiley Face (RJHodges) **4-10-12** PHolley (bit bkwd: hld up: hmpd 5th: bhd fr 6th)	2	**8**	33/1	43	—
1276[10]	**Monty** (GHYardley) **4-10-9**(3) PHenley (plld hrd: prom to 5th)	9	**9**	50/1	35	—
	Glen Garnock (IRE) (RTJuckes) **4-10-12** GaryLyons (bit bkwd: hld up: a bhd)	2½	**10**	33/1	32	—
1594[6]	**Office Hours** (WGMTurner) **4-10-12** WMcFarland (led tl after 1st: prom whn fell 5th)		**F**	8/1	—	—
902[9]	**Ballyhays (IRE)** (NGAyliffe) **7-10-12** RFarrant (s.s: fell 1st)		**F**	50/1	—	—
	Audrey Grace (MissGayKelleway) **5-10-7** DBridgwater (nt j.w: a bhd: t.o whn blnd 2 out: p.u bef last)		**P**	7/1[3]	—	—
1450[9]	**Tomorrows Harvest** (RJHodges) **4-10-7** ILawrence (bkwd: hld up & plld hrd: hdwy after 4th: wknd 6th: t.o whn p.u bef last)		**P**	33/1	—	—
				(SP 121.8%)	**14 Rn**	

4m 10.3 (17.30) CSF £8.91 TOTE £2.20: £1.50 £2.00 £2.10 (£4.50) Trio £15.20 OWNER Mr Simon Lewis (EBBW VALE) BRED Jephanil
Bt in 4,000 gns

1537* Harry, with Willy Star having already franked the form of his Towcester win, scored in the style of a good thing, and could well go on to better things. (11/10)
Lime Street Blues (IRE) was dropped into a seller, but probably came up against a useful sort in this grade. (13/2)
Proud Image had three wins on the Flat at up to a mile, but has been running over twelve furlongs recently. (10/1: op 4/1)
Comeonup, no great shakes on the Flat, is by no means guaranteed to get this trip over timber. (25/1)
Strike-a-Pose was still not fully wound up. (14/1)
Daring Ryde did manage to win a mile claimer at Leicester in June 1995. (50/1)
Audrey Grace (7/1: op 4/1)

1771 BET WITH THE TOTE QUALIFIER NOVICES' CHASE (5-Y.O+) (Class E)
2-10 (2-17) **2m 3f (14 fncs)** £3,243.00 (£984.00: £482.00: £231.00) GOING: 0.24 sec per fur (G)

				SP	RR	SF
1291*	**Mariners Mirror (104)** (NATwiston-Davies) **9-11-0** MrMRimell (hmpd s: hdwy 7th: led after 2 out: sn clr)	—	**1**	11/4[2]	103+	7
1452[3]	**Feel the Power (IRE) (128)** (KCBailey) **8-10-12** CO'Dwyer (lw: hld up: hdwy 5th: wnt 2nd 7th: led 4 out tl mstke 3 out: hmpd & lft in ld 2 out: sn hdd: one pce)	10	**2**	Evens[1]	93	—
1472[U]	**Zaitoon (IRE) (101)** (DNicholson) **5-10-12** DBridgwater (mstke 1st: hdwy 9th: wknd appr 2 out)	10	**3**	8/1	84	—
	Jolly Boat (FJordan) **9-10-12** SWynne (bkwd: prom to 3 out: btn whn mstke 2 out)	2½	**4**	16/1	82	—
1449[6]	**Knowing (69)** (PGWatkins) **9-10-3**(7)ow3 MrAWintle (chsd ldr: hit 4th: wknd 4 out)	dist	**5**	66/1	—	—
1073[P]	**King's Gold (78)** (MrsLRichards) **6-10-12** MRichards (t.o fr 5th)	3	**6**	33/1	—	—
1568[13]	**Irish Perry** (TMorton) **9-10-7** MSharratt (t.o fr 5th)	2½	**7**	66/1	—	—
1449[F]	**Wot No Gin (65)** (AJWilson) **7-10-12** AThornton (hdwy 8th: led 3 out: sn rdn: 1l clr whn fell 2 out)		**F**	33/1	—	—
1456[3]	**Apple John** (RHAlner) **7-10-9**(3) PHenley (swvd lft s: fell 2nd)		**F**	7/1[3]	—	—
1449[4]	**King's Shilling (USA) (79)** (HOliver) **9-10-12** JacquiOliver (prom: wkng whn mstke 10th: t.o whn p.u bef 3 out)		**P**	50/1	—	—
1308[U]	**High Handed (IRE)** (THCaldwell) **5-10-12** BClifford (t.o 5th: p.u bef 9th)		**P**	50/1	—	—
	Ernest Aragorn (MrsSLamyman) **7-10-12v1** TJMurphy (bit bkwd: plld hrd: nt j.w: led & sn clr: hdd & wknd 4 out: t.o whn p.u bef 2 out)		**P**	100/1	—	—
1572[7]	**Bankonit (IRE)** (DJDavies) **8-10-12** ILawrence (bit bkwd: t.o 5th: p.u bef 2 out)		**P**	100/1	—	—
				(SP 120.9%)	**13 Rn**	

4m 49.0 (19.00) CSF £5.61 TOTE £4.00: £1.50 £1.90 £1.50 (£2.90) Trio £6.40 OWNER Mr F. J. Mills (CHELTENHAM) BRED E. J. Praill, Mrs M. Scudamore and M. J. Scudamore

1291* Mariners Mirror, with the runner-up forced wide when the leader fell at the second last, slipped through on the inside to get pole position rounding the home turn. (11/4)
1452 Feel the Power (IRE) seemed in control until belting three out. Forced wide to sidestep Wot No Gin at the next, he then carried his head to one side as he had done at Kempton and gave the impression things were not quite right. (Evens)
Zaitoon (IRE) had been unluckily put out of the race early on his fencing debut and should be better for the experience. (8/1: 4/1-9/1)
Jolly Boat has a good record between the Flags, winning eight times and finishing second in the other four of his twelve completed starts in the last three seasons. (16/1)
1449 Wot No Gin, trying a longer trip, was responding to pressure and forging ahead when coming to grief at the difficult fence, two from home. (33/1)
1456 Apple John (7/1: 4/1-8/1)

1772 INNPLAN INSURANCE NOVICES' AMATEUR H'CAP HURDLE (0-100) (3-Y.O+) (Class E)
2-40 (2-43) **2m 1f (9 hdls)** £2,486.00 (£696.00: £338.00) GOING: 0.24 sec per fur (G)

				SP	RR	SF
1471*	**Wayfarers Way (USA) (89)** (NJHenderson) **5-11-5**(5) MrCVigors (lw: hld up: hdwy 5th: led 3 out: comf)	—	**1**	4/1[2]	81+	37
1470[9]	**The Deaconess (70)** (MrsALMKing) **5-9-12**(7) MrOMcPhail (hld up: hdwy 6th: ev ch 3 out: chsd wnr fr 2 out: no imp)	7	**2**	25/1	55	11
1178[6]	**Irish Wildcard (NZ) (74)** (HOliver) **8-10-2**(7)ow7 MrNHOliver (hld up: lost pl 5th: rallied 3 out: styd on flat: b.b.v)	1	**3**	9/2[3]	59	8
1448[P]	**Country Minstrel (IRE) (78)** (SADouch) **5-10-8**(5) MrJJukes (plld hrd: a.p: ev ch 3 out: sn wknd)	6	**4**	20/1	57	13
1448[2]	**Raven's Roost (IRE) (76)** (GEJones) **5-10-6**(5) MissPJones (plld hrd: a.p: led after 6th to 3 out: sn wknd)	3½	**5**	9/4[1]	52	8
1663[B]	**Alpha Leather (65)** (LPGrassick) **5-9-7**(7) MrJGrassick (hdwy after 4th: wknd 3 out)	4	**6**	50/1	37	—
1178[4]	**Highly Charming (IRE) (87)** (MFBarraclough) **4-11-1**(7) MrAWintle (hld up: hdwy after 4th: led 5th tl after 6th: wknd appr 2 out)	13	**7**	15/2	47	3
1499[5]	**Segala (IRE) (86)** (JJO'Neill) **5-11-0**(7) MrLCorcoran (lw: prom: ev ch appr 3 out: wknd appr 2 out)	1	**8**	15/2	45	1
1536[P]	**Honeybed Wood (70)** (IRBrown) **8-9-12**(7) MrABrown (bkwd: a bhd)	4	**9**	20/1	25	—
128[7]	**Royal Glint (70)** (HEHaynes) **7-9-12**(7) MrPMcAllister (bkwd: a bhd: t.o)	19	**10**	14/1	7	—
	Analogue (IRE) (67) (RJEckley) **4-9-9**(7) MissCThomas (bkwd: prom to 4th: t.o)	10	**11**	20/1	—	—
1274[7]	**Carey's Cottage (IRE) (65)** (MrsPTownsley) **6-9-7**(7) MissCTownsley (t.o fr 3rd)	12	**12**	50/1	—	—
1537[9]	**Follow de Call (73)** (DMcCain) **6-10-1**(7) MrGLake (swtg: prom tl rdn & wknd appr 5th: t.o)	1½	**13**	25/1	—	—
1663[2]	**Skram (84)** (RDickin) **3-10-2**(3) MrCBonner (lw: led to 5th: wknd 6th: t.o whn p.u bef last)		**P**	4/1[2]	—	—
				(SP 145.0%)	**14 Rn**	

4m 4.6 (11.60) CSF £103.11 CT £465.22 TOTE £4.80: £1.80 £13.80 £1.90 (£92.00) Trio £151.80; £106.95 to Sandown 7/12/96 OWNER Lady Tennant (LAMBOURN) BRED Wooden Horse Investments
LONG HANDICAP Carey's Cottage (IRE) 9-13 Alpha Leather 9-11
WEIGHT FOR AGE 3yo-14lb
OFFICIAL EXPLANATION Irish Wildcard (NZ): bled from the nose.
1471* Wayfarers Way (USA) does seem to have finally got his act together, and a 2lb rise in the weights proved no problem. (4/1)

1178 The Deaconess showed improved form on this first run in a handicap. (25/1)
Irish Wildcard (NZ), whose rider gave the impression he was not totally happy with his mount during the race, was subsequently found to have bled from the nose. (9/2: op 5/2)
636 Country Minstrel (IRE), dropped 6lb, refused to settle, but at least ran better than on his last two outings. (20/1)
1448 Raven's Roost (IRE) is another who ran too freely in the first part of the race. (9/4)
1499 Segala (IRE) (15/2: 5/1-8/1)

1773 KINGS CAPLE NOVICES' H'CAP CHASE (0-95) (5-Y.O+) (Class F)

3-10 (3-10) **3m 1f 110y (19 fncs)** £2,866.00 (£868.00: £424.00: £202.00) GOING: 0.24 sec per fur (G)

				SP	RR	SF
1285^{5}	**Ceridwen (74)** (TRGreathead) **6-11-1** NMann (mid div: hit 5th: rdn & hdwy on ins appr 3 out: lft 2nd last: led flat: all out)	—	**1**	20/1	88	—
1596^{5}	**Wixoe Wonder (IRE) (77)** (MBradstock) **6-11-4** PHolley (lw: hld up: hdwy 10th: lft in ld 2 out: hdd flat)	2	**2**	14/1	90	—
1285^{P}	**Market Gossip (63)** (RHAlner) **6-10-1**(3) PHenley (bkwd: a.p: sltly hmpd 12th: hrd rdn after 13th: mstke 3 out: styd on one pce)	1¼	**3**	10/1	75	—
1538^{5}	**Majors Legacy (IRE) (81)** (CaptTAForster) **7-11-8** AThornton (a.p: one pce fr 3 out)	¾	**4**	$8/1^{3}$	93	3
1122^{8}	**Absolatum (62)** (JParfitt) **9-10-3** TJMurphy (bit bkwd: bhd: hdwy 14th: wkng whn mstke 2 out)	7	**5**	33/1	69	—
1385^{4}	**Cool Character (IRE) (69)** (RHBuckler) **8-10-10** BPowell (prom: blnd 9th: bhd fr 4 out: t.o)	dist	**6**	10/1	—	—
1252^{4}	**Golden Drum (IRE) (70)** (TRGeorge) **6-10-11** MAFitzgerald (lw: nt j.w: led to 14th: wknd 3 out: t.o)	11	**7**	16/1	—	—
1538^{4}	**Robsand (IRE) (83)** (GBBalding) **7-11-10** BClifford (bit bkwd: a bhd: t.o fr 12th)	27	**8**	$8/1^{3}$	—	—
1378^{4}	**Bossymoss (IRE) (70)** (AStreeter) **7-10-11** GaryLyons (lw: hld up: mstke 4th: gd hdwy 4 out: 2l 2nd whn fell last)		**F**	$7/1^{2}$	—	—
	Ragged Kingdom (IRE) (60) (CREgerton) **7-10-1** JAMcCarthy (bkwd: fell 1st)		**F**	33/1	—	—
1468^{6}	**Coney Road (75)** (CPEBrooks) **7-11-2** GBradley (hld up & bhd: hdwy 8th: rdn 11th: sn bhd: t.o whn p.u bef 14th)		**P**	$7/1^{2}$	—	—
	Bathwick Bobbie (81) (DLWilliams) **9-11-8** SMcNeill (bkwd: hld up: mstke 8th: bhd fr 10th: t.o whn p.u bef 4 out)		**P**	16/1	—	—
1684^{3}	**Hangover (75)** (RLee) **10-10-13**(3) GHogan (prom to 14th: mstke 3 out: bhd whn p.u bef 2 out)		**P**	$8/1^{3}$	—	—
1291^{2}	**Coverdale Lane (82)** (MrsSJSmith) **9-11-9** MrPMurray (hld up: hdwy after 10th: led 14th: 4l clr whn blnd & uns rdr 2 out)		**U**	16/1	—	—
1038^{*}	**Express Travel (IRE) (78)** (RCurtis) **8-11-5** DMorris (prom: mstkes 2nd & 10th: wkng whn blnd & uns rdr 4 out)		**U**	$2/1^{1}$	—	—
				(SP 144.8%)	**15 Rn**	

6m 39.8 (29.80) CSF £283.20 CT £2,750.44 TOTE £23.40: £3.60 £12.10 £5.00 (£216.80) Trio £638.90 OWNER Mrs S. Greathead (CHIPPING NORTON) BRED William J. Wood
Ceridwen, all the better for a run a month ago, showed just how well she stays in the closing stages. (20/1)
1596 Wixoe Wonder (IRE), stepping up in distance, could not cope with the stamina reserves of the winner from the final fence. (14/1)
1285 Market Gossip, pulled up when favourite for a similar event at Wincanton last month, seems the type to carry plenty of condition. (10/1)
1538 Majors Legacy (IRE) fared much better than at Towcester. (8/1)
Absolatum was in the handicap proper this time. (33/1)
1538 Robsand (IRE) (8/1: op 5/1)
1291 Coverdale Lane was in the driving seat when, as in the earlier novice chase, the awkward penultimate fence reared its ugly head. (16/1)
1038* Express Travel (IRE) (2/1: 4/1-7/4)

1774 SHEPHERDS MEADOW STANDARD OPEN N.H. FLAT RACE (4, 5 & 6-Y.O) (Class H)

3-40 (3-41) **2m 1f** £1,496.00 (£416.00: £200.00)

				SP	RR	SF
1431^{5}	**Dom Beltrano (FR)** (NATwiston-Davies) **4-10-11**(7) LSuthern (a.p: led 4f out to 3f out: led over 1f out: pushed out)	—	**1**	6/1	66 f	—
	Sunday Venture (NZ) (NJHenderson) **4-11-4** MAFitzgerald (bit bkwd: s.s: hld up: stdy hdwy 10f out: led on bit over 3f out: hdd over 1f out: fnd nil: bttr for r)	3½	**2**	$5/2^{1}$	63 f	—
	Bozo (IRE) (BJMRyall) **5-10-11**(7) MGriffiths (w.r.s: hdwy 8f out: rdn over 2f out: styd on fnl f)	¾	**3**	50/1	62 f	—
1275^{9}	**Knight's Crest (IRE)** (RDickin) **6-11-4** BPowell (bit bkwd: a.p: rdn 3f out: r.o one pce)	¾	**4**	16/1	61 f	—
	Just Bayard (IRE) (BdeHaan) **4-11-4** ILawrence (bkwd: hdwy 7f out: wknd 3f out)	17	**5**	50/1	45 f	—
	Crocknamohill (IRE) (KSBridgwater) **5-11-4** DBridgwater (hdwy 8f out: rdn 5f out: wknd 3f out)	2½	**6**	16/1	43 f	—
	Jack (IRE) (JCTuck) **4-11-4** SMcNeill (nvr nr ldrs)	½	**7**	33/1	43 f	—
	Just One Question (IRE) (JJO'Neill) **6-11-11** NWilliamson (bit bkwd: prom: led 9f out to 4f out: eased whn btn 2f out)	1¼	**8**	$7/2^{2}$	48 f	—
1275^{5}	**Aztec Warrior** (KCBailey) **5-11-4** CO'Dwyer (lw: prom: rdn 6f out: wknd 4f out)	4	**9**	$4/1^{3}$	38 f	—
	Camp Head (IRE) (OSherwood) **5-11-4** JAMcCarthy (bkwd: hld up mid div: hdwy 6f out: rdn & wknd over 4f out)	17	**10**	5/1	22 f	—
1203^{13}	**Murray's Million** (JSSmith) **4-11-4** TJMurphy (plld hrd: prom 10f)	9	**11**	33/1	13 f	—
	Cool Harry (USA) (HEHaynes) **5-10-11**(7) MrAWintle (bkwd: a bhd: t.o)	18	**12**	50/1	—	—
	One More Rupee (CPMorlock) **5-11-4** JRKavanagh (rdn 8f out: a bhd: t.o)	2	**13**	50/1	—	—
	Surprise City (AJWilson) **5-11-4** AThornton (bkwd: a bhd: t.o)	27	**14**	33/1	—	—
1579^{14}	**Magslass** (JJO'Neill) **4-10-13** GBradley (led 8f: rdn 7f out: sn wknd: t.o)	dist	**15**	33/1	—	—
				(SP 133.1%)	**15 Rn**	

4m 2.1 CSF £22.11 TOTE £5.70: £1.40 £1.20 £20.50 (£19.80) Trio £166.20; £210.69 to Sandown 7/12/96 OWNER Mr Carl Wright (CHELTENHAM) BRED Daniel Bertrand
Dom Beltrano (FR) found the advantage of a previous outing tipping the scales in his favour. (6/1)
Sunday Venture (NZ), a 26,000 guinea New Zealand import, seemed to blow up in the short home straight and will be hard to beat next time. (5/2)
Bozo (IRE) is out of a half-sister to 2,000 Guineas winner To-Agori-Mou. (50/1)
Knight's Crest (IRE), related to Ten Plus, won a maiden point-to-point at Clonmel. (16/1)
1275 Aztec Warrior (4/1: 3/1-9/2)

T/Jkpt: Not won; £27,479.66 to Wolverhampton 7/12/96. T/Plpt: £832.80 (11.92 Tckts). T/Qdpt: £139.30 (7.6 Tckts). KH

1529-MARKET RASEN (R-H) (Good, Good to soft patches)
Friday December 6th
WEATHER: overcast

1775 BOB KETT CONDITIONAL (S) H'CAP HURDLE (0-95) (4-Y.O+) (Class G)
12-30 (12-30) **2m 3f 110y (10 hdls)** £1,947.00 (£542.00: £261.00) GOING: 1.09 sec per fur (HY)

				SP	RR	SF
1027^{2}	**Glenvally (81)** (BWMurray) **5-11-8** ECallaghan (hld up: pushed along fr 6th: led 3 out: styd on wl appr last)	—	1	11/4^{1}	64	—
	Weather Alert (IRE) (75) (KAMorgan) **5-10-13**(3) MNewton (led 2nd tl after 5th: styd on & ch 2 out: one pce)	4	2	8/1	55	—
819^{2}	**Parish Walk (IRE) (78)** (KJDrewry) **5-11-2**(3) BGrattan (a cl up: ev ch 3 out: nt qckn appr last)	3	3	9/2^{3}	55	—
1562^{9}	**Tharsis (67)** (WJSmith) **11-10-8** STaylor (led to 2nd: lost pl ½-wy: styd on again fr 2 out)	4	4	16/1	41	—
1577^{6}	**In a Moment (USA) (73)** (CGrant) **5-11-0** FLeahy (lw: outpcd fr ½-wy: sme hdwy u.p appr 2 out: sn btn)	2	5	4/1^{2}	45	—
1292^{4}	**Haughton Lad (IRE) (72)** (JParkes) **7-10-13** PMidgley (lw: outpcd & lost tch 6th: sme hdwy again fr 2 out)	2½	6	11/2	42	—
1045^{P}	**Captain Tandy (IRE) (83)** (CSmith) **7-11-10** DJKavanagh (bit bkwd: s.s: sn rcvrd: led after 5th & sn clr: hit 7th: hdd 3 out: sn btn)	27	7	16/1	31	—
	Strephon (IRE) (68) (JPLeigh) **6-10-9** KGaule (prom to 7th: sn t.o)	dist	8	16/1	—	—
1344^{8}	**Troy's Dream (74)** (MDHammond) **5-10-10**(5) RBurns (bhd: rdn 6th: t.o whn p.u between last 2)		P	14/1	—	—
	Tough Character (IRE) (59) (MESowersby) **8-10-0** DParker (bit bkwd: plld hrd: sddle slipped & p.u bef 4th)		P	25/1	—	—

(SP 119.5%) **10 Rn**

5m 14.7 (41.70) CSF £23.94 CT £89.71 TOTE £3.20: £1.30 £3.00 £1.50 (£11.60) Trio £13.40 OWNER Mrs M. Lingwood (MALTON) BRED Norton Grove Stud Ltd

LONG HANDICAP Tough Character (IRE) 9-6

No bid

1027 Glenvally appreciated this longer trip and, after struggling, was well on top at the finish. (11/4)
Weather Alert (IRE) had his chances and kept plugging away, but was never good enough. (8/1)
819 Parish Walk (IRE) had every chance here and just failed to see it out. The soft ground may not have helped. (9/2)
Tharsis showed something this time, staying on when the principals were tiring. (16/1)
1577 In a Moment (USA) looked to have found a poor race, but was not in the mood and, off the bit well over a circuit from home, would have none of it. (4/1)
1292 Haughton Lad (IRE) was always struggling in the soft ground. (11/2)
Troy's Dream (14/1: 8/1-16/1)

1776 CONSTANT SECURITY HURDLE (3-Y.O) (Class E)
1-00 (1-00) **2m 1f 110y (8 hdls)** £2,758.00 (£768.00: £370.00) GOING: 1.09 sec per fur (HY)

				SP	RR	SF
646^{7}	**No More Hassle (IRE)** (MrsMReveley) **3-10-12** PNiven (lw: trckd ldrs: led 3 out: hit next: sn hdd: sn disp ld: r.o flat)	—	1	6/1^{2}	65	11
1370^{4}	**Six Clerks (IRE)** (JGFitzGerald) **3-10-9**(3) FLeahy (lw: a chsng ldrs: led 2 out: hdd & nt qckn flat)	2½	2	7/1^{3}	63	9
	Parrot's Hill (IRE) (MHTompkins) **3-10-12** ADobbin (hld up: hdwy to chal 3 out: nt qckn fr next)	8	3	12/1	55	1
1205^{6}	**Baasm** (JNorton) **3-10-12** WFry (chsd ldrs: effrt 3 out: blnd 2 out: one pce after)	3½	4	16/1	52	—
1370^{6}	**Kingfisher Brave** (MGMeagher) **3-10-12** DerekByrne (prom: effrt 3 out: one pce appr next)	1¾	5	16/1	51	—
1370^{2}	**Belmarita (IRE)** (GAHubbard) **3-10-4**(3) KGaule (lw: mde most tl hdd 3 out: rdn & one pce appr next)	4	6	11/8^{1}	42	—
	Arabian Heights (JMackie) **3-10-12** TEley (in tch: hit 2nd: effrt 3 out: wknd appr next)	1	7	16/1	46	—
1370^{10}	**Pontevedra (IRE)** (KAMorgan) **3-10-7** ASSmith (trckd ldrs tl wknd fr 3 out)	½	8	20/1	41	—
	Mr Gold (IRE) (JMJefferson) **3-10-5**(7) MNewton (hld up & bhd: hdwy 5th: ev ch next: hung lft & wkng whn blnd 2 out)	5	9	20/1	41	—
1205^{P}	**Extremely Friendly** (BobJones) **3-10-12** VSmith (hld up & bhd: n.d)	3½	10	10/1	38	—
	Genuine John (IRE) (JParkes) **3-10-9**(3) PMidgley (mstkes: sme hdwy 3 out: sn wknd)	18	11	9/1	21	—
1526^{5}	**Propolis Power (IRE)** (MWEasterby) **3-10-12** JCallaghan (stdd s: n.d)	10	12	25/1	12	—
	Shoja (MrsVAAconley) **3-10-12** PMcLoughlin (a bhd: t.o)	25	13	33/1	—	—
1526^{12}	**Phantom Dancer (IRE) (70)** (MESowersby) **3-10-12b** DParker (chsd ldrs to 5th: t.o)	dist	14	20/1	—	—
1370^{B}	**Classic Daisy** (RCSpicer) **3-10-7** CMaude (bhd whn p.u bef 5th)		P	33/1	—	—
1652^{7}	**Northern Falcon** (MWEasterby) **3-10-7b** RGarritty (disp ld tl hmpd bnd & lost pl appr 4th: sn rdn & btn: p.u bef 2 out)		P	12/1	—	—
	Society Magic (USA) (CJMann) **3-10-12** JRailton (swtg: plld hrd: uns rdr bnd after 3rd)		U	9/1	—	—

(SP 155.0%) **17 Rn**

4m 33.7 (30.70) CSF £56.07 TOTE £5.10: £2.00 £2.40 £4.70 (£23.40) Trio £51.80 OWNER The No Hassle Partnership (SALTBURN) BRED Declan MacPartlin

646 No More Hassle (IRE) caught the Stewards' eyes last time when having an educational and showed the benefit of it here. After trying to throw it away with a blunder two out, he settled it in good style at the last. (6/1)
1370 Six Clerks (IRE) is improving with each run and can find a modest event in due course. (7/1)
Parrot's Hill (IRE) has yet to win a race of any kind, but this was a decent first effort over hurdles, and improvement is likely. (12/1: op 8/1)
Baasm again showed ability, but his hurdling let him down once more when the pressure was on. (16/1)
1370 Kingfisher Brave, more patiently ridden this time, ran reasonably, but that finishing kick was never there. (16/1)
1370 Belmarita (IRE) was a most frustrating character on the Flat, never quite coming up with the goods, and is beginning to turn out that way at this game. (11/8)
Arabian Heights showed ability and, should he really take to this game, he certainly has enough ability to succeed, but his attitude might be a problem. (16/1)
1652 Northern Falcon (12/1: op 8/1)

1777 CALDERPRINT 'N.H.' NOVICES' HURDLE (4-Y.O+) (Class D)
1-30 (1-30) **2m 1f 110y (8 hdls)** £3,115.00 (£865.00: £415.00) GOING: 1.09 sec per fur (HY)

				SP	RR	SF
1504*	**Good Vibes** (TDEasterby) **4-10-12** RGarritty (lw: cl up: led fr 4th: qcknd clr 2 out: easily)	—	1	11/4^{2}	86++	17
	Alzulu (IRE) (JGFitzGerald) **5-10-12** PNiven (lw: trckd ldrs: effrt appr 2 out: sn outpcd)	9	2	8/13^{1}	78+	9
1341^{F}	**September Breeze (IRE)** (KAMorgan) **5-10-7** ASSmith (led to 4th: cl up tl outpcd appr 2 out)	1	3	25/1	72	3
1536^{11}	**Dark Phoenix (IRE)** (OBrennan) **6-10-7** MBrennan (a in tch: nt qckn fr 3 out)	23	4	10/1^{3}	51	—
1208^{8}	**Ferrers** (MrsPSly) **5-10-12** RMarley (lw: chsd ldrs: effrt 3 out: sn outpcd)	8	5	14/1	49	—

	Horse	Pos	SP	RR	SF
	Minster Boy (JPLeigh) **5-10-12** ADobbin (bit bkwd: mstkes: a bhd) 17	6	25/1	33	—
1457[14]	**Jackho** (MissJBower) **4-10-7**(5) STaylor (reminders 3rd: lost tch 5th) 13	7	66/1	21	—
1339[5]	**Ernest William (IRE) (72)** (GAHubbard) **4-10-9**(3) KGaule (hld up: hdwy & prom after 4th: wknd after 3 out)...¾	8	25/1	20	—
1296[18]	**Karena's Prince** (MrsSJSmith) **4-10-12** RichardGuest (prom to 5th: t.o) ....dist	9	33/1	—	—
	Dougal (BSRothwell) **5-10-12** RSupple (bit bkwd: chsd ldrs to 4th: sn t.o: p.u bef 2 out)....	P	50/1	—	—
			(SP 122.3%)	**10 Rn**	

4m 32.1 (29.10) CSF £4.83 TOTE £4.00: £2.20 £1.00 £4.60 (£2.00) Trio £7.30 OWNER Mr G. E. Shouler (MALTON) BRED Mrs Trisha Dunbar
OFFICIAL EXPLANATION **Dougal: lost his action, but subsequently appeared sound.**
1504* Good Vibes, at his first attempt on soft ground, revelled in it and won his first hurdle race in really useful style. He looks one to keep on the right side. (11/4: 7/4-3/1)
Alzulu (IRE) looked fit enough, but proved a shade disappointing when the pressure was on. He is obviously a stuffy individual who needs a race or two to put him right. (8/13)
September Breeze (IRE), who has changed stables, put in her best effort to date and ought to be able to pick up a race on this showing. (25/1)
1536 Dark Phoenix (IRE), who ran reasonably, was not over-punished when beaten and should come on for the experience. (10/1)
Ferrers showed up well, but this quite testing ground found him out from the third last. (14/1: op 7/1)

1778 ALEXANDRA MOTORS H'CAP CHASE (0-110) (5-Y.O+) (Class E)
2-00 (2-01) **3m 4f 110y (21 fncs)** £3,413.25 (£1,026.00: £495.50: £230.25) GOING: 0.00 sec per fur (G)

	Horse	Pos	SP	RR	SF
1307*	**Ivy House (IRE) (99)** (JJO'Neill) **8-10-12**(5) RMcGrath (lw: hld up & bhd: blnd 13th: hdwy 5 out: led 3 out: styd on u.p)....—	1	9/4 1	110	—
1420*	**Woodlands Boy (IRE) (100)** (RCurtis) **8-11-1**(3) FLeahy (in tch: effrt 15th: sn ev ch: outpcd 3 out: kpt on wl appr last)....5	2	10/1	108	—
1209[4]	**Sparrow Hall (92)** (JGFitzGerald) **9-10-10** PNiven (w ldrs: led 15th to 5 out: r.o one pce) 3	3	14/1	98	—
1338[3]	**Celtic Silver (93)** (MrsSJSmith) **8-10-11** RichardGuest (in tch: blnd 14th & sn outpcd: hdwy & prom 4 out: one pce fr next)....3	4	15/2 3	97	—
1293[4]	**Pennine Pride (93)** (MDHammond) **9-10-11** RGarritty (cl up tl wknd 5 out)....5	5	15/2 3	94	—
1008*	**Sprowston Boy (82)** (MCChapman) **13-10-0** WWorthington (bhd: effrt 15th: sn btn)....22	6	16/1	70	—
1293[3]	**Holy Sting (IRE) (95)** (NATwiston-Davies) **7-10-13b** CMaude (lw: hmpd & b.d bnd appr 7th)....	B	4/1 2	—	—
1313[5]	**Cool Weather (IRE) (82)** (PCheesbrough) **8-10-0b1** ASSmith (in tch: hdwy to chal 15th: led 5 out tl hdd & fell 3 out)....	F	25/1	—	—
1293[10]	**Howcleuch (103)** (JKMOliver) **9-11-7** BStorey (in tch tl p.u lame bef 10th)....	P	16/1	—	—
1209*	**Griffins Bar (85)** (MrsPSly) **8-10-3** RMarley (led to 15th: sn wknd: p.u bef 3 out)....	P	10/1	—	—
1562[7]	**Arrange A Game (82)** (MissJBower) **9-9-9**(5) STaylor (rel to s: t.o whn ref 4 out)....	R	50/1	—	—
1307[5]	**Scrabo View (IRE) (95)** (PBeaumont) **8-10-13b** RSupple (blnd & uns rdr 2nd)....	U	20/1	—	—
			(SP 121.5%)	**12 Rn**	

7m 54.4 CSF £24.25 CT £244.58 TOTE £3.10: £2.00 £5.30 £2.40 (£21.80) Trio £224.50; £221.35 to Sandown 7/12/96 OWNER Mrs L. R. Joughin (PENRITH) BRED Miss Penny Downes
LONG HANDICAP Cool Weather (IRE) 9-10 Arrange A Game 8-12 Sprowston Boy 9-13
OFFICIAL EXPLANATION **Arrange A Game: bled from the nose.**
1307* Ivy House (IRE) cruised round out the back on the bridle, despite one bad mistake. After leading in the home straight, he did not exactly sprint away, but always had the edge on his rivals. (9/4)
1420* Woodlands Boy (IRE) just stays and stays and kept doing that, but never quickly enough to really trouble the winner. (10/1)
1209 Sparrow Hall is off a reasonable mark and is running well, but is short of a change of gear. (14/1: op 8/1)
1338 Celtic Silver would have preferred faster ground, but still ran a sound race and deserves better. (15/2)
1293 Pennine Pride, slow but sure, was left wanting for pace over the last five fences. (15/2)
1008* Sprowston Boy always found this too competitive. (16/1)
1293 Holy Sting (IRE) had the testing conditions he likes, but was brought down on the very sharp bend into the back straight in the early stages. (4/1)
1313 Cool Weather (IRE), in blinkers for the first time, took a serious interest, but had just been collared when coming to grief three out. (25/1)

1779 CLUGSTON H'CAP HURDLE (0-120) (4-Y.O+) (Class D)
2-30 (2-32) **2m 1f 110y (8 hdls)** £2,945.00 (£820.00: £395.00) GOING: 1.09 sec per fur (HY)

	Horse	Pos	SP	RR	SF
1123*	**Centaur Express (113)** (AStreeter) **4-11-12** TEley (lw: mde all: hld on wl fr 2 out) ....—	1	4/5 1	95	22
1542[3]	**Shers Delight (IRE) (87)** (OBrennan) **6-10-0** MBrennan (a.p: ev ch fr 4th: hrd rdn whn mstke last: no ex)....2	2	7/1 3	67	—
1630[4]	**Colorful Ambition (106)** (MrsASwinbank) **6-11-5** JRailton (lw: hld up: hdwy ½-wy: effrt after 3 out: snbtn) 18	3	5/1 2	70	—
1439[6]	**Innocent George (93)** (MissLCSiddall) **7-10-6** RSupple (chsd ldrs: rdn along fr 5th: no imp after) 2½	4	10/1	54	—
1342[7]	**Merilena (IRE) (93)** (GAHubbard) **6-9-13**(7)ow6 NRossiter (prom to 5th: sn outpcd) ....nk	5	20/1	54	—
	New Inn (115) (SGollings) **5-11-11**(3) KGaule (bit bkwd: chsd ldrs tl rdn & wknd fr 3 out) 1¼	6	7/1 3	75	2
	Fred's Delight (IRE) (87) (MrsVAAconley) **5-10-0** PMcLoughlin (bit bkwd: lost tch 4th: sn t.o) ....dist	7	40/1	—	—
			(SP 113.5%)	**7 Rn**	

4m 34.0 (31.00) CSF £6.81 TOTE £1.80: £1.40 £2.00 (£4.00) OWNER Centaur Racing (HEDNESFORD) BRED John Burt and Peter Gordon Partnership
LONG HANDICAP Fred's Delight (IRE) 9-5
1123* Centaur Express loves testing ground and, although shooting up the handicap, was always too determined for this lot. (4/5: evens-11/10)
1542 Shers Delight (IRE), still without the visor, ran well, only to find the winner too tough from the second last. (7/1)
1630 Colorful Ambition has always shown a preference for faster ground, but this was not a bad effort. He will find his mark before long. (5/1)
1439 Innocent George was always struggling in this soft ground and was left behind from the fourth last. (10/1)
Merilena (IRE) had her limitations exposed some way from home. (20/1)
New Inn needed this and should do better in due course. (7/1)

1780 U.K. HYGIENE NOVICES' CHASE (5-Y.O+) (Class E)
3-00 (3-00) **2m 1f 110y (12 fncs)** £3,299.50 (£991.00: £478.00: £221.50) GOING: 1.09 sec per fur (HY)

	Horse	Pos	SP	RR	SF
1563*	**Mister Drum (IRE)** (MJWilkinson) **7-11-5** RSupple (j.rt: mde all: clr fr 3 out)....—	1	Evens 1	114	23
1644[5]	**Bold Boss** (GMMoore) **7-10-12** BStorey (lw: hdwy & prom 5th: ev ch 4 out: outpcd & hung rt whn blnd next: no imp after)....9	2	9/1 3	99	8

				SP	RR	SF
1576^{U}	**Golden Hello** (TDEasterby) **5-11-5** PNiven (lw: blnd 1st: bhd: hung rt most of wy: sme hdwy whn hmpd 3 out: no imp)	1	**3**	9/2^{2}	105	14
1576^{F}	**Fenwick's Brother** (MrsSJSmith) **6-10-5**(7) RWilkinson (bhd: sme hdwy fr 4 out: n.d)	13	**4**	40/1	86	—
1576^{F}	**Fair Ally** (MESowersby) **6-10-12** DParker (prom to 6th: sn wknd)	11	**5**	25/1	76	—
1188^{4}	**Thursday Night (IRE)** (JGFitzGerald) **5-10-12** ADobbin (trckd ldrs: ev ch 4 out: disp 2nd & rdn whn fell 3 out)	.	**F**	9/1^{3}	—	—
1576^{2}	**Uk Hygiene (IRE) (80)** (MDHammond) **6-10-12** RGarritty (lw: chsd ldrs tl lost pl 8th: p.u bef 3 out)		**P**	11/1	—	—
1525^{F}	**Jack Doyle (IRE)** (JJO'Neill) **5-10-12** RichardGuest (trckd ldrs tl wknd appr 4 out: p.u bef next)		**P**	9/2^{2}	—	—
1525^{R}	**Cardinal Sinner (IRE) (56)** (JWade) **7-10-12** ASSmith (mstkes: lost tch 5th: wl t.o whn p.u bef 8th)		**P**	50/1	—	—
				(SP 122.9%)		**9 Rn**

4m 44.7 (29.70) CSF £11.33 TOTE £2.20: £1.10 £2.40 £1.80 (£6.80) Trio £6.30 OWNER Mr Malcolm Batchelor (BANBURY) BRED David Mooney

1563* Mister Drum (IRE), despite going to his right as usual, really attacked his fences and had it sewn up from the third last. (Evens)

1644 Bold Boss put in a determined effort after his unlucky run last time, but just found the winner too good and was tired over the last three fences. (9/1: op 6/1)

1576 Golden Hello, always hanging right, looks to have a problem and being hampered three out made little difference. (9/2: op 3/1)

424 Fenwick's Brother showed a little here and may be improving slightly. (40/1)

1188 Thursday Night (IRE) put in a promising first run over fences. Although not that far off, he looked to be tiring when the winner jumped across him, putting him off, and on the floor, three out. (9/1)

1576 Uk Hygiene (IRE) was found out on this soft ground. (11/1: 8/1-12/1)

1525 Jack Doyle (IRE) (9/2: op 3/1)

1781 'CHRISTMAS IS COMING' INTERMEDIATE CLAIMING N.H. FLAT RACE (4, 5 & 6-Y.O) (Class H)

3-30 (3-30) **2m 1f 110y** £1,217.00 (£337.00: £161.00)

				SP	RR	SF
	The Lady Captain (DTThom) **4-10-1**(3) KGaule (trckd ldrs: racd wd: led 2f out: drvn clr fnl f)	—	**1**	8/1	46 f	—
14317^{7}	**Sprig Muslin** (DRGandolfo) **4-10-1v¹**(5) SophieMitchell (led to 2f out: kpt on)	3	**2**	11/2	45 f	—
1303*	**Poppy's Dream** (JWharton) **6-10-7**(5) MrRThornton (lw: chsd ldrs: drvn 6f out: ev ch 4f out: one pce)	1¾	**3**	6/4^{1}	50 f	—
	Push On Polly (IRE) (JParkes) **6-10-7**(3) PMidgley (bkwd: bhd tl styd on fnl 4f)	17	**4**	10/1	32 f	—
	Game Drive (IRE) (KAMorgan) **4-10-8**(3) ECallaghan (outpcd ½-wy: sn lost pl: styd on fnl 3f)	5	**5**	4/1^{2}	29 f	—
1362^{6}	**Air Bridge** (RMWhitaker) **4-11-0**(5) DJKavanagh (lw: trckd ldrs tl wknd over 4f out)	12	**6**	9/2^{3}	26 f	—
1362^{19}	**Movisa** (WJSmith) **6-9-9**(5) STaylor (wl bhd fr ½-wy)	26	**7**	20/1	—	—
1033^{5}	**Phar Enough (IRE)** (JGFitzGerald) **4-11-6**(3) FLeahy (prom tl outpcd ½-wy: sn wl bhd)	1¼	**8**	11/2	5 f	—
	Dont Tell Marie (TJCarr) **6-9-12**(7)ow3 TJComerford (dwlt: a bhd: t.o)	dist	**9**	14/1	—	—
				(SP 140.6%)		**9 Rn**

4m 38.4 CSF £57.17 TOTE £11.40: £2.90 £2.80 £1.10 (£24.60) Trio £48.20 OWNER Mr D. T. Thom (NEWMARKET) BRED A. W. K. Merriam

The Lady Captain spent most of the race on the bridle but, when off it, she took time to respond. To give her credit though, she did keep on well at the finish. (8/1)

Sprig Muslin tried to gallop her rivals into the ground and almost succeeded. When things are at their most testing, she comes into her own. (11/2: 7/2-6/1)

1303* Poppy's Dream found this ground softer than she prefers, but she did keep on in the closing stages after looking in trouble a long way out. (6/4: tchd 5/2)

Push On Polly (IRE) needed this and, in the circumstances, ran reasonably. (10/1)

1362 Air Bridge, who ran well in a good race last time, was most disappointing here and may well have a problem. (9/2: 8/1-4/1)

T/Plpt: £16.60 (574.92 Tckts). T/Qdpt: £4.10 (198.07 Tckts). AA

1568-CHEPSTOW (L-H) (Chases Good to soft, Hdles Soft)
Saturday December 7th

WEATHER: overcast

1782 DECEMBER MAIDEN HURDLE (I) (4-Y.O+) (Class D)

12-45 (12-46) **2m 110y (8 hdls)** £2,693.50 (£808.00: £389.00: £179.50) GOING: 0.96 sec per fur (S)

				SP	RR	SF
1317^{5}	**Tompetoo (IRE)** (NATwiston-Davies) **5-11-5** CMaude (chsd ldr: led 3rd: rdn appr 3 out: sn clr: r.o wl)	—	**1**	5/2^{2}	78	19
	Three Farthings (JABOld) **6-11-5** GUpton (bit bkwd: hld up: chsd wnr fr 4th: no imp fr 3 out)	10	**2**	9/4^{1}	68	9
	Dannicus (NMBabbage) **5-11-5** VSlattery (plld hrd: prom tl lost pl after 4th: rallied appr 4 out: one pce fr 3 out)	9	**3**	13/2	60	1
1424^{3}	**Mullintor (IRE)** (RRowe) **5-11-5** DO'Sullivan (no hdwy fr 4 out)	20	**4**	10/1	40	—
	Reimei (RAkehurst) **7-11-5** APMcCoy (blnd 1st: sn prom: wknd 3 out: 4th & no ch whn blnd 2 out)	11	**5**	100/30^{3}	30	—
1375^{8}	**Kumari King (IRE) (74)** (AWCarroll) **6-11-5** WMarston (wl bhd fr 4th: t.o)	22	**6**	66/1	8	—
	Stevie's Wonder (IRE) (BJLlewellyn) **6-11-5** MrJLLlewellyn (nt j.w: plld hrd: led tl mstke 3rd: wknd after 4th: t.o)	1¼	**7**	33/1	7	—
	Kevasingo (JLSpearing) **4-11-5** DBridgwater (hld up & bhd: mstke 3rd: gd hdwy after 4th: hit 4 out: wknd qckly: t.o)	hd	**8**	33/1	7	—
	Southernhay Boy (MrsSDWilliams) **5-11-5** SMcNeill (bkwd: hld up: hdwy appr 4th: wknd appr 4 out: t.o)	¾	**9**	11/1	6	—
				(SP 120.6%)		**9 Rn**

4m 15.3 (26.30) CSF £8.68 TOTE £3.90: £1.10 £1.60 £2.20 (£6.50) Trio £14.00 OWNER Tom Pettifer Ltd (CHELTENHAM) BRED Mrs C. Mernagh

1317 Tompetoo (IRE), again showing a liking for testing ground, proved far too good for the runner-up from the third last. (5/2)

Three Farthings, who won a bumper on heavy ground at Newton Abbot in March, was making his hurdling debut. Getting no change out of the winner from the third last, this half-brother to Simpson may appreciate further. (9/4)

Dannicus showed promise on his previous outing at Cheltenham in April, but ran too freely early on here. (13/2)

1424 Mullintor (IRE) found this more competitive than Plumpton, but at least his hurdling seemed better. (10/1: op 11/2)

Reimei did not handle the stamina-sapping conditions and was out on his feet when scrambling over the penultimate flight. (100/30: 2/1-7/2)

1783 TIMBER TOPPERS H'CAP HURDLE (0-140) (4-Y.O+) (Class B)

1-15 (1-16) **2m 4f 110y (11 hdls)** £4,935.50 (£1,484.00: £717.00: £333.50) GOING: 0.96 sec per fur (S)

Form	Horse	Dist	Pos	SP	RR	SF
1636^{4}	**Cadougold (FR) (123)** (MCPipe) **5-10-13** APMcCoy (hld up: hdwy 6th: led on bit 2 out: v.easily)	—	1	$4/1^{3}$	105	60
1429*	**Sparkling Yasmin (125)** (PJHobbs) **4-10-10**(5) DJKavanagh (led to 2 out: no ch w wnr)	3	2	$7/2^{2}$	105	60
1553*	**Nick the Beak (IRE) (110)** (JohnUpson) **7-9-7**(7) GSupple (hld up: hdwy 5th: one pce fr 2 out)	2	3	9/1	88	43
1416^{5}	**Fourth in Line (IRE) (128)** (MJWilkinson) **8-11-4** WMarston (hld up: mstke 1st: hdwy 6th: hrd rdn appr 3 out: sn wknd)	23	4	16/1	88	43
1258^{10}	**Meditator (117)** (APJones) **12-10-7** SMcNeill (prom: lost pl appr 5th: rallied 7th: wknd appr 4 out)	9	5	33/1	70	25
1416^{2}	**Kingdom of Shades (USA) (124)** (AndrewTurnell) **6-11-0** CMaude (prom: rdn & lost pl 7th:t.o fr 4 out: b.b.v)	23	6	$11/8^{1}$	59	14
1556^{4}	**Blazer Moriniere (FR) (138)** (PCRitchens) **7-12-0** SFox (tk keen hold: prom to 7th: t.o)	22	7	100/1	56	11
1571^{B}	**Little Gunner (118)** (RJPrice) **6-10-8** DBridgwater (hld up & plld hrd: bhd fr 5th: t.o)	29	8	11/1	13	—

(SP 112.5%) **8 Rn**

5m 7.0 (20.00) CSF £17.08 CT £105.11 TOTE £4.80: £1.70 £1.10 £1.90 (£6.80) OWNER Mr D. A. Johnson (WELLINGTON) BRED Jacques Seror

LONG HANDICAP Nick the Beak (IRE) 9-12

OFFICIAL EXPLANATION **Kingdom Of Shades (USA): bled from the nose.**

1636 Cadougold (FR) had won here twice before, but never on soft ground, although his other win came at Windsor on heavy. Appreciating the longer trip, he could be named the winner a long way out and the winning margin gives no reflection of his superiority. He can score again. (4/1)

1429* Sparkling Yasmin, raised 6lb, forced the pace over this shorter trip, but the winner was merely toying with her up the long home straight. (7/2: 5/2-4/1)

1553* Nick the Beak (IRE), although raised 8lb, was still 2lb out of the handicap in this stronger company. Despite being flattered by his proximity to the winner, there was no disgrace in this. (9/1: 6/1-10/1)

1154 Fourth in Line (IRE), who does like the mud, did not stay the extra half-mile. (16/1)

1416 Kingdom of Shades (USA) began to struggle at halfway and it subsequently turned out he had bled from the nose. (11/8)

Little Gunner (11/1: 8/1-12/1)

1784 JACK BROWN BOOKMAKER H'CAP CHASE (0-140) (5-Y.O+) (Class B)

1-45 (1-47) **3m 2f 110y (22 fncs)** £7,126.40 (£2,151.20: £1,045.60: £492.80) GOING: 0.96 sec per fur (S)

Form	Horse	Dist	Pos	SP	RR	SF
1662^{U}	**Samlee (IRE) (110)** (PJHobbs) **7-10-4** DBridgwater (hld up: gd hdwy appr 5 out: led 4 out: rdn appr 2 out: r.o wl)	—	1	9/1	117	17
	Dakyns Boy (122) (NATwiston-Davies) **11-11-2** CMaude (bkwd: hld up: lost pl appr 12th: rallied 2 out: hrd rdn & r.o flat)	2½	2	20/1	128	28
	Full of Oats (119) (MissHCKnight) **10-10-10**(3) DFortt (hld up & bhd: lft poor 3rd 4 out: styd on fr 2 out)	s.h	3	7/1	125	25
1383*	**Time Enough (IRE) (111)** (CPEBrooks) **7-10-5** SMcNeill (led to 4 out: 2nd & btn whn blnd 3 out: fin tired)	1½	4	$4/1^{2}$	116	16
	Nazzaro (125) (WGMTurner) **7-11-5b** PHolley (chsd ldr: mstke 13th: 4th & wkng whn fell 5 out)		F	14/1	—	—
1202*	**Bond Jnr (IRE) (115)** (PFNicholls) **7-10-9** APMcCoy (hld up: hdwy 12th: rdn 15th: sn wknd: t.o whn p.u bef 4 out)		P	$11/2^{3}$	—	—
1324^{2}	**Billygoat Gruff (133)** (DNicholson) **7-11-13** WMarston (hld up: hdwy appr 7th: 3rd & wkng whn j.rt, blnd & uns rdr 4 out)		U	$6/4^{1}$	—	—

(SP 109.3%) **7 Rn**

7m 8.7 (38.70) CSF £116.86 TOTE £13.50: £4.10 £8.10 (£63.20) OWNER White Lion Partnership (MINEHEAD) BRED Mrs. E. Moorhead

OFFICIAL EXPLANATION **Bond Jnr (IRE): choked.**

1287 Samlee (IRE) has won on soft ground in the past and put up a good performance to register his first win in a handicap. (9/1: 8/1-12/1)

Dakyns Boy has been dropped 18lb since his last racecourse appearance in the 1995 Scottish National. Finding his second wind in the latter stages, he had quite a hard race in getting up for second on the line, but will come on a lot for the run. (20/1)

Full of Oats, 4lb higher than when completing a hat-trick last season, was no less than 22lb up on the first of those wins. With his stamina coming into play from the second last, this would have put an edge on him. (7/1)

1383* Time Enough (IRE), raised 6lb, is a much-improved performer this season, but one could not help thinking he went off a bit too quickly for such a stamina test. (4/1)

Nazzaro had a fair bit of use made of him in pursuit of Time Enough. (14/1)

1202* Bond Jnr (IRE) did not fence as fluently as one would have liked, and his rider reported that the gelding choked. (11/2: 4/1-6/1)

1324 Billygoat Gruff, who missed last week's Hennessy because of the ground, certainly had some cut here. One of the leading fancies for the Welsh National, he will have to do a lot better than this, and his participation may even be in doubt. (6/4)

1785 REHEARSAL LIMITED H'CAP CHASE (Gd 2) (5-Y.O+) (Class A)

2-20 (2-22) **3m (18 fncs)** £18,822.00 (£7,122.60: £3,486.30: £1,589.10) GOING: 0.96 sec per fur (S)

Form	Horse	Dist	Pos	SP	RR	SF
	Belmont King (IRE) (135) (PFNicholls) **8-10-8** APMcCoy (bit bkwd: hld up: hit 2nd & 6th: hdwy 9th: led 10th: all out)	—	1	6/1	140	73
1454*	**Trying Again (145)** (DRGandolfo) **8-11-1**(3) DFortt (hld up: hdwy 7th: chsd wnr appr 3 out: rdn & r.o wl flat)	1¼	2	$4/1^{2}$	149	82
	St Mellion Fairway (IRE) (134) (DNicholson) **7-10-7** WMarston (hld up: styd on fr 2 out: nvr nrr)	11	3	$5/1^{3}$	131	64
	Mr Mulligan (IRE) (153) (NoelChance) **8-11-12** DBridgwater (bkwd: led 2nd to 4th: blnd 6th: led 7th to 10th: blnd 12th: ev ch appr 5 out: wknd 3 out)	1¼	4	$2/1^{1}$	149	82
1649^{U}	**Grange Brake (132)** (NATwiston-Davies) **10-10-5b** CMaude (led to 2nd: led 4th to 7th: wknd 13th)	3	5	10/1	126	59
	Sister Stephanie (IRE) (132) (GMMcCourt) **7-10-5** BClifford (bit bkwd: hld up: hit 10th: sn bhd: t.o)	dist	6	7/1	—	—
1173^{6}	**Terao (132)** (MCPipe) **10-10-2**(3) GHogan (bit bkwd: a bhd: t.o whn p.u bef 13th)		P	20/1	—	—

(SP 110.6%) **7 Rn**

6m 10.7 (17.70) CSF £27.29 TOTE £7.80: £3.10 £2.10 (£12.30) OWNER Mrs Billie Bond (SHEPTON MALLET) BRED Simon Lambert

LONG HANDICAP Grange Brake 9-12 Sister Stephanie (IRE) 9-10

Belmont King (IRE), bought last autumn from Ireland, missed all last season due to an injury and was running off a mark 5lb higher than when winning the Findus at Leopardstown's 1994 Christmas Meeting. Described by his trainer as as fit as he could get him at home, he did blow quite a bit after the race and has been installed as new favourite for the Welsh National. (6/1)

1454* Trying Again, up 5lb, did not get away from the final fence as quickly as the winner, but certainly seemed to get the trip and lost no caste in defeat. (4/1)

St Mellion Fairway (IRE), graduating to handicaps, loves soft ground and is now far more attractively priced than Belmont King for the Welsh National. (5/1)
Mr Mulligan (IRE) will undoubtedly strip fitter for the outing, but a couple of bad mistakes is far more of a cause for concern. (2/1: 6/4-9/4)
1649 Grange Brake, 7lb out of the handicap, could not repeat last year's rather soft victory in this event. (10/1)
Sister Stephanie (IRE), even taking into consideration that she was 9lb wrong at the weights, ran abysmally on this reappearance. (7/1)

1786 SCUDAMORE CLOTHING 0800 301301 NOVICES' (S) HURDLE (4,5,6 & 7-Y.O) (Class G)
2-50 (2-54) **2m 4f 110y (11 hdls)** £1,954.00 (£544.00: £262.00) GOING: 0.96 sec per fur (S)

				SP	RR	SF
1582U	**Ainsi Soit II (FR) (85)** (GMMcCourt) **5-10-12b** DBridgwater (chsd ldr: led appr 4 out: sn wl clr: eased flat)	—	1	5/1 3	60+	3
1425 4	**Kongies Melody** (KBishop) **5-10-7** RGreene (a.p: wnt poor 2nd appr 3 out: no ch w wnr)	16	2	25/1	43	—
1334 8	**Laura Lye (IRE) (59)** (BdeHaan) **6-10-7** GUpton (plld hrd: led & sn clr: hdd appr 4 out: wknd qckly)	9	3	20/1	36	—
1663P	**Daring Hen (IRE) (85)** (RTJuckes) **6-10-7b1** WMarston (hit 2nd: a bhd)	1	4	20/1	35	—
1419 3	**Miramare (59)** (CLPopham) **6-10-9(3)** TDascombe (prom to 7th)	1½	5	16/1	39	—
1378 6	**Catwalker (IRE) (61)** (HJMWebb) **5-10-9(3)** DFortt (a bhd: t.o)	12	6	16/1	29	—
	Tread the Boards (MCPipe) **5-10-7** APMcCoy (hdwy 6th: wknd qckly after 7th: bhd whn p.u bef 4 out)		P	2/1 1	—	—
1251 3	**Le Baron** (CREgerton) **5-10-12** CMaude (bhd whn p.u after 4 out)		P	7/2 2	—	—
905 5	**Kesanta (83)** (WGMTurner) **6-10-0(7)** JPower (plld hrd: p.u bef 5th: sddle slipped)		P	5/1 3	—	—
1552 7	**Lets Go Now (IRE) (52)** (MrsLCJewell) **6-10-12** DLeahy (prom to 6th: bhd whn rdn after 7th: t.o whn p.u bef 4 out)		P	66/1	—	—
				(SP 115.5%)	**10 Rn**	

5m 22.6 (35.60) CSF £95.91 TOTE £5.70: £1.50 £6.80 £4.10 (£100.90) Trio Not won; £193.93 to Ludlow 9/12/96 OWNER A-Men Partnership (WANTAGE) BRED Jean-Luc Henry and Claude Mayot
Bt in 5,800 gns
OFFICIAL EXPLANATION **Le Baron: the rider reported that the gelding gurgled.**
Kesanta: saddle slipped.
Ainsi Soit II (FR) was dropped into a seller for this return to hurdles and seldom can a horse have gone so far clear in such a short space of time. (5/1: 4/1-6/1)
Kongies Melody, even with such a wide margin of defeat, is still greatly flattered by her proximity to the winner. (25/1)
Laura Lye (IRE) ran too freely and paid the penalty for setting a strong gallop. (20/1)
129 Daring Hen (IRE), bought for 4,600 guineas out of Kim Bailey's stable at the Doncaster Sales, did not find the blinkers doing the trick. (20/1)
Tread the Boards (2/1: op 5/4)
1251 Le Baron (7/2: op 2/1)

1787 FLURRY KNOX NOVICES' CHASE (5-Y.O+) (Class D)
3-20 (3-27) **2m 3f 110y (16 fncs)** £4,549.00 (£1,111.00) GOING: 0.96 sec per fur (S)

				SP	RR	SF
1572*	**Or Royal (FR)** (MCPipe) **5-11-10** APMcCoy (hld up: led 11th to 5 out: led & lft clr 2 out)	—	1	5/4 1	123++	28
1521 2	**Dream Ride (IRE)** (DNicholson) **6-10-12** WMarston (hld up: hdwy 6th: mstke 10th: btn whn lft 2nd & mstke 2 out)	4	2	9/4 2	108	13
1572 2	**Super Coin (120)** (RLee) **8-10-9(3)** GHogan (chsd ldr: led 6th: mstke 7th: hdd 11th: led 5 out: hdd & fell 2 out)		F	9/4 2	—	—
	Sausalito Boy (RJSmith) **8-10-12** DBridgwater (led to 6th: 2nd whn fell 7th)		F	25/1 3	—	—
1573 12	**Saucy's Wolf** (NJHawke) **6-10-12** RGreene (fell 1st)		F	100/1	—	—
1507P	**Ashley House** (BRMillman) **7-10-7(5)** DSalter (hld up & plld hrd: hdwy 6th: wknd 10th: t.o whn p.u bef 4 out)		P	100/1	—	—
				(SP 111.8%)	**6 Rn**	

5m 19.6 (30.60) CSF £4.35 TOTE £2.10: £1.50 £1.20 (£2.60) OWNER Mr D. A. Johnson (WELLINGTON) BRED Haras du Mezeray S. A.
1572* Or Royal (FR) again proved better over the obstacles than Super Coin when the chips were down. (5/4: 4/5-11/8)
1521 Dream Ride (IRE) would only have been third had Super Coin stood up, but a small novice chase would appear there for the taking. (9/4)
1572 Super Coin had been narrowly headed when coming to grief, and may jump better on a less undulating course. (9/4)

1788 DECEMBER MAIDEN HURDLE (II) (4-Y.O+) (Class D)
3-50 (3-56) **2m 110y (8 hdls)** £2,693.50 (£808.00: £389.00: £179.50) GOING: 0.96 sec per fur (S)

				SP	RR	SF
1651P	**Bowcliffe Court (IRE)** (RAkehurst) **4-11-5** APMcCoy (hld up: hdwy 4th: led 4 out: rdn 3 out: r.o wl)	—	1	5/2 2	71	—
	Supreme Genotin (IRE) (97) (JABOld) **7-11-5** GUpton (lw: a.p: led after 4th to 5th: r.o one pce fr 2 out)	1¾	2	15/8 1	69	—
1568 8	**Drakestone (81)** (RLBrown) **5-11-5** PMcLoughlin (led tl after 4th: r.o one pce fr 2 out)	1¼	3	20/1	68	—
1427 2	**Devon Peasant (96)** (LGCottrell) **4-11-0** MrLJefford (prom tl wknd appr last)	3½	4	3/1 3	60	—
1317 10	**Snowshill Harvest (IRE)** (AndrewTurnell) **5-11-5** SMcNeill (bit bkwd: bhd fr 4th: t.o)	dist	5	9/2	—	—
	Emnala (IRE) (EAWheeler) **4-10-7(7)** MrRWakley (a bhd: t.o)	7	6	50/1	—	—
	Astral Invader (IRE) (MSSaunders) **4-11-5** AMcCabe (bit bkwd: sn bhd: t.o whn p.u bef 4 out)		P	33/1	—	—
	Prince of Prey (NJHawke) **8-11-5** WMarston (bkwd: a bhd: t.o whn p.u bef 4 out)		P	50/1	—	—
1380P	**Miss The Beat** (SMellor) **4-11-0** NMann (bit bkwd: prom to 3rd: t.o whn p.u bef 3 out)		P	66/1	—	—
				(SP 119.7%)	**9 Rn**	

4m 21.6 (32.60) CSF £7.65 TOTE £2.60: £1.30 £2.30 £3.40 (£3.60) Trio £14.70 OWNER Mr A. D. Spence (EPSOM) BRED Crest Stud Ltd
IN-FOCUS: The Handicapper will be raising a few question marks about this form because of the proximity of the third to the first two.
Bowcliffe Court (IRE), pulled up early when his saddle slipped at Newbury a week ago, was coming off the Flat in good form. Well suited by the give in the ground, he had to work pretty hard over a trip which only brought his stamina into play because of the testing conditions. (5/2: 11/10-11/4)
Supreme Genotin (IRE) kept battling away, and this Sandown bumper winner would not be inconvenienced by further on heavy ground. (15/8)
974 Drakestone seemed to run above himself in finishing so close. (20/1)
1427 Devon Peasant again appeared to have her stamina limitations exposed in testing ground. (3/1: 9/4-7/2)

T/Plpt: £1,327.90 (10.39 Tckts). T/Qdpt: £339.00 (1.95 Tckts). KH

1269-SANDOWN (R-H) (Good, Good to firm patches)
Saturday December 7th
WEATHER: overcast

1789 EWELL CHASE (5-Y.O+) (Class B)
12-50 (12-50) **3m 110y (22 fncs)** £6,872.50 (£2,080.00: £1,015.00: £482.50) GOING: 0.53 sec per fur (GS)

				SP	RR	SF
1270*	**Aardwolf** (CPEBrooks) **5-10-13** GBradley (led to 9th: led 12th to 17th: led appr 3 out: all out)	—	1	7/2 2	130	42
1637U	**Major Summit (IRE) (134)** (JTGifford) **7-11-7** PHide (chsd wnr to 9th: ev ch fr 3 out: mstke last: r.o wl)	s.h	2	11/10 1	137	50
1155F	**Hill of Tullow (IRE) (139)** (DNicholson) **7-11-10** AMaguire (lw: j.slowly 2nd: led 9th to 12th: hrd rdn 15th: led 17th tl appr 3 out: sn wknd: bhd whn blnd 2 out: t.o)	dist	3	7/2 2	—	—
1367*	**Evangelica (USA) (125)** (MCPipe) **6-11-0** RDunwoody (hld up: cl 4th whn fell 17th: rmntd: t.o)	dist	4	5/1 3	—	—

(SP 108.7%) **4 Rn**

6m 21.3 (19.30) CSF £7.45 TOTE £4.30: (£3.30) OWNER Lady Camilla Dempster (LAMBOURN) BRED Sheikh Mohammed bin Rashid al Maktoum
WEIGHT FOR AGE 5yo-1lb
1270* Aardwolf may have been tackling better opposition and taking a step up in distance, but he jumped soundly in front and made a lot of the running. Showing in front again approaching the Pond Fence, he just held on after a tussle. (7/2)
1637 Major Summit (IRE), racing on ground a bit livelier than he prefers, was just being nudged along in the back straight. Ridden to get to terms at the Pond Fence, he looked to have the measure of the winner going to the last, but a mistake there cost him a length and probably the race. Losses are only lent. (11/10: evens-6/5)
1155 Hill of Tullow (IRE), the winner of this race last year, was very disappointing and still has something to learn about jumping. (7/2: op 9/4)
1367* Evangelica (USA), racing with her tongue tied down, was bang in contention when falling six out. Remounted for fourth, three miles on fast ground is ideal for her. (5/1: 7/2-11/2)

1790 HENRY VIII NOVICES' CHASE (Gd 2) (5-Y.O+) (Class A)
1-20 (1-20) **2m (13 fncs)** £12,941.00 (£4,492.40: £2,206.20) GOING: 0.53 sec per fur (GS)

				SP	RR	SF
1452*	**Mulligan (IRE)** (DNicholson) **6-11-0** AMaguire (lw: j.w: mde virtually all: hrd rdn flat: r.o wl)	—	1	4/6 1	119+	51
1386 2	**Land Afar** (PRWebber) **9-11-0** JOsborne (lw: hld up: ev ch on bit last: rdn & r.o wl nr fin)	nk	2	9/4 2	119+	51
1511*	**Down the Fell** (HowardJohnson) **7-11-4** NWilliamson (chsd wnr: pckd 1st: ev ch 3 out: hrd rdn appr last: unable qckn)	5	3	5/1 3	118?	50

(SP 107.4%) **3 Rn**

4m 1.9 (10.90) CSF £2.32 TOTE £1.70 (£1.60) OWNER Lady Harris (TEMPLE GUITING) BRED Sandford Bloodstock Ltd
1452* Mulligan (IRE) had his first real test over fences and passed with flying colours, putting in a fine exhibition of jumping. He looks a high-class novice and will be suited by some cut. He will win again. (4/6: 8/1-4/5)
1386 Land Afar has shown many times in the past that he has to do it on the bridle and does not find much off it. He travelled supremely well and appeared to be laughing at his rivals going to the last until the winner went a couple of lengths clear of him and he temporarily came off the bit, finding nothing. To his credit, he did get going halfway up the run-in and ran on strongly, if finding the line coming just too soon. (9/4)
1511* Down the Fell was taking on two classy rivals and was tapped for toe at the last. Two and a half miles will probably be more in his favour. (5/1: op 3/1)

1791 THAMES VALLEY EGGS NOVICES' H'CAP HURDLE (4-Y.O+) (Class C)
1-55 (1-55) **2m 110y (8 hdls)** £5,576.00 (£1,688.00: £824.00: £392.00) GOING: 0.53 sec per fur (GS)

				SP	RR	SF
1317*	**Aerion (107)** (OSherwood) **5-11-11** JOsborne (a.p: rdn appr last: led flat: r.o wl)	—	1	7/4 1	89	52
1597*	**Hay Dance (96)** (PJHobbs) **5-10-11**(3) GTormey (plld hrd: hld up: led appr last tl flat: unable qckn)	1½	2	16/1	77	40
1180 2	**Wanstead (IRE) (84)** (JRJenkins) **4-10-2b** NWilliamson (chsd ldr: hrd rdn & ev ch appr last: one pce)	½	3	40/1	64	27
1125*	**El Don (105)** (MJRyan) **4-11-9** JRyan (lost pl appr 2 out: rdn appr last: r.o one pce flat)	¾	4	6/1 3	84	47
1580*	**Lady Peta (IRE) (105)** (NJHenderson) **6-11-9** MAFitzgerald (hdwy appr 2 out: rdn appr last: one pce)	1½	5	15/2	83	46
1517*	**Resist the Force (USA) (110)** (JTGifford) **6-12-0** PHide (lw: hld up: rdn appr last: one pce)	1¼	6	5/2 2	87	50
1323 4	**Bietschhorn Bard (90)** (DRGandolfo) **6-10-8** RDunwoody (hld up: mstke 2 out: sn wknd)	2	7	13/2	65	28
1283*	**Mazzini (IRE) (100)** (RRowe) **5-10-11**(7) MrPO'Keeffe (led tl appr last: sn wknd)	3	8	16/1	72	35

(SP 118.5%) **8 Rn**

4m 4.1 (13.10) CSF £26.43 CT £775.68 TOTE £2.80: £1.50 £3.00 £2.90 (£21.90) Trio £322.80 OWNER P Chamberlain, D Addiscott Partnership (UPPER LAMBOURN) BRED Mrs David Page
IN-FOCUS: **This race was run at a crawl. All the runners were on the bridle and in a heap entering the straight, and it turned into a sprint from the second last. The time was over seven seconds slower than the big handicap hurdle, and the form must be treated with caution.**
1317* Aerion is beginning to look rather useful and showed a nice turn of foot off a slow pace, beating six previous winners in the process. Connections believe he will be better with some cut. (7/4)
1597* Hay Dance took a very keen hold and was still pulling for his head turning for home. He poked a nostril in front, but was put in his place going up the hill. (16/1)
1180 Wanstead (IRE) is exposed and moderate but, in this slowly-run race, he was still there going to the last. The form surely flatters him. (40/1)
1125* El Don stayed on again up the hill, but found it all over bar the shouting. (6/1)
1580* Lady Peta (IRE) moved up sweetly approaching the second last and was almost on terms going to the final flight, before tapped for toe. (15/2)
1517* Resist the Force (USA) was very disappointing under topweight after such an impressive Ascot debut, and the slow pace may well have been against him. (5/2)

1792 MITSUBISHI SHOGUN TINGLE CREEK TROPHY CHASE (Gd 1) (5-Y.O+) (Class A)
2-30 (2-30) **2m (13 fncs)** £33,908.25 (£11,744.50: £5,747.25) GOING: 0.53 sec per fur (GS)

				SP	RR	SF
1737a*	**Sound Man (IRE)** (EJO'Grady,Ireland) **8-11-7** RDunwoody (led 3rd tl blnd bdly & hdd 3 out: rallied appr last: led last: rdn out)	—	1	10/11 1	167	71
	Viking Flagship (174) (DNicholson) **9-11-7** AMaguire (bit bkwd: chsd wnr fr 3rd: blnd 9th: lft in ld 3 out: rdn appr last: hdd last: unable qckn)	5	2	3/1 2	162	66
1509*	**Storm Alert (145)** (DNicholson) **10-11-7** NWilliamson (led tl hdd & blnd bdly 3rd: nt rcvr: t.o fr 4th)	dist	3	4/1 3	—	—

1352[3] **Lord Dorcet (IRE) (133)** (JIACharlton) **6-11-7** JOsborne (lw: 4th whn fell 3rd) .... **F** 8/1 — —
(SP 108.5%) **4 Rn**

3m 59.0 (8.00) CSF £3.76 TOTE £1.80 (£2.20) OWNER Mr David Lloyd (THURLES) BRED P. Scully in Ireland

1737a* Sound Man (IRE) followed up last year's success in this race, but only after a few scary moments. Ultimately engaged in a match with Viking Flagship, he ignored the Pond Fence and it was a wonder he stayed on his feet, although he conceded a good three lengths to his rival. Getting back on terms going to the last, he jumped into the lead over it and stormed clear on the run-in. A step up to three miles for the King George looks a big possibility. (10/11: 8/11-11/10)

Viking Flagship is not easy to get fit, so it was no surprise to see him looking rather tubby for this reappearance. Handed the advantage at the Pond Fence, he began to tire going to the last and lack of a run then took its toll. He will come on in leaps and bounds for this and will be a leading player at Cheltenham again in his bid to regain the two-mile championship crown. Of his twenty-one victories to date, only two have come before the turn of the year. (3/1: 2/1-100/30)

1509* Storm Alert set the pace, but made an almighty blunder at the third and could never recover. (4/1)

1352 Lord Dorcet (IRE) (8/1: 14/1-6/1)

1793 WILLIAM HILL H'CAP HURDLE (0-150) (4-Y.O+) (Class B)

3-05 (3-09) **2m 110y (8 hdls)** £35,316.00 (£10,728.00: £5,264.00: £2,532.00) GOING: 0.53 sec per fur (GS)

				SP	RR	SF
1365[5]	**Make a Stand (123)** (MCPipe) **5-10-5**(3) GTormey (lw: mde all: clr 2nd: hrd rdn appr last: r.o wl)	—	**1**	9/1	105	70
1512[2]	**Master Beveled (132)** (PDEvans) **6-11-3** GBradley (lw: hdwy 3 out: chsd wnr appr last: blnd last: r.o)	2	**2**	20/1	112	77
1752a[7]	**Tidjani (IRE) (115)** (FBerry,Ireland) **4-10-0** JRKavanagh (rdn appr 2 out: hdwy appr last: r.o one pce)	9	**3**	50/1	86	51
1137*	**Silver Groom (IRE) (137)** (RAkehurst) **6-11-3**(5) SRyan (rdn & hdwy after 3 out: chsd wnr appr 2 out tl appr last: sn wknd)	1¾	**4**	5/1[3]	107	72
1267*	**Direct Route (IRE) (133)** (HowardJohnson) **5-11-4** NWilliamson (rdn & hdwy appr 2 out: sn wknd)	3	**5**	9/1	100	65
1365[3]	**Barna Boy (IRE) (133)** (NJHenderson) **8-11-4** MAFitzgerald (lw: hld up: chsd wnr 3 out tl appr 2 out:sn wknd)	¾	**6**	16/1	99	64
1759a[6]	**Mystical City (IRE) (139)** (WPMullins,Ireland) **6-11-7**(3) DJCasey (nvr nr to chal)	1¼	**7**	16/1	104	69
1267[2]	**Urban Dancing (USA) (115)** (BEllison) **7-10-0** GCahill (lw: prom to 3 out)	hd	**8**	20/1	80	45
	Embellished (IRE) (133) (NMeade,Ireland) **4-11-4** RHughes (nvr nrr)	3	**9**	9/2[2]	95	60
	Flying Instructor (124) (PRWebber) **6-10-9** RBellamy (lw: a bhd)	8	**10**	12/1	78	43
1288[5]	**Eskimo Nel (IRE) (137)** (JLSpearing) **5-11-8** AMaguire (bhd fr 3 out)	4	**11**	10/1	87	52
1567*	**Teinein (FR) (137)** (CaptTAForster) **5-11-8** RDunwoody (rdn & hdwy appr 2 out: sn wknd)	1¾	**12**	11/4[1]	85	50
1510[2]	**Charming Girl (USA) (129)** (OSherwood) **5-11-0** JOsborne (a bhd)	9	**13**	12/1	69	34
1365[8]	**Dreams End (136)** (PBowen) **8-11-7** PHide (lw: prom to 3 out)	¾	**14**	20/1	75	40
1439[4]	**Nashville Star (USA) (115)** (RMathew) **5-9-11v**(3) RMassey (lw: chsd wnr to 3 out: sn wknd)	23	**15**	150/1	32	—

(SP 134.7%) **15 Rn**

3m 56.9 (5.90) CSF £169.26 CT £7,635.82 TOTE £11.60: £3.80 £3.70 £8.40 (£106.10) Trio £4,056.10; £628.42 to 9/12/96 OWNER Mr P. A. Deal (WELLINGTON) BRED R. M. West

LONG HANDICAP Tidjani (IRE) 9-11 Urban Dancing (USA) 9-13 Nashville Star (USA) 8-13

IN-FOCUS: **Glenn Tormey gave the winner a superb ride, but it came as something of a surprise that he was allowed to get away quite so far.**

1365 Make a Stand, on a course so well suited to front-runners, was able to dominate. Given a superb ride, he jumped extravagantly and forged clear with a circuit to go. The field came back to him turning out of the back straight, but his rider was only giving him a breather. Kicking on again in the straight, he was not going to be denied. (9/1)

1512 Master Beveled seems well suited by a flat track and, while this course is certainly not that, he still ran a fine race. Cruising through to take second soon after the second last, he made a bad error at the final flight and, but for that, would have finished a lot closer. (20/1)

Tidjani (IRE), 3lb out of the handicap, stayed on from the second last, but the race was already over, and the best he could do was struggle on for a moderate third. (50/1)

1137* Silver Groom (IRE) has never won off a mark as high as this. (5/1)

1267* Direct Route (IRE), 11lb higher for his two recent wins, was tackling stiffer opposition. (9/1: 6/1-10/1)

1365 Barna Boy (IRE), collared for second approaching the penultimate hurdle, was soon done with. A return to two and a half miles is required. (16/1)

1567* Teinein (FR), who has risen 16lb in the handicap for two facile wins, found this far more competitive and the ground a lot faster. As a result, he could never get in a serious blow. (11/4)

1794 DOUG BARROTT H'CAP HURDLE (0-145) (4-Y.O+) (Class B)

3-40 (3-42) **2m 6f (11 hdls)** £5,347.20 (£1,617.60: £788.80: £374.40) GOING: 0.53 sec per fur (GS)

				SP	RR	SF
719[5]	**Cokenny Boy (103)** (MrsJPitman) **11-10-6** NWilliamson (lw: chsd ldr: mstke 3 out: led appr last: rdn: r.o wl)	—	**1**	20/1	85	32
1455*	**Tim (IRE) (110)** (JRJenkins) **6-10-13** JOsborne (hdwy appr 2 out: ev ch last: unable qckn)	2½	**2**	5/2[2]	90	37
1325[4]	**Khalidi (IRE) (113)** (DRGandolfo) **7-11-2** RDunwoody (led tl appr last: one pce)	4	**3**	100/30[3]	90	37
1127[2]	**Tara Rambler (IRE) (119)** (MissSEHall) **7-11-8** AMaguire (lw: hld up: rdn appr 2 out: wknd flat)	6	**4**	10/11[1]	92	39
1647[11]	**Dark Honey (121)** (SDow) **11-11-10** ADicken (lw: bhd fr 8th)	13	**5**	16/1	85	32

(SP 114.7%) **5 Rn**

5m 31.2 (18.20) CSF £65.03 TOTE £15.70: £2.60 £1.70 (£18.40) OWNER Mr S. D. Hemstock (UPPER LAMBOURN) BRED W. McKenzie

Cokenny Boy was very disappointing over fences last season but, reverting to hurdles for the first time since 1994, bounced back to form off a mark of just 103 - his last hurdle win in 1992 came off 129. (20/1)

1455* Tim (IRE), 6lb higher for his comfortable win at Kempton recently, is well suited by a sound surface but found the rise in the handicap stopping him up the hill. (5/2: 7/4-11/4)

1325 Khalidi (IRE) took the field along at a very moderate pace but, collared approaching the final flight, was tapped for toe. (100/30)

1127 Tara Rambler (IRE) was most disappointing and the slow pace may have been against him. (10/11: evens-6/5)

Dark Honey appears on the downgrade. (16/1)

T/Plpt: £1,384.50 (14.21 Tckts). T/Qdpt: £177.50 (8.54 Tckts). AK

1536-TOWCESTER (R-H) (Chases Good, Hdles Good to soft)
Saturday December 7th
WEATHER: overcast & misty

1795 E.B.F. STOKE PARK 'N.H.' (QUALIFIER) NOVICES' HURDLE (4, 5 & 6-Y.O) (Class D)
12-25 (12-30) **2m 5f (11 hdls)** £3,414.00 (£954.00: £462.00) GOING: 0.47 sec per fur (GS)

Form	Horse / details	Dist	Pos	SP	RR	SF
1541*	**Southern Nights** (KCBailey) **6-11-8** AThornton (hdwy 6th: chal & mstke 2 out: led & hit last: rdn out)	—	1	2/1[2]	87	20
1536[2]	**Fine Sir** (TThomsonJones) **6-10-12** DGallagher (w ldr: led 5th tl hdd & mstke last: one pce flat)	1¼	2	15/8[1]	76	9
	Absolutly Equiname (IRE) (MJHeaton-Ellis) **5-10-12** BPowell (bit bkwd: r.o fr 3 out: nvr able to chal)	19	3	9/1[3]	62	—
1476[8]	**Red Bronze (IRE)** (CRBarwell) **5-10-12** BFenton (blnd 1st: hdwy 6th: nvr trbld ldrs)	7	4	16/1	56	—
1438[F]	**Bridled Tern** (JMJefferson) **5-10-7** DerekByrne (trckd ldrs tl wknd appr 2 out)	1	5	12/1	51	—
	Bank Avenue (MrsJPitman) **5-10-12** RFarrant (chsd ldrs to 7th)	17	6	14/1	43	—
1412[5]	**Seymour's Double** (MrsARHewitt) **5-10-12** SWynne (prom to 6th)	5	7	33/1	39	—
	Dingle Wood (IRE) (NMLampard) **6-10-9**(3) PHenley (plld hrd: led to 5th: wknd 3 out)	16	8	10/1	27	—
1323[6]	**Sammorello (IRE)** (NATwiston-Davies) **5-10-12** CLlewellyn (prom tl rdn & wknd appr 3 out)	1	9	10/1	26	—
1580[6]	**The Millmaster (IRE)** (JohnUpson) **5-10-12** DParker (prom to 5th)	dist	10	50/1	—	—
24[11]	**Sonrisa (IRE)** (JWhite) **4-10-12** TJMurphy (bit bkwd: a bhd)	16	11	50/1	—	—
	Cottage Joker (51) (WABethell) **6-10-12** JRailton (a bhd: t.o whn p.u bef 2 out)		P	33/1	—	—
1071[U]	**Lumo (IRE)** (KSBridgwater) **5-10-12** TJenks (in tch to 6th: t.o whn p.u bef 2 out)		P	16/1	—	—
1541[P]	**Musical Hit** (PAPritchard) **5-10-12** LHarvey (a bhd: hit 7th: t.o whn p.u bef 2 out)		P	50/1	—	—
1568[P]	**Happy Jack** (PJJones) **5-10-12b**[1] MrAKinane (sn t.o: p.u bef 3 out)		P	33/1	—	—
1334[7]	**Katharine's Song (IRE)** (DMHyde) **6-10-2**(5) MrRThornton (w ldrs to 5th: t.o whn p.u bef 2 out)		P	50/1	—	—

(SP 139.1%) **16 Rn**

5m 26.2 (24.20) CSF £6.86 TOTE £3.20: £1.60 £1.10 £3.10 (£3.30) Trio £3.30 OWNER Mr J. Perriss (UPPER LAMBOURN) BRED Mrs Patricia Morgan

1541* Southern Nights needed his bridle replacing at the start, but had no saddle problems during the race this time and found too much speed for his rival from the last, despite the drop in trip. (2/1)

1536 Fine Sir does lack a turn of foot, but seems to be unlucky in often running into useful opponents. (15/8)

Absolutly Equiname (IRE), making his hurdles debut, has clearly been hard to train but, after getting outpaced, stayed on well in the home straight and appeared to have plenty left at the line. Once he steps up to three miles, he ought to be a different proposition. (9/1: 5/1-10/1)

Red Bronze (IRE), almost down at the first, never got into contention, but was staying on when most had had enough. (16/1)

1190 Bridled Tern caught the eye, travelling keenly and well on the heels of the leaders, until folding quickly on the steep climb to the second last. A rangy mare with a long stride, she may well be suited by a flatter track. (12/1: op 8/1)

Bank Avenue briefly got loose in the paddock and took a good hold going to post. He looks the sort to do well in time, although firm ground was a necessity for his sire on the Flat. (14/1)

1796 NORTHANTS 96 CONDITIONAL H'CAP HURDLE (0-95) (4-Y.O+) (Class G)
12-55 (12-57) **2m (8 hdls)** £2,094.00 (£584.00: £282.00) GOING: 0.47 sec per fur (GS)

Form	Horse / details	Dist	Pos	SP	RR	SF
1537[3]	**Sprintfayre (82)** (JELong) **8-10-12**(7) AIrvine (chsd ldr: led after 3 out: j.lft last 2: easily)	—	1	5/1[3]	68	25
	Ambidextrous (IRE) (64) (EJAlston) **4-9-10**(5) LCummins (bit bkwd: a.p: ev ch 2 out: swtchd, nt clr run & hit last: sn btn)	6	2	8/1	44	1
1375[7]	**L'Equipe (IRE) (87)** (CJMann) **6-11-10b**[1] JMagee (chsd ldrs: mstke 3rd: rdn & no ex fr 2 out)	4	3	7/2[2]	63	20
1317[12]	**Storm Tiger (IRE) (67)** (SMellor) **5-10-4** EHusband (r.o fr 3 out: nrst fin)	19	4	11/1	24	—
15[3]	**Dr Rocket (90)** (RDickin) **11-11-6**(7) XAizpuru (lw: chsd ldrs tl appr 3 out)	3	5	8/1	44	1
1633[6]	**Reflex Hammer (83)** (JohnUpson) **5-11-6** DParker (lw: plld hrd: chsd ldrs tl rdn & wknd appr 3 out)	½	6	8/1	37	—
1663[U]	**Tomal (73)** (RIngram) **4-10-10** GESmith (a bhd)	nk	7	11/4[1]	26	—
1143[7]	**Bark'n'bite (89)** (MrsMReveley) **4-11-12** GCahill (bhd: rdn 4th: hdwy next: wknd appr 2 out)	½	8	11/2	42	—
	Gymcrak Sovereign (86) (REvans) **8-11-9** PHenley (bit bkwd: led: clr appr 3rd: blnd 5th: hdd after 3 out: wknd)	3½	9	16/1	35	—

(SP 128.5%) **9 Rn**

4m 2.5 (16.50) CSF £44.69 CT £150.74 TOTE £5.60: £2.00 £4.00 £2.10 (£42.90) Trio £54.90; £32.51 to 9/12/96 OWNER Mrs O. C. Foster (WOLDINGHAM) BRED Mrs E. M. Gauvain

STEWARDS' ENQUIRY Obj to Sprintfayre by Cummins overruled.

IN-FOCUS: **winning jockey Andy Irvine was having his first ride.**

1537 Sprintfayre, whose form at the last meeting here is working out particularly well, won with a fair bit in hand, but may have been a little fortunate to keep the race as his inexperienced pilot looked to block his rival approaching the last. He can win again. (5/1)

Ambidextrous (IRE), busy on the Flat this summer, was returning after a twelve-week break. None too fluent at the second last, he was switched inside the winner going to the last, but his rival jumped across him and he made the mistake which ended his chance as a result. (8/1)

L'Equipe (IRE) certainly seemed galvanized by blinkers for the first time in this country, but does not impress with his attitude when the chips are down. (7/2)

Storm Tiger (IRE), last three out, did no more than stay on past beaten horses. (11/1: 6/1-12/1)

15 Dr Rocket is really a chaser and it is very hard to see why he is currently on a higher mark over hurdles. (8/1: op 5/1)

Reflex Hammer took a real grip early on and his best chance would come on an easier track. (8/1)

Bark'n'bite (11/2: 4/1-6/1)

1797 BET WITH THE TOTE QUALIFIER NOVICES' CHASE (5-Y.O+) (Class D)
1-25 (1-25) **2m 6f (16 fncs)** £4,305.00 (£1,290.00: £620.00: £285.00) GOING: 0.21 sec per fur (G)

Form	Horse / details	Dist	Pos	SP	RR	SF
	Credo Is King (IRE) (PRWebber) **6-11-0** AThornton (bit bkwd: prom: blnd 4th: rdn to ld 2 out: edgd rt & hld on wl flat)	—	1	12/1	110	43
1635[3]	**Wisley Wonder (IRE) (122)** (NATwiston-Davies) **6-11-0** CLlewellyn (prom tl j.slowly & lost pl 9th: rallied 11th: rdn 13th: ev ch flat: carried rt & unable qckn)	1½	2	Evens[1]	109	42
1538[6]	**Mr Pickpocket (IRE) (106)** (MissHCKnight) **8-11-0** TJMurphy (led to 3rd: led 4th tl hdd & blnd 4 out: sn rdn & one pce)	5	3	4/1[2]	105	38
	Brogeen Lady (IRE) (DRGandolfo) **6-10-9** RFarrant (led 3rd to 4th: led 4 out to 2 out: kpt on)	½	4	12/1	100	33
1318*	**Goldenswift (IRE) (94)** (GBBalding) **6-11-2** BFenton (hld up: hdwy 7th: wknd appr 2 out)	20	5	4/1[2]	92	25

1566⁵	**Stage Player (82)** (MissCJECaroe) **10-11-0** ILawrence (bhd fr 12th: mstke next)....dist	6	25/1	—	—
1447ᴮ	**Snowdon Lily** (PRWebber) **5-10-6**(3) EHusband (a bhd).......	7	50/1	—	—
	Big Archie (MrsAJBowlby) **6-11-0** BPowell (bit bkwd: fell 1st).......	F	9/1 3	—	—
1646ᴾ	**Proud Toby (IRE)** (GBBalding) **6-11-0** JRailton (bkwd: mstke 6th: sn bhd: t.o whn p.u bef 3 out).......	P	25/1	—	—
1536⁶	**Gemma's Wager (IRE)** (MarkCampion) **6-10-9** LHarvey (blnd & uns rdr 3rd).......	U	50/1	—	—
			(SP 127.0%) **10 Rn**		

5m 39.6 (10.60) CSF £25.63 TOTE £15.10: £2.40 £1.40 £2.10 (£13.30) Trio £35.30 OWNER Mr G. L. Porter (BANBURY) BRED Robert McCarthy

Credo Is King (IRE), the winner of an Irish Point on his latest outing, is a rangy gelding and did look likely to come on for the outing. He jumped well, apart from a mistake at the first ditch, from which his pilot did well to sit tight, and he proved very resolute, finding more when looking likely to be caught from the last. (12/1: 10/1-16/1)
1635 Wisley Wonder (IRE) again ruined his chance by almost refusing at the tricky downhill fence, this time not the open ditch, but the one after. He had the class to get back into the race and looked the winner after the faster jump at the last, but could not get past that rival. The fact that he was carried across the course probably made no difference to the outcome. (Evens)
1538 Mr Pickpocket (IRE) had already been headed when making his mistake, and simply plugged on from that point. He really needs the ground softer to slow rivals down. (4/1)
Brogeen Lady (IRE), an Irish pointer trying regulation fences for the first time, is not over-big, but jumped soundly, and should win races. (12/1: op 6/1)
1318* Goldenswift (IRE), found out by her penalty, was taking lengths out of many of these at the fences and should continue to win her share. (4/1)

1798 PATTISHALL H'CAP HURDLE (0-115) (4-Y.O+) (Class E)
1-55 (1-56) **3m (12 hdls)** £2,547.50 (£710.00: £342.50) GOING: 0.47 sec per fur (GS)

			SP	RR	SF
971*	**Snow Board (86)** (MrsMerritaJones) **7-10-2**ow2 DerekByrne (hld up: hdwy appr 8th: chal last: sn led: rdn & r.o wl)....—	1	5/1 2	67	—
1418³	**Ehtefaal (USA) (87)** (JSKing) **5-10-3** TJMurphy (lw: hdwy 9th: led last: sn hdd & no ex)....2	2	10/1	67	—
861²	**Able Player (USA) (86)** (KJDrewry) **9-10-2** MSharratt (hdwy 7th: led 2 out: hdd last: one pce)....½	3	14/1	65	—
1571ᶠ	**Oatis Rose (97)** (MSheppard) **6-10-8**(5) MrRThornton (a.p: led 9th to 2 out: sn btn)....3	4	6/1 3	74	—
1197*	**Kendal Cavalier (102)** (GBBalding) **6-11-4** BFenton (trckd ldrs: rdn appr 2 out: sn wknd)....8	5	7/2 1	74	—
1586¹⁰	**Strokesaver (IRE) (93)** (CPEBrooks) **6-10-9** DGallagher (hdwy 7th: no imp fr 3 out)....8	6	12/1	60	—
	Grunge (IRE) (87) (DJGMurraySmith) **8-10-3** AThornton (lw: effrt 9th: nvr nr to chal)....6	7	10/1	50	—
1443*	**Haile Derring (112)** (NATwiston-Davies) **6-12-0** CLlewellyn (chsd ldrs to 9th)....1½	8	7/2 1	74	—
1553⁴	**Pettaugh (IRE) (92)** (GAHubbard) **8-10-5**(3) KGaule (prom: led appr 8th: hdd 9th: sn wknd)....5	9	8/1	50	—
	Ronans Glen (87) (MJWilkinson) **9-9-10**(7)ow3 DCO'Connor (a bhd)....dist	10	33/1	—	—
1372⁴	**Rubins Boy (90)** (NJHWalker) **10-10-6** RFarrant (chsd ldrs tl rdn & wknd 9th)....dist	11	20/1	—	—
1564ᴾ	**Tim Soldier (FR) (84)** (MFBarraclough) **9-10-0** AnnStokell (a bhd: t.o whn p.u bef 2 out)....	P	25/1	—	—
1372⁶	**Singlesole (86)** (MrsPSly) **11-10-2** RMarley (trckd ldr: led appr 7th: hdd appr next: sn wknd: p.u bef last)....	P	14/1	—	—
934⁴	**Summer Haven (84)** (NMLampard) **7-9-9**(5) SophieMitchell (led: mstke 4th: hdd & wknd appr 7th: sn t.o: p.u bef 3 out)....	P	33/1	—	—
			(SP 140.2%) **14 Rn**		

6m 14.7 (34.70) CSF £58.37 CT £640.61 TOTE £6.90: £2.40 £3.40 £3.70 (£72.00) Trio £68.10 OWNER Mr F. J. Sainsbury (LAMBOURN) BRED Juddmonte Farms
LONG HANDICAP Snow Board 9-13 Tim Soldier (FR) 9-12 Ronans Glen 9-7 Summer Haven 9-0
971* Snow Board improved again for this step up in trip and, after being pushed along at halfway, won from the last with a telling turn of foot. (5/1: op 3/1)
1418 Ehtefaal (USA) looked in trouble at the top of the hill, but kept staying on, and touched down with the narrowest of advantages at the last, only to be quickly outpaced. This trip suits him and his turn can not be far away. (10/1)
861 Able Player (USA) again ran well, but has been a hard horse to place in recent times, with only one win in his last thirty races. (14/1: op 8/1)
1429 Oatis Rose is rather small and her best effort came under minimum weight, but her stamina appeared to run out on this occasion. (6/1: op 4/1)
1197* Kendal Cavalier certainly looks the part but, although his stamina looked assured, the stiff climb from the third last soon found him out. (7/2)
Strokesaver (IRE) rather ran in snatches and probably was not at home on the track, as he lost ground from the home turn on bothcircuits. (12/1)
Grunge (IRE) (10/1: 8/1-12/1)
1372 Singlesole (14/1: 8/1-16/1)

1799 ALDERTON H'CAP CHASE (0-130) (5-Y.O+) (Class C)
2-25 (2-25) **3m 1f (18 fncs)** £5,150.00 (£1,550.00: £750.00: £350.00) GOING: 0.21 sec per fur (G)

			SP	RR	SF
1175ᴾ	**Harwell Lad (IRE) (120)** (RHAlner) **7-11-4** MrRNuttall (j.w: led tl appr last: sn led again: rdn & r.o gamely)....—	1	14/1	130	51
1540³	**Really a Rascal (105)** (DRGandolfo) **9-10-3** RFarrant (lw: blnd 1st: hit 7th: hdwy 11th: led appr last: sn hdd & unable qckn)....2	2	8/1	114	35
1324³	**King Lucifer (IRE) (130)** (DNicholson) **7-11-9**(5) MrRThornton (lw: pushed along & hdwy 7th: ev ch 2 out: sn rdn & one pce)....2½	3	4/1 2	137	58
1089²	**Court Melody (IRE) (117)** (PFNicholls) **8-11-1b** BPowell (hit 2nd: chsd ldrs: blnd 10th: one pce fr 3 out)....20	4	7/1 3	111	32
1279²	**Rectory Garden (IRE) (113)** (CaptTAForster) **7-10-11** AThornton (prom to 13th)....2½	5	3/1 1	106	27
	Chief Rager (104) (NATwiston-Davies) **7-10-2** CLlewellyn (prom: rdn 11th: sn wknd)....1¾	6	8/1	96	17
1540⁶	**Makes Me Goosey (IRE) (102)** (MrsIMcKie) **8-10-0** LHarvey (chsd ldrs: rdn 11th: wknd next)....11	7	14/1	87	8
957⁷	**Woodlands Genhire (102)** (PAPritchard) **11-10-0** TJMurphy (mstke 6th: sn bhd: t.o)....dist	8	50/1	—	—
1293²	**Ubu Val (FR) (120)** (WABethell) **10-11-4** JRailton (prom to 6th: sn lost pl: t.o whn p.u bef 2 out)....	P	3/1 1	—	—
1420⁷	**Knockaverry (IRE) (102)** (MJWilkinson) **8-10-0** ILawrence (a bhd: t.o whn p.u bef 2 out)....	P	14/1	—	—
			(SP 126.7%) **10 Rn**		

6m 25.5 (10.50) CSF £117.30 CT £499.04 TOTE £20.70: £5.70 £1.90 £1.90 (£113.70) Trio £137.80; £155.38 to Ludlow 9/12/96 OWNER Mr H. Wellstead (BLANDFORD) BRED N. J. Connors
LONG HANDICAP Woodlands Genhire 7-5 Makes Me Goosey (IRE) 9-10
STEWARDS' ENQUIRY Farrant susp. 16-17/12/96 (excessive use of whip).
OFFICIAL EXPLANATION **Harwell Lad (IRE): accounting for the apparent improvement in the gelding's form, his trainer reported that the horse is inconsistent, and when he lost interest last time out he pulled himself up.**

Harwell Lad (IRE) ended 1995 in fine style, but this year had been a fiasco until this sudden return to form. Jumping quite brilliantly, he proved the gamest of the game in a struggle, making his mulish antics all the harder to swallow. (14/1: 10/1-16/1)
1540 Really a Rascal, almost down twice in the first mile, was given time to recover. Produced going to the last, he had no more to give when the winner pulled out all the stops. (8/1)
1324 King Lucifer (IRE) was one of three in line jumping the penultimate fence, but a tired, rather slow jump was the beginning of the end. (4/1)
1089 Court Melody (IRE) made a couple of mistakes, the second at a vital time as the race was hotting up. (7/1)
1279 Rectory Garden (IRE) seemed found out by the course, which puts far more emphasis on stamina than speed. (3/1)
Chief Rager has the action of a horse who will be better suited by softer ground still, although his record to date does not reflect it. He looks short of speed and will do better over further. (8/1)
Knockaverry (IRE) (14/1: 8/1-16/1)

1800 WEATHERBYS 'STARS OF TOMORROW' STANDARD OPEN N.H. FLAT RACE (I) (4, 5 & 6-Y.O) (Class H)
3-00 (3-00) **2m** £1,301.00 (£361.00: £173.00)

	Horse / Details	Dist	Pos	SP	RR	SF
1457[11]	**Lively Encounter (IRE)** (MrsMerritaJones) **5-11-4** DerekByrne (prom: led 9f out: pushed clr appr fnl f: comf)	—	**1**	9/4[2]	71 f	—
1457[2]	**Jack Gallagher** (MissBSanders) **5-11-4** MRichards (chsd ldrs: rdn 3f out: kpt on)	9	**2**	2/1[1]	62 f	—
	Brookhampton Lane (IRE) (MrsAJBowlby) **5-11-4** BPowell (cmpt: bit bkwd: a.p: ev ch 3f out: one pce)	3	**3**	16/1	59 f	—
1289[8]	**Bavardier (IRE)** (GBBalding) **5-11-4** BFenton (bhd tl r.o wl fnl 3f)	11	**4**	8/1	48 f	—
	Clinking (MrsAJPerrett) **5-11-4** MrsAPerrett (hdwy 8f out: wknd over 2f out)	12	**5**	9/2[3]	36 f	—
	Justlikejim (JLHarris) **5-10-11**(7) MGriffiths (hdwy 5f out: nvr rchd ldrs)	1¼	**6**	20/1	35 f	—
	Pealings (IRE) (GAHubbard) **4-11-1**(3) KGaule (bit bkwd: led after 5f to 9f out: wknd 3f out)	1	**7**	12/1	34 f	—
	Northern Star (JAPickering) **5-11-4**(7) MissJWormall (led 5f: wknd 7f out)	1¼	**8**	10/1	40 f	—
	Lucrative Perk (IRE) (MissCJECaroe) **4-10-13** ILawrence (s.i.s: a bhd)	dist	**9**	16/1	—	—
	Sweet Mount (IRE) (NATwiston-Davies) **4-10-6**(7) LSuthern (prom 7f: sn wknd)	7	**10**	11/2	—	—

(SP 142.1%) **10 Rn**

3m 56.7 CSF £8.82 TOTE £3.60: £1.60 £1.80 £4.20 (£6.20) Trio £16.80 OWNER Mr F. J. Sainsbury (LAMBOURN) BRED Thomas L. Burriss
Lively Encounter (IRE), taken down quietly, again pulled for his head early on but, in front by halfway, strode away impressively once given the office in the straight. Not over-big, he nonetheless has a bright future. (9/4)
1457 Jack Gallagher, a long way in front of the winner at Kempton, is clearly flattered by that, for in a fair fight this time he was brushed aside. (2/1: 6/4-9/4)
Brookhampton Lane (IRE), a scopey, deep-girthed newcomer, shaped with some promise without really quickening when popped the question. (16/1)
Bavardier (IRE), fitter for his debut, took a good grip on the way down and was again settled at the back until making late progress. He is learning. (8/1: 6/1-9/1)
Clinking moved forward going well enough, but did not look to stay on this stiff track. (9/2: op 9/4)
Justlikejim, by a sprinter, was ridden to get the trip, but made little impression in the last half-mile. (20/1)
Pealings (IRE) (12/1: op 7/1)
Northern Star (10/1: op 6/1)
Sweet Mount (IRE) (11/2: op 7/2)

1801 WEATHERBYS 'STARS OF TOMORROW' STANDARD OPEN N.H. FLAT RACE (II) (4, 5 & 6-Y.O) (Class H)
3-35 (3-40) **2m** £1,290.50 (£358.00: £171.50)

	Horse / Details	Dist	Pos	SP	RR	SF
	Red Brook (JMJefferson) **4-11-1**(3) ECallaghan (chsd ldrs: rdn 3f out: led over 1f out: r.o)	—	**1**	10/1	54 f	—
1124[2]	**Welsh Silk** (DRGandolfo) **4-10-13**(5) SophieMitchell (a.p: rdn 3f out: kpt on fnl f)	4	**2**	3/1[2]	50 f	—
1289[7]	**Endeavour (FR)** (MJRoberts) **4-11-4** JRailton (hdwy 6f out: rdn over 2f out: no ex ins fnl f)	nk	**3**	16/1	50 f	—
	Jayfcee (MPBielby) **4-11-4** BPowell (led after 2f tl over 1f out: sn wknd)	7	**4**	33/1	43 f	—
	Jet Files (IRE) (MrsJPitman) **5-11-4** RFarrant (hdwy 4f out: wknd over 1f out)	6	**5**	9/2	37 f	—
	Quistaquay (JWMullins) **4-10-13** SCurran (nvr nrr)	hd	**6**	20/1	32 f	—
1296[4]	**The Crooked Oak** (NATwiston-Davies) **4-10-11**(7) MKeighley (led 2f: rdn & wknd over 3f out)	1½	**7**	5/2[1]	35 f	—
1013[3]	**Big Stan's Boy** (CPEBrooks) **5-10-11**(7) MBerry (lw: chsd ldrs: rdn & wknd over 2f out)	1¼	**8**	6/1	34 f	—
1431[2]	**Never In Debt** (AGHobbs) **4-11-4**(7) MrGShenkin (lw: prom 8f)	22	**9**	4/1[3]	19 f	—
	Royal Divide (IRE) (VSoane) **4-11-4** CLlewellyn (bit bkwd: uns rdr bef s: t.o fnl 7f)	dist	**10**	16/1	—	—

(SP 134.6%) **10 Rn**

4m 0.1 CSF £43.77 TOTE £12.60: £3.40 £2.80 £9.10 (£31.40) Trio £152.50; £152.58 to Ludlow 9/12/96 OWNER Dr B. H. Seal (MALTON) BRED Miss Jennifer Mellows
Red Brook, a big, rangy newcomer, is not the best of movers, but stayed on strongly in the home straight after looking short of speed coming up the hill. (10/1: op 6/1)
1124 Welsh Silk, dwarfed by the winner, stuck to his guns in the straight to take second place near the line. (3/1)
Endeavour (FR), a tall, attractive gelding by a sire whose only previous representative here was the Martin Pipe-trained Damas, is a good walker and looked likely to win as he cruised up the hill on the heels of the leaders. Once let down, he quickly went second, but could not make any impression on the winner, and his effort petered out near the finish. More will be heard of him. (16/1)
Jayfcee, the most experienced of these, did much of the donkey-work, but was tiring rapidly when headed. (33/1)
Jet Files (IRE), rather on the leg but a good mover, did not run without promise. (9/2: op 11/4)
Quistaquay, a half-sister to Embley Buoy, was last but one at the bottom of the hill before staying on past the stragglers. (20/1)
1013 Big Stan's Boy (6/1: op 3/1)
1431 Never In Debt (4/1: 3/1-6/1)
Royal Divide (IRE) unseated his rider both in the paddock and on the way to post, and looks a very hairy ride. (16/1)

T/Plpt: £89.90 (79.16 Tckts). T/Qdpt: £39.10 (10.61 Tckts). Dk

1432-WETHERBY (L-H) (Good to soft, Good patches)
Saturday December 7th

One fence omitted, Races 3 & 6 two flights omitted. Vis: poor race 6 - No time taken
WEATHER: foggy

1802 THORP ARCH NOVICES' HURDLE (4-Y.O+) (Class D)
12-40 (12-40) **2m 7f (12 hdls)** £3,178.00 (£883.00: £424.00) GOING: 0.21 sec per fur (G)

	Horse	Dist		SP	RR	SF
1290^{2}	**Ben Cruachan (IRE)** (JMJefferson) **6-11-0** RichardGuest (a.p: led 3 out: styd on wl)	—	1	$3/1^{2}$	66	—
1312^{6}	**Callernish Dan (IRE)** (MartinTodhunter) **6-10-9**(5) MichaelBrennan (led to 3 out: one pce)	7	2	16/1	61	—
1250^{5}	**Barton Ward** (SABrookshaw) **5-11-0** ADobbin (a chsng ldrs: one pce fr 3 out)	12	3	$9/1^{3}$	53	—
1412^{3}	**Ely's Harbour (IRE)** (OSherwood) **5-11-0** JAMcCarthy (in tch: rdn 4 out: no imp)	2½	4	10/1	51	—
1296^{8}	**Larkshill (IRE)** (JGFitzGerald) **5-10-11**(3) FLeahy (in tch: hdwy 4 out: wknd appr next)	2½	5	25/1	49	—
	Pilkington (IRE) (HowardJohnson) **6-11-0** ASSmith (chsd ldrs tl wknd appr 3 out)	10	6	16/1	42	—
	Celtic Duke (MDHammond) **4-11-0** RGarritty (nvr nr ldrs)	2½	7	33/1	41	—
910*	**Share Options (IRE) (101)** (TDEasterby) **5-11-6** JCallaghan (lw: trckd ldrs tl fell 4 out)		F	$13/8^{1}$	—	—
1250^{10}	**Zamorston** (NTinkler) **7-11-0** MBrennan (p.u bef 6th)		P	33/1	—	—
	Pharrambling (IRE) (MrsMReveley) **5-10-9** PNiven (t.o whn p.u bef 3 out)		P	16/1	—	—
	Cairo Prince (IRE) (JJO'Neill) **6-11-0** ARoche (mstkes: a bhd: t.o whn p.u bef 3 out)		P	10/1	—	—
1689^{P}	**Bold'n (70)** (NBMason) **9-10-7**(7) SHaworth (a bhd: wl t.o whn p.u bef 3 out)		P	100/1	—	—
1689^{P}	**Lepton (IRE)** (JWCurtis) **5-11-0** BStorey (cl up tl wknd qckly appr 4 out: p.u bef last)		P	50/1	—	—
	The Alamo (IRE) (RCollins) **5-11-0** BHarding (bit bkwd: broke down & p.u bef 8th)		P	100/1	—	—
1499^{6}	**Star Master** (LLungo) **5-11-0** MFoster (bhd: stdy hdwy appr 4 out: lost pl fr next: blnd & uns rdr last)		U	20/1	—	—

(SP 127.4%) **15 Rn**

5m 51.7 CSF £48.87 TOTE £3.60: £1.70 £4.20 £2.50 (£31.50) Trio £76.90; £76.92 to Ludlow 9/12/96 OWNER The Caledonian Racing Club (MALTON) BRED James Bagnall

STEWARDS' ENQUIRY Guest susp. 16-17/12/96 (improper use of whip).

1290 Ben Cruachan (IRE), obviously improving, stays well and that won him the day, as he certainly does not do anything quickly. (3/1)

1312 Callernish Dan (IRE), warm and edgy beforehand, ran much better this time. Going out in front, he looked very one-paced in the home straight. (16/1)

1250 Barton Ward, unlucky on his previous run, had his chances here, only to prove one-paced in the closing stages. (9/1: 6/1-10/1)

1412 Ely's Harbour (IRE), taking a big step up in distance, was struggling to keep up four out and was soon fighting a lost cause. (10/1)

Larkshill (IRE), after showing little in two bumpers, gave a glimmer of hope here, but did not seem to get home on this occasion. (25/1)

910* Share Options (IRE) was tracking the leaders and going as well as any when falling four out. (13/8: 5/2-6/4)

Cairo Prince (IRE) (10/1: op 5/1)

1803 DICK WARDEN NOVICES' CHASE (5-Y.O+) (Class D)
1-10 (1-12) **2m 4f 110y (14 fncs)** £4,107.00 (£1,236.00: £598.00: £279.00) GOING: 0.21 sec per fur (G)

	Horse	Dist		SP	RR	SF
1511^{F}	**Simply Dashing (IRE)** (TDEasterby) **5-11-10** RGarritty (lw: trckd ldrs: led 9th: r.o strly fr 4 out: easily)	—	1	$10/11^{1}$	127+	60
1691^{F}	**Niki Dee (IRE)** (PBeaumont) **6-11-0** RSupple (bit bkwd: led 2nd to 6th: lost pl 11th: stdy hdwy fr 3 out: r.o)	10	2	20/1	109	42
	River Unshion (IRE) (HowardJohnson) **6-11-0** ASSmith (plld hrd: led 6th: hit 7th: hdd 9th: one pce fr 4 out)	9	3	$12/1^{3}$	102	35
	Cattly Hang (IRE) (98) (JPLeigh) **6-11-0** ADobbin (in tch tl outpcd 9th: kpt on fr 3 out)	¾	4	33/1	102	35
	Black Brook (IRE) (MDHammond) **7-10-11**(3) MrCBonner (in tch tl outpcd fr 8th: n.d after)	16	5	50/1	89	22
1632^{2}	**Lansborough** (GRichards) **6-11-0** BHarding (lw: led to 2nd: cl up tl rdn & wknd 4 out: eased whn btn appr last)	1¼	6	$2/1^{2}$	88	21
	Sireric (IRE) (SBBell) **6-11-0** KJohnson (bit bkwd: lost tch fr 7th)	15	7	100/1	76	9
	Aslan (IRE) (JGFitzGerald) **8-11-0** BStorey (fell 2nd)		F	$12/1^{3}$	—	—
1443^{4}	**Flat Top (95)** (MWEasterby) **5-11-0** PNiven (sn wl bhd: t.o whn p.u bef 4 out)		P	20/1	—	—

(SP 116.5%) **9 Rn**

5m 14.7 (7.70) CSF £18.33 TOTE £1.80: £1.30 £2.50 £2.00 (£17.80) Trio £71.20 OWNER Mr Steve Hammond (MALTON) BRED Eastward Bloodstock Holdings Ltd

1511 Simply Dashing (IRE), none the worse for his fall last time and wearing a tongue-strap for the first time, looked very useful, and plenty more will be seen of him. (10/11: 5/4-5/6)

1691 Niki Dee (IRE), having a confidence-booster, showed a deal of promise under a tender ride and now looks one to follow. (20/1)

River Unshion (IRE), an Irish import, is a free-runner and was on edge here, but he showed enough to suggest that he will pay his way before long. (12/1: 8/1-14/1)

Cattly Hang (IRE) looks just the type for this game and put in a fair first effort over fences. Better will be seen as he gains experience. (33/1)

Black Brook (IRE), the winner of an Irish point, was just getting acclimatised here and, though he showed little, he should have learnt something. (50/1)

1632 Lansborough was a big disappointment, running out of fuel in the home straight as though something was wrong. This was certainly not his true form. (2/1)

Aslan (IRE) (12/1: 8/1-14/1)

1804 ATS H'CAP HURDLE (0-135) (4-Y.O+) (Class C)
1-40 (1-42) **2m (7 hdls)** £3,866.50 (£1,162.00: £561.00: £260.50) GOING: 0.21 sec per fur (G)

	Horse	Dist		SP	RR	SF
	Penny a Day (IRE) (128) (MrsMReveley) **6-11-10** PNiven (lw: a cl up: led 3 out: shkn up & qcknd flat: eased towards fin)	—	1	$Evens^{1}$	111+	10
1305^{5}	**Fassan (IRE) (105)** (MDHammond) **4-10-1** DBentley (in tch: effrt appr 3 out: styd on: nt pce to chal)	3	2	14/1	85	—
1510^{4}	**Kaitak (IRE) (120)** (JMCarr) **5-10-13**(3) FLeahy (a chsng ldrs: effrt 3 out: r.o one pce)	2	3	$11/2^{2}$	98	—
1512^{5}	**Elpidos (119)** (MDHammond) **4-11-1** RGarritty (hld up: effrt appr 3 out: styd on: no imp)	1¼	4	$8/1^{3}$	96	—
1441^{4}	**Mr Bureaucrat (NZ) (117)** (SABrookshaw) **7-10-13** ADobbin (a chsng ldrs: chal 3 out: wknd appr last)	hd	5	10/1	94	—
1656^{R}	**Non Vintage (IRE) (130)** (MCChapman) **5-11-12** WWorthington (outpcd & lost tch appr 3 out: sme late hdwy)	1¼	6	16/1	105	4
1125^{7}	**Dawn Mission (106)** (TDEasterby) **4-10-2** ASSmith (led to 3 out: sn outpcd)	1¼	7	16/1	80	—
1512^{F}	**Thornton Gate (127)** (TDEasterby) **7-11-9** JCallaghan (hld up & bhd: nvr nr to chal)	3½	8	10/1	98	—
1360^{P}	**Bend Sable (IRE) (110)** (FSStorey) **6-10-6** BStorey (in tch tl outpcd appr 3 out)	5	9	50/1	76	—
1656^{6}	**Jazilah (FR) (130)** (RAllan) **8-11-12** RichardGuest (cl up tl lost pl appr 4th)	11	10	33/1	85	—

	Horse	Dist	Pos	SP	RR	SF
	Elation (119) (GRichards) 4-11-1 BHarding (prom tl outpcd & lost tch 4th: n.d after)	1	11	10/1	73	—
				(SP 127.1%)		11 Rn

3m 58.7 (16.70) CSF £17.11 CT £59.64 TOTE £2.00: £1.30 £2.80 £1.90 (£9.60) Trio £40.10 OWNER Mr J. Good (SALTBURN) BRED Mrs Noeleen Roche

Penny a Day (IRE) kept his unbeaten record and did it particularly well, but his hurdling still left something to be desired. If that could be improved, there is obviously a lot more to come. (Evens)

1305 Fassan (IRE) ran well and his style of racing suggests that easier ground and a bit further might well see some improvement, and at last a victory. (14/1: 10/1-16/1)

1510 Kaitak (IRE) ran pretty well and kept staying on when looking beaten. (11/2)

1512 Elpidos keeps running consistently but, as yet, has not quite come into top form. (8/1)

Mr Bureaucrat (NZ) seems to be gradually improving, but just ran out of petrol in the closing stages. He may have just needed this. (10/1)

1271 Non Vintage (IRE), not suited by the sudden increase in pace in the home straight, only decided to run on when it was too late. He needs strongly-run events. (16/1)

1267 Thornton Gate (10/1: 8/1-12/1)

1805 'EMMERDALE' H'CAP CHASE (0-145) (5-Y.O+) (Class B)

2-10 (2-12) **2m 4f 110y (13 fncs)** £6,742.50 (£2,040.00: £995.00: £472.50) GOING: 0.21 sec per fur (G)

	Horse	Dist	Pos	SP	RR	SF
1354[U]	**The Last Fling (IRE) (118)** (MrsSJSmith) **6-10-12** RichardGuest (lw: mstke 1st: cl up: hit 9th: led appr 4 out: rdn & r.o wl flat)	—	1	11/10[1]	130	37
1520[7]	**Cumbrian Challenge (IRE) (125)** (TDEasterby) **7-11-5** RGarritty (a.p: hdwy 4 out: sn rdn: ev ch flat: r.o)	1¼	2	6/1[3]	136	43
1373[6]	**Denver Bay (119)** (JTGifford) **9-10-10**(3) LAspell (led tl appr 4 out: kpt on one pce)	7	3	4/1[2]	125	32
	Wee River (IRE) (125) (GMMoore) **7-11-5** JCallaghan (hld up: smooth hdwy appr 4 out: chsng wnr 2 out: wknd last)	2½	4	7/1	129	36
1361[5]	**All the Aces (134)** (JJO'Neill) **9-12-0** PNiven (bit bkwd: bhd: hit 8th: nvr nr to chal)	7	5	20/1	132	39
1513[F]	**Joe White (119)** (HowardJohnson) **10-10-13** ASSmith (chsd ldrs tl outpcd appr 4 out)	3	6	10/1	115	22
				(SP 108.3%)		6 Rn

5m 18.1 (11.10) CSF £7.31 TOTE £1.80: £1.30 £2.20 (£5.80) OWNER Michael Jackson Bloodstock Ltd (BINGLEY) BRED G. Stewart

1354 The Last Fling (IRE) made mistakes at the same fence on both circuits but, other than that, he did it well and had a bit more in the locker when challenged. (11/10: 11/8-evens)

1520 Cumbrian Challenge (IRE) showed his first real signs of coming back to form here and, although looking in trouble early in the straight, he kept responding well. (6/1)

1373 Denver Bay seems at his best when there is more cut in the ground, and was well tapped for toe over the last four fences. (4/1)

Wee River (IRE) showed definite signs of coming back to form and, put back over the minimum trip, will be one to be kept on the right side. (7/1: 9/2-8/1)

1361 All the Aces had another quiet run and, once he gets some real cut in the ground, better will be seen. (20/1)

1266 Joe White is useful at his best, but his stable is under a bit of a cloud and he stopped quickly entering the straight. (10/1)

1806 WHARFE H'CAP CHASE (0-145) (5-Y.O+) (Class B)

2-40 (2-41) **3m 1f (16 fncs)** £6,944.00 (£2,102.00: £1,026.00: £488.00) GOING: 0.21 sec per fur (G)

	Horse	Dist	Pos	SP	RR	SF
	Island Chief (IRE) (110) (PBeaumont) **7-10-0** RSupple (led 2nd: kpt on wl fr 3 out: comf)	—	1	4/1[2]	126+	—
1655[3]	**Ali's Alibi (114)** (MrsMReveley) **9-10-4** PNiven (bhd: effrt ½-wy: chsng ldrs 4 out: kpt on: nt pce to chal)	5	2	9/2[3]	127	—
1277[2]	**Lord Gyllene (NZ) (120)** (SABrookshaw) **8-10-10** ADobbin (lw: led 1st to 2nd: chsd wnr: kpt on u.p fr 4 ut)	hd	3	7/2[1]	133	—
1558*	**Yorkshire Gale (137)** (JTGifford) **10-11-10**(3) LAspell (lw: chsd ldrs tl wknd fr 4 out)	21	4	7/2[1]	136	—
1315[3]	**Dark Oak (113)** (JWCurtis) **10-10-3** JCallaghan (lw: led to 1st: lost tch fr ½-wy)	6	5	10/1	109	—
	Flashthecash (124) (CREgerton) **10-11-0** JAMcCarthy (prom: effrt whn blnd 11th: n.d after)	1¼	6	16/1	119	—
	Uranus Collonges (FR) (118) (JGFitzGerald) **10-10-8** RGarritty (lost tch fr ½-wy: t.o bef 4 out)		P	20/1	—	—
1655[5]	**Strong Deel (IRE) (116)** (FMurphy) **8-10-6** BHarding (p.u lame after 4th: dead)		P	12/1	—	—
	Astings (FR) (116) (JGFitzGerald) **8-10-6** WDwan (bit bkwd: bhd whn blnd & uns rdr 2nd)		U	6/1	—	—
				(SP 124.3%)		9 Rn

6m 27.4 CSF £22.75 CT £65.47 TOTE £4.40: £1.80 £1.70 £1.40 (£19.20) Trio £19.40 OWNER Mr George Dilger (BRANDSBY) BRED African Bay Syndicate

LONG HANDICAP Island Chief (IRE) 9-10

Island Chief (IRE) looks well handicapped and won this with plenty to spare. Plenty more will be seen of him. (4/1)

1655 Ali's Alibi, wearing a tongue-strap for the first time, saw his race out much better and hopefully his problem is solved. (9/2)

1277 Lord Gyllene (NZ) had his chances and kept plugging away, but was never quite good enough. This may well turn out to be a decent race. (7/2)

1558* Yorkshire Gale, racing off his highest mark to date, found this far too competitive and was left struggling over the last four fences. (7/2)

1315 Dark Oak always found this company too hot. (10/1)

Flashthecash made a real hash of the water jump and can be forgiven this. (16/1)

1807 WALSHFORD NOVICES' H'CAP HURDLE (0-105) (4-Y.O+) (Class D)

3-15 (3-16) **2m 4f 110y (8 hdls)** £3,104.50 (£862.00: £413.50) GOING: 0.21 sec per fur (G)

	Horse	Dist	Pos	SP	RR	SF
1309*	**Ela Mata (101)** (MrsASwinbank) **4-11-3**(7) BGrattan (hld up & bhd: in clr ld after 5th: blnd last: drvn out)	—	1	6/1[3]	75	—
1077*	**Spring Gale (IRE) (102)** (OSherwood) **5-11-11** JAMcCarthy (lw: a chsng ldrs: kpt on wl flat)	2½	2	7/2[2]	74	—
1152[F]	**Dont Forget Curtis (IRE) (84)** (GMMoore) **4-10-7** JCallaghan (hdwy appr 3 out: styd on: nvr able to chal)	8	3	14/1	50	—
	Spritzer (IRE) (91) (JGFitzGerald) **4-11-0** WDwan (bhd: hdwy 3 out: styd on wl towards fin)	3½	4	14/1	54	—
1161[4]	**Hotspur Street (78)** (MWEasterby) **4-10-1b[1]** BHarding (hdwy u.p appr 3 out: no imp)	s.h	5	12/1	41	—
1292[5]	**Menshaar (USA) (86)** (LLungo) **4-10-9** MFoster (nvr nrr)	9	6	14/1	42	—
1517[3]	**Take Cover (IRE) (93)** (MHTompkins) **5-11-2** ADobbin (lw: prom tl rdn & wknd appr 3 out)	3	7	7/1	47	—
1046*	**Highbeath (98)** (MrsMReveley) **5-11-7** PNiven (lw: led to 5th: wknd appr 3 out)	½	8	100/30[1]	51	—
1208[10]	**Corbleu (IRE) (77)** (SBBell) **6-10-0** KJohnson (prom to 5th)	½	9	20/1	30	—
1500[3]	**Auntie Alice (79)** (JGFitzGerald) **6-9-13**(3) FLeahy (in tch tl wknd appr 3 out)	2	10	14/1	30	—
1524[4]	**Joe Jagger (IRE) (77)** (MDHammond) **5-10-0** DBentley (nvr trbld ldrs)	2½	11	16/1	26	—
632[P]	**Anchorena (83)** (DWBarker) **4-10-6** RichardGuest (swtg: n.d)	hd	12	12/1	32	—
1640[13]	**The Other Man (IRE) (77)** (MissLCSiddall) **6-10-0** RSupple (wl bhd fr ½-wy)	2½	13	50/1	24	—
	Ski Path (77) (NBycroft) **7-10-0** ASSmith (a bhd)	9	14	50/1	17	—

				SP	RR	SF
	Brave and Tender (IRE) (77) (HowardJohnson) **7-9-9**(5) GFRyan (p.u after 4th)		P	33/1	—	—
				(SP 131.6%)		**15 Rn**

0m CSF £27.90 CT £274.54 TOTE £6.60: £3.20 £2.20 £3.10 (£14.60) Trio £96.00 OWNER Mr F. J. Sainsbury (RICHMOND) BRED Darley Stud Management Co Ltd

LONG HANDICAP Joe Jagger (IRE) 9-11 Corbleu (IRE) 9-8 The Other Man (IRE) 8-7 Brave and Tender (IRE) 9-12

1309* Ela Mata, from what could be seen in the fog, won this race by quickening clear on the home turn, but then almost threw it away by blundering badly at the final flight. (6/1: op 4/1)

1077* Spring Gale (IRE) stays and stays but, despite a valiant effort, could never make it. Longer trips will suit. (7/2)

Dont Forget Curtis (IRE) certainly appreciated this longer trip, but lacked any real turn of foot to get into contention. (14/1)

Spritzer (IRE), an Irish import having her first run in this country, showed plenty of ability. Better will be seen. (14/1)

1161 Hotspur Street had the blinkers on for the first time, but the effects were not obvious. (12/1: op 8/1)

1292 Menshaar (USA) only got going as the race was over, but does seem to be improving. (14/1)

1517 Take Cover (IRE), stepping up in distance, did not seem to see it out. (7/1)

528* Anchorena (12/1: op 8/1)

T/Plpt: £36.80 (211.79 Tckts). T/Qdpt: £13.60 (41.43 Tckts). AA

1550-FOLKESTONE (R-H) (Good to soft, Soft patches)
Monday December 9th

WEATHER: dull & misty

1808 OTTINGE HURDLE (3-Y.O) (Class E)
1-00 (1-01) **2m 1f 110y (9 hdls)** £2,427.00 (£672.00: £321.00) GOING: 0.47 sec per fur (GS)

				SP	RR	SF
1634[8]	**Red Raja** (PMitchell) **3-10-12** JOsborne (mde all: mstke 1st: clr appr last: easily)	—	1	20/1	81+	31
	Northern Fleet (MrsAJPerrett) **3-10-12** RDunwoody (lw: chsd wnr: mstke 4th: hrd rdn appr last: sn wknd)	14	2	15/8[1]	68+	18
1634[18]	**A Chef Too Far** (RRowe) **3-10-12** DO'Sullivan (lw: hdwy 3 out: rdn appr last: sn wknd)	3	3	15/2[3]	66	16
	Royal Diversion (IRE) (MCPipe) **3-10-7** APMcCoy (a.p: mstke 3 out: rdn appr last: sn wknd)	16	4	15/8[1]	46	—
	Rivers Magic (JWhite) **3-10-12** JRKavanagh (bhd fr 5th: t.o)	dist	5	14/1	—	—
1377[U]	**General Henry** (AMoore) **3-10-12** PHolley (bhd fr 4th: t.o)	18	6	66/1	—	—
	Dark Age (IRE) (RAkehurst) **3-10-12** NWilliamson (lw: plld hrd: hdwy 4th: 4th whn mstke 5th: sn wknd: t.o)	18	7	4/1[2]	—	—
				(SP 114.3%)		**7 Rn**

4m 21.1 (15.10) CSF £55.68 TOTE £21.10: £3.10 £1.10 (£42.20) OWNER Mr J. R. Ali (EPSOM) BRED J. Haine

OFFICIAL EXPLANATION **Dark Age (IRE): finished distressed.**

IN-FOCUS: **This gave Mitchell his first winner over jumps since the 1993-94 season.**

Red Raja was a revelation here, surging clear with the minimum of fuss turning for home to win doing handsprings. (20/1)

Northern Fleet won a two-mile maiden at Beverley on the Flat before finishing second to Fujiyama Crest at Ascot, and has the make and shape for this game. Left for dead by the winner in the straight, he may need further and a sound surface. (15/8)

944 A Chef Too Far, who won in the mud on the Flat, was only battling for second in the home straight, and lost that on the run-in. (15/2)

Royal Diversion (IRE), claimed out of John Dunlop's stable for £18,000 after hacking up in the mud in a Newbury claimer on the Flat at the end on October, was rather disappointing here. After travelling well to two out, she tired going to the last. (15/8: evens-2/1)

Rivers Magic (14/1: op 7/1)

Dark Age (IRE) (4/1: 3/1-9/2)

1809 STALISFIELD GREEN NOVICES' CHASE (5-Y.O+) (Class E)
1-30 (1-30) **2m (12 fncs)** £3,514.50 (£972.00: £463.50) GOING: 0.47 sec per fur (GS)

				SP	RR	SF
1596*	**Greenback (BEL)** (PJHobbs) **5-11-5** CLlewellyn (j.lft: mde virtually all: blnd 3rd: r.o wl)	—	1	8/11[1]	120+	20
1195[3]	**Sunset and Vine** (TCasey) **9-10-12** RDunwoody (chsd wnr after 3rd: ev ch 3 out: 2nd & btn whn blnd last)	11	2	10/1[3]	102?	2
1714[F]	**Minster's Madam** (JNeville) **5-10-4v**(3) TDascombe (lw: hld up: mstke 6th: blnd 7th: rdn appr 2 out: sn wknd)	8	3	11/1	89?	—
1328*	**Porphyrios (105)** (KCBailey) **5-11-5** APMcCoy (hdwy 7th: 3rd whn fell 8th)		F	5/2[2]	—	—
1505[5]	**One More Man (IRE)** (JTGifford) **5-10-12** PHide (lw: chsd wnr tl after 3rd: wknd 6th: wl bhd whn blnd bdly & uns rdr 2 out)		U	12/1	—	—
				(SP 111.6%)		**5 Rn**

4m 9.9 (17.90) CSF £7.54 TOTE £1.70: £1.80 £5.90 (£4.40) OWNER Mr Jack Joseph (MINEHEAD) BRED Patrick Madelein

1596* Greenback (BEL) continually jumped to his left and lost ground at a number of fences as a result, but had the situation in hand from the second last. (8/11)

Sunset and Vine appears to have come on in leaps and bounds for his Kempton run and showed promise. On this evidence, he can find a similar event. (10/1)

1166* Minster's Madam has gained all her wins in the mud. (11/1)

1328* Porphyrios (5/2: 6/4-11/4)

One More Man (IRE) (12/1: 8/1-14/1)

1810 MINSTER MAIDEN HURDLE (4-Y.O+) (Class F)
2-00 (2-02) **2m 6f 110y (11 hdls)** £2,411.40 (£670.40: £322.20) GOING: 0.47 sec per fur (GS)

				SP	RR	SF
1683[2]	**Dantes Cavalier (IRE)** (DRGandolfo) **6-11-5** RDunwoody (hdwy 2nd: lft in ld bnd appr 7th: drvn out)	—	1	4/6[1]	77	7
	Korbell (IRE) (PFNicholls) **7-11-0** APMcCoy (hld up: rdn 7th: chsd wnr fr 3 out: ev ch appr last: r.o)	½	2	6/1[3]	72	2
1422[3]	**Lord Rooble (IRE) (94)** (JTGifford) **5-11-5** PHide (hdwy 2 out: hrd rdn appr last: unable qckn)	10	3	11/2[2]	70	—
	Millmount (IRE) (TPMcGovern) **6-11-0b** NWilliamson (lw: a.p: led 6th tl hmpd by loose horse & hdd bnd appr 7th: hrd rdn appr last: sn wknd)	4	4	10/1	62	—
956[P]	**Hardy Breeze (IRE)** (DMGrissell) **5-11-5** JRKavanagh (hld up: rdn 8th: sn wknd)	12	5	40/1	58	—
	Mel (IRE) (RHBuckler) **6-11-5** BPowell (lw: hld up: rdn 7th: wknd 8th: t.o)	dist	6	14/1	—	—
	Alongwaydown (IRE) (DRGandolfo) **7-11-2**(3) DFortt (bit bkwd: bhd tl fell 2nd)		F	50/1	—	—
	Iades Boy (NZ) (CJMann) **5-11-5** JRailton (a bhd: t.o whn p.u bef last)		P	20/1	—	—
1289[11]	**Stellar Force (IRE)** (OSherwood) **5-11-5** JOsborne (a bhd: t.o whn p.u bef last)		P	14/1	—	—
1187[12]	**Royrace** (WMBrisbourne) **4-11-5** CLlewellyn (led to 6th: hmpd bnd appr 7th: sn wknd: t.o whn p.u bef last)		P	50/1	—	—
	Ginger Maid (MCPipe) **8-11-0** CMaude (prom to 6th: t.o whn p.u bef 3 out)		P	25/1	—	—

				SP	RR	SF
1450^{10}	**Tinker's Cuss** (APJones) **5-11-0** SCurran (prom to 5th: t.o whn p.u bef 7th)		P	50/1	—	—
	Mount Lodge (IRE) (MrsLCJewell) **5-11-5** DLeahy (a bhd: t.o whn p.u bef 7th)		P	66/1	—	—
1550^{P}	**Master Upex** (ASNeaves) **4-11-5** BFenton (a bhd: t.o whn p.u bef 8th)		P	100/1	—	—
				(SP 131.5%)	**14 Rn**	

5m 46.1 (29.10) CSF £6.37 TOTE £1.80: £1.10 £2.60 £1.60 (£6.20) Trio £5.70 OWNER Mr W. H. Dore (WANTAGE) BRED Mrs M. O'Driscoll
1683 Dantes Cavalier (IRE) appreciated the longer trip and, responding to pressure in the straight, managed to keep the persistent runner-up at bay. (4/6: op evens)
Korbell (IRE), who has won ten of her twelve completed outings in the last two seasons in point-to-points, proved a real thorn in the side of the winner in the straight and battled her heart out to the bitter end. An extremely promising debut under Rules, she should have no trouble winning and will come into her own over fences but, whichever code her trainer opts for, she will be better off over three miles. (6/1: op 5/2)
1422 Lord Rooble (IRE) was given a harder ride this time but, after taking closer order two out, failed to find another gear in the straight. (11/2: 3/1-6/1)
Millmount (IRE) looked in very good shape for this first run in over a year. Sent on with a circuit to go, a loose horse then careered in front of her, causing her to lose the advantage. Despite this, she was still not far behind entering the straight before tiring. There is a small race to be found for her. (10/1: 8/1-12/1)
Mel (IRE) (14/1: 33/1-50/1)
1289 Stellar Force (IRE) (14/1: 8/1-16/1)

1811 WHITE HORSE NOVICES' CHASE (5-Y.O+) (Class E)
2-30 (2-32) **3m 2f (19 fncs)** £3,752.50 (£1,120.00: £535.00: £242.50) GOING: 0.47 sec per fur (GS)

				SP	RR	SF
1538^{2}	**Little Martina (IRE) (98)** (DMGrissell) **8-10-11** JRKavanagh (led to 8th: led 10th to 14th: led 3 out: clr appr 2 out: r.o wl)	—	1	$2/1^{1}$	109	27
1571^{3}	**Miss Diskin (IRE) (105)** (RHBuckler) **7-10-7** BPowell (hld up: rdn 4 out: chsd wnr fr 2 out: no imp)	8	2	$9/2^{3}$	100	18
1563^{4}	**Haunting Music (IRE)** (MrsAJPerrett) **8-10-12** RDunwoody (lw: chsd ldr: led 8th to 10th: led 14th to 3 out: 3rd & wkng whn mstke 2 out)	30	3	$5/2^{2}$	87	5
1468^{5}	**Arctic Madam** (PFNicholls) **7-10-7** APMcCoy (hld up: rdn 12th: wknd 14th: t.o)	dist	4	6/1	—	—
1541^{P}	**Alone Home (IRE)** (CJMann) **5-10-8**(3) JMagee (3rd whn blnd 3rd: wknd 6th: t.o fr 8th)	dist	5	40/1	—	—
	Penncaler (IRE) (PJHobbs) **6-10-12** NWilliamson (lw: fell 1st)		F	5/1	—	—
				(SP 113.5%)	**6 Rn**	

6m 43.9 (23.90) CSF £10.78 TOTE £2.50: £2.00 £3.10 (£5.50) OWNER Mr Christopher Newport (ROBERTSBRIDGE) BRED Michael Hickey
WEIGHT FOR AGE 5yo-1lb
1538 Little Martina (IRE) confirmed her recent Towcester promise and made the vast majority of the running, winning in decisive style. (2/1)
1571 Miss Diskin (IRE) made a satisfactory chasing debut, but could never make an impression on the winner. (9/2)
1563 Haunting Music (IRE) quite simply failed to see out this trip. He jumped well in the main and can certainly find a race when dropped in distance. (5/2)
Penncaler (IRE) (5/1: 3/1-11/2)

1812 DENTON H'CAP CHASE (0-105) (5-Y.O+) (Class F)
3-00 (3-00) **2m 5f (15 fncs)** £2,736.00 (£756.00: £360.00) GOING: 0.47 sec per fur (GS)

				SP	RR	SF
1423*	**Mammy's Choice (IRE) (90)** (RHAlner) **6-11-1**(3) PHenley (lw: hld up: led 8th tl appr last: led flat: drvn out)	—	1	$11/10^{1}$	90	7
	Maestro Paul (99) (JTGifford) **10-11-13** PHide (hld up: chsd wnr fr 8th: led appr last tl flat: unable qckn)	1½	2	$3/1^{2}$	98	15
1584^{10}	**Early Drinker (100)** (OSherwood) **8-12-0** JAMcCarthy (hld up: rdn appr 3 out: one pce)	6	3	$13/2^{3}$	94	11
	Rumble (USA) (72) (PRChamings) **8-10-0** BFenton (a wl bhd: t.o)	dist	4	20/1	—	—
1708^{F}	**Hidden Pleasure (79)** (TMJones) **10-10-7** DLeahy (bit bkwd: led to 8th: sn wknd: wl bhd whn fell 10th)		F	16/1	—	—
1708^{3}	**Jacksons Bay (72)** (TCasey) **6-10-0** NWilliamson (hdwy 11th: 4th & btn whn fell 2 out)		F	$13/2^{3}$	—	—
957^{6}	**Fighting Days (USA) (89)** (AMoore) **10-11-3** PHolley (chsd ldr to 8th: wknd 10th: t.o whn p.u bef last)		P	14/1	—	—
				(SP 116.6%)	**7 Rn**	

5m 35.6 (27.60) CSF £4.96 TOTE £1.60: £1.10 £2.50 (£3.40) OWNER Mr David Young (BLANDFORD) BRED J. P. N. Parker
LONG HANDICAP Jacksons Bay 9-5
1423* Mammy's Choice (IRE) needs it soft. Showing good battling qualities, she fought her way back into the lead on the run-in. (11/10)
Maestro Paul, looking big and well for this reappearance, eased his way to the front approaching the last. Lack of a recent run took its toll on the run-in though, and he was unable to prevent the winner going by. (3/1)
Early Drinker has never won beyond two miles and, although leaving his bad Windsor reappearance behind, failed to quicken over the last three fences. (13/2: 4/1-7/1)
1708 Jacksons Bay (13/2: 3/1-7/1)
Fighting Days (USA) (14/1: 12/1-20/1)

1813 SEABROOK H'CAP HURDLE (0-110) (4-Y.O+) (Class E)
3-30 (3-30) **2m 6f 110y (11 hdls)** £2,427.00 (£672.00: £321.00) GOING: 0.47 sec per fur (GS)

				SP	RR	SF
1678*	**General Mouktar (103)** (MCPipe) **6-11-7** 7x APMcCoy (hld up: jnd ldr appr last: led flat: comf)	—	1	$8/11^{1}$	78+	—
1586^{6}	**Jackson Flint (93)** (TThomsonJones) **8-10-11** RDunwoody (chsd ldr: led appr last tl flat: unable qckn)	3	2	$4/1^{2}$	66	—
1661^{9}	**Indian Quest (110)** (NAGaselee) **7-12-0** CLlewellyn (lw: led tl appr last: one pce flat)	5	3	$4/1^{2}$	79	—
1567^{6}	**Maneree (101)** (NACallaghan) **9-11-5** NWilliamson (racd wd: a in rr: t.o)	dist	4	$6/1^{3}$	—	—
				(SP 112.2%)	**4 Rn**	

5m 54.6 (37.60) CSF £3.95 TOTE £1.60 (£4.10) OWNER Mr A. S. Helaissi (WELLINGTON) BRED Stetchworth Park Stud Ltd
IN-FOCUS: The leader set a moderate pace.
1678* General Mouktar, ridden to perfection by McCoy who has won on him on all three occasions this season, has been without the blinkers each time. Brought to join issue on the bridle approaching the last, he sprinted away on the run-in for a comfortable win. The secret seems to be to win with him without letting him know he has had a race. (8/11)
Jackson Flint poked a nostril in front approaching the last, but was only there on sufferance and was firmly put in his place on the run-in. (4/1)
Indian Quest has gained two wins, both in the mud. (4/1)
1567 Maneree (6/1: 7/2-13/2)

T/Plpt: £10.00 (841.78 Tckts). T/Qdpt: £2.10 (362.37 Tckts). AK

1297-LUDLOW (R-H) (Good to firm, Good patches)
Monday December 9th

WEATHER: misty

1814 BIRCHER NOVICES' H'CAP HURDLE (0-100) (4-Y.O+) (Class E)
12-40 (12-42) **2m 5f 110y (11 hdls)** £2,430.00 (£680.00: £330.00) GOING minus 0.28 sec per fur (GF)

				SP	RR	SF
1327[6]	**Colwall (73)** (MissPMWhittle) **5-10-4**(7) KHibbert (bit bkwd: a.p: led appr 2 out: hit 2 out: drvn out)	—	**1**	10/1	54	15
1599[5]	**First Class (82)** (GNAlford) **6-11-6** RGreene (hld up & bhd: gd hdwy 6th: rdn & one pce fr 2 out)	3	**2**	7/2[1]	61	22
1256[8]	**Saltis (IRE) (75)** (ALForbes) **4-10-13** GaryLyons (a.p: led 7th tl appr 2 out: one pce)	4	**3**	7/1[3]	51	12
673[8]	**Tug Your Forelock (67)** (GFJohnsonHoughton) **5-10-5** AMaguire (hld up & bhd: hdwy 8th: rdn appr 2 out: nt pce to chal)	¾	**4**	7/1[3]	42	3
	Quite A Man (83) (SABrookshaw) **8-11-0**(7) TMortimer (bkwd: prom: rdn appr 3 out: wknd next)	nk	**5**	25/1	58	19
1550[6]	**Snowy Petrel (IRE) (86)** (KCBailey) **4-11-10** SMcNeill (mid div: hdwy 6th: rdn after 8th: sn btn)	7	**6**	8/1	56	17
1453[12]	**Shannon Lad (IRE) (77)** (AWCarroll) **6-11-1** DMorris (chsd ldrs tl rdn & wknd appr 3 out: t.o)	17	**7**	4/1[2]	34	—
1251[5]	**Awestruck (62)** (BPreece) **6-9-7b**(7) JMogford (mstke 1st: a bhd: t.o)	8	**8**	14/1	13	—
1260[P]	**The Cheese Baron (65)** (SMellor) **5-10-3** NMann (mid div tl wknd 8th: sn t.o)	2½	**9**	33/1	14	—
1472[F]	**Ferny Ball (IRE) (62)** (CaptTAForster) **8-10-0** SWynne (a bhd: rdn ½-wy: no rspnse: t.o)	24	**10**	33/1	—	—
	Tango Man (IRE) (66) (RJPrice) **4-10-1**(3) GHogan (bolted bef s: led & sn wl clr: wknd & hdd 7th: t.o whn p.u bef 3 out)		**P**	33/1	—	—
	Cravate (FR) (62) (PJHobbs) **6-9-9**(5) DJKavanagh (hdwy 5th: wknd 8th: t.o whn p.u bef 3 out)		**P**	14/1	—	—
				(SP 113.4%)	**12 Rn**	

5m 7.7 (6.70) CSF £40.47 CT £238.32 TOTE £11.70: £3.20 £2.30 £2.70 (£14.10) Trio £46.40 OWNER Mrs Yvonne Allsop (LEDBURY) BRED D. J. and Mrs Eckley

LONG HANDICAP Awestruck 9-10 Ferny Ball (IRE) 9-9 Cravate (FR) 9-13

IN-FOCUS: Trainer Pam Whittle and rider Kevin Hibbert were both enjoying their first winner under Rules.

Colwall, much sharper for the run last month and returning to a more suitable trip, won this with a bit in hand and is now finding his way. (10/1)

1599 First Class posed a serious threat when poised to challenge at the entrance to the straight, but the winner found a better turn of speed and he was well outpointed on the run-in. (7/2)

978 Saltis (IRE) has run his best races over course and distance, and it can only be a matter of time before he does get it together. (7/1)

553 Tug Your Forelock possibly just needed the run after ten weeks out of action, but he was only tapped for toe over the last two and is certainly capable of improvement. (7/1)

Quite A Man put in a better-than-average show on this return to hurdles, but he was definitely in need of at least this outing. There are races to be won with him. (25/1)

1251 Awestruck (14/1: 10/1-16/1)

1815 P & T JONES NOVICES' CHASE (5-Y.O+) (Class E)
1-10 (1-10) **2m (13 fncs)** £3,035.00 (£920.00: £450.00: £215.00) GOING minus 0.28 sec per fur (GF)

				SP	RR	SF
1664[2]	**Scottish Bambi (96)** (PRWebber) **8-11-5** AMaguire (lw: hld up: pckd 2nd: hdwy appr 4 out: led last: r.o wl)	—	**1**	11/4[2]	93	—
	Cheryl's Lad (IRE) (NJHenderson) **6-10-12** MAFitzgerald (w.r.s: sn rcvrd to chse ldrs: led 4 out to last: unable qckn)	1½	**2**	1/3[1]	85+	—
1657[10]	**Monaughty Man (76)** (EMCaine) **10-10-11**(5) DJKavanagh (led tl after 5th: wknd appr 4 out)	19	**3**	25/1[3]	70	—
1644[F]	**The Fence Shrinker (60)** (DMcCain) **5-10-12** TJenks (plld hrd: led after 5th to 4 out: btn whn blnd 2 out)	23	**4**	50/1	43?	—
				(SP 107.5%)	**4 Rn**	

4m 6.9 (14.90) CSF £3.96 TOTE £3.20 (£1.30) OWNER Mr William Kelly (BANBURY) BRED Cheveley Park Stud Ltd

1664 Scottish Bambi had the edge in fitness and experience to call on, and his turn of finishing speed proved decisive in a thrilling duel to the line. (11/4)

Cheryl's Lad (IRE), a class act over hurdles who has won first time out for the past couple of seasons, jumped extremely well on this chasing debut, but the race-fit winner had the legs of him when it mattered most. He should have little trouble making the grade. (1/3)

1816 SHROPSHIRE BUILDING SUPPLIES CONDITIONAL H'CAP HURDLE (0-105) (4-Y.O+) (Class F)
1-40 (1-40) **2m (9 hdls)** £2,788.00 (£844.00: £412.00: £196.00) GOING minus 0.28 sec per fur (GF)

				SP	RR	SF
1502[5]	**Pridewood Picker (88)** (RJPrice) **9-11-2**(3) DJKavanagh (hld up: hdwy 5th: led last: comf)	—	**1**	5/2[1]	69	20
1446*	**Glowing Path (87)** (RJHodges) **6-10-13**(5) JHarris (hld up: stdy hdwy fr 6th: slt ld 2 out: hdd last: no ex flat)	1¾	**2**	11/4[2]	66	17
1663[7]	**Schnozzle (IRE) (89)** (KSBridgwater) **5-11-6** RMassey (bit bkwd: hld up & bhd: hdwy 6th: ev ch fr 2 out: hit last: one pce)	2	**3**	12/1	66	17
1337[5]	**Just for a Reason (73)** (RTJuckes) **4-10-4** EHusband (hld up in rr: hdwy appr 3 out: ev ch 2 out: one pce flat)	¾	**4**	16/1	50	1
1542[5]	**Nothingtodowithme (89)** (CaptTAForster) **6-11-3**(3) ABates (lw: a.p: rn wd appr 3 out: sn rdn: wknd 2 out)	7	**5**	9/2[3]	59	10
1446[7]	**Them Times (IRE) (70)** (FJordan) **7-10-1**ow1 LAspell (bit bkwd: led to 4th: led 6th to 2 out: sn rdn & btn)	2½	**6**	50/1	37	—
1628[9]	**Biya (IRE) (74)** (DMcCain) **4-9-12**(7)ow1 CHoggart (lw: nvr trbld ldrs)	2	**7**	40/1	39	—
1009[4]	**Spring Loaded (77)** (JGMO'Shea) **5-10-5**(3) MichaelBrennan (prom tl rdn & wknd appr 3 out)	1¼	**8**	10/1	41	—
1466[5]	**Hacketts Cross (IRE) (93)** (PEccles) **8-11-10** GHogan (trckd ldrs tl outpcd appr 3 out)	4	**9**	10/1	53	4
1448[7]	**Out of The Blue (69)** (MWEckley) **4-9-9**(5) JMogford (prom to 6th: sn wknd)	1¾	**10**	20/1	27	—
	Britannia Mills (76) (MCChapman) **5-10-2**(5) RossBerry (bkwd: disp ld: led 4th to 6th: sn wknd: t.o whn p.u bef 3 out)		**P**	14/1	—	—
				(SP 121.0%)	**11 Rn**	

3m 42.2 (5.20) CSF £9.74 CT £64.45 TOTE £4.10: £2.20 £1.50 £2.30 (£6.70) Trio £25.80 OWNER Mrs B. Morris (ULLINGSWICK) BRED Mrs J. E. Hodgson

LONG HANDICAP Out of The Blue 9-5 Them Times (IRE) 9-4

1325 Pridewood Picker, ridden with any amount of confidence, won with authority, and this could be the first of many for the season. (5/2)

1446* Glowing Path, produced to win his race at the penultimate flight, could never get away from the pursuing pack and lacked the gears to compete with the winner on the flat. (11/4)

Schnozzle (IRE) has only been lightly-raced, and this very promising effort shows that he possesses the ability to win a similar event. (12/1)

1337 Just for a Reason, winner of his only previous race over course and distance, was fighting for the lead over the last two, but a turn of finishing speed was missing in the dash to the post. He has time on his side. (16/1)

1542 Nothingtodowithme would have taken all the beating had he not run very wide turning for home, giving away substantial ground by doing so. (9/2: op 3/1)
Them Times (IRE), still just short of peak-fitness, was only shaken off approaching the last. She should be kept in mind for any near-at-hand engagements. (50/1)
1466 Hacketts Cross (IRE) (10/1: 6/1-11/1)
Britannia Mills (14/1: 10/1-16/1)

1817 HIS ROYAL HIGHNESS THE PRINCE OF WALES CHALLENGE TROPHY AMATEUR H'CAP CHASE (0-100) (5-Y.O+) (Class F)

2-10 (2-10) **3m (19 fncs)** £3,468.75 (£1,050.00: £512.50: £243.75) GOING minus 0.28 sec per fur (GF)

				SP	RR	SF
1445[5]	**Opal's Tenspot (72)** (JMBradley) **9-9-7**(7) MissVRoberts (hld up: wnt 2nd 9th: led 14th to 15th: led 2 out: r.o strly)	—	**1**	16/1	73	—
1122[P]	**Fairy Park (91)** (HOliver) **11-10-12v**(7) MrNHOliver (bit bkwd: led 3rd to 14th: led 15th to 2 out: one pce)	4	**2**	14/1[3]	89	—
	Just One Canaletto (78) (NATwiston-Davies) **8-9-13**(7) MrJGoldstein (a.p: ev ch 3 out: rdn & one pce appr last)	1¼	**3**	4/1[2]	76	—
1553[2]	**Glen Mirage (93)** (MJCoombe) **11-11-0**(7) MissMCoombe (lft in ld 2nd: hdd next: wknd 3 out)	2½	**4**	4/1[2]	89	—
1472[2]	**Bironi (97)** (CaptTAForster) **7-11-6**(5) MrJJukes (led tl tk wrong crse 2nd: cont wl bhd: hdwy 15th: hrd rdn & btn 4th whn fell last)		**F**	4/5[1]	—	—
				(SP 108.1%)	**5 Rn**	

6m 25.3 (25.30) CSF £129.15 TOTE £17.90: £2.00 £4.30 (£36.20) OWNER Miss Joy Mailes (CHEPSTOW) BRED S. A. Mailes and Mrs R. Bradley
LONG HANDICAP Opal's Tenspot 9-8
STEWARDS' ENQUIRY Jukes susp. 18-21,23,26-28,30-31/12/96 Rule 152 (taking incorrect course) & 1-2/1/97 (incorrect use of whip).
IN-FOCUS: **Ludlow would not be the most difficult course to ride, and Jukes must have been kicking himself.**
1445 Opal's Tenspot came into his own over this extended trip with a comfortably-gained success under a very competent ride. (16/1)
678 Fairy Park enjoyed a very rewarding time last season and he could be on the way back on this showing. (14/1: op 5/1)
Just One Canaletto did not look fully wound up for this return to action, but he ran a fine race in defeat and will be much sharper next time. (4/1: 3/1-9/2)
1553 Glen Mirage, hunting up the leaders when jumping slowly and losing ground five out, did try to rally, but could not muster the pace to do so. (4/1)
1472 Bironi was an extremely unlucky loser, which was all down to jockey error. It is to be hoped he soon recovers from his exertions. (4/5)

1818 MICHAEL PERROTT NOVICES' CLAIMING HURDLE (4-Y.O+) (Class F)

2-40 (2-43) **2m (9 hdls)** £2,486.00 (£696.00: £338.00) GOING minus 0.28 sec per fur (GF)

				SP	RR	SF
392[3]	**First Bee (65)** (FJordan) **5-10-3** SWynne (hld up in rr: hdwy after 6th: led 2 out: r.o wl)	—	**1**	10/1	56	1
956[5]	**Caddy's First (80)** (SMellor) **4-11-0v** NMann (hld up: hdwy 6th: hrd rdn & edgd rt flat: r.o)	1	**2**	10/1	66	11
1438[4]	**Cliburnel News (IRE)** (ALForbes) **6-10-9** GaryLyons (hld up: j.slowly & lost tch 5th: rallied 3 out: one pce appr last)	3	**3**	9/2[3]	58	3
1413[9]	**Tee Tee Too (IRE)** (AWCarroll) **4-10-8** WMarston (a.p: led appr 3 out to 2 out: kpt on same pce)	1¼	**4**	25/1	56	1
1369[7]	**Nashaat (USA) (83)** (MCChapman) **8-10-11** WWorthington (a.p: led after 6th: sn hdd: rdn 2 out: one pce)	3	**5**	2/1[1]	56	1
1332[3]	**Mutawali (IRE) (73)** (RJBaker) **6-10-11**(3) GHogan (hld up: hdwy 5th: wknd appr 2 out)	8	**6**	7/2[2]	51	—
	Mill Dancer (IRE) (JGMO'Shea) **4-9-9**(5) MichaelBrennan (plld hrd: led tl hdd & wknd after 6th: t.o)	9	**7**	25/1	28	—
1663[10]	**Dodgy Dancer (72)** (MrsLWilliamson) **6-10-11** LO'Hara (bit bkwd: hdwy 4th: wknd appr 3 out: t.o)	5	**8**	16/1	34	—
950[F]	**Rub Al Khali** (AStreeter) **5-10-5** TEley (a bhd: t.o)	19	**9**	33/1	9	—
1537[F]	**Polli Pui** (WMBrisbourne) **4-9-11**(3) RMassey (rel to r: a bhd: t.o)	½	**10**	50/1	3	—
1450[13]	**Let You Know (IRE)** (TRGeorge) **6-10-3**ow3 TJenks (a bhd: t.o)	19	**11**	50/1	—	—
1770[F]	**Office Hours** (WGMTurner) **4-10-8** WMcFarland (bhd fr ½-wy: t.o whn p.u bef 3 out)		**P**	8/1	—	—
				(SP 123.5%)	**12 Rn**	

3m 43.2 (6.20) CSF £99.38 TOTE £13.90: £2.00 £1.90 £1.70 (£28.80) Trio £66.30 OWNER Mr D. Pugh (LEOMINSTER)
Nashaat (USA) clmd N Shields £5,000
392 First Bee, brought back to the minimum trip, looked likely to win with ease when she touched down in front at the penultimate flight but, in the end, she had to find a bit more to make sure close home. (10/1: 7/1-11/1)
818 Caddy's First ran much better in his first-time visor and, had he not veered away to the right under pressure on the run-in, he would have gone close to getting off the mark. (10/1)
Cliburnel News (IRE) lost ground when jumping slowly at the fifth and, though she did attempt to rally early in the straight, she used up all her energy in doing so. (9/2: 3/1-5/1)
Tee Tee Too (IRE), showing his first glimpse of form, will hardly need to improve much to find an opening. (25/1)
1204 Nashaat (USA) continues to disappoint over hurdles, but he never won beyond seven on the Flat and it is more than likely that he is not even lasting this minimum trip. (2/1)
1332 Mutawali (IRE) took a keen pull to post and overshot the post by about half a mile. Restrained once in action, his short-lived effort soon after halfway came to little. (7/2)

1819 INVERSHIN NOVICES' H'CAP CHASE (0-100) (5-Y.O+) (Class E)

3-10 (3-10) **3m (19 fncs)** £3,126.00 (£948.00: £464.00: £222.00) GOING minus 0.28 sec per fur (GF)

				SP	RR	SF
1285*	**God Speed You (IRE) (90)** (CPMorlock) **7-11-7b** AMaguire (j.w: mde virtually all: styd on strly)	—	**1**	7/4[1]	111	41
1468*	**Dromhana (IRE) (95)** (PFNicholls) **6-11-12** MAFitzgerald (hld up: hdwy to chse wnr 10th: hrd rdn appr 2 out: kpt on)	1¾	**2**	2/1[2]	115	45
1716[2]	**Record Lover (IRE) (69)** (MCChapman) **6-10-0** WWorthington (chsd ldrs: outpcd 15th: styd on again fr 2 out)	24	**3**	13/2[3]	73	3
1582[6]	**Oxford Quill (69)** (RCurtis) **9-10-0** DMorris (hld up: hdwy 11th: wknd appr 3 out)	10	**4**	12/1	66	—
	Captiva Bay (69) (MrsARHewitt) **7-10-0** SWynne (bkwd: prom to 12th: grad wknd: t.o)	17	**5**	33/1	55	—
1629[P]	**Dormston Boyo (72)** (TWall) **6-10-0**(3) RMassey (prom to 14th: wkng whn pckd 4 out: t.o)	14	**6**	33/1	49	—
1260[7]	**King's Courtier (IRE) (72)** (SMellor) **7-10-3** NMann (bit bkwd: sn wl bhd: t.o whn p.u after 11th)		**P**	33/1	—	—
1638[6]	**Crown Ivory (NZ) (69)** (PCRitchens) **8-10-0** SFox (sn wl bhd & outpcd: t.o whn p.u after 11th)		**P**	10/1	—	—
1582[U]	**Romany Blues (69)** (CPEBrooks) **7-10-0** DGallagher (bit bkwd: prom to 5th: bhd whn blnd & uns rdr 7th)		**U**	8/1	—	—
				(SP 119.7%)	**9 Rn**	

6m 2.8 (2.80) CSF £5.75 CT £14.87 TOTE £2.60: £1.40 £1.70 £1.10 (£2.90) Trio £2.80 OWNER Wallop (WANTAGE) BRED Mrs Vincent O'Brien

LONG HANDICAP Oxford Quill 9-13 Crown Ivory (NZ) 9-11 Romany Blues 9-7
1285* God Speed You (IRE) won this courtesy of a very impressive display both of front-running and jumping. He has not stropped winning yet. (7/4)
1468* Dromhana (IRE) lost no caste in defeat in attempting to concede weight to the winner, and he can soon get back to winning ways. (2/1)

1820 OLDFIELD STANDARD OPEN N.H. FLAT RACE (4, 5 & 6-Y.O) (Class H)
3-40 (3-40) **2m** £1,305.60 (£361.60: £172.80)

				SP	RR	SF
918*	**Mrs Em** (PFNicholls) **4-11-1**(5) OBurrows (a.p: led over 3f out: qckdnd clr fnl f)	—	1	11/8 1	67 f	—
1336 3	**King of The Blues** (JSKing) **4-10-11**(7) LSuthern (chsd ldrs: hdwy & ev ch 3f out: unable qckn fnl f)	4	2	8/1	61 f	—
	Madam Polly (MissPMWhittle) **4-10-6**(7) KHibbert (bit bkwd: chsd ldrs: effrt 3f out: styd on fnl f)	3	3	50/1	53 f	—
	Floosy (TRGeorge) **5-10-13** MAFitzgerald (hld up: hdwy ½-wy: rdn over 2f out: styd on)	nk	4	3/1 2	53 f	—
25 6	**Sarenacare (IRE)** (PJHobbs) **4-11-1**(3) GTormey (bit bkwd: chsd ldrs: rdn over 2f out: nt pce to chal)	2	5	12/1	56 f	—
	Ballina (JGMO'Shea) **4-10-13**(5) MichaelBrennan (bkwd: prom: rdn 4f out: one pce fnl 2f)	hd	6	16/1	56 f	—
1289 5	**Kylami (NZ)** (AGHobbs) **4-10-11**(7) MrGShenkin (hld up & bhd: hdwy over 5f out: wknd 3f out)	7	7	9/2 3	49 f	—
	Chaos And Order (CLPopham) **4-11-4** SMcNeill (prom tl wknd ent st)	¾	8	20/1	48 f	—
	Elly's Dream (PCRitchens) **5-10-13** SFox (hld up: a in rr)	nk	9	40/1	43 f	—
705 6	**Monsieur Pink** (AStreeter) **4-11-4** TEley (led tl hdd & wknd over 3f out)	3½	10	16/1	44 f	—
	Hands Off Millie (JGMO'Shea) **5-10-13** MrNBradley (bkwd: a bhd: t.o fnl 4f)	dist	11	33/1	—	—

(SP 128.0%) **11 Rn**

3m 46.8 CSF £14.08 TOTE £2.50: £1.70 £2.90 £7.60 (£7.60) Trio £167.40; £188.68 to Huntingdon 10/12/96 OWNER Mr G. Z. Mizel (SHEPTON MALLET) BRED Guest Leasing and Bloodstock Co
918* Mrs Em once again left her rivals standing in the latter stages and, in this grade, she looks a class apart. (11/8: evens-2/1)
1336 King of The Blues settled much better on this occasion and ran well. If he can continue his progress, an early success is likely. (8/1: op 5/1)
Madam Polly looked short of a gallop, but she turned in her best race yet and seems to be getting it together. (50/1)
Floosy got closer down the back straight and worked herself into the action turning in but, when the pace lifted, she was unable to respond. She may have needed the run more than was apparent. (3/1)
25 Sarenacare (IRE) will strip fitter for this and will not need to improve much to pick up a small race. (12/1: op 7/1)
Ballina, struggling to hold on on the long run to the straight, did keep staying on and does appear to have some ability. (16/1)

T/Jkpt: Not won; £62,822.40 to Huntingdon 10/12/96. T/Plpt: £349.30 (28.53 Tckts). T/Qdpt: £54.90 (13.08 Tckts). IM

MUSSELBURGH (R-H) (Good to firm, Firm patches)
Monday December 9th
WEATHER: fine

1821 LONGNIDDRY MAIDEN HURDLE (4-Y.O+ F & M) (Class F)
12-20 (12-20) **2m (8 hdls)** £2,115.00 (£590.00: £285.00) GOING minus 0.56 sec per fur (F)

				SP	RR	SF
1667 9	**Kilnamartyra Girl (87)** (JParkes) **6-11-0** AThornton (a cl up: led appr 2 out: clr between last 2: styd on)	—	1	3/1 1	62	—
	Arian Spirit (IRE) (JLEyre) **5-11-0** BStorey (nt j.w: chsd ldrs: rdn fr 5th: styd on: nt pce to chal)	5	2	7/2 2	57	—
	Something Speedy (IRE) (MDHammond) **4-11-0** RGarritty (hld up: hit 5th: styd on fr 2 out: n.d)	10	3	16/1	47	—
1575 P	**Miss Mont (53)** (FPMurtagh) **7-11-0** RHodge (led tl appr 2 out: sn btn)	3	4	100/1	44	—
	Hutchies Lady (RMMcKellar) **4-11-0** DParker (hld up: effrt 5th: n.d)	11	5	33/1	33	—
1666 8	**Jalmaid** (HAlexander) **4-10-9**(5) RMcGrath (prom: blnd 2nd: outpcd fr 5th)	2	6	12/1	31	—
	Fairy-Land (IRE) (HowardJohnson) **4-11-0** ADobbin (in tch tl wknd fr 3 out)	25	7	9/2 3	6	—
1052 13	**North End Lady** (WSCunningham) **5-10-7**(7) LMcGrath (plld hrd: prom whn fell 1st)		F	14/1	—	—
	Moonlight Calypso (MartynWane) **5-11-0** ASSmith (chsd ldrs tl wknd appr 2 out: p.u lame bef last: dead)		P	5/1	—	—
	Swift Move (PMonteith) **4-11-0** GCahill (swtg: mstkes: lost tch 5th: p.u bef 2 out)		P	50/1	—	—
	Celtic Comma (WGReed) **5-11-0** TReed (sn t.o: p.u bef last)		P	66/1	—	—

(SP 109.7%) **11 Rn**

3m 44.8 (5.80) CSF £12.21 TOTE £4.70: £3.90 £1.10 £3.90 (£7.20) Trio £18.00 OWNER Mr P. J. Cronin (MALTON) BRED F. R. Colley
OFFICIAL EXPLANATION **Celtic Comma: may have been feeling the effects of a knock sustained a few days previously.**
1524 Kilnamartyra Girl, after two poor efforts recently, came good in this very moderate race and always had the edge. (3/1)
Arian Spirit (IRE) continually gave ground away by backing off her hurdles and that needs to be rectified. She also needs further. (7/2: op 2/1)
Something Speedy (IRE), a bit novicey at times, stayed on in the closing stages, but never had a hope. (16/1)
Miss Mont ran her best race to date, but this was a moderate event. (100/1)
Hutchies Lady, who is only small, never looked likely to get into it. (33/1)
Jalmaid (12/1: op 33/1)
705 North End Lady again refused to settle and fell at the first. (14/1)

1822 PRESTONPANS CONDITIONAL (S) H'CAP HURDLE (0-95) (4-Y.O+) (Class G)
12-50 (12-50) **3m (13 hdls)** £2,290.00 (£640.00: £310.00) GOING minus 0.56 sec per fur (F)

				SP	RR	SF
1304 5	**Barnstormer (66)** (EAElliott) **10-10-0b**1 DParker (led to 3rd: chsd ldrs: styd on u.p to ld flat)	—	1	50/1	43	—
1671 2	**Trap Dancer (91)** (PMonteith) **8-11-11** GCahill (lw: trckd ldrs: rdn to ld 2 out: hrd rdn & hdd flat)	2	2	4/5 1	67	24
1703 3	**Little Redwing (66)** (MDHammond) **4-10-0v** ECallaghan (lw: hdwy ½-wy: chsng ldrs appr 2 out: hrd rdn & hung rt: styd on)	1¼	3	7/1 2	41	—
1775 4	**Tharsis (67)** (WJSmith) **11-10-1** STaylor (in tch: rdn 4 out: one pce fr 2 out)	9	4	7/1 2	36	—
1047 U	**Yacht Club (67)** (JLEyre) **14-9-10**(5) CElliott (led 3rd to 2 out: sn wknd)	½	5	9/1 3	36	—
	Tancred Mischief (78) (DWBarker) **5-10-12** PMidgley (lw: chsd ldrs tl mstke & wknd 3 out)	8	6	12/1	41	—
1078 6	**Marco Magnifico (USA) (66)** (MissLucindaRussell) **6-10-0v** GLee (t: t.o fr ½-wy: p.u bef 4 out)		P	16/1	—	—
	Charlvic (66) (WSCunningham) **6-9-9**(5) LMcGrath (t.o fr 6th: p.u bef 9th)		P	20/1	—	—
1021 12	**Laurie-O (66)** (DALamb) **12-9-7b**(7) NHannity (prom tl lost tch fr 8th: t.o whn p.u bef last)		P	66/1	—	—

(SP 112.3%) **9 Rn**

5m 42.9 (0.50 under best) (2.90) CSF £85.62 CT £320.23 TOTE £31.20: £2.40 £1.20 £1.50 (£27.30) Trio £56.00 OWNER Mr Eric Elliott (RUSHYFORD) BRED Dr Louis Bann-Murray
LONG HANDICAP Little Redwing 9-12 Barnstormer 9-8 Charlvic 9-5 Laurie-O 9-9

No bid
1304 Barnstormer, who is almost ready to draw his pension, had blinkers on for the first time and they worked the oracle. (50/1)
1671 Trap Dancer looked head and shoulders above this lot, but weight stops trains and it certainly found him out in the closing stages. (4/5)
1703 Little Redwing is not the most enthusiastic-looking individual, but she keeps showing enough to suggest that there could be a race in her. (7/1)
1775 Tharsis is running better at present. (7/1)
805 Yacht Club set the race up, but was done for pace late on. (9/1)
Tancred Mischief looked fit enough but, after a lengthy lay-off, was probably ring-rusty. (12/1)

1823 WEE JIMMY MITCHELL H'CAP CHASE (0-125) (5-Y.O+) (Class D)
1-20 (1-20) **3m (18 fncs)** £3,550.00 (£1,075.00: £525.00: £250.00) GOING minus 0.56 sec per fur (F)

				SP	RR	SF
1268^{2}	**Charming Gale (95)** (MrsSCBradburne) **9-10-2v** MFoster (lw: trckd ldrs: led 13th: styd on wl)	—	**1**	4/1^{1}	106	18
1657^{4}	**Pagliaccio (99)** (MDHammond) **8-10-6** RGarritty (led tl blnd & hdd 5th: cl up: hit 12th: styd on fr 3 out: cl 2nd whn blnd last: nt rcvr)	3	**2**	4/1^{1}	108	20
1657^{5}	**Puritan (CAN) (110)** (NTinkler) **7-11-3b** BStorey (trckd ldrs: effrt 11th: wnt 2nd 14th: one pce fr 4 out)	6	**3**	6/1	115	27
1668^{3}	**Tighter Budget (USA) (104)** (MrsDianneSayer) **9-10-11** MMoloney (led 5th: blnd 6th: blnd & hdd 13th: blnd 14th: one pce after)	1¼	**4**	11/2^{3}	108	20
1578^{3}	**Grand Scenery (IRE) (93)** (HowardJohnson) **8-10-0** ADobbin (mstkes: bhd: hdwy & prom appr 4 out: sn btn)	5	**5**	5/1^{2}	94	6
420^{3}	**The Toaster (97)** (MissMKMilligan) **9-10-4** ASSmith (mstkes: hdwy & prom appr 4 out: sn wknd)	22	**6**	12/1	83	—
1513^{F}	**Greenhill Raffles (117)** (MissLucindaRussell) **10-11-10** AThornton (wl bhd fr ½-wy)	9	**7**	33/1	97	9
	Cornet (107) (DenysSmith) **10-11-0v** PNiven (prom tl lost pl 12th: blnd 4 out: wl btn whn blnd & uns rdr 3 out)		**U**	6/1	—	—
				(SP 111.3%)		**8 Rn**

5m 50.7 (1.90 under best) (-2.30) CSF £18.58 CT £81.98 TOTE £4.00: £1.30 £1.10 £3.40 (£9.20) Trio £77.20 OWNER Mrs John Etherton (CUPAR) BRED Eamonn McCarthy
LONG HANDICAP Grand Scenery (IRE) 9-13
1268 Charming Gale jumps for fun and, when it came down to a struggle, she was always too game for this bunch. (4/1)
1657 Pagliaccio keeps beating himself and, through mistakes, managed to do it again, with the main one being at the last. (4/1)
1657 Puritan (CAN), over a trip longer than his best, was treading water over the last four, (6/1)
1668 Tighter Budget (USA), who should have been more at home on this right-handed track, had been sweating beforehand and made some terrible blunders throughout. He had to give up the struggle over the last five fences. (11/2)
1578 Grand Scenery (IRE) has plenty of ability, but is a funny customer and an iffy jumper. In the circumstances, he did quite well to get into it on the home turn. (5/1)
420 The Toaster, who has changed stables, was having his first run for three and a half months, and his jumping was indifferent. (12/1)

1824 GOREBRIDGE H'CAP HURDLE (0-110) (4-Y.O+) (Class E)
1-50 (1-51) **2m (8 hdls)** £2,584.00 (£724.00: £352.00) GOING minus 0.56 sec per fur (F)

				SP	RR	SF
1669*	**Stash the Cash (IRE) (106)** (MDHammond) **5-12-1** 7x RGarritty (lw: hld up: smooth hdwy to chal last: sn led: rdn out)	—	**1**	6/4^{1}	88	44
1658^{5}	**Fen Terrier (95)** (FPMurtagh) **4-11-4** ADobbin (trckd ldrs: led 2 out tl flat: no ex)	4	**2**	6/4^{1}	73	29
1081^{7}	**Peggy Gordon (77)** (MrsDThomson) **5-10-0** GCahill (chsd ldr: chal 4th: hit 5th: one pce fr 2 out)	12	**3**	6/1^{2}	43	—
538^{6}	**Hee's a Dancer (102)** (MissLucindaRussell) **4-11-11** AThornton (led: hit 3rd: hdd 2 out: one pce)	3	**4**	12/1^{3}	65	21
	Rapid Mover (88) (DANolan) **9-10-11b** MMoloney (prom tl wknd fr 2 out)	6	**5**	20/1	45	1
1666^{11}	**Barik (IRE) (77)** (BMactaggart) **6-10-0** BStorey (bhd: hdwy & ev ch appr 2 out: sn rdn & fnd nil)	4	**6**	66/1	30	—
1686^{P}	**Doon Ridge (77)** (MissLCSiddall) **5-10-0** RSupple (t.o fr 5th)	dist	**7**	50/1	—	—
				(SP 110.2%)		**7 Rn**

3m 36.7 (-2.30) CSF £3.86 TOTE £2.00: £2.20 £1.10 (£1.90) OWNER Mr G. Shiel (MIDDLEHAM) BRED Airlie Stud in Ireland
LONG HANDICAP Barik (IRE) 9-7 Doon Ridge 9-13
1669* Stash the Cash (IRE), given an ideal ride, was produced at the last and, vigorously ridden, quickly settled it. His confidence should now be sky high. (6/4)
1658 Fen Terrier keeps running well, but he had no answer to the winner's turn of foot at the last. (6/4)
1081 Peggy Gordon tried different tactics here, going off in front, and ran better, but was well tapped for toe from the second last. (6/1)
538 Hee's a Dancer, having his first run for his new stable, ran well enough considering his handicap mark. (12/1)
Rapid Mover gave the impression he would be better for this. (20/1)
Barik (IRE) at last showed something here, suddenly coming through on the bridle approaching the second last, but he quickly decided that it was not for him. (66/1)

1825 LEVY BOARD NOVICES' H'CAP HURDLE (0-100) (4-Y.O+) (Class E)
2-20 (2-20) **2m 4f (12 hdls)** £2,542.00 (£712.00: £346.00) GOING minus 0.56 sec per fur (F)

				SP	RR	SF
1360^{5}	**Commander Glen (IRE) (92)** (MDHammond) **4-11-13v** RGarritty (lw: trckd ldrs: smooth hdwy to ld between last 2: rdn & styd on)	—	**1**	5/2^{2}	73	21
1351^{3}	**Leap in the Dark (IRE) (80)** (MissLCSiddall) **7-11-1** AThornton (chsd ldr: chal & blnd 2 out: rdn & nt qckn)	4	**2**	3/1^{3}	58	6
1575*	**Kings Minstral (IRE) (74)** (DALamb) **6-10-9** JBurke (mstkes: led tl between last 2: one pce)	1½	**3**	6/4^{1}	51	—
1687^{15}	**Rubislaw (66)** (MrsKMLamb) **4-9-8**(7)ow1 MissSLamb (sn t.o)	dist	**4**	50/1	—	—
1628^{10}	**Antarctictern (USA) (73)** (GROldroyd) **6-10-8** GCahill (prom tl ref to r bef 7th)		**R**	8/1	—	—
				(SP 106.6%)		**5 Rn**

4m 45.4 (3.40) CSF £9.26 TOTE £2.50: £2.40 £2.50 (£3.80) OWNER Punters Haven Racing Club (MIDDLEHAM) BRED Des Vere Hunt Farming Co
LONG HANDICAP Rubislaw 9-0
1360 Commander Glen (IRE), wearing a visor and a tongue-strap, did all that was asked in this uncompetitive event. (5/2)
1351 Leap in the Dark (IRE) had his chances, but he has yet to win and his attitude would seem to be the problem. (3/1)
1575* Kings Minstral (IRE) again tried to gallop his rivals into the ground, but his jumping was his undoing and he was easily picked off from the second last. (6/4)
Rubislaw needs to go out with a pair of binoculars to keep tabs on the other runners. (50/1)

1826 HUMBIE NOVICES' CHASE (5-Y.O+) (Class E)
2-50 (2-50) **2m 4f (16 fncs)** £2,953.50 (£888.00: £429.00: £199.50) GOING minus 0.56 sec per fur (F)

				SP	RR	SF
	Noyan (RAFahey) **6-10-12** ADobbin (a.p: led & lft wl clr 4 out: easily)	—	1	11/8 1	90+	20
911 6	**Heddon Haugh (IRE)** (PCheesbrough) **8-10-12** RSupple (lw: prom: effrt whn hit 11th: no imp after)	13	2	50/1	80	10
1525 2	**Marble Man (IRE)** (MDHammond) **6-10-12** RGarritty (prom: blnd 6th: outpcd 10th: n.d after)	s.h	3	13/8 2	80	10
1304 7	**Overwhelm (IRE) (88)** (VThompson) **8-11-2** KJones (bhd: sme hdwy 4 out: n.d)	½	4	66/1	83	13
1248 8	**Mountain Fox (IRE) (63)** (VThompson) **6-10-12** MrMThompson (in tch to 8th: sn outpcd)	24	5	100/1	60	—
1138 4	**White Diamond (79)** (MissLucindaRussell) **8-10-12v** MFoster (a outpcd & bhd)	1½	6	25/1	59	—
1576 F	**Highland Way (IRE)** (MartinTodhunter) **8-10-12** ASSmith (lw: led: blnd 8th: hdd & wkng whn fell 4 out)		F	9/2 3	—	—
	Camptosaurus (IRE) (DSAlder) **7-10-12** AThornton (chsd ldrs tl outpcd fr 10th: disp 3rd & no ch whn hmpd & uns rdr 4 out)		U	20/1	—	—
				(SP 111.4%)	**8 Rn**	

4m 56.2 (0.20) CSF £42.83 TOTE £2.50: £1.90 £5.40 £1.00 (£24.40) OWNER Mr C. H. McGhie (MALTON) BRED Oakgrove Stud
Noyan looked lean and fit for this chasing debut and, jumping well, won as he pleased. (11/8: 4/5-6/4)
Heddon Haugh (IRE) gave his usual mulish problems before the start, but then ran quite well, although he never had a hope with the winner.(50/1)
1525 Marble Man (IRE) made an almighty blunder early on and was never really happy thereafter. (13/8)
Overwhelm (IRE) did not impress on looks, but ran reasonably, staying on at the finish. (66/1)
1032 Highland Way (IRE), happy to make it, had just been headed when he went to jelly and took a crashing fall four out. He would seem to have a problem. (9/2)

1827 MUSSELBURGH INTERMEDIATE OPEN N.H. FLAT RACE (4, 5 & 6-Y.O) (Class H)
3-20 (3-20) **2m** £1,196.00 (£331.00: £158.00)

				SP	RR	SF
	Carlisle Bandito's (IRE) (JBerry) **4-11-4** MMoloney (lw: cl up: rdn to ld 3f out: r.o wl)	—	1	7/2 3	55 f	—
	Coble Lane (GPKelly) **4-11-1**(3) GParkin (leggy, attr: lw: hld up & bhd: hdwy 4f out: chsng wnr fnl 2f: rdn & no imp)	6	2	3/1 2	49 f	—
1579 4	**Lord of The Loch (IRE)** (LLungo) **5-11-4** RGarritty (hld up: hdwy 4f out: rdn & nt pce to chal)	2½	3	6/4 1	47 f	—
1692 8	**Deerhunter** (DWBarker) **5-11-4** RMarley (a in tch: effrt 4f out: nt qckn fnl 2f)	2	4	6/1	45 f	—
	Caught At Last (IRE) (MrsMReveley) **5-11-4** GCahill (in tch: effrt 4f out: one pce)	1¼	5	16/1	43 f	—
	Atlantic Sunrise (RMcDonald) **4-10-13** KJones (plld hrd: cl up tl wknd over 4f out)	11	6	50/1	27 f	—
1362 5	**Blood Brother** (JBarclay) **4-10-11**(7) NHorrocks (led tl hdd & wknd 3f out)	s.h	7	8/1	32 f	—
	Blue Chequer (MissMKMilligan) **5-10-13** ADobbin (chsd ldrs tl outpcd fnl 4f)	4	8	50/1	23 f	—
				(SP 122.4%)	**8 Rn**	

3m 40.5 CSF £14.85 TOTE £6.30: £1.10 £1.10 £1.40 (£6.60) OWNER Mr J. Berry (COCKERHAM) BRED Brendan and Sheila Powell
Carlisle Bandito's (IRE), who got warm beforehand, always held a good position and, getting first run, was well on top by the finish.(7/2: 5/2-4/1)
Coble Lane, from a yard that last had a winner in one of these events, was heavily supported and looked quite a useful type. In trying to come from behind, he always had too much on, and the position had to be accepted in the final furlong. (3/1: 4/1-9/4)
1579 Lord of The Loch (IRE) tried to come from off the pace and found things beyond him in the last couple of furlongs. (6/4)
Deerhunter had his chances, but lacked a change of gear. (6/1)
Caught At Last (IRE) showed nothing but temperament last year, and has now changed stables. He ran and behaved a good deal better here. (16/1)
1362 Blood Brother (8/1: op 5/1)

T/Plpt: £5.60 (1,271 Tckts). T/Qdpt: £3.70 (162.98 Tckts). AA

1562-**HUNTINGDON** (R-H) (Good to soft)
Tuesday December 10th
WEATHER: overcast, drizzle

1828 FLAT RACE JOCKEYS CLAIMING HURDLE (4-Y.O+) (Class F)
12-30 (12-30) **2m 110y (8 hdls)** £2,185.00 (£610.00: £295.00) GOING: 0.42 sec per fur (GS)

				SP	RR	SF
1512 4	**Surrey Dancer (128)** (MrsMReveley) **8-11-3**(3) GLee (hld up: hit 4th: led appr 2 out: sn clr: easily)	—	1	6/4 1	79	25
	Fontanays (IRE) (93) (GMMcCourt) **8-10-11** BClifford (prom: led 5th: sn hdd: hit 2 out: kpt on appr last: nt trble wnr)	1¾	2	7/1 3	68	14
1381 8	**Added Dimension (IRE) (90)** (PWinkworth) **5-10-7**(7) XAizpuru (s.i.s: plld hrd: hdwy 2nd: one pce fr 3 out)	3½	3	16/1	68	14
	Eulogy (FR) (82) (KRBurke) **9-10-11** ALarnach (prom: led appr 4th to 5th: rdn & no imp fr next)	4	4	8/1	61	7
	Quillwork (USA) (JPearce) **4-10-3** VSmith (hdwy 4th: led after 5th tl hdd & hit 3 out: sn btn)	1¾	5	20/1	51	—
	Eurolink the Lad (DBurchell) **9-10-7**(7) JPrior (bit bkwd: hld up: hdwy 5th: led next: sn rdn & hdd: wknd 2 out)	4	6	4/1 2	59	5
1288 7	**Arabian Bold (IRE) (123)** (RTJuckes) **8-11-6** PHolley (lw: prom: ev ch 5th: sn wknd: p.u bef 2 out)		P	9/1	—	—
1537 P	**Swing Lucky (63)** (AGBlackmore) **11-10-5b** DSkyrme (led tl appr 4th: sn wknd: t.o whn p.u bef 3 out)		P	20/1	—	—
1086 P	**Woodlands Energy (50)** (PAPritchard) **5-10-6** RBellamy (t.o fr 4th: p.u bef 3 out)		P	33/1	—	—
				(SP 112.0%)	**9 Rn**	

4m 4.3 (16.30) CSF £11.44 TOTE £2.00: £1.10 £1.40 £4.40 (£5.50) Trio £47.40 OWNER Laurel (Leisure) Ltd (SALTBURN) BRED Fonthill Stud
Surrey Dancer, a class apart from most of these, won like it but finished rather sore. (6/4)
Fontanays (IRE), off since finishing third in this race a year ago, returned in good shape and ought to find a race if he stays sound. (7/1: 4/1-8/1)
Added Dimension (IRE), rather keen going down, failed to settle as usual, thus ruining his chance. (16/1)
Eulogy (FR) has won a couple of All-Weather Flat races since his last appearance over hurdles and a step up in trip should break his duck over timber. (8/1)
Quillwork (USA), fit from the Flat, has looked to be struggling to stay the trip over hurdles so far. (20/1)
Eurolink the Lad has changed hands cheaply since his last appearance over hurdles, but moved up promisingly and, for a moment early in the straight, he and the winner looked the only contestants, but lack of a run then found him out. (4/1)
Arabian Bold (IRE) (9/1: op 5/1)

1829 WHAT A BUCK MAIDEN CHASE (5-Y.O+) (Class F)

1-00 (1-03) **3m (19 fncs)** £2,914.50 (£876.00: £423.00: £196.50) GOING: 0.42 sec per fur (GS)

				SP	RR	SF
1564^{2}	**Sugar Hill (IRE) (84)** (JTGifford) **6-11-0** PHide (mde all: rdn clr appr last)	—	**1**	9/2^{3}	100	6
	Slideofhill (IRE) (JJO'Neill) **7-11-0** AThornton (a.p: one pce fr 2 out)	3½	**2**	8/1	98	4
1694^{F}	**Amber Spark (IRE) (94)** (DRGandolfo) **7-11-0** RDunwoody (hld up: hdwy 14th: ev ch 2 out: sn rdn & btn)	s.h	**3**	3/1^{1}	98	4
1371^{5}	**Master Hope (IRE) (73)** (DNicholson) **7-11-0** AMaguire (chsd ldrs: blnd 13th: kpt on appr 2 out)	1¼	**4**	12/1	97	3
1550^{2}	**Forest Musk (IRE)** (PJHobbs) **5-10-13** MAFitzgerald (prom: mstkes 5th & 14th: wknd appr 2 out)	16	**5**	7/1	86	—
	Bolshie Baron (MHWeston) **7-11-0** MrMHarris (bit bkwd: chsd ldrs: blnd 4th: lost pl 11th: n.d after)	16	**6**	20/1	76	—
1417^{8}	**Sakbah (USA)** (JAPickering) **7-10-9** WMarston (prom tl mstke 11th: wkng whn hit 13th)	17	**7**	33/1	59	—
1711^{P}	**Rolled Gold** (MissVenetiaWilliams) **7-11-0** RFarrant (prom: blnd 7th & 13th: wknd 15th)	12	**8**	33/1	56	—
1566^{4}	**Quixall Crossett (56)** (EMCaine) **11-10-9**(5) DJKavanagh (lw: bhd fr 14th: hit next)	9	**9**	33/1	50	—
	Full Shilling (USA) (DLWilliams) **7-11-0** JRaja (hit 3rd: fell 6th)		**F**	33/1	—	—
1563^{5}	**Pearl Epee (90)** (DNicholson) **7-10-9** RBellamy (chsd ldrs tl blnd 12th: fell 14th)		**F**	14/1	—	—
	The Marmalade Cat (MrsDHaine) **7-11-0** JRKavanagh (a bhd: t.o whn p.u bef 15th)		**P**	25/1	—	—
1797^{F}	**Big Archie** (MrsAJBowlby) **6-11-0** CLlewellyn (prom: mstkes 2nd & 8th: sn wknd: p.u bef 15th)		**P**	12/1	—	—
1447^{2}	**Mount Serrath (IRE) (95)** (CREgerton) **8-11-0** JOsborne (uns rdr 1st)		**U**	4/1^{2}	—	—
	Swiss Tactic (IRE) (AEJessop) **7-11-0** VSmith (bit bkwd: nt j.w: bhd tl blnd & uns rdr 4 out)		**U**	33/1	—	—

(SP 132.2%) **15 Rn**

6m 26.5 (29.50) CSF £39.98 TOTE £4.30: £1.50 £2.90 £2.10 (£12.60) Trio £19.10 OWNER Mrs Timothy Pilkington (FINDON) BRED Thomas Thornton

WEIGHT FOR AGE 5yo-1lb

1564 Sugar Hill (IRE), allowed to bowl along, put in a much-improved round of jumping and was well in charge by the last. (9/2)

Slideofhill (IRE), a formerly-useful Irish pointer, has taken time to acclimatise, but should get off the mark before much longer. (8/1: 5/1-10/1)

1423 Amber Spark (IRE) is not over-big, but looked a real danger to the winner approaching the penultimate fence. Not as fast away from the obstacles as that one, he was soon flat to the boards. (3/1)

1371 Master Hope (IRE) continues to progress, staying on nicely late in the day after getting slightly outpaced due to hesitant jumps at a vital stage. (12/1)

1550 Forest Musk (IRE), an ex-Irish pointer, was making his chasing debut after runs in a bumper and a novice hurdle. His jumping was not up to scratch, but he only began to fade on the long run into the home straight. (7/1: 5/1-8/1)

Bolshie Baron, rather small for fences, coped well enough after surviving a dreadful early mistake. (20/1)

1830 FRIENDS OF ISRT NOVICES' HURDLE (4-Y.O+) (Class E)

1-30 (1-38) **2m 110y (8 hdls)** £2,652.50 (£740.00: £357.50) GOING: 0.42 sec per fur (GS)

				SP	RR	SF
	Sharpical (NJHenderson) **4-10-12** MAFitzgerald (lw: hdwy 5th: chal on bit last: qcknd to ld flat: easily)	—	**1**	5/1^{2}	73++	44
	Moonax (IRE) (BWHills) **5-10-12** RDunwoody (bit bkwd: a.p: led appr 3 out: hdd & unable qckn flat)	1¼	**2**	8/13^{1}	72+	43
1499^{3}	**Penrose Lad (NZ)** (DNicholson) **6-10-7**(5) MrRThornton (a.p: ev ch appr 2 out: unable qckn flat)	¾	**3**	12/1	71	42
	Night Dance (KAMorgan) **4-10-12** GTormey (hdwy 4th: one pce fr 2 out)	4	**4**	7/1^{3}	67	38
	Total Joy (IRE) (CJMann) **5-10-12** JRailton (chsd ldrs: no imp appr 2 out)	6	**5**	25/1	61	32
1504^{6}	**Dashanti** (DNicholson) **5-10-9**(3) RMassey (bhd tl r.o fr 2 out)	2½	**6**	33/1	59	30
1517^{4}	**The Stager (IRE)** (JRJenkins) **4-10-12** GBradley (hdwy 5th: wknd appr 2 out)	1¾	**7**	25/1	57	28
	Clinton (IRE) (KCBailey) **5-10-12** CO'Dwyer (mstkes: hdwy appr 3 out: wknd 2 out)	7	**8**	33/1	51	22
1329^{5}	**Symphony's Son (IRE)** (DNicholson) **5-10-12** AMaguire (hdwy 4th: wknd 2 out)	2½	**9**	14/1	48	19
	Bob's Ploy (MHTompkins) **4-10-12** RHughes (lw: prom: led 4th tl appr 3 out: wknd qckly appr next)	17	**10**	20/1	32	3
	Latest Thyne (IRE) (CaptTAForster) **6-10-12** AThornton (bit bkwd: a bhd)	9	**11**	25/1	23	—
1537^{5}	**Al Helal** (JRJenkins) **4-10-12v** WMarston (plld hrd: prom to 5th: sn wknd)	s.h	**12**	50/1	23	—
	Loch Garman (IRE) (FMurphy) **6-10-5**(7) MissElizabethDoyle (in tch to 4th)	27	**13**	50/1	—	—
	Cades Bay (NATwiston-Davies) **5-10-12** CLlewellyn (led to 4th: sn bhd)	25	**14**	33/1	—	—
1555^{12}	**Ballyquintet (IRE)** (HBHodge) **5-10-7** KGaule (bhd fr 4th)	27	**15**	50/1	—	—
	Young Rose (PatMitchell) **4-10-7** TKent (prom to 3rd: wkng whn blnd next)	nk	**16**	50/1	—	—
1091^{P}	**Woodlands Lad Too (65)** (PAPritchard) **4-10-12** RBellamy (a bhd: t.o whn p.u bef last)		**P**	50/1	—	—
1659^{P}	**Talk Back (IRE)** (MissHCKnight) **4-10-12** JOsborne (lw: trckd ldrs tl wknd qckly & blnd 4th: p.u bef next)		**P**	9/1	—	—

(SP 150.4%) **18 Rn**

3m 58.4 (10.40) CSF £9.62 TOTE £8.50: £1.90 £1.20 £2.70 (£5.60) Trio £30.10 OWNER Mr J. A. B. Stafford (LAMBOURN) BRED E. R. W. Stanley and New England Stud Farm Ltd

OFFICIAL EXPLANATION **Talk Back (IRE): gurgled.**

Sharpical, a much sharper, racier horse than the favourite, took to this game like a duck to water and blinded his rivals for speed from the last without knowing he had had a race. He will be a tough nut to crack on sharp tracks. (5/1)

Moonax (IRE), the 1994 St Leger winner, became the first English Classic winner for some time to go jumping. Given his antics on the Flat, he behaved himself well enough, but this sharp track exposed his lack of pace, and a step up in distance looks essential if he is to fulfil his obvious potential. (8/13: 4/5-evens)

1499 Penrose Lad (NZ) has taken a while to find his form this season, but ran really well, doing his best to make a race of it in this exalted company over the last two hurdles. He looks sure to stay further. (12/1)

Night Dance, a formerly useful handicapper from the Flat, had his tongue tied down for his hurdles debut and, although keen going to post, did appear to just about get the trip. (7/1)

Total Joy (IRE), off for over a year, looked fit enough to do himself justice and raced on the heels of the leaders until getting outpaced in the straight. (25/1)

1504 Dashanti did some sterling work in the home straight and looks well worth keeping an eye on, especially over further. (33/1)

Clinton (IRE), making his hurdles debut, jumped rather poorly, but did some eyecatching running to close briefly onto the heels of the leaders turning for home. (33/1)

1329 Symphony's Son (IRE) has hinted at ability in bumpers and Maguire presumably chose him in preference to Penrose Lad. A quite attractive sort, better will come in time. (14/1)

Bob's Ploy has failed to recapture his 1995 Flat form since changing stables and again looked a suspect stayer over timber. (20/1)

1659 Talk Back (IRE), with his tongue tied down, stopped alarmingly in a few strides before the fourth hurdle and clearly has a problem. (9/1: 6/1-10/1)

1831 SIR PETER CROSSMAN ISRT NOVICES' H'CAP CHASE (0-105) (4-Y.O+) (Class D)

2-00 (2-13) **2m 110y (12 fncs)** £3,855.00 (£1,155.00: £555.00: £255.00) GOING: 0.42 sec per fur (GS)

			SP	RR	SF
	River Leven (81) (DRGandolfo) **7-10-5b** RDunwoody (chsd ldr: led appr last: sn rdn clr: eased cl home)......—	1	3/1 [1]	89	22
	Amber Valley (USA) (97) (DLWilliams) **5-11-7** AThornton (bit bkwd: led & sn clr: rdn & hdd appr last: sn btn) .9	2	12/1	96	29
1348[4]	**Jymjam Johnny (IRE) (100)** (JJO'Neill) **7-11-10** AMaguire (lw: hld up: hit 4th: blnd 7th: hdwy 3 out: r.o flat)...¾	3	11/2 [2]	99	32
1563[6]	**Another Venture (IRE) (92)** (FMurphy) **6-10-11**(5) MrRThornton (in tch: mstkes 2nd & 8th: nvr able to chal) .1½	4	20/1	89	22
1254[4]	**Total Asset (78)** (ALForbes) **6-10-2**ow2 GaryLyons (chsd ldrs to 7th) 9	5	10/1 [3]	66	—
1552[F]	**Brazil Or Bust (IRE) (100)** (PRWebber) **5-11-10** JOsborne (chsd ldrs: 3rd & btn whn eased appr last) 30	6	3/1 [1]	59	—
	Serious (97) (KCBailey) **6-11-7** CO'Dwyer (hld up: hit 3 out: eased appr next) 5	7	3/1 [1]	51	—
			(SP 111.9%)		**7 Rn**

4m 16.3 (14.30) CSF £31.41 TOTE £4.10: £1.40 £3.10 (£15.30) OWNER Mr R. E. Brinkworth (WANTAGE) BRED W. Bush
LONG HANDICAP Total Asset 9-3

River Leven seemed the only one in serious pursuit of the leader from a long way out and it paid dividends as that rival came to the end of his tether. He was racing off a 19lb lower mark than he does over hurdles and, given that his jumping now seems sound, he should win again. (3/1)

Amber Valley (USA) excelled himself in the Haydock Champion Hurdle Trial on his latest start, but came here looking just in need of the outing and with his tongue tied down. Not over-big for fences, he jumped soundly and led his rivals a merry dance until tiring in the straight. He should find a race before long. (12/1)

1348 Jymjam Johnny (IRE) did well to get so close after losing many lengths with a dreadful mistake at the water. (11/2: 4/1-6/1)

Another Venture (IRE) could never make much impact and this trip is possibly too sharp. (20/1)

1007 Total Asset, very moderate over hurdles, does now appear somewhat flattered by his chasing debut. (10/1: tchd 16/1)

1179* Brazil Or Bust (IRE) chased the first two at a respectable distance and landed just third at the penultimate fence, but his rider took things very easy and allowed him to coast in, presumably feeling something was not right. (3/1: 2/1-7/2)

Serious has hardly taken the normal route to handicap chases, with just one hurdle run to his name, and his latest outing was in the Schweppes Golden Mile. Not persevered with after a mistake three out, he does not look at all badly handicapped if he can get his act together. (3/1: op 2/1)

1832 NATIONAL HUNT JOCKEYS H'CAP HURDLE (0-125) (4-Y.O+) (Class D)

2-30 (2-38) **2m 110y (8 hdls)** £2,847.00 (£792.00: £381.00) GOING: 0.42 sec per fur (GS)

			SP	RR	SF
	Most Equal (110) (MCPipe) **6-11-5** RHughes (hdwy 4th: chal 2 out: led last: edgd lft: rdn out)......—	1	4/1 [2]	92	56
1567[5]	**Albemine (USA) (119)** (MrsJCecil) **7-12-0** TKent (chsd ldrs: led appr 2 out: hdd last: unable qckn) ......¾	2	9/1	100	64
1374[6]	**Menelave (IRE) (108)** (OSherwood) **6-11-3** JOsborne (lw: chsd ldr tl led 5th: hdd appr 2 out: one pce) 19	3	9/2 [3]	71	35
1567[2]	**Marius (IRE) (112)** (JTGifford) **6-11-7** PHide (lw: led & sn clr: hdd 5th: btn appr next) 5	4	15/8 [1]	70	34
	Glanmerin (IRE) (119) (KAMorgan) **5-12-0** GBradley (hit 4th: a bhd) 21	5	20/1	57	21
	Storm Dust (110) (MissHCKnight) **7-11-5** RDunwoody (bit bkwd: a bhd) 1	6	10/1	47	11
1282[U]	**Jemima Puddleduck (93)** (AStreeter) **5-10-2** TEley (chsd ldrs: pushed along 3rd: wknd next)......16	7	6/1	14	—
1144[7]	**Eden Dancer (105)** (MrsMReveley) **4-10-11**(3) GLee (prom to 4th)......¾	8	7/1	25	—
	Young At Heart (IRE) (91) (MJHaynes) **5-10-0** DSkyrme (bit bkwd: fell 4th)	F	20/1	—	—
			(SP 128.4%)		**9 Rn**

3m 57.2 (9.20) CSF £39.72 CT £158.74 TOTE £5.40: £1.90 £3.40 £1.30 (£26.20) Trio £35.80 OWNER Mr Heeru Kirpalani (WELLINGTON) BRED H. L. Kirpalani
LONG HANDICAP Young At Heart (IRE) 9-10
OFFICIAL EXPLANATION **Jemima Puddleduck: the rider reported that the mare sulked.**

Most Equal looked fit, despite seven months off, and quickened decisively from the last, despite threatening to lean on his rivals. (4/1)

1567 Albemine (USA) ran a terrific race on ground slower than ideal and is clearly in great heart. (9/1)

1374 Menelave (IRE) looked and moved well, leaving her poor effort of last time behind and, although no match for the first two, could have finished somewhat closer. (9/2)

1567 Marius (IRE) could not confirm the form of a fortnight ago with Albemine and gave way tamely on the home turn. (15/8)

Glanmerin (IRE) looked potentially useful in the spring of last year, but has had his problems since. He did enough without getting into the race to suggest that he may yet return to form. (20/1)

Storm Dust, having only his third race in three and a half years, should come on a lot from this. (10/1: 8/1-12/1)

1833 HORSERACE WRITERS CONDITIONAL H'CAP CHASE (0-110) (4-Y.O+) (Class E)

3-00 (3-04) **2m 4f 110y (16 fncs)** £2,968.00 (£889.00: £427.00: £196.00) GOING: 0.42 sec per fur (GS)

			SP	RR	SF
1657[7]	**East Houston (96)** (JJO'Neill) **7-11-10** RMcGrath (lw: hdwy 9th: led 4 out: clr appr 2 out: mstke & lft clr last)—	1	4/1	108	23
	Judicial Field (IRE) (95) (NTinkler) **7-11-9b** EHusband (chsd ldrs: no imp fr 3 out: lft 2nd last)......21	2	3/1 [2]	91	6
1328[P]	**Viaggio (75)** (ALForbes) **8-10-3** MichaelBrennan (prom: pckd 2nd: mstke & lost pl 10th: rallied 12th: ev ch 3 out: sn wknd)......13	3	20/1	61	—
1660[7]	**Count Barachois (USA) (96)** (MrsEHHeath) **8-11-10** KGaule (bit bkwd: led to 4 out: wknd next) ......dist	4	16/1	—	—
1472[3]	**At The Grove (IRE) (96)** (KCBailey) **6-11-5**(5) WWalsh (lw: hdwy whn fell 9th)......	F	9/4 [1]	—	—
1815[3]	**Monaughty Man (72)** (EMCaine) **10-10-0** DJKavanagh (w ldr tl fell 12th)	F	20/1	—	—
1629[5]	**Playing Truant (82)** (DRGandolfo) **8-10-10** LAspell (hld up: hdwy 12th: chsd wnr appr 2 out: btn whn blnd & uns rdr last)	U	7/2 [3]	—	—
			(SP 113.4%)		**7 Rn**

5m 22.5 (22.50) CSF £15.57 TOTE £4.70: £2.10 £2.00 (£3.90) OWNER Highgreen Partnership (PENRITH) BRED J. R. Mitchell
LONG HANDICAP Monaughty Man 9-11

1657 East Houston took charge on the home turn and would still have won well without the last-fence departure of his closest rival. He is a hard horse to predict, but may be best going right-handed. (4/1)

Judicial Field (IRE) looked fit enough, but proved ring-rusty after six months off. (3/1)

1010 Viaggio won a chase at Leicester in December 1993, but had been pulled up in both his runs over fences since. He did well to get back to the leaders by the third last before his stamina failed him. (20/1)

Count Barachois (USA) ran much better than on his comeback and a return to form, probably over the minimum trip, is quite possible. (16/1)

1472 At The Grove (IRE) (9/4: op 6/4)

1629 Playing Truant went in pursuit of the winner on the home turn, but was four lengths down and held when ploughing through the last and unseating his pilot. (7/2)

1834 WEATHERBYS 'STARS OF TOMORROW' INTERMEDIATE N.H. FLAT RACE (4, 5 & 6-Y.O) (Class H)

3-30 (3-36) **2m 110y** £1,385.00 (£385.00: £185.00)

				SP	RR	SF
1362[4]	**Strong Mint (IRE)** (MrsMReveley) **5-11-1**(3) GLee (hdwy 5f out: led over 2f out: rdn out)	—	**1**	Evens[1]	58 f	—
1457[13]	**Feebee Five** (SPCWoods) **4-10-10**(3) PHenley (hld up: hdwy 4f out: chsd wnr fnl 2f: no imp)	2	**2**	14/1	51 f	—
	Bessie Browne (IRE) (GAHubbard) **4-10-13** KGaule (lengthy, unf: bit bkwd: chsd ldrs: one pce fnl 3f)	5	**3**	16/1	46 f	—
1457[15]	**Fiddler's Leap (IRE)** (MissHCKnight) **4-10-11**(7) MrAWintle (bit bkwd: trckd ldrs pllng hrd: ev ch over 2f out: sn btn)	1½	**4**	20/1	50 f	—
	Cosy Ride (IRE) (NATwiston-Davies) **4-10-11**(7) LSuthern (lengthy, unf: lt made: w ldr: led 4f out tl over 2f out: sn btn)	3½	**5**	10/1	46 f	—
	Benvenuto (KCBailey) **5-10-11**(7) MrRWakley (rangy, chsing type: prom 13f)	1¼	**6**	10/1	45 f	—
1450[2]	**Lovely Rascal** (JJO'Neill) **4-10-8**(5) RMcGrath (prom tl wknd 3f out)	3½	**7**	3/1[2]	37 f	—
	Trymyply (HJMWebb) **4-10-13**(5) SophieMitchell (bhd: hdwy 4f out: wknd 2f out)	1½	**8**	50/1	40 f	—
	Quince Bay (JELong) **4-10-13**(5) MrRThornton (cmpt: led over 12f)	5	**9**	33/1	36 f	—
1685[12]	**Social Insecurity (IRE)** (SGollings) **5-10-13**(5) DJKavanagh (chsd ldrs: ev ch 4f out: wknd over 2f out)	2½	**10**	33/1	33 f	—
1329[18]	**Above Suspicion (IRE)** (CJames) **4-11-4** MrEJames (a bhd)	nk	**11**	33/1	33 f	—
1457[12]	**Normandy Duke (NZ)** (CJMann) **4-11-1**(3) JMagee (in tch: hdwy 8f out: rdn 5f out: sn wknd)	10	**12**	25/1	23 f	—
1579[6]	**Run For The Mill** (JMJefferson) **4-10-11**(7) MNewton (lw: chsd ldrs 10f)	3	**13**	15/2[3]	20 f	—
1665[15]	**Toddys Lass** (JAPickering) **4-10-8**(5) MichaelBrennan (a bhd)	dist	**14**	50/1	—	—
	That Man Carter (IRE) (GCBravery) **5-11-1**(3) FLeahy (lt-f, unf: in tch tl rdn & wknd 6f out)	11	**15**	16/1	—	—
	Abfab (KRBurke) **4-10-11**(7) AWatt (attr, small: plld hrd: prom 7f: wknd qckly)	20	**16**	33/1	—	—

(SP 147.7%) **16 Rn**

4m 0.3 CSF £20.83 TOTE £2.00: £1.10 £3.10 £5.10 (£24.00) Trio £136.50 OWNER Mr J. Good (SALTBURN) BRED Dermot and Gerry Mullins

1362 Strong Mint (IRE), brought wide on the home turn in search of the best ground, needed to be shaken up to hold the runner-up at bay. He should continue to go the right way. (Evens)

Feebee Five is on the small size and a moderate mover, but she does have ability, for she was the only one giving chase to the winner from the distance. (14/1)

Bessie Browne (IRE) is well-bred for jumping, but is lengthy and rather unfurnished. She did run respectably, if rather one-paced once in line for home. (16/1)

Fiddler's Leap (IRE) took some settling at the slow early pace and, after looking dangerous turning for home, his stamina seemed to give out. (20/1)

Cosy Ride (IRE) has plenty of growing up to do, but was with the leaders on the home turn. (10/1: op 4/1)

Benvenuto, out of a sister to Celtic Ryde and Ryde Again, is a big, rangy sort who looks the part, and will surely do better in time. (10/1: 5/1-12/1)

Quince Bay, whose sire has yet to produce anything of note under Rules, is a good walker and hinted at some ability, making much of the pace. (33/1)

1579 Run For The Mill (15/2: 10/1-16/1)

T/Jkpt: £37,325.20 (1.99 Tckts). T/Plpt: £69.30 (186.66 Tckts). T/Qdpt: £28.20 (32.75 Tckts). Dk

1419-PLUMPTON (L-H) (Good to soft, Soft patches)

Tuesday December 10th

WEATHER: cold & dull

1835 DITCHLING NOVICES' HURDLE (4-Y.O+) (Class E)

12-40 (12-40) **2m 4f (12 hdls)** £2,616.00 (£726.00: £348.00) GOING: 1.34 sec per fur (HY)

				SP	RR	SF
1550*	**Emerald Statement (IRE)** (DMGrissell) **6-10-9**(3) GHogan (lw: a.p: chsd ldr fr 8th: lft in ld 3 out: clr appr 2 out: easily)	—	**1**	4/7[1]	73+	39
	Sioux To Speak (MissHCKnight) **4-10-12** BFenton (bit bkwd: hdwy 9th: chsd wnr appr 2 out: no imp)	16	**2**	8/1	60	26
1659[5]	**Mazirah** (RCurtis) **5-10-12** DMorris (hdwy 6th: lft 2nd 3 out: rdn: one pce)	½	**3**	20/1	60	26
1651[12]	**English Invader** (RAkehurst) **5-10-12** APMcCoy (lw: 5th whn mstke 4th: bhd fr 8th: t.o)	dist	**4**	7/1[3]	—	—
1568[4]	**Scotby (BEL)** (RHBuckler) **6-11-5** BPowell (a.p: chsd ldr fr 6th: led 8th tl fell 3 out)		**F**	7/2[2]	—	—
1260[P]	**Queen Of The Suir (IRE)** (NRMitchell) **7-10-7** SCurran (lw: chsd ldr to 6th: wknd 7th: t.o whn p.u bef 9th)		**P**	100/1	—	—
	Jack of Diamonds (RJO'Sullivan) **8-10-12** AMcCabe (lw: led to 8th: sn wknd: t.o whn p.u bef 2 out)		**P**	50/1	—	—
1713[U]	**Halam Bell** (WGMTurner) **4-10-0**(7) JPower (tried to ref 1st, 2nd & 3rd: t.o whn ref 4th)		**R**	66/1	—	—
	Kybo's Revenge (IRE) (RRowe) **5-10-12** DO'Sullivan (lw: 5th whn mstke 5th: bhd whn blnd & uns rdr 7th)		**U**	25/1	—	—

(SP 122.5%) **9 Rn**

5m 19.6 (32.60) CSF £6.67 TOTE £1.60: £1.10 £1.60 £3.50 (£4.90) Trio £15.30 OWNER The Hon Mrs C Yeates (ROBERTSBRIDGE) BRED Mrs Mary Doyle

1550* Emerald Statement (IRE), so impressive at Folkestone recently, was right on the heels of the leader, although being pushed along slightly, when that rival crashed to the deck three out, handing him the advantage and ultimately an easy win. This would surely be his minimum trip. (4/7)

Sioux To Speak, who has changed stables since last season, was making his hurdling debut and looked as though the run would do him good. (8/1: op 9/2)

1659 Mazirah was tackling a longer trip. (20/1)

English Invader (7/1: 10/1-6/1)

1568 Scotby (BEL), with a 7lb penalty to contend with, was travelling just as well as the winner when falling at the third last. Compensation should soon be found. (7/2)

1836 HENFIELD (S) H'CAP HURDLE (0-90) (4-Y.O+) (Class G)

1-10 (1-12) **2m 1f (10 hdls)** £1,909.40 (£528.40: £252.20) GOING: 1.34 sec per fur (HY)

				SP	RR	SF
1630[6]	**Kayfaat (USA) (79)** (MCPipe) **8-11-9v** APMcCoy (rdn thrght: chsd ldr: led 7th: clr appr 2 out: r.o)	—	**1**	9/4[1]	72	—
1040[7]	**Slightly Special (IRE) (59)** (BAPearce) **4-10-3** TJMurphy (led tl mstke & hdd 7th: ev ch 3 out: wknd appr 2 out)	14	**2**	33/1	39	—
1707[3]	**Water Hazard (IRE) (73)** (SDow) **4-11-3** ADicken (prom to 6th: poor 3rd whn blnd 2 out)	12	**3**	13/2	42	—
1198[5]	**Al Haal (USA) (71)** (RJO'Sullivan) **7-11-1** DO'Sullivan (lw: prom to 4th)	5	**4**	4/1[2]	35	—

Form	Horse / details	Dist	Pos	SP	RR	SF
	Aldwick Colonnade (80) (MDIUsher) **9-11-10** WMcFarland (nvr nr to chal)	¾	**5**	7/1	43	—
	Fruit Town (IRE) (70) (PButler) **7-11-0** BFenton (lw: mstke 4th: bhd fr 7th)	4	**6**	11/2[3]	29	—
	Trendy Auctioneer (IRE) (64) (MrsLCJewell) **8-10-8v** DLeahy (a bhd)	5	**7**	20/1	19	—
	Persian Bud (IRE) (67) (JRBosley) **8-10-11** MBosley (j.slowly 3rd: a bhd: t.o)	dist	**8**	8/1	—	—

(SP 110.8%) **8 Rn**

4m 35.9 (39.90) CSF £49.82 CT £366.49 TOTE £2.80: £1.80 £6.00 £1.90 (£78.40) Trio £13.80 OWNER Crown Racing (WELLINGTON) BRED James J. Devaney and McMillin Brothers in USA
No bid
IN-FOCUS: **This looked a terrible race.**
1630 Kayfaat (USA) looks a very tricky customer, and praise must be given to his jockey. Never looking happy, McCoy was having to push him along to keep tabs on the leader, but that one tired going to the penultimate hurdle, handing him this quite appalling race on a plate. He looks one to treat with a great deal of caution. (9/4: 7/4-11/4)
Slightly Special (IRE) left his previous form this season well behind in an atrocious race. The soft ground seemed to be to his liking. (33/1)
1707 Water Hazard (IRE) was in trouble early on the final circuit and this ground was probably against him. (13/2: 4/1-7/1)
Al Haal (USA) (4/1: 6/1-3/1)
Aldwick Colonnade (7/1: 3/1-8/1)
Persian Bud (IRE) (8/1: 6/1-9/1)

1837 OWL HOLDINGS H'CAP CHASE (0-120) (4-Y.O+) (Class D)
1-40 (1-40) **2m 5f (16 fncs)** £4,077.50 (£1,220.00: £585.00: £267.50) GOING: 0.96 sec per fur (S)

Form	Horse / details	Dist	Pos	SP	RR	SF
1284[F]	**Beatson (IRE) (95)** (RHBuckler) **7-10-8** BPowell (a.p: mstke 12th: rdn 4 out: led appr 3 out: drvn out)	—	**1**	11/4[2]	108	27
1420[2]	**Mr Matt (IRE) (105)** (DMGrissell) **8-11-4** BFenton (led 3rd to 7th: rdn 11th: led 12th tl appr 3 out: hrd rdn appr last: unable qckn)	9	**2**	7/2	111	30
1570[2]	**Beau Babillard (115)** (PFNicholls) **9-12-0b** APMcCoy (lw: hld up: rdn 11th: one pce fr 12th)	7	**3**	5/2[1]	116	35
1420[U]	**Black Church (92)** (RRowe) **10-10-5** DO'Sullivan (lw: led 7th to 12th: sn wknd: wl bhd whn j.rt 2 out)	2½	**4**	3/1[3]	91	10
1554[3]	**Joker Jack (88)** (RDean) **11-9-12**(3)ow1 TDascombe (lw: led to 3rd: wknd 6th: t.o fr 8th)	dist	**5**	40/1	—	—

(SP 104.9%) **5 Rn**

5m 42.0 (29.00) CSF £10.95 TOTE £4.10: £1.90 £1.60 (£7.10) OWNER Mrs E. B. Gardiner (BRIDPORT) BRED M. Holden in Ireland
LONG HANDICAP Joker Jack 8-3
1284 Beatson (IRE) made up for his Wincanton tumble and responded to pressure to keep the runner-up at bay. (11/4)
1420 Mr Matt (IRE) goes well in the mud. He has not won for two years, but has now run a couple of sound races. (7/2)
1570 Beau Babillard revels in the mud, but was made to look very one-paced under his welter-burden. (5/2)
1420 Black Church looked very well beforehand, but is becoming costly to follow. He seems to find little off the bridle. (3/1)

1838 BRIGHTON NOVICES' CLAIMING HURDLE (4,5,6 & 7-Y.O) (Class F)
2-10 (2-11) **2m 1f (10 hdls)** £1,992.80 (£550.80: £262.40) GOING: 1.34 sec per fur (HY)

Form	Horse / details	Dist	Pos	SP	RR	SF
1762[U]	**Urban Lily (84)** (RJHodges) **6-9-10b**(7) JHarris (lw: chsd ldr: led 4th: clr 2 out: easily)	—	**1**	10/11[1]	60	—
1679[4]	**Fairelaine** (KCBailey) **4-11-1** APMcCoy (hld up: chsd wnr fr 6th: rdn appr 2 out: wknd appr last)	24	**2**	5/4[2]	49	—
	Robin Island (PRHedger) **4-10-1**(7) MClinton (lw: bhd fr 7th: t.o)	dist	**3**	33/1	—	—
	Warspite (PMooney) **6-10-0**(5) SRyan (hdwy 5th: rdn appr 3 out: sn wknd: t.o)	14	**4**	14/1[3]	—	—
	Sir Oliver (IRE) (BAPearce) **7-11-0** TJMurphy (bit bkwd: plld hrd: led to 4th: wknd 6th: bhd whn p.u bef 7th)		**P**	50/1	—	—

(SP 108.4%) **5 Rn**

4m 37.2 (41.20) CSF £2.26 TOTE £1.60: £1.00 £4.40 (£1.70) OWNER Mrs C. J. Cole (SOMERTON) BRED Mrs C. J. Cole
1762 Urban Lily managed to sweep aside the runner-up early in the straight to win this very bad race with plenty in hand. (10/11: 4/5-evens)
1679 Fairelaine, the only danger to the winner three from home, was in trouble in the straight. (5/4)
Warspite (14/1: 10/1-16/1)

1839 'GALLEANO' CHALLENGE CUP H'CAP CHASE (0-110) (5-Y.O+) (Class E)
2-40 (2-40) **3m 1f 110y (20 fncs)** £3,070.20 (£915.60: £436.80: £197.40) GOING: 0.96 sec per fur (S)

Form	Horse / details	Dist	Pos	SP	RR	SF
1420[6]	**Jurassic Classic (109)** (MrsLRichards) **9-12-0** MRichards (chsd ldr 3rd: led 14th: rdn out)	—	**1**	6/1	117	36
1716[5]	**Ring Corbitts (84)** (MJRoberts) **8-10-0**(3) GHogan (lw: hdwy 14th: chsd wnr fr 15th: mstke 4 out: ev ch whn blnd bdly 2 out: unable qckn)	2	**2**	33/1	91	10
1415[2]	**Celtic Town (108)** (OSherwood) **8-11-13** JAMcCarthy (hld up: rdn 15th: wknd 4 out: t.o)	dist	**3**	11/4[1]	—	—
1420[P]	**Mighty Frolic (105)** (MissSEdwards) **9-11-10** MrTHills (bhd fr 7th: t.o fr 14th)	17	**4**	14/1	—	—
	Lay it Off (IRE) (85) (JGO'Neill) **7-10-4** SCurran (lw: blnd 2nd: prom to 13th: t.o fr 15th)	28	**5**	11/2	—	—
1391[F]	**Childhay Chocolate (105)** (PFNicholls) **8-11-10** APMcCoy (3rd whn fell 6th)		**F**	9/2[3]	—	—
1674[P]	**Credon (103)** (SWoodman) **8-11-8** NWilliamson (lw: nt j.w: hdwy 6th: reminders 10th: wknd 14th: t.o whn p.u bef 4 out)		**P**	4/1[2]	—	—
1684[6]	**Titan Empress (81)** (SMellor) **7-10-0v** NMann (bhd whn hmpd 6th: p.u bef 7th)		**P**	10/1	—	—
1389[P]	**Millfrone (IRE) (83)** (RRowe) **6-10-2**ow2 DO'Sullivan (led: mstke 11th: hdd 14th:sn wknd: t.o whn p.u bef 3 out)		**P**	66/1	—	—

(SP 114.7%) **9 Rn**

6m 58.7 (38.70) CSF £128.92 CT £602.83 TOTE £8.80: £1.50 £3.60 £1.40 (£66.10) Trio £58.10 OWNER Brian Seal & Roger Rees (CHICHESTER) BRED C. L. Gilman
LONG HANDICAP Titan Empress 9-13 Millfrone (IRE) 8-7
Jurassic Classic goes well with some cut. Rousted along, he kept going to gain his first victory away from Fontwell. (6/1)
Ring Corbitts, a maiden over hurdles and fences, ran his best race for a very long time and was in with every chance when making an horrendous mistake two from home. He grimly tried to mount another challenge from the last, but failed to find that vital turn of foot. (33/1)
1415 Celtic Town was left for dead from the fourth last. (11/4)
1420 Credon (4/1: 3/1-9/2)
1420 Titan Empress (10/1: op 6/1)

1840 CHAILEY NOVICES' H'CAP HURDLE (0-100) (4-Y.O+) (Class E)
3-10 (3-10) **3m 110y (14 hdls)** £2,364.00 (£654.00: £312.00) GOING: 1.34 sec per fur (HY)

Form	Horse / details	Dist	Pos	SP	RR	SF
1673[5]	**Copper Coil (87)** (WGMTurner) **6-11-4**(7) JPower (a.p: led 10th: drvn out)	—	**1**	10/1	68	—
1539[5]	**Lough Tully (IRE) (74)** (FJordan) **6-10-12** SWynne (lw: hld up: chsd wnr appr 2 out: mstke 2 out:hrd rdn:r.o)	1½	**2**	4/1[1]	54	—

			SP	RR	SF
1476^{6}	**Miss Secret (76)** (CWMitchell) **6-11-0** DBridgwater (hdwy 11th: hrd rdn appr 2 out: unable qckn)....12	**3**	25/1	48	—
1638^{5}	**Honey Mount (90)** (NJHWalker) **5-12-0** NWilliamson (hdwy 11th: hrd rdn appr 2 out: wknd appr last)....8	**4**	5/1 ^{2}	57	—
1673^{4}	**Quinag (89)** (KCBailey) **5-11-13** SMcNeill (lw: led to 6th: wknd 3 out: t.o)....dist	**5**	10/1	—	—
	Equity's Darling (IRE) (79) (DCO'Brien) **4-11-3** DGallagher (rel to r: a bhd: t.o)....10	**6**	14/1	—	—
	Plassy Boy (IRE) (75) (KRBurke) **7-10-13** APMcCoy (lw: bhd fr 10th: t.o)....5	**7**	6/1 ^{3}	—	—
1327^{5}	**Fairies Farewell (82)** (OSherwood) **6-11-6** JAMcCarthy (lw: prom to 11th: t.o whn p.u bef 2 out)....	**P**	10/1	—	—
954^{10}	**Difficult Decision (IRE) (85)** (MrsMerritaJones) **5-11-9** DerekByrne (lw: a.p: led 6th to 10th: 5th & v.tired whn p.u bef last)....	**P**	5/1 ^{2}	—	—
1568^{9}	**Red Branch (IRE) (69)** (JSKing) **7-10-7** TJMurphy (lw: bhd fr 10th: t.o whn p.u bef 3 out)....	**P**	7/1	—	—
			(SP 117.9%)		**10 Rn**

6m 44.8 CSF £47.22 CT £900.84 TOTE £12.80: £2.80 £1.40 £4.10 (£33.10) Trio £72.60 OWNER Mr R. A. Lloyd (SHERBORNE) BRED Eric Saunders

1673 Copper Coil went on with a circuit to race and, responding to pressure, kept the persistent runner-up at bay. (10/1: op 5/1)
1539 Lough Tully (IRE) appreciated this longer trip and kept on well to the line. (4/1: op 10/1)
Miss Secret ran her best race to date. Closing up in the back straight, she was made to look one-paced from the third last. (25/1)
1638 Honey Mount moved up sweetly in the back straight but, under pressure turning for home, the writing was soon on the wall. (5/1)
1673 Quinag (10/1: op 9/2)
Equity's Darling (IRE) (14/1: op 6/1)
Plassy Boy (IRE) (6/1: 8/1-5/1)
1327 Fairies Farewell (10/1: op 4/1)
718 Difficult Decision (IRE) (5/1: 7/1-9/2)

1841 EASTBOURNE H'CAP HURDLE (0-105) (4-Y.O+) (Class F)
3-40 (3-40) **2m 4f (12 hdls)** £1,974.60 (£545.60: £259.80) GOING: 1.34 sec per fur (HY)

			SP	RR	SF
	Ismeno (97) (SDow) **5-11-9** ADicken (led 4th: rdn out)....—	**1**	8/1	80	1
1355^{F}	**Stoney Valley (102)** (JRJenkins) **6-12-0** NWilliamson (hld up: chsd wnr appr 2 out: hrd rdn appr last: unable qckn)....4	**2**	7/1 ^{3}	82	3
1813*	**General Mouktar (103)** (MCPipe) **6-12-1** 7x APMcCoy (lw: hld up: rdn appr 2 out: one pce)....5	**3**	4/6 ^{1}	79	—
1419^{4}	**Do Be Ware (74)** (JFfitch-Heyes) **6-10-0b** BFenton (lw: led 2nd to 3rd: rdn 9th: wknd appr 2 out)....17	**4**	33/1	36	—
1709^{P}	**Raahin (USA) (76)** (SWoodman) **11-10-2** SMcNeill (lw: led to 2nd: led 3rd to 4th: wknd 7th)....26	**5**	25/1	17	—
1553^{P}	**Whistling Buck (IRE) (86)** (RRowe) **8-10-12** DO'Sullivan (lw: prom tl appr 3 out: 5th & wkng whn stumbled after 3 out)....1	**6**	11/2 ^{2}	27	—
1599^{4}	**Little Hooligan (84)** (RJHodges) **5-10-7**(3) TDascombe (lw: hld up: rdn 9th: wknd 3 out: t.o)....dist	**7**	8/1	—	—
			(SP 116.9%)		**7 Rn**

5m 33.4 (46.40) CSF £55.96 TOTE £10.90: £4.80 £1.90 (£33.30) OWNER Mrs A. M. Upsdell (EPSOM) BRED Sheikh Mohammed bin Rashid al Maktoum

LONG HANDICAP Do Be Ware 9-7

Ismeno, whose only victory last term came in the mud, made a winning return to action, despite losing his near-fore plate during the race. (8/1: 6/1-9/1)
1355 Stoney Valley, who has been slipping down the handicap, failed to reel in the winner. (7/1: 5/1-8/1)
1813* General Mouktar was unable to deliver the goods two days running even under the McCoy magic and, once he came off the bridle turning for home, punters knew their fate. (4/6)
819* Do Be Ware, 7lb out of the handicap, was being left for dead by the front three turning for home. (33/1)
Raahin (USA) looked very well beforehand, but was struggling with fully a circuit to race. (25/1)
1419* Whistling Buck (IRE), whose connections reported he did not like the soft ground last time out, not surprisingly flopped again in similar conditions. (11/2: 4/1-6/1)
1599 Little Hooligan (8/1: 6/1-10/1)

T/Plpt: £34.10 (232.38 Tckts). T/Qdpt: £14.30 (49.04 Tckts). AK

1458-SEDGEFIELD (L-H) (Good)
Tuesday December 10th
WEATHER: misty

1842 GOLDEN LION 'N.H.' NOVICES' HURDLE (I) (4-Y.O+) (Class E)
12-20 (12-21) **2m 5f 110y (10 hdls)** £1,952.50 (£540.00: £257.50) GOING minus 0.05 sec per fur (G)

			SP	RR	SF
	Sutherland Moss (TPTate) **5-10-12** JCallaghan (lw: a.p: led appr 2 out: hit last: styd on)....—	**1**	13/8 ^{1}	62	—
1640^{8}	**Grand Cru** (MrsMReveley) **5-10-12** PNiven (cl up: chal 6th: led 3 out: hdd appr next: kpt on)....5	**2**	11/4 ^{3}	58	—
	Basincroft (MissSWilliamson) **6-10-5**(7) ATodd (bit bkwd: mstke 2nd: bhd tl styd on fr 3 out: n.d)....24	**3**	50/1	40	—
1654^{13}	**See More Ghosts (IRE)** (MrsASwinbank) **5-10-12** JSupple (outpcd & mstke 5th: styd on fr 3 out: n.d)....1¾	**4**	20/1	39	—
	Phileas Fogg (IRE) (JSisterson) **7-10-12** BStorey (bit bkwd: led tl hdd & wknd 3 out)....13	**5**	100/1	29	—
1296^{19}	**Boyzontoowa (IRE)** (RCollins) **4-10-12** RichardGuest (bit bkwd: chsd ldrs: ev ch 4 out: wknd next)....10	**6**	66/1	22	—
1362^{13}	**Soundpost** (DMoffatt) **4-10-12** DJMoffatt (mstke 4th: lost tch fr 4 out)....8	**7**	16/1	16	—
1523^{P}	**Akito Racing (IRE)** (MartinTodhunter) **5-10-7** ADobbin (chsd ldrs tl wknd appr 3 out)....2½	**8**	33/1	9	—
1539^{2}	**Jills Joy (IRE)** (JNorton) **5-10-5**(7) BGrattan (trckd ldrs: hdwy to disp ld whn fell 3 out)....	**F**	5/2 ^{2}	—	—
			(SP 111.4%)		**9 Rn**

5m 18.2 (18.20) CSF £6.01 TOTE £2.30: £1.10 £2.00 £27.70 (£6.40) Trio £114.50; £50.02 to Hexham 11/12/96 OWNER Mr C. E. Whiteley (TADCASTER) BRED Ford Farm Bloodstock

Sutherland Moss, who looked fit, won readily enough, but the opposition was not all that great. (13/8)
Grand Cru, who is obviously learning, stays well, but is short of a turn of foot. (11/4)
Basincroft showed his first signs of form and did need the run, but there is still a long way to go. (50/1)
See More Ghosts (IRE), who just seems to stay, never looked likely to get into this. (20/1)
Phileas Fogg (IRE), in need of this, blew up three from home. (100/1)

1843 GOLDEN LION 'N.H.' NOVICES' HURDLE (II) (4-Y.O+) (Class E)

12-50 (12-51) **2m 5f 110y (10 hdls)** £1,935.00 (£535.00: £255.00) GOING minus 0.05 sec per fur (G)

				SP	RR	SF
1640[4]	**Paperising** (GRichards) **4-10-12** ADobbin (lw: a gng wl: led 3 out: easily)	—	1	8/11[1]	77+	8
1527*	**Real Glee (IRE)** (JJQuinn) **7-10-12** TReed (led 3rd to 6th: ev ch tl wknd 2 out)	9	2	4/1[3]	70	1
	Erni (FR) (TPTate) **4-10-6**(7)ow1 RMcCarthy (lw: in tch: outpcd 3 out: styd on fr next)	7	3	16/1	66	—
	Yewcroft Boy (MABarnes) **5-10-12** FPerratt (prom tl outpcd appr 4 out: styd on fr 2 out)	8	4	33/1	59	—
	Maitre de Musique (FR) (105) (MartinTodhunter) **5-10-12** BHarding (led to 3rd: led 6th to 3 out: wknd)	1¼	5	3/1[2]	58	—
	Irish Buzz (IRE) (MrsASwinbank) **4-10-12** MrChrisWilson (outpcd ½-wy: n.d after)	½	6	33/1	58	—
1263[7]	**Persuasive Talent (IRE)** (DALamb) **5-10-12** JBurke (n.d)	8	7	50/1	52	—
	The Mickletonian (JIACharlton) **5-10-12** KJohnson (mstke 6th: sn outpcd & wl bhd)	dist	8	16/1	—	—
	Whitegates Willie (HowardJohnson) **4-10-12** GCahill (prom to 6th: sn t.o: p.u bef 2 out)		P	50/1	—	—

(SP 124.5%) **9 Rn**

5m 14.1 (14.10) CSF £4.74 TOTE £1.90: £1.10 £1.80 £3.80 (£3.00) Trio £7.90 OWNER The Jockeys Whips (PENRITH) BRED Independent British Hospitals

IN-FOCUS: **This was run in a much better time than the first division.**

1640 Paperising made no mistake and won in useful style. (8/11)

1527* Real Glee (IRE), back to hurdling, probably to boost his confidence, ran well, but the winner was always too good. (4/1: op 5/2)

Erni (FR) got tapped for speed when the leading pair went for home, but it was pleasing to see him stay on at the finish. (16/1)

Yewcroft Boy looks a real stayer in the making and was keeping on particularly well at the end. (33/1)

Maitre de Musique (FR) was disappointing here, dropping out tamely when the pressure was applied three out. This run was most likely needed. (3/1)

Irish Buzz (IRE), an Irish import, showed his first signs of form here, making a little late headway. (33/1)

1844 DICKIE DODS MEMORIAL H'CAP HURDLE (0-115) (4-Y.O+) (Class E)

1-20 (1-20) **3m 3f 110y (13 hdls)** £2,337.50 (£650.00: £312.50) GOING minus 0.05 sec per fur (G)

				SP	RR	SF
1528[F]	**Troodos (95)** (MrsASwinbank) **10-11-2** JSupple (lw: hld up: hdwy 4 out: led 2 out: styd on)	—	1	9/4[1]	76	38
1081[5]	**Manettia (IRE) (86)** (MrsMReveley) **7-10-7** GCahill (lw: a.p: ch 3 out: sn rdn: ev ch last: styd on)	1½	2	7/1	66	28
1690[3]	**Act the Wag (IRE) (104)** (MartinTodhunter) **7-11-11** BHarding (chsd ldrs: led 3 out to 2 out: grad wknd)	9	3	9/1	79	41
1671[7]	**D'Arblay Street (IRE) (86)** (WTKemp) **7-10-7b** SMcDougall (led: blnd 4 out: hdd next: wknd 2 out)	nk	4	14/1	61	23
1347[2]	**Huso (99)** (PCHaslam) **8-11-6** MFoster (wnt prom 6th: outpcd 3 out: n.d after)	8	5	4/1[2]	69	31
1528[2]	**Plumbob (IRE) (87)** (LLungo) **7-10-8** RGarritty (chsd ldrs: rdn 4 out: btn next)	13	6	6/1[3]	49	11
1571[7]	**Acrow Line (107)** (DBurchell) **11-12-0** DJBurchell (a outpcd & bhd: t.o fr 4 out)	dist	7	8/1	—	—
937*	**Ilengar (IRE) (93)** (MrsJDGoodfellow) **7-10-11**(3) ECallaghan (outpcd & lost tch 9th: t.o whn p.u bef 2 out)		P	9/1	—	—
	World Without End (USA) (79) (MESowersby) **7-10-0** DParker (bkwd: chsd ldrs tl wknd qckly 8th: t.o whn p.u bef 2 out)		P	33/1	—	—

(SP 118.3%) **9 Rn**

6m 43.3 (8.30) CSF £17.73 CT £110.96 TOTE £2.00: £1.50 £2.20 £2.20 (£10.30) Trio £37.40 OWNER Scotnorth Racing Ltd (RICHMOND) BRED A. G. Forty

LONG HANDICAP World Without End (USA) 9-7

1528 Troodos, at his best when held up, was produced two out, and then stayed on most determinedly. (9/4)

1081 Manettia (IRE), obviously all the better for her educational last time, had made a full recovery from reported lameness and ran really well, making the winner struggle. (7/1)

1690 Act the Wag (IRE), from a yard that can do little right at the moment, had his chances until weakening two out. (9/1)

1304 D'Arblay Street (IRE) showed signs of returning to form here. (14/1)

1347 Huso must have been feeling his hard race of last time, as he found little when pressure was applied on this occasion. (4/1)

1528 Plumbob (IRE) was disappointing, dropping tamely away from the fourth last. (6/1)

1845 NAGS HEAD MAIDEN CHASE (5-Y.O+) (Class E)

1-50 (1-50) **3m 3f (21 fncs)** £3,195.50 (£959.00: £462.00: £213.50) GOING minus 0.05 sec per fur (G)

				SP	RR	SF
1138[F]	**Mister Trick (IRE) (63)** (LLungo) **6-11-5** RGarritty (in tch: hdwy 15th: led 2 out: styd on wl)	—	1	7/1	84	22
1574[5]	**Aylesbury Lad (IRE) (67)** (DALamb) **7-11-5b[1]** JBurke (chsd ldrs: led 13th to 2 out: kpt on)	6	2	33/1	80	18
1574[6]	**Senora d'Or** (BMactaggart) **6-11-0** BStorey (chsd ldrs tl outpcd 14th: styd on again fr 2 out)	10	3	20/1	69	7
	Springhill Quay (IRE) (GRichards) **7-11-5** ADobbin (in tch: hit 9th: effrt 15th: ev ch 4 out: wknd fr next)	18	4	3/1[1]	64	2
1691[F]	**Final Beat (IRE) (82)** (JWCurtis) **7-11-5** PNiven (mstkes: in tch: outpcd 15th: n.d after)	1½	5	9/1	63	1
1357[3]	**Kings Sermon (IRE)** (PBeaumont) **7-11-5** RSupple (led 3rd to 13th: chsd ldrs tl wknd 4 out)	nk	6	7/1	63	1
1689[12]	**Clonroche Lucky (IRE)** (JWade) **6-11-5** KJones (lost tch fr 15th)	3	7	50/1	61	—
1291[3]	**Miss Colette** (MrsDThomson) **8-11-0** LO'Hara (bhd whn blnd 9th: sn t.o)	dist	8	33/1	—	—
802[F]	**Miss Lamplight** (FPMurtagh) **6-11-0** BHarding (in rr whn fell 13th)		F	12/1	—	—
1629[U]	**Choisty (IRE) (92)** (MrsASwinbank) **6-11-5** JSupple (in tch: hdwy 14th: ev ch whn fell 5 out)		F	9/2[2]	—	—
1629[3]	**Kenmare River (IRE) (72)** (RCollins) **6-11-5** KJohnson (chsd ldrs tl lost pl 14th: t.o whn p.u bef last)		P	16/1	—	—
1357[F]	**Royal Paris (IRE)** (MrsSJSmith) **8-11-5** RichardGuest (lw: led to 3rd: chsd ldrs tl wknd qckly & blnd bdly 15th: p.u after next)		P	6/1[3]	—	—
	Liam's Loss (IRE) (JParkes) **7-11-2**(3) PMidgley (sn t.o: p.u bef 14th)		P	100/1	—	—
1138[6]	**Bright Destiny (60)** (JSGoldie) **5-11-5v[1]** DParker (wnt prom 12th: mstke & wknd 16th: t.o whn p.u bef 3 out)		P	50/1	—	—
1668[P]	**Bosworth Field (IRE) (71)** (MrsSarahHorner-Harker) **8-11-5** MFoster (lost tch fr 14th: t.o whn p.u bef 3 out)		P	66/1	—	—
1691[U]	**Broomhill Duker (IRE) (80)** (HowardJohnson) **6-11-5** GCahill (tried to ref & uns rdr 1st)		U	12/1	—	—

(SP 130.8%) **16 Rn**

7m 2.2 (16.20) CSF £194.60 TOTE £11.30: £3.50 £9.90 £7.50 (£100.70) Trio Not won; £154.84 to Hexham 11/12/96 OWNER Mr Edward Birkbeck (CARRUTHERSTOWN) BRED M. Parkhill

WEIGHT FOR AGE 5yo-1lb

1138 Mister Trick (IRE) got it right in good style, showing he really stays. (7/1)

1574 Aylesbury Lad (IRE) is certainly improving. It will surely not be long before he finds a suitable race. (33/1)

1574 Senora d'Or is learning with experience over these fences and was keeping on really well at the end. (20/1)

Springhill Quay (IRE) was a bit novicey at some of the fences, but still had his chances until running out of fuel three out. To give him the benefit, this was his first run for almost two years. (3/1: op 2/1)
1691 Final Beat (IRE) made too many mistakes. (9/1)
1357 Kings Sermon (IRE) jumped better this time, but then stopped quickly four out. He looks likely to be better suited by a more galloping track. (7/1)
Choisty (IRE), from a yard flying this season, was bang in contention when coming to grief five out. (9/2)

1846 LMS MACHINE SERVICES H'CAP CHASE (0-115) (4-Y.O+) (Class E)
2-20 (2-22) **2m 110y (13 fncs)** £2,877.00 (£861.00: £413.00: £189.00) GOING minus 0.05 sec per fur (G)

				SP	RR	SF
1295[4]	**Weaver George (IRE) (99)** (WStorey) **6-11-3** MMoloney (lw: a.p: led 2 out: r.o)	—	1	4/1[2]	109	—
1442[3]	**Rebel King (90)** (MABarnes) **6-10-3**(5) STaylor (chsd ldr: led 8th to 2 out: kpt on wl)	4	2	6/1	96	—
1702*	**Reve de Valse (USA) (93)** (RJohnson) **9-10-11** 8x KJohnson (led to 8th: ev ch tl outpcd fr 3 out)	8	3	7/2[1]	91	—
1688[4]	**One for the Pot (110)** (MrsAMNaughton) **11-12-0** MFoster (lw: hld up: hdwy 8th: effrt & ev ch 4 out: btn 2 out)	2½	4	7/2[1]	106	—
1306[4]	**Master Salesman (82)** (MrsVCWard) **13-10-0** DParker (lw: chsd ldrs tl outpcd & wknd qckly after 6th)	17	5	50/1	62	—
	Bishopdale (85) (SGChadwick) **15-10-3**ow3 FPerratt (chsd ldrs: outpcd whn blnd 7th: sn bhd)	¾	6	25/1	64	—
1702[R]	**Bolaney Girl (IRE) (82)** (FPMurtagh) **7-10-0** ADobbin (lw: hld up: blnd 4th: stdy hdwy to chse ldrs 4 out: 3rd & btn whn fell last)		F	8/1	—	—
1657[9]	**Blazing Dawn (91)** (JSHubbuck) **9-10-9** BStorey (hld up: lost tch fr ½-wy: p.u bef last)		P	5/1[3]	—	—
				(SP 112.3%)	**8 Rn**	

4m 15.3 (17.30) CSF £25.33 CT £81.82 TOTE £5.50: £1.30 £1.10 £2.70 (£6.00) OWNER Regent Decorators Ltd (CONSETT) BRED G. Cashin
LONG HANDICAP Bishopdale 9-7 Bolaney Girl (IRE) 9-7 Master Salesman 8-12
1295 Weaver George (IRE) travelled well on this occasion and, once in front two out, was not going to be denied. (4/1)
696 Rebel King, from a yard out of form, ran well and kept fighting back when looking beaten. (6/1)
1702* Reve de Valse (USA) is honest and struggled on well, but was always fighting a lost cause. (7/2: 5/2-4/1)
1688 One for the Pot just found the weight concession too much and was wisely not over-punished when beaten. The kindness will be repaid. (7/2: 5/2-4/1)
1306 Master Salesman looked very slow. (50/1)
Bishopdale can go out and buy a packet of cigarettes once January comes. (25/1)
1702 Bolaney Girl (IRE) consented to jump off this time and travelled well, but she did not find as much as had looked likely when ridden and then fell at the last. (8/1)

1847 HOPE INN H'CAP CHASE (0-105) (4-Y.O+) (Class F)
2-50 (2-50) **2m 5f (16 fncs)** £2,742.00 (£762.00: £366.00) GOING minus 0.05 sec per fur (G)

				SP	RR	SF
1574[4]	**Dawn Lad (IRE) (72)** (MrsASwinbank) **7-10-0** JSupple (lw: mstke 3rd: in tch: wnt prom 10th: chal 4 out: styd on wl to ld flat)	—	1	6/1	85	—
1578[4]	**Juke Box Billy (IRE) (86)** (MrsJBrown) **8-11-0** ADobbin (lw: trckd ldrs: led 3 out tl hdd & wknd flat)	7	2	4/1[2]	94	2
1248[3]	**Kiltulla (IRE) (72)** (MrsSJSmith) **6-9-7**(7) RWilkinson (a chsng ldrs: kpt on fr 2 out)	3½	3	14/1	77	—
1346[4]	**Music Blitz (80)** (MrsDThomson) **5-10-8** TReed (bhd: hit 11th: styd on fr 3 out: nrst fin)	1¼	4	5/1	84	—
1209[6]	**Son of Iris (100)** (MrsMReveley) **8-12-0** PNiven (lw: trckd ldrs: effrt & ev ch 4 out: wknd fr next)	9	5	3/1[1]	97	5
1578[2]	**Willie Sparkle (79)** (MrsSCBradburne) **10-10-7** MFoster (in tch: outpcd 10th: no imp after)	4	6	9/2[3]	73	—
	Risky Dee (76) (VThompson) **7-10-4** KJones (prom tl outpcd fr 11th)	4	7	25/1	67	—
1702[P]	**Thunderstruck (82)** (HowardJohnson) **10-10-10** BHarding (led: hit 3rd & 11th: hdd 3 out: btn whn blnd 2 out)	15	8	20/1	62	—
	Walls Court (81) (JJBirkett) **9-10-9** LO'Hara (bit bkwd: chsd ldrs tl wknd 3 out)	3	9	20/1	58	—
	Last Refuge (IRE) (96) (TJCarr) **7-11-10** NSmith (outpcd ½-wy: sn lost tch)	2½	10	20/1	72	—
1629[P]	**Karenastino (72)** (MrsSJSmith) **5-10-0** MrPMurray (mstkes: bhd fr ½-wy)	s.h	11	50/1	47	—
				(SP 120.9%)	**11 Rn**	

5m 27.1 (16.10) CSF £29.31 CT £301.42 TOTE £7.30: £1.90 £1.60 £1.50 (£8.70) Trio £77.70 OWNER Mr G. A. Swinbank (RICHMOND) BRED K. Riordan
LONG HANDICAP Kiltulla (IRE) 9-4 Karenastino 9-2
1574 Dawn Lad (IRE) got his act together and did it in good style. Judging by the way he finished, he will stay further. (6/1)
1578 Juke Box Billy (IRE) looked to have this won until stopping in dramatic style on the run-in. (4/1)
1248 Kiltulla (IRE) is improving and showed here he will stay further. (14/1)
1346 Music Blitz, given plenty to do, never looked likely to get into it, despite staying on. (5/1: op 3/1)
1209 Son of Iris, who travelled particularly well until finding little when asked for an effort four out, was then nursed home. (3/1)
1578 Willie Sparkle, an in-and-out performer, never gave his running this time. (9/2: op 3/1)

1848 HARDWICK ARMS NOVICES' H'CAP HURDLE (0-100) (4-Y.O+) (Class E)
3-20 (3-20) **2m 1f (8 hdls)** £2,276.00 (£636.00: £308.00) GOING minus 0.05 sec per fur (G)

				SP	RR	SF
1577[3]	**Court Joker (IRE) (77)** (HAlexander) **4-10-7** BStorey (lw: in tch: hdwy to disp ld 3 out: hdd appr last: rallied to ld cl home)	—	1	12/1	59	2
1249[2]	**Pangeran (USA) (84)** (MrsASwinbank) **4-11-0** JSupple (mde most fr 2nd: j.lft last: ct nr fin)	hd	2	10/1	66	9
1524[3]	**Bowcliffe (81)** (MrsAMNaughton) **5-10-11** MFoster (trckd ldrs: effrt 3 out: one pce appr next)	13	3	12/1	51	—
1772[3]	**Irish Wildcard (NZ) (70)** (HOliver) **8-10-0** VSlattery (plld hrd: in tch: rdn 5th: styd on: no imp)	2	4	9/2[2]	38	—
1687[5]	**Mr Christie (78)** (MissLCSiddall) **4-10-8** RSupple (bhd & drvn along ½-wy: styd on fr 2 out)	1¼	5	12/1	45	—
1667[4]	**Doubling Dice (70)** (RAllan) **5-10-0** BHarding (hld up: hdwy 3 out: nvr rchd ldrs)	4	6	9/2[2]	33	—
1524[5]	**Mullins (IRE) (77)** (DMoffatt) **5-10-7v[1]** DJMoffatt (nvr nr ldrs)	8	7	20/1	32	—
1292[F]	**Corston Joker (86)** (LLungo) **6-11-2** PNiven (bhd: sme hdwy whn blnd 3 out: n.d after)	10	8	14/1	32	—
1466[10]	**Shuttlecock (85)** (MrsNMacauley) **5-11-1** RichardGuest (lw: led to 2nd: lost pl 5th)	¾	9	16/1	30	—
1152[4]	**Durano (98)** (TDEasterby) **5-12-0** RGarritty (lw: trckd ldrs: effrt 3 out: sn rdn & btn)	1	10	5/2[1]	42	—
1049[10]	**Vintage Red (89)** (GRichards) **6-11-5** ADobbin (lw: chsd ldrs tl lost pl appr 3 out)	11	11	6/1[3]	23	—
1659[9]	**Oneoftheoldones (73)** (JNorton) **4-10-0**(3)ow3 ECallaghan (plld hrd: disp ld 4th to 3 out: wknd qckly: fell last)		F	16/1	—	—
				(SP 134.6%)	**12 Rn**	

4m 6.4 (11.40) CSF £127.60 CT £1,384.40 TOTE £20.20: £4.40 £1.80 £2.10 (£78.30) Trio £129.50; £18.24 to Hexham 11/12/96 OWNER Mr James Kennedy (LANCHESTER) BRED Mellon Stud

LONG HANDICAP Doubling Dice 9-13 Irish Wildcard (NZ) 9-11
IN-FOCUS: This looked a moderate event.
1577 Court Joker (IRE) proved determined and, after looking beaten at the last, fought back well. (12/1)
1249 Pangeran (USA) after battling for the lead virtually throughout, then threw it away with a left-handed jump at the last and found little on the run-in. (10/1)
1524 Bowcliffe had his chances but again proved too slow. (12/1)
1772 Irish Wildcard (NZ) took a strongish hold early on and then never really came up with the goods when asked the question. (9/2)
1687 Mr Christie only decided to run on when it was all over. (12/1)
1667 Doubling Dice, dropped out, made a little late headway but basically looked slow. (9/2)
1152 Durano was a big disappointment, stopping as if shot after the third last. (5/2)

T/Plpt: £219.40 (36.38 Tckts). T/Qdpt: £108.10 (7 Tckts). AA

1574-HEXHAM (L-H) (Good)
Wednesday December 11th
WEATHER: cloudy

1849 FEDERATION BREWERY SPECIAL ALE AMATEUR H'CAP HURDLE (0-105) (4-Y.O+) (Class F)
12-50 (12-52) **3m (12 hdls)** £2,480.80 (£688.80: £330.40) GOING: 0.31 sec per fur (GS)

				SP	RR	SF
1080[3]	**Hudson Bay Trader (USA) (79)** (PBeaumont) **9-10-6**(5) MissPRobson (chsd ldrs: led 4 out: kpt on wl flat)	—	1	10/1	60	5
1528[3]	**Ballindoo (83)** (RJArmson) **7-10-8**(7) MrRArmson (lw: hld up & bhd: hdwy 4 out: ev ch last: styd on one pce)	1¾	2	5/1[2]	63	8
1247*	**Belle Rose (IRE) (85)** (GRichards) **6-10-10**(7) MrGElliott (a.p: effrt & blnd last: styd on u.p)	¾	3	3/1[1]	64	9
894[3]	**Scarba (95)** (JMJefferson) **8-11-8**(5) MrRHale (lw: chsd ldrs: outpcd 2 out: kpt on towards fin)	¾	4	13/2	74	19
1642[5]	**Ifallelsefails (94)** (LLungo) **8-11-7**(5) MrMHNaughton (lw: hld up & bhd: hmpd bnd after 8th: gd hdwy 2 out: rdn & nt qckn appr last)	1¼	5	7/1	72	17
	Gymcrak Cyrano (IRE) (90) (NChamberlain) **7-11-1**(7) MissCMetcalfe (j.rt: bhd: hdwy 4 out: outpcd appr 2 out: styd on towards fin)	2½	6	16/1	66	11
1803[P]	**Flat Top (95)** (MWEasterby) **5-11-6**(7) MrMWatson (lw: hld up: gd hdwy 3 out: sn chsng ldrs: one pce whn blnd last)	1½	7	12/1	70	15
	Kings Lane (87) (JMDun) **7-11-2**(3) MrCBonner (a.p: disp ld 2 out: wknd appr last)	1	8	10/1	62	7
1310[6]	**Helens Bay (IRE) (82)** (VThompson) **6-10-11**(3)ow7 MrMThompson (bhd: effrt 3 out: nvr able to chal)	1½	9	33/1	56	—
1562[5]	**Mardood (76)** (SBClark) **11-10-1**(7) MissRClark (chsd ldrs tl outpcd ½-wy: n.d after)	8	10	16/1	44	—
1654[11]	**Cool Steel (IRE) (76)** (MrsJBrown) **4-10-1**(7)ow2 MissJEastwood (led to 5th: cl up tl lost pl 3 out)	1¼	11	25/1	44	—
	Daisy Days (IRE) (84) (HowardJohnson) **6-10-11**(5) MrRThornton (bit bkwd: mstke 1st: cl up: led 5th to 4 out: wkng whn hmpd after 2 out)	8	12	6/1[3]	46	—

(SP 126.2%) **12 Rn**

6m 5.2 (25.20) CSF £58.89 CT £177.31 TOTE £4.10: £1.40 £1.50 £1.10 (£17.60) Trio £43.00 OWNER Mr P. C. N. Curtis (BRANDSBY) BRED Ryedale Farm
1080 Hudson Bay Trader (USA), from a stable now hitting form, proved very determined once in front and was always too strong for this bunch. (10/1)
1528 Ballindoo was produced with what appeared a perfectly-timed run at the last but, when the chips were down, he was just found wanting.(5/1)
1247* Belle Rose (IRE), stepping up in trip, stays well enough, but a blunder at the last certainly did not help. (3/1)
894 Scarba just got outpaced at a vital stage, but was keeping on well at the end, suggesting that the trip suited. (13/2)
Ifallelsefails, given a most patient ride, was produced on the outside of the field approaching two out, but never quite found as much as looked likely. Perhaps this run was still just needed. (7/1)
Gymcrak Cyrano (IRE) ran reasonably without getting into it, and should now improve as a result. (16/1)
1443 Flat Top (12/1: 16/1-25/1)
Kings Lane ran a fair first race of the season until appearing to blow up approaching the last. (10/1)

1850 RACING CHANNEL NOVICES' H'CAP CHASE (0-100) (4-Y.O+) (Class E)
1-20 (1-21) **3m 1f (19 fncs)** £3,452.40 (£1,033.20: £495.60: £226.80) GOING: 0.31 sec per fur (GS)

				SP	RR	SF
1629[4]	**Monymoss (IRE) (97)** (MrsSJSmith) **7-11-11** RichardGuest (chsd ldrs: blnd 11th: led 3 out: styd on wl)	—	1	9/1	108	37
1668*	**Seeking Gold (IRE) (86)** (JBarclay) **7-11-0** 7x BStorey (lw: outpcd ½-wy: styd on fr 3 out: nrst fin)	3½	2	6/1[3]	95	24
1357[4]	**Bold Account (IRE) (85)** (GMMoore) **6-10-13** NBentley (lw: sn prom: led 15th to 3 out: rdn & btn between last 2)	4	3	10/1	91	20
1503[3]	**Slotamatique (IRE) (94)** (GRichards) **7-11-8** ADobbin (lw: chsd ldrs: hmpd 15th: rdn & one pce fr 3 out)	1½	4	7/4[1]	99	28
	Noosa Sound (IRE) (72) (LLungo) **6-10-0** BHarding (hld up: sme hdwy u.p 4 out: nvr rchd ldrs)	¾	5	25/1	77	6
1632[3]	**Shallow River (IRE) (85)** (RCollins) **5-10-7**(5) MrRThornton (mstkes: bhd: gd hdwy 14th: wknd 3 out)	13	6	14/1	81	9
	Desperate Days (IRE) (72) (FKirby) **7-10-0** WDwan (bhd: sme hdwy 14th: wknd appr 3 out)	8	7	16/1	63	—
1578[8]	**Cader Idris (86)** (MrsMReveley) **7-11-0** PNiven (lw: led: hit 8th: disp ld whn fell 15th)		F	10/1	—	—
1691[7]	**Distillery Hill (IRE) (82)** (VThompson) **8-10-10**ow8 MrMThompson (bit bkwd: w ldr tl fell 12th)		F	50/1	—	—
1574[2]	**Mamica (80)** (MDods) **6-10-8** RSupple (hit 6th & 11th: hdwy & in tch whn fell 15th)		F	100/30[2]	—	—
	Avowhat (IRE) (72) (JJO'Neill) **6-9-9**(5) RMcGrath (in tch: hit 5th: wknd 10th: t.o whn p.u after 13th: dead)		P	20/1	—	—
1632[4]	**Gold Pigeon (IRE) (72)** (BSRothwell) **7-10-0** GCahill (blnd 2nd: bhd: t.o whn p.u bef last)		P	20/1	—	—

(SP 129.8%) **12 Rn**

6m 31.0 (20.00) CSF £62.99 CT £524.24 TOTE £10.50: £1.60 £2.40 £2.60 (£24.30) Trio £24.60 OWNER Mrs S. Smith (BINGLEY) BRED Liam and Mary Gaynor
LONG HANDICAP Noosa Sound (IRE) 9-4 Desperate Days (IRE) 9-4
WEIGHT FOR AGE 5yo-1lb
1629 Monymoss (IRE) just stays and stays, and this was certainly the right track for him. (9/1)
1668* Seeking Gold (IRE) was again tapped for speed halfway through the race, but this dour stayer kept on really well in the closing stages. (6/1)
1357 Bold Account (IRE) jumped much better this time, but then ran out of fuel going to the last, which was strange from an out-and-out stayer. (10/1)
1503 Slotamatique (IRE) was badly hampered by a faller five out and, struggling thereafter, was left behind from the second last. (7/4)

Noosa Sound (IRE) hampered five out, kept staying on, but lacked any pace to make his presence felt. From 20lb out of the handicap though, this was not a bad effort. (25/1)
1632 Shallow River (IRE) spoiled his chances with some very erratic jumping. (14/1)
1308* Cader Idris, after making it, was looking in trouble when falling five out. (10/1)
Distillery Hill (IRE) had made just one mistake and was making his effort when falling five out. (50/1)
1574 Mamica (100/30: 2/1-7/2)

1851 BUCHANAN ALES NOVICES' (S) HURDLE (4,5,6 & 7-Y.O) (Class G)
1-50 (1-52) **2m (8 hdls)** £1,794.00 (£494.00: £234.00) GOING: 0.31 sec per fur (GS)

	Horse	Dist	Pos	SP	RR	SF
1628^{3}	**Robsera (IRE) (79)** (JJQuinn) **5-10-12** RGarritty (lw: hld up: smooth hdwy 3 out: led last: styd on u.p)	—	1	$7/2^{2}$	66	19
1628^{*}	**Willy Star (BEL) (92)** (MrsSJSmith) **6-11-12** RichardGuest (lw: in tch: effrt 2 out: styd on flat: nt pce of wnr)	2	2	$11/10^{1}$	78	31
1703^{11}	**Over Stated (IRE) (63)** (PCheesbrough) **6-10-7**(5) GFRyan (trckd ldrs: led after 3 out & qcknd clr: hdd last: no ex)	¾	3	20/1	63	16
	Last Roundup (CWThornton) **4-10-12** MFoster (a chsng ldrs: rdn 3 out: r.o one pce)	3½	4	12/1	60	13
1628^{12}	**Simand (74)** (GMMoore) **4-11-0** JCallaghan (a chsng ldrs: one pce fr 2 out)	8	5	12/1	54	7
1312^{9}	**My Missile (65)** (RGCockburn) **6-10-7** LO'Hara (wl bhd tl styd on fr 3 out)	11	6	33/1	36	—
1687^{14}	**Meesonette** (BEllison) **4-10-7** GCahill (mstkes: bhd: sme hdwy 3 out: n.d)	8	7	20/1	28	—
1628^{5}	**The Final Spark** (GRichards) **5-10-7** BHarding (in tch: stumbled bnd after 4th: effrt 3 out: wknd next)	1	8	$13/2^{3}$	27	—
1245^{4}	**Canonbiebothered** (LLungo) **5-10-7** FPerratt (prom tl wknd fr 5th)	1½	9	12/1	25	—
	Tajar (USA) (MDods) **4-10-12** RSupple (hld up: hdwy ½-wy: ev ch after 3 out: sn wknd)	1	10	10/1	29	—
1349^{9}	**Meadowleck (52)** (WGYoung) **7-10-7** BStorey (mde most tl hdd & wknd after 3 out)	8	11	33/1	16	—
1523^{6}	**About Midnight** (FPMurtagh) **7-10-7** ADobbin (bit bkwd: mstkes: w ldr tl wknd 3 out)	26	12	33/1	—	—
1523^{7}	**Ringrone (IRE)** (VThompson) **7-10-11**ow4 MrMThompson (sn bhd)	6	13	33/1	—	—
1362^{18}	**Roadway Joker** (MABarnes) **5-10-7**(5) STaylor (unruly s: in tch tl wknd appr 2 out: bhd whn fell last: dead)		F	33/1	—	—
1687^{16}	**Safety Tip** (WStorey) **4-10-2**(5) RMcGrath (sn t.o: p.u after 4th)		P	33/1	—	—
	Blow Dry (IRE) (MartynWane) **6-10-12** PNiven (lost tch fr 5th: t.o whn p.u bef last)		P	16/1	—	—
	First in the Field (NBMason) **5-10-0**(7) SHaworth (bit bkwd: blnd & uns rdr 1st)		U	25/1	—	—
				(SP 152.2%)	**17 Rn**	

4m 1.8 (13.80) CSF £8.96 TOTE £4.00: £1.00 £3.10 £11.20 (£5.00) Trio £33.90 OWNER Mr Declan Kinahan (MALTON) BRED Oak Lodge Stud
No bid
1628 Robsera (IRE), given a superb ride, settled it from the last. (7/2)
1628* Willy Star (BEL) did well with a double penalty and was wisely not over-punished. Further successes will be found. (11/10: 6/4-evens)
510 Over Stated (IRE) put in a useful effort and, on an easier track, might well have pinched it. (20/1)
Last Roundup put in a fair first run over hurdles, but proved short of toe. Perhaps more cut will help. (12/1: op 7/1)
893 Simand had her limitations exposed when the pressure was on from two out. (12/1: op 7/1)
My Missile showed her first signs of form, staying on most determinedly to suggest that longer trips should suit. (33/1)

1852 FEDERATION BREWERY H'CAP HURDLE (0-130) (4-Y.O+) (Class C)
2-20 (2-21) **2m (8 hdls)** £3,460.00 (£1,030.00: £490.00: £220.00) GOING: 0.31 sec per fur (GS)

	Horse	Dist	Pos	SP	RR	SF
1658^{3}	**Shining Edge (108)** (TDEasterby) **4-11-2** RGarritty (hld up: effrt 2 out: r.o u.p flat to ld cl home)	—	1	$9/2^{3}$	89	29
1577^{*}	**Anabranch (107)** (JMJefferson) **5-10-8**(7) MNewton (lw: hld up: led on bit between last 2: rdn, hdd & no ex towards fin)	½	2	$6/5^{1}$	88	28
1779^{3}	**Colorful Ambition (106)** (MrsASwinbank) **6-11-0** JRailton (hld up: hdwy 3 out: styd on: nt pce to chal)	6	3	6/1	81	21
	Duke of Perth (92) (HowardJohnson) **5-10-0** GCahill (chsd clr ldr: led 2 out: sn hdd & one pce)	2½	4	10/1	64	4
1658^{2}	**Done Well (USA) (119)** (PMonteith) **4-11-13** ADobbin (hld up: effrt appr 2 out: no imp)	7	5	$5/2^{2}$	84	24
1658^{9}	**Master Hyde (USA) (110)** (WStorey) **7-11-4** MMoloney (led & sn clr: hit 5th: hdd 2 out: sn btn)	1¼	6	16/1	74	14
				(SP 121.5%)	**6 Rn**	

4m 0.4 (12.40) CSF £11.00 TOTE £3.50: £2.40 £1.50 (£3.30) OWNER Mr G. Graham (MALTON) BRED R. B. Warren
LONG HANDICAP Duke of Perth 9-12
1658 Shining Edge is a difficult customer to win with, but he had a man on his back who can do little wrong at present, and he was produced just right. (9/2)
1577* Anabranch looked nailed-on for much of this but, when put under pressure, her response was a shade disappointing and she was worried out of it. (6/5)
1779 Colorful Ambition gave problems before the start, but then ran well. Judging by the way he stayed on, longer trips should suit. (6/1)
Duke of Perth put in a reasonable first effort of the season and should improve as a result. (10/1)
1658 Done Well (USA) seems to be an in-and-out performer this season, and was never really happy once the pace was on. (5/2)
1127 Master Hyde (USA), very disappointing of late, tried different tactics this time and did run a shade better, but it seems his attitude is the problem. (16/1)

1853 BORDER COUNTIES INSURANCE NOVICES' CHASE (5-Y.O+) (Class E)
2-50 (2-50) **2m 110y (12 fncs)** £3,261.30 (£974.40: £466.20: £212.10) GOING: 0.31 sec per fur (GS)

	Horse	Dist	Pos	SP	RR	SF
	Daring Past (112) (MDHammond) **6-10-12** RGarritty (hld up: smooth hdwy 4 out: led appr last: qcknd)	—	1	$8/11^{1}$	89+	21
	Cush Supreme (IRE) (MartinTodhunter) **7-10-12** BHarding (bit bkwd: led tl appr last: sn btn)	6	2	14/1	83	15
1576^{4}	**Bonny Johnny** (DMoffatt) **6-10-12** DJMoffatt (bhd: hdwy 4 out: styd on: nt rch ldrs)	4	3	$13/2^{2}$	79	11
1576^{5}	**Dark Buoy (67)** (BMactaggart) **7-10-12** BStorey (lw: a chsng ldrs: one pce fr 3 out)	1¾	4	$8/1^{3}$	78	10
1718^{5}	**Target Line** (MrsSJSmith) **6-10-5**(7) RWilkinson (prom tl lost pl fr 4 out: sme late hdwy)	7	5	16/1	71	3
1653^{U}	**Fingerhill (IRE)** (VThompson) **7-10-12** MrMThompson (chsd ldrs: blnd 5th: outpcd fr 3 out)	¾	6	16/1	70	2
1576^{6}	**Wee Wizard (IRE) (74)** (MABarnes) **7-10-7**(5) STaylor (drvn along & lost tch 7th: n.d after)	hd	7	$8/1^{3}$	70	2
1346^{11}	**Grand as Owt (65)** (DMcCune) **6-10-12** KJohnson (cl up: blnd 5th: wknd 2 out)	1½	8	50/1	69	1
1703^{P}	**Charlistiona** (JPDodds) **5-10-0**(7) SMelrose (bhd: effrt whn blnd bdly & b.d 6th)		B	33/1	—	—
1020^{4}	**Amber Holly** (JEDixon) **7-10-7** FPerratt (mstkes: in tch whn fell 6th)		F	12/1	—	—
				(SP 124.5%)	**10 Rn**	

4m 10.9 (13.90) CSF £12.96 TOTE £1.60: £1.30 £2.00 £3.00 (£16.70) Trio £11.50 OWNER Mr John Petty (MIDDLEHAM) BRED P. and Mrs Venner
Daring Past, after twenty months off, came back here with a smooth victory on this chasing debut. More should follow. (8/11)
Cush Supreme (IRE) ran well, but just needed this and cried enough going to the last. (14/1: op 8/1)

1576 Bonny Johnny is getting the hang of jumping and again finished well, suggesting that longer trips should help. (13/2)
1576 Dark Buoy had his chances, but is lacking any change of gear. (8/1)
1718 Target Line put in a reasonable first effort over fences and, not given a hard time, was keeping on well at the end. (16/1)
1653 Fingerhill (IRE) keeps showing bits of ability and will no doubt pick up a race, but it will need to be pretty uncompetitive. (16/1)
1020 Amber Holly (12/1: 8/1-14/1)

1854 FEDERATION BREWERY MEDALLION LAGER NOVICES' HURDLE (4-Y.O+) (Class E)
3-20 (3-21) **3m (12 hdls)** £2,679.00 (£744.00: £357.00) GOING: 0.31 sec per fur (GS)

			SP	RR	SF
1807^{6}	**Menshaar (USA) (86)** (LLungo) **4-10-12** RGarritty (lw: hld up: hdwy 4 out: led between last 2: styd on wl).....—	**1**	6/1^{3}	66	12
1541^{3}	**Young Kenny (94)** (PBeaumont) **5-11-5** RSupple (a chsng ldrs: led appr 2 out: hdd between last 2: one pce).3	**2**	2/1^{1}	71	17
1640^{10}	**Adib (USA)** (GMMoore) **6-10-12** NBentley (in tch: hdwy u.p 2 out: nvr able to chal)....3½	**3**	20/1	62	8
1304^{3}	**Blanc Seing (FR) (75)** (JESwiers) **9-10-12b** MrSSwiers (lw: bhd: styd on fr 3 out: nrst fin)....7	**4**	16/1	57	3
	Clontoura (IRE) (MrsCACoward) **8-10-9**(3) PMidgley (lw: chsd ldrs: one pce fr 2 out)....5	**5**	33/1	54	—
	Raining Stairs (IRE) (GRichards) **5-10-12** BHarding (hld up & bhd: stdy hdwy 3 out: nvr plcd to chal)....1½	**6**	9/1	53	—
1345*	**Clare Maid (IRE)** (GRichards) **7-11-0** ADobbin (prom tl hmpd & lost pl bnd appr 4 out: hdwy 3 out: one pce fr 2 out)....½	**7**	2/1^{1}	54	—
1672*	**Pharmistice (IRE) (81)** (MrsASwinbank) **5-11-5** JSupple (lw: hld up: wnt prom 7th: wknd 3 out)....9	**8**	9/2^{2}	53	—
	Carnmoney (IRE) (JSisterson) **8-10-12** TReed (mde most tl hdd & wknd appr 2 out)....1½	**9**	50/1	45	—
1633^{8}	**Kentucky Gold (IRE)** (MrsLWilliamson) **7-10-12** LO'Hara (prom tl wknd appr 2 out)....6	**10**	33/1	41	—
1080^{4}	**Crofton Lake (62)** (JEDixon) **8-11-5** FPerratt (a bhd)....s.h	**11**	20/1	48	—
1672^{9}	**Woodstock Lodge (USA)** (VThompson) **8-10-12** MrMThompson (bit bkwd: prom tl wknd fr 4 out)....8	**12**	50/1	36	—
1654^{17}	**Ruber** (RWThomson) **9-10-12** BStorey (n.d)....hd	**13**	25/1	36	—
1579^{8}	**Boris Brook** (RAllan) **5-10-5**(7) SMelrose (unruly s: wnt prom 5th: wknd 7th: t.o)....4	**14**	33/1	33	—
	Mederic (IRE) (DMForster) **6-10-7**(5) GFRyan (a bhd: p.u bef 2 out: lame)....	**P**	33/1	—	—
1713^{7}	**Ar Aghaidh Abhaile (IRE)** (MissMKMilligan) **5-10-12b1** GCahill (w ldr: disp ld 7th to 4 out: wknd: t.o whn p.u bef 2 out)....	**P**	25/1	—	—
1802^{P}	**Bold'n (70)** (NBMason) **9-10-5**(7) SHaworth (t.o fr 4 out: p.u bef 2 out)....	**P**	50/1	—	—

(SP 149.9%) **17 Rn**

6m 3.2 (23.20) CSF £21.15 TOTE £7.40: £2.30 £2.90 £6.80 (£15.80) Trio £125.70 OWNER Mr G. A. Arthur (CARRUTHERSTOWN) BRED Brereton C. Jones

OFFICIAL EXPLANATION **Raining Stairs (IRE): the rider reported that on the final circuit the gelding began to gurgle, he felt it prudent to hold the horse together on the loose ground, and confirmed that he was distressed on pulling up.**
1807 Menshaar (USA), all the better for his outing in the fog last week, proved a real stayer here and, the further he went, the better he got. (6/1: 4/1-7/1)
1541 Young Kenny is in really good form, but is just short of pace at the business end. Nevertheless, a race will be found. (2/1: tchd 3/1)
Adib (USA), a bumper winner two seasons ago, has been disappointing since, but showed here he is on his way back. (20/1)
1304 Blanc Seing (FR) got the trip well enough this time, but was doing all his running when it was too late. (16/1)
Clontoura (IRE), a point-to-pointer, ran quite well until blowing up two out. (33/1)
Raining Stairs (IRE) put in a real eyecatcher here and, despite reports that he choked during the race, he looks one to keep on the right side once his education is complete. (9/1)
1345* Clare Maid (IRE), handily placed, got messed about no end on the bend into the back straight, and was given an easy time when beaten from the second last. (2/1)

T/Jkpt: Not won; £2,676.83 to Sandown 12/12/96. T/Plpt: £31.60 (344 Tckts). T/Qdpt: £6.40 (146.32 Tckts). AA

1719-LEICESTER (R-H) (Chases Good to firm, Good patches, Hdles Good to soft, Good patches)
Wednesday December 11th
Vis: poor races 5 & 6
WEATHER: misty & cold

1855 ASH NOVICES' HURDLE (4-Y.O+ F & M) (Class E)
1-00 (1-01) **2m (9 hdls)** £2,902.40 (£806.40: £387.20) GOING: 0.01 sec per fur (G)

			SP	RR	SF
1341*	**Potter's Gale (IRE)** (DNicholson) **5-11-3** AMaguire (hld up: hdwy appr 4 out: slt ld 3 out: rdn out)....—	**1**	5/4^{1}	72	27
1030^{2}	**Pip's Dream (84)** (MJRyan) **5-10-10** JRyan (chsd ldr: led 4th to 3 out: hit next: rallied last: unable qckn flat).2½	**2**	14/1	63	18
1679*	**Melstock Meggie** (MrsJPitman) **6-11-3** WMarston (lw: prom: rdn & outpcd 3 out: styd on flat)....1¼	**3**	9/2^{2}	68	23
	Quick Quote (85) (MrsIMcKie) **6-10-10** LHarvey (hld up: hdwy appr 5th: jnd ldrs 4 out: rdn & one pce appr last)....1½	**4**	14/1	60	15
1453^{5}	**Bay Fair** (JRBosley) **4-10-10** MRichards (hld up: hdwy 3 out: nvr nr to chal)....6	**5**	13/2	54	9
1551^{3}	**Fantasy Line** (PRWebber) **5-10-10** JOsborne (racd wd: prom tl wknd appr 4 out: t.o)....20	**6**	5/1^{3}	34	—
1329^{16}	**Lady Foley (IRE)** (CJMann) **4-10-7**(3) JMagee (chsd ldrs to 4 out: sn rdn & outpcd: t.o)....8	**7**	50/1	26	—
	Qualitair Pride (JFBottomley) **4-10-10** GBradley (hld up: a in rr: t.o)....1½	**8**	14/1	24	—
1380^{5}	**Trehane** (NAGraham) **4-10-10** NWilliamson (led to 4th: lost tch 4 out: t.o)....10	**9**	66/1	14	—
	Neptunes Miss (MJWilkinson) **4-10-10** ILawrence (bkwd: hld up mid div: wknd 4 out: sn t.o)....14	**10**	66/1	—	—

(SP 117.6%) **10 Rn**

3m 53.1 (8.10) CSF £18.33 TOTE £1.80: £1.10 £2.20 £1.80 (£12.80) Trio £4.80 OWNER Mr J. E. Potter (TEMPLE GUITING) BRED Colman O'Flynn

1341* Potter's Gale (IRE) will need a stiffer test of stamina to produce her best, but she did nothing wrong here and eventually won going away. (5/4)
1030 Pip's Dream continues to run well. A shade unfortunate to lose her momentum when crashing through the penultimate flight, her attempt to get on terms again was never going to succeed. (14/1: 7/1-16/1)
1679* Melstock Meggie, struggling to keep in touch soon after entering the straight, stayed on really well on meeting the rising ground. She is crying out for a stiffer test of stamina. (9/2: 7/2-6/1)
Quick Quote has shown little to date, but ran well on this seasonal debut. She seems to be getting it together and looks an ideal chaser. (14/1)
1453 Bay Fair did not fare badly, but she found this trip inadequate and was never able to make her presence felt. (13/2: 4/1-15/2)

1551 Fantasy Line had to admit her measure taken on entering the straight after tracking the leaders and looking sure to take a hand in proceedings. (5/1)
Qualitair Pride (14/1: 7/1-16/1)

1856 SPRUCE NOVICES' CHASE (5-Y.O+) (Class E)
1-30 (1-30) **2m 4f 110y (15 fncs)** £3,669.75 (£1,098.00: £526.50: £240.75) GOING: 0.01 sec per fur (G)

				SP	RR	SF
1563^{3}	**Slingsby (IRE) (109)** (NAGaselee) **6-10-12** RDunwoody (led tl appr 4th: blnd 7th: led 2 out: drvn out)	—	**1**	4/5^{1}	103	33
1475^{2}	**Bridepark Rose (IRE) (82)** (PCRitchens) **8-10-7** SFox (a.p: led 11th to 2 out: ev ch last: rdn & no ex flat)	2	**2**	7/1	96	26
1500^{4}	**Curragh Peter** (MrsPBickerton) **9-10-9**(3) GuyLewis (j.b lft: led appr 4th to 11th: outpcd fr 3 out)	24	**3**	50/1	83	13
1538^{U}	**Loch Garman Hotel (IRE)** (PTDalton) **7-10-12** TEley (chsd ldrs to 11th: sn lost tch: t.o)	dist	**4**	8/1	—	—
1680^{F}	**The Booley House (IRE) (97)** (VSoane) **6-10-12** MRichards (bkwd: a bhd: t.o fr 8th)	23	**5**	11/2^{3}	—	—
1394^{8}	**Charter Lane (IRE)** (MrsLCJewell) **6-10-12** DLeahy (a bhd: t.o fr ½-wy)	8	**6**	50/1	—	—
1521^{3}	**Djais (FR)** (JRJenkins) **7-10-12** GBradley (wl bhd whn blnd bdly 2nd: p.u bef next)		**P**	5/1^{2}	—	—
	Typhoon (IRE) (MarkCampion) **6-10-12** MSharratt (bkwd: sn wl bhd: t.o whn blnd & uns rdr 9th)		**U**	50/1	—	—
				(SP 117.1%)	**8 Rn**	

5m 8.9 (7.90) CSF £7.18 TOTE £1.60: £1.10 £2.50 £4.20 (£8.40) Trio £49.00 OWNER Simon Harrap Partnership (LAMBOURN) BRED Peter Murphy
1563 Slingsby (IRE), lucky to find a leg after taking the seventh by the roots, did not have a lot to beat to open his account over fences. He should be able to improve as he learns. (4/5)
1475 Bridepark Rose (IRE), much better suited by this return to a longer trip, gave supporters of the favourite a worrying time until having to admit him too strong for her on the flat. Her turn will come. (7/1: 8/1-12/1)
Curragh Peter may well have made a race of it had he not forfeited so much ground by jumping out to the left. His chances must be respected when he goes the other way round. (50/1)
1281 Loch Garman Hotel (IRE) (8/1: op 5/1)
The Booley House (IRE) (11/2: op 7/2)

1857 CHESTNUT CONDITIONAL (S) HURDLE (4,5,6 & 7-Y.O) (Class G)
2-00 (2-00) **2m (9 hdls)** £2,012.40 (£556.40: £265.20) GOING: 0.01 sec per fur (G)

				SP	RR	SF
913^{4}	**Fleet Cadet (76)** (MCPipe) **5-10-12v**^{1} GSupple (hld up: hdwy 4 out: chal 2 out: sn led: qcknd clr)	—	**1**	4/1^{3}	65	7
	Beechfield Flyer (68) (WClay) **5-10-12** GTormey (bit bkwd: a.p: hrd rdn appr 2 out: kpt on flat: nt pce of wnr)	4	**2**	20/1	61	3
1775^{3}	**Parish Walk (IRE) (78)** (KJDrewry) **5-10-12** BGrattan (led: clr 5th: hdd after 2 out: no ex)	2	**3**	7/2^{2}	59	1
1425^{3}	**Fastini Gold** (MDIUsher) **4-10-12** FLeahy (hld up: hdwy appr 5th: ev ch 2 out: sn rdn: one pce)	2	**4**	11/2	57	—
1345^{3}	**Fenian Court (IRE) (82)** (MissJBower) **5-10-7** KGaule (lw: chsd ldrs: rdn 4 out: btn next)	24	**5**	11/4^{1}	28	—
902^{7}	**Scottish Park** (MCPipe) **7-10-2**(5) BMoore (hld up: rdn along 5th: no ch whn pckd 3 out: sn t.o)	9	**6**	12/1	19	—
	Rosalee Royale (JELong) **4-10-7** GHogan (mstke 1st: a bhd: t.o fr 5th)	19	**7**	7/1	—	—
1679^{7}	**Persian Butterfly** (RMStronge) **4-10-7** MichaelBrennan (prom: 2nd whn sddle slipped & p.u bef 4th)		**P**	25/1	—	—
				(SP 113.1%)	**8 Rn**	

3m 56.7 (11.70) CSF £61.02 TOTE £4.40: £1.90 £2.60 £1.50 (£31.20) OWNER Sir John Swaine (WELLINGTON) BRED R. D. Hollingsworth
No bid
OFFICIAL EXPLANATION **Rosalee Royale: the rider reported that the filly hung badly right in the back straight, so he did not persevere. The Vet reported that the filly returned with a cut on her right stifle.**
913 Fleet Cadet did not need to get serious to win this and it is quite possible that he could succeed in a higher grade when tackling further. (4/1: 5/2-9/2)
Beechfield Flyer performed with credit on this return to action and he was renewing his effort on the flat, suggesting a stiffer test could be what he really needs. (20/1)
1775 Parish Walk (IRE) attempted to gallop his rivals into the ground on this return to the minimum trip, but he had been collared between the last two, and was then short of a turn of speed. (7/2)
1276 Fastini Gold had worked his way into contention by the second last, but was unable to quicken with the principals. He is going to find it increasingly difficult to find an opening. (11/2)
1345 Fenian Court (IRE) looked to be travelling as well as any into the straight but, when push came to shove, she had nothing more to offer. (11/4)
Scottish Park (12/1: op 7/1)

1858 SYCAMORE H'CAP CHASE (0-125) (5-Y.O+) (Class D)
2-30 (2-30) **3m (18 fncs)** £4,796.00 (£1,331.00: £638.00) GOING: 0.01 sec per fur (G)

				SP	RR	SF
1684*	**Lord of the West (IRE) (104)** (JJO'Neill) **7-10-13** 6x AMaguire (hld up: hdwy 4 out: led 2 out: blnd last: drvn clr flat)	—	**1**	2/1^{1}	111	—
1383^{2}	**Philip's Woody (115)** (NJHenderson) **8-11-10** JRKavanagh (lw: hld up: lft in ld 6th: clr 8th: hdd 14th: stumbled appr 3 out: ev ch 2 out: one pce flat)	3½	**2**	13/2	120	8
1637^{3}	**Well Briefed (114)** (RHBuckler) **9-11-2**(7) MGriffiths (led: j.slowly 1st & 5th: tried to ref & hdd next: led 14th to 2 out: wknd appr last)	7	**3**	9/1	114	2
1560*	**Imperial Vintage (IRE) (115)** (MissVenetiaWilliams) **6-11-10** NWilliamson (swtg: fell 1st)		**F**	11/4^{2}	—	—
1468^{2}	**The Shy Padre (IRE) (91)** (MrsJPitman) **7-10-0** WMarston (lw: fell 2nd)		**F**	3/1^{3}	—	—
				(SP 108.3%)	**5 Rn**	

6m 15.5 (21.50) CSF £12.62 TOTE £2.80: £1.80 £3.00 (£7.10) OWNER Anne Duchess of Westminster (PENRITH) BRED Christy Fitzgerald
LONG HANDICAP The Shy Padre (IRE) 9-13
1684* Lord of the West (IRE) had his task simplified by the departure of a couple of his most serious challengers, but he got his wires crossed with his pilot at the last, and only his strength enabled him to recover his momentum and win going away. (2/1)
1383 Philip's Woody had a chance second to none to win a race at this extended trip, but the weight concession to the in-form winner proved just too much of a handicap. (13/2: 9/2-7/1)
1637 Well Briefed did not look to be enjoying the task in hand at times, but he did make his full share of the running until fading rather quickly on the run to the last. (9/1)

1859 BIRCH H'CAP HURDLE (0-120) (4-Y.O+) (Class D)

3-00 (3-00) **2m 4f 110y (11 hdls)** £3,028.30 (£838.80: £400.90) GOING: 0.01 sec per fur (G)

				SP	RR	SF
	Wassl Street (IRE) (95) (KAMorgan) **4-10-13** NWilliamson (bit bkwd: plld hrd: hld up: hdwy 7th: shkn up to ld last: sn clr)	—	**1**	4/1[3]	78	43
	Diwali Dancer (110) (MCPipe) **6-12-0** JOsborne (bkwd: led & sn clr: hdd last: one pce)	4	**2**	7/2[2]	90	55
1374[2]	**Lord Mcmurrough (IRE) (110)** (JNeville) **6-12-0** RFarrant (lw: chsd clr ldr: ev ch fr 3 out: rdn & wknd appr last)	9	**3**	7/4[1]	83	48
	Viscount Tully (84) (CFCJackson) **11-10-2**ow2 MissSJackson (bkwd: nvr nr to chal)	9	**4**	25/1	50	13
1586[2]	**Kalasadi (USA) (106)** (VSoane) **5-11-10b** MRichards (chsd ldng pair to 7th: sn lost tch: t.o fr 3 out)	23	**5**	7/2[2]	54	19
1360[P]	**Royal Citizen (IRE) (94)** (JFBottomley) **7-10-12** GBradley (a bhd: t.o fr 7th: p.u bef 2 out)		**P**	12/1	—	—
187[P]	**Captain My Captain (IRE) (82)** (RBrotherton) **8-10-0** LHarvey (bkwd: a bhd: t.o whn p.u bef 2 out)		**P**	50/1	—	—
				(SP 114.3%)	**7 Rn**	

4m 53.9 (4.90) CSF £17.45 CT £29.29 TOTE £6.20: £2.80 £1.80 (£13.50) OWNER Mr B. Leatherday (MELTON MOWBRAY) BRED Cliveden Stud

LONG HANDICAP Viscount Tully 9-10 Captain My Captain (IRE) 9-12

OFFICIAL EXPLANATION Royal Citizen (IRE): swallowed his tongue.

Wassl Street (IRE), a winner on his hurdling debut last year, needed just one crack of the whip to quicken up into a winning lead. He may be best fresh, although there were excuses on his second run last season. (4/1)

Diwali Dancer ran extremely well after twenty months out of action and, with this badly-needed spin to put an edge on him, he should be back to something like his best. (7/2: op 9/4)

1374 Lord Mcmurrough (IRE) did his best to keep tabs on the clear leader, and looked set to take over at will on the turn into the straight, but he may have had to work harder than he had wished, for he was legless when asked for his effort between the last two. (7/4)

1586 Kalasadi (USA) (7/2: 5/2-4/1)

1860 OAK H'CAP HURDLE (0-110) (4-Y.O+) (Class E)

3-30 (3-31) **2m (9 hdls)** £2,544.00 (£704.00: £336.00) GOING: 0.01 sec per fur (G)

				SP	RR	SF
1658*	**Circus Line (103)** (MWEasterby) **5-11-8** MAFitzgerald (lw: chsd clr ldr: led appr 4 out: mstkes 3 out & 2 out: clr last)	—	**1**	13/8[1]	88	37
1630[3]	**Kintavi (82)** (TWDonnelly) **6-9-12**(3) GHogan (hld up & bhd: hdwy 4 out: chsd wnr appr last: no imp)	5	**2**	7/1[3]	62	11
	Shepherds Rest (IRE) (95) (SMellor) **4-10-7**(7) SHearn (bkwd: hld up: hdwy appr 4 out: nt rch ldrs)	7	**3**	16/1	68	17
1567[4]	**Cawarra Boy (105)** (CJames) **8-11-10** MrEJames (hld up & bhd: sme hdwy fr 3 out: nvr nrr)	2	**4**	15/2	76	25
1642[6]	**Kadari (92)** (WClay) **7-10-11** NWilliamson (bit bkwd: nvr trbld ldrs)	5	**5**	16/1	58	7
1381[3]	**Kelly Mac (90)** (DCO'Brien) **6-10-9** CLlewellyn (chsd clr ldng pair to 5th: wknd 3 out)	2	**6**	7/2[2]	54	3
	Euro Singer (98) (PRWebber) **4-11-3** JOsborne (led & sn clr: hdd appr 4 out: wknd 2 out)	4	**7**	10/1	58	7
	Sheecky (81) (BAMcMahon) **5-10-0** DBridgwater (bkwd: lost tch 5th: t.o)	dist	**8**	33/1	—	—
	Erlking (IRE) (96) (SMellor) **6-11-1** NMann (bkwd: a bhd: t.o)	8	**9**	16/1	—	—
	Alaskan Heir (85) (AStreeter) **5-10-4** TEley (bkwd: fell 1st)		**F**	14/1	—	—
				(SP 120.9%)	**10 Rn**	

3m 51.9 (6.90) CSF £13.59 CT £129.36 TOTE £2.30: £1.10 £2.20 £4.20 (£14.10) Trio £141.60; £125.70 to Taunton 12/12/96 OWNER Mrs P. A. H. Hartley (SHERIFF HUTTON) BRED Havenwood Construction Ltd

LONG HANDICAP Sheecky 9-6

1658* Circus Line had an easier task than was anticipated with so many of his rivals short of peak-fitness. The ease of this success should not be taken at face value. (13/8: evens-2/1)

1630 Kintavi, with the benefit of a run last month, stayed on to chase up the winner in the closing stages, but failed to make any significant impression. (7/1)

Shepherds Rest (IRE) gave notice last term that he was capable of picking up a race, but he needed this to put an edge on him and, in the circumstances, put in a pleasing performance. (16/1)

1567 Cawarra Boy was unable to get himself into the race, despite staying on, but at least he showed he does retain his ability. (15/2: 4/1-8/1)

1381 Kelly Mac had the ground he needs, but ran a bit flat after chasing the leading pair to the end of the back straight. (7/2)

Euro Singer (10/1: op 6/1)

T/Plpt: £57.70 (194.95 Tckts). T/Qdpt: £58.70 (15.65 Tckts). IM

1007-FAKENHAM (L-H) (Good)

Thursday December 12th

WEATHER: dull

1861 FITZWILLIAM (S) H'CAP HURDLE (0-95) (4-Y.O+) (Class G)

12-50 (12-51) **2m (9 hdls)** £2,733.00 (£834.00: £412.00: £201.00) GOING: 0.58 sec per fur (S)

				SP	RR	SF
1628[6]	**Pharly Reef (68)** (DBurchell) **4-10-11** ADobbin (in tch: hdwy 6th: led appr last: rdn out)	—	**1**	7/2[3]	52	6
1727[6]	**Cosmic Star (57)** (PWinkworth) **6-10-0b** JRKavanagh (led tl appr 2nd: hit 5th: led appr 2 out: sn clr: hdd appr last: wknd flat)	3	**2**	40/1	38	—
1703[8]	**Elite Justice (83)** (SGollings) **4-11-12b** KGaule (prom: outpcd appr 2 out: kpt on flat)	1	**3**	10/1	63	17
1390[8]	**Ruth's Gamble (57)** (MrsLCJewell) **8-10-0v** DLeahy (blnd & dropped rr 4th: styd on wl appr 2 out)	2½	**4**	25/1	35	—
1693[3]	**Royal Standard (84)** (PMRich) **9-11-6v**(7) MGriffiths (lw: sn prom: led 5th tl appr 2 out: wknd appr last)	2	**5**	11/4[2]	60	14
1332[6]	**Alosaili (72)** (JCullinan) **9-10-12**(3) GHogan (hld up: rdn & hit 6th: sn btn)	1¾	**6**	8/1	46	—
1562[3]	**Katballou (62)** (KGWingrove) **7-10-5** JRyan (lw: prom to 6th)	11	**7**	7/1	25	—
1569[P]	**Java Shrine (USA) (61)** (JCTuck) **5-10-4b** RBellamy (lw: plld hrd: in tch: effrt 6th: wknd next)	10	**8**	14/1	14	—
1374[8]	**Lucy Tufty (84)** (JPearce) **5-11-13** RDunwoody (in tch to 5th)	25	**9**	5/2[1]	12	—
1390[P]	**Just a Beau (57)** (MrsLCJewell) **5-9-9**(5) SophieMitchell (plld hrd: led appr 2nd: hdd 5th: wknd qckly next)	dist	**10**	66/1	—	—
				(SP 124.6%)	**10 Rn**	

4m 4.9 (20.90) CSF £101.34 CT £1,209.80 TOTE £3.70: £1.70 £6.50 £4.20 (£230.80) Trio £178.20; £175.76 to Cheltenham 13/12/96 OWNER Mr Vivian Guy (EBBW VALE) BRED Limestone Stud

LONG HANDICAP Cosmic Star 9-11 Just a Beau 9-8

No bid
1628 Pharly Reef became another to frank the Bangor form. He takes a good hold, but got home well on this occasion. (7/2)
Cosmic Star, who had worn headgear on the Flat, made a quick reappearance, having been off for nearly three years before her latest run. Kicked clear going to two out, she again ran as if the race would bring her on. (40/1)
334 Elite Justice could not get to the front, but did stay on surprisingly well from the penultimate flight. (10/1: op 6/1)
Ruth's Gamble has not won for almost three years and does appear to run in snatches these days. (25/1)
1693 Royal Standard, most reluctant to line up, set off a couple of lengths behind the others, but quickly made up the ground. His inability to get to the front probably made all the difference. (11/4)
1332 Alosaili continues to disappoint and quickly drew stumps when the pressure was applied. (8/1: 4/1-9/1)
1374 Lucy Tufty is only small and, carrying 12lb more than ever before, never looked up to the task. (5/2)

1862 NEW SMALLER SIZE E.D.P. HURDLE (3-Y.O) (Class D)

1-20 (1-22) **2m (9 hdls)** £2,720.00 (£830.00: £410.00: £200.00) GOING: 0.58 sec per fur (S)

				SP	RR	SF
1634[5]	**Le Teteu (FR)** (BobJones) **3-10-12** RDunwoody (lw: hld up: hdwy 5th: led last: rdn out)	—	1	6/4[1]	79	30
	Desert Mountain (IRE) (NACallaghan) **3-10-12** CLlewellyn (plld hrd: a.p: led 5th to next: led 3 out to last: unable qckn)	2	2	9/4[2]	77	28
	Royal Action (JEBanks) **3-10-12** JRKavanagh (led tl after 1st: led 6th to next: ev ch whn hit 2 out: wknd appr last)	10	3	11/4[3]	67	18
	Forest Boy (JRBosley) **3-10-9**(3) GHogan (in tch: hdwy whn blnd 2 out: sn btn)	nk	4	12/1	67	18
	Haute Cuisine (RJRWilliams) **3-10-12** KGaule (chsd ldrs to 3 out)	21	5	20/1	46	—
	Poetry (IRE) (MHTompkins) **3-10-7** ADobbin (hld up: hit 1st: blnd 5th: no ch after)	5	6	13/2	36	—
1370*	**Fijon (IRE)** (JPearce) **3-10-13** VSmith (lw: prom to 3 out)	1¼	7	10/1	40	—
	Magic Role (JRJenkins) **3-10-5**(7) NTEgan (bit bkwd: nt j.w: a bhd)	15	8	16/1	24	—
1634[P]	**Bright Eclipse (USA)** (MissKWhitehouse) **3-10-12b** TJenks (plld hrd: led after 1st: hdd & wknd 5th: t.o whn p.u bef 2 out)		P	33/1	—	—

(SP 141.1%) **9 Rn**

3m 59.7 (15.70) CSF £6.77 TOTE £2.00: £1.10 £1.80 £1.20 (£9.80) Trio £3.80 OWNER Mrs Judit Woods (NEWMARKET) BRED Pillar Stud
OFFICIAL EXPLANATION **Bright Eclipse (USA): finished distressed and was gulping for air.**
1634 Le Teteu (FR), lightly-made, was not as good as many of these on the level, but seems to have really taken to timber and won in determined style. (6/4: 11/10-7/4)
Desert Mountain (IRE), useful on the Flat in Ireland, looked to just need this first run since May, but was clearly fancied, and made the winner pull out all the stops. (9/4)
Royal Action has always looked the sort to do well over hurdles, but will be better suited by a more galloping track. (11/4)
Forest Boy ran up a hat-trick on the Flat in the summer, but his longest winning distance was Hamilton's extended mile. Given every chance to stay by being dropped in, he was going as well as anything when hitting two out, but then made no further progress. He could be worth another chance on an easy track. (12/1: 7/1-14/1)
Haute Cuisine, being by Petong out of a half-sister to Paris House, hardly has an ideal jumping pedigree, but he did get ten furlongs on the Flat and shaped promisingly for a long way. (20/1)
Poetry (IRE), ideally a front-runner on the Flat, was knocked right back to the rear by her blunder at halfway and was not knocked about. She will be much better than this with a clear round of jumping. (13/2: 4/1-7/1)

1863 STEPHENSON SMART H'CAP CHASE (0-120) (5-Y.O+) (Class D)

1-55 (1-55) **3m 110y (18 fncs)** £4,307.50 (£1,315.00: £650.00: £317.50) GOING: 0.58 sec per fur (S)

				SP	RR	SF
1586[11]	**Dont Tell the Wife (115)** (CREgerton) **10-11-13** JAMcCarthy (hld up: hdwy 8th: chal last: sn led: rdn out)	—	1	7/2[3]	112	27
1279[4]	**Romany Creek (IRE) (116)** (JPearce) **7-12-0** RDunwoody (prom: hit 7th: blnd 4 out: led appr 2 out: hdd & unable qckn flat)	½	2	3/1[2]	113	28
1660[6]	**Pats Minstrel (108)** (RChampion) **11-11-6** ADobbin (chsd ldr: lft in ld 9th: hdd appr 2 out: one pce)	5	3	8/1	101	16
1389[P]	**Victory Gate (USA) (88)** (MrsLCJewell) **11-10-0** DLeahy (effrt 11th: nvr nr ldrs)	dist	4	50/1	—	—
1837[5]	**Joker Jack (89)** (RDean) **11-9-12**(3)ow1 GHogan (prom tl blnd 5th: wl bhd fr 14th)	½	5	16/1	—	—
	Speaker Weatherill (IRE) (108) (OBrennan) **7-11-6** MBrennan (led tl fell 9th)		F	Evens[1]	—	—
	Good Old Chips (88) (JohnWhyte) **9-10-0** JRKavanagh (bit bkwd: t.o fr 8th: p.u bef 13th)		P	33/1	—	—

(SP 119.1%) **7 Rn**

6m 33.5 (30.50) CSF £14.49 TOTE £3.10: £1.40 £2.20 (£6.00) OWNER Elite Racing Club (CHADDLEWORTH) BRED Mrs Brenda Cunningham
LONG HANDICAP Victory Gate (USA) 8-11 Joker Jack 8-2 Good Old Chips 8-13
Dont Tell the Wife was given a confidence-booster over hurdles recently and that clearly did the trick, for this was his best round of fencing in years. He is well handicapped these days, but days when he jumps this well are the exception rather than the rule. (7/2)
1279 Romany Creek (IRE), running without the headgear for the first time in over a year, ran well in a particularly soft race. (3/1)
1660 Pats Minstrel showed surprising stamina for one who has been kept primarily to two miles in recent years. (8/1)
Victory Gate (USA) tried to close on the final circuit without success. (50/1)
1554 Joker Jack tries hard, but is the embodiment of the term paceless and will only ever win when everything else weakens. (16/1)
Speaker Weatherill (IRE), a rangy, attractive sort who really came to himself in the spring when put over fences, suffered his first defeat over the major obstacles, but was still going strongly when coming down. (Evens)

1864 L. L. FIRTH MEMORIAL H'CAP CHASE (0-100) (5-Y.O+) (Class F)

2-30 (2-31) **2m 110y (12 fncs)** £4,307.50 (£1,315.00: £650.00: £317.50) GOING: 0.58 sec per fur (S)

				SP	RR	SF
1696*	**The Lancer (IRE) (90)** (DRGandolfo) **7-11-8** 8x RDunwoody (a.p: led appr last: pushed out)	—	1	6/4[1]	94	36
1796[5]	**Dr Rocket (86)** (RDickin) **11-11-4b** CLlewellyn (a.p: ev ch appr last: unable qckn)	2½	2	12/1	88	30
1769[U]	**Winspit (IRE) (86)** (RHAlner) **6-11-4** JRKavanagh (plld hrd: chsd ldrs: ev ch whn lft in ld 2 out: sn hdd & one pce)	2	3	5/1[3]	86	28
826[3]	**Holy Wanderer (USA) (96)** (TRGeorge) **7-11-11**(3) GHogan (hld up: hdwy 5th: effrt 2 out: hit last: nt qckn)	1½	4	11/2	94	36
	Sounds Golden (73) (JohnWhyte) **8-9-12**(7)ow5 MrRWakley (bit bkwd: hit 3rd: in tch to 4 out)	10	5	33/1	62	—
1328[P]	**The Minister (IRE) (82)** (RChampion) **7-11-0** ADobbin (in tch: rdn whn blnd 3 out: no ch after)	18	6	8/1	53	—
1552[3]	**National Flag (FR) (72)** (KRBurke) **6-10-4** ALarnach (blnd 7th: a bhd)	dist	7	8/1	—	—
1584[5]	**Circulation (76)** (DMcCain) **10-10-5v**(3)ow6 DWalsh (led tl fell 2 out)		F	4/1[2]	—	—

				SP	RR	SF
	Rustic Gent (IRE) (78) (MrsLCJewell) **8-10-10v** DLeahy (bit bkwd: in tch tl blnd & lost pl 8th: t.o whn blnd next: p.u bef 3 out)		**P**	33/1	—	—
				(SP 127.8%)		**9 Rn**

4m 17.1 (17.10) CSF £20.88 CT £74.55 TOTE £1.90: £1.40 £2.40 £3.30 (£7.20) Trio £12.80 OWNER Mr A. E. Frost (WANTAGE) BRED J. O'Keeffe
LONG HANDICAP Sounds Golden 9-6
1696* The Lancer (IRE), on ground very different to last time, again won well and continues on the up. (6/4: tchd 9/4)
1796 Dr Rocket ran a fine race after a pipe-opener over hurdles, but is not as good as he was, and will continue to be difficult to win with. (12/1: op 6/1)
1769 Winspit (IRE), a good mover who takes a hold, had no more to give going to the last. (5/1)
826 Holy Wanderer (USA) has had a few problems over fences so far, not all of his own making, but did appear thrown-in on his hurdles form. He raced with his head rather high when marginally short of room going into the last, but this must still be considered a disappointing effort. (11/2: 4/1-6/1)
Sounds Golden did rather better than in any of his runs last season, but still has some way to go to be a threat. (33/1)
1328 The Minister (IRE) was just beginning to struggle when the mistake three out stopped him in his tracks. (8/1)

1865 COTTESMORE NOVICES' CHASE (5-Y.O+ Mares Only) (Class D)
3-00 (3-00) **2m 5f 110y (16 fncs)** £3,352.70 (£1,022.60: £504.80: £245.90) GOING: 0.58 sec per fur (S)

				SP	RR	SF
	Jasilu (KCBailey) **6-11-2b** CLlewellyn (mde all: j.slowly 3rd & 6th: qcknd 11th: rdn clr appr last)	—	**1**	85/40[2]	94	6
1320[F]	**Scamallach (IRE) (82)** (JRJenkins) **6-10-10b** RDunwoody (trckd wnr: ev ch 4 out tl rdn & btn appr last)	3	**2**	2/1[1]	86	—
1732[9]	**Prize Match (75)** (JCTuck) **7-10-10** RBellamy (trckd ldrs: hit 4 out: kpt on fr next)	5	**3**	5/1[3]	82	—
1552[4]	**Sophie May (88)** (GLMoore) **5-10-10** ADobbin (trckd ldrs: blnd 10th: rdn 4 out: sn btn)	2½	**4**	2/1[1]	80	—
1197[6]	**Pennant Cottage (IRE) (60)** (MissKWhitehouse) **8-10-10b[1]** TJenks (lw: mstkes: a in rr: blnd & lost tch 11th)	dist	**5**	33/1	—	—
				(SP 118.3%)		**5 Rn**

5m 45.4 (30.40) CSF £7.05 TOTE £4.20: £1.60 £1.30 (£3.30) OWNER Mr K. C. Bailey (UPPER LAMBOURN) BRED C. L. Loyd
Jasilu set a steady pace, but took the first circuit to warm up her jumping, putting in some alarmingly slow leaps. (85/40)
1062 Scamallach (IRE) does seem to need to do it all on the bridle, for the moment she came under pressure she was clearly beaten. (2/1)
Prize Match, second in this race a year ago, has cut little ice over fences since and never looked likely to go one better. (5/1)
1552 Sophie May travelled sweetly until the pace quickened on the final circuit. (2/1: op evens)

1866 FAKENHAM RACECOURSE CARAVAN SITE H'CAP HURDLE (0-110) (4-Y.O+) (Class E)
3-30 (3-30) **2m 4f (11 hdls)** £3,386.20 (£1,033.60: £510.80: £249.40) GOING: 0.58 sec per fur (S)

				SP	RR	SF
1418[4]	**Barford Sovereign (104)** (JRFanshawe) **4-11-12** ADobbin (set slow pce tl appr 3rd: led & qcknd appr 8th: clr 2 out: easily)	—	**1**	4/1[2]	91+	8
1727[3]	**Pedaltothemetal (IRE) (90)** (PMitchell) **4-10-9**(3) DWalsh (lw: a.p: rdn & chsd wnr fr 8th: one pce appr 2 out)	9	**2**	13/2	70	—
651[2]	**Wadada (106)** (DBurchell) **5-11-7**(7) JPrior (hdwy appr 7th: kpt on wl fr appr 2 out: nvr able to chal)	2	**3**	6/1[3]	84	1
1798[3]	**Able Player (USA) (86)** (KJDrewry) **9-10-8** MSharratt (chsd ldrs: rdn 8th: kpt on same pce)	1¾	**4**	13/2	63	—
1732[6]	**Durshan (USA) (78)** (JRJenkins) **7-10-0b[1]** JRKavanagh (prom: hit 3rd: lost pl 7th: r.o again fr 2 out)	nk	**5**	11/1	55	—
1585[2]	**Pair of Jacks (IRE) (92)** (GLMoore) **6-11-0** RDunwoody (hdwy 6th: rdn & wknd appr 2 out)	16	**6**	9/4[1]	56	—
1562[10]	**Nagobelia (81)** (JPearce) **8-10-3** KGaule (lw: hld up: hdwy 6th: wknd 8th)	2½	**7**	25/1	43	—
1639[P]	**Lookingforarainbow (IRE) (83)** (BobJones) **8-10-5** VSmith (bhd: effrt 8th: wknd next)	2½	**8**	9/4[1]	43	—
	Ajdar (88) (OBrennan) **5-10-10** MBrennan (plld hrd: led appr 3rd: sn clr: wknd & hdd appr 8th)	dist	**9**	16/1	—	—
				(SP 140.6%)		**9 Rn**

5m 14.7 (29.70) CSF £34.01 CT £156.17 TOTE £5.70: £1.40 £2.40 £1.80 (£14.70) Trio £28.10 OWNER Barford Bloodstock (NEWMARKET) BRED Mrs C. Handscombe
LONG HANDICAP Durshan (USA) 9-12
OFFICIAL EXPLANATION **Lookingforarainbow (IRE): the gelding has physical problems and can be inconsistent if things do not go his own way in a race. The trainer added that the gelding would not run over hurdles again.**
1418 Barford Sovereign, with trip and ground suiting her much better than many of her rivals, was allowed to race close to the pace, and returned to form with a facile victory. (4/1: 5/1-8/1)
1727 Pedaltothemetal (IRE) looked marvellous, but is one-paced and, having had as many chances as Savo Milosevic, is fast becoming frustrating. (13/2)
651 Wadada found this trip too short on such a sharp track and ought to benefit from a step up to three miles. (6/1: op 4/1)
1798 Able Player (USA) did seem to find the trip rather too sharp on such a quick track. (13/2)
Durshan (USA) is something of an in-and-out performer these days and has only won once in his last twenty-seven starts. (11/1: 8/1-12/1)
1585 Pair of Jacks (IRE), stepping up beyond the minimum trip, did not appear to stay. (9/4)

T/Plpt: £59.70 (161.25 Tckts). T/Qdpt: £9.30 (102.28 Tckts). Dk

1789-SANDOWN (R-H) (Good, Good to firm patches)
Thursday December 12th
WEATHER: cold & dull

1867 E.B.F. 'N.H.' QUALIFIER NOVICES' HURDLE (4, 5 & 6-Y.O) (Class D)
1-00 (1-01) **2m 110y (8 hdls)** £2,970.00 (£900.00: £440.00: £210.00) GOING: 0.44 sec per fur (GS)

				SP	RR	SF
1470*	**Hurricane Lamp** (DNicholson) **5-11-10** AMaguire (stdy hdwy 3 out: led 2 out: drvn out)	—	**1**	7/4[1]	96+	52
1651[4]	**Nasone (IRE)** (JTGifford) **5-11-0** PHide (hdwy 4th: ev ch fr 2 out: r.o wl)	nk	**2**	9/4[2]	86+	42
	Friendship (IRE) (NJHenderson) **4-11-0** MAFitzgerald (hdwy 5th: 4th whn mstke 3 out: rdn appr last: 4th whn mstke last: r.o nr fin)	3	**3**	3/1[3]	83+	39
	Award (IRE) (RRowe) **5-11-0** DO'Sullivan (hdwy 3rd: chsd ldr fr 4th: mstke 5th: led appr 2 out: sn hdd: ev ch last: unable qckn)	hd	**4**	50/1	83+	39
1583[4]	**Neat Feat (IRE)** (DRCElsworth) **5-11-0** PHolley (lw: hdwy appr 2 out: sn wknd)	13	**5**	12/1	70	26
1453[11]	**Physical Fun** (AGBlackmore) **5-11-0** DSkyrme (lw: nvr nr to chal)	7	**6**	66/1	63	19
1329[10]	**Loch Na Keal** (CPMorlock) **4-10-9** CMaude (swtg: nvr nrr)	1	**7**	40/1	57	13
1369[B]	**Rossell Island (IRE)** (MrsJPitman) **5-11-0** WMarston (prom to 3 out)	2	**8**	50/1	60	16

	Jazzman (IRE) (APJarvis) **4-11-0** DGallagher (bit bkwd: a bhd)	5 **9**	33/1	56	12
1476P	**Black Statement (IRE)** (APJarvis) **6-10-11**(3) LAspell (prom to 3 out)	16 **10**	50/1	40	—
1471²	**Calvaro (IRE) (70)** (APJarvis) **5-11-0** GBradley (prom to 4th)	2 **11**	25/1	38	—
1659¹⁰	**Gale Wargame (IRE)** (OSherwood) **5-11-0** JOsborne (led tl appr 2 out: sn wknd)	7 **12**	16/1	31	—
			(SP 122.3%)	**12 Rn**	

4m 2.4 (11.40) CSF £6.12 TOTE £2.70: £1.40 £1.30 £1.50 (£3.00) Trio £1.60 OWNER Mr & Mrs F C Welch and Mr R A Barrs (TEMPLE GUITING) BRED Mrs S. C. Welch

IN-FOCUS: **This looked a very decent novice hurdle, with the first four all looking useful individuals.**

1470* Hurricane Lamp was outrageously landed with a 10lb penalty for winning a small novice event at Warwick, but put up a very decent performance. He can complete the hat-trick on his way to better things. (7/4)

1651 Nasone (IRE) is well regarded at home and ran a sound race in defeat. He looks nailed-on for a similar event. (9/4)

Friendship (IRE) looks the type to do well at this game and showed plenty of promise on this hurdling debut. Looking in very good shape in the paddock, he was untidy at the third last. In fourth when again clumsy at the final flight, he looked booked for that position but got his second wind in the closing stages, and ran on to snatch third right on the line. He looks a ready-made winner. (3/1)

Award (IRE), a half-brother to a winning pointer, was given no easy task on this debut, but made a highly-encouraging start. Poking his head in front approaching the second last, he was soon collared by the winner, but his pilot did not ask him any sort of question and the combination still travelled really well. With every chance jumping the final flight, he was only tapped for toe up the hill. He should have no problems finding a race. (50/1)

1583 Neat Feat (IRE) looked extremely well beforehand, but was out of his depth. (12/1)

1868 BOVIS LELLIOTT NOVICES' CHASE (5-Y.O+) (Class C)

1-35 (1-35) **2m 4f 110y (17 fncs)** £5,506.00 (£1,354.00) GOING: 0.44 sec per fur (GS)

				SP	RR	SF
1364*	**Potter's Bay (IRE) (113)** (DNicholson) **7-11-7** AMaguire (lw: chsd ldr: led 10th: mstke 13th: shkn up flat: r.o wl)	—	**1**	2/7¹	112?	14
	Triple Witching (NJHenderson) **10-11-0** MAFitzgerald (led: j.slowly 9th: hdd 10th: ev ch fr 2 out: unable qckn flat)	1	**2**	3/1²	104?	6
				(SP 102.8%)	**2 Rn**	

5m 23.8 (24.80) TOTE £1.20 OWNER Mrs J. E. Potter (TEMPLE GUITING) BRED Colman O'Flynn

1364* Potter's Bay (IRE) will have gained more valuable experience over these tricky obstacles. He went into the second of the Railway Fences on the wrong foot and made a hash of it but, in the sprint from the last, proved too good for his sole opponent. (2/7: op 4/9)

Triple Witching, a useful staying hurdler with David Nicholson, had been off the course since November '94. He appeared pretty straight and, though starting over fences very late on in life, ran a promising race. In front to the tenth, he was back on terms again with his rival from the second last travelling just as well. In the sprint from the final fence, he was just tapped for toe. Given time to get over his exertions, he can certainly win a similar event. (3/1: op 11/8)

1869 BOVIS CROWNGAP H'CAP CHASE (5-Y.O+) (Class B)

2-10 (2-12) **2m 4f 110y (17 fncs)** £6,775.00 (£2,050.00: £1,000.00: £475.00) GOING: 0.44 sec per fur (GS)

				SP	RR	SF
1186²	**Stately Home (IRE) (120)** (PBowen) **5-10-0** AMaguire (lw: j.w: mde all: clr 6th: unchal)	—	**1**	9/4¹	120	32
1637F	**Strong Medicine (134)** (KCBailey) **9-11-0** JOsborne (lw: chsd wnr 2nd to 3rd: chsd wnr fr 10th: rdn appr 2 out: no imp)	12	**2**	9/4¹	125	37
	Bradbury Star (148) (JTGifford) **11-12-0** PHide (nvr nr to chal)	1¼	**3**	7/1³	138	50
1366⁹	**Easthorpe (141)** (MissHCKnight) **8-11-7** MAFitzgerald (lw: chsd wnr tl mstke 2nd: chsd wnr 3rd to 10th: wknd 12th)	1½	**4**	3/1²	130	42
1373P	**Conti D'Estruval (FR) (121)** (GBBalding) **6-10-1** BFenton (hld up: rdn appr 3 out: wknd appr last)	1¾	**5**	9/1	108	20
				(SP 109.0%)	**5 Rn**	

5m 12.7 (13.70) CSF £7.23 TOTE £2.70: £1.40 £1.90 (£2.90) OWNER Mr P. Bowen (HAVERFORDWEST) BRED Ash Hill Stud

LONG HANDICAP Stately Home (IRE) 9-13

1186 Stately Home (IRE) put up a quite staggering performance over these tricky fences that had to be seen to be believed. Jumping like a thing possessed, he dominated in splendid isolation for much of the race. He obviously likes this course and his trainer should take advantage of it. (9/4)

1637 Strong Medicine, 5lb higher than when winning over this course and distance last month, moved into second at the open ditch, the tenth, but never looked like reeling in the tearaway winner. (9/4)

Bradbury Star has had leg problems, but returned looking reasonably straight. He is not the force of old though and is now 20lb lower than when last appearing in a handicap. Nursed round by Hide, he got round in one piece but never threatened to get into it. (7/1: 5/1-8/1)

1016 Easthorpe was most disappointing. (3/1)

811 Conti D'Estruval (FR) is at his best on fast ground over two and a half miles, but could never cut much ice here. (9/1: 6/1-10/1)

1870 BOVIS CROWNGAP WINTER NOVICES' HURDLE (Gd 2) (4-Y.O+) (Class A)

2-40 (2-44) **2m 6f (11 hdls)** £9,645.00 (£3,651.00: £1,788.00: £816.00) GOING: 0.44 sec per fur (GS)

				SP	RR	SF
1639*	**Yahmi (IRE) (116)** (JABOld) **6-11-4** JOsborne (hld up: led last: all out)	—	**1**	4/1²	97	49
1280*	**Jack Tanner (IRE)** (DNicholson) **7-11-7** AMaguire (hld up: mstke 1st: led 2 out to last: hrd rdn: r.o wl)	hd	**2**	1/4¹	100	52
1392³	**Eulogy (IRE) (113)** (RRowe) **6-11-0** DO'Sullivan (lw: w ldr fr 5th: led 3 out to 2 out: unable qckn)	5	**3**	25/1³	89?	41
1351²	**Supermodel (98)** (MrsNMacauley) **4-10-9** SWynne (hld up: hrd rdn appr last: sn wknd)	2½	**4**	100/1	83?	35
1322⁵	**River Room (106)** (KCBailey) **6-11-0** GBradley (lw: w ldr: led 5th: mstke 8th: hdd 3 out: wknd appr 2 out: t.o)	dist	**5**	25/1³	—	—
1476³	**Atavistic (IRE)** (CLPopham) **4-11-0** MAFitzgerald (lw: led to 5th: wknd after 3 out: t.o whn p.u bef 2 out)		**P**	33/1	—	—
				(SP 111.6%)	**6 Rn**	

5m 27.7 (14.70) CSF £5.27 TOTE £4.00: £1.30 £1.30 (£1.60) OWNER Mr W. E. Sturt (WROUGHTON) BRED Barronstown Stud

1639* Yahmi (IRE) had more on his plate on this occasion, but put up a gutsy performance. Cruising alongsides the winner in the straight, he jumped into a narrow lead at the final flight and held on with very little to spare. He is turning into a very useful novice. (4/1: 5/2-9/2)

1280* Jack Tanner (IRE) did not have the race run to suit him and was not convincing at his hurdles - he was awkward and flat at several of them. Despite the slow pace, he gained a narrow lead at the second last but was collared by the winner at the final flight before only just losing out on the run up the hill. He should not be written off and, in a stronger-run race, can bounce back. (1/4)

1392 Eulogy (IRE) ran a very sound race against two classy rivals and should soon open his account over hurdles if his sights are lowered. (25/1)

1351 Supermodel was out of her depth. (100/1)

1871 P & O H'CAP CHASE (5-Y.O+) (Class B)

3-10 (3-14) **3m 5f 110y (24 fncs)** £6,677.50 (£2,020.00: £985.00: £467.50) GOING: 0.44 sec per fur (GS)

				SP	RR	SF
1518*	**Inchcailloch (IRE) (128)** (JSKing) **7-11-7** CMaude (hld up: chsd ldr fr 12th: led appr last: rdn out)	—	**1**	4/6[1]	135	14
1662[2]	**Church Law (107)** (MrsLCTaylor) **9-10-0** AMaguire (hdwy appr 3 out: hrd rdn appr last: unable qckn flat)	1¾	**2**	5/2[2]	113	—
1383[3]	**Frozen Drop (107)** (PCRitchens) **9-10-0** SFox (led: mstke 9th: hdd appr last: sn wknd)	6	**3**	9/2[3]	109	—
1799[8]	**Woodlands Genhire (107)** (PAPritchard) **11-10-0b** WMarston (lw: chsd ldr to 12th: wknd 15th: t.o fr 19th)	dist	**4**	100/1	—	—
				(SP 107.7%)		**4 Rn**

7m 51.0 (36.00) CSF £2.58 TOTE £1.70 (£1.60) OWNER Mr F. J. Carter (SWINDON) BRED Hascombe and Valiant Studs
LONG HANDICAP Church Law 9-12 Frozen Drop 9-9 Woodlands Genhire 7-0

1518* Inchcailloch (IRE) had no problems with this longer trip, but was not really tested as the early pace was slow. Always travelling really well, he cruised into the lead approaching the last and was shaken up on the run-in to assert. (4/6)

1662 Church Law unseated his rider in the paddock and ran back to the stables beforehand. In the race, he moved up going to the Pond Fence, and was snapping at the heels of the winner at the last before put in his place. (5/2)

1383 Frozen Drop is a consistent individual but not really up to this grade, and was racing from 5lb out of the handicap. (9/2)

1872 SURREY RACING HURDLE (3-Y.O) (Class D)

3-40 (3-46) **2m 110y (8 hdls)** £2,905.00 (£880.00: £430.00: £205.00) GOING: 0.44 sec per fur (GS)

				SP	RR	SF
1377*	**Far Dawn (USA)** (MrsAJPerrett) **3-11-7** CMaude (lw: a.p: led appr 2 out: clr appr last: easily)	—	**1**	5/2[2]	84+	40
	Fitzwilliam (USA) (IABalding) **3-11-3** JOsborne (lw: 4th whn mstke 3 out: hdwy appr 2 out: rdn appr last: unable qckn)	12	**2**	6/5[1]	68	24
	Baranov (IRE) (DJGMurraySmith) **3-11-3** DGallagher (led 2nd to 3rd: led 5th tl appr 2 out: mstke 2 out: one pce)	nk	**3**	10/1	68	24
	Spiral Flyer (IRE) (MDIUsher) **3-10-12** WMarston (sme hdwy appr 2 out: sn wknd)	16	**4**	33/1	48	4
1370[3]	**Soldier Mak** (AHide) **3-11-3** PHide (led to 2nd: led 3rd to 5th: 2nd whn mstke 3 out: wknd appr 2 out)	6	**5**	10/1	47	3
	Go With The Wind (CWeedon) **3-11-3** MRichards (nvr nr to chal)	5	**6**	12/1	42	—
1370[9]	**Alarico (FR)** (IPWilliams) **3-11-3** AMaguire (nvr nrr)	nk	**7**	66/1	42	—
	Whispering Dawn (CPEBrooks) **3-10-12** GBradley (4th whn mstke 4th: sn wknd)	3	**8**	8/1[3]	34	—
1712[4]	**Veronica Franco** (BAPearce) **3-10-12** BFenton (a bhd)	6	**9**	33/1	28	—
1519[6]	**Sam Rockett** (PMooney) **3-10-12b**(5) SRyan (lw: sme hdwy appr 2 out: sn wknd)	6	**10**	66/1	27	—
1634[17]	**Hawanafa** (JSMoore) **3-10-12** WMcFarland (mid div whn mstke 2nd: bhd fr 3rd)	9	**11**	66/1	13	—
				(SP 121.4%)		**11 Rn**

4m 4.6 (13.60) CSF £5.82 TOTE £3.10: £1.60 £1.40 £3.00 (£3.10) Trio £21.60 OWNER Mr Peter Wiegand (PULBUROUGH) BRED Galbreath/Phillips Racing Partnership

1377* Far Dawn (USA) had more on his plate under a 4lb penalty, but still put up a highly-impressive display. Cruising into the lead approaching the second last, he scooted clear to win with a ton in hand. He looks very useful and can complete the hat-trick. (5/2)

Fitzwilliam (USA), the easy winner of a Pontefract maiden on the Flat, looked in good shape for this hurdling debut. Clumsy at the third last, he soon picked up ground but, try as he might, never looked like reeling in the winner. A round-bodied gelding, he should soon go one better. (6/5: evens-11/8)

Baranov (IRE), fit from the Flat, should be able to pick up a similar event. (10/1: op 5/1)

Spiral Flyer (IRE), a poor maiden on the Flat, never looked like getting to grips with the principals. (33/1)

1370 Soldier Mak had shot his bolt turning for home. (10/1: 5/1-11/1)

Go With The Wind, sold for 9,500 guineas at Newmarket Autumn Sales, made a little late headway without ever looking likely to get into it. (12/1)

T/Jkpt: £251.20 (38.2 Tckts). T/Plpt: £3.10 (3,773.1 Tckts). T/Qdpt: £2.80 (306.57 Tckts). AK

1594-TAUNTON (R-H) (Good)
Thursday December 12th

WEATHER: dull

1873 WEST HATCH NOVICES' HURDLE (4-Y.O+) (Class C)

1-10 (1-11) **2m 1f (9 hdls)** £3,777.50 (£1,145.00: £560.00: £267.50) GOING minus 0.37 sec per fur (GF)

				SP	RR	SF
1594*	**Yet Again (98)** (MissGayKelleway) **4-11-6** DBridgwater (a.p: led appr last: drvn out)	—	**1**	11/4[2]	89	36
1516*	**Lucia Forte** (KCBailey) **5-11-1** SMcNeill (a.p: ev ch last: unable qckn)	1¼	**2**	5/2[1]	83	30
	Easy Listening (USA) (NJHawke) **4-11-0** GUpton (plld hrd: led 3rd tl appr last: one pce)	4	**3**	8/1	78	25
	Show Faith (IRE) (RHannon) **6-11-0** RHughes (hld up: hdwy appr 6th: hrd rdn appr 2 out: one pce)	2½	**4**	15/2	76	23
1394[6]	**Swan Street (NZ)** (CJMann) **5-11-0** JRailton (lost pl 5th: styd on fr 3 out: n.d)	10	**5**	33/1	66	13
1375[9]	**Sahel (IRE)** (JWMullins) **8-11-0** SCurran (led to 3rd: mstke 3 out: sn wknd)	15	**6**	20/1	52	—
1424[7]	**Galway Boss (IRE)** (IPWilliams) **4-11-0** NWilliamson (hdwy after 4th: wknd 6th)	12	**7**	50/1	41	—
1788[P]	**Astral Invader (IRE)** (MSSaunders) **4-10-11**(3) TDascombe (prom: mstke 5th: sn rdn: wknd 3 out)	8	**8**	66/1	33	—
1633[P]	**Sophies Dream** (JMBradley) **5-11-0** TJMurphy (a bhd)	nk	**9**	100/1	33	—
	Gwithian (NJHawke) **4-11-0** RGreene (bkwd: a bhd)	½	**10**	66/1	33	—
	Deceit the Second (PRRodford) **4-11-0** SBurrough (a bhd)	5	**11**	66/1	28	—
	Maeterlinck (IRE) (GThorner) **4-10-7**(7) ClareThorner (bhd: mstke 1st: t.o whn fell 2 out)		**F**	40/1	—	—
968[2]	**Iktasab (110)** (PFNicholls) **4-11-6** APMcCoy (prom: hrd rdn 5th: wknd after 3 out: 5th & no ch whn fell last)		**F**	7/2[3]	—	—
	Western Playboy (RJBaker) **4-11-0** RFarrant (a bhd: t.o whn p.u bef 2 out)		**P**	40/1	—	—
				(SP 120.3%)		**14 Rn**

3m 53.8 (0.80) CSF £9.52 TOTE £3.00: £1.40 £1.70 £2.60 (£5.00) Trio £28.30 OWNER Mr A. P. Griffin (WHITCOMBE) BRED Aston Park Stud

1594* Yet Again again had the ground on the fast side and proved too good for the runner-up from the final flight. (11/4)

1516* Lucia Forte always in a good position and travelling well, had no answer to the winner's turn of foot going to the last. (5/2)

Easy Listening (USA), bought for 11,800 guineas out of Roger Charlton's stable, was injured at home after making a successful debut as a three-year-old and only ran four times this year. He will win races when he learns to settle. (8/1: op 5/1)

Show Faith (IRE) has yet to prove he really gets the trip over hurdles. (15/2: 5/1-8/1)

968 Iktasab, without the blinkers this time, was never travelling particularly well and is probably one to avoid. (7/2: 3/1-5/1)

1874 CHARD (S) HURDLE (4-Y.O+) (Class G)

1-45 (1-45) **2m 3f 110y (10 hdls)** £1,931.00 (£541.00: £263.00) GOING minus 0.37 sec per fur (GF)

			SP	RR	SF
1770*	**Harry (89)** (DBurchell) **6-11-12** DJBurchell (hld up & bhd: stdy hdwy 5th: led after 3 out: hit 2 out: r.o wl) ......—	**1**	Evens[1]	80	22
1537[7]	**Sleeptite (FR) (81)** (WGMTurner) **6-10-12**(7) JPower (a.p: led 7th tl after 3 out: one pce) 7	**2**	16/1	67	9
1537[4]	**Saracen Prince (USA) (75)** (CLPopham) **4-10-12** RJohnson (hld up: hdwy appr 6th: 4th & btn whn mstke 2 out) 6	**3**	4/1[3]	55	—
	Te Amo (IRE) (MCPipe) **4-10-12** RHughes (led to 7th: wknd appr 2 out) 1¾	**4**	7/2[2]	54	—
1299[5]	**Old Master (IRE) (58)** (RJBaker) **5-10-5**(7) NWillmington (bhd fr 6th) 9	**5**	20/1	47	—
1770[4]	**Comeonup** (JMBradley) **5-10-12** NWilliamson (a bhd: t.o fr 6th) ......dist	**6**	20/1	—	—
	Perfect Bertie (IRE) (NMBabbage) **4-10-5**(7) SO'Shea (plld hrd: prom: 4th & wkng whn fell 3 out)	**F**	16/1	—	—
1786[5]	**Miramare (59)** (CLPopham) **6-10-9**(3) TDascombe (a bhd: t.o whn p.u bef 6th)	**P**	33/1	—	—
1200[P]	**Blakeway** (GAHam) **9-10-7** SBurrough (bhd whn rdn after 5th: sn t.o: p.u bef last)	**P**	50/1	—	—
			(SP 118.4%)	**9 Rn**	

4m 37.2 (6.20) CSF £17.00 TOTE £2.10: £1.10 £3.10 £1.30 (£16.10) Trio £14.90 OWNER Mr Simon Lewis (EBBW VALE) BRED Jephanil
Sold AFear 6,500 gns

1770* Harry defied a double-penalty to complete a hat-trick in this grade. (Evens)
1072 Sleeptite (FR), appreciating this longer trip, finished a lot closer to the winner than he had done at Towcester. (16/1)
1537 Saracen Prince (USA) was a stone better off than when beaten over fifteen lengths by Harry at Towcester last month. (4/1: 8/1-7/2)
Te Amo (IRE) was claimed for £6,000 after winning a claimer over a mile and a half at Leicester in October. (7/2: 2/1-4/1)

1875 STOKE ST MARY NOVICES' H'CAP CHASE (0-100) (5-Y.O+) (Class E)

2-20 (2-21) **2m 3f (15 fncs)** £3,036.60 (£919.80: £449.40: £214.20) GOING minus 0.37 sec per fur (GF)

			SP	RR	SF
1629[P]	**Frontier Flight (USA) (80)** (MissLCSiddall) **6-11-0**(3) EHusband (hld up: hdwy appr 3 out: rdn to ld nr fin).....—	**1**	16/1	88	13
1646[P]	**Brown Robber (71)** (MrsRGHenderson) **8-10-8** RFarrant (mstke & rdr lost irons 3rd: hdwy 10th: lft in ld last: hdd nr fin) ......½	**2**	16/1	79	4
1472[U]	**Cracking Prospect (80)** (BRMillman) **5-10-12**(5) DSalter (hdwy 8th: ev ch flat: unable qckn) 1	**3**	11/1[3]	87	12
1629[W]	**Chris's Glen (80)** (JMBradley) **7-11-3v** NWilliamson (chsd ldr: led 7th to 8th: wknd 4 out) 10	**4**	10/1[2]	78	3
1677[3]	**Koo's Promise (83)** (CLPopham) **5-11-3**(3) TDascombe (lw: hrd rdn 11th: no hdwy) 1¾	**5**	10/1[2]	80	5
1664[4]	**Nautical George (IRE) (83)** (JohnUpson) **6-11-6** RSupple (bhd: blnd 5th: t.o fr 9th) ......dist	**6**	12/1	—	—
	Masked Martin (67) (PRRodford) **5-10-4**ow4 SBurrough (a bhd: t.o) 4	**7**	50/1	—	—
1696[5]	**Nordic Valley (IRE) (88)** (MCPipe) **5-11-11** TJMurphy (prom: hmpd 3 out: 3rd & btn whn fell last)	**F**	7/2[1]	—	—
1378[8]	**Gerry's Pride (IRE) (68)** (JWMullins) **5-10-5** SCurran (fell 1st)	**F**	12/1	—	—
	After The Fox (91) (NJHawke) **9-12-0** GUpton (lw: led to 7th: led 8th tl after 4 out: 2nd whn fell 3 out)	**F**	7/2[1]	—	—
1427[P]	**Saxon Mead (63)** (PJHobbs) **6-10-0b[1]** GTormey (sn prom: led after 4 out: mstke 3 out: 6l clr whn fell last)	**F**	10/1[2]	—	—
1472[4]	**Legal Artist (IRE) (79)** (MissCJohnsey) **6-11-2** LHarvey (swtg: a bhd: t.o whn p.u bef 3 out)	**P**	10/1[2]	—	—
1552[6]	**Anlace (70)** (SMellor) **7-10-7** NMann (bhd: mstke 2nd: t.o whn p.u bef 10th)	**P**	16/1	—	—
1599[6]	**San Diego Charger (IRE) (74)** (ABarrow) **5-10-6**(5) MrRThornton (blnd & uns rdr 2nd)	**U**	16/1	—	—
			(SP 130.0%)	**14 Rn**	

4m 49.0 (7.00) CSF £233.62 CT £2,695.83 TOTE £17.60: £5.40 £4.50 £5.20 (£168.70) Trio £694.20 OWNER Miss L. C. Siddall (TADCASTER)
BRED Aaron U. Jones
LONG HANDICAP Saxon Mead 9-11 Masked Martin 9-11

1060 Frontier Flight (USA), pulled up on soft ground on his fencing debut at Bangor, benefited from the fall of Saxon Mead at the final fence. (16/1)
1328 Brown Robber, dropped in class, could not hold on after being presented a golden opportunity at the final fence. (16/1)
1174 Cracking Prospect was another unable to take advantage of the demise of Saxon Mead. (11/1)
1038 Chris's Glen, dropped 3lb, would only have finished sixth without the grief at the last. (10/1: 7/1-11/1)
1677 Koo's Promise had plenty of weight considering she was a very lucky winner at Wincanton. (10/1)
1331 Nordic Valley (IRE) appreciated this faster ground, but was held when coming down at the last. (7/2: tchd 6/1)
After The Fox caught the eye in the paddock and was well supported in the ring, despite having to concede weight all round on this chasing debut. (7/2)
Saxon Mead, 3lb out of the handicap, was blinkered for his debut over fences and had the race in the bag when departing at the last. It will be interesting to see if the Handicapper raises his mark. (10/1)

1876 GAY SHEPPARD MEMORIAL CHALLENGE TROPHY H'CAP HURDLE (0-120) (4-Y.O+) (Class D)

2-50 (2-50) **3m 110y (12 hdls)** £2,900.00 (£875.00: £425.00: £200.00) GOING minus 0.37 sec per fur (GF)

			SP	RR	SF
891*	**Rosie-B (82)** (NMBabbage) **6-9-9**(5) MrRThornton (a.p: rdn to ld flat: r.o) ......—	**1**	7/4[1]	63	29
1553[5]	**Paddysway (90)** (RHBuckler) **9-10-8** DBridgwater (led tl after 5th: rdn to ld after 3 out: hdd flat) 1	**2**	11/4[2]	70	36
	Lugs Brannigan (IRE) (93) (MBradstock) **7-10-4**(7) KatharineHambidge (hld up & plld hrd: mstke 8th: styd on fr 2 out) 5	**3**	6/1[3]	70	36
1571[9]	**Royal Piper (NZ) (100)** (AJWilson) **9-11-4** RGreene (hld up: hdwy appr 2 out: one pce flat) 1¾	**4**	8/1	76	42
1355[3]	**Staunch Rival (USA) (109)** (GThorner) **9-11-6b**(7) ClareThorner (hld up: hdwy 3 out:rdn appr 2 out: one pce)nk	**5**	20/1	85	51
1562[4]	**Tiger Claw (USA) (84)** (AGHobbs) **10-9-11**(5) OBurrows (prom tl wknd appr 2 out) 6	**6**	16/1	56	22
	Khatir (CAN) (82) (MCPipe) **5-10-0b** NWilliamson (prom: led after 5th: hdd after 3 out: wknd 2 out) 1¼	**7**	10/1	53	19
1598[P]	**Certain Angle (106)** (PJHobbs) **7-11-10** GTormey (bhd fr 9th: t.o whn p.u bef 2 out)	**P**	8/1	—	—
			(SP 119.3%)	**8 Rn**	

5m 49.5 (-2.50) CSF £7.17 CT £21.53 TOTE £3.50: £2.00 £1.50 £1.50 (£4.00) OWNER Internet Racing (CHELTENHAM) BRED J. A. D. Engineering Ltd
LONG HANDICAP Rosie-B 9-10 Khatir (CAN) 9-10

891* Rosie-B, raised 7lb, was still 4lb wrong at the weights and seemed well suited to this slightly longer trip. (7/4)
Paddysway was 3lb lower than when winning in April '93. (11/4: 3/1-100/3)
Lugs Brannigan (IRE), 3lb higher than when scoring under this rider at Wincanton in March, gave the impression he would have gone a lot closer with stronger handling. (6/1)
Royal Piper (NZ), dropped 2lb, ran much better than on his reappearance at Chepstow. (8/1: op 9/2)
1355 Staunch Rival (USA), down 9lb, looked to be going well leaving the back straight, but soon came under pressure. (20/1)

1562 Tiger Claw (USA), stepping up from sellers, was 4lb lower than when fourth at Huntingdon. (16/1)
Khatir (CAN) (10/1: op 5/1)
1598 Certain Angle (8/1: op 5/1)

1877 DUNSTER H'CAP CHASE (0-105) (5-Y.O+) (Class F)
3-20 (3-20) **3m (19 fncs)** £2,788.00 (£844.00: £412.00: £196.00) GOING minus 0.37 sec per fur (GF)

				SP	RR	SF
1582*	**Call Me River (IRE) (77)** (PRHedger) **8-10-0** ILawrence (a.p: led appr 3 out: comf)	—	1	15/8 1	89+	—
1773 6	**Cool Character (IRE) (77)** (RHBuckler) **8-10-0** DBridgwater (bhd tl hdwy appr 3 out: rdn appr last: styd on flat)	2	2	12/1	88	—
1518 3	**Paper Star (99)** (MPMuggeridge) **9-11-3**(5) MrRThornton (lw: led to 5th: led 12th tl appr 3 out: one pce)	2½	3	14/1	108	7
1564*	**Solo Gent (95)** (APJones) **7-11-4** SMcNeill (hld up: rdn after 13th: hdwy 14th: one pce fr 3 out)	1¾	4	9/4 2	103	2
1564 5	**Maxxum Express (IRE) (85)** (GBBalding) **8-10-8** RichardGuest (chsd ldr: led 5th to 12th: hit 14th: blnd 15th: sn wknd)	17	5	16/1	82	—
1674 F	**Rainbow Castle (105)** (PFNicholls) **9-12-0** NWilliamson (hld up: last whn fell 6th)		F	7/1 3	—	—
	Royal Saxon (95) (PBowen) **10-11-4** RJohnson (prom tl mstke 12th (water): t.o 15th: p.u bef 3 out)		P	8/1	—	—
1421 3	**Gallic Girl (IRE) (78)** (CLPopham) **6-9-12**(3)ow1 TDascombe (bhd most of wy: t.o whn p.u & dismntd bef 2 out)		P	12/1	—	—
				(SP 117.1%)		**8 Rn**

6m 9.6 (12.60) CSF £22.38 CT £228.35 TOTE £2.90: £1.50 £2.10 £2.90 (£16.00) OWNER The Larkin Around Partnership (CHICHESTER) BRED S. Banville
LONG HANDICAP Call Me River (IRE) 9-9 Cool Character (IRE) 9-6 Gallic Girl (IRE) 9-6
1582* Call Me River (IRE), raised 8lb, was still 5lb out of the handicap and is clearly on the upgrade. (15/8)
1385 Cool Character (IRE), 8lb wrong at the weights, ran his best race since having a recent wind operation, although he did not bother the winner. (12/1)
1518 Paper Star was 7lb lower than when having an impossible task last time. (14/1: op 8/1)
1564* Solo Gent was running off a mark 3lb higher than when winning at Huntingdon. (9/4)
1473 Rainbow Castle (7/1: 4/1-15/2)
Royal Saxon (8/1: 5/1-9/1)
1421 Gallic Girl (IRE) (12/1: op 8/1)

1878 BICKNOLLER H'CAP HURDLE (0-125) (4-Y.O+) (Class D)
3-50 (3-50) **2m 1f (9 hdls)** £2,794.00 (£784.00: £382.00) GOING minus 0.37 sec per fur (GF)

				SP	RR	SF
1642*	**Out Ranking (FR) (115)** (MCPipe) **4-11-10** RHughes (mde all: rdn out)	—	1	4/5 1	97	19
1709 6	**Lucky Eddie (IRE) (105)** (PJHobbs) **5-11-0** NWilliamson (hld up: chsd wnr fr 2 out: sn hrd rdn: unableqckn)	2½	2	6/1	85	7
	Fabulous Mtoto (91) (MSSaunders) **6-10-0** PHolley (hld up & plld hrd: chsd wnr 6th to 2 out: sn btn)	8	3	4/1 2	63	—
1597 3	**Millcroft Riviera (IRE) (92)** (RHAlner) **5-9-12**(3)ow1 PHenley (chsd wnr tl hit 6th: rdn & wknd appr 2 out)	9	4	11/2 3	56	—
1651 11	**Adonisis (91)** (DRCElsworth) **4-10-0** AProcter (hld up: mstke 3 out: sn bhd: no ch whn blnd last)	10	5	16/1	45	—
				(SP 111.1%)		**5 Rn**

3m 58.4 (5.40) CSF £5.70 TOTE £1.50: £1.20 £1.90 (£3.30) OWNER Knight Hawks Partnership (WELLINGTON) BRED Jacques Beres
LONG HANDICAP Fabulous Mtoto 9-13 Millcroft Riviera (IRE) 9-6 Adonisis 9-6
1642* Out Ranking (FR) registered her fifth win of the season in an uncompetitive handicap. (4/5)
Lucky Eddie (IRE) was already due to go down 3lb. (6/1: op 4/1)
Fabulous Mtoto won twice over a mile and a half during the summer, and has always been inclined to pull too hard over hurdles. (4/1)
1597 Millcroft Riviera (IRE) was still 8lb wrong at the weights. (11/2)

T/Plpt: £255.30 (43.83 Tckts). T/Qdpt: £134.70 (8.06 Tckts). KH

1879a - 1888a : (Irish Racing) - See Computer Raceform

1484a-PUNCHESTOWN (Naas, Ireland) (R-H) (Yielding)
Saturday December 7th

1889a MMI STOCKBROKERS PUNCHESTOWN CHASE (Gd 1) (5-Y.O+)
2-05 (2-06) **2m 4f (14 fncs)** IR £22,750.00 (IR £6,650.00: IR £3,150.00: IR £1,050.00)

				SP	RR	SF
1737a 2	**Royal Mountbrowne** (APO'Brien,Ireland) **8-11-8** CFSwan (chsd ldr to 6th: 4th whn mstke 10th: lft mod 3rd 4 out: nt trble ldrs after 2 out: hdwy appr last: lft 2nd last: styd on u.p to ld flat)	—	1	7/1 3	151?	—
1397a 4	**Merry Gale (IRE)** (JTRDreaper,Ireland) **8-12-0** JPBroderick (led: mstke 9th: jnd briefly next: hdd briefly bef 4 out & bef 2 out: hdd after 2 out: rdn & no ex appr last: lft in ld last: hdd flat)	3	2	8/1	155	—
	Time for a Run (EJO'Grady,Ireland) **9-11-8** JShortt (towards rr: 5th & in tch whn slt mstke 10th: rdn & lft mod 4th 4 out: lft dist 3rd last)	dist	3	25/1	—	—
	Imperial Call (IRE) (FSutherland,Ireland) **7-12-0** CO'Dwyer (trckd ldrs: wnt 2nd after 6th: mstke 8th: disp ld briefly 10th: led briefly bef 4 out & bef 2 out: led after 2 out: j.rt & fell last: rmntd)	7	4	4/6 1	—	—
1410a 2	**Klairon Davis (FR)** (ALTMoore,Ireland) **7-12-0** FWoods (hld up: hdwy to trck ldrs whn fell 4 out)		F	5/2 2	—	—
1737a 5	**Love the Lord (IRE)** (DO'Connell,Ireland) **6-11-9** TPTreacy (towards rr: mstkes: lost tch 6th: t.o & n.d whn p.u after 10th)		P	16/1	—	—
				(SP 121.9%)		**6 Rn**

5m 23.4 (10.40) OWNER Mrs J. O'Kane (PILTOWN) BRED Sidney J. Smith
1737a Royal Mountbrowne, second early, was being left behind when left third four out. A mistake two out saw him further in arrears but, left a moderate if staying on second at the last, he kept on under pressure to get up on the flat. (7/1)
1625a Merry Gale (IRE), without a tongue-strap and allowed to do his own thing in front, showed some signs of his old form. Headed after the second last, he had cried enough before the final fence and was picked off quite easily on the flat. It would not be wise to write him off yet. (8/1: op 5/1)
Time for a Run had lost touch before four out. (25/1)

Imperial Call (IRE), whose jumping was sketchy to say the least, went second at the seventh and hit the next. A peck five out did not stop him going up to dispute it approaching the next and, from that point on, he was always travelling like a winner. He took command between the last two and had only to jump the last for what would have been a fairly impressive win, but he missed his stride at the last, possibly not his own fault, and came down. His jumping will remain a little suspect for many. (4/6)
1410a Klairon Davis (FR) took a strong tug and was a closing third, three lengths behind the leader, when falling four out. (5/2)

1890a - 1899a : (Irish Racing) - See Computer Raceform
NR

1556-CHELTENHAM (L-H) (Good, Good to firm patches)
Friday December 13th
WEATHER: fair

1900 LETHEBY & CHRISTOPHER HURDLE (3-Y.O) (Class C)
12-15 (12-17) **2m 1f (New) (9 hdls)** £3,707.50 (£1,120.00: £545.00: £257.50) GOING: 0.36 sec per fur (GS)

	Horse	Details	Dist	Pos	SP	RR	SF
	Disallowed (IRE)	(MissHCKnight) **3-10-9** MAFitzgerald (led 4th: hit last: drvn out)	—	1	4/1[1]	86+	22
1776[U]	**Society Magic (USA)**	(CJMann) **3-11-0** RDunwoody (hld up: hdwy after 3 out: chsd wnr appr last: one pce flat)	4	2	10/1	87	23
1634[6]	**Pleasureland (IRE)**	(RCurtis) **3-11-0** DMorris (hdwy 3 out: ev ch 2 out: sn rdn & outpcd: styd on flat)	1	3	5/1[3]	86	22
	Mazamet (USA)	(OO'Neill) **3-11-0** VSlattery (hld up: mstke 5th: hdwy 3 out: sn rdn: ev ch 2 out: sn wknd)	11	4	6/1	76	12
1387[5]	**Brandon Magic**	(IABalding) **3-11-0** AMaguire (led to 3rd: ev ch 2 out: wknd appr last)	2½	5	11/2	74	10
	Influence Pedler	(JABOld) **3-11-0** CLlewellyn (prom: blnd 1st: led 3rd to 4th: ev ch 2 out: sn wknd)	2	6	9/2[2]	72	8
1712[5]	**Classy Chief**	(JWhite) **3-11-0** TJMurphy (lw: hld up & plld hrd: hdwy 3 out: ev ch 2 out: sn wknd)	2½	7	14/1	69	5
1064[R]	**Arrogant Heir**	(DHBrown) **3-11-0** MrARebori (mstkes: bhd fr 3 out)	10	8	100/1	60	—
1444[B]	**Noble Colours**	(SGGriffiths) **3-11-0** MrJJukes (lw: prom: ev ch 2 out: sn wknd)	nk	9	100/1	60	—
	Get Tough	(EAWheeler) **3-11-0** CMaude (lw: bhd: mstkes 2nd & 6th: t.o fr 3 out)	dist	10	16/1	—	—
	Benkarosam	(RHollinshead) **3-11-0** GaryLyons (a bhd: t.o fr 3 out)	1½	11	66/1	—	—
1699[3]	**Topaglow (IRE)**	(PTDalton) **3-11-0** NWilliamson (prom: mstke 6th: in tch whn fell 2 out)		F	14/1	—	—
					(SP 116.3%)	**12 Rn**	

4m 11.1 (14.10) CSF £39.31 TOTE £3.60: £2.00 £2.50 £2.00 (£22.60) Trio £45.60 OWNER Million In Mind Partnership (6) (WANTAGE) BRED Dermot Ryan and Partners
Disallowed (IRE), bought for 16,500 guineas out of Michael Bell's yard, managed to win a small race over nine furlongs at Ripon. Forging clear up the hill after rapping the final flight, she seems likely to prove better over hurdles than she did on the Flat. (4/1)
Society Magic (USA), a 16,000 guinea purchase, won over seven at Musselburgh for Ian Balding. Settling much better than when unlucky on his debut, he seemed to get the trip well enough and can soon go one better. (10/1)
1634 Pleasureland (IRE) again showed he needs a stiffer test of stamina. (5/1)
Mazamet (USA), the winner of a Galway mile and a half maiden for John Oxx, was sold for 25,000 guineas at Newmarket Autumn Sales. (6/1)
1387 Brandon Magic did jump better ridden nearer the pace, but did not appear to get the trip. (11/2)
Influence Pedler won twice on the Flat over a mile and three-quarters for Clive Brittain. (9/2: 4/1-6/1)
1712 Classy Chief will need to learn to settle to have any chance of getting the trip (14/1)

1901 CHRIS COLEY RACING NOVICES' CHASE (5-Y.O+) (Class C)
12-45 (12-46) **3m 1f 110y (New) (21 fncs)** £4,980.50 (£1,398.00: £681.50) GOING: 0.36 sec per fur (GS)

	Horse	Details	Dist	Pos	SP	RR	SF
1557[2]	**Flimsy Truth (95)**	(MHWeston) **10-11-4** MrMHarris (mde all: mstke 8th: sn clr: rdn appr 2 out: r.o wl)	—	1	9/1[3]	113	28
1563[2]	**Wee Windy (IRE)**	(JTGifford) **7-11-4** PHide (chsd wnr: hrd rdn appr 2 out: r.o one pce flat)	3	2	4/7[1]	111	26
1858*	**Lord of the West (IRE) (98)**	(JJO'Neill) **7-11-8** AMaguire (hld up: hdwy 3 out: hrd rdn & mstke 2 out: eased whn btn flat)	11	3	15/8[2]	108	23
					(SP 108.4%)	**3 Rn**	

6m 43.8 (22.80) CSF £13.92 TOTE £6.70 (£3.10) OWNER Mr M. H. Weston (WORCESTER) BRED M. H. Weston
1557 Flimsy Truth, stepping up in distance, was quite content to force the pace, and got his trainer off the mark under Rules. (9/1: 6/1-10/1)
1563 Wee Windy (IRE) should have been suited by this longer trip, but never really looked like pegging back the winner. (4/7)
1858* Lord of the West (IRE), making a quick reappearance, found an error at the last putting paid to whatever chance he had. (15/8)

1902 CHUBB FIRE CONDITIONAL H'CAP CHASE (0-125) (5-Y.O+) (Class E)
1-20 (1-20) **2m 5f (New) (17 fncs)** £3,405.00 (£955.00: £465.00) GOING: 0.36 sec per fur (GS)

	Horse	Details	Dist	Pos	SP	RR	SF
1837*	**Beatson (IRE) (101)**	(RHBuckler) **7-10-9** 6x GHogan (lft in ld 4th: shkn up appr 2 out: r.o wl)	—	1	5/4[1]	108	26
1578*	**Buyers Dream (IRE) (92)**	(BEllison) **6-10-0v** GCahill (hld up: chsd wnr fr 10th: blnd 3 out: no imp)	7	2	9/2[2]	94	12
	Linden's Lotto (IRE) (120)	(JWhite) **7-12-0** GuyLewis (bit bkwd: hld up & plld hrd: rdn 11th: sn bhd: lft poor 3rd 4 out)	dist	3	9/2[2]	—	—
	Yeoman Warrior (102)	(RRowe) **9-10-10** LAspell (led tl slipped & uns rdr 4th)		U	9/2[2]	—	—
	Halham Tarn (IRE) (92)	(HJManners) **6-9-9**(5) ADowling (bkwd: plld hrd in rr: gd hdwy & hit 5th: disp ld tl mstke 8th: wknd 11th: poor 3rd whn blnd & uns rdr 4 out)		U	20/1[3]	—	—
					(SP 103.8%)	**5 Rn**	

5m 25.9 (16.90) CSF £6.18 TOTE £1.90: £1.30 £1.60 (£3.00) OWNER Mrs E. B. Gardiner (BRIDPORT) BRED M. Holden in Ireland
LONG HANDICAP Buyers Dream (IRE) 9-8 Halham Tarn (IRE) 9-12
1837* Beatson (IRE), making a quick reappearance, was by no means hard pressed to defy his penalty. (5/4)
1578* Buyers Dream (IRE) could not really bustle up the winner from 6lb out of the handicap. (9/2: 6/1-4/1)
Linden's Lotto (IRE), who rather went off the boil during last season, should at least be sharper for the run. (9/2)

1903 MARLBOROUGH TILES H'CAP HURDLE (0-135) (4-Y.O+) (Class C)
1-55 (1-55) **2m 1f (New) (9 hdls)** £3,468.75 (£1,050.00: £512.50: £243.75) GOING: 0.36 sec per fur (GS)

	Horse	Details	Dist	Pos	SP	RR	SF
1636[2]	**Chai-Yo (119)**	(JABOld) **6-11-10** GUpton (hld up & plld hrd: wnt 2nd after 2 out: swtchd lft & chal on bit whn lft clr last)	—	1	5/4[1]	102	46
71[7]	**Kippanour (USA) (115)**	(CJMann) **4-11-6** RDunwoody (lw: chsd ldr tl rdn & wknd appr last)	12	2	9/1	87	31

	Horse / details	Pos	SP	RR	SF
1510^{7}	**Sovereigns Parade (113)** (NJHenderson) **4-11-4b^{1}** MAFitzgerald (lw: hld up: hrd rdn appr 2 out: no rspnse) 21	**3**	11/2^{3}	65	9
1512^{3}	**Forestal (108)** (SGGriffiths) **4-10-13** MrJJukes (led: rdn & jnd whn fell last: remntd) ....dist	**4**	2/1^{2}	92?	—
			(SP 103.2%)		**4 Rn**

4m 8.7 (11.70) CSF £8.75 TOTE £1.90 (£4.50) OWNER Mr Nick Viney (WROUGHTON) BRED Mrs Audrey Goodwin
1636 Chai-Yo, upped 4lb, looked all over the winner when presented with the race at the last flight. (5/4: evens-4/5)
Kippanour (USA), without the blinkers this time, only got second because of the demise of Forestal. (9/1)
Sovereigns Parade, blinkered for the first time, did not appear very co-operative when coming under the whip. (11/2)
1512 Forestal had the winner galloping all over him when he came down at the last. (2/1)

1904 WRAGGE & CO CHALLENGE H'CAP CHASE (5-Y.O+) (Class B)

2-30 (2-30) **3m 1f 110y (New) (21 fncs)** £12,498.00 (£3,066.00) GOING: 0.36 sec per fur (GS)

	Horse / details	Pos	SP	RR	SF
1806^{4}	**Yorkshire Gale (137)** (JTGifford) **10-11-10** NWilliamson (lw: j.w: mde all: rdn appr 2 out: r.o wl)....—	**1**	11/10^{2}	147	39
1513^{3}	**Glemot (IRE) (135)** (KCBailey) **8-11-8** RDunwoody (lw: trckd wnr: mstke 8th: hit 9th: rdn appr 2 out: no imp) 10	**2**	4/5^{1}	139	31
			(SP 103.2%)		**2 Rn**

6m 41.7 (20.70) TOTE £1.80 OWNER Mr Bill Naylor (FINDON) BRED Miss Y. McClintock and Mrs D. P. O'Brien
1806 Yorkshire Gale, back on one of his favourite courses, put his disappointing run at Wetherby behind him. (11/10: evens-6/5)
1513 Glemot (IRE) has yet to win beyond two miles five furlongs, and the winner had drawn the sting out of him on the final climb. (4/5)

1905 CHELTENHAM SPONSORSHIP CLUB NOVICES' HURDLE (4-Y.O+) (Class C)

3-05 (3-05) **2m 1f (New) (9 hdls)** £3,810.00 (£1,155.00: £565.00: £270.00) GOING: 0.36 sec per fur (GS)

	Horse / details	Pos	SP	RR	SF
1568^{6}	**Daraydan (IRE)** (MCPipe) **4-11-7** RHughes (lw: led 3rd: clr appr last: easily)....—	**1**	6/4^{1}	79	50
1470^{7}	**Mr Darcy** (PRWebber) **4-11-3** RBellamy (hld up & bhd: hdwy 6th: wnt 2nd last: no ch w wnr)....14	**2**	40/1	62	33
1516^{2}	**Beacon Flight (IRE) (103)** (BdeHaan) **5-11-7** CLlewellyn (lw: led to 3rd: lost pl appr 2 out: styd on flat)....2½	**3**	12/1	64	35
1517^{2}	**Carlito Brigante** (PRWebber) **4-11-3** MAFitzgerald (lw: a.p: chsd wnr fr 3 out tl wknd appr last)....¾	**4**	5/2^{2}	59	30
	Shadirwan (IRE) (RAkehurst) **5-11-3** AMaguire (bit bkwd: prom tl rdn & wknd after 2 out)....5	**5**	7/2^{3}	54	25
1424^{2}	**Docklands Courier** (BJMcMath) **4-11-3** NWilliamson (lw: bhd fr 5th: t.o)....dist	**6**	16/1	—	—
1659^{7}	**Sun of Spring** (JWhite) **6-11-3** TJMurphy (bhd fr 5th: t.o)....s.h	**7**	33/1	—	—
	Apollono (RLee) **4-11-3** RJohnson (fell 1st)....	**F**	20/1	—	—
	Amazon Heights (LPGrassick) **4-10-9**(3) GHogan (a bhd: t.o 6th: p.u bef 2 out)....	**P**	100/1	—	—
			(SP 115.5%)		**9 Rn**

4m 7.2 (10.20) CSF £44.53 TOTE £2.50: £1.30 £3.20 £1.80 (£42.20) Trio £53.60 OWNER Mr D. A. Johnson (WELLINGTON) BRED His Highness the Aga Khans Studs S. C.
1568 Daraydan (IRE), back on a sounder surface, was a most impressive winner. (6/4)
Mr Darcy seems to be going the right way and should not always come up against one so smart. (40/1)
1516 Beacon Flight (IRE) gave the impression that he would not be inconvenienced by further. (12/1)
1517 Carlito Brigante seemed to get found out by this stiff course. (5/2)
Shadirwan (IRE) will come on for the outing, but his Flat form suggests he will need further. (7/2)

1906 GOLD CARD (QUALIFIER) H'CAP HURDLE (4-Y.O+) (Class B)

3-40 (3-40) **3m 110y (New) (12 hdls)** £5,138.50 (£1,543.00: £744.00: £344.50) GOING: 0.36 sec per fur (GS)

	Horse / details	Pos	SP	RR	SF
1372*	**Elburg (IRE) (111)** (TRGeorge) **6-10-6** MAFitzgerald (lw: hld up: hdwy 9th: led appr last: edgd rt flat: r.o wl).—	**1**	7/2^{2}	94	23
1698^{2}	**Runaway Pete (USA) (121)** (MCPipe) **6-11-2** RDunwoody (prom: rdn & outpcd appr 2 out: rallied appr last: styd on flat)....1¾	**2**	12/1	103	32
1522*	**Olympian (121)** (JNeville) **9-11-2b** NWilliamson (a.p: led 7th to 8th: ev ch 2 out: btn whn lft 3rd last)....7	**3**	8/1	98	27
1571^{B}	**Glengarrif Girl (IRE) (106)** (MCPipe) **6-10-1v** RHughes (prom tl rdn & outpcd 2 out: rallied appr last: one pce flat)....2	**4**	15/2^{3}	82	11
1372^{3}	**Uluru (IRE) (116)** (CPMorlock) **8-10-11** JRKavanagh (led to 2nd: led 2 out: hdd & wknd appr last)....2½	**5**	16/1	90	19
1384*	**Mister Blake (105)** (RLee) **6-10-0** RJohnson (hld up & bhd: hdwy 9th: ev ch 2 out: sn wknd)....1½	**6**	33/1	78	7
	Erzadjan (IRE) (129) (MrsMReveley) **6-11-10** GCahill (bkwd: blnd 9th: a bhd)....9	**7**	14/1	97	26
1447^{P}	**Swing Quartet (IRE) (105)** (NATwiston-Davies) **6-10-0** CLlewellyn (lw: led 2nd to 7th: led 8th to 2 out: sn wknd)....7	**8**	20/1	68	—
1661*	**Balanak (USA) (124)** (DRGandolfo) **5-11-0**(5) SophieMitchell (hld up & bhd: gd hdwy after 2 out: 3rd & styng on wl whn fell last)....	**F**	8/1	107?	—
1671*	**Lochnagrain (IRE) (120)** (MrsMReveley) **8-11-1** 4x PNiven (hld up: blnd & uns rdr 4th)....	**U**	15/8^{1}	—	—
			(SP 118.9%)		**10 Rn**

6m 1.0 (19.00) CSF £41.01 CT £291.24 TOTE £4.60: £1.60 £2.30 £3.00 (£27.10) Trio £53.80 OWNER Mrs Alison Gamble (ROSS-ON-WYE) BRED Sheikh Mohammed bin Rashid al Maktoum
LONG HANDICAP Swing Quartet (IRE) 9-8 Mister Blake 8-13
1372* Elburg (IRE) defied a 9lb rise in the weights last time and was up the same amount here. One can not help feeling he was helped by the fall of Balanak. (7/2)
1698 Runaway Pete (USA), appreciating this faster ground, could never get his favoured front-running position, but kept plugging away to the end. (12/1: op 8/1)
1522* Olympian, raised 3lb, found this race a bit more competitive than when scoring narrowly at Ascot. (8/1: 5/1-9/1)
1363 Glengarrif Girl (IRE) was 2lb lower than when runner-up here last month. (15/2: 5/1-8/1)
1372 Uluru (IRE) was 10lb better off with the winner than when beaten twenty-three lengths at Huntingdon. (16/1)
1384* Mister Blake was by no means disgraced from over a stone out of the handicap. (33/1)
Erzadjan (IRE) (14/1: 10/1-16/1)
1661* Balanak (USA), raised 4lb and stepping up in trip, had three lengths to make up, but seemed to be coming with a winning run, when unluckily losing his legs upon landing over the last. (8/1: 11/2-9/1)
1671* Lochnagrain (IRE) had favourite-backers going home early. (15/8)

T/Jkpt: £10,069.20 (6.64 Tckts). T/Plpt: £282.20 (42.65 Tckts). T/Qdpt: £11.30 (127.45 Tckts). KH

DONCASTER (L-H) (Good to firm, Good patches)
Friday December 13th
WEATHER: fine

1907 SAUCY KIT NOVICES' HURDLE (4-Y.O+) (Class E)
12-05 (12-06) **2m 4f (10 hdls)** £2,847.00 (£792.00: £381.00) GOING: nil sec per fur (G)

				SP	RR	SF
1689[2]	**Inn At the Top (107)** (JNorton) **4-11-5** WFry (cl up: led 4 out: styd on wl fr next)	—	**1**	6/4[2]	92	38
1639[3]	**Herbert Lodge (IRE) (110)** (KCBailey) **7-11-5** CO'Dwyer (lw: swtg: hld up: hdwy 6th: chsng wnr whn blnd 3 out & 2 out: no imp)	3	**2**	11/10[1]	90	36
1316[8]	**Tweedswood (IRE) (90)** (PBeaumont) **6-10-12** RSupple (lw: plld hrd: led to 4 out: outpcd appr next)	13	**3**	10/1	72	18
1689[5]	**Cypress Avenue (IRE)** (MrsVCWard) **4-10-12** DParker (cl up tl outpcd ½-wy: n.d after)	13	**4**	16/1	62	8
1565[P]	**Mesp (IRE)** (JGMO'Shea) **5-10-2**(5) MichaelBrennan (prom tl outpcd fr 6th)	14	**5**	33/1	46	—
1683[P]	**Gutteridge (IRE)** (TKeddy) **6-10-12** SMcNeill (lw: w ldrs: hit 4 out: sn wknd)	18	**6**	33/1	36	—
1052[10]	**Toshiba House (IRE)** (BEllison) **5-10-7** BHarding (drvn along fr 4th: sn t.o)	dist	**7**	50/1	—	—
1583[3]	**Henrys Port** (MartynMeade) **6-10-12** JRailton (hdwy 6th: hit next: sn chsng ldrs: jst 3rd & wl btn whn fell last)		**F**	8/1[3]	72?	—
1777[P]	**Dougal** (BSRothwell) **5-10-12** BStorey (w bhd fr 5th: t.o whn p.u bef 3 out)		**P**	50/1	—	—
				(SP 123.5%)	**9 Rn**	

4m 47.6 (7.60) CSF £3.71 TOTE £2.60: £1.10 £1.50 £1.40 (£1.50) Trio £4.10 OWNER Mrs Sylvia Blakeley (BARNSLEY) BRED Crest Stud Ltd

1689 Inn At the Top stays well and, after stretching this field going to the third last, the race was his. (6/4)
1639 Herbert Lodge (IRE) was very disappointing with his hurdling when at full stretch, and that made all the difference. (11/10: evens-10/11)
Tweedswood (IRE) needs to learn to settle, and this useful-looking individual should improve. (10/1)
1689 Cypress Avenue (IRE) was struggling for pace halfway through the race and had no further chance. (16/1)
Mesp (IRE) does not do anything quickly and was left struggling fully four out. (33/1)
1583 Henrys Port, patiently ridden, almost got into it three out, but was beaten when falling at the last. (8/1)

1908 GLASGOW PADDOCKS (S) HURDLE (3 & 4-Y.O) (Class G)
12-35 (12-36) **2m 110y (8 hdls)** £2,228.60 (£619.60: £297.80) GOING: nil sec per fur (G)

				SP	RR	SF
	Toulston Lady (IRE) (JWharton) **4-10-11**(5) MrRThornton (lw: nt j.w: gd hdwy to chal appr 3 out: led & j.slowly 2 out: j.v.slowly & hdd last: rallied to ld last 50y)	—	**1**	8/1[3]	47	—
1634[12]	**Laughing Buccaneer** (DNCarey) **3-10-7** SMcNeill (in tch: effrt appr 3 out: lft in ld last: nt qckn towards fin)	nk	**2**	4/1[1]	52	—
1628[15]	**Oakbury (IRE) (64)** (MissLCSiddall) **4-11-7** MRichards (bhd: hdwy 3 out: styd on strly flat)	nk	**3**	8/1[3]	51	—
881[7]	**Song For Jess (IRE)** (FJordan) **3-10-2** SWynne (hdwy ½-wy: ch last: kpt on one pce)	1¼	**4**	4/1[1]	45	—
	Bold Top (BSRothwell) **4-11-7v** ADobbin (led tl hdd 2 out: hrd rdn & no ex)	3	**5**	7/1[2]	47	—
1413[U]	**Arch Angel (IRE)** (GFHCharles-Jones) **3-10-2** DBridgwater (lw: bhd: stdy hdwy appr 3 out: sn rdn: blnd last & no imp)	¾	**6**	16/1	42	—
1369[9]	**Mudlark** (JNorton) **4-11-0**(7) BGrattan (bhd: hdwy 4th: one pce fr 2 out)	½	**7**	4/1[1]	46	—
1413[7]	**Shanoora (IRE)** (MrsNMacauley) **3-9-13**(3) EHusband (hdwy & in tch 4th: wknd 3 out)	5	**8**	8/1[3]	36	—
	Dispol Conqueror (IRE) (PCalver) **3-10-7** BStorey (lw: chsd ldrs tl wknd qckly after 6th: p.u bef last)		**P**	12/1	—	—
	Begger's Opera (PatMitchell) **4-11-7** TKent (bhd whn p.u bef 3 out)		**P**	25/1	—	—
1526[P]	**Ballykissangel** (NBycroft) **3-10-7b[1]** JCallaghan (cl up tl wknd rapidly 3 out: p.u bef last)		**P**	25/1	—	—
				(SP 127.1%)	**11 Rn**	

4m 6.1 (16.10) CSF £40.69 TOTE £13.00: £3.00 £2.30 £2.10 (£31.60) Trio £134.80 OWNER Mr W. Wharton (MELTON MOWBRAY) BRED M. R. Johnson
WEIGHT FOR AGE 3yo-14lb
No bid

Toulston Lady (IRE) took some riding, but was given some splendid assistance. Despite trying to throw it away at her hurdles, she had the speed on the flat. (8/1)
Laughing Buccaneer, taking a real drop in class, had his chances, but proved short of toe when it mattered. (4/1)
1251 Oakbury (IRE) found this ground a bit too fast over this trip, but was certainly finishing well, and the race would have been his in another few strides. (8/1)
589 Song For Jess (IRE) was well enough placed if good enough, but lacked any change of gear. (4/1)
Bold Top had the field stretched entering the straight, but was then very tired and there to be picked off, which he soon was. (7/1)
Arch Angel (IRE) looks to be having problems with her hurdling at the moment. (16/1)

1909 RED RUM NOVICES' CHASE (5-Y.O+) (Class D)
1-10 (1-10) **3m (18 fncs)** £4,048.00 (£1,128.00: £544.00) GOING: nil sec per fur (G)

				SP	RR	SF
1456*	**Berude Not to (IRE)** (OSherwood) **7-11-6** JOsborne (nt j.w to 12th: led 3rd to 7th: sn lost pl: hdwy 12th: led 3 out: pushed out)	—	**1**	1/6[1]	102	22
1680[6]	**Key To Moyade (IRE) (98)** (MJWilkinson) **6-11-0** ILawrence (led to 3rd: led 7th & sn qcknd clr: hdd 3 out: btn whn blnd last)	4	**2**	8/1[2]	93	13
1797[7]	**Snowdon Lily** (PRWebber) **5-10-6**(3) EHusband (outpcd & wl bhd fr 11th)	dist	**3**	50/1	—	—
1150[3]	**Elite Governor (IRE)** (NMLampard) **7-11-0** DBridgwater (cl up whn blnd 3rd: sn bhd: p.u bef 7th)		**P**	10/1[3]	—	—
				(SP 107.9%)	**4 Rn**	

6m 9.4 (15.40) CSF £2.09 TOTE £1.30 (£1.50) OWNER Mr G. Addiscott (UPPER LAMBOURN) BRED Ronald O'Neill in Ireland
WEIGHT FOR AGE 5yo-1lb

1456* Berude Not to (IRE) continually backed off his fences, but his jumping did improve at the end of the race. There still looks to be a question mark about him at present. (1/6)
1340 Key To Moyade (IRE) jumped the favourite silly in the early stages, but tired late on. This was still a good effort. (8/1: op 5/1)
Snowdon Lily was completely outclassed in the final mile. (50/1)
1150 Elite Governor (IRE) made a bad jump at the third, and his rider was anxious from then, before pulling him up at the seventh. (10/1)

1910 VULRORY'S CLOWN LIMITED H'CAP CHASE (0-145) (5-Y.O+) (Class B)

1-45 (1-45) **2m 3f 110y (15 fncs)** £4,838.00 (£1,358.00: £654.00) GOING: nil sec per fur (G)

				SP	RR	SF
1805[2]	**Cumbrian Challenge (IRE) (126)** (TDEasterby) **7-10-7** RGarritty (lw: a.p: chal 2 out: led flat: styd on u.p)	—	1	5/4[1]	132	23
1509[2]	**Callisoe Bay (IRE) (138)** (OSherwood) **7-11-5** JOsborne (lw: led fr 6th: hit 2 out: hdd flat: nt qckn)	½	2	11/8[2]	144	35
	Crystal Spirit (140) (IABalding) **9-11-7** GBradley (led to 6th: hit 9th: kpt on wl fr 2 out)	2½	3	9/2[3]	144	35
				(SP 104.7%)	**3 Rn**	

4m 55.9 (8.90) CSF £2.97 TOTE £2.20 (£1.60) OWNER Cumbrian Industrials Ltd (MALTON) BRED Major V. McCalmont
LONG HANDICAP Cumbrian Challenge (IRE) 10-6

1805 Cumbrian Challenge (IRE) was always having to struggle in the home straight but, with the jockey of the moment on board, he proved too determined for the runner-up. (5/4)

1509 Callisoe Bay (IRE), happy out in front when on the bridle, put down at the second last when asked a question and was worried out of it on the run-in. (11/8: op evens)

Crystal Spirit looked magnificent, but it was just the fact that he had not run for twenty months that made all the difference. He should now be ready to return to his best. (9/2)

1911 DOORKNOCKER NOVICES' CONDITIONAL H'CAP HURDLE (0-100) (4-Y.O+) (Class F)

2-20 (2-20) **2m 110y (8 hdls)** £2,102.00 (£582.00: £278.00) GOING: nil sec per fur (G)

				SP	RR	SF
1594[3]	**Out on a Promise (IRE) (92)** (NJHWalker) **4-11-8**(5) DFinnegan (hld up: gd hdwy 5th: led & blnd 2 out: clr whn hit last)	—	1	7/2[2]	75	35
1705[3]	**Faithful Hand (88)** (MrsSJSmith) **6-11-6**(3) RWilkinson (led: clr fr 3rd tl hdd 2 out: no ch w wnr)	9	2	5/1[3]	62	22
1156[P]	**Past Master (USA) (86)** (SGollings) **8-11-7** KGaule (in tch: effrt appr 3 out: sn rdn & no imp)	7	3	12/1	54	14
1249[3]	**Tiotao (IRE) (70)** (CParker) **6-10-5** DParker (mstkes: chsd ldr tl outpcd after 5th: n.d after)	4	4	7/1	34	—
1144[3]	**Teejay'n'aitch (IRE) (82)** (JSGoldie) **4-11-3** GLee (effrt 5th: sn rdn & n.d)	10	5	5/1[3]	36	—
1451*	**Canary Falcon (93)** (RJO'Sullivan) **5-11-9**(5) NWillmington (hld up: effrt 5th: rdn & no imp fr next: blnd last)	8	6	13/8[1]	39	—
1703[14]	**Ragazzo (IRE) (70)** (JSWainwright) **6-10-5v**[1]ow5 PMidgley (chsd clr ldrs to 5th: sn rdn & wl bhd)	23	7	20/1	—	—
				(SP 118.6%)	**7 Rn**	

3m 58.5 (8.50) CSF £20.57 TOTE £3.80: £2.10 £2.80 (£10.30) OWNER Mr Paul Green (BLEWBURY) BRED H. H. and Mrs Morriss
LONG HANDICAP Ragazzo (IRE) 9-9
OFFICIAL EXPLANATION **Canary Falcon: the rider reported that the gelding felt flat throughout.**

1594 Out on a Promise (IRE) settled quite well but, despite winning decisively, his jumping really needs to improve. (7/2)
1705 Faithful Hand tried hard to make all, but was well short of toe when collared. (5/1)
Past Master (USA) raced with his tongue tied down and looked very slow once asked a question. (12/1)
1249 Tiotao (IRE) has plenty of improvement to find jumping-wise. (7/1)
1144 Teejay'n'aitch (IRE) looked very one-paced in the final mile. (5/1)
1451* Canary Falcon was disappointing, but it was probably the rise in the weights that was responsible. (13/8)

1912 DONCASTER RACECOURSE SPONSORSHIP CLUB H'CAP CHASE (0-130) (5-Y.O+) (Class C)

2-55 (3-05) **2m 110y (9 fncs)** £4,883.00 (£1,363.00: £659.00) GOING: nil sec per fur (G)

				SP	RR	SF
1730*	**Zeredar (NZ) (114)** (KCBailey) **6-11-2b** 6x CO'Dwyer (lw: j.rt: mde all: cleverly)	—	1	13/8[1]	126+	12
1527[4]	**Newhall Prince (110)** (AStreeter) **8-10-12v** TEley (a.p: effrt & ch 4 out: rdn & no imp)	2	2	9/1	120	6
1186*	**Eastern Magic (98)** (GBarnett) **8-10-0** RFarrant (chsd ldrs tl outpcd fr 4 out)	10	3	15/8[2]	98	—
*1660**	***Fine Harvest* (122)** (JLSpearing) **10-11-10** DBridgwater (lw: Withdrawn not under Starter's orders: bolted bef s)		W	3/1[3]	—	—
				(SP 107.9%)	**3 Rn**	

4m 6.9 (11.90) CSF £5.69 TOTE £1.60 (£5.00) OWNER I M S Racing (UPPER LAMBOURN) BRED Miss E. S. Parton
LONG HANDICAP Eastern Magic 9-12

1730* Zeredar (NZ) continually jumped right and would probably be better suited by a right-handed track. He also looks like he needs to do it on the bridle for as long as possible. (13/8)
1527 Newhall Prince looked and ran better, and may be coming back to form. (9/1)
1186* Eastern Magic failed to give his running and was beaten four out. (15/8)

1913 DONCASTER STANDARD OPEN N.H. FLAT RACE (4, 5 & 6-Y.O F & M) (Class H)

3-30 (3-31) **2m 110y** £1,070.00 (£295.00: £140.00)

				SP	RR	SF
1190[3]	**Hurst Flyer** (FPMurtagh) **4-11-4** ADobbin (trckd ldrs: disp ld over 4f out tl led 2f out: hld on wl)	—	1	7/1[3]	61 f	—
	Derring Floss (JAPickering) **6-10-11**(7) MissJWormall (hld up & bhd: hdwy on ins 4f out: disp ld ins fnl f: nt qckn towards fin)	nk	2	33/1	61 f	—
1329[3]	**Rachel Louise** (TKeddy) **4-11-4** DBridgwater (hld up: effrt 4f out: rdn & styd on: nvr able to chal)	5	3	9/2[2]	56 f	—
	Tullow Lady (IRE) (OBrennan) **5-10-11**(7) WWalsh (plld hrd: cl up: disp ld over 4f out tl over 2f out: no ex)	hd	4	12/1	56 f	—
	Ardrom (PRWebber) **4-11-4** MrPScott (trckd ldrs: chal 4f out: one pce fnl 2f)	nk	5	7/1[3]	56 f	—
1190[2]	**Country Orchid** (MrsMReveley) **5-10-11**(7) CMcCormack (lw: hld up: hdwy to disp ld 5f out: rdn & wknd fnl 2f)	1	6	4/7[1]	55 f	—
1692[11]	**Santa Barbara (IRE)** (CGrant) **5-11-4** GBradley (set slow pce: disp ld 5f out tl wknd 2f out)	½	7	8/1	54 f	—
	Primitive Light (ASmith) **6-11-1**(3) PMidgley (bit bkwd: hld up: hdwy to chal 4f out: wknd fnl 2f)	6	8	20/1	48 f	—
1573[5]	**Fine Spirit** (NMLampard) **4-11-1**(3) TDascombe (plld hrd early: outpcd fnl 4f)	7	9	10/1	41 f	—
	Chiappelli (IRE) (TDEasterby) **4-11-4** RGarritty (hld up: outpcd 4f out: n.d)	4	10	8/1	38 f	—
	Restandbejoyful (MrsSLamyman) **4-11-4** RFarrant (outpcd & lost tch fnl 5f)	5	11	33/1	33 f	—
				(SP 156.5%)	**11 Rn**	

4m 7.6 CSF £201.07 TOTE £9.70: £3.00 £18.60 £1.10 (£386.90) Trio £254.70; £215.26 to Haydock 14/12/96 OWNER Mr J. Proudfoot (CARLISLE) BRED Reginald James Castell
OFFICIAL EXPLANATION **Country Orchid: the rider reported that the mare was unsuited by the slow early pace and failed to quicken.**

1190 Hurst Flyer won what turned out to be a five-furlong sprint. (7/1)
Derring Floss, a moderate pointer, ran well in this messy race. (33/1)
1329 Rachel Louise, held up in this slowly-run event, did not have the required turn of foot to get into it. (9/2: 5/2-5/1)
Tullow Lady (IRE), from a yard out of form, pulled too hard for her own good, but still ran pretty well. (12/1)

Ardrom looks the type to be suited by a stronger pace and, in the circumstances, ran well. (7/1)
1190 Country Orchid proved short of toe in the sprint up the straight. (4/7)
Chiappelli (IRE) (8/1: op 5/1)

T/Plpt: £42.50 (178.83 Tckts). T/Qdpt: £13.60 (48.47 Tckts). AA

1900-CHELTENHAM (L-H) (Good to firm, Good patches)
Saturday December 14th
WEATHER: fine

1914 GEORGE STEVENS H'CAP CHASE (5-Y.O+) (Class B)
1-00 (1-01) **2m 110y (New) (14 fncs)** £7,181.00 (£2,016.00: £983.00) GOING: 0.20 sec per fur (G)

				SP	RR	SF
1509[3]	**Dancing Paddy (147)** (KOCunningham-Brown) **8-11-10** ADobbin (hld up: hit 8th: led 4 out: clr appr 2 out: drvn out)	—	1	15/8[2]	148	87
1366[10]	**Kibreet (146)** (PJHobbs) **9-11-9** NWilliamson (chsd ldr: lft in ld 9th: hdd 4 out: hrd rdn appr last: one pce)	3½	2	10/11[1]	144	83
1650[4]	**Sound Reveille (142)** (CPEBrooks) **8-11-5** GBradley (lw: led tl blnd bdly 9th: nt rcvr)	25	3	9/2[3]	115	54
				(SP 105.3%)		**3 Rn**

4m 6.8 (-0.20) CSF £3.62 TOTE £2.40 (£1.30) OWNER Bychance Racing (STOCKBRIDGE) BRED Mrs A. Maclean
1509 Dancing Paddy only made one error this time in what was an uncompetitive handicap. (15/8)
Kibreet continues to struggle off a mark 8lb higher than when winning the Grand Annual here in March. (10/11: evens-11/10)
1650 Sound Reveille took off too soon at the second ditch. (9/2: 3/1-5/1)

1915 BRISTOL NOVICES' HURDLE (Gd 2) (4-Y.O+) (Class A)
1-35 (1-35) **3m 110y (New) (12 hdls)** £9,960.00 (£3,771.75: £1,848.38: £844.88) GOING: 0.20 sec per fur (G)

				SP	RR	SF
1561[2]	**Tarrs Bridge (IRE) (101)** (CJMann) **5-11-4b[1]** JMagee (lw: a gng wl: led on bit last: easily)	—	1	10/1	87	30
1795*	**Southern Nights** (KCBailey) **6-11-4** AThornton (hld up: hdwy after 3 out: led appr 2 out tl pckd last: one pce)	6	2	9/2[3]	83	26
1507*	**Carole's Crusader (115)** (DRGandolfo) **5-10-13** RDunwoody (led: mstke 9th: rdn & hdd appr 2 out: one pce)	4	3	6/4[1]	76	19
1639[6]	**I'm A Chippy (IRE)** (GBBalding) **6-11-0** BFenton (lost pl 7th: rallied 2 out: styd on one pce)	1½	4	20/1	76	19
1561*	**Spaceage Gold (96)** (JABOld) **7-11-4** GUpton (lost pl & hit 5th: bhd whn rdn after 6th: n.d after)	12	5	12/1	72	15
1673*	**Galatasori Jane (IRE) (98)** (PFNicholls) **6-10-9** MAFitzgerald (led appr 2 out: hdd & wknd appr last)	1½	6	16/1	62	5
1774[4]	**Knight's Crest (IRE)** (RDickin) **6-11-0** NWilliamson (hld up & bhd: hdwy appr 7th: wknd 9th)	nk	7	50/1	67	10
1384[2]	**Queen's Award (IRE) (87)** (RHBuckler) **7-11-0** MGriffiths (hld up: hdwy 7th: wknd 9th)	9	8	25/1	61	4
1453*	**Not For Turning (IRE)** (OSherwood) **5-11-0** JOsborne (lw: prom tl wknd qckly appr 2 out: bhd whn p.u bef last)		P	4/1[2]	—	—
				(SP 111.4%)		**9 Rn**

5m 58.6 (16.60) CSF £49.00 TOTE £9.50: £1.90 £1.80 £1.20 (£25.10) Trio £9.20 OWNER The Tuesday Syndicate (UPPER LAMBOURN) BRED David McGrath
1561 Tarrs Bridge (IRE), 8lb better off with the fifth than when beaten a length here last time, proved something of a revelation in the first-time blinkers. (10/1)
1795* Southern Nights had the winner dancing all over him and, when pitching on landing at the final flight, he put all doubts to rest. (9/2: 3/1-5/1)
1507* Carole's Crusader had her limitations exposed but, to her credit, she kept plugging away. (6/4)
I'm A Chippy (IRE) scored between the flags in Ireland last February and got very close in a Tipperary bumper. He needs more cut so that the emphasis is switched to stamina. (20/1)
1561* Spaceage Gold had beaten the winner a length here on 8lb better terms. (12/1)
1673* Galatasori Jane (IRE) had more on her plate here, but gave the impression she may not have got the trip. (16/1)
1774 Knight's Crest (IRE) was highly tried on this hurdling debut. (50/1)
1453* Not For Turning (IRE) (4/1: 3/1-9/2)

1916 BONUSPRINT BULA HURDLE (Gd 2) (4-Y.O+) (Class A)
2-05 (2-10) **2m 1f (New) (9 hdls)** £22,085.00 (£8,358.00: £4,091.50: £1,865.50) GOING: 0.20 sec per fur (G)

				SP	RR	SF
1759a*	**Large Action (IRE) (165)** (OSherwood) **8-11-8** JOsborne (lw: chsd ldr to 4th: shkn up & sltly outpcd after 3 out: led on bit after 2 out: edgd rt flat: drvn out)	—	1	5/4[1]	160	46
	Bimsey (IRE) (146) (RAkehurst) **6-11-0** GBradley (lw: a.p: wnt 2nd 4th: ev ch last: hrd rdn: r.o)	½	2	5/1[3]	152	38
1759a[3]	**Theatreworld (IRE)** (APO'Brien,Ireland) **4-11-2** CFSwan (prom tl wknd appr last)	14	3	11/2	140	26
1508*	**Muse (147)** (DRCElsworth) **9-11-8** PHolley (led tl after 2 out: wknd appr last)	3½	4	14/1	143	29
	Pridwell (MCPipe) **6-11-4** CMaude (lw: reluctant to r: nvr nr ldrs)	4	5	7/2[2]	135	21
	Right Win (IRE) (148) (RHannon) **6-11-4** NWilliamson (lw: hld up: hdwy 3 out: eased whn btn appr last)	9	6	16/1	127	13
	Moorish (155) (JWhite) **6-11-0** MAFitzgerald (bkwd: hmpd s: bhd fr 6th: t.o)	dist	7	50/1	—	—
				(SP 113.2%)		**7 Rn**

4m 5.7 (8.70) CSF £7.67 TOTE £2.20: £1.60 £2.50 (£5.10) OWNER Mr B. T. Stewart-Brown (UPPER LAMBOURN) BRED Mrs J. A. Harold-Barry in Ireland
STEWARDS' ENQUIRY Obj. to Large Action (IRE) by Bradley overruled.
1759a* Large Action (IRE) got caught a shade flat-footed starting down the hill, but came back on the bridle once driven through on the inside to take it up. He had to work harder than had seemed likely to hold the persistent runner-up in the closing stages, and Bradley's objection always seemed optimistic. (5/4: evens-11/8)
Bimsey (IRE) apparently injured his back on his final outing last season. Running a cracker, this will not have done his Official Rating much good, but he could turn out to be better than an average handicapper. (5/1: 7/2-11/2)
1759a Theatreworld (IRE) was 4lb worse off with Large Action than at Fairyhouse, and the faster ground would not have helped either. (11/2)
1508* Muse did not find Large Action's last-minute withdrawal occurring on this occasion. (14/1: 7/1-16/1)
Pridwell, looking big and well, lost more ground at the start than the distance by which he was eventually beaten. (7/2)
Right Win (IRE) was not knocked about once his chance had gone. (16/1)

1917 TRIPLEPRINT GOLD CUP H'CAP CHASE (Gd 3) (5-Y.O+) (Class A)

2-40 (2-43) **2m 5f (New) (17 fncs)** £37,690.00 (£14,110.00: £6,905.00: £2,975.00: £1,337.50: £682.50) GOING: 0.20 sec per fur (G)

				SP	RR	SF
1366[3]	**Addington Boy (IRE) (152)** (GRichards) **8-11-10** ADobbin (lw: hld up: hit 1st: hdwy 12th: rdn to ld appr 2 out: drvn out)	—	1	7/4[1]	160	61
1637[F]	**Go Universal (IRE) (134)** (CPEBrooks) **8-10-6** GBradley (lw: led to 2nd: ev ch appr 2 out: one pce)	6	2	12/1	137	38
	Northern Hide (129) (MSalaman) **10-10-1** PHolley (bit bkwd: led 2nd tl appr 2 out: r.o one pce)	1¼	3	33/1	132	33
1520[4]	**Bertone (IRE) (133)** (KCBailey) **7-10-5** JOsborne (hld up & bhd: hdwy 4 out: r.o one pce fr 2 out)	¾	4	10/1	135	36
1889a*	**Royal Mountbrowne (151)** (APO'Brien,Ireland) **8-11-9** 6x CFSwan (nt j.w: lost pl 11th: bhd whn mstke 13th: styd on fr 2 out)	3	5	9/1	151	52
1366[4]	**Anabatic (IRE) (145)** (MJPO'Brien,Ireland) **8-11-3** TPRudd (hld up: hdwy 12th: ev ch whn pckd 3 out: wknd appr 2 out)	22	6	7/1[3]	128	29
	All for Luck (133) (MCPipe) **11-10-5** CMaude (lw: hld up & bhd: lost tch fr 8th: t.o)	15	7	16/1	104	5
1649[7]	**Old Bridge (IRE) (132)** (AndrewTurnell) **8-10-4** SMcNeill (hld up: mstke 12th: sme hdwy 4 out: sn wknd: t.o)	2½	8	13/2[2]	102	3
1366[6]	**Big Matt (IRE) (144)** (NJHenderson) **8-11-2** MAFitzgerald (bhd fr 9th: t.o whn p.u bef 2 out)		P	15/2	—	—
1737a[3]	**Belvederian (139)** (MFMorris,Ireland) **9-10-11** NWilliamson (blnd & uns rdr 4th)		U	9/1	—	—
				(SP 119.6%)	**10 Rn**	

5m 16.2 (7.20) CSF £22.10 CT £485.16 TOTE £2.90: £1.70 £2.50 £4.90 (£13.90) Trio £206.40 OWNER Gott Foods Ltd (PENRITH) BRED John O'Brien

LONG HANDICAP Royal Mountbrowne 11-6

1366 Addington Boy (IRE), raised 2lb, had a wake-up call at the first, but did not slip here as he had done in the Murphy's. (7/4)

Go Universal (IRE), 4lb higher than when touched off in the John Hughes at Aintree, ran a fine race, but could not go with the winner from the second last. (12/1)

Northern Hide, who won his last two races at Leopardstown for Arthur Moore, looked capable of causing an upset before blowing up in the home straight. To his credit, he appeared to find his second wind on the run-in and looks useful at this sort of trip. He should pay his way this season, even if the Handicapper does raise him a few pounds. (33/1)

1520 Bertone (IRE) gave the impression he may be better over three these days. (10/1)

1889a* Royal Mountbrowne is inclined to make mistakes and these fences certainly found him out. He was not beaten that far in the end though on ground that was plenty fast enough for him. (9/1)

1366 Anabatic (IRE) had finished only five lengths behind the winner on 3lb worse terms in last month's Murphy's. (7/1)

1918 DOUBLEPRINT NOVICES' CHASE (5-Y.O+) (Class C)

3-15 (3-15) **2m 5f (New) (17 fncs)** £6,648.00 (£1,632.00) GOING: 0.20 sec per fur (G)

				SP	RR	SF
1858[F]	**Imperial Vintage (IRE) (115)** (MissVenetiaWilliams) **6-11-10** NWilliamson (hld up: mstke 1st: led 9th: hit 3 out: clr whn hit last: rdn out)	—	1	8/11[1]	116	9
1629*	**General Pongo (97)** (TRGeorge) **7-11-6** MAFitzgerald (led to 9th: hit 12th: one pce flat)	4	2	6/5[2]	109	2
				(SP 103.3%)	**2 Rn**	

5m 32.0 (23.00) TOTE £1.50 OWNER Mr David Williams (HEREFORD) BRED W. J. Mernagh

1560* Imperial Vintage (IRE) is said to jump better in the lead. (8/11)

1629* General Pongo had a squeak when the winner dragged his hind legs through the last, but would have been 11lb better off in a handicap. (6/5: evens-5/4)

1919 LONESOME GLORY SPORT OF KINGS CHALLENGE HURDLE (4-Y.O+) (Class B)

3-45 (3-45) **2m 4f (New) (10 hdls)** £10,162.50 (£3,075.00: £1,500.00: £712.50) GOING: 0.20 sec per fur (G)

				SP	RR	SF
1661[2]	**Karshi (142)** (MissHCKnight) **6-10-12** JOsborne (mde all: nt fluent last: hdd flat: sn led again: r.o wl)	—	1	11/8[1]	122	18
1559*	**Mandys Mantino (135)** (JTGifford) **6-11-7** PHide (chsd ldr: led flat: sn hdd: eased whn btn nr fin)	4	2	7/2[3]	128	24
1559[2]	**Serenity Prayer (USA)** (BruceMiller,USA) **6-11-7** ChipMiller (hld up: wknd after 2 out)	14	3	3/1[2]	117	13
	Ashwell Boy (IRE) (136) (PJHobbs) **5-10-12** RDunwoody (hld up & bhd: hdwy after 3 out: stumbled 2 out: sn wknd)	5	4	9/2	104	—
				(SP 107.5%)	**4 Rn**	

4m 55.3 (15.30) CSF £5.77 TOTE £2.10 (£2.40) OWNER Lord Vestey (WANTAGE) BRED Lord Vestey

1661 Karshi pulled out what was required after getting in too close at the last. (11/8)

1559* Mandys Mantino lost his unbeaten tag and could not take advantage of making the better jump over the last at these weights. (7/2)

1559 Serenity Prayer (USA) has won over nineteen furlongs in the States, but the longer trip did not appear to help here. (3/1)

Ashwell Boy (IRE) is another probably more effective at two miles. (9/2)

T/Plpt: £47.90 (573.83 Tckts). T/Qdpt: £7.00 (216.18 Tckts). KH

1907-DONCASTER (L-H) (Good to firm, Good patches)

Saturday December 14th

WEATHER: cloudy

1920 FORGIVE 'N' FORGET MAIDEN CHASE (4-Y.O+) (Class D)

12-15 (12-15) **2m 3f 110y (15 fncs)** £3,626.00 (£1,088.00: £524.00: £242.00) GOING: 0.01 sec per fur (G)

				SP	RR	SF
1646[F]	**Art Prince (IRE)** (CPEBrooks) **6-11-1**(7) MBerry (mde all: sn clr: hung rt: unchal)	—	1	11/8[1]	111+	55
1596[4]	**Calleva Star (IRE) (79)** (RHAlner) **5-11-5**(3) PHenley (in tch: chsd wnr fr 4 out: no imp: blnd 2 out)	dist	2	9/2[2]	—	—
1680[7]	**Domaine de Pron (FR)** (MrsLCTaylor) **5-11-8** MSharratt (mstkes: a in tch: effrt 9th: no imp)	4	3	33/1	—	—
964[U]	**Glamanglitz** (PTDalton) **6-11-8** TEley (a chsng ldrs: wknd fr 4 out)	1½	4	8/1	—	—
1728[F]	**Dukes Meadow (IRE)** (KCBailey) **6-11-8** JAMcCarthy (blnd 6th: sn t.o)	21	5	6/1[3]	—	—
917[2]	**Royal Hand (67)** (RJArmson) **6-11-8** MrRArmson (mstkes: sn t.o: fell 3 out)		F	16/1	—	—
1664[3]	**Reefa's Mill (IRE)** (JNeville) **4-10-7b**(3) TDascombe (prom tl wknd qckly 9th: p.u bef 2 out)		P	10/1	—	—

Form	Horse	Dist	Pos	SP	RR	SF
1563P	**Old Redwood** (MrsLWilliamson) **9-11-8** LO'Hara (chsd ldrs: blnd 4th: wknd qckly 8th: t.o whn p.u bef 4 out)		P	33/1	—	—
1771P	**High Handed (IRE)** (THCaldwell) **5-11-8** GaryLyons (nt j.w: sn t.o: blnd & uns rdr 10th)		U	16/1	—	—
				(SP 112.4%)	**9 Rn**	

4m 51.2 (4.20) CSF £7.52 TOTE £2.30: £1.50 £1.40 £6.40 (£4.70) Trio £112.80; £143.05 to 16/12/96 OWNER Mr Terry Neill (LAMBOURN)
WEIGHT FOR AGE 4yo-11lb
1646 Art Prince (IRE), who takes a strong hold and is also chancey with his fences, tends to hang right, but he certainly has an engine. (11/8)
1596 Calleva Star (IRE) was completely outclassed and looked clumsy on occasions. (9/2)
Domaine de Pron (FR) has some ability, but there is a lot of work to do on his jumping. (33/1)
Glamanglitz got round at his third attempt and that was probably the aim here. (8/1: op 12/1)
Dukes Meadow (IRE) made one particularly bad error early on, and getting round was the best that could be said of this effort. (6/1)

1921 RACECOURSE MEDICAL OFFICERS ASSOCIATION NOVICES' HURDLE (4-Y.O+) (Class E)

12-45 (12-46) **2m 110y (8 hdls)** £2,679.00 (£744.00: £357.00) GOING: 0.01 sec per fur (G)

Form	Horse	Dist	Pos	SP	RR	SF
	Sea Victor (JLHarris) **4-10-9**(3) RMassey (hld up: hdwy 5th: led last: all out)	—	1	9/1	72	43
1659*	**Ionio (USA)** (MrsVCWard) **5-11-5** BStorey (chsd ldrs: hit 4th: led 3 out tl hdd & mstke last: rallied towards fin)	hd	2	4/1 2	79	50
	Talathath (FR) (DNicholson) **4-10-7**(5) MrRThornton (hdwy 5th: chsng ldrs & rdn 3 out: kpt on wl)	4	3	7/1 3	68	39
1343*	**Endowment** (MrsMReveley) **4-11-5** PNiven (lw: led tl hdd & blnd 3 out: sn btn)	24	4	7/4 1	52	23
1187*	**Advance East** (MDods) **4-11-5** RSupple (lw: hld up: stdy hdwy appr 3 out: fnd nil appr next)	3½	5	4/1 2	48	19
	Ten Past Six (MartynWane) **4-10-12** LO'Hara (chsd ldrs: mstke 2nd & 5th: btn appr 3 out)	21	6	16/1	21	—
	Rising Man (APJarvis) **5-10-12** KGaule (outpcd fr 5th)	9	7	20/1	12	—
1687[7]	**Kildrummy Castle** (JGFitzGerald) **4-10-9**(3) FLeahy (prom tl outpcd 4th: n.d after)	21	8	10/1	—	—
1640[5]	**Rothari** (BSRothwell) **4-10-12** JAMcCarthy (chsd ldrs tl wknd fr 5th)	5	9	20/1	—	—
	Father Gerard (BSRothwell) **5-10-9**(3) GLee (sn wl bhd: t.o)	dist	10	50/1	—	—
	Toshiba Talk (IRE) (99) (BEllison) **4-10-12** GCahill (bit bkwd: lost tch 5th: p.u bef 3 out)		P	14/1	—	—
1042U	**Goatsfut (IRE)** (BPreece) **6-10-9**(3) GHogan (ref & uns rdr 1st)		R	33/1	—	—
				(SP 134.9%)	**12 Rn**	

3m 53.9 (3.90) CSF £47.98 TOTE £8.40: £2.60 £1.70 £1.90 (£17.00) Trio £25.00 OWNER Mr David Abell (MELTON MOWBRAY) BRED Juddmonte Farms
Sea Victor, a tough sort on the Flat, was having his twentieth race of the year and showed all his courage to win. Better things look likely, especially over further. (9/1)
1659* Ionio (USA) has certainly taken to this game and, but for a poor jump at the last, would probably have won. (4/1)
Talathath (FR) looks a tough type for this game and, although always looking held, he kept responding to pressure, and was keeping on particularly well at the end. (7/1: op 4/1)
1343* Endowment went off a bit too freely and was inclined to dive at his hurdles, and then threw in the towel when challenged. (7/4)
1187* Advance East has been a funny customer all his career but, as he showed last time, when things go his way he has more than enough ability. (4/1)
Ten Past Six does not as yet look a natural hurdler, but time may cure that. (16/1)

1922 DONCASTER RACECOURSE SPONSORSHIP CLUB H'CAP HURDLE (0-130) (4-Y.O+) (Class C)

1-20 (1-20) **2m 4f (10 hdls)** £3,626.00 (£1,088.00: £524.00: £242.00) GOING: 0.01 sec per fur (G)

Form	Horse	Dist	Pos	SP	RR	SF
1556*	**Blaze Away (USA) (125)** (IABalding) **5-11-2**(7) MrABalding (lw: hld up: hdwy on bit to ld 2 out: sn clr)	—	1	4/7 1	117?	34
1416[6]	**Monicasman (IRE) (113)** (APJarvis) **6-10-11** PNiven (chsd ldr: hit 5th & 6th: rdn & no imp fr 4 out)	17	2	7/1 3	91	8
1804[7]	**Dawn Mission (105)** (TDEasterby) **4-10-0**(3) FLeahy (led: hit 1st: wl clr fr 6th: rdn & hung rt appr 3 out: wknd, hdd & blnd 2 out)	3½	3	7/1 3	81	—
1661[7]	**Castle Courageous (130)** (LadyHerries) **9-12-0** EMurphy (hld up: effrt 4 out: sn rdn & btn)	5	4	4/1 2	102	19
				(SP 108.6%)	**4 Rn**	

4m 49.9 (9.90) CSF £4.43 TOTE £1.60 (£2.90) OWNER Mr Paul Mellon (KINGSCLERE) BRED Paul Mellon
1556* Blaze Away (USA), ridden with plenty of confidence, won this moderate contest as he pleased. (4/7)
1262 Monicasman (IRE) finished second, but it was not a good effort and he never showed any sparkle. (7/1)
1125 Dawn Mission had his chances to pinch this but, when asked a question, looked thoroughly ungenuine. (7/1)
Castle Courageous failed to impress on looks and ran in similar fashion. (4/1)

1923 THE DIKLER H'CAP CHASE (5-Y.O+) (Class B)

1-50 (1-50) **3m 2f (19 fncs)** £7,366.00 (£2,051.00: £988.00) GOING: 0.01 sec per fur (G)

Form	Horse	Dist	Pos	SP	RR	SF
1501P	**Musthaveaswig (133)** (DNicholson) **10-9-9**(5) MrRThornton (lw: w ldr: led fr 9th: styd on u.p fr 2 out)	—	1	4/1 2	120	33
1302[2]	**Father Sky (134)** (OSherwood) **5-10-0b** JAMcCarthy (trckd ldrs: hdwy & ev ch 4 out: sn rdn: nt qckn appr last)	1¼	2	9/1 3	120	32
1513[4]	**Scotton Banks (IRE) (157)** (TDEasterby) **7-11-10** RGarritty (lw: mstkes: led to 9th: outpcd whn blnd 15th: sn btn)	dist	3	4/9 1	—	—
1670[4]	**Pims Gunner (IRE) (135)** (MDHammond) **8-9-13**(3)ow2 MrCBonner (hld up: mstke & uns rdr 7th)		U	14/1	—	—
				(SP 105.9%)	**4 Rn**	

6m 27.8 (5.80) CSF £23.91 TOTE £5.50 (£11.30) OWNER P R D Fasteners Ltd (TEMPLE GUITING) BRED Patrick Shanahan
LONG HANDICAP Musthaveaswig 9-4 Father Sky 8-4 Pims Gunner (IRE) 8-2
WEIGHT FOR AGE 5yo-1lb
1501 Musthaveaswig likes things to go his way and they did here, but he still had to struggle to beat the second, to whom he should have been giving a stone. (4/1)
1302 Father Sky, who has picked up a fair amount of prizemoney this season, appears very lucky to have done so, and again this was not a good race. (9/1)
1513 Scotton Banks (IRE) has failed to show anything really positive this season, and always seems happier with some cut in the ground, but this was an awful display and his jumping was particularly poor. (4/9)

1924 SEA PIGEON H'CAP HURDLE (4-Y.O+) (Class B)

2-25 (2-25) **2m 110y (8 hdls)** £4,831.50 (£1,452.00: £701.00: £325.50) GOING: 0.01 sec per fur (G)

Form	Horse	Dist	Pos	SP	RR	SF
1779[6]	**New Inn (113)** (SGollings) **5-10-8** KGaule (mde all: hld on wl)	—	1	9/1 3	94	1

				SP	RR	SF
1658^{7}	**Desert Fighter (110)** (MrsMReveley) **5-10-5** PNiven (lw: trckd wnr: ev ch fr 3 out: kpt on towards fin)	nk	**2**	$9/1^{3}$	91	—
1804^{4}	**Elpidos (119)** (MDHammond) **4-11-0** RGarritty (lw: trckd ldrs: effrt & ev ch last: rdn & no ex)	3	**3**	$2/1^{2}$	97	4
1512^{*}	**Tom Brodie (127)** (HowardJohnson) **6-11-8** RSupple (hld up: effrt 3 out: r.o one pce)	2½	**4**	$5/4^{1}$	102	9
1804^{8}	**Thornton Gate (125)** (TDEasterby) **7-11-6** JCallaghan (hld up: hdwy on bit to chal 3 out: wknd between last 2)	nk	**5**	$9/1^{3}$	100	7
1804^{6}	**Non Vintage (IRE) (129)** (MCChapman) **5-11-10** WWorthington (hld up: outpcd 3 out: n.d after)	2½	**6**	10/1	102	9

(SP 116.9%) **6 Rn**

4m 2.5 (12.50) CSF £70.30 TOTE £6.70: £2.70 £2.50 (£19.40) OWNER Mr Ian Stewart (LOUTH) BRED Crockfords Stud

1779 New Inn, in a race run at no pace, was always in the best position and proved game when challenged. (9/1)

1439 Desert Fighter sat on the winner's heels throughout, but an extra effort was always just too much. (9/1)

1804 Elpidos needed a stronger pace than was set here and was basically outbattled. (2/1: 3/1-7/4)

1512* Tom Brodie, from a yard that has just gone of the boil of late, probably found everything against him here, especially the slow pace. (5/4)

1267 Thornton Gate wears a net-muzzle and came there swinging off the bit three out but, soon asked a question, quickly showed his true colours.. (9/1)

1804 Non Vintage (IRE), with no pace, had no chance. (10/1)

1925 BURROUGH HILL LAD NOVICES' CHASE (4-Y.O+) (Class D)

3-00 (3-00) **2m 110y (12 fncs)** £4,020.00 (£1,120.00: £540.00) GOING: 0.01 sec per fur (G)

				SP	RR	SF
1780^{3}	**Golden Hello** (TDEasterby) **5-11-7** RGarritty (lw: j.rt: chsd ldr: lft in ld 4 out: styd on wl fr 2 out)	—	**1**	$9/2^{3}$	121	24
1664^{*}	**Flight Lieutenant (USA) (114)** (TCasey) **7-11-7** JAMcCarthy (trckd ldrs: ev ch fr 4 out tl outpcd fr 2 out)	12	**2**	$9/4^{2}$	109	12
1714^{U}	**Weeheby (USA)** (MFBarraclough) **7-10-13**(3) GHogan (lost tch 4th: sme hdwy appr 4 out: sn wknd)	dist	**3**	25/1	—	—
1365^{4}	**Country Star (IRE)** (CPEBrooks) **5-11-2** DGallagher (swtg: led tl blnd & uns rdr 4 out)		**U**	$8/11^{1}$	—	—

(SP 110.7%) **4 Rn**

4m 5.2 (10.20) CSF £13.55 TOTE £4.30 (£3.70) OWNER Mr G. E. Shouler (MALTON) BRED Bearstone Stud

1780 Golden Hello will never be as fortunate as this again, as everything possible went his way, even down to a loose horse racing upsides him to keep him straight over the last three fences. (9/2)

1664* Flight Lieutenant (USA) had his chances, but also had his limitations exposed. (9/4)

949 Weeheby (USA) got round safely and that should have at least done him some good. (25/1)

1365 Country Star (IRE) really attacked his fences and was still sailing along in front when he stood too far off the fourth last and put his rider on the floor. (8/11)

1926 WEATHERBYS 'STARS OF TOMORROW' INTERMEDIATE N.H. FLAT RACE (4, 5 & 6-Y.O C & G) (Class H)

3-30 (3-30) **2m 110y** £1,259.00 (£349.00: £167.00)

				SP	RR	SF
	King of Camelot (IRE) (DNicholson) **6-11-1**(3) RMassey (hld up: effrt 6f out: styd on to ld wl over 1f out: kpt on strly)	—	**1**	$3/1^{1}$	57 f	—
	Shebang (IRE) (JLDunlop) **4-11-0**(7)ow3 MrHDunlop (lw: hld up: effrt 7f out: outpcd & lost tch 5f out: styd on strly fnl 2f)	2	**2**	$3/1^{1}$	58 f	—
	Bold Action (IRE) (JNorton) **5-10-11**(7) BGrattan (cl up: led 7f out tl wl over 1f out: hrd rdn & one pce)	nk	**3**	$6/1^{3}$	55 f	—
	The Sharrow Legend (IRE) (JSisterson) **4-10-13**(5) STaylor (in tch: hdwy to disp ld over 2f out: wknd over 1f out)	2	**4**	16/1	53 f	—
1692^{6}	**Revolt** (TDEasterby) **4-11-1**(3) GLee (prom tl outpcd 6f out: styd on wl fnl 3f)	1½	**5**	$5/1^{2}$	51 f	—
	Banker Count (MWEasterby) **4-11-1**(3) GParkin (hld up: hdwy to chal 5f out: hrd rdn over 3f out: wknd fnl 2f)	2½	**6**	12/1	49 f	—
	Phar Smoother (IRE) (JGFitzGerald) **4-11-1**(3) FLeahy (bit bkwd: hld up: hdwy ½-wy: grad wknd fnl 4f)	1	**7**	$6/1^{3}$	48 f	—
1296^{15}	**Jennie's Prospect** (JJO'Neill) **5-10-13**(5) RMcGrath (hld up: effrt 7f out: no imp)	9	**8**	16/1	39 f	—
1579^{7}	**Tartan Joy (IRE)** (JAMoore) **5-11-4** MrNWilson (led over 6f: prom tl outpcd 6f out: n.d after)	s.h	**9**	33/1	39 f	—
	Rasin Standards (RCraggs) **6-11-1**(3) GHogan (effrt ½-wy: outpcd 5f out: sn wknd)	23	**10**	25/1	17 f	—
	Caherlow (IRE) (OBrennan) **5-10-11**(7) SPorritt (plld hrd: cl up: led 10f to 7f out: wknd 5f)	1¾	**11**	14/1	15 f	—
	Eastcliffe (IRE) (WMcKeown) **4-11-4** GCahill (plld hrd: rn out 7f out)		**R**	14/1	—	—

(SP 134.8%) **12 Rn**

4m 0.6 CSF £13.78 TOTE £3.90: £2.30 £1.80 £1.90 (£8.30) Trio £7.10 OWNER Mr Jerry Wright (TEMPLE GUITING) BRED Louis Vambeck

King of Camelot (IRE) proved a determined sort in a race that really hotted up from halfway, and looks quite an athletic type. (3/1)

Shebang (IRE), ridden by an inexperienced rider, got left behind at a vital stage, but certainly finished in some style and looks likely to improve. (3/1: op 6/4)

Bold Action (IRE), a tough sort, had a hard race here, but was just outstayed. His turn should come over hurdles. (6/1: op 4/1)

The Sharrow Legend (IRE) has a useful turn of foot and that should stand him in good stead when he tries hurdling. (16/1)

1692 Revolt is a real stayer in the making and his future lies over obstacles, particularly fences. (5/1)

Banker Count, a fair sort, showed some ability and will improve. (12/1)

Phar Smoother (IRE) needed this and better should be seen in time. (6/1)

T/Plpt: £554.00 (15.75 Tckts). T/Qdpt: £170.20 (3.24 Tckts). AA

1640-HAYDOCK (L-H) - Saturday December 14th

1927 Abandoned-Frost

LINGFIELD (L-H) (Good to soft, Chases Good patches)

Saturday December 14th

WEATHER: cold & sunny

1933 TANDRIDGE DISTRICT COUNCIL H'CAP HURDLE (0-130) (4-Y.O+) (Class C)

12-10 (12-10) **2m 110y (8 hdls)** £3,403.75 (£1,030.00: £502.50: £238.75) GOING: 0.92 sec per fur (S)

				SP	RR	SF
1698^{3}	**Ambleside (IRE) (110)** (MrsSDWilliams) **5-10-10** AMaguire (chsd ldr to 4th: hrd rdn appr last: led nr fin)	—	**1**	$8/1^{3}$	93	48
	Kadastrof (FR) (128) (RDickin) **6-12-0** PHide (a.p: chsd ldr fr 4th: led flat: hrd rdn: hdd nr fin)	1½	**2**	$8/1^{3}$	110	65
1262^{*}	**Potentate (USA) (124)** (MCPipe) **5-11-10** CLlewellyn (led: hrd rdn appr last: mstke last: hdd flat: r.o)	s.h	**3**	$4/7^{1}$	106	61

			Pos	SP	RR	SF
	Hawthorne Glen (103) (MrsMELong) **9-9-10**$^{(7)ow1}$ AIrvine (bit bkwd: hld up: shkn up appr last: sn wknd)	10	**4**	20/1	75	29
	Court Nap (IRE) (113) (SMellor) **4-10-13** NMann (lw: bhd tl fell 2 out)		**F**	16/1	—	—
	Tarrock (110) (MrsMerritaJones) **6-10-10** DerekByrne (lw: mstke 5th: bhd tl p.u bef 2 out: lame)		**P**	9/2^{2}	—	—
				(SP 114.7%)		**6 Rn**

4m 2.2 (17.20) CSF £57.66 TOTE £5.10: £1.30 £2.00 (£16.70) OWNER Mr B. M. Yin (SOUTH MOLTON) BRED Mrs Hazel O'Haire
1698 Ambleside (IRE) failed to stay two and three-quarter miles on his reappearance, and was much happier under a fine ride here, getting up near the line. (8/1: op 5/1)
Kadastrof (FR), given a pipe-opener on the Flat a couple of months ago, slipped down the handicap last season after a string of poor efforts, but ran a promising race here, just being worried out of it near the line. (8/1: op 4/1)
1262* Potentate (USA) did not jump fluently in front and was already being nudged along running down the hill as his rivals sat comfortably on his heels. Grimly trying to hold on, he was collared early on the run-in but, to his credit, stuck on well to the bitter end. (4/7)
Hawthorne Glen looked as though he would benefit from this, but nevertheless caught the eye under a considerate ride. He loves the mud and should be kept in mind. (20/1)

1934 PEAK H'CAP CHASE (0-120) (5-Y.O+) (Class D)

12-40 (12-42) **2m 4f 110y (14 fncs)** £3,860.70 (£1,152.60: £550.80: £249.90) GOING: 0.92 sec per fur (S)

				SP	RR	SF
1644^{2}	**Naiysari (IRE) (108)** (PMRich) **8-11-4** TJMurphy (a.p: led 10th: rdn out)	—	**1**	6/1^{2}	119	41
1676^{2}	**Five to Seven (USA) (112)** (PFNicholls) **7-11-8** PHide (lw: led tl after 2nd: rdn & ev ch 4 out: unable qckn)	3½	**2**	Evens^{1}	120	42
	Danger Baby (105) (DLWilliams) **6-11-1** JRKavanagh (hld up: 5th whn mstke 9th: sn wknd)	20	**3**	9/1	98	20
1554^{P}	**Deependable (90)** (MrsLRichards) **9-10-0b** MRichards (lw: hdwy 6th: wknd 8th: t.o)	26	**4**	25/1	62	—
1778^{4}	**Celtic Silver (96)** (MrsSJSmith) **8-10-6**^{ow3} RichardGuest (led after 2nd to 10th: wknd 11th: t.o)	1¾	**5**	7/1	67	—
1584^{4}	**Red Bean (100)** (KVincent) **8-10-10** ADicken (lw: mstke 3rd: a bhd: t.o)	26	**6**	14/1	51	—
1682^{P}	**Kytton Castle (99)** (RDickin) **9-10-9** CLlewellyn (lw: a.p: rdn 4 out: 3rd & btn whn fell 2 out)		**F**	25/1	—	—
1035^{3}	**Seod Rioga (IRE) (114)** (SMellor) **7-11-10** DBridgwater (lw: a bhd: t.o whn p.u bef 3 out)		**P**	13/2^{3}	—	—
959^{P}	**Be Surprised (90)** (AMoore) **10-10-0** NMann (prom to 5th: t.o whn p.u bef 3 out)		**P**	66/1	—	—
1391^{P}	**The Widget Man (105)** (MissLBower) **10-10-8**$^{(7)}$ MrRWakley (j.b: a bhd: t.o fr 4th: p.u bef 9th)		**P**	33/1	—	—
1650^{P}	**Bo Knows Best (IRE) (118)** (GLMoore) **7-11-7**$^{(7)}$ MAttwater (hdwy 6th: sn wknd: bhd whn blnd & uns rdr 7th)		**U**	25/1	—	—
				(SP 122.8%)		**11 Rn**

5m 24.9 (25.90) CSF £12.38 CT £53.61 TOTE £6.70: £1.40 £1.40 £2.80 (£7.20) Trio £12.80 OWNER Mr P. M. Rich (USK) BRED His Highness the Aga Khans Studs S.C
LONG HANDICAP Be Surprised 8-13
1644 Naiysari (IRE) put up a useful display to gain his first win over fences, leading at the fifth last and being ridden along to keep the runner-up at bay. (6/1: op 7/2)
1676 Five to Seven (USA) was a leading player from the outset and had every chance at the fourth last. Once into the straight though, he found the winner always too good. (Evens)
Danger Baby was having his first run of the season and, after a mistake at the sixth last, was soon in trouble. (9/1: 6/1-10/1)
1778 Celtic Silver (7/1: 5/1-8/1)
1584 Red Bean was a classic example of a horse who made an encouraging reappearance after a lengthy lay-off, only to flop badly on his next run. (14/1)

1935 TJH GROUP SUMMIT JUNIOR HURDLE (Gd 2) (3-Y.O) (Class A)

1-10 (1-10) **2m 110y (8 hdls)** £9,735.00 (£3,685.50: £1,805.25: £824.25) GOING: 0.92 sec per fur (S)

				SP	RR	SF
1706*	**Serenus (USA)** (NJHenderson) **3-10-12** JRKavanagh (a.p: led 5th: hrd rdn appr last: r.o wl)	—	**1**	5/2^{2}	81	36
1014^{4}	**Circus Star** (DNicholson) **3-10-12** AMaguire (lw: plld hrd: hld up: lft 3rd 2 out: chsd wnr appr last: nt clr run on ins & swtchd rt: unable qckn)	3	**2**	100/30^{3}	78	33
	Sally's Twins (JSMoore) **3-10-7** WMcFarland (a.p: lft 2nd 2 out: wknd appr last)	8	**3**	50/1	65	20
1706^{3}	**Ben Bowden** (SWoodman) **3-10-12** MRichards (a.p: mstke 5th: wknd 3 out)	14	**4**	25/1	57	12
1712^{3}	**Province** (CJMann) **3-10-12** JRailton (led to 5th: wknd 3 out)	15	**5**	20/1	42	—
	Bigwig (IRE) (AMoore) **3-10-12** NMann (a bhd: t.o)	dist	**6**	66/1	—	—
1158^{4}	**Kerawi** (NATwiston-Davies) **3-11-2** CLlewellyn (hld up: 3rd whn b.d 2 out)		**B**	4/1	—	—
1519^{U}	**Mr Wild (USA)** (RAkehurst) **3-10-12** DBridgwater (plld hrd: j.rt 1st: hdwy 3 out: 2nd & ev ch whn fell 2 out)		**F**	2/1^{1}	—	—
	Apartments Abroad (KMcAuliffe) **3-10-7** DerekByrne (a bhd: hmpd 1st: t.o fr 4th: p.u bef 2 out)		**P**	50/1	—	—
				(SP 119.0%)		**9 Rn**

4m 5.3 (20.30) CSF £11.21 TOTE £3.90: £1.50 £1.10 £5.40 (£3.20) Trio £57.00 OWNER W V & Mrs E S Robins (LAMBOURN) BRED Foxfield
1706* Serenus (USA) was taking a step up in class after his runaway success at Fontwell and, though he battled on really well, the result might have been different had Mr Wild stayed on his feet. (5/2)
1014 Circus Star was again very keen in the early stages. Done no favours in the melee at the second last, he soon moved into second but, despite all Maguire's efforts, was unable to overhaul the winner. There is a race waiting for him once he learns to settle. (100/30: 9/4-7/2)
Sally's Twins made an encouraging start to her hurdling career. Left in second place by the melee at the penultimate hurdle, she tired going to the last. (50/1)
1706 Ben Bowden, a consistent individual so far this season, found this higher class and easier ground against him and was hung out to dry three from home. (25/1)
1712 Province took the field along until past halfway, but his sights need to be lowered. (20/1)
1158 Kerawi had not been asked any real question and was going well in third place when brought down by Mr Wild at the second last. Compensation awaits. (4/1)
Mr Wild (USA) once again failed to complete, but he was going extremely well when taking a crashing fall at the second last. He would surely have gone very close had he stayed on his feet, and looks a ready-made winner. (2/1)

1936 LOWNDES LAMBERT DECEMBER NOVICES' CHASE (Gd 2) (5-Y.O+) (Class A)

1-40 (1-42) **3m (18 fncs)** £13,280.00 (£5,029.00: £2,464.50: £1,126.50) GOING: 0.92 sec per fur (S)

				SP	RR	SF
1646^{2}	**Foodbroker Star (IRE)** (JTGifford) **6-11-0** LAspell (hdwy 8th: swtchd lft appr 3 out: led last: drvn out)	—	**1**	33/1	123	30
1680^{4}	**Stay Lucky (NZ)** (NJHenderson) **7-11-0** JRKavanagh (led to 2nd: led 11th to 13th: hrd rdn appr 2 out: r.o flat)	1½	**2**	8/1	122	29
1805*	**The Last Fling (IRE) (118)** (MrsSJSmith) **6-11-4** RichardGuest (hdwy 9th: blnd 11th: led 13th: blnd bdly 3 out: hdd last: unable qckn)	1¾	**3**	7/1	125	32
	Thermal Warrior (JABOld) **8-11-0** LHarvey (bit bkwd: a bhd: t.o whn p.u bef 3 out: continued)	dist	**4**	50/1	—	—

	Horse		Pos	SP	RR	SF
1646*	**Buckhouse Boy (132)** (NATwiston-Davies) **6-11-4** CLlewellyn (led 4th tl fell 8th)		**F**	5/1[2]	—	—
1680*	**Pharanear (IRE)** (DNicholson) **6-11-0** AMaguire (hld up: rdn 4 out: 4th whn fell 3 out)		**F**	13/2[3]	—	—
1326*	**Pleasure Shared (IRE)** (PJHobbs) **8-11-7** MRichards (lw: fell 2nd)		**F**	3/1[1]	—	—
1632*	**Bankhead (IRE)** (JLSpearing) **7-11-0** DBridgwater (a bhd: mstke 3rd: t.o whn p.u bef 3 out)		**P**	12/1	—	—
1511[3]	**Ah Shush (IRE)** (NoelChance) **8-11-0** DLeahy (lw: nt j.w: a bhd: blnd 4th: t.o whn p.u bef 10th)		**P**	33/1	—	—
1199*	**Punters Overhead (IRE) (124)** (PFNicholls) **8-11-0** JRailton (lw: led 2nd tl mstke & hdd 4th: lft in 8th: hdd 11th: blnd 14th: wknd appr last: p.u flat: dismntd)		**P**	10/1	—	—
1680[2]	**Treasure Again (IRE)** (MrsMerritaJones) **7-11-0b[1]** DerekByrne (mstke 3rd: 4th whn blnd bdly, swvd lft, bmpd & uns rdr 8th)		**U**	5/1[2]	—	—
				(SP 119.9%)	**11 Rn**	

6m 26.8 (32.80) CSF £252.15 TOTE £33.80: £3.50 £2.30 £2.30 (£151.10) Trio £164.30 OWNER Food Brokers Ltd (FINDON) BRED J. O'Leary

IN-FOCUS: **This Grade 2 event turned into a race for survival as one by one they fell by the wayside.**

1646 Foodbroker Star (IRE) appreciated the longer trip and, galvanized into action in the straight, managed to get in front at the final fence before holding on well. (33/1)

1680 Stay Lucky (NZ), appreciating this longer trip, he got his second wind on the run-in and came through for second. He should go one better soon. (8/1: 6/1-9/1)

1805* The Last Fling (IRE) has made a fine start to his chasing career, winning all three of his completed starts, but this was a much tougher assignment. In front at the sixth last, he was lucky to stand up at the third last and, once collared at the last, failed to find another gear. (7/1)

Thermal Warrior, carrying condition for this reappearance, was totally out of his depth. After being pulled up at the third last, he was waved back by connections to complete for fourth prizemoney. (50/1)

1680* Pharanear (IRE) was given a very patient ride but, pushed along from the top of the hill, was staying on and getting on terms when falling at the third last. (13/2)

1199* Punters Overhead (IRE) was far from foot-perfect but, all the same, made his presence felt until tiring before the last. He was then pulled up quickly on the flat as if something was wrong. (10/1: 7/1-11/1)

1937 TJH GROUP LIMITED H'CAP CHASE (0-135) (5-Y.O+) (Class C)

2-10 (2-12) **3m (18 fncs)** £4,878.25 (£1,456.00: £695.50: £315.25) GOING: 0.92 sec per fur (S)

	Horse	Dist	Pos	SP	RR	SF
1469[F]	**Sounds Strong (IRE) (121)** (DNicholson) **7-10-10** AMaguire (blnd 3rd: stdy hdwy whn mstke 3 out: chsd ldr fr 2 out: led flat: drvn out)	—	**1**	15/8[1]	131+	34
	Fellow Countryman (125) (KCBailey) **9-11-0** CLlewellyn (hdwy 4 out: led 3 out tl flat: unable qckn)	1¼	**2**	4/1[3]	134	37
719[2]	**Have to Think (130)** (PFNicholls) **8-11-5b[1]** DBridgwater (lw: led 2nd to 7th: rdn appr 2 out: wknd appr last)	18	**3**	8/1	127	30
1785[P]	**Terao (132)** (MCPipe) **10-11-7** TJMurphy (a.p: mstke 4th: led after 9th to 3 out: wknd appr last)	1¾	**4**	16/1	128	31
1186[F]	**No Pain No Gain (IRE) (123)** (JTGifford) **8-10-9**(3) LAspell (lw: hdwy 13th: wknd appr 2 out)	5	**5**	7/1	116	19
1570*	**Bells Life (IRE) (127)** (PJHobbs) **7-11-2** GTormey (hld up: rdn 12th: wknd 13th)	17	**6**	9/4[2]	108	11
1571[P]	**Lucky Lane (120)** (SEarle) **12-10-9b** ILawrence (a.p: led 7th tl after 9th: wknd 13th)	2½	**7**	33/1	100	3
	Sheer Ability (128) (CJMann) **10-11-3** JRailton (bit bkwd: led to 2nd: wknd 6th: t.o whn p.u bef 11th)		**P**	25/1	—	—
				(SP 121.8%)	**8 Rn**	

6m 24.3 (30.30) CSF £10.24 CT £46.29 TOTE £2.70: £1.40 £2.20 £1.30 (£11.10) OWNER Mrs David Thompson (TEMPLE GUITING) BRED S. Banville

1469 Sounds Strong (IRE) was given a very patient ride and plenty of time to get over a bad error at the third. His jumping faltered a bit when he came under a bit of pressure when asked to get into the race in the straight but, responding to his rider's urgings, he poked his head in front on the flat. (15/8)

Fellow Countryman made a fine return to action. Jumping into the lead at the third last, he made sure the winner fought hard, but was just unable to contain him on the run-in. He finished a long way clear of the rest and should have no trouble going one better. (4/1)

719 Have to Think ran a very sound race and was a leading player until left behind by the front two approaching the last. He is at his best when the mud is really flying. (8/1)

Terao, racing with his tongue tied down, ran better here, but he is still high in the handicap after several bad runs and needs to be dropped a few pounds. (16/1)

1186 No Pain No Gain (IRE) was in trouble approaching the second last. He has never won beyond two miles, five and a half furlongs. (7/1)

1570* Bells Life (IRE) was very disappointing. (9/4)

1938 BIFFA RECYCLING NOVICES' HURDLE (4-Y.O+) (Class E)

2-45 (2-47) **2m 3f 110y (10 hdls)** £2,952.00 (£822.00: £396.00) GOING: 0.92 sec per fur (S)

	Horse	Dist	Pos	SP	RR	SF
890[5]	**The Proms (IRE)** (NATwiston-Davies) **5-10-12** CLlewellyn (hld up: hrd rdn appr last: led flat: r.o wl)	—	**1**	14/1	80	34
1171[U]	**Marching Marquis (IRE)** (NoelChance) **5-10-12** TJMurphy (lw: a.p: led appr 2 out tl flat: unable qckn)	1¼	**2**	7/4[1]	79	33
	Crane Hill (PJHobbs) **6-10-12b** GTormey (hld up: ev ch last: one pce)	4	**3**	8/1[3]	76	30
	Cuthill Hope (IRE) (MHTompkins) **5-10-12** RichardGuest (bit bkwd: hdwy 7th: shkn up appr last: wknd flat)	3	**4**	33/1	73	27
1036[2]	**Mythical Approach (IRE)** (DNicholson) **6-10-12** AMaguire (hdwy 3 out: hrd rdn appr last: sn wknd)	2	**5**	5/2[2]	72	26
	Wristburn (CJMann) **6-10-12** JRailton (stdy hdwy & mstke 2 out: shkn up appr last: nvr nrr)	5	**6**	12/1	68	22
1453[6]	**Strong Paladin (IRE)** (JTGifford) **5-10-9**(3) LAspell (rdn & hdwy 3 out: wknd appr 2 out)	14	**7**	9/1	56	10
1388[3]	**Jakes Justice (IRE)** (JTGifford) **5-10-5**(7) MrPO'Keeffe (prom to 3 out)	8	**8**	14/1	49	3
	Chapilliere (FR) (TThomsonJones) **6-10-12** MRichards (bit bkwd: prom to 5th)	2½	**9**	33/1	47	1
	Tin Pan Alley (DMGrissell) **7-10-12** PMcLoughlin (bit bkwd: hld up: mstke 6th: wknd 7th)	½	**10**	50/1	47	1
1651[10]	**Hi Marble (IRE)** (MrsMerritaJones) **5-10-7** ILawrence (lw: a bhd)	4	**11**	20/1	39	—
	Eau So Sloe (JRPoulton) **5-10-12** ADicken (bhd fr 7th)	20	**12**	50/1	27	—
1707[P]	**Gemini Mist** (MrsPNDutfield) **5-10-7** WMcFarland (a bhd)	hd	**13**	50/1	22	—
	No Matter (IRE) (RRowe) **5-10-12** DO'Sullivan (bit bkwd: a bhd)	13	**14**	33/1	17	—
1583[9]	**Nishaman** (NJHenderson) **5-10-12** JRKavanagh (led to 3rd: led 6th tl appr 2 out: sn wknd)	17	**15**	33/1	3	—
	Jewel Trader (MrsLCJewell) **4-10-12v** DLeahy (bhd fr 5th: t.o fr 6th)	dist	**16**	66/1	—	—
1633[2]	**Market Mayhem** (JLSpearing) **6-10-12** DBridgwater (prom to 4th: p.u bef 5th: lame)		**P**	14/1	—	—
	Jolto (KMcAuliffe) **7-10-12** BClifford (led 3rd to 6th: wknd 7th: t.o whn p.u bef 2 out)		**P**	33/1	—	—
				(SP 140.6%)	**18 Rn**	

4m 58.8 (24.80) CSF £40.99 TOTE £16.00: £3.60 £1.80 £2.60 (£43.40) Trio £82.70 OWNER Mrs J. Mould (CHELTENHAM) BRED Mrs S. Brennan

The Proms (IRE) chased the leaders and, responding well to pressure, managed to get on top on the run-in. (14/1: 8/1-16/1)

1171 Marching Marquis (IRE) managed to get round on this occasion. A leading player from the outset, he showed in front approaching the second last, but was unable to contain the winner on the run-in. His turn is close at hand. (7/4)
Crane Hill looked pretty straight for this first outing in a year. Throwing down his challenge in the straight, he was still in with every chance at the last before tapped for toe. Lack of gears does seem to be his downfall. (8/1)
Cuthill Hope (IRE) made a promising racecourse debut. Taking closer order four out, he was in the thick of things but, as lack of peak fitness finally took its toll, the combination faded on the run-in. Better for this outing, he should find a race. (33/1)
1036 Mythical Approach (IRE), who had a slight muscle enzyme problem after his Worcester reappearance, moved into the action three out, but tired by the final flight. (5/2)
Wristburn caught the eye on this debut until a mistake put paid to his chances. (12/1)
1453 Strong Paladin (IRE) (9/1: 6/1-10/1)
1388 Jakes Justice (IRE) (14/1: 8/1-16/1)

1939 LEVY BOARD H'CAP HURDLE (0-120) (4-Y.O+) (Class D)

3-20 (3-32) **2m 3f 110y (10 hdls)** £2,898.80 (£801.80: £382.40) GOING: 0.92 sec per fur (S)

	Horse / details	Dist	Pos	SP	RR	SF
	Rockcliffe Lad (93) (NATwiston-Davies) **7-10-5** CLlewellyn (led to 5th: led after 3 out: clr appr last: eased flat)	—	1	3/1 3	82+	20
1841 2	**Stoney Valley (102)** (JRJenkins) **6-11-0** AMaguire (hld up: chsd wnr appr 2 out: mstke 2 out: no imp)	10	2	7/2	83	21
	More Dash Thancash (IRE) (92) (MrsMerritaJones) **6-10-4** ILawrence (lw: hld up: ev ch 3 out: wknd appr 2 out)	4	3	9/4 2	70	8
1709 4	**Tickerty's Gift (110)** (GLMoore) **6-11-1v**(7) MAttwater (lw: chsd ldr: led 5th tl after 3 out: sn wknd)	6	4	2/1 1	83	21
	Never Forgotten (88) (AMoore) **11-10-0** NMann (Withdrawn not under Starter's orders: veterinary advice)		W	66/1	—	—
				(SP 112.8%)	**4 Rn**	

5m 0.8 (26.80) CSF £11.86 TOTE £5.20: £3.40 (£4.50) OWNER Mr Simon Keswick (CHELTENHAM) BRED E. J. Praill, Mrs M. Scudamore and M. J. Scudamore
LONG HANDICAP Never Forgotten 9-13
Rockcliffe Lad put up a remarkable performance, considering he had not seen a racecourse since October 1994. Bustled back into the lead soon after the third last, he surged clear going to the final flight and was eased to nearly a walk near the line. (3/1)
1841 Stoney Valley has gained all his wins to date at around two miles, and a return to that trip might help. (7/2)
More Dash Thancash (IRE) missed last season with a tendon strain, but looked in tremendous shape for this return. He looked like playing a serious hand in the outcome three out, but disappointingly dropped away going to the second last. (9/4)
1709 Tickerty's Gift has gained all his four victories to date over hurdles at this course in the mud, but the ground was probably not quite as soft as he requires. He should also be watched for with a stronger pilot. (2/1)

T/Plpt: £267.60 (44.1 Tckts). T/Qdpt: £32.20 (39.37 Tckts). AK

1686-NEWCASTLE (L-H) (Good)
Monday December 16th

One fence omitted
WEATHER: cloudy

1940 NEWCASTLE CULTURAL CAPITAL OF THE NORTH HURDLE (3-Y.O) (Class E)

12-40 (12-41) **2m (9 hdls)** £2,337.00 (£657.00: £321.00) GOING minus 0.19 sec per fur (G)

	Horse / details	Dist	Pos	SP	RR	SF
1652 2	**Son of Anshan** (MrsASwinbank) **3-10-12** JSupple (lw: chsd ldrs: outpcd 5th: hdwy 3 out: styd on strly to ld cl home)	—	1	6/4 1	78	30
1652 3	**Rossel (USA)** (PMonteith) **3-11-5**(7) CMcCormack (cl up: led 4 out & qcknd clr: rdn flat: no ex & hdd towards fin)	½	2	6/1 3	92	44
1652*	**Jackson Park** (TDEasterby) **3-11-5** RDunwoody (lw: w ldrs: outpcd 3 out: no imp after)	7	3	9/4 2	78	30
	J J Baboo (IRE) (MDHammond) **3-10-12** RGarritty (prom: effrt 4 out: outpcd fr next)	12	4	8/1	59	11
1699 2	**Fro** (HAlexander) **3-10-7** BStorey (in tch: outpcd 4 out: styd on towards fin)	10	5	14/1	44	—
1700 8	**Perpetual Light** (JJQuinn) **3-10-7** DerekByrne (nvr nr to chal)	10	6	20/1	34	—
1184 9	**Sousse** (MrsMReveley) **3-10-7** PNiven (hld up & bhd: n.d)	3½	7	14/1	30	—
1699*	**Priddy Fair** (DWBarker) **3-10-11**(3) PMidgley (in tch: grad lost pl fr 4 out)	3	8	20/1	34	—
1652 10	**Nexsis Star** (MrsSJSmith) **3-10-5**(7) RWilkinson (plld hrd: led to 4 out: wknd)	2	9	25/1	30	—
	Amazing Sail (IRE) (MissMKMilligan) **3-10-12** ASSmith (prom to 5th)	12	10	66/1	18	—
	Western Venture (IRE) (RMMcKellar) **3-10-12** ADobbin (a bhd)	7	11	50/1	11	—
1652 17	**Bank On Inland** (JRTurner) **3-10-7** WFry (bhd fr 4th)	4	12	100/1	2	—
1652 6	**Mock Trial (IRE)** (MrsJRRamsden) **3-10-12** MrSSwiers (lw: chsd ldrs: 5th & wkng whn fell 3 out)		F	14/1	—	—
	Blazing Imp (USA) (WSCunningham) **3-10-12** NSmith (wknd qckly 4th: t.o whn p.u bef 4 out)		P	66/1	—	—
	Ramozra (ACWhillans) **3-10-7** BHarding (t.o whn p.u 3 out)		P	100/1	—	—
1356 7	**Sounds Devious** (CParker) **3-10-7** DParker (t.o whn p.u 2 out)		P	100/1	—	—
	Beacon Hill Lady (BEllison) **3-10-7** GCahill (blnd 3rd: t.o whn p.u bef 2 out)		P	100/1	—	—
				(SP 138.4%)	**17 Rn**	

3m 55.7 (3.70) CSF £12.63 TOTE £2.60: £1.10 £1.90 £2.10 (£4.70) Trio £2.60 OWNER Mr G. A. Swinbank (RICHMOND) BRED C. J. R. Trotter
1652 Son of Anshan won this through sheer stamina and should improve as he tries further. (6/4)
1652 Rossel (USA) looked to have pinched this as he quickened clear three out, but he had done too much too quickly and was pegged back late on. He is going to find plenty more opportunities. (6/1)
1652* Jackson Park ran a bit flat this time, being tapped for toe over the last three flights. He was not overpunished when beaten and will be back in top form in due course. (9/4)
J J Baboo (IRE) had bits of form on the Flat in Ireland and this was a fine first effort over here. The experience should stand him in good stead. (8/1)
1699 Fro was tapped for toe, but was keeping on at the end, suggesting that stiffer tests should suit. (14/1)
1652 Mock Trial (IRE) looked a picture, but his limitations had been exposed when he fell three out. (14/1)

1941 NEWCASTLE TYNE BRIDGE ILLUMINATIONS H'CAP CHASE (0-125) (5-Y.O+) (Class D)

1-10 (1-10) **3m (17 fncs)** £3,452.50 (£1,045.00: £510.00: £242.50) GOING minus 0.19 sec per fur (G)

	Horse / details	Dist	Pos	SP	RR	SF
1294[3]	**Stormy Coral (IRE) (97)** (CParker) **6-10-0** BStorey (lw: hld up: effrt 4 out: wnt 2nd next: led flat: r.o wl)	—	1	13/8[1]	103	10
1806[U]	**Astings (FR) (116)** (JGFitzGerald) **8-11-5** RGarritty (mde most tl hdd & nt qckn flat)	3	2	2/1[2]	120	27
1655[P]	**Earlymorning Light (IRE) (115)** (GRichards) **7-11-4** ADobbin (w ldr to 8th: cl up tl wknd appr 3 out)	30	3	10/1	99	6
1657[6]	**Vicaridge (97)** (RBrewis) **9-10-0** KJohnson (lw: mstke 4th: hld up: wnt prom 10th: ev ch fr 12th tl wknd appr 3 out)	7	4	5/2[3]	76	—
1846[P]	**Blazing Dawn (97)** (JSHubbuck) **9-10-0** BHarding (prom tl outpcd & lost tch 13th)	30	5	25/1	56	—

(SP 112.9%) **5 Rn**

6m 9.6 (17.60) CSF £5.24 TOTE £2.70: £1.10 £1.20 (£3.00) OWNER Mr & Mrs Raymond Anderson Green (LOCKERBIE) BRED R. J. McKnight

LONG HANDICAP Stormy Coral (IRE) 9-13 Vicaridge 9-12 Blazing Dawn 9-8

1294 Stormy Coral (IRE), a bit deliberate at some fences, picked up immediately when asked a question and won authoritatively. (13/8)

Astings (FR), looking likely to benefit from this, put in a clear round and should now improve. (2/1)

1315 Earlymorning Light (IRE) is a difficult customer to weigh up and, once the pressure was applied at the third last, he soon cried enough. (10/1: 6/1-11/1)

1657 Vicaridge, trying a longer trip, appeared not to get it, stopping disappointingly over the last three. (5/2)

1307 Blazing Dawn, after a good start to the season, has got back to his old ways. (25/1)

1942 NEWCASTLE INITIATIVE CLAIMING HURDLE (4-Y.O+) (Class F)

1-40 (1-41) **2m (9 hdls)** £2,142.00 (£602.00: £294.00) GOING minus 0.19 sec per fur (G)

	Horse / details	Dist	Pos	SP	RR	SF
	White Willow (130) (MrsMReveley) **7-11-6b** PNiven (lw: mde all: kpt on wl fr 4 out)	—	1	10/11[1]	82	18
1703[4]	**Aide Memoire (IRE) (72)** (RJohnson) **7-10-0** KJohnson (hdwy 4th: outpcd 4 out: styd on wl towards fin)	3½	2	25/1	59?	—
1686[2]	**Auburn Boy (103)** (MWEasterby) **9-11-12** RGarritty (hld up: hdwy 5th: ev ch 3 out: one pce fr next)	1¼	3	7/1[3]	83	19
1804[10]	**Jazilah (FR) (127)** (RAllan) **8-11-12** RDunwoody (hld up & bhd: stdy hdwy 4th: effrt 4 out: rdn & lttl rspnse)	11	4	5/2[2]	72	8
	Artworld (USA) (MWEasterby) **8-10-11**(3) PMidgley (chsd ldrs: ev ch 4 out: wknd after next)	½	5	40/1	60	—
1577[4]	**Nonios (IRE) (97)** (GMMoore) **5-10-13**(7) THogg (in tch: no hdwy fr 4 out)	3½	6	12/1	62	—
1141*	**Stylish Interval (90)** (NWaggott) **4-11-0** ADobbin (nvr bttr than mid div: no ch whn hmpd 2 out)	2½	7	25/1	54	—
1703[16]	**Fly to the End (USA) (72)** (JJQuinn) **6-10-11** DerekByrne (bhd most of wy)	dist	8	200/1	—	—
812[10]	**Mannagar (IRE)** (WStorey) **4-10-11** MMoloney (mstkes: a bhd)	dist	9	200/1	—	—
1577[7]	**Joyrider (88)** (MissMKMilligan) **5-10-5** ASSmith (chsd ldrs: 5th & wkng whn fell 2 out)		F	8/1	—	—
1667[12]	**Percy Parrot** (ACWhillans) **4-10-5b**[1] BHarding (rdn & wknd ½-wy: t.o whn p.u bef 3 out)		P	100/1	—	—
1344[10]	**Circle Boy (64)** (WStorey) **9-10-0**(5) RMcGrath (prom to 3rd: sn bhd: t.o: p.u bef 3 out)		P	200/1	—	—

(SP 124.9%) **12 Rn**

4m (8.00) CSF £25.12 TOTE £2.60: £1.40 £2.90 £1.60 (£14.00) Trio £25.40 OWNER Mr H. North (SALTBURN) BRED Gainsborough Stud Management Ltd

White Willow clmd AGreenhow £8,000

White Willow, dropped in class, found this fairly easy and always had the edge. (10/11)

1703 Aide Memoire (IRE), a funny customer, is running well for her new stable. (25/1)

1686 Auburn Boy had his chances but, when a struggle was required over the last three, it was always too much for him. (7/1)

Jazilah (FR) has the ability to see this lot off but, as yet, has not shown any signs of returning to form. (5/2: op 13/8)

Artworld (USA) showed nothing in two runs last season, but this was a much-improved effort, and he seems to be getting it together. (40/1)

1577 Nonios (IRE) was never giving it his best when asked for an effort in the home straight. (12/1)

1943 NEWCASTLE EDUCATION BUSINESS PARTNERSHIP NOVICES' H'CAP CHASE (0-110) (4-Y.O+) (Class D)

2-10 (2-10) **2m 110y (11 fncs)** £3,452.50 (£1,045.00: £510.00: £242.50) GOING minus 0.19 sec per fur (G)

	Horse / details	Dist	Pos	SP	RR	SF
1346[9]	**Crosshot (75)** (RMcDonald) **9-10-9** KJones (a.p: disp ld 3 out: led flat: r.o)	—	1	9/2	85	17
	Cover Point (IRE) (90) (JGFitzGerald) **5-11-10** RDunwoody (bit bkwd: swtg: led tl hdd & wknd flat)	7	2	7/2[2]	93	25
1346[10]	**Singing Sand (74)** (PMonteith) **6-10-8** GCahill (hld up: hdwy ½-wy: ev ch fr 8th tl blnd & wknd 3 out)	5	3	4/1[3]	72	4
1248[6]	**Islandreagh (IRE) (75)** (GRichards) **5-10-9** ADobbin (chsd ldrs: hit 8th: sn rdn: wknd appr 3 out)	30	4	8/1	44	—
1833[F]	**Monaughty Man (69)** (EMCaine) **10-10-3** KJohnson (outpcd & lost pl 3rd: hit 4th: hmpd 5th: n.d)	10	5	10/1	29	—
1348[F]	**Show Your Hand (IRE) (77)** (LLungo) **8-10-11** BHarding (chsd ldrs tl fell 5th)		F	2/1[1]	—	—
	Coolreny (IRE) (76) (VThompson) **7-10-10**ow4 MrMThompson (bkwd: outpcd whn blnd & uns rdr 11th)		U	40/1	—	—

(SP 116.4%) **7 Rn**

4m 10.3 (12.30) CSF £19.89 CT £62.02 TOTE £5.10: £2.90 £1.80 (£13.40) Trio £17.50 OWNER Mr R. McDonald (DUNS) BRED Robert McDonald

Crosshot was a useful performer almost five years ago over hurdles, and showed here he still has a fair amount of ability. (9/2)

Cover Point (IRE) missed all last season and, at his first attempt over fences, put in a fair effort, and should go one better in due course. (7/2)

Singing Sand has always shown enough ability but, as yet, is unsuccessful. This was a reasonable run though, and the experience should bring him on. (4/1)

733 Islandreagh (IRE) looks the type to do well at this game but, on the whole, is very disappointing. (8/1: op 4/1)

1944 NEWCASTLE CITY OF ENERGY NOVICES' CHASE (5-Y.O+) (Class D)

2-45 (2-45) **2m 4f (14 fncs)** £3,517.50 (£1,065.00: £520.00: £247.50) GOING minus 0.19 sec per fur (G)

	Horse / details	Dist	Pos	SP	RR	SF
1653[6]	**Garbo's Boy** (JRTurner) **6-11-0** WFry (cl up: lft in ld 6th: blnd 8th: kpt on wl fr 3 out)	—	1	14/1	79	—
	Gaelic Blue (MrsSJSmith) **6-10-7**(7) RWilkinson (bit bkwd: in tch: hdwy 7th: styd on one pce fr 4 out)	7	2	25/1	73	—
1563[9]	**Rathfardon (IRE)** (FMurphy) **8-10-7**(7) MrTJBarry (chsd ldrs: ev ch fr 11th tl wknd 2 out)	hd	3	66/1	73	—
1357[2]	**Pantara Prince (IRE)** (JIACharlton) **7-11-0** ADobbin (bdly hmpd 1st: hdwy to jn ldrs 7th: wknd fr 3 out)	17	4	5/1[3]	60	—
	Cullane Lake (IRE) (MissMKMilligan) **6-10-9** ASSmith (effrt ½-wy: nvr trbld ldrs)	4	5	25/1	52	—
1850[F]	**Distillery Hill (IRE) (74)** (VThompson) **8-11-0** KJones (mstkes: lost tch ½-wy: sn t.o)	dist	6	33/1	—	—
1803[F]	**Aslan (IRE)** (JGFitzGerald) **8-11-0** WDwan (led 1st: clr 5th: ref 6th: cont: t.o)	7	7	9/2[2]	—	—
	Celtic Giant (LLungo) **6-11-0** RGarritty (lw: led & fell 1st)		F	4/7[1]	—	—

(SP 117.3%) **8 Rn**

5m 18.1 (25.10) CSF £223.68 TOTE £16.30: £2.40 £1.40 £10.30 (£116.20) OWNER Mr J. R. Turner (HELPERBY) BRED J. R. and T. Turner

911 Garbo's Boy had this simplified after the favourite was on the floor at the first. He beat the rest of this moderate bunch in good style. (14/1)

Gaelic Blue needed this and looked pretty slow, but he does gallop, and was staying on at the end. (25/1)
Rathfardon (IRE) had his chances in this moderate event, but was left struggling over the last couple of fences. (66/1)
1357 Pantara Prince (IRE) did not run too badly considering he was nearly brought down at the first. (5/1)
Cullane Lake (IRE) looked pretty slow, but no doubt the experience should help. (25/1)
Celtic Giant looked to have found a race where remaining upright was the only problem, but he could not manage it. (4/7)

1945 NEWCASTLE STUDENT CITY H'CAP HURDLE (0-120) (4-Y.O+) (Class D)
3-15 (3-16) **2m 4f (11 hdls)** £2,749.00 (£832.00: £406.00: £193.00) GOING: 0.19 sec per fur (G)

				SP	RR	SF
	Livio (USA) (105) (PMonteith) **5-11-5** ADobbin (a gng wl: led 4 out: qcknd clr next: easily)	—	1	5/1[3]	95+	—
1121[F]	**Brancher (91)** (JNorton) **5-10-5** WFry (a.p: drvn along 4 out: kpt on: no ch w wnr)	7	2	5/1[3]	75	—
	Purevalue (IRE) (110) (MWEasterby) **5-11-10** RDunwoody (lw: hld up: shkn up & hdwy appr 4 out: sn chsng ldrs: one pce fr 2 out)	4	3	9/4[1]	91	—
1207[3]	**Keen To The Last (FR) (100)** (MDHammond) **4-11-0** RGarritty (chsd ldrs: effrt 4 out: one pce)	7	4	8/1	76	—
1143*	**Exemplar (IRE) (96)** (MrsSJSmith) **8-10-3**(7) RWilkinson (led tl hdd 4 out: sn outpcd: hit last)	½	5	8/1	71	—
1658[10]	**Dual Image (106)** (JGFitzGerald) **9-11-6** WDwan (hld up & bhd: nvr nr to chal)	2	6	40/1	80	—
1686[3]	**Barton Heights (90)** (MrsMReveley) **4-10-1**(3) GLee (lw: cl up tl wknd after 3 out: eased whn btn)	dist	7	3/1[2]	—	—
62[6]	**Glenugie (102)** (GMMoore) **5-11-2** NBentley (prom tl lost pl 6th: n.d after)	6	8	10/1	—	—

(SP 122.9%) **8 Rn**

5m 17.5 (29.50) CSF £29.97 CT £67.04 TOTE £7.40: £1.60 £1.10 £1.60 (£20.20) Trio £26.50 OWNER The Low Flyers (Thoroughbreds) Ltd (ROSEWELL) BRED Darley Stud Management Co Ltd
Livio (USA) has changed stables and came back to form here with a vengeance, fairly trotting up. (5/1)
1121 Brancher is honest and kept responding to pressure, but always found the winner too good. (5/1)
Purevalue (IRE) looked magnificent, but that spark was never there on this occasion and, although responding to pressure, he was never doing enough to make a serious impression. Despite his appearance, he obviously needed this. (9/4)
1207 Keen To The Last (FR) had his chances, but looked very one-paced over the last four. (8/1: op 5/1)
1143* Exemplar (IRE), after six weeks off, will probably be all the better for this. (8/1: 5/1-9/1)
Dual Image ran much better this time and was sympathetically handled. He seems to be improving nicely. (40/1)
1686 Barton Heights (3/1: 9/4-7/2)

T/Jkpt: Not won; £2,989.67 to Folkestone 17/12/96. T/Plpt: £1,351.40 (7.89 Tckts). T/Qdpt: £544.00 (1.4 Tckts). AA

1693-NEWTON ABBOT (L-H) (Heavy, Soft patches)
Monday December 16th
One fence omitted
WEATHER: cloudy

1946 NOT SO RED (S) HURDLE (4-Y.O+) (Class G)
12-50 (12-51) **2m 6f (10 hdls)** £1,793.00 (£503.00: £245.00) GOING: 1.00 sec per fur (S)

				SP	RR	SF
1645[8]	**Palosanto (IRE) (117)** (MCPipe) **6-11-12b[1]** APMcCoy (mde all: clr appr 2 out: eased flat)	—	1	6/5[2]	89+	31
	Star Performer (IRE) (104) (MrsMReveley) **5-11-5** AMaguire (lw: hld up: hdwy to chse wnr appr 7th: no ch fr 3 out)	24	2	10/11[1]	65	7
1770[5]	**Strike-a-Pose** (BJLlewellyn) **6-11-0** MrJLLlewellyn (in tch tl wknd appr 7th)	3	3	12/1[3]	57	—
1707[4]	**Credit Controller (IRE) (59)** (JFfitch-Heyes) **7-10-12b** BFenton (chsd wnr 5th tl appr 7th: sn wknd: t.o)	dist	4	25/1	—	—
	Bowden Surprise (RJBaker) **6-10-12** BPowell (bit bkwd: bhd 4th: rdn & wknd 6th: t.o whn p.u bef 8th)		P	25/1	—	—

(SP 113.2%) **5 Rn**

5m 46.5 (34.50) CSF £2.67 TOTE £2.50: £2.30 £1.00 (£1.10) OWNER Mr B. A. Kilpatrick (WELLINGTON) BRED W. R. Jackson
No bid
1441 Palosanto (IRE), equipped with the blinkers for the first time, was taking a step down in class and scored easily. (6/5)
Star Performer (IRE), making the 350-mile journey south in search of suitable ground, could never get on terms with the winner. (10/11)
1770 Strike-a-Pose has run disappointingly in two similar events so far this season. (12/1: op 8/1)
1707 Credit Controller (IRE) is still a maiden after contesting some very poor events. (25/1)

1947 E.B.F. TATTERSALLS (IRELAND) QUALIFIER NOVICES' CHASE (5-Y.O+ Mares Only) (Class E)
1-20 (1-20) **2m 5f 110y (14 fncs)** £2,995.65 (£907.20: £443.10: £211.05) GOING: 1.00 sec per fur (S)

				SP	RR	SF
1811[2]	**Miss Diskin (IRE) (105)** (RHBuckler) **7-10-10** BPowell (lw: hdwy to ld 7th: hdd 12th: led 2 out: styd on wl flat)	—	1	2/1[1]	91	22
1443[3]	**Country Store** (APJones) **7-10-10** DBridgwater (hld up: hdwy to chse ldrs 8th: ev ch 2 out tl no ex flat)	2½	2	14/1	89	20
1557[4]	**Pearl's Choice (IRE) (87)** (JCMcConnochie) **8-10-10** AThornton (led to 2nd: led 3rd to next: led 5th to 7th: mstke 8th: led 12th to next: no ex last)	1¼	3	12/1	88	19
	Wonderfull Polly (IRE) (PFNicholls) **8-10-5**(5) OBurrows (bhd 6th: mstke 11th: hdwy 12th: ev ch 2 out: wknd appr last)	1	4	14/1	88	19
	Lorna-Gail (RHAlner) **10-10-7**(3) PHenley (bhd: hdwy 8th: sn in tch: wknd appr 2 out)	2½	5	3/1[2]	86	17
	Ardent Love (IRE) (DNicholson) **7-10-10** AMaguire (bit bkwd: bhd: hdwy 9th: rdn appr 2 out: outpcd)	3½	6	11/1	83	14
1582[9]	**Bournel (76)** (CRBarwell) **8-10-10v** BFenton (bit bkwd: a bhd: t.o 9th)	dist	7	33/1	—	—
	Carmel's Joy (IRE) (TRGeorge) **7-10-10** LHarvey (chsd ldrs tl mstke 11th: nt rcvr: t.o)	nk	8	5/1[3]	—	—
1811[4]	**Arctic Madam** (PFNicholls) **7-10-3**(7) MrJTizzard (j.slowly 1st: mstke 6th: in tch tl wknd 8th: t.o)	26	9	25/1	—	—
1677[4]	**Mistress Rosie (72)** (MHill) **9-10-10** SFox (led 2nd to next: prom tl wknd 9th: t.o whn p.u bef last)		P	25/1	—	—
	Kingsmill Quay (MissJduPlessis) **7-10-10** GUpton (bit bkwd: chsd ldr: led 4th to next: mstke 7th: p.u after next)		P	50/1	—	—
1771[5]	**Knowing (69)** (PGWatkins) **9-10-3**(7) MrAWintle (a mid div: bhd 9th: t.o whn p.u bef 2 out)		P	66/1	—	—

(SP 118.4%) **12 Rn**

5m 49.6 (32.60) CSF £28.00 TOTE £2.90: £1.20 £2.40 £1.70 (£9.80) Trio £47.40 OWNER Mr Martyn Forrester (BRIDPORT) BRED John Neary
1811 Miss Diskin (IRE) relished the underfoot conditions. She has improved with racing this season, shows a great attitude, and could go for the Final of this at Uttoxeter in March. (2/1)
1443 Country Store put in a very good effort on this chasing debut and, appreciating the soft conditions, was only beaten on the

run-in. (14/1: 10/1-16/1)
1557 Pearl's Choice (IRE) is still to win after twenty-four attempts, but has figured prominently on occasions and this effort was enough to suggest that there is a race for her. (12/1: 8/1-14/1)
Wonderfull Polly (IRE), not seen out since June 1995, would have appreciated this outing, her first over fences. She may have finished closer but for a mistake down the back straight, but this was still a good effort, and she is sure to improve on it. (14/1: op 7/1)
Lorna-Gail has been out of action for almost a year and will almost certainly come on for the run. (3/1)
Ardent Love (IRE) (11/1: 7/1-12/1)

1948 LES SEWARD MEMORIAL CHALLENGE TROPHY H'CAP HURDLE (0-110) (4-Y.O+) (Class E)

1-50 (1-50) **2m 1f (8 hdls)** £2,190.00 (£615.00: £300.00) GOING: 1.00 sec per fur (S)

				SP	RR	SF
	Friendly House (IRE) (91) (MCPipe) **7-11-10** APMcCoy (mde all: qcknd appr 5th: rdn appr last: styd on wl)	—	1	$7/4^{1}$	73	21
1709^{7}	**Muhtashim (IRE) (87)** (JFfitch-Heyes) **6-11-6** BFenton (mid div: hdwy 5th: chsd wnr after next: rdn appr 2 out: wknd appr last)	2½	2	$9/2^{2}$	67	15
1727^{5}	**Daily Sport Girl (90)** (BJLlewellyn) **7-11-9** MrJLLlewellyn (bhd: hdwy to chse ldrs 6th: no imp)	24	3	$9/2^{2}$	47	—
1382^{5}	**Hullo Mary Doll (79)** (AJChamberlain) **7-10-7**(5) SophieMitchell (bhd: styd on fr 6th: nvr nrr)	¾	4	$9/2^{2}$	35	—
1768^{P}	**Chili Heights (82)** (KBishop) **6-11-1** RGreene (bit bkwd: prom tl rdn & wknd appr 5th: t.o)	dist	5	14/1	—	—
	Tilt Tech Flyer (82) (IRJones) **11-10-8**(7) MissEJJones (bit bkwd: chsd wnr tl after 6th: sn wknd: t.o)	7	6	$7/1^{3}$	—	—
	Queens Curate (67) (MrsEBScott) **9-10-0** BPowell (bit bkwd: prom early: bhd 5th: sn t.o)	dist	7	66/1	—	—
				(SP 111.6%)	**7 Rn**	

4m 21.4 (28.40) CSF £9.40 TOTE £2.30: £1.30 £2.90 (£7.50) OWNER Mrs Sarah Buckley (WELLINGTON) BRED Miss S. Von Schilcher
LONG HANDICAP Queens Curate 9-12
Friendly House (IRE) has improved considerably from his earlier efforts, but this was a weak contest. Making all the running, he only had one serious rival to contend with, and did it comfortably. (7/4: Evens-2/1)
Muhtashim (IRE) improved on his first two efforts this season, and should be able to pick up a race. (9/2: op 3/1)
1630 Daily Sport Girl was always behind and was beaten from some way out. (9/2)

1949 WEATHERBYS 1997 DIARY H'CAP CHASE (0-125) (5-Y.O+) (Class D)

2-20 (2-20) **2m 110y (11 fncs)** £3,424.20 (£1,035.60: £504.80: £239.40) GOING: 1.00 sec per fur (S)

				SP	RR	SF
1430^{2}	**James the First (115)** (PFNicholls) **8-11-11b** APMcCoy (lw: led tl mstke 2nd: led 4th: clr appr 2 out: unchal)	—	1	$6/5^{1}$	119	15
	Aal El Aal (105) (PJHobbs) **9-11-1** GTormey (lw: a.p: chsd wnr 8th: lost tch appr 2 out: fin tired: dismtnd)	22	2	$9/4^{2}$	88	—
1769^{P}	**Star of Italy (90)** (CPMorlock) **9-10-0** LHarvey (chsd wnr: led 2nd to 4th: hdd next: chsd wnr to 8th: sn wknd: t.o)	dist	3	16/1	—	—
	Allo George (113) (AGNewcombe) **10-11-9** AThornton (bit bkwd: in tch to 5th: t.o next)	dist	4	$11/4^{3}$	—	—
				(SP 108.8%)	**4 Rn**	

4m 29.9 (29.90) CSF £4.04 TOTE £1.80 (£2.00) OWNER Mr B. L. Blinman (SHEPTON MALLET) BRED Stetchworth Park Stud Ltd
LONG HANDICAP Star of Italy 9-10
1430 James the First, wearing blinkers for the first time over fences, scored in convincing style. He carries a reputation of being a rogue, but although patchy in the early stages, he soon put his best foot forward. (6/5)
Aal El Aal, who beat James the First in April, was now on 10lb worse terms. Keeping tabs on the winner, he weakened quickly and finished very tired in these heavy conditions. (9/4)
Allo George improved considerably last season, but was running over a trip short of his best. He will need at least another outing to his name and a longer distance to regain winning ways. (11/4)

1950 TOM HOLT AND REALITY NOVICES' HURDLE (4-Y.O+) (Class D)

2-50 (2-51) **2m 1f (8 hdls)** £2,911.90 (£818.40: £399.70) GOING: 1.00 sec per fur (S)

				SP	RR	SF
	Deano's Beeno (MCPipe) **4-10-12** CMaude (lw: hdwy to ld 5th: clr after next: unchal)	—	1	$100/30^{2}$	93+	44
$1757a^{6}$	**Lake Kariba (122)** (PFNicholls) **5-11-12** APMcCoy (lw: led to 2nd: led 4th: hdd next: wknd fr 6th)	dist	2	$Evens^{1}$	—	—
	Raffles Rooster (AGNewcombe) **4-10-12** AThornton (prom to 5th: grad wknd: t.o)	30	3	12/1	—	—
	Blade of Fortune (VGGreenway) **8-10-5**(7) MrJTizzard (bit bkwd: in rr: styd on fr 6th: nvr nrr: t.o)	24	4	33/1	—	—
	Spirit Level (73) (JRPayne) **8-11-2**ow9 MrRPayne (bkwd: a wl bhd: t.o 3rd)	dist	5	66/1	—	—
	Il Trastevere (FR) (MissGayKelleway) **4-10-12** DBridgwater (bit bkwd: led 2nd to 4th: wknd next: t.o whn p.u bef 2 out)		P	9/1	—	—
	Lees Please (IRE) (NGAyliffe) **4-10-12** GUpton (bkwd: a bhd: t.o 5th: p.u bef 2 out)		P	66/1	—	—
	Typhoon Eight (IRE) (BWHills) **4-10-12** BPowell (bit bkwd: chsd ldrs tl wknd 5th: t.o whn p.u bef 2 out)		P	$5/1^{3}$	—	—
133^{15}	**Jackamus (IRE)** (GAHam) **5-10-5**(7) MrMFrith (bit bkwd: bhd: rdn 4th: t.o next: p.u bef 6th)		P	100/1	—	—
				(SP 114.4%)	**9 Rn**	

4m 13.6 (20.60) CSF £6.69 TOTE £4.00: £1.50 £1.10 £2.20 (£3.20) Trio £15.20 OWNER The Blue Chip Group (WELLINGTON) BRED E. Gregory
Deano's Beeno, an average handicapper on the Flat, went clear with three left to jump and was never going to be caught. He looks a decent novice prospect. (100/30: 6/4-7/2)
1757a Lake Kariba was under a double-penalty, but met a useful debutant and may need a longer trip. (Evens)
Raffles Rooster, prominent in the early stages, weakened significantly after halfway. (12/1: op 6/1)
Il Trastevere (FR) (9/1: 5/1-10/1)
Typhoon Eight (IRE) (5/1: 3/1-11/2)

1951 POT BLACK CHILDCRAFT H'CAP CHASE (0-110) (5-Y.O+) (Class E)

3-20 (3-20) **2m 5f 110y (14 fncs)** £2,886.45 (£873.60: £426.30: £202.65) GOING: 1.00 sec per fur (S)

				SP	RR	SF
1839^{P}	**Titan Empress (81)** (SMellor) **7-10-0v** NMann (hld up: hdwy 9th: chsd ldr 11th: led next: clr 2 out: drvn out)	—	1	14/1	94	13
1697^{P}	**Country Keeper (84)** (BJMRyall) **8-10-3**ow3 GUpton (bhd: hdwy 11th: styd on wl fr 2 out)	2	2	20/1	96	12
1697^{4}	**Jailbreaker (93)** (BRMillman) **9-10-7**(5) DSalter (hdwy to ld 4th to 12th: sn outpcd: wknd 2 out)	12	3	$9/2^{3}$	96	15
	Giventime (105) (AndrewTurnell) **8-11-10** LHarvey (bit bkwd: chsd ldrs tl wknd appr 11th)	14	4	$4/1^{2}$	97	16
835^{*}	**Bit of A Touch (92)** (RGFrost) **10-10-11** CMaude (in tch to 9th: grad wknd)	19	5	5/1	70	—
1697^{*}	**Bramblehill Buck (IRE) (109)** (PFNicholls) **7-12-0b** APMcCoy (lw: chsd ldr tl reminder 5th: bhd 8th: sn t.o)	dist	6	$5/2^{1}$	—	—
1697^{P}	**Golden Opal (90)** (RHBuckler) **11-10-2**(7) MGriffiths (mid div: hdwy to chse ldr 9th: wknd appr 12th: p.u bef last: dismntd)		P	16/1	—	—

				SP	RR	SF
1598[2]	**Scotoni (95)** (RJO'Sullivan) **10-11-0** BPowell (led to 4th: wknd 8th: t.o whn p.u bef 11th)		**P**	7/1	—	—
				(SP 113.2%)		**8 Rn**

5m 49.5 (32.50) CSF £192.31 CT £1,325.87 TOTE £12.60: £2.60 £3.60 £1.20 (£76.60) OWNER Mr T. D. J. Syder (SWINDON) BRED Mrs John Thorneloe

LONG HANDICAP Titan Empress 9-12 Country Keeper 8-12

1420 Titan Empress took advantage of the below-par performances of some of her well-fancied opponents. Clear with two to jump, she had to battle to hold her lead to the line, but this form may prove deceptive. (14/1)

1426 Country Keeper was the only one close enough to put in a challenge to the winner on the run-in. (20/1)

Jailbreaker is a consistent individual and hinted at a return to form with this appearance. (9/2)

1697* Bramblehill Buck (IRE) had the unenviable task of carrying topweight in this heavy ground and backers knew their fate from some way out. (5/2: op 6/4)

1598 Scotoni (7/1: 4/1-8/1)

1952 BULPIN CHALLENGE CUP AMATEUR H'CAP HURDLE (0-120) (4-Y.O+) (Class E)

3-50 (3-51) **2m 6f (10 hdls)** £2,305.50 (£648.00: £316.50) GOING: 1.00 sec per fur (S)

				SP	RR	SF
1571[6]	**Top Javalin (NZ) (98)** (NJHawke) **9-10-2**(7) MrGShenkin (a.p: led appr 2 out: rdn out to hld on flat)	—	**1**	13/2 [3]	82	16
1681*	**Big Strand (IRE) (112)** (MCPipe) **7-11-4**(5) MrAFarrant (hld up: hdwy 7th: in tch 2 out: hrd rdn & ev ch last: styd on)	½	**2**	9/4 [1]	96	30
	Texan Baby (BEL) (115) (NATwiston-Davies) **7-11-9**(3) MrMRimell (in tch: ev ch 8th tl wknd appr 2 out)	19	**3**	10/1	85	19
1767[7]	**Fontainerouge (IRE) (89)** (GBBalding) **6-9-7**(7) MrEBabington (in tch tl wknd appr 8th)	2½	**4**	20/1	57	—
1794*	**Cokenny Boy (108)** (MrsJPitman) **11-10-12**(7) MrPCosgrave (prom: rdn to ld briefly after 8th: wknd appr 2 out)	4	**5**	15/2	73	7
1798[4]	**Oatis Rose (97)** (MSheppard) **6-10-1**(7) MrRWakley (bhd tl hdwy 7th: sn wknd)	4	**6**	4/1 [2]	59	—
1571[8]	**St Ville (96)** (RHBuckler) **10-10-0**(7) MissMCoombe (bhd: sme hdwy 7th: nvr nrr)	6	**7**	16/1	54	—
1568[5]	**Kings Cherry (IRE) (95)** (JABOld) **8-9-13**(7) MrGBaines (hdwy 6th: wknd 8th)	8	**8**	9/1	47	—
1659[P]	**Web of Steel (89)** (CJHemsley) **6-9-7**(7) MissADudley (bkwd: a bhd: mstke 5th: sn t.o)	dist	**9**	200/1	—	—
	Highly Decorated (94) (MissAMNewton-Smith) **11-9-12**(7)ow5 MissCJElliott (bkwd: a bhd: t.o 5th)	dist	**10**	100/1	—	—
	Pennymoor Prince (101) (RGFrost) **7-10-5**(7) MrAHoldsworth (bit bkwd: led: hdd 3rd: wknd after 6th: t.o whn p.u bef 2 out)		**P**	12/1	—	—
1681[P]	**Major Nova (95)** (NASmith) **7-9-13**(7) MrNBradley (bit bkwd: led 3rd: hdd 6th: sn wknd: t.o whn p.u bef 2 out)		**P**	25/1	—	—
1330[7]	**Zip Your Lip (89)** (MrsPTownsley) **6-9-7**(7) MissCTownsley (bhd fr 5th: t.o whn p.u bef 2 out)		**P**	33/1	—	—
1695[2]	**Hello Me Man (IRE) (89)** (BJLlewellyn) **8-9-7**(7) MissEJJones (in tch: led 6th: hdd 8th: wknd qckly: p.u bef 2 out)		**P**	8/1	—	—
				(SP 132.7%)		**14 Rn**

5m 46.5 (34.50) CSF £22.42 CT £146.43 TOTE £7.70: £2.20 £2.90 £3.50 (£14.30) Trio £75.00 OWNER Mrs Valerie Thum (CHARD) BRED Ainsley Downs No 3 Breeding Partnership

LONG HANDICAP Fontainerouge (IRE) 9-10 Highly Decorated 9-5 Web of Steel 8-4 Zip Your Lip 9-10

STEWARDS' ENQUIRY Cosgrave susp. 26-28 & 30-31/12/96 (excessive use of whip).

IN-FOCUS: This was a first winner as a trainer for Nigel Hawke, who won the Grand National on Seagram.

1571 Top Javalin (NZ), who has been lightly-raced in the last three seasons, had not won for nearly four years. Stepping up on his seasonal debut at Chepstow last month, he had to rally to hold his closest challenger on the run-in. (13/2)

1681* Big Strand (IRE) has creditable form to his name and travelled well throughout the race, but was found wanting on the run-in. (9/4)

Texan Baby (BEL) had a difficult task here under topweight in these conditions. (10/1: op 6/1)

1794* Cokenny Boy (15/2: 5/1-8/1)

1695 Hello Me Man (IRE) (8/1: op 14/1)

T/Plpt: £52.70 (149.48 Tckts). T/Qdpt: £56.60 (11.32 Tckts). T

1659-WARWICK (L-H) (Good to firm, Good patches)

Monday December 16th

WEATHER: overcast

1953 HAMPTON HURDLE (3-Y.O) (Class E)

12-30 (12-30) **2m (8 hdls)** £3,036.00 (£846.00: £408.00) GOING minus 0.29 sec per fur (GF)

				SP	RR	SF
	Name of Our Father (USA) (PBowen) **3-10-9**(3) DWalsh (hld up: hdwy appr 4th: wnt 2nd appr 3 out: led appr last: drvn out)	—	**1**	33/1	59	20
1595*	**Theme Arena** (MCPipe) **3-11-0** RHughes (lw: a.p: led appr 4th: clr 5th: hdd appr last: one pce)	3	**2**	2/1 [1]	58	19
640[7]	**Sheath Kefaah** (JRJenkins) **3-11-5v[1]** GBradley (hld up: hdwy appr 3 out: r.o flat)	4	**3**	14/1	59	20
1377[11]	**Impending Danger** (KSBridgwater) **3-10-9**(3) RMassey (hdwy after 3rd: one pce fr 3 out)	6	**4**	50/1	46	7
1634[11]	**Warning Reef** (CLPopham) **3-10-9**(3) TDascombe (mstke 2nd: hdwy appr 4th: wknd 5th)	10	**5**	14/1	36	—
640[6]	**Balmoral Princess** (JHPeacock) **3-11-0b** RBellamy (nvr nrr)	1¾	**6**	25/1	36	—
	Code Red (WRMuir) **3-10-12** JAMcCarthy (lw: nvr trbld ldrs)	6	**7**	16/1	28	—
1675*	**Lady Magnum (IRE)** (JNeville) **3-11-0** PHide (prom tl wknd after 3 out)	2	**8**	12/1 [3]	28	—
	Angus McCoatup (IRE) (MDHammond) **3-10-12** DBentley (bhd fr 5th)	7	**9**	14/1	19	—
1444*	**Crown And Cushion** (TRGreathead) **3-11-5** PHolley (bhd fr 5th)	1½	**10**	14/1	25	—
1862[P]	**Bright Eclipse (USA)** (MissKWhitehouse) **3-10-12** CLlewellyn (bhd fr 5th)	18	**11**	33/1	—	—
	Decision Maker (IRE) (KRBurke) **3-10-12** NWilliamson (bit bkwd: mstke 2nd: j.slowly 5th: sn bhd)	8	**12**	20/1	—	—
	Red Tie Affair (USA) (JMBradley) **3-10-12** DGallagher (led to 2nd: tried to run out 3rd: wknd 4th)	8	**13**	33/1	—	—
	Loch Dancer (MrsNMacauley) **3-10-7** SWynne (bit bkwd: a bhd: t.o fr 4th)	25	**14**	50/1	—	—
	Saucy Dancer (JCTuck) **3-10-7** SMcNeill (bkwd: a bhd: t.o fr 5th)	½	**15**	33/1	—	—
	Supergold (IRE) (CMurray) **3-10-12** KGaule (chsd ldrs to 4th: bhd whn blnd 3 out: t.o)	9	**16**	33/1	—	—
1712[8]	**Reem Fever (IRE)** (DWPArbuthnot) **3-10-8**ow1 MAFitzgerald (a bhd: t.o fr 5th)	18	**17**	50/1	—	—
	Toby Brown (DNicholson) **3-10-12** RJohnson (bhd whn fell 3rd)		**F**	14/1	—	—
1595[2]	**Jammy Jenny** (NATwiston-Davies) **3-10-7** TJenks (led 2nd tl appr 4th: p.u lame bef 5th)		**P**	8/1 [2]	—	—
	Extra Hour (IRE) (WRMuir) **3-10-12** MRichards (chsd ldrs tl wknd qckly 4th: p.u bef 5th)		**P**	25/1	—	—

	Horse	Dist	Pos	SP	RR	SF
	Albaha (USA) (JEBanks) **3-10-12** JRKavanagh (w.r.s: t.n.p)		**R**	2/1[1]	—	—
				(SP 157.7%)		**21 Rn**

3m 46.0 (4.00) CSF £113.15 TOTE £106.80: £17.10 £1.30 £7.30 (£64.60) Trio Not won; £178.84 to Folkestone 17/12/96 OWNER Mr T. M. Morris (HAVERFORDWEST) BRED Thomas P. Tatham

OFFICIAL EXPLANATION **Balmoral Princess: the rider explained that his instructions were to settle the filly in midfield and to finish as close as he could. He added that she was outpaced early on, and stayed on past beaten horses.**

Name of Our Father (USA) rather disappointed on the Flat after finishing second as a juvenile, but had apparently been working and schooling well. His trainer admitted to having had £2 win on the Tote! (33/1)

1595* Theme Arena found one too good on this step up from winning a seller. (2/1)

640 Sheath Kefaah, tried in a visor, finished in a style which suggested he would not be inconvenienced by a longer trip. (14/1)

Impending Danger showed considerable improvement on his hurdling debut last month. (50/1)

1444 Warning Reef (14/1: op 25/1)

458 Balmoral Princess caught the eye of the Stewards who accepted the explanation given at the subsequent enquiry, although her trainer did admit the filly ran as if she needed further. (25/1)

Angus McCoatup (IRE) (14/1: 10/1-16/1)

Toby Brown (14/1: 8/1-16/1)

1595 Jammy Jenny (8/1: 6/1-10/1)

Albaha (USA), who reached the frame on the Flat three times this year, is obviously far more used to starting stalls and seemed to get spooked by the tapes. (2/1)

1954 GOG BROOK H'CAP HURDLE (0-125) (4-Y.O+) (Class D)

1-00 (1-00) **2m (8 hdls)** £2,786.00 (£771.00: £368.00) GOING minus 0.29 sec per fur (GF)

	Horse	Dist	Pos	SP	RR	SF
1727*	**Severn Gale (96)** (JSAllen) **6-10-7**(7) XAizpuru (hld up: led appr 4th: rdn appr 2 out: r.o wl)	—	1	5/2[2]	85	24
1816*	**Pridewood Picker (88)** (RJPrice) **9-10-1**(5) DJKavanagh (hld up: hdwy 5th: ev ch 2 out: hung lft appr last: nt r.o)	8	2	10/11[1]	69	8
1715[P]	**Isaiah (110)** (MrsJCecil) **7-12-0** TKent (chsd ldrs: led after 3rd: sn hdd: hit 5th: sn rdn: wknd appr last)	1¾	3	10/1	89	28
1860[7]	**Euro Singer (98)** (PRWebber) **4-11-2** MAFitzgerald (led tl after 3rd: rdn appr 2 out: wknd appr last)	nk	4	9/2[3]	77	16
				(SP 108.2%)		**4 Rn**

3m 45.4 (3.40) CSF £4.99 TOTE £3.10 (£1.70) OWNER Mrs Carol Allen (ALCESTER) BRED Broomhill Stud

1727* Severn Gale proved far more resolute than the favourite off a 4lb higher mark. (5/2)

1816* Pridewood Picker likes to do it all on the bridle and certainly did not relish a battle. (10/11: evens-11/10)

1715 Isaiah, dropped 3lb, jumped better this time and at least showed he retains some ability. (10/1: op 6/1)

Euro Singer was ridden with a little more restraint here, but needs to come down in the weights. (9/2)

1955 BUDBROOKE NOVICES' CHASE (5-Y.O+) (Class D)

1-30 (1-30) **3m 2f (20 fncs)** £4,648.00 (£1,132.00) GOING minus 0.29 sec per fur (GF)

	Horse	Dist	Pos	SP	RR	SF
1522[3]	**Gysart (IRE)** (MCPipe) **7-11-0b** NWilliamson (mde all: wl clr 14th: blnd 3 out: eased flat)	—	1	8/15[1]	88+	—
1771[7]	**Irish Perry** (TMorton) **9-10-9** ILawrence (lft 3rd 5th: sn wl bhd: lft poor 2nd 14th)	dist	2	50/1	—	—
1423[3]	**Ramstown Lad (IRE)** (KCBailey) **7-11-0** CO'Dwyer (hld up: disp 2nd whn fell 5th)		F	7/4[2]	—	—
1829[P]	**The Marmalade Cat** (MrsDHaine) **7-10-11**(3) GHogan (chsd wnr: hit 11th: wkng whn fell 14th)		F	40/1[3]	—	—
				(SP 106.0%)		**4 Rn**

6m 52.5 (27.50) CSF £10.52 TOTE £1.40 (£5.90) OWNER The Hon Mrs R Cobbold (WELLINGTON) BRED J. Ward

1522 Gysart (IRE) found a soft race for his chasing debut, but gave those who had laid the odds a heart-stopping moment three out. (8/15)

1423 Ramstown Lad (IRE) made his exit at the second ditch. (7/4)

1956 ETTINGTON H'CAP HURDLE (0-120) (4-Y.O+) (Class D)

2-00 (2-00) **2m 3f (9 hdls)** £2,884.00 (£799.00: £382.00) GOING minus 0.29 sec per fur (GF)

	Horse	Dist	Pos	SP	RR	SF
1681[2]	**Reaganesque (USA) (107)** (PGMurphy) **4-11-8** JRKavanagh (chsd ldr: led appr 3 out: hit 2 out: drvn out)	—	1	3/1[2]	89	20
1859[3]	**Lord Mcmurrough (IRE) (110)** (JNeville) **6-11-11** NWilliamson (hld up: chsd wnr after 3 out: hrd rdn & hung lft appr last: r.o one pce flat)	2	2	3/1[2]	90	21
1661[5]	**Domappel (112)** (MrsJCecil) **4-11-13** TKent (hld up: mske & lost pl 6th: no hdwy fr 2 out)	6	3	13/8[1]	87	18
1767*	**Dominion's Dream (104)** (MCPipe) **4-10-12v**(7) GSupple (led tl appr 3 out: wknd appr 2 out)	12	4	7/2[3]	69	—
				(SP 110.3%)		**4 Rn**

4m 26.8 (6.80) CSF £10.82 TOTE £4.00 (£5.80) OWNER Mrs John Spielman (BRISTOL) BRED Gainsborough Farm Inc

1681 Reaganesque (USA), up 2lb, was only declared when the race was re-opened at the overnight stage, and Kavanagh has now won on both occasions he has ridden the gelding. (3/1)

1859 Lord Mcmurrough (IRE) needs softer ground than he encountered here. (3/1)

1661 Domappel, dropped 2lb, was still 7lb higher than when scoring here last month. (13/8)

1767* Dominion's Dream found this much tougher off a 6lb higher mark. (7/2: 9/4-4/1)

1957 STONELEIGH H'CAP CHASE (0-130) (5-Y.O+) (Class C)

2-30 (2-30) **2m 4f 110y (17 fncs)** £4,599.50 (£1,391.00: £678.00: £321.50) GOING minus 0.29 sec per fur (GF)

	Horse	Dist	Pos	SP	RR	SF
1731[2]	**Rex to the Rescue (IRE) (100)** (RHAlner) **8-10-4**(5) MrRThornton (led to 6th: led 4 out: drvn out)	—	1	4/1[2]	108	24
1641[2]	**Mr President (IRE) (102)** (CPEBrooks) **7-10-11** GBradley (hld up: hit 10th: hdwy appr 11th: outpcd 3 out: rallied appr last: nvr trbld wnr)	5	2	11/8[1]	106	22
1641[4]	**Crafty Chaplain (97)** (DMcCain) **10-10-3**(3) DWalsh (swtg: plld hrd: chsd ldr: led 6th to 4 out: hit 2 out: one pce)	1¾	3	10/1	100	16
1660[2]	**Bally Parson (112)** (RDickin) **10-11-7** NWilliamson (mstkes: a.p: btn whn hit 2 out & last)	3	4	5/1[3]	112	28
1660[4]	**Lake of Loughrea (IRE) (104)** (KCBailey) **6-10-13** CO'Dwyer (lw: hld up: hdwy 12th: mstke 3 out: wknd qckly)	21	5	6/1	88	4
1631[3]	**Andrelot (115)** (PBowen) **9-11-10b** RJohnson (s.i.s. rdn & sn prom: lost pl 8th: t.o fr 11th)	dist	6	10/1	—	—
1641[5]	**Nickle Joe (102)** (MTate) **10-10-11** WMarston (hdwy 5th: hrd rdn 10th: wknd 11th: sn t.o)	21	7	25/1	—	—
				(SP 115.1%)		**7 Rn**

5m 7.8 (3.80) CSF £9.80 TOTE £4.70: £2.30 £1.40 (£5.90) OWNER Mr Tony Thomas & Mr Stewart McDonald (BLANDFORD)

1731 Rex to the Rescue (IRE) gained just reward for some consistent performances. (4/1)

1641 Mr President (IRE) is finding things difficult off a rating 19lb higher than when winning at Newbury in March. (11/8)
1641 Crafty Chaplain was back down to the mark off which he had won at Fakenham. (10/1)
1660 Bally Parson found his jumping coming apart at the seams once the race began in earnest. (5/1: 3/1-11/2)
1660 Lake of Loughrea (IRE), without the blinkers this time, travelled well until halted by an error. (6/1: 4/1-13/2)
1063 Andrelot (10/1: 5/1-11/1)

1958 HOECHST ROUSSEL PANACUR E.B.F. 'N.H.' QUALIFIER NOVICES' HURDLE (4-Y.O+ F & M) (Class D)
3-00 (3-00) **2m 4f 110y (11 hdls)** £3,251.50 (£904.00: £434.50) GOING minus 0.29 sec per fur (GF)

			SP	RR	SF
1679^{P} **Konvekta Queen (IRE)** (OSherwood) **5-10-10** JOsborne (hld up: hdwy appr 7th: led on bit after 3 out: shkn up & wnt clr 2 out: easily)	—	**1**	$11/4^{1}$	62+	—
1539^{P} **Joy For Life (IRE) (60)** (RMStronge) **5-10-7**(3) DWalsh (chsd ldr to 7th: hrd rdn appr 2 out: styd on flat: no ch w wnr)	10	**2**	25/1	54	—
1341^{8} **Maylin Magic** (TCasey) **5-10-10** MAFitzgerald (hld up: hdwy appr 7th: hrd rdn appr 2 out: wknd flat)	6	**3**	$7/2^{2}$	50	—
1565^{P} **Briery Gale** (CaptTAForster) **6-10-10** SWynne (hld up: lost pl appr 7th: styd on flat)	2	**4**	10/1	48	—
Di's Last (MCPipe) **6-10-10** RHughes (swtg: led: clr 6th: hdd after 3 out: sn hrd rdn: wknd appr last)	2	**5**	$11/4^{1}$	46	—
1323^{8} **Wise 'n' Shine (64)** (NMLampard) **5-10-10** MrAKinane (wl bhd fr 6th)	12	**6**	50/1	37	—
1536^{P} **Nero's Gem** (CFCJackson) **5-10-10** WMcFarland (a bhd: t.o fr 7th)	dist	**7**	50/1	—	—
1341^{4} **Bridge Delight** (MJWilkinson) **7-10-3**(7) DCO'Connor (a bhd: t.o fr 7th)	nk	**8**	$9/2^{3}$	—	—
1467^{5} **Rosehall (73)** (MrsTDPilkington) **5-11-0**(3) GHogan (lw: dropped rr 6th: t.o whn p.u bef 7th)		**P**	14/1	—	—
1289^{16} **Special Topic** (APJones) **6-10-10** SCurran (prom: hit 5th: rdn 6th: sn bhd: t.o whn p.u bef 7th)		**P**	50/1	—	—
			(SP 119.2%)	**10 Rn**	

5m 3.3 (16.30) CSF £57.76 TOTE £4.30: £1.50 £4.70 £1.50 (£53.50) Trio £88.20 OWNER Konvekta Ltd (UPPER LAMBOURN) BRED Mrs E. Skelly

Konvekta Queen (IRE) presumably failed to handle the yielding ground at Worcester and made short work of these, despite being untidy at the last. (11/4: 2/1-3/1)
Joy For Life (IRE) seems to need further and this was very much a case of being best of the rest. (25/1)
Maylin Magic may do better back at two miles. (7/2)
Briery Gale gave the impression that the object was to get round in one piece. (10/1)
Di's Last, in the frame in all three of her bumpers, did not impress in the paddock. (11/4: 2/1-3/1)
1341 Bridge Delight (9/2: 5/2-5/1)
1180* Rosehall (14/1: 8/1-16/1)

1959 TEMPLE GRAFTON NOVICES' H'CAP HURDLE (0-105) (4-Y.O+) (Class D)
3-30 (3-30) **2m 3f (9 hdls)** £2,999.40 (£838.40: £406.20) GOING minus 0.29 sec per fur (GF)

			SP	RR	SF
1732* **Lets Be Frank (95)** (NoelChance) **5-11-4** RJohnson (a.p: led appr 2 out: drvn out)	—	**1**	$6/5^{1}$	79	—
1638^{2} **The Captain's Wish (108)** (DNicholson) **5-11-12**(5) MrRThornton (hld up: hdwy appr 6th: ev ch appr 2 out: hrd rdn appr last: r.o flat)	1	**2**	$5/2^{2}$	91	11
1251* **Always Greener (IRE) (79)** (JWMullins) **5-10-2** SCurran (led 3rd tl appr 2 out: rdn & r.o one pce)	¾	**3**	12/1	62	—
1663^{5} **Smart Lord (86)** (JRBosley) **5-10-9** MBosley (bhd tl r.o fr 3 out: nt rch ldrs)	4	**4**	16/1	65	—
1659^{4} **Evezio Rufo (87)** (NPLittmoden) **4-10-10v** JRKavanagh (prom tl ev ch 3 out: sn rdn & wknd)	10	**5**	$10/1^{3}$	58	—
1642^{7} **Sweet Trentino (IRE) (82)** (MTate) **5-10-5** WMarston (bhd whn mstke 4th: nvr trbld ldrs)	1¾	**6**	25/1	51	—
1451^{8} **Red Light (82)** (JRJenkins) **4-10-5b** GBradley (hld up: hdwy appr 5th: wknd appr 3 out)	2½	**7**	12/1	49	—
1726^{12} **Not To Panic (IRE) (77)** (KRBurke) **6-10-0** NWilliamson (mstke 6th: a bhd)	¾	**8**	33/1	44	—
1517^{5} **Blue And Royal (IRE) (84)** (VSoane) **4-10-7** CLlewellyn (prom tl wknd appr 5th)	8	**9**	33/1	44	—
1539^{4} **Positivo (77)** (MissCJECaroe) **5-10-0** DLeahy (a bhd)	6	**10**	12/1	32	—
1679^{9} **Becky's Girl (77)** (RBrotherton) **6-10-0** PHolley (led to 3rd: wknd appr 5th)	7	**11**	33/1	26	—
Sleazey (77) (JGO'Neill) **5-10-0** JOsborne (bkwd: prom tl wknd 6th: bhd whn p.u bef 2 out)		**P**	25/1	—	—
1278^{11} **Mr Gordon Bennett (77)** (RDickin) **5-9-7**(7) XAizpuru (plld hrd: bhd fr 5th: t.o whn p.u bef 2 out)		**P**	33/1	—	—
			(SP 131.5%)	**13 Rn**	

4m 31.6 (11.60) CSF £5.10 CT £22.75 TOTE £2.30: £1.10 £1.90 £2.70 (£3.80) Trio £19.90 OWNER Mrs M. M. Stobart (LAMBOURN) BRED Malcolm Armitage Penney
LONG HANDICAP Not To Panic (IRE) 9-2 Positivo 9-10 Becky's Girl 8-11 Mr Gordon Bennett 9-2
1732* Lets Be Frank did not find a further 5lb hike in the weights preventing him from completing a hat-trick. (6/5)
1638 The Captain's Wish had been raised 6lb for his good second at Sandown and lost nothing in defeat. (5/2)
1251* Always Greener (IRE) deserves full marks for a plucky effort in better company. (12/1)
1663 Smart Lord was never going to get to the leaders in time. (16/1)
1659 Evezio Rufo did not appear suited to this extended trip. (10/1: 7/1-11/1)
1539 Positivo (12/1: op 8/1)

T/Plpt: £189.30 (42.88 Tckts). T/Qdpt: £23.30 (25.62 Tckts). KH

1808-FOLKESTONE (R-H) (Chases Good, Good to soft patches, Hdles Good to soft)
Tuesday December 17th
WEATHER: dull

1960 LEVY BOARD H'CAP HURDLE (0-110) (4-Y.O+) (Class E)
12-30 (12-30) **2m 1f 110y (8 hdls)** £2,259.00 (£624.00: £297.00) GOING: 0.87 sec per fur (S)

			SP	RR	SF
1630^{5} **Zingibar (78)** (JMBradley) **4-10-6** NWilliamson (mde all: hrd rdn appr last: r.o wl)	—	**1**	$5/1^{3}$	62	19
1772* **Wayfarers Way (USA) (96)** (NJHenderson) **5-11-10** MAFitzgerald (lw: hdwy 3 out: chsd wnr fr 2 out: rdn appr last: wknd flat)	8	**2**	$Evens^{1}$	73	30
1828^{2} **Fontanays (IRE) (93)** (GMMcCourt) **8-11-7** DBridgwater (chsd wnr to 2 out: rdn & one pce)	1	**3**	11/2	69	26
1732^{4} **August Twelfth (86)** (DCO'Brien) **8-11-0** CLlewellyn (lw: bhd fr 3 out)	16	**4**	$3/1^{2}$	47	4
			(SP 107.1%)	**4 Rn**	

4m 29.5 (23.50) CSF £9.89 TOTE £5.80 (£2.70) OWNER Mr D. Holpin (CHEPSTOW) BRED Charlton Down Stud

1630 Zingibar was given a canny ride by Williamson. Setting a very moderate pace, he quickened things up entering the back straight and, responding to pressure, had the favourite beaten going to the last. This ended a losing sequence of sixteen. (5/1)
1772* Wayfarers Way (USA), who has been raised 7lb for his recent success, appeared to be travelling really well running down the hill but, when asked for an effort approaching the final flight, his stamina gave way. This trip on tacky ground is too far for him, and he really needs two miles on a sound surface. (Evens)
1828 Fontanays (IRE) could only plod on at the one pace from two out. Both his wins to date have come with more cut. (11/2: op 5/2)
1732 August Twelfth really needs the mud and a faster-run race to be seen to any real affect. (3/1)

1961 HEATHFIELD H'CAP CHASE (0-110) (5-Y.O+) (Class E)

1-00 (1-00) **3m 2f (19 fncs)** £3,590.00 (£1,070.00: £510.00: £230.00) GOING: 0.87 sec per fur (S)

				SP	RR	SF
1598^{3}	**Bally Clover (107)** (MissVenetiaWilliams) **9-11-12** NWilliamson (lw: hld up: 4th whn mstke 13th: led 15th: clr appr 2 out: all out)	—	1	7/4^{1}	107	20
833^{5}	**Banntown Bill (IRE) (90)** (MCPipe) **7-10-9v** CMaude (led tl j.slowly & hdd 2nd: chsd wnr fr 3 out: rdn appr 2 out: r.o flat)	2½	2	20/1	89	2
1817^{4}	**Glen Mirage (93)** (MJCoombe) **11-10-12** MissMCoombe (hdwy 11th: unable qckn fr 3 out)	3½	3	9/1	89	2
1839^{P}	**Credon (103)** (SWoodman) **8-11-8v^{1}** RDunwoody (lw: mstke 6th: hdwy 12th: one pce fr 14th)	1¼	4	15/2^{3}	99	12
1643^{4}	**Diamond Fort (109)** (JCMcConnochie) **11-12-0** BPowell (lw: hdwy 11th: wknd 13th)	10	5	4/1^{2}	98	11
1765^{10}	**Mr Invader (99)** (NAGaselee) **9-11-4** CLlewellyn (lw: prom to 15th: t.o)	dist	6	8/1	—	—
1684^{P}	**Sorbiere (95)** (NJHenderson) **9-11-0b** MAFitzgerald (lw: mstke 5th: 6th whn fell 9th)		F	12/1	—	—
23^{P}	**Vicar of Bray (90)** (LWells) **9-10-9** BClifford (a bhd: t.o whn p.u bef 8th)		P	20/1	—	—
1819^{P}	**King's Courtier (IRE) (81)** (SMellor) **7-10-0v^{1}** NMann (led 2nd to 15th: wknd appr 3 out: t.o whn p.u bef 2 out)		P	40/1	—	—
1863^{5}	**Joker Jack (83)** (RDean) **11-9-13**(3)ow2 TDascombe (lw: bhd fr 7th: t.o whn p.u bef 13th)		P	40/1	—	—
				(SP 111.3%)	**10 Rn**	

7m 2.1 (42.10) CSF £30.45 CT £219.04 TOTE £2.70: £1.30 £5.40 £2.40 (£14.90) Trio £47.90 OWNER Mr James Williams (HEREFORD) BRED Peter Magnier
LONG HANDICAP King's Courtier (IRE) 9-5 Joker Jack 8-9
1598 Bally Clover is well suited by the mud, but this tacky ground proved exhausting. Leading at the fifth last, he had nothing left in the tank at the end. (7/4)
Banntown Bill (IRE) bounced back to form. Taking second place three from home, he began to make inroads on the winner when that rival tired from the last, but was unable to peg him back in time. (20/1)
1817 Glen Mirage did not get much help from the saddle and, when the chips were down, his rider was unable to offer any real assistance. (9/1: 6/1-10/1)
1420 Credon looked in good shape beforehand and ran better than on his two previous outings, if made to look one-paced over the last six fences. (15/2: 5/1-8/1)
Diamond Fort (4/1: op 9/4)
1391 Sorbiere (12/1: op 6/1)

1962 SELLINDGE H'CAP HURDLE (0-105) (4-Y.O+) (Class F)

1-30 (1-31) **2m 6f 110y (11 hdls)** £2,156.60 (£597.60: £285.80) GOING: 0.87 sec per fur (S)

				SP	RR	SF
1786*	**Ainsi Soit II (FR) (94)** (GMMcCourt) **5-11-11b** DBridgwater (a.p: led 2 out: drvn out)	—	1	7/2^{2}	80	8
1561^{3}	**Rare Spread (IRE) (75)** (MCPipe) **6-10-6** CMaude (stdy hdwy 3 out: chsd wnr after 2 out: ev ch last: hrd rdn: nt r.o)	4	2	13/2	58	—
1541^{P}	**Roskeen Bridge (IRE) (69)** (CWeedon) **5-10-0** MRichards (a.p: rdn 8th: one pce)	4	3	25/1	49	—
1798^{P}	**Summer Haven (70)** (NMLampard) **7-10-1** MrAKinane (led after 1st to 2 out: sn wknd)	6	4	25/1	46	—
1786^{P}	**Lets Go Now (IRE) (69)** (MrsLCJewell) **6-9-9**(5) SophieMitchell (nvr nr to chal)	2½	5	100/1	43	—
1581^{5}	**Dream Leader (IRE) (96)** (MJRoberts) **6-11-13** JRailton (lw: led tl after 1st: rdn 2 out: sn wknd)	10	6	6/1^{3}	63	—
1841^{5}	**Raahin (USA) (85)** (SWoodman) **11-11-2** MBosley (lw: bhd fr 6th)	2	7	25/1	51	—
1582^{8}	**Its Grand (74)** (JMBradley) **7-10-5** RJohnson (prom to 6th)	1¾	8	10/1	39	—
1040^{8}	**Script (73)** (JRJenkins) **5-9-11**(7) NTEgan (a bhd)	14	9	25/1	28	—
1466^{2}	**Bright Sapphire (75)** (DBurchell) **10-10-6** DJBurchell (hdwy 6th: wknd 2 out)	4	10	9/1	27	—
1866^{5}	**Durshan (USA) (72)** (JRJenkins) **7-10-3b** JOsborne (lw: hdwy 5th: rdn 2 out: sn wknd)	13	11	10/1	14	—
1840^{6}	**Equity's Darling (IRE) (79)** (DCO'Brien) **4-10-10** CLlewellyn (lw: virtually ref to r: t.o whn b.d 3 out)		B	20/1	—	—
	Sweetly Disposed (IRE) (97) (NJHenderson) **8-11-7**(7) TCMurphy (bit bkwd: a bhd: t.o whn fell 3 out)		F	20/1	—	—
1536^{3}	**El Freddie (90)** (JABOld) **6-11-7** GUpton (bhd fr 6th: t.o whn p.u bef 7th)		P	3/1^{1}	—	—
				(SP 128.9%)	**14 Rn**	

5m 56.5 (39.50) CSF £26.94 CT £477.49 TOTE £5.80: £4.70 £1.50 £10.10 (£24.00) Trio £491.80; £561.17 to Catterick 18/12/96 OWNER A-Men Partnership (WANTAGE) BRED Jean-Luc Henry and Claude Mayot
LONG HANDICAP Lets Go Now (IRE) 8-10 Roskeen Bridge (IRE) 9-13
OFFICIAL EXPLANATION **El Freddie: the rider reported that the gelding felt flat and was never going. On pulling up he was found to be distressed.**
1786* Ainsi Soit II (FR) is obviously far happier back over hurdles and followed up his recent Chepstow seller victory, leading at the second last and proving far more resolute than the runner-up on the run-in. (7/2)
1561 Rare Spread (IRE) is definitely not one to trust and, not for the first time, proved very unco-operative. Cruising turning for home, he appeared to be laughing at the winner and was on level terms jumping the final flight but, asked for an effort, failed to go through with it. He should be left well alone. (13/2)
397 Roskeen Bridge (IRE) ran better here, if looking woefully one-paced over the last four hurdles. He has achieved little under Rules to date. (25/1)
Summer Haven again adopted front-running tactics but, collared two from home, was soon a spent force. She is a very poor performer. (25/1)
Lets Go Now (IRE), still carrying 13lb more than his long-handicap weight despite his rider's claim, struggled on past tired rivals to be nearest at the finish. Not too much should be read into this as he his basically a very bad performer. (100/1)
1581 Dream Leader (IRE) looked in tremendous shape, but he has been raised 11lb for scraping home at Windsor last month and has since been beaten at the same venue. He needs to come down in the weights. (6/1: op 4/1)
1866 Durshan (USA) (10/1: 7/1-11/1)
1536 El Freddie (3/1: 5/1-100/30)

1963 BET WITH THE TOTE (QUALIFIER) NOVICES' CHASE (5-Y.O+) (Class E)

2-00 (2-01) **2m 5f (15 fncs)** £4,175.00 (£1,250.00: £600.00: £275.00) GOING: 0.87 sec per fur (S)

Form	Horse	Dist	Pos	SP	RR	SF
	Melnik (MrsAJPerrett) **5-10-12** CMaude (lw: chsd ldr: led 2 out: rdn out)	—	1	9/1	109	15
	Conquering Leader (IRE) (NJHenderson) **7-10-7** MAFitzgerald (lw:a.p: chsd wnr fr 2 out: rdn appr last: r.o)	1¼	2	10/11[1]	103	9
	Sir Leonard (IRE) (OSherwood) **6-10-12** JOsborne (led to 2 out: unable qckn)	5	3	5/1[3]	104	10
	Sleetmore Gale (IRE) (TPMcGovern) **6-10-7** NWilliamson (hdwy 9th: 5th whn blnd 10th: wknd appr 2 out)	12	4	16/1	90	—
1196[4]	**Givus a Call (IRE)** (JTGifford) **6-10-12** PHide (lw: lost pl 10th: r.o one pce fr 2 out)	3	5	12/1	93	—
1596[2]	**Jovial Man (IRE)** (RJO'Sullivan) **7-10-12** DBridgwater (hdwy 11th: rdn appr 2 out: 4th & btn whn blnd bdly last)	3	6	4/1[2]	91	—
	Night Fancy (69) (MrsAMWoodrow) **8-10-12** PMcLoughlin (prom tl appr 2 out)	21	7	100/1	75	—
1728[P]	**Sheriffmuir (100)** (MrsLWadham) **7-10-9**(3) GHogan (a.p: 3rd whn blnd 10th: sn wknd)	17	8	16/1	62	—
1772[12]	**Carey's Cottage (IRE)** (MrsPTownsley) **6-10-12** LHarvey (a bhd)	13	9	100/1	52	—
	Lift and Load (USA) (80) (MJBolton) **9-10-9**(3) LAspell (bkwd: hdwy 9th: wknd 11th: t.o whn p.u bef 2 out: dismntd)		P	66/1	—	—
				(SP 122.0%)	**10 Rn**	

5m 39.8 (31.80) CSF £17.73 TOTE £12.20: £3.20 £1.60 £2.60 (£18.60) Trio £23.90 OWNER Mr Peter Wiegand (PULBUROUGH) BRED Sheikh Mohammed bin Rashid al Maktoum

IN-FOCUS: **This was a decent novice chase, especially by Folkestone standards and it would be a surprise if several winners did not come out of this race.**

Melnik looked extremely well for his reappearance and put up a good show on this chasing debut, leading at the second last and being ridden along to keep the runner-up at bay. Further success awaits him. (9/1: 6/1-10/1)

Conquering Leader (IRE), who has reportedly had knee problems, looked in good shape for this first run in over a year and made a very encouraging debut over fences. Given softer ground and a bit further, she should have no problems finding a race. (10/11: evens-11/10)

Sir Leonard (IRE) made an encouraging start to his chasing career on this reappearance. He is sure to come on for the run and should soon be winning. (5/1: op 5/2)

Sleetmore Gale (IRE) is an ex-Irish mare who won a maiden point-to-point in April before winning a maiden hurdle three months later. (16/1)

1196 Givus a Call (IRE), who failed to take to fences last season, returned to them here and managed to get round, staying on again over the last two fences having got outpaced a mile from home. This will hopefully have done his confidence some good. (12/1: 8/1-14/1)

1596 Jovial Man (IRE) had ground and trip more in his favour this time. Pushed along turning for home, he was held in fourth place when all but falling at the final fence. (4/1)

1964 LYMPNE NOVICES' HURDLE (4-Y.O+) (Class E)

2-30 (2-31) **2m 4f 110y (10 hdls)** £2,805.00 (£780.00: £375.00) GOING: 0.87 sec per fur (S)

Form	Horse	Dist	Pos	SP	RR	SF
	Rough Quest (TCasey) **10-10-12** MAFitzgerald (lw: stdy hdwy 7th: 4th whn mstke 3 out: chsd ldr appr last: mstke last: rdn to ld nr fin)	—	1	5/1[2]	97+	—
	Destin d'Estruval (FR) (DNicholson) **5-10-12** DBridgwater (a.p: led 2 out: rdn appr last: hdd nr fin)	½	2	11/4[1]	97+	—
1659[2]	**Royal Event** (DRGandolfo) **5-10-12** RDunwoody (a.p: led 3 out to 2 out: wknd appr last)	25	3	11/4[1]	77	—
1317[7]	**Safeglide (IRE)** (JTGifford) **6-10-12** PHide (mstke 1st: lost pl 6th: rallied 2 out: wknd appr last)	5	4	11/1[3]	73	—
1766[6]	**Flaxley Wood** (RHBuckler) **5-10-12** BPowell (lw: nvr nr to chal)	10	5	33/1	65	—
1151*	**Danzante (IRE)** (RMStronge) **4-10-7**(5) MrRThornton (a bhd)	8	6	20/1	59	—
1835[U]	**Kybo's Revenge (IRE)** (RRowe) **5-10-12** DO'Sullivan (lw: a bhd)	hd	7	50/1	59	—
1795[8]	**Dingle Wood (IRE)** (NMLampard) **6-10-12** MrAKinane (a.p: led appr 5th to 3 out: sn wknd: t.o)	dist	8	16/1	—	—
	Sullamell (RJHodges) **5-10-5**(7) JHarris (led tl appr 5th: sn wknd: t.o whn p.u bef 6th)		P	33/1	—	—
1476[2]	**Captain Jack** (MCPipe) **6-10-12b** RHughes (prom to 7th: t.o whn p.u bef 2 out)		P	11/4[1]	—	—
1640[15]	**Noquita (NZ)** (JCMcConnochie) **9-10-12** JRKavanagh (lw: a bhd: t.o whn p.u bef 6th)		P	40/1	—	—
1766[7]	**Master Bomber (IRE)** (RHAlner) **5-10-12** JOsborne (bhd fr 3 out: t.o whn p.u bef last)		P	50/1	—	—
	Pett Lad (JSHomewood) **8-10-12** MRichards (bkwd: a bhd: t.o whn p.u bef 6th)		P	50/1	—	—
	Over The Water (IRE) (RHAlner) **4-10-9**(3) PHenley (bit bkwd: a bhd: t.o whn p.u bef last)		P	20/1	—	—
				(SP 134.6%)	**14 Rn**	

5m 13.0 CSF £20.35 TOTE £6.00: £1.30 £2.80 £1.40 (£17.50) Trio £37.60 OWNER Mr A. T. A. Wates (DORKING)

IN-FOCUS: **This novice hurdle would not have been out of place at one of the big tracks and featured several useful sorts, not least of all the Grand National winner.**

Rough Quest, whose only previous run over hurdles was back in May 1991, was only running here because of the abandonment of Haydock on Saturday, and his trainer was desperate to get a run into him before the King George. Looking on very good terms with himself beforehand, he oozed class and travelled really well throughout the race, stylishly picking up his rivals in the last mile. Drawing alongside the leader approaching the last, he made a mistake at the final flight and gave the best part of two lengths to his rival on the run-in. Galvanized into action, he rallied splendidly to poke his head in front with 10 yards to go. This should have put a nice edge on him for the Christmas showdown with One Man. (5/1: 3/1-11/2)

Destin d'Estruval (FR), an ex-French gelding who won on the Flat in 1994 and a two-mile chase at Auteuil, was in the frame on both his runs over hurdles earlier this year. Bought by Martin Pipe for owner Darren Mercer, he was making his British debut for David Nicholson and did extremely well. He managed to go two lengths up on Rough Quest on the run-in but, despite all his efforts, was just worried out of it in the last 10 yards. He looks a ready-made winner and could turn out to be pretty useful. (11/4)

1659 Royal Event had been shaping as though this longer trip would suit, and a race should soon be found. (11/4)

Safeglide (IRE), who lost his pitch setting out on the final circuit, got back into it two from home before tiring. (11/1: 6/1-12/1)

1965 SHADDOXHURST CONDITIONAL H'CAP CHASE (0-100) (5-Y.O+) (Class F)

3-00 (3-02) **2m (12 fncs)** £2,710.80 (£748.80: £356.40) GOING: 0.87 sec per fur (S)

Form	Horse	Dist	Pos	SP	RR	SF
1584[7]	**Pegmarine (USA) (79)** (MrsAMWoodrow) **13-11-7** GHogan (hdwy 3 out: led appr last: r.o wl)	—	1	13/2	89	7
1170[5]	**Soleil Dancer (IRE) (84)** (DMGrissell) **8-11-12** PHenley (hdwy 8th: rdn appr 2 out: r.o flat)	1½	2	11/1	93	11
1769[2]	**Fichu (USA) (79)** (MrsLRichards) **8-11-4**(3) MClinton (chsd ldr fr 5th: led appr 2 out: mstke 2 out: hdd appr last: wknd flat)	9	3	15/8[1]	79	—
1423[P]	**Cruise Control (81)** (RRowe) **10-11-6**(3) AGarrity (bit bkwd: nvr nr to chal)	½	4	20/1	80	—
1714[4]	**Shalik (IRE) (79)** (JRJenkins) **6-11-4**(3) NTEgan (led & sn clr: hdd appr 2 out: sn wknd)	16	5	7/1	62	—
1421*	**Dawn Chance (79)** (RJHodges) **10-11-7** TDascombe (chsd ldr to 5th: wknd 6th: t.o)	dist	6	5/1[3]	—	—
1708[2]	**Willie Makeit (IRE) (83)** (RTPhillips) **6-11-11** MartinSmith (lw: mstke & uns rdr 1st)		U	7/2[2]	—	—

(SP 112.6%) **7 Rn**
4m 19.9 (27.90) CSF £60.71 TOTE £9.30: £3.00 £5.50 (£24.90) OWNER Mrs Ann Woodrow (HIGH WYCOMBE) BRED Dr Archie Donaldson
Pegmarine (USA) bounced back to form, leading approaching the last and keeping on too well for his rivals. (13/2)
Soleil Dancer (IRE), returning to fences for the first time since the 1994-95 season, ran better and stuck on well for second. (11/1: 8/1-12/1)
1769 Fichu (USA) was much happier on this return to the minimum trip and moved to the front approaching the second last. However, he was untidy at that fence and, soon headed, tired in the tacky ground. (15/8)
Cruise Control, still looking in need of the outing, stayed on when it was all over, and needs a return to three miles. (20/1)
1714 Shalik (IRE) stormed off in front but, in these energy-sapping conditions, was collared approaching the second last. (7/1: 9/2-8/1)
1708 Willie Makeit (IRE) (7/2: op 9/4)

1966 WEATHERBYS 'STARS OF TOMORROW' STANDARD OPEN N.H. FLAT RACE (4, 5 & 6-Y.O) (Class H)
3-30 (3-31) **2m 1f 110y** £1,322.00 (£367.00: £176.00)

			SP	RR	SF
	Guido (IRE) (MissVenetiaWilliams) **5-11-4** NWilliamson (stdy hdwy over 7f out: chsd ldr over 2f out: led 1f out: all out)......—	**1**	12/1	67 f	—
	Brownes Hill Lad (IRE) (RJO'Sullivan) **4-12-0** DBridgwater (lw: led to 1f out: hrd rdn: r.o wl)......nk	**2**	4/1 2	77 f	—
1457[10]	**Mike's Music (IRE)** (DMGrissell) **5-11-1**(3) GHogan (a.p: rdn over 2f out: sn wknd)......19	**3**	20/1	49 f	—
1555[2]	**Supreme Troglodyte (IRE)** (CPMorlock) **4-10-13** JRKavanagh (a.p: rdn over 2f out: sn wknd)......½	**4**	3/1 1	44 f	—
	Hurricane Jane (IRE) (MJRoberts) **4-10-13** JRailton (lw: hdwy 5f out: rdn over 2f out: sn wknd)......2	**5**	33/1	42 f	—
1177[5]	**Jaydeebee** (MMadgwick) **5-10-13** GUpton (a.p: rdn over 2f out: sn wknd)......5	**6**	25/1	38 f	—
	Christchurch (FR) (SEarle) **6-11-4** MrDBreen (hdwy over 9f out: wknd over 4f out)......9	**7**	40/1	34 f	—
	Benji (TCasey) **5-11-4** MAFitzgerald (hdwy over 9f out: wknd over 2f out)......11	**8**	12/1	24 f	—
	Kilshey (JTGifford) **5-10-13** PHide (hdwy over 3f out: wknd over 2f out)......½	**9**	8/1	19 f	—
	Roman Actor (JJSheehan) **4-11-4** DO'Sullivan (bit bkwd: nvr nrr)......7	**10**	40/1	17 f	—
	Full of Bounce (IRE) (RJHodges) **5-11-1**(3) TDascombe (bit bkwd: prom 12f)......2	**11**	20/1	16 f	—
	Eurochief (RMStronge) **5-10-13**(5) MrRThornton (hdwy over 9f out: wknd over 6f out)......3	**12**	33/1	13 f	—
1685[16]	**Spirit of Success** (NMLampard) **6-11-4** MrAKinane (lw: prom over 4f)......10	**13**	50/1	4 f	—
1573[7]	**St Mellion Leisure (IRE)** (MCPipe) **4-11-4** CMaude (w ldr over 11f)......6	**14**	5/1 3	—	—
	Young Manny (AEJessop) **5-11-4** RJohnson (lw: a bhd: t.o fnl 6f)......13	**15**	50/1	—	—
	Saras Delight (DNicholson) **4-11-1**(3) RMassey (bhd fnl 4f: t.o)......28	**16**	4/1 2	—	—
	Colonel Jack (RJHodges) **4-10-11**(7) JHarris (lw: a bhd: t.o fnl 7f)......dist	**17**	33/1	—	—

(SP 139.2%) **17 Rn**
4m 26.0 CSF £62.59 TOTE £13.60: £2.20 £2.50 £6.40 (£41.70) Trio Not won; £349.12 to Catterick 18/12/96 OWNER Mr P. Tompsett (HEREFORD) BRED Dermot O'Reilly Hyland
Guido (IRE), in a tremendous battle with the runner-up, just managed to prevail with little left in the tank. (12/1)
Brownes Hill Lad (IRE), an ex-Irish gelding who won bumpers at Tralee in August and Limerick in October, was faced with a stiff 10lb penalty for those successes, but ran extremely well on his first outing for his new stable. Showing a never-say-die attitude, he just failed to get back up, and his new connections should not have to wait long for a trip to the winner's enclosure. (4/1)
Mike's Music (IRE) was left for dead by the front two in the straight. (20/1)
1555 Supreme Troglodyte (IRE) had shot her bolt early in the short straight. (3/1)
Hurricane Jane (IRE) had cooked her goose entering the short straight. (33/1)
Jaydeebee is a half-sister to Master Oats. (25/1)
Kilshey (8/1: 5/1-10/1)
St Mellion Leisure (IRE) (5/1: 5/2-11/2)
Saras Delight (4/1: 2/1-9/2)

T/Jkpt: Not won; £5,937.25 to Bangor-On-Dee 18/12/96. T/Plpt: £2,135.70 (4.72 Tckts). T/Qdpt: £103.70 (20.83 Tckts). AK

1821-MUSSELBURGH (R-H) (Firm, Good to firm patches)
Tuesday December 17th
WEATHER: fine

1967 TABLE MAIDEN HURDLE (4-Y.O+) (Class E)
12-20 (12-22) **2m 4f (12 hdls)** £2,263.50 (£636.00: £310.50) GOING minus 0.56 sec per fur (F)

			SP	RR	SF
	Invest Wisely (MDHammond) **4-11-5** RGarritty (lw: w ldr: led 7th: slipped bdly 3 out: hdd 2 out: rallied to ld cl home)......—	**1**	5/6 1	74	7
1470[2]	**Smolensk (IRE)** (JBerry) **4-11-5** MMoloney (lw: trckd ldrs: hmpd 3 out: led 2 out: clr whn hit last: sn rdn: hdd & no ex towards fin)......nk	**2**	6/5 2	74	7
1666[9]	**Nizaal (USA)** (RAllan) **5-10-12**(7) SMelrose (in tch: hdwy & ch 3 out: outpcd fr next)......18	**3**	16/1 3	59	—
1821[P]	**Celtic Comma** (WGReed) **5-11-0** TReed (led 2nd to 7th: sn rdn: wknd after 3 out)......20	**4**	66/1	38	—
1667[11]	**Super Guy** (JBarclay) **4-11-5** ADobbin (led to 2nd: t.o fr ½-wy)......3	**5**	50/1	41	—
1666[U]	**Royal Palm** (VThompson) **4-11-5** KJones (t.o fr ½-wy)......dist	**6**	66/1	—	—

(SP 110.8%) **6 Rn**
4m 47.1 (5.10) CSF £2.08 TOTE £1.80: £1.00 £1.50 (£1.10) OWNER Mr A. G. Chappell (MIDDLEHAM) BRED Littleton Stud
Invest Wisely won this through sheer stamina and, as he tries further, he should improve. (5/6: evens-4/5)
1470 Smolensk (IRE) seemed to have this sewn up going to the last, but did not stay anything like as well as the winner and was worried out of it. (6/5: evens-5/4)
Nizaal (USA) showed something and will probably be happier over the minimum trip. (16/1)
Celtic Comma was beaten a long way but, considering she had been pulled up on her previous three starts, this was an improvement. (66/1)

1968 BATHING COACH NOVICES' CHASE (5-Y.O+) (Class E)
12-50 (12-51) **3m (18 fncs)** £2,831.85 (£856.80: £417.90: £198.45) GOING minus 0.56 sec per fur (F)

			SP	RR	SF
1826[2]	**Heddon Haugh (IRE)** (PCheesbrough) **8-10-12** RSupple (lw: led 4th to 4 out: chal & hit 2 out: styd on to ld cl home)......—	**1**	100/30 2	83	—
1853[6]	**Fingerhill (IRE)** (VThompson) **7-10-12** MrMThompson (j.lft: a.p: led 4 out: sn rdn: hdd & no ex towards fin)..½	**2**	7/1	83	—
1845[F]	**Miss Lamplight (72)** (FPMurtagh) **6-10-7** ADobbin (hld up: stdy hdwy fr 12th: ev ch 3 out: nt qckn appr last)..3	**3**	7/1	76	—

1826[4] **Overwhelm (IRE) (88)** (VThompson) **8-11-2** KJones (in tch tl wknd appr 4 out: blnd bdly 3 out)....................18 **4** 5/1[3] 73 —
1691[6] **The Energiser (67)** (DALamb) **10-10-12** JBurke (swtg: hld up: hdwy ½-wy: ev ch 14th: sn wknd).....................9 **5** 20/1 63 —
1576[8] **Mister Casual (72)** (WGReed) **7-10-12** TReed (a bhd: t.o whn p.u lame flat)....................................... **P** 8/1 — —
1691[4] **Corporal Kirkwood (IRE)** (MartinTodhunter) **6-10-12** PNiven (lw: mstkes: cl up tl mstke & uns rdr 11th).......... **U** 3/1[1] — —
8[P] **Establish (IRE) (76)** (JPDodds) **8-10-7** KJohnson (swtg: led to 4th: chsd ldrs tl outpcd 14th: 4th & styng on whn blnd & uns rdr 4 out).. **U** 16/1 — —
(SP 111.5%) **8 Rn**

6m 5.6 (12.60) CSF £23.77 TOTE £3.40: £1.10 £2.20 £2.30 (£22.20) OWNER Mr I. D. Cheesbrough (BISHOP AUCKLAND) BRED James Keegan

1826 Heddon Haugh (IRE), a shade fractious at the start, jumped off on terms and proved very determined in a driving finish to win a very poor race. (100/30)

1853 Fingerhill (IRE) had a golden chance here, but did not help matters by continually jumping left, and was just outsprinted. (7/1)

802 Miss Lamplight got round for the first time over fences and looked a big danger, but she failed to see it out when pressure was applied. (7/1)

1826 Overwhelm (IRE), the only one in the field to have won any sort of race, looked very slow. (5/1)

1691 Corporal Kirkwood (IRE), the paddock pick, was clumsy at his fences from the outset and finally shook his rider off with a mistake at the first fence in the back straight. (3/1)

Establish (IRE) has ability, but sweats badly beforehand. To give her credit, she was staying on in fourth place when she blundered her rider out of the saddle four out. (16/1)

1969 SEA HOLE (S) H'CAP HURDLE (0-95) (4-Y.O+) (Class G)

1-20 (1-20) **2m (8 hdls)** £2,083.20 (£585.20: £285.60) GOING minus 0.56 sec per fur (F)

SP RR SF

1686[4] **Triennium (USA) (79)** (PMonteith) **7-11-13** ADobbin (t: lw: trckd ldrs: led 2 out: r.o).......................................— **1** 10/11[1] 62 25
1703[10] **Seconds Away (53)** (JSGoldie) **5-9-12**(3) GLee (hld up: hdwy appr 2 out: sn chsng wnr: nt qckn flat)...............3 **2** 7/1[3] 33 —
1703[12] **Catton Lady (52)** (RCraggs) **6-9-7**(7) BGrattan (prom: outpcd 2 out: kpt on wl towards fin)...............................1 **3** 16/1 31 —
1775[P] **Troy's Dream (67)** (MDHammond) **5-11-1** RGarritty (bhd: gd hdwy & prom 3 out: ch between last 2: sn rdn & btn)...1½ **4** 10/1 45 8
School of Science (58) (DANolan) **6-10-6** SMcDougall (nvr bttr than mid div)...4 **5** 25/1 32 —
1666[7] **Greek Gold (IRE) (54)** (DWBarker) **7-10-2** RMarley (lw: cl up: led 5th to 2 out: wknd).................................11 **6** 5/1[2] 17 —
1703[13] **Dark Midnight (IRE) (58)** (DALamb) **7-10-6bow3** JBurke (effrt & mstke 4th: n.d).....................................1¾ **7** 33/1 19 —
1824[6] **Barik (IRE) (62)** (BMactaggart) **6-10-10** BStorey (led to 5th: wknd appr 2 out)..11 **8** 12/1 12 —
1821[4] **Miss Mont (53)** (FPMurtagh) **7-10-1** GCahill (chsd ldrs tl mstke & uns rdr 3rd).. **U** 12/1 — —
(SP 118.7%) **9 Rn**

3m 40.4 (1.40) CSF £8.11 CT £59.84 TOTE £2.50: £1.20 £1.40 £3.20 (£9.00) Trio £82.80 OWNER Mr M. C. Boyd (ROSEWELL) BRED Fittocks Stud Ltd

LONG HANDICAP Catton Lady 9-13

No bid

1686 Triennium (USA), tubed for the first time and dropped in grade, did it in decent enough style. (10/11)

1141 Seconds Away looked dangerous for a stride or two at the second last but, once pressure was applied, his limitations were quickly exposed. (7/1)

1078 Catton Lady shaped pretty well and, judging by the way she finished, she will do better when tried over further. (16/1)

Troy's Dream, happier at this shorter trip, almost got into contention two out, only then to run out of steam. (10/1: op 4/1)

Greek Gold (IRE) travels well, but had trouble in staying the trip, and needs more patient handling. (5/1)

1821 Miss Mont (12/1: op 8/1)

1970 MUSSELBURGH LINKS H'CAP CHASE (0-120) (5-Y.O+) (Class D)

1-50 (1-50) **2m 4f (16 fncs)** £3,485.00 (£1,055.00: £515.00: £245.00) GOING minus 0.56 sec per fur (F)

SP RR SF

1361[4] **Montrave (99)** (PMonteith) **7-11-3** ADobbin (hld up: hdwy to ld 4 out: r.o).......................................— **1** 5/1[3] 109 30
1823[3] **Puritan (CAN) (110)** (NTinkler) **7-12-0b** MissPJones (lw: trckd ldrs: chal 4 out: blnd 2 out: rallied towards fin)..¾ **2** 7/2[2] 119 40
1823[2] **Pagliaccio (99)** (MDHammond) **8-11-3** RGarritty (w ldr: led 7th: hit 9th: hdd & mstke 4 out: blnd 3 out: one pce after)...6 **3** 9/4[1] 104 25
1847[7] **Risky Dee (85)** (VThompson) **7-10-3ow3** KJones (in tch: kpt on fr 3 out: no imp)..6 **4** 66/1 85 3
1268[3] **Cross Cannon (110)** (JWade) **10-12-0** TReed (hld up: hdwy ½-wy: outpcd 12th: n.d after)...........................1¾ **5** 5/1[3] 108 29
1823* **Charming Gale (101)** (MrsSCBradburne) **9-11-0v**(5) 6x GFRyan (lw: led to 7th: cl up tl rdn & wknd 4 out: hit 3 out)...4 **6** 7/2[2] 96 17
(SP 110.0%) **6 Rn**

4m 54.6 (-1.40) CSF £20.65 TOTE £5.90: £2.90 £2.70 (£8.20) OWNER Mr D. St Clair (ROSEWELL) BRED Miss C. E. J. Dawson

LONG HANDICAP Risky Dee 9-8

1361 Montrave, from a yard in from, was trying this trip for the first time over fences and, getting it well, won most convincingly. (5/1)

1823 Puritan (CAN), back to his optimum trip, spoilt his chances with a bad mistake at the second last. (7/2)

1823 Pagliaccio did his usual and beat himself. (9/4)

Risky Dee, over a trip a bit on the sharp side, ran quite well without seriously getting into it. (66/1)

1268 Cross Cannon is good on his day, but he does not have them very often. (5/1)

1823* Charming Gale was never able to dominate and was already struggling three out when a blunder three out finished her chances. (7/2)

1971 GAS H'CAP HURDLE (0-125) (4-Y.O+) (Class D)

2-20 (2-20) **3m (13 hdls)** £2,705.00 (£815.00: £395.00: £185.00) GOING minus 0.56 sec per fur (F)

SP RR SF

1701[5] **Supertop (105)** (LLungo) **8-11-5** RGarritty (lw: hld up: hdwy to chse ldr 9th: led on bit after 2 out: r.o)...........— **1** 5/2[3] 89 28
1844[4] **D'Arblay Street (IRE) (86)** (WTKemp) **7-10-0b** SMcDougall (lw: led tl after 2 out: kpt on same pce)..................6 **2** 4/1 66 5
1671[6] **Tallywagger (114)** (GMMoore) **9-11-7**(7) THogg (chsd ldr: effrt 3 out: r.o one pce)...1¼ **3** 2/1[1] 93 32
1344* **Latin Leader (86)** (CParker) **6-10-0b** DParker (lw: mstkes: chsd ldrs: outpcd 9th: wknd fr 2 out)...................dist **4** 9/4[2] — —
(SP 112.7%) **4 Rn**

5m 39.1 (4.30 under best) (-0.90) CSF £10.97 TOTE £2.90 (£8.90) OWNER Mr G. A. Arthur (CARRUTHERSTOWN) BRED Limestone Stud

1701 Supertop, given a fine ride, enjoyed the strong pace. Kept on the bridle, there were never any doubts about the result. (5/2)

1844 D'Arblay Street (IRE) stays forever and tried to make that tell. In doing so, he set the race up for the winner. (4/1)

1671 Tallywagger is just a stayer and was well tapped for toe in the closing stages. (2/1)

1344* Latin Leader, trying a longer trip, did not help matters with some sloppy hurdling. His measure had been taken by the second last, from which point he was given an easy time. (9/4)

1972 HOLE ACROSS H'CAP CHASE (0-95) (5-Y.O+) (Class F)

2-50 (2-50) **2m (12 fncs)** £2,734.10 (£767.60: £374.30) GOING minus 0.56 sec per fur (F)

				SP	RR	SF
975^{2}	**Cardenden (IRE) (68)** (JBarclay) **8-10-1** BStorey (mde most: hld on wl)	—	1	5/2^{2}	74	7
1824^{5}	**Rapid Mover (91)** (DANolan) **9-11-10b** MMoloney (trckd wnr: chal 4 out: slt ld 2 out: hdd last: kpt on towards fin)	½	2	4/1^{3}	97	30
1833^{2}	**Judicial Field (IRE) (95)** (NTinkler) **7-12-0b** RGarritty (trckd ldrs: blnd 8th: sn rdn: nt qckn fr 3 out)	6	3	11/10^{1}	95	28
1306^{5}	**Flash of Realm (FR) (95)** (BMactaggart) **10-11-7**(7) IJardine (nvr wnt pce)	13	4	8/1	82	15

(SP 107.3%) **4 Rn**

3m 54.8 (0.80) CSF £10.48 TOTE £2.80 (£5.30) OWNER Kinneston Farmers (LESLIE) BRED Ronald McKelvey

975 Cardenden (IRE), although not very quick, is honest and, made plenty of use of, was too tough for the runner-up. (5/2)

1824 Rapid Mover, always in the right position, looked to be going best two out but, when it came down to a struggle, he just found the winner too determined. (4/1)

1833 Judicial Field (IRE) showed enough to suggest that there is another race or two in him, but a mistake five out finished his hopes. (11/10)

1306 Flash of Realm (FR) has yet to show anything positive this season. (8/1: op 4/1)

1973 SHORT HOLE STANDARD N.H. FLAT RACE (4, 5 & 6-Y.O) (Class H)

3-20 (3-20) **2m** £1,070.00 (£295.00: £140.00)

				SP	RR	SF
1827*	**Carlisle Bandito's (IRE)** (JBerry) **4-11-11** MMoloney (hld up: hdwy on bit to ld over 1f out: shkn up & qcknd)	—	1	6/4^{2}	53 f	—
787*	**Sioux Warrior** (NTinkler) **4-11-8**(3) EHusband (lw: led tl over 1f out: nt pce of wnr)	6	2	7/2^{3}	47 f	—
1692^{4}	**Nutty Solera** (CParker) **6-11-11** BStorey (trckd ldr: chal ½-wy: rdn & one pce fnl 3f)	nk	3	5/4^{1}	47 f	—
1692^{17}	**Salem Beach** (MartinTodhunter) **4-10-13** PNiven (lw: in tch tl outpcd fnl 3f)	10	4	20/1	25 f	—

(SP 111.4%) **4 Rn**

3m 38.0 CSF £6.48 TOTE £2.20 (£2.60) OWNER Mr Chris Deuters (COCKERHAM) BRED Brendan and Sheila Powell

1827* Carlisle Bandito's (IRE) settles well, has a good turn of foot, and was always travelling too strongly for the opposition. (6/4)

787* Sioux Warrior tried hard to make all, but had no answer to the winner's turn of speed in the last furlong and a half. (7/2)

1692 Nutty Solera raced a bit too freely early on and then failed to quicken at the business end. (5/4)

Salem Beach is improving, but there is still some way to go. (20/1)

T/Plpt: £188.90 (33.6 Tckts). T/Qdpt: £114.10 (5.63 Tckts). AA

1713-SOUTHWELL (L-H) - Tuesday December 17th

1974 Abandoned-Fog

1628-BANGOR-ON-DEE (L-H) (Chase Good, Good to soft patches, Hdles Good) Wednesday December 18th

Vis: poor races 6 & 7
WEATHER: overcast & dull

1980 MAESFAN NOVICES' (S) HURDLE (3, 4 & 5-Y.O) (Class G)

12-30 (12-30) **2m 1f (9 hdls)** £2,088.50 (£586.00: £285.50) GOING: 0.69 sec per fur (S)

				SP	RR	SF
	D'naan (IRE) (MCPipe) **3-10-5b** APMcCoy (mde all: wl clr 4th: hit 2 out: unchal)	—	1	13/8^{1}	71	14
1770^{2}	**Lime Street Blues (IRE) (79)** (CPEBrooks) **5-11-5b** GBradley (a.p: rdn 2 out: kpt on: no ch w wnr)	4	2	11/4^{2}	67	24
1857^{4}	**Fastini Gold** (MDIUsher) **4-11-5b**^{1} WMcFarland (hld up: hdwy 5th: chsd wnr appr 3 out: no imp)	11	3	10/1	57	14
1770^{8}	**Smiley Face** (RJHodges) **4-10-12**(7) JHarris (hld up & bhd: styd on fr 3 out: nvr nrr)	11	4	33/1	47	4
	Analogical (DMcCain) **3-10-0** SWynne (bkwd: hld up mid div: hdwy appr 5th: wknd appr 2 out)	4	5	33/1	38	—
1413^{8}	**Admiral's Guest (IRE)** (WClay) **4-11-5** RFarrant (in tch: effrt 5th: wknd appr 2 out)	hd	6	33/1	43	—
1168^{P}	**Spitfire Bridge (IRE)** (GMMcCourt) **4-10-12**(7) RHobson (bit bkwd: hld up: hdwy 6th: wknd 3 out)	s.h	7	33/1	43	—
1652^{14}	**Rattle** (JJO'Neill) **3-10-0b**(5) RMcGrath (hld up: hdwy 5th: wknd after 3 out)	3	8	5/1^{3}	40	—
1118^{2}	**Night Boat (73)** (WClay) **5-11-5** TEley (a in rr: t.o)	13	9	8/1	28	—
1788^{P}	**Miss The Beat** (SMellor) **4-10-11**(3) EHusband (swtg: a in rr: t.o)	3	10	50/1	20	—
1149^{13}	**Chillington** (WMBrisbourne) **3-10-5b** CLlewellyn (prom: rdn & wknd 5th: sn t.o)	dist	11	33/1	—	—
	Nafertiti (IRE) (JWMullins) **4-11-0** SCurran (swtg: bkwd: a bhd: t.o)	3	12	25/1	—	—
962^{F}	**Indian Wolf** (BJLlewellyn) **3-10-5v**^{1} ILawrence (racd wd: prom to 4th: wknd qckly: t.o whn p.u after next)		P	33/1	—	—
	Persian Dawn (RTPhillips) **3-10-0** RJohnson (bhd fr 5th: t.o whn p.u bef 2 out)		P	20/1	—	—

(SP 129.8%) **14 Rn**

4m 15.7 (20.70) CSF £6.97 TOTE £2.80: £2.00 £1.30 £2.50 (£3.90) Trio £24.40 OWNER Mrs P. B. Browne (WELLINGTON) BRED Blandford Bloodstock

WEIGHT FOR AGE 3yo-14lb

No bid

D'naan (IRE) did not have a lot to beat on this hurdling debut and, making sure he put the emphasis on stamina, was never in any danger. (13/8: 9/4-6/4)

1770 Lime Street Blues (IRE) gives the impression he hates the job, but he did keep staying on, if having to admit the winner much too good. (11/4)

1857 Fastini Gold tried hard to make inroads into the winner's clear lead inside the last half-mile, but the effort proved in vain. (10/1)

Smiley Face made some late progress, but was unable to get himself into contention. (33/1)

Analogical did not shape badly on her racecourse debut and will improve with this experience under her belt. (33/1)

1981 ST. HELENS FORD NOVICES' CHASE (5-Y.O+) (Class D)

1-00 (1-00) **2m 4f 110y (15 fncs)** £4,357.50 (£1,320.00: £645.00: £307.50) GOING: 1.00 sec per fur (S)

				SP	RR	SF
1326[2]	**Around The Gale (IRE) (122)** (DRGandolfo) **5-11-6** RDunwoody (led to 2nd: led 10th: lft clr next: eased flat)	—	1	4/7 1	112+	45
1541[P]	**Bayline Star (IRE) (96)** (MissHCKnight) **6-11-0** GBradley (bit bkwd: lost tch 9th: styd on fr 3 out: no ch w wnr)	8	2	14/1	100	33
1646[B]	**Garnwin (IRE)** (NJHenderson) **6-11-0** JRKavanagh (bit bkwd: prom tl outpcd 9th: hdwy to chse wnr 2 out: no imp)	2	3	16/1	98	31
	Decyborg (FR) (MCPipe) **5-11-6** APMcCoy (led 2nd to 10th: wknd appr 3 out: fin tired)	27	4	8/1 2	83	16
1653[4]	**Chipped Out** (MartinTodhunter) **6-11-0** CLlewellyn (lw: trckd ldrs to 8th: sn rdn & wknd: t.o)	dist	5	8/1 2	—	—
1680[5]	**Macgeorge (IRE)** (RLee) **6-11-0** RJohnson (a.p: 2nd & ev ch whn fell 11th)		F	14/1	—	—
1632[U]	**Naughty Future** (JJO'Neill) **7-11-6** ARoche (j.b: t.o whn p.u bef 5th: lame)		P	10/1 3	—	—
	Valley Garden (JJO'Neill) **6-11-0** NWilliamson (bkwd: sn t.o: reminders 6th: p.u bef 2 out)		P	20/1	—	—
				(SP 118.9%)	**8 Rn**	

5m 27.2 (27.20) CSF £9.92 TOTE £1.50: £1.10 £3.80 £2.70 (£10.90) OWNER Mr T. J. Whitley (WANTAGE) BRED Mrs M. O'Driscoll

OFFICIAL EXPLANATION **Naughty Future: was lame.**

1326 Around The Gale (IRE), going easily in the lead when left clear five out, could have won by a distance had he not been eased to a walk on the run-in. (4/7)

Bayline Star (IRE), a winner between the flags in Ireland, coped adequately with the regulation fences and should be able to find an opening over a longer trip. (14/1: op 8/1)

Garnwin (IRE) did not enjoy the best of luck on his chasing debut last month, but he completed the course on this occasion and is sure to strip fitter next time. (16/1)

Decyborg (FR), a winner over fences in France, ran as if he needed this first run in two months and should have no trouble in improving on this. (8/1: 6/1-10/1)

Macgeorge (IRE) had jumped boldly and was still the most serious threat to the winner when he crashed out at the fifth last. (14/1: 10/1-16/1)

1632 Naughty Future (10/1: 7/1-12/1)

1982 ASTBURY WREN H'CAP HURDLE (0-140) (4-Y.O+) (Class B)

1-30 (1-31) **3m (12 hdls)** £4,765.25 (£1,442.00: £703.50: £334.25) GOING: 0.69 sec per fur (S)

				SP	RR	SF
1067[2]	**Freddie Muck (120)** (NATwiston-Davies) **6-11-0** CLlewellyn (lw: a.p: led appr 2 out: clr whn hit last)	—	1	3/1 1	100	47
1571[10]	**Yes Man (IRE) (110)** (MissHCKnight) **7-10-4** RJohnson (led tl appr 2 out: rdn whn hit last: kpt on)	3½	2	8/1	88	35
1661[6]	**Sun Surfer (FR) (134)** (CaptTAForster) **8-12-0** SWynne (chsd ldrs: mstke 9th: sn rdn & outpcd: styd on towards fin)	4	3	5/1	109	56
1571*	**General Tonic (109)** (DRGandolfo) **9-10-3** RDunwoody (hld up: hdwy 7th: rdn after 3 out: sn btn)	½	4	100/30 2	84	31
1783[8]	**Little Gunner (112)** (RJPrice) **6-10-6** DGallagher (hld up & bhd: effrt appr 2 out: no imp)	10	5	25/1	80	27
	Nahthen Lad (IRE) (130) (MrsJPitman) **7-11-10** NWilliamson (bit bkwd: hld up: effrt & pushed along 8th: wknd appr 3 out: eased)	8	6	7/2 3	93	40
948[2]	**Call My Guest (IRE) (125)** (REPeacock) **6-11-5** APMcCoy (chsd ldr to 9th: wknd appr 2 out: eased whn btn)	1½	7	14/1	87	34
				(SP 108.6%)	**7 Rn**	

6m 0.1 (21.10) CSF £22.82 TOTE £3.20: £1.50 £4.80 (£18.70) OWNER Cheltenham Racing Ltd (CHELTENHAM) BRED N. A. Twiston-Davies

1067 Freddie Muck, much happier back over this extended trip, won with any amount in hand. He is thriving this season. (3/1)

1571 Yes Man (IRE) turned the tables on General Tonic on these more favourable terms and showed a welcome return to form. (8/1)

1661 Sun Surfer (FR), feeling the pinch when awkward four out, was soon hard at work and, though he did stay on, was only ever fighting for the places. (5/1: 7/2-11/2)

1571* General Tonic possibly made his move a bit too soon, for he was struggling to hold on before reaching the straight. (100/30: 2/1-7/2)

Nahthen Lad (IRE) did not sparkle on this seasonal pipe-opener back over hurdles, but the outing is sure to prove beneficial and chasing is his game nowadays. (7/2)

1983 CHALIE RICHARDS MALT WHISKY H'CAP CHASE (0-115) (5-Y.O+) (Class E)

2-00 (2-01) **4m 1f (24 fncs)** £4,162.50 (£1,260.00: £615.00: £292.50) GOING: 0.69 sec per fur (S)

				SP	RR	SF
1778[5]	**Pennine Pride (91)** (MDHammond) **9-10-1v** NWilliamson (w ldr: led 9th to 15th: led 17th: styd on strly)	—	1	5/1 3	106	8
1684[4]	**Glenfinn Princess (96)** (MrsMerritaJones) **8-10-6** DerekByrne (lw: hld up & bhd: mstke 15th: hdwy 18th: chsd wnr 4 out: one pce fr 2 out)	7	2	10/1	107	9
1662[3]	**Stop the Waller (IRE) (114)** (FMurphy) **7-11-5**(5) MrRThornton (j.w: led 2nd to 9th: led 15th to 17th: wknd 4 out)	18	3	6/1	114	16
1697[6]	**Shamarphil (90)** (RHAlner) **10-10-0** MissSBarraclough (swtg: chsd ldrs: j.slowly 10th: wknd 19th)	1¼	4	20/1	89	—
1778[B]	**Holy Sting (IRE) (95)** (NATwiston-Davies) **7-10-5b** CLlewellyn (lw: prom tl rdn & wknd appr 4 out: t.o)	24	5	11/4 1	80	—
1711[4]	**Keep it Zipped (IRE) (99)** (OSherwood) **6-10-9b** JAMcCarthy (hld up: hdwy 14th: 5th & rdn whn fell 20th)		F	10/1	—	—
1684[5]	**Leinthall Princess (92)** (JLNeedham) **10-9-13**(3)ow2 GHogan (led to 2nd: wknd 12th: t.o whn fell 3 out)		F	33/1	—	—
1655[4]	**Front Line (112)** (JJO'Neill) **9-11-8** MMoloney (bit bkwd: a in rr: t.o whn p.u bef 4 out)		P	12/1	—	—
1662[4]	**Desperate (95)** (AGFoster) **8-10-5** MRichards (hld up: hdwy 9th: rdn 19th: sn wknd: t.o whn p.u bef 4 out)		P	7/1	—	—
1765[2]	**Rocky Park (95)** (GBBalding) **10-10-5** APMcCoy (mstke 3rd: chsd ldrs tl blnd & uns rdr 16th)		U	4/1 2	—	—
				(SP 123.7%)	**10 Rn**	

9m 5.1 (54.10) CSF £51.48 CT £287.64 TOTE £7.20: £2.20 £2.70 £1.80 (£33.80) Trio £77.60 OWNER Mrs W. A. Beaumont (MIDDLEHAM)

LONG HANDICAP Leinthall Princess 9-1

1778 Pennine Pride put himself in the big time with a gutsy display over this marathon trip, and the Pintail and Eider Chases at Newcastle have been pencilled in. (5/1)

1684 Glenfinn Princess, travelling every bit like a winner half a mile out, gave the impression she did not quite see out the trip. (10/1: 12/1-8/1)

1662 Stop the Waller (IRE) turned in another bold display of jumping and was in the firing-line until the final half-mile appeared to catch him out. (6/1)

1202 Shamarphil jumps and stays, but she was unable to compete with the leading pair inside the last mile. (20/1)

1778 Holy Sting (IRE), on the heels of the leaders, looked to be delaying his effort, but he came off the bridle out in the country and could do little to prevent the principals leaving him for dead. (11/4)

1984 RED COAT CONDITIONAL H'CAP HURDLE (0-100) (4-Y.O+) (Class F)

2-30 (2-32) **2m 1f (9 hdls)** £2,640.00 (£740.00: £360.00) GOING: 0.69 sec per fur (S)

				SP	RR	SF
1860^{2}	**Kintavi (82)** (TWDonnelly) **6-10-13** GHogan (chsd ldrs: led after 3 out: sn clr: comf)	—	**1**	$2/1^{1}$	76	26
1816^{2}	**Glowing Path (87)** (RJHodges) **6-11-1**(3) JHarris (plld hrd: chsd ldrs: one pce fr 2 out)	7	**2**	$5/2^{2}$	74	24
1772^{4}	**Country Minstrel (IRE) (76)** (SADouch) **5-10-7** DFortt (a chsng ldrs: rdn & one pce fr 3 out)	5	**3**	12/1	59	9
1860^{5}	**Kadari (92)** (WClay) **7-11-9v** GuyLewis (chsd ldr: led 6th tl after next: sn rdn & outpcd)	6	**4**	12/1	69	19
1816^{7}	**Biya (IRE) (73)** (DMcCain) **4-10-4** DWalsh (swtg: hld up: drvn along 5th: effrt appr 3 out: no imp)	3½	**5**	33/1	47	—
1816^{3}	**Schnozzle (IRE) (89)** (KSBridgwater) **5-11-6** RMassey (hld up: a in rr)	10	**6**	$5/1^{3}$	53	3
	Sheep Stealer (87) (REPeacock) **8-11-4** MichaelBrennan (bit bkwd: led & sn clr: hdd 6th: wknd 3 out: t.o)	10	**7**	14/1	42	—
	Never so Blue (IRE) (93) (PBradley) **5-11-10** DJKavanagh (a bhd: t.o fr 6th)	1	**8**	16/1	47	—
1814^{P}	**Tango Man (IRE) (69)** (RJPrice) **4-10-0** TDascombe (hld up & bhd: hdwy appr 5th: wknd appr 2 out: t.o)	3½	**9**	50/1	20	—
1860^{F}	**Alaskan Heir (85)** (AStreeter) **5-11-2** LAspell (swvd s: a in rr: t.o)	2½	**10**	16/1	33	—

(SP 117.3%) **10 Rn**

4m 14.6 (19.60) CSF £7.22 CT £41.98 TOTE £3.00: £1.30 £1.80 £2.50 (£4.40) Trio £34.10 OWNER Mr S. Taberner (SWADLINCOTE) BRED S. Taberner

LONG HANDICAP Tango Man (IRE) 9-11

1860 Kintavi landed some hefty wagers on this step down in class and should have little trouble in following up. (2/1)

1816 Glowing Path, swinging off the bridle for much of the way, obviously did too much too soon, for he had shot his bolt on reaching the straight. (5/2)

1772 Country Minstrel (IRE), still to get off the mark, ran well enough to suggest his turn will come. (12/1)

Kadari had little chance of gaining revenge on the winner, but she did her best until calling enough soon after turning in. (12/1)

1816 Schnozzle (IRE) should have been thereabouts, but he ran a very lack-lustre race and was never really in contention. (5/1)

1985 CLWYD H'CAP CHASE (0-120) (5-Y.O+) (Class D)

3-00 (3-01) **2m 4f 110y (15 fncs)** £4,065.00 (£1,230.00: £600.00: £285.00) GOING: 1.00 sec per fur (S)

				SP	RR	SF
1564^{3}	**Distinctive (IRE) (96)** (MJWilkinson) **7-10-9** CLlewellyn (swtg: led & sn clr: hdd after 2 out: btn whn lft in ld last)	—	**1**	5/1	107	39
1540*	**Fools Errand (IRE) (115)** (GBBalding) **6-12-0** APMcCoy (chsd ldrs: outpcd 9th: hdwy 3 out: styng on whn bdly hmpd last)	4	**2**	$7/2^{2}$	123	55
1799^{2}	**Really a Rascal (106)** (DRGandolfo) **9-11-5** RDunwoody (hld up: hdwy appr 9th: rdn 3 out: styng on whn sltly hmpd last)	2½	**3**	$11/4^{1}$	112	44
1295^{3}	**Solba (USA) (110)** (CParker) **7-11-9** BStorey (bit bkwd: hld up: pushed along 7th: rdn appr 2 out: no imp)	12	**4**	$9/2^{3}$	107	39
959^{2}	**Mine's an Ace (NZ) (95)** (MissVenetiaWilliams) **9-10-8** NWilliamson (prom: mstkes 11th & 4 out: wkng whn fell 3 out)		**F**	13/2	—	—
1769*	**Sister Rosza (IRE) (96)** (MrsSLamyman) **8-10-9** RFarrant (hld up: hdwy 9th: chal 2 out: sn led: 2l clr whn fell last)		**F**	11/1	—	—
1442^{4}	**Potato Man (100)** (BEllison) **10-10-13** RJohnson (chsd ldrs: rdn 7th: sn wknd: t.o whn p.u bef 3 out)		**P**	20/1	—	—
	Dolikos (98) (THCaldwell) **9-10-11** TEley (bkwd: a bhd: t.o whn p.u bef 3 out)		**P**	40/1	—	—

(SP 112.6%) **8 Rn**

5m 25.9 (25.90) CSF £21.19 CT £51.38 TOTE £6.60: £1.60 £1.80 £1.10 (£9.80) Trio £8.60 OWNER Mr Jeremy Hancock (BANBURY) BRED Capt D. G. Swan

1564 Distinctive (IRE) again gave his rivals a lesson in jumping, but he was nearing the end of his tether when headed, and was most fortunate to be handed the race. (5/1)

1540* Fools Errand (IRE) looks to be a hard ride and definitely needs a stiffer test of stamina, but he was finding top gear when forced to take avoiding action at the last. (7/2)

1799 Really a Rascal had reached the heels of the leaders three out, but was under strong pressure and staying on when he needed to side-step a falling rival at the final obstacle. (11/4)

1295 Solba (USA), nudged along at halfway, was never able to get within striking range of the principals. This run could have been needed to put an edge on him. (9/2)

1769* Sister Rosza (IRE) took the measure of Distinctive between the last two and was set for victory when capsizing at the last. (11/1: 8/1-12/1)

1986 YELLOW COLLAR INTERMEDIATE OPEN N.H. FLAT RACE (4, 5 & 6-Y.O) (Class H)

3-30 (3-30) **2m 1f** £1,658.00 (£463.00: £224.00)

				SP	RR	SF
1336^{D}	**Scoring Pedigree (IRE)** (JWMullins) **4-11-4** SCurran (hld up: hdwy ½-wy: led 6f out: drvn clr 3f out: v.easily)	—	**1**	$5/4^{1}$	68 f	—
1124^{4}	**Callindoe (IRE)** (JLNeedham) **6-10-13** NWilliamson (hld up: hdwy 7f out: chsd wnr over 2f out: no imp)	7	**2**	7/1	56 f	—
	Chasing The Moon (IRE) (GBBalding) **4-11-4** APMcCoy (attr: bit bkwd: hld up & bhd: hdwy 6f out: nt rch ldrs)	8	**3**	$9/2^{2}$	54 f	—
	Gower-Slave (PBowen) **4-11-4** RJohnson (chsd ldrs: one pce fnl 3f)	3½	**4**	15/2	51 f	—
	The Eens (DMcCain) **4-11-1**(3) DWalsh (bit bkwd: hld up in tch: rdn over 3f out: nt rch ldrs)	4	**5**	33/1	47 f	—
	Maggie Strait (MrsALMKing) **4-10-6**(7) MrOMcPhail (hld up & bhd: hdwy 4f out: nvr nrr)	nk	**6**	20/1	42 f	—
1665^{8}	**Mistress Tudor** (SMellor) **5-10-10**(3) EHusband (bit bkwd: in tch tl wknd over 3f out)	½	**7**	33/1	41 f	—
1665^{4}	**The Croppy Boy** (JNeville) **4-11-1**(3) TDascombe (w ldr tl wknd over 4f out)	6	**8**	12/1	40 f	—
898^{P}	**Water Font (IRE)** (JJO'Neill) **4-11-4** ARoche (chsd ldrs over 10f)	6	**9**	12/1	35 f	—
	Dancing Ranger (MissSJWilton) **5-11-4** TEley (prom tl rdn & wknd over 4f out)	nk	**10**	50/1	35 f	—
1336*	**Midas** (KRBurke) **5-11-11** RDunwoody (hld up: hdwy 6f out: wknd over 3f out)	3½	**11**	$6/1^{3}$	38 f	—
	Just Andy (BPreece) **5-11-4** TJenks (mid div tl wknd over 4f out: t.o)	15	**12**	50/1	17 f	—
1504^{10}	**Cashel Quay (IRE)** (MrsPBickerton) **6-11-1**(3) GuyLewis (a in rr: t.o)	26	**13**	100/1	—	—
1124^{14}	**Glendronach** (BRCambidge) **4-10-13** GaryLyons (led 11f: sn rdn & wknd: t.o)	10	**14**	66/1	—	—

(SP 133.6%) **14 Rn**

4m 18.1 CSF £12.08 TOTE £2.10: £1.40 £2.40 £2.10 (£8.90) Trio £15.30 OWNER Mr Seamus Mullins (AMESBURY) BRED M. Walsh

1336 Scoring Pedigree (IRE) made amends for an unlucky disqualification on his racecourse debut with a clear-cut success that could be the first of many. (5/4: op 5/2)

1124 Callindoe (IRE) showed she is going the right way with another improved performance and she should be able to find an opening. (7/1)

Chasing The Moon (IRE) will benefit considerably from the experience and should be much sharper next time. (9/2: 5/2-5/1)

Gower-Slave ran well on this debut and only faded inside the last half-mile. He will win races. (15/2: 5/1-10/1)

705 Water Font (IRE) (12/1: op 8/1)
1336* Midas took closer order out in the country, but the pace was quickening all the time, and the penalty helped take its toll on the turn for home. (6/1: op 4/1)

T/Jkpt: £7,222.30 (0.94 Tckts); £610.34 to Towcester 19/12/96. T/Plpt: £25.10 (491.38 Tckts). T/Qdpt: £11.40 (83.97 Tckts). IM

1699-CATTERICK (L-H) (Good)
Wednesday December 18th

Race 1 - No time taken
WEATHER: foggy

1987 GLEBE NOVICES' CHASE (5-Y.O+) (Class E)
12-50 (12-50) **2m (12 fncs)** £3,042.90 (£907.20: £432.60: £195.30) GOING: 0.56 sec per fur (S)

				SP	RR	SF
1511^{2}	**Monyman (IRE) (97)** (MDHammond) **6-11-5** RGarritty (a.p: effrt 3 out: led last: styd on wl)	—	**1**	11/8^{1}	106	—
1525*	**Twin Falls (IRE) (93)** (GMMoore) **5-11-5** JCallaghan (chsd ldrs: led 8th tl hdd last: no ex)	5	**2**	3/1^{3}	101	—
1780^{4}	**Fenwick's Brother** (MrsSJSmith) **6-10-12** RichardGuest (bhd: hit 4 out: gd hdwy 3 out: nvr plcd to chal)	4	**3**	14/1	90	—
1831^{2}	**Amber Valley (USA) (97)** (DLWilliams) **5-10-12** PHolley (led to 8th: ev ch tl wknd fr 3 out)	14	**4**	2/1^{2}	76	—
1701^{9}	**Friendly Knight** (JSHaldane) **6-10-12** TReed (chsd ldrs: 2nd whn fell 3 out)		**F**	40/1	—	—
1249^{7}	**Gone Ashore (IRE)** (MABarnes) **5-10-7**(5) STaylor (blnd & uns rdr 1st)		**U**	50/1	—	—
				(SP 111.5%)		**6 Rn**

Time Not Taken CSF £5.70 TOTE £2.70: £4.50 £1.10 (£3.40) OWNER Mr Trevor Hemmings (MIDDLEHAM) BRED Lady Naylor Leyland
1511 Monyman (IRE), patiently ridden, won most authoritatively and looked to be back on the right track. (11/8)
1525* Twin Falls (IRE) ran well but he was no match for the winner in the closing stages. (3/1)
1780 Fenwick's Brother is learning fast and was given a most sympathetic ride here. He looks one to watch. (14/1)
1831 Amber Valley (USA), who wears a tongue-strap, is useful when things go his way, but he was never allowed to settle here and decided he had had enough three out. (2/1)
Friendly Knight was running well and was still just in second place when coming down three out. (40/1)

1988 CATTERICK RACE CLUB 1997 'JOIN UP NOW' AMATEUR H'CAP HURDLE (0-100) (4-Y.O+) (Class F)
1-20 (1-20) **2m 3f (10 hdls)** £2,120.20 (£587.20: £280.60) GOING: 0.39 sec per fur (GS)

				SP	RR	SF
1701^{6}	**Fryup Satellite (79)** (MrsJBrown) **5-10-2**(5) MissPRobson (a.p: led 2 out: all out)	—	**1**	6/1	58	4
1852^{4}	**Duke of Perth (90)** (HowardJohnson) **5-10-13**(5) MissPJones (chsd ldrs: disp ld last: kpt on)	hd	**2**	9/2^{2}	69	15
1718*	**Fawley Flyer (91)** (WGMTurner) **7-10-12**(7) MrEBabington (led to 2nd: led 6th to 2 out: kpt on)	hd	**3**	5/1^{3}	70	16
1849^{7}	**Flat Top (95)** (MWEasterby) **5-11-2**(7) MrMWatson (lost tch ½-wy: hdwy 3 out: hit 2 out: styd on wl towards fin)	½	**4**	6/1	73	19
	High Penhowe (75) (JJQuinn) **8-10-0**(3) MrCBonner (nvr nr ldrs)	dist	**5**	8/1	—	—
1417^{9}	**Cuillin Caper (75)** (TRWatson) **4-9-10**(7) MissRClark (chsd ldrs tl wknd appr 2 out)	16	**6**	50/1	—	—
1807^{14}	**Ski Path (76)** (NBycroft) **7-9-11**(7)ow4 MrPMurray (prom to 5th: sn t.o)	dist	**7**	50/1	—	—
1796^{9}	**Gymcrak Sovereign (84)** (REvans) **8-10-5**(7) MissCEvans (plld hrd: led 2nd: sn clr: hdd & wknd 6th: t.o)		**8**	25/1	—	—
1825^{4}	**Rubislaw (72)** (MrsKMLamb) **4-9-7**(7) MissSLamb (bhd fr ½-wy: t.o)		**9**	200/1	—	—
1344^{2}	**Tall Measure (92)** (DGSwindlehurst) **10-10-13b**(7)ow6 MrDSwindlehurst (rr div whn fell 4th)		**F**	12/1	—	—
1701^{3}	**Sudden Spin (100)** (JNorton) **6-11-9**(5) MrMHNaughton (in tch whn fell 6th)		**F**	9/4^{1}	—	—
				(SP 121.3%)		**11 Rn**

4m 46.1 (21.10) CSF £32.14 CT £135.72 TOTE £5.30: £1.20 £3.60 £1.50 (£14.90) Trio £48.20 OWNER Mr John Lees (YORK) BRED John Lees
LONG HANDICAP Rubislaw 8-7 Ski Path 9-12
1701 Fryup Satellite looked particularly well and, given a fine ride, did just enough to hang on. (6/1)
1852 Duke of Perth, from a stable out of form of late, just found the final struggle too much. (9/2: op 3/1)
1718* Fawley Flyer is game and consistent but, despite a valiant effort, just lacked a turn of foot to take it. (5/1)
1443 Flat Top got outpaced at one stage and then put in a poor jump two out, but for which he would probably have won. (6/1)
High Penhowe never got into this and obviously needed it. (8/1)
1344 Tall Measure (12/1: op 8/1)
1701 Sudden Spin loves this track and was not far away when falling. (9/4)

1989 GOOD LUCK PAUL ALSTER NOVICES' CHASE (5-Y.O+) (Class E)
1-50 (1-50) **3m 1f 110y (19 fncs)** £3,179.40 (£949.20: £453.60: £205.80) GOING: 0.56 sec per fur (S)

				SP	RR	SF
1716^{F}	**Gems Lad (86)** (MrsSJSmith) **9-11-5** RichardGuest (led 3rd: hit 9th: hdd 12th: outpcd appr 3 out: styng on whn blnd last: swtchd & rallied to ld last strides)	—	**1**	9/2^{3}	98	25
1691^{F}	**Tico Gold (77)** (PCheesbrough) **8-10-12** ASSmith (chsd ldrs tl blnd 12th & 13th & lost pl: hdwy 4 out: led 3 out: blnd last: hdd & nt qckn towards fin)	hd	**2**	3/1^{2}	91	18
1691^{2}	**Shawwell (81)** (JIACharlton) **9-10-12** KJohnson (led to 3rd: hit 4th: lft in ld 14th: hdd & blnd 3 out: wknd next)	22	**3**	3/1^{2}	77	4
1845^{7}	**Clonroche Lucky (IRE)** (JWade) **6-10-12** KJones (chsd ldrs: blnd 2nd: outpcd 11th: n.d after)	26	**4**	33/1	61	—
	Dorlin Castle (93) (LLungo) **8-10-12** TReed (hld up: smooth hdwy to ld 12th: fell 14th)		**F**	7/4^{1}	—	—
1845^{U}	**Broomhill Duker (IRE) (80)** (HowardJohnson) **6-10-12** ADobbin (a bhd: t.o whn p.u bef 12th)		**P**	16/1	—	—
				(SP 113.4%)		**6 Rn**

6m 49.2 (31.20) CSF £17.40 TOTE £4.60: £1.80 £2.20 (£5.80) OWNER Miss J. Wood (BINGLEY) BRED Miss J. U. Wood
1716 Gems Lad just stays and stays and, after looking well beaten turning into the straight, his stamina won the day. (9/2)
1691 Tico Gold made his usual amount of mistakes, but still looked to have it won three out, only to find one who stayed better than himself. (3/1)
1691 Shawwell was always in the thick of things, but he was clumsy at various stages and finally gave up after a mistake three out. (3/1)
Clonroche Lucky (IRE) looked both slow and clumsy at times. (33/1)
Dorlin Castle cruised into the lead setting out on the final circuit and just had to remain on his feet to win this, but yet again he lost concentration and fell. (7/4: op 11/10)

1990 RAFFYARD HOUSE (S) HURDLE (4, 5 & 6-Y.O) (Class G)
2-20 (2-21) **2m 3f (10 hdls)** £1,943.00 (£538.00: £257.00) GOING: 0.39 sec per fur (GS)

				SP	RR	SF
1628^{7}	**Tirmizi (USA) (86)** (MrsASwinbank) **5-11-5** JSupple (sn drvn along: hdwy 4 out: led appr 2 out: styd on wl)	—	**1**	7/1^{3}	60	1
1569^{F}	**Furietto (IRE) (98)** (MDHammond) **6-11-5** RGarritty (trckd ldrs: led after 3 out tl appr 2 out: rdn & no ex)	5	**2**	1/2^{1}	56	—
1703^{6}	**Heavens Above (56)** (FMurphy) **4-10-12** KWhelan (a.p: ev ch 3 out: sn rdn & one pce)	5	**3**	25/1	45	—
1775^{5}	**In a Moment (USA) (70)** (CGrant) **5-11-5** JCallaghan (outpcd ½-wy: styd on fr 3 out: n.d)	7	**4**	14/1	46	—
1849^{11}	**Cool Steel (IRE) (74)** (MrsJBrown) **4-10-12** ADobbin (led to 4th: chsd ldrs tl wknd 4 out)	6	**5**	20/1	34	—
1701^{4}	**Anorak (USA) (89)** (GMMoore) **6-10-12**(7) NHannity (led 4th tl after 3 out: wknd qckly)	½	**6**	5/1^{2}	40	—
1672^{8}	**Nenagh Gunner** (JJQuinn) **6-10-7** RichardGuest (bhd: hdwy ½-wy: wknd 4 out)	26	**7**	20/1	6	—
1705^{4}	**Robert The Brave** (JMJefferson) **4-10-9**(3) ECallaghan (lost tch fr 6th)	20	**8**	25/1	—	—
1781^{8}	**Phar Enough (IRE)** (JGFitzGerald) **4-10-12** PNiven (chsd ldrs to 6th: wknd qckly: t.o whn p.u bef 2 out)		**P**	20/1	—	—
1851^{7}	**Meesonette** (BEllison) **4-10-7v^{1}** ASSmith (t.o fr ½-wy: p.u bef 3 out)		**P**	16/1	—	—

(SP 130.4%) **10 Rn**

4m 50.0 (25.00) CSF £11.77 TOTE £15.70: £3.70 £1.30 £3.60 (£6.90) Trio £89.30 OWNER Mr S. Smith (RICHMOND) BRED H. H. Aga Khan
No bid
OFFICIAL EXPLANATION **Nenagh Gunner: the rider reported that he had been told to give the mare every chance, but not be too hard on her, and that from three out had no chance of improving her placing. The trainer added that the mare was unlikely to run again.**
1628 Tirmizi (USA) just seems to stay as he was off the bit with well over a circuit to go, but he then kept answering his rider's every call and, once he struck the front approaching the penultimate flight, it was soon his. (7/1)
1569 Furietto (IRE) travelled particularly well but, once asked for a real effort on the home turn, his response was a shade disappointing. He will find a race in due course. (1/2)
1703 Heavens Above took the eye in the paddock and had his chances, but looked one-paced from the home turn. (25/1)
1775 In a Moment (USA) runs when in the mood and was never doing enough. (14/1: 10/1-20/1)
911 Cool Steel (IRE) looks in tremendous condition but, as yet, his ability does not match his looks. (20/1)
1701 Anorak (USA) showed just what a funny customer he is and ran no sort of race. (5/1)
99 Nenagh Gunner should improve in due course. (20/1)

1991 BOVILLE H'CAP CHASE (0-105) (4-Y.O+) (Class F)
2-50 (2-50) **2m 3f (15 fncs)** £2,786.40 (£770.40: £367.20) GOING: 0.56 sec per fur (S)

				SP	RR	SF
1798^{P}	**Tim Soldier (FR) (79)** (MFBarraclough) **9-10-10** RSupple (racd wd: a.p: led 2 out: styd on wl)	—	**1**	25/1	89	21
1847^{11}	**Karenastino (69)** (MrsSJSmith) **5-10-0** MrPMurray (led 3rd: hit 4 out: hdd 2 out: one pce)	5	**2**	33/1	75	7
1846^{2}	**Rebel King (90)** (MABarnes) **6-11-2**(5) STaylor (chsd ldrs: outpcd 3 out: kpt on flat)	½	**3**	5/2^{2}	95	27
1823^{6}	**The Toaster (97)** (MissMKMilligan) **9-12-0** ASSmith (in tch: effrt 4 out: one pce fr 2 out)	5	**4**	9/2	98	30
1847^{2}	**Juke Box Billy (IRE) (86)** (MrsJBrown) **8-11-3** ADobbin (in tch: effrt 4 out: rdn & btn next)	9	**5**	7/4^{1}	80	12
9^{P}	**Funny Old Game (78)** (DMcCune) **9-10-9** KJohnson (wnt prom 5th: outpcd 8th: 6th whn fell 11th)		**F**	20/1	—	—
1943^{F}	**Show Your Hand (IRE) (77)** (LLungo) **8-10-8** MFoster (led to 3rd: lost tch fr 7th: p.u bef 4 out)		**P**	7/2^{3}	—	—

(SP 116.9%) **7 Rn**

5m 0.9 (21.90) CSF £386.88 TOTE £19.40: £4.50 £9.00 (£54.40) OWNER Mr Ken Dale (CLAVERDON) BRED Bernard Geffroy
LONG HANDICAP Karenastino 9-5
Tim Soldier (FR), suited by the rain during the afternoon, came back to form and won his first race for nearly three years. (25/1)
Karenastino put in a much-improved effort, particularly from 9lb out of the handicap. (33/1)
1846 Rebel King is running well at present, but just lacks that vital dash. (5/2)
1823 The Toaster was always close enough if good enough, but looked very one-paced in the home straight. (9/2)
1847 Juke Box Billy (IRE) ran most disappointingly, and the rain-softened ground was against him. (7/4)

1992 HUTTON WANDESLEY NOVICES' H'CAP HURDLE (0-95) (4-Y.O+) (Class F)
3-20 (3-21) **2m (8 hdls)** £2,138.40 (£592.40: £283.20) GOING: 0.39 sec per fur (GS)

				SP	RR	SF
1524*	**Last Try (IRE) (92)** (BSRothwell) **5-12-0** ASSmith (cl up: led 3 out: all out)	—	**1**	4/1^{2}	78	35
1575^{5}	**Environmental Law (67)** (WMcKeown) **5-10-3b^{1}** ADobbin (chsd ldrs: ev ch flat: kpt on)	hd	**2**	11/2	53	10
1772^{7}	**Highly Charming (IRE) (84)** (MFBarraclough) **4-10-13**(7) MrAWintle (in tch: hdwy 3 out: sn chsng ldrs: one pce fr next)	6	**3**	20/1	64	21
1851^{5}	**Simand (74)** (GMMoore) **4-10-3**(7) NHannity (bhd: styd on fr 2 out: nvr nrr)	2½	**4**	20/1	51	8
1911^{3}	**Past Master (USA) (86)** (SGollings) **8-11-8** KGaule (chsd ldrs: outpcd 3 out: no imp after)	hd	**5**	7/1	63	20
1183^{6}	**Ranger Sloane (75)** (AStreeter) **4-10-4**(7) SLycett (bhd: styd on fr 3 out: nrst fin)	2	**6**	25/1	50	7
1848^{3}	**Bowcliffe (81)** (MrsAMNaughton) **5-11-3** MFoster (prom: outpcd after 3 out: no imp after)	1	**7**	14/1	55	12
1667^{8}	**Dr Edgar (80)** (MDods) **4-11-2** RSupple (led to 3 out: wknd)	15	**8**	14/1	39	—
	Maple Bay (IRE) (70) (BEllison) **7-10-3**(3) MrCBonner (bhd: hdwy 3 out: no imp whn blnd 2 out)	1¼	**9**	15/2	28	—
1081^{6}	**Jonaem (IRE) (80)** (MrsESlack) **6-11-2** KJohnson (bhd: effrt 3 out: sn btn)	4	**10**	16/1	34	—
1768^{6}	**My Shenandoah (IRE) (68)** (HOliver) **5-10-4** VSlattery (lost tch & wl bhd ½-wy: n.d after)	2½	**11**	3/1^{1}	20	—
1686^{7}	**Appearance Money (IRE) (78)** (FMurphy) **5-10-7**(7) MissElizabethDoyle (prom tl outpcd fr 5th)	1¼	**12**	12/1	28	—
1663^{R}	**Aydisun (64)** (RCurtis) **4-10-0** DMorris (n.d)	28	**13**	5/1^{3}	—	—
1667^{10}	**Jarrow (65)** (MrsAMNaughton) **5-10-1** JSupple (rr div whn fell 4th)		**F**	66/1	—	—

(SP 143.1%) **14 Rn**

3m 57.7 (14.70) CSF £29.84 CT £401.23 TOTE £4.50: £4.10 £2.60 £3.90 (£37.30) Trio £278.70 OWNER Mr H. J. Harenberg (MALTON) BRED H. J. Harenberg
OFFICIAL EXPLANATION **Aydisun: swallowed his tongue.**
1524* Last Try (IRE) proved a game sort and refused to give in once in front. (4/1)
1575 Environmental Law had the blinkers on for the first time and they certainly improved him. (11/2: op 10/1)
1178 Highly Charming (IRE) had his chances, but lacked a change of gear in the home straight. (20/1)
1851 Simand ran quite well and was putting in her best work when the race was virtually over. (20/1)
1911 Past Master (USA) is running reasonably, but lacked the ability to make any real mark on the race. (7/1)
950 Ranger Sloane just seems to stay and was finishing well, but always too late. (25/1)
Maple Bay (IRE) (15/2: 9/2-8/1)

T/Plpt: £8,447.70 (0.55 Tckts); £5,137.16 to Towcester 19/12/96. T/Qdpt: £468.50 (1.7 Tckts). AA

1762-EXETER (R-H) (Good becoming Soft)
Wednesday December 18th

Race 7: No comments due to poor visibility
WEATHER: rain & thick fog

1993 GEMINI RADIO CLAIMING HURDLE (4, 5 & 6-Y.O) (Class F)
12-40 (12-41) **2m 2f (8 hdls)** £2,102.00 (£582.00: £278.00) GOING: 1.02 sec per fur (HY)

				SP	RR	SF
1304*	**Top Skipper (IRE) (69)** (VGGreenway) **4-10-7**(7) MrJTizzard (a.p: led appr 2 out: clr last: comf)	—	1	12/1 3	49	6
1715 3	**Peter Monamy (102)** (MCPipe) **4-11-3b** CMaude (mid div: hdwy 5th: ev ch 2 out: hrd rdn appr last: wknd flat)	5	2	1/2 1	48	5
1569 4	**Fortunes Rose (IRE) (63)** (JSKing) **4-10-0** TJMurphy (bhd: hdwy 6th: styd on fr 2 out)	6	3	20/1	25	—
1876 7	**Khatir (CAN) (78)** (MCPipe) **5-11-3b** CO'Dwyer (bit bkwd: chsd ldrs tl led 3rd: hdd appr 2 out: wknd appr last)	nk	4	5/1 2	42	—
	Borjito (SPA) (CRBarwell) **5-11-12** BFenton (bhd tl styd on fr 2 out)	hd	5	25/1	51	8
971 P	**Allahrakha (70)** (MHill) **5-11-6** SFox (bit bkwd: led to 3rd: rdn & wknd 5th: t.o whn p.u bef 2 out)		P	14/1	—	—
1628 14	**My Harvinski (69)** (IRJones) **6-10-5** MAFitzgerald (a bhd: t.o whn p.u bef 2 out)		P	14/1	—	—
1838 3	**Robin Island** (PRHedger) **4-9-12b**(7) MClinton (in tch tl wknd 4th: t.o whn p.u bef 2 out)		P	66/1	—	—
1569 P	**Norfolk Glory** (DFBassett) **4-10-5** MrAHoldsworth (bit bkwd: bhd whn blnd & uns rdr 2nd)		U	66/1	—	—

(SP 116.0%) **9 Rn**

4m 42.3 (32.30) CSF £17.98 TOTE £13.90: £2.90 £1.00 £3.70 (£5.20) Trio £21.50 OWNER Mr V. G. Greenway (TAUNTON) BRED G. J. Cullinan

1304* Top Skipper (IRE), on his first appearance for his new stable, was running over a distance nearly a mile shorter than his only previous win. (12/1: op 8/1)

1715 Peter Monamy, a course and distance winner earlier in the year, had a good opportunity here on the book and this was reflected in the betting. (1/2)

1569 Fortunes Rose (IRE) showed her first signs form and was staying on well towards the finish. (20/1)

Khatir (CAN), who looked useful as a three-year-old, is disappointing nowadays and has been known to be rather temperamental. (5/1: tchd 8/1)

Allahrakha (14/1: op 8/1)

1446 My Harvinski (14/1: op 8/1)

1994 CHILDCRAFT NOVICES' CHASE (4-Y.O+) (Class D)
1-10 (1-11) **2m 2f (12 fncs)** £4,958.00 (£1,484.00: £712.00: £326.00) GOING: 0.71 sec per fur (S)

				SP	RR	SF
1270 F	**Grooving (IRE)** (JTGifford) **7-11-2** PHide (hld up & bhd: hdwy 8th: chsd ldr next: ev ch last: rdn to ld nr fin)	—	1	7/2 2	97	30
1646 4	**Court Master (IRE)** (RHBuckler) **8-11-2** BPowell (led tl rdn & hdd nr fin)	hd	2	11/1	97	30
	Dante's View (USA) (91) (PRHedger) **8-11-2** DO'Sullivan (hld up: hdwy to chse ldrs 10th: one pce 2 out)	11	3	50/1	87	20
1423 4	**Tellicherry** (MissHCKnight) **7-10-11** JOsborne (chsd ldrs 5th: wknd fr 8th)	15	4	16/1	69	2
	Dodgy Dealer (IRE) (MrsSusanNock) **6-11-2** CO'Dwyer (prom: chsd ldrs 6th: wknd)	29	5	66/1	48	—
	Boots N All (IRE) (GBBalding) **6-11-2** BClifford (bit bkwd: prom to 6th)	¾	6	40/1	47	—
1677 2	**Josifina** (AGFoster) **5-10-11** AThornton (hdwy 5th: in tch tl wknd 8th)	3	7	20/1	40	—
1552 2	**Reeshloch (90)** (AndrewTurnell) **7-11-2** SMcNeill (hdwy 4th: in tch next to 7th: hmpd & fell 3 out)		F	12/1	—	—
	Kimanicky (IRE) (NJHenderson) **6-11-2** MAFitzgerald (lw: bhd: hdwy 7th: p.u bef 2 out)		P	6/4 1	—	—
1759a 4	**Castlekellyleader (IRE)** (PFNicholls) **7-11-2** CMaude (lw: bhd: hdwy 5th: prom & mstke 8th: wknd & p.u bef 2 out)		P	4/1 3	—	—
	Uncle Algy (MissHCKnight) **7-11-2** TJMurphy (bit bkwd: prom to 10th: p.u bef 2 out)		P	25/1	—	—
	Bullanguero (IRE) (HSHowe) **7-11-2** GTormey (bit bkwd: nvr trbld ldrs: p.u bef 2 out)		P	100/1	—	—

(SP 119.6%) **12 Rn**

4m 42.6 (21.60) CSF £38.67 TOTE £5.00: £1.40 £2.40 £23.00 (£21.00) Trio £233.90; £270.15 to Towcester 19/12/96 OWNER Mrs T. Brown (FINDON) BRED T. Simmons

Grooving (IRE), who fell at the first on his chasing debut, was the subject of some good support in the betting. The ground, very much on the softer side of good, seemed to his liking and he would appreciate a little further. Cheltenham is being mentioned by connections, with the Sun Alliance Chase the main target. (7/2)

1646 Court Master (IRE), a maiden under Rules, just lost out in the slog to the line. There would seem to be a race for him on this show. (11/1)

Dante's View (USA), who showed decent form over hurdles, looked one-paced in the closing stages, but this was a creditable effort on his first attempt at the larger obstacles after a fourteen-month lay-off. (50/1)

1552 Reeshloch (12/1: 6/1-14/1)

Kimanicky (IRE) was expected to do a lot better and, although jumping well enough, found the ground too testing, and was wisely pulled up. (6/4)

1759a Castlekellyleader (IRE) was a leading novice hurdler in Ireland last season, but was prone to jumping errors. Making a mistake five out, he was nearly brought down at the next and, with all chances gone approaching the second last, was pulled up. If he could master jumping, he would surely be a force to be reckoned with over fences. (4/1: 5/2-9/2)

1995 HENRIETTA KNIGHT 50TH BIRTHDAY NOVICES' H'CAP HURDLE (0-105) (4-Y.O+) (Class D)
1-40 (1-41) **2m 2f (8 hdls)** £3,129.00 (£869.00: £417.00) GOING: 1.02 sec per fur (HY)

				SP	RR	SF
1427 6	**Cool Gunner (73)** (JSKing) **6-10-0** CMaude (a.p: chsd ldr 6th tl led appr last: sn clr: easily)	—	1	8/1	60+	7
1788 2	**Supreme Genotin (IRE) (97)** (JABOld) **7-11-10** GUpton (lw: led tl appr last: sn wknd)	6	2	6/4 1	79	26
1539 6	**Winnow (75)** (AndrewTurnell) **6-10-2** LHarvey (hdwy to chse ldrs 4th: ev ch 2 out: wknd appr last)	3½	3	6/1 3	54	1
	Tudor Town (77) (KBishop) **8-10-4**ow4 SBurrough (bit bkwd: in tch to ½-wy)	3½	4	16/1	52	—
1568 7	**Blazing Miracle (75)** (MrsRGHenderson) **4-9-11**(5)ow2 DSalter (in tch tl lost pl 4th: styd on wl fr 2 out)	nk	5	7/1	50	—
1470 6	**Above the Cut (USA) (88)** (CPMorlock) **4-11-1** AMaguire (hld up: hdwy 6th: sn ev ch: wknd qckly appr 2 out: t.o)	dist	6	6/1 3	—	—
1693 2	**Tap Shoes (IRE) (73)** (RJBaker) **6-10-0** BPowell (nvr trbld ldrs: t.o)	1¾	7	7/2 2	—	—
1788 P	**Prince of Prey (73)** (NJHawke) **8-10-0** SMcNeill (bit bkwd: chsd ldr tl wknd qckly 6th: t.o)	dist	8	33/1	—	—

(SP 123.2%) **8 Rn**

4m 38.6 (28.60) CSF £21.28 CT £76.30 TOTE £7.50: £1.40 £1.70 £1.90 (£7.50) Trio £20.30 OWNER Mr Richard Peterson (SWINDON) BRED R. Burton

LONG HANDICAP Tudor Town 9-10 Blazing Miracle 9-6 Cool Gunner 9-11 Tap Shoes (IRE) 9-9 Prince of Prey 9-6

Cool Gunner has improved considerably on last season and succeeded in this first attempt at a handicap. (8/1)
1788 Supreme Genotin (IRE) has still to win over hurdles and carrying topweight did not help his cause. He will find himself up against it in similar events off his current mark. (6/4)
1539 Winnow put up an improved effort. She was staying on at the one pace in the home straight but, although due to go up 7lb after this, can find a race over a longer distance. (6/1: op 4/1)
1375 Above the Cut (USA) (6/1: op 7/2)

1996 SCOTTISH EQUITABLE/JOCKEYS ASSOCIATION (QUALIFIER) H'CAP HURDLE (0-130) (5-Y.O+) (Class C)

2-10 (2-10) **2m 2f (8 hdls)** £3,590.00 (£1,070.00: £510.00: £230.00) GOING: 1.02 sec per fur (HY)

	Horse / details	Dist	Pos	SP	RR	SF
1351P	**Edgemoor Prince (96)** (PJHobbs) **5-10-0** AMaguire (lw: hdwy to ld 3rd: hdd 5th: led after next: clr last: easily)	—	1	4/1 2	80+	4
	Spring Saint (107) (MissCHorler) **7-10-11** GUpton (hld up & bhd: hdwy 5th: sn prom: ev ch 2 out: wknd appr last)	8	2	5/1 3	84	8
	Bell One (USA) (106) (AJKDunn) **7-10-10** SMcNeill (bit bkwd: bhd: hdwy 3rd: chsd ldr next: led tl mstke 5th: rallied & ev ch 2 out: wknd appr last)	15	3	100/30 1	70	—
1794³	**Khalidi (IRE) (113)** (DRGandolfo) **7-10-12**(5) SophieMitchell (chsd ldr to 3rd: prom to 6th: r.o fr 2 out: nvr nrr)	9	4	4/1 2	69	—
1599*	**Road to Au Bon (USA) (96)** (RJBaker) **8-10-0** BPowell (led to 3rd: led 5th: hdd after next: sn wknd)	1¾	5	16/1	50	—
	Slew Man (FR) (120) (MCPipe) **5-11-10** CMaude (bit bkwd: chsd ldrs tl wknd fr 6th)	16	6	11/2	60	—
51aP	**Decide Yourself (IRE) (107)** (TThomsonJones) **6-10-11** MAFitzgerald (bhd fr 3rd: t.o whn p.u bef last)		P	7/1	—	—

(SP 113.5%) **7 Rn**

4m 39.4 (29.40) CSF £22.27 TOTE £3.30: £1.80 £4.20 (£18.70) OWNER The Racing Hares (MINEHEAD) BRED Mrs A. C. Wakeham
LONG HANDICAP Road to Au Bon (USA) 8-12
1351 Edgemoor Prince, unlucky last time at Cheltenham, made amends. Looking well treated for this handicap debut, he used the weight advantage to its full and, clear over the last, won comfortably. (4/1: op 5/2)
Spring Saint twice a course and distance winner, ran respectably for this seasonal debut. If he can find his favoured heavy ground, he can return to winning ways again this season. (5/1)
Bell One (USA), who has been off for thirteen months, goes well fresh but, after having every chance two out, found this tacky ground too much in the closing stages. With this run under his belt, he can find improvement on a sounder surface. (100/30: op 6/1)
1794 Khalidi (IRE) (4/1: 3/1-9/2)
Slew Man (FR) (11/2: op 3/1)

1997 EDIMBOURG H'CAP CHASE (0-130) (5-Y.O+) (Class C)

2-40 (2-41) **2m 7f 110y (17 fncs)** £4,867.00 (£1,456.00: £698.00: £319.00) GOING: 0.71 sec per fur (S)

	Horse / details	Dist	Pos	SP	RR	SF
	Full of Fire (111) (KCBailey) **9-10-11** CO'Dwyer (bit bkwd: hld up & bhd: hdwy 10th: chsd ldr fr 15th: led flat: styd on wl)	—	1	6/1 3	120	—
1373*	**Shining Light (IRE) (106)** (DNicholson) **7-10-6** AMaguire (lw: hdwy 9th: mstke & chsd ldr 12th to 15th: in tch last: styd on flat)	1½	2	2/1 1	114	—
1175⁴	**Oatis Regrets (128)** (MissHCKnight) **8-12-0** JOsborne (lw: led tl hdd & wknd flat)	9	3	7/2 2	130	—
	Sunley Bay (123) (PFNicholls) **10-11-9** PHide (chsd ldrs tl wknd 12th)	10	4	8/1	118	—
1428³	**Dom Samourai (FR) (117)** (MCPipe) **5-11-3b** CMaude (chsd ldr to 12th: rdn & wknd next)	1	5	7/2 2	111	—
1598*	**Duhallow Lodge (113)** (CRBarwell) **9-10-13** BFenton (lw: in tch tl wknd 13th: p.u bef last)		P	12/1	—	—
	Master Jolson (105) (NJHenderson) **8-10-5** MAFitzgerald (bit bkwd: in tch tl wknd fr 15th: p.u bef 2 out)		P	14/1	—	—

(SP 117.5%) **7 Rn**

6m 25.0 (38.00) CSF £18.38 TOTE £7.10: £2.60 £1.10 (£9.70) OWNER Mr Michael Gillow (UPPER LAMBOURN) BRED Tom and Brian Groarke
Full of Fire stayed on the better of the two main contenders on the run-in. His target for the season would seem to be more of the same at this level. (6/1)
1373* Shining Light (IRE) ran well on ground softer than he would prefer and stayed on well, although never getting to the winner. (2/1)
1175 Oatis Regrets holds a King George entry and a lot more was expected of him in this company. He held the lead until over the last, but could find little on the flat. (7/2)
Sunley Bay (8/1: tchd 12/1)
1598* Duhallow Lodge (12/1: op 6/1)
Master Jolson (14/1: 10/1-16/1)

1998 HOECHST ROUSSEL PANACUR 'N.H.' E.B.F. QUALIFIER NOVICES' HURDLE (4-Y.O+ F & M) (Class D)

3-10 (3-14) **2m 3f 110y (9 hdls)** £3,631.70 (£1,085.60: £519.80: £236.90) GOING: 1.02 sec per fur (HY)

	Horse / details	Dist	Pos	SP	RR	SF
1580²	**River Bay (IRE)** (MissHCKnight) **5-10-10** BFenton	—	1	9/4 2	63	11
	Fiddling The Facts (IRE) (NJHenderson) **5-10-10** MAFitzgerald (lw)	nk	2	5/1 3	63	11
1541P	**Moonlighter (56)** (CFCJackson) **6-10-5**(5) OBurrows	20	3	100/1	46	—
1565*	**Gaye Fame** (KCBailey) **5-11-3** CO'Dwyer	13	4	2/1 1	43	—
1583⁷	**O My Love** (MissHCKnight) **5-10-10** JOsborne	14	5	20/1	24	—
	Country Style (RHAlner) **7-10-7**(3) PHenley	12	6	33/1	14	—
1810P	**Ginger Maid** (MCPipe) **8-10-3**(7) GSupple	½	7	50/1	14	—
	Half Moon Girl (RGFrost) **4-10-10** MrAHoldsworth (bit bkwd)	12	8	100/1	4	—
1573⁹	**Vansell** (RHBuckler) **5-10-10** BPowell (bit bkwd)	16	9	40/1	—	—
	Brown Wren (PJHobbs) **5-10-10** GTormey	¾	10	20/1	—	—
	Country Town (APJones) **6-10-10** SMcNeill	2	11	100/1	—	—
	Bonita Blakeney (60) (GBBalding) **6-10-10** BClifford (bit bkwd)	dist	12	50/1	—	—
1695P	**Zen Or** (JWMullins) **5-10-3**(7) DavidTurner		13	100/1	—	—
1177¹¹	**Pharmorefun (IRE)** (GBBalding) **4-10-10** TJMurphy		14	50/1	—	—
1766P	**Lilly The Filly** (MrsBarbaraWaring) **5-10-10** RGreene		P	100/1	—	—
1555⁴	**Royal Ruler (IRE)** (JTGifford) **5-10-10** PHide		P	6/1	—	—
1695P	**Dolce Notte (IRE)** (MCPipe) **6-10-10** CMaude		P	16/1	—	—

(SP 126.7%) **17 Rn**

5m 4.7 (32.70) CSF £13.85 TOTE £3.10: £1.20 £2.10 £10.20 (£12.00) Trio Not won; £423.69 to Towcester 19/12/96 OWNER Riverwood Racing (WANTAGE) BRED D. P. O'Brien

1580 River Bay (IRE) would have appreciated this stiff test of stamina, and emerged from the mist in the final 25 yards to hold off the persistent runner-up. She is qualified to run in the final of this series at Newbury in March, and that is apparently her main target for the season. (9/4: 3/1-2/1)
Fiddling The Facts (IRE) drifted in the betting, but made a very impressive debut. Making the winner fight to the line and finishing well clear of the rest of the field, she is sure to improve from this introduction. (5/1: 5/2-6/1)
Moonlighter has shown very little in novice hurdles to date and would seem to have appreciated this step back in distance. (100/1)
1565* Gaye Fame, a well-bred mare, made a promising start on her hurdling debut this season, but ran disappointingly here. (2/1: op 5/4)

T/Plpt: £94.30 (97.82 Tckts). T/Qdpt: £25.80 (30.1 Tckts). T

1987-CATTERICK (L-H) (Soft)
Thursday December 19th
WEATHER: unsettled

1999 PICTON 'N.H.' NOVICES' HURDLE (4-Y.O+) (Class E)
12-20 (12-22) **2m 3f (10 hdls)** £2,742.00 (£762.00: £366.00) GOING: 0.94 sec per fur (S)

				SP	RR	SF
1666[3]	**King Pin** (PBeaumont) **4-10-12** RSupple (lw: hld up: stdy hdwy 3 out: hung lft: led last: comf)	—	**1**	9/4[1]	62+	—
1705*	**Lagen Bridge (IRE) (95)** (DMoffatt) **7-11-5** DJMoffatt (jnd ldrs 5th: led appr 2 out: hung bdly lft & hdd last: one pce)	1½	**2**	3/1[2]	68	6
	Major Harris (IRE) (MDHammond) **4-10-12** RGarritty (lw: hld up & bhd: hdwy 6th: chsng ldrs 2 out: cl 3rd whn blnd bdly last: nt rcvr)	11	**3**	12/1	52+	—
	Don't Tell Tom (IRE) (72) (JWade) **6-10-12** KJones (bit bkwd: chsd ldrs: led after 3 out tl appr next: one pce)	3½	**4**	50/1	49	—
1343[F]	**Fils de Cresson (IRE) (92)** (JRAdam) **6-10-12** MMoloney (hld up: hdwy ½-wy: ev ch after 3 out: wknd 2 out)	4	**5**	11/2	45	—
1705[5]	**Silver Minx** (MrsMReveley) **4-10-12** RHodge (led tl hdd & wknd after 3 out)	26	**6**	20/1	23	—
1633[3]	**Gazanali (IRE)** (GMMoore) **5-10-12** NBentley (hld up: hdwy & prom 6th: wknd appr 2 out)	1¼	**7**	5/1[3]	22	—
1633[9]	**Joe Luke (IRE)** (GMMoore) **4-10-12** JCallaghan (bhd: pushed along ½-wy: n.d)	6	**8**	33/1	17	—
636[5]	**Eternal City (90)** (GRichards) **5-11-5** ADobbin (sme hdwy ½-wy: sn wknd)	nk	**9**	14/1	24	—
	Fort Zeddaan (IRE) (MrsSJSmith) **6-10-12** RichardGuest (chsd ldrs tl wknd 3 out)	14	**10**	33/1	5	—
1654[14]	**Element of Risk (IRE) (63)** (WSCunningham) **6-10-12** NSmith (prom tl wknd 4 out)	½	**11**	16/1	5	—
1654[P]	**Blond Moss** (SEKettlewell) **6-10-9(3)** GLee (chsd ldrs tl wknd qckly 6th)	7	**12**	100/1	—	—
1687[10]	**Edstone (IRE)** (JWCurtis) **4-10-12** BStorey (bit bkwd: outpcd & bhd fr ½-wy)	nk	**13**	100/1	—	—
31[P]	**Matachon** (MSmith) **6-10-12** JSupple (in tch: effrt 6th: sn lost pl)	3½	**14**	100/1	—	—
1523[4]	**Philbecky** (JMJefferson) **5-10-4(3)** ECallaghan (sn bhd: p.u bef 4 out)		**P**	50/1	—	—
	Meesons Express (MrsSarahHorner-Harker) **6-10-12** MFoster (bit bkwd: wknd qckly 5th: p.u bef next)		**P**	100/1	—	—
872[3]	**Hutcel Loch** (RDEWoodhouse) **5-10-7** RJohnson (prom tl rdn & wknd 4 out: p.u bef 2 out)		**P**	12/1	—	—
				(SP 134.3%)		**17 Rn**

4m 58.5 (33.50) CSF £10.02 TOTE £3.00: £1.10 £1.10 £6.40 (£7.50) Trio £61.80 OWNER Exors of the late Mr J N Hinchliffe (BRANDSBY) BRED C. C. Bromley and Son
1666 King Pin appreciated this soft ground and won particularly well. There looks to be more to come, especially when he gets over his problem of hanging. (9/4)
1705* Lagen Bridge (IRE) put in another decent effort but, yet again, spoilt the performance by hanging badly left throughout the closing stages. (3/1)
Major Harris (IRE) was closing on the leaders, although he still had something to do, when he almost fell at the last. This was not a bad debut. (12/1)
Don't Tell Tom (IRE) ran a useful first race of the season and would seem to be improving. (50/1)
Fils de Cresson (IRE) ran a fair race after he fell last time and appeared to blow up in the closing stages. (11/2)
1705 Silver Minx showed again what a headstrong individual he is, and soon gave up once collared. (20/1)

2000 ST PAULS MAIDEN CHASE (5-Y.O+) (Class F)
12-50 (12-51) **2m 3f (15 fncs)** £2,561.40 (£763.20: £363.60: £163.80) GOING: 0.94 sec per fur (S)

				SP	RR	SF
1845[P]	**Bosworth Field (IRE) (71)** (MrsSarahHorner-Harker) **8-11-5b** MFoster (chsd ldrs: led 7th: styd on wl fr 3 out)	—	**1**	33/1	84	9
	Brigadier John (IRE) (JRAdam) **7-11-5** MMoloney (bit bkwd: blnd 3rd: bhd tl styd on fr 4 out: nrst fin)	6	**2**	20/1	79	4
1780[5]	**Fair Aily** (MESowersby) **6-11-5** DParker (j.rt: in tch: hdwy 3 out: one pce fr next)	5	**3**	7/2[3]	75	—
1853[2]	**Cush Supreme (IRE)** (MartinTodhunter) **7-11-5** RJohnson (lw: cl up: blnd 7th & 4 out: wknd appr last)	1	**4**	9/4[2]	74	—
1853[8]	**Grand as Owt (65)** (DMcCune) **6-11-5** KJohnson (in tch tl outpcd fr 8th)	29	**5**	16/1	50	—
	Periroyal (MrsSJSmith) **6-10-12(7)** RWilkinson (bhd: shkn up & hdwy appr 8th: disp ld whn fell 10th)		**F**	20/1	—	—
1920[F]	**Royal Hand (67)** (RJArmson) **6-11-5** MrRArmson (mstkes: a bhd: t.o whn fell 3 out)		**F**	20/1	—	—
1705[11]	**Make A Buck** (LLungo) **6-11-5b[1]** RichardGuest (blnd 1st: fell 2nd)		**F**	16/1	—	—
1845[4]	**Springhill Quay (IRE)** (GRichards) **7-11-5** ADobbin (chsd ldrs tl wknd qckly 8th: p.u bef 11th)		**P**	2/1[1]	—	—
1780[P]	**Cardinal Sinner (IRE) (56)** (JWade) **7-11-5** KJones (led: hit 5th: hdd 7th: wknd qckly next: p.u bef 4 out)		**P**	25/1	—	—
				(SP 119.2%)		**10 Rn**

5m 12.5 (33.50) CSF £463.09 TOTE £35.70: £9.80 £8.10 £1.10 (£179.00) Trio £109.80; £109.84 to Hereford 20/12/96 OWNER Mrs Sarah Horner-Harker (YARM)
Bosworth Field (IRE) had shown nothing previously, but obviously appreciated this soft ground, and there was certainly no fluke about it. (33/1)
Brigadier John (IRE), a decent type, ran well, staying on steadily in the closing stages. This should have taught him plenty. (20/1)
1576 Fair Ally had his chances, but was always inclined to jump right, and was well short of pace in the closing stages. (7/2)
1853 Cush Supreme (IRE) made some bad mistakes but, given a most determined ride, was bang in contention until his stamina gave out in the home straight. (9/4)
Periroyal was putting in a most impressive round on his first time over fences when he came down six out. (20/1)
1845 Springhill Quay (IRE) was a big disappointment, dropping tamely away setting out on the final circuit, and then being pulled up. (2/1)

2001 AMPLEFORTH H'CAP HURDLE (0-105) (4-Y.O+) (Class F)
1-20 (1-20) **2m (8 hdls)** £2,065.60 (£571.60: £272.80) GOING: 0.94 sec per fur (S)

				SP	RR	SF
1824[2]	**Fen Terrier (97)** (FPMurtagh) **4-11-13** ADobbin (trckd ldrs: led appr 2 out: pushed clr: eased flat)	—	**1**	9/4[2]	82	32

Opera Fan (IRE) (83) (KAMorgan) 4-10-13 ASSmith (lw: bhd: hdwy appr 2 out: no ch w wnr)...5 2 4/1 63 13
1729[5] I'm a Dreamer (IRE) (98) (MissMERowland) 6-11-7(7) RWilkinson (lw: trckd ldrs: effrt appr 2 out: sn rdn & btn)...10 3 7/2[3] 68 18
1779[7] Fred's Delight (IRE) (78) (MrsVAAconley) 5-10-8 BStorey (led to 2nd: cl up: led 3 out tl appr next: sn btn)...½ 4 12/1 48 —
1848[2] Pangeran (USA) (84) (MrsASwinbank) 4-11-0 JSupple (lw: led 2nd to 3 out: rdn & wknd qckly: t.o)...dist 5 7/4[1] — —
(SP 117.0%) 5 Rn

4m 7.0 (24.00) CSF £11.17 TOTE £4.30: £1.30 £1.40 (£11.70) OWNER Mr K. G. Fairbairn (CARLISLE) BRED Racing Thoroughbreds P L C
OFFICIAL EXPLANATION **Pangeran (USA): did not act on the soft ground.**
1824 Fen Terrier was always going well within herself and quickly put it beyond doubt going to the second last. (9/4)
Opera Fan (IRE) somehow got left behind early on and, although making useful progress approaching two out, he was never going anything like well enough to trouble the winner. (4/1)
I'm a Dreamer (IRE) sat handy but, once the pace increased on the home turn, he found himself stuck in the mud. (7/2)
Fred's Delight (IRE) showed some ability and may well be coming back to form. (12/1)
1848 Pangeran (USA) seemingly failed to act on this ground. (7/4)

2002 HAPPY CHRISTMAS H'CAP CHASE (0-105) (5-Y.O+) (Class F)

1-50 (1-50) **2m (12 fncs)** £2,635.20 (£727.20: £345.60) GOING: 0.94 sec per fur (S)

SP RR SF
1987[2] **Twin Falls (IRE) (93)** (GMMoore) **5-11-6** JCallaghan (lw: cl up fr 5th: led flat: styd on wl)...— 1 13/8[2] 100 18
1704[P] **Port in a Storm (88)** (MDHammond) **7-10-12**(3) MrCBonner (lw: cl up: lft in ld appr 5th: rdn 3 out: hdd flat: kpt on)...¾ 2 11/8[1] 94 12
1702[4] **Positive Action (85)** (MABarnes) **10-10-7**(5) STaylor (outpcd & lost tch 7th)...dist 3 7/2[3] — —
1943[5] **Monaughty Man (73)** (EMCaine) **10-10-0** KJohnson (lw: led tl rn out bnd appr 5th)... R 12/1 — —
(SP 110.1%) 4 Rn

4m 18.1 (26.10) CSF £4.14 TOTE £2.00 (£1.90) OWNER Mrs Susan Moore (MIDDLEHAM) BRED Newgate Stud Co
LONG HANDICAP Monaughty Man 9-10
1987 Twin Falls (IRE), having his second run in consecutive days, had a real battle and did it well. (13/8: 4/5-7/4)
1704 Port in a Storm had the ground and the trip he likes but, despite trying hard, was not quite up to it. (11/8)
1702 Positive Action has lost his way altogether at present. (7/2)
1566 Monaughty Man was happy out in front when he jumped a piece of string the racecourse had put to close off the hurdle track. (12/1)

2003 LEVY BOARD H'CAP HURDLE (0-115) (4-Y.O+) (Class E)

2-20 (2-21) **3m 1f 110y (12 hdls)** £2,364.00 (£654.00: £312.00) GOING: 0.94 sec per fur (S)

SP RR SF
1347[3] **Pharare (IRE) (93)** (RDEWoodhouse) **6-11-3** ASSmith (lw: mde all: styd on gamely fr 3 out)...— 1 2/1[1] 76 7
1310[3] **Smart Approach (IRE) (89)** (MrsMReveley) **6-10-6**(7) CMcCormack (a.p: hdwy u.p appr 2 out: ch last: nt qckn)1¾ 2 4/1[3] 71 2
1849[5] **Ifallelsefails (94)** (LLungo) **8-11-4** RichardGuest (lw: hld up: smooth hdwy fr 8th: chal after 3 out: wknd next)19 3 3/1[2] 64 —
690[P] **Moobakkr (USA) (87)** (KAMorgan) **5-10-8**(3) ECallaghan (chsd ldrs tl outpcd fr 3 out)...15 4 20/1 48 —
Absalom's Pillar (100) (JMackie) **6-11-10** TEley (bit bkwd: trckd ldrs pllng hrd: mstke 5th: hit 3 out: sn btn)....7 5 9/2 56 —
Denticulata (76) (PSpottiswood) **8-10-0** DParker (hdwy & prom 8th: wknd 3 out)...2 6 25/1 31 —
1807[12] **Anchorena (78)** (DWBarker) **4-10-2** ADobbin (plld hrd: lost pl & mstke 8th: p.u bef 2 out)... P 8/1 — —
(SP 116.2%) 7 Rn

6m 51.7 (44.70) CSF £10.27 CT £21.07 TOTE £2.40: £1.60 £1.70 (£4.40) Trio £7.00 OWNER Mr C. F. Colquhoun (YORK) BRED N. O'Brian
LONG HANDICAP Denticulata 9-11
1347 Pharare (IRE) had his own way out in front. He loves the soft and stays forever, and would not be denied. (2/1)
1310 Smart Approach (IRE) acted well on this very soft ground and looked a big danger going to the last, only to find the winner too tough. (4/1)
1849 Ifallelsefails improved swinging off the bit in the back straight but, when an effort was required approaching the second last, his response was disappointing. Perhaps he just did not stay. (3/1: 9/4-7/2)
690 Moobakkr (USA) got round for the first time this season and is obviously happier on this ground. (20/1)
Absalom's Pillar, having his first run for well over a year, was far too free for his own good. (9/2: 3/1-5/1)
Denticulata is happier on faster ground. (25/1)

2004 CATTERICK RACE CLUB 1997 'JOIN UP NOW' H'CAP CHASE (0-120) (5-Y.O+) (Class D)

2-50 (2-50) **3m 1f 110y (19 fncs)** £3,595.50 (£1,071.00: £510.00: £229.50) GOING: 0.94 sec per fur (S)

SP RR SF
Heavenly Citizen (IRE) (89) (JLGledson) **8-10-2** BStorey (mde most: kpt on wl fr 3 out)...— 1 16/1 98 —
1704* **Kenmore-Speed (100)** (MrsSJSmith) **9-10-13** RichardGuest (trckd ldr gng wl: led 15th to 3 out: kpt on one pce)...8 2 13/8[1] 104 —
1778[3] **Sparrow Hall (92)** (JGFitzGerald) **9-10-5** RJohnson (chsd ldrs: drvn along most of wy: outpcd fr 4 out)...14 3 9/2[3] 87 —
1863* **Dont Tell the Wife (121)** (CREgerton) **10-12-1**(5) 6x MrRThornton (lw: bhd: outpcd 12th: sme hdwy appr 3 out: sn btn)...23 4 9/2[3] 102 —
1923[U] **Pims Gunner (IRE) (107)** (MDHammond) **8-11-6** RGarritty (in tch tl outpcd 14th: hdwy u.p appr 3 out: snbtn) .4 5 2/1[2] 85 —
1704[F] **Marchwood (98)** (NChamberlain) **9-10-11** TReed (bhd: hdwy & prom 12th: 2l 3rd & rdn whn fell last)... F 25/1 — —
(SP 117.5%) 6 Rn

7m 4.8 (46.80) CSF £42.57 CT £132.72 TOTE £26.80: £7.80 £3.50 (£18.10) OWNER Mr J. L. Gledson (HEXHAM) BRED Louis Hill
Heavenly Citizen (IRE), who loves the soft, always runs well on this track, and won his first race for three years here in most determined style. (16/1)
1704* Kenmore-Speed put in another decent effort and is going to win his fair share of races. (13/8)
1778 Sparrow Hall jumps deliberately and is slow, but he keeps galloping, though his one pace was never enough here. (9/2)
1863* Dont Tell the Wife won a poor even last time and always found this too competitive. (9/2)
1670 Pims Gunner (IRE) was never happy this time, and something was obviously wrong with him. (2/1)
Marchwood ran well and was not far away when coming down three out. (25/1)

2005 GARRISON INTERMEDIATE N.H. FLAT RACE (4, 5 & 6-Y.O) (Class H)

3-20 (3-20) **2m** £1,343.00 (£373.00: £179.00)

SP RR SF
Point Reyes (IRE) (CWThornton) **4-10-11**(7) NHorrocks (in tch: effrt 5f out: rdn 3f out: kpt on wl fnl f to ld nr fin)...— 1 2/1[1] 43 f —
1033[2] **Nifaaf (USA)** (KAMorgan) **4-10-8**(5) MrRThornton (cl up: led 7f out: rdn over 2f out: kpt on wl: jst ct)...s.h 2 10/1 38 f —

				SP	RR	SF
1362[9]	**Harfdecent** (MrsMReveley) **5-11-1**(3) GLee (plld hrd: led after 2f to 7f out: chal 4f out: kpt on wl)	s.h	**3**	9/4 [2]	43 f	—
1362[8]	**The Stuffed Puffin (IRE)** (LLungo) **4-10-11**(7) IJardine (lw: in tch: hdwy 5f out: ev ch 3f out: kpt on)	¾	**4**	10/1	42 f	—
	Monsieur Darcy (IRE) (JRAdam) **5-11-4** MrCStorey (bit bkwd: prom tl wknd fnl 3f)	6	**5**	20/1	36 f	—
	Brandsby Minster (PBeaumont) **5-10-11**(7) BGrattan (bkwd: a.p: ev ch 4f out: wknd fnl 3f)	5	**6**	14/1	31 f	—
1296[17]	**Brook House** (BBousfield) **5-10-6**(7) CMcCormack (bit bkwd: bhd: gd hdwy ½-wy: sn chsng ldrs: rdn & btn 2f out)	½	**7**	100/1	26 f	—
1504[11]	**Dantes Amour (IRE)** (MDHammond) **5-10-11**(7) RBurns (bhd: hdwy 4f out: no imp)	1¾	**8**	25/1	29 f	—
	Hunting Slane (CGrant) **4-11-1**(3) FLeahy (in tch: hdwy 6f out: sn chsng ldrs: wknd fnl 3f)	2½	**9**	50/1	26 f	—
1781[4]	**Push On Polly (IRE)** (JParkes) **6-10-10**(3) ECallaghan (led 2f: chsd ldrs tl wknd 6f out)	21	**10**	10/1	—	—
	Recca (IRE) (DenysSmith) **4-11-1**(3) MrCBonner (lost tch fnl 5f)	6	**11**	11/2 [3]	—	—
1781[7]	**Movisa** (WJSmith) **6-10-8**(5) STaylor (sn bhd)	16	**12**	200/1	—	—
	Henbrig (GROldroyd) **6-10-10**(3) GParkin (w ldrs tl wknd fr ½-wy)	s.h	**13**	100/1	—	—
				(SP 126.5%)	**13 Rn**	

4m 6.6 CSF £22.82 TOTE £2.40: £1.30 £3.90 £1.50 (£9.40) Trio £24.70 OWNER Mr I. Bray (MIDDLEHAM) BRED Mrs Norah O'Connor

Point Reyes (IRE), a decent mover, had to struggle to win this and battled on well. He should do even better on faster ground. (2/1: 5/4-9/4)

1033 Nifaaf (USA) got the trip well in this soft ground and this was probably her best run to date. (10/1: op 5/1)

Harfdecent, despite running a bit free, showed here he is improving. He should find his mark in due course. (9/4)

The Stuffed Puffin (IRE) is improving with experience and this was a decent effort. (10/1)

Monsieur Darcy (IRE), a good-looking sort, ran well and should now improve. (20/1)

Brandsby Minster, looking likely to benefit from this, should now do better. (14/1)

T/Plpt: £246.70 (34.96 Tckts). T/Qdpt: £11.00 (81.47 Tckts). AA

1795-TOWCESTER (R-H) (Chases Good to soft, Hdles Soft, Heavy patches)
Thursday December 19th

WEATHER: raining

2006 TURKEY (S) H'CAP HURDLE (0-95) (4-Y.O+) (Class G)

12-40 (12-43) **2m (8 hdls)** £2,094.00 (£584.00: £282.00) GOING: 1.08 sec per fur (HY)

				SP	RR	SF
1796[2]	**Ambidextrous (IRE) (67)** (EJAlston) **4-10-5**(7) LCummins (hdwy appr 4th: led after 5th: pckd 3 out: clr appr next: rdn out)	—	**1**	6/1 [3]	56	22
1536[9]	**Polo Pony (IRE) (66)** (JohnUpson) **4-10-4**(7) GSupple (bhd: hdwy 3 out: r.o flat)	9	**2**	16/1	46	12
1299[10]	**Saymore (74)** (WClay) **10-11-5** SWynne (hdwy appr 3 out: chsd wnr appr next: sn no imp)	1¾	**3**	12/1	52	18
1466*	**Sir Pageant (79)** (KSBridgwater) **7-11-10b** DBridgwater (hld up: hdwy appr 3 out: nvr rchd ldrs)	8	**4**	11/2 [2]	49	15
1390[2]	**Kashan (IRE) (64)** (PHayward) **8-10-9** BFenton (led 2nd to 4th: hit next: wknd 3 out)	4	**5**	7/4 [1]	30	—
1836[2]	**Slightly Special (IRE) (59)** (BAPearce) **4-10-4** TJMurphy (prom: led 4th to next: sn lost pl: rdn & r.o flat)	20	**6**	16/1	5	—
1861[4]	**Ruth's Gamble (57)** (MrsLCJewell) **8-10-2v** DLeahy (hdwy appr 4th: wknd 3 out)	1¼	**7**	12/1	2	—
	Wickens One (69) (DPGeraghty) **6-11-0** NWilliamson (bkwd: nvr rchd ldrs)	1¼	**8**	16/1	13	—
1707[2]	**Lanesra Breeze (71)** (TJNaughton) **4-11-2** CMaude (chsd ldrs tl rdn & wknd appr 2 out)	5	**9**	14/1	10	—
1072[7]	**Antiguan Flyer (68)** (GProdromou) **7-10-13** WMarston (prom: led & hit 5th: sn hdd & wknd)	8	**10**	25/1	—	—
1775[7]	**Captain Tandy (IRE) (78)** (CSmith) **7-11-4**(5) DJKavanagh (a bhd)	5	**11**	33/1	4	—
1628[4]	**Sharmoor (74)** (MissLCSiddall) **4-11-5** AThornton (hdwy appr 4th: ev ch 5th: sn wknd: t.o whn p.u bef 2 out)		**P**	10/1	—	—
1771[P]	**Bankonit (IRE) (73)** (DJDavies) **8-11-4b** ILawrence (sn rdn & t.o: p.u bef 2 out)		**P**	16/1	—	—
1299[13]	**Bill and Win (70)** (TWall) **5-10-12v**[1](3) RMassey (prom to 3rd: t.o whn p.u bef 2 out)		**P**	33/1	—	—
1795[P]	**Cottage Joker (55)** (WABethell) **6-10-0** AMaguire (led to 2nd: wknd 5th: t.o whn p.u bef 2 out)		**P**	33/1	—	—
				(SP 133.4%)	**15 Rn**	

4m 11.5 (25.50) CSF £96.62 CT £1,046.26 TOTE £7.40: £1.70 £5.10 £3.10 (£75.40) Trio £235.90; £272.50 to Hereford 20/12/96 OWNER Mrs Carol McPhail (PRESTON) BRED Saeed Manana

LONG HANDICAP Cottage Joker 9-10

Bt in 3,000 gns

1796 Ambidextrous (IRE), whose form here twelve days ago looks to be really working out, was in the process of going clear when a peck at the third last halted his progress for a few strides. (6/1)

Polo Pony (IRE), taking a drop in class and trip, did all his best work in the last half-mile and ought to find a race at this level, despite his lack of size. (16/1)

Saymore has come tumbling down the handicap in recent weeks and finally offered some hope by chasing the winner up the hill. He is now on a mark almost two stone lower than when he last won three years ago. (12/1: 7/1-14/1)

1466* Sir Pageant needs further than the minimum, even on such a stiff track, and finished with petrol left in the tank. (11/2)

1390 Kashan (IRE) looked to have the beating of the winner on a line through Sprintfayre, but found this track too stiff for him. He deserves a chance to reproduce his debut effort on a flatter course. (7/4)

1836 Slightly Special (IRE) was kept up to his work to pass a couple of beaten horses on the run-in and, if anything, this flatters him. (16/1)

1707 Lanesra Breeze (14/1: 7/1-16/1)

1628 Sharmoor (10/1: 5/1-12/1)

2007 HOLLY NOVICES' CHASE (5-Y.O+) (Class D)

1-10 (1-12) **2m 6f (16 fncs)** £4,059.75 (£1,218.00: £586.50: £270.75) GOING: 0.91 sec per fur (S)

				SP	RR	SF
	Whattabob (IRE) (NJHenderson) **7-10-12** MAFitzgerald (bit bkwd: trckd ldrs: led 9th: mstke next: hdd 12th: led appr last: rdn & r.o wl)	—	**1**	7/2 [2]	111	36
1596[3]	**Ramallah (90)** (MissHCKnight) **7-10-12** BFenton (hld up: hdwy appr 2 out: r.o wl appr last)	3	**2**	10/1	109	34
1856[2]	**Bridepark Rose (IRE) (82)** (PCRitchens) **8-10-7** SFox (chsd ldrs: led 3 out: hit next: hdd appr last: sn btn)	2½	**3**	10/1	102	27
	See Enough (RHBuckler) **8-10-12** SMcNeill (prom: led 6th to 8th: one pce appr 2 out)	nk	**4**	12/1	107	32
1764[2]	**Lively Knight (IRE) (120)** (JTGifford) **7-11-5** PHide (hld up: hdwy 9th: rdn & no imp whn hit last)	2	**5**	11/4 [1]	112	37
1829[2]	**Slideofhill (IRE)** (JJO'Neill) **7-10-12** CO'Dwyer (hld up: nvr plcd to chal)	17	**6**	7/2 [2]	93	18
	Furry Fox (IRE) (RCurtis) **8-10-12** DMorris (nvr trbld ldrs)	15	**7**	25/1	82	7
	Ivy Boy (IRE) (CJMann) **6-10-12** JRailton (chsd ldrs tl hit 11th)	3	**8**	20/1	80	5

				SP	RR	SF
	Chiappucci (IRE) (87) (MrsEHHeath) **6-10-12** AThornton (bkwd: led appr 3rd to 6th: led 8th to 9th: led 12th to 3 out: sn wknd)	dist	9	33/1	—	—
	Huge Mistake (NATwiston-Davies) **7-10-12** CLlewellyn (bit bkwd: prom to 5th: rdn 7th: in tch whn fell 10th)		F	11/1	—	—
1572[3]	**Gordon (90)** (PRWebber) **5-10-12** JOsborne (a bhd: t.o whn p.u bef 2 out)		P	8/1 3	—	—
1798[6]	**Strokesaver (IRE)** (CPEBrooks) **6-10-12** GBradley (chsd ldrs: blnd & lost tch 10th: t.o whn p.u bef 12th)		P	14/1	—	—
	Bucket of Gold (OBrennan) **6-10-12** MBrennan (bit bkwd: plld hrd: prom: wknd 10th: t.o whn p.u bef 2 out)		P	16/1	—	—
	Volleyball (IRE) (PRHedger) **7-10-12** MRichards (bhd fr 7th: blnd 13th: t.o whn p.u bef 2 out)		P	33/1	—	—
	Saint Keyne (DLWilliams) **6-10-12** PHolley (bit bkwd: led tl after 2nd: j.slowly next: wkng whn mstke 13th: t.o whn p.u bef 3 out)		P	33/1	—	—
				(SP 146.4%)	**15 Rn**	

5m 56.4 (27.40) CSF £43.91 TOTE £5.20: £2.70 £2.70 £3.60 (£25.30) Trio £209.00 OWNER Mrs Margaret Turner (LAMBOURN) BRED Dr F. J. Healy

Whattabob (IRE), who beat Yahmi and finished third in the Persian War over hurdles last season, was not entirely convincing at his hurdles, but stayed on in fine style when challenged, and gives every indication of making up into a good three-mile chaser. (7/2)
1596 Ramallah, who ran well over hurdles here earlier in the year, suddenly began to make giant strides on the stiff climb to the straight, and stayed on well to the line without unduly troubling the winner. (10/1: 7/1-12/1)
1856 Bridepark Rose (IRE), who had only one race in two years from October 1994, has now blown away the cobwebs and is getting her act together. She would be a good thing in a novices' handicap off her present mark. (10/1)
See Enough loves the ground and is capable of very useful form, but also has broken blood-vessels. He jumped more than adequately, and this effort suggests he should be winning over fences if he stays healthy. (12/1: 8/1-14/1)
1764 Lively Knight (IRE) looked to be found wanting for stamina in these conditions, but this was by no means a bad effort under a penalty. (11/4)
1798 Strokesaver (IRE) (14/1: 10/1-16/1)

2008 PLUM PUDDING CLAIMING HURDLE (4-Y.O+) (Class F)
1-40 (1-43) **2m 5f (11 hdls)** £2,199.00 (£614.00: £297.00) GOING: 1.08 sec per fur (HY)

				SP	RR	SF
1642[2]	**Roberty Lea (118)** (MrsMReveley) **8-11-12** PNiven (chsd ldr: led 6th: drew clr appr 2 out: blnd last: eased nr fin)	—	1	Evens 1	98	—
1698[U]	**Stac-Pollaidh (87)** (KCBailey) **6-10-9** CO'Dwyer (hld up: hdwy 6th: chsd wnr appr 2 out: no imp)	19	2	8/1	67	—
1562[2]	**Quiet Mistress (81)** (WABethell) **6-10-6b** AMaguire (lw: prom: rdn after 5th: chsd wnr fr next: wknd qckly after 3 out: r.o again flat)	17	3	5/2 2	51	—
1304[2]	**Snowy Lane (IRE) (68)** (JNeville) **8-10-11hb** NWilliamson (lw: chsd ldrs: lost tch 6th: n.d after)	1¼	4	7/1 3	55	—
1334[5]	**Frank Naylar** (RHBuckler) **5-10-13**(7) MGriffiths (bhd fr 6th)	17	5	16/1	51	—
1828[5]	**Quillwork (USA)** (JPearce) **4-10-3** VSmith (s.i.s: sme hdwy 7th: btn whn blnd 2 out: p.u bef last)		P	14/1	—	—
1814[10]	**Ferny Ball (IRE) (57)** (CaptTAForster) **8-10-8b** SWynne (nt j.w: prom to 5th: t.o whn p.u bef 8th)		P	20/1	—	—
1729[12]	**Seminole Wind (55)** (CRBarwell) **5-10-11v** BFenton (led tl hdd & wknd qckly 6th: p.u bef next)		P	33/1	—	—
1056[4]	**Imperial Honors (IRE)** (NMLampard) **5-10-7**(7) MrLBaker (lw: mstke 4th: a bhd: t.o whn p.u bef 8th)		P	33/1	—	—
	Escadaro (USA) (50) (MrsVCWard) **7-10-5v** JRKavanagh (a bhd: t.o whn p.u bef 8th)		P	33/1	—	—
1685[18]	**Bit 'o' Sunshine** (CASmith) **5-10-2**(7)ow9 BClarke (s.i.s: a bhd: p.u bef 7th)		P	33/1	—	—
				(SP 131.3%)	**11 Rn**	

5m 49.8 (47.80) CSF £10.98 TOTE £1.90: £1.70 £2.20 £1.10 (£16.70) Trio £6.70 OWNER Wentdale Const Ltd (SALTBURN) BRED Stud-On-The-Chart

OFFICIAL EXPLANATION **Seminole Wind: swallowed his tongue and finished distressed.**
1642 Roberty Lea outclassed the opposition and pulled right away on the climb to two out. (Evens)
Stac-Pollaidh went a distant third with a mile left but, despite staying on, never never made any impression on the winner. He has done his winning on faster ground. (8/1: 6/1-9/1)
1562 Quiet Mistress went clear with the winner early on the final circuit, but the blinkers seemed to work nothing like as well this time. Needing reminders passing the Stands, she stopped alarmingly on the stiff climb to two out and, with further reminders, consented to run on again to grab third place close home. (5/2)
1304 Snowy Lane (IRE) would have been two and a half stone better off with the winner in a handicap and was easily outpaced on the final circuit. (7/1)
Frank Naylar has not had much experience, but does look rather slow. (16/1)
1828 Quillwork (USA) (14/1: op 7/1)

2009 CHRISTMAS CRACKER H'CAP CHASE (0-125) (5-Y.O+) (Class D)
2-10 (2-11) **2m 110y (12 fncs)** £4,565.00 (£1,370.00: £660.00: £305.00) GOING: 0.91 sec per fur (S)

				SP	RR	SF
1902*	**Beatson (IRE) (101)** (RHBuckler) **7-11-1** 6x BPowell (a.p: led appr 2 out: easily)	—	1	6/4 1	111+	44
	Juleit Jones (IRE) (90) (JTGifford) **7-10-1**(3) LAspell (bit bkwd: plld hrd: led 3rd: hdd appr 2 out: sn wknd)	19	2	4/1	82	15
1864[2]	**Dr Rocket (86)** (RDickin) **11-10-0** CLlewellyn (chsd ldrs tl mstke 9th)	8	3	100/30 3	70	3
1833[4]	**Count Barachois (USA) (96)** (MrsEHHeath) **8-10-10** AThornton (led to 3rd: wknd 6th: t.o fr 8th)	dist	4	14/1	—	—
	Jacob's Wife (106) (PRWebber) **6-11-6** JOsborne (bit bkwd: chsd ldrs: hit 4th & 5th: 2nd & rdn whn fell 2 out)		F	5/2 2	—	—
				(SP 118.3%)	**5 Rn**	

4m 21.4 (19.40) CSF £7.96 TOTE £2.50: £1.60 £1.40 (£8.20) OWNER Mrs E. B. Gardiner (BRIDPORT) BRED M. Holden in Ireland
1902* Beatson (IRE), a winner without a penalty, was dropping over half a mile in trip. Always close to the pace, his stamina was proving decisive when he was left clear two out. (6/4)
Juleit Jones (IRE), arguably very well in on a couple of her efforts in novice chases last year, pulled far too hard on the uphill stretch over the first three fences and that, coupled with lack of peak-fitness, found her out on the uphill run to the straight. She has joined the powerful Gifford team during her 600 day lay-off and looks well worth keeping an eye on, particularly on an easier track. (4/1)
1864 Dr Rocket frequently runs well here, but was found out by the fast pace in the first half of the race. (100/30)
1833 Count Barachois (USA) could never dominate and was beaten by halfway. (14/1: op 8/1)
Jacob's Wife is far from fully exposed as yet, and was in the process of finishing a clear second when capsizing two from home. She was a couple of lengths down on the winner and looking held at the time. (5/2)

2010 SANTA CLAUS NOVICES' HURDLE (4-Y.O+) (Class E)
2-40 (2-42) **2m (8 hdls)** £2,897.50 (£810.00: £392.50) GOING: 1.08 sec per fur (HY)

				SP	RR	SF
	Red Blazer (MissHCKnight) **5-10-12** JOsborne (bit bkwd: hld up: hdwy 5th: led 2 out: edgd rt appr last: lft clr: easily)	—	1	9/4 1	81+	28

				SP	RR	SF
1796*	**Sprintfayre (90)** (JELong) **8-10-12**(7) AIrvine (led tl hdd & hit 2 out: btn whn lft 2nd last)	12	**2**	12/1	76	23
1777[5]	**Ferrers** (MrsPSly) **5-10-12** RMarley (hdwy 4th: ev ch whn blnd 3 out: kpt on same pce)	½	**3**	33/1	69	16
1505*	**Royal Raven (IRE) (109)** (JTGifford) **5-10-9**(3) LAspell (hdwy 5th: one pce appr last)	2	**4**	5/1 3	67	14
	Vitaman (IRE) (MrsJPitman) **7-10-12** WMarston (bkwd: chsd ldrs: nt qckn fr 3 out)	1¾	**5**	33/1	65	12
1317[8]	**Strathminster** (KCBailey) **5-10-12** CO'Dwyer (bit bkwd: hdwy appr 3 out: btn appr next)	nk	**6**	9/1	64	11
	Captain Walter (IRE) (JABOld) **6-10-12** GUpton (bkwd: hdwy 5th: wknd appr 2 out)	18	**7**	10/1	46	—
	Ekeus (IRE) (JSKing) **6-10-12** CMaude (bkwd: prom to 3 out)	8	**8**	33/1	38	—
1651*	**Hoh Warrior (IRE)** (CPEBrooks) **5-11-5** GBradley (hld up: hdwy & blnd 5th: wkng whn hit 2 out)	16	**9**	5/2 2	29	—
1640[9]	**Foxies Lad** (NMBabbage) **5-10-12** VSlattery (swtg: plld hrd: chsd ldr tl wknd appr 3 out)	5	**10**	25/1	17	—
	Legible (SMellor) **8-10-12** NMann (bkwd: in tch to 5th)	nk	**11**	9/1	17	—
1810[F]	**Alongwaydown (IRE)** (DRGandolfo) **7-10-12** DLeahy (bkwd: a bhd)	8	**12**	33/1	9	—
1855[9]	**Trehane** (NAGraham) **4-10-7** NWilliamson (a bhd)	nk	**13**	33/1	4	—
	Milwaukee (IRE) (OBrennan) **7-10-7** MBrennan (bkwd: in tch to 5th)	15	**14**	16/1	—	—
	Motoqua (DNicholson) **4-10-7** AMaguire (hdwy 5th: ev ch whn fell last)		**F**	8/1	—	—
1729[11]	**Ki Chi Saga (USA)** (MMadgwick) **4-10-12** DMorris (lw: mstke 3rd: a bhd: t.o whn p.u bef 3 out)		**P**	33/1	—	—
				(SP 151.3%)	**16 Rn**	

4m 10.3 (24.30) CSF £34.12 TOTE £4.10: £1.60 £2.00 £11.60 (£31.80) Trio Not won; £359.18 to Hereford 20/12/96 OWNER Mr T. H. Shrimpton (WANTAGE) BRED Sir Stanley Grinstead

STEWARDS' ENQUIRY Obj. to Red Blazer by Irvine overruled. Irvine fined £60 (no good or reasonable grounds for objection).

Red Blazer, who broke down at Aintree twenty months ago, looked back to something like his best on this hurdles debut. He would have won without the last-flight departure of his main rival and could take high rank. (9/4)

1796* Sprintfayre, beaten in one of the best selling races here in a long time last month, showed just how good that form is. Marginally squeezed out by Motoqua going to the last, he lost nothing in defeat in this company. (12/1: op 20/1)

1777 Ferrers lost a good pitch with a mistake three out, but for which he would have finished even closer. (33/1)

1505* Royal Raven (IRE), a very good mover, got to the back of the leading group going to three out, but found little from that point. (5/1: op 3/1)

Vitaman (IRE) did not look fit, but ran his best race over hurdles without being knocked about, and is clearly learning. (33/1)

Strathminster again showed promise, and there will be more to come as he gets race-fit. (9/1: 6/1-10/1)

Captain Walter (IRE) (10/1: 20/1-8/1)

1651* Hoh Warrior (IRE) was let down by his jumping, but again flopped on soft ground as he had on his only start last season. (5/2: 2/1-100/30)

Legible (9/1: 6/1-10/1)

Motoqua won an Irish bumper last time, after finishing seventh in a Newmarket maiden for James Fanshawe as a two-year-old. Fighting fit, despite six months off, she was getting the worst of a good race with the winner when taking a heavy fall at the last. Provided this fall has not put her off, she looks the sort to do well over hurdles. (8/1: 6/1-10/1)

2011 LADBROKE H'CAP CHASE (0-125) (5-Y.O+) (Class D)

3-10 (3-12) **3m 1f (18 fncs)** £7,262.50 (£2,200.00: £1,075.00: £512.50) GOING: 0.91 sec per fur (S)

				SP	RR	SF
1674[2]	**Price's Hill (107)** (KCBailey) **9-10-10** CO'Dwyer (swtg: hdwy 8th: mstke 13th: led 4 out to next: led appr 2 out: hit last: styd on strly)	—	**1**	4/1 2	116	37
1631*	**River Mandate (125)** (CaptTAForster) **9-12-0** AThornton (chsd ldrs: rdn 15th: kpt on flat)	4	**2**	5/2 1	131	52
1765[5]	**Spuffington (113)** (JTGifford) **8-11-2** PHide (chsd ldrs: lost pl 10th: rallied 14th: nt qckn flat)	s.h	**3**	11/1	119	40
1765[8]	**Special Account (97)** (CRBarwell) **10-10-0** BFenton (hit 8th: a bhd)	dist	**4**	14/1	—	—
1631[2]	**Even Blue (IRE) (117)** (DMcCain) **8-11-6** RDunwoody (j.w: led 15th: led 3 out: sn hdd & wknd)	1½	**5**	5/2 1	—	—
1287[U]	**Big Ben Dun (112)** (CPEBrooks) **10-11-1** GBradley (lw: a bhd: t.o whn p.u bef 2 out)		**P**	11/1	—	—
1765[9]	**Ghia Gneuiagh (110)** (NATwiston-Davies) **10-10-13** CMaude (bhd whn mstke 13th: t.o whn p.u bef 2 out)		**P**	25/1	—	—
	Brave Buccaneer (105) (AndrewTurnell) **9-10-8** SMcNeill (bkwd: hld up: hdwy 11th: mstke 14th: hit 3 out: sn wknd: p.u bef last)		**P**	16/1	—	—
	Celtic Barle (102) (HBHodge) **12-10-5** AMaguire (bkwd: hdwy 11th: rdn & wknd appr 2 out: p.u bef last)		**P**	10/1 3	—	—
1805[5]	**All the Aces (125)** (JJO'Neill) **9-12-0** PNiven (a bhd: t.o whn p.u bef last)		**P**	16/1	—	—
	Sheelin Lad (IRE) (100) (MrsTJMcInnesSkinner) **8-10-3**ow3 GUpton (chsd ldr: hit 12th: wknd appr 3 out: p.u bef 2 out)		**P**	25/1	—	—
	Mweenish (97) (PRWebber) **14-10-0** RBellamy (bkwd: bhd fr 8th: blnd 11th: t.o whn p.u bef 2 out)		**P**	33/1	—	—
				(SP 132.0%)	**12 Rn**	

6m 45.1 (30.10) CSF £15.44 CT £102.42 TOTE £4.70: £1.30 £2.40 £4.30 (£7.10) Trio £52.60 OWNER Mr G. D. W. Swire (UPPER LAMBOURN) BRED Mrs P. Hawkes

LONG HANDICAP Special Account 9-12 Sheelin Lad (IRE) 9-3 Mweenish 9-3

1674 Price's Hill put in a fine round of jumping by his standards, and his stamina came to the fore in the final mile. (4/1)

1631* River Mandate was rather deliberate over some of the early fences and was in trouble some way out, but kept battling away, and was rewarded with snatching second place right on the line. (5/2: 7/4-11/4)

1540 Spuffington lost his place going out on the final circuit, but recovered within half a mile. Just about the last on the bridle, the tank emptied shortly before the penultimate fence, although he only forfeited second close home. (11/1: 7/1-12/1)

1057* Special Account never left the trailing group on this occasion. (14/1)

1631 Even Blue (IRE) jumped impeccably, but was found out by the testing conditions, and his front-running efforts folded rapidly going to two out. (5/2)

1287 Big Ben Dun (11/1: 7/1-12/1)

Brave Buccaneer, having only his second race since February 1995, looked burly, but ran well for a long way, although a tired jump three out finished him completely. He is still handicapped to win a staying chase. (16/1)

Celtic Barle, off a mark 7lb lower than when winning last time, had the small matter of a 665-day absence to overcome. Moving up threateningly in the final mile, lack of a race told at the top of the hill. He is long in the tooth now, but the Handicapper has given him a chance. (10/1)

2012 IVY STANDARD OPEN N.H. FLAT RACE (4, 5 & 6-Y.O) (Class H)

3-40 (3-43) **2m** £1,416.50 (£394.00: £189.50)

				SP	RR	SF
	Princeful (IRE) (MrsJPitman) **5-11-8**(3) GHogan (bit bkwd: plld hrd: led after 2f: pushed clr fnl f)	—	**1**	7/2 2	64 f	—
1685*	**Billingsgate** (DrDChesney) **4-11-4**(7) NWillmington (a.p: ev ch 4f out: one pce appr fnl f)	2½	**2**	7/1 3	62 f	—
	King Mole (JABOld) **5-11-4** GUpton (lt-f: lengthy, unf: q lt made: hdwy 6f out: rdn 2f out: r.o fnl f)	3	**3**	7/1 3	52 f	—
	Mr Moonlight (IRE) (CPEBrooks) **4-11-4** GBradley (q gd st: tall, leggy: bkwd: in tch: hdwy 7f out: wknd over 2f out)	14	**4**	12/1	38 f	—

1573^{2}	**Shore Party (IRE)** (NATwiston-Davies) **4-10-11**(7) LSuthern (prom tl rdn & wknd 4f out)	hd	**5**	7/4 [1]	37 f	—
1800^{3}	**Brookhampton Lane (IRE)** (MrsAJBowlby) **5-11-4** BPowell (chsd ldrs 9f)	27	**6**	9/1	10 f	—
	Jolly Heart (IRE) (OBrennan) **6-11-4** MBrennan (q attr, chsing type: hld up: hdwy 7f out: wknd 3f out)	4	**7**	20/1	6 f	—
1573^{8}	**Willows Roulette** (AGHobbs) **4-11-4** RGreene (plld hrd: prom 10f)	½	**8**	33/1	6 f	—
	Belvento (IRE) (JTGifford) **4-11-4** PHide (cmpt, rather neat: bit bkwd: a bhd)	18	**9**	8/1	—	—
	Sheet Lightning (RJSmith) **4-11-4** CMaude (plain: chsd ldrs 10f)	dist	**10**	25/1	—	—
	Bartholomew Fair (CADwyer) **5-11-4** ILawrence (q neat, wl made: bkwd: bhd: hdwy 7f out: wknd over 3f out)	1¼	**11**	8/1	—	—
	Thetwokays (OBrennan) **5-10-11**(7) SPorritt (unf: bkwd: a bhd)	½	**12**	33/1	—	—
	Mr Robstee (AJChamberlain) **5-11-4** LHarvey (fair sort: bit bkwd: led 2f: wknd 8f out)	4	**13**	33/1	—	—
	Benjamin Jones (CJHemsley) **4-11-4** BFenton (w'like, fair sort: bkwd: a bhd: t.o)	dist	**14**	20/1	—	—
	Birdietoo (MrsPSly) **4-10-13** RMarley (unf, lt made: bkwd: chsd ldrs 8f: wknd qckly: t.o)	19	**15**	33/1	—	—

(SP 148.6%) **15 Rn**

4m 12.4 CSF £32.82 TOTE £5.00: £1.70 £3.70 £2.10 (£21.30) Trio £64.00 OWNER Robert & Elizabeth Hitchins (UPPER LAMBOURN) BRED J. S. Bellingham

Princeful (IRE) pulled hard until getting in front and won, once again, with some authority. (7/2: 6/4-4/1)

1685* Billingsgate looked fit this time and gave the winner something to think about in the straight. (7/1: op 7/2)

King Mole is rather lightly-made, but showed plenty, moving up on the outside and staying on in the final furlong. (7/1)

Mr Moonlight (IRE), unruly and green in the paddock, behaved himself in the race and should have learnt much. (12/1: 6/1-14/1)

1573 Shore Party (IRE) is not over-big and had done his running before the home turn. (7/4: 9/4-6/4)

1800 Brookhampton Lane (IRE) was left behind soon after halfway and never looked likely to get back in contention. (9/1: 6/1-10/1)

Jolly Heart (IRE), an eyecatching son of a winning hurdler, shaped with more promise than his finishing position suggests. (20/1)

Belvento (IRE) (8/1: op 4/1)

Bartholomew Fair has a Flat pedigree, but was sold unraced from the Gosden yard in 1994. Not over-big, he briefly got to the leading group and may not have got the trip. (8/1)

2013a - 2033a : (Irish Racing) - See Computer Raceform

T/Jkpt: £7,100.00 (0.88 Tckts); £463.94 to Hereford 20/12/96. T/Plpt: £163.30 (132.25 Tckts). T/Qdpt: £9.70 (167.59 Tckts) Dk

1768-HEREFORD (R-H) (Good to soft)
Friday December 20th

WEATHER: overcast

2034 THYME MAIDEN HURDLE (I) (4-Y.O+) (Class E)

12-50 (12-52) **2m 1f (9 hdls)** £2,192.00 (£612.00: £296.00) GOING: 0.50 sec per fur (GS)

				SP	RR	SF
1659^{3}	**Star Selection** (JMackie) **5-11-2**(3) EHusband (mde all: clr fr 3 out: r.o wl)	—	**1**	11/2	77	36
974^{5}	**King Rat (IRE)** (JGMO'Shea) **5-11-0v**(5) MichaelBrennan (hld up: hdwy 5th: styd on fr 2 out: no ch w wnr)	12	**2**	16/1	66	25
1788^{3}	**Drakestone (90)** (RLBrown) **5-11-0**(5) MrRThornton (swtg: chsd wnr: no imp fr 3 out)	4	**3**	9/2 [3]	62	21
900^{10}	**Frome Lad** (WGMTurner) **4-10-12**(7) JPower (bit bkwd: prom tl wknd appr 2 out)	23	**4**	33/1	40	—
1726^{4}	**Night City** (LadyHerries) **5-11-5** JOsborne (swtg: bhd: j.slowly 1st: hdwy appr 5th: wknd qckly 3 out)	7	**5**	2/1 [1]	34	—
	Lasto Adree (IRE) (GThorner) **5-11-5** BPowell (bkwd: hld up: mstke 2nd: hdwy 4th: wknd 6th: t.o)	26	**6**	7/1	9	—
1726^{9}	**Mr Hemp** (AGFoster) **4-11-5** DerekByrne (bhd fr 5th: t.o)	10	**7**	50/1	—	—
22^{3}	**Bramley May** (TRGeorge) **6-11-5** APMcCoy (prom tl wknd rapidly appr 3 out: t.o)	1¼	**8**	5/2 [2]	—	—
1336^{9}	**Aqua Amber** (JMBradley) **4-11-5** DWalsh (bit bkwd: mstkes: bhd fr 4th: t.o 5th: p.u bef 2 out)		**P**	50/1	—	—
1250^{P}	**Shady Emma** (FJordan) **4-11-0** SWynne (bhd whn p.u & dismntd bef 4th)		**P**	66/1	—	—
1830^{P}	**Woodlands Lad Too (65)** (PAPritchard) **4-11-5** RBellamy (a bhd: t.o whn mstke 6th: p.u bef 2 out)		**P**	100/1	—	—
1905^{P}	**Amazon Heights** (LPGrassick) **4-10-11**(3) GHogan (a bhd: t.o 4th: p.u bef 2 out)		**P**	100/1	—	—

(SP 124.2%) **12 Rn**

4m 8.3 (15.30) CSF £82.68 TOTE £7.00: £2.50 £2.00 £1.50 (£31.40) Trio £30.60; £6.03 to Uttoxeter 21/12/96 OWNER Mr R. M. Mitchell (CHURCH BROUGHTON) BRED Stanley Estate and Stud Co

1659 Star Selection, given a breather at halfway, found his front-running tactics paying off on this softer ground. (11/2)

974 King Rat (IRE), tried in a visor, had give in the ground this time and gave the impression he requires further. (16/1)

1788 Drakestone, rather warm in the paddock, could not go with the winner from the third last. (9/2: op 3/1)

Frome Lad is a half-brother to chaser Nazzaro. (33/1)

1726 Night City was noted swishing his tail when his chance had already gone, and gave the impression he was hating every minute of it. (2/1: op evens)

Lasto Adree (IRE) (7/1: 4/1-10/1)

2035 THYME MAIDEN HURDLE (II) (4-Y.O+) (Class E)

1-20 (1-20) **2m 1f (9 hdls)** £2,178.00 (£608.00: £294.00) GOING: 0.50 sec per fur (GS)

				SP	RR	SF
	Mid Day Chaser (IRE) (PRWebber) **5-11-0** JOsborne (hld up: hdwy appr 5th: led appr 2 out: clr appr last: comf)	—	**1**	5/2 [2]	82+	33
1830^{5}	**Total Joy (IRE)** (CJMann) **5-11-5** JRailton (hld up: hdwy to ld 5th: hdd appr 2 out: one pce)	10	**2**	4/1 [3]	78	29
1782^{8}	**Kevasingo** (JLSpearing) **4-11-5** TJMurphy (hld up: hdwy appr 5th: one pce fr 3 out)	4	**3**	50/1	74	25
	Tantara Lodge (IRE) (KCBailey) **5-11-5** CO'Dwyer (hld up: hdwy 5th: mstke 6th: sn lost pl & eased)	26	**4**	11/1	49	—
1810^{P}	**Royrace** (WMBrisbourne) **4-11-5** SWynne (prom to 6th)	nk	**5**	100/1	49	—
1633^{7}	**Milling Brook** (JMBradley) **4-11-2**(3) TDascombe (hld up: hdwy appr 5th: rdn & wknd 6th)	hd	**6**	50/1	49	—
1151^{6}	**Nanjizal** (KSBridgwater) **4-11-2**(3) RMassey (a bhd: t.o fr 6th)	dist	**7**	100/1	—	—
	Daunt (FJordan) **4-11-5** APMcCoy (plld hrd: nt j.w: led & j.rt 3rd: clr 4th: hdd 5th: wknd rapidly: t.o)	2½	**8**	10/11 [1]	—	—
1282^{3}	**Eurolink Shadow (83)** (DMcCain) **4-11-5b**[1] DWalsh (led tl hdd & carried rt 3rd: hrd rdn & wknd 6th: t.o)	1¼	**9**	50/1	—	—
	Red Phantom (IRE) (SMellor) **4-11-5** NMann (a bhd: t.o fr 6th)	3	**10**	25/1	—	—

(SP 121.0%) **10 Rn**

4m 7.8 (14.80) CSF £12.95 TOTE £3.50: £1.10 £2.00 £9.40 (£9.80) Trio £40.20 OWNER Tavern Racing (BANBURY) BRED J. Duddy

Mid Day Chaser (IRE) had shown plenty of ability in bumpers last season, and connections are thinking in terms of the Mares Only Series. (5/2: 2/1-4/1)

1830 Total Joy (IRE) may do better over a longer trip. (4/1: op 9/4)
Kevasingo had presumably got bogged down in soft ground on his hurdling debut at Chepstow. (50/1)
Tantara Lodge (IRE) was not knocked about after a mistake four out. (11/1: 5/1-12/1)
Daunt, bought for 100,000 guineas out of John Gosden's yard, is going to have to revert to the Flat to repay some of his purchase price on this evidence. (10/11: 1/2-evens)

2036 CLOVES NOVICES' CONDITIONAL H'CAP HURDLE (0-100) (4-Y.O+) (Class F)

1-50 (1-50) **2m 3f 110y (11 hdls)** £2,087.00 (£582.00: £281.00) GOING: 0.50 sec per fur (GS)

				SP	RR	SF
	Mahler (90) (NATwiston-Davies) **6-11-7**(3) DWalsh (a.p: rdn 8th: led 2 out: all out)	—	1	100/30[2]	69	—
1814*	**Colwall (80)** (MissPMWhittle) **5-10-4**(10) 7x KHibbert (a.p: led appr 6th: hdd 2 out: sn rdn: one pce)	2½	2	4/1[3]	57	—
1537[8]	**Ecu de France (IRE) (66)** (PCRitchens) **6-9-11**(3) MichaelBrennan (sn wl bhd: styd on fr 3 out: nvr nrr)	7	3	50/1	37	—
1838*	**Urban Lily (87)** (RJHodges) **6-10-11b**(10) 7x JHarris (prom tl wknd 7th)	6	4	2/1[1]	53	—
1762[2]	**Time Leader (75)** (RDickin) **4-9-13**(10) XAizpuru (prom: wkng whn mstke 8th)	3	5	100/30[2]	39	—
1638[10]	**Lyphard's Fable (USA) (70)** (TRGeorge) **5-9-8**(10) CHynes (chsd ldr tl appr 7th: sn wknd)	3½	6	14/1	31	—
1762[5]	**Madam Rose (IRE) (66)** (JWMullins) **6-9-4**(10) DavidTurner (led tl appr 6th: wknd rapidly: sn t.o)	dist	7	50/1	—	—
1814[9]	**The Cheese Baron (66)** (SMellor) **5-9-4**(10) SHearn (a bhd: t.o fr 6th: p.u bef 3 out)		P	50/1	—	—
1772[11]	**Analogue (IRE) (66)** (RJEckley) **4-9-11**(3) DJKavanagh (sn t.o: p.u & dismntd bef 5th)		P	16/1	—	—
				(SP 117.9%)	**9 Rn**	

5m 3.1 (32.10) CSF £16.57 CT £498.00 TOTE £5.80: £2.70 £1.30 £6.40 (£15.40) Trio £46.70 OWNER English Badminton Partnership (CHELTENHAM) BRED E. Peary
LONG HANDICAP Ecu de France (IRE) 9-13 Madam Rose (IRE) 9-4 The Cheese Baron 9-13 Analogue (IRE) 9-10
OFFICIAL EXPLANATION **Analogue (IRE): was found to have a fractured pelvis the next morning.**
Mahler finished very tired and strength from the saddle helped tip the scales in his favour. (100/30: 9/4-7/2)
1814* Colwall found one too good under his penalty on this softer surface. (4/1)
Ecu de France (IRE) came from the next parish, but could not reel in the leg-weary leading pair in time. (50/1)
1838* Urban Lily found this more competitive than at Plumpton last time. (2/1)
1762 Time Leader did not stay this extended trip on ground as soft as this. (100/30: 9/4-7/2)

2037 CARAWAY NOVICES' H'CAP CHASE (0-100) (5-Y.O+) (Class E)

2-20 (2-22) **2m (12 fncs)** £2,995.65 (£907.20: £443.10: £211.05) GOING: 0.50 sec per fur (GS)

				SP	RR	SF
1763[P]	**Captain Stockford (69)** (PWegmann) **9-10-0** SWynne (mde all: mstke 4th: lft clr & hit 2 out: r.o wl)	—	1	33/1	77	4
1815*	**Scottish Bambi (103)** (PRWebber) **8-12-6** 7x JOsborne (hld up: mstke 6th (water): hdwy 8th: r.o flat: nt trble wnr)	4	2	3/1[1]	107	34
1449[3]	**Northern Singer (71)** (RJHodges) **6-9-13**(3) TDascombe (hld up: mstke 2nd: hdwy 7th: btn whn lft 2nd & hit 2 out)	6	3	3/1[1]	69	—
1708[5]	**Bold Acre (81)** (JMBradley) **6-10-12** NWilliamson (hld up: rdn after 4 out: nvr nr to chal)	5	4	9/2[2]	74	1
1875[U]	**San Diego Charger (IRE) (74)** (ABarrow) **5-10-0**(5) MrRThornton (nvr nr ldrs)	11	5	20/1	56	—
1449[C]	**Ashmead Rambler (IRE) (70)** (PJHobbs) **6-10-1**ow1 CMaude (hld up: hdwy 8th: btn whn hmpd 2 out)	5	6	3/1[1]	47	—
	Pandora's Prize (69) (JLSpearing) **10-10-0** TJMurphy (a bhd)	1	7	50/1	45	—
1680[P]	**Il Bambino (89)** (HJManners) **8-11-6** MrACharles-Jones (a bhd: t.o fr 8th)	22	8	14/1	43	—
1680[P]	**Caracol (71)** (JNeville) **7-9-13**(3)ow2 GHogan (hld up: stdy hdwy 8th: cl 6th whn fell 3 out)		F	16/1	—	—
1572[U]	**The Wayward Bishop (IRE) (71)** (MrsLCTaylor) **7-9-9b**[1](7)ow2 DCO'Connor (chsd wnr: hit 4th: ev ch whn fell 2 out)		F	33/1	—	—
	Dunnicks View (72) (FGTucker) **7-10-3**ow1 GUpton (mstke 2nd: t.o 7th: p.u bef 3 out)		P	11/1[3]	—	—
				(SP 126.7%)	**11 Rn**	

4m 9.0 (18.00) CSF £130.75 CT £376.31 TOTE £68.20: £10.40 £1.70 £1.40 (£58.60) Trio £90.50; £65.04 to Uttoxeter 21/12/96 OWNER Mr P. Wegmann (GLOUCESTER) BRED Mrs A. C. Wakeham
LONG HANDICAP Captain Stockford 9-5 Pandora's Prize 9-5 Caracol 9-5 The Wayward Bishop (IRE) 9-5 Ashmead Rambler (IRE) 9-12
OFFICIAL EXPLANATION **Captain Stockford: accounting for the horse's apparent improvement in form, the trainer and jockey said the gelding is very boisterous and likes to dominate, which he was unable to do on his previous run. It was also suggested that the shorter distance suited him also.**
1414 Captain Stockford was the subject of an enquiry into his apparent improvement in form. The Stewards accepted the explanation that the gelding was very boisterous, likes to dominate and probably appreciated this shorter distance. (33/1)
1815* Scottish Bambi was no less than 25lb higher than when beating Poucher here last month. (3/1: op 2/1)
1449 Northern Singer was fitter than when finishing twenty-two lengths behind Scottish Bambi on 25lb better terms a month ago. (3/1)
1708 Bold Acre could not take advantage of a 3lb lower mark. (9/2)
1449 Ashmead Rambler (IRE) had no excuses, but would have finished closer but for being hampered at the penultimate fence. (3/1)
Il Bambino (14/1: 10/1-16/1)
Caracol, twice a winner between the Flags, would have been in the money had he stood up. (16/1)

2038 COWSLIP (S) HURDLE (4-Y.O+) (Class G)

2-50 (2-50) **2m 1f (9 hdls)** £2,052.00 (£572.00: £276.00) GOING: 0.50 sec per fur (GS)

				SP	RR	SF
	My Man in Dundalk (IRE) (BJCurley) **7-10-12** EMurphy (led tl appr 3rd: led 3 out: r.o wl)	—	1	2/1[2]	64	8
1857*	**Fleet Cadet (76)** (MCPipe) **5-10-12v** APMcCoy (hld up: hdwy appr 5th: rdn & ev ch 2 out: r.o flat)	nk	2	Evens[1]	64	8
1630[8]	**Scottish Wedding (75)** (TWall) **6-10-11**(3) RMassey (hdwy 3rd: rdn & ev ch 3 out: wknd appr last)	11	3	5/1[3]	55	—
1874[6]	**Comeonup** (JMBradley) **5-10-12** NWilliamson (led appr 3rd: hdd 3 out: rdn & wknd 2 out)	14	4	10/1	40	—
1902[U]	**Halham Tarn (IRE)** (HJManners) **6-10-12**(7) ADowling (hld up: hdwy appr 5th: wknd 6th)	5	5	11/1	43	—
	Lajadhal (FR) (KBishop) **7-11-5** LHarvey (bit bkwd: prom: wkng whn mstke 6th)	4	6	14/1	39	—
	Nordic Flight (RJEckley) **8-10-7**(5) DJKavanagh (a bhd)	nk	7	50/1	31	—
1782[7]	**Stevie's Wonder (IRE)** (BJLlewellyn) **6-10-12** MrJLLlewellyn (a bhd)	9	8	25/1	23	—
	Applianceofscience (66) (KOWarner) **9-11-12** JRyan (a bhd)	4	9	33/1	33	—
1828[P]	**Woodlands Energy (50)** (PAPritchard) **5-10-7** RBellamy (a bhd: t.o)	dist	10	25/1	—	—
1663[9]	**Bold Charlie (60)** (SMellor) **4-10-12** NMann (prom to 5th: t.o)	3½	11	25/1	—	—
1680[R]	**Tibbs Inn (54)** (ABarrow) **7-10-7b**[1](5) MrRThornton (rel to r: wl bhd most of wy: t.o whn p.u bef 3 out)		P	33/1	—	—
				(SP 143.5%)	**12 Rn**	

4m 13.2 (20.20) CSF £5.28 TOTE £3.50: £2.30 £1.20 £1.70 (£4.40) Trio £12.40 OWNER Mrs B. J. Curley (NEWMARKET) BRED J. G. Groome

Bt in 5,400 gns
Comeonup clmd T Connop £5,750
My Man in Dundalk (IRE), off the course for exactly 1,000 days, showed his trainer has not lost his touch. (2/1)
1857* Fleet Cadet found the winner always had the edge, but lost nothing in defeat. (Evens)
1034 Scottish Wedding was running in a seller for the first time this season. (5/1)
1770 Comeonup did not see out the trip in this yielding ground. (10/1)
Halham Tarn (IRE) (11/1: 6/1-12/1)
Lajadhal (FR) (14/1: op 8/1)

2039 COMFREY MAIDEN CHASE (5-Y.O+) (Class E)

3-20 (3-21) **3m 1f 110y (19 fncs)** £3,200.40 (£970.20: £474.60: £226.80) GOING: 0.50 sec per fur (GS)

				SP	RR	SF
	Indian Tracker (MCPipe) **6-11-5** CMaude (lw: led to 2nd: w ldr: led 13th: r.o wl fr 2 out)	—	**1**	5/1[3]	107	20
1797[4]	**Brogeen Lady (IRE)** (DRGandolfo) **6-11-0** APMcCoy (led 2nd to 13th: ev ch 3 out: one pce fr 2 out)	16	**2**	9/4[1]	92	5
1468[3]	**Anythingyoulike** (CASmith) **7-11-5** MRichards (wl bhd tl sme hdwy 12th: bdly hmpd 14th: n.d after)	16	**3**	14/1	87	—
1711[P]	**Apatura Hati** (RHAlner) **7-10-9**(5) MrRThornton (prom: mstke 15th: wknd 4 out)	6	**4**	14/1	78	—
1275[14]	**Thunder Road (IRE)** (RDickin) **5-11-5** BPowell (a bhd)	7	**5**	50/1	80	—
1538[P]	**Rainbow Fountain** (NMLampard) **9-11-0** MrAKinane (prom: 4th whn blnd 14th: sn wknd)	2½	**6**	50/1	72	—
1683[13]	**Greenfield George (IRE)** (PJHobbs) **5-11-5** NWilliamson (bhd whn j.slowly 9th: hmpd 14th: sn t.o)	dist	**7**	25/1	—	—
	Wandering Light (IRE) (CaptTAForster) **7-11-5** SWynne (hdwy 12th: cl 5th whn bdly hmpd bend appr 14th: nt rcvr)	2	**8**	9/2[2]	—	—
	Mr Lovely (IRE) (JNeville) **5-11-2**(3) TDascombe (bit bkwd: fell 1st)		**F**	12/1	—	—
1331[3]	**Lord Nitrogen (USA) (78)** (BJLlewellyn) **6-11-5** SCurran (prom: 5th whn fell 14th)		**F**	20/1	—	—
1787[F]	**Saucy's Wolf** (NJHawke) **6-11-5** LHarvey (j.bdly: t.o 4th: blnd 9th: p.u bef 10th)		**P**	50/1	—	—
1829[U]	**Mount Serrath (IRE) (95)** (CREgerton) **8-11-5** JOsborne (bhd fr 10th: t.o whn p.u bef 4 out)		**P**	13/2	—	—
1711[F]	**Langton Parmill** (WGMTurner) **11-10-12**(7) NWillmington (mstke 11th: sn bhd: t.o whn p.u bef 4 out)		**P**	33/1	—	—
1955[F]	**Ramstown Lad (IRE)** (KCBailey) **7-11-5** CO'Dwyer (blnd 2nd: a bhd: t.o whn p.u bef 2 out)		**P**	15/2	—	—
581[3]	**Dustys Trail (IRE) (66)** (PBowen) **7-11-5** DWalsh (rdn 7th: t.o 11th: p.u bef 4 out)		**P**	20/1	—	—
1771[4]	**Jolly Boat** (FJordan) **9-11-5** JRKavanagh (mid div: mstke 5th: blnd & uns rdr 8th)		**U**	8/1	—	—

(SP 145.0%) **16 Rn**

6m 39.5 (29.50) CSF £18.79 TOTE £4.30: £2.40 £1.70 £5.10 (£16.40) Trio £57.10 OWNER Joe & Joanne Richards (WELLINGTON)
WEIGHT FOR AGE 5yo-1lb

Indian Tracker won a bumper on the soft at Lingfield in March, and the bold policy of going straight over fences certainly paid off. He can defy a penalty. (5/1: op 3/1)
1797 Brogeen Lady (IRE) could not live with the winner from the penultimate fence. (9/4)
1468 Anythingyoulike would probably have finished closer with better luck in running. (14/1)
Wandering Light (IRE) won three of his four point-to-points in Ireland in 1995, and this first run over fences can be safely ignored. (9/2)
1447 Mount Serrath (IRE) (13/2: 4/1-7/1)
1955 Ramstown Lad (IRE) (15/2: 4/1-8/1)

2040 ROSEMARY H'CAP HURDLE (0-120) (4-Y.O+) (Class D)

3-50 (3-51) **2m 1f (9 hdls)** £2,857.00 (£802.00: £391.00) GOING: 0.50 sec per fur (GS)

				SP	RR	SF
1791[2]	**Hay Dance (98)** (PJHobbs) **5-10-11** NWilliamson (hld up: hdwy 5th: led appr last: shkn up: r.o)	—	**1**	5/2[1]	77	15
1791[7]	**Bietschhorn Bard (88)** (DRGandolfo) **6-9-10**(5) SophieMitchell (hld up & bhd: gd hdwy appr 3 out: ev ch last: r.o)	½	**2**	3/1[2]	67	5
1726[2]	**Sailep (FR) (100)** (RJHodges) **4-10-10**(3) TDascombe (a.p: led 6th tl wknd appr last)	9	**3**	4/1	70	8
1866[3]	**Wadada (106)** (DBurchell) **5-11-5** DJBurchell (hld up: hdwy 4th: led after 5th to 6th: hrd rdn appr 2 out: sn wknd)	6	**4**	5/1	70	8
1793[15]	**Nashville Star (USA) (100)** (RMathew) **5-10-13v** RBellamy (w ldr to 4th: wknd appr 3 out)	18	**5**	12/1	48	—
	River Island (USA) (103) (JABOld) **8-10-9**(7) EGreehy (hld up: a bhd)	1¾	**6**	20/1	49	—
1663[P]	**Ethbaat (USA) (90)** (MJHeaton-Ellis) **5-10-3** MRichards (hld up & plld hrd: hit 2nd: a bhd)	11	**7**	20/1	26	—
1382[2]	**Robert's Toy (IRE) (115)** (MCPipe) **5-12-0** APMcCoy (led tl after 5th: wknd appr 3 out)	5	**8**	7/2[3]	46	—

(SP 129.7%) **8 Rn**

4m 11.4 (18.40) CSF £11.64 CT £28.06 TOTE £2.50: £2.00 £1.10 £1.60 (£8.30) OWNER Wessex Go Racing Partnership (MINEHEAD) BRED Limestone Stud

1791 Hay Dance, in no hurry to strike the front, ran out a decisive, if narrow, winner. (5/2)
1323 Bietschhorn Bard came with a well-timed challenge, but found the winner traveling strongly, and was not so quickly away from the final flight. (3/1)
1726 Sailep (FR) was 12lb higher than when second to Canary Falcon at Kempton. (4/1)
1866 Wadada has never won on ground as soft as this. (5/1)
1439 Nashville Star (USA) (12/1: op 8/1)

T/Jkpt: Not won; £2,965.07 to Ascot 21/12/96. T/Plpt: £120.00 (81.07 Tckts). T/Qdpt: £22.10 (36.16 Tckts). KH

1849-HEXHAM (L-H) (Good to soft)

Friday December 20th

WEATHER: overcast

2041 MINCE PIE NOVICES' HURDLE (4-Y.O+) (Class E)

12-30 (12-30) **2m (8 hdls)** £2,700.00 (£750.00: £360.00) GOING: 0.65 sec per fur (S)

				SP	RR	SF
1687[3]	**Qattara (IRE)** (WMcKeown) **6-10-12** GCahill (lw: chsd ldrs: led after 2 out: sn clr: hit last)	—	**1**	6/1[2]	82	23
	Elastic (RGCockburn) **10-10-7** LO'Hara (led tl hdd 2 out: kpt on same pce)	6	**2**	16/1	71	12
1804[2]	**Fassan (IRE) (108)** (MDHammond) **4-10-12** RGarritty (hld up: smooth hdwy ½-wy: led 2 out: sn hdd & btn)	2	**3**	1/2[1]	74	15
1802[P]	**Cairo Prince (IRE)** (JJO'Neill) **6-10-12** ARoche (in tch tl lost pl 3 out: styd on again towards fin)	11	**4**	20/1	63	4
1666[6]	**Calder King** (JLEyre) **5-10-12b** BStorey (in tch: effrt 3 out: rdn & no imp)	s.h	**5**	10/1	63	4

Form	Horse	Dist	Pos	SP	RR	SF
	Storm Call (DWWhillans) **5-10-7** DBentley (lw: in tch: effrt 3 out: no imp)	3	**6**	20/1	55	—
	Posted Abroad (IRE) (HowardJohnson) **4-10-12** ADobbin (in tch tl wknd appr last)	2	**7**	14/1	58	—
1802[U]	**Star Master** (LLungo) **5-10-12** PNiven (chsd ldrs: hit 4th: blnd 3 out: sn wknd: t.o)	dist	**8**	8/1[3]	—	—
	Robara (80) (SJLeadbetter) **6-11-5** NLeach (t.o fr ½-wy)	16	**9**	20/1	—	—
1309[P]	**Rustic Warrior** (JWade) **6-10-12** KJones (chsd ldrs to 4th: sn t.o)	dist	**10**	50/1	—	—
1579[10]	**Guile Point** (DALamb) **5-10-7** JBurke (bit bkwd: t.o fr ½-wy: p.u bef 2 out)		**P**	50/1	—	—

(SP 131.9%) **11 Rn**

4m 6.6 (18.60) CSF £93.70 TOTE £8.50: £2.20 £3.90 £1.00 (£33.50) Trio £44.40; £56.39 to Uttoxeter 21/12/96 OWNER Mr W. McKeown (NEWCASTLE-UPON-TYNE) BRED Michael O'Keeffe

1687 Qattara (IRE), suited by the stiff track and easy ground, was made plenty of use of. He got better as the race progressed and won particularly well (6/1)

Elastic ran well after an absence of almost two years and, by the look of things, this front-running, soft-ground specialist will be back on the winning trail soon. (16/1)

1804 Fassan (IRE), on a stiffer track which should have suited, showed his true colours and failed to come up with the goods when the pressure was applied. (1/2: 4/6-4/9)

Cairo Prince (IRE), a one-time fourth in the Derby, showed absolutely nothing on his hurdling debut. This time there was some encouragement and, judging by the way he finished, longer trips should suit. (20/1)

1666 Calder King had the blinkers on this time, but they failed to have the desired effect, and he never offered a threat. (10/1: 5/1-12/1)

Storm Call, making his hurdles debut, ran reasonably without getting into it, and looks the type to improve with experience. (20/1)

Posted Abroad (IRE), from an out-of-form yard, ran really well until blowing up going to the last. (14/1: 10/1-16/1)

Star Master (8/1: op 12/1)

2042 HOLLY NOVICES' HURDLE (4-Y.O+) (Class E)

1-00 (1-00) **3m (12 hdls)** £2,805.00 (£780.00: £375.00) GOING: 0.65 sec per fur (S)

Form	Horse	Dist	Pos	SP	RR	SF
1843*	**Paperising** (GRichards) **4-11-5** ADobbin (lw: a.gng wl: led appr 2 out: easily)	—	**1**	3/1[2]	78+	5
1640[2]	**Swanbister (IRE) (99)** (LLungo) **6-11-5** RGarritty (lw: wnt prom 7th: led 4 out to 3 out: rdn & no ch w wnr fr 2 out)	¾	**2**	5/4[1]	78	5
1689[9]	**Boston Man** (RDEWoodhouse) **5-10-12** BStorey (hdwy & in tch ½-wy: outpcd 4 out: kpt on wl fr 2 out)	2½	**3**	33/1	69	—
1640[6]	**Glenbower** (MDHammond) **4-10-9**(3) MrCBonner (in tch: effrt 3 out: styd on one pce)	2½	**4**	12/1	67	—
1849[8]	**Kings Lane (87)** (JMDun) **7-11-0**(5) MrMHNaughton (a chsng ldrs: one pce fr 3 out)	1¼	**5**	12/1	73	—
1768[7]	**Old Cavalier** (JJO'Neill) **5-10-12** PNiven (w ldr: led 3 out tl appr next: one pce)	3½	**6**	10/1	64	—
1713[6]	**Farmers Subsidy** (GMMoore) **4-10-12** NBentley (a.p: outpcd 3 out: kpt on one pce fr next)	nk	**7**	33/1	64	—
1851[6]	**My Missile (65)** (RGCockburn) **6-10-7** LO'Hara (lw: bhd: hdwy & in tch 4 out: wknd fr next)	18	**8**	50/1	47	—
1654[19]	**South Coast Star (IRE)** (HowardJohnson) **6-10-7**(5) GFRyan (in tch tl wknd fr 3 out)	3	**9**	33/1	50	—
1654[12]	**Clongour (IRE)** (FMurphy) **6-10-12** KWhelan (in tch tl outpcd fr 3 out)	7	**10**	6/1[3]	45	—
	Barney Rubble (DWWhillans) **11-10-12** DBentley (led tl hdd 4 out: wknd)	hd	**11**	20/1	45	—
1654[P]	**Cragnabuoy (IRE) (96)** (WGReed) **6-10-12** TReed (a wl bhd)	10	**12**	14/1	38	—
1672[7]	**Crashballoo (IRE)** (PCheesbrough) **5-10-12** ASSmith (sn bhd)	10	**13**	14/1	32	—
1692[24]	**Samite (IRE)** (SJLeadbetter) **5-10-12** NLeach (bhd fr 6th: t.o whn p.u bef 4 out)		**P**	33/1	—	—
1907[7]	**Toshiba House (IRE)** (BEllison) **5-10-7** GCahill (chsd ldrs tl blnd & wknd 3 out: p.u bef last)		**P**	50/1	—	—

(SP 142.0%) **15 Rn**

6m 16.2 (36.20) CSF £8.06 TOTE £3.30: £2.70 £1.10 £32.90 (£3.50) Trio £40.80; £46.56 to Uttoxeter 21/12/96 OWNER The Jockeys Whips (PENRITH) BRED Independent British Hospitals

1843* Paperising turned the tables on the runner-up on their Haydock running in some style, and he looks to be a very useful stayer. (3/1: op 2/1)

1640 Swanbister (IRE) did everything right, but was completely outclassed by the winner, and was greatly flattered by his proximity at the end. He is just a stayer with no real turn of foot. (5/4)

Boston Man had shown nothing previously over hurdles, but the further he went here, the stronger he got. Staying is certainly going to be his forte. (33/1)

1640 Glenbower is gradually improving, but he does not do anything quickly. (12/1: op 7/1)

1849 Kings Lane is running well this season and his turn will come in due course. (12/1)

1026 Old Cavalier was made a lot of use of this time and that told in the closing stages. The experience should have taught him plenty. (10/1: 8/1-12/1)

1851 My Missile ran a fair race and, if her sights are lowered, she can pick up a modest event. (50/1)

Clongour (IRE) (6/1: op 12/1)

2043 ROAST TURKEY NOVICES' CHASE (5-Y.O+) (Class E)

1-30 (1-30) **2m 4f 110y (15 fncs)** £3,234.00 (£966.00: £462.00: £210.00) GOING: 0.65 sec per fur (S)

Form	Horse	Dist	Pos	SP	RR	SF
	Lien de Famille (IRE) (97) (JJQuinn) **6-10-12** PNiven (prom: mstke 7th: hdwy to ld 3 out: styd on)	—	**1**	4/1[2]	92	22
1944[F]	**Celtic Giant** (LLungo) **6-10-12** RGarritty (blnd 6th: hdwy u.p 4 out: sn chsng ldrs: one pce appr last)	5	**2**	4/5[1]	88	18
1803[7]	**Sireric (IRE)** (SBBell) **6-10-12** KJohnson (mstkes: led fr 2nd & sn clr: hdd 3 out: no ex)	3½	**3**	16/1	85	15
1691[3]	**Royal Surprise (75)** (WGReed) **9-10-12b** TReed (led to 2nd: chsd ldr to 10th: wknd 3 out)	20	**4**	12/1	70	—
1853[3]	**Bonny Johnny** (DMoffatt) **6-10-12** DJMoffatt (mstkes: a bhd: fell 10th)		**F**	7/1	—	—
1576*	**Elliott's Wish (IRE)** (HowardJohnson) **5-11-5** ADobbin (s.s: hdwy whn blnd 8th: sn t.o: p.u bef 4 out)		**P**	6/1[3]	—	—

(SP 115.9%) **6 Rn**

5m 21.3 (24.30) CSF £7.76 TOTE £4.50: £2.40 £1.10 (£5.10) Trio £53.90; £30.41 to Uttoxeter 21/12/96 OWNER Mrs Marie Taylor (MALTON) BRED G. J. King in Ireland

Lien de Famille (IRE) won on his first attempt over fences here and did it well. There is no doubt more races are in the pipe-line. (4/1)

1944 Celtic Giant managed to get round this time, but he looked short of pace at times, and will need real stamina tests to bring out the best in him. (4/5)

Sireric (IRE) showed his first signs of form over fences and, once he gets his jumping together, he should improve. (16/1)

1691 Royal Surprise helped force the pace until his limitations were exposed over the last three fences. (12/1: op 6/1)

1853 Bonny Johnny is clumsy and needs to improve his jumping a good deal. (7/1)

1576* Elliott's Wish (IRE) (6/1: op 4/1)

2044 ST NICHOLAS H'CAP HURDLE (0-105) (4-Y.O+) (Class F)
2-00 (2-00) **2m (8 hdls)** £2,259.00 (£624.00: £297.00) GOING: 0.65 sec per fur (S)

				SP	RR	SF
	Brumon (IRE) (88) (DMoffatt) **5-11-7b** DJMoffatt (blnd 3rd: hdwy 5th: led 2 out: hung lft & styd on flat)	—	**1**	14/1	72	16
1686*	**Kemo Sabo (92)** (CParker) **4-11-11** DParker (chsd ldr: led appr 2 out: sn hdd: one pce)	5	**2**	6/4 ^{1}	71	15
506 ^{3}	**Here Comes Herbie (84)** (WStorey) **4-11-3** MMoloney (mstke 1st: effrt & hit 5th: one pce fr 2 out)	13	**3**	9/2 ^{2}	50	—
1772 ^{8}	**Segala (IRE) (83)** (JJO'Neill) **5-11-2** PNiven (led: clr fr 4th tl hdd appr 2 out: grad wknd)	¾	**4**	6/1 ^{3}	48	—
1826 ^{F}	**Highland Way (IRE) (95)** (MartinTodhunter) **8-12-0** ASSmith (lw: in tch: hit 5th: effrt 3 out: sn btn)	9	**5**	13/2	51	—
1703 ^{7}	**Familiar Art (75)** (DMoffatt) **5-10-8** RGarritty (lost tch fr 5th: p.u bef 2 out)		**P**	8/1	—	—
1718 ^{R}	**Tashreef (72)** (JJBirkett) **6-10-5b** BStorey (rel to r: t.o whn p.u bef 3rd)		**P**	20/1	—	—

(SP 108.3%) **7 Rn**

4m 10.1 (22.10) CSF £32.80 CT £90.74 TOTE £14.20: £3.80 £2.60 (£13.10) OWNER Mr Mike Flynn (CARTMEL) BRED Warner L. Jones

Brumon (IRE) won what was a poor race, but did it well, despite hanging badly left in the closing stages. (14/1: 8/1-20/1)

1686* Kemo Sabo, up 8lb in the weights, showed little of his dash from last time and, struggling some way out, was always fighting a lost cause. (6/4: op 4/5)

506 Here Comes Herbie, from a yard that has not really hit top form, ran reasonably without looking likely to get into it. (9/2: 6/1-4/1)

1499 Segala (IRE) tried different tactics this time but, once caught approaching two out, soon cried enough. (6/1)

1826 Highland Way (IRE), back to hurdling, presumably to get his confidence back, was left struggling from three out. (13/2)

2045 CHRISTMAS BARGAIN CONDITIONAL (S) H'CAP HURDLE (0-95) (4-Y.O+) (Class G)
2-30 (2-31) **2m 4f 110y (10 hdls)** £1,725.00 (£475.00: £225.00) GOING: 0.65 sec per fur (S)

				SP	RR	SF
1718 ^{6}	**Precipice Run (82)** (JJBirkett) **11-11-10** GCahill (in tch: hdwy appr 2 out: led flat: styd on)	—	**1**	16/1	61	10
1822 ^{5}	**Yacht Club (67)** (JLEyre) **14-10-4**(5) CElliott (lw: hdwy & prom 6th: led 3 out tl hdd flat: hrd rdn & no ex)	¾	**2**	8/1	45	—
1807 ^{9}	**Corbleu (IRE) (74)** (SBBell) **6-11-2** ECallaghan (led tl hdd 3 out: r.o one pce)	2	**3**	5/1 ^{3}	51	—
1822 ^{4}	**Tharsis (65)** (WJSmith) **11-10-7** STaylor (hdwy 3 out: sn rdn & no imp)	8	**4**	12/1	36	—
1575 ^{2}	**Dashmar (65)** (MsLCPlater) **9-10-7** DParker (lw: cl up to 5th: sn bhd)	6	**5**	100/30 ^{2}	31	—
	Mr Sloan (58) (JSGoldie) **6-10-0** GLee (bit bkwd: hdwy 4 out: wknd after next)	3½	**6**	33/1	21	—
1523 ^{F}	**Nawtinookey (60)** (MartinTodhunter) **6-9-11b** ^{1}(5) CMcCormack (trckd ldrs: chal 4 out: rdn & wknd appr 2 out)	30	**7**	7/1	—	—
1942 ^{P}	**Circle Boy (64)** (WStorey) **9-10-6** RMcGrath (cl up to 6th: wknd qckly 3 out)	15	**8**	7/1	—	—
1854 ^{4}	**Blanc Seing (FR) (75)** (JESwiers) **9-11-3b** FLeahy (prom tl p.u lame appr 6th)		**P**	5/2 ^{1}	—	—

(SP 120.9%) **9 Rn**

5m 18.6 (30.60) CSF £126.95 CT £680.85 TOTE £25.80: £3.50 £3.00 £1.60 (£22.80) Trio £107.10; £34.71 to Uttoxeter 21/12/96 OWNER Mr C. Warwick (WORKINGTON) BRED P. Neary

No bid

OFFICIAL EXPLANATION **Blanc Seing (FR): was lame in front.**

1718 Precipice Run won this very poor event by sticking doggedly to his task. (16/1)

1822 Yacht Club looked to have them all in trouble two out but, despite some very vigorous driving, just failed to quicken enough. (8/1)

Corbleu (IRE) forced the pace, but looked very slow once tackled over the last three flights. (5/1)

1822 Tharsis is running reasonably, but was always left wanting for speed. (12/1: op 7/1)

1575 Dashmar has ability, but seems to possess his own ideas about how to use it. (100/30)

1344 Nawtinookey had his chances until stopping as if something was wrong approaching the second last. (7/1: 5/1-8/1)

Circle Boy (7/1: op 9/2)

2046 SANTA CLAUS H'CAP CHASE (0-110) (5-Y.O+) (Class E)
3-00 (3-00) **3m 1f (19 fncs)** £3,070.20 (£915.60: £436.80: £197.40) GOING: 0.65 sec per fur (S)

				SP	RR	SF
1704 ^{3}	**Off The Bru (89)** (MrsSCBradburne) **11-10-2**(7)ow4 MrMBradburne (led 6th to 9th: lost pl 15th: hdwy 2 out: led appr last: styd on wl)	—	**1**	6/1 ^{3}	99	27
1670 ^{6}	**Gala Water (90)** (TDCDun) **10-10-10**ow6 TReed (lw: prom tl outpcd & lost pl 11th: gd hdwy 4 out: led 3 out tl appr last: no ex)	8	**2**	7/1	95	21
1655 ^{2}	**Road by the River (IRE) (97)** (PCheesbrough) **8-11-3** BStorey (bhd: hdwy 14th: ch 2 out: one pce)	14	**3**	3/1 ^{2}	93	25
1304 ^{P}	**Jendee (IRE) (88)** (BEllison) **8-10-5**(3) MrCBonner (bhd: hdwy & prom 14th: ev ch appr 3 out: sn wknd)	½	**4**	10/1	84	16
1863 ^{3}	**Pats Minstrel (108)** (RChampion) **11-12-0** ADobbin (lw: led to 4th: led 9th to 13th: led next to 3 out: sn wknd)	dist	**5**	8/1	—	—
1704 ^{P}	**Snook Point (84)** (DALamb) **9-10-4**ow4 JBurke (led 4th to 6th: led 13th to 14th: wknd 3 out: blnd 2 out: p.u bef last)		**P**	20/1	—	—
1670 ^{3}	**Westwell Boy (107)** (PBeaumont) **10-11-13** RSupple (lw: cl up tl blnd & uns rdr 13th)		**U**	11/8 ^{1}	—	—

(SP 118.9%) **7 Rn**

6m 37.9 (26.90) CSF £43.27 CT £138.85 TOTE £8.40: £3.30 £1.60 (£22.90) OWNER The Fife Steeplechasing Partnership (CUPAR) BRED J. O'Donnell

LONG HANDICAP Snook Point 9-9

1704 Off The Bru, in this real test of stamina, came into his own in the last half-mile and won most decisively. (6/1)

1307 Gala Water had the track and the ground she likes, but was just outbattled in the closing stages. (7/1)

1655 Road by the River (IRE) had his chances, but he might still just have needed this, and cried enough two out. (3/1: op 2/1)

1304 Jendee (IRE) runs when in the mood, and this was a better effort. (10/1: 8/1-12/1)

1863 Pats Minstrel made this a real test of stamina and that found him out three from home. (8/1)

2047 LEVY BOARD INTERMEDIATE OPEN N.H. FLAT RACE (4, 5 & 6-Y.O) (Class H)
3-30 (3-32) **2m** £1,406.00 (£391.00: £188.00)

				SP	RR	SF
1579 ^{3}	**Bobby Grant** (CGrant) **5-11-4** PNiven (cl up: led 4f out: rdn & r.o wl fnl f)	—	**1**	9/1	55 f	—
1296 ^{9}	**Magpie Melody (IRE)** (LLungo) **5-11-4** ARoche (prom: effrt 3f out: kpt on wl fnl f)	2½	**2**	5/1	53 f	—
	Roman Outlaw (MDHammond) **4-11-4** DBentley (bit bkwd: hld up: hdwy 3f out: styd on wl: nrst fin)	1	**3**	16/1	52 f	—
	Sir Bob (IRE) (WMcKeown) **4-11-4** GCahill (w ldr: led ½-wy to 4f out: r.o one pce)	hd	**4**	7/2 ^{2}	51 f	—
1504 ^{2}	**First Light** (JJQuinn) **4-11-4** RGarritty (wnt prom after 6f: ev ch over 1f out: nt qckn)	¾	**5**	9/4 ^{1}	51 f	—
	Derannie (IRE) (GRichards) **4-11-4** ADobbin (in tch: effrt 3f out: chsng ldrs 2f out: wknd 1f out)	4	**6**	4/1 ^{3}	47 f	—

1834[7]	**Lovely Rascal** (JJO'Neill) **4-10-8**(5) RMcGrath (chsd ldrs tl grad wknd fnl 2f) 3½	**7**	16/1	38 f	—
1692[13]	**Top Ace** (GFWhite) **4-11-4** MrARobson (chsd ldrs tl wknd appr fnl f) ....½	**8**	33/1	43 f	—
	Houselope Spring (HowardJohnson) **4-10-13**(5) GFRyan (prom tl wknd fnl 3f) 6	**9**	20/1	37 f	—
	Snooty Eskimo (IRE) (JSHaldane) **4-11-4** ASSmith (bit bkwd: in tch: no imp fnl 4f) 2½	**10**	20/1	34 f	—
1579[9]	**Queens Brigade** (FTWalton) **4-11-4** BStorey (nvr rchd ldrs) ....½	**11**	20/1	34 f	—
	Johnneys Spirit (RGCockburn) **4-11-4** LO'Hara (in tch tl wknd fnl 4f) 19	**12**	16/1	15 f	—
1692[10]	**Alan's Pride (IRE)** (WMcKeown) **5-10-13** KWhelan (unruly s: wnt prom ½-wy: wknd over 2f out) 12	**13**	25/1	—	—
	The Burglar (IRE) (RHGoldie) **4-11-4** RSupple (a wl bhd) 14	**14**	33/1	—	—
	Banner Year (IRE) (TJCarr) **5-11-4** NSmith (t.o fr ½-wy) 2	**15**	33/1	—	—
1692[18]	**Ottadini (IRE)** (WGReed) **4-10-13** TReed (led to ½-wy: wknd 4f out) ....s.h	**16**	33/1	—	—
1362[10]	**Teelin Bay (IRE)** (CParker) **4-11-4** DParker (t.o fr ½-wy) 1¼	**17**	25/1	—	—
	Montein (SJLeadbetter) **5-11-4** NLeach (bkwd: t.o fnl 6f) 3½	**18**	33/1	—	—

(SP 154.0%) **18 Rn**

4m 5.4 CSF £60.66 TOTE £11.30: £3.80 £1.80 £10.90 (£34.90) Trio £135.70; £114.71 to Uttoxeter 21/12/96 OWNER Mr John Thompson (BILLINGHAM) BRED Mrs D. Jenks

IN-FOCUS: This was the first winner trained by former top jockey Chris Grant.

1579 Bobby Grant certainly stays well and, after looking in trouble with a furlong to go, found another gear. (9/1)

Magpie Melody (IRE) is improving fast and was keeping on particularly well in the closing stages. (5/1)

Roman Outlaw should have learnt plenty from this, and looks a real stayer in the making. (16/1)

Sir Bob (IRE), up with the pace throughout, proved to be a real battler, but was short of a turn of speed at the business end. (7/2)

1504 First Light travelled quite well, but then failed to pick up in closing stages. He looks one to watch when he tries hurdling. (9/4: 2/1-3/1)

Derannie (IRE) showed ability, but seemed to blow up in the closing stages. (4/1: op 2/1)

T/Plpt: £42.90 (168.43 Tckts). T/Qdpt: £37.50 (12.97 Tckts). AA

1600-UTTOXETER (L-H) (Soft)
Friday December 20th

WEATHER: overcast & very cold

2048 STREBEL BOILERS & RADIATORS H'CAP HURDLE (0-130) (4-Y.O+) (Class C)

1-10 (1-10) **2m (9 hdls)** £3,550.00 (£1,075.00: £525.00: £250.00) GOING: 0.68 sec per fur (S)

			SP	RR	SF
1374[4]	**Tejano Gold (USA) (111)** (PBradley) **6-11-0** RDunwoody (bit bkwd: chsd ldr: led 6th: clr 2 out: v.easily) ....—	**1**	9/2[3]	94+	25
1636[8]	**Master Tribe (IRE) (120)** (MrsJPitman) **6-11-9** WMarston (bit bkwd: chsd ldrs: wnt 2nd 6th: outpcd 2 out: sn btn) 5	**2**	10/1	98	29
1832*	**Most Equal (115)** (MCPipe) **6-11-4** 5x RHughes (hld up: hdwy appr 3 out: shkn up appr next: nvr able to chal) 1½	**3**	3/1[2]	92	23
1804[5]	**Mr Bureaucrat (NZ) (117)** (SABrookshaw) **7-11-6** RJohnson (hld up: effrt appr 3 out: sn rdn: no imp) 6	**4**	7/1	88	19
	Moving Out (121) (MissHCKnight) **8-11-3**(7) MrAWintle (bkwd: led & sn clr: hdd 6th: wknd appr 2 out) 1¼	**5**	16/1	90	21
1439*	**Saint Ciel (USA) (110)** (FJordan) **8-10-13** MAFitzgerald (hld up in tch: lost pl appr 3 out: sn btn) 3	**6**	11/4[1]	76	7
1828[6]	**Eurolink the Lad (106)** (DBurchell) **9-10-9** DJBurchell (racd wd: hdwy 6th: rdn 3 out: sn wknd: t.o) ....dist	**7**	10/1	—	—

(SP 106.4%) **7 Rn**

3m 59.8 (18.80) CSF £38.34 CT £116.43 TOTE £5.40: £2.30 £3.80 (£13.90) OWNER Mr Paul Bradley (FORSBROOK) BRED W. D. & D. Fishback, L. R. French, & B. Beal

1374 Tejano Gold (USA), in the leading pair from the start, began to assert his superiority from the penultimate flight and could not have won any easier in the end. (9/2)

Master Tribe (IRE) still had a bit left to work on, but he ran up to his mark, and this outing should have put him spot on. (10/1)

1832* Most Equal has not yet won on ground as soft as this, and his attempt to deliver a challenge at the second last came to little. (3/1)

1804 Mr Bureaucrat (NZ) failed to muster the speed to get serious. He could be worth waiting for for when his attentions are switched to fences. (7/1)

Moving Out would have found this trip inadequate, but it should have put an edge on him. (16/1)

1439* Saint Ciel (USA) had everything in his favour but, not for the first time, ran very flat. In this sort of mood, he is one to avoid. (11/4)

2049 LEFLEY'S HOG ROAST NOVICES' CHASE (5-Y.O+) (Class D)

1-40 (1-40) **2m 4f (15 fncs)** £3,826.25 (£1,160.00: £567.50: £271.25) GOING: 0.40 sec per fur (GS)

			SP	RR	SF
1389*	**Oban** (MissHCKnight) **6-11-6** GBradley (hld up: hdwy to chal 2 out: led last: drvn clr flat) ....—	**1**	100/30[1]	115	56
1809[2]	**Sunset and Vine** (TCasey) **9-11-0** RDunwoody (led appr 3rd to 4th: led 6th to last: rdn & swtchd rt flat: no imp) 6	**2**	4/1[3]	104	45
	Major Look (NZ) (SABrookshaw) **8-11-4** RJohnson (bit bkwd: hld up: hdwy 7th: wknd appr 4 out) 5	**3**	14/1	104	45
1646[3]	**Take the Buckskin** (TThomsonJones) **9-11-0** MAFitzgerald (hld up in rr: j.slowly 10th: rdn next: effrt 4 out: wknd 3 out) 4	**4**	7/2[2]	97	38
1771[3]	**Zaitoon (IRE) (101)** (DNicholson) **5-11-0** AMaguire (hld up: hdwy 7th: 2nd & ev ch whn fell 4 out)	**F**	8/1	—	—
1673[2]	**Slipmatic** (AndrewTurnell) **7-10-9** SMcNeill (lw: hmpd & fell 1st)	**F**	10/1	—	—
1780[F]	**Thursday Night (IRE)** (JGFitzGerald) **5-11-0** AThornton (led & j.b rt 1st: hdd appr 3rd: led 4th to 6th: fell next)	**F**	4/1[3]	—	—

(SP 112.2%) **7 Rn**

5m 14.3 CSF £15.80 TOTE £3.40: £1.70 £2.00 (£3.60) OWNER Lord Hartington (WANTAGE) BRED Willingham House Stud

1389* Oban let the leaders cut their own throats and, swooping to take it up at the last, strode clear for another impressive performance. (100/30)

1809 Sunset and Vine is gradually getting it together over fences and, though the winner proved too much of a handful on this occasion, his turn can not be far away. (4/1)

Major Look (NZ) ran in hunter chases when he last appeared on a racecourse in the spring of 1995 and, though he was too backward to do himself justice, he should have no trouble in making the grade. (14/1)

1646 Take the Buckskin was again novicey on occasions with his jumping and, over this inadequate trip, was unable to make his presence felt. (7/2)

1771 Zaitoon (IRE) was gradually creeping into the picture when he crumpled on landing four from home. (8/1)

1673 Slipmatic (10/1: op 20/1)

2050 BURTON ALBION FOOTBALL CLUB (S) HURDLE (3-Y.O) (Class G)
2-10 (2-12) **2m** **(9 hdls)** £2,025.50 (£568.00: £276.50) GOING: 0.68 sec per fur (S)

				SP	RR	SF
1675[3]	**Stonecutter** (MRChannon) **3-10-10v** RHughes (a w ldrs: led appr 3 out: all out)	—	**1**	9/4[1]	65	5
1652[21]	**Boy Blakeney** (MrsSJSmith) **3-10-10** RichardGuest (led: j.b rt & hdd 2nd: ev ch 3 out: hmpd last: swtchd rt & rallied cl home)	nk	**2**	7/1	65	5
1149[3]	**How Could-I (IRE)** (MrsNMacauley) **3-10-5b** AThornton (hld up: hdwy appr 6th: nt rch ldrs)	12	**3**	6/1[3]	48	—
1444[F]	**Come On In** (RDickin) **3-10-10** CLlewellyn (hld up: styd on fr 2 out: nvr nrr)	3	**4**	33/1	50	—
1872[4]	**Spiral Flyer (IRE)** (MDIUsher) **3-10-5** WMarston (prom: drvn along 6th: wknd appr 2 out)	2	**5**	4/1[2]	43	—
1444[4]	**Paulton** (KBishop) **3-10-10** RGreene (nvr nr to chal)	1¼	**6**	50/1	46	—
1706[7]	**Tathmin** (JRBosley) **3-10-10v[1]** MBosley (w ldrs early: wknd appr 3 out)	2½	**7**	25/1	44	—
1908[6]	**Arch Angel (IRE)** (GFHCharles-Jones) **3-10-5** DGallagher (hld up: hdwy 5th: wknd after 3 out)	4	**8**	12/1	35	—
1595[F]	**Appeal Again (IRE)** (DBurchell) **3-10-7(3)** GuyLewis (hld up: hdwy 6th: wknd 3 out: t.o)	16	**9**	40/1	24	—
1370[8]	**Lebedinski (IRE) (74)** (MrsPSly) **3-10-5v[1]** RMarley (a in rr: t.o)	6	**10**	14/1	13	—
1172[3]	**Flash In The Pan (IRE)** (JSMoore) **3-10-5** WMcFarland (a.p: rdn & ev ch whn fell last)		**F**	7/1	60?	—
501[7]	**Indian Sunset** (CREgerton) **3-10-10b[1]** JAMcCarthy (bkwd: lft in ld 2nd: hdd & wknd appr 3 out: p.u bef 2 out)		**P**	12/1	—	—
1413[P]	**Nordic Hero (IRE)** (APJarvis) **3-10-3(7)** CDavies (hdwy 5th: wknd appr 3 out: p.u bef next)		**P**	50/1	—	—
	Rebounder (DJSffrenchDavis) **3-10-7(3)** JMagee (chsd ldrs to 5th: bhd whn p.u bef next)		**P**	50/1	—	—
				(SP 127.2%)	**14 Rn**	

4m 3.4 (22.40) CSF £18.82 TOTE £2.40: £1.10 £3.50 £3.20 (£13.80) Trio £67.00 OWNER Miss S. Deburiatte (UPPER LAMBOURN) BRED Worksop Manor Stud Farm
Bt in 5,000 gns

1675 Stonecutter, who ran with his tongue tied down, sat closer to the pace, but needed Hughes at his strongest to succeed with not an ounce to spare. (9/4)
1413 Boy Blakeney, gaining experience all the time, would have won but for a rival falling right in his path at the last. (7/1)
1149 How Could-I (IRE) struggled to get her feet out of the mud and, despite staying on well, was never going to reach the principals. (6/1)
Come On In, given time to regain his confidence, was doing all his best work when the race was all but over. (33/1)
1872 Spiral Flyer (IRE), nudged along to hold her place at the end of the back straight, kept plugging away, but she was brushed aside with ease when the battle to the finish really got under way. (4/1)
Flash In The Pan (IRE), never far away, was flat to the boards but disputing the lead when falling at the last. She would have taken a great deal of beating, and deserves a chance to make amends. (7/1)
501 Indian Sunset (12/1: op 7/1)

2051 ST MODWEN LIMITED H'CAP CHASE (0-135) (5-Y.O+) (Class C)
2-40 (2-40) **2m** **(12 fncs)** £4,448.50 (£1,348.00: £659.00: £314.50) GOING: 0.40 sec per fur (GS)

				SP	RR	SF
1454[4]	**Super Tactics (IRE) (128)** (RHAlner) **8-11-0(3)** PHenley (lw: hld up: effrt & pushed along 4 out: led last: drvn clr)	—	**1**	9/2	138	53
1682*	**Mister Oddy (128)** (JSKing) **10-11-3** MAFitzgerald (lw: j.w: led to 4th: led after 4 out to last: unable qckn)	3	**2**	5/4[1]	135	50
	Native Mission (132) (JGFitzGerald) **9-11-7** RDunwoody (bit bkwd: hld up: hdwy appr 4 out: rdn 2 out: one pce)	1¼	**3**	3/1[2]	138	53
1682[3]	**Random Assault (NZ) (132)** (DNicholson) **7-11-7** AMaguire (plld hrd: led 4th tl after 4 out: hit next: sn btn)	28	**4**	7/2[3]	110	25
				(SP 109.8%)	**4 Rn**	

3m 59.0 (9.00) CSF £10.10 TOTE £6.00 (£3.20) OWNER Mr H. V. Perry (BLANDFORD) BRED James Robinson

1454 Super Tactics (IRE) is a useful individual on his day and, despite being the outsider in the market, showed what he is made of with a fairly comfortable success under a very competent ride. (9/2)
1682* Mister Oddy turned in another bold display of jumping and was only forced to give best at the last. He is a credit to his connections. (5/4)
Native Mission has won first time out for the past couple of seasons, but he did have a long absence from the racecourse to overcome and for him to run so well gives every indication that he is as good as ever. (3/1)
1682 Random Assault (NZ) again refused to settle and a mistake three out on being headed took the stuffing out of him. (7/2: 5/2-4/1)

2052 ALAN POVEY SIGNS NOVICES' H'CAP CHASE (0-100) (5-Y.O+) (Class E)
3-10 (3-10) **3m 2f** **(20 fncs)** £3,022.00 (£916.00: £448.00: £214.00) GOING: 0.40 sec per fur (GS)

				SP	RR	SF
1773[U]	**Coverdale Lane (82)** (MrsSJSmith) **9-10-11** MrPMurray (in tch: rdn appr 4 out: led appr last: styd on strly)	—	**1**	9/2[2]	96	—
1773[4]	**Majors Legacy (IRE) (81)** (CaptTAForster) **7-10-10** AThornton (disp ld: led 16th to 3 out: one pce appr last)	6	**2**	8/1[3]	91	—
1680[P]	**Be Brave (78)** (TJEtherington) **6-10-7** RRourke (trckd ldrs: led 3 out tl appr last: one pce)	1½	**3**	33/1	87	—
1819[U]	**Romany Blues (71)** (CPEBrooks) **7-10-0** DGallagher (prom: disp ld 16th to next: sn wknd)	18	**4**	25/1	69	—
1716*	**Ocean Leader (95)** (MrsDHaine) **9-11-10** AMaguire (hld up & bhd: hdwy 12th: wknd appr 3 out)	16	**5**	5/2[1]	84	—
1252[6]	**Dominie (IRE) (90)** (KCBailey) **8-11-5b** CLlewellyn (lw: a bhd: t.o fr 14th)	dist	**6**	20/1	—	—
827[6]	**George Ashford (IRE) (89)** (PRJohnson) **6-11-4** MSharratt (a bhd: t.o)	10	**7**	25/1	—	—
	Oats N Barley (88) (PRRodford) **7-11-3** SBurrough (bkwd: hld up: stdy hdwy 12th: fell next)		**F**	14/1	—	—
1773[F]	**Ragged Kingdom (IRE) (74)** (CREgerton) **7-10-0(3)ow3** LAspell (bkwd: a bhd: t.o whn fell 13th)		**F**	50/1	—	—
1582[5]	**The Brud (76)** (OSherwood) **8-10-5** JAMcCarthy (bit bkwd: a bhd: t.o whn p.u bef 4 out)		**P**	9/1	—	—
1778[P]	**Griffins Bar (85)** (MrsPSly) **8-11-0** RMarley (mde most to 16th: rdn & mstke 3 out: bhd whn p.u bef last)		**P**	11/1	—	—
1773[F]	**Bossymoss (IRE) (71)** (AStreeter) **7-10-0** TEley (lw: trckd ldrs: pckd 13th: mstke 3 out: p.u bef next)		**P**	9/1	—	—
				(SP 110.2%)	**12 Rn**	

7m 1.0 (34.00) CSF £34.55 CT £891.54 TOTE £4.20: £2.00 £2.00 £7.80 (£17.70) Trio £135.80; £135.82 to Uttoxeter 21/12/96 OWNER Mr Jim Pilkington (BINGLEY) BRED Mrs M. J. Cole
LONG HANDICAP Ragged Kingdom (IRE) 9-3 Romany Blues 9-5 Bossymoss (IRE) 9-13

1773 Coverdale Lane made ample amends for an unlucky defeat on her previous outing. She stays well, and we have not seen the last of her yet. (9/2: op 3/1)
1773 Majors Legacy (IRE) helped force the pace and showed that he is approaching his peak. That initial success can not be far away. (8/1: 6/1-9/1)
Be Brave put the experience gained on his previous outing to full use, and only faded as lack of peak-fitness caught up with him. He looks a ready-made winner at this game. (33/1)
Romany Blues did at least complete the course, and raced with the pace until weakening early in the straight. (25/1)

1716* Ocean Leader is not so effective on soft ground, but he ran well below what he is capable of and, unless something comes out in the wash, this can only be deemed as an off-day. (5/2)
1209* Griffins Bar, a bold front-runner, had company all the way and was unable to take a breather. He was a spent force when untidy at the final ditch, and was eventually pulled up. (11/1)

2053 E.B.F. 'N.H.' (QUALIFIER) NOVICES' HURDLE (4, 5 & 6-Y.O) (Class E)
3-40 (3-40) **2m 4f 110y (10 hdls)** £2,536.50 (£714.00: £349.50) GOING: 0.68 sec per fur (S)

	Horse	Details	Dist	Pos	SP	RR	SF
1654*	**Agistment**	(JGFitzGerald) **5-11-10** RDunwoody (lw: chsd ldrs: led 7th to 2 out: rdn to ld flat: r.o wl)	—	1	5/2 2	92+	7
1568*	**Mighty Moss (IRE)**	(DNicholson) **5-11-3**(7) MrFHutsby (hld up & bhd: gd hdwy appr 3 out: slt ld 2 out tl flat: hrd rdn: unable qckn)	½	2	4/6 1	92+	7
1802³	**Barton Ward**	(SABrookshaw) **5-11-0** RJohnson (a.p: rdn appr 2 out: kpt on one pce)	6	3	25/1	77	—
	Seabrook Lad	(MJWilkinson) **5-11-0** ILawrence (bit bkwd: bhd: styd on fr 2 out: nvr nrr)	10	4	100/1	69	—
1802F	**Share Options (IRE) (104)**	(TDEasterby) **5-11-10** AMaguire (prom: led appr 6th to 7th: wknd appr 2 out)	9	5	8/1 3	72	—
1683³	**Aut Even (IRE)**	(CaptTAForster) **6-11-0** AThornton (hld up: hdwy 6th: rdn & outpcd appr 3 out)	14	6	14/1	51	—
	Colonel Blazer	(MissHCKnight) **4-11-0** MAFitzgerald (hld up: hdwy 6th: wknd 3 out)	6	7	12/1	47	—
1507⁶	**Coole Cherry**	(CRBarwell) **6-11-0** BFenton (led tl appr 6th: wknd appr 3 out)	nk	8	100/1	46	—
1438⁵	**Scally Hicks**	(BPJBaugh) **5-10-9** GaryLyons (a bhd: t.o)	7	9	100/1	36	—
1713⁴	**Carly-J**	(FSJackson) **5-10-9** MrNKent (bit bkwd: chsd ldrs: mstke 4th: wknd appr 3 out: t.o)	11	10	100/1	27	—
1777⁶	**Minster Boy**	(JPLeigh) **5-11-0** CLlewellyn (a bhd: t.o)	4	11	100/1	29	—
1639¹²	**Chatergold (IRE)**	(APJarvis) **4-10-7**(7) CDavies (lost tch ½-wy: t.o)	2	12	100/1	28	—
1867¹⁰	**Black Statement (IRE)**	(APJarvis) **6-10-11**(3) LAspell (prom tl wknd qckly appr 3 out: t.o)	hd	13	100/1	27	—

(SP 124.8%) **13 Rn**

5m 15.9 (31.90) CSF £4.57 TOTE £3.10: £1.40 £1.00 £3.50 (£1.30) Trio £7.70 OWNER Marquesa de Moratalla (MALTON) BRED Dunchurch Lodge Stud Co
1654* Agistment, under an inspired ride from Dunwoody, showed he is capable of winning at a trip some way short of his best. (5/2)
1568* Mighty Moss (IRE) has looked destined for the top, and it must be said he did very little wrong here, but strength from the saddle was the deciding factor in such a tight finish. (4/6)
1802 Barton Ward had to admit the big guns too good for him in the closing stages, but this may well have been his best effort yet. His future looks bright. (25/1)
Seabrook Lad seemed much better suited to this extended trip but, even so, the company was far too good, and his final placing was as close as he could manage. (100/1)
1802 Share Options (IRE) sat in behind the leaders, travelling well within himself but, once off the bridle turning for home, dropped away tamely. (8/1)
1683 Aut Even (IRE) edged closer at the end of the back straight, but he failed to maintain the progress and had been hung out to dry approaching the penultimate flight. (14/1)
Colonel Blazer (12/1: 8/1-14/1)

T/Plpt: £217.90 (56.56 Tckts). T/Qdpt: £17.90 (50.33 Tckts). IM

1517-ASCOT (R-H) (Good to firm, Hdles Good patches)
Saturday December 21st
WEATHER: very cold

2054 'BOOK OF MUSIC' NOVICES' CHASE (Gd 2) (5-Y.O+) (Class A)
12-35 (12-36) **2m 3f 110y (16 fncs)** £12,320.00 (£4,661.00: £2,280.50: £1,038.50) GOING: 0.37 sec per fur (GS)

	Horse	Details	Dist	Pos	SP	RR	SF
1803*	**Simply Dashing (IRE)**	(TDEasterby) **5-11-7** RDunwoody (a.p: led appr last: rdn out)	—	1	13/8 1	137	62
1787*	**Or Royal (FR)**	(MCPipe) **5-11-10** APMcCoy (a.p: led 12th tl hrd rdn, hung rt & hdd appr last: unable qckn)	3	2	7/2 2	138	63
1521*	**Oh So Risky**	(DRCElsworth) **9-11-10** PHolley (lw: hld up: rdn appr 2 out: one pce)	10	3	5/1 3	129	54
1815²	**Cheryl's Lad (IRE)**	(NJHenderson) **6-11-3** MAFitzgerald (bhd fr 10th: mstke 11th)	7	4	13/2	117	42
1925U	**Country Star (IRE)**	(CPEBrooks) **5-11-3** GBradley (swtg: j.lft: led to 12th: wknd 4 out)	7	5	7/1	111	36
1829⁶	**Bolshie Baron**	(MHWeston) **7-11-3** MrMHarris (a bhd: t.o fr 8th)	dist	6	66/1	—	—
1716³	**Lucky Dollar (IRE) (99)**	(KCBailey) **8-11-3** CLlewellyn (lw: 5th whn fell 8th)		F	25/1	—	—
1965⁵	**Shalik (IRE) (79)**	(JRJenkins) **6-11-3** NTEgan (bhd whn mstke 5th: t.o fr 8th: p.u bef 3 out)		P	100/1	—	—

(SP 109.1%) **8 Rn**

4m 56.0 (9.00) CSF £7.03 TOTE £2.10: £1.30 £1.60 £1.30 (£3.10) OWNER Mr Steve Hammond (MALTON) BRED Eastward Bloodstock Holdings Ltd
1803* Simply Dashing (IRE) was facing his first real test over fences, but proved more than up to the task, thanks to some help from the runner-up. Unbeaten in four completed outings over fences, he looks a very exciting novice and is certainly Cheltenham material. (13/8)
1787* Or Royal (FR), winner of both his outings so far this season, moved to the front five out and appeared to have the measure of the winner jumping the second last. However, when his rider hit him, his stride began to shorten, he drifted right and did not look over-enthusiastic. Losing the advantage as a result, he was then unable to cope with Simply Dashing. Nevertheless, he still looks a very useful novice chaser and, given some rain - he has done all his winning with some cut - he should soon be back in the winner's enclosure. Indeed, he would probably be helped if he could be held up until the last possible minute. (7/2: 2/1-4/1)
1521* Oh So Risky was taking on much better opposition on this occasion and, after travelling and jumping well for much of the race, his jockey started to niggle him in the last half-mile and he began to lunge at his fences. It is unlikely he is going to make the top-grade over fences. (5/1)
1815 Cheryl's Lad (IRE) was very disappointing. (13/2: 9/2-7/1)
1925 Country Star (IRE) sweated up badly on a bitterly cold afternoon. Jumping to his left at many of the fences, he led the way to the fifth last before soon calling it a day. Three of his four victories to date have come on a left-handed track. (7/1: 5/1-15/2)

2055 MITIE GROUP KENNEL GATE NOVICES' HURDLE (Gd 2) (4-Y.O+) (Class A)
1-10 (1-10) **2m 110y (9 hdls)** £9,212.00 (£3,488.10: £1,709.05: £780.85) GOING: 0.37 sec per fur (GS)

	Horse	Details	Dist	Pos	SP	RR	SF
1793*	**Make a Stand (132)**	(MCPipe) **5-11-7** APMcCoy (lw: j.w: mde all: clr 3rd: unchal)	—	1	8/13 1	98+	56
	Eagles Rest (IRE)	(NJHenderson) **5-11-0** MAFitzgerald (hdwy 6th: chsd wnr fr 3 out: no imp)	5	2	20/1	86	44
1788*	**Bowcliffe Court (IRE) (100)**	(RAkehurst) **4-11-0** AMaguire (mstke 3rd: no hdwy fr 3 out)	16	3	8/1 3	71	29

	Horse	Dist	Pos	SP	RR	SF
	Bahamian Sunshine (USA) (RAkehurst) **5-11-0** GBradley (mstke 5th: chsd wnr after 2nd to 3 out: sn wknd)	10	**4**	12/1	61	19
1507[4]	**Supreme Charm (IRE)** (KCBailey) **4-11-0** CLlewellyn (lw: chsd wnr tl after 2nd: wknd 5th)	8	**5**	14/1	53	11
	Super High (PHowling) **4-11-0** NWilliamson (lw: bhd fr 3rd)	3	**6**	50/1	50	8
	Latahaab (USA) (JTGifford) **5-11-0** PHide (bit bkwd: hld up: 3rd whn mstke 6th: wknd 3 out: bhd whn blnd 2 out: t.o whn p.u bef last)		**P**	10/1	—	—
	Perfect Pal (IRE) (MissGayKelleway) **5-11-0** RDunwoody (bit bkwd: bhd whn blnd, hmpd & uns rdr 2nd)		**U**	7/1[2]	—	—
	Dances With Hooves (DJSffrenchDavis) **4-11-0** SMcNeill (bhd whn mstke & uns rdr 1st)		**U**	33/1	—	—
				(SP 118.6%)	**9 Rn**	

3m 58.8 (8.80) CSF £14.02 TOTE £1.70: £1.10 £3.60 £1.90 (£16.20) Trio £26.90 OWNER Mr P. A. Deal (WELLINGTON) BRED R. M. West

1793* Make a Stand, so impressive at Sandown recently, was returning to novice company and turned this into a non-event. Jumping really cleanly and efficiently as he has done with great success this season, he made all the running and, forging clear on the final circuit, never looked like being caught. He was eased down considerably on the run-in and was value for at least twenty lengths. He is turning into an extremely useful novice. (8/13: op 11/10)

Eagles Rest (IRE), looking reasonably straight for his first run in nine months, was given no easy task on this hurdling debut. He had no hope with the winner and was greatly flattered to finish so close, but he should soon be winning. (20/1)

1788* Bowcliffe Court (IRE) found the trip too sharp and the ground too lively. Two and a half miles on soft ground will be much more to his liking. (8/1: 5/1-9/1)

Bahamian Sunshine (USA), who finished fourth in the Queen Alexandra at the Royal Meeting for David Loder this year, had been off the course for nearly four months. (12/1: 7/1-14/1)

1507 Supreme Charm (IRE) (14/1: op 8/1)

Latahaab (USA) (10/1: 6/1-12/1)

Perfect Pal (IRE) (7/1: 4/1-8/1)

2056 LONG WALK HURDLE (Gd 1) (4-Y.O+) (Class A)

1-45 (1-45) **3m 1f 110y (14 hdls)** £25,240.00 (£9,552.00: £4,676.00: £2,132.00) GOING: 0.37 sec per fur (GS)

	Horse	Dist	Pos	SP	RR	SF
1522[2]	**Ocean Hawk (USA) (142)** (NATwiston-Davies) **4-11-7** CLlewellyn (lw: mde all: rdn appr 2 out: r.o wl)	—	**1**	7/1	140	33
1647[3]	**Trainglot (148)** (JGFitzGerald) **9-11-7** RDunwoody (lw: hdwy 8th: hrd rdn appr 2 out: r.o one pce)	4	**2**	9/4[1]	138	31
1936[F]	**Pleasure Shared (IRE) (164)** (PJHobbs) **8-11-7** NWilliamson (lw: hld up: chsd wnr fr 11th: ev ch 3 out: hrd rdn appr 2 out: one pce)	2	**3**	5/2[2]	136	29
1647[6]	**Top Spin (134)** (JRJenkins) **7-11-7** AMaguire (nvr nr to chal)	5	**4**	33/1	133?	26
1647*	**What a Question (IRE)** (MFMorris) **8-11-2** GBradley (lw: mstke 6th: pckd 7th: chsd wnr to 11th: sn wknd)	4	**5**	7/2[3]	126	19
1922*	**Blaze Away (USA) (125)** (IABalding) **5-11-7** APMcCoy (lw: hdwy 8th: collapsed after 10th: dead)		**F**	6/1	—	—
				(SP 111.3%)	**6 Rn**	

6m 22.8 (21.80) CSF £21.80 TOTE £7.70: £3.00 £1.60 (£9.70) OWNER Mr Matt Archer & Miss Jean Broadhurst (CHELTENHAM) BRED Brereton C. Jones

1522 Ocean Hawk (USA) put his disappointing defeat here last month behind him, showing that form to be all wrong. Enjoying being in front, he was given a masterful ride by Llewellyn. He is turning into a very serious candidate for the Stayers' Hurdle at the Cheltenham Festival. (7/1)

1647 Trainglot, who lost out to What a Question by nearly eight lengths on 7lb worse terms at Newbury last time, was back on the same terms with that rival as when beating her eight lengths at Wetherby the time before, and duly confirmed that form. (9/4)

1326* Pleasure Shared (IRE), reverting to hurdles, was on level terms with the winner jumping three out and appeared to be going well. However, soon under pressure, he could then only struggle on at one pace. It will be interesting to see if his trainer decides to keep him to the minor obstacles or return him to fences. (5/2)

1647 Top Spin is not in the same league as these rivals. (33/1)

1647* What a Question (IRE) gave chase to the winner to the fourth last before tiring. (7/2)

1922* Blaze Away (USA) looked extremely well in the paddock but, after closing on the leaders early on the final circuit, he sadly collapsed soon after the tenth, having suffered a heart attack. (6/1: 10/1-11/2)

2057 BETTERWARE CUP H'CAP CHASE (5-Y.O+) (Class B)

2-20 (2-21) **3m 110y (20 fncs)** £24,378.75 (£7,380.00: £3,602.50: £1,713.75) GOING: 0.37 sec per fur (GS)

	Horse	Dist	Pos	SP	RR	SF
1518[2]	**Go Ballistic (128)** (JGMO'Shea) **7-10-0** APMcCoy (lw: hld up: mstkes 2nd & 15th: w ldr fr 3 out: led 2 out: rdn out)	—	**1**	4/1[1]	141	57
1440*	**Unguided Missile (IRE) (153)** (GRichards) **8-11-11** RDunwoody (plld hrd: led to 4th: mstke 11th: led 4 out to 2 out: ev ch last: unable qckn)	1¾	**2**	9/2[2]	165	81
1520[2]	**Major Bell (135)** (ACWhillans) **8-10-7** NWilliamson (lw: a.p: mstke 11th: hrd rdn appr 3 out: wknd appr 2 out)	20	**3**	9/2[2]	134	50
1655*	**Turning Trix (128)** (DNicholson) **9-10-0** AMaguire (lw: blnd 2nd: bhd whn blnd bdly 3rd: 6th & no ch whn blnd 3 out)	13	**4**	6/1	118	34
1869[2]	**Strong Medicine (134)** (KCBailey) **9-10-6** CLlewellyn (lw: led 4th to 4 out: wknd appr 2 out)	1¼	**5**	25/1	124	40
1871*	**Inchcailloch (IRE) (133)** (JSKing) **7-10-5** 5x CMaude (bhd fr 11th: t.o)	dist	**6**	5/1[3]	—	—
1869[3]	**Bradbury Star (148)** (JTGifford) **11-11-6** PHide (lw: prom to 14th: 6th & btn whn fell 16th)		**F**	33/1	—	—
1173[4]	**Travado (156)** (NJHenderson) **10-12-0** MAFitzgerald (lw: bhd fr 11th: t.o whn p.u bef last)		**P**	25/1	—	—
1649[5]	**Dextra Dove (137)** (SEarle) **9-10-9** GBradley (mstke 2nd: lost pl 5th: rallied 11th: ev ch 4 out: wknd 3 out: t.o whn p.u bef last)		**P**	6/1	—	—
				(SP 112.2%)	**9 Rn**	

6m 11.1 (6.10) CSF £20.35 CT £74.61 TOTE £4.60: £1.70 £1.70 £1.80 (£9.10) Trio £14.20 OWNER Mrs B. J. Lockhart (WESTBURY-ON-SEVERN) BRED J. Bowen

LONG HANDICAP Go Ballistic 9-13 Turning Trix 9-13

1518 Go Ballistic, whose two previous victories came over this course and distance on this ground, completed the hat-trick. Matching strides with the leader from the third last, he gained a very slender advantage two out and, rousted along on the run-in, asserted his authority. (4/1)

1440* Unguided Missile (IRE), winner of this race last year, lost nothing in defeat, considering he was conceding 25lb to the winner. In with every chance jumping the final fence before his welter burden took its toll, he should soon gain compensation. (9/2)

1520 Major Bell has been hiked up another 6lb for finishing second here last month, but still ran well, if left for dead by the front two turning for home. (9/2)

1655* Turning Trix was badly let down by his jumping and a very bad error at the third almost had him on the deck. He could never really recover from that, but did struggle on to finish a very moderate fourth. (6/1)

1869 Strong Medicine, soon at the head of affairs, was collared at the fourth last and had come to the end of his tether turning for home. Although he has won two small races over three miles, two and a half miles is probably his trip. (25/1)
1871* Inchcailloch (IRE) has been in sparkling form this season, but he was totally lifeless on this occasion, and punters knew their fate early on the final circuit. This was too bad to be true. (5/1)
1173 Travado, who fell on his only two previous attempts at this trip, showed no sparkle whatsoever and was in trouble setting out on the final circuit. (25/1)

2058 FROGMORE H'CAP CHASE (5-Y.O+) (Class B)

2-50 (2-51) **2m (12 fncs)** £9,457.70 (£2,861.60: £1,395.80: £662.90) GOING: 0.37 sec per fur (GS)

				SP	RR	SF
1792[3]	**Storm Alert (150)** (DNicholson) **10-11-11** AMaguire (lw: chsd ldr: lft in ld 4th: rdn out)	—	1	3/1[2]	155	85
1650*	**Ask Tom (IRE) (153)** (TPTate) **7-12-0** RGarritty (lw: hld up: chsd wnr fr 2 out: ev ch last: r.o)	½	2	Evens[1]	158	88
1637[2]	**Around the Horn (135)** (JTGifford) **9-10-10** SMcNeill (hld up: lft 2nd 4th: ev ch 3 out: 2nd whn mstke 2 out: sn wknd)	26	3	10/1	114	44
	Sybillin (140) (JGFitzGerald) **10-11-1** RDunwoody (mstke 1st: a bhd)	16	4	16/1	103	33
1912*	**Zeredar (NZ) (125)** (KCBailey) **6-10-0b** CLlewellyn (led tl fell 4th)		F	4/1[3]	—	—
				(SP 110.0%)		**5 Rn**

3m 54.2 (3.20) CSF £6.23 TOTE £3.30: £1.40 £1.40 (£2.20) OWNER Mrs Dawn Perrett (TEMPLE GUITING) BRED John Hennessy
LONG HANDICAP Zeredar (NZ) 9-13
1792 Storm Alert loves Ascot and was gaining his fifth victory here, and his third this season. A return trip for the Victor Chandler next month is on the cards but, with a 4lb penalty, he may well struggle to confirm the form with the runner-up. (3/1)
1650* Ask Tom (IRE) did not have as much use made of him as one would have expected. He will face a rematch with Storm Alert in the Victor Chandler here next month and, with that rival having to shoulder a 4lb penalty, he should be able to reverse the placings, especially if more forcing tactics are applied. (Evens)
1637 Around the Horn was on level terms with the winner jumping the third last, but was just beginning to feel the pinch when a mistake at the second last sealed his fate. (10/1: 7/1-12/1)
Sybillin, sent to France last year for a change of scenery, was going to be retired, but it was decided to bring him back into training. Unfortunately, it was a very sad sight to see this one-time high-class individual unenthusiastically trail round. He gave very little hope to connections and should surely be retired. (16/1)

2059 KNIGHTS ROYAL HURDLE (4 & 5-Y.O) (Class B)

3-20 (3-24) **2m 110y (9 hdls)** £8,559.00 (£2,592.00: £1,266.00: £603.00) GOING: 0.37 sec per fur (GS)

				SP	RR	SF
1508[2]	**Mistinguett (IRE) (134)** (NATwiston-Davies) **4-10-11** CLlewellyn (lw: mde all: rdn out)	—	1	11/2[3]	116	63
1793[11]	**Eskimo Nel (IRE) (135)** (JLSpearing) **5-10-11** RGarritty (lw: hdwy 5th: cshd wnr appr 2 out: ev ch last: unable qckn)	4	2	8/1	112	59
1648[F]	**Mr Percy (IRE) (118)** (JTGifford) **5-10-12** SMcNeill (lw: hld up: shkn up appr 2 out: one pce)	9	3	9/2[1]	104	51
	Tibetan (132) (LadyHerries) **4-11-2** MAFitzgerald (mstke 1st: chsd wnr tl mstke 6th: 3rd whn mstke 3 out: sn wknd)	10	4	5/1[2]	99	46
1924[6]	**Non Vintage (IRE) (129)** (MCChapman) **5-11-5** WWorthington (lw: a bhd)	11	5	25/1	91	38
	Tragic Hero (140) (MCPipe) **4-11-10b** APMcCoy (hld up: rdn 3 out: sn wknd)	1¾	6	9/2[1]	94	41
1661[8]	**Alltime Dancer (IRE) (121)** (OSherwood) **4-11-2** GBradley (lw: a bhd)	4	7	33/1	83	30
1017[3]	**Paddy's Return (IRE) (141)** (FMurphy) **4-11-10b** RDunwoody (a.p: chsd wnr 6th tl appr 2 out: 3rd & btn whn fell last)		F	5/1[2]	110?	—
1919[4]	**Ashwell Boy (IRE) (136)** (PJHobbs) **5-11-2** NWilliamson (lw: blnd 2nd: a bhd: t.o whn p.u bef 2 out)		P	11/2[3]	—	—
				(SP 118.4%)		**9 Rn**

3m 55.3 (5.30) CSF £45.13 TOTE £6.20: £1.90 £1.90 £1.80 (£21.20) Trio £60.10 OWNER Mr John Duggan (CHELTENHAM) BRED Michael Quirke
1508 Mistinguett (IRE), given a lovely ride by Llewellyn, bounced back to form, despite the fast ground, and jumped much better than on her last appearance here. (11/2)
1288 Eskimo Nel (IRE) bounced back to form. She had every chance jumping the final flight before done for toe by the winner. (8/1)
1369* Mr Percy (IRE) was not given a hard time and did not race as prominently as he has done so far this season. Looked after by his jockey, he was looking very one-paced from the third last, but was left in third place at the last by the fall of Paddy's Return. The winner of two novice hurdles already this season, he looks one to note with interest. (9/2)
Tibetan, who looked a promising juvenile last season, looked tired when making an error at the third last and soon capitulated. The run should bring him on. (5/1)
1924 Non Vintage (IRE) could never get into it. (25/1)
Tragic Hero, off the course since running on the Flat at Salisbury in July, was disappointing on this return and had shot his bolt turning for home. (9/2)
1017 Paddy's Return (IRE), from an out-of-form stable, had the blinkers back on, which was a help, but would have been better suited by a stiffer test of stamina. He was well held in third when taking a bad fall at the final flight. (5/1)

T/Jkpt: £3,273.80 (2.98 Tckts). T/Plpt: £20.80 (1,571.37 Tckts). T/Qdpt: £15.90 (102.3 Tckts). AK

1927-HAYDOCK (L-H) (Good to soft)
Saturday December 21st

One fence omitted
WEATHER: fine

2060 WIRRAL HURDLE (3-Y.O) (Class D)

12-15 (12-15) **2m (8 hdls)** £2,955.00 (£830.00: £405.00) GOING: 0.37 sec per fur (GS)

				SP	RR	SF
	Shu Gaa (IRE) (OSherwood) **3-10-12** JOsborne (mde all: clr 3 out: unchal)	—	1	11/10[1]	72+	24
1652[9]	**What Jim Wants (IRE)** (JJO'Neill) **3-10-7**(5) RMcGrath (lw: a.p: chsd wnr appr 3 out: no imp)	12	2	12/1	60	12
	Tagatay (MJCamacho) **3-10-9**(3) ECallaghan (chsd ldrs: rdn 2 out: kpt on one pce)	9	3	14/1	51	3
1776[4]	**Baasm** (JNorton) **3-10-12** WFry (hld up in tch: hdwy 3 out: rdn & one pce fr next)	2	4	10/1	49	1
1776[7]	**Arabian Heights** (JMackie) **3-10-9**(3) EHusband (prom tl appr 3 out: sn rdn & wknd)	¾	5	10/1	48	—
1776[9]	**Mr Gold (IRE)** (JMJefferson) **3-10-12** RichardGuest (hld up & bhd: effrt 3 out: wknd next: t.o)	21	6	14/1	27	—

				SP	RR	SF
	Palamon (USA) (JWhite) **3-10-12** PCarberry (bkwd: hld up in tch tl rdn & wknd appr 3 out: t.o)	8	**7**	7/2[2]	19	—
1526[4]	**Thorntoun Estate (IRE)** (MartinTodhunter) **3-10-12** ASSmith (a bhd: t.o)	5	**8**	16/1	14	—
1444[7]	**Irish Kinsman** (GHYardley) **3-10-12** WMcFarland (hld up & bhd: effrt & rdn 5th: no imp: t.o)	5	**9**	33/1	9	—
1652[15]	**Joe Shaw** (MrsMReveley) **3-10-12** PNiven (lw: in rr whn fell 3rd)		**F**	7/1[3]	—	—
1444[6]	**Worth The Bill** (FJordan) **3-10-12** SWynne (nt j.w: sn t.o: p.u after 5th)		**P**	25/1	—	—
	Sharp Command (PEccles) **3-10-7**(5) MichaelBrennan (chsd wnr to 5th: wkng whn blnd & uns rdr 3 out)		**U**	14/1	—	—
				(SP 140.9%)		**12 Rn**

3m 55.6 (13.60) CSF £18.69 TOTE £2.20: £1.10 £2.50 £4.50 (£20.00) Trio £65.00 OWNER Mr Ali K Al Jafleh (UPPER LAMBOURN) BRED Ali K. Al Jafleh

Shu Gaa (IRE) never reached the heights expected of him on the Flat, but he found a very easy race to begin his hurdling career, and looks set to do well at this game. (11/10)

1652 What Jim Wants (IRE) obviously needs a stiffer test of stamina, for he was unable to make the slightest impression on the winner, despite staying on. (12/1)

Tagatay, a middle-distance performer on the Flat, showed promise on this hurdling debut, and there is plenty of room for improvement. (14/1)

1776 Baasm, still carrying plenty of condition, tried hard to mount a challenge early in the straight, but lacked the pace to do so. (10/1)

1776 Arabian Heights sat in behind the leaders, but did not find a lot when let down, and was in trouble soon after entering the straight. (10/1)

1652 Joe Shaw (7/1: 9/1-6/1)

Sharp Command shared the lead down the back straight, but he was struggling to hold his pitch when he blundered away his jockey at the third last. (14/1)

2061 SOUTHPORT NOVICES' CHASE (5-Y.O+) (Class C)

12-45 (12-55) **2m 4f (13 fncs)** £4,485.75 (£1,356.00: £660.50: £312.75) GOING: 0.37 sec per fur (GS)

				SP	RR	SF
1850[4]	**Slotamatique (IRE) (94)** (GRichards) **7-11-0** ADobbin (lw: chsd ldr: lft in ld 9th: hrd rdn flat: all out)	—	**1**	9/2[2]	108	16
1586[8]	**Spinnaker** (NAGaselee) **6-11-0** JOsborne (bit bkwd: hld up: hdwy 8th: rdn to chal last: no ex cl home)	¾	**2**	11/2[3]	107	15
	Cariboo Gold (USA) (KCBailey) **7-11-0** JRailton (bkwd: chsd ldrs: effrt & rdn appr 2 out: sn wknd)	18	**3**	9/2[2]	93	1
1803[5]	**Black Brook (IRE)** (MDHammond) **7-11-0** PNiven (bit bkwd: a bhd: t.o ½-wy)	dist	**4**	12/1	—	—
1644*	**Oat Couture** (LLungo) **8-11-5** RichardGuest (led: sn clr: mstke 5th: blnd 9th: sn hdd: blnd 4 out: btn whn fell 2 out)		**F**	Evens[1]	—	—
				(SP 109.4%)		**5 Rn**

5m 17.6 (20.60) CSF £23.97 TOTE £4.70: £2.00 £2.80 (£19.00) OWNER Slotamatics (Bolton) Ltd (PENRITH)

1850 Slotamatique (IRE), always jumping well, looked set to forge clear at the end of the back straight, but he needed to be kept up to his work in the closing stages to ward off a persistent challenger. (9/2)

Spinnaker, a half-brother to Grand National winner Party Politics, did not look fully tuned up for this chasing debut, but he made the winner pull out all the stops. This could be the making of him. (11/2: op 7/2)

Cariboo Gold (USA) wore blinkers over hurdles and needed time to strike form, so this first outing since April 1994, which was understandably badly needed, should go a long way towards putting an edge on him. He jumped well enough and should make the grade over fences. (9/2)

1803 Black Brook (IRE) (12/1: op 8/1)

1644* Oat Couture, in contrast to his debut, jumped appallingly, and was in a poor fourth when he came to grief at the penultimate obstacle. (Evens)

2062 WIDNES H'CAP HURDLE (0-135) (4-Y.O+) (Class C)

1-20 (1-22) **2m (8 hdls)** £3,485.00 (£1,055.00: £515.00: £245.00) GOING: 0.37 sec per fur (GS)

				SP	RR	SF
1852*	**Shining Edge (111)** (TDEasterby) **4-10-9** JOsborne (chsd ldrs: chal last: sn led: r.o wl)	—	**1**	2/1[1]	91	40
1924*	**New Inn (116)** (SGollings) **5-11-0** KGaule (lw: led to 3rd: led 5th tl flat: rdn & unable qckn cl home)	2	**2**	7/2[3]	94	43
	House Captain (118) (JGFitzGerald) **7-10-13**(3) FLeahy (bkwd: hld up: hdwy 5th: outpcd appr 2 out: styd on strly towards fin)	½	**3**	12/1	96	45
1656[5]	**Marchant Ming (IRE) (130)** (MDHammond) **4-12-0** PNiven (led 3rd to 5th: wknd appr 2 out)	6	**4**	3/1[2]	102	51
1010[6]	**Watch My Lips (102)** (MHTompkins) **4-10-0** DBridgwater (hld up: mstke 3rd: lost tch 3 out: t.o)	18	**5**	8/1	56	5
	Albertito (FR) (102) (RHollinshead) **9-10-0** SWynne (bkwd: dropped rr ½-wy: sn t.o)	14	**6**	20/1	42	—
1804[11]	**Elation (119)** (GRichards) **4-11-3** ADobbin (bit bkwd: hld up in tch: wknd 3 out: t.o)	4	**7**	13/2	55	4
				(SP 117.5%)		**7 Rn**

3m 51.6 (9.60) CSF £9.46 TOTE £2.90: £1.90 £2.40 (£4.60) OWNER Mr G. Graham (MALTON) BRED R. B. Warren

LONG HANDICAP Albertito (FR) 9-7

1852* Shining Edge, delaying his effort to the last, had no trouble taking command on the run-in, and the rest was pretty straightforward. (2/1)

1924* New Inn has done all his winning on a sounder surface, but he gave it his best shot, only to find the winner too strong for him when the whips were cracking. (7/2)

House Captain, having only the fifth run of his career at the age of almost eight, looked to have shot his bolt when fading early in the straight. Getting his second wind, he was galloping on to some purpose towards the finish, and can return to form when tackling another half-mile. (12/1)

1656 Marchant Ming (IRE) helped share the lead, but he had company all the way and, with the weight taking its toll, had shot his bolt soon after turning in. (3/1)

Elation had had a year's break before returning to action earlier in the month and, with this run still needed, called enough entering the straight. (13/2)

2063 ST HELENS H'CAP CHASE (0-145) (5-Y.O+) (Class B)

1-55 (1-55) **4m 110y (22 fncs)** £6,684.00 (£2,022.00: £986.00: £468.00) GOING: 0.37 sec per fur (GS)

				SP	RR	SF
	Pink Gin (107) (MDHammond) **9-10-11** PNiven (hld up: hdwy 13th: led 4 out: clr fr 2 out: comf)	—	**1**	7/1	115+	—
1961[5]	**Diamond Fort (109)** (JCMcConnochie) **11-10-13** SWynne (led 5th to 6th: lost pl 11th: wl bhd tl styd on fr 3 out)	14	**2**	11/2[3]	109	—
1877[3]	**Paper Star (97)** (MPMuggeridge) **9-10-1**ow1 WMcFarland (led to 5th: led 6th to 12th: led 13th: j.b rt next: hdd 4 out: wknd after next)	20	**3**	10/1	85	—
1806[P]	**Uranus Collonges (FR) (116)** (JGFitzGerald) **10-11-6b** ADobbin (bkwd: sn chsng ldrs: lost tch 4 out: t.o)	6	**4**	10/1	100	—
1662*	**Christmas Gorse (120)** (NAGaselee) **10-11-10** JOsborne (chsd ldr fr 8th: led 12th: hdd & fell next)		**F**	11/8[1]	—	—
1829[9]	**Quixall Crossett (96)** (EMCaine) **11-9-9**(5) STaylor (wl bhd tl hdwy 13th: rdn & lost tch 17th: t.o: fell last)		**F**	100/1	—	—
1799[6]	**Chief Rager (104)** (NATwiston-Davies) **7-10-8** DBridgwater (nt j.w: t.o whn p.u after 10th)		**P**	100/30[2]	—	—

(SP 112.2%) **7 Rn**

8m 56.9 (50.90) CSF £40.13 TOTE £5.10: £2.20 £2.70 (£18.90) OWNER Mrs Margaret Francis (MIDDLEHAM) BRED Simpson Crowden Bloodstock

LONG HANDICAP Paper Star 9-12 Quixall Crossett 7-2

OFFICIAL EXPLANATION **Chief Rager: the rider reported that the gelding needs softer ground.**

Pink Gin has paid his way in the past and stamina is his strong suit. After thirteen months on the sidelines, to have been produced fit enough to win as he did means a lot of credit is due to his able trainer. (7/1)

Diamond Fort relishes these long-distance chases, but is getting no younger, and it was only his proven stamina that enabled him to pick up a worthy runner-up prize. (11/2)

1877 Paper Star made her share of the running, but may have done too much too soon over this marathon trip, for she was treading ground from the turn into the straight. (10/1)

1662* Christmas Gorse did appear to be enjoying himself and was lobbing along contentedly when taking a chance too many at the thirteenth. (11/8)

1799 Chief Rager could not cope with these big fences, but somehow survived a circuit before calling it a day. (100/30)

2064 E.B.F. 'N.H.' (QUALIFIER) NOVICES' HURDLE (4, 5 & 6-Y.O) (Class D)

2-30 (2-30) **2m (8 hdls)** £3,025.00 (£850.00: £415.00) GOING: 0.37 sec per fur (GS)

				SP	RR	SF
1777^{2}	**Alzulu (IRE)** (JGFitzGerald) **5-11-0** PCarberry (lw: a chsng ldrs: led 3 out: hit 2 out & last: hld on cl home)	—	1	6/4^{2}	82+	39
1777*	**Good Vibes** (TDEasterby) **4-11-10** JOsborne (lw: led & sn clr: rn v.wd & hdd after 2nd: chsd wnr fr 3 out: hrd rdn: unable qckn flat)	1¾	2	Evens^{1}	90+	47
1687^{2}	**Pentland Squire** (JMJefferson) **5-11-0** RichardGuest (lft in ld after 2nd: hdd 3 out: sn btn)	18	3	9/1^{3}	62	19
1692^{9}	**Eirespray (IRE)** (MDHammond) **5-11-0** DBentley (bit bkwd: hld up: outpcd 5th: sn bhd: t.o)	11	4	33/1	51	8
1187^{4}	**Galen (IRE)** (MrsMReveley) **5-11-0** PNiven (hld up in rr: t.o fr 5th)	4	5	12/1	47	4
	Dan de Man (IRE) (MissLCSiddall) **5-11-0** ADobbin (bkwd: plld hrd: hld up: lost tch 5th: t.o)	5	6	25/1	42	—
1795^{7}	**Seymour's Double** (MrsARHewitt) **5-11-0** SWynne (hld up & bhd: t.o fr ½-wy)	3	7	66/1	39	—

(SP 116.0%) **7 Rn**

3m 52.8 (10.80) CSF £3.36 TOTE £2.50: £1.60 £1.10 (£1.50) OWNER Mr D. Buckle (MALTON) BRED Ardenode Stud Ltd

1777 Alzulu (IRE) gained his revenge over the favourite on these better terms, but there was an element of luck attached. For one who is sure to be better when tackling a more suitable trip, there is plenty to like about the commitment he puts into the job. (6/4)

1777* Good Vibes almost threw the race away when failing to negotiate the bend at Aintree, and identical problems at an earlier stage here proved costly. Until he masters going left-handed, he will be better kept to tracks going the other way round. (Evens)

1687 Pentland Squire, taken to post early, had the misfortune to be left in front far too soon, and had run himself out when collared at the third last. (9/1)

2065 BOSTON PIT H'CAP CHASE (0-135) (5-Y.O+) (Class C)

3-00 (3-01) **2m 4f (13 fncs)** £4,711.00 (£1,321.00: £643.00) GOING: 0.37 sec per fur (GS)

				SP	RR	SF
1024*	**General Command (IRE) (123)** (GRichards) **8-11-2** PCarberry (lw: j.w: mde all: clr 2 out: unchal)	—	1	8/11^{1}	141+	12
	Valiant Warrior (133) (MDHammond) **8-11-12** PNiven (bkwd: hld up: hdwy to chse wnr appr 2 out: no imp)	16	2	2/1^{2}	138	9
1869^{5}	**Conti D'Estruval (FR) (117)** (GBBalding) **6-10-10** ADobbin (lw: chsd wnr fr 6th tl rdn & wknd 3 out)	23	3	9/2^{3}	104	—

(SP 109.4%) **3 Rn**

5m 19.3 (22.30) CSF £2.41 TOTE £1.70 (£1.40) OWNER Mr Robert Ogden (PENRITH) BRED Miss M. Fenton

1024* General Command (IRE) turned in a fine display of jumping from the front and provided his jockey with another winner on his return after injury. He has certainly got his act together this term. (8/11)

Valiant Warrior has won first time out in the past, but will strip fitter with this run under his belt and there was no disgrace in this defeat. (2/1)

1869 Conti D'Estruval (FR) performs best when he can bounce off the ground, and that was not the case this time. (9/2)

2066 THELWALL STANDARD OPEN N.H. FLAT RACE (4, 5 & 6-Y.O) (Class H)

3-30 (3-30) **2m** £1,292.00 (£362.00: £176.00)

				SP	RR	SF
	Slide On (PDEvans) **6-11-4** GaryLyons (bkwd: hld up in tch: hdwy to ld 4f out: sn clr: rdn out)	—	1	16/1	76 f	—
1692^{7}	**Meadow Hymn (IRE)** (JGFitzGerald) **5-11-4** WDwan (a chsng ldrs: effrt & rdn 2f out: nt pce of wnr)	5	2	16/1	71 f	—
	Merry Masquerade (IRE) (MrsMReveley) **5-11-4** RHodge (wl grwn, chsng type: bit bkwd: wl bhd tl styd on fnl 3f)	13	3	20/1	58 f	—
1692^{3}	**Billy Buckskin** (JNorton) **4-11-4** WFry (chsd ldrs: rdn 3f out: styd on same pce)	nk	4	14/1	58 f	—
	Ben Eiger (IRE) (NATwiston-Davies) **4-11-4** DBridgwater (bit bkwd: hld up & bhd: hdwy 6f out: wknd 2f out)	3	5	10/1	55 f	—
	Breath of Scandal (IRE) (OSherwood) **5-11-4** JOsborne (lw: hld up mid div: gd hdwy 5f out: outpcd over 2f out)	13	6	9/4^{1}	42 f	—
	No Finer Man (IRE) (GRichards) **5-11-4** ADobbin (hld up: hdwy 7f out: wknd over 2f out)	1	7	4/1^{3}	41 f	—
1913^{8}	**Primitive Light** (ASmith) **6-10-6**(7) NHorrocks (bit bkwd: chsd ldrs: led 6f out to 4f out: grad wknd)	½	8	33/1	35 f	—
	Badger's Lane (KCBailey) **5-11-11** JRailton (bkwd: led after 2f to 10f out: wknd ent st: t.o)	13	9	5/1	34 f	—
	Back On The Lash (IRE) (FMurphy) **4-11-4** PCarberry (a in rr: eased whn btn fnl 3f: t.o)	12	10	20/1	15 f	—
1834*	**Strong Mint (IRE)** (MrsMReveley) **5-11-11** PNiven (lw: hld up: hdwy ½-wy: wknd over 4f out: t.o)	26	11	11/4^{2}	—	—
1774^{8}	**Just One Question (IRE)** (JJO'Neill) **6-11-11** RichardGuest (led 2f: led 10f out to 6f out: wknd over 3f out: t.o)	1¾	12	16/1	—	—
1834^{10}	**Social Insecurity (IRE)** (SGollings) **5-11-4** KGaule (prom tl wknd over 3f out: t.o)	1	13	33/1	—	—
1665^{7}	**Scholar Green** (GHYardley) **4-11-4** WMcFarland (lost pl 6f out: t.o)	dist	14	33/1	—	—

(SP 145.9%) **14 Rn**

3m 46.8 CSF £256.47 TOTE £24.40: £4.10 £4.30 £6.70 (£148.20) Trio Not won; £348.38 to 23/12/96 OWNER Mr P. D. Evans (WELSHPOOL) BRED R. W. Morris

OFFICIAL EXPLANATION **Strong Mint (IRE): was unsuited by the ground.**

Slide On was not disgraced on his only previous outing in the spring and showed his true worth when set alight to draw clear below the distance. He looks a useful individual. (16/1)

1692 Meadow Hymn (IRE), fitter than most, was unable to match strides with the winner in the latter stages, but showed enough to suggest we have not seen the best of him yet. (16/1)

Merry Masquerade (IRE), a well-grown debutante with plenty of scope for improvement, stayed on strongly from off the pace to grab the minor prize right on the line. (20/1)

1692 Billy Buckskin ran another promising race, but he is slow, and will probably come into his own when his attentions are switched to hurdles. (14/1)
Ben Eiger (IRE), a strongly-made half-brother to Wisley Wonder, could only plug on at the one pace in the latter stages, but the experience will not be lost, and he does look a progressive type. (10/1: op 5/1)
Breath of Scandal (IRE), a winner between the Flags in Ireland, was carrying a summer bloom on his coat. Patiently ridden, he came through on the inside to look the likely winner three furlongs out, but lack of peak-fitness took its toll and he was not knocked about when beaten. The kindness will be repaid. (9/4: 7/4-3/1)
No Finer Man (IRE) (4/1: 6/1-7/2)
Badger's Lane (5/1: 4/1-7/1)
1834* Strong Mint (IRE) would not let himself down on the frozen ground down the back straight according to his jockey. This poor performance can safely be ignored. (11/4)

T/Plpt: £87.20 (116.46 Tckts). T/Qdpt: £17.40 (31.96 Tckts). IM

1933-LINGFIELD (L-H) (Good to soft, Hdles Soft patches)
Saturday December 21st

WEATHER: overcast

2067 BRANDY BUTTER CONDITIONAL H'CAP HURDLE (0-110) (4-Y.O+) (Class E)
12-30 (12-30) **2m 110y (8 hdls)** £2,364.00 (£654.00: £312.00) GOING: 1.52 sec per fur (HY)

				SP	RR	SF
1860³	**Shepherds Rest (IRE) (95)** (SMellor) **4-10-9**(7) SHearn (a.p: led 2 out: rdn out)	—	**1**	100/30 ²	75	37
1663⁶	**Museum (IRE) (79)** (PWinkworth) **5-9-10**(4) XAizpuru (hld up: hdwy 3 out: rdn appr 2 out: styd on flat)	2½	**2**	10/1	57	19
1939⁴	**Tickerty's Gift (107)** (GLMoore) **6-11-10**(4) MAttwater (chsd ldrs: rdn & outpcd appr 2 out: kpt on one pce fr next)	5	**3**	13/2	80	42
1933⁴	**Hawthorne Glen (100)** (MrsMELong) **9-11-3**(4) AIrvine (nt fluent: led: hdd & mstke 2 out: sn wknd)	8	**4**	15/8 ¹	65	27
1866²	**Pedaltothemetal (IRE) (90)** (PMitchell) **4-10-11** DJKavanagh (hld up: sme hdwy after 3 out: sn rdn: one pce)	10	**5**	9/2 ³	45	7
	Derisbay (IRE) (80) (JJBridger) **8-10-1b** SophieMitchell (bit bkwd: prom tl wknd 5th: t.o)	12	**6**	25/1	24	—
590ᴾ	**Father Power (IRE) (79)** (SABowen) **8-10-0** CRae (bhd fr 4th: t.o)	s.h	**7**	50/1	23	—
	Wide Support (90) (AMoore) **11-10-7**(4) MBatchelor (bit bkwd: prom tl wknd after 3 out: t.o in 6th whn fell last)		**F**	33/1	—	—
	Ballymgyr (IRE) (79) (EAWheeler) **7-9-10**(4) MGriffiths (bit bkwd: w ldr to 2nd: wknd 4th: t.o whn p.u after 3 out)		**P**	20/1	—	—
				(SP 112.0%)	**9 Rn**	

4m 15.9 (30.90) CSF £31.65 CT £183.84 TOTE £3.60: £2.00 £2.80 £1.30 (£17.70) Trio £66.90 OWNER The Odd Dozen (SWINDON) BRED Mrs M. Dunny
LONG HANDICAP Father Power (IRE) 9-5
IN-FOCUS: Simon Hearn was riding his first winner.
1860 Shepherds Rest (IRE) travelled well throughout and, although having to be pushed out on the run-in, always had the matter firmly in hand. (100/30)
1663 Museum (IRE) kept on well on the flat and is gradually finding some form. (10/1)
1939 Tickerty's Gift is in the grasp of the Handicapper at present. (13/2: 3/1-7/1)
1933 Hawthorne Glen jumped poorly and was beaten by the second last. (15/8: 3/1-7/4)
1866 Pedaltothemetal (IRE) never threatened to take a hand in proceedings. (9/2: 11/4-5/1)

2068 PORT & STILTON NOVICES' H'CAP CHASE (0-95) (4-Y.O+) (Class F)
1-00 (1-02) **2m (12 fncs)** £2,584.80 (£770.40: £367.20: £165.60) GOING: 1.52 sec per fur (HY)

				SP	RR	SF
1797⁶	**Stage Player (82)** (MissCJECaroe) **10-11-4** DLeahy (chsd ldrs: led appr 3 out: clr last: rdn out)	—	**1**	16/1	91	17
1831*	**River Leven (88)** (DRGandolfo) **7-11-7b**(3) DFortt (chsd ldr: mstke 6th: hrd rdn & ev ch 3 out: one pce)	4	**2**	11/8 ¹	93	19
1732⁵	**Policemans Pride (FR) (72)** (MMadgwick) **7-10-8** BFenton (led: clr to 8th: hdd appr 3 out: grad wknd)	20	**3**	8/1	57	—
	Bayrak (USA) (84) (PAKelleway) **6-11-1**(5) ABates (a bhd: t.o fr 4th)	dist	**4**	7/2 ²	—	—
1708ᴾ	**Kentavrus Way (IRE) (64)** (AMoore) **5-10-0** NMann (ref to r: t.n.p)		**R**	33/1	—	—
1771⁶	**King's Gold (78)** (MrsLRichards) **6-11-0** MRichards (blnd & uns rdr 2nd)		**U**	14/1	—	—
1763*	**Castleconner (IRE) (82)** (RGFrost) **5-11-4b** MrAHoldsworth (last whn blnd & uns rdr 5th)		**U**	4/1 ³	—	—
				(SP 110.9%)	**7 Rn**	

4m 27.3 (35.30) CSF £36.52 CT £172.54 TOTE £13.30: £3.50 £1.30 (£4.60) Trio £18.30 OWNER Miss C. J. E. Caroe (THURLEIGH) BRED White Lodge Stud Ltd
LONG HANDICAP Kentavrus Way (IRE) 9-7
1566 Stage Player jumped quite soundly and recorded his first win for over five years. (16/1)
1831* River Leven was not particularly fluent at some of his fences and found the weight concession telling in the closing stages. (11/8: op 4/5)
1732 Policemans Pride (FR) set the pace, but was a spent force turning for home. (8/1)
Bayrak (USA) was never a factor. (7/2: op 6/1)
1763* Castleconner (IRE) was at the back and not going very well when unseating his rider at the fifth. (4/1)

2069 H.B.L.B. CHRISTMAS H'CAP HURDLE (0-130) (4-Y.O+ F & M) (Class C)
1-35 (1-35) **2m 3f 110y (10 hdls)** £3,492.50 (£1,040.00: £495.00: £222.50) GOING: 1.52 sec per fur (HY)

				SP	RR	SF
1698*	**Sail by the Stars (115)** (CaptTAForster) **7-10-13** AThornton (lw: chsd ldr: led appr 2 out: pushed clr flat)	—	**1**	9/4 ²	97+	33
1571⁵	**Fortunes Course (IRE) (110)** (JSKing) **7-10-8** TJMurphy (led: hdd & outpcd appr 2 out: sn rdn: r.o one pce flat)	4	**2**	6/1	89	25
	Handy Lass (102) (JSSmith) **7-9-7**(7) MGriffiths (bit bkwd: hld up: rdn 6th: hdwy to chse wnr 2 out: sn rdn: wknd flat)	5	**3**	20/1	77	13
1258³	**Silver Shred (130)** (MCPipe) **5-11-9**(5) OBurrows (hld up: rdn appr 3 out: wknd appr next)	dist	**4**	5/4 ¹	—	—
1586³	**Lessons Lass (IRE) (103)** (MissHCKnight) **4-10-1** BFenton (chsd ldrs tl wknd 3 out)	dist	**5**	9/2 ³	—	—
				(SP 112.4%)	**5 Rn**	

5m 11.0 (37.00) CSF £13.83 TOTE £3.20: £1.50 £2.40 (£7.20) OWNER Mr T. F. F. Nixon (LUDLOW) BRED T. F. F. Nixon
LONG HANDICAP Handy Lass 9-10
OFFICIAL EXPLANATION Lessons Lass (IRE): gurgled.

1698* Sail by the Stars is in great form at present and recorded her third win of the season here in fine style. (9/4: op 6/4)
1571 Fortunes Course (IRE) finds this trip the bare minimum and stayed on again having been outpaced approaching the second last. (6/1: op 4/1)
Handy Lass ran well until lack of condition told. (20/1)
1258 Silver Shred, well supported in the Ring, was very disappointing here and is possibly better on a sounder surface. (5/4: op 2/1)
1586 Lessons Lass (IRE) dropped away disappointingly in the closing stages and was reported to have gurgled. (9/2)

2070 JARDINE INSURANCE SERVICES HURDLE (3-Y.O) (Class E)

2-10 (2-13) **2m 110y (8 hdls)** £2,616.00 (£726.00: £348.00) GOING: 1.52 sec per fur (HY)

	Horse	Dist	Pos	SP	RR	SF
	Roseberry Avenue (IRE) (RAkehurst) **3-10-7**(5) SRyan (a.p: mstke 3 out: led 2 out: edgd lft appr last: veered rt & lft flat: r.o)	—	**1**	9/4 2	75	40
1808*	**Red Raja** (PMitchell) **3-11-5** MRichards (led: hdd 2 out: hmpd appr last: hrd rdn flat: r.o)	¾	**2**	13/8 1	81	46
1634 7	**Sterling Fellow** (DLWilliams) **3-10-12v** MClarke (rr: rdn 3rd: mod late hdwy: nvr nrr: t.o)	dist	**3**	12/1	—	—
	Brighton Road (IRE) (GBBalding) **3-10-12** BClifford (lw: prom tl wknd appr 2 out: t.o)	hd	**4**	14/1	—	—
1935 6	**Bigwig (IRE)** (AMoore) **3-10-12** NMann (bhd fr 4th: t.o)	13	**5**	66/1	—	—
	Scottish Hero (MissHCKnight) **3-10-12** BFenton (prom tl wknd 3 out: t.o)	3	**6**	7/1 3	—	—
1712 7	**Embroidered** (RMFlower) **3-10-0**(7) JKMcCarthy (a bhd: t.o: lame)	19	**7**	66/1	—	—
1706 4	**Hanbitooh (USA)** (MrsAJPerrett) **3-10-12** GUpton (prom to 3rd: t.o)	9	**8**	12/1	—	—
1377 14	**Half An Inch (IRE)** (TMJones) **3-10-12b** DLeahy (in tch: rdn 3rd: sn wknd: t.o)	3	**9**	33/1	—	—
1872 10	**Sam Rockett** (PMooney) **3-10-7b**(5) DJKavanagh (rr: hdwy 4th: wknd next: t.o)	11	**10**	50/1	—	—
	Bailiwick (NAGraham) **3-10-12** SCurran (in tch to 5th: t.o)	10	**11**	25/1	—	—
	Eskimo Kiss (IRE) (GFJohnsonHoughton) **3-10-7** AThornton (mstke 1st: a bhd: t.o)	5	**12**	25/1	—	—
	Jamies First (IRE) (RIngram) **3-10-12** DO'Sullivan (a bhd: t.o)	3½	**13**	25/1	—	—
	Induna Mkubwa (CFWall) **3-10-12** LHarvey (prom to 5th: t.o)	1¼	**14**	14/1	—	—
1872 9	**Veronica Franco** (BAPearce) **3-10-7** TJMurphy (prom to 5th: sn t.o)	dist	**15**	50/1	—	—
				(SP 131.5%)	**15 Rn**	

4m 14.4 (29.40) CSF £6.59 TOTE £2.80: £1.60 £1.30 £2.80 (£3.90) Trio £10.70 OWNER Mr P. D. Savill (EPSOM) BRED Lowquest Ltd
OFFICIAL EXPLANATION **Embroidered: pulled up very sore.**
Roseberry Avenue (IRE) did not jump particularly fluently at one or two and wandered alarmingly in the closing stages when put under pressure, causing slight interference to the runner-up in the process. Nonetheless, he was a winner on merit. (9/4: 6/4-3/1)
1808* Red Raja ran very well again, but found his penalty beating him on the run-in. (13/8)
1377 Sterling Fellow kept on for a distant third, having been off the bridle from the start. (12/1)
Brighton Road (IRE) ran alright, but did not get home on this softer ground. (14/1)
Scottish Hero ran better than his finishing position suggests, travelling well until crying enough at the third from home. (7/1)
1706 Hanbitooh (USA) (12/1: 7/1-14/1)
Induna Mkubwa (14/1: 7/1-16/1)

2071 E.B.F. 'N.H.' (QUALIFIER) NOVICES' HURDLE (4, 5 & 6-Y.O) (Class E)

2-40 (2-41) **2m 110y (8 hdls)** £2,532.00 (£702.00: £336.00) GOING: 1.52 sec per fur (HY)

	Horse	Dist	Pos	SP	RR	SF
1551*	**Boardroom Shuffle (IRE)** (JTGifford) **5-11-2**(3) LAspell (a.p: led & hit 2 out: sn clr: easily)	—	**1**	8/15 1	87+	49
1782 2	**Three Farthings** (JABOld) **6-11-0** GUpton (a.p: led 4th: hdd 2 out: one pce)	14	**2**	9/2 3	68	30
	Master Pilgrim (GBBalding) **4-11-0** BFenton (bit bkwd: keen hold: hld up: sme hdwy 3 out: rdn appr next: one pce)	12	**3**	33/1	57	19
1810*	**Dantes Cavalier (IRE)** (DRGandolfo) **6-11-2**(3) DFortt (led to 4th: wknd next)	4	**4**	4/1 2	58	20
1651 8	**John Drumm** (PRWebber) **5-11-0** AThornton (prom to 5th)	2½	**5**	10/1	51	13
1695 4	**Shanagore Warrior (IRE)** (SMellor) **4-11-0** NMann (bhd fr 3rd: t.o)	dist	**6**	33/1	—	—
344 5	**Belle Perk (IRE)** (TPMcGovern) **5-10-9** TJMurphy (hld up: sme hdwy after 3 out: mod 3rd whn blnd & uns rdr 2 out)		**U**	50/1	—	—
				(SP 120.3%)	**7 Rn**	

4m 13.9 (28.90) CSF £3.95 TOTE £1.50: £1.00 £2.70 (£3.50) OWNER Mr A. D. Weller (FINDON) BRED Stonethorn Stud Farms Ltd
1551* Boardroom Shuffle (IRE) won this in really smart fashion, and is a very useful novice. (8/15)
1782 Three Farthings ran well here, but met a smart rival. He looked one-paced in the closing stages, and is essentially a stayer who will improve when put over further. (9/2)
Master Pilgrim ran quite well and will come on for the run. (33/1)
1810* Dantes Cavalier (IRE) dropped away disappointingly from the top of the hill. (4/1: 3/1-5/1)

2072 MAC VIDI NOVICES' CHASE (5-Y.O+) (Class E)

3-10 (3-12) **3m (18 fncs)** £3,691.80 (£1,024.80: £491.40) GOING: 1.52 sec per fur (HY)

	Horse	Dist	Pos	SP	RR	SF
1771*	**Mariners Mirror (118)** (NATwiston-Davies) **9-11-7** MrMRimell (led 7th: rdn & lft clr 2 out: easily)	—	**1**	6/5 1	115+	28
1798 5	**Kendal Cavalier** (GBBalding) **6-10-12** BFenton (hld up: rdn & outpcd 13th: closed sltly appr 3 out. lft 2nd & sltly hmpd 2 out: kpt on one pce flat)	4	**2**	5/2 3	103	16
1797 U	**Gemma's Wager (IRE)** (MarkCampion) **6-10-7** LHarvey (a bhd: mstke 8th: t.o fr 10th)	dist	**3**	40/1	—	—
1797 3	**Mr Pickpocket (IRE) (106)** (MissHCKnight) **8-10-12** TJMurphy (led to 7th: mstke 11th: disp ld whn fell 2 out)		**F**	2/1 2	—	—
1632 P	**Benbulbin (IRE)** (JWMullins) **6-10-12** SCurran (bit bkwd: a bhd: t.o fr 14th: p.u bef 3 out)		**P**	40/1	—	—
				(SP 112.2%)	**5 Rn**	

6m 44.1 (50.10) CSF £4.55 TOTE £1.80: £1.40 £1.40 (£2.60) OWNER Mr F. J. Mills (CHELTENHAM) BRED E. J. Praill, Mrs M. Scudamore and M. J. Scudamore
1771* Mariners Mirror cut out a lot of the running, but was being strongly challenged when left clear two from home, and looked a shade fortunate. (6/5)
1798 Kendal Cavalier was making a little headway but was only booked for third when slightly hampered at the second last. He looks an out-and-out stayer. (5/2)
1797 Mr Pickpocket (IRE) had a ding-dong battle with the winner throughout and was upsides and going just the better when falling at the second last. (2/1)

2073 HOLLY & IVY MAIDEN OPEN N.H. FLAT RACE (4, 5 & 6-Y.O) (Class H)

3-40 (3-42) **2m 110y** £1,311.50 (£364.00: £174.50)

				SP	RR	SF
	Arkley Royal (JABOld) **5-11-5** GUpton (lw: hld up: hdwy ½-wy: led 2f out: sn clr: r.o wl)	—	**1**	4/6^{1}	62 f	—
1329^{9}	**Shariakanndi (FR)** (JSKing) **4-11-5** TJMurphy (hld up: hdwy 6f out: rdn 3f out: kpt on one pce fnl 2f)	10	**2**	10/1	52 f	—
1573^{4}	**Repeat Offer** (PDCundell) **4-11-5** SCurran (plld hrd: a.p: led 6f out: hdd 2f out: one pce)	½	**3**	4/1^{2}	52 f	—
1685^{6}	**Irish Delight** (RCurtis) **4-11-5** DMorris (rr: hdwy ½-wy: rdn 4f out: one pce)	24	**4**	8/1^{3}	29 f	—
	Peace Initiative (KVincent) **4-11-5** ADicken (bit bkwd: prom tl wknd 3f out)	11	**5**	20/1	18 f	—
	Bebe Grey (PRHedger) **5-10-7v^{1}**(7) MClinton (bit bkwd: a bhd)	8	**6**	14/1	5 f	—
	Huish (IRE) (GFHCharles-Jones) **5-11-5** MrACharles-Jones (bit bkwd: plld hrd: led: hdd 6f out: wknd qckly: t.o)	dist	**7**	25/1	—	—
	Pitarry (DMGrissell) **6-11-5** BFenton (prom to ½-wy: t.o)	18	**8**	16/1	—	—
	Chemin-de-Fer (BAPearce) **4-11-5** MrsKHills (bit bkwd: prom tl wknd 7f out: t.o)	11	**9**	25/1	—	—
1801^{10}	**Royal Divide (IRE)** (VSoane) **4-11-5** MRichards (a bhd: t.o fr ½-wy)	dist	**10**	20/1	—	—
				(SP 130.0%)	**10 Rn**	

4m 14.9 CSF £9.89 TOTE £1.60: £1.20 £2.30 £1.20 (£3.90) Trio £15.10 OWNER Mr John Bickel (WROUGHTON) BRED S. Pike

Arkley Royal, well supported in the Ring and the pick of the paddock, ran out an emphatic winner. (4/6: Evens-4/7)

Shariakanndi (FR) stayed on up the straight and will probably want a trip when switched to hurdles. (10/1: op 6/1)

1573 Repeat Offer took a keen hold, but nonetheless ran well until tiring in the last two furlongs. (4/1: tchd 6/1)

1685 Irish Delight (8/1: 4/1-9/1)

Bebe Grey (14/1: 8/1-16/1)

T/Plpt: £16.20 (499.51 Tckts). T/Qdpt: £3.70 (146.02 Tckts). SM

2048-UTTOXETER (L-H) (Good to soft, Good patches)

Saturday December 21st

one flight omitted due to frost

WEATHER: fine

2074 TECHNICAL HIGH SCHOOL PAST PUPILS NOVICES' HURDLE (4-Y.O+) (Class E)

12-25 (12-28) **2m (7 hdls)** £2,631.00 (£741.00: £363.00) GOING: 0.64 sec per fur (S)

				SP	RR	SF
1382^{4}	**Mister Rm (109)** (NATwiston-Davies) **4-11-5** DWalsh (a.p: led 3 out: sn clr: easily)	—	**1**	4/1^{2}	91+	46
1695*	**Stormy Passage (IRE) (105)** (PJHobbs) **6-11-5** GTormey (lw: a.p: ev ch 3 out: no imp)	6	**2**	15/8^{1}	85	40
1253^{3}	**Prussia (98)** (WClay) **5-11-5** DGallagher (a.p: led 4th to 3 out: sn wknd)	4	**3**	8/1^{3}	81	36
	Percy Braithwaite (IRE) (MissPMWhittle) **4-10-5**(7) KHibbert (a.p: ev ch appr 3 out: wknd appr 2 out)	4	**4**	12/1	70	25
1353^{3}	**Samanid (IRE) (110)** (MissLCSiddall) **4-11-5** OPears (hld up & bhd: stdy hdwy fr 3 out: nvr plcd to chal)	6	**5**	9/1	71+	26
	Banny Hill Lad (CPMorlock) **6-10-12** JRKavanagh (hld up: hdwy appr 3 out: eased whn btn appr 2 out)	8	**6**	33/1	56	11
1907^{6}	**Gutteridge (IRE)** (TKeddy) **6-10-12b^{1}** ILawrence (prom: nt fluent 4th: wknd appr 3 out)	7	**7**	33/1	49	4
1369^{8}	**Rood Music** (MGMeagher) **5-10-12** DerekByrne (led to 4th: wknd after 5th)	16	**8**	50/1	33	—
1659^{P}	**Our Tom** (JWharton) **4-10-7**(5) MrRThornton (a bhd)	s.h	**9**	50/1	33	—
1280^{3}	**Manasis (NZ)** (SABrookshaw) **5-10-12** RJohnson (prom: rdn after 4th: wknd after 5th)	4	**10**	14/1	29	—
	Ballyranter (MDHammond) **7-10-9**(3) MrCBonner (bkwd: rdn 4th: bhd fr 5th)	nk	**11**	12/1	29	—
1250^{2}	**Victoria Day** (BAMcMahon) **4-10-4**(3) TDascombe (bhd fr 4th: t.o)	13	**12**	12/1	11	—
955^{12}	**Racing Telegraph** (CNAllen) **6-10-9**(3) GHogan (s.s: plld hrd: a bhd: t.o whn p.u bef 3 out)		**P**	50/1	—	—
				(SP 117.4%)	**13 Rn**	

3m 55.6 (14.60) CSF £11.04 TOTE £4.80: £2.50 £1.20 £1.90 (£3.40) Trio £8.40 OWNER Mr F J Mills & Mr W Mills (CHELTENHAM) BRED Major and Mrs R. B. Kennard

OFFICIAL EXPLANATION **Samanid (IRE): the rider reported that his instructions were to settle the colt as he had run too freely last time. However, he considered the colt's action was not right, and added that the horse gurgled in the closing stages.**

1382 Mister Rm clearly appreciated this return to novice company. (4/1)

1695* Stormy Passage (IRE) proved no match for the winner, having previously raced in the mud this season. (15/8)

1253 Prussia, still kept to two miles, would have been 11lb better off with the winner in a handicap. (8/1)

Percy Braithwaite (IRE), a ten-furlong winner in July for Mark Johnston, was bought for 6,000 guineas and made a satisfactory debut. (12/1: 8/1-14/1)

1353 Samanid (IRE) ran an eyecatching race without being knocked about. He is one to note. (9/1)

Banny Hill Lad has been off course since finishing third in a Huntingdon bumper in March 1995. With his rider readily accepting the situation early in the home straight, he is another who gave the impression he will do a lot better in time. (33/1)

1280 Manasis (NZ) (14/1: op 8/1)

Ballyranter (12/1: 8/1-14/1)

2075 CHRIS TALBOT 39TH BIRTHDAY H'CAP CHASE (0-120) (5-Y.O+) (Class D)

12-55 (12-55) **3m (18 fncs)** £3,663.75 (£1,110.00: £542.50: £258.75) GOING: 0.38 sec per fur (GS)

				SP	RR	SF
1806^{3}	**Lord Gyllene (NZ) (119)** (SABrookshaw) **8-12-0** RJohnson (wnt 2nd 6th: hit 14th: led 3 out: sn clr: eased flat)	—	**1**	6/4^{1}	133+	—
1641^{3}	**Sailor Jim (107)** (PTDalton) **9-11-2** WMarston (led: mstke 4th: hdd 3 out: sn btn: eased flat)	16	**2**	5/1^{2}	110	—
1564^{P}	**Carlingford Lakes (IRE) (91)** (TThomsonJones) **8-10-0** BPowell (prom: outpcd 11th: wknd 13th)	5	**3**	9/1	91	—
1342^{6}	**Braes of Mar (110)** (NJHenderson) **6-11-5** JRKavanagh (prom: nt fluent 11th: wkng whn hit 13th)	½	**4**	6/1	110	—
1839^{3}	**Celtic Town (108)** (OSherwood) **8-11-3** JAMcCarthy (bhd: reminder after 10th: sn t.o)	29	**5**	11/2^{3}	88	—
	My Main Man (99) (TRGeorge) **8-10-8** DWalsh (bhd whn p.u after 6th)		**P**	10/1	—	—
				(SP 105.4%)	**6 Rn**	

6m 20.8 CSF £8.14 TOTE £2.10: £1.50 £1.90 (£3.20) OWNER Mr Stanley Clarke (SHREWSBURY) BRED Mrs N. M. Taylor

LONG HANDICAP Carlingford Lakes (IRE) 9-10

1806 Lord Gyllene (NZ) found this much less competitive than at Wetherby last time off a 1lb lower mark. (6/4)

1641 Sailor Jim, dropped 3lb, found his front-running tactics leaving him vulnerable over this longer trip. (5/1)

Carlingford Lakes (IRE), 4lb out of the handicap, was apparently knocked into on her comeback race last month. (9/1)

1342 Braes of Mar, reverting to fences, was in trouble after being hesitant at the first on the far side on the final circuit. (6/1)
1839 Celtic Town fell on the only previous occasion he has worn blinkers, but they would appear to be worth another try. (11/2)

2076 MANNY BERNSTEIN BOOKMAKERS NOVICES' H'CAP HURDLE (0-100) (4-Y.O+) (Class E)

1-30 (1-30) **3m 110y (10 hdls)** £2,473.50 (£696.00: £340.50) GOING: 0.64 sec per fur (S)

				SP	RR	SF
1854*	**Menshaar (USA) (90)** (LLungo) **4-11-4** RSupple (lw: a.p: hit 7th: led appr last: drvn out)	—	**1**	7/2^{1}	73	14
1654^{4}	**Coole Hill (IRE) (93)** (DNicholson) **5-11-2**(5) MrRThornton (a.p: ev ch 2 out: one pce)	3	**2**	7/2^{1}	74	15
	Tilty (USA) (96) (AStreeter) **6-11-10v^{1}** TEley (bit bkwd: chsd ldr to 7th: lost pl 9th: rallied 2 out: styd on flat)	1¼	**3**	12/1	76	17
1959^{5}	**Evezio Rufo (87)** (NPLittmoden) **4-11-1v** BPowell (hld up: hdwy 7th: led after 8th tl appr last: one pce)	2	**4**	16/1	66	7
1320^{4}	**Felloo (IRE) (91)** (TRGeorge) **7-11-5** TJenks (lft in ld 2nd: hdd after 8th: wknd appr last)	7	**5**	16/1	65	6
1768^{5}	**Burntwood Melody (72)** (PTDalton) **5-10-0** JSupple (nvr nr ldrs)	5	**6**	14/1	43	—
1814^{5}	**Quite A Man (83)** (SABrookshaw) **8-10-4**(7) TMortimer (bit bkwd: hld up: hdwy 5th: rdn appr 8th: sn wknd: t.o)	dist	**7**	20/1	—	—
1906^{6}	**Mister Blake (94)** (RLee) **6-11-8** RJohnson (bhd whn p.u bef 3 out)		**P**	5/1^{2}	—	—
1768^{11}	**Nunson (72)** (RDickin) **7-10-0** DGallagher (bhd fr 8th: t.o whn p.u bef 3 out)		**P**	50/1	—	—
1654^{10}	**Jigginstown (84)** (JJO'Neill) **9-10-12** ARoche (a bhd: t.o whn p.u bef 3 out)		**P**	14/1	—	—
1417^{3}	**Riverbank Rose (72)** (WClay) **5-10-0** GTormey (prom tl wknd appr 7th: t.o 8th: p.u bef 3 out)		**P**	12/1	—	—
	Ballydougan (IRE) (73) (RMathew) **8-10-1v** RBellamy (bit bkwd: bhd: rdn 5th: t.o 8th: p.u bef 3 out)		**P**	25/1	—	—
1807^{5}	**Hotspur Street (78)** (MWEasterby) **4-10-6b** WMarston (led tl mstke & uns rdr 2nd)		**U**	7/1^{3}	—	—

(SP 124.7%) **13 Rn**

6m 14.9 (32.90) CSF £16.08 CT £126.61 TOTE £4.40: £1.50 £2.20 £3.60 (£11.70) Trio £88.60 OWNER Mr G. A. Arthur (CARRUTHERSTOWN) BRED Brereton C. Jones

LONG HANDICAP Riverbank Rose 9-12 Nunson 9-7 Burntwood Melody 9-13

1854* Menshaar (USA) again showed he possesses plenty of abiltiy for one so young and was 4lb higher than when last seen in a handicap. (7/2)
1654 Coole Hill (IRE), a model of consistency, was unable to cope with the winner. (7/2)
Tilty (USA) found his second wind in the later stages and will be sharper for the run. (12/1)
1959 Evezio Rufo seemed to get this stamina test well enough, but could not produce an extra gear. (16/1)
Felloo (IRE) was reverting to timber after being well beaten on his fencing debut at Newbury last month. (16/1)

2077 HEATHYARDS ENGINEERING NOVICES' H'CAP CHASE (0-100) (5-Y.O+) (Class E)

2-05 (2-05) **2m 5f (16 fncs)** £3,087.00 (£936.00: £458.00: £219.00) GOING: 0.38 sec per fur (GS)

				SP	RR	SF
1920*	**Art Prince (IRE) (100)** (CPEBrooks) **6-11-7**(7) MBerry (lw: j.w: led 2nd: wl clr fr 10th: unchal)	—	**1**	8/11^{1}	117+	50
1840^{7}	**Plassy Boy (IRE) (72)** (KRBurke) **7-10-0** RSupple (mstke 8th: sn wl bhd: styd on fr 3 out: no ch w wnr)	dist	**2**	12/1	—	—
	Baroncelli (72) (MJWilkinson) **6-10-0** ILawrence (wl bhd 9th: styd on fr 3 out: n.d)	1½	**3**	14/1	—	—
1829^{F}	**Pearl Epee (90)** (DNicholson) **7-11-4** RJohnson (hld up: hit 8th: chsd wnr fr 10th: hit 11th & 12th: no imp)	4	**4**	9/2^{2}	—	—
1539^{8}	**Spearhead Again (IRE) (89)** (KSBridgwater) **7-11-0v^{1}**(3) RMassey (led to 2nd: hit 8th: wknd 10th: t.o whn fell 4 out)		**F**	11/1^{3}	—	—
1798^{10}	**Ronans Glen (77)** (MJWilkinson) **9-10-5** TJO'Sullivan (bhd whn fell 7th)		**F**	12/1	—	—
1847^{9}	**Walls Court (76)** (JJBirkett) **9-10-4** LO'Hara (bit bkwd: bhd fr 4th: mstke 7th: t.o 9th: p.u bef 2 out)		**P**	12/1	—	—
1629^{P}	**Heathyards Boy (72)** (DMcCain) **6-10-0b** DWalsh (prom: hit 8th: wknd qckly 10th: t.o whn ref 3 out)		**R**	33/1	—	—

(SP 117.1%) **8 Rn**

5m 20.2 (15.20) CSF £10.22 CT £68.15 TOTE £1.60: £1.40 £1.60 £3.00 (£15.80) Trio £45.40 OWNER Mr Terry Neill (LAMBOURN)

LONG HANDICAP Plassy Boy (IRE) 9-12 Heathyards Boy 9-10

1920* Art Prince (IRE) jumped pretty well for a novice, especially when considering he was out on his own for most of the second circuit. (8/11)
Plassy Boy (IRE), on his chasing debut, plugged on to win the separate race for second. (12/1)
Baroncelli was another graduating to fences. (14/1)
1563 Pearl Epee, 5lb higher than when second over course and distance in May, got the worst of a finish of tired horses for the place money, after trying in vain to go after the winner. (9/2)
Spearhead Again (IRE) (11/1: 8/1-12/1)
Walls Court (12/1: op 8/1)

2078 HOUGHTON VAUGHAN H'CAP HURDLE (0-145) (4-Y.O+) (Class B)

2-35 (2-35) **2m 4f 110y (8 hdls)** £5,070.10 (£1,535.80: £750.40: £357.70) GOING: 0.64 sec per fur (S)

				SP	RR	SF
1372^{2}	**Arithmetic (115)** (MrsJPitman) **6-10-0** WMarston (led to 3rd: led 5th: rdn appr 2 out: all out)	—	**1**	5/2^{2}	92	18
1645^{3}	**Dally Boy (115)** (TDEasterby) **4-9-9**(5) MrRThornton (a.p: wnt 2nd 6th: rdn & ev ch 2 out: r.o)	¾	**2**	3/1^{3}	91	17
	Express Gift (139) (MrsMReveley) **7-11-10** NSmith (hld up: lost pl 7th: stdy hdwy appr 3 out: nvr plcd to chal)	13	**3**	11/2	105+	31
1645^{4}	**Outset (IRE) (127)** (MDHammond) **6-10-9**(3) MrCBonner (led 3rd to 5th: wknd 6th)	8	**4**	2/1^{1}	87	13
1258^{7}	**Dr Leunt (IRE) (134)** (PJHobbs) **5-11-5** GTormey (prom tl rdn & wknd after 7th)	nk	**5**	7/1	94	20
1645^{7}	**Beachy Head (123)** (JJO'Neill) **8-10-8** ARoche (bit bkwd: lost pl 4th: wl bhd fr 7th)	3½	**6**	25/1	80	6

(SP 118.6%) **6 Rn**

5m 5.6 (21.60) CSF £10.57 CT £34.48 TOTE £2.60: £1.40 £1.80 (£4.60) OWNER Robert & Elizabeth Hitchins (UPPER LAMBOURN) BRED P. M. Prior-Wandesforde

LONG HANDICAP Arithmetic 9-12 Dally Boy 9-12

OFFICIAL EXPLANATION **Beachy Head: the rider reported that he could not make more effort as the gelding was hanging right, and would be better suited by better ground.**

1372 Arithmetic, just out of the handicap proper, got the better of a protracted tussle with the runner-up. (5/2)
1645 Dally Boy, like the winner 2lb wrong at the weights, did not jump the second last quite as well as his rival when seemingly just about to poke his head in front. (3/1)
Express Gift, coming back from injury problems, had a pipe-opener on the Flat last month and his rider did not appear bothered when the tempo quickened towards the end of the back straight. He can do much better than this. (11/2)
1645 Outset (IRE), raised 2lb, was in trouble fully a mile from home. (2/1)
1258 Dr Leunt (IRE) is on the comeback trail after cracking a pedal-bone when disqualified from second place in the 1995 Triumph Hurdle. (7/1)
Beachy Head, remaining over hurdles, was inclined to run in snatches. (25/1)

2079 WELLMAN PLC NOVICES' CHASE (5-Y.O+) (Class D)

3-05 (3-06) **2m (12 fncs)** £3,877.50 (£1,090.00: £532.50) GOING: 0.38 sec per fur (GS)

				SP	RR	SF
1644[3]	**Garolo (FR)** (CPEBrooks) **6-11-0** DGallagher (lw: led: j.rt 5th: hdd 6th: led on bit 2 out: sn clr)	—	**1**	4/7[1]	117?	19
1764[P]	**Robins Pride (IRE)** (CLPopham) **6-10-11**(3) TDascombe (chsd ldr: led 6th to 2 out: btn whn hit last)	12	**2**	8/1[3]	105?	7
1340[P]	**Rolfe (NZ)** (DNicholson) **6-11-0b** RJohnson (nt j.w: lft 3rd 4th: rdn 5th: bhd whn j.rt 7th: t.o)	dist	**3**	2/1[2]	—	—
	Glenmavis (DrPPritchard) **9-11-0** DrPPritchard (3rd whn mstke & uns rdr 4th)		**U**	40/1	—	—
				(SP 110.5%)	**4 Rn**	

4m 5.5 (15.50) CSF £4.94 TOTE £1.50: £1.40 (£2.40) OWNER Lady Lloyd Webber (LAMBOURN) BRED Alec Weisweiller

1644 Garolo (FR) proved too smart for these rivals. (4/7)

Robins Pride (IRE), pulled up on his chasing debut, was rated over a stone below the winner over hurdles. (8/1: tchd 16/1)

2080 WEATHERBYS 'STARS OF TOMORROW' STANDARD OPEN N.H. FLAT RACE (4, 5 & 6-Y.O) (Class H)

3-35 (3-35) **2m** £1,474.00 (£414.00: £202.00)

				SP	RR	SF
	Cherrymore (IRE) (MrsJPitman) **5-11-1**(3) GHogan (a.p: led over 3f out: shkn up & clr 2f out: eased wl ins fnl f)	—	**1**	Evens[1]	66 f	—
	Benefit-In-Kind (IRE) (MissHCKnight) **4-10-11**(7) MrAWintle (bkwd: a.p: r.o one pce fnl 2f)	6	**2**	8/1	60 f	—
1289[3]	**Pot Black Uk** (PJHobbs) **5-11-4** GTormey (plld hrd: led over 12f: one pce)	nk	**3**	4/1[2]	60 f	—
	Mr Montague (IRE) (TWDonnelly) **4-11-4** TEley (bkwd: hld up & bhd: hdwy 5f out: rdn 2f out: one pce)	3	**4**	33/1	57 f	—
	Blowing Rock (IRE) (RDickin) **4-11-4** DGallagher (bit bkwd: prom tl wknd over 2f out)	8	**5**	33/1	49 f	—
	Ledburian (MissPMWhittle) **6-10-11**(7) KHibbert (bkwd: rdn 8f out: no hdwy fnl 4f)	5	**6**	66/1	44 f	—
1800[6]	**Justlikejim** (JLHarris) **5-10-13**(5) MrRThornton (lw: hdwy 6f out: wknd over 3f out)	nk	**7**	33/1	43 f	—
	Justjim (NATwiston-Davies) **4-11-4** DWalsh (prom tl rdn & wknd 4f out)	8	**8**	15/2[3]	35 f	—
	Tom Tugg (IRE) (WGMcKenzie-Coles) **6-11-4** RJohnson (bkwd: bhd fnl 5f)	8	**9**	20/1	27 f	—
	Go For The Doctor (BAMcMahon) **6-11-1**(3) TDascombe (plld hrd: prom tl wknd 3f out)	1¼	**10**	50/1	26 f	—
	The Bug (JPLeigh) **6-11-4** BPowell (plld hrd: a bhd)	10	**11**	50/1	16 f	—
	Park End (CLPopham) **4-10-11**(7) TO'Connor (bit bkwd: a bhd)	2	**12**	40/1	14 f	—
	May Rose (PJHobbs) **6-10-6**(7) MrSDurack (plld hrd: prom 10f: t.o)	17	**13**	33/1	—	—
	Gem's Precious (TWall) **5-11-1**(3) RMassey (bit bkwd: prom 10f: t.o)	23	**14**	33/1	—	—
	The Muckle Quine (JJO'Neill) **5-10-13** ARoche (a bhd: t.o)	dist	**15**	25/1	—	—
				(SP 124.0%)	**15 Rn**	

4m 1.0 CSF £9.99 TOTE £1.80: £1.20 £2.50 £1.50 (£8.10) Trio £8.30 OWNER Robert & Elizabeth Hitchins (UPPER LAMBOURN) BRED Jeremiah Dunne

Cherrymore (IRE), from a stable finding some form, is a half-brother to winning chaser Cherry Ripe. (Evens)

Benefit-In-Kind (IRE), bought for 23,000 guineas, secured the runner-up spot at the death and will come on for the outing. (8/1: op 5/1)

1289 Pot Black Uk took a strong hold early on and could not go with the winner in the home straight. (4/1: 5/2-9/2)

Mr Montague (IRE), a half-brother to a winning sprinter, is out of a mare who won over six. Not surprisingly ridden to get the trip, he will strip fitter next time. (33/1)

Blowing Rock (IRE) ran well until the winner went for home. (33/1)

Justjim (15/2: 5/1-8/1)

T/Plpt: £8.40 (1,063.34 Tckts). T/Qdpt: £7.90 (76.22 Tckts). KH

1666-KELSO (L-H) - Monday December 23rd

2081 Abandoned-Frost

1814-LUDLOW (R-H) (Good to firm, Firm patches)
Monday December 23rd

WEATHER: overcast

2088 TANNERS CAVA CONDITIONAL (S) H'CAP HURDLE (0-95) (3-Y.O+) (Class G)

1-00 (1-02) **2m 5f 110y (11 hdls)** £2,146.00 (£596.00: £286.00) GOING minus 0.61 sec per fur (F)

				SP	RR	SF
1874[2]	**Sleeptite (FR) (81)** (WGMTurner) **6-11-0**(5) JPower (led tl appr 3rd: led 4th tl appr 6th: led appr 3 out: clr last)	—	**1**	3/1[1]	65+	25
737[3]	**Lovelark (62)** (RLee) **7-9-9**(5) MGriffiths (bit bkwd: a chsng ldrs: outpcd appr 3 out: rallied u.p towards fin)	4	**2**	33/1	43	3
1962[10]	**Bright Sapphire (75)** (DBurchell) **10-10-8**(5) JPrior (a.p: led appr 6th tl appr 3 out: kpt on one pce)	1½	**3**	9/1	55	15
1786[P]	**Le Baron (73)** (CREgerton) **5-10-11** SophieMitchell (a chsng ldrs: rdn 3 out: nt pce to chal)	10	**4**	15/2[3]	46	6
1962[8]	**Its Grand (74)** (JMBradley) **7-10-12** TDascombe (chsd ldrs: rdn appr 2 out: one pce)	1¼	**5**	12/1	46	6
1874[F]	**Perfect Bertie (IRE) (63)** (NMBabbage) **4-9-10**(5)ow1 MKeighley (hdwy 8th: nt rch ldrs)	10	**6**	10/1	27	—
1770[7]	**Quick Decision (IRE) (62)** (JKCresswell) **5-9-9**(5) NTEgan (bit bkwd: chsd ldrs tl outpcd after 8th)	1¾	**7**	25/1	25	—
1786[6]	**Catwalker (IRE) (62)** (HJMWebb) **5-9-9b**(5) CRae (hld up: effrt 6th: wknd appr 3 out)	7	**8**	25/1	20	—
1466[7]	**Gunmaker (78)** (BJLlewellyn) **7-10-13**(3) DJKavanagh (dropped rr ½-wy: t.o)	6	**9**	14/1	31	—
1251[8]	**Beths Wish (62)** (GMPrice) **7-10-0** GuyLewis (a bhd: t.o)	nk	**10**	33/1	15	—
1814[4]	**Tug Your Forelock (67)** (GFJohnsonHoughton) **5-10-5** MichaelBrennan (hld up in tch: rdn & wknd 3 out: t.o)	3	**11**	9/2[2]	18	—
1786[4]	**Daring Hen (IRE) (69)** (RTJuckes) **6-10-7b** GTormey (a bhd: t.o)	3	**12**	16/1	17	—
1466[9]	**King of Babylon (IRE) (70)** (FJordan) **4-10-8** LAspell (rel to r: a wl bhd: t.o)	1¾	**13**	16/1	17	—
899[7]	**Celcius (67)** (MCPipe) **12-10-0b**(5) BMoore (hld up in tch: wknd after 8th: t.o)	¾	**14**	20/1	14	—
1638[11]	**Bite the Bullet (62)** (AJChamberlain) **5-10-0** RMassey (prom: led appr 3rd to 4th: wknd appr 8th: t.o)	14	**15**	20/1	—	—
1816[9]	**Hacketts Cross (IRE) (90)** (PEccles) **8-12-0** GHogan (bhd fr ½-wy: t.o whn p.u bef 3 out)		**P**	10/1	—	—
				(SP 132.4%)	**16 Rn**	

4m 59.8 (-1.20) CSF £92.83 CT £779.85 TOTE £3.80: £1.10 £6.90 £2.40 £2.30 (£65.30) Trio £362.10; £413.17 to Ayr 26/12/96 OWNER Mr David Chown (SHERBORNE) BRED Ronald Reeves in France

LONG HANDICAP Beths Wish 9-9 Perfect Bertie (IRE) 9-10 Catwalker (IRE) 9-12 Lovelark 9-8 Bite the Bullet 9-8 Quick Decision (IRE) 9-11

Sold C Brasher 3,600 gns

1874 Sleeptite (FR) made sure this was a true test of stamina and, forging clear in the straight, won very easily indeed. (3/1)

Lovelark, an improving sort, looked about to drop right away when the leading pair quickened away on the approach to the straight, but she stayed on strongly after getting her second wind, and an even longer trip looks within her grasp. (33/1)
1466 Bright Sapphire, fighting for the lead from the start, had to admit younger rivals had the legs of him when the battle to the finish really developed. (9/1)
1251 Le Baron tried hard to get himself into the action turning in but, with the pace being maintained, was soon struggling and in trouble. (15/2)
1285 Its Grand found this ground much too lively and could do little to prevent the principals drawing away. (12/1)
1466 Hacketts Cross (IRE) (10/1: op 5/1)

2089 TANNERS CHAMPAGNE H'CAP CHASE (0-120) (5-Y.O+) (Class D)

1-30 (1-30) **3m (19 fncs)** £3,517.50 (£1,065.00: £520.00: £247.50) GOING minus 0.61 sec per fur (F)

	Horse	Details	Btn	Pos	SP	RR	SF
1731*	**Act of Parliament (IRE) (107)**	(KCBailey) **8-11-2b** CO'Dwyer (lw: j.w: led tl appr 3rd: chsd ldr: chal 2 out: sn led: rdn out)	—	**1**	9/4 2	121	54
1819*	**God Speed You (IRE) (97)**	(CPMorlock) **7-10-6b** AMaguire (j.w: led appr 3rd: pckd 3 out: hdd after next: rallied u.p flat)	½	**2**	8/13 1	111	44
256 9	**Harristown Lady (108)**	(GBBalding) **9-11-3b** APMcCoy (bit bkwd: lost pl 5th: tk poor 3rd 12th: no imp)	30	**3**	10/1 3	102	35
1445 P	**Foxgrove (91)**	(RJPrice) **10-9-9**(5) MrRThornton (prom to 10th: sn outpcd: n.d after)	½	**4**	66/1	84	17
	Pant Llin (91)	(FJordan) **10-10-0** SWynne (bkwd: a bhd: t.o fr 12th)	14	**5**	25/1	75	8
1817 2	**Fairy Park (91)**	(HOliver) **11-9-7v**(7) MrHJOliver (lost tch whn mstke 7th: chsd ldng pair 10th to 12th: sn wknd: t.o)	4	**6**	16/1	72	5

(SP 113.0%) **6 Rn**

5m 48.8 (1.30 under best) (-11.20) **CSF £3.94 CT £6.87 TOTE £3.30: £2.90 £1.00 (£2.00)** OWNER **Mr J. Perriss (UPPER LAMBOURN)** BRED Mrs Susan Bury
LONG HANDICAP Foxgrove 8-6 Pant Llin 9-3 Fairy Park 9-9
1731* Act of Parliament (IRE) had a head-to-head with the favourite all the way and, in a spirited battle to the finish, always just had the edge. (9/4)
1819* God Speed You (IRE) had more on his plate this time but, had he not landed on his head at the third last, may well have prevailed. (8/13)
Harristown Lady acts well on fast ground, but she needed this first run in six months, and was unable to get within striking range of the principals. (10/1)

2090 HOECHST ROUSSEL PANACUR E.B.F. 'N.H.' (QUALIFIER) NOVICES' HURDLE (4-Y.O+ F & M) (Class E)

2-00 (2-01) **2m 5f 110y (11 hdls)** £2,724.00 (£764.00: £372.00) GOING minus 0.61 sec per fur (F)

	Horse	Details	Btn	Pos	SP	RR	SF
1317 6	**Maid For Adventure (IRE)**	(MissHCKnight) **5-10-12** BFenton (hld up: hdwy to ld 3 out: sn clr: comf)	—	**1**	9/4 2	73+	6
1915 6	**Galatasori Jane (IRE) (98)**	(PFNicholls) **6-11-5** APMcCoy (led to 2nd: led 7th tl after next: rdn & outpcd appr 3 out: rallied flat)	10	**2**	11/4 3	73	6
1958 5	**Di's Last**	(MCPipe) **6-10-5**(7) GSupple (hld up: hdwy 6th: led after 8th: hdd & blnd 3 out: sn btn)	¾	**3**	14/1	65	—
1998 P	**Dolce Notte (IRE)**	(MCPipe) **6-10-5**(7) BMoore (lft in ld 5th: sn hdd: wknd 3 out)	11	**4**	25/1	57	—
	Gi Moss	(PRHarriss) **9-10-12b**1 WMarston (bkwd: plld hrd: led 2nd tl appr 3rd: led appr 6th to 7th: wknd next: t.o)	27	**5**	100/1	37	—
1873 2	**Lucia Forte (102)**	(KCBailey) **5-11-5** CO'Dwyer (led appr 3rd tl fell 5th)		**F**	11/10 1	—	—
	Lucy's Choice	(MrsRGHenderson) **5-10-7**(5) DSalter (bkwd: a bhd: t.o fr 7th: p.u bef 3 out)		**P**	100/1	—	—
1685 P	**Alright Guvnor**	(NASmith) **6-10-12** JRyan (a bhd: t.o fr ½-wy: p.u bef 3 out)		**P**	100/1	—	—

(SP 118.5%) **8 Rn**

5m 3.6 (2.60) CSF £8.94 TOTE £3.00: £1.10 £1.10 £2.10 (£5.20) Trio £7.50 OWNER Mr Chris Brasher (WANTAGE) BRED Mrs Marie Crean
1317 Maid For Adventure (IRE) seems to have appreciated this extended trip and, left with a clear advantage after leading three out, was able to take things easy nearing the finish. (9/4)
1915 Galatasori Jane (IRE) could do little to prevent the leaders going away from her on the run to the straight, but she stayed on again in the closing stages. She does need all of three miles on such a fast track. (11/4: 2/1-3/1)
1958 Di's Last had just been headed when she all but got rid of her pilot three out, and had little hope of recovering. (14/1: op 7/1)
1873 Lucia Forte pulled her way into the lead on the long run to the third and was bowling along a few lengths clear when she departed the scene at the fifth. Although she had more than a circuit to cover, it is doubtful if any of these rivals would have been able to reel her in. (11/10: evens-5/4)

2091 TANNERS WINES NOVICES' CHASE (5-Y.O+) (Class C)

2-30 (2-30) **2m (13 fncs)** £4,688.00 (£1,318.00: £644.00) GOING minus 0.61 sec per fur (F)

	Horse	Details	Btn	Pos	SP	RR	SF
1787 F	**Super Coin (120)**	(RLee) **8-10-12** RJohnson (led 3rd to 4th: led 4 out: rdn whn lft clr last: eased)	—	**1**	4/11 1	85+	—
1828 4	**Eulogy (FR)**	(KRBurke) **9-10-12** APMcCoy (led 4th: rn wd after next: hdd 4 out: sn btn)	15	**2**	10/1 3	70	—
1828 P	**Arabian Bold (IRE)**	(RTJuckes) **8-10-12** WMarston (led to 3rd: outpcd appr 4 out: styd on flat)	½	**3**	25/1	70?	—
1864 4	**Holy Wanderer (USA) (96)**	(TRGeorge) **7-10-9**(3) GHogan (lw: hld up in rr: stdy hdwy 9th: ev ch whn blnd & uns rdr last)		**U**	3/1 2	—	—

(SP 111.3%) **4 Rn**

3m 58.3 (6.30) CSF £4.26 TOTE £1.30 (£3.00) OWNER Mr George Brookes (PRESTEIGNE) BRED J. R. Heatley
1787 Super Coin has suffered his share of bad luck in the past, but fortune certainly favoured him here, and it was not coming out of turn. (4/11)
1828 Eulogy (FR) should not be long in getting off the mark over fences if this promising debut is anything to go by. (10/1)
Arabian Bold (IRE), a useful individual over hurdles in the past, has been out of sorts since the spring of 1995, but he did not fare badly on this debut over fences and should be able to pay his way. (25/1)
1864 Holy Wanderer (USA) had worked his way into the action and looked to be travelling much the better when an untidy mistake at the last gave his jockey little chance of retaining his seat. (3/1)

2092 TANNERS BURGUNDY H'CAP CHASE (0-115) (5-Y.O+) (Class E)

3-00 (3-00) **2m 4f (17 fncs)** £3,100.00 (£940.00: £460.00: £220.00) GOING minus 0.61 sec per fur (F)

	Horse	Details	Btn	Pos	SP	RR	SF
1542 4	**Too Sharp (100)**	(MissHCKnight) **8-10-13** JFTitley (lw: j.w: chsd ldr: led appr 2 out: drvn out)	—	**1**	15/8 1	110	22
1302 4	**Corrarder (100)**	(JGSmyth-Osbourne) **12-10-13** JRailton (j.w: hld up in rr: hdwy 13th: rdn to chal last: unable qckn)	1¾	**2**	20/1	109	21
1509 F	**Spinning Steel (99)**	(PRRodford) **9-10-12** SBurrough (lw: j.w: led: clr 4th: hdd & wknd appr 2 out)	20	**3**	10/1	92	4
1465 3	**Channel Pastime (88)**	(DBurchell) **12-9-12**(3) GuyLewis (chsd ldrs: pushed along 10th: outpcd appr 3 out)	2½	**4**	9/2 3	79	—

				SP	RR	SF
1704[5]	**Comedy Road (93)** (RLee) **12-10-6** RJohnson (trckd ldrs: mstke 10th: rdn whn hit 3 out: sn btn)......9	5		8/1	76	—
1717[F]	**Celtino (97)** (CaptTAForster) **8-10-10** SWynne (lw: nt j.w: a bhd: t.o 13th: p.u bef 3 out)......	P		2/1 [2]	—	—

(SP 111.3%) **6 Rn**

4m 50.8 (-1.20) CSF £26.75 CT £262.27 TOTE £2.70: £1.20 £8.00 (£14.10) OWNER Sir Anthony Scott (WANTAGE) BRED Lady Scott

OFFICIAL EXPLANATION Celtino: was outpaced early on and lost interest when he became detached.

1542 Too Sharp turned in an impressive display of jumping and found more when challenged to win readily in a good time. (15/8)

Corrarder, produced from off the pace, delivered a determined challenge at the last, but the winner had kept a bit more up her sleeve and she had the legs when it mattered. This was more like his old self. (20/1)

1298 Spinning Steel, a very free-running, bold jumper, showed here that anything other than the minimum trip is beyond him, and he was down to a walk when negotiating the penultimate fence. (10/1)

1465 Channel Pastime, much better when faced with a stiffer test of stamina, did not shape badly, but he was struggling to hold on from early in the straight. (9/2: op 7/1)

1717 Celtino is lacking in confidence with his jumping after hitting the deck in his previous race and, always being taken along too fast, had made more than the odd mistake before being wisely pulled up. (2/1)

2093 TANNERS CLARET 'N.H.' NOVICES' HURDLE (4-Y.O+) (Class E)

3-30 (3-31) **2m (9 hdls)** £2,528.00 (£708.00: £344.00) GOING minus 0.61 sec per fur (F)

			SP	RR	SF
1633[4]	**Ultimate Smoothie** (MCPipe) **4-10-12** APMcCoy (hld up in tch: chal 2 out: sn led: rdn out)......—	1	5/4 [1]	67	—
	Joshua's Vision (IRE) (90) (RLee) **5-10-12** RJohnson (bkwd: hld up in tch: effrt appr 2 out: str run flat: r.o) .1½	2	6/1 [2]	66	—
1633[P]	**Manvulane (IRE) (92)** (MrsCJBlack) **6-10-12v** JRailton (led & sn clr: hdd after 2 out: kpt on u.p) 2	3	16/1 [3]	64	—
931*	**Sounds Like Fun (96)** (MissHCKnight) **5-11-5** JFTitley (chsd ldr: rdn appr 2 out: sn outpcd) 3½	4	5/4 [1]	67	—
	South West Express (IRE) (DJWintle) **4-10-12** WMarston (bit bkwd: chsd ldrs: pushed along appr 3 out: sn lost tch)......10	5	33/1	50	—
1683[14]	**Derrys Prerogative** (AWCarroll) **6-10-12** DBridgwater (a bhd: t.o fr 5th)......22	6	100/1	28	—
1033[9]	**Baba Sam (IRE)** (PEccles) **5-10-12** BFenton (a bhd: t.o fr 6th)......1	7	50/1	27	—
1683[7]	**Loughdoo (IRE)** (RLee) **8-10-12** MRichards (bit bkwd: a bhd: t.o fr 6th) 17	8	33/1	10	—
1685[17]	**Private Memories** (AWCarroll) **6-10-12** TJMurphy (a bhd: lost tch 6th: t.o) 13	9	100/1	—	—

(SP 118.9%) **9 Rn**

3m 41.9 (4.90) CSF £9.40 TOTE £2.70: £1.10 £1.20 £2.50 (£7.10) Trio £13.50 OWNER Isca Bloodstock (WELLINGTON) BRED Fares Stables Ltd

1633 Ultimate Smoothie had far more use made of him than he did on his hurdling debut and, always traveling smoothly, could be called the winner from some way out. (5/4)

Joshua's Vision (IRE), having her first run in over seven months, ran extremely well considering he looked short of peak fitness, and there is no reason why he should not be better suited to a longer trip. (6/1)

Manvulane (IRE) does perform best when allowed to stretch the opposition, but he still had surplus flesh to get rid of and, in the circumstances, ran one of his best races yet. An early success would come as just reward. (16/1)

931* Sounds Like Fun could not hold his pitch when the tempo quickened soon after turning in, and another half-mile would not go amiss on such a tight track. (5/4: 10/11-11/8)

South West Express (IRE) was unable to match the leaders for pace from the turn into the straight, and he will benefit from further, but will be a good deal sharper next time he appears. He hurdled well though on this debut. (33/1)

T/Jkpt: £1,162.00 (6.11 Tckts). T/Plpt: £38.90 (677.08 Tckts). T/Qdpt: £15.70 (126.64 Tckts). IM

1356-AYR (L-H) - Thursday December 26th

2094 Abandoned-Frost

2034-HEREFORD (R-H) - Thursday December 26th

2100 Abandoned-Frost

1828-HUNTINGDON (R-H) - Thursday December 26th

2106 Abandoned-Frost

1451-KEMPTON (R-H) (Good to firm)

Thursday December 26th

WEATHER: cold

2112 GOOD JOB NOVICES' HURDLE (4-Y.O+) (Class B)

12-40 (12-41) **2m (8 hdls)** £7,262.50 (£2,200.00: £1,075.00: £512.50) GOING minus 0.06 sec per fur (G)

			SP	RR	SF
	Sanmartino (IRE) (DNicholson) **4-11-5** AMaguire (lw: a.p: mstke 3rd: led 2 out to last: rdn: led nr fin) ......—	1	100/30 [2]	101+	51
1594[2]	**Secret Spring (FR) (109)** (PRHedger) **4-11-5** MRichards (stdy hdwy 3 out: led last: qcknd: hdd nr fin)......1	2	6/1	100	50
1729*	**Proton** (RAkehurst) **6-11-5** RDunwoody (lw: chsd ldr: led 3 out to 2 out: wknd appr last)......9	3	4/1 [3]	91	41
1368*	**Kailash (USA) (120)** (MCPipe) **5-11-10** APMcCoy (lw: hld up: ev ch 2 out: wknd appr last)......2	4	2/1 [1]	94	44
	Leading Spirit (IRE) (CFWall) **4-11-5** GBradley (hdwy 5th: ev ch 3 out: wknd appr 2 out)......11	5	11/1	78	28
1679[2]	**Moor Hall Lady** (NMBabbage) **5-11-0** CMaude (a bhd) 15	6	50/1	58	8
1726[11]	**Mansur (IRE)** (NJHenderson) **4-11-5** MAFitzgerald (led: mstkes 3rd & 4th: hdd 3 out: sn wknd: t.o)......dist	7	33/1	—	—
1729[2]	**Desert Green (FR)** (RHannon) **7-11-5** NWilliamson (lw: bhd tl p.u bef 3 out: lame)......	P	12/1	—	—

(SP 111.6%) **8 Rn**

3m 44.4 (2.40) CSF £21.18 TOTE £4.50: £1.70 £1.80 £1.10 (£18.00) Trio £16.50 OWNER Mr K. Abdulla (TEMPLE GUITING) BRED Juddmonte Farms

IN-FOCUS: Frost and lack of rain had made the ground decidedly fast, leading to 16 non-runners during the afternoon. There were also a number of horses which failed to jump with any fluency and the ground may well have played a part in this.

Sanmartino (IRE), winner of the 1995 Tote Ebor and a head second to Celeric in the Jockey Club Cup at Newmarket in October when trained by Barry Hills, at last made his eagerly-awaited hurdling debut after three abandonments. He poked a whisker in front two out and appeared to be travelling well, but was collared at the final flight. He looked in serious trouble when left two lengths behind, but rallied to get back up. He has the potential to be a very classy novice, and will probably be seen to better effect over further or on a stiffer course. (100/30: 9/4-4/1)
1594 Secret Spring (FR) is well regarded at home and, travelling really well throughout the race, looked likely to succeed as he led at the last and quickened away. The winner rallied really well though, and he was worried out of it near the line. He only just gets two miles and needs a flat track and ground no worse than good. He might head for Aintree, and can win again. (6/1)
1729* Proton ran well against two potentially classy rivals. Sent on three from home, he was collared at the second last, and then left for dead. (4/1)
1368* Kailash (USA) was facing much stiffer opposition here, and lost his unbeaten record which he had managed to extend to seven. Still with every chance at the second last, he tired going to the last. (2/1)
Leading Spirit (IRE), winner of a couple of mile and a half handicaps here on the Flat this year, was coming back after nearly four months off, and did not help matters before the start by unseating Bradley and getting loose. He still had every chance three out, before lack of race fitness and his earlier antics took their toll. He will come on for this. (11/1: 8/1-12/1)
1729 Desert Green (FR) had not been asked any sort of question at the back when pulled up before the third last with a slightly injured hock. (12/1)

2113 PERTEMPS RECRUITMENT PARTNERSHIP FELTHAM NOVICES' CHASE (Gd 1) (5-Y.O+) (Class A)

1-10 (1-10) **3m (19 fncs)** £25,067.50 (£8,705.00: £4,277.50) GOING minus 0.06 sec per fur (G)

	Horse	Details	Dist	Pos	SP	RR	SF
	Djeddah (FR)	(FDoumen,France) **5-11-7** AKondrat (lw: chsd ldr 3rd to 9th: chsd ldr 11th tl pckd 13th: chsd ldr fr 15th: led 4 out: rdn out)	—	1	9/2	130	75
1653[2]	**Solomon's Dancer (USA)**	(GRichards) **6-11-7** RDunwoody (lw: chsd ldr 9th to 11th: chsd ldr fr 13th: led 15th to 4 out: ev ch fr 3 out: pckd last: unable qckn flat)	1	2	9/2	128	74
1789*	**Aardwolf**	(CPEBrooks) **5-11-7** GBradley (lw: led after 2nd: mstke 5th: mstke & hdd 15th: 3rd whn mstke 3 out: r.o flat)	¾	3	9/4[1]	129	74
1936[F]	**Buckhouse Boy (122)**	(NATwiston-Davies) **6-11-7** CMaude (led tl after 2nd: 4th whn fell 8th)		F	100/30[2]	—	—
1635*	**Hatcham Boy (IRE)**	(DNicholson) **6-11-7** AMaguire (5th whn mstke & uns rdr 6th)		U	4/1[3]	—	—
					(SP 110.2%)	**5 Rn**	

5m 51.5 (-3.50) CSF £21.32 TOTE £5.90: £2.30 £1.30 (£10.20) OWNER Mrs Stella Elkaim (LAMORLAYE) BRED In France
WEIGHT FOR AGE 5yo-1lb
Djeddah (FR), whose trainer has a good record at this course, has won three times this year, all on soft, but his trainer says he does not have much choice in France and the gelding is better on this faster ground. Sent on four out, he had a real scrap with the runner-up in the straight, but held on. He may well go to the Cheltenham Festival. (9/2)
1653 Solomon's Dancer (USA) was taking a step up in class and distance, but ran a fine race. Engaged in a tremendous tussle with the winner in the straight, he gave his all, but was tapped for toe on the run-in. He should soon regain the winning thread. (9/2)
1789* Aardwolf failed to jump with the same fluency he had to win twice over Sandown's fences and this may have been due to the very fast ground here. Setting the pace to the fifth last, he was in trouble when making a blunder three out. To his credit, he was sticking on again at the end. On a slightly easier surface, he can regain the winning thread. (9/4)

2114 NETWORK PERSONNEL H'CAP HURDLE (4-Y.O+) (Class B)

1-40 (1-40) **2m (8 hdls)** £6,827.00 (£2,066.00: £1,008.00: £479.00) GOING minus 0.06 sec per fur (G)

	Horse	Details	Dist	Pos	SP	RR	SF
1832[2]	**Albemine (USA) (122)**	(MrsJCecil) **7-10-10** TKent (lw: mde all: rdn appr 2 out: r.o wl)	—	1	6/4[1]	101	18
1903*	**Chai-Yo (124)**	(JABOld) **6-10-12** GUpton (hld up: chsd wnr fr 2 out: rdn appr last: unable qckn)	1¼	2	7/4[2]	102	19
1873*	**Yet Again (112)**	(MissGayKelleway) **4-10-0** DBridgwater (hld up: rdn appr last: one pce)	3	3	11/4[3]	87	4
1732[12]	**Pyrrhic Dance (113)**	(MJHaynes) **6-10-1**ow1 DSkyrme (chsd wnr to 3 out: wknd appr 2 out: t.o)	dist	4	20/1	—	—
					(SP 107.8%)	**4 Rn**	

3m 49.6 (7.60) CSF £4.23 TOTE £2.60: £2.80 (£2.30) OWNER Mrs J. Cecil (NEWMARKET) BRED Peter E. Burrell Trust
LONG HANDICAP Yet Again 9-10 Pyrrhic Dance 7-5
1832 Albemine (USA), who had been aimed at this race for some time, did not let his supporters down under a fine ride. Making all, he was bustled along approaching the second last to gain a valuable length or so on his rivals, and found far more off the bridle than his opponents. He loves this ground. (6/4)
1903* Chai-Yo has been in tremendous form this season, winning on the bridle, but does not find much off it if this run is anything to go by. Despite a 20lb rise since his first win of the season, it seemed to be a matter of time before he cruised past the winner, but his effort when let down was disappointing. (7/4: op evens)
1873* Yet Again, 4lb out of the weights and taking on handicappers for the first time, had the ground in his favour. He appeared to be travelling just as well as the runner-up but, when asked for his effort at the penultimate obstacle, failed to find what was required. (11/4)

2115 PERTEMPS KING GEORGE VI CHASE (Gd 1) (5-Y.O+) (Class A)

2-15 (2-15) **3m (19 fncs)** £63,325.00 (£23,966.25: £11,733.13: £5,350.63) GOING minus 0.06 sec per fur (G)

	Horse	Details	Dist	Pos	SP	RR	SF
1157*	**One Man (IRE) (177)**	(GRichards) **8-11-10** RDunwoody (stdy hdwy 14th: led 3 out: clr appr last: rdn out)	—	1	8/13[1]	173	97
1964*	**Rough Quest (168)**	(TCasey) **10-11-10** MAFitzgerald (no hdwy fr 4 out: lft mod 2nd last)	12	2	4/1[2]	165	89
1366[5]	**Barton Bank (157)**	(DNicholson) **10-11-10** AMaguire (lw: chsd ldr tl blnd 15th: sn wknd)	9	3	10/1	159	83
1520*	**Strong Promise (IRE) (144)**	(GAHubbard) **5-11-10** KGaule (lw: bhd fr 15th: t.o)	dist	4	6/1[3]	—	—
1785[4]	**Mr Mulligan (IRE) (153)**	(NoelChance) **8-11-10** APMcCoy (lw: led: pckd 15th: hdd 3 out: 2nd & btn whn fell last)		F	13/2	—	—
					(SP 118.6%)	**5 Rn**	

5m 45.3 (0.50 under best) (-9.70) CSF £3.94 TOTE £1.90: £1.10 £2.00 (£2.80) OWNER Mr J. Hales (PENRITH) BRED Hugh J. Holohan
WEIGHT FOR AGE 5yo-1lb
IN-FOCUS: Richard Dunwoody gained a record-breaking fourth King George, all coming on greys, and also broke the course record time by half a second set by Cuddy Dale five years ago.

1157* One Man (IRE) did not let his army of supporters down. Steadily creeping into the action in the last mile, he led at the third last and was already well in command when Mr Mulligan fell at the last. Whether he idled or was getting tired on the run-in is arguable, and Dunwoody really had to keep him going. There is still a doubt about his ability to handle Cheltenham, but he goes there for the Pillar Chase next month. He may well turn out to be a King George specialist and there is no reason why he should not come back next year and complete the hat-trick. (8/13)
1964* Rough Quest certainly found the ground too fast and his pilot reported he was off the bridle from halfway. Having moved into third after the fourth last, he was making little impression, but was left a moderate second at the last. A return match with the winner in the Pillar Chase next month is on the cards. (4/1)
1366 Barton Bank, winner of this race in 1993 and nearly in 1994, is still prone to making errors and was in second when a mistake five out spelt the end for him. While still useful, he is not the force of old and has won only once in the last three years. (10/1: 7/1-11/1)
1520* Strong Promise (IRE) has been in the form of his life this season and had the ground in his favour. He ran no race at all here though and it looked as though something was amiss. (6/1)
1785 Mr Mulligan (IRE) has had an interrupted programme of late, but left his Chepstow reappearance well behind. He really seemed to be enjoying himself out in front, and had the field nicely strung out, jumping far better than he had previously. Headed three out, he found the winner too good and was booked for second, about six lengths behind, when falling at the last. He is back on song and a decent prize awaits him. (13/2: 12/1-6/1)

2116 NETWORK DESIGN INTERNATIONAL WAYWARD LAD NOVICES' CHASE (5-Y.O+) (Class B)

2-45 (2-50) **2m 4f 110y (17 fncs)** £10,308.75 (£3,120.00: £1,522.50: £723.75) GOING minus 0.06 sec per fur (G)

	Horse / details	Dist	Pos	SP	RR	SF
1809*	**Greenback (BEL)** (PJHobbs) **5-11-7** NWilliamson (hdwy 13th: led 2 out: hrd rdn appr last: r.o wl)	—	1	11/2^{3}	121+	54
1780*	**Mister Drum (IRE)** (MJWilkinson) **7-11-7** RDunwoody (led: mstke 11th: hdd 2 out: unable qckn)	1¾	2	13/8^{2}	120+	53
1868*	**Potter's Bay (IRE) (119)** (DNicholson) **7-11-7** AMaguire (lw: mstke 4th: stdy hdwy 12th: chsd ldr 13th tl mstke 4 out: 4th & btn whn mstke 3 out)	10	3	11/8^{1}	112	45
1714*	**Sublime Fellow (IRE) (122)** (NJHenderson) **6-11-7** MAFitzgerald (lw: mstke 8th: chsd ldr to 13th: wknd 3 out)	5	4	6/1	108	41
				(SP 109.9%)		**4 Rn**

5m 4.0 (3.00) CSF £13.82 TOTE £6.10 (£4.70) OWNER Mr Jack Joseph (MINEHEAD) BRED Patrick Madelein
1809* Greenback (BEL) once again showed a tendency to jump to his left. He led at the second last though and, given a few reminders, proved too strong for the runner-up. Williamson thinks he will get further. (11/2)
1780* Mister Drum (IRE) did a fine job of pacemaking but, collared at the second last, found the winner too strong. He is suited to a right-handed track and should soon return to the winner's enclosure. (13/8)
1868* Potter's Bay (IRE) made a number of jumping errors and this may have been due to the ground. He is better than this and is well worth another chance to redeem himself. (11/8)
1714* Sublime Fellow (IRE) finds little off the bridle and was quickly left for dead when things got serious. (6/1)

2117 PERTEMPS CRACK CLUB H'CAP HURDLE (4-Y.O+) (Class B)

3-15 (3-17) **3m 110y (12 hdls)** £6,911.50 (£2,092.00: £1,021.00: £485.50) GOING minus 0.06 sec per fur (G)

	Horse / details	Dist	Pos	SP	RR	SF
1794^{2}	**Tim (IRE) (112)** (JRJenkins) **6-10-8** MAFitzgerald (a gng wl: hld up: led last: shkn up: r.o wl)	—	1	7/2	90	27
1067^{4}	**Peatswood (119)** (MRChannon) **8-11-1** GBradley (chsd ldr: led 9th to last: unable qckn)	4	2	2/1^{1}	94	31
	Ealing Court (107) (NMBabbage) **7-10-3**^{ow3} GUpton (hld up: rdn 3 out: sn wknd)	10	3	16/1	76?	10
1661^{3}	**Mytton's Choice (IRE) (128)** (DNicholson) **5-11-10** AMaguire (lw: hld up: rdn appr 2 out: sn wknd)	nk	4	11/4^{2}	97	34
1906^{5}	**Uluru (IRE) (115)** (CPMorlock) **8-10-11** RDunwoody (led to 9th: wknd 3 out: t.o)	dist	5	100/30^{3}	—	—
				(SP 111.2%)		**5 Rn**

5m 54.2 (8.20) CSF £10.42 TOTE £3.70: £1.80 £1.70 (£4.80) Trio £24.80 OWNER The Crack Club (ROYSTON) BRED C. Farrell
LONG HANDICAP Ealing Court 9-1
1794 Tim (IRE), appearing to enjoy this longer trip, looked the winner from a long way out and, leading at the last, had no problems in sprinting clear. (7/2)
1067 Peatswood, all the better for a recent outing, was well treated on his old form and appreciated the return to a longer trip. Leading four out, he was easily brushed aside by the winner at the last. (2/1)
Ealing Court faced an awesome task in carrying 16lb more than his long-handicap weight after a lengthy lay-off. (16/1)
1661 Mytton's Choice (IRE) has been a model of consistency, but quite simply failed to stay the three miles here. (11/4: 7/4-3/1)
1906 Uluru (IRE) had the ground and trip in his favour, but is a bit high in the handicap at present. (100/30: 5/1-3/1)

T/Jkpt: £11,804.30 (0.6 Tckts); £6,650.32 to Kempton 27/12/96. T/Plpt: £372.30 (133.99 Tckts). T/Qdpt: £29.30 (89.33 Tckts). AK

1775-MARKET RASEN (R-H) - Thursday December 26th

2118 Abandoned-Frost

1946-NEWTON ABBOT (L-H) - Thursday December 26th

2125 Abandoned-Frost

1842-SEDGEFIELD (L-H) - Thursday December 26th

2131 Abandoned-Frozen ground

1802-WETHERBY (L-H) - Thursday December 26th

2138 Abandoned-Snow & frost

1673-WINCANTON (R-H) - Thursday December 26th

2144 Abandoned-Frost

WOLVERHAMPTON (L-H) - Thursday December 26th

2150 Abandoned-Frost

1782-CHEPSTOW (L-H) - Friday December 27th

2156 Abandoned-Frost

2112-KEMPTON (R-H) - Friday December 27th

2163 Abandoned-Frost

1855-LEICESTER (R-H) - Friday December 27th

2169 Abandoned-Frost

1967-MUSSELBURGH (R-H) (Good to firm)

Friday December 27th

WEATHER: fine

2175 CARBERRY TOWER HURDLE (3-Y.O) (Class E)

12-35 (12-35) **2m (8 hdls)** £1,815.50 (£508.00: £246.50) GOING minus 0.28 sec per fur (GF)

				SP	RR	SF
1940[2]	**Rossel (USA)** (PMonteith) **3-11-12** ADobbin (lw: a.p: led appr 3rd: hdd 2 out: led flat: styd on wl)	—	**1**	4/9[1]	92	42
	Honeyschoice (IRE) (MDHammond) **3-10-12** RGarritty (hld up: hdwy to chse wnr 4th: led & hit 2 out: clr whn blnd last: sn hdd: nt rcvr)	3	**2**	4/1[2]	75+	25
1700[3]	**Noir Esprit** (JMCarr) **3-10-9**(3) FLeahy (hld up: stdy hdwy 5th: r.o fr last: nrst fin)	1½	**3**	25/1	74?	24
1940[8]	**Priddy Fair** (DWBarker) **3-10-11**(3) PMidgley (a chsng ldrs: nt qckn fr 3 out)	3	**4**	40/1	73?	23
	Catherine's Choice (MDHammond) **3-10-9**(3) MrCBonner (mstkes: prom tl lost pl 3 out: n.d after)	14	**5**	33/1	57	7
	Mountain Dream (RAllan) **3-10-12** BStorey (hdwy 4th: hit 3 out: n.d)	10	**6**	14/1[3]	47	—
	Miletrian City (JBerry) **3-10-12** MMoloney (prom: outpcd & blnd 5th: n.d after)	17	**7**	20/1	30	—
	Respecting (JAMoore) **3-10-12** NSmith (plld hrd: led tl after 2nd: sn lost pl)	¾	**8**	50/1	29	—
1940[11]	**Western Venture (IRE)** (RMMcKellar) **3-10-12** DParker (cl up: led after 2nd: hdd appr next: sn wknd & t.o)	4	**9**	200/1	25	—
1526[7]	**Brogans Brush** (JSHaldane) **3-10-12** GCahill (sn t.o: p.u bef 2 out)		**P**	100/1	—	—
				(SP 113.3%)	**10 Rn**	

3m 41.0 (2.00) CSF £2.63 TOTE £1.50: £1.10 £1.20 £3.30 (£2.20) Trio £14.30 OWNER Mr Allan Melville (ROSEWELL) BRED Allen E. Paulson

1940 Rossel (USA) looked as though his double penalty had beaten him again when headed going to the last, but he was quick to seize on the leader's blunder and regain the advantage soon after landing. (4/9)

Honeyschoice (IRE) did everything right until a terrible blunder at the last cost him the race. Plenty of other opportunities will be found. (4/1)

1700 Noir Esprit is improving fast. This was a fair effort and he finished to some purpose. (25/1)

1699* Priddy Fair ran really well in this company and there is another modest race or two in her. (40/1)

Catherine's Choice just needs to brush up on his hurdling and should improve a good bit. (33/1)

Mountain Dream was showing a little when a mistake three out stopped him. (14/1: 10/1-20/1)

2176 RUSTY NAIL NOVICES' CHASE (5-Y.O+) (Class E)

1-05 (1-07) **3m (18 fncs)** £2,455.90 (£743.20: £362.60: £172.30) GOING minus 0.28 sec per fur (GF)

				SP	RR	SF
1653[3]	**Blue Charm (IRE) (110)** (MrsSCBradburne) **6-11-5** RGarritty (lw: mde most: shkn up & r.o wl fr 3 out)	—	**1**	9/4[2]	102	24
1668[2]	**Winter Belle (USA)** (HowardJohnson) **8-10-9**(3) MrCBonner (bhd: hdwy 12th: wnt 2nd 2 out: kpt on wl)	2½	**2**	16/1	93	15
1576[7]	**Fine Tune (IRE) (60)** (MrsSCBradburne) **6-10-12** AThornton (j.lft thrght: chsd ldrs: effrt 4 out: one pce)	19	**3**	100/1	81	3
1968[2]	**Fingerhill (IRE) (80)** (VThompson) **7-10-12** MrMThompson (in tch: rdn to chse ldrs appr 4 out: sn btn)	19	**4**	33/1	68	—
1968[U]	**Establish (IRE) (76)** (JPDodds) **8-10-7** KJohnson (b.d 1st)		**B**	66/1	—	—
1826*	**Noyan** (RAFahey) **6-11-5** ADobbin (bdly hmpd & fell 1st)		**F**	5/6[1]	—	—
1968*	**Heddon Haugh (IRE) (86)** (PCheesbrough) **8-11-5** RSupple (unruly s: disp ld to 6th: cl up tl outpcd 11th: mstkes after: t.o whn p.u bef 3 out)		**P**	33/1	—	—
1668[F]	**Tough Test (IRE)** (MrsJDGoodfellow) **6-10-12** GCahill (bdly hmpd 1st & p.u bef next)		**P**	8/1[3]	—	—
				(SP 110.7%)	**8 Rn**	

6m 0.7 (7.70) CSF £30.55 TOTE £3.10: £1.50 £1.40 £8.10 (£13.20) Trio £145.30 OWNER Mrs M. C. Lindsay (CUPAR) BRED Patrick Coghlan

1653 Blue Charm (IRE), winning at his longest trip to date, was not really tested as the main opposition went out at the first. (9/4)

1668 Winter Belle (USA) is running well and certainly seems to stay but is just short of a turn of foot. (16/1)

Fine Tune (IRE) jumped badly left throughout and caused all sorts of mayhem at the first but still had a chance until being found out in the home straight. (100/1)

1968 Fingerhill (IRE) was always finding this company too quick and finally gave up four out. (33/1)

1826* Noyan was given no room at all at the first and not surprisingly finished up on the floor. (5/6: 4/5-evens)

1968* Heddon Haugh (IRE) gave problems at the start and then suddenly bottomed out soon after halfway and, stopping as though something was wrong, was pulled up. (33/1)

1668 Tough Test (IRE) (8/1: 6/1-9/1)

2177 MILLER HILL MAIDEN HURDLE (4-Y.O+) (Class E)

1-35 (1-35) **2m 4f (12 hdls)** £1,878.50 (£526.00: £255.50) GOING minus 0.28 sec per fur (GF)

				SP	RR	SF
1967[2]	**Smolensk (IRE)** (JBerry) **4-11-5** MMoloney (lw: hld up: a.gng wl: led on bit appr last: qcknd)	—	**1**	7/4[1]	70+	32
1672[5]	**Cheater (IRE)** (HowardJohnson) **5-11-5** ASSmith (a.p: led after 3 out tl between last 2: no ch w wnr)	11	**2**	14/1	61	23
1822[3]	**Little Redwing (67)** (MDHammond) **4-10-11v**(3) MrCBonner (led fr 6th tl after 3 out: one pce)	4	**3**	50/1	53	15
	Arctic Sandy (IRE) (JKMOliver) **6-11-5** BStorey (hld up: hdwy & prom 3 out: rdn & btn between last 2)	7	**4**	9/4[2]	52	14
1821[3]	**Something Speedy (IRE)** (MDHammond) **4-11-0** RGarritty (hld up: hdwy 7th: no imp fr 3 out)	2	**5**	16/1	46	8
	Canaan Valley (85) (DRobertson) **8-11-5** JBurke (led to 6th: chsd ldrs tl outpcd fr 4 out)	10	**6**	25/1	43	5
	Penny Peppermint (REBarr) **4-11-0** NSmith (lost tch ½-wy: sn t.o)	11	**7**	200/1	29	—
1851[13]	**Ringrone (IRE)** (VThompson) **7-11-0b**[1] MrMThompson (blnd 6th: sn t.o)	23	**8**	200/1	11	—
1499[2]	**Three Wild Days (95)** (TPTate) **4-11-5** AThornton (lw: prom tl fell 8th: dead)		**F**	3/1[3]	—	—
1689[8]	**Jaunty General** (CParker) **5-11-5** DParker (prom to ½-wy: wl bhd whn p.u bef last)		**P**	16/1	—	—
				(SP 117.4%)	**10 Rn**	

4m 45.6 (3.60) CSF £24.45 TOTE £2.30: £1.30 £2.20 £3.30 (£32.30) Trio £41.10 OWNER Mrs Chris Deuters (COCKERHAM) BRED Miss B. Galway-Greer

1967 Smolensk (IRE), given a more patient ride, got it right this time and did it in some style. (7/4)

1672 Cheater (IRE) tried hard and had his chances but his lack of pace was well exposed by the winner after the last. (14/1)

1822 Little Redwing did her usual and was in contention throughout but was well short of speed when it mattered. (50/1)

Arctic Sandy (IRE) looked big and well but, judging by his performance, he needed it and should improve. (9/4)
1821 Something Speedy (IRE) has some ability and will find a modest race in due course. (16/1)

2178 PINKIE HILL H'CAP HURDLE (0-125) (4-Y.O+) (Class D)

2-05 (2-05) **3m (13 hdls)** £2,633.60 (£739.60: £360.80) GOING minus 0.28 sec per fur (GF)

				SP	RR	SF
1671[3]	**Trump (113)** (CParker) **7-11-10** DParker (chsd clr ldr: effrt 3 out: led flat: r.o)	—	1	6/5[1]	95	33
1971[2]	**D'Arblay Street (IRE) (89)** (WTKemp) **7-10-0** SMcDougall (led & sn wl clr: hrd rdn appr last: hdd & no ex flat)	4	2	6/1	68	6
2003[3]	**Ifallelsefails (94)** (LLungo) **8-10-5** RSupple (hld up: effrt appr 2 out: ch appr last: no ex)	1¾	3	7/2[3]	72	10
1849[9]	**Helens Bay (IRE) (89)** (VThompson) **6-10-0b** KJohnson (outpcd ½-wy: n.d after)	11	4	50/1	60?	—
1945[7]	**Barton Heights (90)** (MrsMReveley) **4-9-8**(7) CMcCormack (lw: mstkes: hld up: effrt 3 out: btn appr last: virtually p.u flat)	dist	5	5/2[2]	—	—

(SP 112.5%) **5 Rn**

5m 45.6 (5.60) CSF £8.08 TOTE £2.00: £1.50 £1.90 (£3.10) OWNER Mr & Mrs Raymond Anderson Green (LOCKERBIE) BRED Cheveley Park Stud Ltd
LONG HANDICAP Helens Bay (IRE) 9-0 D'Arblay Street (IRE) 9-11
1671 Trump, on his favourite track, won well and is now likely to go chasing. (6/5)
1971 D'Arblay Street (IRE) made this a real test of stamina but, reeled in going to the last, his lack of pace was then well exposed. (6/1: 9/2-7/1)
2003 Ifallelsefails travelled well yet again but when it came down to a struggle, he was again disappointing. (7/2)
Helens Bay (IRE) was left struggling at halfway but did keep on at the finish and this was not a bad effort from a stone out of the handicap. (50/1)
1686 Barton Heights looks well but is obviously not right at present and, never jumping fluently, was then eased considerably when beaten. (5/2)

2179 COL W. L. M. MONTEITH H'CAP CHASE (0-120) (5-Y.O+) (Class D)

2-40 (2-42) **3m (18 fncs)** £2,697.00 (£816.00: £398.00: £189.00) GOING minus 0.28 sec per fur (GF)

				SP	RR	SF
1578[6]	**Hurricane Andrew (IRE) (87)** (JAMoore) **8-10-0** NSmith (led fr 3rd: hld on wl fr 4 out)	—	1	4/1[3]	92	5
1704[4]	**Forward Glen (87)** (PCheesbrough) **9-10-0b** RSupple (bhd: hdwy & prom ½-wy: chsd ldrs fr 4 out: kpt on wl towards fin)	¾	2	16/1	92	5
1641*	**Wayuphill (92)** (CParker) **9-10-5** BStorey (lw: hld up: gd hdwy 14th: ev ch whn blnd bdly 3 out: one pce after)	1	3	6/4[1]	96	9
1970[4]	**Risky Dee (87)** (VThompson) **7-10-0** KJohnson (chsd ldrs tl wknd fr 4 out)	19	4	20/1	78	—
1847[6]	**Willie Sparkle (87)** (MrsSCBradburne) **10-10-0** MFoster (chsd ldrs tl blnd bdly 13th: n.d after)	7	5	7/1	74	—
1805[6]	**Joe White (115)** (HowardJohnson) **10-12-0** ASSmith (prom tl rdn & lost pl 13th: p.u bef 4 out: lame)		P	11/4[2]	—	—
1846[6]	**Bishopdale (87)** (SGChadwick) **15-10-0** FPerratt (led to 3rd: outpcd & lost tch ½-wy: t.o whn p.u bef 4 out)		P	25/1	—	—

(SP 113.7%) **7 Rn**

6m 1.3 (8.30) CSF £50.03 CT £123.02 TOTE £5.10: £2.00 £7.10 (£62.40) OWNER Mr J. A. Moore (DARLINGTON) BRED Mitchelstown Stud
LONG HANDICAP Hurricane Andrew (IRE) 9-13 Forward Glen 9-0 Risky Dee 9-1 Willie Sparkle 9-4 Bishopdale 9-2
OFFICIAL EXPLANATION Joe White: was lame behind.
1578 Hurricane Andrew (IRE) appreciated the trip and, in front virtually throughout, was not going to stop. (4/1)
1704 Forward Glen, a stone out of the handicap, ran one of his better races and was keeping on well in the closing stages but he is never one to rely on. (16/1)
1641* Wayuphill, having her first run for her new stable, again travelled well but, when it came down to a struggle, she made a particularly bad blunder three out, and was fighting a lost cause thereafter. (6/4)
1970 Risky Dee, 13lb wrong in the handicap, is running quite well at present but he had been found out early in the straight here. (20/1)
1847 Willie Sparkle was 10lb out of the handicap but it was a terrible blunder that finished his hopes six from home. (7/1)
1805 Joe White stopped as though something was wrong six from home and was then pulled up. (11/4)

2180 PRESTON TOWER STANDARD OPEN N.H. FLAT RACE (4, 5 & 6-Y.O) (Class H)

3-15 (3-15) **2m** £1,138.00 (£318.00: £154.00)

				SP	RR	SF
	Lord Lamb (MrsMReveley) **4-11-11** PNiven (h.d.w: hld up: hdwy 5f out: disp ld 3f out: hung rt & r.o wl fnl f: comf)	—	1	1/4[1]	50 f	—
1973[3]	**Nutty Solera** (CParker) **6-11-11** BStorey (trckd ldrs: hdwy to disp ld 3f out: nt pce of wnr fnl f)	3	2	6/1[2]	47 f	—
1973[4]	**Salem Beach** (MartinTodhunter) **4-10-13** ADobbin (hld up: hdwy 5f out: sn chsng ldrs: one pce fnl 2½f)	9	3	16/1	26 f	—
2005[8]	**Dantes Amour (IRE)** (MDHammond) **5-11-4** RGarritty (cl up: effrt 4f out: wknd fnl 2f)	1¼	4	14/1[3]	30 f	—
	The Early Bird (PMonteith) **5-10-13** GCahill (led tl hdd & wknd 3f out)	5	5	14/1[3]	20 f	—
	Jimmy Sprite (REBarr) **5-11-4** NSmith (bit bkwd: cl up tl wknd 6f out)	10	6	66/1	15 f	—

(SP 115.0%) **6 Rn**

3m 49.4 CSF £2.68 TOTE £1.30: £1.10 £1.70 (£1.60) OWNER Mr A Sharratt & Mr J Renton (SALTBURN) BRED Mrs T. Hall
Lord Lamb has changed stables and has done particularly well physically, winning this with something to spare, but he still looks more than a bit of a character. (1/4)
1973 Nutty Solera did his utmost but proved short of a turn of foot and always found the winner too strong. (6/1: op 4/1)
1973 Salem Beach tried to come from off the pace but had her limitations well exposed in the final three furlongs. (16/1)
Dantes Amour (IRE), wearing a tongue-strap, had his chances until crying enough in the last couple of furlongs. (14/1)
The Early Bird (14/1: op 33/1)

T/Plpt: £124.90 (123.31 Tckts). T/Qdpt: £63.30 (16.56 Tckts). AA

2138-WETHERBY (L-H) - Friday December 27th

2181 Abandoned-Snow & frost

2187a - 2193a : (Irish Racing) - See Computer Raceform

1960-FOLKESTONE (R-H) - Saturday December 28th

2194 Abandoned-Snow & frost

2106-HUNTINGDON (R-H) - Saturday December 28th

2200 Abandoned-Frost

1646-NEWBURY (L-H) - Saturday December 28th
2207 **Abandoned**-Frost

1940-NEWCASTLE (L-H) - Saturday December 28th
2213 **Abandoned**-Frost

1587-CARLISLE (R-H) - Monday December 30th
2219 **Abandoned**-Frozen in places

2207-NEWBURY (L-H) - Monday December 30th
2226 **Abandoned**-Frost

1835-PLUMPTON (L-H) - Monday December 30th
2233 **Abandoned**-Frost

1085-STRATFORD-ON-AVON (L-H) - Monday December 30th
2239 **Abandoned**-Frost

1999-CATTERICK (L-H) - Tuesday December 31st
2246 **Abandoned**-Snow

1706-FONTWELL (Fig. 8) - Tuesday December 31st
2253 **Abandoned**-Frost

1873-TAUNTON (R-H) - Tuesday December 31st
2259 **Abandoned**-Frozen ground

1953-WARWICK (L-H) - Tuesday December 31st
2265 **Abandoned**-Frozen ground

2246-CATTERICK (L-H) - Wednesday January 1st
2272 **Abandoned**-Snow

1914-CHELTENHAM (L-H) - Wednesday January 1st
2278 **Abandoned**-Frost

1993-EXETER (R-H) - Wednesday January 1st
2284 **Abandoned**-Frost

2169-LEICESTER (R-H) - Wednesday January 1st
2291 **Abandoned**-Snow & frost

2074-UTTOXETER (L-H) - Wednesday January 1st
2297 **Abandoned**-Snow & frost

1726-WINDSOR (Fig. 8) - Wednesday January 1st
2304 **Abandoned**-Frost

2094-AYR (L-H) - Thursday January 2nd
2311 **Abandoned**-Frost

2118-MARKET RASEN (R-H) - Thursday January 2nd
2318 **Abandoned**-Snow

2325a - 2332a : (Irish Racing) - See Computer Raceform

1409a-LEOPARDSTOWN (Dublin, Ireland) (L-H) (Good to soft)
Thursday December 26th

2333a DENNY HURDLE (Gd 2) (3-Y.O)
1-30 (1-32) **2m** **(8 hdls)** IR £9,675.00 (IR £2,775.00: IR £1,275.00: IR £375.00)

				SP	RR	SF
1747a[15]	**Grimes** (CRoche,Ireland) **3-10-9** CO'Dwyer (hld up in rr: hdwy 3 out: led appr last: mstke last: jst hld on)	—	**1**	9/1	90	30
1747a[3]	**Greenhue (IRE)** (MJPO'Brien,Ireland) **3-10-6**(3) KLO'Brien (hld up towards rr: stdy hdwy fr 3 out: c wd st: styd on wl u.p flat: jst failed)	s.h	**2**	7/1[2]	90	30
	Rescue Time (IRE) (KPrendergast,Ireland) **3-10-9** JShortt (mid div: hdwy appr 5th: led early st: sn jnd: ev ch last: no ex flat)	5½	**3**	8/1[3]	84	24
1747a[11]	**Choosey's Treasure (IRE)** (APO'Brien,Ireland) **3-10-6**(3) RPO'Brien (cl up fr 3rd: styd on u.p fr bef last)	hd	**4**	14/1	84	24
1747a[4]	**Miss Pennyhill (IRE)** (ASadik,Ireland) **3-9-11**(7) JMMaguire (mid div: hdwy 5th: led appr 2 out: hdd early st: one pce u.p appr last)	1½	**5**	14/1	78	18

Miss Roberto (IRE) (MBrassil,Ireland) **3-10-9** KFO'Brien (cl up: hdwy after 4th: led next: 2nd 3 out: lost pl & 5th 2 out: one pce u.p appr last: kpt on flat) ....s.h **6** 7/1[2] 83 23
Hard News (USA) (DPKelly,Ireland) **3-10-6**(3) GCotter (prom: 2nd whn bd mstke 4th: mid div next: 6th on outside 2 out: rdn & no imp appr last: kpt on) 1 **7** 16/1 82 22
1747a* **Spirit Dancer (IRE)** (GMLyons,Ireland) **3-11-0** SCLyons (led: jnd 5th: led 3 out: sn hdd: btn appr 2 out) 3½ **8** 10/1 83 23
1747a[13] **Iacchus (IRE)** (APO'Brien,Ireland) **3-10-4**(5) JButler (in tch: lost pl after 3rd: n.d fr 5th) 9 **9** 20/1 69 9
1747a[6] **Corn Abbey (IRE)** (MissSCollins,Ireland) **3-10-9** FWoods (in tch: 5th whn slt mstke 3 out: 3rd appr next: 4th st: sn wknd) ....s.h **10** 7/1[2] 69 9
Go Sasha (IRE) (PMartin,Ireland) **3-10-4**(5) TMartin (in tch: lost pl after 3rd: n.d fr 5th) ....¾ **11** 10/1 69 9
1747a[8] **Tax Reform (USA)** (DGMcArdle,Ireland) **3-10-9** HRogers (hdwy 4th: wnt 4th next: wkng whn slt mstke 2 out: sn n.d) 2 **12** 12/1 67 7
Apache Twist (IRE) (SJTreacy,Ireland) **3-10-9** TPTreacy (a bhd) ....dist **13** 11/1 — —
Slightly Speedy (IRE) (JTGorman,Ireland) **3-10-9** RHughes (towards rr whn b.d 3rd) .... **B** 16/1 — —
1747a[2] **Highly Motivated** (APO'Brien,Ireland) **3-10-4** CFSwan (hld up: mid div whn b.d 3rd) .... **B** 9/4[1] — —
1747a[5] **Evriza (IRE)** (APO'Brien,Ireland) **3-10-9** JOsborne (prom: 2nd whn fell 3rd) .... **F** 10/1 — —
(SP 162.5%) **16 Rn**

3m 57.1 (-3.90) OWNER John McManus
Grimes put his initial outing over hurdles well behind him with a smart performance. Always travelling well, he led before the last, got away with a mistake and battled really well to the line. (9/1)
1747a Greenhue (IRE) had plenty to do until making headway before two out. Fifth into the straight, he was kept up to deliver his challenge, but the effort just failed. (7/1)
Rescue Time (IRE), an odds-on disappointment at Punchestown when found to be lame, ran to his mark here. Challenging and holding every chance over the last, he could not quicken with the other pair on the flat. (8/1)
1747a Choosey's Treasure (IRE), the outsider of the stable's four runners, put in a strong run from the last after being given plenty to do. (14/1)
1747a Miss Pennyhill (IRE) got to the front two out, but had her limitations exposed on the run to the last. (14/1)
Miss Roberto (IRE) lost her place two out, but stayed on again in the straight. (7/1)
1747a Highly Motivated was brought down at the third by the fall of stable-companion Evriza. (9/4)

2335a DENNY GOLD MEDAL NOVICES' CHASE (Gd 1) (4-Y.O+)
2-40 (2-42) **2m 1f (11 fncs)** IR £22,750.00 (IR £6,650.00: IR £3,150.00: IR £1,050.00)

SP RR SF

1758a[F] **Danoli (IRE)** (TFoley,Ireland) **8-11-6** TPTreacy (sn chsng ldr: mstke 4th: lft in ld 6th: jnd appr 4 out: hdd next: led after 2 out: edgd lft appr last: drew clr flat: styd on wl) ....— **1** 5/2[1] 124+ 32
1790[2] **Land Afar** (PRWebber) **9-11-6** JOsborne (cl up: 2nd whn j.slowly & lost pl 7th: 4th whn j.v.slowly & lost pl next: hdwy after 3 out: wnt 3rd appr last: styd on flat: nt rch wnr) ....6 **2** 3/1[2] 118 26
1486a[4] **Beakstown (IRE)** (PMullins,Ireland) **7-11-6** GCotter (a cl up: disp ld bef 4 out: led 3 out tl hdd after next: swtchd rt & ev ch appr last: one pce flat) ....1 **3** 20/1 117+ 25
1405a[4] **Headbanger** (MMLynch,Ireland) **9-11-6** DHO'Connor (hld up: hdwy 4 out: wnt 4th 3 out: wnt 3rd wl bef last: no imp flat) 3½ **4** 20/1 114 22
The Carrig Rua (IRE) (MichaelFlynn,Ireland) **6-11-6** APowell (in tch: hdwy 7th: 4th appr 3 out: sn lost pl: in tch 2 out: rdn & one pce appr last) 3 **5** 8/1 111 19
1486a* **Jeffell** (ALTMoore,Ireland) **6-11-6** FWoods (slt mstke 1st: cl up: lft 2nd after 6th: 3rd next: ev ch 2 out: sn rdn & btn) ....1½ **6** 5/2[1] 110 18
Penndara (IRE) (APO'Brien,Ireland) **7-11-6** CFSwan (a rr: wl bhd fr 6th: t.o) ....dist **7** 14/1 — —
Kharasar (IRE) (AMullins,Ireland) **6-11-6** CO'Dwyer (hld up: hdwy fr 4 out: trckng ldrs whn stumbled & fell 2 out) .... **F** 6/1[3] — —
1405a[2] **Crossfarnogue (IRE)** (APO'Brien,Ireland) **7-11-6** JButler (led: j.rt: fell 6th) .... **F** 25/1 — —
(SP 127.6%) **9 Rn**

4m 16.2 (-6.80) OWNER D. J. O'Neill (BAGENALSTOWN) BRED W. Austin in Ireland
1758a Danoli (IRE), apart from a mistake at the fourth, was almost foot-perfect and was literally running away turning into the straight. He seems to appreciate some aggression from his opponents, but this was very easy for him. He has the experience now to take on the more experienced chasers. (5/2)
1790 Land Afar was certainly not foot-perfect and a bad mistake four out saw him lose his place completely. With plenty to do turning into the straight, he landed third over the last and stayed on to go second close home. There still has to be a doubt regarding his attitude. (3/1)
1216a Beakstown (IRE) is only a handicapper, but was able to go with the winner once the pressure was on. Weakening from the last, the Handicapper has chosen to ignore this improved performance and he can soon score back in his own grade. (20/1)
Headbanger ran above his mark, and he too can score again in his grade. (20/1)
1486a* Jeffell was a real disappointment. Seemingly travelling well on the outside at the second last, he punctured quickly in the straight and had dropped right away before the last. (5/2)
Kharasar (IRE) had only just began to mount his effort and was a closing fourth when coming down two out. (6/1)

NR

2336a - 2340a : (Irish Racing) - See Computer Raceform

0999a-LIMERICK (Ireland) (R-H) (Good to soft)
Thursday December 26th

2341a MURPHYS IRISH STOUT NOVICES' CHASE (Gd 3) (5-Y.O+)
2-35 (2-39) **2m 4f (14 fncs)** IR £6,850.00 (IR £1,550.00: IR £650.00: IR £350.00)

SP RR SF

Dun Belle (IRE) (PAFahy,Ireland) **7-11-9** TJMitchell (chsd ldr: led 2 out: rdn & styd on whn chal) ....— **1** 9/2[3] 94 —
1234a[5] **Ultra Flutter** (MHourigan,Ireland) **9-11-9** JPBroderick (sn led: mstke & hdd 2 out: 3rd & rdn st: chal last: styd on u.p: nt rch wnr) ....1½ **2** Evens[1] 93 —
Woodville Star (IRE) (WJBurke,Ireland) **7-11-4** THorgan (hld up in tch: cl 4th 4 out: trckd ldrs: wnt 2nd after 2 out: rdn & chal appr last: no ex flat) ....nk **3** 3/1[2] 88 —
Irish Peace (IRE) (JABerry,Ireland) **8-11-6** CO'Brien (cl up early: mstkes: last fr 5th: reminders 8th: rdn & lost tch bef 4 out: n.d) ....20 **4** 10/1 74 —

				SP	RR	SF
	Moussahim (USA) (GACusack,Ireland) **6-11-9** LPCusack (hld up towards rr: sme early mstkes: 5th & in tch 10th: rdn & lost tch 4 out: sn n.d)	15	5	9/1	65	—
	Minella Gold (IRE) (JohnNallen,Ireland) **7-11-6** DJCasey (in tch: 4th at 8th: 3rd 4 out: rdn next: 4th u.p st: styng on but btn whn fell last)		F	6/1	—	—
				(SP 126.6%)		**6 Rn**

5m 12.6 OWNER Mrs A. Connolly (LEIGHLINBRIDGE)
Dun Belle (IRE) continues her rate of improvement and made it four in a row, leading two out and staying on strongly. Her jumping is very solid. (9/2: op 4/5)
1234a Ultra Flutter was in front until a mistake two out, and his renewed effort from the last was not enough. (Evens)
Woodville Star (IRE), well held by the winner on previous Navan form, went in pursuit after the last, but was well held from there. (3/1)
Moussahim (USA) (9/1: op 6/1)

NR

2342a - 2344a : (Irish Racing) - See Computer Raceform

2331a-LEOPARDSTOWN (Dublin, Ireland) (L-H) (Good to soft)
Friday December 27th

2345a CHELTENHAM GOLD CARD (QUALIFIER) H'CAP HURDLE (4-Y.O+)
12-55 (12-58) **3m (12 hdls)** IR £5,480.00 (IR £1,240.00: IR £520.00: IR £280.00)

				SP	RR	SF
	Miltonfield (JEMulhern,Ireland) **7-10-4** CO'Dwyer (hld up in rr: hdwy 8th: good hdwy on outside to jn ldrs 2 out: closing 3rd appr last: landed 2nd: led early flat: hands & heels)	—	1	3/1 1	97	48
	Collon Leader (IRE) (AJMartin,Ireland) **7-9-8** JRBarry (mid div: hdwy on ins 7th: 6th 3 out: 5th 2 out: wnt 2nd st: disp ld: led appr last: hdd early flat: styd on)	hd	2	11/1	87	38
	Casey Jane (IRE) (WPMullins,Ireland) **5-10-0** DJCasey (hld up: mid div: hdwy appr 2 out: 5th st: 4th & rdn appr last: styd on)	7	3	8/1	88	39
	Tell The Nipper (IRE) (MHourigan,Ireland) **5-10-5b1** JPBroderick (mid div: hdwy after 7th: 5th 3 out: sn disp ld: led 2 out: jnd appr last: sn hdd: one pce flat)	s.h	4	5/1 2	93	44
1405a6	**Amble Speedy (IRE)** (ALTMoore,Ireland) **6-10-1** FWoods (bhd: hdwy 3 out: wnt 6th st: styd on flat: nrst fin)	s.h	5	5/1 2	89	40
1759a5	**Padashpan (USA)** (WPMullins,Ireland) **7-11-6** TPTreacy (hld up in rr: hdwy to mid div 4 out: wd st: styd on: nrst fin)	3½	6	14/1	106	57
	Sir John (IRE) (APO'Brien,Ireland) **7-9-2**(5) JButler (led: jnd appr 7th: hdd 4 out: disp ld again appr 2 out: 4th st: no imp appr last)	3	7	12/1	77	28
	Young Mrs Kelly (IRE) (EMcNamara,Ireland) **6-9-7** JJones (cl up: fair 3rd appr 8th: sn clsd on ldrs tl lost pl appr 2 out: styd on at fin)	½	8	12/1	77	28
	Liscahill Fort (IRE) (JMcLoughney,Ireland) **7-9-4**(3) BBowens (wnt 2nd appr 2nd: disp ld bef 7th: led 4 out: pushed along after next: hdd bef 2 out: one pce appr st: kpt on)	s.h	9	14/1	77	28
	Vicar Street (IRE) (APO'Brien,Ireland) **6-9-13** CFSwan (in tch: losing pl whn mstke 8th: n.d fr 3 out: styd on at fin)	1½	10	11/2 3	82	33
	Dark Swan (IRE) (TJO'Mara,Ireland) **6-9-9** RHughes (cl up: 4th 3 out: no imp appr next: kpt on same pce)	s.h	11	25/1	78	29
	Total Confusion (GMLyons,Ireland) **9-10-2**ow3 PCarberry (prom: lost pl after 5th: 7th & rdn 3 out: n.d fr next)	2	12	10/1	83	31
	Balawhar (IRE) (EJO'Grady,Ireland) **6-12-0** RDunwoody (n.d: wl bhd fr 3 out)	13	13	14/1	101	52
321a8	**Shankorak** (FBerry,Ireland) **9-10-12**(7) RPHogan (n.d)	dist	14	20/1	—	—
	Mr Boal (IRE) (JHScott,Ireland) **7-10-7** KFO'Brien (a bhd: t.o)	dist	15	33/1	—	—
				(SP 149.2%)		**15 Rn**

6m 14.1 (-12.90) OWNER J. C. Savage (CURRAGH)
Miltonfield, cruising on the outside at the second last, continued his progress in the straight and got to the front early on the run-in. Pushed out with hands and heels, he had a lot more in hand than the official verdict suggests, a view which the handicapper obviously shared by putting him up 10lb. (3/1)
Collon Leader (IRE) popped on over the last but was no match for the winner when tackled. (11/1)
Casey Jane (IRE) stayed on under pressure on the flat without ever looking a possibility. (8/1)
Tell The Nipper (IRE) got to the front two out until being outpaced from the last. (5/1)
Amble Speedy (IRE) stayed on well on the flat but his future lies over fences. (5/1)
Padashpan (USA) gave away some ground when taking a wide detour in the straight, and he is worth keeping on the right side of. (14/1)

2346a MCCAIN H'CAP CHASE (5-Y.O+)
1-25 (1-29) **2m 2f (12 fncs)** IR £6,850.00 (IR £1,550.00: IR £650.00: IR £350.00)

				SP	RR	SF
1889a2	**Merry Gale (IRE)** (JTRDreaper,Ireland) **8-10-13** RDunwoody (mde all: slt mstke 4th: rdn clr appr last: styd on wl)	—	1	5/4 2	140+	—
1889aF	**Klairon Davis (FR)** (ALTMoore,Ireland) **7-12-0** FWoods (hld up in tch: slt mstkes 5th & 6th: 2nd next: hdwy appr 3 out: rdn after 2 out: no imp appr last)	8	2	4/5 1	148	—
1410a*	**Fiftysevenchannels (IRE)** (EBolger,Ireland) **7-10-0** CFSwan (rn 4th: wnt 3rd after 3 out: no imp fr 2 out)	13	3	8/1 3	108	—
1750a3	**Jassu** (JEKiely,Ireland) **10-10-1**ow1 APowell (rn 2nd tl 7th: 3rd & lost tch after 3 out)	3	4	14/1	107	—
	Pyr Four (JTRDreaper,Ireland) **9-9-9**(5) JButler (a bhd: t.o fr 5th)	dist	5	25/1	—	—
				(SP 121.6%)		**5 Rn**

4m 26.0 OWNER Herb Stanley (KILSALLAGHAN) BRED Noel O'Brien in Ireland
1889a Merry Gale (IRE), given a chance by the Handicapper, had a smashing confidence-booster here. Making all the running, he stretched away before the last to win quite impressively. The Hennessy Cognac Gold Cup here would be an obvious target, but he can take another handicap en route, despite being raised 5lb. (5/4)
1889a Klairon Davis (FR) was travelling particularly well but his jumping certainly lacked the fluency of the winner's. He was destined for the runner-up position from two out and there might be a tendency to believe that he is not as good as he was, but there will still be plenty willing to give him another chance. (4/5)
1410a* Fiftysevenchannels (IRE) was making no impression from the third last. (8/1)

1750a Jassu was another with no chance at these weights. (14/1)

2347a 1ST CHOICE NOVICES' HURDLE (Gd 3) (4-Y.O+)
2-00 (2-00) **2m 2f (9 hdls)** IR £9,675.00 (IR £2,775.00: IR £1,275.00: IR £375.00)

				SP	RR	SF
1757a*	**Istabraq (IRE)** (APO'Brien,Ireland) **4-11-3** CFSwan (hld up: wnt 2nd over 5th: hdwy appr 3 out: led 2 out: c wd st: clr appr last: easily)	—	1	30/100 1	115+	24
1757a2	**Palette (IRE)** (WPMullins,Ireland) **4-11-1** DJCasey (hld up: rdn appr 2 out: mstke 2 out: wnt fair 2nd appr last: kpt on: no imp)	5½	2	100/30 2	108	17
	Delphi Lodge (IRE) (TJTaaffe,Ireland) **6-11-8** MrAJMartin (hld up: last 3 out: fair 4th 2 out: 3rd appr last: kpt on: n.d)	1	3	33/1	109	23
1757a5	**Three Scholars** (WPMullins,Ireland) **5-11-8** RDunwoody (led: clr bef 3rd to 3 out: hdd 2 out: sn rdn & btn)	14	4	12/1 3	97	11
	All the Vowels (IRE) (JEMulhern,Ireland) **5-11-4** JPBroderick (wnt 2nd appr 2nd: lost pl 5th: 3rd next: dropped bhd after 3 out: t.o)	20	5	20/1	75	—
				(SP 115.4%)		**5 Rn**

4m 28.3 (-0.70) OWNER John McManus (PILTOWN) BRED Shadwell Estate Company Limited

1757a* Istabraq (IRE) confirmed the improvement he made at Fairyhouse and looks a serious Sun Alliance Novice Hurdle prospect. He allowed Three Scholars the luxury of a long lead, but was always poised to pounce and led before two out with his rider looking around for dangers. Clear into the straight, he went on to win with any amount in hand and will come back here for another event in February. He certainly stays and has toe. (30/100)

1757a Palette (IRE), runner-up to the winner at Fairyhouse earlier in the month, again faced an impossible task. She went second before the last, but was never on terms to challenge. (100/30)

Delphi Lodge (IRE) kept on to go third in the straight, but was totally out of his depth in trying to concede 5lb. (33/1)

2348a PADDY POWER H'CAP CHASE (Gd 2) (4-Y.O+)
2-35 (2-35) **3m (17 fncs)** IR £44,050.00 (IR £15,250.00: IR £7,250.00: IR £2,450.00: IR £1,650.00: IR £850.00)

				SP	RR	SF
1759aF	**New Co (IRE)** (MFMorris,Ireland) **8-10-6** CO'Dwyer (hld up in rr: stdy hdwy 11th: lft 5th after 3 out: wnt 3rd 2 out: 2nd st: disp ld appr last: rdn & styd on u.p flat)	—	1	11/4 1	128	60
	Wylde Hide (ALTMoore,Ireland) **9-11-2** FWoods (prom: led 3rd to 5th: rn 2nd tl appr 8th: 6th 3 out: hdwy on ins to ld after 2 out: sn rdn: jnd appr last: kpt on)	1	2	8/1	137	69
1889a3	**Time for a Run** (EJO'Grady,Ireland) **9-10-4** RDunwoody (hld up: mid div fr 8th: hdwy appr 3 out: 6th 2 out: 4th & rdn st: 3rd appr last: styd on: nt trble ldrs)	7	3	6/1 2	121	53
	Back Bar (IRE) (ALTMoore,Ireland) **8-10-5** JPBroderick (a cl up: 3rd 4 out: no ex u.p appr last: styd on wl flat)	½	4	20/1	121	53
1397a5	**Antonin (FR)** (MrsSABramall,Ireland) **8-11-7**(3) KWhelan (cl up: wnt 2nd over 8th: led appr 3 out: hdd 2 out: 5th & no imp appr last: kpt on)	6	5	14/1	136	68
1350*	**Dancing Vision (IRE)** (EMcNamara,Ireland) **6-9-12** JJones (bhd: sme hdwy whn mstke 5 out: hdwy & 7th 2 out: no imp appr last)	11	6	25/1	103	35
16496	**Feathered Gale** (ALTMoore,Ireland) **9-11-9**(5) MrJTMcNamara (in tch: lost pl bef 4 out: no imp after next: styd on)	3½	7	16/1	131	63
1495a2	**Heist** (NMeade,Ireland) **7-10-9** KFO'Brien (towards rr whn mstke 10th: sme hdwy fr 2 out: n.d)	5½	8	10/1	108	40
1003a6	**Beat The Second (IRE)** (APO'Brien,Ireland) **8-9-13** CFSwan (mid div whn mstke 4th: n.d fr 4 out: styd on fr 2 out)	hd	9	7/1 3	98	30
1495a4	**Second Schedual** (MissAMMcMahon,Ireland) **11-11-3** MrGJHarford (bhd: nvr nrr)	1	10	14/1	115	47
	Whale of a Knight (IRE) (ALTMoore,Ireland) **7-10-7** PCarberry (hld up mid div: hdwy 5 out: 6th next: hmpd 3 out: sme hdwy after 2 out: no imp appr last: eased flat)	5½	11	7/1 3	102	34
1495a*	**Lord Singapore (IRE)** (JJWalsh,Ireland) **8-11-7** DJCasey (towards rr: kpt on fr 2 out: n.d)	3	12	8/1	114	46
1750a6	**Ballyhire Lad (IRE)** (APO'Brien,Ireland) **7-10-9**(3) MrBMCash (cl up: 4th 4 out: lft 2nd next: ev ch 2 out: sn wknd)	s.h	13	33/1	105	37
1750a4	**Topical Tip (IRE)** (JEMulhern,Ireland) **7-10-3** TPTreacy (disp ld tl appr 2nd: slt mstke 4th: prom tl lost pl after 9th: n.d fr 12th)	11	14	16/1	88	20
1495aP	**Love and Porter (IRE)** (JJO'Connor,Ireland) **8-10-9** DHO'Connor (bhd: j.slowly 12th: n.d: t.o)	20	15	25/1	81	13
1752a9	**Tryfirion (IRE)** (VBowens,Ireland) **7-10-8**(3) BBowens (mid div: towards rr whn fell 11th)		F	14/1	—	—
1495aP	**Nuaffe** (PAFahy,Ireland) **11-11-6b1** TJMitchell (led appr 2nd to next: led 5th: slt mstke 4 out: hdd & cl 2nd whn blnd bdly & uns rdr next)		U	40/1	—	—
				(SP 146.9%)		**17 Rn**

6m 18.1 (-16.90) OWNER Exors the Late Mrs L C Ronan (FETHARD)

1234a New Co (IRE), well treated at the weights, running from a mark 9lb lower than his reassessment following his Navan win, made heavy enough weather of it. In front after two out, he battled on bravely from the last to resist the persistent challenge of Wylde Hide. He will be a Grand National entry, but a more realistic target might be another tilt over the smaller obstacles in the Coral Cup Hurdle at Cheltenham, a race in which he finished third last season. (11/4)

Wylde Hide put his previous run this season behind him and there might have been a different result had he got his favoured heavy ground. He seems as good as ever and the Handicapper has edged him up 4lb for this. (8/1)

1889a Time for a Run could yet redeem his reputation over fences, this being by far his best effort. He made steady headway from five out and went third approaching the last without ever being able to deliver a challenge. (6/1)

Back Bar (IRE) also showed signs of a return to form, keeping on well under pressure. (20/1)

1397a Antonin (FR) was left in front when Nuaffe crashed three out, but was headed at the next. (14/1)

Whale of a Knight (IRE) was travelling well behind the leaders five out and, for a few strides before the second last, looked as though he was going to prove a threat. He dropped away before the turn in, but there is a major prize waiting for him somewhere. (7/1)

NR

2349a - 2358a : (Irish Racing) - See Computer Raceform

2344a-LEOPARDSTOWN (Dublin, Ireland) (L-H) (Good to soft)
Saturday December 28th

2359a O'DWYERS STILLORGAN ORCHARD NOVICES' HURDLE (4-Y.O+)
1-05 (1-08) **2m 6f (11 hdls)** IR £4,410.00 (IR £930.00: IR £390.00)

			SP	RR	SF
1757a3	**Noble Thyne (IRE)** (PMullins,Ireland) **6-11-8** TPTreacy (disp ld tl led 4 out: slt mstke last: sn rdn: styd on u.p) —	1	Evens 1	106	10
319a*	**Ask The Butler (IRE)** (CRoche,Ireland) **5-11-11** CO'Dwyer (hld up: wnt 3rd appr 3rd: slt mstke 6th: wnt 2nd after 3 out: waited w: effrt after last: ev ch: styd on u.p) s.h	2	9/4 3	109	13
	Buggy (IRE) (KFarrelly,Ireland) **7-11-8** TJMitchell (led & disp ld tl hdd 4 out: 3rd & btn sn after next) dist	3	20/1	—	—
1751a*	**Tarthooth (IRE)** (ALTMoore,Ireland) **5-12-0** FWoods (hld up: rn 3rd tl appr 3rd: slt mstke 6th: last & in tch whn fell 7th)	F	2/1 2	—	—
			(SP 118.9%)		**4 Rn**

5m 45.0 (1.00) OWNER C. Maye (GORESBRIDGE)
1757a Noble Thyne (IRE) took over three from home and made the rest. He held on well under pressure from the last, but it transpired afterwards that he had bled. His trainer was at pains to underline his opinion that the race had turned into a sprint and that that did not suit him. That idea is not backed up by a bit of sectional timing. The Sun Alliance is the target, but he has bled before and there will always be a niggling doubt. (Evens)
Ask The Butler (IRE) appeared to be cruising all over the winner from the turn in, but found precious little when asked a serious question near the finish. It is unusual to see O'Dwyer so confident before the last and yet be beaten. The horse goes up 7lb for this effort. (9/4)
1751a* Tarthooth (IRE) was a close fourth when falling five out. (2/1)

2360a WILLIAM NEVILLE & SONS NOVICES' CHASE (Gd 3) (5-Y.O+)
1-35 (1-39) **3m (17 fncs)** IR £6,850.00 (IR £1,550.00: IR £650.00: IR £350.00)

			SP	RR	SF
1758a*	**Dorans Pride (IRE)** (MHourigan,Ireland) **7-11-13** JPBroderick (mde all: qcknd after 3 out: clr fr next: unchal) —	1	1/5 1	133+	46
	Le Ginno (FR) (TFoley,Ireland) **9-11-7** TPTreacy (sn 3rd: wnt 2nd over 4th: hdwy appr 3 out: sn rdn & outpcd: n.d fr 2 out) dist	2	9/2 2	—	—
	Garabagh (IRE) (JHScott,Ireland) **7-11-4** PCarberry (wnt 2nd appr 2nd tl j.slowly & lost pl 4th: fair 3rd whn slt mstke 8th: slt mstke 13th: sme hdwy bef 3 out: sn wknd) 25	3	25/1 3	—	—
	Cavallo (FR) (MrsSABramall,Ireland) **6-11-4** FWoods (bhd: mstke 8th: wl t.o fr next) dist	4	25/1 3	—	—
			(SP 109.2%)		**4 Rn**

6m 24.5 (-10.50) OWNER T. J. Doran (PATRICKSWELL) BRED Hugh Suffern Bloodstock Ltd
1758a* Dorans Pride (IRE) does jump a bit high and carefully, but was able to set his own pace and warmed up gradually. Going clear before the second last, he won totally unextended, but this was not a great field and connections have all the options. (1/5)
Le Ginno (FR), in second place virtually throughout, lost touch from two out. (9/2)

2361a LEOPARDSTOWN CHRISTMAS HURDLE (Gd 3) (4-Y.O+)
2-05 (2-08) **3m (12 hdls)** IR £6,850.00 (IR £1,550.00: IR £650.00: IR £350.00)

			SP	RR	SF
20565	**What a Question (IRE)** (MFMorris,Ireland) **8-11-7** CO'Dwyer (mde all: sn clr: rdn wl bef last: styd on) —	1	5/2 2	132	58
16472	**Antapoura (IRE)** (APO'Brien,Ireland) **4-10-8** CFSwan (disp 2nd: lft clr 2nd at 8th: no imp on wnr tl hdwy u.p between last 2: slt mstke last: no imp flat) 4	2	4/7 1	122	42
	Rathgibbon (IRE) (SJTreacy,Ireland) **5-11-2** TPTreacy (hld up: lft 3rd & mstke 8th: sme hdwy after 3 out: no imp fr 2 out) 15	3	20/1	114	40
	Dee Ell (ALTMoore,Ireland) **10-10-9**(7) JDMoore (mstke 1st: a bhd: t.o fr 3 out) dist	4	14/1	—	—
1759aF	**Radanpour (IRE)** (WPMullins,Ireland) **4-10-13** DJCasey (disp 2nd: slt mstke 4th: fell 8th)	F	7/1 3	—	—
			(SP 116.1%)		**5 Rn**

6m 9.5 (-17.50) OWNER Mrs Miles Valentine (FETHARD) BRED R. A. and Mrs St George
2056 What a Question (IRE), soon clear, just ran these into the ground. Her jumping was much more fluent than it had been at Ascot and she stayed on strongly under pressure from the last. The Stayers' Hurdle is her objective again. (5/2)
1647 Antapoura (IRE), very well fancied to confirm Newbury placings with the winner, still has plenty of time on her side. (4/7)
Rathgibbon (IRE) is only a handicapper and, although close before two out, was done with before the straight. (20/1)
Dee Ell, on 12lb better terms, looked to have every chance of turning Newbury form around with the winner but he was all of twelve lengths in arrears until beginning to close two out. He had reduced the deficit to two lengths at the last, but had been under pressure to do so and had nothing left on the flat. (14/1)
1492a Radanpour (IRE) was in second place when falling five out. (7/1)

2362a ERICSSON CHASE (Gd 2) (5-Y.O+)
2-40 (2-41) **3m (17 fncs)** IR £32,500.00 (IR £9,500.00: IR £4,500.00: IR £1,500.00)

			SP	RR	SF
1750a*	**Johnny Setaside (IRE)** (NMeade,Ireland) **7-12-0** RDunwoody (led tl appr 2nd: rn 2nd: disp ld 11th: led next: hdd briefly bef 4 out: hdd again appr 3 out: led 2 out: rdn appr last: drvn out: dead) —	1	2/1 1	145	62
1397a6	**King of the Gales** (ALTMoore,Ireland) **9-12-0** FWoods (bhd: mod 3rd fr 5 out: styd on u.p fr 2 out: wnt 2nd early flat: kpt on: nrst fin) 3	2	16/1	143	60
1216a3	**Opera Hat (IRE)** (JRHFowler,Ireland) **8-11-9** APowell (led appr 2nd: mstke 6th: jnd 11th: hdd next: led again briefly appr 4 out: led again appr 3 out tl slt mstke & hdd 2 out: sn rdn & btn) 15	3	7/2 3	128	45
1917U	**Belvederian** (MFMorris,Ireland) **9-12-0** CO'Dwyer (j.slowly & dropped bhd briefly 5th: j.slowly 10th: fair 3rd 12th: no imp whn blnd next: styd on fr last) 10	4	8/1	126	43
1750a2	**Son Of War** (PMcCreery,Ireland) **9-12-0** USmyth (cl up tl dropped bhd after 9th: n.d fr 5 out: kpt on fr 2 out) 4½	5	15/2	123	40
1758aU	**Macallister (IRE)** (VBowens,Ireland) **6-11-11** BBowens (hld up: lft 3rd 11th: 5th whn mstke next: n.d fr 5 out) 2½	6	40/1	119	36
	Idiots Venture (APO'Brien,Ireland) **9-12-0** CFSwan (hld up in tch: slt mstke 4th: wnt 3rd appr 7th tl bd mstke & uns rdr 11th)	U	5/2 2	—	—
			(SP 115.3%)		**7 Rn**

6m 18.5 (-16.50) OWNER John O'Meara (NAVAN) BRED Sean Kinsella

1750a* Johnny Setaside (IRE) went on two out for a brave win, but collapsed and died after the race. (2/1)
King of the Gales, without a win since scoring in a handicap here at this meeting three years ago, showed signs of a return to form, coming from off the pace two out to be nearest at the finish. (16/1)
1625a* Opera Hat (IRE) again showed her dislike for Leopardstown. Leading and disputing until the winner led two out, she stayed in contention until approaching the last, but then downed tools. (7/2)
1737a Belvederian made a bad mistake five out and was no danger from the next. (8/1)
1750a Son Of War was trailing and under pressure from eight out. (15/2)
1625a Idiots Venture was a fair third and had not been asked when blundering badly and unseating his rider seven out. (5/2)

NR

2363a - 2370a : (Irish Racing) - See Computer Raceform

2067-LINGFIELD (L-H) - Friday January 3rd
2371 Abandoned-Frost & snow

2131-SEDGEFIELD (L-H) - Friday January 3rd
2378 Abandoned-Snow

2006-TOWCESTER (R-H) - Friday January 3rd
2384 Abandoned-Snow

2060-HAYDOCK (L-H) - Saturday January 4th
2391 Abandoned-Frost

2175-MUSSELBURGH (R-H) - Saturday January 4th
2397 Abandoned-Frost

1867-SANDOWN (R-H) - Saturday January 4th
2404 Abandoned-Frozen ground

2265-WARWICK (L-H) - Saturday January 4th
2411 Abandoned-Frozen ground & snow

2194-FOLKESTONE (R-H) - Monday January 6th
2417 Abandoned-Snow & frost

2291-LEICESTER (R-H) - Tuesday January 7th
2424 Abandoned-Snow

2081-KELSO (L-H) - Wednesday January 8th
2430 Abandoned-Snow

2233-PLUMPTON (L-H) - Wednesday January 8th
2436 Abandoned-Frost

2181-WETHERBY (L-H) - Thursday January 9th
2442 Abandoned-Snow

2144-WINCANTON (R-H) - Thursday January 9th
2448 Abandoned-Frost

2454a - 2460a : (Irish Racing) - See Computer Raceform

2358a-LEOPARDSTOWN (Dublin, Ireland) (L-H) (Yielding)
Monday December 30th
Rescheduled from 29/12/96

2461a DECEMBER FESTIVAL HURDLE (Gd 2) (4-Y.O+)
1-15 (1-17) **2m (8 hdls)** IR £9,675.00 (IR £2,775.00: IR £1,275.00: IR £375.00)

				SP	RR	SF
1916[3]	**Theatreworld (IRE)** (APO'Brien,Ireland) **4-11-2** CFSwan (mde all: j.w: rdn clr bef last: eased bef fin)	—	1	2/1[2]	120+	67
1487a[2]	**Hill Society (IRE)** (NMeade,Ireland) **4-11-2** RDunwoody (hld up in tch: lft 2nd after 4th: rdn & no imp on ldr appr last: slt mstke: kpt on)	5	2	8/1	115	62
1759a[2]	**Cockney Lad (IRE)** (NMeade,Ireland) **7-11-7** PCarberry (hld up in tch: lft 3rd after 4th: in tch: rdn after 2 out: no imp appr last)	1½	3	6/4[1]	114	66
	Slaney Glow (IRE) (JSCullen,Ireland) **5-11-2** FWoods (bhd & in tch tl after 3 out: t.o: kpt on to go 4th after last)	dist	4	33/1	—	—
1487a[4]	**Mayasta (IRE)** (FBerry,Ireland) **6-11-2** CO'Dwyer (in tch: hdwy 4th tl rdn & wknd appr 2 out: eased whn btn: t.o)	3½	5	12/1	—	—

			SP	RR	SF
	Guest Performance (IRE) (DTHughes,Ireland) **4-11-2** RHughes (rn 2nd tl blnd bdly & uns rdr 4th)	**U**	5/2 3	—	—
			(SP 123.6%)		**6 Rn**

3m 56.2 (-4.80) OWNER Mrs John Magnier (PILTOWN) BRED I. Allen, K. C. Choo and Calogo Bloodstock Ag
1916 Theatreworld (IRE), with his tongue tied down this time, made all the running and was travelling like a winner from two out. Pushed clear before the straight, he was unchallenged on the flat although being kept up to his work. A tilt at the Irish Champion Hurdle here in January is the next objective. (2/1)
1487a Hill Society (IRE), in second place from the fourth flight, could make no impression two out but kept on determinedly to keep his stable companion out of the runner-up spot. (8/1: op 5/1)
1759a Cockney Lad (IRE), third from the fourth, was unable to challenge the winner from two out and had a hard enough race for the minor spot against his stable companion. (6/4)
Mayasta (IRE) (12/1: op 8/1)
Guest Performance (IRE) was in second place when blundering badly at the fourth, giving his jockey no chance. (5/2)

2462a - 2494a : (Irish Racing) - See Computer Raceform

CAGNES-SUR-MER (Nice, France) (L-H) (Very Soft)
Tuesday December 31st

2495a PRIX JACQUES PINEL DE GRANDCHAMP HURDLE (4-Y.O+)
1-45 (1-48) **2m 55y** £7,905.00 (£3,953.00: £2,372.00)

				SP	RR	SF
	La Gougouline (FR) (AHosselet,France) **4-9-6** EDiard	—	**1**		98	—
2079*	**Garolo (FR)** (CPEBrooks) **6-10-4** GBradley	nk	**2**		110	—
	Funny Spirit (FR) (France) **7-8-10** PHavas	6½	**3**		81	—
						13 Rn

4m 0.5 P-M 6.00F: 2.00F 2.00F 1.60F (12.70F) OWNER R. Notari BRED Noel Pelat
2079* Garolo (FR) looked to have the race in his grasp but was caught near the line. He is due to return here on Sunday, and compensation may well come his way.

2495a-CAGNES-SUR-MER (Nice, France) (L-H) (Heavy)
Sunday January 5th

2496a PRIX DU RESTAURANT LA CRAVACHE D'OR - ROGER DUCHENE HURDLE (5-Y.O+)
2-50 (2-52) **2m 2f** £7,246.00

				SP	RR	SF
2495a2	**Garolo (FR)** (CPEBrooks) **7-10-8** GBradley	—	**1**		—	—
	Bikalamoun (FR) (France) **7-10-8** YBouche	s.h	**2**		—	—
	Kariver (FR) (France) **6-10-1** FCheyer	7	**3**		—	—
						9 Rn

0m P-M 1.70F: 1.50F 1.30F 1.80F (3.70F) OWNER Lady Lloyd Webber (LAMBOURN) BRED Alec Weisweiller
2495a Garolo (FR), making a quick reappearance after being beaten a short head here on Tuesday, justified favouritism. Striking the front approaching the final flight, he kept on well to the line despite the strong finish of the runner-up.

2054-ASCOT (R-H) - Friday January 10th
2497 Abandoned-Frozen ground

2397-MUSSELBURGH (R-H) (Good to firm, Firm patches)
Friday January 10th
WEATHER: fine

2503 DYEWATER MAIDEN HURDLE (I) (4-Y.O+) (Class F)
12-40 (12-43) **2m (8 hdls)** £1,928.80 (£531.80: £252.40) GOING minus 0.13 sec per fur (G)

				SP	RR	SF
	Best of All (IRE) (JBerry) **5-11-2** MMoloney (hld up: hdwy 3 out: led flat: r.o)	—	**1**	16/1	70	13
16662	**Shinerolla** (CParker) **5-11-7** DParker (plld hrd: hdwy 4th: disp ld between last 2: hdd & no ex flat)	4	**2**	2/1 1	71	14
9062	**Falcon's Flame (USA)** (MrsJRRamsden) **4-10-9** APMcCoy (plld hrd: wnt prom after 2nd: disp ld between last 2: hdd & wknd flat)	s.h	**3**	9/4 2	71	2
1800*	**Lively Encounter (IRE)** (MrsMerritaJones) **6-11-7** DerekByrne (lw: hld up: hdwy on bit to chal 5th: effrt 2 out: sn outpcd & hmpd: no ch after)	12	**4**	2/1 1	59	2
19997	**Gazanali (IRE)** (GMMoore) **6-11-7** NBentley (cl up: led fr 3rd tl between last 2: wknd)	6	**5**	14/1 3	53	—
18216	**Jalmaid** (HAlexander) **5-10-11**(5) RMcGrath (nvr trbld ldrs)	4	**6**	50/1	44	—
152611	**Bridlington Bay** (BEllison) **4-10-9** GCahill (cl up tl wknd 5th)	¾	**7**	200/1	48	—
	Kings High (IRE) (WTKemp) **7-11-7** SMcDougall (led to 3rd: cl up tl wknd 3 out)	12	**8**	100/1	36	—
	Our Wilma (MrsDThomson) **8-11-2** TReed (prom to 5th)	4	**9**	200/1	27	—
6986	**Welburn Boy** (RDEWoodhouse) **5-11-7** ASSmith (cl up to 3rd: sn lost pl)	1¼	**10**	50/1	31	—
	Desert Lore (RMMcKellar) **6-11-7** ADobbin (wl bhd fr 3rd)	dist	**11**	100/1	—	—
				(SP 116.9%)		**11 Rn**

3m 47.7 (8.70) CSF £45.56 TOTE £16.80: £4.50 £1.60 £1.00 (£22.00) Trio £24.40 OWNER Mr Robert Aird (COCKERHAM) BRED Mrs D. Hutch
WEIGHT FOR AGE 4yo-12lb
Best of All (IRE) took well to hurdling on this first attempt and, seeing the trip out well on this fast ground, won authoritatively. (16/1)
1666 Shinerolla had his chances, but just failed to pick up at the business end. He is going to find a race, but it is not going to be anything special. (2/1)
906 Falcon's Flame (USA), off the track for three months, ran well and looks likely to benefit from the outing. (9/4)
1800* Lively Encounter (IRE), a bumper winner, found this a different game and ran as though longer trips would help. He is an excitable type who needs to learn to settle. (2/1)

1633 Gazanali (IRE) failed to impress on looks, but ran quite well until getting outpaced from the second last. (14/1: 10/1-16/1)
Jalmaid is not very big, but is improving slightly with experience. (50/1)

2504 DYEWATER MAIDEN HURDLE (II) (4-Y.O+) (Class F)
1-10 (1-10) **2m (8 hdls)** £1,909.90 (£526.40: £249.70) GOING minus 0.13 sec per fur (G)

				SP	RR	SF
1999^{P}	**Hutcel Loch** (RDEWoodhouse) **6-11-2** ASSmith (cl up: led fr 3rd to flat: rallied to ld cl home)	—	**1**	9/1	67	17
1992^{9}	**Maple Bay (IRE) (70)** (BEllison) **8-11-7** GCahill (lw: hld up: hdwy 5th: slt ld flat: kpt on u.p: jst ct)	s.h	**2**	12/1	72	22
2180^{2}	**Nutty Solera** (CParker) **7-11-7** BStorey (hld up: hdwy 3 out: chsng ldrs next: one pce appr last)	9	**3**	$5/1^{2}$	63	13
1312^{4}	**Lumback Lady** (BMactaggart) **7-10-13**(3) GLee (hld up: jnd ldrs 3rd: one pce fr 2 out)	4	**4**	$8/1^{3}$	54	4
1726^{6}	**Music Please** (KCBailey) **5-11-7** CO'Dwyer (bit bkwd: trckd ldrs: ev ch 2 out: sn rdn & wknd)	4	**5**	$11/8^{1}$	55	5
	Unprejudice (95) (MDHammond) **6-11-7** RGarritty (lw: rr div: effrt appr 2 out: nvr nr to chal)	1	**6**	$5/1^{2}$	54	4
	Decent Penny (IRE) (MrsRichardArthur) **8-11-2** AThornton (lw: prom tl wknd after 3 out)	11	**7**	16/1	38	—
1026^{8}	**Jed Abbey** (RShiels) **5-11-2** DBentley (outpcd fr ½-wy)	9	**8**	50/1	29	—
906^{13}	**Most Respectful** (DenysSmith) **4-10-9** PNiven (chsd ldrs tl wknd qckly appr 2 out)	25	**9**	11/1	9	—
1851^{12}	**About Midnight (63)** (FPMurtagh) **8-11-2b**[1] ADobbin (led to 3rd: sn wknd: t.o whn p.u bef 2 out)		**P**	200/1	—	—
				(SP 120.9%)		**10 Rn**

3m 46.8 (7.80) CSF £100.58 TOTE £8.10: £1.80 £2.30 £2.20 (£191.20) Trio £48.90 OWNER Mr W. H. Jackson (YORK) BRED W. H. Jackson and G. Leatham
WEIGHT FOR AGE 4yo-12lb
872 Hutcel Loch, much happier on this fast ground, got a bit warm beforehand and showed a great deal of determination late on. There looks to be some improvement in her. (9/1: op 6/1)
Maple Bay (IRE) put in by far his best effort over hurdles here and there is surely a race to be found. (12/1)
2180 Nutty Solera was tapped for speed late on and will probably need further. (5/1)
1312 Lumback Lady ran well after two months off and should find a race in due course. (8/1)
1726 Music Please seemed to blow up, and probably needed this. (11/8: evens-6/4)
Unprejudice, off the track for almost a year, should improve for this. (5/1)

2505 LINKS (S) H'CAP HURDLE (0-95) (4-Y.O+) (Class G)
1-45 (1-45) **2m (8 hdls)** £2,406.00 (£666.00: £318.00) GOING minus 0.13 sec per fur (G)

				SP	RR	SF
1969*	**Triennium (USA) (85)** (PMonteith) **8-11-10** ADobbin (lw: t: a gng wl: led 3 out: comf)	—	**1**	$2/1^{1}$	68+	23
1911^{4}	**Tiotao (IRE) (70)** (CParker) **7-10-9** DParker (trckd ldrs: effrt 2 out: kpt on one pce)	4	**2**	11/1	49	4
1969^{3}	**Catton Lady (61)** (RCraggs) **7-9-7**(7) BGrattan (chsd ldrs: outpcd appr 2 out: kpt on towards fin)	1½	**3**	20/1	39	—
	Blue Domain (71) (RCraggs) **6-10-10** NSmith (hld up & bhd: gd hdwy to chse wnr 2 out: wknd appr last)	½	**4**	20/1	48	3
1969^{5}	**School of Science (61)** (DANolan) **7-10-0** SMcDougall (cl up: led 4th to 3 out: r.o one pce)	5	**5**	25/1	33	—
1969^{4}	**Troy's Dream (67)** (MDHammond) **6-10-6** RGarritty (hld up: hdwy appr 2 out: no imp)	½	**6**	8/1	39	—
1848^{6}	**Doubling Dice (70)** (RAllan) **6-10-2**(7) SMelrose (hld up: hdwy & prom appr 2 out: sn btn)	6	**7**	10/1	36	—
32^{9}	**Bud's Bet (IRE) (77)** (MissJFCraze) **9-11-2** RJohnson (nvr trbld ldrs)	3	**8**	$7/1^{3}$	40	—
1980^{8}	**Rattle (73)** (JJO'Neill) **4-9-9**(5) RMcGrath (pushed along fr 4th: n.d)	hd	**9**	16/1	36	—
1992^{4}	**Simand (74)** (GMMoore) **5-10-13** JCallaghan (chsd ldrs tl wknd u.p 3 out)	9	**10**	$9/2^{2}$	28	—
1578^{13}	**See You Always (IRE) (62)** (MABarnes) **7-9-10b**(5) STaylor (led to 4th: wknd appr 2 out)	3½	**11**	33/1	12	—
1969^{U}	**Miss Mont (61)** (FPMurtagh) **8-10-0** GCahill (prom to 4th: p.u bef 2 out)		**P**	33/1	—	—
				(SP 117.7%)		**12 Rn**

3m 46.9 (7.90) CSF £22.70 CT £310.50 TOTE £2.80: £1.40 £1.60 £5.00 (£12.00) Trio £64.40 OWNER Mr M. C. Boyd (ROSEWELL) BRED Fittocks Stud Ltd
LONG HANDICAP Catton Lady 9-6 School of Science 9-11 Miss Mont 9-9
WEIGHT FOR AGE 4yo-12lb
No bid
1969* Triennium (USA) has been completely transformed since being tubed and there were never any doubts about the result. (2/1)
1911 Tiotao (IRE), whose jumping has improved, had his chances, but was made to look very one-paced by the winner. (11/1: 8/1-12/1)
1969 Catton Lady, who ran as though a stiffer test would help, was also 8lb wrong in the handicap. (20/1)
Blue Domain travels well, but just seems to have trouble in seeing out the trip at present. (20/1)
School of Science is not really coming up with the goods at the business end yet. (25/1)
1969 Troy's Dream (8/1: 6/1-10/1)
1848 Doubling Dice (10/1: op 4/1)

2506 HOPESWATER NOVICES' CHASE (5-Y.O+) (Class E)
2-15 (2-15) **2m (12 fncs)** £3,097.50 (£924.00: £441.00: £199.50) GOING minus 0.13 sec per fur (G)

				SP	RR	SF
1987*	**Monyman (IRE) (99)** (MDHammond) **7-12-2** RGarritty (trckd ldrs: led & hmpd 3 out: easily)	—	**1**	$8/11^{1}$	105+	32
1346^{12}	**Devilry (100)** (RCraggs) **7-11-10** NSmith (hld up: hdwy appr 4 out: blnd last: styd on: no ch w wnr)	10	**2**	$12/1^{3}$	89	16
1987^{U}	**Gone Ashore (IRE) (60)** (MABarnes) **6-10-13**(5) STaylor (led tl hdd 3 out: btn whn blnd next)	6	**3**	66/1	77	4
2043^{P}	**Elliott's Wish (IRE) (81)** (HowardJohnson) **6-11-10b**[1] RJohnson (mstkes: cl up tl blnd & wknd 8th)	26	**4**	20/1	57	—
1672^{P}	**Alicharger (58)** (PMonteith) **7-11-4v**[1] ADobbin (sn wl bhd: p.u bef 4 out)		**P**	50/1	—	—
1907^{2}	**Herbert Lodge (IRE)** (KCBailey) **8-11-4** CO'Dwyer (blnd & uns rdr 2nd)		**U**	$7/4^{2}$	—	—
				(SP 110.2%)		**6 Rn**

4m 2.0 (8.00) CSF £8.85 TOTE £2.10: £1.10 £3.60 (£5.00) OWNER Mr Trevor Hemmings (MIDDLEHAM) BRED Lady Naylor Leyland
1987* Monyman (IRE) had a simple task once his only serious rival came to grief. (8/11: evens-11/10)
1009* Devilry struggled on late for second place, despite ploughing through the last. (12/1)
Gone Ashore (IRE) ran his best race to date, but was very tired when hitting the second last. (66/1)
1576* Elliott's Wish (IRE) was clumsy throughout and, after a particularly bad blunder five from home, his rider deserved a medal for getting him round. (20/1)
1907 Herbert Lodge (IRE) (7/4: 5/4-2/1)

2507 MUSSELBURGH 10TH ANNIVERSARY H'CAP HURDLE (0-115) (4-Y.O+) (Class E)
2-45 (2-46) **3m (13 hdls)** £3,692.75 (£1,112.00: £538.50: £251.75) GOING minus 0.13 sec per fur (G)

				SP	RR	SF
1344^{3}	**Highland Park (85)** (RCraggs) **11-10-0** ADobbin (chsd ldrs: led 2 out: all out)	—	**1**	16/1	68	3

1798* **Snow Board (91)** (MrsMerritaJones) **8-10-6** DerekByrne (lw: hld up: hdwy 9th: hrd rdn 2 out: styd on wl towards fin)	nk	**2**	11/4[2]	74	9
1971* **Supertop (111)** (LLungo) **9-11-12** RGarritty (hld up & bhd: smooth hdwy appr 2 out: sn rdn: kpt on flat: nvr able to chal)	1	**3**	6/4[1]	93	28
1854[13] **Ruber (85)** (RWThomson) **10-10-0** DParker (prom tl outpcd 4 out: hdwy u.p 2 out: kpt on wl towards fin)	s.h	**4**	66/1	67?	2
2178[2] **D'Arblay Street (IRE) (86)** (WTKemp) **8-10-1** SMcDougall (led to 4th: cl up: led 3 out to 2 out: sn outpcd: kpt on towards fin)	¾	**5**	8/1	68	3
2042[3] **Boston Man (85)** (RDEWoodhouse) **6-10-0** BStorey (in tch: hdwy to disp ld 2 out: wknd last)	2	**6**	15/2[3]	65	—
2052[6] **Dominie (IRE) (99)** (KCBailey) **9-11-0b** CO'Dwyer (chsd ldrs: outpcd 4 out: wknd between last 2)	24	**7**	12/1	63	—
1971[3] **Tallywagger (113)** (GMMoore) **10-11-7**(7) THogg (led fr 4th to 3 out: wknd between last 2)	5	**8**	10/1	74	9
			(SP 113.7%)	**8 Rn**	

5m 52.1 (12.10) CSF £56.23 CT £98.14 TOTE £14.90: £2.40 £2.30 £1.10 (£20.60) Trio £24.30 OWNER Mr Ray Craggs (SEDGEFIELD) BRED Newsells Park Stud
LONG HANDICAP Highland Park 9-10 Boston Man 9-13 Ruber 8-8
1344 Highland Park, trying the trip for the first time, was well suited to it and proved most determined once in front. (16/1)
1798* Snow Board took some riding to get going from the second last, but all he does is stay and he was beginning to peg back the winner. (11/4: 2/1-3/1)
1971* Supertop travelled well as usual but, once off the bit between the last two, failed to come up with the goods. (6/4: 2/1-5/4)
1290 Ruber, who has been hobdayed, ran a cracker from 20lb out of the handicap, and looks one to keep an eye on. (66/1)
2178 D'Arblay Street (IRE) did not go off as fast as usual and his hurdling left something to be desired, but this real stayer kept fighting back when all seemed lost. (8/1)
2042 Boston Man ran pretty well on his first attempt in handicap company. (15/2)
Dominie (IRE) has plenty of ability when he decides to use it. (12/1: op 7/1)
1971 Tallywagger (10/1: op 6/1)

2508 MUSSELBURGH 10TH ANNIVERSARY H'CAP CHASE (0-115) (5-Y.O+) (Class E)

3-15 (3-15) **2m 4f (16 fncs)** £3,535.60 (£1,058.80: £508.40: £233.20) GOING minus 0.13 sec per fur (G)

			SP	RR	SF
2179[3] **Wayuphill (92)** (CParker) **10-10-11** BStorey (lw: trckd ldrs: chal whn lft in ld 3 out: r.o)	—	**1**	5/1[3]	108	12
1970[2] **Puritan (CAN) (109)** (NTinkler) **8-12-0b** RGarritty (lw: bhd: mstke 9th: sn drvn along: hdwy appr 4 out: one pce fr 2 out)	8	**2**	9/4[1]	119	23
1525[3] **Val de Rama (IRE) (89)** (DenysSmith) **8-10-8** PNiven (cl up tl outpcd 12th: no imp after)	9	**3**	8/1	91	—
1823[5] **Grand Scenery (IRE) (89)** (HowardJohnson) **9-10-8** APMcCoy (bhd: hdwy 12th: chsng ldrs 4 out: hrd rdn & nt qckn)	nk	**4**	7/1	91	—
1972[2] **Rapid Mover (91)** (DANolan) **10-10-10b** MMoloney (in tch tl outpcd appr 4 out: n.d after)	17	**5**	14/1	80	—
1991[3] **Rebel King (90)** (MABarnes) **7-10-4**(5) STaylor (mstkes: chsd ldrs tl outpcd fr 10th)	24	**6**	14/1	59	—
1970* **Montrave (99)** (PMonteith) **8-11-4** ADobbin (led: rdn & disp ld whn fell 3 out)		**F**	5/2[2]	—	—
			(SP 113.0%)	**7 Rn**	

5m 7.0 (11.00) CSF £15.91 TOTE £5.00: £2.60 £1.90 (£10.60) OWNER Mr & Mrs Raymond Anderson Green (LOCKERBIE)
2179 Wayuphill found everything going her way and did it well. (5/1)
1970 Puritan (CAN) looks a moody customer. He needed some strong riding to get him into contention in the straight, but it then quickly proved beyond him. (9/4)
1525 Val de Rama (IRE), having his first outing for seven weeks, showed up well until blowing up five out. (8/1)
1823 Grand Scenery (IRE), a law unto himself, almost got into it on the home turn but, soon ridden, showed his true colours. (7/1)
1972 Rapid Mover was not in a going mood and dropped out. (14/1)

2509 WHITEWATER NOVICES' H'CAP HURDLE (0-100) (4-Y.O+) (Class E)

3-45 (3-48) **2m 4f (12 hdls)** £2,637.00 (£732.00: £351.00) GOING minus 0.13 sec per fur (G)

			SP	RR	SF
Kalisko (FR) (77) (RAllan) **7-10-4**(7) SMelrose (hdwy 8th: led 2 out: r.o wl)	—	**1**	16/1	59	22
1703* **Flyaway Blues (89)** (MrsMReveley) **5-11-9** PNiven (hld up & bhd: hdwy ½-wy: chsng wnr appr last: rdn & no imp)	2½	**2**	5/1[2]	69	32
1848[5] **Mr Christie (77)** (MissLCSiddall) **5-10-11** AThornton (outpcd & lost tch ½-wy: hdwy 2 out: styd on wl)	1	**3**	25/1	56	19
1848* **Court Joker (IRE) (83)** (HAlexander) **5-11-3** BStorey (in tch: effrt 4 out: btn 2 out)	20	**4**	10/1	46	9
2003[P] **Anchorena (73)** (DWBarker) **5-10-7** RJohnson (mid div: effrt ½-wy: styd on fr 2 out: nvr rchd ldrs)	hd	**5**	12/1	36	—
2060[2] **What Jim Wants (IRE) (86)** (JJO'Neill) **4-10-2**(5) RMcGrath (chsd ldrs tl outpcd fr 7th)	1½	**6**	6/1[3]	48	—
1807[3] **Dont Forget Curtis (IRE) (84)** (GMMoore) **5-11-4** JCallaghan (in tch tl rdn & btn appr 2 out)	hd	**7**	7/1	46	9
1700[4] **Alwarqa (81)** (MDHammond) **4-10-2** DBentley (hld up: effrt ½-wy: btn whn blnd 2 out)	1¼	**8**	100/30[1]	27	—
1825[3] **Kings Minstral (IRE) (73)** (DALamb) **7-10-7** JBurke (led: hit 7th & 4 out: hdd & wknd after 3 out)	9	**9**	14/1	27	—
2177[6] **Canaan Valley (83)** (DRobertson) **9-11-3** FPerratt (plld hrd: cl up tl wknd fr 8th)	2	**10**	20/1	35	—
1942[7] **Stylish Interval (90)** (NWaggott) **5-11-10** APMcCoy (chsd ldrs: led after 3 out tl hdd next: wknd)	1¼	**11**	20/1	51	14
1310[5] **Millies Image (66)** (FPMurtagh) **6-10-0** ADobbin (lost tch 7th)	6	**12**	100/1	13	—
1988* **Fryup Satellite (82)** (MrsJBrown) **6-10-13**(3) ECallaghan (lw: hld up: effrt ½-wy: hdwy u.p 3 out: sn btn)	8	**13**	12/1	—	—
1840[P] **Difficult Decision (IRE) (80)** (MrsMerritaJones) **6-11-0** CO'Dwyer (trckd ldrs: blnd 4 out: sn wknd & eased)	6	**14**	10/1	—	—
1672[4] **More Champagne (66)** (MrsDThomson) **7-10-0** GCahill (bhd fr ½-wy: p.u bef 4 out)		**P**	14/1	—	—
			(SP 133.7%)	**15 Rn**	

4m 49.5 (7.50) CSF £95.97 CT £1,896.49 TOTE £54.00: £13.60 £2.90 £6.20 (£339.50) Trio £147.00 OWNER Miss Louise Davis (CORNHILL-ON-TWEED) BRED Haras de Coudraies in France
LONG HANDICAP Millies Image 9-13 More Champagne 9-11
WEIGHT FOR AGE 4yo-13lb
STEWARDS' ENQUIRY J Callaghan susp. 20-23/1/97 (careless riding).
Kalisko (FR), who has changed stables yet again, won this in most emphatic style. (16/1)
1703* Flyaway Blues, given a most patient ride, had his chance going to the last, but failed to respond when seriously ridden. (5/1)
1848 Mr Christie has ability, but only runs when in the mood and, despite staying on here, it was always too late. (25/1)
1848* Court Joker (IRE) won a poor race last time and had his limitations exposed here. (10/1)
528* Anchorena showed her first signs of form for her new stable. (12/1)
2060 What Jim Wants (IRE) found this ground too fast. (6/1)

T/Plpt: £32.10 (425.79 Tckts). T/Qdpt: £8.40 (189.85 Tckts). AA

1974-**SOUTHWELL** (L-H) (Standard)

Friday January 10th

Other races under Rules of Flat Racing
WEATHER: overcast WIND: almost nil

2510 LEVY BOARD STANDARD OPEN N.H. FLAT RACE (4,5,6 & 7-Y.O) (Class H)

12-55 (12-57) **2m** £1,318.50 (£366.00: £175.50)

				SP	RR	SF
	Edge Ahead (IRE) (TThomsonJones) **7-11-4** MAFitzgerald (hld up: effrt 4f out: styd on wl u.p to ld wl ins fnl f)	—	**1**	12/1	72 f	—
	In The Van (MrsDHaine) **5-11-4** JFTitley (hdwy ½-wy: drvn along 4f out: led 1f out tl nr fin)	1	**2**	9/2^{2}	71 f	—
2066^{2}	**Meadow Hymn (IRE)** (JGFitzGerald) **6-11-4** WDwan (lw: trckd ldrs: ev ch over 1f out: nt qckn)	1½	**3**	6/1^{3}	70 f	—
1820*	**Mrs Em** (PFNicholls) **5-11-4**(5) OBurrows (lw: trckd ldrs: led over 3f out to 1f out: kpt on one pce)	2½	**4**	9/2^{2}	72 f	—
2066*	**Slide On** (PDEvans) **7-11-11** GaryLyons (hld up: hdwy ½-wy: sn chsng ldrs: rdn & n.m.r 2f out: one pce)	2	**5**	11/4^{1}	72 f	—
	Fern Leader (IRE) (MrsASwinbank) **7-11-4** JSupple (bit bkwd: in tch: drvn along over 4f out: one pce fnl 3f)	2½	**6**	10/1	63 f	—
	Cyber King (RDEWoodhouse) **4-10-6** NWilliamson (plld hrd: trckd ldrs: chal over 3f out: wknd over 1f out)	2½	**7**	20/1	60 f	—
	Super Saffron (BSmart) **7-10-13** CLlewellyn (trckd ldrs: led over 5f out tl over 3f out: wknd)	16	**8**	10/1	39 f	—
	Lost In The Post (IRE) (CWThornton) **4-9-13**(7) NHorrocks (bit bkwd: chsd ldrs: ev ch tl wknd over 2f out)	6	**9**	6/1^{3}	38 f	—
	Moon Devil (IRE) (MarkCampion) **7-11-4** MRichards (lw: led tl over 5f out: sn lost pl: t.o)	dist	**10**	10/1	—	—
	Port Valenska (IRE) (JLHarris) **4-10-6** DGallagher (bkwd: drvn along 7f out: t.o 5f out)	15	**11**	40/1	—	—
	Silver Gull (IRE) (HSHowe) **6-11-4** GTormey (t.o 6f out)	nk	**12**	40/1	—	—
	Hyperion Lad (TTBill) **5-11-4** JRailton (chsd ldrs tl lost pl 5f out: sn t.o)	dist	**13**	33/1	—	—
	Rush Me Not (IRE) (SWCampion) **4-10-1**(5) MichaelBrennan (t.o 6f out)	9	**14**	40/1	—	—
	Ifafa Beach (IRE) (JNorton) **5-10-13**(5) DJKavanagh (sn wl bhd: reminders & t.o ½-wy)	9	**15**	16/1	—	—
	Gymcrak Pharoah (GHolmes) **4-10-6** AMaguire (prom to ½-wy: t.o 5f out)	2½	**16**	16/1	—	—

(SP 153.4%) **16 Rn**

3m 56.8 CSF £75.85 TOTE £23.30: £4.90 £2.10 £3.00 (£44.20) Trio £99.30; £114.72 to Leopardstown 11/1/97 OWNER Mrs Carol Edge (UPPER LAMBOURN) BRED F. Latham
WEIGHT FOR AGE 4yo-12lb

Edge Ahead (IRE), who is very stoutly-bred, stuck on under pressure to show ahead near the line. Over hurdles, he will need every inch of two and a half miles. (12/1)

In The Van, a tall, chasing type, stuck on under pressure to show ahead a furlong out, but was outstayed near the line. He stays alright but looks one-paced. (9/2: 2/1-5/1)

2066 Meadow Hymn (IRE) ran another sound race. (6/1)

1820* Mrs Em took it up traveling strongly but, under a double-penalty, could find no more when headed a furlong out. (9/2: op 2/1)

2066* Slide On, on his toes beforehand, was under pressure and only staying on at one pace in the final quarter-mile. (11/4)

Fern Leader (IRE), winner of three of his four starts in points, looked in need of the outing. Over hurdles, he will need two and a half miles. (10/1)

Cyber King, a narrow type, would not settle, but gave a good account of himself until tiring approaching the final furlong. (20/1)

T/Jkpt: Not won; £23,409.76 to Wolverhampton 11/1/97. T/Plpt: £282.00 (46.53 Tckts). T/Qdpt: £32.20 (42.3 Tckts). WG

2497-**ASCOT (R-H) - Saturday January 11th**

2511 Abandoned-Frozen ground

2213-**NEWCASTLE (L-H) - Saturday January 11th**

2517 Abandoned-Frost

2411-**WARWICK (L-H) - Saturday January 11th**

2524 Abandoned-Frost

2253-**FONTWELL (Fig. 8) - Monday January 13th**

2532 Abandoned-Frost

2219-**CARLISLE** (R-H) (Good, Good to firm patches)

Tuesday January 14th

WEATHER: fine

2539 SEAN GRAHAM NOVICES' HURDLE (I) (4-Y.O+) (Class E)

12-30 (12-31) **2m 1f (9 hdls)** £2,108.00 (£588.00: £284.00) GOING: 0.13 sec per fur (G)

				SP	RR	SF
	Quango (JGFitzGerald) **5-11-5** PCarberry (hld up: hdwy on bit to ld 2 out: easily)	—	**1**	4/1^{3}	79+	—
	Cumbrian Maestro (TDEasterby) **4-10-7** RGarritty (lw: a.p: ev ch 3 out: styd on: nt pce of wnr)	3	**2**	11/4^{2}	76	—
	Butterwick King (IRE) (RAFahey) **5-11-5** PNiven (hld up & bhd: hdwy appr 3 out: sn prom: one pce appr last)	1½	**3**	14/1	75	—
1689^{P}	**Clavering (IRE)** (HowardJohnson) **7-11-5** ADobbin (trckd ldrs: led 4 out to 2 out: sn outpcd)	4	**4**	5/2^{1}	71	—
1692^{15}	**Political Millstar** (RNixon) **5-11-5** BStorey (bhd tl styd on fr 3 out)	1¾	**5**	50/1	69	—
	Gaelic Charm (IRE) (JIACharlton) **9-11-0** KJohnson (bit bkwd: chsd ldrs: effrt appr 3 out: sn outpcd)	4	**6**	33/1	61	—
1921^{6}	**Ten Past Six** (MartynWane) **5-11-5** ASSmith (w ldrs tl wknd 3 out)	1¼	**7**	12/1	64	—
1999^{4}	**Don't Tell Tom (IRE) (75)** (JWade) **7-11-5** KJones (led tl after 1st: chsd ldrs tl wknd fr 4 out)	3½	**8**	11/1	61	—
2047^{13}	**Alan's Pride (IRE)** (WMcKeown) **6-11-0** GCahill (dwlt: hdwy to ld after 1st: hdd 4 out: wknd next)	6	**9**	20/1	51	—
1652^{20}	**Hobbs Choice** (GMMoore) **4-10-9** NBentley (bhd: effrt 5th: sn wknd)	2½	**10**	14/1	55	—
	Meadow Bee (WGReed) **5-11-5** TReed (bkwd: t.o fr 5th)	dist	**11**	100/1	—	—

				SP	RR	SF
	Martha Buckle (JSGoldie) **8-10-11**(3) GLee (stdd s: a bhd: t.o)	½	**12**	66/1	—	—
	Jock (MissSWilliamson) **5-10-12**(7) ATodd (bkwd: t.o whn p.u bef 3 out)		**P**	50/1	—	—
	Hiltons Travel (IRE) (EJAlston) **6-11-5** MFoster (mstkes: t.o whn p.u bef 4 out)		**P**	50/1	—	—
				(SP 120.7%)	**14 Rn**	

4m 19.3 (18.30) CSF £14.58 TOTE £3.80: £1.90 £2.00 £5.40 (£12.00) Trio £106.40 OWNER Mr L. Milligan (MALTON) BRED Lord Fairhaven
WEIGHT FOR AGE 4yo-12lb

Quango, a useful performer on the level two years ago, put off many would-be supporters by getting warm in the paddock. His performance in the race was a delight and, given a super ride, he won as he pleased. (4/1: op 7/4)
Cumbrian Maestro, a long way behind the winner on their best Flat form, looked quite handy at this game and showed enough to suggest that a race or two can be found. (11/4)
Butterwick King (IRE), well supported in a bumper last year, was having his first run since and showed enough promise to give hope for the future. (14/1)
Clavering (IRE) put his poor run six weeks ago behind him here, and this should have put him straight. (5/2)
Political Millstar was staying on well, suggesting that longer trips will bring out the best in him. (50/1)
Gaelic Charm (IRE) ran well on this track until being brought down last season and, needing this, again showed ability. (33/1)

2540 SEAN GRAHAM NOVICES' CHASE (5-Y.O+) (Class D)

1-00 (1-01) **3m** **(18 fncs)** £3,842.50 (£1,165.00: £570.00: £272.50) GOING: 0.13 sec per fur (G)

				SP	RR	SF
1845F	**Choisty (IRE) (92)** (MrsASwinbank) **7-11-3** JSupple (lw: a cl up: mstke 10th: disp ld 2 out: styd on wl flat)	—	**1**	9/2[2]	100	6
	Brandy Cross (IRE) (HowardJohnson) **8-11-3** PCarberry (lw: j.w: led fr 4th tl disp ld 2 out: nt qckn flat)	2½	**2**	6/1	98	4
1579[2]	**For Cathal (IRE)** (MrsMReveley) **6-11-3** PNiven (lw: hld up: wnt prom 11th: rdn to chal 2 out: no ex flat)	1½	**3**	2/1[1]	97	3
1850F	**Mamica (80)** (MDods) **7-11-3** NSmith (bhd: blnd 9th: hdwy 12th: styd on: nvr able to chal)	12	**4**	9/1	89	—
1981P	**Naughty Future** (JJO'Neill) **8-11-9** ARoche (chsd ldrs: j.slowly 2nd: one pce fr 4 out)	12	**5**	11/2[3]	87	—
1778F	**Cool Weather (IRE) (78)** (PCheesbrough) **9-11-3b** ASSmith (chsd ldrs: btn whn blnd bdly 2 out)	11	**6**	12/1	74	—
1246[6]	**Deise Marshall (IRE) (76)** (JWade) **9-11-3** BStorey (prom tl lost pl & blnd 10th: n.d after)	¾	**7**	25/1	74	—
2045[6]	**Mr Sloan** (JSGoldie) **7-11-0**(3) GLee (mstkes & bhd: n.d)	17	**8**	100/1	62	—
1944[3]	**Rathfardon (IRE)** (FMurphy) **9-10-10**(7) MrTJBarry (outpcd fr 12th: blnd 4 out)	½	**9**	25/1	62	—
1989[4]	**Clonroche Lucky (IRE)** (JWade) **7-11-3** KJones (a bhd)	1¼	**10**	100/1	61	—
938[2]	**Woodford Gale (IRE) (83)** (MissLucindaRussell) **7-11-3** AThornton (chsd ldrs: drvn along fr 12th: wknd next)	1½	**11**	14/1	60	—
1713[2]	**Dry Hill Lad** (JNorton) **6-11-3** WFry (fell 1st)		**F**	14/1	—	—
1944[4]	**Pantara Prince (IRE)** (JIACharlton) **8-11-3** ADobbin (lost tch 11th: t.o whn p.u bef 4 out)		**P**	20/1	—	—
2043[4]	**Royal Surprise (75)** (WGReed) **10-11-3b** TReed (led tl blnd & hdd 4th: rdn 10th: sn lost pl: p.u bef last)		**P**	33/1	—	—
	Wild Game (IRE) (MissSWilliamson) **6-10-10**(7) ATodd (bit bkwd: mstkes: t.o whn p.u after 10th)		**P**	100/1	—	—
				(SP 130.6%)	**15 Rn**	

6m 15.2 (23.20) CSF £32.11 TOTE £7.90: £2.90 £3.20 £2.10 (£28.50) Trio £14.20 OWNER Hotel Brokers International (RICHMOND) BRED Mrs Nancy Doyle

1845 Choisty (IRE), suited by this galloping track, jumped much better and proved a tough sort when the pressure was on. (9/2)
Brandy Cross (IRE) won plenty of point-to-points in Ireland, and looked a useful recruit to this game after a year off. He should find suitable opportunities. (6/1)
1579 For Cathal (IRE) took the eye in the paddock, and ran a useful race, only to get outbattled late on. Better now looks likely. (2/1)
1574 Mamica made one particularly bad blunder and then ran well, coming from way behind to be nearest at the finish. (9/1)
1632 Naughty Future backed off one fence in particular early on, but then ran reasonably. This should have done his confidence some good. (11/2)
1778 Cool Weather (IRE) ran a fine race, but his measure had been taken when he almost fell two out. (12/1)

2541 SEAN GRAHAM NOVICES' HURDLE (II) (4-Y.O+) (Class E)

1-30 (1-37) **2m 1f** **(9 hdls)** £2,122.00 (£592.00: £286.00) GOING: 0.13 sec per fur (G)

				SP	RR	SF
1921[4]	**Endowment (105)** (MrsMReveley) **5-11-12b** PNiven (lw: mde most: hit 4 out: lft clr 3 out: drvn out: sddle slipped)	—	**1**	3/1[2]	81	24
1689[7]	**Lostris (IRE)** (MDods) **6-11-0** BStorey (in tch: styd on fr 2 out: nt pce to chal)	5	**2**	16/1	64	7
	Barefoot Landing (USA) (CParker) **6-11-0** DParker (hld up & bhd: stdy hdwy 4 out: nvr plcd to chal)	14	**3**	50/1	51	—
2060[6]	**Mr Gold (IRE)** (JMJefferson) **4-10-4**(3) ECallaghan (slt ld 2nd to 4th: grad wknd fr 3 out)	3	**4**	33/1	53	—
1345[6]	**Golf Land (IRE)** (LLungo) **5-11-5** AThornton (mstkes: chsd ldrs: one pce fr 4 out)	18	**5**	16/1	36	—
1992F	**Jarrow (65)** (MrsAMNaughton) **6-11-5** MFoster (in tch tl outpcd fr ½-wy)	15	**6**	200/1	22	—
	Tsanga (GMMoore) **5-11-5** NBentley (a in rr)	2	**7**	33/1	20	—
1524[8]	**Coquet Gold (60)** (FTWalton) **6-11-0** KJohnson (bhd & rdn ½-wy: t.o)	dist	**8**	200/1	—	—
2047[18]	**Montein** (SJLeadbetter) **6-11-5** NLeach (bit bkwd: blnd 1st: a bhd: t.o)	3	**9**	200/1	—	—
1940*	**Son of Anshan** (MrsASwinbank) **4-11-0** JSupple (lw: chsd ldrs: 2nd & rdn whn fell 3 out)		**F**	Evens[1]	—	—
1687[12]	**Hawk Hill Boy** (FPMurtagh) **6-11-5** ADobbin (t.o fr 4th: p.u bef 3 out)		**P**	100/1	—	—
2041*	**Qattara (IRE) (100)** (WMcKeown) **7-11-12** GCahill (in tch: effrt & mstke 4 out: 2nd & styng on whn broke leg & p.u after 2 out: dead)		**P**	7/2[3]	—	—
	Spectre Brown (FJestin) **7-11-5** TReed (Withdrawn not under Starter's orders: v.unruly & uns rdr twice)		**W**	100/1	—	—
	Shirley's Time (MrsJBrown) **6-11-5** PCarberry (Withdrawn not under Starter's orders: bolted gng to s)		**W**	50/1	—	—
				(SP 122.3%)	**12 Rn**	

4m 14.6 (13.60) CSF £45.48 TOTE £4.20: £1.40 £2.10 £5.00 (£45.40) Trio £200.10 OWNER Mr R. Hilley (SALTBURN) BRED Bloomsbury Stud
WEIGHT FOR AGE 4yo-12lb

1921 Endowment had the blinkers, which seem a must, back on. Everything went his way and he was always just doing enough under pressure. (3/1)
1689 Lostris (IRE), a real stayer, kept on well over the last three flights, but just lacked a change of gear to get to the winner. (16/1)
Barefoot Landing (USA), given a lot to do, was noted finishing well, and this should have taught her plenty. (50/1)
Mr Gold (IRE) raced a bit too freely, but still ran well until blowing up from three out. (33/1)
1345 Golf Land (IRE) jumped sloppily and failed to make any serious impression. (16/1)
1940* Son of Anshan proved disappointing, as he was struggling in second place when falling heavily three out. (Evens)
2041* Qattara (IRE) had just gone into second and looked dangerous when he broke a leg two out. (7/2)

2542 SEAN GRAHAM H'CAP CHASE (0-140) (5-Y.O+) (Class B)

2-00 (2-03) **3m (18 fncs)** £6,963.50 (£2,108.00: £1,029.00: £489.50) GOING: 0.13 sec per fur (G)

				SP	RR	SF
1941*	**Stormy Coral (IRE) (103)** (CParker) **7-10-7** BStorey (hld up: jnd ldr 13th: led 4 out: j.lft last 3: hdd flat: r.o wl to ld towards fin)	—	1	13/8[1]	117	6
1806[2]	**Ali's Alibi (114)** (MrsMReveley) **10-11-4** PNiven (a.p: blnd 11th: disp ld 3 out: led flat: hdd & nt qckn towards fin)	2	2	3/1[2]	127	16
1670[5]	**Aly Daley (IRE) (103)** (HowardJohnson) **9-10-7** ADobbin (mde most tl hdd 4 out: outpcd fr 2 out)	13	3	7/1	107	—
1799[P]	**Ubu Val (FR) (120)** (WABethell) **11-11-10** ASSmith (lw: lost pl 7th: hdwy & prom 11th: wknd 13th: hmpd 4 out)	8	4	4/1[3]	119	8
1983*	**Pennine Pride (96)** (MDHammond) **10-9-11v**(3) MrCBonner (w ldr: outpcd fr 10th: wknd 14th: 4th & btn whn fell 4 out)		F	4/1[3]	—	—

(SP 115.6%) **5 Rn**

6m 12.1 (20.10) CSF £6.90 TOTE £2.60: £1.40 £1.90 (£3.00) OWNER Mr & Mrs Raymond Anderson Green (LOCKERBIE) BRED R. J. McKnight

1941* Stormy Coral (IRE), who wears a pricker on his near-side, did this really well on ground certainly fast enough. (13/8)
1806 Ali's Alibi put in another sound run but, despite a valiant effort, was tapped for speed late on. He deserves a change of luck. (3/1)
1307 Aly Daley (IRE), back to form here after six weeks off, should continue to pay his way. (7/1)
1293 Ubu Val (FR) looked a moody customer and was going nowhere when being hampered four out. (4/1)
1983* Pennine Pride found this ground too fast and, although still within sight of the leaders, was going nowhere when falling four out. (4/1)

2543 SEAN GRAHAM H'CAP HURDLE (0-135) (5-Y.O+) (Class C)

2-30 (2-32) **2m 1f (9 hdls)** £3,420.00 (£1,035.00: £505.00: £240.00) GOING: 0.13 sec per fur (G)

				SP	RR	SF
	Rallegio (94) (PMonteith) **8-10-0** ADobbin (prom: rdn 3 out: styd on to ld appr last: kpt on wl flat)	—	1	10/1	79	8
1658[6]	**Cittadino (98)** (CWThornton) **7-10-4** MFoster (bhd: hdwy 3 out: sn chsng ldrs & rdn: kpt on u.p flat)	3½	2	10/1	80	9
2062[2]	**New Inn (118)** (SGollings) **6-11-5**(5) MichaelBrennan (lw: led tl hdd appr last: no ex)	1	3	4/1[3]	99	28
2062*	**Shining Edge (114)** (TDEasterby) **5-11-6** RGarritty (lw: trckd ldrs: effrt 3 out: rdn & btn appr last)	2	4	11/4[1]	93	22
1988[2]	**Duke of Perth (94)** (HowardJohnson) **6-10-0** PCarberry (chsd ldrs tl wknd appr last)	6	5	7/1	67	—
1163[5]	**Once More for Luck (IRE) (112)** (MrsMReveley) **6-11-4** PNiven (in tch: mstke 3rd: effrt 3 out: outpcd fr ext)	7	6	15/2	79	8
1846[F]	**Bolaney Girl (IRE) (94)** (FPMurtagh) **8-10-0** ARoche (hld up & bhd: n.d)	9	7	33/1	52	—
1852[2]	**Anabranch (110)** (JMJefferson) **6-10-9**(7) MNewton (a.p: ev ch 4 out: wknd appr 2 out: wl btn whn blnd & uns rdr last)		U	3/1[2]	—	—

(SP 117.1%) **8 Rn**

4m 12.6 (11.60) CSF £91.23 CT £428.12 TOTE £15.80: £2.80 £2.70 £1.30 (£85.10) OWNER Mr Guthrie Robertson (ROSEWELL) BRED Mrs Florence C. McCaw

LONG HANDICAP Rallegio 9-13 Bolaney Girl (IRE) 9-5 Duke of Perth 9-12

Rallegio, from a yard bang in form, responded to some strong driving in splendid style and won authoritatively. (10/1)
1658 Cittadino kept staying on to suggest that he is now getting his act together. (10/1)
2062 New Inn, on the fast ground he loves, put up a gallant attempt to make all, but the weight just anchored him late on. (4/1)
2062* Shining Edge had his chances, but the struggle this time proved beyond him. (11/4)
1988 Duke of Perth, from a yard that is showing signs of coming back to form, ran well until stopping going to the last. (7/1)
1163 Once More for Luck (IRE) likes things to go his way and they never did here. (15/2)

2544 SEAN GRAHAM BOOKMAKERS H'CAP CHASE (0-120) (5-Y.O+) (Class D)

3-00 (3-01) **2m 4f 110y (16 fncs)** £3,566.25 (£1,080.00: £527.50: £251.25) GOING: 0.13 sec per fur (G)

				SP	RR	SF
1506[4]	**Random Harvest (IRE) (93)** (MrsMReveley) **8-10-11** PNiven (in tch: hdwy to ld 7th: r.o wl fr 2 out: eased flat)	—	1	Evens[1]	105+	47
1657[8]	**Rustic Air (104)** (JGFitzGerald) **10-11-8** PCarberry (hdwy on ins whn hmpd bnd after 8th: sn cl up: one pce fr 2 out)	6	2	9/1	111	53
	Russian Castle (IRE) (105) (JWade) **8-11-9** KJones (led to 7th: outpcd & lost pl fr 10th: styd on u.p fr 2 out)	6	3	16/1	108	50
2046[3]	**Road by the River (IRE) (96)** (PCheesbrough) **9-11-0** ASSmith (a chsng ldrs: wknd fr 2 out)	3½	4	9/1	96	38
1831[3]	**Jymjam Johnny (IRE) (99)** (JJO'Neill) **8-10-12**(5) RMcGrath (hld up & bhd: blnd 10th: hdwy next: rdn & no imp fr 3 out)	3½	5	8/1[3]	96	38
1578[11]	**Super Sandy (83)** (FTWalton) **10-10-1** KJohnson (bhd tl sme late hdwy)	1¾	6	33/1	79	21
1985[4]	**Solba (USA) (109)** (CParker) **8-11-13** BStorey (mstkes: nvr trbld ldrs)	nk	7	6/1[2]	105	47
	Popeshall (110) (MissSWilliamson) **10-11-7**(7) ATodd (bit bkwd: chsd ldrs tl lost pl 10th: hdwy appr 4 out: wknd 2 out)	3½	8	20/1	103	45
1831[4]	**Another Venture (IRE) (90)** (FMurphy) **7-10-8** RGarritty (lost tch fr 9th: p.u bef 2 out)		P	12/1	—	—

(SP 116.7%) **9 Rn**

5m 9.2 (6.20) CSF £10.46 CT £85.86 TOTE £1.70: £1.10 £1.80 £3.80 (£10.00) Trio £35.70 OWNER Mr C. C. Buckley (SALTBURN) BRED T. N. Tanner

1506 Random Harvest (IRE) made no mistake this time and won in useful style. This should have boosted his confidence a great deal. (Evens)
1657 Rustic Air ran his best race of the season and would seem to be coming to hand. (9/1)
Russian Castle (IRE) found this trip too sharp and, after getting well outpaced, was picking up in good style at the finish. (16/1)
2046 Road by the River (IRE) keeps running well and gave the impression that he should be all the better for this. (9/1)
1831 Jymjam Johnny (IRE) needs things to go just right, and was always finding the struggle too much on this occasion. (8/1)
1295 Super Sandy has only ever won at Hexham over the minimum trip on testing ground and, in the circumstances, this was a fair effort. (33/1)
1985 Solba (USA) seems to have lost his confidence at his fences for the time being, and was never able to get into the race here. (6/1)
Popeshall, needing this, did not run too badly. (20/1)

2545 SEAN GRAHAM BOOKMAKERS H'CAP HURDLE (0-125) (4-Y.O+) (Class D)

3-30 (3-30) **2m 4f 110y (11 hdls)** £2,997.00 (£842.00: £411.00) GOING: 0.13 sec per fur (G)

				SP	RR	SF
1945*	**Livio (USA) (115)** (PMonteith) **6-11-8** ADobbin (lw: trckd ldrs tl blnd 6th: hdwy & mstke 4 out: rdn to ld 2 out: r.o wl: eased towards fin)	—	1	13/8[1]	99+	37
1906[U]	**Lochnagrain (IRE) (121)** (MrsMReveley) **9-12-0** PNiven (lw: hld up: hdwy 4 out: styd on wl fr 2 out: nrst fin)	2½	2	4/1[2]	103	41
2049[F]	**Thursday Night (IRE) (108)** (JGFitzGerald) **6-11-1** PCarberry (trckd ldrs: effrt 3 out: kpt on: nt pce to chal)	5	3	7/1[3]	86	24

2178* **Trump (115)** (CParker) **8-11-8** DParker (lw: a chsng ldrs: ev ch 3 out: one pce fr next)....nk **4** 8/1 93 31
1671[5] **Nicholas Plant (93)** (JSGoldie) **8-9-11**(3) GLee (hld up: hdwy to ld 3 out: hdd next: wknd last)....4 **5** 14/1 68 6
1945[8] **Glenugie (100)** (GMMoore) **6-10-7** NBentley (a.p: ev ch 3 out: sn wknd)....18 **6** 20/1 61 —
1701[8] **Danbys Gorse (93)** (JMJefferson) **5-9-7**(7) MNewton (hld up: sme hdwy u.p 3 out: n.d)....2 **7** 33/1 52 —
Old Habits (IRE) (108) (JLEyre) **8-11-1** BStorey (bit bkwd: w ldr: led 6th to 7th: ev ch tl wknd fr 3 out)....1 **8** 14/1 66 4
1988F **Sudden Spin (100)** (JNorton) **7-10-4**(3) ECallaghan (lost tch 6th: n.d after)....14 **9** 8/1 48 —
Farney Glen (95) (JJO'Neill) **10-9-11**(5) RMcGrath (bit bkwd: in tch tl outpcd fr 4 out)....11 **10** 66/1 34 —
Peep O Day (100) (JLEyre) **6-10-7** AThornton (mde most tl hdd & wknd qckly 3 out)....24 **11** 14/1 20 —
Johnny Kelly (110) (JMCarr) **10-11-0**(3) FLeahy (bit bkwd: sn bhd: p.u bef 2 out).... **P** 50/1 — —
(SP 124.0%) **12 Rn**

5m 2.7 (11.70) CSF £8.86 CT £35.17 TOTE £2.80: £1.30 £1.50 £2.60 (£4.20) Trio £14.60 OWNER The Low Flyers (Thoroughbreds) Ltd (ROSEWELL) BRED Darley Stud Management Co Ltd
LONG HANDICAP Danbys Gorse 9-7 Nicholas Plant 9-13
1945* Livio (USA) won well despite a couple of mistakes, and still seems to be improving. (13/8)
1906 Lochnagrain (IRE) is in tremendous heart at present, and ran a super race here without being given too hard a time. (4/1)
1780 Thursday Night (IRE), after falling twice over fences, had a nice run here. This should have done him no end of good. (7/1)
2178* Trump ran well, but was short of toe when the pressure was on over the last three flights. (8/1)
1671 Nicholas Plant, ridden with restraint for a change, put up a reasonable effort after six weeks off. (14/1)
Glenugie is taking time to find his form this season, but there were slight signs of encouragement here. (20/1)
Danbys Gorse, on ground much faster than he would really like, never got into it, but should benefit as a result. (33/1)
Old Habits (IRE) had a really good blow until weakening three out. (14/1)

T/Jkpt: £20,933.60 (3.13 Tckts). T/Plpt: £158.50 (81.6 Tckts). T/Qdpt: £36.00 (26.89 Tckts). AA

2424-LEICESTER (R-H) (Chases Good to firm, Good patches, Hdles Good to soft, Good patches)
Tuesday January 14th

Race 3: one fence omitted
WEATHER: fine & dry

2546 LYRIC NOVICES' HURDLE (I) (5-Y.O+) (Class E)
12-40 (12-40) **3m (13 hdls)** £2,018.50 (£566.00: £275.50) GOING: 0.11 sec per fur (G)

SP RR SF
1810[2] **Korbell (IRE)** (PFNicholls) **8-10-7** APMcCoy (a.p: pushed along ½-wy: chal 3 out: led appr last: all out)....— **1** 11/4[2] 77 19
1507[2] **Flying Gunner (110)** (DNicholson) **6-11-4** AMaguire (a.p: rdn & outpcd 3 out: chal & hit last: rallied u.p cl home)....nk **2** 11/2[3] 88 30
1654[2] **Hand Woven (123)** (NATwiston-Davies) **5-11-4** CLlewellyn (lw: led tl appr last: rdn & one pce flat)....4 **3** 7/4[1] 85 27
1766[5] **Quini Eagle (FR)** (MCPipe) **5-10-12** CMaude (a.p: rdn 2 out: sn btn)....10 **4** 16/1 73 15
Music Master (IRE) (CREgerton) **7-10-12** JOsborne (bkwd: hld up: hdwy 7th: btn whn mstke 3 out)....5 **5** 33/1 69 11
1854[3] **Adib (USA)** (GMMoore) **7-10-12** JCallaghan (nvr nr to chal)....10 **6** 16/1 63 5
1867[8] **Rossell Island (IRE)** (MrsJPitman) **6-10-12** WMarston (hld up: hdwy appr 7th: wknd 4 out)....6 **7** 14/1 59 1
1639[4] **Jobsagoodun** (NJHenderson) **6-10-12** MAFitzgerald (bit bkwd: hld up mid div: bhd fr 4 out)....5 **8** 7/1 55 —
1907[4] **Cypress Avenue (IRE)** (MrsVCWard) **5-10-12v1** JRKavanagh (prom to 6th: sn wknd)....3½ **9** 20/1 53 —
Sergent Kay (MrsCACoward) **7-10-9**(3) PMidgley (bkwd: a bhd: t.o)....8 **10** 100/1 48 —
1842* **Sutherland Moss (111)** (TPTate) **6-11-4** NWilliamson (swtg: hld up in tch: rdn 4 out: grad wknd: t.o)....1 **11** 12/1 53 —
1329[11] **Hills Gamble** (PJBevan) **7-10-12** WWorthington (bkwd: plld hrd: prom tl wknd appr 4 out: t.o)....1¾ **12** 50/1 46 —
1685[14] **Burfords For Scrap** (RDickin) **5-10-12** BPowell (lw: a bhd: t.o)....8 **13** 100/1 40 —
2038[7] **Nordic Flight (62)** (RJEckley) **9-10-7**(5) DJKavanagh (bkwd: a bhd: t.o)....¾ **14** 100/1 40 —
1959[11] **Becky's Girl (60)** (RBrotherton) **7-10-7** LHarvey (a bhd: mstke 8th: t.o)....dist **15** 100/1 — —
Sovereign Pass (RDEWoodhouse) **5-10-12** DGallagher (bkwd: plld hrd: lost pl 5th: t.o whn p.u bef 4 out).... **P** 100/1 — —
1124[17] **Kyle David (IRE)** (FJordan) **5-10-12** SWynne (bkwd: bhd & rdn 3rd: t.o whn ref 5th).... **R** 100/1 — —
(SP 132.6%) **17 Rn**

5m 55.6 (14.60) CSF £18.97 TOTE £3.10: £1.70 £2.70 £1.50 (£11.00) Trio £4.30 OWNER Mr K. J. Mitchell (SHEPTON MALLET) BRED Seamus Kennedy
1810 Korbell (IRE) found this extended trip ideal, but needed to pull out all the stops to hang on close home. (11/4)
1507 Flying Gunner, prone to making the odd mistake when the pressure is on, only just failed to concede 11lb to the winner, and he certainly lost no caste in defeat. (11/2)
1654 Hand Woven again attempted to gallop his rivals into the ground, but he was unable to get away and was easily outpointed on the run-in. (7/4: 5/4-2/1)
1766 Quini Eagle (FR) should have been in his element over this extended trip, but he was throwing out distress signals jumping the penultimate flight and his measure had been taken. (16/1)
Music Master (IRE), a fine stamp of a horse who has chaser written all over him, ran extremely well on this hurdling debut, but had already blown up when untidy at the third last. (33/1)
1854 Adib (USA) could have found the ground livelier than he cares for and was unable to get himself into the action, but he will find easier opportunities to open his account at this game. (16/1)
Rossell Island (IRE) (14/1: 10/1-16/1)
1639 Jobsagoodun, still with a bit left to work on having had an interrupted schedule, sat in behind the leaders to the end of the back straight and was not unduly punished when all chance had gone. A grand-looking individual, he could be anything when he is fully wound up. (7/1)

2547 PENWICK NOVICES' HURDLE (4-Y.O+) (Class E)
1-10 (1-10) **2m (9 hdls)** £2,725.50 (£768.00: £376.50) GOING: 0.11 sec per fur (G)

SP RR SF
2010[9] **Hoh Warrior (IRE)** (CPEBrooks) **6-11-11** GBradley (hld up: hdwy 6th: chal last: rdn to ld flat)....— **1** 6/1[3] 92 45
Avanti Express (IRE) (CREgerton) **7-11-5** JOsborne (hld up in tch: hdwy 5th: led appr 2 out tl flat: unable qckn)....1 **2** 11/1 85 38

	Horse		Dist	Pos	SP	RR	SF
18[4]	**Just Bruce (88)** (MrsEHHeath) **8-11-5** DGallagher (mde most tl hdd & wknd appr 2 out)		10	**3**	20/1	75	28
	Milford Sound (PJHobbs) **4-10-7** RJohnson (lw: hld up: hdwy 5th: one pce fr 2 out)		2½	**4**	10/1	73	14
1283[4]	**Silver Thyne (IRE)** (MrsJPitman) **5-11-5** WMarston (lw: plld hrd: prom: rdn appr 4 out: wknd appr 2 out)		2½	**5**	6/1[3]	70	23
1782*	**Tompetoo (IRE) (105)** (NATwiston-Davies) **6-11-11** CLlewellyn (chsd ldr: rdn appr 4 out: grad wknd)		1½	**6**	3/1[1]	75	28
	Morpheus (DNicholson) **8-11-5** AMaguire (swtg: hld up: hdwy 6th: wknd 3 out)		¾	**7**	10/1	68	21
1855[6]	**Fantasy Line** (PRWebber) **6-11-0** RBellamy (plld hrd: w ldrs to 4 out: sn wknd)		2½	**8**	16/1	60	13
1375[4]	**Laburnum Gold (IRE)** (MrsJPitman) **6-11-5** RFarrant (lw: nvr trbld ldrs)		¾	**9**	10/1	65	18
1665[3]	**Tristram's Image (NZ)** (NJHenderson) **6-11-5** MAFitzgerald (nvr plcd to chal)		5	**10**	10/1	60	13
1830[14]	**Cades Bay** (NATwiston-Davies) **6-11-5** DBridgwater (swtg: a in rr)		3	**11**	20/1	57	10
974[2]	**Todd (USA)** (AHHarvey) **6-11-5** JAMcCarthy (a bhd)		4	**12**	20/1	53	6
1071*	**Tidal Force (IRE)** (PJHobbs) **6-11-5** NWilliamson (a in rr)		3½	**13**	9/2[2]	49	2
	Cottesmore (MissAEEmbiricos) **6-11-5** JRKavanagh (bit bkwd: prom to ½-wy: sn wknd)		½	**14**	100/1	49	2
1180[6]	**Brown And Mild** (MissAEEmbiricos) **6-11-5** JRyan (w ldrs tl wknd appr 4 out)		3	**15**	66/1	46	—
1808[4]	**Royal Diversion (IRE)** (MCPipe) **4-10-2** APMcCoy (hld up: hdwy 4th: rdn & wknd appr 4 out: t.o)		1¾	**16**	8/1	39	—
1835[3]	**Mazirah** (RCurtis) **6-11-5** DMorris (bhd fr 4 out: t.o)		2½	**17**	20/1	41	—
1699[8]	**Gautby Henpecked** (GMMoore) **4-10-2** JCallaghan (bhd fr ½-wy: t.o)		23	**18**	50/1	13	—
	Serious Option (IRE) (RCurtis) **6-11-5** DWalsh (chsd ldrs to 5th: sn lost tch: t.o)		14	**19**	50/1	4	—
	Never Time (IRE) (MrsVAAconley) **5-11-0(5)** MrRThornton (mstke 1st: a bhd: t.o whn p.u bef last)			**P**	100/1	—	—

(SP 159.9%) **20 Rn**

3m 52.6 (7.60) CSF £82.66 TOTE £5.50: £1.90 £5.40 £16.10 (£27.60) Trio £55.80; £70.80 to Windsor 15/1/97 OWNER Mr D. F. Allport (LAMBOURN) BRED T. Horgan

WEIGHT FOR AGE 4yo-12lb

2010 Hoh Warrior (IRE), much happier back on this more suitable ground, won this readily. On his day he is more than a shade useful. (6/1)

Avanti Express (IRE), sure to strip fitter with this first outing in thirteen months under his belt, turned in a most impressive performance, and looks a ready-made winner. (11/1: 7/1-12/1)

18 Just Bruce, a free-running individual, hurdled fluently and forced the pace until lack of a recent run caught him out on the approach to the second last. He has struggled to find an opening in the past, but he has the ability, and his turn will come. (20/1)

Milford Sound, a mile winner on the Flat, was having his first outing for his new connections. He showed plenty of promise on this hurdling debut and should go on from here. (10/1)

1283 Silver Thyne (IRE) took a keen tug and sat closer to the pace this time, but he was hard at work soon after turning in and could do little to prevent the principals from pulling away. More patient tactics over a longer trip could be what he needs. (6/1)

1782* Tompetoo (IRE) travelled strongly, tucked in behind the leaders. Once he came off the bridle on the home turn though, he was soon in dire trouble, and his chance had gone. (3/1)

Morpheus, returning after a long absence from the racecourse, ran much better than his final placing suggests, and can only improve on this. (10/1)

1808 Royal Diversion (IRE) (8/1: 6/1-9/1)

2548 DANNY NOVICES' H'CAP CHASE (0-105) (5-Y.O+) (Class E)

1-40 (1-40) **2m 4f 110y (14 fncs)** £3,057.75 (£927.00: £453.50: £216.75) GOING minus 0.14 sec per fur (G)

	Horse	Dist	Pos	SP	RR	SF
1981[3]	**Garnwin (IRE) (95)** (NJHenderson) **7-11-4** MAFitzgerald (lw: led tl appr 4th: led 2 out: hrd rdn flat: r.o wl)	—	**1**	9/4[2]	101	3
1875[F]	**Nordic Valley (IRE) (86)** (MCPipe) **6-10-9** APMcCoy (lw: hld up: hdwy 8th: ev ch last: rdn & unable qckn flat)	¾	**2**	7/2[3]	91	—
2077[F]	**Ronans Glen (77)** (MJWilkinson) **10-10-0** RSupple (plld hrd: led appr 4th to 6th: one pce fr 2 out)	6	**3**	25/1	78	—
	Gipsy Rambler (77) (PJBevan) **12-10-0** WWorthington (bit bkwd: prom: ev ch 3 out: rdn & one pce appr last)	1½	**4**	50/1	77	—
1811[3]	**Haunting Music (IRE) (105)** (MrsAJPerrett) **9-12-0** CMaude (j.w: chsd ldr: led 6th to 3 out: rdn & wknd next)	3	**5**	2/1[1]	102	4
1465[4]	**River Red (77)** (KFrost) **11-10-0** PMcLoughlin (hld up: hdwy 7th: led 3 out to 2 out: rdn & wknd appr next)	10	**6**	25/1	66	—
1412[7]	**Smart Casanova (77)** (MJWilkinson) **8-10-0** ILawrence (lw: b.d 1st)		**B**	50/1	—	—
1944[7]	**Aslan (IRE) (95)** (JGFitzGerald) **9-11-4** NWilliamson (fell 1st: broke back: dead)		**F**	4/1	—	—

(SP 117.9%) **8 Rn**

5m 16.6 (15.60) CSF £10.52 CT £138.01 TOTE £3.40: £1.60 £1.70 £9.00 (£6.50) OWNER Pioneer Heat-Treatment (LAMBOURN) BRED John Kehoe

LONG HANDICAP Gipsy Rambler 8-11 River Red 9-11 Smart Casanova 8-11 Ronans Glen 9-9

OFFICIAL EXPLANATION Haunting Music (IRE): was later found to have been suffering from a virus.

1981 Garnwin (IRE) has now grasped what is required, and this first success over fences is only the beginning. (9/4)

1875 Nordic Valley (IRE) looked to be travelling best when joining issue at the last, but the winner had a bit more to give and had the legs of him in the duel to the line. (7/2: op 9/4)

Ronans Glen got left behind early in the straight, but this was a step up on recent outings this term and he is capable of picking up a chase. (25/1)

Gipsy Rambler performed with credit on this return to action after an extended break, and does look to have retained some ability. (50/1)

1811 Haunting Music (IRE) turned in a bold display of jumping, but he appeared to find the trip inadequate and was well outpaced when the battle to the finish really got under way. (2/1)

Aslan (IRE) (4/1: op 6/1)

2549 MADERIA QUEEN NOVICES' CHASE (5-Y.O+) (Class E)

2-10 (2-10) **2m 1f (12 fncs)** £3,126.50 (£879.00: £429.50) GOING minus 0.14 sec per fur (G)

	Horse	Dist	Pos	SP	RR	SF
1270[2]	**Amancio (USA) (119)** (MrsAJPerrett) **6-11-3** MAFitzgerald (lw: j.w: led 3rd: drew clr fr 4 out: eased)	—	**1**	1/2[1]	112+	19
1981[4]	**Decyborg (FR)** (MCPipe) **6-11-9** APMcCoy (led to 3rd: outpcd & rdn appr 3 out: sn bhd)	dist	**2**	7/4[2]	—	—
1309[P]	**Alicat (IRE)** (JWCurtis) **6-11-3** DerekByrne (bkwd: j.lft: mstke 1st: a t.o)	dist	**3**	50/1	—	—
1768[P]	**Mr Motivator** (TKeddy) **7-11-3** SMcNeill (fell 1st)		**F**	33/1[3]	—	—

(SP 107.9%) **4 Rn**

4m 18.7 (8.70) CSF £1.66 TOTE £1.40: (£1.20) OWNER Mr Paul Locke (PULBOROUGH) BRED Hill'N Dale Farm

1270 Amancio (USA) gives his fences plenty of air and, faced with nothing more than a solo school round, sauntered home at his leisure. (1/2)

1981 Decyborg (FR) did his best to keep tabs on the winner, but he found the task beyond him from the turn into the straight. (7/4)

2550 LYRIC NOVICES' HURDLE (II) (5-Y.O+) (Class E)

2-40 (2-40) **3m (13 hdls)** £2,018.50 (£566.00: £275.50) GOING: 0.11 sec per fur (G)

	Horse	Dist	Pos	SP	RR	SF
1854[2]	**Young Kenny (95)** (PBeaumont) **6-11-4** RSupple (chsd ldrs: rdn appr 4 out: mstke 3 out: chal & swtchd rt last: styd on to ld nr fin)	—	**1**	12/1[3]	103	20

				SP	RR	SF
	Montecot (FR) (SMellor) **8-10-12** NMann (lost pl 6th: hdwy 9th: ev ch last: rdn & r.o wl)	nk	**2**	12/1^{3}	97+	14
1964^{2}	**Destin d'Estruval (FR)** (DNicholson) **6-10-12** DBridgwater (hld up: stdy hdwy ½-wy: led 3 out: hrd rdn & ct nr fin)	hd	**3**	8/13^{1}	97	14
1768*	**Boots Madden (IRE) (104)** (MissVenetiaWilliams) **7-11-4** NWilliamson (hld up: hdwy & rdn appr 4 out: wknd next)	15	**4**	9/2^{2}	93	10
	Paris Fashion (FR) (NATwiston-Davies) **6-10-7** TJenks (bit bkwd: led to 3 out: wknd next)	5	**5**	14/1	78	—
1261^{3}	**Mendip Prince (IRE)** (PJHobbs) **7-10-12** AMaguire (bit bkwd: w ldr: rdn appr 9th: wknd appr 3 out)	13	**6**	14/1	75	—
1580^{3}	**Dark Challenger (IRE)** (MrsJPitman) **5-10-12** WMarston (a in rr)	3	**7**	16/1	73	—
1575^{3}	**Clever Boy (IRE) (67)** (JWCurtis) **6-11-4** DerekByrne (hdwy 8th: wknd appr 4 out)	3	**8**	25/1	77?	—
1683^{6}	**Rathkeal (IRE)** (MJHeaton-Ellis) **6-10-12** DGallagher (in tch to 8th: sn wknd: t.o)	14	**9**	25/1	61	—
1795^{6}	**Bank Avenue** (MrsJPitman) **6-10-12** RFarrant (hld up: hdwy 8th: wknd 4 out: t.o)	nk	**10**	25/1	61	—
	Brownscroft (MissPMWhittle) **9-10-0**(7) KHibbert (a bhd: t.o)	30	**11**	100/1	36	—
	Itspenshams (JCTuck) **8-10-7** SMcNeill (bkwd: a bhd: t.o)	9	**12**	100/1	30	—
	So Far Bold (IRE) (IPWilliams) **7-10-12b** JOsborne (bkwd: plld hrd: prom tl wknd 9th: t.o)	1¼	**13**	16/1	34	—
2053^{11}	**Minster Boy** (JPLeigh) **6-10-12** CLlewellyn (chsd ldrs to ½-wy: sn lost tch: t.o)	s.h	**14**	100/1	34	—
	Balcony Boy (RDEWoodhouse) **5-10-12** JCallaghan (bkwd: a bhd: t.o whn p.u bef 3 out)		**P**	50/1	—	—
1873^{11}	**Deceit the Second** (PRRodford) **5-10-12** SBurrough (bit bkwd: a bhd: mstke 6th: t.o: p.u bef 3 out)		**P**	100/1	—	—
1665^{11}	**Moor Dance Man** (NPLittmoden) **7-10-12** MrDVerco (chsd ldrs to 8th: wknd qckly: t.o whn p.u bef 4 out)		**P**	25/1	—	—
				(SP 141.9%)	**17 Rn**	

5m 58.5 (17.50) CSF £152.88 TOTE £20.40: £2.30 £3.70 £1.10 (£230.10) Trio £216.90 OWNER Mr J. G. Read (BRANDSBY) BRED Mowbray Properties Ltd

OFFICIAL EXPLANATION **Moor Dance Man: swallowed his tongue.**

1854 Young Kenny stays extremely well and, though he needed to be switched to deliver his challenge at the last, he found all that was necessary to be top dog at the finish. (12/1)

Montecot (FR), who has been chasing in France, turned in a very promising effort on this hurdling debut in this country and should have little trouble in going one better. (12/1: op 25/1)

1964 Destin d'Estruval (FR) again got tapped for speed after looking all over the winner at the last, and it may well be advisable to let him take his chance over a shorter trip with the same tactics employed. (8/13)

1768* Boots Madden (IRE), patiently ridden on this first attempt at this extended trip, tried to get himself into the action turning in, but he was soon being bustled along and the task proved beyond him. (9/2: op 11/4)

Paris Fashion (FR), three times a winner over fences, ran well on her initial outing over hurdles in this country and, with this run to put an edge on her, should be able to win at this game. (14/1: 10/1-16/1)

1261 Mendip Prince (IRE) lost out in the battle to make the running, but he gave chase to the leader until weakening rather quickly early in the straight. (14/1: op 8/1)

2551 THUNDERBOLT NOVICES' CHASE (5-Y.O+) (Class E)

3-10 (3-10) **3m (18 fncs)** £3,161.75 (£959.00: £469.50: £224.75) GOING minus 0.14 sec per fur (G)

				SP	RR	SF
1819^{2}	**Dromhana (IRE) (99)** (PFNicholls) **7-11-11** APMcCoy (lw: a.p: led 6th: lft clr 10th: unchal)	—	**1**	100/30^{3}	103+	36
1845^{5}	**Final Beat (IRE) (78)** (JWCurtis) **8-11-5** DerekByrne (hdwy 6th: hrd rdn to go 2nd nr fin: no ch w wnr)	25	**2**	25/1	80	13
1909^{2}	**Key To Moyade (IRE) (98)** (MJWilkinson) **7-11-5** ILawrence (chsd ldrs: lft mod 2nd 12th: no imp)	½	**3**	8/1	80	13
1811^{F}	**Penncaler (IRE)** (PJHobbs) **7-11-5** RJohnson (sn t.o)	dist	**4**	8/1	—	—
1875^{7}	**Masked Martin (60)** (PRRodford) **6-11-5** SBurrough (a t.o)	9	**5**	100/1	—	—
1955*	**Gysart (IRE)** (MCPipe) **8-11-11b** CMaude (prom: j.slowly 5th: lft 2nd 10th: fell 12th)		**F**	11/4^{2}	—	—
	Dispol Dancer (MrsVAAconley) **6-11-0**(5) MrRThornton (t.o whn p.u bef 11th)		**P**	100/1	—	—
1456^{4}	**Ourownfellow (IRE)** (RCurtis) **8-11-5** DMorris (j.b lft: sn t.o: p.u bef 11th)		**P**	10/1	—	—
1797^{2}	**Wisley Wonder (IRE) (115)** (NATwiston-Davies) **7-11-5b^{1}** CLlewellyn (led to 6th: cl 2nd whn blnd & uns rdr 10th)		**U**	2/1^{1}	—	—
				(SP 120.2%)	**9 Rn**	

6m 3.0 (9.00) CSF £66.47 TOTE £2.70: £1.10 £4.50 £1.80 (£67.20) Trio £67.00; £68.00 to Windsor 15/1/97 OWNER Mr John Blackwell (SHEPTON MALLET) BRED Lawson Burriss

1819 Dromhana (IRE) had his task simplified when Wisley Wonder departed a mile out, and had only to negotiate the remaining obstacles to come home alone. (100/30: 9/4-7/2)

1845 Final Beat (IRE) got up close home to pick up a worthy runner-up prize, but was never within striking range of the winner. (25/1)

1909 Key To Moyade (IRE), always in the chasing group, looked assured of the runner-up prize turning for home, but he does not quite see out this trip and was found wanting nearing the finish. (8/1)

1797 Wisley Wonder (IRE), happy enough to let the winner give him a lead, was still full of running when he got too close to the penultimate ditch and pitched his rider out of the side-door. (2/1)

2552 MAJOR LEAGUE NOVICES' H'CAP HURDLE (0-105) (4-Y.O+) (Class E)

3-40 (3-41) **2m 4f 110y (11 hdls)** £2,473.50 (£696.00: £340.50) GOING: 0.11 sec per fur (G)

				SP	RR	SF
1940^{F}	**Mock Trial (IRE) (90)** (MrsJRRamsden) **4-10-0** BFenton (hld up in tch: hdwy to ld 4 out: rdn & r.o wl)	—	**1**	7/1	73	17
1713*	**Lance Armstrong (IRE) (103)** (GMMcCourt) **7-11-12** AMaguire (lw: a.p: ev ch 3 out: one pce flat)	3	**2**	10/1	84	41
1840^{2}	**Lough Tully (IRE) (79)** (FJordan) **7-10-2** SWynne (hld up: effrt appr 4 out: styd on appr last)	1½	**3**	9/1	59	16
1841^{3}	**General Mouktar (105)** (MCPipe) **7-12-0** APMcCoy (hld up in tch: stdy hdwy 4 out: rdn & one pce fr 2 out)	2	**4**	6/1^{3}	83	40
1855^{3}	**Melstock Meggie (90)** (MrsJPitman) **7-10-13** WMarston (prom: rdn 4 out: one pce)	hd	**5**	9/4^{1}	68	25
2036^{2}	**Colwall (82)** (MissPMWhittle) **6-9-12**(7) KHibbert (prom to 3 out: sn rdn: wknd appr next)	6	**6**	14/1	55	12
2036*	**Mahler (95)** (NATwiston-Davies) **7-11-4** DWalsh (mde most to 4 out: wknd 2 out)	1¼	**7**	5/1^{2}	67	24
	Snowshill Shaker (85) (NATwiston-Davies) **8-10-8** CLlewellyn (bkwd: hld up: nvr plcd to chal)	1¼	**8**	12/1	56	13
1995^{2}	**Supreme Genotin (IRE) (97)** (JABOld) **8-11-6** GUpton (nvr nr to chal)	nk	**9**	10/1	68	25
1663*	**Rovestar (89)** (JSKing) **6-10-12** TJMurphy (a in rr)	4	**10**	14/1	57	14
2036^{5}	**Time Leader (77)** (RDickin) **5-10-0** BPowell (a bhd: t.o)	8	**11**	25/1	39	—
1681^{5}	**Glistening Dawn (95)** (TKeddy) **7-11-4b** SMcNeill (w ldrs: ev ch 4 out: wknd next)	1½	**12**	14/1	55	12
1842^{2}	**Grand Cru (91)** (MrsMReveley) **6-11-0** DGallagher (chsd ldrs tl wknd appr 4 out)	1¼	**13**	14/1	51	8
	No Morals (78) (PRWebber) **6-10-1** JOsborne (bkwd: a bhd: t.o whn p.u bef 2 out)		**P**	33/1	—	—
2053^{10}	**Carly-J (79)** (FSJackson) **6-10-2**ow2 MrNKent (bhd fr 7th: t.o whn p.u bef 2 out)		**P**	33/1	—	—

				SP	RR	SF
1664P	**Lothian Jem (77)** (JWharton) **8-9-9**(5) MrRThornton (w ldrs: j.slowly 6th: wknd appr 4 out: t.o whn p.u bef 2 out)		**P**	50/1	—	—

(SP 148.5%) **16 Rn**

5m 0.1 (11.10) CSF £83.66 CT £624.20 TOTE £14.80: £1.90 £1.70 £3.40 £2.10 (£72.80) Trio £560.80; £315.95 to Windsor 15/1/97 OWNER Mr P. A. Leonard (THIRSK) BRED Sheikh Mohammed Bin Rashid Al Maktoum

LONG HANDICAP Mock Trial (IRE) 9-13 Time Leader 9-12 Carly-J 9-10 Lothian Jem 9-4

WEIGHT FOR AGE 4yo-13lb

1940 Mock Trial (IRE), well suited to this stiffer test of stamina, took advantage of his lenient handicap mark and won this more or less as he pleased. He will not be hard pressed to defy a penalty. (7/1)

1713* Lance Armstrong (IRE) showed with the pace from the start, but found the weight concession too much when the chips were down. He does stay extra well and is very versatile. (10/1: op 6/1)

1840 Lough Tully (IRE) just appears to stay and stay and, finding this trip a bit on the short side, was never closer than at the finish. (9/1)

1841 General Mouktar looked to be cantering when joining the leaders three out, but he decided a concession of two stone to the winner was asking too much, and enough was enough between the last two. (6/1: op 4/1)

1855 Melstock Meggie, in more or less the same place throughout, failed to make any further progress in the last half-mile and may well need even further. (9/4: op 7/2)

2036* Mahler had far more use made of him and, in the end, these forceful tactics backfired somewhat, as he had shot his bolt before reaching the second last. He is a very fluent jumper and could make a name for himself when his attentions are switched to fences. (5/1)

1995 Supreme Genotin (IRE) (10/1: op 6/1)

1842 Grand Cru (14/1: op 8/1)

T/Plpt: £149.90 (62.08 Tckts). T/Qdpt: £10.00 (64.85 Tckts). IM

2200-HUNTINGDON (R-H) - Wednesday January 15th

2553 Abandoned-Frost

2304-WINDSOR (Fig. 8) - Wednesday January 15th

2559 Abandoned-Frost

2088-LUDLOW (R-H) (Good to firm, Firm patches)
Thursday January 16th

WEATHER: overcast

2566 MARSHBROOK MAIDEN HURDLE (4-Y.O+) (Class E)

1-10 (1-11) **2m (9 hdls)** £2,682.00 (£752.00: £366.00) GOING minus 0.37 sec per fur (GF)

				SP	RR	SF
2074[4]	**Percy Braithwaite (IRE)** (MissPMWhittle) **5-11-1**(7) KHibbert (hld up: hdwy 6th: chal 2 out: lft in ld last: rdn out)	—	**1**	8/1	71	23
1872[2]	**Fitzwilliam (USA)** (IABalding) **4-10-10** GBradley (lw: chsd ldr: led appr 3 out: rdn & hit last: sn hdd: rallied towards fin)	1¼	**2**	5/4 1	70	10
1905[2]	**Mr Darcy** (PRWebber) **5-11-8** RBellamy (chsd ldrs: rdn appr 2 out: unable qckn)	3	**3**	3/1 2	67	19
1470[8]	**Break the Rules** (MCPipe) **5-11-8** CMaude (hld up: hdwy 6th: one pce fr 3 out)	4	**4**	5/1 3	63	15
	Meg's Memory (IRE) (AStreeter) **4-10-5** TEley (hld up in tch: effrt 6th: one pce fr 2 out)	¾	**5**	50/1	57	—
1523[5]	**Best Friend** (JWCurtis) **5-11-3** DerekByrne (led & sn clr: wknd & hdd appr 3 out)	7	**6**	66/1	50	2
	Alistover (RDickin) **4-9-12**(7) XAizpuru (bkwd: chsd ldrs tl wknd appr 3 out)	1¼	**7**	100/1	49	—
1333[5]	**Questan** (MCPipe) **5-11-1**(7) GSupple (bit bkwd: prom tl wknd after 6th: t.o)	dist	**8**	12/1	—	—
	Red Lane (JDDownes) **7-11-8** MrADalton (bkwd: mstke 1st: a bhd: t.o)	8	**9**	100/1	—	—
	Time Goes On (RJHodges) **5-11-0**(3) TDascombe (bkwd: trckd ldrs to 6th: grad wknd: t.o)	1¾	**10**	66/1	—	—
2038[8]	**Stevie's Wonder (IRE)** (BJLlewellyn) **7-11-8** MrJLLlewellyn (ref to r: t.n.p)		**R**	66/1	—	—

(SP 113.3%) **11 Rn**

3m 40.7 (3.70) CSF £16.80 TOTE £8.70: £1.50 £1.10 £1.70 (£5.00) Trio £8.40 OWNER Glass Pig Racing Syndicate (LEDBURY) BRED J. G. O'Brien in Ireland

WEIGHT FOR AGE 4yo-12lb

2074 Percy Braithwaite (IRE), well suited by this fast ground, was able to take advantage of the favourite's error at the last and found more than enough to repel his renewed challenge. (8/1: op 4/1)

1872 Fitzwilliam (USA) did not jump any of the final three hurdles with any fluency, otherwise he would have won. (5/4: op 4/5)

1905 Mr Darcy looked a live threat from the turn into the straight, but he just lacked that bit extra when the battle to the line really developed. He should not be too hard to place. (3/1)

1470 Break the Rules, sure to benefit when he can get his toe in, had reached the heels of the leaders on the home turn, but he was soon at full stretch and lacked the speed to do anything about it. (5/1)

Meg's Memory (IRE) performed best of the newcomers and, with this experience under her belt, should be able to make her mark. (50/1)

1333 Questan (12/1: op 8/1)

2567 NEENTON (S) H'CAP HURDLE (0-95) (4-Y.O+) (Class G)

1-40 (1-40) **2m (9 hdls)** £2,024.00 (£564.00: £272.00) GOING minus 0.37 sec per fur (GF)

				SP	RR	SF
1980[3]	**Fastini Gold (70)** (MDIUsher) **5-10-7** MAFitzgerald (hld up: hdwy appr 3 out: qcknd u.p to ld cl home)	—	**1**	4/1 1	54	1
1542[6]	**Astral Invasion (USA) (81)** (GMMcCourt) **6-10-11b**(7) RHobson (led 2nd: clr fr 4th: hrd rdn & ct nr fin)	1½	**2**	14/1	64	11
1861[2]	**Cosmic Star (63)** (PWinkworth) **7-9-7b**(7) XAizpuru (chsd ldrs: chal on bit 3 out: ev ch flat: unable qckn)	nk	**3**	6/1 3	45	—
1816[6]	**Them Times (IRE) (63)** (FJordan) **8-10-0** SWynne (led to 2nd: rdn appr 2 out: one pce)	5	**4**	8/1	40	—
1841[7]	**Little Hooligan (81)** (RJHodges) **6-11-1**(3) TDascombe (hld up: hdwy 6th: rdn appr 3 out: nt pce to chal)	nk	**5**	4/1 1	58	5
1818[4]	**Tee Tee Too (IRE) (76)** (AWCarroll) **5-10-13** WMarston (prom tl rdn & wknd appr 3 out)	¾	**6**	6/1 3	52	—
1693F	**Denomination (USA) (87)** (MCPipe) **5-11-10** CMaude (hld up: hdwy after 6th: wknd 3 out: t.o)	11	**7**	9/2 2	52	—
2038[6]	**Lajadhal (FR) (71)** (KBishop) **8-10-8** LHarvey (bkwd: a bhd: t.o)	6	**8**	14/1	30	—
1446[8]	**Against The Clock (63)** (PBowen) **5-10-0** RJohnson (trckd ldrs: rdn & btn appr 3 out: t.o)	20	**9**	14/1	2	—

1446[3] **Scalp 'em (IRE) (63)** (DrPPritchard) **9-10-0** DrPPritchard (bit bkwd: chsd ldrs to 6th: sn lost tch: p.u bef last) .... **P** 25/1 — —
(SP 121.7%) **10 Rn**

3m 42.6 (5.60) CSF £54.40 CT £311.34 TOTE £4.00: £1.40 £4.30 £3.20 (£56.10) Trio £99.80; £113.96 to Kempton 17/1/97 OWNER Mr G. A. Summers (WANTAGE) BRED Miss D. J. Day
LONG HANDICAP Them Times (IRE) 9-13 Cosmic Star 9-11 Against The Clock 9-3 Scalp 'em (IRE) 9-8
Sold A & P Price 6,000 gns
1980 Fastini Gold, without the blinkers this time, landed something of a gamble, producing a devastating turn of speed to take control inside the last 50 yards. (4/1: op 7/1)
1542 Astral Invasion (USA) had to show his true grit to hold off the persistent Cosmic Star and did not deserve to get collared in the shadow of the post. (14/1)
1861 Cosmic Star, still full of running when delivering her challenge three out, was still in with every chance on the flat, but was always coming out second best until the winner swooped to conquer. (6/1: op 4/1)
1816 Them Times (IRE) had nothing more to give when the pressure was on and, as yet, seems to be having trouble lasting the trip. (8/1)
1599 Little Hooligan, back in his own class on this return to the minimum trip, could not muster the pace to mount a challenge and was always being held. (4/1)
1818 Tee Tee Too (IRE), hard at work to hold his pitch on the long home turn, was fighting a lost cause on reaching the straight. (6/1)
1425 Denomination (USA) (9/2: 3/1-5/1)

2568 TENBURY H'CAP CHASE (0-125) (5-Y.O+) (Class D)

2-10 (2-10) **3m (19 fncs)** £3,566.25 (£1,080.00: £527.50: £251.25) GOING minus 0.37 sec per fur (GF)

				SP	RR	SF
1918*	**Imperial Vintage (IRE) (115)** (MissVenetiaWilliams) **7-11-5** NWilliamson (mstke 1st: blnd 4th: led 12th: hrd rdn appr last: hld on gamely)	—	**1**	7/2[2]	118	60
2069[2]	**Fortunes Course (IRE) (96)** (JSKing) **8-10-0** TJMurphy (led tl after 2nd: outpcd 9th: blnd 13th: rallied next: sustained run flat: jst failed)	hd	**2**	5/1[3]	99	41
1806[5]	**Dark Oak (111)** (JWCurtis) **11-11-1** DerekByrne (lw: hld up & bhd: hdwy 12th: chal 3 out: str run flat: r.o)	hd	**3**	16/1	114	56
1501[2]	**Fiveleigh Builds (124)** (MissLucindaRussell) **10-12-0** AThornton (bit bkwd: lost pl 5th: hdwy 12th: rdn & ev ch whn hit 3 out: one pce appr last)	4	**4**	11/1	124	66
1731[3]	**Coolree (IRE) (110)** (PFNicholls) **9-11-0** MAFitzgerald (j.w: hdwy 8th: ev ch fr 4 out tl one pce appr last)	nk	**5**	5/1[3]	110	52
2089[2]	**God Speed You (IRE) (101)** (CPMorlock) **8-10-5b** JRKavanagh (j.w: led after 2nd tl rn out after 11th: continued wl bhd)	25	**6**	13/8[1]	84	26
1957[6]	**Andrelot (113)** (PBowen) **10-11-3b** RJohnson (chsd ldr: lft in ld after 11th: hdd next: sn rdn & wknd: t.o)	30	**7**	25/1	76	18
1858[3]	**Well Briefed (113)** (RHBuckler) **10-11-3** BPowell (a bhd: t.o whn p.u bef 3 out: b.b.v)		**P**	16/1	—	—
				(SP 117.6%)	**8 Rn**	

5m 53.5 (-6.50) CSF £20.38 CT £226.52 TOTE £6.00: £1.70 £1.80 £2.20 (£7.70) Trio £40.90 OWNER Mr David Williams (HEREFORD) BRED W. J. Mernagh
LONG HANDICAP Fortunes Course (IRE) 9-13
OFFICIAL EXPLANATION **Well Briefed: had bled from the nose.**
IN-FOCUS: **This was a competitive race run in a very fast time and the form should hold up well.**
1918* Imperial Vintage (IRE) made more than his share of mistakes, but his heart is in the right place and, answering his jockey's every call, he found the line arriving not a stride too soon. (7/2)
2069 Fortunes Course (IRE) is only small but she is courageous and, turning in by far her best performance over fences, only just failed to pull the race out of the fire. (5/1)
1806 Dark Oak came to win his race at the final ditch, but the winner kept pulling out more, and his strong, determined, late challenge only just failed to get him there. Compensation awaits. (16/1)
1501 Fiveleigh Builds could have just needed this first run in almost two months, but he was fighting for supremacy when he clouted the third last, and his measure had been taken between the last two. This was a brave try under topweight. (11/1: 8/1-12/1)
1731 Coolree (IRE) turned in a very bold display of fencing and joined issue turning for home but, as yet, is unproven at this extended trip, and he was forced to call enough approaching the last. He should not be long in returning to form. (5/1)
2089 God Speed You (IRE), bowling along in a clear lead, tried to duck into the stable yard soon after passing the Stands and, though he did eventually continue, he had no chance at all of recovering. This effort can safely be forgotten. (13/8)

2569 LONGMYND NOVICES' H'CAP CHASE (0-105) (5-Y.O+) (Class E)

2-40 (2-42) **2m (13 fncs)** £2,948.75 (£890.00: £432.50: £203.75) GOING minus 0.37 sec per fur (GF)

				SP	RR	SF
2037[3]	**Northern Singer (79)** (RJHodges) **7-9-13**(3)ow2 TDascombe (j.w: chsd ldrs: led 8th: lft clr 4 out)	—	**1**	16/1	87	15
2037[4]	**Bold Acre (77)** (JMBradley) **7-10-0b** RJohnson (a.p: chal & blnd 4 out: nt rcvr)	3½	**2**	14/1	82+	12
1714[3]	**Lobster Cottage (88)** (KCBailey) **9-10-11** SMcNeill (led to 8th: outpcd 4 out: hit next: sn btn)	5	**3**	11/2	88	18
1780[P]	**Uk Hygiene (IRE) (82)** (MDHammond) **7-10-5**ow2 RGarritty (hld up: hdwy 8th: one pce fr 4 out)	nk	**4**	9/2[3]	81	9
1994[3]	**Dante's View (USA) (91)** (PRHedger) **9-11-0** DO'Sullivan (hld up & bhd: hdwy appr 4 out: nt rch ldrs)	3	**5**	4/1[2]	87	17
2091[U]	**Holy Wanderer (USA) (96)** (TRGeorge) **8-11-2**(3) GHogan (lw: hld up in rr: hdwy 9th: wkng whn hit 3 out:t.o)	20	**6**	7/2[1]	72	2
	Dara's Course (IRE) (77) (MissPMWhittle) **8-10-0** TJMurphy (bkwd: prom tl outpcd 8th: sn t.o)	8	**7**	25/1	45	—
1179[F]	**Ice Magic (77)** (FJYardley) **10-10-0v** BFenton (bkwd: hld up: hdwy 6th: wknd 4 out: t.o)	dist	**8**	33/1	—	—
2037[2]	**Scottish Bambi (105)** (PRWebber) **9-12-0** AThornton (lw: swvd lft s: effrt appr 4 out: no imp whn p.u bef 2 out)		**P**	4/1[2]	—	—
2076[P]	**Nunson (77)** (RDickin) **8-10-0** BPowell (a bhd: t.o fr ½-wy: p.u bef 4 out)		**P**	50/1	—	—
				(SP 117.1%)	**10 Rn**	

3m 54.1 (2.10) CSF £183.08 CT £1,271.05 TOTE £20.80: £2.70 £1.80 £2.40 (£48.00) Trio £91.70 OWNER Mr Joe Panes (SOMERTON) BRED N. J. Dent
LONG HANDICAP Bold Acre 9-13 Dara's Course (IRE) 9-11 Ice Magic 9-6 Northern Singer 9-8 Nunson 8-11
OFFICIAL EXPLANATION **Scottish Bambi: was found to have pulled muscles in his quarters.**
2037 Northern Singer, winning from 6lb out of the handicap, was already in complete control when his most serious rival missed out at the fourth last. From then on, the prize was his. (16/1)
2037 Bold Acre is not so effective when the ground is lively, but he did his best to make a race of it, and he is at the right age to go on improving. (14/1)
1714 Lobster Cottage, a faller here on his previous appearance, was already getting the worst of the battle when he made another untidy mistake at the same obstacle, three out. (11/2)
1780 Uk Hygiene (IRE) failed to get close enough to cause concern, but he never stopped trying. This run should have put an edge on him. (9/2)

1994 Dante's View (USA) may well need further on such a fast track, for he could never summon the pace to land a blow. (4/1)
2091 Holy Wanderer (USA) has won round here, but he has also had his share of grief. He was already feeling the strain when untidy at the third last, and the position was accepted. (7/2)

2570 WELSHPOOL H'CAP HURDLE (0-100) (5-Y.O+) (Class F)

3-10 (3-10) **3m 2f 110y (13 hdls)** £2,528.00 (£708.00: £344.00) GOING minus 0.37 sec per fur (GF)

				SP	RR	SF
2088^{9}	**Gunmaker (72)** (BJLlewellyn) **8-10-4** NWilliamson (chsd ldrs: lost pl 8th: rallied 3 out: styd on to ld nr fin)	—	**1**	$5/1^{2}$	56	—
1122^{P}	**Brindley House (90)** (RCurtis) **10-11-8** DWalsh (led to 3 out: rallied & ev ch flat: r.o)	1¼	**2**	25/1	73	—
1718^{4}	**First Crack (84)** (FJordan) **12-11-2** SWynne (hld up: hdwy 9th: led 3 out: hrd rdn & edgd rt flat: hdd nr fin)	1¼	**3**	10/1	67	—
257^{5}	**Derring Bridge (86)** (MrsSMJohnson) **7-11-4** AThornton (bit bkwd: hld up in tch: effrt appr 3 out: nvr nr to chal)	20	**4**	12/1	56	—
1814^{P}	**Cravate (FR) (68)** (PJHobbs) **7-9-7**(7) MMoran (wl bhd tl styd on fr 3 out)	1	**5**	50/1	38	—
1814^{8}	**Awestruck (70)** (BPreece) **7-10-2b**ow2 TJenks (chsd ldr: hrd rdn 10th: wknd 3 out)	1¼	**6**	25/1	39	—
1962^{2}	**Rare Spread (IRE) (78)** (MCPipe) **7-10-10** CMaude (a in rr)	3	**7**	$9/2^{1}$	45	—
1876^{6}	**Tiger Claw (USA) (81)** (AGHobbs) **11-10-6**(7) MrGShenkin (chsd ldrs to 10th: sn wknd)	¾	**8**	12/1	48	—
1582^{F}	**Westerly Gale (IRE) (86)** (NJHenderson) **7-11-4** MAFitzgerald (prom to 10th: sn lost tch: t.o)	5	**9**	$7/1^{3}$	50	—
2076^{4}	**Evezio Rufo (85)** (NPLittmoden) **5-11-3v** BPowell (hdwy appr 5th: rdn 9th: wknd appr 3 out: t.o)	1½	**10**	$9/2^{1}$	48	—
2076^{P}	**Mister Blake (92)** (RLee) **7-11-10** RJohnson (hld up: hdwy 7th: wknd 10th: t.o whn p.u bef 3 out)		**P**	$5/1^{2}$	—	—

(SP 116.3%) **11 Rn**

6m 17.7 (18.70) CSF £105.98 CT £1,096.16 TOTE £4.30: £2.20 £3.90 £1.90 (£191.40) Trio £118.70; £33.46 to Kempton 17/1/97 OWNER Mr B. J. Llewellyn (BARGOED) BRED J. Neville and R. J. Holder
LONG HANDICAP Cravate (FR) 9-1 Awestruck 9-3
725 Gunmaker, winning for the first time at the trip, made relentless progress inside the last half-mile and found the better turn of foot to forge ahead nearing the finish. He is much improved with stronger handling. (5/1)
957 Brindley House ran extremely well on this return to hurdles and, on more suitable ground, would have taken all the beating. (25/1)
1718 First Crack looked set to score another win at her favourite track when jumping the last with a two-length advantage, but she drifted right under a very strong ride and was worn down close home. This trip could have been stretching her stamina to the limit. (10/1)
95* Derring Bridge stays forever, but he has not been out since July and lack of peak-fitness took its toll when he did try to get himself into the action. (12/1)
1962 Rare Spread (IRE), buried in the pack, never promised to get himself into contention and proved most disapppointing. (9/2)
1876 Tiger Claw (USA) (12/1: 8/1-14/1)
2076 Evezio Rufo has never won over hurdles and had his full quota of weight in this competitive handicap, but punters must have thought he was the value and once again burnt their fingers. (9/2)
1906 Mister Blake (5/1: op 3/1)

2571 TELFORD NOVICES' CHASE (5-Y.O+) (Class E)

3-40 (3-42) **2m 4f (17 fncs)** £3,013.75 (£910.00: £442.50: £208.75) GOING minus 0.37 sec per fur (GF)

				SP	RR	SF
1468^{P}	**Inch Emperor (IRE)** (AWCarroll) **7-11-5** TJMurphy (j.w: mde virtually all: styd on strly)	—	**1**	11/2	84	10
2039^{U}	**Jolly Boat** (FJordan) **10-11-5** SWynne (bit bkwd: chsd wnr fr 3rd: ev ch 4 out: one pce fr next)	3	**2**	$11/8^{1}$	82	8
	Aeolian (MissPMWhittle) **6-10-12**(7) KHibbert (bit bkwd: hld up: hdwy 6th: wknd appr 4 out: btn whn blnd last)	20	**3**	66/1	66	—
1909^{3}	**Snowdon Lily (61)** (PRWebber) **6-11-0** RBellamy (lost pl 4th: t.o 11th: n.d afterwards)	13	**4**	20/1	50	—
1206^{6}	**Merryhill Gold** (JWCurtis) **6-11-5** DerekByrne (nvr trbld ldrs: t.o)	1¼	**5**	20/1	54	—
1826^{6}	**White Diamond (79)** (MissLucindaRussell) **9-11-5v** MFoster (dropped rr 7th: sn t.o)	2½	**6**	$9/2^{3}$	52	—
2091^{3}	**Arabian Bold (IRE)** (RTJuckes) **9-11-5** WMarston (prom tl lost pl 11th: t.o)	25	**7**	$4/1^{2}$	32	—

(SP 106.7%) **7 Rn**

5m 0.6 (8.60) CSF £11.18 TOTE £6.50: £2.10 £1.30 (£9.80) OWNER Mr T. V. Cullen (WORCESTER) BRED Catherine O'Brien
Inch Emperor (IRE) appreciated this step down in distance and, making sure it was a true test of stamina, galloped his rivals into the ground.(11/2)
1771 Jolly Boat still has something left to work on and, though he joined issue four out, he was in trouble at the next. (11/8)
Aeolian did not shape badly on this chasing debut and there could be a small race in him. (66/1)
2091 Arabian Bold (IRE) only just got the minimum trip over hurdles and showed here that stamina is not his strong suit. (4/1: op 5/2)

2572 WEATHERBYS 'STARS OF TOMORROW' INTERMEDIATE N.H. FLAT RACE (4, 5 & 6-Y.O) (Class H)

4-10 (4-10) **2m** £1,413.00 (£393.00: £189.00)

				SP	RR	SF
	Mountain Storm (IRE) (NJHenderson) **5-10-12**(7) THagger (chsd ldrs: rdn to ld 2f out: drvn clr)	—	**1**	$4/1^{2}$	76 f	—
1926^{2}	**Shebang (IRE)** (JLDunlop) **5-10-12**(7) MrHDunlop (chsd clr ldr: rdn & ev ch 2f out: nt pce of wnr)	5	**2**	$7/4^{1}$	71 f	—
	Jim's Quest (PJHobbs) **4-10-0**(7) MMoran (bit bkwd: hdwy over 4f out: styd on wl fnl f)	2	**3**	$6/1^{3}$	69 f	—
	Certain Shot (GMMcCourt) **6-10-12**(7) RHobson (bhd: hdwy 6f out: rdn over 2f out: styd on)	4	**4**	14/1	65 f	—
1820^{2}	**King of The Blues** (JSKing) **5-10-12**(7) MGriffiths (hdwy ½-wy: rdn 2f out: kpt on same pce)	5	**5**	$6/1^{3}$	60 f	—
2080^{5}	**Blowing Rock (IRE)** (RDickin) **5-10-12**(7) XAizpuru (bit bkwd: a in rr)	8	**6**	12/1	52 f	—
	Itsahardlife (IRE) (MDHammond) **6-10-12**(7) RBurns (bit bkwd: nvr plcd to chal)	3	**7**	12/1	49 f	—
	Society Times (USA) (MCPipe) **4-10-0**(7) GSupple (plld hrd: sn wl clr: rdn 3f out: hdd 2f out: wknd qckly)	1	**8**	$6/1^{3}$	48 f	—
1800^{10}	**Sweet Mount (IRE)** (NATwiston-Davies) **5-10-7**(7) LSuthern (a in rr)	1¼	**9**	12/1	42 f	—
1986^{12}	**Just Andy** (BPreece) **6-10-12**(7) MissLBoswell (prom: rdn & wknd over 6f out: t.o)	25	**10**	66/1	22 f	—
	Vita Nuova (IRE) (WJenks) **6-11-0** MrAMitchell (bkwd: s.v.s: a wl bhd: t.o)	1	**11**	20/1	16 f	—
	Jimsue (CHJones) **6-11-5** MrLLay (bkwd: dropped rr 7f out: t.o)	dist	**12**	33/1	—	—

(SP 138.2%) **12 Rn**

3m 33.1 CSF £12.13 TOTE £7.40: £2.50 £1.40 £2.70 (£6.10) Trio £44.60 OWNER Mr Anthony Speelman (LAMBOURN) BRED Michael Lysaght
WEIGHT FOR AGE 4yo-12lb
Mountain Storm (IRE) needed to be well forward in condition to succeed in this fast-run event, but he did win going away and could be set to go places. (4/1: op 5/2)
1926 Shebang (IRE) may have poked her nose in front for a few strides passing the quarter-mile marker, but the winner was able to quicken up, and he was left in his wake. (7/4)
Jim's Quest, a good-looking half-brother to two winners, was beginning to grasp what was needed in the latter stages, and will know more next time. (6/1)

Certain Shot, a half-brother to prolific winner Celtic Shot, was unable to mount a challenge, but he did keep staying on, and the experience will not be lost. (14/1)
1820 King of The Blues, more experienced than most of his rivals, was at full stretch early in the straight and did not possess the pace to prove troublesome. (6/1: 4/1-13/2)
Itsahardlife (IRE) (12/1: op 8/1)
Society Times (USA) took a very keen tug and soon opened up a commanding lead. Almost a furlong to the good at halfway, he still looked the winner entering the straight, but earlier efforts took their toll and he was legless when headed. If he can be taught to settle, he will not remain a maiden for long. (6/1)

T/Plpt: £435.20 (22.53 Tckts). T/Qdpt: £257.10 (2.81 Tckts). IM

2259-TAUNTON (R-H) (Good to firm, Good patches)
Thursday January 16th

WEATHER: fine

2573 LEVY BOARD JANUARY CONDITIONAL H'CAP HURDLE (0-115) (4-Y.O+) (Class E)
1-20 (1-20) **2m 3f 110y (10 hdls)** £2,221.50 (£624.00: £304.50) GOING minus 0.31 sec per fur (GF)

				SP	RR	SF
1960*	**Zingibar (83)** (JMBradley) **5-10-2** MichaelBrennan (hld up: hdwy 6th: lft in ld 7th: sn clr: rdn out)	—	**1**	8/1	63	3
1762*	**Burlington Sam (NZ) (89)** (AGHobbs) **9-10-8** OBurrows (hld up: hdwy after 6th: chsd wnr fr 7th: r.o one pce flat)	2½	**2**	9/2^{2}	67	7
1599^{3}	**Fleur de Tal (94)** (WGMTurner) **6-10-8**$^{(5)}$ JPower (prom tl wknd appr 7th)	16	**3**	9/2^{2}	59	—
1954^{4}	**Euro Singer (95)** (PRWebber) **5-11-0** EHusband (lw: led tl appr 6th: wknd 7th)	8	**4**	13/2^{3}	53	—
1474^{4}	**Vision of Freedom (IRE) (105)** (PBowen) **9-11-10** DJKavanagh (lw: a bhd: t.o fr 6th)	28	**5**	13/2^{3}	40	—
1187^{2}	**Nordic Breeze (IRE) (102)** (MCPipe) **5-11-2b**$^{(5)}$ BMoore (lw: w ldr: led appr 6th: mstke & uns rdr 7th)		**U**	7/4^{1}	—	—

(SP 110.5%) **6 Rn**

4m 37.6 (6.60) CSF £37.45 TOTE £7.40: £3.10 £1.90 (£16.00) OWNER Mr D. Holpin (CHEPSTOW) BRED Charlton Down Stud
1960* Zingibar defied a 5lb higher mark, having been taken to Southwell for a blow-out last week. (8/1)
1762* Burlington Sam (NZ) could not complete a four-timer, having gone up 6lb since his last win and 19lb in all. (9/2: op 3/1)
1599 Fleur de Tal began to struggle going to the fourth last. (9/2)
1474 Vision of Freedom (IRE) (13/2: 5/1-8/1)
1187 Nordic Breeze (IRE) was blinkered for the first time on this debut in handicap company and seemed to be going well when unshipping his rider four out. (7/4)

2574 PICKERIDGE (S) HURDLE (4, 5 & 6-Y.O) (Class G)
1-50 (1-50) **2m 1f (9 hdls)** £1,857.50 (£520.00: £252.50) GOING minus 0.31 sec per fur (GF)

				SP	RR	SF
2070^{10}	**Sam Rockett (70)** (PMooney) **4-10-2b**$^{(5)}$ SRyan (hdwy appr 6th: led appr 2 out: easily)	—	**1**	16/1	73+	2
1980*	**D'naan (IRE)** (MCPipe) **4-11-0b** APMcCoy (led tl appr 2 out: one pce)	9	**2**	4/6^{1}	72	1
2050^{6}	**Paulton** (KBishop) **4-10-7** RGreene (hdwy 6th: r.o one pce fr 2 out)	8	**3**	10/1^{3}	57	—
	Rose of Glenn (BPalling) **6-11-0** RFarrant (bit bkwd: s.s: nvr nr to chal)	6	**4**	16/1	46	—
	Contract Bridge (IRE) (PGMurphy) **4-10-3**^{ow1} WMcFarland (s.s: mstke 5th: nvr nr ldrs)	5	**5**	6/1^{2}	43	—
1878^{5}	**Adonisis (80)** (DRCElsworth) **5-11-5** PHolley (lw: chsd ldrs: wkng whn hit 3 out)	1½	**6**	10/1^{3}	45	—
1980^{4}	**Smiley Face (65)** (RJHodges) **5-10-12**$^{(7)}$ JHarris (chsd ldr: 3rd & wkng whn mstke 3 out)	1½	**7**	11/1	44	—
1377^{U}	**Aavasaksa (FR)** (AGNewcombe) **4-10-7** JOsborne (bkwd: sme hdwy 6th: wknd appr 3 out)	8	**8**	12/1	36	—
2093^{7}	**Baba Sam (IRE)** (PEccles) **6-11-0**$^{(5)}$ MrRThornton (mstke 6th: a bhd: t.o)	15	**9**	40/1	22	—
	Prince Rudolf (IRE) (WGMTurner) **5-10-12**$^{(7)}$ NWillmington (fell 3rd)		**F**	20/1	—	—
2038^{10}	**Woodlands Energy (48)** (PAPritchard) **6-11-0** CLlewellyn (a bhd: t.o whn p.u bef 2 out)		**P**	50/1	—	—
1993^{U}	**Norfolk Glory (55)** (DFBassett) **5-11-5** MrAHoldsworth (swtg: s.s: blnd & uns rdr 3rd)		**U**	100/1	—	—

(SP 130.4%) **12 Rn**

3m 59.8 (6.80) CSF £27.69 TOTE £18.60: £2.80 £1.40 £1.60 (£11.80) Trio £70.20 OWNER Mr P. M. Mooney (ASTON UPTHORPE) BRED C. J. Rowlands
WEIGHT FOR AGE 4yo-12lb
Bt in 5,500 gns
Sam Rockett, who finished second to Yet Again on the Sand at Lingfield at the end of last month, appreciated this drop in class. (16/1)
1980* D'naan (IRE), reported to have gurgled in the home straight when making a successful debut at Bangor, had no answer to the winner here. (4/6)
1444 Paulton ran his best race to date over hurdles, which unfortunately is not saying a lot. (10/1: 14/1-25/1)
Rose of Glenn will need a stiffer test of stamina over timber. (16/1)
Contract Bridge (IRE) (6/1: 9/4-13/2)
1333 Adonisis (10/1: op 6/1)
Aavasaksa (FR) (12/1: 16/1-10/1)

2575 STEPHEN LITTLE AND DICK REYNOLDS BOOKMAKERS H'CAP CHASE (0-145) (5-Y.O+) (Class B)
2-20 (2-21) **4m 2f 110y (27 fncs)** £6,937.50 (£2,100.00: £1,025.00: £487.50) GOING minus 0.31 sec per fur (GF)

				SP	RR	SF
1871^{4}	**Woodlands Genhire (105)** (PAPritchard) **12-10-0b** CLlewellyn (chsd ldr: led 23rd: clr appr 3 out: drvn out)	—	**1**	100/1	110?	—
1789^{4}	**Evangelica (USA) (125)** (MCPipe) **7-11-6** APMcCoy (lw: hld up: stdy hdwy 10th: chsd wnr fr 2 out: one pce flat)	2½	**2**	11/4^{1}	129	15
1871^{3}	**Frozen Drop (105)** (PCRitchens) **10-10-0** SFox (prom: outpcd 22nd: rallied 3 out: hit last: one pce)	1½	**3**	9/1	108	—
1997^{4}	**Sunley Bay (123)** (PFNicholls) **11-11-4** PHide (prom: mstke 13th: outpcd 22nd: rallied 3 out: one pce flat)	s.h	**4**	13/2^{3}	126	12
1674*	**Badastan (IRE) (115)** (PJHobbs) **8-10-10b** GTormey (led: mstke 22nd: hdd 23rd: wknd appr last)	6	**5**	11/4^{1}	114	—
1643^{5}	**Killeshin (133)** (HJManners) **11-11-7**$^{(7)}$ ADowling (nt j.w: t.o 6th: p.u bef 17th)		**P**	9/1	—	—
1937^{3}	**Have to Think (128)** (PFNicholls) **9-11-9** DBridgwater (lw: bhd fr 21st: t.o whn p.u bef 4 out)		**P**	6/1^{2}	—	—
	Distillation (105) (GFEdwards) **12-9-9**$^{(5)}$ MrRThornton (bit bkwd: nt j.w: a bhd: mstkes 15th & 21st: sn t.o: p.u bef 3 out)		**P**	66/1	—	—
1778^{2}	**Woodlands Boy (IRE) (105)** (RCurtis) **9-10-0** DMorris (rdn & some hdwy 19th: wknd 21st: t.o whn p.u bef 3 out)		**P**	13/2^{3}	—	—

2551[5] **Masked Martin (111)** (PRRodford) **6-10-6b**ow6 SBurrough (blnd 8th: bhd whn mstkes 11th & 12th: t.o 14th: p.u bef 21st) .... **P** 200/1 — —
(SP 117.3%) **10 Rn**

9m 1.5 (12.00 under best) (16.50) CSF £344.51 CT £2,582.02 TOTE £97.00: £10.70 £1.10 £2.40 (£93.70) Trio £124.20; £12.25 to Kempton 17/1/97 OWNER Woodlands (Worcestershire) Ltd (SHIPSTON-ON-STOUR) BRED W. J. Barnett and Sons
LONG HANDICAP Frozen Drop 9-11 Woodlands Genhire 7-2 Distillation 8-0 Woodlands Boy (IRE) 9-11 Masked Martin 6-11
Woodlands Genhire caused quite a shock from no less than 40lb out of the handicap and was his trainer's first winner for some three and a half years. (100/1)
1789 Evangelica (USA) seemed to get this marathon trip well enough, but could not peg back the winner. (11/4)
1871 Frozen Drop, 3lb wrong at the weights, was effectively 9lb higher than when winning at Fontwell in September. (9/1)
Sunley Bay seems to be jumping better these days and ran well on ground really too lively for him. (13/2)
1674* Badastan (IRE), raised 5lb, likes to force the pace, but seemed to find this trip beyond him, and collapsed through sheer exhaustion immediately after the finish. (11/4)
Killeshin was soon taken off his legs on this fast surface. (9/1: 6/1-10/1)
1937 Have to Think (6/1: 4/1-13/2)
1778 Woodlands Boy (IRE) could only manage a brief effort with a circuit to go. (13/2)

2576 E.B.F. 'N.H.' (QUALIFIER) NOVICES' HURDLE (5, 6 & 7-Y.O) (Class D)
2-50 (2-50) **2m 3f 110y (10 hdls)** £3,137.00 (£882.00: £431.00) GOING minus 0.31 sec per fur (GF)

	Horse / details	Dist	Pos	SP	RR	SF
1807[2]	**Spring Gale (IRE) (106)** (OSherwood) **6-11-10** JOsborne (a.p: chal whn hit 6th: led 2 out: pushed out)	—	**1**	6/5 [1]	82	26
1996*	**Edgemoor Prince (106)** (PJHobbs) **6-11-10** AMaguire (led: hit 3 out: hrd rdn & hdd 2 out: one pce)	2	**2**	2/1 [2]	80	24
1536[4]	**Weather Wise** (WGMTurner) **5-10-7**(7) JPower (a.p: rdn 3 out: r.o one pce)	3	**3**	12/1	68	12
2090[3]	**Di's Last** (MCPipe) **7-10-9** APMcCoy (a.p: no hdwy fr 7th)	11	**4**	5/1 [3]	54	—
1762[4]	**Eleanora Muse (65)** (PaddyFarrell) **7-10-6**(3) GuyLewis (nvr trbld ldrs)	9	**5**	14/1	47	—
1998[10]	**Brown Wren** (PJHobbs) **6-10-9** GTormey (prom to 7th)	¾	**6**	16/1	46	—
2093[6]	**Derrys Prerogative** (AWCarroll) **7-11-0** DBridgwater (rdn 5th: a bhd)	7	**7**	66/1	45	—
1998[P]	**Lilly The Filly** (MrsBarbaraWaring) **6-10-9** RGreene (a bhd)	7	**8**	100/1	34	—
1573[13]	**Missed The Match** (REPocock) **7-11-0** PMcLoughlin (prom to 6th: t.o)	22	**9**	100/1	21	—
	Piccolina (RTPhillips) **5-10-9** JRailton (a bhd: t.o)	¾	**10**	14/1	16	—
1036[12]	**Sierra Nevada** (PFNicholls) **6-10-9**(5) OBurrows (bhd fr 6th: t.o)	5	**11**	16/1	17	—
1810[P]	**Tinker's Cuss** (APJones) **6-10-9** SCurran (prom to 3rd: t.o)	3	**12**	66/1	9	—
	Big Theo (MrsPNDutfield) **6-11-0** PHolley (bkwd: hdwy 6th: 5th & wkng whn p.u bef 2 out)		**P**	20/1	—	—

(SP 138.0%) **13 Rn**

4m 36.7 (5.70) CSF £4.10 TOTE £2.00: £1.30 £1.50 £2.20 (£2.20) Trio £21.90 OWNER Crabb, Ead, Moore (UPPER LAMBOURN) BRED T. J. Hurley
1807 Spring Gale (IRE) found this a lot easier then when shouldering topweight in a novices' handicap last time. (6/5)
1996* Edgemoor Prince, unable to cope with the winner, is a shade flattered by the margin of defeat. (2/1: 6/4-9/4)
1536 Weather Wise finished a highly respectable third and should be suited by a return to further. (12/1)
2090 Di's Last was galloping on the spot from the fourth last. (5/1)

2577 BICKENHALL NOVICES' H'CAP CHASE (0-110) (5-Y.O+) (Class D)
3-20 (3-20) **2m 3f (15 fncs)** £3,550.00 (£1,075.00: £525.00: £250.00) GOING minus 0.31 sec per fur (GF)

	Horse / details	Dist	Pos	SP	RR	SF
1257[5]	**Olliver Duckett (76)** (CLPopham) **8-10-6** GTormey (led after 4th: j.lft 3 out: drvn out)	—	**1**	14/1	84	—
1676[3]	**The Mine Captain (98)** (OSherwood) **10-12-0** JOsborne (hld up: hdwy 9th: hrd rdn & ev ch 3 out: nt qckn flat)	1	**2**	2/1 [2]	105	12
1995[3]	**Winnow (70)** (AndrewTurnell) **7-9-7**(7) CRae (led tl after 4th: one pce fr 3 out)	7	**3**	13/2 [3]	71	—
1875[4]	**Chris's Glen (77)** (JMBradley) **8-10-2v**(5) MichaelBrennan (prom: hit 10th: wknd 3 out)	6	**4**	13/2 [3]	73	—
2007[3]	**Bridepark Rose (IRE) (82)** (PCRitchens) **9-10-12** SFox (hld up: mstkes 8th & 9th: hdwy appr 3 out: rdn & wknd 2 out)	5	**5**	6/4 [1]	74	—
2007[P]	**Gordon (90)** (PRWebber) **6-11-6** AMaguire (hld up in rr: stdy hdwy 10th: wkng whn mstke 3 out)	17	**6**	8/1	68	—

(SP 117.8%) **6 Rn**

4m 53.7 (11.70) CSF £41.87 TOTE £15.50: £5.10 £1.70 (£16.40) OWNER Mr M. A. Long (TAUNTON) BRED The Earl of Ronaldshay
LONG HANDICAP Winnow 9-13
Olliver Duckett, having his first run for Chris Popham, seems to have benefited from professional handling. (14/1)
1676 The Mine Captain found the weight concession beyond him off a mark 7lb higher than when winning at Southwell last May. (2/1)
1995 Winnow appears likely to need a stiffer test of stamina, especially now she has graduated to fences. (13/2)
1875 Chris's Glen, down another 3lb, seems to be struggling to find the right trip over fences. (13/2)
2007 Bridepark Rose (IRE) is beginning to look the type who is difficult to win with. (6/4)

2578 YARCOMBE NOVICES' H'CAP HURDLE (0-100) (4-Y.O+) (Class E)
3-50 (3-50) **2m 1f (9 hdls)** £2,475.50 (£693.00: £336.50) GOING minus 0.31 sec per fur (GF)

	Horse / details	Dist	Pos	SP	RR	SF
1380[4]	**Little Shefford (75)** (MPMuggeridge) **5-10-6** ILawrence (mde all: clr appr 2 out: rdn out)	—	**1**	20/1	61	27
1772[P]	**Skram (87)** (RDickin) **4-10-6** AMaguire (a.p: chsd wnr after 3 out: r.o flat)	2½	**2**	14/1	71	25
1715[4]	**Ath Cheannaithe (FR) (82)** (JNeville) **5-10-13** DBridgwater (chsd wnr tl after 3 out: one pce)	8	**3**	16/1	58	24
1693*	**Shift Again (IRE) (84)** (OSherwood) **5-10-10b**(5) SophieMitchell (hld up: hdwy appr 5th:rdn 3 out: wknd 2 out)	4	**4**	13/2 [3]	56	22
2093*	**Ultimate Smoothie (97)** (MCPipe) **5-12-0** APMcCoy (lw: hld up: hdwy 5th: mstkes 6th & 3 out: n.d after)	5	**5**	13/8 [1]	65	31
2035[6]	**Milling Brook (75)** (JMBradley) **5-10-1**(5) MichaelBrennan (bhd: t.o 5th: late hdwy)	1¾	**6**	20/1	41	7
1873[4]	**Show Faith (IRE) (95)** (RHannon) **7-11-12** JAMcCarthy (hld up: hdwy 5th: wknd 6th)	½	**7**	5/1 [2]	61	27
1091[3]	**Almapa (82)** (RJHodges) **5-10-6**(7) JHarris (bhd fr 6th: blnd last)	2	**8**	14/1	46	12
1873[6]	**Sahel (IRE) (85)** (JWMullins) **9-11-2** SCurran (lw: bhd fr 6th)	3	**9**	14/1	46	12
1948[5]	**Chili Heights (77)** (KBishop) **7-10-8b**1 RGreene (t.o fr 5th)	dist	**10**	33/1	—	—
	Sober Island (71) (MrsDThomas) **8-9-13**(3)ow2 GuyLewis (s.s: a bhd: t.o fr 6th)	9	**11**	66/1	—	—
1984[3]	**Country Minstrel (IRE) (76)** (SADouch) **6-10-0**(7) CRae (hld up: hdwy 5th: 5th & no ch whn fell 2 out)		**F**	14/1	—	—
1569[2]	**Parade Racer (72)** (PGMurphy) **6-10-3** WMcFarland (a bhd: t.o whn fell 3 out)		**F**	10/1	—	—

(SP 123.7%) **13 Rn**

3m 53.7 (0.70) CSF £245.69 CT £4,149.40 TOTE £42.50: £8.70 £2.90 £4.10 (£134.50) Trio £183.00; £103.12 to Kempton 17/1/97 OWNER Mr John Liddiard (LAMBOURN) BRED Mrs P. Waldron

LONG HANDICAP Sober Island 9-10
WEIGHT FOR AGE 4yo-12lb
1380 Little Shefford could be the type who is best when fresh. (20/1)
1663 Skram looked much more at home back on this sounder surface. (14/1: 7/1-16/1)
1715 Ath Cheannaithe (FR), dropped 5lb, seems at his best when allowed to dictate matters. (16/1)
1693* Shift Again (IRE), only raised 2lb, found this ground in total contrast to the heavy at Newton Abbot. (13/2: 9/2-7/1)
2093* Ultimate Smoothie had topweight to contend with and was not helped by some indifferent hurdling. (13/8)
Milling Brook came from the next parish to reach his finishing position. (20/1)
1873 Show Faith (IRE) (5/1: 7/2-11/2)
1091 Almapa (14/1: 10/1-16/1)

2579 CURLAND H'CAP HURDLE (0-120) (4-Y.O+) (Class D)

4-20 (4-20) **2m 1f (9 hdls)** £2,759.00 (£774.00: £377.00) GOING minus 0.31 sec per fur (GF)

				SP	RR	SF
	Le Khoumf (FR) (110) (JNeville) **6-11-6** JOsborne (a.p: led appr 5th: j.lft 2 out: easily)	—	1	100/30[2]	89+	40
71*	**Nine O Three (IRE) (105)** (AGNewcombe) **8-11-1** DGallagher (bit bkwd: a.p: chsd wnr appr 2 out: sn rdn: no imp)	5	2	100/30[2]	79	30
1984[2]	**Glowing Path (90)** (RJHodges) **7-9-7**(7) JHarris (hld up: stdy hdwy appr 5th: one pce fr 3 out)	7	3	7/1	58	9
1585[4]	**Yubralee (USA) (114)** (MCPipe) **5-11-10** APMcCoy (led: sn clr: hdd appr 5th: rdn & wknd 2 out)	6	4	3/1[1]	76	27
	Chantry Beath (93) (PGMurphy) **6-9-12**(5) SophieMitchell (bit bkwd: a bhd)	5	5	16/1	50	1
1767[9]	**First Century (IRE) (102)** (BPalling) **8-10-12** AMaguire (bit bkwd: a bhd: t.o fr 5th)	dist	6	33/1	—	—
1954[2]	**Pridewood Picker (94)** (RJPrice) **10-9-13**(5) DJKavanagh (hld up: sme hdwy appr 6th: 5th & no ch whn fell last)		F	4/1[3]	—	—
				(SP 112.5%)	**7 Rn**	

3m 53.8 (0.80) CSF £13.33 TOTE £3.50: £1.60 £3.80 (£22.50) OWNER Mr David Lewis (NEWPORT, GWENT) BRED Jean-Marc Boudrelle
Le Khoumf (FR), a respectable twelfth in last season's Supreme Novices' Hurdle at Cheltenham, made short work of these rivals. (100/30)
71* Nine O Three (IRE) would probably not have beaten the winner had he been fully fit. (100/30)
1984 Glowing Path had to contend with a 3lb rise in the weights in this better company. (7/1)
1585 Yubralee (USA) probably went off too fast for his own good. (3/1)
Chantry Beath, bought for 7,200 guineas, needed this first run for his new stable. (16/1)

T/Plpt: £823.20 (11.76 Tckts). T/Qdpt: £223.60 (4.03 Tckts). KH

2580a - 2595a : (Irish Racing) - See Computer Raceform

2580a-THURLES (Ireland) (R-H) (Good)

Thursday January 9th

Rescheduled from Naas 4/1/97

2596a SLANEY NOVICES' HURDLE (Gd 3) (5-Y.O+)

2-45 (2-45) **2m 4f (12 hdls)** IR £6,850.00 (IR £1,550.00: IR £650.00: IR £350.00)

				SP	RR	SF
1492a[F]	**Liss De Paor (IRE)** (APO'Brien,Ireland) **6-11-6** CFSwan (hld up towards rr: hdwy to disp ld briefly 4 out: led 2 out: rdn & styd on)	—	1	11/10[1]	96	—
1751a[4]	**Mullover** (MrsJHarrington,Ireland) **6-11-8** JShortt (disp ld: mstkes 5th & 6th: outpcd 4 out: rdn & nt rch ldr appr last: styd on)	2½	2	16/1	96	—
2361a[F]	**Radanpour (IRE)** (WPMullins,Ireland) **5-11-7** DJCasey (led & disp ld: mstke & hdd 2 out: rdn & no ex nr last: kpt on same pce)	s.h	3	5/1[3]	99	—
2359a[2]	**Ask The Butler (IRE)** (CRoche,Ireland) **6-11-11** CO'Dwyer (hld up: in tch whn j.slowly 7th: dropped bhd & p.u after next)		P	5/4[2]	—	—
				(SP 114.6%)	**4 Rn**	

4m 51.4 OWNER J. C. Dempsey (PILTOWN)
1492a Liss De Paor (IRE), held up for the first two miles, went second four out. She led two out and was in total command from that point. Her jumping problems appear to have been sorted out. (11/10)
Mullover ran second until getting left behind early in the straight. He ran on again from the last to go second close home, but is flattered by this result. (16/1)
2361a Radanpour (IRE) made the running until headed after a mistake two out. (5/1)
2359a Ask The Butler (IRE), weak in the market, was losing touch when making a slow jump over the sixth from home and was pulled up after the next. There appeared to be little wrong with him on his return to the ring. (5/4)

2597a - 2599a & 2601a : (Irish Racing) - See Computer Raceform

2460a-LEOPARDSTOWN (Dublin, Ireland) (L-H) (Good to yielding)

Saturday January 11th

2600a FITZPATRICK HOTEL GROUP NOVICES' CHASE (5-Y.O+)

1-05 (1-05) **2m 5f (14 fncs)** IR £5,480.00 (IR £1,240.00: IR £520.00: IR £280.00)

				SP	RR	SF
2341a[2]	**Ultra Flutter** (MHourigan,Ireland) **10-11-8** APMcCoy (disp early: mde virtually all: rdn appr last: styd on u.p whn chal flat)	—	1	5/4[1]	112	—
	Miracle Man (CWeedon) **9-11-4** NWilliamson (cl up: mstke 3rd: wnt 2nd briefly 7th & 4 out: 3rd, rdn & chsd ldrs bef 3 out: lft 2nd next: chsd wnr: styd on u.p)	½	2	5/1	108	—
2335a[5]	**The Carrig Rua (IRE)** (MichaelFlynn,Ireland) **7-11-8** RDunwoody (2nd & disp early: cl up: 2nd fr 6th: rdn & chsd wnr whn mstke 2 out: 3rd u.p st: nt trble ldrs appr last: kpt on)	6	3	5/2[2]	107	—
	Man of Arran (IRE) (PO'Leary,Ireland) **7-11-4** KFO'Brien (hld up in tch: sme mstkes: 4th whn mstke 9th: 5th & rdn 4 out: n.d next)	25	4	7/2[3]	84	—

	Horse	Dist	Pos	SP	RR	SF
2360a[3]	**Garabagh (IRE)** (JHScott,Ireland) **8-11-4** PatrickMcWilliams (mstke 1st: wnt 2nd after 2nd to 5th: 4th whn mstke next: last whn mstke 7th: sn lost tch: n.d)	20	**5**	33/1	69	—
	Radiant River (IRE) (JEMulhern,Ireland) **7-11-1**(3) GCotter (towards rr: wnt 4th at 10th: rdn & lost tch bef 3 out: dropped bhd: t.o)	25	**6**	33/1	50	—
				(SP 117.8%)	**6 Rn**	

5m 41.2 (4.20) OWNER Donal Higgins (PATRICKSWELL)

2341a Ultra Flutter made all the running at a pace that suited him and few others. He looked a bit vulnerable between the last two, but was holding the runner-up all the way on the flat. His jumping was sound and, despite his age, he could still be a lively enough contender in the Sun Alliance Chase. (5/4)

Miracle Man, never out of the first three, was a serious challenger from two out and, although apparently held on the run-in, kept on under a strong ride. For a horse absent since November 1995, this was a smart enough performance and improvement is anticipated. (5/1)

The Carrig Rua (IRE) tracked the winner throughout, but was under pressure when blundering at the second last. (5/2)

Man of Arran (IRE), whose jumping was not fluent, was being driven along five out before dropping right out of contention. (7/2)

Radiant River (IRE) had lost touch before four out and finished completely tailed off. (33/1)

2602a PIERSE LEOPARDSTOWN H'CAP CHASE (Gd 2) (5-Y.O+)

2-05 (2-07) **3m (17 fncs)** IR £16,250.00 (IR £4,750.00: IR £2,250.00: IR £750.00)

	Horse	Dist	Pos	SP	RR	SF
2348a[3]	**Time for a Run** (EJO'Grady,Ireland) **10-10-0** NWilliamson (hld up in tch: 4th at 10th: wnt 3rd 5 out: 2nd after 3 out: 3rd & chal early st: led nr last: rdn clr flat: styd on wl)	—	**1**	4/1[2]	124	10
2348a[11]	**Whale of a Knight (IRE)** (ALTMoore,Ireland) **8-10-0** FWoods (hld up in rr: slt mstke 12th: lft 5th 3 out: trckd ldrs: 2nd & chal early st: adv briefly appr last: hdd after last)	10	**2**	6/4[1]	117	3
2362a[2]	**King of the Gales** (ALTMoore,Ireland) **10-11-7** CO'Brien (hld up in rr: 6th & rdn after 3 out: 5th & no imp appr last: styd on: 3rd nr fin)	7	**3**	9/2[3]	134	20
	The Crazy Bishop (IRE) (AMullins,Ireland) **9-10-3** APMcCoy (ran 3rd: mstke 4th: lft 2nd & bdly hmpd 8th: disp briefly 10th: led 3 out: hdd u.p appr last: 3rd whn mstke last: one pce flat)	¾	**4**	16/1	115	1
2362a[U]	**Idiots Venture** (APO'Brien,Ireland) **10-11-11** CFSwan (hld up: ran 4th: 3rd after 3 out: chsd ldrs 2 out: 3rd & rdn st: no imp appr last: one pce)	12	**5**	5/1	129	15
1917[5]	**Royal Mountbrowne** (APO'Brien,Ireland) **9-12-0** THorgan (ld: mstke 3rd & 7th: j.slwly & jnd 10th: mstke & hdd 3 out: 5th & btn whn mstke next)	15	**6**	9/1	122	8
2348a[F]	**Tryfirion (IRE)** (VBowens,Ireland) **8-10-1**(3) BBowens (hld up: 5th whn mstke 5th: chsd ldrs fr 12th: 4th & rdn whn blnd & uns rdr 3 out)		**U**	14/1	—	—
1495a[6]	**Fissure Seal** (ALTMoore,Ireland) **11-10-13** RDunwoody (racd in 2nd tl blnd & uns rdr 8th)		**U**	20/1	—	—
				(SP 122.2%)	**8 Rn**	

6m 22.4 (-12.60) OWNER John McManus (THURLES)

2348a Time for a Run jumped much better here than he has done so far this season and cruised through to dispute the lead approaching the straight. He went on before the last and literally sprinted clear. From a mark 3lb out of the handicap, this was certainly impressive and he has gone up 9lb. (4/1)

2348a Whale of a Knight (IRE) made smooth headway from three out and touched down in third place after the next. Apparently going well turning into the straight upsides the winner, he was left standing after the last. (6/4)

2362a King of the Gales got himself a long way behind, staying on in the straight without ever threatening. (9/2)

The Crazy Bishop (IRE) was badly hampered before halfway, but still got back into it to lead after three out. Soon under pressure, he dropped away after the second last and was a well beaten third when blundering at the last. (16/1)

2362a Idiots Venture, kept wide from five out, went third after three out. He had his chance at the next, but dropped away quite tamely in the straight. (5/1)

2603a THE LADBROKE LIMITED H'CAP HURDLE (Gd 1) (4-Y.O+)

2-35 (2-42) **2m (8 hdls)** IR £39,200.00 (IR £11,500.00: IR £5,500.00: IR £1,900.00)

	Horse	Dist	Pos	SP	RR	SF
2048[2]	**Master Tribe (IRE)** (MrsJPitman) **7-10-4** NWilliamson (hld up in tch: imp 3 out: 3rd & trckd ldrs 2 out: led appr last: hld on u.p)	—	**1**	18/1	101	18
	Black Queen (IRE) (JEKiely,Ireland) **6-10-0**ow1 AO'Brien (hld up in rr: hdwy 4th: chal appr last: rdn & r.o)	hd	**2**	12/1	97	13
1804*	**Penny a Day (IRE)** (MrsMReveley) **7-11-10** PNiven (hld up: chsd ldrs 3 out: styd on fr appr last)	6	**3**	7/1[2]	115	32
1752a[2]	**Family Way** (ALTMoore,Ireland) **10-10-11** FWoods (mid div: hdwy & 4th 2 out: r.o one pce)	1½	**4**	15/2[3]	100	17
1752a[5]	**Metastasio** (DGMcArdle,Ireland) **5-10-10b** HRogers (mid div: hdwy 3 out: mstke 2 out: styd on u.p flat)	3	**5**	33/1	100	13
318a[4]	**Khayrawani (IRE)** (CRoche,Ireland) **5-11-4** CO'Dwyer (hld up: imp 5th: disp ld fr 3 out: rdn appr last: mstke & btn)	hd	**6**	5/1[1]	108	21
1510*	**Executive Design** (MrsMReveley) **5-11-5** GCahill (rr of mid div: prog 3 out: 10th, rdn & no imp after 2 out: kpt on)	4½	**7**	16/1	105	18
2461a[U]	**Guest Performance (IRE)** (DTHughes,Ireland) **5-11-10** RHughes (hld up in tch: 4th at 4th: 9th & chsd ldrs 3 out: 10th 2 out: no imp appr last: kpt on)	hd	**8**	14/1	110	23
	Magical Lady (IRE) (MJPO'Brien,Ireland) **5-11-3** TPRudd (sn in tch: 3rd after 3rd: led bef 5th: jnd after 3 out: hdd st: rdn & nt qckn appr last: one pce)	½	**9**	33/1	102	15
2461a[2]	**Hill Society (IRE)** (NMeade,Ireland) **5-11-6** RDunwoody (hld up in tch: 4th at 5th: cl 4th 3 out: 6th, rdn & chsd ldrs 2 out: no imp appr last: one pce)	3	**10**	16/1	102	15
1804[3]	**Kaitak (IRE)** (JMCarr) **6-10-4** FLeahy (mid div: prog to 7th at 5th: 5th & chsd ldrs 3 out: rdn & nt rch ldrs after next: no imp appr last)	nk	**11**	40/1	82	—
	King Of Kerry (IRE) (APO'Brien,Ireland) **6-10-13** CFSwan (mid div early: bhd after 3rd: kpt on fr 2 out: n.d)	12	**12**	11/1	79	—
1510[6]	**Palacegate King** (ACWhillans) **8-10-4** THorgan (in tch early: mid div: rdn & no imp 2 out: kpt on)	1½	**13**	50/1	68	—
2333a[3]	**Rescue Time (IRE)** (KPrendergast,Ireland) **4-9-12** GCotter (hld up in rr: prog 3 out: rdn & nt rch ldrs after 2 out: no impr last)	1½	**14**	40/1	75	—
	Fontaine Lodge (IRE) (AMullins,Ireland) **7-10-2**ow1 APowell (in rr: nvr bttr than mid div: kpt on)	1½	**15**	40/1	63	—
2078[3]	**Express Gift** (MrsMReveley) **8-11-10** NSmith (nvr bttr than mid div)	2	**16**	20/1	83	—
	Clifdon Fog (IRE) (JSBolger,Ireland) **6-10-8b** APMcCoy (hld up in tch: 5th & rdn 4th: 8th at 5th: wknd next: n.d appr 2 out)	2½	**17**	7/1[2]	65	—
1234a[3]	**Notcomplainingbut (IRE)** (PMullins,Ireland) **6-11-12** TPTreacy (in tch: 4th at 3rd: lost pl bef 5th: no imp fr 3 out)	5	**18**	25/1	78	—
	Shanes Hero (IRE) (PMcCreery,Ireland) **7-10-13** JPBroderick (mid div: mstke 2nd: prog next: wnt 2nd at 5th: 3rd 3 out: 7th, rdn & chsd ldrs 2 out: sn no imp)	3	**19**	50/1	62	—

			Pos	SP	RR	SF
1779*	**Centaur Express** (AStreeter) **5-10-4** TEley (led & disp ld: hdd briefly bef 4th: hdd appr next: wknd bef 3 out: sn n.d)	13	**20**	25/1	44	—
1752a[10]	**Lady Arpel (IRE)** (PO'Leary,Ireland) **5-10-9** KFO'Brien (sn 2nd & disp ld: adv briefly bef 4th: hdd 5th: wknd bef next: dropped bhd)	14	**21**	14/1	35	—
	Reasilvia (IRE) (EJO'Grady,Ireland) **7-10-10** GBradley (in rr: mstke 2nd: bhd fr next: n.d)	8	**22**	50/1	24	—
	Glint Of Eagles (IRE) (WPMullins,Ireland) **8-10-9** DJCasey (hld up: mid div: prog 4th: 8th & trckd ldrs whn s.u after 3 out: dead)		**S**	25/1	—	—
				(SP 135.2%)	**23 Rn**	

3m 50.0 (-11.00) OWNER Jebel Ali Racing Stables (UPPER LAMBOURN) BRED Lord Harrington
2048 Master Tribe (IRE) looked to be galloping over his rivals two out and led well before the last. He was not going away at the end, but neither was he giving in. (18/1)
Black Queen (IRE), kidded and cajoled along on the outside from two out, went second on the flat and, despite hanging left, showed more than her usual enthusiasm to give the winner a real battle. It was afterwards disclosed that she was in season. (12/1)
1804* Penny a Day (IRE) started to make headway two out and landed fifth over the last. He stayed on, but was never getting on terms. (7/1)
1752a Family Way went in pursuit of the leaders on the inside from two out. He held a chance briefly before the last, but was done with early on the flat. (15/2)
1752a Metastasio, whose rider lost an iron two out, finished best of all. (33/1)
Khayrawani (IRE) came through to lead before the last bend, but was under pressure and going nowhere well before the last. (5/1)
1510* Executive Design got himself well behind and, although staying on from two out, was never going to get into serious contention. (16/1)
1804 Kaitak (IRE) had his chance three out, but had dropped away after the next. (40/1)
1347 Palacegate King never got out of mid-division. (50/1)
2078 Express Gift never got into contention. (20/1)
1779* Centaur Express led and shared the lead until approaching the fifth and dropped out fairly quickly before the next. (25/1)

2604a - 2612a : (Irish Racing) - See Computer Raceform

2496a-CAGNES-SUR-MER (Nice, France) (L-H) (Heavy)
Wednesday January 8th

2613a GRANDE HAIES DE CAGNES HURDLE (5-Y.O+)
2-33 (2-32) **2m 4f** £22,447.00

			Pos	SP	RR	SF
	Pampajim (FR) (TCivel,France) **8-10-7** TPelerin	—	**1**		—	—
	Mon Domino (RCollet,France) **8-10-9** PHaves	3½	**2**		—	—
	Chinese Gordon (IRE) (J-PGallorini,France) **7-10-7** HBlois	4	**3**		—	—
2496a*	**Garolo (FR)** (CPEBrooks) **7-10-6** GBradley (btn dist)		**7**		—	—
						13 Rn

5m 3.03 P-M 15.30F: 4.20F 1.70F 10.40F (33.30F) OWNER Ecurie Partners BRED Mlle D. Platt
2496a* Garolo (FR) raced in third position until weakening three out. He appeared not to get the trip.

2430-KELSO (L-H) (Good)
Friday January 17th
WEATHER: overcast

2614 E.B.F. TATTERSALLS (IRELAND) (QUALIFIER) NOVICES' CHASE (6-Y.O+ Mares Only) (Class E)
1-00 (1-01) **2m 6f 110y (17 fncs)** £3,436.25 (£1,040.00: £507.50: £241.25) GOING: 0.21 sec per fur (G)

			Pos	SP	RR	SF
1850[2]	**Seeking Gold (IRE) (89)** (JBarclay) **8-11-8** BStorey (led to 2nd: chsd ldrs: outpcd 12th: hdwy 2 out: led flat: styd on strly)	—	**1**	11/4[2]	97	30
1947[6]	**Ardent Love (IRE) (84)** (DNicholson) **8-10-10** AMaguire (mstkes: reminders thrght: in tch: hdwy u.p 3 out: outpcd appr last: styd on flat)	4	**2**	7/2[3]	82	15
	Call Me Black (IRE) (MDHammond) **8-10-10** RGarritty (hmpd 5th: hdwy & mstke 10th: effrt 3 out: chal whn blnd last: nt qckn)	1	**3**	6/1	81	14
1944[5]	**Cullane Lake (IRE)** (MissMKMilligan) **7-10-10** ASSmith (led 2nd: mstke last: sn hdd & btn)	2	**4**	20/1	80	13
	Old Betsy (MrsSJSmith) **7-10-10** RichardGuest (chsd ldrs: ev ch fr 11th tl blnd & wknd 2 out)	13	**5**	33/1	71	4
2176[B]	**Establish (IRE) (76)** (JPDodds) **9-10-10** KJohnson (hmpd 5th: bhd tl fell 13th)		**F**	16/1	—	—
	Game Point (DALamb) **8-10-10** JBurke (chsd ldrs tl fell 5th)		**F**	66/1	—	—
	Weejumpawud (MrsJStorey) **7-10-10** MrCStorey (fell 1st)		**F**	33/1	—	—
1994[4]	**Tellicherry** (MissHCKnight) **8-10-10** BFenton (prom whn bdly hmpd & uns rdr 5th)		**U**	2/1[1]	—	—
				(SP 114.5%)	**9 Rn**	

5m 49.4 (17.40) CSF £11.49 TOTE £3.30: £1.30 £1.70 £2.30 (£4.90) Trio £10.00 OWNER Gilry (LESLIE) BRED John Bourke
1850 Seeking Gold (IRE), although short of pace, jumps, stays and is genuine. Against this opposition, that was all that was required. (11/4)
Ardent Love (IRE) beat herself by continually backing off her fences and her rider had to work hard throughout. To her credit, she did keep on when all looked lost. (7/2: 5/2-4/1)
Call Me Black (IRE), making both her debut in this country and over fences, ran reasonably and no doubt a modest race will be found. (6/1)
1944 Cullane Lake (IRE) ran much better this time, but probably still needed it. (20/1)
Old Betsy had no real form to recommend her, but she did show something until a blunder two out stopped her dead. (33/1)
1423 Tellicherry, in a race that would have taken little winning, got tangled up with a faller early on and her rider had no chance of staying aboard. (2/1)

2615 GLASSEDIN SCOTTISH HURDLE (4-Y.O) (Class C)
1-30 (1-33) **2m 110y (8 hdls)** £3,582.50 (£1,085.00: £530.00: £252.50) GOING: 0.21 sec per fur (G)

			Pos	SP	RR	SF
2175*	**Rossel (USA)** (PMonteith) **4-11-9** ADobbin (lw: trckd ldrs: led fr 5th: hld on wl flat)	—	**1**	5/1[2]	92	25
	Soldat (USA) (DNicholson) **4-11-9** DBridgwater (hld up: hdwy 5th: hit 3 out: sn rdn: styd on u.p flat: nrst fin)	nk	**2**	1/2[1]	92+	25
1940[3]	**Jackson Park (105)** (TDEasterby) **4-11-5** AMaguire (lw: led fr 1st to 5th: ev ch last: nt qckn towards fin)	¾	**3**	8/1[3]	87	20
1940[4]	**J J Baboo (IRE)** (MDHammond) **4-11-0** RGarritty (hld up: wnt prom 4th: nt qckn fr 2 out)	4	**4**	25/1	78	11

				SP	RR	SF
1652^{4}	**Meltemison** (MDHammond) **4-10-11**(3) MrCBonner (bit bkwd: swtg: plld hrd: cl up tl outpcd fr 2 out)	3½	**5**	12/1	75+	8
	Double Agent (HowardJohnson) **4-11-0** PCarberry (nt j.w: led to 1st: cl up tl wknd appr last)	2	**6**	25/1	73	6
1940^{7}	**Sousse** (MrsMReveley) **4-10-9** PNiven (hld up & bhd: n.d)	7	**7**	40/1	61	—
1356^{8}	**Cry Baby** (ACWhillans) **4-10-9**(5) STaylor (chsd ldrs tl outpcd fr 5th)	2½	**8**	200/1	64	—
1700^{6}	**Double Dash (IRE)** (DMoffatt) **4-11-5** DJMoffatt (n.d)	18	**9**	100/1	51	—
1940^{6}	**Perpetual Light** (JJQuinn) **4-10-9** DerekByrne (prom to ½-wy: grad lost pl: lame)	10	**10**	66/1	31	—
2175^{6}	**Mountain Dream** (RAllan) **4-11-0** BStorey (a bhd)	5	**11**	66/1	32	—
1356^{6}	**Mapleton** (MrsSJSmith) **4-11-0** RichardGuest (prom tl wknd fr 3 out)	2½	**12**	66/1	29	—
				(SP 118.2%)	**12 Rn**	

3m 59.4 (13.40) CSF £7.20 TOTE £6.10: £1.50 £1.10 £2.90 (£2.50) Trio £4.20 OWNER Mr Allan Melville (ROSEWELL) BRED Allen E. Paulson

OFFICIAL EXPLANATION **Perpetual Light: the trainer reported that the filly was lame behind.**

2175* Rossel (USA) goes from strength to strength and, jumping well, put up a really game performance. (5/1)

Soldat (USA), an expensive French purchase, certainly has the look of a decent type and moved really well, but his hurdling was the difference as he made mistakes at vital stages. Much better is to come from him, especially when the going eases. (1/2)

1940 Jackson Park keeps running well but, try as he might, the game winner had just got the edge on him. (8/1)

1940 J J Baboo (IRE) is on the upgrade and will surely not be long in picking up a similar race. (25/1)

1652 Meltemison caught everybody's eye last time and, despite sweating profusely, ran well again and after seven weeks off. He looked likely to need it. (12/1: op 8/1)

Double Agent would not have a cut at his hurdles and, once he gets confidence in his jumping, the improvement should be immense. (25/1)

1184 Sousse is obviously a funny customer as she was taken to post early, but she did show a little without being given a hard time. (40/1)

2616 SCOTTISH BORDERS NATIONAL H'CAP CHASE (5-Y.O+) (Class B)

2-00 (2-03) **4m (24 fncs)** £20,902.50 (£6,345.00: £3,110.00: £1,492.50) GOING: 0.21 sec per fur (G)

				SP	RR	SF
1670*	**Seven Towers (IRE) (125)** (MrsMReveley) **8-10-0** BStorey (bhd: hdwy & prom 18th: chal 2 out: led flat: styd on wl)	—	**1**	11/2 2	134	—
1670^{2}	**Mony-Skip (IRE) (128)** (MrsSJSmith) **8-10-3**ow3 RichardGuest (wnt prom 12th: led 2 out tl hdd flat: kpt on)	4	**2**	16/1	135	—
1649^{3}	**Lo Stregone (150)** (TPTate) **11-11-11** CFSwan (in tch tl outpcd 19th: gd hdwy 3 out: kpt on one pce fr last)	8	**3**	11/2 2	152	—
1513*	**Into the Red (133)** (MrsMReveley) **13-10-8** PNiven (bhd: hdwy 15th: hit 5 out: sn chsng ldrs: nt qckn fr 2 out)	3½	**4**	5/1 1	133	—
1785^{3}	**St Mellion Fairway (IRE) (134)** (DNicholson) **8-10-9** AMaguire (hld up: hdwy & prom 17th: hit 5 out: one pce fr 2 out)	5	**5**	11/2 2	131	—
1941^{2}	**Astings (FR) (125)** (JGFitzGerald) **9-10-0** PCarberry (lw: trckd ldrs tl blnd bdly & lost pl 11th: hdwy 18th: nt qckn fr 2 out)	4	**6**	9/1	119	—
1784^{F}	**Nazzaro (128)** (WGMTurner) **8-10-3b**ow3 AThornton (mde most to 2 out: wknd)	4	**7**	16/1	120	—
1655^{6}	**Ceilidh Boy (125)** (MrsJDGoodfellow) **11-10-0** ASSmith (prom tl outpcd 14th: hit 18th: n.d after)	22	**8**	25/1	104	—
1501^{P}	**Whaat Fettle (130)** (GRichards) **12-10-5** ADobbin (cl up tl wknd fr 4 out)	6	**9**	20/1	105	—
1578^{12}	**Side of Hill (125)** (BMactaggart) **12-9-11**(3) GLee (cl up tl rdn & wknd fr 18th)	12	**10**	200/1	93	—
2063*	**Pink Gin (125)** (MDHammond) **10-10-0** DBridgwater (a outpcd & bhd)	dist	**11**	14/1	—	—
1784^{3}	**Full of Oats (125)** (MissHCKnight) **11-10-0** BFenton (lw: hdwy & prom whn fell 17th)		**F**	7/1 3	—	—
1823^{7}	**Greenhill Raffles (125)** (MissLucindaRussell) **11-10-0v** MFoster (prom tl blnd 13th: sn wl bhd: p.u bef 2 out)		**P**	100/1	—	—
				(SP 113.8%)	**13 Rn**	

8m 7.4 CSF £72.84 CT £458.79 TOTE £7.60: £2.60 £4.30 £1.70 (£78.30) Trio £138.30 OWNER Mrs E. A. Murray (SALTBURN) BRED J. Mernagh

LONG HANDICAP Seven Towers (IRE) 9-6 Astings (FR) 9-7 Ceilidh Boy 9-9 Mony-Skip (IRE) 9-4 Side of Hill 7-8 Pink Gin 9-2 Full of Oats 9-9 Greenhill Raffles 8-13

1670* Seven Towers (IRE) looks none too happy early on in a race, but he does stay forever and this marathon trip proved right up his street. He won it most emphatically. (11/2)

1670 Mony-Skip (IRE) is certainly game and, despite making the odd mistake, kept staying on, but just found the winner too strong in the closing stages. (16/1)

1649 Lo Stregone has worn blinkers on the last three occasions and was without them here, but still put up a good performance. Should they be refitted, he looks one to side with. (11/2)

1513* Into the Red, a stable-companion of the winner, had his chances, but was always struggling with the pace on the last circuit. After a mistake five out, he was fighting a lost cause. (5/1)

1785 St Mellion Fairway (IRE) ran well on ground faster than he really prefers and this should have put him straight. (11/2)

1941 Astings (FR) was a virtual faller at the eleventh, but his brilliant rider picked him off the floor and amazingly got him back into the race. Not surprisingly this told late on. (9/1)

1784 Nazzaro, happier on much softer ground, ran a cracker to the second last. (16/1)

1501 Whaat Fettle, a Kelso specialist, had apparently been held up in his work and it showed over the last four fences. (20/1)

2617 TIM DOODY WHITE LINE MOREBATTLE LIMITED H'CAP HURDLE (4-Y.O+) (Class B)

2-30 (2-34) **2m 110y (8 hdls)** £4,769.80 (£1,443.40: £704.20: £334.60) GOING: 0.21 sec per fur (G)

				SP	RR	SF
1793^{5}	**Direct Route (IRE) (133)** (HowardJohnson) **6-10-12** PCarberry (a gng wl: led on bit fnl 100y: easily)	—	**1**	100/30 1	109+	31
1690^{5}	**Uncle Doug (127)** (MrsMReveley) **6-10-6** PNiven (lw: w ldrs: led 2 out: hdd fnl 100y: no ch w wnr)	1	**2**	16/1	102	24
1924^{5}	**Thornton Gate (125)** (TDEasterby) **8-10-4** JCallaghan (plld hrd: hdwy 5th: chsng ldrs 2 out: rdn & styd on one pce)	½	**3**	10/1	100	22
	Ingletonian (121) (BMactaggart) **8-10-0** BStorey (bit bkwd: chsd ldrs: styng on whn bdly hmpd appr last: nt rcvr)	3½	**4**	150/1	92?	14
1656^{4}	**Home Counties (IRE) (142)** (DMoffatt) **8-11-7v** DJMoffatt (lw: chsd ldrs: hit 3 out: rdn & no imp after)	9	**5**	5/1 2	104	26
2062^{4}	**Marchant Ming (IRE) (129)** (MDHammond) **5-10-8** RGarritty (mde most tl mstke & hdd 2 out: ducked lft appr last: sn btn & eased)	30	**6**	5/1 2	62	—
	Aragon Ayr (121) (PMonteith) **9-10-0** ADobbin (bit bkwd: outpcd ½-wy: lost tch 5th)	4	**7**	11/2 3	51	—
1314^{5}	**Common Sound (IRE) (121)** (JBarclay) **6-9-9**(5) MrRThornton (mstke 2nd: prom tl outpcd 5th)	7	**8**	33/1	44	—
1017^{2}	**Hatta Breeze (129)** (DNicholson) **5-10-8** AMaguire (lw: in tch: 6th & btn whn fell 2 out)		**F**	100/30 1	—	—
1942^{4}	**Jazilah (FR) (121)** (RAllan) **9-10-0** DBridgwater (a bhd: p.u bef 3 out)		**P**	50/1	—	—
				(SP 115.4%)	**10 Rn**	

3m 55.7 (9.70) CSF £47.16 CT £441.09 TOTE £4.30: £1.20 £2.20 £3.70 (£19.40) Trio £236.90; £43.38 to Kempton 18/1/97 OWNER Mr Chris Heron (CROOK) BRED Mrs Noeleen Roche

LONG HANDICAP Common Sound (IRE) 9-9 Ingletonian 8-7 Jazilah (FR) 9-13
1793 Direct Route (IRE), given what is now a typical Carberry ride, never came off the bit at any stage and just laughed at the opposition. (100/30)
1690 Uncle Doug, made plenty of use of over this shorter trip, did his best, but the winner was different class. (16/1)
1924 Thornton Gate took his customary strong hold and came later this time but, when off the bit, he was never quite doing enough. There is certainly ability there if he can be persuaded. (10/1)
Ingletonian, from 21lb out of the handicap, ran an amazing race and, but for almost being carried out at the last, would have been in the first three. (150/1)
1656 Home Counties (IRE) has lost his edge of late and never really looked likely to make any impression once off the bit. (5/1)
2062 Marchant Ming (IRE), happier on softer ground, was disappointing and almost ran out at the last when beaten. (5/1)
Aragon Ayr needed this and ran moderately. (11/2)

2618 ANDREW HAMILTON & CO. RUTHERFORD H'CAP CHASE (0-135) (5-Y.O+) (Class C)
3-00 (3-02) **2m 1f (12 fncs)** £4,421.80 (£1,338.40: £653.20: £310.60) GOING: 0.21 sec per fur (G)

	Horse		Pos	SP	RR	SF
1805[4]	**Wee River (IRE) (125)** (GMMoore) **8-11-4** JCallaghan (lw: hld up: hit 8th: hdwy on bit 3 out: led last: rdn & r.o)	—	**1**	7/4[2]	133	43
1688[3]	**Regal Romper (IRE) (112)** (MrsSJSmith) **9-10-5** RichardGuest (led tl mstke & hdd 5th: led 8th: hdd last: kpt on gamely)	2	**2**	9/2[3]	118	28
1792[F]	**Lord Dorcet (IRE) (133)** (JIACharlton) **7-11-12** ADobbin (trckd ldrs: effrt 3 out: sn rdn: kpt on flat: nvr able to chal)	3½	**3**	6/4[1]	136	46
1846[4]	**One for the Pot (107)** (MrsAMNaughton) **12-10-0** MFoster (cl up: led fr 5th: hit 7th: hdd 8th: outpcd fr 3 out)	9	**4**	20/1	101	11
2058[4]	**Sybillin (135)** (JGFitzGerald) **11-12-0** PCarberry (hld up: effrt & hdwy 3 out: sn btn)	9	**5**	10/1	121	31
1702[2]	**Uncle Bert (IRE) (111)** (MissLucindaRussell) **7-10-4**ow4 AThornton (prom tl outpcd 4 out: sn bhd)	3½	**6**	50/1	94	—

(SP 110.4%) **6 Rn**

4m 15.8 (8.80) CSF £8.94 TOTE £3.40: £1.60 £2.00 (£7.40) OWNER Mr Sean Graham (MIDDLEHAM) BRED William P. Delaney
LONG HANDICAP One for the Pot 9-13 Uncle Bert (IRE) 9-6
1805 Wee River (IRE), looking particularly well, took a strong hold and, despite one mistake, there were never any doubts about the result. (7/4)
1688 Regal Romper (IRE) ran his usual game race, only to find the winner too strong in the closing stages. (9/2)
1352 Lord Dorcet (IRE) was always well enough placed, but he was off the bit some way out and, although keeping on, was never quite good enough. He left the impression that he should be all the better for this. (6/4)
1846 One for the Pot ran a fine race until finding this company too hot from the third last. (20/1)
2058 Sybillin, taken out early and mounted on the course, showed little encouragement in the race. (10/1: 8/1-12/1)
1702 Uncle Bert (IRE), from an out-of-form yard, looked pretty slow once the pressure was on over the last five fences. (50/1)

2619 E.B.F. 'N.H.' (QUALIFIER) NOVICES' HURDLE (5, 6 & 7-Y.O) (Class E)
3-30 (3-32) **2m 2f (10 hdls)** £2,584.00 (£724.00: £352.00) GOING: 0.21 sec per fur (G)

	Horse		Pos	SP	RR	SF
2064*	**Alzulu (IRE) (114)** (JGFitzGerald) **6-11-10** PCarberry (disp ld & hit 1st: cl up: led fr 7th: clr whn blnd last: easily)	—	**1**	4/5[1]	89+	24
1926[5]	**Revolt** (TDEasterby) **5-11-0** CFSwan (chsd ldrs: ev ch 4 out: rdn & blnd last: one pce after)	7	**2**	12/1	73	8
1938[5]	**Mythical Approach (IRE)** (DNicholson) **7-11-0** AMaguire (hld up: hdwy 4 out: chsng ldrs 2 out: kpt on one pce)	1¼	**3**	9/2[2]	72	7
1667[2]	**Malta Man (IRE)** (PCheesbrough) **7-11-0** ASSmith (hld up: stdy hdwy appr 2 out: nvr plcd to chal)	1¼	**4**	14/1	71+	6
1633[11]	**Judicious Norman (IRE)** (JRAdam) **6-11-0** TReed (lw: stdd s: bhd tl hdwy 4 out: nrst fin)	hd	**5**	33/1	71+	6
1854[14]	**Boris Brook** (RAllan) **6-10-7**(7) SMelrose (chsd ldrs: rdn 4 out: wknd 2 out)	¾	**6**	200/1	70	5
	Nordic Prince (IRE) (TPTate) **6-11-0** RGarritty (chsd ldrs: outpcd & hit 7th: no imp fr 3 out)	1¼	**7**	6/1[3]	69	4
1431[3]	**April Seventh (IRE)** (JNeville) **6-11-0** DBridgwater (mde most to 7th: cl up tl wknd appr 2 out)	9	**8**	16/1	61	—
1843[7]	**Persuasive Talent (IRE) (67)** (DALamb) **6-11-0** JBurke (in tch tl outpcd fr 7th)	8	**9**	200/1	54	—
1692[12]	**Smiddy Lad** (RShiels) **6-11-0** DBentley (in tch tl outpcd 4 out: btn whn hit 2 out)	1¼	**10**	100/1	53	—
	Solsgirth (JBarclay) **6-11-0** AThornton (prom: hit 2nd: wknd fr 7th)	2	**11**	200/1	51	—
1667[7]	**Sunny Leith** (PMonteith) **6-11-0** ADobbin (bhd fr ½-wy)	25	**12**	50/1	29	—
	My Mavourneen (MrsSCBradburne) **5-10-9** MFoster (n.d)	2½	**13**	100/1	21	—
1926[4]	**The Sharrow Legend (IRE)** (JSisterson) **5-11-0** BStorey (n.d)	hd	**14**	33/1	26	—
	Great Gable (IRE) (DMoffatt) **6-11-0** DJMoffatt (prom tl wknd fr 4 out)	14	**15**	200/1	14	—
2000[F]	**Make A Buck (67)** (LLungo) **7-11-0b** RSupple (prom: shkn up ½-wy: sn wknd)	18	**16**	200/1	—	—
	Glacial Girl (IRE) (DSAlder) **5-10-9** KJohnson (a bhd)	2	**17**	200/1	—	—
1827[8]	**Blue Chequer** (MissMKMilligan) **6-10-9** PNiven (lost tch 6th: wl t.o whn p.u bef 2 out)		**P**	100/1	—	—
2503[8]	**Kings High (IRE)** (WTKemp) **7-11-0** SMcDougall (bhd fr ½-wy: p.u flat: lame)		**P**	200/1	—	—

(SP 122.6%) **19 Rn**

4m 28.2 (15.20) CSF £11.32 TOTE £1.70: £1.10 £2.40 £1.60 (£9.00) Trio £13.90 OWNER Mr D. Buckle (MALTON) BRED Ardenode Stud Ltd
OFFICIAL EXPLANATION The Sharrow Legend (IRE): was not suited by the going.
2064* Alzulu (IRE), ridden with plenty of confidence, almost threw it away by blundering at the last, but he was soon back on the bridle. He is still learning. (4/5)
1926 Revolt ran a super race at his first attempt over hurdles here and more will be heard of him, especially over the bigger obstacles. (12/1)
1938 Mythical Approach (IRE) ran well in this useful heat and should pick up his share of races. (9/2)
1667 Malta Man (IRE) had another educational and looks one to keep on the right side. (14/1)
Judicious Norman (IRE), who made the running last time, was ridden completely the opposite way here and showed plenty. (33/1)
Boris Brook has the look of a decent sort and showed something this time, but he did appear slow and may need further yet. (200/1)

T/Plpt: £32.00 (404.47 Tckts). T/Qdpt: £19.60 (43.55 Tckts). AA

2163-KEMPTON (R-H) (Good to firm)
Friday January 17th
WEATHER: raining becoming sunny

2620 RUNNYMEDE NOVICES' CONDITIONAL H'CAP HURDLE (0-110) (5-Y.O+) (Class E)
1-40 (1-40) **3m 110y (12 hdls)** £2,780.00 (£780.00: £380.00) GOING: 0.14 sec per fur (G)

	Horse		Pos	SP	RR	SF
1964[P]	**Captain Jack (103)** (MCPipe) **7-11-11** DWalsh (nt j.w: w ldr: led 8th: rdn out)	—	**1**	6/4[1]	78	23

1995[5] **Blazing Miracle (78)** (MrsRGHenderson) **5-10-0** DSalter (hld up: rdn appr 2 out: r.o flat)....5 **2** 13/2[3] 50 —
Cardinal Gayle (IRE) (78) (RHAlner) **7-10-0** PHenley (bit bkwd: hld up: chsd wnr appr 2 out tl flat: sn wknd)...3 **3** 7/1 48 —
883[P] **Lodestone Lad (IRE) (78)** (RDickin) **7-9-9b**(5) XAizpuru (bit bkwd: led to 8th: wknd after 3 out)....30 **4** 10/1 28 —
1791[3] **Wanstead (IRE) (86)** (JRJenkins) **5-10-3b**(5) NTEgan (lw: hld up: chsd wnr 3 out to appr 2 out: sn wknd).....1½ **5** 9/4[2] 35 —
(SP 105.7%) **5 Rn**

6m 5.9 (19.90) CSF £9.11 TOTE £1.60: £1.40 £3.00 (£4.00) OWNER Mr Clive Smith (WELLINGTON) BRED Highclere Stud Ltd
LONG HANDICAP Cardinal Gayle (IRE) 9-4 Lodestone Lad (IRE) 9-7 Blazing Miracle 9-2
OFFICIAL EXPLANATION **Wanstead (IRE): Regarding the apparent tender handling, the rider reported that the gelding was very tired on the run-in and had no more to give.**
1476 Captain Jack seems better without the blinkers and on a sound surface. However, his jumping left a great deal to be desired and his jockey had to bustle him into many of the hurdles. Either he has not mastered the art of hurdling yet or he did not want to jump them but, rousted along, he asserted in the straight to win this bad event. He has ability, but may well be worth avoiding. (6/4: op evens)
1327 Blazing Miracle, 12lb out of the handicap, was helped by this much longer trip and stayed on to take second on the run-in. (13/2)
Cardinal Gayle (IRE), who looked big and well for his first run since April 1995, was racing from 10lb out of the handicap. He looked a real danger to the winner before lack of a recent run took its toll, and he was looking tired when collared for the runner-up spot on theflat. (7/1)
Lodestone Lad (IRE), not looking fully fit for this first run in three months, was reverting to hurdles. (10/1)
1791 Wanstead (IRE) failed to stay this much longer trip. He is extremely moderate and exposed, and is not one to trust. (9/4)

2621 EASTER HERO H'CAP CHASE (0-135) (5-Y.O+) (Class C)

2-10 (2-10) **2m (13 fncs)** £4,463.00 (£1,349.00: £657.00: £311.00) GOING: 0.14 sec per fur (G)

SP RR SF

2051* **Super Tactics (IRE) (131)** (RHAlner) **9-11-9**(3) PHenley (hdwy 5th: led appr last: rdn out)....— **1** 5/2[1] 143 38
1912[W] **Fine Harvest (122)** (JLSpearing) **11-11-3** TJMurphy (a.p: led 6th: mstke 9th: j.lft 3 out: hdd appr last: unable qckn flat)....1¾ **2** 7/2[2] 132 27
1520[P] **Senor El Betrutti (IRE) (133)** (MrsSusanNock) **8-12-0** GBradley (lost pl 4th: rallied appr 3 out: rdn & ev ch appr 2 out: one pce)....1¼ **3** 7/1 142 37
1730[2] **Dear Do (108)** (NJHenderson) **10-10-3**ow3 MAFitzgerald (hdwy 7th: rdn appr 2 out: one pce)....6 **4** 4/1[3] 111 3
1957[4] **Bally Parson (110)** (RDickin) **11-10-5** NWilliamson (mstke 3rd: chsd ldr to 6th: 3rd whn mstke 7th: wknd appr 3 out)....12 **5** 6/1 101 —
1570[F] **Armala (110)** (JTGifford) **12-10-2**(3)ow2 LAspell (lw: a bhd)....8 **6** 6/1 93 —
2009[4] **Count Barachois (USA) (105)** (MrsEHHeath) **9-10-0** KGaule (lw: led to 6th: ev ch 4 out: wknd appr 3 out).....3 **7** 50/1 85 —
(SP 113.8%) **7 Rn**

3m 53.8 (9.80) CSF £10.90 CT £47.55 TOTE £3.40: £1.50 £2.70 (£4.50) OWNER Mr H. V. Perry (BLANDFORD) BRED James Robinson
LONG HANDICAP Dear Do 9-12 Count Barachois (USA) 8-9
2051* Super Tactics (IRE) has steadily been rising in the weights, but that was not going to stop his terrific form this season. (5/2)
1660* Fine Harvest seems better on a right-handed track and ran a fine race, despite a rise of 12lb in the handicap since the beginning of the season. He has yet to win on ground worse than good and, as long as the rain stays away, he should soon regain the winning thread. (7/2)
1520 Senor El Betrutti (IRE) is a quirky customer and that was again evident here as he dropped himself out of it setting out on the final circuit and was almost tailed off at one point. Making up tremendous ground to get back into it turning for home, he was tapped for toe over the last two fences. He needs a right-handed track and two and a half miles on a sound surface. However, he must have everything going his way and, whilst he has plenty of ability, he looks one to avoid. (7/1)
1730 Dear Do was carrying 5lb more than his long-handicap weight. (4/1: 3/1-9/2)
1957 Bally Parson had the ground in his favour, but is very exposed. (6/1)

2622 WALTON HURDLE (4-Y.O) (Class B)

2-40 (2-42) **2m (8 hdls)** £6,246.00 (£1,908.00: £944.00: £462.00) GOING: 0.14 sec per fur (G)

SP RR SF

1634[3] **Summer Spell (USA)** (NJHenderson) **4-10-10** MAFitzgerald (hdwy 4th: led appr last: rdn out)....— **1** 11/4[1] 89+ 52
1935[F] **Mr Wild (USA)** (RAkehurst) **4-10-10** APMcCoy (a.p: led 3 out tl appr last: unable qckn)....3 **2** 9/2[3] 86 49
Quality (IRE) (PJHobbs) **4-10-10** RDunwoody (hdwy 5th: rdn appr last: one pce)....4 **3** 10/1 82+ 45
1872* **Far Dawn (USA)** (MrsAJPerrett) **4-11-2** CMaude (lw: hld up: hrd rdn appr 2 out: one pce)....1¾ **4** 3/1[2] 86 49
Sulawesi (IRE) (NATwiston-Davies) **4-10-5** CLlewellyn (gd hdwy 3 out: wknd appr 2 out)....16 **5** 33/1 59 22
Brilliant Red (PRHedger) **4-10-10** MRichards (hdwy 5th: wknd appr 2 out)....3½ **6** 10/1 61 24
1900* **Disallowed (IRE)** (MissHCKnight) **4-11-1** JFTitley (prom tl after 3 out)....3 **7** 7/1 63 26
1387[6] **Seattle Alley (USA)** (PRWebber) **4-10-10** JOsborne (nvr nr to chal)....12 **8** 14/1 46 9
1900[5] **Brandon Magic** (IABalding) **4-10-10** GBradley (a.p: led 4th tl hdd & mstke 3 out: sn wknd)....15 **9** 16/1 31 —
Brecon (WRMuir) **4-10-10** JRKavanagh (a bhd)....1 **10** 100/1 30 —
Scathebury (KRBurke) **4-10-10** ALarnach (lw: a bhd)....6 **11** 66/1 24 —
1862[8] **Magic Role** (JRJenkins) **4-10-10** JRailton (prom to 4th)....½ **12** 100/1 23 —
2070[11] **Bailiwick** (NAGraham) **4-10-10** NWilliamson (bit bkwd: a bhd)....8 **13** 100/1 15 —
1953[15] **Saucy Dancer** (JCTuck) **4-10-5** SMcNeill (lw: bhd fr 4th)....7 **14** 100/1 3 —
Mr Hacker (GThorner) **4-10-10** BPowell (bit bkwd: bhd fr 3rd)....28 **15** 100/1 — —
1872[3] **Baranov (IRE)** (DJGMurraySmith) **4-10-10** DGallagher (led: mstke 1st: hdd 4th: sn wknd: t.o whn p.u bef 2 out).... **P** 20/1 — —
(SP 127.2%) **16 Rn**

3m 45.6 (3.60) CSF £14.53 TOTE £3.80: £2.10 £1.60 £2.20 (£12.90) Trio £122.60 OWNER W V & Mrs E S Robins (LAMBOURN) BRED Jim Robinson, Pam Robinson and Walmac Internationa
IN-FOCUS: **This looked a very useful Juvenile event and it would be a big surprise if several winners did not come out of this.**
1634 Summer Spell (USA) would have preferred some cut in the ground, but that was not enough to stop him putting up a polished display in this hot event. He has now been made joint-favourite for the Triumph Hurdle. (11/4)
1935 Mr Wild (USA) at last got his jumping together and ran a fine race. He looks sure to win a race before long. (9/2: op 5/2)
Quality (IRE), who won two races for Bill O'Gorman last year, was sold for 25,000 guineas at the Newmarket Autumn Sales. Given no easy task on this hurdling debut, he showed a lot of promise and was bang there two out before tapped for toe going to the last. He should have no problems opening his account. (10/1: 6/1-12/1)
1872* Far Dawn (USA), faced with a 6lb penalty for two impressive victories, was meeting some potentially useful rivals. Rather outpaced after the third last, his jockey surprisingly failed to get down to work until entering the straight, by which time he had quite a bit of ground to make up. Not surprisingly under his penalty, he could only go up and down in the same place. Under a more forceful ride, he can regain winning ways. (3/1)

Sulawesi (IRE), sold out of Willie Jarvis's stable for 7,500 guineas at the Newmarket Autumn Sales, made up a tremendous amount of ground three from home before lack of a recent outing took its toll. She should come on for this. (33/1)
Brilliant Red, sold out of Paul Cole's stable for 24,000 guineas at the Newmarket Autumn Sales, had shot his bolt turning for home. He will strip fitter for the run and should progress from this. (10/1: 6/1-12/1)
1900* Disallowed (IRE) (7/1: 5/1-8/1)

2623 HANWORTH H'CAP CHASE (0-140) (5-Y.O+) (Class B)

3-10 (3-10) **3m (19 fncs)** £5,006.40 (£1,516.20: £740.60: £352.80) GOING: 0.14 sec per fur (G)

				SP	RR	SF
2057^{P}	**Dextra Dove (137)** (SEarle) **10-11-11** CMaude (w ldr: led 5th to 6th: led 9th to 10th: ev ch whn lft in ld 3 out: hrd rdn appr 2 out: r.o wl)	—	1	11/4^{2}	144	52
1858^{2}	**Philip's Woody (115)** (NJHenderson) **9-10-3** JRKavanagh (lw: hld up: n.m.r on ins after 4 out: swtchd rt appr 3 out: ev ch fr 3 out: unable qckn flat)	3	2	100/30	120	28
	Rose King (117) (MissSEdwards) **10-10-2**(3)ow5 LAspell (hld up: ev ch 4 out: wknd appr 3 out)	8	3	16/1	88 t	20
1473^{4}	**Le Meille (IRE) (112)** (KRBurke) **8-10-0** NWilliamson (lw: hld up: ev ch whn mstke 3 out: 3rd & rdn whn blnd bdly 2 out: nt rcvr)	2½	4	3/1^{3}	86 t	18
1558^{4}	**Grey Smoke (129)** (MissHCKnight) **7-11-3** JFTitley (led tl mstke & hdd 5th: led 6th to 9th: led 10th tl fell 3 out)		F	9/4^{1}	—	—
				(SP 111.4%)		**5 Rn**

6m 5.2 (10.20) CSF £11.23 TOTE £3.20: £1.20 £1.30 (£6.20) OWNER Dextra Lighting Systems (STURMINSTER NEWTON) BRED G. H. and Mrs V. E. Price
LONG HANDICAP Rose King 8-7
1649 Dextra Dove bounced back to form. Level with Grey Smoke when that rival departed three from home, he managed to dispose of the runner-up on the flat to win off his highest ever mark. (11/4)
1858 Philip's Woody, very consistent, was having his ninth consecutive run off a mark of 115. Forced to settle for second for the fourth time in a row, he deserves a change of luck. (100/30)
Rose King, carrying 23lb more than his long-handicap weight, had been hung out to dry turning for home. (16/1)
1473 Le Meille (IRE), who has changed stables since last season, was just beginning to look held in third when another bad error two out brought him to a standstill. (3/1)

2624 ASHFORD NOVICES' HURDLE (5-Y.O+) (Class B)

3-40 (3-40) **2m (8 hdls)** £6,376.00 (£1,948.00: £964.00: £472.00) GOING: 0.14 sec per fur (G)

				SP	RR	SF
2112^{2}	**Secret Spring (FR) (118)** (PRHedger) **5-11-4** MRichards (stdy hdwy 5th: led appr last: rdn flat: r.o wl)	—	1	3/1^{3}	100	59
1830*	**Sharpical** (NJHenderson) **5-11-4** MAFitzgerald (stdy hdwy 5th: ev ch appr last: unable qckn flat)	2½	2	11/4^{2}	98	57
1905*	**Daraydan (IRE) (118)** (MCPipe) **5-11-8** APMcCoy (led: clr 3rd: rdn 4th: hdd appr last: one pce)	1¾	3	5/2^{1}	100	59
1905^{4}	**Carlito Brigante** (PRWebber) **5-10-12** JOsborne (a.p: ev ch appr last: one pce)	2½	4	25/1	87	46
1651^{3}	**Nordance Prince (IRE) (112)** (MissGayKelleway) **6-10-12** RDunwoody (hld up: rdn 3 out: wknd appr 2 out)	12	5	10/1	75	34
	Peetsie (IRE) (NATwiston-Davies) **5-10-7** CLlewellyn (prom to 3 out)	10	6	50/1	60	19
	Blomberg (IRE) (JRFanshawe) **5-10-12** PHide (prom tl after 3 out)	1¼	7	9/2	64	23
1729^{3}	**Battleship Bruce (95)** (TCasey) **5-10-12** DGallagher (mid div whn hmpd 2nd: bhd fr 3rd: t.o fr 4th)	25	8	50/1	39	—
	At Liberty (IRE) (RHannon) **5-10-12** NWilliamson (bhd fr 5th: t.o)	3	9	50/1	36	—
	Clock Watchers (68) (JJBridger) **9-10-12** DMorris (bit bkwd: mid div whn hmpd 2nd: bhd fr 3rd: t.o fr 4th)	dist	10	100/1	—	—
1905^{5}	**Shadirwan (IRE)** (RAkehurst) **6-10-12** GBradley (2nd whn fell 2nd)		F	33/1	—	—
1791^{6}	**Resist the Force (USA) (109)** (JTGifford) **7-11-8** LAspell (a bhd: t.o whn p.u bef 2 out)		P	20/1	—	—
	Itani (MJWilkinson) **5-10-12** ILawrence (a bhd: t.o whn p.u bef 2 out)		P	100/1	—	—
				(SP 126.9%)		**13 Rn**

3m 45.6 (3.60) CSF £11.12 TOTE £4.80: £1.90 £1.60 £3.00 (£4.50) Trio £3.60 OWNER Mr M. K. George (CHICHESTER) BRED Timothy D. Rootes
IN-FOCUS: **This was another useful Novice event.**
2112 Secret Spring (FR) looks a useful individual and paid a big compliment to Sanmartino who beat him here on Boxing Day. Travelling well, he cruised into the lead approaching the last and, woken up on the run-in, stormed clear. He must have two miles on a flat track on fast ground, and his trainer remarked afterwards that he was concerned that the ground might have been too soft for him here, as although the official going was good to firm, the times suggested it was good. He can win again. (3/1)
1830* Sharpical, who beat Moonax on his debut, appeared to be travelling really well in the straight. However, once let down after the last, he failed to find as much as looked likely and had to settle for second. He should regain the winning thread. (11/4: 2/1-7/2)
1905* Daraydan (IRE), who had a 10lb penalty to shoulder, stormed off in front and was soon clear. His jockey was bustling him along from halfway, although he was not collared until approaching the final flight. (5/2)
1905 Carlito Brigante was much happier on this easier track and was close enough if good enough going to the last before tapped for toe. He can pick up a race before long if not put in such a competitive event. (25/1)
1651 Nordance Prince (IRE) had given his all turning for home. (10/1)
Peetsie (IRE), fit from the Flat, was making his hurdling debut and showed up well until tiring three from home. (50/1)

2625 ROYAL MAIL H'CAP HURDLE (0-135) (4-Y.O+) (Class C)

4-10 (4-11) **3m 110y (12 hdls)** £3,615.00 (£1,095.00: £535.00: £255.00) GOING: 0.14 sec per fur (G)

				SP	RR	SF
1952^{5}	**Cokenny Boy (108)** (MrsJPitman) **12-10-11** NWilliamson (hld up: mstke 7th: led appr last: rdn out)	—	1	5/1	86	12
1906^{3}	**Olympian (121)** (JNeville) **10-11-10b** RDunwoody (led 2nd to 8th: ev ch appr last: unable qckn flat)	1½	2	7/2^{3}	98	24
1859^{2}	**Diwali Dancer (113)** (MCPipe) **7-11-2** APMcCoy (led to 2nd: led 8th: rdn appr 2 out: hdd appr last: one pce flat)	1¼	3	11/4^{2}	89	15
2117*	**Tim (IRE) (115)** (JRJenkins) **7-11-4** JOsborne (hld up: n.m.r & swtchd lft appr last: rdn: one pce)	2	4	2/1^{1}	90	16
1961^{F}	**Sorbiere (100)** (NJHenderson) **10-10-3** MAFitzgerald (lw: bhd fr 3 out)	14	5	20/1	66	—
1982^{5}	**Little Gunner (110)** (RJPrice) **7-10-13** DGallagher (lw: hld up: rdn after 3 out: sn wknd)	14	6	10/1	67	—
				(SP 112.7%)		**6 Rn**

6m 5.1 (19.10) CSF £20.89 TOTE £6.00: £2.50 £2.40 (£5.80) OWNER Mr S. D. Hemstock (UPPER LAMBOURN) BRED W. McKenzie
1794* Cokenny Boy was much happier back on this sounder surface. (5/1)
1906 Olympian ran a fine race under topweight and cut out much of the running to the eighth. Still in with every chance going to the final flight, he found the winner too strong on the run-in. (7/2)
1859 Diwali Dancer had no problems with this longer trip. (11/4)

2117* Tim (IRE) tried to mount a challenge going to the last, but was tapped for toe. (2/1)

T/Jkpt: £7,100.00 (0.59 Tckts); £3,741.33 to Kempton 18/1/97. T/Plpt: £61.10 (242.31 Tckts). T/Qdpt: £13.40 (91.36 Tckts). AK

0065-SOUTHWELL (L-H) (Standard)
Friday January 17th
Other races under Rules of Flat Racing.
WEATHER: overcast & misty WIND: almost nil

2626 LEVY BOARD STANDARD OPEN N.H. FLAT RACE (4,5,6 & 7-Y.O) (Class H)
12-45 (12-45) **2m** £1,213.50 (£336.00: £160.50)

	Horse / Trainer / Age-Wt / Jockey (comment)	Dist	Pos	SP	RR	SF
	The Khoinoa (IRE) (MrsASwinbank) **7-11-4** JSupple (hld up: jnd ldrs 6f out: led over 4f out: drvn along & styd on strly fnl f)	—	1	10/1	69 f	—
2510[5]	**Slide On** (PDEvans) **7-11-6**(5) MichaelBrennan (lw: led 1f: led 6f out tl over 4f out: nt qckn fnl f)	10	2	6/4[1]	66 f	—
	Sir Boston (RDEWoodhouse) **4-10-6** RJohnson (hdwy ½-wy: chal 5f out: styd on same pce fnl 2f)	1	3	16/1	58 f	—
	Rudolphine (IRE) (BobJones) **6-11-4** NMann (hld up & plld hrd: hdwy 6f out: ev ch over 2f out: sn wknd & eased)	18	4	5/1	40 f	—
	Roll Again (MCPipe) **6-10-11**(7) GSupple (in tch: outpcd 6f out: grad wknd)	10	5	4/1[3]	30 f	—
	Stone The Crows (IRE) (JGFitzGerald) **7-11-4** WDwan (bit bkwd: hld up & plld hrd: jnd ldrs ½-wy: ev ch tl wknd 3f out)	6	6	7/2[2]	24 f	—
	Our Carol (IRE) (JParkes) **5-10-13** VSmith (bit bkwd: sn trckng ldrs: drvn along 7f out: sn lost pl)	12	7	20/1	7 f	—
1151[5]	**Abyss** (NPLittmoden) **5-11-4** LHarvey (trckd ldrs: drvn along & lost pl 6f out)	10	8	20/1	2 f	—
	Gift Star (USA) (CMurray) **4-10-6** OPears (hld up: bhd fnl 6f)	7	9	12/1	—	—
2073[7]	**Huish (IRE)** (GFHCharles-Jones) **6-11-4** MrACharles-Jones (led after 1f to 6f out: sn lost pl)	2½	10	20/1	—	—
1013[9]	**Holkham Bay** (LWordingham) **5-10-11**(7) CRae (trckd ldrs tl lost pl 7f out: t.o 3f out)	19	11	14/1	—	—
	Red Oassis (HOliver) **6-10-11**(7) MrHJOliver (bkwd: racd wd: a bhd: t.o fr ½-wy)	7	12	14/1	—	—
				(SP 149.2%)	**12 Rn**	

3m 59.9 CSF £28.46 TOTE £22.90: £4.40 £1.20 £3.00 (£15.90) Trio £36.40 OWNER Mr M. Allison (RICHMOND) BRED J. A. Weld
WEIGHT FOR AGE 4yo-12lb

The Khoinoa (IRE), on his toes beforehand, looked fit, despite an absence of 657 days. Staying on really strongly, he pulled right away in the final furlong. This was just an ordinary bumper. (10/1)
2510 Slide On, who looked very fit, was left behind by the winner in the final furlong. (6/4)
Sir Boston, who carried plenty of condition, gave a good account of himself first time. (16/1)
Rudolphine (IRE), nicely backed to make a winning debut, did not settle as a result of the modest pace. After having every chance, he dropped away over a furlong out and was eased up. (5/1: op 12/1)
Roll Again (4/1: op 5/2)
Stone The Crows (IRE) looked to be carrying plenty of condition on his first outing for 629 days and ran as if in need of it. (7/2: 5/2-4/1)

T/Plpt: £15.40 (472.45 Tckts). T/Qdpt: £6.10 (125.13 Tckts). WG

2272-CATTERICK (L-H) (Good)
Saturday January 18th
Vis: poor races 1, 2 & 3 - no times taken
WEATHER: misty

2627 SWALE NOVICES' HURDLE (5-Y.O+) (Class E)
1-00 (1-01) **3m 1f 110y (12 hdls)** £2,931.00 (£816.00: £393.00) GOING: 0.40 sec per fur (GS)

	Horse / Trainer / Age-Wt / Jockey (comment)	Dist	Pos	SP	RR	SF
2053[5]	**Share Options (IRE) (104)** (TDEasterby) **6-11-4** JCallaghan (lw: lft in ld 1st: hdd 2nd: w ldrs: in ld 3 out: kpt on wl flat)	—	1	7/4[1]	76	—
2003[2]	**Smart Approach (IRE) (90)** (MrsMReveley) **7-10-6**(7) CMcCormack (lw: a.p: disp ld 2 out: nt qckn towards fin)	½	2	7/2[2]	71	—
1654[8]	**Chill Factor** (MrsMReveley) **7-10-9**(3) GLee (hld up: hdwy 4 out: styd on wl: nrst fin)	18	3	25/1	58	—
1654[7]	**Phar Echo (IRE)** (LLungo) **6-10-12** RSupple (chsd ldrs: ev ch 3 out: one pce appr next)	9	4	20/1	53	—
2177[2]	**Cheater (IRE)** (HowardJohnson) **6-10-12** ASSmith (a chsng ldrs: one pce fr 3 out)	9	5	13/2[3]	47	—
1843[3]	**Erni (FR)** (TPTate) **5-10-5**(7) RMcCarthy (lw: a.p: effrt 3 out: btn appr next)	1	6	11/1	47	—
2042[10]	**Clongour (IRE)** (FMurphy) **7-10-5**(7) MissElizabethDoyle (bhd: sme hdwy fr 4 out: n.d)	nk	7	25/1	46	—
1842[F]	**Jills Joy (IRE)** (JNorton) **6-10-12** WFry (chsd ldrs to 3 out)	1¼	8	7/1	46	—
	King Fly (MrsSarahHorner-Harker) **7-10-12** MFoster (chsd ldrs: chal 3 out: sn wknd)	22	9	50/1	32	—
1687[6]	**Prince of Saints (IRE)** (MDHammond) **6-10-12** ADobbin (in tch: hdwy 8th: wknd after 3 out)	6	10	7/1	28	—
1842[3]	**Basincroft** (MissSWilliamson) **7-10-5**(7) ATodd (rr div whn b.d 1st)		B	100/1	—	—
2047[16]	**Ottadini (IRE)** (WGReed) **5-10-11**ow4 TReed (led tl fell 1st)		F	200/1	—	—
1565[P]	**Off Piste Sally** (FMurphy) **5-10-2**(5) MrRThornton (bit bkwd: wl t.o whn p.u bef 8th)		P	50/1	—	—
1854[9]	**Carnmoney (IRE) (75)** (JSisterson) **9-10-12** GCahill (led fr 2nd tl lost pl 4 out: p.u bef last)		P	66/1	—	—
1666[10]	**Political Bill** (JIACharlton) **6-10-12** KJohnson (bit bkwd: bhd fr 7th: p.u bef 2 out)		P	100/1	—	—
	Just Polly (HAlexander) **5-10-0**(7) MrTJBarry (bit bkwd: t.o fr ½-wy: p.u after 3 out)		P	100/1	—	—
	Kambletree (IRE) (MESowersby) **6-10-7** DParker (bit bkwd: t.o fr ½-wy: p.u bef 8th)		P	100/1	—	—
1999[13]	**Edstone (IRE)** (JWCurtis) **5-10-12** DerekByrne (bit bkwd: jnd ldrs 6th: lost pl 4 out: p.u bef 2 out)		P	200/1	—	—
	Daring Magic (JHetherton) **5-10-4**(3) ECallaghan (bit bkwd: a wl bhd: p.u after 8th)		P	200/1	—	—
	My Young Pet (RMcDonald) **8-10-12** KJones (bhd fr ½-wy: p.u after 3 out)		P	200/1	—	—
1845[P]	**Liam's Loss (IRE)** (JParkes) **8-10-12** VSmith (bit bkwd: bhd fr 7th: p.u bef 2 out)		P	200/1	—	—
69[P]	**Classic Jester (IRE)** (RChampion) **6-10-12** MMoloney (bit bkwd: lost tch fr ½-wy: p.u bef 2 out)		P	200/1	—	—
2503[10]	**Welburn Boy** (RDEWoodhouse) **5-10-12b[1]** BStorey (lost tch fr ½-wy: p.u bef 2 out)		P	50/1	—	—
				(SP 132.0%)	**23 Rn**	

Time Not Taken CSF £6.86 TOTE £2.90: £1.70 £1.60 £3.10 (£5.50) Trio £77.50 OWNER Mr Steve Hammond (MALTON) BRED John Walsh
2053 Share Options (IRE), trying his longest trip to date, needed every yard of it to get home. (7/4)

2003 Smart Approach (IRE) put in another good effort, but was again worried out of it in the closing stages. (7/2)
1654 Chill Factor, a stable-companion of the runner-up, was given a patient ride, but was making no further impression from the second last. (25/1)
1654 Phar Echo (IRE), after six weeks off, ran quite well until appearing to blow up on the home turn. (20/1)
2177 Cheater (IRE) was a shade disappointing, dropping out when the race really began from the third last. (13/2)

2628 BEDALE NOVICES' CHASE (5-Y.O+) (Class E)

1-30 (1-31) **2m (12 fncs)** £3,336.75 (£999.00: £479.50: £219.75) GOING: 0.40 sec per fur (GS)

				SP	RR	SF
2176[F]	**Noyan** (RAFahey) **7-11-4**(5) MrRThornton (a.p: chal 4 out: led last: styd on wl)	—	**1**	11/4[2]	110+	—
1780[2]	**Bold Boss (100)** (GMMoore) **8-11-3** BStorey (lw: chsd ldrs: led 8th tl hdd last: no ex)	5	**2**	11/4[2]	99	—
865[4]	**El Crank Senor** (RDEWoodhouse) **5-10-7** DerekByrne (hdwy whn mstke 8th: styd on wl fr 3 out: nrst fin)	7	**3**	16/1	92	—
1126[2]	**Chorus Line (IRE) (79)** (PBeaumont) **8-10-12** RSupple (in tch: chsng ldrs 4 out: one pce fr next)	3½	**4**	20/1	84	—
	Royal Crimson (97) (MDHammond) **6-11-0**(3) MrCBonner (nvr rchd ldrs)	14	**5**	20/1	75	—
1925[3]	**Weeheby (USA) (89)** (MFBarraclough) **8-11-3** TJMurphy (chsd ldrs tl outpcd fr 4 out)	1½	**6**	50/1	73	—
1793[8]	**Urban Dancing (USA) (107)** (BEllison) **8-11-3** GCahill (n.d)	5	**7**	7/1[3]	68	—
584[8]	**Childsway** (SJRobinson) **9-10-12**(5) MichaelBrennan (mde most to 8th: sn wknd)	4	**8**	66/1	64	—
1856[3]	**Curragh Peter (72)** (MrsPBickerton) **10-11-0**(3) GuyLewis (prom to ½-wy)	3½	**9**	50/1	61	—
1987[3]	**Fenwick's Brother (87)** (MrsSJSmith) **7-10-10**(7) RWilkinson (in tch: outpcd whn fell 7th)		**F**	12/1	—	—
	Diddy Rymer (MrsSJSmith) **7-10-12** MrPMurray (fell 1st)		**F**	66/1	—	—
	Dandy des Plauts (FR) (MrsSJSmith) **6-11-3** KJohnson (bit bkwd: bhd whn fell 8th)		**F**	66/1	—	—
1853*	**Daring Past (112)** (MDHammond) **7-11-9** ADobbin (lw: chsd ldrs: rdn 4 out: 3rd & btn whn fell 3 out)		**F**	5/2[1]	—	—
2000[P]	**Cardinal Sinner (IRE) (56)** (JWade) **8-11-3b** KJones (fell 1st)		**F**	200/1	—	—
2042[9]	**South Coast Star (IRE)** (HowardJohnson) **7-11-3** ASSmith (t.o whn p.u bef 3 out)		**P**	100/1	—	—
2506[3]	**Gone Ashore (IRE) (60)** (MABarnes) **6-10-12**(5) STaylor (w ldrs to 5th: t.o whn p.u bef 3 out)		**P**	200/1	—	—
1802[P]	**Lepton (IRE)** (JWCurtis) **6-11-3** JCallaghan (t.o whn p.u bef last)		**P**	66/1	—	—
1771[P]	**Ernest Aragorn** (MrsSLamyman) **8-11-3v** BClifford (rn out 1st)		**R**	200/1	—	—

(SP 129.9%) **18 Rn**

Time Not Taken CSF £10.28 TOTE £4.30: £2.10 £1.60 £3.90 (£10.70) Trio Not won; £204.07 to Newton Abbot 20/1/97 OWNER Mr C. H. McGhie (MALTON) BRED Oakgrove Stud
WEIGHT FOR AGE 5yo-10lb
2176 Noyan, back to form here after his mishap last time, won in good style and is going to find more success. (11/4)
1780 Bold Boss put up a useful effort here, only to find the winner too good from the last. He really does deserve a change of luck. (11/4)
865 El Crank Senor showed plenty on this chasing debut and, on what could be seen in the fog, he just needs to brush up a bit on his jumping for there to be plenty of improvement to come. (16/1)
1126 Chorus Line (IRE), having her first run for over two and a half months, showed enough and should find a modest race in due course. (20/1)
1853* Daring Past was in third place and looking in a deal of trouble when coming to grief three out. (5/2)

2629 DARLINGTON CONDITIONAL (S) H'CAP HURDLE (0-90) (4-Y.O+) (Class G)

2-00 (2-00) **2m (8 hdls)** £2,057.50 (£570.00: £272.50) GOING: 0.40 sec per fur (GS)

				SP	RR	SF
1666[13]	**Kierchem (IRE) (65)** (CGrant) **6-10-5** MichaelBrennan (lw: a.p: led appr last: r.o)	—	**1**	25/1	50	—
1990[6]	**Anorak (USA) (88)** (GMMoore) **7-11-7**(7) NHannity (chsd ldrs: led 3 out: sn hdd: kpt on appr last)	3	**2**	25/1	70	—
1703[5]	**Arthur Bee (61)** (BBousfield) **10-9-11**(4)ow1 CMcCormack (bhd: hdwy 5th: chsng ldrs appr 2 out: kpt on u.p)	1¼	**3**	16/1	42	—
1992[12]	**Appearance Money (IRE) (72)** (FMurphy) **6-10-8**(4) THogg (lw: hld up: hdwy ½-wy: led after 3 out tl appr last: wknd)	¾	**4**	16/1	52	—
1703[2]	**Chummy's Saga (73)** (LLungo) **7-10-9**(4) IJardine (hld up: hdwy 3 out: chsng ldrs appr 2 out: one pce appr last)	1¼	**5**	5/1[3]	52	—
2503[6]	**Jalmaid (66)** (HAlexander) **5-10-6** RMcGrath (prom: one pce fr 3 out)	½	**6**	12/1	44	—
2505[8]	**Bud's Bet (IRE) (77)** (MissJFCraze) **9-11-3** MNewton (lw: nvr trbld ldrs)	9	**7**	12/1	46	—
1908[5]	**Bold Top (67)** (BSRothwell) **5-10-7b** ECallaghan (led 2nd to 5th: wknd 3 out)	¾	**8**	12/1	36	—
1992[2]	**Environmental Law (72)** (WMcKeown) **6-10-12b** GCahill (chsd ldrs tl outpcd fr 3 out)	¾	**9**	7/2[1]	40	—
2505[11]	**See You Always (IRE) (60)** (MABarnes) **7-10-0b** STaylor (chsd ldrs tl wknd appr 2 out)	1¼	**10**	20/1	27	—
1969[2]	**Seconds Away (60)** (JSGoldie) **6-10-0** GLee (hld up: hit 5th: n.d)	9	**11**	50/1	18	—
1775[2]	**Weather Alert (IRE) (75)** (KAMorgan) **6-11-1** RMassey (led to 2nd: chsd ldrs tl wknd fr 3 out)	3½	**12**	5/1[3]	29	—
2050[2]	**Boy Blakeney (88)** (MrsSJSmith) **4-11-2b** RWilkinson (w ldr: led 5th to 3 out: hrd rdn & wknd qckly)	13	**13**	4/1[2]	29	—
2044[P]	**Familiar Art (70)** (DMoffatt) **6-10-3**(7) IPike (s.s: a bhd)	2	**14**	33/1	9	—
1775[P]	**Tough Character (IRE) (60)** (MESowersby) **9-9-10**(4) NHorrocks (sn t.o)	dist	**15**	200/1	—	—

(SP 128.3%) **15 Rn**

Time Not Taken CSF £484.81 CT £8,995.21 TOTE £49.80: £7.40 £4.40 £5.70 (£180.80) Trio £225.20; £285.50 to Newton Abbot 20/1/97
OWNER Mrs M. Hunter (BILLINGHAM) BRED T. Coughlan
LONG HANDICAP Arthur Bee 9-11 See You Always (IRE) 9-13 Seconds Away 9-9 Tough Character (IRE) 9-5
WEIGHT FOR AGE 4yo-12lb
No bid
Kierchem (IRE) won this well and seems to be on the upgrade. (25/1)
1990 Anorak (USA), from a stable flying at the moment, came back to form, but was always finding the struggle too much in the closing stages. (25/1)
1703 Arthur Bee, who takes some riding, was keeping on well under vigorous pressure at the finish, but was never doing enough to offer a threat. (16/1)
1523 Appearance Money (IRE) hit the front going really well after the third last and looked the likely winner, only to run out of fuel going to the final flight. Perhaps more patient tactics could be needed. (16/1)
1703 Chummy's Saga has the ability but, just when he looked likely to get into it, he then failed to prolong the effort. He may have just needed this after six weeks off. (5/1)
1992 Environmental Law (7/2: op 6/1)

2630 LEEMING H'CAP CHASE (0-110) (5-Y.O+) (Class E)

2-30 (2-30) **3m 1f 110y (19 fncs)** £3,159.75 (£948.00: £456.50: £210.75) GOING: 0.40 sec per fur (GS)

				SP	RR	SF
1991*	**Tim Soldier (FR) (84)** (MFBarraclough) **10-10-2** RSupple (a chsng ldrs: led 2 out: blnd last: styd on)	—	1	14/1	93	—
1845P	**Kenmare River (IRE) (82)** (RCollins) **7-9-9b**1(5) MrRThornton (led tl mstke & hdd 2 out: kpt on same pce)	3½	2	100/1	89	—
2046P	**Snook Point (86)** (DALamb) **10-10-4**ow4 JBurke (in tch: hdwy 8th: ev ch 4 out: disp 2nd whn blnd 3 out: n.d after)	7	3	33/1	88	—
1985F	**Sister Rosza (IRE) (97)** (MrsSLamyman) **9-11-1** DerekByrne (in tch: hdwy 11th: no imp fr 4 out)	7	4	9/2[2]	95	2
2004*	**Heavenly Citizen (IRE) (95)** (JLGledson) **9-10-13** BStorey (chsd ldrs: drvn along 11th: wknd 14th)	1¾	5	6/1[3]	92	—
2544³	**Russian Castle (IRE) (105)** (JWade) **8-11-6**(3) MrCBonner (chsd ldrs: hit 7th: outpcd fr 12th)	8	6	9/2[2]	97	4
1845P	**Bright Destiny (82)** (JSGoldie) **6-9-11**(3) GLee (bhd: hdwy ½-wy: no imp)	3	7	200/1	72	—
2004F	**Marchwood (98)** (NChamberlain) **10-11-2** KJohnson (bhd: hdwy 8th: sn in tch: hit 13th: sn wknd)	hd	8	12/1	88	—
1704²	**Gale Ahead (IRE) (98)** (GMMoore) **7-11-2** NBentley (hdwy & prom 8th: rdn & lost pl 11th: n.d after)	dist	9	7/2[1]	—	—
1991⁴	**The Toaster (95)** (MissMKMilligan) **10-10-13** ASSmith (bhd: sme hdwy 11th: sn wknd: p.u bef 3 out)		P	14/1	—	—
1662P	**Far Senior (108)** (PWegmann) **11-11-12b** GaryLyons (chsd ldrs tl lost pl 8th: t.o whn p.u bef 13th)		P	33/1	—	—
1985P	**Potato Man (99)** (BEllison) **11-11-3** ADobbin (hit 7th: sn wl bhd: t.o whn p.u bef 13th)		P	20/1	—	—
1704U	**Twin States (98)** (JRTurner) **8-11-2** WFry (nvr gng wl: bhd whn p.u after 13th: b.b.v)		P	12/1	—	—
1307³	**Ole Ole (82)** (MrsEMoscrop) **11-10-0** JCallaghan (in tch: hit 11th: sn lost pl: p.u bef 4 out)		P	9/1	—	—
2046⁴	**Jendee (IRE) (85)** (BEllison) **9-10-3** GCahill (a bhd: t.o whn p.u bef 2 out)		P	14/1	—	—
	I'm in Clover (IRE) (82) (JNorton) **8-9-7**(7) BGrattan (bhd fr ½-wy: blnd & uns rdr 15th)		U	33/1	—	—

(SP 133.3%) **16 Rn**

6m 47.1 (29.10) CSF £931.79 CT £32,713.64 TOTE £22.00: £3.20 £4.60 £8.50 £2.70 (£667.20) Trio Not won; £265.41 to Newton Abbot 20/1/97 OWNER Mr Ken Dale (CLAVERDON) BRED Bernard Geffroy

LONG HANDICAP Kenmare River (IRE) 9-4 Bright Destiny 8-6 Snook Point 9-7 I'm in Clover (IRE) 9-4

OFFICIAL EXPLANATION Twin States: bled from the nose.

1991* Tim Soldier (FR) proved his previous win here was no fluke. (14/1)

1629 Kenmare River (IRE) put up his best ever performance here from 10lb out of the handicap. (100/1 op. 16/1)

Snook Point does not do anything quickly, but had his chances here, only to throw them away with a blunder three out. (33/1)

1985 Sister Rosza (IRE) is probably better with more give in the ground. This trip may also have been stretching her stamina. (9/2)

2004* Heavenly Citizen (IRE) failed to reproduce his running of last time, and was struggling a long way out. (6/1)

2544 Russian Castle (IRE) was having only his second run of the season, both of which have been this week, and this seemed to be too much. (9/2)

2631 LEYBURN H'CAP HURDLE (0-110) (4-Y.O+) (Class E)

3-00 (3-01) **2m (8 hdls)** £2,553.00 (£708.00: £339.00) GOING: 0.40 sec per fur (GS)

				SP	RR	SF
	Mr Moriarty (IRE) (92) (SRBowring) **6-11-0** MFoster (swtg: led fr 2nd tl appr 2 out: chal whn lft in ld last: styd on)	—	1	14/1	75	33
2001²	**Opera Fan (IRE) (83)** (KAMorgan) **5-10-5** ASSmith (cl up: rdn appr 2 out: kpt on same pce)	1½	2	6/1[3]	65	23
1832⁷	**Jemima Puddleduck (93)** (AStreeter) **6-11-1v** TEley (chsd ldrs: drvn along fr 4th: lost pl next: styd on wl fr 2 out)	nk	3	14/1	74	32
1942³	**Auburn Boy (103)** (MWEasterby) **10-11-6**(5) MichaelBrennan (hld up & bhd: effrt 3 out: styd on: no imp)	2½	4	10/1	82	40
	Shahgram (IRE) (98) (PBeaumont) **9-10-13**(7) BGrattan (bit bkwd: hld up: hdwy 3 out: n.m.r last: r.o)	1	5	33/1	76	34
1700*	**Russian Rascal (IRE) (95)** (TDEasterby) **4-10-0**(5) MrRThornton (w ldrs tl outpcd fr 2 out)	½	6	9/2[2]	72	18
	Tapatch (IRE) (98) (MWEasterby) **9-11-3**(3) PMidgley (sn trckng ldrs: led appr 2 out: sn hdd & wknd)	hd	7	25/1	75	33
1851*	**Robsera (IRE) (84)** (JJQuinn) **6-10-6** DerekByrne (hdwy 4th: chsng ldrs 3 out: wknd next)	hd	8	14/1	61	19
2034*	**Star Selection (98)** (JMackie) **6-11-3**(3) EHusband (lw: led & hit 1st: sn hdd: outpcd 4th: n.d after)	6	9	3/1[1]	69	27
2044³	**Here Comes Herbie (83)** (WStorey) **5-10-5** MMoloney (wnt prom 4th: wknd appr 2 out)	2	10	20/1	52	10
1630⁷	**Grandman (IRE) (88)** (DMoffatt) **6-10-10** DJMoffatt (a bhd)	¾	11	16/1	56	14
1852⁶	**Master Hyde (USA) (106)** (WStorey) **8-11-9**(5) RMcGrath (chsd ldrs: rdn fr 4th: wknd 3 out)	hd	12	25/1	74	32
1628P	**Gallardini (IRE) (86)** (BSRothwell) **8-10-8** RSupple (effrt ½-wy: sn rdn & btn)	19	13	33/1	35	—
1715²	**Shifting Moon (84)** (FJordan) **5-10-6b** SWynne (chsd ldrs to 3 out: wknd)	9	14	11/1	24	—
1312³	**Mithraic (IRE) (102)** (WSCunningham) **5-11-3**(7) LMcGrath (t: chsd ldrs: outpcd whn hit 5th: sn wknd)	6	15	10/1	36	—
	All Clear (IRE) (96) (HowardJohnson) **6-11-4** DParker (bkwd: a wl bhd: t.o)	17	16	33/1	13	—
1804⁹	**Bend Sable (IRE) (105)** (FSStorey) **7-11-13** BStorey (hld up: gd hdwy 5th: led 2 out tl fell last)		F	10/1	88?	—
1667⁶	**Del Piero (IRE) (95)** (MDHammond) **6-11-3** ADobbin (p.u lame bef 3rd: dead)		P	14/1	—	—
871⁶	**Beau Matelot (85)** (MissMKMilligan) **5-10-7b**1 GCahill (bhd whn p.u bef 2 out)		P	33/1	—	—

(SP 149.8%) **19 Rn**

3m 55.5 (12.50) CSF £99.52 CT £1,154.25 TOTE £20.20: £4.80 £2.70 £2.30 £2.80 (£80.90) Trio £161.80 OWNER Mr D. H. Bowring (EDWINSTOWE) BRED Joseph Hernon and Partners

WEIGHT FOR AGE 4yo-12lb

Mr Moriarty (IRE) proved very determined and, after being headed, was fighting back when presented with the race at the last. (14/1)

2001 Opera Fan (IRE) goes particularly well on this track and gives the impression that he should stay further. (6/1)

Jemima Puddleduck, with a visor on this time, gave her best performance of the season, but she does like this track. (14/1)

1942 Auburn Boy was only staying on when it was too late and is proving difficult to win with these days. (10/1)

Shahgram (IRE), from a yard in form, ran well and, though he is not one to trust fully, he should improve from this. (33/1)

1700* Russian Rascal (IRE) raced up with this frenetic pace until it all proved too much over the last two flights. (9/2)

Tapatch (IRE), having his first run of the season, gave the impression that he should be all the better for it. (25/1)

2034* Star Selection would have preferred softer ground and there were also too many to take him on here. (3/1)

1312 Mithraic (IRE) (10/1: 8/1-12/1)

Bend Sable (IRE) was in front when he fell at the last. (10/1)

1667 Del Piero (IRE) (14/1: 10/1-16/1)

2632 SEAMER NOVICES' H'CAP CHASE (0-105) (5-Y.O+) (Class E)

3-30 (3-31) **2m 3f (16 fncs)** £2,235.88 (£2,235.88: £495.50: £227.75) GOING: 0.40 sec per fur (GS)

				SP	RR	SF
1629P	**Monnaie Forte (IRE) (90)** (JRAdam) **7-11-2** MMoloney (a.p: led 3 out: jst hld on)	—	1	33/1	99	28
1653⁷	**Marlingford (78)** (MrsJJordan) **10-9-11**(7)ow4 LMcGrath (in tch: outpcd 4 out: hdwy 2 out: str run flat)	—	1	20/1	87	12

Form	Horse	Dist	Pos	SP	RR	SF
1847[3]	**Kiltulla (IRE) (74)** (MrsSJSmith) **7-9-7**(7) RWilkinson (chsd ldrs: chal 8th: blnd 4 out: one pce fr 2 out)	9	**3**	14/1	75	4
1991[2]	**Karenastino (74)** (MrsSJSmith) **6-10-0** MrPMurray (mstkes: led fr 4th tl blnd & hdd 3 out: hit next: sn btn)	½	**4**	20/1	75	4
2002*	**Twin Falls (IRE) (94)** (GMMoore) **6-11-6** JCallaghan (bhd: effrt ½-wy: styd on fr 4 out: n.d)	12	**5**	3/1[2]	85	14
1944*	**Garbo's Boy (79)** (JRTurner) **7-10-5** WFry (mstkes: outpcd fr ½-wy)	8	**6**	10/1	63	—
2043*	**Lien de Famille (IRE) (102)** (JJQuinn) **7-12-0** BStorey (nt j.w: n.d)	8	**7**	5/1[3]	79	8
1826[U]	**Camptosaurus (IRE) (75)** (DSAlder) **8-10-1** KJohnson (a bhd)	9	**8**	33/1	45	—
1853[7]	**Wee Wizard (IRE) (74)** (MABarnes) **8-9-9**(5) STaylor (nvr gng wl: a wl bhd)	15	**9**	25/1	31	—
1844[P]	**World Without End (USA) (80)** (MESowersby) **8-10-6** DParker (bhd whn fell 3rd)		**F**	50/1	—	—
2000*	**Bosworth Field (IRE) (78)** (MrsSarahHorner-Harker) **9-10-4b** MFoster (prom: wkng whn fell 12th: dead)		**F**	14/1	—	—
	Know-No-No (IRE) (83) (MDHammond) **8-10-9** ADobbin (in tch: effrt 4 out: wknd next: 5th & wl btn whn fell last)		**F**	10/1	—	—
1248*	**Abbeylands (IRE) (91)** (HowardJohnson) **9-11-3** ASSmith (led to 4th: p.u bef next: lame)		**P**	11/4[1]	—	—
	Most Rich (IRE) (74) (BEllison) **9-10-0** GCahill (chsd ldrs: hit 3rd: wknd 10th: p.u bef 2 out)		**P**	50/1	—	—
2052[P]	**Bossymoss (IRE) (74)** (AStreeter) **8-10-0** TEley (a bhd: blnd & uns rdr 12th)		**U**	14/1	—	—

(SP 129.7%) **15 Rn**

4m 56.2 (17.20) CSF MF, M £254.23 M, MF £244.01 CT MF, M, K £4,237.57 M, MF, K £4,178.95 TOTE MF £16.20 M £24.70: MF £10.20 M £7.40 £2.90 (£361.10) Trio Not won; £311.91 to Newton Abbot 20/1/97 OWNER Mr James Adam (GORDON)/Miss J. Seaton (YARM) BRED E. Stuart Knape/John Kelly

LONG HANDICAP Marlingford 9-6 Karenastino 9-9 Wee Wizard (IRE) 9-11 Kiltulla (IRE) 9-5 Most Rich (IRE) 9-13 Bossymoss (IRE) 9-10

1348* Monnaie Forte (IRE), back to form after a mishap last time, found the post coming just in time here. (33/1)

Marlingford last won a race in 1991, and his form of late has been moderate to say the least, but another stride would have seen him with the outright advantage. (20/1)

1847 Kiltulla (IRE) keeps showing enough to suggest there is a race to be found, but his jumping was on the clumsy side here at times. (14/1)

1991 Karenastino went off at a strong pace, but his jumping left something to be desired, and that finally sapped all reserves in the home straight. (20/1)

2002* Twin Falls (IRE) failed to impress on looks and never appeared happy in the race, only staying on when it was all over. (3/1)

2633 CATTERICK MAIDEN N.H. FLAT RACE (4,5,6 & 7-Y.O) (Class H)

4-00 (4-01) **2m** £1,360.50 (£378.00: £181.50)

Form	Horse	Dist	Pos	SP	RR	SF
	Autumn Lord (PBeaumont) **4-10-5**(7) BGrattan (trckd ldrs: led 3f out: r.o: comf)	—	**1**	6/1[2]	73 f	—
2066[4]	**Billy Buckskin** (JNorton) **5-11-5**(5) MrRThornton (chsd ldrs: disp ld 3 out: styd on: nt pce of wnr)	7	**2**	6/1[2]	66 f	—
1926[7]	**Phar Smoother (IRE)** (JGFitzGerald) **5-11-7**(3) FLeahy (a.p: effrt 4f out: kpt on: nt pce to chal)	11	**3**	6/1[2]	55 f	—
	Supreme Target (IRE) (MrsMReveley) **5-11-2**(3) GLee (lw: sn chsng ldrs: effrt over 3f out: r.o one pce)	½	**4**	2/1[1]	50 f	—
	Buddleia (JRTurner) **4-10-0**(7) NHorrocks (a.p: effrt 5f out: nt qckn fnl 3f)	4	**5**	25/1	46 f	—
	Nosam (NBMason) **7-11-3**(7) SHaworth (bit bkwd: plld hrd: trckd ldrs tl outpcd fnl 3f)	2½	**6**	14/1	48 f	—
1926[R]	**Eastcliffe (IRE)** (WMcKeown) **5-11-10** GCahill (cl up: led after 6f to 3f out: grad wknd)	4	**7**	8/1[3]	44 f	—
	Sunstrike (RMcDonald) **5-11-3**(7) CMcCormack (hld up: hdwy to chal ½-wy: wknd 3f out)	5	**8**	100/1	39 f	—
2005[4]	**The Stuffed Puffin (IRE)** (LLungo) **5-11-3**(7) IJardine (lw: hld up & bhd: sme hdwy ½-wy: n.d)	3½	**9**	6/1[2]	36 f	—
	Stonesby (IRE) (GMMoore) **5-11-3**(7) NHannity (bit bkwd: hld up & bhd: hdwy 6f out: hung rt ent st: n.d)	s.h	**10**	10/1	35 f	—
	Helperby (IRE) (HowardJohnson) **5-11-5**(5) GFRyan (bkwd: in tch: outpcd 5f out: n.d after)	2½	**11**	14/1	33 f	—
2005[9]	**Hunting Slane** (CGrant) **5-11-5**(5) MichaelBrennan (bhd & hung bdly rt appr st: t.o)	21	**12**	12/1	12 f	—
2005[11]	**Recca (IRE)** (DenysSmith) **5-11-3**(7) RBurns (rdn & wknd 6f out: t.o)	4	**13**	12/1	8 f	—
2047[10]	**Snooty Eskimo (IRE)** (JSHaldane) **5-11-7**(3) ECallaghan (bhd fr ½-wy: t.o)	12	**14**	20/1	—	—
	Jo Lightning (IRE) (BEllison) **4-10-12** MrRHale (bkwd: wl t.o fr ½-wy)	dist	**15**	33/1	—	—
2080[15]	**The Muckle Quine** (JJO'Neill) **6-11-0**(5) RMcGrath (swtg: wl t.o fr ½-wy)	3	**16**	50/1	—	—
1692[22]	**Tidal Race (IRE)** (JSHaldane) **5-11-7**(3) PMidgley (wl t.o fr ½-wy)	dist	**17**	100/1	—	—
	Hawkers Deal (DANolan) **4-10-9**(3) RMassey (unruly s: led 6f: sn t.o)	dist	**18**	14/1	—	—
1692[23]	**Miss Fortina** (JWCurtis) **5-10-12**(7) MNewton (bkwd: wl t.o fnl 10f)	½	**19**	200/1	—	—

(SP 162.1%) **19 Rn**

3m 50.8 CSF £49.02 TOTE £7.40: £2.30 £1.50 £3.10 (£30.10) Trio £70.00; £50.34 to Newton Abbot 20/1/97 OWNER Mr A. R. Boocock (BRANDSBY) BRED A. R. Boocock

WEIGHT FOR AGE 4yo-12lb

Autumn Lord is not the best of lookers, but he certainly won this in style. (6/1)

2066 Billy Buckskin keeps trying hard, but the winner always had too many gears for him. (6/1: op 4/1)

1926 Phar Smoother (IRE) does not do anything quickly, but does stay really well, and that will come into force over hurdles. (6/1)

Supreme Target (IRE) travelled well, but proved green when asked for an effort early in the straight, and obviously still needs experience.(2/1)

Buddleia is only small, but she did run well. (25/1)

Nosam, a real National Hunt type, took a strong hold and ran well. He looks a real stayer. (14/1)

Stonesby (IRE) (10/1: op 20/1)

Hunting Slane (12/1: op 25/1)

T/Plpt: £12,342.80 (1 Tckt). T/Qdpt: £714.60 (0.1 Tckt); £869.11 to Newton Abbot 20/1/97. AA

2391-HAYDOCK (L-H) (Good to firm)

Saturday January 18th

WEATHER: overcast

2634 NORTH WEST RACING CLUB NOVICES' HURDLE (4-Y.O+) (Class E)

12-45 (12-45) **2m 4f (10 hdls)** £2,778.00 (£783.00: £384.00) GOING: 0.19 sec per fur (G)

Form	Horse	Dist	Pos	SP	RR	SF
	Harbour Island (MCPipe) **5-11-6** CMaude (chsd ldr: led 7th: clr 2 out: eased flat)	—	**1**	3/1[2]	82+	36
2509[3]	**Mr Christie (77)** (MissLCSiddall) **5-11-6** AThornton (lw: bhd: hdwy 3 out: styd on appr last: no ch w wnr)	16	**2**	14/1	69	23
1689[6]	**Tremendisto (98)** (CaptJWilson) **7-11-11** RichardGuest (led & sn clr: hdd 7th: one pce fr 3 out)	1¾	**3**	12/1	73	27
1964[5]	**Flaxley Wood** (RHBuckler) **6-11-6** BPowell (chsd ldrs: effrt appr 3 out: nvr nr to chal)	3	**4**	25/1	65	19
1958*	**Konvekta Queen (IRE)** (OSherwood) **6-11-6** RDunwoody (hld up: hdwy 6th: rdn after 3 out: sn btn)	¾	**5**	5/2[1]	65	19
1810[6]	**Mel (IRE) (76)** (RHBuckler) **7-11-6** LHarvey (bkwd: chsd ldng pair to 7th: sn lost tch)	6	**6**	33/1	60	14
1825[2]	**Leap in the Dark (IRE) (80)** (MissLCSiddall) **8-11-6** OPears (hdwy & rdn 6th: nvr nr to chal)	8	**7**	25/1	54	8

1180[5]	**Club Caribbean** (PJHobbs) **5-11-1** NWilliamson (hld up: effrt 7th: wknd 3 out: t.o) 24	**8**	20/1	29	—
2064[5]	**Galen (IRE)** (MrsMReveley) **6-11-6** PNiven (a bhd: t.o) 4	**9**	9/1	31	—
	Benfleet (MCPipe) **6-11-6** DWalsh (bit bkwd: mstke 5th: a bhd: t.o) 4	**10**	12/1	28	—
1900[3]	**Pleasureland (IRE) (102)** (RCurtis) **4-10-7** DMorris (chsd ldrs tl wknd 7th: t.o) 11	**11**	7/2 3	19	—
	La Mon Dere (IRE) (PJHobbs) **6-11-6** WMarston (bkwd: a bhd: rdn 4th: t.o fr 7th) ....dist	**12**	16/1	—	—
	Niyaka (62) (CaptJWilson) **10-11-6** JRKavanagh (bkwd: a bhd: t.o whn p.u bef 3 out)	**P**	33/1	—	—
	Givry (IRE) (GMMcCourt) **7-11-6** DBridgwater (bit bkwd: a bhd: t.o whn p.u bef 2 out)	**P**	33/1	—	—

(SP 135.0%) **14 Rn**

4m 49.1 (12.10) CSF £41.61 TOTE £3.60: £1.60 £3.70 £3.40 (£43.20) Trio £143.80 OWNER Mr Malcolm Jones (WELLINGTON) BRED W. and R. Barnett Ltd
WEIGHT FOR AGE 4yo-13lb
OFFICIAL EXPLANATION **Pleasureland (IRE): blew up.**
Harbour Island, a very lightly-made individual who proved disappointing on the Flat, made full use of his undoubted stamina and quite simply outclassed the opposition. (3/1)
2509 Mr Christie stayed on well to gain the runner-up prize, but had to admit the winner in a class of his own. (14/1)
1689 Tremendisto set a scorching gallop, but could never get away from the winner and had met his match early in the straight. (12/1: op 8/1)
Flaxley Wood, running his best race yet, could never get close enough to cause concern, but he did keep staying on, and all is not lost. (25/1)
1958* Konvekta Queen (IRE) took closer order at the end of the back straight, but she was under pressure after jumping three out and her chance had gone. (5/2)
1187 Galen (IRE) (9/1: op 6/1)
Benfleet (12/1: op 8/1)
1900 Pleasureland (IRE) (7/2: 5/2-4/1)

2635 BELLCHARM MITSUBISHI CHAMPION HURDLE TRIAL (Gd 2) (5-Y.O+) (Class A)
1-15 (1-15) **2m (8 hdls)** £18,860.00 (£7,168.00: £3,534.00: £1,638.00) GOING: 0.19 sec per fur (G)

			SP	RR	SF
2059*	**Mistinguett (IRE) (138)** (NATwiston-Davies) **5-11-2** CLlewellyn (mde all: sn clr: r.o strly) ....—	**1**	8/1	141?	84
1656[3]	**Dato Star (IRE) (148)** (JMJefferson) **6-11-7** RichardGuest (a.p: chsd wnr fr 5th: kpt on: nt pce to chal) 4	**2**	7/2 2	142	85
1916[2]	**Bimsey (IRE) (150)** (RAkehurst) **7-11-3** RDunwoody (prom tl outpcd & rdn 5th: n.d afterwards) 11	**3**	5/4 1	127	70
1916[5]	**Pridwell (157)** (MCPipe) **7-11-7** CMaude (hld up in rr: styd on fr 3 out: nvr nrr) 8	**4**	5/1 3	123	66
1916[6]	**Right Win (IRE) (148)** (RHannon) **7-11-10** JAMcCarthy (chsd ldrs: outpcd 5th: sn bhd) 12	**5**	33/1	114	57
2059[2]	**Eskimo Nel (IRE) (135)** (JLSpearing) **6-10-12** DBridgwater (hld up: effrt & rdn 5th: no imp: t.o) 23	**6**	12/1	79	22
	Edipo Re (PJHobbs) **5-11-3** PCarberry (bit bkwd: rdn & dropped rr 3rd: sn t.o) 1¼	**7**	40/1	83?	26
2059[6]	**Tragic Hero (140)** (MCPipe) **5-11-10b** DWalsh (trckd ldrs to ½-wy: sn lost tch: t.o) 9	**8**	25/1	81	24
2603a*	**Master Tribe (IRE) (120)** (MrsJPitman) **7-11-3** NWilliamson (hld up: hdwy 5th: btn whn p.u after last)	**P**	10/1	—	—

(SP 120.5%) **9 Rn**

3m 40.9 (-1.10) CSF £34.44 TOTE £9.10: £2.20 £1.40 £1.50 (£29.40) Trio £10.50 OWNER Mr John Duggan (CHELTENHAM) BRED Michael Quirke
OFFICIAL EXPLANATION **Master Tribe: had lost his action approaching the final obstacle. He appeared to return sound, but was found to have bruised a foot the next day.**
2059* Mistinguett (IRE) did not allow her rivals to get within striking range and she had the race won from some way out. With a featherweight to carry in the Tote Gold Trophy at Newbury next month, she will be the one to beat. (8/1)
1656 Dato Star (IRE) has not got the speed to win such a hot contest at this trip on fast ground, but it would be different if it came up hock-deep on a stiff track like Cheltenham. In the meantime he is crying out to be given a chance to take on our top staying hurdlers. (7/2)
1916 Bimsey (IRE) is not very big and was at full stretch here to keep tabs on the leader and, losing that battle turning out of the back straight, was never going to get back into it. (5/4)
1916 Pridwell stayed on from the rear in the latter stages, but could not lift his pace on such lively ground. (5/1)
2603a* Master Tribe (IRE) had moved into third place approaching the penultimate flight and looked assured of finishing there, but his jockey felt him lose his action approaching the last and tried to pull him up. He had no option but to jump that hurdle, and he was found to be sound when he was eventually brought to a halt. (10/1)

2636 PETER MARSH LIMITED H'CAP CHASE (Gd 2) (5-Y.O+) (Class A)
1-45 (1-47) **3m (18 fncs)** £24,776.00 (£9,435.80: £4,667.90: £2,180.30) GOING: 0.19 sec per fur (G)

			SP	RR	SF
1359[2]	**Jodami (162)** (PBeaumont) **12-11-10** NWilliamson (lw: hld up: hdwy 8th: chal 3 out: styd on strly to ld nr fin)—	**1**	9/2 2	169	69
2057[2]	**Unguided Missile (IRE) (158)** (GRichards) **9-11-6** RDunwoody (lw: j.w: chsd ldr: led 12th: hrd rdn & hdd cl home) ....nk	**2**	8/11 1	165	65
	Avro Anson (145) (MJCamacho) **9-10-7** PNiven (bit bkwd: hld up: hdwy 7th: ev ch fr 3 out: kpt on u.p flat) ....½	**3**	9/1	152	52
1923[3]	**Scotton Banks (IRE) (153)** (TDEasterby) **8-11-1v[1]** PCarberry (led & sn clr: hdd 12th: rdn next: sn lost tch: t.o) ....dist	**4**	10/1	—	—
1982[6]	**Nahthen Lad (IRE) (156)** (MrsJPitman) **8-11-4** WMarston (chsd ldrs: pushed along 10th: sn wknd: p.u bef 14th)	**P**	5/1 3	—	—
1785[5]	**Grange Brake (145)** (NATwiston-Davies) **11-10-7b** DWalsh (mstke 1st: chsd ldrs: reminders & lost pl 6th: t.o: p.u bef 4 out)	**P**	33/1	—	—

(SP 114.8%) **6 Rn**

6m 3.5 (4.80 under best) (5.50) CSF £8.20 TOTE £4.50: £1.90 £1.40 (£2.80) OWNER Mr J. N. Yeadon (BRANDSBY) BRED Eamon Phelan
LONG HANDICAP Avro Anson 10-0 Grange Brake 9-1
STEWARDS' ENQUIRY Williamson susp. 27-30/1/97 (improper use of whip).
OFFICIAL EXPLANATION **Nahthen Lad (IRE): was found to have a sore near-fore foot on returning to the yard.**
1359 Jodami, a previous winner of this event, was thought to need this outing after being held up in his work but, with the assistance of a new jockey, he turned in one of his best ever performances to break the course record, which had stood for over twenty years, by over four seconds. (9/2)
2057 Unguided Missile (IRE) did everything right and certainly did not deserve to lose out, but the winner proved the stronger in a thrilling battle to the post. When he recovers from this hard race, he will continue to show he is not far behind the best. (8/11: 10/11-evens)
Avro Anson lacks experience in this class over fences, but he almost defied his burly looks with a performance that stamps him as a very progressive chaser. It is no surprise to see that he has entered the Grand National betting. (9/1: op 6/1)
1923 Scotton Banks (IRE) had totally different ground when successful twelve months ago and, though he did attempt to run his rivals off their legs, he was brushed aside with ease down the back straight. This fast ground is not for him. (10/1)

2637 TOTE PREMIER LONG DISTANCE HURDLE (Gd 2) (5-Y.O+) (Class A)

2-15 (2-16) **2m 7f 110y (12 hdls)** £12,740.00 (£4,822.00: £2,361.00: £1,077.00) GOING: 0.19 sec per fur (G)

	Horse	Details	Dist	Pos	SP	RR	SF
2056*	**Ocean Hawk (USA) (156)**	(NATwiston-Davies) **5-11-10** CLlewellyn (led to 8th: led 3 out: hrd drvn flat: all out)	—	**1**	Evens[1]	140	32
2056[3]	**Pleasure Shared (IRE) (151)**	(PJHobbs) **9-11-10** RDunwoody (lw: a.p: led 8th to 3 out: rallied u.p nr fin)	¾	**2**	6/4[2]	140	32
2056[4]	**Top Spin (134)**	(JRJenkins) **8-11-3** PCarberry (hld up: outpcd appr 3 out: sn btn)	15	**3**	9/1[3]	122?	14
	Mudahim (146)	(MrsJPitman) **11-11-3** WMarston (bkwd: hld up: hdwy to jn ldrs 7th: rdn & outpcd 9th)	2½	**4**	10/1	121	13
1647[7]	**Ruling (USA)**	(KRBurke) **11-11-3** NWilliamson (bit bkwd: w ldrs to 3 out: sn wknd: t.o)	7	**5**	20/1	116	8
					(SP 113.9%)		**5 Rn**

5m 48.8 (16.80) CSF £2.78 TOTE £2.00: £1.20 £1.20 (£1.60) OWNER Mr Matt Archer & Miss Jean Broadhurst (CHELTENHAM) BRED Brereton C. Jones

2056* Ocean Hawk (USA) carries plenty of condition, but he wins his races by burning the opposition off and he did need the full treatment here to ward off a persistent challenger nearing the finish. (Evens)

2056 Pleasure Shared (IRE) gave the winner a much harder race than he did on identical terms last month, but it was still not good enough to exact revenge. He will now return to fences. (6/4)

2056 Top Spin obviously needs more cut in the ground as he gets older and, unable to hold his pitch on the home turn, was soon fighting a lost cause. (9/1)

Mudahim needed this first run since changing stables and, as he has also shown a liking for the mud, this effort was probably better than it looked. (10/1: op 6/1)

2638 ST. HELENS COLLEGE STUDENTS NOVICES' CHASE (5-Y.O+) (Class B)

2-45 (2-47) **2m 4f (15 fncs)** £11,715.00 (£3,570.00: £1,760.00: £855.00) GOING: 0.19 sec per fur (G)

	Horse	Details	Dist	Pos	SP	RR	SF
2054*	**Simply Dashing (IRE)**	(TDEasterby) **6-11-12** RDunwoody (chsd ldr: hmpd 11th: led appr 2 out: sn clr: canter)	—	**1**	2/7[1]	123++	30
1557[F]	**Ballyline (IRE) (88)**	(WTKemp) **6-11-9** NWilliamson (led: j.lft 11th & 4 out: hdd & wknd appr 2 out)	10	**2**	9/1[3]	112	19
1901*	**Flimsy Truth (100)**	(MHWeston) **11-11-9** MrMHarris (a chsng ldng pair: effrt appr last: no imp)	3½	**3**	9/2[2]	109	16
1582[7]	**La Mezeray (76)**	(MrsJEHawkins) **9-11-4** DWalsh (bit bkwd: hld up in rr: lost tch appr 3 out: t.o)	25	**4**	25/1	84	—
					(SP 109.8%)		**4 Rn**

5m 13.1 (16.10) CSF £3.30 TOTE £1.10: (£1.80) OWNER Mr Steve Hammond (MALTON) BRED Eastward Bloodstock Holdings Ltd

2054* Simply Dashing (IRE) did not need to get serious to maintain his winning sequence and will now be aimed at the Cheltenham Festival where he will have a choice of engagements. (2/7)

1557 Ballyline (IRE), although inclined to jump left, did a good job of pacemaking until the winner said go, and then the only race on was for the places. (9/1)

1901* Flimsy Truth failed to get in a blow against the principals and this step back in distance on such fast ground was not in his favour. (9/2)

2639 OLD HALL COUNTRY CLUB H'CAP CHASE (5-Y.O+) (Class B)

3-15 (3-16) **2m (12 fncs)** £7,162.80 (£2,162.40: £1,051.20: £495.60) GOING: 0.19 sec per fur (G)

	Horse	Details	Dist	Pos	SP	RR	SF
1682[W]	**Konvekta King (IRE) (128)**	(OSherwood) **9-10-13** RDunwoody (a.p: hit 6th: led & qcknd flat: sn clr)	—	**1**	5/2[1]	134	59
1869[4]	**Easthorpe (138)**	(MissHCKnight) **9-11-9b[1]** JFTitley (lw: j.w: led to 2nd: led 5th to 7th: led appr 3 out tl flat: sn outpcd)	2½	**2**	3/1[2]	142	67
1688*	**Political Tower (130)**	(RNixon) **10-11-1** PNiven (lw: hld up: hdwy 8th: rdn appr last: one pce)	2½	**3**	7/2[3]	131	56
	Time Won't Wait (IRE) (137)	(RTPhillips) **8-11-8** JRailton (bit bkwd: hld up & bhd: hit 2nd: hdwy appr 3 out: blnd last: nt rcvr)	1½	**4**	4/1	137	62
1914[3]	**Sound Reveille (139)**	(CPEBrooks) **9-11-3**(7) MBerry (j.w: led 2nd to 5th: led 7th tl appr 3 out: sn wknd)	2½	**5**	8/1	136	61
					(SP 106.9%)		**5 Rn**

3m 58.5 (3.50) CSF £8.93 TOTE £2.90: £1.50 £1.70 (£3.70) OWNER Konvekta Ltd (UPPER LAMBOURN) BRED Peter Kehoe in Ireland

1352* Konvekta King (IRE) showed no signs of rustiness after a two-month break with a smoothly-gained success in a very truly-run race. He is thriving this term. (5/2)

1869 Easthorpe, wearing blinkers for this return to the minimum trip, ran up to his best and an early return to form is earmarked. (3/1)

1688* Political Tower has never won on ground as lively as this, but he gave it his best shot and certainly lost no caste in defeat. (7/2)

Time Won't Wait (IRE) usually needs a pipe-opener, but he may well have taken a deal of beating had he not made an almighty blunder when in full flight at the last. (4/1)

1914 Sound Reveille is taking time to recover his true form and may well do so when the ground eases to his liking. (8/1)

2640 HAYDOCK STANDARD OPEN N.H. FLAT RACE (4, 5 & 6-Y.O) (Class H)

3-45 (3-45) **2m** £1,633.50 (£456.00: £220.50)

	Horse	Details	Dist	Pos	SP	RR	SF
1296*	**Colour Code**	(MrsASwinbank) **5-11-11** JSupple (mde all: sn wl clr: unchal)	—	**1**	10/11[1]	100 f	—
	Ballad Minstrel (IRE)	(JGFitzGerald) **5-11-11** PCarberry (bit bkwd: hld up: hdwy to chse wnr 6f out: rdn 2f out: no imp)	19	**2**	7/4[2]	81 f	—
	Into The Black (IRE)	(MrsMReveley) **6-11-4** PNiven (bit bkwd: hld up: hdwy 6f out: nvr nr to chal)	9	**3**	8/1[3]	65 f	—
2005[5]	**Monsieur Darcy (IRE)**	(JRAdam) **6-11-4** JRailton (bkwd: hdwy 6f out: rdn over 2f out: nvr nr ldrs)	1¼	**4**	20/1	64 f	—
1834[5]	**Cosy Ride (IRE)**	(NATwiston-Davies) **5-11-4** CLlewellyn (chsd ldrs 10f: sn wknd: t.o)	15	**5**	8/1[3]	49 f	—
	Champs-Girl (IRE)	(BWMurray) **4-10-1** WDwan (bkwd: a bhd: t.o fnl 6f)	dist	**6**	50/1	—	—
					(SP 117.7%)		**6 Rn**

3m 42.3 CSF £2.69 TOTE £1.90: £1.30 £1.40 (£1.50) OWNER Mr Bill Walker (RICHMOND) BRED Meon Valley Stud

WEIGHT FOR AGE 4yo-12lb

1296* Colour Code had more use made of him than he did on his debut, but the outcome was just the same and, whilst the company was nothing to write home about, he annihilated them. (10/11: 5/4-4/5)

Ballad Minstrel (IRE) won on his racecourse debut last season, but he looked to have plenty left to work on this time and that proved the deciding factor inside the last half-mile. (7/4)

Into The Black (IRE), a brother to winning chasers Into the Red and Over the Road, was unable to make his presence felt, but the experience will not be lost. (8/1)

2005 Monsieur Darcy (IRE) will do much better when he tackles fences, for he has the size to make even those obstacles look small. (20/1)

1834 Cosy Ride (IRE), as fit as a flea, could not go the pace on this fast ground and was going in reverse before reaching the end of the back straight. (8/1)

T/Plpt: £18.10 (875.27 Tckts). T/Qdpt: £2.70 (330.73 Tckts). IM

2620-KEMPTON (R-H) (Good to firm)
Saturday January 18th

WEATHER: overcast & damp

2641 TWICKENHAM NOVICES' CHASE (5-Y.O+) (Class B)
12-40 (12-40) **2m (13 fncs)** £9,240.50 (£2,819.00: £1,392.00: £678.50) GOING: 0.16 sec per fur (G)

				SP	RR	SF
2335a[2]	**Land Afar (133)** (PRWebber) **10-11-7** JOsborne (lw: mstke 6th: stdy hdwy 9th: led on bit appr 2 out: clr appr last: pushed out)	—	1	5/4[1]	140	47
2116[2]	**Mister Drum (IRE) (124)** (MJWilkinson) **8-11-7** APMcCoy (led to 2nd: blnd 6th: led 8th to 4 out: led appr 3 out tl appr 2 out: 2nd & btn whn mstke last)	5	2	4/1[3]	135	42
1919[2]	**Mandys Mantino** (JTGifford) **7-11-3** PHide (stdy hdwy 7th: lost pl 4 out: 3rd & styng on whn mstke last)	3	3	100/30[2]	128	35
1790[3]	**Down the Fell** (HowardJohnson) **8-11-11** AMaguire (w ldr: led 2nd to 8th: led 4 out tl appr 3 out: sn wknd)	26	4	7/1	110	17
1925*	**Golden Hello** (TDEasterby) **6-11-7** RGarritty (lw: 4th whn fell 7th)		F	10/1	—	—
				(SP 109.1%)		**5 Rn**

3m 51.1 (7.10) CSF £5.99 TOTE £2.10: £1.20 £1.70 (£3.40) OWNER Mr T. J. Ford (BANBURY) BRED Grange Stud (UK)

2335a Land Afar had the race run to suit him, for the fast pace meant he could easily be put to sleep in the rear and had no problems picking off his rivals as they tired. He will be entered for the Arkle Chase at the Cheltenham Festival, but that course does not suit him and he would be far better waiting for Liverpool. (5/4)

2116 Mister Drum (IRE), at his best on a right-handed track, likes to make the running but, with Down the Fell also liking to dominate, the two of them went off like scalded cats. Nevertheless, he held on well until collared by the winner approaching the penultimate fence. He has been in fine form this season and should soon add to his tally if remaining on a right-handed track. (4/1)

1919 Mandys Mantino has suffered just one defeat over hurdles, but this big, strapping individual has always looked a chaser in the making. Chucked in at the deep-end on this chasing debut, he is sure to have learnt a lot from this and will be much better suited by two and a half miles. He should have no problems opening his account over the larger obstacles. (100/30: 7/4-7/2)

1790 Down the Fell, along with Mister Drum, went off at a very fast pace and it was no surprise to see him fold up badly going to the third last. He is much better than this. (7/1)

1925* Golden Hello has had real problems with his jumping this season and that was once again evident here as he fell at the seventh when close up. (10/1: 7/1-11/1)

2642 JOHN COURT OF MARGATE QUALITY DECORATORS NOVICES' HURDLE (5-Y.O+) (Class B)
1-10 (1-12) **2m 5f (10 hdls)** £6,285.00 (£1,920.00: £950.00: £465.00) GOING: 0.16 sec per fur (G)

				SP	RR	SF
1921*	**Sea Victor (113)** (JLHarris) **5-11-4** DGallagher (hld up: led appr 2 out: mstke last: drvn out)	—	1	2/1[1]	97	30
2550[2]	**Montecot (FR)** (SMellor) **8-11-0** NMann (chsd ldr to 2nd: mstke 7th: rdn appr 2 out: unable qckn flat)	1¼	2	11/2	92	25
1556[2]	**Courbaril (124)** (MCPipe) **5-11-7** APMcCoy (led: clr 2nd: hdd appr 2 out: one pce flat)	5	3	5/2[2]	95	28
1583*	**Ready Money Creek (IRE) (110)** (OSherwood) **6-11-4** JOsborne (lw: chsd ldr 2nd to 3 out: wknd appr 2 out)	16	4	11/4[3]	80	13
1594[9]	**Country Tarquin** (RJHodges) **5-11-0** TDascombe (lw: rdn 6th: hdwy 7th: wknd after 3 out)	8	5	50/1	70	3
1505[3]	**Adilov (94)** (JJBridger) **5-11-0** AMaguire (lw: hld up: rdn 7th: sn wknd: t.o)	dist	6	25/1	—	—
1820[5]	**Sarenacare (IRE)** (PJHobbs) **5-11-0** GTormey (7th & wkng whn mstke 6th: sn t.o)	6	7	50/1	—	—
1873[10]	**Gwithian** (NJHawke) **5-11-0** RGreene (bit bkwd: plld hrd: bhd fr 4th: t.o fr 6th)	3	8	100/1	—	—
	Honest Dave (60) (BAPearce) **7-11-0** KGaule (bhd fr 5th: t.o fr 6th)	dist	9	100/1	—	—
1958[3]	**Maylin Magic** (TCasey) **6-10-9** MAFitzgerald (a bhd: t.o fr 6th: p.u bef 2 out)		P	25/1	—	—
				(SP 117.6%)		**10 Rn**

5m 5.4 (13.40) CSF £12.01 TOTE £2.90: £1.10 £1.70 £1.50 (£10.40) Trio £9.20 OWNER Mr David Abell (MELTON MOWBRAY) BRED Juddmonte Farms

STEWARDS' ENQUIRY Maguire susp. 27-31/1 & 1/2/97 (irresponsible riding).

1921* Sea Victor was well suited by the step up in trip and once again demonstrated what a tough individual he is. A real credit to his trainer, he looks a useful recruit to hurdling and can complete the hat-trick. (2/1)

2550 Montecot (FR), making a quick reappearance, was on the heels of the winner jumping the last, but failed to find another gear. (11/2: 4/1-6/1)

1556 Courbaril has been in sparkling form this season on fast ground, winning five of his eight races, but he did look rather temperamental last time. There was no sign of that here and, setting the pace, he was soon clear until caught two out. (5/2)

1583* Ready Money Creek (IRE), taking a step up in distance, was collared three from home and then tired as lack of a recent run - this was his first outing in seven and a half weeks - rather than lack of stamina proved his undoing. He is worth another chance at this sort of trip, but would prefer some cut in the ground. (11/4)

1431 Country Tarquin, taking a step up in trip, had shot his bolt soon after the third last. (50/1)

1505 Adilov has run well to be placed in several hurdles this season, but this was not his day and he was beaten three-quarters of a mile out. Whether the Stewards had a rush of blood to the head is debatable, but Maguire was amazingly suspended for six days for irresponsible riding over an incident going to the first flight. (25/1)

2643 SUNBURY NOVICES' CHASE (5-Y.O+) (Class B)
1-40 (1-41) **3m (19 fncs)** £8,165.00 (£2,495.00: £1,235.00: £605.00) GOING: 0.16 sec per fur (G)

				SP	RR	SF
1456*	**Fine Thyne (IRE)** (MrsAJPerrett) **8-11-10** MAFitzgerald (lw: chsd ldr: led 15th: clr 3 out: v.easily)	—	1	4/11[1]	99++	32
	Pavi's Brother (PRHedger) **9-11-10** ILawrence (wl bhd fr 10th: hdwy appr 3 out: chsd wnr appr 2 out: no imp)	6	2	12/1[3]	95	28
2007[P]	**Volleyball (IRE) (77)** (PRHedger) **8-11-5** MRichards (lw: blnd 1st: mstke 6th: bhd fr 7th: t.o fr 10th)	27	3	50/1	72	5
2049[2]	**Sunset and Vine (103)** (TCasey) **10-11-5** APMcCoy (j.lft: led: mstke 1st: hdd 15th: wknd appr 3 out: virtually p.u flat: t.o)	dist	4	11/4[2]	—	—
				(SP 109.7%)		**4 Rn**

6m 12.3 (17.30) CSF £4.63 TOTE £1.40: (£2.30) OWNER Mr Peter Wiegand (PULBOROUGH) BRED Minch Bloodstock in Ireland

1456* Fine Thyne (IRE) had little more than an afternoon's stroll to pick up some valuable prize money, gain more experience and blow away a few cobwebs. This was his first run in over eight weeks. (4/11)

Pavi's Brother, who looked a tricky ride in point-to-points, looks extremely moderate but, after being nearly tailed off at one point, struggled on to finish a moderate second. (12/1)
Volleyball (IRE) was far from fluent at a number of fences and appears to have little ability. (50/1)
2049 Sunset and Vine set the pace, despite jumping to his left at many of his fences, but was collared five out and tired badly in the straight as this longer trip proved well beyond him. (11/4)

2644 VICTOR CHANDLER H'CAP HURDLE (0-135) (5-Y.O+) (Class C)

2-10 (2-14) **2m 5f (10 hdls)** £3,745.00 (£1,135.00: £555.00: £265.00) GOING: 0.16 sec per fur (G)

				SP	RR	SF
1832^{6}	**Storm Dust (107)** (MissHCKnight) **8-10-5** BFenton (hld up: rdn 2 out: led last: r.o wl)	—	**1**	25/1	88	27
1876^{4}	**Royal Piper (NZ) (102)** (AJWilson) **10-10-0** RGreene (gd hdwy appr 2 out: str run flat: fin wl)	nk	**2**	25/1	83	22
1678^{2}	**Morstock (112)** (RJHodges) **7-10-7**$^{(3)}$ TDascombe (hdwy 7th: led appr 2 out to last: unable qckn)	1¼	**3**	8/1^{3}	92	31
1866^{*}	**Barford Sovereign (109)** (JRFanshawe) **5-10-7** PHide (led tl appr 2 out: wknd appr last)	8	**4**	7/2^{1}	83	22
1859^{5}	**Kalasadi (USA) (104)** (VSoane) **6-10-2b** MRichards (hdwy appr last: nvr nrr)	6	**5**	16/1	73	12
1709^{3}	**Smuggler's Point (USA) (107)** (JJBridger) **7-10-5** AMaguire (a.p: chsd ldr 3rd tl appr 2 out: sn wknd)	4	**6**	10/1	73	12
1924^{3}	**Elpidos (118)** (MDHammond) **5-11-2** RGarritty (rdn 7th: hdwy 3 out: wknd appr 2 out)	4	**7**	7/1^{2}	81	20
1982^{7}	**Call My Guest (IRE) (123)** (REPeacock) **7-11-7** APMcCoy (prom to 7th)	20	**8**	14/1	71	10
1856^{P}	**Djais (FR) (119)** (JRJenkins) **8-11-3v^{1}** GBradley (hdwy 3rd: wknd appr 2 out)	hd	**9**	20/1	67	6
1934^{P}	**Seod Rioga (IRE) (106)** (SMellor) **8-10-4v^{1}** NMann (lw: a bhd)	10	**10**	33/1	46	—
2059^{7}	**Alltime Dancer (IRE) (119)** (OSherwood) **5-11-3** JOsborne (lw: lost pl 3rd: sme hdwy 3 out: sn wknd)	1	**11**	14/1	58	—
1597^{2}	**Rosencrantz (IRE) (108)** (MissVenetiaWilliams) **5-10-6** RJohnson (lw: stdy hdwy 7th: 3rd whn fell 3 out)		**F**	7/2^{1}	—	—
	Lucky Blue (130) (SEarle) **10-12-0** MAFitzgerald (bit bkwd: prom to 4th: t.o whn p.u bef 3 out)		**P**	16/1	—	—

(SP 117.6%) **13 Rn**

5m 2.6 (10.60) CSF £459.32 CT £4,872.80 TOTE £34.50: £5.40 £4.10 £2.20 (£384.80) Trio £766.20 OWNER Mr Sunley Tice (WANTAGE) BRED Sunley Stud
LONG HANDICAP Royal Piper (NZ) 9-11
1832 Storm Dust, all the better for his recent run after a lengthy lay-off, has had his problems, but showed none of them here, leading at the final flight and just managing to hold on from the fast-finishing runner-up. (25/1)
1876 Royal Piper (NZ), 3lb out of the handicap, is no easy horse to win with. Producing a whirlwind finish, he would surely have prevailed with a little further to go. Both his wins to date have come in the mud. (25/1)
1678 Morstock, whose three wins to date have come at Wincanton over two miles on good ground, seems just as happy over this longer trip. (8/1)
1866* Barford Sovereign had the trip and ground in her favour, although she has been raised 5lb for her recent victory. (7/2)
1586 Kalasadi (USA) is not very consistent. (16/1)
1709 Smuggler's Point (USA), in a much more competitive event, showed in second place for a long way. (10/1)
1597 Rosencrantz (IRE), taking a step up in trip, was travelling well and was close up in third when falling at the third last. He should soon make amends. (7/2)

2645 SUN 'KING OF THE PUNTERS' LANZAROTE H'CAP HURDLE (4-Y.O+) (Class B)

2-40 (2-43) **2m (8 hdls)** £14,278.00 (£4,324.00: £2,112.00: £1,006.00) GOING: 0.16 sec per fur (G)

				SP	RR	SF
2055^{*}	**Make a Stand (132)** (MCPipe) **6-10-3** APMcCoy (lw: mde all: clr 2nd: unchal)	—	**1**	2/1^{1}	118+	54
1566^{2}	**Gales Cavalier (IRE) (129)** (DRGandolfo) **9-10-0** JOsborne (lost pl 3rd: hdwy appr 2 out: r.o)	4	**2**	10/1	111	47
1793^{4}	**Silver Groom (IRE) (137)** (RAkehurst) **7-10-3**$^{(5)}$ SRyan (hdwy 3 out: chsd wnr appr 2 out tl flat: unable qckn)	2	**3**	10/1	117	53
1924^{4}	**Tom Brodie (129)** (HowardJohnson) **7-10-0** BFenton (hld up: rdn appr 2 out: r.o one pce)	1¼	**4**	11/1	108	44
1365^{6}	**Chief's Song (136)** (SDow) **7-10-7** DGallagher (lw: chsd wnr to 4th: wknd 3 out)	5	**5**	7/1^{3}	110	46
2117^{4}	**Mytton's Choice (IRE) (129)** (DNicholson) **6-10-0** AMaguire (hld up: mstkes 2nd & 5th: wknd 3 out)	6	**6**	11/1	97	33
1793^{2}	**Master Beveled (139)** (PDEvans) **7-10-10** GBradley (lw: chsd wnr 4th tl appr 2 out: sn wknd)	9	**7**	5/1^{2}	98	34
1793^{14}	**Dreams End (134)** (PBowen) **9-10-5** RFarrant (hdwy 3 out: wknd appr 2 out)	6	**8**	14/1	87	23
	Kissair (IRE) (134) (NJHenderson) **6-10-5** MAFitzgerald (bit bkwd: a bhd)	1	**9**	25/1	86	22
	Roll a Dollar (129) (DRCElsworth) **11-10-0** PHolley (bhd fr 3 out)	2	**10**	20/1	79	15
$318a^{18}$	**Ros Castle (129)** (RJHodges) **6-10-0** ILawrence (bit bkwd: bhd fr 2nd)	15	**11**	33/1	64	—
2059^{P}	**Ashwell Boy (IRE) (134)** (PJHobbs) **6-10-5** RJohnson (lw: bhd tl fell 4th)		**F**	25/1	—	—

(SP 119.4%) **12 Rn**

3m 44.1 (2.10) CSF £19.74 CT £153.43 TOTE £2.90: £1.90 £3.10 £3.20 (£18.20) Trio £77.00 OWNER Mr P. A. Deal (WELLINGTON) BRED R. M. West
LONG HANDICAP Tom Brodie 9-12 Mytton's Choice (IRE) 9-12 Roll a Dollar 9-12 Ros Castle 9-11
IN-FOCUS: **Martin Pipe took full advantage of a loophole in the Rules to doubly declare top weight Pridwell here and at Haydock, where he actually ran, thus ensuring there would not be a rise of 14lb in the weights, helping his other runner Make a Stand and keeping four opponents out of the handicap.**
2055* Make a Stand, 9lb higher than when winning the William Hill Handicap Hurdle at Sandown last month, turned another competitive handicap into a mockery, tearing off in front at such a rate of knots that there was no hope for his rivals of living with him. They just had to hope that he would come back to them, but McCoy had no intention of letting them do that and the combination won without being challenged. He continues to impress and there seems to be no stopping this exciting novice at present. (2/1)
1566 Gales Cavalier (IRE) was reverting to hurdles for the first time since March 1994 because of his attractive mark of 129 compared to 159 over fences. Finding his feet approaching the second last, he ran on nicely to take second on the run-in. This was a very encouraging run and, although his trainer has said he will go back chasing, he could win over hurdles with an attractive handicap mark such as this, especially if stepping up to two and a half miles. (10/1)
1793 Silver Groom (IRE) was meeting the winner on 9lb better terms for being beaten nearly thirteen lengths at Sandown. (10/1)
1924 Tom Brodie has been in tremendous form this season but has risen steadily in the weights as a result. Two miles on fast ground are his ideal requirements. (11/1)
1365 Chief's Song had no chance of pacemaking with Make a Stand in the field and was a spent force three out. (7/1)
2117 Mytton's Choice (IRE), who failed to stay three miles last time, was in trouble jumping the third last. (11/1)
1793 Master Beveled, fit from the All-Weather and 2lb better off with the winner for being beaten two lengths at Sandown, was very disappointing. (5/1)

2646 VICTOR CHANDLER H'CAP CHASE (Gd 2) (5-Y.O+) (Class A)
3-10 (3-14) **2m (13 fncs)** £21,560.00 (£8,203.00: £4,051.50: £1,885.50) GOING: 0.16 sec per fur (G)

Form	Horse	Dist	Pos	SP	RR	SF
2058[2]	**Ask Tom (IRE) (156)** (TPTate) **8-10-10** RGarritty (a.p: chsd ldr 4th tl appr 3 out: hrd rdn appr 2 out: chsd ldr appr last: led flat: r.o wl)	—	1	9/4[1]	162	58
943[2]	**Clay County (146)** (MDHammond) **12-10-0** APMcCoy (lw: led: mstke 9th: rdn appr 2 out: hdd flat: r.o)	¾	2	11/1	151	47
1917[P]	**Big Matt (IRE) (148)** (NJHenderson) **9-10-2**[ow2] MAFitzgerald (lw: stdy hdwy fr 8th: 4th whn mstke 2 out: r.o flat)	2	3	13/2	151	45
1792[2]	**Viking Flagship (170)** (DNicholson) **10-11-10** AMaguire (bit bkwd: a.p: chsd ldr appr 3 out tl appr last: unable qckn)	hd	4	4/1[2]	173	69
1914[2]	**Kibreet (146)** (PJHobbs) **10-10-0** GTormey (lw: chsd ldr to 4th: wknd 6th)	17	5	14/1	132	28
2058*	**Storm Alert (154)** (DNicholson) **11-10-8** RJohnson (nvr gng wl: a bhd: t.o fr 6th)	15	6	11/2[3]	125	21
1914*	**Dancing Paddy (148)** (KOCunningham-Brown) **9-10-2** PHide (lw: blnd 1st: bhd whn fell 2nd)		F	6/1	—	—
1910[2]	**Callisoe Bay (IRE) (146)** (OSherwood) **8-10-0** JOsborne (bhd whn blnd & uns rdr 1st)		U	14/1	—	—
				(SP 115.4%)	**8 Rn**	

3m 46.5 (2.80 under best) (2.50) CSF £24.12 CT £125.60 TOTE £2.80: £1.50 £2.50 £1.70 (£14.40) OWNER Mr B. T. Stewart-Brown (TADCASTER) BRED Capt S. H. Walford

LONG HANDICAP Kibreet 9-11 Big Matt (IRE) 9-12 Clay County 9-13 Callisoe Bay (IRE) 9-6

2058 Ask Tom (IRE) put up a tremendous performance to show that he is now in the top league of two-mile chasers. He looked in trouble turning for home but, battling his heart out, eventually managed to get on top on the run-in, and smashed the course record by over two seconds. His action and head-carriage suggested that this fast ground was not really to his liking which makes this performance even more commendable. The Queen Mother Champion Chase must definitely be on the agenda now, although he still needs to show further improvement, as he will be meeting Viking Flagship on level terms. (9/4)

943 Clay County, off the track for three months, ran a tremendous race against some high-class rivals. Tearing off in front, he simply refused to give way and was only overhauled on the run-in. A real two-mile specialist, his turn is not far away. (11/1: 8/1-12/1)

1366 Big Matt (IRE), whose two flops at Cheltenham recently confirmed that he does not like that course, found this track over two miles on fast ground too sharp. Having steadily moved into the action in the back straight, he was rather tapped for toe once in line for home until running on on the flat to snatch third on the line. (13/2: 9/2-7/1)

1792 Viking Flagship was fitter than at Sandown last month, but still gave the impression in the paddock that this run would do him good. Moving into second approaching the third last appearing to be travelling nicely, he was soon being pushed along and, collared for the runner-up berth going to the last, failed to find another gear. He is still right on course for the Queen Mother Champion Chase, and must again have a leading chance. (4/1)

1914 Kibreet, 3lb out of the handicap, has never won off a mark as high as this and was struggling entering the back straight. He needs to drop in the weights. (14/1: 10/1-16/1)

2058* Storm Alert, who would have been much happier if this race had been run at Ascot, ran appallingly and was never travelling. (11/2: 4/1-6/1)

1914* Dancing Paddy (6/1: op 10/1)

2647 SUN PUNTERS CLUB FULWELL H'CAP CHASE (0-145) (5-Y.O+) (Class B)
3-40 (3-43) **2m 4f 110y (17 fncs)** £7,080.50 (£2,144.00: £1,047.00: £498.50) GOING: 0.16 sec per fur (G)

Form	Horse	Dist	Pos	SP	RR	SF
1765[7]	**Garrylough (IRE) (111)** (DRGandolfo) **8-10-1b[1]** AMaguire (mde all: clr appr 3 out: easily)	—	1	11/2	125+	57
1934[2]	**Five to Seven (USA) (117)** (PFNicholls) **8-10-7** APMcCoy (lw: hld up: chsd wnr fr 11th: unable qckn fr 4 out)	14	2	3/1[1]	120	52
1454[3]	**Lackendara (118)** (MissHCKnight) **10-10-8** BFenton (lw: chsd wnr 3rd to 11th: wknd 12th: 4th & no ch whn blnd 4 out)	19	3	5/1[3]	106	38
2009*	**Beatson (IRE) (112)** (RHBuckler) **8-9-13**(3) GHogan (a.p: cl 3rd whn blnd 13th: nt rcvr)	10	4	100/30[2]	92	24
2057[5]	**Strong Medicine (134)** (KCBailey) **10-11-10** SMcNeill (lw: blnd 4th: a bhd: t.o)	21	5	10/1	98	30
1917[2]	**Go Universal (IRE) (134)** (CPEBrooks) **9-11-10** GBradley (a bhd: t.o whn p.u bef 3 out)		P	100/30[2]	—	—
				(SP 112.3%)	**6 Rn**	

5m 2.1 (1.10) CSF £20.60 TOTE £7.60: £3.00 £1.80 (£10.40) OWNER Mr T. J. Whitley (WANTAGE) BRED John Clarke

1119 Garrylough (IRE) found the application of blinkers working the oracle and, making all the running, forged clear turning for home to win with a ton in hand. (11/2)

1934 Five to Seven (USA) was left for dead by the winner turning for home and, for the third consecutive time this season, had to settle for second. (3/1)

1454 Lackendara has had his problems and has not won for nearly two years. Punters knew their fate halfway down the back straight. (5/1)

2009* Beatson (IRE) has been in tremendous form this season but has been raised 11lb for his last victory. Nevertheless, he was close up in third place when an horrendous error at the fifth last knocked the stuffing out of him. (100/30)

2057 Strong Medicine, back over his ideal trip and on ground he likes, ran no race at all. (10/1)

1917 Go Universal (IRE), who ran so well in the Tripleprint Gold Cup at Cheltenham, showed nothing here and it may well have been because he was travelling right-handed. A return to a left-handed track is a must. (100/30)

2648 WEATHERBYS 'STARS OF TOMORROW' STANDARD OPEN N.H. FLAT RACE (4, 5 & 6-Y.O) (Class H)
4-10 (4-14) **2m** £1,696.50 (£474.00: £229.50)

Form	Horse	Dist	Pos	SP	RR	SF
1800[5]	**Clinking** (MrsAJPerrett) **6-11-5** MrsAPerrett (hdwy 6f out: led over 2f out: rdn out)	—	1	8/1	53 f	—
25[2]	**Tanglefoot Tipple** (RHAlner) **6-11-2**(3) PHenley (lw: hld up: chsd wnr wl over 1f out: unable qckn fnl f)	7	2	2/1[1]	46 f	—
	Ten Times (USA) (MCPipe) **4-10-7** APMcCoy (led over 12f: wknd over 1f out)	9	3	2/1[1]	37 f	—
	Currer Bell (CMurray) **4-10-2** KGaule (chsd ldr: led over 3f out tl over 2f out: sn wknd)	6	4	7/1[3]	26 f	—
	Embargo (IRE) (JLDunlop) **5-10-12**(7) MrHDunlop (bit bkwd: uns rdr & bolted bef s: bhd fnl 6f)	4	5	13/2[2]	27 f	—
	Star Island (DRCElsworth) **4-10-0**(7) MrNMoran (hdwy 6f out: wknd over 4f out)	2½	6	7/1[3]	25 f	—
	Grematic (NJHawke) **6-11-5** RGreene (bit bkwd: bhd fnl 5f)	12	7	25/1	13 f	—
	Shavano (MMadgwick) **5-11-5** BFenton (t: lw: bhd fnl 4f: t.o)	30	8	33/1	—	—
				(SP 122.9%)	**8 Rn**	

3m 51.1 CSF £24.03 TOTE £9.60: £2.00 £1.10 £1.30 (£10.00) Trio £5.40 OWNER Mr G. Harwood (PULBOROUGH) BRED Juddmonte Farms

WEIGHT FOR AGE 4yo-12lb

1800 Clinking found the better ground and flat track much more to his liking and putting less emphasis on stamina. Sent on over a quarter of a mile from home, he was rousted along to assert. (8/1: 5/1-10/1)

25 Tanglefoot Tipple, who has changed stables since finishing second at Worcester in June, is a big, unfurnished gelding who needs plenty of time. Looking in really good shape in the paddock, he looked rather green and failed to find a turn of foot, but will have learnt from this, and can find a similar event before long. (2/1)
Ten Times (USA), a half-brother to six Flat winners, was in training with Bill O'Gorman last year, but never made it to the racecourse. (2/1)
Currer Bell, a half-sister to sprinter Samson-Agonistes and miler Inderaputeri, showed in front early in the straight but, collared approaching the final quarter-mile, soon had bellows to mend. (7/1: 5/1-8/1)
Embargo (IRE) (13/2: 2/1-7/1)
Star Island (7/1: 5/1-8/1)

T/Jkpt: £8,420.50 (0.4 Tckts); £7,115.95 to Newton Abbot 20/1/97. T/Plpt: £64.40 (362.95 Tckts). T/Qdpt: £42.70 (34.37 Tckts). AK

2539-CARLISLE (R-H) (Good to firm, Good patches)
Monday January 20th

WEATHER: fine

2649 GOSSIP HOLME NOVICES' HURDLE (4-Y.O+) (Class E)
1-25 (1-26) **2m 1f (9 hdls)** £2,612.00 (£732.00: £356.00) GOING: 0.08 sec per fur (G)

	Horse / details	Dist	Pos	SP	RR	SF
1666*	**Mister Ross (IRE) (98)** (HowardJohnson) **7-11-11** PCarberry (lw: mde virtually all: pushed clr between last 2: eased flat)	—	**1**	Evens 1	76+	6
	Northern Union (CAN) (CParker) **6-11-5** DParker (chsd ldrs: wnt 2nd 6th: kpt on fr 2 out: no ch w wnr)	1¼	**2**	5/1 2	69	—
	Forever Noble (IRE) (MDHammond) **4-10-7** RGarritty (bhd: hdwy 6th: styd on fr 2 out)	hd	**3**	10/1	69	—
2175⁵	**Catherine's Choice** (MDHammond) **4-10-4**(3) MrCBonner (mid div: kpt on fr 3 out: nvr nr to chal)	9	**4**	33/1	60	—
2504⁴	**Lumback Lady** (BMactaggart) **7-10-11**(3) GLee (in tch: no imp fr 3 out)	1	**5**	20/1	54	—
1843⁴	**Yewcroft Boy** (MABarnes) **6-11-0**(5) STaylor (bit bkwd: a.p: drvn along 5th: outpcd fr 3 out)	4	**6**	50/1	56	—
1700¹⁰	**Recruitment** (JRTurner) **4-10-7** WFry (unruly s: sn prom: wknd 3 out)	11	**7**	100/1	45	—
1700⁷	**Crabbie's Pride** (MGMeagher) **4-10-7b¹** DerekByrne (hld up: hdwy 4th: rdn & wkng whn blnd 2 out)	3½	**8**	16/1	42	—
1672³	**Black Ice (IRE)** (TPTate) **6-11-5** PNiven (w ldrs: rdn & outpcd 6th: wknd next)	nk	**9**	15/2 3	42	—
	Henry Hoolet (PMonteith) **8-11-5** GCahill (swvd rt s: sn mid div: sme hdwy 3 out: sn wknd)	5	**10**	25/1	37	—
1652¹⁶	**Whothehellisharry** (JBerry) **4-10-7b¹** MMoloney (prom: rdn 5th: wknd next)	4	**11**	20/1	33	—
1305⁴	**Bollin Frank** (TDEasterby) **5-11-5** ASSmith (lw: plld hrd: trckd ldrs tl wknd qckly after 6th)	11	**12**	11/1	23	—
1851⁸	**The Final Spark** (GRichards) **6-11-0** LO'Hara (bhd fr 5th)	8	**13**	50/1	10	—
1654ᴾ	**Triona's Hope (IRE)** (EMCaine) **8-10-12**(7) TristanDavidson (hmpd s: a bhd: t.o 4th)	hd	**14**	1000/1	15	—
	Millers Goldengirl (IRE) (MrsSJSmith) **6-11-0** RichardGuest (bhd fr 5th)	6	**15**	100/1	5	—
	Aunt Piquee (GRichards) **8-11-0** ADobbin (wl bhd fr 4th: t.o)	26	**16**	25/1	—	—
2175⁷	**Miletrian City** (JBerry) **4-10-0**(7) SHaworth (b.d 1st)		**B**	50/1	—	—
1699⁷	**Needle Match** (JJO'Neill) **4-10-2**(5) RMcGrath (fell 1st)		**F**	33/1	—	—
	Coeur Francais (FR) (NWaggott) **5-11-0**(5) MichaelBrennan (j.rt: prom to 3rd: t.o whn blnd next: rn out 5th)		**R**	100/1	—	—
				(SP 133.8%)	**19 Rn**	

4m 18.1 (17.10) CSF £5.26 TOTE £1.90: £1.30 £1.80 £4.40 (£8.20) Trio £64.30 OWNER Mr Gordon Brown (CROOK) BRED Mrs Kathleen Creedon and Con O'Leary
WEIGHT FOR AGE 4yo-12lb
1666* Mister Ross (IRE), who won a maiden point-to-point in Ireland last year, found this simple, and but for being eased right down on the run-in, would probably have had ten lengths to spare. (Evens)
Northern Union (CAN), highly tried in his only outing over hurdles last season, is greatly flattered by the margin of defeat. (5/1)
Forever Noble (IRE) stuck on strongly up the hill and will be suited by two and a half miles. (10/1)
2175 Catherine's Choice might have some improvement in him. (33/1)

2650 BRICK KILN NOVICES' CHASE (5-Y.O+) (Class E)
1-55 (1-57) **2m 4f 110y (16 fncs)** £3,308.75 (£970.00: £472.50: £223.75) GOING: 0.08 sec per fur (G)

	Horse / details	Dist	Pos	SP	RR	SF
1357ᴾ	**Crown Equerry (IRE)** (GRichards) **7-11-4** PCarberry (sn trckng ldrs: hit 11th: led 4 out: clr last: eased)	—	**1**	8/13 1	93+	33
1850³	**Bold Account (IRE) (86)** (GMMoore) **7-11-4** ADobbin (led 4th to 4 out: blnd last: kpt on)	2	**2**	7/1 3	91	31
1989²	**Tico Gold (77)** (PCheesbrough) **9-11-4** ASSmith (chsd ldrs: outpcd & mstke 10th: styd on fr 2 out)	1¼	**3**	6/1 2	91	31
	Gone Away (IRE) (MDHammond) **8-11-4** RGarritty (hld up: hdwy 10th: hit next: sn wknd: t.o 3 out)	dist	**4**	20/1	—	—
1853⁴	**Dark Buoy (72)** (BMactaggart) **8-11-4** BStorey (sn bhd: t.o whn p.u bef last: b.b.v)		**P**	14/1	—	—
1991ᴾ	**Show Your Hand (IRE) (77)** (LLungo) **9-11-10** MFoster (led to 4th: wknd after 12th: bhd whn mstke 2 out: p.u bef last)		**P**	16/1	—	—
1944²	**Gaelic Blue (73)** (MrsSJSmith) **7-11-4** RichardGuest (hld up: hdwy 11th: 3rd & prom whn uns rdr 4 out)		**U**	7/1 3	—	—
				(SP 118.5%)	**7 Rn**	

5m 14.2 (11.20) CSF £5.86 TOTE £1.70: £1.50 £1.80 (£5.00) OWNER Mr Robert Ogden (PENRITH) BRED Thomas O'Connor
OFFICIAL EXPLANATION **Dark Buoy: bled from the nose.**
Crown Equerry (IRE), who had to be pulled up after a bad mistake at the first on his chasing debut, is by no means a natural jumper. Making only one serious mistake, he had his race well won at the last and was then eased, otherwise he would have won by ten lengths. (8/13)
1850 Bold Account (IRE) was completely outpaced by the winner. He was blowing hard afterwards and the outing should bring him on, but he really needs three miles. (7/1)
1989 Tico Gold, struggling when making an error at the tenth, stuck on over the last two. All he does is stay and he will be suited by three miles and beyond. (6/1: 4/1-13/2)
1853 Dark Buoy (14/1: 12/1-20/1)
1944 Gaelic Blue was in third when he blundered badly and gave his rider no chance. He would not have beaten the winner under any circumstances. (7/1)

2651 MARY BROW H'CAP HURDLE (0-115) (4-Y.O+) (Class E)
2-25 (2-27) **2m 4f 110y (11 hdls)** £2,416.00 (£676.00: £328.00) GOING: 0.08 sec per fur (G)

	Horse / details	Dist	Pos	SP	RR	SF
1807*	**Ela Mata (110)** (MrsASwinbank) **5-11-2**(7) BGrattan (hld up & bhd: gd hdwy 6th: led 8th: clr next: easily)	—	**1**	6/5 1	101+	42
2044²	**Kemo Sabo (92)** (CParker) **5-10-5** DParker (chsd ldrs: shkn up 5th: styd on fr 3 out)	16	**2**	11/2 2	71	12

2545^{6}	**Glenugie (100)** (GMMoore) **6-10-13** NBentley (chsd ldrs: rdn & outpcd appr 3 out: styd on fr next)................s.h	**3**	13/2 ^{3}	79	20
1945^{4}	**Keen To The Last (FR) (99)** (MDHammond) **5-10-12** RGarritty (led 2nd to 8th: wknd towards fin).................3½	**4**	9/1	75	16
1294^{9}	**Dockmaster (88)** (MissMKMilligan) **6-10-1** ASSmith (in rr fr 7th)...21	**5**	12/1	47	—
2062^{7}	**Elation (115)** (GRichards) **5-12-0** ADobbin (chsd ldrs tl lost pl 8th)...6	**6**	13/2 ^{3}	70	11
1945^{5}	**Exemplar (IRE) (95)** (MrsSJSmith) **9-10-8** RichardGuest (led to 2nd: lost pl 8th)..11	**7**	13/2 ^{3}	41	—
	Eurolink the Rebel (USA) (96) (SBClark) **5-10-2**(7) MissRClark (hld up: lost tch 7th: t.o whn p.u bef 2 out)........	**P**	66/1	—	—
			(SP 120.0%)		**8 Rn**

5m 0.6 (9.60) CSF £8.52 CT £29.90 TOTE £2.00: £1.10 £2.20 £2.00 (£2.20) OWNER Mr F. J. Sainsbury (RICHMOND) BRED Darley Stud Management Co Ltd

1807* Ela Mata, on his toes beforehand, was dropped out at the start. After moving up to take charge, he won very easily indeed. Raised 9lb after Wetherby, he is due for another hike in the weights. (6/5)

2044 Kemo Sabo stuck on under pressure and seemed to stay the trip alright. (11/2)

2545 Glenugie, badly outpaced on the home turn, stuck on and might be worth a try over three miles. (13/2)

1945 Keen To The Last (FR) does not find a great deal under pressure. (9/1)

2652 TODD HILLS H'CAP CHASE (0-120) (5-Y.O+) (Class D)

2-55 (2-55) **3m (18 fncs)** £3,818.00 (£1,154.00: £562.00: £266.00) GOING: 0.08 sec per fur (G)

			SP	RR	SF
1847^{5}	**Son of Iris (98)** (MrsMReveley) **9-11-3** PNiven (trckd ldrs: blnd 14th: led 3 out: drvn clr flat: eased towards fin)..—	**1**	6/1 ^{3}	110	—
2046^{U}	**Westwell Boy (105)** (PBeaumont) **11-11-10** RSupple (lw: led to 8th: rdn to ld 4 out: hdd next: no ch w wnr) 7	**2**	6/5 ^{1}	112	—
2061*	**Slotamatique (IRE) (102)** (GRichards) **8-11-7** ADobbin (lw: blnd 5th: mstke next: led 8th tl 4 out: wknd next)2½	**3**	2/1 ^{2}	108	—
1578^{14}	**Supposin (92)** (MrsSJSmith) **9-10-11** RichardGuest (trckd ldrs: one pce fr 3 out)...½	**4**	7/1	97	—
2179^{2}	**Forward Glen (81)** (PCheesbrough) **10-10-0b** ASSmith (chsd ldrs tl fell 3 out)..	**F**	9/1	—	—
			(SP 115.6%)		**5 Rn**

6m 18.6 (26.60) CSF £13.74 TOTE £6.40: £2.20 £1.10 (£6.80) OWNER M H G Systems Ltd (SALTBURN) BRED James Roche
LONG HANDICAP Forward Glen 9-9

1847 Son of Iris, who has a history of breaking blood-vessels, put his poor run of last time behind him. Surviving his one bad mistake five out, in the end he won with plenty to spare. (6/1)

1670 Westwell Boy was unable to dominate, and in the end, proved no match. (6/5)

2061* Slotamatique (IRE) was sloppy in his jumping and faded from three out. (2/1)

1024 Supposin had his tongue tied down as usual, and was left behind up the hill. (7/1)

2653 HOARY TOM NOVICES' CHASE (5-Y.O+) (Class D)

3-25 (3-25) **2m (12 fncs)** £3,737.50 (£1,120.00: £545.00: £257.50) GOING: 0.08 sec per fur (G)

			SP	RR	SF
1653*	**Sparky Gayle (IRE)** (CParker) **7-11-13** BStorey (lw: bhd: hdwy 7th: rdn to ld 2 out: styd on wl flat)..............—	**1**	4/7 ^{1}	117+	42
	Chief Minister (IRE) (MDHammond) **8-11-3** RGarritty (lw: trckd ldrs: chal 3 out: r.o wl u.p flat)....................1¼	**2**	9/4 ^{2}	106+	31
1943^{3}	**Singing Sand (74)** (PMonteith) **7-11-3** ADobbin (trckd ldrs: lft in ld 6th: mstke & hdd 2 out: sn wknd).............20	**3**	40/1	86	11
1574^{U}	**Nijway (73)** (MABarnes) **7-10-12**(5) STaylor (chsd ldrs: drvn along 6th: outpcd fr 9th)..3	**4**	150/1	83	8
2628^{F}	**Fenwick's Brother (87)** (MrsSJSmith) **7-11-3** RichardGuest (trckd ldrs tl grad wknd fr 4 out) 2	**5**	40/1	81	6
1500^{2}	**Killbally Boy (IRE) (81)** (HowardJohnson) **7-11-3** PCarberry (led: reminders after 5th: fell next)	**F**	9/1 ^{3}	—	—
1578^{9}	**Movac (IRE) (86)** (MissLucindaRussell) **8-11-8v**[1] GCahill (bhd fr 7th: p.u bef 4 out)	**P**	25/1	—	—
			(SP 113.8%)		**7 Rn**

4m 2.5 (8.50) CSF £2.06 TOTE £1.50: £1.00 £2.50 (£1.80) OWNER Mr & Mrs Raymond Anderson Green (LOCKERBIE) BRED Thomas Walsh

1653* Sparky Gayle (IRE) took time to warm to his task, but time may prove he had plenty on his plate giving the runner-up 10lb. Though capable of winning over two miles, another half-mile would suit him better. (4/7)

Chief Minister (IRE), a useful Handicap Hurdler, looked, ran and jumped well on this debut over the major obstacles. He should find plenty of opportunities. (9/4: op 6/4)

1943 Singing Sand raced keenly. Tiring when making a mistake two out, an easier track may suit him better. (40/1)

1346 Nijway, though beaten a long way, seemed to run his best race so far over fences. (150/1)

1987 Fenwick's Brother, who fell just two days earlier, shaped nicely and was by no means knocked about. He will be an interesting proposition under a low weight in a novices' handicap. (40/1)

2654 BELLS FIELD NOVICES' H'CAP HURDLE (0-105) (4-Y.O+) (Class E)

3-55 (3-55) **3m 110y (12 hdls)** £2,458.00 (£688.00: £334.00) GOING: 0.08 sec per fur (G)

			SP	RR	SF
1160^{P}	**Bardaros (74)** (MissLucindaRussell) **8-10-8** MFoster (sn trckng ldrs: led appr 2 out: sn pushed clr)..............—	**1**	20/1	66	3
1290^{3}	**Pebble Beach (IRE) (87)** (GMMoore) **7-11-7** NBentley (trckd ldrs: led 9th tl appr 2 out: kpt on same pce)......13	**2**	11/2 ^{2}	71	8
1775^{6}	**Haughton Lad (IRE) (69)** (JParkes) **8-10-3** VSmith (hdwy 8th: styd on fr 3 out)..¾	**3**	16/1	52	—
2507^{4}	**Ruber (75)** (RWThomson) **10-10-9** DParker (outpcd & drvn along 8th: hdwy 3 out: styd on one pce).............1¼	**4**	7/1	57	—
2045^{5}	**Dashmar (67)** (MsLCPlater) **10-9-10v**[1](5)ow1 MichaelBrennan (bhd: hdwy 3 out: wnt 2nd flat: sn eased: fin lame)..nk	**5**	25/1	49	—
1316^{4}	**Movie Man (74)** (JRTurner) **5-10-8** ADobbin (hld up: stdy hdwy 8th: one pce fr 3 out) ....¾	**6**	16/1	56	—
1654^{18}	**Fenloe Rambler (IRE) (80)** (RJohnson) **6-11-0** KJohnson (chsd ldrs: drvn along to ld 8th: hdd next: one pce fr 3 out)...s.h	**7**	14/1	62	—
1672^{6}	**The Next Waltz (IRE) (75)** (LLungo) **6-10-9** RSupple (trckd ldrs: chal 3 out: wknd appr next).........................3½	**8**	8/1	54	—
1689^{11}	**Pocaire Gaoithe (IRE) (72)** (WStorey) **7-10-6v**[1] MMoloney (chsd ldrs: drvn along 6th: wknd appr 3 out)..........4	**9**	12/1	49	—
2042^{5}	**Kings Lane (89)** (JMDun) **8-11-4**(5) MrMHNaughton (in tch: drvn along 6th: hdwy 8th: wknd 3 out) 13	**10**	12/1	57	—
1988^{6}	**Cuillin Caper (69)** (TRWatson) **5-10-3** OPears (sn bhd: t.o) ....dist	**11**	33/1	—	—
1292^{2}	**Baher (USA) (90)** (MrsASwinbank) **8-11-10** JSupple (bhd & pushed along: hdwy 8th: ev ch whn fell 3 out)........	**F**	6/1 ^{3}	—	—
2042^{7}	**Farmers Subsidy (75)** (GMMoore) **5-10-9** RGarritty (led to 8th: sn lost pl: p.u bef 2 out)................................	**P**	14/1	—	—
2507^{6}	**Boston Man (84)** (RDEWoodhouse) **6-11-4** BStorey (j.lft: nvr gng wl: blnd 5th: t.o whn p.u after next)................	**P**	7/2 ^{1}	—	—
2509^{6}	**What Jim Wants (IRE) (85)** (JJO'Neill) **4-10-0**(5) RMcGrath (lost pl 6th: sme hdwy 9th: p.u lame after 2 out)	**P**	7/1	—	—
	Busy Boy (70) (DALamb) **10-10-4** JBurke (w ldrs tl lost pl 7th: t.o whn p.u bef 3 out)	**P**	20/1	—	—
			(SP 144.8%)		**16 Rn**

6m 3.9 (19.90) CSF £132.10 CT £1,738.12 TOTE £22.50: £3.60 £1.80 £4.70 £3.50 (£44.10) Trio £184.50; £189.70 to Market Rasen 21/1/97
OWNER Mr Peter Russell (KINROSS) BRED Aiden Murphy
LONG HANDICAP Dashmar 9-11

WEIGHT FOR AGE 4yo-14lb

1160 Bardaros, winner of three of his four starts in point-to-points last season, had not distinguished himself in three outings over regulation fences this time. Having his first outing for well over two months, he stuck on strongly after hitting the front to pull well clear. (20/1)
1290 Pebble Beach (IRE) had his tongue tied down. After making the best of his way home, he was left for dead by the winner. (11/2)
1775 Haughton Lad (IRE) certainly seemed to appreciate the step up in distance. (16/1)
2507 Ruber, who ran so well at Musselburgh when a long way out of the handicap, was struggling fully a mile from home. Keeping on up the hill, he never looked like posing a threat. (7/1)
2045 Dashmar was a clear second on the run-in when his rider sat up. It transpired that he had gone lame. (25/1)
1316 Movie Man certainly seemed to stay this trip alright. (16/1)
2507 Boston Man ran as if something was amiss. Again fitted with a tongue-strap, he never looked happy and lost ground jumping to his left. Falling through the fifth, he clambered over the next and his rider sensibly called it a day. (7/2)

T/Plpt: £12.80 (707.72 Tckts). T/Qdpt: £10.30 (66.5 Tckts). WG

2125-NEWTON ABBOT (L-H) (Heavy)

Monday January 20th

WEATHER: unsettled

2655 TEIGNMOUTH MAIDEN HURDLE (4-Y.O+) (Class F)

1-35 (1-36) **2m 1f (8 hdls)** £2,344.60 (£660.60: £323.80) GOING: 1.20 sec per fur (HY)

	Horse	Dist	Pos	SP	RR	SF
	Juyush (USA) (JABOld) **5-11-8** JOsborne (lw: a.p: led 5th: pckd 2 out: clr last: easily)	—	**1**	Evens[1]	86+	23
2010[F]	**Motoqua** (DNicholson) **5-11-3** AMaguire (hld up: hdwy appr 5th: ev ch appr 2 out: no imp)	7	**2**	11/4[2]	74	11
	Country Lover (MCPipe) **6-11-8v** APMcCoy (hld up: hdwy after 4th: ev ch appr 2 out: sn wknd)	10	**3**	6/1[3]	70	7
	Ashtar (USA) (MCPipe) **7-11-8** CMaude (hld up: mstke 4th: hdwy 5th: hrd rdn & wknd 3 out)	30	**4**	16/1	42	—
	Fencer's Quest (IRE) (CaptTAForster) **4-10-10** NWilliamson (hld up & plld hrd: stdy hdwy appr 4th: wknd after 3 out)	2½	**5**	33/1	39	—
1950[4]	**Blade of Fortune** (VGGreenway) **9-11-1**(7) MrJTizzard (led to 5th: wknd after 3 out)	3	**6**	33/1	37	—
	Alpine Joker (PJHobbs) **4-10-10** RDunwoody (hit 3rd: hdwy 4th: wknd 3 out)	¾	**7**	16/1	36	—
2035[3]	**Kevasingo** (JLSpearing) **5-11-8** TJMurphy (prom tl wknd 5th: t.o)	25	**8**	33/1	12	—
	Piper's Rock (IRE) (GBBalding) **6-11-8** BClifford (bkwd: t.o fr 6th)	dist	**9**	33/1	—	—
2034[4]	**Frome Lad** (WGMTurner) **5-11-1**(7) JPower (prom tl after 4th: t.o whn p.u bef 2 out)		**P**	25/1	—	—
	Chalcuchima (NJHawke) **4-10-10** RGreene (bkwd: bhd fr 5th: t.o whn p.u bef 2 out)		**P**	33/1	—	—
1336[10]	**Miss Night Owl** (RGFrost) **6-11-3** JFrost (a bhd: t.o whn p.u bef 2 out)		**P**	66/1	—	—
	Win I Did (IRE) (RHAlner) **7-11-0**(3) PHenley (a bhd: t.o whn p.u bef 3 out)		**P**	33/1	—	—
1333[8]	**Klosters** (RJHodges) **5-11-0**(3) TDascombe (prom to 3rd: t.o whn p.u bef 2 out)		**P**	100/1	—	—
	Lord Regal (IRE) (MrsJPitman) **6-11-8** WMarston (Withdrawn not under Starter's orders: inj in paddock)		**W**	14/1	—	—
				(SP 133.4%)	**14 Rn**	

4m 23.8 (30.80) CSF £3.30 TOTE £2.00: £1.10 £1.40 £2.00 (£3.10) Trio £2.80 OWNER Mr W. E. Sturt (WROUGHTON) BRED Corbin J. Robertson

WEIGHT FOR AGE 4yo-12lb

Juyush (USA), bought for 70,000 guineas at Newmarket Autumn Sales, was a useful performer for Barry Hills on the Flat. He had been waiting for this ground, having had a couple of hairline fractures. (Evens)
2010 Motoqua would have finished second to the highly-regarded Red Blazer but for a last flight fall at Towcester last month. Coming up against another useful sort here, her turn will come. (11/4)
Country Lover, claimed for £12,000 having become disappointing on the Flat, did not get home in this very heavy ground. It will be interesting to see which way he goes from here. (6/1: op 5/2)
Ashtar (USA) had disappointed in the second of his bumpers in similar conditions to here, and probably needs better ground. (16/1)
Fencer's Quest (IRE), bought for 10,000 guineas out of Roger Charlton's stable, only had one run on the Flat and shaped well enough until the testing going began to take its toll. (33/1)
Lord Regal (IRE) (14/1: op 8/1)

2656 JANUARY 'N.H.' NOVICES' HURDLE (4-Y.O+) (Class E)

2-05 (2-06) **2m 6f (10 hdls)** £2,652.00 (£747.00: £366.00) GOING: 1.20 sec per fur (HY)

	Horse	Dist	Pos	SP	RR	SF
1835[F]	**Scotby (BEL) (106)** (RHBuckler) **7-11-10** BPowell (hld up: hdwy 5th: rdn & outpcd 3 out: rallied to ld appr 2 out: r.o wl)	—	**1**	9/2[3]	78	50
1695[3]	**Defendtherealm** (RGFrost) **6-11-4** JFrost (hld up & bhd: hdwy 6th: ev ch appr 2 out: one pce)	4	**2**	33/1	69	41
2071[6]	**Shanagore Warrior (IRE)** (SMellor) **5-10-11**(7) SHearn (lw: hld up: hdwy 5th: r.o one pce fr 3 out)	5	**3**	33/1	66	38
2073[2]	**Shariakanndi (FR)** (JSKing) **5-11-4** TJMurphy (hld up: hdwy appr 6th: ev ch appr 2 out: one pce)	nk	**4**	16/1	65	37
	St Mellion Drive (MCPipe) **7-11-4** APMcCoy (led tl appr 2 out: sn wknd)	19	**5**	2/1[1]	51	23
1966[11]	**Full of Bounce (IRE)** (RJHodges) **6-11-1**(3) TDascombe (rdn & hdwy appr 7th: wknd appr 3 out: t.o)	dist	**6**	33/1	—	—
1939*	**Rockcliffe Lad (100)** (NATwiston-Davies) **8-11-10** CLlewellyn (prom tl wknd 3 out: t.o)	26	**7**	11/4[2]	—	—
1685[9]	**Classic Chat** (JLSpearing) **5-11-4** DBridgwater (a bhd: t.o whn p.u bef 2 out)		**P**	33/1	—	—
1200[3]	**One For Navigation (IRE)** (PFNicholls) **5-11-4** PHide (chsd ldr tl mstke 3 out: 5th & no ch whn p.u bef 2 out)		**P**	7/1	—	—
1820[3]	**Madam Polly** (MissPMWhittle) **5-10-6**(7) KHibbert (a bhd: t.o whn p.u bef 2 out)		**P**	33/1	—	—
	Summit Else (NATwiston-Davies) **6-10-13** TJenks (hld up: hdwy appr 5th: wknd appr 7th: t.o whn p.u bef 2 out)		**P**	20/1	—	—
	Alpine Song (MissVAStephens) **12-10-13** MissVStephens (a bhd: t.o whn p.u bef 2 out)		**P**	33/1	—	—
	Camillas Legacy (HTCole) **6-10-13** DGallagher (bkwd: sn t.o: p.u bef 2 out)		**P**	33/1	—	—
	Lady of Mine (PBowen) **7-10-13** RJohnson (bkwd: a bhd: t.o whn p.u bef 2 out)		**P**	33/1	—	—
	Vancouver Lad (IRE) (WGMTurner) **8-10-11**(7) JPower (hdwy 5th: wknd appr 7th: t.o whn p.u bef 2 out)		**P**	66/1	—	—
1177[12]	**Alice Shorelark** (SGKnight) **6-10-13** MrTGreed (a bhd: t.o whn p.u bef 2 out)		**P**	66/1	—	—
				(SP 127.8%)	**16 Rn**	

5m 44.7 (32.70) CSF £134.64 TOTE £5.50: £1.60 £2.80 £6.60 (£43.20) Trio £116.60 OWNER Mrs E. B. Gardiner (BRIDPORT) BRED P. Madelein

1835 Scotby (BEL) again showed his liking for the mud and much of this victory is down to his ability to get the trip. His trainer thinks he will make a chaser next season. (9/2)

1695 Defendtherealm showed improved form over this longer distance. (33/1)
1695 Shanagore Warrior (IRE), twice placed between the Flags in Ireland, was stepping up in trip, and shaped as though he needs even further. (33/1)
2073 Shariakandi (FR) made a reasonable enough start to his hurdling career. (16/1)
St Mellion Drive won a couple of bumpers in the soft, but paid the penalty for forcing the pace in these testing conditions. (2/1)

2657 NEWTON ABBOT H'CAP CHASE (0-100) (5-Y.O+) (Class F)

2-35 (2-36) **2m 110y (13 fncs)** £2,696.60 (£757.60: £369.80) GOING: 1.20 sec per fur (HY)

			SP	RR	SF
	Indian Arrow (NZ) (90) (MCPipe) **9-11-5** CMaude (led after 1st to 4th: led 6th: clr 3 out: easily) —	**1**	12/1	104+	—
1199[4]	**Mr Playfull (91)** (RGFrost) **7-11-6** JFrost (hld up: hdwy 8th: chsd wnr fr 2 out: no imp) 9	**2**	6/1[2]	96	—
1328[7]	**Good for a Laugh (88)** (AGHobbs) **13-10-10**(7) MrGShenkin (bit bkwd: prom: mstke 3rd: sn lost pl: rallied appr 2 out: one pce) 6	**3**	12/1	88	—
1951[2]	**Country Keeper (75)** (BJMRyall) **9-10-4** GUpton (wl bhd 6th: styd on fr 3 out: nvr nrr) ½	**4**	8/1[3]	74	—
1864*	**The Lancer (IRE) (95)** (DRGandolfo) **8-11-10** RDunwoody (lw: led tl after 1st: lft 2nd 4 out: wknd appr last) 3½	**5**	5/2[1]	91	—
1947[4]	**Wonderfull Polly (IRE) (87)** (PFNicholls) **9-11-2** PHide (lw: blnd 4 out: no hdwy) 3½	**6**	6/1[2]	79	—
1783[7]	**Blazer Moriniere (FR) (90)** (PCRitchens) **8-11-5** SFox (bit bkwd: bhd fr 4 out) 13	**7**	25/1	70	—
1694[3]	**Colette's Choice (IRE) (76)** (GAHam) **8-10-0**(5) MrRThornton (a bhd: t.o fr 7th) dist	**8**	20/1	—	—
	Hanson Street (NZ) (71) (PJHobbs) **10-10-0** NWilliamson (bhd tl fell 8th)	**F**	20/1	—	—
1947[P]	**Mistress Rosie (72)** (MHill) **10-10-1** JRKavanagh (bhd fr 8th: t.o whn p.u bef 2 out)	**P**	33/1	—	—
1764[P]	**Kino's Cross (98)** (AJWilson) **8-11-13** AThornton (bhd fr 7th: t.o whn p.u bef last)	**P**	10/1	—	—
1696[4]	**Benjamin Lancaster (97)** (MAGriffin) **13-11-5**(7) MGriffiths (led 4th to 6th: wknd 9th: t.o whn p.u bef 2 out)	**P**	14/1	—	—
1584[8]	**Miss Marigold (93)** (RJHodges) **8-11-8** BPowell (nvr gng wl: mstke 3rd: a bhd: t.o whn p.u bef 9th)	**P**	20/1	—	—
1763[3]	**Fenwick (85)** (RJHodges) **10-10-11**(3) TDascombe (prom: 2nd whn blnd & uns rdr 4 out)	**U**	16/1	—	—
			(SP 126.4%)	**14 Rn**	

4m 35.7 (35.70) CSF £74.11 CT £831.45 TOTE £16.10: £4.70 £2.70 £4.80 (£80.30) Trio £159.90; £67.58 to Market Rasen 21/1/97 OWNER Joe & Joanne Richards (WELLINGTON) BRED Mrs M.E. and R.E. Lee
LONG HANDICAP Hanson Street (NZ) 9-5

Indian Arrow (NZ) made a successful debut over fences for his new stable, and won with great ease after a twenty-month lay-off. He can score again. (12/1)
1199 Mr Playfull does not mind the mud, but proved no match for the winner over this trip, which is on the short side for him. (6/1)
1328 Good for a Laugh, who has dropped 22lb this season, has changed stables, and though a bit long in the tooth, may have benefited from a change of scenery. (12/1)
1951 Country Keeper, well out of the handicap when runner-up here last time, was totally unsuited to this shorter trip. (8/1)
1864* The Lancer (IRE), raised 5lb for his Fakenham win, was 13lb higher than when successful over course and distance in similar ground at the start of last month. (5/2)
1947 Wonderfull Polly (IRE), dropping back in distance, again missed out at the last ditch. (6/1)
1570 Benjamin Lancaster (14/1: 10/1-16/1)
1763 Fenwick gave his rider little chance of staying aboard at the final ditch. (16/1)

2658 BET WITH THE TOTE (QUALIFIER) NOVICES' CHASE (6-Y.O+) (Class E)

3-05 (3-06) **3m 2f 110y (20 fncs)** £3,121.75 (£946.00: £462.50: £220.75) GOING: 1.20 sec per fur (HY)

			SP	RR	SF
	Cyborgo (FR) (MCPipe) **7-10-12** APMcCoy (lw: led to 2nd: mstke 3rd: led appr 14th to 16th: led 4 out: clr 2 out: r.o wl) —	**1**	8/11[1]	118+	11
1694[2]	**Well Timed (93)** (RGFrost) **7-11-5** JFrost (a.p: led 16th to 4 out: wknd appr 2 out: lft 2nd last) 20	**2**	33/1	113	6
2007[4]	**See Enough (110)** (RHBuckler) **9-10-12** SMcNeill (mid div: lost pl 13th: n.d after) 22	**3**	5/1[2]	93	—
2072[2]	**Kendal Cavalier** (GBBalding) **7-10-12** BFenton (mid div: lost pl 13th: bhd whn rdn 16th) 4	**4**	14/1	90	—
1947*	**Miss Diskin (IRE) (100)** (RHBuckler) **8-11-0** BPowell (lw: led 3rd to 6th: led 8th tl appr 14th: wknd 15th) 2½	**5**	14/1	91	—
1711*	**Flaked Oats** (PFNicholls) **8-11-5** PHide (hld up: stdy hdwy 14th: ev ch 4 out: 2nd & btn whn fell last)	**F**	10/1	—	—
1447[F]	**What's Your Story (IRE) (111)** (DNicholson) **8-10-12** AMaguire (fell 2nd)	**F**	13/2[3]	—	—
1426[2]	**Foxtrot Romeo (104)** (CPEBrooks) **7-10-12** GBradley (prom tl wknd 15th: t.o whn p.u bef 2 out)	**P**	12/1	—	—
1936[P]	**Bankhead (IRE) (115)** (JLSpearing) **8-11-12** DBridgwater (a bhd: reminders after 4th: t.o whn p.u bef 11th)	**P**	16/1	—	—
1865*	**Jasilu** (KCBailey) **7-11-7b** AThornton (lw: led 2nd to 3rd: led 6th to 8th: wknd 12th: p.u after 13th)	**P**	25/1	—	—
2076[P]	**Ballydougan (IRE) (78)** (RMathew) **9-10-12v** RBellamy (hmpd s: a bhd: t.o whn p.u bef 15th)	**P**	100/1	—	—
1765[3]	**Red Parade (NZ) (97)** (NJHawke) **9-10-12** RGreene (a bhd: t.o whn p.u bef 4 out)	**P**	14/1	—	—
1694[4]	**Sorrel Hill (97)** (PJHobbs) **10-10-12** MAFitzgerald (prom to 11th: t.o whn p.u bef 16th)	**P**	33/1	—	—
2039[3]	**Anythingyoulike (87)** (CASmith) **8-10-12** MRichards (bhd fr 13th: t.o whn p.u bef 4 out)	**P**	33/1	—	—
	Golden Drops (NZ) (AGHobbs) **9-10-12** CMaude (bhd fr 13th: t.o whn p.u bef 4 out)	**P**	50/1	—	—
2007[F]	**Huge Mistake (95)** (NATwiston-Davies) **8-10-12** CLlewellyn (a bhd: mstke 9th: blnd & uns rdr 15th)	**U**	25/1	—	—
			(SP 150.0%)	**16 Rn**	

7m 24.5 (50.50) CSF £45.94 TOTE £2.10: £1.50 £7.00 £1.90 (£85.60) Trio £32.50 OWNER County Stores (Somerset) Holdings Ltd (WELLINGTON) BRED Francois Cottin and Alfred Lefevre

Cyborgo (FR), the winner of last year's Cheltenham Stayers' Hurdle, is entered in the Gold Cup and barely put a foot wrong on this start to his chasing career. (8/11)
1694 Well Timed was battling it out for second place when Flaked Oats departed at the last. (33/1)
2007 See Enough found the leaders beginning to get away with fully a circuit to go. (5/1: op 10/1)
1947* Miss Diskin (IRE) paid the penalty for forcing the pace over this extended trip. (14/1)
1711* Flaked Oats was engaged in a good battle for the runner-up spot when departing at the last. (10/1)

2659 HORSERACE BETTING LEVY BOARD H'CAP HURDLE (0-125) (4-Y.O+) (Class D)

3-35 (3-40) **3m 3f (12 hdls)** £3,039.00 (£854.00: £417.00) GOING: 1.20 sec per fur (HY)

			SP	RR	SF
	Maid Equal (97) (MCPipe) **6-9-7**(7) GSupple (hld up: hdwy appr 9th: led appr 2 out: drvn out) —	**1**	25/1	78	9
2117[3]	**Ealing Court (97)** (NMBabbage) **8-10-0** NWilliamson (hld up: hdwy 7th: ev ch appr 2 out: sn rdn: one pce) 3	**2**	8/1[3]	76	7
1798[7]	**Grunge (IRE) (97)** (DJGMurraySmith) **9-10-0** DGallagher (hdwy 9th: rdn appr 2 out: one pce) 8	**3**	25/1	71	2
1798[2]	**Ehtefaal (USA) (97)** (JSKing) **6-10-0** TJMurphy (hld up: hdwy & hit 5th: one pce fr 2 out) 1¼	**4**	10/1	71	2
	Rakazona Beau (116) (SEarle) **7-11-5** CMaude (bit bkwd: hld up: hdwy 3 out: 4th & btn whn blnd last) 6	**5**	25/1	86	17
1938[3]	**Crane Hill (105)** (PJHobbs) **7-10-8b** GTormey (prom: led 9th tl appr 2 out: sn wknd) 2	**6**	8/1[3]	74	5

				SP	RR	SF
1952[6]	**Oatis Rose (98)** (MSheppard) **7-9-10**(5)ow1 MrRThornton (mstke 9th: a bhd)	18	**7**	9/1	56	—
1571[4]	**Lansdowne (125)** (PFNicholls) **9-11-7**(7) LCummins (lw: hdwy appr 7th: wknd after 3 out)	4	**8**	10/1	81	12
1952[3]	**Texan Baby (BEL) (115)** (NATwiston-Davies) **8-11-4** CLlewellyn (lw: prom: rdn 9th: sn wknd)	5	**9**	11/2[1]	68	—
1952[7]	**St Ville (97)** (RHBuckler) **11-10-0** BPowell (bhd fr 6th: t.o fr 8th)	20	**10**	7/1[2]	38	—
	Mountain Reach (97) (PRWebber) **7-10-0** JOsborne (bit bkwd: led to 2nd: wknd 9th: t.o whn p.u bef 2 out)		**P**	20/1	—	—
1783[5]	**Meditator (112)** (APJones) **13-11-1b** SMcNeill (bhd fr 8th: t.o whn p.u bef 2 out)		**P**	20/1	—	—
1586[9]	**Jadidh (99)** (ABarrow) **9-9-11**(5)ow2 DSalter (a bhd: t.o 6th: p.u after 8th)		**P**	20/1	—	—
	Flyer's Nap (110) (RHAlner) **11-10-10**(3) PHenley (bkwd: hdwy 9th: rdn & wknd after 3 out: p.u bef 2 out)		**P**	9/1	—	—
1962*	**Ainsi Soit Il (FR) (101)** (GMMcCourt) **6-10-4b** DBridgwater (prom: led appr 8th to 9th: wknd 3 out: p.u bef 2 out)		**P**	8/1[3]	—	—
	Montagnard (97) (MBradstock) **13-10-0** PHolley (bit bkwd: led 2nd tl appr 8th: wknd qckly appr 9th: t.o whn p.u bef 2 out)		**P**	25/1	—	—
1787[F]	**Sausalito Boy (99)** (RJSmith) **9-10-2** DWalsh (bhd whn p.u after 8th)		**P**	50/1	—	—

(SP 131.0%) **17 Rn**

7m 10.0 (47.00) CSF £190.41 CT £4,624.73 TOTE £34.50: £4.80 £2.10 £6.70 £1.90 (£177.50) Trio £1,346.00 OWNER Mr Heeru Kirpalani (WELLINGTON) BRED H. L. Kirpalani

LONG HANDICAP Maid Equal 9-3 Ealing Court 9-13 Mountain Reach 9-11 Oatis Rose 9-13 Jadidh 9-4 Ehtefaal (USA) 9-6 St Ville 9-11 Montagnard 9-11 Grunge (IRE) 9-4

Maid Equal, 11lb out of the handicap, had not seen a racecourse for the best part of two years and was yet another feather in Martin Pipe's cap. (25/1)

2117 Ealing Court, only just out of the handicap this time, travelled really well through the race and is knocking on the door. (8/1)

Grunge (IRE), carrying 10lb more than his long-handicap mark, could not sustain his run. (25/1)

1798 Ehtefaal (USA) ran a sound race from 8lb wrong in the handicap. (10/1)

Rakazona Beau, off course since finishing lame when winning a novice hurdle at Ascot in April, was contesting third place when making a hash of the last. This was a pleasing comeback. (25/1)

2660 ARGYLE BOOKMAKERS OF PLYMOUTH H'CAP CHASE (0-125) (5-Y.O+) (Class D)

4-05 (4-09) **2m 5f 110y (16 fncs)** £3,696.25 (£1,120.00: £547.50: £261.25) GOING: 1.20 sec per fur (HY)

				SP	RR	SF
1765[4]	**Orswell Lad (105)** (PJHobbs) **8-10-8** NWilliamson (a.p: led 10th to 4 out: rallied appr 2 out: led last: drvn out)	—	**1**	10/1	118	10
	Montebel (IRE) (113) (NATwiston-Davies) **9-11-2** DWalsh (hdwy 4th: led 4 out to last: one pce)	2	**2**	11/2[1]	125	17
1937[6]	**Bells Life (IRE) (125)** (PJHobbs) **8-12-0** GTormey (hld up: stdy hdwy 4th: one pce fr 3 out)	9	**3**	12/1	130	22
1952*	**Top Javalin (NZ) (98)** (NJHawke) **10-10-1** RGreene (prom: mstke 6th: wknd 11th)	23	**4**	8/1[3]	86	—
1985[2]	**Fools Errand (IRE) (115)** (GBBalding) **7-11-4** APMcCoy (prom: mstke 4th: sn lost pl: no ch whn mstke 4 out)	6	**5**	6/1[2]	98	—
2039[2]	**Brogeen Lady (IRE) (100)** (DRGandolfo) **7-10-3** RDunwoody (led to 10th: wknd 4 out: t.o)	27	**6**	11/2[1]	63	—
1635[5]	**Madison County (IRE) (110)** (PJHobbs) **7-10-13v** MAFitzgerald (bhd fr 10th: t.o whn p.u bef 3 out)		**P**	8/1[3]	—	—
	Cantoris Frater (101) (MrsJPitman) **10-10-4** WMarston (a bhd: t.o whn p.u bef 4 out)		**P**	12/1	—	—
1763[P]	**Tapageur (97)** (MCPipe) **12-9-7**(7) GSupple (j.b: a bhd: t.o whn p.u bef 11th)		**P**	16/1	—	—
2009[F]	**Jacob's Wife (106)** (PRWebber) **7-10-9** JOsborne (a bhd: t.o whn p.u bef 11th)		**P**	6/1[2]	—	—
1837[3]	**Beau Babillard (113)** (PFNicholls) **10-11-2b** PHide (prom tl wknd qckly 10th: t.o whn p.u bef 4 out)		**P**	16/1	—	—
1812*	**Mammy's Choice (IRE) (98)** (RHAlner) **7-9-12**(3)ow1 PHenley (hdwy 5th: mstke 10th: sn wknd: t.o whn p.u bef 2 out)		**P**	10/1	—	—
	Silverino (102) (SEarle) **11-10-5b**ow5 CMaude (prom tl mstke 3rd: t.o 9th: p.u bef 4 out)		**P**	25/1	—	—
1951[P]	**Golden Opal (97)** (RHBuckler) **12-9-7**(7) MGriffiths (mstke 3rd: sn bhd: t.o whn p.u bef last)		**P**	50/1	—	—
1682[4]	**Newlands-General (118)** (PFNicholls) **11-11-2**(5) OBurrows (hld up: hdwy 7th: blnd & uns rdr 11th)		**U**	20/1	—	—

(SP 137.5%) **15 Rn**

5m 57.1 (40.10) CSF £66.56 CT £646.83 TOTE £12.50: £3.00 £3.10 £4.70 (£80.30) Trio £187.50 OWNER Mr R. M. E. Wright (MINEHEAD) BRED G. Amey

LONG HANDICAP Tapageur 9-8 Silverino 9-3 Golden Opal 9-1 Mammy's Choice (IRE) 9-12

1426* Orswell Lad repeated November's game course and distance win off a 6lb higher mark. (10/1)

Montebel (IRE) made a fine comeback after nearly two years off and is one to bear in mind. (11/2)

1937 Bells Life (IRE) bounced back after a disappointing run last time and gave a good account of himself under a big weight for these conditions. (12/1)

1952* Top Javalin (NZ) was making a belated debut over fences. (8/1)

1985 Fools Errand (IRE) had ground conditions in his favour, but has gone up 10lb for his two wins this season. (6/1)

2039 Brogeen Lady (IRE), trying to make all in these stamina-sapping conditions, ran much better than her final placing suggests. (11/2)

2661 WEATHERBYS 'STARS OF TOMORROW' INTERMEDIATE OPEN N.H. FLAT RACE (4,5,6 & 7-Y.O) (Class H)

4-35 (4-38) **2m 1f** £1,271.00 (£356.00: £173.00)

				SP	RR	SF
1431*	**Iranos (FR)** (MCPipe) **5-11-12** APMcCoy (led 14f: hrd rdn to ld over 1f out: all out)	—	**1**	4/5[1]	52 f	—
1774*	**Dom Beltrano (FR)** (NATwiston-Davies) **5-11-5**(7) LSuthern (lw: a.p: led 3f out: hrd rdn & hdd over 1f out: r.o)	¾	**2**	10/1[3]	51 f	—
	Royal Pot Black (IRE) (PJHobbs) **6-11-5** GTormey (bit bkwd: chsd ldrs: outpcd 5f out: styd on fnl 2f)	6	**3**	10/1[3]	39 f	—
	Hot 'n Saucy (APJones) **5-11-0** MrSBush (nvr nr to chal)	6	**4**	66/1	28 f	—
	Dublin Freddy (MissVenetiaWilliams) **6-11-12** NWilliamson (plld hrd: prom 13f)	5	**5**	5/2[2]	35 f	—
	Country Beau (JSKing) **5-11-5** TJMurphy (nvr nr ldrs)	4	**6**	20/1	25 f	—
	Heidiqueenofclubs (IRE) (NATwiston-Davies) **6-11-0** DBridgwater (a bhd: t.o)	dist	**7**	10/1[3]	—	—
1431[8]	**Mr Agriwise** (RGFrost) **6-11-5** JFrost (bit bkwd: bhd fnl 6f: t.o)	½	**8**	40/1	—	—
	Brave Edwin (IRE) (JABOld) **7-11-5** JOsborne (bkwd: trckd ldrs tl wknd qckly 4f out: t.o)	2½	**9**	10/1[3]	—	—
	Slack Alice (JLSpearing) **6-11-0** DWalsh (bit bkwd: prom 13f: t.o)	nk	**10**	40/1	—	—
	Splash of Blakeney (SGKnight) **6-10-9**(5) DSalter (bhd fnl 7f: t.o)	2½	**11**	66/1	—	—
	Joyful Pabs (KBishop) **5-11-0** RGreene (bit bkwd: a bhd: t.o)		**12**	66/1	—	—
	St Mabyn Inn Boy (PRRodford) **5-11-5** SBurrough (bit bkwd: a bhd: t.o)		**13**	66/1	—	—
1820[9]	**Elly's Dream** (PCRitchens) **6-11-0** SFox (bit bkwd: prom: rdn 6f out: sn wknd: t.o)		**14**	66/1	—	—
1573[11]	**Baby Lancaster** (MAGriffin) **6-10-12**(7) MGriffiths (prom 11f: t.o)		**15**	66/1	—	—

(SP 139.1%) **15 Rn**

4m 22.5 (261.50) CSF £11.99 TOTE £2.20: £1.00 £2.80 £4.60 (£9.50) Trio £62.20 OWNER Mr B. A. Kilpatrick (WELLINGTON) BRED Patrick Champion

1431* Iranos (FR) had to dig deep to get the better of a dour struggle. (4/5: op evens)
1774* Dom Beltrano (FR) had finished behind the winner on his debut, but forced the favourite to pull out all the stops this time. (10/1: op 7/2)
Royal Pot Black (IRE) will not suffer from a lack of stamina on this evidence. (10/1)
Hot 'n Saucy shaped really well after not being given a hard time. (66/1)
Dublin Freddy, trained by David Nicholson when winning on similar ground last season, must have settled better there. (5/2)
Heidiqueenofclubs (IRE) (10/1: 5/1-12/1)

T/Jkpt: Not won; £10,194.70 to Market Rasen 21/1/97. T/Plpt: £1,319.70 (10.35 Tckts). T/Qdpt: £410.20 (5.89 Tckts). KH

2546-LEICESTER (R-H) (Chases - good to firm, good patches. Hurdles good to soft, good patches)
Tuesday January 21st
WEATHER: overcast

2662 STONESBY NOVICES' HURDLE (I) (4-Y.O+) (Class E)
1-00 (1-00) **2m 4f 110y (11 hdls)** £2,329.00 (£644.00: £307.00) GOING: 0.27 sec per fur (GS)

Form	Horse	Btn	Pos	SP	RR	SF
1640^{7}	**Hurdante (IRE)** (GBBalding) **7-11-6** APMcCoy (lw: chsd ldrs: led appr 4 out: sn clr: comf)	—	**1**	10/1	84+	34
1369^{2}	**Mentmore Towers (IRE)** (MrsJPitman) **5-11-6** WMarston (led: mstke 3rd: slipped on landing next: hdd appr 4 out: kpt on u.p: no ch w wnr)	9	**2**	5/2^{2}	77	27
1830^{3}	**Penrose Lad (NZ) (92)** (DNicholson) **7-11-6** AMaguire (hdwy 4th: chsd wnr fr 3 out: rdn & no ex flat)	hd	**3**	15/2^{3}	77	27
2509^{7}	**Dont Forget Curtis (IRE) (83)** (GMMoore) **5-11-6** NBentley (hld up: hdwy 6th: rdn & wknd appr last)	10	**4**	25/1	69	19
1683^{12}	**Spring Double (IRE)** (NATwiston-Davies) **6-11-6** DBridgwater (hld up in tch: effrt appr 4 out: sn rdn & wknd)	1½	**5**	20/1	68	18
2055^{2}	**Eagles Rest (IRE)** (NJHenderson) **6-11-6** MAFitzgerald (lw: hld up: stdy hdwy appr 4 out: rdn & wknd appr 2 out)	¾	**6**	10/11^{1}	67	17
1250^{7}	**Fancy Nancy (IRE)** (MissCJohnsey) **6-11-1** LHarvey (bkwd: lost pl & hmpd 5th: t.o)	24	**7**	100/1	44	—
	Westcote Lad (WJenks) **8-11-6** TJenks (bkwd: w ldr: hrd rdn & wknd appr 3 out: t.o)	18	**8**	33/1	35	—
1835^{2}	**Sioux To Speak** (MissHCKnight) **5-11-6** BFenton (hld up: effrt 7th: wknd 4 out: t.o)	14	**9**	20/1	24	—
2053^{4}	**Seabrook Lad** (MJWilkinson) **6-11-6** ILawrence (bit bkwd: prom tl fell 5th)		**F**	20/1	—	—
1329^{12}	**Firecrown** (MrsPRobeson) **7-11-6** MRichards (lw: bhd whn mstke 7th: t.o whn p.u bef 4 out)		**P**	100/1	—	—
1654^{P}	**Knockbride (IRE)** (FMurphy) **8-11-6** MFoster (bit bkwd: hld up: rdn & lost pl 7th: t.o whn p.u bef 4 out)		**P**	100/1	—	—

(SP 125.9%) **12 Rn**

5m 3.7 (14.70) CSF £32.60 TOTE £10.90: £1.90 £1.50 £1.90 (£15.90) Trio £25.10 OWNER TJA Consultants Ltd (ANDOVER) BRED P.Moakley
OFFICIAL EXPLANATION **Hurdante (IRE): regarding the improved form, the trainer reported that the gelding made a mistake at the last on the far side on his previous run, became unbalanced and could not handle the bend.**
1640 Hurdante (IRE) proved much more manageable on this occasion, and duly got off the mark over hurdles with a very easily-gained success. He should in time prove just as effective over fences. (10/1: 8/1-12/1)
1369 Mentmore Towers (IRE) ran well after a two-month break, especially as he almost departed the scene when losing his footing at the fourth. As he stays particularly well, it is only a matter of time before he shows his true worth. (5/2)
1830 Penrose Lad (NZ) tried hard to reel in the winner inside the last half-mile, but he was always getting the worst of the argument, and was forced to forfeit the runner-up spot nearing the finish. (15/2)
1807 Dont Forget Curtis (IRE) has yet to prove he really stays this trip and had met his match between the last two. (25/1)
1191 Spring Double (IRE), given a more patient ride, did not find a lot when asked for an effort early in the straight. As yet he is not getting it together over hurdles. (20/1)
2055 Eagles Rest (IRE), a very attractive type who looks every bit a chaser, looked to be cantering when closing up on the home turn. When the button was pressed approaching the penultimate flight, there was no response at all and he was beaten in a matter of strides. (10/11: 8/11-evens)

2663 STONESBY NOVICES' HURDLE (II) (4-Y.O+) (Class E)
1-30 (1-30) **2m 4f 110y (11 hdls)** £2,329.00 (£644.00: £307.00) GOING: 0.27 sec per fur (GS)

Form	Horse	Btn	Pos	SP	RR	SF
	Special Beat (NJHenderson) **5-10-10**(5) MrCVigors (a.p: rdn 3 out: btn whn lft in ld last: rdn out)	—	**1**	8/1^{3}	72	26
	Edredon Bleu (FR) (MissHCKnight) **5-11-6** RDunwoody (led to 3 out: rallied u.p flat: no imp)	2½	**2**	5/2^{1}	75	29
1830^{9}	**Symphony's Son (IRE)** (DNicholson) **6-11-6** AMaguire (hld up & bhd: stdy hdwy 7th: wknd 3 out)	7	**3**	7/1^{2}	70	24
2074^{6}	**Banny Hill Lad** (CPMorlock) **7-11-6** JRKavanagh (hld up: hdwy 7th: wknd appr 3 out)	27	**4**	33/1	49	3
2055^{P}	**Latahaab (USA)** (JTGifford) **6-11-6** PHide (hld up: hdwy 6th: mstke next: wknd 4 out)	4	**5**	12/1	45	—
1250^{8}	**Supremo (IRE)** (MJWilkinson) **8-11-6** TJO'Sullivan (bhd fr 6th: t.o)	dist	**6**	25/1	—	—
1867^{4}	**Award (IRE)** (RRowe) **6-11-6** DO'Sullivan (hld up: hdwy 6th: led 3 out: 6l clr whn fell last)		**F**	5/2^{1}	83?	—
1470^{4}	**Kilcarne Bay (IRE)** (OSherwood) **7-11-6** JOsborne (prom tl wknd 4 out: 5th & no ch whn p.u bef 2 out)		**P**	5/2^{1}	—	—
1938^{9}	**Chapilliere (FR)** (TThomsonJones) **7-11-6** MAFitzgerald (hld up in tch: wknd 6th: t.o whn p.u bef 2 out)		**P**	33/1	—	—
2010^{12}	**Alongwaydown (IRE)** (DRGandolfo) **8-11-6** DLeahy (bit bkwd: a bhd: t.o whn p.u bef 2 out)		**P**	50/1	—	—
1683^{9}	**Don't Mind If I Do (IRE)** (PRWebber) **6-11-6** MrPScott (bhd fr 7th: t.o whn p.u bef last)		**P**	50/1	—	—
	Belgran (USA) (BPreece) **8-11-6v**^{1} TJenks (chsd ldrs: rdn 5th: sn lost tch: t.o whn p.u bef 4 out)		**P**	100/1	—	—
	Antarctica (USA) (JHetherton) **5-10-8**(7) MNewton (hld up & bhd: sme hdwy appr 4 out: 6th & no ch whn p.u bef 2 out)		**P**	100/1	—	—

(SP 132.6%) **13 Rn**

5m 4.8 (15.80) CSF £28.71 TOTE £11.00: £3.00 £1.30 £2.10 (£30.90) Trio £40.50 OWNER Mr C. Marner (LAMBOURN) BRED Christian Marner
OFFICIAL EXPLANATION **Kilcarne Bay (IRE): the rider reported reported that he was unhappy with the gelding's action.**
Special Beat, a winning stayer on the Flat, made a very impressive debut over hurdles. Though she was lucky to score, she would have been a worthy runner-up even if the leader had not departed at the last. (8/1)
Edredon Bleu (FR), a prolific winner over fences in France, having his first outing in this country, attempted to make all. He lost control early in the straight, and though he stayed on again on the Flat, was never going to get there. Built more like a hurdler than a chaser, he should not be long in paying in his way. (5/2: 7/4-11/4)
1830 Symphony's Son (IRE) began a forward move on the home turn, but lack of a recent race took its toll and he was rather fortunate to run into the prizes. (7/1)

1867 Award (IRE), travelling strongly when taking over at the third last, had left his rivals for dead when he crashed through the final flight. He is short of experience and was trying this trip for the first time. (5/2)
1470 Kilcarne Bay (IRE) dropped away tamely once into the straight and was pulled up when all chance had gone. His jockey could offer no excuse for this below-par performance. (5/2)

2664 BROOK CONDITIONAL (S) H'CAP HURDLE (0-90) (4-Y.O+) (Class G)
2-00 (2-00) **2m (9 hdls)** £2,145.00 (£595.00: £285.00) GOING: 0.27 sec per fur (GS)

				SP	RR	SF
2038[2]	**Fleet Cadet (82)** (MCPipe) **6-11-12v** GSupple (hld up: hdwy 5th: led 2 out: clr last: easily)	—	**1**	5/4[1]	64+	12
1767[8]	**Indian Temple (69)** (KBishop) **6-10-13** EHusband (chsd ldrs: led appr 4 out: rdn & hdd 2 out: sn btn)	4	**2**	9/1[3]	47	—
2006[6]	**Slightly Special (IRE) (63)** (BAPearce) **5-10-2**(5)ow6 GordonGallagher (led tl appr 4 out: sn rdn: one pce)	2½	**3**	12/1	39	—
1332[7]	**Remember Star (68)** (ADSmith) **4-10-0** ABates (hld up & bhd: r.o fr 3 out: nrst fin)	2½	**4**	16/1	41	—
1836[7]	**Trendy Auctioneer (IRE) (57)** (MrsLCJewell) **9-10-1v** SophieMitchell (bit bkwd: a bhd: t.o)	23	**5**	25/1	7	—
	Berts Choice (65) (JGMO'Shea) **6-10-9** MichaelBrennan (a bhd: t.o fr 5th)	3	**6**	20/1	12	—
2038[11]	**Bold Charlie (56)** (SMellor) **5-9-9v**(5) SHearn (chsd ldrs tl wknd appr 3 out: t.o)	25	**7**	25/1	—	—
1980[2]	**Lime Street Blues (IRE) (79)** (CPEBrooks) **6-11-9b** MBerry (lw: chsd ldr to 5th: wknd appr 4 out: t.o)	dist	**8**	13/8[2]	—	—
1707[6]	**Mini Fete (FR) (62)** (KRBurke) **8-10-6** RPainter (a bhd: t.o bef 2 out)		**P**	20/1	—	—
2552[P]	**Lothian Jem (67)** (JWharton) **8-10-11b[1]** GHogan (lw: chsd clr ldrs: j.slowly 4th: sn bhd: t.o whn p.u bef 4 out)		**P**	33/1	—	—
1120[P]	**Hugh Daniels (72)** (BPreece) **9-10-11**(5) JMogford (a bhd: t.o ½-wy: p.u bef 4 out)		**P**	16/1	—	—
				(SP 132.2%)		**11 Rn**

4m 2.7 (17.70) CSF £13.16 CT £103.84 TOTE £2.50: £1.10 £1.20 £2.20 (£17.10) Trio £42.20 OWNER Sir John Swaine (WELLINGTON) BRED R. D. Hollingsworth
LONG HANDICAP Remember Star 8-13 Bold Charlie 9-12
WEIGHT FOR AGE 4yo-12lb
Bt in 3,000 gns
2038 Fleet Cadet, always cantering, outclassed this opposition with an effortless success and would hardly have realized he had been in a race. (5/4)
Indian Temple ran much better on this step down in class, but was a shade unlucky to come up against one as useful as the winner. (9/1)
2006 Slightly Special (IRE) had to work hard to shake off a persistent rival in the first mile, and it left him with very little more in the locker. He had run his race when the winner cruised past him, but there is certainly a race in him. (12/1)
Remember Star never got into the race, but she stayed on from off the pace in the latter stages, and from 15lb out of the handicap this was not a bad effort. (16/1)

2665 RABBIT H'CAP CHASE (0-105) (5-Y.O+) (Class F)
2-30 (2-31) **3m (18 fncs)** £3,566.50 (£994.00: £479.50) GOING: 0.04 sec per fur (G)

				SP	RR	SF
1122[P]	**Bendor Mark (90)** (MJWilkinson) **8-11-1** APMcCoy (hld up: hdwy 10th: lft in ld 4 out: clr next: r.o)	—	**1**	10/1[3]	10[illegible]	34
1902[U]	**Yeoman Warrior (102)** (RRowe) **10-11-13** DO'Sullivan (lw: prom: led 7th tl after next: blnd & lost pl 14th: rallied 3 out: r.o wl flat)	2	**2**	16/1	112	45
1877*	**Call Me River (IRE) (79)** (PRHedger) **9-10-4** ILawrence (lw: hld up: stdy hdwy 10th: rdn 13th: wknd after 2 out)	20	**3**	2/1[1]	75	8
1812[2]	**Maestro Paul (99)** (JTGifford) **11-11-10** PHide (lw: hld up & bhd: gd hdwy 4 out: wknd appr last)	5	**4**	8/1[2]	92	25
1817[3]	**Just One Canaletto (78)** (NATwiston-Davies) **9-10-3** TJMurphy (in tch: no hdwy fr 4 out)	5	**5**	10/1[3]	68	1
1839[5]	**Lay it Off (IRE) (85)** (JGO'Neill) **8-10-10** SCurran (led to 5th: reminders 8th: wknd appr 3 out)	1½	**6**	16/1	74	7
1877[4]	**Solo Gent (95)** (APJones) **8-11-6** SMcNeill (lost pl 8th: sn t.o)	8	**7**	8/1[2]	78	11
1961[6]	**Mr Invader (90)** (NAGaselee) **10-11-1** WMarston (bhd: hmpd 2nd: hdwy 6th: blnd bdly 14th: nt rcvr: t.o)	dist	**8**	16/1	—	—
395[P]	**Hurryup (91)** (RDickin) **10-11-2** RDunwoody (led 5th to 7th: led after next tl fell 4 out)		**F**	12/1	—	—
1773[P]	**Coney Road (75)** (CPEBrooks) **8-10-0b[1]** DGallagher (prom tl fell 12th)		**F**	10/1[3]	—	—
1717[3]	**Houghton (94)** (WJenks) **11-10-12**(7) MrRBurton (fell 2nd)		**F**	16/1	—	—
2052[P]	**Griffins Bar (85)** (MrsPSly) **9-10-10** RMarley (prom tl wknd 10th: t.o whn p.u bef 4 out)		**P**	16/1	—	—
2089[5]	**Pant Llin (80)** (FJordan) **11-10-5** SWynne (mstke 1st: rdn & t.o 8th: p.u bef 4 out)		**P**	25/1	—	—
	Royal Square (CAN) (95) (MissJBower) **11-11-6** DBridgwater (bit bkwd: p.u bef 6th & dismntd)		**P**	16/1	—	—
1817*	**Opal's Tenspot (75)** (JMBradley) **10-10-0** RFarrant (a bhd: t.o whn p.u bef 4 out)		**P**	11/1	—	—
1731[P]	**Call Me Early (92)** (MissJFCraze) **12-11-3** MrJRees (bit bkwd: blnd & uns rdr 5th)		**U**	33/1	—	—
1961[P]	**King's Courtier (IRE) (77)** (SMellor) **8-9-13v**(3)ow2 EHusband (hmpd 2nd: bhd whn blnd & uns rdr 6th)		**U**	33/1	—	—
				(SP 143.9%)		**17 Rn**

6m 4.7 (10.70) CSF £164.89 CT £425.92 TOTE £10.30: £3.00 £3.10 £1.50 £2.30 (£105.40) Trio £54.60 OWNER Mr C. J. Courage (BANBURY) BRED J. W. Purves
LONG HANDICAP Opal's Tenspot 9-8 King's Courtier (IRE) 9-6
Bendor Mark opened his account when McCoy last partnered him and, staying on when left with the advantage four out, tied up on the flat but was never in any danger of being caught. (10/1)
Yeoman Warrior, a desperately unlucky loser, completed a gloomy day for his stable and, after such a game effort, thoroughly deserves to find consolation. (16/1)
1877* Call Me River (IRE) edged closer in the final mile and was poised to challenge entering the straight, but he was unable to land a blow and had shot his bolt after negotiating the second last. (2/1)
1812 Maestro Paul made stealthy progress and went in pursuit of the winner three out, but lack of stamina took its toll and he was galloping on the spot over the last two. (8/1)
1817 Just One Canaletto waited on the leaders, but failed to pick up when popped the question on the home turn, and was never a factor. (10/1)
Mr Invader had no luck at all, but he had worked his way onto the heels of the leaders when a bad mistake five out all but severed the partnership. (16/1)
190* Hurryup helped force the pace and was still the one to catch when he misjudged the final ditch, four out, and took a heavy fall. (12/1)
1817* Opal's Tenspot (11/1: 8/1-12/1)

2666 DANIEL LAMBERT H'CAP HURDLE (0-120) (5-Y.O+) (Class D)
3-00 (3-03) **2m 4f 110y (11 hdls)** £3,652.00 (£1,096.00: £528.00: £244.00) GOING: 0.27 sec per fur (GS)

				SP	RR	SF
1727[4]	**Henrietta Howard (IRE) (109)** (MrsDHaine) **7-11-2**(3) GHogan (hld up in tch: rdn 3 out: led last: styd on strly)	—	**1**	14/1	94	45
1841*	**Ismeno (105)** (SDow) **6-11-1** ADicken (hld up: hdwy appr 4 out: led 3 out: hdd & hit last: unable qckn)	1¾	**2**	10/1[3]	89	40

				SP	RR	SF
1678^{3}	**Silver Standard (102)** (CaptTAForster) **7-10-12b** SWynne (hld up: hdwy appr 4 out: hrd rdn appr 2 out: styd on)	2	**3**	10/1^{3}	84	35
1710^{6}	**Cassio's Boy (90)** (RJEckley) **6-10-0** DGallagher (hdwy 5th: wknd appr last)	8	**4**	16/1	66	17
2069^{3}	**Handy Lass (98)** (JSSmith) **8-10-8** TJMurphy (bhd tl styd on fr 3 out)	7	**5**	20/1	68	19
1956*	**Reaganesque (USA) (112)** (PGMurphy) **5-11-8** RFarrant (chsd ldrs: rdn appr 4 out: sn btn)	7	**6**	10/1^{3}	77	28
	Selatan (IRE) (111) (DRGandolfo) **5-11-4**(3) DFortt (bit bkwd: prom to 6th: sn wknd)	4	**7**	16/1	73	24
1878*	**Out Ranking (FR) (118)** (MCPipe) **5-12-0** APMcCoy (j.rt: led to 3 out: sn rdn & wknd)	nk	**8**	7/1^{2}	80	31
1870^{3}	**Eulogy (IRE) (112)** (RRowe) **7-11-8** DO'Sullivan (mstke 5th: sn bhd: hdwy appr 4 out: wknd 3 out)	¾	**9**	4/1^{1}	73	24
1732^{8}	**Cambo (USA) (91)** (MCBanks) **11-10-1** DSkyrme (hdwy 4th: wknd 3 out)	hd	**10**	20/1	52	3
1860^{4}	**Cawarra Boy (105)** (CJames) **9-11-1** MrEJames (hld up & bhd: stdy hdwy 7th: wknd 4 out: t.o)	16	**11**	16/1	53	4
1903^{2}	**Kippanour (USA) (112)** (CJMann) **5-11-8b** RDunwoody (trckd ldrs tl wknd 4 out: t.o)	10	**12**	10/1^{3}	53	4
	Musical Monarch (NZ) (112) (NJHawke) **11-11-8** MRichards (bkwd: a bhd: t.o)	3	**13**	33/1	50	1
	Boyfriend (90) (MrsJPitman) **7-10-0** WMarston (prom to 7th: sn wknd: t.o)	24	**14**	20/1	10	—
	Garaiyba (IRE) (96) (DNicholson) **6-10-6** AMaguire (hld up: hdwy appr 4 out: rdn whn collapsed after 3 out)		**F**	4/1^{1}	—	—
	Hoodwinker (IRE) (110) (WJenks) **8-11-6** TJenks (bkwd: bhd fr ½-wy: t.o whn p.u bef 4 out)		**P**	16/1	—	—
1355^{2}	**Ramsdens (IRE) (100)** (NATwiston-Davies) **5-10-10** DBridgwater (prom: reminders after 1st: rdn & wknd 7th: t.o whn p.u after 3 out)		**P**	10/1^{3}	—	—

(SP 145.4%) **17 Rn**

5m 0.5 (11.50) CSF £151.32 CT £1,392.14 TOTE £27.50: £3.40 £3.50 £2.20 £4.10 (£146.50) Trio £223.00; £254.50 to Lingfield 22/1/97 OWNER Mrs Solna ThomsonJones (NEWMARKET) BRED Mrs N. Johnston

LONG HANDICAP Cassio's Boy 9-9 Boyfriend 9-13

1727 Henrietta Howard (IRE), in no hurry to take on the leaders, had to be shaken up to go about her business three out, but she responded willingly and, landing in front at the last, proved too strong for the hard-driven runner-up. (14/1)

1841* Ismeno kicked for home early in the straight and tried to pinch a winning lead, but he was unable to get away, and had already been collared when he clobbered the final hurdle. (10/1)

1678 Silver Standard, a very consistent individual who invariably makes the frame, could not summon up the speed to deliver a challenge despite staying on. (10/1)

1710 Cassio's Boy had reached a challenging position at halfway, but he was unable to quicken up when the pace lifted entering the straight, although he did not admit defeat until approaching the last. (16/1)

2069 Handy Lass made up quite a lot of ground in the last half-mile, but never threatened to reach the leaders. She is one to bear in mind from now on. (20/1)

1878* Out Ranking (FR), not for the first time, jumped badly right, but set a testing gallop until feeling the strain and dropping out approaching the penultimate flight. (7/1)

Garaiyba (IRE), winner of four races on the Flat and a maiden hurdle in Ireland, probably needed this first run in three months. Patiently ridden, she moved up on the home turn, but was under pressure and done for when she collapsed approaching the second last. (4/1)

2667 DICK CHRISTIAN NOVICES' CHASE (5-Y.O+) (Class E)

3-30 (3-31) **2m 4f 110y (15 fncs)** £3,561.60 (£1,066.80: £512.40: £235.20) GOING: 0.04 sec per fur (G)

				SP	RR	SF
1856*	**Slingsby (IRE) (109)** (NAGaselee) **7-11-10** AThornton (hld up: mstke 2nd: hdwy 8th: led 11th: wl clr fr 3 out: eased flat)	—	**1**	3/1^{2}	103+	2
1994^{P}	**Uncle Algy (85)** (MissHCKnight) **8-11-4** BFenton (bhd: hdwy u.p 3 out: chsd wnr appr last: no imp)	7	**2**	20/1	92	—
1732^{7}	**Super Ritchart** (BPalling) **9-11-4** RFarrant (hld up: hdwy & hit 9th: blnd next: hmpd 11th: sn btn)	3	**3**	20/1	89	—
1571^{2}	**Karar (IRE)** (RRowe) **7-11-4** DO'Sullivan (bhd: sme hdwy 11th: j.slowly next: n.d)	8	**4**	4/1^{3}	83	—
1771^{F}	**Wot No Gin (65)** (AJWilson) **8-11-4** MAFitzgerald (mstke 4th: a bhd)	3½	**5**	13/2	80	—
1565^{P}	**Primitive Penny** (MrsDHaine) **6-10-10**(3) GHogan (mstke 1st: a bhd)	3	**6**	33/1	73	—
1864^{5}	**Sounds Golden (60)** (JohnWhyte) **9-11-4** PHide (prom: lft in ld 8th: hdd 11th: 2nd & btn whn mstke 3 out: t.o)	29	**7**	50/1	55	—
1680^{3}	**Three Philosophers (IRE) (115)** (CaptTAForster) **8-11-4** SWynne (lw: led: sn clr: fell 8th)		**F**	11/8^{1}	—	—
1865^{5}	**Pennant Cottage (IRE) (60)** (WJenks) **9-10-13** TJenks (mstke 1st: bhd tl fell 2 out)		**F**	50/1	—	—
2571^{4}	**Snowdon Lily (61)** (PRWebber) **6-10-10**(3) EHusband (prom: mstke & hmpd 8th: 3rd whn fell 11th)		**F**	66/1	—	—

(SP 118.3%) **10 Rn**

5m 22.2 (21.20) CSF £51.17 TOTE £3.10: £1.60 £4.30 £3.20 (£53.40) Trio £90.20 OWNER Simon Harrap Partnership (LAMBOURN) BRED Peter Murphy

1856* Slingsby (IRE) gained the advantage five out and, gradually forging clear, was eased right down near the finish. He appears to have got his act together now. (3/1)

Uncle Algy showed much improved form on this second outing over fences, and it is possible he will stay further. (20/1)

1418 Super Ritchart, three times a winner here over hurdles, did not fare badly on this chasing debut but he made a few novicey mistakes. He will be all the wiser after this. (20/1)

1571 Karar (IRE) needs a test of stamina over hurdles and he could not go the pace on this chasing debut over this inadequate trip. He will be all the better for the experience, and an increase in distance. (4/1)

1771 Wot No Gin (13/2: op 4/1)

1680 Three Philosophers (IRE) again had a lapse of concentration, and crumpled on landing after setting a telling gallop to the eighth. He had not made a semblance of a mistake and was clear when he keeled over. (11/8)

2668 CROXTON PARK NOVICES' HURDLE (4-Y.O+) (Class E)

4-00 (4-01) **2m (9 hdls)** £3,372.00 (£942.00: £456.00) GOING: 0.27 sec per fur (GS)

				SP	RR	SF
2112*	**Sanmartino (IRE)** (DNicholson) **5-11-11** AMaguire (lw: a.p: led 2 out: rdn & r.o wl)	—	**1**	8/15^{1}	101+	46
	High In The Clouds (IRE) (CaptTAForster) **5-11-5** SWynne (lw: trckd ldrs: hdwy 5th: led appr 2 out: sn hdd: rdn & kpt on flat)	1½	**2**	20/1	94+	39
1830^{2}	**Moonax (IRE)** (BWHills) **6-11-5** RDunwoody (chsd ldrs: j.slowly 4th: ev ch appr 2 out: unable qckn)	4	**3**	9/4^{2}	90	35
1808^{2}	**Northern Fleet** (MrsAJPerrett) **4-10-7** MAFitzgerald (prom: ev ch appr 2 out: sn rdn & wknd)	13	**4**	16/1	77	10
1953^{4}	**Impending Danger** (KSBridgwater) **4-10-4**(3) RMassey (prom: led 4th tl appr 2 out: sn wknd)	11	**5**	25/1	66	—
1634^{9}	**Apache Park (USA)** (MSheppard) **4-10-7** DGallagher (plld hrd: led to 4th: wknd 3 out)	7	**6**	66/1	59	—
2035^{8}	**Daunt** (FJordan) **5-11-5** APMcCoy (hld up & bhd: mstke 5th: sme hdwy fr 3 out: nvr nrr)	2½	**7**	14/1^{3}	56+	1
1801^{2}	**Welsh Silk** (DRGandolfo) **5-11-2**(3) DFortt (bhd: sme hdwy fr 3 out: nvr nrr)	½	**8**	33/1	56	1
1782^{5}	**Reimei** (RAkehurst) **8-11-5** DBridgwater (hld up: hdwy 5th: wknd appr 2 out)	2½	**9**	20/1	53	—
1980^{7}	**Spitfire Bridge (IRE)** (GMMcCourt) **5-10-12**(7) RHobson (a bhd)	½	**10**	66/1	53	—

	Horse			SP	RR	SF
	Knockbrit Lady (IRE) (AGFoster) **6-11-0** AThornton (t.o)	20	**11**	66/1	28	—
2060[P]	**Worth The Bill** (FJordan) **4-10-7** PHide (bhd fr 5th: t.o)	4	**12**	66/1	29	—
	Man of The Match (MrsJPitman) **7-11-5** RFarrant (hld up: hdwy 4th: mstke next: sn wknd: t.o)	3½	**13**	40/1	25	—
1675[6]	**Stone Island** (JohnWhyte) **4-10-13** LHarvey (t.o)	3	**14**	66/1	28	—
2035[10]	**Red Phantom (IRE)** (SMellor) **5-11-2**(3) EHusband (t.o)	2½	**15**	66/1	20	—
1959[P]	**Sleazey (70)** (JGO'Neill) **6-11-5** SCurran (hdwy 3rd: rdn & wknd appr 4 out: t.o)	7	**16**	66/1	13	—
	It'sthebusiness (MSheppard) **5-11-5** GUpton (hld up & bhd: hdwy 5th: btn whn fell 2 out: dead)		**F**	66/1	—	—
1938[14]	**No Matter (IRE)** (RRowe) **6-11-5** DO'Sullivan (chsd ldrs to ½-wy: sn wknd: t.o whn p.u bef 3 out)		**P**	66/1	—	—

(SP 140.7%) **18 Rn**

3m 54.9 (9.90) CSF £19.72 TOTE £1.60: £1.00 £7.30 £1.10 (£49.60) Trio £32.70 OWNER Mr K. Abdulla (TEMPLE GUITING) BRED Juddmonte Farms

WEIGHT FOR AGE 4yo-12lb

2112* Sanmartino (IRE) had to work to make sure of victory on the run-in and, unless the runner-up is very useful, this can only be described as a workmanlike performance. (8/15)

High In The Clouds (IRE), three times successful over middle distances in Ireland on the Flat, almost caused a major upset on this hurdling debut. His trainer reckoned this was the best novice hurdle seen so far this term, so obviously he thinks highly of this fellow and he could be anything. (20/1)

1830 Moonax (IRE) was cruising when he lengthened up to join issue approaching the second last, but as on his debut, was tapped for toe when the battle to the finish really developed. We are likely to see him in a different light when and if he tackles the best in staying events. (9/4)

1808 Northern Fleet may well have trouble winning at this minimum trip, but he was fighting for the lead until getting outpaced from the penultimate flight. (16/1)

1953 Impending Danger could not match strides with the principals when the race began in earnest, but he is a progressive sort who should be able to win a race in his own company. (25/1)

2035 Daunt was not allowed to run himself into the ground this time, and if he does learn to settle as he did here, then he should repay some of his purchase price. (14/1)

T/Plpt: £220.80 (46.18 Tckts). T/Qdpt: £25.50 (41.18 Tckts) IM

2318-MARKET RASEN (R-H) (Good, Chases good to soft patches straight, Hurdles good to firm patches back straight)

Tuesday January 21st

WEATHER: dry & cloudy

2669 MIDDLE RASEN NOVICES' HURDLE (4-Y.O+) (Class E)

1-10 (1-16) **2m 1f 110y (8 hdls)** £2,559.50 (£717.00: £348.50) GOING minus 0.08 sec per fur (G)

	Horse			SP	RR	SF
1830[4]	**Night Dance** (KAMorgan) **5-11-5** ASSmith (lw: mde all: all out)	—	**1**	11/2[3]	78	23
1953[F]	**Toby Brown** (DNicholson) **4-10-7** RJohnson (mstkes: bhd tl hdwy u.p after 3 out: str run flat: jst failed)	½	**2**	20/1	78	11
1940[9]	**Nexsis Star** (MrsSJSmith) **4-10-7** RichardGuest (mstkes: a.p: ev ch 2 out: nt qckn)	1½	**3**	33/1	76	9
2035[2]	**Total Joy (IRE) (92)** (CJMann) **6-11-5** JRailton (a chsng ldrs: one pce fr 2 out)	8	**4**	14/1	69	14
1855[2]	**Pip's Dream (85)** (MJRyan) **6-11-0** JRyan (chsd ldrs: effrt 3 out: outpcd fr next)	1	**5**	12/1	63	8
1276[4]	**Barton Scamp** (SABrookshaw) **5-11-5** NWilliamson (hdwy 5th: sn prom: wknd between last 2)	3	**6**	33/1	65	10
1953[9]	**Angus McCoatup (IRE)** (MDHammond) **4-10-7** DBentley (stdy hdwy 5th: nvr plcd to chal)	4	**7**	50/1	62	—
	Indicator (96) (JJQuinn) **5-11-5** PNiven (bhd: stdy hdwy appr 2 out: nvr nr to chal)	hd	**8**	12/1	62	7
	White Plains (IRE) (MCPipe) **4-10-7** DWalsh (chsd ldrs: ev ch 3 out: wknd appr next)	1¾	**9**	7/2[2]	60	—
1776[8]	**Pontevedra (IRE)** (KAMorgan) **4-9-11**(5) MrRThornton (bhd tl sme late hdwy)	4	**10**	33/1	51	—
	Skip to Somerfield (BSRothwell) **5-11-0** ADobbin (cl up tl lost pl after 5th)	1¼	**11**	33/1	50	—
2175[2]	**Honeyschoice (IRE)** (MDHammond) **4-10-7** RGarritty (uns rdr & bolted bef s: hld up: hdwy 5th: rdn appr 2 out: sn wknd)	1¼	**12**	2/1[1]	54	—
1992[3]	**Highly Charming (IRE) (84)** (MFBarraclough) **5-10-12**(7) MrAWintle (lw: bhd fr ½-wy)	3	**13**	33/1	51	—
	Suranom (IRE) (MrsDHaine) **5-11-5** JFTitley (trckd ldrs tl wknd fr 5th)	13	**14**	6/1	39	—
1873[3]	**Easy Listening (USA)** (NJHawke) **5-11-5** CMaude (cl up tl rdn & wknd qckly 5th)	16	**15**	6/1	25	—
1699[5]	**Swynford Supreme** (JFBottomley) **4-10-7** DerekByrne (a bhd: t.o)	6	**16**	25/1	19	—
	Shaagni Ana (USA) (JGSmyth-Osbourne) **6-11-5** RSupple (bit bkwd: a bhd: wl t.o fr 5th)	dist	**17**	50/1	—	—
2541[W]	**Shirley's Time** (MrsJBrown) **6-11-5** PCarberry (prom to 4th: bhd whn fell 2 out: rmntd)		**18**	50/1	—	—
2629[15]	**Tough Character (IRE) (51)** (MESowersby) **9-11-5** LO'Hara (a bhd: t.o whn p.u bef 5th)		**P**	100/1	—	—

(SP 151.7%) **19 Rn**

4m 11.7 (8.70) CSF £113.83 TOTE £5.10: £2.80 £11.10 £8.60 (£711.10; £50.08 to Lingfield 22/1/97) Trio Not won; £320.98 to Lingfield 22/1/97 OWNER Racecourse Medical Officers Association (MELTON MOWBRAY) BRED Miss J. A. Challen

WEIGHT FOR AGE 4yo-12lb

1830 Night Dance, wearing a tongue strap, enjoyed being out in front and, although tiring at the finish, he was always going to hold on. (11/2: 6/1-4/1)

Toby Brown jumped stickily early on, but once he got into his stride from the home turn, he really powered home. (20/1)

1652 Nexsis Star ran well, but his jumping left something to be desired, and once that improves better should be seen. (33/1)

2035 Total Joy (IRE) has his chances but lacked a turn of foot, and may well need a little further. (14/1: op 8/1)

1855 Pip's Dream keeps running well. (12/1)

Angus McCoatup (IRE) should improve over a little further. (50/1)

Indicator only got going when the race was over, and left the impression that he wants further or more testing ground. (12/1)

White Plains (IRE), a useful performer on the Flat, disappointingly ran out of petrol in the home straight. (7/2)

2175 Honeyschoice (IRE) got loose before the race which must have upset him. (2/1: op 3/1)

2670 SCOTHERN H'CAP HURDLE (0-120) (4-Y.O+) (Class D)

1-40 (1-46) **2m 1f 110y (8 hdls)** £2,987.00 (£832.00: £401.00) GOING minus 0.08 sec per fur (G)

	Horse			SP	RR	SF
1860*	**Circus Line (114)** (MWEasterby) **6-11-10** PCarberry (lw: trckd ldrs: led on bit appr 2 out: clr whn blnd last: eased flat)	—	**1**	2/1[1]	97+	32

1954[3]	**Isaiah (108)** (MrsJCecil) **8-11-4** TKent (chsd ldrs: rdn 3 out: kpt on: nt pce of wnr)	2	**2**	16/1	89	24
1775*	**Glenvally (94)** (BWMurray) **6-10-1**(3)ow4 ECallaghan (chsd clr ldrs: hdwy u.p 3 out: one pce fr next)	¾	**3**	20/1	75	6
1582[P]	**Sassiver (USA) (92)** (PAKelleway) **7-10-2** KGaule (effrt 4th: sn hrd drvn: styd on fr 2 out: nvr nrr)	3	**4**	12/1	70	5
1502[7]	**Indian Jockey (105)** (MCPipe) **5-11-1b[1]** DWalsh (lw: led: rdn 5th: hdd appr 2 out: sn btn)	3	**5**	11/1	80	15
1207[4]	**Gymcrak Tiger (IRE) (90)** (GHolmes) **7-10-0** NWilliamson (hld up & bhd: stdy hdwy fr 3 out: nrst fin)	2½	**6**	14/1	63+	—
1832[5]	**Glanmerin (IRE) (116)** (KAMorgan) **6-11-12** ASSmith (bhd: sme hdwy appr 2 out: nvr plcd to chal)	6	**7**	25/1	83	18
2041[3]	**Fassan (IRE) (105)** (MDHammond) **5-11-1** RGarritty (effrt 5th: no imp)	1	**8**	9/1	71	6
1642[3]	**Eurotwist (104)** (SEKettlewell) **8-11-0** RJohnson (lw: mstkes: effrt 4th: n.d)	5	**9**	13/2[3]	66	1
1681[P]	**Manolete (99)** (MrsMerritaJones) **6-10-9** DerekByrne (effrt ½-wy: n.d)	1	**10**	12/1	60	—
815[P]	**Star of David (IRE) (103)** (MissAEEmbiricos) **9-10-13** JRyan (bit bkwd: wl bhd fr ½-wy)	18	**11**	33/1	47	—
1353[2]	**Mim-Lou-and (115)** (MissHCKnight) **5-11-4**(7) MrAWintle (lw: chsd clr ldrs: effrt 5th: sn btn)	3½	**12**	3/1[2]	56	—
	Major Yaasi (USA) (93) (JAGlover) **7-10-3** TEley (sme hdwy 3 out: 7th & wl btn whn fell last)		**F**	33/1	—	—
	Jungle Knife (118) (KAMorgan) **11-12-0** ADobbin (t.o whn p.u bef 3 out)		**P**	33/1	—	—

(SP 135.4%) **14 Rn**

4m 10.7 (7.70) CSF £34.45 CT £503.33 TOTE £3.80: £1.60 £4.50 £5.90 (£25.00) Trio £111.60 OWNER Mrs P. A. H. Hartley (SHERIFF HUTTON) BRED Havenwood Construction Ltd

LONG HANDICAP Glenvally 9-8 Gymcrak Tiger (IRE) 9-12

1860* Circus Line is certainly improving but his jumping is his weak point. (2/1)

1954 Isaiah is being given a chance by the Handicapper and is running well. (16/1)

1775* Glenvally is improving and put up another good show from 6lb out of the handicap. (20/1)

1371 Sassiver (USA) never really looked happy, but decided to run on when it was all too late. (12/1)

1193 Indian Jockey tried to gallop his rivals into the ground, but could never shake them off and once passed approaching two out, he quickly decided it was not for him. (11/1)

1207 Gymcrak Tiger (IRE), after a lengthy lay-off, showed enough to suggest that he can improve, especially over a bit further. (14/1)

1832 Glanmerin (IRE) never got into this but left the impression he should do better as a result. (25/1)

1353 Mim-Lou-and (3/1: op 9/2)

2671 ERIC & LUCY PAPWORTH H'CAP CHASE (0-110) (5-Y.O+) (Class E)

2-10 (2-15) **3m 4f 110y (21 fncs)** £3,047.75 (£917.00: £443.50: £206.75) GOING: 0.00 sec per fur (G)

				SP	RR	SF
1961[2]	**Banntown Bill (IRE) (90)** (MCPipe) **8-10-8v** DWalsh (led to 3rd: cl up: led 17th: kpt on wl flat)	—	**1**	6/1	102	—
1307[4]	**Call the Shots (IRE) (90)** (JWade) **8-10-8** NWilliamson (a cl up: ev ch last: no ex)	4	**2**	4/1[1]	100	—
1089[4]	**Change the Reign (107)** (MissAEEmbiricos) **10-11-6**(5) MrRThornton (hdwy 14th: sn chsng ldrs & pushed along: no imp fr 4 out)	22	**3**	14/1	103	—
2004[3]	**Sparrow Hall (90)** (JGFitzGerald) **10-10-8b** RJohnson (led fr 3rd: hit 5th: blnd 16th: blnd & hdd 17th: ev ch tl blnd & wknd 3 out)	1½	**4**	11/2	86	—
1983[5]	**Holy Sting (IRE) (95)** (NATwiston-Davies) **8-10-13b** CMaude (chsd ldrs tl outpcd & lost tch 14th: styd on again towards fin)	hd	**5**	9/2[2]	90	—
2540[6]	**Cool Weather (IRE) (82)** (PCheesbrough) **9-10-0b** ASSmith (chsd ldrs tl rdn & wknd 16th)	dist	**6**	10/1	—	—
2179*	**Hurricane Andrew (IRE) (88)** (JAMoore) **9-10-6** NSmith (bit bkwd: prom tl blnd 11th & 12th: sn wl bhd: blnd 17th & p.u)		**P**	13/2	—	—
2052[5]	**Ocean Leader (92)** (MrsDHaine) **10-10-10** JFTitley (lw: bhd: hdwy & prom 14th: blnd 16th: p.u bef next)		**P**	5/1[3]	—	—
1819[3]	**Record Lover (IRE) (82)** (MCChapman) **7-10-0** WWorthington (a bhd: t.o whn p.u bef 4 out)		**P**	33/1	—	—
1778[6]	**Sprowston Boy (82)** (MCChapman) **14-9-7**(7) RossBerry (a bhd: no ch whn blnd & uns rdr last)		**U**	20/1	—	—

(SP 121.3%) **10 Rn**

7m 44.2 CSF £29.57 CT £301.96 TOTE £9.40: £2.40 £1.80 £3.10 (£19.50) Trio £82.30 OWNER Mr Eric Scarth (WELLINGTON) BRED Thomas Conroy

LONG HANDICAP Cool Weather (IRE) 9-10 Record Lover (IRE) 9-1 Sprowston Boy 9-13

1961 Banntown Bill (IRE) does not win very often, but he is in good form at present and did this determinedly. (6/1)

1307 Call the Shots (IRE) ran well again and should find his mark in due course. (4/1)

1089 Change the Reign was off the bit throughout the final circuit and proved too slow to get into it. (14/1)

2004 Sparrow Hall was let down by some poor jumping. (11/2)

1983 Holy Sting (IRE) finished well and obviously needs things at their most testing. (9/2)

2052 Ocean Leader seems to have a problem, as just when he improved, he ploughed through the sixteenth and his rider pulled him up. (5/1)

2672 BET WITH THE TOTE (QUALIFIER) NOVICES' CHASE (6-Y.O+) (Class E)

2-40 (2-47) **2m 6f 110y (15 fncs)** £3,421.50 (£1,032.00: £501.00: £235.50) GOING: 0.92 sec per fur (S)

				SP	RR	SF
	Kamikaze (KCBailey) **7-10-10b[1]** CO'Dwyer (trckd ldrs: a gng wl: led 3 out: easily)	—	**1**	6/1	103+	26
1850*	**Monymoss (IRE) (103)** (MrsSJSmith) **8-11-2** RichardGuest (cl up tl outpcd appr 3 out)	11	**2**	7/2[2]	101	24
	Miss Optimist (DNicholson) **7-10-5** RJohnson (j.rt 4th: hdwy 10th: c wd & ch 3 out: one pce)	2	**3**	100/30[1]	89	12
2049[3]	**Major Look (NZ) (113)** (SABrookshaw) **9-11-0** ADobbin (w ldrs: led 9th to 4 out: sn outpcd)	15	**4**	4/1[3]	87	10
2546[10]	**Sergent Kay** (MrsCACoward) **7-10-10** PCarberry (hmpd 4th: outpcd 9th: nvr trbld ldrs)	7	**5**	50/1	78	1
1850[7]	**Desperate Days (IRE) (62)** (FKirby) **8-10-10** WDwan (lost tch fr 9th)	6	**6**	66/1	74	—
2000[3]	**Fair Ally (77)** (MESowersby) **7-10-10** DParker (w.r.s: wnt prom 3rd: hit 9th & sn wknd: p.u bef 3 out)		**P**	25/1	—	—
	Halkopous (MissVenetiaWilliams) **11-10-10** NWilliamson (lw: cl up: hit 4th & 10th: led 4 out to next: wknd qckly & p.u bef 2 out)		**P**	7/2[2]	—	—
2628[P]	**Lepton (IRE)** (JWCurtis) **6-10-10** DerekByrne (mde most to 9th: wknd fr 11th: p.u bef 3 out)		**P**	66/1	—	—
1829[7]	**Sakbah (USA) (64)** (JAPickering) **8-10-2**(3) PHenley (sn bhd: t.o whn p.u bef 9th)		**P**	50/1	—	—
	General Giggs (IRE) (JPLeigh) **9-11-0** KGaule (bit bkwd: a bhd: t.o whn p.u bef 3 out)		**P**	33/1	—	—
2551[P]	**Dispol Dancer** (MrsVAAconley) **6-10-5**(5) MrRThornton (j.rt & mstkes: a wl bhd: p.u bef 9th)		**P**	66/1	—	—
2632[F]	**World Without End (USA) (80)** (MESowersby) **8-10-5**(5) STaylor (mstkes: blnd & uns rdr 5th)		**U**	50/1	—	—
	Hawker Hunter (USA) (CREgerton) **6-10-10** JAMcCarthy (bit bkwd: bhd whn blnd & uns rdr 10th)		**U**	12/1	—	—

(SP 126.6%) **14 Rn**

5m 57.8 (30.80) CSF £26.05 TOTE £8.20: £1.80 £1.40 £1.70 (£8.30) Trio £42.60 OWNER Major B. Gatensbury (UPPER LAMBOURN) BRED Gerald W. Leigh

Kamikaze, wearing blinkers for this first try over the bigger obstacles, looked a very useful prospect and fairly trotted up. He is one to follow. (6/1)

1850* Monymoss (IRE) is honest and has fair ability, but was completely outclassed here. (7/2)

Miss Optimist is useful on her day, but lack of experience over fences was probably her undoing here, and this should have taught her something. (100/30)
2049 Major Look (NZ) was in the thick of things until running out of fuel from the fourth last. He may well have needed this. (4/1)
Sergent Kay, a winning pointer, looked pretty slow in this company. (50/1)
Halkopous seems to have a problem, as he stopped extremely quickly three out and was pulled up, though he was certainly not lame. (7/2)

2673 E.B.F. 'N.H.' (QUALIFIER) NOVICES' HURDLE (5, 6 & 7-Y.O) (Class E)

3-10 (3-19) **2m 3f 110y (10 hdls)** £2,700.30 (£750.80: £360.90) GOING minus 0.08 sec per fur (G)

				SP	RR	SF
	Spendid (IRE) (DNicholson) **5-11-0** RJohnson (in tch: stdy hdwy to ld 2 out: r.o wl)	—	**1**	9/1	82+	1
1369[3]	**Peace Lord (IRE) (100)** (MrsDHaine) **7-11-0** JFTitley (lw: hdwy 6th: sn chsng ldrs: disp ld 2 out: nt qckn)	6	**2**	6/1[3]	77	—
1583[2]	**Darakshan (IRE) (104)** (MissHCKnight) **5-11-0** JRailton (cl up: led fr 5th tl hdd 2 out: no ex)	4	**3**	13/8[1]	74	—
1692[5]	**Southern Cross** (MWEasterby) **5-11-0** PCarberry (lw: mstke 1st: bhd tl hdwy 6th: hit 3 out: hung rt & styd on: n.d)	2	**4**	9/1	72	—
1905[3]	**Beacon Flight (IRE) (102)** (BdeHaan) **6-11-5** NWilliamson (a.p: effrt 3 out: one pce)	7	**5**	5/1[2]	71	—
1913[2]	**Derring Floss** (JAPickering) **7-10-2**(7) MissJWormall (led to 5th: cl up tl wknd appr 3 out)	11	**6**	20/1	52	—
1801[7]	**The Crooked Oak** (NATwiston-Davies) **5-11-0** CMaude (bhd: rdn & sme hdwy 3 out: n.d)	½	**7**	14/1	57	—
1842[6]	**Boyzontoowa (IRE)** (RCollins) **5-11-0** RichardGuest (bit bkwd: in tch to 5th)	25	**8**	66/1	37	—
2005[3]	**Harfdecent** (MrsMReveley) **6-11-0** PNiven (nvr nr to chal)	hd	**9**	10/1	36	—
1654[9]	**Menaldi (IRE)** (PCheesbrough) **7-11-0** ASSmith (nvr plcd to chal)	nk	**10**	33/1	36	—
1801[4]	**Jayfcee** (MPBielby) **5-11-0** BPowell (prom tl wknd fr 6th)	3½	**11**	33/1	33	—
1966[14]	**St Mellion Leisure (IRE)** (MCPipe) **5-11-0** DWalsh (chsd ldrs: hit 6th: sn rdn & wknd)	28	**12**	14/1	10	—
1926[3]	**Bold Action (IRE)** (JNorton) **6-11-0** WFry (mstkes: bhd fr 6th: t.o)	3	**13**	14/1	8	—
1683[8]	**Cast of Thousands** (CREgerton) **6-11-0** JAMcCarthy (bhd: hdwy 6th: wknd 3 out: p.u bef next)		**P**	8/1	—	—
	Redwood Lad (JWCurtis) **7-11-0** DerekByrne (bit bkwd: wknd rapidly 6th: wl t.o whn p.u bef 3 out)		**P**	50/1	—	—
				(SP 143.3%)		**15 Rn**

4m 47.7 (14.70) CSF £65.61 TOTE £11.70: £3.50 £2.30 £1.70 (£25.60) Trio £32.70 OWNER Mrs Stewart Catherwood (TEMPLE GUITING) BRED Liam Ormsby
Spendid (IRE), having his first run in this country, won most authoritatively and looks a progressive sort. (9/1: 6/1-10/1)
1369 Peace Lord (IRE) keeps running well and will find a race or two in due course, (6/1: 4/1-7/1)
1583 Darakshan (IRE) was again in the thick of things throughout, but when it came down to a struggle, he was found wanting. (13/8: op 3/1)
1692 Southern Cross has the ability but is a character and also his jumping needs to improve. (9/1)
1905 Beacon Flight (IRE), trying further, failed to get home, but he has had six weeks off which could have made the difference. (5/1)

2674 MARKET RASEN H'CAP CHASE (0-115) (5-Y.O+) (Class E)

3-40 (3-50) **2m 1f 110y (12 fncs)** £2,891.75 (£869.00: £419.50: £194.75) GOING: 0.92 sec per fur (S)

				SP	RR	SF
1717*	**Netherby Said (97)** (PBeaumont) **7-11-1** RSupple (mde all: hit 3rd: sn clr: hit last: kpt on wl)	—	**1**	7/4[1]	111+	30
1826[3]	**Marble Man (IRE) (85)** (MDHammond) **7-10-3** DBentley (lw: chsd wnr thrght: hdwy u.p 3 out: nvr able to chal)	4	**2**	9/1	95	14
1657[3]	**Aljadeer (USA) (110)** (MWEasterby) **8-12-0b** PCarberry (mstkes: in tch fr 6th: 3rd & styng on u.p whn blnd 3 out: one pce after)	2	**3**	3/1[2]	119	38
1843[2]	**Real Glee (IRE) (106)** (JJQuinn) **8-11-10** CMaude (mstkes: lost tch 6th: hdwy u.p 4 out: nvr able to chal)	12	**4**	8/1[3]	104	23
2009[3]	**Dr Rocket (86)** (RDickin) **12-10-4** NWilliamson (lw: prom tl wknd fr 9th)	19	**5**	12/1	66	—
1846[3]	**Reve de Valse (USA) (91)** (RJohnson) **10-10-9** KJohnson (mstke 5th: sn outpcd & lost tch)	8	**6**	14/1	64	—
1957[3]	**Crafty Chaplain (94)** (DMcCain) **11-10-12** DWalsh (prom tl outpcd 7th: sn lost pl)	21	**7**	10/1	48	—
1769[3]	**Lasata (107)** (RMCarson) **12-11-11** DMorris (dwlt: wnt prom 6th: wknd fr 8th)	18	**8**	14/1	44	—
1765[P]	**Kindle's Delight (98)** (MissHCKnight) **9-11-2** JFTitley (bhd fr ½-wy)	13	**9**	10/1	23	—
1717[2]	**Copper Cable (82)** (CSmith) **10-10-0** MRanger (sn bhd: wl t.o whn p.u after 4 out)		**P**	50/1	—	—
				(SP 123.6%)		**10 Rn**

4m 39.0 (24.00) CSF £18.20 CT £44.16 TOTE £2.80: £1.20 £2.50 £1.30 (£17.00) Trio £13.10 OWNER Mrs S. Sunter (BRANDSBY) BRED J. Sunter
LONG HANDICAP Copper Cable 9-2
1717* Netherby Said has changed stables, and won really well, leaving nothing to chance, although he still tended to go to his right. (7/4)
1826 Marble Man (IRE) put up a decent show but always found the winner too good. Nevertheless this should stand him in good stead. (9/1)
1657 Aljadeer (USA) never looked all that happy but was given a strong ride. His jumping leaves plenty to be desired. (3/1)
1843 Real Glee (IRE) spoilt his chance by making mistakes throughout. (8/1: op 5/1)
2009 Dr Rocket was soon found out once the pace lifted. (12/1)

2675 WEST RASEN STANDARD OPEN N.H. FLAT RACE (4, 5 & 6-Y.O) (Class H)

4-10 (4-15) **1m 5f 110y** £1,287.00 (£357.00: £171.00)

				SP	RR	SF
	Invercargill (NZ) (CJMann) **5-10-11**(7) DKiernan (a.p: led over 1f out: r.o)	—	**1**	10/1	55 f	—
	Noble Tom (IRE) (RCollins) **5-11-4** RJohnson (prom: led 2f out tl over 1f out: kpt on wl)	¾	**2**	16/1	54 f	—
	Alisande (IRE) (JAGlover) **5-10-10**(3) MrCBonner (lw: hld up: hdwy 3f out: styd on: nt pce to chal)	1¾	**3**	8/1	47 f	—
1296[11]	**Jessica One (IRE)** (MrsMReveley) **6-10-13** PNiven (rr div: hdwy 5f out: prom 2f out: kpt on one pce)	1¾	**4**	7/4[1]	45 f	—
	Juniper Hill (KAMorgan) **5-11-4** ASSmith (chsd ldrs: nt qckn fnl 3f)	1¼	**5**	9/2[2]	49 f	—
	Donnegale (IRE) (TPTate) **5-10-11**(7) RMcCarthy (plld hrd: prom tl outpcd 5f out: n.d after)	2	**6**	8/1	46 f	—
	Blaster Watson (CSmith) **6-11-4** MRanger (led 2f: cl up: led 6f out to 2f out: wknd)	6	**7**	16/1	39 f	—
2510[9]	**Lost In The Post (IRE)** (CWThornton) **4-9-13**(7) NHorrocks (led after 2f to 6f out: cl up tl wknd fnl 2f)	1¾	**8**	8/1	30 f	—
	Dig For Gold (MissSEHall) **4-10-6** NBentley (bit bkwd: hld up: hdwy ½-wy: outpcd fnl 4f)	¾	**9**	5/1[3]	29 f	—
	My Vantage (MWEasterby) **4-10-3**(3) GParkin (bhd: effrt 5f out: c wd st: n.d)	8	**10**	16/1	20 f	—
	Gymcrak-Gypsy (GHolmes) **5-10-13** RGarritty (hld up: n.d)	2½	**11**	14/1	19 f	—
	Tycoon Prince (DShaw) **4-10-6b**[1] MBrennan (chsd ldrs: hrd rdn 5f out: sn btn)	9	**12**	16/1	6 f	—
	Farm Talk (MESowersby) **5-11-4** DParker (bit bkwd: bhd fnl 5f)	28	**13**	25/1	—	—
	Magnus Maximus (MrsSLamyman) **5-11-4** BClifford (bhd most of wy)	3½	**14**	25/1	—	—
1665[12]	**Byhookorbycrook (IRE)** (JCullinan) **5-10-13** VSlattery (plld hrd: rdn 6f out: sn lost tch)	hd	**15**	33/1	—	—
				(SP 154.5%)		**15 Rn**

3m 20.2 CSF £182.08 TOTE £21.60: £4.70 £4.20 £2.70 (£156.60) Trio Not won; £133.45 to Lingfield 22/1/97 OWNER Mrs P. Dodd (UPPER LAMBOURN) BRED R. A. and T. C. Williams

WEIGHT FOR AGE 4yo-5lb
Invercargill (NZ) won this well and should have the speed for the minimum trip over hurdles. (10/1: op 6/1)
Noble Tom (IRE), from a yard whose horses are running well at present, showed plenty and should be all the better for the run. (16/1)
Alisande (IRE), a decent type, should improve and may well prefer easier ground. (8/1: op 5/1)
Jessica One (IRE) got into the race turning for home, only then to lack a finishing kick. (7/4)
Juniper Hill looks the type to improve as he gains experience. (9/2)
Donnegale (IRE) spoilt his chances by running too freely in the early stages. (8/1)

T/Jkpt: £9,638.80 (0.09 Tckts); £12,354.07 to Lingfield 22/1/97. T/Plpt: £69.10 (171.28 Tckts). T/Qdpt: £6.50 (177.8 Tckts) AA

2371-LINGFIELD (L-H) (Soft)
Wednesday January 22nd

Race 7- due to bad light placings confirmed for first 5 only.
WEATHER: damp

2676 PORTCULLIS NOVICES' AMATEUR HURDLE (4-Y.O+) (Class E)
1-10 (1-12) **2m 7f (12 hdls)** £2,687.50 (£750.00: £362.50) GOING: 1.33 sec per fur (HY)

				SP	RR	SF
1568^{3}	**Kind Cleric** (PJHobbs) **6-11-5**(7) MrSMulcaire (rdn & hdwy appr 2 out: blnd last: led flat: r.o wl)	—	**1**	8/1	75	41
1835*	**Emerald Statement (IRE) (107)** (DMGrissell) **7-12-0**(5) MrRThornton (hdwy 4th: rdn 7th: led 3 out: hrd rdn appr last: hdd flat: r.o)	¾	**2**	5/2^{1}	82	48
2546^{4}	**Quini Eagle (FR)** (MCPipe) **5-11-7**(5) MrAFarrant (lw: a.p: led 7th to 3 out: wknd appr last: t.o)	dist	**3**	9/1	—	—
	Clarkes Gorse (IRE) (JTGifford) **6-11-5**(7) MrPO'Keeffe (bit bkwd: a bhd: t.o)	7	**4**	7/1^{3}	—	—
2552^{7}	**Mahler (95)** (NATwiston-Davies) **7-11-9**(3) MrMRimell (led 2nd to 7th: wknd appr 3 out: t.o)	¾	**5**	16/1	—	—
1639^{P}	**Drum Battle (92)** (WGMTurner) **5-11-5**(7) MrEBabington (prom to 9th: t.o)	18	**6**	25/1	—	—
1260*	**Minella Derby (IRE)** (PFNicholls) **7-11-12**(7) MrJTizzard (prom to 9th: t.o)	10	**7**	7/2^{2}	—	—
1795^{2}	**Fine Sir (103)** (TThomsonJones) **7-11-12** MrMArmytage (hdwy 6th: wknd 9th: t.o whn p.u bef 2 out)		**P**	7/1^{3}	—	—
1638^{7}	**Bayerd (IRE) (97)** (CREgerton) **6-11-12b^{1}**(7) MrEJames (a bhd: t.o whn p.u bef 2 out)		**P**	20/1	—	—
	Ryder Cup (IRE) (NJHenderson) **5-11-7**(5) MrCVigors (lw: led to 2nd: wknd 4th: t.o whn p.u bef 3 out)		**P**	10/1	—	—
1729^{4}	**Zadok** (JFfitch-Heyes) **5-11-5**(7) MrGShenkin (a bhd: t.o whn p.u bef 3 out)		**P**	50/1	—	—
	Letmo Warrior (IRE) (KRBurke) **5-11-7**(5) MrLEBalogh (a bhd: t.o whn p.u bef 2 out)		**P**	50/1	—	—
1633^{10}	**Lucky Tanner** (MissHCKnight) **6-11-5**(7) MrAWintle (prom to 9th: t.o whn p.u bef 2 out)		**P**	50/1	—	—
1938^{12}	**Eau So Sloe** (JRPoulton) **6-11-5**(7) MrJGoldstein (bhd fr 5th: t.o whn p.u bef 2 out)		**P**	100/1	—	—
1573^{14}	**Fortunes Gleam (IRE)** (JSKing) **6-11-2**(5) MrASansome (bhd fr 4th: t.o fr 7th: p.u bef 3 out)		**P**	100/1	—	—
	Rakaposhi Imp (CHJones) **7-11-0**(7) MissBSmall (a bhd: mstke 5th: t.o whn p.u bef 7th)		**P**	100/1	—	—

(SP 129.3%) **16 Rn**

6m 3.6 (40.60) CSF £26.89 TOTE £8.30: £1.70 £1.20 £3.10 (£11.30) Trio £48.90 OWNER The Hammer Partnership (MINEHEAD) BRED Woodfield Stables

1568 Kind Cleric was well-suited by this thorough test of stamina. Picking up ground running down the hill, it looked as if he had thrown his chances away when making a bad error at the last. He kept on really well and managed to get the better of the runner-up on the flat. (8/1: op 5/1)
1835* Emerald Statement (IRE) looked like maintaining his unbeaten record as he moved to the front three from home. He became very leg-weary in the testing conditions and was collared on the run-in, but finished miles clear of the third. He should soon regain the winning thread. (5/2)
2546 Quini Eagle (FR) went on early on the final circuit but he was collared three out, and was left for dead by the front two going to the last. (9/1)
Clarkes Gorse (IRE) won an Irish Point-To-Point in the mud last year. Not looking fully wound up for this debut over hurdles, he never threatened to get into it. (7/1)
2552 Mahler found this trip too far and, after making the running for the first circuit, was very tired going to the third last. (16/1)
1795 Fine Sir (7/1: 5/1-8/1)
Ryder Cup (IRE) (10/1: 6/1-12/1)

2677 RAMPART 'N.H.' MAIDEN HURDLE (4-Y.O+) (Class D)
1-40 (1-43) **2m 110y (8 hdls)** £3,091.40 (£870.40: £426.20) GOING: 1.33 sec per fur (HY)

				SP	RR	SF
1551^{2}	**Splendid Thyne** (TCasey) **5-11-7** MAFitzgerald (hld up: rdn appr 2 out: led appr last: r.o wl)	—	**1**	4/1^{1}	80	33
	Sursum Corda (CaptTAForster) **6-11-7** RDunwoody (hdwy 5th: led after 3 out tl appr last: ev ch flat: unable qckn)	1¼	**2**	4/1^{1}	79	32
1938^{8}	**Jakes Justice (IRE)** (JTGifford) **6-11-7** PHide (a.p: ev ch 2 out: wknd appr last)	11	**3**	14/1	68	21
1685^{2}	**Dark Orchard (IRE)** (WRMuir) **6-11-7** MRichards (hdwy 4th: ev ch 2 out: wknd appr last)	¾	**4**	10/1	67	20
2503^{4}	**Lively Encounter (IRE)** (MrsMerritaJones) **6-11-7** DerekByrne (led to 4th: wknd 3 out)	10	**5**	5/1^{2}	58	11
1551^{4}	**Charlie's Folly** (BdeHaan) **6-11-7** JOsborne (hdwy 4th: wknd 3 out)	6	**6**	25/1	52	5
	Uprising (IRE) (JABOld) **7-11-7** SMcNeill (a.p: led 4th tl appr 3 out: wknd appr 2 out)	¾	**7**	25/1	51	4
2012^{6}	**Brookhampton Lane (IRE)** (MrsAJBowlby) **6-11-7** BPowell (a.p: led appr 3 out tl after 3 out: wknd 2 out)	2	**8**	25/1	49	2
1044^{4}	**Cyphratis (IRE)** (MrsJPitman) **6-11-7** WMarston (hdwy 3rd: wknd appr 2 out)	9	**9**	9/1	41	—
1665^{2}	**Zander** (NATwiston-Davies) **5-11-7** DBridgwater (bit bkwd: prom to 3 out)	18	**10**	12/1	23	—
1966^{4}	**Supreme Troglodyte (IRE)** (CPMorlock) **5-11-2** JRKavanagh (nvr nrr)	s.h	**11**	20/1	18	—
1966^{8}	**Benji** (TCasey) **6-11-7** NWilliamson (a bhd)	nk	**12**	50/1	23	—
1782^{4}	**Mullintor (IRE)** (RRowe) **6-11-7** DO'Sullivan (bhd fr 5th)	6	**13**	20/1	17	—
	Zaisan (IRE) (JTGifford) **4-10-6**(3) LAspell (bit bkwd: a bhd)	2½	**14**	25/1	14	—
	Thirty Below (IRE) (JABOld) **8-11-7** GUpton (bit bkwd: a bhd)	1¾	**15**	25/1	13	—
	Double Achievement (IRE) (MCPipe) **7-11-7** APMcCoy (a bhd: t.o)	20	**16**	14/1	—	—
	Ilewinit (IRE) (PCRitchens) **8-11-7** SFox (bit bkwd: a bhd: t.o)	2½	**17**	50/1	—	—
	Calm Down (IRE) (TCasey) **6-11-7** AThornton (bit bkwd: prom to 3rd: reins broke: t.o)	½	**18**	33/1	—	—
	Shouldhavesaidno (IRE) (THind) **6-11-2** PMcLoughlin (bhd fr 4th: t.o whn p.u after 3 out)		**P**	50/1	—	—
	Single Sourcing (IRE) (MissHCKnight) **6-11-7** JFTitley (bhd whn p.u bef 5th: b.b.v)		**P**	15/2^{3}	—	—

(SP 146.1%) **20 Rn**

4m 14.5 (29.50) CSF £18.30 TOTE £4.10: £1.80 £2.50 £3.50 (£13.90) Trio £259.70; £102.45 to Huntingdon 23/1/97 OWNER Mr John Galvanoni (DORKING) BRED Mrs S. C. Welch

WEIGHT FOR AGE 4yo-12lb
OFFICIAL EXPLANATION **Single Sourcing (IRE): bled from the nose.**
1551 Splendid Thyne stalked the leaders. Bustled along in the straight, he had a tremendous duel to get on top approaching the last, but kept on too well for the runner-up. (4/1: 3/1-9/2)
Sursum Corda made a very pleasing debut over hurdles. Sent to the front soon after the third last, he had a tremendous battle with the winner from the penultimate hurdle, and may even have got his head in front again for a few strides on the run-in before the winner asserted. He should soon be winning. (4/1: 6/1-7/2)
1388 Jakes Justice (IRE) had every chance at the second last before being left for dead by the front two going to the final flight. (14/1)
1685 Dark Orchard (IRE), one of several with every chance jumping the penultimate hurdle, had come to the end of his tether going to the last. (10/1: 7/1-12/1)
2503 Lively Encounter (IRE), in front to halfway, had bellows to mend three from home. (5/1)
1044 Cyphratis (IRE) (9/1: 5/1-10/1)

2678 MOAT (S) HURDLE (4,5,6 & 7-Y.O) (Class G)

2-10 (2-13) **2m 110y (8 hdls)** £2,219.10 (£617.60: £297.30) GOING: 1.33 sec per fur (HY)

Form	Horse	Dist	Pos	SP	RR	SF
1451[6]	**Bella Sedona (92)** (LadyHerries) **5-11-0** RDunwoody (bdly hmpd 1st: gd hdwy fr 2 out: str run flat: led last strides)	—	1	5/2[1]	56+	—
	One In The Eye (JRPoulton) **4-10-7** ADicken (hdwy 3rd: j.rt 2 out: hrd rdn appr last: led flat: hdd last strides)	nk	2	50/1	61	—
2050[8]	**Arch Angel (IRE)** (GFHCharles-Jones) **4-10-3**[ow1] MrACharles-Jones (lw: hdwy 3 out: led last tl flat: r.o)	½	3	20/1	56	—
1786[3]	**Laura Lye (IRE) (70)** (BdeHaan) **7-11-0** GUpton (hdwy 4th: led 2 out: hrd drvn: hdd last: unable qckn)	4	4	20/1	51	—
2574[4]	**Rose of Glenn** (BPalling) **6-11-0** RFarrant (a.p: led 5th to 2 out: ev ch flat: one pce)	nk	5	9/1	51	—
1786[P]	**Tread the Boards (85)** (MCPipe) **6-11-0** APMcCoy (hdwy 3 out: ev ch 2 out: hrd rdn: one pce)	2	6	13/2[3]	49	—
	Celtic Lilley (53) (JFfitch-Heyes) **7-11-0b** BFenton (nvr nr to chal)	8	7	50/1	41	—
1953[7]	**Code Red** (WRMuir) **4-10-7** MRichards (lw: prom tl appr 2 out)	12	8	7/1	35	—
1595[U]	**Ewar Bold** (KOCunningham-Brown) **4-10-7** DGallagher (j.rt 1st: nvr nrr)	3	9	20/1	32	—
27[7]	**Jobber's Fiddle (69)** (DLWilliams) **5-11-0** NWilliamson (bit bkwd: a mid div)	3	10	20/1	24	—
295[7]	**Dr Dave (IRE)** (PRChamings) **6-11-5** AThornton (hdwy appr 3 out: sn wknd)	2	11	16/1	27	—
2050[F]	**Flash In The Pan (IRE)** (JSMoore) **4-10-2** WMcFarland (bhd fr 4th)	14	12	4/1[2]	8	—
2070[9]	**Half An Inch (IRE)** (TMJones) **4-10-7b** BPowell (led to 3rd: wknd 5th)	8	13	25/1	6	—
	Another Fiddle (IRE) (BAPearce) **7-11-5** TJMurphy (bit bkwd: bhd fr 5th)	8	14	20/1	—	—
73[P]	**Sayitagain** (JRJenkins) **5-11-5** JOsborne (bit bkwd: bhd fr 4th: t.o)	24	15	33/1	—	—
1424[P]	**Franks Jester** (MrsJPitman) **6-11-5** WMarston (prom to 4th: t.o)	dist	16	25/1	—	—
1862[5]	**Haute Cuisine** (RJRWilliams) **4-10-7** JRKavanagh (a.p: led 3rd to 5th: wknd appr 3 out: t.o whn p.u bef last)		P	14/1	—	—
1964[P]	**Sullamell** (RJHodges) **6-11-5** SBurrough (bhd fr 4th: t.o whn p.u bef 2 out)		P	33/1	—	—
1953[16]	**Supergold (IRE)** (CMurray) **4-10-7b** KGaule (prom tl appr 3 out: t.o whn p.u bef last)		P	33/1	—	—
476[P]	**Kirkie Cross** (KGWingrove) **5-11-0b[1]** JRyan (prom to 5th: t.o whn p.u bef last)		P	50/1	—	—
1770[P]	**Tomorrows Harvest** (RJHodges) **5-10-11**(3) TDascombe (a bhd: t.o fr 3rd: p.u bef 2 out)		P	50/1	—	—
				(SP 145.1%)	**21 Rn**	

4m 21.7 (36.70) CSF £156.86 TOTE £2.90: £1.60 £25.50 £46.00 (£424.30) Trio £191.80; £216.12 to Huntingdon 23/1/97 OWNER Mr E. Reitel (LITTLEHAMPTON) BRED Mrs E. Longton
WEIGHT FOR AGE 4yo-12lb
Bt in 5,000 gns
STEWARDS' ENQUIRY Upton susp. 31/1-1/2 & 3-4/2/97 (excessive use of whip).
1451 Bella Sedona was given a tremendous ride. Badly hampered at the first, she was well adrift of her rivals and still appeared to have no chance entering the straight - only disputing eighth place and with plenty of ground to make up. She sprouted wings and came flying through despite the testing conditions, to snatch the spoils in the last couple of strides. (5/2)
One In The Eye made a pleasing debut over hurdles. Despite jumping to his right at the second last as he began to get on terms, he eventually managed to force his head in front on the run-in, only to be caught by the whirlwind finish of the winner. (50/1)
1908 Arch Angel (IRE) moved up to the leaders three out and showed with a narrow advantage at the last. Collared by the runner-up on the run-in, she grimly stuck on but, in the end, had to settle for third. (20/1)
1786 Laura Lye (IRE) went to the front two out and came under extreme pressure from her rider. Wandering about slightly, she was collared at the last and failed to find another gear. (20/1)
2574 Rose of Glenn appreciated the underfoot conditions. Showing in front at the fifth, she was collared two out, but refused to give way without a fight. Still in with every chance on the run-in, she was then just tapped for toe. (9/1)
Tread the Boards, one of a host of horses with every chance at the penultimate hurdle, then just lacked that vital turn of foot. (13/2)

2679 FORT NOVICES' H'CAP CHASE (0-105) (5-Y.O+) (Class E)

2-40 (2-43) **2m 4f 110y (14 fncs)** £3,570.75 (£1,071.00: £515.50: £237.75) GOING: 1.33 sec per fur (HY)

Form	Horse	Dist	Pos	SP	RR	SF
1865[4]	**Sophie May (82)** (LMontagueHall) **6-10-13b[1]** APMcCoy (hdwy 9th: led appr 3 out: r.o wl)	—	1	10/1	98	31
1552*	**Scoresheet (IRE) (93)** (JTGifford) **7-11-10** PHide (a.p: rdn appr last: unable qckn)	4	2	4/1[3]	106	39
1829[3]	**Amber Spark (IRE) (88)** (DRGandolfo) **8-11-5** RDunwoody (lw: hdwy 9th: chsd wnr 3 out tl flat: one pce)	3	3	3/1[1]	99	32
1680[8]	**Bonnifer (IRE) (69)** (MJWilkinson) **8-10-0** WMarston (mstke 8th: hdwy 4 out: sn wknd)	17	4	20/1	66	—
2077[3]	**Baroncelli (69)** (MJWilkinson) **7-10-0** ILawrence (a bhd)	8	5	25/1	60	—
2009[2]	**Juleit Jones (IRE) (90)** (JTGifford) **8-11-4**(3) LAspell (led: sn clr: hdd appr 3 out: wknd appr 2 out)	½	6	14/1	81	14
1994[B]	**Reeshloch (90)** (AndrewTurnell) **8-11-0**(7) CRae (hdwy 4 out: wknd appr 3 out)	5	7	9/1	77	10
2048[5]	**Moving Out (87)** (MissHCKnight) **9-11-4** GBradley (lw: lost pl 9th: rallied 4 out: wknd appr 3 out: t.o)	23	8	100/30[2]	56	—
1863[4]	**Victory Gate (USA) (71)** (MrsLCJewell) **12-10-2** DLeahy (a bhd: t.o whn p.u bef 9th)		P	33/1	—	—
1773[P]	**Bathwick Bobbie (81)** (DLWilliams) **10-10-9**(3) GHogan (bit bkwd: mid div whn mstke 6th: bhd fr 10th: t.o whn p.u bef 3 out)		P	20/1	—	—
1468[7]	**Parliamentarian (IRE) (85)** (TCasey) **8-11-2b[1]** MAFitzgerald (bit bkwd: prom to 6th: t.o whn p.u bef 3 out)		P	25/1	—	—
2067[P]	**Ballymgyr (IRE) (87)** (EAWheeler) **8-11-4** DGallagher (a bhd: t.o whn p.u bef 3 out)		P	20/1	—	—
	Oneofus (69) (MrsLRichards) **8-10-0** MRichards (prom to 4 out: t.o whn p.u bef 3 out)		P	33/1	—	—
1563[7]	**Bassenhally (83)** (MrsPSly) **7-11-0** RMarley (7th whn blnd & uns rdr 5th)		U	11/1	—	—
				(SP 130.0%)	**14 Rn**	

5m 34.9 (35.90) CSF £46.01 CT £143.25 TOTE £13.20: £2.90 £1.50 £1.50 (£20.00) Trio £22.10 OWNER Mr J. Daniels (EPSOM) BRED J. Daniels
LONG HANDICAP Bonnifer (IRE) 9-12

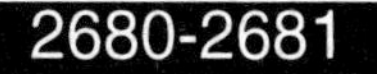

1865 Sophie May, beaten twenty one and a half lengths at Folkestone in November by Scoresheet, reversed the form on 16lb better terms. Fitted with blinkers for the first time, she moved to the front approaching the third last and soon had things nicely under control. (10/1)
1552* Scoresheet (IRE) was not given a particularly hard ride under top weight, but managed to win the battle for second prize on the run-in. (4/1)
1829 Amber Spark (IRE) is well suited by testing conditions and went in pursuit of the winner three out. He was unable to reel in that rival and was caught for the runner-up berth on the flat. (3/1)
Bonnifer (IRE) made an effort four from home but it came to little. (20/1)
2009 Juleit Jones (IRE) could not cope with this longer trip, and after setting the pace was collared approaching the third last and soon in trouble. (14/1)
1253* Bassenhally (11/1: 8/1-12/1)

2680 KEEP NOVICES' H'CAP HURDLE (0-105) (4-Y.O+) (Class E)

3-10 (3-13) **2m 110y (8 hdls)** £2,407.50 (£670.00: £322.50) GOING: 1.33 sec per fur (HY)

				SP	RR	SF
1581[3]	**None Stirred (IRE) (98)** (JTGifford) **7-11-12** PHide (a.p: hrd rdn appr last: 2nd & btn whn lft in ld last: r.o wl)	—	1	6/1[3]	80	21
2040[3]	**Sailep (FR) (97)** (RJHodges) **5-11-8**(3) TDascombe (hld up: rdn appr 2 out: lft 2nd last: unable qckn)	2½	2	8/1	77	18
	Fionans Flutter (IRE) (92) (DRCElsworth) **9-11-6** PHolley (hdwy 2 out: rdn appr last: r.o one pce)	4	3	12/1	68	9
1565[P]	**Gentle Breeze (IRE) (80)** (JTGifford) **5-10-5**(3) LAspell (hdwy 3 out: rdn appr 2 out: one pce)	¾	4	14/1	55	—
2068[U]	**King's Gold (79)** (MrsLRichards) **7-10-7** MRichards (hdwy 3 out: wknd appr last)	3	5	16/1	51	—
1998[5]	**O My Love (79)** (MissHCKnight) **6-10-7** JOsborne (lw: hdwy 3 out: rdn appr 2 out: one pce)	hd	6	12/1	51	—
1663[8]	**That Old Feeling (IRE) (72)** (JWhite) **5-10-0** TJMurphy (lw: prom to 3rd)	3½	7	16/1	41	—
2067[2]	**Museum (IRE) (82)** (PWinkworth) **6-10-3**(7) XAizpuru (a mid div)	10	8	6/1[3]	41	—
1766[3]	**Sir Dante (IRE) (85)** (RRowe) **6-10-13** DO'Sullivan (lw: bhd fr 4th)	8	9	11/2[2]	36	—
1872[11]	**Hawanafa (86)** (JSMoore) **4-10-2b**1ow2 WMcFarland (prom to 5th)	8	10	33/1	29	—
1583[6]	**Ilewin Janine (IRE) (83)** (PCRitchens) **6-10-11** SFox (led to 3 out: sn wknd)	14	11	12/1	13	—
1388[4]	**Topanga (84)** (JABennett) **5-10-12b** DBridgwater (bit bkwd: a bhd)	5	12	11/1	9	—
1729[8]	**Master Goodenough (IRE) (78)** (AGFoster) **6-9-13**(7)ow6 DCreech (hdwy 2nd: blnd 4th: sn wknd)	23	13	33/1	—	—
1772[10]	**Royal Glint (72)** (HEHaynes) **8-10-0** NWilliamson (bit bkwd: bhd fr 3rd)	8	14	16/1	—	—
1726[14]	**Murphy's Run (IRE) (72)** (PEccles) **7-9-9**(5) MrRThornton (a bhd)	hd	15	33/1	—	—
1995*	**Cool Gunner (81)** (JSKing) **7-10-9** CMaude (a.p: led 3 out tl stumbled & uns rdr last)		U	9/2[1]	—	—
				(SP 137.8%)	**16 Rn**	

4m 18.3 (33.30) CSF £55.05 CT £535.07 TOTE £6.60: £1.60 £3.20 £3.00 £4.40 (£17.20) Trio £65.20 OWNER Mr Colin Frewin (FINDON) BRED Double Wrapped Syndicate
LONG HANDICAP Hawanafa 9-0 Master Goodenough (IRE) 9-7 Royal Glint 9-7 Murphy's Run (IRE) 9-4
WEIGHT FOR AGE 4yo-12lb
OFFICIAL EXPLANATION Sir Dante (IRE): the rider reported that the gelding was unsuited by the ground and hung left throughout. When the gelding tired, he held him together. The trainer added that he would run the horse over further and on faster ground next time.
1581 None Stirred (IRE) can count himself very lucky. A leading player from the off, he was held in second when the leader got rid of his rider at the last, presenting him with the race. (6/1)
2040 Sailep (FR) has been running consistently this season. Chasing the leaders, she was booked for third when the leader unseated his rider at the last, handing him second prize. (8/1)
Fionans Flutter (IRE), without a run in thirteen months, struggled on in the straight to take third prize. (12/1)
Gentle Breeze (IRE) took closer order three out, but was only treading water in the straight. (14/1: 10/1-16/1)
King's Gold, reverting to hurdles after an unsuccessful time over fences this season, took closer order three out, but had cooked his goose soon after the penultimate hurdle. (16/1)
O My Love moved up onto the heels of the leaders three from home, but despite her rider's efforts, could only go up and down in the same place in the straight. (12/1: 8/1-16/1)
1995* Cool Gunner moved to the front three out, and had mastered None Stirred when stumbling on landing at the final flight, torpedoing his rider out of the saddle. Compensation awaits. (9/2)

2681 DAVE FREEMAN MEMORIAL H'CAP CHASE (0-105) (5-Y.O+) (Class F)

3-40 (3-43) **3m (18 fncs)** £3,014.50 (£847.00: £413.50) GOING: 1.33 sec per fur (HY)

				SP	RR	SF
2011[P]	**Brave Buccaneer (105)** (AndrewTurnell) **10-11-7**(7) CRae (hdwy 13th: hrd rdn appr last: led flat: r.o wl)	—	1	25/1	118	24
1684[2]	**Eastern River (85)** (CaptTAForster) **11-10-8** SWynne (lw: a.p: led after 4 out tl flat: unable qckn)	2½	2	4/1[1]	96	2
1837[4]	**Black Church (90)** (RRowe) **11-10-13** DO'Sullivan (hdwy 4 out: rdn appr last: r.o one pce)	1¼	3	14/1	101	7
2075[3]	**Carlingford Lakes (IRE) (87)** (TThomsonJones) **9-10-10** MAFitzgerald (hld up: hrd rdn appr last: r.o one pce)	¾	4	16/1	97	3
	Darren the Brave (100) (CPEBrooks) **9-11-9** GBradley (a.p: ev ch whn stumbled 3 out: ev ch whn stumbled bdly 2 out: nt rcvr)	21	5	6/1[3]	96	2
1829*	**Sugar Hill (IRE) (90)** (JTGifford) **7-10-13** PHide (led tl after 4 out: sn wknd)	2	6	11/2[2]	85	—
	Little-Nipper (95) (RJSmith) **12-11-4** CMaude (hdwy 7th: wknd 4 out)	16	7	33/1	79	—
	Keano (IRE) (93) (PJHobbs) **8-11-2** APMcCoy (bhd fr 4 out)	2½	8	7/1	75	—
1717[P]	**Zambezi Spirit (IRE) (96)** (MrsMerritaJones) **8-11-5** DerekByrne (a bhd)	3½	9	10/1	76	—
2052[F]	**Oats N Barley (88)** (PRRodford) **8-10-11** SBurrough (bit bkwd: a bhd)	16	10	8/1	57	—
	Valnau (FR) (81) (MCPipe) **10-9-11b**(7) GSupple (bhd whn fell 8th)		F	16/1	—	—
1839[4]	**Mighty Frolic (100)** (MissSEdwards) **10-11-9** MrTHills (hdwy 6th: wknd appr 3 out: t.o whn p.u bef last)		P	33/1	—	—
2011[P]	**Sheelin Lad (IRE) (86)** (MrsTJMcInnesSkinner) **9-10-9** GUpton (prom to 9th: t.o whn p.u bef 3 out)		P	20/1	—	—
2011[P]	**Mweenish (86)** (PRWebber) **15-10-9** RBellamy (mstke 12th: bhd fr 13th: t.o whn p.u bef 3 out)		P	50/1	—	—
487[4]	**Spikey (NZ) (85)** (JRJenkins) **11-10-8** JOsborne (bhd tl p.u bef 7th: dismntd)		P	25/1	—	—
2063[P]	**Chief Rager (104)** (NATwiston-Davies) **8-11-13** DBridgwater (mid div whn mstke 2nd: bhd whn mstke 9th: t.o whn p.u bef 10th)		P	14/1	—	—
	Professor Strong (IRE) (103) (PFNicholls) **9-11-12** NWilliamson (bit bkwd: t.o whn p.u bef 10th)		P	8/1	—	—
1711[P]	**Little Rowley (77)** (MrsLRichards) **8-10-0** MRichards (bhd fr 12th: t.o whn p.u bef 3 out)		P	50/1	—	—
				(SP 140.8%)	**18 Rn**	

6m 43.4 (49.40) CSF £123.56 CT £1,417.05 TOTE £38.20: £4.50 £1.70 £3.80 £2.50 (£190.20) Trio £681.20 OWNER Mr R. C. Watts (WANTAGE) BRED Gerard McMahon
LONG HANDICAP Little Rowley 8-11
OFFICIAL EXPLANATION Professor Strong (IRE): finished distressed.

2011 Brave Buccaneer bounced back to form on ground he loves, despite his welter burden. Taking closer order a mile out, he eventually managed to get on top on the flat. (25/1)
1684 Eastern River went to the front soon after the fourth last, and grimly fought off his rivals until caught by the winner on the run-in. (4/1: 5/2-9/2)
1837 Black Church moved up smoothly four from home, but did not find a great deal off the bridle. (14/1)
2075 Carlingford Lakes (IRE) chased the leaders and stayed on for fourth. (16/1)
Darren the Brave, off the course since May '95, did not have luck on his side. A leading player from the off, he did not help his cause by stumbling three out and at the next, from which he failed to recover. On this evidence he is certainly up to winning a small race. (6/1)
1829* Sugar Hill (IRE) took the field along but, collared at the top of the hill, was soon in trouble. (11/2)
Keano (IRE) (7/1: 5/1-8/1)
1717 Zambezi Spirit (IRE) (10/1: 7/1-12/1)
Professor Strong (IRE) (8/1: op 5/1)

2682 WEATHERBYS 'STARS OF TOMORROW' STANDARD OPEN N.H. FLAT RACE (4, 5 & 6-Y.O) (Class H)
4-10 (4-15) **2m 110y** £1,306.00 (£366.00: £178.00)

				SP	RR	SF
2073*	**Arkley Royal** (JABOld) **6-11-11** GUpton (lw: hdwy 6f out: led over 1f out tl ins fnl f: rdn: led last stride)	—	1	13/8 1	62 f	—
	Edmond (FR) (CaptTAForster) **5-11-4** AThornton (hdwy 8f out: led over 3f out tl over 1f out: led ins fnl f: hdd last stride)	s.h	2	9/1	55 f	—
	Mister Ermyn (LMontagueHall) **4-10-6** DMorris (hdwy 7f out: rdn over 1f out: r.o)	1	3	33/1	54 f	—
	Rasak (LadyHerries) **5-11-4** EMurphy (lw: gd hdwy 6f out: shkn up over 2f out: r.o ins fnl f)	1½	4	100/30 2	53 f	—
	Bigsound (IRE) (MissVenetiaWilliams) **5-11-4** NWilliamson (bit bkwd: hld up: ev ch over 1f out: wknd fnl f)	5	5	8/1 3	48 f	—
	Wisley Warrior (NATwiston-Davies) **6-11-4** CMaude (a.p: led over 6f out tl over 3f out: sn wknd)	6	6	12/1	42 f	—
	Bold Leap (PRWebber) **5-11-4** MrASansome (rangy: lost pl 11f out: r.o one pce fnl 3f)	21	7	33/1	22 f	—
	Welsh Asset (KGWingrove) **6-10-11**(7) MrAWintle (nvr nrr)	2	8	40/1	20 f	—
	Dante's Gold (IRE) (CREgerton) **6-11-4** JOsborne (hdwy over 7f out: wknd over 5f out)	2½	9	14/1	17 f	—
	Fred Moth (THind) **4-10-6** PMcLoughlin (bit bkwd: led 10f: wknd over 3f out)	6	10	40/1	11 f	—
	Norlandic (NZ) (PJHobbs) **5-11-4** MAFitzgerald (hld up: rdn over 3f out: sn wknd)	5	11	16/1	7 f	—
1203 10	**Frankie Muck** (NATwiston-Davies) **5-11-4** DBridgwater (bit bkwd: prom 14f)	1	12	20/1	6 f	—
	Caldebrook (IRE) (JTGifford) **6-10-11**(7) SLaird (bit bkwd: hld up: rdn over 3f out: sn wknd)		13	20/1	—	—
	Kaz Kalem (IRE) (PJHobbs) **5-11-4** GTormey (bit bkwd: bhd fnl 4f)		14	10/1	—	—
	Good Time Dancer (PRWebber) **5-10-13** MrPScott (rather unf: prom over 9f)		15	16/1	—	—
	Whod of Thought It (IRE) (PRChamings) **6-10-13**(5) MrCVigors (hdwy over 11f out: wknd over 5f out)		16	100/1	—	—
	Tedross (MissAMNewton-Smith) **6-10-13**(5) MrRThornton (bit bkwd: w ldr over 8f: t.o)		17	40/1	—	—
	Beckamere (PButler) **5-10-13** TJMurphy (bhd fnl 10f: t.o)		18	66/1	—	—
	X-Ray (IRE) (JRJenkins) **4-10-6** GBradley (w.r.s: a bhd: t.o)		19	33/1	—	—
				(SP 145.6%)	**19 Rn**	

4m 14.9 CSF £17.67 TOTE £2.70: £1.60 £4.80 £11.30 (£22.40) Trio £193.40; £92.64 to Huntingdon 23/1/97 OWNER Mr John Bickel (WROUGHTON) BRED S. Pike
WEIGHT FOR AGE 4yo-12lb
2073* Arkley Royal, travelling smoothly turning into the straight, took control below the distance, but he certainly did not have things as easy as he had here last month, and was collared inside the final furlong. With his pilot having to get serious he managed to force a nostril in front on the line. (13/8: 5/4-2/1)
Edmond (FR), a half-brother to several winners in France, gained a narrow lead early in the straight. Collared below the distance, he put his head back in front again in the final furlong. In a desperate finish, the photo revealed he had been beaten a whisker. (9/1)
Mister Ermyn took closer order soon after halfway, and stayed on in the final quarter-mile to finish on the heels of the front two. (33/1)
Rasak is bred in the purple being by Kris out of a French Oaks winner. He showed plenty of promise on this debut, making giant strides to get into the action at the top of the hill. Shaken up in the straight, he kept on nicely inside the final furlong to finish a pleasing fourth. He will have learnt a lot here and can step up on this before long. (100/30: 2/1-7/2)
Bigsound (IRE), a nice type, looked as though the run would do him good and so it proved. Throwing down his challenge in the straight, he still had every chance below the distance before tiring in the testing conditions. (8/1: op 4/1)
Wisley Warrior was sent to the front going to the top of the hill, but he was collared and soon in trouble entering the straight. (12/1: 8/1-14/1)
Dante's Gold (IRE) (14/1: 8/1-16/1)

T/Jkpt: Not won; £15,891.71 to Huntingdon 23/1/97. T/Plpt: £93.60 (177.06 Tckts). T/Qdpt: £28.50 (44.89 Tckts) AK

2378-SEDGEFIELD (L-H) - Wednesday January 22nd
2683 Abandoned-Frost

2553-HUNTINGDON (R-H) (Good becoming Good to soft)
Thursday January 23rd
WEATHER: misty

2690 OFFORD 'N.H.' NOVICES' HURDLE (4-Y.O+) (Class E)
1-20 (1-20) **2m 110y (8 hdls)** £3,055.00 (£855.00: £415.00) GOING: 0.57 sec per fur (S)

				SP	RR	SF
2010 11	**Legible (105)** (SMellor) **9-11-5** RJohnson (bit bkwd: hdwy 4th: led flat: jst hld on)	—	1	14/1	80	49
1830 8	**Clinton (IRE)** (KCBailey) **6-11-5** AThornton (hit 1st: hdwy appr 2 out: str run flat: jst failed)	hd	2	25/1	80	49
	Sierra Bay (IRE) (OSherwood) **7-11-5** JOsborne (bit bkwd: in tch: hdwy 4th: led 2 out tl flat: wknd)	1¾	3	15/8 1	78+	47
1457 3	**Shekels (IRE)** (CPEBrooks) **6-11-5** DGallagher (lw: plld hrd: a.p: ev ch 2 out: one pce)	3	4	16/1	75	44
1867 2	**Nasone (IRE)** (JTGifford) **6-11-5** PHide (lw: chsd ldr: led 3rd to next: led 5th to 2 out: wknd flat)	hd	5	2/1 2	75	44
1907 F	**Henrys Port (95)** (MartynMeade) **7-11-5** MRichards (in tch: outpcd 4th: kpt on wl fr 2 out)	3	6	40/1	72	41
2080*	**Cherrymore (IRE)** (MrsJPitman) **6-11-5** WMarston (plld hrd: chsd ldrs: hit 5th: btn whn mstke 2 out)	3	7	4/1 3	69	38
1867 6	**Physical Fun** (AGBlackmore) **6-11-5** DSkyrme (bit bkwd: nvr nrr)	5	8	50/1	65	34
	Harlequin Chorus (JABOld) **7-11-5** GUpton (chsd ldrs: no imp fr 3 out)	5	9	25/1	60	29
1964 7	**Kybo's Revenge (IRE)** (RRowe) **6-11-5** DO'Sullivan (nvr nr to chal)	nk	10	50/1	59	28
1729 7	**Reverse Thrust** (PRHedger) **6-10-12**(7) MClinton (in tch: hdwy & ev ch 5th: wknd next)	1¼	11	33/1	58	27
	Libertarian (IRE) (OSherwood) **7-11-2**(3) GHogan (a bhd)	2	12	33/1	56	25

2079[U]	**Glenmavis** (DrPPritchard) **10-11-5** DrPPritchard (hdwy whn hit 4th: sn wknd)	7	**13**	50/1	50	19
2010[3]	**Ferrers (90)** (MrsPSly) **6-11-5** RMarley (lw: led to 3rd: led 4th to next: wknd after 3 out)	4	**14**	20/1	46	15
2547[13]	**Tidal Force (IRE)** (PJHobbs) **6-11-5** MAFitzgerald (nvr nr ldrs)	1¼	**15**	12/1	44	13
2055[5]	**Supreme Charm (IRE)** (KCBailey) **5-11-5** SMcNeill (prom to 5th)	¾	**16**	16/1	44	13
1913[4]	**Tullow Lady (IRE)** (OBrennan) **6-11-0** MBrennan (a bhd: t.o whn mstke 3 out)	dist	**17**	33/1	—	—
2572[10]	**Just Andy** (BPreece) **6-11-5** TJenks (bhd fr 3rd: t.o whn p.u bef 2 out)		**P**	50/1	—	—
1583[10]	**Reach The Clouds (IRE)** (JohnUpson) **5-11-5** CMaude (bit bkwd: t.o whn p.u bef 2 out)		**P**	33/1	—	—
24[7]	**Blue Havana** (GraemeRoe) **5-11-0** JRKavanagh (a bhd: t.o whn p.u bef 2 out)		**P**	50/1	—	—
1830[13]	**Loch Garman (IRE)** (FMurphy) **7-11-5** BFenton (w ldr tl mstke 2nd: p.u lame)		**P**	50/1	—	—

(SP 152.7%) **21 Rn**

4m 1.2 (13.20) CSF £315.88 TOTE £18.20: £3.30 £8.20 £1.90 (£182.60) Trio £238.90; £235.57 to Folkestone 24/1/97 OWNER Mr S. P. Tindall (SWINDON) BRED Kiltinan Farms Inc

IN-FOCUS: Jockey Roger Marley retired after riding Ferrers in this race.

Legible has been lightly-raced over the years, but clearly has plenty of ability when right. Flat out on the run-in, he showed plenty of tenacity to hold on. (14/1)

1830 Clinton (IRE) hurdled better this time after his early error. Doing an awful lot of running in the straight, he just failed to get there in time. Opportunities await. (25/1)

Sierra Bay (IRE) missed last season with leg trouble. He covers a lot of ground and, when he hit the front early in the straight, it simply looked a matter of how far, but he did not look fully wound up and lack of a race eventually took its toll. If he can be kept sound, he remains a very interesting prospect. (15/8)

1457 Shekels (IRE), on his hurdles debut, seemed to pull too hard, but stuck to his task surprisingly well and might stay further. (16/1)

1867 Nasone (IRE) was made quite a bit more use of this time, but the tactics seemed to have found him out as he was out on his feet on the run-in. He may have needed this more than it appeared after the bad weather. (2/1)

1907 Henrys Port continues to run respectably and may do better over further. (40/1)

2080* Cherrymore (IRE) did not jump well in the second half of the race, but will hopefully have learnt plenty. (4/1)

Physical Fun is gradually getting his act together and has ability. (50/1)

Reverse Thrust was travelling strongly when making his move, but faded quickly turning for home. He could just have needed this after seven weeks off, and is well worth keeping an eye on. (33/1)

1071* Tidal Force (IRE) (12/1: op 8/1)

2691 KITTY WARD-THOMAS NOVICES' CHASE (5-Y.O+) (Class D)

1-50 (1-51) **2m 110y (12 fncs)** £4,142.50 (£1,240.00: £595.00: £272.50) GOING: 0.57 sec per fur (S)

					SP	RR	SF
1271[2]	**Lightening Lad** (JSKing) **9-11-4** CMaude (chsd ldr: led after 5th: j.rt last: rdn & r.o wl)	—	**1**	3/1[2]	117	40
1764*	**Guinda (IRE) (111)** (NATwiston-Davies) **7-11-6** DWalsh (lw: chsd ldrs: pckd 9th: ev ch appr 2 out: unable qckn flat)	3½	**2**	4/1[3]	116	39
1365[7]	**Crack On** (PJHobbs) **7-11-4** RJohnson (lw: hld up: hdwy 6th: hmpd 8th: mstke 3 out: hit last 2: kpt on)	2	**3**	9/4[1]	112	35
	Who Is Equiname (IRE) (NJHenderson) **7-11-4** MAFitzgerald (hld up: pckd 6th: stdy hdwy 3 out: nvr plcd to chal)	dist	**4**	11/1	—	—
2547[3]	**Just Bruce (83)** (MrsEHHeath) **8-11-4** KGaule (chsd ldrs to 8th)	4	**5**	33/1	—	—
	Althrey Blue (IRE) (60) (AndrewTurnell) **8-11-4** SMcNeill (bit bkwd: a bhd)	4	**6**	100/1	—	—
2549[F]	**Mr Motivator** (TKeddy) **7-11-4** ILawrence (s.i.s: a bhd)	26	**7**	50/1	—	—
1838[4]	**Warspite** (PMooney) **7-10-13**(5) SRyan (bit bkwd: hit 4th: sn bhd)	19	**8**	66/1	—	—
1994*	**Grooving (IRE)** (JTGifford) **8-11-11** PHide (swtg: in tch: hdwy & 3rd whn fell 8th)		**F**	4/1[3]	—	—
	Blair Castle (IRE) (GBBalding) **6-11-4** BFenton (bkwd: fell 1st)		**F**	12/1	—	—
	Mheanmetoo (DLWilliams) **6-11-1**(3) GHogan (bkwd: plld hrd: led & sn clr: hdd after 5th: sn wknd: mstke 8th: p.u bef next)		**P**	66/1	—	—

(SP 120.7%) **11 Rn**

4m 17.2 (15.20) CSF £14.73 TOTE £5.20: £1.60 £1.60 £1.70 (£7.80) Trio £14.80 OWNER Mr Richard Peterson (SWINDON) BRED John Brookman

1271 Lightening Lad, belatedly sent chasing after missing most of last season, jumped well apart from landing askew at the last, and looks a useful recruit. (3/1)

1764* Guinda (IRE), not as good as the winner over timber, did her best to put her experience to good use, but could not seriously trouble the winner in the final furlong. (4/1)

1365 Crack On looks the sort to take to this game, but when the chips were down his jumping was very novicey, and that spoilt his chance. (9/4)

Who Is Equiname (IRE), having only his second run in twenty-one months, jumped adequately and was not knocked about in the last mile. (11/1)

2547 Just Bruce, very keen going down, could not keep tabs much on the leaders much past halfway. (33/1)

1994* Grooving (IRE) looked rather unlucky to come down, as he appeared to jump into the back of a rival when falling. (4/1)

2692 YELLING NOVICES' H'CAP HURDLE (0-100) (4-Y.O+) (Class E)

2-20 (2-20) **2m 110y (8 hdls)** £2,582.50 (£720.00: £347.50) GOING: 0.57 sec per fur (S)

					SP	RR	SF
2006*	**Ambidextrous (IRE) (75)** (EJAlston) **5-10-1**(7) LCummins (hdwy 5th: hit next: led last: r.o wl)	—	**1**	4/1[3]	64	27
1796[4]	**Storm Tiger (IRE) (67)** (SMellor) **6-9-11v[1]**(3) EHusband (chsd ldrs: led appr 2 out: hdd last: r.o)	3	**2**	10/1	53	16
1990[3]	**Heavens Above (67)** (FMurphy) **5-10-0** BFenton (led to 3rd: sn led again: clr 5th: hdd appr 2 out: sn btn)	7	**3**	20/1	46	9
2060[4]	**Baasm (80)** (JNorton) **4-9-10**(5) BGrattan (bhd: hdwy 3 out: nvr nrr)	2½	**4**	12/1	57	8
1959[7]	**Red Light (80)** (JRJenkins) **5-10-13b** JOsborne (prom tl appr 3 out)	8	**5**	16/1	49	12
1770[6]	**Daring Ryde (72)** (JPSmith) **6-10-5**ow5 AThornton (mstke 1st: hdwy appr 3 out: nvr rchd ldrs)	1	**6**	33/1	40	—
2040[2]	**Bietschhorn Bard (90)** (DRGandolfo) **7-11-6**(3) DFortt (nvr nr to chal)	3½	**7**	9/4[1]	55	18
1729[6]	**Ottavio Farnese (91)** (AHide) **5-11-10** PHide (hdwy 4th: wknd 3 out)	1½	**8**	8/1	54	17
	Millenium Lass (IRE) (93) (MissMERowland) **9-11-12** GaryLyons (bkwd: chsd ldrs tl appr 2 out)	s.h	**9**	33/1	56	19
1768[9]	**The Brewer (67)** (JCTuck) **5-10-0** SMcNeill (swtg: n.d)	s.h	**10**	25/1	30	—
955[F]	**Nagara Sound (87)** (BPreece) **6-11-6** TJenks (a bhd)	½	**11**	14/1	50	13
1857[P]	**Persian Butterfly (67)** (RMStronge) **5-9-7**(7) GSupple (w ldr: led briefly 3rd: wknd 3 out)	15	**12**	40/1	15	—
1959[P]	**Mr Gordon Bennett (67)** (RDickin) **6-9-7**(7) XAizpuru (wl bhd fr 5th)	6	**13**	33/1	9	—
2574*	**Sam Rockett (79)** (PMooney) **4-9-9b**(5) 7x SRyan (in tch tl appr 3 out)	4	**14**	3/1[2]	18	—
1864[P]	**Rustic Gent (IRE) (67)** (MrsLCJewell) **9-10-0v** DLeahy (bkwd: in tch: wkng whn blnd 3 out)	5	**15**	33/1	1	—

	Horse		Pos	SP	RR	SF
	Marrowfat Lady (IRE) (84) (NEBerry) **6-10-10**(7) SMelrose (fell 3rd)		**F**	33/1	—	—
				(SP 142.0%)	**16 Rn**	

4m 3.8 (15.80) CSF £43.25 CT £714.90 TOTE £5.20: £1.20 £1.80 £2.60 £2.30 (£17.50) Trio £158.70; £67.08 to Folkestone 24/1/97 OWNER Mrs Carol McPhail (PRESTON) BRED Saeed Manana

LONG HANDICAP Heavens Above 9-9 The Brewer 9-12 Daring Ryde 9-8 Persian Butterfly 9-2 Mr Gordon Bennett 9-7 Sam Rockett 9-5 Rustic Gent (IRE) 9-12 Storm Tiger (IRE) 9-9

WEIGHT FOR AGE 4yo-12lb

OFFICIAL EXPLANATION **Bietschhorn Bard: had gurgled**

2006* Ambidextrous (IRE) took longer to find his stride on this sharper track, but was going away well at the finish. (4/1)

1796 Storm Tiger (IRE) got much closer to the winner than he had at Towcester, and really stuck to the task on the run-in. (10/1)

1990 Heavens Above, dropped back in trip, tried to force the pace and slip the field down the back, but he had been collared by the straight. (20/1)

2060 Baasm did his running late in the day and, despite his pedigree, does shape as though he will stay further. (12/1)

1183 Red Light does not seem to have held the form of his two runs earlier this season. (16/1)

1770 Daring Ryde, knocked back almost to last by a mistake at the first, was ridden with plenty of patience and is unlikely to ever stay beyond this trip. (33/1)

1369 Ottavio Farnese (8/1: 6/1-9/1)

Millenium Lass (IRE), ex-Irish, looked well in her coat, but in need of the run. She is not very big and so did well under topweight. (33/1)

2693 BET WITH THE TOTE (QUALIFIER) NOVICES' CHASE (6-Y.O+) (Class D)

2-50 (2-50) **3m (19 fncs)** £4,141.00 (£1,243.00: £599.00: £277.00) GOING: 0.57 sec per fur (S)

	Horse	Dist	Pos	SP	RR	SF
1963[3]	**Sir Leonard (IRE)** (OSherwood) **7-10-10** JOsborne (lw: a.p: led 9th to 14th: led 4 out to next: led last: rdn out)	—	**1**	9/2[2]	93	17
1680[U]	**The Reverend Bert (IRE)** (GBBalding) **9-10-10** BFenton (j.w: hld up: hdwy 9th: led 3 out to last: one pce)	5	**2**	10/1	90	14
1901[2]	**Wee Windy (IRE) (110)** (JTGifford) **8-10-10** PHide (lw: chsd ldrs: hit 15th: rdn 3 out: one pce)	3½	**3**	9/4[1]	87	11
2072[F]	**Mr Pickpocket (IRE) (106)** (MissHCKnight) **9-10-10** JFTitley (chsd ldrs to 4 out: styd on again fr 2 out)	7	**4**	9/2[2]	83	7
1635[P]	**Claymore Lad (60)** (JSKing) **7-10-10** TJMurphy (bit bkwd: led to 9th: led 14th to 4 out: wknd appr 2 out)	nk	**5**	50/1	83	7
1357[P]	**The Bird O'Donnell** (FMurphy) **11-10-3**(7) MrTJBarry (nt j.w: chsd ldrs to 14th)	12	**6**	14/1	75	—
1858[F]	**The Shy Padre (IRE) (90)** (MrsJPitman) **8-10-10** RFarrant (hdwy 11th: blnd 4 out: nt rcvr)	3	**7**	9/1[3]	73	—
1920[5]	**Dukes Meadow (IRE) (78)** (KCBailey) **7-10-10** AThornton (lw: chsd ldrs: hit 4th: mstkes 12th & next: sn wknd)	2½	**8**	33/1	71	—
1994[6]	**Boots N All (IRE)** (GBBalding) **7-10-10** BClifford (bit bkwd: rdn 10th: a bhd)	6	**9**	33/1	67	—
2077[4]	**Pearl Epee (85)** (DNicholson) **8-10-5** RJohnson (nt j.w: blnd bdly 5th: sn t.o: p.u bef 2 out)		**P**	16/1	—	—
2007[P]	**Strokesaver (IRE) (88)** (CPEBrooks) **7-10-10** DGallagher (bhd fr 12th: t.o whn p.u bef 3 out)		**P**	25/1	—	—
1963*	**Melnik** (MrsAJPerrett) **6-11-3** CMaude (lw: nvr gng wl: a bhd: t.o whn p.u bef 2 out)		**P**	9/2[2]	—	—
2007[P]	**Saint Keyne** (DLWilliams) **7-10-10** JRKavanagh (bkwd: a bhd: t.o whn p.u bef 2 out)		**P**	40/1	—	—
				(SP 131.1%)	**13 Rn**	

6m 24.7 (27.70) CSF £46.49 TOTE £4.20: £1.30 £3.60 £1.60 (£38.30) Trio £35.60 OWNER Mrs Jean Bishop (UPPER LAMBOURN) BRED Jeremy Hill

OFFICIAL EXPLANATION **Melnik: was later found to have been suffering from a virus.**

1963 Sir Leonard (IRE), never out of the first two, jumped soundly and stayed on best of all after looking in trouble on the home turn. (9/2)

1260 The Reverend Bert (IRE) put in a couple of marvellous leaps to join issue going down the back. After looking likely to win, he proved very one-paced once the winner rallied. (10/1)

1901 Wee Windy (IRE) was again rather a disappointment, and for one who managed to win three handicap hurdles, he looks surprisingly lacking in gears over fences so far. (9/4)

2072 Mr Pickpocket (IRE), outpaced at a vital stage, then stayed on and will come into his own when set a real test of stamina. (9/2)

Claymore Lad showed his first sign of ability and ought to be able to find a little race. (50/1)

1357 The Bird O'Donnell, a useful hunter last term, gave the impression that he might have gone quite close but for some dreadful jumping.(14/1)

1468 The Shy Padre (IRE) (9/1: 6/1-10/1)

1963* Melnik (9/2: op 5/2)

2694 SAPLEY CONDITIONAL H'CAP HURDLE (0-105) (5-Y.O+) (Class F)

3-20 (3-24) **2m 5f 110y (10 hdls)** £2,286.50 (£639.00: £309.50) GOING: 0.57 sec per fur (S)

	Horse	Dist	Pos	SP	RR	SF
1586[4]	**Madame President (IRE) (83)** (CPMorlock) **6-10-10** DFortt (a.p: led flat: rdn & r.o wl)	—	**1**	12/1	65	23
1638[3]	**Wreckless Man (86)** (JABOld) **10-10-6**(7) EGreehy (bhd: gd hdwy appr 2 out: fin fast)	1½	**2**	5/1[2]	67	25
1174[4]	**Luke Warm (73)** (DRGandolfo) **7-9-11**(3) SophieMitchell (bit bkwd: hdwy 5th: led next: clr whn hit 2 out: wknd & hdd flat)	1	**3**	12/1	53	11
1873[5]	**Swan Street (NZ) (83)** (CJMann) **6-10-7**(3) JMagee (lw: racd wd: mstke 2nd: hdwy 7th: hit 3 out: wknd next)	15	**4**	10/1	52	10
1810[3]	**Lord Rooble (IRE) (94)** (JTGifford) **6-10-11**(10) WGreatrex (lw: hdwy 5th: btn whn mstke 2 out)	6	**5**	13/2	59	17
1945[2]	**Brancher (91)** (JNorton) **6-11-4** ECallaghan (in tch: jnd ldrs 6th: wknd appr 2 out)	s.h	**6**	4/1[1]	56	14
	Bigwheel Bill (IRE) (89) (JRJenkins) **8-10-6**(10) DYellowlees (bit bkwd: chsd ldrs to 3 out)	2	**7**	33/1	52	5
2006[2]	**Polo Pony (IRE) (73)** (JohnUpson) **5-10-0** BGrattan (lw: wl bhd: sme hdwy fr 7th: n.d)	7	**8**	16/1	31	—
1958[2]	**Joy For Life (IRE) (73)** (RMStronge) **6-9-10**(4) GSupple (chsd ldrs: rdn appr 3 out: sn wknd)	2½	**9**	16/1	29	—
1718[3]	**We're in the Money (73)** (MissJBower) **13-9-4**(10) ClaudineFroggitt (prom to 4th)	11	**10**	33/1	21	—
1906[8]	**Swing Quartet (IRE) (99)** (NATwiston-Davies) **7-11-9**(3) DWalsh (prom: led after 5th to next: wknd 7th)	18	**11**	14/1	33	—
1694[6]	**Icantelya (IRE) (92)** (JWMullins) **8-11-5** PHenley (sn rdn along: prom: hit 3rd: bhd fr 5th)	15	**12**	33/1	15	—
1732[11]	**Dahlia's Best (USA) (90)** (MissMERowland) **7-11-3** GHogan (fell 1st)		**F**	33/1	—	—
2003[4]	**Moobakkr (USA) (82)** (KAMorgan) **6-10-9** RMassey (lw: led tl after 5th: wknd 7th: t.o whn p.u bef last)		**P**	8/1	—	—
1813[4]	**Maneree (94)** (NACallaghan) **10-11-7** MichaelBrennan (hmpd 1st: sn bhd: hdwy 6th: wkng whn p.u bef 2 out)		**P**	11/2[3]	—	—
1962[5]	**Lets Go Now (IRE) (73)** (MrsLCJewell) **7-10-0** GTormey (rdn 5th: sn t.o: p.u bef 2 out)		**P**	33/1	—	—
1256[6]	**Batty's Island (73)** (BPreece) **8-9-10**(4) JMogford (bit bkwd: prom to 5th: t.o whn p.u bef 2 out)		**P**	20/1	—	—
				(SP 138.9%)	**17 Rn**	

5m 22.4 (22.40) CSF £69.74 CT £698.21 TOTE £15.00: £3.80 £2.20 £2.00 £2.10 (£43.30) Trio £194.00 OWNER Sir Peter Miller (WANTAGE) BRED Godfrey Deacon

LONG HANDICAP Luke Warm 9-12 Polo Pony (IRE) 9-8 Joy For Life (IRE) 9-10 We're in the Money 9-2 Lets Go Now (IRE) 9-6

OFFICIAL EXPLANATION **Wreckless Man: the rider's instructions were to hold his mount up and make his move as late as possible. The trainer, who was happy with the ride, added that the gelding was moody and would run over further next time.**

1586 Madame President (IRE) probably found the sticky ground in her favour as stamina proved her top card. (12/1: op 7/1)

1638 Wreckless Man, detached and going nowhere down the far side, suddenly took hold of his bit turning for home, only just failing to get up. He certainly has ability. (5/1)
1174 Luke Warm seemed to have it won by the second last, but looked to need this race and again finished weakly. (12/1)
1276 Swan Street (NZ), stepping up in trip, did not seem to last home after some sloppy jumping. (10/1)
1810 Lord Rooble (IRE) was already beginning to struggle when landing on all fours at the penultimate flight. (13/2: 7/2-7/1)
1945 Brancher joined issue on the final circuit, but was under pressure and finding little on the run-in. (4/1: op 5/2)
2003 Moobakkr (USA) (8/1: op 12/1)

2695 MARCH H'CAP CHASE (0-120) (5-Y.O+) (Class D)
3-50 (3-52) **2m 110y (12 fncs)** £3,981.50 (£1,054.00: £504.50) GOING: 0.57 sec per fur (S)

				SP	RR	SF
1996^{4}	**Khalidi (IRE) (106)** (DRGandolfo) **8-11-2** JOsborne (prom: led appr 2 out to last: rallied to ld nr fin)	—	**1**	$85/40^{2}$	104	7
1949^{2}	**Aal El Aal (105)** (PJHobbs) **10-11-1** GTormey (lw: hld up: mstke 9th: led & blnd last: no ex & ct nr fin)	1	**2**	$2/1^{1}$	102	5
2621^{7}	**Count Barachois (USA) (90)** (MrsEHHeath) **9-10-0** KGaule (led: pckd 5th: hdd appr 2 out: wknd appr last)	12	**3**	$7/1^{3}$	75	—
1660^{3}	**Man Mood (FR) (110)** (CPEBrooks) **6-11-6b¹** MrEJames (chsd ldrs tl wknd qckly 8th: t.o whn p.u bef last)		**P**	$85/40^{2}$	—	—
1584^{9}	**The Flying Footman (97)** (RDickin) **11-10-7** PHide (bit bkwd: prom: hit 3rd: rdn & wknd appr 2 out: p.u bef last)		**P**	9/1	—	—
				(SP 119.8%)		**5 Rn**

4m 24.8 (22.80) CSF £7.10 TOTE £3.50: £1.90 £2.00 (£3.30) OWNER Mr T. J. Whitley (WANTAGE) BRED H. H. Aga Khan in Ireland
LONG HANDICAP Count Barachois (USA) 9-10
OFFICIAL EXPLANATION Man Mood (FR): the rider reported that the gelding gurgled and appeared unsuited by the good to soft ground.
1794 Khalidi (IRE) looked to have been let in lightly for this chasing debut, but had to pull out all the stops after jumping well for a beginner.(85/40)
1949 Aal El Aal made his move on the home turn, but after not being entirely fluent two out, jumped to the front at the last and landed in a heap in the process. He did not exactly impress with his attitude and failed to last home. (2/1: 6/4-9/4)
2009 Count Barachois (USA) is taking time to come to hand, but ought to find a race once the ground dries up. (7/1)
1660 Man Mood (FR), with his tongue tied down as usual and with first-time blinkers, went from coasting to tailing off in a matter of strides. He clearly has big problems. (85/40: 6/4-9/4)

2696 HUNTINGDON MAIDEN OPEN N.H. FLAT RACE (4, 5 & 6-Y.O) (Class H)
4-20 (4-22) **2m 110y** £1,602.00 (£447.00: £216.00)

				SP	RR	SF
2012^{3}	**King Mole** (JABOld) **6-11-5** GUpton (racd wd: hld up: hdwy 6f out: led 2f out: rdn out)	—	**1**	$85/40^{1}$	63 f	—
1329^{8}	**New Leaf (IRE)** (DRGandolfo) **5-11-2**(3) DFortt (bit bkwd: hdwy 6f out: ev ch over 1f out: r.o wl nr fin)	1¾	**2**	11/1	61 f	—
2012^{4}	**Mr Moonlight (IRE)** (CPEBrooks) **5-11-5** DGallagher (hld up: hdwy to ld 4f out: hdd 2f out: kpt on)	1	**3**	14/1	60 f	—
2066^{3}	**Merry Masquerade (IRE)** (MrsMReveley) **6-11-5** RHodge (hdwy 4f out: styd on wl appr fnl f)	1¼	**4**	$6/1^{3}$	59 f	—
	Tappers Knapp (IRE) (OSherwood) **5-11-5** JOsborne (w'like: hdwy 4f out: rdn & racd alone st: no imp)	2	**5**	$4/1^{2}$	57 f	—
	The Clarsach (CaptTAForster) **5-11-0** SWynne (neat, q str: in tch: pushed along 6f out: kpt on fnl 2f)	¾	**6**	20/1	52 f	—
	Tailormade (CaptTAForster) **5-11-5** AThornton (unf: lw: hdwy 7f out: rdn 4f out: wknd 2f out)	14	**7**	16/1	43 f	—
1966^{12}	**Eurochief** (RMStronge) **6-11-5** DWalsh (bkwd: prom: led 6f out to 4f out: wknd over 2f out)	¾	**8**	20/1	42 f	—
	Royal Team (MJWilkinson) **5-11-5** MSharratt (str: bkwd: hdwy 5f out: wknd over 2f out)	nk	**9**	33/1	42 f	—
	Pedlar's Cross (IRE) (GMMcCourt) **5-10-12**(7) RStudholme (w'like, leggy: bkwd: chsd ldrs 11f)	3	**10**	33/1	39 f	—
	Folding (MrsABarclay) **6-11-5** PHide (hunting type: prom tl wknd 4f out)	2	**11**	33/1	37 f	—
1834^{11}	**Above Suspicion (IRE)** (CJames) **5-11-5** MrEJames (bhd: hdwy 5f out: nvr trbld ldrs)	3½	**12**	33/1	34 f	—
	Green King (APJones) **5-11-5** MAFitzgerald (w'like: nvr nr ldrs)	16	**13**	20/1	18 f	—
1834^{4}	**Fiddler's Leap (IRE)** (MissHCKnight) **5-10-12**(7) MrAWintle (bit bkwd: chsd ldr 8f)	hd	**14**	20/1	18 f	—
1913^{3}	**Rachel Louise** (TKeddy) **5-11-0** SMcNeill (chsd ldrs tl rdn & wknd over 3f out)	2	**15**	12/1	11 f	—
1986^{3}	**Chasing The Moon (IRE)** (GBBalding) **5-11-5** BFenton (a bhd)	15	**16**	8/1	2 f	—
	Stonehenge Sam (IRE) (JWMullins) **5-11-5** SCurran (not big, lt made: in tch 8f)	5	**17**	33/1	—	—
2012^{11}	**Bartholomew Fair** (CADwyer) **6-11-5** ILawrence (bkwd: chsd ldrs: led 8f out to 6f out: sn wknd)	1¼	**18**	12/1	—	—
	Ardleigh Venture (MHTompkins) **4-10-2** KGaule (w'like, lengthy: bkwd: a bhd)	3½	**19**	20/1	—	—
1555^{11}	**Blameless** (MrsDHaine) **5-11-0** JFTitley (bit bkwd: a bhd)	6	**20**	25/1	—	—
2080^{8}	**Justjim** (NATwiston-Davies) **5-10-12**(7) LSuthern (prom 8f)	8	**21**	16/1	—	—
	Tupenny Smoke (GraemeRoe) **5-10-7**(7) MartinSmith (led over 8f)	19	**22**	33/1	—	—
				(SP 164.8%)		**22 Rn**

4m 0.2 CSF £28.88 TOTE £4.50: £2.90 £3.80 £4.30 (£42.90) Trio £128.10 OWNER Mrs J. Fowler (WROUGHTON) BRED W. D. Hockenhull
WEIGHT FOR AGE 4yo-12lb
2012 King Mole franked the form of last month's Towcester bumper in good style after racing wide in search of the best ground. (85/40)
New Leaf (IRE) ran much better than on his debut and will clearly stay well. (11/1)
2012 Mr Moonlight (IRE), quite a keen sort, got very much closer to the winner than he had at Towcester. (14/1: op 7/1)
2066 Merry Masquerade (IRE) again took a long time to get going, and was doing his best work at the finish. (6/1)
Tappers Knapp (IRE) crept forward on the home turn, but then went badly right-handed and raced a long way to the inside of his rivals. (4/1: op 5/2)
The Clarsach, not very big but strongly-made, did not shape too badly. (20/1)
Royal Team, quite a keen sort, was noted making good headway leaving the back straight before the effort petered out. (33/1)
1913 Rachel Louise (12/1: 7/1-14/1)
2012 Bartholomew Fair (12/1: 8/1-14/1)

T/Jkpt: Not won; £22,942.93 to Uttoxeter 24/1/97. T/Plpt: £69.70 (166.63 Tckts). T/Qdpt: £11.80 (64.06 Tckts). Dk/IM

2442-WETHERBY (L-H) (Good)
Thursday January 23rd
WEATHER: cloudy

2697 ARCTIC TERN NOVICES' HURDLE (4-Y.O+) (Class E)
1-35 (1-35) **2m (9 hdls)** £2,517.50 (£705.00: £342.50) GOING: 0.48 sec per fur (GS)

				SP	RR	SF
1504^{4}	**Whip Hand (IRE)** (JGFitzGerald) **6-11-5** PCarberry (trckd ldrs: led last: qcknd)	—	**1**	$7/2^{2}$	79+	1
1848^{10}	**Durano (96)** (TDEasterby) **6-11-5** PNiven (a cl up: led 3 out to last: no ex)	3	**2**	12/1	76	—

Khalikhoum (IRE) (SirJohnBarlowBt) **4-10-7** ADobbin (a chsng ldrs: rdn appr 3 out: one pce)........................25 **3** 14/1 51 —
Future's Trader (MDHammond) **4-10-7** RGarritty (in tch: effrt 4 out: styd on: nt pce to chal)..........................1¼ **4** 25/1 50 —
1992[7] **Bowcliffe (78)** (MrsAMNaughton) **6-11-5** MFoster (led to 3 out: grad wknd)......................................1½ **5** 20/1 48 —
2074[11] **Ballyranter** (MDHammond) **8-11-2**(3) MrCBonner (mstke 2nd: in tch: outpcd 4 out: styd on fr next)..............1¾ **6** 50/1 47 —
Noble Canonire (DShaw) **5-11-0** ASSmith (a bhd)..21 **7** 50/1 21 —
Prince Baltasar (NBycroft) **8-11-5** OPears (lost tch fr 5th)..10 **8** 100/1 16 —
Petrico (PBeaumont) **5-11-5** RSupple (a bhd: wl t.o)..dist **9** 50/1 — —
King of Sparta (OSherwood) **4-10-7** DBridgwater (prom tl mstke 4th: p.u bef next).......................... **P** 11/2[3] — —
1689[P] **Magic Times** (CGrant) **6-11-5** BStorey (lost tch fr 4th: p.u bef last).. **P** 50/1 — —
Bonny Rigg (IRE) (LLungo) **5-11-0** TReed (a bhd: p.u bef last).. **P** 50/1 — —
1305[P] **Selectric (IRE)** (JWade) **6-11-5** GCahill (chsd ldrs tl wknd qckly 4 out: p.u bef 3 out)........................ **P** 50/1 — —
1935[2] **Circus Star** (DNicholson) **4-10-7** AMaguire (lw: in tch: hdwy u.p 4 out: 5th & struggling whn blnd 3 out: p.u bef last).. **P** 4/5[1] — —
(SP 128.9%) **14 Rn**

4m 3.9 (21.90) CSF £39.25 TOTE £5.00: £1.20 £1.90 £2.50 (£16.90) Trio £85.50 OWNER Lady Lloyd Webber (MALTON) BRED Carrigbeg Stud Co Ltd

WEIGHT FOR AGE 4yo-12lb

1504 Whip Hand (IRE) looked useful on his first attempt over hurdles and, always on the bridle, won with something in hand. (7/2)

1848 Durano put up a vastly-improved performance, despite never being a match for the winner. A repeat of this will surely find him a race. (12/1: op 6/1)

Khalikhoum (IRE) looked very fit for this debut over hurdles but, once the pressure was applied approaching three out, he looked one-paced. (14/1)

Future's Trader ran a reasonable first race over hurdles, but was well tapped for speed over the last three, and may need further. (25/1)

1848 Bowcliffe keeps running reasonably and is the sort to pick up a race or two when things get easier in the spring. (20/1)

Ballyranter needs to brush up on his hurdling. Once he does, there should be significant improvement. (50/1)

King of Sparta did not seem too keen on this game and, stopping quickly after hitting the fourth, was wisely pulled up. (11/2: 7/2-6/1)

2698 WOOLLY MAMMOTH NOVICES' CHASE (5-Y.O+) (Class E)

2-05 (2-05) **3m 1f (18 fncs)** £3,047.75 (£917.00: £443.50: £206.75) GOING: 0.48 sec per fur (GS)

SP RR SF

2540* **Choisty (IRE) (92)** (MrsASwinbank) **7-11-10** JSupple (lw: mde all: clr to 14th: hld on wl fr 2 out)....................— **1** 5/2[2] 112? —
2113[U] **Hatcham Boy (IRE)** (DNicholson) **7-11-10** AMaguire (lw: chsd wnr fr 7th: ev ch fr 4 out: hrd rdn & hit last: kpt on)..nk **2** 1/2[1] 112? —
2540[10] **Clonroche Lucky (IRE)** (JWade) **7-11-5** BStorey (a outpcd & bhd)..dist **3** 50/1 — —
2571[5] **Merryhill Gold** (JWCurtis) **6-11-5** DerekByrne (lw: chsd ldrs to 9th: wknd qckly)..¾ **4** 50/1 — —
1845[P] **Royal Paris (IRE) (75)** (MrsSJSmith) **9-11-5** TReed (mstkes: a bhd: t.o)..dist **5** 20/1[3] — —
1691[5] **Monymax (IRE) (68)** (MrsSJSmith) **8-11-5** RichardGuest (bhd whn fell 6th).. **F** 25/1 — —
Manor Court (IRE) (DALamb) **9-11-5** JBurke (hdwy & prom ½-wy: hit 11th & sn wknd: p.u bef 4 out)................ **P** 33/1 — —
(SP 110.7%) **7 Rn**

6m 41.0 CSF £3.70 TOTE £3.00: £1.50 £1.30 (£1.70) OWNER Hotel Brokers International (RICHMOND) BRED Mrs Nancy Doyle

2540* Choisty (IRE) made this a real test of stamina and proved game under pressure. (5/2)

1635* Hatcham Boy (IRE), who was novicey at some fences, was off the bit to chase the winner throughout the final circuit and, despite some of the strongest attentions from the saddle, he could never quite make it. A poor jump at the last probably made all the difference. (1/2)

1989 Clonroche Lucky (IRE) was never going the pace at any stage. (50/1)

854 Merryhill Gold got well outpaced with a circuit to go and looked very moderate thereafter. (50/1)

1357 Royal Paris (IRE) jumped moderately and his rider did a good job in getting him round safely. (20/1)

2699 ARCTIC FOX NOVICES' H'CAP CHASE (0-110) (5-Y.O+) (Class D)

2-35 (2-37) **2m 4f 110y (15 fncs)** £3,480.00 (£1,050.00: £510.00: £240.00) GOING: 0.48 sec per fur (GS)

SP RR SF

1981[F] **Macgeorge (IRE) (100)** (RLee) **7-11-12** AMaguire (lw: mde all: hld on wl fr 4 out)..— **1** 11/2[2] 120 52
2544* **Random Harvest (IRE) (99)** (MrsMReveley) **8-11-11** 6x PNiven (lw: chsd ldrs: pushed along fr 10th: ev ch 4 out: hung lft: nt qckn flat)..2 **2** 8/11[1] 117 49
1803[4] **Cattly Hang (IRE) (98)** (JPLeigh) **7-11-10** ADobbin (chsd ldrs: chal 4 out: sn rdn: eased whn btn appr last)...18 **3** 15/2[3] 102 34
2052[3] **Be Brave (79)** (TJEtherington) **7-10-5** RRourke (mstke 2nd: a bhd)..13 **4** 12/1 73 5
2632* **Marlingford (74)** (MrsJJordan) **10-9-7**(7) 6x LMcGrath (lw: in tch tl outpcd fr 10th)..................................¾ **5** 8/1 68 —
Master of Troy (80) (CParker) **9-10-6** DParker (a bhd)..25 **6** 25/1 54 —
2650[U] **Gaelic Blue (77)** (MrsSJSmith) **7-10-3**ow3 RichardGuest (5th & in tch whn fell 7th).. **F** 9/1 — —
(SP 117.7%) **7 Rn**

5m 22.9 (15.90) CSF £10.04 CT £28.49 TOTE £6.50: £1.90 £1.20 (£4.10) OWNER Mr J. H. Watson (PRESTEIGNE) BRED Mrs B. Brady

LONG HANDICAP Marlingford 9-6 Gaelic Blue 9-13

1981 Macgeorge (IRE), who has always looked made for this game, put in a fine performance and won in determined style. This should have done him no end of good. (11/2)

2544* Random Harvest (IRE) had his chances throughout, but rather spoilt them by continually hanging left when put under pressure in the home straight. (8/11)

1803 Cattly Hang (IRE) looked likely to be all the better for this and jumped and ran well. He was wisely not knocked about when beaten and better will be seen in due course. (15/2)

2052 Be Brave, in a useful race, got round safely after mistakes early on and that seemed to be the object of the exercise. (12/1: op 8/1)

2632* Marlingford found this company too hot and dropped away over the last six fences. (8/1: op 5/1)

2650 Gaelic Blue was handy enough, although the race had yet to begin, when he came down at the seventh fence. (9/1)

2700 SNOW LEOPARD H'CAP CHASE (0-130) (5-Y.O+) (Class C)

3-05 (3-06) **2m (12 fncs)** £4,337.50 (£1,300.00: £625.00: £287.50) GOING: 0.48 sec per fur (GS)

SP RR SF

1912[3] **Eastern Magic (100)** (GBarnett) **9-10-0** DBridgwater (cl up: led fr 6th: hld on gamely flat)................................— **1** 6/1[3] 107 —
1846* **Weaver George (IRE) (102)** (WStorey) **7-10-2** MMoloney (chsd ldrs tl outpcd appr 4 out: styd on appr last: chal flat: kpt on)..hd **2** 4/1[2] 109 —

				SP	RR	SF
2506*	**Monyman (IRE) (105)** (MDHammond) **7-10-5** RGarritty (trckd ldrs: effrt 4 out: ev ch 3 out: hrd rdn & nt qckn appr last)	2½	**3**	Evens[1]	109	—
2051[4]	**Random Assault (NZ) (128)** (DNicholson) **8-12-0** AMaguire (led: mstke 5th: hdd next: ev ch tl outpcd 3 out: styd on appr last)	2½	**4**	7/1	130	13
1702[3]	**Full O'Praise (NZ) (101)** (PCalver) **10-10-1** BStorey (hld up: effrt 4 out: sn btn)	23	**5**	13/2	80	—
				(SP 110.1%)		**5 Rn**

4m 13.2 (21.20) CSF £25.81 TOTE £6.00: £2.50 £2.30 (£12.10) OWNER Mrs Christine Smith (STOKE-ON-TRENT) BRED C. Wiggins
LONG HANDICAP Eastern Magic 9-10

1912 Eastern Magic left his moderate run of last time way behind and proved very determined, fighting off several challengers in the home straight. (6/1)

1846* Weaver George (IRE) is obviously in particularly good heart this season and, after looking well beaten early in the straight, came again approaching the last to only just fail. (4/1)

2506* Monyman (IRE), at his first attempt in handicap company, was a shade disappointing, but his stable is not really sparkling at the moment. He should find plenty of other opportunities. (Evens)

2051 Random Assault (NZ) settled better this time and put up a fine performance under topweight. He has a peculiar action, but seems to be at last getting it together. (7/1)

1702 Full O'Praise (NZ) has lost his edge for this sort of race and was firmly put in his place over the last three fences. (13/2)

2701 YETI NOVICES' HURDLE (5-Y.O+) (Class E)

3-35 (3-35) **2m 4f 110y (10 hdls)** £2,587.50 (£725.00: £352.50) GOING: 0.48 sec per fur (GS)

				SP	RR	SF
2047*	**Bobby Grant** (CGrant) **6-10-12** PNiven (lw: trckd ldrs: led appr 3 out: hung rt: r.o wl)	—	**1**	9/1	68+	—
790[7]	**Love The Blues (106)** (DNicholson) **5-10-7** AMaguire (mid div: hrd drvn 4 out: hdwy & mstke next: r.o appr last: nrst fin)	4	**2**	3/1[1]	60	—
	Cherokee Chief (OSherwood) **6-10-12** JAMcCarthy (hld up & bhd: wnt prom 4 out: chal next: nt qckn fr 2 out)	1½	**3**	12/1	64	—
1305[3]	**Suas Leat (IRE) (102)** (JMJefferson) **7-11-6**(7) MNewton (a.p: effrt & ev ch 3 out: one pce)	2½	**4**	8/1	77	5
2042[4]	**Glenbower** (MDHammond) **5-10-9**(3) MrCBonner (a.p: outpcd 4 out: kpt on fr next)	2½	**5**	14/1	60	—
2539[8]	**Don't Tell Tom (IRE) (75)** (JWade) **7-10-12** GCahill (chsd ldrs: outpcd 4 out: kpt on fr 2 out)	2	**6**	25/1	58	—
1689[3]	**Antarctic Wind (IRE) (102)** (MDHammond) **7-11-3** RGarritty (led fr 5th tl hdd appr 3 out: grad wknd)	10	**7**	8/1	55	—
1594[5]	**Sparkling Buck** (OSherwood) **5-10-0**(7) DThomas (nvr bttr than mid div)	5	**8**	16/1	42	—
1692[2]	**Cherry Dee** (PBeaumont) **6-10-7** RSupple (mstkes: bhd tl stdy late hdwy)	2	**9**	5/1[3]	40	—
1807[13]	**The Other Man (IRE) (56)** (MissLCSiddall) **7-10-12** OPears (nvr trbld ldrs)	2	**10**	50/1	43	—
1802[5]	**Larkshill (IRE)** (JGFitzGerald) **6-10-12** PCarberry (prom to 4 out)	4	**11**	7/2[2]	40	—
1854[10]	**Kentucky Gold (IRE) (57)** (MrsLWilliamson) **8-10-12** LO'Hara (chsd ldrs tl mstke & wknd 4 out)	2	**12**	50/1	39	—
2546[P]	**Sovereign Pass** (RDEWoodhouse) **5-10-12** BStorey (a bhd)	25	**13**	50/1	19	—
	Corrimulzie (IRE) (KAMorgan) **6-10-12** ASSmith (mstkes: a bhd)	9	**14**	25/1	12	—
	Persian Grange (IRE) (DALamb) **7-10-12** JBurke (led to 5th: wknd qckly next: t.o)	dist	**15**	50/1	—	—
	Joss Bay (TPTate) **5-10-12** RichardGuest (bhd tl fell 3 out)		**F**	20/1	—	—
854[5]	**Palace of Gold (73)** (LLungo) **7-10-5**(7) WDowling (sddle slipped & p.u after 4th)		**P**	25/1	—	—
2539[7]	**Ten Past Six** (MartynWane) **5-10-12** ADobbin (chsd ldrs tl wknd fr 6th: p.u bef 3 out)		**P**	25/1	—	—
	Black Ice Boy (IRE) (RBastiman) **6-10-9**(3) HBastiman (a bhd: p.u bef last)		**P**	50/1	—	—
1579[12]	**Only A Sioux** (JRTurner) **5-10-12** WFry (bhd fr ½-wy: p.u bef last)		**P**	50/1	—	—
				(SP 148.3%)		**20 Rn**

5m 15.0 (28.00) CSF £36.53 TOTE £13.30: £2.50 £2.40 £4.10 (£51.10) Trio £101.20 OWNER Mr John Thompson (BILLINGHAM) BRED Mrs D. Jenks

2047* Bobby Grant looks a really good recruit to the game, but the only blot on an otherwise useful performance was the fact that he was continually hanging right. (9/1)

790 Love The Blues took some riding to get her going, but she obviously stays forever and she really picked up from the second last, albeit too late. Stiffer tests would seem what she needs. (3/1: 5/2-4/1)

Cherokee Chief, a real chasing sort, showed plenty and much more will be seen of him. (12/1: op 8/1)

1305 Suas Leat (IRE) never seems to run a bad race, but the weight concession proved beyond him in the home straight. (8/1)

2042 Glenbower, slow but sure, will find his mark in due course. (14/1)

1999 Don't Tell Tom (IRE) stays well, but is short of a turn of foot. (25/1)

1692 Cherry Dee jumped moderately early on and just had an educational. Time will see plenty of improvement. (5/1)

2702 POLAR BEAR H'CAP HURDLE (0-135) (4-Y.O+) (Class C)

4-05 (4-07) **2m 7f (12 hdls)** £3,395.50 (£1,024.00: £497.00: £233.50) GOING: 0.48 sec per fur (GS)

				SP	RR	SF
1783[3]	**Nick the Beak (IRE) (108)** (JohnUpson) **8-10-5** RSupple (a.p: led 3 out: hld on wl)	—	**1**	12/1	88	—
1906[7]	**Erzadjan (IRE) (128)** (MrsMReveley) **7-11-11** PNiven (hld up: hdwy 4 out: chal 2 out: nt qckn towards fin)	hd	**2**	7/1	108	—
1455[3]	**The Toiseach (IRE) (112)** (JRFanshawe) **6-10-9** AMaguire (lw: a cl up: led fr 8th to 3 out: outpcd fr 2 out)	9	**3**	11/2[3]	86	—
1265*	**Jocks Cross (IRE) (117)** (GRichards) **6-11-0** ADobbin (cl up: disp ld 4 out: rdn & grad wknd fr next)	10	**4**	9/2[1]	84	—
2078[2]	**Dally Boy (115)** (TDEasterby) **5-10-12** RGarritty (chsd ldrs: rdn 4 out: sn outpcd)	1¾	**5**	5/1[2]	81	—
	Disco des Mottes (FR) (131) (GRichards) **6-12-0** PCarberry (prom: mstke 3rd: rdn & outpcd 4 out: sn btn & eased)	30	**6**	25/1	76	—
2003*	**Pharare (IRE) (103)** (RDEWoodhouse) **7-10-0** BStorey (led to 8th: sn rdn: outpcd fr 4 out)	2	**7**	16/1	46	—
1645[5]	**Izza (108)** (WStorey) **6-10-0**(5) RMcGrath (hld up & bhd: fell 7th: dead)		**F**	15/2	—	—
2008*	**Roberty Lea (118)** (MrsMReveley) **9-11-1** GCahill (prom tl lost pl 5th: wl bhd whn p.u bef 3 out)		**P**	12/1	—	—
1859*	**Wassl Street (IRE) (103)** (KAMorgan) **5-10-0** ASSmith (hld up: effrt 4 out: sn btn & p.u bef 3 out)		**P**	9/2[1]	—	—
				(SP 117.8%)		**10 Rn**

5m 53.9 CSF £85.92 CT £475.40 TOTE £18.50: £4.40 £2.30 £2.50 (£54.50) Trio £119.10 OWNER Sir Nicholas Wilson (TOWCESTER) BRED Mrs R. Fitzgerald
LONG HANDICAP Wassl Street (IRE) 9-12 Pharare (IRE) 9-8

1783 Nick the Beak (IRE), back to something like his old form, travelled particularly well and pulled out just enough when challenged. (12/1)

Erzadjan (IRE) had to work hard to get into it and kept staying on, but was always being held in the closing stages. He is certainly not the easiest of rides, but will always find plenty of opportunities. (7/1)

1455 The Toiseach (IRE) travelled and jumped well, but was short of pace when ridden three out. He looks the type to do better over fences.(11/2)

1265* Jocks Cross (IRE), from a yard out of form at the moment, ran a super race until blowing up in the home straight. (9/2)

2078 Dally Boy was a shade disappointing, coming off the bit four from home and making no impression thereafter. (5/1)
Disco des Mottes (FR) ran reasonably to the fourth last and was then eased a good deal when well beaten. (25/1)
2003* Pharare (IRE) had plenty on here and was well tapped for speed over the last four flights. (16/1)
1859* Wassl Street (IRE) seems at his best with much more give in the ground, and was a big disappointment on this occasion. (9/2: 6/1-4/1)

T/Plpt: £449.50 (19.56 Tckts). T/Qdpt: £57.80 (13.63 Tckts). AA

2448-WINCANTON (R-H) (Good to firm, Firm patches)
Thursday January 23rd

Race 2: one fence omitted
WEATHER: fine

2703 PAINTERS H'CAP HURDLE (0-125) (4-Y.O+) (Class D)

1-30 (1-30) **2m (8 hdls)** £3,243.00 (£888.00: £429.00) GOING minus 0.22 sec per fur (G)

				SP	RR	SF
2040*	**Hay Dance (102)** (PJHobbs) **6-10-5** NWilliamson (lw: hld up in rr: hdwy 3 out: led on bit nr fin: hrd hld)	—	**1**	8/11[1]	83+	33
2644[3]	**Morstock (112)** (RJHodges) **7-10-12**(3) TDascombe (led to nr fin: no ch w wnr)	1¼	**2**	9/4[2]	92	42
2578[7]	**Show Faith (IRE) (97)** (RHannon) **7-10-0b** RHughes (a.p: rdn & ev ch 2 out: wknd flat)	7	**3**	5/1[3]	70	20
2040[5]	**Nashville Star (USA) (97)** (RMathew) **6-10-0v** RBellamy (prom tl rdn & wknd appr 2 out)	15	**4**	16/1	55	5
638[F]	**Windward Ariom (108)** (PMitchell) **11-10-11b** ALarnach (bkwd: bhd fr 5th: t.o)	25	**5**	25/1	41	—
				(SP 115.1%)		**5 Rn**

3m 40.8 (0.80) CSF £2.85 TOTE £1.70: £1.30 £1.40 (£1.70) OWNER Wessex Go Racing Partnership (MINEHEAD) BRED Limestone Stud
LONG HANDICAP Show Faith (IRE) 9-12 Nashville Star (USA) 9-13
2040* Hay Dance defied a 4lb rise in the weights with the cheeky Williamson not moving a muscle. (8/11)
2644 Morstock found the winner simply toying with him and is greatly flattered by the margin of defeat. (9/4: op 5/4)
1873 Show Faith (IRE), tried in blinkers, was just out of the handicap. (5/1)

2704 MAURICE LISTER MAIDEN CHASE (6-Y.O+) (Class E)

2-00 (2-00) **3m 1f 110y (19 fncs)** £3,847.00 (£1,156.00: £558.00: £259.00) GOING minus 0.22 sec per fur (G)

				SP	RR	SF
1199[F]	**Stormy Sunset (72)** (WWDennis) **10-10-7**(7) MrTDennis (lw: a.p: hmpd 1st: led appr 8th: r.o wl)	—	**1**	8/1[3]	88	—
2054[6]	**Bolshie Baron** (MHWeston) **8-11-5** MrMHarris (hdwy 10th: hit 11th: ev ch 3 out: btn whn mstke last)	9	**2**	10/1	87	—
	Glendine (IRE) (CJMann) **7-11-5** JRailton (prom tl j.slowly 13th: rallied appr 2 out: mstke last: styd on)	6	**3**	8/1[3]	84	—
1582[2]	**Jac Del Prince (60)** (PFNicholls) **7-11-5** BPowell (prom tl wknd 3 out)	26	**4**	5/2[1]	67	—
2077[2]	**Plassy Boy (IRE) (70)** (KRBurke) **8-11-5** ALarnach (prom tl mstke 11th: t.o)	9	**5**	9/1	62	—
	Withycombe Hill (PJHobbs) **7-10-12**(7) MrSDurack (wl bhd whn hit 8th: sme hdwy 13th: wknd 15th: t.o)	2	**6**	12/1	60	—
903[4]	**Speedy Snapsgem (IRE) (70)** (PJHobbs) **7-11-5** APMcCoy (fell 1st: dead)		**F**	7/1[2]	—	—
	Fortria Rosie Dawn (MissVenetiaWilliams) **7-11-0** NWilliamson (bit bkwd: fell 6th)		**F**	20/1	—	—
1835[P]	**Jack of Diamonds** (RJO'Sullivan) **9-11-5** AMcCabe (prom: hmpd 3rd: wknd 9th: bhd whn fell 10th)		**F**	50/1	—	—
2575[P]	**Masked Martin (60)** (PRRodford) **6-11-5b** SBurrough (t.o whn fell 6th)		**F**	50/1	—	—
1829[F]	**Full Shilling (USA) (64)** (DLWilliams) **8-11-2v**(3) GuyLewis (bkwd: prom: mstke 4th: bhd whn mstke 13th: t.o whn p.u bef 15th)		**P**	16/1	—	—
1773[7]	**Golden Drum (IRE) (69)** (TRGeorge) **7-11-0b**(5) MrRThornton (led: blnd 3rd: hdd appr 8th: rdn 13th: blnd 14th: sn wknd: t.o whn p.u bef 3 out)		**P**	16/1	—	—
1874[P]	**Miramare (60)** (CLPopham) **7-11-2**(3) TDascombe (bhd fr 5th: t.o whn p.u bef 12th)		**P**	33/1	—	—
	Waipiro (MrsSDWilliams) **7-11-5** LHarvey (bhd fr 7th: t.o whn p.u bef 16th)		**P**	20/1	—	—
2052[4]	**Romany Blues (62)** (CPEBrooks) **8-10-7**(7) MBerry (blnd & uns rdr 3rd)		**U**	8/1[3]	—	—
				(SP 129.3%)		**15 Rn**

6m 41.0 (22.00) CSF £78.67 TOTE £11.60: £3.10 £2.80 £2.90 (£38.60) Trio £213.00 OWNER Mrs Jill Dennis (BUDE) BRED J. J. Howlett
Stormy Sunset, who has won both her points on yielding ground, stayed on well enough in the home straight. (8/1)
1829 Bolshie Baron has registered both his victories between the flags on this sort of ground. (10/1)
Glendine (IRE), who finally managed to win an Irish point last May, had shown little in three hunter chases. (8/1)
1582 Jac Del Prince, in trouble at the cross fence, is certainly not as good as his half-brother Royal Mountbrowne. (5/2)

2705 ELITE RACING CLUB CLAIMING HURDLE (4-Y.O) (Class F)

2-30 (2-33) **2m (8 hdls)** £2,197.50 (£610.00: £292.50) GOING: 0.22 sec per fur (G)

				SP	RR	SF
1953[8]	**Lady Magnum (IRE)** (JNeville) **4-10-12** NMann (chsd ldr: led after 3 out: rdn out)	—	**1**	4/1[3]	65	18
2574[2]	**D'naan (IRE)** (MCPipe) **4-11-3b** RBellamy (led tl after 3 out: one pce flat)	7	**2**	5/2[1]	63	16
2070[12]	**Eskimo Kiss (IRE)** (GFJohnsonHoughton) **4-10-6** JRailton (prom tl outpcd 5th: styd on fr 2 out)	11	**3**	10/1	41	—
	El Bardador (IRE) (RJHodges) **4-10-10**(7) JHarris (hdwy 3 out: one pce fr 2 out)	5	**4**	9/1	47	—
2050[7]	**Tathmin** (JRBosley) **4-11-0v** MBosley (nvr trbld ldrs)	3½	**5**	20/1	41	—
1908[4]	**Song For Jess (IRE) (74)** (FJordan) **4-10-6** RGreene (nvr nr ldrs)	6	**6**	12/1	27	—
1872[5]	**Soldier Mak** (AHide) **4-11-3**(3) LAspell (prom tl rdn & wknd appr 2 out)	¾	**7**	100/30[2]	40	—
1595[8]	**Red Time** (MSSaunders) **4-10-11** PHolley (hdwy 4th: mstke 5th: sn wknd)	11	**8**	25/1	20	—
1900[11]	**Benkarosam** (MrsSDWilliams) **4-10-5** LHarvey (a bhd)	hd	**9**	40/1	14	—
2622[11]	**Scathebury** (KRBurke) **4-11-6** NWilliamson (prom to 5th)	6	**10**	14/1	23	—
1808[5]	**Rivers Magic** (JWhite) **4-11-3**(3) TDascombe (bhd whn fell 3 out)		**F**	12/1	—	—
1377[10]	**It's Dawan** (PMitchell) **4-11-12** RHughes (a bhd: t.o whn p.u bef 5th)		**P**	20/1	—	—
1014[7]	**Seven Crowns (USA)** (CLPopham) **4-10-11** BPowell (a bhd: t.o whn p.u bef 2 out)		**P**	25/1	—	—
1706[F]	**Bold Start Lady** (EAWheeler) **4-11-0**(7) MGriffiths (bhd: mstke 3rd: t.o 4th: p.u bef 2 out)		**P**	33/1	—	—
				(SP 135.4%)		**14 Rn**

3m 45.5 (5.50) CSF £14.07 TOTE £4.10: £2.10 £1.60 £3.40 (£7.30) Trio £32.10 OWNER Magnum Construction Ltd (NEWPORT, GWENT) BRED M. B. O'Toole
IN-FOCUS: **Martin Bosley announced his retirement after partnering Tathmin.**
1675* Lady Magnum (IRE) again showed she is useful in this sort of company. (4/1)
2574 D'naan (IRE) could not take advantage of a hesitant jump by the winner at the final flight. (5/2)
Eskimo Kiss (IRE) seemed to need blinkers to show her best in this type of event on the Flat. (10/1: op 20/1)

El Bardador (IRE), a 6,000 guineas purchase at Doncaster November Sales, needed first-time blinkers to win a ten-furlong seller for William Jarvis at Yarmouth last September. (9/1)
1908 Song For Jess (IRE) (12/1: 8/1-14/1)

2706 PAT RUTHVEN AND GUY NIXON MEMORIAL VASE AMATEUR H'CAP CHASE (0-115) (5-Y.O+) (Class E)
3-00 (3-00) **3m 1f 110y (21 fncs)** £2,822.00 (£1,136.00: £548.00) GOING minus 0.22 sec per fur (G)

Form	Horse	Dist	Pos	SP	RR	SF
2089*	**Act of Parliament (IRE) (112)** (KCBailey) **9-11-4b**(7) MrRWakley (chsd ldr to 14th: rdn to chal 3 out: led flat: rdn out)	—	1	9/4[2]	123	—
2551*	**Dromhana (IRE) (105)** (PFNicholls) **7-10-11**(7) 6x MrJTizzard (led 2nd: rdn appr 3 out: hdd flat)	1	2	10/11[1]	115	—
1287[P]	**Tug of Peace (113)** (GBBalding) **10-11-5**(7) MrABalding (hld up: wnt 2nd 14th: ev ch 3 out: wknd appr last)	7	3	12/1	119	—
1877[2]	**Cool Character (IRE) (87)** (RHBuckler) **9-9-9**(5) MrRThornton (hld up: hdwy 10th: hit 12th & 14th: sn wknd)	19	4	10/1	81	—
2575[3]	**Frozen Drop (102)** (PCRitchens) **10-10-8**(7) MrGShenkin (led to 2nd: dropped rr & rdn 9th: t.o 12th: p.u bef 17th)		P	6/1[3]	—	—

(SP 114.2%) **5 Rn**

6m 40.8 (21.80) CSF £4.73 TOTE £2.60: £1.50 £1.50 (£2.10) OWNER Mr J. Perriss (UPPER LAMBOURN) BRED Mrs Susan Bury
LONG HANDICAP Cool Character (IRE) 8-13
2089* Act of Parliament (IRE), raised 5lb, was 7lb higher than for the first leg of his hat-trick. (9/4)
2551* Dromhana (IRE) was 10lb higher than when second to God Speed You at Ludlow. (10/11)
Tug of Peace was more like his old self here off a mark 7lb lower than when successful over course and distance in November 1995. (12/1: 7/1-14/1)
2575 Frozen Drop (6/1: op 4/1)

2707 ARTISTS H'CAP CHASE (0-135) (5-Y.O+) (Class C)
3-30 (3-31) **2m (13 fncs)** £6,184.00 (£1,516.00) GOING minus 0.22 sec per fur (G)

Form	Horse	Dist	Pos	SP	RR	SF
2660[U]	**Newlands-General (118)** (PFNicholls) **11-11-4** BPowell (j.lft: mde all: clr 3 out: comf)	—	1	11/8[2]	126+	18
1682[2]	**Thumbs Up (128)** (GMMcCourt) **11-12-0** JRailton (hld up: rdn appr 3 out: no imp)	11	2	4/7[1]	125	17

(SP 105.7%) **2 Rn**

4m 0.1 (7.10) TOTE £1.70 OWNER Mr C. Murphy (SHEPTON MALLET) BRED J. M. Castle
1682 Newlands-General, jumping left, was scoring for the first time over fences on a right-handed course. (11/8: op evens)
1682 Thumbs Up could not make a race of it in the home straight. (4/7)

2708 POTTERS H'CAP HURDLE (0-105) (4-Y.O+) (Class F)
4-00 (4-01) **2m 6f (11 hdls)** £2,372.50 (£660.00: £317.50) GOING minus 0.22 sec per fur (G)

Form	Horse	Dist	Pos	SP	RR	SF
1448[3]	**Clod Hopper (IRE) (77)** (WRMuir) **7-9-9**(5) ABates (lw: mde all: drvn out)	—	1	10/1	63	8
1673[P]	**Mr Strong Gale (IRE) (88)** (PFNicholls) **6-10-8**(3) LAspell (lw: hld up & bhd: hdwy 3 out: ev ch last: r.o)	1	2	11/2[2]	73	18
2008[2]	**Stac-Pollaidh (88)** (KCBailey) **7-10-4**(7)ow1 MrRWakley (hld up: hdwy appr 2 out: styd on flat)	8	3	9/1	68	12
2552[4]	**General Mouktar (105)** (MCPipe) **7-12-0** JRailton (hld up: stdy hdwy 6th: one pce fr 2 out)	hd	4	11/4[1]	84	29
1814[2]	**First Class (85)** (GNAlford) **7-10-8** RGreene (lw: mstke 1st: lost pl 5th: hdwy 7th: rdn & wknd appr 2 out)	5	5	11/2[2]	61	6
1961[3]	**Glen Mirage (84)** (MJCoombe) **12-10-7** MissMCoombe (sme hdwy appr 2 out: nt rch ldrs)	5	6	11/1	56	1
	Quelque Chose (92) (BJMeehan) **7-11-1** RHughes (bit bkwd: hld up: hdwy 3 out: wknd appr 2 out)	2	7	25/1	63	8
2036[4]	**Urban Lily (80)** (RJHodges) **7-9-10b**(7) JHarris (prom: wnt 2nd 3 out: wknd appr 2 out)	17	8	12/1	38	—
1993*	**Top Skipper (IRE) (87)** (VGGreenway) **5-10-3**(7)ow7 MrJTizzard (chsd wnr to 3 out: sn wknd)	4	9	13/2[3]	42	—
2574[6]	**Adonisis (80)** (DRCElsworth) **5-10-3** PHolley (lw: a bhd)	4	10	33/1	33	—
2552[12]	**Glistening Dawn (95)** (TKeddy) **7-11-4b** NMann (a bhd: t.o fr 7th)	dist	11	14/1	—	—
1996[5]	**Road to Au Bon (USA) (80)** (RJBaker) **9-10-3** BPowell (lw: prom tl wknd 6th: t.o fr 8th)	dist	12	14/1	—	—
1875[P]	**Legal Artist (IRE) (98)** (MissCJohnsey) **7-11-2**(5) MrRThornton (bhd whn mstke 7th: t.o)	dist	13	25/1	—	—
	Fane Park (IRE) (85) (CLPopham) **9-10-5**(3) TDascombe (bkwd: fell 1st)		F	33/1	—	—

(SP 132.8%) **14 Rn**

5m 16.5 (7.50) CSF £63.20 CT £489.78 TOTE £15.70: £3.50 £2.30 £3.50 (£80.60) Trio £223.60 OWNER Mr T. J. Parrott (LAMBOURN) BRED P. and D. James
LONG HANDICAP Clod Hopper (IRE) 9-10
1448 Clod Hopper (IRE) seems to need fast ground to show his best. (10/1)
1673 Mr Strong Gale (IRE), still lightly-raced, was inclined to run about a bit, but stayed on to the end. (11/2)
2008 Stac-Pollaidh was never a threat to the two principals. (9/1)
2552 General Mouktar is the type who likes to do it all on the bridle. (11/4)
1814 First Class was 3lb higher than when second in a novice handicap at Ludlow. (11/2)
2036 Urban Lily (12/1: op 8/1)

T/Plpt: £73.90 (102.18 Tckts). T/Qdpt: £22.90 (23.28 Tckts). KH

2709a - 2737a : (Irish Racing) - See Computer Raceform

2599a-LEOPARDSTOWN (Dublin, Ireland) (L-H) (Good to yielding)
Sunday January 19th

2738a WATERFORD CRYSTAL HURDLE (4-Y.O)
1-35 (1-35) **2m (8 hdls)** IR £4,110.00 (IR £930.00: IR £390.00: IR £210.00)

Form	Horse	Dist	Pos	SP	RR	SF
1747a[12]	**Dr Bones (IRE)** (MJPO'Brien,Ireland) **4-10-7** TPRudd (mid div: hld up: 7th 3 out: 3rd 2 out: led appr last: styd on)	—	1	25/1	85	28
	Afarka (IRE) (SJTreacy,Ireland) **4-10-2** TPTreacy (rn 2nd tl appr 5th: 2nd again 2 out: rdn & ev ch appr last: kpt on flat: no ex nr fin)	nk	2	10/1	80	23
2333a[8]	**Spirit Dancer (IRE)** (GMLyons,Ireland) **4-10-13** SCLyons (hld up towards rr: hdwy 3 out: hdwy & 7th whn mstke 2 out: 5th & chsd ldrs nr last: rdn & styd on: nt rch ldrs)	2½	3	12/1	88	31

Snow Falcon (TJTaaffe,Ireland) **4-10-7** RDunwoody (towards rr: hld up: 9th at 5th: 6th & chsd ldrs 2 out: nt rch ldrs appr last: styd on)........2½ **4** 14/1 80 23

Marlonette (IRE) (WPMullins,Ireland) **4-10-8** DJCasey (hld up in tch: 3rd at 5th: disp ld next: sn led: hdd appr last: 4th over last: one pce flat)........4 **5** 8/1 77 20

Namoodaj (DNicholson) **4-10-7** PCarberry (hld up: nt fluent: 7th at 4th: closing 5th 2 out: effrt st: 3rd u.p & no ex nr last: one pce & nt trble ldrs flat)........1½ **6** 5/4 1 74 17

2333aB **Highly Motivated** (APO'Brien,Ireland) **4-10-8** CFSwan (hld up in tch: 5th 3 out: 4th & chsd ldrs 2 out: effrt early st: 6th & n.m.r nr last: kpt on same pce)........2 **7** 100/30 2 73 16

Family Project (IRE) (JSBolger,Ireland) **4-9-9**(7) MWMartin (hld up in tch: mstke 3rd: 4th at 5th: 8th & chsd ldrs 2 out: nt rch ldrs appr last: kpt on)........½ **8** 12/1 67 10

The Swan (NMeade,Ireland) **4-10-2** RHughes (towards rr: rdn after 3 out: no imp early st: kpt on)........3 **9** 12/1 64 7

Victory Bound (USA) (GTHourigan,Ireland) **4-10-7** FWoods (hld up towards rr: sme hdwy bef 2 out: nvr nrr).2 **10** 6/1 3 67 10

Lough Slania (IRE) (KPrendergast,Ireland) **4-10-7** JShortt (cl up: 2nd briefly at 5th: 3rd 3 out: btn & wknd bef 2 out)........6 **11** 14/1 61 4

2333aF **Evriza (IRE)** (APO'Brien,Ireland) **4-11-0** THorgan (led: rdn & jnd 3 out: sn hdd: wknd appr next: sn n.d)........12 **12** 10/1 56 —

Nascimento (USA) (FBerry,Ireland) **4-10-7** CO'Dwyer (towards rr: n.d 2 out)........1 **13** 16/1 48 —

(SP 157.2%) **13 Rn**

3m 53.1 (-7.90) OWNER Mrs Denis Fortune (NAAS)

Dr Bones (IRE), an ordinary maiden on the Flat, showed improved form here, having a first outing for his new stable. He battled on well from the last and was always holding the runner-up. He will be entered in the Triumph Hurdle but the stable has better. (25/1)

Afarka (IRE), more experienced over flights than the winner, had every chance. (10/1)

1747a* Spirit Dancer (IRE) is inconsistent but this is the level of his form. (12/1: op 8/1)

Snow Falcon, having his first run since leaving Michael Bell's Newmarket yard, put in a promising enough performance and will be placed to win. (14/1)

Marlonette (IRE) failed to confirm Thurles superiority over Afarka. (8/1)

Namoodaj, looking big and well for his jumping debut, came out of midfield to track the leaders on the outside from two out. Fourth and wide into the straight, he wasn't making any impression in third place over the last and dropped away on the level. Lack of race fitness or stamina limitations might be put forward but this was a disappointing effort. (5/4)

2333a Highly Motivated went fourth four out but appeared to meet with every bit of trouble going and was done with well before the last. (100/30)

2739a BAILEYS ARKLE PERPETUAL CHALLENGE CUP NOVICES' CHASE (Gd 2) (5-Y.O+)

2-05 (2-05) **2m 1f (11 fncs)** IR £9,675.00 (IR £2,775.00: IR £1,275.00: IR £375.00)

SP RR SF

1790* **Mulligan (IRE)** (DNicholson) **7-12-0** AMaguire (mde all: j.w: rdn clr flat: styd on wl: eased nr fin)........— **1** 2/1 2 125+ 44

2335a3 **Beakstown (IRE)** (PMullins,Ireland) **8-11-11**(3) GCotter (lft 3rd at 2nd: wnt 2nd st: rdn & nt rch wnr nr last: kpt on same pce flat)........9 **2** 14/1 117 36

2335a7 **Penndara (IRE)** (APO'Brien,Ireland) **8-11-7** CFSwan (rn 2nd: mstke 2 out: 3rd & rdn st: 3rd, edgd rt & no ex nr last: kpt on same pce flat)........1 **3** 20/1 109 28

2335aF **Kharasar (IRE)** (AMullins,Ireland) **7-11-7** CO'Dwyer (hld up towards rr: 4th whn mstke 4 out: pushed along & mstke next: rdn & no imp early st: j.rt last)........9 **4** 5/1 3 100 19

2335a4 **Headbanger** (MMLynch,Ireland) **10-11-7** DHO'Connor (hld up towards rr: mstke 5th: wnt 4th 3 out: 5th & rdn st: no imp appr last)........1½ **5** 16/1 99 18

2335a* **Danoli (IRE)** (TFoley,Ireland) **9-12-0** TPTreacy (hld up: cl up: 3rd whn fell 2nd)........ **F** 9/10 1 — —

(SP 119.9%) **6 Rn**

4m 16.0 (-7.00) OWNER Lady Harris (TEMPLE GUITING) BRED Sandford Bloodstock Ltd

1790* Mulligan (IRE), made all the running, edging on in the straight and going clear from the last. There was no semblance of a mistake but it would have been more interesting had Danoli stood up. A Warwick outing in mid-February is the next step before the Arkle at Cheltenham. (2/1)

2335a Beakstown (IRE), ridden along in third place three out, went second after two out but was no threat well before the last. (14/1)

Penndara (IRE) put in an improved performance, tracking the leader and apparently going well until a mistake two out. Three lengths in arrears at the last, he hung right on the flat. There is plenty of scope here. (20/1)

2335a Kharasar (IRE) was making some headway from the rear when blundering four out, and another mistake at the next saw him out of contention. (5/1)

2335a* Danoli (IRE) was close up in fourth place when clouting the second fence hard and paying the penalty. (9/10)

2740a A I G EUROPE CHAMPION HURDLE (Gd 1) (4-Y.O+)

2-40 (2-40) **2m (8 hdls)** IR £34,000.00 (IR £9,500.00: IR £4,500.00: IR £1,500.00)

SP RR SF

2461a3 **Cockney Lad (IRE)** (NMeade,Ireland) **8-11-10** RHughes (hld up: 6th at 5th: 5th & chsd ldrs appr 2 out: 4th & clsd st: 3rd, rdn & chal last: sn chsng ldr: styd on u.p: led nr fin)........— **1** 10/1 130 51

2461a* **Theatreworld (IRE)** (APO'Brien,Ireland) **5-11-6** CFSwan (led & disp ld: outjmpd 3rd, 5th & 3 out: rdn after 3 out: narrow ld nr last: kpt on u.p: hdd nr fin)........1 **2** 13/8 1 129 46

1752a* **Dardjini (USA)** (NMeade,Ireland) **7-11-10** PCarberry (cl up: hld up: mostly 3rd: mstke 3 out: chal st: cl 2nd u.p & ev ch whn bad mstke last: rdn & kpt on same pce)........2 **3** 25/1 127 48

16482 **Urubande (IRE)** (APO'Brien,Ireland) **7-11-10** RDunwoody (prom: led & disp ld fr 3rd: hdd after 3 out: disp ld 2 out: 2nd, rdn & nt qckn st: one pce & no imp appr last)........9 **4** 4/1 3 118 39

Escartefigue (FR) (DNicholson) **5-11-6** DBridgwater (plld hrd: cl up: 4th whn mstke 3rd: rdn 5th: 4th 3 out: lost pl u.p appr next: 6th & no imp st: one pce)........4½ **5** 7/1 114 31

2603a18 **Notcomplainingbut (IRE)** (PMullins,Ireland) **6-11-5** TPTreacy (towards rr: lost tch 3 out: n.d st: kpt on)........1 **6** 25/1 108 29

1648* **Zabadi (IRE)** (DNicholson) **5-11-6** AMaguire (hld up: 5th & trckd ldrs 3 out: closing 4th 2 out: 5th & rdn st: sn no imp)........5½ **7** 100/30 2 107 24

(SP 110.5%) **7 Rn**

3m 51.4 (-9.60) OWNER D. Daly (NAVAN)

2461a Cockney Lad (IRE) with the race run to suit him, was able to use his undoubted turn of foot to good effect. Fifth and going well two out, he went third on the outside before the last and despite edging left on the run-in, stayed on under pressure to lead near the finish. (10/1)

2461a* Theatreworld (IRE) with his tongue tied down again, was soon disputing the lead. Never particularly fluent, he was being ridden along three out. With the advantage after a mistake at the second last, he boxed on relentlessly under pressure but had to give best near the finish. He made it hard for himself this time and a little rest might do him no harm. (13/8)

1752a* Dardjini (USA) held up in third place, came to challenge before the last. He miffed it when holding every chance and could not raise another effort on the flat. His enthusiasm just might be questionable. (25/1)
1648 Urubande (IRE) took his stable companion on from the start and didn't weaken until the approach to the second last. Fourth and beaten well before the last, he looks almost certain to head now for the Stayers' Hurdle. (4/1)
Escartefigue (FR) looked very big but went with them until weakening three out. Soon out of contention, he kept on again on the flat. (7/1: op 3/1)
1234a Notcomplainingbut (IRE) got herself a long way behind and was completely tailed off from four out. She stayed on again in the straight but remains a rather enigmatic mare. (25/1)
1648* Zabadi (IRE) would give the outside to no-one. Ridden along after three out, he dropped right away from the next and undoubtedly needed this run. (100/30)

2741a FOXROCK H'CAP CHASE (5-Y.O+)
3-10 (3-11) **2m 3f (11 fncs)** IR £5,480.00 (IR £1,240.00: IR £520.00: IR £280.00)

	Horse			SP	RR	SF
	Manhattan Castle (IRE) (ALTMoore,Ireland) **8-9-13** FWoods (hld up towards rr: 7th & clsd st: chal to disp ld last: led early flat: styd on)	—	1	4/1 2	136	24
1737a4	**Arctic Weather (IRE)** (MJPO'Brien,Ireland) **8-9-7** TPRudd (hld up towards rr: 6th at 8th: hdwy & 6th 2 out: chal on ins early st: disp ld & ev ch last: hdd & no ex early flat: kpt on)	1½	2	5/1 3	129	17
1277*	**Call it a Day (IRE)** (DNicholson) **7-10-3** AMaguire (in tch: 5th at 8th: 4th 3 out: 2nd & chal on ins st: disp ld appr last: 3rd & no ex early flat: rdn & styd on wl)	½	3	100/30 1	138	26
2362a4	**Belvederian** (MFMorris,Ireland) **10-10-5** PCarberry (rn 2nd: led 6th: jnd early st: ev ch last: rdn & no ex flat: kpt on same pce)	2	4	10/1	139	27
15663	**Kadi (GER)** (DNicholson) **8-10-4** RJohnson (cl up: 3rd at 8th: 2nd 3 out: 3rd & rdn st: no ex appr last: 5th early flat: kpt on same pce)	1½	5	7/1	136	24
2362a3	**Opera Hat (IRE)** (JRHFowler,Ireland) **9-11-2** CO'Dwyer (hld up in tch: 5th at 6th: 4th whn slt mstke 4 out: 3rd 3 out: 2nd bef 2 out: 4th & rdn st: nt rch ldrs appr last: one pce)	7	6	4/1 2	143	31
2346a3	**Fiftysevenchannels (IRE)** (EBolger,Ireland) **8-9-10** CFSwan (hld up towards rr: hdwy & 7th 3 out: 5th st: rdn & no ex appr last: no imp flat)	4	7	7/1	119	7
2602a6	**Royal Mountbrowne** (APO'Brien,Ireland) **9-11-3** THorgan (led: hit 4th: hdd 6th: 5th whn mstke & lost pl 3 out: no imp appr next)	15	8	10/1	128	16

(SP 122.9%) **8 Rn**

4m 41.9 (-10.10) OWNER P. Fitzpatrick (NAAS) BRED F. Feeney
Manhattan Castle (IRE) showed the benefit of a run over hurdles at Christmas with a snug win here. Seventh into the straight, he got a nice run through on the inside to dispute it at the last, took over early on the flat and, quickening, put the issue beyond doubt. (4/1)
Arctic Weather (IRE) started to get into it after the second last, got all the breaks on the inner to dispute it over the last but just could not quicken on the flat. (5/1)
1277* Call it a Day (IRE) never far off the pace, went second after two out and got his head in front just before the last. With the pressure on he didn't find a lot on the run-in but was staying on again towards the line. (100/30)
2362a Belvederian showed a bit of zest here, leading from seven out until headed on the run to the last. He kept on at one pace on the flat, and a return to three miles might suit now he appears to have got some of his jumping confidence back. (10/1)
1566 Kadi (GER), always with the pace, went second three out but had cried enough before the last. (7/1)
2362a Opera Hat (IRE) again demonstrated her disdain for the Leopardstown fences. (4/1)

NR

2742a - 2743a : (Irish Racing) - See Computer Raceform

1920-DONCASTER (L-H) (Good, Good to firm patches)
Friday January 24th
WEATHER: dry & bright

2744 SELBY NOVICES' CONDITIONAL H'CAP HURDLE (0-110) (4-Y.O+) (Class F)
1-00 (1-00) **2m 110y (8 hdls)** £2,156.60 (£597.60: £285.80) GOING: 0.41 sec per fur (GS)

	Horse			SP	RR	SF
20013	**I'm a Dreamer (IRE) (94)** (MissMERowland) **7-11-9** PMidgley (a.p: led 2 out: hld on wl)	—	1	8/1	74	25
13094	**Silly Money (87)** (TDEasterby) **6-11-2** ECallaghan (lw: trckd ldrs: ev ch 2 out: disp ld flat: nt qckn cl home)	nk	2	6/1 3	67	18
	Rare Occurance (80) (JGMO'Shea) **7-10-9** MichaelBrennan (lw: hdwy 5th: ev ch 3 out: rdn & one pce)	6	3	20/1	54	5
165211	**Lucky Bea (84)** (MWEasterby) **4-10-1** GLee (in tch: outpcd 5th: hdwy 3 out: blnd 2 out: nt pce to chal)	1¾	4	9/2 2	56	—
17774	**Dark Phoenix (IRE) (87)** (OBrennan) **7-11-2** RMassey (chsd ldrs: rdn & one pce fr 3 out)	2½	5	4/1 1	57	8
18512	**Willy Star (BEL) (95)** (MrsSJSmith) **7-11-7(3)** RWilkinson (lw: chsd ldrs: rdn appr 3 out: no imp after)	2½	6	7/1	62	13
19925	**Past Master (USA) (83)** (SGollings) **9-10-9(3)** GSupple (led tl hdd & wknd 2 out)	½	7	10/1	50	1
21126	**Moor Hall Lady (88)** (NMBabbage) **6-11-3** GTormey (mstke 3rd: hdwy 4th: outpcd 5th: n.d after)	12	8	9/2 2	43	—
1776P	**Northern Falcon (87)** (MWEasterby) **4-10-4b** FLeahy (outpcd & lost tch 5th: n.d after)	13	9	11/1	30	—
25416	**Jarrow (71)** (MrsAMNaughton) **6-10-0** GFRyan (prom tl outpcd 5th: sn bhd)	7	10	50/1	7	—

(SP 118.4%) **10 Rn**

4m 6.7 (16.70) CSF £51.61 CT £853.41 TOTE £8.70: £1.80 £2.50 £2.90 (£39.50) Trio £189.90; £187.30 to Doncaster 25/1/97 OWNER Miss M. E. Rowland (LOWER BLIDWORTH) BRED A. Watkins
LONG HANDICAP Jarrow 9-8
WEIGHT FOR AGE 4yo-12lb
2001 I'm a Dreamer (IRE), happier on this faster ground, showed fine resolution to hold on. (8/1)
1309 Silly Money at last showed what he can do here, but it has to be said this was a moderate event. (6/1)
Rare Occurance has obviously had his problems, judging by his lack of action over the last two seasons. Considering this was his first run for almost a year, it was a fair effort. (20/1)
1159 Lucky Bea looked short of pace when the tempo increased here, but he was keeping on at the end and gives the impression that easier ground might well help. (9/2: 3/1-5/1)
1777 Dark Phoenix (IRE), well supported, had her chances, only to prove one-paced in the closing stages. Her stable has yet to hit any sort of form. (4/1)
1851 Willy Star (BEL) looks to have his fair share of weight. (7/1: op 9/2)

2745 BALBY NOVICES' CHASE (6-Y.O+) (Class D)
1-35 (1-35) **2m 110y (12 fncs)** £3,960.00 (£1,080.00: £520.00) GOING: 0.41 sec per fur (GS)

	Horse / details	Dist	Pos	SP	RR	SF
1066[2]	**Jathib (CAN) (128)** (MrsMerritaJones) **6-11-12** DerekByrne (cl up: led fr 6th: comf)	—	1	4/5[1]	125+	49
2641[F]	**Golden Hello** (TDEasterby) **6-11-12** RGarritty (lw: j.rt: trckd ldrs: effrt & ch 3 out: nt qckn)	4	2	100/30[2]	121	45
1831[6]	**Brazil Or Bust (IRE) (99)** (PRWebber) **6-11-6** MAFitzgerald (hld up: effrt 4 out: sn rdn & one pce)	9	3	7/2[3]	106?	30
1414*	**Sigma Run (IRE) (81)** (JGMO'Shea) **8-11-1**(5) MichaelBrennan (led to 6th: ev ch tl fell 4 out)		F	14/1	—	—
				(SP 107.5%)		**4 Rn**

4m 7.1 (12.10) CSF £3.51 TOTE £1.80 (£1.70) OWNER Crown Pkg & Mailing Svs Ltd (LAMBOURN) BRED Hill 'N Dale Farms

1066 Jathib (CAN) had no problems going left-handed this time and, although getting a bit warm beforehand, he always had this situation well in hand. (4/5: op evens)

2641 Golden Hello was wearing a pricker on his off-side, but it had little effect as he continually jumped right and the winner was always far too good for him. (100/30)

1831 Brazil Or Bust (IRE) spent the early part of the race being bumped by Golden Hello at every fence. His rider eventually caught on, but his mount then cried enough four out. (7/2)

1414* Sigma Run (IRE) ran well and was still pestering the winner when meeting the fourth last all wrong. (14/1: 8/1-16/1)

2746 CUSWORTH NOVICES' HURDLE (5-Y.O+) (Class D)
2-05 (2-07) **3m 110y (11 hdls)** £3,353.00 (£933.00: £449.00) GOING: 0.41 sec per fur (GS)

	Horse / details	Dist	Pos	SP	RR	SF
1539*	**Salmon Breeze (IRE) (95)** (NJHenderson) **6-11-4** MAFitzgerald (lw: a.p: led 3 out: ran on u.p)	—	1	7/1[2]	92	43
1795[3]	**Absolutly Equiname (IRE)** (MJHeaton-Ellis) **6-10-12** DGallagher (hdwy 5th: sn trckng ldrs: ev ch fr 3 out: kpt on wl)	nk	2	12/1	86	37
1505[4]	**Satcotino (IRE)** (MHTompkins) **6-10-7** KGaule (bhd: hdwy 7th: hrd rdn & chsng ldrs appr 3 out: kpt on)	7	3	16/1	76	27
2076[2]	**Coole Hill (IRE) (95)** (DNicholson) **6-10-7** AMaguire (a.p: effrt & ev ch 3 out: r.o one pce)	2	4	7/1[2]	75	26
1998[4]	**Gaye Fame (92)** (KCBailey) **6-10-13** PCarberry (hdwy 7th: sn chsng ldrs: effrt 3 out: no imp)	11	5	7/1[2]	74	25
2550[8]	**Clever Boy (IRE) (67)** (JWCurtis) **6-11-4** DerekByrne (lw: chsd ldrs: outpcd 4 out: kpt on fr 2 out: no mp)	11	6	25/1	72	23
1907[5]	**Mesp (IRE) (69)** (JGMO'Shea) **6-10-2v**[1](5) MichaelBrennan (a.p: disp ld 4 out to 3 out: wknd)	5	7	50/1	57	8
2546[3]	**Hand Woven (123)** (NATwiston-Davies) **5-11-4** CLlewellyn (lw: chsd ldr: led 5th tl hdd & blnd 3 out: sn btn)	nk	8	10/11[1]	68	19
1795[9]	**Sammorello (IRE)** (NATwiston-Davies) **6-10-12** DBridgwater (bhd: pushed along ½-wy: n.d)	25	9	25/1	46	—
1782[3]	**Dannicus** (NMBabbage) **6-10-12** VSlattery (prom tl rdn & wknd 7th)	22	10	14/1	31	—
730[P]	**Rushen Raider** (KWHogg) **5-10-12** MFoster (mstkes: prom tl wknd 4 out)	3	11	10/1[3]	29	—
1774[13]	**One More Rupee** (CPMorlock) **6-10-5**(7) MHandley (racd wd: led to 5th: wknd qckly & sn wl t.o)	dist	12	66/1	—	—
1579[5]	**Nautilus The Third (IRE)** (MDHammond) **6-10-12** RGarritty (lost tch fr 4 out: p.u bef 2 out)		P	20/1	—	—
1818[8]	**Dodgy Dancer (70)** (MrsLWilliamson) **7-10-12** LO'Hara (chsd ldrs tl wknd fr 7th: p.u bef 3 out)		P	66/1	—	—
2576[8]	**Lilly The Filly** (MrsBarbaraWaring) **6-10-7** RGreene (a bhd: p.u bef 3 out)		P	100/1	—	—
	Book of Dreams (IRE) (60) (JGMO'Shea) **9-10-12** RichardGuest (bhd: hdwy 6th: wknd 4 out: p.u bef 3 out)		P	100/1	—	—
	Kickcashtal (MrsCMBowman) **8-10-12** WFry (wl t.o whn p.u bef 4 out)		P	100/1	—	—
				(SP 139.6%)		**17 Rn**

6m 0.4 (17.40) CSF £85.53 TOTE £7.70: £2.40 £2.90 £4.00 (£32.70) Trio £232.10 OWNER The Salmon Racing Partnership (LAMBOURN) BRED William Kavanagh

OFFICIAL EXPLANATION **Hand Woven: ran flat and may not have recovered from a hard race last time.**

1539* Salmon Breeze (IRE), a good-looking sort, enjoyed this longer trip and did it well. When he goes chasing, he will really come into his own. (7/1)

1795 Absolutly Equiname (IRE), who has always looked a stayer, kept fighting away here and further tests of stamina will bring its rewards.(12/1)

Satcotino (IRE) certainly does not do anything quickly, but she does respond to pressure and seems to stay forever. (16/1)

2076 Coole Hill (IRE) keeps running well, but she is just failing to get home at present. To give her the benefit, her yard is not in the best of form right now. (7/1)

1998 Gaye Fame, close enough if good enough from the fourth last, failed to pick up when ridden. (7/1)

1575 Clever Boy (IRE) had a stiff task and, in the circumstances, ran pretty well. (25/1)

2546 Hand Woven was a big disappointment and was already in trouble when a bad blunder three out stopped him altogether. (10/11)

2747 ROSSINGTON MAIN NOVICES' HURDLE (Gd 2) (4-Y.O+) (Class A)
2-35 (2-37) **2m 110y (8 hdls)** £9,901.00 (£3,677.80: £1,796.40: £814.80) GOING: 0.41 sec per fur (GS)

	Horse / details	Dist	Pos	SP	RR	SF
1862*	**Le Teteu (FR)** (BobJones) **4-10-7** RGarritty (trckd ldrs: led 3 out: r.o wl appr last)	—	1	5/2[2]	85	49
1867*	**Hurricane Lamp (117)** (DNicholson) **6-11-5** AMaguire (hdwy 4th: led after next: hdd & mstke 3 out: ev ch tl outpcd appr last)	5	2	11/8[1]	80	56
1368[3]	**Green Green Desert (FR)** (OSherwood) **6-11-5** DBridgwater (lw: hld up: ev ch 3 out: rdn & fnd nil next)	7	3	5/1[3]	73	49
2074*	**Mister Rm (110)** (NATwiston-Davies) **5-11-5** CLlewellyn (lw: in tch: effrt 5th: one pce)	6	4	5/1[3]	68	44
2506[U]	**Herbert Lodge (IRE) (110)** (KCBailey) **8-11-5b**[1] PCarberry (led & sn wl clr: hit 3rd: blnd bdly 5th & sn hdd: nt rcvr)	dist	5	10/1	—	—
				(SP 113.1%)		**5 Rn**

3m 58.2 (8.20) CSF £6.20 TOTE £4.10: £2.20 £1.30 (£4.10) OWNER Mrs Judit Woods (NEWMARKET) BRED Pillar Stud

WEIGHT FOR AGE 4yo-12lb

1862* Le Teteu (FR) is not very big, but has what some of his opponents lack, namely a heart for the game. Always going nicely, he showed a useful turn of foot to settle it. (5/2)

1867* Hurricane Lamp looked the type to pick up the winner and carry him but, when it came down to a struggle, found that size is no match for guts. (11/8)

1368 Green Green Desert (FR) has made a career out of being beaten and showed just how it is done again. (5/1)

2074* Mister Rm looked well short of pace in this company and was fighting a lost cause from some way out. (5/1)

1907 Herbert Lodge (IRE) was, not for the first time, very awkward beforehand and went off at breakneck speed. After virtually falling at the fifth flight, that was it. (10/1)

2748 DONCASTER SPONSORSHIP CLUB H'CAP CHASE (0-135) (5-Y.O+) (Class C)
3-10 (3-11) **2m 3f 110y (15 fncs)** £4,597.50 (£1,380.00: £665.00: £307.50) GOING: 0.41 sec per fur (GS)

	Horse	Dist	Pos	SP	RR	SF
	Bell Staffboy (IRE) (110) (JGMO'Shea) **8-10-9**(5) MichaelBrennan (lw: cl up: led 8th: drew clr fr 4 out: eased flat)	—	1	2/1[2]	125+	53
2508[2]	**Puritan (CAN) (109)** (NTinkler) **8-10-13b** RGarritty (lw: trckd ldrs: pushed along 8th: sn chsng wnr: rdn & no imp fr 4 out)	7	2	Evens[1]	118	46
	In Truth (119) (SGollings) **9-11-9** KGaule (led tl hdd & outpcd 8th: hit 9th: sn btn)	28	3	8/1	105	33
1902[3]	**Linden's Lotto (IRE) (120)** (JWhite) **8-11-10** AMaguire (sn wl bhd)	dist	4	5/1[3]	—	—

(SP 111.1%) **4 Rn**

4m 57.5 (10.50) CSF £4.32 TOTE £3.60: (£2.40) OWNER K W Bell & Son Ltd (WESTBURY-ON-SEVERN) BRED Maurice Fenton
Bell Staffboy (IRE), who looked superb, won this in useful fashion and looks worth following. (2/1)
2508 Puritan (CAN), who loves this track, is well handicapped, but simply met one far too good. (Evens)
In Truth ran well after almost two years off and will be happier with more give in the ground. (8/1)
1902 Linden's Lotto (IRE) showed absolutely nothing. (5/1)

2749 SANDALL BEAT NOVICES' H'CAP CHASE (0-115) (5-Y.O+) (Class D)
3-40 (3-41) **3m (18 fncs)** £3,704.50 (£1,081.00: £518.00: £236.50) GOING: 0.41 sec per fur (GS)

	Horse	Dist	Pos	SP	RR	SF
2568[6]	**God Speed You (IRE) (101)** (CPMorlock) **8-11-5b** AMaguire (mde all: mstkes 4th & 11th: kpt on wl fr 4 out)	—	1	11/8[1]	118	41
1923[2]	**Father Sky (110)** (OSherwood) **6-12-0b** PNiven (lw: chsd wnr fr 5th: rdn 13th: no imp fr 4 out)	16	2	85/40[2]	116	39
1856[5]	**The Booley House (IRE) (97)** (VSoane) **7-11-1** DerekByrne (bhd: sme hdwy 12th: n.d)	19	3	13/2	91	14
2548[3]	**Ronans Glen (82)** (MJWilkinson) **10-10-0** RSupple (chsd ldrs: drvn along fr 9th: wknd 12th: blnd bdly 13th)	5	4	5/1[3]	72	—
	Lord Vick (IRE) (82) (MissAEEmbiricos) **8-10-0b[1]** JRyan (chsd ldrs: reminders 5th & 7th: mstke 11th: sn wknd)	25	5	14/1	56	—

(SP 110.8%) **5 Rn**

6m 12.5 (18.50) CSF £4.51 TOTE £2.40: £1.30 £1.40 (£1.80) OWNER Wallop (WANTAGE) BRED Mrs Vincent O'Brien
LONG HANDICAP Ronans Glen 9-4 Lord Vick (IRE) 9-1
STEWARDS' ENQUIRY Ryan susp. 3/4/2/97 (improper use of whip)
2568 God Speed You (IRE) did nothing wrong this time, apart from getting in a bit close to some fences, and won in really good style. (11/8)
1923 Father Sky finished in the prizemoney yet again and ran a fair race, but was completely outclassed over the last four fences.(85/40)
The Booley House (IRE) is a big boat of a horse who never looked likely to get into this. (13/2)
2548 Ronans Glen last won almost four years ago. 10lb wrong in the handicap, he was done with a mile from home. (5/1)

2750 WEATHERBYS 'STARS OF TOMORROW' STANDARD OPEN N.H. FLAT RACE (4, 5 & 6-Y.O) (Class H)
4-10 (4-10) **2m 110y** £1,507.50 (£420.00: £202.50)

	Horse	Dist	Pos	SP	RR	SF
1692*	**Mr Lurpak** (MrsMReveley) **5-11-12** PNiven (lw: a gng wl: smooth hdwy to ld 2f out: shkn up & r.o)	—	1	6/5[1]	84 f	—
	Potter Again (IRE) (DNicholson) **5-10-11**(3) RMassey (trckd ldrs fr ½-wy: disp ld 4f out to 2f out: r.o: nt pce of wnr)	4	2	4/1[2]	68 f	—
	The Snow Burn (TPTate) **4-10-7** JCallaghan (hld up: hdwy ½-wy: disp ld 4f out to 2f out: kpt on same pce)	5	3	20/1	68 f	—
	Jack Robbo (IRE) (JGFitzGerald) **5-11-5** WDwan (bhd: pushed along ½-wy: styd on fnl 4f: nrst fin)	19	4	10/1	50 f	—
1289[4]	**Wentworth (USA)** (GThorner) **5-11-5** DBridgwater (cl up: ev ch & rdn 4f out: sn wknd)	2	5	12/1	48 f	—
	Polo Ridge (IRE) (OSherwood) **5-10-12**(7) DThomas (hld up: hdwy 7f out: sn prom: one pce fnl 4f)	2½	6	10/1	46 f	—
	My Buster (MissSEHall) **5-11-5** AMaguire (bit bkwd: trckd ldrs: led 7f out to 4f out: grad lost pl)	2	7	6/1[3]	44 f	—
	Chasing Dreams (CGrant) **6-11-5** RGarritty (lw: trckd ldrs tl wknd fnl 4f)	1½	8	20/1	42 f	—
	Coromandel (AHHarvey) **5-11-0** ASSmith (bhd: gd hdwy 7f out: chsng ldrs 4f out: sn rdn & wknd)	6	9	25/1	31 f	—
	Brief Suspence (IRE) (RAFahey) **4-10-7** DerekByrne (nvr nr to chal)	2½	10	20/1	34 f	—
1275[3]	**Prototype** (GFJohnsonHoughton) **6-11-12** MAFitzgerald (disp ld after 3f tl lost pl 3f out: shkn up 3f out: n.d)	7	11	7/1	34 f	—
	Pearl Silk (TTBill) **4-9-13**(3) GLee (chsd ldrs tl wknd fnl 6f)	2	12	33/1	20 f	—
	Connel's Croft (JMackie) **5-11-5** RSupple (hdwy ½-wy: outpcd fnl 5f)	6	13	33/1	19 f	—
2066[13]	**Social Insecurity (IRE)** (SGollings) **6-11-5** KGaule (led tl hdd 7f out: sn rdn & wknd: t.o)	30	14	50/1	—	—
	Woodhouse Lane (NChamberlain) **5-10-12**(7) MissCMetcalfe (a bhd: t.o)	s.h	15	50/1	—	—
	Seven Four Seven (MrsLWilliamson) **6-11-0** LO'Hara (a bhd: t.o)	20	16	50/1	—	—

(SP 148.0%) **16 Rn**

3m 58.1 CSF £6.14 TOTE £2.10: £1.30 £1.60 £7.00 (£4.50) Trio £68.80 OWNER MD Foods Plc (SALTBURN) BRED Exors of the late Countess of Durham
WEIGHT FOR AGE 4yo-12lb
1692* Mr Lurpak again looked useful, and his turn of foot will stand him in good stead in any company. (6/5)
Potter Again (IRE) put up a good performance against a useful rival and surely compensation awaits. (4/1)
The Snow Burn, one of the best lookers in the field, ran pretty well and the future looks bright, especially when he goes over obstacles. (20/1)
Jack Robbo (IRE), a real jumping type, proved too slow in this company, but was keeping on well at the end. (10/1: op 6/1)
1289 Wentworth (USA) had his chances, but was firmly put in his place when the pressure was on in the last half-mile. (12/1: op 8/1)
Polo Ridge (IRE) looks a stayer and ran accordingly. (10/1: op 6/1)
My Buster was not knocked about and is one to watch when put over hurdles. (6/1)
1275 Prototype (7/1: op 4/1)
T/Plpt: £199.10 (44.67 Tckts). T/Qdpt: £27.40 (27 Tckts). AA

2417-FOLKESTONE (R-H) (Chases Good to soft, Hdles Soft)
Friday January 24th
Race 6: two fences omitted first circuit, three fences omitted second circuit
WEATHER: sunny & mild

2751 VALENTINE GORTON MAIDEN HURDLE (4-Y.O) (Class E)
1-10 (1-11) **2m 1f 110y (8 hdls)** £2,749.30 (£764.80: £367.90) GOING: 0.72 sec per fur (S)

	Horse	Dist	Pos	SP	RR	SF
1862[2]	**Desert Mountain (IRE)** (NACallaghan) **4-11-5** RHughes (plld hrd: a.p: led appr last: rdn out)	—	1	3/1[2]	77	23

Prev	Horse / details	Dist	Pos	SP	RR	SF
	Melt The Clouds (CAN) (MCPipe) **4-11-5** RDunwoody (lw: hdwy 3 out: ev ch last: unable qckn)	1¾	2	100/30[3]	75	21
	Anna Soleil (IRE) (OSherwood) **4-11-5** JAMcCarthy (led to 2nd: led 3 out tl appr last: sn wknd)	5	3	16/1	71	17
2622[2]	**Mr Wild (USA)** (RAkehurst) **4-11-0**(5) SRyan (hld up: 5th whn mstke 2 out: wknd appr last)	12	4	6/4[1]	60	6
	Illuminate (DCO'Brien) **4-11-5** TJMurphy (lw: nvr nr to chal)	nk	5	33/1	60	6
	Daydreamer (USA) (RHBuckler) **4-11-5** BPowell (hdwy 3rd: wknd 5th)	16	6	25/1	45	—
1634[13]	**Claire's Dancer (IRE)** (AndrewTurnell) **4-11-5b**[1] LHarvey (swtg: plld hrd: led 2nd to 3 out: sn wknd: t.o)	dist	7	50/1	—	—
2574[8]	**Aavasaksa (FR)** (AGNewcombe) **4-11-2**(3) TDascombe (a bhd: t.o whn fell last)		F	100/1	—	—
	Elite Force (IRE) (MMadgwick) **4-11-5** DMorris (bhd fr 4th: t.o whn p.u bef 3 out)		P	50/1	—	—
	Queens Fancy (SDow) **4-11-0** ADicken (a bhd: t.o whn p.u bef last)		P	66/1	—	—
	Prospero (MrsAJPerrett) **4-11-5** MRichards (bit bkwd: a.p: ev ch 2 out: sn wknd: p.u bef last)		P	7/1	—	—
2070[13]	**Jamies First (IRE)** (RIngram) **4-11-5** DO'Sullivan (lw: bhd fr 4th: t.o whn p.u bef 3 out)		P	100/1	—	—
				(SP 120.6%)	**12 Rn**	

4m 28.9 (22.90) CSF £12.43 TOTE £4.40: £1.20 £1.20 £4.40 (£14.30) Trio £25.30 OWNER Easy Monk Partnership (NEWMARKET) BRED Ron Con Ltd

1862 Desert Mountain (IRE) confirmed the promise shown on his debut, despite taking a keen hold. He will now be entered for the Triumph Hurdle. (3/1)

Melt The Clouds (CAN), placed several times on the Flat but never successful, was sold out of Peter Harris' stable for 25,000 guineas. Looking in good shape for this hurdling debut, he now looks set to open his account. (100/30: 5/1-3/1)

Anna Soleil (IRE), a one-paced maiden on the Flat for Mick Channon, has been off the course since last April but still showed plenty of promise on this hurdling debut. A rangy gelding, he should be able to find a race before long. (16/1)

2622 Mr Wild (USA) looked nailed-on for an ordinary novice event like this after showing good form in better company, which makes this performance very disappointing. An uneasy favourite, he was not travelling particularly well in the back straight and flattened the second last. (6/4: op 4/5)

Prospero (7/1: 7/2-8/1)

2752 MANSTON NOVICES' H'CAP CHASE (0-100) (5-Y.O+) (Class E)

1-45 (1-47) **2m (12 fncs)** £3,128.75 (£935.00: £447.50: £203.75) GOING: 0.72 sec per fur (S)

Prev	Horse / details	Dist	Pos	SP	RR	SF
	Key Player (IRE) (71) (RRowe) **8-10-4** DO'Sullivan (a.p: chsd ldr appr last: led flat: r.o wl)	—	1	16/1	82	12
	Mr Bean (87) (KRBurke) **7-11-6** ALarnach (a.p: led appr last tl flat: unable qckn)	1	2	16/1	97	27
2068[3]	**Policemans Pride (FR) (67)** (MMadgwick) **8-10-0** DMorris (led to 6th: lft in ld 2 out: sn hdd & wknd)	10	3	12/1	67	—
2068[2]	**River Leven (91)** (DRGandolfo) **8-11-10b** RDunwoody (nvr nr to chal)	6	4	5/2[1]	85	15
	Virbazar (FR) (69) (JGSmyth-Osbourne) **10-10-2**ow2 GUpton (bit bkwd: blnd 2nd: hdwy 6th: wknd 3 out)	2½	5	16/1	61	—
406[3]	**Brigadier Supreme (IRE) (72)** (PButler) **8-10-5** TJMurphy (a bhd: hmpd 4th: t.o fr 5th)	dist	6	33/1	—	—
1582[F]	**Master Pangloss (IRE) (68)** (AndrewTurnell) **7-9-8**(7)ow1 CRae (mid div whn b.d 4th)		B	33/1	—	—
2569[2]	**Bold Acre (76)** (JMBradley) **7-10-9b** PHide (a.p: led 6th tl fell 2 out)		F	3/1[2]	—	—
1677[F]	**Relkowen (80)** (AndrewTurnell) **7-10-13** MRichards (fell 1st)		F	13/2	—	—
2037[F]	**Caracol (67)** (JNeville) **8-9-11**(3) TDascombe (4th whn fell 4th)		F	6/1[3]	—	—
1708[7]	**Full of Tricks (67)** (JJBridger) **9-10-0** LHarvey (lw: a bhd: t.o whn p.u bef 8th)		P	33/1	—	—
1812[F]	**Hidden Pleasure (76)** (TMJones) **11-10-9** DLeahy (bit bkwd: s.s: t.o whn virtually ref 3rd: p.u bef 5th)		P	33/1	—	—
2548[B]	**Smart Casanova (67)** (MJWilkinson) **8-10-0** TJO'Sullivan (in rr: hdwy 3 out: sn wknd: 5th & no ch whn blnd & uns rdr last)		U	33/1	—	—
				(SP 121.2%)	**13 Rn**	

4m 12.7 (20.70) CSF £204.62 CT £2,856.93 TOTE £47.40: £7.90 £2.70 £2.30 (£187.40) Trio £229.00; £290.30 to Doncaster 25/1/97 OWNER Mr W. Packham (PULBOROUGH) BRED William. J. Hamilton

LONG HANDICAP Master Pangloss (IRE) 9-9 Caracol 9-7 Full of Tricks 9-7 Virbazar (FR) 9-7 Smart Casanova 9-7

Key Player (IRE), who had shown little to date, caused quite a shock as he made a winning debut over fences, despite an absence of over a year. (16/1)

Mr Bean, fit from the Flat, made a very pleasing debut over fences and was rated 14lb lower than on his only outing over hurdles last season. (16/1)

2068 Policemans Pride (FR) ran better here. He is, though, a poor, exposed gelding who remains a maiden after twenty-three attempts. (12/1: 6/1-14/1)

2068 River Leven was very disappointing. (5/2)

1677 Relkowen (13/2: 3/1-7/1)

2753 NORTH FORELAND (S) HURDLE (4,5,6 & 7-Y.O) (Class G)

2-15 (2-16) **2m 1f 110y (8 hdls)** £2,074.20 (£576.20: £276.60) GOING: 0.72 sec per fur (S)

Prev	Horse / details	Dist	Pos	SP	RR	SF
836[5]	**Yellow Dragon (IRE)** (BAPearce) **4-10-5** RHughes (hdwy 3rd: led appr last: comf)	—	1	7/1[3]	60	13
	Chocolate Ice (RJO'Sullivan) **4-10-5** DO'Sullivan (lost pl 3rd: rallied to chse wnr appr last: unable qckn)	9	2	5/1[2]	52	5
1990[2]	**Furietto (IRE) (95)** (MDHammond) **7-11-10** RDunwoody (led tl appr last: sn wknd)	8	3	11/10[1]	52	17
1679[5]	**Quaker Waltz (80)** (JCTuck) **7-10-12** SMcNeill (a.p: chsd ldr 3 out tl appr last: sn wknd)	4	4	5/1[2]	36	1
1707[F]	**Memory's Music (68)** (MMadgwick) **5-11-3** DMorris (hld up: rdn 2 out: sn wknd: t.o whn p.u bef last)		P	8/1	—	—
1818[P]	**Office Hours** (WGMTurner) **5-11-3** WMcFarland (lw: stdy hdwy 3 out: wknd after 2 out: t.o whn p.u bef last)		P	14/1	—	—
1333[P]	**Saboteuse** (JCPoulton) **5-10-12** TJMurphy (chsd ldr tl appr 4th: sn wknd: t.o whn p.u bef 2 out)		P	20/1	—	—
	Tennyson Bay (JRPoulton) **5-11-3** ADicken (mstke 1st: a bhd: t.o whn p.u bef last: dismntd)		P	25/1	—	—
1149[10]	**Storm Wind (IRE)** (KRBurke) **4-10-5** ALarnach (hdwy 3rd: chsd ldr appr 4th to 3 out: wknd 2 out: t.o whn p.u bef last)		P	33/1	—	—
2678[15]	**Sayitagain** (JRJenkins) **5-10-10**(7) NTEgan (bhd fr 3rd: t.o whn p.u bef last)		P	33/1	—	—
				(SP 125.7%)	**10 Rn**	

4m 28.1 (22.10) CSF £39.75 TOTE £18.40: £3.40 £1.70 £1.50 (£18.20) Trio £9.10 OWNER Mr C. M. Kwai (LIMPSFIELD) BRED J. N. McCaffrey

WEIGHT FOR AGE 4yo-12lb

Bt in 5,500 gns

654 Yellow Dragon (IRE) made no mistake in this bad race, cruising into the lead approaching the last and asserting with the minimum of fuss. (7/1)

Chocolate Ice, fit from the Flat where he remained a maiden, was dropped in class for this hurdling debut. (5/1: 6/1-4/1)

1990 Furietto (IRE), whose only victory to date came over three miles, was taking a drop in distance and decided to force the pace in order to wear out his rivals on this testing ground. However, collared on the long run to the final flight, he soon tired. (11/10: 8/11-6/5)

1679 Quaker Waltz was taking a drop in class. (5/1)

2754 KENT H'CAP CHASE (0-125) (5-Y.O+) (Class D)

2-45 (2-47) **3m 2f (19 fncs)** £4,760.00 (£1,430.00: £690.00: £320.00) GOING: 0.72 sec per fur (S)

Form	Horse	Dist	Pos	SP	RR	SF
1799[4]	**Court Melody (IRE) (115)** (PFNicholls) **9-10-11b**(7) MrJTizzard (hdwy 8th: led 13th: hrd rdn appr last: r.o wl)	—	1	8/1	124	32
1811*	**Little Martina (IRE) (105)** (DMGrissell) **9-10-8** JRKavanagh (lw: led after 3rd to 6th: led 10th to 12th: rdn 3 out: r.o wl flat)	½	2	5/2[1]	114	22
2011[3]	**Spuffington (113)** (JTGifford) **9-10-13**(3) LAspell (hdwy 5th: rdn appr 2 out: unable qckn)	4	3	13/2[3]	119	27
2075[5]	**Celtic Town (104)** (OSherwood) **9-10-7b** JAMcCarthy (nvr nr to chal)	18	4	20/1	99	7
1662[P]	**Beaurepaire (IRE) (108)** (RHAlner) **9-10-11** SMcNeill (lw: led 6th to 10th: led 12th to 13th: wknd 14th: t.o)	dist	5	11/1	—	—
2011[P]	**Celtic Barle (102)** (HBHodge) **13-10-5** ILawrence (lw: hdwy 11th: rdn 3 out: 4th & btn whn mstke 2 out: t.o)	6	6	8/1	—	—
1937[P]	**Sheer Ability (125)** (CJMann) **11-12-0** RDunwoody (bit bkwd: a bhd: t.o fr 7th)	dist	7	12/1	—	—
2063[2]	**Diamond Fort (105)** (JCMcConnochie) **12-10-8** RFarrant (lw: a bhd: t.o fr 7th: p.u bef 13th)		P	14/1	—	—
1806[6]	**Flashthecash (122)** (CREgerton) **11-11-11** MRichards (lw: hdwy 13th: wknd 4 out: wl bhd whn p.u bef last)		P	10/1	—	—
	Top Brass (IRE) (103) (KCBailey) **9-10-6** TJMurphy (led tl after 3rd: wknd 13th: t.o whn p.u bef 15th)		P	9/1	—	—
1728*	**Flow (105)** (RHBuckler) **8-10-8** BPowell (bhd fr 7th: t.o whn p.u bef 3 out)		P	9/2[2]	—	—
	Veryvel (CZE) (97) (JNeville) **6-10-0** NMann (bhd whn blnd & uns rdr 1st)		U	20/1	—	—

(SP 133.6%) **12 Rn**

6m 50.9 (30.90) CSF £30.24 CT £135.87 TOTE £14.40: £5.30 £1.40 £2.00 (£37.80) Trio £102.10 OWNER J W Aplin, P K Barber & Mick Coburn (SHEPTON MALLET) BRED Miss E. Charlton

1799 Court Melody (IRE), a real mudlark, had some cut in the ground for the first time this season and duly returned to the winner's enclosure. (8/1)

1811* Little Martina (IRE) showed the right attitude here. After appearing to get tapped for toe from the third last, she refused to give in without a struggle and may well have prevailed with a little further to go. A progressive mare, she should not take long to get back into the winner's enclosure. (5/2)

2011 Spuffington goes well with some give in the ground, but found lack of acceleration his undoing early in the straight. He has not won for nearly two years. (13/2)

2075 Celtic Town had the blinkers on this time, but they failed to have the desired effect and he never threatened to get into it. (20/1)

1662 Beaurepaire (IRE) again ran badly, and was hung out to dry the best part of a mile from home. (11/1: 8/1-12/1)

2011 Celtic Barle was held in fourth pace when making an error two from home. (8/1)

1728* Flow (9/2: op 3/1)

2755 H.B.L.B. GOODWINS H'CAP HURDLE (0-105) (4-Y.O+) (Class F)

3-20 (3-20) **2m 1f 110y (8 hdls)** £2,180.00 (£605.00: £290.00) GOING: 0.72 sec per fur (S)

Form	Horse	Dist	Pos	SP	RR	SF
1828[3]	**Added Dimension (IRE) (89)** (PWinkworth) **6-10-8**(7) XAizpuru (swtg: hdwy to ld appr last: r.o wl)	—	1	11/1	74	—
1767[P]	**Classic Pal (USA) (75)** (NRMitchell) **6-10-1**ow1 DSkyrme (hld up: chsd wnr appr last: no imp)	6	2	10/1	55	—
1791[8]	**Mazzini (IRE) (97)** (RRowe) **6-11-2**(7) MrPO'Keeffe (led to 2nd: led 3rd to 3 out: rdn appr last: one pce)	1¾	3	13/2	75	1
1675[2]	**Always Happy (93)** (MissGayKelleway) **4-10-7** SMcNeill (lw: a.p: led 3 out tl appr last: sn wknd)	4	4	7/2[2]	67	—
2573*	**Zingibar (83)** (JMBradley) **5-10-9** RDunwoody (led 2nd to 3rd: wknd appr 2 out)	4	5	3/1[1]	54	—
816[9]	**Circus Colours (97)** (JRJenkins) **7-11-9** RHughes (bit bkwd: stdy hdwy 5th: wknd after 2 out)	10	6	14/1	59	—
1707*	**Zesti (80)** (TTClement) **5-10-6** NMann (hld up: rdn 2 out: sn wknd: t.o)	dist	7	5/1[3]	—	—
2067*	**Shepherds Rest (IRE) (101)** (SMellor) **5-11-6**(7) SHearn (lw: a.p: ev ch whn mstke & uns rdr 2 out)		U	11/2	—	—

(SP 116.7%) **8 Rn**

4m 33.9 (27.90) CSF £101.46 CT £709.28 TOTE £17.50: £3.10 £1.80 £2.60 (£54.60) Trio £98.40; £112.27 to Doncaster 25/1/97 OWNER Mr N. A. Dunger (DUNSFOLD) BRED Swettenham Stud and Ron Con Limited

WEIGHT FOR AGE 4yo-12lb

1828 Added Dimension (IRE) won his first race over hurdles. Making giant strides to lead approaching the last, he soon pulled away. (11/1)

Classic Pal (USA), having only his second outing after a lengthy lay-off, ran much better here. Taking second place approaching the final flight, he had no hope of reeling-in the winner. (10/1: 20/1-8/1)

1283* Mazzini (IRE), who made the majority of the running to the third last, looked like dropping out of it running down the hill, but did plod on to recapture third prize. (13/2)

1675 Always Happy, formerly with Martin Pipe, moved sweetly to the front three from home but, collared approaching the final flight, she had little more to offer. The soft ground may well have been too much for her. (7/2)

2573* Zingibar, set to rise 4lb in future handicaps, had shot his bolt approaching the second last. (3/1)

657 Circus Colours, looking big and well for this first run in nearly four months, crept closer a mile from home but decided he had done enough on the long downhill run. (14/1)

2756 CANTERBURY H'CAP CHASE (0-100) (5-Y.O+) (Class F)

3-50 (3-52) **2m 5f (10 fncs)** £3,064.90 (£851.40: £408.70) GOING: 0.72 sec per fur (S)

Form	Horse	Dist	Pos	SP	RR	SF
1819[4]	**Oxford Quill (71)** (RCurtis) **10-10-0** DMorris (lw: hdwy 6th: mstke 7th: led appr 2 out: hung lft appr last: drvn out)	—	1	25/1	84	20
1833[U]	**Playing Truant (81)** (DRGandolfo) **9-10-10** RDunwoody (hdwy 4 out: chsd wnr fr 2 out: mstke last: nt qckn)	8	2	9/2[1]	88	24
1947[3]	**Pearl's Choice (IRE) (87)** (JCMcConnochie) **9-11-2** BPowell (a.p: rdn appr 2 out: one pce)	2	3	13/2	92	28
2092[4]	**Channel Pastime (85)** (DBurchell) **13-10-11**(3) GuyLewis (a.p: rdn appr 2 out: sn wknd)	1¾	4	9/1	89	25
1710[3]	**Pavlova (IRE) (75)** (RRowe) **7-10-4** DO'Sullivan (7th whn mstke 4 out: no hdwy fr 3 out)	5	5	14/1	75	11
2665[P]	**Opal's Tenspot (71)** (JMBradley) **10-10-0** RFarrant (prom to 3 out)	27	6	25/1	51	—
1951*	**Titan Empress (81)** (SMellor) **8-10-10v** NMann (mid div whn b.d 4th: dead)		B	11/2[2]	—	—
1865[3]	**Prize Match (75)** (JCTuck) **8-10-4** SMcNeill (lw: bhd whn fell 4th)		F	12/1	—	—
1965[4]	**Cruise Control (78)** (RRowe) **11-10-0**(7) AGarrity (a bhd: mstke 3rd: t.o whn p.u bef last)		P	14/1	—	—
1934[4]	**Deependable (88)** (MrsLRichards) **10-11-3b** MRichards (lw: a bhd: t.o whn p.u bef 2 out)		P	12/1	—	—
286[3]	**Forest Feather (IRE) (87)** (CWeedon) **9-11-2b** BClifford (lw: bhd fr 6th: t.o whn p.u bef 4 out)		P	6/1[3]	—	—
70[5]	**Spy Dessa (71)** (AGNewcombe) **9-9-11**(3) PHenley (bit bkwd: mid div whn blnd bdly 4th: t.o fr 5th: p.u bef last)		P	12/1	—	—
	Retail Runner (90) (MissSEdwards) **12-11-5** MrTHills (bit bkwd: led tl appr 2 out: sn wknd: t.o whn p.u bef last)		P	7/1	—	—

(SP 127.8%) **13 Rn**

5m 31.7 (23.70) CSF £133.81 CT £774.68 TOTE £20.90: £5.40 £1.70 £2.40 (£114.50) Trio £409.00 OWNER Mr T. F. Parrett (LAMBOURN) BRED Mrs A. Bailey

LONG HANDICAP Oxford Quill 9-11 Spy Dessa 9-6 Opal's Tenspot 9-12

IN-FOCUS: First two fences running away from the stands were omitted due to the low positioning of the sun. In addition, the third last was omitted on the final circuit due to an injured horse.

1331 Oxford Quill liked the soft ground and lack of fences - normally they would have to jump fifteen. (25/1)

1833 Playing Truant crept steadily closer in the last mile, but after taking second place two from home, was unable to get on terms with the winner. (9/2)

1947 Pearl's Choice (IRE) has shown promise on both her previous starts this season, but once again was tapped for toe over the last two fences. (13/2)

2092 Channel Pastime has just one win to his name over fences, despite reaching the frame on all nine previous outings this season. Age is not on his side. (9/1)

1710 Pavlova (IRE), making her chasing debut against experienced rivals, made little impression over the last three fences. (14/1)

1817* Opal's Tenspot, pulled up at Leicester on Tuesday, had been hung out to dry three from home. (25/1)

1951* Titan Empress (11/2: 4/1-6/1)

286 Forest Feather (IRE) (6/1: 4/1-13/2)

Spy Dessa (12/1: 25/1-10/1)

Retail Runner (7/1: op 12/1)

2757 ASHFORD STANDARD N.H. FLAT RACE (4, 5 & 6-Y.O F & M) (Class H)

4-20 (4-22) **2m 1f 110y** £1,266.00 (£351.00: £168.00)

				SP	RR	SF
	Tara Gale (IRE) (JNeville) **5-10-11**(7) XAizpuru (hdwy over 2f out: led 1f out: r.o wl)	—	**1**	14/1	55 f	—
1450^{4}	**Where's Miranda** (GMMcCourt) **5-10-11**(7) RHobson (hld up: led wl over 1f out to 1f out: unable qckn)	3	**2**	7/4 1	52 f	—
1801^{6}	**Quistaquay** (JWMullins) **5-11-1**(3) PHenley (rdn over 6f out: hdwy over 2f out: r.o)	2	**3**	9/1	50 f	—
1966^{6}	**Jaydeebee** (MMadgwick) **6-10-11**(7) JPower (hdwy 12f out: ev ch wl over 1f out: wknd fnl f)	1¾	**4**	14/1	49 f	—
1966^{5}	**Hurricane Jane (IRE)** (MJRoberts) **5-11-4** MrsAPerrett (chsd ldr early: led 10f out tl wl over 1f out: sn wknd)	9	**5**	11/2 3	41 f	—
2073^{6}	**Bebe Grey** (PRHedger) **6-10-11v**(7) MClinton (lost pl 9f out: r.o one pce fnl 2f)	6	**6**	25/1	35 f	—
1913^{5}	**Ardrom** (PRWebber) **5-11-4** MrPScott (lw: prom 15f)	10	**7**	3/1 2	26 f	—
	Folesclave (IRE) (JSKing) **5-10-11**(7) MrJTizzard (hdwy 6f out: wknd 4f out)	9	**8**	10/1	18 f	—
1986^{7}	**Mistress Tudor** (SMellor) **6-11-1**(3) EHusband (led: sn clr: hdd 10f out: wknd 7f out)	9	**9**	20/1	10 f	—
1555^{10}	**Aintgotwon** (AHide) **6-11-1**(3) LAspell (hdwy 9f out: wknd 5f out)	16	**10**	25/1	—	—
1986^{6}	**Maggie Strait** (MrsALMKing) **5-10-11**(7) MrOMcPhail (bhd fnl 6f)	2	**11**	6/1	—	—
	Nelly Blanche (DRCElsworth) **6-10-11**(7) MrNMoran (hdwy 7f out: wknd 5f out)	26	**12**	16/1	—	—
				(SP 141.8%)	**12 Rn**	

4m 34.3 CSF £41.40 TOTE £12.50: £2.20 £1.20 £2.50 (£27.50) Trio £73.20 OWNER Mr A. J. Williams (NEWPORT, GWENT) BRED T. Coughlan

Tara Gale (IRE) began to pick up ground running down the hill and, sent on a furlong from home, proved too strong for the runner-up. (14/1)

1450 Where's Miranda, who showed promise on her debut, was sent to the front early in the short straight, but found the winner too good. (7/4)

1801 Quistaquay, as on her debut, was doing all her best work in the latter stages. Two and a half miles will probably be better for her. (9/1: 5/1-10/1)

1966 Jaydeebee ran better than she had done here last month, and had every chance before tiring in the final furlong. (14/1: 10/1-20/1)

1966 Hurricane Jane (IRE) went on with a circuit to race, but soon back-pedalled when collared early in the straight. Two miles on a sound surface will probably suit her better. (11/2: 4/1-7/1)

1913 Ardrom (3/1: 6/4-100/30)

Folesclave (IRE) (10/1: op 6/1)

Maggie Strait (6/1: op 10/1)

T/Plpt: £1,207.20 (7.15 Tckts). T/Qdpt: £43.00 (20.56 Tckts). AK

2297-UTTOXETER (L-H) (Good, Hdles Good to firm home st)

Friday January 24th

WEATHER: cloudy, becoming bright

2758 BRAKE BROS. FOOD SERVICES H'CAP CHASE (0-125) (5-Y.O+) (Class D)

1-15 (1-16) **3m 2f (20 fncs)** £3,647.50 (£1,105.00: £540.00: £257.50) GOING: 0.04 sec per fur (G)

				SP	RR	SF
2075*	**Lord Gyllene (NZ) (125)** (SABrookshaw) **9-12-0** ADobbin (led to 3rd: lft in ld 5th: qcknd 13th: clr 3 out: styd on strly)	—	**1**	8/1 3	143	56
1784*	**Samlee (IRE) (115)** (PJHobbs) **8-11-4** NWilliamson (lw: swtg: hld up in tch: effrt & rdn 4 out: styd on: no ch w wnr)	15	**2**	9/2 1	124	37
1799^{5}	**Rectory Garden (IRE) (111)** (CaptTAForster) **8-11-0** AThornton (a.p: pushed along 12th: styd on one pce fr 3 out)	3	**3**	11/2 2	118	31
1923*	**Musthaveaswig (123)** (DNicholson) **11-11-12** RJohnson (chsd ldrs: wnt 2nd 14th: rdn 3 out: sn btn)	2½	**4**	9/1	128	41
2011^{P}	**Big Ben Dun (107)** (CPEBrooks) **11-10-3**(7) MBerry (hld up & bhd: effrt 16th: wknd 3 out: t.o)	18	**5**	16/1	101	14
1765*	**Ballyea Boy (IRE) (113)** (DNicholson) **7-10-11**(5) MrRThornton (chsd ldrs: rdn 15th: sn wknd: t.o)	6	**6**	9/2 1	104	17
2089^{3}	**Harristown Lady (107)** (GBBalding) **10-10-10b** BFenton (a in rr: t.o)	s.h	**7**	20/1	98	11
1856^{4}	**Loch Garman Hotel (IRE) (99)** (PTDalton) **8-10-2**ow2 CMaude (lost pl 7th: sn bhd: t.o)	1½	**8**	66/1	89	—
1871^{2}	**Church Law (105)** (MrsLCTaylor) **10-10-8** JRailton (lw: hld up in rr: hdwy 15th: sn rdn: outpcd fr 3 out)	1½	**9**	8/1 3	94	7
1558^{3}	**Copper Mine (120)** (OSherwood) **11-11-9** JOsborne (bit bkwd: led 3rd: blnd & hdd 5th: wknd 14th: t.o)	17	**10**	14/1	98	11
2004^{4}	**Dont Tell the Wife (119)** (CREgerton) **11-11-8** JFTitley (lw: hld up in rr: reminders 11th: lost tch 13th: t.o)	12	**11**	16/1	90	3
				(SP 108.7%)	**11 Rn**	

6m 34.9 (7.90) CSF £37.30 CT £175.19 TOTE £7.10: £2.90 £1.80 £1.90 (£14.60) Trio £49.90 OWNER Mr Stanley Clarke (SHREWSBURY) BRED Mrs N. M. Taylor

LONG HANDICAP Loch Garman Hotel (IRE) 8-12

2075* Lord Gyllene (NZ) made sure this was a true test of stamina. Increasing the tempo a mile from home, he had broken his pursuers early in the straight. He can jump and, with stamina not a problem, he is now finding his way in this country. (8/1: op 5/1)

1784* Samlee (IRE) had to admit the winner much too good for him at the weights, and was never able to get within striking range. (9/2)

1799 Rectory Garden (IRE) was making hard work of it from a long way out, but he did keep plugging away and could be about to find his form. (11/2)

1923* Musthaveaswig went after the winner inside the final mile, but was fighting a lost cause from the turn into the straight. His stable seems to one of the worst sufferers from the bad weather at the turn of the year. (9/1)
1765* Ballyea Boy (IRE) travelled well in behind the leaders, but he was beginning to struggle at the end of the back straight and dropped away tamely. (9/2: op 3/1)

2759 ADDISON OF NEWPORT NOVICES' HURDLE (4-Y.O+) (Class E)
1-50 (1-51) **2m 4f 110y (10 hdls)** £2,652.00 (£747.00: £366.00) GOING: 0.04 sec per fur (G)

				SP	RR	SF
2053[3]	**Barton Ward** (SABrookshaw) **6-11-5** ADobbin (hld up: hdwy 7th: led appr 2 out: r.o strly)	—	**1**	8/1	77	40
1581*	**Sparkling Spring (IRE) (102)** (KCBailey) **6-11-11** CO'Dwyer (lw: chsd ldrs: ev ch 3 out: one pce fr next)	5	**2**	13/2	79	42
1768[2]	**Supreme Flyer (IRE)** (KCBailey) **7-10-12**(7) MrRWakley (a.p: mstke 7th: ev ch 2 out: nt pce of wnr)	2½	**3**	20/1	71	34
1959[2]	**The Captain's Wish (112)** (DNicholson) **6-11-11** RJohnson (hld up in tch: ev ch fr 3 out: rdn & one pce appr last)	2	**4**	6/1[3]	76	39
	The Bargeman (NZ) (DRGandolfo) **9-11-2**(3) DFortt (hld up & bhd: styd on fr 3 out: nvr nrr)	3	**5**	50/1	67	30
2642[2]	**Montecot (FR)** (SMellor) **8-11-5** JRailton (trckd ldrs: effrt & drvn along 3 out: no imp)	1½	**6**	15/8[1]	66	29
	Blazing Storm (IRE) (CREgerton) **5-11-0**(5) MrRThornton (bit bkwd: chsd ldrs tl wknd appr 2 out)	2½	**7**	25/1	64	27
2076[6]	**Burntwood Melody (70)** (PTDalton) **6-11-5** BFenton (prom to 3 out: sn rdn & wknd)	9	**8**	66/1	57	20
2074[3]	**Prussia (98)** (WClay) **6-11-11** AThornton (prom tl wknd appr 3 out)	6	**9**	25/1	58	21
1900[F]	**Topaglow (IRE)** (PTDalton) **4-10-6** TEley (lw: chsd ldrs tl wknd appr 2 out)	s.h	**10**	33/1	52	2
1801[5]	**Jet Files (IRE)** (MrsJPitman) **6-11-5** WMarston (hld up: a bhd: t.o)	6	**11**	20/1	48	11
2060*	**Shu Gaa (IRE)** (OSherwood) **4-10-12** JOsborne (lw: mde most tl hdd & wknd appr 2 out)	2	**12**	5/1[2]	52	2
2074[12]	**Victoria Day** (BAMcMahon) **5-11-0** SWynne (a bhd: t.o fr ½-wy)	dist	**13**	33/1	—	—
900[9]	**Connaught's Pride** (PJHobbs) **6-11-0** NWilliamson (swtg: bit bkwd: bhd: t.o)	2	**14**	25/1	—	—
1090[3]	**Madam's Walk** (NATwiston-Davies) **7-11-0** CMaude (bkwd: a bhd: t.o fr ½-wy: p.u bef 2 out)		**P**	25/1	—	—
1921[R]	**Goatsfut (IRE)** (BPreece) **7-11-5** TJenks (a bhd: t.o & p.u bef 2 out)		**P**	100/1	—	—
				(SP 125.4%)	**16 Rn**	

4m 51.9 (7.90) CSF £48.63 TOTE £9.80: £2.30 £2.60 £5.20 (£29.60) Trio £171.20; £171.25 to Doncaster 25/1/97 OWNER Mrs H. J. Clarke (SHREWSBURY) BRED Barton Stallion Partnership
WEIGHT FOR AGE 4yo-13lb
2053 Barton Ward completed a quick double for connections. This was a most impressive first success over hurdles, and he is definitely on the upgrade. (8/1: op 5/1)
1581* Sparkling Spring (IRE) had more use made of him than he did on his debut, but found the concession of weight to the winner more than he could manage from the penultimate flight. He should not be long in recovering his true form. (13/2)
1768 Supreme Flyer (IRE) did very little wrong on this occasion. He was still a live danger two out, but once the winner lifted the pace was left in his wake. (20/1)
1959 The Captain's Wish, content to delay his challenge, looked to hold all the aces three out, but he could do little more than stay on at the one pace. (6/1)
The Bargeman (NZ), a maiden over hurdles having his first outing in over twenty months, was never put into the race. He made significant progress in the last half mile though, and is open to improvement. (50/1)
2642 Montecot (FR) has been forced to have three quick runs in an attempt to get him handicapped for a return to fences, and that is where his future lies. (15/8)
Blazing Storm (IRE), a newcomer from Ireland, pushed the leaders until blowing up early in the straight. He may well need all of three miles, but he is certainly one to keep in mind. (25/1)

2760 ROGER ASTON NOVICES' CHASE (5-Y.O+) (Class E)
2-20 (2-20) **2m 5f (16 fncs)** £3,123.75 (£935.00: £457.50: £218.75) GOING: 0.04 sec per fur (G)

				SP	RR	SF
1764[3]	**Wild West Wind (IRE)** (MissHCKnight) **7-11-4** JFTitley (chsd ldr: disp ld fr 10th: led appr 3 out: rdn out)	—	**1**	5/1	116	49
1771[2]	**Feel the Power (IRE) (128)** (KCBailey) **9-11-4** CO'Dwyer (lw: hld up: hdwy 11th: ev ch fr 3 out: one pce flat)	3½	**2**	3/1[2]	113	46
	Him of Praise (IRE) (OSherwood) **7-11-4** JOsborne (j.w: racd keenly: mde most tl wknd appr 3 out)	18	**3**	6/5[1]	100	33
1680[U]	**Easy Breezy** (CJMann) **7-11-4** JRailton (bit bkwd: chsd ldrs: mstke 8th: hit 12th: sn wknd)	9	**4**	20/1	93	26
1716[6]	**Dunlir (69)** (PRRodford) **7-10-11**(7) MGriffiths (bit bkwd: nt j.w: t.o fr 6th)	30	**5**	50/1	70	3
2061[2]	**Spinnaker (101)** (NAGaselee) **7-11-4** AThornton (trckd ldng pair: ev ch 3 out: wkng whn fell next: broke back: destroyed)		**F**	9/2[3]	—	—
				(SP 112.0%)	**6 Rn**	

5m 10.7 (5.70) CSF £18.71 TOTE £4.50: £2.20 £1.40 (£4.50) OWNER Lord Vestey (WANTAGE) BRED Martin Nestor
1764 Wild West Wind (IRE) benefited from a very forceful ride, and in the end won going away. He is now getting the hang of fences and will win more races. (5/1)
1771 Feel the Power (IRE) threw down his challenge at the final ditch and momentarily looked to have the edge, but the winner would not be denied. (3/1)
Him of Praise (IRE), successful between the Flags in Ireland in 1995 and a winner in his only run over hurdles just over ten months ago, raced freely and jumped for fun. Lack of peak fitness caught up with him soon after turning in and he was then allowed to complete in his own time. He has the making of a high-class chaser once he learns to settle. (6/5)

2761 JENKINSONS CATERERS H'CAP HURDLE (0-135) (4-Y.O+) (Class C)
2-50 (2-53) **3m 110y (12 hdls)** £3,436.25 (£1,040.00: £507.50: £241.25) GOING: 0.04 sec per fur (G)

				SP	RR	SF
1798[8]	**Haile Derring (112)** (NATwiston-Davies) **7-11-7** CMaude (a.p: led after 9th: clr 2 out: eased towards fin)	—	**1**	5/4[1]	95	34
	Rimouski (97) (BRCambidge) **9-10-6** NWilliamson (chsd ldrs: effrt & rdn 3 out: chsd wnr fr next: no imp)	5	**2**	5/1[3]	77	16
2570[4]	**Derring Bridge (91)** (MrsSMJohnson) **7-10-0** RJohnson (lw: hld up: outpcd appr 3 out: styd on u.p fr last)	2½	**3**	8/1	69	8
1681[4]	**Fast Thoughts (106)** (DRGandolfo) **10-10-10**(5) SophieMitchell (led 3rd tl after 9th: sn rdn & outpcd)	5	**4**	14/1	81	20
	Sparkling Cone (112) (OSherwood) **8-11-7** JOsborne (bkwd: hld up in tch: effrt appr 3 out: wknd next)	2	**5**	9/2[2]	86	25
	Smith Too (IRE) (115) (MrsJPitman) **9-11-7**(3) GHogan (bkwd: led to 3rd: mstke 8th: sn wknd: t.o)	12	**6**	5/1[3]	81	20
				(SP 113.7%)	**6 Rn**	

5m 54.3 (12.30) CSF £7.60 TOTE £2.20: £1.40 £1.70 (£3.30) OWNER Mrs V. Stockdale (CHELTENHAM) BRED Mrs V. Stockdale
LONG HANDICAP Derring Bridge 9-9
1443* Haile Derring was always travelling like a winner. Taking over on the home turn, he was able to take things easy in the closing stages. (5/4)
Rimouski, much sharper after a recent outing on the All-Weather, was not allowed to drop himself out this time. Staying on strongly in the latter stages, he had to admit the winner too much of a handful. (5/1)

2570 Derring Bridge, struggling with the pace for much of the trip, was beginning to peg back the leaders towards the finish but the post was always beating him. (8/1)
1428 Fast Thoughts has not quite come to himself yet this term, and his front-running tactics had come to an end turning out of the back straight. (14/1)
Sparkling Cone had a twenty-two-month absence from the racecourse to overcome, but he showed up with every chance until weakening approaching the second last. He can only improve on this. (9/2: 7/2-11/2)
Smith Too (IRE) (5/1: 3/1-11/2)

2762 JOHN PARTRIDGE ENGLISH CLOTHING H'CAP CHASE (0-130) (5-Y.O+) (Class C)
3-25 (3-26) **2m 5f (16 fncs)** £4,435.50 (£1,344.00: £657.00: £313.50) GOING: 0.04 sec per fur (G)

				SP	RR	SF
	Mely Moss (FR) (126) (CREgerton) **6-12-0** JOsborne (bit bkwd: mde virtually all: drew clr fr 3 out: unchal)	—	**1**	4/1[2]	134+	56
1465[2]	**Flapjack Lad (98)** (NATwiston-Davies) **8-10-0** DWalsh (chsd wnr: disp ld appr 4 out: rdn & wknd appr 3 out)	14	**2**	6/1[3]	95	17
1637[B]	**River Bounty (126)** (CPEBrooks) **11-11-7**(7) MBerry (bkwd: chsd ldrs: rdn & outpcd fr 3 out)	¾	**3**	11/1	123	45
2075[2]	**Sailor Jim (107)** (PTDalton) **10-10-9** CMaude (lw: hld up & bhd: effrt 4 out: styd on u.p fr next: nvr nrr)	1	**4**	11/4[1]	103	25
2092*	**Too Sharp (105)** (MissHCKnight) **9-10-7** JFTitley (lw: hld up: hdwy 10th: pushed along appr 4 out: sn btn)	2	**5**	4/1[2]	100	22
1676[F]	**The Caumrue (IRE) (108)** (GBBalding) **9-10-10** BFenton (swtg: a in rr: lost tch 11th: t.o)	dist	**6**	10/1	—	—
	Postman's Path (103) (CaptTAForster) **11-10-5** AThornton (bkwd: in rr: t.o: p.u bef 11th)		**P**	20/1	—	—
1985*	**Distinctive (IRE) (98)** (MJWilkinson) **8-10-0** WMarston (lw: uns rdr s: t.n.p)		**U**	8/1	—	—
				(SP 114.2%)	**8 Rn**	

5m 11.3 (6.30) CSF £25.64 CT £220.48 TOTE £4.20: £1.10 £2.20 £2.50 (£31.60) OWNER Mr Darren Mercer (CHADDLEWORTH) BRED Mrs Philippe Morruzzi and Jean Kaas
LONG HANDICAP Flapjack Lad 9-11 Distinctive (IRE) 9-13
Mely Moss (FR), a winner over hurdles and fences in France, was forced to miss the whole of last season with injury. A powerful-looking individual, he belied his burly looks and landed quite a touch with a comfortable success. He looks set to go places. (4/1)
1465 Flapjack Lad continues to run well and moved upsides on the home turn. However the winner outjumped him at the fourth last, and he was soon hard at work and outpaced. (6/1)
River Bounty, brought down on his seasonal debut in November, still looked to need this, and he was feeling the strain soon after reaching the straight. (11/1)
2075 Sailor Jim, much more effective when pushing the pace, tried to come from behind. He did not appear to be putting much effort into his work and in the end had a hard race to reach his finishing position. (11/4)
2092* Too Sharp could not quite cope with this step up in class, and was never in a position to give her supporters much hope. (4/1)

2763 RAM FM NOVICES' HURDLE (4-Y.O+) (Class E)
3-55 (3-55) **2m (9 hdls)** £2,463.00 (£693.00: £339.00) GOING: 0.04 sec per fur (G)

				SP	RR	SF
1651[5]	**Donnington (IRE)** (OSherwood) **7-11-5** JOsborne (hld up: hdwy 6th: led after 2 out: rdn out)	—	**1**	3/1[2]	80	48
1766*	**Wade Road (IRE)** (MissHCKnight) **6-11-11** JFTitley (lw: hld up: smooth hdwy 6th: jnd ldrs appr 3 out: chal last: unable qckn)	2	**2**	4/7[1]	84	52
	Bonjour (100) (CJMann) **7-11-5** JRailton (hld up & bhd: hdwy appr 6th: mstke 3 out: sn rdn: one pce)	6	**3**	20/1	72	40
2090[F]	**Lucia Forte (102)** (KCBailey) **6-11-6** CO'Dwyer (lw: chsd ldr: led 5th tl after 2 out: sn rdn & wknd)	4	**4**	6/1[3]	69	37
2035[4]	**Tantara Lodge (IRE)** (KCBailey) **6-11-5** AThornton (hld up: hdwy 6th: rdn & outpcd next: t.o)	27	**5**	40/1	41	9
1699[4]	**Tarry (88)** (AStreeter) **4-10-8** TEley (bhd: hdwy on ins appr 5th: outpcd next: sn t.o)	5	**6**	33/1	37	—
1329[7]	**Eurofast Pet (IRE)** (SABrookshaw) **7-11-5** ADobbin (bit bkwd: hld up: a bhd: t.o fr 3 out)	9	**7**	33/1	27	—
2053[9]	**Scally Hicks** (BPJBaugh) **6-11-0** GaryLyons (chsd ldrs to 5th: sn lost tch: t.o)	4	**8**	100/1	18	—
2550[P]	**Deceit the Second** (PRRodford) **5-10-12b**(7) MGriffiths (led to 5th: wknd qckly: t.o)	dist	**9**	100/1	—	—
				(SP 118.0%)	**9 Rn**	

3m 45.5 (4.50) CSF £4.80 TOTE £4.90: £1.50 £1.40 £4.10 (£3.10) Trio £12.70 OWNER Mr B. T. Stewart-Brown (UPPER LAMBOURN) BRED Michael O'Keeffe
WEIGHT FOR AGE 4yo-12lb
1651 Donnington (IRE), who will stay further, showed the benefit of the experience gained on his hurdling debut in the Autumn with a very workmanlike display, and he looks a progressive type. (3/1)
1766* Wade Road (IRE) was unable to produce his best over what could prove an inadequate trip, and this highly-promising individual will soon leave this form behind. (4/7)
Bonjour looked as though he had been well prepared for this belated seasonal debut, and turned in a very promising display until lack of a previous run took its toll on the approach to the penultimate flight. (20/1)
2090 Lucia Forte, dropping back to the minimum trip, did not give best without a struggle, and she only admitted defeat approaching the last. (6/1)

T/Jkpt: Not won; £42,951.57 to Cheltenham 25/1/97. T/Plpt: £101.70 (116.2 Tckts). T/Qdpt: £16.50 (55.58 Tckts). IM

2311-AYR (L-H) (Good, Good to soft bk st)
Saturday January 25th
WEATHER: overcast

2764 ALBERT BARTLETT & SONS H'CAP HURDLE (0-125) (4-Y.O+) (Class D)
12-30 (12-30) **2m (9 hdls)** £2,901.50 (£872.00: £421.00: £195.50) GOING: 0.76 sec per fur (S)

				SP	RR	SF
1824*	**Stash the Cash (IRE) (110)** (MDHammond) **6-11-6** RGarritty (lw: hld up: stdy hdwy 5th: led 2 out: rdn & r.o wl)	—	**1**	100/30[2]	100	56
	Supreme Soviet (92) (ACWhillans) **7-9-11**(5) STaylor (chsd ldr: led 5th to 2 out: no ex)	5	**2**	8/1	77	33
1314*	**Adamatic (IRE) (98)** (RAllan) **6-10-8** JCallaghan (chsd ldrs: blnd 5th: effrt appr 3 out: nt qckn)	6	**3**	4/1[3]	77	33
2617[8]	**Common Sound (IRE) (114)** (JBarclay) **6-11-10** BStorey (bhd: hdwy 5th: wnt prom 3 out: one pce after)	8	**4**	50/1	85	41
2541*	**Endowment (105)** (MrsMReveley) **5-11-1b** PNiven (lw: led to 5th: sn rdn & wknd)	28	**5**	2/1[1]	48	4
2631[16]	**All Clear (IRE) (93)** (HowardJohnson) **6-10-3** DParker (chsd ldrs to 5th: sn wknd)	nk	**6**	100/1	36	—
	Fox Sparrow (107) (NTinkler) **7-11-3** ASSmith (outpcd & hit 4th: wl bhd after)	4	**7**	25/1	46	2

				SP	RR	SF
2505*	**Triennium (USA) (90)** (PMonteith) **8-10-0** GCahill (t: trckd ldrs: rdn 4 out: sn btn: p.u bef 3 out)		**P**	6/1	—	—

(SP 108.6%) **8 Rn**

3m 51.6 (14.60) CSF £23.59 CT £87.28 TOTE £4.10: £1.40 £1.70 £1.50 (£33.30) OWNER Mr G. Shiel (MIDDLEHAM) BRED Airlie Stud in Ireland

OFFICIAL EXPLANATION **Endowment: was found to be lame on the near-fore after the race.**

Triennium (USA): had lost his action.

1824* Stash the Cash (IRE), suited by the strong pace, won well again and is in tremendous heart. (100/30)

Supreme Soviet did his utmost to gallop his rivals into the ground from halfway, but in so doing set up the race for the winner. This consistent sort deserves a change of luck. (8/1)

1314* Adamatic (IRE), who is on a decent mark at present, ran pretty well considering he made one pretty bad mistake. He should continue to pay his way. (4/1)

1314 Common Sound (IRE) is now coming down the handicap, and this was a much better effort. (50/1)

2541* Endowment did not seem to like being taken on for the lead and, once headed at the fifth, quickly lost all interest. He was later reported to be lame. (2/1)

2505* Triennium (USA), who found this softish ground against him, lost his action altogether and was wisely pulled up. (6/1)

2765 STAKIS CASINOS H'CAP CHASE (0-130) (5-Y.O+) (Class C)

1-00 (1-00) **3m 1f (19 fncs)** £5,735.00 (£1,730.00: £840.00: £395.00) GOING: 0.76 sec per fur (S)

				SP	RR	SF
2568[4]	**Fiveleigh Builds (122)** (MissLucindaRussell) **10-11-6** MFoster (lw: led fr 2nd to 4 out: rallied to ld 2 out: styd on wl)	—	**1**	4/1[2]	128	44
	Whispering Steel (127) (GRichards) **11-11-11** BStorey (trckd ldrs: led 4 out to 2 out: kpt on flat)	1½	**2**	6/1[3]	132	48
2542[2]	**Ali's Alibi (114)** (MrsMReveley) **10-10-12** PNiven (lw: hld up: hdwy 11th: sn chsng ldrs: mstke 14th: rdn appr 4 out: no imp after)	4	**3**	6/4[1]	117	33
2616[8]	**Ceilidh Boy (120)** (MrsJDGoodfellow) **11-11-4b** ASSmith (bhd: outpcd 13th: styd on fr 3 out: n.d)	7	**4**	12/1	118	34
2542[3]	**Aly Daley (IRE) (103)** (HowardJohnson) **9-10-1** GCahill (led to 2nd: sn drvn along: mstke 10th: bhd after)	16	**5**	14/1	91	7
2544[7]	**Solba (USA) (106)** (CParker) **8-10-4** DParker (chsd ldrs tl mstke & outpcd fr 15th)	1½	**6**	10/1	93	9
1657[2]	**Deep Decision (102)** (PCheesbrough) **11-10-0** KJohnson (prom to 12th: sn outpcd & bhd)	13	**7**	8/1	81	—

(SP 108.8%) **7 Rn**

6m 34.3 (27.30) CSF £22.71 TOTE £5.20: £2.20 £2.80 (£10.50) OWNER Miss Lucinda Russell (KINROSS) BRED Peter Magnier

LONG HANDICAP Deep Decision 9-12

2568 Fiveleigh Builds, from a yard at last coming back to form, showed just what a tough individual he is and won well. (4/1)

Whispering Steel, back with the yard that made him, has now slipped back down the handicap and ran a super race, if just giving the impression that he may well have blown up. He looks one to side with from now on. (6/1)

2542 Ali's Alibi had his chances throughout the final circuit but, once asked for a real effort, his jumping deteriorated, and he failed to come up with the goods. (6/4)

1655 Ceilidh Boy was always finding things happening too quickly, but to give him credit he did stick on well at the finish. (12/1: op 8/1)

2542 Aly Daley (IRE), off the bit virtually throughout, found proceedings beyond him with fully a circuit left. (14/1: op 8/1)

2544 Solba (USA) gave signs of coming back to form but, once the pressure was on over the last six fences, his response was disappointing. (10/1)

2766 CLIENT ENTERTAINMENT SERVICES E.B.F. 'N.H.' (QUALIFIER) NOVICES' HURDLE (5, 6 & 7-Y.O) (Class B)

1-30 (1-30) **2m 4f (11 hdls)** £5,108.00 (£1,514.00: £742.00: £356.00) GOING: 0.76 sec per fur (S)

				SP	RR	SF
1999*	**King Pin (96)** (PBeaumont) **5-11-10** RSupple (lw: hld up: smooth hdwy 4 out: slt ld 2 out: hit last: hung lft: r.o: comf)	—	**1**	3/1[3]	92	39
2042*	**Paperising (109)** (GRichards) **5-11-10** BStorey (trckd ldrs: led appr 3 out to 2 out: ev ch tl outpcd flat)	3	**2**	5/2[1]	90	37
2552[2]	**Lance Armstrong (IRE) (105)** (GMMcCourt) **7-11-2**(3) DFortt (led tl hdd appr 3 out: sn outpcd: kpt on u.p fr 2 out)	3	**3**	11/4[2]	82	29
1640*	**Shanavogh (106)** (GMMoore) **6-11-10** JCallaghan (chsd ldrs: rdn after 4 out: sn btn)	12	**4**	5/2[1]	78	25
2619[5]	**Judicious Norman (IRE)** (JRAdam) **6-11-0** TReed (lw: bhd: hdwy 7th: wknd next: p.u bef 3 out)		**P**	14/1	—	—
	Apollo Colosso (JRAdam) **7-11-0** MMoloney (bit bkwd: prom tl wknd qckly 7th: p.u bef 3 out)		**P**	100/1	—	—

(SP 116.5%) **6 Rn**

5m 4.7 (23.70) CSF £10.71 TOTE £3.90: £1.80 £2.10 (£6.10) OWNER Mr J. R. Hinchliffe (BRANDSBY) BRED C. C. Bromley and Son

OFFICIAL EXPLANATION **Judicious Norman (IRE): the trainer reported that the gelding was unsuited by the going.**

1999* King Pin, the pick of these on looks, again tended to hang left, but showed just how useful he is by winning authoritatively. (3/1)

2042* Paperising, from a yard not quite in top form, ran well only to be tapped for foot over the last three flights. He needs a longer trip. (5/2)

2552 Lance Armstrong (IRE) is a game and consistent sort. Although his limitations were exposed, he stayed on particularly well when headed, and will obviously get further. (11/4)

1640* Shanavogh had the beating of the runner-up on their Haydock form, but was the first to crack. This was a disappointing display. (5/2)

2619 Judicious Norman (IRE) disappointed, and was said to be unsuited by the soft surface. (14/1)

2767 SCOTTISH SUN MADE IN SCOTLAND FOR SCOTLAND NOVICES' CHASE (6-Y.O+) (Class B)

2-00 (2-00) **3m 1f (19 fncs)** £7,304.00 (£2,132.00: £1,036.00: £488.00) GOING: 0.76 sec per fur (S)

				SP	RR	SF
	Santa Concerto (IRE) (LLungo) **8-10-12** RSupple (cl up: chal & hit 14th: blnd next: led 3 out: clr whn j.slowly last: eased flat)	—	**1**	7/4[1]	109+	23
2614*	**Seeking Gold (IRE) (89)** (JBarclay) **8-10-12** GCahill (bhd: hdwy 4 out: styd on strly: no ch w wnr)	1¾	**2**	16/1	108	22
2638[2]	**Ballyline (IRE) (88)** (WTKemp) **6-11-3** ASSmith (led tl hdd 3 out: wknd)	6	**3**	14/1	109	23
	Ask Me Later (IRE) (MrsSCBradburne) **8-10-12** MFoster (chsd ldrs: outpcd 12th: no imp after)	dist	**4**	50/1	—	—
1901[3]	**Lord of the West (IRE) (107)** (JJO'Neill) **8-11-3** PNiven (lw: bhd: blnd bdly 9th & 10th: t.o whn p.u bef 15th)		**P**	7/2[3]	—	—
2650*	**Crown Equerry (IRE)** (GRichards) **7-11-3** BStorey (bhd: blnd 8th: p.u bef 4 out)		**P**	9/4[2]	—	—
1669[3]	**Coqui Lane** (JMDun) **10-10-12** TReed (cl up tl 11th: grad lost pl: p.u bef 15th)		**P**	20/1	—	—

(SP 108.6%) **7 Rn**

6m 38.9 (31.90) CSF £22.10 TOTE £2.60: £1.80 £3.10 (£16.30) OWNER Mr John Corr (CARRUTHERSTOWN) BRED Mrs Gladys Bourke

OFFICIAL EXPLANATION **Crown Equerry (IRE): was unsuited by the going.**

Santa Concerto (IRE), having his first look at fences, made some mistakes but got stronger as the race progressed, and should have learnt plenty. (7/4)

2614* Seeking Gold (IRE) got left behind as usual when the pace picked up, but her stamina then came into play, and she was eating up ground late on. Greatly flattered by her proximity to the winner, she will be very interesting when trying marathon trips on soft ground. (16/1)
2638 Ballyline (IRE) ran a super race, but left the impression that this trip was beyond him. (14/1)
Ask Me Later (IRE), likely be all the better for this, ran reasonably until weakening over the last six fences. (50/1)
1901 Lord of the West (IRE) has always looked very clumsy and appeared lucky to find some easy opportunities earlier this season. His jumping put paid to any hopes here. (7/2)
2650* Crown Equerry (IRE), having his second race of the week, never looked happy on this softish ground. Not jumping with any fluency, he was wisely pulled up. (9/4)
1669 Coqui Lane ran well for over a circuit and was then given an easy time before being pulled up. This should have taught him something.(20/1)

2768 HIGHLAND MARY NOVICES' H'CAP HURDLE (0-110) (5-Y.O+) (Class D)

2-35 (2-36) **3m 110y (12 hdls)** £2,290.00 (£640.00: £310.00) GOING: 0.76 sec per fur (S)

				SP	RR	SF
2546^{6}	**Adib (USA) (85)** (GMMoore) **7-10-9** NBentley (a.p: led after 4 out: hrd rdn & hit last: all out)	—	**1**	13/8^{2}	67	—
1849^{3}	**Belle Rose (IRE) (85)** (GRichards) **7-10-9** LO'Hara (cl up: led 4 out: sn hdd: kpt on u.p)	4	**2**	4/1^{3}	64	—
2076*	**Menshaar (USA) (100)** (LLungo) **5-11-10** RSupple (prom: effrt 4 out: sn rdn & no imp)	7	**3**	5/4^{1}	75	—
1851^{11}	**Meadowleck (76)** (WGYoung) **8-10-0** GCahill (led to 4 out: hrd rdn & one pce)	1¼	**4**	200/1	50?	—
1854^{11}	**Crofton Lake (76)** (JEDixon) **9-10-0** BStorey (outpcd fr 7th: n.d after)	12	**5**	25/1	42	—
1822^{P}	**Charlvic (76)** (WSCunningham) **7-9-7**(7) LMcGrath (chsd ldrs to 8th: sn t.o)	18	**6**	50/1	30	—
				(SP 108.8%)	**6 Rn**	

6m 30.1 (44.10) CSF £7.19 TOTE £2.70: £1.50 £1.50 (£5.80) OWNER N B Mason (Farms) Ltd (MIDDLEHAM) BRED North Ridge Farm
LONG HANDICAP Meadowleck 8-5 Crofton Lake 9-0 Charlvic 8-8
2546 Adib (USA) looked well in. He did the business in determined style, but it was never easy. (13/8)
1849 Belle Rose (IRE) ran a game race. Always in contention, she always looked second best from the home turn, but would not give in. (4/1: op 5/2)
2076* Menshaar (USA), set a very stiff task by the Handicapper, was beaten come the fourth last. (5/4)
Meadowleck ran her best race for a long time, despite being 19lb out of the handicap. (200/1)
1080 Crofton Lake again looked very slow. (25/1)

2769 LAND OF BURNS H'CAP CHASE (0-115) (5-Y.O+) (Class E)

3-10 (3-11) **2m 4f (17 fncs)** £3,090.00 (£930.00: £450.00: £210.00) GOING: 0.76 sec per fur (S)

				SP	RR	SF
2508^{F}	**Montrave (99)** (PMonteith) **8-11-9** RSupple (trckd ldrs: led 12th: qcknd clr 4 out: easily)	—	**1**	5/2^{1}	112+	11
1972^{3}	**Judicial Field (IRE) (93)** (NTinkler) **8-11-3b** RGarritty (lw: hld up: effrt 12th: sn chsng ldrs: hit 4 out: no imp after)	2½	**2**	5/1^{2}	104	3
1266^{7}	**Golden Fiddle (IRE) (100)** (JKMOliver) **9-11-10** BStorey (chsd ldrs: hit 10th: outpcd 12th: styd on again fr 2 out)	5	**3**	5/1^{2}	107	6
1991^{F}	**Funny Old Game (78)** (DMcCune) **10-10-2** KJohnson (chsd ldrs: led 11th tl mstke & hdd 12th: outpcd next: styd on fr 2 out)	hd	**4**	25/1	85	—
1991^{5}	**Juke Box Billy (IRE) (84)** (MrsJBrown) **9-10-8** ASSmith (hld up: effrt 9th: chsng ldrs fr 12th: disp 2nd & btn whn blnd 3 out: wknd next)	hd	**5**	5/1^{2}	91	—
2179^{5}	**Willie Sparkle (77)** (MrsSCBradburne) **11-10-1** MFoster (blnd 2nd: in tch tl outpcd fr 11th)	1¾	**6**	12/1^{3}	82	—
1972*	**Cardenden (IRE) (76)** (JBarclay) **9-10-0** DParker (led to 11th: wknd qckly: t.o)	dist	**7**	14/1	—	—
2545^{5}	**Nicholas Plant (87)** (JSGoldie) **8-10-11** GCahill (blnd & uns rdr 2nd)		**U**	5/1^{2}	—	—
				(SP 113.4%)	**8 Rn**	

5m 27.3 (32.30) CSF £14.17 CT £51.57 TOTE £3.00: £1.30 £1.70 £2.00 (£4.90) Trio £10.30 OWNER Mr D. St Clair (ROSEWELL) BRED Miss C. E. J. Dawson
LONG HANDICAP Cardenden (IRE) 9-7
1970* Montrave, ridden with more patience this time, won particularly well and had been eased down to a walk at the post. (5/2)
1972 Judicial Field (IRE) had his chances in the final mile but, when put under pressure, was never doing anything like enough. (5/1)
1142 Golden Fiddle (IRE), after two and a half months off, ran reasonably and was battling back at the end. (5/1)
Funny Old Game, who last won three years ago, on this track, has shown little since, but did give slight signs of encouragement. (25/1)
1991 Juke Box Billy (IRE) is proving very difficult to win with and was fitted with a tongue-strap on this occasion. (5/1)
2179 Willie Sparkle (12/1: 7/1-14/1)
1972* Cardenden (IRE) (14/1: 7/1-16/1)

2770 AYRSHIRE POST STANDARD N.H. FLAT RACE (4, 5 & 6-Y.O) (Class H)

3-40 (3-42) **2m** £1,329.00 (£369.00: £177.00)

				SP	RR	SF
	Lord Podgski (IRE) (PMonteith) **6-11-5** GCahill (a cl up: led over 3f out: rdn & styd on strly)	—	**1**	9/4^{1}	67 f	—
2047^{2}	**Magpie Melody (IRE)** (LLungo) **6-11-0**(5) BGrattan (trckd ldrs: led 5f out tl over 3f out: kpt on same pce)	6	**2**	11/4^{2}	61 f	—
	Woodfield Vision (IRE) (MrsMReveley) **6-10-12**(7) CMcCormack (hld up: hdwy to disp ld 5f out: rdn & wknd fnl 3f)	7	**3**	11/1^{3}	54 f	—
	Portman (WMcKeown) **5-10-12**(7) NHorrocks (hld up & bhd: stdy hdwy 5f out: rdn 3f out: nvr rchd ldrs)	3½	**4**	14/1	51 f	—
	Andy Clyde (ABailey) **4-10-0**(7) SMelrose (hld up: hdwy ½-wy: rdn 5f out: no imp)	11	**5**	16/1	40 f	—
	Wellswood (IRE) (JMJefferson) **4-10-0**(7) MNewton (bkwd: in tch: outpcd 5f out: no imp after)	3½	**6**	11/4^{2}	36 f	—
	Royal Spruce (IRE) (GMMoore) **6-10-12**(7) NHannity (effrt 7f out: no imp)	½	**7**	25/1	36 f	—
2626^{3}	**Sir Boston** (RDEWoodhouse) **4-10-0**(7) GSupple (in tch tl outpcd fnl 6f)	1½	**8**	12/1	34 f	—
	Cottstown Boy (IRE) (MrsSCBradburne) **6-10-12**(7) MrMBradburne (bit bkwd: plld hrd: mde most tl hdd 5f out: wknd)	7	**9**	100/1	27 f	—
	Sunset Flash (MrsJDGoodfellow) **5-11-5** MrRHale (cl up: disp ld 10f out to 7f out: wknd 5f out)	12	**10**	50/1	15 f	—
705^{11}	**The Vale (IRE)** (RMMcKellar) **5-11-0**(5) RMcGrath (rdn 7f out: sn bhd)	10	**11**	200/1	5 f	—
				(SP 120.0%)	**11 Rn**	

3m 52.3 CSF £7.87 TOTE £3.60: £2.30 £1.30 £1.50 (£5.90) Trio £6.80 OWNER Mrs G. Smyth (ROSEWELL) BRED Gerald Smyth
WEIGHT FOR AGE 4yo-12lb
Lord Podgski (IRE) does not do anything quickly, but he stays particularly well. Keeping up the gallop when ridden, he forged clear in the last two furlongs. (9/4)
2047 Magpie Melody (IRE) travelled well but, when it came down to a fight, the winner was always too strong. (11/4: 2/1-3/1)

Woodfield Vision (IRE) moved really well until the race really began in the last three furlongs, from which point he visibly tired. The experience should improve him. (11/1: 8/1-14/1)
Portman looks the type to improve with experience and was given a nice ride here. (14/1)
Andy Clyde is a real Flat type and never offered a serious threat, but looks the sort to benefit from experience. (16/1)
Wellswood (IRE), a weak-looking individual, showed some ability and obviously needs time. (11/4)
2626 Sir Boston (12/1: op 8/1)

T/Plpt: £120.70 (93.77 Tckts). T/Qdpt: £19.60 (40.19 Tckts). AA

2278-CHELTENHAM (L-H) (Good to firm)
Saturday January 25th
WEATHER: fine

2771 JOHN SIMPSON GOLDEN JUBILEE NOVICES' H'CAP HURDLE (0-120) (5-Y.O+) (Class D)
1-00 (1-01) **2m 1f (New) (8 hdls)** £3,647.50 (£1,105.00: £540.00: £257.50) GOING: 0.08 sec per fur (G)

				SP	RR	SF
2071*	**Boardroom Shuffle (IRE) (120)** (JTGifford) **6-12-0** PHide (hld up: stdy hdwy 5th: led appr last: sn hdd: rdn to ld flat: r.o wl)	—	1	5/2 1	108	62
1855*	**Potter's Gale (IRE) (98)** (DNicholson) **6-10-6** AMaguire (hld up: hdwy 5th: led last: hrd rdn & hdd flat)	1½	2	6/1	85	39
1726*	**Danegold (IRE) (105)** (MRChannon) **5-10-13** JOsborne (hld up: hit 2nd: rdn & hdwy on ins appr 2 out: ev ch last: wknd)	5	3	12/1	87	41
1640³	**Rangitikei (NZ) (103)** (CJMann) **6-10-11** RDunwoody (a.p: led 3 out: mstke 2 out: hdd appr last: one pce)	½	4	8/1	84	38
2703*	**Hay Dance (109)** (PJHobbs) **6-11-3** 7x NWilliamson (lw: hld up & bhd: hdwy appr 2 out: rdn & wknd appr last)	3½	5	4/1 2	87	41
1766P	**Palladium Boy (92)** (MrsJGRetter) **7-10-0** TJMurphy (no hdwy fr 3 out)	8	6	100/1	63	17
2624³	**Daraydan (IRE) (120)** (MCPipe) **5-12-0b1** CMaude (lw: led: rdn & hdd 4th: wknd after 2 out)	2½	7	9/2 3	88	42
2074⁵	**Samanid (IRE) (105)** (MissLCSiddall) **5-10-13** OPears (bhd fr 5th: t.o)	19	8	25/1	55	9
2578F	**Country Minstrel (IRE) (92)** (SADouch) **6-9-7**(7) CRae (hld up mid div: wknd appr 2 out: fell last)		F	100/1	—	—
1791⁴	**El Don (105)** (MJRyan) **5-10-13** JRyan (chsd ldr: led 4th: mstke 5th: hdd 3 out: wknd after 2 out: p.u bef last)		P	11/1	—	—
1709²	**Iron N Gold (95)** (TCasey) **5-10-3** DBridgwater (bhd: mstkes 2nd & 3rd: t.o whn p.u bef 3 out)		P	20/1	—	—
2093⁴	**Sounds Like Fun (96)** (MissHCKnight) **6-10-4** JFTitley (a bhd: t.o whn p.u bef 2 out)		P	20/1	—	—
				(SP 123.5%)	**12 Rn**	

4m 1.2 (4.20) CSF £16.48 CT £144.44 TOTE £3.20: £1.80 £1.90 £2.90 (£7.40) Trio £42.70 OWNER Mr A. D. Weller (FINDON) BRED Stonethorn Stud Farms Ltd
LONG HANDICAP Palladium Boy 8-1 Country Minstrel (IRE) 8-10
2071* Boardroom Shuffle (IRE) maintained his unbeaten record with another good performance. He is likely to go to the Supreme Novices' Hurdle, but will also be left in the Champion Hurdle. (5/2)
1855* Potter's Gale (IRE) produced a fine leap to lead at the final flight, but could not take advantage of the weight concession from the winner. (6/1)
1726* Danegold (IRE), a springer in the market, found the stiff uphill finish too much for him. (12/1)
1640 Rangitikei (NZ) gave a good account of himself off a mark 6lb higher than when winning a less competitive race at Towcester in November. (8/1: op 14/1)
2703* Hay Dance, attempting a quick follow-up, could not do it all on the bridle this time. (4/1)
2624 Daraydan (IRE) derived no benefit from the blinkers. (9/2: op 9/4)

2772 FINESSE HURDLE (Gd 2) (4-Y.O) (Class A)
1-35 (1-35) **2m 1f (New) (8 hdls)** £9,779.99 (£3,702.75: £1,813.88: £828.38) GOING: 0.08 sec per fur (G)

				SP	RR	SF
1634²	**Shooting Light (IRE)** (PGMurphy) **4-11-0** RDunwoody (lw: a.p: led on bit appr last: rdn out)	—	1	10/11 1	98	43
1514²	**Noble Lord** (RHBuckler) **4-11-0** BPowell (led tl rdn & hdd appr last: one pce)	6	2	7/1	92	37
2070*	**Roseberry Avenue (IRE)** (RAkehurst) **4-11-0** AMaguire (a.p: rdn & ev ch appr last: one pce)	1½	3	11/2 2	91	36
1900⁴	**Mazamet (USA)** (OO'Neill) **4-11-0** VSlattery (a.p: rdn appr 2 out: one pce)	6	4	33/1	85?	30
1519*	**Lear Jet (USA)** (BobJones) **4-11-4** JOsborne (prom: mstke 5th: rdn & wknd after 2 out: t.o)	27	5	6/1 3	64	9
1935³	**Sally's Twins** (JSMoore) **4-10-9** WMcFarland (swtg: bhd: hit 2nd: mstke 4th: t.o fr 3 out)	¾	6	33/1	54	—
	Macmorris (USA) (DRCElsworth) **4-11-0** PHolley (prom tl wknd qckly after 3 out: t.o whn p.u bef last)		P	20/1	—	—
1444P	**Fursan (USA)** (NATwiston-Davies) **4-11-0** DBridgwater (lw: hld up & plld hrd: hdwy 3 out: rdn & wknd 2 out: t.o whn p.u bef last)		P	10/1	—	—
				(SP 114.3%)	**8 Rn**	

4m 2.5 (5.50) CSF £7.08 TOTE £2.00: £1.30 £1.80 £1.70 (£5.40) Trio £6.40 OWNER Mr J. M. Brown (BRISTOL) BRED The Earl of Harrington
OFFICIAL EXPLANATION **Lear Jet (USA): trainer reported that the colt had gurgled.**
1634 Shooting Light (IRE) confirmed his position as one of the leading juvenile hurdlers, and gained some valuable experience over the Triumph Hurdle course. (10/11)
1514 Noble Lord does not seem to know how to run a bad race, but the winner was much too sharp. (7/1)
2070* Roseberry Avenue (IRE) won over a mile and three-quarters on good to firm at Sandown, but would have found softer ground putting more of an emphasis on stamina. (11/2: op 3/1)
1900 Mazamet (USA) did enough to suggest he will get off the mark when his sights are lowered. (33/1)
1519* Lear Jet (USA) was subsequently reported by his trainer to have gurgled. (6/1)

2773 LADBROKE TROPHY H'CAP CHASE (5-Y.O+) (Class B)
2-10 (2-10) **2m 5f (New) (17 fncs)** £16,937.50 (£5,125.00: £2,500.00: £1,187.50) GOING: 0.08 sec per fur (G)

				SP	RR	SF
1566*	**Dublin Flyer (168)** (CaptTAForster) **11-12-0** BPowell (lw: mde all: rdn & r.o wl flat)	—	1	15/8 1	171	78
1917*	**Addington Boy (IRE) (158)** (GRichards) **9-11-4** ADobbin (a.p: lft 2nd 10th: ev ch 3 out: rdn appr last: no imp)	2	2	2/1 2	160	67
1789³	**Hill of Tullow (IRE) (140)** (DNicholson) **8-10-0b1** AMaguire (bhd: mstke 12th: styd on fr 2 out: n.d)	17	3	16/1	129	36
2647P	**Go Universal (IRE) (140)** (CPEBrooks) **9-10-0** NWilliamson (lw: chsd wnr tl blnd 10th: wknd appr 2 out)	4	4	16/1	126	33
	Pashto (140) (NJHenderson) **10-10-0** JOsborne (prom tl wknd appr 2 out)	¾	5	50/1	125	32
1649F	**Challenger du Luc (FR) (153)** (MCPipe) **7-10-13b** RDunwoody (lw: hld up in rr: stdy hdwy whn j.slowly & reminders 12th: wknd appr 3 out)	7	6	11/4 3	133	40

2057F **Bradbury Star (145)** (JTGifford) **12-10-5** PHide (lw: bhd fr 7th) 5 **7** 20/1 121 28
(SP 113.3%) **7 Rn**

5m 9.8 (0.80) CSF £5.69 CT £36.85 TOTE £2.70: £2.10 £1.50 (£2.60) OWNER Mr J. B. Sumner (LUDLOW) BRED Marston Stud
LONG HANDICAP Pashto 9-4 Hill of Tullow (IRE) 9-11 Go Universal (IRE) 9-8

1566* Dublin Flyer goes well fresh and looked trained to the minute. Connections feel there was something amiss in last year's Gold Cup, and think he deserves another crack. (15/8)

1917* Addington Boy (IRE), raised 6lb, will have to meet the winner at level weights in the Gold Cup. His trainer believes that the stiffer test of stamina will help. (2/1: 11/8-9/4)

1789 Hill of Tullow (IRE), tried in blinkers and 3lb out of the handicap, stayed on past beaten rivals up the hill. (16/1)

2647 Go Universal (IRE), 6lb wrong at the weights, made a mess of the first ditch and gave the impression he may have pulled up rather feelingly. (16/1)

Pashto, 10lb out of the handicap, ran well for a long way on this belated seasonal appearance. (50/1)

1649 Challenger du Luc (FR) was trying to close when putting in an indifferent jump at the final ditch. (11/4)

1869 Bradbury Star could well have connections pondering his retirement. (20/1)

2774 CLEEVE HURDLE (Gd 1) (4-Y.O+) (Class A)

2-45 (2-46) **2m 5f 110y (New) (10 hdls)** £25,640.00 (£9,552.00: £4,676.00: £2,132.00) GOING: 0.08 sec per fur (G)

				SP	RR	SF
1916*	**Large Action (IRE) (163)** (OSherwood) **9-11-8** JOsborne (lw: chsd ldr: led after 2 out: r.o wl)	—	**1**	8/15 1	136+	39
2635 4	**Pridwell (157)** (MCPipe) **7-11-8** RDunwoody (lw: hld up: ev ch after 2 out: r.o flat)	1¾	**2**	7/1 3	135	38
1656 2	**Castle Sweep (IRE) (149)** (DNicholson) **6-11-8** AMaguire (hld up: nt fluent 2 out: rdn & wnt 2nd appr last: one pce)	1¼	**3**	3/1 2	134	37
1916 4	**Muse (143)** (DRCElsworth) **10-11-8** PHolley (led tl after 2 out: virtually p.u flat: fin lame: dismntd)	dist	**4**	14/1	—	—
				(SP 109.4%)		**4 Rn**

5m 10.5 (10.50) CSF £4.33 TOTE £1.50: (£2.40) OWNER Mr B. T. Stewart-Brown (UPPER LAMBOURN) BRED Mrs J. A. Harold-Barry in Ireland

1916* Large Action (IRE) looked a bit more at home over this longer trip and did enough to ensure he will go for the Champion Hurdle. However, like Mysilv last year, he may also run in the Stayers' event. (8/15)

2635 Pridwell was going as well as the winner turning in, and although no match for the winner regained second place on the flat. (7/1)

1656 Castle Sweep (IRE) tried to mount a challenge on the long run to the final flight, but could never quite get to grips with the winner. (3/1)

1916 Muse was dismounted immediately after crossing the line looking very lame, and might easily have run his last race. (14/1)

2775 PILLAR PROPERTY INVESTMENTS CHASE (6-Y.O+) (Class B)

3-20 (3-21) **3m 1f 110y (New) (21 fncs)** £16,775.00 (£5,075.00: £2,475.00: £1,175.00) GOING: 0.08 sec per fur (G)

				SP	RR	SF
2115*	**One Man (IRE) (177)** (GRichards) **9-11-12** RDunwoody (hld up: hdwy 13th: wnt 2nd 16th: led flat: pushed out)	—	**1**	2/5 1	166	70
2115 3	**Barton Bank (157)** (DNicholson) **11-11-12** AMaguire (led 3rd tl flat: hrd rdn: r.o wl)	hd	**2**	4/1 2	166	70
1904*	**Yorkshire Gale (137)** (JTGifford) **11-11-6** NWilliamson (lw: hld up: hit 2nd & 4th: lft 2nd 6th: rdn after 3 out: sn wknd: eased flat)	dist	**3**	6/1 3	—	—
1367 3	**Martomick (140)** (KCBailey) **10-11-5** JOsborne (lw: led to 3rd: 2nd whn blnd 6th: bhd whn mstke 10th: sn t.o)	dist	**4**	16/1	—	—
				(SP 111.6%)		**4 Rn**

6m 24.2 (3.20) CSF £2.48 TOTE £1.40: (£2.10) OWNER Mr J. Hales (PENRITH) BRED Hugh J. Holohan

2115* One Man (IRE) finally broke his Cheltenham bogey and had more in hand over the persistent runner-up than the margin indicates. However, it appeared afterwards that his trainer may be thinking in terms of the two-mile Queen Mother Champion Chase prior to the Martell Cup at Aintree. (2/5)

2115 Barton Bank probably ran his best race ever on this course and, allowed to have his own way in front, never put a foot wrong. The problem will be that the Gold Cup field seems unlikely to be short of front runners. (4/1: 3/1-9/2)

1904* Yorkshire Gale was surprisingly supported in the ring, but it only goes to show that punters can be a sentimental bunch. (6/1: op 10/1)

2776 '50 YEARS OF TIMEFORM' NOVICES' H'CAP CHASE (5-Y.O+) (Class C)

3-55 (3-55) **2m 5f (New) (17 fncs)** £7,520.75 (£2,276.00: £1,110.50: £527.75) GOING: 0.08 sec per fur (G)

				SP	RR	SF
2577 2	**The Mine Captain (100)** (OSherwood) **10-10-5** JOsborne (hld up: hdwy 5th: led 3 out: all out)	—	**1**	6/1	107	39
2116 3	**Potter's Bay (IRE) (119)** (DNicholson) **8-11-10** AMaguire (hld up in rr: hdwy 11th: ev ch 2 out: hrd rdn & r.o flat)	nk	**2**	100/30 2	126	58
2007 5	**Lively Knight (IRE) (115)** (JTGifford) **8-11-6** PHide (swtg: hld up: mstke 11th: hdwy 12th: hit 4 out: sn wknd)	15	**3**	7/2 3	110	42
2568*	**Imperial Vintage (IRE) (118)** (MissVenetiaWilliams) **7-11-9** NWilliamson (led: mstkes 2nd, 3rd & 5th: hdd 6th: led 7th to 3 out: wknd 2 out)	6	**4**	11/4 1	109	41
2638 4	**La Mezeray (95)** (MrsJEHawkins) **9-10-0** WMarston (lw: w ldr: led 6th to 7th: wknd 3 out)	6	**5**	50/1	81	13
1925 2	**Flight Lieutenant (USA) (109)** (TCasey) **8-11-0** RDunwoody (hld up: blnd 10th: mstke 11th: hdwy after 3 out: 5th & wkng whn mstke 2 out: t.o)	dist	**6**	11/2	—	—
1875F	**After The Fox (95)** (NJHawke) **10-10-0** BPowell (lw: hld up: mstke 4th: p.u bef 9th: rdn lost irons)		**P**	11/2	—	—
				(SP 119.0%)		**7 Rn**

5m 14.8 (5.80) CSF £25.74 CT £74.96 TOTE £7.10: £2.10 £1.90 (£11.00) OWNER Mr Gerald Evans (UPPER LAMBOURN) BRED A. D. Forster
LONG HANDICAP La Mezeray 8-9 After The Fox 9-10

2577 The Mine Captain, raised 2lb, had to work hard to get the better of a good tussle up the final climb. (6/1)

2116 Potter's Bay (IRE) jumped better this time, and lost no caste in defeat under top weight. (100/30)

2007 Lively Knight (IRE) was in trouble after clouting the tricky fourth-last fence. (7/2)

2568* Imperial Vintage (IRE), up 3lb, jumped better as the race progressed, but this was more competitive than he is used to. (11/4)

1335* La Mezeray fared as well as could be expected from 19lb out of the handicap. (50/1)

2777 D. J. EQUINE H'CAP HURDLE (0-145) (4-Y.O+) (Class B)

4-30 (4-32) **2m 1f (New) (8 hdls)** £5,589.00 (£1,692.00: £826.00: £393.00) GOING: 0.08 sec per fur (G)

				SP	RR	SF
1903 4	**Forestal (109)** (SGGriffiths) **5-10-1** TJMurphy (lost pl after 2nd: hdwy after 2 out: led flat: r.o wl)	—	**1**	10/1	97	36
1636 5	**Bolivar (IRE) (114)** (RAkehurst) **5-10-1**(5) SRyan (lw: hld up: hdwy 5th: led appr last: hdd flat)	2½	**2**	8/1	100	39
	Star Rage (IRE) (126) (JLHarris) **7-11-4** DGallagher (lw: a.p: led appr last: sn hdd: one pce)	4	**3**	11/4 1	108	47
1559 3	**Chicodari (127)** (DNicholson) **5-11-5b** AMaguire (hld up: hdwy appr 2 out: one pce appr last)	2½	**4**	11/2 3	107	46

			Pos	SP	RR	SF
1783[4]	**Fourth in Line (IRE) (125)** (MJWilkinson) **9-11-3** WMarston (lw: hld up & bhd: hdwy appr 2 out: sn rdn: styd on flat)	2½	**5**	16/1	102	41
2078[5]	**Dr Leunt (IRE) (130)** (PJHobbs) **6-11-8** GTormey (led to 2nd: wknd appr last)	nk	**6**	14/1	107	46
2645[10]	**Roll a Dollar (125)** (DRCElsworth) **11-11-3** PHolley (nvr nr to chal)	1¼	**7**	25/1	101	40
2048[3]	**Most Equal (117)** (MCPipe) **7-10-9** RDunwoody (lw: hld up: hdwy 3 out: wknd 2 out)	2	**8**	5/1 [2]	91	30
1933[2]	**Kadastrof (FR) (128)** (RDickin) **7-11-6** BPowell (lw: plld hrd early: prom: j.slowly 5th: wknd qckly 3 out)	2½	**9**	14/1	100	39
2059[5]	**Non Vintage (IRE) (126)** (MCChapman) **6-11-4** WWorthington (bhd fr 3 out)	6	**10**	14/1	92	31
2703[4]	**Nashville Star (USA) (108)** (RMathew) **6-10-0v** DBridgwater (led 2nd: rdn clr appr 2 out: hdd appr last:wknd)	9	**11**	50/1	65	4
1636[3]	**Intermagic (111)** (JCFox) **7-10-3** SFox (hld up: hdwy 3 out: eased whn btn appr last)	8	**12**	10/1	61	—
1636[9]	**Thinking Twice (USA) (134)** (NJHenderson) **8-11-12** NWilliamson (plld hrd early: prom: shkn up appr 2 out: eased whn btn appr last)	2½	**13**	25/1	82	21
1636[6]	**Abbey Street (IRE) (122)** (OSherwood) **5-11-0** JOsborne (lw: hld up: hdwy after 5th: wknd after 3 out: t.o whn p.u bef last: lame)		**P**	7/1	—	—

(SP 136.0%) **14 Rn**

4m 1.3 (4.30) CSF £89.42 CT £268.10 TOTE £14.50: £3.20 £4.10 £2.00 (£158.10) Trio £178.60 OWNER Mr S. G. Griffiths (CARMARTHEN) BRED Mrs M. T. Dawson
LONG HANDICAP Nashville Star (USA) 9-2
OFFICIAL EXPLANATION **Thinking Twice (USA): the rider reported that the gelding had been feeling the ground and lost his action going to the last. The trainer added that the gelding was slightly lame afterwards.**
1903 Forestal, adopting totally different tactics, was brought with a well-timed run. (10/1)
Bolivar (IRE), suited by this stiff course, will stay further. (8/1: 11/2-9/1)
Star Rage (IRE), having tuned up on the All-Weather, was 9lb higher than when winning last season's County Hurdle. (11/4)
1559 Chicodari, back in blinkers, was 6lb better off with the winner than when beaten five lengths at Haydock last May. (11/2)
1783 Fourth in Line (IRE) needs softer ground than this. (16/1)
2078 Dr Leunt (IRE) has already been dropped 6lb since his comeback. (14/1)
1636 Intermagic ran better than his finishing position suggests on ground plenty lively enough for him. (10/1)
1340 Thinking Twice (USA) was another who could have finished much closer, but the Stewards accepted the explanation as to why he was eased on the long run to the final flight. (25/1)
Abbey Street (IRE) (7/1: op 12/1)

T/Jkpt: £412.40 (183.67 Tckts). T/Plpt: £8.70 (3,335.88 Tckts). T/Qdpt: £5.30 (225.56 Tckts). KH

2744-DONCASTER (L-H) (Good, Good to firm patches)
Saturday January 25th
WEATHER: fine & sunny

2778 'GREAT YORKSHIRE MEETING' NOVICES' CHASE (5-Y.O+) (Class D)
12-45 (12-46) **2m 3f 110y (15 fncs)** £4,422.00 (£1,212.00: £586.00) GOING: 0.16 sec per fur (G)

			Pos	SP	RR	SF
	Woodbridge (IRE) (FMurphy) **8-11-4** PCarberry (w ldr: hit 9th: led 11th: styd on u.p flat)	—	**1**	20/1	95	28
2061[3]	**Cariboo Gold (USA)** (KCBailey) **8-11-4b** AThornton (trckd ldrs: blnd 10th: chal 3 out: mstke next: kpt on same pce)	2	**2**	1/4 [1]	93	26
2628[9]	**Curragh Peter (72)** (MrsPBickerton) **10-11-1**(3) GuyLewis (mde most tl mstke & hdd 11th: wknd 3 out)	24	**3**	14/1 [3]	74	7
1031[P]	**Just Supposen (IRE)** (BSRothwell) **6-11-1**(3) ECallaghan (prom tl fell 7th)		**F**	10/1 [2]	—	—
1920[3]	**Domaine de Pron (FR)** (MrsLCTaylor) **6-11-4** TJO'Sullivan (trckd ldrs: effrt 11th: outpcd whn blnd & uns rdr next)		**U**	10/1 [2]	—	—

(SP 109.6%) **5 Rn**

5m 0.6 (13.60) CSF £25.49 TOTE £10.90: £2.10 £1.30 (£4.20) OWNER Mr Sonny Purcell (MIDDLEHAM) BRED P. F. and L. Quirke
Woodbridge (IRE), who had come to grief on his only previous outing over fences, seized the initiative when the favourite made a mistake two out, and kept right up to his work, was never going to be overhauled. This gave his trainer a welcome change of luck. All he does is stay. (20/1)
2061 Cariboo Gold (USA), with the blinkers back on, blundered badly at the tenth and his rider did remarkably well to keep the partnership intact. Almost upsides when hitting two out, he was never really putting his heart into his work. (1/4: op 1/6)
1856 Curragh Peter who led on sufferance, was out on a limb three from home. (14/1)
1920 Domaine de Pron (FR) was feeling the pace when he parted company four out. (10/1)

2779 BESSACARR H'CAP HURDLE (0-135) (4-Y.O+) (Class C)
1-20 (1-20) **2m 110y (8 hdls)** £3,678.00 (£1,104.00: £532.00: £246.00) GOING: 0.16 sec per fur (G)

			Pos	SP	RR	SF
2543[4]	**Shining Edge (114)** (TDEasterby) **5-10-12** GBradley (chsd ldrs: led after last: rdn out)	—	**1**	11/1	96	44
2543[3]	**New Inn (118)** (SGollings) **6-11-2** KGaule (led: qcknd appr 3 out: hdd after last: nt qckn)	1¼	**2**	14/1	99	47
1954*	**Severn Gale (102)** (JSAllen) **7-9-7**(7) XAizpuru (chsd ldrs: one pce fr 3 out)	9	**3**	14/1	74	22
2603a[11]	**Kaitak (IRE) (119)** (JMCarr) **6-11-0**(3) FLeahy (chsd ldrs: drvn along 5th: one pce fr next)	¾	**4**	14/1	90	38
1924[2]	**Desert Fighter (112)** (MrsMReveley) **6-10-7**(3) GLee (racd wd: hld up: hdwy 5th: wknd after 3 out)	12	**5**	14/1	72	20
1793[13]	**Charming Girl (USA) (129)** (OSherwood) **6-11-13** JAMcCarthy (hld up: hdwy 5th: wknd next)	8	**6**	14/1	81	29
2048[4]	**Mr Bureaucrat (NZ) (115)** (SABrookshaw) **8-10-13** RJohnson (chsd ldrs: wkng whn mstke 3 out)	1	**7**	12/1	66	14
	Nijmegen (130) (JGFitzGerald) **9-12-0** PCarberry (bhd whn hmpd 4th: n.d)	11	**8**	25/1	70	18
2114*	**Albemine (USA) (124)** (MrsJCecil) **8-11-8** TKent (trckd ldrs tl lost pl 5th)	7	**9**	11/2 [3]	58	6
2048[6]	**Saint Ciel (USA) (108)** (FJordan) **9-10-6** SWynne (prom tl wknd 5th)	9	**10**	20/1	33	—
	Celestial Choir (114) (JLEyre) **7-10-12** RichardGuest (hld up: effrt whn fell 5th)		**F**	5/1 [2]	—	—
2048*	**Tejano Gold (USA) (119)** (PBradley) **7-11-3** AThornton (lw: mid div whn fell 4th)		**F**	7/1	—	—
2579*	**Le Khoumf (FR) (117)** (JNeville) **6-11-1** MAFitzgerald (lw: in tch tl lost pl appr 3 out: bhd whn p.u bef last)		**P**	11/4 [1]	—	—

(SP 129.2%) **13 Rn**

3m 56.1 (6.10) CSF £150.81 CT £2,007.53 TOTE £14.30: £3.80 £3.80 £4.20 (£48.00) Trio £226.40 OWNER Mr G. Graham (MALTON) BRED R. B. Warren
2543 Shining Edge, under a strong ride, did just enough. (11/1)
2543 New Inn, as when he won here three runs ago, tried to pinch it from the front. Quickening the pace and seizing the initiative on the home turn, he gave his all in willing fashion. (14/1)

1954* Severn Gale, 6lb higher, was unable to dominate. (14/1)
2603a Kaitak (IRE) looks to be in the grip of the Handicapper. (14/1)
1924 Desert Fighter, having his first outing for forty-two days, possibly just needed it. (14/1)
2579* Le Khoumf (FR), from a 7lb higher mark, looked particularly well, but ran no race at all. Connections were unable to offer any explanation. (11/4)

2780 DONCASTER SPONSORSHIP CLUB H'CAP HURDLE (0-135) (4-Y.O+) (Class C)

1-50 (1-51) **2m 4f (10 hdls)** £3,834.00 (£1,152.00: £556.00: £258.00) GOING: 0.16 sec per fur (G)

			SP	RR	SF
1945^{6}	**Dual Image (104)** (JGFitzGerald) **10-10-2** PCarberry (hld up: stdy hdwy 7th: led last: drvn out) ....—-	1	11/1	88	25
1956^{3}	**Domappel (111)** (MrsJCecil) **5-10-9** TKent (led: hit 5th & 6th: hdd last: kpt on u.p) 1¾	2	$7/2^{2}$	94	31
2644^{11}	**Alltime Dancer (IRE) (117)** (OSherwood) **5-11-1b** JAMcCarthy (chsd ldrs: rdn appr 3 out: styd on same pce)1½	3	14/1	98	35
1945^{3}	**Purevalue (IRE) (110)** (MWEasterby) **6-10-8** RJohnson (hld up: hdwy 6th: rdn & outpcd next: wknd 3 out) ..dist	4	$7/4^{1}$	—	—
1267^{6}	**Our Kris (120)** (MESowersby) **5-11-4** JRKavanagh (chsd ldrs tl rdn & lost pl appr 3 out) 13	5	20/1	—	—
2062^{6}	**Albertito (FR) (102)** (RHollinshead) **10-10-0** SWynne (chsd ldrs tl drvn along & lost pl 6th: t.o 3 out) 6	6	33/1	—	—
	Blast Freeze (IRE) (126) (NJHenderson) **8-11-10** MAFitzgerald (hld up: hdwy 7th: 3rd & ev ch whn fell 2 out)...	F	6/1	—	—
1701^{2}	**Ralitsa (IRE) (105)** (MDHammond) **5-9-10**(7) RBurns (drvn along & lost pl 6th: sn bhd & p.u)....	P	$9/2^{3}$	—	—

(SP 113.8%) **8 Rn**

4m 49.9 (9.90) CSF £45.20 CT £498.57 TOTE £10.90: £1.90 £1.90 £2.70 (£24.60) OWNER Datum Building Supplies Ltd (MALTON) BRED T. Brennan
LONG HANDICAP Albertito (FR) 9-4
OFFICIAL EXPLANATION **Ralitsa (IRE): was sore after making a mistake.**
1945 Dual Image, as usual, travelled strongly, but it took all his brilliant rider's skill to persuade him to do enough on the run-in. He will probably revert to fences now. (11/1)
1956 Domappel, having his first outing for forty days, proved most willing. His hurdling here was not up to scratch. (7/2)
1125 Alltime Dancer (IRE), who has rather lost his way, showed a return to form in blinkers for the first time. (14/1)
1945 Purevalue (IRE) ran a poor race. Badly tapped for toe a mile from home, his rider gave up after three out. (7/4)
Blast Freeze (IRE), having her first outing for two seasons, was bang in contention when she fell at the second last flight. With the winner finding little under pressure, she may well have won. (6/1)

2781 NAPOLEONS RACING RIVER DON NOVICES' HURDLE (Gd 2) (4-Y.O+) (Class A)

2-25 (2-25) **2m 4f (10 hdls)** £9,883.99 (£3,736.45: £1,825.73: £828.83) GOING: 0.16 sec per fur (G)

			SP	RR	SF
1907*	**Inn At the Top (112)** (JNorton) **5-11-6** DerekByrne (mde all: styd on wl fr 2 out)....—-	1	$5/1^{3}$	92	53
2053^{2}	**Mighty Moss (IRE) (122)** (DNicholson) **6-11-10** MrFHutsby (lw: trckd ldrs: chal 3 out: edgd lft & nt qckn flat)...2	2	$11/10^{1}$	94	55
2547*	**Hoh Warrior (IRE) (115)** (CPEBrooks) **6-11-10** GBradley (lw: sn chsng ldr: nt qckn appr last) 2½	3	6/1	92	53
1921^{2}	**Ionio (USA) (118)** (MrsVCWard) **6-11-10** JRKavanagh (outpcd & reminder 6th: lost pl after next)....27	4	$9/4^{2}$	71	32
1519^{4}	**Squire's Occasion (CAN)** (RAkehurst) **4-10-11** RJohnson (wnt prom 6th: hit next: sn rdn: wknd after 7th) .dist	5	16/1	—	—

(SP 115.2%) **5 Rn**

4m 47.1 (7.10) CSF £10.92 TOTE £5.70: £2.00 £1.20 (£6.10) OWNER Mrs Sylvia Blakeley (BARNSLEY) BRED Crest Stud Ltd
WEIGHT FOR AGE 4yo-13lb
1907* Inn At the Top, given a determined ride, stayed on in really game fashion. (5/1)
2053 Mighty Moss (IRE) moved upsides three out looking to be travelling much the better but, under pressure on the run-in, he edged left in behind the winner. He almost certainly needs some give under foot to be seen at his best. (11/10)
2547* Hoh Warrior (IRE) appreciated this decent ground. He does not seem to like the soft. (6/1)
1921 Ionio (USA) ran no race at all. (9/4)
1519 Squire's Occasion (CAN), a winner on the All-Weather Flat a week earlier, was virtually pulled up when all chance had gone. (16/1)

2782 PERTEMPS GREAT YORKSHIRE H'CAP CHASE (0-145) (5-Y.O+) (Class B)

3-00 (3-00) **3m (18 fncs)** £23,315.00 (£7,070.00: £3,460.00: £1,655.00) GOING: 0.16 sec per fur (G)

			SP	RR	SF
2065*	**General Command (IRE) (130)** (GRichards) **9-11-10** PCarberry (w ldr: led 10th: styd on wl fr 2 out) ....—-	1	$5/2^{1}$	148	60
1799^{3}	**King Lucifer (IRE) (130)** (DNicholson) **8-11-5**(5) MrRThornton (a chsng ldrs: wnt 2nd 3 out: no imp) 5	2	14/1	145	57
1637*	**Golden Spinner (130)** (NJHenderson) **10-11-10** MAFitzgerald (chsd ldrs: ev ch 4 out: nt qckn fr next)....6	3	$9/2^{2}$	141	53
2057^{4}	**Turning Trix (127)** (DNicholson) **10-11-7** JRKavanagh (chsd ldrs: outpcd & hit 12th: styd on fr 4 out) ....½	4	10/1	137	49
1558^{2}	**Betty's Boy (IRE) (127)** (KCBailey) **8-11-7** AThornton (in tch: hdwy & ev ch 4 out: wknd appr next) 4	5	14/1	135	47
1937*	**Sounds Strong (IRE) (127)** (DNicholson) **8-11-7** RJohnson (hld up: hdwy 11th: no imp fr 14th) 1¼	6	$9/2^{2}$	134	46
1287^{4}	**Run Up the Flag (122)** (JTGifford) **10-10-13**(3) MrCBonner (in tch: hit 9th: hdwy 12th: wknd after 4 out)....3	7	12/1	127	39
1997^{P}	**Duhallow Lodge (113)** (CRBarwell) **10-10-7** BFenton (bhd fr 8th: sme hdwy 4 out: n.d) 1¾	8	33/1	117	29
2004^{5}	**Pims Gunner (IRE) (106)** (MDHammond) **9-10-0** DBentley (bhd fr 8th: kpt on fr 4 out)....s.h	9	20/1	110	22
1655^{F}	**Merry Master (119)** (GMMoore) **13-10-13b** SMcNeill (j.rt: led to 10th: wknd qckly 13th: t.o 3 out) ....dist	10	33/1	—	—
1657*	**Easby Joker (129)** (SEKettlewell) **9-11-9** GBradley (t: lw: nvr gng wl: lost tch 8th: t.o whn p.u bef last)	P	$13/2^{3}$	—	—
1863^{2}	**Romany Creek (IRE) (119)** (JPearce) **8-10-13** KGaule (swtg: blnd & uns rdr 2nd)....	U	16/1	—	—

(SP 124.9%) **12 Rn**

6m 1.6 (7.60) CSF £35.11 CT £143.00 TOTE £3.50: £1.90 £5.30 £2.70 (£43.90) Trio £88.70 OWNER Mr Robert Ogden (PENRITH) BRED Miss M. Fenton
LONG HANDICAP Pims Gunner (IRE) 9-13
2065* General Command (IRE) who has gone up 16lb after winning his three previous outings this season, jumps for fun. Given a positive ride, he stayed on really strongly over the last two to score in most convincing fashion. He will stay, acts on fast ground and looks made to measure for the Scottish National. (5/2)
1799 King Lucifer (IRE) was the only one to make a real race of it. He would have been even better suited by some give underfoot. (14/1)
1637* Golden Spinner, from a 5lb higher mark, possibly ran out of stamina in the closing stages. (9/2)
2057 Turning Trix, 4lb higher than when winning at Newcastle two runs ago, was struggling to go the pace when he hit the twelfth. Staying on again at the finish, he will be suited by further. (10/1)
1558 Betty's Boy (IRE) is probably only as good as he showed here. (14/1)
1937* Sounds Strong (IRE), from a 6lb higher mark, was getting nowhere with three-quarters of a mile left to run. (9/2)

2783 MANSION HOUSE H'CAP CHASE (5-Y.O+) (Class B)

3-35 (3-35) **2m 110y (12 fncs)** £6,932.00 (£2,081.00: £1,003.00: £464.00) GOING: 0.16 sec per fur (G)

Form	Horse / Details	Dist	Pos	SP	RR	SF
2618[3]	**Lord Dorcet (IRE) (130)** (JIACharlton) **7-11-6** RJohnson (trckd ldr: led 8th: qcknd next: styd on wl fr 2 out)	—	**1**	7/2[2]	141	45
2051[3]	**Native Mission (132)** (JGFitzGerald) **10-11-8** PCarberry (hld up: jnd ldr 7th: ev ch 2 out: hung lft: kpt on flat)	1½	**2**	4/1[3]	142	46
2639[4]	**Time Won't Wait (IRE) (135)** (RTPhillips) **8-11-11** JRailton (lw: hld up: hdwy 5th: effrt 4 out: 4th & no imp whn mstke 2 out)	7	**3**	3/1[1]	138	42
2058[3]	**Around the Horn (130)** (JTGifford) **10-11-6** SMcNeill (chsd ldrs: one pce fr 3 out)	¾	**4**	8/1	132	36
2639[3]	**Political Tower (129)** (RNixon) **10-11-5** RichardGuest (prom: outpcd 8th: kpt on fr 2 out)	nk	**5**	15/2	131	35
2116[4]	**Sublime Fellow (IRE) (118)** (NJHenderson) **7-10-8** MAFitzgerald (led to 8th: wknd after 4 out)	2	**6**	8/1	118	22
2618[5]	**Sybillin (125)** (JGFitzGerald) **11-11-1** DerekByrne (prom: reminders 5th: rdn 7th: sn lost pl: t.o 3 out)	26	**7**	20/1	100	4
2646[U]	**Callisoe Bay (IRE) (138)** (OSherwood) **8-12-0** JAMcCarthy (j.rt: lost tch 5th: t.o 4 out)	9	**8**	9/1	104	8

(SP 116.0%) **8 Rn**

4m 2.6 (7.60) CSF £17.04 CT £42.10 TOTE £4.20: £1.80 £2.00 £1.70 (£10.10) OWNER Mr John Hogg (STOCKSFIELD) BRED Mrs Ann Fitzgerald

2618 Lord Dorcet (IRE) presumably needed the outing at Kelso after the freeze up. Ridden with plenty of enterprise, he outbattled the runner-up. (7/2)

2051 Native Mission landed almost upsides two out, but persisted in hanging left, and proved less determined than the winner. (4/1)

2639 Time Won't Wait (IRE) seems to be a spring horse and should improve on this effort. (3/1)

2058 Around the Horn is possibly better over two and a half miles nowadays. (8/1)

2639 Political Tower looks to have his fair share of weight at present. (15/2)

1910 Callisoe Bay (IRE) is a gutless sort. Persistently jumping right, he lost all interest after only five fences. (9/1)

2784 SOUTH YORKSHIRE TIMES BREWERS HURDLE (4-Y.O) (Class C)

4-10 (4-10) **2m 110y (8 hdls)** £4,588.00 (£1,384.00: £672.00: £316.00) GOING: 0.16 sec per fur (G)

Form	Horse / Details	Dist	Pos	SP	RR	SF
2615[3]	**Jackson Park (105)** (TDEasterby) **4-11-6** RJohnson (trckd ldr: styd on fr 3 out: led flat: drvn out)	—	**1**	13/8[2]	87	35
1862[3]	**Royal Action** (JEBanks) **4-11-0** JRKavanagh (nt j.w: led: blnd last: edgd lft: hdd flat: kpt on same pce)	1¼	**2**	6/4[1]	80	28
2622[8]	**Seattle Alley (USA)** (PRWebber) **4-11-0** AThornton (hld up: stdy hdwy 5th: ev ch 2 out: r.o one pce)	3½	**3**	12/1	76	24
1776[3]	**Parrot's Hill (IRE)** (MHTompkins) **4-11-0** RichardGuest (trckd ldrs tl outpcd fr 3 out)	13	**4**	7/1[3]	64	12
	Apache Len (USA) (MDHammond) **4-10-7**(7) RBurns (in rr fr 5th)	25	**5**	16/1	40	—
	Mighty Keen (MCBanks) **4-11-0** DSkyrme (bhd: sme hdwy 5th: sn wknd)	21	**6**	25/1	19	—
	Society Girl (JGMO'Shea) **4-10-4**(5) MichaelBrennan (prom: hit 5th: sn lost pl)	1½	**7**	14/1	13	—
	Classic Colours (USA) (ICampbell) **4-11-0** KGaule (plld hrd: wnt prom 5th: wknd appr 3 out)	14	**8**	33/1	4	—
	Little Murray (FMurphy) **4-11-0** PCarberry (prom to 4th: sn bhd: t.o)	dist	**9**	33/1	—	—

(SP 120.6%) **9 Rn**

3m 59.7 (9.70) CSF £4.35 TOTE £2.60: £1.10 £1.50 £2.40 (£2.00) Trio £5.10 OWNER Mr C. H. Stevens (MALTON) BRED M. H. Easterby

2615 Jackson Park is a real battler. His young rider was again seen to great effect. (13/8)

1862 Royal Action who has broken his duck on the All-Weather Flat since Fakenham, did not jump fluently. Holding a narrow advantage when falling through the final flight, the winner then proved just too strong. He will need to brush up his hurdling. (6/4)

Seattle Alley (USA) moved up on the bridle at halfway, but was flat out and only keeping on at the same pace from two out. He does not lack ability, but is not one to have on your side in a tight battle. (12/1)

1776 Parrot's Hill (IRE) was given an easy time of it when it was clear he was only booked for fourth. (7/1)

Apache Len (USA) struggled to go the pace from halfway. On the Flat he showed his best form in blinkers. (16/1)

T/Plpt: £112.80 (145.15 Tckts). T/Qdpt: £12.20 (101.42 Tckts). WG

2764-AYR (L-H) (Good, Good to soft bk st)

Monday January 27th

WEATHER: fine

2785 ALLOWAY VILLAGE 'N.H.' NOVICES' HURDLE (4-Y.O+) (Class E)

1-40 (1-43) **2m (9 hdls)** £2,556.00 (£716.00: £348.00) GOING: 0.79 sec per fur (S)

Form	Horse / Details	Dist	Pos	SP	RR	SF
1296[12]	**Jervaulx (IRE)** (GRichards) **6-11-5** PCarberry (lw: a cl up: hit 4 out: led appr 3 out: rdn & r.o wl)	—	**1**	8/1	81+	37
1362*	**Ardarroch Prince** (MrsMReveley) **6-11-5** PNiven (lw: hld up & bhd: gd hdwy ½-wy: chal appr 3 out: rdn & nt qckn)	4	**2**	9/4[1]	77+	33
1306[F]	**Parson's Lodge (IRE) (77)** (LLungo) **9-11-0** RSupple (bhd: hdwy 5th: styd on wl fr 2 out: nrst fin)	1½	**3**	66/1	71	27
1999[5]	**Fils de Cresson (IRE) (85)** (JRAdam) **7-11-5** MMoloney (lw: in tch: effrt 4 out: sn chsng ldrs: one pce appr last)	nk	**4**	5/1[3]	75	31
1843[5]	**Maitre de Musique (FR) (104)** (MartinTodhunter) **6-11-0**(5) MichaelBrennan (cl up: led 4th tl appr 3 out: wknd between last 2)	½	**5**	10/1	75	31
2615[12]	**Mapleton** (MrsSJSmith) **4-10-7** RichardGuest (chsd ldrs tl outpcd fr 3 out)	1¼	**6**	33/1	73	17
1999[3]	**Major Harris (IRE)** (MDHammond) **5-11-5** RGarritty (stdy hdwy fr 3 out: nvr nr to chal)	nk	**7**	100/30[2]	73	29
2649[10]	**Henry Hoolet** (PMonteith) **8-11-5** GCahill (mid div: effrt appr 3 out: nvr nr to chal)	1¾	**8**	100/1	71	27
2041[6]	**Storm Call** (DWWhillans) **6-11-0** DBentley (nvr trbld ldrs)	8	**9**	25/1	58	14
2619[13]	**My Mavourneen** (MrsSCBradburne) **5-11-0** MFoster (chsd ldrs tl wknd after 4 out)	1	**10**	200/1	57	13
	Sharp Sand (PMonteith) **7-11-5** TReed (effrt 5th: sn in tch: wknd appr 3 out)	5	**11**	100/1	57	13
2649[14]	**Triona's Hope (IRE)** (EMCaine) **8-10-12**(7) TristanDavidson (a bhd: t.o)	23	**12**	500/1	34	—
2649[16]	**Aunt Piquee** (GRichards) **8-11-0** ADobbin (sn bhd: t.o)	16	**13**	200/1	13	—
1973[2]	**Sioux Warrior** (NTinkler) **5-11-2**(3) EHusband (a bhd: t.o)	2½	**14**	25/1	16	—
1705[10]	**Smart In Satin** (MissLucindaRussell) **7-11-5** LO'Hara (in tch to 4th: t.o)	1¾	**15**	200/1	14	—
1290[P]	**Kirtle Monstar** (LLungo) **6-11-5** FPerratt (led to 4th: wknd qckly next: t.o)	23	**16**	100/1	—	—
1827[7]	**Blood Brother** (JBarclay) **5-11-5** AThornton (prom to 5th: t.o)	2½	**17**	25/1	—	—
1579*	**Bold Statement** (GMMoore) **5-11-5** NBentley (lw: hmpd & uns rdr after 1st)		**U**	5/1[3]	—	—

	Horse		Pos	SP	RR	SF
1940^{P}	**Sounds Devious**	(CParker) **4-10-2** DParker (hmpd & uns rdr 1st)	**U**	200/1	—	—
				(SP 128.5%)		**19 Rn**

3m 55.7 (18.70) CSF £24.63 TOTE £9.30: £5.30 £1.20 £8.60 (£13.30) Trio £150.90; £172.17 to Warwick 28/1/97 OWNER Mr Robert Ogden (PENRITH) BRED Vincent Byrne
WEIGHT FOR AGE 4yo-12lb

1296 Jervaulx (IRE), who disappointed in his bumper, looked quite useful here. The further they went the better he got. (8/1: 5/1-10/1)
1362* Ardarroch Prince, patiently ridden, moved up looking to be going better than the winner on the home turn, only then to prove short of a real turn of foot. His turn will come. (9/4)
Parson's Lodge (IRE), back to hurdling here after winning a chase and then falling last season, showed plenty of promise, finishing strongly after being set a very stiff task. (66/1)
1999 Fils de Cresson (IRE), an eye-catching sort, ran pretty well and is gradually coming to hand. (5/1: 4/1-6/1)
1843 Maitre de Musique (FR), who disappointed last time, failed to impress on looks here but still ran much better. (10/1: op 6/1)
Mapleton, who had shown little previously, gave signs of hope here. (33/1)
1999 Major Harris (IRE) never got into this, but left the impression that he is still learning. There ought to be better to come. (100/30)
Henry Hoolet ran reasonably, and should benefit from the outing. (100/1)
1579* Bold Statement was unlucky as his rider got knocked out of the saddle two strides after jumping the first flight. (5/1)

2786 TAM O'SHANTER NOVICES' CHASE (5-Y.O+) (Class D)

2-10 (2-11) **2m (12 fncs)** £3,688.00 (£1,114.00: £542.00: £256.00) GOING: 0.79 sec per fur (S)

	Horse		Dist	Pos	SP	RR	SF
2628^{2}	**Bold Boss (100)**	(GMMoore) **8-11-3** BStorey (lw: in tch: hit 5th & 6th: pushed along & hdwy next: led 2 out: rdn & r.o)	—	**1**	4/5^{1}	99	30
1316^{9}	**Nooran**	(ACWhillans) **6-11-3** PCarberry (cl up: led 6th tl blnd & hdd 8th: led 4 out to 2 out: kpt on)	2½	**2**	33/1	97	28
2543*	**Rallegio (90)**	(PMonteith) **8-11-3** ADobbin (lw: a.p: led 8th to 4 out: one pce fr 2 out)	2	**3**	5/2^{2}	95	26
1943*	**Crosshot (82)**	(RMcDonald) **10-11-9** KJones (lw: chsd ldrs tl hmpd & lost pl after 8th: n.d after)	16	**4**	11/1^{3}	85	16
2653^{5}	**Fenwick's Brother (87)**	(MrsSJSmith) **7-11-3** RichardGuest (lw: in tch tl outpcd 7th: styd on again fr 2 out)	½	**5**	11/1^{3}	78	9
2632^{F}	**Know-No-No (IRE) (83)**	(MDHammond) **8-11-3** RGarritty (in tch: outpcd appr 4 out: no ch whn blnd 2 out)	1¼	**6**	14/1	77	8
1848^{8}	**Corston Joker (83)**	(LLungo) **7-11-3** RSupple (mstkes: bhd fr ½-wy)	3	**7**	16/1	74	5
1987^{F}	**Friendly Knight**	(JSHaldane) **7-11-3** TReed (sn wl bhd: sme late hdwy)	14	**8**	16/1	60	—
2629^{10}	**See You Always (IRE) (59)**	(MABarnes) **7-10-12b**(5) STaylor (outpcd fr ½-wy)	nk	**9**	66/1	59	—
	Emerald Sea (USA) (85)	(JBarclay) **10-11-3** AThornton (prom tl blnd bdly 4th: sn wknd)	dist	**10**	25/1	—	—
	Moss Pageant (60)	(FTWalton) **7-11-3** KJohnson (led & sn clr: hdd 6th: wknd next: p.u bef 2 out)		**P**	66/1	—	—
1667^{F}	**Glint of Ayr**	(RHGoldie) **7-10-12** GCahill (sn t.o: p.u bef 6th)		**P**	200/1	—	—
					(SP 129.5%)		**12 Rn**

4m 5.2 (20.20) CSF £38.84 TOTE £1.30: £1.10 £3.70 £1.50 (£15.50) Trio £15.70 OWNER Mr John Robson (MIDDLEHAM) BRED Dr O. Zawawi

2628 Bold Boss was never travelling or jumping that fluently, but he responded to pressure and eventually won well enough. (4/5: op evens)
1316 Nooran put in a decent first effort over fences here. He will surely find a race or two before long. (33/1)
2543* Rallegio ran quite well on this his chasing debut, but failed to pick up when ridden in the home straight. The experience should stand him in good stead. (5/2: 7/2-9/4)
1943* Crosshot appeared unlucky, as he clipped another runner's heels after the fifth last and lost all momentum. (11/1: 7/1-12/1)
2653 Fenwick's Brother was staying on after getting outpaced at a vital stage. He would seem to need a bit further. (11/1)
Know-No-No (IRE) seems to be going the wrong way at the moment. (14/1: 10/1-16/1)

2787 SOUTAR JOHNNY NOVICES' HURDLE (5-Y.O+) (Class E)

2-40 (2-42) **3m 110y (12 hdls)** £2,430.00 (£680.00: £330.00) GOING: 0.79 sec per fur (S)

	Horse		Dist	Pos	SP	RR	SF
2042^{2}	**Swanbister (IRE) (103)**	(LLungo) **7-11-4** RSupple (lw: a cl up: led appr 3 out: styd on wl)	—	**1**	5/4^{1}	78	19
2619^{10}	**Smiddy Lad**	(RShiels) **6-10-12** DBentley (hld up: hdwy on bit to chal whn hit 3 out: ev ch tl outpcd flat)	2	**2**	50/1	71	12
1802^{7}	**Celtic Duke**	(MDHammond) **5-10-12** RGarritty (mid div: styd on wl fr 3 out: nrst fin)	16	**3**	25/1	60	1
	Allerbank	(MrsJStorey) **6-10-12** MrCStorey (lw: bhd & mstke 5th: pushed along & hdwy 7th: styd on: n.d)	3½	**4**	100/1	58	—
2626*	**The Khoinoa (IRE)**	(MrsASwinbank) **7-10-12** JSupple (lw: mstkes: bhd: hdwy 7th: chsng ldrs 4 out: wknd next)	18	**5**	4/1^{2}	46	—
1705^{7}	**Four From Home (IRE)**	(JJO'Neill) **5-10-12** ARoche (cl up: led 8th tl appr 3 out: grad wknd)	3½	**6**	50/1	44	—
2504^{7}	**Decent Penny (IRE)**	(MrsRichardArthur) **8-10-7** AThornton (led to 8th: sn wknd)	4	**7**	50/1	36	—
2541^{2}	**Lostris (IRE)**	(MDods) **6-10-7** BStorey (trckd ldrs: effrt after 4 out: sn btn & wknd qckly)	21	**8**	9/2^{3}	23	—
1666^{12}	**Obvious Risk**	(EMCaine) **6-10-5**(7) TristanDavidson (a bhd)	4	**9**	200/1	25	—
2654^{6}	**Movie Man (74)**	(JRTurner) **5-10-12** TReed (prom tl wknd fr 7th)	2½	**10**	20/1	23	—
2654^{2}	**Pebble Beach (IRE) (87)**	(GMMoore) **7-11-4** JCallaghan (chsd ldrs: wkng whn fell 4 out)		**F**	6/1	—	—
2654^{P}	**Busy Boy (70)**	(DALamb) **10-10-12** JBurke (a bhd: t.o whn p.u bef 3 out)		**P**	100/1	—	—
2619^{6}	**Boris Brook**	(RAllan) **6-10-5**(7) SMelrose (a bhd: t.o whn p.u bef 3 out)		**P**	25/1	—	—
2541^{P}	**Hawk Hill Boy**	(FPMurtagh) **6-10-12** ADobbin (in tch tl mstke & lost pl 7th: t.o whn p.u bef 3 out)		**P**	100/1	—	—
					(SP 118.7%)		**14 Rn**

6m 21.0 (35.00) CSF £82.47 TOTE £2.00: £1.50 £57.70 £1.90 (£86.30) Trio £236.80; £150.10 to Warwick 28/1/97 OWNER Col D. C. Greig (CARRUTHERSTOWN) BRED Ned Sullivan

2042 Swanbister (IRE) gained the win he deserved here, but needed all his staying power to do so. (5/4)
Smiddy Lad had shown next to nothing previously, but put in an eye-catching performance here, only losing out due to greenness late on. Better now seems likely. (50/1)
Celtic Duke seems to stay forever and is gradually improving, but he needs time. (25/1)
Allerbank looks a real stayer, and may well come into his own on more testing ground. (100/1)
2626* The Khoinoa (IRE) needs to improve his hurdling, and once he does better should be seen. (4/1)
Four From Home (IRE) showed his first real signs of form, only to weaken rapidly in the closing stages. (50/1)
2541 Lostris (IRE) was a big disappointment, and stopped as though shot once she came off the bridle on the home turn. (9/2)
2654 Pebble Beach (IRE) had already shot his bolt when he fell heavily four out. (6/1)

2788 HAPPY BIRTHDAY MAY MILLAR NOVICES' H'CAP CHASE (0-105) (5-Y.O+) (Class E)

3-10 (3-11) **3m 1f (19 fncs)** £3,281.75 (£989.00: £479.50: £224.75) GOING: 0.79 sec per fur (S)

	Horse		Dist	Pos	SP	RR	SF
1845^{6}	**Kings Sermon (IRE) (78)**	(PBeaumont) **8-10-5** RSupple (mstkes: cl up: led fr 13th: kpt on wl fr 4 out)	—	**1**	10/1	89	21
1850^{5}	**Noosa Sound (IRE) (73)**	(LLungo) **7-10-0** BStorey (a.p: chsd wnr fr 14th: kpt on wl towards fin)	1	**2**	6/1	83	15

				SP	RR	SF
2052*	**Coverdale Lane (90)** (MrsSJSmith) **10-11-3** MrPMurray (bhd & drvn along ½-wy: styd on fr 14th: 3rd & no imp whn blnd 2 out)	17	**3**	3/1[1]	90	22
2632[6]	**Garbo's Boy (79)** (JRTurner) **7-10-6** WFry (mstkes: hdwy u.p 13th: nvr trbld ldrs)	3	**4**	14/1	77	9
2630[7]	**Bright Destiny (73)** (JSGoldie) **6-10-0v** GCahill (chsd ldrs tl outpcd fr 14th)	10	**5**	33/1	64	—
	Abbey Lamp (IRE) (93) (MissLucindaRussell) **8-11-6** AThornton (chsd ldrs to 8th: sn outpcd & bhd)	dist	**6**	25/1	—	—
2063[F]	**Quixall Crossett (75)** (EMCaine) **12-9-9**(7)[ow2] TristanDavidson (a wl bhd)	25	**7**	50/1	—	—
1845*	**Mister Trick (IRE) (79)** (LLungo) **7-10-6**[ow1] RGarritty (mid div whn fell 7th)		**F**	7/2[2]	—	—
2540[8]	**Mr Sloan (73)** (JSGoldie) **7-9-11**(3) GLee (chsd ldrs: outpcd whn fell 14th)		**F**	66/1	—	—
1981[P]	**Valley Garden (97)** (JJO'Neill) **7-11-10b** PCarberry (chsd ldrs: rdn & wkng whn blnd bdly 15th: p.u bef 3 out)		**P**	16/1	—	—
	Ansuro Again (78) (MrsMReveley) **8-10-5** PNiven (effrt 10th: rdn & mstke 12th: sn wknd: p.u bef 3 out)		**P**	6/1	—	—
2540[4]	**Mamica (80)** (MDods) **7-10-7** NSmith (bhd: hdwy whn blnd 11th: sn wknd: p.u bef 3 out)		**P**	5/1[3]	—	—
1845[2]	**Aylesbury Lad (IRE) (75)** (DALamb) **8-10-2b**[ow2] JBurke (led: blnd 8th: blnd bdly & hdd 13th: sn p.u: dead)		**P**	10/1	—	—
2632[9]	**Wee Wizard (IRE) (73)** (MABarnes) **8-9-9b**(5) STaylor (nvr gng wl: almost ref 13th: p.u bef next)		**P**	50/1	—	—
				(SP 135.4%)	**14 Rn**	

6m 38.0 (31.00) CSF £69.71 CT £216.09 TOTE £15.70: £4.70 £3.20 £2.40 (£59.40) Trio £88.90 OWNER Mrs P. A. H. Hartley (BRANDSBY) BRED Nicholas Morrissey

LONG HANDICAP Mr Sloan 9-7 Quixall Crossett 8-11 Noosa Sound(IRE) 9-12 Bright Destiny 9-1 Aylesbury Lad(IRE) 9-13 Wee Wizard(IRE) 9-12

1845 Kings Sermon (IRE), happier on this track, really attacked his fences. Although chancy at times, he never looked in danger of falling and won well. (10/1)

1850 Noosa Sound (IRE), from a yard just coming to form, put in an improved effort, sticking grimly to his task at the finish. He seems to stay forever. (6/1)

2052* Coverdale Lane is only slow and was off the bridle with over a circuit to go. Despite keeping on, she was never anything like good enough. (3/1)

1944* Garbo's Boy spoiled his chances by making mistakes. He really must improve his jumping. (14/1)

802 Bright Destiny ran reasonably until finding things too much from the sixth last. (33/1)

Valley Garden ran quite well, but seemed to be struggling when a blunder stopped him altogether five out. (16/1)

2540 Mamica has the ability, but jumping is the problem. (5/1)

2789 BURNS' COTTAGE NOVICES' CHASE (5-Y.O+) (Class D)

3-40 (3-46) **2m 4f (17 fncs)** £3,824.50 (£1,156.00: £563.00: £266.50) GOING: 0.79 sec per fur (S)

				SP	RR	SF
1669[2]	**Mr Knitwit** (PMonteith) **10-11-4** ADobbin (trckd ldrs: led 4 out: sn qcknd clr)	—	**1**	6/1[3]	113+	34
1803[6]	**Lansborough** (GRichards) **7-11-4** PCarberry (lw: hld up: effrt 10th: chsng ldrs 4 out whn sltly hmpd: one pce after)	11	**2**	4/1[2]	104	25
	Judicious Captain (74) (MrsJStorey) **10-11-4** MrCStorey (in tch tl outpcd 10th: styd on fr 4 out: no imp)	1¾	**3**	66/1	103	24
2061[F]	**Oat Couture** (LLungo) **9-11-10** AThornton (hit 9th: hdwy u.p whn blnd 11th: n.d after)	dist	**4**	4/1[2]	—	—
1807[8]	**Highbeath** (MrsMReveley) **6-11-4** PNiven (lw: bhd fr ½-wy)	20	**5**	14/1	—	—
	Rifawan (USA) (MrsMReveley) **6-11-4** DWalsh (w ldrs: led appr 4 out: hdd & fell 4 out: dead)		**F**	5/4[1]	—	—
2653[3]	**Singing Sand (74)** (PMonteith) **7-11-4** RSupple (led: blnd 11th: hdd appr 4 out: sn btn: 4th & no ch whn fell last)		**F**	33/1	—	—
2176[3]	**Fine Tune (IRE) (60)** (MrsSCBradburne) **7-11-4** MFoster (fell 2nd)		**F**	100/1	—	—
2000[5]	**Grand as Owt (65)** (DMcCune) **7-11-4** KJohnson (in tch tl outpcd 9th: t.o whn p.u bef 13th)		**P**	50/1	—	—
1714[6]	**Ethical Note (IRE)** (MrsSJSmith) **6-11-4** RichardGuest (prom to 4th: sn wl bhd: t.o whn p.u bef 3 out)		**P**	100/1	—	—
				(SP 113.8%)	**10 Rn**	

5m 19.7 (24.70) CSF £26.85 TOTE £6.80: £1.80 £1.10 £13.30 (£5.20) Trio £97.10 OWNER Coupar Capital Racing (ROSEWELL) BRED William Corrigan

1669 Mr Knitwit, having his first attempt over fences, won in really useful style. Plenty more opportunities should come his way. (6/1: op 4/1)

1803 Lansborough was slightly hampered by a couple of fallers, but this was no real excuse as he was simply never good enough. (4/1: op 5/2)

Judicious Captain ran a reasonable first race of the season, and he should be all the better for this. (66/1)

2061 Oat Couture was never all that happy and, after a blunder at the open ditch (seven out), he soon found things beyond him. (4/1: 3/1-9/2)

1046* Highbeath got round safely in his own time, and the experience should see a little improvement. (14/1: 10/1-16/1)

Rifawan (USA) came with a big reputation, but it all went wrong at the fourth last, where he fell fatally. (5/4)

2653 Singing Sand is a chancy jumper, but ran a fair race to the fourth last. He was out on his feet when falling heavily at the last. (33/1)

2790 AULD BRIG NOVICES' H'CAP HURDLE (0-110) (4-Y.O+) (Class D)

4-10 (4-17) **2m 4f (11 hdls)** £3,218.00 (£898.00: £434.00) GOING: 0.79 sec per fur (S)

				SP	RR	SF
2627[4]	**Phar Echo (IRE) (85)** (LLungo) **6-11-6** RSupple (lw: cl up: led 3 out: sn hdd: rallied to ld flat: r.o)	—	**1**	5/1[2]	67	26
1575[4]	**Lifebuoy (IRE) (83)** (JRTurner) **6-11-4** TReed (trckd ldrs: led after 3 out & qcknd: hdd flat: kpt on)	1	**2**	100/30[1]	64	23
	Pariah (IRE) (89) (MartinTodhunter) **8-11-10** PNiven (hld up: stdy hdwy appr 3 out: chsng ldrs & rdn 3 out: kpt on)	3	**3**	20/1	68	27
2619[12]	**Sunny Leith (78)** (PMonteith) **6-10-13** ADobbin (lw: led tl hdd 3 out: one pce)	10	**4**	9/1	49	8
537[3]	**Blazing Trail (IRE) (89)** (MissLucindaRussell) **9-11-10** AThornton (chsd ldrs tl rdn & btn appr 3 out)	3	**5**	10/1	57	16
1911[5]	**Teejay'n'aitch (IRE) (79)** (JSGoldie) **5-10-11**(3) GLee (in tch: effrt appr 3 out: no imp)	nk	**6**	10/1	47	6
2541[3]	**Barefoot Landing (USA) (76)** (CParker) **6-10-11** DParker (lw: trckd ldrs: effrt 4 out: rdn & btn appr next)	1	**7**	5/1[2]	43	2
1672[P]	**Kasirama (IRE) (78)** (MDHammond) **6-10-13** RGarritty (hld up: hdwy appr 3 out: sn wknd)	½	**8**	11/2[3]	45	4
2509[9]	**Kings Minstral (IRE) (73)** (DALamb) **7-10-8** JBurke (chsd ldrs to 6th: t.o whn p.u bef 3 out)		**P**	9/1	—	—
2539[12]	**Martha Buckle (65)** (JSGoldie) **8-10-0** GCahill (lost tch fr ½-wy: t.o whn p.u bef 3 out)		**P**	50/1	—	—
				(SP 116.7%)	**10 Rn**	

5m 8.0 (27.00) CSF £20.55 CT £280.54 TOTE £5.20: £1.80 £1.50 £3.90 (£10.80) Trio £32.60 OWNER S H C Racing (CARRUTHERSTOWN) BRED John O'Connor

2627 Phar Echo (IRE), looking particularly fit, was well suited by the drop in trip, showing fine courage to gain the upper hand after the last. (5/1)

1575 Lifebuoy (IRE) looked the likely winner when quickening into a useful lead at the third last, but was just worried out of it. After a two-month lay-off, he may have needed this. (100/30)

Pariah (IRE), returning after almost two years off, ran a super race and was not overpunished when obviously not good enough. He should benefit no end from this. (20/1)

1345 Sunny Leith, having his first run in handicap company, tried to gallop his rivals into the ground, but was tapped for toe over the last three. (9/1)

537 Blazing Trail (IRE), back over hurdles, showed enough to suggest that he is in good heart. He will appreciate a return to chasing, especially on soft ground. (10/1)
2541 Barefoot Landing (USA) looked to be going quite well for much of the race but, once off the bridle turning for home, her response was most disappointing. (5/1)
1316 Kasirama (IRE) (11/2: 4/1-6/1)
1825 Kings Minstral (IRE) (9/1: 6/1-10/1)

T/Plpt: £31.50 (384.29 Tckts). T/Qdpt: £12.60 (63 Tckts) AA

2436-PLUMPTON (L-H) (Good, Good to soft patches)
Monday January 27th
WEATHER: overcast

2791 HICKSTEAD MAIDEN HURDLE (I) (4-Y.O+) (Class F)
1-30 (1-31) **2m 1f (10 hdls)** £1,917.20 (£529.20: £251.60) GOING: 1.08 sec per fur (HY)

				SP	RR	SF
	Pomme Secret (FR) (MCPipe) **4-10-10** CMaude (mde virtually all: rdn out)	—	**1**	9/2^{3}	89+	14
2547^{2}	**Avanti Express (IRE)** (CREgerton) **7-11-8** JOsborne (hdwy 6th: w wnr fr 3 out: ev ch 2 out: rdn appr last: unable qckn)	4	**2**	11/10^{1}	85	22
	Eau de Cologne (MrsLRichards) **5-11-8** MRichards (w wnr to 5th: wknd appr 2 out)	11	**3**	20/1	75	12
1581^{7}	**Ivory Coaster (NZ)** (BdeHaan) **6-11-8** CLlewellyn (hld up: rdn 3 out: sn wknd)	14	**4**	25/1	62	—
2624^{10}	**Clock Watchers (68)** (JJBridger) **9-11-8** DMorris (swtg: bit bkwd: prom to 7th)	12	**5**	100/1	50	—
	Barbary Falcon (PJJones) **7-11-8** SMcNeill (lw: hdwy 5th: chsd wnr 6th tl appr 3 out: sn wknd)	nk	**6**	25/1	50	—
	Burn Out (JPearce) **5-11-8** RDunwoody (hld up: rdn 7th: wknd 3 out)	12	**7**	3/1^{2}	39	—
2071^{U}	**Belle Perk (IRE)** (TPMcGovern) **6-11-3** MAFitzgerald (lw: hdwy 7th: wknd 3 out)	½	**8**	20/1	33	—
1774^{11}	**Murray's Million** (JSSmith) **5-11-8** TJMurphy (bhd whn mstke 6th: t.o)	18	**9**	100/1	21	—
	The Bizzo (50) (JFPanvert) **6-11-0**(3) PHenley (a bhd: t.o fr 6th)	21	**10**	100/1	—	—
2055^{U}	**Perfect Pal (IRE)** (MissGayKelleway) **6-11-8** DBridgwater (a bhd: mstke 2nd: t.o fr 6th)	8	**11**	12/1	—	—
2574^{F}	**Prince Rudolf (IRE)** (WGMTurner) **5-11-1**(7) NWillmington (a bhd: t.o fr 7th)	28	**12**	100/1	—	—
				(SP 119.7%)	**12 Rn**	

4m 24.5 (28.50) CSF £8.81 TOTE £4.20: £1.80 £1.10 £4.90 (£4.20) Trio £26.30 OWNER Elite Racing Club (WELLINGTON) BRED Ewar Stud Farms
WEIGHT FOR AGE 4yo-12lb
IN-FOCUS: This was not your usual Plumpton maiden hurdle - with several Cheltenham Festival prospects taking part, this was a decent little race.
Pomme Secret (FR), claimed out of Jonathan Pease's stable after winning at Clairefontaine in August, has not raced since. That did not stop him from making a very pleasing start to his hurdling career. Dictating matters from the front, he was strongly pressed by the runner-up from three out, but managed to assert his authority going to the last. Further success awaits, and the Triumph Hurdle is very much on the cards. (9/2)
2547 Avanti Express (IRE) moved up to dispute the advantage with the winner three from home, but the concession of 12lb proved too much, and he had to settle for second best once again. Nevertheless this was a good performance, and he looks a ready-made winner. (11/10)
Eau de Cologne, who won on the Flat for Chris Thornton last April, was bought privately for 30,000 guineas at the Doncaster November Sales. Playing an active role, he was only shaken off by the front two turning for home. He will come on for this first run in three and a half months. (20/1)
1203 Ivory Coaster (NZ), who failed to stay two and a half miles on his hurdling debut, was left for dead from the third last. (25/1)
Clock Watchers still did not look fully fit, but was close up until the fourth last. He is no better than a plater. (100/1)
Barbary Falcon, who won a bumper for Toby Balding back in July '95 on his only previous outing, moved into second place early on the final circuit. He was collared for that position approaching the third last and soon done with. (25/1)
Burn Out, who won a valuable bumper at Aintree last March, was having his first outing since flopping at Punchestown the following month. Chasing the leaders, he had given his all three out, and may now step up to two and a half miles. (3/1: 2/1-100/30)
Perfect Pal (IRE), who looked a really exciting bumper horse two seasons ago, has had his problems and appears to have gone completely. Tailed off on the All-Weather at Lingfield recently, he gave not the slightest glimmer of hope here. (12/1: 8/1-14/1)

2792 POYNINGS (S) H'CAP HURDLE (0-90) (6-Y.O+) (Class G)
2-00 (2-01) **2m 1f (10 hdls)** £2,042.40 (£566.40: £271.20) GOING: 1.08 sec per fur (HY)

				SP	RR	SF
1841^{4}	**Do Be Ware (69)** (JFfitch-Heyes) **7-10-8** BFenton (hdwy 7th: led after 3 out: all out)	—	**1**	20/1	54	—
1861^{*}	**Pharly Reef (75)** (DBurchell) **5-11-0** DJBurchell (hdwy 7th: rdn appr 2 out: ev ch last: r.o)	¾	**2**	9/2^{2}	59	4
490^{3}	**Summer Villa (65)** (KGWingrove) **5-10-4b** JRyan (hdwy appr 2 out: ev ch fr 2 out: r.o)	hd	**3**	9/1	49	—
1962^{9}	**Script (68)** (JRJenkins) **6-10-7** JOsborne (chsd ldr: led 3 out: sn hdd: unable qckn)	2½	**4**	16/1	50	—
1836^{3}	**Water Hazard (IRE) (69)** (SDow) **5-10-8** ADicken (hld up: rdn 7th: sn wknd)	14	**5**	10/1	38	—
1809^{3}	**Minster's Madam (89)** (JNeville) **6-11-11v**(3) TDascombe (led to 3 out: sn wknd)	1	**6**	7/2^{1}	57	2
2567^{8}	**Lajadhal (FR) (68)** (KBishop) **8-10-7** LHarvey (nvr nrr)	7	**7**	20/1	29	—
2067^{6}	**Derisbay (IRE) (76)** (JJBridger) **9-11-1b** DMorris (prom to 7th)	5	**8**	33/1	32	—
2006^{7}	**Ruth's Gamble (61)** (MrsLCJewell) **9-10-0v** DLeahy (lw: hdwy 7th: sn wknd)	1¼	**9**	16/1	16	—
2036^{3}	**Ecu de France (IRE) (65)** (PCRitchens) **7-10-4** SFox (prom to 7th)	1	**10**	12/1	19	—
1861^{9}	**Lucy Tufty (81)** (JPearce) **6-11-6** RDunwoody (hdwy 7th: wknd 3 out)	6	**11**	7/1^{3}	30	—
1939^{W}	**Never Forgotten (86)** (GLMoore) **12-11-11** NMann (bit bkwd: a bhd)	12	**12**	33/1	23	—
1952^{10}	**Highly Decorated (80)** (MissAMNewton-Smith) **12-10-12b**(7) JKMcCarthy (bhd fr 7th)	6	**13**	33/1	12	—
1836^{5}	**Aldwick Colonnade (75)** (MDIUsher) **10-11-0** WMcFarland (bit bkwd: a bhd)	4	**14**	12/1	3	—
2067^{F}	**Wide Support (84)** (GLMoore) **12-11-9** PHolley (bhd fr 6th)	1¼	**15**	33/1	11	—
1675^{7}	**Four Weddings (USA) (75)** (MissKMGeorge) **4-10-2** JRKavanagh (bit bkwd: bhd fr 4th)	23	**16**	20/1	—	—
				(SP 125.2%)	**16 Rn**	

4m 27.5 (31.50) CSF £95.70 CT £806.30 TOTE £15.60: £2.70 £1.50 £3.10 £2.00 (£26.00) Trio £163.60; £34.57 to Warwick 28/1/97 OWNER Mr John Ffitch-Heyes (LEWES) BRED R. and Mrs J. Digby-Ware
LONG HANDICAP Ruth's Gamble 9-7
WEIGHT FOR AGE 4yo-12lb
No bid

1841 Do Be Ware was back in his proper class. Sent to the front soon after the third last, he was given no peace whatsoever, and had nothing left to spare at the line. (20/1)
1861* Pharly Reef, 7lb higher than when winning at Fakenham last month, threw down his challenge in the straight, and was a real danger despite his rider losing his whip. He kept on well to the line, but was unable to master the winner. (9/2)
490 Summer Villa, fit from a recent run on the Flat, ran much better here. Throwing down her challenge in the straight, she kept on to the bitter end. (9/1)
828 Script is certainly no better than this class and, having moved to the front three out, was promptly collared. (16/1)
1836 Water Hazard (IRE) found this ground against him (it was certainly easier than the official report) and was a spent force in the back straight. (10/1)
1809 Minster's Madam, reverting to hurdles, goes well here and has won two races in this grade over course and distance. With the ground in her favour, this effort was rather disappointing. (7/2)
Aldwick Colonnade (12/1: op 8/1)

2793 LEWES NOVICES' CHASE (5-Y.O+) (Class E)

2-30 (2-30) **2m (13 fncs)** £3,198.00 (£943.00: £451.00: £205.00) GOING: 0.70 sec per fur (S)

	Horse / details	Dist	Pos	SP	RR	SF
2549*	**Amancio (USA) (124)** (MrsAJPerrett) **6-11-9** MAFitzgerald (mde virtually all: v.easily)	—	**1**	2/9 1	121+	32
2079²	**Robins Pride (IRE)** (CLPopham) **7-11-0**(3) TDascombe (lw: hld up: rdn to chse wnr 4 out: unable qckn fr 2 out)	10	**2**	5/1 2	105?	16
2007⁷	**Furry Fox (IRE)** (RCurtis) **9-11-3** DMorris (mstke 1st: a bhd: t.o fr 8th)	dist	**3**	25/1 3	—	—
2752⁶	**Brigadier Supreme (IRE) (72)** (PButler) **8-11-3** TJMurphy (lw: a bhd: t.o whn fell 9th: rmntd)	dist	**4**	100/1	—	—
1764⁶	**Purbeck Cavalier** (RHAlner) **8-11-0b1**(3) PHenley (chsd wnr tl blnd & uns rdr 4 out)		**U**	33/1	—	—
				(SP 106.3%)		**5 Rn**

4m 11.6 (19.60) CSF £1.46 TOTE £1.10: £1.10 £1.30 (£1.60) OWNER Mr Paul Locke (PULBOROUGH) BRED Hill'N Dale Farm
2549* Amancio (USA) had little more than a gentle stroll to win this atrocious race. This was another confidence-boosting run, as connections prepare him for the Arkle Chase at the Festival. (2/9: 1/3-1/5)
2079 Robins Pride (IRE) moved up to take second place four from home, and grimly tried to get on terms with the winner. It was a futile exercise however, and he was left for dead from the penultimate fence. (5/1)

2794 HICKSTEAD MAIDEN HURDLE (II) (4-Y.O+) (Class F)

3-00 (3-00) **2m 1f (10 hdls)** £1,917.20 (£529.20: £251.60) GOING: 1.08 sec per fur (HY)

	Horse / details	Dist	Pos	SP	RR	SF
1375³	**No Pattern** (GLMoore) **5-11-8** DGallagher (lw: hld up: led 2 out: rdn out)	—	**1**	7/2 3	80	—
	Cotteir Chief (IRE) (JNeville) **6-11-8** RDunwoody (bit bkwd: hdwy 7th: ev ch 2 out: rdn & swtchd lft appr last: 2nd whn blnd last: unable qckn)	1¾	**2**	9/4 1	78+	—
1555*	**Bula Vogue (IRE)** (RRowe) **7-11-3** DO'Sullivan (a.p: led 3 out to 2 out: one pce)	nk	**3**	10/1	73	—
	Persian Elite (IRE) (CREgerton) **6-11-8** JOsborne (lw: led to 4th: n.m.r on ins bnd after 3 out: one ce)	½	**4**	12/1	78	—
	Worthy Memories (MrsMerritaJones) **8-11-3** DerekByrne (nvr nr to chal)	23	**5**	100/1	51	—
	Voila Premiere (IRE) (MHTompkins) **5-11-8** KGaule (lw: bhd fr 5th)	11	**6**	100/30 2	46	—
2648²	**Tanglefoot Tipple** (RHAlner) **6-11-5**(3) PHenley (lw: chsd ldr: led 4th to 3 out: wkng whn nt clr run on ins bnd after 3 out)	9	**7**	15/2	37	—
1555⁷	**Yarsley Jester** (DMGrissell) **5-11-3** JRKavanagh (a bhd)	6	**8**	50/1	27	—
	Speedy Snaps Pride (PDCundell) **5-11-8** LHarvey (mstke 3rd: a bhd)	1¼	**9**	50/1	30	—
2642⁶	**Adilov (94)** (JJBridger) **5-11-8** DMorris (lw: 5th whn fell 6th)		**F**	20/1	—	—
	Crampscastle (IRE) (NoelChance) **7-11-8** RJohnson (bit bkwd: hld up: rdn 3 out: wknd appr 2 out: bhd whn p.u bef last)		**P**	20/1	—	—
				(SP 119.1%)		**11 Rn**

4m 32.3 (36.30) CSF £10.70 TOTE £4.40: £1.60 £1.70 £2.30 (£5.30) Trio £15.80 OWNER Mr K. Higson (BRIGHTON) BRED Mrs N. F. M. Sampson
OFFICIAL EXPLANATION **Voila Premiere (IRE): finished distressed.**
1375 No Pattern, fit from the Flat, gained a slender advantage at the second last and asserted on the run-in. He would not want the ground any softer than this. (7/2: op 7/4)
Cotteir Chief (IRE), who finished in the frame in the Lockinge Stakes and the Diomed Stakes in 1994 for Martin Pipe, has had his problems and been off the course since July 1995. Nevertheless, he is being aimed at the Champion Hurdle, despite this being his debut over obstacles. He was switched going to the final flight and, not helped by making a serious error there, he failed to find what was required. Sure to benefit a great deal from this, he is capable of winning at this game, but the thought of him running in the Champion Hurdle is quite ridiculous. (9/4)
1555* Bula Vogue (IRE), winner of a bumper in November, made a pleasing debut over hurdles. Sent on three out, she was collared at the penultimate hurdle and then just tapped for toe. (10/1: 4/1-11/1)
Persian Elite (IRE), tailed off on both his starts on the Flat last year, ran much better on his hurdling debut, following an absence of over four months. Short of room turning out of the back straight, he was always just tapped for toe. (12/1)
Worthy Memories has shown nothing to date, and only plodded on past a few tired rivals. (100/1)
Voila Premiere (IRE) was in good form on the Flat last year, but was disappointing on this hurdling debut. He reportedly finished distressed. (100/30)
2648 Tanglefoot Tipple (15/2: 5/1-8/1)

2795 PLUMPTON NOVICES' H'CAP CHASE (0-100) (5-Y.O+) (Class E)

3-30 (3-30) **2m 5f (16 fncs)** £3,503.45 (£1,049.60: £504.30: £231.65) GOING: 0.70 sec per fur (S)

	Horse / details	Dist	Pos	SP	RR	SF
1582³	**Cardinal Rule (IRE) (66)** (MissVenetiaWilliams) **8-10-1** RJohnson (a.p: led 10th: rdn out)	—	**1**	10/1	74	26
2577³	**Winnow (69)** (AndrewTurnell) **7-9-11**(7) CRae (hdwy 10th: ev ch 2 out: unable qckn)	5	**2**	15/2	73	25
2569⁵	**Dante's View (USA) (89)** (PRHedger) **9-11-10** MAFitzgerald (lw: stdy hdwy 12th: rdn appr last: one pce)	1	**3**	11/2 2	92	44
1936⁴	**Thermal Warrior (79)** (JABOld) **9-11-0** GUpton (hdwy appr 2 out: nvr nrr)	4	**4**	10/1	79	31
1773ᴾ	**Hangover (75)** (RLee) **11-10-7**(3) GHogan (hdwy 9th: wknd appr 2 out)	1¾	**5**	16/1	74	26
1694⁵	**Purbeck Rambler (68)** (GBBalding) **6-10-3v1** BFenton (nvr nr to chal)	9	**6**	20/1	60	12
1875⁵	**Koo's Promise (80)** (CLPopham) **6-10-12**(3) TDascombe (prom tl appr 3 out)	17	**7**	12/1	59	11
2634⁶	**Mel (IRE) (71)** (RHBuckler) **7-10-6** BPowell (lw: led tl after 3rd: led 5th to 10th: mstke 11th: wknd 12th)	9	**8**	6/1 3	43	—
	Rolleston Blade (79) (JRBest) **10-10-7**(7) MrPO'Keeffe (lw: prom to 11th)	4	**9**	20/1	48	—
1252⁷	**Sense of Value (87)** (JSSmith) **8-11-8** WMarston (a bhd)	14	**10**	25/1	46	—

1875[F]	**Gerry's Pride (IRE) (68)** (JWMullins) **6-10-3** SCurran (hdwy appr 2 out: 6th & no ch whn fell last)		F	20/1	—	—
1875[F]	**Saxon Mead (65)** (PJHobbs) **7-10-0** GTormey (hdwy 9th: 3rd & rdn whn fell 2 out)		F	5/1[1]	—	—
2657[F]	**Hanson Street (NZ) (65)** (PJHobbs) **10-10-0** KGaule (bhd fr 9th: t.o whn p.u bef 2 out)		P	25/1	—	—
1506[3]	**Minor Key (IRE) (87)** (JRJenkins) **7-11-8** GBradley (led after 3rd to 5th: wknd 10th: t.o whn p.u bef 11th)		P	14/1	—	—
1839[2]	**Ring Corbitts (84)** (MJRoberts) **9-11-5** JRailton (lw: 7th whn blnd & uns rdr 6th)		U	11/2[2]	—	—
				(SP 133.9%)		**15 Rn**

5m 34.8 (21.80) CSF £78.08 CT £430.93 TOTE £10.20: £2.70 £2.70 £2.50 (£23.80) Trio £132.50 OWNER Mr Peter Burch (HEREFORD) BRED Mrs Patricia Mackean

LONG HANDICAP Hanson Street (NZ) 9-11 Saxon Mead 9-12

OFFICIAL EXPLANATION Minor Key (IRE): had choked.

1582 Cardinal Rule (IRE) at last came good, leading early on the final circuit and being ridden along to beat a moderate bunch. (10/1)

2577 Winnow again showed promise over a more suitable trip, having every chance at the second last, before getting tapped for toe. (15/2)

2569 Dante's View (USA) appreciated the longer trip, and gradually eased his way into the action in the last mile. Ridden along soon after the second last, he made no impression. (11/2: 4/1-6/1)

1936 Thermal Warrior is a very poor performer these days, although he did run better than on his reappearance, staying on in the straight to be nearest at the line. (10/1: 8/1-12/1)

1684 Hangover, another poor performer, has not won for five years. (16/1)

1875 Saxon Mead (5/1: 3/1-11/2)

1839 Ring Corbitts (11/2: 4/1-6/1)

2796 ALBOURNE H'CAP CHASE (0-105) (5-Y.O+) (Class F)

4-00 (4-01) **2m (13 fncs)** £2,733.50 (£756.00: £360.50) GOING: 0.70 sec per fur (S)

				SP	RR	SF
1731[5]	**Whippers Delight (IRE) (87)** (GFHCharles-Jones) **9-10-10** MrACharles-Jones (lw: a.p: led last: rdn out)	—	1	20/1	99	9
1952[8]	**Kings Cherry (IRE) (104)** (JABOld) **9-11-13** GUpton (hdwy appr 2 out: r.o)	4	2	14/1	112	22
2577*	**Olliver Duckett (82)** (CLPopham) **8-10-5** GTormey (led to last: unable qckn)	1½	3	2/1[1]	89	—
1864[3]	**Winspit (IRE) (86)** (RHAlner) **7-10-9** JRKavanagh (hld up: chsd ldr fr 4 out: ev ch whn mstke 2 out: sn wknd)	10	4	9/2[2]	83	—
1841[6]	**Whistling Buck (IRE) (81)** (RRowe) **9-10-4** DO'Sullivan (nvr nrr)	6	5	10/1	72	—
1306[P]	**Shrewd John (91)** (MissKMGeorge) **11-11-0** DGallagher (nvr nr to chal)	½	6	20/1	81	—
	Churchtown Port (IRE) (99) (PButler) **7-11-8** MAFitzgerald (hld up: pckd 2nd: rdn 9th: sn wknd)	8	7	8/1	81	—
2692[15]	**Rustic Gent (IRE) (78)** (MrsLCJewell) **9-10-1v** DLeahy (a bhd: t.o fr 7th)	23	8	50/1	37	—
1965*	**Pegmarine (USA) (81)** (MrsAMWoodrow) **14-10-4** JAMcCarthy (a bhd: t.o fr 7th)	16	9	10/1	24	—
2038[5]	**Halham Tarn (IRE) (90)** (HJManners) **7-10-6**(7) ADowling (prom to 4 out: t.o whn fell 2 out)		F	20/1	—	—
1965[2]	**Soleil Dancer (IRE) (84)** (DMGrissell) **9-10-4**(3) PHenley (a bhd: mstke 5th: t.o whn p.u bef 9th)		P	13/2[3]	—	—
	Young Alfie (79) (JFPanvert) **12-9-13b**(3)ow2 GHogan (bit bkwd: a wl bhd: t.o whn p.u bef 4 out)		P	50/1	—	—
				(SP 119.0%)		**12 Rn**

4m 14.4 (22.40) CSF £225.26 CT £742.23 TOTE £21.30: £4.10 £6.50 £1.20 (£172.50) Trio £117.40 OWNER Mr S. P. Tindall (WANTAGE) BRED Mrs John Lonergan

Whippers Delight (IRE) as usual looked very well beforehand, and bounced back to form after a string of appalling runs this season. Appearing beaten turning for home, he stayed on to lead at the last and forged right away. (20/1)

Kings Cherry (IRE), since coming over from Ireland, had completed just once in five starts over fences, and has been hurdling this season. Lumbered with top weight on this return to the larger obstacles, he stayed on to take second place on the run-in. He has done all his winning in the mud. (14/1)

2577* Olliver Duckett once again ran better for his new trainer. Tearing off in front, he appeared to have set a suicidal pace, but was not overhauled until the last. (2/1)

1864 Winspit (IRE) makes errors and that was again evident here. He was within a length of the leader, when a mistake two out sealed his fate. (9/2)

1841 Whistling Buck (IRE) was making his chasing debut, but could never get into it. (10/1)

951 Shrewd John, sold for a mere 1,550 guineas since his last outing, never threatened. (20/1)

1965* Pegmarine (USA) (10/1: 7/1-11/1)

2797 PYECOMBE H'CAP HURDLE (0-110) (4-Y.O+) (Class E)

4-30 (4-30) **2m 4f (12 hdls)** £2,490.00 (£690.00: £330.00) GOING: 1.08 sec per fur (HY)

				SP	RR	SF
2634[4]	**Flaxley Wood (83)** (RHBuckler) **6-10-4** BPowell (a.p: led 5th: rdn out)	—	1	11/2[3]	65	27
1988[3]	**Fawley Flyer (92)** (WGMTurner) **8-10-6**(7) JPower (led to 3rd: chsd wnr fr 3 out: unable qckn)	1½	2	8/1	73	35
2669[4]	**Total Joy (IRE) (92)** (CJMann) **6-10-13** RDunwoody (hdwy 9th: rdn appr 2 out: one pce)	4	3	4/1[1]	70	32
1586[5]	**Claireswan (IRE) (98)** (MHTompkins) **5-11-5** KGaule (lw: a.p: rdn appr 2 out: sn wknd)	8	4	7/1	69	31
2644[6]	**Smuggler's Point (USA) (105)** (JJBridger) **7-11-12** DMorris (led 3rd to 5th: wknd appr 3 out)	6	5	14/1	71	33
1813[3]	**Indian Quest (104)** (NAGaselee) **8-11-11** CLlewellyn (lw: hdwy 9th: wknd appr 3 out)	nk	6	8/1	70	32
1698[R]	**Kilcoran Bay (98)** (JWMullins) **5-11-5** RGreene (nvr nr to chal)	3	7	20/1	62	24
1709[5]	**Bon Voyage (USA) (95)** (DMGrissell) **5-11-2b** JRKavanagh (hdwy 7th: wknd appr 3 out)	7	8	16/1	53	15
1810[4]	**Millmount (IRE) (93)** (TPMcGovern) **7-11-0b** MAFitzgerald (lw: bhd fr 7th: t.o)	10	9	9/2[2]	43	5
1962[B]	**Equity's Darling (IRE) (79)** (DCO'Brien) **5-9-9**(5) MrRThornton (lw: virtually ref to r: a t.o)	1¾	10	33/1	28	—
2666[5]	**Handy Lass (98)** (JSSmith) **8-11-5** TJMurphy (a bhd: virtually p.u flat: t.o)	23	11	12/1	28	—
2659[P]	**Sausalito Boy (87)** (RJSmith) **9-10-8** DBridgwater (s.s: t.o tl p.u bef 4th)		P	20/1	—	—
1985[F]	**Mine's an Ace (NZ) (96)** (MissVenetiaWilliams) **10-11-3** RJohnson (hld up: rdn appr 3 out: sn wknd: t.o whn p.u bef last)		P	16/1	—	—
				(SP 126.9%)		**13 Rn**

5m 15.6 (28.60) CSF £46.77 CT £184.90 TOTE £6.20: £2.50 £1.80 £2.20 (£27.70) Trio £45.80 OWNER Mrs La Trobe (BRIDPORT) BRED P. M. Prior-Wandesforde

LONG HANDICAP Equity's Darling (IRE) 9-9

2634 Flaxley Wood confirmed the promise shown at Haydock, leading at the fifth and being ridden along to maintain the advantage (11/2: 7/2-6/1)

1988 Fawley Flyer has steadily been rising in the weights following a string of good efforts, but that did not stop him putting in another solid performance. Taking second place three out, he grimly tried to get on terms with the winner, but was always lacking that turn of foot. (8/1)

2669 Total Joy (IRE) saw out this longer trip, but failed to find the necessary acceleration in the straight. (4/1)

1394* Claireswan (IRE) was close up until calling it a day early in the straight. (7/1)

2644 Smuggler's Point (USA) was back in his own league, but was a spent force going to the third last. (14/1: 8/1-16/1)

1813 Indian Quest has been badly out of form for a long time (he was flattered by his previous performance in a slowly run race) and again ran poorly. (8/1)
1810 Millmount (IRE) (9/2: op 8/1)

T/Jkpt: Not won; £2,638.79 to Warwick 28/1/97. T/Plpt: £25.30 (435.7 Tckts). T/Qdpt: £12.10 (45.57 Tckts) AK

2503-MUSSELBURGH (R-H) (Good to firm, Firm bk st)
Tuesday January 28th
WEATHER: fine

2798 MCEWANS EXPORT NOVICES' HURDLE (4-Y.O+) (Class E)
1-20 (1-20) **2m (8 hdls)** £2,574.00 (£714.00: £342.00) GOING minus 0.42 sec per fur (GF)

Form	Horse	Dist	Pos	SP	RR	SF
2504[2]	**Maple Bay (IRE) (84)** (BEllison) **8-11-5** ADobbin (a.p: led after 2 out: r.o wl flat)	—	1	11/2	73	11
2503*	**Best of All (IRE)** (JBerry) **5-11-7** MMoloney (hld up: wnt 2nd 3 out: stdd after next: effrt appr last: kpt on one pce)	2	2	3/1[2]	73	11
2503[3]	**Falcon's Flame (USA)** (MrsJRRamsden) **4-10-7** PCarberry (lw: hld up: hdwy 3 out: chal & hit last: kpt on towards fin)	½	3	11/4[1]	71	—
	High Hope Henry (USA) (MDHammond) **4-10-7** RGarritty (hld up: hdwy 3 out: one pce fr next)	7	4	10/1	64	—
2503[2]	**Shinerolla** (CParker) **5-11-5** DParker (lw: in tch: effrt appr 2 out: one pce appr last)	nk	5	7/2[3]	63	1
	Nancys Choice (MrsNHope) **7-11-5** JBurke (plld hrd: led fr 2nd & sn clr: blnd 2 out: sn hdd & btn)	9	6	100/1	54	—
2619[14]	**The Sharrow Legend (IRE)** (JSisterson) **5-11-0(5)** STaylor (chsd ldrs tl wknd fr 2 out)	2	7	50/1	52	—
	Knave (PMonteith) **4-10-7** GCahill (a bhd)	12	8	25/1	40	—
1705[9]	**Primitive Heart** (HowardJohnson) **5-11-5** ASSmith (led to 2nd: chsd ldrs tl wknd qckly 3 out)	7	9	25/1	33	—
	On The Off Chance (LLungo) **5-11-5** RSupple (mstke 2nd: a bhd)	12	10	66/1	21	—
1942[9]	**Mannagar (IRE)** (WStorey) **5-11-0(5)** RMcGrath (wl bhd fr ½-wy)	5	11	100/1	16	—
2503[11]	**Desert Lore** (RMMcKellar) **6-11-5** BStorey (chsd ldrs to 5th: sn bhd)	30	12	200/1	—	—

(SP 112.0%) **12 Rn**

3m 44.2 (5.20) CSF £19.02 TOTE £4.30: £1.30 £1.80 £1.50 (£6.80) Trio £7.00 OWNER Ferrograph Ltd (LANCHESTER) BRED Berkshire Equestrian Services Ltd
WEIGHT FOR AGE 4yo-12lb
OFFICIAL EXPLANATION **Mannagar (IRE) finished distressed**
2504 Maple Bay (IRE) got it right this time, and responded to pressure to score decisively. He is sure to pick up more races. (11/2)
2503* Best of All (IRE) appeared to be going particularly well when her rider took a pull after the second last, but when it came down to a struggle on the flat, she was found wanting. (3/1)
2503 Falcon's Flame (USA) looked the part here and was produced just right but, once off the bit, he fiddled the last and failed to come up with the goods. The ability is there if he can ever be persuaded. (11/4)
High Hope Henry (USA) ran well, but returned with a badly injured tendon and will be out for some time. (10/1)
2503 Shinerolla was always struggling to get in a blow from the third last. This was a most disappointing effort. (7/2)
Nancys Choice ran well after almost a year off, and would have been a fair bit closer but for a blunder two out. (100/1)

2799 BEAMISH RED IRISH ALE NOVICES' CHASE (5-Y.O+) (Class E)
1-50 (1-53) **2m (12 fncs)** £3,070.20 (£915.60: £436.80: £197.40) GOING minus 0.42 sec per fur (GF)

Form	Horse	Dist	Pos	SP	RR	SF
2628[7]	**Urban Dancing (USA) (99)** (BEllison) **8-11-3** KJohnson (chsd ldrs: outpcd 3 out: styd on appr last: led flat)..	—	1	5/1[3]	86	30
2629[4]	**Appearance Money (IRE)** (FMurphy) **6-10-12** PCarberry (hld up: stdy hdwy to chse ldr 7th: led 3 out: stumbled last: sn hdd: rdn & fnd nil)	2½	2	10/1	79	23
2177[4]	**Arctic Sandy (IRE)** (JKMOliver) **7-11-3** BStorey (wnt 2nd 5th: lft in ld 7th: blnd & hdd 3 out: no ex)	1½	3	5/2[1]	82	26
2653[P]	**Movac (IRE) (86)** (MissLucindaRussell) **8-11-10** MMoloney (chsd ldrs to 6th: sn wknd)	dist	4	10/1	—	—
2631[7]	**Tapatch (IRE)** (MWEasterby) **9-11-3b** RGarritty (2nd whn fell 4th)		F	11/2	—	—
2543[7]	**Bolaney Girl (IRE) (75)** (FPMurtagh) **8-10-12** ADobbin (ref to r: t.n.p)		R	10/1	—	—
2628[4]	**Chorus Line (IRE) (84)** (PBeaumont) **8-10-12** RSupple (lw: led tl blnd & uns rdr 7th)		U	7/2[2]	—	—

(SP 110.1%) **7 Rn**

3m 55.1 (1.10) CSF £41.36 TOTE £5.60: £3.90 £1.50 (£36.60) OWNER Mr Ronald McCulloch (LANCHESTER)
1267 Urban Dancing (USA) seemed to find this trip on the sharp side, but proved game and in the end won well. Better should be seen over further. (5/1)
2629 Appearance Money (IRE) threw a hurdle race away last time, and managed to snatch defeat from the jaws of victory again here. She obviously needs very patient handling. (10/1)
2177 Arctic Sandy (IRE), a real chasing type, just needs experience and better will be seen. (5/2)
1138 Movac (IRE) was outpaced on the final circuit and may well need further, but also needs to improve. (10/1: 8/1-12/1)
2631 Tapatch (IRE) (11/2: 4/1-6/1)
2628 Chorus Line (IRE) was happy bowling along in front, until meeting the sixth last all wrong and giving his rider no chance of staying aboard. (7/2)

2800 GILLESPIE MALT STOUT NOVICES' H'CAP HURDLE (0-100) (4-Y.O+) (Class E)
2-20 (2-22) **2m 4f (12 hdls)** £2,616.00 (£726.00: £348.00) GOING minus 0.42 sec per fur (GF)

Form	Horse	Dist	Pos	SP	RR	SF
2692[3]	**Heavens Above (62)** (FMurphy) **5-10-1** PCarberry (lw: led to 2nd: trckd ldrs: led on bit 2 out: rdn out flat).....	—	1	7/2[1]	45	7
1652[19]	**Prelude To Fame (USA) (89)** (MissMKMilligan) **4-11-1** ADobbin (cl up: led 8th to 2 out: kpt on u.p flat)	¾	2	8/1	71	20
2631[10]	**Here Comes Herbie (80)** (WStorey) **5-11-5** MMoloney (hld up & bhd: hdwy ½-wy: hit 8th: sn chsng ldrs: nt qckn fr last)	1	3	14/1	62	24
2060[8]	**Thorntoun Estate (IRE) (74)** (MartinTodhunter) **4-9-7b(7)** CMcCormack (lw: mstkes: hdwy ½-wy: sn chsng ldrs & hrd rdn: styd on fr 2 out: no imp)	8	4	15/2[3]	49	—
1821[2]	**Arian Spirit (IRE) (80)** (JLEyre) **6-11-5** BStorey (hld up: effrt 7th: sn rdn & styd on: nvr able to chal)	¾	5	5/1[2]	55	17
2177[3]	**Little Redwing (69)** (MDHammond) **5-10-8v** RGarritty (lw: effrt 7th: styd on u.p fr 3 out: nvr rchd ldrs)	nk	6	12/1	43	5
1959[8]	**Not To Panic (IRE) (65)** (KRBurke) **7-10-4** ASSmith (prom: ev ch 3 out: wknd next)	1¼	7	14/1	38	—
2505[7]	**Doubling Dice (68)** (RAllan) **6-10-0(7)** SMelrose (hit 8th & outpcd: sme hdwy appr 2 out: n.d)	1¼	8	16/1	40	2
2001[5]	**Pangeran (USA) (88)** (MrsASwinbank) **5-11-13** JSupple (lw: in tch tl outpcd fr 4 out)	14	9	8/1	49	11

				SP	RR	SF
2654[8]	**The Next Waltz (IRE) (75)** (LLungo) **6-11-0** RSupple (lw: in tch tl outpcd 7th: n.d after)	2	**10**	8/1	35	—
2505[5]	**School of Science (61)** (DANolan) **7-10-0b** SMcDougall (led fr 2nd to 8th: wknd)	4	**11**	50/1	17	—
2629[11]	**Seconds Away (61)** (JSGoldie) **6-10-0** GCahill (a bhd)	1	**12**	33/1	17	—
1524[7]	**Flaming Hope (IRE) (78)** (MrsNHope) **7-11-3v[1]** JBurke (prom to 7th: sn wknd)	2½	**13**	10/1	32	—
	Greenfield Manor (72) (JSisterson) **10-10-6**(5) STaylor (a bhd)	2	**14**	33/1	24	—
1988[9]	**Rubislaw (61)** (MrsKMLamb) **5-9-7**(7) MissSLamb (a bhd)	19	**15**	100/1	—	—
				(SP 128.8%)		**15 Rn**

4m 45.4 (3.40) CSF £30.64 CT £338.53 TOTE £4.20: £1.40 £2.80 £7.40 (£35.00) Trio £179.40; £103.61 to Windsor 29/1/97 OWNER R & G Leonard (MIDDLEHAM) BRED C. T. and Mrs Bletsoe
LONG HANDICAP Seconds Away 9-7 Thorntoun Estate (IRE) 9-13 School of Science 9-10 Rubislaw 9-4
WEIGHT FOR AGE 4yo-13lb
2692 Heavens Above looked as well as ever, and with plenty of use made of him was always travelling well. He had enough in hand to settle it when ridden after the last, and should get further. (7/2)
646 Prelude To Fame (USA), back to form, appreciated this longer trip and, judged on this effort, will get even further. (8/1)
2044 Here Comes Herbie likes to come from off the pace, but on this occasion had to struggle to get anywhere near, and to give him credit he did stick on well. He is a tricky customer to win with, but there is plenty of ability there. (14/1)
1526 Thorntoun Estate (IRE) looks a funny customer, and his hurdling was sloppy to say the least. He was given plenty of help from the saddle, and did keep struggling on. (15/2)
1821 Arian Spirit (IRE) never got going until too late, and is not the most natural of jumpers, but she is learning. (5/1)
2177 Little Redwing was never doing enough to make the slightest impression. (12/1)

2801 KILMANY CUP H'CAP CHASE (0-120) (5-Y.O+) (Class D)
2-50 (2-50) **2m 4f (16 fncs)** £3,525.00 (£1,050.00: £500.00: £225.00) GOING minus 0.42 sec per fur (GF)

				SP	RR	SF
2508*	**Wayuphill (98)** (CParker) **10-10-7** BStorey (hld up: hdwy ½-wy: led 4 out: r.o)	—	**1**	13/8[1]	112	19
1941[4]	**Vicaridge (93)** (RBrewis) **10-10-2** ASSmith (lw: j.lft: chsd ldrs: led 9th to 4 out: btn whn blnd 2 out)	10	**2**	7/1[3]	99	6
1970[6]	**Charming Gale (98)** (MrsSCBradburne) **10-10-7** MFoster (led to 9th: cl up tl outpcd fr 4 out)	3½	**3**	8/1	101	8
2508[5]	**Rapid Mover (91)** (DANolan) **10-10-0b** MMoloney (chsd ldrs tl rdn & btn appr 4 out)	1¾	**4**	50/1	93	—
1688[2]	**Timbucktoo (119)** (JKMOliver) **10-12-0** ADobbin (chsd ldrs tl outpcd fr 4 out)	18	**5**	9/2[2]	106	13
2748[2]	**Puritan (CAN) (109)** (NTinkler) **8-11-4b** MissPJones (lw: bhd: hdwy u.p & prom 4 out: 3rd & btn whn hmpd & uns rdr last)		**U**	9/2[2]	—	—
2508[4]	**Grand Scenery (IRE) (91)** (HowardJohnson) **9-10-0** PCarberry (cl up whn blnd & uns rdr 2nd)		**U**	8/1	—	—
				(SP 111.1%)		**7 Rn**

4m 58.0 (2.00) CSF £11.56 CT £60.17 TOTE £1.90: £1.80 £3.50 (£19.90) OWNER Mr & Mrs Raymond Anderson Green (LOCKERBIE)
LONG HANDICAP Grand Scenery (IRE) 9-11 Rapid Mover 9-12
2508* Wayuphill has hit a rich vein of form of late, and won this moderate contest in good style. (13/8)
1941 Vicaridge was not helped by the attentions of a loose horse for much of the race, but threw his chance away by continually jumping left.(7/1)
1970 Charming Gale, racing without the visor this time, ran reasonably to the fourth last. (8/1: op 5/1)
1688 Timbucktoo probably found this ground a bit too quick, and he was left behind over the last four fences. (9/2)

2802 MCEWANS 70/- H'CAP HURDLE (0-125) (4-Y.O+) (Class D)
3-20 (3-21) **3m (13 hdls)** £3,659.00 (£1,024.00: £497.00) GOING: 0.42 sec per fur (GS)

				SP	RR	SF
2627[5]	**Cheater (IRE) (86)** (HowardJohnson) **6-10-0b[1]** PCarberry (mde all: r.o wl u.p flat)	—	**1**	10/1	71	—
2507*	**Highland Park (86)** (RCraggs) **11-10-0** ADobbin (lw: prom: pushed along 3 out: ev ch fr 2 out: nt qckn flat)	4	**2**	11/2[3]	68	—
2507[3]	**Supertop (111)** (LLungo) **9-11-11** RSupple (lw: hld up: stdy hdwy to chal 2 out: sn rdn & no ex)	1¾	**3**	9/4[2]	92	15
1967*	**Invest Wisely (97)** (MDHammond) **5-10-11** RGarritty (lw: chsd wnr tl outpcd & hmpd 2 out: sn rdn & btn)	4	**4**	11/8[1]	76	—
2545[8]	**Old Habits (IRE) (108)** (JLEyre) **8-11-8** BStorey (hld up: effrt 8th: prom & mstke 3 out: sn drvn along & no imp after)	¾	**5**	16/1	86	9
2627[P]	**Carnmoney (IRE) (86)** (JSisterson) **9-9-9**(5) STaylor (prom tl outpcd 8th: no imp fr 4 out)	11	**6**	100/1	57	—
1690[2]	**Leading Prospect (100)** (MrsJDGoodfellow) **10-11-0** ASSmith (prom: drvn along fr 8th: wknd appr 2 out)	6	**7**	16/1	67	—
				(SP 110.1%)		**7 Rn**

5m 48.3 (8.30) CSF £52.79 TOTE £11.00: £4.60 £2.30 (£15.90) OWNER Mr Gordon Brown (CROOK) BRED J. Ward
LONG HANDICAP Carnmoney (IRE) 9-3 Cheater (IRE) 9-8
2627 Cheater (IRE) had blinkers on for the first time and they made all the difference. (10/1)
2507* Highland Park is an honest sort, but is just short of a turn of foot. (11/2)
2507 Supertop likes things to go his way, and once he came off the bit going to the last that was it. (9/4)
1967* Invest Wisely was a shade disappointing here, and being hampered two out made little difference. To give him the benefit his stable is not really firing at present. (11/8: Evens-6/4)
2545 Old Habits (IRE), still likely to benefit from this, ran quite well in the circumstances . (16/1)
Carnmoney (IRE), 11lb wrong in the handicap, looked pretty slow throughout the final circuit. (100/1)

2803 MCEWANS LAGER NOVICES' CHASE (5-Y.O+) (Class E)
3-50 (3-50) **3m (18 fncs)** £2,988.30 (£890.40: £424.20: £191.10) GOING minus 0.42 sec per fur (GF)

				SP	RR	SF
2000[4]	**Cush Supreme (IRE) (77)** (MartinTodhunter) **8-11-5** PCarberry (lw: plld hrd: led fr 3rd & sn clr: kpt on wl fr 2 out: comf)	—	**1**	6/1[3]	92	—
2176[P]	**Tough Test (IRE)** (MrsJDGoodfellow) **7-11-5** GCahill (chsd wnr fr 4th: hdwy 4 out: sn prom: nt qckn fr 2 out)	4	**2**	2/1[2]	89	—
2545[4]	**Trump** (CParker) **8-11-5** DParker (lw: j.deliberately: bhd: hdwy 4 out: no imp)	14	**3**	5/4[1]	80	—
	Kalajo (BMactaggart) **7-11-5** BStorey (led to 3rd: outpcd ½-wy: n.d after)	3	**4**	25/1	78	—
1716[4]	**Tactix (65)** (MissMKMilligan) **7-11-0** ASSmith (chsd ldrs tl outpcd fr 13th: 5th & wl btn whn fell last)		**F**	16/1	—	—
1989[P]	**Broomhill Duker (IRE) (77)** (HowardJohnson) **7-11-5** ADobbin (in tch to 7th: t.o whn p.u bef 11th)		**P**	50/1	—	—
892[2]	**Classic Crest (IRE)** (MissLucindaRussell) **6-11-5v** MFoster (in tch whn blnd & uns rdr 8th)		**U**	16/1	—	—
2507[5]	**D'Arblay Street (IRE)** (WTKemp) **8-11-5** SMcDougall (lw: mstke & uns rdr 5th)		**U**	14/1	—	—
				(SP 116.3%)		**8 Rn**

6m 9.9 (16.90) CSF £17.88 TOTE £4.70: £1.70 £1.60 £2.30 (£10.70) OWNER Mr Robert Ogden (ULVERSTON) BRED Con Troy
2000 Cush Supreme (IRE), whose rider gave up trying to keep hold of him, was allowed to stride on from the third and the issue was never in doubt from that point. He won with something in hand. (6/1)
1668 Tough Test (IRE) put up a decent effort after two unlucky runs, and will obviously find a race in due course. (2/1)

2545 Trump had a good look at his fences and is certainly not a natural. He would seem to need time to get the hang of this game. (5/4)
Kalajo, a winning pointer, was not beaten too far after getting completely outpaced with a circuit to go, and will obviously benefit from the experience. (25/1)

2804 WEATHERBYS 'STARS OF TOMORROW' STANDARD OPEN N.H. FLAT RACE (4, 5 & 6-Y.O) (Class H)
4-20 (4-20) **2m** £1,516.00 (£426.00: £208.00)

				SP	RR	SF
1913[6]	**Country Orchid** (MrsMReveley) **6-11-0** PNiven (hld up: hdwy 4f out: led over 1f out: r.o)	—	**1**	4/1[3]	41 f	—
	Es Go (RBastiman) **4-10-4**(3) HBastiman (led after 5f tl hdd over 1f out: kpt on)	2½	**2**	11/4[1]	44 f	—
	Delightfool (RNixon) **6-11-0** ADobbin (hdwy & prom ½-wy: one pce fnl 3f)	9	**3**	20/1	30 f	—
	Just Ned (JSHaldane) **6-11-5** ASSmith (bit bkwd: led 5f: a chsng ldrs: one pce fnl 4f)	nk	**4**	100/1	34 f	—
	Castle Bay (IRE) (LLungo) **6-11-5** RSupple (lw: plld hrd & prom early: lost pl after 5f: hdwy appr st: hung bdly rt & styd on)	hd	**5**	3/1[2]	34 f	—
1827[6]	**Atlantic Sunrise** (RMcDonald) **5-10-7**(7) CMcCormack (in tch: effrt appr st: no imp)	1¼	**6**	50/1	28 f	—
	Sunrise Sensation (RMcDonald) **4-10-7** KJones (prom tl outpcd fnl 4f)	s.h	**7**	20/1	33 f	—
59[9]	**Chief of Khorassan (FR)** (SEKettlewell) **5-11-2**(3) GLee (hld up: nvr nr to chal)	s.h	**8**	12/1	33 f	—
1986[11]	**Midas** (KRBurke) **6-11-12** PCarberry (lw: hld up: hdwy 6f out: chsng ldrs 3f out: sn btn)	1¼	**9**	7/1	39 f	—
2770[9]	**Cottstown Boy (IRE)** (MrsSCBradburne) **6-11-5** MFoster (plld hrd: prom to st)	9	**10**	100/1	23 f	—
2633[5]	**Buddleia** (JRTurner) **4-9-9**(7) NHorrocks (chsd ldrs: effrt 6f out: wknd 3f out)	6	**11**	20/1	12 f	—
	Chief Chippie (WTKemp) **4-10-7** SMcDougall (bit bkwd: chsd ldrs tl wknd fnl 5f)	8	**12**	33/1	9 f	—
	Katsar (IRE) (MDHammond) **5-11-5** RGarritty (outpcd fnl 5f)	2	**13**	12/1	7 f	—
	Far Pasture (MrsNHope) **5-11-0** JBurke (bhd & hmpd over 3f out: p.u ins fnl f)		**P**	100/1	—	—
	Buster Two (IRE) (JSHaldane) **4-10-7** MMoloney (bit bkwd: prom tl lost pl ent st: s.u over 3f out)		**S**	100/1	—	—
				(SP 122.7%)	**15 Rn**	

3m 44.6 CSF £13.02 TOTE £4.40: £1.70 £1.10 £3.40 (£14.00) Trio £247.90; £24.45 to Windsor 29/1/97 OWNER Mrs J. V. Kehoe (SALTBURN) BRED W. Ginzel
WEIGHT FOR AGE 4yo-12lb
1913 Country Orchid, suited by the stronger gallop this time, saw it out most determinedly. (4/1: op 5/2)
Es Go was warm in the preliminaries, but put up a useful performance only to be tapped for foot late on. His turn will come. (11/4)
Delightfool ran reasonably well, but was short of speed when the pace was on in the last three furlongs. (20/1)
Just Ned put up a fair performance, having looked in need of the run. (100/1)
Castle Bay (IRE) took the eye in the paddock, but spoiled his chances by running very green. Once he realises what is required plenty of improvement will be seen. (3/1)
1986 Midas (7/1: 5/1-8/1)
Katsar (IRE) (12/1: op 7/1)

T/Plpt: £631.30 (17.21 Tckts). T/Qdpt: £49.90 (20.19 Tckts) AA

2524-**WARWICK (L-H) (Good to firm, Good patches)**
Tuesday January 28th
WEATHER: fine

2805 'HIGH FRONT' NOVICES' HURDLE (4-Y.O+) (Class E)
1-10 (1-11) **2m (8 hdls)** £2,909.50 (£817.00: £398.50) GOING minus 0.23 sec per fur (G)

				SP	RR	SF
2624[4]	**Carlito Brigante** (PRWebber) **5-11-5** JOsborne (a.p: led appr last: comf)	—	**1**	10/11[1]	87+	38
2622[7]	**Disallowed (IRE)** (MissHCKnight) **4-10-8** MAFitzgerald (lw: led tl appr last: one pce)	1¾	**2**	9/2[3]	86	25
2655[3]	**Country Lover** (MCPipe) **6-11-5v** RDunwoody (prom tl rdn & wknd 2 out)	10	**3**	4/1[2]	75	26
1583[5]	**Tree Creeper (IRE)** (AndrewTurnell) **5-11-5** LHarvey (prom: lost pl appr 4th: rallied 5th: outpcd appr 2 out: styd on flat)	1	**4**	10/1	74	25
2504[5]	**Music Please** (KCBailey) **5-11-5** AThornton (lw: prom: ev ch appr 2 out: 3rd & btn whn pckd last)	1	**5**	16/1	73	24
2080[3]	**Pot Black Uk** (PJHobbs) **6-11-5** GTormey (prom tl wknd 3 out)	10	**6**	20/1	63	14
1184[7]	**Star Blakeney** (GBarnett) **4-10-7** RFarrant (bit bkwd: hdwy appr 5th: wknd appr 2 out)	5	**7**	25/1	58	—
2060[7]	**Palamon (USA)** (JWhite) **4-10-7** BClifford (nvr nrr)	1¼	**8**	20/1	57	—
1873[7]	**Galway Boss (IRE)** (IPWilliams) **5-11-5** BPowell (nvr nrr)	6	**9**	100/1	51	2
	Fred Jeffrey (IRE) (AndrewTurnell) **6-10-12**(7) CRae (bhd fr 4th)	1	**10**	50/1	50	1
2547[12]	**Todd (USA)** (AHHarvey) **6-11-5** JAMcCarthy (hld up: hdwy 4th: wknd 3 out)	5	**11**	33/1	45	—
2661[8]	**Mr Agriwise** (RGFrost) **6-11-5** JFrost (a bhd)	5	**12**	100/1	40	—
161[12]	**Mollie Silvers** (JKCresswell) **5-10-7**(7) NTEgan (bhd fr 4th)	1	**13**	100/1	34	—
	Classic Model (JCTuck) **6-11-5** SMcNeill (swtg: bhd fr 4th)	s.h	**14**	66/1	39	—
	Nicky Wilde (CPEBrooks) **7-11-5** GBradley (t: bkwd: prom: reminders appr 4th: wkng whn mstke 3 out)	2½	**15**	25/1	36	—
	Cuillin (RJSmith) **5-11-0** DWalsh (swtg: s.s: a bhd: t.o)	14	**16**	100/1	17	—
1693[P]	**Nuns Lucy (56)** (FJordan) **6-11-0** SWynne (bit bkwd: bhd: rdn after 3rd: t.o)		**17**	100/1	—	—
	Brightling Fair (MissAMNewton-Smith) **5-10-7**(7) JKMcCarthy (bkwd: s.s: a bhd: t.o)		**18**	100/1	—	—
1276[P]	**Scboo** (REPeacock) **8-11-0**(5) MichaelBrennan (swtg: bkwd: bhd fr 4th: t.o whn p.u bef 2 out)		**P**	100/1	—	—
				(SP 136.1%)	**19 Rn**	

3m 44.3 (2.30) CSF £4.91 TOTE £1.70: £1.40 £1.30 £1.50 (£5.50) Trio £3.70 OWNER Lady Bamford (BANBURY) BRED Whitsbury Manor Stud
WEIGHT FOR AGE 4yo-12lb
2624 Carlito Brigante won with something in hand, and will be entered in both novice events at Cheltenham because his rider thinks he will stay an extra half-mile. (10/11: evens-11/10)
1900* Disallowed (IRE) seems suited by front-running tactics, but was unable to cope with the winner. (9/2)
2655 Country Lover, despite much faster ground this time, was again in trouble at the penultimate hurdle. (4/1: 3/1-9/2)
Tree Creeper (IRE), the first foal of a sister to Buck Willow, would be better suited to a more galloping track with the emphasis switched to stamina. (10/1: 8/1-12/1)
2504 Music Please does not seem to be getting the trip at the moment. (16/1)
2080 Pot Black Uk, graduating to hurdles, will probably need further on a course as sharp as this. (20/1)

2806 'LOW PRESSURE' NOVICES' H'CAP HURDLE (0-105) (4-Y.O+) (Class E)
1-40 (1-40) **2m (8 hdls)** £2,447.50 (£685.00: £332.50) GOING minus 0.23 sec per fur (G)

Form	Horse	Dist	Pos	SP	RR	SF
	Trouvaille (IRE) (89) (AndrewTurnell) **6-11-3** LHarvey (lw: chsd ldr: led 5th: r.o wl)	—	1	7/1	71	25
2567*	**Fastini Gold (75)** (RJPrice) **5-10-3** JOsborne (hld up: hdwy appr 5th: r.o one pce fr 2 out)	3½	2	9/2[3]	54	8
	Beaumont (IRE) (96) (JEBanks) **7-11-10** JRKavanagh (hld up: hdwy appr 3 out: ev ch appr 2 out: swtchd lft & stumbled appr last: one pce)	½	3	3/1[1]	74	28
	Tilaal (USA) (88) (MDHammond) **5-11-2** RDunwoody (bkwd: hld up: hdwy appr 4th: ev ch appr 2 out: one pce)	1¾	4	9/2[3]	64	18
2552[11]	**Time Leader (73)** (RDickin) **5-9-8**(7) XAizpuru (hld up: hdwy 4th: one pce fr 3 out)	4	5	8/1	45	—
2578[6]	**Milling Brook (73)** (JMBradley) **5-10-1** RJohnson (prom to 3 out: no ch whn mstke last)	3½	6	16/1	42	—
1640[14]	**Lothian Commander (75)** (DMcCain) **5-10-3**ow2 DWalsh (bit bkwd: nvr nr to chal)	2½	7	33/1	41	—
1772[6]	**Alpha Leather (72)** (LPGrassick) **6-10-0** MrJGrassick (hdwy appr 4th: wknd 3 out)	5	8	33/1	33	—
1762[U]	**Upham Rascal (72)** (DRGandolfo) **6-10-0** DLeahy (bit bkwd: hld up: hdwy appr 4th: wknd appr 3 out)	s.h	9	33/1	33	—
1908[2]	**Laughing Buccaneer (84)** (DNCarey) **4-10-0** BPowell (bhd fr 5th)	9	10	12/1	36	—
2034[2]	**King Rat (IRE) (85)** (JGMO'Shea) **6-10-8v**(5) MichaelBrennan (hld up: hdwy after 3rd: 2nd whn mstke 3 out: sn wknd)	1¾	11	7/2[2]	35	—
1327[P]	**Kings Vision (75)** (WJenks) **5-10-3**ow3 TJenks (t: bkwd: a bhd: t.o)	17	12	50/1	8	—
2692[13]	**Mr Gordon Bennett (72)** (RDickin) **6-10-0b1** CLlewellyn (lw: led to 5th: wknd 3 out: t.o)	9	13	50/1	—	—
	Urshi-Jade (83) (JGMO'Shea) **9-10-4**(7)ow11 JTNolan (bit bkwd: a bhd: t.o fr 4th)	8	14	50/1	—	—
2578[11]	**Sober Island (73)** (MrsDThomas) **8-9-12**(3)ow1 GuyLewis (bkwd: bhd fr 4th: t.o)	13	15	50/1	—	—

(SP 137.4%) **15 Rn**

3m 46.8 (4.80) CSF £39.31 CT £111.09 TOTE £16.50: £4.40 £2.40 £2.10 (£42.50) Trio £66.70 OWNER Mr G. Payne (WANTAGE) BRED John Quane

LONG HANDICAP Upham Rascal 9-2 Laughing Buccaneer 9-3 Alpha Leather 9-4 Kings Vision 9-12 Mr Gordon Bennett 9-2 Urshi-Jade 9-7 Sober Island 9-7

WEIGHT FOR AGE 4yo-12lb

Trouvaille (IRE), positively ridden, kept on well in the home straight, and his trainer hopes he will make a chaser next season. (7/1)
2567* Fastini Gold could not defy a 5lb hike in the ratings for winning a seller last time. (9/2)
Beaumont (IRE), twice a winner on the Flat in the autumn, may have found two miles on this course too sharp. (3/1)
Tilaal (USA) looked to be going best on the home turn, but lack of a recent run appeared to find him out. (9/2)
2036 Time Leader could not sustain his effort on this return to two miles. (8/1)
2578 Milling Brook, ridden much closer to the pace this time, might be worth a try in a seller. (16/1)

2807 ROSCOE HARVEY MEMORIAL NOVICES' CHASE (5-Y.O+) (Class D)
2-10 (2-10) **2m 4f 110y (17 fncs)** £4,202.00 (£1,216.00: £588.00: £274.00) GOING minus 0.23 sec per fur (G)

Form	Horse	Dist	Pos	SP	RR	SF
1787[2]	**Dream Ride (IRE) (115)** (DNicholson) **7-11-4** RJohnson (swtg: led 3rd to 5th: led 12th to 3 out: led appr 2 out: sn clr: comf)	—	1	2/5[1]	95+	24
1840[P]	**Red Branch (IRE) (60)** (JSKing) **8-11-4** TJMurphy (led 5th to 12th: led 3 out: sn hdd: one pce)	10	2	33/1	87?	16
2010[8]	**Ekeus (IRE)** (JSKing) **7-11-4** CMaude (led to 3rd: wknd 12th)	19	3	20/1[3]	72?	1
2088[7]	**Quick Decision (IRE)** (JKCresswell) **6-10-11**(7) NTEgan (lw: chsd ldrs: rdn after 10th: wknd 4 out)	20	4	40/1	57?	—
1856[U]	**Typhoon (IRE)** (MarkCampion) **7-11-4** MSharratt (bit bkwd: sn t.o: blnd 10th: blnd & uns rdr 3 out: rmntd)	dist	5	66/1	—	—
1429[2]	**Holdimclose** (RGFrost) **7-11-4** JFrost (bit bkwd: fell 3rd)		F	11/4[2]	—	—
	Starlight Fool (67) (KCBailey) **8-11-4b1** AThornton (bit bkwd: fell 2nd)		F	20/1[3]	—	—

(SP 114.5%) **7 Rn**

5m 11.4 (7.40) CSF £16.75 TOTE £1.30: £1.30 £7.80 (£26.70) OWNER C G Clarke and G C Mordaunt (TEMPLE GUITING) BRED Mrs Concepta Dormer-Lewis

1787 Dream Ride (IRE) had been kept for this race run in the memory of his trainer's former patron. (2/5)
Red Branch (IRE) made a real race of it until the second last, and this was a big improvement on anything he had achieved over timber. (33/1)
Ekeus (IRE) was another making his debut over fences. (20/1)

2808 MACKENZIE CONSULTING NOVICES' HURDLE (4-Y.O+) (Class E)
2-40 (2-41) **2m 4f 110y (11 hdls)** £2,640.00 (£740.00: £360.00) GOING minus 0.23 sec per fur (G)

Form	Horse	Dist	Pos	SP	RR	SF
2655[2]	**Motoqua** (DNicholson) **5-11-0** RJohnson (hld up: hdwy appr 7th: rdn 3 out: led 2 out: sn clr)	—	1	3/1[2]	65	—
1457[6]	**Stormyfairweather (IRE)** (NJHenderson) **5-11-5** MAFitzgerald (hld up: mstke 5th: styd on fr 2 out: nt trble wnr)	6	2	16/1[3]	74	—
1659[6]	**The Brewmaster (IRE)** (IPWilliams) **5-11-5** BPowell (bit bkwd: led to 7th: ev ch 2 out: one pce)	1	3	33/1	74	—
	Sweet Lord (IRE) (MBradstock) **6-11-5** PHolley (bkwd: chsd ldr: led 7th to 2 out: btn whn mstke last)	hd	4	25/1	74	—
1706[5]	**Quiet Moments (IRE)** (PGMurphy) **4-10-6** RFarrant (rdn 8th: sn bhd)	6	5	100/1	69	—
1959[6]	**Sweet Trentino (IRE) (80)** (MTate) **6-11-5** WMarston (bhd fr 8th)	11	6	40/1	60	—
1867[12]	**Gale Wargame (IRE)** (OSherwood) **6-11-5** JOsborne (prom tl wknd 7th: t.o whn p.u bef 2 out)		P	25/1	—	—
2634*	**Harbour Island** (MCPipe) **5-11-11** RDunwoody (stmbld, hmpd & uns rdr 1st)		U	4/9[1]	—	—

(SP 114.2%) **8 Rn**

5m 2.1 (15.10) CSF £30.66 TOTE £3.90: £1.40 £1.70 £2.10 (£15.10) Trio £58.70 OWNER Mrs Claire Smith (TEMPLE GUITING) BRED Darley Stud Management Co Ltd

WEIGHT FOR AGE 4yo-13lb

2655 Motoqua had her task made simpler by the early departure of Harbour Island. (3/1: 9/4-7/2)
1457 Stormyfairweather (IRE), out of a full sister to Western Sunset, finished third in a maiden Irish point last spring, and should do better when tackling further. (16/1)
1659 The Brewmaster (IRE) tried to bring his stamina into play over this longer trip. (33/1)
Sweet Lord (IRE) is out of a mare placed in bumpers. (25/1)
2634* Harbour Island stumbled at the first, and Dunwoody was apparently knocked out of the saddle from behind. (4/9)

2809 'WIND CHILL' NOVICES' CHASE (5-Y.O+) (Class D)
3-10 (3-10) **3m 2f (20 fncs)** £3,813.00 (£1,134.00: £552.00: £261.00) GOING minus 0.23 sec per fur (G)

Form	Horse	Dist	Pos	SP	RR	SF
2638[3]	**Flimsy Truth (100)** (MHWeston) **11-11-10** MrMHarris (led: hit 12th: hdd 14th: led 15th: all out)	—	1	5/6[1]	113	31

				SP	RR	SF
1447[U]	**Jultara (IRE) (98)** (IPWilliams) **8-11-5** BPowell (lw: chsd wnr: mstke 10th: led 14th to 15th: blnd 16th: rallied & ev ch 2 out: hrd rdn: r.o)	1	**2**	6/5[2]	107	25
1795[P]	**Musical Hit** (PAPritchard) **6-11-5** RBellamy (blnd 3rd: t.o fr 8th)	dist	**3**	40/1	—	—
1371[7]	**Arr Eff Bee (60)** (JPSmith) **10-11-5** AThornton (bkwd: blnd 6th: t.o fr 8th)	½	**4**	25/1[3]	—	—
	Wessex Milord (60) (JABennett) **12-11-5** LHarvey (bkwd: pckd 8th: sn t.o: p.u bef 15th)		**P**	66/1	—	—

(SP 107.8%) **5 Rn**

6m 34.0 (9.00) CSF £1.94 TOTE £1.80: £1.10 £1.10 (£1.10) OWNER Mr M. H. Weston (WORCESTER) BRED M. H. Weston
2638 Flimsy Truth had to work hard to hold the renewed effort of the runner-up. (5/6: 4/7-10/11)
1447 Jultara (IRE) lost ground with an error five out, but fought back well in the home straight. (6/5)
Musical Hit got the better of the separate duel for the minor honours. (40/1)

2810 'LONG RANGE' NOVICES' H'CAP CHASE (0-105) (5-Y.O+) (Class E)

3-40 (3-40) **2m (12 fncs)** £2,849.75 (£863.00: £421.50: £200.75) GOING minus 0.23 sec per fur (G)

				SP	RR	SF
1714[P]	**Flaming Miracle (IRE) (72)** (GBarnett) **7-10-1b** RFarrant (plld hrd: hdwy appr 6th: j.slowly & lost pl 4 out: rallied appr last: str run to ld nr fin)	—	**1**	5/1	86	18
2745[3]	**Brazil Or Bust (IRE) (99)** (PRWebber) **6-12-0** JOsborne (lw: hld up: hdwy 7th: rdn to ld 2 out: clr last: hrd rdn & hdd nr fin)	1¾	**2**	11/4[2]	111	43
1814[6]	**Snowy Petrel (IRE) (89)** (KCBailey) **5-10-8b** AThornton (led after 5th to 8th: wknd appr last)	7	**3**	10/1	94	16
1943[2]	**Cover Point (IRE) (92)** (JGFitzGerald) **6-11-7** RDunwoody (lw: a.p: led 8th to 2 out: wknd flat)	4	**4**	2/1[1]	93	25
2077[R]	**Heathyards Boy (74)** (DMcCain) **7-10-3b**ow3 DWalsh (led tl after 5th: wknd 7th)	9	**5**	50/1	66	—
1878[2]	**Lucky Eddie (IRE) (99)** (PJHobbs) **6-12-0** CMaude (lw: blnd 2nd: sn bhd: t.o)	15	**6**	7/2[3]	76	8
1552[5]	**Coolteen Hero (IRE) (83)** (RHAlner) **7-10-12** WMcFarland (bit bkwd: chsd ldr tl mstke 5th: bhd whn mstke 6th: blnd & uns rdr 8th)		**U**	10/1	—	—

(SP 119.0%) **7 Rn**

3m 57.4 (3.40) CSF £19.02 TOTE £5.90: £2.70 £1.70 (£10.20) OWNER Mr George Barnett (STOKE-ON-TRENT) BRED Stockwell Ltd
LONG HANDICAP Heathyards Boy 9-10
WEIGHT FOR AGE 5yo-10lb
OFFICIAL EXPLANATION **Flaming Miracle (IRE): accounting for the horse's apparent improvement in form, it was reported that the gelding is suited by a strongly-run race, but had been too keen early on in a slowly run race at Southwell and had tired in the closing stages.**
1254 Flaming Miracle (IRE) jumped better this time, and made up four lengths from the final fence to win going away. (5/1)
2745 Brazil Or Bust (IRE) seemed to have this in the bag, but the weight concession proved too much on the run-in. (11/4)
1550 Snowy Petrel (IRE) was dropping back in trip, and had the headgear refitted for this chasing debut. (10/1)
1943 Cover Point (IRE), raised 2lb, appeared to be travelling like a winner on the home turn, but the way he capitulated reflected the state of English cricket at the moment. (2/1: 5/4-9/4)
1878 Lucky Eddie (IRE), on his chasing debut, seemed to lose confidence after his early blunder. (7/2: 5/2-4/1)

2811 'SLOW THAW' STANDARD OPEN N.H. FLAT RACE (4, 5 & 6-Y.O) (Class H)

4-10 (4-10) **2m** £1,476.00 (£411.00: £198.00)

				SP	RR	SF
898[2]	**Big Perks (IRE)** (PTDalton) **5-11-4** CMaude (hld up: hdwy 5f out: led ins fnl f: rdn out)	—	**1**	7/1	57 f	—
	Spunkie (RFJohnsonHoughton) **4-10-6** RJohnson (gd hdwy 6f out: led over 1f out tl ins fnl f: hrd rdn: r.o)	½	**2**	14/1	57 f	—
1827[2]	**Coble Lane** (IPWilliams) **5-11-4** JOsborne (hld up: hdwy 9f out: ev ch 2f out: one pce)	8	**3**	8/1	49 f	—
	Sheepcote Hill (IRE) (DNicholson) **6-11-1**(3) RMassey (bit bkwd: hld up & bhd: hdwy 7f out: r.o one pce fnl 2f)	nk	**4**	11/2[2]	48 f	—
	Master Pip (AGFoster) **5-11-4** SMcNeill (bit bkwd: hld up: hdwy 5f out: one pce fnl 3f)	1	**5**	20/1	47 f	—
	Silent Cracker (RDickin) **5-11-4** BPowell (unf: bit bkwd: prom: led 8f out: c wd st: hdd over 1f out: wknd)	2	**6**	33/1	45 f	—
1665*	**Lord Foley (NZ)** (JGMO'Shea) **5-11-6**(5) MichaelBrennan (plld hrd: prom tl wknd over 1f out)	1	**7**	11/4[1]	51 f	—
1457[5]	**Stanmore (IRE)** (CPEBrooks) **5-11-4** GBradley (hld up & bhd: hdwy 6f out: one pce fnl 3f)	3½	**8**	6/1[3]	41 f	—
2012[10]	**Sheet Lightning** (RJSmith) **5-10-11**(7) LSuthern (prom 11f)	8	**9**	50/1	33 f	—
	Bulko Boy (NZ) (PJHobbs) **5-11-4** DBridgwater (prom 11f)	s.h	**10**	8/1	33 f	—
1800[9]	**Lucrative Perk (IRE)** (MissCJECaroe) **5-10-13** ILawrence (bit bkwd: hdwy 8f out: wknd over 4f out)	3	**11**	100/1	25 f	—
	Bucks Reef (AJWilson) **5-11-4** AThornton (a bhd)	¾	**12**	33/1	29 f	—
2648[7]	**Grematic** (NJHawke) **6-11-4** RDunwoody (prom over 12f)	6	**13**	50/1	23 f	—
	Royal Mist (IRE) (MrsJPitman) **6-11-1**(3) GHogan (bhd fnl 4f)	1¼	**14**	7/1	22 f	—
	Sandville Lad (MrsDThomas) **5-11-1**(3) GuyLewis (bkwd: prom 10f)	7	**15**	50/1	15 f	—
	Tingrith Lad (JABennett) **5-11-4** LHarvey (a bhd)	¾	**16**	100/1	14 f	—
	Super Nova (CJHemsley) **6-11-4** BFenton (bkwd: s.s: a bhd: t.o)	dist	**17**	50/1	—	—
	Miss Mighty (JHPeacock) **4-10-1** RBellamy (bkwd: led 8f: wknd qckly 6f out: t.o)	9	**18**	100/1	—	—

(SP 131.7%) **18 Rn**

3m 51.1 CSF £93.48 TOTE £11.50: £3.40 £3.80 £1.70 (£110.10) Trio £176.50 OWNER Mr R. A. H. Perkins (BURTON-ON-TRENT) BRED Thomas Joyce
WEIGHT FOR AGE 4yo-12lb
OFFICIAL EXPLANATION **Stanmore (IRE): the rider explained his instructions were to drop the gelding out in the rear, get him settled and to put him into the race from halfway. He added that the gelding is highly-strung and tends to run too freely. He was able to settle him quite well in the slow-run race and asked the gelding for an effort on the home turn, but by then he was a tired horse.**
898 Big Perks (IRE) changed hands for 20,000 guineas after his promising debut. (7/1: op 12/1)
Spunkie, the second foal of a selling hurdle winner, lived up to his name in the closing stages. (14/1)
1827 Coble Lane has changed stables since finishing second at Musselburgh. (8/1)
Sheepcote Hill (IRE), bought for 22,000 guineas as a four year old, is a half-brother to a winning Irish pointer out of a mare who won both an Irish bumper and a point. (11/2: 7/2-6/1)
Master Pip is a full-brother to seven-furlong winner Karen Louise. (20/1)
Silent Cracker is the first foal of successful hurdler and chaser Silent Surrender. (33/1)
1665* Lord Foley (NZ) proved difficult to settle in a race run at a dawdle to halfway. (11/4)
1457 Stanmore (IRE) (6/1: op 5/2)

T/Jkpt: £2,232.70 (3.18 Tckts). T/Plpt: £23.70 (422.64 Tckts). T/Qdpt: £20.10 (25.96 Tckts) KH

2662-LEICESTER (R-H) (Chases Good to firm, Good patches, Hurdles Good to soft)
Wednesday January 29th
One fence omitted final circuit 5th race
WEATHER: overcast

2812 E.B.F. 'N.H.' (QUALIFIER) NOVICES' HURDLE (5, 6 & 7-Y.O) (Class D)
1-40 (1-40) **2m 4f 110y (11 hdls)** £3,548.00 (£1,064.00: £512.00: £236.00) GOING: 0.56 sec per fur (S)

				SP	RR	SF
2010*	**Red Blazer** (MissHCKnight) **6-11-10** JOsborne (hld up: stdy hdwy appr 4 out: led appr last: readily)	—	**1**	5/4^{1}	93	49
1683^{4}	**Denham Hill (IRE)** (CJMann) **6-10-11**$^{(3)}$ JMagee (led after 4th: sn clr: hdd appr last: kpt on u.p)	3	**2**	14/1	81	37
1633*	**Crimson King (IRE)** (CaptTAForster) **6-11-10** AThornton (hld up: hdwy 7th: ev ch 2 out: sn rdn: one pce)	1¼	**3**	9/1	90	46
1867^{3}	**Friendship (IRE)** (NJHenderson) **5-11-0** MAFitzgerald (hld up in tch: effrt & ev ch 4 out: wknd next)	6	**4**	4/1^{2}	75	31
2012*	**Princeful (IRE)** (MrsJPitman) **6-11-0** WMarston (lw: chsd ldrs: hit 5th: wknd appr 2 out)	6	**5**	11/2^{3}	70	26
1867^{9}	**Jazzman (IRE)** (APJarvis) **5-11-0** JFTitley (bit bkwd: hld up in rr: styd on fr 3 out: nvr nrr)	1	**6**	25/1	70	26
2662^{F}	**Seabrook Lad** (MJWilkinson) **6-11-0** PNiven (hdwy 5th: wknd appr 2 out)	½	**7**	20/1	69	25
1766^{2}	**The Land Agent** (JWMullins) **6-11-0** SCurran (chsd ldrs tl wknd appr 4 out)	10	**8**	11/1	61	17
1802^{4}	**Ely's Harbour (IRE)** (OSherwood) **6-11-0** JAMcCarthy (nvr nr to chal)	2	**9**	25/1	60	16
2668^{8}	**Welsh Silk** (DRGandolfo) **5-10-9**$^{(5)}$ SophieMitchell (a in rr)	8	**10**	33/1	54	10
	Charley Lambert (IRE) (JMackie) **6-11-0** RSupple (bkwd: prom tl wknd appr 7th: t.o)	17	**11**	33/1	40	—
2080^{9}	**Tom Tugg (IRE)** (WGMcKenzie-Coles) **7-11-0** CMaude (bkwd: led: hit 1st & 4th: sn hdd: wknd 4 out: t.o)	½	**12**	66/1	40	—
1536^{10}	**Hit The Bid (IRE)** (IPWilliams) **6-11-0** PCarberry (prom tl wknd appr 4 out: t.o)	10	**13**	100/1	32	—
	Axo Sport (IRE) (APJarvis) **5-11-0** SWynne (bkwd: chsd ldrs to 7th: sn lost tch: t.o)	19	**14**	100/1	17	—
2053^{12}	**Chatergold (IRE)** (APJarvis) **5-10-7**$^{(7)}$ CDavies (bit bkwd: prom to 6th: bhd whn p.u bef 2 out)		**P**	100/1	—	—
1583^{P}	**Mr Goonhilly** (RHAlner) **7-10-9**$^{(5)}$ MrRThornton (a bhd: t.o whn p.u bef 2 out)		**P**	100/1	—	—
	Team Princess (AGNewcombe) **7-10-9** RJohnson (t.o fr 5th: p.u bef 4 out)		**P**	100/1	—	—

(SP 129.6%) **17 Rn**

5m 6.6 (17.60) CSF £19.96 TOTE £2.10: £1.10 £3.30 £2.10 (£19.70) Trio £15.80 OWNER Mr T. H. Shrimpton (WANTAGE) BRED Sir Stanley Grinstead

2010* Red Blazer, ridden with supreme confidence, showed his true class with another very smooth success. It is the intention to give him one more run, prior to being thrown in at the deep end in the Royal SunAlliance at Cheltenham. (5/4)

1683 Denham Hill (IRE) had more use made of him, and ran by far his best race yet. He will not always come up against one as good as the winner. (14/1: 10/1-16/1)

1633* Crimson King (IRE) probably made his ground up far too quickly on the approach to the straight. Having looked a serious threat at the penultimate flight, he was unable to match strides when the winner kicked for home. This was a very encouraging performance, and he looks the type to go on improving. (9/1: op 5/1)

1867 Friendship (IRE) had much more on his plate here, but he joined issue four out before finding the quickening tempo too much for him. (4/1: op 2/1)

2012* Princeful (IRE) was unable to maintain his winning sequence on this hurdling debut, but he sat on the heels of the leaders until fading early in the straight. Sure to be wiser for the experience, he looks a real racehorse. (11/2)

Jazzman (IRE), still looking to have a bit left to work on, was doing all his best work late on. He is gaining experience all the time. (25/1)

1766 The Land Agent (11/1: 7/1-12/1)

2813 BURTON LAZARS CONDITIONAL (S) H'CAP HURDLE (0-90) (4, 5 & 6-Y.O) (Class G)
2-10 (2-12) **2m (9 hdls)** £1,952.50 (£540.00: £257.50) GOING: 0.56 sec per fur (S)

				SP	RR	SF
1857^{2}	**Beechfield Flyer (77)** (WClay) **6-11-9** GTormey (mde all: j.rt 2 out: clr last)	—	**1**	7/2^{2}	63	21
1860^{8}	**Sheecky (71)** (BAMcMahon) **6-11-3** SRyan (chsd ldrs: effrt & ev ch 3 out: rdn & btn appr last)	7	**2**	9/1	50	8
2664*	**Fleet Cadet (89)** (MCPipe) **6-12-7v** ^{7x} GSupple (hld up & bhd: stdy hdwy 5th: rdn appr 2 out: sn btn)	4	**3**	13/8^{1}	64	22
1984^{9}	**Tango Man (IRE) (62)** (RJPrice) **5-10-8** BGrattan (hld up & bhd: hdwy 4 out: nt rch ldrs)	2	**4**	33/1	35	—
1816^{8}	**Spring Loaded (73)** (JGMO'Shea) **6-11-0v**$^{1(5)}$ JTNolan (hld up: hdwy appr 4 out: rdn & wknd 3 out)	8	**5**	9/1	38	—
2664^{6}	**Berts Choice (65)** (JGMO'Shea) **6-10-11** GLee (chsd ldrs to 4 out: sn wknd: t.o)	15	**6**	33/1	15	—
2574^{7}	**Smiley Face (65)** (RJHodges) **5-10-6**$^{(5)}$ JHarris (hld up: hdwy & hit 4 out: sn wknd: t.o)	4	**7**	12/1	11	—
2574^{3}	**Paulton (72)** (KBishop) **4-10-6** EHusband (lw: hld up: hdwy 4th: hit next: sn lost tch: t.o)	3	**8**	4/1^{3}	15	—

(SP 113.9%) **8 Rn**

4m 4.6 (19.60) CSF £30.71 CT £61.37 TOTE £7.20: £2.10 £2.50 £1.20 (£29.40) OWNER Mrs M. Robertson (STOKE-ON-TRENT)
WEIGHT FOR AGE 4yo-12lb
No bid

1857 Beechfield Flyer gained his revenge over the favourite on these more favourable terms, due in no small way to the switch to forcing tactics. He should have no trouble in winning again. (7/2)

Sheecky, a previous winner here, threw down a determined challenge, but the winner would not be denied. (9/1: 8/1-12/1)

2664* Fleet Cadet cruised up to the leaders three out, but he was off the bridle before reaching the next. Despite staying on, his measure had been taken. (13/8: 4/5-7/4)

1980 Smiley Face (12/1: op 20/1)

2574 Paulton (4/1: op 8/1)

2814 MARSHALL H'CAP CHASE (0-125) (5-Y.O+) (Class D)
2-40 (2-40) **2m 4f 110y (15 fncs)** £3,850.00 (£1,150.00: £550.00: £250.00) GOING: 0.17 sec per fur (G)

				SP	RR	SF
1997^{2}	**Shining Light (IRE) (109)** (DNicholson) **8-11-3** RJohnson (hld up: hdwy 9th: chal last: led flat: drvn out)	—	**1**	7/2^{2}	118	43
1957*	**Rex to the Rescue (IRE) (105)** (RHAlner) **9-10-8**$^{(5)}$ MrRThornton (j.w: led to 7th: led 2 out: hdd & no ex flat)	2½	**2**	7/2^{2}	112	37
2544^{2}	**Rustic Air (104)** (JGFitzGerald) **10-10-12** PCarberry (lw: prom tl rdn & outpcd appr 2 out: styd on flat)	2½	**3**	3/1^{1}	109	34
1520^{5}	**Plunder Bay (USA) (115)** (NJHenderson) **6-11-9** MAFitzgerald (lw: hld up: hdwy on ins appr 3 out: rdn & one pce fr next)	3	**4**	9/2^{3}	118	43
1350^{4}	**Cropredy Lad (96)** (PRWebber) **10-10-4** JOsborne (lw: j.w: chsd ldr: led 7th to 2 out: sn rdn & btn)	5	**5**	16/1	95	20
23^{2}	**Howgill (94)** (CaptTAForster) **11-10-2** SWynne (bkwd: chsd ldrs: mstke 4 out: wknd next: t.o)	7	**6**	14/1	87	12
	Mugoni Beach (117) (MCPipe) **12-11-11** CMaude (hld up: pckd 3rd: lost tch 9th: t.o fr 3 out)	2½	**7**	9/1	108	33

(SP 110.2%) **7 Rn**

5m 10.8 (9.80) CSF £13.95 TOTE £4.50: £3.00 £1.60 (£5.00) OWNER The Deeley Partnership (TEMPLE GUITING) BRED Mrs A. Furlong

1997 Shining Light (IRE), was back over possibly his ideal trip. He needed to battle before asserting his superiority on the run-in, but won going away in the end. (7/2)
1957* Rex to the Rescue (IRE) turned in a bold display of jumping, and made his share of the running. He just found the winner too strong in the battle to the line. (7/2)
2544 Rustic Air lost his pitch approaching the second last, but rallied again in the latter stages. He has won over further, and stamina is probably his strong suit. (3/1)
1520 Plunder Bay (USA) made his move on the inside soon after entering the straight. He had every chance until failing to quicken when the chips were down. (9/2)
1350 Cropredy Lad looked sure to take a hand in proceedings approaching the penultimate fence, but he tied up rather quickly after being headed. It seems he finds this trip inadequate. (16/1)
Mugoni Beach (9/1: 5/1-10/1)

2815 CHARNWOOD NOVICES' CLAIMING HURDLE (4-Y.O+) (Class F)

3-10 (3-10) **2m (9 hdls)** £2,679.00 (£744.00: £357.00) GOING: 0.56 sec per fur (S)

				SP	RR	SF
1305*	**Brambles Way (112)** (MrsMReveley) **8-11-12b** PNiven (hld up: hdwy appr 4 out: led on bit next: clr whn blnd last)	—	**1**	6/4^{1}	78+	31
1413^{2}	**Bluntswood Hall** (RHollinshead) **4-10-9** GaryLyons (led to 3rd: rdn & outpcd appr last)	15	**2**	9/1	58	—
1872^{8}	**Whispering Dawn** (CPEBrooks) **4-11-0** GBradley (a.p: led 3rd to 3 out: rdn appr last: one pce)	½	**3**	4/1^{2}	63	4
	Sahhar (PJBevan) **4-10-11** WWorthington (hdwy 4th: rdn 3 out: kpt on appr last)	s.h	**4**	50/1	59	—
936^{P}	**Re Roi (IRE) (99)** (WGMTurner) **5-10-13(7)** JPower (bit bkwd: hld up: hdwy 6th: one pce fr 3 out)	2	**5**	7/1	54	7
2074^{9}	**Our Tom** (JWharton) **5-11-3(5)** MrRThornton (chsd ldrs: mstke 4th: one pce fr 3 out)	nk	**6**	66/1	56	9
2090^{5}	**Gi Moss** (PRHarriss) **10-11-1b** WMarston (bit bkwd: chsd ldrs to 3 out: sn lost tch)	½	**7**	66/1	49	2
2567^{7}	**Denomination (USA) (86)** (MCPipe) **5-10-13(7)** GSupple (chsd ldrs: ev ch 4 out: outpcd fr next)	12	**8**	20/1	42	—
	Kaye's Secret (JLHarris) **4-10-8** RSupple (rdn 4th: a in rr)	nk	**9**	50/1	41	—
2060^{9}	**Irish Kinsman** (GHYardley) **4-10-11b^{1}** VSlattery (lw: lost pl ½-wy: t.o)	24	**10**	66/1	20	—
1149^{11}	**Bites** (TTBill) **4-10-0** TEley (bhd fr 4th: t.o)	¾	**11**	66/1	9	—
1966^{17}	**Colonel Jack** (RJHodges) **5-10-13(7)** JHarris (a bhd: t.o)	8	**12**	66/1	9	—
	First Gold (JWharton) **8-11-8** RJohnson (lw: j.b lft 3rd: a bhd: t.o)	1½	**13**	20/1	9	—
1595^{P}	**Trianna** (RBrotherton) **4-10-4** SCurran (bhd fr 5th: t.o)	2	**14**	50/1	1	—
	The Oddfellow (NBycroft) **4-11-1** JSupple (a bhd: t.o fr ½-wy)	6	**15**	66/1	6	—
1862^{7}	**Fijon (IRE)** (JPearce) **4-10-2** JOsborne (b.d 1st)		**B**	9/2^{3}	—	—
	A Million Watts (GMMcCourt) **6-10-9(7)** RHobson (b.d 1st)		**B**	66/1	—	—
498^{P}	**Masruf (IRE)** (KCBailey) **5-11-8** CO'Dwyer (bkwd: hdwy 4th: wknd appr 4 out: t.o whn p.u after next)		**P**	33/1	—	—
1200^{P}	**Tolcarne Lady** (KBishop) **8-10-13** RGreene (bkwd: prom to 5th: sn wknd: t.o whn p.u bef 2 out)		**P**	66/1	—	—
				(SP 131.0%)	**19 Rn**	

4m 3.1 (18.10) CSF £14.78 TOTE £2.00: £1.30 £2.50 £1.30 (£7.20) Trio £42.80 OWNER Mr Nigel Jones (SALTBURN) BRED W. P. S. Johnson
WEIGHT FOR AGE 4yo-12lb
STEWARDS' ENQUIRY Bradley susp. 7-8/2/97 (careless riding).
1305* Brambles Way, a drifter in the market, completed the hat-trick in the easiest possible fashion, although he may not have had a lot to beat. (6/4: op 4/7)
1413 Bluntswood Hall is only a selling plater but he is improving with experience. There is a race waiting for him. (9/1)
Whispering Dawn attracted all the money in the ring and made the majority of the running but, once the winner cruised past, she must have realised this was not going to be her day. (4/1: op 7/1)
Sahhar looked well tuned-up for his hurdling debut, and performed with credit after being off the racecourse for almost five months. A seller is well within his grasp. (50/1)
936 Re Roi (IRE), given a break after a couple of successes in August, could not make his presence felt but will strip fitter for the run. (7/1)
Our Tom, a winner three times on the All-Weather, ran his best race yet over hurdles, and seems to be getting the hang of the game. (66/1)
1370* Fijon (IRE) (9/2: op 3/1)

2816 SILVER BELL MAIDEN CHASE (6-Y.O+) (Class F)

3-40 (3-40) **3m (17 fncs)** £3,195.50 (£959.00: £462.00: £213.50) GOING: 0.17 sec per fur (G)

				SP	RR	SF
2667^{6}	**Primitive Penny** (MrsDHaine) **6-11-0** JFTitley (hld up: hdwy 11th: led 4 out: clr whn blnd 2 out: hld on towards fin)	—	**1**	16/1	85	27
1639^{7}	**Deel Quay (IRE)** (KCBailey) **6-11-5** CO'Dwyer (hld up: hdwy 8th: rdn 2 out: styd on wl flat)	½	**2**	9/4^{1}	90	32
1920^{2}	**Calleva Star (IRE) (79)** (RHAlner) **6-11-5** MAFitzgerald (hld up: hdwy 9th: blnd & lost pl 12th: rallied 2 out: r.o wl towards fin)	¾	**3**	6/1^{3}	89	31
2758^{8}	**Loch Garman Hotel (IRE) (81)** (PTDalton) **8-11-5** CMaude (j.w: led to 4 out: rdn next: rallied last: r.o)	nk	**4**	7/1	89	31
1795^{10}	**The Millmaster (IRE)** (JohnUpson) **6-11-5** RSupple (prom tl wknd 14th: t.o)	29	**5**	25/1	70	12
2039^{5}	**Thunder Road (IRE)** (RDickin) **6-11-5** PNiven (hmpd 6th: a in rr: t.o)	½	**6**	16/1	69	11
2000^{F}	**Royal Hand (67)** (RJArmson) **7-11-5** MrRArmson (nt.j.w: a in rr: t.o)	s.h	**7**	50/1	69	11
2704^{2}	**Bolshie Baron** (MHWeston) **8-11-5** MrMHarris (chsd ldrs: mstke 10th: wknd 4 out: t.o)	13	**8**	11/1	61	3
970^{U}	**Rent Day** (JWMullins) **8-11-0** SCurran (bit bkwd: hld up: hmpd 6th: hdwy 9th: rdn & hld whn rn out 2 out: continued: t.o)	dist	**9**	16/1	—	—
1829^{4}	**Master Hope (IRE) (80)** (DNicholson) **8-11-5** RJohnson (chsd ldrs: mstke 5th: fell next: dead)		**F**	3/1^{2}	—	—
1596^{P}	**Paddy Burke (IRE)** (AGNewcombe) **7-11-5** AThornton (mid div: fell 7th)		**F**	50/1	—	—
1829^{8}	**Rolled Gold (64)** (MissVenetiaWilliams) **8-11-0(5)** MrRThornton (chsd ldrs: mstke 9th: fell 12th)		**F**	33/1	—	—
2569^{8}	**Ice Magic (69)** (FJYardley) **10-11-5v** JSupple (nt j.w: a bhd: t.o: ref 4 out)		**R**	25/1	—	—
				(SP 123.1%)	**13 Rn**	

6m 9.8 (15.80) CSF £48.99 TOTE £12.50: £3.30 £2.50 £1.20 (£19.90) Trio £93.40; £42.13 to Towcester 30/1/97 OWNER Mrs Peter Mason (NEWMARKET) BRED Miss F. Geddes
Primitive Penny, successful between the Flags, had to work hard to keep her head in front. It would have been so much easier had she not taken the penultimate fence by the roots. (16/1)
Deel Quay (IRE) did not appear fully wound up for this first look at fences, but he ran extremely well, and will be hard to beat from now on. (9/4)
1920 Calleva Star (IRE) still has plenty to learn about jumping fences, but this extended trip could be what he requires, and an early success should follow. (6/1)
1281 Loch Garman Hotel (IRE) gave a good display of jumping from the front, and then rallied bravely in the closing stages to go down fighting. His turn will come. (7/1)

1829 Master Hope (IRE) unnerved himself with a mistake at the first ditch, and he had not regained his confidence when he fell at the next. (3/1)

2817 GOLDEN MILLER H'CAP HURDLE (0-120) (4-Y.O+) (Class D)

4-10 (4-11) **2m 4f 110y (11 hdls)** £3,054.00 (£912.00: £436.00: £198.00) GOING: 0.56 sec per fur (S)

				SP	RR	SF
2543[2]	**Cittadino (100)** (CWThornton) **7-10-10** MFoster (chsd ldrs: led appr 2 out: hrd rdn: all out)	—	**1**	6/1[2]	82	41
1522[4]	**Moment of Glory (IRE) (114)** (DRGandolfo) **6-11-10** GBradley (hld up & bhd: hdwy appr 4 out: ev ch fr 2 out: r.o)	hd	**2**	9/1	96	55
2644[F]	**Rosencrantz (IRE) (108)** (MissVenetiaWilliams) **5-11-4** RJohnson (hld up: hdwy 7th: hrd rdn appr last: unable qckn)	2	**3**	11/4[1]	88	47
1638*	**Allow (IRE) (93)** (BLlewellyn) **6-9-12**(5) MrRThornton (hld up: hdwy appr 4 out: one pce appr last)	3½	**4**	8/1	71	30
	Wings Cove (118) (LadyHerries) **7-12-0** JOsborne (a.p: ev ch appr 2 out: btn whn blnd last)	1¾	**5**	20/1	94	53
1767[2]	**Jefferies (101)** (JABOld) **8-10-11** GUpton (bkwd: hld up mid div: effrt 7th: no imp fr 3 out)	1	**6**	7/1	77	36
2625[3]	**Diwali Dancer (113)** (MCPipe) **7-11-2**(7) GSupple (led tl hdd & wknd appr 2 out)	4	**7**	9/1	85	44
2666[12]	**Kippanour (USA) (112)** (CJMann) **5-11-5b**(3) JMagee (hld up: hdwy 7th: ev ch 3 out: wknd next)	2½	**8**	20/1	82	41
	The Glow (IRE) (106) (MrsJPitman) **9-11-2** WMarston (chsd ldrs tl wknd appr 4 out)	7	**9**	20/1	71	30
	Chill Wind (91) (NBycroft) **8-10-1** RSupple (a bhd: t.o)	dist	**10**	50/1	—	—
2630[P]	**Far Senior (95)** (PWegmann) **11-10-5** GaryLyons (lost pl ½-wy: sn t.o)	dist	**11**	66/1	—	—
2003[5]	**Absalom's Pillar (96)** (JMackie) **7-10-6** TEley (plld hrd: hld up: fell 5th)		**F**	14/1	—	—
2670*	**Circus Line (120)** (MWEasterby) **6-12-2** 6x MAFitzgerald (mstkes early: prom tl p.u after 7th: dismntd)		**P**	13/2[3]	—	—
1996[2]	**Spring Saint (107)** (MissCHorler) **8-11-3** CMaude (a in rr: p.u bef 2 out)		**P**	20/1	—	—
1934[F]	**Kytton Castle (109)** (RDickin) **10-10-12**(7) XAizpuru (hld up in tch: wknd & p.u appr 4 out: collapsed: dead)		**P**	33/1	—	—
1794[5]	**Dark Honey (109)** (SDow) **12-11-5** ADicken (bhd whn hmpd & uns rdr 5th)		**U**	25/1	—	—
				(SP 133.9%)	**16 Rn**	

5m 5.01 (16.01) CSF £53.23 CT £174.53 TOTE £5.50: £1.80 £3.90 £1.10 £2.00 (£44.60) Trio £52.00 OWNER Mr D. B. Dennison (MIDDLEHAM)

2543 Cittadino showed his appreciation for this extra half-mile with a hard-fought success that was a credit to all concerned. (6/1)

1522 Moment of Glory (IRE) looked to have timed his effort to perfection when delivering his challenge at the second last. Hard as he tried, he had to admit the concession of 14lb too much. (9/1: 6/1-10/1)

2644 Rosencrantz (IRE) took closer order turning in, and was poised to challenge at the penultimate flight, but a turn of finishing speed was missing once the whips started cracking. (11/4)

1638* Allow (IRE) was close enough if good enough two out, but he was always being stretched, and could not summon the pace to mount a challenge. (8/1)

Wings Cove ran a fine race considering he had not been on a racecourse for twenty-one months. He is sure to strip fitter for the run, and does not seem to have lost his ability. (20/1)

1767 Jefferies may well need a slightly stiffer test of stamina, for he was unable to muster enough speed to concern the principals. (7/1)

2625 Diwali Dancer (9/1: op 6/1)

2670* Circus Line (13/2: 4/1-7/1)

T/Plpt: £13.00 (844.39 Tckts). T/Qdpt: £7.00 (96.29 Tckts) IM

2559-WINDSOR (Fig. 8) (Good to firm)
Wednesday January 29th

WEATHER: overcast

2818 BURNHAM (S) HURDLE (4,5,6 & 7-Y.O) (Class G)

1-30 (1-30) **2m (8 hdls)** £2,090.50 (£583.00: £281.50) GOING minus 0.15 sec per fur (G)

				SP	RR	SF
1770[3]	**Proud Image** (GMMcCourt) **5-11-5** BClifford (a.p: chsd ldr fr 5th: led 2 out: j.b rt last: rdn out)	—	**1**	5/1[2]	63	21
2578[8]	**Almapa (80)** (RJHodges) **5-11-9**(3) TDascombe (hdwy 3 out: rdn appr 2 out: ev ch whn pckd last: unable qckn)	3½	**2**	12/1	67	25
2678[6]	**Tread the Boards (85)** (MCPipe) **6-11-0b[1]** BPowell (a.p: rdn appr 3 out: one pce)	3	**3**	6/1[3]	52	10
2692[12]	**Persian Butterfly (55)** (RMStronge) **5-11-0** PHide (chsd ldr: led 4th to 2 out: one pce flat)	5	**4**	33/1	47	5
2678[10]	**Jobber's Fiddle (69)** (DLWilliams) **5-11-0** MClarke (rdn 5th: hdwy 3 out: one pce)	5	**5**	33/1	42	—
2678[9]	**Ewar Bold** (KOCunningham-Brown) **4-10-7** DGallagher (nvr nr to chal)	10	**6**	33/1	37	—
	Classic Delight (USA) (ICampbell) **4-10-2** KGaule (7th whn blnd 2 out: nvr nrr)	1¾	**7**	33/1	30	—
2006[P]	**Sharmoor (72)** (MissLCSiddall) **5-11-0** MRichards (nvr nrr)	2½	**8**	10/1	27	—
	Espla (JSMoore) **6-11-5** WMcFarland (a bhd)	7	**9**	12/1	25	—
2692[F]	**Marrowfat Lady (IRE) (84)** (NEBerry) **6-10-7**(7) SMelrose (hdwy 5th: wknd appr 3 out)	11	**10**	16/1	9	—
1772[13]	**Follow de Call (68)** (DMcCain) **7-11-5** DWalsh (prom tl appr 3 out)	3	**11**	33/1	11	—
	Tauten (IRE) (PBurgoyne) **7-11-0** ILawrence (a bhd)	1¼	**12**	25/1	5	—
	Just Flamenco (MJRyan) **6-11-5** JRKavanagh (lw: bhd fr 5th)	22	**13**	33/1	—	—
2668[15]	**Red Phantom (IRE)** (SMellor) **5-11-5v** NMann (lw: hdwy 4th: 6th whn b.d 5th)		**B**	25/1	—	—
	Rockville Pike (IRE) (JGMO'Shea) **5-11-0**(5) MichaelBrennan (led to 4th: sn wknd: t.o whn fell 2 out)		**F**	20/1	—	—
2624[8]	**Battleship Bruce (95)** (TCasey) **5-11-5** DBridgwater (lw: hld up: rdn 4th: ev ch 2 out: 3rd whn fell last)		**F**	15/8[1]	57?	—
2678[5]	**Rose of Glenn** (BPalling) **6-11-0** RFarrant (hdwy whn fell 5th)		**F**	8/1	—	—
	Stark Lomond (USA) (THind) **4-10-7** PMcLoughlin (bit bkwd: a bhd: t.o whn p.u bef 2 out)		**P**	12/1	—	—
2050[5]	**Spiral Flyer (IRE)** (MDIUsher) **4-10-2** LHarvey (bhd fr 4th: t.o whn p.u bef 2 out)		**P**	8/1	—	—
				(SP 156.1%)	**19 Rn**	

3m 55.7 (7.70) CSF £67.14 TOTE £7.50: £2.10 £4.70 £2.50 (£27.80) Trio £162.00; £25.11 to Towcester 30/1/97 OWNER Town and Country Tyre Services Ltd (WANTAGE) BRED Miss S. E. Jarvis

WEIGHT FOR AGE 4yo-12lb

No bid

1770 Proud Image confirmed the promise shown on his hurdling debut in this class. Leading at the second last, he jumped violently to his right at the final flight but, despite that, he only needed to be ridden along to assert. (5/1)

1091 Almapa was much happier back in his own class. Throwing down his challenge in the straight and holding every chance, he pecked on landing at the final flight and was then left standing. (12/1: op 8/1)

2678 Tread the Boards was never far away, but was once again tapped for toe in the straight. (6/1)

Persian Butterfly ran by far her best race over hurdles. Leading at halfway, she was collared two out, but remained in contention until left behind on the run-in. (33/1)
Jobber's Fiddle improved on her Lingfield run of last week, which followed a lengthy lay-off, but was made to look very pedestrian in the straight. (33/1)
1628 Sharmoor (10/1: 8/1-12/1)
1729 Battleship Bruce was taking a drop in class, but was being nudged along at halfway. Nevertheless, he threw down a challenge in the straight and had every chance at the penultimate hurdle. He was about a length down and looking to be getting the worst of the argument when falling at the final flight. He is becoming disappointing. (15/8)
2678 Rose of Glenn was getting closer in fifth place when falling at the fifth. She needs a stiffer test of stamina, and some give underfoot, to be seen to best effect. (8/1)

2819 OAKSIDE NOVICES' CHASE (5-Y.O+) (Class E)

2-00 (2-01) **3m (18 fncs)** £3,614.75 (£1,088.00: £526.50: £245.75) GOING minus 0.15 sec per fur (G)

				SP	RR	SF
1946*	**Palosanto (IRE)** (MCPipe) **7-11-5** DWalsh (chsd ldr: led 9th: clr 10th: blnd 2 out: unchal)	—	1	11/4[2]	113+	45
1538[3]	**Hawaiian Sam (IRE) (98)** (AndrewTurnell) **7-11-5** GCrone (a.p: chsd wnr fr 13th: no imp)	10	2	9/2[3]	106	38
2667[3]	**Super Ritchart (84)** (BPalling) **9-11-5** DerekByrne (t.o fr 11th: nvr nr to chal)	dist	3	14/1	—	—
2679[P]	**Ballymgyr (IRE) (87)** (EAWheeler) **8-11-5b** DGallagher (lw: prom to 4 out: t.o)	14	4	25/1	—	—
2643[3]	**Volleyball (IRE) (77)** (PRHedger) **8-11-5** MRichards (a bhd: t.o fr 10th)	18	5	33/1	—	—
1839[P]	**Millfrone (IRE) (60)** (RRowe) **7-11-5** DO'Sullivan (lw: led: clr 3rd: hdd 9th: wknd 13th: t.o)	2	6	50/1	—	—
1728[2]	**Secret Bid (IRE) (100)** (RHAlner) **7-11-5** JRKavanagh (lw: poor 5th whn blnd 11th: t.o fr 12th)	20	7	5/2[1]	—	—
1998[12]	**Bonita Blakeney (60)** (GBBalding) **7-11-0** BClifford (bit bkwd: a bhd: t.o fr 10th)	21	8	33/1	—	—
	Napoleon's Gold (IRE) (AGFoster) **7-10-12**(7) DCreech (a bhd: t.o fr 3rd)	dist	9	50/1	—	—
1962[6]	**Dream Leader (IRE)** (MJRoberts) **7-11-5** BPowell (lw: a bhd: t.o fr 10th: p.u bef 14th)		P	10/1	—	—
1728[P]	**Lord Antrim (IRE)** (RMStronge) **8-11-5** PHide (t: bhd fr 10th: t.o whn p.u bef 4 out)		P	50/1	—	—
	Mystic Manna (AndrewTurnell) **11-11-5** LHarvey (bit bkwd: bhd fr 6th: t.o fr 10th: p.u bef 14th)		P	20/1	—	—
1963[5]	**Givus a Call (IRE)** (JTGifford) **7-11-2**(3) LAspell (lw: bhd whn blnd & uns rdr 8th)		U	13/2	—	—
				(SP 122.9%)	**13 Rn**	

5m 58.5 (3.50) CSF £14.13 TOTE £4.00: £1.40 £1.80 £2.70 (£8.80) Trio £30.50 OWNER Mr B. A. Kilpatrick (WELLINGTON) BRED W. R. Jackson
1946* Palosanto (IRE) made a fine start to his chasing career. Leading with a circuit to go, he soon went clear and, despite a bad error at the penultimate fence, managed to win this very poor event in glorious isolation. He can win again. (11/4)
1538 Hawaiian Sam (IRE) moved into second place six out but the winner had long gone. Not even a bad error by that rival at the penultimate fence could help him to get closer. (9/2)
2667 Super Ritchart was tailed off for the final circuit, but plodded on to take third prize. (14/1)
Ballymgyr (IRE), pulled up on both his starts so far this term, ran better with the blinkers back on. Racing in third or fourth place although at a respectable distance, he was left further behind in the straight. (25/1)
Millfrone (IRE), pulled up on all three of his starts this season, stormed off in front and soon had the field well strung out. Collared with a circuit to go, he had shot his bolt a mile from home. He is a very poor performer. (50/1)
1962 Dream Leader (IRE) (10/1: op 6/1)
1963 Givus a Call (IRE) (13/2: 7/2-7/1)

2820 LEVY BOARD NOVICES' H'CAP HURDLE (0-100) (4-Y.O+) (Class E)

2-30 (2-35) **2m 6f 110y (11 hdls)** £2,915.00 (£815.00: £395.00) GOING minus 0.15 sec per fur (G)

				SP	RR	SF
1274[8]	**Montel Express (IRE) (95)** (KCBailey) **5-11-6**(7) MrRWakley (stdy hdwy 8th: led flat: rdn out)	—	1	10/1	79	46
2708*	**Clod Hopper (IRE) (80)** (WRMuir) **7-10-7**(5) 7x ABates (led 2nd: mstke 6th: rdn appr 2 out: hdd flat: unable qckn)	1¾	2	5/1[2]	63	30
2552[6]	**Colwall (82)** (MissPMWhittle) **6-10-7**(7) KHibbert (a.p: rdn appr 2 out: wknd appr last)	9	3	11/1	58	25
1952[P]	**Zip Your Lip (82)** (MrsPTownsley) **7-11-0** DerekByrne (hdwy appr 3 out: rdn appr 2 out: wknd appr last)	¾	4	33/1	58	25
2634[2]	**Mr Christie (83)** (MissLCSiddall) **5-11-1** BPowell (lw: nvr nr to chal)	5	5	9/2[1]	55	22
	Jay Em Ess (NZ) (83) (AGHobbs) **8-10-8**(7) MrGShenkin (lw: hdwy 3 out: one pce)	3	6	33/1	53+	20
1388[2]	**Nordic Spree (IRE) (92)** (GLMoore) **5-11-10** PHolley (prom tl appr 3 out)	7	7	14/1	57	24
1762[3]	**Karen's Typhoon (IRE) (72)** (TPMcGovern) **6-10-4** DGallagher (nvr nrr)	1½	8	16/1	36	3
1640[11]	**Reluckino (80)** (JGMO'Shea) **7-10-7v**[1](5) MichaelBrennan (nvr nrr)	8	9	16/1	38	5
	Farleyer Rose (IRE) (69) (MrsLRichards) **8-10-1** MRichards (hdwy 7th: wknd appr 2 out)	9	10	14/1	21	—
1550[3]	**Ross Dancer (IRE) (86)** (JSMoore) **5-11-4** WMcFarland (hdwy 8th: wknd appr 3 out)	5	11	12/1	34	1
2567[P]	**Scalp 'em (IRE) (68)** (DrPPritchard) **9-10-0** DrPPritchard (prom to 8th)	nk	12	33/1	16	—
2665[U]	**King's Courtier (IRE) (74)** (SMellor) **8-10-6v** CLlewellyn (led to 2nd: wknd 5th)	s.h	13	33/1	22	—
1673[7]	**Young Tycoon (NZ) (78)** (AJWilson) **6-10-10** LHarvey (a bhd)	nk	14	33/1	26	—
2620[3]	**Cardinal Gayle (IRE) (69)** (RHAlner) **7-9-12**(3)ow1 PHenley (hdwy 6th: wknd 8th)	21	15	11/1	2	—
2620[4]	**Lodestone Lad (IRE) (68)** (RDickin) **7-10-0** TJMurphy (bhd fr 8th)	1½	16	33/1	—	—
2010[13]	**Trehane (75)** (NAGraham) **5-10-7** KGaule (lw: prom to 8th)	4	17	33/1	4	—
2070[3]	**Sterling Fellow (88)** (DLWilliams) **4-10-7v** DBridgwater (rdn 4th: hdwy 5th: wknd 8th)	hd	18	15/2[3]	17	—
2546[7]	**Rossell Island (IRE) (81)** (MrsJPitman) **6-10-10**(3) GHogan (bhd fr 3rd: t.o whn p.u bef 3 out)		P	14/1	—	—
2074[7]	**Gutteridge (IRE) (76)** (PDEvans) **7-10-8** DWalsh (prom to 3 out: t.o whn p.u bef 2 out)		P	5/1[2]	—	—
1707[8]	**Flaming Rose (IRE) (70)** (RRowe) **7-10-2**ow2 DO'Sullivan (a bhd: t.o fr 5th: p.u bef 3 out)		P	33/1	—	—
				(SP 152.0%)	**21 Rn**	

5m 28.2 (5.20) CSF £62.27 CT £537.85 TOTE £11.10: £2.40 £1.80 £4.80 £16.00 (£38.80) Trio £196.10 OWNER Mrs Jacqueline Conroy (UPPER LAMBOURN)
LONG HANDICAP Clod Hopper (IRE) 10-12 Scalp 'em (IRE) 9-2 Flaming Rose (IRE) 9-11
WEIGHT FOR AGE 4yo-13lb
OFFICIAL EXPLANATION Jay Em Ess (NZ): rider reported that the gelding seemed to lose his action after the first in the back straight and felt it prudent to ease him. The trainer added that the horse had lost his confidence over fences last year and, having hung left here, would race left-handed in future.
859* Montel Express (IRE) left his poor run at Sandown in November well behind. Creeping into the action in the last three-quarters of a mile, he managed to get on top on the run-in to win this moderate event. (10/1: op 6/1)
2708* Clod Hopper (IRE) has gained both his victories to date on a fast surface, so this ground was ideal. Soon at the head of affairs, he grimly tried to hold on, but was eventually overhauled on the run-in. (5/1)

2036 Colwall goes well on a sound surface, and played an active role until left for dead by the front two soon after the second last. (11/1: 8/1-12/1)
Zip Your Lip seems rather high in the handicap. He moved into the action going to the third last, before weakening after the penultimate flight. A slightly shorter trip might help. (33/1)
Jay Em Ess (NZ) was handled very tenderly. Noted taking closer order three out, his jockey did not move and the combination came home in their own time. The Stewards recorded the explanation. (33/1)
1388 Nordic Spree (IRE) (14/1: 10/1-16/1)
Gutteridge (IRE) (5/1: op 8/1)

2821 SCANIA APPROVED USED VEHICLES H'CAP CHASE (0-125) (5-Y.O+) (Class D)
3-00 (3-04) **3m (18 fncs)** £4,053.25 (£1,216.00: £585.50: £270.25) GOING minus 0.15 sec per fur (G)

	Horse	Dist	Pos	SP	RR	SF
2681[9]	**Zambezi Spirit (IRE) (97)** (MrsMerritaJones) **8-10-0** DerekByrne (lw: hld up: shkn up appr 2 out: led flat: drvn out)	—	1	13/2	106	24
2647[2]	**Five to Seven (USA) (117)** (PFNicholls) **8-11-6** DBridgwater (a.p: mstke 1st: led 3 out tl flat: hrd rdn: r.o)	½	2	7/2[1]	126	44
1501*	**Bas de Laine (FR) (125)** (MDHammond) **11-12-0v[1]** RGarritty (lw: led tl blnd & hdd 3 out: hrd rdn appr last: unable qckn)	5	3	7/2[1]	130	48
1934[3]	**Danger Baby (105)** (DLWilliams) **7-10-8** PHolley (hdwy 9th: rdn 4 out: one pce)	¾	4	4/1[2]	110	28
2665[8]	**Mr Invader (97)** (NAGaselee) **10-10-0b[1]** CLlewellyn (a.p: rdn 4 out: one pce)	¾	5	16/1	101	19
1985[3]	**Really a Rascal (105)** (DRGandolfo) **10-10-5(3)** DFortt (stdy hdwy 4 out: rdn appr 3 out: one pce: lame)	½	6	6/1[3]	109	27
	Claxton Greene (97) (CPEBrooks) **13-10-0** DGallagher (a bhd)	17	7	25/1	90	8
1799[P]	**Knockaverry (IRE) (100)** (MJWilkinson) **9-10-3** ILawrence (hdwy 9th: wknd 14th)	22	8	16/1	78	—
2621[5]	**Bally Parson (105)** (RDickin) **11-10-8** TJMurphy (lw: 2nd whn blnd 6th: bhd whn blnd 12th)	2½	9	14/1	81	—
1876[5]	**Staunch Rival (USA) (115)** (GThorner) **10-11-4b** BPowell (bhd fr 12th)	7	10	12/1	87	5
2660[5]	**Fools Errand (IRE) (115)** (GBBalding) **7-11-4** BClifford (a bhd: mstke 9th: t.o whn p.u bef 10th)		P	7/1	—	—

(SP 134.5%) **11 Rn**

5m 59.6 (4.60) CSF £31.96 CT £91.57 TOTE £8.20: £1.80 £1.40 £2.00 (£25.70) Trio £46.70 OWNER Mr P. C. Townsend (LAMBOURN) BRED Patrick Day
LONG HANDICAP Mr Invader 9-7 Zambezi Spirit (IRE) 9-13
OFFICIAL EXPLANATION **Fools Errand (IRE): lost his action and was then pulled up.**
1717 Zambezi Spirit (IRE) regained the winning thread on ground that was ideal for him, responding to pressure to keep the runner-up at bay. He likes the ground on either side of good according to his trainer. (13/2)
2647 Five to Seven (USA) had no problems with this longer trip, looking set to break his run of seconditis as he led at the third last. Despite giving his all he was worried out of it on the run-in. There is nothing wrong with his attitude, and he richly deserves a change of luck. (7/2)
1501* Bas de Laine (FR), wearing a visor for the first time, has found a new lease of life this season which has resulted in a 14lb rise in the weights. In front until a mistake cost him the advantage three from home, he then found top weight anchoring him. He has yet to win on ground worse than good. (7/2)
1934 Danger Baby took closer order with a circuit to race, but was tapped for toe over the last four fences. The Handicapper appears to have his measure, as he is on a mark 9lb higher than he has ever won off before. (4/1)
2665 Mr Invader, 7lb out of the handicap, ran much better here and was a leading player until tapped for toe in the straight. His only victory to date came over two years ago. (16/1)
1985 Really a Rascal crept into the action early in the straight, but could only go up and down in the same place over the last three fences. His trainer later reported that the gelding was lame behind. Both his victories to date have come with some cut. (6/1)
2660 Fools Errand (IRE) (7/1: 5/1-8/1)

2822 EXTERIOR PROFILES NOVICES' HURDLE (4-Y.O+) (Class E)
3-30 (3-33) **2m 4f (10 hdls)** £2,757.50 (£770.00: £372.50) GOING minus 0.15 sec per fur (G)

	Horse	Dist	Pos	SP	RR	SF
980*	**Scoundrel** (KCBailey) **6-11-4** SMcNeill (stdy hdwy 5th: led 3 out to last: led flat: all out)	—	1	6/5[1]	69	7
1800[2]	**Jack Gallagher** (MissBSanders) **6-11-4** MRichards (a.p: led 5th to 3 out: led last tl flat: hrd rdn: r.o wl)	s.h	2	6/1[3]	69	7
1998*	**River Bay (IRE) (99)** (MissHCKnight) **6-11-5** BFenton (hld up: ev ch 3 out: wknd appr 2 out)	9	3	7/4[2]	63	1
2053[8]	**Coole Cherry** (CRBarwell) **7-11-4** JRKavanagh (led to 5th: wknd 3 out)	2	4	25/1	60	—
2624[9]	**At Liberty (IRE)** (RHannon) **5-11-4** DGallagher (prom to 3 out)	10	5	20/1	52	—
865[16]	**Captain Navar (IRE)** (JGMO'Shea) **7-10-13(5)** MichaelBrennan (bit bkwd: a bhd)	6	6	50/1	47	—
1873[F]	**Maeterlinck (IRE)** (GThorner) **5-10-11(7)** ClareThorner (hdwy 3rd: wknd 7th)	2	7	50/1	46	—
1685[7]	**Daydream Believer** (MSalaman) **5-10-13** WMcFarland (bhd fr 7th)	16	8	50/1	28	—
1964[6]	**Danzante (IRE)** (RMStronge) **5-11-4** DWalsh (blnd 5th: bhd fr 6th: t.o whn p.u bef 2 out)		P	12/1	—	—

(SP 118.3%) **9 Rn**

4m 59.4 (13.40) CSF £8.21 TOTE £2.20: £1.10 £1.60 £1.30 (£3.80) Trio £2.10 OWNER Mrs J. M. Corbett (UPPER LAMBOURN) BRED Mrs P. Nicholson
OFFICIAL EXPLANATION **Daydream Believer: returned with a twisted plate.**
980* Scoundrel, a comfortable winner of two bumpers this season, had a real fight on his hands on his hurdling debut. Engaged in a tremendous tussle with the runner-up, he had just enough left in the locker to hold on. He can win again. (6/5: 4/5-11/8)
1800 Jack Gallagher, runner-up in both his bumpers this season, made a very pleasing debut over hurdles. Going at it hammer and tongs with the winner over the last three, he responded admirably to pressure and failed by only a whisker. He should soon be winning. (6/1)
1998* River Bay (IRE) probably found this ground too lively and, after having every chance three out, was left for dead by the front two. She needs some cut in the ground to bring her stamina to the fore. (7/4)
Coole Cherry, in front to the fifth, had bellows to mend early in the straight. Both his wins in Irish points have come in the mud. (25/1)
At Liberty (IRE), racing with his tongue tied down, was close up until left standing from the third last. (20/1)
1151* Danzante (IRE) (12/1: 7/1-14/1)

2823 HOLYPORT CONDITIONAL H'CAP CHASE (0-115) (5-Y.O+) (Class E)
4-00 (4-01) **2m 5f (15 fncs)** £3,068.75 (£920.00: £442.50: £203.75) GOING minus 0.15 sec per fur (G)

	Horse	Dist	Pos	SP	RR	SF
1696[2]	**Hawaiian Youth (IRE) (99)** (GMMcCourt) **9-10-12** DFortt (lw: hdwy 2nd: led 7th to 10th: led 11th: clr appr last: r.o wl)	—	1	5/2[1]	102	14
2657[3]	**Good for a Laugh (88)** (AGHobbs) **13-10-1** OBurrows (hdwy 6th: mstke 9th: ev ch 3 out: unable qckn fr 2 out)	4	2	10/1[3]	88	—
1389[3]	**Mr Conductor (IRE) (108)** (RHAlner) **6-11-7** PHenley (rdn & hdwy appr 2 out: r.o one pce)	10	3	5/2[1]	100	12

				SP	RR	SF
1951^{3}	**Jailbreaker (87)** (BRMillman) **10-10-0** DSalter (hdwy 11th: wknd appr 2 out)	1¼	**4**	5/1^{2}	78	—
1934^{P}	**Be Surprised (87)** (GLMoore) **11-10-0** MBatchelor (led to 3rd: led 6th to 7th: led 10th to 11th: wknd appr last)	nk	**5**	33/1	78	—
2621^{6}	**Armala (105)** (JTGifford) **12-11-4** LAspell (lw: led 3rd to 6th: wkng whn mstke 11th)	10	**6**	5/1^{2}	89	1
2679^{P}	**Bathwick Bobbie (87)** (DLWilliams) **10-10-0** GHogan (a bhd)	7	**7**	33/1	65	—
	Tribal Ruler (90) (DMcCain) **12-10-3** DWalsh (bkwd: hdwy 11th: wknd appr 2 out)	1	**8**	20/1	67	—
2660^{P}	**Beau Babillard (113)** (PFNicholls) **10-11-12b** LCummins (lw: hdwy 6th: wknd 11th)	½	**9**	10/1^{3}	90	2
2704^{P}	**Full Shilling (USA) (87)** (DLWilliams) **8-10-0b** GuyLewis (prom to 11th)	1	**10**	33/1	63	—
1684^{P}	**Coasting (87)** (GBBalding) **11-10-0** ABates (prom to 5th: mstke 9th)	½	**11**	14/1	63	—
2704^{U}	**Romany Blues (89)** (CPEBrooks) **8-10-2**^{ow2} MBerry (hdwy 11th: 4th whn fell 4 out)		**F**	33/1	—	—
				(SP 131.9%)		**12 Rn**

5m 19.7 (10.70) CSF £26.71 CT £65.31 TOTE £3.70: £1.80 £2.00 £1.70 (£24.50) Trio £23.10 OWNER Mr G. Redford (WANTAGE) BRED Owen Farrell

LONG HANDICAP Bathwick Bobbie 9-8 Be Surprised 9-2 Full Shilling (USA) 8-5 Romany Blues 8-3

1696 Hawaiian Youth (IRE) was happier back over this longer trip. Leading for much of the final circuit, he forged clear from the second last to win in decisive style. (5/2)

2657 Good for a Laugh had every chance three from home, before the winner found extra over the last two. He has not won for three years.(10/1)

1389 Mr Conductor (IRE) stayed on over the last three fences without looking likely to get to the principals. (5/2)

1951 Jailbreaker probably found this surface too fast, as he has never won on ground better than good. He has not won for over two years. (5/1)

Be Surprised, 12lb out of the handicap and without a win in five years, has shown no form whatsoever for a long time, so this was something of a surprise, as he made a lot of the running and only tired going to the final fence. (33/1)

2824 COPPER HORSE H'CAP HURDLE (0-120) (4-Y.O+) (Class D)

4-30 (4-30) **2m (8 hdls)** £2,945.00 (£820.00: £395.00) GOING minus 0.15 sec per fur (G)

				SP	RR	SF
1964^{3}	**Royal Event (100)** (DRGandolfo) **6-10-5**$^{(3)}$ DFortt (mde all: all out)	—	**1**	2/1^{1}	79	18
1767^{4}	**Handson (93)** (BRMillman) **5-9-10**$^{(5)ow1}$ DSalter (hdwy appr 2 out: hrd rdn appr last: ev ch flat: r.o)	½	**2**	6/1^{3}	72	10
1599^{7}	**Supermick (92)** (WRMuir) **6-10-0** MRichards (chsd wnr: ev ch 3 out: rdn appr 2 out: unable qckn flat)	5	**3**	7/1	66	5
2657^{P}	**Miss Marigold (96)** (RJHodges) **8-10-4b** BPowell (hdwy 3rd: once pce fr 3 out)	¾	**4**	25/1	69	8
1860^{6}	**Kelly Mac (92)** (DCO'Brien) **7-10-0** CLlewellyn (lw: prom to 3 out)	6	**5**	8/1	59	—
1732^{10}	**Dontdressfordinner (93)** (RJHodges) **7-9-12**$^{(3)ow1}$ TDascombe (hld up: hrd rdn appr 2 out: wknd flat)	¾	**6**	11/1	59	—
1325^{U}	**Society Guest (118)** (AndrewTurnell) **11-11-5**$^{(7)}$ CRae (bhd fr 5th)	10	**7**	6/1^{3}	74	13
1860^{9}	**Erlking (IRE) (93)** (SMellor) **7-10-1b** DBridgwater (hdwy appr 3 out: wknd appr 2 out)	7	**8**	12/1	42	—
	Flying Eagle (108) (THind) **6-11-2** PMcLoughlin (lw: plld hrd: hld up: rdn 3 out: sn wknd)	23	**9**	9/2^{2}	34	—
1962^{7}	**Raahin (USA) (93)** (SWoodman) **12-10-1**^{ow1} SMcNeill (bhd fr 2nd: t.o fr 4th)	16	**10**	50/1	3	—
				(SP 125.5%)		**10 Rn**

3m 54.1 (6.10) CSF £14.95 CT £69.67 TOTE £2.70: £2.40 £2.60 £2.30 (£10.20) Trio £21.60 OWNER Mr T. J. Whitley (WANTAGE) BRED W. D. Hockenhull

LONG HANDICAP Kelly Mac 9-11 Handson 9-12 Supermick 9-8 Dontdressfordinner 9-12 Raahin (USA) 8-6

1964 Royal Event, returning to the minimum trip, made every post a winning one, and had a little left in the locker to keep the determined runner-up at bay. (2/1)

1382* Handson threw down a very determined challenge in the straight. Despite giving his all, he was unable to get past the winner. (6/1: op 4/1)

1381* Supermick, 6lb out of the handicap, loomed up alongside the winner in the straight. Not far behind that rival jumping the last, he was tapped for toe. (7/1: 5/1-15/2)

Miss Marigold, reverting back to hurdles, could only keep on in her own time over the last three flights. (25/1)

1860 Kelly Mac, 3lb out of the handicap, played an active role until coming to the end of his tether three from home. (8/1: 6/1-9/1)

1585* Dontdressfordinner, who failed to stay two and half miles last time, tried to get on terms in the straight, but had run out of gas from the last. (11/1: 7/1-12/1)

Society Guest (6/1: 4/1-7/1)

Erlking (IRE) (12/1: op 8/1)

Flying Eagle (9/2: 6/1-4/1)

T/Jkpt: Not won; £2,229.82 to Sedgefield 30/1/97. T/Plpt: £20.00 (586.62 Tckts). T/Qdpt: £6.30 (157.39 Tckts) AK

2751-FOLKESTONE (R-H) (Chases Good, Hurdles Good to soft, Good patches)

Thursday January 30th

WEATHER: overcast

2825 GIBBONS BROOK NOVICES' HURDLE (4-Y.O+) (Class E)

1-45 (1-45) **2m 1f 110y (9 hdls)** £2,368.50 (£666.00: £325.50) GOING: 0.46 sec per fur (GS)

				SP	RR	SF
	Shadow Leader (CREgerton) **6-11-3** JAMcCarthy (stdy hdwy 3 out: led appr last: rdn out)	—	**1**	3/1^{1}	80+	30
	Grief (IRE) (DRCElsworth) **4-10-7** PHolley (bkwd: hdwy 3rd: ev ch flat: unable qckn)	3	**2**	10/1	79?	17
	Wise King (JABOld) **7-11-3** GUpton (hdwy 5th: rdn 2 out: one pce)	1¾	**3**	7/2^{2}	76?	26
	Kings Witness (USA) (PFNicholls) **4-10-7** BPowell (lw: nt j.w: hld up: rdn 3 out: one pce)	4	**4**	4/1^{3}	74?	12
	Fresh Fruit Daily (PAKelleway) **5-10-12** DGallagher (w ldr: led 3rd tl appr last: sn wknd)	8	**5**	12/1	60?	10
	Geisway (CAN) (NJHWalker) **7-11-3** RFarrant (bit bkwd: hld up: hrd rdn appr 2 out: wknd appr last)	24	**6**	16/1	43	—
	Salaman (FR) (DCO'Brien) **5-11-3** CLlewellyn (lw: j.slowly 1st & 3rd: a bhd)	6	**7**	4/1^{3}	37	—
	Envocamanda (IRE) (DMGrissell) **8-11-3** JRKavanagh (bit bkwd: bhd fr 6th)	19	**8**	20/1	20	—
413^{3}	**Lord Tomanico (FR) (90)** (CJMann) **5-11-9** JRailton (led to 3rd: wknd 6th: t.o whn p.u bef last: lame)		**P**	15/2	—	—
	Courting Danger (DRGandolfo) **4-10-7** MAFitzgerald (swtg: bhd fr 6th: t.o whn p.u bef last)		**P**	20/1	—	—
				(SP 131.2%)		**10 Rn**

4m 22.1 CSF £35.34 TOTE £4.00: £5.20 £2.10 £1.70 (£27.10) Trio £28.80 OWNER Mr James Blackshaw (CHADDLEWORTH) BRED A. J. Sexton

WEIGHT FOR AGE 4yo-12lb

OFFICIAL EXPLANATION Envocamanda (IRE): finished distressed.

Lord Tomanico (FR): finished lame.

IN-FOCUS: The final flight was moved to a position only 100 yards from the winning post, therefore the distance between the second last and the final flight was nearly five furlongs.
Shadow Leader, placed at Royal Ascot in 1995 and winner of a handicap at Ascot in October, made a pleasing start to his hurdling career. Creeping into the action in the last mile, he led approaching the final flight and was rousted along to dispose of the runner-up in the closing stages. (3/1)
Grief (IRE), an ex-Irish gelding who won a maiden at Roscommon, was sold out of John Oxx's stable for 17,000gns. Carrying plenty of surplus condition for this hurdling debut, he showed a lot of promise and managed to poke his head in front for a few yards entering the straight before passed by the winner. Refusing to give way, he still had every chance early on the run-in before lack of race-fitness took its toll. Sure to come on a great deal for this, he should soon pick up a race. (10/1)
Wise King, who ran well in bumpers last season, has been off the track for nine months. Nevertheless, he got into the action on the final circuit if tapped for toe from the second last. (7/2)
Kings Witness (USA), sold out of Willie Haggas's yard for 22,000 guineas, was really let down by his jumping on this hurdling debut. Losing ground at many of his hurdles, this proved a real handicap for him and he could only struggle on at one pace from the top of the hill. He will improve once his hurdling is sorted out. (4/1: op 5/2)
Fresh Fruit Daily, who won an All-Weather maiden on the Flat at the beginning of the month, was rather free in front, and once collared approaching the last had little left in the locker. (12/1)
Geisway (CAN), not surprisingly, looked in need of this first run since October 1995 and after tracking the leaders was a spent force on the long downhill run to the final flight. (16/1)
413 Lord Tomanico (FR) (15/2: 5/1-8/1)

2826 STELLING MINNIS NOVICES' HURDLE (4-Y.O+) (Class E)
2-15 (2-15) **2m 6f 110y (11 hdls)** £2,326.50 (£654.00: £319.50) GOING: 0.46 sec per fur (GS)

	Horse / details	Dist	Pos	SP	RR	SF
1998^{2}	**Fiddling The Facts (IRE)** (NJHenderson) **6-10-13** MAFitzgerald (hld up: chsd ldr fr 7th: led appr last: comf)	—	1	7/4^{1}	69+	—
2010^{4}	**Royal Raven (IRE) (100)** (JTGifford) **6-11-1**(3) LAspell (bit bkwd: hld up: chsd wnr appr last: no imp)	10	2	4/1^{3}	67	—
	Unsinkable Boxer (IRE) (NJHWalker) **8-11-4** ILawrence (bit bkwd: hdwy to ld 7th: hdd appr last: sn wknd)	15	3	14/1	56+	—
2546^{5}	**Music Master (IRE)** (CREgerton) **7-11-4** JAMcCarthy (lw: hmpd bnd after 1st: hdwy 7th: wknd appr 2 out)	24	4	7/2^{2}	39	—
	Kingswood Manor (MissVenetiaWilliams) **5-11-4** RFarrant (prom to 3 out)	2½	5	12/1	37	—
1810^{5}	**Hardy Breeze (IRE)** (DMGrissell) **6-11-4** JRKavanagh (prom to 7th)	3½	6	16/1	35	—
1840^{5}	**Quinag (89)** (KCBailey) **6-10-13** SMcNeill (lw: bhd fr 8th)	5	7	14/1	26	—
	Upham Surprise (JABOld) **9-11-4** GUpton (swtg: bit bkwd: bhd fr 7th: t.o whn p.u bef last)		P	8/1	—	—
	Gentle Tune (IRE) (JRBest) **7-10-11**(7) MrPO'Keeffe (led tl hdd & mstke 7th: wknd qckly: t.o whn p.u bef 3 out)		P	33/1	—	—
2663^{P}	**Alongwaydown (IRE)** (DRGandolfo) **8-11-4** DLeahy (bhd fr 8th: t.o whn p.u bef last)		P	66/1	—	—
				(SP 121.0%)	**10 Rn**	

5m 56.3 (39.30) CSF £8.56 TOTE £2.70: £1.60 £1.10 £9.80 (£3.80) Trio £36.60 OWNER Mrs E. Roberts (LAMBOURN) BRED E. Hamilton
1998 Fiddling The Facts (IRE) put up a very polished display, cruising into the lead approaching the final flight and surging clear to win with the minimum of fuss. She loves soft ground according to her trainer, and can certainly follow up. (7/4)
2010 Royal Raven (IRE) may have run five weeks ago, but he appeared to be carrying plenty of condition, maybe he was held up at home during the cold spell. Better suited by this longer trip, he moved into second place approaching the final flight, but had no hope of reeling in the winner. Sure to come on for this, he should soon go one better. (4/1)
Unsinkable Boxer (IRE), off the course since April 1995, unsurprisingly did not look fully fit, but that did not stop him making a very promising reappearance. Leading early on the final circuit, he was collared approaching the final flight and tired as lack of a recent run took its toll. Given time to get over his exertions after a lengthy lay-off, he should soon find a race. (14/1)
2546 Music Master (IRE) managed to get into the action on the final circuit but had shot his bolt going to the penultimate hurdle.(7/2: 5/2-4/1)
Kingswood Manor, off the course since finishing third on his hurdling debut nearly a year ago, played an active role until forced to give way three from home. (12/1)
1673 Quinag (14/1: 8/1-16/1)

2827 PADDLESWORTH NOVICES' CHASE (5-Y.O+) (Class D)
2-45 (2-45) **2m 5f (15 fncs)** £3,550.00 (£1,075.00: £525.00: £250.00) GOING: 0.46 sec per fur (GS)

	Horse / details	Dist	Pos	SP	RR	SF
2693^{2}	**The Reverend Bert (IRE)** (GBBalding) **9-11-3** BFenton (lw: hdwy 9th: led 2 out: lft clr last)	—	1	7/2^{2}	106	42
901^{2}	**Frazer Island (IRE)** (RRowe) **8-11-3** DO'Sullivan (bit bkwd: a.p: rdn 3 out: lft 2nd last: unable qckn)	9	2	14/1	99	35
	Normarange (IRE) (DMGrissell) **7-11-3** MRichards (hld up: rdn 3 out: one pce)	1¼	3	20/1	98	34
1764^{4}	**Flippance (98)** (NAGaselee) **7-11-3** CLlewellyn (hld up: rdn 3 out: sn wknd)	6	4	8/1^{3}	94	30
1994^{2}	**Court Master (IRE)** (RHBuckler) **9-11-3** BPowell (led: mstke 8th: hdd 11th: rdn 3 out: wknd 2 out)	13	5	8/1^{3}	84	20
1568^{11}	**Harry the Horse** (JABOld) **9-11-3** GUpton (a bhd)	10	6	14/1	76	12
	Welsh Cottage (73) (JTGifford) **10-10-10**(7) MrPO'Keeffe (bit bkwd: a bhd)	nk	7	33/1	76	12
1856^{6}	**Charter Lane (IRE) (63)** (MrsLCJewell) **7-11-3** DLeahy (bhd fr 4 out)	hd	8	50/1	76	12
1963^{2}	**Conquering Leader (IRE)** (NJHenderson) **8-10-12** MAFitzgerald (lw: hdwy 2nd: led 11th to 2 out: 2nd whn fell last)		F	4/5^{1}	—	—
1812^{4}	**Rumble (USA) (69)** (PRChamings) **9-11-3** SMcNeill (prom to 6th: t.o whn p.u bef 8th: b.b.v)		P	33/1	—	—
				(SP 125.9%)	**10 Rn**	

5m 24.2 (16.20) CSF £44.57 TOTE £4.60: £1.10 £3.20 £3.80 (£23.00) Trio £114.10; £53.07 to Lingfield 31/1/97 OWNER The Bollie Club (ANDOVER) BRED Lady Rathdonnell
OFFICIAL EXPLANATION **Rumble (USA): bled from the nose.**
2693 The Reverend Bert (IRE) jumped into the lead at the second last, but the favourite was gamely coming back at him when departing at the final fence, leaving him to come home in his own time. (7/2)
901 Frazer Island (IRE), looking as though this first run in three and a half months was needed, was never far away but was well held in third place when left in second at the final fence. (14/1)
Normarange (IRE) ran well considering his only previous run was over hurdles back in November 1995. Chasing the leaders, he was tapped for toe over the last three fences. (20/1)
Flippance (8/1: op 5/1)
1994 Court Master (IRE), in front to the fifth last, grimly tried to hold on but was a spent force jumping the second last (8/1)
Harry the Horse (14/1: op 8/1)

1963 Conquering Leader (IRE) has only run once so far this season because there have been no opportunities for her on soft ground. Leading five out, she lost the advantage at the penultimate fence, but was grimly trying to get back on terms when capsizing at the last. Given the soft ground she likes and a longer trip, she should have no problems winning. (4/5)

2828 SIX MILE BOTTOM H'CAP HURDLE (0-115) (4-Y.O+) (Class E)

3-15 (3-15) **2m 1f 110y (9 hdls)** £2,158.50 (£606.00: £295.50) GOING: 0.46 sec per fur (GS)

				SP	RR	SF
1832^{4}	**Marius (IRE) (110)** (JTGifford) **7-11-11**$^{(3)}$ LAspell (chsd ldr: led appr 5th: clr appr 2 out: easily)	—	**1**	9/4^{1}	89+	23
1960^{4}	**August Twelfth (85)** (DCO'Brien) **9-10-3** CLlewellyn (lw: lost pl 5th: rallied 3 out: chsd wnr fr 2 out: no imp)	17	**2**	5/1	49	—
2670^{4}	**Sassiver (USA) (92)** (PAKelleway) **7-10-7**$^{(3)}$ GHogan (lost pl 5th: rallied 3 out: wknd appr last)	8	**3**	7/2^{2}	48	—
2040^{6}	**River Island (USA) (98)** (JABOld) **9-11-2** GUpton (led tl appr 5th: sn wknd)	26	**4**	10/1	30	—
	Thefieldsofathenry (IRE) (109) (CREgerton) **7-11-13** JAMcCarthy (lw: hld up: chsd wnr appr 5th to 2 out: sn wknd)	17	**5**	4/1^{3}	26	—
	Play Games (USA) (95) (LadyElizaMays-Smith) **9-10-13** DGallagher (bkwd: bhd fr 5th: t.o whn p.u bef 3 out)		**P**	5/1	—	—
				(SP 115.4%)		**6 Rn**

4m 26.4 CSF £13.05 TOTE £3.20: £1.40 £1.60 (£4.10) OWNER Mrs Anthony Andrews (FINDON) BRED James O'Sullivan

1832 Marius (IRE), looking big and well beforehand, had a nice leisurely stroll round. Leading with a circuit to go, he forged clear going to the penultimate hurdle. (9/4)

1960 August Twelfth was outpaced as the tempo increased on the final circuit, but he struggled into second place two from home, if having no hope of reeling in the winner. He is in his element in the mud. (5/1)

2670 Sassiver (USA) wast outpaced early on the final circuit, but moved up to dispute second place two out before tiring going to the last. His four wins to date have come on ground good or faster. (7/2: 5/2-4/1)

River Island (USA) set a moderate pace but, collared with a circuit to race, soon tired. (10/1)

Thefieldsofathenry (IRE), an ex-Irish gelding, has not run since August 1995 but looked in good shape in the paddock. Taking second place on the final circuit, he was collared for that position two out, and tired as lack of a recent run took its toll. (4/1: 3/1-9/2)

Play Games (USA) (5/1: op 8/1)

2829 NEWINGTON PEENE H'CAP CHASE (0-115) (5-Y.O+) (Class E)

3-45 (3-45) **3m 2f (19 fncs)** £2,862.75 (£867.00: £423.50: £201.75) GOING: 0.46 sec per fur (GS)

				SP	RR	SF
	Simpson (87) (JABOld) **12-10-6** GUpton (lost pl 7th: rallied 13th: lost pl appr 3 out: rallied appr last: led flat: r.o wl)	—	**1**	4/1^{2}	96	23
1983^{U}	**Rocky Park (95)** (GBBalding) **11-11-0** BFenton (j.lft: chsd ldr: led 4th: hrd rdn & j.b lft last: hdd flat: unable qckn)	2½	**2**	5/1^{3}	103	30
1773^{U}	**Express Travel (IRE) (81)** (RCurtis) **9-10-0** DMorris (hdwy 7th: rdn 3 out: ev ch last: one pce)	4	**3**	4/1^{2}	86	13
2665^{4}	**Maestro Paul (99)** (JTGifford) **11-11-1**$^{(3)}$ LAspell (hdwy 15th: rdn 3 out: sn wknd)	17	**4**	10/1	94	21
1798^{11}	**Rubins Boy (81)** (NJHWalker) **11-9-7**$^{(7)}$ DFinnegan (prom to 13th)	6	**5**	25/1	72	—
2665^{2}	**Yeoman Warrior (102)** (RRowe) **10-11-7** DO'Sullivan (lw: led tl mstke & hdd 4th: wknd 13th)	12	**6**	5/4^{1}	86	13
1997^{P}	**Master Jolson (105)** (NJHenderson) **9-11-10** JRKavanagh (lw: hdwy 15th: rdn 3 out: sn wknd)	16	**7**	16/1	79	6
				(SP 119.9%)		**7 Rn**

6m 43.5 (23.50) CSF £23.43 TOTE £5.70: £3.70 £2.00 (£11.70) OWNER Mr John Bickel (WROUGHTON) BRED K. Britten and J. Old

LONG HANDICAP Rubins Boy 9-13 Express Travel (IRE) 9-11

Simpson, well below his best in novice chases in the spring, was a staggering 66lb lower for his handicap debut over fences compared with his run in an Ascot Handicap Hurdle last term. Getting outpaced on two occasions, he renewed his effort from the second last, and came with a spirited run to get up on the flat. Not suited by this course and ground according to his trainer, he needs a galloping track and a soft surface. (4/1)

1765 Rocky Park jumped left at a number of his fences as he made the running. Jumping violently left at the final fence, he soon threw away the advantage. Both his wins have come on soft ground. (5/1)

1038* Express Travel (IRE) managed to get on terms with the leader when that rival jumped violently to his left at the last, but was then tapped for toe on the run-in. (4/1)

2665 Maestro Paul found this trip much too sharp for him, and was a spent force soon after the third last. (10/1: op 6/1)

2665 Yeoman Warrior ran no race at all, and was very hesitant at many fences. (5/4)

2830 WEST WOOD STANDARD OPEN N.H. FLAT RACE (4, 5 & 6-Y.O) (Class H)

4-15 (4-17) **2m 1f 110y** £1,182.00 (£327.00: £156.00)

				SP	RR	SF
	Top Note (IRE) (JTGifford) **5-11-1**$^{(3)}$ LAspell (rdn over 3f out: hdwy over 1f out: led ins fnl f: r.o wl)	—	**1**	9/4^{1}	50 f	—
2682^{9}	**Dante's Gold (IRE)** (CREgerton) **6-11-4** JAMcCarthy (lw: led 16f out: rdn over 2f out: hdd ins fnl f: r.o)	¾	**2**	14/1	49 f	—
	Squaddie (JWPayne) **5-11-4** ILawrence (hdwy 6f out: hrd rdn over 1f out: r.o)	1¾	**3**	8/1	48 f	—
1966^{3}	**Mike's Music (IRE)** (DMGrissell) **6-11-1**$^{(3)}$ GHogan (a.p: ev ch 1f out: unable qckn)	2½	**4**	5/1^{2}	45 f	—
	Your Fellow (IRE) (CPEBrooks) **5-11-4** DGallagher (hdwy over 4f out: ev ch over 2f out: wknd wl over 1f out)	7	**5**	9/4^{1}	39 f	—
1774^{5}	**Just Bayard (IRE)** (BdeHaan) **5-11-4** CLlewellyn (bit bkwd: hld up: rdn over 2f out: 5th & btn whn n.m.r 1f out)	½	**6**	13/2^{3}	39 f	—
2648^{6}	**Star Island** (DRCElsworth) **4-10-8** PHolley (bit bkwd: a bhd)	18	**7**	9/1	24 f	—
	Don'tcallmegeorge (JRBest) **6-10-11**$^{(7)}$ MrPO'Keeffe (led over 1f: wknd over 4f out)	17	**8**	33/1	7 f	—
	Unforgetable (JRJenkins) **5-11-4** JRailton (lw: prom 12f)	½	**9**	11/1	6 f	—
				(SP 130.6%)		**9 Rn**

4m 33.5 CSF £40.84 TOTE £2.30: £1.30 £5.90 £2.70 (£35.60) Trio £101.80 OWNER Mrs S. N. J. Embiricos (FINDON) BRED William Flood

WEIGHT FOR AGE 4yo-12lb

Top Note (IRE), a full-brother to No Pain No Gain, cost 26,000 guineas and recovered a small part of that here. Quite a good-looking gelding, he was rather tapped for toe as the tempo increased running down the hill, but he came into his own in the straight, and produced a nice run to snatch the spoils inside the final furlong. He will be much better served by a faster-run race. (9/4: 6/4-5/2)

Dante's Gold (IRE), a good-sized individual who will make a chaser in time, looked extremely well in the paddock and left his initial run on soft ground well behind. Setting a very moderate pace, he quickened up the tempo running down the hill and, despite being challenged by a whole host of rivals, was only passed inside the final furlong. (14/1)

Squaddie looked in good shape for this debut, and kept on well under pressure in the straight for third prize. (8/1: 6/1-10/1)

1966 Mike's Music (IRE) is improving with each race, and threw down a very dangerous challenge in the straight. He might have even poked his head in front for a few strides, but was tapped for toe in the final furlong. (5/1)

Your Fellow (IRE) had every chance entering the straight before tiring. (9/4)

Just Bayard (IRE), a nice sort, did not look fit enough to do himself justice and so it proved. Chasing the leaders, he was beginning to feel the pinch when tightened up for room a furlong from home. (13/2)
Star Island (9/1: 6/1-10/1)

T/Plpt: £184.90 (51.37 Tckts). T/Qdpt: £73.50 (7.6 Tckts) AK

2683-SEDGEFIELD (L-H) - Thursday January 30th

2831 Abandoned - Patch of false ground

2384-TOWCESTER (R-H) (Chases Good, Hurdles Good to soft)

Thursday January 30th

All races put back 5 mins
WEATHER: cloudy

2838 CANONS ASHBY (S) H'CAP HURDLE (0-95) (4-Y.O+) (Class G)

1-30 (1-35) **2m 5f (11 hdls)** £2,232.50 (£620.00: £297.50) GOING: 0.97 sec per fur (S)

				SP	RR	SF
2578[F]	**Parade Racer (70)** (PGMurphy) **6-10-9** WMcFarland (hld up & plld hrd: stdy hdwy appr 7th: led after 3 out: rdn out)	—	1	5/2[1]	57	16
1553[7]	**Whitebonnet (IRE) (82)** (CREgerton) **7-11-7b** JOsborne (a.p: ev ch appr 2 out: one pce)	5	2	6/1[2]	65	24
1859[4]	**Viscount Tully (78)** (CFCJackson) **12-11-3** MissSJackson (hld up: stdy hdwy 6th: r.o one pce fr 3 out)	7	3	20/1	56	15
1984[4]	**Kadari (88)** (WClay) **8-11-10v**(3) GuyLewis (hdwy 7th: ev ch 3 out: wknd appr 2 out)	10	4	9/1	58	17
1993[3]	**Fortunes Rose (IRE) (63)** (JSKing) **5-10-2** TJMurphy (prom: mstke 4th: rdn appr 8th: wknd after 3 out)	7	5	14/1	28	—
2088[2]	**Lovelark (61)** (RLee) **8-9-7**(7) MGriffiths (lft in ld 2nd: hdd after 3 out: sn wknd)	1¾	6	8/1[3]	25	—
2546[14]	**Nordic Flight (62)** (RJEckley) **9-10-1b** RJohnson (prom to 6th: t.o)	26	7	33/1	6	—
2694[8]	**Polo Pony (IRE) (67)** (JohnUpson) **5-10-6** RSupple (lw: bhd fr 8th: t.o)	1½	8	9/1	10	—
2576[7]	**Derrys Prerogative (65)** (AWCarroll) **7-10-4v1** DBridgwater (hdwy 6th: wknd 7th: t.o)	hd	9	40/1	8	—
	Annabel's Baby (IRE) (66) (DJWintle) **8-10-5** WMarston (bkwd: hdwy 6th: ev ch 3 out: wknd qckly: t.o)	4	10	33/1	6	—
2628[F]	**Diddy Rymer (80)** (MrsSJSmith) **7-11-5** RichardGuest (hdwy 5th: wknd appr 3 out: t.o)	30	11	16/1	—	—
1772[9]	**Honeybed Wood (66)** (IRBrown) **9-10-5** MrABrown (bit bkwd: hdwy appr 7th: wknd 8th: t.o)	4	12	33/1	—	—
2579[5]	**Chantry Beath (89)** (PGMurphy) **6-12-0** EMurphy (led tl fell 2nd)		F	12/1	—	—
1798[P]	**Singlesole (84)** (MrsPSly) **12-11-4**(5) SophieMitchell (bkwd: a bhd: t.o whn p.u & dismntd bef last)		P	16/1	—	—
	Dugort Strand (IRE) (77) (OBrennan) **6-11-2** MBrennan (bhd: blnd 5th: t.o whn p.u bef 6th)		P	33/1	—	—
	Chilly Lad (71) (RTJuckes) **6-10-10v** GaryLyons (prom tl wknd 6th: t.o whn p.u bef 3 out)		P	40/1	—	—
	Corns Little Fella (65) (DPGeraghty) **9-9-11**(7) THagger (bit bkwd: bhd whn p.u bef 6th)		P	40/1	—	—
2088[12]	**Daring Hen (IRE) (63)** (RTJuckes) **7-9-13**(3) RMassey (prom tl blnd 5th: t.o whn p.u bef last)		P	40/1	—	—
1448[5]	**Killing Time (75)** (DBurchell) **6-11-0** DJBurchell (bit bkwd: a bhd: t.o whn p.u bef last)		P	8/1[3]	—	—
1786[2]	**Kongies Melody (74)** (KBishop) **6-10-13** RGreene (bhd whn p.u after 6th)		P	33/1	—	—
1446[5]	**Alice's Mirror (73)** (KBishop) **8-10-9**(3) PHenley (bit bkwd: prom tl mstke 6th: t.o whn p.u bef last)		P	16/1	—	—

(SP 146.3%) **21 Rn**

5m 34.3 (32.30) CSF £16.68 CT £256.93 TOTE £4.70: £2.10 £2.30 £4.00 £1.80 (£31.80) Trio £346.70 OWNER LM Racing (BRISTOL) BRED Mrs J. L. Edwards
No bid
1569 Parade Racer, disappointing on fast ground last time, justified a good deal of support in the ring. (5/2: op 5/1)
Whitebonnet (IRE), who has been slipping down the ratings, was only 1lb higher than when winning a similar event here a year ago.(6/1)
Viscount Tully, dropped in class, has descended to a mark 18lb lower than when he last won back in April 1994. (20/1)
1984 Kadari, a springer in the market, was dropped 4lb on this return to selling company. (9/1)

2839 LAMPORT HALL H'CAP CHASE (0-130) (5-Y.O+) (Class C)

2-00 (2-05) **3m 1f (18 fncs)** £4,955.00 (£1,380.00: £665.00) GOING: 0.49 sec per fur (GS)

				SP	RR	SF
1785[6]	**Sister Stephanie (IRE) (123)** (GMMcCourt) **8-11-12** DBridgwater (nt j.w: hld up: reminder after 4th: hdwy 11th: blnd 12th: hrd rdn appr 2 out: led last: edgd lft: all out)	—	1	6/4[2]	132	49
2011[2]	**River Mandate (125)** (CaptTAForster) **10-12-0** AThornton (led 2nd to 3rd: pushed along 6th: led appr 2 out: hrd rdn & hdd last: r.o)	½	2	Evens[1]	134	51
2658[P]	**Red Parade (NZ) (98)** (NJHawke) **9-10-1ow1** CMaude (plld hrd: led to 2nd: led 6th: hit 3 out: hrd rdn & hdd appr 2 out: sn btn)	7	3	9/1[3]	102	18
2075[P]	**My Main Man (99)** (TRGeorge) **9-10-2** RJohnson (bit bkwd: led 3rd to 6th: j.slowly 10th: wkng whn j.slowly 4 out: t.o whn p.u bef 2 out)		P	11/1	—	—

(SP 108.3%) **4 Rn**

6m 35.9 (20.90) CSF £3.22 TOTE £2.20: (£1.50) OWNER The Antwick Partnership (WANTAGE) BRED Mrs Breda Allen in Ireland
1785 Sister Stephanie (IRE), rather taken off her legs early on, took time to warm to her task but the tacky ground brought her stamina into play. (6/4)
2011 River Mandate, 5lb higher than when successful on his comeback, went down with all guns blazing. (Evens)
1765 Red Parade (NZ) settled better when allowed to lead, but that made him a sitting target on this stiff course. (9/1: op 4/1)

2840 DRAYTON HOUSE NOVICES' HURDLE (4-Y.O+) (Class E)

2-30 (2-36) **2m (8 hdls)** £2,810.00 (£785.00: £380.00) GOING: 0.97 sec per fur (S)

				SP	RR	SF
2655*	**Juyush (USA)** (JABOld) **5-11-10** JOsborne (led to 3rd: led 5th: edgd rt appr last: rdn & r.o wl flat)	—	1	4/11[1]	86	60
1667*	**Dana Point (IRE)** (MrsSJSmith) **5-11-10** RichardGuest (a.p: ev ch whn hit 2 out: sltly hmpd appr last: eased whn btn flat)	5	2	10/1[3]	81	55
1453[3]	**Halona (96)** (CPEBrooks) **7-10-12** GBradley (bit bkwd: plld hrd: hdwy to ld 3rd: hdd 5th: one pce fr 3 out)	15	3	13/2[2]	54	28
	Absolute Limit (JTGifford) **5-11-3** PHide (bkwd: no hdwy fr 3 out)	4	4	33/1	55	29
2624[5]	**Nordance Prince (IRE) (108)** (MissGayKelleway) **6-11-3** DBridgwater (plld hrd: prom to 3 out)	6	5	10/1[3]	49	23
2050[4]	**Come On In** (RDickin) **4-10-7** TJMurphy (hdwy whn wandered 4th: wknd 3 out)	10	6	66/1	41	3
	Time To Parlez (CJDrewe) **6-11-3** SCurran (bkwd: nvr nrr ldrs)	7	7	66/1	32	6

	Horse	Dist	Pos	SP	RR	SF
	Over Zealous (IRE) (JohnUpson) **5-11-3** RSupple (bit bkwd: hdwy 5th: wknd 3 out)	3	**8**	50/1	29	3
191[8]	**Smart Remark** (THind) **5-11-3** PMcLoughlin (bkwd: hdwy 3rd: wknd 5th)	10	**9**	50/1	19	—
2566[7]	**Alistover** (RDickin) **4-9-9**(7) XAizpuru (prom to 4th)	1¾	**10**	50/1	14	—
2690[P]	**Reach The Clouds (IRE)** (JohnUpson) **5-11-3** CMaude (bkwd: s.s: a bhd)	1	**11**	66/1	16	—
2574[5]	**Contract Bridge (IRE)** (PGMurphy) **4-10-2** WMcFarland (bhd fr 5th)	1	**12**	50/1	12	—
1683[P]	**Ragdon** (MrsARHewitt) **6-11-3** SWynne (bit bkwd: prom to 4th)	3½	**13**	66/1	12	—
2649[15]	**Millers Goldengirl (IRE)** (MrsSJSmith) **6-10-12** TReed (a bhd: t.o fr 4th)	12	**14**	66/1	—	—
	Party Lady (IRE) (AJWilson) **8-10-12** LHarvey (bkwd: a bhd: t.o 4th: blnd last)		**15**	66/1	—	—
	Bally Wonder (MrsEHHeath) **5-10-12** AThornton (prom to 4th: t.o whn p.u after 2 out)		**P**	66/1	—	—
	Balladur (USA) (MrsJPitman) **4-10-7** RDunwoody (lw: plld hrd: hdwy appr 4th: wknd 5th: t.o whn p.u bef 2 out)		**P**	12/1	—	—
22[5]	**Out For A Duck** (HEHaynes) **6-11-3** RJohnson (bkwd: a bhd: t.o whn p.u bef 2 out)		**P**	50/1	—	—
				(SP 135.7%)		**18 Rn**

4m 3.9 (17.90) CSF £5.52 TOTE £1.40: £1.20 £3.10 £1.50 (£5.80) Trio £8.10 OWNER Mr W. E. Sturt (WROUGHTON) BRED Corbin J. Robertson

WEIGHT FOR AGE 4yo-12lb

2655* Juyush (USA) took quite a while to dispose of the runner-up, and this stuffy entire is likely to have one more run before the Supreme Novices' at Cheltenham. (4/11: 1/2-1/3)

1667* Dana Point (IRE) proved to be no pushover for the hot-pot favourite, and further success awaits him. (10/1)

1453 Halona should be suited by a longer trip. (13/2)

Absolute Limit, a well-made chasing type, will strip fitter for the outing and improvement can be expected. (33/1)

2624 Nordance Prince (IRE) ran too freely to get home up the stiff final climb. (10/1)

Balladur (USA) (12/1: op 8/1)

2841 CANONS ASHBY NOVICES' CHASE (5-Y.O+) (Class E)

3-00 (3-05) **2m 6f** **(16 fncs)** £3,873.00 (£1,164.00: £562.00: £261.00) GOING: 0.49 sec per fur (GS)

	Horse	Dist	Pos	SP	RR	SF
	Druid's Brook (KCBailey) **8-11-4** AThornton (hld up: stdy hdwy 7th: rdn & outpcd appr 2 out: rallied & hit last: led last stride: all out)	—	**1**	6/1[2]	102	34
1728[3]	**Garethson (IRE)** (MissHCKnight) **6-11-4** DBridgwater (led 3rd: hrd rdn 2 out: hdd last stride)	s.h	**2**	6/1[2]	102	34
2614[2]	**Ardent Love (IRE) (76)** (DNicholson) **8-10-13** RJohnson (mstke 7th: styd on appr 2 out: nvr nrr)	8	**3**	8/1[3]	91	23
1773[8]	**Robsand (IRE) (79)** (GBBalding) **8-11-4** BClifford (hld up: mstke 8th: styd on fr 2 out: hmpd by loose horse flat)	1	**4**	16/1	95	27
1964[4]	**Safeglide (IRE) (88)** (JTGifford) **7-11-4** PHide (a.p: blnd 3rd: jnd ldr after 9th: 3rd & btn whn mstke 2 out)	2½	**5**	12/1	94	26
2072[3]	**Gemma's Wager (IRE)** (MarkCampion) **7-10-13** LHarvey (mstke 6th: bhd fr 12th)	16	**6**	50/1	77	9
2698[5]	**Royal Paris (IRE) (75)** (MrsSJSmith) **9-11-4** TReed (bhd fr 13th)	5	**7**	33/1	78	10
2658[P]	**Ballydougan (IRE) (78)** (RMathew) **9-11-4v** RBellamy (hld up: hdwy 8th: wknd 4 out)	hd	**8**	50/1	78	10
2571[2]	**Jolly Boat (90)** (FJordan) **10-11-4** SWynne (prom tl wknd 3 out)	5	**9**	14/1	75	7
	Fortytwo Dee (IRE) (NASmith) **7-10-13** JRyan (bkwd: a bhd: t.o fr 8th)	24	**10**	50/1	52	—
2614[5]	**Old Betsy (60)** (MrsSJSmith) **7-10-13** RichardGuest (blnd 9th: bhd fr 11th: t.o)	nk	**11**	25/1	52	—
1875[2]	**Brown Robber (69)** (MrsRGHenderson) **9-11-4** MrWHenderson (a bhd: t.o 8th: p.u bef 2 out)		**P**	33/1	—	—
2010[14]	**Milwaukee (IRE)** (OBrennan) **8-10-13** MBrennan (bkwd: nt j.w: s.s: t.o 8th: p.u bef 2 out)		**P**	33/1	—	—
2072[P]	**Benbulbin (IRE)** (JWMullins) **7-11-4** SCurran (led to 3rd: 2nd whn blnd & uns rdr 7th)		**U**	50/1	—	—
2007*	**Whattabob (IRE)** (NJHenderson) **8-11-10** JOsborne (lw: hld up: hit 6th: chsd ldr 4 out: 2l 2nd whn blnd & uns rdr 2 out)		**U**	Evens[1]	—	—
				(SP 130.4%)		**15 Rn**

5m 49.7 (20.70) CSF £39.43 TOTE £6.10: £2.70 £2.40 £2.00 (£28.00) Trio £24.40 OWNER Racing Club KCB (UPPER LAMBOURN) BRED Mrs D. B. Johnstone

Druid's Brook, an impressive winner of both his points, stayed on gamely to snatch the verdict on the line. (6/1)

1728 Garethson (IRE) looked set to score when the favourite departed at the penultimate fence, but was pipped on the post. (6/1)

2614 Ardent Love (IRE) seems to need three miles even on a course as testing as this. (8/1)

1538 Robsand (IRE) is another who looks an out-and-out stayer. (16/1)

1964 Safeglide (IRE) made a respectable start to his chasing career. (12/1)

2007* Whattabob (IRE) may well have prevailed given subsequent events. (Evens)

2842 LEVY BOARD H'CAP HURDLE (0-110) (4-Y.O+) (Class E)

3-30 (3-36) **2m** **(8 hdls)** £2,477.50 (£690.00: £332.50) GOING: 0.97 sec per fur (S)

	Horse	Dist	Pos	SP	RR	SF
1776*	**No More Hassle (IRE) (95)** (MrsMReveley) **4-10-12** PNiven (chsd ldr tl j.slowly 3rd: mstke 2 out: led flat: r.o)	—	**1**	6/4[1]	76	13
2545[7]	**Danbys Gorse (86)** (JMJefferson) **5-10-12**(3) ECallaghan (hld up & bhd: shkn up & gd hdwy fr 3 out: n.m.r flat: swtchd rt: r.o)	nk	**2**	12/1[3]	67	16
2692*	**Ambidextrous (IRE) (82)** (EJAlston) **5-10-4**(7) 7x LCummins (hld up: hdwy 5th: led flat: sn hdd: nt qckn)	½	**3**	15/8[2]	62	11
1830[10]	**Bob's Ploy (80)** (MHTompkins) **5-10-9v[1]** RichardGuest (lw: led tl flat)	2½	**4**	12/1[3]	58	7
1467[4]	**Winsford Hill (90)** (PJHobbs) **6-11-5** GTormey (a.p: wnt 2nd 3rd: ev ch 2 out: wknd last)	5	**5**	12/1[3]	63	12
1718[8]	**Rain-N-Sun (78)** (JLHarris) **11-10-7** AThornton (prom tl wknd 2 out)	2½	**6**	12/1[3]	48	—
2670[F]	**Major Yaasi (USA) (93)** (JAGlover) **7-11-8** RJohnson (bkwd: hdwy after 3rd: wknd 4th)	17	**7**	16/1	46	—
961[7]	**Bowles Patrol (IRE) (71)** (JohnUpson) **5-10-0** RSupple (a bhd)	2½	**8**	33/1	22	—
1866[9]	**Ajdar (80)** (OBrennan) **6-10-9** MBrennan (hld up & plld hrd: bhd fr 5th)	3½	**9**	20/1	27	—
1984[10]	**Alaskan Heir (84)** (AStreeter) **6-10-13** TEley (prom tl rdn & wknd)	3	**10**	16/1	28	—
	Karline Ka (FR) (95) (RDickin) **6-11-3**(7) XAizpuru (bkwd: prom tl wknd after 4th: t.o)	dist	**11**	25/1	—	—
	Mrs Jawleyford (USA) (88) (CSmith) **9-11-3** MRanger (bkwd: bhd fr 5th: t.o whn p.u bef 2 out)		**P**	33/1	—	—
				(SP 131.8%)		**12 Rn**

4m 11.9 (25.90) CSF £20.63 CT £36.93 TOTE £2.60: £1.30 £1.80 £1.70 (£17.90) Trio £7.90 OWNER The No Hassle Partnership (SALTBURN) BRED Declan MacPartlin

LONG HANDICAP Ambidextrous (IRE) 10-11 Bowles Patrol (IRE) 9-8

WEIGHT FOR AGE 4yo-12lb

1776* No More Hassle (IRE) won over two miles on the Flat, and found his stamina coming into play in a well-contested finish. (6/4)

2545 Danbys Gorse had been running over further, and found himself with an awful lot to do from the third last. (12/1)

2692* Ambidextrous (IRE), off a mark 15lb higher than the first of his two wins, was due to go up a further 2lb in the future. (15/8)

1830 Bob's Ploy showed much-improved form in the visor. (12/1: op 8/1)
Winsford Hill, dropped 4lb, is only lightly-raced and fared much better this time. (12/1: op 8/1)
Rain-N-Sun has slipped to a mark 4lb lower than when scoring over course and distance last April. (12/1)

2843 ALTHORP HOUSE H'CAP CHASE (0-120) (5-Y.O+) (Class D)

4-00 (4-05) **2m 110y (12 fncs)** £3,497.50 (£1,045.00: £500.00: £227.50) GOING: 0.49 sec per fur (GS)

	Horse / details	Dist	Pos	SP	RR	SF
	Arfer Mole (IRE) (110) (JABOld) **9-11-11** JOsborne (chsd ldr: hit 3 out: led 2 out: sn rdn: r.o wl)	—	1	11/4[2]	119	45
1677*	**Second Call (108)** (CaptTAForster) **8-11-9** RDunwoody (hld up: j.rt 2nd: led after 3 out to 2 out: nt qckn flat)	2	2	Evens[1]	115	41
1521[F]	**Prince Skyburd (93)** (MrsPMAAvison) **6-10-8** DBridgwater (hld up: hdwy 6th: ev ch 3 out: wknd 2 out)	25	3	11/4[2]	76	2
2695[3]	**Count Barachois (USA) (86)** (MrsEHHeath) **9-10-1** KGaule (lw: led: j.lft 4th: hdd after 3 out: sn wknd)	2½	4	10/1[3]	66	—
				(SP 112.4%)	**4 Rn**	

4m 16.4 (14.40) CSF £5.86 TOTE £3.90: (£3.10) OWNER Mr W. E. Sturt (WROUGHTON) BRED M. Parkhill
Arfer Mole (IRE) made a successful transition to fences off a mark 5lb lower than his hurdles rating. (11/4)
1677* Second Call found herself beaten by a chasing debutant on her first venture in handicap company. (Evens)
1521 Prince Skyburd may not have been suited by the sticky ground. (11/4)
2695 Count Barachois (USA), dropped 4lb, was set to go down a further 3lb before this effort.. (10/1: 6/1-12/1)

2844 CASTLE ASHBY INTERMEDIATE OPEN N.H. FLAT RACE (4, 5 & 6-Y.O) (Class H)

4-30 (4-36) **2m** £1,371.00 (£381.00: £183.00)

	Horse / details	Dist	Pos	SP	RR	SF
1801*	**Red Brook** (JMJefferson) **5-11-7**(3) ECallaghan (hld up: hdwy 6f out: led over 2f out: all out)	—	1	5/1[2]	68 f	—
2661[3]	**Royal Pot Black (IRE)** (PJHobbs) **6-11-3** GTormey (hdwy 9f out: jnd wnr over 2f out: hrd rdn: nt qckn fnl f)	¾	2	3/1[1]	60 f	—
	Crackon Jake (IRE) (JSMoore) **4-10-7** WMcFarland (hld up & bhd: hdwy 6f out: r.o ins fnl f)	1	3	33/1	61 f	—
	Skycab (IRE) (JTGifford) **5-10-10**(7) WGreatrex (hld up & bhd: hdwy 5f out: c wd st: wknd 2f out)	13	4	6/1[3]	46 f	—
1781*	**The Lady Captain** (DTThom) **5-11-5** KGaule (prom tl wknd 3f out)	12	5	14/1	36 f	—
	Cool As A Cucumber (IRE) (OSherwood) **6-11-3** JOsborne (bkwd: plld hrd: led after 5f: hdd over 2f out: eased whn btn)	3½	6	6/1[3]	31 f	—
	Jupiter Probe (IRE) (RWaley-Cohen) **6-11-3** WMarston (bkwd: sn prom: rdn & wknd over 4f out)	nk	7	33/1	30 f	—
	Hijack (MissHCKnight) **6-11-3** JFTitley (tall: led 5f: wknd 4f out)	1	8	16/1	29 f	—
	Forbidden Waters (IRE) (MissVenetiaWilliams) **6-11-3** AThornton (hdwy 7f out: wknd 4f out)	6	9	33/1	23 f	—
	Ludo's Orchestra (IRE) (MarkCampion) **6-11-3** LHarvey (bkwd: prom 11f)	2½	10	33/1	21 f	—
	Coltibuono (IRE) (MBradstock) **5-11-3** GBradley (bkwd: prom 10f)	5	11	33/1	16 f	—
	Bomba Charger (AGHobbs) **5-11-3** RGreene (bit bkwd: prom 10f)	14	12	33/1	2 f	—
	Old Man of Ramas (NMBabbage) **5-10-10**(7) SO'Shea (bit bkwd: a bhd)	8	13	13/2	—	—
24[3]	**Boundtohonour (IRE)** (HOliver) **5-11-3** RDunwoody (bkwd: a bhd)	5	14	13/2	—	—
2648[5]	**Embargo (IRE)** (JLDunlop) **5-10-10**(7) MrHDunlop (bhd fnl 6f)	8	15	8/1	—	—
	Oriental Boy (IRE) (RLee) **5-11-3** RJohnson (bkwd: a bhd: t.o)	12	16	20/1	—	—
	Query Line (JMCastle) **6-10-12** SCurran (bit bkwd: tried to run out bnd 10f out: sn bhd: t.o)	20	17	33/1	—	—
	The Gadfly (RDickin) **5-11-3** TJMurphy (bit bkwd: a bhd: t.o)	24	18	33/1	—	—
				(SP 148.9%)	**18 Rn**	

4m 0.8 CSF £20.71 TOTE £8.60: £3.30 £1.60 £19.90 (£14.80) Trio Not won; £346.81 to Lingfield 31/1/97 OWNER Dr B. H. Seal (MALTON)
BRED Miss Jennifer Mellows
WEIGHT FOR AGE 4yo-12lb
1801* Red Brook stayed on dourly to repeat last month's course win. (5/1: 4/1-6/1)
2661 Royal Pot Black (IRE) showed just how well he stays, but the winner just had the edge. (3/1)
Crackon Jake (IRE) showed stamina was certainly not a problem, and will be all the better for the experience. (33/1)
Skycab (IRE) is a half-brother to Grooving. (6/1)
1781* The Lady Captain found this more competitive than the claimer last time. (14/1: op 8/1)
Cool As A Cucumber (IRE) was bought out of Chris Thornton's stable for 21,000gns after finishing second at Sedgefield in April 1995. (6/1: 4/1-7/1)
Old Man of Ramas (13/2: 20/1-6/1)
Embargo (IRE) (8/1: 6/1-9/1)

T/Plpt: £92.70 (116.92 Tckts). T/Qdpt: £13.30 (47.11 Tckts) KH

2845a - 2847a : (Irish Racing) - See Computer Raceform

1219a-GOWRAN PARK (Kilkenny, Ireland) (R-H) (Good)

Thursday January 23rd

2848a BURGER KING THYESTES H'CAP CHASE (Gd 2) (5-Y.O+)

2-45 (2-46) **3m (16 fncs)** IR £16,125.00 (IR £4,625.00: IR £2,125.00: IR £625.00) GOING: 0.00 sec per fur (G)

	Horse / details	Dist	Pos	SP	RR	SF
1649[8]	**Couldnt Be Better** (CPEBrooks) **10-12-0** GBradley (hld up in tch: 5th at 8th: cl 3rd whn mstke 4 out: 2nd & chal 3 out: 3rd 2 out: disp ld last: led early flat: styd on u.p)	—	1	7/1[3]	154	77
	Corymandel (IRE) (HdeBromhead,Ireland) **8-10-0** TPRudd (led bef 2nd: mstke 2 out: hdd last: rdn & one pce flat)	2½	2	40/1	124	47
2348a*	**New Co (IRE)** (MFMorris,Ireland) **9-10-5** CO'Dwyer (hld up: towards rr early: wnt 7th at 9th: bad mstke next: hdwy & 5th 4 out: chal 3 out: narrow ld briefly last: no ex u.p)	½	3	7/4[1]	129	52
2341a*	**Dun Belle (IRE)** (PAFahy,Ireland) **8-10-0** TJMitchell (towards rr: wnt 6th at 11th: rdn & chsd ldrs 4 out: sit mstke next: 4th & nt trble ldrs between last 2: styd on flat)	1½	4	13/2[2]	123	46
2602a[4]	**The Crazy Bishop (IRE)** (AMullins,Ireland) **9-10-2b**1ow2 RDunwoody (plld hrd early: cl up: 3rd at 9th: 4th & chsd ldrs 4 out: 6th & btn appr next)	3½	5	8/1	123	44
	Monkey Ago (MrsSABramall,Ireland) **10-9-7**(7) MDMurphy (mid div: 8th at 8th: wnt 5th whn mstke 11th: 7th appr 4 out: rdn & one pce bef 3 out: no imp)	15	6	40/1	111	34
2348a[4]	**Back Bar (IRE)** (ALTMoore,Ireland) **9-10-0** JPBroderick (in tch: 4th at 8th: 3rd at 10th: wknd after next: no imp appr 4 out)	10	7	13/2[2]	104	27

	Horse	Dist	Pos	SP	RR	SF
2602a^{U}	**Fissure Seal** (ALTMoore,Ireland) **11-10-8b^{1}** FWoods (rn 2nd fr 3rd tl after 4 out: 4th & btn 3 out: one pce)	nk	**8**	11/1	112	35
	Bart Owen (PMullins,Ireland) **12-10-0** THorgan (towards rr: mstke 10th: never a danger)	5	**9**	40/1	101	24
2348a^{U}	**Nuaffe** (PAFahy,Ireland) **12-10-4b**(3) GCotter (led early: cl up: 3rd at 8th: wknd next: sn n.d)	6	**10**	14/1	104	27
2346a^{4}	**Jassu** (JEKiely,Ireland) **11-10-5** TPTreacy (towards rr: pushed along½-wy: dropped bhd: t.o)	25	**11**	14/1	85	8
2602a^{5}	**Idiots Venture** (APO'Brien,Ireland) **10-11-5** CFSwan (hld up: towards rr whn fell 11th)		**F**	9/1	—	—
	Shanagarry (IRE) (PHeffernan,Ireland) **8-10-8** KFO'Brien (in tch: 5th at 4th: mid div 8th: towards rr 11th: dropped bhd 5 out: sn p.u)		**P**	14/1	—	—
1758a^{R}	**The Outback Way (IRE)** (JJO'Connor,Ireland) **7-10-1b^{ow1}** DHO'Connor (hld up towards rr: never a danger: bhd whn p.u bef 2 out)		**P**	16/1	—	—

(SP 138.2%) **14 Rn**

6m 9.9 (-40.10) OWNER R. A. B. Whittle (LAMBOURN) BRED Queenford Stud Ltd

IN-FOCUS: The going was believed to have been on the Yielding side of Soft, rather than the Official Good description.

1649 Couldnt Be Better, always travelling well, responded to a bit of urging from the fourth last and went second with three to jump. Ridden to lead at the last, he stayed on well on the flat. The ground conditions undoubtedly played a major role. In hindsight, he had a comparatively easy task at these weights for a Cheltenham Gold Cup third. (7/1)

Corymandel (IRE), 19lb out of the handicap, took them along from the third. Under pressure three out, he blundered at the second last and relinquished his advantage at the final fence, but still kept on on the flat. (40/1)

2348a* New Co (IRE) made a dreadful blunder seven out and despite another mistake four out, was still going strongly in the straight. He was not fluent at the second last and made another mistake at the last. Given a clear round, he might have proved himself still in front of the Handicapper. (7/4)

2341a* Dun Belle (IRE), the only novice and 5lb out of the handicap, stayed on well from two out without ever threatening. (13/2)

Fissure Seal made a bad mistake eight out and dropped right away early in the straight. (11/1)

2849a - 2855a : (Irish Racing) - See Computer Raceform

2481a-NAAS (Ireland) (L-H) (Good)
Saturday January 25th

2856a NAAS NOVICES' CHASE (Gd 3) (5-Y.O+)

3-15 (3-17) **3m** **(16 fncs)** IR £6,850.00 (IR £1,550.00: IR £650.00: IR £350.00) GOING minus 0.07 sec per fur (G)

	Horse	Dist	Pos	SP	RR	SF
2600a*	**Ultra Flutter** (MHourigan,Ireland) **10-11-11** JPBroderick (j.w: led & disp ld: led 8th: clr 12th: styd on wl)	—	**1**	6/4^{1}	119+	45
2345a^{5}	**Amble Speedy (IRE)** (ALTMoore,Ireland) **7-11-11** FWoods (hld up: mid div: 6th & hdwy 11th: hdwy & 5th 4 out: wnt mod 2nd bef 2 out: stydon: no ch with wnr)	11	**2**	100/30^{2}	112	38
2360a^{2}	**Le Ginno (FR)** (TFoley,Ireland) **10-11-8** TPTreacy (towards rr: hdwy 11th: dist 6th after 3 out: 5th 2 out: landed 3rd over last: styd on: nt trble wnr)	5½	**3**	12/1	105	31
1758a^{3}	**Executive Options (IRE)** (JMcCaghy,Ireland) **8-11-5** JShortt (hld up: wnt mod at 6th: mstke 10th: mod 3rd 4 out: 4th & no imp bef 2 out: kpt on)	9	**4**	7/1^{3}	96	22
	Folly Road (IRE) (DHarvey,Ireland) **7-11-8** PLMalone (led & disp ld: mstke 2nd: hdd 8th: 3rd whn mstke 10th: wkng 4th whn hit 4 out: no imp: kpt on same pce fr 2 out)	2½	**5**	7/1^{3}	97	23
	Ferrycarrigcrystal (IRE) (SJLambert,Ireland) **9-11-8** KFO'Brien (rn 3rd: mstke 9th: wnt 2nd bef next: lost tch with wnr 12th: mod 3rd & no imp 2 out: one pce: mstke last)	2	**6**	8/1	96	22
2341a^{4}	**Irish Peace (IRE)** (JABerry,Ireland) **9-11-5** CO'Dwyer (in tch: lft 5th at 9th: 8th at 12th: no imp 3 out)	3	**7**	8/1	91	17
	Baileys Bridge (IRE) (MrsSABramall,Ireland) **6-10-12**(7) MDMurphy (mid div: lft 6th at 9th: 7th at 12th: n.d fr next)	13	**8**	66/1	82	8
	Brave Fountain (IRE) (APO'Brien,Ireland) **9-11-5** CFSwan (in tch: j. slowly: towards rr 7th: towards rr whn slow 11th: n.d)	12	**9**	8/1	74	—
	Penny Pot (MrsSABramall,Ireland) **5-9-13**(7)ow1 MrJLCullen (towards rr: mstkes: hdwy to mod 4th at 11th: 6th over next: n.d 3 out: p.u between last 2)		**P**	66/1	—	—
2600a^{6}	**Radiant River (IRE)** (JEMulhern,Ireland) **7-11-2**(3) GCotter (a towards rr: n.d: bhd whn p.u after 3 out)		**P**	25/1	—	—
	Cesar du Manoir (FR) (MrsSABramall,Ireland) **7-11-2**(3) KWhelan (5th at 6th & whn blnd & uns rdr 9th)		**U**	20/1	—	—

(SP 140.7%) **12 Rn**

6m 45.0 (10.00) OWNER Donal Higgins (PATRICKSWELL)

2600a* Ultra Flutter missed the Thyestes because of a minor setback and was easy to back here. He belied that lack of confidence, making virtually all and going clear from four out. Age might be against him, but he will still make plenty of appeal in the Sun Alliance Chase. (6/4)

2345a Amble Speedy (IRE) stayed on from the ruck to go second from two out, without ever posing the slightest threat. (100/30)

2360a Le Ginno (FR) stayed on at one pace from four out without ever posing a threat. (12/1)

2857a IRISH RACING WRITERS NOVICES' HURDLE (4-Y.O+)

3-45 (3-45) **2m** **(8 hdls)** IR £3,082.50 (IR £697.50: IR £292.50: IR £157.50) GOING minus 0.07 sec per fur (G)

	Horse	Dist	Pos	SP	RR	SF
	I'm Supposin (IRE) (KPrendergast,Ireland) **5-11-7** JShortt (hld up in tch: 4th at 4th: trckd ldrs 3 out: jnd ldrs 2 out: led last: qcknd clr: comf)	—	**1**	7/2^{1}	110+	10
	Finnegan's Hollow (IRE) (APO'Brien,Ireland) **7-11-11** CFSwan (hld up in tch: wnt 2nd briefly at 5th: 3rd whn slight mstke 3 out: chal & ev ch 2 out: nt qckn with wnr flat: kpt on same pce)	7	**2**	4/1^{2}	103	7
	Graphic Equaliser (IRE) (FJLacy,Ireland) **5-11-7** DTEvans (hld up: 6th & trckd ldrs 5th: cl 5th 2 out: effrt appr last: kpt on flat: nt trble wnr)	nk	**3**	7/2^{1}	103	3
2359a^{3}	**Buggy (IRE)** (KFarrelly,Ireland) **8-11-11** TJMitchell (led: jnd 2 out: hdd last: nt qckn flat: one pce)	1½	**4**	12/1	101	5
2347a^{3}	**Delphi Lodge (IRE)** (TJTaaffe,Ireland) **7-11-11** MrAJMartin (cl up: hld up: mostly 3rd: 2nd 3 out: cl 4th & ev ch 2 out: rdn & no ex whn sltly hmpd last: kpt on)	1	**5**	8/1^{3}	100	4
	Blushing Sand (IRE) (PTLeonard,Ireland) **7-10-12**(7) MrTJBeattie (sn towards rr: 7th & in tch 5th: chsd ldrs 3 out: nt trble ldrs between last 2: one pce)	7	**6**	14/1	87	—
	Ennel Gale (IRE) (JTRDreaper,Ireland) **7-10-7**(7) DAMcLoughlin (mod 8th at 4th: no imp appr 2 out)	20	**7**	33/1	62	—
	Afghani (IRE) (WPMullins,Ireland) **8-11-0**(5) PMorris (towards rr: mstke 2nd: mod 7th at 4th: n.d)	¾	**8**	25/1	66	—
	Harry Heaney (IRE) (PMartin,Ireland) **8-11-0**(5) TMartin (n.d)	15	**9**	100/1	51	—

Singers Corner (DCarroll,Ireland) **5-10-8**(3)ow1 USmyth (rn 2nd tl appr 5th: 6th 3 out: sn wknd & n.d: dropped bhd)....5 **10** 200/1 42 —
(SP 98.2%) **10 Rn**

4m 6.8 (12.80) OWNER Nicholas Cooper
I'm Supposin (IRE), unsuited by the sticky underfoot conditions, always seemed to be enjoying himself. He landed in front over the last and quickened right away. Despite the lack of experience, he is a definite Champion Hurdle candidate. (7/2: op 8/11)
Finnegan's Hollow (IRE) would not be too far off the top rank in the novice brigade but was made to look very slow by the winner. (4/1: op 5/2)
Graphic Equaliser (IRE) was switched for no apparent reason from the wide outside at the second last to find the inside rail before the final flight. This was not a bad effort in the circumstances. (7/2)
Buggy (IRE) took on a lot of the donkey work, and was still in contention at the last before being outpaced. (12/1)

2858a (Irish Racing) - See Computer Raceform

2627-CATTERICK (L-H) (Good, Good to firm patches)
Friday January 31st
WEATHER: Overcast

2859 HARTLEPOOL HURDLE (4-Y.O) (Class E)
1-40 (1-42) **2m (8 hdls)** £2,565.00 (£715.00: £345.00) GOING: 0.45 sec per fur (GS)

	Horse / details	Dist	Pos	SP	RR	SF
2631[6]	**Russian Rascal (IRE) (95)** (TDEasterby) **4-11-5** PNiven (a.p: led 2 out: r.o wl)	—	**1**	5/1[2]	87	44
2615[4]	**J J Baboo (IRE)** (MDHammond) **4-10-12** RGarritty (mde most fr 2nd tl hdd 2 out: no ex)	8	**2**	5/2[1]	72	29
2060[5]	**Arabian Heights** (JMackie) **4-10-12** TEley (hld up & bhd: hdwy 5th: styd on steadily fr 2 out)	1¼	**3**	20/1	71+	28
699[3]	**Silverdale Knight** (KWHogg) **4-11-5** MFoster (chsd ldrs: rdn 3 out: kpt on wl)	¾	**4**	6/1[3]	77	34
2175[4]	**Priddy Fair** (DWBarker) **4-10-12**(3)ow1 PMidgley (hld up: stdy hdwy 5th: sn trckng ldrs: nt qckn fr 2 out)	nk	**5**	20/1	73	29
	Formidable Partner (MrsVCWard) **4-10-7**(5) MrRThornton (led to 2nd: chsd ldrs tl lost pl 5th: hdwy u.p after 3 out: nt qckn fr next)	¾	**6**	25/1	69	26
2175[3]	**Noir Esprit** (JMCarr) **4-10-9**(3) FLeahy (lw: in tch: outpcd 3 out: no imp after)	2½	**7**	10/1	66	23
2060[3]	**Tagatay** (MJCamacho) **4-10-9**(3) ECallaghan (trckd ldrs: nt qckn appr 2 out)	nk	**8**	14/1	66	23
2669[7]	**Angus McCoatup (IRE)** (MDHammond) **4-10-12** DBentley (mid div: outpcd after 3 out: kpt on towards fin)	nk	**9**	25/1	66	23
1699[6]	**Radmore Brandy** (GRichards) **4-10-7** ADobbin (nvr nr to chal)	8	**10**	25/1	53	10
2539[10]	**Hobbs Choice** (GMMoore) **4-11-0b1** JCallaghan (jnd ldr 3rd: wknd appr 2 out)	s.h	**11**	50/1	60	17
2669[3]	**Nexsis Star** (MrsSJSmith) **4-10-12** RichardGuest (hld up: stdy hdwy ½-wy: effrt appr 2 out: sn wknd)	1	**12**	6/1[3]	57	14
2744[4]	**Lucky Bea (84)** (MWEasterby) **4-10-12** PCarberry (hld up & bhd: n.d)	17	**13**	12/1	40	—
1940[12]	**Bank On Inland** (JRTurner) **4-10-7** WFry (a bhd)	20	**14**	100/1	15	—
2503[7]	**Bridlington Bay (65)** (BEllison) **4-10-12** GCahill (chsd ldrs to 5th)	5	**15**	100/1	15	—
1940[P]	**Beacon Hill Lady** (BEllison) **4-10-7** KJohnson (bhd fr ½-wy)	22	**16**	200/1	—	—
	Match The Colour (CGrant) **4-10-12** BStorey (mstkes: a wl bhd: t.o whn p.u 3 out)		**P**	50/1	—	—
	Principal Boy (IRE) (TJEtherington) **4-10-12** RRourke (plld hrd: a bhd: p.u bef 2 out)		**P**	50/1	—	—
1700[9]	**Diamond Beach** (GMMoore) **4-10-12** NBentley (prom tl mstke & uns rdr 5th)		**U**	50/1	—	—
				(SP 128.6%)	**19 Rn**	

3m 55.0 (12.00) CSF £15.37 TOTE £5.60: £2.50 £1.10 £11.10 (£7.90) Trio £107.80 OWNER Mr C. H. Stevens (MALTON) BRED R. M. Fox
2631 Russian Rascal (IRE), having to sit in just behind the leaders this time, travelled well, and was always going much better than the opposition at the business end. (5/1)
2615 J J Baboo (IRE), from a yard not really firing, was made plenty of use of and in the circumstances ran really well. (5/2: op 6/4)
2060 Arabian Heights, dropped out, showed plenty this time and looks to be getting the hang of things. (20/1)
699 Silverdale Knight, off the track for over four months, ran a super race and, by the way he was keeping on at the finish, he should stay further. (6/1)
2175 Priddy Fair keeps running well and she is likely to be better treated in handicaps. (20/1)
Formidable Partner ran in snatches here. He wore both blinkers and a visor on the Flat and may well need some headgear at this game. (25/1)
2060 Tagatay showed enough after six weeks off to suggest there is better to come. (14/1)
2669 Angus McCoatup (IRE) ran well enough on this sharp track over a trip which would seem too short. (25/1)
2669 Nexsis Star was a shade disappointing here. Not helped by receiving a bump at the second last when making his move, he was then allowed to come home in his own time. (6/1)

2860 STAYERS' NOVICES' CHASE (5-Y.O+) (Class D)
2-10 (2-10) **3m 1f 110y (19 fncs)** £3,678.00 (£1,104.00: £532.00: £246.00) GOING: 0.45 sec per fur (GS)

	Horse / details	Dist	Pos	SP	RR	SF
2650[3]	**Tico Gold (77)** (PCheesbrough) **9-11-5** ASSmith (trckd ldr: hit 13th: led 3 out: hit last: all out)	—	**1**	6/4[1]	96	2
2693[6]	**The Bird O'Donnell** (FMurphy) **11-10-12b1**(7) MrTJBarry (racd wd: led tl hdd 3 out: kpt on towards fin)	1½	**2**	13/8[2]	95	1
2509[12]	**Millies Image (60)** (FPMurtagh) **6-11-0** ADobbin (chsd ldrs: drvn along fr 11th: lost tch fr 14th)	dist	**3**	20/1	—	—
1574[8]	**Dear Jean** (MESowersby) **7-11-0** DParker (sn bhd)	dist	**4**	33/1	—	—
2540[F]	**Dry Hill Lad** (JNorton) **6-11-5** WFry (in tch: pushed along fr 11th: 3rd & outpcd whn fell 15th)		**F**	7/2[3]	—	—
				(SP 108.0%)	**5 Rn**	

6m 53.4 (35.40) CSF £3.94 TOTE £1.90: £3.90 £1.10 (£3.90) OWNER Miss S. J. Turner (BISHOP AUCKLAND) BRED T. K. Knox
2650 Tico Gold found a moderate contest here and travelled well, but needed keeping up to his work after making a mess of the last. (6/4)
2693 The Bird O'Donnell jumped well. Racing wide trying to find ground which was not cut up, he got tapped for foot from the second last and, despite fighting back, was always second best. (13/8)
Millies Image looked slow over hurdles and is shaping in similar fashion over fences. (20/1)
Dear Jean apparently won a Point-to-Point in very testing conditions, and is going to need a lot of luck to make it at this game. (33/1)
1713 Dry Hill Lad showed a little but was struggling in third when falling five from home. (7/2)

2861 E.B.F. 'N.H.' (QUALIFIER) NOVICES' HURDLE (5, 6 & 7-Y.O) (Class E)
2-40 (2-45) **2m 3f (10 hdls)** £2,477.50 (£690.00: £332.50) GOING: 0.45 sec per fur (GS)

	Horse / details	Dist	Pos	SP	RR	SF
1807[4]	**Spritzer (IRE) (91)** (JGFitzGerald) **5-10-6**(3) FLeahy (lw: hdwy 6th: led appr 2 out: sn clr)	—	**1**	5/1[2]	73+	2
1807[7]	**Take Cover (IRE) (92)** (MHTompkins) **6-11-0** RichardGuest (a chsng ldrs: effrt 3 out: styd on: no ch w wnr)	11	**2**	12/1	69	—

				Pos	SP	RR	SF
2619^{7}	**Nordic Prince (IRE)**	(TPTate) **6-11-0** JCallaghan (a.p: led after 3 out tl appr 2 out: no ex)	3½	**3**	5/1^{2}	66	—
1777^{3}	**September Breeze (IRE)**	(KAMorgan) **6-10-9** ASSmith (lw: a chsng ldrs: rdn 3 out: r.o one pce)	1¾	**4**	7/1	59	—
1516^{3}	**Hydro (IRE)**	(MDHammond) **6-11-0** RGarritty (cl up: led 4 out tl after 3 out: sn outpcd)	2	**5**	14/1	63	—
1685^{3}	**Ardrina**	(FMurphy) **6-10-9** PCarberry (in tch: outpcd 4 out: no imp after)	14	**6**	5/2^{1}	46	—
2690^{14}	**Ferrers (90)**	(MrsPSly) **6-11-0** MBrennan (lw: in tch: effrt 4 out: sn chsng ldrs: btn appr 2 out)	1¼	**7**	14/1	50	—
2043^{F}	**Bonny Johnny**	(DMoffatt) **7-11-0** DJMoffatt (chsd ldrs: effrt 3 out: sn btn)	2	**8**	50/1	48	—
1827^{5}	**Caught At Last (IRE)**	(MrsMReveley) **6-11-0** GCahill (hld up & bhd: sme hdwy fr 3 out: n.d)	nk	**9**	50/1	48	—
2675^{6}	**Donnegale (IRE)**	(TPTate) **5-11-0** PNiven (lw: hld up & bhd: n.d)	23	**10**	14/1	29	—
2504*	**Hutcel Loch**	(RDEWoodhouse) **6-11-0** ADobbin (led to 4 out: sn rdn & wknd)	9	**11**	11/2^{3}	21	—
2541^{7}	**Tsanga**	(GMMoore) **5-11-0** NBentley (in tch: hdwy & ch 3 out: sn rdn & btn)	10	**12**	66/1	13	—
2701^{P}	**Only A Sioux**	(JRTurner) **5-11-0** DParker (in tch to 6th)	12	**13**	100/1	2	—
2539^{11}	**Meadow Bee**	(WGReed) **5-11-0** TReed (sn t.o: p.u bef 2 out)		**P**	200/1	—	—
	Florrie Gunner	(JJQuinn) **7-10-9** BStorey (in tch whn mstke, stumbled & uns rdr 6th)		**U**	50/1	—	—
2673^{P}	***Redwood Lad***	(JWCurtis) **7-11-0b^{1}** DerekByrne (Withdrawn not under Starter's orders: veterinary advice at s)		**W**	200/1	—	—

(SP 126.8%) **15 Rn**

4m 47.9 (22.90) CSF £59.25 TOTE £6.10: £2.60 £2.30 £1.90 (£28.00) Trio £19.00 OWNER Mrs R. A. G. Haggie (MALTON)

1807 Spritzer (IRE), obviously all the better for her debut run in this country last time, was always going much the best here and won in really useful style. (5/1)

1807 Take Cover (IRE) never looked to be going all that well but does keep responding to pressure, if always fighting a lost cause here. (12/1: op 8/1)

Nordic Prince (IRE) seems to be improving and there should be a race or two in the pipeline. (5/1)

1777 September Breeze (IRE) likes to race up with the pace but was short of toe at the business end and ought to stay further yet. (7/1)

1516 Hydro (IRE) had his chances, but on this sharp track he proved well short of speed when it mattered. (14/1)

1685 Ardrina is a real stayer and this track proved too sharp for her. (5/2: op 9/2)

2504* Hutcel Loch (11/2: 7/2-6/1)

2862 DINSDALE CONDITIONAL (S) H'CAP HURDLE (0-95) (4-Y.O+) (Class G)

3-10 (3-12) **2m 3f (10 hdls)** £1,642.50 (£455.00: £217.50) GOING: 0.45 sec per fur (GS)

				Pos	SP	RR	SF
2045^{2}	**Yacht Club (71)**	(JLEyre) **15-10-0**(4)ow4 CElliott (a.p: led after 3 out: drvn out)	—	**1**	10/1	52	—
2629^{6}	**Jalmaid (67)**	(HAlexander) **5-10-0** RMcGrath (mid div: pushed along fr ½-wy: styd on wl fr 3 out: nrst fin)	1	**2**	9/1	47	—
2006^{3}	**Saymore (74)**	(WClay) **11-10-7** RMassey (led tl after 3rd: led 6th tl after 3 out: r.o one pce)	3	**3**	4/1^{1}	52	—
1990^{4}	**In a Moment (USA) (70)**	(CGrant) **6-10-3** MichaelBrennan (outpcd & bhd tl styd on fr 3 out)	11	**4**	4/1^{1}	38	—
	Ijab (CAN) (78)	(JParkes) **7-10-11** ECallaghan (lost pl ½-wy: styd on fr 2 out: n.d)	1¾	**5**	8/1^{3}	45	—
2629^{3}	**Arthur Bee (68)**	(BBousfield) **10-9-11**(4)ow1 CMcCormack (chsd ldrs: rdn 3 out: one pce)	1½	**6**	11/1	34	—
2629^{2}	**Anorak (USA) (90)**	(GMMoore) **7-11-2**(7) NHannity (hdwy 6th: sn rdn & no imp)	1½	**7**	6/1^{2}	54	—
1942^{5}	**Artworld (USA) (80)**	(MWEasterby) **9-10-13** PMidgley (lw: hld up: smooth hdwy to trck ldrs 3 out: ch & effrt next: 4th & btn whn blnd last)	½	**8**	6/1^{2}	44	—
	Kismetim (67)	(GPKelly) **7-10-0** BGrattan (bhd: sme hdwy u.p 3 out: sn btn)	6	**9**	50/1	26	—
2672^{U}	**World Without End (USA) (72)**	(MESowersby) **8-10-5b^{1}** GCahill (hdwy to ld after 3rd: hdd 6th: sn lost pl)	30	**10**	50/1	6	—
783*	**Ilewin (95)**	(RBastiman) **10-12-0** HBastiman (hld up: hdwy ½-wy: effrt 3 out: sn wknd)	15	**11**	6/1^{2}	16	—
1942^{F}	**Joyrider (85)**	(MissMKMilligan) **6-11-4b^{1}** MNewton (chsd ldrs tl outpcd fr 6th)	3	**12**	10/1	4	—
	Dolly Prices (67)	(WJSmith) **12-10-0** STaylor (sn t.o: p.u bef 5th)		**P**	33/1	—	—
1776^{14}	**Phantom Dancer (IRE) (79)**	(MESowersby) **4-9-10**(4) NHorrocks (prom to ½-wy: t.o whn p.u bef 2 out)		**P**	100/1	—	—

(SP 138.3%) **14 Rn**

4m 50.0 (25.00) CSF £100.21 CT £402.19 TOTE £12.50: £3.20 £3.90 £4.40 (£70.60) Trio £110.00 OWNER Mr Ernest Spencer (HAMBLETON) BRED Capt M. A. Phillips

LONG HANDICAP Jalmaid 9-13 Arthur Bee 9-8 Yacht Club 9-11 Kismetim 9-3 Dolly Prices 9-1 Phantom Dancer (IRE) 9-5

WEIGHT FOR AGE 4yo-12lb

No bid

2045 Yacht Club likes to be up with the pace, and as all the opposition began to falter in the straight he galloped on relentlessly. (10/1)

2503 Jalmaid is a tough little mare who just stays, but her effort was always that bit too late here. (9/1)

2006 Saymore is in good heart at the moment and is slipping down the handicap, which should bring him a similar event in due course. (4/1)

1990 In a Moment (USA) has plenty of ability when he decides to use it but was always too late when he consented to run here. (4/1)

Ijab (CAN) is a real character, who has the ability if only he can be persuaded. (8/1)

2629 Arthur Bee raced up with the pace on this occasion and seems better suited when coming from behind. (11/1)

1942 Artworld (USA) looked to be hacking up when moving up behind the leaders three out, but once asked for an effort over the next his engine fell out, and he almost came to grief at the last. (6/1)

783* Ilewin (6/1: op 12/1)

2863 STOKESLEY H'CAP CHASE (0-120) (5-Y.O+) (Class D)

3-40 (3-40) **2m 3f (15 fncs)** £3,740.00 (£1,040.00: £500.00) GOING: 0.45 sec per fur (GS)

				Pos	SP	RR	SF
2700^{2}	**Weaver George (IRE) (102)**	(WStorey) **7-11-6** MMoloney (hld up: hdwy to ld 9th: r.o u.p fr 2 out)	—	**1**	11/8^{1}	112	32
2630*	**Tim Soldier (FR) (89)**	(MFBarraclough) **10-10-7** RSupple (a.p: hdwy 10th: sn chsng wnr: kpt on same pce fr 2 out)	2	**2**	9/4^{2}	97	17
2632^{5}	**Twin Falls (IRE) (94)**	(GMMoore) **6-10-12** JCallaghan (chsd ldrs tl wl outpcd 4 out)	25	**3**	5/2^{3}	81	1
2002^{2}	**Port in a Storm (88)**	(MDHammond) **8-10-3**(3) MrCBonner (led to 9th: blnd 10th & 11th: wknd qckly: p.u bef 4 out)		**P**	7/1	—	—

(SP 113.9%) **4 Rn**

4m 57.0 (18.00) CSF £4.77 TOTE £2.70 (£2.60) OWNER Regent Decorators Ltd (CONSETT) BRED G. Cashin

2700 Weaver George (IRE) is running consistently well at present and, although always going best here, needed to be kept up to his work to make sure of it. (11/8)

2630* Tim Soldier (FR) is a persistent sort who was always second best but would not accept it. (9/4)

2632 Twin Falls (IRE) has lost his way at the moment. (5/2)

2002 Port in a Storm made two diabolical errors in the back straight and was then pulled up injured. (7/1: op 9/2)

2864 COWTON H'CAP HURDLE (0-115) (5-Y.O+) (Class E)

4-10 (4-10) **3m 1f 110y (12 hdls)** £2,407.50 (£670.00: £322.50) GOING: 0.45 sec per fur (GS)

				SP	RR	SF
2076^{3}	**Tilty (USA) (97)** (AStreeter) **7-11-2v** TEley (lw: led: reminders 7th: mstke 8th: hdd 4 out: led after 3 out: styd on)	—	**1**	6/4^{1}	77	19
1718^{7}	**Soloman Springs (USA) (81)** (MrsVCWard) **7-9-9**(5) MrRThornton (outpcd & lost tch ½-wy: hdwy after 3 out: chal 2 out: btn appr last)	8	**2**	8/1	56	—
1988^{5}	**High Penhowe (82)** (JJQuinn) **9-9-10**(5)ow1 MichaelBrennan (chsd ldrs: chal 3 out: sn rdn & one pce)	11	**3**	7/1^{3}	50	—
2178^{5}	**Barton Heights (85)** (MrsMReveley) **5-10-4** PNiven (lw: racd wd: trckd ldr: led 4 out tl after next: wknd appr 2 out: virtually p.u flat)	dist	**4**	13/8^{2}	—	—
	Johnny's Turn (109) (JNorton) **12-12-0** MrNKent (in tch tl fell 5th)		**F**	16/1	—	—
				(SP 107.6%)		**5 Rn**

6m 34.2 (27.20) CSF £10.90 TOTE £1.90: £1.50 £1.30 (£23.00) OWNER Cheadle Racing (UTTOXETER) BRED Mrs Emory A. Hamilton
LONG HANDICAP High Penhowe 9-8 Soloman Springs (USA) 9-6

2076 Tilty (USA) never looked happy with things but kept responding to pressure as the others fell apart. (6/4)
Soloman Springs (USA) looked out of it for most of the trip but then suddenly decided to run turning for home, only to cry enough soon afterwards. (8/1: 7/1-12/1)
1988 High Penhowe had her chances but, once the pressure was seriously on approaching the second last, she soon decided it was not for her. (7/1: op 9/2)
2178 Barton Heights has lost his way altogether and, stopping dead from the second last, walked home. (13/8)

T/Plpt: £71.60 (107.72 Tckts). T/Qdpt: £34.50 (12.6 Tckts) AA

2676-LINGFIELD (L-H) (Hurdles Soft, Chase Good to soft)
Friday January 31st

WEATHER: Overcast becoming sunny

2865 ASHURST HURDLE (4-Y.O) (Class E)

1-30 (1-30) **2m 3f 110y (10 hdls)** £2,279.50 (£637.00: £308.50) GOING: 1.13 sec per fur (HY)

				SP	RR	SF
	Cheerful Aspect (IRE) (CaptTAForster) **4-10-10** NWilliamson (hld up: mstke 5th: led appr last: shkn up: comf)	—	**1**	5/1^{3}	84+	20
	Ela Agapi Mou (USA) (GLMoore) **4-10-10** PHolley (hdwy 3 out: rdn 2 out: unable qckn)	10	**2**	33/1	76	12
2634^{11}	**Pleasureland (IRE) (98)** (RCurtis) **4-10-10** DMorris (rdn & hdwy 3 out: one pce)	2	**3**	7/1	74	10
	Chabrol (CAN) (TTClement) **4-10-10** VSmith (hld up: rdn appr 2 out: one pce)	½	**4**	20/1	74	10
2070^{2}	**Red Raja** (PMitchell) **4-11-3** JOsborne (led tl mstke & hdd 5th: led appr 2 out tl appr last: wknd flat)	nk	**5**	15/8^{1}	81	17
	Major Dundee (IRE) (MCPipe) **4-10-10** RDunwoody (chsd ldr: led 5th tl appr 2 out: sn wknd)	22	**6**	3/1^{2}	55	—
1370^{P}	**Royal Then (FR)** (JNeville) **4-10-10** JRKavanagh (a bhd)	25	**7**	33/1	35	—
2070^{5}	**Bigwig (IRE)** (GLMoore) **4-10-10** NMann (mstke 3rd: bhd fr 5th)	3	**8**	66/1	33	—
1595^{3}	**Dark Truffle** (TRGeorge) **4-9-12**(7) CHynes (hld up: rdn appr 3 out: sn wknd: t.o)	dist	**9**	25/1	—	—
	Harbet House (FR) (RJO'Sullivan) **4-10-10** DBridgwater (bit bkwd: mstke 2nd: hdwy 3 out: 3rd & ev ch whn fell 2 out)		**F**	25/1	—	—
654^{4}	**Lord Ellangowan (IRE)** (RIngram) **4-10-10b** KGaule (lw: prom to 6th: t.o whn p.u bef 2 out)		**P**	33/1	—	—
1712*	**Jelali (IRE)** (DJGMurraySmith) **4-11-3** DGallagher (bhd fr 6th: t.o whn p.u bef 2 out)		**P**	12/1	—	—
	Gulliver (NJHWalker) **4-10-10** ILawrence (lw: hdwy 5th: wknd 7th: t.o whn p.u after 2 out)		**P**	16/1	—	—
				(SP 125.3%)		**13 Rn**

5m 6.1 (32.10) CSF £146.90 TOTE £5.30: £3.00 £3.50 £1.90 (£457.40) Trio £121.10; £136.56 to Chepstow 1/2/97 OWNER Lady Pilkington (LUDLOW) BRED Gainsborough Stud Management Ltd

Cheerful Aspect (IRE), who won at Pontefract in April for Ed Dunlop, enjoyed the ground and made a very pleasing debut over hurdles. Leading approaching the last, he needed only to be woken up to pull right away for a very convincing victory. Sure to come on for this first run in four months, he can win again. (5/1)
Ela Agapi Mou (USA), a poor plater on the Flat, looked very pedestrian in the straight but just managed to win the battle for second prize. (33/1)
1900 Pleasureland (IRE) ran better here but he had to be bustled along to take closer order three from home, and was then made to look woefully onepaced. His main problem is lack of acceleration. (7/1: 5/1-8/1)
Chabrol (CAN), who won a claimer at Yarmouth in August, chased the leaders, but could only go up and down in the same place in the straight. (20/1)
2070 Red Raja found this longer trip in this ground too much for him. Showing in front for a second time approaching the penultimate hurdle, he was collared going to the last, and although still second early on the run-in then tired. A return to two miles is needed. (15/8)
Major Dundee (IRE) was placed numerous times on the Flat for Richard Hannon, but managed only one success, that coming here when Willie Carson hit the headlines, getting caught on the line when trying to be too clever. Looking straight for this hurdling debut, his first run in over four months, he was sent on at halfway but was collared approaching the second last and soon had bellows to mend. Two miles may well suit him better. (3/1)
Harbet House (FR), who won a handicap on the Flat last summer for Charles Cyzer, looked just in need of this hurdling debut, his first run in over three months. Nevertheless he showed promise and had every chance when capsizing at the penultimate hurdle. He can win a small novice event before long. (25/1)
1712* Jelali (IRE) (12/1: op 8/1)

2866 WORTH WOOD (S) H'CAP HURDLE (0-95) (4-Y.O+) (Class G)

2-00 (2-00) **2m 110y (8 hdls)** £1,852.50 (£515.00: £247.50) GOING: 1.13 sec per fur (HY)

				SP	RR	SF
2792^{4}	**Script (68)** (JRJenkins) **6-10-7** JOsborne (lw: racd wd: lost pl appr 2 out: rallied appr last: led flat: r.o wl)	—	**1**	5/1^{3}	48	7
2664^{3}	**Slightly Special (IRE) (61)** (BAPearce) **5-10-0** TJMurphy (led: mstke 5th: hrd rdn appr last: hdd flat: unable qckn)	2	**2**	6/1	39	—
2068^{R}	**Kentavrus Way (IRE) (61)** (GLMoore) **6-9-7**(7) MBatchelor (hld up: mstke 1st: rdn 5th: one pce)	7	**3**	14/1	32	—
2792^{8}	**Derisbay (IRE) (76)** (JJBridger) **9-11-1b** DO'Sullivan (chsd ldr: ev ch appr 2 out: sn wknd)	1	**4**	20/1	46	5
2579^{3}	**Glowing Path (89)** (RJHodges) **7-11-7**(7) JHarris (hdwy 2nd: rdn 5th: wknd appr 2 out)	9	**5**	9/4^{1}	51	10
1729^{P}	**Callonescy (IRE) (61)** (DCO'Brien) **5-10-0** CLlewellyn (bhd fr 3rd)	5	**6**	33/1	18	—

				SP	RR	SF
357*	**Nord Lys (IRE) (69)** (BJLlewellyn) **6-10-1**(7) MissEJJones (lw: hdwy 4th: wknd appr 3 out)	17	**7**	7/1	9	—
1796^{7}	**Tomal (70)** (RIngram) **5-10-9** DGallagher (hld up: hrd rdn appr 2 out: 3rd & wkng whn fell last)		**F**	$5/2^{2}$	41?	—
				(SP 117.2%)	**8 Rn**	

4m 14.3 (29.30) CSF £32.55 CT £361.26 TOTE £6.80: £1.70 £1.70 £1.90 (£10.50) Trio £79.90; £15.77 to Chepstow 1/2/97 OWNER Electronic & Software Publications Ltd (ROYSTON) BRED R. M. West
LONG HANDICAP Slightly Special (IRE) 9-10
No bid
OFFICIAL EXPLANATION Glowing Path: was not suited by the soft ground.
2792 Script, making a quick reappearance, was given a very sensible ride by Osborne who took him wide throughout in search of the better ground. Picking up ground going to the final flight, the gelding managed to get on top on the run-in to win his first race in this country. (5/1: op 3/1)
2664 Slightly Special (IRE) attempted to make all the running but, despite giving his all, was eventually overhauled on the run-in. There is a small seller in him if the ground remains soft. (6/1)
Kentavrus Way (IRE) was much happier with this return to hurdling and low-grade event but he was made to look very pedestrian in the straight. He is a very poor individual, and it is absolutely no surprise he has failed to open his account at the winter game. (14/1)
Derisbay (IRE) ran his best race for a very long time, and had every chance running down the hill before tiring early in the straight. All three of his victories have come in this grade but he is not won for over three years. (20/1)
2579 Glowing Path has been in fine form this season but he failed to handle this soft ground, and the writing was on the wall a long way from home. (9/4)

2867 ADVENTURE NOVICES' CHASE (5-Y.O+) (Class D)

2-30 (2-30) **2m (12 fncs)** £3,597.00 (£1,086.00: £528.00: £249.00) GOING: 0.97 sec per fur (S)

				SP	RR	SF
1568^{2}	**Glitter Isle (IRE) (96)** (JTGifford) **7-11-4** PHide (led to 2nd: chsd ldr fr 6th: led appr last: rdn out)	—	**1**	13/2	112	44
$2613a^{7}$	**Garolo (FR)** (CPEBrooks) **7-11-10b**[1] GBradley (a.p: hrd rdn appr last: r.o one pce)	2	**2**	$11/2^{3}$	116	48
	As du Trefle (FR) (MCPipe) **9-11-4** JOsborne (lw: pckd 1st: led 3rd tl appr last: wknd flat)	5	**3**	14/1	105	37
1664^{F}	**Exterior Profiles (IRE)** (NATwiston-Davies) **7-11-4** TJMurphy (lw: led 2nd to 3rd: 4th whn blnd bdly 4th: nt rcvr)	1¾	**4**	$11/2^{3}$	103	35
1572^{F}	**Mouse Bird (IRE) (116)** (DRGandolfo) **7-11-4** RDunwoody (mstke 5th: stdy hdwy fr 4 out: nvr plcd to chal)	s.h	**5**	$9/2^{2}$	103	35
1963^{6}	**Jovial Man (IRE)** (RJO'Sullivan) **8-11-4** DO'Sullivan (bit bkwd: bhd fr 4th: t.o)	dist	**6**	12/1	—	—
2752^{P}	**Full of Tricks (60)** (JJBridger) **9-11-4** DMorris (lw: chsd ldr after 3rd to 6th: wknd 8th: t.o)	12	**7**	100/1	—	—
1793^{12}	**Teinein (FR)** (CaptTAForster) **6-11-4** NWilliamson (hdwy appr 3 out: 4th & btn whn fell 2 out)		**F**	$9/4^{1}$	—	—
2680^{3}	**Fionans Flutter (IRE)** (DRCElsworth) **9-11-4** PHolley (bhd tl fell 4th: dead)		**F**	12/1	—	—
2628^{R}	**Ernest Aragorn** (MrsSLamyman) **8-11-4** BClifford (a bhd: t.o whn p.u bef 5th)		**P**	100/1	—	—
2672^{U}	**Hawker Hunter (USA)** (CREgerton) **6-11-4b** JAMcCarthy (mstke & uns rdr 2nd)		**U**	33/1	—	—
				(SP 120.0%)	**11 Rn**	

4m 12.2 (20.20) CSF £39.74 TOTE £6.90: £2.00 £2.30 £4.40 (£28.20) Trio £80.80 OWNER Mrs Timothy Pilkington (FINDON) BRED Pat Hickey
1568 Glitter Isle (IRE), who has always looked like a chaser, made a winning debut over the larger obstacles. Gaining control over the final fence, he was rousted along for victory. (13/2)
2613a Garolo (FR), who has won and been placed over hurdles in France since scoring over fences at Uttoxeter last month, ran well considering he was conceding 6lb to all his rivals. Never far away, he was only about a length down jumping the final fence and, although unable to cope with the winner, pulled clear of the third. All three of his victories to date have come in the mud and he should soon return to the winner's enclosure. (11/2: 4/1-6/1)
As du Trefle (FR) may not have raced since April 1993 but his trainer is a master at getting his horses fit, and this gelding looked in fine shape considering his lengthy lay-off. Showing a great deal of promise, he was soon at the head of affairs and was not overhauled until approaching the final fence. Given time to get over his exertions here he should have no problems winning. (14/1: op 7/1)
1664 Exterior Profiles (IRE) made an horrendous blunder at the fourth, from which his rider did well to recover. Unfortunately the gelding lost a lot of ground and, although staying on again in the closing stages, could never get into it. Once he gets his jumping sorted out he can certainly win over fences given the right conditions - he has yet to win on ground worse than good. (11/2)
1572 Mouse Bird (IRE), who fell on his chasing debut, had no more than a confidence-boosting run as his jockey sat as quiet as a church mouse all the way round. Despite this he made eyecatching headway in the straight to be nearest at the line, and it was something of a surprise that the Stewards did not hold an enquiry into this running. At his best in the mud, he should have learnt a lot from this and is surely now ready to strike. (9/2)

2868 HOLTYE MAIDEN HURDLE (4-Y.O+) (Class E)

3-00 (3-00) **2m 110y (8 hdls)** £2,685.50 (£753.00: £366.50) GOING: 1.13 sec per fur (HY)

				SP	RR	SF
2071^{2}	**Three Farthings** (JABOld) **7-11-8** CLlewellyn (hld up: rdn appr last: led flat: r.o wl)	—	**1**	$13/8^{1}$	68	43
	Mutanassib (IRE) (MCPipe) **4-10-10** RDunwoody (lw: led 2nd: rdn appr last: hdd flat: unable qckn)	2	**2**	$4/1^{3}$	66	29
	Magic Combination (IRE) (BJCurley) **4-10-7**(3) LAspell (hld up: rdn appr last: sn wknd)	6	**3**	$7/2^{2}$	60	23
2566^{3}	**Mr Darcy** (PRWebber) **5-11-8** JOsborne (nvr nr to chal)	13	**4**	9/2	48	23
2071^{3}	**Master Pilgrim** (GBBalding) **5-11-8** BFenton (a.p: rdn appr 2 out: sn wknd)	1	**5**	14/1	47	22
1726^{13}	**Night Flare (FR)** (SWoodman) **5-11-8** NWilliamson (lw: hdwy 3 out: wknd appr 2 out)	2½	**6**	50/1	44	19
1998^{P}	**Royal Ruler (IRE)** (JTGifford) **6-11-3** PHide (lw: led to 2nd: wknd 3 out: t.o)	dist	**7**	16/1	—	—
1938^{15}	**Nishaman** (NJHenderson) **6-11-8** JRKavanagh (a bhd: t.o)	6	**8**	25/1	—	—
	Bon Luck (IRE) (JABennett) **5-11-8** LHarvey (a bhd: t.o)	14	**9**	14/1	—	—
	She Said No (GLMoore) **5-10-10**(7) MAttwater (prom to 3 out: t.o whn p.u bef last)		**P**	33/1	—	—
				(SP 126.5%)	**10 Rn**	

4m 9.3 (24.30) CSF £8.49 TOTE £2.50: £1.30 £1.50 £1.60 (£5.60) Trio £16.10 OWNER Mr K. R. Britten (WROUGHTON) BRED K. Britten and J. Old
WEIGHT FOR AGE 4yo-12lb
2071 Three Farthings was not going to be short-changed here. Throwing down his challenge in the straight, he managed to get on top on the run-in. A half-brother to Simpson, he likes this ground and will come into his own over further. (13/8)
Mutanassib (IRE), a maiden on the Flat for Alec Stewart due to lack of acceleration, was sold for 20,000 guineas. Looking in good shape for this hurdling debut, he cut out the donkey-work but was eventually collared on the run-in. He should soon be winning. (4/1: op 2/1)
Magic Combination (IRE), an ex-Irish gelding who won three times on the Flat early last year for Kevin Prendergast, was a beaten favourite on his hurdling debut at Fairyhouse back in October, but subsequently split Theatreworld and Antapoura in a two-mile handicap on the level. Well supported in the market, he was one of three battling for honours in the straight before tiring approaching the final flight. A lightly-made gelding, he has a rather scratchy action and may be better suited by a sounder surface. (7/2)

2566 Mr Darcy never threatened to get into it and only plodded on past beaten rivals. (9/2: 7/1-4/1)
2071 Master Pilgrim played an active role until coming to the end of his tether early in the straight. (14/1)

2869 FELCOURT H'CAP CHASE (0-125) (5-Y.O+) (Class D)

3-30 (3-31) **3m (18 fncs)** £3,808.00 (£1,144.00: £552.00: £256.00) GOING: 0.97 sec per fur (S)

				SP	RR	SF
1951[4]	**Giventime (105)** (AndrewTurnell) **9-11-2** LHarvey (lw: hld up: led 4 out: rdn out)	—	**1**	7/2[1]	115	23
1697[3]	**A N C Express (110)** (JSKing) **9-11-7** TJMurphy (hdwy 7th: rdn 11th: lost pl appr 3 out: rallied 2 out: chsd wnr appr last: r.o)	2	**2**	4/1[2]	119	27
	Plastic Spaceage (115) (JABOld) **14-11-12** CLlewellyn (bit bkwd: lost pl 9th: rallied flat: r.o)	4	**3**	8/1	121	29
2630[4]	**Sister Rosza (IRE) (96)** (MrsSLamyman) **9-10-7** RFarrant (hld up: hmpd 2nd: mstke 7th: rdn appr 2 out: unable qckn)	nk	**4**	8/1	102	10
1839*	**Jurassic Classic (112)** (MrsLRichards) **10-11-9** MRichards (lft in ld 2nd: mstke & hdd 4 out: wknd appr last)	3	**5**	7/1	116	24
1799[7]	**Makes Me Goosey (IRE) (96)** (MrsIMcKie) **9-10-7b** PHide (hld up: mstke 9th: hrd rdn appr 2 out: sn wknd)	nk	**6**	16/1	100	8
1997[5]	**Dom Samourai (FR) (117)** (MCPipe) **6-12-0b** RDunwoody (a bhd: t.o)	dist	**7**	12/1	—	—
2754[U]	**Veryvel (CZE) (97)** (JNeville) **6-10-8** NWilliamson (lw: pckd 3rd: mstke 10th: a bhd: t.o)	1½	**8**	25/1	—	—
2075[4]	**Braes of Mar (106)** (NJHenderson) **7-11-3b[1]** JOsborne (led tl fell 2nd)		**F**	10/1	—	—
1697[2]	**Three Saints (IRE) (96)** (CaptTAForster) **8-10-7** SWynne (2nd whn blnd & uns rdr 11th)		**U**	5/1[3]	—	—
				(SP 120.1%)	**10 Rn**	

6m 31.0 (37.00) CSF £17.50 CT £97.36 TOTE £4.60: £1.20 £1.60 £3.60 (£7.80) Trio £23.90 OWNER Mr L. G. Kimber (WANTAGE) BRED C. L. Loyd

Giventime loves the mud, and looked an absolute picture in the paddock. Sent on four from home, he was rousted along in the straight to register his fourth victory here. He can win again. (7/2)
1697 A N C Express got outpaced on the long downhill run to the third last but he rallied to go into second place approaching the final fence, and although unable to get on terms with the winner finished a clear second best. He has gained all three victories to date with some cut in the ground, and should soon be winning. (4/1)
Plastic Spaceage, looking in need of this first run in nearly ten months, is certainly an o.a.p but, despite losing his pitch with a circuit to race, stayed on nicely on the run-in to take third prize. He has not won for nearly four years. (8/1)
2630 Sister Rosza (IRE) was much better suited by the underfoot conditions and appeared to get home over this trip, if failing to find another gear over the last two fences. (8/1: op 14/1)
1839* Jurassic Classic, well suited by some give, cut out the majority of the running until making a mistake four from home. He grimly tried to hold on but was a spent force soon after the penultimate fence. (7/1)
1540 Makes Me Goosey (IRE) chased the leaders but had been hung out to dry two from home. All three of his victories to date have come at Towcester. (16/1)
1428 Dom Samourai (FR) (12/1: 8/1-14/1)
1697 Three Saints (IRE) (5/1: 7/2-11/2)

2870 HEDDON NOVICES' H'CAP HURDLE (0-100) (5-Y.O+) (Class E)

4-00 (4-03) **2m 3f 110y (10 hdls)** £2,419.50 (£677.00: £328.50) GOING: 1.13 sec per fur (HY)

				SP	RR	SF
2797[10]	**Equity's Darling (IRE) (74)** (DCO'Brien) **5-10-6b[1]** PHide (hdwy 6th: led appr last: mstke last: drvn out)	—	**1**	20/1	57	18
1565[3]	**Lady High Sheriff (IRE) (72)** (CaptTAForster) **7-10-4** SWynne (lw: hdwy 6th: led appr 2 out tl appr last: unable qckn)	1½	**2**	5/1[2]	54	15
1448[6]	**Steel Gem (IRE) (74)** (PMRich) **8-9-13(7)** MGriffiths (hdwy 5th: led 7th tl appr 2 out: wknd appr last)	13	**3**	4/1[1]	45	6
2547[8]	**Fantasy Line (87)** (PRWebber) **6-11-5** JOsborne (hdwy 3 out: wknd appr 2 out)	9	**4**	16/1	51	12
1855[4]	**Quick Quote (85)** (MrsIMcKie) **7-11-3** LHarvey (nvr nr to chal)	5	**5**	6/1	45	6
2552[8]	**Snowshill Shaker (85)** (NATwiston-Davies) **8-11-3** CLlewellyn (hld up: rdn appr 2 out: sn wknd)	2	**6**	11/2[3]	43	4
2552[10]	**Rovestar (89)** (JSKing) **6-11-7** TJMurphy (prom tl appr 2 out)	26	**7**	12/1	26	—
1448[8]	**Otter Prince (68)** (TRGeorge) **8-9-7b[1](7)** CHynes (prom to 6th)	8	**8**	25/1	—	—
	Kennett Square (IRE) (70) (LadyElizaMays-Smith) **8-10-2** JAMcCarthy (bkwd: a.p: led 4th tl mstke & hdd 7th: sn wknd)	21	**9**	33/1	—	—
	Hanging Grove (IRE) (89) (PGMurphy) **7-11-7** NMann (led 3rd to 4th: wknd 6th: t.o)	dist	**10**	14/1	—	—
2076[5]	**Felloo (IRE) (90)** (TRGeorge) **8-11-8** RDunwoody (prom to 4th: t.o whn p.u bef 2 out)		**P**	10/1	—	—
	Torch Vert (IRE) (92) (NJHWalker) **5-11-10** RFarrant (led to 3rd: wknd 7th: t.o whn p.u bef 2 out)		**P**	14/1	—	—
1952[P]	**Hello Me Man (IRE) (84)** (BJLlewellyn) **9-11-2** MrJLLlewellyn (bit bkwd: swtg: a bhd: t.o whn p.u after 6th)		**P**	20/1	—	—
1729[9]	**Braydon Forest (73)** (CJDrewe) **5-10-5b[ow5]** AThornton (a bhd: t.o whn p.u bef 2 out)		**P**	33/1	—	—
2038*	**My Man in Dundalk (IRE) (84)** (BJCurley) **8-10-13(3)** LAspell (bhd fr 5th: t.o whn p.u bef 2 out)		**P**	13/2	—	—
				(SP 134.9%)	**15 Rn**	

5m 5.7 (31.70) CSF £113.75 CT £461.83 TOTE £28.20: £6.50 £1.40 £1.60 (£54.60) Trio £318.10 OWNER Mrs V. O'Brien (TONBRIDGE) BRED Pat Doyle

LONG HANDICAP Braydon Forest 9-11 Otter Prince 9-6

OFFICIAL EXPLANATION **Equity's Darling (IRE): the trainer stated the mare has always been reluctant to start in her races, but with the application of blinkers for the first time she consented to start and hold her position.**

Equity's Darling (IRE) had virtually refused to start on all three of her previous outings this season, but the application of blinkers worked wonders and she was well behaved on this occasion. Traveling nicely, she struck the front approaching the last, and although hitting that flight hard responded to pressure to hold on well. Nevertheless, she is still one to steer well clear of. (20/1)
1565 Lady High Sheriff (IRE) appeared to enjoy the underfoot conditions and went on approaching the second last. Collared going to the final flight, she found the winner always had a bit too much up her sleeve. (5/1: 4/1-6/1)
Steel Gem (IRE) was very well backed and moved to the front four from home. Collared approaching the second last, he had bellows to mend soon after that flight. (4/1: 10/1-7/2)
1855 Fantasy Line took closer order three from home but had been seen off entering the straight. This longer trip appeared beyond her. (16/1)
Torch Vert (IRE) (14/1: 10/1-16/1)
2038* My Man in Dundalk (IRE) (13/2: 5/2-7/1)

2871 H.B.L.B. EDENBRIDGE H'CAP HURDLE (0-110) (4-Y.O+) (Class E)

4-30 (4-32) **2m 3f 110y (10 hdls)** £2,251.50 (£629.00: £304.50) GOING: 1.13 sec per fur (HY)

				SP	RR	SF
2067[3]	**Tickerty's Gift (107)** (GLMoore) **7-11-7(7)** MAttwater (chsd ldr: led 5th: clr appr last: r.o wl)	—	**1**	9/2	90	18
2755[U]	**Shepherds Rest (IRE) (101)** (SMellor) **5-11-8** AThornton (lw: hld up: lft 2nd 2 out: wknd appr last)	8	**2**	11/4[2]	77	5

	Horse / details	Dist	Pos	SP	RR	SF
1948^{3}	**Daily Sport Girl (88)** (BJLlewellyn) **8-10-9** MrJLLlewellyn (lw: lost pl 5th: r.o one pce fr 2 out)	7	**3**	12/1	59	—
2755^{5}	**Zingibar (87)** (JMBradley) **5-10-8** NWilliamson (hld up: reminders 4th: wknd appr 3 out)	20	**4**	11/1	41	—
1948*	**Friendly House (IRE) (97)** (MCPipe) **8-11-4** RDunwoody (lw: led: mstke 1st: hdd 5th: rdn 6th: sn wknd)	24	**5**	5/2^{1}	32	—
2753*	**Yellow Dragon (IRE) (94)** (BAPearce) **4-9-10**$^{(7)}$ 6x GordonGallagher (lw: hld up: chsd wnr fr 7th: ev ch whn pckd 3 out: 2nd whn fell 2 out)		**F**	7/2^{3}	—	—
				(SP 111.7%)		**6 Rn**

5m 11.1 (37.10) CSF £15.77 TOTE £5.00: £1.90 £1.80 (£9.60) OWNER Mr K. Higson (BRIGHTON) BRED K. Higson
WEIGHT FOR AGE 4yo-12lb

2067 Tickerty's Gift loves these conditions and this course - his four previous victories have all come here in the mud. Gaining a slender lead at the fifth, he forged clear from the second last, despite his rider looking extremely unstylish, to win in decisive fashion. (9/2)
2067* Shepherds Rest (IRE), left in second place two from home, was not far behind the winner at that stage, but tired in the testing conditions going to the last. (11/4: 2/1-3/1)
1948 Daily Sport Girl dropped right away early on the final circuit, but did plod on past beaten rivals to finish a moderate third. (12/1)
2755 Zingibar, who was given a couple of reminders with a full circuit to race, had shot his bolt going to the third last. (11/1: 6/1-12/1)
1948* Friendly House (IRE), racing with his tongue tied down, had more on his plate here but still put up a lacklustre performance. (5/2)
2753* Yellow Dragon (IRE), successful in a seller in the mud at Folkestone last week, had more to do here, but he looked a serious threat three from home and was only about a length down on the winner when falling at the penultimate hurdle. (7/2)

T/Jkpt: Not won; £5,324.43 to Chepstow 1/2/97. T/Plpt: £307.40 (37.6 Tckts). T/Qdpt: £19.60 (46.91 Tckts). AK

2573-TAUNTON (R-H) (Good)
Friday January 31st
WEATHER: Cloudy

2872 MARTIN PIPE WINNERS GALORE NOVICES' HURDLE (4-Y.O+) (Class E)
1-45 (1-46) **2m 1f (9 hdls)** £2,442.00 (£687.00: £336.00) GOING minus 0.20 sec per fur (G)

	Horse / details	Dist	Pos	SP	RR	SF
2669^{15}	**Easy Listening (USA)** (NJHawke) **5-11-3** JRailton (a.p: wnt 2nd 6th: led 2 out: clr last: r.o wl)	—	**1**	14/1	74	30
2566^{4}	**Break the Rules** (MCPipe) **5-10-10**$^{(7)}$ GSupple (lw: hld up: hdwy appr 2 out: r.o flat)	2	**2**	16/1	72	28
	Merawang (IRE) (PFNicholls) **4-10-7** RJohnson (hld up: hdwy 6th: one pce fr 2 out)	4	**3**	4/1^{2}	70+	14
2622^{6}	**Brilliant Red** (PRHedger) **4-10-7** BPowell (lw: a.p: one pce fr 2 out)	½	**4**	5/1^{3}	70	14
1519^{3}	**Doctor Green (FR) (110)** (MCPipe) **4-12-0v** DWalsh (led: sn clr: blnd 3 out: hdd 2 out: sn wknd)	s.h	**5**	16/1	91	35
1634^{10}	**Chief Mouse (105)** (MissHCKnight) **4-11-7** JFTitley (chsd ldr to 6th: wknd 2 out)	2	**6**	20/1	82	26
2751^{2}	**Melt The Clouds (CAN)** (MCPipe) **4-10-7** CMaude (hld up: hdwy appr 2 out: wknd appr last)	2½	**7**	5/4^{1}	66	10
1782^{9}	**Southernhay Boy** (MrsSDWilliams) **6-11-3** WMcFarland (mstke 5th: sn bhd)	18	**8**	16/1	47	3
	Mystic Hill (RGFrost) **6-11-3** JFrost (blnd 1st: a bhd)	1¼	**9**	14/1	46	2
	Qu'appelle (SEarle) **4-10-7** SMcNeill (mstke 2nd: sn bhd: t.o fr 5th)	dist	**10**	100/1	—	—
2566^{10}	**Time Goes On** (RJHodges) **5-10-9**$^{(3)}$ DFortt (a bhd: t.o fr 5th)	11	**11**	100/1	—	—
2655^{P}	**Chalcuchima** (NJHawke) **4-10-7** RGreene (bhd: mstke 5th: sn t.o)	28	**12**	100/1	—	—
1283^{6}	**Gale Spring (IRE)** (RJHodges) **5-10-9**$^{(3)}$ TDascombe (bhd fr 6th: fell last)		**F**	50/1	—	—
				(SP 121.8%)		**13 Rn**

3m 57.4 (4.40) CSF £189.25 TOTE £17.30: £2.30 £3.90 £1.80 (£63.50) Trio £191.30; £242.60 to Chepstow 1/2/97 OWNER Mr Derek Kacy Flint (CHARD) BRED Juddmonte Farms
WEIGHT FOR AGE 4yo-12lb
OFFICIAL EXPLANATION **Easy Listening (USA): is a nervous type who, with hindsight, was not at all suited by the long overnight journey to Market Rasen.**

1873 Easy Listening (USA) confirmed the promise of his debut, and the Stewards inquired into his disappointing run last time. They accepted the explanation that the gelding was unsettled by the long journey to Market Rasen and by having to stay away overnight. (14/1: op 8/1)
2566 Break the Rules kept on without troubling the winner and seems to be getting the hang of things. (16/1)
Merawang (IRE), a 54,000 guineas Irish import, was lightly-raced after winning at the Curragh as a juvenile. Considered to be a Triumph Hurdle contender, he will have to improve a lot on this. (4/1: op 5/2)
2622 Brilliant Red failed to raise his game sufficiently in the home straight. (5/1)
1519 Doctor Green (FR) adopted his usual front-running tactics but his 21lb in penalties was anchoring him from the penultimate hurdle. (16/1)
1205* Chief Mouse was trying to overcome a double penalty. (20/1)
Mystic Hill (14/1: 8/1-16/1)

2873 ALISON FARRANT PRETTY WOMAN NOVICES' H'CAP CHASE (0-110) (5-Y.O+) (Class D)
2-15 (2-19) **2m 110y (13 fncs)** £3,517.50 (£1,065.00: £520.00: £247.50) GOING minus 0.20 sec per fur (G)

	Horse / details	Dist	Pos	SP	RR	SF
2670^{5}	**Indian Jockey (108)** (MCPipe) **5-11-10** DWalsh (j.w: mde all: easily)	—	**1**	6/1	124	31
1875^{3}	**Cracking Prospect (77)** (BRMillman) **6-9-12b1**$^{(5)}$ DSalter (hld up: hdwy 7th: chsd wnr fr 4 out: no imp)	8	**2**	5/1	85	2
2548^{2}	**Nordic Valley (IRE) (86)** (MCPipe) **6-10-12** CMaude (chsd wnr to 4th: lft 2nd 9th: btn whn hit 2 out)	1	**3**	7/2^{2}	93	10
1763^{6}	**October Brew (USA) (84)** (MCPipe) **7-10-3b**$^{(7)}$ GSupple (chsd wnr 4th tl blnd 9th: wkng whn mstke 4 out: t.o)	dist	**4**	9/1	—	—
1449^{U}	**Bishops Castle (IRE) (87)** (RGFrost) **9-10-13** JFrost (wl bhd fr 7th: t.o)	4	**5**	9/2^{3}	—	—
2036^{7}	**Madam Rose (IRE) (74)** (JWMullins) **7-10-0** SCurran (bhd: hmpd 2nd: t.o fr 7th)	dist	**6**	50/1	—	—
1596^{P}	**Baxworthy Lord (74)** (CLPopham) **6-10-0** GTormey (hld up: 5th & wkng whn fell 8th)		**F**	66/1	—	—
1787^{P}	**Ashley House (74)** (BRMillman) **8-10-0** BPowell (bhd: hmpd 2nd: t.o whn p.u bef 8th)		**P**	50/1	—	—
2569*	**Northern Singer (81)** (RJHodges) **7-10-4**$^{(3)}$ TDascombe (blnd & uns rdr 2nd)		**U**	3/1^{1}	—	—
				(SP 111.8%)		**9 Rn**

4m 6.0 (6.00) CSF £31.58 CT £107.76 TOTE £6.40: £2.70 £1.20 £1.70 (£40.70) Trio £41.70 OWNER Mr Stuart Mercer (WELLINGTON) BRED John Hayter
LONG HANDICAP Baxworthy Lord 9-0 Ashley House 9-0 Madam Rose (IRE) 9-0
WEIGHT FOR AGE 5yo-10lb

2670 Indian Jockey was reported to have schooled well and made an impressive start to his chasing career. (6/1: 3/1-13/2)
1875 Cracking Prospect dropped 3lb, was tried in blinkers over this shorter trip. (5/1)
2548 Nordic Valley (IRE) reverting to two miles, was not helped by clouting the second last in the battle for the runner-up spot. (7/2: op 9/4)

2874 MARTIN PIPE RACING IS THE LIFE NOVICES' H'CAP HURDLE (0-105) (4-Y.O+) (Class E)

2-45 (2-45) **2m 1f (9 hdls)** £2,253.00 (£633.00: £309.00) GOING minus 0.20 sec per fur (G)

	Horse	Dist	Pos	SP	RR	SF
2705[2]	**D'naan (IRE) (88)** (MCPipe) **4-10-7b** CMaude (mde virtually all: hrd rdn appr 2 out: all out)	—	1	100/30[2]	72	16
2818[2]	**Almapa (80)** (RJHodges) **5-10-8**(3) TDascombe (hld up: hdwy 3 out: ev ch last: nt qckn)	2	2	4/1[3]	62	18
2578[5]	**Ultimate Smoothie (97)** (MCPipe) **5-11-7**(7) GSupple (lw: hld up: hdwy 3 out: one pce fr 2 out)	8	3	3/1[1]	72	28
2806[10]	**Laughing Buccaneer (81)** (DNCarey) **4-10-0** BPowell (rn in snatches: wl bhd 4th: hdwy 5th: lost pl 6th: n.d after)	7	4	12/1	49	—
915[2]	**Lonicera (89)** (RHAlner) **7-11-3**(3) PHenley (plld hrd: chsd wnr: ev ch 3 out: wknd appr 2 out)	4	5	11/2	53	9
2680[14]	**Royal Glint (69)** (HEHaynes) **8-9-7**(7) MrLBaker (hld up: hrd rdn appr 6th: bhd fr 3 out)	13	6	12/1	21	—
2692[11]	**Nagara Sound (87)** (BPreece) **6-11-4** TJenks (hld up: hrd rdn appr 3 out: wknd appr 2 out)	2½	7	11/2	37	—
	Concinnity (USA) (69) (BScriven) **8-9-7**(7) MrOMcPhail (mstke 4th: t.o fr 5th)	22	8	33/1	—	—
				(SP 117.2%)		**8 Rn**

3m 58.5 (5.50) CSF £16.33 CT £40.05 TOTE £3.00: £1.60 £1.10 £1.70 (£9.20) OWNER Mrs P. B. Browne (WELLINGTON) BRED Blandford Bloodstock
LONG HANDICAP Royal Glint 9-10 Laughing Buccaneer 9-6 Concinnity (USA) 9-10
WEIGHT FOR AGE 4yo-12lb
2705 D'naan (IRE) suffers from a wind problem, but the way he battled on this occasion could not be faulted. (100/30)
2818 Almapa came with a dangerous-looking challenge but the winner would not be denied. (4/1)
2578 Ultimate Smoothie jumped better this time but his challenge failed to materialize. (3/1)
1908 Laughing Buccaneer was 8lb out of the handicap but gave the impression he may he be a bit of a monkey. (12/1: op 7/1)
915 Lonicera may have led briefly three from home. (11/2)
Royal Glint (12/1: 6/1-16/1)

2875 CHESTER BARNES 50TH BIRTHDAY 'N.H.' NOVICES' HURDLE (I) (4-Y.O+) (Class E)

3-15 (3-15) **2m 3f 110y (10 hdls)** £1,945.00 (£545.00: £265.00) GOING minus 0.20 sec per fur (G)

	Horse	Dist	Pos	SP	RR	SF
1870[P]	**Atavistic (IRE)** (CLPopham) **5-11-1**(3) TDascombe (lw: a.p: led 3 out: rdn out)	—	1	2/1[1]	72	10
1964[P]	**Over The Water (IRE)** (RHAlner) **5-11-1**(3) PHenley (chsd ldr: led 7th to 3 out: rdn & one pce fr 2 out)	9	2	33/1	65	3
1507[5]	**Charlie Parrot (IRE)** (MCPipe) **7-11-4** DWalsh (hld up: hdwy 5th: rdn appr 2 out: one pce)	3½	3	3/1[3]	62	—
2576[6]	**Brown Wren** (PJHobbs) **6-10-13** GTormey (hld up: sme hdwy 6th: nvr nr ldrs)	15	4	13/2	44	—
	Annie Ruth (IRE) (MrsJPitman) **6-10-10**(3) GHogan (bit bkwd: mstke 5th: sn bhd)	13	5	14/1	34	—
2655[4]	**Ashtar (USA)** (MCPipe) **7-11-4** CMaude (led: wl clr 4th: hdd 7th: wknd after 3 out)	1¾	6	9/4[2]	37	—
2656[P]	**Alice Shorelark** (SGKnight) **6-10-13** MrTGreed (bhd whn mstke 6th: sn t.o)	dist	7	66/1	—	—
1323[P]	**Sula's Dream** (GAHam) **8-10-10**(3) DFortt (a bhd: t.o fr 6th)	11	8	50/1	—	—
1329[17]	**Becky's Lad** (MrsDThomas) **7-11-1**(3) GuyLewis (a bhd: t.o fr 6th)	9	9	33/1	—	—
1200[P]	**Moreceva (IRE)** (PaddyFarrell) **7-11-4** WMarston (swtg: bhd: rdn after 5th: sn t.o)	1¾	10	33/1	—	—
				(SP 121.4%)		**10 Rn**

4m 41.7 (10.70) CSF £63.93 TOTE £2.60: £1.10 £3.70 £1.80 (£37.70) Trio £109.30; £30.81 to Chepstow 1/2/97 OWNER Mrs Mr Mr Jill Emery, Staple, Morris (TAUNTON) BRED S. Ross
1476 Atavistic (IRE), the paddock pick, bounced back after being highly tried when pulled up at Sandown last time. (2/1)
Over The Water (IRE) had taken a real walk in the market when pulled up on his debut. (33/1)
1283 Charlie Parrot (IRE) could not overhaul the runner-up let alone the winner. (3/1: 2/1-7/2)
Brown Wren, out of a staying chaser, may do better when tackling further. (13/2)

2876 DAVID JOHNSON CHALLENGER H'CAP CHASE (0-110) (5-Y.O+) (Class E)

3-45 (3-45) **3m (19 fncs)** £2,887.10 (£873.80: £426.40: £202.70) GOING minus 0.20 sec per fur (G)

	Horse	Dist	Pos	SP	RR	SF
2671*	**Banntown Bill (IRE) (97)** (MCPipe) **8-11-5v** 7x DWalsh (w ldr: led 6th: hit 7th: hdd 8th: rdn to ld 3 out: r.o wl)	—	1	3/1[1]	108	25
	Mozemo (84) (MCPipe) **10-10-6** CMaude (hld up: stdy hdwy 8th: led 13th to 3 out: sn btn)	11	2	7/2[2]	88	5
1839[F]	**Childhay Chocolate (102)** (PFNicholls) **9-11-10** RJohnson (led: hdd & hit 6th: hit 7th: led 8th to 13th: wknd 3 out)	6	3	6/1	102	19
2706[4]	**Cool Character (IRE) (78)** (RHBuckler) **9-10-0** BPowell (hdwy 10th: wknd 14th)	1½	4	13/2	77	—
1697[5]	**Steeple Jack (82)** (KBishop) **10-10-4** RGreene (t.o fr 5th)	dist	5	17/2	—	—
2708[6]	**Glen Mirage (90)** (MJCoombe) **12-10-12** MissMCoombe (bhd tl hdwy 11th: wknd qckly & p.u bef 14th)		P	6/1	—	—
1763[4]	**Glentower (IRE) (88)** (CLPopham) **9-10-10** GTormey (p.u lame after 5th)		P	5/1[3]	—	—
				(SP 116.3%)		**7 Rn**

6m 6.6 (9.60) CSF £13.49 TOTE £3.80: £2.50 £2.60 (£10.30) OWNER Mr Eric Scarth (WELLINGTON) BRED Thomas Conroy
LONG HANDICAP Cool Character (IRE) 9-8
2671* Banntown Bill (IRE) defied his penalty despite being only due to go up 5lb in future handicaps. (3/1: 5/2-4/1)
Mozemo, having his first run for his new stable, looked straight enough, but gave the impression he may have blown up once in line for home. (7/2)
1391 Childhay Chocolate, still 4lb higher than when winning at Southwell last May, at least got round in one piece. (6/1: op 4/1)
1877 Cool Character (IRE) was out of the handicap yet again. (13/2)

2877 MARTIN PIPE AM I THAT DIFFICULT? H'CAP HURDLE (0-110) (5-Y.O+) (Class E)

4-15 (4-15) **3m 110y (12 hdls)** £2,284.50 (£642.00: £313.50) GOING minus 0.20 sec per fur (G)

	Horse	Dist	Pos	SP	RR	SF
2659*	**Maid Equal (93)** (MCPipe) **6-10-4**(7) 7x GSupple (hld up: hdwy 5th: led 9th: rdn & r.o wl flat)	—	1	2/1[2]	79	48
2708[2]	**Mr Strong Gale (IRE) (88)** (PFNicholls) **6-10-6** RJohnson (hld up: hdwy 8th: ev ch last: hrd rdn: nt qckn)	1	2	Evens[1]	73	42
2570[8]	**Tiger Claw (USA) (82)** (AGHobbs) **11-10-0** RGreene (hld up: lost pl appr 9th: styd on fr 2 out: n.d)	19	3	20/1	55	24
2694[P]	**Batty's Island (82)** (BPreece) **8-9-7**(7) JMogford (prom tl wknd appr 2 out)	3	4	20/1	53	22
2570*	**Gunmaker (82)** (BJLlewellyn) **8-10-0** SCurran (prom: led after 7th to 9th: sn wknd: t.o)	29	5	13/2[3]	34	3
2659[P]	**Jadidh (87)** (ABarrow) **9-10-0v**(5) DSalter (lost pl 5th: t.o fr 8th)	2½	6	12/1	37	6
485[5]	**Passed Pawn (107)** (MCPipe) **10-11-11** CMaude (led tl after 7th: wknd qckly appr 8th: t.o whn p.u bef 2 out)		P	12/1	—	—
				(SP 121.6%)		**7 Rn**

5m 50.7 (-1.30) CSF £4.53 TOTE £3.10: £2.50 £1.10 (£2.00) OWNER Mr Heeru Kirpalani (WELLINGTON) BRED H. L. Kirpalani
LONG HANDICAP Gunmaker 9-10 Tiger Claw (USA) 9-12 Batty's Island 9-5
2659* Maid Equal was effectively on a 4lb lower mark here despite her penalty, and was due to go up a further 7lb in the ratings.(2/1)

2708 Mr Strong Gale (IRE) was already due to go up 4lb following his second last week. (Evens)
1876 Tiger Claw (USA) was effectively racing off a mark 1lb higher than when winning a seller at Huntingdon on his seasonal debut. (20/1)
Jadidh (12/1: 8/1-14/1)
Passed Pawn (12/1: op 8/1)

2878 CHESTER BARNES 50TH BIRTHDAY 'N.H.' NOVICES' HURDLE (II) (4-Y.O+) (Class E)

4-45 (4-46) **2m 3f 110y (10 hdls)** £1,934.50 (£542.00: £263.50) GOING minus 0.20 sec per fur (G)

				SP	RR	SF
1878[4]	**Millcroft Riviera (IRE) (82)** (RHAlner) **6-11-1**(3) PHenley (prom: mstke & lost pl 7th: rallied appr last: styd on to ld nr fin)	—	**1**	7/1	68	9
2549[2]	**Decyborg (FR)** (MCPipe) **6-11-4** CMaude (led: clr 2nd: rdn & hdd whn lft clr 2 out: ct nr fin)	2	**2**	13/2[3]	66	7
408*	**Miss Foxy (85)** (RGFrost) **7-11-5** JFrost (hld up: lost pl 7th: n.d after)	dist	**3**	8/1	—	—
	Lauren's Treasure (IRE) (80) (MrsSDWilliams) **6-11-4** WMcFarland (t.o whn mstke 6th)	¾	**4**	20/1	—	—
	Landsker Star (FGHollis) **7-10-8**(5) DSalter (bhd fr 6th: t.o)	14	**5**	66/1	—	—
1573[15]	**Mingay** (GrahamRichards) **6-10-11**(7) JPrior (mstke 1st: t.o fr 3rd)	29	**6**	100/1	—	—
1998[13]	**Zen Or (67)** (JWMullins) **6-10-6**(7) DavidTurner (bhd fr 6th)	27	**7**	66/1	—	—
2662[9]	**Sioux To Speak** (MissHCKnight) **5-11-4** JFTitley (chsd ldr: led & fell 2 out)		**F**	4/1[2]	—	—
2510[4]	**Mrs Em** (PFNicholls) **5-10-13** RJohnson (hld up: hdwy 6th: 2nd & ev ch whn fell 2 out)		**F**	10/11[1]	—	—
69[P]	**Rory'm (IRE)** (LWaring) **8-11-4** DLeahy (nt j.w: t.o 3rd: p.u bef 2 out)		**P**	100/1	—	—

(SP 119.1%) **10 Rn**

4m 42.0 (11.00) CSF £45.93 TOTE £9.70: £1.70 £1.10 £1.70 (£13.70) Trio £17.40 OWNER Mr John Carter (BLANDFORD) BRED J. S. Bellingham

1878 Millcroft Riviera (IRE), trying a longer trip, looked well held until the grief at the penultimate flight. (7/1: 4/1-15/2)
2549 Decyborg (FR), reverting to hurdles, looked booked for third until apparently being presented the race at the second last. (13/2)
408* Miss Foxy (8/1: 5/1-9/1)
1835 Sioux To Speak looked set for a good battle with the favourite when they both departed simultaneously. (4/1)
2510 Mrs Em was upsides Sioux To Speak with the race in the balance when disaster struck the pair of them. (10/11: 5/4-5/6)

T/Plpt: £43.00 (227.47 Tckts). T/Qdpt: £2.20 (326.01 Tckts) KH

2156-CHEPSTOW (L-H) (Good)
Saturday February 1st

WEATHER: unsettled

2879 BBC CEEFAX AND MARCIA-ANN COOPER H'CAP CHASE (0-135) (5-Y.O+) (Class C)

1-15 (1-17) **2m 3f 110y (16 fncs)** £7,555.00 (£2,290.00: £1,120.00: £535.00) GOING: 0.50 sec per fur (GS)

				SP	RR	SF
2660[3]	**Bells Life (IRE) (125)** (PJHobbs) **8-11-4** GTormey (j.w: hld up: hdwy 9th: led 3 out: clr 2 out: easily)	—	**1**	7/2[1]	140+	72
1682[5]	**Seek The Faith (USA) (107)** (MSheppard) **8-10-0** BPowell (hld up & bhd: hdwy appr 5 out: chsd wnr fr 2 out: no imp)	7	**2**	14/1	116	48
2072*	**Mariners Mirror (120)** (NATwiston-Davies) **10-10-13** MrMRimell (swtg: hld up: hdwy appr 5 out: led 4 out to 3 out: one pce)	3	**3**	11/2[2]	127	59
2065[3]	**Conti D'Estruval (FR) (115)** (GBBalding) **7-10-8** BClifford (hld up: hdwy 9th: one pce fr 3 out)	hd	**4**	10/1	122	54
1805[3]	**Denver Bay (119)** (JTGifford) **10-10-9**(3) LAspell (hld up & bhd: hdwy appr 5 out: one pce fr 3 out)	½	**5**	11/2[2]	125	57
2621[3]	**Senor El Betrutti (IRE) (133)** (MrsSusanNock) **8-11-12** CLlewellyn (no hdwy fr 5 out)	11	**6**	8/1	130	62
2657[P]	**Benjamin Lancaster (107)** (MAGriffin) **13-9-7**(7) MGriffiths (prom: hit 8th: sn wknd)	6	**7**	33/1	99	31
	General Pershing (135) (DNicholson) **11-12-0** RJohnson (bit bkwd: led to 8th: wknd appr 5 out)	1¾	**8**	12/1	126	58
1937[4]	**Terao (127)** (MCPipe) **11-11-6** TJMurphy (j.rt: plld hrd: hdwy 5th: led 8th to 4 out: sn wknd)	6	**9**	13/2[3]	113	45
1934[U]	**Bo Knows Best (IRE) (115)** (GLMoore) **8-10-8** CMaude (a bhd: t.o 5th: p.u bef 5 out)		**P**	25/1	—	—
2639[5]	**Sound Reveille (135)** (CPEBrooks) **9-11-7**(7) MBerry (lw: chsd ldr to 3rd: wknd 6th: bhd whn blnd & uns rdr 4 out)		**U**	12/1	—	—

(SP 115.4%) **11 Rn**

4m 57.2 (8.20) CSF £45.16 CT £241.41 TOTE £4.40: £1.80 £3.20 £1.90 (£33.30) Trio £63.60 OWNER Mr R. Gibbs (MINEHEAD) BRED Dr Welby Henry

LONG HANDICAP Benjamin Lancaster 9-4

2660 Bells Life (IRE) showed he does not necessarily have to have the ground on the soft side, with an emphatic win. This was his fourth course victory, and he will probably return here in a fortnight. (7/2)
1682 Seek The Faith (USA) got the longer distance well enough but is never one to find much off the bridle. (14/1)
2072* Mariners Mirror was by no means disgraced on this transition to handicap company. (11/2)
2065 Conti D'Estruval (FR) has slipped back down to a mark off which he won at Stratford last April. (10/1)
1805 Denver Bay had to contend with unusually fast ground by Chepstow's standards. (11/2)
General Pershing (12/1: op 8/1)

2880 PRESTIGE NOVICES' HURDLE (Gd 2) (5-Y.O+) (Class A)

1-45 (1-46) **3m (12 hdls)** £9,915.00 (£3,754.50: £1,839.75: £840.75) GOING: 0.50 sec per fur (GS)

				SP	RR	SF
2550*	**Young Kenny (107)** (PBeaumont) **6-11-0** RSupple (hld up & bhd: hdwy 8th: sn rdn: led 2 out: r.o wl)	—	**1**	11/2	103	58
2546*	**Korbell (IRE) (102)** (PFNicholls) **8-10-9** RJohnson (prom: rdn 6th: outpcd appr 4 out: rallied & swtchd lft appr last: nt qckn flat)	1¾	**2**	5/1[3]	97	52
1639[2]	**Menesonic (IRE) (106)** (RHAlner) **7-11-0** JCulloty (hld up: hdwy 4 out: one pce fr 2 out)	3	**3**	12/1	100	55
2550[3]	**Destin d'Estruval (FR)** (DNicholson) **6-11-0** DBridgwater (chsd ldr: led 7th: clr appr 4 out: hdd 2 out: one pce)	4	**4**	100/30[2]	97	52
1768[4]	**Warner For Players (IRE)** (PJHobbs) **6-11-0** CLlewellyn (lw: hld up: lost tch 8th: gd hdwy appr 4 out: 5th & btn whn mstke 2 out)	10	**5**	20/1	91	46
2662*	**Hurdante (IRE) (115)** (GBBalding) **7-11-0** BClifford (lw: hld up: hdwy 5th: hit 6th: wknd qckly 3 out)	8	**6**	3/1[1]	85	40
2666[9]	**Eulogy (IRE) (112)** (RRowe) **7-11-0** LAspell (led: hit 4th: hdd 7th: wknd appr 4 out: t.o)	22	**7**	12/1	71	26
2656*	**Scotby (BEL) (100)** (RHBuckler) **7-11-0** BPowell (hld up: hdwy 7th: wknd 4 out: t.o)	1¼	**8**	12/1	70	25
2576[2]	**Edgemoor Prince (108)** (PJHobbs) **6-11-3** CMaude (plld hrd: prom 7th: t.o)	12	**9**	14/1	65	20

1581[2] **Best of Friends (IRE) (100)** (MissHCKnight) **7-11-0** JFTitley (lw: a bhd: t.o fr 8th)..dist **10** 12/1 — —
(SP 122.3%) **10 Rn**

5m 53.3 (13.30) CSF £32.24 TOTE £6.40: £1.70 £1.70 £3.20 (£10.10) Trio £31.50 OWNER Mr J. G. Read (BRANDSBY) BRED Mowbray Properties Ltd

2550* Young Kenny continues to improve and is thought to be a potentially nice chaser for next season. (11/2)
2546* Korbell (IRE) again showed how well she stays, and one cannott help thinking she will really come into her own when put over fences. (5/1)
1639 Menesonic (IRE) should have little difficulty taking a run-of-the-mill staying novice hurdle. (12/1: op 8/1)
2550 Destin d'Estruval (FR) threw down the gauntlet entering the long home straight and may be more effective on softer ground. (100/30)
1768 Warner For Players (IRE) continues to disappoint. (20/1)
2662* Hurdante (IRE) did not appear to get the trip but it may be he requires more give underfoot. (3/1)

2881 JOHN HUGHES GRAND NATIONAL TRIAL H'CAP CHASE (7+) (Class B)
2-15 (2-16) **3m 5f 110y (22 fncs)** £10,201.50 (£3,087.00: £1,506.00: £715.50) GOING: 0.50 sec per fur (GS)

	Horse / details			SP	RR	SF
2659[P]	**Flyer's Nap (130)** (RHAlner) **11-11-7** DBridgwater (lw: hld up: hdwy 11th: led appr 5 out: sn clr: lft wl clr 2 out: eased flat)	—	**1**	11/1	141	46
2575[4]	**Sunley Bay (120)** (PFNicholls) **11-10-11** RJohnson (hld up: hit 6th: hdwy appr 12th: outpcd 15th: btn whn lft 2nd 2 out)	8	**2**	9/2[3]	126	31
2616[F]	**Full of Oats (120)** (MissHCKnight) **11-10-11** JCulloty (hld up: hdwy 15th: one pce fr 4 out)	3	**3**	13/8[1]	124	29
1784[2]	**Dakyns Boy (124)** (NATwiston-Davies) **12-11-1** CLlewellyn (led to 11th: outpcd appr 5 out: n.d after)	3½	**4**	7/2[2]	126	31
2575[P]	**Killeshin (133)** (HJManners) **11-11-10** SCurran (bhd: j.slowly 13th: t.o fr 17th)	29	**5**	16/1	118	23
2754[3]	**Spuffington (113)** (JTGifford) **9-10-1**(3) LAspell (lw: hld up: hdwy 11th: btn whn b.d 2 out)		**B**	11/2	—	—
2658[3]	**See Enough (110)** (RHBuckler) **9-10-1** SMcNeill (chsd ldr: led 11th tl appr 5 out: 2nd & btn whn fell 2 out)		**F**	10/1	—	—
2575[P]	**Distillation (109)** (GFEdwards) **12-9-11**(3) TDascombe (j.slowly 1st: sn bhd: t.o 15th: p.u bef 5 out)		**P**	100/1	—	—

(SP 118.2%) **8 Rn**

7m 43.9 (23.90) CSF £56.79 CT £113.62 TOTE £12.70: £3.70 £1.60 £1.10 (£21.00) OWNER Mr R. J. Tory (BLANDFORD) BRED R. J. and Mrs Tory
LONG HANDICAP Distillation 7-10

Flyer's Nap, back to a mark only 1lb higher than when he last won in April 1995, bounced back to form with a vengeance. He will be entered for the Astec Buzz Shop National Hunt Handicap Chase at Cheltenham, and could go for the Scottish National if the ground is not too fast. (11/1: 8/1-12/1)
2575 Sunley Bay was only battling it out for fourth place until the melee at the penultimate fence. (9/2)
1784 Full of Oats never really threatened to take a serious hand, and only finished in the money because of the misfortune of others. (13/8)
1784 Dakyns Boy has never scored on ground better than good to soft. (7/2)
2754 Spuffington was booked for third when brought down by the horse who would have been destined to finish runner-up. (11/2)
2658 See Enough has never won on ground better than soft and was clearly playing second fiddle when coming to grief. (10/1)

2882 POACHERS (S) H'CAP HURDLE (0-95) (4-Y.O+) (Class G)
2-50 (2-51) **2m 110y (8 hdls)** £2,192.00 (£612.00: £296.00) GOING: 0.50 sec per fur (GS)

	Horse / details			SP	RR	SF
2038[3]	**Scottish Wedding (75)** (TWall) **7-10-10** RJohnson (j.slowly 2nd: hdwy 4th: outpcd 3 out: hrd rdn & rallied appr last: led flat: r.o)	—	**1**	7/1[3]	60	22
1960[3]	**Fontanays (IRE) (89)** (GMMcCourt) **9-11-3**(7) RHobson (lw: hld up: hdwy appr 4 out: led 3 out: 4l clr whn blnd bdly last: hdd flat)	2	**2**	5/1[1]	72+	34
1946[3]	**Strike-a-Pose (76)** (BJLlewellyn) **7-10-11** MrJLLlewellyn (a.p: led 4th to 3 out: one pce)	2	**3**	14/1	57	19
2680[10]	**Hawanafa (75)** (JSMoore) **4-10-0b** SMcNeill (a.p: ev ch 3 out: one pce)	3½	**4**	20/1	53	5
2708[8]	**Urban Lily (77)** (RJHodges) **7-10-5b**(7) JHarris (a.p: ev ch 3 out: wknd appr last)	½	**5**	6/1[2]	54	16
2664[8]	**Lime Street Blues (IRE) (79)** (CPEBrooks) **6-10-7b**(7) MBerry (plld hrd: prom: ev ch whn mstke 3 out: sn wknd)	2½	**6**	6/1[2]	54	16
1993[4]	**Khatir (CAN) (78)** (MCPipe) **6-10-13v** CMaude (sn wl bhd: nvr nrr)	6	**7**	8/1	47	9
2567[5]	**Little Hooligan (80)** (RJHodges) **6-10-12**(3) TDascombe (j.slowly 2nd: hdwy 4 out: wknd 3 out)	2	**8**	6/1[2]	47	9
1390[6]	**Jonjas Chudleigh (78)** (RGFrost) **10-10-13** JFrost (sn wl bhd: nrst fin)	nk	**9**	10/1	45	7
1984[8]	**Never so Blue (IRE) (88)** (PBradley) **6-11-4**(5) SophieMitchell (swtg: prom to 3 out)	½	**10**	14/1	54	16
	Mick The Yank (IRE) (73) (HOliver) **7-10-1**(7) MrHOliver (bit bkwd: a bhd)	11	**11**	20/1	29	—
2567[6]	**Tee Tee Too (IRE) (75)** (AWCarroll) **5-10-3**(7) MGriffiths (prom: hrd rdn after 3rd: wknd 3 out)	4	**12**	16/1	27	—
2792[15]	**Wide Support (84)** (GLMoore) **12-11-5v**[1] NMann (j.slowly 2nd: sn bhd)	1	**13**	33/1	35	—
488[P]	**Anotherone to Note (67)** (HJManners) **6-9-9**(7)ow2 ADowling (plld hrd in rr: gd hdwy after 4th: mskte 4 out: sn wknd)	8	**14**	50/1	10	—
	Deep Isle (75) (BJLlewellyn) **11-10-10** RSupple (w ldr: led 3rd: hdd & mstke 4th: sn wknd)	6	**15**	33/1	12	—
2006[P]	**Bill and Win (65)** (TWall) **6-10-0v** RFarrant (bhd fr 4th: t.o)		**16**	50/1	—	—
	Gilbert (IRE) (65) (DNCarey) **9-10-0** BPowell (bkwd: led to 3rd: wknd qckly 4th: t.o whn p.u bef 2 out)		**P**	33/1	—	—

(SP 133.7%) **17 Rn**

4m 5.2 (16.20) CSF £39.57 CT £460.63 TOTE £8.00: £1.70 £1.10 £2.90 £5.30 (£21.90) Trio £103.90 OWNER G A Weetman, Reynolds & Dean (CHURCH STRETTON) BRED A. Goddard
LONG HANDICAP Hawanafa 9-7 Anotherone to Note 9-9 Bill and Win 9-12 Gilbert (IRE) 9-4
WEIGHT FOR AGE 4yo-10lb
Bt in 4,600 gns

2038 Scottish Wedding really responded to pressure but would have not prevailed without the favourite making a real hash of the final flight. (7/1)
1960 Fontanays (IRE), dropped in class, threw it away at the last and can be considered a winner without a penalty. (5/1)
1946 Strike-a-Pose, who had a run on the Flat last week, was dropping back to a more suitable trip over hurdles. (14/1)
Hawanafa, dropped in grade, ran a sound race from 7lb out of the handicap. (20/1)
2036 Urban Lily would probably have preferred more cut in the ground. (6/1)
1980 Lime Street Blues (IRE) did himself no favours by running too freely. (6/1)

2883 TONY PRESTON ASPIRING CHAMPIONS NOVICES' CHASE (5-Y.O+) (Class C)

3-20 (3-21) **3m (18 fncs)** £5,411.75 (£1,634.00: £794.50: £374.75) GOING: 0.50 sec per fur (GS)

Form	Horse / details	Dist	Pl	SP	RR	SF
1326P	**Tennessee Twist (IRE)** (MrsJPitman) **7-11-2** RFarrant (prom: outpcd 12th: rdn & rallied appr 5 out: led flat: drvn out)	—	1	13/2	128	53
2039*	**Indian Tracker** (MCPipe) **7-11-7** CMaude (j.w: led: clr 11th: pckd last: sn hdd: hrd rdn: nt qckn)	2	2	2/1 1	132	57
1503*	**Baronet (IRE) (115)** (DNicholson) **7-11-11** RJohnson (a.p: j.slowly 2nd: mstke 6th: rdn appr 5 out: wknd 3 out)	17	3	8/1	124	49
1909*	**Berude Not to (IRE)** (OSherwood) **8-11-11** JAMcCarthy (prom: j.rt 5th: rdn appr 5 out: wknd 4 out)	nk	4	100/30 2	124	49
1797*	**Credo Is King (IRE) (116)** (PRWebber) **7-11-7** AThornton (chsd ldr: blnd 4th: rdn appr 5 out: wknd qckly appr 3 out: t.o)	30	5	11/2 3	100	25
1936*	**Foodbroker Star (IRE)** (JTGifford) **7-11-8(3)** LAspell (no ch fr 12th: t.o)	24	6	6/1	88	13
2658 4	**Kendal Cavalier** (GBBalding) **7-11-2** BClifford (j.slowly 1st: a bhd: t.o fr 8th)	29	7	20/1	60	—
2551 4	**Penncaler (IRE)** (PJHobbs) **7-11-2** CLlewellyn (a bhd: t.o fr 8th)	dist	8	33/1	—	—
2681 10	**Oats N Barley (85)** (PRRodford) **8-11-2** BPowell (a bhd: t.o 11th: p.u bef 4 out)		P	40/1	—	—
1952P	**Major Nova (86)** (NASmith) **8-11-2** JRyan (a bhd: t.o 8th: p.u bef 13th)		P	50/1	—	—
1639 11	**Dextra (IRE)** (SEarle) **7-11-2** SCurran (a bhd: t.o 11th: p.u bef 4 out)		P	66/1	—	—
	Swift Pokey (DLWilliams) **7-11-2** MClarke (bit bkwd: a bhd: t.o 8th: p.u bef 12th)		P	66/1	—	—
				(SP 125.6%)	**12 Rn**	

6m 8.4 (15.40) CSF £19.36 TOTE £7.30: £1.80 £1.40 £2.10 (£10.80) Trio £27.40 OWNER Halewood International Ltd (UPPER LAMBOURN) BRED John Brophy

Tennessee Twist (IRE) is thought to be better on softer ground, but showed the right sort of attitude to collar the bold front-runner, and can go on from here. (13/2)
2039* Indian Tracker, strongly pressed when nodding at the final fence, lost no caste in defeat. (2/1)
1503* Baronet (IRE) could not live with the two principals over the last three obstacles. (8/1: op 5/1)
1909* Berude Not to (IRE) began to feel the strain jumping the final ditch. (100/30)
1797* Credo Is King (IRE) ran much better than his finishing position suggests. (11/2)

2884 GAMEKEEPERS H'CAP HURDLE (0-130) (4-Y.O+) (Class C)

3-55 (3-56) **2m 110y (8 hdls)** £3,715.50 (£1,119.00: £542.00: £253.50) GOING: 0.50 sec per fur (GS)

Form	Horse / details	Dist	Pl	SP	RR	SF
2777 9	**Kadastrof (FR) (128)** (RDickin) **7-11-5(7)** XAizpuru (chsd ldr: led 3rd: mstke 3 out: r.o wl)	—	1	12/1	112	67
1933*	**Ambleside (IRE) (112)** (MrsSDWilliams) **6-10-10** DBridgwater (prom: lost pl after 4th: rallied appr 2 out: r.o one pce)	3	2	11/10 1	93	48
	Doctoor (USA) (108) (MCPipe) **7-9-13(7)** BMoore (hld up: stdy hdwy fr 3 out: nvr plcd to chal)	hd	3	25/1	89+	44
2646 5	**Kibreet (118)** (PJHobbs) **10-11-2** RJohnson (a.p: ev ch 4 out: wknd appr last)	6	4	9/1	93	48
	Brave Tornado (125) (GBBalding) **6-11-9** BClifford (hdwy 4 out: one pce fr 3 out)	¾	5	20/1	99	54
2645 8	**Dreams End (130)** (PBowen) **9-12-0** RFarrant (hld up: hdwy after 4th: wknd appr 3 out)	8	6	16/1	97	52
1952P	**Pennymoor Prince (110)** (RGFrost) **8-10-8ow8** JFrost (nvr nr to chal)	1¼	7	40/1	76	23
2645 11	**Ros Castle (124)** (RJHodges) **6-11-1(7)** JHarris (nvr trbld ldrs)	1	8	20/1	89	44
1996 6	**Slew Man (FR) (120)** (MCPipe) **6-10-11(7)** GSupple (hld up: hdwy after 4th: wknd 4 out)	2½	9	16/1	82	37
1455 4	**Chaprassi (IRE) (121)** (MCPipe) **8-11-5** CMaude (lw: led to 3rd: hit 4th: wknd 4 out)	½	10	11/4 2	83	38
2670 10	**Manolete (102)** (MrsMerritaJones) **6-9-7(7)** MLane (a bhd: t.o)	12	11	33/1	52	7
1996 3	**Bell One (USA) (105)** (AJKDunn) **8-10-3** SMcNeill (prom to 3rd)	7	12	7/1 3	48	3
1933F	**Court Nap (IRE) (112)** (SMellor) **5-10-10** CLlewellyn (a bhd: t.o)	¾	13	14/1	54	9
1942*	**White Willow (125)** (TWall) **8-11-6v(3)** RMassey (a bhd: t.o)	7	14	16/1	61	16
				(SP 147.5%)	**14 Rn**	

3m 58.5 (9.50) CSF £27.94 CT £382.01 TOTE £14.30: £3.40 £1.40 £9.90 (£22.90) Trio £176.90 OWNER Mr A. P. Paton (STRATFORD) BRED Roland Lepeau in France

LONG HANDICAP Manolete 9-7 Pennymoor Prince 9-9

STEWARDS' ENQUIRY Moore susp. 10-13/2/97 (failure to ensure best possible placing).

1933 Kadastrof (FR) turned around last month's Lingfield form with Ambleside with the aid of his rider's allowance. (12/1: op 8/1)
1933* Ambleside (IRE) was surprisingly strongly supported in the ring on ground not soft enough for him. (11/10: 3/1-evens)
Doctoor (USA), off the course for the best part of three years, looked straight enough and should have won this. His rider gave the impression rigor mortis had set in and was suspended for four days for not obtaining the best possible placing. No doubt the Handicapper will take note. (25/1)
2646 Kibreet was reverting to timber off a mark considerably lower than his chasing rating. (9/1)
Brave Tornado fared reasonably well on his comeback especially when considering he needs the mud. (20/1)
1288* Dreams End does not seem to find it easy to carry big weights. (16/1)

T/Jkpt: Not won; £10,846.01 to Newcastle 3/2/97. T/Plpt: £74.00 (307.66 Tckts). T/Qdpt: £18.60 (48.63 Tckts). KH

2404-SANDOWN (R-H) (Chases Good to firm, Hdles Good, Gd to firm bk st)

Saturday February 1st

WEATHER: Cold

2885 SCILLY ISLES NOVICES' CHASE (Gd 1) (5-Y.O+) (Class A)

12-45 (12-45) **2m 4f 110y (17 fncs)** £23,881.60 (£8,275.60: £4,052.80) GOING: 0.20 sec per fur (G)

Form	Horse / details	Dist	Pl	SP	RR	SF
1869*	**Stately Home (IRE) (126)** (PBowen) **6-11-6** NWilliamson (j.w: mde all: clr 3rd: pckd 12th: hrd rdn appr last: r.o wl)	—	1	5/1 3	141	22
2641*	**Land Afar (140)** (PRWebber) **10-11-6** JOsborne (lw: hld up: lft 2nd 13th: ev ch 3 out: unable qckn fr 2 out)	1½	2	11/4 2	140	21
1987 4	**Amber Valley (USA) (97)** (DLWilliams) **6-11-6** AThornton (lw: a bhd: t.o fr 11th)	dist	3	66/1	—	—
2638*	**Simply Dashing (IRE) (135)** (TDEasterby) **6-11-6** RDunwoody (chsd wnr tl fell 13th)		F	5/6 1	—	—
2691F	**Grooving (IRE)** (JTGifford) **8-11-6** PNiven (3rd whn fell 12th)		F	12/1	—	—
2641 2	**Mister Drum (IRE) (124)** (MJWilkinson) **8-11-6** WMarston (3rd whn fell 1st)		F	14/1	—	—
				(SP 113.7%)	**6 Rn**	

5m 16.3 (17.30) CSF £18.13 TOTE £5.90: £2.40 £1.60 (£7.10) OWNER Mr P. Bowen (HAVERFORDWEST) BRED Ash Hill Stud

1869* Stately Home (IRE) showed his liking for this course in no uncertain terms in December, and again appeared to enjoy himself. Despite taking a step up in class, he stormed off in front and gave a fine exhibition of jumping, his only mistake coming when pecking at the sixth last. His task was greatly helped as three of his rivals came to grief, but he was given a severe test by Land Afar. He proved far more resolute than that rival though and kept on well up the hill. This is his trip and he will now go for the Cathcart at the Festival. (5/1)
2641* Land Afar has never won over this trip but he did see it out. After being on level terms with the winner jumping the Pond Fence three out, appearing to be traveling well, he was asked for his effort at the next and, as usual, failed to produce the goods. He has to do it on the bridle but that is very difficult against such rivals. His record for the season is now four seconds from six starts which says it all. (11/4)
1987 Amber Valley (USA) was out of his depth here but did at least complete in his own time to pick up a valuable third prize. (66/1)
2638* Simply Dashing (IRE) had jumped well and had still not been asked any sort of question in second place, when capsizing at the fifth last. He is still very much Cheltenham material and must have a very good chance if the ground remains sound. (5/6: 8/11-evens)
2691 Grooving (IRE), who would have preferred some cut in the ground, had jumped alright until coming to grief at the second of the railway fences, five out. He has now fallen on three of his four starts over fences. (12/1)
2641 Mister Drum (IRE) (14/1: op 7/1)

2886 AGFA HURDLE (5-Y.O+) (Class B)

1-20 (1-20) **2m 110y (8 hdls)** £10,162.50 (£3,075.00: £1,500.00: £712.50) GOING: 0.20 sec per fur (G)

	Horse	Dist	Pos	SP	RR	SF
	Double Symphony (IRE) (128) (CPEBrooks) **9-10-4** JOsborne (hld up: swtchd lft appr last: led flat: pushed out)	—	1	13/2 3	102	41
2645 5	**Chief's Song (135)** (SDow) **7-11-4** RDunwoody (chsd ldr: led 2 out tl flat: unable qckn)	5	2	10/11 1	111	50
1510 5	**Ground Nut (IRE) (124)** (RHBuckler) **7-11-0** PHolley (lw: led: mstke 4th: hdd 2 out: ev ch last: sn wknd)	4	3	10/1	103	42
	Florid (USA) (CPEBrooks) **6-10-9** GBradley (lw: plld hrd: hld up: shkn up appr 2 out: sn wknd)	21	4	7/2 2	78+	17
2781 4	**Ionio (USA) (118)** (MrsVCWard) **6-11-0** JRKavanagh (lw: a bhd: t.o fr 4th)	6	5	11/1	77	16
2668 7	**Daunt** (FJordan) **5-10-9** AThornton (a bhd: t.o)	dist	6	16/1	—	—
				(SP 111.2%)	**6 Rn**	

3m 56.8 (5.80) CSF £12.04 TOTE £5.30: £1.80 £1.30 (£3.90) OWNER Mr Anthony Pye-Jeary (LAMBOURN) BRED J. H. Kidd
OFFICIAL EXPLANATION **Daunt: was reported to have lost a front shoe.**
Florid (USA): gurgled during the race.
Double Symphony (IRE), a very useful hurdler and chaser in Ireland, was switched back to hurdles on this first run for her new stable. Despite not having conditions in her favour - she goes well with some cut and had never won on ground better than good - she put up a very impressive display and needed only to be shaken up to gain control early on the run-in. This run will have done her a lot of good and she will revert to fences for the Game Spirit Chase at Newbury next Saturday, before a crack at the Queen Mother Champion Chase. She looks set to make her mark in this country. (13/2)
2645 Chief's Song had been reportedly working well at home, and raced in second place until gaining control two out. Despite his pilot working hard, he was overhauled on the run-in. A useful individual who has won six times, he has yet to win on ground worse than good. (10/11)
1510 Ground Nut (IRE) adopted his usual front-running role and took the field along to the second last. Refusing to give way, he was only brushed aside on the run-in. This was a sound effort especially considering that the ground was probably too lively for him. Given some cut and a step up to two and a half, he should soon open his account for the season. (10/1: 6/1-11/1)
Florid (USA), a useful Flat performer who won a conditions race for Henry Cecil at Newmarket last May, was certainly pitched in at the deep end on this hurdling debut. Looking very well for this first run in three months, he took a very keen hold indeed in behind the leaders and, not surprisingly, his earlier antics caused him to drop away in the straight. He reportedly gurgled and next time he runs his tongue will be tied. This run is best forgotten and he should have little trouble in finding a race. (7/2: 2/1-9/2)
2781 Ionio (USA) looks one to avoid. (11/1: 6/1-12/1)
2668 Daunt has been a complete waste of money for connections. (16/1)

2887 AGFA DIAMOND H'CAP CHASE (Gd 2) (5-Y.O+) (Class A)

1-50 (1-52) **3m 110y (22 fncs)** £24,058.80 (£7,081.20) GOING: 0.20 sec per fur (G)

	Horse	Dist	Pos	SP	RR	SF
2623*	**Dextra Dove (137)** (SEarle) **10-11-2** NWilliamson (lw: hld up: reminder 4th: lft 2nd 11th: reminder 15th: led 16th: lft clr 2 out: rdn out)	—	1	8/1	145	23
1917 3	**Northern Hide (127)** (MSalaman) **11-10-6** PHolley (lw: led after 1st to 16th: ev ch 3 out: rdn: unable qckn)	2½	2	12/1	133	11
1649*	**Coome Hill (IRE) (147)** (WWDennis) **8-11-12** JOsborne (lw: 2nd whn fell 2nd)		F	11/4 1	—	—
1789 2	**Major Summit (IRE) (134)** (JTGifford) **8-10-13** PHide (lw: led tl after 1st: mstke 10th: lft 2nd 18th: ev ch 3 out: fell 2 out: dead)		F	4/1	—	—
2057*	**Go Ballistic (135)** (JGMO'Shea) **8-11-0** RDunwoody (hld up: mstke 7th: blnd 17th: 2nd whn fell 18th)		F	3/1 2	—	—
2636 3	**Avro Anson (143)** (MJCamacho) **9-11-8** PNiven (w ldr 5th tl blnd & uns rdr 11th)		U	100/30 3	—	—
				(SP 113.5%)	**6 Rn**	

6m 21.1 (19.10) CSF £73.21 TOTE £9.20: £2.70 £4.20 (£40.80) OWNER Dextra Lighting Systems (STURMINSTER NEWTON) BRED G. H. and Mrs V. E. Price
2623* Dextra Dove loves this ground but he does take the mickey out of his rider and Williamson was giving him a reminder as early as the fourth. At least he stayed on his feet, which is more than can be said for his rivals, and the fatal fall of Major Summit, when about a length down at the second last, handed him the race on a plate. In the end this valuable event took little winning. He might not run again before the Grand National as his trainer wants him to be fresh. (8/1: 6/1-9/1)
1917 Northern Hide cut out most of the running until the water jump, seven out. Still in with every chance jumping the Pond Fence, he was then tapped for toe. He appeared to stay this trip well enough. (12/1: op 8/1)
2057* Go Ballistic has done all his winning over fences at Ascot on fast ground, and made a bad mistake at the first of the Railway Fences, six out. With those fences coming so close it is often hard for a horse to correct himself before the next fence, and that's what happened here as he capsized at the next. (3/1)

2888 TOTE BOOKMAKERS SANDOWN H'CAP HURDLE (Gd 3) (4-Y.O+) (Class A)

2-25 (2-27) **2m 6f (11 hdls)** £27,700.00 (£10,495.00: £5,147.50: £2,357.50) GOING: 0.20 sec per fur (G)

	Horse	Dist	Pos	SP	RR	SF
1441*	**Tullymurry Toff (IRE) (127)** (JMJefferson) **6-10-12**(3) ECallaghan (a.p: led appr 2 out: hung rt flat: rdn out)	—	1	7/2 2	113	54
1870*	**Yahmi (IRE) (124)** (JABOld) **7-10-12** JOsborne (a.p: ev ch 2 out: 2nd & btn whn n.m.r nr fin)	1¾	2	100/30 1	109	50
2078 4	**Outset (IRE) (124)** (MDHammond) **7-10-9**(3) MrCBonner (led to 3rd: led 5th tl appr 2 out: one pce)	3½	3	16/1	106	47
2702 2	**Erzadjan (IRE) (128)** (MrsMReveley) **7-11-2** PNiven (rdn & hdwy appr 2 out: r.o one pce)	½	4	5/1 3	110	51
1915*	**Tarrs Bridge (IRE) (121)** (CJMann) **6-10-9b** JRailton (a.p: rdn appr last: one pce)	1¾	5	13/2	102	43

				SP	RR	SF
1906[2]	**Runaway Pete (USA) (124)** (MCPipe) **7-10-12** RDunwoody (lw: w ldr: led 3rd to 5th: rdn 3 out: wknd appr 2 out)	2	**6**	9/1	103	44
2625[4]	**Tim (IRE) (115)** (JRJenkins) **7-10-3** PHide (hdwy 6th: mstke 7th: wknd appr 2 out)	½	**7**	16/1	94	35
1522[W]	**Fired Earth (IRE) (130)** (JRFanshawe) **9-11-4** NWilliamson (bit bkwd: a mid div)	hd	**8**	12/1	109	50
1645[2]	**Burnt Imp (USA) (131)** (GMMoore) **7-11-5** JCallaghan (a bhd)	14	**9**	20/1	100	41
2545[2]	**Lochnagrain (IRE) (124)** (MrsMReveley) **9-10-9**(3) GLee (hdwy 4th: wknd 3 out)	2½	**10**	12/1	91	32
2603a[16]	**Express Gift (136)** (MrsMReveley) **8-11-10** NSmith (mstke 6th: hdwy 3 out: wknd appr 2 out)	11	**11**	33/1	95	36
1019[6]	**Mr Kermit (125)** (AJWilson) **6-10-13** LHarvey (bhd fr 4th)	½	**12**	25/1	83	24
2659[8]	**Lansdowne (124)** (PFNicholls) **9-10-7**(5) OBurrows (lw: bhd fr 6th)	5	**13**	25/1	79	20
				(SP 127.8%)	**13 Rn**	

5m 20.0 (7.00) CSF £14.97 CT £160.81 TOTE £5.20: £2.30 £2.30 £3.90 (£12.60) Trio £121.40 OWNER Mr John H Wilson and Mr J H Riley (MALTON) BRED Con Troy and David Fenton

1441* Tullymurry Toff (IRE) continues to do everything that is asked of him. Facing his stiffest task to date, he gained control just before the second last and already had the measure of the runner-up when cutting right across him in the closing stages. The Coral Cup at the Festival is very much on the cards for this progressive individual, who is yet to win on ground worse than good. (7/2)

1870* Yahmi (IRE), a much better performer this season, threw down his challenge in the straight but was second best when slightly tightened up by the winner in the closing stages. He loves this ground but would prefer three miles. (100/30)

2078 Outset (IRE) ran better here and moved to the front at halfway. Collared approaching the second last, he could only go up and down in the same place. (16/1)

2702 Erzadjan (IRE), 10lb higher than when last successful, is not the easiest of rides, but with his jockey bustling away at him he stayed on in the straight to be nearest at the line. (5/1)

1915* Tarrs Bridge (IRE) had far more on his plate in this very competitive event but appeared to be cruising early in the straight. Once asked for his effort between the last two hurdles, he failed to find another gear. (13/2)

1906 Runaway Pete (USA), who disputed the lead to halfway, was eventually done with going to the second last. He loves this ground but has never won off a mark as high as this. (9/1)

2889 RIPLEY HURDLE (4-Y.O) (Class C)

3-00 (3-01) **2m 110y (8 hdls)** £3,517.50 (£1,065.00: £520.00: £247.50) GOING: 0.20 sec per fur (G)

				SP	RR	SF
	Hayaain (KCBailey) **4-10-10** JRailton (hld up: led appr 2 out: sn clr: r.o wl)	—	**1**	8/1	82+	30
2668[4]	**Northern Fleet** (MrsAJPerrett) **4-11-0** GBradley (lw: hdwy 5th: hrd rdn appr 2 out: chsd wnr fr last: no imp)	9	**2**	2/1[1]	77	25
1953*	**Name of Our Father (USA)** (PBowen) **4-11-4** DWalsh (lw: a.p: led 5th tl appr 2 out: wknd appr last)	6	**3**	12/1	76	24
1872[6]	**Go With The Wind** (CWeedon) **4-11-0** MRichards (hld up: 4th whn mstke 3 out: sn wknd)	4	**4**	33/1	68	16
1776[6]	**Belmarita (IRE)** (GAHubbard) **4-10-9** NWilliamson (lw: chsd ldr: led 4th to 5th: wknd appr 2 out)	5	**5**	12/1	58	6
	Silvretta (IRE) (JTGifford) **4-10-5** PHide (a bhd)	10	**6**	7/1	44	—
1900[2]	**Society Magic (USA)** (CJMann) **4-11-0** RDunwoody (mstke 5th: hdwy 3 out: wknd appr 2 out)	nk	**7**	3/1[2]	53	1
2772[P]	**Macmorris (USA)** (DRCElsworth) **4-11-0b1** PHolley (lw: led: clr 3rd: swvd bdly lft & hdd 4th: sn wknd: t.o whn fell 2 out)		**F**	14/1	—	—
	Heart (MissHCKnight) **4-10-5** JOsborne (lw: hdwy 3 out: wknd appr 2 out: t.o whn p.u bef last)		**P**	9/2[3]	—	—
2622[12]	**Magic Role** (JRJenkins) **4-11-0** WMarston (hld up: 4th whn blnd 3rd: wknd 5th: t.o whn p.u bef last)		**P**	50/1	—	—
				(SP 127.1%)	**10 Rn**	

4m 0.5 (9.50) CSF £24.95 TOTE £10.00: £2.00 £1.30 £2.60 (£20.60) Trio £80.60 OWNER Quicksilver Racing Partnership (UPPER LAMBOURN) BRED Shadwell Estate Company Limited

Hayaain, who won a maiden at Bath for Dick Hern before disappointing twice, made a winning start to his hurdling career. Despite being off the track for six and a half months, he could not have made a better start to his hurdling career, leading at the second last and soon forging clear for a decisive win. This race was not as strongly contested as it has been in the past. (8/1: op 3/1)

2668 Northern Fleet, under vigorous driving entering the straight, stayed on to take second place jumping the last but had no hope of reeling in the winner. He is better served by this fast ground but needs further. (2/1)

1953* Name of Our Father (USA) had more to do here under a penalty, but nevertheless showed up in front soon after halfway. Collared approaching the second last, he was quickly beaten. (12/1: op 8/1)

1872 Go With The Wind ran a bit better here but he made a mistake three out and was soon a spent force. (33/1)

1776 Belmarita (IRE) showed in front briefly at halfway, but had been brushed aside turning for home. (12/1)

Heart, a maiden on the Flat for Michael Stoute, was sold for 17,000 guineas. Moving up nicely three from home, she tamely dropped away entering the straight, being pulled up before the last. (9/2: 9/4-5/1)

2890 ELMBRIDGE H'CAP CHASE (5-Y.O+) (Class B)

3-30 (3-32) **2m (13 fncs)** £6,938.90 (£1,950.40: £952.70) GOING: 0.20 sec per fur (G)

				SP	RR	SF
	Certainly Strong (IRE) (135) (DNicholson) **7-10-3**ow3 RDunwoody (mde all: blnd 2nd: clr appr last: rdn out)	—	**1**	9/4[1]	140	36
2618*	**Wee River (IRE) (132)** (GMMoore) **8-10-0** JCallaghan (lw: chsd wnr fr 6th: rdn appr 2 out: unable qckn)	3	**2**	5/2[2]	134	33
2645[2]	**Gales Cavalier (IRE) (159)** (DRGandolfo) **9-11-13** JOsborne (chsd wnr to 6th: lost pl appr 3 out: one pce)	4	**3**	3/1[3]	157	56
2621*	**Super Tactics (IRE) (135)** (RHAlner) **9-10-0**(3) PHenley (lw: 3rd whn fell 3rd)		**F**	7/2	—	—
				(SP 106.6%)	**4 Rn**	

3m 57.6 (6.60) CSF £7.18 TOTE £2.50 (£4.80) OWNER Mr Nick Skelton (TEMPLE GUITING) BRED Patrick Moakley in Ireland
LONG HANDICAP Wee River (IRE) 9-10 Certainly Strong (IRE) 9-9

Certainly Strong (IRE) won two Grade Two novice chases last season, and was being prepared for the Arkle when splitting a cannon bone, which had to be pinned, on the gallops. Looking very fit for this first run in just over a year, she forged clear at the second last for a convincing victory. The Grand Annual is a possibility at Cheltenham. (9/4)

2618* Wee River (IRE), 4lb out of the handicap, moved into second at halfway but, try as he might, found the winner too strong over the last two fences. (5/2)

2645 Gales Cavalier (IRE), reverting to fences, despite being on a very attractive mark over hurdles, really does need two and a half and so it was absolutely no surprise as he got outpaced turning for home. Try as he might, he could never really get back into it. Over a more suitable trip, he can open his account for the season. (3/1)

2891 FEBRUARY MAIDEN HURDLE (5-Y.O+) (Class D)

4-05 (4-07) **2m 6f (11 hdls)** £3,087.00 (£936.00: £458.00: £219.00) GOING: 0.20 sec per fur (G)

				SP	RR	SF
1962[P]	**El Freddie (90)** (JABOld) **7-11-7** LHarvey (lost pl appr 6th: rallied 7th: w ldr appr 2 out: led flat: r.o wl)	—	**1**	9/2[2]	71	47
2690[8]	**Physical Fun (78)** (AGBlackmore) **6-11-4**(3) PHenley (lw: hld up: led appr 2 out to flat: unable qckn)	1¼	**2**	13/2	70	46

1639[5] **Riding Crop (IRE)** (NJHenderson) **7-11-7** PNiven (led tl appr 2 out: sn wknd)....23 **3** 2/1[1] 53 29
Camera Man (NJHenderson) **7-11-7** JRKavanagh (lw: nvr nr to chal)....20 **4** 7/1 39 15
1551[5] **Arctic Triumph** (MBradstock) **6-11-7** PHolley (mstke 6th: prom tl appr 2 out)....1 **5** 10/1 38 14
1795[4] **Red Bronze (IRE)** (CRBarwell) **6-11-7** GBradley (hdwy 7th: wknd appr 2 out: t.o)....15 **6** 12/1 27 3
1550[4] **Lord Khalice (IRE)** (GAHubbard) **6-11-0**(7) NRossiter (prom to 3 out: t.o)....½ **7** 16/1 27 3
2620[2] **Blazing Miracle (70)** (MrsRGHenderson) **5-10-11**(5) DSalter (a bhd: t.o fr 7th)....21 **8** 20/1 7 —
2642[5] **Country Tarquin** (RJHodges) **5-11-7** RDunwoody (lw: prom to 8th: t.o)....3½ **9** 11/2[3] 9 —
(SP 120.2%) **9 Rn**

5m 23.6 (10.60) CSF £32.23 TOTE £6.10: £1.90 £1.80 £1.70 (£22.20) Trio £14.60 OWNER Mr Martin Lovatt (WROUGHTON)
IN-FOCUS: This looked a very poor event by Sandown standards.
1536 El Freddie left his poor run at Folkestone well behind. Having a protracted battle with the leader over the last two hurdles, he eventually got on top on the run-in. (9/2: 9/4-5/1)
2690 Physical Fun really came into his own over this much longer trip. Gaining a slender advantage approaching the second last, he had a ding-dong battle with the winner, but just found that rival too good on the run-in. (13/2: 12/1-6/1)
1639 Riding Crop (IRE) took the field along but, collared approaching the second last, was soon left for dead. A drop in distance may well be needed. (2/1)
Camera Man, off the track for nearly fourteen months, was tailed off in the back straight but plodded on past beaten horses, although never threatening to get back into the picture. (7/1: 6/1-9/1)
1551 Arctic Triumph failed to see out this much longer trip and was very tired entering the straight. (10/1)
2642 Country Tarquin (11/2: op 3/1)

T/Plpt: £1,090.70 (21.36 Tckts). T/Qdpt: £191.90 (6.82 Tckts) AK

2239-STRATFORD-ON-AVON (L-H) (Good)
Saturday February 1st
WEATHER: Dull & cold

2892 MERRY HILL SHOPPING CENTRE NOVICES' CHASE (5-Y.O+) (Class E)
1-05 (1-05) **2m 1f 110y (13 fncs)** £2,875.75 (£871.00: £425.50: £202.75) GOING: 0.25 sec per fur (GS)

SP RR SF

Eudipe (FR) (MCPipe) **5-11-11** SWynne (j.w: a.p: chsd ldr fr 7th: led appr 2 out: sn clr: canter)....— **1** 4/9[1] 128++ 51
2691[F] **Blair Castle (IRE)** (GBBalding) **6-11-2** BFenton (chsd ldrs: styd on to go 2nd flat: no ch w wnr)....12 **2** 9/1[3] 99 31
1386[4] **Clifton Game** (MRChannon) **7-11-2** DGallagher (led after 3rd: sn clr: wknd & hdd appr 2 out: btn whn hit last)....4 **3** 7/2[2] 95 27
2068* **Stage Player (89)** (MissCJECaroe) **11-11-8** ILawrence (bit bkwd: bhd: reminders 3rd: nvr nr to chal)....25 **4** 16/1 79 11
1633[12] **The Secret Grey** (DMcCain) **6-11-2** TJenks (a in rr: t.o)....2 **5** 100/1 71 3
2691[8] **Warspite** (PMooney) **7-10-11**(5) SRyan (chsd ldrs: mstke 3rd: sn lost tch: t.o)....dist **6** 100/1 — —
2657[P] **Kino's Cross (95)** (AJWilson) **8-10-13**(3) GHogan (mid div: reminders 5th: fell 7th).... **F** 33/1 — —
2574[P] **Woodlands Energy** (PAPritchard) **6-10-11** RBellamy (a bhd: t.o whn p.u bef 4 out).... **P** 200/1 — —
1062[P] **Win a Hand** (BJMRyall) **7-10-11** RGreene (bkwd: blnd & uns rdr 2nd).... **U** 100/1 — —
2778[3] **Curragh Peter (72)** (MrsPBickerton) **10-10-13**(3) GuyLewis (nt j.w: led tl after 3rd: pckd 7th: bhd whn blnd & uns rdr last).... **U** 33/1 — —
(SP 116.7%) **10 Rn**

4m 18.3 (9.30) CSF £5.05 TOTE £1.60: £1.20 £1.10 £1.20 (£4.10) Trio £10.80 OWNER Mr D. A. Johnson (WELLINGTON) BRED Mme Andre & Bruno Vagne
WEIGHT FOR AGE 5yo-9lb
Eudipe (FR), a useful recruit from France with winning form on the Flat, over hurdles, and over fences, was never out of a canter to win this poor event, but he showed that he can jump, and will have a choice of engagements at the Festival. (4/9)
Blair Castle (IRE) succeeded in getting round this time, but he is still short of peak fitness and the experience should not be lost. (9/1)
1386 Clifton Game tried hard to get the winner off the bridle with a brave attempt at front-running, but he only succeeded in beating himself. He has got the hang of the game now and will surely find easier opportunities. (7/2)

2893 E.B.F. 'N.H.' (QUALIFIER) NOVICES' HURDLE (5, 6 & 7-Y.O) (Class E)
1-35 (1-38) **2m 110y (9 hdls)** £2,253.00 (£633.00: £309.00) GOING: 0.68 sec per fur (S)

SP RR SF

1926* **King of Camelot (IRE)** (DNicholson) **7-10-11**(3) RMassey (hld up: 2nd whn blnd 4th: led appr 3 out: sn clr: easily)....— **1** 2/5[1] 72+ —
971[9] **Winter Rose (76)** (MissPMWhittle) **6-10-7**(7) KHibbert (bit bkwd: set slow pce tl appr 3 out: kpt on appr last: no ch w wnr)....4 **2** 5/1[2] 68 —
1583[8] **Freno (IRE)** (KCBailey) **6-11-0** WMcFarland (bit bkwd: hld up & bhd: mstke 5th: hdwy next: one pce fr 2 out).5 **3** 6/1[3] 63 —
Elgintorus (IRE) (CJMann) **7-10-11**(3) JMagee (prom tl rdn & wknd after 3 out: sn btn)....8 **4** 100/1 56 —
Cumberland Youth (MissCJECaroe) **6-11-0** ILawrence (bkwd: hld up: hdwy 5th: outpcd after next: t.o: p.u bef 2 out).... **P** 100/1 — —
(SP 104.4%) **5 Rn**

4m 12.4 (25.40) CSF £2.26 TOTE £1.40: £1.00 £4.20 (£1.90) OWNER Mr Jerry Wright (TEMPLE GUITING) BRED Louis Vambeck
1926* King of Camelot (IRE) was certainly not helped by such a slow pace being set on this hurdling debut. He all but paid the penalty when standing off too far at the fourth flight, but in such a weak contest he was always running away and came home at his own leisure. (2/5: op 1/4)
718 Winter Rose, who has been pitted against handicap company in his last couple of races, gave the winner a lead from halfway but was fighting a lost cause from the turn into the straight and is flattered to finish so close. (5/1: op 8/1)
Freno (IRE), still carrying surplus condition after two months on the sidelines, showed a glimpse of form and should continue to progress. (6/1: op 7/2)

2894 A.H.P. TRAILERS WOMBOURNE H'CAP CHASE (0-125) (5-Y.O+) (Class D)
2-05 (2-05) **2m 5f 110y (16 fncs)** £3,582.50 (£1,085.00: £530.00: £252.50) GOING: 0.25 sec per fur (GS)

SP RR SF

2762[U] **Distinctive (IRE) (97)** (MJWilkinson) **8-10-6** ILawrence (lw: j.w: a.w ldrs: led 10th: clr appr 2 out: rdn out)....— **1** 4/1[1] 107 34
2644[10] **Seod Rioga (IRE) (110)** (SMellor) **8-11-2**(3) DFortt (led 3rd to 10th: hrd rdn appr last: r.o)....1¾ **2** 8/1[3] 119 46

1769P	**Over the Pole (107)** (PRChamings) **10-11-2** TJenks (bit bkwd: j.w: a.p: one pce fr 2 out)....5	3	16/1	112	39
2092P	**Celtino (97)** (CaptTAForster) **9-10-6** SWynne (hld up: hdwy 11th: rdn appr 2 out: nvr able to chal)....2½	4	7/1 2	100	27
1731F	**Merry Panto (IRE) (100)** (CPEBrooks) **8-10-9** DGallagher (hld up & bhd: hdwy 11th: j.slowly next: mstke 4 out: sn btn)....10	5	4/1 1	96	23
1951P	**Scotoni (95)** (RJO'Sullivan) **11-10-4** DO'Sullivan (led to 3rd: mstke 6th: lost pl 9th: t.o)....16	6	12/1	79	6
2665P	**Royal Square (CAN) (95)** (NPLittmoden) **11-10-4** MrDVerco (bit bkwd: prom: mstke & rdn 4th: wknd 9th: t.o)27	7	20/1	59	—
2748[4]	**Linden's Lotto (IRE) (115)** (JWhite) **8-11-5b1(5)** SRyan (lw: chsd ldrs to 11th: sn lost tch: t.o)....dist	8	14/1	—	—
2762[6]	**The Caumrue (IRE) (105)** (GBBalding) **9-11-0** BFenton (hld up: hdwy 9th: 4th whn fell next)....	F	7/1 2	—	—
	Artic Wings (IRE) (103) (OBrennan) **9-10-12** MBrennan (hld up in rr: effrt 9th: sn no imp: t.o: p.u bef 4 out)....	P	4/1 1	—	—

(SP 121.1%) **10 Rn**

5m 23.5 (11.50) CSF £34.29 CT £431.04 TOTE £4.50: £1.70 £3.80 £5.60 (£19.20) Trio £90.70; £89.51 to Newcastle 3/2/97 OWNER Mr Jeremy Hancock (BANBURY) BRED Capt D. G. Swan

1985* Distinctive (IRE) can jump and stay and, gaining a healthy lead with a spectacular leap three out, only needed to be kept up to his work to score. (4/1)

1035 Seod Rioga (IRE), had far more use made of him without the visor he wore on his previous outing, and showed a return to form with a very promising performance. (8/1)

Over the Pole, much more at home on this sounder surface, ran well, and with this race to put an edge on him should be more the finished article next time. (16/1)

2092 Celtino putting up his best performance this term, lacked the pace to mount a challenge, but he did keep battling away and he would seem to be on the way back. (7/1)

1731 Merry Panto (IRE) appeared to have lost his confidence after hitting the deck on his previous outing, and although he had anything but a fault-free round here, at least survived. (4/1)

Artic Wings (IRE), well supported in the market on this seasonal debut, ran very flat indeed and was never in striking range of the leaders. (4/1)

2895 HARTSHORNE MOTOR SERVICES LTD. (WALSALL) H'CAP HURDLE (0-120) (4-Y.O+) (Class D)

2-35 (2-35) **2m 6f 110y (12 hdls)** £2,920.00 (£820.00: £400.00) GOING: 0.68 sec per fur (S)

			SP	RR	SF
2666[3]	**Silver Standard (104)** (CaptTAForster) **7-11-3b** SWynne (chsd ldr: led after 8th: clr 2 out: v.easily)....—	1	4/7 1	78+	30
2761[6]	**Smith Too (IRE) (113)** (MrsJPitman) **9-11-9(3)** DFortt (bit bkwd: led tl after 8th: rdn appr 2 out: sn btn)....2½	2	100/30 2	85	37
2666[10]	**Cambo (USA) (89)** (MCBanks) **11-10-2** DSkyrme (nt j.w: reminders 8th: hdwy & ev ch 4 out: outpcd fr next)...5	3	9/2 3	58	10

(SP 104.9%) **3 Rn**

5m 41.7 (25.70) CSF £2.40 TOTE £1.60 (£1.40) OWNER Mr G. W. Lugg (LUDLOW) BRED Marquess & Marchioness of Tavistock & Lord Howland

2666 Silver Standard always waiting to pounce, stepped up a gear to forge clear on the home turn and won as an odds-on favourite should do. (4/7)

Smith Too (IRE) did his best to make a race of it and stuck on willingly in the latter stages after getting his second wind. This run should put an edge on him. (100/30: 7/4-7/2)

Cambo (USA) did not really have a cut at his hurdles, but he was rousted up to give himself every chance four out, before getting left behind once the tempo increased. (9/2)

2896 RICHARDSON'S MERLIN PARK NOVICES' CHASE (5-Y.O+) (Class E)

3-05 (3-05) **3m (18 fncs)** £2,927.75 (£887.00: £433.50: £206.75) GOING: 0.25 sec per fur (GS)

			SP	RR	SF
2778U	**Domaine de Pron (FR)** (MrsLCTaylor) **6-11-4** RBellamy (led 3rd to 6th: led last: rdn out)....—	1	25/1	102	31
1711[2]	**Parahandy (IRE)** (GBBalding) **7-11-4** BFenton (led: pckd 2nd: hdd next: led 3 out to last: hrd rdn & no ex flat)....2	2	2/1 2	101	30
1694*	**Poucher (IRE) (100)** (CaptTAForster) **7-11-10** SWynne (lw: nt j.w: hld up: hdwy 11th: blnd 13th: gd hdwy to chal last: unable qckn flat)....1½	3	11/8 1	106	35
2660[4]	**Top Javalin (NZ) (98)** (NJHawke) **10-11-4** RGreene (mstke & lost pl 4th: rdn 11th: rallied 14th: wknd 3 out)..20	4	5/1 3	86	15
1829P	**Big Archie** (MrsAJBowlby) **7-11-4** DLeahy (prom: rdn whn j.slowly 4 out: wknd next: t.o)....14	5	20/1	77	6
2052[7]	**George Ashford (IRE) (86)** (PRJohnson) **7-11-10** MSharratt (a bhd: rdn 7th: mstke next: sn t.o)....dist	6	16/1	—	—
2569[7]	**Dara's Course (IRE) (74)** (MissPMWhittle) **8-10-6(7)** KHibbert (bit bkwd: led 6th tl mstke & hdd 3 out: 4th & btn whn fell next)....	F	25/1	—	—
2657[8]	**Colette's Choice (IRE) (70)** (GAHam) **8-10-10(3)** DFortt (hld up & bhd: t.o 11th: p.u bef 4 out)....	P	20/1	—	—

(SP 115.2%) **8 Rn**

6m 9.6 (17.60) CSF £68.81 TOTE £20.40: £5.80 £1.50 £1.10 (£86.20) OWNER Mrs L. C. Taylor (CHIPPING WARDEN) BRED Jacques Cypres

2778 Domaine de Pron (FR) appreciated this step up to three miles and at last got his jumping together. One of three in the air at the last, he was the quickest away and stayed on dourly to open his account. (25/1)

1711 Parahandy (IRE), in the firing line from the start, was only forced to give best on the run-in and should not be long in finding an opening. (2/1)

1694* Poucher (IRE) found the ground plenty fast enough for him and as a result his jumping suffered. With plenty to do inside the last half mile, he rallied to join issue at the final obstacle, but was tapped for toe on the flat. (11/8)

2660 Top Javalin (NZ) struggled to get back into it after an early mistake and, though he did reach the heels of the principals five out, quickly got outpaced when the battle to the finish really got underway. (5/1)

Big Archie was totally unsuited by this tight track, but he did race prominently, despite jumping slowly on occasions, until losing touch inside the last half-mile. (20/1)

2897 STRATFORD-ON-AVON RACECOURSE COMPANY LTD. 75TH ANNIVERSARY NOVICES' H'CAP HURDLE (0-105) (4-Y.O+) (Class E)

3-40 (3-40) **2m 3f (10 hdls)** £2,368.50 (£666.00: £325.50) GOING: 0.68 sec per fur (S)

			SP	RR	SF
868[8]	**River Wye (IRE) (87)** (GHYardley) **5-11-7** VSlattery (chsd ldrs: led after 3 out: sn clr: eased nr fin)....—	1	14/1	76+	17
2578*	**Little Shefford (83)** (MPMuggeridge) **5-11-3** ILawrence (lw: led: clr 4th: wknd & hdd after 3 out: sn outpcd) ..13	2	7/1	61	2
2634[7]	**Leap in the Dark (IRE) (80)** (MissLCSiddall) **8-11-0** OPears (lw: hld up & bhd: rdn & hdwy 7th: nvr nr to chal)....1¼	3	12/1	57	—
1569*	**Dragonmist (IRE) (72)** (DBurchell) **7-10-6** DJBurchell (trckd ldrs tl lost pl ½-wy: rallied appr 3 out: too much to do)....2	4	7/2 1	47	—
2067[5]	**Pedaltothemetal (IRE) (89)** (PMitchell) **5-11-9** DGallagher (hld up: rdn ½-wy: hdwy 7th: wknd appr 2 out)....3	5	10/1	62	3
77[3]	**High Post (81)** (GAHam) **8-10-12(3)** DFortt (bit bkwd: hld up & bhd: sme hdwy fr 3 out: nt rch ldrs)....3	6	12/1	51	—
2578[2]	**Skram (90)** (RDickin) **4-11-0** DLeahy (lw: prom to 7th: sn wknd: t.o)....18	7	5/1 2	45	—

Form	Horse and details	Dist	Pl	SP	RR	SF
2692^{14}	**Sam Rockett (85)** (PMooney) **4-10-4**(5) SRyan (hld up: hdwy appr 6th: wknd after next: t.o)	1	**8**	12/1	39	—
2692^{9}	**Millenium Lass (IRE) (90)** (MissMERowland) **9-11-10** GaryLyons (bit bkwd: lost pl 5th: sn bhd: t.o)	2½	**9**	25/1	42	—
2680^{7}	**That Old Feeling (IRE) (70)** (JWhite) **5-10-4** TJMurphy (swtg: prom: rdn 5th: sn wknd: t.o)	1¼	**10**	16/1	21	—
1952^{4}	**Fontainerouge (IRE) (84)** (GBBalding) **7-11-4** BFenton (a in rr: t.o)	16	**11**	6/1^{3}	22	—
2547^{11}	**Cades Bay (82)** (NATwiston-Davies) **6-11-2** TJenks (hld up: hdwy 5th: 3rd whn fell 3 out)		**F**	12/1	—	—
				(SP 121.9%)	**12 Rn**	

4m 43.9 (25.90) CSF £102.46 CT £1,124.39 TOTE £22.80: £7.40 £2.10 £2.70 (£153.10) Trio £112.20 OWNER Mr S. Ho (MALVERN) BRED Rathbarry Stud and Miss S. Ryan

WEIGHT FOR AGE 4yo-10lb

River Wye (IRE), who has had a soft-palate operation since disappointing on his seasonal debut in the autumn, outclassed the opposition in the closing stages and this success could be the first of many. (14/1: 10/1-16/1)

2578* Little Shefford again attempted to gallop his rivals into the ground, but over this extended trip lack of stamina appeared the biggest problem. (7/1)

1825 Leap in the Dark (IRE) looked absolutely magnificent, but took far too long to warm up and his spirited late flourish was to no avail.(12/1)

1569* Dragonmist (IRE) had the blinds left off on this step up from selling company and, inclined to drop herself out from halfway, had little chance of getting back despite staying on when it was all over. (7/2)

2067 Pedaltothemetal (IRE) appears to need a longer trip, for she was narrowly beaten over two miles on the Flat and stamina seems to be her strong suit. (10/1: 6/1-11/1)

77 High Post, one of three who had lost touch a mile out, did extremely well to get so close at the finish and with this outing to sharpen him up is one to keep in mind. (12/1)

Cades Bay, trying a slightly longer trip, was just getting into the action, travelling well, when falling at the third last. He does look capable of winning a race or two. (12/1)

T/Plpt: £27.60 (188.83 Tckts). T/Qdpt: £48.10 (4.6 Tckts). IM

2697-**WETHERBY (L-H) (Good)**
Saturday February 1st
WEATHER: Overcast

2898 DEMMY IN WETHERBY NOVICES' HURDLE (4-Y.O+) (Class D)
1-10 (1-12) **2m (9 hdls)** £3,239.50 (£976.00: £473.00) GOING: 0.48 sec per fur (GS)

Form	Horse and details	Dist	Pl	SP	RR	SF
2697^{2}	**Durano (98)** (TDEasterby) **6-11-3** DerekByrne (lw: trckd ldrs: rdn to ld last: r.o)	—	**1**	9/1	76	17
2649^{3}	**Forever Noble (IRE)** (MDHammond) **4-10-7** RGarritty (led to 2nd: cl up: led after 4 out to last: kpt on)	2	**2**	14/1	74	5
	New Century (USA) (DNicholls) **5-11-0**(3) FLeahy (lw: hld up: hdwy 4 out: sn chsng ldrs: hung lft & nt qckn flat)	1¼	**3**	14/1	73	14
	Chopwell Drapes (IRE) (HowardJohnson) **7-11-3** MMoloney (hld up & bhd: stdy hdwy & mstke 3 out: r.o: nvr plcd to chal)	14	**4**	100/1	59+	—
1908^{7}	**Mudlark** (JNorton) **5-11-3** WDwan (styd on fr 3 out: nvr nrr)	d.h	**4**	100/1	59	—
2697^{6}	**Ballyranter** (MDHammond) **8-11-3** DBentley (lw: hit 5th: styd on fr 3 out: nvr rchd ldrs)	¾	**6**	50/1	58	—
2060^{F}	**Joe Shaw** (MrsMReveley) **4-10-7** RHodge (hld up & bhd: hdwy on bit 3 out: nvr plcd to chal)	2	**7**	33/1	56+	—
2738a^{6}	**Namoodaj** (DNicholson) **4-10-2**(5) MrRThornton (lw: mstkes: in tch: effrt 4 out: rdn & one pce fr next)	1¼	**8**	5/2^{2}	55	—
	Royal York (GRichards) **5-10-12** PCarberry (lw: in tch: kpt on one pce fr 3 out)	½	**9**	7/1^{3}	49	—
1907^{P}	**Dougal** (BSRothwell) **6-10-12**(5) BGrattan (wl bhd tl styd on fr 3 out)	4	**10**	100/1	50	—
2634^{3}	**Tremendisto (95)** (CaptJWilson) **7-11-8** RichardGuest (chsd ldrs: blnd 2nd: ev ch & hit 4 out: sn btn)	2	**11**	16/1	53	—
2649^{12}	**Bollin Frank** (TDEasterby) **5-11-3** ASSmith (hld up & bhd: stdy hdwy 3 out: nvr nr to chal)	3½	**12**	25/1	45	—
1802^{6}	**Pilkington (IRE) (88)** (HowardJohnson) **7-10-12**(5) MichaelBrennan (chsd ldrs to 4 out)	1¼	**13**	25/1	44	—
2663^{P}	**Antarctica (USA)** (JHetherton) **5-10-12** DParker (hld up: stdy hdwy 4 out: sn rdn & no imp)	¾	**14**	100/1	38	—
2539*	**Quango** (JGFitzGerald) **5-11-8** ADobbin (lw: chsd ldrs: rdn 4 out: sn btn)	1	**15**	6/4^{1}	47	—
2746^{11}	**Rushen Raider** (KWHogg) **5-11-3** MFoster (chsd ldrs tl rdn & btn 4 out)	3	**16**	33/1	39	—
2177^{5}	**Something Speedy (IRE)** (MDHammond) **5-10-5**(7) RBurns (nvr bttr than mid div)	¾	**17**	50/1	33	—
1843^{6}	**Irish Buzz (IRE)** (MrsASwinbank) **5-11-3** JSupple (wl bhd fr 4th: t.o)	21	**18**	66/1	17	—
	The Road West (IRE) (JLEyre) **8-11-3** BStorey (drvn along 4 out: sn wl bhd)	hd	**19**	33/1	17	—
2697^{P}	**Bonny Rigg (IRE)** (LLungo) **5-10-12** TReed (bit bkwd: mstkes: a bhd)	13	**20**	66/1	—	—
2798^{10}	**On The Off Chance** (LLungo) **5-11-3** NBentley (a bhd: t.o)	dist	**21**	100/1	—	—
	Shadows of Silver (MrsMReveley) **9-10-12** GCahill (bit bkwd: led fr 2nd tl hdd after 4 out: sn wknd: fell last)		**F**	33/1	—	—
1208^{P}	**Mubariz (IRE)** (CSmith) **5-11-3** MRanger (blnd & lost pl 5th: t.o whn p.u bef 3 out)		**P**	100/1	—	—
				(SP 142.6%)	**23 Rn**	

3m 59.9 (17.90) CSF £121.69 TOTE £10.30: £2.40 £3.10 £3.70 (£54.90) Trio £121.50 OWNER Mr C. H. Stevens (MALTON) BRED A. M. Wragg

WEIGHT FOR AGE 4yo-10lb

OFFICIAL EXPLANATION Joe Shaw: the rider reported the gelding had gurgled and so forced him to hold on to his head.

2697 Durano is in really good heart. Well handled, he put in a fast jump at the last, which gave him the advantage, and he then responded to pressure in good style. (9/1: 6/1-10/1)

2649 Forever Noble (IRE) stays well but on this occasion he was just tapped for toe. Opportunities will be found, especially when he comes back to form. (14/1)

New Century (USA) got the trip well enough and showed plenty here to suggest that he will find a race before long. (14/1)

Chopwell Drapes (IRE) had shown absolutely nothing before, but he put up a most eye-catching performance here and finished to some purpose. He looks one to keep on the right side of. (100/1)

Mudlark was beaten in what appeared a poor seller last time, but this was a much-improved performance and he is learning fast. (100/1)

2697 Ballyranter is learning but there is still some improvement needed in his jumping. (50/1)

1652 Joe Shaw is on the upgrade and was given a most sympathetic ride here, apearing to finish full of running. Despite what the Stewards were told later, he is full of promise. (33/1)

2738a Namoodaj jumped sloppily and that put paid to his chances. (5/2)

Royal York showed enough to suggest that there is better to come. (7/1: op 4/1)

Dougal is improving. (100/1)

2899 DEMMY THE BOOKMAKER NOVICES' CHASE (5-Y.O+) (Class D)

1-40 (1-40) **2m 4f 110y (15 fncs)** £3,585.25 (£1,072.00: £513.50: £234.25) GOING: 0.48 sec per fur (GS)

				SP	RR	SF
2699[3]	**Cattly Hang (IRE) (97)** (JPLeigh) **7-11-3** ADobbin (lw: mde all: hld on gamely fr 4 out)	—	1	11/1	107	44
2653[2]	**Chief Minister (IRE)** (MDHammond) **8-11-3** RGarritty (lw: prom: pushed along fr 7th: ch 3 out: kpt on u.p)	1½	2	4/6 1	106	43
1646[P]	**Colonel In Chief (IRE)** (GRichards) **7-11-3** PCarberry (trckd ldrs: chal whn blnd bdly 4 out: sn hrd drvn: no ex flat)	nk	3	3/1 2	106	43
2745[2]	**Golden Hello (116)** (TDEasterby) **6-11-13** ASSmith (j.rt: chsd ldrs tl wknd fr 4 out)	dist	4	5/1 3	—	—
2778[F]	**Just Supposen (IRE)** (BSRothwell) **6-11-3** BStorey (sn outpcd: blnd 8th & 10th: p.u bef 11th)		P	50/1	—	—
2540[P]	**Wild Game (IRE)** (MissSWilliamson) **6-10-10**(7) ATodd (mstkes: racd wd: lost tch fr 7th: p.u bef 11th)		P	100/1	—	—

(SP 113.0%) **6 Rn**

5m 22.8 (15.80) CSF £18.65 TOTE £8.20: £1.70 £1.30 (£4.50) OWNER Mr W. G. N. Morgan (GAINSBOROUGH)

2699 Cattly Hang (IRE) showed what a game performer he is and kept fighting off all comers. (11/1)

2653 Chief Minister (IRE) never looked to be going all that well, but he kept responding to pressure and is obviously learning with experience.(4/6)

Colonel In Chief (IRE) looked likely to take this until making a diabolical blunder four out, and the fact that he remained in contention is remarkable. (3/1)

2745 Golden Hello is always worth opposing. (5/1)

2900 DEMMY CREDIT H'CAP HURDLE (0-135) (4-Y.O+) (Class C)

2-10 (2-11) **2m 7f (12 hdls)** £2,861.00 (£796.00: £383.00) GOING: 0.48 sec per fur (GS)

				SP	RR	SF
2780[4]	**Purevalue (IRE) (109)** (MWEasterby) **6-10-5** RichardGuest (led fr 2nd: blnd 3 out: hld on wl)	—	1	7/1	88	—
2627*	**Share Options (IRE) (104)** (TDEasterby) **6-10-0** ASSmith (trckd ldrs: chal 7th: rdn 3 out: kpt on)	1½	2	5/2 2	82	—
	Campaign (111) (MDHammond) **6-10-7** RGarritty (lw: trckd ldrs: effrt 3 out: styd on: nt pce to chal)	½	3	10/1	89	—
2059[4]	**Tibetan (132)** (LadyHerries) **5-11-9**(5) MrRThornton (lw: hld up: hdwy to chal 4 out: effrt next: wknd fr 2 out)	8	4	2/1 1	104	—
2702[6]	**Disco des Mottes (FR) (132)** (GRichards) **6-12-0** PCarberry (trckd ldrs: effrt 4 out: sn btn)	21	5	20/1	89	—
2636[4]	**Scotton Banks (IRE) (130)** (TDEasterby) **8-11-12** BStorey (outpcd & lost tch fr ½-wy)	5	6	16/1	84	—
2702[4]	**Jocks Cross (IRE) (115)** (GRichards) **6-10-11** ADobbin (led to 2nd: w ldrs: hit 8th: rdn & btn after 4 out)	6	7	4/1 3	65	—

(SP 114.1%) **7 Rn**

5m 50.9 CSF £23.07 TOTE £7.70: £2.80 £2.00 (£11.00) OWNER Mr A. D. Simmons (SHERIFF HUTTON) BRED Limestone Stud

LONG HANDICAP Disco des Mottes (FR) 73-13 Share Options (IRE) 9-12

2780 Purevalue (IRE), stepped up in trip and ridden forcibly this time, decided to put his best foot forward and won it really well. (7/1)

2627* Share Options (IRE) was always in the firing-line but, despite staying on, was just short of that vital change of gear. (5/2)

Campaign put in a useful first effort of the season and, when his stable really comes into form, he will come into his own. (10/1)

2059 Tibetan, a stayer off the Flat, was trying a much longer trip over hurdles this time and did not appear to get it, but this was his first run for six weeks. (2/1)

2702 Disco des Mottes (FR) is finding hurdling hard work at the moment and a return to chasing might well help. (20/1)

2636 Scotton Banks (IRE) has been most disappointing over the bigger obstacles and, although never going the pace, had a confidence-booster over hurdles here. (16/1)

2702 Jocks Cross (IRE) was most disappointing after his promising effort last week, and this may have been just a bit quick for him. (4/1)

2901 MARSTON MOOR H'CAP CHASE (5-Y.O+) (Class B)

2-40 (2-41) **2m 4f 110y (15 fncs)** £8,183.25 (£2,466.00: £1,195.50: £560.25) GOING: 0.48 sec per fur (GS)

				SP	RR	SF
2639*	**Konvekta King (IRE) (132)** (OSherwood) **9-11-4** ADobbin (a.p: pushed along 8th: led 4 out: styd on strly)	—	1	5/2 1	135	55
2741a[5]	**Kadi (GER) (138)** (DNicholson) **8-11-5**(5) MrRThornton (lw: prom: rdn along fr 9th: ev ch fr 3 out: nt qckn flat)	5	2	9/2	137	57
2641[4]	**Down the Fell (123)** (HowardJohnson) **8-10-9** PCarberry (led tl hdd 4 out: sn rdn & btn)	7	3	4/1 3	117	37
2748[3]	**In Truth (119)** (SGollings) **9-10-5** KGaule (chsd ldrs: outpcd 9th: hmpd 11th: sn lost touch: styd on towards fin)	2	4	33/1	111	31
2065[2]	**Valiant Warrior (133)** (MDHammond) **9-11-5** RGarritty (lw: prom tl mstkes & lost pl 7th & 8th: styd on towards fin)	1¾	5	7/2 2	124	44
1936[3]	**The Last Fling (IRE) (124)** (MrsSJSmith) **7-10-10** RichardGuest (lw: trckd ldrs: hdwy to disp ld whn fell 10th)		F	4/1 3	—	—

(SP 111.9%) **6 Rn**

5m 19.9 (12.90) CSF £12.76 TOTE £3.30: £1.90 £2.00 (£8.10) OWNER Konvekta Ltd (UPPER LAMBOURN) BRED Peter Kehoe in Ireland

2639* Konvekta King (IRE) ran as though he needed this extra distance and is still ahead of the Handicapper. (5/2)

2741a Kadi (GER) was always struggling with the pace, but he did keep on and, with more give in the ground, his turn will come. (9/2)

2641 Down the Fell beat himself by not having a cut at his fences. (4/1)

2748 In Truth ran reasonably after becoming well outpaced turning for home, and there is still a race or two in him. (33/1)

2065 Valiant Warrior, from a yard not really firing, never looked happy. Despite this, he was keeping on at the finish. (7/2)

1936 The Last Fling (IRE) is certainly very useful but his jumping remains a problem. Until that is solved, he can never be fully relied upon. (4/1)

2902 DEMMY SWITCH H'CAP HURDLE (0-145) (5-Y.O+) (Class B)

3-15 (3-15) **2m (9 hdls)** £5,585.50 (£1,684.00: £817.00: £383.50) GOING: 0.48 sec per fur (GS)

				SP	RR	SF
1636[F]	**Edelweis du Moulin (FR) (127)** (GRichards) **5-11-9** PCarberry (a.gng wl: hdwy on bit to ld last: hrd hld)	—	1	11/4 2	112+	25
2645[4]	**Tom Brodie (128)** (HowardJohnson) **7-11-10** ADobbin (hld up: smooth hdwy to ld 3 out: hdd last: no ch w wnr)	5	2	7/1 3	108	21
2779[F]	**Celestial Choir (114)** (JLEyre) **7-10-10** BStorey (a.p: outpcd 3 out: kpt on wl appr last)	nk	3	5/2 1	94	7
453[2]	**Ham N'Eggs (110)** (MDHammond) **6-10-6** DBentley (trckd ldrs: effrt 3 out: r.o one pce)	2	4	16/1	88	1
2779[5]	**Desert Fighter (113)** (MrsMReveley) **6-10-2**(7)ow1 MHerrington (lw: chsd ldrs: disp ld appr 3 out: outpcd & blnd 2 out: sn btn)	4	5	14/1	87	—
2617[3]	**Thornton Gate (124)** (TDEasterby) **8-11-6** ASSmith (trckd ldrs: hdwy & ev ch 3 out: sn rdn & no ex)	5	6	7/1 3	93	6
2644[7]	**Elpidos (117)** (MDHammond) **5-10-13** RGarritty (w ldr: led 4 out to 3 out: sn btn & eased)	10	7	10/1	76	—
1439[F]	**Holders Hill (IRE) (108)** (MGMeagher) **5-10-4** DerekByrne (a last)	s.h	8	20/1	67	—
2617[2]	**Uncle Doug (127)** (MrsMReveley) **6-11-9** GCahill (lw: mde most to 4 out: wknd next: p.u bef last)		P	9/1	—	—

(SP 116.6%) **9 Rn**

3m 59.4 (17.40) CSF £20.82 CT £48.95 TOTE £3.60: £1.60 £2.20 £1.40 (£11.20) Trio £19.80 OWNER Mr Robert Ogden (PENRITH) BRED Simon Philibert

1636 Edelweis du Moulin (FR), given a typical Carberry ride, showed just what a useful performer he is and won without ever coming off the bridle. He has to be respected in any company. (11/4)
2645 Tom Brodie has been in tremendous form this season, but was made to look pedestrian by the classy winner. (7/1)
Celestial Choir is a tough sort, who was staying on after getting outpaced. Her turn should come before long, and she ought to stay further. (5/2)
453 Ham N'Eggs ran quite well, but did rather tend to hang badly left all the way up the home straight. (16/1)
2779 Desert Fighter was in the thick of things but, once it got too competitive, he blundered two out and that was it. (14/1)
2617 Thornton Gate travelled well until an effort was required early in the straight, from which point he was found wanting. (7/1)
1924 Elpidos tried different tactics here, and was then given an easy time once beaten. (10/1)
2617 Uncle Doug (9/1: 6/1-10/1)

2903 HAROLD CHARLTON MEMORIAL HUNTERS' CHASE (6-Y.O+) (Class H)
3-45 (3-45) **3m 1f (18 fncs)** £1,192.50 (£330.00: £157.50) GOING: 0.48 sec per fur (GS)

				SP	RR	SF
	Cab on Target (MrsMReveley) **11-11-10** MrSSwiers (lw: hld up: hdwy 10th: led flat: r.o)	—	**1**	8/13[1]	110	—
	Teaplanter (MissCSaunders) **14-11-13**(5) MrBPollock (lw: led to 5th: led fr 10th tl hdd flat: r.o)	2	**2**	7/2[2]	117	—
	Matt Reid (JPLeigh) **13-11-11**(7) MrWMorgan (lw: a.p: chsd ldr fr 10th tl outpcd fr 3 out)	22	**3**	20/1	103	—
	Fordstown (IRE) (JamieAlexander) **8-11-11**(7) MrJamieAlexander (outpcd & bhd: sme hdwy fr 12th: n.d)	14	**4**	33/1	94	—
	Southern Minstrel (NChamberlain) **14-11-7**(7) MissCMetcalfe (prom tl outpcd fr 11th: n.d after)	2	**5**	14/1	88	—
	Peajade (MissJillWormall) **13-11-3**(7) MissJWormall (bhd: sme hdwy 4 out: n.d)	s.h	**6**	20/1	84	—
	Highlandman (JSHaldane) **11-11-3**(7) MrMBradburne (nvr trbld ldrs)	2	**7**	50/1	83	—
	Tom Log (WMBurnell) **10-11-3**(7) MrWBurnell (bit bkwd: chsd ldrs: blnd 6th: sn bhd)	dist	**8**	50/1	—	—
1024[4]	**Kushbaloo** (CParker) **12-11-11**(7) MrAParker (chsd ldrs to ½-wy: grad lost pl: virtually p.u flat)	nk	**9**	6/1[3]	—	—
	No Word (IBaker) **10-11-3**(7) MrIBaker (racd wd: plld hrd: led fr 5th to 10th: wknd qckly: t.o whn blnd 4 out: p.u)		**P**	100/1	—	—
				(SP 122.5%)		**10 Rn**

6m 43.8 CSF £2.94 TOTE £1.80: £1.10 £1.10 £7.20 (£2.30) Trio £17.80 OWNER Mr N. Hurst (SALTBURN) BRED W. Lombard
Cab on Target was obviously going to take all the beating if he jumped, and he hardly put a foot wrong. (8/13)
Teaplanter, trying to win this for the fourth consecutive year, put up a game performance, but his younger rival was just too quick for him after the last. He will again find his share of these events. (7/2: op 9/4)
Matt Reid ran well in this company until finding things too hot from the third last. (20/1)
Fordstown (IRE) certainly does not do anything quickly, but he did stay on, albeit too late. (33/1)
Southern Minstrel was always finding things happening too quickly for his liking. (14/1)

2904 WEATHERBYS 'STARS OF TOMORROW' STANDARD OPEN N.H. FLAT RACE (4, 5 & 6-Y.O) (Class H)
4-20 (4-20) **2m** £1,413.00 (£393.00: £189.00)

				SP	RR	SF
2633[3]	**Phar Smoother (IRE)** (JGFitzGerald) **5-11-2** WDwan (in tch: effrt 5f out: rdn to ld 1f out: styd on wl)	—	**1**	10/1	56 f	—
	Wynyard Knight (MrsMReveley) **5-11-2** RHodge (tall: hld up & bhd: smooth hdwy to ld 5f out: qcknd 4f out: hdd 1f out: kpt on)	1½	**2**	7/4[1]	55 f	—
	Generous Streak (FR) (JNorton) **4-10-1**(5) MrRThornton (hld up: hdwy u.p ½-wy: ch 4f out: r.o one pce)	6	**3**	6/1[3]	49 f	—
2047[3]	**Roman Outlaw** (MDHammond) **5-11-2** RGarritty (a chsng ldrs: ev ch 5f out: one pce fnl 3f)	nk	**4**	9/2[2]	48 f	—
	Sprightley Pip (IRE) (MissCJohnsey) **6-10-11**(5) MichaelBrennan (bkwd: prom: hrd rdn 4f out: kpt on one pce)	2	**5**	33/1	46 f	—
1926[6]	**Banker Count** (MWEasterby) **5-11-2** ADobbin (lw: plld hrd: hdwy to trck ldrs ½-wy: effrt & one pce fnl 4f)	9	**6**	7/1	37 f	—
	Thunderpoint (IRE) (TDEasterby) **5-11-2** ASSmith (bit bkwd: trckd ldrs: chal 6f out: wknd fnl 3f)	1½	**7**	9/1	36 f	—
	Strong Magic (IRE) (MissCJohnsey) **5-11-2** DerekByrne (bkwd: in tch tl outpcd fnl 5f)	6	**8**	25/1	30 f	—
2626[7]	**Our Carol (IRE)** (JParkes) **5-10-11** VSmith (led tl hdd 5f out: wknd fnl 4f)	7	**9**	50/1	18 f	—
2675[2]	**Noble Tom (IRE)** (RCollins) **5-11-2** PCarberry (hld up & bhd: hdwy ½-wy: hung lft 4f out: sn wknd)	4	**10**	13/2	19 f	—
	Shannon Shoon (IRE) (HowardJohnson) **5-10-11**(5) GFRyan (chsd ldrs tl wknd fnl 6f)	4	**11**	20/1	15 f	—
	Lady's Pet (MissSWilliamson) **6-10-9**(7) ATodd (prom: wkng whn sltly hmpd 8f out)	½	**12**	33/1	14 f	—
2675[7]	**Blaster Watson** (CSmith) **6-11-2** MRanger (a bhd)	6	**13**	50/1	8 f	—
	Stan's Pride (MrsVAAconley) **5-11-2** BStorey (plld hrd: a bhd)	22	**14**	33/1	—	—
	Coquettish (JHetherton) **4-10-1** DParker (a bhd)	1	**15**	33/1	—	—
	Ceejayell (NChamberlain) **4-9-8**(7) MissCMetcalfe (bkwd: plld hrd: jnd ldrs after 5f: wknd 6f out)	1	**16**	50/1	—	—
				(SP 140.0%)		**16 Rn**

4m 0.2 CSF £27.05 TOTE £12.00: £2.70 £1.80 £2.30 (£20.40) Trio £170.10; £148.62 to Newcastle 3/2/97 OWNER John Smith's Ltd (MALTON) BRED J. J. Harty
WEIGHT FOR AGE 4yo-10lb
2633 Phar Smoother (IRE), better suited by this galloping track, showed that he is improving and won most decisively. (10/1)
Wynyard Knight looked the best horse here, but it was basically inexperience that beat him and he should soon make amends. (7/4)
Generous Streak (FR), although off the bit some way out, kept plugging away and will obviously have learnt from this. (6/1: op 4/1)
2047 Roman Outlaw had his chances throughout and kept trying hard, only to prove short of speed when it mattered. (9/2)
Sprightley Pip (IRE) had a hard race, but kept responding to pressure and was always lacking that vital turn of speed. (33/1)
1926 Banker Count must learn to settle. (7/1)
Thunderpoint (IRE) (9/1: op 6/1)
2675 Noble Tom (IRE) (13/2: op 4/1)

T/Plpt: £109.60 (83.83 Tckts). T/Qdpt: £13.30 (44.5 Tckts). AA

2532-FONTWELL (Fig. 8) (Good to firm)
Monday February 3rd
Race 1: 1 flight omitted fnl circ
WEATHER: sunny & cold

2905 PAGHAM (S) H'CAP HURDLE (0-95) (4-Y.O+) (Class G)
1-40 (1-41) **2m 6f 110y (10 hdls)** £2,160.00 (£600.00: £288.00) GOING: 0.13 sec per fur (G)

				SP	RR	SF
2708[7]	**Quelque Chose (90)** (BJMeehan) **7-11-10** RHughes (lw: hdwy 7th: led appr last: r.o wl)	—	**1**	2/1[1]	76	17

				SP	RR	SF
2792*	**Do Be Ware (76)** (JFfitch-Heyes) **7-10-10** 7x BFenton (a.p: lft in ld 6th: hdd after 7th: led after 2 out tl appr last: unable qckn)	11	**2**	10/1	54	—
	Mull House (85) (GPEnright) **10-11-5v** AMaguire (hdwy 6th: wknd appr last)	4	**3**	10/1	60	1
2824[10]	**Raahin (USA) (70)** (SWoodman) **12-10-4** SMcNeill (lw: nvr nr to chal)	hd	**4**	16/1	45	—
2570[5]	**Cravate (FR) (66)** (PJHobbs) **7-9-7**(7) MMoran (hdwy 8th: wknd appr last)	nk	**5**	16/1	41	—
1786[P]	**Kesanta (83)** (WGMTurner) **7-10-10**(7) JPower (hdwy 7th: wknd appr last)	3	**6**	7/1[3]	56	—
1563[U]	**Scorpion Bay (69)** (DJSffrenchDavis) **9-10-0**(3)ow3 JMagee (a.p: led after 7th tl after 2 out: sn wknd)	18	**7**	33/1	29	—
1710[5]	**Roger's Pal (73)** (PEccles) **10-10-7** DGallagher (bhd fr 8th)	14	**8**	10/1	23	—
2792[13]	**Highly Decorated (80)** (MissAMNewton-Smith) **12-10-7b**(7) JKMcCarthy (hdwy 6th: wknd 8th: t.o)	dist	**9**	50/1	—	—
2680[13]	**Master Goodenough (IRE) (72)** (AGFoster) **6-9-13**(7)ow6 DCreech (led 2nd tl fell 6th)		**F**	33/1	—	—
1836*	**Kayfaat (USA) (84)** (MCPipe) **9-11-4v** CMaude (rdn thrght: prom to 4th: t.o whn p.u after 7th)		**P**	11/2[2]	—	—
2664[4]	**Remember Star (77)** (ADSmith) **4-10-0** BPowell (a bhd: t.o whn p.u bef last)		**P**	14/1	—	—
1963[9]	**Carey's Cottage (IRE) (66)** (MrsPTownsley) **7-10-0b**[1] DBridgwater (a bhd: t.o whn p.u bef 6th)		**P**	33/1	—	—
2669[17]	**Shaagni Ana (USA) (67)** (JGSmyth-Osbourne) **6-10-1** WMarston (lw: led to 2nd: mstke 4th: wknd 6th: t.o whn p.u bef last)		**P**	25/1	—	—
1710[P]	**Profession (66)** (FGray) **6-10-0** RFarrant (t: wl bhd whn p.u bef 8th)		**P**	33/1	—	—
2088[11]	**Tug Your Forelock (66)** (GFJohnsonHoughton) **6-9-7**(7) DFinnegan (mid div whn hmpd & uns rdr 6th)		**U**	12/1	—	—

(SP 132.2%) **16 Rn**

5m 35.7 (19.70) CSF £21.57 CT £167.62 TOTE £3.70: £1.40 £2.10 £1.80 £1.80 (£26.00) Trio £45.10 OWNER Mr Nigel Stafford (UPPER LAMBOURN) BRED E. A. Badger

LONG HANDICAP Scorpion Bay 8-11 Master Goodenough (IRE) 9-13 Remember Star 9-0 Carey's Cottage (IRE) 9-5 Cravate (FR) 9-3 Profession 9-1 Tug Your Forelock 9-10

WEIGHT FOR AGE 4yo-11lb

Quelque Chose appreciated the drop in class and coped with the fast ground, leading approaching the final flight and pulling clear for a decisive victory. (2/1)

2792* Do Be Ware, taking a step up in distance, went on turning out of the back straight. Collared approaching the final flight, he found the winner far too good. He may be more effective over a slightly shorter trip. (10/1: 6/1-11/1)

Mull House, who disappointed on the Flat last year, was having his first run over hurdles for nearly two and a half years. Taking closer order at halfway, he had shot his bolt going to the final flight. (10/1: 7/1-12/1)

1841 Raahin (USA) has been badly out of form this season, but this was by far his easiest task. He never threatened to get into it though, although he did stay on to fight out the minor placings. (16/1)

Cravate (FR), carrying 4lb more than her long handicap weight despite her rider's claim, was in trouble going to the final flight. (16/1)

832 Kesanta took closer order with a circuit to race, but was a spent force on the extremely long run from the second last to the last flight. (7/1: 5/1-8/1)

1710 Roger's Pal (10/1: 8/1-12/1)

2906 SIDLESHAM H'CAP CHASE (0-110) (6-Y.O+) (Class E)

2-10 (2-10) **2m 2f (15 fncs)** £2,943.80 (£877.40: £418.20: £188.60) GOING: 0.13 sec per fur (G)

				SP	RR	SF
2796[6]	**Shrewd John (91)** (MissKMGeorge) **11-10-12** DGallagher (chsd ldr fr 3rd: led 10th: rdn out)	—	**1**	16/1	101	16
2621[4]	**Dear Do (103)** (NJHenderson) **10-11-10** JRKavanagh (hld up: chsd wnr fr 11th: rdn appr 2 out: unable qckn)	1¾	**2**	11/10[1]	111	26
2796*	**Whippers Delight (IRE) (94)** (GFHCharles-Jones) **9-11-1** 7x MrACharles-Jones (lw: led tl blnd & hdd 10th: wknd 11th)	16	**3**	11/4[2]	88	3
2068[U]	**Castleconner (IRE) (85)** (RGFrost) **6-10-6b**ow3 JFrost (chsd ldr to 3rd: wknd 9th)	12	**4**	11/2[3]	69	—
1934[6]	**Red Bean (96)** (KVincent) **9-11-3** DBridgwater (lw: a bhd)	5	**5**	13/2	75	—

(SP 108.9%) **5 Rn**

4m 35.5 (13.50) CSF £32.12 TOTE £12.20: £3.20 £1.30 (£7.80) OWNER Mr Geo Taylor (ASTON ROWANT) BRED Major R. H. Dening

2796 Shrewd John, beaten 22 lengths by Whippers Delight at Plumpton last week, decisively turned the tables on 7lb better terms. Leading at the sixth last, he was rousted along to win his first race in seventeen months. (16/1)

2621 Dear Do was poised to challenge in the straight but, when his rider asked him for an effort, he failed to find the necessary turn of foot. (11/10)

2796* Whippers Delight (IRE), who bounced back to form last week, narrowly bowled along in front, but a bad mistake at the sixth from home knocked the stuffing out of him. (11/4: 2/1-3/1)

2068 Castleconner (IRE) (11/2: op 3/1)

2907 CHICHESTER NOVICES' CLAIMING HURDLE (5-Y.O+) (Class F)

2-40 (2-40) **2m 2f 110y (9 hdls)** £2,249.00 (£624.00: £299.00) GOING: 0.13 sec per fur (G)

				SP	RR	SF
1726[7]	**Jovie King (IRE)** (RHBuckler) **5-11-0** BPowell (lw: a.p: led 6th: rdn out)	—	**1**	11/2[3]	65	10
2677[13]	**Mullintor (IRE) (85)** (RRowe) **6-11-3** DO'Sullivan (hdwy 6th: hrd rdn appr 2 out: r.o flat)	3	**2**	11/2[3]	65	10
1838[2]	**Fairelaine** (KCBailey) **5-10-2**(7) MrRWakley (lw: mstke 1st: stdy hdwy appr 2 out: r.o wl flat)	nk	**3**	11/2[3]	57+	2
1193[5]	**Night in a Million (71)** (SWoodman) **6-11-6** JOsborne (bit bkwd: lost pl 6th: r.o one pce fr 2 out)	2½	**4**	16/1	66	11
2794[F]	**Adilov (94)** (JJBridger) **5-11-3** AMaguire (lw: hld up: hrd rdn appr 2 out: 2nd & btn whn mstke last)	1¼	**5**	7/2[1]	62	7
2755[7]	**Zesti (77)** (TTClement) **5-10-8** NMann (a.p: 2nd whn mstke 3 out: rdn appr 2 out: wknd last)	4	**6**	5/1[2]	49	—
	Olivipet (FGray) **8-9-9**(5) MrRThornton (hdwy 6th: rdn appr 2 out: wknd appr last)	2½	**7**	50/1	39	—
1539[12]	**Noddadante (IRE)** (NRMitchell) **7-10-6**(5) SophieMitchell (nvr nrr)	4	**8**	25/1	47	—
546[5]	**Just-Mana-Mou (IRE) (80)** (WGMTurner) **5-9-12**(7) NWillmington (hdwy 5th: wknd 6th)	8	**9**	7/1	34	—
2676[P]	**Zadok** (JFfitch-Heyes) **5-11-0**(3) PHenley (prom to 3rd)	14	**10**	20/1	34	—
1958[P]	**Special Topic** (APJones) **7-10-3** SCurran (a bhd)	26	**11**	66/1	—	—
1861[10]	**Just a Beau (50)** (MrsLCJewell) **6-10-8** DLeahy (a bhd)	7	**12**	66/1	—	—
2574[9]	**Baba Sam (IRE)** (PEccles) **6-10-11** DGallagher (prom to 4th)	s.h	**13**	50/1	—	—
1766[P]	**Fair Haul** (RGFrost) **6-11-0** JFrost (a bhd)	12	**14**	66/1	—	—
2763[9]	**Deceit the Second** (PRRodford) **5-10-1b**(7) MGriffiths (led to 6th: sn wknd: t.o whn p.u bef 2 out)		**P**	66/1	—	—
2704[F]	**Jack of Diamonds** (RJO'Sullivan) **9-10-5** PHolley (lw: a bhd: t.o whn p.u bef 2 out)		**P**	50/1	—	—

(SP 123.9%) **16 Rn**

4m 33.4 (15.40) CSF £31.52 TOTE £7.80: £2.10 £1.90 £2.60 (£15.00) Trio £83.30 OWNER Mr R. H. Buckler (BRIDPORT) BRED John B. Hughes

Jovie King (IRE) made a winning debut for his new stable in this lower grade event. Looking in good shape beforehand, he went on at the fourth last and, ridden along, managed to keep his rivals at bay. (11/2)

1782 Mullintor (IRE) found things happening a bit too quickly for him on this lively ground, but he did stay on on for second. He is worth a try over further. (11/2)
1838 Fairelaine was given a terrible ride. Out with the washing and apparently with no chance whatsoever in the back straight, she began to make eye-catching headway going to the second last, despite her jockey doing very little. The jockey at last decided to ride her on the run-in and the mare ran on really strongly, only just failing to take second place. With a professional on board and over further, she can do a lot better than this. (11/2: op 5/2)
Night in a Million, looking in need of this first run for three months, would have been much better off had this been a handicap. Outpaced in the back straight, he struggled on again in the closing stages for fourth place. (16/1)
2642 Adilov was disappointing considering his good placed efforts in much better company. He was already held when making a bad error at the last. (7/2)
1707* Zesti, back in a more suitable class, played an active role until calling it a day jumping the final flight. (5/1)

2908 BET WITH THE TOTE (QUALIFIER) NOVICES' CHASE (6-Y.O+) (Class D)

3-10 (3-11) **3m 2f 110y (22 fncs)** £4,010.00 (£1,110.00: £530.00) GOING: 0.13 sec per fur (G)

				SP	RR	SF
	Vol Par Nuit (USA) (FDoumen,France) **6-10-7**(5)ow2 MrTDoumen (lw: chsd ldr fr 3rd: led 8th: clr appr last: r.o wl)	—	1	4/6[1]	93+	41
1983[F]	**Keep it Zipped (IRE) (99)** (OSherwood) **7-11-3b** JOsborne (lw: led to 8th: chsd wnr fr 2 out: unable qckn)	7	2	3/1[2]	94	44
2693[P]	**Strokesaver (IRE) (88)** (CPEBrooks) **7-10-10** DGallagher (lw: chsd ldr to 3rd: chsd wnr 4 out to 2 out: 3rd & btn whn blnd & uns rdr last: rmntd)	dist	3	12/1	—	—
2816[6]	**Thunder Road (IRE)** (RDickin) **6-10-10** JCulloty (stdy hdwy 12th: 4th whn fell 17th)		F	7/1[3]	—	—
2760[5]	**Dunlir (69)** (PRRodford) **7-10-3**(7) MGriffiths (lw: 5th whn fell 17th)		F	50/1	—	—
2681[P]	**Little Rowley (60)** (MrsLRichards) **8-10-10** MRichards (a bhd: t.o whn p.u bef 17th)		P	50/1	—	—
2704[6]	**Withycombe Hill** (PJHobbs) **7-10-3**(7) MrSDurack (mstkes: a bhd: t.o whn ref 3 out)		R	14/1	—	—
2756[5]	**Pavlova (IRE) (75)** (RRowe) **7-10-5** DO'Sullivan (lw: uns rdr & bolted bef s: mstkes: blnd 14th: bhd fr 16th: t.o whn blnd & uns rdr next)		U	10/1	—	—
				(SP 124.9%)	**8 Rn**	

6m 50.5 (10.50) CSF £3.41 TOTE £1.60: £1.20 £1.10 £2.60 (£3.00) OWNER Mr D. O. McIntyre (LAMORLAYE) BRED Vinery & Flamingo Partnership
Vol Par Nuit (USA) quickly got the hang of British fences and, leading at the eighth, asserted his authority going to the last. He is now bound for the Cheltenham Festival. (4/6)
1711 Keep it Zipped (IRE) ran better here. The early leader, he moved into second place two out, but found the winner far too strong. (3/1)
1798 Strokesaver (IRE) ran much better here and had every chance early in the straight. He was held when getting rid of his rider at the last. (12/1)
Thunder Road (IRE) (7/1: 8/1-12/1)

2909 STREBEL BOILERS AND RADIATORS SERIES (QUALIFIER) H'CAP HURDLE (0-115) (4-Y.O+) (Class E)

3-40 (3-40) **2m 2f 110y (9 hdls)** £2,301.00 (£636.00: £303.00) GOING: 0.13 sec per fur (G)

				SP	RR	SF
2069[5]	**Lessons Lass (IRE) (100)** (LadyHerries) **5-11-8** JOsborne (a.p: led 5th: clr appr last: eased flat)	—	1	100/30[2]	86+	34
1867[5]	**Neat Feat (IRE) (94)** (DRCElsworth) **6-11-2** PHolley (lw: hld up: chsd wnr fr 6th: ev ch appr 2 out: wknd appr last)	12	2	2/1[1]	70	18
	Flow Back (78) (GPEnright) **5-10-0** RJohnson (a.p: rdn 6th: wknd appr 2 out)	20	3	16/1	36	—
2062[5]	**Watch My Lips (98)** (MHTompkins) **5-11-6** AMaguire (lw: led to 5th: wknd 6th)	6	4	11/2	51	—
1956[4]	**Dominion's Dream (102)** (MCPipe) **5-11-3v**(7) GSupple (lw: rdn thrght: chsd ldr 2nd to 5th: sn wknd)	14	5	7/2[3]	43	—
1948[2]	**Muhtashim (IRE) (90)** (JFfitch-Heyes) **7-10-12** BFenton (lw: a bhd: t.o fr 6th)	dist	6	9/2	—	—
				(SP 118.1%)	**6 Rn**	

4m 29.2 (11.20) CSF £10.44 TOTE £3.90: £2.00 £1.90 (£6.40) OWNER Mr V. McCalla (LITTLEHAMPTON) BRED James Campbell
LONG HANDICAP Flow Back 9-13
2069 Lessons Lass (IRE), with ground and trip in her favour, made a winning debut for her new stable. Sent on with a circuit to race, she stormed clear going to the last and was eased considerably on the run-in. The winning distance is certainly no true reflection of her superiority. (100/30)
1867 Neat Feat (IRE) appeared to be absolutely cruising turning for home alongside the winner. When asked for an effort, he found disappointingly little and was left for dead going to the last. (2/1)
Flow Back, fit from the Flat, was left standing by the front two turning for home. (16/1)
1010 Watch My Lips took the field along but, collared with a circuit to go, disappointingly dropped away. (11/2: 4/1-6/1)
1956 Dominion's Dream looked far from happy, and her jockey was having to badger her along for much of the race. She gave up early on the final circuit. (7/2)

2910 BOGNOR REGIS H'CAP CHASE (0-100) (5-Y.O+) (Class F)

4-10 (4-10) **3m 2f 110y (22 fncs)** £2,929.50 (£812.00: £388.50) GOING: 0.13 sec per fur (G)

				SP	RR	SF
2681[3]	**Black Church (90)** (RRowe) **11-11-9** BFenton (mstke 3rd: stdy hdwy 13th: led appr 2 out: easily)	—	1	11/2[2]	103	36
1554[4]	**Master Comedy (72)** (MissLBower) **13-10-5b** AMaguire (bit bkwd: a.p: led 4 out tl appr 2 out: unable qckn)	7	2	6/1[3]	81	14
2752[3]	**Policemans Pride (FR) (67)** (MMadgwick) **8-10-0** DMorris (led to 10th: led 13th: blnd 17th: hdd 4 out: wknd appr last)	14	3	10/1	67	—
2679[P]	**Victory Gate (USA) (67)** (MrsLCJewell) **12-10-0** DLeahy (a bhd)	9	4	66/1	62	—
2623[3]	**Rose King (95)** (MissSEdwards) **10-12-0** MrTHills (bhd fr 18th)	11	5	15/8[1]	83	16
2756[F]	**Prize Match (75)** (JCTuck) **8-10-8** SMcNeill (lw: stdy hdwy 16th: wknd 18th: t.o)	dist	6	16/1	—	—
1582[4]	**Mingus (USA) (76)** (RHBuckler) **10-10-9** BPowell (hld up: mstke 4th: cl 6th whn fell 17th)		F	9/1	—	—
1877[P]	**Royal Saxon (95)** (PBowen) **11-12-0** RJohnson (lw: prom to 17th: wkng whn blnd 18th: t.o whn p.u bef last)		P	12/1	—	—
2039[6]	**Rainbow Fountain (72)** (NMLampard) **10-10-5** MrAKinane (lw: mstke 2nd: bhd fr 3rd: t.o whn p.u bef 4 out)		P	33/1	—	—
1708[4]	**Albury Grey (67)** (TPMcGovern) **10-10-0** GCrone (lw: a bhd: blnd 11th: t.o fr 12th: p.u bef last)		P	16/1	—	—
2660[P]	**Silverino (86)** (SEarle) **11-11-5b** CMaude (bhd fr 6th: t.o whn p.u bef 18th)		P	16/1	—	—
2694[12]	**Icantelya (IRE) (85)** (JWMullins) **8-11-4v[1]** SCurran (a.p: led 10th to 13th: wknd 17th: t.o whn ref 2 out)		R	20/1	—	—
				(SP 118.1%)	**12 Rn**	

6m 56.7 (16.70) CSF £34.96 CT £296.20 TOTE £5.80: £2.00 £1.10 £3.90 (£9.90) Trio £19.40 OWNER Dr B. Alexander (PULBOROUGH) BRED A. E. Hanbidge
LONG HANDICAP Albury Grey 9-7 Victory Gate (USA) 9-13

2681 Black Church, who has been expensive to follow this season, at long last came good. Given a very patient ride, he led approaching the second last and stormed clear without looking like he had had a race. (11/2)
1076 Master Comedy, looking in need of this first run in ten weeks, did not run badly. Jumping into the lead at the water, four out, he was collared approaching the second last and then left for dead. He has not won for the best part of three years. (6/1)
2752 Policemans Pride (FR) was taking a big step up in distance no doubt to offset his lack of pace, but having shown in front for the majority of the race, he was collared four from home. He grimly tried to hold on, but had run out of stamina going to the last. (10/1: 6/1-12/1)

2911 LEVY BOARD STANDARD N.H. FLAT RACE (4, 5 & 6-Y.O) (Class H)
4-40 (4-42) **2m 2f** £1,213.50 (£336.00: £160.50)

	Horse		Pos	SP	RR	SF
	Macy (IRE) (RDickin) **4-10-1**(7) XAizpuru (lw: lost pl 6f out: rallied over 1f out: led wl ins fnl f: r.o wl)	—	**1**	7/1	52 f	—
1986[4]	**Gower-Slave** (PBowen) **5-10-13**(5) MrRThornton (led over 13f: rdn over 2f out: swtchd rt 1f out: ev ch ins fnl f: unable qckn)	1	**2**	2/1[2]	51 f	—
	Kingswood Imperial (RJO'Sullivan) **4-10-1**(7) NWillmington (lw: chsd ldr 13f out: led over 4f out tl over 1f out: ev ch ins fnl f: one pce)	1½	**3**	10/1	50 f	—
2682[13]	**Caldebrook (IRE)** (JTGifford) **6-10-11**(7) SLaird (lw: hdwy 6f out: led over 1f out tl wl ins fnl f: one ce)	1½	**4**	7/4[1]	48 f	—
	Hulalea (NZ) (MissSEdwards) **5-11-6**ow2 MrTHills (chsd ldr 5f: one pce fnl 2f)	4	**5**	8/1	47 f	—
	Claregary (IRE) (RRowe) **4-9-10**(7) AGarrity (prom over 10f)	11	**6**	5/1[3]	30 f	—
2682[17]	**Tedross** (MissAMNewton-Smith) **6-11-1**(3) PHenley (hdwy 6f out: wknd 4f out: t.o)	dist	**7**	33/1	—	—
	See Minnow (MissSWaterman) **4-9-12**(5) DSalter (a bhd: t.o fnl 6f)	dist	**8**	33/1	—	—

(SP 124.9%) **8 Rn**

4m 52.7 CSF £21.48 TOTE £5.70: £1.60 £1.30 £2.80 (£7.50) OWNER Mrs M. Payne (STRATFORD) BRED James Devereux
WEIGHT FOR AGE 4yo-10lb
IN-FOCUS: **This race was run at a farcical pace - they went so slowly early on, it looked as though the crowd was set in for the night - and the tempo only increased in the last three-quarters of a mile.**
Macy (IRE), out of a dam who won the Norwegian Oaks and from the same family as Jodami, got outpaced as the tempo increased in the back straight. Getting his second wind from below the distance, he came through to win the scrap in the closing stages. (7/1: 7/2-8/1)
1986 Gower-Slave set nothing more than a crawl. Collared over half a mile from home, he was still battling for honours inside the final furlong before the winner asserted. (2/1: 6/4-5/2)
Kingswood Imperial looked very fit in the paddock and eased his way to the front over half a mile from home. Collared below the distance, he refused to give way and kept on to the end. (10/1: 5/1-12/1)
Caldebrook (IRE) showed in front below the distance, but was worried out of it in the dash to the line. (7/4: 5/2-6/4)
Hulalea (NZ), who got loose in the paddock, was given an extremely quiet ride with his jockey doing virtually nothing on him in the straight. (8/1: 4/1-10/1)

T/Plpt: £35.50 (275.01 Tckts). T/Qdpt: £7.60 (102.3 Tckts) AK

2517-NEWCASTLE (L-H) (Good, Good to firm patches)
Monday February 3rd
Final fence omitted
WEATHER: overcast, windy & cold

2912 KENTON NOVICES' CHASE (5-Y.O+) (Class E)
1-50 (1-50) **3m (18 fncs)** £2,901.75 (£879.00: £429.50: £204.75) GOING: 0.02 sec per fur (G)

	Horse		Pos	SP	RR	SF
2540[3]	**For Cathal (IRE)** (MrsMReveley) **6-11-4** PNiven (lw: nt j.w. w ldr: led after 3 out: hit last: all out)	—	**1**	7/4[1]	94	4
2540[P]	**Pantara Prince (IRE) (86)** (JIACharlton) **8-11-4** ADobbin (trckd ldrs: chal 3 out: nt qckn flat)	1¼	**2**	33/1	93	3
2061[4]	**Black Brook (IRE)** (MDHammond) **8-11-4** RGarritty (mde most tl after 3 out: wknd last)	14	**3**	14/1	84	—
1668[F]	**Strongalong (IRE) (64)** (PCheesbrough) **7-11-4** ASSmith (chsd ldrs: outpcd 13th: sn wknd)	4	**4**	100/1	81	—
2043[2]	**Celtic Giant (97)** (LLungo) **7-11-4** RSupple (lw: hld up & plld hrd: hdwy 7th: hit 9th & 12th: wknd 14th: blnd 2 out)	27	**5**	9/4[3]	63	—
2654[9]	**Pocaire Gaoithe (IRE) (65)** (WStorey) **7-11-4** MMoloney (mstkes: sn drvn along: lost tch 9th: t.o 13th)	30	**6**	50/1	43	—
1668[F]	**Aristodemus (85)** (MrsLMarshall) **8-11-4** KJohnson (mstkes: in tch: wkng whn blnd 14th: t.o whn p.u bef last)	..	**P**	33/1	—	—
1441[3]	**Turnpole (IRE)** (MrsMReveley) **6-11-4** NSmith (hld up: hit 2nd: in tch whn blnd & uns rdr 7th)		**U**	2/1[2]	—	—

(SP 116.0%) **8 Rn**

6m 13.6 (21.60) CSF £42.83 TOTE £2.60: £1.40 £2.90 £1.60 (£19.70) Trio £44.00 OWNER Mr D. S. Hall (SALTBURN) BRED Donal Sheahan
OFFICIAL EXPLANATION **Celtic Giant: finished distressed.**
2540 For Cathal (IRE), on this fast ground, would not have a cut at his fences and, under maximum pressure, scraped home with not an ounce to spare. He gives the impression that all he does is stay. (7/4)
1944 Pantara Prince (IRE) put two poor runs behind him to give the winner a real battle. (33/1)
1803 Black Brook (IRE), who has won a point-to-point in Ireland, ran well until fading at the last. This stable is struggling to find form at present. (14/1)
Strongalong (IRE) jumped better than on some occasions in the past. (100/1)
2043 Celtic Giant struggled on this fast ground and, as a result, his jumping suffered and he finished distressed. Well-named, he will be suited by some give underfoot. (9/4)
1441 Turnpole (IRE) hit the second then put in an awkward jump at the seventh, parting company with his rider. (2/1)

2913 ADVENT CATERING AT THE PAVILION CONDITIONAL (S) H'CAP HURDLE (0-95) (4-Y.O+) (Class G)
2-20 (2-20) **2m (9 hdls)** £1,983.50 (£556.00: £270.50) GOING: 0.02 sec per fur (G)

	Horse		Pos	SP	RR	SF
2701[P]	**Palace of Gold (73)** (LLungo) **7-10-1**(10) WDowling (w ldrs: led 3rd tl appr 3 out: led between last 2: hrd rdn: hld on wl)	—	**1**	25/1	55	21
	Brackenthwaite (88) (JLEyre) **7-11-4**(8) CElliott (bkwd: hld up: stdy hdwy 3 out: chal last: nt qckn)	1¼	**2**	14/1	69	35
1908[3]	**Oakbury (IRE) (68)** (MissLCSiddall) **5-9-12**(8) TSiddall (bhd: hdwy 6th: styd on fr next)	6	**3**	14/1	43	9
2744[9]	**Northern Falcon (82)** (MWEasterby) **4-10-10b** FLeahy (chsd ldrs: outpcd 3 out: kpt on between last 2)	½	**4**	20/1	56	12
2629*	**Kierchem (IRE) (71)** (CGrant) **6-10-9** MichaelBrennan (lw: trckd ldrs: led appr 3 out: hdd between last 2: wknd flat)	3	**5**	7/1[3]	42	8
2800[8]	**Doubling Dice (68)** (RAllan) **6-10-3**(3) SMelrose (chsd ldrs: one pce fr 3 out)	6	**6**	12/1	33	—

2768[6] **Charlvic (62)** (WSCunningham) **7-9-6**(8) LMcGrath (sn bhd: t.o 4th: sme hdwy 3 out: n.d)....7 **7** 66/1 20 —
1990[5] **Cool Steel (IRE) (67)** (MrsJBrown) **5-10-5b** ECallaghan (nt j.w: led to 3rd: wknd appr 3 out)....2½ **8** 14/1 23 —
Nosmo King (IRE) (67) (MrsMAKendall) **6-10-5** EHusband (bit bkwd: in tch: drvn along 5th: wknd next)....5 **9** 50/1 18 —
2768[4] **Meadowleck (65)** (WGYoung) **8-10-3** GLee (chsd ldrs: drvn along 4th: wknd after next)....2½ **10** 50/1 13 —
1701[7] **Doolar (USA) (78)** (PTDalton) **10-11-2b** MNewton (in tch: rdn 4th: wknd after next)....s.h **11** 9/1 26 —
2785[8] **Henry Hoolet (77)** (PMonteith) **8-11-1** GCahill (lw: in tch: drvn along 4th: wknd 3 out)....1¾ **12** 11/4[1] 23 —
1851[3] **Over Stated (IRE) (76)** (PCheesbrough) **7-11-0** GFRyan (a in rr)....1½ **13** 14/1 21 —
1310[P] **Storming Lorna (IRE) (65)** (WMcKeown) **7-9-12**(5)ow2 CMcCormack (hld up: gd hdwy 5th: ev ch tl wknd appr 3 out)....16 **14** 50/1 — —
2541[8] **Coquet Gold (62)** (FTWalton) **6-10-0** STaylor (chsd ldrs: drvn along 4th: wknd next: t.o)....dist **15** 100/1 — —
Fanadiyr (IRE) (66) (WStorey) **5-10-4** RMcGrath (bit bkwd: stdd s: nt j.w: a bhd: t.o 4th)....25 **16** 10/1 — —
2505[6] **Troy's Dream (68)** (MDHammond) **6-9-12**(8)ow1 RBurns (sn bhd: t.o whn p.u bef last).... **P** 14/1 — —
2505[2] **Tiotao (IRE) (69)** (CParker) **7-9-11**(10) TristanDavidson (lw: hld up: mid div & styng on whn rn out 3 out).... **R** 11/1 — —
1686[5] **Skiddaw Samba (84)** (MrsMReveley) **8-10-12**(10) DWebb (uns rdr 1st).... **U** 6/1[2] — —
(SP 138.9%) **19 Rn**

4m 0.9 (8.90) CSF £332.46 CT £4,635.93 TOTE £67.20: £9.20 £2.20 £2.70 £4.50 (£402.60) Trio £237.40; £267.55 to Lingfield 4/2/97 OWNER Mrs Barbara Lungo (CARRUTHERSTOWN) BRED Cheveley Park Stud Ltd
LONG HANDICAP Coquet Gold 9-12 Charlvic 9-8
WEIGHT FOR AGE 4yo-10lb
No bid
IN-FOCUS: **This was Willie Dowling's first winner.**
854 Palace of Gold pulled up early last time after his saddle slipped. He did not lack assistance from his rider, whose use of the whip looked brutal at times. (25/1)
Brackenthwaite, reappearing after an absence of 388 days, looked as a big as the proverbial bull but still ran really well, giving the winner a real fight. (14/1)
1908 Oakbury (IRE) was again putting in his best work in the closing stages. (14/1)
1652 Northern Falcon seemed to run his best race over hurdles so far. (20/1)
2629* Kierchem (IRE), raised 6lb, possibly hit the front too soon and, treading water between the last two, faded on the run-in. (7/1)
2785 Henry Hoolet, who looked to have a good chance at the weights, dropped away once in line for home. (11/4)
Fanadiyr (IRE) (10/1: op 6/1)

2914 FENHAM NOVICES' CHASE (5-Y.O+) (Class E)
2-50 (2-50) **2m 110y (12 fncs)** £2,771.75 (£839.00: £409.50: £194.75) GOING: 0.02 sec per fur (G)

SP RR SF
2786* **Bold Boss (100)** (GMMoore) **8-11-9** BStorey (lw: lft in ld 4th: clr 8th: comf)....— **1** 4/5[1] 91+ 28
2786[8] **Friendly Knight** (JSHaldane) **7-11-2** ASSmith (lw: chsd ldrs: kpt on fr 3 out: no ch w wnr)....5 **2** 25/1 79 16
1920[4] **Glamanglitz** (PTDalton) **7-11-2** RSupple (a chsng ldrs: one pce fr 3 out)....4 **3** 16/1[3] 75 12
2628[F] **Daring Past (110)** (MDHammond) **7-11-9** RGarritty (nt j.w: hit 6th: sn drvn along: wl btn whn blnd 3 out)....dist **4** 6/4[2] — —
2041[9] **Robara** (SJLeadbetter) **7-11-2** NLeach (nt j.w: sn bhd: t.o 5th)....dist **5** 20/1 — —
2628[F] **Dandy des Plauts (FR)** (MrsSJSmith) **6-10-9**(7) RWilkinson (sn outpcd & bhd: t.o 5th)....3 **6** 50/1 — —
2786[P] **Moss Pageant (60)** (FTWalton) **7-11-2** KJohnson (bit bkwd: led tl fell 4th).... **F** 100/1 — —
2002[R] **Monaughty Man (62)** (EMCaine) **11-11-6** MMoloney (sn drvn along: lost pl 8th: bhd whn p.u bef 3 out).... **P** 33/1 — —
(SP 115.9%) **8 Rn**

4m 8.1 (10.10) CSF £21.06 TOTE £1.70: £1.30 £1.80 £1.20 (£11.70) OWNER Mr John Robson (MIDDLEHAM) BRED Dr O. Zawawi
2786* Bold Boss has finally got the hang of things, and was never out of second gear here. (4/5: evens-11/10)
1987 Friendly Knight, well-beaten behind Bold Boss at Ayr seven days earlier, showed the benefit of that outing. (25/1)
1920 Glamanglitz, an ex-Irish pointer, has had trouble with his jumping so far but shaped better here. He will be suited by further and softer ground. (16/1)
2628 Daring Past, from a stable bang out of form, lacked confidence in his jumping. Struggling after a mistake at the sixth, he was dropping out when he got the third last all wrong. (6/4)

2915 MELTON H'CAP HURDLE (0-105) (4-Y.O+) (Class F)
3-20 (3-20) **3m (13 hdls)** £2,144.50 (£602.00: £293.50) GOING: 0.02 sec per fur (G)

SP RR SF
1849[4] **Scarba (95)** (JMJefferson) **9-11-3**(3) ECallaghan (lw: hld up: stdy hdwy 8th: led 3 out: lft clr next: blnd last: drvn out)....— **1** 8/1 80 4
2654[10] **Kings Lane (85)** (JMDun) **8-10-10** DParker (a chsng ldrs: drvn along 7th: kpt on wl fr 2 out)....3 **2** 20/1 68 —
2076[P] **Jigginstown (77)** (JJO'Neill) **10-9-9**(7) LCooper (hld up & bhd: stdy hdwy 9th: styd on one pce fr 2 out)....3 **3** 20/1 58 —
1942[2] **Aide Memoire (IRE) (76)** (RJohnson) **8-10-1** KJohnson (chsd ldrs: led after 10th: hdd 3 out: one pce)....2 **4** 16/1 56 —
1849* **Hudson Bay Trader (USA) (84)** (PBeaumont) **10-10-9** MissPRobson (lw: prom: outpcd 9th: kpt on fr 2 out)....5 **5** 7/1[2] 60 —
2634[9] **Galen (IRE) (89)** (MrsMReveley) **6-11-0** PNiven (lw: hld up: hdwy 8th: ev ch 10th: 4th & wkng whn blnd last)3½ **6** 5/1[1] 63 —
2701[10] **The Other Man (IRE) (75)** (MissLCSiddall) **7-10-0** OPears (hdwy & prom 8th: one pce fr 10th)....s.h **7** 33/1 49 —
2651[5] **Dockmaster (83)** (MissMKMilligan) **6-10-8** ADobbin (bhd: reminders 6th: sme hdwy 9th: n.d)....9 **8** 15/2[3] 51 —
2651[7] **Exemplar (IRE) (90)** (MrsSJSmith) **9-11-1** RichardGuest (hdwy 7th: ev ch 10th: sn wknd)....½ **9** 12/1 58 —
1849[10] **Mardood (75)** (SBClark) **12-10-0** JSupple (bit bkwd: chsd ldrs: drvn along 6th: sn wl outpcd)....2½ **10** 50/1 41 —
2076[U] **Hotspur Street (78)** (MWEasterby) **5-10-0b**(3) FLeahy (w ldrs: led 10th: sn hdd & wknd)....6 **11** 12/1 40 —
2008[3] **Quiet Mistress (81)** (WABethell) **7-10-6b** ASSmith (mde most to 10th: sn lost pl)....1¾ **12** 14/1 42 —
Suvla Bay (IRE) (82) (OBrennan) **9-10-7** MBrennan (plld hrd: trckd ldrs tl wknd 9th)....8 **13** 25/1 38 —
2631[11] **Grandman (IRE) (85)** (DMoffatt) **6-10-10** DJMoffatt (nt j.w: a bhd)....s.h **14** 16/1 40 —
1850[6] **Shallow River (IRE) (93)** (RCollins) **6-11-4** AThornton (chsd ldrs tl lost pl 9th)....26 **15** 14/1 31 —
2543[5] **Duke of Perth (91)** (HowardJohnson) **6-11-2** PCarberry (lw: hld up: stdy hdwy 8th: ev ch & rdn whn fell 2 out).. **F** 7/1[2] — —
1989[F] **Dorlin Castle (94)** (LLungo) **9-11-5** RSupple (sn bhd & drvn along: reminders 5th: t.o whn p.u bef 2 out).... **P** 8/1 — —
2654[3] **Haughton Lad (IRE) (75)** (JParkes) **8-10-0** VSmith (w ldrs tl wknd after 8th: bhd whn p.u bef 2 out).... **P** 16/1 — —
2654[P] **Farmers Subsidy (79)** (GMMoore) **5-10-4**ow4 NBentley (bhd tl p.u bef 3 out).... **P** 50/1 — —
Moonshine Dancer (100) (DWBarker) **7-11-8**(3) PMidgley (hdwy 8th: wknd 10th: p.u after 3 out).... **P** 33/1 — —
2697[8] **Prince Baltasar (75)** (NBycroft) **8-10-0** GCahill (sn bhd: t.o 6th: p.u bef 9th).... **P** 500/1 — —
(SP 145.4%) **21 Rn**

6m 3.6 (21.60) CSF £161.08 CT £2,912.27 TOTE £7.90: £1.80 £6.80 £19.70 £3.90 (£247.90) Trio Not won; £655.42 to Lingfield 4/2/97 OWNER Yorkshire Racing Club Owners Group (MALTON) BRED Bryan Gordon

LONG HANDICAP The Other Man (IRE) 9-4 Haughton Lad (IRE) 9-9 Farmers Subsidy 9-9 Mardood 9-10 Prince Baltasar 8-7
OFFICIAL EXPLANATION Moonshine Dancer: gurgled during the race.
1849 Scarba, closely matched with Hudson Bay Trader on Hexham running, gave his under-rated trainer and his promising young rider another success. (8/1: 6/1-9/1)
2042 Kings Lane put a poor effort last time behind him. (20/1)
1654 Jigginstown has ability, but obviously some sort of problem. He probably ran his best race over hurdles so far here. (20/1)
1942 Aide Memoire (IRE) is running well for her new stable. (16/1)
1849* Hudson Bay Trader (USA), raised 5lb, was in trouble four out, but to his credit kept on all the way to the line. (7/1)
1187 Galen (IRE), well-supported in the market, might be capable of better. (5/1)
2543 Duke of Perth moved up travelling as well as the winner, and was a length behind and had just come under pressure when he fell two out. Whether he would have stayed on as well as the winner is doubtful. (7/1)

2916 GOSFORTH DECORATING AND BUILDING SERVICES H'CAP CHASE (0-120) (5-Y.O+) (Class D)
3-50 (3-50) **3m (18 fncs)** £3,420.00 (£1,035.00: £505.00: £240.00) GOING: 0.02 sec per fur (G)

				SP	RR	SF
1934[5]	**Celtic Silver (95)** (MrsSJSmith) **9-10-3**ow3 RichardGuest (mde all: clr 13th: blnd last: drvn out)	—	1	4/1[2]	105	6
2630[9]	**Gale Ahead (IRE) (97)** (GMMoore) **7-10-5** BStorey (lw: prom tl blnd 12th: mstke & lost pl next: hdwy 4 out: kpt on between last 2: no imp)	4	2	11/2	104	8
2652[3]	**Slotamatique (IRE) (102)** (GRichards) **8-10-10** ADobbin (lw: trckd ldrs: effrt 4 out: wknd between last 2)	10	3	7/2[1]	103	7
1670[F]	**Kilcolgan (104)** (MrsJDGoodfellow) **10-10-12** GCahill (mstkes: rdn & wnt prom 8th: blnd 10th: outpcd 13th: wknd last)	10	4	4/1[2]	98	2
2544[4]	**Road by the River (IRE) (96)** (PCheesbrough) **9-10-4** ASSmith (chsd ldrs: drvn along 13th: mstke & wknd 4 out)	dist	5	9/2[3]	—	—
	Over the Stream (120) (MissMKMilligan) **11-12-0** AThornton (bit bkwd: reminders & lost pl 8th: t.o fr 14th)	dist	6	20/1	—	—
2063[4]	**Uranus Collonges (FR) (111)** (JGFitzGerald) **11-11-5b** RGarritty (sn bhd: p.u bef 9th)		P	8/1	—	—
2630[3]	**Snook Point (96)** (DALamb) **10-10-4**ow4 JBurke (prom tl lost pl 9th: mstke next: bhd whn p.u bef 11th)		P	25/1	—	—

(SP 115.5%) **8 Rn**

6m 7.9 (15.90) CSF £24.34 CT £76.31 TOTE £5.20: £1.70 £1.80 £1.70 (£22.00) Trio £20.10 OWNER Mrs S. Smith (BINGLEY) BRED A. Baylis
LONG HANDICAP Snook Point 8-11
1778 Celtic Silver made this a test of stamina and his jumping was blemish-free apart from the last, but the race was already won by then. (4/1)
1704 Gale Ahead (IRE) seemed to stumble on landing at the twelfth, and it must have knocked his confidence as he hit the next. Sticking on to show clear second between the last two, this was another more encouraging effort. (11/2)
2652 Slotamatique (IRE) went in pursuit of the winner, but his stamina seemed to give out between the last two. (7/2)
1670 Kilcolgan, having his first outing for 63 days, made several mistakes, when normally he is sure-footed. Struggling to keep up three-quarters of a mile from home, he tired badly at the last as if in need of the outing. (4/1)
2544 Road by the River (IRE) ran another of his poor races. (9/2)

2917 NORTHERN RACING 'N.H.' NOVICES' HURDLE (4-Y.O+) (Class E)
4-20 (4-23) **2m (9 hdls)** £2,368.50 (£666.00: £325.50) GOING: 0.02 sec per fur (G)

				SP	RR	SF
2697*	**Whip Hand (IRE)** (JGFitzGerald) **6-11-10** PCarberry (lw: hld up: stdy hdwy 6th: swtchd lft & led after 2 out: pushed clr flat)	—	1	2/7[1]	88+	28
2744[5]	**Dark Phoenix (IRE) (86)** (OBrennan) **7-10-13v[1]** MBrennan (hld up: drvn along & gd hdwy 5th: ev ch 2 out: hung rt: kpt on: no ch w wnr)	3½	2	25/1[3]	74	14
2673[10]	**Menaldi (IRE) (73)** (PCheesbrough) **7-11-4** ASSmith (a chsng ldrs: styd on one pce fr 3 out)	7	3	33/1	72	12
2539[4]	**Clavering (IRE)** (HowardJohnson) **7-11-4** JFTitley (lw: chsd ldrs: led 5th tl after 2 out: hung lft & one pce flat)	½	4	8/1[2]	71	11
2066[7]	**No Finer Man (IRE)** (GRichards) **6-11-4** ADobbin (in tch: outpcd appr 3 out: kpt on appr last)	1½	5	25/1[3]	70	10
2539[9]	**Alan's Pride (IRE)** (WMcKeown) **6-10-13** GCahill (unruly: chsd ldrs tl wknd 3 out)	10	6	50/1	55	—
1672[10]	**La Riviera (IRE)** (JIACharlton) **5-11-4** KJohnson (prom tl rdn & wknd appr 3 out)	1½	7	200/1	58	—
2627[10]	**Prince of Saints (IRE)** (MDHammond) **6-11-4** RGarritty (bhd: kpt on fr 3 out: n.d)	1¾	8	25/1[3]	56	—
	Dromore Dream (IRE) (MrsJBrown) **8-11-4** MrSSwiers (bit bkwd: wl bhd: sme hdwy 3 out: n.d)	2	9	25/1[3]	54	—
2539[3]	**Butterwick King (IRE)** (RAFahey) **5-11-4** DerekByrne (chsd ldrs tl wknd appr 2 out)	1¾	10	8/1[2]	53	—
2785[14]	**Sioux Warrior** (NTinkler) **5-11-1b[1](3)** EHusband (mid div: hdwy 4th: wknd after 6th)	½	11	100/1	52	—
	Master Flashman (MrsMReveley) **8-11-4** PNiven (a bhd)	16	12	50/1	36	—
2064[6]	**Dan de Man (IRE)** (MissLCSiddall) **6-11-4** AThornton (in tch tl outpcd appr 3 out: sn wknd)	6	13	50/1	30	—
	Grampsawinna (GROldroyd) **9-10-10**(3) ECallaghan (bit bkwd: a bhd)	5	14	200/1	20	—
2005[13]	**Henbrig** (GROldroyd) **7-10-13** BStorey (a in rr)	5	15	200/1	15	—
1999[6]	**Silver Minx** (MrsMReveley) **5-11-4** RHodge (plld hrd: led: blnd 1st: hdd 5th: wknd qckly next)	2	16	50/1	18	—
2572[7]	**Itsahardlife (IRE)** (MDHammond) **6-10-11**(7) RBurns (sn bhd)	10	17	66/1	8	—
	Rambling Lane (RAllan) **8-10-11**(7) SMelrose (rr div: sme hdwy ½-wy: sn wknd)	12	18	200/1	—	—
1263[10]	**Un Poco Loco** (MrsJBrown) **5-11-1**(3) GLee (prom: drvn along 5th: wknd next)	1	19	200/1	—	—
2541[9]	**Montein** (SJLeadbetter) **6-11-4** NLeach (a bhd)	8	20	200/1	—	—

(SP 131.6%) **20 Rn**

4m 2.0 (10.00) CSF £15.75 TOTE £1.40: £1.20 £2.00 £9.00 (£7.40) Trio £109.90 OWNER Lady Lloyd Webber (MALTON) BRED Carrigbeg Stud Co Ltd
2697* Whip Hand (IRE) was not as impressive as the betting suggested he might be, but once sent about his business, quickened clear of some moderate rivals on the run-in. (2/7)
2744 Dark Phoenix (IRE), winner of two bumpers two seasons ago, wore a visor for the first time. Hanging under pressure, she was never giving her rider full co-operation. (25/1)
1654 Menaldi (IRE), a fair sort, ran easily his best race so far. (33/1)
2539 Clavering (IRE) tended to hang under pressure and is not the finished article yet. (8/1)
No Finer Man (IRE), a half-brother to Addington Boy, showed ability on his hurdling debut, and will be suited by a step up to two and a half miles. (25/1)
Dromore Dream (IRE), who won a maiden point-to-point two years ago, showed some promise. (25/1)
2539 Butterwick King (IRE), who wore a tongue-strap, is still on the weak side and he dropped away over the last two. (8/1)

T/Jkpt: £13,006.50 (0.1 Tckts); £16,487.21 to Carlisle 4/2/97. T/Plpt: £74.80 (153.91 Tckts). T/Qdpt: £14.30 (70.43 Tckts) WG

2649-CARLISLE (R-H) (Ch Good to soft, Good patches, Hdles Soft)
Tuesday February 4th

One obstacle omitted each race
WEATHER: fine but cloudy

2918 WETHERAL NOVICES' HURDLE (4-Y.O+) (Class E)
1-40 (1-41) **2m 4f 110y (9 hdls)** £2,738.00 (£768.00: £374.00) GOING: 0.85 sec per fur (S)

				SP	RR	SF
2766^{2}	**Paperising (112)** (GRichards) **5-12-1** ADobbin (trckd ldrs: hit 4 out: led 2 out: styd on wl)	—	1	4/7^{1}	78+	36
2649^{4}	**Catherine's Choice** (MDHammond) **4-10-7** RGarritty (chsd ldrs: led 5th to 2 out: no ex)	4	2	20/1	64	11
2654*	**Bardaros (83)** (MissLucindaRussell) **8-11-9** MFoster (lw: a.p: outpcd 3 out: kpt on appr last)	18	3	8/1^{3}	55	13
1187^{8}	**Pentlands Flyer (IRE)** (HowardJohnson) **6-11-3** ASSmith (lw: plld hrd: wnt prom 4th: chal next: wknd appr 2 out)	hd	4	20/1	49	7
	Cool Game (MrsMReveley) **7-11-3** PNiven (outpcd after 4th: sme late hdwy)	13	5	66/1	39	—
2504^{3}	**Nutty Solera** (CParker) **7-11-3** BStorey (a.p: effrt 4 out: sn outpcd)	1¼	6	11/2^{2}	38	—
	Paparazzo (GMMoore) **6-11-3** JCallaghan (nvr bttr than mid div)	½	7	16/1	37	—
2785^{12}	**Triona's Hope (IRE)** (EMCaine) **8-10-10**(7) TristanDavidson (prom to 5th)	dist	8	1000/1	—	—
1921^{8}	**Kildrummy Castle** (JGFitzGerald) **5-11-3** PCarberry (mid div: effrt 4 out: wknd next)	11	9	20/1	—	—
2180^{4}	**Dantes Amour (IRE)** (MDHammond) **6-11-0**(3) MrCBonner (lost tch ½-wy: p.u bef 2 out)		P	66/1	—	—
2649^{F}	**Needle Match** (JJO'Neill) **4-10-2**(5) RMcGrath (mstkes: t.o whn p.u after 3 out)		P	100/1	—	—
1672^{P}	**Lyford Cay (IRE)** (JRBewley) **7-11-3** DBentley (bkwd: led: blnd 1st: hdd 5th: wknd qckly: p.u bef 2 out)		P	200/1	—	—
2785^{16}	**Kirtle Monstar** (LLungo) **6-11-3** RSupple (mstkes: a bhd: p.u bef 2 out)		P	200/1	—	—
1999^{14}	**Matachon** (MSmith) **7-11-6**ow3 GHarker (lost tch 4th: t.o whn p.u bef 3 out)		P	500/1	—	—
	Bunny Buck (IRE) (HowardJohnson) **7-11-3** GCahill (lost tch ½-wy: p.u bef 2 out)		P	33/1	—	—
				(SP 118.5%)	**15 Rn**	

5m 19.4 (28.40) CSF £16.64 TOTE £1.50: £1.20 £2.70 £1.70 (£8.10) Trio £18.70 OWNER The Jockeys Whips (PENRITH) BRED Independent British Hospitals
WEIGHT FOR AGE 4yo-11lb
2766 Paperising stays and likes testing ground and, against this opposition, he still had something to spare. (4/7)
2649 Catherine's Choice, stepping up in trip, got it well enough but just found the winner too classy. (20/1)
2654* Bardaros won a poor race on fast ground here last time, but found it more difficult in these conditions. (8/1)
1036 Pentlands Flyer (IRE) is far too keen for his own good, and must learn to settle. (20/1)
Cool Game looks the type to stay for ever, and only got going when the race was over. (66/1)
2504 Nutty Solera had his chance but did not seem suited to these soft conditions, and was unable to cope when the pace was on from the fourth last. (11/2)

2919 BET WITH THE TOTE (QUALIFIER) NOVICES' CHASE (6-Y.O+) (Class D)
2-10 (2-10) **3m (16 fncs)** £3,861.00 (£1,170.00: £572.00: £273.00) GOING: 0.85 sec per fur (S)

				SP	RR	SF
2767^{P}	**Crown Equerry (IRE)** (GRichards) **7-11-3** PCarberry (mde all: mstkes 3rd & 11th: clr last: rdn out)	—	1	7/1^{2}	111	28
2767*	**Santa Concerto (IRE)** (LLungo) **8-11-3** RSupple (a chsng wnr: rdn fr 13th: kpt on wl towards fin)	2	2	4/9^{1}	110	27
2803^{3}	**Trump** (CParker) **8-10-10** DParker (hld up: mstke 9th: effrt next: no imp)	dist	3	7/1^{2}	—	—
2614^{3}	**Call Me Black (IRE)** (MDHammond) **8-10-7**ow2 RGarritty (hld up: sme hdwy 11th: wknd fr 13th)	12	4	12/1^{3}	—	—
2551^{2}	**Final Beat (IRE) (78)** (JWCurtis) **8-10-10** DerekByrne (in tch tl mstke & outpcd 10th: n.d after)	7	5	20/1	—	—
1653^{8}	**Seldom But Severe (IRE)** (EAElliott) **7-10-5**(5) GFRyan (bit bkwd: chsd clr ldrs tl outpcd fr 9th)	3½	6	33/1	—	—
2788^{P}	**Mamica (80)** (MDods) **7-10-10** NSmith (lw: a bhd: t.o whn p.u bef 2 out)		P	16/1	—	—
2614^{F}	**Establish (IRE) (76)** (JPDodds) **9-10-5** KJohnson (mstkes: a bhd: t.o whn p.u bef 12th)		P	100/1	—	—
				(SP 116.5%)	**8 Rn**	

6m 24.9 (32.90) CSF £10.33 TOTE £8.80: £1.90 £1.40 £1.10 (£4.70) Trio £6.60 OWNER Mr Robert Ogden (PENRITH) BRED Thomas O'Connor
OFFICIAL EXPLANATION **Crown Equerry (IRE): the gelding enjoyed being able to dictate, and goes extremely well for Carberry.**
2767 Crown Equerry (IRE) was a different proposition this time despite the similar ground and, allowed to dictate things, enjoyed himself and kept on really well. (7/1: 5/1-8/1)
2767* Santa Concerto (IRE) was always nipping at the winner's heels, but when off the bridle he was very one-paced and just looks a dour stayer. (4/9)
2803 Trump is far too careful at his fences as yet, and gets left behind once there is any pace on. (7/1: 5/1-8/1)
2614 Call Me Black (IRE) could never make any real impression in this event, but she was wisely not over-punished and the kindness should be repaid. (12/1)

2920 HOECHST ROUSSEL PANACUR E.B.F. 'N.H.' (QUALIFIER) NOVICES' HURDLE (5-Y.O+ Mares Only) (Class E)
2-40 (2-41) **2m 4f 110y (9 hdls)** £2,626.00 (£736.00: £358.00) GOING: 0.85 sec per fur (S)

				SP	RR	SF
1849^{12}	**Daisy Days (IRE) (82)** (HowardJohnson) **7-11-5** ASSmith (trckd ldr: led fr 5th: styd on wl fr 3 out)	—	1	9/2^{3}	72	13
1654^{15}	**Lippy Louise** (MrsMReveley) **5-10-12** PNiven (lw: bhd: hdwy appr 3 out: styd on wl towards fin)	10	2	14/1	57	—
1807^{10}	**Auntie Alice (76)** (JGFitzGerald) **7-10-12** PCarberry (wnt prom 4th: chsd wnr fr 6th: rdn 3 out: btn next)	1¼	3	3/1^{2}	56	—
2785^{3}	**Parson's Lodge (IRE) (77)** (LLungo) **9-10-12** RSupple (hld up: hdwy 5th: chsng ldrs appr 3 out: sn rdn & btn)	18	4	5/2^{1}	42	—
1021^{P}	**Clairabell (IRE)** (JIACharlton) **6-10-12** BStorey (prom to 5th: sme hdwy again fr 2 out)	½	5	14/1	42	—
2047^{7}	**Lovely Rascal** (JJO'Neill) **5-10-12** ARoche (mstkes: bhd tl hdd & prom appr 6th: sn wknd)	16	6	8/1	29	—
2566^{6}	**Best Friend** (JWCurtis) **5-10-12** DerekByrne (lost tch fr 5th: t.o whn blnd last)	dist	7	16/1	—	—
	Sandrift (90) (CParker) **8-10-12** DParker (in tch: effrt & mstke 4 out: sn wknd: p.u bef last)		P	11/1	—	—
	Good Venture (LRLloyd-James) **6-10-9**(3) ECallaghan (bkwd: led: hit 1st & 4th: hdd 5th: wknd qckly: p.u bef 3 out)		P	50/1	—	—
1692^{20}	**Whatyeronabout (IRE)** (GMMoore) **5-10-12** JCallaghan (t.o fr ½-wy: p.u bef last)		P	50/1	—	—
2627^{F}	**Ottadini (IRE)** (WGReed) **5-10-12** JBurke (prom to 4th: sn bhd: t.o whn p.u bef 4 out)		P	200/1	—	—
				(SP 114.8%)	**11 Rn**	

5m 23.7 (32.70) CSF £56.50 TOTE £4.10: £2.20 £1.80 £1.80 (£12.60) Trio £17.30 OWNER The Sun Punters Club (CROOK) BRED A. Sherwood
STEWARDS' ENQUIRY Roche susp. 13-15 & 17/2/97 (excessive use of whip).
Daisy Days (IRE) won this moderate race in good style, having it sewn up over the last three flights. (9/2)

1190 Lippy Louise, on her second attempt over hurdles, is obviously learning fast and made up heaps of ground over the last four. She should certainly stay a lot further. (14/1: 10/1-16/1)
1500 Auntie Alice was close enough from halfway but, flat-out turning for home, she failed to come up with the goods. (3/1)
2785 Parson's Lodge (IRE), trying a longer trip, almost got into it on the home turn, but then disappointed, finding nothing under pressure. (5/2: 6/4-11/4)
Clairabell (IRE) looked pretty slow here, but does seem to stay well as she was keeping on at the finish. (14/1)
1450 Lovely Rascal has ability but still has plenty to learn and needs to brush up her hurdling. (8/1: tchd 14/1)
Sandrift (11/1: 7/1-14/1)

2921 JOHN BROCK MEMORIAL H'CAP CHASE (0-125) (5-Y.O+) (Class D)

3-10 (3-11) **2m (11 fncs)** £3,747.20 (£1,133.60: £552.80: £262.40) GOING: 0.85 sec per fur (S)

				SP	RR	SF
2674^{2}	**Marble Man (IRE) (92)** (MDHammond) **7-10-0** DBentley (lw: led to 3 out: rallied flat to ld cl home)	—	**1**	5/1	100	6
2618^{2}	**Regal Romper (IRE) (112)** (MrsSJSmith) **9-11-6** RichardGuest (w ldr: led 3 out: hrd rdn flat & ct cl home)	¾	**2**	$13/8^{1}$	119	25
2801^{5}	**Timbucktoo (117)** (JKMOliver) **10-11-11** BStorey (mstkes: chsd ldrs tl outpcd 8th: n.d after)	27	**3**	$9/4^{2}$	97	3
2002^{3}	**Positive Action (92)** (MABarnes) **11-9-9b**(5) STaylor (nt j.w: lost tch 5th: t.o)	dist	**4**	25/1	—	—
2632*	**Monnaie Forte (IRE) (92)** (JRAdam) **7-10-0** MMoloney (lw: trckd ldrs: effrt & ev ch whn hmpd, tried to run out & fell 3 out)		**F**	$100/30^{3}$	—	—
				(SP 112.5%)		**5 Rn**

4m 17.3 (23.30) CSF £13.08 TOTE £4.80: £2.20 £1.80 (£4.40) OWNER Mr D. J. Lever (MIDDLEHAM) BRED E. Farrell
LONG HANDICAP Marble Man (IRE) 9-7 Positive Action 9-0 Monnaie Forte (IRE) 9-12
2674 Marble Man (IRE) showed here he is learning fast at this game, and proved to be most determined to get back up after looking beaten going to the last. (5/1)
2618 Regal Romper (IRE), on ground slower than he really prefers, ran his usual game race but just failed to last home. (13/8)
2801 Timbucktoo had easier ground this time but was still disappointing, not having a cut at his fences when the pace was on. (9/4)
2002 Positive Action has lost his way altogether, and got slower and slower at his fences as the race progressed. (25/1)
2632* Monnaie Forte (IRE) might well have just won this, but when making his move three out he received a slight bump from Regal Romper which gave him the idea to duck out. Although he did get over the fence, he hit the wing hard and fell. (100/30: 9/4-7/2)

2922 HETHERSGILL CONDITIONAL H'CAP HURDLE (0-115) (4-Y.O+) (Class E)

3-40 (3-40) **3m 110y (10 hdls)** £2,293.50 (£641.00: £310.50) GOING: 0.85 sec per fur (S)

				SP	RR	SF
	Northern Squire (97) (JMJefferson) **9-11-10** ECallaghan (lw: hdwy to ld 1st: hdd 3 out: lft in ld last: styd on gamely)	—	**1**	$11/4^{1}$	75	1
	Hobkirk (83) (ACWhillans) **8-10-10** STaylor (trckd ldrs: chal 4 out: hrd rdn next: wl outpcd 2 out: styd on to disp ld flat: nt qckn)	hd	**2**	$3/1^{2}$	61	—
1844^{2}	**Manettia (IRE) (89)** (MrsMReveley) **8-11-2** GCahill (lw: led to 1st: w ldr: led 3 out: 3l clr whn blnd & hdd last: nt rcvr)	12	**3**	$11/4^{1}$	59+	—
	Five Flags (IRE) (88) (MrsSJSmith) **9-11-1** RWilkinson (in tch: outpcd 4 out: styd on: no imp)	5	**4**	$10/1^{3}$	55	—
	Linkside (90) (MGMeagher) **12-11-3** MichaelBrennan (bhd: drvn along fr 6th: no imp)	2½	**5**	$10/1^{3}$	55	—
2545^{10}	**Farney Glen (88)** (JJO'Neill) **10-11-1** RMcGrath (bit bkwd: chsd ldrs: effrt & ev ch 4 out: sn rdn & btn)	18	**6**	12/1	41	—
2800^{6}	**Little Redwing (73)** (MDHammond) **5-9-9b**(5) RBurns (in tch tl wl outpcd fr 6th)	13	**7**	$10/1^{3}$	18	—
693^{4}	**Blooming Spring (IRE) (77)** (MrsDThomson) **8-10-1**(3) NHorrocks (prom tl wknd fr 4 out)	19	**8**	16/1	10	—
				(SP 119.2%)		**8 Rn**

6m 28.7 (44.70) CSF £11.29 CT £22.51 TOTE £5.40: £1.70 £1.20 £1.10 (£7.40) Trio £12.40 OWNER Mrs J. M. Davenport (MALTON) BRED J. M. Jefferson and Mrs M. E. Dixon
LONG HANDICAP Little Redwing 9-10
STEWARDS' ENQUIRY Taylor susp. 13-15/2/97 + 1 day (excessive use of whip).
Northern Squire was turned out in tremendous condition for his first run of the season. He was never all that happy in the race, but is as game as they come and that won him the day. He will certainly know he has had a race. (11/4)
Hobkirk, having his first run since changing stables, looked a tough sort and kept battling away when all appeared lost. His tenacity should find him success. (3/1)
1844 Manettia (IRE) looked to have this won when forging into a clear lead going to the last, but the whole race had been a battle, and when she ploughed through the final flight she lost all her momentum and her chance. (11/4: 5/2-4/1)
Five Flags (IRE) is slow but sure and could never get into this. (10/1)
Linkside has obviously had problems as this was his first run for well over a year. In the circumstances it was not too bad. (10/1: 6/1-11/1)
Farney Glen, still needing this, blew up from the fourth last. (12/1)
2800 Little Redwing (10/1: 12/1-8/1)

2923 LIBRA GRAVURE CYLINDERS H'CAP CHASE (0-110) (5-Y.O+) (Class E)

4-10 (4-12) **2m 4f 110y (14 fncs)** £3,230.90 (£978.20: £477.60: £227.30) GOING: 0.85 sec per fur (S)

				SP	RR	SF
2652*	**Son of Iris (105)** (MrsMReveley) **9-11-10** PNiven (lw: in tch: rdn fr 11th: styd on wl appr last to ld last 100y)	—	**1**	7/1	114	47
2803*	**Cush Supreme (IRE) (84)** (MartinTodhunter) **8-10-3** 7x PCarberry (lw: led: j.slowly 6th & 7th: stumbled last: hrd rdn, hdd & no ex fnl 100y)	1¾	**2**	$100/30^{2}$	92	25
2650^{2}	**Bold Account (IRE) (86)** (GMMoore) **7-10-5b**[1] ADobbin (a chsng ldrs: ev ch & rdn 3 out: one pce appr last)	1¾	**3**	11/2	92	25
2801^{U}	**Grand Scenery (IRE) (88)** (HowardJohnson) **9-10-7** ASSmith (bhd: hdwy appr 3 out: rdn & no imp)	13	**4**	10/1	84	17
2801*	**Wayuphill (105)** (CParker) **10-11-10** 7x BStorey (lw: in tch: effrt 9th: one pce fr 3 out)	½	**5**	$3/1^{1}$	101	34
2508^{6}	**Rebel King (88)** (MABarnes) **7-10-2**(5) STaylor (prom: rdn fr 10th: wknd after 3 out)	11	**6**	12/1	75	8
1847*	**Dawn Lad (IRE) (81)** (MrsASwinbank) **8-10-0** JSupple (lw: effrt ½-wy: rdn & btn fr 9th)	22	**7**	$7/2^{3}$	51	—
2179^{P}	**Bishopdale (82)** (SGChadwick) **16-10-1**ow1 FPerratt (prom to 6th: sn bhd: blnd 9th)	1¾	**8**	50/1	51	—
2665^{U}	**Call Me Early (89)** (MissJFCraze) **12-10-8** ILawrence (chsd ldrs: blnd 7th: hit next: wknd 3 out: p.u bef last)		**P**	25/1	—	—
530^{P}	**Kelpie the Celt (81)** (MrsDThomson) **10-10-0** LO'Hara (chsd ldrs tl wknd rapidly: p.u bef 8th)		**P**	100/1	—	—
				(SP 121.8%)		**10 Rn**

5m 27.5 (24.50) CSF £29.86 CT £130.18 TOTE £8.10: £2.30 £1.40 £1.70 (£19.90) Trio £36.70 OWNER M H G Systems Ltd (SALTBURN) BRED James Roche
LONG HANDICAP Dawn Lad (IRE) 9-10 Bishopdale 9-8 Kelpie the Celt 9-3
OFFICIAL EXPLANATION Dawn Lad (IRE): was unsuited by the soft ground.
2652* Son of Iris has suddenly found a purple patch and, after looking in real trouble here, he stayed on to lead halfway up the run-in.(7/1: 5/1-8/1)

2803* Cush Supreme (IRE) tried to dominate again, but a stumble a stride after landing at the last did not help matters, and he was just run out of it. (100/30)
2650 Bold Account (IRE) had the blinkers on to sharpen him up and he raced in contention throughout, but just lacked that final dash. (11/2)
2508 Grand Scenery (IRE) is a law unto himself, but has the ability if ever caught in the mood. (10/1)
2801* Wayuphill has gone up 13lb for his last two victories and that seemed to find him out on this occasion. (3/1)
1991 Rebel King, from a yard that can do little right at present, was left struggling over the last three fences. (12/1)
1847* Dawn Lad (IRE), after eight weeks off, put up a poor display, never giving any hope. (7/2)

2924 DURDAR INTERMEDIATE N.H. FLAT RACE (4, 5 & 6-Y.O) (Class H)
4-40 (4-40) **2m 1f** £1,035.00 (£285.00: £135.00)

				SP	RR	SF
	Tom's River (IRE) (MrsMReveley) **5-11-1**(3) GLee (bit bkwd: bhd: hdwy 6f out: led 1½f out: styd on wl)	—	**1**	10/1	60 f	—
	One Stop (MABarnes) **4-9-12**(5) STaylor (chsd ldrs: ev ch 2f out: kpt on wl)	2½	**2**	12/1	53 f	—
1986[9]	**Water Font (IRE)** (JJO'Neill) **5-10-13**(5) RMcGrath (mde most tl hdd & wknd 1½f out)	13	**3**	20/1	45 f	—
2633[7]	**Eastcliffe (IRE)** (WMcKeown) **5-10-11**(7) CMcCormack (plld hrd: sn cl up: chal 4f out: wknd fnl 2f)	1½	**4**	20/1	44 f	—
1296[14]	**Jessolle** (GRichards) **5-10-13** MrRHale (trckd ldrs tl grad wknd fnl 2f)	1	**5**	20/1	38 f	—
	What A Tale (IRE) (MrsMReveley) **5-11-4** GCahill (bhd: drvn along ½-wy: hdwy 6f out: no imp fnl 3f)	2½	**6**	Evens[1]	41 f	—
	Superexalt (JGFitzGerald) **5-11-1**(3) FLeahy (hld up: hdwy 6f out: sn in tch: wknd 3f out)	9	**7**	100/30[2]	32 f	—
	Sabu (JIACharlton) **5-11-1**(3) ECallaghan (bkwd: cl up tl wknd 4f out)	22	**8**	50/1	12 f	—
	Jumbo's Dream (JEDixon) **6-11-4** MissPRobson (bkwd: wl bhd fr ½-wy)	4	**9**	50/1	8 f	—
	Border Image (FPMurtagh) **6-10-11**(7) NHorrocks (in tch tl wknd fnl 5f)	3½	**10**	50/1	5 f	—
2804[5]	**Castle Bay (IRE)** (LLungo) **6-10-13**(5) BGrattan (hld up & bhd: effrt 6f out: no rspnse)	3½	**11**	9/2[3]	1 f	—
	Ferrino Fruits (IRE) (MGMeagher) **6-10-13**(5) MichaelBrennan (bkwd: sn drvn along: lost tch ½-wy: t.o)	dist	**12**	33/1	—	—
				(SP 131.2%)	**12 Rn**	

4m 32.6 CSF £112.98 TOTE £8.30: £2.20 £2.80 £5.80 (£43.50) Trio £175.40; £172.94 to Ludlow 5/2/97 OWNER Jemm Partnership (SALTBURN) BRED Ted O'Rourke
WEIGHT FOR AGE 4yo-10lb
Tom's River (IRE) came from behind to win this in useful style. He looks a real stayer in the making. (10/1)
One Stop ran well and looks the type to improve as a result. (12/1)
705 Water Font (IRE) put up by far his best effort to date, but was just tapped for toe late on. (20/1)
Eastcliffe (IRE) is learning with every run. (20/1)
Jessolle showed little in a red hot bumper here last time, but gave plenty of hope for the future this time. (20/1)
What A Tale (IRE) came with a big reputation but showed little of it - he probably needed the experience. (Evens)
2804 Castle Bay (IRE) (9/2: op 5/2)

T/Jkpt: £24,269.00 (1 Tckt). T/Plpt: £14.80 (827.61 Tckts). T/Qdpt: £8.50 (74.6 Tckts) AA

2805-WARWICK (L-H) (Good to firm)
Tuesday February 4th
WEATHER: rain

2925 RYTON HURDLE (4-Y.O) (Class E)
1-30 (1-30) **2m (8 hdls)** £2,670.00 (£745.00: £360.00) GOING: 0.05 sec per fur (G)

				SP	RR	SF
2566[2]	**Fitzwilliam (USA)** (IABalding) **4-10-12** GBradley (lw: a.p: led after 3rd: clr appr 2 out: drvn out)	—	**1**	11/4[1]	73	28
	Exalted (IRE) (WJenks) **4-10-12** TJenks (bit bkwd: hdwy appr 4th: chsd wnr appr 2 out: no imp)	6	**2**	14/1	67	22
	Takeamemo (IRE) (OSherwood) **4-10-7** JOsborne (bit bkwd: hld up & bhd: mstke 3rd: hdwy 3 out: j.slowly last: nt rch ldrs)	4	**3**	8/1	58	13
	Tiutchev (MissHCKnight) **4-10-12** JFTitley (bkwd: a.p: ev ch 3 out: sn wknd)	5	**4**	6/1	58	13
2805[8]	**Palamon (USA)** (JWhite) **4-10-12** BClifford (nvr nrr)	1¼	**5**	16/1	57	12
2622[10]	**Brecon** (WRMuir) **4-10-12** MRichards (led to 2nd: wknd appr 3 out)	2	**6**	50/1	55	10
2669[2]	**Toby Brown** (DNicholson) **4-10-12** AMaguire (nvr trbld ldrs)	6	**7**	3/1[2]	49	4
1158[P]	**Gulf of Siam** (JMackie) **4-10-12** TEley (bkwd: hld up & bhd: hdwy appr 4th: wknd 3 out)	1½	**8**	50/1	47	2
736[7]	**Still Here (IRE)** (PBowen) **4-10-12** RJohnson (prom to 3rd)	10	**9**	50/1	37	—
2784[6]	**Mighty Keen** (MCBanks) **4-10-12** DSkyrme (bkwd: a bhd)	3	**10**	33/1	34	—
2070[14]	**Induna Mkubwa** (CFWall) **4-10-12** KGaule (bit bkwd: hdwy after 3rd: wknd appr 3 out)	hd	**11**	33/1	34	—
	Green Bopper (USA) (CPMorlock) **4-10-12** CMaude (bit bkwd: plld hrd: led 2nd tl after 3rd: wknd 5th)	1	**12**	33/1	33	—
2622[5]	**Sulawesi (IRE)** (NATwiston-Davies) **4-10-7** CLlewellyn (hdwy 5th: wknd 3 out: bhd whn fell 2 out)		**F**	5/1[3]	—	—
2668[6]	**Apache Park (USA)** (MSheppard) **4-10-12** DGallagher (a bhd: t.o 4th: p.u bef last)		**P**	25/1	—	—
2668[5]	**Impending Danger (85)** (KSBridgwater) **4-10-12** DBridgwater (prom to 3rd: t.o whn p.u bef 2 out)		**P**	14/1	—	—
	Alana's Ballad (IRE) (BPJBaugh) **4-10-7** GaryLyons (a bhd: t.o 4th: p.u bef 2 out)		**P**	100/1	—	—
				(SP 132.5%)	**16 Rn**	

3m 49.5 (7.50) CSF £39.96 TOTE £3.80: £1.40 £5.20 £2.90 (£26.40) Trio £105.70; £89.40 to Ludlow 5/2/97 OWNER Mr Paul Mellon (KINGSCLERE)
2566 Fitzwilliam (USA) was reported by his pilot to have found Ludlow too sharp last time, and Bradley made more use of him on this more galloping course. He can score again. (11/4)
Exalted (IRE), a 30,000 guineas purchase out of Sir Mark Prescott's stable, was disappointing after winning once as a juvenile. Entered in the Triumph Hurdle, normal improvement should see him off the mark. (14/1)
Takeamemo (IRE) dead-heated in a two-mile maiden at Clonmel last September, then finished fifth in useful company on her hurdling debut shortly after. Left a lot to do, she gave the impression there are better things to come. (8/1: 6/1-9/1)
Tiutchev, bought for 31,000 guineas at Newmarket Autumn Sales, only ran three times on the Flat. A Triumph Hurdle entry, he ran a fine race until blowing up and should last longer next time. (6/1: 4/1-13/2)
Palamon (USA), a former inmate of Roger Charlton's, was a ten furlong auction race winner at Leicester. He is shaping as though he needs further. (16/1)
2622 Sulawesi (IRE) (5/1: op 11/4)

2926 PRINCETHORPE NOVICES' CHASE (5-Y.O+) (Class D)

2-00 (2-02) **2m 4f 110y (17 fncs)** £3,777.50 (£1,145.00: £560.00: £267.50) GOING minus 0.11 sec per fur (G)

				SP	RR	SF
2548*	**Garnwin (IRE) (100)** (NJHenderson) **7-11-9** JRKavanagh (lw: hld up: stdy hdwy 8th: led appr 2 out: drvn out)	—	1	9/4[1]	121	49
2776[6]	**Flight Lieutenant (USA) (109)** (TCasey) **8-11-9** AThornton (hld up: hdwy 10th: hit 3 out: ev ch 2 out: hrd rdn: nt qckn flat)	1¾	2	4/1[3]	120	48
2569[3]	**Lobster Cottage (87)** (KCBailey) **9-11-9** SMcNeill (chsd ldrs: blnd 2nd: led 8th tl appr 2 out: sn wknd)	22	3	11/1	103	31
1829[U]	**Swiss Tactic (IRE) (64)** (AEJessop) **8-11-3** VSmith (bit bkwd: sme hdwy whn j.lft 11th: n.d)	18	4	66/1	82	10
2628[6]	**Weeheby (USA) (84)** (MFBarraclough) **8-11-3** TJMurphy (chsd ldrs: rdn after 7th: mstke 8th: wknd qckly after 3 out)	1¾	5	25/1	81	9
2793[3]	**Furry Fox (IRE)** (RCurtis) **9-11-3** DMorris (lw: wl bhd fr 10th: t.o)	18	6	25/1	67	—
2679[8]	**Moving Out (84)** (MissHCKnight) **9-11-3** GBradley (prom: wkng whn blnd 12th: t.o)	s.h	7	3/1[2]	67	—
2667[5]	**Wot No Gin (65)** (AJWilson) **8-11-3** RJohnson (blnd 6th: a bhd: t.o)	3	8	7/1	65	—
1909[P]	**Elite Governor (IRE)** (NMLampard) **8-10-10**(7) MrLBaker (hld up: hdwy 10th: wkng & mstke 4 out: fell 3 out)	...	F	25/1	—	—
2550[11]	**Brownscroft** (MissPMWhittle) **9-10-5**(7) MrRWakley (mstke 4th: sn bhd: t.o whn p.u bef 3 out)		P	100/1	—	—
2571[3]	**Aeolian** (MissPMWhittle) **6-10-10**(7) KHibbert (lw: a bhd: t.o whn p.u bef 11th)		P	50/1	—	—
	Dandie Imp (AWCarroll) **9-11-3** BPowell (bkwd: prom tl wknd appr 11th: t.o whn p.u bef 4 out)		P	14/1	—	—
1261[P]	**Eventsinternashnal** (MSheppard) **8-11-3b** MrJMPritchard (sn t.o: p.u after 10th)		P	100/1	—	—
2691[P]	**Mheanmetoo** (DLWilliams) **6-11-3** PHolley (bit bkwd: led: clr whn mstke 6th: hdd 8th: sn wknd: t.o whn p.u bef 11th)		P	100/1	—	—
2807[5]	**Typhoon (IRE)** (MarkCampion) **7-11-3** MSharratt (ref to r: t.n.p)		R	100/1	—	—
	Convamore Queen (IRE) (NMBabbage) **8-10-12** VSlattery (bkwd: bhd whn blnd & uns rdr 5th)		U	50/1	—	—

(SP 124.2%) **16 Rn**

5m 8.0 (4.00) CSF £10.25 TOTE £2.70: £1.80 £2.20 £1.80 (£6.40) Trio £10.00 OWNER Pioneer Heat-Treatment (LAMBOURN) BRED John Kehoe

2548* Garnwin (IRE), in no hurry to take on the leaders, again looked the type who tends to idle in front. (9/4: op 6/4)
1925 Flight Lieutenant (USA) jumped much better than at Cheltenham last time, and was only forced to give best on the run-in. (4/1: 9/4-9/2)
2569 Lobster Cottage would have been much better off at the weights with the first two had this been a handicap. (11/1: 8/1-12/1)

2927 E.B.F. 'N.H.' (QUALIFIER) NOVICES' HURDLE (5, 6 & 7-Y.O) (Class D)

2-30 (2-31) **2m 4f 110y (11 hdls)** £3,377.50 (£940.00: £452.50) GOING: 0.05 sec per fur (G)

				SP	RR	SF
1938[2]	**Marching Marquis (IRE)** (NoelChance) **6-11-0** RJohnson (chsd ldr: led after 6th: wl clr appr 2 out: eased flat)	—	1	5/6[1]	83+	13
2676[P]	**Ryder Cup (IRE)** (NJHenderson) **5-11-0** JRKavanagh (bkwd: hld up & bhd: rdn & hdwy 8th: wnt 2nd 2 out: no ch w wnr)	15	2	14/1	71	1
2673[11]	**Jayfcee** (MPBielby) **5-11-0** BPowell (plld hrd: prom tl lost pl 7th: sme hdwy fr 3 out)	3	3	33/1	69	—
2090*	**Maid For Adventure (IRE)** (MissHCKnight) **6-11-5** JCulloty (hld up: chsd wnr fr 7th: wknd appr 2 out)	1¾	4	3/1[2]	73	3
	Tidebrook (KCBailey) **7-11-0** CO'Dwyer (bit bkwd: hld up: stdy hdwy 6th: mstke 7th: wkng whn mstke 3 out: blnd 2 out)	3	5	9/2[3]	65	—
	Commuter Country (CRBarwell) **6-11-0** BFenton (bkwd: wl bhd fr 7th: t.o)	21	6	33/1	49	—
1964[8]	**Dingle Wood (IRE)** (NMLampard) **7-11-0** MrAKinane (hld up & plld hrd: hdwy 5th: wknd appr 7th: t.o)	5	7	33/1	45	—
2093[3]	**Manvulane (IRE) (92)** (MrsCJBlack) **7-11-0v** JRailton (led tl after 6th: wknd qckly: 5th & no ch whn p.u bef 2 out)		P	12/1	—	—

(SP 120.9%) **8 Rn**

5m 1.6 (14.60) CSF £14.25 TOTE £2.00: £1.10 £2.40 £9.30 (£21.60) OWNER Michael And Gerry Worcester (LAMBOURN) BRED Martin Kenirons

1938 Marching Marquis (IRE) proved far too good for these rivals and will now go for the Persian War at Chepstow, prior to the Royal SunAlliance at Cheltenham. (5/6)
Ryder Cup (IRE), who won a maiden point-to-point in Ireland last year, was presumably all at sea in the mud at Lingfield on his debut. (14/1: op 8/1)
1801 Jayfcee looks slow and is probably going to need three miles. (33/1)
2090* Maid For Adventure (IRE) could not go with the winner from the third last. (3/1: op 7/4)
Tidebrook, supported in the ring, looked very novicey once the race began in earnest a mile from home. (9/2)
2093 Manvulane (IRE) (12/1: op 6/1)

2928 GEORGE CONEY CHALLENGE CUP H'CAP CHASE (0-130) (5-Y.O+) (Class C)

3-00 (3-01) **3m 5f (22 fncs)** £6,212.00 (£1,732.00: £836.00) GOING minus 0.11 sec per fur (G)

				SP	RR	SF
2758[4]	**Musthaveaswig (121)** (DNicholson) **11-11-10** AMaguire (hld up: outpcd 15th: rallied 17th: rdn appr 2 out: led appr last: drvn out)	—	1	9/2	128	5
2665*	**Bendor Mark (98)** (MJWilkinson) **8-10-1**ow1 JFTitley (prom: j.slowly 6th: led 13th tl j.slowly 16th: lft in ld 3 out: hdd appr last: one pce)	5	2	4/1[3]	102	—
2706[3]	**Tug of Peace (113)** (GBBalding) **10-11-2** BFenton (hld up: j.slowly 9th: t.o whn mstke 17th)	28	3	6/1	100	—
	Limonaire (FR) (125) (JPeromingo,France) **11-12-0b**[1] AVieira (led to 5th: lost pl 15th: t.o whn fell 17th)		F	12/1	—	—
2063[F]	**Christmas Gorse (120)** (NAGaselee) **11-11-9** CLlewellyn (led 5th: clr 8th: hdd 13th: led 16th: 4l clr whn blnd & uns rdr 3 out)		U	3/1[1]	—	—
2821[4]	**Danger Baby (105)** (DLWilliams) **7-10-8** PHolley (lw: hld up: mstke & uns rdr 6th)		U	100/30[2]	—	—
2758[5]	**Big Ben Dun (105)** (CPEBrooks) **11-10-1**(7) MBerry (2nd whn mstke & uns rdr 2nd)		U	10/1	—	—

(SP 117.3%) **7 Rn**

7m 45.5 (25.50) CSF £21.87 TOTE £3.50: £2.20 £2.50 (£11.20) OWNER P R D Fasteners Ltd (TEMPLE GUITING) BRED Patrick Shanahan
LONG HANDICAP Bendor Mark 9-12

2758 Musthaveaswig has been entered in the Grand National, and could end up at Aintree given fast ground. (9/2)
2665* Bendor Mark, still out of the handicap despite being raised 7lb, was probably stretching his stamina to the limit. (4/1)
2706 Tug of Peace was never in the hunt. (6/1)
2063 Christmas Gorse would have taken some catching given how well he stays. (3/1)

2929 EBRINGTON H'CAP HURDLE (0-130) (4-Y.O+) (Class C)
3-30 (3-32) **2m 4f 110y (11 hdls)** £3,454.00 (£1,042.00: £506.00: £238.00) GOING: 0.05 sec per fur (G)

	Horse / details		Pos	SP	RR	SF
2666[6]	**Reaganesque (USA) (111)** (PGMurphy) **5-10-11** RFarrant (lw: hld up: hdwy 3rd: led appr 7th: clr 2 out: drvn out)	—	**1**	9/4[2]	96	19
2644[4]	**Barford Sovereign (109)** (JRFanshawe) **5-10-9** AMaguire (swtg: led tl appr 7th: hrd rdn appr last: one pce)	4	**2**	7/4[1]	91	14
2779[9]	**Albemine (USA) (124)** (MrsJCecil) **8-11-10** TKent (chsd ldr tl after 6th: wknd 3 out)	15	**3**	9/2[3]	94	17
	Amillionmemories (100) (MrsBarbaraWaring) **7-10-0** RGreene (bkwd: wl bhd tl r.o fr 2 out: n.d)	1	**4**	14/1	69	—
1903[3]	**Sovereigns Parade (110)** (NJHenderson) **5-10-10** JRKavanagh (lw: wl bhd tl hdwy 8th: wknd appr 2 out: t.o)	30	**5**	7/1	56	—
2573[5]	**Vision of Freedom (IRE) (100)** (PBowen) **9-10-0** NWilliamson (prom: 4th whn blnd 7th: bhd whn fell 3 out)		**F**	11/1	—	—
				(SP 112.8%)		**6 Rn**

4m 59.1 (12.10) CSF £6.30 TOTE £3.70: £1.40 £1.50 (£2.40) OWNER Mrs John Spielman (BRISTOL) BRED Gainsborough Farm Inc
LONG HANDICAP Amillionmemories 9-6
1956* Reaganesque (USA), supported in the offices, made it five winners in ten days for his stable. (9/4)
2644 Barford Sovereign tried her best but could not cope with the winner. (7/4)
2114* Albemine (USA) did not appear suited by this extra half-mile. (9/2)
Amillionmemories, 8lb out of the handicap, may need further nowadays and will strip fitter for this. (14/1)

2930 AIR WEDDING TROPHY HUNTERS' CHASE (5-Y.O+) (Class H)
4-00 (4-00) **3m 2f (20 fncs)** £1,114.00 (£309.00: £148.00) GOING minus 0.11 sec per fur (G)

Horse / details		Pos	SP	RR	SF
The Malakarma (MissCSaunders) **11-12-3**(5) MrBPollock (bkwd: chsd ldr: j.slowly 6th & 8th: pushed along after 10th: jnd ldr & pckd 15th: sn outpcd: rallied to ld flat)	—	**1**	4/6[1]	83	16
Out For Fun (PeterKing) **11-11-9**(7) MrNRMitchell (bkwd: led: clr 8th: j.slowly 14th: mstke last: hdd flat)	2	**2**	6/4[2]	76	9
Sirisat (MissTOBlazey) **13-11-10**(7)ow1 MissTBlazey (lw: hld up: hit 12th & 13th: sn bhd)	15	**3**	9/1[3]	68	—
Corn Exchange (DGDuggan) **9-11-9**(7) MrMFitzgerald (bkwd: blnd & uns rdr 3rd)		**U**	25/1	—	—
			(SP 113.8%)		**4 Rn**

6m 47.2 (22.20) CSF £2.11 TOTE £1.40 (£1.90) OWNER Mr Charles Dixey (NORTHAMPTON) BRED C. R. Dixey
The Malakarma finds this trip on the short side these days, but eventually found stamina coming to his aid. (4/6)
Out For Fun was coming to the end of his tether when missing out at the final fence, which proved the last straw. (6/4)

2931 FEBRUARY MAIDEN N.H. FLAT RACE (4, 5 & 6-Y.O F & M) (Class H)
4-30 (4-30) **2m** £1,028.00 (£278.00: £128.00)

	Horse / details		Pos	SP	RR	SF
	Erintante (IRE) (FDoumen,France) **4-10-9**(5) MrTDoumen (leggy: hld up: plld hrd: qcknd to ld wl over 1f out: pushed out)	—	**1**	6/4[1]	91 f	—
	Melody Maid (NJHenderson) **5-11-3**(7) THagger (hdwy 8f out: led 5f out tl wl over 1f out: one pce)	3	**2**	9/1	88 f	—
	Castle Mews (IRE) (GCBravery) **6-11-5**(5) SRyan (leggy, lt-f: a.p: r.o one pce fnl 2f)	11	**3**	16/1	77 f	—
	Good Job (CJMann) **5-11-3**(7) DKiernan (s.s: gd hdwy 8f out: one pce fnl 2f)	hd	**4**	9/1	77 f	—
	Wise Gunner (MCPipe) **4-11-0** DWalsh (a.p: no hdwy fnl 3f)	3	**5**	9/1	74 f	—
	Miss Match (LGCottrell) **6-11-5**(5) OBurrows (prom: ev ch over 2f out: sn wknd)	4	**6**	33/1	70 f	—
	Suilven (KCBailey) **5-11-3**(7) MrRWakley (w'like: bit bkwd: swvd rt s: hld up: hdwy 6f out: one pce fnl 3f)	1½	**7**	7/1[2]	68 f	—
	Fruitation (MJWilkinson) **6-11-7**(3) LAspell (bkwd: hld up: hdwy 8f out: wknd 4f out)	4	**8**	7/1[2]	64 f	—
	Nearly A Score (GBBalding) **5-11-5**(5) ABates (nvr nr to chal)	s.h	**9**	14/1	64 f	—
1504[8]	**Night Escapade (IRE)** (CWeedon) **5-11-3**(7) LSuthern (hdwy 7f out: wknd over 3f out)	5	**10**	9/1	59 f	—
2757[2]	**Where's Miranda** (GMMcCourt) **5-11-3**(7) RStudholme (lw: prom 10f)	8	**11**	8/1[3]	51 f	—
	Gems Lass (JAPickering) **6-11-3**(7) MissJWormall (prom 10f)	6	**12**	66/1	45 f	—
	Geisha (PRWebber) **5-11-10** MrPScott (lw: prom: led 9f out to 5f out: sn wknd)	7	**13**	14/1	38 f	—
	Artic Meadow (AEJessop) **6-11-5**(5) MrRThornton (bkwd: wl bhd after 4f)	1½	**14**	100/1	37 f	—
	Storm Queen (IRE) (APJarvis) **6-11-3**(7) CDavies (bit bkwd: a bhd)	11	**15**	14/1	26 f	—
1913[9]	**Fine Spirit** (NMLampard) **5-11-10** MrAKinane (led 7f: wknd over 7f out)	2½	**16**	33/1	23 f	—
	Sunsword (MFBarraclough) **6-11-3**(7) MrAWintle (bkwd: s.s: wl bhd fnl 10f)	4	**17**	66/1	19 f	—
	Welsh Daisy (JSAllen) **5-11-3**(7) XAizpuru (lengthy, unf: bkwd: s.s: a bhd: t.o)	10	**18**	66/1	9 f	—
	Pollys Sister (GHYardley) **5-11-10** MrAPhillips (bhd fnl 8f: t.o)	19	**19**	66/1	—	—
1986[14]	**Glendronach** (BRCambidge) **5-11-10** GTormey (prom 8f: t.o)		**20**	100/1	—	—
	Grand Fiasco (LPGrassick) **4-11-0** MrJGrassick (bkwd: t.o whn p.u 4f out)		**P**	50/1	—	—
	Paper Tigress (IRE) (DNicholson) **6-11-7**(3) RMassey (bhd tl p.u lame 8f out)		**P**	14/1	—	—
				(SP 164.5%)		**22 Rn**

3m 42.7 CSF £19.60 TOTE £2.80: £1.30 £2.70 £9.10 (£11.10) Trio £138.70; £175.82 to Ludlow 5/2/97 OWNER Haras D'Ecouves (LAMORLAYE) BRED Mrs Hugh Baird
WEIGHT FOR AGE 4yo-10lb
Erintante (IRE), a leggy, sparely-made individual, was turned out trained to the minute. She took a keen hold, but quickened up well in the straight. (6/4)
Melody Maid beat the others easily enough, and may have caught a tartar in the winner. (9/1: 6/1-10/1)
Castle Mews (IRE) looked fit. (16/1)
Good Job is from a stable that does pretty well in these events. (9/1: op 5/1)
Wise Gunner is the first foal of a dual bumper winner who later scored once over fences. (9/1: 5/1-10/1)
Miss Match is a half-sister to a winner between the Flags. (33/1)
Fruitation (7/1: op 4/1)

T/Plpt: £25.70 (338.61 Tckts). T/Qdpt: £11.10 (48.79 Tckts) KH

2511-ASCOT (R-H) (Good to firm, Firm patches)
Wednesday February 5th

Race 5: 1 fence omitted final circuit
WEATHER: sunny

2932 KILFANE CONDITIONAL H'CAP HURDLE (0-120) (5-Y.O+) (Class E)
1-30 (1-30) **2m 4f (11 hdls)** £3,533.75 (£1,070.00: £522.50: £248.75) GOING: 0.33 sec per fur (GS)

	Horse	Dist	Pos	SP	RR	SF
1710[4]	**Flying Fiddler (IRE) (89)** (MJRoberts) **6-10-2b** PHenley (lw: hdwy 6th: led 3 out: clr appr last: r.o wl)	—	1	16/1	82?	18
	Can Can Charlie (100) (JPearce) **7-10-13** LAspell (hdwy 6th: rdn appr 2 out: chsd wnr appr last: no imp)	14	2	9/2 [2]	82	18
2824[2]	**Handson (90)** (BRMillman) **5-10-3** DSalter (lw: hdwy 6th: chsd wnr appr 2 out tl appr last: sn wknd)	6	3	5/1 [3]	67	3
2797[5]	**Smuggler's Point (USA) (105)** (JJBridger) **7-11-4** SophieMitchell (a.p: led 5th to 7th: led 8th to 3 out: sn wknd)	2½	4	16/1	80	16
1958[P]	**Rosehall (87)** (MrsTDPilkington) **6-9-11(3)** LSuthern (wl bhd to 3 out: nvr nrr)	2½	5	66/1	60	—
2703[2]	**Morstock (115)** (RJHodges) **7-12-0** TDascombe (hdwy 6th: pckd 8th: wknd appr 2 out)	½	6	8/1	88	24
2817[8]	**Kippanour (USA) (109)** (CJMann) **5-11-8b** JMagee (bhd fr 8th)	12	7	14/1	72	8
1418[6]	**Shahrani (110)** (MCPipe) **5-11-9** GSupple (swtg: led to 5th: led 7th to 8th: wknd 3 out)	11	8	12/1	64	—
2631[4]	**Auburn Boy (103)** (MWEasterby) **10-11-2** PMidgley (sme hdwy 8th: sn wknd: t.o whn p.u bef 2 out)		P	11/2	—	—
1661[4]	**Hooded Hawk (IRE) (109)** (NJHenderson) **6-11-8** TCMurphy (mstkes: a.p: blnd 7th: wknd 8th: wl bhd whn p.u bef 2 out)		P	100/30 [1]	—	—

(SP 112.0%) **10 Rn**

4m 57.5 (15.50) CSF £76.96 CT £379.25 TOTE £24.00: £4.00 £1.80 £1.40 (£36.40) Trio £47.60 OWNER Mr Mike Roberts (HAILSHAM) BRED Thomas Tormey
LONG HANDICAP Rosehall 8-12

1710 Flying Fiddler (IRE), from a stable that has had the virus, scooted up on this fast ground. Leading at the third last, he forged clear in the straight for a very decisive victory. (16/1)
Can Can Charlie eventually managed to win the battle for second prize, but had no hope of catching the runaway winner. This is his ground. (9/2)
2824 Handson moved up to take second place turning for home, but he was collared for that berth approaching the final flight and soon tired. This longer trip appeared to stretch him, and a return to a shorter distance will probably suit. (5/1)
2797 Smuggler's Point (USA) cut out the running from halfway but, collared three from home, was soon done with. (16/1)
1180* Rosehall, carrying 13lb more than her long handicap mark despite her rider's allowance, was soon well adrift of her rivals, but was noted making eye-catching late headway. It will be interesting to see how she does when lowered in class and allowed to run off her proper mark. (66/1)
2703 Morstock may only have won over two miles, but he can cope with this longer trip. The problem on this occasion was his weight - he was 5lb higher than he has ever won off before - and he was a spent force turning for home. (8/1)

2933 STANLAKE NOVICES' CHASE (5-Y.O+) (Class B)
2-00 (2-00) **2m (12 fncs)** £12,405.00 (£3,045.00) GOING: 0.33 sec per fur (GS)

	Horse	Dist	Pos	SP	RR	SF
2793*	**Amancio (USA) (124)** (MrsAJPerrett) **6-11-4** RDunwoody (mde all: blnd 8th: clr appr 3 out: shkn up appr last: easily)	—	1	11/10 [2]	126+	56
2745*	**Jathib (CAN) (128)** (MrsMerritaJones) **6-11-8** DerekByrne (lw: chsd wnr: pckd 4 out: rdn appr 2 out: no imp)	5	2	8/11 [1]	125	55

(SP 105.5%) **2 Rn**

3m 58.4 (7.40) TOTE £1.80 OWNER Lady Harrison (PULBOROUGH) BRED Hill'N Dale Farm
2793* Amancio (USA), rather warm beforehand, was quite keen early on as he set the pace. His one error came when misjudging the fifth last, but he had pulled clear by the home turn. Connections must have been absolutely delighted to pick up so much prize-money with the minimum of fuss. The Arkle is the likely Cheltenham Festival target if the horse is well, but life will be a lot tougher for him there. (11/10)
2745* Jathib (CAN) did not jump as well as the winner and lunged at several of his fences. Nodding on landing at the fourth last did not help his cause and, from that point, he was unable to prevent his rival from pulling away. (8/11)

2934 SHENLEY ENTERPRISES LIMITED H'CAP HURDLE (4-Y.O+) (Class B)
2-30 (2-30) **3m (13 hdls)** £8,083.20 (£2,445.60: £1,192.80: £566.40) GOING: 0.33 sec per fur (GS)

	Horse	Dist	Pos	SP	RR	SF
2761*	**Haile Derring (117)** (NATwiston-Davies) **7-10-7** TJenks (lw: mde all: clr 2 out: rdn appr last: r.o wl)	—	1	9/4 [1]	100+	12
1783[2]	**Sparkling Yasmin (125)** (PJHobbs) **5-11-1** RDunwoody (lw: chsd wnr: hrd rdn appr 2 out: sn wknd)	9	2	7/2 [3]	102	14
2625*	**Cokenny Boy (114)** (MrsJPitman) **12-10-4** NWilliamson (lw: hld up: rdn appr 2 out: sn wknd)	8	3	4/1	86	—
2637[3]	**Top Spin (134)** (JRJenkins) **8-11-10** AMaguire (a bhd)	2½	4	8/1	104	16
2117[2]	**Peatswood (119)** (MRChannon) **9-10-9** RHughes (hld up: rdn 10th: wknd 3 out)	10	5	11/4 [2]	82	—

(SP 110.8%) **5 Rn**

6m 1.0 (22.00) CSF £9.56 TOTE £3.10: £1.60 £1.80 (£4.60) OWNER Mrs V. Stockdale (CHELTENHAM) BRED Mrs V. Stockdale
LONG HANDICAP Cokenny Boy 10-0
IN-FOCUS: **Tom Jenks was riding a belated first winner of the season.**
2761* Haile Derring continues to defy the Handicapper - he has risen to a mark of 117 from 69 since his first win of last season. Merrily bowling along in front, he forged clear in the straight for a very decisive victory. He has now won eight of his last eleven starts and will head for the Gold Card Final at the Festival. (9/4)
1783 Sparkling Yasmin did not have the ground in her favour - she has never won on ground better than good to soft - but still ran creditably if unable to contain the winner over the last two. Given the mud she loves, she can regain winning ways. (7/2)
2625* Cokenny Boy had the ground in his favour, and moved up to dispute second place soon after the third last, but he was beaten early in the straight. (4/1)
2637 Top Spin was not in the mood on this occasion and never threatened to get into it. (8/1)
2117 Peatswood ran no race at all after his promising effort at Kempton on Boxing Day, and was beaten fully three out. (11/4)

2935 COMET CHASE (Gd 1) (5-Y.O+) (Class A)
3-05 (3-07) **2m 3f 110y (16 fncs)** £37,032.00 (£14,010.60: £6,855.30: £3,122.10) GOING: 0.33 sec per fur (GS)

	Horse	Dist	Pos	SP	RR	SF
2115[4]	**Strong Promise (IRE) (148)** (GAHubbard) **6-11-7** NWilliamson (chsd ldr: led 4 out: rdn out)	—	1	10/1 [3]	167	93
2775*	**One Man (IRE) (177)** (GRichards) **9-11-7** RDunwoody (lw: led to 4 out: rdn appr 2 out: unable qckn)	1	2	4/7 [1]	166	92

1792* **Sound Man (IRE) (168)** (EJO'Grady,Ireland) **9-11-7** CFSwan (nt j.w: hld up: blnd bdly 8th: hrd rdn appr 2 out: sn wknd)....10 **3** 9/4^{2} 158 84
2646^{3} **Big Matt (IRE) (144)** (NJHenderson) **9-11-7** JOsborne (lw: a bhd: t.o whn blnd 12th)....dist **4** 25/1 — —
(SP 107.3%) **4 Rn**

4m 47.2 (0.20) CSF £15.72 TOTE £8.30 (£2.80) OWNER Mr G. A. Hubbard (WOODBRIDGE) BRED William McCarthy

2115 Strong Promise (IRE) showed his King George running to be all wrong, and caused a major upset. Jumping into the lead at the fourth last, this top-class novice was always keeping his two very experienced rivals at bay in the straight. He is in the Queen Mother Champion Chase and the Cathcart, with his trainer keen to run him in the former. (10/1)

2775* One Man (IRE) was a major disappointment, for the whole idea of running him over this trip was so that connections could decide whether to run him in the Queen Mother or the Gold Cup. Electing to make the running on this occasion, he was collared four from home but was still only a length down in the straight. Despite all Dunwoody's efforts, the gelding could not muster another gear. He travels supremely well on the bridle, but is increasingly finding less than expected once off it. While connections are keen to run at Cheltenham, they would be well advised to by-pass the Festival and bring him out fresh and well for the Martell Cup at Aintree, where the flat track will be in his favour. (4/7)

1792* Sound Man (IRE) totally ruined his chance with some very sloppy jumping. His worst error came when almost getting rid of his rider at the eighth and, under pressure turning for home, he was soon a spent force. If he is to be a serious contender for the Queen Mother his jumping must improve dramatically. (9/4)

2646 Big Matt (IRE) was totally outclassed from start to finish. (25/1)

2936 HSBC JAMES CAPEL REYNOLDSTOWN NOVICES' CHASE (Gd 2) (5-Y.O+) (Class A)

3-35 (3-36) **3m 110y (19 fncs)** £20,087.50 (£5,912.50) GOING: 0.33 sec per fur (GS)

			SP	RR	SF
2113*	**Djeddah (FR) (132)** (FDoumen,France) **6-11-12** AKondrat (lw: hld up: led 4 out: clr appr 2 out: easily)....—	**1**	13/8^{1}	138+	63
2706^{2}	**Dromhana (IRE) (110)** (PFNicholls) **7-11-5** RDunwoody (lw: chsd ldr: mstke 12th: ev ch 3 out: wknd appr 2 out)....24	**2**	9/1	115	40
2776^{2}	**Potter's Bay (IRE) (124)** (DNicholson) **8-11-9** AMaguire (a wl bhd: t.o whn fell last)....	**F**	7/2^{3}	—	—
2540^{2}	**Brandy Cross (IRE)** (HowardJohnson) **8-11-5** PCarberry (led: mstke 15th: hdd 4 out: ev ch whn fell 3 out)....	**F**	13/2	—	—
2616^{2}	**Mony-Skip (IRE) (125)** (MrsSJSmith) **8-11-9** RichardGuest (4th whn fell 6th: dead)....	**F**	3/1^{2}	—	—
			(SP 108.7%)		**5 Rn**

6m 16.5 (11.50) CSF £12.86 TOTE £2.60: £1.50 £2.00 (£6.10) OWNER Mrs Stella Elkaim (LAMORLAYE) BRED In France

2113* Djeddah (FR) put up a very good display, leading at the fourth last and cruising clear in the straight to win doing handsprings. The Royal SunAlliance Chase at the Festival is his target. (13/8)

2706 Dromhana (IRE) raced in second place, and had every chance three out before being left for dead by the winner. He should soon regain the winning thread. (9/1)

2776 Potter's Bay (IRE) ran no race at all. (7/2)

2540 Brandy Cross (IRE), taking a step up in class, took the field along until making a mistake at the first fence out of Swinley Bottom. Headed four out, he was still close up when crashing to the deck at the next. He should soon recoup losses. (13/2)

2937 FERNBANK NOVICES' HURDLE (4-Y.O+) (Class C)

4-05 (4-10) **2m 110y (9 hdls)** £3,501.25 (£1,060.00: £517.50: £246.25) GOING: 0.33 sec per fur (GS)

			SP	RR	SF
2642^{3}	**Courbaril (124)** (MCPipe) **5-11-7b^{1}** CFSwan (lw: led to 3rd: led 5th to 6th: hrd rdn 3 out: led flat: r.o wl)....—	**1**	6/1^{3}	95	56
2662^{6}	**Eagles Rest (IRE)** (NJHenderson) **6-11-4** NWilliamson (hdwy 5th: led 2 out tl flat: unable qckn)....½	**2**	12/1	92	53
2112^{5}	**Leading Spirit (IRE)** (CFWall) **5-11-4** KGaule (hld up: led appr 2 out: sn hdd: wknd appr last)....12	**3**	8/1	80	41
2112^{3}	**Proton** (RAkehurst) **7-11-4** RDunwoody (lw: a.p: rdn appr 2 out: sn wknd)....7	**4**	5/1^{2}	73	34
2649*	**Mister Ross (IRE) (108)** (HowardJohnson) **7-11-4** PCarberry (chsd ldr: mstke 1st: led 3rd to 5th: led 6th tl appr 2 out: sn wknd)....½	**5**	5/1^{2}	73	34
	Blaze of Song (DJWintle) **5-11-4** WMarston (bhd fr 6th: t.o)....dist	**6**	33/1	—	—
2566*	**Percy Braithwaite (IRE) (100)** (MissPMWhittle) **5-10-11(7)** KHibbert (hld up: rdn 3 out: sn wknd)....s.h	**7**	14/1	—	—
2690^{3}	**Sierra Bay (IRE)** (OSherwood) **7-11-4** JOsborne (lw: blnd bdly 4th: hdwy 6th: wknd 3 out: t.o whn p.u bef 2 out)....	**P**	7/4^{1}	—	—
2772^{5}	**Lear Jet (USA)** (BobJones) **4-10-11** RGarritty (prom to 6th: t.o whn p.u bef 2 out)....	**P**	16/1	—	—
2624^{7}	**Blomberg (IRE)** (JRFanshawe) **5-11-4** RHughes (a bhd: t.o whn p.u bef 2 out: collapsed: dead)....	**P**	12/1	—	—
			(SP 126.0%)		**10 Rn**

3m 58.1 (8.10) CSF £72.51 TOTE £8.40: £2.10 £3.10 £2.20 (£43.20) Trio £153.80 OWNER Richard Green (Fine Paintings) (WELLINGTON) BRED George & Mrs Steinberg

WEIGHT FOR AGE 4yo-10lb

OFFICIAL EXPLANATION **Lear Jet (USA): had gurgled.**

2642 Courbaril, fitted with blinkers for the first time, was given an excellent ride for the gelding had to be stoked along for much of the final circuit. Under strong pressure three out, he looked held, but Swan conjured a tremendous run out of him, to get him up in the closing stages. (6/1: 4/1-13/2)

2662 Eagles Rest (IRE), so disappointing at Leicester last time out, showed that to be all wrong here. Returning to the minimum trip, he gained a slender advantage two out, but was given no peace by the winner and was eventually worried out of it near the line. His turn is not far away. (12/1: op 7/1)

2112 Leading Spirit (IRE) again showed promise, and moved to the front approaching the second last. Soon collared, he was beaten going to the final flight. (8/1)

2112 Proton played an active role until left for dead turning for home. (5/1: 7/2-11/2)

2649* Mister Ross (IRE), taking a step up in class, showed in front at various stages during the race but, collared approaching the second last, was soon beaten. (5/1: 7/2-11/2)

2690 Sierra Bay (IRE) made an horrendous mistake that nearly got rid of Osborne at the fourth hurdle. He was wisely not given a hard time after that, and was eventually pulled up. He is well worth another chance. (7/4)

Blomberg (IRE) (12/1: 8/1-14/1)

2938 ASCOT STANDARD OPEN N.H. FLAT RACE (4, 5 & 6-Y.O) (Class H)

4-35 (4-46) **2m 110y** £2,274.00 (£639.00: £312.00)

			SP	RR	SF
2682^{3}	**Mister Ermyn** (LMontagueHall) **4-10-7** RHughes (led 4f: led over 4f out tl over 3f out: led 2f out: r.o wl)....—	**1**	2/1^{1}	60 f	—
1289^{10}	**Borodino (IRE)** (RRowe) **5-11-0(3)** LAspell (bit bkwd: hld up: hrd rdn over 1f out: r.o)....2½	**2**	10/1^{3}	58 f	—

				SP	RR	SF
	Tuckers Town (IRE) (OSherwood) **5-11-3** JOsborne (lw: a.p: led over 3f out to 2f out: wknd fnl f)	10	**3**	2/1[1]	48 f	—
2648*	**Clinking** (MrsAJPerrett) **6-11-10** MrsAPerrett (hdwy over 4f out: ev ch 2f out: wknd fnl f)	2	**4**	3/1[2]	53 f	—
	Enigma Bell (SGollings) **4-10-7** KGaule (bit bkwd: bhd fnl 4f)	18	**5**	16/1	29 f	—
1774[7]	**Jack (IRE)** (JCTuck) **5-11-3** SMcNeill (swtg: a.p: led over 12f out tl over 4f out: wknd 3f out)	8	**6**	33/1	21 f	—
	Evening Dancer (RJHodges) **4-10-4**(3) TDascombe (bhd fnl 4f)	6	**7**	25/1	15 f	—
	Yonder Star (GRSmith) **5-10-10**(7) CHynes (bit bkwd: plld hrd: hdwy over 6f out: wknd 4f out: t.o)	dist	**8**	33/1	—	—
1124[11]	***Jemaro (IRE)*** (WJenks) **6-11-3** TJenks (Withdrawn under Starter's orders: bolted bef s)		**W**	33/1	—	—

(SP 119.3%) **8 Rn**

4m 1.08 CSF £21.48 TOTE £2.90: £1.20 £2.40 £1.10 (£11.40) Trio £16.00 OWNER Mr J. Daniels (EPSOM) BRED J. Daniels
WEIGHT FOR AGE 4yo-10lb

2682 Mister Ermyn confirmed the promise shown at Lingfield recently, despite racing on a completely different surface. Showing in front early in the straight, he forged clear for a decisive victory. He is a stayer, and the softer the ground the better according to his trainer. (2/1)

Borodino (IRE) looked as though this run would just do him good, but still left his initial outing three months ago well behind, responding to pressure and keeping on in good style for second prize. (10/1: 7/1-14/1)

Tuckers Town (IRE) was the subject of encouraging reports, and certainly looked in good shape beforehand. Moving sweetly to the front turning for home, he was collared a quarter of a mile out and soon left for dead. With this experience under his belt, he should soon be winning. (2/1: 5/4-9/4)

2648* Clinking moved up stylishly turning for home and looked a serious threat. His 7lb penalty found him out though, and he tired in the final furlong. (3/1)

T/Plpt: £2,117.40 (8.71 Tckts). T/Qdpt: £498.10 (2.35 Tckts) AK

2566-LUDLOW (R-H) (Good to firm, Firm patches)
Wednesday February 5th

Race 6: 2 fences omitted
WEATHER: fine

2939 BULL RING MAIDEN HURDLE (4-Y.O+) (Class E)
1-40 (1-42) **2m** **(9 hdls)** £2,542.00 (£712.00: £346.00) GOING minus 0.60 sec per fur (F)

				SP	RR	SF
2668[2]	**High In The Clouds (IRE)** (CaptTAForster) **5-11-8** SWynne (lw: a gng wl: led 3 out: comf)	—	**1**	8/11[1]	87+	14
1921[3]	**Talathath (FR)** (DNicholson) **5-11-8** RJohnson (hld up: hdwy 6th: ev ch 2 out: rdn & nt qckn flat)	2	**2**	5/2[2]	85	12
	Rory (MrsJCecil) **6-11-8** TKent (a.p: led appr 6th: hdd 3 out: one pce fr 2 out)	4	**3**	7/1[3]	81	8
2805[5]	**Music Please** (KCBailey) **5-11-8** CO'Dwyer (hld up: hdwy 6th: ev ch appr 3 out: wknd 2 out)	8	**4**	20/1	73	—
	Pinkerton's Pal (MCPipe) **6-11-8** CMaude (plld hrd: led 3rd tl appr 6th: wknd appr 3 out)	3	**5**	14/1	70	—
1770[10]	**Glen Garnock (IRE)** (RTJuckes) **5-11-8** GaryLyons (plld hrd: prom tl wknd after 6th)	4	**6**	100/1	66	—
2784[7]	**Society Girl** (JGMO'Shea) **4-10-2**(5) MichaelBrennan (hld up: hdwy 6th: nvr nr to chal)	5	**7**	66/1	56	—
1953[11]	**Bright Eclipse (USA)** (JGMO'Shea) **4-10-6**(7)ow1 JTNolan (nvr trbld ldrs)	1½	**8**	66/1	61	—
1628[13]	**Riverbank Red** (WClay) **6-11-3** TEley (plld hrd: led 3rd tl appr 6th: sn wknd)	½	**9**	100/1	54	—
1905[F]	**Apollono** (RLee) **5-11-8** LHarvey (bhd fr 5th)	9	**10**	33/1	50	—
	Mellow Master (NJHWalker) **4-10-5**(7) DFinnegan (bhd: blnd 4th: sn t.o)	12	**11**	66/1	38	—
	Julian Oliver (WGMTurner) **5-11-1**(7) NWillmington (bhd: mstke 1st: t.o fr 5th)	dist	**12**	100/1	—	—
2080[14]	**Gem's Precious** (TWall) **6-11-5**(3) RMassey (a bhd: t.o 4th: p.u bef 3 out)		**P**	100/1	—	—

(SP 121.8%) **13 Rn**

3m 39.0 (2.00) CSF £2.43 TOTE £1.70: £1.00 £1.30 £2.90 (£1.30) Trio £3.30 OWNER Mrs J G Griffith & Lady Barlow (LUDLOW)
WEIGHT FOR AGE 4yo-10lb

2668 High In The Clouds (IRE) showed his debut to be no fluke with a most convincing win. He can go on from here, but judging by his trainer's post-race comment, the gelding will not be seen at the Cheltenham Festival. (8/11)

1921 Talathath (FR) came up against a useful sort and will not always meet one so smart. (5/2)

Rory, four times a winner on the Flat, is a half-brother to a useful point-to-pointer. He can take a similar event on this evidence. (7/1)

2805 Music Please again ran out of steam in the latter stages. (20/1)

Pinkerton's Pal, who won once as a juvenile on the Flat, was bought out of Clive Brittain's yard for 9,000 gns at Newmarket Autumn Sales. He will do better when he learns to settle. (14/1: op 6/1)

Glen Garnock (IRE), last of ten finishers in a seller on his debut, showed he has ability on this faster ground despite running too freely.(100/1)

2940 BRIDGNORTH NOVICES' CHASE (5-Y.O+) (Class E)
2-10 (2-10) **3m** **(19 fncs)** £2,932.50 (£885.00: £430.00: £202.50) GOING minus 0.60 sec per fur (F)

				SP	RR	SF
2054[F]	**Lucky Dollar (IRE) (99)** (KCBailey) **9-11-8** CO'Dwyer (hld up: hdwy after 12th: led 3 out: sn clr: easily)	—	**1**	100/30[2]	103+	47
1771[P]	**King's Shilling (USA) (79)** (HOliver) **10-11-2** JacquiOliver (hld up: stdy hdwy 4th: led appr 4 out to 3 out: no ch w wnr)	9	**2**	25/1	91	35
2571*	**Inch Emperor (IRE)** (AWCarroll) **7-11-8** TJMurphy (lw: j.lft: led tl appr 4 out: wknd 3 out)	19	**3**	8/1[3]	84	28
2816[8]	**Bolshie Baron** (MHWeston) **8-11-2** MrMHarris (j.rt: sn wl bhd)	2	**4**	20/1	77	21
2776[5]	**La Mezeray (76)** (MrsJEHawkins) **9-11-3** DWalsh (blnd 1st: lost pl 4th: reminder after 6th: bhd fr 10th: t.o)	24	**5**	14/1	62	6
2693[8]	**Dukes Meadow (IRE) (78)** (KCBailey) **7-11-2** AThornton (prom: rdn 9th: 3rd whn fell 15th)		**F**	16/1	—	—
2667[F]	**Three Philosophers (IRE) (115)** (CaptTAForster) **8-11-2** SWynne (chsd ldr tl blnd bdly & uns rdr 12th: dead)		**U**	4/5[1]	—	—
2819[P]	**Lord Antrim (IRE)** (RMStronge) **8-11-2** SCurran (t: hld up: mstke & uns rdr 8th)		**U**	66/1	—	—

(SP 112.4%) **8 Rn**

5m 53.3 (-6.70) CSF £61.12 TOTE £4.30: £1.20 £2.80 £1.90 (£15.90) OWNER Mr G. P. D. Milne (UPPER LAMBOURN) BRED Edward Vaughan

1716 Lucky Dollar (IRE), apparently unsighted when falling last time, gained due reward for some consistent efforts, although he did not have much to beat with the favourite out of the contest. (100/30)

1449 King's Shilling (USA) made his bid for glory entering the home straight, but this trip stretched his stamina to the limits. (25/1)

2571* Inch Emperor (IRE) won a weak event over two and a half miles here last month, but may be better going left-handed on this evidence.(8/1)

2667 Three Philosophers (IRE) unfortunately broke his pelvis. (4/5)

2941 ASHFORD H'CAP HURDLE (0-110) (4-Y.O+ F & M) (Class E)
2-40 (2-40) **2m 5f 110y (11 hdls)** £2,304.00 (£644.00: £312.00) GOING minus 0.60 sec per fur (F)

	Horse / details	Dist	Pos	SP	RR	SF
2882*	**Scottish Wedding (81)** (TWall) **7-10-10**(3) 6x RMassey (a.p: led 8th: sn hdd: led 3 out: drvn out)	—	1	7/1	64	17
2570[3]	**First Crack (86)** (FJordan) **12-11-4** SWynne (hld up: hit 4th: hdwy 6th: ev ch whn hit 2 out: one pce)	2½	2	7/2[2]	67	20
2573[3]	**Fleur de Tal (92)** (WGMTurner) **6-11-3**(7) JPower (hld up: hdwy to ld after 8th: hdd 3 out: one pce)	3½	3	9/1	71	24
2694*	**Madame President (IRE) (90)** (CPMorlock) **6-11-5**(3) DFortt (hld up: rdn & wknd appr 3 out)	7	4	9/2[3]	63	16
2708[3]	**Stac-Pollaidh (87)** (KCBailey) **7-11-5** CO'Dwyer (reminders after 3rd: bhd fr 7th)	5	5	11/4[1]	57	10
1865[2]	**Scamallach (IRE) (89)** (JRJenkins) **7-11-7b** GBradley (a bhd)	7	6	8/1	53	6
2694[9]	**Joy For Life (IRE) (69)** (RMStronge) **6-10-1** RJohnson (led: rdn & hdd 8th: sn wknd)	1¼	7	20/1	33	—
	Go Frolic (77) (MissCPhillips) **9-10-9** BPowell (prom: j.slowly 2nd: wknd qckly 6th: t.o)	28	8	11/1	20	—

(SP 113.8%) **8 Rn**

5m 1.0 (Equals Standard) CSF £29.08 CT £202.46 TOTE £6.50: £1.30 £1.90 £4.30 (£15.80) OWNER G A Weetman, Reynolds & Dean (CHURCH STRETTON) BRED A. Goddard

2882* Scottish Wedding defied a penalty for her lucky Chepstow selling win despite her trainer being concerned about the faster ground. She was certainly not inconvenienced by the longer trip. (7/1)
2570 First Crack, raised 2lb, looked a threat until flattening the penultimate hurdle. (7/2)
2573 Fleur de Tal, dropped 2lb, probably needs to come down a few pounds more. (9/1)
2694* Madame President (IRE), raised 7lb, also had faster ground to contend with. (9/2)
2708 Stac-Pollaidh ran a dismal race. (11/4)
1865 Scamallach (IRE) was reverting to hurdles. (8/1)

2942 ATTWOOD MEMORIAL TROPHY H'CAP CHASE (0-120) (5-Y.O+) (Class D)
3-15 (3-15) **2m 4f (17 fncs)** £3,650.00 (£1,025.00: £500.00) GOING minus 0.60 sec per fur (F)

	Horse / details	Dist	Pos	SP	RR	SF
2568[5]	**Coolree (IRE) (109)** (PFNicholls) **9-11-3** DBridgwater (chsd ldr: rdn 13th: led 2 out: r.o wl)	—	1	11/4[3]	111	11
1631[4]	**Spanish Light (IRE) (120)** (SirJohnBarlowBt) **8-12-0** CMaude (led: clr 4th: mstke 3 out: sn hrd rdn: mstke & hdd 2 out: one pce)	2½	2	14/1	120	20
	Norse Raider (112) (MCPipe) **7-11-6** DWalsh (nt j.w: hld up: rdn 13th: wknd appr 4 out)	21	3	11/8[1]	95	—
2623[2]	**Philip's Woody (112)** (NJHenderson) **9-11-6b** JRKavanagh (hld up: hdwy 10th: j.slowly & lost pl 11th: rallied appr 4 out: hrd rdn appr 3 out: 3rd & btn whn fell 2 out)		F	2/1[2]	—	—

(SP 108.8%) **4 Rn**

4m 55.4 (3.40) CSF £21.04 TOTE £4.20 (£7.60) OWNER Mr B. T. R. Weston (SHEPTON MALLET) BRED Joe Logan
2568 Coolree (IRE) seems to have sorted out his jumping problems, although he did run down the final fence. (11/4)
1631 Spanish Light (IRE) appeared to be pressurized into jumping errors when the chips were down. (14/1)
Norse Raider was only having his third outing over fences and it showed. (11/8)
2623 Philip's Woody, dropped 3lb, took a real bone-crunching fall. (2/1)

2943 CHURCH STRETTON (S) H'CAP HURDLE (0-95) (4-Y.O+) (Class G)
3-45 (3-46) **2m (9 hdls)** £2,038.00 (£568.00: £274.00) GOING minus 0.60 sec per fur (F)

	Horse / details	Dist	Pos	SP	RR	SF
2813[4]	**Tango Man (IRE) (61)** (RJPrice) **5-10-5** CMaude (hld up & bhd: gd hdwy appr 3 out: led on bit 2 out: rdn out)	—	1	10/1	47	3
2792[9]	**Ruth's Gamble (56)** (MrsLCJewell) **9-10-0v** DLeahy (a.p: led appr 3 out to 2 out: one pce)	3½	2	50/1	39	—
2678[11]	**Dr Dave (IRE) (67)** (PRChamings) **6-10-11** AThornton (trckd ldrs: ev ch whn hmpd 2 out: nt rcvr)	½	3	20/1	49	5
1816[4]	**Just for a Reason (73)** (RTJuckes) **5-11-0**(3) EHusband (bit bkwd: hdwy fr 3 out: nt rch ldrs)	5	4	6/1[2]	50	6
2668[10]	**Spitfire Bridge (IRE) (65)** (GMMcCourt) **5-10-9** DBridgwater (nvr nr to chal)	6	5	5/2[1]	36	—
2664[2]	**Indian Temple (69)** (KBishop) **6-10-13** RGreene (hdwy appr 3 out: nvr nr to chal)	s.h	6	12/1	40	—
2818[11]	**Follow de Call (68)** (DMcCain) **7-10-12** DWalsh (hdwy appr 4th: wknd appr 3 out)	3½	7	50/1	35	—
	Spanish Arch (IRE) (70) (CRMillington) **8-11-0** JCulloty (bkwd: prom to 4th)	2	8	33/1	35	—
1585[P]	**Kalzari (USA) (78)** (AWCarroll) **12-11-3**(5) MichaelBrennan (hdwy 5th: wknd appr 3 out)	s.h	9	10/1	43	—
2567[4]	**Them Times (IRE) (62)** (FJordan) **8-10-6** SWynne (led tl after 3rd: wknd after 6th)	2½	10	12/1	25	—
2838[P]	**Killing Time (75)** (DBurchell) **6-11-5** DJBurchell (hit 4th: a bhd)	1½	11	10/1	36	—
2818[4]	**Persian Butterfly (56)** (RMStronge) **5-10-0** DGallagher (led after 3rd: hit 4th: hdd appr 3 out: sn wknd)	2	12	6/1[2]	15	—
2567[2]	**Astral Invasion (USA) (83)** (TWall) **6-11-10v**(3) RMassey (prom tl rdn & wknd appr 3 out)	3½	13	8/1[3]	39	—
2818[5]	**Jobber's Fiddle (69)** (DLWilliams) **5-10-13b** RJohnson (prom tl rdn & wknd after 6th)	3½	14	14/1	21	—
2034[P]	**Woodlands Lad Too (56)** (PAPritchard) **5-10-0** RBellamy (a bhd: t.o)	28	15	66/1	—	—
1980[9]	**Night Boat (71)** (WClay) **6-11-1** TEley (hld up: hdwy 6th: ev ch whn blnd & uns rdr 2 out)		U	16/1	—	—

(SP 136.6%) **16 Rn**

3m 38.0 (1.00) CSF £425.09 CT £8,668.34 TOTE £16.40: £2.60 £4.10 £3.20 £1.70 (£181.30) Trio Not won; £1,182.74 to Kelso 6/2/97 OWNER My Left Foot Racing Syndicate (ULLINGSWICK) BRED Hugh McGahon
LONG HANDICAP Persian Butterfly 9-13 Woodlands Lad Too 9-11 Ruth's Gamble 9-12
Sold J O'Shea 8,400 gns
Tango Man (IRE), very patiently ridden, found his task made easier by the departure of Night Boat, who was going just as well. (10/1)
1861 Ruth's Gamble, 2lb out of the handicap, benefited from the incident at the penultimate hurdle. (50/1)
210 Dr Dave (IRE) was interfered with by the falling Night Boat, but he was not travelling as well as the leaders at the time. (20/1)
1816 Just for a Reason stayed on late in the day, and this run will have sharpened him up. (6/1)
Spitfire Bridge (IRE) was returning to selling company for his handicap debut. (5/2)
2664 Indian Temple may have found the ground too lively. (12/1)
2567 Them Times (IRE) (12/1: op 8/1)

2944 PONTRILAS HUNTERS' CHASE (6-Y.O+) (Class H)
4-15 (4-15) **2m 4f (15 fncs)** £1,171.50 (£324.00: £154.50) GOING minus 0.60 sec per fur (F)

	Horse / details	Dist	Pos	SP	RR	SF
	Beau Dandy (MissCSaunders) **10-11-7**(7) MrTMarks (a.p: hmpd 8th: led after 9th: shkn up flat: r.o)	—	1	5/6[1]	98	—
	Hennerwood Oak (LadySusanBrooke) **7-11-2**(7) MrMMunrowd (hld up: hdwy 13th: ev ch 2 out: hrd rdn & nt qckn flat)	½	2	33/1	93	—
	Billy Bathgate (BRHughes) **11-11-7**(7) MrDSJones (hld up: hdwy 7th: lft in ld after 8th: hdd after 9th: hit 4 out: sn wknd)	dist	3	7/1[3]	—	—

	Horse / details	Dist	Pos	SP	RR	SF
	Hickelton Lad (DLWilliams) **13-11-11**(3) MrMRimell (mstkes: bhd fr 15th: t.o)	30	**4**	9/1	—	—
	Al Hashimi (NTRidout) **13-11-7**(7) MrNRidout (chsd ldr tl fell 8th)		**F**	10/1	—	—
	Pastoral Pride (USA) (MissPollyCurling) **13-11-9**(5) MissPCurling (led tl p.u after 8th: b.b.v)		**P**	11/4[2]	—	—
				(SP 115.7%)	**6 Rn**	

5m 2.2 (10.20) CSF £20.78 TOTE £1.70: £1.60 £4.40 (£17.30) OWNER Mr Shand Kydd (NORTHAMPTON) BRED R. J. McKenna
OFFICIAL EXPLANATION **Pastoral Pride (USA): bled from the nose.**
Beau Dandy won a shade more decisively than the margin suggests. (5/6: 8/11-evens)
Hennerwood Oak did nothing wrong, but the winner had the edge. (33/1)

2945 WINSTANSTOW NOVICES' HURDLE (5-Y.O+) (Class E)

4-45 (4-45) **2m 5f 110y (11 hdls)** £2,444.00 (£684.00: £332.00) GOING minus 0.60 sec per fur (F)

	Horse / details	Dist	Pos	SP	RR	SF
2676[6]	**Drum Battle (92)** (WGMTurner) **5-10-12** AThornton (a.p: led appr 3 out: lft clr last)	—	**1**	6/1[3]	67	—
2763[5]	**Tantara Lodge (IRE)** (KCBailey) **6-10-12** CO'Dwyer (hld up: hdwy 6th: one pce fr 3 out)	7	**2**	12/1	62	—
2634[10]	**Benfleet** (MCPipe) **6-10-12** DWalsh (lw: hld up in rr: gd hdwy appr 3 out: btn whn hit 2 out: t.m.t.d)	hd	**3**	7/2[2]	62	—
2822[6]	**Captain Navar (IRE)** (JGMO'Shea) **7-10-7**(5) MichaelBrennan (hld up: hdwy 7th: hung lft & hit 2 out: lft 2nd & blnd bdly last)	1¼	**4**	25/1	61	—
2822[P]	**Danzante (IRE)** (RMStronge) **5-10-12** DGallagher (hld up: j.rt 4th: hdwy 6th: rdn 8th: wknd appr 3 out)	7	**5**	25/1	56	—
2093[8]	**Loughdoo (IRE)** (RLee) **9-10-12** OPears (a bhd)	hd	**6**	14/1	56	—
2746[P]	**Dodgy Dancer (65)** (MrsLWilliamson) **7-10-12b** LO'Hara (led: hit 6th: hdd & wknd appr 3 out)	11	**7**	50/1	47	—
2676[7]	**Minella Derby (IRE)** (PFNicholls) **7-11-5** RJohnson (chsd ldr: rdn appr 3 out: hung lft appr 2 out: ev ch whn ran out last)		**R**	5/6[1]	74?	—
				(SP 115.1%)	**8 Rn**	

5m 6.8 (5.80) CSF £60.83 TOTE £5.20: £1.10 £1.10 £2.70 (£9.50) OWNER Mr David Chown (SHERBORNE) BRED Berkshire Equestrian Services Ltd
Drum Battle was fighting it out with the reluctant Minella Derby when the favourite ran out at the last. (6/1)
2035 Tantara Lodge (IRE), stepping up in distance, did not look over-blessed with finishing speed. (12/1)
Benfleet, a 17,000 guineas purchase out of Robert Armstrong's stable, was a come-from-behind stayer on the Flat, but the tactics were overdone here. (7/2)
679 Captain Navar (IRE) looked a most difficult ride, and Brennan had to come around the home turn on one rein. (25/1)
1260* Minella Derby (IRE) really blotted his copybook, and it remains to be seen if it was simply the fact he did not like going right-handed. (5/6)

T/Jkpt: £7,100.00 (0.2 Tckts); £3,480.99 to Huntingdon 6/2/97. T/Plpt: £133.90 (72.13 Tckts). T/Qdpt: £60.30 (8.72 Tckts) KH

2690-HUNTINGDON (R-H) (Good)
Thursday February 6th
WEATHER: fine

2946 GLATTON CLAIMING HURDLE (4-Y.O+) (Class F)

1-30 (1-32) **2m 110y (8 hdls)** £2,230.50 (£623.00: £301.50) GOING: 0.04 sec per fur (G)

	Horse / details	Dist	Pos	SP	RR	SF
2744[6]	**Willy Star (BEL) (94)** (MrsSJSmith) **7-10-11**(7) RWilkinson (chsd ldrs: led 2 out: clr last: comf)	—	**1**	8/1	84	18
2543[6]	**Once More for Luck (IRE) (110)** (MrsMReveley) **6-11-12** JOsborne (lw: hld up & bhd: hdwy 3 out: rdn & r.o flat)	2	**2**	5/2[1]	90	24
2670[9]	**Eurotwist (104)** (SEKettlewell) **8-11-2** RSupple (hdwy appr 3 out: rdn appr next: kpt on)	7	**3**	6/1[3]	73	7
1993[2]	**Peter Monamy (102)** (MCPipe) **5-11-6b** DWalsh (chsd ldrs: lft 2nd & hmpd 3 out: sn rdn & no imp)	8	**4**	5/1[2]	70	4
1328[P]	**High Low (USA)** (WJenks) **9-11-8** TJenks (bit bkwd: led to 2 out: sn btn)	2	**5**	16/1	70	4
2815[2]	**Bluntswood Hall** (RHollinshead) **4-10-5** GaryLyons (prom: mstke 5th: sn rdn: btn whn hit last)	¾	**6**	9/1	62	—
2755[6]	**Circus Colours (95)** (JRJenkins) **7-11-6** AMaguire (lw: chsd ldrs to 5th)	10	**7**	12/1	57	—
2815[13]	**First Gold** (JWharton) **8-11-6** RJohnson (prom to 5th)	7	**8**	33/1	50	—
2815[6]	**Our Tom** (JWharton) **5-11-3**(5) MrRThornton (chsd ldrs tl appr 3 out)	18	**9**	33/1	35	—
1337[7]	**Autumn Flame (IRE)** (OBrennan) **6-10-11** MBrennan (bhd fr 4th)	nk	**10**	33/1	24	—
	Dolliver (USA) (CADwyer) **5-11-2** ILawrence (bhd fr 3rd)	15	**11**	33/1	14	—
1836[4]	**Al Haal (USA) (66)** (JJoseph) **8-11-0** JCulloty (blnd 3rd: nvr trbld ldrs)	1½	**12**	14/1	11	—
	Broughtons Relish (WJMusson) **4-10-4** PHide (mstke 1st: a bhd)	2½	**13**	33/1	8	—
2818[7]	**Classic Delight (USA)** (ICampbell) **4-10-0** KGaule (chsd ldrs tl rdn & wknd appr 5th)	2	**14**	33/1	2	—
2818[13]	**Just Flamenco** (MJRyan) **6-11-4** JRyan (lw: hld up: a bhd)	20	**15**	33/1	—	—
	Friendly Coast (DTThom) **11-11-0** BFenton (bkwd: t.o fr 5th)	24	**16**	33/1	—	—
2048[7]	**Eurolink the Lad (102)** (DBurchell) **10-11-0** DJBurchell (hdwy appr 4th: wnt 2nd & fell 3 out)		**F**	9/1	—	—
1595[4]	**Hayling-Billy** (PRHedger) **4-10-0**(7) MClinton (hdwy 4th: rdn 3 out: in tch whn uns rdr next)		**U**	16/1	—	—
				(SP 140.3%)	**18 Rn**	

3m 59.2 (11.20) CSF £27.93 TOTE £12.40: £3.50 £1.60 £2.70 (£21.90) Trio £27.00 OWNER Mrs S. Smith (BINGLEY) BRED Madame W. Verwey
WEIGHT FOR AGE 4yo-10lb
2744 Willy Star (BEL) looked in great heart on the way down and won with a fair bit in hand. (8/1: 6/1-9/1)
2543 Once More for Luck (IRE) was being niggled along in the rear group until closing going on to the final circuit. Suddenly beginning to run on on the home turn, he finished strongly but too late to trouble the winner. (5/2)
1642 Eurotwist did not find much once ridden, just staying on in his own time. (6/1)
1993 Peter Monamy was flat out when losing all momentum when hampered three out. He would have been much closer but for this. (5/1: op 11/4)
High Low (USA) has been in action on the All-Weather but failed to last home after having most of the field at full stretch by the third last. (16/1)
2815 Bluntswood Hall, a very poor mover, was in contention when the mistake four out got him off the bridle. (9/1)
2755 Circus Colours (12/1: op 8/1)
1828 Eurolink the Lad (9/1: 6/1-10/1)
1595 Hayling-Billy would not have won but would probably have finished fourth or fifth but for his mishap. (16/1)

2947 WHITTLESEY NOVICES' H'CAP CHASE (0-110) (5-Y.O+) (Class D)

2-00 (2-03) **3m (19 fncs)** £4,313.25 (£1,296.00: £625.50: £290.25) GOING: 0.04 sec per fur (G)

Form	Horse	Dist	Pos	SP	RR	SF
2778[2]	**Cariboo Gold (USA) (92)** (KCBailey) **8-11-1b** JOsborne (lw: chsd ldrs: led 13th to 3 out: led appr 2 out: rdn clr flat)	—	1	4/1[1]	106	8
1797[5]	**Goldenswift (IRE) (94)** (GBBalding) **7-11-3** BFenton (hdwy 15th: rdn appr last: unable qckn)	3½	2	5/1[3]	106	8
2658[P]	**Foxtrot Romeo (104)** (CPEBrooks) **7-11-13** GBradley (prom: led 9th to 13th: led 3 out tl appr next: one pce)	1¼	3	12/1	115	17
2693[5]	**Claymore Lad (77)** (JSKing) **7-10-0** TJMurphy (led to 9th: hit 12th: mstke 15th: wknd appr 2 out)	15	4	9/2[2]	78	—
1981[2]	**Bayline Star (IRE) (96)** (MissHCKnight) **7-11-5** JCulloty (lw: hld up: hdwy 8th: no imp fr 15th)	4	5	4/1[1]	94	—
2643[2]	**Pavi's Brother (95)** (PRHedger) **9-11-4** MRichards (bit bkwd: hld up & bhd: hdwy 14th: nvr rchd ldrs)	18	6	14/1	81	—
2679[4]	**Bonnifer (IRE) (77)** (MJWilkinson) **8-10-0** ILawrence (chsd ldrs tl blnd 12th)	6	7	33/1	59	—
2671[P]	**Record Lover (IRE) (77)** (MCChapman) **7-10-0** WWorthington (bhd fr 15th)	24	8	33/1	43	—
2816[5]	**The Millmaster (IRE) (77)** (JohnUpson) **6-10-0** RSupple (chsd ldrs to 14th)	nk	9	33/1	43	—
2704[4]	**Jac Del Prince (81)** (PFNicholls) **7-10-4**ow4 PHide (prom: hit 9th: wkng whn blnd 15th)	5	10	33/1	44	—
2667[2]	**Uncle Algy (85)** (MissHCKnight) **8-10-8** JFTitley (lw: mstke 9th: hdwy next: wknd 13th: j.lft 3 out: p.u bef 2 out)		P	8/1	—	—
2665[5]	**Just One Canaletto (78)** (NATwiston-Davies) **9-10-1**ow1 DWalsh (in tch: hit 4th: blnd 12th: p.u bef next)		P	25/1	—	—
1318[4]	**The Go Ahead (IRE) (90)** (CaptTAForster) **7-10-13** AThornton (bit bkwd: disp ld tl hit 8th: wknd next: p.u bef 11th: b.b.v)		P	9/1	—	—
2807[F]	**Starlight Fool (79)** (KCBailey) **8-10-2b**ow2 WMcFarland (hdwy 3rd: rdn 9th: wkng whn j.slowly 11th: p.u bef 15th)		P	33/1	—	—
2679[U]	**Bassenhally (83)** (MrsPSly) **7-10-6** MBrennan (bhd fr 11th: p.u bef 15th)		P	20/1	—	—

(SP 133.6%) **15 Rn**

6m 17.0 (20.00) CSF £23.57 CT £207.22 TOTE £4.70: £2.20 £2.00 £5.20 (£12.10) Trio £71.50 OWNER Mrs Sharon Nelson (UPPER LAMBOURN) BRED Regal Oak Farm & Albert G. Clay

LONG HANDICAP The Millmaster (IRE) 9-6 Bonnifer (IRE) 9-4 Claymore Lad 9-7 Just One Canaletto 9-12 Jac Del Prince 8-11 Starlight Fool 9-4 Record Lover (IRE) 9-6

OFFICIAL EXPLANATION **The Go Ahead (IRE): bled from the nose.**

2778 Cariboo Gold (USA) missed last season and would not let himself down on the ground last time. There was just enough cut for him here and he looks useful in this mood. (4/1)

1797 Goldenswift (IRE) ran a fine race after a two-month break and should soon regain winning ways. (5/1)

1426 Foxtrot Romeo got stuck in the mud last time but bounced back to form on this better ground. (12/1: 8/1-14/1)

2693 Claymore Lad looked a handicap certainty on his last run but must have been flattered by it as he never looked like winning. (9/2: op 3/1)

1981 Bayline Star (IRE) was a fraction disappointing and remains hard to weigh up. (4/1)

2643 Pavi's Brother dropped himself out early on and by the time he got going the leaders were well away. (14/1)

2948 SIDNEY BANKS MEMORIAL NOVICES' HURDLE (4-Y.O+) (Class B)

2-30 (2-32) **2m 4f 110y (10 hdls)** £7,181.00 (£2,168.00: £1,054.00: £497.00) GOING: 0.04 sec per fur (G)

Form	Horse	Dist	Pos	SP	RR	SF
2053*	**Agistment (122)** (JGFitzGerald) **6-11-4** RDunwoody (lw: hld up: led appr 3 out: hdd appr next: sn led again: rdn & edgd lft last: hld on wl)	—	1	6/5[1]	92	—
1683*	**Forest Ivory (NZ)** (DNicholson) **6-11-4** AMaguire (a.p: led after 3 out: hit next & hdd: swtchd flat: r.o)	nk	2	11/4[2]	92	—
2676[2]	**Emerald Statement (IRE) (114)** (DMGrissell) **7-11-4** BFenton (lw: lost pl & pushed along appr 4th: rallied 7th: rdn appr 2 out: r.o wl flat)	½	3	6/1	91	—
2805*	**Carlito Brigante** (PRWebber) **5-11-4** AThornton (lw: hld up: hdwy 7th: wknd 2 out: fin lame)	20	4	9/1	76	—
2576*	**Spring Gale (IRE) (114)** (OSherwood) **6-11-4** JOsborne (lw: chsd ldr to 7th)	dist	5	11/2[3]	—	—
	Monks Soham (IRE) (102) (GAHubbard) **9-11-4** RJohnson (bkwd: in tch to 7th)	11	6	33/1	—	—
2677[15]	**Thirty Below (IRE)** (JABOld) **8-11-4** GUpton (bit bkwd: a bhd: t.o fr 5th)	8	7	50/1	—	—
2663[2]	**Edredon Bleu (FR)** (MissHCKnight) **5-11-4** JCulloty (led tl hdd & wknd appr 3 out: virtually p.u appr last)	dist	8	14/1	—	—

(SP 123.4%) **8 Rn**

4m 49.6 CSF £4.88 TOTE £1.90: £1.20 £1.30 £2.30 (£3.10) OWNER Marquesa de Moratalla (MALTON) BRED Dunchurch Lodge Stud Co

STEWARDS' ENQUIRY Obj. to Agistment by Maguire overruled.

2053* Agistment has a long, raking stride but, despite giving the impression that he would not want the ground too much firmer, did the job well and was probably value for a little further. This trip is probably his minimum on such a sharp track and last year's Festival Bumper remains the only blemish on his record. (6/5)

1683* Forest Ivory (NZ) twice finished behind the winner in Bumpers last year, but looked like making a good race of it when a mistake two out cost him a narrow lead and much of his chance. Switched round the winner after the last, he was never interfered with but stuck to his task right to the line. (11/4)

2676 Emerald Statement (IRE) shapes like a true stayer and may have found a rather muddling race against him, for he finished to great effect and there appeared plenty left in the tank. (6/1)

2805* Carlito Brigante, cruising on the heels of the leaders until the tempo picked up going to three out, faded badly in the straight. Pulling up rather feelingly, he was dismounted soon after the line. (9/1)

2576* Spring Gale (IRE) was dropped immediately the tempo quickened (11/2)

Monks Soham (IRE) is lightly-raced for a nine-year-old and is well below this class. (33/1)

2663 Edredon Bleu (FR) was a disappointment in so much that he flaked out totally once headed, as if something was amiss. (14/1)

2949 FARCET FEN H'CAP CHASE (0-120) (5-Y.O+) (Class D)

3-00 (3-03) **2m 4f 110y (16 fncs)** £3,582.00 (£1,071.00: £513.00: £234.00) GOING: 0.04 sec per fur (G)

Form	Horse	Dist	Pos	SP	RR	SF
2894*	**Distinctive (IRE) (103)** (MJWilkinson) **8-11-3** 6x RDunwoody (lw: mde all: hit 7th: clr 12th: easily)	—	1	100/30[2]	114+	24
2796[2]	**Kings Cherry (IRE) (104)** (JABOld) **9-11-4** GUpton (hld up & bhd: hdwy 11th: rdn & wnt 2nd appr 2 out: kpt on)	5	2	4/1[3]	111	21
2657[5]	**The Lancer (IRE) (95)** (DRGandolfo) **8-10-6**(3) DFortt (in tch tl mstke & lost pl 9th: rallied 11th: no imp fr 3 out)	11	3	4/1[3]	94	4
2762[2]	**Flapjack Lad (95)** (NATwiston-Davies) **8-10-9** DWalsh (lw: chsd wnr fr 4th: rdn & wknd appr 2 out)	8	4	5/2[1]	87	—
2039[P]	**Ramstown Lad (IRE) (91)** (KCBailey) **8-9-12**(7)ow5 MrRWakley (lw: mstke 6th: a bhd)	13	5	10/1	73	—

Pharsilk (IRE) (110) (THind) **8-11-10** PMcLoughlin (bkwd: plld hrd: chsd wnr to 4th: hit 6th: wkng whn mstke 10th: t.o whn p.u bef 3 out)........ **P** 10/1 — —
2756* **Oxford Quill (86)** (RCurtis) **10-10-0** DMorris (lw: hdwy 9th: wkng whn blnd & uns rdr 3 out)........ **U** 14/1 — —
(SP 116.5%) **7 Rn**

5m 12.9 (12.90) CSF £16.37 TOTE £3.60: £2.20 £2.40 (£9.10) OWNER Mr Jeremy Hancock (BANBURY) BRED Capt D. G. Swan
LONG HANDICAP Oxford Quill 9-5

2894* Distinctive (IRE) is fast although sometimes quite low over his fences and none of these could live with him on the final circuit. He is still on the upgrade. (100/30)
2796 Kings Cherry (IRE) went second turning for home but the winner was well in command by then. (4/1)
2657 The Lancer (IRE) ran in snatches and seems better on softer ground. This trip ought to suit. (4/1)
2762 Flapjack Lad has been knocking on the door but was below his best here, for he admitted defeat after two miles of chasing the winner. (5/2)
1955 Ramstown Lad (IRE) (10/1: 7/1-12/1)
Pharsilk (IRE), having his first run in this country, looks a rather hairy ride as he pulls extremely hard. He will probably prove best when able to dominate, the winner denying him the chance here. (10/1)

2950 HUNTINGDON GOLD CARD (QUALIFIER) H'CAP HURDLE (4-Y.O+) (Class B)
3-30 (3-30) **2m 5f 110y (10 hdls)** £4,799.05 (£1,452.40: £708.70: £336.85) GOING: 0.04 sec per fur (G)

SP RR SF

2666* **Henrietta Howard (IRE) (115)** (MrsDHaine) **7-10-2** JFTitley (lw: chsd clr ldrs: led appr 2 out: clr last: easily) — **1** 5/1[1] 102+ 15
2880[2] **Korbell (IRE) (113)** (PFNicholls) **8-10-0** RJohnson (lw: w ldr: mstke 1st: led after 7th tl appr 2 out: rdn & no imp)........4 **2** 3/1[2] 97 10
2888[7] **Tim (IRE) (115)** (JRJenkins) **7-10-2** JOsborne (in tch tl lost pl & rdn after 5th: rallied next: no imp fr 2 out)........9 **3** 9/2[3] 92 5
Uron V (FR) (119) (CFWall) **11-10-6** KGaule (bkwd: hld up: hdwy 5th: rdn appr 7th: one pce fr 3 out)........1½ **4** 16/1 95 8
2779[8] **Nijmegen (130)** (JGFitzGerald) **9-11-3** RDunwoody (bit bkwd: bhd: styd on fr 7th: nvr nr ldrs)........11 **5** 6/1 98 11
1710* **Mirador (113)** (RCurtis) **6-10-0** DMorris (lw: hld up: effrt 6th: wknd next)........8 **6** 9/1 75 —
2777[10] **Non Vintage (IRE) (125)** (MCChapman) **6-10-12** WWorthington (in tch to 7th)........3½ **7** 14/1 85 —
2644[P] **Lucky Blue (128)** (SEarle) **10-11-1** AMaguire (bkwd: led tl after 7th: sn wknd)........7 **8** 14/1 82 —
2644[9] **Djais (FR) (115)** (JRJenkins) **8-10-2** RSupple (a bhd: t.o fr 7th)........12 **9** 16/1 60 —
Sweet Glow (FR) (137) (MCPipe) **10-11-10** DWalsh (bkwd: a bhd: t.o fr 6th: p.u bef 2 out)........ **P** 14/1 — —
(SP 127.8%) **10 Rn**

5m 11.2 (11.20) CSF £10.98 CT £31.60 TOTE £3.00: £1.70 £1.80 £1.50 (£3.90) Trio £7.10 OWNER Mrs Solna ThomsonJones (NEWMARKET) BRED Mrs N. Johnston
LONG HANDICAP Mirador 8-9 Korbell (IRE) 9-3

2666* Henrietta Howard (IRE) has made great strides since being stepped up in trip. Some fifteen lengths behind the two leaders on the final circuit, she closed up at halfway and was in total charge in the straight. (5/2)
2880 Korbell (IRE), dropping in trip and reappearing quickly after Saturday's fine effort, did not go down without a fight but could not find the pace to trouble the winner, having an unnecessarily hard race on the run-in. Stamina is her strong suit. (3/1)
2625 Tim (IRE) stayed on in the last mile but lost his pitch at a vital stage and really needs further. (9/2)
Uron V (FR), back over hurdles for a new yard, caught the eye, running well despite looking some way from fitness. (16/1)
Nijmegen, set an awful lot to do in the final mile, has yet to prove he stays the trip. (6/1)
1710* Mirador, a long way out of the handicap, really needs a much stiffer test of stamina. (9/1)
Lucky Blue took the field along for almost two miles and was clear of all except Korbell for the first circuit. Unfortunately, he did appear slightly sore on his return. (14/1)

2951 DUCK'S CROSS NOVICES' HUNTERS' CHASE (5-Y.O+) (Class H)
4-00 (4-00) **3m (19 fncs)** £1,044.90 (£313.20: £150.60: £69.30) GOING: 0.04 sec per fur (G)

SP RR SF

Orchestral Suite (IRE) (MissJenniferPidgeon) **9-11-7**(7) MrFHutsby (a.p: led 3 out: rdn out)........— **1** 2/1[1] 103? —
Lurriga Glitter (IRE) (RJSmith) **9-11-7**(7) MrRWakley (bhd: hdwy 11th: led 13th to 3 out: ev ch last: unable qckn)........3½ **2** 16/1 101? —
Symbol of Success (IRE) (DLWilliams) **6-11-11v**(3) MrMRimell (mstke 1st: chsd ldrs: one pce fr 3 out)........hd **3** 14/1 101? —
Stede Quarter (RDench) **10-11-11**(7) MrPBull (prom: lost pl briefly 6th: led 12th to 13th: wknd 3 out)........dist **4** 16/1 — —
Amazon Lily (MrsJEEales) **10-11-2**(7) MrMGorman (bkwd: led 4th to 10th: fell next)........ **F** 9/2[3] — —
Green's Van Goyen (IRE) (MrsDHMcCarthy) **9-11-9**(5) MrTMcCarthy (bkwd: led to 2nd: lost pl 6th: rallied 11th: wknd 12th: t.o whn p.u bef 15th)........ **P** 3/1[2] — —
Not My Line (IRE) (AndyMorgan) **8-11-9**(5) MrASansome (chsd ldrs: led 10th to 12th: wkng whn p.u bef next). **P** 16/1 — —
Rising Sap (JDDownes) **7-11-7**(7) MrADalton (bit bkwd: hld up: hdwy 9th: wknd 16th: p.u bef 3 out)........ **P** 10/1 — —
Mediane (USA) (MissAnnabelWilson) **12-11-11**(3) MrSimonAndrews (bhd: blnd 8th: mstke next: sn t.o: p.u bef 15th)........ **P** 33/1 — —
No Joker (IRE) (NAGaselee) **9-11-7**(7) CaptRHall (bit bkwd: blnd 1st: led 2nd to 4th: sltly hmpd, swvd & uns rdr 11th)........ **U** 6/1 — —
(SP 127.1%) **10 Rn**

6m 27.6 (30.60) CSF £35.21 TOTE £2.40: £1.10 £4.50 £4.40 (£24.90) Trio £93.80 OWNER Exors of the late Mr G Pidgeon (BRACKLEY) BRED G. Browne

Orchestral Suite (IRE), lightly-raced but successful in point to points, jumped soundly and never looked in much danger. (2/1)
Lurriga Glitter (IRE), the winner of an Irish point, did well on his debut over regulation fences. He looked to blow up on the home turn, but his pilot gave him a breather and did his best to mount a challenge at the last. (16/1)
Symbol of Success (IRE) hardly looked a guaranteed stayer on his previous form but plugged on to the line. (14/1)
Stede Quarter is pretty moderate and did well to last so long with his penalty. (16/1)
Amazon Lily had jumped well until the open ditch in front of the stands caught her out. (9/2)
No Joker (IRE) (6/1: op 4/1)

2952 LONG STANTON H'CAP HURDLE (0-120) (5-Y.O+) (Class D)
4-30 (4-30) **2m 110y (8 hdls)** £2,863.00 (£793.00: £379.00) GOING: 0.04 sec per fur (G)

SP RR SF

1939[3] **More Dash Thancash (IRE) (92)** (MrsMerritaJones) **7-10-5** DerekByrne (lw: chsd ldrs: led 3 out: j.rt last: rdn out)........— **1** 5/1[2] 76 38
2670[7] **Glanmerin (IRE) (115)** (KAMorgan) **6-12-0** GBradley (lw: hdwy 4th: ev ch 3 out: rdn & unable qckn flat)........4 **2** 11/1 96 57

Form	Horse (Rating) (Trainer) Age-Wt Jockey (comment)	Btn	Pos	SP	RR	SF
908[3]	**Prizefighter (114)** (JLEyre) **6-11-13** AMaguire (hdwy 4th: rdn appr 2 out: one pce)	3	**3**	9/4[1]	92	53
2694[7]	**Bigwheel Bill (IRE) (87)** (JRJenkins) **8-9-7**(7) DYellowlees (bhd: styd on fr appr 3 out: r.o wl flat)	3	**4**	14/1	63	23
2543[U]	**Anabranch (110)** (JMJefferson) **6-11-2**(7) MNewton (hld up: hdwy 4th: led 5th to 3 out: sn wknd)	22	**5**	5/1[2]	68	25
208[5]	**Chieftain's Crown (USA) (90)** (THind) **6-10-3** PMcLoughlin (chsd ldrs to 5th)	19	**6**	20/1	33	—
	Lucayan Cay (IRE) (88) (MrsAJBowlby) **6-10-1** DLeahy (bkwd: in tch tl appr 5th)	1¾	**7**	16/1	30	—
	Storm Falcon (USA) (95) (SMellor) **7-10-8** JOsborne (bkwd: led after 1st tl after 3rd: wknd qckly 5th)	dist	**8**	11/2[3]	—	—
221[3]	**Green Lane (USA) (110)** (JJoseph) **9-11-9** JCulloty (bkwd: bhd fr 4th)	15	**9**	20/1	—	—
2815[5]	**Re Roi (IRE) (99)** (WGMTurner) **5-10-12** RDunwoody (a bhd: t.o)	7	**10**	10/1	—	—
2779[3]	**Severn Gale (102)** (JSAllen) **7-10-8**(7) XAizpuru (led tl after 1st: led after 3rd to 5th: btn whn fell last)		**F**	5/1[2]	—	—
				(SP 135.7%)	**11 Rn**	

3m 52.0 (4.00) CSF £61.66 CT £150.24 TOTE £6.40: £1.90 £3.10 £2.00 (£27.60) Trio £48.50 OWNER Mr F. J. Sainsbury (LAMBOURN) BRED Miss Roseanne Millett & Paul McEnery

LONG HANDICAP Bigwheel Bill (IRE) 9-11

1939 More Dash Thancash (IRE) took this in good style despite a crooked jump at the last, and can win again. (5/1)

2670 Glanmerin (IRE) now back to something approaching his best, looks likely to win before too long. (11/1)

908 Prizefighter, in what looked a truly-run race, could not preserve his turn of foot. Ideally he wants fast ground. (9/4)

Bigwheel Bill (IRE) made giant strides approaching three out and again after the last. He probably wants another half-mile. (14/1)

1852 Anabranch cruised to the front four out but does appear to struggle to get the trip in a fast-run race. (5/1)

208 Chieftain's Crown (USA) could not live with the pace back over the minimum trip. (20/1)

Storm Falcon (USA) looked burly after a long lay-off but is potentially well handicapped over hurdles, almost two stone below his chase rating. (11/2)

T/Jkpt: £2,211.80 (3.21 Tckts). T/Plpt: £24.00 (515.64 Tckts). T/Qdpt: £5.90 (125.78 Tckts) Dk/IM

2614-KELSO (L-H) (Good)
Thursday February 6th

WEATHER: unsettled

2953 WEATHERBYS BULLETIN MAGAZINE MAIDEN HURDLE (4-Y.O+) (Class D)

1-50 (1-51) **2m 110y (8 hdls)** £3,022.00 (£916.00: £448.00: £214.00) GOING: 0.43 sec per fur (GS)

Form	Horse (Rating) (Trainer) Age-Wt Jockey (comment)	Btn	Pos	SP	RR	SF
	Secret Service (IRE) (CWThornton) **5-11-5** MFoster (lw: in tch: effrt 3 out: hmpd last: styd on to ld fnl 150y)	—	**1**	6/1	73	4
2649[5]	**Lumback Lady** (BMactaggart) **7-11-0** BStorey (a chsng ldrs: led last: hdd & nt qckn towards fin)	3	**2**	16/1	65	—
	Billy Bushwacker (MrsMReveley) **6-11-5** PNiven (lw: mstkes: bhd: gd hdwy 3 out: one pce appr last)	7	**3**	11/8[1]	63	—
	Swift Riposte (IRE) (110) (PMonteith) **6-11-5** ADobbin (hmpd 1st: wnt prom ½-wy: hit 5th: wknd 2 out: hmpd after last)	19	**4**	11/2[3]	45	—
2744[10]	**Jarrow (65)** (MrsAMNaughton) **6-11-0**(5) MichaelBrennan (chsd ldrs tl wknd fr 5th)	2	**5**	100/1	43	—
2787[9]	**Obvious Risk** (EMCaine) **6-10-12**(7) TristanDavidson (nvr nr ldrs)	3½	**6**	500/1	40	—
	Western General (MissMKMilligan) **6-11-5** ASSmith (hld up: nvr trbld ldrs)	6	**7**	16/1	34	—
2633[8]	**Sunstrike** (RMcDonald) **5-11-5** KJones (lw: nvr bttr than mid div)	1¼	**8**	100/1	33	—
	Chain Line (JWFAynsley) **7-11-2**(3) MrCBonner (sn wl bhd: sme late hdwy)	1¾	**9**	300/1	31	—
	Point Duty (FPMurtagh) **7-11-5** DBentley (bit bkwd: prom: wkng whn blnd 3 out)	nk	**10**	100/1	31	—
	Pearls of Thought (IRE) (ACWhillans) **4-10-4** KJohnson (wl t.o)	dist	**11**	100/1	—	—
	Solway King (MABarnes) **7-11-0**(5) STaylor (fell 1st)		**F**	100/1	—	—
1973*	**Carlisle Bandito's (IRE)** (JBerry) **5-11-5** MMoloney (lw: trckd ldrs: led 5th tl hdd & fell last)		**F**	3/1[2]	—	—
	Brockville Bairn (MrsASwinbank) **4-10-9** JSupple (chsd ldrs to ½-wy: t.o whn p.u bef 2 out)		**P**	66/1	—	—
2785[17]	**Blood Brother** (JBarclay) **5-10-12**(7) NHorrocks (cl up tl wknd qckly 3 out: p.u bef 2 out)		**P**	100/1	—	—
	Evening Dusk (IRE) (JKMOliver) **5-11-0** RGarritty (bit bkwd: sn wl bhd: p.u bef 2 out)		**P**	50/1	—	—
				(SP 118.5%)	**16 Rn**	

4m 6.9 (20.90) CSF £83.19 TOTE £6.80: £1.70 £3.30 £1.30 (£28.80) Trio £28.00 OWNER Mr Guy Reed (MIDDLEHAM) BRED E. O'Leary

WEIGHT FOR AGE 4yo-10lb

Secret Service (IRE), given a patient ride, did the job required well and, getting stronger as the race progressed, won going away. He will certainly not be inconvenienced by a bit further. (6/1: op 4/1)

2504 Lumback Lady is running consistently well and will surely break her duck before long. (16/1)

Billy Bushwacker, always a bit of a monkey on the Flat,showed his true colours here by treating his hurdles with far too much caution. Continually giving ground away, he found his reserves sapped late on. (11/8: 11/10-evens)

Swift Riposte (IRE) almost got brought down at the first but then ran well until blowing up two out. (11/2: 4/1-6/1)

Jarrow put in his best effort to date but there is still plenty more needed. (100/1)

1973* Carlisle Bandito's (IRE), who has the look of a chaser, ran well at his first attempt over hurdles here and, although he had just been headed, he was fighting back when he was over-brave at the last and came to grief. (3/1)

2954 BET WITH THE TOTE (QUALIFIER) NOVICES' H'CAP CHASE (0-110) (6-Y.O+) (Class D)

2-20 (2-23) **3m (19 fncs)** £3,663.75 (£1,110.00: £542.50: £258.75) GOING: 0.43 sec per fur (GS)

Form	Horse (Rating) (Trainer) Age-Wt Jockey (comment)	Btn	Pos	SP	RR	SF
2803[U]	**D'Arblay Street (IRE) (72)** (WTKemp) **8-10-3** PCarberry (w ldr: led 14th: clr fr 3 out: eased flat)	—	**1**	8/1	88+	31
2767[4]	**Ask Me Later (IRE) (79)** (MrsSCBradburne) **8-10-10** MFoster (chsd ldrs: no imp fr 4 out)	11	**2**	12/1	88	31
2803[2]	**Tough Test (IRE) (84)** (MrsJDGoodfellow) **7-11-1** GCahill (lw: a chsng ldrs: one pce fr 14th)	5	**3**	6/1[2]	89	33
2788[F]	**Mister Trick (IRE) (78)** (LLungo) **7-10-9** RGarritty (lw: bhd: hdwy u.p 13th: 4th whn blnd 4 out: no imp after)	3	**4**	9/2[1]	81	25
2671[6]	**Cool Weather (IRE) (78)** (PCheesbrough) **9-10-9b** ASSmith (in tch to 12th: sn wknd)	dist	**5**	12/1	—	—
1691*	**Majority Major (IRE) (84)** (PCheesbrough) **8-10-10**(5) GFRyan (bit bkwd: hit 4th: blnd 6th: wl bhd fr 14th)	3½	**6**	10/1	—	—
2630[2]	**Kenmare River (IRE) (72)** (RCollins) **7-10-3b** BStorey (led to 14th: wknd 3 out)	7	**7**	9/2[1]	—	—
1968[3]	**Miss Lamplight (72)** (FPMurtagh) **7-10-3** ADobbin (sn bhd: t.o fr 14th)	dist	**8**	33/1	—	—
2788[F]	**Mr Sloan (69)** (JSGoldie) **7-9-11**(3) GLee (mstkes: bhd whn fell 11th)		**F**	100/1	—	—
2540[5]	**Naughty Future (93)** (JJO'Neill) **8-11-10** ARoche (mstkes: in tch whn fell 12th)		**F**	7/1[3]	—	—
1968[U]	**Corporal Kirkwood (IRE) (76)** (MartinTodhunter) **7-10-7** JCallaghan (lost tch fr ½-wy: p.u bef 3 out)		**P**	12/1	—	—
2803[U]	**Classic Crest (IRE) (74)** (MissLucindaRussell) **6-10-0v**(5)ow5 MichaelBrennan (prom to 10th: sn t.o: p.u bef 4 out)		**P**	33/1	—	—
2788[P]	**Ansuro Again (78)** (MrsMReveley) **8-10-9** PNiven (bit bkwd: nt j.w: sn t.o: p.u bef 11th)		**P**	12/1	—	—

2788[7] **Quixall Crossett (70)** (EMCaine) **12-9-8**(7)ow1 TristanDavidson (a bhd: t.o whn blnd & uns rdr 15th) .... **U** 200/1 — —
(SP 121.5%) **14 Rn**

6m 28.1 (21.10) CSF £89.79 CT £570.74 TOTE £9.30: £2.90 £3.20 £1.90 (£103.20) Trio £207.30 OWNER Green For Luck (DUNS) BRED Mrs Kathleen Flood

LONG HANDICAP Mr Sloan 9-11 Quixall Crossett 9-1

2507 D'Arblay Street (IRE) had the right man on board and, given a superb ride, won with ease. This should have done his confidence no end of good. (8/1)

2767 Ask Me Later (IRE) ran well but was never a match for the winner. Nevertheless, he is still improving. (12/1)

2803 Tough Test (IRE) does not do anything quickly and, after being in the chasing group throughout, he looked very onepaced over the last six fences. (6/1)

1845* Mister Trick (IRE) was always having to work to improve. Just when he got within sight of the leaders, he made his customary blunder four out and that was it. (9/2)

2540 Cool Weather (IRE) was going quite well until an effort was required with a circuit to go. (12/1: op 8/1)

1691* Majority Major (IRE), off the track for over two months, needed this. (10/1)

2630 Kenmare River (IRE) tried to take the winner on throughout, but the effort of that found him out in these very sticky conditions and he stopped quickly over the last three fences. (9/2)

2540 Naughty Future would not have a cut at his fences at any stage. (7/1)

2955 FORRESTERS H'CAP HURDLE (0-125) (4-Y.O+) (Class D)

2-50 (2-51) **2m 6f 110y (11 hdls)** £2,745.00 (£770.00: £375.00) GOING: 0.43 sec per fur (GS)

				SP	RR	SF
1081*	**Tribune (94)** (CWThornton) **6-10-13** MFoster (mde all: hit 2nd: kpt on u.p fr 2 out)	—	**1**	5/4[1]	74	17
	Turkish Tower (86) (RNixon) **6-10-5** ADobbin (lw: chsd wnr fr 5th: rdn: ev ch & hit 2 out: no ex flat)	12	**2**	9/4[2]	58	1
2769[6]	**Willie Sparkle (87)** (MrsSCBradburne) **11-10-6v** GCahill (chsd ldrs tl outpcd fr 7th: sn t.o)	dist	**3**	12/1	—	—
2780[P]	**Ralitsa (IRE) (105)** (MDHammond) **5-11-10** RGarritty (prom tl rdn & wknd rapidly 3rd: p.u bef next)		**P**	3/1[3]	—	—

(SP 107.9%) **4 Rn**

5m 40.2 (23.20) CSF £4.07 TOTE £2.20 (£3.10) OWNER Hexagon Racing (MIDDLEHAM) BRED R. G. Bonson

OFFICIAL EXPLANATION **Ralitsa (IRE): the gelding appeared to have had a recurrence of a back problem.**

1081* Tribune was racing in the most testing conditions he has come across here, as the ground was sticky and there was also a strong headwind, although never looking all that happy, he proved to be most determined and that won the day. (5/4)

Turkish Tower is not the most natural of hurdlers but he keeps galloping only to find the winner too strong after the last. (9/4)

2179 Willie Sparkle showed little enthusiasm once the pace was stepped up with a circuit to go. (12/1: op 8/1)

1701 Ralitsa (IRE) seems to have a big problem as he just refused to go at all after only three flights. (3/1: op 2/1)

2956 ISLE OF SKYE BLENDED SCOTCH WHISKY H'CAP CHASE (0-115) (5-Y.O+) (Class E)

3-20 (3-21) **3m 1f (19 fncs)** £3,241.25 (£980.00: £477.50: £226.25) GOING: 0.43 sec per fur (GS)

				SP	RR	SF
	Davy Blake (105) (TNDalgetty) **10-11-6** ADobbin (lw: mde all: lft clr 3 out: styd on wl)	—	**1**	16/1	118	40
2046*	**Off The Bru (93)** (MrsSCBradburne) **12-10-1**(7)ow6 MrMBradburne (prom tl outpcd 14th: styd on strly fr last)	11	**2**	6/1	99	15
2767[2]	**Seeking Gold (IRE) (92)** (JBarclay) **8-10-7** BStorey (lw: a chsng ldrs: outpcd 14th: no imp after)	s.h	**3**	11/4[2]	98	20
2916*	**Celtic Silver (98)** (MrsSJSmith) **9-10-13** 6x RichardGuest (hld up: gd hdwy 15th: 3rd & styng on whn bdly hmpd 3 out: nt rcvr)	12	**4**	9/4[1]	96	18
2630[P]	**Jendee (IRE) (85)** (BEllison) **9-10-0** KJohnson (nvr gng wl: chsd ldrs tl wknd fr 14th)	16	**5**	16/1	73	—
	Acajou III (FR) (110) (GRichards) **9-11-11** PCarberry (lw: w ldr fr 4th tl rdn & fell 3 out)		**F**	9/2[3]	—	—
2630[P]	**The Toaster (95)** (MissMKMilligan) **10-10-10** ASSmith (sn bhd: sme hdwy u.p 12th: sn wknd: p.u bef 3 out)		**P**	33/1	—	—
2616[10]	**Side of Hill (91)** (BMactaggart) **12-10-3**(3) GLee (in tch: outpcd & lost pl: blnd 11th: p.u bef 3 out)		**P**	33/1	—	—
	Stoney Burke (IRE) (100) (MissLucindaRussell) **8-11-1** MFoster (sn outpcd & bhd: t.o whn p.u bef 13th)		**P**	14/1	—	—

(SP 114.2%) **9 Rn**

6m 30.3 (20.30) CSF £98.09 CT £315.12 TOTE £20.80: £3.80 £2.10 £1.60 (£42.40) Trio £75.60 OWNER Mr T. N. Dalgetty (JEDBURGH) BRED R. G. Thompson

LONG HANDICAP Jendee (IRE) 9-11

Davy Blake has only ever won on this track under Rules and, returning here after seventeen months off with various problems, was as good as ever. (16/1)

2046* Off The Bru just stays and stays these days and only got going when the race was over. (6/1)

2767 Seeking Gold (IRE) ran her usual game race but was short of toe over the last three. (11/4)

2916* Celtic Silver, ridden with restraint this time, was given plenty to do. Just when he began to eat up the ground, he was almost brought down three out and that was it. (9/4)

2046 Jendee (IRE) has two ways of running and the best is not seen very often these days. (16/1)

Acajou III (FR) took the winner on but was a bit iffy at some fences, and was really being stretched when he met the third last all wrong and came to grief. (9/2)

2957 BELTANE PARTNERS H'CAP HURDLE (0-115) (4-Y.O+) (Class E)

3-50 (3-52) **2m 110y (8 hdls)** £2,316.00 (£651.00: £318.00) GOING: 0.43 sec per fur (GS)

				SP	RR	SF
2617[4]	**Ingletonian (105)** (BMactaggart) **8-11-7** BStorey (lw: mde all: hld on wl)	—	**1**	6/1[3]	85	19
2509[2]	**Flyaway Blues (93)** (MrsMReveley) **5-10-9** PNiven (lw: hld up: hdwy 3 out: ch last: sn hrd rdn: styd on towards fin)	nk	**2**	4/1[1]	73	7
	Summerhill Special (IRE) (112) (DWBarker) **6-12-0** RichardGuest (hld up: gd hdwy 3 out: ch last: no ex)	1¼	**3**	50/1	91	25
2780*	**Dual Image (110)** (JGFitzGerald) **10-11-12** PCarberry (hld up: effrt & hit 3 out: sn rdn & no imp)	7	**4**	4/1[1]	82	16
1658[8]	**Cool Luke (IRE) (100)** (FMurphy) **8-10-11**(5) MichaelBrennan (trckd ldrs: effrt 2 out: rdn & fnd nil)	1¼	**5**	6/1[3]	71	5
2764[3]	**Adamatic (IRE) (98)** (RAllan) **6-10-7**(7) SMelrose (lw: hld up: hdwy & prom 5th: rdn 2 out: sn btn)	21	**6**	6/1[3]	48	—
2798*	**Maple Bay (IRE) (91)** (BEllison) **8-10-7** 7x KJohnson (hld up: effrt 3 out: sn btn)	4	**7**	11/2[2]	37	—
1824[4]	**Hee's a Dancer (98)** (MissLucindaRussell) **5-11-0** MFoster (prom tl outpcd fr 5th)	4	**8**	12/1	40	—
1848[11]	**Vintage Red (87)** (GRichards) **7-10-3** ADobbin (hdwy 4th: outpcd fr next)	3	**9**	25/1	27	—
	Going Public (95) (PCheesbrough) **10-10-11** ASSmith (trckd ldrs tl wknd appr 3 out)	1½	**10**	40/1	33	—
2800[15]	**Rubislaw (84)** (MrsKMLamb) **5-9-7v**(7) MissSLamb (cl up tl wknd fr 5th: hit 3 out)	17	**11**	200/1	6	—

(SP 114.7%) **11 Rn**

4m 3.8 (17.80) CSF £26.79 CT £992.59 TOTE £6.30: £1.80 £1.50 £12.50 (£16.60) Trio £219.60; £278.49 to Bangor 7/2/97 OWNER Mrs Hilary MacTaggart (HAWICK) BRED A. D. Redhead

LONG HANDICAP Rubislaw 7-9
2617 Ingletonian confirmed his promise of the previous meeting and, leaving nothing to chance, showed fine courage to hold on. (6/1)
2509 Flyaway Blues showed what a frustrating character he is here, and it was only when his rider put his stick down late on that he condescended to run on. (4/1)
Summerhill Special (IRE) had fair form a couple of seasons ago and came back to something like her best on the Flat last year. She showed here she is in good heart after an absence of three and a half months. (50/1)
2780* Dual Image likes things to go his way and, after a poor jump three out, was never doing enough. (4/1)
1360 Cool Luke (IRE) travelled well as usual but, when it came down to an effort, he was yet again disappointing. (6/1)
2764 Adamatic (IRE) ran moderately here. (6/1)

2958 MOET & CHANDON NOVICES' HURDLE (4-Y.O+) (Class D)

4-20 (4-21) **2m 6f 110y (11 hdls)** £2,996.00 (£908.00: £444.00: £212.00) GOING: 0.43 sec per fur (GS)

	Horse / details	Dist	Pos	SP	RR	SF
2510³	**Meadow Hymn (IRE)** (JGFitzGerald) **6-11-4** PNiven (a in tch: effrt 7th: styd on to ld 2 out: drvn out)	—	1	7/1	80	—
1580⁵	**Grosvenor (IRE)** (GRichards) **6-11-4** PCarberry (hld up: hdwy 7th: prom & mstke 3 out: sn rdn: styd on appr last: nt pce to chal)	4	2	9/4 1	77	—
2787²	**Smiddy Lad** (RShiels) **6-11-4** DBentley (a.p: outpcd 3 out: kpt on appr last: wknd flat)	9	3	9/2	71	—
2764²	**Supreme Soviet (94)** (ACWhillans) **7-11-4** ADobbin (lw: hld up: hdwy to ld appr 7th: hit 8th: hdd after 3 out: sn btn)	½	4	4/1 3	70	—
2619⁴	**Malta Man (IRE) (94)** (PCheesbrough) **7-11-4** ASSmith (lw: trckd ldrs: led after 3 out tl hdd & mstke 2 out: wknd flat)	3½	5	7/2 2	68	—
2627P	**Liam's Loss (IRE)** (JParkes) **8-11-4** VSmith (outpcd & lost pl ½-wy: hit 7th: n.d after)	dist	6	200/1	—	—
2673⁸	**Boyzontoowa (IRE)** (RCollins) **5-11-4** RichardGuest (cl up tl wknd fr 7th)	nk	7	100/1	—	—
	Stepdaughter (MrsDThomson) **11-10-13** LO'Hara (bit bkwd: cl up to 4th: sn bhd)	11	8	100/1	—	—
	Royal Rank (USA) (65) (DSAlder) **7-11-4** KJohnson (bkwd: bhd fr ½-wy: wl t.o)	dist	9	100/1	—	—
2614F	**Weejumpawud** (MrsJStorey) **7-10-13** MrCStorey (led tl hdd appr 7th: wknd qckly & wl t.o)	17	10	200/1	—	—
2701¹⁵	**Persian Grange (IRE)** (DALamb) **7-11-4** JBurke (in tch: outpcd whn fell 7th)		F	100/1	—	—
1687⁴	**Pappa Charlie (USA)** (CParker) **6-11-4** BStorey (fell 2nd)		F	12/1	—	—
	Rye Rum (IRE) (JWFAynsley) **6-11-4** MMoloney (bkwd: cl up to 3rd: t.o whn p.u bef 7th)		P	200/1	—	—

(SP 116.8%) **13 Rn**

5m 49.5 (32.50) CSF £21.53 TOTE £5.60: £2.10 £1.50 £1.50 (£9.60) Trio £33.00 OWNER Mrs M. Nowell (MALTON) BRED Dermot O'Mahony
2510 Meadow Hymn (IRE) is certainly a stayer, as some of his opponents looked to be going much better than him for much of the race, but he kept galloping and that was what mattered. (7/1)
Grosvenor (IRE), patiently ridden, spoiled his chances with a mistake three out, but it s doubtful whether he would have beaten the winner anyway. (9/4)
2787 Smiddy Lad put in another decent effort here but was always finding this company too hot from the second last. (9/2)
2764 Supreme Soviet, held up to get the trip, did not seem to stay. (4/1: 3/1-9/2)
2619 Malta Man (IRE), stepping up in trip, travelled particularly well but failed to get home and seemingly just did not stay. (7/2)

T/Plpt: £131.20 (58.44 Tckts). T/Qdpt: £16.20 (35.42 Tckts) AA

2703-WINCANTON (R-H) (Good to firm, Firm patches)
Thursday February 6th
WEATHER: unsettled

2959 HOECHST ROUSSEL PANACUR E.B.F. (QUALIFIER) NOVICES' HURDLE (5-Y.O+ Mares Only) (Class E)

1-40 (1-41) **2m 6f (11 hdls)** £2,784.00 (£774.00: £372.00) GOING: 0.23 sec per fur (G)

	Horse / details	Dist	Pos	SP	RR	SF
2090²	**Galatasori Jane (IRE) (94)** (PFNicholls) **7-10-10**(7) LCummins (a.p: led 7th: pckd 3 out: edgd rt flat: all out)	—	1	2/1 1	73	31
1453⁷	**Tremplin (IRE)** (NJHenderson) **6-10-10** JRKavanagh (lw: hld up: hdwy 7th: chsd wnr fr 3 out: sn rdn: j.rt 2 out: rallied appr last: r.o)	1¼	2	2/1 1	65	23
2655P	**Win I Did (IRE)** (RHAlner) **7-10-7**(3) PHenley (hdwy 6th: wknd after 3 out)	dist	3	11/1 3	—	—
1341⁹	**Bel-de-Moor** (MPMuggeridge) **5-10-10** WMarston (prom to 3 out)	3½	4	33/1	—	—
1680P	**Dunnicks Country (67)** (FGTucker) **7-10-3**(7) MGriffiths (led 3rd tl after 5th: wknd after 3 out: t.o)	1¼	5	50/1	—	—
2822⁸	**Daydream Believer** (MSalaman) **5-10-10** PHolley (hdwy 5th: wknd after 3 out: t.o)	29	6	33/1	—	—
2701⁸	**Sparkling Buck** (OSherwood) **5-10-10** JAMcCarthy (led to 3rd: led after 5th to 7th: wknd 3 out: t.o)	1¾	7	100/30 2	—	—
1555⁹	**Castle Lynch (IRE)** (RHAlner) **5-10-10** SMcNeill (a bhd: t.o fr 8th)	14	8	25/1	—	—
2661¹²	**Joyful Pabs** (KBishop) **5-10-10** RGreene (a bhd: t.o fr 8th)	4	9	50/1	—	—
	Gay Time (PJHobbs) **5-10-3**(7) MrSDurack (t.o fr 5th)		10	20/1	—	—
2656P	**Camillas Legacy** (HTCole) **6-10-10** DGallagher (bit bkwd: prom tl mstkes 4th & 5th: t.o whn p.u bef 2 out)		P	33/1	—	—
	Westwood Treat (BRMillman) **5-10-5**(5) DSalter (t.o 4th: p.u bef 7th)		P	33/1	—	—
2676P	**Fortunes Gleam (IRE)** (JSKing) **6-10-10** CMaude (bhd whn mstke 4th: sn t.o: p.u bef 7th)		P	33/1	—	—
1835P	**Queen Of The Suir (IRE)** (NRMitchell) **8-10-5**(5) SophieMitchell (s.s: a bhd: t.o whn p.u bef 3 out)		P	50/1	—	—

(SP 127.3%) **14 Rn**

5m 24.1 (15.10) CSF £5.28 TOTE £2.80: £1.10 £1.60 £2.30 (£3.00) Trio £11.90 OWNER Mr B. L. Blinman (SHEPTON MALLET)
2090 Galatasori Jane (IRE) ran here instead of the Premiere Auction later in the afternoon, and judging by the way she made hard work of winning, it was a shrewd move. (2/1: op 3/1)
Tremplin (IRE) got within striking distance of the winner turning for home and caused her to pull out all the stops. Better ground may help. (2/1: 6/4-9/4)
Win I Did (IRE) (11/1: 8/1-12/1)

2960 BET WITH THE TOTE (QUALIFIER) NOVICES' CHASE (6-Y.O+) (Class D)

2-10 (2-10) **2m 5f (17 fncs)** £4,284.00 (£1,156.00) GOING: 0.23 sec per fur (G)

	Horse / details	Dist	Pos	SP	RR	SF
2795⁷	**Koo's Promise (80)** (CLPopham) **6-10-9**(3) TDascombe (chsd ldr to 7th: lost pl 8th: lft 2nd 12th: rdn to ld 3 out: sn clr: rdn out)	—	1	9/1 3	86	—
2776P	**After The Fox (91)** (NJHawke) **10-10-10** BPowell (hld up: wnt 2nd 7th: led 11th tl wknd & hdd 3 out)	4	2	15/8 2	81	—

2819* **Palosanto (IRE)** (MCPipe) **7-11-3** CMaude (j.lft: led: pushed along after 4th: sn clr: hit 6th: hdd 11th: blnd 12th: 3rd & wkng whn fell 13th) .... **F** 1/2^{1} — —
(SP 111.4%) **3 Rn**

5m 31.0 (23.00) CSF £20.77 TOTE £4.50 (£5.60) OWNER G A Warren Ltd (TAUNTON)
1875 Koo's Promise had been finding life difficult in little novice handicaps on her last two outings. (9/1)
1875 After The Fox completed at the third time of asking over fences. He seemed in control until the picture suddenly changed three out. (15/8)
2819* Palosanto (IRE) never looked particularly happy. (1/2)

2961 PREMIERE 'N.H.' NOVICES' AUCTION HURDLE (5, 6 & 7-Y.O) (Class B)

2-40 (2-42) **2m 6f (11 hdls)** £12,200.00 (£3,325.00: £1,575.00: £700.00) GOING: 0.23 sec per fur (G)

Form	Horse / details	Dist	Pos	SP	RR	SF
2763^{4}	**Lucia Forte (102)** (KCBailey) **6-10-11** JRailton (hld up in rr: stdy hdwy fr 3 out: led on bit appr last: rdn out)	—	**1**	4/1^{1}	83	26
1791^{5}	**Lady Peta (IRE) (104)** (NJHenderson) **7-11-11** JRKavanagh (lw: hld up: hdwy 8th: ev ch last: hrd rdn & edgd lft flat: nt qckn)	1¼	**2**	13/2^{3}	96	39
2791^{6}	**Barbary Falcon** (PJJones) **7-10-9** CMaude (a.p: rdn appr 2 out: one pce)	6	**3**	33/1	76	19
1507^{3}	**Dacelo (FR) (92)** (OSherwood) **6-10-12** JAMcCarthy (hld up: rdn appr 2 out: no hdwy)	6	**4**	11/1	74	17
1581^{4}	**Millersford** (NAGaselee) **6-11-4** DGallagher (hld up: hdwy 7th: blnd 3 out: rdn to ld appr 2 out: hdd & wknd appr last)	1	**5**	5/1^{2}	80	23
2690^{16}	**Supreme Charm (IRE)** (KCBailey) **5-10-6** SMcNeill (chsd ldr: rdn appr 2 out: wknd appr last)	5	**6**	5/1^{2}	64	7
2547^{5}	**Silver Thyne (IRE)** (MrsJPitman) **5-11-4** NWilliamson (hld up: mstke 1st:sme hdwy whn mstke 8th: sn wknd)	5	**7**	4/1^{1}	72	15
2808^{3}	**The Brewmaster (IRE)** (IPWilliams) **5-10-12** BPowell (plld hrd: led: mstke 3 out: hdd appr 2 out: sn wknd)	2	**8**	12/1	65	8
2677^{9}	**Cyphratis (IRE)** (MrsJPitman) **6-11-1** WMarston (hld up: hdwy 5th: lost pl bnd appr 6th: dropped rr 7th: sn t.o)	dist	**9**	14/1	—	—
792^{8}	**Regal Gem (IRE) (74)** (CRBarwell) **6-10-4** RFarrant (a bhd: t.o fr 8th)	18	**10**	50/1	—	—
2656^{P}	**One For Navigation (IRE)** (PFNicholls) **5-10-6** DBridgwater (lw: hld up: hdwy 7th: rdn 8th: wknd qckly appr 2 out: p.u bef last)		**P**	14/1	—	—

(SP 120.9%) **11 Rn**

5m 23.7 (14.70) CSF £28.57 TOTE £4.90: £2.30 £2.70 £5.00 (£12.70) Trio £259.10; £218.98 to Bangor 7/2/97 OWNER Mrs Lucia Farmer (UPPER LAMBOURN) BRED Mrs K. I. Hayward
OFFICIAL EXPLANATION **One for Navigation (IRE): finished distressed.**
2763 Lucia Forte was switched off in last place after being thought to have run too freely last time. Brought with a well-timed challenge, she found enough to hold the runner-up who had been travelling equally as well. (4/1: 3/1-9/2)
1791 Lady Peta (IRE), looking particularly well, was still cruising nearing the penultimate hurdle, but the winner was going just as strongly. A sound effort in trying to concede a stone. (13/2)
2791 Barbary Falcon seemed to appreciate this longer trip. (33/1)
1507 Dacelo (FR) again did nothing wrong. (11/1: 7/1-12/1)
1581 Millersford could well have found this ground too lively. (5/1)
1507 Supreme Charm (IRE) is another who may benefit from some good ground. (5/1)
1044 Cyphratis (IRE) (14/1: op 8/1)
1200 One For Navigation (IRE) was reported by his trainer to have been distressed. (14/1: 8/1-16/1)

2962 RACING IN WESSEX CHASE (5-Y.O+) (Class B)

3-10 (3-11) **2m 5f (17 fncs)** £6,612.50 (£2,000.00: £975.00: £462.50) GOING: 0.23 sec per fur (G)

Form	Horse / details	Dist	Pos	SP	RR	SF
2773^{6}	**Challenger du Luc (FR) (150)** (MCPipe) **7-12-0b** CMaude (hld up in rr: hdwy 11th: led on bit last: shkn up: qcknd clr: easily)	—	**1**	1/3^{1}	107++	14
2647^{4}	**Beatson (IRE) (112)** (RHBuckler) **8-11-6** BPowell (w ldr: led 8th to 9th: led 10th: rdn 2 out: hdd last: no ch w wnr)	5	**2**	11/4^{2}	95	2
2756^{4}	**Channel Pastime (82)** (DBurchell) **13-11-6** GuyLewis (led to 8th: led 9th to 10th: hrd rdn & ev ch 3 out: hit 2 out: one pce)	2	**3**	25/1^{3}	94	1
2657^{U}	**Fenwick (85)** (RJHodges) **10-11-6** TDascombe (bhd fr 11th: t.o)	26	**4**	25/1^{3}	74	—

(SP 109.4%) **4 Rn**

5m 31.0 (23.00) CSF £1.62 TOTE £1.50 (£1.50) OWNER Mr D. A. Johnson (WELLINGTON) BRED Mme Jeanne-Marie Bizard
2773 Challenger du Luc (FR) proved different class to these. He will go to Cheltenham and probably runs in the Gold Cup. (1/3)
2647 Beatson (IRE) would have been 30lb better off with the winner in a handicap. (11/4)
2756 Channel Pastime is rated 30lb inferior to Beatson, let alone the winner. (25/1)

2963 GILLINGHAM H'CAP HURDLE (0-125) (4-Y.O+) (Class D)

3-40 (3-40) **2m (8 hdls)** £2,826.00 (£786.00: £378.00) GOING: 0.23 sec per fur (G)

Form	Horse / details	Dist	Pos	SP	RR	SF
	Northern Starlight (99) (MCPipe) **6-10-3** CMaude (led: sn clr: hit 5th & 3 out: rdn appr 2 out: unchal)	—	**1**	9/2^{2}	88	40
	Goldingo (104) (GMPrice) **10-10-8** JRKavanagh (hld up: rdn to chse wnr appr 2 out: no imp)	9	**2**	7/1	84	36
2771^{5}	**Hay Dance (109)** (PJHobbs) **6-10-13** NWilliamson (lw: chsd wnr tl wknd appr 2 out: eased appr last)	7	**3**	8/13^{1}	82	34
	Keep Me in Mind (IRE) (108) (NRMitchell) **8-10-12** DSkyrme (bit bkwd: hld up: 4th & no ch whn rn wd bnd appr 2 out)	20	**4**	6/1^{3}	61	13
2884^{8}	**Ros Castle (124)** (RJHodges) **6-11-7**(7) JHarris (reluctant to r: a t.o)	dist	**5**	25/1	—	—

(SP 110.7%) **5 Rn**

3m 46.0 (6.00) CSF £28.23 TOTE £5.00: £1.70 £1.80 (£20.00) OWNER Mr Arthur Souch (WELLINGTON) BRED R. J. Glenn and K. Leadbetter
Northern Starlight, with the hot-pot favourite liking to do it all on the bit, adopted extremely effective tactics. (9/2)
Goldingo looked pretty straight for this belated reappearance. (7/1)
2771 Hay Dance did not have the race run to suit him, thanks to the tactics of the winner. His trainer thought this race may have come too quickly after his previous run. (8/13)
Keep Me in Mind (IRE) (6/1: op 4/1)

2964 SOMERSET HUNTERS' CHASE (6-Y.O+) (Class H)

4-10 (4-10) **3m 1f 110y (21 fncs)** £1,119.00 (£309.00: £147.00) GOING: 0.23 sec per fur (G)

Form	Horse / details	Dist	Pos	SP	RR	SF
	Double Silk (RCWilkins) **13-12-10**(3) MrRTreloggen (led 2nd: clr 4 out: r.o wl)	—	**1**	4/9^{1}	110	4
	Visaga (MrsAIHellstenius) **11-12-6**(7) MrSLloyd (bit bkwd: led to 2nd: mstke 12th: one pce fr 4 out)	16	**2**	5/1^{2}	100	—

	Horse			SP	RR	SF
	Sonofagipsy (JWDufosee) **13-12-6**(7) MrRNuttall (bkwd: hld up: rdn 15th: outpcd 4 out: styd on flat)	2	3	6/1 3	99	—
	Upham Close (MrsMandyHand) **11-11-7**(7) MrsAHand (bit bkwd: lost tch 9th: rdn & hdwy 17th: chsd wnr appr 3 out: 3rd & wkng whn fell last)		F	11/1	—	—
	Furry Knowe (DavidPritchard) **12-12-6**(7) MrDPritchard (hld up: hit 9th: 4th whn fell 11th)		F	66/1	—	—
	Jupiter Moon (MrsCHicks) **8-12-3**(7) MrRHicks (j.lft: sn prom: dropped rr 6th: sn t.o: p.u bef 12th)		P	20/1	—	—
				(SP 114.8%)	**6 Rn**	

6m 56.1 (37.10) CSF £3.32 TOTE £1.50: £1.30 £1.90 (£3.10) OWNER Mr R. C. Wilkins (BATH) BRED Mrs P. M. Eyre
Double Silk will have one more run after a final decision is made about his participation in the Foxhunters'. (4/9)
Visaga, making his debut in this sphere, should at least be sharper for the outing. (5/1)
Sonofagipsy seemed to find his second wind in the closing stages after possibly blowing up. (6/1)

2965 WINCANTON STANDARD OPEN CLAIMING N.H. FLAT RACE (4, 5 & 6-Y.O) (Class H)
4-40 (4-41) **2m** £1,150.50 (£318.00: £151.50)

	Horse			SP	RR	SF
2572[8]	**Society Times (USA)** (MCPipe) **4-10-6** CMaude (lw: plld hrd: sn chsng ldr: led 6f out: easily)	—	1	11/4 2	49 f	—
1820[7]	**Kylami (NZ)** (AGHobbs) **5-11-7** RGreene (led 10f: rdn & ev ch over 2f out: one pce)	4	2	11/4 2	50 f	—
	Golden Lily (MissGayKelleway) **4-10-2**(7) LReynolds (lt-f: unf: hld up: hdwy 8f out: one pce fnl 3f)	2	3	9/2 3	46 f	—
	Country Cousin (PFNicholls) **5-11-4** DBridgwater (hld up: hdwy 5f out: hrd rdn over 2f out: one pce)	6	4	5/2 1	39 f	—
1336[7]	**Boozys Dream** (NBThomson) **6-10-12**(3) GuyLewis (hdwy 8f out: wknd 5f out: t.o)	dist	5	33/1	—	—
2661[11]	**Splash of Blakeney** (SGKnight) **6-10-5**(5) DSalter (prom tl rdn over 6f out: t.o)	6	6	40/1	—	—
1834[15]	**That Man Carter (IRE)** (GCBravery) **6-11-3**(5) SRyan (lw: plld hrd: prom tl rdn & wknd over 4f out: t.o)	7	7	8/1	—	—
				(SP 116.6%)	**7 Rn**	

3m 49.0 CSF £10.19 TOTE £2.90: £1.40 £2.50 (£7.10) OWNER Mr M. C. Pipe (WELLINGTON) BRED Robert A. McMillan
WEIGHT FOR AGE 4yo-10lb
2572 Society Times (USA) settled better once he got to the front and proved too sharp for what was probably a moderate bunch. (11/4)
1289 Kylami (NZ) found the winner toying with him. (11/4)
Golden Lily was making her debut in a poor race. (9/2: op 9/4)
Country Cousin does not possess much scope. (5/2)
That Man Carter (IRE) (8/1: 7/1-12/1)

T/Plpt: £211.10 (30.13 Tckts). T/Qdpt: £11.20 (46 Tckts) KH

2966a - 2992a : (Irish Racing) - See Computer Raceform

2737a-LEOPARDSTOWN (Dublin, Ireland) (L-H) (Good to yielding)
Sunday February 2nd

2993a SPRING HURDLE (Gd 3) (4-Y.O)
1-35 (1-35) **2m (8 hdls)** IR £6,850.00 (IR £1,550.00: IR £650.00: IR £350.00) GOING: Not Established

	Horse			SP	RR	SF
	Commanche Court (IRE) (TMWalsh,Ireland) **4-10-11** NWilliamson (hld up: 7th whn mstke 4th: 4th whn slight mstke 3 out: 2nd bef st: chal appr last: led early flat: styd on: hands & heels)	—	1	6/1	99	41
2333a[7]	**Hard News (USA)** (DPKelly,Ireland) **4-10-11** PCarberry (rn freely: disp ld: led 2nd: jnd last: hdd & no ex early flat: kpt on)	2	2	14/1	97	39
	Strategic Ploy (JohnMcKay,Ireland) **4-10-6** TJMitchell (towards rr early: wnt 5th at 4th: 7th & rdn 3 out: 4th 2 out: 3rd, rdn & nt trble ldrs appr last: kpt on same pce)	5½	3	5/2 2	87	29
2738a[5]	**Marlonette (IRE)** (WPMullins,Ireland) **4-10-6** DJCasey (in tch early: lost pl bef 4th: towards rr & sme hdwy 3 out: 8th 2 out: no imp appr last: styd on)	7	4	14/1	80	22
2738a[12]	**Evriza (IRE)** (APO'Brien,Ireland) **4-10-12b**[1] THorgan (towards rr: 9th at 5th: 7th & chsd ldrs 2 out: no imp appr last: kpt on)	5	5	20/1	81	23
	Keal Ryan (IRE) (DTHughes,Ireland) **4-10-4**(7) PJDobbs (disp ld early: rn 2nd fr 2nd to 3 out: sn rdn: wkng 5th 2 out: nt trble ldrs appr last: kpt on same pce)	3	6	25/1	77	19
2333a[5]	**Miss Pennyhill (IRE)** (ASadik,Ireland) **4-9-13b**(7) JMMaguire (hld up: hdwy & 4th at 5th: 2nd after 3 out: 3rd 2 out: rdn & nt qckn st: no imp appr last)	nk	7	14/1	71	13
2333a*	**Grimes** (CRoche,Ireland) **4-11-3** CO'Dwyer (hld up towards rr: hdwy 3 out: 6th, rdn & chsd ldrs 2 out: sn no imp)	9	8	9/4 1	73	15
2333a[6]	**Miss Roberto (IRE)** (MBrassil,Ireland) **4-10-12** JShortt (cl up: 3rd at 4th: 5th 3 out: sn rdn: wknd appr next: no imp)	2	9	10/1	66	8
	Bavario (USA) (DKWeld,Ireland) **4-10-11** RDunwoody (cl up early: 4th at 4th: 6th 3 out: sn rdn & wknd: n.d next)	3	10	5/1 3	62	4
2738a[7]	**Highly Motivated** (APO'Brien,Ireland) **4-10-6** CFSwan (hld up: 7th at 3rd: 8th at 5th: no imp appr 2 out)	4½	11	8/1	53	—
2738a[13]	**Nascimento (USA)** (FBerry,Ireland) **4-10-11** FrancisFlood (towards rr: mstke 3rd: never a danger)	15	12	33/1	43	—
	Marchaway (IRE) (FBerry,Ireland) **4-10-4**(7) RPHogan (towards rr: nt fluent: never a danger)	11	13	20/1	32	—
				(SP 146.8%)	**13 Rn**	

3m 52.9 (-8.10) OWNER D. F. Desmond (KILL) BRED Cambremont Ltd Partnership
Commanche Court (IRE), winner of the Austrian Derby last year, when trained by Nicolas Clement, certainly looked the part in a contest which attracted eight previous winners. He wasn't fluent but, moving into second before two out, was always travelling like a winner. He will have another run in this sort of company before Cheltenham. (6/1: op 4/1)
Hard News (USA) tried to make all but was a sitting duck all the way up the straight. (14/1)
Strategic Ploy, previously impressive, could make no impression on the first two here. (5/2)
2333a* Grimes (9/4: op 6/4)
Bavario (USA) (5/1: op 5/2)
2738a Highly Motivated (8/1: op 16/1)

2994a SCALP NOVICES' CHASE (Gd 2) (5-Y.O+)

2-05 (2-07) **2m 5f (14 fncs)** IR £9,750.00 (IR £2,850.00: IR £1,350.00: IR £450.00) GOING: Not Established

SP RR SF

2360a* **Dorans Pride (IRE)** (MHourigan,Ireland) **8-12-0** JPBroderick (mde all: j.w: clr 2nd to 6th: rdn clr flat: styd on wl) ....— **1** 8/11[1] 148 30
1758a[2] **See More Business (IRE)** (PFNicholls) **7-12-0** RDunwoody (hld up towards rr early: 2nd fr 2nd: trckd wnr fr 6th: chsd wnr whn hit 3 out: sn rdn: u.p st: nt rch wnr) ....6 **2** 11/8[2] 143 25
2848a[4] **Dun Belle (IRE)** (PAFahy,Ireland) **8-11-9** TJMitchell (sn mod 3rd: slow 5th: cld sltly bef 7th: rdn & n.d 3 out) ....dist **3** 11/1[3] — —
Kaldan Khan (APO'Brien,Ireland) **6-11-7** CFSwan (j.slowly: sn towards rr: n.d: wl t.o) ....dist **4** 40/1 — —
(SP 110.8%) **4 Rn**

5m 33.0 (-4.00) OWNER T. J. Doran (PATRICKSWELL) BRED Hugh Suffern Bloodstock Ltd

2360a* Dorans Pride (IRE), virtually foot-perfect apart from a slight mistake four out, made all the running. He was travelling particularly strongly from two out and this was impressive. Whether he has the experience for the Gold Cup remains to be seen and his connections are very mindful of his novice status. (8/11)

1758a See More Business (IRE), in second place from the third, was always fighting a losing battle. He lost ground to the winner six out, and made another mistake three from home. It might be unfair to call him unenthusiastic but he certainly seemed a bit demoralized in the straight. The SunAlliance remains his target. (11/8)

2848a Dun Belle (IRE), useful in her own right, was a trailer after five from home. (11/1: op 7/1)

Kaldan Khan was tailed off from the fifth. (40/1)

2995a DELOITTE AND TOUCHE NOVICES' HURDLE (Gd 2) (5-Y.O+)

2-35 (2-35) **2m 2f (9 hdls)** IR £13,000.00 (IR £3,800.00: IR £1,800.00: IR £600.00) GOING: Not Established

SP RR SF

2347a* **Istabraq (IRE)** (APO'Brien,Ireland) **5-11-10** CFSwan (dwlt briefly: hld up: 5th at 6th: wnt 3rd after 3 out: led appr next: mstke: jnd nr last: slt mstke: hdd briefly flat: rdn & styd on last 100y) ....— **1** 4/11[1] 124 59
2857a[2] **Finnegan's Hollow (IRE)** (APO'Brien,Ireland) **7-11-7** CO'Dwyer (hld up towards rr: hdwy after 3 out: 3rd 2 out: 2nd & trckd wnr st: chal to disp ld last: narrow ld briefly flat: no ex last 100y: hands & heels) ......hd **2** 14/1 118 56
2347a[2] **Palette (IRE)** (WPMullins,Ireland) **5-10-13** DJCasey (rn 4th: 5th & rdn after 3 out: mod 3rd & nt trble ledrs appr last) ....10 **3** 13/2[2] 104 39
2347a[4] **Three Scholars** (WPMullins,Ireland) **6-11-7** RDunwoody (hld up: hdwy 3 out: cl 2nd whn slight mstke 2 out: 3rd & rdn st: one pce & no imp appr last) 5 **4** 20/1 105 43
Dudley Do Right (IRE) (TJTaaffe,Ireland) **5-11-4** NWilliamson (rn 2nd tl after 3 out: mod 4th 2 out: one pce appr last: no imp) 3½ **5** 33/1 102 37
2359a[F] **Tarthooth (IRE)** (ALTMoore,Ireland) **6-11-13** FWoods (led: mstke 3rd: hdd after 3 out: sn wknd & n.d) ....6 **6** 13/2[2] 102 40
2596a* **Liss De Paor (IRE)** (APO'Brien,Ireland) **6-11-8** THorgan (rn 3rd tl wknd qckly after 3 out: sn dropped bhd: t.o) ....dist **7** 8/1[3] — —
(SP 125.5%) **7 Rn**

4m 22.2 (-6.80) OWNER John McManus (PILTOWN) BRED Shadwell Estate Company Limited

2347a* Istabraq (IRE) faced the toughest task of his career so far, and appeared to struggle a bit to hold his stable companion, but Swan, taking it up before the second last, did not have to resort to any real punishment. Now that he has had a proper race, there might be further improvement to come. (4/11)

2857a Finnegan's Hollow (IRE), in the same ownership and a stable-companion of the winner, was an improving second after two out. Although not fluent when jumping the last, he still managed to get his head in front briefly on the flat but, under a hands and heels ride, was denied victory. (14/1)

2347a Palette (IRE), always in touch, was in third place and had cried enough early in the straight. (13/2)

Three Scholars made headway after three out, but was done with early in the straight. (20/1)

2359a Tarthooth (IRE) made the running until weakening quickly after three out. (13/2)

2996a : (Irish Racing) - See Computer Raceform

2997a HENNESSY COGNAC GOLD CUP CHASE (Gd 1) (5-Y.O+)

3-40 (3-41) **3m (17 fncs)** IR £59,000.00 (IR £19,000.00: IR £9,000.00: IR £3,000.00) GOING: Not Established

SP RR SF

2739a[F] **Danoli (IRE)** (TFoley,Ireland) **9-12-0** TPTreacy (led: hdd 2nd: disp ld 4th: hdd next: led & disp ld 7th: hdd briefly 10th & after 5 out: rdn 2 out: styd on u.p whn chal flat) ....— **1** 6/1[3] 170 93
2636* **Jodami** (PBeaumont) **12-12-0** NWilliamson (hld up: mod 6th whn mstke 8th: slight mstke 11th: 4th 4 out: 3rd, rdn & clsd after next: 2nd & chsd wnr early st: nt rch wnr u.p flat: no ex last 100y: kpt on: lame)...1½ **2** 5/1[2] 169 92
1889a[4] **Imperial Call (IRE)** (FSutherland,Ireland) **8-12-0** CO'Dwyer (hld up: 4th fr 4th: 2nd after 12th: led briefly after next: cl 2nd 3 out: rdn bef next: lost tch with wnr after 2 out: 3rd, one pce & no imp appr last) ....20 **3** Evens[1] 156 79
2346a* **Merry Gale (IRE)** (JTRDreaper,Ireland) **9-12-0** RDunwoody (led 2nd: jnd 4th: led again 5th tl appr 7th: 3rd at 10th: lft 2nd briefly 12th: mod 3rd whn mstke 4 out: no imp next) 25 **4** 7/1 139 62
2602a[3] **King of the Gales** (ALTMoore,Ireland) **10-12-0** CO'Brien (towards rr: nt fluent early: n.d: t.o) ....dist **5** 50/1 — —
1649[2] **The Grey Monk (IRE)** (GRichards) **9-12-0** ADobbin (cl up: 3rd at 6th: 2nd after next: led briefly 10th: cl 2nd whn fell 12th) .... **F** 7/1 — —
1785* **Belmont King (IRE)** (PFNicholls) **9-12-0** DBridgwater (in tch: mod 6th & reminders 6th: 5th at 10th: hmpd 12th: rdn & no imp 4 out: p.u bef next) .... **P** 20/1 — —
2848a[F] **Idiots Venture** (APO'Brien,Ireland) **10-12-0** CFSwan (hld up towards rr: trailing 10th: bhd & n.d whn p.u bef 3 out) .... **P** 50/1 — —
(SP 114.6%) **8 Rn**

6m 10.2 (-24.80) OWNER D. J. O'Neill (BAGENALSTOWN) BRED W. Austin in Ireland

2739a Danoli (IRE) really appreciated an aggressive ride. He is no pet lamb himself and, under a strong ride from Treacy, he answered all the calls. He wasn't foot-perfect but never looked like being in trouble with his jumping, and forcing tactics are obviously what he enjoys. Going on from two out, he was always resisting Jodami in the straight. The intention is to give him another run at Gowran Park on the 15th. He does not need to be any fitter than this though. (6/1)

2636* Jodami ran one of his better races in defeat, but was pulled up and dismounted after the line and was found to have badly damaged his off-fore tendon. He has been retired after a memorable career. (5/1)

1889a Imperial Call (IRE), well-supported despite misgivings about his race-fitness, looked to have every chance when leading five out. He had relinquished the advantage at the next, and from that point on was fighting a losing battle, with his jockey reporting that he blew up. Certainly he dropped out quickly on the approach to the straight. He returned to the parade ring with some slight cuts behind and he too looks like going to Gowran. He should not be written off yet. (Evens)
2346a* Merry Gale (IRE) dropped right away after a mistake four out, but was a spent force before then. (7/1)
1649 The Grey Monk (IRE) was running with plenty of zest in second place, when meeting the sixth from home all wrong, and paid the penalty. (7/1: op 4/1)

2998a LEOPARDSTOWN HUNTERS CHASE (5-Y.O+)
4-10 (4-16) **3m (17 fncs)** IR £6,850.00 (IR £1,550.00: IR £650.00: IR £350.00) GOING: Not Established

Horse	Dist	Pos	SP	RR	SF
What A Hand (EJO'Grady,Ireland) **9-11-13** MrPFenton (rn 2nd early: 3rd at 6th: lost tch 9th: 6th & rdn 5 out: hdwy 3 out: hdwy & 4th 2 out: 2nd st: sn chal: led appr last: rdn clr)	—	1	7/2^{3}	109+	59
Aiguille (IRE) (AHeffernan,Ireland) **8-11-8** MrBMCash (hld up in tch: 3rd at 10th: wnt 2nd 12th: led bef 3 out: rdn & hdd nr last: one pce flat)	5	2	9/1	101	51
Mr K's Winterblues (IRE) (JJMangan,Ireland) **7-10-6**(7) MrWEwing (towards rr: mstkes 6th & 4 out: rdn & hdwy next: 5th st: mod 3rd appr last: styd on u.p flat: nt rch ldrs)	3½	3	20/1	89	39
Life of a King (IRE) (WPMullins,Ireland) **9-11-9** MrJANash (led tl appr 3 out: 2nd 2 out: 3rd & one pce early st: no imp appr last)	8	4	7/4^{1}	94	44
Stay In Touch (IRE) (JJCostello,Ireland) **7-11-10**(3) MrDPCostello (2nd fr 2nd: mstke 10th: 3rd whn mstkes 12th & 4 out: 3rd & rdn 2 out: 4th & one pce appr last)	6	5	9/4^{2}	94	44
Caddy Man (IRE) (LCashman,Ireland) **8-11-2**(7) MrPCashman (hld up: slt mstke 3rd: wnt 4th at 9th: chsd ldrs whn mstke 3 out: no imp after 2 out: one pce)	8	6	7/1	85	35
No Mistake VI (IRE) (TMWalsh,Ireland) **9-11-6**(3) MrRWalsh (towards rr: 6th at 8th: 5th 5 out: no imp whn mstke 2 out: one pce)	5½	7	14/1	81	31
Lineker (IRE) (NSMcGrath,Ireland) **10-11-9** MrAJMartin (in tch: 5th at 7th: lost pl next: towards rr 10th: lost tch: t.o 4 out: p.u bef next)		P	20/1	—	—

(SP 128.0%) **8 Rn**

6m 22.9 (-12.10) OWNER Mrs L. J. Roberts (THURLES) BRED J. S. Hoare
What A Hand, given plenty of time to warm up, came through in the straight to take the advantage at the last. The form does not amount to much, but he certainly has not gone backward since coming over to Ireland. (7/2: op 2/1)
Aiguille (IRE) flattered from three out but was comfortably held on the flat. (9/1)
Life of a King (IRE), the surprise favourite, ran in front to four out but dropped right away in the straight. (7/4)
Stay In Touch (IRE) (9/4: op Evens)
Caddy Man (IRE) (7/1: op 4/1)

2999a - (Irish Racing) - See Computer Raceform

1980-BANGOR-ON-DEE (L-H) (Chase Good, Hdles Good, Good to firm patches)
Friday February 7th
One fence omitted 6th race.
WEATHER: fine & sunny

3000 E.B.F. 'N.H.' (QUALIFIER) NOVICES' HURDLE (5, 6 & 7-Y.O) (Class E)
1-45 (1-45) **2m 1f (9 hdls)** £2,836.00 (£796.00: £388.00) GOING: 0.12 sec per fur (G)

Form	Horse	Dist	Pos	SP	RR	SF
2673^{3}	**Darakshan (IRE) (104)** (MissHCKnight) **5-11-0** JCulloty (lw: chsd ldrs: led last: rdn & r.o wl)	—	1	7/4^{2}	75	32
	Gods Squad (JMackie) **5-11-0** RSupple (bkwd: a.p: led appr 2 out to last: rdn & unable qckn flat)	2	2	7/1^{3}	73	30
2656^{5}	**St Mellion Drive** (MCPipe) **7-11-0** DWalsh (swtg: led: j.slowly 1st: hdd appr 2 out: sn rdn & outpcd)	14	3	5/4^{1}	60	17
	Althrey Pilot (IRE) (AndrewTurnell) **6-11-0** SMcNeill (bkwd: hld up in rr: hdwy 3 out: styd on)	½	4	20/1	60	17
1938^{P}	**Market Mayhem** (JLSpearing) **7-10-9**(5) MichaelBrennan (chsd ldrs: no hdwy fr 3 out)	3½	5	12/1	56	13
2668^{16}	**Sleazey (70)** (JGO'Neill) **6-11-0b^{1}** SCurran (hdwy 4th: wknd appr 3 out: t.o)	27	6	50/1	31	—
1986^{5}	**The Eens** (DMcCain) **5-11-0** RGarritty (bit bkwd: hdwy 5th: wknd appr 3 out: t.o)	1½	7	33/1	29	—
	Fred Fuggles (CFCJackson) **5-10-9**(5) OBurrows (a bhd: t.o)	8	8	50/1	22	—
2503^{5}	**Gazanali (IRE)** (GMMoore) **6-11-0** NBentley (a bhd: t.o)	14	9	16/1	9	—
1659^{U}	**Countess Millie** (LJBarratt) **5-10-9** SWynne (bit bkwd: fell 1st)		F	100/1	—	—
2066^{12}	**Just One Question (IRE)** (JJO'Neill) **7-11-0** PNiven (prom: mstke 6th: wknd & p.u 2 out)		P	16/1	—	—
1768^{P}	**Althrey Gale (IRE)** (FLloyd) **6-11-0** TEley (bkwd: a bhd: t.o fr 6th: p.u bef 2 out)		P	100/1	—	—

(SP 126.4%) **12 Rn**

4m 3.8 (8.80) CSF £13.98 TOTE £2.90: £1.10 £2.30 £1.10 (£6.90) Trio £3.80 OWNER Mr Michael Watt (WANTAGE) BRED His Highness the Aga Khans Studs S. C.
2673 Darakshan (IRE) readily accepted a lead and, moving up smoothly to take charge at the last, quickly put the issue beyond doubt. (7/4)
Gods Squad ran extremely well on this hurdling debut and, as he is sure to strip fitter for it, can only go one way after this. (7/1)
2656 St Mellion Drive needs a stiffer test of stamina but, though he tried to stretch his rivals, he always had company, and was tapped for toe when the battle to the line really developed. (5/4)
Althrey Pilot (IRE), given time to get the hang of things on his racecourse debut, was finding his stride in the closing stages and will be all the wiser next time. (20/1)
1633 Market Mayhem sat in behind the leaders travelling comfortably but, when the pace lifted on the turn for home, he could do little more than stay on at the one pace. (12/1: 7/1-14/1)

3001 EDWARD SYMMONS HOTEL & LEISURE NOVICES' H'CAP CHASE (0-110) (5-Y.O+) (Class D)
2-20 (2-22) **2m 1f 110y (12 fncs)** £3,745.00 (£1,135.00: £555.00: £265.00) GOING: Not Established

Form	Horse	Dist	Pos	SP	RR	SF
2862^{3}	**Saymore (76)** (WClay) **11-10-0** SWynne (lw: hld up: hdwy 7th: blnd 4 out: rallied appr last: styng on whn n.m.r & swtchd flat: jst failed: fin 2nd, s.h: awrdd r)	—	1	33/1	91	13
1780^{P}	**Jack Doyle (IRE) (94)** (JJO'Neill) **6-11-4** PNiven (hld up & bhd: hdwy 8th: led appr 2 out: rdn & edgd rt flat: all out: fin 1st: disq: plcd 2nd)		2	14/1	109	31

1830[11] **Latest Thyne (IRE) (90)** (CaptTAForster) **7-11-0** AThornton (bit bkwd: chsd ldrs: ev ch whn mstke 2 out: kpt on u.p) 1¼ **3** 16/1 104 26
1629[2] **Whirly (IRE) (95)** (RHAlner) **8-11-5** SMcNeill (bit bkwd: prom: ev ch 3 out: wknd appr next)....19 **4** 11/2[2] 91 13
2759[8] **Burntwood Melody (76)** (PTDalton) **6-10-0** PMcLoughlin (lw: bhd: reminders 5th: nvr nrr) ....7 **5** 50/1 66 —
1572[5] **Glendoe (IRE) (84)** (AndrewTurnell) **6-10-8** LHarvey (chsd ldrs: mstke 7th: sn lost tch)....nk **6** 14/1 74 —
2657* **Indian Arrow (NZ) (100)** (MCPipe) **9-11-10** DWalsh (lw: led to 8th: led 3 out: sn hdd & wknd) ....2 **7** 9/4[1] 88 10
2666[11] **Cawarra Boy (98)** (CJames) **9-11-8** MrEJames (a bhd: t.o)....2½ **8** 20/1 84 6
2752[2] **Mr Bean (92)** (KRBurke) **7-11-2** ALarnach (lw: hld up: hdwy 7th: wknd 4 out: t.o) ....2½ **9** 16/1 75 —
2631[5] **Shahgram (IRE) (86)** (PBeaumont) **9-10-10** RSupple (bit bkwd: a bhd t.o) ....1½ **10** 14/1 68 —
2506[2] **Devilry (93)** (AStreeter) **7-11-3** TEley (mid div: mstke 6th: sn lost pl: t.o)....dist **11** 20/1 — —
2793[2] **Robins Pride (IRE) (100)** (CLPopham) **7-11-7**(3) TDascombe (prom: led 8th to 3 out: sn rdn & wknd: p.u bef next) .... **P** 16/1 — —
2752[F] **Bold Acre (80)** (JMBradley) **7-10-4b** JCulloty (in tch to 7th: t.o whn p.u bef 3 out) .... **P** 9/1[3] — —
2745[F] **Sigma Run (IRE) (81)** (JGMO'Shea) **8-10-0v1**(5) MichaelBrennan (prom: mstke 7th: rdn & wknd appr 4 out: p.u bef 2 out) .... **P** 9/1[3] — —
1732[2] **Rachael's Owen (80)** (CWeedon) **7-10-4** MRichards (a in rr: t.o: p.u bef 2 out) .... **P** 11/1 — —
(SP 126.6%) **15 Rn**

4m 30.6 (20.60) CSF £398.34 CT £6,824.72 TOTE £57.30: £6.10 £3.70 £5.50 (£1,050.40; £1,080.09 to Newbury 8/2/97) Trio Not won; £413.00 to Newbury 8/2/97 OWNER P Morris & G Evans (STOKE-ON-TRENT) BRED Airlie Stud
LONG HANDICAP Burntwood Melody 9-3 Saymore 9-12
STEWARDS' ENQUIRY Niven susp. 17-18/2/97 (careless riding). Thornton susp. 17-18/2/97 (improper use of whip).
2862 Saymore, returning to fences, would have been a very unlucky loser even if the decision had gone against him, and he again showed his liking for this track. (33/1)
1525 Jack Doyle (IRE) always looked to have it under control after gaining command into the straight, but he rather carelessly made a bee-line for the stands' rail inside the final 100 yards and disqualification was a formality. (14/1)
Latest Thyne (IRE) made a promising debut over fences over a trip which could be short of his best, and if he had been more fluent he would have taken all the beating. (16/1)
1629 Whirly (IRE) was just short of a run after ten weeks off, and ran accordingly. (11/2)
1572 Glendoe (IRE) (14/1: op 8/1)
2657* Indian Arrow (NZ), given no peace at the head of affairs, regained command three out but, overtaken almost immediately, was soon hard at work and done for. (9/4)

3002 BERMANS H'CAP HURDLE (0-110) (4-Y.O+) (Class E)

2-50 (2-53) **2m 1f (9 hdls)** £3,517.50 (£1,065.00: £520.00: £247.50) GOING: 0.12 sec per fur (G)

SP RR SF
2777[11] **Nashville Star (USA) (92)** (RMathew) **6-11-4v** AThornton (lw: led to 5th: led appr next: rdn & r.o wl) ....— **1** 7/1[2] 75 37
2838[4] **Kadari (88)** (WClay) **8-10-11v**(3) GuyLewis (lw: chsd ldrs: styd on flat: no ch w wnr)....2½ **2** 15/2[3] 69 31
2859* **Russian Rascal (IRE) (102)** (TDEasterby) **4-11-4** 7x RGarritty (lw: hld up: hdwy to chal 2 out: sn rdn: one pce: b.b.v) ....1¼ **3** 4/7[1] 82 34
2631[14] **Shifting Moon (79)** (FJordan) **5-10-5b** SWynne (prom: effrt & mstke 3 out: sn btn) 6 **4** 8/1 53 15
2842[10] **Alaskan Heir (84)** (AStreeter) **6-10-10** TEley (swtg: a in rr: reminders ½-wy: no imp) 3½ **5** 25/1 55 17
Nipper Reed (98) (THind) **7-11-10** PMcLoughlin (bit bkwd: chsd wnr: led 5th: sn hdd & wknd: t.o) ....dist **6** 15/2[3] — —
2665[F] **Houghton (95)** (WJenks) **11-11-0**(7) MrRBurton (chsd ldrs to 5th: sn wknd: t.o) ....9 **7** 33/1 — —
(SP 117.6%) **7 Rn**

4m 3.4 (8.40) CSF £52.44 TOTE £9.70: £4.00 £2.00 (£56.60) OWNER Mr Robin Mathew (BURFORD) BRED Eaglestone Farm Inc
WEIGHT FOR AGE 4yo-10lb
OFFICIAL EXPLANATION Russian Rascal (IRE): bled from the nose.
1439 Nashville Star (USA) is not afraid to force the pace and, prepared to do battle when pressed into the penultimate flight, he deservedly retained his advantage to the post. (7/1)
2838 Kadari probably found the ground too lively, but she ran her race out to the finish and another success will not come out of turn. (15/2)
2859* Russian Rascal (IRE), restrained off the pace, made steady progress to mount a challenge two out but once there was made to work and, with no response forthcoming, was forced to admit defeat. He was found to have bled. (4/7)
1715 Shifting Moon, waiting on the leaders, missed out completely at the third last and, with the stuffing taken out of him, was soon beaten. (8/1)

3003 OLD HALL ESTATES H'CAP CHASE (0-115) (6-Y.O+) (Class E)

3-20 (3-22) **3m 6f (21 fncs)** £4,630.50 (£1,404.00: £687.00: £328.50) GOING: 0.71 sec per fur (S)

SP RR SF
1773* **Ceridwen (80)** (TRGreathead) **7-10-0** NMann (hld up: hdwy 16th: led 2 out: styd on strly)....— **1** 9/2[2] 91 —
2816[4] **Loch Garman Hotel (IRE) (81)** (PTDalton) **8-10-1** RSupple (lw: lost pl 6th: hdwy 11th: lft in ld 4 out: hdd 2 out: styd on one pce)....5 **2** 7/1 89 —
2658[P] **Anythingyoulike (87)** (CASmith) **8-10-7** MRichards (hld up: hdwy 12th: rdn appr 2 out: sn btn) ....5 **3** 20/1 92 —
2869[U] **Three Saints (IRE) (96)** (CaptTAForster) **8-11-2** SWynne (chsd ldrs: hit 10th: rdn 16th: sn wknd) ....23 **4** 8/1 87 —
2876* **Banntown Bill (IRE) (99)** (MCPipe) **8-11-5v** 4x DWalsh (chsd ldr: led 17th tl mstke & hdd 4 out: rdn & wknd next) ....6 **5** 9/4[1] 87 —
2681[8] **Keano (IRE) (93)** (PJHobbs) **8-10-13** GTormey (led to 17th: wkng whn blnd 4 out: t.o)....25 **6** 6/1[3] 66 —
2754[4] **Celtic Town (104)** (OSherwood) **9-11-10b** JAMcCarthy (mstke 3rd: lost pl 9th: t.o: p.u bef 16th) .... **P** 14/1 — —
2821[7] **Claxton Greene (97)** (CPEBrooks) **13-11-3** DGallagher (chsd ldrs: mstke 13th: t.o: p.u bef 4 out) .... **P** 25/1 — —
2667[F] **Pennant Cottage (IRE) (84)** (WJenks) **9-10-4**ow4 MrAMitchell (mstkes: bhd tl p.u bef 9th) .... **P** 66/1 — —
(SP 103.6%) **9 Rn**

8m 9.5 (49.50) CSF £26.25 CT £385.84 TOTE £4.30: £1.30 £1.90 £3.00 (£15.20) Trio £26.20 OWNER Mrs S. Greathead (CHIPPING NORTON) BRED William J. Wood
LONG HANDICAP Ceridwen 9-13 Pennant Cottage (IRE) 8-8
1773* Ceridwen, ridden with any amount of confidence, cruised into the lead at the second last and did not need to be let down to win with plenty in hand. She stays well and is at the right end of the handicap. (9/2)
2816 Loch Garman Hotel (IRE) looked set to open his account when presented with the lead four out, but the winner was waiting to pounce and took his measure without much trouble. (7/1)
2039 Anythingyoulike put in his best-ever effort under Rules, but was only playing for the places from the turn for home. (20/1)
2876* Banntown Bill (IRE) was the one to catch when bowling along with a two-length advantage approaching the last ditch, but he failed to jump as well as he had been doing and, forfeiting the lead, had soon shot his bolt. (9/4: op 6/4)

3004 TBR CONSTRUCTION NOVICES' H'CAP HURDLE (0-105) (4-Y.O+) (Class E)

3-50 (3-53) **2m 4f (11 hdls)** £3,004.00 (£844.00: £412.00) GOING: 0.12 sec per fur (G)

	Horse and details	Dist	Pos	SP	RR	SF
2806[6]	**Milling Brook (76)** (JMBradley) **5-10-0** SWynne (a.p: led appr 3 out: sn clr: hrd rdn & jst hld on)	—	1	16/1	49	—
866[3]	**Vallingale (IRE) (85)** (MissHCKnight) **6-10-9** JCulloty (hld up in tch: gd hdwy appr 2 out: hrd rdn & fin strly)	hd	2	7/1[2]	58	—
31[5]	**Mrs Robinson (IRE) (76)** (JMackie) **6-9-11**(3) EHusband (chsd ldrs: outpcd appr 3 out: styd on strly flat)	nk	3	20/1	49	—
2806[7]	**Lothian Commander (78)** (DMcCain) **5-10-2**ow2 DWalsh (bit bkwd: chsd ldrs: wnt 2nd 6th: rdn 3 out: rallied u.p cl home)	¾	4	16/1	50	—
2662[4]	**Dont Forget Curtis (IRE) (88)** (GMMoore) **5-10-12** JCallaghan (lw: hld up: hdwy 7th: rdn appr 2 out: no imp)	25	5	15/2[3]	40	—
2763[8]	**Scally Hicks (76)** (BPJBaugh) **6-10-0** TEley (nvr nr to chal)	1	6	66/1	27?	—
1523*	**Anglesey Sea View (104)** (ABailey) **8-12-0** TKent (bhd: effrt 8th: nt rchd ldrs)	hd	7	9/2[1]	55	—
2744[3]	**Rare Occurance (80)** (JGMO'Shea) **7-9-13**(5) MichaelBrennan (hld up: hdwy 6th: wknd appr 3 out: t.o)	8	8	7/1[2]	25	—
2053[6]	**Aut Even (IRE) (96)** (CaptTAForster) **7-11-6** AThornton (hld up in rr: t.o)	24	9	9/2[1]	22	—
2676[P]	**Bayerd (IRE) (97)** (CREgerton) **6-11-7b** JAMcCarthy (lw: led tl hdd & wknd qckly appr 3 out: t.o)	dist	10	20/1	—	—
2690[12]	**Libertarian (IRE) (90)** (OSherwood) **7-11-0** MRichards (hld up: hdwy 6th: wknd 8th: t.o: p.u bef 2 out)		P	11/1	—	—
2649[8]	**Crabbie's Pride (87)** (MGMeagher) **4-9-11b**(3) FLeahy (lw: hld up mid div: p.u bef 2 out)		P	16/1	—	—
2665[F]	**Coney Road (76)** (CPEBrooks) **8-10-0v[1]** DGallagher (j.b rt: chsd ldrs to 7th: bhd whn p.u 2 out)		P	16/1	—	—
1953[10]	**Crown And Cushion (87)** (TRGreathead) **4-10-0** NMann (lw: a bhd: t.o ½-wy: p.u bef 3 out)		P	20/1	—	—
1250[14]	**Lastoftheidiots (76)** (TWall) **8-9-11**(3) RMassey (lost pl 5th: t.o: p.u bef 7th)		P	100/1	—	—

(SP 121.8%) **15 Rn**

4m 54.7 (18.70) CSF £108.15 CT £2,076.36 **TOTE** £27.50: £6.10 £2.00 £3.50 (£58.80) Trio £1,155.60; £32.55 to Newbury 8/2/97 OWNER Mr Martyn James (CHEPSTOW) BRED G. Lucas

LONG HANDICAP Milling Brook 9-11 Scally Hicks 8-4 Mrs Robinson (IRE) 9-5 Lothian Commander 9-11 Crabbie's Pride 9-10 Crown And Cushion 9-5 Lastoftheidiots 8-4

WEIGHT FOR AGE 4yo-11lb

2806 Milling Brook, appreciating this return to a longer trip, won the race by kicking clear on the home turn and, though it was getting tight late on, the line arrived in time. (16/1)

866 Vallingale (IRE), fresh and well after four months on the easy list, threw down a determined challenge on the flat and, given a stiffer test of stamina, should have little trouble going one better. (7/1)

Mrs Robinson (IRE) made a very promising return to action after a lengthy break and, if there is any more improvement to follow, she should soon be paying her way. (20/1)

Lothian Commander, behind the winner on his previous outing, finished marginally closer here. He is not short of stamina. (16/1)

1523* Anglesey Sea View has been ridden up with the pace on her previous outings over hurdles, and she did not take to being restrained. (9/2)

2053 Aut Even (IRE) would seem to be going the wrong way. His future might lie over fences. (9/2)

Libertarian (IRE) (11/1: 8/1-12/1)

3005 GILBERT COTTON MEMORIAL HUNTERS' CHASE (6-Y.O+) (Class H)

4-20 (4-21) **2m 4f 110y (14 fncs)** £1,530.00 (£430.00: £210.00) GOING: Not Established

	Horse and details	Dist	Pos	SP	RR	SF
	Inch Maid (SABrookshaw) **11-11-9**(7) MissHBrookshaw (hld up: hdwy 7th: led 3 out: styd on strly)	—	1	10/1	123	16
	Lord Relic (NZ) (SABrookshaw) **11-12-0**(7) MrRFord (chsd ldrs: led 8th: j.slowly & hdd 3 out: rdn & no ex appr last)	3	2	7/2[2]	126	19
	My Nominee (DENicholls) **9-12-0b**(7) MrRBurton (chsd ldrs: led 7th to 8th: rdn 10th: sn lost tch)	dist	3	5/2[1]	—	—
	Driving Force (MrsHMobley) **11-12-4b**(3) MrMRimell (led 6th to 7th: blnd 10th: sn t.o)	25	4	8/1[3]	—	—
	King of Shadows (MissCMCarden) **10-11-7**(7) MrSPrior (bkwd: bhd whn b.d 5th)		B	20/1	—	—
977[4]	**Native Rambler (IRE)** (MrsAPrice) **7-11-7**(7) MissEJames (fell 5th)		F	50/1	—	—
	Barkisland (JRSuthern) **13-12-0**(7) MrJMPritchard (sn t.o: p.u bef 11th)		P	33/1	—	—
	Kino (AJMartin,Ireland) **10-12-0**(7) MrAndrewMartin (bkwd: led to 4th: wknd 7th: t.o: p.u bef 9th)		P	33/1	—	—
	Palm Reader (PHMorris) **13-12-0**(7) MrCJBBarlow (sn wl bhd: t.o: p.u bef 10th)		P	33/1	—	—
	My Young Man (CPEBrooks) **12-12-0**(7) MrEJames (bit bkwd: led 4th to 6th: wknd 10th: t.o: p.u bef 3 out)		P	5/2[1]	—	—
	Spy's Delight (MrsARHewitt) **11-11-7**(7) MrEWoolley (bit bkwd: blnd & uns rdr 2nd)		U	33/1	—	—

(SP 118.1%) **11 Rn**

5m 32.2 (32.20) CSF £39.29 TOTE £7.00: £2.50 £1.10 £1.30 (£22.10) Trio £59.60 OWNER Mr S. A. Brookshaw (SHREWSBURY) BRED James Bradbury

Inch Maid, twice a winner between the flags last season, has bonded well with her young rider and beat her more fancied stable-mate with the minimum of fuss. (10/1: 8/1-12/1)

Lord Relic (NZ) does most of his winning when there is more cut, but he had his chance here before having to admit the winner too smart for him. (7/2)

My Nominee was not as forward in condition as the leading pair, for he was under pressure starting down the back straight, and backers soon knew their fate. (5/2)

Driving Force, a useful individual under Rules, got into the bottom of a fence out in the country and that knocked the stuffing out of him. (8/1)

3006 DENBIGH INTERMEDIATE N.H. FLAT RACE (4, 5 & 6-Y.O F & M) (Class H)

4-50 (4-50) **2m 1f** £1,371.00 (£381.00: £183.00)

	Horse and details	Dist	Pos	SP	RR	SF
2750[2]	**Potter Again (IRE)** (DNicholson) **5-11-0**(3) RMassey (hld up in tch: hdwy 3f out: led over 2f out: sn clr: eased nr fin)	—	1	4/7[1]	61 f	—
	All Done (SMellor) **4-10-7** MrPScott (bit bkwd: hld up: hdwy 5f out: str run fnl f: jst failed)	nk	2	14/1	61 f	—
2661[4]	**Hot 'n Saucy** (APJones) **5-11-3** MrSBush (a.p: led 3f out tl over 2f out: sn rdn: one pce)	2½	3	9/1	58 f	—
	Crystal Jewel (PJHobbs) **5-11-3** GTormey (bit bkwd: trckd ldrs: ev ch 3f out: outpcd fnl 2f)	6	4	8/1[3]	53 f	—
	Side By Side (IRE) (CWThornton) **4-10-0**(7) NHorrocks (hld up & bhd: sme late hdwy: n.d)	5	5	14/1	48 f	—
2757[9]	**Mistress Tudor** (SMellor) **6-11-0**(3) EHusband (led 14f: sn rdn & wknd)	7	6	33/1	41 f	—
2633[4]	**Supreme Target (IRE)** (MrsMReveley) **5-11-0**(3) GLee (hld up: hdwy ½-wy: wknd 3f out)	1¾	7	6/1[2]	40 f	—
2750[12]	**Pearl Silk** (TTBill) **4-10-2**(5) OBurrows (hld up: hdwy 4f out: wknd over 2f out)	1¾	8	66/1	38 f	—
1275[6]	**Saucy Nun (IRE)** (IPWilliams) **5-10-10**(7) FBogle (chsd ldrs: rdn & wknd over 3f out)	1	9	10/1	37 f	—
	Ta-Ra-Abit (IRE) (TWall) **4-10-4**(3) LAspell (w ldr tl wknd 4f out: t.o)	8	10	33/1	30 f	—
	Be In Space (MissPMWhittle) **6-10-10**(7) KHibbert (w'like: bkwd: chsd ldrs 10f: sn wknd: t.o)	4	11	50/1	26 f	—

Diamond Time (CaptTAForster) **6-10-12**(5) ABates (mid div tl wknd 5f out: t.o)	1¾	**12**	20/1	24 f	—
Tafzalette (PWegmann) **5-10-10**(7) SFowler (bkwd: prom 9f: sn wknd: t.o)	7	**13**	50/1	18 f	—
			(SP 137.5%)	**13 Rn**	

4m 7.1 CSF £12.30 TOTE £1.80: £1.10 £2.30 £3.10 (£15.10) Trio £32.50 OWNER Mr J. E. Potter (TEMPLE GUITING) BRED Colman O'Flynn
WEIGHT FOR AGE 4yo-10lb

2750 Potter Again (IRE) lengthened up to take charge entering the final quarter-mile and gained a healthy lead. She would probably have won by six or so lengths had she not been eased. (4/7)

All Done, lobbing along in the rear until past halfway, took closer order on the approach to the straight and, despite hanging and looking green, produced a sustained late challenge that almost caught the winner unawares. (14/1: op 8/1)

2661 Hot 'n Saucy had the advantage of a recent run, but that was on different ground to this. In finishing so close she gave notice that she is getting to know what is required. (9/1: 4/1-11/1)

Crystal Jewel, close enough to prove a threat on the approach to the straight, found lack of peak fitness a problem when the pace lifted. She will come on for this. (8/1: 5/1-9/1)

Side By Side (IRE) stayed on steadily in the latter stages and is open to improvement. (14/1: op 8/1)

Mistress Tudor again forced the pace, and did not give in when challenged. Her stride shortened entering the last two furlongs, and she quickly beat a retreat. (33/1)

2633 Supreme Target (IRE) (6/1: op 3/1)

1275 Saucy Nun (IRE) (10/1: 14/1-8/1)

T/Jkpt: Not won; £3,019.72 to Newbury 8/02/97. T/Plpt: £4,992.80 (2 Tckts). T/Qdpt: £113.70 (6.33 Tckts) IM

2226-NEWBURY (L-H) (Good)
Friday February 7th
WEATHER: showers

3007 STROUD GREEN HURDLE (4-Y.O) (Class C)
1-30 (1-30) **2m 110y (8 hdls)** £3,980.00 (£1,190.00: £570.00: £260.00) GOING: 0.76 sec per fur (S)

	Horse	Dist	Pos	SP	RR	SF
1935B	**Kerawi** (NATwiston-Davies) **4-11-5** CLlewellyn (a.p: rdn 5th: chsd ldr appr 2 out: led flat: r.o wl)	—	**1**	12/1	101	63
1634*	**White Sea (IRE)** (MCPipe) **4-11-0** CFSwan (led: clr appr 3 out: j.slowly last: hdd flat: unable qckn)	1¾	**2**	2/1 1	94+	56
2772²	**Noble Lord** (RHBuckler) **4-11-0** BPowell (a.p: rdn appr 3 out: wknd 2 out)	16	**3**	14/1	79	41
2615²	**Soldat (USA)** (DNicholson) **4-11-5** DBridgwater (hdwy 4th: rdn appr 3 out: wknd appr 2 out)	13	**4**	13/2	71	33
2622*	**Summer Spell (USA)** (NJHenderson) **4-11-5** RDunwoody (bit bkwd: hld up: chsd ldr appr 5th tl appr 2 out: sn wknd)	1	**5**	100/30 2	70	32
	Fly Fishing (USA) (FDoumen,France) **4-11-5** AKondrat (lw: chsd ldr after 1st tl appr 5th: sn wknd)	9	**6**	5/1 3	62	24
2751*	**Desert Mountain (IRE)** (NACallaghan) **4-11-0** RHughes (hld up: rdn appr 3 out: wknd appr 2 out)	4	**7**	11/1	53	15
	Full Throttle (MHTompkins) **4-11-0** RichardGuest (sme hdwy 3 out: sn wknd)	s.h	**8**	33/1	53	15
	Muhtadi (IRE) (LadyHerries) **4-11-0** PHide (prom to 5th)	7	**9**	33/1	46	8
2781⁵	**Squire's Occasion (CAN)** (RAkehurst) **4-10-12**(7) XAizpuru (lw: a bhd)	8	**10**	50/1	43	5
	Kutman (USA) (GBBalding) **4-11-0** BFenton (bit bkwd: a bhd)	1	**11**	33/1	37	—
	Bold Buster (IABalding) **4-11-0** JFTitley (bhd fr 2nd: t.o whn p.u bef 2 out)		**P**	50/1	—	—
	Sassy Street (IRE) (RFJohnsonHoughton) **4-11-0** NWilliamson (a bhd: t.o whn p.u bef 2 out)		**P**	66/1	—	—
				(SP 123.3%)	**13 Rn**	

4m 3.3 (13.30) CSF £33.94 TOTE £14.90: £3.20 £1.60 £4.30 (£20.60) Trio £105.20 OWNER Mr Matt Archer & Miss Jean Broadhurst (CHELTENHAM) BRED Juddmonte Farms

OFFICIAL EXPLANATION **White Sea (IRE): the rider reported that the filly is light-framed and had raced keenly early on, and that he gave her a breather turning for home. He added that she fiddled the last two and landed flat-footed at the last and, although she did pick up on the flat, could not have caught the winner who was idling in front.**

1935 Kerawi was given a fine ride, as the cause looked hopeless in the straight when the runner-up surged well clear and was cruising. Swan was far too confident and Llewellyn seized the opportunity, making giant strides on that rival going to the last. Gaining control early on the run-in, he had managed to catch Swan napping and kept on well. The first two will meet once more in the Triumph Hurdle. (12/1)

1634* White Sea (IRE) was given a nightmare ride by Swan, there was no question she should have won this. Bowling along in front, the filly forged clear in the straight with little fuss, travelling well and with her pilot oozing confidence. After two out, Swan was quite happy to allow her to coast home, despite Kerawi making significant headway to the last. A slow jump there lost her momentum and her rival swept by. Panic set in and Swan tried to conjure another run out of the filly, to no avail. Losses should soon be recouped, and White Sea has been installed favourite for the Triumph Hurdle in many books. (2/1)

2772 Noble Lord has been in fine form this season and ran a sound race here, if left for dead two out. (14/1: 10/1-16/1)

2615 Soldat (USA) was very disappointing on ground that should have been to his liking. Moving into contention at halfway, he tamely dropped away approaching the second last. (13/2: 9/2-7/1)

2622* Summer Spell (USA) was very disappointing, considering the rain-softened ground should have been in his favour. After racing in second turning for home, he was a spent force going to the penultimate flight. (100/30)

Fly Fishing (USA), winner of two races in France this season in the mud, had been hung out to dry turning into the straight. (5/1)

3008 ALDERMASTON NOVICES' CHASE (5-Y.O+) (Class D)
2-00 (2-00) **2m 1f (13 fncs)** £3,543.34 (£1,131.33: £595.33) GOING: 0.76 sec per fur (S)

	Horse	Dist	Pos	SP	RR	SF
1764⁷	**Squire Silk** (AndrewTurnell) **8-11-2** PCarberry (lw: a gng wl: hld up: chsd ldr fr 9th: led appr 3 out: pckd 3 out: hrd hld)	—	**1**	11/8 2	135+	68
2892*	**Eudipe (FR)** (MCPipe) **5-11-1** CFSwan (led: rdn 4 out: hdd appr 3 out: unable qckn flat)	1½	**2**	8/11 1	142?	66
2777¹²	**Intermagic** (JCFox) **7-11-2** SFox (lw: blnd 8th: chsd ldr tl mstke 9th: sn wknd: 3rd & no ch whn mstke 3 out: t.o)	dist	**3**	14/1 3	—	—
				(SP 106.7%)	**3 Rn**	

4m 15.9 (11.90) CSF £2.56 TOTE £2.50 (£1.70) OWNER Mr Robert Ogden (WANTAGE) BRED R. Ogden
WEIGHT FOR AGE 5yo-9lb

1764 Squire Silk, a high-class hurdler, could not have had a better spin following his mishap at Exeter nine weeks ago. Jumping and travelling well, he enjoyed himself and had no more than an exercise gallop. He must be a serious candidate for the Arkle. (11/8)

2892* Eudipe (FR) has shown himself to be a useful individual, but was no match for the winner who played with him in the straight. He can regain the winning thread before long. (8/11)
2777 Intermagic, given a baptism of fire on his chasing debut, got round to collect third prize. (14/1: 10/1-16/1)

3009 ARKELL BREWERY H'CAP CHASE (0-135) (5-Y.O+) (Class C)

2-30 (2-30) **2m 1f (13 fncs)** £4,532.50 (£1,360.00: £655.00: £302.50) GOING: 0.76 sec per fur (S)

				SP	RR	SF
2051[2]	**Mister Oddy (128)** (JSKing) **11-11-4**(3) DFortt (lw: mde all: pushed out)	—	1	11/4[1]	133	71
1321[F]	**High Alltitude (IRE) (107)** (MJHeaton-Ellis) **9-10-0** BPowell (hld up: rdn appr 3 out: r.o one pce flat)	1¼	2	7/1	111	49
2783[2]	**Native Mission (135)** (JGFitzGerald) **10-12-0** PCarberry (lw: hld up: chsd wnr appr 2 out tl flat: one pce)	5	3	3/1[2]	134	72
2707[2]	**Thumbs Up (127)** (GMMcCourt) **11-11-6** RDunwoody (chsd wnr 3rd tl appr 2 out: wknd appr last)	2½	4	13/2	124	62
2700*	**Eastern Magic (107)** (GBarnett) **9-10-0** RFarrant (3rd whn blnd bdly 9th: nt rcvr: t.o)	dist	5	9/2[3]	—	—
2796[7]	**Churchtown Port (IRE) (107)** (PButler) **7-10-0** NWilliamson (bit bkwd: 2nd whn fell 2nd)		F	16/1	—	—
1949*	**James the First (121)** (PFNicholls) **9-11-0b** PHide (lw: 3rd whn blnd bdly 2nd: nt rcvr: bhd whn mstke 6th: t.o fr 8th: p.u bef last)		P	12/1	—	—
				(SP 109.3%)		**7 Rn**

4m 16.4 (12.40) CSF £18.01 TOTE £3.60: £1.60 £3.00 (£17.90) OWNER Mrs R. M. Hill (SWINDON) BRED V. N. F. Tjolle
LONG HANDICAP High Alltitude (IRE) 9-9 Eastern Magic 9-10 Churchtown Port (IRE) 9-6
2051 Mister Oddy really enjoyed himself in front and, never seriously threatened, came home at his leisure to score with plenty in hand. All his wins have come at around two miles, and he has yet to win on ground better than good. He is a real credit to his trainer, and will now be aimed at the Grand Annual at the Festival. (11/4)
1321 High Alltitude (IRE), off the track since his fall here in November, was racing from 5lb out of the handicap but, bustled along in the straight, stayed on well on the flat to finish a promising second. His turn is not far away. (7/1)
2783 Native Mission, conceding weight all-round, moved into second place approaching the second last, but he could never get in a serious blow at the winner, and was caught for second on the flat. (3/1)
2707 Thumbs Up is not the force of old. (13/2)
2700* Eastern Magic, winner of three of his four races this season, was 4lb out of the handicap and had not been asked a question in third place, when all but falling at the cross-fence, five out. (9/2)

3010 CHARLES HIGGINS MEMORIAL FOXHUNTERS' CUP HUNTERS' CHASE (5-Y.O+) (Class H)

3-00 (3-00) **2m 4f (16 fncs)** £1,604.00 (£444.00: £212.00) GOING: Not Established

				SP	RR	SF
	Slievenamon Mist (VictorDartnall) **11-12-2**(5) MrJJukes (hdwy 7th: chsd ldr fr 12th: led 4 out: r.o wl)	—	1	5/2[2]	122	48
	Principle Music (USA) (MrsPGrainger) **9-11-5**(7) MrAPhillips (a.p: led 11th to 4 out: unable qckn fr 2 out)	6	2	25/1	108	34
	Hobnobber (JHDocker) **10-11-5**(7) MrJDocker (no hdwy fr 4 out)	26	3	14/1	87	13
	Flowing River (USA) (NRMitchell) **11-11-5**(7) MrNRMitchell (hdwy 11th: hmpd 12th: sn wknd)	3½	4	33/1	85	11
	Tea Cee Kay (COKing) **7-11-7**(5) MrASansome (a bhd)	s.h	5	16/1	85	11
	Flame O'Frensi (KCumings) **11-11-9**(7) MissJCumings (led to 6th: wknd 11th)	26	6	12/1	68	—
	Orujo (IRE) (MissCGordon) **9-11-5**(7) MrPTYoung (bkwd: a.p: led 6th to 11th: wknd 12th)	4	7	33/1	61	—
	Charlies Delight (IRE) (MrsCHicks) **9-11-11**(7)ow1 MrRHicks (blnd 1st: prom to 5th: t.o)	dist	8	50/1	—	—
	Idiotic (PRChamings) **9-11-12**(5) MrCVigors (lw: fell 2nd)		F	2/1[1]	—	—
	Pro Bono (IRE) (PCCaudwell) **7-11-10**(7) MrADalton (lw: a.p: mstke 2nd: 3rd whn fell 12th)		F	12/1	—	—
	Birchall Boy (PLSouthcombe) **9-11-5**(7) MissWSouthcombe (lw: a bhd: t.o whn p.u bef 3 out)		P	33/1	—	—
1076[3]	**Ramstar** (MissPollyCurling) **9-12-5**(5) MissPCurling (hld up: shkn up 12th: sn wknd: t.o whn p.u bef last)		P	10/1[3]	—	—
				(SP 113.6%)		**12 Rn**

5m 19.7 (24.70) CSF £59.67 TOTE £2.90: £1.60 £7.50 £3.70 (£108.60) Trio £391.20; £165.32 to Newbury 8/2/97 OWNER Mr Nick Viney (BARNSTAPLE) BRED James Mulcahy
Slievenamon Mist, who wears a copper band because of an arthritic problem, is a useful pointer. He gained a slender advantage four out, and proved too strong for the runner-up from the penultimate fence. Liverpool is his target. (5/2)
Principle Music (USA) looked reasonably straight for his first run in a year, and was the only one to make a race of it with the winner. Leading at the sixth last, he was collared two fences later but only shaken off from the second last. (25/1)
Hobnobber, racing towards the back of the field, did manage to struggle into third, but the front two were already home and dry. (14/1: 10/1-16/1)
Flowing River (USA) made an effort turning out of the back straight, but he was done no favours by the faller at the cross-fence, and was soon in trouble. (33/1)
Flame O'Frensi (12/1: 8/1-14/1)
Pro Bono (IRE) (12/1: 8/1-14/1)
1076 Ramstar (10/1: op 6/1)

3011 MAYOR OF BOSTON H'CAP HURDLE (5-Y.O+) (Class B)

3-30 (3-30) **2m 5f (11 hdls)** £4,858.40 (£1,467.20: £713.60: £336.80) GOING: 0.76 sec per fur (S)

				SP	RR	SF
1586*	**Copper Boy (119)** (RHBuckler) **8-10-3** BPowell (lw: mde all: clr 5th: mstke 3 out: blnd 2 out: all out)	—	1	11/4[1]	94	43
1783[6]	**Kingdom of Shades (USA) (124)** (AndrewTurnell) **7-10-8** PCarberry (hld up: chsd wnr appr 3 out: rdn appr 2 out: unable qckn flat)	1	2	13/2[3]	98	47
1919*	**Karshi (142)** (MissHCKnight) **7-11-12** JFTitley (lw: chsd wnr tl appr 3 out: wknd appr 2 out)	17	3	7/2[2]	103	52
1793[6]	**Barna Boy (IRE) (132)** (NJHenderson) **9-11-2** RDunwoody (lw: rdn 8th: nvr nr to chal)	9	4	10/1	86	35
2635[5]	**Right Win (IRE) (144)** (RHannon) **7-12-0** NWilliamson (lw: rdn 5th: bhd fr 8th)	6	5	9/1	94	43
2777[2]	**Bolivar (IRE) (118)** (RAkehurst) **5-9-11**(5) SRyan (hld up: mstke 3rd: rdn 8th: sn wknd)	4	6	7/2[2]	65	14
2817[2]	**Moment of Glory (IRE) (116)** (DRGandolfo) **6-10-0v**[1] RHughes (mstke 8th: a bhd: t.o: lame)	dist	7	8/1	—	—
				(SP 114.6%)		**7 Rn**

5m 12.3 (18.30) CSF £18.92 TOTE £4.10: £2.00 £3.50 (£11.80) OWNER Mr C. Raymond (BRIDPORT) BRED C. H. Raymond
LONG HANDICAP Moment of Glory (IRE) 9-12
STEWARDS' ENQUIRY Titley susp. 17-22/2 & 24-27/2/97 (intentional interference).
1586* Copper Boy may be eight years old, but he is still pretty much unexposed as this was only his fifth-ever race. He put up an extremely gutsy performance for, after making a mistake at the first hurdle in the straight, he then made an even worse one at the second last and was beginning to look extremely tired. He dug deep to keep the runner-up at bay, and will come on for this run. Held in extremely high regard by his trainer, he has a choice of engagements at the Festival. (11/4)

1783 Kingdom of Shades (USA) moved into second place approaching the third last, and his rider must have been hopeful as the winner looked extremely leg-weary. Try as he might, he failed to get on terms with his tenacious rival. He goes well in the mud and should soon find a race. (13/2)
1919* Karshi raced in second place but, collared for that position early in the straight, he was soon in trouble. His pilot was later suspended for 10 days for intentional interference. (7/2)
1793 Barna Boy (IRE) was racing over a far more suitable trip, but he could only plod past tired rivals. (10/1)
1916 Right Win (IRE), a one-time high-class Flat performer, has gone totally the wrong way. (9/1)
2777 Bolivar (IRE) was disappointing over a trip that should have suited, and was a spent force turning into the straight. (7/2)

3012 FEBRUARY NOVICES' H'CAP HURDLE (0-115) (4-Y.O+) (Class D)

4-00 (4-00) **2m 110y (8 hdls)** £3,054.00 (£912.00: £436.00: £198.00) GOING: 0.76 sec per fur (S)

Form	Horse	Dist	Pos	SP	RR	SF
2771^{4}	**Rangitikei (NZ) (104)** (CJMann) **6-11-10** RDunwoody (led 3rd: comf)	—	**1**	$2/1^{1}$	91+	44
2909^{2}	**Neat Feat (IRE) (94)** (DRCElsworth) **6-11-0** PHolley (lw: hdwy 3 out: rdn appr 2 out: chsd wnr fr last: no imp)	.8	**2**	$5/1^{3}$	73	26
2692^{7}	**Bietschhorn Bard (90)** (DRGandolfo) **7-10-7b**$^{1(3)}$ DFortt (hdwy appr 3 out: chsd wnr 3 out to last: one pce)	.2½	**3**	11/2	67	20
1651^{9}	**I Recall (IRE) (80)** (PHayward) **6-10-0** BFenton (chsd ldr to 3rd: wknd 5th)	2½	**4**	33/1	54	7
2690^{11}	**Reverse Thrust (84)** (PRHedger) **6-9-11**$^{(7)}$ MClinton (hld up: rdn appr 2 out: wknd)	11	**5**	16/1	48	1
2690^{6}	**Henrys Port (98)** (MartynMeade) **7-11-4** NWilliamson (hld up: rdn appr 2 out: wkng whn blnd 2 out)	3	**6**	$4/1^{2}$	59	12
217^{2}	**Zahid (USA) (96)** (KRBurke) **6-11-2** RHughes (lw: hdwy 3 out: wknd appr 2 out)	18	**7**	10/1	39	—
2547^{17}	**Mazirah (83)** (RCurtis) **6-10-3** DMorris (bhd fr 5th)	16	**8**	10/1	11	—
	Lagham Lad (84) (DWPArbuthnot) **8-10-4** PCarberry (bkwd: led to 3rd: wknd 4th: t.o)	dist	**9**	16/1	—	—
				(SP 118.3%)	**9 Rn**	

4m 8.5 (18.50) CSF £12.09 CT £44.13 TOTE £2.20: £1.20 £1.90 £1.90 (£4.80) Trio £12.10 OWNER Mrs J. M. Mayo (UPPER LAMBOURN) BRED D. P. and Mrs S. G. Price
LONG HANDICAP I Recall (IRE) 9-2
2771 Rangitikei (NZ), fitted with a tongue-strap for the first time, put up a very polished display. In front halfway down the back straight, he always had the situation well in hand. He needs a stiff two miles, and his trainer says he will make a lovely chaser next term. (2/1)
2909 Neat Feat (IRE), making a quick reappearance, eventually struggled into second at the final flight but had no hope with the winner. (5/1)
2040 Bietschhorn Bard ran better in the first-time blinkers and moved into second three out. He failed to reel in the winner, and was collared for the runner-up berth at the last. (11/2)
I Recall (IRE), 12lb out of the handicap, was in trouble at the cross-hurdle, four out. (33/1)
2690 Henrys Port (4/1: op 5/2)

3013 LEVY BOARD H'CAP HURDLE (0-130) (4-Y.O+) (Class C)

4-30 (4-31) **3m 110y (12 hdls)** £3,727.00 (£1,126.00: £548.00: £259.00) GOING: 0.76 sec per fur (S)

Form	Horse	Dist	Pos	SP	RR	SF
2658^{P}	**Bankhead (IRE) (116)** (JLSpearing) **8-11-3**$^{(7)}$ MissCSpearing (a.p: led appr 9th: r.o wl)	—	**1**	33/1	99	61
2817^{4}	**Allow (IRE) (93)** (BLlewellyn) **6-9-10**$^{(5)}$ DJKavanagh (hdwy 5th: ev ch last: unable qckn)	3	**2**	$7/1^{2}$	74	36
2659^{2}	**Ealing Court (99)** (NMBabbage) **8-10-7** NWilliamson (hdwy 8th: ev ch 2 out: wknd appr last)	7	**3**	$4/1^{1}$	76	38
2708^{4}	**General Mouktar (105)** (MCPipe) **7-10-13** CFSwan (lw: stdy hdwy 3 out: wknd appr last)	4	**4**	9/1	79	41
2644^{2}	**Royal Piper (NZ) (108)** (AJWilson) **10-11-2** RGreene (hdwy fr 3 out: nvr nr to chal)	5	**5**	10/1	79	41
2761^{4}	**Fast Thoughts (101)** (DRGandolfo) **10-10-9b** RDunwoody (led tl appr 9th: wknd appr 3 out)	6	**6**	12/1	68	30
2761^{3}	**Derring Bridge (92)** (MrsSMJohnson) **7-10-0** BFenton (nvr nrr)	11	**7**	25/1	52	14
2644^{5}	**Kalasadi (USA) (103)** (VSoane) **6-10-11b** JFTitley (bhd fr 8th)	6	**8**	16/1	59	21
2625^{5}	**Sorbiere (95)** (NJHenderson) **10-10-3** JRKavanagh (lw: a bhd)	nk	**9**	33/1	50	12
2702^{3}	**The Toiseach (IRE) (112)** (JRFanshawe) **6-11-6** PHide (bhd fr 3 out)	2	**10**	$8/1^{3}$	66	28
1476^{5}	**Hunters Rock (IRE) (115)** (KCBailey) **8-11-2**$^{(7)}$ MrRWakley (prom to 3 out)	4	**11**	14/1	67	29
1429^{6}	**Better Bythe Glass (IRE) (97)** (NATwiston-Davies) **8-10-5** TJenks (prom to 9th)	12	**12**	12/1	41	3
2761^{2}	**Rimouski (97)** (BRCambidge) **9-10-5** GaryLyons (hdwy 5th: wknd 6th)	8	**13**	10/1	35	—
2117^{5}	**Uluru (IRE) (111)** (CPMorlock) **9-11-2**$^{(3)}$ DFortt (prom to 5th: t.o whn p.u bef 2 out)		**P**	20/1	—	—
1915^{8}	**Queen's Award (IRE) (92)** (RHBuckler) **8-10-0** BPowell (lw: hdwy 6th: wknd 7th: t.o whn p.u bef 3 out)		**P**	$8/1^{3}$	—	—
				(SP 125.3%)	**15 Rn**	

6m 8.1 (22.10) CSF £230.30 CT £1,050.17 TOTE £95.40: £13.70 £3.20 £2.20 (£678.20) Trio £606.00; £435.31 to Newbury 8/2/97 OWNER Mrs Liz Brazier (ALCESTER) BRED Ronald O'Neill
LONG HANDICAP Derring Bridge 9-7 Queen's Award (IRE) 9-12
1632* Bankhead (IRE) reverting to hurdles after being pulled up in his last two chases, looked harshly treated but caused a real surprise. Moving to the front approaching the cross-hurdle, he kept up the gallop and managed to hold the persistent runner-up at bay. (33/1)
2817 Allow (IRE) saw out this longer trip and threw down his challenge in the straight. On level terms with the winner jumping the final flight, he found that rival had a bit extra up his sleeve. (7/1)
2659 Ealing Court ran another sound race, and had every chance two out before tiring. There is a race waiting for him on soft ground. (4/1)
2708 General Mouktar found this trip just beyond him and, after steadily moving into the action in the straight, was a tired animal going to the last. (9/1)
2644 Royal Piper (NZ) is no easy horse to win with and needs exaggerated waiting tactics. As usual he was doing all his best work at the finish, but the principals were already home and dry. (10/1)
2761 Fast Thoughts dictated matters from the front but, collared approaching the fourth last, he was soon in trouble. (12/1)
1476 Hunters Rock (IRE) (14/1: op 8/1)
1384 Queen's Award (IRE) (8/1: op 5/1)

T/Plpt: £182.10 (67.32 Tckts). T/Qdpt: £40.10 (21.84 Tckts) AK

2838-TOWCESTER (R-H) (Chase Good to Soft, Hdles Soft)

Friday February 7th

WEATHER: fine

3014 WOODCOCK NOVICES' HURDLE (I) (4-Y.O+) (Class E)

1-10 (1-12) **2m (8 hdls)** £1,976.50 (£554.00: £269.50) GOING: 0.63 sec per fur (S)

Form	Horse	Dist	Pos	SP	RR	SF
2673*	**Spendid (IRE)** (DNicholson) **5-11-9** AMaguire (lw: chsd clr ldrs: wnt prom 4th: hit 3 out: led last: rdn out)	—	**1**	$5/4^{1}$	80	45

Form	Horse	Dist	Pos	SP	RR	SF
2642[4]	**Ready Money Creek (IRE) (110)** (OSherwood) **6-11-9** JOsborne (chsd ldr tl led appr 3 out: hdd last: unable qckn nr fin)	hd	**2**	13/8[2]	80	45
1260[6]	**Logical Step (IRE) (100)** (DRGandolfo) **7-11-3** DLeahy (hdwy 5th: rdn appr 2 out: one pce)	11	**3**	14/1	63	28
1208[2]	**Shared Risk** (JNorton) **5-11-0**(3) ECallaghan (hdwy 4th: one pce fr 3 out)	hd	**4**	16/1	63	28
2690[9]	**Harlequin Chorus (95)** (JABOld) **7-11-3** GUpton (bhd fr 5th)	10	**5**	12/1	53	18
	Fire on Ice (IRE) (MrsDHaine) **5-11-3** TJMurphy (hld up: hdwy 5th: wkng whn mstke 2 out)	3	**6**	14/1	50	15
2546[12]	**Hills Gamble** (PJBevan) **7-11-3** WWorthington (led tl appr 3 out: wknd appr next)	½	**7**	50/1	49	14
2677[18]	**Calm Down (IRE)** (TCasey) **6-11-3** RJohnson (hdwy 4th: wknd appr 3 out)	dist	**8**	33/1	—	—
	Gentleman James (IRE) (MrsMerritaJones) **7-11-3** DerekByrne (bit bkwd: sn wl bhd: t.o whn p.u bef 5th)		**P**	25/1	—	—
2697[3]	**Khalikhoum (IRE)** (SirJohnBarlowBt) **4-10-7** CMaude (lw: hdwy 4th: rdn 3 out: sn wknd: p.u bef last)		**P**	10/1[3]	—	—
	Red River (IRE) (CJDrewe) **6-10-7**(5) MrRThornton (t.o fr 3rd: p.u bef 2 out)		**P**	50/1	—	—
				(SP 129.2%)	**11 Rn**	

4m 1.4 (15.40) CSF £3.58 TOTE £2.30: £1.50 £1.10 £2.30 (£1.70) Trio £5.40 OWNER Mrs Stewart Catherwood (TEMPLE GUITING) BRED Liam Ormsby

WEIGHT FOR AGE 4yo-10lb

2673* Spendid (IRE) quickened clear with the runner-up on the long haul into the straight, but had to pull out all the stops to prevail. Not over-big, the penalty in this ground almost found him out. (5/4)

2642 Ready Money Creek (IRE), on this stiff track and with plenty of cut in the ground, bounced back from his Kempton flop despite the return to two miles. An attractive, good-moving sort, his future probably lies over further and fences. (13/8: 6/4-9/4)

1260 Logical Step (IRE), much fitter this time, shaped with promise and ought to find a race. (14/1)

1208 Shared Risk was hard at work and finding little extra in the final half-mile. Handling such conditions gives hope that he may get further. (16/1)

Harlequin Chorus dropped off the main bunch at halfway, but did stay on past beaten horses late in the day. He looks to need further. (12/1)

Fire on Ice (IRE), highly-tried on the level, was not knocked about on his hurdles debut and is worth keeping an eye on. (14/1: op 8/1)

3015 PARTRIDGE NOVICES' CHASE (5-Y.O+) (Class E)

1-40 (1-40) **2m 110y (12 fncs)** £2,875.75 (£871.00: £425.50: £202.75) GOING: 0.63 sec per fur (S)

Form	Horse	Dist	Pos	SP	RR	SF
2691*	**Lightening Lad** (JSKing) **9-11-8** CMaude (j.w: mde virtually all: drvn out flat)	—	**1**	11/8[1]	112	39
2091*	**Super Coin (120)** (RLee) **9-11-8** RJohnson (a.p: rdn appr 2 out: kpt on wl flat)	1¼	**2**	5/2[2]	111	38
1542[2]	**Dominos Ring (IRE)** (MrsHLWalton) **8-11-2** MrAWalton (hld up: blnd 4th: hdwy 6th: r.o fr 2 out)	2	**3**	14/1[3]	103	30
2807*	**Dream Ride (IRE) (115)** (DNicholson) **7-11-8** AMaguire (prom: hit 7th: 3rd & btn whn mstke 2 out)	3	**4**	5/2[2]	106	33
2007[P]	**Bucket of Gold** (OBrennan) **7-11-2** MBrennan (in tch tl mstke 6th: rallied & ev ch appr 3 out: sn wknd)	14	**5**	20/1	86	13
1920[P]	**Old Redwood (60)** (MrsLWilliamson) **10-11-2** LO'Hara (prom: hit 6th: ev ch appr 3 out: sn rdn & wknd)	2	**6**	50/1	79 t	11
2867[U]	**Hawker Hunter (USA) (110)** (CREgerton) **6-11-2b** JRailton (swtg: j.b: prom to 8th)	3	**7**	25/1	77 t	9
2672[P]	**Sakbah (USA) (64)** (JAPickering) **8-10-11** WMarston (mstke 4th: bhd whn mstke 3 out)	dist	**8**	50/1	—	—
1994[5]	**Dodgy Dealer (IRE)** (MrsSusanNock) **7-11-2** DerekByrne (bit bkwd: bhd whn p.u bef 5th)		**P**	40/1	—	—
2701[12]	**Kentucky Gold (IRE)** (MrsLWilliamson) **8-11-2** ASSmith (t.o fr 6th: p.u bef 3 out)		**P**	50/1	—	—
				(SP 122.8%)	**10 Rn**	

4m 19.3 (17.30) CSF £4.91 TOTE £2.50: £1.10 £1.60 £1.70 (£4.60) Trio £16.60 OWNER Mr Richard Peterson (SWINDON) BRED John Brookman

OFFICIAL EXPLANATION **Dodgy Dealer (IRE): finished lame.**

2691* Lightening Lad jumped like an old hand, and stayed on stoutly to move into the Arkle picture, the runner-up having finished third in that race last year. (11/8)

2091* Super Coin seemed well-suited by the stiff uphill finish which helped offset his lack of finishing speed, and ran his best race of the season. Given the chance, he could develop a liking for this place. (5/2)

1542 Dominos Ring (IRE), given time to recover after an early mistake, stayed on well once in line for home. This was a promising start over bigger obstacles. (14/1)

2807* Dream Ride (IRE) was not quite up to this class, but there will be plenty of easier chases between now and the end of the season. (5/2: op 5/4)

Bucket of Gold, dropped back in trip, rather ran in snatches, fading after briefly looking dangerous at the bottom of the hill. (20/1)

Old Redwood at least completed. (50/1)

3016 TEAL H'CAP HURDLE (0-115) (4-Y.O+) (Class E)

2-10 (2-10) **3m (12 hdls)** £2,410.50 (£678.00: £331.50) GOING: 0.63 sec per fur (S)

Form	Horse	Dist	Pos	SP	RR	SF
2659[3]	**Grunge (IRE) (94)** (DJGMurraySmith) **9-10-7** AMaguire (lw: hld up: hdwy appr 7th: led 3 out: rdn out)	—	**1**	5/1[2]	74	—
2659[4]	**Ehtefaal (USA) (92)** (JSKing) **6-10-5** TJMurphy (lw: in tch: hdwy appr 7th: rdn 9th: kpt on wl flat)	1½	**2**	11/2[3]	71	—
2507[2]	**Snow Board (92)** (MrsMerritaJones) **8-10-5** DerekByrne (hld up: hdwy whn mstke 3 out: styd on flat)	2	**3**	9/4[1]	70	—
2570[P]	**Mister Blake (90)** (RLee) **7-10-3** RJohnson (hdwy 4th: rdn appr 3 out: no imp)	15	**4**	16/1	58	—
2838[2]	**Whitebonnet (IRE) (87)** (CREgerton) **7-9-9b**(5) SophieMitchell (prom: led 8th to 3 out: sn wknd)	9	**5**	9/1	49	—
2659[P]	**Mountain Reach (92)** (PRWebber) **7-10-5** JOsborne (prom to 3 out)	14	**6**	14/1	44	—
2659[10]	**St Ville (91)** (RHBuckler) **11-10-4** PHolley (led 2nd to 6th: rdn 8th: sn wknd)	s.h	**7**	14/1	43	—
	Cunninghams Ford (IRE) (112) (AHHarvey) **9-11-11** ASSmith (bkwd: chsd ldrs to 5th: sn bhd: t.o whn p.u bef 8th)		**P**	33/1	—	—
2550[6]	**Mendip Prince (IRE) (93)** (PJHobbs) **7-10-6** CO'Dwyer (plld hrd: w ldrs: j.lft 6th: wknd next: t.o whn p.u bef 3 out)		**P**	13/2	—	—
2681[P]	**Chief Rager (104)** (NATwiston-Davies) **8-11-3** TJenks (led to 2nd: led 6th to 8th: wknd 3 out: p.u bef next)		**P**	14/1	—	—
2658[U]	**Huge Mistake (96)** (NATwiston-Davies) **8-10-9** CMaude (sn rdn along: bhd fr 5th: t.o whn p.u bef 3 out)		**P**	10/1	—	—
2864[F]	**Johnny's Turn (109)** (JNorton) **12-11-8** MrNKent (bhd fr 8th: t.o whn p.u bef 2 out)		**P**	33/1	—	—
				(SP 127.0%)	**12 Rn**	

6m 16.8 (36.80) CSF £32.56 CT £74.04 TOTE £6.00: £2.50 £2.00 £1.30 (£15.60) Trio £9.90 OWNER Mrs R. D. Cowell (LAMBOURN) BRED P. P. Dunphy

LONG HANDICAP Whitebonnet (IRE) 9-9

2659 Grunge (IRE), worse off with both second and third for being well behind them here earlier in the season, took this by the scruff of the neck three out and would not be caught. (5/1)

2659 Ehtefaal (USA), ridden along from some way out, chased the winner for all he was worth, but to no avail. (11/2)

2507 Snow Board was tracking the winner when he clouted the third last with his hind legs. He lost a couple of lengths and would otherwise have gone close. (9/4)

1906 Mister Blake left his last two runs behind, but was easily dropped on the run to two out. (16/1)
2838 Whitebonnet (IRE) likes it here but, once the winner jumped past him three out, was quickly in trouble. (9/1)
Mountain Reach ran well for a long way after a considerable absence. (14/1)
2063 Chief Rager (14/1: op 8/1)
Huge Mistake (10/1: 8/1-12/1)

3017 SPORTING LIFE CHAMPION TRIAL HURDLE (5-Y.O+) (Class B)

2-40 (2-40) **2m (8 hdls)** £4,872.00 (£1,367.00: £666.00) GOING: 0.63 sec per fur (S)

				SP	RR	SF
	Collier Bay (175) (JABOld) **7-11-8** JOsborne (bit bkwd: w ldr: led 4th to 5th: led appr 2 out: sn hdd: led flat: rdn out)	—	**1**	8/11^{1}	141+	67
	Relkeel (160) (DNicholson) **8-11-0** AMaguire (bkwd: hld up: hdwy 3 out: led next: hdd & unable qckn flat)	¾	**2**	11/8^{2}	132+	58
2740a^{5}	**Escartefigue (FR) (148)** (DNicholson) **5-11-0** DBridgwater (led: j.slowly 3rd: hdd next: led 5th tl appr 2 out: sn btn)	15	**3**	11/2^{3}	117	43
				(SP 115.4%)		**3 Rn**

3m 56.6 (10.60) CSF £2.15 TOTE £1.50 (£1.30) OWNER Mr W. E. Sturt (WROUGHTON) BRED Stanley Estate and Stud Co
Collier Bay had been marking time waiting for some cut, but will still come on plenty for this. Made to work hard by the runner-up, he stayed on to great purpose on the flat, but his action suggests that now even good ground could prove too fast for him at the Festival. (8/11: 1/2-4/5)
Relkeel looked the least fit of the three, and the decent pace might have been expected to find him out earlier than it did. Fresh and keen on the way to post, he cruised through to lead two out but, shaken up, he blew up going to the last and had a rather easier race than the winner. If he gets his ground, he would make them all go in the Champion. (11/8)
2740a Escartefigue (FR) is useful in his own right and looked the fittest of the three, but was brushed aside by two very good horses once the taps were turned on. (11/2)

3018 DUCK H'CAP CHASE (0-135) (5-Y.O+) (Class C)

3-10 (3-10) **3m 1f (18 fncs)** £4,401.25 (£1,330.00: £647.50: £306.25) GOING: 0.63 sec per fur (S)

				SP	RR	SF
2681*	**Brave Buccaneer (110)** (AndrewTurnell) **10-10-3** DBridgwater (hld up: mstke 10th: hdwy 13th: led after 3 out: clr 2 out: rdn out)	—	**1**	9/4^{2}	118	41
	Camelot Knight (117) (NATwiston-Davies) **11-10-10** CMaude (bit bkwd: prom: hit 11th: outpcd 3 out: hrd rdn & rallied appr last: r.o flat)	1½	**2**	16/1	124	47
2762*	**Mely Moss (FR) (135)** (CREgerton) **6-12-0** JOsborne (lw: hld up: stdy hdwy 10th: led 3 out: sn hdd & rdn: one pce)	1¾	**3**	6/4^{1}	141	64
2754^{5}	**Beaurepaire (IRE) (107)** (RHAlner) **9-10-0** RJohnson (lw: prom: outpcd 3 out: styd on fr 2 out)	2	**4**	14/1	112	35
2758^{6}	**Ballyea Boy (IRE) (113)** (DNicholson) **7-10-6** AMaguire (prom: rdn 12th: lft in ld 4 out: hdd 3 out: sn btn)	2	**5**	4/1^{3}	116	39
2575^{P}	**Woodlands Boy (IRE) (108)** (RCurtis) **9-9-12**$^{(3)ow1}$ PHenley (lw: hld up & bhd: styd on fr 3 out: n.d)	s.h	**6**	12/1	111	33
1985^{P}	**Dolikos (107)** (THCaldwell) **10-10-0** TJMurphy (bit bkwd: hld up: hdwy 4 out: wknd 3 out: t.o)	dist	**7**	40/1	—	—
	Invasion (107) (OBrennan) **13-10-0b** MBrennan (nvr gng wl: sn t.o: p.u bef 2 out)		**P**	14/1	—	—
1937^{7}	**Lucky Lane (110)** (SEarle) **13-10-3b** ILawrence (prom: mstke & rdn 6th: bhd fr 11th: t.o whn p.u bef 4 out)		**P**	33/1	—	—
2550^{13}	**So Far Bold (IRE) (110)** (IPWilliams) **7-10-3b** CO'Dwyer (led tl j.slowly 4 out: sn wknd: t.o whn p.u bef 2 out)		**P**	16/1	—	—
				(SP 128.9%)		**10 Rn**

6m 34.3 (19.30) CSF £37.56 CT £68.48 TOTE £2.80: £1.20 £6.30 £1.60 (£25.90) Trio £36.80 OWNER Mr R. C. Watts (WANTAGE) BRED Gerard McMahon
LONG HANDICAP Woodlands Boy (IRE) 9-9 Invasion 9-10 Beaurepaire (IRE) 9-13 Dolikos 9-4
2681* Brave Buccaneer, raised 5lb, was well-supported and had to be kept up to his work after apparently having it sewn up two out. (9/4)
Camelot Knight, dropped 7lb, found his second wind under strong pressure. This will have blown away a few cobwebs. (16/1)
2762* Mely Moss (FR), upped 9lb, did not seem bothered by this stiffer test of stamina, and stayed on after seemingly held at the second last. (6/4)
2754 Beaurepaire (IRE) was much more like his old self here, and kept on up the hill. (14/1)
2758 Ballyea Boy (IRE), again 7lb higher than on the second of his wins, ran better here. (4/1)

3019 WOODCOCK NOVICES' HURDLE (II) (4-Y.O+) (Class E)

3-40 (3-40) **2m (8 hdls)** £1,976.50 (£554.00: £269.50) GOING: 0.63 sec per fur (S)

				SP	RR	SF
	My Cheeky Man (DNicholson) **6-11-3** RJohnson (hld up: hdwy 5th: led 2 out: drvn out)	—	**1**	12/1	78	19
1938*	**The Proms (IRE)** (NATwiston-Davies) **6-11-9** CLlewellyn (lw: led tl after 2nd: hrd rdn & ev ch 2 out: one pce)	4	**2**	11/8^{1}	80	21
	Tonka (DRGandolfo) **5-11-3** DLeahy (plld hrd: mstkes 1st and 2nd: sn led: clr 3rd: hdd 2 out: btn whn mstke & sltly hmpd last)	5	**3**	14/1	69	10
2680^{U}	**Cool Gunner (86)** (JSKing) **7-11-9** CMaude (swtg: hld up: hdwy 4th: one pce fr 3 out)	3	**4**	9/2^{2}	72	13
2010^{7}	**Captain Walter (IRE)** (JABOld) **7-11-3** JOsborne (hld up: hdwy 3 out: wkng whn hit last)	8	**5**	6/1	58	—
2759^{7}	**Blazing Storm (IRE)** (CREgerton) **5-10-12**$^{(5)}$ MrRThornton (nvr trbld ldrs)	3	**6**	11/2^{3}	55	—
2794^{5}	**Worthy Memories** (MrsMerritaJones) **8-10-12** DerekByrne (nvr nr ldrs)	4	**7**	25/1	46	—
2812^{10}	**Welsh Silk** (DRGandolfo) **5-10-12**$^{(5)}$ SophieMitchell (a bhd)	3	**8**	10/1	48	—
	Music Class (IRE) (CPEBrooks) **6-11-3** AMaguire (bit bkwd: hdwy appr 4th: wknd after 3 out)	6	**9**	12/1	42	—
	Orchard King (OBrennan) **7-11-3** MBrennan (prom tl wknd after 3 out: t.o)	13	**10**	14/1	29	—
	Tudor Falcon (PBradley) **4-10-7** TJMurphy (prom tl mstke 3 out: t.o)	15	**11**	25/1	14	—
2861^{7}	**Ferrers (88)** (MrsPSly) **6-11-3** WMarston (hld up: hdwy 3 out: sn hrd rdn: 2nd & btn whn fell last)		**F**	14/1	69?	—
2677^{12}	**Benji** (TCasey) **6-11-3** CO'Dwyer (prom tl wknd 3 out: t.o whn p.u bef last)		**P**	25/1	—	—
	A Badge Too Far (IRE) (MrsLWilliamson) **7-10-12** LO'Hara (bkwd: mstke 2nd: sn bhd: t.o whn p.u bef 3 out)		**P**	33/1	—	—
				(SP 148.9%)		**14 Rn**

4m 6.1 (20.10) CSF £32.28 TOTE £25.90: £4.10 £1.30 £4.00 (£15.20) Trio £132.70 OWNER Mrs A. A. Shutes (TEMPLE GUITING) BRED Mrs Diana Shutes
WEIGHT FOR AGE 4yo-10lb
My Cheeky Man had shown signs of promise on one run over hurdles a year ago, having run well in a couple of bumpers. (12/1)
1938* The Proms (IRE), dropping back in trip, is probably going to need a course as stiff as this over two miles. (11/8)
Tonka jumped better as the race progressed and, despite running much too freely, still looked capable of winning two out. Three times a winner on the Flat, he should not take long to get off the mark. (14/1)
2680 Cool Gunner had much more to do this time, and would have been receiving 23lb from the runner-up had this been a handicap. (9/2)

Captain Walter (IRE) was feeling the strain at the second last. (6/1)
2759 Blazing Storm (IRE), the drop back in distance would probably not have been in his favour. (11/2: 6/1-4/1)
1801 Welsh Silk (10/1: 8/1-12/1)
Music Class (IRE) (12/1: 6/1-14/1)

3020 PHEASANT NOVICES' CHASE (5-Y.O+) (Class E)
4-10 (4-10) **3m 1f (18 fncs)** £3,044.75 (£923.00: £451.50: £215.75) GOING: 0.63 sec per fur (S)

				SP	RR	SF
1258[9]	**Jet Rules (IRE)** (MrsJPitman) **7-11-4** RFarrant (a.p: hit 4 out: styd on to ld nr fin)	—	**1**	3/1[2]	115	45
2841[4]	**Robsand (IRE) (79)** (GBBalding) **8-11-4** BClifford (led after 5th tl hdd nr fin)	¾	**2**	20/1	115	45
2551[U]	**Wisley Wonder (IRE) (115)** (NATwiston-Davies) **7-11-4b** CLlewellyn (hld up: hdwy 14th: ev ch appr 2 out: wknd flat)	13	**3**	7/2[3]	106	36
2672*	**Kamikaze** (KCBailey) **7-11-10b** CO'Dwyer (blnd bdly 1st: wl bhd tl hdwy 9th: mstke 12th: 4th & btn whn blnd last)	7	**4**	6/4[1]	108+	38
2841[3]	**Ardent Love (IRE) (76)** (DNicholson) **8-10-13** AMaguire (lw: hit 6th: hdwy 4 out: wknd after 3 out)	5	**5**	10/1	94	24
2841[10]	**Fortytwo Dee (IRE)** (NASmith) **7-10-13** TJMurphy (bhd fr 3 out)	¾	**6**	50/1	93	23
1326[F]	**Cool Runner (99)** (MrsSusanNock) **7-11-4** DerekByrne (bhd whn mstke 14th)	1¼	**7**	20/1	97	27
2795[U]	**Ring Corbitts (84)** (MJRoberts) **9-11-1**(3) PHenley (prom: rdn 12th: sn wknd)	10	**8**	25/1	91	21
1195[2]	**Mystic Isle (IRE)** (NAGaselee) **7-11-4** WMarston (mstkes: prom: rdn 12th: wknd appr 3 out)	10	**9**	11/1	84	14
2883[P]	**Major Nova (86)** (NASmith) **8-11-4** JRyan (lw: bhd whn bdly hmpd 8th: sn t.o)	26	**10**	40/1	68	—
	Prince Canute (MrsRGHenderson) **7-10-13**(5) DSalter (bkwd: j.b: bhd whn j.rt & blnd 8th: t.o whn p.u bef 10th)		**P**	33/1	—	—
2809[3]	**Musical Hit** (PAPritchard) **6-11-4** RBellamy (lw: t.o whn p.u bef 3 out)		**P**	40/1	—	—
2704[3]	**Glendine (IRE)** (CJMann) **7-11-4b**[1] JRailton (chsd ldrs: blnd & rdn 9th: sn wknd: t.o whn p.u bef 13th)		**P**	33/1	—	—
2816[7]	**Royal Hand (67)** (RJArmson) **7-11-4** MrRArmson (blnd 11th: sn bhd: t.o whn blnd bdly 3 out: p.u bef 2 out)		**P**	50/1	—	—
2839[3]	**Red Parade (NZ) (97)** (NJHawke) **9-11-4** CMaude (lw: led tl after 5th: hit 13th: 5th & wkng whn blnd & uns rdr 2 out)		**U**	16/1	—	—
				(SP 138.6%)	**15 Rn**	

6m 38.1 (23.10) CSF £62.85 TOTE £3.70: £2.50 £4.40 £1.60 (£102.10) Trio £114.00 OWNER The Jet Stationery Company Ltd (UPPER LAMBOURN) BRED Gus Bourke

Jet Rules (IRE) made a successful debut over fences, and showed just how well he stays in the closing stages. (3/1: op 6/4)
2841 Robsand (IRE) made sure this would be a real test of stamina and hardly deserved to be caught at the death. (20/1)
2551 Wisley Wonder (IRE) adopted different tactics, and still ran out of gas after the final fence, but his jumping was much improved. (7/2)
2672* Kamikaze nearly fell at the first and this outing is probably best forgotten. (6/4)
2841 Ardent Love (IRE) was rather disappointing. (10/1)
1195 Mystic Isle (IRE) (11/1: 8/1-12/1)

3021 SNIPE STANDARD OPEN N.H. FLAT RACE (4, 5 & 6-Y.O) (Class H)
4-40 (4-41) **2m** £1,276.50 (£354.00: £169.50)

				SP	RR	SF
1801[3]	**Endeavour (FR)** (MJRoberts) **5-11-4** JRailton (a.p: rdn to ld 3f out: r.o wl)	—	**1**	9/1	66 f	—
2696*	**King Mole** (JABOld) **6-11-11** GUpton (hld up: hdwy after 6f: ev ch 3f out: rdn over 1f out: nt qckn ins fnl f)	1¼	**2**	4/6[1]	72 f	—
	Sir Prize (IRE) (GBBalding) **4-10-8** BClifford (cmpt: a.p: rdn over 2f out: styd on ins fnl f)	½	**3**	7/1[3]	64 f	—
	Prussian Steel (IRE) (MBradstock) **6-11-4** CO'Dwyer (unf: bit bkwd: hdwy 8f out: rdn 3f out: r.o one pce fnl 2f)	1	**4**	16/1	63 f	—
2811[3]	**Coble Lane** (IPWilliams) **5-11-4** JOsborne (plld hrd: hdwy after 5f: led 6f out to 3f out: eased whn btn fnl f)	21	**5**	8/1	42 f	—
2633[2]	**Billy Buckskin** (JNorton) **5-10-13**(5) MrRThornton (prom: led 9f out to 6f out: wknd over 2f out)	3	**6**	11/2[2]	39 f	—
	Regency Leisure (RJEckley) **5-11-4** VSlattery (w ldrs tl wknd over 4f out)	5	**7**	20/1	34 f	—
2844[10]	**Ludo's Orchestra (IRE)** (MarkCampion) **6-11-4** DBridgwater (led 7f: wknd over 3f out)	2	**8**	16/1	32 f	—
	Wilma's Choice (DPGeraghty) **6-10-13** JSupple (tall: bhd fnl 7f)	11	**9**	25/1	16 f	—
	Denstar (IRE) (JWhite) **4-10-8** TJMurphy (neat: a bhd)	9	**10**	12/1	12 f	—
	Caractacus Potts (TWDonnelly) **5-11-4** AMaguire (cmpt: bit bkwd: a bhd)	½	**11**	12/1	12 f	—
2750[16]	**Seven Four Seven** (MrsLWilliamson) **6-10-13** LO'Hara (bit bkwd: bhd fnl 5f: t.o)	22	**12**	25/1	—	—
	Coolest By Phar (IRE) (MSheppard) **5-11-4** RJohnson (unf: lw: prom 10f: bhd whn swvd lft & uns rdr ins fnl f)		**U**	14/1	—	—
				(SP 155.3%)	**13 Rn**	

4m 8.3 CSF £17.84 TOTE £13.80: £2.40 £1.40 £2.60 (£10.10) Trio £32.40 OWNER Mr Mike Roberts (HAILSHAM) BRED Patrice Vagne
WEIGHT FOR AGE 4yo-10lb

1801 Endeavour (FR) is clearly going the right way. (9/1)
2696* King Mole had a good duel with the winner under his penalty. (4/6)
Sir Prize (IRE) fought back well after appearing held, and would appear to have a bright future. (7/1: 4/1-8/1)
Prussian Steel (IRE) kept plugging away up the hill and did not appear short of stamina. (16/1)
2811 Coble Lane ran much better than the margin of his defeat suggests. (8/1)
2633 Billy Buckskin (11/2: 7/2-6/1)
Denstar (IRE) (12/1: 7/1-16/1)
Caractacus Potts (12/1: 6/1-14/1)

T/Plpt: £5.00 (1444.59 Tckts). T/Qdpt: £4.80 (91.22 Tckts) Dk/ KH

2785-AYR (L-H) (Soft)
Saturday February 8th
WEATHER: unsettled

3022 GALLOWAY GAZETTE HURDLE (4-Y.O) (Class E)
1-00 (1-01) **2m (9 hdls)** £2,290.00 (£640.00: £310.00) GOING: 0.99 sec per fur (S)

				SP	RR	SF
2615[8]	**Cry Baby** (ACWhillans) **4-10-7**(5) STaylor (trckd ldrs: led appr last: styd on)	—	**1**	7/1	68	17
	Clash of Swords (PCalver) **4-10-12** TReed (j.lft: trckd ldrs: effrt 3 out: j.b lft last: styd on towards fin)	2½	**2**	6/1[3]	66	15
906[3]	**Phantom Haze** (CParker) **4-10-12** DParker (lw: mde most tl hdd appr last: no ex)	¾	**3**	7/4[2]	65	14

				SP	RR	SF
2784[4]	**Parrot's Hill (IRE)** (MHTompkins) **4-10-12** BStorey (chsd ldr fr 4th: slt ld 3 out: hdd next: one pce appr last)	½	**4**	6/4[1]	64	13
	Known Secret (USA) (PMonteith) **4-10-12** ADobbin (bit bkwd: mstkes: t.o fr 5th)	dist	**5**	20/1	—	—
				(SP 107.9%)		**5 Rn**

4m 1.8 (24.80) CSF £37.28 TOTE £11.10: £2.80 £3.60 (£27.20) OWNER Mr Allan Gilchrist (HAWICK) BRED Mrs M. Tinkler

Cry Baby had shown little previously but obviously appreciated these testing conditions and, as the others threw it away, he seized the opportunity. (7/1)

Clash of Swords looked likely to trot up turning for home, but then threw away all chance by jumping badly left. (6/1)

906 Phantom Haze, having is first run for his new stable and racing on testing ground for the first time, failed to see it out. (7/4)

2784 Parrot's Hill (IRE) had his chance, but it all proved too much in the testing conditions when the pressure was seriously on going to the last. (6/4)

Known Secret (USA) needed this quite badly. (20/1)

3023 EVENING TIMES NOVICES' CHASE (6-Y.O+) (Class D)

1-30 (1-30) **2m 4f (17 fncs)** £3,808.00 (£1,144.00: £552.00: £256.00) GOING: 0.99 sec per fur (S)

				SP	RR	SF
2653*	**Sparky Gayle (IRE)** (CParker) **7-11-8** BStorey (lw: j.w: a.p: led 4 out: easily)	—	**1**	2/5[1]	123+	36
2789[2]	**Lansborough** (GRichards) **7-10-12** ADobbin (lw: a chsng ldrs: mstke 11th: wnt 2nd 2 out: no ch w wnr)	11	**2**	3/1[2]	104	17
2767[P]	**Coqui Lane** (JMDun) **10-10-12** TReed (led: mstke 8th: hdd 4 out: btn whn hit next)	8	**3**	14/1[3]	98	11
1653[5]	**Le Denstan (84)** (MrsDThomson) **10-11-3** DParker (hld up: lost tch ½-wy: n.d after)	dist	**4**	25/1	—	—
2914[P]	**Monaughty Man (62)** (EMCaine) **11-10-12** MMoloney (a outpcd & bhd)	1¾	**5**	100/1	—	—
2788[P]	**Valley Garden (97)** (JJO'Neill) **7-10-12b** GCahill (mstkes: t.o whn p.u bef 11th)		**P**	33/1	—	—
				(SP 110.9%)		**6 Rn**

5m 24.2 (29.20) CSF £1.83 TOTE £1.40: £1.20 £1.40 (£1.50) OWNER Mr & Mrs Raymond Anderson Green (LOCKERBIE) BRED Thomas Walsh

2653* Sparky Gayle (IRE) got the conditions he revels in here and, jumping like an old hand, won most impressively. (2/5)

2789 Lansborough struggling some way out, his limitations were well exposed. (3/1)

2767 Coqui Lane improved on his educational at the last meeting, and is obviously going the right way. (14/1)

1653 Le Denstan, having his first run for over two and a half months, never took any interest and this was obviously well-needed. (25/1)

3024 D. M. HALL 'N.H.' NOVICES' HURDLE (5-Y.O+) (Class E)

2-00 (2-01) **2m 4f (11 hdls)** £2,696.00 (£756.00: £368.00) GOING: 0.99 sec per fur (S)

				SP	RR	SF
1999[2]	**Lagen Bridge (IRE) (98)** (DMoffatt) **8-11-4** DJMoffatt (trckd ldrs: led 4 out: clr whn mstke last: pushed out)	—	**1**	7/2[2]	79	39
2047[4]	**Sir Bob (IRE)** (WMcKeown) **5-10-12** GCahill (lw: chsd ldrs: pushed along fr 6th: styd on wl fr 3 out: nrst fin)	1½	**2**	9/2[3]	72	32
2047[6]	**Derannie (IRE)** (GRichards) **5-10-12** ADobbin (in tch: hit 6th: hdwy 4 out: one pce appr last)	7	**3**	7/2[2]	66	26
1938[4]	**Cuthill Hope (IRE)** (MHTompkins) **6-10-12** BStorey (hld up: hdwy ½-wy: wnt 2nd 4 out: rdn & btn next)	5	**4**	2/1[1]	62	22
2640[4]	**Monsieur Darcy (IRE)** (JRAdam) **6-10-12** MrCStorey (in tch tl outpcd 7th: n.d after)	14	**5**	40/1	51	11
2785[9]	**Storm Call** (DWWhillans) **6-10-7** DBentley (in tch tl wknd fr 4 out)	4	**6**	25/1	43	3
2913[10]	**Meadowleck (65)** (WGYoung) **8-10-2**(5) STaylor (led tl hdd & wknd qckly 4 out)	19	**7**	100/1	28	—
2918[8]	**Triona's Hope (IRE) (52)** (EMCaine) **8-10-5**(7) TristanDavidson (a bhd: t.o)	dist	**8**	500/1	—	—
2785[11]	**Sharp Sand** (PMonteith) **7-10-12** MMoloney (chsd ldrs tl rdn & wknd 7th: p.u bef 3 out)		**P**	40/1	—	—
	Thromedownsometing (MrsDThomson) **7-10-10**ow3 TReed (sn t.o: p.u bef 6th)		**P**	50/1	—	—
	Ashgrove Dancer (IRE) (LLungo) **7-10-5**(7) IJardine (bit bkwd: prom to 5th: wknd qckly next: p.u bef 3 out)		**P**	100/1	—	—
	Cream O The Border (ACWhillans) **5-10-7** FPerratt (bit bkwd: prom tl wknd rapidly appr 6th: p.u bef 3 out)		**P**	100/1	—	—
				(SP 109.8%)		**12 Rn**

5m 7.9 (26.90) CSF £16.00 TOTE £3.70: £1.40 £1.50 £2.20 (£6.30) Trio £9.70 OWNER Mrs Eileen Milligan (CARTMEL) BRED James Flahavan

1999 Lagen Bridge (IRE) did not hang as badly this time, and always looked the winner, but a couple of sloppy jumps when in command did not help. (7/2)

2047 Sir Bob (IRE), having his first run over hurdles, just needs to sort out his jumping and this real stayer will improve a fair bit. (9/2)

2047 Derannie (IRE), patiently ridden on this hurdles debut, got into it in the straight, only to run out of petrol in these testing conditions. (7/2)

1938 Cuthill Hope (IRE) was dropped out and given every chance to get the trip, but just when he got into contention turning for home, he ran into the marathon runners' wall. (2/1: 6/4-9/4)

2640 Monsieur Darcy (IRE) showed promise in bumpers but was a shade disappointing here, being left behind in the final mile. (40/1)

2041 Storm Call was stepped up in trip, but it failed to bring any improvement. (25/1)

3025 STRACHAN KERR H'CAP CHASE (0-140) (5-Y.O+) (Class B)

2-30 (2-31) **3m 1f (19 fncs)** £6,490.00 (£1,945.00: £935.00: £430.00) GOING: 0.99 sec per fur (S)

				SP	RR	SF
2765[2]	**Whispering Steel (128)** (GRichards) **11-11-2** BStorey (lw: a gng wl: led fr 14th: styd on wl fr 4 out)	—	**1**	11/8[1]	133	7
2916[4]	**Kilcolgan (117)** (MrsJDGoodfellow) **10-10-5b**1ow5 NBentley (swtg: led tl hdd 14th: sn outpcd: styd on wl fr 3 out)	3	**2**	16/1	120	—
	Northants (124) (WStorey) **11-10-12** MMoloney (hld up: effrt 11th: mstke next: chal 15th: wknd 3 out)	8	**3**	3/1[3]	122	—
2078[6]	**Beachy Head (128)** (JJO'Neill) **9-11-2** GCahill (chsd ldrs: hit 13th: wknd appr 4 out)	¾	**4**	20/1	126	—
1647[10]	**Better Times Ahead (140)** (GRichards) **11-12-0** ADobbin (cl up: outpcd 12th: wknd 14th)	11	**5**	5/2[2]	130	4
				(SP 106.3%)		**5 Rn**

6m 51.9 (44.90) CSF £14.89 TOTE £2.20: £1.60 £2.60 (£9.30) OWNER Mr Michael Gillow (PENRITH) BRED B. Thompson

LONG HANDICAP Kilcolgan 9-6

2765 Whispering Steel jumped and travelled well and, given a fine ride, stamped his authority on the race four out. He was always in command despite a couple of deliberate jumps over the last two. (11/8)

2916 Kilcolgan just stays and, despite having the blinkers on for the first time, he got outpaced at a vital stage and it was far too late when he ran on again. (16/1)

Northants looked in good condition for his first outing of the season, but obviously still needed it, tiring in the closing stages.(3/1)

2078 Beachy Head, back to chasing for the first time this season, had the soft ground he loves and ran reasonably. (20/1)

1359 Better Times Ahead ran as though this was needed. (5/2)

3026 MARTNAHAM NOVICES' HURDLE (5-Y.O+) (Class E)

3-00 (3-03) **2m (9 hdls)** £2,430.00 (£680.00: £330.00) GOING: 0.99 sec per fur (S)

				SP	RR	SF
	Foresworn (USA) (DWWhillans) **5-10-12** DBentley (a.p: shkn up 3 out: led between last 2: r.o wl)	—	**1**	16/1	82+	14
2785*	**Jervaulx (IRE)** (GRichards) **6-11-4** ADobbin (hld up: hdwy 4 out: chal next: led 2 out: sn hdd & nt qckn)	7	**2**	5/4[1]	81	13

Form	Horse	Dist	Pos	SP	RR	SF
2649[2]	**Northern Union (CAN)** (CParker) **6-10-12** DParker (lw: trckd ldrs: mstke 5th: led appr 3 out tl hdd next: sn btn)	9	**3**	6/4[2]	66	—
2633[9]	**The Stuffed Puffin (IRE)** (LLungo) **5-10-12** NBentley (mstke 1st: led tl hdd appr 3 out: sn btn)	15	**4**	14/1[3]	51	—
2953[6]	**Obvious Risk (56)** (EMCaine) **6-10-5**(7) TristanDavidson (effrt 5th: nvr trbld ldrs)	1½	**5**	33/1	50	—
	Nordisk Legend (MrsDThomson) **5-10-12** TReed (plld hrd: a bhd)	26	**6**	200/1	24	—
	De-Veers Currie (IRE) (DMoffatt) **5-10-7** DJMoffatt (mstkes: a bhd)	18	**7**	25/1	1	—
	Mr Medley (ACWhillans) **5-10-12** BStorey (prom to 5th: sn wknd: p.u bef 3 out)		**P**	16/1	—	—
2917[6]	**Alan's Pride (IRE)** (WMcKeown) **6-10-7** GCahill (cl up tl wknd 4 out: p.u bef last)		**P**	14/1[3]	—	—
	Operatic Dancer (RMMcKellar) **6-10-12** MMoloney (mstkes: rdn & lost tch 5th: p.u bef 3 out)		**P**	200/1	—	—

(SP 117.3%) **10 Rn**

4m 2.4 (25.40) CSF £34.49 TOTE £29.60: £3.50 £1.10 £1.30 (£22.20) Trio £14.90 OWNER Mr D. W. Whillans (HAWICK) BRED Terry Heidman
Foresworn (USA), who only ran once on the Flat before changing stables, revelled in these testing conditions and won in really useful style. (16/1)
2785* Jervaulx (IRE) won well here at the last meeting, but the form of that race is not as yet working out and he was put in his place here. (5/4)
2649 Northern Union (CAN) won on testing ground on the level but, after holding every chance, he found conditions here too much. (6/4)
2005 The Stuffed Puffin (IRE) had shown ability on the soft in bumpers, but he disappointingly stopped when the pressure was on over the last three flights. (14/1: 10/1-16/1)
Obvious Risk looked slow when the pace was really on from the fourth last. (33/1)

3027 FIELD AND LAWN (MELLERAYS BELLE CHALLENGE CUP) H'CAP CHASE (0-125) (5-Y.O+) (Class D)

3-30 (3-31) **2m 4f (17 fncs)** £3,522.00 (£1,056.00: £508.00: £234.00) GOING: Not Established

Form	Horse	Dist	Pos	SP	RR	SF
2769[U]	**Nicholas Plant (97)** (JSGoldie) **8-10-0** GCahill (mde all: styd on wl fr 4 out)	—	**1**	8/1	110	4
2769[2]	**Judicial Field (IRE) (98)** (NTinkler) **8-9-12b**(3)ow1 EHusband (lw: chsd wnr most of wy: hit 12th: btn whn blnd 2 out)	8	**2**	9/2[3]	105	—
1645[P]	**Village Reindeer (NZ) (107)** (PCalver) **10-10-10** TReed (hld up: hdwy 9th: chsng ldrs 12th: rdn 4 out: 3rd whn blnd & hmpd 2 out: n.d after)	13	**3**	5/1	103	—
2765[6]	**Solba (USA) (100)** (CParker) **8-10-3** DParker (prom tl mstke & outpcd 10th: hdwy to chse ldrs 4 out: btn whn blnd 3 out)	19	**4**	4/1[2]	81	—
2769[3]	**Golden Fiddle (IRE) (97)** (JKMOliver) **9-10-0** BStorey (prom tl wknd fr 11th)	7	**5**	3/1[1]	72	—
2954[U]	**Quixall Crossett (98)** (EMCaine) **12-9-8**(7)ow1 TristanDavidson (t.o fr 5th)	dist	**6**	300/1	—	—
2616[9]	**Whaat Fettle (125)** (GRichards) **12-12-0** ADobbin (prom tl wknd fr 10th: p.u bef 4 out)		**P**	10/1	—	—
	Island Gale (98) (DMcCune) **12-10-1**ow1 FPerratt (lost tch fr 8th: wl t.o whn p.u bef 4 out)		**P**	50/1	—	—
	Peter (97) (DWWhillans) **9-10-0** DBentley (prom whn blnd bdly & uns rdr 8th)		**U**	12/1	—	—

(SP 110.0%) **9 Rn**

5m 27.5 (32.50) CSF £37.82 CT £168.98 TOTE £9.50: £1.40 £1.40 £2.00 (£31.60) Trio £117.90; £21.60 to Hereford 10/2/97. OWNER Mrs M. F. Paterson (GLASGOW) BRED Mrs J. A. Armstrong
LONG HANDICAP Nicholas Plant 9-4 Judicial Field (IRE) 9-10 Quixall Crossett 7-1 Island Gale 9-3 Peter 9-8
2545 Nicholas Plant loves this ground and jumped pretty well and, out in front where he likes to be, was never going to stop. Further successes look likely. (8/1)
2769 Judicial Field (IRE) was always in the thick of things but, when it came to a struggle, he was found wanting yet again. (9/2: op 3/1)
Village Reindeer (NZ), a soft-ground specialist, was having his first run for two and a half months, and although he had his chances, he looked slightly ring-rusty and was beaten when jumping into the back of the second horse. (5/1)
2765 Solba (USA) ran in snatches, and was done with when almost falling three out. (4/1)
2769 Golden Fiddle (IRE) ran moderately, dropping out in the final mile. (3/1)
2616 Whaat Fettle last won on softish ground over four years ago. (10/1: 8/1-12/1)
Peter was going well enough with a circuit to go when he gave his rider no chance of staying on. (12/1)

3028 GAIETY THEATRE H'CAP HURDLE (0-120) (4-Y.O+) (Class D)

4-00 (4-01) **2m 4f (11 hdls)** £3,057.50 (£920.00: £445.00: £207.50) GOING: 0.99 sec per fur (S)

Form	Horse	Dist	Pos	SP	RR	SF
2789[4]	**Oat Couture (115)** (LLungo) **9-11-9** ADobbin (a cl up: led appr 3 out tl hdd flat: sn led again: r.o u.p)	—	**1**	8/1[3]	97	15
2790[3]	**Pariah (IRE) (92)** (MartinTodhunter) **8-10-0** GCahill (hld up: stdy hdwy appr 3 out: rdn to ld flat: sn hdd: kpt on wl)	½	**2**	7/2[1]	74	—
2603a[13]	**Palacegate King (116)** (ACWhillans) **8-11-5**(5) STaylor (in tch: rdn & hdwy 4 out: chal next: no ex flat)	5	**3**	7/2[1]	94	12
2817*	**Cittadino (106)** (CWThornton) **7-10-7**(7) NHorrocks (a.p: chal 3 out: hit 2 out: no ex)	2	**4**	7/2[1]	82	—
2651[2]	**Kemo Sabo (92)** (CParker) **5-10-0** DParker (led tl hdd appr 3 out: sn btn)	20	**5**	5/1[2]	52	—
	New Charges (97) (PBeaumont) **10-10-0**(5) BGrattan (cl up tl wknd appr 3 out)	hd	**6**	20/1	57	—
	Bang in Trouble (IRE) (106) (JJO'Neill) **6-10-7**(7) DJewett (prom tl wknd appr 3 out)	7	**7**	12/1	60	—
2651[3]	**Glenugie (99)** (GMMoore) **6-10-7v** NBentley (in tch: drvn along fr 6th: hrd rdn & wknd 4 out)	dist	**8**	5/1[2]	—	—
	Kirstenbosch (93) (LLungo) **10-9-8**(7)ow1 WDowling (a bhd: p.u bef 3 out)		**P**	66/1	—	—

(SP 125.1%) **9 Rn**

5m 16.0 (35.00) CSF £36.42 CT £110.79 TOTE £7.00: £3.50 £2.10 £1.30 (£23.50) Trio £39.10 OWNER Mackinnon Mills (CARRUTHERSTOWN) BRED Springhill Bloodstock Ltd
LONG HANDICAP Pariah (IRE) 9-12 Kirstenbosch 9-3
2789 Oat Couture, back to hurdling after two disappointing efforts over fences recently, and back in top form, showed fine courage to hold on.(8/1)
2790 Pariah (IRE) loves plenty of cut in the ground, and put in another useful effort here to show he is going the right way. (7/2)
2603a Palacegate King loves these conditions, but has yet to win over this distance and was outstayed from the last. He is off a useful mark at present. (7/2)
2817* Cittadino, upped 6lb in the weights, ran well, but was struggling when a blunder two out finished him. (7/2)
2651 Kemo Sabo seemed to find this trip in this ground all too much. (5/1)
New Charges ran as though he blew up. (20/1)
2651 Glenugie was never happy in this ground. (5/1)

T/Plpt: £137.10 (48.58 Tckts). T/Qdpt: £6.00 (89.54 Tckts) AA

2859-CATTERICK (L-H) (Good)
Saturday February 8th
One fence omitted fnl circ 2nd race.
WEATHER: overcast & windy

3029 LEVY BOARD NOVICES' HURDLE (4-Y.O+ F & M) (Class E)
1-30 (1-30) **2m (9 hdls)** £2,458.00 (£688.00: £334.00) GOING: 0.37 sec per fur (GS)

				SP	RR	SF
2566[5]	**Meg's Memory (IRE)** (AStreeter) **4-10-4** TEley (lw: trckd ldrs: effrt 2 out: styd on to ld flat: drvn out)	—	**1**	8/1	67	14
2861*	**Spritzer (IRE) (91)** (JGFitzGerald) **5-11-7** PNiven (hdwy 4th: rdn to ld 2 out: hdd flat: no ex nr fin)	¾	**2**	7/4[2]	73	30
872[2]	**Nishamira (IRE)** (TDBarron) **5-11-0** DGallagher (lw: trckd ldrs: led after 3 out: hdd next: styd on same pce flat)	1¾	**3**	6/4[1]	65	22
2673[6]	**Derring Floss** (JAPickering) **7-10-7**(7) MissJWormall (a in tch: one pce fr 3 out)	10	**4**	20/1	55	12
1980[5]	**Analogical** (DMcCain) **4-10-4** RSupple (chsd ldrs: wkng whn blnd 2 out)	14	**5**	50/1	41	—
1940[5]	**Fro** (HAlexander) **4-9-13**(5) RMcGrath (lw: led 1st to 5th: wknd next)	9	**6**	6/1[3]	32	—
2547[18]	**Gautby Henpecked** (GMMoore) **4-10-4b[1]** JCallaghan (j.b: sn bhd: t.o 4th: sme hdwy 2 out: n.d)	13	**7**	50/1	19	—
2552[P]	**Carly-J (72)** (FSJackson) **6-11-0** MrNKent (chsd ldrs tl lost pl 3 out)	3	**8**	50/1	16	—
	Marjimel (MrsAMNaughton) **6-11-0** MFoster (lw: bhd fr 4th)	nk	**9**	50/1	15	—
2815[9]	**Kaye's Secret** (JLHarris) **4-10-4** JSupple (drvn & lost pl 4th: sn wl bhd)	10	**10**	50/1	5	—
2669[11]	**Skip to Somerfield** (BSRothwell) **5-11-0** ASSmith (plld hrd: trckd ldrs: led 5th tl after next: sn wknd)	4	**11**	20/1	1	—
	Allerbeck (JLGoulding) **7-11-0** LO'Hara (bit bkwd: s.s: nt j.w: a t.o)	dist	**12**	50/1	—	—
1679[P]	**Persian Sunset (IRE)** (MissJBower) **5-11-0** KGaule (t.o fr 5th)	12	**13**	50/1	—	—
1821[7]	**Fairy-Land (IRE)** (HowardJohnson) **5-10-9**(5) GFRyan (led to 1st: lost pl & blnd 4th: sn t.o)	5	**14**	25/1	—	—
2066[8]	**Primitive Light** (ASmith) **7-10-7**(7) MNewton (hld up: hdwy 4th: sn prom: outpcd appr 2 out: 6th whn fell last)		**F**	20/1	—	—
	Regal Jest (BWMurray) **7-10-11**(3) ECallaghan (lw: lost pl after 3rd: sn wl t.o: p.u bef last)		**P**	50/1	—	—
				(SP 135.6%)	**16 Rn**	

3m 57.1 (14.10) CSF £21.21 TOTE £6.50: £1.50 £1.10 £1.10 (£7.40) Trio £5.20 OWNER Centaur Racing (UTTOXETER) BRED Golden Vale Stud
WEIGHT FOR AGE 4yo-10lb

2566 Meg's Memory (IRE) may lack size, but certainly has the heart for a battle. (8/1: op 5/1)
2861* Spritzer (IRE), carrying a 7lb penalty, is probably better suited by an extra half-mile. (7/4)
872 Nishamira (IRE), winner of a bumper and a maiden on the Flat, jumped soundly. After taking it up travelling smoothly, she was run out of it on the Flat. An extra half-mile will not come amiss. (6/4)
1913 Derring Floss, who showed poor form in points, would probably be better suited by fences. (20/1)
1940 Fro (6/1: op 10/1)

3030 WHITBY NOVICES' CHASE (5-Y.O+) (Class E)
2-05 (2-05) **2m (11 fncs)** £2,989.25 (£899.00: £434.50: £202.25) GOING: 0.37 sec per fur (GS)

				SP	RR	SF
2702[P]	**Roberty Lea** (MrsMReveley) **9-11-2** PNiven (j.slowly: sn bhd: gd hdwy 9th: led last: drvn out)	—	**1**	7/2[2]	83	31
2628[5]	**Royal Crimson (89)** (MDHammond) **6-11-2** RGarritty (lw: in tch: hdwy 9th: led 2 out to last: nt qckn)	2½	**2**	7/2[2]	81	29
2699[5]	**Marlingford (74)** (MrsJJordan) **10-11-2**(7) LMcGrath (swtg: led to 5th: lft in ld 9th: hdd nxt: btn whn mstke last)	9	**3**	8/1[3]	79	27
1943[U]	**Coolreny (IRE) (72)** (VThompson) **8-11-2** MrMThompson (bit bkwd: s.s: nt j.w: a wl bhd)	dist	**4**	100/1	—	—
1815[4]	**The Fence Shrinker (60)** (DMcCain) **6-11-2** JSupple (chsd ldrs: wkng whn blnd 7th: t.o 9th)	dist	**5**	33/1	—	—
2672[P]	**Lepton (IRE)** (JWCurtis) **6-11-2b[1]** DerekByrne (b.d 2nd)		**B**	50/1	—	—
1253[9]	**Dash To The Phone (USA)** (KAMorgan) **5-10-7** ASSmith (in tch: hdwy 5th: led 7th tl fell 9th)		**F**	14/1	—	—
2628[8]	**Childsway** (SJRobinson) **9-10-11**(5) DJKavanagh (w ldrs: led 5th to 7th: ev ch whn fell next)		**F**	20/1	—	—
2619[15]	**Great Gable (IRE)** (DMoffatt) **6-11-2** LO'Hara (bit bkwd: fell 2nd)		**F**	50/1	—	—
2799[U]	**Chorus Line (IRE) (84)** (PBeaumont) **8-10-11** RSupple (lw: chsd ldrs tl fell 5th)		**F**	9/4[1]	—	—
2842[6]	**Rain-N-Sun (73)** (JLHarris) **11-11-2** DGallagher (sn bhd: t.o whn tried to ref 6th: p.u bef 8th)		**P**	16/1	—	—
2632[P]	**Most Rich (IRE) (73)** (BEllison) **9-11-2** KJohnson (sn bhd: sme hdwy whn blnd & uns rdr 9th)		**U**	33/1	—	—
				(SP 114.4%)	**12 Rn**	

4m 5.1 (13.10) CSF £13.77 TOTE £4.00: £1.60 £1.50 £2.20 (£7.00) Trio £6.50 OWNER Wentdale Const Ltd (SALTBURN) BRED Stud-On-The-Chart
WEIGHT FOR AGE 5yo-9lb

2008* Roberty Lea took time to get his eye in. Coming from off the pace, he will be better suited by an extra half-mile and easier ground. (7/2: op 6/4)
Royal Crimson, from a stable that can do no right at present, was outstayed by the winner on the run-in. (7/2)
2699 Marlingford ran as well as could be expected, considering he would have been receiving 15lb from the runner-up if this had been handicap. (8/1)
1049 Dash To The Phone (USA) showed ability, and was still travelling nicely when he came down at the last in the back straight. (14/1)
2799 Chorus Line (IRE) came down at the water. (9/4)

3031 BRIDGE (S) HURDLE (4-Y.O+) (Class G)
2-35 (2-39) **2m (8 hdls)** £2,066.00 (£576.00: £278.00) GOING: 0.37 sec per fur (GS)

				SP	RR	SF
2859[13]	**Lucky Bea (84)** (MWEasterby) **4-10-7** PNiven (hld up: hdwy 5th: styd on u.p fr 2 out: led flat: all out)	—	**1**	6/1[3]	62	6
1940[10]	**Amazing Sail (IRE)** (MissMKMilligan) **4-10-7** ASSmith (led 3rd to last: edgd lft u.p: kpt on wl)	nk	**2**	33/1	62	6
2920[3]	**Auntie Alice (76)** (JGFitzGerald) **7-10-12** WDwan (lw: bhd: hdwy 4th: ev ch & rdn 2 out: nt qckn flat)	¾	**3**	7/2[1]	56	10
2631[8]	**Robsera (IRE) (84)** (JJQuinn) **6-11-10** RGarritty (lw: hld up: hdwy 5th: led last: sn hdd & nt qckn)	s.h	**4**	4/1[2]	68	22
2859[10]	**Radmore Brandy** (GRichards) **4-9-13**(3) GLee (trckd ldrs: ev ch 2 out: nt qckn appr last)	2	**5**	15/2	54	—
2882[10]	**Never so Blue (IRE) (84)** (PBradley) **6-11-3**(7) RWilkinson (hdwy 4th: ev ch whn hmpd appr 2 out: chal last: styd on)	¾	**6**	14/1	65	19
2913[8]	**Cool Steel (IRE) (67)** (MrsJBrown) **5-11-0**(3) ECallaghan (hld up & bhd: gd hdwy 3 out: styd on flat: nt rch ldrs)	2½	**7**	20/1	56	10
	Beauman (PDEvans) **7-11-3** KGaule (led to 3rd: drvn along 3 out: wknd appr next)	23	**8**	6/1[3]	33	—
2862[7]	**Anorak (USA) (89)** (GMMoore) **7-11-3**(7) NHannity (lw: chsd ldrs tl lost pl after 5th)	hd	**9**	12/1	40	—

	Horse / details	Dist	Pos	SP	RR	SF
2510^{11}	**Port Valenska (IRE)** (JLHarris) **4-10-7** DGallagher (t.o fr 5th)	28	**10**	50/1	5	—
2628^{P}	**South Coast Star (IRE) (68)** (HowardJohnson) **7-11-3** MFoster (chsd ldrs: reminders 4th: wknd 3 out)	½	**11**	50/1	4	—
2859^{16}	**Beacon Hill Lady** (BEllison) **4-9-11**(5) RMcGrath (sn bhd: t.o 2 out)	4	**12**	50/1	—	—
1699^{9}	**Lomond Lassie (USA)** (TKersey) **4-9-13**(7)ow4 MNewton (sn t.o)	1¼	**13**	50/1	—	—
2649^{B}	**Miletrian City** (JBerry) **4-10-7** DerekByrne (in tch tl wknd after 5th)	2	**14**	20/1	—	—
	Sun Mark (IRE) (MrsASwinbank) **6-11-3** JSupple (bit bkwd: prom early: bhd fr 4th)	s.h	**15**	8/1	—	—
2818^{8}	**Sharmoor (69)** (MissLCSiddall) **5-10-12** RSupple (chsd ldrs tl lost pl 4th: t.o 3 out)	21	**16**	14/1	—	—
2899^{P}	**Just Supposen (IRE) (90)** (BSRothwell) **6-11-10b^{1}** JCallaghan (trckd ldrs: 6th & rdn whn fell 3 out)		**F**	20/1	—	—
	Badger Hill (MissSWilliamson) **4-10-0**(7) ATodd (bit bkwd: bhd whn fell 5th)		**F**	50/1	—	—

(SP 141.7%) **18 Rn**

3m 59.7 (16.70) CSF £191.88 TOTE £8.10: £1.60 £8.00 £1.60 (£535.00) Trio Not won; £214.13 to Hereford 10/2/97. OWNER Bee Health Ltd (SHERIFF HUTTON) BRED Mrs L. M. Tong

WEIGHT FOR AGE 4yo-10lb

Bt in 4,200 gns

2744 Lucky Bea, called unreliable by his trainer, did just enough under a forceful ride. (6/1: op 4/1)

Amazing Sail (IRE), tailed off on the All-Weather last time, ran surprisingly well, helping to set a strong pace. (33/1)

2920 Auntie Alice appreciated the drop in class. (7/2)

1851* Robsera (IRE) seemed to run up to his best. (4/1)

1699 Radmore Brandy ran easily her best race over hurdles so far. (15/2)

Never so Blue (IRE) staged a revival, and would have finished a fraction closer but for being hampered. (14/1)

1990 Cool Steel (IRE), given a patient ride, had it all to do three out. He was sticking on at the finish and possibly has more ability than he cares to show. (20/1)

3032 IAN HUTCHINSON MEMORIAL CHALLENGE CUP NOVICES' AMATEUR H'CAP HURDLE (0-105) (4-Y.O+) (Class F)

3-05 (3-05) **3m 1f 110y (12 hdls)** £2,202.50 (£615.00: £297.50) GOING: Not Established

	Horse / details	Dist	Pos	SP	RR	SF
2654^{4}	**Ruber (75)** (RWThomson) **10-9-13**(5) MissPRobson (lw: chsd ldrs: drvn along 7th: led 3 out: styd on wl flat)	—	**1**	8/1	57	—
2669^{8}	**Indicator (96)** (JJQuinn) **5-11-4**(7) MrABalding (hld up: stdy hdwy 9th: ev ch whn blnd next: nt qckn flat)	1½	**2**	13/2	77	7
2669^{10}	**Pontevedra (IRE) (88)** (KAMorgan) **4-9-12**(7)ow5 MrRWakley (hld up: gd hdwy 9th: one pce appr 2 out)	8	**3**	14/1	64	—
1847^{10}	**Last Refuge (IRE) (86)** (TJCarr) **8-10-8**(7) MrCMulhall (trckd ldrs: outpcd 8th: sme hdwy 3 out: n.d)	8	**4**	25/1	57	—
2649^{9}	**Black Ice (IRE) (72)** (TPTate) **6-9-8**(7) MrWBurnell (trckd ldrs tl grad wknd fr 3 out)	4	**5**	10/1	41	—
1988^{7}	**Ski Path (73)** (NBycroft) **8-9-9**(7)ow2 MissRClark (blnd 1st: hdwy & prom 5th: wknd 7th)	24	**6**	33/1	27	—
2820^{P}	**Gutteridge (IRE) (76)** (PDEvans) **7-9-12**(7)ow5 MrWMcLaughlin (chsd ldrs tl wknd after 3 out)	½	**7**	12/1	29	—
2701^{5}	**Glenbower (85)** (MDHammond) **5-10-11**(3) MrCBonner (mstkes: mde most to 3 out: wknd qckly & p.u bef next)		**P**	7/2^{2}	—	—
2768^{2}	**Belle Rose (IRE) (88)** (GRichards) **7-10-12**(5) MrRHale (w ldrs tl wknd qckly 7th: t.o 3 out: p.u bef next)		**P**	4/1^{3}	—	—
2860^{F}	**Dry Hill Lad (87)** (JNorton) **6-10-9**(7) MrPScott (bhd fr 8th: t.o whn p.u bef 2 out)		**P**	16/1	—	—
2898^{18}	**Irish Buzz (IRE) (81)** (MrsASwinbank) **5-10-3**(7)ow10 MrChrisWilson (jnd ldrs 7th: wknd appr 3 out: t.o whn p.u bef 2 out)		**P**	25/1	—	—
2790^{2}	**Lifebuoy (IRE) (86)** (JRTurner) **6-11-1** MrSSwiers (lw: bhd & drvn along 7th: p.u after 2 out)		**P**	3/1^{1}	—	—
	Strong Character (71) (DALamb) **11-9-7**(7) MissSLamb (bkwd: mstkes: chsd ldrs: lost pl & blnd 8th: t.o whn p.u bef 2 out)		**P**	50/1	—	—

(SP 133.6%) **13 Rn**

6m 40.2 (33.20) CSF £59.14 CT £687.50 TOTE £10.80: £2.20 £2.90 £4.60 (£51.60) Trio £137.70; £174.63 to Hereford 10/2/97. OWNER Mr R. W. Thomson (HAWICK) BRED C. H. Bell

LONG HANDICAP Pontevedra (IRE) 9-9 Irish Buzz (IRE) 8-12 Ski Path 9-8 Strong Character 9-2

WEIGHT FOR AGE 4yo-12lb

OFFICIAL EXPLANATION Lifebuoy (IRE): did not like the loose going or stay the extended three miles.

2654 Ruber, given a positive ride by his highly-capable partner, never looked being overhauled. (8/1)

2669 Indicator appreciated the step-up in distance. Even if he had not blundered three out, he would still not have beaten the winner. (13/2)

Pontevedra (IRE), 5lb out of the handicap and with his rider only able to claim 2lb of his allowance, was nibbled at in the market. (14/1)

Last Refuge (IRE), who has clearly had his problems, shaped as if on the way back. (25/1)

1672 Black Ice (IRE), a keen-going sort, will probably not be seen to best effect until he goes over fences. (10/1)

2701 Glenbower, from a stable badly out of form, hardly jumped a flight and, after making the running, was legless on the final turn. (7/2)

3033 RED ONION GRAND NATIONAL TRIAL H'CAP CHASE (0-130) (5-Y.O+) (Class C)

3-35 (3-35) **3m 6f (23 fncs)** £7,302.50 (£2,195.00: £1,060.00: £492.50) GOING: 0.37 sec per fur (GS)

	Horse / details	Dist	Pos	SP	RR	SF
1844^{3}	**Act the Wag (IRE) (108)** (MartinTodhunter) **8-11-8** PNiven (lw: chsd ldrs: led 4 out: drvn along & styd on wl)	—	**1**	13/2	117	—
2630^{5}	**Heavenly Citizen (IRE) (93)** (JLGledson) **9-10-7** KJohnson (led 4th to 7th: drvn along 16th: styd on same pce fr 3 out: no imp)	6	**2**	9/1	98	—
2782^{9}	**Pims Gunner (IRE) (102)** (MDHammond) **9-11-2** RGarritty (trckd ldrs: outpcd & drvn along 16th: rdn & sltly hmpd 4 out: one pce fr next)	1	**3**	11/2^{3}	107	—
2568^{3}	**Dark Oak (110)** (JWCurtis) **11-11-10** DerekByrne (blnd 10th: mstke 14th: drvn along & outpcd 16th:t.o 18th)	dist	**4**	7/1	—	—
2652^{2}	**Westwell Boy (105)** (PBeaumont) **11-11-5** RSupple (lw: led 7th: hdd & fell 4 fr home)		**F**	100/30^{2}	—	—
2698*	**Choisty (IRE) (108)** (MrsASwinbank) **7-11-8** JSupple (lw: mstkes: led: blnd 3rd: hdd next: chsd ldrs: drvn along & outpcd 17th: blnd & uns rdr next)		**U**	7/4^{1}	—	—

(SP 110.7%) **6 Rn**

8m 7.7 CSF £48.48 TOTE £6.00: £1.80 £3.20 (£19.00) OWNER Mr Robert Ogden (ULVERSTON) BRED J. R. Kidd

1844 Act the Wag (IRE), given a couple of outings over hurdles to get his confidence, was always travelling nicely and had only to be kept up to his work. (13/2)

2630 Heavenly Citizen (IRE) usually runs well round here. (9/1)

2004 Pims Gunner (IRE) showed a return to something like his best form after some poor efforts. (11/2: 7/2-6/1)

2568 Dark Oak ran badly. (7/1)

2652 Westwell Boy had just been headed when he took a crashing fall three from home. (100/30)

2698* Choisty (IRE) did not put in a blemish-free round, and he looked to be struggling badly when parting company with his rider. (7/4)

3034 ASKE H'CAP HURDLE (0-130) (4-Y.O+) (Class C)

4-05 (4-06) **2m (8 hdls)** £3,413.25 (£1,026.00: £495.50: £230.25) GOING: 0.37 sec per fur (GS)

				SP	RR	SF
2777[3]	**Star Rage (IRE) (127)** (JLHarris) **7-12-0** DGallagher (j.lft: sddle slipped: shkn up 4th: led appr 2 out: r.o wl u.p flat)	—	1	9/4[1]	108	53
2902[5]	**Desert Fighter (111)** (MrsMReveley) **6-10-12** PNiven (trckd ldrs: effrt 3 out: nt qckn flat)	2½	2	5/1	90	35
2603a[20]	**Centaur Express (118)** (AStreeter) **5-11-5** TEley (lw: led tl appr 2 out: kpt on same pce appr last)	¾	3	3/1[3]	96	41
2799[F]	**Tapatch (IRE) (99)** (MWEasterby) **9-9-11b**(3) GLee (trckd ldrs tl wknd appr 2 out: eased)	dist	4	16/1	—	—
2669*	**Night Dance (104)** (KAMorgan) **5-10-5** ASSmith (lw: plld hrd: trckd ldrs: drvn along & hit 5th: sn wknd & eased)	28	5	5/2[2]	—	—
2902[7]	**Elpidos (115)** (MDHammond) **5-11-2** RGarritty (lost tch 4th: t.o whn p.u bef 2 out)		P	10/1	—	—
				(SP 116.0%)	**6 Rn**	

3m 53.6 (10.60) CSF £13.12 TOTE £2.50: £1.50 £2.50 (£10.20) OWNER Mr David Abell (MELTON MOWBRAY) BRED Killarkin Stud

LONG HANDICAP Tapatch (IRE) 9-13

2777 Star Rage (IRE) is as tough as old boots. Making light of the handicap, and with a saddle that had slipped with a circuit to go, he knuckled down willingly on the run-in. The plan is to run him in the Imperial Cup before he attempts to win the County Hurdle at the Festival for the second year running. (9/4)

2902 Desert Fighter as usual travelled strongly, but did not find as much as expected when he came off the bridle. The cut-up ground may not have been in his favour. (5/1)

2603a Centaur Express, 5lb higher than when winning at Market Rasen two runs ago, was as usual taken to post early. He seemed to run up to his best. (3/1)

2631 Tapatch (IRE) as usual found nothing off the bridle. (16/1)

2669* Night Dance, unable to dominate, would not settle and, after dropping right out, was allowed to come home in his own time. (5/2)

3035 BROUGH H'CAP HURDLE (0-105) (4-Y.O+) (Class F)

4-35 (4-36) **2m 3f (10 hdls)** £2,132.50 (£595.00: £287.50) GOING: 0.37 sec per fur (GS)

				SP	RR	SF
2800[3]	**Here Comes Herbie (82)** (WStorey) **5-10-4**(5) RMcGrath (hld up: hdwy 6th: led 2 out: hit last: drvn out)	—	1	11/2[2]	69	—
	Topsawyer (93) (MissSEHall) **9-11-6** KGaule (bit bkwd: hld up: hdwy 6th: chal 2 out: nt qckn flat)	3	2	7/1	78	—
2509[13]	**Fryup Satellite (82)** (MrsJBrown) **6-10-9** MissPRobson (lw: w ldrs: led 6th to 2 out: kpt on one pce)	6	3	14/1	61	—
1779[4]	**Innocent George (87)** (MissLCSiddall) **8-11-0** RSupple (hdwy 6th: drvn along & prom 3 out: one pce)	s.h	4	14/1	66	—
2744[2]	**Silly Money (91)** (TDEasterby) **6-11-4** RGarritty (lw: chsd ldrs: chal 3 out: wknd next)	6	5	11/2[2]	65	—
2701[6]	**Don't Tell Tom (IRE) (86)** (JWade) **7-10-10**(3) ECallaghan (hdwy 6th: sn prom: wknd 3 out)	8	6	16/1	54	—
2631[2]	**Opera Fan (IRE) (86)** (KAMorgan) **5-10-13** ASSmith (lw: led tl mstke & hdd 6th: wknd qckly 3 out: t.o)	26	7	4/1[1]	32	—
1701*	**Tip it In (90)** (ASmith) **8-10-10**(7) MNewton (chsd ldrs: hit 7th: wknd qckly 3 out: t.o)	1¼	8	6/1[3]	35	—
1249*	**Apollo's Daughter (73)** (JLGoulding) **9-10-0** JSupple (hmpd 4th: sn drvn along: t.o fr 3 out)	20	9	20/1	1	—
2509[4]	**Court Joker (IRE) (82)** (HAlexander) **5-10-9** PNiven (lw: hld up: b.d 4th)		B	12/1	—	—
2631[3]	**Jemima Puddleduck (95)** (AStreeter) **6-11-8v** TEley (chsd ldrs: drvn along 7th: outpcd whn fell next)		F	6/1[3]	—	—
	Birthplace (IRE) (73) (RTate) **7-10-0** KJohnson (bkwd: plld hrd: trckd ldrs tl fell 4th)		F	33/1	—	—
	Queen Buzzard (88) (EWeymes) **9-11-1** MrJWeymes (bkwd: prom tl lost pl 7th: t.o whn p.u bef 2 out)		P	25/1	—	—
				(SP 130.3%)	**13 Rn**	

4m 50.3 (25.30) CSF £43.24 CT £490.76 TOTE £6.40: £1.70 £2.20 £4.60 (£41.10) Trio £208.90; £214.82 to Hereford 10/2/97. OWNER Mr H. S. Hutchinson (CONSETT) BRED H. Hutchinson

LONG HANDICAP Apollo's Daughter 9-11 Birthplace (IRE) 9-13

2800 Here Comes Herbie, a winner on the Flat here, recovered well after flattening the last. (11/2: op 7/2)

Topsawyer, a grand type, was having his first outing for thirteen months. Despite looking burly, he was the only one to seriously trouble the winner. Provided he stays sound, he is sure to add to his record. (7/1)

1988* Fryup Satellite had much more use made of him this time and ran better for it. (14/1)

1779 Innocent George is slipping down the weights. (14/1)

2744 Silly Money looked a real danger three out, but called it a day at the next. (11/2)

2631 Opera Fan (IRE) seemed to run out of stamina and, with all chance gone, was virtually pulled up. (4/1)

T/Plpt: £488.20 (17.89 Tckts). T/Qdpt: £180.20 (2.27 Tckts) WG

3007-NEWBURY (L-H) (Good)

Saturday February 8th

WEATHER: fine

3036 CATHAY PACIFIC AIRWAYS H'CAP CHASE (0-145) (6-Y.O+) (Class B)

1-15 (1-15) **3m 2f 110y (21 fncs)** £7,670.40 (£2,134.40: £1,027.20) GOING: 0.74 sec per fur (S)

				SP	RR	SF
2741a[3]	**Call it a Day (IRE) (138)** (DNicholson) **7-11-12** AMaguire (hld up: stdy hdwy 16th: shkn up after 2 out: led last: drvn out)	—	1	11/4[2]	148	70
2839[2]	**River Mandate (125)** (CaptTAForster) **10-10-13b[1]** AThornton (chsd ldr: lft in ld appr 17th: hrd rdn appr 3 out: hdd 2 out: swtchd rt flat: r.o)	1¼	2	100/30[3]	134	56
2623[4]	**Le Meille (IRE) (112)** (KRBurke) **8-10-0** NWilliamson (hld up: stdy hdwy 16th: led 2 out to last: wknd)	5	3	10/1	118	40
2773[7]	**Bradbury Star (135)** (JTGifford) **12-11-9** PHide (mstke 3rd: lost pl 6th: hit 16th: sn t.o: p.u bef 2 out)		P	20/1	—	—
2881[2]	**Sunley Bay (120)** (PFNicholls) **11-10-8** DBridgwater (hld up: reminders after 5th: rdn 10th: j.slowly 12th: t.o whn hit 14th: p.u bef 17th)		P	6/1	—	—
2660[2]	**Montebel (IRE) (118)** (NATwiston-Davies) **9-10-6** CLlewellyn (led tl p.u lame appr 17th)		P	2/1[1]	—	—
				(SP 111.2%)	**6 Rn**	

6m 55.7 (20.70) CSF £11.22 TOTE £3.00: £1.90 £1.50 (£5.50) OWNER Mrs Jane Lane (TEMPLE GUITING) BRED Mrs Kathleen Banville

LONG HANDICAP Le Meille (IRE) 9-11

2741a Call it a Day (IRE), who has been running over inadequate trips, was patiently ridden and will now go to Cheltenham. (11/4)

2839 River Mandate, blinkered for the first time, gave everything but the winner had that edge in finishing speed. (100/30)

2623 Le Meille (IRE), 3lb out of the handicap, was going well when touching down ahead at the penultimate fence but this extended trip found him out. He would appear to have recaptured his form of last season. (10/1)

2660 Montebel (IRE) had yet to be asked a question when breaking down at the cross-fence. He has reportedly been retired. (2/1)

3037 MITSUBISHI SHOGUN GAME SPIRIT CHASE (Gd 2) (5-Y.O+) (Class A)

1-45 (1-45) **2m 1f (13 fncs)** £23,643.00 (£6,957.00) GOING: 0.74 sec per fur (S)

				SP	RR	SF
2886*	**Double Symphony (IRE) (139)** (CPEBrooks) **9-10-12** JOsborne (hld up: led on bit last: rdn out)	—	1	4/5^{1}	144	69
2646^{F}	**Dancing Paddy (147)** (KOCunningham-Brown) **9-11-3** DWalsh (w ldr: hit 2nd: lft in ld 5th: mstke 6th: hit 4 out: rdn 2 out: hdd last: one pce)	3½	2	100/30^{3}	146	71
	Arctic Kinsman (145) (NATwiston-Davies) **9-11-10** CLlewellyn (bit bkwd: led tl blnd & uns rdr 5th)		U	9/4^{2}	—	—
				(SP 109.4%)	**3 Rn**	

4m 14.6 (10.60) CSF £3.28 TOTE £1.70 (£2.00) OWNER Mr Anthony Pye-Jeary (LAMBOURN) BRED J. H. Kidd

2886* Double Symphony (IRE) could do nothing more than win what turned out to be a soft race in the way she did. She will probably go for the Cathcart. (4/5)

1914* Dancing Paddy again made his fair share of jumping errors. (100/30: 9/2-3/1)

Arctic Kinsman appeared to put a foot in the ditch. (9/4)

3038 TOTE GOLD TROPHY H'CAP HURDLE (Gd 3) (4-Y.O+) (Class A)

2-20 (2-27) **2m 110y (8 hdls)** £58,796.00 (£21,914.00: £10,644.50: £4,497.50: £1,936.25: £911.75) GOING: 0.74 sec per fur (S)

				SP	RR	SF
2645*	**Make a Stand (136)** (MCPipe) **6-11-7**^{4x} CMaude (mde all: clr 3rd: rdn appr 3 out: unchal)	—	1	6/1^{2}	125+	86
1474^{3}	**Hamilton Silk (126)** (MCPipe) **5-10-11** JamieEvans (hld up & bhd: gd hdwy 3 out: r.o flat)	9	2	40/1	106	67
2617*	**Direct Route (IRE) (133)** (HowardJohnson) **6-11-4** NWilliamson (hld up: stdy hdwy 3rd: r.o one pce fr 2 out)	1	3	7/1^{3}	112	73
2635*	**Mistinguett (IRE) (138)** (NATwiston-Davies) **5-11-9**^{4x} JOsborne (lw: hld up: stdy hdwy fr 3 out: nt rch ldrs)	nk	4	7/1^{3}	117	78
2645^{3}	**Silver Groom (IRE) (137)** (RAkehurst) **7-11-3**$^{(5)}$ SRyan (hld up: hdwy 4th: chsd wnr 3 out tl wknd flat)	2½	5	33/1	114	75
2902*	**Edelweis du Moulin (FR) (127)** (GRichards) **5-10-12** PCarberry (lw: hld up: hdwy 4th: wknd appr last)	6	6	5/2^{1}	98	59
1636*	**Mister Morose (IRE) (138)** (NATwiston-Davies) **7-11-9** DWalsh (prom: chsd wnr 5th to 3 out: sn wknd)	5	7	12/1	104	65
2645^{9}	**Kissair (IRE) (134)** (NJHenderson) **6-11-5** JFTitley (lw: prom tl wknd appr last)	3½	8	50/1	97	58
2617^{F}	**Hatta Breeze (129)** (DNicholson) **5-10-11**$^{(3)}$ RMassey (nvr nrr)	1¾	9	20/1	90	51
2777^{6}	**Dr Leunt (IRE) (134)** (PJHobbs) **6-11-5** GTormey (rdn 3rd: n.d)	2½	10	50/1	92	53
2059^{F}	**Paddy's Return (IRE) (141)** (FMurphy) **5-11-12b** RDunwoody (prom tl wknd 3 out)	10	11	11/1	90	51
2635^{6}	**Eskimo Nel (IRE) (135)** (JLSpearing) **6-11-3**$^{(3)}$ LAspell (hdwy 3rd: wknd 3 out)	3	12	25/1	81	42
2777^{7}	**Roll a Dollar (127)** (DRCElsworth) **11-10-12** PHolley (lw: a bhd)	3½	13	66/1	69	30
2886^{2}	**Chief's Song (136)** (SDow) **7-11-7** ADicken (lw: rdn 3rd: sn bhd)	3½	14	33/1	75	36
2740a^{7}	**Zabadi (IRE) (143)** (DNicholson) **5-12-0** AMaguire (hld up & bhd: sme hdwy 5th: sn wknd)	4	15	20/1	78	39
	Romancer (IRE) (139) (NATwiston-Davies) **6-11-10b** MRichards (prom: chsd wnr to 5th: wknd 3 out)	7	16	10/1	67	28
	Storm Damage (IRE) (136) (PFNicholls) **5-11-7** DBridgwater (hld up: rdn 4th: sn bhd)	½	17	14/1	64	25
	Clifton Beat (USA) (141) (PJHobbs) **6-11-12** RHughes (lw: a bhd: t.o whn p.u bef last)		P	33/1	—	—
				(SP 129.7%)	**18 Rn**	

3m 58.5 (8.50) CSF £215.83 CT £1,605.09 TOTE £8.00: £2.10 £3.90 £2.20 £1.80 (£151.30) Trio £384.20 OWNER Mr P. A. Deal (WELLINGTON) BRED R. M. West

LONG HANDICAP Make a Stand 10-8

2645* Make a Stand, carrying 7lb less than the Handicapper would have liked, turned a supposedly-competitive handicap into a procession. He is entered for both novice events at the Festival as well as the Champion Hurdle. (6/1)

1474 Hamilton Silk came from well off the pace to take second on the run-in and chase his stable-companion home. (40/1)

2617* Direct Route (IRE) did not have to carry the 5lb he has been raised, as the weights were published early. (7/1)

2635* Mistinguett (IRE), raised a stone for beating Dato Star at Haydock, only had to carry a 4lb penalty. (7/1)

2645 Silver Groom (IRE) paid the penalty on the run-in for going in vain pursuit of the winner in the final half-mile. (33/1)

2902* Edelweis du Moulin (FR) was able to run off his old mark here but, like the others, could never get near the winner. (5/2)

1636* Mister Morose (IRE), 10lb higher than when winning over course and distance at the Hennessy meeting. (12/1)

Kissair (IRE) gave notice he might be on the way back. (50/1)

3039 HARWELL H'CAP CHASE (0-145) (5-Y.O+) (Class B)

2-50 (2-56) **2m 4f (16 fncs)** £6,807.50 (£2,060.00: £1,005.00: £477.50) GOING: 0.74 sec per fur (S)

				SP	RR	SF
2782^{3}	**Golden Spinner (128)** (NJHenderson) **10-10-11** RDunwoody (lw: a.p: led 8th to 10th: led 11th: drvn out)	—	1	6/4^{1}	139	52
2639^{2}	**Easthorpe (138)** (MissHCKnight) **9-11-7b** JFTitley (lw: led to 8th: led 10th to 11th: ev ch 3 out: hrd rdn appr last: fin tired)	10	2	11/2^{2}	141	54
2762^{3}	**River Bounty (124)** (CPEBrooks) **11-10-7** NWilliamson (mstke 2nd: rdn 11th: sn bhd: lft poor 3rd 3 out)	13	3	9/1	117	30
1917^{7}	**All for Luck (130)** (MCPipe) **12-10-13** CMaude (blnd 2nd: wl bhd fr 5th)	3	4	10/1	120	33
	Forest Sun (125) (GBBalding) **12-10-8** BClifford (bhd fr 5th)	nk	5	25/1	115	28
1917^{8}	**Old Bridge (IRE) (132)** (AndrewTurnell) **9-11-1** SMcNeill (hld up: hdwy 12th: 3rd whn fell 4 out)		F	6/1^{3}	—	—
1650^{P}	**Front Street (135)** (OSherwood) **10-11-4** JOsborne (a bhd: lost tch 10th: p.u bef 4 out)		P	14/1	—	—
2783^{4}	**Around the Horn (129)** (JTGifford) **10-10-12** PHide (lw: prom to 12th: lft 3rd & sltly hmpd 4 out: p.u bef 3 out)		P	6/1^{3}	—	—
				(SP 113.6%)	**8 Rn**	

5m 11.8 (16.80) CSF £9.57 CT £49.06 TOTE £2.10: £1.30 £1.90 £1.70 (£5.80) Trio £14.00 OWNER Mrs Hugh Maitland-Jones (LAMBOURN) BRED Mrs C. I. Henty

LONG HANDICAP River Bounty 10-5

2782 Golden Spinner, dropped 2lb, was back to his best trip and registered his third course and distance win. (6/4)

2639 Easthorpe has yet to score over two-and-a-half miles. (11/2: 4/1-6/1)

2762 River Bounty only finished third due to a couple of defections in the straight. (9/1)

1649 Old Bridge (IRE) was stalking the first two and had still to be asked a question when coming to grief. (6/1)

1650 Front Street (14/1: op 8/1)

3040 YEAR OF THE OX NOVICES' CHASE (5-Y.O+) (Class C)

3-20 (3-26) **3m (18 fncs)** £5,085.00 (£1,530.00: £740.00: £345.00) GOING: 0.74 sec per fur (S)

				SP	RR	SF
2658*	**Cyborgo (FR)** (MCPipe) **7-11-8** RDunwoody (lw: led to 2nd: led after 13th: reminders appr 3 out: drvn out)	—	1	10/11^{1}	121+	64
2113^{F}	**Buckhouse Boy (132)** (NATwiston-Davies) **7-11-12** CMaude (lw: a.p: blnd 4th: hrd rdn & chsd wnr appr last: no imp)	6	2	8/1^{3}	121	64

				SP	RR	SF
1868[2]	**Triple Witching** (NJHenderson) **11-11-2** NWilliamson (bit bkwd: a.p: ev ch 3 out: sn rdn: mstke 2 out: wkng whn j.lft last)	11	**3**	8/1[3]	104	47
1423[F]	**Just 'n Ace (IRE) (102)** (MissSEdwards) **6-11-2** PHide (bhd fr 13th)	18	**4**	50/1	92	35
2614[U]	**Tellicherry** (MissHCKnight) **8-10-11** JFTitley (mstke 3rd: a bhd)	2	**5**	50/1	85	28
2113[3]	**Aardwolf (128)** (CPEBrooks) **6-11-12** JOsborne (lw: led 2nd tl after 13th: wknd appr 4 out: t.o whn p.u bef last)		**P**	9/4[2]	—	—
2947[P]	**Uncle Algy (85)** (MissHCKnight) **8-11-2** BFenton (bhd: mstke 11th: sn t.o: p.u bef 3 out)		**P**	66/1	—	—
				(SP 110.8%)	**7 Rn**	

6m 9.6 (19.60) CSF £7.57 TOTE £1.70: £1.30 £2.60 (£5.50) OWNER County Stores (Somerset) Holdings Ltd (WELLINGTON) BRED Francois Cottin and Alfred Lefevre

2658* Cyborgo (FR) was subsequently described by Pipe as the best former hurdler he has had going to the Gold Cup. He added he will have one more run, but also has a Royal SunAlliance entry. (10/11: 4/6-evens)

1646* Buckhouse Boy would have preferred more cut, but at least got round in one piece, and was taking on a potentially high-class sort in the winner. (8/1)

1868 Triple Witching looked very leg-weary at the last. (8/1)

3041 KUNG HEI FAT CHOY NOVICES' HURDLE (4-Y.O+) (Class C)

3-50 (3-57) **2m 110y (8 hdls)** £4,019.50 (£1,216.00: £593.00: £281.50) GOING: 0.74 sec per fur (S)

				SP	RR	SF
2825*	**Shadow Leader** (CREgerton) **6-11-9** NWilliamson (lw: hld up in rr: hdwy 5th: led on bit appr last: rdn out)	—	**1**	5/1[2]	95+	56
2059[3]	**Mr Percy (IRE) (127)** (JTGifford) **6-11-12** PHide (led to 3rd: rdn to ld 2 out: sn hdd: one pce)	4	**2**	5/1[2]	94	55
	Polydamas (KCBailey) **5-11-4** RHughes (lw: a.p: rdn & ev ch 3 out: one pce fr 2 out)	7	**3**	15/2[3]	79	40
	Andanito (IRE) (LadyHerries) **6-11-4** RDunwoody (a.p: led appr 3 out to 2 out: sn wknd)	4	**4**	7/2[1]	76+	37
2763*	**Donnington (IRE) (110)** (OSherwood) **7-11-9** JOsborne (lw: plld hrd early: prom: eased whn btn appr last)	8	**5**	7/2[1]	73	34
	Get Real (IRE) (NJHenderson) **6-10-13**(5) MrCVigors (lw: plld hrd: a.p: led 3rd tl appr 3 out: sn wknd)	nk	**6**	16/1	67+	28
2055[3]	**Bowcliffe Court (IRE) (100)** (RAkehurst) **5-11-4**(5) SRyan (hld up: hdwy 4th: wknd 2 out)	2	**7**	14/1	71	32
	The Flying Doctor (IRE) (GBBalding) **7-11-4** BFenton (bkwd: plld hrd: nvr nr ldrs)	10	**8**	33/1	56	17
	Umberston (IRE) (PRHedger) **4-10-8** MRichards (lw: n.d)	3½	**9**	33/1	52	3
2547[7]	**Morpheus (99)** (DNicholson) **8-11-4** AMaguire (bit bkwd: hld up & bhd: hdwy 3 out: wknd appr last)	8	**10**	20/1	45	6
2791[11]	**Perfect Pal (IRE)** (MissGayKelleway) **6-10-11**(7) LReynolds (a bhd: t.o)	13	**11**	66/1	32	—
	Mister Goodguy (IRE) (RCurtis) **8-11-4** DMorris (bkwd: a bhd: t.o)	2½	**12**	50/1	30	—
2872[10]	**Qu'appelle** (SEarle) **4-10-8** ILawrence (a bhd: t.o)	10	**13**	200/1	20	—
	Immense (IRE) (MrsAJPerrett) **7-11-4** CMaude (bkwd: a bhd: t.o)	28	**14**	14/1	—	—
1788[5]	**Snowshill Harvest (IRE)** (AndrewTurnell) **6-11-4** SMcNeill (plld hrd: bhd whn hmpd & fell 5th)		**F**	50/1	—	—
				(SP 125.3%)	**15 Rn**	

4m 5.3 (15.30) CSF £27.77 TOTE £5.20: £2.40 £1.80 £2.00 (£9.00) Trio £34.80 OWNER Mr James Blackshaw (CHADDLEWORTH) BRED A. J. Sexton

WEIGHT FOR AGE 4yo-10lb

2825* Shadow Leader, pulling double in the home straight, put up an impressive performance and deserves a chance to take on the best. (5/1)

2059 Mr Percy (IRE) did nothing wrong, and could have been taking on quite a useful novice. (5/1)

Polydamas, a 41,000 guineas purchase at Newmarket Autumn Sales, should not be hard to place. (15/2: 5/1-8/1)

Andanito (IRE), one of the top bumper horses last season, made a satisfactory hurdling debut and may be better over further. (7/2)

2763* Donnington (IRE) again proved disappointing on this course. (7/2: op 9/4)

Get Real (IRE) needs to settle and some cut may help. (16/1)

2055 Bowcliffe Court (IRE), he needs further unless it is bottomless. (14/1: 10/1-16/1)

Immense (IRE) (14/1: op 33/1)

3042 WEATHERBYS 'STARS OF TOMORROW' SERIES FINAL STANDARD OPEN N.H. FLAT RACE (4,5,6 & 7-Y.O) (Class H)

4-20 (4-25) **2m 110y** £7,006.00 (£2,128.00: £1,044.00: £502.00)

				SP	RR	SF
1275*	**Mr Markham (IRE)** (JTGifford) **5-11-9** PHide (hld up: hdwy 10f out: n.m.r & swtchd lft 3f out: led 2f out: r.o wl)	—	**1**	7/2[1]	80 f	—
2661[2]	**Dom Beltrano (FR)** (NATwiston-Davies) **5-11-9** CMaude (chsd ldr: led over 3f out to 2f out: one pce)	6	**2**	11/2[3]	74 f	—
2682*	**Arkley Royal** (JABOld) **6-12-0** GUpton (lw: hld up: hdwy 5f out: ev ch 2f out: one pce)	nk	**3**	6/1	79 f	—
2012[2]	**Billingsgate** (DrDChesney) **5-11-2**(7) NWillmington (hld up: hdwy 8f out: hrd rdn over 4f out: ev ch 2f out: one pce)	1¼	**4**	9/1	73 f	—
2661*	**Iranos (FR)** (MCPipe) **5-12-0** RHughes (led tl over 3f out: one pce)	1½	**5**	11/2[3]	76 f	—
2696[2]	**New Leaf (IRE)** (DRGandolfo) **5-11-4** RDunwoody (hdwy 11f out: rdn 5f out: ev ch 2f out: wknd fnl f)	½	**6**	4/1[2]	66 f	—
2510[2]	**In The Van** (MrsDHaine) **5-11-4** JFTitley (rdn 7f out: eased whn no ch over 4f out)	dist	**7**	6/1	—	—
2510[10]	**Moon Devil (IRE)** (MarkCampion) **7-11-4** JOsborne (hld up: eased whn no ch over 4f out)	17	**8**	33/1	—	—
1665[6]	**Bellidium** (AEJessop) **5-10-13** GTormey (a bhd: t.o fnl 8f)	17	**9**	50/1	—	—
2904[5]	**Sprightley Pip (IRE)** (MissCJohnsey) **6-11-4** BFenton (prom: rdn 9f out: sn wknd: t.o)	9	**10**	33/1	—	—
2804[9]	**Midas** (KRBurke) **6-11-9** NWilliamson (bhd fnl 6f: t.o)	6	**11**	33/1	—	—
				(SP 122.3%)	**11 Rn**	

4m 3.6 CSF £21.31 TOTE £3.70: £1.80 £2.00 £2.40 (£12.10) Trio £24.50 OWNER Felix Rosenstiel's Widow & Son (FINDON) BRED M. Ryan

1275* Mr Markham (IRE), well-backed, was squeezed for room on the stands' rails three furlongs out, but soon got back on an even keel. (7/2)

2661 Dom Beltrano (FR) found the winner far too strong in the final furlong. (11/2: 7/2-6/1)

2682* Arkley Royal found these conditions far removed from Lingfield's mud. (6/1: op 7/2)

2012 Billingsgate was another to find the emphasis more on speed than stamina this time. (9/1)

2661* Iranos (FR) (11/2: 7/2-6/1)

T/Jkpt: £282.50 (30.08 Tckts). T/Plpt: £19.40 (1452.42 Tckts). T/Qdpt: £7.50 (187.43 Tckts) KH

2758-UTTOXETER (L-H) (Good)
Saturday February 8th
WEATHER: fine & sunny

3043 E.B.F. TATTERSALLS (IRELAND) (QUALIFIER) NOVICES' CHASE (6-Y.O+ Mares Only) (Class D)
1-40 (1-40) **2m 4f (15 fncs)** £3,631.25 (£1,100.00: £537.50: £256.25) GOING minus 0.17 sec per fur (G)

	Horse		Pos	SP	RR	SF
	Harvest View (IRE) (88) (CPEBrooks) **7-10-7**(7) MBerry (hld up: hdwy 7th: led appr 4 out: rdn out)	—	1	8/1^{3}	106	—
2691^{2}	**Guinda (IRE) (111)** (NATwiston-Davies) **7-11-6** TJMurphy (lw: chsd ldrs: rdn 4 out: wnt 2nd next: no imp)	2½	2	8/11^{1}	110	—
2658^{P}	**Jasilu** (KCBailey) **7-11-12b** JRailton (lw: led tl appr 4 out: rdn & outpcd fr next)	13	3	10/1	106	—
2756^{3}	**Pearl's Choice (IRE) (87)** (JCMcConnochie) **9-11-0** BPowell (chsd ldr: blnd 11th: wknd appr 4 out)	1½	4	10/1	92	—
2657^{6}	**Wonderfull Polly (IRE) (87)** (PFNicholls) **9-10-9**(5) OBurrows (hld up: effrt appr 4 out: nt rch ldrs)	6	5	10/1	88	—
1819^{5}	**Captiva Bay (69)** (MrsARHewitt) **8-11-0** SWynne (swtg: prom to 10th: grad faded: t.o)	18	6	66/1	73	—
2660^{P}	**Mammy's Choice (IRE) (95)** (RHAlner) **7-11-9**(3) PHenley (lw: chsd ldrs: wkng whn mstke 10th: t.o)	12	7	7/1^{2}	76	—
	Lambrini (IRE) (DMcCain) **7-11-0** TJenks (bit bkwd: hld up in rr: mstke 8th: t.o)	5	8	66/1	60	—
1947^{7}	**Bournel (76)** (CRBarwell) **9-11-0v** RichardGuest (bit bkwd: bhd: reminders 6th: pckd 8th: t.o)	17	9	66/1	46	—
2546^{15}	**Becky's Girl** (RBrotherton) **7-11-0** LHarvey (a bhd: t.o)	hd	10	66/1	46	—
2664^{P}	**Mini Fete (FR)** (KRBurke) **8-11-0** ALarnach (a bhd: t.o fr 9th)	8	11	66/1	40	—
				(SP 116.2%)	**11 Rn**	

5m 2.7 CSF £13.55 TOTE £8.00: £1.70 £1.20 £2.00 (£8.60) Trio £14.20 OWNER Dr P. P. Brown (LAMBOURN) BRED Mrs F. P. Downes

Harvest View (IRE), out of action since falling over hurdles in the spring of last year, overcame her burly appearance to make an ideal start to her chasing career. She looks a promising recruit. (8/1: 6/1-9/1)

2691 Guinda (IRE), tackling a longer trip for the first time this season, was making hard work of it from the turn into the straight and, though she never stopped trying, found the concession of so much weight beyond her. (8/11)

1865* Jasilu tried to put the emphasis on stamina, but was in trouble approaching the third last and could do nothing more. (10/1)

2756 Pearl's Choice (IRE), determined to keep tabs on the leader, was beginning to feel the strain when a bad mistake was the final straw for her. (10/1)

2657 Wonderfull Polly (IRE) has yet to prove she stays this trip, and although she was nursed round in an attempt to make sure, she could not get close enough to cause concern. (10/1: 5/1-11/1)

3044 PERTEMPS CREAM NOVICES' H'CAP CHASE (5-Y.O+) (Class C)
2-10 (2-11) **2m 5f (16 fncs)** £8,793.00 (£2,664.00: £1,302.00: £621.00) GOING minus 0.17 sec per fur (G)

	Horse		Pos	SP	RR	SF
2748*	**Bell Staffboy (IRE) (117)** (JGMO'Shea) **8-11-5**(5) MichaelBrennan (lw: hld up: hdwy 8th: led 4 out: clr 2 out: drvn out)	—	1	2/1^{1}	125	33
2628*	**Noyan (110)** (RAFahey) **7-10-12**(5) MrRThornton (lw: swtg: hld up: hdwy 8th: j.rt 11th: chsd wnr fr 3 out: no imp)	9	2	2/1^{1}	111	19
2691^{4}	**Who Is Equiname (IRE) (105)** (NJHenderson) **7-10-12** JRKavanagh (hld up & bhd: styd on fr 3 out: nvr nrr)	11	3	8/1^{3}	98	6
2695*	**Khalidi (IRE) (107)** (DRGandolfo) **8-11-0** RJohnson (w ldr tl outpcd 12th: sn btn)	1½	4	6/1^{2}	99	7
1951^{5}	**Bit of A Touch (93)** (RGFrost) **11-10-0** BPowell (bit bkwd: prom: lost pl whn blnd 8th: t.o fr 10th)	dist	5	14/1	—	—
2867^{4}	**Exterior Profiles (IRE) (110)** (NATwiston-Davies) **7-11-3** TJMurphy (lw: led to 4 out: 3rd whn blnd & uns rdr next)		U	6/1^{2}	—	—
				(SP 113.0%)	**6 Rn**	

5m 12.5 (7.50) CSF £6.23 TOTE £3.20: £1.80 £1.90 (£3.10) OWNER K W Bell & Son Ltd (WESTBURY-ON-SEVERN) BRED Maurice Fenton

LONG HANDICAP Bit of A Touch 9-13

2748* Bell Staffboy (IRE) is back to his best this term, and gained another runaway success from the top of the handicap. It only goes to show what a really useful individual he is. (2/1)

2628* Noyan is no slouch himself, but the winner handed out a comprehensive beating and there was no excuse. (2/1)

2691 Who Is Equiname (IRE) had little more than a school round, and his final placing was as close as he got. (8/1)

2695* Khalidi (IRE) had plenty of use made of him over him over this longer trip and, after being shaken off at the end of the back straight, was no further danger. (6/1)

2867 Exterior Profiles (IRE), still a bit hairy with his jumping, looked to have shot his bolt when he blundered away his pilot at the final ditch. (6/1)

3045 LADBROKE H'CAP HURDLE (0-145) (4-Y.O+) (Class B)
2-40 (2-40) **2m 6f 110y (12 hdls)** £10,679.25 (£3,234.00: £1,579.50: £752.25) GOING minus 0.17 sec per fur (G)

	Horse		Pos	SP	RR	SF
1709*	**Supreme Lady (IRE) (119)** (MissHCKnight) **6-11-0** JCulloty (lw: hld up in rr: stdy hdwy appr 3 out: chal 2 out: sn led: comf)	—	1	5/1^{3}	103+	47
2062^{3}	**House Captain (120)** (JGFitzGerald) **8-10-12**(3) FLeahy (hld up: hdwy 8th: rdn appr last: kpt on)	3½	2	7/2^{1}	102	46
1982*	**Freddie Muck (129)** (NATwiston-Davies) **7-11-10** TJenks (a.p: led 3 out tl after next: rdn & no ex flat)	hd	3	13/2	110	54
1316	**All On (109)** (JHetherton) **6-10-4** TJMurphy (dropped rr ½-wy: styd on again fr 3 out)	6	4	33/1	86	30
1959*	**Lets Be Frank (105)** (NoelChance) **6-10-0** RJohnson (chsd ldrs: disp ld 4 out & next: rdn & wknd 2 out)	5	5	6/1	79	23
	Linton Rocks (120) (TThomsonJones) **8-11-1** BPowell (bkwd: chsd ldrs tl wknd appr 3 out)	4	6	20/1	91	35
2078*	**Arithmetic (117)** (MrsJPitman) **7-10-12** WMarston (lw: led to 3 out: sn rdn & wknd: t.o)	28	7	9/2^{2}	68	12
2644^{8}	**Call My Guest (IRE) (119)** (REPeacock) **7-11-0b^{1}** RichardGuest (hdwy 5th: sn chsng ldrs: wknd 4 out: t.o)	12	8	33/1	61	5
2702*	**Nick the Beak (IRE) (111)** (JohnUpson) **8-9-13**(7) GSupple (lw: prom tl wknd appr 4 out: t.o)	s.h	9	13/2	53	—
2637^{5}	**Ruling (USA) (127)** (KRBurke) **11-11-3**(5) MrRThornton (bit bkwd: bhd: pushed along ½-wy: no ch whn p.u flat: lame)		P	33/1	—	—
208*	**Gimme (IRE) (105)** (JGMO'Shea) **7-9-9v**(5) MichaelBrennan (bit bkwd: lost pl 6th: t.o: p.u bef 4 out)		P	33/1	—	—
				(SP 114.5%)	**11 Rn**	

5m 17.7 (0.70) CSF £19.36 CT £102.36 TOTE £6.60: £1.80 £1.50 £1.90 (£10.20) Trio £21.50 OWNER The Supreme Lady Partnership (WANTAGE) BRED Mrs Anne Kerr

LONG HANDICAP Lets Be Frank 9-10 Gimme (IRE) 9-13

1709* Supreme Lady (IRE) continued to step up in distance with a very smoothly-gained success, and will now be aimed at the Coral Cup at the Festival. (5/1)

2062 House Captain ran well and, though he had little chance with the easy winner, showed he is coming back to something like his best. (7/2)

1982* Freddie Muck threw down the gauntlet turning in, but could not get away from the winner and, though he kept battling away, had met his match from the last. (13/2)

16 All On lost her pitch going out into the country and was soon shuffled back to the rear, but she was picking up in the latter stages and, if lowered in class, could return to form. (33/1)
1959* Lets Be Frank, taking a big step-up in class and running from 4lb out of the handicap, shared the lead three out and only got left behind from the next. He is capable of winning again, but as yet it would not be at this level. (6/1)
Linton Rocks had not run for 21 months, and though he was leg-weary inside the last half-mile, does look to have retained his ability. (20/1)

3046 SINGER & FRIEDLANDER NATIONAL TRIAL H'CAP CHASE (6-Y.O+) (Class B)

3-10 (3-10) **4m 2f (24 fncs)** £24,136.80 (£9,031.20: £4,415.60: £1,898.00: £849.00: £429.40) GOING minus 0.17 sec per fur (G)

				SP	RR	SF
2758*	**Lord Gyllene (NZ) (132)** (SABrookshaw) **9-11-9** RJohnson (lw: j.w: mde all: clr 2 out: styd on strly)	—	1	11/8 1	152+	39
2637 4	**Mudahim (125)** (MrsJPitman) **11-11-2** WMarston (bit bkwd: chsd wnr fr 5th: rdn & outpcd appr 4 out: styd on again flat)	8	2	6/1	140	27
2754*	**Court Melody (IRE) (120)** (PFNicholls) **9-10-11b** JCulloty (chsd ldr fr 7th: wnt 2nd appr 4 out: one pce fr 2 out)	1½	3	10/1	134	21
2758 2	**Samlee (IRE) (115)** (PJHobbs) **8-10-6** JRKavanagh (lw: hld up mid div: no hdwy fr 19th)	17	4	11/2 3	119	6
2782 5	**Betty's Boy (IRE) (124)** (KCBailey) **8-11-1** JRailton (hld up: stdy hdwy 18th: wknd appr 4 out)	15	5	9/1	119	6
1513 U	**Andros Prince (109)** (MissAEEmbiricos) **12-9-9**(5) MrRThornton (bit bkwd: prom tl wknd 19th: t.o)	dist	6	66/1	—	—
2881*	**Flyer's Nap (137)** (RHAlner) **11-12-0** BPowell (lw: hld up & bhd: rdn 17th: t.o whn p.u bef 2 out)		P	9/2 2	—	—
2758 9	**Church Law (109)** (MrsLCTaylor) **10-9-9**(5) SophieMitchell (a bhd: rdn 16th: t.o & p.u bef 20th)		P	25/1	—	—
2575*	**Woodlands Genhire (109)** (PAPritchard) **12-10-0b** RBellamy (t.o fr ½-wy: p.u bef 16th)		P	33/1	—	—

(SP 117.3%) **9 Rn**

8m 34.3 (12.10 under best) (9.30) CSF £9.68 CT £55.41 TOTE £2.40: £1.20 £2.50 £2.80 (£7.10) Trio £76.20 OWNER Mr Stanley Clarke (SHREWSBURY) BRED Mrs N. M. Taylor
LONG HANDICAP Andros Prince 8-12 Church Law 9-7 Woodlands Genhire 7-10
OFFICIAL EXPLANATION **Church Law: was later found to have a throat infection.**
Woodlands Genhire: finished with a sore foot.
2758* Lord Gyllene (NZ) gave another exhibition of jumping from the front and, staying on far too strongly for his pursuers, now intends to keep his record intact with a tilt at the Midlands National next month, where there is a valuable bonus to be gained. (11/8)
2637 Mudahim needs the most testing conditions to produce his best, so this promising display on ground far too lively shows that he is coming to himself and, if he gets conditions to suit, there are plenty of prizes to be had. (6/1)
2754* Court Melody (IRE), unable to get his toe in here, nevertheless was far from disgraced in this company, and he still has a good future ahead of him. (10/1)
2758 Samlee (IRE), meeting the winner on 7lb better terms for a fifteen-length beating here last month, was never really racing with any zest, and had been hung out to dry in the final mile. (11/2)
2782 Betty's Boy (IRE) did not give any encouragement as to his chances of staying the National trip. (9/1)

3047 DONCASTER BLOODSTOCK SALES BREEDERS' TROPHY NOVICES' H'CAP CHASE (6-Y.O+) (Class C)

3-40 (3-44) **3m 2f (20 fncs)** £14,720.00 (£4,460.00: £2,180.00: £1,040.00) GOING minus 0.17 sec per fur (G)

				SP	RR	SF
1918 2	**General Pongo (100)** (TRGeorge) **8-10-0** RFarrant (sn prom: led 15th: styd on strly)	—	1	8/1	111	—
2767 P	**Lord of the West (IRE) (107)** (JJO'Neill) **8-10-7** AThornton (hld up: hit 8th: hdwy 14th: styd on appr last)	1½	2	25/1	117	6
2658 F	**What's Your Story (IRE) (111)** (DNicholson) **8-10-11** RJohnson (hld up mid div: hdwy 16th: styd on one pce fr 3 out)	6	3	14/1	117	6
2809*	**Flimsy Truth (104)** (MHWeston) **11-9-13**(5) MrRThornton (led 4th to 5th: wknd appr 4 out)	6	4	10/1	107	—
2667 4	**Karar (IRE) (101)** (RRowe) **7-10-1**ow1 DO'Sullivan (hld up & bhd: stdy hdwy fr 16th: nt rch ldrs)	11	5	11/1	97	—
2760 2	**Feel the Power (IRE) (128)** (KCBailey) **9-12-0** JRailton (lw: hld up in rr: hdwy 16th: blnd 4 out & 3 out: sn wknd: t.o)	28	6	16/1	107	—
2693*	**Sir Leonard (IRE) (117)** (OSherwood) **7-11-3** JAMcCarthy (wl bhd: hdwy 13th: sn drvn along: wknd appr 4 out: t.o)	12	7	11/2 2	88	—
2660*	**Orswell Lad (112)** (PJHobbs) **8-10-12** LHarvey (lw: trckd ldrs: lost pl ½-wy: t.o: p.u bef 4 out)		P	8/1	—	—
2749*	**God Speed You (IRE) (108)** (CPMorlock) **8-10-5b**(3) DFortt (lw: led to 4th: led 5th to 15th: wknd qckly: t.o: p.u bef 2 out)		P	7/1 3	—	—
2698 2	**Hatcham Boy (IRE) (114)** (DNicholson) **7-11-0** WMarston (chsd ldrs to 15th: wkng whn blnd next: p.u bef 4 out)		P	10/1	—	—
2658 2	**Well Timed (100)** (RGFrost) **7-10-0** BPowell (prom to 4 out: p.u bef next)		P	14/1	—	—
2672 4	**Major Look (NZ) (107)** (SABrookshaw) **9-10-7** RichardGuest (trckd ldrs to 16th: bhd whn p.u bef 2 out)		P	16/1	—	—
2754 2	**Little Martina (IRE) (109)** (DMGrissell) **9-10-9** JRKavanagh (prom to 6th: t.o: p.u bef 10th)		P	5/1 1	—	—

(SP 122.2%) **13 Rn**

6m 41.1 (14.10) CSF £165.77 CT £2,513.03 TOTE £11.10: £3.10 £6.60 £3.80 (£114.10) Trio £576.70; £341.18 to Hereford 10/2/97. OWNER Mrs J. K. Powell (ROSS-ON-WYE) BRED R. R. Evans Bloodstock Ltd
LONG HANDICAP Well Timed 9-7 General Pongo 9-11
OFFICIAL EXPLANATION **Little Martina (IRE): lost her action after putting her back legs in the water jump.**
1918 General Pongo, always travelling well within himself, took over just inside the last mile and, staying on particularly well, was always holding the challenge of the runner-up. This extended trip could be what he needs. (8/1)
2767 Lord of the West (IRE) made the odd mistake but never looked like falling and, with his undoubted stamina coming into play, kept the winner up to his work right to the end. (25/1)
1447 What's Your Story (IRE) took closer order on the home turn, but could not get himself into the action, although it must be said a clear round was the main objective, after failing to complete on his only outings over fences. (14/1)
2809* Flimsy Truth, always prepared to take on the leaders, had to admit the quickening tempo too much for him from the turn into the straight. (10/1)
2667 Karar (IRE) had everything in his favour here, but he was never put into the race with a serious chance. (11/1)
2760 Feel the Power (IRE) ran no race at all. (16/1)
2749* God Speed You (IRE) pressed the leaders for the first mile, but dropped away and was pulled up at halfway. (7/1)

3048 BBC RADIO STOKE NOVICES' HURDLE (5-Y.O+) (Class C)

4-10 (4-14) **3m 110y (14 hdls)** £3,891.25 (£1,180.00: £577.50: £276.25) GOING minus 0.17 sec per fur (G)

				SP	RR	SF
2662 2	**Mentmore Towers (IRE)** (MrsJPitman) **5-10-12** RFarrant (lw: chsd ldrs: led 10th: clr appr last: comf)	—	1	9/4 1	85+	12
2759*	**Barton Ward (108)** (SABrookshaw) **6-11-3** RichardGuest (lw: hld up: hdwy 8th: chsd wnr 3 out: no imp)	12	2	3/1 2	82	9

	Horse	Details	Dist	Pos	SP	RR	SF
2663[4]	**Banny Hill Lad**	(CPMorlock) **7-10-9**(3) DFortt (hld up: hdwy 6th: wknd appr 2 out)	20	**3**	25/1	64	—
	Stormy Session	(NATwiston-Davies) **7-10-12** TJMurphy (bkwd: hld up: hdwy 7th: wknd 3 out)	6	**4**	20/1	60	—
1840*	**Copper Coil (94)**	(WGMTurner) **7-10-10**(7) JPower (chsd ldrs tl wknd appr 3 out)	1¾	**5**	14/1	64	—
2701[2]	**Love The Blues (105)**	(DNicholson) **5-10-7** RJohnson (hld up: nvr nr to chal)	9	**6**	7/2[3]	48	—
2656[P]	**Classic Chat**	(JLSpearing) **5-10-7**(5) MichaelBrennan (lost pl 5th: sn t.o)	19	**7**	66/1	41	—
2546[8]	**Jobsagoodun**	(NJHenderson) **6-10-12** JRKavanagh (prom to 9th: sn rdn & lost pl: t.o)	s.h	**8**	11/2	41	—
2042[6]	**Old Cavalier**	(JJO'Neill) **6-10-12** AThornton (led to 10th: wknd appr 3 out: t.o)	3	**9**	20/1	39	—
2662[8]	**Westcote Lad**	(WJenks) **8-10-12** TJenks (hdwy 5th: wknd 10th: t.o)	30	**10**	66/1	19	—
2822[4]	**Coole Cherry**	(CRBarwell) **7-10-12** BPowell (disp ld to 10th: wknd qckly: t.o)	8	**11**	33/1	14	—
	Granham Pride (IRE)	(KCBailey) **7-10-12** JRailton (bkwd: hld up in rr: t.o: p.u bef 3 out)		**P**	10/1	—	—
2037[F]	**The Wayward Bishop (IRE) (75)**	(MrsLCTaylor) **8-10-12b** DLeahy (trckd ldrs to 8th: t.o: p.u bef 3 out)		**P**	66/1	—	—
1541[P]	**Southsea Scandals (IRE)**	(KBishop) **6-10-12** RGreene (chsd ldrs to 9th: sn wknd: t.o: p.u bef 4 out)		**P**	40/1	—	—

(SP 132.4%) **14 Rn**

5m 53.7 (11.70) CSF £8.69 TOTE £3.60: £1.60 £1.60 £9.60 (£3.90) Trio £238.10; £137.51 to Hereford 10/2/97. OWNER Mr Philip Matton (UPPER LAMBOURN) BRED Pat Hickey

OFFICIAL EXPLANATION **The Wayward Bishop: was later found to have a throat infection.**

2662 Mentmore Towers (IRE), in his element over this longer trip, shook off the challenge of the runner-up with ease, and won going away. (9/4)

2759* Barton Ward, full of running when moving onto the heels of the leaders turning in, could not respond when popped the question, and is not yet seeing the trip out. (3/1)

2074 Banny Hill Lad had to admit the principals too strong for him in the last half-mile, but is still short of experience and there could be better to come. (25/1)

Stormy Session was unable to get near enough to land a blow, but he will improve for this run. (20/1)

1840* Copper Coil was a live threat until feeling the strain on the turn for home. (14/1)

2701 Love The Blues tried to get herself into contention on the approach to the third last, but she did not appear to be putting much effort into it and was never a serious factor. (7/2)

Granham Pride (IRE) (10/1: op 6/1)

3049 WELLMAN PLC NOVICES' H'CAP HURDLE (0-105) (4-Y.O+) (Class E)

4-40 (4-43) **2m (10 hdls)** £2,347.50 (£660.00: £322.50) GOING minus 0.17 sec per fur (G)

	Horse	Details	Dist	Pos	SP	RR	SF
1356[P]	**Globe Runner (91)**	(JJO'Neill) **4-10-6** ARoche (a.p: led 2 out: drvn clr flat)	—	**1**	6/1[3]	76	—
2771[8]	**Samanid (IRE) (99)**	(MissLCSiddall) **5-11-10** OPears (lw: hld up & bhd: hdwy 7th: ev ch 2 out: hrd rdn & unable qckn flat)	2½	**2**	14/1	82	9
2861[2]	**Take Cover (IRE) (92)**	(MHTompkins) **6-11-3** RichardGuest (a.p: led appr 3 out to 2 out: rdn & btn last)	7	**3**	4/1[2]	68	—
2859[3]	**Arabian Heights (89)**	(JMackie) **4-10-4** WMarston (lw: chsd ldrs: outpcd 4 out: rallied 3 out: no imp fr next)	7	**4**	5/2[1]	58	—
2806[8]	**Alpha Leather (75)**	(LPGrassick) **6-10-0** MrJGrassick (bhd: rdn 5th: no imp)	7	**5**	33/1	37	—
2874[7]	**Nagara Sound (80)**	(BPreece) **6-9-12**(7) JMogford (nvr nr to chal)	2½	**6**	12/1	39	—
2759[9]	**Prussia (98)**	(WClay) **6-11-9** RJohnson (led tl appr 3 out: sn rdn & outpcd)	nk	**7**	13/2	57	—
2870[6]	**Snowshill Shaker (85)**	(NATwiston-Davies) **8-10-10** TJenks (chsd ldrs: rdn & wknd after 4 out: t.o)	9	**8**	9/1	35	—
2842[8]	**Bowles Patrol (IRE) (75)**	(JohnUpson) **5-9-7**(7) GSupple (mid div tl wknd appr 3 out: t.o)	4	**9**	20/1	21	—
1908*	**Toulston Lady (IRE) (75)**	(JWharton) **5-9-9b**(5) MrRThornton (lw: a.p: 3rd & btn whn fell last)		**F**	8/1	51?	—
1816[10]	**Out of The Blue (75)**	(MWEckley) **5-10-0** PMcLoughlin (blnd & uns rdr 1st)		**U**	33/1	—	—

(SP 122.3%) **11 Rn**

3m 51.6 (10.60) CSF £77.61 CT £346.23 TOTE £8.80: £2.60 £3.50 £1.60 (£48.00) Trio £48.70 OWNER G & P Barker Ltd/Globe Engineering (PENRITH) BRED Badger Hill Stud

LONG HANDICAP Alpha Leather 9-1 Bowles Patrol (IRE) 9-3 Toulston Lady (IRE) 9-11 Out of The Blue 8-13

WEIGHT FOR AGE 4yo-10lb

1356 Globe Runner had far more use made of him and, after taking command two out, only had to be kept up to his work to get off the mark. (6/1)

2074 Samanid (IRE) looked to be going best when making smooth progress entering the straight, but he did not find the expected amount when let down. Edging left under pressure on the flat, he was never going to trouble the winner. (14/1)

2861 Take Cover (IRE), well placed throughout the race, was always going to be the one to beat, but he proved very one-paced after being collared, and may need matters all his own way. (4/1)

2859 Arabian Heights, inclined to run in snatches, was in trouble in the straight, and could have two ways of running. (5/2)

Nagara Sound (12/1: op 8/1)

1908* Toulston Lady (IRE) pushed the pace all the way, but appeared to be getting the worst of the battle when she crash-landed at the last. She has got plenty to learn about hurdling, but has ability and may benefit from racing over further. (8/1)

T/Plpt: £53.70 (440.88 Tckts). T/Qdpt: £29.50 (32.97 Tckts) IM

2100-HEREFORD (R-H) (Good to soft, Good patches)

Monday February 10th

WEATHER: rain

3050 EWYAS HAROLD NOVICES' H'CAP HURDLE (0-90) (4-Y.O+) (Class F)

2-00 (2-00) **2m 1f (9 hdls)** £2,570.00 (£720.00: £350.00) GOING: 0.55 sec per fur (S)

	Horse	Details	Dist	Pos	SP	RR	SF
1992[6]	**Ranger Sloane (74)**	(GFierro) **5-10-13** RFarrant (hld up: stdy hdwy 4th: led after 2 out: r.o wl)	—	**1**	25/1	61	31
1581[6]	**Operetto (IRE) (76)**	(MrsSusanNock) **7-11-1** GBradley (a.p: rdn & ev ch 3 out: r.o one pce fr 2 out)	5	**2**	8/1	58	28
1327[P]	**Sylvester (IRE) (73)**	(MissAEBroyd) **7-10-7**(5) MichaelBrennan (hld up: hdwy appr 5th: ev ch 3 out: one pce fr 2 out)	1	**3**	40/1	54	24
2680[6]	**O My Love (78)**	(MissHCKnight) **6-11-3** JOsborne (a.p: led 5th tl after 2 out: one pce)	1¼	**4**	8/1	58	28
2806[2]	**Fastini Gold (77)**	(RJPrice) **5-11-2** RJohnson (hld up: hdwy 6th: ev ch 3 out: wknd appr last)	4	**5**	13/2[3]	53	23
2874[2]	**Almapa (83)**	(RJHodges) **5-11-5**(3) TDascombe (hld up: hdwy appr 5th: wknd appr 2 out)	3	**6**	10/1	57	27
1393[3]	**The Carrot Man (85)**	(PWinkworth) **9-11-3**(7) XAizpuru (bit bkwd: prom to 6th)	9	**7**	8/1	50	20
2813[3]	**Fleet Cadet (87)**	(MCPipe) **6-11-12v** JamieEvans (hld up: stdy hdwy appr 5th: wknd appr 2 out)	12	**8**	6/1[2]	41	11
	Happy Brave (78)	(PDCundell) **5-11-3** LHarvey (bkwd: hld up: hdwy appr 5th: wknd appr 3 out)	7	**9**	14/1	25	—
1427[U]	**Saafi (IRE) (75)**	(RJBaker) **6-11-0** VSlattery (bkwd: a bhd)	11	**10**	33/1	12	—

2578[3] **Ath Cheannaithe (FR) (82)** (JNeville) **5-11-7** NWilliamson (led 2nd tl 4th: wknd after 6th)....1¼ **11** 10/1 18 —
Flashman (80) (BJLlewellyn) **7-11-5** MrJLLlewellyn (bkwd: a bhd: t.o fr 5th)....12 **12** 14/1 4 —
2897[6] **High Post (80)** (GAHam) **8-11-2**(3) RMassey (bhd tl fell 6th).... **F** 12/1 — —
2705* **Lady Magnum (IRE) (93)** (JNeville) **4-11-8** NMann (a bhd: t.o whn p.u bef 3 out).... **P** 5/1[1] — —
2690[13] **Glenmavis (80)** (DrPPritchard) **10-11-5** DrPPritchard (led to 2nd: led 4th to 5th: wknd appr 3 out: bhd whn p.u bef last).... **P** 40/1 — —
2692[2] **Storm Tiger (IRE) (75)** (SMellor) **6-10-11v**(3) EHusband (prom to 6th: t.o whn p.u bef 2 out).... **P** 5/1[1] — —
(SP 145.2%) **16 Rn**

4m 9.1 (16.10) CSF £225.18 CT £7,226.51 TOTE £38.60: £5.30 £2.90 £8.30 £2.10 (£108.80) Trio Not won; £256.14 to Leicester 11/2/97
OWNER Mr G. Fierro (HEDNESFORD) BRED T. Barratt
WEIGHT FOR AGE 4yo-10lb
OFFICIAL EXPLANATION Lady Magnum (IRE): made a mistake at the first flight and was not suited by the ground.
1992 Ranger Sloane is considered to need further - so the morning rain helped. (25/1)
Operetto (IRE), dropping back in distance, was trying his luck in a handicap. (8/1)
Sylvester (IRE) ran by far his best race to date. (40/1)
2680 O My Love, a sister to a winner between the flags, may do better on really good ground. (8/1)
2806 Fastini Gold was not helped by the easing in the ground. (13/2)
2874 Almapa, up 3lb, is another who prefers top of the ground. (10/1)
2705* Lady Magnum (IRE) was reported not to have been suited by the soft ground. (5/1)
2692 Storm Tiger (IRE) had been raised 8lb after his good effort in a first-time visor. (5/1)

3051 WORMELOW NOVICES' H'CAP CHASE (0-100) (5-Y.O+) (Class E)

2-30 (2-30) **2m 3f (14 fncs)** £3,100.00 (£940.00: £460.00: £220.00) GOING: 0.55 sec per fur (S)

SP RR SF
2795* **Cardinal Rule (IRE) (73)** (MissVenetiaWilliams) **8-10-7** NWilliamson (mde all: mstke 3rd: clr whn pckd last).— **1** 4/1[1] 90 20
2693[9] **Boots N All (IRE) (70)** (GBBalding) **7-10-4** WMarston (a.p: ev ch 3 out: sn rdn: one pce)....4 **2** 16/1 84 14
2577[4] **Chris's Glen (75)** (JMBradley) **8-10-9v** RJohnson (lw: prom: wknd appr 3 out: 3rd & no ch whn blnd 2 out) .dist **3** 14/1 — —
2796[3] **Olliver Duckett (84)** (CLPopham) **8-11-4** GTormey (prom tl wknd 10th)....1¾ **4** 11/2[2] — —
2884[11] **Manolete (87)** (MrsMerritaJones) **6-11-7** DerekByrne (a bhd: t.o fr 8th)....2½ **5** 9/1 — —
2091[2] **Eulogy (FR) (82)** (KRBurke) **10-11-2** ALarnach (rdn after 5th: bhd fr 8th: t.o)....7 **6** 10/1 — —
2841[9] **Jolly Boat (90)** (FJordan) **10-11-10** SWynne (bhd fr 7th: t.o)....5 **7** 14/1 — —
2906[4] **Castleconner (IRE) (82)** (RGFrost) **6-11-2** JFrost (bhd: mstke 2nd: t.o fr 7th)....2½ **8** 10/1 — —
2823[7] **Bathwick Bobbie (78)** (DLWilliams) **10-10-12** SMcNeill (bhd fr 8th: t.o)....20 **9** 20/1 — —
1963[7] **Night Fancy (69)** (MrsAMWoodrow) **9-10-3** JRKavanagh (a bhd: t.o fr 8th)....2½ **10** 25/1 — —
2940[2] **King's Shilling (USA) (79)** (HOliver) **10-10-13** JacquiOliver (chsd ldrs: wknd appr 3 out: 3rd & no ch whn fell last).... **F** 7/1[3] — —
2870[P] **Hello Me Man (IRE) (74)** (BJLlewellyn) **9-10-8** ILawrence (bhd fr 7th: t.o whn p.u bef 3 out).... **P** 20/1 — —
2076[7] **Quite A Man (83)** (SABrookshaw) **9-11-3** TEley (bit bkwd: t.o whn blnd 10th: p.u bef 4 out).... **P** 9/1 — —
2795[8] **Mel (IRE) (71)** (RHBuckler) **7-10-5** BPowell (t.o fr 7th: p.u bef 4 out).... **P** 20/1 — —
Colonel Colt (75) (RDickin) **6-10-9** JCulloty (bkwd: bhd: mstke 6th: t.o whn p.u bef 4 out).... **P** 16/1 — —
2577[6] **Gordon (87)** (PRWebber) **6-11-7** JOsborne (lw: a bhd: t.o whn p.u bef 4 out).... **P** 14/1 — —
(SP 136.0%) **16 Rn**

4m 49.5 (19.50) CSF £63.67 CT £797.57 TOTE £3.80: £2.10 £2.70 £2.80 £2.70 (£45.50) Trio £150.60; £171.83 to Leicester 11/2/97 OWNER Mr Peter Burch (HEREFORD) BRED Mrs Patricia Mackean
2795* Cardinal Rule (IRE), raised 7lb, really finds this trip on the short side, but his trainer thought that the cut in the ground helped. (4/1)
Boots N All (IRE) finished second in four of his five Irish point-to-points, and was the only one to make a race of it. (16/1)
2577 Chris's Glen, not suited by the rain-softened ground, was out on his feet when losing third at the penultimate fence, only to be handed it back at the last. (14/1)
2796 Olliver Duckett, 8lb higher than when winning at Taunton, wants faster ground than he encountered here. (11/2)
Manolete (9/1: 12/1-8/1)
2940 King's Shilling (USA), dropping back in trip, has once won on soft but is better on good or faster ground. (7/1)

3052 HOECHST ROUSSEL PANACUR E.B.F. 'N.H.' (QUALIFIER) NOVICES' HURDLE (5-Y.O+ Mares Only) (Class E)

3-00 (3-01) **2m 3f 110y (11 hdls)** £2,598.00 (£728.00: £354.00) GOING: 0.55 sec per fur (S)

SP RR SF
2840[3] **Halona (96)** (CPEBrooks) **7-10-12** GBradley (lw: led 2nd: sn clr: blnd 2 out: rdn out).... — **1** 11/10[1] 73 —
1998[3] **Moonlighter (66)** (CFCJackson) **7-10-7**(5) OBurrows (hld up: hdwy 6th: chsd wnr after 8th: rdn & r.o one pce flat)....2 **2** 10/1 71 —
1685[8] **Kosheen (IRE)** (MissHCKnight) **6-10-12** JCulloty (bit bkwd: a.p: one pce fr 8th)....17 **3** 6/1[3] 57 —
2870[5] **Quick Quote (85)** (MrsIMcKie) **7-10-12** LHarvey (hld up: stdy hdwy 6th: one pce fr 8th)....3 **4** 5/1[2] 55 —
1450[7] **Fun While It Lasts** (CaptTAForster) **6-10-12** SWynne (bhd fr 6th: t.o)....26 **5** 20/1 34 —
Arctic Muse (PJHobbs) **6-10-12** GTormey (bit bkwd: lost pl 6th: sme hdwy whn mstke 7th: sn wknd: t.o) .....30 **6** 33/1 9 —
2656[P] **Madam Polly** (MissPMWhittle) **5-10-5**(7) KHibbert (prom to 6th: t.o)....12 **7** 33/1 — —
2634[8] **Club Caribbean** (PJHobbs) **5-10-12** NWilliamson (prom: chsd wnr fr 6th tl wknd after 8th: t.o)....2½ **8** 14/1 — —
2656[P] **Lady of Mine** (PBowen) **7-10-12** RJohnson (led to 2nd: wkng whn blnd 8th: t.o)....½ **9** 33/1 — —
Faithlegg (IRE) (NJHenderson) **6-10-12** JRKavanagh (bkwd: hld up: hdwy 5th: wknd 8th: bhd whn p.u bef last).... **P** 13/2 — —
1998[14] **Pharmorefun (IRE)** (GBBalding) **5-10-12** BClifford (bhd: mstke 5th: t.o whn p.u bef 2 out).... **P** 33/1 — —
1450[8] **Lady Rosebury** (RJPrice) **7-10-9**(3) TDascombe (bhd whn rdn after 5th: t.o whn p.u bef 7th).... **P** 33/1 — —
Pennyahei (SABrookshaw) **6-10-12** TEley (a bhd: t.o whn p.u bef 2 out).... **P** 33/1 — —
2661[14] **Elly's Dream** (PCRitchens) **6-10-12** SFox (bhd: mstke 1st: t.o whn p.u bef 7th).... **P** 33/1 — —
1177[10] **Miss Starteam** (RGFrost) **7-10-12** JFrost (bkwd: a bhd: t.o whn p.u bef 3 out).... **P** 50/1 — —
2875[8] **Sula's Dream** (GAHam) **8-10-9**(3) RMassey (a bhd: t.o whn p.u bef 3 out).... **P** 50/1 — —
(SP 136.9%) **16 Rn**

4m 58.2 (27.20) CSF £13.20 TOTE £2.10: £1.60 £3.10 £2.20 (£6.90) Trio £29.10 OWNER Mrs Z. S. Clark (LAMBOURN) BRED Mrs Z. S. Clark
2840 Halona, wearing a net muzzle and with a longer trip to help, has been coming up against a better-class animal than these. (11/10: op 4/6)
1998 Moonlighter showed her Exeter run to be no fluke, and would appear to be on the upgrade. (10/1)
1450 Kosheen (IRE) had previously shown form in bumpers. (6/1)
1855 Quick Quote looks short of pace, and those who finished well-beaten behind her are probably very moderate. (5/1)

3053 WEATHERBYS LEASING DIRECTORY H'CAP CHASE (0-100) (5-Y.O+) (Class F)
3-30 (3-31) **2m (12 fncs)** £2,840.00 (£860.00: £420.00: £200.00) GOING: 0.55 sec per fur (S)

				SP	RR	SF
1696[P]	**Thats the Life (75)** (TRGeorge) **12-10-3** RJohnson (mde all: mstkes 3 out & 2 out: sn hrd rdn: r.o wl)	—	1	14/1	86	16
2674[5]	**Dr Rocket (82)** (RDickin) **12-10-3b**(7) XAizpuru (chsd wnr: hrd rdn appr last: no imp)	3½	2	6/1[2]	90	20
2657[7]	**Blazer Moriniere (FR) (84)** (PCRitchens) **8-10-12** SFox (a.p: outpcd 8th: rallied appr 3 out: one pce)	4	3	16/1	88	18
2962[4]	**Fenwick (85)** (RJHodges) **10-10-10**(3) TDascombe (prom: hrd rdn & wknd appr 4 out)	14	4	8/1[3]	75	5
2796[9]	**Pegmarine (USA) (79)** (MrsAMWoodrow) **14-10-7** NWilliamson (lw: a bhd: t.o)	dist	5	14/1	—	—
	Swahili Run (82) (JGMO'Shea) **9-10-5**(5) MichaelBrennan (bkwd: fell 1st)		F	14/1	—	—
1769[4]	**Monks Jay (IRE) (88)** (GThorner) **8-11-2** ILawrence (bit bkwd: bhd: mstke 4th: t.o whn p.u bef 2 out)		P	8/1[3]	—	—
2796[F]	**Halham Tarn (IRE) (90)** (HJManners) **7-10-11**(7) ADowling (mstke 2nd: bhd whn hit 7th: t.o whn p.u bef last)		P	20/1	—	—
2873[U]	**Northern Singer (81)** (RJHodges) **7-10-9** BPowell (hld up: mstke 4th: hdwy 7th: wknd 4 out: p.u bef last)		P	5/2[1]	—	—
1983[F]	**Leinthall Princess (77)** (JLNeedham) **11-10-5** MissPJones (bit bkwd: a bhd: t.o 7th: p.u bef last)		P	16/1	—	—
2796[8]	**Rustic Gent (IRE) (72)** (MrsLCJewell) **9-10-0v** DLeahy (prom to 8th: bhd whn blnd bdly 3 out: p.u bef 2 out)		P	33/1	—	—
2796[4]	**Winspit (IRE) (86)** (RHAlner) **7-11-0** JRKavanagh (lw: bhd fr 6th: blnd & uns rdr 4 out)		U	6/1[2]	—	—
2089[6]	**Fairy Park (84)** (HOliver) **12-10-5v**(7) MrHJOliver (bhd tl blnd & uns rdr 3 out)		U	12/1	—	—
1696[6]	**Prudent Peggy (72)** (RGFrost) **10-10-0** MrAHoldsworth (prom to 7th: bhd whn blnd & uns rdr 2 out)		U	14/1	—	—

(SP 133.2%) **14 Rn**

4m 7.7 (16.70) CSF £98.05 CT £1,290.50 TOTE £17.80: £3.60 £1.90 £3.10 (£62.20) Trio £847.30 OWNER Ms Liz Kilfeather (ROSS-ON-WYE) BRED B. J. Maye

LONG HANDICAP Prudent Peggy 9-11

OFFICIAL EXPLANATION **Thats The Life: had been unsuited by the heavy ground on his previous run.**

1328 Thats the Life was considered to have been unsuited by the heavy ground when pulled up at Newton Abbot at the beginning of December. (14/1)

2674 Dr Rocket, dropped 4lb, tried his best but could not take advantage of the winner's two mistakes. (6/1)

Blazer Moriniere (FR), five times a winner over hurdles and fences in France, gave a good account of himself off a 6lb lower mark than when making his chasing debut in this country on heavy ground. (16/1)

2657 Fenwick had been outclassed at Wincanton last week. (8/1)

2569* Northern Singer may be better on a sounder surface. (5/2)

3054 ARROW MAIDEN CLAIMING HURDLE (4-Y.O+) (Class F)
4-00 (4-00) **2m 3f 110y (11 hdls)** £2,178.00 (£608.00: £294.00) GOING: Not Established

				SP	RR	SF
2752[F]	**Caracol** (JNeville) **8-11-3**(3) TDascombe (led to 3rd: led 5th: clr 6th: hit 2 out & last: rdn & edgd lft flat: r.o)	—	1	6/1	50	—
1448[4]	**Arioso (60)** (JLNeedham) **9-10-6**(5) MichaelBrennan (hld up: hdwy 6th: chsd wnr fr 7th: styng on whn n.m.r flat)	1¼	2	14/1	40	—
2805[15]	**Nicky Wilde** (CPEBrooks) **7-11-10** GBradley (t: bit bkwd: hld up: hdwy 6th: mstke 7th: j.lft 3 out: one pce)	9	3	10/1	46	—
2840[6]	**Come On In** (RDickin) **4-10-11** JCulloty (hdwy appr 7th: 4th & no ch whn mstke 2 out)	3½	4	7/1	40	—
2907[3]	**Fairelaine** (KCBailey) **5-10-12**(7) MrRWakley (bkwd: bhd tl sme hdwy fr 7th: n.d)	14	5	11/4[1]	26	—
2656[P]	**Alpine Song** (MissVAStephens) **12-10-13** MissVStephens (prom: wkng whn blnd 8th)	6	6	33/1	15	—
2818[3]	**Tread the Boards (70)** (MCPipe) **6-10-11b** JamieEvans (lw: hld up: hdwy appr 7th: mstke 8th: sn rdn & wknd)	s.h	7	7/2[2]	13	—
2655[6]	**Blade of Fortune** (VGGreenway) **9-11-8** BPowell (prom tl wknd appr 7th)	6	8	14/1	19	—
2926[P]	**Brownscroft** (MissPMWhittle) **9-10-10**(7) KHibbert (a bhd: t.o)	dist	9	33/1	—	—
1900[9]	**Noble Colours** (SGGriffiths) **4-11-5** MrJJukes (bit bkwd: prom to 8th: t.o)	5	10	11/1	—	—
2705[3]	**Eskimo Kiss (IRE)** (GFJohnsonHoughton) **4-10-6** NWilliamson (reminders appr 6th: sn bhd: t.o)	dist	11	11/2[3]	—	—
2546[13]	**Burfords For Scrap** (RDickin) **5-11-6** WMarston (prom to 6th: t.o)		12	20/1	—	—
2815[B]	**A Million Watts** (GMMcCourt) **6-11-2b** BClifford (led 3rd to 5th: wknd appr 7th: t.o)		13	14/1	—	—
2678[P]	**Tomorrows Harvest** (RJHodges) **5-10-11** ILawrence (t.o 6th: p.u bef 3 out)		P	33/1	—	—
2840[15]	**Party Lady (IRE)** (AJWilson) **8-10-13v[1]** LHarvey (t.o 5th: p.u bef 3 out)		P	33/1	—	—
1329[21]	**Arklow King (IRE)** (PWegmann) **5-12-0** GaryLyons (bkwd: a bhd: t.o 5th: p.u bef 8th)		P	50/1	—	—

(SP 147.0%) **16 Rn**

5m 3.3 (32.30) CSF £89.24 TOTE £9.10: £2.30 £4.50 £4.30 (£57.70) Trio £128.50; £81.48 to Leicester 11/2/97 OWNER Mr C. G. Bolton (NEWPORT, GWENT) BRED Mrs David Gordon Lennox

WEIGHT FOR AGE 4yo-10lb

STEWARDS' ENQUIRY Obj. to Caracol by Brennan overruled.

2037 Caracol, twice a winner between the flags, had been let down by his jumping over fences, and the return to hurdles worked. (6/1)

1448 Arioso looked a shade unlucky from the stands, but the head-on camera revealed a different story. (14/1)

Nicky Wilde was taking a drop in class. (10/1)

2050 Come On In has already been beaten in a seller. (7/1)

2907 Fairelaine never threatened to take a hand. (11/4)

3055 GOLDEN VALLEY HUNTERS' CHASE (6-Y.O+) (Class H)
4-30 (4-32) **3m 1f 110y (19 fncs)** £1,339.50 (£372.00: £178.50) GOING: 0.55 sec per fur (S)

				SP	RR	SF
	Miss Millbrook (DTGoldsworthy) **9-11-2**(7) MrEWilliams (hld up: hdwy 7th: led 12th: clr fr 4 out: blnd last: rdn out)	—	1	4/1[3]	110	15
	Cape Cottage (DJCaro) **13-11-7**(7) MrAPhillips (hld up: hdwy 8th: chsd wnr fr 4 out: no imp)	25	2	12/1	99	4
256[U]	**Rusty Bridge** (MrsSMJohnson) **10-12-3**(7) MrRBurton (led tl blnd 6th: mstke 8th: bhd fr 11th)	22	3	20/1	96	1
2951[P]	**Not My Line (IRE)** (AndyMorgan) **8-11-2**(5) MrASansome (prom: lft in ld 6th: hdd 12th: wknd 4 out)	2½	4	33/1	77	—
	Catchapenny (MrsDEHTurner) **12-12-3b**(7) MrWTellwright (prom to 12th: t.o)	5	5	12/1	91	—
	Some-Toy (JohnSquire) **11-11-7**(7) MissLBlackford (bkwd: a bhd: t.o fr 10th)	dist	6	8/1	—	—
	Celtic Abbey (MrsChristineHardinge) **9-12-0**(7) MrDSJones (bkwd: blnd 9th & 11th: sn bhd: t.o whn p.u bef 15th: b.b.v)		P	9/4[1]	—	—
	Lighten the Load (JSPayne) **10-11-0**(7) MrAWintle (a bhd: t.o whn p.u bef 4 out)		P	11/1	—	—
	The Rum Mariner (MrsJASkelton) **10-11-2**(5) MrJJukes (chsd ldrs tl wknd 13th: mstke 14th: t.o whn p.u bef 3 out)		P	8/1	—	—
	Fiddlers Pike (MrsRGHenderson) **16-12-3**(7) MrsRHenderson (lw: bhd fr 10th: sn t.o: p.u bef 3 out)		P	20/1	—	—
	Forest Fountain (IRE) (JDCallow) **6-11-0**(7) MrADalton (lw: a bhd: t.o 10th: p.u bef 3 out)		P	7/2[2]	—	—

Form	Horse / details	Dist	Pl	SP	RR	SF
	J B Lad (HRTuck) **11-11-0**(7) MissPGundry (blnd 1st: sn bhd: t.o 10th: p.u bef 3 out)		**P**	25/1	—	—
	Boddington Hill (BAHall) **9-10-11**(5) MrCVigors (t.o whn p.u bef 11th)		**P**	25/1	—	—
597^{P}	**Pharrago (IRE)** (LSaunders) **8-11-0**(7) MissEJJones (lw: t.o whn blnd 7th: p.u bef 8th)		**P**	33/1	—	—
2930^{U}	**Corn Exchange** (DGDuggan) **9-11-4**(3) MrMRimell (lw: a bhd: t.o 10th: p.u bef 3 out)		**P**	33/1	—	—
	Ross Venture (RWCrank) **12-12-3**(7) MrCStockton (prom: mstke 10th: wknd 13th: t.o whn p.u bef 2 out)		**P**	33/1	—	—
	Judy Line (GWLewis) **8-10-9**(7) MissVRoberts (mstke 1st: sn t.o: p.u bef 3 out)		**P**	33/1	—	—
	Kettles (MRDaniell) **10-10-9**(7) MrRWakley (sme hdwy 13th: wknd 15th: blnd & uns rdr 3 out)		**U**	10/1	—	—
				(SP 159.9%)	**18 Rn**	

6m 43.9 (33.90) CSF £55.27 TOTE £7.30: £2.00 £6.90 £2.90 (£146.70) Trio £173.60; £198.12 to Leicester 11/2/97 OWNER Mr D. T. Goldsworthy (BRIDGEND) BRED C. Parker

OFFICIAL EXPLANATION **Celtic Valley: bled from the nose.**

Miss Millbrook had made a successful debut under Rules on soft ground at Chepstow last April. (4/1)

Cape Cottage had registered his only win under Rules on soft ground, over this course and distance, nearly three years ago. (12/1)

94 Rusty Bridge could have done with another mile. (20/1)

Celtic Abbey made two bad mistakes and was reported to have broken a blood-vessel. (9/4)

3056 LEDBURY H'CAP HURDLE (0-105) (4-Y.O+) (Class F)

5-00 (5-00) **2m 1f (9 hdls)** £2,318.00 (£648.00: £314.00) GOING: 0.55 sec per fur (S)

Form	Horse / details	Dist	Pl	SP	RR	SF
2755*	**Added Dimension (IRE) (93)** (PWinkworth) **6-11-3**(7) XAizpuru (plld hrd: a.p: led 3 out: clr whn blnd last)	—	**1**	9/2^{3}	78	28
2824^{6}	**Dontdressfordinner (89)** (RJHodges) **7-11-3**(3) TDascombe (prom: lost pl 4th: rdn 6th: sn rallied: chsd wnr appr 2 out: one pce)	4	**2**	7/1	70	20
2882^{2}	**Fontanays (IRE) (91)** (GMMcCourt) **9-11-1**(7) RHobson (lw: hld up: hdwy fr 2 out: nvr plcd to chal)	2	**3**	2/1^{1}	70	20
2824^{3}	**Supermick (88)** (WRMuir) **6-11-5** NWilliamson (led tl hdd 3 out: wknd appr 2 out: 3rd whn mstke last)	7	**4**	11/4^{2}	61	11
2842^{P}	**Mrs Jawleyford (USA) (80)** (CSmith) **9-10-11** MRanger (plld hrd: wnt prom 3rd: rdn 6th: sn wknd)	nk	**5**	33/1	53	3
2871^{3}	**Daily Sport Girl (85)** (BJLlewellyn) **8-11-2** MrJLLlewellyn (hld up: rdn 5th: sn bhd)	15	**6**	11/2	43	—
2824^{8}	**Erlking (IRE) (90)** (SMellor) **7-11-7v^{1}** JOsborne (lw: bhd: rdn 6th: sn t.o)	20	**7**	12/1	30	—
2842^{11}	**Karline Ka (FR) (90)** (RDickin) **6-11-7** JCulloty (fell 3rd)		**F**	20/1	—	—
				(SP 121.5%)	**8 Rn**	

4m 12.0 (19.00) CSF £34.40 CT £76.32 TOTE £7.00: £1.40 £3.40 £1.80 (£33.30) OWNER Mr N. A. Dunger (DUNSFOLD) BRED Swettenham Stud and Ron Con Limited

2755* Added Dimension (IRE) defied a 4lb hike in the ratings, but gave his supporters an anxious moment at the final flight. (9/2: op 3/1)

2824 Dontdressfordinner, dropped 4lb, would not have been suited by the morning rain. (7/1)

2882 Fontanays (IRE), upped 2lb, was not so positively ridden this time. (2/1)

2824 Supermick dropped away tamely after the third last. (11/4)

T/Jkpt: Not won; £2,231.77 to Leicester 11/2/97. T/Plpt: £13,692.90 (0.5 Tckts); £9,252.02 to Leicester 11/2/97. T/Qdpt: £392.30 (2.8 Tckts) KH

2791-PLUMPTON (L-H) (Good to soft, Soft home st)

Monday February 10th

WEATHER: rain becoming clear

3057 COWFOLD CONDITIONAL (S) H'CAP HURDLE (0-95) (4-Y.O+) (Class G)

1-50 (1-50) **2m 1f (10 hdls)** £1,924.80 (£532.80: £254.40) GOING: 1.89 sec per fur (HY)

Form	Horse / details	Dist	Pl	SP	RR	SF
2866^{3}	**Kentavrus Way (IRE) (61)** (GLMoore) **6-9-9**(5) MBatchelor (rdn 4th: hdwy appr 2 out: led appr last: r.o)	—	**1**	14/1	43	—
2792^{3}	**Summer Villa (67)** (KGWingrove) **5-10-6b** LAspell (hdwy 5th: chsd wnr appr last: unable qckn)	13	**2**	9/2^{1}	37	—
2866^{4}	**Derisbay (IRE) (74)** (JJBridger) **9-10-13b** SophieMitchell (hdwy 3rd: lost pl 6th: r.o one pce fr 3 out)	4	**3**	25/1	40	—
2907^{10}	**Zadok (66)** (JFfitch-Heyes) **5-10-5b^{1}** PHenley (lw: hdwy 5th: led 6th tl appr last: sn wknd)	6	**4**	12/1	26	—
1390^{11}	**Precious Wonder (63)** (PButler) **8-10-2** ABates (nvr nr to chal)	1¼	**5**	14/1	22	—
961^{6}	**Deptford Belle (68)** (RCurtis) **7-10-7** DWalsh (prom to 3 out)	5	**6**	14/1	23	—
2866^{2}	**Slightly Special (IRE) (64)** (BAPearce) **5-10-3** SRyan (led: sn clr: hdd 6th: wknd 3 out)	1½	**7**	6/1^{3}	17	—
2792^{6}	**Minster's Madam (88)** (JNeville) **6-11-8v**(5) JHarris (lw: nvr gng wl: a bhd)	11	**8**	9/2^{1}	31	—
2070^{7}	**Embroidered (77)** (RMFlower) **4-9-13**(7)ow6 JKMcCarthy (a bhd: t.o)	dist	**9**	33/1	—	—
2818^{F}	**Battleship Bruce (89)** (TCasey) **5-12-0b** DFortt (a.p: chsd ldr appr 3 out tl appr 2 out: sn wknd: bhd whn p.u bef last)		**P**	9/1	—	—
1864^{7}	**National Flag (FR) (70)** (KRBurke) **7-10-4v**(5) AWatt (6th whn p.u bef 3 out: dead)		**P**	12/1	—	—
2678^{14}	**Another Fiddle (IRE) (72)** (BAPearce) **7-10-4**(7)ow3 GordonGallagher (a bhd: t.o whn p.u bef 2 out)		**P**	33/1	—	—
2791^{8}	**Belle Perk (IRE) (61)** (TPMcGovern) **6-10-0** CRae (lw: bhd fr 7th: p.u bef last)		**P**	5/1^{2}	—	—
2753^{P}	**Memory's Music (68)** (MMadgwick) **5-10-2**(5) JPower (bhd fr 7th: p.u bef last)		**P**	14/1	—	—
2907^{P}	**Deceit the Second (61)** (PRRodford) **5-9-9v^{1}**(5) MGriffiths (lw: mstke 4th: chsd ldr to 5th: sn wknd: bhd whn p.u bef last)		**P**	33/1	—	—
				(SP 132.0%)	**15 Rn**	

4m 44.9 (48.90) CSF £74.25 CT £1,472.93 TOTE £26.80: £5.80 £1.90 £2.90 (£36.80) Trio £79.60 OWNER Mr F. L. Hill (BRIGHTON) BRED Churchtown House Stud

LONG HANDICAP Embroidered 9-13 Kentavrus Way (IRE) 9-13 Deceit the Second 9-3

WEIGHT FOR AGE 4yo-10lb

No bid

OFFICIAL EXPLANATION **Minster's Madam: was unable to dominate and lost interest as a result.**

IN-FOCUS: **After a substantial amount of rain before racing, the ground on the hurdles course was undoubtedly heavy. Considering the conditions, the horses went off far too fast and, as a result, most of them could hardly put one foot in front of the other from the home turn.**

2866 Kentavrus Way (IRE) actually managed to win this desperate race. Miles behind the principals turning out of the back straight, they all faded in front of him in the heavy ground, and he plodded past them and into the lead approaching the final flight. (14/1)

2792 Summer Villa managed to struggle into second place approaching the last, but she was very tired and never looked like mustering another gear. (9/2)

2866 Derisbay (IRE) may have been very tired in the last half-mile, but the majority of the opposition were legless, and he was able to struggle by. He is greatly flattered to finish so close. (25/1)

1729 Zadok, fitted with blinkers for the first time, went on early on the final circuit, but he was out on his feet when collared approaching the final flight. (12/1)
Precious Wonder is a very poor maiden who seems better suited by the mud, but never threatened to get into it. (14/1)
2818 Battleship Bruce (9/1: 5/1-10/1)

3058 DYKE CLAIMING HURDLE (4-Y.O) (Class F)

2-20 (2-20) **2m 1f (10 hdls)** £2,176.20 (£603.20: £288.60) GOING: Not Established

				SP	RR	SF
	Supreme Illusion (AUS) (JohnBerry) **4-10-0** VSmith (bhd: hdwy appr 2 out: led last: all out)	—	**1**	50/1	54	—
2882[4]	**Hawanafa (68)** (JSMoore) **4-10-2b**[ow2] WMcFarland (plld hrd: a.p: led 6th: clr 7th: blnd 2 out: wkng whn blnd bdly & hdd last)	3½	**2**	4/1 [3]	53	—
1712[P]	**Petros Gem** (MJBolton) **4-9-13**(7) JHarris (hld up: 4th whn mstke 6th: chsd ldr appr 3 out tl appr last: sn wknd)	3	**3**	50/1	54	—
2815[3]	**Whispering Dawn** (CPEBrooks) **4-11-1** DGallagher (led to 6th: wknd 3 out: t.o)	dist	**4**	2/1 [2]	—	—
2784[8]	**Classic Colours (USA)** (ICampbell) **4-11-3** KGaule (prom to 6th: t.o)	dist	**5**	12/1	—	—
	Noblesse Oblige (KCBailey) **4-11-3** AThornton (lw: hld up: rdn 5th: 5th & wkng whn blnd 6th: t.o whn p.u bef 7th)		**P**	15/8 [1]	—	—
1634[P]	**Petros Pride** (MJBolton) **4-10-3**(3) LAspell (a bhd: t.o fr 7th: p.u bef 2 out)		**P**	50/1	—	—
	Simply Seven (PButler) **4-10-5** PHolley (a bhd: t.o whn p.u bef 7th)		**P**	50/1	—	—
1712[6]	**Ember** (RTPhillips) **4-10-6** DBridgwater (a bhd: t.o whn p.u bef 7th)		**P**	8/1	—	—
				(SP 114.8%)	**9 Rn**	

4m 55.4 (59.40) CSF £218.63 TOTE £105.60: £8.20 £1.20 £5.70 (£213.20) Trio Not won; £127.67 to Leicester 11/2/97 OWNER Mr John Berry (NEWMARKET) BRED Swettenham Stud

IN-FOCUS: **Once again the leaders went off far too quickly considering the ground. The time was almost 11 seconds slower than the first race.**

Supreme Illusion (AUS), a poor maiden on the Flat, made a winning debut over hurdles, but she is greatly flattered as her rivals were out on their feet in the straight. A good twenty lengths behind the leader turning for home, she did little more than plod on past legless rivals to strike the front jumping the last. She had nothing in reserve, and was all out to hold on. Bizarrely, she figured amongst the entries for the Dubai World Cup. (50/1)
2882 Hawanafa moved to the front setting out on the final circuit and soon forged clear. She made a bad error two out though and, completely out on her feet, came to a grinding halt when ploughing through the final fight. (4/1)
Petros Gem moved into second place running down the hill, but she was very tired when collared for the runner-up berth going to the last. (50/1)
2815 Whispering Dawn (2/1: op 5/4)
Classic Colours (USA) (12/1: 8/1-16/1)
Ember (8/1: 6/1-9/1)

3059 HASSOCKS NOVICES' CHASE (5-Y.O+) (Class E)

2-50 (2-50) **2m (13 fncs)** £3,183.65 (£951.20: £455.10: £207.05) GOING: 1.51 sec per fur (HY)

				SP	RR	SF
2810[U]	**Coolteen Hero (IRE) (81)** (RHAlner) **7-11-7** WMcFarland (mde all: mstkes 3 out & 2 out: rdn out)	—	**1**	13/2	90	23
2793[U]	**Purbeck Cavalier** (RHAlner) **8-11-0** AThornton (hld up: chsd wnr appr 2 out: unable qckn)	6	**2**	7/2 [1]	77	10
	Buckland Lad (IRE) (78) (DMGrissell) **6-11-0** BFenton (hdwy fr 2 out: r.o one pce)	7	**3**	4/1 [2]	70	3
1708[6]	**Dress Dance (IRE) (80)** (NRMitchell) **7-10-9**(5) SophieMitchell (chsd wnr to 4th: lost pl 6th: rallied 9th: one pce)	1¾	**4**	5/1 [3]	68	1
2703[3]	**Show Faith (IRE)** (RHannon) **7-11-0** JAMcCarthy (chsd wnr 4th tl appr 2 out: wkng whn mstke last)	14	**5**	7/2 [1]	54	—
	Regal Aura (IRE) (DCO'Brien) **7-11-0** PHide (lw: bhd fr 8th)	6	**6**	25/1	48	—
2703[5]	**Windward Ariom** (PMitchell) **11-11-0** JFTitley (hdwy 9th: wknd 4 out: t.o)	25	**7**	10/1	23	—
2793[4]	**Brigadier Supreme (IRE) (63)** (PButler) **8-11-0** TJMurphy (lw: reluctant to r: a bhd: t.o fr 7th)	dist	**8**	33/1	—	—
2676[P]	**Eau So Sloe** (JRPoulton) **6-11-0** ADicken (bhd fr 7th: fell 4 out)		**F**	33/1	—	—
				(SP 113.3%)	**9 Rn**	

4m 26.4 (34.40) CSF £26.58 TOTE £9.30: £2.60 £1.50 £1.80 (£10.10) Trio £15.90 OWNER J P M & J W Cook (BLANDFORD) BRED T. Simmons

IN-FOCUS: **Whilst the ground appeared to be slightly better on the chase course in the straight, the time still suggested the ground was heavy and not as officially given out.**

1169 Coolteen Hero (IRE) handled the testing ground. Making all the running, he was untidy at two of the last three fences but, despite this, he proved too strong for his rivals. (13/2)
Purbeck Cavalier managed to take second place approaching the second last but, in the testing conditions, never looked like getting on terms with the winner. (7/2)
Buckland Lad (IRE), having his first run of the season and making his chasing debut, got round safely in these very testing conditions and, after being a long way behind turning for home, stayed on well to take third prize. He is sure to benefit from this. (4/1: op 9/4)
1708 Dress Dance (IRE) was made to look very pedestrian over the last five fences. (5/1)
2703 Show Faith (IRE), making his chasing debut, struggles to get two miles so he had no chance of getting it in these conditions. Nevertheless, he showed promise until inevitably tiring. (7/2)
Windward Ariom (10/1: 8/1-12/1)

3060 BET WITH THE TOTE (QUALIFIER) NOVICES' CHASE (6-Y.O+) (Class E)

3-20 (3-20) **3m 1f 110y (20 fncs)** £3,290.25 (£984.00: £471.50: £215.25) GOING: 1.51 sec per fur (HY)

				SP	RR	SF
	High Learie (AHHarvey) **7-10-10** JAMcCarthy (mde virtually all: drvn out)	—	**1**	14/1	110	14
2760[4]	**Easy Breezy** (CJMann) **7-10-10** JRailton (hdwy 5th: chsd wnr fr 12th: ev ch appr 2 out: unable qckn flat)	2	**2**	16/1	109	13
2039[4]	**Apatura Hati (80)** (RHAlner) **8-10-5** AThornton (hdwy 13th: rdn 16th: wknd last)	9	**3**	10/1	98	2
2908[F]	**Dunlir (69)** (PRRodford) **7-10-3**(7) MGriffiths (blnd 3rd: a t.o)	dist	**4**	33/1	—	—
	Nikkis Pet (JNeville) **10-10-5** DWalsh (chsd wnr 2nd to 12th: mstke 13th: wknd 15th: t.o whn p.u bef 2 out)		**P**	14/1	—	—
2693[P]	**Melnik** (MrsAJPerrett) **6-11-3** CMaude (prom to 10th: t.o whn p.u bef 2 out)		**P**	6/4 [1]	—	—
2819[U]	**Givus a Call (IRE) (93)** (JTGifford) **7-10-7**(3) LAspell (mstke 3rd: a bhd: t.o whn p.u bef 15th)		**P**	9/2 [3]	—	—
1708[P]	**Pinoccio (80)** (DCO'Brien) **10-10-10** PHide (mstke 5th: prom to 8th: t.o whn p.u bef 14th)		**P**	50/1	—	—

			Pos	SP	RR	SF
2795[4]	**Thermal Warrior (78)** (JABOld) **9-10-10** GUpton (hdwy 14th: 4th & btn whn blnd & uns rdr 2 out)		**U**	5/2[2]	—	—

(SP 120.0%) **9 Rn**

7m 14.8 (54.80) CSF £183.56 TOTE £27.50: £3.80 £2.00 £1.70 (£94.80) Trio £133.40 OWNER Mr Edward Harvey (BISHOP'S STORTFORD) BRED P. Rawson

High Learie, formerly with Oliver Sherwood, may have been off the course since last April but that was not going to stop him making a winning debut over fences. Making virtually all the running, he managed to hold off the persistent runner-up to give his first-season trainer his first winner. (14/1: 6/1-16/1)

Easy Breezy showed he stays this longer trip in these very testing conditions. Moving into second place soon after halfway, he proved a real thorn in the side of the winner, but just failed to muster another turn of foot on the run-in. (16/1)

Apatura Hati took closer order with a circuit to go and, although staying on early in the straight, that run had come to an end jumping the final fence. (10/1)

Nikkis Pet (14/1: 10/1-16/1)

1963* Melnik was again not in the mood, and punters knew their fate soon after halfway. (6/4)

3061 SHEFFIELD PARK NOVICES' HURDLE (4-Y.O+ F & M) (Class E)

3-50 (3-50) **2m 1f (10 hdls)** £2,679.00 (£744.00: £357.00) GOING: 1.89 sec per fur (HY)

			Pos	SP	RR	SF
2794[3]	**Bula Vogue (IRE)** (RRowe) **7-11-0** DO'Sullivan (lw: led 2nd: clr appr last: rdn out)	—	**1**	10/11[1]	73	—
2642[P]	**Maylin Magic (76)** (TCasey) **6-11-0** DBridgwater (hdwy 7th: chsd wnr appr last: mstke last: unable qckn)	5	**2**	14/1	68	—
1966[9]	**Kilshey** (JTGifford) **6-11-0** PHide (led to 2nd: ev ch tl appr 2 out: wknd appr last)	4	**3**	14/1	65	—
	Finlana (MrsDHaine) **4-10-4** JFTitley (hdwy 5th: wknd appr 2 out)	18	**4**	5/1[2]	48	—
1726[5]	**Ilandra (IRE)** (RAkehurst) **5-11-0** AMaguire (hdwy 7th: wknd appr 2 out)	9	**5**	6/1[3]	39	—
1820[4]	**Floosy** (TRGeorge) **6-11-0** TJenks (hmpd s: a wl bhd: t.o fr 7th)	25	**6**	16/1	16	—
	Knot True (JohnBerry) **7-11-0** PHolley (9th whn b.d 3rd)		**B**	40/1	—	—
2680[11]	**Ilewin Janine (IRE) (78)** (PCRitchens) **6-11-0** DGallagher (7th whn fell 3rd)		**F**	8/1	—	—
	Tapestry Rose (JRPoulton) **6-11-0** ADicken (bkwd: prom to 6th: t.o whn p.u bef 2 out)		**P**	66/1	—	—
	Our Emma (JJoseph) **8-11-0** DSkyrme (bkwd: 3rd whn blnd bdly 2nd: wknd 6th: t.o whn p.u bef 2 out)		**P**	66/1	—	—
	Orchid House (NRMitchell) **5-11-0** GUpton (w.r.s & uns rdr)		**U**	33/1	—	—

(SP 122.0%) **11 Rn**

4m 45.3 (49.30) CSF £15.33 TOTE £2.00: £1.60 £2.60 £3.60 (£5.30) Trio £82.20 OWNER The In Vogue Partnership (PULBOROUGH) BRED Daniel J. O'Keeffe

WEIGHT FOR AGE 4yo-10lb

2794 Bula Vogue (IRE) confirmed the promise shown here two weeks ago. Soon in front, her jockey very sensibly made sure she set only a moderate pace in the testing conditions, and the combination forged clear from the second last to win in clear-cut style. (10/11: 4/6-evens)

1958 Maylin Magic eventually struggled into second place approaching the last, but she made a mistake there and never looked like getting on terms. (14/1: op 6/1)

Kilshey ran much better on this hurdling debut. Settling in second place, she looked a real threat to the winner turning for home, before tiring soon after the second last. (14/1: op 8/1)

Finlana, sold out of Michael Stoute's stable for a mere 1,300 guineas, was close up turning out of the back straight, but was a spent force going to the penultimate hurdle. (5/1)

Ilewin Janine (IRE) (8/1: 12/1-7/1)

3062 FLYAWAY CHALLENGE CUP HUNTERS' CHASE (5-Y.O+) (Class H)

4-20 (4-20) **3m 1f 110y (20 fncs)** £1,590.00 (£440.00: £210.00) GOING: 1.51 sec per fur (HY)

			Pos	SP	RR	SF
	Loyal Note (SRAndrews) **9-12-2**(3) MrSimonAndrews (led 5th to 7th: led 9th to 10th: led 11th to 13th: j.slowly 15th: mstke 16th: led appr last: r.o wl)	—	**1**	7/1	106	—
	Trifast Lad (MJRoberts) **12-11-11**(3) MrPHacking (led 3rd to 5th: led 7th to 9th: led 10th to 11th: led 13th: mstke 16th: hdd appr last: unable qckn)	2½	**2**	7/2[2]	99	—
	Sunny Mount (MissCSaunders) **11-11-7**(7) MrSMorris (lw: hdwy 13th: chsd ldrs fr 4 out: ev ch 2 out: one pce)	¾	**3**	8/13[1]	99	—
	Annio Chilone (RChampion) **11-11-7**(7) MrPO'Keeffe (bit bkwd: hld up: rdn appr 2 out: sn wknd)	22	**4**	11/2[3]	85	—
	Colonel Kenson (RobertBarr) **11-11-7**(7) MrMGingell (led to 3rd: lost pl 6th: bhd whn fell 8th)		**F**	33/1	—	—

(SP 115.0%) **5 Rn**

7m 30.0 (70.00) CSF £28.62 TOTE £8.30: £1.60 £1.80 (£7.70) OWNER Mr R. Andrews (LUTON) BRED Mrs E. M. Andrews

Loyal Note, in and out of the lead, managed to show in front again approaching the last, much to the delight of his pilot, who was also enjoying his first winner as a trainer. (7/1: op 9/2)

Trifast Lad, a useful but lightly-raced pointer, made a very promising debut under Rules. In and out of the lead, he showed in front again with a circuit to race but, collared approaching the last, failed to find another gear. He should soon find a similar event. (7/2: op 6/1)

Sunny Mount, a useful individual in this sphere, won a point-to-point last month. Content to bide his time off the pace, he got into the action on the final circuit, and had every chance jumping the second last before failing to find another gear. He needs more use made of him. (8/13: 2/5-4/6)

Annio Chilone, an unreliable character for Josh Gifford, did not look fully fit and had given his all entering the straight. (11/2: 4/1-6/1)

3063 FIRLE PLACE H'CAP HURDLE (0-105) (4-Y.O+) (Class F)

4-50 (4-50) **2m 4f (12 hdls)** £2,194.40 (£608.40: £291.20) GOING: 1.89 sec per fur (HY)

			Pos	SP	RR	SF
934[5]	**Mayb-Mayb (68)** (JNeville) **7-10-1** TJMurphy (lw: led to 5th: led 9th: clr 2 out: rdn out)	—	**1**	6/1	51	11
2792[7]	**Lajadhal (FR) (69)** (KBishop) **8-10-2**ow2 WMcFarland (lost pl 9th: rallied appr last: chsd wnr fr last: no imp)	9	**2**	20/1	45	3
2797[9]	**Millmount (IRE) (89)** (TPMcGovern) **7-11-1b**(7) CRae (lw: a.p: led 6th to 9th: rdn appr 3 out: 3rd & btn whn mstke last)	4	**3**	4/1[3]	62	22
2952[6]	**Chieftain's Crown (USA) (90)** (THind) **6-11-9** DBridgwater (lw: hdwy 7th: ev ch 3 out: wknd appr 2 out)	17	**4**	8/1	49	9
2797[7]	**Kilcoran Bay (95)** (JWMullins) **5-11-7v**(7) MrABalding (a bhd)	3	**5**	12/1	52	12
2690[10]	**Kybo's Revenge (IRE) (68)** (RRowe) **6-10-1**ow1 DO'Sullivan (mstke 2nd: bhd fr 7th)	6	**6**	100/30[2]	20	—
2871[F]	**Yellow Dragon (IRE) (95)** (BAPearce) **4-11-3** KGaule (hld up: rdn appr 3 out: sn wknd)	2½	**7**	5/2[1]	45	—
1072[5]	**Cavo Greco (USA) (70)** (JJoseph) **8-10-3** DSkyrme (a.p: led 5th to 6th: wknd 9th: t.o whn p.u bef 2 out)		**P**	33/1	—	—

(SP 112.4%) **8 Rn**

5m 35.6 (48.60) CSF £90.01 CT £484.02 TOTE £4.30: £1.10 £2.60 £3.30 (£79.20) Trio £110.00; £82.12 to Leicester 11/2/97 OWNER Mr J. Neville (NEWPORT, GWENT) BRED Bram Davies and R. J. Holder

LONG HANDICAP Lajadhal (FR) 9-12
WEIGHT FOR AGE 4yo-11lb
Mayb-Mayb regained the advantage four out, and forged clear in the straight for a clear-cut success. (6/1: op 4/1)
Lajadhal (FR) lost his pitch in the back straight but, with his rivals tired in the straight, he struggled to take second jumping the last. (20/1)
1810 Millmount (IRE) was being tapped for toe in the last mile. (4/1)
2952 Chieftain's Crown (USA), making a quick reappearance, did not have conditions in his favour, but actually managed to poke a nostril in front for a few strides turning out of the back straight, before tiring. He has gained all his wins on fast ground. (8/1: op 4/1)
Kilcoran Bay showed no promise and was always at the back. (12/1: 8/1-14/1)
Kybo's Revenge (IRE) appeared to hate the ground, and punters soon knew their fate. (100/30: 2/1-7/2)
2871 Yellow Dragon (IRE) (5/2: 2/1-3/1)

T/Plpt: £1,567.60 (5.97 Tckts). T/Qdpt: £57.20 (14.34 Tckts) AK

3022-AYR (L-H) (Soft, Heavy patches bk st)
Tuesday February 11th
WEATHER: unsettled

3064 LEVY BOARD NOVICES' H'CAP HURDLE (0-100) (4-Y.O+) (Class E)
1-40 (1-41) **2m (9 hdls)** £2,626.50 (£729.00: £349.50) GOING: 1.41 sec per fur (HY)

	Horse / details	Dist	Pos	SP	RR	SF
2619^{11}	**Solsgirth (69)** (JBarclay) **6-10-8** AThornton (a.p: pushed along fr 5th: led 2 out: styd on wl)	—	1	20/1	51	13
2898^{7}	**Joe Shaw (85)** (MrsMReveley) **4-11-0** PNiven (lw: hld up: hdwy 5th: ev ch & rdn fr 3 out: nt qckn towards fin)	1¼	2	11/4^{2}	66	18
2783^{5}	**Political Tower (85)** (RNixon) **10-11-10** BStorey (trckd ldr fr 4th: led 4 out to 2 out: sn btn)	8	3	5/2^{1}	58	20
2798^{6}	**Nancys Choice (75)** (MrsNHope) **7-11-0** JBurke (plld hrd: led to 4 out: sn wknd)	dist	4	20/1	—	—
2044^{4}	**Segala (IRE) (79)** (JJO'Neill) **6-11-4** PCarberry (chsd ldrs: blnd 4 out: sn hrd drvn: btn appr next)	26	5	14/1	—	—
1666^{5}	**Bill's Pride (78)** (PMonteith) **6-11-3** ADobbin (prom tl wknd appr 4 out: p.u bef 3 out)		P	20/1	—	—
2785^{4}	**Fils de Cresson (IRE) (85)** (JRAdam) **7-11-10** MMoloney (lw: chsd ldrs tl wknd & blnd 4 out: p.u bef next)		P	4/1^{3}	—	—
2697^{5}	**Bowcliffe (78)** (MrsAMNaughton) **6-11-3** MFoster (lost pl 4th: t.o whn p.u bef 3 out)		P	14/1	—	—
2790^{6}	**Teejay'n'aitch (IRE) (78)** (JSGoldie) **5-11-3** GCahill (prom to 5th: t.o whn p.u bef 3 out)		P	14/1	—	—
	Running Green (64) (DMoffatt) **6-10-3**ow2 DJMoffatt (bhd: hdwy 5th: sn in tch: wknd 3 out: p.u bef last)		P	25/1	—	—
				(SP 113.4%)	**10 Rn**	

4m 8.6 (31.60) CSF £64.70 CT £173.58 TOTE £59.10: £13.80 £1.50 £1.20 (£113.80) Trio £117.70 OWNER Kinneston Farmers (LESLIE) BRED C. J. T. Alexander
WEIGHT FOR AGE 4yo-10lb
OFFICIAL EXPLANATION **Fils de Cresson (IRE): has been found to have a heart problem.**
Solsgirth, who had shown nothing previously, took to these testing conditions and, although off the bit some way out, all he did was stay. (20/1)
2898 Joe Shaw, patiently ridden, was put into the race this time from three out and in the end was just outstayed. (11/4)
2783 Political Tower, having a change from chasing, put up a decent show until the testing conditions found him out late on. (5/2)
2798 Nancys Choice, a headstrong individual, raced freely in front until running himself into the ground four out. (20/1)
2044 Segala (IRE) showed up until his lack of stamina was exposed from the fourth last. (14/1)

3065 RIVER DOON H'CAP HURDLE (0-125) (4-Y.O+) (Class D)
2-10 (2-10) **2m (9 hdls)** £2,777.00 (£772.00: £371.00) GOING: 1.41 sec per fur (HY)

	Horse / details	Dist	Pos	SP	RR	SF
2631^{9}	**Star Selection (97)** (JMackie) **6-10-4**(3) EHusband (lw: disp ld tl led 4 out: clr whn blnd 2 out)	—	1	11/4^{2}	79+	36
	Merry Mermaid (96) (BMactaggart) **7-10-6** BStorey (disp ld to 4 out: rdn & btn appr next)	21	2	7/2^{3}	57	14
	Monica's Choice (IRE) (116) (MrsMReveley) **6-11-12** PNiven (lw: hld up: effrt 5th: no imp)	4	3	5/2^{1}	73	30
	Our Robert (95) (JGFitzGerald) **5-10-5** PCarberry (effrt 5th: shkn up 4 out: wknd appr next)	6	4	9/1	46	3
2764^{4}	**Common Sound (IRE) (110)** (JBarclay) **6-11-6** AThornton (chsd clr ldrs to ½-wy: wknd 4 out)	30	5	9/2	31	—
				(SP 105.6%)	**5 Rn**	

4m 3.6 (26.60) CSF £10.47 TOTE £2.50: £1.30 £1.80 (£8.20) OWNER Mr R. M. Mitchell (CHURCH BROUGHTON) BRED Stanley Estate and Stud Co
2631 Star Selection had the ground he loves and really asserted his authority from the fourth last. (11/4)
Merry Mermaid really likes this ground but this was her first run of the season which probably made all the difference. (7/2)
Monica's Choice (IRE), an Irish import having his first run in this country, looked to have quite a stiff task on here and failed to get into it, but does look the sort to do better in time. (5/2)
Our Robert found these testing conditions all to much from the home turn. (9/1: op 5/1)
2764 Common Sound (IRE) has won twice on soft ground in Ireland but was most disappointing here. (9/2)

3066 RIVER CREE NOVICES' HURDLE (4-Y.O+) (Class E)
2-40 (2-41) **2m 6f (12 hdls)** £2,582.50 (£720.00: £347.50) GOING: 1.41 sec per fur (HY)

	Horse / details	Dist	Pos	SP	RR	SF
1654^{3}	**Military Academy** (GRichards) **8-12-0** PCarberry (lw: trckd ldrs: led appr 3 out: easily)	—	1	8/11^{1}	81+	—
2790^{4}	**Sunny Leith (77)** (PMonteith) **6-11-7** ADobbin (a.p: chal 4 out: kpt on: no ch w wnr)	7	2	33/1	69	—
2768*	**Adib (USA) (92)** (GMMoore) **7-12-0** NBentley (a.p: effrt 4 out: one pce)	12	3	11/2^{2}	67	—
1667^{5}	**Drakewrath (IRE)** (RABartlett) **7-11-7** DParker (chsd ldr: led 7th tl appr 3 out: wknd)	8	4	16/1	54	—
2701^{9}	**Cherry Dee** (PBeaumont) **6-10-11**(5) BGrattan (mstkes: bhd & outpcd tl styd on fr 4 out)	nk	5	10/1^{3}	49	—
2787^{4}	**Allerbank** (MrsJStorey) **6-11-7** MrCStorey (mid div: effrt ½-wy: outpcd fr 8th)	5	6	14/1	51	—
2615^{9}	**Double Dash (IRE) (85)** (DMoffatt) **4-11-3** DJMoffatt (in tch tl mstke & wknd 8th)	6	7	12/1	53	—
	Fayette County (IRE) (JJO'Neill) **6-11-7** AThornton (bhd: hdwy 7th: btn whn mstke & wknd 4 out)	2½	8	10/1^{3}	44	—
2045^{7}	**Nawtinookey (54)** (MartinTodhunter) **7-10-13b**(3) GLee (in tch tl wknd fr 4 out)	16	9	100/1	28	—
3024^{7}	**Meadowleck (65)** (WGYoung) **8-11-2** GCahill (led to 7th: lost pl & fell 4 out)		F	100/1	—	—
2673^{9}	**Harfdecent** (MrsMReveley) **6-11-7** PNiven (bhd: hdwy 7th: ev ch & rdn appr 4 out: mstke 4 out: wknd qckly & p.u bef next)		P	16/1	—	—
2924^{10}	**Border Image** (FPMurtagh) **6-11-7** ARoche (bhd: gd hdwy to jn ldrs 6th: hrd rdn & wknd 8th: p.u bef 4 out)		P	66/1	—	—
2770^{7}	**Royal Spruce (IRE)** (GMMoore) **6-11-7** JCallaghan (nvr gng wl: wl t.o whn p.u bef 8th)		P	50/1	—	—

Just Eve (MrsDThomson) **10-11-2** TReed (lost tch 7th: t.o whn p.u bef 3 out) .... **P** 500/1 — —
(SP 126.2%) **14 Rn**

6m 7.1 (56.10) CSF £36.37 TOTE £1.80: £1.10 £5.00 £1.20 (£17.70) Trio £53.70 OWNER Mr Robert Ogden (PENRITH) BRED P. M. Prior-Wandesforde
WEIGHT FOR AGE 4yo-11lb
OFFICIAL EXPLANATION Fayette County (IRE): hung badly right throughout.
1654 Military Academy looked different class in the paddock and proved to be so in the race, winning as he liked. (8/11)
2790 Sunny Leith tried hard to take the winner on but was completely outclassed. He will not always meet one so useful. (33/1)
2768* Adib (USA) is slow but sure and his one pace was well exposed here. (11/2)
1667 Drakewrath (IRE) won point-to-points last year and ran reasonably here until finding it all too much going to the third last. (16/1)
2701 Cherry Dee has a lot to learn about jumping and once she does there should be plenty of improvement. (10/1: 6/1-12/1)
2787 Allerbank had the ground at its most testing here but yet again looked very slow. (14/1)
Fayette County (IRE) (10/1: 7/1-12/1)

3067 RIVER GIRVAN NOVICES' CHASE (6-Y.O+) (Class D)

3-10 (3-12) **3m 3f 110y (21 fncs)** £3,704.00 (£1,112.00: £536.00: £248.00) GOING: 1.41 sec per fur (HY)

				SP	RR	SF
2789^{3}	**Judicious Captain (81)** (MrsJStorey) **10-10-10** MrCStorey (lw: a.p: blnd 6th & 11th: led 3 out: styd on wl flat)	—	1	4/1	96	—
2954^{F}	**Naughty Future (93)** (JJO'Neill) **8-11-3** RSupple (mstkes: hdwy ½-wy: chsng ldrs 4 out: chal last: rdn & nt qckn)	1¾	2	100/30^{2}	102	—
2954*	**D'Arblay Street (IRE) (72)** (WTKemp) **8-11-3** PCarberry (led fr 4th: blnd 15th: hdd 3 out: wknd)	21	3	7/2^{3}	89	—
2698^{3}	**Clonroche Lucky (IRE) (67)** (JWade) **7-10-10** KJones (prom: mstke 10th: wknd fr 15th)	dist	4	100/1	—	—
2788^{6}	**Abbey Lamp (IRE) (93)** (MissLucindaRussell) **8-10-10** AThornton (chsd ldrs tl wknd 5 out)	dist	5	33/1	—	—
2788^{2}	**Noosa Sound (IRE) (79)** (LLungo) **7-10-10** BStorey (lw: hld up: hdwy & prom 12th: rdn, wknd & mstke 4 out: fell next)		F	3/1^{1}	—	—
3027^{6}	**Quixall Crossett (56)** (EMCaine) **12-10-3**(7) TristanDavidson (led to 4th: chsd ldrs tl wknd & blnd 14th: fell next)		F	300/1	—	—
2919^{6}	**Seldom But Severe (IRE)** (EAElliott) **7-10-5**(5) GFRyan (mstkes: rdn & lost tch 12th: bdly hmpd 15th: p.u bef 3 out)		P	50/1	—	—
2788^{5}	**Bright Destiny (60)** (JSGoldie) **6-10-10v** GCahill (stdd s: a bhd: p.u bef 4 out)		P	66/1	—	—
2000^{P}	**Springhill Quay (IRE)** (GRichards) **8-10-10** ADobbin (prom: blnd bdly 3rd: wknd qckly & p.u bef 13th)		P	11/1	—	—
2912^{6}	**Pocaire Gaoithe (IRE) (65)** (WStorey) **7-10-5**(5) RMcGrath (nt j.w: t.o whn p.u bef 16th)		P	50/1	—	—

(SP 108.3%) **11 Rn**

7m 51.2 (68.20) CSF £14.70 TOTE £6.60: £1.20 £1.80 £2.30 (£8.40) Trio £13.20 OWNER Mr James Adam (KELSO) BRED Mrs V. Lippiatt
2789 Judicious Captain, at his first attempt at marathon distances, got the trip particularly well and, but for a couple of iffy jumps at the open ditches, there was a lot to like about this performance. (4/1)
2954 Naughty Future again spoiled his chances by continually backing off his fences, but he does go particularly well on this track and in these conditions. He obviously still has plenty of ability when in the mood. (100/30)
2954* D'Arblay Street (IRE) put up a useful effort, but the testing conditions just found him out and he ran out of fuel from the third last. (7/2)
2698 Clonroche Lucky (IRE) has yet to give any real signs of encouragement this season. (100/1)
2788 Noosa Sound (IRE), who had previously looked an out-and-out stayer, was found out over this extended trip in these testing conditions, and he was out on his feet when falling at the third last, where he lay for some time. (3/1)
2000 Springhill Quay (IRE) seems to have a problem, as he stopped as though shot setting out on the final circuit and was later said to be distressed. (11/1)

3068 RIVER TIG NOVICES' CHASE (5-Y.O+) (Class E)

3-40 (3-42) **2m 5f 110y (18 fncs)** £3,307.50 (£920.00: £442.50) GOING: 1.41 sec per fur (HY)

				SP	RR	SF
2899^{3}	**Colonel In Chief (IRE)** (GRichards) **7-11-4** PCarberry (led 3rd to 6th: led 9th: clr fr 14th: hit 2 out: unchal)	—	1	5/4^{1}	116	—
2789*	**Mr Knitwit** (PMonteith) **10-11-11** ADobbin (chsd ldrs: wnt 2nd 10th: no ch w wnr fr 13th)	dist	2	11/8^{2}	—	—
2672^{6}	**Desperate Days (IRE) (62)** (FKirby) **8-11-4** WDwan (wl bhd fr 8th)	dist	3	100/1	—	—
2767^{3}	**Ballyline (IRE) (88)** (WTKemp) **6-11-11** ASSmith (mde most to 9th: wknd qckly next: t.o whn p.u bef 4 out)		P	7/1^{3}	—	—
2632^{7}	**Lien de Famille (IRE) (102)** (JJQuinn) **7-11-11** BStorey (mstkes: prom tl blnd 10th: wknd qckly: t.o whn p.u bef 3 out)		P	12/1	—	—

(SP 107.7%) **5 Rn**

6m 5.2 (53.20) CSF £3.02 TOTE £3.00: £1.50 £1.10 (£1.20) OWNER Mr Robert Ogden (PENRITH) BRED John Noonan
2899 Colonel In Chief (IRE), helping to force the pace, ran his rivals ragged setting out on the final circuit and it was just a case of standing up to win. (5/4)
2789* Mr Knitwit was put in his place in these conditions and had no chance with the winner throughout the final mile. (11/8)
Desperate Days (IRE) looked extremely slow throughout. (100/1)
2767 Ballyline (IRE) had a battle with the winner for the lead and had run himself into the ground setting out on the final circuit. (7/1)
2043* Lien de Famille (IRE) has lost his way altogether for the time being. (12/1: op 8/1)

3069 LOCH ENOCH H'CAP CHASE (0-110) (5-Y.O+) (Class E)

4-10 (4-10) **2m (12 fncs)** £3,163.00 (£949.00: £457.00: £211.00) GOING: 1.41 sec per fur (HY)

				SP	RR	SF
2786^{3}	**Rallegio (90)** (PMonteith) **8-11-0** ADobbin (lw: bhd: hdwy ½-wy: led 3 out: r.o wl)	—	1	7/2^{1}	107	20
3027*	**Nicholas Plant (94)** (JSGoldie) **8-11-4** 7x GCahill (chsd ldrs tl wl outpcd 4th: hdwy 4 out: styd on strly)	5	2	7/2^{1}	106	19
2674*	**Netherby Said (104)** (PBeaumont) **7-12-0** RSupple (lw: cl up: led 4th tl mstke & hdd 8th: lft in ld 4 out: hdd 3 out: sn btn)	1½	3	7/2^{1}	115	28
2769^{4}	**Funny Old Game (76)** (DMcCune) **10-9-11**(3) MichaelBrennan (sme hdwy 4th: outpcd fr 7th)	8	4	25/1	79	—
2618^{4}	**One for the Pot (100)** (MrsAMNaughton) **12-11-10** MFoster (lw: chsd ldrs: hit 6th: outpcd fr next: blnd 2 out)	13	5	9/2^{2}	90	3
3023^{5}	**Monaughty Man (76)** (EMCaine) **11-10-0** MMoloney (prom tl outpcd fr 6th)	17	6	100/1	49	—
2544^{6}	**Super Sandy (78)** (FTWalton) **10-10-2** KJohnson (led to 4th: chsd ldrs: wkng whn blnd 8th)	5	7	7/1^{3}	46	—
2790^{5}	**Blazing Trail (IRE) (103)** (MissLucindaRussell) **9-11-13** AThornton (chsd ldrs: led 8th tl fell next)		F	10/1	—	—
2786^{10}	**Emerald Sea (USA) (82)** (JBarclay) **10-10-6** BStorey (a bhd: t.o whn p.u bef 7th)		P	50/1	—	—

(SP 113.2%) **9 Rn**

4m 16.6 (31.60) CSF £14.75 CT £40.49 TOTE £3.10: £1.30 £3.10 £1.20 (£9.20) Trio £11.70 OWNER Mr Guthrie Robertson (ROSEWELL) BRED Mrs Florence C. McCaw

LONG HANDICAP Monaughty Man 9-0 Funny Old Game 9-13
2786 Rallegio loved this ground and won in useful style. He is certainly going the right way at this game. (7/2)
3027* Nicholas Plant ran a cracker over a trip far too short, and will be back in the winner's enclosure before long. (7/2)
2674* Netherby Said, who looked magnificent, had plenty on here, and was chasing a lost cause over the last three fences. (7/2)
2769 Funny Old Game is running reasonably well at the moment, despite lacking the pace to make an impression here. (25/1)
2618 One for the Pot ran as though a bit stuffy here, and may be all the better for this. (9/2)
2790 Blazing Trail (IRE) got the ground he loves but, meeting the fourth last on the wrong stride, he failed to put himself right. (10/1)

3070 RIVER AYR MAIDEN N.H. FLAT RACE (4, 5 & 6-Y.O) (Class H)
4-40 (4-41) **2m** £1,380.00 (£380.00: £180.00)

	Horse / details	Dist	Pos	SP	RR	SF
2696[4]	**Merry Masquerade (IRE)** (MrsMReveley) **6-11-5**(3) GLee (in tch: outpcd over 3f out: hdwy & hung lft 2f out: led over 1f out: r.o wl)	—	**1**	11/8[1]	58 f	—
	Prime Example (IRE) (MartinTodhunter) **6-11-5**(3) MichaelBrennan (trckd ldrs fr ½-wy: led over 2f out tl over 1f out: r.o)	3	**2**	4/1[2]	55 f	—
	No Gimmicks (IRE) (JGFitzGerald) **5-11-5**(3) FLeahy (hld up: hdwy & ev ch over 2f out: r.o one pce)	3½	**3**	9/2[3]	52 f	—
	Linwood (GRichards) **6-11-3** MrRHale (mid div: pushed along 7f out: styd on: nvr nr to chal)	3	**4**	12/1	44 f	—
	Easby Blue (SEKettlewell) **5-11-5**(3) MrCBonner (w ldrs: effrt 3f out: btn whn bmpd 2f out)	4	**5**	6/1	45 f	—
	Cool Kevin (MrsMAKendall) **4-10-12** MrsMKendall (bit bkwd: cl up: led over 3f out tl over 2f out: wknd)	11	**6**	100/1	34 f	—
2804[4]	**Just Ned** (JSHaldane) **6-11-1**(7) NHorrocks (led tl hdd & wknd over 3f out)	5	**7**	20/1	29 f	—
	Young Semele (JRAdam) **5-11-3** MrCStorey (cl up tl wknd fnl 3f)	7	**8**	10/1	17 f	—
2804[3]	**Delightfool** (RNixon) **6-11-3** GCahill (prom 3f: sn outpcd & wl bhd)	29	**9**	14/1	—	—
2804[12]	**Chief Chippie** (WTKemp) **4-10-5**(7) SHaworth (lost tch 7f out)	2	**10**	100/1	—	—
2640[6]	**Champs-Girl (IRE)** (BWMurray) **4-10-4**(3) ECallaghan (prom tl wknd 7f out)	dist	**11**	100/1	—	—
	Chan Move (WJSmith) **5-11-3**(5) STaylor (bit bkwd: a bhd: wl t.o)	dist	**12**	100/1	—	—

(SP 126.7%) **12 Rn**

4m 6.4 CSF £6.73 TOTE £2.10: £1.20 £1.70 £1.40 (£4.60) Trio £14.60 OWNER Mr G. S. Brown (SALTBURN) BRED James MacMahon
WEIGHT FOR AGE 4yo-10lb
2696 Merry Masquerade (IRE) needed these conditions to bring out the best in him, and he is going to make up into a nice staying chaser one day. (11/8)
Prime Example (IRE) ran a useful first race, but just found his more experienced rival too good late on. (4/1: 3/1-9/2)
No Gimmicks (IRE) looks a real staying type, and showed enough to suggest that more will be seen of him. (9/2: 3/1-5/1)
Linwood, a tall, long-striding mare, did well in these conditions and should make her mark once put over hurdles. (12/1: 8/1-14/1)
Eashy Blue looked to be going well for much of the trip, but lack of experience told in the straight in these testing conditions. Better will be seen of him once the ground dries out a bit. (6/1: op 3/1)

T/Plpt: £9.10 (950.33 Tckts). T/Qdpt: £2.40 (240.9 Tckts) AA

2812-LEICESTER (R-H) (Ch Good-firm, Good ptchs, Hdles Good-soft, Good ptchs) Tuesday February 11th
WEATHER: overcast

3071 WREN H'CAP CHASE (0-115) (5-Y.O+) (Class E)
2-00 (2-01) **2m 4f 110y (15 fncs)** £3,179.40 (£949.20: £453.60: £205.80) GOING: 0.28 sec per fur (GS)

	Horse / details	Dist	Pos	SP	RR	SF
2699*	**Macgeorge (IRE) (107)** (RLee) **7-11-6** AMaguire (j.w: mde virtually all: clr 2 out: eased nr fin)	—	**1**	7/4[1]	125+	53
2762[4]	**Sailor Jim (105)** (PTDalton) **10-11-4** NWilliamson (lw: hld up: hdwy 10th: jnd wnr 4 out: wknd appr 2 out)	18	**2**	4/1[3]	109	37
2814[6]	**Howgill (94)** (CaptTAForster) **11-10-7b** SWynne (chsd ldrs: outpcd appr 4 out: hrd rdn appr 2 out: no imp)	5	**3**	12/1	94	22
2011[5]	**Even Blue (IRE) (115)** (MrsCJBlack) **9-12-0** JRailton (chsd ldrs: lost tch whn mstkes 10th & next: styd on u.p fr 2 out)	1	**4**	7/2[2]	114	42
2814[5]	**Cropredy Lad (92)** (PRWebber) **10-10-5** JOsborne (lw: nvr nr ldrs)	1¼	**5**	11/2	90	18
2077[F]	**Spearhead Again (IRE) (87)** (KSBridgwater) **8-10-0** BPowell (mstke 7th: a bhd)	4	**6**	25/1	82	10
2843[4]	**Count Barachois (USA) (87)** (MrsEHHeath) **9-10-0** KGaule (lw: w wnr to 10th: wknd qckly: t.o)	30	**7**	33/1	59	—
2823[8]	**Tribal Ruler (87)** (DMcCain) **12-10-0** DWalsh (bit bkwd: bhd: blnd 9th: p.u bef next)		**P**	25/1	—	—

(SP 112.3%) **8 Rn**

5m 10.9 (9.90) CSF £8.27 CT £54.78 TOTE £1.70: £1.10 £2.00 £2.90 (£4.70) OWNER Mr J. H. Watson (PRESTEIGNE) BRED Mrs B. Brady
LONG HANDICAP Spearhead Again (IRE) 9-11 Count Barachois (USA) 9-7 Tribal Ruler 9-11
2699* Macgeorge (IRE), at the top of his form just now, galloped these rivals into the ground and won very easily indeed. (7/4)
2762 Sailor Jim made smooth progress to put himself in with every chance on the approach to the straight but, once the winner quickened things up, he was soon struggling to hold on. (4/1)
23 Howgill got tapped for toe turning out of the back straight and, though he did keep persevering under pressure, had to admit the principals too strong for him. (12/1: op 8/1)
2011 Even Blue (IRE) was given no chance to adopt his usual front-running tactics and, inclined to run his race in snatches, was fighting a lost cause from halfway. (7/2)
2814 Cropredy Lad, settled in rear, never got into the race, but he was staying on and these tactics over three miles could bring about an upturn in his fortunes. (11/2)

3072 VICARAGE CLAIMING HURDLE (4-Y.O+) (Class F)
2-30 (2-32) **2m (9 hdls)** £2,595.00 (£720.00: £345.00) GOING: 0.28 sec per fur (GS)

	Horse / details	Dist	Pos	SP	RR	SF
2925[P]	**Apache Park (USA)** (MSheppard) **4-10-5b[1]** DGallagher (a.p: led appr 4 out: j.b rt: blnd last: rdn & hld on)	—	**1**	14/1	59	23
	Threesocks (BSmart) **4-10-3** ILawrence (hld up: hdwy 4th: chsd wnr fr 4 out: rdn 2 out: r.o towards fin)	1¼	**2**	12/1	56	20
	Tulu (115) (MrsJRRamsden) **6-11-9** RGarritty (bkwd: hld up: hdwy appr 5th: ev ch 4 out: rdn & wknd appr last)	13	**3**	2/1[1]	53	27
2884[14]	**White Willow (118)** (TWall) **8-11-8v**(3) RMassey (hld up: hdwy appr 4 out: wknd 3 out)	23	**4**	4/1[2]	32	6
2946[5]	**High Low (USA)** (WJenks) **9-11-8b[1]** TJenks (swtg: chsd ldr: led appr 5th: sn hdd: wknd 3 out)	4	**5**	6/1[3]	25	—
2815[7]	**Gi Moss** (PRHarriss) **10-10-11b** WMarston (rdn 4 out: nvr nr to chal)	1¼	**6**	20/1	13	—
2867[P]	**Ernest Aragorn** (MrsSLamyman) **8-11-5v** RFarrant (hdwy 4th: rdn & wkng whn bdly hmpd 3 out)	1¾	**7**	50/1	19	—

Form	Horse / details	Dist	Pos	SP	RR	SF
185^{P}	**Khazari (USA) (65)** (RBrotherton) **9-11-5** LHarvey (bkwd: a in rr)	6	**8**	25/1	13	—
2815^{11}	**Bites** (TTBill) **4-10-0** TEley (nvr nr ldrs)	½	**9**	66/1	3	—
1770^{9}	**Monty** (GHYardley) **5-11-5** VSlattery (t.o)	6	**10**	50/1	6	—
1818^{7}	**Mill Dancer (IRE)** (PWHiatt) **5-10-8** SWynne (led: mstke 2nd: hdd & wknd appr 5th: t.o)	¾	**11**	33/1	—	—
1980^{6}	**Admiral's Guest (IRE)** (WClay) **5-11-5v** RJohnson (chsd ldrs to 5th: sn wknd: t.o)	14	**12**	33/1	—	—
	Brick Court (IRE) (RFJohnsonHoughton) **5-10-8** NWilliamson (bkwd: b.d 2nd)		**B**	10/1	—	—
2813^{2}	**Sheecky (72)** (BAMcMahon) **6-11-3**(5) SRyan (chsd ldrs: rdn appr 4 out: btn whn fell 3 out)		**F**	9/1	—	—
2818^{9}	**Espla** (JSMoore) **6-11-8** WMcFarland (bit bkwd: fell 2nd)		**F**	14/1	—	—
2873^{P}	**Ashley House (70)** (BRMillman) **8-10-11b**^{1}(5) DSalter (chsd ldrs to ½-wy: bhd whn p.u bef 4 out)		**P**	66/1	—	—
	Arabian Design (JRinger) **5-11-5** BPowell (bit bkwd: t.o: p.u bef 4 out)		**P**	33/1	—	—
939^{11}	**Backhander (IRE)** (RTPhillips) **5-11-2** JRailton (a in rr: t.o whn p.u bef 2 out)		**P**	20/1	—	—
	Manabar (MJPolglase) **5-11-5** VSmith (bhd whn blnd & uns rdr 3 out)		**U**	33/1	—	—

(SP 139.8%) **19 Rn**

3m 56.1 (11.10) CSF £158.32 TOTE £17.60: £3.50 £2.80 £2.50 (£101.90) Trio £253.10 OWNER Mr M. G. Hynes (LEDBURY) BRED Echo Valley Horse Farm and Swettenham Stud

WEIGHT FOR AGE 4yo-10lb

Apache Park (USA) clmd T Pearson £3,000.

Apache Park (USA) was able to open his account on this step down in company and had he not jumped violently right at three of the last four flights, would have won more or less as he pleased. (14/1)

Threesocks, fit from the Flat, made her move with the winner early in the straight but he was always going that bit better and she is flattered to finish so close. (12/1)

Tulu looked more like a mare in foal for this return to action but she is better class than this when she is fully tuned up and should be a different proposition next time. (2/1: op evens)

2946 High Low (USA) adopted his usual forceful tactics in his first time blinkers but he was unable to match strides when the winner cruised past early in the straight and gradually dropped away. (6/1: op 4/1)

3073 THURNBY MAIDEN CHASE (5-Y.O+) (Class F)

3-00 (3-03) **2m 1f (12 fncs)** £2,626.75 (£784.00: £374.50: £169.75) GOING: 0.28 sec per fur (GS)

Form	Horse / details	Dist	Pos	SP	RR	SF
2691^{5}	**Just Bruce (83)** (MrsEHHeath) **8-11-5** KGaule (led 2nd to 5th: outpcd appr 4 out: lft in ld 2 out: rdn out)	—	**1**	7/1^{3}	98	30
	Frank Knows (60) (TRGeorge) **7-11-5** RJohnson (bit bkwd: prom: outpcd 8th: rallied appr last: r.o)	2½	**2**	100/1	96	28
2875^{3}	**Charlie Parrot (IRE)** (MCPipe) **7-11-5** JamieEvans (hld up: stdy hdwy 4th: hit 4 out: rdn appr 2 out: wknd flat)	17	**3**	9/2^{2}	80	12
2823^{10}	**Full Shilling (USA) (64)** (DLWilliams) **8-11-2b**(3) GuyLewis (chsd ldrs to 7th: sn lost tch: t.o)	10	**4**	25/1	70	2
1683^{P}	**Althrey Aristocrat (IRE) (60)** (FLloyd) **7-11-5** SMcNeill (a bhd: t.o)	dist	**5**	100/1	—	—
2746^{10}	**Dannicus** (NMBabbage) **6-11-5** VSlattery (hmpd 1st: sn t.o: carried out 6th)		**C**	11/1	—	—
	Elzoba (FR) (MCPipe) **5-10-10** CMaude (led to 2nd: hit 4th: led next: clr fr 4 out: fell 2 out)		**F**	4/6^{1}	—	—
2892^{5}	**The Secret Grey** (DMcCain) **6-11-5** DWalsh (fell 1st)		**F**	50/1	—	—
	Pleasure Cruise (JKCresswell) **7-10-12**(7) NTEgan (fell 1st)		**F**	66/1	—	—
2682^{16}	**Whod of Thought It (IRE)** (PRChamings) **6-11-0**(5) MrCVigors (fell 6th)		**F**	50/1	—	—
2752^{5}	**Virbazar (FR) (60)** (JGSmyth-Osbourne) **10-11-5** GUpton (bit bkwd: sn wl bhd: t.o whn fell 7th: dead)		**F**	25/1	—	—

(SP 114.1%) **11 Rn**

4m 23.6 (13.60) CSF £412.91 TOTE £7.90: £1.10 £8.10 £1.40 (£75.30) Trio £144.20 OWNER Mr A. M. Heath (ROYSTON) BRED A. M. Heath

WEIGHT FOR AGE 5yo-9lb

2691 Just Bruce was a very fortunate winner but the name of the game is jumping and it enabled him to get off the mark. (7/1)

Frank Knows, making his chasing bow on this belated seasonal debut, ran well in the circumstances and should be much wiser and fitter when he next appears. (100/1)

2875 Charlie Parrot (IRE), far from foot-perfect at the final ditch, was left with every chance at the penultimate fence but he was unable to take it and proved very onepaced when the battle to the finish really developed. At least he showed he can jump. (9/2)

1782 Dannicus (11/1: 8/1-12/1)

Elzoba (FR), another Pipe import from France, recovered from an early mistake and drew clear from the turn into the straight. He was still full of running with the prize safely wrapped up when he knuckled over on landing at the second last. (4/6)

3074 TRIAL H'CAP CHASE (0-125) (5-Y.O+) (Class D)

3-30 (3-30) **3m (18 fncs)** £5,481.00 (£1,638.00: £784.00: £357.00) GOING: 0.28 sec per fur (GS)

Form	Horse / details	Dist	Pos	SP	RR	SF
1043*	**Merlins Dream (IRE) (108)** (OSherwood) **8-11-3** JOsborne (lw: led to 3rd: led 3 out: hrd drvn flat: hld on wl)	—	**1**	11/2^{3}	114	46
2782^{U}	**Romany Creek (IRE) (116)** (JPearce) **8-11-11v** NWilliamson (hld up & bhd: hdwy 10th: mstke 12th: blnd & lost pl 4 out: rallied & ev ch last: r.o)	¾	**2**	7/1	122	54
2706*	**Act of Parliament (IRE) (119)** (KCBailey) **9-11-7b**(7) MrRWakley (hld up: hdwy 8th: lost pl 4 out: styd on appr last)	8	**3**	9/2^{2}	119	51
2814^{7}	**Mugoni Beach (117)** (MCPipe) **12-11-12** JamieEvans (hld up: effrt & ev ch 3 out: sn rdn: wknd last)	1¼	**4**	16/1	116	48
2814*	**Shining Light (IRE) (114)** (DNicholson) **8-11-9** AMaguire (hld up: mstke 10th: hdwy 12th: chal & hit 2 out: sn rdn & wknd)	5	**5**	9/4^{1}	110	42
2817^{9}	**The Glow (IRE) (113)** (MrsJPitman) **9-11-8b** RFarrant (bit bkwd: plld hrd: prom: mstke 12th: ev ch 3 out: wknd qckly appr last)	8	**6**	7/1	104	36
2758^{11}	**Dont Tell the Wife (116)** (CREgerton) **11-11-4**(7) MBerry (lw: hld up: hdwy 8th: outpcd 10th: hrd rdn & hit 13th: n.d after)	4	**7**	16/1	104	36
2568^{P}	**Well Briefed (110)** (RHBuckler) **10-11-5** BPowell (j.w: led 3rd to 3 out: wknd qckly next: t.o)	dist	**8**	20/1	—	—
2869^{6}	**Makes Me Goosey (IRE) (96)** (MrsIMcKie) **9-10-5b** LHarvey (j.b: prom whn j.v.slowly 9th: t.o whn p.u bef next: dead)		**P**	10/1	—	—

(SP 115.0%) **9 Rn**

6m 7.0 (13.00) CSF £39.49 CT £170.64 TOTE £6.20: £1.60 £1.80 £1.60 (£20.70) Trio £59.20 OWNER Mr W. S. Watt (UPPER LAMBOURN) BRED Neville Bourke

1043* Merlins Dream (IRE), produced in tip top condition after a mid-season holiday, had to work in the latter stages but he always appeared to have the edge and could now be on a roll. (11/2)

1863 Romany Creek (IRE) had the visor back on but a series of mistakes inside the final mile caused him to lose ground at a crucial stage, otherwise he would have won. He will be on a recovery mission in the coming weeks. (7/1: 5/1-8/1)

2706* Act of Parliament (IRE) became detached on the approach to the straight and though he did find his stride again in the closing stages was never going to reach the leading pair. (9/2)
Mugoni Beach, much sharper than on his initial outing last month, ran a race full of promise and is coming to hand. (16/1)
2814* Shining Light (IRE) waited on the leaders and never left the inside rail but he clouted the penultimate fence when in full flight and that took the stuffing out of him. This trip could be stretching his stamina. (9/4)
The Glow (IRE) ran much better than his finishing position would suggest and, back over a slightly shorter trip, could well return to form. (7/1)

3075 SOMMERBY HURDLE (4-Y.O) (Class E)

4-00 (4-01) **2m (9 hdls)** £2,721.00 (£756.00: £363.00) GOING: 0.28 sec per fur (GS)

	Horse	Details	Dist	Pos	SP	RR	SF
	Font Romeu (FR)	(MCPipe) **4-10-12** JamieEvans (chsd ldrs: rdn after 5th: led 2 out: r.o strly)	—	**1**	25/1	83	18
2697[P]	**Circus Star**	(DNicholson) **4-10-12** AMaguire (hld up: hdwy 5th: led 3 out to 2 out: one pce)	5	**2**	6/1[2]	78	13
2759[10]	**Topaglow (IRE)**	(PTDalton) **4-10-12** BFenton (hld up: hdwy appr 4 out: rdn appr 2 out: r.o wl flat)	½	**3**	50/1	73	13
2889[2]	**Northern Fleet**	(MrsAJPerrett) **4-10-12** CMaude (lw: a.p: led appr 5th to 3 out: sn rdn: one pce)	1¾	**4**	8/1[3]	71	11
1712[2]	**Siberian Henry**	(BSmart) **4-10-12** ILawrence (hld up: hdwy 5th: ev ch 3 out: btn whn hit last)	3	**5**	25/1	68	8
2889[3]	**Name of Our Father (USA)**	(PBowen) **4-11-5** RJohnson (chsd ldrs: rdn & no hdwy fr 3 out)	3	**6**	25/1	72	12
2751[6]	**Daydreamer (USA)**	(RHBuckler) **4-10-12** BPowell (nvr nr to chal)	1	**7**	66/1	64	4
1370[5]	**Precious Island**	(PTDalton) **4-10-7** JSupple (hld up: hdwy appr 4 out: wknd 3 out)	5	**8**	50/1	54	—
	Ezanak (IRE)	(MissHCKnight) **4-10-12** JCulloty (nvr nrr)	¾	**9**	14/1	58	—
2925[10]	**Mighty Keen**	(MCBanks) **4-10-12** DSkyrme (chsd ldrs tl wknd appr 3 out: t.o)	16	**10**	50/1	42	—
2868[3]	**Magic Combination (IRE)**	(BJCurley) **4-10-9**[(3)] LAspell (a in rr: t.o)	5	**11**	10/1	37	—
2820[18]	**Sterling Fellow (83)**	(DLWilliams) **4-10-12v** MClarke (sn t.o)	4	**12**	66/1	33	—
2655[5]	**Fencer's Quest (IRE)**	(CaptTAForster) **4-10-12** NWilliamson (nvr trbld ldrs: t.o)	hd	**13**	25/1	33	—
2815[15]	**The Oddfellow**	(NBycroft) **4-10-12** OPears (t.o)		**14**	66/1	—	—
2791*	**Pomme Secret (FR)**	(MCPipe) **4-11-5** JOsborne (lw: prom: rdn 5th: wknd appr 4 out: t.o)		**15**	11/10[1]	—	—
	Circled (USA)	(JohnHarris) **4-10-7** DGallagher (prom tl mstke 5th: sn bhd: t.o)		**16**	25/1	—	—
1862[6]	**Poetry (IRE)**	(MHTompkins) **4-10-7** JRailton (t.o whn p.u bef 2 out)		**P**	33/1	—	—
	Gemini Dream	(RFJohnsonHoughton) **4-10-12** RBellamy (bhd fr ½-wy: t.o whn p.u bef 4 out)		**P**	50/1	—	—
2825[P]	**Courting Danger**	(DRGandolfo) **4-10-9b1**[(3)] DFortt (led tl after 5th: sn wknd: t.o whn p.u bef 2 out)		**P**	66/1	—	—
2751[3]	**Anna Soleil (IRE)**	(OSherwood) **4-10-12** JAMcCarthy (lw: blnd & uns rdr 2nd)		**U**	8/1[3]	—	—

(SP 135.9%) **20 Rn**

3m 58.6 (13.60) CSF £156.37 TOTE £54.80: £12.10 £1.70 £18.70 (£47.20) Trio Not won; £315.28 to Lingfield 12/2/97 OWNER Pond House Gold (WELLINGTON) BRED Mrs A. Daubin
OFFICIAL EXPLANATION **Pomme Secret (FR): rider reported that the colt was never on the bridle and made jumping errors.**
Font Romeu (FR), another recruit from France, made up for the disappointing performance of his better-fancied stable-mate with a very smooth success and he looks a promising juvenile. (25/1)
1935 Circus Star, still struggling to make his mark over hurdles, did look to be travelling best when showing in front three out but once the winner threw down his challenge the writing was on the wall. (6/1)
1699 Topaglow (IRE) does need a stiffer test of stamina then he had here and was only finding top gear when the race was as good as over. (50/1)
2889 Northern Fleet made sure the pace was strong and was in the firing line, going as well as any, until failing to pick up as the tempo increased between the last two. (8/1: op 4/1)
1712 Siberian Henry found this company stronger than he met on his hurdling debut but he had only just given best when he ploughed through the last. (25/1)
2889 Name of Our Father (USA) pushed the pace but he was being made to work turning in and found the task beyond him. (25/1)
2868 Magic Combination (IRE) (10/1: op 3/1)
2791* Pomme Secret (FR) let his Cheltenham hopes down with a bang on this most disappointing display, and the only visible excuse could be that he had not been given sufficient time to recover from his Plumpton race. (11/10: evens-5/4)

3076 OADBY H'CAP HURDLE (0-110) (4-Y.O+) (Class E)

4-30 (4-30) **2m (9 hdls)** £2,406.00 (£666.00: £318.00) GOING: 0.28 sec per fur (GS)

	Horse	Details	Dist	Pos	SP	RR	SF
1963[8]	**Sheriffmuir (105)**	(MrsLWadham) **8-12-0** JFTitley (lw: hld up: hdwy 4th: led 2 out: r.o wl)	—	**1**	16/1	93	35
1984*	**Kintavi (90)**	(TWDonnelly) **7-10-13** TEley (lw: mstke 2nd: hdwy 4th: ev ch 2 out: one pce)	2	**2**	3/1[2]	76	18
2813*	**Beechfield Flyer (85)**	(WClay) **6-10-8** GTormey (hdwy 4th: one pce fr 2 out)	6	**3**	11/2	65	7
2817[10]	**Chill Wind (86)**	(NBycroft) **8-10-9** RJohnson (bit bkwd: hdwy 4th: led 3 out to 2 out: sn hrd rdn & wknd)	¾	**4**	33/1	65	7
2631*	**Mr Moriarty (IRE) (97)**	(SRBowring) **6-11-6** AMaguire (led to 2nd: led 3rd tl hit 3 out: wknd appr last)	3½	**5**	7/2[3]	73	15
2744[7]	**Past Master (USA) (81)**	(SGollings) **9-10-4** KGaule (lw: rdn & hdwy after 5th: hit 4 out: sn wknd: t.o)	21	**6**	10/1	36	—
2842[4]	**Bob's Ploy (81)**	(MHTompkins) **5-10-4v** NWilliamson (lw: led 2nd to 3rd: wknd qckly appr 2 out: t.o)	6	**7**	11/4[1]	30	—
2828[4]	**River Island (USA) (92)**	(JABOld) **9-11-1** GUpton (hld up & bhd: lost tch ½-wy: t.o whn p.u bef 2 out)		**P**	16/1	—	—

(SP 113.1%) **8 Rn**

3m 58.2 (13.20) CSF £57.92 CT £276.87 TOTE £21.10: £4.20 £1.20 £2.00 (£26.70) OWNER Mr J. J. W. Wadham (NEWMARKET) BRED Stetchworth Park Stud Ltd
Sheriffmuir appreciated this return to hurdles and, with the going in his favour, was able to succeed at the minimum trip for the first time. (16/1)
1984* Kintavi looked the likely winner when jumping the penultimate flight upsides, but he did not pick up when pressure was applied, although to his credit he did stay on. (3/1)
2813* Beechfield Flyer had more on his plate here and, though he did well to make the frame, did not give his supporters much hope of success. (11/2: 7/2-6/1)
Chill Wind looked set to produce a big upset when showing ahead in the straight but he ran out of steam approaching the last. He is worth keeping in mind from now on. (33/1)
2842 Bob's Ploy looked well in at the weights and was in with every chance until calling enough approaching the second last. He looks to have a mind of his own. (11/4)

T/Jkpt: Not won; £7,011.98 to Lingfield 12/2/97. T/Plpt: £264.50 (108.39 Tckts). T/Qdpt: £28.70 (34.21 Tckts) IM

2831-SEDGEFIELD (L-H) - Tuesday February 11th

3077 - 3083 Abandoned - Course Unfit

2865-LINGFIELD (L-H) (Heavy)

Wednesday February 12th

One fence, one hurdle omitted. Racing delayed 20 mins after 2nd - crse inspection.

3084 ORPINGTON NOVICES' HURDLE (4-Y.O+) (Class D)

2-00 (2-00) **2m 110y (7 hdls)** £3,224.60 (£895.60: £429.80) GOING: 1.89 sec per fur (HY)

				SP	RR	SF
2865[F]	**Harbet House (FR)** (RJO'Sullivan) **4-10-7** NWilliamson (plld hrd: a.p: led 4th: clr appr last: rdn out)	—	**1**	6/1[3]	82	27
2791[3]	**Eau de Cologne** (MrsLRichards) **5-11-3** MRichards (hld up: rdn appr 2 out: unable qckn)	7	**2**	12/1	75	30
2791[4]	**Ivory Coaster (NZ)** (BdeHaan) **6-11-3** JOsborne (hdwy 4th: hrd rdn appr last: one pce)	1½	**3**	33/1	74	29
790[6]	**Rising Dough (IRE)** (GLMoore) **5-11-3** DGallagher (bit bkwd: hdwy 3rd: ev ch 2 out: wknd flat)	7	**4**	3/1[2]	67	22
	Frys No Fool (JABOld) **7-11-3** GUpton (hdwy 3rd: wknd 2 out)	9	**5**	8/1	58	13
2806*	**Trouvaille (IRE) (96)** (AndrewTurnell) **6-11-9** LHarvey (bhd fr 3rd)	28	**6**	14/1	37	—
1768[3]	**Balleswhidden (95)** (BSmart) **5-11-3** CLlewellyn (bit bkwd: n.d)	3	**7**	8/1	28	—
2868[2]	**Mutanassib (IRE)** (MCPipe) **4-10-7** RDunwoody (a.p: led 3rd to 4th: wknd 3 out)	6	**8**	7/4[1]	22	—
	Cheeky Charlie (JFfitch-Heyes) **5-11-3** BFenton (a bhd)	17	**9**	66/1	6	—
	Otto E Mezzo (MJPolglase) **5-11-3** VSmith (bkwd: prom to 3 out)	10	**10**	25/1	—	—
	Barbara's Jewel (ABailey) **5-11-3** TKent (led to 3rd: sn wknd: t.o whn p.u bef 3 out)		**P**	50/1	—	—
	Dia Georgy (CADwyer) **6-11-3** ILawrence (a bhd: t.o whn p.u bef 2 out)		**P**	50/1	—	—
2791[5]	**Clock Watchers (68)** (JJBridger) **9-11-3** DMorris (bhd fr 3rd: t.o whn p.u bef 2 out)		**P**	66/1	—	—
1830[15]	**Ballyquintet (IRE)** (HBHodge) **6-10-12** KGaule (bhd fr 3rd: t.o whn p.u bef 4th)		**P**	66/1	—	—
	Anif (USA) (JJoseph) **6-11-3** DSkyrme (a bhd: t.o whn p.u bef 3 out)		**P**	66/1	—	—
				(SP 128.9%)	**15 Rn**	

4m 22.3 (37.30) CSF £69.11 TOTE £8.80: £2.80 £2.30 £5.00 (£47.30) Trio £171.10; £168.69 to Taunton 13/2/97 OWNER Mr C. A. Washbourn (WHITCOMBE) BRED S. Niarchos

WEIGHT FOR AGE 4yo-10lb

2865 Harbet House (FR), who showed plenty of promise when falling here twelve days ago, loves the mud and, leading at the fourth, had no problems forging clear from the second last for a decisive victory. A real chasing type, staying is his game and he would need two and three-quarter miles on good to soft ground, according to his trainer. (6/1)

2791 Eau de Cologne, who showed a lot of promise on his Plumpton debut, coped with the energy-sapping conditions and struggled on in the straight to win the battle for second prize. (12/1: op 6/1)

2791 Ivory Coaster (NZ) has shown that he goes well on this ground but, try as he might, failed to muster another gear in the straight. (33/1)

790 Rising Dough (IRE) can handle this ground, but he did not look fully wound up after a four and a half month absence, and that told against him in these severe conditions for, having every chance at the second last, he tired on the run-in. He should soon be winning. (3/1: 4/1-5/2)

Frys No Fool, off the course for nearly a year, was making his hurdling debut, and did not run badly until lack of a recent run took its toll early in the straight. (8/1: 6/1-10/1)

2806* Trouvaille (IRE), whose win last month came on fast ground, totally failed to handle these extremely testing conditions. (14/1: op 8/1)

2868 Mutanassib (IRE) (7/4: op evens)

3085 SANDERSTEAD MAIDEN HURDLE (4-Y.O+) (Class E)

2-30 (2-33) **2m 7f (10 hdls)** £2,729.00 (£759.00: £365.00) GOING: 1.89 sec per fur (HY)

				SP	RR	SF
2880[5]	**Warner For Players (IRE)** (PJHobbs) **6-11-8** NWilliamson (hdwy 4th: led 6th: clr 2 out: eased flat)	—	**1**	10/11[1]	68+	—
1683[5]	**Dancetillyoudrop (IRE)** (PFNicholls) **6-11-8** DBridgwater (lw: hdwy 6th: chsd wnr after 3 out: unable qckn)	5	**2**	9/2[2]	65	—
1323[P]	**Credo Boy** (KBishop) **8-11-8** BPowell (nvr nr to chal: t.o)	dist	**3**	25/1	—	—
2012[8]	**Willows Roulette** (AGHobbs) **5-11-8** RGreene (hdwy 6th: wknd appr 2 out: t.o)	2	**4**	50/1	—	—
	Greg's Profiles (NATwiston-Davies) **6-11-8** TJMurphy (a bhd: t.o)	dist	**5**	12/1	—	—
2661[9]	**Brave Edwin (IRE)** (JABOld) **7-11-8** JOsborne (hdwy 6th: wknd appr 2 out: t.o)	12	**6**	15/2[3]	—	—
	Forest Mill (80) (JLSpearing) **5-11-3** RJohnson (bit bkwd: bhd fr 6th: t.o)	dist	**7**	25/1	—	—
1536[7]	**High Mood (61)** (TRGeorge) **7-11-8** RFarrant (hdwy 6th: wknd appr 3 out: t.o)	1¾	**8**	50/1	—	—
2626[5]	**Roll Again** (MCPipe) **6-11-8** CMaude (prom to 6th: t.o whn p.u bef 2 out)		**P**	20/1	—	—
2039[F]	**Mr Lovely (IRE)** (JNeville) **6-11-8** WMarston (prom to 6th: t.o whn p.u bef 3 out)		**P**	9/1	—	—
	Paprika (IRE) (88) (AGNewcombe) **8-11-3** DGallagher (a bhd: t.o whn p.u bef 2 out)		**P**	14/1	—	—
1077[P]	**Fashion Leader (IRE)** (CWeedon) **6-11-8** BFenton (bit bkwd: prom tl mstke 4th: t.o whn p.u bef 6th)		**P**	50/1	—	—
	King's Affair (PRHedger) **7-11-1**(7) MClinton (chsd ldr to 6th: sn wknd: t.o whn p.u bef 3 out)		**P**	50/1	—	—
1679[8]	**Derrybelle** (DLWilliams) **6-11-3** MClarke (a bhd: t.o whn p.u bef 2 out)		**P**	50/1	—	—
2826[P]	**Gentle Tune (IRE)** (JRBest) **7-11-1**(7) MrPO'Keeffe (led to 6th: sn wknd: t.o whn p.u bef 3 out)		**P**	50/1	—	—
2677[6]	**Charlie's Folly** (BdeHaan) **6-11-8** CLlewellyn (bhd fr 6th: t.o whn p.u bef 2 out)		**P**	20/1	—	—
				(SP 135.7%)	**16 Rn**	

6m 31.4 (68.40) CSF £4.76 TOTE £2.40: £1.10 £1.80 £10.50 (£4.30) Trio £71.00 OWNER Terry Warner Sports (MINEHEAD) BRED Hugh Suffern Bloodstock Ltd

2880 Warner For Players (IRE) was in his element in these conditions. Leading early on the final circuit, he forged clear with the minimum of fuss in the straight to win doing handsprings. He was eased considerably on the run-in and was certainly value for at least fifteen lengths. He must have conditions like this and, if the rain continues to fall, will have no problems winning again. (10/11: 8/11-evens)

1683 Dancetillyoudrop (IRE) appreciated the longer trip, and was the only one to make a race of it with the winner. He was easily brushed aside in the straight, and is greatly flattered by the margin as the winner was eased down considerably. (9/2)

Mr Lovely (IRE) (9/1: 12/1-8/1)

Paprika (IRE) (14/1: 10/1-16/1)

3086 OXTED NOVICES' CHASE (5-Y.O+) (Class D)

3-00 (3-20) **2m 4f 110y (13 fncs)** £3,996.60 (£1,195.80: £573.40: £262.20) GOING: 2.16 sec per fur (HY)

				SP	RR	SF
2867*	**Glitter Isle (IRE) (112)** (JTGifford) **7-11-10** PHide (a.p: chsd ldr fr 7th: led 2 out: comf)	—	**1**	13/8[1]	112+	44

	Horse (Trainer) Age-Wt Jockey (comment)	Dist	Pos	SP	RR	SF
	Angelo's Double (IRE) (RHBuckler) **9-11-4** BPowell (bit bkwd: led: mstke 9th: hdd 2 out: wknd last)	12	**2**	$5/2^{2}$	97+	29
	Indian Delight (MCPipe) **7-11-4** CMaude (lw: prom to 4 out: t.o)	dist	**3**	25/1	—	—
	Plumbridge (PRChamings) **9-11-4** BFenton (a bhd: t.o)	22	**4**	25/1	—	—
2679^{7}	**Reeshloch (90)** (AndrewTurnell) **8-11-4b** NWilliamson (a.p: 4th whn mstke 4 out: sn wknd: t.o)	29	**5**	12/1	—	—
	With Impunity (102) (PFNicholls) **8-11-4** DBridgwater (5th whn fell 8th)		**F**	$9/2^{3}$	—	—
2049^{F}	**Slipmatic** (AndrewTurnell) **8-10-13** LHarvey (bhd whn fell 8th)		**F**	16/1	—	—
2657^{4}	**Country Keeper (75)** (BJMRyall) **9-11-4** GUpton (a bhd: blnd 7th: t.o whn fell 2 out)		**F**	20/1	—	—
2691^{6}	**Althrey Blue (IRE) (60)** (AndrewTurnell) **8-11-4** SMcNeill (bhd fr 6th: t.o whn fell 2 out)		**F**	50/1	—	—
	Sound Statement (IRE) (MissSEdwards) **8-11-4** MrTHills (bhd fr 9th: t.o whn p.u bef 3 out)		**P**	20/1	—	—
2795^{P}	**Minor Key (IRE) (87)** (JRJenkins) **7-11-4** JOsborne (a bhd: blnd 7th: t.o whn p.u bef 9th)		**P**	33/1	—	—
2756^{P}	**Spy Dessa (63)** (AGNewcombe) **9-11-4** DGallagher (bhd fr 9th: t.o whn p.u bef 3 out)		**P**	50/1	—	—
1568^{12}	**Lucky Call (NZ)** (AGHobbs) **6-11-4** RGreene (bhd tl blnd & uns rdr 6th)		**U**	50/1	—	—
				(SP 124.5%)	**13 Rn**	

5m 51.0 (52.00) CSF £5.10 TOTE £2.50: £1.80 £1.70 £4.30 (£8.30) Trio £33.20 OWNER Mrs Timothy Pilkington (FINDON) BRED Pat Hickey

2867* Glitter Isle (IRE) seemed well suited by the return to two and a half miles, and was perfectly at home in the mud. Putting up a polished display, he led at the second last, and had no problems forging clear for a decisive victory. Despite his having run only twice over fences, connections are contemplating a trip to Cheltenham for the Royal SunAlliance Chase. (13/8)

Angelo's Double (IRE), not surprisingly, did not look fully wound up for this first run in a year, but still showed a great deal of promise on this chasing debut. Bowling along in front, he was collared at the second last, but grimly tried to hold on until lack of a recent run took its toll going over the final fence. He goes well in the mud and should soon open his account over the larger obstacles.(5/2: 9/4-7/2)

Indian Delight looked in good shape for his chasing debut, his first run in ten months, and played an active role until left standing from the fourth last. (25/1)

1552 Reeshloch (12/1: 8/1-14/1)

3087 THREE COUNTIES H'CAP HURDLE (0-110) (4-Y.O+) (Class E)

3-30 (3-50) **2m 110y (7 hdls)** £2,201.20 (£608.20: £289.60) GOING: 2.16 sec per fur (HY)

	Horse (Trainer) Age-Wt Jockey (comment)	Dist	Pos	SP	RR	SF
3002^{6}	**Nipper Reed (98)** (THind) **7-11-2** RDunwoody (s.s: plld hrd: hdwy to ld 1st: hrd rdn flat: r.o wl)	—	**1**	7/1	81	31
2828^{2}	**August Twelfth (85)** (DCO'Brien) **9-10-3**ow1 PHide (lw: hld up: chsd wnr appr last: unable qckn)	3½	**2**	$11/4^{2}$	65	14
2871*	**Tickerty's Gift (110)** (GLMoore) **7-11-7**(7) MAttwater (lw: led to 1st: chsd wnr fr 4th: ev ch 2 out: wknd appr last)	9	**3**	$6/4^{1}$	81	31
551^{P}	**El Grando (83)** (KOCunningham-Brown) **7-10-1** DGallagher (chsd wnr 2nd tl mstke 4th: wknd appr 2 out)	22	**4**	5/1	33	—
2842^{5}	**Winsford Hill (89)** (PJHobbs) **6-10-7** GTormey (lw: s.s: bhd fr 3 out)	19	**5**	$9/2^{3}$	20	—
				(SP 114.0%)	**5 Rn**	

4m 27.7 (42.70) CSF £24.60 TOTE £5.80: £1.70 £2.00 (£10.00) OWNER Mr G. Piper (WENDOVER) BRED Witham Land and Leisure Services Ltd

OFFICIAL EXPLANATION **Nipper Reed: trainer reported that the gelding's run last time had been his first for two years, and that he relished the heavy going here.**

Nipper Reed was given a lovely ride by Dunwoody, who kept searching out the better ground all the way round. Soon in front having whipped round at the start, he kept up the gallop in the straight to give his trainer his first-ever winner. (7/1)

2828 August Twelfth revels in these conditions but, despite struggling into second place approaching the last, was unable to get on terms with the winner. (11/4)

2871* Tickerty's Gift has gained all five of his victories to date here in the mud, and had every chance two out before top-weight found him out. (6/4: evens-13/8)

223 El Grando, without a run in five-and-a-half months, had bellows to mend turning into the straight. (5/1)

2842 Winsford Hill (9/2: 3/1-5/1)

3088 WARLINGHAM H'CAP HURDLE (0-100) (4-Y.O+) (Class F)

4-00 (4-17) **2m 3f 110y (9 hdls)** £2,250.00 (£625.00: £300.00) GOING: 2.16 sec per fur (HY)

	Horse (Trainer) Age-Wt Jockey (comment)	Dist	Pos	SP	RR	SF
2797^{3}	**Total Joy (IRE) (92)** (CJMann) **6-11-13** RDunwoody (hdwy 5th: led 3 out: clr appr last: comf)	—	**1**	$5/1^{2}$	78	—
2694^{5}	**Lord Rooble (IRE) (93)** (JTGifford) **6-11-7**(7) SLaird (hdwy 3 out: chsd wnr appr last: no imp)	11	**2**	$6/1^{3}$	70	—
1962^{3}	**Roskeen Bridge (IRE) (69)** (CWeedon) **6-10-4** NWilliamson (hdwy 5th: led appr 3 out: sn hdd: wknd appr last)	3½	**3**	$5/1^{2}$	43	—
2656^{3}	**Shanagore Warrior (IRE) (86)** (SMellor) **5-11-0**(7) SHearn (lw: a.p: rdn 3 out: 4th & btn whn mstke 2 out)	8	**4**	$5/1^{2}$	54	—
	Red Lighter (70) (JABOld) **8-10-5** GUpton (led to 3rd: hmpd bnd appr 5th: wknd 3 out)	10	**5**	20/1	29	—
2818^{6}	**Ewar Bold (75)** (KOCunningham-Brown) **4-10-0** DGallagher (a wl bhd)	11	**6**	20/1	25	—
1683^{P}	**Miss Mylette (IRE) (65)** (DJWintle) **6-10-0** WMarston (led 3rd tl appr 3 out: sn wknd: t.o)	dist	**7**	33/1	—	—
2678^{7}	**Celtic Lilley (66)** (JFfitch-Heyes) **7-9-12b**(3)ow1 PHenley (hld up: rdn 6th: sn wknd t.o)	7	**8**	16/1	—	—
2870*	**Equity's Darling (IRE) (82)** (DCO'Brien) **5-11-3b** PHide (lw: reluctant to r: a bhd: t.o whn p.u bef 2 out)		**P**	$6/1^{3}$	—	—
2897^{11}	**Fontainerouge (IRE) (80)** (GBBalding) **7-11-1** BFenton (mid div whn mstke 4th: bhd fr 5th: t.o whn p.u bef 2 out)		**P**	15/2	—	—
1047^{6}	**Dancing Dancer (73)** (DPGeraghty) **8-10-8** JSupple (a bhd: t.o whn p.u bef 2 out)		**P**	14/1	—	—
1131^{2}	**Amber Ring (75)** (MissKMGeorge) **4-10-0** JRKavanagh (bhd fr 5th: t.o whn p.u bef 2 out)		**P**	14/1	—	—
2820^{8}	**Karen's Typhoon (IRE) (72)** (TPMcGovern) **6-10-7** RJohnson (2nd whn s.u bnd appr 5th)		**S**	16/1	—	—
2870^{P}	***My Man in Dundalk (IRE) (89)*** (BJCurley) **8-11-7**(3) LAspell (Withdrawn not under Starter's orders: trainer's protest against Handicapper)		**W**	$9/2^{1}$	—	—
				(SP 146.1%)	**13 Rn**	

5m 36.0 (62.00) CSF £33.83 CT £151.07 TOTE £9.00: £2.30 £3.60 £1.90 (£13.10) Trio £42.80 OWNER Mr P. M. Warren (UPPER LAMBOURN) BRED Mrs Kiki Ward Platt

LONG HANDICAP Miss Mylette (IRE) 9-9

WEIGHT FOR AGE 4yo-10lb

STEWARDS' ENQUIRY Curley fined £1,400 (wilful disregard of the interest of racegoers).

2797 Total Joy (IRE) coped extremely well with the energy-sapping conditions, leading at the third last and forging clear from the penultimate hurdle to win with plenty in hand. (5/1)

2694 Lord Rooble (IRE) lacks pace and, although struggling into second place approaching the final flight, had no hope of reeling in the winner. He needs to come down in the handicap. (6/1)

1962 Roskeen Bridge (IRE) managed to force his head in front approaching the third last, only to be passed by the winner soon afterwards. He grimly tried to hold on, but was a spent force soon after jumping the penultimate hurdle. (5/1)

3089 R.E. SASSOON MEMORIAL HUNTERS' CHASE (5-Y.O+) (Class H)

4-30 (4-45) **3m (16 fncs)** £1,110.00 (£310.00: £150.00) GOING: 2.16 sec per fur (HY)

Horse / details		Pos	SP	RR	SF
Vicompt de Valmont (PFNicholls) **12-12-2**(5) MrTMitchell (lw: hdwy 9th: chsd ldr fr 10th: led last: r.o wl)	—	1	3/1[2]	113	6
Avostar (MissCSaunders) **10-12-2**(5) MrBPollock (led to last: unable qckn)	12	2	8/1	105	—
Fifth Amendment (CJMann) **12-12-0b**(7) MrAHales (bit bkwd: nvr nr to chal: t.o)	dist	3	12/1	—	—
Centre Stage (MrsSWarr) **11-11-7**(7) MrAWarr (a bhd: t.o fr 5th)	dist	4	33/1	—	—
Ell Gee (MrsPTownsley) **7-11-2**(7) MissCTownsley (3rd whn fell 7th)		F	50/1	—	—
Faringo (MrsDMGrissell) **12-12-0**(7) MrWGowlett (a bhd: t.o fr 5th: p.u bef 4 out)		P	20/1	—	—
Amadeus (FR) (RobertBarr) **9-11-7**(7) MrCWard (bit bkwd: bhd fr 9th: t.o whn p.u bef 12th)		P	20/1	—	—
Over the Edge (CSporborg) **11-12-0**(7) MrSSporborg (lw: bhd fr 8th: t.o whn p.u bef 3 out)		P	8/1	—	—
Colonial Kelly (MrsDMGrissell) **9-11-11**(3) MrPHacking (lw: a bhd: blnd 10th: t.o whn p.u bef 11th)		P	9/2[3]	—	—
Gambling Royal (DrPPritchard) **14-12-0**(7) DrPPritchard (bit bkwd: swtg: chsd ldr to 10th: sn wknd: t.o whn p.u bef 3 out)		P	33/1	—	—
Major Mac (DLWilliams) **10-11-7**(7) MrSDurack (bit bkwd: bhd fr 10th: t.o whn p.u bef 4 out)		P	50/1	—	—
Castlebay Lad (MichaelAppleby) **14-11-7**(7) MrMAppleby (mstke 4th: bhd whn ref 11th)		R	50/1	—	—
Holland House (PRChamings) **11-12-2**(5) MrCVigors (lw: hdwy 6th: mstke 10th: 3rd whn slipped & uns rdr bnd appr 3 out)		U	11/8[1]	—	—

(SP 136.5%) **13 Rn**

7m 12.0 (78.00) CSF £27.11 TOTE £5.30: £1.30 £3.40 £2.70 (£19.40) Trio £121.80; £137.28 to Taunton 13/2/97 OWNER Mrs Bridget Nicholls (SHEPTON MALLET) BRED Roland Rothwell

Vicompt de Valmont, last seen out in the Grand National, had a much easier task on this reappearance. Taking second place at the tenth, he jumped into the lead at the final fence and soon pulled away. (3/1: 9/4-7/2)

Avostar ran a really promising race in these gruelling conditions, especially considering he has not run since finishing lame at Uttoxeter back in May 1995. Bowling along in front, he had only the winner to worry about in the straight but, when collared by that rival jumping the final fence, had little more to offer. As long as he is given time to get over his exertions, he should not be hard-pressed to find a race. (8/1: 4/1-10/1)

Fifth Amendment (12/1: 10/1-20/1)

Over the Edge (8/1: op 5/1)

Holland House had conditions in his favour for this first run in ten months, and was in third place when slipping badly turning into the straight, giving his rider no chance of staying on board. (11/8: op evens)

3090 LEVY BOARD INTERMEDIATE OPEN N.H. FLAT RACE (4, 5 & 6-Y.O) (Class H)

5-00 (5-09) **2m 110y** £1,318.50 (£366.00: £175.50)

Form	Horse / details		Pos	SP	RR	SF
2682[4]	**Rasak** (LadyHerries) **5-11-4** RDunwoody (a.p: led over 1f out: hrd rdn: r.o wl)	—	1	2/1[2]	66 f	—
1177*	**Curraduff Moll (IRE)** (NATwiston-Davies) **6-11-6** CLlewellyn (led tl over 1f out: rdn: r.o)	nk	2	6/4[1]	68 f	—
	Fin Bec (FR) (APJones) **4-10-8** SCurran (a.p: rdn over 3f out: wknd 2f out)	12	3	20/1	54 f	—
2844[2]	**Royal Pot Black (IRE)** (PJHobbs) **6-11-4** GTormey (lw: hdwy 7f out: wknd over 4f out)	17	4	6/1[3]	38 f	—
2682[10]	**Fred Moth** (THind) **4-10-8** DSkyrme (prom over 11f)	nk	5	33/1	37 f	—
	Brook Bee (NAGaselee) **5-11-4** WMarston (hdwy 7f out: wknd over 4f out)	1¼	6	12/1	36 f	—
2844[3]	**Crackon Jake (IRE)** (JSMoore) **4-10-8** WMcFarland (hld up: rdn over 6f out: wknd)	16	7	6/1[3]	21 f	—
2757[6]	**Bebe Grey** (PRHedger) **6-10-6**(7) MClinton (prom over 8f)	9	8	25/1	7 f	—
	Monmouth Way (IRE) (PRChamings) **5-11-4** BFenton (prom over 8f)	2½	9	33/1	9 f	—
	Overrunning (AHHarvey) **5-10-13** MRichards (unf: t.o fnl 11f)	dist	10	25/1	—	—
	Paperprince (NZ) (AGHobbs) **5-10-11**(7) MrGShenkin (a bhd: t.o)	20	11	14/1	—	—
2830[8]	**Don'tcallmegeorge** (JRBest) **6-10-11**(7) MrPO'Keeffe (a bhd: t.o)	9	12	33/1	—	—
	Hold My Hand (PRChamings) **6-11-4** NWilliamson (angular: a bhd: t.o)	½	13	12/1	—	—
	Muallaf (IRE) (MrsAMWoodrow) **5-11-4** JAMcCarthy (rangy: unf: bkwd: plld hrd: hdwy 12f out: wknd over 6f out: t.o)	3½	14	33/1	—	—

(SP 148.2%) **14 Rn**

4m 20.4 CSF £5.91 TOTE £3.30: £1.70 £1.70 £2.90 (£7.20) Trio Not won; £126.28 to Taunton 13/2/97 OWNER Lady Herries (LITTLEHAMPTON) BRED Sheikh Mohammed Bin Rashid Al Maktoum

WEIGHT FOR AGE 4yo-10lb

2682 Rasak confirmed the promise shown here three weeks ago. Launching his challenge in the straight, he poked a nostril in front below the distance but, in these very gruelling conditions, his rider had to keep him going all the way to the line. A big, backward individual, he has further improvement in him. (2/1: op evens)

1177* Curraduff Moll (IRE) ran a fine race under his penalty. Bowling along in front, she was marginally passed by the winner below the distance, but proved a tough nut to crack and kept on commendably all the way to the line. (6/4)

Fin Bec (FR) played an active role until tiring entering the final quarter-mile. (20/1)

2844 Royal Pot Black (IRE) moved up soon after halfway, but had been snookered running down the hill. (6/1: op 5/2)

Fred Moth had put up the flag five furlongs from home. (33/1)

2844 Crackon Jake (IRE) (6/1: op 7/2)

Paperprince (NZ) (14/1: 12/1-20/1)

T/Jkpt: £10,327.30 (0.4 Tckts); £8,727.32 to Taunton 13/2/97. T/Plpt: £258.40 (53.19 Tckts). T/Qdpt: £28.20 (38.97 Tckts) AK

2798-MUSSELBURGH (R-H) (Good to firm, Good patches becoming Good to soft)
Wednesday February 12th

WEATHER: rain

3091 MUSSELBURGH CONDITIONAL (S) H'CAP HURDLE (0-95) (4-Y.O+) (Class G)

2-10 (2-10) **2m (8 hdls)** £2,427.00 (£672.00: £321.00) GOING minus 0.24 sec per fur (G)

Form	Horse / details		Pos	SP	RR	SF
2913*	**Palace of Gold (80)** (LLungo) **7-10-9**(8) 7x WDowling (mde all: hit last: r.o wl)	—	1	9/2[1]	64	—

			Pos	SP	RR	SF
2913[3]	**Oakbury (IRE) (68)** (MissLCSiddall) **5-9-11**(8) TSiddall (prom tl outpcd & lost pl 3rd: styd on fr 2 out to chse wnr last: kpt on)	1¼	**2**	9/2[1]	51	—
2913[6]	**Doubling Dice (66)** (RAllan) **6-10-0**(3) SMelrose (bhd: hdwy 5th: styd on one pce fr 2 out)	9	**3**	11/1	40	—
2913[12]	**Henry Hoolet (77)** (PMonteith) **8-10-9**(5) CMcCormack (lw: a.p: ev ch 2 out: wknd last)	2½	**4**	7/1	48	—
2862[9]	**Kismetim (63)** (GPKelly) **7-10-0** BGrattan (rr div: styd on appr last: nvr able chal)	2½	**5**	16/1	32	—
2913[R]	**Tiotao (IRE) (69)** (CParker) **7-9-10**(10) TristanDavidson (w wnr: mstkes 4th & 5th: outpcd appr 2 out)	1¾	**6**	6/1[3]	36	—
2953[5]	**Jarrow (65)** (MrsAMNaughton) **6-10-2** MichaelBrennan (trckd ldrs: ev ch 3 out: wknd after next)	2	**7**	9/1	30	—
2957[9]	**Vintage Red (87)** (GRichards) **7-11-10** ECallaghan (lw: trckd ldrs: ch 3 out: wknd next)	3	**8**	11/2[2]	49	—
2629[7]	**Bud's Bet (IRE) (74)** (MissJFCraze) **9-10-11** MNewton (a rr div)	5	**9**	12/1	31	—
2800[12]	**Seconds Away (63)** (JSGoldie) **6-10-0** GCahill (a bhd)	7	**10**	25/1	13	—
				(SP 114.3%)	**10 Rn**	

3m 49.9 (10.90) CSF £22.71 CT £189.26 TOTE £4.90: £2.80 £1.70 £3.00 (£10.10) Trio £29.60 OWNER Mrs Barbara Lungo (CARRUTHERSTOWN) BRED Cheveley Park Stud Ltd
LONG HANDICAP Kismetim 9-7 Seconds Away 9-5
No bid
2913* Palace of Gold, well handled, did the job in good style and ought to stay further. (9/2: op 5/2)
2913 Oakbury (IRE) keeps running as though longer trips would help. (9/2)
1848 Doubling Dice keeps running reasonably, but lacks that final dash to make any serious impression. (11/1)
2913 Henry Hoolet, who ran dismally last time, did better here only to run out of fuel in the closing stages. (7/1)
Kismetim, from 7lb out of the handicap, showed some ability, staying on at the end. (16/1)
2505 Tiotao (IRE) is his own worst enemy, and does not seem to like jumping hurdles. Perhaps some sort of headgear might help. (6/1)

3092 ANDERSON STRATHERN NOVICES' H'CAP CHASE (0-100) (5-Y.O+) (Class E)
2-40 (2-40) **2m** **(12 fncs)** £2,976.00 (£888.00: £424.00: £192.00) GOING minus 0.24 sec per fur (G)

			Pos	SP	RR	SF
2789[F]	**Singing Sand (74)** (PMonteith) **7-10-11** RSupple (lw: mstkes 1st & 2nd: mde most: r.o wl fr 3 out)	—	**1**	6/4[1]	81	28
2957[8]	**Hee's a Dancer (100)** (MissLucindaRussell) **5-12-0** AThornton (led to 2nd: chsd ldr: mstke 6th: ev ch & hit 4 out: one pce fr next)	9	**2**	12/1	98	36
2786[6]	**Know-No-No (IRE) (80)** (MDHammond) **8-11-3** BStorey (hdwy 7th: ev ch 4 out: wknd fr 3 out: 2nd whn blnd last)	2	**3**	5/1[3]	76	23
2541[W]	**Spectre Brown (72)** (FJestin) **7-10-9**ow5 TReed (chsd ldrs tl wknd fr 7th)	20	**4**	33/1	48	—
1703[17]	**Shut Up (63)** (MrsEMoscrop) **8-10-0** FPerratt (prom tl wknd 8th: 5th & btn whn fell 3 out)		**F**	50/1	—	—
2799[2]	**Appearance Money (IRE) (87)** (FMurphy) **6-11-10** PCarberry (lw: hld up & bhd: effrt appr 4 out: 4th & no imp whn fell 2 out)		**F**	5/2[2]	—	—
1943[4]	**Islandreagh (IRE) (72)** (GRichards) **6-10-9** ADobbin (prom tl blnd bdly 8th: p.u bef 4 out)		**P**	16/1	—	—
2505[P]	**Miss Mont (63)** (FPMurtagh) **8-10-0** DBentley (mstkes: a bhd: t.o whn p.u bef 4 out)		**P**	50/1	—	—
3030[U]	**Most Rich (IRE) (73)** (BEllison) **9-10-10** KJohnson (lw: prom tl blnd & uns rdr 8th)		**U**	9/1	—	—
				(SP 115.7%)	**9 Rn**	

3m 57.2 (3.20) CSF £17.66 CT £66.77 TOTE £2.40: £1.20 £2.00 £2.10 (£19.30) Trio £15.00 OWNER Hamilton House Ltd (ROSEWELL) BRED Miss H. B. Hamilton
LONG HANDICAP Shut Up 9-11 Miss Mont 9-11
WEIGHT FOR AGE 5yo-9lb
2789 Singing Sand found a moderate contest here, and won it in good style. This should have boosted his confidence. (6/4)
1824 Hee's a Dancer, who looked harshly treated over hurdles, has his fair share of weight at this game but he did show enough to suggest that he will improve. (12/1)
2786 Know-No-No (IRE) ran his best race for a while, but looked very one-paced over the last four fences. (5/1)
2799 Appearance Money (IRE), ridden from behind this time, could never make any impression when asked a question and was a well beaten fourth when falling. (5/2)
Most Rich (IRE) has yet to get round in three attempts so far this season, but he looks to have ability. (9/1)

3093 TOM MCCONNELL MEMORIAL HURDLE (4-Y.O) (Class E)
3-10 (3-10) **2m** **(8 hdls)** £2,399.00 (£664.00: £317.00) GOING: 0.30 sec per fur (GS)

			Pos	SP	RR	SF
2615[6]	**Double Agent** (HowardJohnson) **4-10-12** PCarberry (mde all: r.o wl flat)	—	**1**	15/8[2]	73	4
2615[5]	**Meltemison (100)** (MDHammond) **4-10-9**(3) MrCBonner (swtg: hld up: hdwy on bit to chal 3 out: disp ld 2 out: rdn last: nt pce of wnr)	1¼	**2**	7/4[1]	72	3
2859[6]	**Formidable Partner** (MrsVCWard) **4-10-12v** BStorey (lw: trckd ldrs: effrt appr 2 out: hrd rdn & nt pce to chal)	8	**3**	4/1[3]	64	—
2798[3]	**Falcon's Flame (USA) (94)** (VThompson) **4-10-12** MrMThompson (lw: plld hrd: jnd ldr 2nd: wknd appr 2 out)	18	**4**	6/1	46	—
2798[8]	**Knave** (PMonteith) **4-10-12** ADobbin (bhd: effrt 3 out: no imp)	8	**5**	25/1	38	—
2785[U]	**Sounds Devious** (CParker) **4-10-7** DParker (cl up tl mstke & wknd 3 out: p.u bef last)		**P**	100/1	—	—
				(SP 110.3%)	**6 Rn**	

3m 55.9 (16.90) CSF £5.04 TOTE £3.50: £1.80 £1.10 (£2.80) OWNER Hertford Offset Ltd (CROOK) BRED Mrs R. D. Peacock
2615 Double Agent jumped much better this time and, given a superb ride, held on tenaciously. There is plenty of improvement in him yet, especially when he tries further. (15/8)
2615 Meltemison never impresses on looks but he has an engine, and after spending much of the race swinging off the bit, his response when ridden was a shade disappointing. (7/4)
2859 Formidable Partner had the visor on, but needed a stronger pace than was set here and was never doing enough when it mattered. (4/1)
2798 Falcon's Flame (USA) has changed stables, but raced far too freely and was completely unsuited by the slow early pace. (6/1)
Knave could never get into this and is still learning. (25/1)

3094 J.R. MCNAIR H'CAP CHASE (0-105) (5-Y.O+) (Class F)
3-40 (3-40) **3m** **(18 fncs)** £2,950.00 (£880.00: £420.00: £190.00) GOING: 0.30 sec per fur (GS)

			Pos	SP	RR	SF
2923[2]	**Cush Supreme (IRE) (84)** (MartinTodhunter) **8-11-2** PCarberry (lw: j.lft: mde all: lft clr 14th: unchal)	—	**1**	10/11[1]	96	22
1902[2]	**Buyers Dream (IRE) (89)** (BEllison) **7-11-7v** TReed (hdwy & in tch ½-wy: styd on fr 4 out: nvr able to chal)	7	**2**	6/1[2]	96	22
2179[4]	**Risky Dee (74)** (VThompson) **8-10-6** DBentley (prom: mstke 11th: effrt appr 4 out: sn btn)	5	**3**	16/1	78	4
2803[F]	**Tactix (68)** (MissMKMilligan) **7-10-0** BStorey (bhd: blnd 11th: sme late hdwy)	8	**4**	25/1	67	—
2652[F]	**Forward Glen (76)** (PCheesbrough) **10-10-8b** ASSmith (mstkes: bhd: effrt whn blnd 12th: n.d)	15	**5**	7/1[3]	65	—

			Pos	SP	RR	SF
	Oakley (88) (DenysSmith) **8-11-6** AThornton (chsd wnr: 4l 2nd whn fell 14th)		**F**	10/1	—	—
	Rusty Blade (92) (PMonteith) **8-11-10** ADobbin (bit bkwd: prom to 6th: sn wl bhd: p.u bef 4 out)		**P**	16/1	—	—
2671[P]	**Hurricane Andrew (IRE) (88)** (JAMoore) **9-11-6** NSmith (chsd ldrs tl hit 13th & sn wknd: p.u bef 2 out)		**P**	9/1	—	—
				(SP 113.9%)	**8 Rn**	

6m 14.3 (21.30) CSF £6.66 CT £46.27 TOTE £1.90: £1.40 £1.70 £2.60 (£2.10) OWNER Mr Robert Ogden (ULVERSTON) BRED Con Troy
LONG HANDICAP Tactix 9-11
2923 Cush Supreme (IRE) had his task simplified when his only serious rival fell at the fifth last, leaving him to win with something in hand, despite showing a tendency to run down his fences. (10/11: evens-4/5)
1902 Buyers Dream (IRE) does not do anything quickly but he does try hard, though it was always in vain here. (6/1)
2179 Risky Dee ran reasonably, but was never good enough to make a serious impression. (16/1)
1716 Tactix made mistakes, and was out the back until picking up when it was all too late. (25/1)
2179 Forward Glen was certainly not in the mood on this occasion. (7/1)
Oakley was the only one able to lay up with the winner, and seemed to be going just as well, although a few lengths down, when falling five out. (10/1)

3095 FIFE HUNT CLUB CUP HUNTERS' CHASE (5-Y.O+) (Class H)

4-10 (4-10) **3m (18 fncs)** £1,576.00 (£436.00: £208.00) GOING: 0.30 sec per fur (GS)

		Dist	Pos	SP	RR	SF
	Howayman (KAnderson) **7-11-7**(7) MrAParker (prom: led 4 out: styd on u.p)	—	**1**	7/2[2]	107	—
	Murder Moss (IRE) (SColtherd) **7-11-7**(7) MrMJRuddy (hdwy 7th: chal 10th: led after 14th to 4 out: styd on: no ex flat)	7	**2**	7/1[3]	102	—
	Free Transfer (IRE) (DJFairbairn) **8-11-9**(5) MrCStorey (chsd ldrs: blnd 12th: sn outpcd & no imp after)	12	**3**	8/1	94	—
	Fish Quay (MrsKMLamb) **14-11-7**(7) MissSLamb (led 2nd to 5th: wknd & mstke 10th: sn t.o)	dist	**4**	100/1	—	—
	Master Kit (IRE) (JNRBillinge) **8-12-0**(7) MrJBillinge (bit bkwd: led fr 7th tl hdd fr 14th: disp 2nd & v.tired whn fell last)		**F**	10/11[1]	—	—
	Little Wenlock (MrsDSCGibson) **13-12-2**(5) MrsVJackson (sn bhd: t.o whn p.u bef 2 out)		**P**	16/1	—	—
	Political Issue (TLARobson) **13-11-9**(5) MrPJohnson (led to 2nd: led 5th to 7th: wknd 9th: t.o whn p.u bef 4 out)		**P**	12/1	—	—
	Kilminfoyle (SHShirley-Beavan) **10-11-7**(7) MrTScott (bhd whn mstke 4th: mstke & uns rdr 5th)		**U**	14/1	—	—
				(SP 119.4%)	**8 Rn**	

6m 26.3 (33.30) CSF £26.65 TOTE £4.70: £1.40 £1.60 £1.20 (£29.60) Trio £55.10 OWNER Mr Dennis Waggott (LOCKERBIE) BRED Rockhouse Farms Ltd
Howayman got it right this time, but it was a gruelling event and he needed plenty of help from the saddle to hold on. (7/2)
Murder Moss (IRE) has already won a point-to-point this year and obviously had fitness on his side, but in the end he was just not good enough. (7/1)
Free Transfer (IRE) was well up with the pace until a terrible blunder seven out put paid to him. (8/1)
Master Kit (IRE) showed last season that he is a very good horse indeed, but he did look in need of this and blew up turning for home. He kept fighting back, but was extremely tired when he took a crashing fall at the last, and lay winded for a long time. (10/11: 4/5-evens)

3096 GOOSEGREEN NOVICES' H'CAP HURDLE (0-100) (4-Y.O+) (Class E)

4-40 (4-40) **3m (13 hdls)** £2,807.00 (£777.00: £371.00) GOING: 0.30 sec per fur (GS)

		Dist	Pos	SP	RR	SF
2820[5]	**Mr Christie (83)** (MissLCSiddall) **5-11-5** AThornton (a.p: effrt 2 out: chal last: rdn to ld fnl 50y)	—	**1**	7/2[2]	69	21
1999[9]	**Eternal City (84)** (GRichards) **6-11-6** ADobbin (trckd ldrs gng wl: hdwy to chal appr last: led flat: hdd & nt qckn towards fin)	1	**2**	12/1	69	21
2800*	**Heavens Above (70)** (FMurphy) **5-10-6** PCarberry (lw: led fr 4th tl hdd flat: no ex)	1¼	**3**	11/4[1]	55	7
2768[5]	**Crofton Lake (64)** (JEDixon) **9-10-0** BStorey (a chsng ldrs: one pce fr 3 out)	14	**4**	20/1	39	—
2922[7]	**Little Redwing (68)** (MDHammond) **5-10-1v**(3) MrCBonner (lw: chsd ldrs: ev ch 3 out: outpcd fr next)	3½	**5**	8/1	41	—
2922[8]	**Blooming Spring (IRE) (77)** (MrsDThomson) **8-10-13** DParker (led to 4th: chsd ldrs tl outpcd 4 out: hrd rdn & no imp after)	15	**6**	16/1	40	—
1021[9]	**Dalusman (IRE) (75)** (FPMurtagh) **9-10-11** RSupple (effrt 8th: nvr trbld ldrs)	12	**7**	12/1	30	—
	Frisky Thyne (IRE) (88) (MDHammond) **8-11-10** DBentley (a bhd: blnd 3 out)	1¾	**8**	12/1	42	—
2619[9]	**Persuasive Talent (IRE) (67)** (DALamb) **6-10-3** JBurke (bhd: hit 9th: t.o)	dist	**9**	10/1	—	—
1672[2]	**Cash Box (IRE) (78)** (TJCarr) **9-11-0** NSmith (a.p: hit 4th: cl 3rd whn fell 2 out)		**F**	4/1[3]	—	—
1851[9]	**Canonbiebothered (64)** (LLungo) **6-10-0** FPerratt (plld hrd: gd hdwy to chal 4th: sddle slipped: rn wd & p.u after 7th)		**P**	33/1	—	—
				(SP 125.8%)	**11 Rn**	

6m 2.3 (22.30) CSF £44.02 CT £125.20 TOTE £5.40: £1.70 £2.90 £1.50 (£38.80) Trio £9.90 OWNER David Mann Partnership (TADCASTER) BRED Hesmonds Stud Ltd
LONG HANDICAP Crofton Lake 9-12 Canonbiebothered 9-7
OFFICIAL EXPLANATION **Canonbiebothered: saddle slipped.**
2634 Mr Christie has always possessed the ability to win a race such as this and, given a fine ride here, did it determinedly. (7/2)
636 Eternal City, after six weeks off, spent most of the race on the bridle only to fail to quicken late on. He should benefit from the run. (12/1: op 5/1)
2800* Heavens Above, despite being 8lb higher and on much softer ground, ran a fine race to be only just touched off. (11/4)
2768 Crofton Lake had his chances but lacked the turn of foot to take them. (20/1)
2800 Little Redwing ran her usual race, chasing the leaders but failing come up with the goods when the pressure was on . (8/1)
Frisky Thyne (IRE) (12/1: op 8/1)
1672 Cash Box (IRE) was bang in contention and looking likely to be in the frame when taking a heavy fall at the penultimate flight. (4/1)

T/Plpt: £17.20 (567.44 Tckts). T/Qdpt: £5.10 (136.43 Tckts) AA

3029-CATTERICK (L-H) (Good, Good to soft patches)
Thursday February 13th

WEATHER: blustery & overcast

3097 WEST OF YORE NOVICES' CHASE (5-Y.O+) (Class E)
1-50 (1-50) **2m 3f (15 fncs)** £3,042.50 (£855.00: £417.50) GOING: 0.89 sec per fur (S)

				SP	RR	SF
2810[4]	**Cover Point (IRE) (90)** (JGFitzGerald) **6-11-2** PCarberry (lw: chsd ldr: shkn up after 4 out: led & lft wl clr 2 out: eased flat)	—	**1**	4/7 [1]	69+	30
	Stealing Home (IRE) (MrsMReveley) **7-10-11** PNiven (in tch: mstke 9th: sn outpcd & n.d after)	5	**2**	9/2 [2]	60	21
2549[3]	**Alicat (IRE)** (JWCurtis) **6-11-2** DerekByrne (chsd ldrs: mstke 2nd: outpcd fr 8th & sn wl bhd)	dist	**3**	50/1	—	—
2047[15]	**Banner Year (IRE)** (TJCarr) **6-11-2** NSmith (lw: blnd 1st: sn bhd: t.o whn p.u bef 3 out)		**P**	50/1	—	—
2899[P]	**Wild Game (IRE)** (MissSWilliamson) **6-11-2** BStorey (sn wl bhd: t.o whn p.u bef 11th)		**P**	50/1	—	—
2632[4]	**Karenastino (65)** (MrsSJSmith) **6-11-2** TReed (led tl hdd, stumbled & uns rdr 2 out)		**U**	11/2 [3]	—	—
	Don't Tell Judy (IRE) (MissMKMilligan) **9-11-2** ASSmith (mstke & uns rdr 2nd)		**U**	12/1	—	—
				(SP 110.8%)	**7 Rn**	

5m 5.0 (26.00) CSF £3.16 TOTE £1.30: £1.10 £1.70 (£2.20) OWNER Mrs Anne Henson (MALTON) BRED Gay O'Callaghan

2810 Cover Point (IRE) found a poor race here, and was just getting the better of his only serious rival when the latter came to grief two out. (4/7)

Stealing Home (IRE), having her first run in this country, never looked likely to get into it, but she was not knocked about and should pick up a modest race in due course. She does not look anything special. (9/2: op 3/1)

Alicat (IRE) got round in his own time, and that seems to be all he can manage for the time being. (50/1)

2632 Karenastino ran well here and his jumping was much improved and, although he had just marginally been headed, the race was certainly not over when he came to grief two out. His luck should change. (11/2)

3098 SINNINGTON MAIDEN HURDLE (4-Y.O+) (Class F)
2-20 (2-21) **2m (8 hdls)** £2,029.00 (£569.00: £277.00) GOING: 0.89 sec per fur (S)

				SP	RR	SF
1776[2]	**Six Clerks (IRE) (92)** (JGFitzGerald) **4-10-9** PCarberry (lw: hld up: hdwy 5th: led 2 out: rdn & styd on)	—	**1**	4/9 [1]	63	21
698[4]	**Tawafij (USA) (85)** (MDHammond) **8-11-2**(3) MrCBonner (lw: hld up: hdwy 5th: styd on & ev ch last: nt qckn)	1¾	**2**	7/1 [2]	61	29
2838[11]	**Diddy Rymer (75)** (MrsSJSmith) **7-11-0** TReed (chsd ldrs: kpt on one pce fr 2 out)	7	**3**	12/1 [3]	49	17
2917[16]	**Silver Minx** (MrsMReveley) **5-11-5** PNiven (unruly s: led tl hdd 2 out: btn whn blnd last)	4	**4**	16/1	50	18
1692[14]	**Milenberg Joys** (PCalver) **5-11-2**(3) PMidgley (hld up: stdy hdwy appr 2 out: nvr rchd ldrs)	13	**5**	66/1	37	5
2633[11]	**Helperby (IRE)** (HowardJohnson) **5-11-0**(5) GFRyan (chsd ldrs tl rdn & wknd qckly after 3 out)	7	**6**	33/1	30	—
2861[12]	**Tsanga** (GMMoore) **5-11-5** NBentley (prom tl outpcd fr 3 out)	10	**7**	50/1	20	—
2177[7]	**Penny Peppermint** (REBarr) **5-11-0** GCahill (a bhd)	6	**8**	100/1	9	—
2180[3]	**Salem Beach** (MartinTodhunter) **5-11-0** ADobbin (lw: j.bdly: bhd fr 3 out)	12	**9**	12/1 [3]	—	—
1687[13]	**Parry** (SBBell) **5-11-0** BStorey (fell 1st)		**F**	50/1	—	—
	Red-Stoat (IRE) (MrsJStorey) **8-11-0** KJohnson (s.s: a bhd: t.o whn p.u bef 2 out)		**P**	50/1	—	—
1821[F]	**North End Lady** (WSCunningham) **6-11-0** NSmith (wknd rapidly appr 4th: j.v.slowly next 2: p.u bef 3 out)		**P**	14/1	—	—
2953[10]	**Point Duty** (FPMurtagh) **7-11-5** DBentley (in tch to 5th: p.u bef 2 out)		**P**	14/1	—	—
				(SP 127.6%)	**13 Rn**	

4m 4.9 (21.90) CSF £4.20 TOTE £1.40: £1.10 £1.30 £1.40 (£2.20) Trio £13.80 OWNER Marquesa de Moratalla (MALTON) BRED Blue Blood Investments

WEIGHT FOR AGE 4yo-10lb

1776 Six Clerks (IRE) struggled to win this and was a shade disappointing. (4/9)

698 Tawafij (USA) put in a determined effort from the second last, but always found the winner too strong. (7/1)

Diddy Rymer, dropped back in trip here, ran much better, and there ought to be a modest race to be picked up. (12/1)

1999 Silver Minx, a headstrong individual, ran reasonably and may at last be getting the hang of this game. (16/1)

Milenberg Joys, who showed little in bumpers, gave his first signs of hope here but there is still some way to go. (66/1)

2180 Salem Beach (12/1: op 8/1)

3099 ZETLAND H'CAP CHASE (0-115) (5-Y.O+) (Class E)
2-55 (2-55) **3m 1f 110y (19 fncs)** £2,986.50 (£839.00: £409.50) GOING: 0.89 sec per fur (S)

				SP	RR	SF
1850[P]	**Gold Pigeon (IRE) (75)** (BSRothwell) **8-10-0** BStorey (mde all: hld on wl fr 3 out)	—	**1**	14/1	88	—
2860*	**Tico Gold (84)** (PCheesbrough) **9-10-9b1** ASSmith (hld up: hdwy 9th: mstkes 13th & 14th: sn rdn: ev ch 3 out: r.o one pce)	5	**2**	6/4 [1]	94	2
2671[4]	**Sparrow Hall (87)** (JGFitzGerald) **10-10-12** PCarberry (mstkes: chsd ldrs: outpcd 13th: no imp fr 4 out)	18	**3**	6/4 [1]	86	—
2545[P]	**Johnny Kelly (99)** (JMCarr) **10-11-7**(3) FLeahy (wkng whn blnd bdly 12th: p.u bef next)		**P**	12/1 [3]	—	—
2916[P]	**Snook Point (77)** (DALamb) **10-10-2**ow2 JBurke (prom tl wknd qckly appr 12th: p.u bef 13th)		**P**	9/2 [2]	—	—
				(SP 112.5%)	**5 Rn**	

7m 0.2 (42.20) CSF £34.12 TOTE £13.10: £3.60 £1.10 (£9.30) OWNER Contrac Promotions Ltd (MALTON) BRED L. Woods

LONG HANDICAP Gold Pigeon (IRE) 9-6

OFFICIAL EXPLANATION Gold Pigeon (IRE): the mare had been incubating a virus when pulled up last time.

Gold Pigeon (IRE) won his first race, and did it the hard way. She showed fine courage to keep going, but the form certainly has holes in it. (14/1)

2860* Tico Gold, tried in blinkers this time, did not seem to co-operate when asked to take the winner on. (6/4)

2671 Sparrow Hall gets clumsier as he gets older. (6/4)

Johnny Kelly (12/1: 6/1-16/1)

2630 Snook Point obviously has a problem, as he stopped as though shot turning into the back straight on the final circuit. (9/2)

3100 CLEVELAND NOVICES' HURDLE (5-Y.O+) (Class E)
3-30 (3-30) **3m 1f 110y (12 hdls)** £2,232.00 (£627.00: £306.00) GOING: 0.89 sec per fur (S)

				SP	RR	SF
2958*	**Meadow Hymn (IRE)** (JGFitzGerald) **6-11-4** PCarberry (lw: a cl up: led 2 out: eased flat)	—	**1**	Evens [1]	72+	17
2746[6]	**Clever Boy (IRE) (75)** (JWCurtis) **6-11-4** DerekByrne (lw: cl up: led 6th to 2 out: no ch w wnr)	2	**2**	7/1 [3]	71	16
2506[4]	**Elliott's Wish (IRE) (60)** (HowardJohnson) **6-10-12** ADobbin (chsd ldrs: hit 9th: sn btn)	dist	**3**	20/1	—	—
2627[3]	**Chill Factor (90)** (MrsMReveley) **7-10-12** PNiven (hld up: hdwy ½-wy: rdn 8th: sn btn)	dist	**4**	85/40 [2]	—	—

				SP	RR	SF
2047[9]	**Houselope Spring** (HowardJohnson) **5-10-7**(5) GFRyan (prom to 8th: sn wknd)	18	**5**	20/1	—	—
1539[11]	**La Chance** (MrsHLWalton) **7-10-12** MrAWalton (t.o fr 7th)	8	**6**	66/1	—	—
3020[P]	**Royal Hand (67)** (RJArmson) **7-10-12** MrRArmson (a bhd: poor 4th whn fell last)		**F**	100/1	—	—
2924[3]	**Water Font (IRE)** (JJO'Neill) **5-10-7**(5) RMcGrath (mstke 6th: sn wl bhd: p.u bef 2 out)		**P**	20/1	—	—
2746[P]	**Kickcashtal** (MrsCMBowman) **8-10-12** MSharratt (wl t.o whn p.u after 7th)		**P**	100/1	—	—
2627[B]	**Basincroft** (MissSWilliamson) **7-10-5**(7) ATodd (mde most to 6th: wknd 8th: p.u bef 2 out)		**P**	100/1	—	—
	Beltino (MrsJStorey) **6-10-12** KJohnson (wl t.o whn p.u after 7th)		**P**	100/1	—	—
2958[F]	**Persian Grange (IRE) (50)** (DALamb) **7-10-12** JBurke (blnd 2nd: t.o whn p.u bef 8th)		**P**	100/1	—	—
	Al Jinn (MartynWane) **6-10-12** ASSmith (lost tch 8th: t.o whn p.u bef 2 out)		**P**	100/1	—	—
	Monnedell (IRE) (EWeymes) **5-10-12** DBentley (in tch tl wknd fr 7th: p.u bef 4 out)		**P**	100/1	—	—
2627[P]	**Kambletree (IRE)** (MESowersby) **6-10-7** DParker (lost tch fr 6th: t.o whn p.u bef 3 out)		**P**	200/1	—	—
				(SP 117.7%)	**15 Rn**	

6m 46.9 (39.90) CSF £7.41 TOTE £1.80: £1.80 £1.10 £2.60 (£2.60) Trio £35.60 OWNER Mrs M. Nowell (MALTON) BRED Dermot O'Mahony
2958* Meadow Hymn (IRE), suited by this trip, won well and is certainly going the right way. (Evens)
2746 Clever Boy (IRE) ran well here although he was completely outclassed by the winner. (7/1)
2506 Elliott's Wish (IRE), returning to hurdling after disappointing over fences, looked very slow from the fourth last. (20/1)
2627 Chill Factor had his limitations exposed here, and was disappointing once off the bridle. (85/40)

3101 BEDALE H'CAP CHASE (0-110) (5-Y.O+) (Class E)

4-05 (4-05) **2m 3f (15 fncs)** £2,916.50 (£819.00: £399.50) GOING: 0.89 sec per fur (S)

				SP	RR	SF
2863*	**Weaver George (IRE) (104)** (WStorey) **7-11-8** MMoloney (lw: led fr 4th: qcknd 3 out: r.o)	—	**1**	11/8[1]	114	11
2674[3]	**Aljadeer (USA) (110)** (MWEasterby) **8-12-0b** PCarberry (lw: hld up: blnd 8th: effrt 3 out: kpt on: nt pce of wnr)	2	**2**	13/8[2]	118	15
3069[F]	**Blazing Trail (IRE) (103)** (MissLucindaRussell) **9-11-7** MFoster (lw: led: j.slowly 3rd: j.slowly & hdd 4th: cl up tl wknd 3 out)	23	**3**	11/4[3]	92	—
				(SP 106.9%)	**3 Rn**	

5m 11.8 (32.80) CSF £3.50 TOTE £1.90 (£1.60) OWNER Regent Decorators Ltd (CONSETT) BRED G. Cashin
2863* Weaver George (IRE) is in tremendous heart and, jumping well, was always going best. (11/8)
2674 Aljadeer (USA), patiently ridden, found the sprint over the last four fences too much. (13/8)
3069 Blazing Trail (IRE), who fell only two days ago, appears to have lost his confidence as he was always tending to back off his fences. (11/4)

3102 GOATHLAND NOVICES' H'CAP HURDLE (0-105) (4-Y.O+) (Class E)

4-35 (4-35) **2m 3f (10 hdls)** £2,211.00 (£621.00: £303.00) GOING: 0.89 sec per fur (S)

				SP	RR	SF
	Enchanted Cottage (75) (JMJefferson) **5-10-13**(3) ECallaghan (hld up: stdy hdwy 3 out: slt ld next: hit last: all out)	—	**1**	5/1[2]	54	3
2898[13]	**Pilkington (IRE) (82)** (HowardJohnson) **7-11-6**(3) MichaelBrennan (trckd ldrs: hit 3 out: ev ch 2 out: hung lft flat: kpt on towards fin)	hd	**2**	8/1	61	10
3035[3]	**Fryup Satellite (82)** (MrsJBrown) **6-11-9** MissPRobson (lw: a.p: ev ch 2 out: kpt on)	½	**3**	4/1[1]	61	10
2915[11]	**Hotspur Street (78)** (MWEasterby) **5-11-5b** PNiven (led fr 3rd to 2 out: styd on same pce)	nk	**4**	6/1[3]	56	5
2669[13]	**Highly Charming (IRE) (80)** (MFBarraclough) **5-11-7** RSupple (in tch: effrt 3 out: ev ch next: one pce)	3	**5**	8/1	56	5
2692[4]	**Baasm (80)** (JNorton) **4-10-11** DerekByrne (hld up: hdwy 3 out: chal next: hit last: wknd)	1½	**6**	6/1[3]	55	—
2918[9]	**Kildrummy Castle (83)** (JGFitzGerald) **5-11-10** PCarberry (lw: led to 3rd: bhd fr 5th)	dist	**7**	10/1	—	—
2701[P]	**Ten Past Six (74)** (MartynWane) **5-11-1** ASSmith (prom tl wknd after 3 out: p.u bef next)		**P**	15/2	—	—
2898[10]	**Dougal (76)** (BSRothwell) **6-10-12**(5) BGrattan (lw: bhd: hdwy & prom ½-wy: outpcd 6th: t.o whn p.u bef 2 out)		**P**	6/1[3]	—	—
510[6]	**Ahbejaybus (IRE) (59)** (TKersey) **8-10-0** KJohnson (cl up to 3rd: t.o fr 6th: p.u bef 2 out)		**P**	100/1	—	—
				(SP 123.6%)	**10 Rn**	

4m 57.6 (32.60) CSF £43.25 CT £164.68 TOTE £6.60: £3.20 £1.20 £2.70 (£35.50) Trio £54.20 OWNER Mrs J. M. Davenport (MALTON) BRED Alan G. Byrne
LONG HANDICAP Ahbejaybus (IRE) 9-13
WEIGHT FOR AGE 4yo-10lb
Enchanted Cottage, from a stable in form, travelled well but, this being his first run of the season, he seemed to blow up late on and it was a desperate thing at the end. (5/1)
Pilkington (IRE) looked his own worst enemy here, as he was hanging into the rails when the pressure was on after the last. To give him credit, he was keeping on well as the line approached. (8/1)
3035 Fryup Satellite looked superb and ran his usual game race on this his favourite track, but he is just short of a turn of foot. (4/1)
1807 Hotspur Street tried to force the pace from a long way out and, after looking well beaten at the second last, decided to run again at the finish to show that there is more ability there if the key can be found. (6/1)
1992 Highly Charming (IRE) had his chances, but lacks a change of gear. (8/1)
2692 Baasm looked to be going quite well for much of the trip, but disappointed under pressure and tired late on. (6/1)
Kildrummy Castle (10/1: op 6/1)
2898 Dougal, who showed a glimmer of hope last time, did just the opposite here . (6/1)

T/Plpt: £9.00 (670.21 Tckts). T/Qdpt: £7.50 (41.71 Tckts) AA

2885-SANDOWN (R-H) (Ch Good, Good-soft ptchs, Hdles Good-sft, Gd ptchs)
Thursday February 13th

WEATHER: v.windy

3103 VILLAGE NOVICES' HURDLE (4-Y.O+) (Class D)

2-00 (2-01) **2m 110y (8 hdls)** £2,905.00 (£880.00: £430.00: £205.00) GOING: 0.83 sec per fur (S)

				SP	RR	SF
2840*	**Juyush (USA)** (JABOld) **5-11-12** JOsborne (a.p: led appr 2 out: clr appr last: blnd last: shkn up: easily)	—	**1**	1/6[1]	90	39
	Glide Path (USA) (JRJenkins) **8-11-4** AMaguire (lw: hdwy to chse wnr appr 2 out: wknd flat)	21	**2**	14/1[2]	62	11
	Keen Bid (IRE) (MrsLRichards) **6-11-4** MRichards (bkwd: led: mstke 1st: hdd 4th: wknd appr 2 out)	2	**3**	33/1	60	9
2840[4]	**Absolute Limit** (JTGifford) **5-11-4** PHide (chsd ldr appr 2nd: led 4th tl appr 2 out: sn wknd)	5	**4**	14/1[2]	55	4
	He Knows The Rules (RHBuckler) **5-11-4** BPowell (hdwy 3 out: ev ch appr 2 out: sn wknd)	5	**5**	33/1	50	—

				SP	RR	SF
2663P	**Kilcarne Bay (IRE)** (OSherwood) **7-11-4** JAMcCarthy (prom to 5th)	10	**6**	16/1 3	40	—
	Modajjaj (MissLBower) **5-11-4** LHarvey (bit bkwd: a bhd)	½	**7**	66/1	40	—
2889 4	**Go With The Wind** (CWeedon) **4-10-8** DO'Sullivan (a bhd: t.o: lame)	29	**8**	14/1 2	12	—
	Zipalong (MrsPTownsley) **6-11-4** WMcFarland (bkwd: a bhd: t.o)	26	**9**	66/1	—	—
1953 12	**Decision Maker (IRE)** (KRBurke) **4-10-8** NWilliamson (mstke 1st: a bhd: t.o)	4	**10**	66/1	—	—
1800 7	**Pealings (IRE)** (GAHubbard) **5-10-11**(7) NRossiter (3rd whn j.slowly & uns rdr 3rd)		**U**	66/1	—	—
				(SP 123.4%)	**11 Rn**	

4m 12.2 (21.20) CSF £4.11 TOTE £1.20: £1.10 £1.90 £5.50 (£4.60) Trio £24.50 OWNER Mr W. E. Sturt (WROUGHTON) BRED Corbin J. Robertson

WEIGHT FOR AGE 4yo-10lb

2840* Juyush (USA) had a very simple task, but gave his supporters one anxious moment, for after having the race nicely sewn up he made a dreadful mess of the last. Quite rightly thoughts of the Champion Hurdle were quickly dismissed, and he will contest one of the novices' hurdles at the Festival, depending on the ground. He may have another run before then. (1/6)

Glide Path (USA), disappointing on the Flat last year, was sold out of John Hills' yard for 11,000 guineas and failed to sparkle on the All-Weather for his new connections. He picked up ground to take second place, but never looked like getting on terms, and tired up the hill. (14/1: op 6/1)

Keen Bid (IRE), sold out of Willie Jarvis' stable for 17,000 guineas in 1994, had not raced since, and not surprisingly looked very tubby in the paddock. Nevertheless he still showed up well until tiring approaching the second-last. (33/1)

2840 Absolute Limit, fitter than when twenty-four lengths behind the winner at Towcester, actually finished further behind. In front at halfway, he soon tired once collared approaching the second-last. (14/1: 10/1-16/1)

He Knows The Rules, off the course since pulling up at Warwick thirteen months ago, was on level terms with the winner approaching the second last before lack of a recent run took its toll. (33/1)

2889 Go With The Wind (14/1: 8/1-16/1)

3104 FIRST HALF CLUB NOVICES' H'CAP CHASE (0-120) (5-Y.O+) (Class D)

2-35 (2-36) **3m 110y (22 fncs)** £4,175.00 (£1,025.00) GOING: 0.83 sec per fur (S)

				SP	RR	SF
2819 2	**Hawaiian Sam (IRE) (98)** (AndrewTurnell) **7-11-2** GCrone (lft 2nd 4th: led 5th: mstke 16th: r.o wl)	—	**1**	2/1 3	106	5
2049 4	**Take the Buckskin (98)** (TThomsonJones) **10-11-2** RDunwoody (lw: hld up: lft 2nd 10th: j.slowly 5th: rdn appr 3 out: btn whn j.slowly last)	18	**2**	15/8 2	94	—
2693 3	**Wee Windy (IRE) (110)** (JTGifford) **8-12-0** PHide (lw: led tl blnd & uns rdr 4th)		**U**	7/4 1	—	—
2679P	**Oneofus (82)** (MrsLRichards) **8-10-0** MRichards (chsd ldr: lft in ld 4th: hdd 5th: 2nd whn blnd & uns rdr 10th) ...		**U**	25/1	—	—
				(SP 108.3%)	**4 Rn**	

6m 43.0 (41.00) CSF £5.66 TOTE £3.20 (£2.10) OWNER Mr Robert Russell (WANTAGE) BRED Mrs Paul Finegan

LONG HANDICAP Oneofus 9-1

2819 Hawaiian Sam (IRE) had his task greatly simplified by the departure of two of his rivals before halfway, and after the runner-up's slow jump at the fifteenth he always had the situation in hand. (2/1)

2049 Take the Buckskin was racing over his optimum trip, but was rather deliberate at some of his fences, especially at the last ditch where he was very slow. Close enough jumping the Pond fence, he was already held when slow at the last. He needs to improve his jumping. (15/8)

3105 FAIRMILE CONDITIONAL H'CAP HURDLE (0-120) (4-Y.O+) (Class E)

3-10 (3-10) **2m 110y (8 hdls)** £2,640.00 (£740.00: £360.00) GOING: 0.83 sec per fur (S)

				SP	RR	SF
2884 3	**Doctoor (USA) (113)** (MCPipe) **7-11-9** DWalsh (3rd whn mstke 4th: chsd ldr appr 3 out: mstke last: led flat: easily)	—	**1**	11/8 1	95+	40
2824*	**Royal Event (102)** (DRGandolfo) **6-10-12** DFortt (led: hrd rdn appr last: hdd flat: unable qckn)	5	**2**	100/30 3	79	24
2932 2	**Can Can Charlie (100)** (JPearce) **7-10-10** SRyan (hld up: rdn 5th: wknd appr 2 out: t.o)	30	**3**	11/4 2	48	—
2755 3	**Mazzini (IRE) (96)** (RRowe) **6-10-6** LAspell (chsd ldr tl appr 3 out: wknd appr 2 out: t.o)	22	**4**	13/2	23	—
2884 13	**Court Nap (IRE) (108)** (SMellor) **5-10-11**(7) SHearn (lw: bhd fr 3 out: t.o whn blnd & uns rdr 2 out)		**U**	20/1	—	—
				(SP 109.9%)	**5 Rn**	

4m 11.3 (20.30) CSF £5.88 TOTE £2.30: £1.20 £1.40 (£3.60) OWNER Mr Alfred Walls (WELLINGTON) BRED Mrs Charles A. Martin

2884 Doctoor (USA), whose jockey was banned under the non-triers rule on his reappearance, absolutely hacked up this time. Toying with the leader in the straight, he made a complete mess of the last, but was soon in front, and pulled away without turning a hair. He was value for far more than the official distance. (11/8: evens-6/4)

2824* Royal Event took the field along, but the winner was cruising upsides in the straight. Collared early on the run-in, he soon bowed to the inevitable. On breeding he needs further, and is worth another try at two-and-a-half miles. (100/30)

2932 Can Can Charlie found the recent rain against him, and was already looking in trouble in the back straight. (11/4)

2755 Mazzini (IRE) raced in second place for much of the contest, but was left for dead early in the straight. (13/2)

3106 LONDESBOROUGH H'CAP CHASE (0-130) (5-Y.O+) (Class C)

3-45 (3-45) **2m 4f 110y (17 fncs)** £5,929.00 (£1,456.00) GOING: 0.83 sec per fur (S)

				SP	RR	SF
1676*	**Too Plush (109)** (AndrewTurnell) **8-10-13** LHarvey (chsd ldr fr 4th: lft in ld 13th: rdn out)	—	**1**	6/1 3	108	19
1937 5	**No Pain No Gain (IRE) (120)** (JTGifford) **9-11-10** PHide (lw: chsd ldr to 4th: lft 2nd 13th: ev ch appr 2 out: unable qckn)	2½	**2**	3/1 2	117	28
2647*	**Garrylough (IRE) (118)** (DRGandolfo) **8-11-8b** RDunwoody (led tl fell 13th)		**F**	8/11 1	—	—
2665 7	**Solo Gent (96)** (APJones) **8-10-0** NWilliamson (a bhd: t.o whn p.u bef 10th)		**P**	8/1	—	—
				(SP 108.3%)	**4 Rn**	

5m 28.0 (29.00) CSF £20.07 TOTE £6.20 (£9.40) OWNER Mrs C. C. Williams (WANTAGE) BRED Miss B. Sykes

LONG HANDICAP Solo Gent 9-12

1676* Too Plush completed the hat-trick, but after being left in front five out had only one rival to worry about. Rousted along, he proved too good for the runner-up from the penultimate fence. (6/1: 3/1-13/2)

1937 No Pain No Gain (IRE), who failed to stay three miles last time, had every chance going to the second last, but found the winner too good. (3/1)

2647* Garrylough (IRE) set the pace, but got too close to several fences, and finally paid the price five out. (8/11)

3107 WILFRED JOHNSTONE HUNTERS' CHASE (6-Y.O+) (Class H)

4-15 (4-15) **2m 4f 110y (17 fncs)** £1,604.00 (£444.00: £212.00) GOING: 0.83 sec per fur (S)

	Horse	Dist	Pos	SP	RR	SF
	Mr Boston (MrsMReveley) **12-12-1** MrSSwiers (hld up: rdn appr last: led flat: r.o wl)	—	**1**	13/8[1]	111	6
	Howaryasun (IRE) (MrsChristineHardinge) **9-11-11v**(7) MrDSJones (lw: led to 4th: led 3 out tl flat: unable qckn)	5	**2**	9/2[2]	110	5
	Wild Illusion (MissJenniferPidgeon) **13-11-11**(7) MrRLawther (lw: a.p: rdn appr 2 out: r.o flat)	½	**3**	13/8[1]	110	5
	Poors Wood (SBreen) **10-11-3**(7) MrPO'Keeffe (hdwy to ld 4th: hdd 3 out: wknd appr last)	12	**4**	12/1	92	—
	Amari King (JWall) **13-11-8**(7) MrCWardThomas (hld up: rdn appr 3 out: sn wknd: t.o)	dist	**5**	15/2[3]	—	—
	Royal Irish (ACAyres) **13-10-13**(7) MissCTownsley (mstke 2nd: prom to 4th: t.o whn p.u bef 10th)		**P**	40/1	—	—

(SP 116.3%) **6 Rn**

5m 36.6 (37.60) CSF £9.24 TOTE £2.10: £1.40 £2.20 (£5.40) OWNER Mr M. K. Oldham (SALTBURN) BRED Mrs D. M. Hurndall-Waldron

Mr Boston, who had to have a piece of bone removed from a hock after falling here last March, was competing in this sphere for the first time. Although this trip was well short of his best, he was rated far superior to the rest, and despite having ground to make up turning in, he was in front soon after the last. (13/8)

Howaryasun (IRE) looked in good shape for his first run in nine months, and showed plenty of promise. Moving into the lead again at the Pond fence, he failed to find another gear when collared on the run-in (9/2)

Wild Illusion, who won a point-to-point twelve days ago, looked in great shape in the paddock. He was rather tapped for toe from the Pond fence, but stayed on again up the hill, and would have taken second place in another few strides. He has never won over a distance as short as this and, with age blunting his speed, three miles is definitely required. (13/8)

Poors Wood moved to the front at the fourth but, collared three out, had soon shot his bolt. (12/1)

3108 SPRING NOVICES' H'CAP HURDLE (0-110) (4-Y.O+) (Class D)

4-50 (4-51) **2m 6f (11 hdls)** £3,035.00 (£920.00: £450.00: £215.00) GOING: 0.83 sec per fur (S)

	Horse	Dist	Pos	SP	RR	SF
2552[3]	**Lough Tully (IRE) (80)** (FJordan) **7-10-3** JOsborne (lw: led 2nd: clr 4th: rdn out)	—	**1**	6/1[3]	67	46
2891[7]	**Lord Khalice (IRE) (79)** (GAHubbard) **6-10-2** NWilliamson (a.p: mstke 2 out: unable qckn)	8	**2**	14/1	60	39
2891[2]	**Physical Fun (89)** (AGBlackmore) **6-10-12** DSkyrme (rdn & hdwy appr 2 out: swtchd rt appr last: one pce)	1	**3**	9/2[2]	70	49
2676[5]	**Mahler (94)** (NATwiston-Davies) **7-11-3** DWalsh (a.p: rdn 3 out: wknd appr 2 out)	18	**4**	14/1	61	40
3013[2]	**Allow (IRE) (93)** (BLlewellyn) **6-11-2** AMaguire (led to 2nd: rdn 7th: wknd appr last)	¾	**5**	2/1[1]	60	39
	Vintage Claret (101) (JTGifford) **8-11-7**(3) LAspell (rdn 8th: nvr nr to chal)	4	**6**	25/1	65	44
1915[5]	**Spaceage Gold (99)** (JABOld) **8-11-8** GUpton (j.slowly: bhd fr 4th)	11	**7**	10/1	55	34
2550[9]	**Rathkeal (IRE) (83)** (MJHeaton-Ellis) **6-10-6v**[1] BPowell (reminders 4th: hdwy 6th: sn wknd)	3½	**8**	25/1	36	15
2820[10]	**Farleyer Rose (IRE) (77)** (MrsLRichards) **8-10-0** MRichards (rdn & hdwy after 3 out: eased whn btn appr 2 out)	7	**9**	25/1	25	4
2663*	**Special Beat (96)** (NJHenderson) **5-11-0**(5) MrCVigors (prom tl appr 2 out)	dist	**10**	7/1	—	—
2826[2]	**Royal Raven (IRE) (97)** (JTGifford) **6-11-6** PHide (lw: prom to 8th: 6th & no ch whn p.u bef 2 out)		**P**	13/2	—	—

(SP 125.6%) **11 Rn**

5m 32.7 (19.70) CSF £79.47 CT £379.15 TOTE £6.90: £1.90 £4.70 £2.30 (£31.00) Trio £81.30 OWNER Mr R. A. Hancocks (LEOMINSTER) BRED Seamus Richmond

LONG HANDICAP Farleyer Rose (IRE) 9-6

2552 Lough Tully (IRE) was soon in front, and galloped on relentlessly in the straight. (6/1)

1550 Lord Khalice (IRE), miles behind Physical Fun here twelve days ago, reversed that form, but had no chance with the winner. (14/1)

2891 Physical Fun began his effort in the straight, and had a real battle for second, but just lost out. (9/2)

2676 Mahler once again failed to stay the trip and, after racing up with the pace, came to the end of his tether approaching the second-last. A return to two-and-a half miles is needed. (14/1: 10/1-16/1)

3013 Allow (IRE) may have found this coming too soon after his hard race at Newbury last Friday, and after being a leading player dropped away going to the final flight. (2/1)

1915 Spaceage Gold (10/1: op 6/1)

2663* Special Beat (7/1: 4/1-8/1)

T/Plpt: £356.80 (27.21 Tckts). T/Qdpt: £92.30 (7.7 Tckts) AK

2872-TAUNTON (R-H) (Good)

Thursday February 13th

WEATHER: v.windy

3109 BLACKDOWN MAIDEN HURDLE (I) (4-Y.O+) (Class F)

1-40 (1-41) **2m 1f (9 hdls)** £1,707.00 (£477.00: £231.00) GOING: 0.25 sec per fur (GS)

	Horse	Dist	Pos	SP	RR	SF
2872[2]	**Break the Rules** (MCPipe) **5-10-12**(7) GSupple (hld up: hdwy 3 out: led appr 2 out: comf)	—	**1**	13/8[1]	72	—
1788[4]	**Devon Peasant (95)** (LGCottrell) **5-11-0** MrLJefford (a.p: led after 3 out tl appr 2 out: one pce)	3½	**2**	5/2[2]	64	—
	Kinnescash (IRE) (PBowen) **4-10-9** RJohnson (hld up: hdwy 5th: ev ch appr 2 out: one pce)	1¼	**3**	14/1	68	—
2872[9]	**Mystic Hill** (RGFrost) **6-11-5** JFrost (prom tl wknd appr 2 out)	11	**4**	11/1	57	—
1427[7]	**Walter's Destiny** (CWMitchell) **5-11-5** SMcNeill (prom to 3 out)	4	**5**	33/1	53	—
	Rumpelstiltskin (HSHowe) **5-11-5** RFarrant (hdwy 6th: mstke 3 out: wknd appr 2 out)	2½	**6**	66/1	51	—
2655[7]	**Alpine Joker** (PJHobbs) **4-10-9** GTormey (hld up: hdwy 5th: ev ch appr 2 out: sn wknd)	2	**7**	14/1	49	—
	Soldier Cove (USA) (MartynMeade) **7-11-5** CMaude (mstke 1st: a bhd)	5	**8**	25/1	45	—
	Vanborough Lad (MJBolton) **8-11-2**(3) TDascombe (prom: ev ch 3 out: wknd appr 2 out)	2½	**9**	33/1	42	—
2093[5]	**South West Express (IRE)** (DJWintle) **5-11-5** WMarston (led tl after 3 out: sn wknd)	4	**10**	20/1	38	—
	Venice Beach (CPEBrooks) **5-11-5** GBradley (prom tl mstke 5th: j.lft 6th: sn bhd)	10	**11**	9/2[3]	29	—
	Master-H (RHAlner) **4-10-9** AThornton (bit bkwd: hld up: hdwy appr 6th: wknd after 3 out: t.o)	dist	**12**	20/1	—	—
	Jobie (RTPhillips) **7-11-5** JRailton (lw: bhd whn blnd 2 out: p.u bef last)		**P**	33/1	—	—

(SP 130.2%) **13 Rn**

4m 13.5 (20.50) CSF £5.36 TOTE £2.60: £1.60 £1.40 £1.90 (£4.80) Trio £10.20 OWNER Mr A. J. Lomas (WELLINGTON) BRED Cleaboy Farms Co

WEIGHT FOR AGE 4yo-10lb

OFFICIAL EXPLANATION **Venice Beach: finished distressed.**
2872 Break the Rules probably had a bit less to do this time, and confirmed he is going the right way. (13/8)
1788 Devon Peasant ran another sound race on the fastest ground she has encountered. (5/2)
Kinnescash (IRE) scored twice on the Flat as a juvenile including a win over ten furlongs. Campaigned on the All-Weather until a month ago, he should not be inconvenienced by further. (14/1)
Mystic Hill, bought for 14,000 guineas, won on the Flat for Guy Harwood and fared much better than when blundering at the first on his debut here last month. (11/1: op 7/1)

3110 PORLOCK (S) H'CAP HURDLE (0-95) (4-Y.O+) (Class G)
2-10 (2-11) **2m 1f (9 hdls)** £2,004.50 (£562.00: £273.50) GOING: 0.25 sec per fur (GS)

				SP	RR	SF
1638[12]	**Dissolve (71)** (NMLampard) **5-10-1**(7) MrLBaker (a.p: led flat: edgd rt: all out)	—	**1**	33/1	54	1
2874*	**D'naan (IRE) (93)** (MCPipe) **4-11-6b** CMaude (lw: led 2nd: reminders appr 5th: hit last: sn hdd: hrd rdn: r.o)	nk	**2**	3/1[1]	76	13
2818*	**Proud Image (84)** (GMMcCourt) **5-11-7** DBridgwater (led to 2nd: ev ch whn hit 2 out: one pce)	4	**3**	5/1[2]	63	10
1174[7]	**Steer Point (72)** (RGFrost) **6-10-9** JFrost (hld up & bhd: gd hdwy 3 out: one pce fr 2 out)	10	**4**	20/1	42	—
2006[5]	**Kashan (IRE) (63)** (PHayward) **9-10-0** BFenton (lw: hld up: gd hdwy fr 2 out: r.o)	4	**5**	6/1[3]	29	—
2866[5]	**Glowing Path (87)** (RJHodges) **7-11-3**(7) JHarris (prom tl wknd appr 2 out)	1¼	**6**	10/1	52	—
	Shanakee (73) (BJLlewellyn) **10-10-10** MrJLLlewellyn (hld up: hdwy appr 6th: ev ch 3 out: wknd appr 2 out)	2	**7**	20/1	36	—
2882[6]	**Lime Street Blues (IRE) (76)** (CPEBrooks) **6-10-13b** GBradley (bhd tl gd hdwy 5th: mstke 6th: wknd 3 out)	3½	**8**	9/1	35	—
2866[7]	**Nord Lys (IRE) (67)** (BJLlewellyn) **6-10-4** ILawrence (a bhd)	15	**9**	16/1	12	—
186[6]	**General Shirley (IRE) (80)** (PRHedger) **6-10-10**(7) MClinton (bkwd: hld up: hdwy appr 6th: wknd qckly after 3 out)	¾	**10**	10/1	25	—
2818[10]	**Marrowfat Lady (IRE) (68)** (NEBerry) **6-10-5** JRailton (lw: bhd fr 4th)	1½	**11**	25/1	11	—
2882[11]	**Mick The Yank (IRE) (68)** (HOliver) **7-10-5** JacquiOliver (a bhd: t.o)	10	**12**	12/1	2	—
2792[14]	**Aldwick Colonnade (70)** (MDIUsher) **10-10-7** WMarston (prom to 5th: t.o)	hd	**13**	25/1	4	—
2882[8]	**Little Hooligan (76)** (RJHodges) **6-10-10b**(3) TDascombe (bhd fr 4th: t.o)	5	**14**	14/1	5	—
	Courage-Mon-Brave (63) (TRGeorge) **9-10-0** RJohnson (bkwd: bhd fr 5th: t.o whn p.u bef 2 out)		**P**	12/1	—	—
	Bold Reine (FR) (63) (ABarrow) **8-10-0** AProcter (bkwd: a bhd: t.o 5th: p.u bef 2 out)		**P**	33/1	—	—
				(SP 135.2%)	**16 Rn**	

4m 9.8 (16.80) CSF £124.69 CT £571.04 TOTE £65.60: £6.90 £1.70 £2.10 £6.20 (£113.60) Trio £691.10 OWNER Western Solvents Ltd (MARLBOROUGH) BRED Enterprise Bloodstock Ltd
LONG HANDICAP Courage-Mon-Brave 9-11 Bold Reine (FR) 9-7
WEIGHT FOR AGE 4yo-10lb
Bt in 5,200 gns
Dissolve had to survive a Stewards' Enquiry before getting both her trainer and jockey off the mark under Rules. (33/1)
2874* D'naan (IRE), raised 5lb, fought back despite the winner leaning on him in the closing stages. (3/1)
2818* Proud Image seems pretty consistent in this grade. (5/1)
968 Steer Point could not take advantage of a drop in class. (20/1)
2006 Kashan (IRE) gave the impression the trip was inadequate. (6/1)
2866 Glowing Path was still 5lb higher than when winning a similar event at Hereford in November. (10/1)
2567 Little Hooligan (14/1: op 8/1)
Courage-Mon-Brave (12/1: op 33/1)

3111 HENLADE NOVICES' CHASE (5-Y.O+) (Class D)
2-45 (2-45) **2m 3f (15 fncs)** £3,517.50 (£1,065.00: £520.00: £247.50) GOING: 0.25 sec per fur (GS)

				SP	RR	SF
2885[F]	**Mister Drum (IRE) (124)** (MJWilkinson) **8-12-0** WMarston (lw: led 3rd: clr appr last: comf)	—	**1**	11/10[1]	97+	21
2867[2]	**Garolo (FR) (117)** (CPEBrooks) **7-11-8b** GBradley (lw: a.p: chsd wnr fr 4 out: btn whn mstke last)	6	**2**	5/4[2]	86	10
2810[6]	**Lucky Eddie (IRE) (97)** (PJHobbs) **6-11-2b**[1] CMaude (a.p: one pce fr 4 out)	2½	**3**	10/1[3]	78	2
2037[P]	**Dunnicks View (71)** (FGTucker) **8-10-9**(7) MGriffiths (led to 2nd: slipped bnd appr 9th: sn wknd: t.o)	dist	**4**	40/1	—	—
2943[13]	**Astral Invasion (USA)** (TWall) **6-10-13v**(3) RMassey (bhd: t.o fr 7th)	12	**5**	33/1	—	—
2676[P]	**Lucky Tanner** (MissHCKnight) **6-11-2** JCulloty (fell 1st)		**F**	20/1	—	—
	Sydney Boon (DRCElsworth) **6-11-2** PHolley (led 2nd to 3rd: t.o 7th: p.u bef 10th)		**P**	33/1	—	—
1938[13]	**Gemini Mist** (MrsPNDutfield) **6-10-11** MrLJefford (mstke 1st: sn t.o: p.u bef 9th)		**P**	40/1	—	—
	Rustic Flight (LWaring) **10-11-2** DLeahy (sn t.o: blnd 5th: p.u bef 3 out)		**P**	66/1	—	—
2892[U]	**Win a Hand (67)** (BJMRyall) **7-10-8**(3) TDascombe (j.slowly 1st: ref & uns rdr 2nd)		**R**	40/1	—	—
				(SP 120.6%)	**10 Rn**	

5m 1.4 (19.40) CSF £2.60 TOTE £2.00: £1.40 £1.30 £1.40 (£1.80) Trio £3.50 OWNER Mr Malcolm Batchelor (BANBURY) BRED David Mooney
2641 Mister Drum (IRE) is entered in several events at Cheltenham, and may go to Kempton next weekend first. (11/10)
2867 Garolo (FR) was not helped by the strong wind drying the ground. (5/4: op evens)
2810 Lucky Eddie (IRE) did much better in the blinkers than on his fencing debut at Warwick last month. (10/1)

3112 CRANMORE H'CAP HURDLE (0-100) (4-Y.O+ F & M) (Class F)
3-20 (3-20) **3m 110y (12 hdls)** £2,400.00 (£675.00: £330.00) GOING: 0.25 sec per fur (GS)

				SP	RR	SF
2877*	**Maid Equal (100)** (MCPipe) **6-11-7**(7) GSupple (hld up: gd hdwy to ld 8th: lft clr last)	—	**1**	9/4[1]	89	59
1553[8]	**Apachee Flower (74)** (HSHowe) **7-10-2** RJohnson (rdn 8th: hdwy appr 2 out: styd on flat)	12	**2**	16/1	55	25
2941[3]	**Fleur de Tal (92)** (WGMTurner) **6-10-13**(7) JPower (a.p: one pce fr 3 out)	1½	**3**	16/1	72	42
2941*	**Scottish Wedding (85)** (TWall) **7-10-10**(3) 7x RMassey (lw: a.p: no hdwy fr 3 out)	1½	**4**	8/1[3]	64	34
1840[3]	**Miss Secret (76)** (CWMitchell) **7-10-4** DBridgwater (nvr nr ldrs)	29	**5**	10/1	36	6
2838[P]	**Alice's Mirror (72)** (KBishop) **8-9-7b**(7) MGriffiths (prom tl wknd 8th)	3	**6**	33/1	30	—
2896[P]	**Colette's Choice (IRE) (85)** (GAHam) **8-10-13** AThornton (lw: led to 2nd: wknd 8th)	1½	**7**	25/1	42	12
	Stray Harmony (73) (RJSmith) **7-10-1**ow1 CMaude (a bhd)	2½	**8**	50/1	29	—
2882[3]	**Strike-a-Pose (74)** (BJLlewellyn) **7-10-2** ILawrence (hdwy 7th: rdn & wknd 9th)	½	**9**	20/1	29	—
2875[4]	**Brown Wren (72)** (PJHobbs) **6-10-0** GTormey (hdwy 5th: wknd 8th: t.o)	dist	**10**	10/1	—	—
1962[4]	**Summer Haven (72)** (NMLampard) **8-10-0** MrAKinane (lw: led 2nd to 8th: 6th & wkng whn fell 3 out)		**F**	33/1	—	—
792[3]	**Myblackthorn (IRE) (92)** (PFNicholls) **7-11-1**(5) OBurrows (lw: hdwy 7th: btn whn lft 2nd last: p.u & dismntd flat: lame)		**P**	12/1	—	—
2897[4]	**Dragonmist (IRE) (72)** (DBurchell) **7-10-0h** DJBurchell (a bhd: t.o 7th: p.u bef 2 out)		**P**	4/1[2]	—	—

Form	Horse	Dist	Pos	SP	RR	SF
2838P	**Kongies Melody (72)** (KBishop) **6-10-0** RGreene (hit 4th: sn bhd: t.o 9th: p.u bef 2 out)		P	50/1	—	—
28244	**Miss Marigold (92)** (RJHodges) **8-11-3b(3)** TDascombe (lw: hld up: hdwy 7th: ev ch whn blnd & uns rdr last)		U	16/1	77?	—

(SP 123.8%) **15 Rn**

6m 3.6 (11.60) CSF £33.60 CT £445.85 TOTE £2.80: £1.90 £3.60 £4.20 (£55.30) Trio £220.60 OWNER Mr Heeru Kirpalani (WELLINGTON) BRED H. L. Kirpalani

LONG HANDICAP Brown Wren 9-7 Summer Haven 9-12 Alice's Mirror 9-10 Kongies Melody 9-9 Stray Harmony 9-12

2877* Maid Equal, off a 7lb higher mark, was already due to go up a further 3lb. She looked to be going just the better when the only danger departed at the final flight. (9/4)

1256 Apachee Flower, tried in a visor last time, got going far too late in the day off this 2lb lower rating. (16/1)

2941 Fleur de Tal may have found this longer trip beyond her best. (16/1)

2941* Scottish Wedding, carrying 2lb more than her new rating, did not look so happy over three miles, but she has been busy of late. (8/1)

792 Myblackthorn (IRE), left a well-beaten second at the last, broke down on the run-in. (12/1)

2824 Miss Marigold, dropped 4lb, was upsides, possibly not going quite so well as the winner, when unshipping her rider at the last. (16/1)

3113 CHEDDAR H'CAP CHASE (0-115) (5-Y.O+) (Class E)

3-55 (3-57) **3m (19 fncs)** £3,712.50 (£1,125.00: £550.00: £262.50) GOING: 0.25 sec per fur (GS)

Form	Horse	Dist	Pos	SP	RR	SF
26934	**Mr Pickpocket (IRE) (106)** (MissHCKnight) **9-11-7** JFTitley (lw: led to 5th: led 7th: clr 2 out: comf)	—	1	11/4[1]	116+	18
27828	**Duhallow Lodge (110)** (CRBarwell) **10-11-11** BFenton (lw: hld up & bhd: hdwy 7th: lost pl 13th: rallied to chse wnr 3 out: hrd rdn appr last: no imp)	4	2	12/1	117	19
28234	**Jailbreaker (86)** (BRMillman) **10-9-10(5)ow1** DSalter (a.p: chsd wnr 4 out to 3 out: one pce)	6	3	12/1	89	—
26653	**Call Me River (IRE) (85)** (PRHedger) **9-10-0** ILawrence (lw: prom: hrd rdn & wknd appr 3 out)	7	4	11/2[2]	84	—
	Jason's Boy (85) (JMBradley) **7-10-0** RJohnson (bkwd: prom to 4 out)	8	5	11/1	78	—
28944	**Celtino (94)** (CaptTAForster) **9-10-9** SWynne (prom: mstke 6th: wknd 4 out)	5	6	13/2	84	—
28216	**Really a Rascal (105)** (DRGandolfo) **10-11-6** MAFitzgerald (hld up & bhd: sme hdwy 13th: wkng whn fell 15th)		F	6/1[3]	—	—
28797	**Benjamin Lancaster (97)** (MAGriffin) **13-10-5(7)** MGriffiths (prom: led 5th to 7th: dropped rr 14th: t.o whn p.u bef 3 out)		P	16/1	—	—
	Spring to it (95) (MCPipe) **11-10-10** JamieEvans (sme hdwy 11th: wknd 13th: t.o whn p.u bef 3 out)		P	10/1	—	—
	Aswamedh (85) (PJHobbs) **9-10-0** GTormey (hld up: mstke 6th: bhd whn bdly hmpd 15th: t.o whn p.u bef 3 out)		P	20/1	—	—
2881P	**Distillation (86)** (GFEdwards) **12-9-12(3)ow1** TDascombe (bhd: rdn 8th: sn t.o: p.u bef 3 out)		P	66/1	—	—
2910F	**Mingus (USA) (85)** (RHBuckler) **10-10-0** SMcNeill (hld up: hdwy 12th: wknd & uns rdr 14th)		U	16/1	—	—

(SP 120.5%) **12 Rn**

6m 20.4 (23.40) CSF £33.48 CT £320.59 TOTE £3.10: £1.80 £4.00 £3.00 (£31.80) Trio £45.10 OWNER Mr John Holmes (WANTAGE) BRED Thomas Larkin

LONG HANDICAP Call Me River (IRE) 9-8 Jason's Boy 9-11 Jailbreaker 9-10 Distillation 9-6 Mingus (USA) 9-5

2693 Mr Pickpocket (IRE), well backed in the offices, duly obliged on his handicap debut. (11/4)

1598* Duhallow Lodge, down 3lb, was still 1lb higher then when winning over course and distance in November. (12/1: op 6/1)

2823 Jailbreaker gave a reasonable account of himself from 4lb out of the handicap, but has not won for over two years. (12/1: op 8/1)

2665 Call Me River (IRE), 6lb wrong at the weights, was effectively 8lb higher than when scoring over course and distance in December. (11/2)

Jason's Boy, yet to win over three miles, will strip fitter for the outing. (11/1)

2894 Celtino could not take advantage of a 3lb lower mark. (13/2: op 4/1)

2821 Really a Rascal (6/1: 4/1-13/2)

Spring to it (10/1: op 6/1)

3114 FEBRUARY H'CAP HURDLE (0-120) (4-Y.O+) (Class D)

4-25 (4-25) **2m 3f 110y (10 hdls)** £2,814.00 (£852.00: £416.00: £198.00) GOING: 0.25 sec per fur (GS)

Form	Horse	Dist	Pos	SP	RR	SF
28176	**Jefferies (101)** (JABOld) **8-11-5** CLlewellyn (hld up: stdy hdwy 5th: led 3 out: rdn & hdd 2 out: lft in ld last: edgd rt: r.o)	—	1	5/2[2]	84	26
25792	**Nine O Three (IRE) (105)** (AGNewcombe) **8-11-9** AThornton (hld up: stdy hdwy 7th: rdn to ld 2 out: blnd & hdd last: swtchd lft: rallied nr fin)	¾	2	7/4[1]	87	29
27972	**Fawley Flyer (94)** (WGMTurner) **8-10-5(7)** JPower (a.p: led after 6th to 3 out: one pce fr 2 out)	4	3	5/1[3]	73	15
27448	**Moor Hall Lady (85)** (NMBabbage) **6-10-3v1** WMarston (led 2nd tl after 6th: wknd qckly 3 out: t.o)	dist	4	13/2	—	—
10398	**Spring to Glory (102)** (PHayward) **10-11-6** BFenton (led to 2nd: 3rd whn fell 6th)		F	14/1	—	—
2817P	**Spring Saint (106)** (MissCHorler) **8-11-10** CMaude (bhd whn rdn after 5th: sn t.o: p.u bef 2 out)		P	8/1	—	—
2797P	**Sausalito Boy (82)** (RJSmith) **9-10-0b1** DBridgwater (a bhd: t.o whn p.u bef 6th)		P	66/1	—	—

(SP 114.2%) **7 Rn**

4m 46.4 (15.40) CSF £6.87 CT £17.00 TOTE £4.10: £2.30 £1.90 (£4.90) OWNER Miss S. Blumberg (WROUGHTON) BRED R. D. & Mrs J. S. Chugg

LONG HANDICAP Sausalito Boy 9-9

2817 Jefferies benefited from the favourite's sloppy jump at the last, and looked a fortunate winner. (5/2)

2579 Nine O Three (IRE) did not find as much as anticipated when let down going to the penultimate hurdle, but would still have won had he jumped the last properly. (7/4)

2797 Fawley Flyer remains a model of consistency despite having gone up no less than 20lb this season. (5/1: 100/30-11/2)

3115 BLACKDOWN MAIDEN HURDLE (II) (4-Y.O+) (Class F)

4-55 (4-57) **2m 1f (9 hdls)** £1,696.50 (£474.00: £229.50) GOING: 0.25 sec per fur (GS)

Form	Horse	Dist	Pos	SP	RR	SF
254710	**Tristram's Image (NZ)** (NJHenderson) **6-11-5** MAFitzgerald (lw: a.p: mstke 3 out: led after 2 out: drvn out)	—	1	2/1[1]	64	—
	Welton Arsenal (KBishop) **5-11-5** RGreene (hld up: stdy hdwy 6th: r.o flat)	¾	2	6/1[3]	63	—
	Give And Take (MCPipe) **4-10-9** JamieEvans (led 2nd: reminders after 5th: wandered, j.rt & rdr lost iron 2 out: sn hdd: nt rcvr)	2	3	9/4[2]	61+	—
	Dormy Three (RJHodges) **7-11-2(3)** TDascombe (bkwd: a.p: one pce fr 2 out)	5	4	16/1	57	—
2634P	**Givry (IRE)** (GMMcCourt) **7-11-0(5)** SophieMitchell (prom tl wknd appr 2 out)	3½	5	25/1	53	—
962	**Cuban Nights (USA)** (BJLlewellyn) **5-11-5** RJohnson (plld hrd: prom to 3 out)	11	6	7/1	43	—
17066	**Princely Affair** (JMBradley) **4-10-9** SWynne (led to 2nd: wknd 3 out)	½	7	16/1	43	—
	Pearl Hart (RTPhillips) **5-10-7(7)** MartinSmith (bit bkwd: nvr trbld ldrs)	5	8	20/1	33	—
	Langtonian (GFEdwards) **8-11-5** BFenton (a bhd)	6	9	33/1	32	—

				SP	RR	SF
	Song of Kenda (BRMillman) **5-10-9**(5) DSalter (bkwd: a bhd)	1	**10**	33/1	26	—
504[6]	**Abbeydoran** (MrsJEHawkins) **6-11-0** WMarston (a bhd: t.o)	28	**11**	66/1	—	—
589[11]	**Rapid Liner** (RJBaker) **4-10-9** VSlattery (nt j.w: a bhd: t.o fr 6th)	1	**12**	50/1	4	—
743[P]	**Fiery Footsteps** (CLPopham) **5-10-7**(7) TO'Connor (hld up & plld hrd: hdwy 4th: wknd 6th)	¾	**13**	66/1	—	—
	Moor Dutch (RGFrost) **6-11-5** MrAHoldsworth (lost pl 5th: bhd whn p.u bef 2 out)		**P**	50/1	—	—
				(SP 124.1%)	**14 Rn**	

4m 12.5 (19.50) CSF £12.92 TOTE £2.40: £1.90 £1.70 £2.20 (£9.20) Trio £6.90 OWNER Mr S. Keeling (LAMBOURN) BRED D. F. Fuge
WEIGHT FOR AGE 4yo-10lb
1665 Tristram's Image (NZ), better for the experience gained last time, greatly benefited from the antics of Give And Take. (2/1)
Welton Arsenal made a promising start to his hurdling career but, although he did manage two victories on the Flat, it should be remembered he was very difficult to win with. (6/1: 4/1-13/2)
Give And Take was gelded after being bought out of Lord Huntingdon's yard for 12,000 guineas. Despite causing his own trouble, he did look desperately unlucky, and his rider would probably have been better riding without his iron rather than wasting so much time in regaining it. (9/4)
Dormy Three was certainly not disgraced considering he was carrying condition. (16/1)
Givry (IRE) finished third of four in a point-to-point in April 1995. (25/1)

T/Jkpt: Not won; £12,757.54 to Newcastle 14/2/97. T/Plpt: £13.10 (913.27 Tckts). T/Qdpt: £9.50 (74.97 Tckts) KH

3116a - 3125a : (Irish Racing) - See Computer Raceform

2606a-NAVAN (Ireland) (L-H) (Yielding to soft)
Saturday February 8th

3126a BOYNE E.B.F. HURDLE (Gd 2) (5-Y.O+)
2-30 (2-33) **3m (13 hdls)** IR £9,675.00 (IR £2,775.00: IR £1,275.00: IR £375.00) GOING: Not Established

				SP	RR	SF
2361a*	**What a Question (IRE)** (MFMorris,Ireland) **9-11-9** CO'Dwyer (rn 3rd: disp ld 4 out: led 3 out: rdn appr last: styd on flat: drew clr last 100 yds)	—	**1**	4/1[2]	133	56
2361a[2]	**Antapoura (IRE)** (APO'Brien,Ireland) **5-10-10** CFSwan (rn 2nd: disp ld 4 out: hdd next: cl 2nd & ev ch appr last: rdn & no ex flat)	2½	**2**	2/1[1]	122	41
1487a[6]	**Derrymoyle (IRE)** (MCunningham,Ireland) **8-11-5** JPBroderick (hld up: wnt 3rd 3 out: chsd ldrs next: rdn & styd on appr last)	3½	**3**	5/1[3]	125	48
2740a[6]	**Notcomplainingbut (IRE)** (PMullins,Ireland) **6-11-0** TPTreacy (hld up: chsd ldrs 3 out: rdn & no imp between last 2)	10	**4**	8/1	113	36
2857a[6]	**Blushing Sand (IRE)** (PTLeonard,Ireland) **7-10-9**(7) MrTJBeattie (towards rr: hdwy bef 3 out: nvr nrr)	3	**5**	25/1	113	36
1156[3]	**Difficult Times (IRE)** (GMLyons,Ireland) **5-10-13**ow1 SCLyons (rn 4th: rdn after 4 out: no imp between last 2)	4½	**6**	12/1	111	29
	Chance Coffey (PFO'Donnell,Ireland) **12-11-5** GMO'Neill (towards rr: n.d)	15	**7**	33/1	103	26
2740a[4]	**Urubande (IRE)** (APO'Brien,Ireland) **7-11-9** THorgan (bhd: plld hrd: clsd bef 8th: 6th 3 out: no imp appr next: eased)	3	**8**	4/1[2]	105	28
2348a[15]	**Love and Porter (IRE)** (JJO'Connor,Ireland) **9-11-0** DHO'Connor (led: hdd bef 4 out: sn wknd)	dist	**9**	33/1	—	—
				(SP 118.5%)	**9 Rn**	

6m 5.7 (0.70) OWNER Mrs Miles Valentine (FETHARD) BRED R. A. and Mrs St George
2361a* What a Question (IRE) again confirmed superiority over Antapoura. Leading four out, she made the rest and was going best from two out. Third in the Stayers' last year, she now goes for that again, but would prefer better ground than this. (4/1: op 5/2)
2361a Antapoura (IRE), once again found the winner too strong. She had every chance in the duel from four out, but really needs the heavy ground to show her best. (2/1)
1487a Derrymoyle (IRE) showed distinct signs of a return to form, appearing to be cruising on the bridle three out but not making much improvement between the last two flights. He is certainly going the right way, and better ground would suit him in the Cheltenham race. (5/1)
2740a Notcomplainingbut (IRE) put in one of her less inspired runs here. (8/1)
1156 Difficult Times (IRE) (12/1: op 20/1)
2740a Urubande (IRE), discarded by Charlie Swan for stable companion Antapoura, was given an extraordinary ride. Pulling hard and way off the pace at the rear of the field, he improved to go sixth with three to jump, but the progress wasn't maintained and he trailed in. Admittedly, the ground was against him, as he undoubtedly needs a much sounder surface, but all his best form has been shown when allowed to run in front. There was no official inquiry held into this performance. (4/1)

3128a NOBBER H'CAP CHASE (5-Y.O+)
3-30 (3-35) **2m 1f (10 fncs)** IR £5,480.00 (IR £1,240.00: IR £520.00: IR £280.00) GOING: Not Established

				SP	RR	SF
2346a[2]	**Klairon Davis (FR)** (ALTMoore,Ireland) **8-12-0** FWoods (led bef 2nd: jnd 3 out: led 2 out: drew clr between last 2: styd on wl)	—	**1**	4/9[1]	162+	80
2997a[P]	**Idiots Venture** (APO'Brien,Ireland) **10-10-7** CFSwan (sn chsg ldr: disp ld 3 out: hdd 2 out: sn rdn: kpt on same pce)	8	**2**	4/1[2]	134	52
2848a[P]	**Shanagarry (IRE)** (PHeffernan,Ireland) **8-10-7** CO'Dwyer (a bhd: n.d)	15	**3**	9/1	119	37
	Monalee River (IRE) (WPMullins,Ireland) **9-10-7** TPTreacy (sn 3rd: lost tch bef 5th)	7	**4**	5/1[3]	113	31
				(SP 115.9%)	**4 Rn**	

4m 19.7 (-4.30) OWNER C. Jones (NAAS) BRED M. C. Quellier in France
2346a Klairon Davis (FR) had nothing to beat. He was a bit slow at some fences, notably four and three out, but was able to draw clear between the last two. This was not an impressive performance but there is plenty left to work on, and he definitely goes in defence of his two-mile Champion crown. (4/9)
2602a Idiots Venture, totally out of form to date this season, was running over an inadequate trip and 7lb out of the handicap. He was less than a length behind the winner three out and was not shaken off until after the next. (4/1: op 5/2)
Shanagarry (IRE), 17lb out of the handicap, was trailing before halfway and kept on without threatening. (9/1: op 6/1)
Monalee River (IRE), 22lb out of the handicap, was never a factor after blundering at the fourth and fifth. (5/1: op 3/1)

3129a - 3130a : (Irish Racing) - See Computer Raceform

1861-FAKENHAM (L-H) (Good)
Friday February 14th
WEATHER: fine & sunny

3131 SHERINGHAM (S) H'CAP HURDLE (0-90) (4-Y.O+) (Class G)
1-45 (1-45) **2m (9 hdls)** £2,739.50 (£836.00: £413.00: £201.50) GOING: 0.13 sec per fur (G)

				SP	RR	SF
2943[2]	**Ruth's Gamble (54)** (MrsLCJewell) **9-10-2v** DLeahy (trckd ldrs: led appr last: rdn clr flat)	—	**1**	6/1	39	4
1866[7]	**Nagobelia (76)** (JPearce) **9-11-10** NMann (led tl after 3rd: led 2 out: hdd appr last: one pce flat)	3	**2**	14/1	58	23
	Captain Marmalade (73) (DTThom) **8-11-7** KGaule (chsd ldrs: pushed along 5th: ev ch 2 out: one pce appr last)	3	**3**	9/1	52	17
2615[7]	**Sousse (80)** (MrsMReveley) **4-11-4** PNiven (lw: hld up: rdn & hdwy appr 6th: ev ch 3 out: wknd next)	11	**4**	7/4[1]	48	3
	Emerald Venture (68) (FCoton) **10-11-2** JFTitley (nvr nrr)	6	**5**	12/1	30	—
2668[14]	**Stone Island (80)** (JohnWhyte) **4-10-11**(7) MrRWakley (prom to 6th)	4	**6**	16/1	38	—
2943[3]	**Dr Dave (IRE) (67)** (PRChamings) **6-11-1** BFenton (hld up & plld hrd: hdwy to ld after 3rd: sn clr: hit 3 out: hdd next: sn wknd)	1½	**7**	9/2[2]	24	—
355[U]	**Wordy's Wind (67)** (LWordingham) **8-10-8**(7) CRae (a bhd)	1¾	**8**	20/1	22	—
3057[2]	**Summer Villa (67)** (KGWingrove) **5-11-1b** JRyan (nvr nr to chal)	5	**9**	11/2[3]	17	—
879[11]	**Pocono Knight (64)** (CHJones) **7-10-12** JAMcCarthy (in tch: wkng whn mstke 6th: bhd whn fell 2 out)		**F**	20/1	—	—

(SP 124.0%) **10 Rn**

3m 56.2 (12.20) CSF £80.71 CT £690.88 TOTE £7.60: £1.30 £3.50 £2.50 (£20.50) Trio £53.50 OWNER Mrs A. Emanuel (SUTTON VALENCE) BRED D. W. Chapman
WEIGHT FOR AGE 4yo-10lb
No bid

2943 Ruth's Gamble returned to top form last time and showed his liking for the course. (6/1)
Nagobelia looked well in his coat, but might just have needed this after two months off. He has had a long spell in the wilderness but, now that he has returned to form, he should soon be winning. (14/1)
Captain Marmalade, fit from the All-Weather, ran a respectable race but has yet to break his duck over timber. (9/1: op 5/1)
2615 Sousse, on her toes beforehand, was anchored at the back until let down on the final circuit. She needed reminders to get her running and does not look an easy ride. (7/4)
Emerald Venture usually runs well fresh, but never looked likely to get going in time on this occasion. (12/1: 6/1-14/1)
1675 Stone Island has lost his form since changing yards. (16/1)
2943 Dr Dave (IRE), held up at the back, fought uncontrollably for his head until the brakes failed after the first half-mile. (9/2: 6/1-7/2)

3132 PRINCE CARLTON H'CAP CHASE (0-100) (5-Y.O+) (Class F)
2-20 (2-21) **3m 110y (18 fncs)** £4,036.00 (£1,228.00: £604.00: £292.00) GOING: 0.13 sec per fur (G)

				SP	RR	SF
2894[P]	**Artic Wings (IRE) (100)** (OBrennan) **9-12-0** MBrennan (a.p: led 3 out: sn clr: j.rt last: drvn out flat)	—	**1**	11/2	103+	35
2906[3]	**Whippers Delight (IRE) (92)** (GFHCharles-Jones) **9-10-13**(7) XAizpuru (lw: led tl blnd & hdd 13th: kpt on fr 4 out)	7	**2**	7/1	90	22
2681[5]	**Darren the Brave (100)** (CPEBrooks) **9-12-0** GBradley (chsd ldrs: hit 5th: wknd 4 out)	19	**3**	100/30[1]	86	18
1773[2]	**Wixoe Wonder (IRE) (79)** (MBradstock) **7-10-7** PHolley (lw: prom: led 13th: hdd 3 out: wknd qckly next)	12	**4**	6/1	57	—
2823[2]	**Good for a Laugh (82)** (AGHobbs) **13-10-3**(7) MrGShenkin (lw: hdwy 5th: wkng whn blnd 2 out)	1½	**5**	9/2[2]	59	—
2876[P]	**Glen Mirage (90)** (MJCoombe) **12-11-4** MissMCoombe (lw: mstkes: sn wl bhd: sme hdwy fr 3 out)	1½	**6**	11/1	66	—
2923[P]	**Call Me Early (89)** (MissJFCraze) **12-11-3** ILawrence (a bhd)	10	**7**	33/1	59	—
2910[4]	**Victory Gate (USA) (72)** (MrsLCJewell) **12-10-0** DLeahy (a bhd: t.o fr 12th)	11	**8**	40/1	35	—
2821[5]	**Mr Invader (90)** (NAGaselee) **10-11-4b** WMarston (disp ld tl blnd 8th: mstke 11th: wknd 14th: virtually p.u flat)	17	**9**	5/1[3]	41	—

(SP 113.8%) **9 Rn**

6m 20.1 (17.10) CSF £39.10 CT £133.82 TOTE £7.20: £2.00 £1.60 £1.80 (£14.90) Trio £14.50 OWNER Lady Anne Bentinck (WORKSOP) BRED E. D. and Mrs Martin Smith
LONG HANDICAP Victory Gate (USA) 9-8
OFFICIAL EXPLANATION **Artic Wings (IRE): accounting for the winner's apparent improvement in form, the trainer reported that Artic Wings had failed to sparkle after a nine month lay-off, and many of the horses in the yard had been 'wrong' before her last run.**

2894 Artic Wings (IRE) left her seasonal debut behind, and won in the style of a well-handicapped horse to give the yard their first winner of the season, winning easily until slowing up at the final fence. She scored off higher marks in her hurdling days, and ought to do so again if a similar soft race can be found. (11/2)
2906 Whippers Delight (IRE) is surely better over shorter, but is game and stuck to his task. (7/1)
2681 Darren the Brave may have been unsuited by the track, for he failed to last home despite regaining third place late in the day. (100/30: 9/4-7/2)
1773 Wixoe Wonder (IRE), ridden more aggressively this time, patently failed to get the trip. (6/1)
2823 Good for a Laugh, very well-handicapped even on efforts this season, has never threatened to stay three miles, but gave the impression that he would have struggled to win this at any trip. (9/2)
1961 Glen Mirage looked less than fully co-operative, and only ran on when the race was over. (11/1: 8/1-12/1)

3133 E.B.F. 'N.H.' (QUALIFIER) NOVICES' HURDLE (5, 6 & 7-Y.O) (Class D)
2-55 (2-55) **2m 4f (11 hdls)** £2,700.50 (£824.00: £407.00: £198.50) GOING: 0.13 sec per fur (G)

				SP	RR	SF
2673[2]	**Peace Lord (IRE) (105)** (MrsDHaine) **7-11-0** JFTitley (lw: mstke 1st: w ldr: led 8th: clr appr last: pushed out)	—	**1**	7/4[2]	77	31
2690[2]	**Clinton (IRE)** (KCBailey) **6-11-0** CO'Dwyer (lw: hld up: hdwy appr 8th: chsng wnr whn j.slowly 2 out: rdn & hit last: no imp)	5	**2**	6/4[1]	73	27
1551[6]	**Super Rapier (IRE)** (GAHubbard) **5-11-0** BFenton (chsd ldrs: one pce fr 3 out)	23	**3**	14/1	55	9
2891[5]	**Arctic Triumph** (MBradstock) **6-11-0** PHolley (lw: prom: rdn 7th: btn next)	2½	**4**	14/1	53	7
2626[11]	**Holkham Bay** (LWordingham) **5-11-0** JRyan (mstke 4th: bhd fr 7th)	23	**5**	33/1	34	—
2619[8]	**April Seventh (IRE)** (JNeville) **6-11-0** WMarston (mde most to 8th: wknd 3 out)	5	**6**	9/2[3]	30	—
58[P]	**Clashawan (IRE)** (OBrennan) **7-10-9** MBrennan (j.b: t.o whn p.u bef 8th)		**P**	25/1	—	—

2844^{5} **The Lady Captain** (DTThom) **5-10-9** KGaule (mstke 1st: bhd fr 7th: t.o whn p.u bef last)	**P**	14/1	—	—
		(SP 121.3%)	**8 Rn**	

4m 55.9 (10.90) CSF £4.87 TOTE £3.40: £1.00 £1.70 £3.30 (£1.80) OWNER Sir Peter & Lady Gibbings (NEWMARKET) BRED Ronald Scanlon
OFFICIAL EXPLANATION **April Seventh (IRE): gurgled**
2673 Peace Lord (IRE) got due reward for perseverance, winning in good style. (7/4)
2690 Clinton (IRE), whose Huntingdon form has taken a few knocks recently, jumped moderately when the chips were down and was no match for the winner. (6/4: op evens)
1551 Super Rapier (IRE) ran a very respectable race, as he undoubtedly needs a stiffer test of stamina. (14/1: op 8/1)
2891 Arctic Triumph was outpaced in the last half-mile, but seemed to be running out of gas as well. (14/1: op 8/1)
Holkham Bay is rather unfurnished, and again showed precious little. (33/1)
1431 April Seventh (IRE), gambled on presumably as the Kelso form is working out well, was easily outpaced by the two principals and wasn't knocked about once out of contention. (9/2: 8/1-4/1)
2844 The Lady Captain (14/1: 12/1-20/1)

3134 BET WITH THE TOTE (QUALIFIER) NOVICES' CHASE (6-Y.O+) (Class D)

3-30 (3-30) **3m 110y (18 fncs)** £3,378.00 (£1,029.00: £507.00: £246.00) GOING: 0.13 sec per fur (G)

		SP	RR	SF
2827^{4} **Flippance (98)** (NAGaselee) **7-10-10** WMarston (lw: prom: lft in ld 12th: hdd & hit next: ev ch whn hit 2 out: led appr last: rdn out) —	**1**	4/5^{1}	93	—
2795^{9} **Rolleston Blade (72)** (JRBest) **10-10-3**$^{(7)}$ MrPO'Keeffe (blnd 1st: mstke 8th: hdwy 10th: led 13th: mstke next: hit 2 out: sn hdd & btn) 8	**2**	8/1^{3}	88	—
2827^{8} **Charter Lane (IRE) (63)** (MrsLCJewell) **7-10-10** DLeahy (lw: chsd ldrs: 3rd whn blnd 4 out: no ch after) 15	**3**	40/1	78	—
2841^{P} **Milwaukee (IRE)** (OBrennan) **8-10-5** MBrennan (in tch: dropped rr 10th: no imp fr 4 out) 1¼	**4**	12/1	72	—
1961^{P} **Joker Jack (62)** (RDean) **12-10-7**$^{(3)}$ TDascombe (led to 8th: lost pl 11th: hit 13th: sn bhd) 3	**5**	25/1	75	—
Sharrow Bay (NZ) (AGHobbs) **10-10-10** RGreene (fell 3rd)	**F**	11/1	—	—
1779^{5} **Merilena (IRE)** (GAHubbard) **7-10-5** BFenton (w ldr: led 8th tl blnd & uns rdr 12th)	**U**	3/1^{2}	—	—
		(SP 114.0%)	**7 Rn**	

6m 27.7 (24.70) CSF £7.50 TOTE £1.90: £1.30 £3.50 (£5.30) OWNER Exors of the late Mr C L Rykens (LAMBOURN) BRED Mrs E. J. Floyd
Flippance found a poor race and won cosily enough in the end, but did not entirely impress, getting very low at both four and three out, though losing no ground on either occasion. He looked somewhat reluctant when left in front, and needed to lead on the bridle to go on again. (4/5: 1/2-evens)
Rolleston Blade is only moderate, but gave the impression that he might have won but for a string of mistakes. (8/1)
Charter Lane (IRE), well behind the winner at Folkestone, already looked held when the mistake finished him. (40/1)
Milwaukee (IRE), a winning Irish pointer, looked fitter this time but is shaping as if very moderate. (12/1: op 8/1)
1863 Joker Jack was outpaced once the tempo increased. (25/1)
1779 Merilena (IRE), a lengthy mare who ought to take to this game, was bowling along happily in the lead when unseating with a circuit left. She would probably have gone close. (3/1)

3135 WALTER WALES MEMORIAL CUP HUNTERS' CHASE (5-Y.O+) (Class H)

4-05 (4-05) **2m 5f 110y (16 fncs)** £2,566.00 (£726.00: £358.00) GOING: 0.13 sec per fur (G)

		SP	RR	SF
2903* **Cab on Target** (MrsMReveley) **11-11-10** MrSSwiers (hld up: hdwy 10th: rdn to ld flat) —	**1**	4/6^{1}	115	30
Arise (IRE) (AWVarey) **8-11-3**$^{(7)}$ MrEJames (prom: led 4 out: hdd & unable qckn flat) 1¼	**2**	40/1	114	29
3010^{F} **Pro Bono (IRE)** (PCCaudwell) **7-11-3**$^{(7)}$ MrADalton (prom: led 10th to 13th: wknd appr 2 out) 11	**3**	8/1^{3}	106	21
Just Jack (PJonason) **11-11-3**$^{(7)}$ MrRWakley (chsd ldrs tl wknd 3 out) 18	**4**	16/1	93	8
3010^{F} **Idiotic** (PRChamings) **9-11-5**$^{(5)}$ MrCVigors (mstkes 1st, 5th & 11th: bhd fr 13th) ½	**5**	3/1^{2}	92	7
Emsee-H (JMTurner) **12-11-5**$^{(5)}$ MrASansome (a bhd) dist	**6**	25/1	—	—
Icarus (USA) (DHBrown) **11-11-3b**$^{(7)}$ MrARebori (bit bkwd: prom: lft in ld 8th: hdd 10th: fell next: dead)	**F**	33/1	—	—
Spartan Silver (MBloom) **11-11-5**$^{(7)ow2}$ MrNBloom (a bhd: t.o whn p.u bef 11th)	**P**	20/1	—	—
96^{4} **Prinzal** (GMMcCourt) **10-11-3**$^{(7)}$ MrMEmmanuel (nt j.w: led: sn clr: blnd & uns rdr 8th)	**U**	9/1	—	—
No More Trix (WMBurnell) **11-11-3**$^{(7)}$ MrWBurnell (blnd & uns rdr 4th)	**U**	25/1	—	—
		(SP 129.8%)	**10 Rn**	

5m 30.2 (15.20) CSF £44.35 TOTE £1.60: £1.10 £4.80 £2.00 (£25.50) Trio £82.50 OWNER Mr N. Hurst (SALTBURN) BRED W. Lombard
2903* Cab on Target had probably never seen a track as sharp as this, never mind raced on one. However, he did the job in good style once ridden, despite never travelling notably well. The jury is still out on just how much of his ability he retains, but at his best he would be the one to beat in the Foxhunters' at the Festival. (4/6: 2/5-8/11)
Arise (IRE), given a good, enterprising ride, nearly pulled off a surprise. He recently returned between the flags after a year off, and is clearly up to winning in this sphere. (40/1)
Pro Bono (IRE) ran as if this may have been needed more than it appeared, although it was still not a bad effort. (8/1)
Just Jack, a recent winner between the flags, could not keep up the gallop going to two out. (16/1)
Idiotic describes his price, as his jumping remains a problem. (3/1: 5/1-11/4)
96 Prinzal went well for a much more experienced pilot last year, but shot off uncontrollably from the start, and was a fence clear when unseating. He has ability but needs to be kept in check. (9/1)

3136 CROMER H'CAP HURDLE (0-115) (4-Y.O+) (Class E)

4-40 (4-40) **2m (9 hdls)** £2,988.00 (£909.00: £447.00: £216.00) GOING: 0.13 sec per fur (G)

		SP	RR	SF
3076^{2} **Kintavi (90)** (TWDonnelly) **7-10-7** PNiven (lw: hld up: hdwy to ld appr 3 out: qcknd clr 2 out: mstke last: easily) —	**1**	13/8^{1}	81+	31
2842^{9} **Ajdar (83)** (OBrennan) **6-10-0** MBrennan (hld up: hdwy 3 out: r.o flat: no ch w wnr) 10	**2**	16/1	64	14
1956^{2} **Lord Mcmurrough (IRE) (111)** (JNeville) **7-11-11**$^{(3)}$ TDascombe (chsd ldrs: ev ch 6th: rdn next: outpcd 2 out) 2	**3**	7/2^{2}	90	40
Irish Emerald (87) (GCBravery) **10-10-4** KGaule (bkwd: trckd ldrs: led 6th: sn hdd & btn) 24	**4**	5/1	42	—
1832^{3} **Menelave (IRE) (107)** (OSherwood) **7-11-10** JAMcCarthy (chsd clr ldr: lost pl 5th: n.d afterwards) 2½	**5**	9/2^{3}	60	10
2828^{5} **Thefieldsofathenry (IRE) (105)** (CREgerton) **7-11-1**$^{(7)}$ MBerry (led: sn clr: wknd & hdd 6th) 30	**6**	5/1	28	—
		(SP 117.7%)	**6 Rn**	

3m 51.3 (7.30) CSF £22.55 TOTE £2.20: £1.80 £3.20 (£14.10) OWNER Mr S. Taberner (SWADLINCOTE) BRED S. Taberner
LONG HANDICAP Ajdar 9-6

3076 Kintavi looked a picture of health in the paddock and, having found a much easier race than the one in which he was beaten three days ago, fairly scooted in. (13/8)
Ajdar confirmed that the Brennan yard may well be on the way back, for he ran very much his best race since joining the stable. (16/1)
1956 Lord Mcmurrough (IRE) needs more of a test of stamina, but did not show much heart for a battle once things were not going his way. (7/2: 2/1-4/1)
Irish Emerald, returning after a very long absence, looked to need the race, but moved well and ran promisingly for a long way. (5/1)
1832 Menelave (IRE) had another non-going day and is certainly not consistent. (9/2: 3/1-5/1)
2828 Thefieldsofathenry (IRE) raced far too freely, but has only just returned from a spell on the sidelines. He had the form to do well off this sort of mark when he last raced in Ireland. (5/1: 4/1-6/1)

T/Plpt: £28.60 (282.51 Tckts). T/Qdpt: £3.00 (226.21 Tckts) Dk

2912-NEWCASTLE (L-H) (Good, Good to soft patches)
Friday February 14th

one fence omitted each circuit
WEATHER: fine

3137 NORTHERN RACING H'CAP HURDLE (0-115) (4-Y.O+) (Class E)
2-05 (2-05) **2m (9 hdls)** £2,284.50 (£642.00: £313.50) GOING: 0.24 sec per fur (G)

				SP	RR	SF
3049²	**Samanid (IRE) (99)** (MissLCSiddall) **5-11-3** OPears (hld up: smooth hdwy to ld 2 out: r.o wl)	—	1	100/30³	90	34
2842²	**Danbys Gorse (90)** (JMJefferson) **5-10-5**(3) ECallaghan (hld up: hdwy 4 out: led 3 out to 2 out: nt pce of wnr)	9	2	5/2¹	72	16
2631F	**Bend Sable (IRE) (109)** (FSStorey) **7-11-13** BStorey (hld up: effrt appr 3 out: styd on: no imp)	3½	3	3/1²	88	32
2041²	**Elastic (93)** (RGCockburn) **11-10-11** LO'Hara (lw: led tl hdd 3 out: one pce)	6	4	8/1	66	10
2651⁶	**Elation (110)** (GRichards) **5-12-0** ADobbin (prom tl lost pl 5th: sme late hdwy)	1½	5	16/1	81	25
2913U	**Skiddaw Samba (84)** (MrsMReveley) **8-9-13**(3) GLee (chsd ldrs tl wknd 3 out)	13	6	14/1	42	—
2764⁷	**Fox Sparrow (105)** (NTinkler) **7-11-9** ASSmith (cl up tl wknd fr 3 out)	2	7	20/1	61	5
2764⁶	**All Clear (IRE) (86)** (HowardJohnson) **6-10-4** PCarberry (hld up: gd hdwy to chse ldr 4th: wknd 4 out)	dist	8	14/1	—	—
				(SP 111.7%)		**8 Rn**

4m 2.7 (10.70) CSF £10.79 CT £23.39 TOTE £3.80: £1.10 £1.40 £1.90 (£4.40) OWNER Magnum Construction Ltd (TADCASTER) BRED H. H. The Aga Khans Studs S.C.
3049 Samanid (IRE) is in tremendous form at the moment and won this really well. He looks likely to follow up. (100/30)
2842 Danbys Gorse looked to have done everything right, only to get tapped for speed going to the last. He would probably benefit from a stronger pace or a little bit further. (5/2)
2631 Bend Sable (IRE) travelled well, but he was no match for the front pair when the race began in earnest three out. (3/1)
2041 Elastic looked in good condition after almost two months off, and ran a fine race over a distance too short. This should have put her right. (8/1)
2062 Elation is coming to himself looks-wise and this was not a bad effort, but his real future looks to be chasing. (16/1)

3138 BORDER MINSTREL SUNDAY LUNCH NOVICES' CHASE (5-Y.O+) (Class D)
2-40 (2-40) **2m 4f (13 fncs)** £3,533.75 (£1,070.00: £522.50: £248.75) GOING: 0.24 sec per fur (G)

				SP	RR	SF
2923³	**Bold Account (IRE) (86)** (GMMoore) **7-11-3b** ADobbin (chsd ldr: led fr 7th: hld on wl cl home)	—	1	3/1²	82	—
3023³	**Coqui Lane** (JMDun) **10-11-3** TReed (lw: nt j.w: led to 7th: drvn along fr 11th: ev ch tl outpcd 3 out: styd on wl flat: no ex towards fin)	nk	2	7/4¹	82	—
2632³	**Kiltulla (IRE) (65)** (MrsSJSmith) **7-11-3** RichardGuest (a chsng ldrs: ev ch fr 11th: one pce fr 3 out)	6	3	16/1³	77	—
3023⁴	**Le Denstan (84)** (MrsDThomson) **10-11-8** DParker (in tch tl outpcd fr 12th)	11	4	33/1	73	—
2914⁵	**Robara** (SJLeadbetter) **7-11-3** NLeach (mstke 1st: prom tl wknd & hit 4 out)	5	5	100/1	64	—
2912P	**Aristodemus (85)** (MrsLMarshall) **8-11-3** KJohnson (in tch tl blnd 7th: blnd bdly 9th: wl bhd after)	14	6	150/1	53	—
	Real Tonic (GRichards) **7-11-3** PCarberry (plld hrd: prom whn fell 5th)		F	7/4¹	—	—
2650P	**Dark Buoy (72)** (BMactaggart) **8-11-3** BStorey (bhd whn bdly hmpd 5th: sme hdwy 9th: wknd 12th: p.u bef 3 out)		P	33/1	—	—
3030⁴	**Coolreny (IRE) (72)** (VThompson) **8-11-3** MrMThompson (sn bhd: p.u lame appr 8th: dead)		P	150/1	—	—
				(SP 111.8%)		**9 Rn**

5m 17.0 (24.00) CSF £7.86 TOTE £4.00: £1.30 £1.60 £1.40 (£4.30) Trio £8.00 OWNER Mr John Robson (MIDDLEHAM) BRED John A. Codd
OFFICIAL EXPLANATION Coqui Lane: spread a plate.
2923 Bold Account (IRE) had his task simplified when the runner-up jumped erratically and the favourite came to grief early on, but he did the job in stout fashion. (3/1: op 7/1)
3023 Coqui Lane should have won this, but threw it away by continually backing off his fences and jumping the ditches far too big, and in the circumstances did well to make a race of it. (7/4)
2632 Kiltulla (IRE) is an honest sort but lacks a turn of foot. There are modest races to be found. (16/1)
3023 Le Denstan is gradually coming back to form with this being his second outing after a lengthy lay-off. (33/1)
Robara jumped better this time only to tire over the last four fences. (100/1)
Real Tonic looked in tremendous condition for his first race of the season, but he was very fresh and, taking a keen hold, completely missed out the fifth fence and took a crashing fall. (7/4)

3139 HENNESSY COGNAC SPECIAL SERIES NOVICES' HURDLE (4-Y.O+) (Class B)
3-15 (3-15) **2m (9 hdls)** £6,148.00 (£1,864.00: £912.00: £436.00) GOING: 0.24 sec per fur (G)

				SP	RR	SF
2619*	**Alzulu (IRE) (118)** (JGFitzGerald) **6-11-7** ADobbin (lw: led fr 3rd: hung lft fr 3 out: pushed out flat)	—	1	13/8¹	90	59
2840²	**Dana Point (IRE)** (MrsSJSmith) **5-11-3** RichardGuest (lw: trckd ldrs: chsd wnr fr 3 out: r.o: nt pce to chal)	5	2	9/4³	81	50
2064²	**Good Vibes (120)** (TDEasterby) **5-11-7** RGarritty (lw: trckd ldrs: effrt 3 out: sn btn)	14	3	7/4²	71	40
2918²	**Catherine's Choice** (MDHammond) **4-10-7** MrCBonner (lw: in tch: effrt 4 out: no imp)	7	4	33/1	60	19
2917³	**Menaldi (IRE) (73)** (PCheesbrough) **7-11-3** ASSmith (led to 3rd: cl up tl mstke & wknd qckly 4 out)	dist	5	50/1	—	—
	Jungle Fresh (MrsDThomson) **4-10-7** TReed (plld hrd: a bhd: t.o whn p.u bef 3 out)		P	200/1	—	—
				(SP 110.6%)		**6 Rn**

3m 57.9 (5.90) CSF £5.15 TOTE £2.50: £2.80 £1.20 (£4.60) OWNER Mr D. Buckle (MALTON) BRED Ardenode Stud Ltd
WEIGHT FOR AGE 4yo-10lb

2619* Alzulu (IRE) won this in tremendous style, but he tended to hang left three out and, on pulling up, was slightly lame. (13/8)
2840 Dana Point (IRE) is improving all the time and put in a most determined effort here, but always found the winner too strong. He deserves to find further success. (9/4)
2064 Good Vibes, wearing a pricker to stop him hanging, gave no serious problems this time but, after almost two months off, ran as though he was a bit ring-rusty. (7/4)
2918 Catherine's Choice ran as well as could be expected in this company. (33/1)
2917 Menaldi (IRE) still gives the impression that there is something to work on. (50/1)

3140 NEW CHAMPAGNE & SEAFOOD RESTAURANT H'CAP CHASE (0-125) (5-Y.O+) (Class D)

3-50 (3-50) **2m 110y (10 fncs)** £3,650.00 (£1,025.00: £500.00) GOING: 0.24 sec per fur (G)

Form	Horse	Dist	Pos	SP	RR	SF
2957[4]	**Dual Image (103)** (JGFitzGerald) **10-11-5** RGarritty (hld up: mstkes 7th & 8th: hmpd 4 out: smooth hdwy 3 out: led last: styd on u.p)	—	1	6/4[1]	113	—
2923[6]	**Rebel King (88)** (MABarnes) **7-10-4** BStorey (disp ld to 4th: led 8th to last: kpt on u.p)	2	2	11/2[2]	96	—
2630[P]	**Potato Man (95)** (BEllison) **11-10-11v[1]** ADobbin (disp ld tl led 4th: hdd 8th: ev ch tl outpcd fr 2 out)	18	3	9/1[3]	86	—
2921[F]	**Monnaie Forte (IRE) (90)** (JRAdam) **7-10-6** MMoloney (lw: trckd ldrs: chal whn fell 4 out)		F	6/4[1]	—	—
				(SP 105.4%)		**4 Rn**

4m 17.7 (19.70) CSF £7.69 TOTE £2.10 (£3.30) OWNER Datum Building Supplies Ltd (MALTON) BRED T. Brennan
2957 Dual Image is not the most natural of chasers, and after two careful jumps was hampered by a faller four out. However, this seemed to galvanize him into action, and he was always doing just enough. (6/4)
2923 Rebel King ran a smashing race, only to be tapped for speed on the flat, but this was still an encouraging effort. (11/2: 7/2-7/1)
1295 Potato Man had both a visor and a tongue strap, but when it came down to a battle over the last three fences, he was found wanting. (9/1: 6/1-10/1)
2921 Monnaie Forte (IRE) is proving most frustrating, as he was going particularly well when falling four out. (6/4)

3141 ST MODWEN NOVICES' CHASE (5-Y.O+) (Class D)

4-20 (4-20) **3m (17 fncs)** £3,680.00 (£1,115.00: £545.00: £260.00) GOING: 0.24 sec per fur (G)

Form	Horse	Dist	Pos	SP	RR	SF
2954[2]	**Ask Me Later (IRE) (79)** (MrsSCBradburne) **8-11-4** MFoster (lw: a.p: effrt & hit 12th: led 2 out: r.o u.p)	—	1	11/2[3]	99	32
1803[3]	**River Unshion (IRE) (105)** (HowardJohnson) **7-11-4** RichardGuest (a chsng ldrs: ev ch 3 out: cl 2nd & rdn whn blnd last: no ex)	12	2	10/11[1]	91	24
2954[6]	**Majority Major (IRE) (84)** (PCheesbrough) **8-11-9** ASSmith (lw: hld up: hdwy 10th: outpcd 13th: styd on again fr 2 out)	9	3	16/1	90	23
2614[4]	**Cullane Lake (IRE)** (MissMKMilligan) **7-10-13** RSupple (led: blnd 12th: hdd & wknd 2 out)	¾	4	8/1	80	13
2912[2]	**Pantara Prince (IRE) (86)** (JIACharlton) **8-11-4** ADobbin (hld up: hdwy 11th: sn chsng ldrs: rdn & btn appr 3 out)	8	5	9/2[2]	79	12
2788[4]	**Garbo's Boy (79)** (JRTurner) **7-11-9** KJohnson (mstkes: chsd ldrs: rdn fr 13th: btn appr 3 out)	3	6	10/1	82	15
2803[4]	**Kalajo** (BMactaggart) **7-11-4** BStorey (bhd: sme hdwy whn blnd bdly 13th: sn wknd)	9	7	33/1	71	4
	Oykel River (IRE) (MissSWilliamson) **9-11-4** JSupple (shkn up 3rd: wl t.o fr 8th)	dist	8	100/1	—	—
1944[6]	**Distillery Hill (IRE) (67)** (VThompson) **9-11-4** MrMThompson (outpcd fr ½-wy: t.o whn p.u bef 3 out)		P	66/1	—	—
2841[7]	**Royal Paris (IRE) (75)** (MrsSJSmith) **9-11-4** TReed (mstkes: lost tch fr 10th: p.u bef 3 out)		P	25/1	—	—
				(SP 121.3%)		**10 Rn**

6m 9.2 (17.20) CSF £10.79 TOTE £6.00: £1.80 £1.50 £2.40 (£4.50) Trio £32.20 OWNER Mr Timothy Hardie (CUPAR) BRED Andrew Conway
2954 Ask Me Later (IRE) looked a picture and proved to be a game sort, winning most authoritatively. (11/2)
1803 River Unshion (IRE) had his chances two out, but looked held, although a handy second, when a blunder at the last finished any hopes. (10/11: op 6/4)
2954 Majority Major (IRE) is on his way back to form, and this was an encouraging effort. (16/1)
2614 Cullane Lake (IRE) tried to gallop her rivals into the ground, but after a bad error at the twelfth she was soon struggling, and gave up altogether two from home. (8/1: 6/1-10/1)
2912 Pantara Prince (IRE), given a patient ride, looked dangerous four out only to run out of petrol when asked for a real effort from the next. (9/2)
2788 Garbo's Boy spoilt any chances he had by making several mammoth blunders. (10/1)

3142 BE MY VALENTINE STANDARD OPEN N.H. FLAT RACE (4, 5 & 6-Y.O) (Class H)

4-55 (4-56) **2m** £1,402.50 (£390.00: £187.50)

Form	Horse	Dist	Pos	SP	RR	SF
1504[5]	**Mac's Supreme (IRE)** (FMurphy) **5-11-1**(3) MichaelBrennan (trckd ldrs: led over 3f out: r.o wl)	—	1	3/1[1]	67 f	—
2640[3]	**Into The Black (IRE)** (MrsMReveley) **6-11-4** GCahill (bhd: drvn along ½-wy: hdwy 5f out: kpt on wl)	2	2	8/1	65 f	—
2904[7]	**Thunderpoint (IRE)** (TDEasterby) **5-11-4** RGarritty (a.p: effrt & ch 3f out: hrd drvn: r.o one pce)	3½	3	9/1	62 f	—
2904[3]	**Generous Streak (FR)** (JNorton) **4-10-5**(3) ECallaghan (a.p: effrt 4f out: 3rd whn eased & ct cl home)	hd	4	6/1	61 f	—
	Major Hage (IRE) (HowardJohnson) **6-11-4** RichardGuest (hld up: smooth hdwy to trck ldr 6f out: effrt 3f out: sn btn)	14	5	11/2[3]	47 f	—
	Miss Moneypenny (MrsAJFindlay) **5-10-6**(7) RBurns (hdwy ½-wy: chsng ldrs 4f out: wknd over 2f out)	½	6	100/1	42 f	—
	Lord Knows (IRE) (JIACharlton) **6-11-4** KJohnson (outpcd 6f out: styd on fnl 2f)	2½	7	16/1	44 f	—
2804[7]	**Sunrise Sensation** (RMcDonald) **4-10-8** KJones (hdwy ½-wy: sn chsng ldrs: outpcd fnl 3f)	½	8	20/1	44 f	—
2750[4]	**Jack Robbo (IRE)** (JGFitzGerald) **5-11-1**(3) GLee (trckd ldrs tl outpcd 5f out: n.d after)	3½	9	5/1[2]	40 f	—
2924[2]	**One Stop** (MABarnes) **4-10-3** BStorey (cl up: led 6f out tl over 3f out: grad wknd)	nk	10	6/1	35 f	—
	Lord of The Rings (FMurphy) **5-10-11**(7) MrTJBarry (bhd: effrt ½-wy: n.d)	2	11	33/1	38 f	—
	Hollow Palm (IRE) (LLungo) **6-11-4** RSupple (hld up & bhd: effrt ½-wy: nvr rchd ldr)	2	12	33/1	36 f	—
	Allforus (IRE) (MrsDThomson) **5-10-13** TReed (prom 10f: sn bhd)	18	13	100/1	13 f	—
2904[11]	**Shannon Shoon (IRE)** (HowardJohnson) **5-10-13**(5) GFRyan (led & sn clr: hdd 6f out: sn lost pl)	½	14	33/1	18 f	—
2633[15]	**Jo Lightning (IRE)** (BEllison) **4-10-8** MrRHale (chsd ldrs tl lost pl 5f out)	15	15	200/1	3 f	—
	Political Mandate (RNixon) **4-10-3** ADobbin (bhd fnl 6f)	8	16	20/1	—	—
	Romaldkirk (VThompson) **5-11-4** MrMThompson (bit bkwd: bhd fr ½-wy)	14	17	200/1	—	—
	Michandra Boy (MartynWane) **4-10-8** ASSmith (bhd fnl 6f: t.o)	23	18	20/1	—	—
				(SP 138.7%)		**18 Rn**

3m 58.0 CSF £26.72 TOTE £5.20: £1.80 £2.00 £3.50 (£10.30) Trio £183.80; £235.61 to Newcastle 15/2/97 OWNER Mr B. McEntaggart (MIDDLEHAM) BRED Tom Harty
WEIGHT FOR AGE 4yo-10lb
STEWARDS' ENQUIRY Callaghan susp. 24-26/2/96 (failure to ensure best possible placing)

1504 Mac's Supreme (IRE) moved well throughout, and once he stepped up the pace in the straight, was always in command. (3/1)
2640 Into The Black (IRE) is a stayer and a half and, although off-the-bit by halfway, he kept galloping on, but lacked a turn of foot to peg the winner back. (8/1)
Thunderpoint (IRE) is obviously improving with experience, but does not do anything quickly. (9/1)
2904 Generous Streak (FR) had his chances, but was short of speed though he would have been third had his rider not dropped his hands. (6/1: 4/1-7/1)
Major Hage (IRE) sat in behind the leaders and it looked a question of when and how far, but he suddenly ran out of fuel three from home. He looks one to keep in mind when put over hurdles. (11/2: op 10/1)
Lord Knows (IRE), a decent type, looks a stayer in the making, only running on when it was too late. (16/1)
2750 Jack Robbo (IRE) (5/1: op 5/2)
2924 One Stop (6/1: 4/1-13/2)

T/Jkpt: £10,673.50 (1.9 Tckts). T/Plpt: £7.90 (1,444.01 Tckts). T/Qdpt: £7.90 (102.97 Tckts) AA

3103-SANDOWN (R-H) (Good, Chases Good to firm patches)
Friday February 14th

WEATHER: overcast & raining

3143 FOX 'N.H.' NOVICES' HURDLE (5-Y.O+) (Class D)

1-30 (1-30) **2m 110y (8 hdls)** £3,035.00 (£920.00: £450.00: £215.00) GOING: 0.65 sec per fur (S)

				SP	RR	SF
1651^{2}	**Queen of Spades (IRE) (116)** (NATwiston-Davies) **7-11-4** CLlewellyn (j.w: mde all: clr 3rd: eased flat)	—	**1**	15/8^{1}	89+	46
2677^{5}	**Lively Encounter (IRE)** (MrsMerritaJones) **6-11-0** DerekByrne (hdwy appr 2 out: r.o one pce)	6	**2**	20/1	79	36
2677*	**Splendid Thyne** (TCasey) **5-11-4** RDunwoody (hdwy appr 2 out: hrd rdn appr last: one pce)	3	**3**	100/30^{2}	80	37
	Star Mystery (CREgerton) **6-11-0** JOsborne (bit bkwd: chsd wnr tl flat: sn wknd)	3	**4**	13/2	73	30
	Father Henry (IRE) (NJHenderson) **6-11-0** MAFitzgerald (lw: 3rd whn blnd & lost pl 4th: rallied appr 2 out: 3rd & btn whn mstke last)	5	**5**	12/1	69	26
2948^{7}	**Thirty Below (IRE)** (JABOld) **8-11-0** SMcNeill (a bhd)	18	**6**	50/1	51	8
1457^{7}	**Charlie Banker (IRE)** (KRBurke) **5-11-0** ALarnach (bit bkwd: mstke 2nd: bhd fr 4th: t.o)	dist	**7**	33/1	—	—
2677^{4}	**Dark Orchard (IRE)** (WRMuir) **6-11-0** MRichards (hld up: rdn appr 2 out: sn wknd: t.o)	7	**8**	14/1	—	—
2012^{9}	**Belvento (IRE)** (JTGifford) **5-10-11**(3) LAspell (bhd fr 3 out: t.o)	8	**9**	33/1	—	—
1317^{2}	**Tower Street** (JTGifford) **6-11-0** PHide (hld up: 3rd whn p.u after 3 out: lame)		**P**	4/1^{3}	—	—
	Maenad (DJSffrenchDavis) **6-10-9** BPowell (a bhd: t.o whn p.u bef 2 out)		**P**	50/1	—	—
				(SP 120.1%)	**11 Rn**	

4m 6.0 (15.00) CSF £40.53 TOTE £2.90: £1.90 £4.00 £1.20 (£19.50) Trio £35.60 OWNER Mrs R. Vaughan (CHELTENHAM) BRED William McCarthy

OFFICIAL EXPLANATION **Tower Street: was lame.**

1651 Queen of Spades (IRE) put up a very impressive display. Jumping very fluently, she forged clear early on the final circuit and never looked like being caught. A good seventeen lengths clear jumping the final flight, she was eased considerably on the run-in and is value for three times the official distance. She reminds her trainer of Arctic Kinsman whom he trained to win the Supreme Novices' Hurdle at 50/1 and that is where she will now head. (15/8: 11/10-2/1)
2677 Lively Encounter (IRE) who got bogged down in the mud last time out, stayed on in the straight to snatch second place on the run-in but, by then, the winner was already home and dried. A step up to two-and-a-half miles might be in his favour. (20/1)
2677* Splendid Thyne did not have the soft ground this time, and found it all happening too quickly for him after being pushed along to pick up ground entering the straight. He was then labouring and would be better served by some mud. (100/30)
Star Mystery looked big and well for this hurdling debut - his first run in eleven months - and showed a great deal of promise. Racing in second place, he had no hope of reeling in the winner, but held on to that position until tiring on the run-in. Sure to come on for this, he should have no problems finding a race. (13/2)
Father Henry (IRE), who looks a chaser in the making, was turned out looking very well for his racecourse debut and showed plenty of promise. A very bad error at the fourth cost him a lot of ground, but he rallied splendidly to dispute second place going to the penultimate hurdle. Unable to make any further impression, he was held when flattening the final flight. Sure to be a lot wiser for this, he should find a novice event before long. (12/1: 8/1-14/1)

3144 SABRINA GOODWILL 'I LOVE YOU ALWAYS' H'CAP CHASE (0-145) (5-Y.O+) (Class B)

2-00 (2-00) **2m (13 fncs)** £6,789.00 (£1,904.00: £927.00) GOING: 0.65 sec per fur (S)

				SP	RR	SF
3009*	**Mister Oddy (133)** (JSKing) **11-11-8**(3) 5x DFortt (lw: chsd ldr: lft in ld 4th: clr appr 2 out: comf)	—	**1**	7/2^{3}	145+	48
2783*	**Lord Dorcet (IRE) (136)** (JIACharlton) **7-12-0** RJohnson (lft 2nd 4th: mstke 9th: rdn 4 out: no imp)	13	**2**	3/1^{2}	135	38
3009^{4}	**Thumbs Up (127)** (GMMcCourt) **11-11-5** RDunwoody (lost pl 6th: rallied 9th: wknd appr 3 out)	4	**3**	16/1	122	25
2890*	**Certainly Strong (IRE) (134)** (DNicholson) **7-11-12** AMaguire (led tl fell 4th)		**F**	8/11^{1}	—	—
				(SP 111.0%)	**4 Rn**	

4m 6.8 (15.80) CSF £12.40 TOTE £4.90 (£7.30) OWNER Mrs R. M. Hill (SWINDON) BRED V. N. F. Tjolle

3009* Mister Oddy continues in tremendous form. Left in front at the fourth, he forged clear in the last half-mile to win with plenty in hand. If there is some cut in the ground he could well make a bold showing in the Grand Annual at the Festival. (7/2)
2783* Lord Dorcet (IRE) is now very high in the handicap having been raised 6lb for his recent success and, try as he might, he failed to make any impression on the winner over the last three fences. Connections are undecided whether to go for the Queen Mother Champion Chase or the Grand Annual at the Festival with the latter looking by far the more sensible option. (3/1)
3009 Thumbs Up is not the force of old. Looking in trouble early in the back straight, he managed to get back into it five from home only to lose touch again going to the Pond Fence. (16/1)

3145 BADGER NOVICES' CHASE (5-Y.O+) (Class D)

2-35 (2-35) **2m 4f 110y (17 fncs)** £3,420.00 (£1,035.00: £505.00: £240.00) GOING: 0.65 sec per fur (S)

				SP	RR	SF
2843*	**Arfer Mole (IRE) (115)** (JABOld) **9-11-7** JOsborne (reminder 7th: hdwy 8th: rdn appr 3 out: led appr 2 out: r.o wl)	—	**1**	Evens^{1}	107	26
2880^{7}	**Eulogy (IRE)** (RRowe) **7-11-3** RDunwoody (lw: lost pl 9th: rallied appr 2 out: ev ch last: r.o one pce)	2	**2**	8/1	101	20
2759^{4}	**The Captain's Wish** (DNicholson) **6-11-3** AMaguire (hld up: lft 2nd 12th: nt clr run on ins appr 2 out: ev ch flat: unable qckn)	hd	**3**	4/1^{2}	101	20

				SP	RR	SF
2679^{6}	**Juleit Jones (IRE) (87)** (JTGifford) **8-10-9**$^{(3)}$ LAspell (led tl appr 2 out: wknd appr last)	12	**4**	33/1	87	6
2841^{5}	**Safeglide (IRE) (88)** (JTGifford) **7-11-3** PHide (mstkes 8th & 9th: a bhd)	12	**5**	12/1	83	2
2667*	**Slingsby (IRE) (109)** (NAGaselee) **7-11-10** AThornton (lw: 4th whn fell 6th: dead)		**F**	9/2^{3}	—	—
2807^{2}	**Red Branch (IRE) (69)** (JSKing) **8-11-3** TJMurphy (lw: chsd ldr tl blnd & uns rdr 12th)		**U**	25/1	—	—
				(SP 113.8%)	**7 Rn**	

5m 24.4 (25.40) CSF £8.99 TOTE £1.90: £1.40 £2.20 (£7.10) OWNER Mr W. E. Sturt (WROUGHTON) BRED M. Parkhill

2843* Arfer Mole (IRE) looks a lazy individual if this run is anything to go by. With his jockey having to niggle him along in the back straight for the final time, the gelding eventually got to the front approaching the second last and, pushed along, asserted his authority on the run-in. (Evens)

1870 Eulogy (IRE), making his chasing debut, got outpaced early in the back straight, but managed to pick up ground again going to the second last. Running to the final fence he looked as if he might almost win the race, but he failed to land running and that could have made all the difference. (8/1)

2759 The Captain's Wish, making his chasing debut, threw down his challenge approaching the last. With every chance early on the run-in, he carried his head rather high and failed to find any extra. (4/1)

2679 Juleit Jones (IRE), who failed to get home over this trip in the mud last time out, bowled along in front. Collared approaching the second last, she was soon done with, and a return to two miles would help. (33/1)

2841 Safeglide (IRE) (12/1: 8/1-14/1)

2667* Slingsby (IRE) (9/2: 3/1-5/1)

3146 SCOTTISH EQUITABLE/JOCKEYS ASSOCIATION SERIES (QUALIFIER) H'CAP HURDLE (0-120) (4-Y.O+) (Class D)

3-10 (3-12) **2m 6f (11 hdls)** £3,615.00 (£1,095.00: £535.00: £255.00) GOING: 0.65 sec per fur (S)

				SP	RR	SF
2659^{7}	**Oatis Rose (96)** (MSheppard) **7-10-7** AMaguire (led 3rd to 8th: led 3 out tl flat: hrd drvn: led last stride)	—	**1**	10/1	78	40
2071^{4}	**Dantes Cavalier (IRE) (105)** (DRGandolfo) **7-11-2** RDunwoody (stdy hdwy 3 out: w wnr appr 2 out: led flat: hrd drvn: hdd last stride)	s.h	**2**	2/1^{1}	87	49
1813^{2}	**Jackson Flint (90)** (TThomsonJones) **9-10-1** JCulloty (hdwy 7th: rdn appr 2 out: wknd flat)	14	**3**	10/1	62	24
1876*	**Rosie-B (89)** (NMBabbage) **7-10-0** NWilliamson (led to 3rd: led 8th to 3 out: wknd appr 2 out)	hd	**4**	3/1^{2}	61	23
1673^{6}	**Kilmington (IRE) (106)** (JTGifford) **8-11-3** PHide (a.p: rdn appr 2 out: sn wknd)	½	**5**	7/1	77	39
2817^{U}	**Dark Honey (104)** (SDow) **12-11-1** ADicken (bhd fr 6th)	16	**6**	12/1	64	26
2666^{4}	**Cassio's Boy (90)** (RJEckley) **6-10-1** RJohnson (lw: hdwy 6th: wknd appr 2 out)	½	**7**	13/2^{3}	49	11
2869^{F}	**Braes of Mar (113)** (NJHenderson) **7-11-10** MAFitzgerald (lw: bhd fr 7th)	5	**8**	20/1	69	31
				(SP 114.8%)	**8 Rn**	

5m 31.9 (18.90) CSF £28.64 CT £191.64 TOTE £12.90: £2.50 £1.50 £1.80 (£19.40) Trio £48.50 OWNER Mrs John Redvers (LEDBURY) BRED O. C. Morris

LONG HANDICAP Rosie-B 9-12

1798 Oatis Rose was given a marvellous ride by her jockey, but will not forget this race in a hurry. Engaged in a tremendous battle with the runner-up over the last two hurdles, she looked set to finish second best on the run-in, but Maguire managed to conjure a little bit extra from the mare and she lunged a nostril in front on the line. (10/1)

2071 Dantes Cavalier (IRE) was happier on this return to a longer trip. Joining the winner approaching the second last, he had a real set-to but looked likely to prevail as he went nearly half a length up on the run-in. With Dunwoody throwing absolutely everything at him, he was caught right on the line. Compensation is richly deserved. (2/1)

1813 Jackson Flint, off the track for nearly ten weeks, moved into third place approaching the second last, but he failed to contain the first two and tired on the run-in. (10/1: 7/1-11/1)

1876* Rosie-B, in fine form this season, showed in front for a second time halfway down the back straight. Collared three from home, she had shot her bolt early in the straight. (3/1)

1673 Kilmington (IRE) played an active role until calling it a day going to the second last. (7/1: 5/1-15/2)

3147 STAG H'CAP CHASE (0-145) (5-Y.O+) (Class B)

3-45 (3-46) **3m 110y (22 fncs)** £6,469.50 (£1,956.00: £953.00: £451.50) GOING: 0.65 sec per fur (S)

				SP	RR	SF
2879^{5}	**Denver Bay (115)** (JTGifford) **10-10-0**$^{(3)}$ LAspell (hld up: led 15th: drvn out)	—	**1**	100/30^{3}	125	10
2773^{3}	**Hill of Tullow (IRE) (134)** (DNicholson) **8-11-8b** AMaguire (lw: hld up: swtchd rt appr 3 out: chsd wnr appr 2 out: hrd rdn appr last: ev ch flat: nt r.o)	hd	**2**	2/1^{1}	144	29
	Superior Finish (140) (MrsJPitman) **11-12-0** RFarrant (bit bkwd: led 8th to 10th: lost pl 15th: r.o one pce fr 2 out)	23	**3**	10/1	135	20
2887*	**Dextra Dove (140)** (SEarle) **10-12-0** CMaude (led to 4th: led 7th to 8th: led 10th to 15th: mstke 17th: hrd rdn 4 out: wknd appr 2 out)	1½	**4**	9/4^{2}	134	19
	Sibton Abbey (138) (GAHubbard) **12-11-12v** AThornton (bit bkwd: hld up: rdn 18th: wknd appr 3 out)	8	**5**	16/1	127	12
	James Pigg (130) (PFNicholls) **10-11-4** DBridgwater (led 4th to 7th: wknd 12th: t.o)	dist	**6**	10/1	—	—
				(SP 111.2%)	**6 Rn**	

6m 32.5 (30.50) CSF £9.71 TOTE £4.20: £1.80 £1.60 (£4.50) OWNER Mr Bill Naylor (FINDON) BRED Marston Stud

2879 Denver Bay had no problems seeing out this longer trip and, leading at the open ditch, responded far better to pressure than the runner-up. (100/30)

2773 Hill of Tullow (IRE) moved into second place approaching the second last and threw down a challenge on the run-in. However, try as Maguire might, the gelding would not go past his rival and was not putting it all in. (2/1)

Superior Finish, third in last year's Grand National, looked as though the run would do him good, and after getting detached from the fifteenth, was staying on again over the last two fences, snatching third prize near the line. Sure to come on for the outing, he needs much further than this, but is not easy to win with as he has been successful only twice in nearly four years. (10/1: 6/1-11/1)

2887* Dextra Dove, who made a lot of the running to the fifteenth, came under pressure soon after the fourth-last and eventually called it a day going to the penultimate fence. This was a disappointing performance, and his trainer blames himself for not being as hard on him as he should have been, as the gelding is as lazy at home as he is on the racecourse. He will now have another run before the Grand National. (9/4: 6/4-5/2)

Sibton Abbey did not look fully tuned up for this reappearance and dropped away going to the Pond Fence. He is not the force of old.(16/1)

3148 CAT & MOUSE CLAIMING HURDLE (5-Y.O+) (Class F)

4-15 (4-15) **2m 110y (8 hdls)** £2,262.00 (£632.00: £306.00) GOING: 0.65 sec per fur (S)

				SP	RR	SF
2888[11]	**Express Gift (134)** (MrsMReveley) **8-11-10** RDunwoody (hld up: chsd ldr fr 5th: led 2 out: clr appr last: eased flat)	—	**1**	4/11[1]	93+	22
	Dance King (100) (TTClement) **5-11-2** VSmith (bit bkwd: hld up: chsd wnr appr last: unable qckn)	6	**2**	12/1[3]	79	8
2897[5]	**Pedaltothemetal (IRE) (88)** (PMitchell) **5-10-7** GTormey (chsd ldr to 5th: rdn 3 out: r.o one pce fr 2 out)	hd	**3**	14/1	70	—
2937[6]	**Blaze of Song** (DJWintle) **5-11-7** CLlewellyn (led to 2 out: sn wknd)	1½	**4**	25/1	83?	12
1939[2]	**Stoney Valley (102)** (JRJenkins) **7-10-9** NWilliamson (a bhd)	19	**5**	7/2[2]	52	—
	Micky Brown (MissLBower) **6-10-12** WMcFarland (a bhd: mstke 4th: t.o fr 5th)	dist	**6**	66/1	—	—

(SP 115.3%) **6 Rn**

4m 12.8 (21.80) CSF £6.14 TOTE £1.40: £1.70 £3.20 (£8.00) OWNER M W Horner, H Young, and D S Arnold (SALTBURN) BRED H. Young

2603a Express Gift was taking a huge drop in class, and had no problems in winning this. Leading at the second last, he forged clear with the minimum of fuss. He was eased down considerably on the run-in and is value for at least twelve lengths. (4/11)

Dance King, who has changed stables since last season, did not look fully fit, but managed to struggle into second place approaching the last if having no hope with the winner. He is greatly flattered to finish so close. (12/1)

2897 Pedaltothemetal (IRE) lacks pace and definitely needs further, as she was staying on again from the second last. (14/1)

Blaze of Song took the field along but, collared at the second last, soon capitulated. (25/1)

3149 OTTER STANDARD OPEN N.H. FLAT RACE (4, 5 & 6-Y.O) (Class H)

4-50 (4-51) **2m 110y** £1,448.00 (£403.00: £194.00)

				SP	RR	SF
	Dawn Leader (IRE) (JABOld) **6-11-10** GUpton (hdwy over 6f out: led over 3f out: clr over 1f out: easily)	—	**1**	7/4[1]	92 f	—
705[3]	**Damien's Choice (IRE)** (MrsMerritaJones) **5-11-3** DerekByrne (lw: hdwy over 5f out: chsd wnr wl over 1f out: no imp)	13	**2**	14/1	72 f	—
2572[2]	**Shebang (IRE)** (JLDunlop) **5-10-10**(7) MrHDunlop (lost pl over 6f out: r.o one pce fnl 3f)	7	**3**	9/1	66 f	—
1071[2]	**Countryman (IRE)** (TRGeorge) **6-11-3** RDunwoody (bit bkwd: a.p: rdn over 3f out: one pce)	3	**4**	10/1	63 f	—
1052[3]	**Little Crumplin** (OSherwood) **5-11-3** JOsborne (led over 11f out tl over 3f out: wknd over 2f out)	3½	**5**	6/1[3]	59 f	—
	Zephyrelle (IRE) (NJHenderson) **5-10-12** NWilliamson (rdn & hdwy over 4f out: nvr nrr)	1¾	**6**	14/1	53 f	—
2012[5]	**Shore Party (IRE)** (NATwiston-Davies) **5-11-3** CLlewellyn (prom over 13f)	1	**7**	9/2[2]	57 f	—
2811[8]	**Stanmore (IRE)** (CPEBrooks) **5-11-3** DGallagher (swtg: hmpd on ins 5f out: nvr nrr)	4	**8**	16/1	53 f	—
	Cinnamon Club (NAGaselee) **5-10-12** AThornton (w'like: scope: hdwy over 5f out: wknd 3f out)	hd	**9**	20/1	48 f	—
2911[2]	**Gower-Slave** (PBowen) **5-11-3** RJohnson (prom 13f)	12	**10**	25/1	41 f	—
	Editorial (RRowe) **5-11-0**(3) LAspell (bit bkwd: hdwy over 4f out: wknd over 3f out)	4	**11**	33/1	37 f	—
	The Phantom Farmer (IRE) (NJHenderson) **6-11-3** MAFitzgerald (bhd whn hmpd 5f out)	1½	**12**	14/1	36 f	—
	Thunderbird (AHHarvey) **5-10-12** MRichards (bkwd: bhd fnl 8f)	17	**13**	50/1	14 f	—
2811[9]	**Sheet Lightning** (RJSmith) **5-10-10**(7) LSuthern (led 5f: wknd 6f out: t.o)	27	**14**	66/1	—	—
	Fire Opal (NJHenderson) **5-11-3** JRKavanagh (lw: a bhd: t.o)	6	**15**	20/1	—	—
2811[5]	**Master Pip** (AGFoster) **5-11-3** SMcNeill (a.p: stumbled 4f out: chsd wnr 3f out tl broke leg 2f out: p.u: dead)		**P**	25/1	—	—

(SP 137.4%) **16 Rn**

4m 5.8 CSF £29.22 TOTE £3.20: £1.60 £5.00 £2.40 (£49.20) Trio £148.80 OWNER Bonusprint (WROUGHTON) BRED William Deacon

Dawn Leader (IRE) made a very impressive debut for his new stable. Cruising into the lead early in the straight, he forged clear with the minimum of fuss to win doing handsprings. He looks a very useful individual and will now go for the Festival Bumper. (7/4: 3/1-6/4)

705 Damien's Choice (IRE), who has changed stables since his last run nearly five months ago, looked in fine shape but, although taking second place early inside the final quarter-mile, had no hope of reeling in the winner. (14/1: 12/1-33/1)

2572 Shebang (IRE) got outpaced towards the end of the back straight, but did struggle on again in the last three furlongs to take a moderate third place. (9/1: 7/1-12/1)

1071 Countryman (IRE), who has changed stables since his last outing three-and-a-half months ago, was carrying some condition. After racing with the leaders, he could only go up and down in the same place in the straight. (10/1: 5/1-11/1)

1052 Little Crumplin, formerly with Mick Easterby, moved to the front early on the final circuit but, collared over three furlongs from home, was soon done with as lack of a recent run took its toll. (6/1: op 5/2)

Zephyrelle (IRE), an unfurnished sister to Winter Squall, struggled on in the last half-mile to be nearest at the line. (14/1: 10/1-16/1)

2012 Shore Party (IRE) (9/2: 4/1-7/1)

The Phantom Farmer (IRE) (14/1: op 5/1)

T/Plpt: £74.40 (168.02 Tckts). T/Qdpt: £7.30 (134.58 Tckts) AK

2879-CHEPSTOW (L-H) (Soft)

Saturday February 15th

WEATHER: fine

3150 M & N GROUP LIMITED H'CAP HURDLE (4-Y.O+) (Class B)

1-15 (1-16) **2m 4f 110y (11 hdls)** £7,022.00 (£2,126.00: £1,038.00: £494.00) GOING: Not Established

				SP	RR	SF
2884[5]	**Brave Tornado (125)** (GBBalding) **6-10-12** BFenton (a.p: led 4 out: all out)	—	**1**	8/1[3]	103	64
1916[7]	**Moorish (135)** (NATwiston-Davies) **7-11-8** CLlewellyn (hld up: gd hdwy appr 4 out: ev ch last: r.o)	1	**2**	11/1	112	73
1645*	**Anzum (137)** (DNicholson) **6-11-10** RJohnson (chsd ldrs: rdn 3rd: outpcd 3 out: hrd rdn & rallied flat)	¾	**3**	15/2[2]	114	75
1783*	**Cadougold (FR) (130)** (MCPipe) **6-11-3** RDunwoody (hld up: stdy hdwy 5th: ev ch 2 out: sn rdn: one pce)	2	**4**	11/10[1]	105	66
3038[10]	**Dr Leunt (IRE) (127)** (PJHobbs) **6-11-0** GTormey (plld hrd: prom tl wknd 3 out)	12	**5**	12/1	93	54
	Lying Eyes (123) (WGMTurner) **6-10-3**(7) JPower (bit bkwd: prom tl wknd 3 out)	nk	**6**	20/1	89	50
2884*	**Kadastrof (FR) (134)** (RDickin) **7-11-0**(7) XAizpuru (led: clr 3rd: hdd 4 out: sn wknd)	8	**7**	10/1	93	54
2617[5]	**Home Counties (IRE) (139)** (DMoffatt) **8-11-12** DJMoffatt (a bhd: t.o fr 4 out)	dist	**8**	16/1	—	—
2777[13]	**Thinking Twice (USA) (133)** (NJHenderson) **8-11-6** RFarrant (lw: bhd fr 6th: t.o fr 4 out)	5	**9**	12/1	—	—
3038[17]	**Storm Damage (IRE) (136)** (PFNicholls) **5-11-9** DBridgwater (prom: j.slowly 5th: sn wknd: t.o fr 4 out)	4	**10**	12/1	—	—
2777[P]	**Abbey Street (IRE) (122)** (OSherwood) **5-10-9** JOsborne (lw: hld up & bhd: hdwy after 7th: sn wknd: t.o whn p.u bef last)		**P**	16/1	—	—

	Horse	Dist	Pos	SP	RR	SF
2761[5]	**Sparkling Cone (118)** (OSherwood) **8-10-5** CMaude (a bhd: t.o 4 out: p.u bef 2 out)		**P**	40/1	—	—
				(SP 130.0%)		**12 Rn**

4m 58.5 (11.50) CSF £91.99 CT £647.38 TOTE £9.80: £2.30 £3.70 £2.60 (£95.80) Trio £118.50 OWNER Miss B. Swire (ANDOVER) BRED Miss B. Swire
LONG HANDICAP Sparkling Cone 9-13
STEWARDS' ENQUIRY Fenton Susp: 24-27/2/97 (excessive use of whip).
OFFICIAL EXPLANATION Abbey Street (IRE): made a noise during the race.
2884 Brave Tornado had softer ground and a longer trip this time, and held on well under a ride which got his pilot in hot water. (8/1)
Moorish, another to relish this soft ground, was trying a new trip, and bounced back to form on his first run since changing stables. (11/1)
1645* Anzum, raised 7lb, certainly made Johnson earn his fee, but in the end this trip proved on the short side. (15/2: 5/1-8/1)
1783* Cadougold (FR), up 7lb, was supported at all rates from 11/4 in the morning, but found disappointingly little when the chips were down. (11/10)
2777 Dr Leunt (IRE) ran much too freely in the first half-mile. (12/1)
Lying Eyes ran well until apparently blowing up. (20/1)
2777 Thinking Twice (USA) (12/1: op 8/1)

3151 FLEDGLING CHASE (6-Y.O+) (Class B)
1-45 (1-45) **2m 3f 110y (16 fncs)** £6,775.00 (£2,050.00: £1,000.00: £475.00) GOING: 1.01 sec per fur (HY)

	Horse	Dist	Pos	SP	RR	SF
	Air Shot (128) (DNicholson) **7-11-0** RJohnson (bit bkwd: hld up & plld hrd: hdwy 6th: led 2 out: drvn out)	—	**1**	5/2[2]	143	62
2636[P]	**Nahthen Lad (IRE) (150)** (MrsJPitman) **8-11-12** RFarrant (lw: led: rdn & hdd 5 out: led 3 out to 2 out: one pce)	6	**2**	100/30[3]	150	69
2879*	**Bells Life (IRE) (132)** (PJHobbs) **8-11-3** GTormey (hld up: led 5 out: sn rdn: hdd 3 out: hit 2 out: eased whn btn flat)	9	**3**	13/8[1]	134	53
2759[6]	**Montecot (FR) (120)** (SMellor) **8-11-3** BFenton (hit 2nd: bhd fr 5th: t.o fr 9th)	dist	**4**	7/1	—	—
2942*	**Coolree (IRE) (112)** (PFNicholls) **9-11-0b[1]** DBridgwater (chsd ldr tl hit 6th: t.o 9th: p.u bef 11th)		**P**	14/1	—	—
				(SP 108.9%)		**5 Rn**

5m 8.7 (19.70) CSF £9.93 TOTE £3.50: £1.70 £1.40 (£5.10) OWNER Mrs Peter Prowting (TEMPLE GUITING) BRED Mrs E. A. Prowting
Air Shot, who returned from summer grass with a slight tendon strain, looked as though the outing would do him good, but his market support proved to be spot on. He will try to go one better than last year in the Cathcart at Cheltenham. (5/2)
1982 Nahthen Lad (IRE) was found to have sore shins and a low blood count when pulled up at Haydock. He looked far more like his old self here over a trip short of his best. (100/30: 5/2-4/1)
2879* Bells Life (IRE) lost his unbeaten record at Chepstow, but this was a step up in class. (13/8)

3152 COLIN DAVIES PERSIAN WAR PREMIER NOVICES' HURDLE (Gd 2) (4-Y.O+) (Class A)
2-15 (2-15) **2m 4f 110y (11 hdls)** £9,735.00 (£3,685.50: £1,805.25: £824.25) GOING: 0.61 sec per fur (S)

	Horse	Dist	Pos	SP	RR	SF
2771*	**Boardroom Shuffle (IRE) (130)** (JTGifford) **6-11-6** PHide (lw: hld up: stdy hdwy after 7th: led flat: rdn out)	—	**1**	6/4[1]	96+	66
2781[2]	**Mighty Moss (IRE) (122)** (DNicholson) **6-11-6** MrFHutsby (a.p: led 5th: clr 2 out: mstke last: hdd flat)	2½	**2**	9/2[3]	94	64
2927*	**Marching Marquis (IRE)** (NoelChance) **6-11-6** RJohnson (a.p: rdn appr 4 out: ev ch 3 out: one pce)	5	**3**	8/1	90	60
2826*	**Fiddling The Facts (IRE) (107)** (NJHenderson) **6-11-1** JOsborne (lw: hld up: hdwy 6th: wknd 3 out)	3½	**4**	11/1	82	52
3024*	**Lagen Bridge (IRE) (112)** (DMoffatt) **8-11-6** DJMoffatt (hld up: hdwy after 7th: hit 3 out: wkng whn hit 2 ut)	1	**5**	20/1	87	57
2808[U]	**Harbour Island** (MCPipe) **5-11-6** RDunwoody (lw: w ldr: led after 4th tl j.slowly 5th: lost pl 7th: rallied appr 4 out: wknd 3 out: t.o)	dist	**6**	7/2[2]	—	—
3007[4]	**Soldat (USA)** (DNicholson) **4-11-1** DBridgwater (a bhd: t.o whn p.u bef 6th)		**P**	11/1	—	—
2550[5]	**Paris Fashion (FR)** (NATwiston-Davies) **6-11-1** TJenks (lw: led tl after 4th: wknd 6th: t.o whn p.u after 7th)		**P**	25/1	—	—
				(SP 116.8%)		**8 Rn**

4m 59.9 (12.90) CSF £8.14 TOTE £2.20: £1.20 £1.50 £2.70 (£4.60) OWNER Mr A. D. Weller (FINDON) BRED Stonethorn Stud Farms Ltd
WEIGHT FOR AGE 4yo-11lb
2771* Boardroom Shuffle (IRE), very confidently ridden, may be the type who does not do a lot once hitting the front, and the runner-up's error at the last helped settle it. His trainer stated that, whatever happens at the Festival, this exciting prospect will go chasing next season. (6/4)
2781 Mighty Moss (IRE) lost nothing in defeat, but the winner was already bearing down on him when he dragged his hind legs through the last. (9/2)
2927* Marching Marquis (IRE) found this company too hot, and was well held when untidy at the final flight. (8/1)
2826* Fiddling The Facts (IRE) could not cope with this step up in class. (11/1)
3024* Lagen Bridge (IRE) was another who failed to make the grade. (20/1)
2808 Harbour Island stayed well and liked this sort of ground on the Flat, but it should also be remembered he needed blinkers. (7/2)

3153 ASHFIELDS FARM H'CAP CHASE (0-125) (5-Y.O+) (Class D)
2-45 (2-48) **3m 2f 110y (22 fncs)** £3,715.50 (£1,119.00: £542.00: £253.50) GOING: 1.01 sec per fur (HY)

	Horse	Dist	Pos	SP	RR	SF
2869*	**Giventime (111)** (AndrewTurnell) **9-11-0** LHarvey (a.p: mstke 16th: hrd rdn appr last: led flat: r.o)	—	**1**	4/1[1]	123	18
2829[2]	**Rocky Park (97)** (GBBalding) **11-10-0** BFenton (led: hit 2 out: hdd flat: r.o)	1¼	**2**	14/1	108	3
2881[B]	**Spuffington (113)** (JTGifford) **9-11-2** PHide (lw: a.p: one pce fr 3 out)	14	**3**	8/1	116	11
2011[4]	**Special Account (98)** (CRBarwell) **11-9-12**(3)ow1 PHenley (rdn & hdwy 14th: 4th & btn whn hit 3 out)	nk	**4**	20/1	101	—
2869[7]	**Dom Samourai (FR) (113)** (MCPipe) **6-11-2v[1]** BPowell (bhd: rdn 11th: hdwy appr 5 out: wknd 4 out)	8	**5**	20/1	111	6
2869[3]	**Plastic Spaceage (115)** (JABOld) **14-11-4** GUpton (nvr nr ldrs)	2½	**6**	11/2[3]	111	6
2671[5]	**Holy Sting (IRE) (97)** (NATwiston-Davies) **8-10-0b** CMaude (a bhd)	24	**7**	16/1	79	—
2869[2]	**A N C Express (114)** (JSKing) **9-11-3** TJMurphy (swtg: mstkes: hdwy 9th: rdn 13th: wknd qckly 3 out)	2½	**8**	9/2[2]	94	—
1983[4]	**Shamarphil (97)** (RHAlner) **11-10-0** MissSBarraclough (mstkes 1st & 3rd: sn wl bhd: t.o)	10	**9**	50/1	71	—
	Space Cappa (97) (MissVAStephens) **9-10-0** MissVStephens (a bhd: t.o)	hd	**10**	33/1	71	—
2881[4]	**Dakyns Boy (122)** (NATwiston-Davies) **12-11-11** CLlewellyn (lw: a bhd: t.o)	2	**11**	8/1	95	—
	Scribbler (121) (GMMcCourt) **11-11-10** DBridgwater (a bhd: t.o)	10	**12**	25/1	88	—
2575[P]	**Have to Think (125)** (PFNicholls) **9-12-0b** RJohnson (prom to 14th: t.o whn p.u bef 4 out)		**P**	20/1	—	—
2754[7]	**Sheer Ability (120)** (CJMann) **11-11-6b[1]**(3) JMagee (hld up mid div: mstke 7th: blnd 10th: sn bhd: t.o whn p.u bef 3 out)		**P**	25/1	—	—
2616[7]	**Nazzaro (125)** (WGMTurner) **8-12-0b** RDunwoody (prom to 11th: t.o whn p.u bef 5 out)		**P**	14/1	—	—

				SP	RR	SF
2754[P]	**Top Brass (IRE) (103)** (KCBailey) **9-10-6** JOsborne (prom tl wknd 12th: t.o whn p.u bef 17th)		P	20/1	—	—
				(SP 126.6%)	**16 Rn**	

7m 13.3 (43.30) CSF £47.62 CT £407.52 TOTE £4.40: £1.90 £2.80 £1.60 £4.50 (£32.90) Trio £239.70 OWNER Mr L. G. Kimber (WANTAGE) BRED C. L. Loyd

LONG HANDICAP Rocky Park 9-12 Special Account 9-11 Shamarphil 9-0 Space Cappa 9-9 Holy Sting (IRE) 9-9

2869* Giventime is certainly in top form at the moment and defied a 6lb hike in the weights. (4/1)

2829 Rocky Park, just out of the handicap, jumped much better than of late, but a slight mistake at the penultimate fence helped to tip the scales in the winner's favour. (14/1)

2881 Spuffington seemed to be travelling well until finding little in the final half-mile. (8/1)

2011 Special Account could not live with the two principals in the long home straight. (20/1)

1428 Dom Samourai (FR), dropped 4lb, did not find the switch to a visor doing the trick. (20/1)

3154 E.B.F. 'N.H.' (QUALIFIER) NOVICES' HURDLE (5, 6 & 7-Y.O) (Class E)

3-15 (3-19) **2m 110y (8 hdls)** £2,514.00 (£704.00: £342.00) GOING: 0.61 sec per fur (S)

				SP	RR	SF
2812[5]	**Princeful (IRE)** (MrsJPitman) **6-11-0** RFarrant (swtg: a.p: led appr 4 out: hung lft 2 out: rdn & r.o flat)	—	1	7/2[2]	78	6
2071[5]	**John Drumm** (PRWebber) **6-11-0** JOsborne (led appr 2nd tl appr 4 out: ev ch flat: nt qckn)	¾	2	8/1	77	5
	Belmorebruno (MCPipe) **7-11-0** CMaude (j.lft: a.p: ev ch 4 out: btn whn mstke 2 out)	7	3	8/1	71	—
2547[6]	**Tompetoo (IRE) (105)** (NATwiston-Davies) **6-11-10** CLlewellyn (lw: led tl appr 2nd: j.slowly 3rd: mstke & lost pl 4th: styd on fr 2 out)	3	4	6/1	78	6
1171[7]	**Rhythm And Blues** (RHBuckler) **7-11-0** BPowell (prom: lost pl 4th: styd on fr 2 out)	2½	5	25/1	65	—
	Close Harmony (NJHenderson) **5-10-9** RDunwoody (lw: hld up & plld hrd: hdwy 4th: wknd appr 3 out: eased whn btn)	27	6	4/1[3]	34	—
	Hightech Touch (LPGrassick) **7-11-0** MrJGrassick (sme hdwy after 4th: wknd 4 out)	¾	7	50/1	38	—
1336[2]	**Little Jake (IRE)** (NoelChance) **7-11-0** RJohnson (mstke 3rd: a bhd)	¾	8	10/1	38	—
1334[F]	**Dukes Castle (IRE)** (RGFrost) **6-11-0** JFrost (bit bkwd: bhd fr 4th)	2½	9	50/1	35	—
	Lizzys First (BRMillman) **5-10-9**(5) DSalter (bkwd: hdwy 3rd: wknd after 4th: t.o)	28	10	50/1	8	—
2825[3]	**Wise King** (JABOld) **7-11-0** GUpton (hdwy 4th: 4th & btn whn fell last)		F	2/1[1]	76?	—
				(SP 130.9%)	**11 Rn**	

4m 11.5 (22.50) CSF £31.70 TOTE £4.20: £1.30 £1.60 £3.20 (£24.60) Trio £91.10 OWNER Robert & Elizabeth Hitchins (UPPER LAMBOURN) BRED J. S. Bellingham

2812 Princeful (IRE) certainly carries plenty of condition, and did not help his rider from the second last. However, he did find a bit more when strongly challenged on the run-in, and definitely has the scope to go over fences. (7/2)

1651 John Drumm, apparently not one hundred per cent last time, may have forced his head back in front briefly on the run-in, and can take a similar event on this evidence. (8/1)

Belmorebruno, a half-brother to a couple of winning hurdlers, has a few jumping problems to be ironed out, but ran well in the circumstances. (8/1: op 4/1)

2547 Tompetoo (IRE) was not helped by some indifferent hurdling. (6/1)

1036 Rhythm And Blues may do better over a longer trip. (25/1)

Close Harmony, who showed plenty of promise in a Sandown bumper nearly a year ago, fared much better than her finishing position suggests, but needs to learn to settle. (4/1)

3155 CLIVE GRAHAM NOVICES' CHASE (5-Y.O+) (Class E)

3-50 (3-50) **3m (18 fncs)** £3,512.50 (£1,060.00: £515.00: £242.50) GOING: 1.01 sec per fur (HY)

				SP	RR	SF
3040*	**Cyborgo (FR)** (MCPipe) **7-12-0** RDunwoody (lw: chsd ldr: led 12th: clr 3 out: r.o wl)	—	1	4/7[1]	135++	51
3040[2]	**Buckhouse Boy (132)** (NATwiston-Davies) **7-11-8** CMaude (lw: a.p: hit 2nd: chsd wnr fr 5 out: one pce fr 3 out)	9	2	4/1[2]	123	39
2760[3]	**Him of Praise (IRE)** (OSherwood) **7-11-2** JOsborne (lw: led: pckd 5th: hdd 12th: wknd qckly 3 out)	21	3	8/1[3]	103	19
2896[2]	**Parahandy (IRE)** (GBBalding) **7-11-0**(7)ow5 MrABalding (no hdwy fr 5 out)	10	4	16/1	101	12
2658[P]	**Golden Drops (NZ)** (AGHobbs) **9-11-2** RGreene (swtg: bhd fr 11th)	7	5	66/1	92	8
2883[6]	**Foodbroker Star (IRE)** (JTGifford) **7-11-8** PHide (prom: 4th whn blnd bdly 10th: nt rcvr)	8	6	20/1	92	8
1854[5]	**Clontoura (IRE)** (IPWilliams) **9-11-2** BPowell (hdwy 10th: wknd 12th: t.o)	24	7	50/1	70	—
2841[8]	**Ballydougan (IRE) (74)** (RMathew) **9-11-2v** TJMurphy (a bhd: t.o)	28	8	100/1	52	—
	Better Future (IRE) (TKeddy) **8-11-2** RJohnson (a bhd: t.o)	s.h	9	50/1	52	—
2039[8]	**Wandering Light (IRE)** (CaptTAForster) **8-11-2** CLlewellyn (a bhd: t.o)	10	10	25/1	45	—
2883[5]	**Credo Is King (IRE) (112)** (PRWebber) **7-11-8** DBridgwater (prom tl wknd 8th: t.o whn p.u bef 5 out)		P	20/1	—	—
2039[7]	**Greenfield George (IRE)** (PJHobbs) **6-11-2** LHarvey (hld up: hdwy 10th: wknd appr 5 out: bhd whn p.u bef 2 out)		P	66/1	—	—
	Sound Carrier (USA) (CLPopham) **9-11-2** GTormey (bkwd: bhd fr 10th: t.o whn p.u bef 5 out)		P	66/1	—	—
2819[P]	**Mystic Manna** (AndrewTurnell) **11-11-2** GCrone (a bhd: t.o whn p.u bef 5 out)		P	50/1	—	—
				(SP 125.3%)	**14 Rn**	

6m 25.4 (32.40) CSF £2.75 TOTE £1.60: £2.50 £1.60 £1.60 (£3.00) Trio £10.20 OWNER County Stores (Somerset) Holdings Ltd (WELLINGTON) BRED Francois Cottin and Alfred Lefevre

3040* Cyborgo (FR) made a slight blemish at the final fence, but it was all over bar the shouting by then. (4/7)

3040 Buckhouse Boy was 10lb better off with the winner than when beaten six lengths at Newbury a week ago. (4/1)

2760 Him of Praise (IRE), an impressive winner of his only point in Ireland, did not seem to get the trip in this soft ground. (8/1)

2896 Parahandy (IRE) was taking on some useful sorts this time. (16/1)

3156 FLYOVER H'CAP HURDLE (0-135) (4-Y.O+) (Class C)

4-25 (4-25) **3m (12 hdls)** £3,715.50 (£1,119.00: £542.00: £253.50) GOING: 0.61 sec per fur (S)

				SP	RR	SF
3013*	**Bankhead (IRE) (122)** (JLSpearing) **8-10-8**(7) MissCSpearing (led appr 2nd: hdd 8th: led appr 4 out: r.o wl fr 2 out: t.o)	—	1	15/2[3]	99	10
2880[8]	**Scotby (BEL) (107)** (RHBuckler) **7-10-0** BPowell (jnd ldrs 5th: sn stdd: hdwy 8th: ev ch whn mstke 2 out: nt qckn)	2	2	12/1	83	—
1906[4]	**Glengarrif Girl (IRE) (107)** (MCPipe) **7-10-0v** GTormey (a.p: one pce fr 4 out)	6	3	8/1	79	—
	My Rossini (116) (PJBevan) **8-10-6**(3) JMagee (bit bkwd: a.p: led 8th tl rdn & hdd appr 4 out: wknd appr 2 out)	4	4	12/1	85	—

				SP	RR	SF
2880[3]	**Menesonic (IRE) (112)** (RHAlner) **7-10-5** JCulloty (swtg: led after 1st: sn hdd: wknd appr 4 out)	1	**5**	7/2[2]	80	—
2884[7]	**Pennymoor Prince (112)** (RGFrost) **8-10-5**ow5 JFrost (swtg: led tl after 1st: wknd appr 4 out)	26	**6**	14/1	63	—
2869[8]	**Veryvel (CZE) (112)** (JNeville) **6-10-5** TJMurphy (lw: bhd fr 8th: t.o)	14	**7**	14/1	54	—
1647[9]	**Hebridean (135)** (PRWebber) **10-12-0** JOsborne (bit bkwd: hdwy 6th: wknd 8th: eased whn no ch 3 out)	15	**8**	20/1	67	—
2659[9]	**Texan Baby (BEL) (112)** (NATwiston-Davies) **8-10-5** CLlewellyn (bhd fr 7th: t.o)	12	**9**	14/1	36	—
1950[5]	**Spirit Level (107)** (JRPayne) **9-9-7**(7) MrSDurack (a bhd: t.o fr 6th)	dist	**10**	100/1	—	—
2950[2]	**Korbell (IRE) (111)** (PFNicholls) **8-10-4** RJohnson (w ldrs whn fell 3rd: dead)		**F**	2/1[1]	—	—
	The Mexicans Gone (107) (DPGeraghty) **9-10-0** VSlattery (bit bkwd: a bhd: t.o whn p.u bef 2 out)		**P**	14/1	—	—
				(SP 126.2%)	**12 Rn**	

6m 12.1 (32.10) CSF £90.36 CT £691.64 TOTE £7.10: £2.20 £4.30 £2.10 (£47.80) Trio £190.90 OWNER Mrs Liz Brazier (ALCESTER) BRED Ronald O'Neill

LONG HANDICAP Glengarrif Girl (IRE) 9-12 Pennymoor Prince 9-8 Scotby (BEL) 9-7 Spirit Level 7-5

3013* Bankhead (IRE) defied a 6lb rise in the ratings. (15/2: 5/1-8/1)

2656* Scotby (BEL), 7lb out of the handicap, seemed about to land in the lead when missing out at the penultimate hurdle, and from then on the winner had the edge. (12/1)

1906 Glengarrif Girl (IRE) prefers a sounder surface. (8/1)

My Rossini should be sharper for the outing. (12/1: 8/1-14/1)

2880 Menesonic (IRE) was stepping up from novice company. (7/2)

Pennymoor Prince (14/1: op 25/1)

2950 Korbell (IRE) unfortunately broke her pelvis. (2/1)

T/Plpt: £80.70 (220.23 Tckts). T/Qdpt: £12.20 (71.03 Tckts) KH

3137-NEWCASTLE (L-H) (Good, Good to soft in places)

Saturday February 15th

One fence omitted all races. Two fences omitted 5th race.

WEATHER: fine

3157 NORTHERN RACING CONDITIONAL H'CAP HURDLE (0-105) (4-Y.O+) (Class F)

1-25 (1-26) **3m (13 hdls)** £2,267.00 (£637.00: £311.00) GOING: 0.23 sec per fur (G)

				SP	RR	SF
2915[8]	**Dockmaster (81)** (MissMKMilligan) **6-9-13**(5) NHorrocks (cl up: disp ld 7th tl led 4 out: clr after next: kpt on)	—	**1**	14/1	63	8
1988[4]	**Flat Top (95)** (MWEasterby) **6-11-4** PMidgley (hld up: hdwy 9th: 4th whn bdly hmpd 3 out: sn chsng wnr: r.o)	1½	**2**	10/1	76+	21
1645[9]	**Give Best (100)** (JJO'Neill) **6-11-9** RMcGrath (styd on fr 4 out: nrst fin)	1½	**3**	9/1	80	25
2654[P]	**What Jim Wants (IRE) (89)** (JJO'Neill) **4-9-7**(7) DJewett (sn chsng ldrs: outpcd 4 out: kpt on wl fr 2 out)	8	**4**	33/1	64	—
2955[2]	**Turkish Tower (86)** (RNixon) **6-10-9** FLeahy (lw: hdwy & prom 4 out: sn rdn: 4th & btn whn blnd last)	nk	**5**	12/1	61	6
2915[5]	**Hudson Bay Trader (USA) (84)** (PBeaumont) **10-10-7** GSupple (lw: chsd ldrs: pushed along fr ½-wy: lost pl 9th: styd on again towards fin)	6	**6**	12/1	55	—
2954[P]	**Ansuro Again (82)** (MrsMReveley) **8-10-0**(5) MHerrington (hdwy to chal 8th: sn rdn: btn whn hmpd 3 out)	1½	**7**	25/1	52	—
2915[3]	**Jigginstown (77)** (JJO'Neill) **10-9-7**(7) LCooper (bhd: sme hdwy fr 8th: nvr rchd ldrs)	½	**8**	12/1	46	—
2800[5]	**Arian Spirit (IRE) (82)** (JLEyre) **6-10-0**(5)ow2 CElliott (mstke 3rd: effrt 8th: no imp)	2½	**9**	7/1[2]	50	—
2915[2]	**Kings Lane (86)** (JMDun) **8-10-4**(5) CMcCormack (chsd ldrs: disp ld 7th to 4 out: wknd)	1¾	**10**	8/1[3]	52	—
3032[6]	**Ski Path (77)** (NBycroft) **8-9-9**(5) AScholes (prom to ½-wy: sn bhd: t.o)	dist	**11**	200/1	—	—
3028[6]	**New Charges (95)** (PBeaumont) **10-11-4** BGrattan (a bhd: b.d 3 out)		**B**	16/1	—	—
2915*	**Scarba (100)** (JMJefferson) **9-11-9** ECallaghan (lw: hld up: stdy hdwy ½-wy: 2nd & effrt whn fell 3 out)		**F**	8/1[3]	—	—
2922[3]	**Manettia (IRE) (91)** (MrsMReveley) **8-11-0** GCahill (prom tl lost pl 5th: sn rdn & bhd: p.u lame bef 3 out)		**P**	5/1[1]	—	—
2820*	**Montel Express (IRE) (105)** (KCBailey) **5-11-9**(5) WWalsh (swtg: hld up: p.u lame bef 7th: dead)		**P**	9/1	—	—
1671[4]	**Dig Deeper (95)** (RAllan) **10-11-4** SMelrose (led to 7th: sn lost pl: p.u bef 4 out)		**P**	14/1	—	—
	Murphaideez (77) (RAFahey) **10-10-0** MNewton (a wl bhd: t.o whn p.u bef 3 out)		**P**	100/1	—	—
2003[6]	**Denticulata (77)** (PSpottiswood) **9-9-9**(5) SHaworth (chsd ldrs tl wknd qckly 9th: p.u bef 3 out)		**P**	100/1	—	—
1796[8]	**Bark'n'bite (87)** (MrsMReveley) **5-10-10** GLee (chsd ldrs: rdn fr 8th: wknd 4 out: p.u bef 2 out)		**P**	25/1	—	—
2954[F]	**Mr Sloan (77)** (JSGoldie) **7-9-7**(7) NHannity (sn bhd & drvn along: t.o whn p.u bef 3 out)		**P**	200/1	—	—
				(SP 136.4%)	**20 Rn**	

6m 2.4 (20.40) CSF £143.36 CT £1,252.69 TOTE £30.20: £5.00 £3.20 £2.80 £3.50 (£107.10) Trio £233.50; £263.18 to Hereford 17/2/97

OWNER Mr J. D. Gordon (LEYBURN) BRED Cleaboy Farms Co

LONG HANDICAP What Jim Wants (IRE) 9-10 Ski Path 9-2 Murphaideez 9-2 Denticulata 9-8 Mr Sloan 8-4

WEIGHT FOR AGE 4yo-12lb

OFFICIAL EXPLANATION **Dockmaster: accounting for the improved form, the trainer reported that the gelding has had wind problems, had taken time to come to himself and acted on the softer ground here. The jockey who rode him last time added that the gelding had been left at the start and did not seem to like being covered up.**

Dockmaster bounced back to form here after some disappointing efforts, and was given a fine ride. (14/1)

1988 Flat Top is difficult to win with these days but, on this occasion, it was not his fault, and he deserves a change of luck. (10/1)

Give Best is fast coming to form and is one to keep an eye on. (9/1)

2509 What Jim Wants (IRE) does not seem to have a trip, as yet again he got outpaced at a vital stage before staying on. (33/1)

2955 Turkish Tower had his chances, but his limitations had been exposed when he almost came to grief at the last. (12/1)

2915 Hudson Bay Trader (USA) has plenty more ability when in the mood, but he lost all interest halfway through the race, and only stayed on when it was too late. (12/1)

Ansuro Again has been most disappointing over fences, and this was a much better effort. (25/1)

2915* Scarba was looking dangerous in second place when falling three out. (8/1)

3158 NEWSHAM NOVICES' HURDLE (4-Y.O+) (Class E)

1-55 (1-57) **2m (9 hdls)** £2,484.00 (£699.00: £342.00) GOING: 0.23 sec per fur (G)

				SP	RR	SF
1438*	**Marello** (MrsMReveley) **6-11-5** PNiven (lw: hld up: a gng wl: hdwy 5th: mstke 2 out: led last: shkn up: comf)	—	**1**	1/2[1]	90+	61
	Nigel's Lad (IRE) (PCHaslam) **5-11-4** MFoster (lw: chsd ldr tl lft clr 3rd: hdd last: kpt on)	2½	**2**	12/1	87	58
2898*	**Durano (100)** (TDEasterby) **6-11-10** RGarritty (lw: a chsng ldrs: no imp fr 3 out)	17	**3**	6/1[2]	76	47
	Far Ahead (JLEyre) **5-11-4** BStorey (hdwy 5th: styd on wl fr 2 out: nvr rchd ldrs)	1¼	**4**	16/1	68	39

				SP	RR	SF
2898[15]	**Quango** (JGFitzGerald) **5-11-10** DGallagher (chsd ldrs tl rdn & btn after 4 out)	1	**5**	6/1[2]	73	44
2669[6]	**Barton Scamp** (SABrookshaw) **5-11-4** TEley (hdwy 4 out: nvr rchd ldrs)	nk	**6**	20/1	67	38
	Gospel Song (108) (ACWhillans) **5-11-4** ASSmith (lw: trckd ldrs: effrt 4 out: wknd & eased fr next)	16	**7**	9/1[3]	51+	22
2859[U]	**Diamond Beach** (GMMoore) **4-10-8** NBentley (hld up & bhd: sme late hdwy)	2	**8**	66/1	49	10
2924[5]	**Jessolle** (GRichards) **5-10-13** ADobbin (hld up: nvr nr to chal)	5	**9**	33/1	39	10
1921[P]	**Toshiba Talk (IRE) (99)** (BEllison) **5-11-4** TReed (effrt 5th: sn in tch: wknd 3 out)	11	**10**	25/1	33	4
2917[11]	**Sioux Warrior** (NTinkler) **5-11-1b**(3) EHusband (chsd ldrs tl wknd fr 4 out)	3	**11**	50/1	30	1
	Greenfinch (CAN) (65) (MrsAMNaughton) **6-11-4v** JSupple (mid div: pushed along ½-wy: sn wknd)	1¾	**12**	200/1	28	—
2750[8]	**Chasing Dreams** (CGrant) **6-11-4** JCallaghan (chsd ldrs to 5th)	4	**13**	100/1	24	—
	Craigie Boy (NBycroft) **7-11-4** OPears (bhd fr ½-wy)	1¼	**14**	200/1	23	—
2898[21]	**On The Off Chance** (LLungo) **5-10-11**(7) IJardine (a bhd)	5	**15**	200/1	18	—
	African Sun (IRE) (MCChapman) **4-10-8** KGaule (a bhd: t.o)	dist	**16**	50/1	—	—
1990[8]	**Robert The Brave** (JMJefferson) **5-11-1**(3) ECallaghan (bhd & reminders 3rd: p.u bef last)		**P**	200/1	—	—
2669[18]	**Shirley's Time** (MrsJBrown) **6-11-4** GCahill (a bhd: p.u bef 2 out)		**P**	66/1	—	—
	Jamaican Flight (USA) (MrsSLamyman) **4-10-8** JAMcCarthy (led & sn clr: tried to run out, j.slowly & uns rdr 3rd)		**U**	33/1	—	—
				(SP 143.2%)	**19 Rn**	

3m 56.8 (4.80) CSF £9.64 TOTE £1.50: £1.00 £3.10 £3.40 (£9.50) Trio £33.10 OWNER Mrs M. Williams (SALTBURN) BRED R. Chugg
WEIGHT FOR AGE 4yo-10lb

OFFICIAL EXPLANATION Gospel Song: accounting for the apparent tender handling, the rider reported that his instructions were to settle the gelding and then make the best of his way home from three out, but the gelding landed flat-footed at the third last and blew up. The trainer added that the horse had been difficult to get fit, compared to last season when it had had three prior outings on the Flat.

1438* Marello, who has been laid off with a virus and various other ailments for three months, did the job well in the circumstances here and better should follow. (1/2)

Nigel's Lad (IRE), given a most positive ride on his hurdling debut, put up a super performance, and a repeat of this will surely find him a race. (12/1: op 7/1)

2898* Durano had his chances, but also had his limitations exposed over the last four flights. (6/1)

Far Ahead ran a fair first race over hurdles, and ought to pick up a prize or two in time. (16/1)

2539* Quango looks a moody individual, and always found the effort required here beyond him. (6/1)

1276 Barton Scamp has ability but seems to lack a turn of foot. (20/1)

Gospel Song travelled well, but after fiddling the third last it was obvious he was not going to make an impression. He was given a very kind ride thereafter and should benefit from it. (9/1: op 6/1)

3159 LEVY BOARD NOVICES' HURDLE (4-Y.O+) (Class E)

2-25 (2-28) **2m 4f (11 hdls)** £2,473.50 (£696.00: £340.50) GOING: 0.23 sec per fur (G)

				SP	RR	SF
2701*	**Bobby Grant** (CGrant) **6-11-10** PNiven (lw: hld up: hdwy 6th: led appr 3 out: mstke 2 out: styd on strly)	—	**1**	3/1[1]	74+	22
3024[P]	**Ashgrove Dancer (IRE)** (LLungo) **7-10-11**(7) IJardine (wl bhd: hdwy 4 out: styd on wl: nrst fin)	4	**2**	200/1	65	13
3014[4]	**Shared Risk** (JNorton) **5-11-1**(3) ECallaghan (hdwy & prom 6th: ev ch fr 2 out: blnd last: nt rcvr)	2½	**3**	8/1[3]	63	11
2812[11]	**Charley Lambert (IRE)** (JMackie) **6-11-1**(3) EHusband (hld up & bhd: hdwy 7th: styd on fr 3 out: nrst fin)	½	**4**	16/1	62	10
2917[5]	**No Finer Man (IRE)** (GRichards) **6-11-4** ADobbin (prom whn blnd 4th: smooth hdwy 6th: chsng ldrs 4 out: one pce fr next)	3	**5**	7/2[2]	60	8
2673[13]	**Bold Action (IRE)** (JNorton) **6-11-1**(3) GLee (chsd ldrs: chal 7th: outpcd fr 3 out)	2	**6**	20/1	58	6
2958[F]	**Pappa Charlie (USA)** (CParker) **6-11-4** BStorey (hld up: sme hdwy 4 out: no ch whn blnd 2 out)	4	**7**	20/1	55	3
2958[5]	**Malta Man (IRE) (94)** (PCheesbrough) **7-11-4** ASSmith (lw: hld up: hdwy 5th: rdn 3 out: sn btn)	2½	**8**	7/2[2]	53	1
3035[6]	**Don't Tell Tom (IRE) (86)** (JWade) **7-11-4** GCahill (prom: rdn fr 6th: grad wknd)	6	**9**	33/1	48	—
2546[11]	**Sutherland Moss (100)** (TPTate) **6-11-10** RGarritty (jnd ldrs 5th: led 7th: hdd appr 3 out: wknd)	15	**10**	12/1	42	—
316a[4]	**Well Armed (IRE)** (JJO'Neill) **6-10-13**(5) RMcGrath (in tch tl 4 out: blnd 2 out)	3	**11**	10/1	34	—
2918[4]	**Pentlands Flyer (IRE)** (HowardJohnson) **6-11-4** RichardGuest (nvr trbld ldrs: blnd 3 out)	16	**12**	16/1	21	—
2918[7]	**Paparazzo** (GMMoore) **6-11-4** JCallaghan (cl up tl wknd fr 7th)	2½	**13**	20/1	19	—
2898[20]	**Bonny Rigg (IRE)** (LLungo) **5-10-13** TReed (a bhd)	1½	**14**	100/1	13	—
1843[P]	**Whitegates Willie** (HowardJohnson) **5-11-4** DParker (w ldrs tl wknd fr 7th)	25	**15**	200/1	—	—
	Rachael's Dawn (71) (JLEyre) **7-10-13** MMoloney (t.o whn p.u bef 6th)		**P**	50/1	—	—
680[5]	**War Whoop (89)** (MissLucindaRussell) **5-11-10** LO'Hara (chsd ldrs to ½-wy: p.u bef 3 out)		**P**	33/1	—	—
2627[9]	**King Fly** (MrsSarahHorner-Harker) **7-11-4** MFoster (led to 7th: sn wknd: t.o whn p.u bef 3 out)		**P**	66/1	—	—
2918[P]	**Lyford Cay (IRE)** (JRBewley) **7-11-4** DBentley (sn t.o: p.u bef 3 out)		**P**	500/1	—	—
				(SP 134.9%)	**19 Rn**	

5m 6.4 (18.40) CSF £625.18 TOTE £3.50: £2.00 £28.70 £2.70 (£260.70) Trio Not won; £400.53 to Hereford 17/2/97 OWNER Mr John Thompson (BILLINGHAM) BRED Mrs D. Jenks

2701* Bobby Grant had to work for this, but he does stay and, apart from a poor jump two out, there was a lot to like about the way he did it. (3/1)

Ashgrove Dancer (IRE) seemed happier on this slightly better ground and, given plenty of time to find his stride, he made up a tremendous amount from the fourth last, but was making no further impression on the winner late on. He is obviously learning fast. (200/1)

3014 Shared Risk, trying a longer trip, gave the winner a race, but was getting the worst of the exchanges when a blunder at the last finished him. Nevertheless this was an improved effort. (8/1)

Charley Lambert (IRE) is fast coming to hand, and this was a much improved effort, as he was staying on nicely at the end. (16/1)

2917 No Finer Man (IRE) ran a useful race considering he made a bad blunder early on. In time there would seem to be plenty more to come from him. (7/2)

1926 Bold Action (IRE) ran a deal better than on his hurdling debut, and is obviously on the upgrade. (20/1)

2958 Malta Man (IRE) is proving disappointing at the moment, but he still gives the impression that he will do better in time. (7/2)

1842* Sutherland Moss (12/1: 8/1-14/1)

Well Armed (IRE) (10/1: op 6/1)

3160 BBC RADIO NEWCASTLE BREAKFAST SHOW H'CAP CHASE (0-140) (5-Y.O+) (Class B)

3-00 (3-02) **2m 4f (15 fncs)** £8,557.00 (£2,581.00: £1,253.00: £589.00) GOING: Not Established

				SP	RR	SF
2011[P]	**All the Aces (120)** (JJO'Neill) **10-10-13** SMcNeill (bit bkwd: hld up: stdy hdwy 3 out: led flat: comf)	—	**1**	14/1	133+	35
2765*	**Fiveleigh Builds (124)** (MissLucindaRussell) **10-11-3** MFoster (chsd ldr: hit 11th: led last: hdd & no ex flat)	2½	**2**	3/1[2]	135	37

2901[F] **The Last Fling (IRE) (124)** (MrsSJSmith) **7-11-3** RichardGuest (lw: mstkes: led chsng group fr 6th: hdwy & ch 3 out: hrd rdn flat: nt qckn) ....1½ **3** 5/2[1] 134 36
1970[5] **Cross Cannon (107)** (JWade) **11-10-0** BStorey (led tl hdd & wknd last)....3½ **4** 14/1 114 16
2901[5] **Valiant Warrior (133)** (MDHammond) **9-11-12** RGarritty (lw: in tch tl outpcd fr 9th)....dist **5** 7/1[3] — —
3025[5] **Better Times Ahead (133)** (GRichards) **11-11-12** ADobbin (chsd ldrs tl lost pl 6th: sn wl bhd)....dist **6** 14/1 — —
2782[P] **Easby Joker (129)** (SEKettlewell) **9-11-8** PNiven (t: prom chsng group tl blnd bdly 8th: p.u bef 10th).... **P** 5/2[1] — —
(SP 114.6%) **7 Rn**

5m 4.9 (11.90) CSF £52.11 CT £130.22 TOTE £18.50: £4.40 £2.10 (£19.20) OWNER Mr J. P. McManus (PENRITH) BRED Mrs M. A. Shirley
STEWARDS' ENQUIRY Guest susp. 24-26/2/97 (excessive use of whip).
OFFICIAL EXPLANATION All the Aces: the horse had jumped better this time and the yard was running into form.
1805 All the Aces has always looked the type to win races such as this, and he did it here under a very kind ride. There would seem to be plenty more to come. (14/1)
2765* Fiveleigh Builds, as usual, ran his heart out, only to find the winner far too good on the run-in. (3/1)
2901 The Last Fling (IRE) was continually diving through his fences and did remarkably well to remain upright and in contention, but in doing so had a very hard race. (5/2)
1970 Cross Cannon was in tremendous form here, and it is a pity that his favourite track, Sedgefield, is out of action for the time being. (14/1)
2901 Valiant Warrior was disappointing and was never really firing, but no doubt he will come back to form when his stable does.(7/1)
3025 Better Times Ahead ran no sort of race, and seems to have lost the thread for the time being. (14/1: op 8/1)
1657* Easby Joker almost destroyed the eighth fence, injuring himself quite badly. (5/2)

3161 GORDON ARMSTRONG WINES NOVICES' CHASE (5-Y.O+) (Class C)
3-35 (3-35) **2m 110y (11 fncs)** £5,044.75 (£1,528.00: £746.50: £355.75) GOING: 0.23 sec per fur (G)
SP RR SF
2899[2] **Chief Minister (IRE)** (MDHammond) **8-11-3** RGarritty (lw: a cl up: led 3 out: styd on under str pressure flat)— **1** 11/10[1] 114 46
2914* **Bold Boss (106)** (GMMoore) **8-11-13** BStorey (lw: disp ld: hit 5th: hdd 4 out: ev ch tl outpcd flat)....16 **2** 11/4[2] 109 41
2786[2] **Nooran** (ACWhillans) **6-11-3** ASSmith (disp ld tl led 4 out: hdd 3 out: wknd)....30 **3** 5/1[3] 69 1
2786[4] **Crosshot (88)** (RMcDonald) **10-11-9** KJones (mstkes: in tch tl blnd 5th: wl bhd after)....28 **4** 16/1 48 —
2779[7] **Mr Bureaucrat (NZ)** (SABrookshaw) **8-11-3** ADobbin (in tch tl blnd bdly 7th: sn t.o: p.u bef 3 out).... **P** 11/2 — —
(SP 112.2%) **5 Rn**

4m 5.9 (7.90) CSF £4.38 TOTE £2.20: £1.20 £1.40 (£2.20) OWNER Mr G. Shiel (MIDDLEHAM) BRED The Mount Coote Partnership
2899 Chief Minister (IRE) is happier on faster ground, but he still did the business this time and his rider left nothing to chance, driving him vigorously clear after the last. (11/10)
2914* Bold Boss did his best, but in the end the weight concession proved beyond him. (11/4)
2786 Nooran had his chances, but then disappointingly tired badly from the third last. (5/1)
2786 Crosshot never looked happy, and after a terrible blunder at the fifth it was all he could do to get round. (16/1)
2048 Mr Bureaucrat (NZ) was running a fair first race over fences, until a blunder and a half five out stopped him. (11/2: 4/1-6/1)

3162 TOTE EIDER H'CAP CHASE (0-140) (5-Y.O+) (Class B)
4-10 (4-10) **4m 1f (24 fncs)** £22,053.49 (£8,256.50: £4,040.75: £1,741.25: £783.13: £399.88) GOING: 0.23 sec per fur (G)
SP RR SF
2616* **Seven Towers (IRE) (127)** (MrsMReveley) **8-11-8** PNiven (hld up: effrt 16th: led on bit after 3 out: drvn clr flat)....— **1** 2/1[1] 136 50
1778* **Ivy House (IRE) (106)** (JJO'Neill) **9-9-10**(5) RMcGrath (lw: hld up & bhd: hdwy 18th: chsng ldrs 2 out: nt qckn flat)....8 **2** 5/1[3] 110 24
2881[5] **Killeshin (130)** (HJManners) **11-11-11** SCurran (bhd: gd hdwy 15th: sn w ldrs: led 5 out tl after 3 out: one pce)....nk **3** 25/1 134 48
2841* **Druid's Brook (105)** (KCBailey) **8-10-0** JAMcCarthy (hdwy to trck ldrs 14th: effrt 5 out: one pce fr next)....7 **4** 8/1 105 19
3025[2] **Kilcolgan (105)** (MrsJDGoodfellow) **10-10-0b** NBentley (disp ld tl lft in ld 14th: hdd 15th: blnd next: outpcd & n.d after)....12 **5** 6/1 98 12
2903[3] **Matt Reid (110)** (JPLeigh) **13-10-5** KGaule (chsd ldrs: led 16th tl rdn & hdd 5 out: wknd appr 3 out)....11 **6** 40/1 96 10
2542[F] **Pennine Pride (105)** (MDHammond) **10-10-0** DBentley (in tch tl outpcd fr 6 out)....15 **7** 25/1 82 —
2881[F] **See Enough (110)** (RHBuckler) **9-10-5** SMcNeill (w ldrs: led 15th to 16th: wknd 5 out)....5 **8** 10/1 84 —
1643* **Parsons Boy (127)** (GRichards) **8-11-8** ADobbin (lw: in tch: outpcd fr 15th: btn whn blnd 5 out)....1¾ **9** 9/2[2] 100 14
1983[P] **Front Line (112)** (JJO'Neill) **10-10-7b** RichardGuest (hld up & bhd: blnd 10th: n.d)....3 **10** 20/1 83 —
2616[11] **Pink Gin (113)** (MDHammond) **10-10-8** BStorey (outpcd fr 15th: sn wl bhd: p.u bef 3 out).... **P** 25/1 — —
2765[4] **Ceilidh Boy (117)** (MrsJDGoodfellow) **11-10-12v1** ASSmith (disp ld tl blnd, hmpd & uns rdr 14th).... **U** 20/1 — —
(SP 126.2%) **12 Rn**

8m 32.5 (2.60 under best) (16.50) CSF £11.31 CT £189.04 TOTE £3.30: £1.30 £2.10 £6.10 (£8.40) Trio £100.80 OWNER Mrs E. A. Murray (SALTBURN) BRED J. Mernagh
LONG HANDICAP Pennine Pride 9-5 Druid's Brook 9-9 Kilcolgan 9-13
2616* Seven Towers (IRE) is on the upgrade and he loves these extra long trips, and always had more in hand when it mattered. (2/1)
1778* Ivy House (IRE) tried his usual come-from-behind tactics, but just when he began to look dangerous, he ran out of fuel. (5/1)
2575 Killeshin won this last year, but has done nothing this season until now, although this is the first time he has had the cut in the ground which he really loves. (25/1)
2841* Druid's Brook was really thrown in at the deep end here against seasoned handicappers, but he acquitted himself well and should be all the better for it. (8/1: op 5/1)
3025 Kilcolgan forced the pace, but he made one poor jump setting out on the final circuit and was tapped for speed thereafter. (6/1: op 10/1)
2903 Matt Reid ran a fair race, but his stamina gave out from the fourth last. (40/1)
1643* Parsons Boy, after almost two months off, was most disappointing here, and there was obviously something wrong with him. (9/2: 3/1-5/1)

3163 GOSFORTH H'CAP HURDLE (0-140) (4-Y.O+) (Class B)
4-45 (4-46) **2m 4f (11 hdls)** £6,937.50 (£2,100.00: £1,025.00: £487.50) GOING: 0.23 sec per fur (G)
SP RR SF
2902[3] **Celestial Choir (114)** (JLEyre) **7-10-12** BStorey (trckd ldrs: led appr 3 out: r.o wl)....— **1** 9/2[2] 96 17
2912[U] **Turnpole (IRE) (128)** (MrsMReveley) **6-11-12** PNiven (lw: hld up: hdwy to chal 4 out: r.o: nt pce of wnr)....2½ **2** 5/1[3] 108 29
2902[2] **Tom Brodie (128)** (HowardJohnson) **7-11-12** ASSmith (hld up: smooth hdwy to chse ldrs 3 out: rdn & nt qckn)4 **3** 7/1 105 26
2779[4] **Kaitak (IRE) (119)** (JMCarr) **6-11-0**(3) FLeahy (trckd ldrs tl outpcd 4 out: styd on appr last)....7 **4** 12/1 90 11
2702[5] **Dally Boy (114)** (TDEasterby) **5-10-12** JCallaghan (led tl hdd 4 out: sn outpcd)....1 **5** 10/1 84 5
2802[5] **Old Habits (IRE) (106)** (JLEyre) **8-10-4** TEley (prom tl outpcd fr 4 out)....5 **6** 25/1 72 —

	Horse	Details	Dist	Pos	SP	RR	SF
2950^{5}	**Nijmegen (128)**	(JGFitzGerald) **9-11-12** WDwan (cl up tl rdn & btn appr 3 out)	1¼	**7**	14/1	93	14
2617^{6}	**Marchant Ming (IRE) (128)**	(MDHammond) **5-11-12** ADobbin (mstke 1st: w ldr: led 4 out tl appr next: wknd)	nk	**8**	33/1	93	14
2642*	**Sea Victor (118)**	(JLHarris) **5-11-2** DGallagher (trckd ldrs: chal 4 out: wknd next)	23	**9**	11/8^{1}	65	—
394*	**Viardot (IRE) (107)**	(HAlexander) **8-10-0**$^{(5)}$ RMcGrath (lw: hld up: mstke 4 out: a bhd)	14	**10**	20/1	51	—
					(SP 124.5%)		**10 Rn**

5m 4.5 (16.50) CSF £26.42 CT £147.61 TOTE £4.20: £1.60 £2.60 £2.40 (£13.40) Trio £26.60 OWNER Mrs Carole Sykes (HAMBLETON) BRED J. L. Eyre

2902 Celestial Choir, trying a longer trip, was well-suited by the steady pace and always had the edge in the sprint up the straight. (9/2)
2912 Turnpole (IRE) back to hurdling after disappointing over fences last time, ran a fine race, and would seem to be coming to form. (5/1)
2902 Tom Brodie travelled on the bridle, but this extra distance seemed to find him out. (7/1)
2779 Kaitak (IRE), stepping up in trip, surprisingly got outpaced when things hotted up, but he was keeping on at the end. (12/1)
2702 Dally Boy ran better than last time, but basically did not set a strong enough pace, and was outspeeded form the fourth last. (10/1)
2802 Old Habits (IRE) did not have the required speed when the race really began approaching the last three flights. (25/1)
2950 Nijmegen (14/1: 7/1-16/1)
2642* Sea Victor went out like a light from the third last and would seem to have a problem. (11/8)

T/Jkpt: Not won; £4,562.79 to 17/2/97. T/Plpt: £219.40 (98.38 Tckts). T/Qdpt: £10.30 (125.44 Tckts) AA

2925-WARWICK (L-H) (Good)
Saturday February 15th

WEATHER: fine & sunny

3164 MICHAEL PAGE GROUP H'CAP HURDLE (0-135) (4-Y.O+) (Class C)
1-50 (1-51) **2m (8 hdls)** £4,150.00 (£1,150.00: £550.00) GOING: 0.14 sec per fur (G)

	Horse	Details	Dist	Pos	SP	RR	SF
2963^{2}	**Goldingo (106)**	(GMPrice) **10-10-0** JRKavanagh (lw: hld up: hdwy appr 2 out: chal last: sn led: rdn out)	—	1	9/2^{3}	86	29
2902^{6}	**Thornton Gate (122)**	(TDEasterby) **8-11-2** PCarberry (chsd ldrs tl led on bit 3 out: rdn 2 out: hdd & unable qckn flat)	1½	2	9/2^{3}	101	44
2777^{4}	**Chicodari (127)**	(DNicholson) **5-11-7b** AMaguire (chsd ldrs: rdn appr 2 out: edgd lft & r.o flat)	¾	3	100/30^{1}	105	48
2779^{2}	**New Inn (122)**	(SGollings) **6-10-13**$^{(3)}$ MichaelBrennan (lw: led: sn clr: hdd 3 out: ev ch last: sn btn)	nk	4	4/1^{2}	99	42
1201^{5}	**Frogmarch (USA) (130)**	(RTPhillips) **7-11-10** NWilliamson (bit bkwd: hld up: hdwy 5th: no imp fr 2 out)	5	5	8/1	102	45
2892^{F}	**Kino's Cross (114)**	(AJWilson) **8-10-8** JCulloty (lw: chsd ldrs: dropped rr 5th: n.d afterwards)	9	6	20/1	77	20
2779^{10}	**Saint Ciel (USA) (106)**	(FJordan) **9-10-0** RSupple (a bhd)	8	7	12/1	61	4
1996^{P}	**Decide Yourself (IRE) (110)**	(TThomsonJones) **7-10-4**^{ow3} AThornton (bit bkwd: mstkes: prom to 3 out: wkng whn blnd 2 out: iron broke)	dist	8	20/1	—	—
					(SP 107.8%)		**8 Rn**

3m 48.4 (6.40) CSF £20.37 CT £58.52 TOTE £4.40: £1.50 £1.90 £1.40 (£9.50) OWNER Mr G. M. Price (BRECON) BRED G. Price
LONG HANDICAP Goldingo 9-12

2963 Goldingo, taking this for the second year running, handled the fairly quick ground well and seems to be still improving. He loves this track. (9/2)
2902 Thornton Gate looked likely to win on the turn, but the Handicapper still has the better of him as he is higher than his last win, despite fourteen subsequent defeats. (9/2)
2777 Chicodari, a very good mover, ran on well after the last without quite keeping straight. He tended to carry his head a littlehigh. (100/30)
2779 New Inn, as a front runner, is always vulnerable to something with a turn of foot, and seems to have the unfortunate habit of going up in the handicap without winning that often. (4/1)
Frogmarch (USA) looked to still need this, but ran well without threatening in the straight. A stocky sort, he does not look tall enough to excel with big weights, but has done well under such burdens. He is worth another chance in better company with a low weight. (8/1: op 5/1)
1179 Kino's Cross had little more than a confidence booster after a torrid time over fences. (20/1)
2048 Saint Ciel (USA) (12/1: op 8/1)

3165 MICHAEL PAGE LEGAL NOVICES' CHASE (5-Y.O+) (Class B)
2-20 (2-20) **3m 2f (20 fncs)** £7,197.50 (£2,180.00: £1,065.00: £507.50) GOING: 0.14 sec per fur (G)

	Horse	Details	Dist	Pos	SP	RR	SF
1915^{3}	**Carole's Crusader (106)**	(DRGandolfo) **6-10-11** AMaguire (led 2nd to 5th: ev ch whn pckd 15th: sn outpcd: rallied 2 out: hrd rdn to ld flat)	—	1	3/1^{2}	113	30
2879^{3}	**Mariners Mirror (120)**	(NATwiston-Davies) **10-11-5** MrMRimell (prom: lft in ld 8th: hit 15th: clr 4 out: hdd & unable qckn flat)	¾	2	3/1^{2}	121	38
3020*	**Jet Rules (IRE) (120)**	(MrsJPitman) **7-11-6** NWilliamson (lw: sn rdn: hdwy to ld 5th: blnd & hdd 8th: hit 13th: btn 4 out)	dist	3	Evens^{1}	—	—
2749^{3}	**The Booley House (IRE) (92)**	(VSoane) **7-11-2** PCarberry (led to 2nd: wknd 14th)	27	4	25/1	—	—
1068^{2}	**Capo Castanum (86)**	(MissHCKnight) **8-11-6** JCulloty (t: hld up: hdwy 9th: wknd 11th: fell 13th)		F	12/1^{3}	—	—
	Top it All (69)	(PRHarriss) **9-11-2** DWalsh (bkwd: in tch: rdn 10th: sn lost pl: p.u bef 13th)		P	100/1	—	—
					(SP 112.5%)		**6 Rn**

6m 39.2 (14.20) CSF £11.64 TOTE £3.70: £1.80 £1.90 (£8.60) OWNER Mrs C. Skipworth (WANTAGE) BRED D. J. and Mrs Deer

1915 Carole's Crusader, a long-backed mare, made a winning chasing debut in battling style without really impressing at the obstacles. (3/1)
2879 Mariners Mirror is in fine form at present and looked in complete control on the home turn, but her stamina just ran out. (3/1)
3020* Jet Rules (IRE), with the ground faster than ideal, was always finding these going a shade too fast for him on this track. His jumping suffered as a result. (Evens)
2749 The Booley House (IRE) was immediately in trouble when Mariners Mirror turned the taps on in the final mile. (25/1)
1068 Capo Castanum (12/1: 10/1-16/1)

3166 MICHAEL PAGE SALES AND MARKETING H'CAP HURDLE (0-115) (4-Y.O+) (Class E)
2-50 (2-52) **2m 4f 110y (11 hdls)** £2,433.50 (£681.00: £330.50) GOING: 0.14 sec per fur (G)

	Horse	Details	Dist	Pos	SP	RR	SF
3045^{5}	**Lets Be Frank (104)**	(NoelChance) **6-11-6** NWilliamson (hld up: hdwy 8th: led appr 2 out: clr last: comf)	—	1	3/1^{1}	86+	31
2806^{3}	**Beaumont (IRE) (98)**	(JEBanks) **7-11-0** PCarberry (hdwy 7th: led after 3 out sn hdd: rdn & one pce)	5	2	3/1^{1}	76	21
2708^{5}	**First Class (84)**	(GNAlford) **7-9-9**$^{(5)}$ ABates (prom: led 7th tl after 3 out: one pce)	1¾	3	10/1	61	6

	Horse	Dist	Pos	SP	RR	SF
2662[3]	**Penrose Lad (NZ) (100)** (DNicholson) **7-11-2** AMaguire (lw: chsd ldrs: no hdwy fr 3 out)	7	**4**	11/2[3]	71	16
2932[P]	**Hooded Hawk (IRE) (103)** (NJHenderson) **6-11-5** JRKavanagh (nvr nr to chal)	12	**5**	13/2	65	10
3016[P]	**Chief Rager (99)** (NATwiston-Davies) **8-11-1** DWalsh (led tl after 3rd: wknd 7th)	¾	**6**	20/1	60	5
	No Fiddling (IRE) (93) (GMMcCourt) **6-10-2**(7) RStudholme (lw: blnd 2nd: rdn 6th: sn no ch)	½	**7**	14/1	54	—
	Doualago (FR) (110) (MCPipe) **7-11-12b** JamieEvans (prom tl appr 7th)	3	**8**	5/1[2]	69	14
	Needwood Poppy (94) (BCMorgan) **9-10-10** BClifford (bit bkwd: in tch to 7th)	¾	**9**	33/1	52	—
2625[6]	**Little Gunner (108)** (RJPrice) **7-11-10** RBellamy (lw: bhd fr 7th)	3½	**10**	16/1	63	8
	Finnigan Free (93) (GAHam) **7-10-2**(7)ow9 MrMFrith (rapid hdwy to ld after 3rd: clr whn mstke next: hdd 7th: wknd qckly)	23	**11**	66/1	30	—
1701[10]	**Mill Thyme (90)** (PBeaumont) **5-10-6** RSupple (prom to 6th)	26	**12**	33/1	7	—
1693[4]	**Celtic Emerald (84)** (RJEckley) **9-9-11**(3) MichaelBrennan (t.o fr 4th: p.u bef 7th)		**P**	100/1	—	—
				(SP 130.2%)		**13 Rn**

4m 59.8 (12.80) CSF £12.13 CT £79.66 TOTE £3.80: £1.80 £1.60 £2.80 (£6.20) Trio £36.20 OWNER Mrs M. M. Stobart (LAMBOURN) BRED Malcolm Armitage Penney

LONG HANDICAP Finnigan Free 9-7 Celtic Emerald 8-1

3045 Lets Be Frank, whose moderate effort last week was his first run in nearly two months, quickly bounced back and is still improving. (3/1)

2806 Beaumont (IRE) looked sure to win when nipping up the inside in the back straight, but was very clearly second best once the winner made his move. There will be other days for him. (3/1)

2708 First Class ran a good race, but could not quicken like the principals. (10/1)

2662 Penrose Lad (NZ) seemed to be travelling better than anything with a mile left, but lacks gears and a stiffer track might help. (11/2)

1661 Hooded Hawk (IRE), in touch to the fifth last, found nothing once the tempo quickened. (13/2)

2063 Chief Rager looks to have lost his way for the moment. (20/1)

3167 MICHAEL PAGE GROUP KINGMAKER NOVICES' CHASE (Gd 2) (5-Y.O+) (Class A)

3-20 (3-21) **2m (12 fncs)** £11,540.00 (£4,362.00: £2,131.00: £967.00) GOING: 0.14 sec per fur (G)

	Horse	Dist	Pos	SP	RR	SF
2739a*	**Mulligan (IRE) (141)** (DNicholson) **7-11-12** AMaguire (j.w: mde all: qcknd appr last: impressive)	—	**1**	5/6[1]	141++	87
3008*	**Squire Silk** (AndrewTurnell) **8-11-5** PCarberry (lw: hld up: blnd 4th & 5th: hdwy 7th: ev ch 2 out: wknd flat)	6	**2**	Evens[2]	128	74
1793[10]	**Flying Instructor** (PRWebber) **7-11-5** RBellamy (chsd wnr to 3 out: r.o flat)	1	**3**	25/1	127+	73
2892[2]	**Blair Castle (IRE)** (GBBalding) **6-11-5** BClifford (prom to 3 out)	11	**4**	16/1[3]	116?	62
				(SP 114.3%)		**4 Rn**

3m 53.3 (-0.70) CSF £2.09 TOTE £1.90 (£1.20) OWNER Lady Harris (TEMPLE GUITING) BRED Sandford Bloodstock Ltd

2739a* Mulligan (IRE), on ground faster than ideal, put in another superb display of jumping and won in tremendous style. He really does look a star in the making, and will take all the beating in the Arkle. (5/6: evens-11/10)

3008* Squire Silk has never looked a natural jumper and was found sorely wanting by the two fences (the second an open ditch) on the steep rise towards the back straight, standing too far off both and doing well to stay upright. Along the back straight he certainly looked a faster horse than the favourite, but jumping is all-important and his mistakes eventually took their toll. On this evidence, a flat course will suit him best. (Evens)

Flying Instructor, a decent hurdler making his chasing debut, loved this ground which looked a little faster than the official good. The way he matched strides with the winner down the back until clipping the top of five out, and then spending too much time in the air at the next, suggests he will prove very useful indeed. (25/1)

2892 Blair Castle (IRE) was in the thick of things until a slight mistake four out signalled the end. (16/1)

3168 QUESTOR INTERNATIONAL TRIAL NOVICES' HURDLE (4-Y.O+) (Class B)

3-55 (3-56) **2m 4f 110y (11 hdls)** £7,100.00 (£2,150.00: £1,050.00: £500.00) GOING: 0.14 sec per fur (G)

	Horse	Dist	Pos	SP	RR	SF
1900[6]	**Influence Pedler** (JABOld) **4-10-6** NWilliamson (lw: w ldr tl led after 5th: qcknd clr appr 2 out: rdn out)	—	**1**	16/1	86?	7
2771[2]	**Potter's Gale (IRE) (105)** (DNicholson) **6-11-7** AMaguire (lw: hld up: hdwy appr 3 out: one pce appr next)	7	**2**	13/8[2]	85	17
2766*	**King Pin (118)** (PBeaumont) **5-11-12** RSupple (nt j.w: hld up: rdn appr 2 out: no imp)	7	**3**	5/4[1]	84	16
2893*	**King of Camelot (IRE)** (DNicholson) **7-11-8** RMassey (hld up & plld hrd: btn appr 2 out)	8	**4**	7/1[3]	74	6
2656[7]	**Rockcliffe Lad (100)** (NATwiston-Davies) **8-11-8** DWalsh (lw: led: hdd after 5th: hit next: 2nd whn p.u bef 7th: dismntd)		**P**	9/1	—	—
				(SP 110.9%)		**5 Rn**

5m 3.1 (16.10) CSF £39.73 TOTE £16.70: £2.20 £1.40 (£10.70) OWNER Miss S. Blumberg (WROUGHTON) BRED Stetchworth Park Stud Ltd

WEIGHT FOR AGE 4yo-11lb

1900 Influence Pedler, on Flat form, would have been suited by a true test of stamina as much as the others, but Williamson elected to wait in front and rode a marvellous race, kicking decisively off the bend going to two out. (16/1)

2771 Potter's Gale (IRE), restrained at the back, moved onto the leader's heels turning for home before being beaten for speed. (13/8)

2766* King Pin did not jump very quickly and lost a little ground at most of the flights. He was clearly not suited by such a falsely-run race and tended to hang left late in the day. (5/4)

2893* King of Camelot (IRE) showed his inexperience by failing to settle and looked a difficult ride, wandering around in the home straight. (7/1: 3/1-15/2)

1939* Rockcliffe Lad (9/1: 6/1-10/1)

3169 MICHAEL PAGE FINANCE H'CAP CHASE (5-Y.O+) (Class B)

4-30 (4-31) **2m 4f 110y (17 fncs)** £6,944.00 (£1,934.00: £942.00) GOING: 0.14 sec per fur (G)

	Horse	Dist	Pos	SP	RR	SF
2879[6]	**Senor El Betrutti (IRE) (129)** (MrsSusanNock) **8-10-12** NWilliamson (chsd ldr: led 11th: drew clr fr 13th: easily)	—	**1**	9/4[2]	136	56
1520[3]	**Southampton (123)** (GBBalding) **7-10-6v** BClifford (lw: hld up: lost tch 10th: r.o again appr last)	10	**2**	10/11[1]	122	42
2879[8]	**General Pershing (135)** (DNicholson) **11-11-4** AMaguire (led: sn clr: hdd 11th: hit 3 out: sn btn)	11	**3**	100/30[3]	126	46
				(SP 106.2%)		**3 Rn**

5m 8.0 (4.00) CSF £4.25 TOTE £2.50 (£2.30) OWNER Mr Gerard Nock (STOW-ON-THE-WOLD) BRED Bretton Blood Stock PLC

2621 Senor El Betrutti (IRE) loves this ground but is normally at his best when able to dominate. Sensibly allowing General Pershing to go clear at halfway, he cheekily nipped up his inside turning into the back straight for the final time and quickly had the race won. (9/4)

1520 Southampton was able to race upsides the winner for the first mile and a half, but once that rival made his move he became detached in last place and quickly lost interest. (10/11: 4/6-evens)

General Pershing was again very free and took a hair-raising dive at the first. Settling down after the first half-mile, he tired over the last five fences. (100/30)

3170 MICHAEL PAGE TECHNOLOGY STANDARD N.H. FLAT RACE (4, 5 & 6-Y.O) (Class H)

5-00 (5-02) **2m** £1,028.00 (£278.00: £128.00)

Form	Horse	Dist	Pos	SP	RR	SF
	Samuel Wilderspin (DNicholson) **5-11-0**(3) RMassey (w'like: a gng wl: jnd ldrs 4f out: led on bit wl over 1f out: sn pushed clr)	—	**1**	Evens^{1}	81 f	—
	Light The Fuse (IRE) (KCBailey) **5-10-10**(7) CScudder (cmpt: bit bkwd: gd hdwy fnl 3f: nrst fin)	11	**2**	12/1	70 f	—
2682^{7}	**Bold Leap** (PRWebber) **5-11-3** MrASansome (hdwy 7f out: sn rdn: kpt on wl appr fnl f)	3	**3**	33/1	67 f	—
	War Paint (IRE) (MrsJPitman) **5-10-10**(7) MrGBaines (scope: w'like: attr: trckd ldrs: ev ch over 2f out: one pce)	nk	**4**	15/2^{3}	67 f	—
2811^{7}	**Lord Foley (NZ)** (JGMO'Shea) **5-11-7**(3) MichaelBrennan (hdwy 8f out: rdn 3f out: sn btn)	5	**5**	6/1^{2}	69 f	—
	River Dawn (IRE) (CPEBrooks) **5-10-10**(7) MBerry (q attr: bit bkwd: a.p: led 3f out tl wl over 1f out: sn btn)	2½	**6**	15/2^{3}	59 f	—
2938^{W}	**Jemaro (IRE)** (WJenks) **6-11-3** MrAMitchell (led 13f)	3½	**7**	50/1	56 f	—
	Weapons Free (TPTate) **6-10-10**(7) RMcCarthy (tall: bkwd: prom: ev ch over 2f out: wknd over 1f out)	1¾	**8**	12/1	54 f	—
	Proper Primitive (CJDrewe) **4-9-9**(7) CRae (lt-f: unf: s.i.s: hld up: hdwy 3f out: nvr rchd ldrs)	nk	**9**	66/1	49 f	—
2682^{15}	**Good Time Dancer** (PRWebber) **5-10-5**(7) DThomas (plld hrd: chsd ldrs: rdn 4f out: sn wknd & eased)	8	**10**	33/1	41 f	—
2811^{6}	**Silent Cracker** (RDickin) **5-10-10**(7) XAizpuru (w ldr 10f)	13	**11**	8/1	33 f	—
	Captain Culpepper (IRE) (JKCresswell) **6-10-10**(7) NTEgan (tall: unf: bkwd: in tch 10f)	2½	**12**	100/1	30 f	—
2844^{8}	**Hijack** (MissHCKnight) **6-10-10**(7) MrAWintle (hdwy 8f out: wknd 4f out)	1¼	**13**	16/1	29 f	—
	Paypnutsgetmonkeys (IRE) (CASmith) **4-10-2** MrsDSmith (neat: sn bhd)	2	**14**	66/1	22 f	—
	Celtic Carrot (RJPrice) **5-11-0**(3) GuyLewis (w'like: hdwy after 6f: wknd 6f out)	½	**15**	33/1	26 f	—
	Miss Foley (JHPeacock) **4-9-10**(7)ow1 LSuthern (lengthy: a bhd)	nk	**16**	100/1	22 f	—
	Haberdasher (MissPMWhittle) **6-10-10**(7) KHibbert (big: bkwd: a bhd)	8	**17**	50/1	18 f	—
1555^{14}	**Tabbitts Hill** (PRWebber) **5-10-12** MrPScott (plld hrd: in tch 10f)	15	**18**	33/1	—	—
	Newski Lass (PWegmann) **5-10-5**(7) JPower (cmpt: bkwd: plld hrd: chsd ldrs 10f)	hd	**19**	66/1	—	—
	Sweet Perry (AWCarroll) **6-11-3** DWalsh (leggy: plld hrd: trckd ldrs 9f)	11	**20**	50/1	—	—
	Ginger Watt (IRE) (RJPrice) **5-11-0**(3) TDascombe (q. tall: prom: sddle slipped after 4f: t.o 6f out)	dist	**21**	33/1	—	—
1151^{7}	**Honest George** (KSBridgwater) **6-10-10**(7) MGriffiths (swtg: dwlt: a bhd: t.o)	5	**22**	25/1	—	—
				(SP 151.1%)		**22 Rn**

3m 43.4 CSF £16.33 TOTE £2.40: £1.40 £4.00 £17.20 (£21.30) Trio £92.60 OWNER County Graphix Colour Ltd (TEMPLE GUITING) BRED Midshires Frozen Foods Ltd

WEIGHT FOR AGE 4yo-10lb

Samuel Wilderspin, whose dam comes from a good jumping family, wore a cross noseband but settled well, and was always travelling. Sent on early in the straight, he strode away in the manner of a decent horse once given the office. (Evens)

Light The Fuse (IRE) is a poor mover and took time to get going before finishing as well as any. (12/1: 5/1-14/1)

Bold Leap was hard at work some way from home, but stuck to his task and snatched third on the line. (33/1)

War Paint (IRE), an attractive newcomer, challenged on the home turn before failing to last home. (15/2: 7/2-8/1)

2811 Lord Foley (NZ) briefly looked a threat on the home turn, but was soon hard at work. (6/1)

River Dawn (IRE), a likeable newcomer, looked green and in need of the experience but shaped really well. (15/2: 5/1-8/1)

Weapons Free, a big, tall newcomer, looked a long way from the finished article but showed promise. (12/1: 6/1-14/1)

T/Plpt: £497.20 (29.48 Tckts). T/Qdpt: £116.70 (6.36 Tckts) Dk

2818-WINDSOR (Fig. 8) (Good)

Saturday February 15th

Race 5 - One fence omitted fnl circ

WEATHER: sunny

3171 KING JOHN NOVICES' HURDLE (I) (5-Y.O+) (Class D)

1-30 (1-30) **2m 6f 110y (11 hdls)** £2,679.00 (£744.00: £357.00) GOING: 0.26 sec per fur (GS)

Form	Horse	Dist	Pos	SP	RR	SF
2812^{4}	**Friendship (IRE)** (NJHenderson) **5-11-0** MAFitzgerald (lw: mstke 6th: stdy hdwy 8th: led appr 2 out: clr appr last: easily)	—	**1**	8/15^{1}	83+	37
	Riot Leader (IRE) (TRGeorge) **7-10-7**(7) CHynes (bit bkwd: a.p: led 7th tl appr 2 out: unable qckn)	11	**2**	66/1	75?	29
2825^{7}	**Salaman (FR)** (DCO'Brien) **5-11-0** GBradley (lw: led 2nd to 7th: ev ch 3 out: wknd appr 2 out)	6	**3**	10/1	71?	25
865^{3}	**Bombadil** (MrsSLamyman) **5-11-0** JRailton (hdwy 8th: wknd appr 3 out)	5	**4**	10/1	67?	21
2656^{4}	**Shariakanndi (FR)** (JSKing) **5-11-0** WMarston (prom 7th)	13	**5**	7/1^{2}	58	12
2663^{P}	**Chapilliere (FR)** (TThomsonJones) **7-11-0** MRichards (hdwy 2nd: wknd 3 out: 5th & no ch whn blnd last)	3	**6**	50/1	56	10
2668^{13}	**Man of The Match** (MrsJPitman) **7-11-0** DLeahy (hdwy 7th: wknd appr 3 out)	1½	**7**	16/1	55	9
2878*	**Millcroft Riviera (IRE) (82)** (RHAlner) **6-11-6** JFTitley (lw: prom tl appr 3 out)	¾	**8**	8/1^{3}	60	14
2656^{6}	**Full of Bounce (IRE)** (RJHodges) **6-10-11**(3) TDascombe (led to 2nd: wknd 6th)	7	**9**	66/1	49	3
	Grizzly Bear (IRE) (RMStronge) **7-11-0** SWynne (bhd fr 6th)	28	**10**	16/1	30	—
2677^{17}	**Ilewinit (IRE)** (PCRitchens) **8-11-0** SFox (nt j.w: a bhd: t.o fr 6th: p.u bef 3 out)		**P**	66/1	—	—
	Uckerby Lad (MissJduPlessis) **6-10-11**(3) DFortt (bit bkwd: a bhd: mstke 5th: t.o fr 6th: p.u bef 3 out)		**P**	66/1	—	—
				(SP 126.7%)		**12 Rn**

5m 36.5 (13.50) CSF £65.06 TOTE £1.50: £1.20 £16.10 £2.10 (£46.50) Trio £168.90; £171.30 to Hereford 17/2/97 OWNER Mr T Benfield and Mr W Brown (LAMBOURN) BRED G. Merrigan

2812 Friendship (IRE) was far from fluent at his hurdles, but he was in a different league to these rivals and, cruising into the lead approaching the second last, forged clear with the minimum of fuss to win doing handsprings. He does need to improve his jumping. (8/15)

Riot Leader (IRE), in need of this first run in nearly a year, nevertheless showed up well and gained control at the seventh. Collared approaching the second last, he was firmly put in his place by the winner. (66/1)

Salaman (FR) ran much better here, and was still in with every chance early in the straight before tiring. (10/1: 5/1-11/1)

865 Bombadil was making his hurdling debut having been of the course for four months, but failed to stay this much longer trip and had given his all early in the straight. A half-brother to two sprint winners, he needs to return to two miles. (10/1)

2656 Shariakanndi (FR) (7/1: 7/2-8/1)

2878* Millcroft Riviera (IRE) (8/1: 5/1-9/1)

3172 KING JOHN NOVICES' HURDLE (II) (5-Y.O+) (Class D)

2-00 (2-02) **2m 6f 110y (11 hdls)** £2,658.00 (£738.00: £354.00) GOING: 0.26 sec per fur (GS)

Form	Horse	Dist	Pos	SP	RR	SF
2812[6]	**Jazzman (IRE)** (APJarvis) **5-11-0** JFTitley (a.p: led appr 2 out: all out)	—	1	4/1[2]	78	39
2759[2]	**Sparkling Spring (IRE) (108)** (KCBailey) **6-11-6** JRailton (a.p: ev ch fr 2 out: unable qckn flat)	½	2	13/8[1]	84	45
	High Patriarch (IRE) (NJHWalker) **5-11-0** ILawrence (bkwd: stdy hdwy 7th: ev ch 3 out: wknd 2 out)	15	3	16/1	67	28
2677[8]	**Brookhampton Lane (IRE)** (MrsAJBowlby) **6-11-0** DLeahy (plld hrd: hdwy appr 3 out: wknd appr 2 out)	5	4	33/1	63	24
	Professor Page (IRE) (TThomsonJones) **7-11-0** DerekByrne (lw: nvr nr to chal)	2½	5	16/1	62	23
2875[2]	**Over The Water (IRE)** (RHAlner) **5-11-0** WMarston (a.p: led 8th tl appr 2 out: sn wknd)	9	6	20/1	55	16
2808[2]	**Stormyfairweather (IRE)** (NJHenderson) **5-11-0** MAFitzgerald (prom tl appr 2 out)	10	7	13/2	48	9
2872[F]	**Gale Spring (IRE)** (RJHodges) **5-10-6**(3) TDascombe (a bhd: t.o)	dist	8	66/1	—	—
2053[13]	**Black Statement (IRE)** (JTGifford) **7-10-11**(3) LAspell (plld hrd: hdwy 2nd: wknd appr 3 out: t.o)	dist	9	50/1	—	—
3021[4]	**Prussian Steel (IRE)** (MBradstock) **6-11-0** PHolley (bhd fr 7th: t.o whn p.u bef 3 out)		P	20/1	—	—
1565[2]	**Marlousion (IRE) (93)** (CPEBrooks) **5-10-9** GBradley (led to 8th: sn wknd: t.o whn p.u bef 2 out)		P	6/1[3]	—	—
	Mrs Barty (IRE) (CWeedon) **7-10-9** MRichards (prom to 3rd: t.o whn p.u bef 3 out)		P	20/1	—	—
3084[P]	**Anif (USA)** (JJoseph) **6-11-0** DSkyrme (prom to 6th: t.o whn p.u bef 8th)		P	66/1	—	—
				(SP 119.7%)	**13 Rn**	

5m 35.8 (12.80) CSF £9.43 TOTE £5.20: £1.60 £1.50 £4.70 (£6.20) Trio £34.00 OWNER Mr L. Fust (ASTON UPTHORPE) BRED Tom McDonald

2812 Jazzman (IRE) appreciated the step up in distance. Gaining control approaching the second last, he had a tremendous battle with the runner-up and had little left in reserve. (4/1)

2759 Sparkling Spring (IRE), tackling a slightly longer trip, threw down a very determined challenge over the last two hurdles. Going at it hammer-and-tongs with the winner, he once again found his penalty taking its toll on the run-in. He should soon return to the winner's enclosure. (13/8)

High Patriarch (IRE) looked very tubby for his first run in thirteen months, but still showed promise, having every chance early in the straight before a lack of peak-fitness took its toll jumping the penultimate hurdle. (16/1)

2012 Brookhampton Lane (IRE) took a very keen hold. Beginning a forward move early in the straight, he failed to get on terms with the principals and was a tired animal going to the second-last. (33/1)

Professor Page (IRE) looked in good shape considering this was his first run since November 1995, and struggled on past beaten rivals to be nearest at the line. (16/1)

2875 Over The Water (IRE), taking a step up in trip. moved to the front four out but, collared approaching the second last, soon had bellows to mend. (20/1)

2808 Stormyfairweather (IRE) (13/2: 3/1-7/1)

3173 MAGNA CARTA NOVICES' CHASE (5-Y.O+) (Class E)

2-30 (2-34) **2m 5f (15 fncs)** £3,340.25 (£1,007.00: £488.50: £229.25) GOING: 0.26 sec per fur (GS)

Form	Horse	Dist	Pos	SP	RR	SF
2069*	**Sail by the Stars** (CaptTAForster) **8-10-12** SWynne (a.p: led 2 out: edgd rt appr last: rdn out)	—	1	5/2[1]	97	31
2908[3]	**Strokesaver (IRE) (88)** (CPEBrooks) **7-11-3b[1]** GBradley (a.p: lft in ld 3rd: hdd 2 out: unable qckn)	7	2	16/1	97	31
1922[2]	**Monicasman (IRE)** (APJarvis) **7-11-3** JFTitley (a.p: blnd 2nd: w ldr fr 3rd: ev ch 2 out: one pce)	4	3	9/2[3]	94	28
2816[3]	**Calleva Star (IRE) (82)** (RHAlner) **6-11-3** MAFitzgerald (a.p: rdn appr 3 out: one pce)	5	4	8/1	90	24
1998[11]	**Country Town** (APJones) **7-10-12** PHolley (nvr nr to chal)	17	5	33/1	72	6
2756[P]	**Cruise Control (78)** (RRowe) **11-11-3** DO'Sullivan (a mid div)	8	6	33/1	71	5
2819[5]	**Volleyball (IRE) (77)** (PRHedger) **8-11-3** MRichards (lw: bhd fr 10th)	18	7	33/1	57	—
1963[4]	**Sleetmore Gale (IRE)** (TPMcGovern) **7-10-9**(3) TDascombe (prom to 10th)	2½	8	13/2	50	—
	Multi Line (MrsPTownsley) **7-10-12** DerekByrne (a bhd)	6	9	66/1	46	—
2926[U]	**Convamore Queen (IRE)** (NMBabbage) **8-10-12** WMarston (bhd fr 6th: t.o)	25	10	66/1	27	—
2660[6]	**Brogeen Lady (IRE) (100)** (DRGandolfo) **7-10-9**(3) DFortt (led tl fell 3rd)		F	4/1[2]	—	—
1423[U]	**The Weatherman** (AEJessop) **9-11-3** TKent (bit bkwd: bhd whn fell 6th)		F	66/1	—	—
1417[2]	**Jolis Absent** (MJRyan) **7-10-12** JRyan (bit bkwd: a bhd: mstke 5th: t.o whn p.u after 11th)		P	10/1	—	—
2838[9]	**Derrys Prerogative** (AWCarroll) **7-11-3** DLeahy (a bhd: t.o whn p.u bef 4 out)		P	50/1	—	—
1563[8]	**My Warrior** (MarkCampion) **9-11-3** JRailton (blnd & uns rdr 2nd)		U	50/1	—	—
1572[6]	**Mystic Court (IRE) (72)** (AndrewTurnell) **6-11-3** ILawrence (bhd whn blnd & uns rdr 3rd)		U	25/1	—	—
				(SP 127.2%)	**16 Rn**	

5m 23.1 (14.10) CSF £40.07 TOTE £3.60: £1.90 £2.60 £2.40 (£31.00) Trio £71.20 OWNER Mr T. F. F. Nixon (LUDLOW) BRED T. F. F. Nixon

2069* Sail by the Stars, unbeaten over hurdles this season, made a winning debut over fences. Leading at the second last and being rousted along to assert her authority, she will be better suited by some mud. (5/2: 7/4-11/4)

2908 Strokesaver (IRE) showed further improvement in the first-time blinkers. Left in front at the third, he disputed the lead until the winner asserted. (16/1)

1922 Monicasman (IRE) has been disappointing over hurdles this season, but the switch to fences appears to have done the trick if this initial run is anything to go by. Disputing the lead from the third, he still had every chance jumping the second last before tapped for toe. (9/2: 3/1-5/1)

2816 Calleva Star (IRE) was not helped by the drop in distance, and was made to look very pedestrian over the last four fences. (8/1)

1417 Jolis Absent (10/1: 6/1-12/1)

3174 HATCH BRIDGE HURDLE (4-Y.O) (Class B)

3-05 (3-05) **2m (8 hdls)** £7,546.25 (£2,270.00: £1,097.50: £511.25) GOING: 0.26 sec per fur (GS)

Form	Horse	Dist	Pos	SP	RR	SF
2865[5]	**Red Raja** (PMitchell) **4-11-0** MRichards (lw: mde all: j.rt 2nd: rdn 3 out: clr appr 2 out: r.o wl)	—	1	13/2	87	49
2622[4]	**Far Dawn (USA)** (MrsAJPerrett) **4-11-0** DerekByrne (lw: a.p: bmpd 2nd: mstke 3 out: unable qckn)	6	2	11/4[1]	81	43
	Infamous (USA) (RJO'Sullivan) **4-11-0** DO'Sullivan (a.p: one pce fr 3 out)	2	3	16/1	79	41
2889*	**Hayaain** (KCBailey) **4-11-4** JRailton (a.p: rdn 3 out: one pce)	3½	4	3/1[2]	80	42
2865[2]	**Ela Agapi Mou (USA)** (GLMoore) **4-11-0** PHolley (prom tl appr 3 out)	6	5	14/1	70	32
	Salty Girl (IRE) (JSMoore) **4-10-9** WMcFarland (lw: hdwy appr 3 out: sn wknd)	5	6	33/1	60	22
2751[4]	**Mr Wild (USA)** (RAkehurst) **4-11-0** WMarston (mstke 1st: bhd fr 5th)	12	7	11/2[3]	53	15
	Fasil (IRE) (NJHWalker) **4-11-0** ILawrence (hdwy 4th: wknd 5th)	1½	8	12/1	51	13
	Hisar (IRE) (CPEBrooks) **4-11-0** GBradley (plld hrd: hld up: shkn up appr 3 out: sn wknd)	9	9	9/1	42	4
2925[5]	**Palamon (USA)** (JWhite) **4-11-0** SRyan (a bhd)	21	10	33/1	21	—

				SP	RR	SF
1935*	**Serenus (USA)** (NJHenderson) **4-11-7** MAFitzgerald (lw: prom whn hmpd & fell 2nd)		**F**	15/2	—	—
				(SP 128.3%)		**11 Rn**

3m 54.9 (6.90) CSF £25.25 TOTE £7.80: £1.80 £1.80 £6.60 (£21.40) Trio £167.60 OWNER Mr J. R. Ali (EPSOM) BRED J. Haine
2865 Red Raja, who failed to stay two-and-a-half miles last time out, was much happier with the return to the minimum trip and, making all the running, was ridden clear from the third last. (13/2)
2622 Far Dawn (USA) may have won twice this season but, because of the conditions of the race, he managed to escape a penalty. Bang on the heels of the winner three out, he failed to muster another gear. (11/4)
Infamous (USA), formerly with Paul Cole, has had a couple of runs on the All-Weather recently. Never far away, he was nicely placed jumping the third last but, under considerate handling, failed to find another gear. He can improve on this. (16/1)
2889* Hayaain had more on his plate here and, after being in a good position jumping the third last, could then only go up and down in the same place. (3/1)
2865 Ela Agapi Mou (USA) had far more to do here, and had given best going to the third last. (14/1)
2751 Mr Wild (USA) (11/2: 7/2-6/1)
Fasil (IRE) (12/1: 8/1-14/1)
Hisar (IRE) (9/1: 6/1-10/1)
1935* Serenus (USA) (15/2: 4/1-8/1)

3175 FAIRLAWNE H'CAP CHASE (0-125) (5-Y.O+) (Class D)

3-40 (3-40) **3m (17 fncs)** £3,848.50 (£1,153.00: £554.00: £254.50) GOING: 0.26 sec per fur (GS)

				SP	RR	SF
	Equity Player (102) (RCurtis) **12-10-13** DMorris (rdn & hdwy appr 4 out: led 3 out: clr 2 out: r.o wl)	—	**1**	4/1[2]	115	26
2928[U]	**Big Ben Dun (105)** (CPEBrooks) **11-11-2** GBradley (lw: hld up: w ldr fr 11th: led 4 out to 3 out: unable qckn)	12	**2**	5/1[3]	110	21
2910[P]	**Royal Saxon (94)** (PBowen) **11-10-5** WMarston (lw: w ldr: led 11th to 4 out: wknd 3 out)	4	**3**	25/1	96	7
3013[6]	**Fast Thoughts (107)** (DRGandolfo) **10-11-1b**(3) DFortt (led: mstke 6th: hdd 11th: sn wknd: t.o)	26	**4**	13/2	92	3
2821*	**Zambezi Spirit (IRE) (98)** (MrsMerritaJones) **8-10-9** DerekByrne (hld up: ev ch 13th: sn wknd: t.o whn j.lft 3 out: p.u bef 2 out)		**P**	7/4[1]	—	—
2814[4]	**Plunder Bay (USA) (113)** (NJHenderson) **6-11-10** MAFitzgerald (lw: blnd & uns rdr 1st)		**U**	4/1[2]	—	—
				(SP 110.2%)		**6 Rn**

6m 13.1 (18.10) CSF £20.59 TOTE £4.40: £1.50 £2.20 (£11.40) OWNER The Mrs S Partnership (LAMBOURN) BRED R. A. Steele
Equity Player, a model of consistency last season, looked fit for this first run in eleven months and did not let his supporters down. Galvanized into action on the long loop to the fourth last, he jumped into the lead three from home and soon asserted. (4/1)
1287 Big Ben Dun, 2lb lower than when last successful, ran much better here and managed to show in front four from home. Collared by the winner at the next, he then failed to find the necessary turn of foot. (5/1)
Royal Saxon, pulled up on both his starts this season, ran better here and showed in front at the eleventh. Collared four from home, he was soon beaten. (25/1)
3013 Fast Thoughts, reverting to fences, gave up quickly once headed at the eleventh. (13/2)
2821* Zambezi Spirit (IRE) should have been suited by the ground but ran as though something was amiss. With every chance five from home, he then stopped as if shot and was eventually pulled up before the second last. He has broken blood-vessels in the past and, although there were no obvious signs that that had happened this time, it is possible he broke internally. (7/4: 5/4-15/8)
2814 Plunder Bay (USA) (4/1: 3/1-9/2)

3176 STAINES H'CAP CHASE (0-110) (5-Y.O+) (Class E)

4-15 (4-15) **2m 5f (15 fncs)** £3,028.25 (£911.00: £440.50: £205.25) GOING: 0.26 sec per fur (GS)

				SP	RR	SF
2823*	**Hawaiian Youth (IRE) (104)** (GMMcCourt) **9-11-9**(3) DFortt (lw: rdn & hdwy appr 3 out: chsd ldr fr 2 out: led flat: all out)	—	**1**	9/4[1]	115	30
2867[6]	**Jovial Man (IRE) (94)** (RJO'Sullivan) **8-11-2** PHolley (led 3rd tl flat: r.o)	nk	**2**	7/1	105	20
2752*	**Key Player (IRE) (79)** (RRowe) **8-10-1**ow1 DO'Sullivan (lw: lost pl 7th: rallied appr 3 out: r.o one pce)	3	**3**	8/1	88	2
2823[5]	**Be Surprised (78)** (GLMoore) **11-9-7**(7) MBatchelor (led to 3rd: lost pl 8th: rallied 4 out: wknd 2 out)	11	**4**	16/1	78	—
2762[5]	**Too Sharp (102)** (MissHCKnight) **9-11-10** JFTitley (hdwy 5th: lost pl 8th: chsd ldr appr 3 out to 2 out: wknd appr last)	3	**5**	5/1[3]	100	15
2829[5]	**Rubins Boy (78)** (NJHWalker) **11-9-7**(7) DFinnegan (bhd fr 9th)	10	**6**	33/1	68	—
3009[F]	**Churchtown Port (IRE) (99)** (PButler) **7-11-4**(3) LAspell (lw: chsd ldr fr 6th: mstke 11th: wknd appr 3 out: bhd whn fell 2 out)		**F**	10/1	—	—
2679*	**Sophie May (89)** (LMontagueHall) **6-10-11b** WMarston (mstke 2nd: bhd whn fell 5th)		**F**	7/2[2]	—	—
2894[F]	**The Caumrue (IRE) (105)** (GBBalding) **9-11-13** GBradley (lw: bhd whn mstke 8th: t.o whn p.u bef 10th)		**P**	11/1	—	—
2756[P]	**Deependable (88)** (MrsLRichards) **10-10-10v** MRichards (lw: a bhd: t.o whn p.u bef 4 out)		**P**	20/1	—	—
2820[13]	**King's Courtier (IRE) (78)** (SMellor) **8-10-0v** NMann (bhd fr 3rd: t.o whn p.u bef 4 out)		**P**	50/1	—	—
				(SP 126.2%)		**11 Rn**

5m 27.2 (18.20) CSF £18.51 CT £105.80 TOTE £3.30: £1.30 £2.80 £2.50 (£19.60) Trio £25.40 OWNER Mr G. Redford (WANTAGE) BRED Owen Farrell
LONG HANDICAP Rubins Boy 9-13 Key Player (IRE) 9-13 Be Surprised 9-11 King's Courtier (IRE) 9-3
2823* Hawaiian Youth (IRE) had it all to do as the first two strode clear in the last mile. However, he picked up ground in the straight and, gradually reeling in the runner-up, managed to get on top halfway up the run-in. (9/4)
1963 Jovial Man (IRE) was very well handicapped - he won over hurdles off 108, but was on a mark of just 94 here. Soon at the head of affairs, he looked likely to succeed in the straight, but the winner eventually overhauled him on the run-in. (7/1: 5/1-15/2)
2752* Key Player (IRE) got outpaced early on the final circuit, but he stayed on again in the straight for third prize. (8/1: op 5/1)
2823 Be Surprised lost his pitch early on the final circuit, but managed to struggle back into it early in the straight before weakening two from home. He is a very bad performer. (16/1)
2762 Too Sharp, having lost her pitch, managed to take second place approaching the third last, but she was collared for that position two from home and was soon beaten. She has yet to win on ground worse than good. (5/1)
1515* The Caumrue (IRE) (11/1: 8/1-12/1)

3177 RUNNYMEDE H'CAP HURDLE (0-125) (4-Y.O+) (Class D)

4-50 (4-57) **2m (8 hdls)** £2,819.00 (£784.00: £377.00) GOING: 0.26 sec per fur (GS)

				SP	RR	SF
2952*	**More Dash Thancash (IRE) (101)** (MrsMerritaJones) **7-10-5** DerekByrne (lw: a.p: led appr 2 out: qcknd flat: easily)	—	**1**	11/10[1]	86+	41

				SP	RR	SF
2871[2]	**Shepherds Rest (IRE) (101)** (SMellor) **5-10-5** NMann (lw: hld up: chsd wnr appr 2 out: ev ch last: unable qckn)	3½	**2**	5/1[3]	83	38
	Colossus of Roads (100) (TThomsonJones) **8-10-4** MRichards (uns rdr & bolted bef s: hld up: rdn appr last: sn wknd)	7	**3**	11/2	75	30
2824[5]	**Kelly Mac (96)** (DCO'Brien) **7-10-0** WMarston (chsd ldr: ev ch 3 out: wknd appr 2 out)	1½	**4**	10/1	69	24
2963[5]	**Ros Castle (120)** (RJHodges) **6-11-10b** JRailton (nvr nr to chal)	½	**5**	25/1	93	48
2929[3]	**Albemine (USA) (124)** (MrsJCecil) **8-12-0** TKent (lw: led tl appr 2 out: wknd appr last)	1¾	**6**	9/2[2]	95	50
1519[5]	**Hever Golf Diamond (112)** (JRBest) **4-9-13**(7)ow6 MrPO'Keeffe (lw: bhd fr 5th)	17	**7**	10/1	66	5
2894[8]	**Linden's Lotto (IRE) (103)** (JWhite) **8-10-0**(7) SParker (a bhd)	¾	**8**	33/1	56	11
2952[9]	**Green Lane (USA) (105)** (JJoseph) **9-10-9** DSkyrme (lw: a bhd)	19	**9**	25/1	39	—
				(SP 126.7%)	**9 Rn**	

3m 54.9 (6.90) CSF £7.65 CT £22.90 TOTE £2.00: £1.10 £1.50 £3.00 (£3.60) Trio £16.10 OWNER Mr F. J. Sainsbury (LAMBOURN) BRED Miss Roseanne Millett & Paul McEnery

LONG HANDICAP Hever Golf Diamond 9-8 Kelly Mac 9-6

WEIGHT FOR AGE 4yo-10lb

2952* More Dash Thancash (IRE) may have been raised 9lb for his win last week, but he was even more impressive here. Leading approaching the second last, he showed a fine turn of foot on the run-in to sprint away. (11/10)

2871 Shepherds Rest (IRE), more at home over the minimum trip, threw down his challenge approaching the second last. Still in with every chance at the final flight, he was left standing by his rival. (5/1: 3/1-11/2)

Colossus of Roads ran extremely well considering he has been off the course since May 1995, and his exertions before the race. Chasing the leaders, he was still not far away early in the straight before his earlier antics took their toll going to the last. (11/2: 8/1-5/1)

2824 Kelly Mac, 8lb out of the handicap, had every chance early in the straight before tiring. (10/1)

Ros Castle never looked like posing a threat. (25/1)

2929 Albemine (USA) loves to hear his feet rattle and make the running, and that is what he did until collared approaching the second last. (9/2: 7/2-11/2)

T/Plpt: £109.80 (78.75 Tckts). T/Qdpt: £29.80 (16.47 Tckts) AK

2905-FONTWELL (Fig. 8) (Ch Good, Hdles Good to soft; becoming Soft after race 2) Monday February 17th

WEATHER: rain

3178 FEBRUARY NOVICES' HURDLE (4-Y.O+) (Class E)

2-20 (2-20) **2m 6f 110y (11 hdls)** £3,099.00 (£864.00: £417.00) GOING: 1.11 sec per fur (HY)

				SP	RR	SF
2812[2]	**Denham Hill (IRE)** (CJMann) **6-11-4** JRailton (mde all: clr appr 2 out: r.o wl)	—	**1**	5/6[1]	81	18
1422[7]	**Brackenheath (IRE)** (DMGrissell) **6-11-4** BFenton (hld up: chsd wnr appr 2 out: 2nd & btn whn mstke last)	14	**2**	33/1	71	8
2794[4]	**Persian Elite (IRE)** (CREgerton) **6-11-4** JAMcCarthy (chsd wnr to 7th: wknd 3 out)	8	**3**	5/1[3]	65	2
2945*	**Drum Battle (93)** (WGMTurner) **5-11-3**(7) JPower (lw: a.p: chsd wnr 7th tl appr 2 out: sn wknd)	2	**4**	12/1	70	7
1938[10]	**Tin Pan Alley** (DMGrissell) **8-11-4** MRichards (bhd fr 8th: t.o)	dist	**5**	50/1	—	—
3054[6]	**Alpine Song** (MissVAStephens) **12-10-13** MissVStephens (prom to 3rd: t.o)	dist	**6**	50/1	—	—
2676[4]	**Clarkes Gorse (IRE)** (JTGifford) **6-11-4** PHide (bhd fr 7th: t.o whn p.u bef 2 out)		**P**	4/1[2]	—	—
	Lord Love (IRE) (PRChamings) **5-11-4** SMcNeill (a bhd: t.o whn p.u bef 8th)		**P**	50/1	—	—
2008[5]	**Frank Naylar** (RHBuckler) **6-11-4b[1]** DBridgwater (rdn & hdwy 3rd: wknd 7th: t.o whn p.u bef 2 out)		**P**	50/1	—	—
	Charlie Bee (70) (RHBuckler) **8-11-4** BPowell (a bhd: t.o whn p.u bef 2 out)		**P**	50/1	—	—
1317[15]	**Millcroft Regatta (IRE)** (RHAlner) **5-11-4** JCulloty (bit bkwd: a bhd: t.o whn p.u bef last)		**P**	50/1	—	—
2820[7]	**Nordic Spree (IRE) (92)** (GLMoore) **5-11-4** PHolley (bhd whn p.u bef 4th)		**P**	14/1	—	—
1998[6]	**Country Style** (RHAlner) **8-10-13** AMaguire (bhd fr 6th: t.o whn p.u bef 3 out)		**P**	50/1	—	—
				(SP 122.2%)	**13 Rn**	

5m 55.5 (39.50) CSF £38.01 TOTE £1.80: £1.10 £5.50 £1.60 (£23.40) Trio £74.90 OWNER Mr J. E. Brown (UPPER LAMBOURN) BRED J. Griffin

2812 Denham Hill (IRE), with less on his plate on this occasion, was in his element in the mud. He once again adopted forceful tactics, making all the running and surging clear in the straight for a decisive victory. He will go chasing next season. (5/6: evens-11/10)

Brackenheath (IRE) left his hurdling debut at Plumpton three months ago well behind. Moving into second place approaching the second last, he failed to reel in the winner and was held when clouting the final flight. (33/1)

2794 Persian Elite (IRE) failed to see out this much longer trip and, after racing in second place until the final circuit, was out on his feet turning out of the back straight. (5/1: op 3/1)

2945* Drum Battle had a 6lb penalty to contend with and, after moving into second place with a circuit to go, was collared for that position turning for home. (12/1: 5/1-14/1)

3179 WITTERING (S) H'CAP CHASE (0-95) (5-Y.O+) (Class G)

2-50 (2-51) **2m 3f (16 fncs)** £2,553.00 (£708.00: £339.00) GOING: 1.11 sec per fur (HY)

				SP	RR	SF
2756[6]	**Opal's Tenspot (69)** (JMBradley) **10-10-5** BFenton (a.p: led 3 out: r.o wl)	—	**1**	10/1	80	15
2660[P]	**Golden Opal (84)** (RHBuckler) **12-11-6** DBridgwater (mstke 10th: hdwy appr 3 out: r.o one pce)	8	**2**	25/1	88	23
2796[5]	**Whistling Buck (IRE) (81)** (RRowe) **9-11-3** DO'Sullivan (led to 3rd: led 6th: mstke 12th: hdd 3 out: wknd appr last)	3	**3**	13/2[3]	83	18
2910[2]	**Master Comedy (72)** (MissLBower) **13-10-8b** AMaguire (hld up: one pce fr 4 out)	2½	**4**	11/4[1]	72	7
1554[2]	**Rhoman Fun (IRE) (69)** (RHBuckler) **8-10-5** BPowell (nvr nr to chal)	nk	**5**	5/1[2]	68	3
3073[4]	**Full Shilling (USA) (66)** (DLWilliams) **8-9-13b**(3)ow2 GuyLewis (hld up: rdn appr 3 out: sn wknd)	1½	**6**	16/1	64	—
1445[P]	**Salcombe Harbour (NZ) (64)** (DrPPritchard) **13-10-0** DrPPritchard (lw: a bhd)	8	**7**	33/1	55	—
2813[5]	**Spring Loaded (77)** (JGMO'Shea) **6-10-10v**(3) MichaelBrennan (3rd whn fell 11th)		**F**	10/1	—	—
1812[P]	**Fighting Days (USA) (86)** (GLMoore) **11-11-8v** PHolley (led 3rd to 6th: wknd 8th: t.o whn p.u after 4 out)		**P**	20/1	—	—
2660[P]	**Tapageur (91)** (MCPipe) **12-11-13** DWalsh (t.o whn p.u bef 10th)		**P**	10/1	—	—
2892[6]	**Warspite (67)** (PMooney) **7-9-12b[1]**(5) SRyan (5th whn mstke 6th: sn wknd: t.o whn p.u bef 10th)		**P**	25/1	—	—
2910[P]	**Albury Grey (64)** (TPMcGovern) **10-10-0** GCrone (a wl bhd: t.o whn p.u bef 7th)		**P**	25/1	—	—
2905[U]	**Tug Your Forelock (64)** (GFJohnsonHoughton) **6-10-0** JCulloty (bhd tl blnd & uns rdr 12th)		**U**	11/1	—	—

				SP	RR	SF
3001[9]	**Mr Bean (92)** (KRBurke) **7-11-7**(7) AWatt (lw: mstke 4th: mid div whn blnd & unr rdr 3 out)		**U**	9/1	—	—

(SP 127.4%) **14 Rn**

5m 10.4 (31.40) CSF £220.79 CT £1,613.98 TOTE £12.00: £3.20 £6.90 £2.20 (£106.30) Trio £187.40; £134.63 to Market Rasen 18/2/97
OWNER Miss Joy Mailes (CHEPSTOW) BRED S. A. Mailes and Mrs R. Bradley
LONG HANDICAP Albury Grey 9-10 Tug Your Forelock 9-10 Salcombe Harbour (NZ) 9-6
No bid
IN-FOCUS: **This was a quite desperate event, with virtually the whole field having absolutely no hope for the future.**
2756 Opal's Tenspot jumped into the lead three out and plodded on better than his poor rivals. (10/1)
Golden Opal, pulled up in seven of his last nine starts, showed just how frightful this race was, as he actually managed to struggle on for second prize. (25/1)
2796 Whistling Buck (IRE), whose connections reported earlier in the season that he does not like it soft, nevertheless showed the way to the third last, before being put in his place. (13/2)
2910 Master Comedy looked pretty dreadful in the paddock, and was made to appear extremely slow, even in this appalling race. (11/4)
1554 Rhoman Fun (IRE), without a run in nearly three months, needs further and could never get into it. (5/1)
2752 Mr Bean (9/1: 5/1-10/1)

3180 BRITISH EQUESTRIAN INSURANCE BROKERS H'CAP HURDLE (0-115) (4-Y.O+) (Class E)

3-20 (3-20) **2m 6f 110y (11 hdls)** £2,929.50 (£812.00: £388.50) GOING: 1.11 sec per fur (HY)

				SP	RR	SF
1876[2]	**Paddysway (92)** (RHBuckler) **10-10-6** DBridgwater (chsd ldr: led 6th to 3 out: rdn: led nr fin)	—	**1**	9/2[3]	67	—
2820[9]	**Reluckino (88)** (JGMO'Shea) **7-9-13v**(3)ow2 MichaelBrennan (lw: reminder 4th: hdwy 6th: led 3 out: clr appr 2 out: wknd & hdd nr fin)	½	**2**	25/1	63	—
3016[7]	**St Ville (88)** (RHBuckler) **11-10-2b** BPowell (lost pl 8th: rallied flat: r.o wl)	½	**3**	14/1	62	—
2950[6]	**Mirador (94)** (RCurtis) **6-10-8** DMorris (hld up: chsd ldr after 7th tl appr 3 out: rdn: wknd flat)	6	**4**	2/1[1]	64	—
3016[P]	**Cunninghams Ford (IRE) (105)** (AHHarvey) **9-11-5** JAMcCarthy (bhd fr 6th: t.o whn p.u bef 8th)		**P**	33/1	—	—
2817[3]	**Rosencrantz (IRE) (110)** (MissVenetiaWilliams) **5-11-10** AMaguire (hdwy 8th: wknd 3 out: 5th & no ch whn p.u bef 2 out)		**P**	7/2[2]	—	—
1645[P]	**Arabian Sultan (107)** (MCPipe) **10-11-7** DWalsh (led to 6th: wknd 7th: t.o whn p.u bef 8th)		**P**	8/1	—	—
1710[2]	**Daring King (87)** (MJBolton) **7-9-12**(3) LAspell (bhd fr 7th: t.o whn p.u bef 2 out)		**P**	7/1	—	—
816[8]	**Punch's Hotel (97)** (RRowe) **12-10-11b** DO'Sullivan (prom to 5th: t.o whn p.u bef 2 out)		**P**	10/1	—	—

(SP 119.9%) **9 Rn**

6m 1.8 (45.80) CSF £90.80 CT £1,342.60 TOTE £6.90: £1.20 £7.70 £1.90 (£209.00) Trio £54.40 OWNER Mr R. T. C. Searle (BRIDPORT)
BRED Miss H. and Mrs P. Day
LONG HANDICAP Reluckino 9-6
OFFICIAL EXPLANATION **Rosencrantz (IRE): the rider reported that the gelding was unable to handle the soft ground.**
1876 Paddysway was given a lovely ride. Sent on at halfway, he was collared three out and looked in serious trouble as the leader stormed clear. Hopes of success looked pretty remote in the straight, but with the leader tiring badly, he managed to find another effort and got up near the line. (9/2)
Reluckino was given a fine ride and looked to have stolen the race as he led at the third last, and soon forged clear. The danger signs started showing going to the final flight, and he was incredibly tired when eventually collared near the line. (25/1)
St Ville is described by his trainer as a 'real old monkey' and it is not hard to see why. Losing his pitch in the back straight for the final time, he appeared to have no hope going to the second last but he decided to have another go at it on the run-in and finished with a real flourish. (14/1)
2950 Mirador was disappointing for, after taking second place with a circuit to go, she was collared for that position going to the third last and soon in trouble. (2/1)
2817 Rosencrantz (IRE) has done all his winning on a fast surface, and quite simply failed to handle the mud. (7/2: 9/4-4/1)
Arabian Sultan (8/1: 5/1-10/1)

3181 AMBERLEY NOVICES' H'CAP CHASE (0-100) (5-Y.O+) (Class E)

3-50 (3-50) **3m 2f 110y (22 fncs)** £3,183.65 (£951.20: £455.10: £207.05) GOING: 1.11 sec per fur (HY)

				SP	RR	SF
2926[6]	**Furry Fox (IRE) (72)** (RCurtis) **9-11-6** DMorris (hdwy 12th: rdn appr 3 out: led last: drvn out)	—	**1**	7/2[1]	86	18
2947[10]	**Jac Del Prince (60)** (PFNicholls) **7-10-8** PHide (led tl after 1st: mstke 12th: 3rd whn mstke 2 out: r.o one pce)	4	**2**	4/1[2]	72	4
2704[5]	**Plassy Boy (IRE) (70)** (KRBurke) **8-11-4** AMaguire (a.p: led 16th tl blnd & hdd last: sn wknd)	5	**3**	12/1	77	11
3043[9]	**Bournel (76)** (CRBarwell) **9-11-10** BFenton (a.p: mstke 2nd: lft in ld 7th: hdd 13th: rdn appr 3 out: sn wknd)	8	**4**	25/1	78	12
1199[F]	**Bells Wood (60)** (AJKDunn) **8-10-8** SMcNeill (a.p: mstke 3rd: led 13th to 16th: rdn appr 3 out: sn wknd)	2	**5**	20/1	61	—
2819[6]	**Millfrone (IRE) (60)** (RRowe) **7-10-8** DO'Sullivan (led after 1st tl fell 7th)		**F**	16/1	—	—
2749[4]	**Ronans Glen (72)** (MJWilkinson) **10-11-6** TJO'Sullivan (a bhd: mstke 5th: blnd 10th: t.o whn p.u bef 15th)		**P**	8/1	—	—
2876[4]	**Cool Character (IRE) (72)** (RHBuckler) **9-11-6** BPowell (a bhd: t.o whn p.u bef 17th)		**P**	9/2[3]	—	—
2947[9]	**The Millmaster (IRE) (69)** (JohnUpson) **6-11-0**(3) MichaelBrennan (t.o whn p.u bef 16th)		**P**	16/1	—	—
1763[7]	**Akiymann (USA) (69)** (MCPipe) **7-11-3b** DWalsh (5th whn p.u bef 16th)		**P**	10/1	—	—
	Quaker Bob (60) (MissJBower) **12-10-8** KGaule (bkwd: bhd fr 7th: t.o whn p.u bef 13th)		**P**	9/1	—	—
2795[F]	**Gerry's Pride (IRE) (65)** (JWMullins) **6-10-13** SCurran (bhd whn blnd 18th: t.o whn p.u bef 3 out)		**P**	16/1	—	—
3104[U]	**Oneofus (69)** (MrsLRichards) **8-11-3** MRichards (6th whn s.u bnd after 12th)		**S**	14/1	—	—

(SP 131.2%) **13 Rn**

7m 28.4 (48.40) CSF £18.81 CT £149.86 TOTE £4.80: £1.70 £2.20 £4.30 (£16.70) Trio £53.70 OWNER Four Play Racing (LAMBOURN) BRED C. Ronaldson
Furry Fox (IRE) appreciated the longer trip for all he does is stay, and that is exactly what he did here, getting to the front at the last. (7/2)
2704 Jac Del Prince appeared to be travelling quite nicely on the final circuit, but he was quite a few lengths off the leader when a mistake two out did his cause no good. Nevertheless, he did struggle on to take second on the run-in. (4/1: 3/1-9/2)
2077 Plassy Boy (IRE) moved to the front on the final circuit, but a bad error cost him the lead at the last and he was soon beaten. (12/1: op 7/1)
Bournel goes well in the mud, and ran her best race so far this season, only giving best early in the straight. (25/1)
Bells Wood managed to get round for the first time under Rules, but was in trouble early in the straight. (20/1)
2876 Cool Character (IRE) (9/2: 6/1-4/1)
546 Akiymann (USA) (10/1: 6/1-12/1)

3182 JOHN ROGERSON MEMORIAL CHALLENGE TROPHY H'CAP CHASE (0-120) (5-Y.O+) (Class D)

4-20 (4-21) **3m 2f 110y (22 fncs)** £4,010.00 (£1,110.00: £530.00) GOING: 1.11 sec per fur (HY)

	Horse		Pos	SP	RR	SF
2658^{F}	**Flaked Oats (101)** (PFNicholls) **8-11-8** DBridgwater (mstke 12th: hdwy 13th: chsd ldr appr 16th: led & mstke 17th: all out)	—	**1**	Evens^{1}	111	28
3018^{6}	**Woodlands Boy (IRE) (102)** (RCurtis) **9-11-9** DMorris (led: mstke 16th: hdd 17th: rdn appr last: r.o one pce)	1¼	**2**	9/2^{2}	111	28
1961^{4}	**Credon (100)** (SWoodman) **9-11-7** SMcNeill (chsd ldr tl appr 16th: rdn appr last: wknd flat)	30	**3**	20/1	91	8
1947^{5}	**Lorna-Gail (95)** (RHAlner) **11-11-2** AMaguire (a bhd: t.o fr 6th: fell 14th)		**F**	5/1^{3}	—	—
2928^{U}	**Danger Baby (103)** (DLWilliams) **7-11-10** BPowell (hdwy 13th: wknd 16th: p.u bef 17th)		**P**	11/2	—	—
2910*	**Black Church (97)** (RRowe) **11-11-4** DO'Sullivan (a bhd: t.o whn mstke 2 out: p.u bef last)		**P**	13/2	—	—
				(SP 118.3%)		**6 Rn**

7m 25.3 (45.30) CSF £6.22 TOTE £2.00: £1.60 £1.90 (£4.70) OWNER Mr E. B. Swaffield (SHEPTON MALLET) BRED E. B. Swaffield

2658 Flaked Oats moved to the front six out despite making a mistake there but, with the runner-up working away at him, he had a little left in the locker at the line. (Evens)

2575 Woodlands Boy (IRE) is an out-and-out stayer who revels in the mud, and he took the field along. Collared six out, he kept beavering away to make sure the winner had a far from easy race. (9/2)

1961 Credon goes well in the mud and certainly had conditions in his favour. In second place for the first two circuits, he was feeling the pinch going to the last and, very tired on the run-in, was virtually pulled up. (20/1)

1947 Lorna-Gail (5/1: 9/2-8/1)

2821 Danger Baby (11/2: op 3/1)

2910* Black Church was not having a going day. (13/2: 7/2-7/1)

3183 STREBEL BOILERS AND RADIATORS SERIES (QUALIFIER) H'CAP HURDLE (0-125) (5-Y.O+) (Class D)

4-50 (4-50) **2m 2f (9 hdls)** £3,172.50 (£945.00: £450.00: £202.50) GOING: 1.11 sec per fur (HY)

	Horse		Pos	SP	RR	SF
1467^{3}	**Grouseman (113)** (MissHCKnight) **11-11-7b** JCulloty (a.p: led appr 2 out: rdn out)	—	**1**	7/2^{3}	96	—
2828*	**Marius (IRE) (118)** (JTGifford) **7-11-9**(3) LAspell (mstke 3rd: chsd ldr 5th: ev ch 3 out: unable qckn)	11	**2**	13/8^{2}	91	—
	Walking Tall (IRE) (106) (TPMcGovern) **6-11-0** DBridgwater (nvr nr to chal)	10	**3**	14/1	70	—
2792^{12}	**Never Forgotten (92)** (GLMoore) **12-10-0** PHolley (bhd fr 3 out)	19	**4**	40/1	39	—
2670^{2}	**Isaiah (109)** (MrsJCecil) **8-11-3** TKent (led tl appr 2 out: sn wknd)	14	**5**	11/8^{1}	44	—
				(SP 111.5%)		**5 Rn**

4m 58.8 (49.80) CSF £9.15 TOTE £5.10: £2.10 £1.30 (£3.90) OWNER Aquarius (WANTAGE) BRED Robert McCarthy

LONG HANDICAP Never Forgotten 9-2

1467 Grouseman, without a run in three months, went to the front approaching the second last and, rousted along, asserted his authority. (7/2)

2828* Marius (IRE), 8lb higher than he has won off before, had every chance at the third-last, but was unable to contain the winner from the penultimate hurdle. (13/8)

Walking Tall (IRE), off the course for nearly a year, has yet to win on ground worse than good and could never get into it. (14/1: 3/1-16/1)

Never Forgotten, 12lb out of the handicap, was being left behind from the third last. (40/1)

2670 Isaiah has won on this ground but, after setting the pace, tamely dropped away once collared. (11/8)

T/Plpt: £282.30 (38.29 Tckts). T/Qdpt: £31.80 (23.49 Tckts) AK

3050-HEREFORD (R-H) (Good to Soft becoming Soft)

Monday February 17th

WEATHER: rain

3184 PRIMROSE NOVICES' HURDLE (4-Y.O+) (Class E)

2-10 (2-13) **2m 1f (9 hdls)** £2,347.50 (£660.00: £322.50) GOING: 0.97 sec per fur (S)

	Horse		Pos	SP	RR	SF
2791^{2}	**Avanti Express (IRE)** (CREgerton) **7-11-3** JOsborne (mde all: clr 2 out: r.o wl)	—	**1**	4/5^{1}	85	51
	Into The Web (IRE) (MrsMerritaJones) **6-11-3** DerekByrne (bit bkwd: hld up & bhd: stdy hdwy fr 6th: r.o flat: no ch w wnr)	22	**2**	16/1	64+	30
2872^{3}	**Merawang (IRE)** (PFNicholls) **4-10-7** RJohnson (a.p: chsd wnr after 6th: wknd appr 2 out)	2½	**3**	7/2^{2}	62	18
2945^{3}	**Benfleet** (MCPipe) **6-11-3** CMaude (plld hrd: prom: j.slowly 2nd: wknd qckly appr 3 out)	½	**4**	7/1^{3}	62	28
1986^{2}	**Callindoe (IRE)** (JLNeedham) **7-10-12** NWilliamson (bit bkwd: bhd tl sme hdwy appr 5th: wknd 6th)	10	**5**	16/1	47	13
186^{5}	**Backview** (BJLlewellyn) **5-11-3** MrJLLlewellyn (bkwd: prom: chsd wnr 5th tl wknd appr 3 out)	¾	**6**	50/1	51	17
1504^{9}	**Look In The Mirror** (NATwiston-Davies) **6-11-3** CLlewellyn (bhd fr 5th)	9	**7**	33/1	43	9
2840^{10}	**Alistover** (RDickin) **4-9-9**(7) XAizpuru (a bhd)	6	**8**	33/1	32	—
1774^{12}	**Cool Harry (USA)** (HEHaynes) **6-10-10**(7) MrSDurack (bkwd: a bhd: t.o)		**9**	100/1	—	—
	Lucky Escape (CaptTAForster) **6-11-3** SWynne (bit bkwd: bhd fr 6th: t.o)		**10**	33/1	—	—
3004^{P}	**Crown And Cushion (72)** (TRGreathead) **4-10-13b^{1}** NMann (a bhd: t.o whn p.u bef 2 out)		**P**	25/1	—	—
2872^{6}	**Chief Mouse (105)** (MissHCKnight) **4-11-5** GBradley (prom: wkng whn mstke 6th: t.o whn p.u bef 2 out)		**P**	8/1	—	—
	T'Niel (GFierro) **6-10-5**(7) SLycett (s.s: a bhd: t.o whn p.u bef 3 out)		**P**	100/1	—	—
2663^{P}	**Belgran (USA)** (BPreece) **8-11-3** TJenks (a bhd: t.o 5th: p.u bef 3 out)		**P**	100/1	—	—
2035^{7}	**Nanjizal** (KSBridgwater) **5-11-0**(3) RMassey (bit bkwd: bhd fr 4th: t.o whn p.u bef 3 out)		**P**	100/1	—	—
				(SP 131.7%)		**15 Rn**

4m 12.4 (19.40) CSF £17.01 TOTE £1.60: £1.10 £4.20 £1.30 (£14.70) Trio £43.70 OWNER Mrs Sarah Stevens (CHADDLEWORTH) BRED Jim Browne

WEIGHT FOR AGE 4yo-10lb

2791 Avanti Express (IRE) had things pretty much his own way this time. He will miss Cheltenham and go chasing next season. (4/5: op 5/4)

Into The Web (IRE), a winner between the flags in Ireland, ran a race full of promise over an inadequate trip. He is one to keep an eye on. (16/1)

2872 Merawang (IRE) could not live with the winner from the third last. (7/2)

2945 Benfleet should not have been suited by this shorter trip but, running too freely, found the rain-softened ground an even bigger problem. (7/1: op 9/2)

1986 Callindoe (IRE), making her hurdling debut, is bred to need further. (16/1)

Backview looked in need of this. (50/1)

3185 DAFFODIL H'CAP CHASE (0-115) (5-Y.O+) (Class E)

2-40 (2-42) **3m 1f 110y (19 fncs)** £2,875.75 (£871.00: £425.50: £202.75) GOING: 0.97 sec per fur (S)

				SP	RR	SF
2896[3]	**Poucher (IRE) (100)** (CaptTAForster) **7-11-5** SWynne (hld up & bhd: hdwy 11th: hit 15th: led appr 2 out: sn clr: easily)	—	1	9/4[1]	112	8
	Alice Smith (85) (BJEckley) **10-10-4** RJohnson (w ldr: led 7th to 9th: led 3 out: sn hdd: one pce)	14	2	12/1	88	—
1194[5]	**Nevada Gold (98)** (FJYardley) **11-11-3** WMarston (led to 7th: led 9th to 3 out: one pce)	hd	3	12/1	101	—
2665[P]	**Pant Llin (81)** (FJordan) **11-10-0b** RSupple (hdwy 11th: wknd 4 out: t.o)	30	4	20/1	65	—
1951[6]	**Bramblehill Buck (IRE) (109)** (PFNicholls) **8-11-7b**(7) MrJTizzard (prom tl wknd 14th: t.o)	5	5	8/1	90	—
2908[2]	**Keep it Zipped (IRE) (99)** (OSherwood) **7-11-4b** JOsborne (mstke 3rd: lost pl 10th: t.o whn p.u bef 15th)		P	9/2[3]	—	—
2829[7]	**Master Jolson (102)** (NJHenderson) **9-11-7** JRKavanagh (bhd fr 8th: t.o whn p.u bef 3 out)		P	20/1	—	—
3003[2]	**Loch Garman Hotel (IRE) (82)** (PTDalton) **8-10-1**ow1 CMaude (prom tl wknd 11th: t.o whn p.u bef 3 out)		P	100/30[2]	—	—
2754[P]	**Diamond Fort (100)** (JCMcConnochie) **12-11-5** NWilliamson (bhd whn rdn 10th: t.o whn p.u bef 15th)		P	5/1	—	—
	Tirley Missile (81) (JSSmith) **11-10-0** TJMurphy (bhd: mstke 6th: t.o whn p.u bef 15th)		P	33/1	—	—
				(SP 127.7%)	**10 Rn**	

6m 55.9 (45.90) CSF £28.31 CT £264.74 TOTE £2.90: £1.10 £3.00 £2.80 (£8.90) Trio £55.20 OWNER Mrs A. L. Wood (LUDLOW) BRED John Ryan

LONG HANDICAP Pant Llin 9-13 Tirley Missile 9-5

2896 Poucher (IRE) confirmed his trainer's opinion that he wants three miles in testing ground. (9/4)
Alice Smith was left to battle it out for the runner-up spot once the winner went for home. (12/1)
1194 Nevada Gold at least made the prize money this time. (12/1)

3186 COWSLIP NOVICES' H'CAP HURDLE (0-105) (4-Y.O+) (Class E)

3-10 (3-15) **2m 3f 110y (11 hdls)** £2,337.00 (£657.00: £321.00) GOING: Not Established

				SP	RR	SF
2662[5]	**Spring Double (IRE) (91)** (NATwiston-Davies) **6-11-6** CLlewellyn (hld up: hdwy appr 8th: led appr 3 out: hdd last: sn led again: r.o wl)	—	1	12/1	78	1
2634[5]	**Konvekta Queen (IRE) (90)** (OSherwood) **6-11-5** JOsborne (hld up & bhd: hdwy 6th: led last: sn hdd: nt qckn)	1¾	2	6/1	76	—
2552[5]	**Melstock Meggie (90)** (MrsJPitman) **7-11-5** NWilliamson (a.p: led 7th tl appr 3 out: wknd appr last)	9	3	4/1[2]	68	—
2893[2]	**Winter Rose (76)** (MissPMWhittle) **6-9-12**(7) KHibbert (bhd tl hdwy 8th: nt rch ldrs)	15	4	16/1	42	—
3050[5]	**Fastini Gold (77)** (RJPrice) **5-10-6** CMaude (a bhd: t.o)	24	5	16/1	23	—
2897[2]	**Little Shefford (83)** (MPMuggeridge) **5-10-12** ILawrence (led to 7th: wknd 8th: t.o)	14	6	12/1	18	—
2870[10]	**Hanging Grove (IRE) (85)** (PGMurphy) **7-11-0** NMann (a bhd: t.o)	16	7	25/1	7	—
3050*	**Ranger Sloane (81)** (GFierro) **5-10-10** 7x RFarrant (mid div whn fell 5th)		F	8/1	—	—
2878[F]	**Sioux To Speak (89)** (MissHCKnight) **5-11-4** GBradley (chsd ldr to 6th: wknd 7th: t.o whn p.u bef 2 out)		P	11/2[3]	—	—
3000[5]	**Market Mayhem (88)** (JLSpearing) **7-11-3** TJMurphy (a bhd: t.o whn p.u bef 3 out)		P	14/1	—	—
3050[F]	**High Post (80)** (GAHam) **8-10-6**(3) RMassey (plld up lame after 4th)		P	33/1	—	—
3004*	**Milling Brook (82)** (JMBradley) **5-10-11** RJohnson (hmpd 5th: sn bhd: t.o whn p.u bef 3 out)		P	12/1	—	—
2897*	**River Wye (IRE) (95)** (GHYardley) **5-11-10** VSlattery (hld up: hdwy appr 7th: rdn & wknd appr 8th: t.o whn p.u bef 3 out)		P	7/2[1]	—	—
2771[F]	**Country Minstrel (IRE) (74)** (SADouch) **6-9-10**(7) CRae (hld up: hdwy appr 7th: wknd appr 3 out: p.u bef last)		P	14/1	—	—
3050[3]	**Sylvester (IRE) (73)** (MissAEBroyd) **7-9-13**(3) PHenley (bhd: mstke 8th: t.o whn p.u bef 3 out)		P	16/1	—	—
2865[9]	**Dark Truffle (82)** (TRGeorge) **4-10-1** SWynne (prom to 6th: t.o whn p.u bef 3 out)		P	16/1	—	—
				(SP 149.7%)	**16 Rn**	

5m 1.9 (30.90) CSF £92.72 CT £334.46 TOTE £23.20: £3.20 £4.10 £1.50 £3.50 (£55.90) Trio £115.30 OWNER Mrs Lorna Berryman (CHELTENHAM) BRED Mrs Catherine Kenneally

WEIGHT FOR AGE 4yo-10lb

OFFICIAL EXPLANATION River Wye (IRE): lost a shoe during the race.

2662 Spring Double (IRE), who tends to idle in front, quickly responded when taken on at the final flight. (12/1)
2634 Konvekta Queen (IRE) showed that soft ground was not the problem when she was pulled up on her hurdling debut. (6/1)
2552 Melstock Meggie had a stiffer test of stamina this time due to the ground. (4/1)
2893 Winter Rose was 6lb lower than when last in a handicap. (16/1)

3187 SNOWDROP NOVICES' CHASE (5-Y.O+) (Class E)

3-40 (3-42) **2m (12 fncs)** £2,986.50 (£839.00: £409.50) GOING: 1.14 sec per fur (HY)

				SP	RR	SF
3073[F]	**Elzoba (FR)** (MCPipe) **5-10-7** CMaude (mde all: led clr 4 out: unchal)	—	1	Evens[2]	104+	42
2810[5]	**Heathyards Boy (67)** (DMcCain) **7-11-2b** TJenks (prom: mstke & rdn 5th: mstke 7th: sn wknd: lft poor 2nd 2 out)	dist	2	66/1	—	—
	Relaxed Lad (JHPeacock) **8-11-2** RBellamy (hld up & plld hrd: mstke 3rd: lost tch fr 6th: t.o)	21	3	200/1	—	—
3059[2]	**Purbeck Cavalier (77)** (RHAlner) **8-11-2b** RJohnson (prom: ev ch whn blnd bdly 4 out: nt rcvr: wknd & no ch whn fell 2 out)		F	10/1[3]	—	—
2635[P]	**Master Tribe (IRE)** (MrsJPitman) **7-11-2** NWilliamson (hld up: hdwy 4th: mstke 6th (water): 3rd & wkng whn mstke 8th: p.u bef 4 out)		P	10/11[1]	—	—
				(SP 113.5%)	**5 Rn**	

4m 12.2 (21.20) CSF £23.20 TOTE £2.00: £1.10 £8.90 (£9.50) OWNER Mr M. C. Pipe (WELLINGTON) BRED Mme Etiennette Dubois

WEIGHT FOR AGE 5yo-9lb

3073 Elzoba (FR) made amends for his unlucky defeat last week in what turned out to be another bad contest. (Evens)
Heathyards Boy was lucky to finish second. (66/1)
2635 Master Tribe (IRE), who bruised a foot at Haydock, was a bitter disappointment on his chasing debut. His rider considered he was not happy on the soft ground, and added that the gelding was never jumping after landing on the lip of the water. (10/11: tchd evens)

3188 BLUEBELL NOVICES' H'CAP CHASE (0-105) (5-Y.O+) (Class E)

4-10 (4-12) **2m 3f (14 fncs)** £2,875.75 (£871.00: £425.50: £202.75) GOING: 1.14 sec per fur (HY)

				SP	RR	SF
3051*	**Cardinal Rule (IRE) (80)** (MissVenetiaWilliams) **8-10-13** 7x NWilliamson (mde virtually all: clr 2 out: r.o wl)	—	1	6/4[1]	95	21
2819[3]	**Super Ritchart (84)** (BPalling) **9-11-3** TJenks (a.p: chsd wnr 4 out: wknd appr 2 out)	13	2	14/1	88	14

3051[3] **Chris's Glen (75)** (JMBradley) **8-10-8v** RJohnson (chsd wnr to 4 out: sn wknd) ....13 **3** 16/1 68 —
2795[2] **Winnow (71)** (AndrewTurnell) **7-9-11**(7) CRae (hld up: hdwy 4th: wknd 10th) ....16 **4** 11/2[3] 51 —
3001[5] **Burntwood Melody (67)** (PTDalton) **6-10-0** RSupple (a bhd: t.o) ....dist **5** 25/1 — —
2873[6] **Madam Rose (IRE) (68)** (JWMullins) **7-9-8**(7)ow1 DavidTurner (hdwy 5th: wknd 8th: t.o whn blnd & uns rdr 2 out: rmntd) ....dist **6** 50/1 — —
Mindyerownbusiness (IRE) (67) (RLee) **8-10-0** SWynne (hmpd 4th: fell 5th) .... **F** 20/1 — —
2795[F] **Saxon Mead (67)** (PJHobbs) **7-10-0b** GTormey (fell 4th) .... **F** 10/1 — —
2896[F] **Dara's Course (IRE) (74)** (MissPMWhittle) **8-10-7** MrAPhillips (a bhd: t.o whn p.u bef 3 out) .... **P** 20/1 — —
2807[3] **Ekeus (IRE) (67)** (JSKing) **7-10-0** TJMurphy (mstke 3rd: bhd fr 10th: t.o whn p.u bef 3 out) .... **P** 20/1 — —
Little Gains (69) (RLee) **8-9-13**(3)ow2 PHenley (bit bkwd: a bhd: t.o whn p.u bef 3 out) .... **P** 33/1 — —
3001[3] **Latest Thyne (IRE) (95)** (CaptTAForster) **7-12-0** CLlewellyn (bhd: mstke 9th: t.o whn p.u bef 3 out) .... **P** 7/2[2] — —
3051[P] **Colonel Colt (75)** (RDickin) **6-10-8** WMarston (a bhd: t.o whn p.u bef 4 out) .... **P** 20/1 — —
2548[4] **Gipsy Rambler (67)** (PJBevan) **12-10-0** WWorthington (bit bkwd: a bhd: t.o whn p.u bef 3 out) .... **P** 16/1 — —
2876[2] **Mozemo (84)** (MCPipe) **10-11-3** CMaude (prom tl blnd & uns rdr 6th) .... **U** 13/2 — —
(SP 146.3%) **15 Rn**

5m 2.1 (32.10) CSF £24.63 CT £286.57 TOTE £2.90: £1.80 £3.20 £4.30 (£29.60) Trio £54.30 OWNER Mr Peter Burch (HEREFORD) BRED Mrs Patricia Mackean

LONG HANDICAP Mindyerownbusiness (IRE) 9-13 Ekeus (IRE) 9-7 Little Gains 9-7 Burntwood Melody 9-12 Madam Rose (IRE) 9-7 Saxon Mead 9-10

3051* Cardinal Rule (IRE) had it even softer than last week, and completed the hat-trick without too much fuss. (6/4)
2819 Super Ritchart came up against a rival in top form. (14/1)
3051 Chris's Glen, 7lb better off with the winner than a week ago, had to contend with even more give underfoot. (16/1)
2795 Winnow was 12lb better off with the winner than when beaten five lengths at Plumpton. (11/2)
1875 Saxon Mead (10/1: op 6/1)
2876 Mozemo (13/2: op 7/2)

3189 CROCUS NOVICES' HURDLE (I) (5-Y.O+) (Class E)
4-40 (4-41) **3m 2f (13 hdls)** £1,882.00 (£527.00: £256.00) GOING: 1.14 sec per fur (HY)

SP RR SF

2662[7] **Fancy Nancy (IRE) (75)** (MissCJohnsey) **6-10-7** CMaude (hld up: hdwy 8th: led 9th: r.o wl) ....— **1** 7/1 51 —
2820[15] **Cardinal Gayle (IRE) (68)** (RHAlner) **7-10-9**(3) PHenley (hld up: hdwy 7th: rdn & wnt 2nd appr 2 out: btn whn hit last) ....13 **2** 3/1[1] 48 —
3072[6] **Gi Moss** (PRHarriss) **10-10-7b** WMarston (dropped rr & rdn 8th: mstke 10th: rallied appr 3 out: btn whn mstke 2 out) ....10 **3** 15/2 37 —
1297[3] **One More Dime (IRE) (74)** (JLNeedham) **7-10-7** NWilliamson (led to 9th: wknd appr 2 out) ....16 **4** 7/2[2] 27 —
2006[8] **Wickens One (67)** (DPGeraghty) **7-10-7** RSupple (hld up: hdwy 7th: wknd 9th) ....14 **5** 16/1 18 —
1431[9] **Zaggy Lane** (MrsRGHenderson) **5-10-7**(5) DSalter (bit bkwd: prom to 10th) ....14 **6** 33/1 15 —
1995[4] **Tudor Town (69)** (KBishop) **9-10-12** LHarvey (hld up: hdwy appr 9th: wknd after 10th: t.o) ....18 **7** 7/1 4 —
Woldsman (NATwiston-Davies) **7-10-12** CLlewellyn (lw: hld up: hdwy whn p.u after 6th) .... **P** 4/1[3] — —
2546[R] **Kyle David (IRE)** (FJordan) **5-10-12** RJohnson (bit bkwd: prom tl hrd rdn & wknd qckly after 7th: p.u after 8th) .... **P** 20/1 — —
1562[8] **Milly le Moss (IRE) (58)** (RJEckley) **8-10-7v** VSlattery (dropped rr & rdn 5th: t.o 7th: p.u bef 9th) .... **P** 9/1 — —
(SP 127.6%) **10 Rn**

7m 11.7 (68.70) CSF £28.99 TOTE £10.60: £2.10 £1.30 £2.60 (£32.10) Trio £111.60 OWNER Mr T. A. Johnsey (CHEPSTOW) BRED Millhill Stud

Fancy Nancy (IRE) handled the testing conditions well, but this was a poor event. (7/1)
2620 Cardinal Gayle (IRE) could not go with the winner in what became a slog in the mud. (3/1)
Gi Moss was stepping up considerably in distance. (15/2)
1297 One More Dime (IRE), carrying condition, did not last home in the rain-softened ground. (7/2)
Woldsman caught the eye in the paddock, and had just moved up when pulled up before halfway. (4/1: op 5/2)

3190 CROCUS NOVICES' HURDLE (II) (5-Y.O+) (Class E)
5-10 (5-10) **3m 2f (13 hdls)** £1,871.50 (£524.00: £254.50) GOING: 1.14 sec per fur (HY)

SP RR SF

2746[9] **Sammorello (IRE)** (NATwiston-Davies) **6-10-12** CLlewellyn (hld up: hdwy appr 9th: btn whn lft in ld 2 out: r.o) ....— **1** 11/4[2] 49 —
2905[5] **Cravate (FR) (63)** (PJHobbs) **7-10-0**(7) MMoran (led 2nd to 10th: one pce) ....5 **2** 9/2[3] 41 —
2870[8] **Otter Prince (60)** (TRGeorge) **8-10-12** RJohnson (prom: hit 9th: wknd after 10th: t.o) ....dist **3** 7/1 — —
2891[8] **Blazing Miracle (70)** (MrsRGHenderson) **5-10-2**(5) DSalter (a.p: led 10th: 15l clr whn fell 2 out) .... **F** 2/1[1] — —
2080[6] **Ledburian** (MissPMWhittle) **7-10-5**(7) KHibbert (prom tl wknd after 8th: t.o whn p.u bef 3 out) .... **P** 6/1 — —
1766[8] **Shrimp** (RHAlner) **6-10-7** NWilliamson (bit bkwd: bhd fr 3rd: t.o whn p.u bef 3 out) .... **P** 9/1 — —
2088[10] **Beths Wish (55)** (GMPrice) **8-10-7** JRKavanagh (led to 2nd: lost pl 5th: t.o whn p.u bef 3 out) .... **P** 16/1 — —
2878[6] **Mingay** (GrahamRichards) **6-10-5**(7) MrSPrior (lost pl 3rd: reminder after 7th: t.o whn p.u bef 9th) .... **P** 25/1 — —
(SP 124.7%) **8 Rn**

7m 20.9 (77.90) CSF £16.01 TOTE £3.40: £2.10 £1.20 £2.60 (£16.60) Trio £15.90 OWNER Mrs S. A. MacEchern (CHELTENHAM) BRED Park Enterprises

Sammorello (IRE) was a most fortunate winner. (11/4)
2905 Cravate (FR) is blessed with stamina rather than speed. (9/2)
Otter Prince, trying a longer trip, had been tried in blinkers last time. (7/1)
2620 Blazing Miracle had this in the bag when crumpling on landing at the penultimate flight. (2/1: op evens)
Shrimp (9/1: 6/1-10/1)

T/Jkpt: £7,100.00 (0.1 Tckts); £7,789.49 to Market Rasen 18/2/97. T/Plpt: £99.60 (137.55 Tckts). T/Qdpt: £41.40 (17.37 Tckts) KH

2918-CARLISLE (R-H) - Tuesday February 18th
3191 Abandoned-Waterlogged

2669-MARKET RASEN (R-H) (Good, Good to soft st)
Tuesday February 18th
One fence omitted each circ 4th & 6th race
WEATHER: windy with snow showers

3197 LOUTH NOVICES' HURDLE (4-Y.O+) (Class D)
2-00 (2-00) **2m 1f 110y (8 hdls)** £3,300.20 (£917.20: £440.60) GOING: 0.82 sec per fur (S)

				SP	RR	SF
3019*	**My Cheeky Man** (DNicholson) **6-11-9** RJohnson (hld up: stdy hdwy 4th: hit 2 out: styd on wl u.p flat: led post)	—	1	15/2[3]	82	64
2917*	**Whip Hand (IRE)** (JGFitzGerald) **6-12-1** JOsborne (lw: hld up: stdy hdwy 4th: led appr 2 out: jst ct)	s.h	2	6/5[1]	88	70
3041[10]	**Morpheus (99)** (DNicholson) **8-11-3** AMaguire (stdd s: hld up & wl bhd: stdy hdwy 3 out: styd on between last 2)	19	3	11/1	59	41
2805[3]	**Country Lover** (MCPipe) **6-11-3b[1]** CMaude (lw: chsd ldr: led appr 3 out: hdd appr next: sn wknd)	¾	4	11/1	58	40
2794[2]	**Cotteir Chief (IRE)** (JNeville) **6-11-3** RDunwoody (hld up & bhd: stdy hdwy 4th: rdn & wknd appr 2 out)	24	5	9/2[2]	36	18
2953[3]	**Billy Bushwacker** (MrsMReveley) **6-11-3** NSmith (lw: j.slowly: hdwy 4th: sn prom: wknd appr 2 out)	½	6	10/1	36	18
	Tonto (WHTinning) **4-10-7** DerekByrne (sn bhd)	6	7	50/1	30	2
2859[12]	**Nexsis Star** (MrsSJSmith) **4-10-7** RGuest (nt j.w: chsd ldrs tl wknd 3 out)	7	8	16/1	24	—
2946[8]	**First Gold** (JWharton) **8-11-3** JRKavanagh (lw: sn bhd: t.o)	dist	9	50/1	—	—
2626[2]	**Slide On** (PDEvans) **7-11-3** NWilliamson (mstkes: blnd bdly & lost pl 4th: t.o whn p.u lame bef last)		P	14/1	—	—
	Marigliano (USA) (KAMorgan) **4-10-7** ASSmith (lw: set str pce: hdd appr 3 out: wknd qckly appr last: t.o whn p.u bef last)		P	17/2	—	—
2861[U]	**Florrie Gunner** (JJQuinn) **7-10-12** JCallaghan (lw: mstkes: sn wl bhd & drvn along: t.o whn p.u bef last)		P	50/1	—	—
	O K Kealy (MCChapman) **7-11-3** WWorthington (sn bhd: t.o whn p.u bef last)		P	100/1	—	—

(SP 131.1%) **13 Rn**

4m 18.8 (15.80) CSF £17.29 TOTE £11.50: £1.90 £1.90 £2.50 (£10.10) Trio £68.30 OWNER Mrs A. A. Shutes (TEMPLE GUITING) BRED Mrs Diana Shutes
WEIGHT FOR AGE 4yo-10lb

OFFICIAL EXPLANATION **Morpheus: the rider stated that his instructions were to settle his mount at the back, as he had been too keen in his previous two races, and to gradually move through the field. However, the gelding hung right, especially when under pressure in the closing stages. The trainer's representative added that the horse has had leg problems in the past, and that he was satisfied with the ride given here.**

3019* My Cheeky Man was already under pressure when he met the second last flight all wrong. Responding to his rider's urgings, he put his head in front right on the line. He may have had luck on his side here, but he looks essentially a stayer. (15/2: 9/2-8/1)

2917* Whip Hand (IRE) travelled well in a strongly-run race. Taking a decisive advantage at the second last, his rider seemed unconcerned by My Cheeky Man and allowed him to fiddle the last. Coming under pressure in the final 75 yards, he was pipped on the post. Conceding the winner 6lb, he really ought to have won this. (6/5)

2547 Morpheus was dropped right out at the start. Only asked to do enough to secure third, he looks capable of better than this and will be an interesting proposition in a novices' handicap. (11/1)

2805 Country Lover, in blinkers as opposed to a visor, sat upsides the leader who seemed to go very fast. It was no surprise to see him run out of petrol going to two out. (11/1: 8/1-12/1)

2794 Cotteir Chief (IRE), who was never the most consistent of animals on the Flat, moved up on the bridle at halfway, but found next to nothing when asked to join issue. (9/2)

2953 Billy Bushwacker jumped hesitantly. He certainly has the ability to win a run-of-the-mill novices' event, but his jumping would have to improve. (10/1: op 6/1)

Marigliano (USA), very keen going to post, seemed to set a suicidal pace. (17/2: 5/1-9/1)

3198 QUEENS ROYAL LANCERS H'CAP CHASE (0-120) (5-Y.O+) (Class D)
2-30 (2-30) **2m 4f (15 fncs)** £3,522.00 (£1,056.00: £508.00: £234.00) GOING: 0.82 sec per fur (S)

				SP	RR	SF
3101[2]	**Aljadeer (USA) (110)** (MWEasterby) **8-11-10** NWilliamson (hld up: hdwy 8th: led 3 out: rdn clr last: drvn out)	—	1	7/1	125	36
2814[3]	**Rustic Air (104)** (JGFitzGerald) **10-11-4** PCarberry (lw: led 2nd: blnd 4 out: hdd next: rdn & wknd 2 out)	17	2	6/1	105	16
3069[3]	**Netherby Said (104)** (PBeaumont) **7-11-4** RSupple (lw: mstkes: plld hrd: trckd ldrs: blnd 7th & 10th: kpt on fr 3 out)	hd	3	4/1[3]	105	16
2660[P]	**Jacob's Wife (106)** (PRWebber) **7-11-6** JOsborne (hdwy 11th: kpt on one pce fr 4 out)	6	4	14/1	103	14
2922[6]	**Farney Glen (87)** (JJO'Neill) **10-9-10(5)** RMcGrath (sn bhd: sme hdwy 3 out: nvr nr ldrs)	5	5	20/1	80	—
3018[7]	**Dolikos (97)** (THCaldwell) **10-10-11** TJMurphy (hld up: effrt 9th: n.d)	10	6	25/1	82	—
2899*	**Cattly Hang (IRE) (105)** (JPLeigh) **7-11-5** ADobbin (lw: outpcd & drvn along 8th: n.d)	1	7	2/1[1]	89	—
2949*	**Distinctive (IRE) (109)** (MJWilkinson) **8-11-9** RDunwoody (led to 2nd: trckd ldrs tl wknd qckly 10th: t.o whn p.u bef 3 out)		P	3/1[2]	—	—
2695[P]	**The Flying Footman (90)** (RDickin) **11-10-4** JCulloty (in tch: blnd 4th: p.u bef 8th)		P	33/1	—	—

(SP 123.3%) **9 Rn**

5m 17.2 (26.20) CSF £45.80 CT £179.11 TOTE £7.50: £1.30 £2.00 £1.80 (£19.60) Trio £15.20 OWNER Miss V. Foster (SHERIFF HUTTON) BRED Arthur I. Appleton

OFFICIAL EXPLANATION **Cattly Hang (IRE): the trainer reported that the gelding finished distressed.**

3101 Aljadeer (USA) responded favourably to a more positive ride than usual. Meeting the last well, he soon pulled way clear, but despite the wide margin, was very tired at the line. (7/1)

2814 Rustic Air set a strong pace. He ploughed through the fourth last, breaking the rail on the landing side, but his brilliant jockey did not move an inch. (6/1)

3069 Netherby Said, 13lb higher than when successful on his reappearance at Southwell, made several bad mistakes, and it was surprising to see him keep going all the way to the line. (4/1)

2009 Jacob's Wife seemed to stay this extended trip alright. (14/1)

2922 Farney Glen may be capable of slightly better over further. (20/1)

2899* Cattly Hang (IRE) seemed to sulk. His trainer said he finished distressed. (2/1)

2949* Distinctive (IRE), off a 6lb higher mark, was taken on for the lead and seemed to resent it. (3/1)

3199 SHERWOOD RANGERS YEOMANRY H'CAP HURDLE (0-120) (4-Y.O+) (Class D)
3-00 (3-00) **2m 1f 110y (8 hdls)** £2,796.20 (£773.20: £368.60) GOING: 0.82 sec per fur (S)

				SP	RR	SF
2950[7]	**Non Vintage (IRE) (120)** (MCChapman) **6-12-0** WWorthington (hdwy 3 out: led between last 2: sn clr)	—	1	4/1[3]	105	53
3035[8]	**Tip it In (92)** (ASmith) **8-9-7**(7) NHorrocks (chsd ldrs: outpcd after 3 out: styd on appr last)	7	2	4/1[3]	71	19
2780[5]	**Our Kris (116)** (MESowersby) **5-11-10b** JRKavanagh (lw: chsd ldr: rdn to ld 2 out: sn hdd: one pce)	2½	3	12/1	92	40
3034[4]	**Tapatch (IRE) (95)** (MWEasterby) **9-10-3** NWilliamson (hld up: mstke 2nd: rdn 3 out: hung rt: nt run on)	2	4	7/1	70	18
2957[3]	**Summerhill Special (IRE) (113)** (DWBarker) **6-11-7** RGuest (hld up: pckd bdly 3rd: rdn 3 out: no rspnse)	2	5	5/2[1]	86	34
2040[8]	**Robert's Toy (IRE) (115)** (MCPipe) **6-11-9b** CMaude (lw: led to 2 out: wknd last)	1	6	3/1[2]	87	35
				(SP 113.8%)		**6 Rn**

4m 22.4 (19.40) CSF £18.72 TOTE £4.20: £2.30 £2.10 (£5.70) OWNER Mr Alan Mann (MARKET RASEN) BRED Leon O'Coileain
LONG HANDICAP Tip it In 9-12
2059 Non Vintage (IRE), given a real chance at the weights, was suited by the strongly-run race. (4/1)
1701* Tip it In, who likes sharp tracks, presumably needed it last time after a two-month break. (4/1)
945 Our Kris ran his best race for some time. (12/1)
3034 Tapatch (IRE) wanted nothing to do with it. (7/1)
2957 Summerhill Special (IRE) pecked badly at the third and ran no race at all. (5/2)
1382 Robert's Toy (IRE), with the blinkers back on, was soon setting a strong pace but was legless in the straight. (3/1)

3200 E.B.F. TATTERSALLS (IRELAND) (QUALIFIER) NOVICES' CHASE (6-Y.O+ Mares Only) (Class E)
3-30 (3-30) **2m 1f 110y (11 fncs)** £3,094.75 (£928.00: £446.50: £205.75) GOING: 0.82 sec per fur (S)

				SP	RR	SF
1310[4]	**Chadwick's Ginger** (WHTinning) **9-10-12** DerekByrne (mde all: styd on wl fr 2 out)	—	1	2/1[1]	101	—
2861[11]	**Hutcel Loch** (RDEWoodhouse) **6-10-12** ASSmith (wnt 2nd 7th: no imp whn blnd 2 out)	6	2	8/1	96	—
3134[U]	**Merilena (IRE)** (GAHubbard) **7-10-12** BFenton (lw: lost pl 5th: blnd next: sn t.o: styd on fr 3 out)	7	3	9/2[3]	89	—
3031[3]	**Auntie Alice** (JGFitzGerald) **7-10-12** JOsborne (chsd ldrs: outpcd whn blnd 7th: n.d after)	12	4	9/2[3]	78	—
3030[F]	**Chorus Line (IRE) (84)** (PBeaumont) **8-10-12** RSupple (lw: chsd ldrs: j.slowly 5th: wknd appr 3 out: poor 3rd whn blnd last)	21	5	4/1[2]	59	—
	Knockreigh Cross (IRE) (BSRothwell) **8-10-12** JSupple (swtg: sn wl bhd)	8	6	50/1	52	—
2864[3]	**High Penhowe** (JJQuinn) **9-10-12** WMarston (nt j.w: sn bhd: t.o fr 6th)	dist	7	11/1	—	—
93[2]	**Morcat** (CIRatcliffe) **8-10-12** MrCMulhall (in tch: effrt 7th: sn wknd: p.u bef 2 out)		P	12/1	—	—
2939[9]	**Riverbank Red** (WClay) **6-10-9**(3) GuyLewis (chsd ldrs: drvn along 6th: lost pl next: p.u bef 2 out)		P	33/1	—	—
				(SP 121.7%)		**9 Rn**

4m 47.2 (32.20) CSF £18.59 TOTE £3.00: £1.30 £1.90 £2.20 (£25.20) Trio £44.20 OWNER Mr W. H. Tinning (THORNTON-LE-CLAY) BRED Ian Hunter and A. Knight
1310 Chadwick's Ginger, who likes to get her toe in, jumped soundly and never looked in any real danger in this poor mares' race. (2/1: op 3/1)
2504* Hutcel Loch, making her debut over fences, was well held when she fell through the second last. (8/1)
3134 Merilena (IRE), having her second race in four days, struggled badly to go the pace. She needs at least another half-mile. (9/2)
3031 Auntie Alice, on her chasing debut, was already struggling when she blundered at the seventh. (9/2)
3030 Chorus Line (IRE) jumped hesitantly at the water. Very tired from the home turn, she almost fell at the last. (4/1)

3201 LEVY BOARD H'CAP HURDLE (0-105) (4-Y.O+) (Class F)
4-00 (4-01) **2m 5f 110y (10 hdls)** £2,442.50 (£680.00: £327.50) GOING: 0.82 sec per fur (S)

				SP	RR	SF
2654[P]	**Boston Man (84)** (RDEWoodhouse) **6-10-11** PCarberry (sn chsng ldr: led after 5th: drvn out: hld on towards fin)	—	1	16/1	69	19
1563[F]	**Hancock (73)** (JHetherton) **5-10-0** WMarston (in tch: wnt 2nd after 3 out: kpt on wl flat)	1	2	50/1	57	7
2915[6]	**Galen (IRE) (89)** (MrsMReveley) **6-11-2** RDunwoody (mid div: drvn along & outpcd 6th: kpt on fr 2 out)	27	3	13/2[2]	53	3
2702[P]	**Wassl Street (IRE) (101)** (KAMorgan) **5-12-0** ASSmith (chsd ldrs tl wknd after 3 out)	4	4	9/1	62	12
3002[5]	**Alaskan Heir (79)** (AStreeter) **6-10-6** TEley (lw: chsd ldrs: drvn along 7th: sn wknd)	2	5	20/1	39	—
3002[2]	**Kadari (87)** (WClay) **8-10-11v**(3) GuyLewis (in tch: drvn along 7th: sn wl outpcd)	¾	6	8/1[3]	46	—
2915[9]	**Exemplar (IRE) (88)** (MrsSJSmith) **9-11-1** RGuest (hdwy & drvn along 6th: outpcd fr next)	3	7	16/1	45	—
3004[3]	**Mrs Robinson (IRE) (78)** (JMackie) **6-10-2**(3) EHusband (sn bhd: sme hdwy 2 out: n.d)	nk	8	8/1[3]	35	—
2842[7]	**Major Yaasi (USA) (85)** (JAGlover) **7-10-12b**[1] JOsborne (chsd ldrs tl wknd 3 out)	9	9	16/1	35	—
2828[3]	**Sassiver (USA) (88)** (PAKelleway) **7-11-1** KGaule (hmpd & lost pl 5th: sme hdwy 7th: n.d)	5	10	10/1	34	—
	Shoofe (USA) (75) (KAMorgan) **9-10-2** RJohnson (in rr fr 6th)	5	11	20/1	18	—
2882[16]	**Bill and Win (73)** (TWall) **6-9-11v**(3) RMassey (sn bhd & drvn along)	1¼	12	66/1	15	—
2552[13]	**Grand Cru (89)** (MrsMReveley) **6-10-13**(3) GLee (bhd: sme hdwy whn hmpd 5th: blnd 3 out: sn wknd)	7	13	14/1	25	—
3031[F]	**Just Supposen (IRE) (83)** (BSRothwell) **6-10-10** JSupple (sn bhd)	7	14	50/1	14	—
2919[5]	**Final Beat (IRE) (76)** (JWCurtis) **8-10-3** BFenton (lw: bhd & drvn along 5th)	12	15	33/1	—	—
	Grace Card (95) (BRCambidge) **11-11-8** NWilliamson (sn bhd: t.o fr 6th)	20	16	20/1	2	—
2877[P]	**Passed Pawn (101)** (MCPipe) **10-11-7**(7) GSupple (led: clr 3rd: hdd & wknd qckly after 5th: t.o 7th)	dist	17	20/1	—	—
2670[6]	**Gymcrak Tiger (IRE) (87)** (GHolmes) **7-11-0** AMaguire (hld up: b.d 5th)		B	9/1	—	—
3063*	**Mayb-Mayb (75)** (JNeville) **7-10-2** 7x TJMurphy (prom whn fell 5th)		F	11/4[1]	—	—
				(SP 143.0%)		**19 Rn**

5m 33.3 (29.30) CSF £639.97 CT £5,176.91 TOTE £25.50: £3.00 £92.40 £2.00 £2.60 (£1,477.30; £1,040.39 to Folkestone 19/2/97) Trio Not won; £1,213.33 to Folkestone 19/2/97 OWNER Mr M. K. Oldham (YORK) BRED Miss A. L. M. King
LONG HANDICAP Bill and Win 8-9 Hancock 9-11
2654 Boston Man ran very badly indeed at Carlisle, and again had the tongue-strap left off. Given a most positive ride, he showed the right sort of spirit and is a chaser in the making. (16/1)
Hancock, having his first outing for 77 days, belied his odds, sticking on really strongly, and was the only one to make a race of it. (50/1)
2915 Galen (IRE), in trouble a long way out, looks a bit high in the weights. (13/2)
2702 Wassl Street (IRE), pulled up 26 days earlier, suddenly became legless on the home turn. (9/1)
Alaskan Heir, suited by the give underfoot - the going looked a good deal softer than the official version - ran his best race so far this time. (20/1)
3063* Mayb-Mayb took a crashing fall. (11/4)

3202 ALFORD NOVICES' CHASE (5-Y.O+) (Class E)
4-30 (4-31) **3m 1f (17 fncs)** £3,068.75 (£920.00: £442.50: £203.75) GOING: 0.82 sec per fur (S)

				SP	RR	SF
2699[2]	**Random Harvest (IRE) (104)** (MrsMReveley) **8-11-10** RDunwoody (lw: w ldrs: led 9th: qcknd clr appr 2 out: easily)	—	**1**	11/10[1]	119+	15
2007[6]	**Slideofhill (IRE)** (JJO'Neill) **8-11-4** MrPFenton (bit bkwd: outpcd & pushed along 12th: hdwy 3 out: styd on flat)	23	**2**	9/1[3]	98	—
2841[U]	**Whattabob (IRE) (105)** (NJHenderson) **8-11-10** NWilliamson (mstkes: trckd ldrs: ev ch tl rdn & wknd appr 3 out: 2nd & tired whn hit last)	28	**3**	2/1[2]	86	—
2789[5]	**Highbeath** (MrsMReveley) **6-11-4** NSmith (outpcd & drvn along 12th: sn bhd: t.o)	dist	**4**	20/1	—	—
2788*	**Kings Sermon (IRE) (85)** (PBeaumont) **8-11-10** RSupple (led to 9th: outpcd & drvn along whn blnd 12th: poor 4th whn fell 2 out)		**F**	11/1	—	—
	Claverhouse (IRE) (JGFitzGerald) **8-11-4** JOsborne (plld hrd: trckd ldrs: hit 10th: wknd 12th: bhd whn p.u bef 14th)		**P**	10/1	—	—
2630[U]	**I'm in Clover (IRE) (72)** (JNorton) **8-11-4v** WMarston (blnd 2nd: sn drvn along & bhd: t.o whn p.u bef 12th)		**P**	50/1	—	—
2037[7]	**Pandora's Prize (60)** (JLSpearing) **11-10-6b**(7) MrSJoynes (trckd ldrs tl lost pl 12th: t.o whn p.u bef last)		**P**	50/1	—	—
				(SP 117.1%)	**8 Rn**	

6m 51.6 (40.60) CSF £11.08 TOTE £2.20: £1.10 £1.70 £1.60 (£10.70) Trio £7.20 OWNER Mr C. C. Buckley (SALTBURN) BRED T. N. Tanner

2699 Random Harvest (IRE) has taken a while to get the hang of fences but, judging by this display, he is improving fast. Stamina will not be a problem, and he will now take in the four-mile National Hunt Chase at Cheltenham with good prospects. (11/10)

1829 Slideofhill (IRE), who made his name in Irish points, looked in need of the outing. He shaped like a real stayer here, putting in his best work on the run-in. He too could give a good account of himself in the NH Chase at the Festival. (9/1: 6/1-10/1)

2841 Whattabob (IRE) totally lacked confidence in his jumping. After looking a real danger to the winner at one stage, he stopped in two strides on the final turn, and was out on his feet when he fell through the last. He must brush up his jumping considerably if he is to progress. (2/1)

2788* Kings Sermon (IRE) was well-beaten when he took a heavy fall two out. (11/1: 8/1-12/1)

3203 MARKET RASEN INTERMEDIATE OPEN N.H. FLAT RACE (4, 5 & 6-Y.O) (Class H)
5-00 (5-02) **1m 5f 110y** £1,339.50 (£372.00: £178.50)

				SP	RR	SF
2633*	**Autumn Lord** (PBeaumont) **4-10-10**(5) BGrattan (mde all: rn green over 1f out: hld on wl)	—	**1**	6/4[1]	71 f	—
1966*	**Guido (IRE)** (MissVenetiaWilliams) **6-11-11** NWilliamson (hld up: smooth hdwy ½-wy: chal 2f out: sn hrd rdn: r.o)	nk	**2**	5/1[2]	77 f	—
2675[3]	**Alisande (IRE)** (JAGlover) **5-10-10**(3) MrCBonner (lw: hld up: hdwy 6f out: sn drvn along: styd on)	11	**3**	8/1	52 f	—
2911*	**Macy (IRE)** (RDickin) **4-10-8**(7) XAizpuru (trckd ldrs tl outpcd fnl 4f)	½	**4**	12/1	57 f	—
	Brother Harry (JWharton) **5-11-1**(3) RMassey (gd sort: hld up: hdwy 5f out: rdn over 2f out: no imp)	18	**5**	40/1	35 f	—
2931[8]	**Fruitation** (MJWilkinson) **6-10-13** RDunwoody (hdwy 5f out: kpt on: nvr nr ldrs)	3½	**6**	12/1	26 f	—
	Pause For Thought (MrsMReveley) **4-10-8** RHodge (hld up: styd on fnl 4f: nvr nr ldrs)	6	**7**	11/2[3]	17 f	—
	The Country Don (MrsPSly) **5-11-4** WMarston (chsd ldrs tl lost pl 5f out)	4	**8**	33/1	19 f	—
2626[12]	**Red Oassis** (HOliver) **6-11-4** JacquiOliver (bhd tl kpt on fnl 4f: n.d)	1¾	**9**	33/1	17 f	—
	Phone The Pipeline (MCPipe) **4-10-1**(7) GSupple (prom: sn pushed along: lost pl 6f out)	10	**10**	16/1	—	—
	Sister Jane (PDEvans) **4-10-3** MrWMcLaughlin (nvr bttr than mid div)	hd	**11**	33/1	—	—
2675[10]	**My Vantage** (MWEasterby) **4-10-8** LWyer (hld up & bhd: n.d)	1½	**12**	40/1	—	—
2770[8]	**Sir Boston** (RDEWoodhouse) **4-10-8** ASSmith (chsd wnr tl wknd 4f out)	½	**13**	20/1	—	—
2675[13]	**Farm Talk** (MESowersby) **5-11-4** JRKavanagh (t.o fr ½-wy)	19	**14**	50/1	—	—
	Withy Close (IRE) (NoelChance) **4-10-8** RJohnson (sme hdwy ½-wy: sn wknd: t.o)	6	**15**	11/1	—	—
	Landler (JNorton) **4-10-5**(3) GLee (lengthy: a wl bhd: t.o)	20	**16**	16/1	—	—
2904[14]	**Stan's Pride** (MrsVAAconley) **5-11-4** BFenton (t.o fnl 5f)	2	**17**	33/1	—	—
	Frugal (BWMurray) **4-10-8** WDwan (bit bkwd: prom 5f: t.o fnl 3f)	14	**18**	33/1	—	—
1926[11]	**Caherlow (IRE)** (OBrennan) **6-11-4** MBrennan (sn bhd & drvn along: t.o 8f out: virtually p.u)	dist	**19**	40/1	—	—
				(SP 147.4%)	**19 Rn**	

3m 19.7 CSF £8.78 TOTE £2.20: £1.20 £2.80 £2.50 (£6.40) Trio £13.80 OWNER Mr A. R. Boocock (BRANDSBY) BRED A. R. Boocock
WEIGHT FOR AGE 4yo-4lb

2633* Autumn Lord, who set a good gallop, showed definite signs of inexperience when challenged over a furlong out, but produced the right sort of spirit and pulled a neck clear near the line. He will now step up and go for the bumper at Aintree. (6/4: 2/1-5/4)

1966* Guido (IRE) certainly has an engine. Moving up on the bridle, he never flinched under hard riding but, with the weight concession, had to give best near the line. (5/1: 7/2-11/2)

2675 Alisande (IRE), the paddock pick, should find an ordinary bumper. (8/1)

2911* Macy (IRE) could not live with the first two in the final half-mile, but he finished a long way clear of the remainder. (12/1: op 8/1)

Fruitation (12/1: 8/1-14/1)

Withy Close (IRE) (11/1: 8/1-12/1)

Landler showed a round action, and swished his tail. (16/1)

T/Jkpt: Not won; £13,733.88 to Folkestone 19/2/97. T/Plpt: £153.90 (113.87 Tckts). T/Qdpt: £29.10 (39.99 Tckts) WG

2825-FOLKESTONE (R-H) (Chase Soft, Hdles Heavy)
Wednesday February 19th
All races put back 5 mins
WEATHER: gale force wind

3204 DAVID BENGE NOVICES' H'CAP HURDLE (0-95) (4-Y.O+) (Class F)
2-10 (2-19) **2m 1f 110y (9 hdls)** £1,777.50 (£490.00: £232.50) GOING: 1.22 sec per fur (HY)

				SP	RR	SF
2680[8]	**Museum (IRE) (82)** (PWinkworth) **6-11-1**(7) XAizpuru (lw: a.p: led 3 out: rdn out)	—	**1**	8/1	68	27
3110*	**Dissolve (78)** (NMLampard) **5-10-11**(7) 7x MrLBaker (a.p: chsd wnr after 2 out: no imp)	11	**2**	9/1	54	13
2705[5]	**Tathmin (70)** (MRBosley) **4-10-0v** ILawrence (rdn 6th: hdwy appr last: r.o)	¾	**3**	11/1	45	—
1953[2]	**Theme Arena (93)** (MCPipe) **4-11-9** APMcCoy (lw: a.p: led 6th to 3 out: wknd appr last)	24	**4**	3/1[1]	46	—

				SP	RR	SF
	Swinging Sixties (IRE) (79) (GLMoore) **6-11-5** DGallagher (hdwy 3 out: wknd appr last)	9	**5**	5/1[3]	24	—
1953[5]	**Warning Reef (76)** (CLPopham) **4-10-6b[1]** GTormey (sme hdwy 4th: wknd appr 2 out)	9	**6**	10/1	13	—
2909[3]	**Flow Back (75)** (GPEnright) **5-11-1** RJohnson (led to 3rd: wknd 6th)	½	**7**	16/1	11	—
859[P]	**Danny Gale (IRE) (88)** (GMMcCourt) **6-12-0b[1]** SMcNeill (a.p: led 3rd to 6th: sn wknd)	5	**8**	10/1	20	—
3057*	**Kentavrus Way (IRE) (60)** (GLMoore) **6-9-7**(7) MBatchelor (unruly bef s: s.s: hdwy 3rd: wknd appr last)	½	**9**	9/2[2]	—	—
1905[6]	**Docklands Courier (84)** (BJMcMath) **5-11-10** CLlewellyn (prom to 4th: t.o)	dist	**10**	8/1	—	—
	Patong Beach (64) (PCRitchens) **7-10-4** SFox (a bhd: t.o whn p.u bef last)		**P**	33/1	—	—
2035[5]	**Royrace (65)** (WMBrisbourne) **5-10-2**(3) RMassey (hld up: rdn 3 out: wknd 2 out: t.o whn p.u bef last)		**P**	12/1	—	—
				(SP 135.1%)		**12 Rn**

4m 37.4 (31.40) CSF £81.04 CT £757.68 TOTE £9.70: £3.10 £3.90 £4.70 (£30.40) Trio £214.40 OWNER R D Barber & R J B Blake (DUNSFOLD) BRED M. Ryan and Miss M. Davison

WEIGHT FOR AGE 4yo-10lb

2067 Museum (IRE) was well-suited by the mud and, jumping into the lead at the third last, was ridden along to assert. (8/1)

3110* Dissolve, carrying a 7lb penalty for last week's Taunton success, moved into second place on the long downhill run to the final flight, but was unable to get on terms with the winner. (9/1: 9/2-10/1)

Tathmin, making his handicap debut, ran his best race to date, staying on past tired rivals for third prize. (11/1)

1953 Theme Arena, whose two runs to date over hurdles have both been on fast ground, found this too testing. In front at the fourth last, she was collared at the next and then tired as the mud found her out. (3/1: 5/2-9/2)

Swinging Sixties (IRE) has form in the mud, but had not been out since finishing second at Hamilton on the Flat last May. Taking closer order in the back straight, he had shot his bolt on the long downhill run to the final flight. (5/1: 7/1-9/2)

1444 Warning Reef (10/1: op 6/1)

859 Danny Gale (IRE) (10/1: 8/1-14/1)

3057* Kentavrus Way (IRE), whose win at Plumpton last week amounted to little, was not in a co-operative mood at all, and it took a great deal of patience and persuasion to get him to line up. After losing ground as the tape went up, he soon moved up to race in midfield, but was eventually hung out to dry on the run downhill. He should be left well alone. (9/2)

1424 Docklands Courier (8/1: op 5/1)

3205 LYMPNE NOVICES' CLAIMING HURDLE (4-Y.O+) (Class F)

2-40 (2-51) **2m 6f 110y (11 hdls)** £2,232.50 (£620.00: £297.50) GOING: 1.22 sec per fur (HY)

				SP	RR	SF
2570[7]	**Rare Spread (IRE) (76)** (MCPipe) **7-11-12** APMcCoy (hdwy 5th: chsd ldr appr 7th: led appr last: r.o wl)	—	**1**	9/4[1]	58	—
2905[7]	**Scorpion Bay (60)** (DJSffrenchDavis) **9-10-11**(3) JMagee (hdwy 3 out: 3rd & btn whn blnd bdly last)	16	**2**	16/1	35	—
1781[2]	**Sprig Muslin** (DRGandolfo) **5-10-12v**(5) SophieMitchell (led & pckd 1st: mstke 2 out: hdd & wknd appr last)	1	**3**	11/4[2]	37	—
	Teoroma (JRJenkins) **7-11-8** MrMGingell (prom tl appr 2 out)	20	**4**	16/1	28	—
3088[6]	**Ewar Bold (75)** (KOCunningham-Brown) **4-10-9** BFenton (led to 1st: wknd 7th)	1½	**5**	8/1[3]	25	—
2792[10]	**Ecu de France (IRE) (62)** (PCRitchens) **7-11-2** SFox (bhd fr 7th: t.o)	dist	**6**	10/1	—	—
1958[6]	**Wise 'n' Shine (62)** (NMLampard) **6-10-4**(7) MrLBaker (a bhd: t.o fr 7th)	19	**7**	14/1	—	—
133[7]	**Double Trouble** (DRGandolfo) **6-11-1**(3) DFortt (bhd fr 5th: t.o fr 7th)	28	**8**	16/1	—	—
2673[12]	**St Mellion Leisure (IRE)** (MCPipe) **5-10-9**(7) GSupple (hdwy 6th: wkng whn p.u bef 7th)		**P**	14/1	—	—
2907[13]	**Baba Sam (IRE)** (PEccles) **6-11-2** DGallagher (bhd fr 2nd: t.o whn p.u bef 7th)		**P**	16/1	—	—
2655[9]	**Piper's Rock (IRE)** (GBBalding) **6-11-12** RGreene (a bhd: t.o whn p.u bef 7th)		**P**	8/1[3]	—	—
2547[19]	**Serious Option (IRE)** (RCurtis) **6-11-4** DMorris (bhd fr 5th: t.o whn p.u bef 7th)		**P**	16/1	—	—
2705[P]	**Seven Crowns (USA)** (CLPopham) **4-10-7** GTormey (bhd fr 4th: t.o whn p.u bef 7th)		**P**	25/1	—	—
2946[11]	**Dolliver (USA)** (CADwyer) **5-11-0** ILawrence (prom to 5th: t.o whn p.u bef 7th)		**P**	33/1	—	—
				(SP 138.3%)		**14 Rn**

6m 25.6 (68.60) CSF £44.05 TOTE £3.40: £1.50 £12.40 £1.50 (£162.30) Trio £18.80 OWNER Mr Malcolm Jones (WELLINGTON) BRED J. A. Doherty

WEIGHT FOR AGE 4yo-11lb

2570 Rare Spread (IRE) was in a good mood on this occasion and, leading approaching the last, kept on well to give McCoy a winner on his first day back from injury. (9/4)

Scorpion Bay, whose seventh last time out was the best position he had so far managed to obtain, ran by far and away his best race to date. Taking closer order three from home, he was battling for minor honours when flattening the final flight. (16/1)

1781 Sprig Muslin, who won a bumper last season in the mud, lacks scope but ran well on this hurdling debut. Soon at the head of affairs, she grimly tried to hold on, but was very leg-weary when overhauled going to the final flight. These conditions suit her. (11/4: 2/1-3/1)

Teoroma, of little consequence on the Flat, played an active role on this hurdling debut until a lack of a recent run took its toll going to the penultimate hurdle. (16/1)

Ewar Bold (8/1: op 14/1)

2036 Ecu de France (IRE) (10/1: op 6/1)

3206 'GAY RECORD' CHALLENGE TROPHY H'CAP CHASE (0-100) (5-Y.O+) (Class F)

3-10 (3-18) **2m (12 fncs)** £2,612.70 (£722.20: £344.10) GOING: 1.22 sec per fur (HY)

				SP	RR	SF
3059[3]	**Buckland Lad (IRE) (78)** (DMGrissell) **6-11-2** BFenton (hld up: led 7th: mstke 8th: clr appr last: all out)	—	**1**	15/8[1]	86	27
3053[4]	**Fenwick (85)** (RJHodges) **10-11-6**(3) TDascombe (hdwy 3 out: chsd wnr appr 2 out: mstke 2 out: r.o flat)	1¾	**2**	13/2	91	32
2756[P]	**Retail Runner (90)** (MissSEdwards) **12-12-0** MrTHills (chsd ldr to 6th: lost pl 3 out: rallied appr last: r.o)	2½	**3**	4/1[2]	94	35
2906[5]	**Red Bean (90)** (KVincent) **9-12-0v[1]** AMaguire (lw: led to 7th: wknd appr 2 out)	15	**4**	15/2	79	20
3053[P]	**Rustic Gent (IRE) (72)** (MrsLCJewell) **9-10-10v** DLeahy (a bhd: t.o)	24	**5**	25/1	37	—
2949[U]	**Oxford Quill (77)** (RCurtis) **10-11-1** DMorris (lw: bhd fr 7th: t.o whn p.u bef last)		**P**	5/1[3]	—	—
	Drewitts Dancer (67) (TPMcGovern) **10-10-5** DBridgwater (3rd whn blnd & uns rdr 3rd)		**U**	7/1	—	—
				(SP 112.9%)		**7 Rn**

4m 19.8 (27.80) CSF £12.89 TOTE £2.30: £1.20 £4.10 (£7.00) OWNER Mrs R. M. Hepburn (ROBERTSBRIDGE) BRED Patrick Moore

OFFICIAL EXPLANATION Oxford Quill: the trainer reported that the gelding finished distressed.

3059 Buckland Lad (IRE), all the better for his Plumpton run last week, led at the sixth last and forged clear from the penultimate fence with the race appearing to be safely in the bag. He tired badly on the flat and, with the second and third closing, found the line only just saving him. (15/8)

3053 Fenwick ran better here. Moving into second place approaching the second last, he appeared to be well held by the winner but, with that rival tiring on the flat, he kept on really well. (13/2: 9/2-7/1)

Retail Runner, in second place early on, did not have much help from the saddle and lost his pitch three out. With the winner tiring though, he kept on really well and would have been even closer with a more experienced pilot up. (4/1)

1934 Red Bean, 10lb lower than at the beginning of the season, set the pace to the sixth last and then tired under his welter burden going to the penultimate fence. (15/2: 5/1-8/1)
2756* Oxford Quill is not the best of jumpers and was later reported to have finished distressed. (5/1)

3207 STANFORD (S) H'CAP HURDLE (0-90) (5-Y.O+) (Class G)

3-40 (3-48) **2m 1f 110y (9 hdls)** £1,639.50 (£452.00: £214.50) GOING: 1.22 sec per fur (HY)

				SP	RR	SF
2943[11]	**Killing Time (72)** (DBurchell) **6-10-10** DJBurchell (hdwy 4th: led appr last: rdn out)	—	**1**	14/1	55	—
1562[P]	**Parisian (62)** (JABennett) **12-9-7**(7) ALucas (gd hdwy appr last: r.o)	¾	**2**	16/1	44	—
3057[5]	**Precious Wonder (63)** (PButler) **8-10-1** TJMurphy (lost pl 4th: rallied appr 2 out: wknd flat)	3	**3**	7/1	43	—
3061[F]	**Ilewin Janine (IRE) (78)** (PCRitchens) **6-11-2** DGallagher (mstke 6th: hdwy 3 out: hrd rdn appr last: wknd flat)	1	**4**	6/1[3]	57	2
3057[3]	**Derisbay (IRE) (74)** (JJBridger) **9-10-12b** AMaguire (hld up: hrd rdn appr 2 out: sn wknd)	21	**5**	5/1[2]	34	—
3088[8]	**Celtic Lilley (65)** (JFfitch-Heyes) **7-10-3b** BFenton (prom to 3 out)	1	**6**	14/1	24	—
2946[12]	**Al Haal (USA) (66)** (JJoseph) **8-10-4** DSkyrme (lw: a.p: led 6th tl appr last: sn wknd: collapsed after r)	3½	**7**	16/1	21	—
	Valianthe (USA) (90) (MCPipe) **9-11-7b**(7) GSupple (hdwy 4th: wknd appr last)	1½	**8**	7/1	44	—
3110[13]	**Aldwick Colonnade (70)** (MDIUsher) **10-10-8** WMcFarland (bhd fr 3 out)	10	**9**	16/1	15	—
2866*	**Script (74)** (JRJenkins) **6-10-12** JOsborne (lw: a bhd)	14	**10**	9/4[1]	6	—
66[16]	**Side Bar (62)** (MissKMGeorge) **7-10-0b** JRKavanagh (lw: led 2nd to 6th: sn wknd)	13	**11**	20/1	—	—
3057[6]	**Deptford Belle (68)** (RCurtis) **7-10-6** DMorris (a bhd)	24	**12**	16/1	—	—
1948[6]	**Tilt Tech Flyer (82)** (IRJones) **12-11-6** MissEJJones (led to 2nd: wknd 5th: t.o whn p.u bef 3 out)		**P**	9/1	—	—
				(SP 138.3%)	**13 Rn**	

4m 41.4 (35.40) CSF £224.00 CT £1,590.76 TOTE £15.70: £3.90 £12.00 £1.80 (£250.80) Trio £505.10 OWNER Mr Simon Lewis (EBBW VALE) BRED L. H. J. Ward
LONG HANDICAP Side Bar 9-13 Parisian 9-3
No bid

1448 Killing Time, whose only previous victory came on firm ground, coped with the mud and, leading approaching the last, just managed to hold the others at bay. (14/1: 10/1-16/1)
Parisian, still carrying 4lb more than his long handicap mark despite his rider's allowance, was having his first run in three months and might have won this under a better ride. Still out with the washing at the top of the hill, he did not receive much assistance from the saddle, but despite this, made up a tremendous amount of ground in the final quarter-mile, to finish right on the heels of the leader. (16/1)
3057 Precious Wonder, a maiden plater, goes well in the mud and managed to get back into the action at the top of the hill. One of four vying for honours jumping the last, he tired on the run-in. (7/1)
Ilewin Janine (IRE), taking a drop in class, was one of four within a length or so jumping the last, before tiring. (6/1)
3057 Derisbay (IRE) likes the mud but had been hung out to dry at the top of the hill. He has not won since December 1993. (5/1)
Valianthe (USA) (7/1: op 4/1)
2866* Script may have won recently, but was not in the mood here. (9/4)
Tilt Tech Flyer (9/1: 6/1-10/1)

3208 FLISHER FOODS MAIDEN HUNTERS' CHASE (5-Y.O+) (Class H)

4-10 (4-15) **2m 5f (15 fncs)** £1,067.30 (£319.40: £153.20: £70.10) GOING: Not Established

				SP	RR	SF
3062[2]	**Trifast Lad** (MJRoberts) **12-12-5**(3) MrPHacking (chsd ldr: led 2 out: r.o wl)	—	**1**	11/10[1]	99	32
	Sands of Gold (IRE) (CNNimmo) **9-12-1**(7) MrLLay (lw: led to 2 out: unable qckn)	2½	**2**	12/1	97	30
	King High (NigelWrighton) **10-12-1**(7) MrCWard (hdwy 10th: 3rd & no ch whn blnd 2 out)	8	**3**	33/1	91	24
	Astound (IRE) (MrsSallyMullins) **7-12-1**(7) Lt-ColRWebb-Bowen (hdwy fr 2 out: nvr nr to chal)	4	**4**	16/1	88	21
	Gypsy King (IRE) (GICooper) **9-12-1**(7) MrACoe (bit bkwd: hdwy 7th: 4th & no ch whn blnd 2 out)	1	**5**	9/2[2]	87	20
3089[F]	**Ell Gee** (MrsPTownsley) **7-11-10**(7) MissCTownsley (prom to 6th: t.o)	dist	**6**	33/1	—	—
3089[4]	**Centre Stage** (MrsSWarr) **11-12-1**(7) MrAWarr (bhd whn blnd 2nd: t.o fr 9th)	16	**7**	10/1	—	—
	Joctor Don (IRE) (GBBalding) **5-11-5**(7) MrEBabington (fell 1st)		**F**	20/1	—	—
	Dashboard Light (MrsCharlotteCooke) **7-12-5**(3) MrSimonAndrews (hdwy 3rd: wknd 11th: t.o whn p.u bef 2 out)		**P**	8/1	—	—
	Greybury Lane (IRE) (MrsDBASilk) **9-12-1**(7) MrPBull (lw: blnd & uns rdr 2nd)		**U**	11/2[3]	—	—
				(SP 125.6%)	**10 Rn**	

5m 48.6 (40.60) CSF £15.87 TOTE £2.00: £1.10 £3.30 £20.40 (£20.00) Trio £243.40 OWNER Mr Mike Roberts (HAILSHAM) BRED Wilfred White
WEIGHT FOR AGE 5yo-10lb

3062 Trifast Lad confirmed the promise shown at Plumpton last week and, jumping into the lead two out, soon had the race in safe-keeping. He can win again. (11/10)
Sands of Gold (IRE) looked in good shape for this first run since March '95, and ran well, taking the field along until put in his place two out. He should soon find a race. (12/1: 5/1-14/1)
King High, whose last outing was on the Flat on the All-Weather at Southwell back in January 1992, ran quite well. Taking closer order with a mile to race, he was held in third pitch when making a bad error two from home. (33/1)
Astound (IRE) goes in this ground but was given a hopeless ride. With his jockey doing nothing more than sitting on him, the gelding was left to his own devices, but made eye-catching late headway to take fourth place. He is capable of winning a race but needs a step up in trip and a jockey on him. (16/1)
Gypsy King (IRE), looking in need of this first run in a year, was held in fourth place when clouting the penultimate fence. (9/2)
Dashboard Light (8/1: 5/1-10/1)
Greybury Lane (IRE) (11/2: op 5/2)

3209 FOLKESTONE H'CAP HURDLE (0-115) (4-Y.O+) (Class E)

4-40 (4-46) **2m 6f 110y (11 hdls)** £2,363.60 (£654.60: £312.80) GOING: 1.22 sec per fur (HY)

				SP	RR	SF
3063[3]	**Millmount (IRE) (89)** (TPMcGovern) **7-10-13b** DBridgwater (lw: hdwy 5th: hrd rdn appr 2 out: led appr last: r.o wl)	—	**1**	5/1[3]	73	—
2659[P]	**Ainsi Soit Il (FR) (99)** (GMMcCourt) **6-11-6b**(3) DFortt (led tl appr last: unable qckn)	4	**2**	3/1[2]	80	—
2905[8]	**Roger's Pal (76)** (PEccles) **10-10-0** DGallagher (hld up: rdn appr 2 out: sn wknd)	18	**3**	20/1	44	—
3087[2]	**August Twelfth (84)** (DCO'Brien) **9-10-8** CLlewellyn (lw: hdwy 6th: stumbled bnd appr 7th: wknd appr last: t.o)	dist	**4**	11/4[1]	—	—

				SP	RR	SF
2948^{6}	**Monks Soham (IRE) (100)** (GAHubbard) **9-11-10** NWilliamson (hdwy 6th: hrd rdn 3 out: wknd appr last: t.o)	10	**5**	5/1 ^{3}	—	—
3063^{2}	**Lajadhal (FR) (76)** (KBishop) **8-10-0** LHarvey (chsd ldr to 6th: sn wknd: t.o)	5	**6**	8/1	—	—
500^{3}	**Celtic Laird (85)** (DBurchell) **9-10-9** DJBurchell (prom to 5th: t.o whn p.u bef 3 out)		**P**	25/1	—	—
2907^{2}	**Mullintor (IRE) (85)** (RRowe) **6-10-9** DO'Sullivan (hdwy 6th: wknd 2 out: p.u bef last)		**P**	5/1 ^{3}	—	—
				(SP 121.4%)	**8 Rn**	

6m 16.1 (59.10) CSF £20.28 CT £259.57 TOTE £6.00: £2.30 £1.60 £4.20 (£13.40) OWNER Mr Tommy Breen (LEWES) BRED J. F. O'Malley
LONG HANDICAP Lajadhal (FR) 9-3 Roger's Pal 9-9

3063 Millmount (IRE), under pressure in the back straight, nevertheless managed to get on top approaching the last and kept on well. (5/1)
1962* Ainsi Soit Il (FR), back over a more suitable trip, took the field along but, collared by the winner approaching the final flight, had nothing more to give. (3/1)
1710 Roger's Pal is a poor plater and was in trouble at the top of the hill. He has now won just twice from fifty starts. (20/1)
3087 August Twelfth is in his element on this ground, but this longer trip was against him, and he was legless turning for home. A drop in distance is needed. (11/4: 2/1-7/2)
2948 Monks Soham (IRE) found this trip too far. (5/1: 7/2-11/2)

T/Jkpt: £14,680.20 (0.1 Tckts); £18,608.81 to Wincanton 20/2/97. T/Plpt: £1,219.80 (14.93 Tckts). T/Qdpt: £128.40 (11.32 Tckts) AK

2041-HEXHAM (L-H) - Wednesday February 19th
3210 Abandoned-Waterlogged

3077-SEDGEFIELD (L-H) - Wednesday February 19th
3216 Abandoned-Course Unfit

2946-HUNTINGDON (R-H) (Good to soft, Soft in home st)
Thursday February 20th
WEATHER: unsettled and windy

3222 UNIQUE CONSULTANTS NOVICES' H'CAP HURDLE (0-105) (4-Y.O+) (Class E)
1-50 (1-52) **2m 4f 110y (10 hdls)** £3,176.00 (£886.00: £428.00) GOING: 0.40 sec per fur (GS)

				SP	RR	SF
2870^{2}	**Lady High Sheriff (IRE) (78)** (CaptTAForster) **7-11-1** SWynne (in tch: hdwy to ld 7th: clr 2 out: rdn out)	—	**1**	9/2 ^{2}	67	—
2812^{7}	**Seabrook Lad (79)** (MJWilkinson) **6-11-2** WMarston (lw: hld up: hdwy 5th: led 6th to next: ev ch 3 out: kpt on flat)	10	**2**	11/8 ^{1}	60	—
2897^{F}	**Cades Bay (82)** (NATwiston-Davies) **6-11-5** TJenks (hld up: hdwy 6th: chsd wnr appr 2 out: no imp)	nk	**3**	16/1	63	—
1861^{7}	**Katballou (63)** (KGWingrove) **8-9-7**(7) MrOMcPhail (hdwy 6th: one pce fr 3 out)	1¼	**4**	33/1	43	—
2925^{7}	**Toby Brown (98)** (DNicholson) **4-11-10** RJohnson (lw: in tch: hdwy 6th: ev ch 3 out: sn btn)	½	**5**	9/1 ^{3}	78	—
3054^{4}	**Come On In (76)** (RDickin) **4-9-9**(7) XAizpuru (prom: hit 5th: no imp fr 7th)	17	**6**	16/1	42	—
2870^{P}	**Torch Vert (IRE) (87)** (NJHWalker) **5-11-10** ILawrence (chsd ldrs: ev ch whn hit 3 out: sn wknd)	½	**7**	25/1	53	—
3004^{6}	**Scally Hicks (65)** (BPJBaugh) **6-10-2**ow2 GaryLyons (bhd fr 5th)	29	**8**	50/1	8	—
2805^{10}	**Fred Jeffrey (IRE) (79)** (AndrewTurnell) **6-11-2** LHarvey (prom to 5th: sn lost pl)	9	**9**	25/1	15	—
1562^{P}	**Our Rainbow (81)** (MrsPSly) **5-11-4** MBrennan (chsd ldrs: rdn appr 6th: sn wknd)	2½	**10**	33/1	15	—
3019^{9}	**Music Class (IRE) (85)** (CPEBrooks) **6-11-8** DGallagher (a bhd)	11	**11**	16/1	11	—
2692^{5}	**Red Light (76)** (JRJenkins) **5-10-13b** PCarberry (lw: chsd ldrs tl rdn & wknd appr 3 out)	1	**12**	20/1	1	—
2805^{11}	**Todd (USA) (77)** (AHHarvey) **6-11-0** JAMcCarthy (hdwy 5th: wknd 7th: t.o whn p.u bef 2 out)		**P**	25/1	—	—
2547^{15}	**Brown And Mild (67)** (MissAEEmbiricos) **6-10-4** KGaule (chsd ldrs: rdn 6th: wknd qckly: t.o whn p.u bef 3 out)		**P**	33/1	—	—
2680^{9}	**Sir Dante (IRE) (84)** (RRowe) **6-11-7** DO'Sullivan (led to 6th: sn wknd: t.o whn p.u bef 2 out)		**P**	14/1	—	—
3085^{7}	**Forest Mill (80)** (JLSpearing) **5-11-3** DBridgwater (prom to 5th: bhd whn p.u bef 7th)		**P**	33/1	—	—
				(SP 124.6%)	**16 Rn**	

5m 4.9 CSF £9.24 CT £89.08 TOTE £4.40: £1.10 £1.20 £1.90 £5.10 (£5.30) Trio £27.70 OWNER Mrs Michael Ward-Thomas (LUDLOW) BRED Tony Mullins
LONG HANDICAP Scally Hicks 9-11 Katballou 9-11
WEIGHT FOR AGE 4yo-11lb

2870 Lady High Sheriff (IRE) found this slog through tacky ground was just what the doctor ordered. She stays well. (9/2)
2053 Seabrook Lad looked something of a steering job, as four of the six in front of him last time had won in the last week. This did not prove the case however and, flat out on the home turn, he looked unlikely to be placed. He kept plugging away though and may have been found out by the tacky surface. (11/8)
2897 Cades Bay was waited with, and looked a threat on the home turn before petering out late on. He is gradually getting his act together, but looked to finish rather sore. (16/1)
1562 Katballou is only moderate, but ran well and would seem to have found his trip. He looks up to winning a seller. (33/1)
2669 Toby Brown was not helped by the step up in trip. (9/1: op 5/1)
3054 Come On In never threatened to take a hand. (16/1)

3223 HORSELEY FEN H'CAP CHASE (0-110) (5-Y.O+) (Class E)
2-20 (2-22) **3m (19 fncs)** £3,228.00 (£969.00: £467.00: £216.00) GOING: 0.83 sec per fur (S)

				SP	RR	SF
2754^{6}	**Celtic Barle (100)** (HBHodge) **13-11-4** SMcNeill (in tch: rdn to chse ldr after 3 out: led flat: r.o)	—	**1**	10/1	111	13
2681^{2}	**Eastern River (86)** (CaptTAForster) **11-10-4** SWynne (a.p: led 11th: clr 16th: rdn appr last: hdd flat: r.o)	½	**2**	13/8 ^{1}	97	—
3106^{P}	**Solo Gent (94)** (APJones) **8-10-12** SCurran (chsd ldrs: kpt on u.p flat)	4	**3**	9/1	102	4
2863^{2}	**Tim Soldier (FR) (89)** (MFBarraclough) **10-10-7** RSupple (blnd 1st: hdwy 12th: one pce appr 2 out)	1½	**4**	4/1 ^{2}	96	—
2665^{P}	**Griffins Bar (85)** (MrsPSly) **9-10-3b^{1}** JCulloty (led 2nd to 11th: wknd 3 out)	dist	**5**	16/1	—	—
2681^{P}	**Sheelin Lad (IRE) (88)** (MrsTJMcInnesSkinner) **9-10-3**(3)ow2 DFortt (led to 2nd: wknd 15th)	18	**6**	33/1	—	—
2829^{6}	**Yeoman Warrior (106)** (RRowe) **10-11-10** DO'Sullivan (j.b: prom tl lost pl 11th: rallied briefly 3 out: wkng whn blnd last)	8	**7**	10/1	—	—
2652^{4}	**Supposin (91)** (MrsSJSmith) **9-10-9** RichardGuest (mstke 2nd: bhd fr 5th: hmpd 12th: t.o whn p.u bef 15th)		**P**	14/1	—	—
3018^{P}	**Invasion (103)** (OBrennan) **13-11-7** MBrennan (sn t.o: p.u bef 10th)		**P**	25/1	—	—
3020^{7}	**Cool Runner (92)** (MrsSusanNock) **7-10-10** DerekByrne (blnd 3rd: sn rdn & bhd: t.o whn p.u bef 4 out)		**P**	8/1 ^{3}	—	—
2681^{P}	**Mighty Frolic (95)** (MissSEdwards) **10-10-13** PHide (lw: chsd ldrs: blnd 10th: wknd 14th: t.o whn p.u bef 3 out)		**P**	25/1	—	—

				SP	RR	SF
2821^{8}	**Knockaverry (IRE) (97)** (MJWilkinson) **9-11-1** WMarston (chsd ldrs: rdn 13th: wkng whn blnd & uns rdr 4 out)	.	**U**	20/1	—	—
				(SP 125.3%)		**12 Rn**

6m 35.2 (38.20) CSF £25.73 CT £151.87 TOTE £8.80: £1.80 £1.90 £1.80 (£13.70) Trio £46.70 OWNER Mrs Irene Hodge (WARE) BRED Mrs I. Hodge

2754 Celtic Barle turned the clock back with a marvellously game effort, for his pilot was pushing him along some way out, yet he still found enough to burst through on the inside of the leader on the run-in. (10/1)

2681 Eastern River is becoming unlucky but he does contribute to his own downfall, as he was idling in front with the race looking safe going to the last. When passed by the winner, he did not have time to produce an effort. (13/8)

1877 Solo Gent continues to save most of his best runs for this track, but the sticky ground would not have been ideal. (9/1: op 6/1)

2863 Tim Soldier (FR) remains in good form although he did look spent after the last. This trip on the ground may just stretch him. (4/1: op 5/2)

2052 Griffins Bar, blinkered for the first time, lasted longer than he has been doing of late. (16/1)

Sheelin Lad (IRE) is taking time to get back to full fitness after a long lay-off, and gives the impression that he would like the chance to dictate the pace. (33/1)

2829 Yeoman Warrior is built like a tank and jumped like one on this occasion. It says much for his powers of recovery that he was able to stay in contention for so long. (10/1: op 6/1)

3224 EQUITABLE HOUSE HURDLE (4-Y.O) (Class C)

2-50 (2-52) **2m 110y (8 hdls)** £3,601.75 (£1,084.00: £524.50: £244.75) GOING: 0.40 sec per fur (GS)

				SP	RR	SF
2825^{4}	**Kings Witness (USA)** (PFNicholls) **4-10-12** DBridgwater (hdwy 4th: led after 3 out: hit next: sn clr:easily)	—	**1**	$6/4^{1}$	78+	13
2925^{F}	**Sulawesi (IRE)** (NATwiston-Davies) **4-10-7** CMaude (hld up: hdwy appr 3 out: r.o appr last)	14	**2**	10/1	59	—
3022^{4}	**Parrot's Hill (IRE)** (MHTompkins) **4-10-12** RichardGuest (w ldrs: led appr 4th: hdd after 3 out: sn btn)	1	**3**	$6/1^{3}$	64	—
2925^{2}	**Exalted (IRE)** (WJenks) **4-10-12** TJenks (lw: trckd ldrs: ev ch 3 out: rdn & wknd appr next)	17	**4**	$11/4^{2}$	47	—
2889^{6}	**Silvretta (IRE)** (JTGifford) **4-10-7** PHide (lw: j.b: plld hrd: hdwy 4th: wknd after next)	18	**5**	10/1	25	—
2889^{P}	**Magic Role** (JRJenkins) **4-10-12**v^{1} PCarberry (w ldrs to 5th)	dist	**6**	33/1	—	—
	Caballus (USA) (MrsJPitman) **4-10-12** RFarrant (plld hrd: prom: wkng whn hit 5th)	dist	**7**	8/1	—	—
2865^{P}	**Gulliver** (NJHWalker) **4-10-12**b^{1} ILawrence (led tl hdd & lost tch appr 4th: t.o whn p.u bef 3 out)		**P**	25/1	—	—
				(SP 117.0%)		**8 Rn**

4m 4.9 (16.90) CSF £16.77 TOTE £2.80: £1.40 £2.10 £1.10 (£8.10) OWNER Mr Jeffrey Hordle (SHEPTON MALLET) BRED T. Holmes, M. Levy & R. Trontz

2825 Kings Witness (USA) does not impress as a natural jumper, but is getting his act together slowly and was certainly impressive in the end. Whether he could handle the hustle and bustle of the Triumph is another matter. (6/4)

2622 Sulawesi (IRE) has taken time to learn to settle, but should be winning soon as this was a promising effort. (10/1)

3022 Parrot's Hill (IRE) was again found out by conditions underfoot, but a nasty gash could also have contributed to his downfall. (6/1)

2925 Exalted (IRE) did not get the trip in this ground. (11/4)

Silvretta (IRE) is going to have to jump a good deal better to have any future at this game. (10/1)

Magic Role, visored for the first time, raced up with the leaders early on but was in trouble a long way out. (33/1)

Caballus (USA) (8/1: 6/1-9/1)

3225 LONGWOOD FEN H'CAP CHASE (0-125) (5-Y.O+) (Class D)

3-20 (3-21) **2m 110y (8 fncs)** £5,367.00 (£1,308.00) GOING: 0.83 sec per fur (S)

				SP	RR	SF
3144^{3}	**Thumbs Up (125)** (GMMcCourt) **11-11-7**(7) RHobson (w ldr: led 8th to next: led 3 out: lft clr last)	—	**1**	5/1	135	29
2921^{2}	**Regal Romper (IRE) (111)** (MrsSJSmith) **9-11-0** RichardGuest (w ldrs to 8th: btn whn lft 2nd last)	15	**2**	$9/4^{2}$	107	1
2700^{4}	**Random Assault (NZ) (125)** (DNicholson) **8-12-0** RJohnson (lw: led to 8th: led 9th to 3 out: sn rdn: 2nd & btn whn fell last)		**F**	$3/1^{3}$	—	—
1066^{4}	**Lowawatha (99)** (MrsEHHeath) **9-10-2** KGaule (mstke 3rd: j.slowly next: sn t.o: p.u bef 2 out)		**P**	12/1	—	—
3009^{5}	**Eastern Magic (103)** (GBarnett) **9-10-6** DBridgwater (bhd: blnd 1st: hdwy whn mstke 6th: wknd 4 out: hmpd & uns rdr last)		**U**	$2/1^{1}$	—	—
				(SP 113.5%)		**5 Rn**

4m 26.3 (24.30) CSF £15.81 TOTE £5.80: £1.70 £1.50 (£4.60) OWNER Mrs B. Taylor (WANTAGE) BRED Peader McCoy

IN-FOCUS: **Young rider Richard Hobson was partnering his first winner.**

3144 Thumbs Up, back on the mark he won off five outings ago, found a very ordinary race, jumping soundly apart from a slight peck five from home. (5/1)

2921 Regal Romper (IRE) has a terrific record but on ground faster than this and, hard as he tried, ran some way below his best. (9/4)

2700 Random Assault (NZ) went head-to-head with the winner, but finally gave way on the long run to two out. His cause looked lost and he was under strong pressure when falling at the last. Thankfully, he appeared unscathed after lying prone for several minutes. (3/1)

862 Lowawatha (12/1: op 6/1)

3226 PIDLEY FEN MAIDEN HURDLE (4-Y.O+ F & M) (Class E)

3-50 (3-51) **2m 110y (16 hdls)** £2,810.00 (£785.00: £380.00) GOING: 0.40 sec per fur (GS)

				SP	RR	SF
3029^{3}	**Nishamira (IRE)** (TDBarron) **5-11-5** DGallagher (racd wd: led appr 3 out: hdd appr next: lft in ld last: rdn out)	—	**1**	$3/1^{1}$	65	22
2861^{6}	**Ardrina** (FMurphy) **6-11-5** PCarberry (lw: prom: rdn appr 2 out: styd on wl flat)	2	**2**	5/1	63	20
2925^{3}	**Takeamemo (IRE)** (OSherwood) **4-10-9** JAMcCarthy (racd wd: a.p: ev ch whn hmpd last: nt rcvr)	1½	**3**	$7/2^{2}$	62+	9
2878^{F}	**Mrs Em** (PFNicholls) **5-11-5** RJohnson (lw: hdwy 4th: rdn appr 2 out: one pce)	4	**4**	$9/2^{3}$	58	15
2677^{11}	**Supreme Troglodyte (IRE)** (CPMorlock) **5-11-2**(3) DFortt (hld up: hdwy 5th: btn appr 2 out)	13	**5**	16/1	45	2
	Ring For Rosie (CaptTAForster) **6-11-5** JCulloty (bhd: pushed along 3rd: hdwy next: nvr rchd ldrs)	14	**6**	33/1	32	—
	Summer Princess (GFierro) **4-10-9** GaryLyons (bit bkwd: hld up & bhd: hdwy appr 3 out: nvr plcd to chal)	1½	**7**	40/1	30	—
2889^{5}	**Belmarita (IRE)** (GAHubbard) **4-10-9** RichardGuest (led tl appr 3 out: sn wknd)	7	**8**	10/1	23	—
3029^{4}	**Derring Floss** (JAPickering) **7-10-12**(7) MissJWormall (chsd ldrs to 5th)	1¼	**9**	20/1	22	—
	Callermine (MissHDay) **8-11-5** MFoster (plld hrd: prom to 5th)	14	**10**	66/1	9	—
2811^{11}	**Lucrative Perk (IRE)** (MissCJECaroe) **5-11-5** DLeahy (in tch to 4th)	6	**11**	50/1	3	—
2661^{10}	**Slack Alice** (JLSpearing) **6-11-5** TJMurphy (stumbled s: nvr nr ldrs)	2½	**12**	50/1	—	—
3006^{12}	**Diamond Time** (CaptTAForster) **6-11-5** SWynne (a bhd)	8	**13**	20/1	—	—
3006^{6}	**Mistress Tudor** (SMellor) **6-11-5** NMann (lw: in tch to 4th)	2	**14**	40/1	—	—
2805^{13}	**Mollie Silvers** (JKCresswell) **5-10-12**v^{1}(7) NTEgan (a bhd)	hd	**15**	50/1	—	—
2875^{5}	**Annie Ruth (IRE)** (MrsJPitman) **6-11-5** RFarrant (prom to 4th: sn wknd)	hd	**16**	25/1	—	—
3072^{2}	**Threesocks** (BSmart) **4-10-9** ILawrence (hdwy appr 3 out: led appr next: fell last)		**F**	7/1	65?	—

				SP	RR	SF
3029^{11}	**Skip to Somerfield** (BSRothwell) **5-11-5** ASSmith (hld up: no imp whn p.u bef 3 out)		P	40/1	—	—
2677^{P}	**Shouldhavesaidno (IRE)** (THind) **6-11-5** DO'Sullivan (in tch to 4th: t.o whn p.u bef 3 out)		P	50/1	—	—
2840^{P}	**Bally Wonder** (MrsEHHeath) **5-11-5** KGaule (plld hrd: prom to 4th: t.o whn p.u bef 2 out)		P	66/1	—	—
2572^{9}	**Sweet Mount (IRE)** (NATwiston-Davies) **5-11-5** CMaude (chsd ldrs to 4th: t.o whn p.u bef 2 out)		P	25/1	—	—
3061^{P}	**Our Emma** (JJoseph) **8-11-5** LHarvey (t.o fr 4th: p.u bef 2 out)		P	66/1	—	—
				(SP 149.3%)	**22 Rn**	

4m 4.3 (16.30) CSF £17.82 TOTE £4.60: £2.30 £2.20 £2.00 (£12.10) Trio £18.30 OWNER M P Burke Developments Ltd (THIRSK) BRED His Highness the Aga Khans Studs S. C.

WEIGHT FOR AGE 4yo-10lb

3029 Nishamira (IRE), taken wide in search of better ground, was a slightly fortunate winner but should stay further. (3/1)

2861 Ardrina kept responding to pressure and, after looking likely to finish fourth at best, stayed on strongly near the finish. She will stay further. (5/1: op 8/1)

2925 Takeamemo (IRE), another taken wide, jumped better on this occasion and was unfortunate that the leader fell in her path at the last, otherwise she may well have prevailed. (7/2)

2878 Mrs Em made a forward move travelling well, but lacked the pace over this shorter trip. (9/2: 3/1-5/1)

1966 Supreme Troglodyte (IRE) is not very big, and weakened suddenly on the home turn after making up a lot of ground to get into contention. (16/1)

Ring For Rosie looks the type to do better in time. (33/1)

Summer Princess was ridden with considerable restraint in an attempt to get the trip, and was not knocked about once her measure had been taken. She has shown moderate form on the level at up to seven furlongs, and it might be unwise to read too much into this eye-catching display. (40/1)

2889 Belmarita (IRE) (10/1: 7/1-11/1)

3072 Threesocks had taken charge, and was a couple of lengths up and travelling like the winner, when overjumping at the last and turning over on landing. (7/1)

3227 EUXIMOOR FEN NOVICES' CHASE (5-Y.O+) (Class E)

4-25 (4-27) **2m 4f 110y (16 fncs)** £3,023.25 (£906.00: £435.50: £200.25) GOING: 0.83 sec per fur (S)

				SP	RR	SF
2827^{2}	**Frazer Island (IRE)** (RRowe) **8-11-3** DO'Sullivan (lw: mde all: rdn appr last: hld on wl)	—	1	14/1 3	117?	42
2641^{3}	**Mandys Mantino** (JTGifford) **7-11-3** PHide (lw: trckd ldrs: ev ch appr 2 out: rdn & no ex flat)	2	2	2/5 1	115?	40
2843^{2}	**Second Call (110)** (CaptTAForster) **8-11-10** SWynne (hld up: hdwy 9th: blnd next: no imp appr 2 out)	20	3	7/2 2	107?	32
2819^{P}	**Dream Leader (IRE)** (MJRoberts) **7-11-3** JRailton (lw: prom: wkng whn mstke 3 out)	dist	4	33/1	—	—
3202^{P}	**Pandora's Prize (60)** (JLSpearing) **11-10-12** TJMurphy (prom to 10th: sn wknd)	dist	5	150/1	—	—
3015^{5}	**Bucket of Gold** (OBrennan) **7-11-3** MBrennan (prom: blnd 6th, 7th & 8th: p.u bef 9th)		P	20/1	—	—
	The Eloper (MissEMEngland) **9-10-10**(7) NTEgan (bkwd: hld up & plld hrd: blnd 3rd: lost tch & blnd 8th: p.u bef next)		P	150/1	—	—
				(SP 109.3%)	**7 Rn**	

5m 23.4 (23.40) CSF £18.35 TOTE £8.90: £2.00 £1.20 (£3.40) OWNER Dr B. Alexander (PULBOROUGH) BRED John Thompson

2827 Frazer Island (IRE) ruined any hopes of a lenient handicap mark with a game front-running display, outbattling the favourite in the straight. (14/1: op 8/1)

2641 Mandys Mantino found this tacky ground right against him and, despite nipping through on the winner's inside turning for home, could not be coaxed home. (2/5)

2843 Second Call often seems to spoil her chance with a bad jump, as she did on this occasion. (7/2)

1962 Dream Leader (IRE) was going nowhere when the mistake sealed his fate. (33/1)

3228 WIMBLINGTON FEN AMATEUR H'CAP HURDLE (0-115) (4-Y.O+) (Class E)

4-55 (4-59) **2m 110y (8 hdls)** £2,337.50 (£650.00: £312.50) GOING: 0.40 sec per fur (GS)

				SP	RR	SF
3076*	**Sheriffmuir (119)** (MrsLWadham) **8-11-10**(7) 7x MrPScott (lw: hld up: hdwy 4th: led appr 2 out: rdn clr flat)	—	1	13/8 1	93	42
	Alka International (88) (MrsPTownsley) **5-9-7**(7) MissCTownsley (bit bkwd: trckd ldrs: r.o flat)	9	2	50/1	53	2
2952^{4}	**Bigwheel Bill (IRE) (92)** (JRJenkins) **8-10-1**(3) MrCBonner (lw: led 4th tl appr 2 out: hit last: rdn & wknd flat)	¾	3	2/1 2	57	6
1984^{5}	**Biya (IRE) (88)** (DMcCain) **5-9-7**(7) MrGLake (led after 1st to 4th: rdn appr 3 out: one pce)	7	4	12/1	46	—
3053^{P}	**Halham Tarn (IRE) (88)** (HJManners) **7-9-7**(7) MissADudley (trckd ldrs: no ex fr 3 out)	1	5	16/1	45	—
2946*	**Willy Star (BEL) (110)** (MrsSJSmith) **7-11-1**(7) MrEBabington (hld up: hdwy 4th: hit next: sn btn)	19	6	3/1 3	48	—
	Paula's Boy (IRE) (91) (DFBassett) **7-9-10**(7)ow3 MissKDiMarte (bit bkwd: led tl after 1st: t.o fr 5th)	dist	7	66/1	—	—
	Silent Sovereign (103) (PCClarke) **8-10-8b**(7)ow15 MrPClarke (bkwd: s.s: rapid hdwy & rn wd 1st: rn out next)		R	150/1	—	—
				(SP 114.1%)	**8 Rn**	

4m 2.3 (14.30) CSF £50.90 CT £157.96 TOTE £2.80: £1.50 £5.10 £1.10 (£38.60) OWNER Mr J. J. W. Wadham (NEWMARKET) BRED Stetchworth Park Stud Ltd

LONG HANDICAP Willy Star (BEL) 11-1 Bigwheel Bill (IRE) 9-11 Alka International 8-12 Biya (IRE) 8-8 Halham Tarn (IRE) 9-6 Paula's Boy (IRE) 9-3 Silent Sovereign 7-6

STEWARDS' ENQUIRY Clarke referred to Portman Square (incompetent riding).

3076* Sheriffmuir, well ridden, had already had his Leicester win franked by the second, and made light of his penalty. (13/8)

Alka International looked to need the run, but tried hard despite hanging away from the stands. (50/1)

2952 Bigwheel Bill (IRE), who wore headgear for his two wins over timber, did not look entirely in love with this game. (2/1)

Biya (IRE) won on the All-Weather three weeks ago, and kept trying to the line. His rider makes plenty of use of his stick. (12/1: 8/1-14/1)

Halham Tarn (IRE) had lost his way over fences recently, but this effort was a little more promising. (16/1)

2946* Willy Star (BEL) was sending out distress signals after the mistake four out. (3/1)

Silent Sovereign was not controlled round the first turn by Mr Clarke, which saw racing's 'Galloping Gaucho' referred to Portman Square. (150/1)

T/Plpt: £17.80 (778.33 Tckts). T/Qdpt: £10.70 (58.98 Tckts) Dk

2959-WINCANTON (R-H) (Good)
Thursday February 20th
WEATHER: unsettled

3229 GEORGIE NEWALL NOVICES' CHASE (5-Y.O+) (Class D)
2-05 (2-07) **2m (13 fncs)** £3,852.00 (£1,072.00: £516.00) GOING: 0.19 sec per fur (G)

				SP	RR	SF
2873*	**Indian Jockey (117)** (MCPipe) **5-10-13** NWilliamson (led after 1st tl mstke 9th: led 4 out: sn rdn clr: r.o wl)	—	1	11/8[2]	109	19
2960[2]	**After The Fox (84)** (NJHawke) **10-11-2** GUpton (led tl after 1st: mstke 6th: led 9th to 4 out: one pce)	7	2	11/1[3]	96	15
3001[P]	**Robins Pride (IRE) (100)** (CLPopham) **7-10-13**(3) TDascombe (bdly hmpd 4th: rdn & hdwy 8th: btn whn mstkes 3 out & 2 out)	11	3	16/1	85	4
	Shankar (IRE) (DNicholson) **6-11-2** AMaguire (bit bkwd: hld up & plld hrd: fell 4th)		F	5/4[1]	—	—
2812[P]	**Mr Goonhilly** (RHAlner) **7-11-2** AThornton (fell 2nd)		F	100/1	—	—
3053[F]	**Swahili Run (82)** (JGMO'Shea) **9-10-13**(3) MichaelBrennan (mstke 3rd: 3rd whn fell 4th)		F	100/1	—	—
	Hold Your Ranks (79) (RGFrost) **10-11-2** JFrost (a bhd: t.o whn blnd & uns rdr 7th)		U	20/1	—	—

(SP 107.5%) **7 Rn**

4m 5.4 (12.40) CSF £12.27 TOTE £2.10: £1.40 £2.30 (£4.90) OWNER Mr Stuart Mercer (WELLINGTON) BRED John Hayter
WEIGHT FOR AGE 5yo-9lb

2873* Indian Jockey did not have an awful lot to beat following the departure of the favourite. (11/8)
2960 After The Fox, dropping back in distance, found the winner too strong from the cross-fence. (11/1: 8/1-12/1)
2793 Robins Pride (IRE) was lucky not to be brought down at the fourth. (16/1)
Shankar (IRE) did not help his rider by proving a handful to settle. (5/4)

3230 JIM FORD CHALLENGE CUP CHASE (5-Y.O+) (Class B)
2-35 (2-35) **3m 1f 110y (21 fncs)** £12,055.00 (£3,640.00: £1,770.00: £835.00) GOING: 0.19 sec per fur (G)

				SP	RR	SF
2887[F]	**Coome Hill (IRE) (147)** (WWDennis) **8-11-2** JOsborne (lw: led to 4 out: led 3 out: r.o wl)	—	1	7/4[2]	160+	36
2636[2]	**Unguided Missile (IRE) (157)** (GRichards) **9-11-8** RDunwoody (lw: w wnr: led 4 out to 3 out: mstke 2 out: r.o one pce)	1¼	2	11/8[1]	165	41
1560[U]	**Hanakham (IRE) (118)** (RJHodges) **8-11-2** BPowell (hld up & bhd: hdwy 11th: one pce fr 3 out)	10	3	33/1	153	29
	Maamur (USA) (145) (CaptTAForster) **9-11-2** AThornton (bit bkwd: prom: j.slowly 5th: hit 15th & 17th: rdn & wknd appr 3 out)	5	4	9/2[3]	150	26
2901[2]	**Kadi (GER) (138)** (DNicholson) **8-11-2** AMaguire (hld up: hdwy after 4 out: 3rd whn blnd 3 out: nt rcvr)	7	5	10/1	145	21
3039[4]	**All for Luck (126)** (MCPipe) **12-11-2** BFenton (bhd fr 5th: t.o)	26	6	50/1	129	5
1324*	**Cherrynut (130)** (PFNicholls) **8-11-2** NWilliamson (mstkes: bhd whn fell 4 out)		F	16/1	—	—

(SP 116.5%) **7 Rn**

6m 33.7 (14.70) CSF £4.55 TOTE £3.00: £2.00 £1.50 (£2.80) OWNER Mrs Jill Dennis (BUDE) BRED Mrs S. O'Connell

1649* Coome Hill (IRE), who would have been getting another 4lb from the runner-up had this been a handicap, looked to be getting on top when making much the better jump at the second last. He has certainly earned his place in the Gold Cup line-up, but looks thrown in with only 10st 6lb in the National. (7/4)
2636 Unguided Missile (IRE), his trainer's first runner at the course, apparently spent seven hours in the horse-box due to bad weather. He seemed to be getting the worse of the argument when a bad error at the penultimate fence settled it. (11/8)
1560 Hanakham (IRE) was by no means disgraced in this company. (33/1)
Maamur (USA) needs softer ground, and it was touch and go as to whether he ran. This will have sharpened him up. (9/2)
2901 Kadi (GER) still seemed capable of taking a hand when making a real nonsense of the third last, which knocked all the stuffing out of him. (10/1)

3231 K.J. PIKE & SONS KINGWELL HURDLE (Gd 2) (4-Y.O+) (Class A)
3-05 (3-07) **2m (8 hdls)** £15,625.00 (£5,912.50: £2,893.75: £1,318.75) GOING: 0.19 sec per fur (G)

				SP	RR	SF
2884[6]	**Dreams End (129)** (PBowen) **9-11-10** RDunwoody (hld up: hdwy 3 out: led appr 2 out: r.o wl)	—	1	16/1	132	60
3038[16]	**Romancer (IRE) (139)** (NATwiston-Davies) **6-11-2b** CLlewellyn (lw: hld up: hdwy 3 out: rdn appr 2 out: wnt 2nd appr last: no imp)	8	2	11/4[1]	116	44
2780[F]	**Blast Freeze (IRE) (126)** (NJHenderson) **8-10-11** JRKavanagh (lw: hld up: mstke & lost pl 3 out: styd on flat)	7	3	4/1[2]	104	32
2884[2]	**Ambleside (IRE) (116)** (MrsSDWilliams) **6-11-2** NWilliamson (hmpd s: bhd tl r.o fr 2 out: n.d)	½	4	20/1	109?	37
3038[15]	**Zabadi (IRE) (139)** (DNicholson) **5-11-10** AMaguire (hld up: hdwy after 3 out: wknd appr last)	s.h	5	4/1[2]	116	44
2886[3]	**Ground Nut (IRE) (124)** (RHBuckler) **7-11-2** BPowell (led to 5th: wknd appr 2 out)	14	6	7/1	94	22
1933[3]	**Potentate (USA) (128)** (MCPipe) **6-11-2** APMcCoy (w ldr: led 5th tl appr 2 out: sn wknd)	5	7	5/1[3]	89	17
2886[4]	**Florid (USA)** (CPEBrooks) **6-11-2** GBradley (ref to r: t.n.p)		R	9/1	—	—

(SP 116.5%) **8 Rn**

3m 45.4 (5.40) CSF £56.83 TOTE £13.50: £2.90 £1.40 £2.50 (£16.30) Trio £65.80 OWNER Mr T. G. Price (HAVERFORDWEST) BRED Hascombe and Valiant Studs

2884 Dreams End, well suited by the strong pace, bounced back to the form which saw him beat Space Trucker over course and distance in November. He really prefers a flat course, but will take his chance in the Champion Hurdle. (16/1)
Romancer (IRE) was brought up the stands' side in the home straight, but the winner proved too much of a handful. (11/4)
2780 Blast Freeze (IRE) may not have been suited by this shorter trip. (4/1: 3/1-9/2)
2884 Ambleside (IRE) needed softer ground to have any sort of chance in this company. (20/1)
2740a Zabadi (IRE) looked a threat racing down the hill to the home turn, but dropped away after going second briefly at the penultimate flight. (4/1)
2886 Ground Nut (IRE) was 8lb better off than when beaten just over ten lengths by the winner here in November, but was not helped by being taken on for the lead by Potentate. (7/1)
1933 Potentate (USA) needs softer ground, and it was a case of him and Ground Nut cutting their own throats by battling for the lead. (5/1)
2886 Florid (USA) (9/1: op 6/1)

3232 LADBROKE H'CAP CHASE (0-125) (5-Y.O+) (Class D)

3-35 (3-37) **2m 5f (17 fncs)** £6,840.00 (£2,070.00: £1,010.00: £480.00) GOING: 0.19 sec per fur (G)

				SP	RR	SF
2829[4]	**Maestro Paul (96)** (JTGifford) **11-10-0**(3) LAspell (hld up: rdn 12th: rallied appr 2 out: led appr last: sn clr: drvn out)	—	**1**	13/2	103	—
2894[6]	**Scotoni (93)** (RJO'Sullivan) **11-10-0** NWilliamson (w ldr: lft in ld 7th: blnd 8th: hdd appr 2 out: r.o one pce)	2	**2**	16/1	99	—
3043*	**Harvest View (IRE) (100)** (CPEBrooks) **7-10-7** GBradley (hld up: mstkes 1st & 8th: hdwy 10th: led appr 2 out tl appr last: one pce)	hd	**3**	13/8[1]	105	—
2962[3]	**Channel Pastime (95)** (DBurchell) **13-9-13**(3)ow2 GuyLewis (hld up: rdn 13th: one pce)	3	**4**	25/1	98	—
3050[7]	**The Carrot Man (107)** (PWinkworth) **9-11-0** JRKavanagh (hit 13th: a bhd)	2½	**5**	14/1	108	—
	Chief Joseph (102) (NATwiston-Davies) **10-10-9** CLlewellyn (hld up: mstke 3rd: fell 6th: dead)		**F**	6/1[3]	—	—
2821[2]	**Five to Seven (USA) (117)** (PFNicholls) **8-11-10b**[1] RDunwoody (led tl fell 7th: dead)		**F**	2/1[2]	—	—
				(SP 115.4%)		**7 Rn**

5m 34.9 (26.90) CSF £78.56 TOTE £8.10: £2.20 £3.70 (£36.10) OWNER Mr H. T. Pelham (FINDON) BRED Stackallan Stud
LONG HANDICAP Scotoni 9-13 Channel Pastime 9-3
2829 Maestro Paul, dropped 3lb, was back to the right sort of trip. (13/2)
1598 Scotoni, down 3lb, was just out of the handicap here. (16/1)
3043* Harvest View (IRE) looked rather novicey at some of her fences on this switch to handicap company. (13/8)
2962 Channel Pastime was carrying 10lb more than his long handicap mark. (25/1)

3233 MERE MAIDEN HURDLE (4-Y.O+) (Class E)

4-05 (4-09) **2m (8 hdls)** £2,862.50 (£800.00: £387.50) GOING: 0.19 sec per fur (G)

				SP	RR	SF
	The Flying Phantom (MHTompkins) **6-11-5** RDunwoody (chsd ldr: led appr 2 out: wandered appr last: all out)	—	**1**	5/1[2]	83	36
3115[3]	**Give And Take** (MCPipe) **4-10-9** APMcCoy (led: mstke 4th: rdn & hdd appr 2 out: r.o one pce)	1½	**2**	6/4[1]	82	25
	Crandon Boulevard (MrsJPitman) **4-10-9** JOsborne (hld up: stdy hdwy 5th: one pce fr 2 out)	5	**3**	20/1	77	20
	Embankment (IRE) (NJHenderson) **7-11-0**(5) MrCVigors (lw: hld up & bhd: hdwy after 3 out: btn whn j.rt last)	3	**4**	12/1	74	27
	Spread The Word (LGCottrell) **5-10-9**(5) DSalter (hld up: hdwy after 3 out: one pce fr 2 out)	1¼	**5**	33/1	67	20
1726[3]	**Fairy Knight** (RHannon) **5-11-5** NWilliamson (bit bkwd: nvr nr to chal)	11	**6**	11/2[3]	61	14
	Zidac (PJMakin) **5-11-5** BFenton (no hdwy fr 3 out)	3	**7**	25/1	58	11
3109[3]	**Kinnescash (IRE)** (PBowen) **4-10-9** AMaguire (prom tl wknd appr 2 out)	2½	**8**	12/1	56	—
1867[7]	**Loch Na Keal** (CPMorlock) **5-11-0** CLlewellyn (nvr nr ldrs)	1¼	**9**	20/1	50	3
3115[9]	**Langtonian** (GFEdwards) **8-11-2**(3) MichaelBrennan (prom to 3rd)	8	**10**	100/1	47	—
	Artistic Plan (IRE) (RHAlner) **5-11-5** BPowell (lw: prom to 5th)	½	**11**	12/1	46	—
2750[11]	**Prototype** (GFJohnsonHoughton) **6-11-5** AThornton (a bhd)	1	**12**	16/1	45	—
3115[4]	**Dormy Three** (RJHodges) **7-11-2**(3) TDascombe (chsd ldrs: rdn 3 out: sn wknd)	6	**13**	33/1	39	—
	Freeline Fontaine (IRE) (NJHenderson) **5-11-5** JRKavanagh (mstke 4th: a bhd)	1¾	**14**	33/1	37	—
3115[P]	**Moor Dutch** (RGFrost) **6-11-5** JFrost (plld hrd: a bhd: t.o)	28	**15**	100/1	9	—
	Elraas (USA) (RJO'Sullivan) **5-10-12**(7) NWillmington (bhd fr 5th: t.o)	½	**16**	50/1	9	—
2965[5]	**Boozys Dream** (NBThomson) **6-11-2**(3) GuyLewis (bhd: mstke 5th: t.o whn p.u bef 3 out)		**P**	100/1	—	—
3115[2]	**Welton Arsenal** (KBishop) **5-11-5** RGreene (nt j.w: a bhd: t.o whn p.u bef 2 out)		**P**	7/1	—	—
				(SP 140.6%)		**18 Rn**

3m 49.5 (9.50) CSF £12.78 TOTE £7.30: £2.80 £1.50 £6.10 (£9.20) Trio £22.00 OWNER P H Betts (Holdings) Ltd (NEWMARKET) BRED P. J. and R. M. Lane
WEIGHT FOR AGE 4yo-10lb
The Flying Phantom, who ran in the 1994 Derby and finished third in the 1995 Chester Cup, was well suited by the strong pace. He won an event where only two horses were ever really in it. (5/1: 3/1-11/2)
3115 Give And Take, backed as if defeat was out of the question, set a strong pace and kept on grimly to the end. His hurdling can still be improved. (6/4)
Crandon Boulevard, lightly-raced on the Flat, ought to be capable of improvement but may be better over further. (20/1)
Embankment (IRE), four times a winner at up to a mile on the Flat, should be better for the experience. (12/1)
Spread The Word never managed a win on the Flat, but showed her best form in headgear. (33/1)
1726 Fairy Knight (11/2: 7/2-6/1)
Artistic Plan (IRE) (12/1: 20/1-10/1)
3115 Welton Arsenal (7/1: 5/1-8/1)

3234 ILCHESTER H'CAP HURDLE (0-105) (4-Y.O+) (Class F)

4-35 (4-43) **2m (8 hdls)** £2,250.00 (£625.00: £300.00) GOING: 0.19 sec per fur (G)

				SP	RR	SF
2755[4]	**Always Happy (93)** (MissGayKelleway) **4-10-11** AMaguire (hld up: gd hdwy appr 2 out: led flat: drvn out)	—	**1**	7/2[1]	75	29
2755[2]	**Classic Pal (USA) (74)** (NRMitchell) **6-10-2** DSkyrme (hld up: hdwy 3 out: led appr 2 out: hdd flat: r.o)	1½	**2**	7/2[1]	55	19
2692[10]	**The Brewer (72)** (JCTuck) **5-10-0** RBellamy (swtg: a.p: ev ch appr last: one pce)	2½	**3**	66/1	50	14
2952[7]	**Lucayan Cay (IRE) (88)** (MrsAJBowlby) **6-11-2** BPowell (a.p: ev ch appr 2 out: one pce)	1¼	**4**	14/1	65	29
3056[5]	**Mrs Jawleyford (USA) (80)** (CSmith) **9-10-8** MRanger (hld up: hdwy after 3 out: mstke 2 out: one pce)	2½	**5**	33/1	54	18
	Tissisat (USA) (92) (JKirby) **8-11-6** GUpton (hld up & bhd: hdwy appr 2 out: bttr for r)	4	**6**	16/1	62+	26
3012[4]	**I Recall (IRE) (78)** (PHayward) **6-10-6** BFenton (prom to 3 out)	5	**7**	7/1[3]	43	7
3056[2]	**Dontdressfordinner (89)** (RJHodges) **7-11-3** RDunwoody (prom tl wknd appr 2 out)	½	**8**	11/2[2]	54	18
3002*	**Nashville Star (USA) (96)** (RMathew) **6-11-10v** AThornton (led 2nd tl appr 2 out: sn wknd)	5	**9**	8/1	56	20
1427[F]	**Imalight (82)** (RGFrost) **8-10-10** JFrost (bkwd: s.i.s: nvr nrr)	1¼	**10**	20/1	41	5
3050[10]	**Saafi (IRE) (75)** (RJBaker) **6-10-0b**[1](3) TDascombe (hld up: hdwy after 3 out: sn wknd)	nk	**11**	50/1	33	—
	Gladys Emmanuel (78) (REPocock) **10-10-3**(3) PHenley (bit bkwd: led to 2nd: rdn & wknd appr 2 out)	1½	**12**	25/1	35	—
3087[4]	**El Grando (83)** (KOCunningham-Brown) **7-10-11** NWilliamson (hit 5th: sn bhd)	2	**13**	10/1	38	2
2708[F]	**Fane Park (IRE) (82)** (CLPopham) **9-10-10** GTormey (hld up: hdwy 5th: wknd after 3 out)	¾	**14**	33/1	36	—
3031[6]	**Never so Blue (IRE) (87)** (PBradley) **6-10-10**(5) SophieMitchell (a bhd)	3	**15**	16/1	38	2
3056[6]	**Daily Sport Girl (85)** (BJLlewellyn) **8-10-13** MrJLLlewellyn (prom tl wknd qckly appr 2 out)	1½	**16**	16/1	34	—
2040[7]	**Ethbaat (USA) (87)** (MJHeaton-Ellis) **6-11-1** MRichards (unruly s: plld hrd: dropped rr 5th: t.o)	15	**17**	33/1	21	—

				SP	RR	SF
1595[7]	**In Cahoots (83)** (ADSmith) **4-9-12**(3)ow1 MichaelBrennan (plld hrd: bhd fr 3rd: t.o whn p.u bef 2 out)		**P**	50/1	—	—
2874[8]	**Concinnity (USA) (72)** (BScriven) **8-10-0** MrAHoldsworth (prom to 4th: t.o whn p.u bef 2 out)		**P**	66/1	—	—
1678[5]	**Mu-Tadil (72)** (RJBaker) **5-10-0** VSlattery (sn rdn: a bhd: t.o whn p.u bef 2 out)		**P**	66/1	—	—

(SP 142.7%) **20 Rn**

3m 49.4 (9.40) CSF £14.97 CT £705.33 TOTE £3.70: £1.50 £1.50 £19.90 £3.10 (£14.70) Trio £1,625.40; £938.67 to Haydock 21/2/97 OWNER Mr C. R. Fleet (WHITCOMBE) BRED Cheveley Park Stud Ltd
LONG HANDICAP The Brewer 9-4 In Cahoots 9-7 Concinnity (USA) 9-4 Mu-Tadil 9-7
WEIGHT FOR AGE 4yo-10lb
2755 Always Happy came with a well-timed run, and looked more at home on this sounder surface. (7/2)
2755 Classic Pal (USA) could not confirm the Folkestone form with the winner on this better ground. (7/2)
The Brewer, 10lb wrong at the weights, had shown form in bumpers last season but this was his first sign of ability over hurdles. (66/1)
Lucayan Cay (IRE) was obviously all the better for his run a fortnight ago. (14/1: 10/1-16/1)
Mrs Jawleyford (USA), already due to drop 3lb, would have preferred softer ground. (33/1)
Tissisat (USA), reported to have been suffering leg problems, ran a race full of promise. (16/1)
3002* Nashville Star (USA) (8/1: 5/1-9/1)

3235 GOLF COURSE STANDARD N.H. FLAT RACE (4, 5 & 6-Y.O) (Class H)

5-05 (5-11) **2m** £1,264.00 (£354.00: £172.00)

				SP	RR	SF
	Noisy Miner (IRE) (DNicholson) **5-11-1**(3) RMassey (unf: hld up: hdwy over 4f out: led over 2f out: sn clr: pushed out)	—	**1**	15/8[1]	75 f	—
	Filscot (WGMTurner) **5-10-11**(7) JPower (a.p: led over 3f out tl over 2f out: r.o one pce)	12	**2**	33/1	63 f	—
	Redgrave Wolf (KBishop) **4-9-10**(7) GSupple (a.p: r.o one pce fnl 2f)	s.h	**3**	33/1	58 f	—
	Racketball (NATwiston-Davies) **4-10-1**(7) LSuthern (a.p: one pce fnl 3f)	2	**4**	10/1	61 f	—
	Gorman (IRE) (MissHCKnight) **5-11-1**(3) PHenley (lw: prom tl wknd over 2f out)	8	**5**	5/1[3]	53 f	—
	Moonraker's Mirage (DRCElsworth) **6-10-11**(7) MrNMoran (s.s: hdwy whn rn wd bnd over 3f out: nt rcvr)	3½	**6**	12/1	49 f	—
	Wild Native (IRE) (PFNicholls) **5-10-11**(7) LCummins (s.s: nvr trbld ldrs)	13	**7**	4/1[2]	36 f	—
	Spruce Lodge (JSKing) **4-10-3**(5) SophieMitchell (no hdwy fnl 4f)	3½	**8**	16/1	33 f	—
	Act In Time (IRE) (TRGeorge) **5-10-11**(7) CHynes (led over 12f: sn wknd)	3	**9**	12/1	30 f	—
	Two Lords (GAHam) **5-11-4** GTormey (s.s: rdn after 6f: nvr nr ldrs)	6	**10**	33/1	24 f	—
99[2]	**Arrange** (JCABatchelor) **5-10-11**(7) MrSWalker (hld up & plld hrd: n.d)	1½	**11**	20/1	22 f	—
	Salix (NJHawke) **5-10-13**(5) OBurrows (a bhd)	6	**12**	50/1	16 f	—
	Cathay (IRE) (MrsJPitman) **5-10-11**(7) MrGBaines (w'like: bkwd: s.s: a bhd)	8	**13**	6/1	8 f	—
	General Killiney (IRE) (DJCaro) **5-11-4** MrAPhillips (bkwd: bhd fnl 5f)	6	**14**	50/1	2 f	—
	Tom Diamond (LASnook) **5-11-1**(3) MichaelBrennan (bkwd: bhd fnl 5f)	13	**15**	33/1	—	—
	Mac'smyuncle (RGFrost) **6-11-4b1** MrAHoldsworth (prom 8f: t.o)	10	**16**	50/1	—	—
	Charlie Pip (RCurtis) **5-11-4** MrMAppleby (a bhd: t.o)	dist	**17**	33/1	—	—

(SP 141.4%) **17 Rn**

3m 45.2 CSF £85.78 TOTE £3.60: £2.30 £12.70 £7.90 (£107.40) Trio Not won; £292.79 to Haydock 21/2/97 OWNER Mrs R. J. Skan (TEMPLE GUITING) BRED Andrew Kavanagh
WEIGHT FOR AGE 4yo-10lb
Noisy Miner (IRE) hails from a stable with a strong hand in these events. (15/8)
Filscot is out of a winning pointer. (33/1)
Redgrave Wolf is the first foal of Redgrave Rose. (33/1)
Racketball is a brother of Tain Ton. (10/1: op 5/1)
Gorman (IRE) cost IR3,000 guineas as a four-year-old. (5/1: 7/2-6/1)
Moonraker's Mirage would have finished closer had he not taken the scenic route. (12/1: op 6/1)
Wild Native (IRE) (4/1: 2/1-9/2)
Cathay (IRE) (6/1: op 4/1)

T/Jkpt: Not won; £37,485.63 to Haydock 21/2/97. T/Plpt: £231.60 (94.37 Tckts). T/Qdpt: £79.40 (12.97 Tckts) KH

3236a - 3244a : (Irish Racing) - See Computer Raceform

2593a-THURLES (Ireland) (R-H) (Soft)

Thursday February 13th

3245a KINLOCH BRAE CHASE (Gd 2) (6-Y.O+)

3-00 (3-04) **2m 4f** **(14 fncs)** IR £9,675.00 (IR £2,775.00: IR £1,275.00: IR £375.00) GOING: Not Established

				SP	RR	SF
2997a[4]	**Merry Gale (IRE)** (JTRDreaper,Ireland) **9-12-0** CO'Dwyer (cl up: led briefly 2nd: hmpd & lost pl 8th: chsd ldr whn lft cl 2nd 2 out: shaken up to ld flat)	—	**1**	9/4[2]	155	—
2741a[8]	**Royal Mountbrowne** (APO'Brien,Ireland) **9-12-0** CFSwan (led & disp ld: 2nd whn mstke 8th: chsd ldr whn lft in ld 2 out: hdd last: no ex)	¾	**2**	7/1[3]	154	—
	The Real Article (IRE) (GStack,Ireland) **8-11-4** LPCusack (mstke 1st: towards rr: mstke & rdn 10th: 4th & no imp next: t.o)	dist	**3**	33/1	—	—
1231a[3]	**Corston Dancer (IRE)** (JABerry,Ireland) **9-10-13b** THorgan (towards rr: lost tch 8th: wl t.o.)	dist	**4**	100/1	—	—
2994a*	**Dorans Pride (IRE)** (MHourigan,Ireland) **8-12-0** JPBroderick (cl up: disp ld fr 3rd: led 7th: clr fr next to 4 out: fell 2 out)		**F**	1/2[1]	—	—

(SP 113.9%) **5 Rn**

5m 30.9 OWNER Herb Stanley (KILSALLAGHAN) BRED Noel O'Brien in Ireland
2997a Merry Gale (IRE), with his tongue tied down, was presented with this by the fall of Dorans Pride two out. He got the better of the runner-up early on the flat, and was just pushed out to win. This was not impressive and one has to go along with his trainer's opinion that he is just not as good as he was. (9/4)
1917 Royal Mountbrowne, meeting the winner on very disadvantageous terms, was readily held on the flat. (7/1)
2994a* Dorans Pride (IRE) led at halfway and looked assured of victory when falling two out. His jumping had been without blemish over these easy fences, and no harm was done. (1/2)

3246a - 3253a : (Irish Racing) - See Computer Raceform

2845a-GOWRAN PARK (Kilkenny, Ireland) (R-H) (Yielding)
Saturday February 15th

3254a RED MILLS TRIAL HURDLE (Gd 3) (4-Y.O+)
3-30 (3-35) **2m (9 hdls)** IR £6,850.00 (IR £1,550.00: IR £650.00: IR £350.00) GOING: Not Established

	Horse / details	Dist	Pos	SP	RR	SF
2740a[2]	**Theatreworld (IRE)** (APO'Brien,Ireland) **5-11-9** CFSwan (in tch: reminders after 6th: wnt 3rd st: chal 2 out: led appr last: r.o wl)	—	1	9/4[1]	137	30
2603a[8]	**Guest Performance (IRE)** (DTHughes,Ireland) **5-11-9** RHughes (sn chsng ldr: led after 6th: hdd & rdn appr last: nt qckn w wnr flat)	1½	2	7/2[2]	136	29
	Lady Daisy (IRE) (AMullins,Ireland) **8-10-5**(7) AO'Shea (cl up: rdn 2 out: nt qckn w ldrs between last 2)	8	3	7/1[3]	114	10
2740a[3]	**Dardjini (USA)** (NMeade,Ireland) **7-11-6** KFO'Brien (hld up: 3rd 3 out: rdn 2 out: sn btn)	12	4	9/4[1]	110	6
2603a[9]	**Magical Lady (IRE)** (JohnMcKay,Ireland) **5-11-1** FWoods (led: hdd after 6th: no ex fr 3 out)	6	5	10/1	102	—
1752a[4]	**Bolino Star (IRE)** (SJTreacy,Ireland) **6-11-7** TPTreacy (hld up towards rr: hdwy appr 2 out: nvr nr to chal)	1½	6	10/1	103	—
2848a[3]	**New Co (IRE)** (MFMorris,Ireland) **9-11-3** CO'Dwyer (hld up: nt qckn & lost tch appr 3 out: n.d)	6	7	11/1	93	—
	Anusha (WJLanigan,Ireland) **7-10-12** DTEvans (mid div: mod 8th after 3 out: n.d)	7	8	33/1	81	—
2461a[5]	**Mayasta (IRE)** (FBerry,Ireland) **7-10-5**(7) RPHogan (hld up: 8th at 4th: n.d appr 3 out)	8	9	33/1	73	—
	Pas Possible (IRE) (ALeahy,Ireland) **5-11-3** GMO'Neill (towards rr: sme hdwy 5th: sn wknd: towards rr whn pckd bdly 3 out: rdr lost iron: t.o)	dist	10	100/1	—	—

(SP 129.6%) **10 Rn**

3m 51.4 (-3.60) OWNER Mrs John Magnier (PILTOWN) BRED I. Allen, K. C. Choo and Calogo Bloodstock Ag

2740a Theatreworld (IRE) did not have much confidence surrounding him, but his toughness saw him through with some style. Closing in third place before the straight, he had taken the measure of the runner-up before the last and maintained his advantage on the flat without being asked to do too much. He is not Champion Hurdle class and the trip would seem to rule him out of the Stayers', nevertheless he may take his chance in one of them. (9/4)

2461a Guest Performance (IRE) went ahead three out but was readily outpaced from the last by the winner. This was his best effort to date, and he has gone up 5lb, a move which would rather dim his prospects in the Coral Cup, but he will appreciate the longer trip and really needs better ground. (7/2)

Lady Daisy (IRE) is only a handicapper, but an improving one, and she has an ambitious Imperial Cup/County Hurdle double bid in her sights.(7/1)

2740a Dardjini (USA) was very disappointing and did not want to know about it from three out. (9/4)

Magical Lady (IRE) found this competition just too warm. (10/1: op 6/1)

1752a Bolino Star (IRE) has handicapping aspirations at Cheltenham, and put in a fair effort here considering she had eight stitches in a gashed hind leg after her Navan second in December. She will come on from this. (10/1: op 4/1)

2848a New Co (IRE) (11/1: op 7/1)

3255a RED MILLS TRIAL CHASE (5-Y.O+)
4-00 (4-02) **3m (16 fncs)** IR £4,110.00 (IR £930.00: IR £390.00: IR £210.00) GOING: Not Established

	Horse / details	Dist	Pos	SP	RR	SF
2848a[10]	**Nuaffe** (PAFahy,Ireland) **12-11-6b** TJMitchell (cl up: led 5th: mstke 9th: rdn 2 out: mstke last: styd on u.p)	—	1	9/2[2]	117	40
2856a[3]	**Le Ginno (FR)** (TFoley,Ireland) **10-11-3** TPTreacy (cl up: mstkes: lft 2nd at 7th: effrt fr 3 out: u.p appr last: styd on flat: no ex)	1	2	5/1[3]	113	36
	Cheslock (IRE) (JMonroe,Ireland) **8-11-0b** PARoche (sn bhd: mstke 5th: wl t.o)	dist	3	50/1	—	—
	Harcon (IRE) (JTRDreaper,Ireland) **9-11-12** CFSwan (led: hdd & mstke 5th: cl 2nd whn fell 7th)		F	4/9[1]	—	—

(SP 106.0%) **4 Rn**

6m 28.8 (-21.20) OWNER John Doyle (LEIGHLINBRIDGE) BRED T. Logan

Nuaffe blundered his way round after going to the front at the fifth. He made a serious mistake at the last, but still had enough in hand to repel his novice opponent. (9/2)

Harcon (IRE) made a mistake at the fifth, and came down two fences later. He was in a sorry state when led away. (4/9)

3256a - 3257a : (Irish Racing) - See Computer Raceform

2966a-PUNCHESTOWN (Naas, Ireland) (R-H) (Soft)
Sunday February 16th

3258a JUVENILE HURDLE (Gd 3) (4-Y.O)
2-10 (2-11) **2m (9 hdls)** IR £6,850.00 (IR £1,550.00: IR £650.00: IR £350.00) GOING: Not Established

	Horse / details	Dist	Pos	SP	RR	SF
2993a*	**Commanche Court (IRE)** (TMWalsh,Ireland) **4-11-0** NWilliamson (rn 2nd: led 6th: rdn & styd on fr 2 out: clr flat)	—	1	4/6[1]	99+	—
2993a[8]	**Grimes** (CRoche,Ireland) **4-11-3** CO'Dwyer (hld up: mstke 5th: wnt 2nd appr 3 out: rdn & chsd wnr 2 out: j.slwly last: one pce)	5	2	13/2[3]	97	—
2993a[9]	**Miss Roberto (IRE)** (MBrassil,Ireland) **4-10-2**(7) RPHogan (led: clr early: hdd 6th: rdn 3 out: mstke next: r.o appr last)	1	3	16/1	88	—
2738a[3]	**Spirit Dancer (IRE)** (GMLyons,Ireland) **4-11-0** SCLyons (hld up towards rr: chsd ldrs 3 out: no imp after 2 out)	9	4	9/1	84	—
2603a[14]	**Rescue Time (IRE)** (KPrendergast,Ireland) **4-11-0** JShortt (hld up: nt fluent: 6th 3 out: no imp next)	10	5	10/1	74	—
2993a[11]	**Highly Motivated** (APO'Brien,Ireland) **4-10-9** CFSwan (rn 3rd: mstke 3rd: chsd ldrs bef 3 out: no imp fr 2 out)	2½	6	14/1	67	—
2993a[7]	**Miss Pennyhill (IRE)** (ASadik,Ireland) **4-10-4**(5) TMartin (5th at 4th: towards rr 6th: no imp 3 out)	s.h	7	33/1	66	—
2738a*	**Dr Bones (IRE)** (MJPO'Brien,Ireland) **4-11-0** TPRudd (hld up towards rr: rdn bef 3 out: dropped bhd: t.o: virtually p.u: lame)	dist	8	5/1[2]	—	—

(SP 124.6%) **8 Rn**

4m 20.1 OWNER D. F. Desmond (KILL) BRED Cambremont Ltd Partnership

2993a* Commanche Court (IRE) went ahead four out and made the rest. Collected nicely at the last, he went clear on the flat and, although not inconvenienced by the heavy ground, would certainly prefer sounder conditions. He is going the right way, and seems to have a good attitude towards the game, but there is a feeling that the English juvenile hurdlers are a long way in front. (4/6)
2333a* Grimes, in second place from three out, was making no impression well before the last, and his mistake there made no difference to the result. (13/2: op 4/1)
2333a Miss Roberto (IRE) ran in front until headed by the winner. She was in third and totally outpaced when blundering two out, yet stayed on again with real purpose from the last. (16/1)

3260a I.A.W.S. NOVICES' CHASE (Gd 2) (5-Y.O+)
3-10 (3-12) **2m (11 fncs)** IR £13,800.00 (IR £3,800.00: IR £1,800.00) GOING: Not Established

Form	Horse	Dist	Pos	SP	RR	SF
2335a[6]	**Jeffell** (ALTMoore,Ireland) **7-11-7** FWoods (j.w: mde all: lft clr 2 out: unchal)	—	1	5/2[1]	120+	32
	Papillon (IRE) (TMWalsh,Ireland) **6-11-4** NWilliamson (towards rr: wnt mod 4th 3 out: lft dist 2nd 2 out: no imp whn bad mstke last)	15	2	10/1	102	14
2739a[4]	**Kharasar (IRE)** (AMullins,Ireland) **7-11-4** CO'Dwyer (hld up: reminders after 7th: chsd ldrs 4 out: lft mod 3rd & n.d whn mstke 2 out: one pce)	¾	3	7/2[2]	101	13
	Currency Basket (IRE) (PO'Leary,Ireland) **8-11-0** JShortt (towards rr: fell 2nd)		F	20/1	—	—
2739a[3]	**Penndara (IRE)** (APO'Brien,Ireland) **8-11-4** CFSwan (rn 2nd: mstke 7th: chsd wnr whn fell 2 out)		F	5/2[1]	—	—
	Rocketts Castle (IRE) (MrsSABramall,Ireland) **7-11-0** PCarberry (chsd ldrs: mstke 7th: no imp 4 out: p.u bef next)		P	16/1	—	—
2739a[2]	**Beakstown (IRE)** (PMullins,Ireland) **8-11-10** TPTreacy (rn 3rd: slow 5th: rdn after 7th: losing tch whn slow 4 out: p.u bef next)		P	9/2[3]	—	—

(SP 117.3%) **7 Rn**

4m 31.7 (22.70) OWNER Thomas Bailey (NAAS)
2335a Jeffell got his act together in no uncertain manner. He made all, jumping well, and appeared to have it sewn up when left clear two out. Cheltenham is not on his agenda. (5/2)
Papillon (IRE), making steady headway from five out, was left second two out, but was no threat when blundering at the last. He needs much further. (10/1)
2739a Kharasar (IRE) attracted plenty of support in the market, and flattered in third place before four out, but looked well beaten in fourth place when losing ground two out. Left in third place from there, he was very one-paced after. (7/2)
2739a Penndara (IRE), only a length in arrears when coming down two out, would not have beaten the winner. He needs better ground. (5/2)
2739a Beakstown (IRE) had a stiff task on paper, and his jumping also let him down. Fading from five out, he was pulled up with three to jump. (9/2)

3261a ERICSSON GSM GRAND NATIONAL TRIAL H'CAP CHASE (Gd 3) (5-Y.O+)
3-40 (3-42) **3m 2f (18 fncs)** IR £20,700.00 (IR £5,700.00: IR £2,700.00) GOING: Not Established

Form	Horse	Dist	Pos	SP	RR	SF
2348a[5]	**Antonin (FR)** (MrsSABramall,Ireland) **9-10-0** CO'Dwyer (in tch: wnt 2nd at 5th: lft in ld 7th: drew clr after 5 out: styd on wl: unchal)	—	1	6/1	136+	—
2997a[5]	**King of the Gales** (ALTMoore,Ireland) **10-10-6** CFSwan (hld up: mod 3rd 5 out: dist 2nd bef next: n.d fr 3 out: one pce)	dist	2	9/2[2]	—	—
1750a[5]	**Carrigeen Kerria (IRE)** (RHLalor,Ireland) **9-9-7** DJCasey (in tch: mstkes 9th & 10th: bd mstke 12th: dist 4th 5 out: n.d)	5	3	20/1	—	—
2848a[8]	**Fissure Seal** (ALTMoore,Ireland) **11-9-8** FWoods (hld up towards rr: mstke 8th: fell 10th)		F	12/1	—	—
2348a[10]	**Second Schedual** (MissAMMcMahon,Ireland) **12-9-8**ow1 TPTreacy (cl up early: lost pl 4th: mstke next: dropped bhd 6th: p.u after 7th)		P	9/1	—	—
2848a[2]	**Corymandel (IRE)** (HdeBromhead,Ireland) **8-9-7** TPRudd (led: bad mstke & hdd 7th: 2nd to 11th: wknd next: dist 5th whn mstke 5 out: p.u bef next)		P	10/1	—	—
	Master Oats (KCBailey) **11-12-0** NWilliamson (hld up: wnt 3rd at 9th: 2nd at 12th: reminders bef next: rdn & chsd wnr 5 out: sn wknd: p.u bef 3 out)		P	7/4[1]	—	—
2362a[5]	**Son Of War** (PMcCreery,Ireland) **10-10-7** RDunwoody (cl up: mstkes: lost tch 11th: mstke & uns rdr 2 out)		U	5/1[3]	—	—
2856a[4]	**Executive Options (IRE)** (JMcCaghy,Ireland) **8-9-10**ow3 PCarberry (plld hrd: hld up: blnd & uns rdr 4th)		U	20/1	—	—

(SP 121.8%) **9 Rn**

7m 27.2 OWNER G R Bailey Ltd BRED Pierre Sayet & Maurice Marlin
2348a Antonin (FR) did everything right this time, taking over after the seventh and steadily drawing clear. Unchallenged from five out, he made no mistakes and seemed to really appreciate the heavy ground. Successful off 120 at Wexford earlier this season, he was running off 134 and has gone up 9lb. On paper, he would have a chance at Aintree but he is an enigmatic character. (6/1)
2602a King of the Gales went a remote second four out, and stayed on without making any impression. (9/2)
Carrigeen Kerria (IRE) went round in her own time, and was a remote third when blundering two out. (20/1)
2848a Fissure Seal (12/1: op 8/1)
Master Oats has run like this first-time-out before for, after going second seven out, he was out-jumped at the next. He dropped right out before four out and pulled up before the next. Despite market support, he looks a light of other days. (7/4)

3262a - 3264a : (Irish Racing) - See Computer Raceform

2634-HAYDOCK (L-H) (Good to soft becoming Good)
Friday February 21st
WEATHER: fine

3265 TWEEDLE DUM 'N.H.' NOVICES' H'CAP HURDLE (4-Y.O+) (Class C)
2-00 (2-00) **2m (8 hdls)** £3,533.75 (£1,070.00: £522.50: £248.75) GOING: 0.53 sec per fur (GS)

Form	Horse	Dist	Pos	SP	RR	SF
3019[2]	**The Proms (IRE) (109)** (NATwiston-Davies) **6-11-10** CLlewellyn (lw: hld up: lost pl 5th: rallied appr 2 out: led last: drvn out)	—	1	7/2[2]	89	49
3035[5]	**Silly Money (90)** (TDEasterby) **6-10-5** RGarritty (hld up: stdy hdwy 5th: hrd rdn & r.o flat)	¾	2	8/1[3]	69	29
2790*	**Phar Echo (IRE) (94)** (LLungo) **6-10-9** RSupple (led tl after 1st: led after 2 out: hdd last: wknd)	6	3	8/1[3]	67	27
3014[3]	**Logical Step (IRE) (97)** (DRGandolfo) **7-10-12** RDunwoody (hld up: hdwy 5th: ev ch 2 out: one pce)	¾	4	7/2[2]	70	30
2917[8]	**Prince of Saints (IRE) (85)** (MDHammond) **6-10-0** DBentley (no hdwy fr 3 out)	6	5	10/1	52	12

2785[6] **Mapleton (95)** (MrsSJSmith) **4-9-7**(7) RWilkinson (prom: led appr 5th tl after 2 out: sn wknd)....................2½ **6** 12/1 59 9
3026[2] **Jervaulx (IRE) (96)** (GRichards) **6-10-11** PCarberry (w ldr tl rdn & wknd after 3 out)....................16 **7** 15/8[1] 44 4
Whiter Morn (85) (CaptJWilson) **7-9-7**(7) NHorrocks (led after 1st: hdd appr 5th: sn wknd)....................½ **8** 100/1 33 —
(SP 119.2%) **8 Rn**

3m 55.0 (13.00) CSF £29.57 CT £194.26 TOTE £3.60: £1.10 £1.70 £2.00 (£11.50) OWNER Mrs J. Mould (CHELTENHAM) BRED Mrs S. Brennan
LONG HANDICAP Prince of Saints (IRE) 9-9 Mapleton 9-7 Whiter Morn 8-1
WEIGHT FOR AGE 4yo-10lb
3019 The Proms (IRE) defied top weight but had to work hard over a course and trip which barely brought his stamina into play. He will go for the Royal SunAlliance at Cheltenham. (7/2)
3035 Silly Money has not been getting home over extended trips, but one could see why he has been tried over them here. (8/1)
2790* Phar Echo (IRE), dropping back in trip, could not defy a 9lb hike in the weights. (8/1)
3014 Logical Step (IRE) did not find a lot when the chips were down and may need softer ground. (7/2)
1687 Prince of Saints (IRE), 5lb wrong on his handicap debut, comes from a stable that has been out of sorts. (10/1)
3026 Jervaulx (IRE) was most disappointing, and his trainer could offer the Stewards no explanation. (15/8)

3266 WHITE RABBIT H'CAP CHASE (0-135) (5-Y.O+) (Class C)

2-30 (2-30) **3m (18 fncs)** £4,531.25 (£1,370.00: £667.50: £316.25) GOING: 0.53 sec per fur (GS)

SP RR SF

General Wolfe (135) (CaptTAForster) **8-12-0** RDunwoody (hld up: hdwy to chse ldr 13th: hrd rdn to ld last strides)....................— **1** 7/2[2] 152 50
1385* **McGregor The Third (125)** (GRichards) **11-11-4** ADobbin (chsd ldr: led 11th: hrd rdn flat: hdd last trides).....nk **2** 4/1[3] 142 40
2880[4] **Destin d'Estruval (FR) (123)** (DNicholson) **6-11-2** DBridgwater (hld up: hit 1st: hdwy 14th: ev ch 3 out: sn rdn: wknd last: eased whn btn)....................16 **3** 11/4[1] 129 27
3018[2] **Camelot Knight (119)** (NATwiston-Davies) **11-10-12** CLlewellyn (lw: hld up: reminder after 7th: hdwy 13th: wknd 4 out)....................dist **4** 13/2 — —
Camitrov (FR) (133) (TKeddy) **7-11-12** PCarberry (bit bkwd: led to 10th: wknd qckly 13th: t.o)....................dist **5** 16/1 — —
3025[3] **Northants (121)** (WStorey) **11-10-9**(5) RMcGrath (hld up: mstkes 3rd & 5th: wl bhd 10th: t.o whn p.u lame flat). **P** 4/1[3] — —
3039[3] **River Bounty (119)** (CPEBrooks) **11-10-12b**[1] GBradley (prom: led 10th to 11th: wknd qckly & p.u bef 12th: lame).................... **P** 14/1 — —
(SP 114.8%) **7 Rn**

6m 19.3 (21.30) CSF £16.69 TOTE £4.00: £2.30 £1.30 (£5.40) OWNER Winning Line Racing Ltd (LUDLOW) BRED Mrs M. Easton
General Wolfe goes well when fresh and repeated last year's victory in this event off a 12lb higher mark. He will now go for the Astec Buzz Shop at Cheltenham prior to the Grand National. (7/2)
1385* McGregor The Third, helped by the drying ground, could not quite hold the winner on the long run-in. (4/1)
2880 Destin d'Estruval (FR) was making his debut over fences in this country, having won on very soft ground at Auteuil. (11/4)

3267 QUEEN OF HEARTS H'CAP HURDLE (0-145) (4-Y.O+) (Class B)

3-00 (3-00) **2m 4f (10 hdls)** £4,815.30 (£1,457.40: £711.20: £338.10) GOING: 0.53 sec per fur (GS)

SP RR SF

1645[6] **Allegation (132)** (MCPipe) **7-11-1v** JamieEvans (chsd ldr: led appr last: sn clr)....................— **1** 25/1 120 45
3163[4] **Kaitak (IRE) (119)** (JMCarr) **6-9-13**(3) FLeahy (hld up: hdwy 6th: led after 7th: hdd appr last: sn btn)....................10 **2** 14/1 99 24
3011[2] **Kingdom of Shades (USA) (127)** (AndrewTurnell) **7-10-10** PCarberry (hld up: hdwy 6th: rdn appr 3 out: styd on fr 2 out)....................2½ **3** 7/4[1] 105 30
2888[3] **Outset (IRE) (127)** (MDHammond) **7-10-7**(3) MrCBonner (hld up: hdwy whn mstke 7th: one pce fr 3 out)....................5 **4** 11/2 101 26
2888[9] **Burnt Imp (USA) (130)** (GMMoore) **7-10-13** JCallaghan (bhd whn rdn 5th: sme late hdwy)....................1½ **5** 9/1 103 28
3038[7] **Mister Morose (IRE) (135)** (NATwiston-Davies) **7-11-4** CLlewellyn (hld up: rdn & bhd 6th: rallied 3 out: 4th & btn whn hit 2 out)....................6 **6** 3/1[2] 103 28
2900[4] **Tibetan (131)** (LadyHerries) **5-11-0** RDunwoody (hld up: stdy hdwy 6th: wknd appr 3 out: t.o)....................22 **7** 5/1[3] 81 6
2817[7] **Diwali Dancer (117)** (MCPipe) **7-9-7**(7) GSupple (led tl after 7th: wknd qckly appr 3 out: t.o)....................11 **8** 16/1 59 —
3160[6] **Better Times Ahead (145)** (GRichards) **11-12-0** ADobbin (t.o 4th: p.u bef 3 out).................... **P** 25/1 — —
(SP 123.7%) **9 Rn**

4m 52.2 (15.20) CSF £302.06 CT £858.79 TOTE £27.50: £4.40 £2.50 £1.30 (£108.30) Trio £151.90 OWNER Martin Pipe Racing Club (WELLINGTON) BRED Newgate Stud Co
LONG HANDICAP Diwali Dancer 9-9
Allegation, dropped 5lb, was a convincing winner in the end, and now goes for either the Coral Cup or the Gold Card at the Festival. (25/1)
3163 Kaitak (IRE), 4lb higher than when winning over course and distance in December 1995, was already due to go down 2lb. (14/1)
3011 Kingdom of Shades (USA), up 3lb, was not suited by the drying ground. (7/4)
2888 Outset (IRE) was 9lb higher than when scoring at Aintree last March. (11/2)
1645 Burnt Imp (USA) looks in the Handicapper's grip, having gone up 15lb this winter. (9/1)
3038 Mister Morose (IRE) may have found the ground a bit lively. (3/1)

3268 GLENGOYNE HIGHLAND MALT TAMEROSIA SERIES (QUALIFIER) NOVICES' CHASE (5-Y.O+) (Class D)

3-30 (3-30) **2m 4f (15 fncs)** £3,631.25 (£1,100.00: £537.50: £256.25) GOING: Not Established

SP RR SF

3008[2] **Eudipe (FR)** (MCPipe) **5-11-4** RDunwoody (lw: hld up: mstke 7th (water): wnt 2nd appr 3 out: rdn appr 2 out: r.o to ld flat)....................— **1** 11/10[1] 139 28
2885[F] **Simply Dashing (IRE) (135)** (TDEasterby) **6-12-0** RGarritty (chsd ldr: hit 9th: led 11th: clr 2 out: mstke last: wknd & hdd flat)....................2½ **2** 11/10[1] 137 36
2841[2] **Garethson (IRE)** (MissHCKnight) **6-11-4** DBridgwater (lw: led to 11th: wknd 3 out)....................dist **3** 10/1[2] — —
3047[P] **Major Look (NZ) (107)** (SABrookshaw) **9-11-8** ADobbin (sn wl bhd: t.o)....................9 **4** 33/1[3] — —
2650[4] **Gone Away (IRE) (64)** (MDHammond) **8-11-1**(3) MrCBonner (sn t.o: pckd 10th)....................28 **5** 100/1 — —
(SP 108.3%) **5 Rn**

5m 18.4 (21.40) CSF £2.41 TOTE £2.10: £1.20 £1.30 (£1.40) OWNER Mr D. A. Johnson (WELLINGTON) BRED Mme Andre & Bruno Vagne
WEIGHT FOR AGE 5yo-10lb
3008 Eudipe (FR) took advantage of a weight concession from the runner-up in the closing stages. (11/10)
2885 Simply Dashing (IRE) was just starting to look a little leg-weary when missing out at the last. (11/10: evens-6/5)
2841 Garethson (IRE) was allowed to come home in his own time once his chance had gone. (10/1)

3269 SCOTTISH EQUITABLE/JOCKEYS ASSOCIATION SERIES (QUALIFIER) H'CAP HURDLE (0-120) (4-Y.O+) (Class D)

4-00 (4-01) **2m 4f (10 hdls)** £2,853.00 (£864.00: £422.00: £201.00) GOING: 0.53 sec per fur (GS)

	Horse	Dist	Pos	SP	RR	SF
1952²	**Big Strand (IRE) (115)** (MCPipe) **8-11-10** JamieEvans (lw: hld up & bhd: hdwy appr 3 out: swtchd rt appr 2 out: str run to ld nr fin)	—	1	11/2 ²	96	33
3048²	**Barton Ward (105)** (SABrookshaw) **6-11-0** ADobbin (hld up: hdwy after 7th: led appr 2 out: ct nr fin)	1¼	2	11/4 ¹	85	22
2666⁷	**Selatan (IRE) (110)** (DRGandolfo) **5-11-5** RDunwoody (led tl appr 2 out: wknd flat)	8	3	10/1	84	21
3035²	**Topsawyer (95)** (MissSEHall) **9-10-4** KGaule (hld up: hdwy 6th: ev ch 2 out: wknd flat)	1¾	4	7/1	67	4
3146⁷	**Cassio's Boy (91)** (RJEckley) **6-10-0** PCarberry (hld up & bhd: hdwy 7th: wknd appr 2 out: mstke last)	7	5	12/1	58	—
2900*	**Purevalue (IRE) (112)** (MWEasterby) **6-11-7** RichardGuest (lw: prom: ev ch 2 out: sn wknd)	6	6	6/1 ³	74	11
2808⁶	**Sweet Trentino (IRE) (91)** (MTate) **6-10-0** CLlewellyn (nvr nr ldrs)	1¼	7	50/1	52	—
3028*	**Oat Couture (119)** (LLungo) **9-12-0** RSupple (lw: rdn 6th: a bhd)	½	8	9/1	79	16
2929⁴	**Amillionmemories (93)** (MrsBarbaraWaring) **7-10-2** PHolley (lw: mstke 4th: a bhd)	6	9	16/1	49	—
2666ᴾ	**Hoodwinker (IRE) (109)** (WJenks) **8-11-4** DBridgwater (lw: chsd ldr: reminders after 2nd: wknd appr 3 out)	10	10	14/1	57	—
1681ᴾ	**Nuns Cone (91)** (REPeacock) **9-9-11**(3) RMassey (bhd fr 7th)	3	11	33/1	36	—
3028⁷	**Bang in Trouble (IRE) (104)** (JJO'Neill) **6-10-8**(5) RMcGrath (p.u lame bef 4th)		P	14/1	—	—
3034ᴾ	**Elpidos (115)** (MDHammond) **5-11-7**(3) MrCBonner (prom to 6th: t.o whn p.u bef 2 out)		P	25/1	—	—
				(SP 123.6%)	**13 Rn**	

4m 57.8 (20.80) CSF £19.92 CT £140.85 TOTE £5.80: £2.40 £1.70 £3.90 (£5.40) Trio £88.80 OWNER Mr E. C. Jones (WELLINGTON) BRED M. Parkhill

LONG HANDICAP Nuns Cone 9-11 Cassio's Boy 9-13 Sweet Trentino (IRE) 8-12

1952 Big Strand (IRE), 8lb higher than when winning at Worcester in December, needed every yard of this trip on ground as fast as this. (11/2)
3048 Barton Ward was back to his best distance for his handicap debut. (11/4)
Selatan (IRE) is more effective with some give underfoot. (10/1)
3035 Topsawyer had been raised 2lb for finishing second last time. (7/1)
2666 Cassio's Boy would have preferred a softer surface. (12/1)
2900* Purevalue (IRE), raised 3lb, folded up tamely over this shorter trip. (6/1)

3270 WALRUS HUNTERS' CHASE (5-Y.O+) (Class H)

4-30 (4-32) **3m (18 fncs)** £1,544.00 (£434.00: £212.00) GOING: 0.53 sec per fur (GS)

	Horse	Dist	Pos	SP	RR	SF
3005²	**Lord Relic (NZ)** (SABrookshaw) **11-12-0**(7) MrRFord (a.p: led 2 out: r.o wl)	—	1	9/4 ¹	118	20
	Country Tarrogen (TDWalford) **8-12-2**(5) MrNWilson (hld up & bhd: hdwy 11th: carried lft appr last: hrd rdn flat: one pce)	6	2	7/2 ²	114	16
	Glen Oak (DGDuggan) **12-11-7**(7) MrMPFitzgerald (lw: hld up: mstkes: hdwy 11th: rdn 12th: wknd 2 out)	13	3	33/1	98	—
3005³	**My Nominee** (DENicholls) **9-12-0b**(7) MrRBurton (led 4th to 2 out: rdn & wnt lft appr last: sn wknd)	5	4	5/1	102	4
	Travel Bound (MichaelMullineaux) **12-11-9b**¹(7)ow2 MrDBarlow (prom to 10th: t.o)	dist	5	50/1	—	—
1075ᴾ	**Mobile Messenger (NZ)** (TRGeorge) **9-11-7**(7) MissSSamworth (led to 4th: 5th whn fell 9th)		F	20/1	—	—
3010⁸	**Charlies Delight (IRE)** (MrsCHicks) **9-11-13**(5) MrASansome (hld up: hdwy 10th: 6th whn fell 14th)		F	66/1	—	—
	Will it Last (FLMatthews) **11-11-2**(7) MrLBrown (t.o 8th: p.u bef 11th)		P	100/1	—	—
	Mhemeanles (FrankNicholls) **7-11-7**(7) MrNRMitchell (t.o 8th: p.u bef 14th)		P	50/1	—	—
	The Major General (GRichards) **10-12-0**(7) CaptAOgden (lw: hld up in rr: hdwy 9th: blnd 13th & 14th: wknd 4 out: p.u bef 3 out)		P	9/2 ³	—	—
3095ᶠ	**Master Kit (IRE)** (JNRBillinge) **8-11-11**(7) MrJBillinge (lw: hld up & plld hrd: mstke 1st: hdwy 5th: 6th whn blnd & uns rdr 4 out)		U	9/2 ³	—	—
				(SP 120.1%)	**11 Rn**	

6m 32.1 (34.10) CSF £9.56 TOTE £2.90: £1.30 £1.60 £4.80 (£7.10) Trio £37.10 OWNER Mrs H. J. Clarke (SHREWSBURY) BRED E. B. Champion in New Zealand

3005 Lord Relic (NZ) did the business this time, despite the fact the ground was again good. (9/4)
Country Tarrogen, already in good form between the flags, should not be considered unlucky. (7/2)
Glen Oak had trouble handling these fences, and did well in the circumstances. (33/1)
3005 My Nominee has yet to recapture the form which saw him win three hunter chases last season. (5/1)

3271 LEVY BOARD NOVICES' HURDLE (4-Y.O+) (Class D)

5-00 (5-00) **2m (8 hdls)** £3,039.00 (£854.00: £417.00) GOING: 0.53 sec per fur (GS)

	Horse	Dist	Pos	SP	RR	SF
3109*	**Break the Rules (98)** (MCPipe) **5-11-2**(7) GSupple (hld up & bhd: hdwy 5th: led appr last: rdn out)	—	1	5/1 ³	75	45
	Royal Scimitar (USA) (MrsAJPerrett) **5-11-4** RDunwoody (chsd ldr: ev ch 3 out: edgd lft appr last: hrd rdn & styd on flat)	1½	2	11/8 ¹	69	39
3084⁸	**Mutanassib (IRE)** (MCPipe) **4-10-8** JamieEvans (led tl appr last: hrd rdn: r.o one pce)	2½	3	6/1	66	26
2696³	**Mr Moonlight (IRE)** (CPEBrooks) **5-11-4** GBradley (prom: ev ch 3 out: sn rdn: 4th & btn whn mstke last)	16	4	7/1	50	20
2763⁷	**Eurofast Pet (IRE)** (SABrookshaw) **7-11-4** CLlewellyn (hld up: mstkes 3rd & 5th: no hdwy fr 3 out)	8	5	50/1	42	12
2917¹⁰	**Butterwick King (IRE)** (RAFahey) **5-11-4** PNiven (hld up & bhd: hdwy appr 3 out: wknd appr 2 out)	3	6	14/1	39	9
	Riveaux (IRE) (GRichards) **7-11-4** PCarberry (hld up: hdwy 5th: wknd 3 out)	9	7	16/1	30	—
2844⁶	**Cool As A Cucumber (IRE)** (OSherwood) **6-11-4** MRichards (hld up & bhd: hdwy appr 3 out: rdn & wknd appr 2 out)	1¾	8	9/2 ²	28	—
3158⁹	**Jessolle** (GRichards) **5-10-13** ADobbin (a bhd: t.o)	16	9	33/1	7	—
	Praise Be (FR) (TPTate) **7-11-4** RGarritty (bhd fr 3rd: t.o)	hd	10	33/1	12	—
				(SP 124.1%)	**10 Rn**	

3m 55.8 (13.80) CSF £12.23 TOTE £4.00: £1.10 £1.90 £3.10 (£4.30) Trio £9.60 OWNER Mr A. J. Lomas (WELLINGTON) BRED Cleaboy Farms Co

WEIGHT FOR AGE 4yo-10lb

3109* Break the Rules went smoothly to the front, but had to be kept up to his work on the run-in. (5/1)
Royal Scimitar (USA), a Listed winner at Chester last August, was bought out of Paul Cole's yard for 30,000 guineas at Newmarket December Sales. He will be better for the experience and may appreciate a longer trip. (11/8)
2868 Mutanassib (IRE) had faster ground this time, and can take a small novice hurdle on this evidence. (6/1)
2696 Mr Moonlight (IRE), on his hurdling debut, found disappointingly little in the home straight. (7/1)

1329 Eurofast Pet (IRE) needs to polish up his hurdling. (50/1)
2844 Cool As A Cucumber (IRE) (9/2: 7/1-4/1)

T/Jkpt: £53,466.00 (1 Tckt). T/Plpt: £36.10 (519.88 Tckts). T/Qdpt: £6.00 (135.08 Tckts) KH

2641-**KEMPTON (R-H) (Good)**
Friday February 21st
WEATHER: sunny

3272 BEDFONT NOVICES' HURDLE (5-Y.O+) (Class D)
2-10 (2-12) **2m 5f (10 hdls)** £2,969.00 (£834.00: £407.00) GOING: 0.62 sec per fur (S)

				SP	RR	SF
	Royaltino (IRE) (FDoumen,France) **5-11-5** AKondrat (lw: a.p: led 2 out: rdn out)	—	**1**	5/2[2]	93	19
2663[F]	**Award (IRE)** (RRowe) **6-10-10** NWilliamson (mstke 7th: gd hdwy 3 out: wandered & ev ch appr last: r.o flat)	¾	**2**	6/4[1]	83	9
3014[2]	**Ready Money Creek (IRE) (112)** (OSherwood) **6-11-0** JOsborne (lw: led 2nd to 2 out: unable qckn)	7	**3**	7/2[3]	82	8
2663[5]	**Latahaab (USA)** (JTGifford) **6-10-10** PHide (lw: led to 2nd: ev ch appr 2 out: sn wknd)	3	**4**	33/1	76	2
2961[5]	**Millersford (101)** (NAGaselee) **6-11-0** JCulloty (lw: hld up: rdn 3 out: wknd appr 2 out)	nk	**5**	10/1	80	6
2663[3]	**Symphony's Son (IRE)** (DNicholson) **6-10-10** AMaguire (hdwy 3 out: wknd appr 2 out)	7	**6**	16/1	70	—
2932[5]	**Rosehall (76)** (MrsTDPilkington) **6-10-2**(7) LSuthern (prom tl appr 2 out)	8	**7**	66/1	63	—
2840[7]	**Time To Parlez** (CJDrewe) **6-10-10** SCurran (lw: a bhd)	23	**8**	66/1	47	—
2771[P]	**Iron N Gold (92)** (TCasey) **5-11-0** DGallagher (hdwy 3 out: wknd appr 2 out)	3	**9**	40/1	48	—
216[4]	**Mister Generosity (IRE)** (CWeedon) **6-10-10** BPowell (prom to 5th: t.o)	dist	**10**	100/1	—	—
	Smart Rookie (IRE) (NJHenderson) **7-10-10** JRKavanagh (bit bkwd: hld up: rdn appr 2 out: wkng whn fell 2 out)		**F**	14/1	—	—
3085[5]	**Greg's Profiles** (NATwiston-Davies) **6-10-10** CMaude (bhd fr 7th: t.o whn p.u bef 2 out)		**P**	50/1	—	—
				(SP 123.7%)	**12 Rn**	

5m 18.5 (26.50) CSF £6.44 TOTE £3.40: £1.70 £1.30 £1.40 (£4.10) Trio £3.50 OWNER Henri de Pracomtal BRED Andrew Murphy

Royaltino (IRE), a useful French novice who has won three times, one of those coming last season in a bumper at Warwick, finished third in a £40,000 hurdle at Enghien in November. Looking really well beforehand, despite a four-and-a-half hour wait for the ferry at Calais the previous day, he gained a slender lead two out, but was immediately challenged by the runner-up. Rousted along on the run-in, he proved just too good for his rivals. An angular individual, this was an impressive display, giving 10lb, and he will now head for the Royal SunAlliance Novices' Hurdle at Cheltenham. (5/2)

2663 Award (IRE), so unlucky not to collect last time out, had the misfortune to come up against a really useful tool. Making giant strides to get into the action at the end of the back straight, he joined issue with the winner two out but tended to wander about a little through greenness going to the last. Nevertheless, he stuck on really well in the closing stages, if not looking likely to overhaul his rival. He looks a ready-made winner. (6/4)

3014 Ready Money Creek (IRE), an attractive individual, looked in fine fettle and soon established himself at the head of affairs. Collared two out, he was then left standing by the front two. Staying is his game and with some more cut in the ground he can return to the winner's enclosure. However his future undoubtedly lies over fences. (7/2)

Latahaab (USA) left his two previous runs over hurdles well behind and, playing an active role, still had every chance early in the straight before tiring. (33/1)

2961 Millersford, an attractive gelding, looked extremely well beforehand and hunted up the leaders until tiring approaching the second last. A big, strapping individual, his future undoubtedly lies over fences. (10/1)

Smart Rookie (IRE) (14/1: 10/1-16/1)

3273 CORINTHIAN HUNTERS' CHASE (5-Y.O+) (Class H)
2-40 (2-51) **3m (19 fncs)** £1,548.00 (£428.00: £204.00) GOING: 0.62 sec per fur (S)

				SP	RR	SF
	The Jogger (CLTizzard) **12-12-0**(7) MrJTizzard (led 3rd to 13th: led 14th: clr appr 3 out: easily)	—	**1**	9/2[2]	109+	41
2951[P]	**Mediane (USA)** (MissAnnabelWilson) **12-11-11**(3) MrSimonAndrews (hdwy 6th: chsd wnr fr 9th: led 13th to 14th: chsd wnr appr last: no imp)	13	**2**	150/1	93	25
3107[4]	**Poors Wood** (SBreen) **10-11-7**(7) MrPO'Keeffe (hdwy 10th: 3rd whn blnd bdly 12th: 2nd whn blnd 4 out: wknd appr last)	14	**3**	11/1[3]	84	16
2903[2]	**Teaplanter** (MissCSaunders) **14-12-2**(5) MrBPollock (lw: led to 3rd: j.slowly 6th: wknd 10th)	14	**4**	2/5[1]	82	14
3107[5]	**Amari King** (JWall) **13-12-0**(7) MrCWardThomas (lw: prom to 9th: t.o fr 13th: p.u bef 2 out)		**P**	33/1	—	—
3089[3]	**Fifth Amendment** (CJMann) **12-12-0b**(7) MrAHales (bit bkwd: prom to 6th: t.o whn blnd & uns rdr 14th)		**U**	25/1	—	—
				(SP 105.4%)	**6 Rn**	

6m 23.6 (28.60) CSF £255.55 TOTE £3.40: £1.20 £10.40 (£89.60) OWNER Mrs P. Tizzard (SHERBORNE) BRED Pierce Molony

OFFICIAL EXPLANATION **Teaplanter: no explanation offered.**

The Jogger, who impressively won a point-to-point recently, had little to beat with the favourite running so badly. Soon at the head of affairs, he had no problems forging clear turning for home to win doing handsprings. He will now head for the Cheltenham Foxhunters'. (9/2: op 3/1)

Mediane (USA) has not won a race for six years, and one has to go back a long way to find any sort of form, which makes this performance extremely surprising. (150/1)

3107 Poors Wood made an horrendous mistake early on the final circuit but, despite this, had moved into second place when making another bad error four out. Unable to get on terms with the winner, he was collared for the runner-up berth soon after the second last. This trip is too far for him. (11/1: 7/1-12/1)

2903 Teaplanter has been an admirable servant over the years, and has established himself as one of the leading hunter chasers during the nineties. To say he has been a model of consistency would be something of an understatement for in his thirty-five outings prior to this, he has won a staggering twenty-two races and finished second in another eight. Unfortunately he was not himself on this occasion, and punters knew their fate setting out on the final circuit. Hopefully there are still more races to be won with this grand old campaigner but age is not on his side. (2/5: 4/7-4/11)

3274 MANOR NOVICES' CHASE (5-Y.O+) (Class D)
3-10 (3-16) **3m (19 fncs)** £3,485.00 (£1,055.00: £515.00: £245.00) GOING: 0.62 sec per fur (S)

				SP	RR	SF
2883[4]	**Berude Not to (IRE)** (OSherwood) **8-11-12b** JOsborne (w ldr: led appr 2 out: clr appr last: comf)	—	**1**	13/2	130+	61
2049*	**Oban (115)** (MissHCKnight) **7-11-12** JCulloty (lw: hld up: rdn appr 3 out: unable qckn)	7	**2**	6/1	125	56

3040[P]	**Aardwolf (128)** (CPEBrooks) **6-11-12** DGallagher (lw: led tl appr 2 out: wknd appr last)	¾	**3**	9/2[3]	125	56
3040[3]	**Triple Witching** (NJHenderson) **11-11-5** NWilliamson (hld up: mstke 4 out: sn wknd: t.o)	dist	**4**	7/2[2]	—	—
2637[2]	**Pleasure Shared (IRE)** (PJHobbs) **9-11-12** CMaude (lw: bhd tl fell 5th)		**F**	6/4[1]	—	—
2926[4]	**Swiss Tactic (IRE) (64)** (AEJessop) **8-11-5** TKent (lw: a wl bhd: t.o fr 6th: p.u bef 11th)		**P**	100/1	—	—

(SP 109.0%) **6 Rn**

6m 14.0 (19.00) CSF £36.15 TOTE £5.40: £2.80 £1.90 (£8.10) OWNER Mr G. Addiscott (UPPER LAMBOURN) BRED Ronald O'Neill in Ireland
2883 Berude Not to (IRE) was far more convincing with the blinkers on for the first time over fences. Concentrating much better on the job in hand, he disputed the lead with Aardwolf and, gaining a definite advantage approaching the second last, forged clear to win with plenty in hand. He can progress further if the blinds remain on and they continue to have the desired effect. (13/2)
2049* Oban, taking a step up in class having won two small novice chases, saw out this longer trip under a patient ride. With quite a few lengths to make up on the two leaders turning for home, his jockey pushed him along and, although he eventually came through to take second place on the run-in, he never looked like posing a serious threat. (6/1)
2113 Aardwolf, on ground that was ideal for him - there was some cut - ran much better than at Newbury last time out, if not quite returning to the form he showed at Sandown earlier in the season. Disputing the lead until approaching the second-last, he was then soon beaten. He seems to prefer going right-handed. (9/2: op 3/1)
3040 Triple Witching was very disappointing, and punters knew their fate soon after he made a mistake four from home. It might be worth trying him back over two-and-a-half miles. (7/2)
2637 Pleasure Shared (IRE) looked extremely well beforehand, but did not make a very happy return to fences as he departed as early as the fifth. His record over fences now reads one win and two falls, and it will be interesting to see if his trainer perseveres with him over the major obstacles or reverts back to hurdles. (6/4)

3275 KEMPTON PARK 'N.H.' NOVICES' HURDLE (5-Y.O+) (Class D)
3-40 (3-45) **2m (8 hdls)** £2,843.00 (£798.00: £389.00) GOING: 0.62 sec per fur (S)

				SP	RR	SF
2763[2]	**Wade Road (IRE) (115)** (MissHCKnight) **6-11-8** JCulloty (a.p: jnd ldr 2 out: mstke last: rdn: led nr fin)	—	**1**	15/8[2]	95	36
2112[4]	**Kailash (USA) (118)** (MCPipe) **6-11-8** CMaude (lw: hld up: led 2 out: rdn flat: hdd nr fin)	1	**2**	11/10[1]	94	35
2805[4]	**Tree Creeper (IRE)** (AndrewTurnell) **5-11-0** LHarvey (a.p: led 3 out to 2 out: one pce)	4	**3**	12/1	82	23
	In The Rough (IRE) (DNicholson) **6-11-0** AMaguire (stdy hdwy appr 2 out: one pce)	2½	**4**	13/2[3]	80	21
2750[5]	**Wentworth (USA)** (GThorner) **5-11-0** BPowell (w ldr: led 4th to 3 out: wknd appr last)	2½	**5**	33/1	77	18
3014[8]	**Calm Down (IRE)** (TCasey) **6-11-0** JOsborne (hdwy 3 out: shkn up appr 2 out: wknd appr last)	7	**6**	66/1	70	11
	Fleeting Mandate (IRE) (NJHenderson) **5-11-0** JRKavanagh (mstke 3rd: bhd fr 5th)	8	**7**	20/1	62	3
2626[10]	**Huish (IRE)** (GFHCharles-Jones) **6-11-0** MrACharles-Jones (a bhd)	1½	**8**	100/1	61	2
2840[9]	**Smart Remark** (THind) **5-11-0** DSkyrme (lw: led to 4th: wknd 3 out)	28	**9**	100/1	33	—
2690[P]	**Blue Havana** (GraemeRoe) **5-10-9** PHide (bhd fr 3 out: t.o)	dist	**10**	100/1	—	—

(SP 115.6%) **10 Rn**

3m 58.9 (16.90) CSF £3.90 TOTE £2.40: £1.10 £1.40 £1.60 (£2.20) Trio £4.40 OWNER Lord Chelsea (WANTAGE) BRED John O'Connor
2763 Wade Road (IRE), a headstrong individual who was fitted with a cross-noseband and needed to be led round by two handlers, was racing over an easy two miles on a sharp, flat track, which on the face of it did not look ideal. He joined issue with the leader two out but, after making a mistake at the final flight, it looked as if he was going to have to settle for second best. His jockey conjured up a lovely run out of the gelding and the combination got up near the line. The stiff two miles of the Citroen Supreme Novices' Hurdle at Cheltenham should suit him much better. (15/8)
2112 Kailash (USA) came up against a smart individual here and lost absolutely nothing in defeat. Gaining a narrow advantage two from home, he looked to have the measure of his rival early on the run-in after Wade Road had made a mistake. Despite doing nothing wrong he was just worried out of it near the line. He should soon regain the winning thread. (11/10: op 7/4)
2805 Tree Creeper (IRE) poked a nostril in front three from home, but he was collared two out and left standing by the front two. He is worth a step up in distance. (12/1: 8/1-14/1)
In The Rough (IRE), winner of a bumper at Ludlow last March on his only previous outing, was given a quiet debut over hurdles but still showed promise. Creeping closer turning for home, Maguire was very sympathetic on the gelding, but the combination stayed on to finish an eye-catching fourth. Sure to have learnt a lot from this, he should not be difficult to win with. (13/2: 4/1-7/1)
2750 Wentworth (USA) showed some promise on this hurdling debut, and disputed the lead until the second-last before calling it a day. (33/1)

3276 PORTLANE H'CAP CHASE (0-135) (5-Y.O+) (Class C)
4-10 (4-14) **2m 4f 110y (17 fncs)** £5,389.00 (£1,321.00) GOING: 0.62 sec per fur (S)

				SP	RR	SF
3169[3]	**General Pershing (135)** (DNicholson) **11-12-0** AMaguire (plld hrd: mde all: clr 3rd: mstke last: easily)	—	**1**	11/10[2]	135	51
2647[3]	**Lackendara (115)** (MissHCKnight) **10-10-8** BFenton (lw: chsd wnr: mstkes 5th & 4 out: rdn appr 3 out: unable qckn)	4	**2**	8/11[1]	112	28

(SP 105.5%) **2 Rn**

5m 20.5 (19.50) TOTE £1.70: OWNER Mr J. E. Potter (TEMPLE GUITING) BRED Snailwell Stud Co Ltd
OFFICIAL EXPLANATION **Lakendara: the trainer reported that the gelding had bled from the nose.**
3169 General Pershing, awash with sweat at the start, once again took a fierce hold and had soon established a useful advantage. No doubt his rival was expecting him to tire, but he kept up the gallop and, with Maguire oozing confidence in the straight, not even making a hash of the last was going to stop him. (11/10: evens-6/5)
2647 Lackendara looked really well beforehand, but he has not won for nearly two years and, try as he might in the straight, he could not get to his sole rival. (8/11)

3277 LITTLETON H'CAP HURDLE (0-125) (5-Y.O+) (Class D)
4-40 (4-43) **2m 5f (10 hdls)** £2,866.00 (£868.00: £424.00: £202.00) GOING: 0.62 sec per fur (S)

				SP	RR	SF
2909*	**Lessons Lass (IRE) (110)** (LadyHerries) **5-11-2** JOsborne (mde all: rdn out)	—	**1**	100/30[2]	93	18
1455[2]	**High Grade (114)** (MissSJWilton) **9-11-6** NWilliamson (bit bkwd: hld up: chsd wnr fr 2 out: unable qckn)	1½	**2**	10/1	96	21
3013[5]	**Royal Piper (NZ) (107)** (AJWilson) **10-10-13** RGreene (hdwy appr last: r.o)	4	**3**	10/1	86	11
3114[F]	**Spring to Glory (102)** (PHayward) **10-10-8** BFenton (chsd wnr to 2 out: sn wknd)	4	**4**	33/1	78	3
2950[3]	**Tim (IRE) (113)** (JRJenkins) **7-11-5** AMaguire (nvr nr to chal)	½	**5**	5/1[3]	88	13
3114[2]	**Nine O Three (IRE) (105)** (AGNewcombe) **8-10-11** DGallagher (hld up: rdn 3 out: sn wknd)	1	**6**	5/2[1]	80	5
	Purple Splash (117) (PJMakin) **7-11-9v** JRKavanagh (hdwy appr 2 out: wknd appr last)	8	**7**	9/1	86	11
2817[5]	**Wings Cove (118)** (LadyHerries) **7-11-7(3)** LAspell (bhd fr 3 out)	24	**8**	11/2	68	—

				SP	RR	SF
2884[12]	**Bell One (USA) (102)** (AJKDunn) **8-10-8** SMcNeill (prom to 3 out)	9	**9**	25/1	45	—
				(SP 118.7%)	**9 Rn**	

5m 17.8 (25.80) CSF £33.80 CT £279.83 TOTE £3.40: £1.80 £2.10 £1.60 (£23.00) Trio £69.60 OWNER Mr V. McCalla (LITTLEHAMPTON) BRED James Campbell

2909* Lessons Lass (IRE) may have been hiked up 10lb for her recent success, but that was not going to stop her, as she made all the running and relentlessly kept up the gallop in the straight. (100/30)
1455 High Grade, carrying some condition for this first run in three months, is not the easiest of individuals and, although moving into second place two from home, once again had to settle for being the bridesmaid. He has not won since December 1993 and is one to oppose. (10/1)
3013 Royal Piper (NZ) is a very frustrating individual, and once again was only running on at the death. (10/1)
Spring to Glory ran much better here and raced in second place to the penultimate flight before tiring. (33/1)
2950 Tim (IRE), successful twice here already this season, never looked like making it three. (5/1)
3114 Nine O Three (IRE) has been running well of late, which makes this performance disappointing, and punters knew their fate turning out of the back straight. (5/2)
Purple Splash (9/1: 6/1-10/1)
2817 Wings Cove (11/2: op 7/2)

T/Plpt: £74.30 (160.18 Tckts). T/Qdpt: £17.60 (36.32 Tckts) AK

0110-SOUTHWELL (L-H) (Good)
Friday February 21st

one fence omitted fnl circ 1st race
WEATHER: fine & sunny with str winds

3278 NIGHTINGALE NOVICES' H'CAP CHASE (0-110) (5-Y.O+) (Class D)
2-20 (2-20) **2m (12 fncs)** £3,452.50 (£1,045.00: £510.00: £242.50) GOING: 0.29 sec per fur (GS)

				SP	RR	SF
2926[5]	**Weeheby (USA) (81)** (MFBarraclough) **8-11-2** GTormey (lw: chsd ldrs: hit 9th: styng on whn lft in ld 2 out: drvn out)	—	**1**	6/1[3]	94	27
2947[8]	**Record Lover (IRE) (69)** (MCChapman) **7-10-4** WWorthington (chsd ldrs: rdn & outpcd 7th: styd on fr 2 out: no imp)	2½	**2**	16/1	80	13
3051[P]	**Gordon (87)** (PRWebber) **6-11-5**(3) EHusband (lw: prom: hmpd 3rd: sn drvn along: kpt on fr 3 out)	3	**3**	20/1	95	28
2810[3]	**Snowy Petrel (IRE) (89)** (KCBailey) **5-11-1b** AThornton (hld up: effrt 9th: nvr nr ldrs)	10	**4**	7/2[1]	87	11
3001*	**Saymore (83)** (WClay) **11-11-4** SWynne (hld up: rdn 9th: sn wknd)	½	**5**	11/2[2]	80	13
3015[6]	**Old Redwood (67)** (MrsLWilliamson) **10-10-2** RBellamy (lft in ld 3rd: hdd after 9th: wknd appr next)	2	**6**	11/1	62	—
3179[U]	**Mr Bean (92)** (KRBurke) **7-11-13** ALarnach (chsd ldrs: blnd 2nd: drvn along 7th: led after 9th: hdd appr 3 out: wkng whn hmpd 2 out)	½	**7**	20/1	87	20
2926[P]	**Dandie Imp (78)** (AWCarroll) **9-10-13** TJMurphy (cl up whn b.d 3rd)		**B**	10/1	—	—
2810*	**Flaming Miracle (IRE) (78)** (GBarnett) **7-10-13b** RFarrant (trckd ldrs: led appr 3 out: 2l clr whn fell next)		**F**	7/2[1]	—	—
	Rinus Major (IRE) (67) (DMcCain) **6-10-2**ow2 TJenks (led tl fell 3rd)		**F**	33/1	—	—
				(SP 109.9%)	**10 Rn**	

4m 5.9 (12.90) CSF £74.49 CT £1,514.81 TOTE £6.40: £1.20 £4.50 £2.70 (£88.30) Trio £130.00; £40.29 to Kempton 22/2/97 OWNER The DANA Partnership (CLAVERDON) BRED Courtney & Congleton
WEIGHT FOR AGE 5yo-9lb

1925 Weeheby (USA) took advantage of the leader's fall at the second-last fence. He was staying on strongly at the time, and it would not have been plain sailing for Flaming Miracle. (6/1)
1716 Record Lover (IRE) usually runs well, but rarely gets his head in front. (16/1)
1572 Gordon was always making hard work of this. He needs plenty of driving and might be suited by another half-mile. (20/1)
2810 Snowy Petrel (IRE) had a lot less use made of him, but his response to pressure four out was very tame indeed. (7/2)
2810* Flaming Miracle (IRE), from a 6lb higher mark, set sail once in line for home. He was two lengths up and travelling strongly when he fell at the second-last fence. Weeheby was staying on well at the time, and it was by no means a foregone conclusion. (7/2: op 2/1)

3279 PHOENIX NOVICES' CHASE (5-Y.O+) (Class D)
2-50 (2-54) **3m 110y (19 fncs)** £3,485.00 (£1,055.00: £515.00: £245.00) GOING: 0.29 sec per fur (GS)

				SP	RR	SF
2867[3]	**As du Trefle (FR) (111)** (MCPipe) **9-11-4** APMcCoy (lw: j.w: mde all: easily)	—	**1**	1/2[1]	102+	56
3043[4]	**Pearl's Choice (IRE) (86)** (JCMcConnochie) **9-10-13** AThornton (chsd wnr: blnd 6th: kpt on fr 3 out: no ch w wnr)	8	**2**	12/1	92	46
2693[P]	**Pearl Epee (85)** (DNicholson) **8-10-13** RJohnson (chsd ldrs: hit 12th: wkng whn hit 4 out)	dist	**3**	16/1	—	—
3060[2]	**Easy Breezy** (CJMann) **7-11-4** JRailton (in tch: bhd fr 12th)	1¾	**4**	10/1[3]	—	—
3020[6]	**Fortytwo Dee (IRE)** (NASmith) **7-10-13** JRyan (t.o fr 12th: p.u bef 2 out)		**P**	33/1	—	—
1582[P]	**Damcada (IRE) (67)** (AWCarroll) **9-11-4** SWynne (t.o fr 13th: p.u bef 4 out)		**P**	33/1	—	—
	Lisnavaragh (JParkes) **11-11-4** VSmith (s.s: a t.o: p.u bef 3 out)		**P**	66/1	—	—
3015[P]	**Kentucky Gold (IRE) (60)** (MrsLWilliamson) **8-11-4** RBellamy (sn bhd: drvn along 5th: t.o 10th: p.u bef 3 out)		**P**	66/1	—	—
1318[2]	**Lottery Ticket (IRE) (101)** (TRGeorge) **8-11-4** JAMcCarthy (blnd & uns rdr 2nd)		**U**	5/1[2]	—	—
				(SP 114.9%)	**9 Rn**	

6m 17.3 (10.30) CSF £6.90 TOTE £1.40: £1.30 £1.80 £2.20 (£6.00) Trio £16.00 OWNER Mr D. A. Johnson (WELLINGTON) BRED Louis Chaignon in France

2867 As du Trefle (FR) proved different class to this lot. Turning in some spectacular leaps, he was never out of third gear. (1/2)
3043 Pearl's Choice (IRE) survived a shocking blunder at the sixth. He kept on gamely in pursuit of the winner and this was easily his best effort so far. (12/1: 8/1-14/1)
2077 Pearl Epee, whose jumping was not blemish-free, was legless four out. (16/1)
3060 Easy Breezy was struggling throughout the final circuit. (10/1)
1318 Lottery Ticket (IRE) hit the second fence hard, and gave his rider no chance. (5/1: op 5/2)

3280 ADELPHI FOR CNC MACHINING H'CAP CHASE (0-120) (5-Y.O+) (Class D)

3-20 (3-21) **3m 110y (19 fncs)** £3,355.00 (£1,015.00: £495.00: £235.00) GOING: 0.29 sec per fur (GS)

	Horse	Dist	Pos	SP	RR	SF
2749^{2}	**Father Sky (110)** (OSherwood) **6-11-7b** JAMcCarthy (trckd ldrs: led after 4 out: drvn out)	—	**1**	100/30^{2}	120	39
	Young Miner (94) (MrsTJMcInnesSkinner) **11-10-5** GUpton (trckd ldrs: kpt on wl fr 2 out: no imp)	5	**2**	20/1	101	20
2876^{3}	**Childhay Chocolate (99)** (PFNicholls) **9-10-10** RJohnson (lw: led: drvn along 13th: hdd after 4 out: one pce fr next)	1¾	**3**	6/1	105	24
3113^{F}	**Really a Rascal (105)** (DRGandolfo) **10-10-13**(3) DFortt (hld up: effrt 15th: 3rd & rdn whn blnd 3 out: sn wknd)	10	**4**	4/1^{3}	104	23
3074^{4}	**Mugoni Beach (117)** (MCPipe) **12-12-0** APMcCoy (lw: hit 6th: drvn along 12th: bhd fr 15th: t.o: fin lame)	dist	**5**	5/2^{1}	—	—
3071^{5}	**Cropredy Lad (92)** (PRWebber) **10-10-3** AThornton (lw: chsd ldrs: outpcd 12th: bhd fr 4 out: t.o)	4	**6**	5/1	—	—

(SP 107.4%) **6 Rn**

6m 24.3 (17.30) CSF £40.21 TOTE £3.70: £2.30 £5.20 (£28.30) OWNER Mr Kenneth Kornfeld (UPPER LAMBOURN) BRED Sheikh Mohammed

OFFICIAL EXPLANATION **Mugoni Beach: was found to be lame behind after the race.**

2749 Father Sky, who is not normally the greatest of battlers, found this plain-sailing after going for home after four out. (100/30)

Young Miner, having his first outing for 709 days, ran really well despite looking as if the race was needed. He kept on stoutly over the last two and, providing he stands racing, he should add to his record. (20/1)

2876 Childhay Chocolate was given a positive ride and for once his jumping was blemish-free. (6/1)

2821 Really a Rascal was hard at work, and not looking to relish a struggle, when he fell through the third last. (4/1)

3074 Mugoni Beach, who is a renowned front-runner, was ridden from the back this time and he did not like it. After hitting the sixth, he was driven along setting out on to the final circuit, and called it a day completely five from home. (5/2: op 6/4)

3281 EAST MIDLANDS ELECTRICITY (LINCOLN) H'CAP HURDLE (0-120) (4-Y.O+) (Class D)

3-50 (3-50) **3m 110y (13 hdls)** £2,745.00 (£770.00: £375.00) GOING: 0.68 sec per fur (S)

	Horse	Dist	Pos	SP	RR	SF
2877^{2}	**Mr Strong Gale (IRE) (95)** (PFNicholls) **6-10-3** RJohnson (rel to go to s: chsd ldrs: styd on to ld between last 2: drvn out)	—	**1**	11/4^{1}	73	16
3045^{6}	**Linton Rocks (120)** (TThomsonJones) **8-11-7**(7) XAizpuru (sn trckng ldrs: led appr 2 out: hdd between last 2: r.o)	1	**2**	4/1^{2}	97	40
3201^{6}	**Kadari (93)** (WClay) **8-9-12v**(3)ow1 GuyLewis (chsd ldrs: led after 9th tl appr 2 out: kpt on wl appr last)	1¾	**3**	14/1	69	11
2702^{7}	**Pharare (IRE) (102)** (RDEWoodhouse) **7-10-10** ASSmith (led tl after 9th: wknd appr 3 out)	13	**4**	12/1	70	13
2932^{7}	**Kippanour (USA) (103)** (CJMann) **5-10-4b**(7) DKiernan (sn bhd: sme hdwy 3 out: nvr nr ldrs)	9	**5**	12/1	65	8
3013^{13}	**Rimouski (94)** (BRCambidge) **9-10-2**ow1 GaryLyons (sn bhd & pushed along: sme hdwy 3 out: n.d)	9	**6**	12/1	50	—
3045^{9}	**Nick the Beak (IRE) (110)** (JohnUpson) **8-11-4** JSupple (outpcd & pushed along 9th: n.d after)	1½	**7**	11/2^{3}	65	8
2568^{2}	**Fortunes Course (IRE) (110)** (JSKing) **8-11-4** APMcCoy (w ldrs: reminder 7th: sn drvn along: wknd after 9th)	1½	**8**	4/1^{2}	64	7
2915^{13}	**Suvla Bay (IRE) (92)** (OBrennan) **9-10-0** MBrennan (bit bkwd: sme hdwy 8th: wknd 10th)	24	**9**	20/1	30	—
2694^{10}	**We're in the Money (92)** (MissJBower) **13-9-7**(7) ClaudineFroggitt (sn bhd & pushed along: t.o fr 8th)	17	**10**	100/1	19	—
3016^{P}	**Johnny's Turn (94)** (JNorton) **12-10-2** MrNKent (bhd fr 7th: t.o whn p.u bef 2 out)		**P**	33/1	—	—

(SP 120.5%) **11 Rn**

6m 14.6 (28.60) CSF £13.37 CT £122.05 TOTE £3.00: £2.20 £2.90 £3.90 (£5.30) Trio £16.30 OWNER Mr T. G. A. Chappell (SHEPTON MALLET) BRED Thomas F. Bourke

LONG HANDICAP Suvla Bay (IRE) 9-1 We're in the Money 7-10 Kadari 9-9

2877 Mr Strong Gale (IRE) would not parade in front of the stands before the start, but once the race was under way he did nothing wrong. From a 7lb higher mark, he had to be kept right up to his work. (11/4)

3045 Linton Rocks confirmed the promise of his initial outing after missing a season. He proved willing under pressure and deserves to go one better soon. (4/1)

3002 Kadari, having his second outing in four days, ran much better and stayed on all the way to the line. (14/1)

2702 Pharare (IRE), a confirmed front-runner, called it a day three from home. (12/1)

2568 Fortunes Course (IRE) (4/1: op 5/2)

3282 ALBATROSS NOVICES' HURDLE (4-Y.O+) (Class D)

4-20 (4-21) **2m (9 hdls)** £2,829.00 (£794.00: £387.00) GOING: 0.68 sec per fur (S)

	Horse	Dist	Pos	SP	RR	SF
3084^{10}	**Otto E Mezzo** (MJPolglase) **5-11-2** VSmith (sn trckng ldrs: styd on u.p to ld between last 2: r.o)	—	**1**	9/1^{3}	72	15
2939^{5}	**Pinkerton's Pal** (MCPipe) **6-11-2** APMcCoy (lw: led tl hdd between last 2: hrd rdn & kpt on same pce)	2½	**2**	13/8^{2}	70	13
2953^{F}	**Carlisle Bandito's (IRE)** (JBerry) **5-11-2** MMoloney (trckd ldrs fr 4th: rdn & btn appr 2 out)	13	**3**	6/5^{1}	57	—
	Nebaal (USA) (GBarnett) **7-11-2** SWynne (t.o fr 4th: blnd 3 out)	dist	**4**	50/1	—	—
2945^{7}	**Dodgy Dancer (64)** (MrsLWilliamson) **7-11-2b** RBellamy (chsd ldrs tl wknd qckly 4th: sn t.o)	12	**5**	50/1	—	—
3084^{P}	**Dia Georgy** (CADwyer) **6-10-13**(3) MBrennan (swtg: t.o fr 4th: p.u bef 2 out)		**P**	33/1	—	—
	Risky Tu (PAKelleway) **6-10-11** RJohnson (lw: trckd ldrs: reminders 4th: lost pl & p.u after 6th)		**P**	11/1	—	—
	Greenacres Star (WClay) **7-10-8**(3) GuyLewis (bhd whn blnd 3rd: sn t.o: p.u bef 5th)		**P**	33/1	—	—

(SP 111.7%) **8 Rn**

4m 3.3 (21.30) CSF £21.61 TOTE £10.50: £1.40 £1.10 £1.20 (£10.70) Trio £4.30 OWNER J P M & J W Cook (NEWMARKET) BRED Normanby Stud Ltd

Otto E Mezzo, who was lost in the mud first time, appreciated this much better going and, answering his rider's calls, gained the upper hand at the final flight. (9/1: op 6/1)

2939 Pinkerton's Pal, allowed to get on with it this time, came under severe pressure between the last two but found the winner too good. (13/8)

2953 Carlisle Bandito's (IRE) was carrying plenty of condition. In trouble going to two out, he was given a relatively easy time of it and is better than he showed here. (6/5: evens-11/8)

Risky Tu (11/1: op 7/1)

3283 VULTURE NOVICES' HURDLE (4-Y.O+) (Class D)

4-50 (4-50) **2m 4f 110y (11 hdls)** £2,997.00 (£842.00: £411.00) GOING: 0.68 sec per fur (S)

	Horse	Dist	Pos	SP	RR	SF
3088*	**Total Joy (IRE) (90)** (CJMann) **6-11-10** JRailton (mde all: clr fr 5th: eased flat)	—	**1**	2/1^{1}	76+	19
3076^{3}	**Beechfield Flyer (85)** (WClay) **6-11-4** GTormey (chsd wnr fr 7th: kpt on fr 2 out: no imp)	7	**2**	9/1	65	8

				SP	RR	SF
2177*	**Smolensk (IRE) (100)** (JBerry) **5-11-10** MMoloney (lw: outpcd & drvn along 7th: sme hdwy 3 out: sn rdn & wknd)	15	**3**	9/4[2]	59	2
2825[6]	**Geisway (CAN)** (NJHWalker) **7-11-4** RJohnson (hdwy 6th: sn chsng ldrs: wknd appr 2 out)	16	**4**	11/1	40	—
3032[P]	**Dry Hill Lad (80)** (JNorton) **6-11-1b[1]**(3) EHusband (chsd ldr to 6th: bhd fr 3 out)	18	**5**	20/1	26	—
2898[14]	**Antarctica (USA)** (JHetherton) **5-10-13** DParker (bhd fr 6th)	5	**6**	33/1	17	—
2840[8]	**Over Zealous (IRE)** (JohnUpson) **5-11-4** JSupple (t.o fr 6th)	23	**7**	20/1	4	—
1301[3]	**Welsh Loot (IRE)** (OSherwood) **6-11-4** JAMcCarthy (hdwy 6th: sn drvn along & no imp: poor 4th whn fell last)		**F**	11/1	—	—
2865[P]	**Jelali (IRE)** (DJGMurraySmith) **4-10-13** APMcCoy (blnd 2nd: hdwy 6th: wknd qckly 3 out: p.u bef next)		**P**	15/2[3]	—	—
	Fradicant (GBarnett) **8-11-4** SWynne (bit bkwd: plld hrd: sn trckng wnr: wknd 5th: t.o 7th: p.u bef 3 ut)		**P**	50/1	—	—
2945[4]	**Captain Navar (IRE)** (JGMO'Shea) **7-11-1**(3) MichaelBrennan (mstkes: bhd whn blnd 5th: t.o whn p.u bef 8th).		**P**	10/1	—	—
2893[P]	**Cumberland Youth** (MissCJECaroe) **6-11-4b[1]** DLeahy (t.o fr 6th: p.u bef 2 out)		**P**	50/1	—	—
2005[10]	**Push On Polly (IRE)** (JParkes) **7-10-13** VSmith (blnd & uns rdr 1st)		**U**	25/1	—	—

(SP 131.9%) **13 Rn**

5m 14.5 (28.50) CSF £19.91 TOTE £3.50: £1.70 £2.50 £1.30 (£16.20) Trio £3.60 OWNER Mr P. M. Warren (UPPER LAMBOURN) BRED Mrs Kiki Ward Platt

WEIGHT FOR AGE 4yo-11lb

3088* Total Joy (IRE) found this different going no problem and, forcing the gallop throughout, was in no danger two from home and won easing up. (2/1)

3076 Beechfield Flyer, who usually spends his time running in selling races, finished a clear second best, emphasising the low grade of this contest. (9/1: 6/1-10/1)

2177* Smolensk (IRE), like his stable-mate Carlisle Bandito's in the previous race, ran a flat race, and is surely capable of better than he showed here. (9/4)

2825 Geisway (CAN) is on the decline, Dropped in class, he weakened going to two out. (11/1: 8/1-12/1)

Welsh Loot (IRE) (11/1: 8/1-12/1)

1712* Jelali (IRE) (15/2: 5/1-8/1)

T/Plpt: £174.40 (50.92 Tckts). T/Qdpt: £4.90 (152.31 Tckts) WG

2778-DONCASTER (L-H) (Good, Good to firm patches)
Saturday February 22nd

WEATHER: overcast & windy

3284 'OPEN MORNING' (S) HURDLE (4, 5 & 6-Y.O) (Class G)

2-00 (2-01) **2m 110y (8 hdls)** £1,639.50 (£452.00: £214.50) GOING: 0.02 sec per fur (G)

				SP	RR	SF
3131[4]	**Sousse (80)** (MrsMReveley) **4-9-13**(3) GLee (trckd ldrs: led after 3 out: hung lft: drvn out)	—	**1**	4/1[1]	54	2
3110[3]	**Proud Image (85)** (GMMcCourt) **5-11-6**(3) DFortt (lw: trckd ldrs: ev ch 2 out: nt qckn flat)	2	**2**	4/1[1]	63	21
2076[P]	**Riverbank Rose (66)** (WClay) **6-10-9v**(3) GuyLewis (chsd ldrs: led 5th tl after 3 out: kpt on same pce fr next)	1½	**3**	14/1	51	9
2678[3]	**Arch Angel (IRE)** (GFHCharles-Jones) **4-9-9**(7) XAizpuru (bhd: gd hdwy appr 3 out: wandered appr last: kpt on)	4	**4**	12/1	47	—
2629[13]	**Boy Blakeney (85)** (MrsSJSmith) **4-10-7** RichardGuest (chsd ldrs tl outpcd fr 3 out)	6	**5**	9/1[3]	46	—
	Dame Prospect (79) (MissMERowland) **6-11-1**(3) PMidgley (lw: hdwy 5th: kpt on fr 2 out: nvr nr to chal)	s.h	**6**	20/1	47	5
2696[13]	**Green King** (APJones) **5-11-3** SMcNeill (hdwy 5th: styd on fr 3 out: nvr rchd ldrs)	¾	**7**	33/1	45	3
3091[2]	**Oakbury (IRE) (70)** (MissLCSiddall) **5-10-10**(7) TSiddall (sn bhd & pushed along: sme hdwy 3 out: n.d)	15	**8**	9/1[3]	31	—
2946[10]	**Autumn Flame (IRE)** (OBrennan) **6-10-12** MBrennan (bhd: sme hdwy 3 out: n.d)	2½	**9**	50/1	23	—
3058[2]	**Hawanafa (70)** (JSMoore) **4-10-2b** WMcFarland (trckd ldrs: ev ch 3 out: sn wknd)	2½	**10**	8/1[2]	21	—
2946[6]	**Bluntswood Hall** (RHollinshead) **4-10-7** GaryLyons (in tch: effrt appr 3 out: sn wknd)	1	**11**	8/1[2]	25	—
3031[16]	**Sharmoor (68)** (MissLCSiddall) **5-10-12** OPears (sn bhd)	3	**12**	20/1	17	—
1309[5]	**Culrain (78)** (THCaldwell) **6-11-6**(3) MichaelBrennan (a in rr)	nk	**13**	16/1	28	—
3072[11]	**Mill Dancer (IRE)** (PWHiatt) **5-10-9**(3) EHusband (led: j.b rt: hdd 5th: sn lost pl)	2½	**14**	33/1	14	—
	Quixotry (JMackie) **6-11-3** TEley (bit bkwd: hld up: hdwy 5th: wkng whn hmpd next)	17	**15**	50/1	3	—
2815[14]	**Trianna** (RBrotherton) **4-10-2** LHarvey (bhd fr 5th)	29	**16**	50/1	—	—
	Reno's Treasure (USA) (JohnHarris) **4-10-2** DGallagher (j.b: sn bhd: t.o 5th)	29	**17**	50/1	—	—
	Magical Blues (IRE) (MissAEEmbiricos) **5-11-3** JRyan (hdwy 5th: prom & styng on whn fell 3 out)		**F**	11/1	—	—
2678[8]	**Code Red** (WRMuir) **4-10-2**(5) ABates (hdwy 5th: sn rdn: cl up whn blnd & uns rdr 3 out)		**U**	12/1	—	—

(SP 141.7%) **19 Rn**

4m 1.3 (11.30) CSF £17.24 TOTE £4.30: £2.00 £2.30 £5.20 (£9.00) Trio £79.70 OWNER Wentdale Racing Partnership (SALTBURN) BRED Manor Grange Stud Co Ltd

WEIGHT FOR AGE 4yo-10lb

No bid

3131 Sousse, who had two handlers in the paddock, tended to hang and, though scoring decisively in the end, is clearly a bit of a madam. (4/1)

3110 Proud Image probably ran right up to his best. (4/1)

1417 Riverbank Rose could not match the first two from three out, and will be better suited by a more severe test of stamina. (14/1)

2678 Arch Angel (IRE) ran about badly going to the final flight. (12/1)

2050 Boy Blakeney, who had the blinkers left off this time, found himself outpaced up the straight on this fast ground. (9/1)

Dame Prospect, absent for 799 days after winning a novice selling handicap at Market Rasen, looked fit and ran accordingly. (20/1)

3091 Oakbury (IRE) (9/1: op 6/1)

Magical Blues (IRE), given time to get his eye in, was a couple of lengths behind and closing when he fell very heavily. (11/1: 5/1-12/1)

Code Red was almost upsides but under strong pressure when he parted company three out. He would not have finished in the first three. (12/1)

3285 'COME BEHIND THE SCENES' NOVICES' CHASE (6-Y.O+) (Class E)

2-30 (2-31) **3m (18 fncs)** £3,668.00 (£887.00) GOING: 0.02 sec per fur (G)

				SP	RR	SF
3044*	**Bell Staffboy (IRE) (124)** (JGMO'Shea) **8-11-7**(3) MichaelBrennan (lw: j.rt: led 3rd: hit 4 out: clr 2 out: drvn out)	—	**1**	4/9[1]	120	30

Form	Horse	Details	Dist	Pos	SP	RR	SF
2672[2]	**Monymoss (IRE) (105)**	(MrsSJSmith) **8-11-4** RichardGuest (wnt 2nd 9th: hit 12th: rdn 3 out: no imp)	9	**2**	5/2[2]	108	18
1038[8]	**Seymour Spy (85)**	(MrsARHewitt) **8-10-12** SWynne (led to 3rd: outpcd 12th: mod 3rd whn p.u lame bef 4 out)		**P**	14/1[3]	—	—
2691[7]	**Mr Motivator**	(TKeddy) **7-10-12** SMcNeill (disp 3rd & outpcd whn blnd & uns rdr 13th)		**U**	50/1	—	—
					(SP 106.4%)	**4 Rn**	

6m 8.6 (14.60) CSF £1.76 TOTE £1.40 (£1.30) OWNER K W Bell & Son Ltd (WESTBURY-ON-SEVERN) BRED Maurice Fenton
3044* Bell Staffboy (IRE), who had to make his own running, jumped badly right as a consequence but had only to be kept up to his work. He returned with blood oozing from an artery but hopefully should be none the worse. (4/9)
2672 Monymoss (IRE) was not good enough to seriously trouble the winner. (5/2)

3286 DONCASTER RACECOURSE SPONSORSHIP CLUB H'CAP HURDLE (0-140) (4-Y.O+) (Class B)

3-05 (3-06) **2m 110y (8 hdls)** £4,896.50 (£1,472.00: £711.00: £330.50) GOING: Not Established

Form	Horse	Details	Dist	Pos	SP	RR	SF
2779*	**Shining Edge (121)**	(TDEasterby) **5-11-3** BFenton (lw: hld up: stdy hdwy 5th: styd on fr 3 out: rdn to ld flat: r.o)	—	**1**	7/2[2]	100	36
3034*	**Star Rage (IRE) (130)**	(JLHarris) **7-11-12** DGallagher (sn trckng ldrs: led appr 3 out tl flat: rallied & r.o)	1¼	**2**	11/4[1]	108	44
3034[2]	**Desert Fighter (111)**	(MrsMReveley) **6-10-7** PNiven (trckd ldrs: ev ch tl outpcd fr 2 out)	6	**3**	11/2[3]	83	19
2929[2]	**Barford Sovereign (109)**	(JRFanshawe) **5-10-5** RichardGuest (lw: led tl appr 3 out: sn outpcd: styd on fr 2 out)	hd	**4**	6/1	81	17
	Sesame Seed (IRE) (119)	(NJHenderson) **9-11-1** WMcFarland (effrt 5th: kpt on same pce fr out)	¾	**5**	14/1	90	26
3164[8]	**Decide Yourself (IRE) (107)**	(TThomsonJones) **7-10-3** JCulloty (effrt & drvn along 5th: outpcd fr next)	6	**6**	33/1	72	8
	Frickley (130)	(GRichards) **11-11-9**(3) MichaelBrennan (trckd ldrs: effrt appr 3 out: wknd next)	6	**7**	16/1	90	26
2783[8]	**Callisoe Bay (IRE) (132)**	(OSherwood) **8-12-0** JAMcCarthy (hld up: pushed along after 5th: no rspnse)	4	**8**	11/1	88	24
1644[4]	**Speedwell Prince (IRE) (129)**	(NATwiston-Davies) **7-11-11** TJenks (chsd ldrs: outpcd & drvn along 5th: wknd next)	19	**9**	8/1	66	2
					(SP 113.5%)	**9 Rn**	

3m 56.5 (6.50) CSF £12.44 CT £45.69 TOTE £4.20: £1.70 £1.50 £1.30 (£4.50) Trio £9.20 OWNER Mr G. Graham (MALTON) BRED R. B. Warren
STEWARDS' ENQUIRY Fenton susp. 3-4/3/97 (excessive use of whip).
2779* Shining Edge, from a 7lb higher mark, was given a patient ride in what was a moderately-run race. Showing the right sort of spirit to get his head in front on the run-in, he is a much improved performer. (7/2)
3034* Star Rage (IRE), raised 3lb, found himself in front a long way from home in what was a falsely-run race. After being headed after the last, he battled back well, and a stronger gallop and stiffer track will suit him a lot better. (11/4)
3034 Desert Fighter, outpaced by the first two from two out, tended to wander about under pressure. (11/2)
2929 Barford Sovereign, who is better over an extra half-mile, made the running but made the mistake of not forcing the pace. After being left behind, she was staying on again at the finish. (6/1)
Sesame Seed (IRE), having his first outing for a year and over a trip short of his best, ran a pleasing first race. (14/1)

3287 'RACING IS FUN' HURDLE (4-Y.O) (Class E)

3-40 (3-40) **2m 4f (10 hdls)** £2,485.40 (£689.40: £330.20) GOING: 0.02 sec per fur (G)

Form	Horse	Details	Dist	Pos	SP	RR	SF
2805[2]	**Disallowed (IRE)**	(MissHCKnight) **4-10-13** JCulloty (lw: trckd ldrs: styd on u.p fr 2 out: hung lft: led fnl 75y)	—	**1**	2/1[2]	81	21
3075[3]	**Topaglow (IRE)**	(PTDalton) **4-10-12** BFenton (trckd ldrs: led after 7th to 3 out: led flat: sn hdd: r.o)	1½	**2**	9/1	79	19
2925*	**Fitzwilliam (USA)**	(IABalding) **4-10-12**(7)ow1 MrABalding (led 2nd to 3rd: led 3 out tl flat: r.o same pce)	2	**3**	6/4[1]	84	23
3075[8]	**Precious Island**	(PTDalton) **4-10-7** JSupple (jnd ldrs 5th: wknd appr 2 out)	5	**4**	25/1	68	8
3075[U]	**Anna Soleil (IRE)**	(OSherwood) **4-10-12** JAMcCarthy (sn trckng ldrs: outpcd fr 3 out)	3	**5**	11/2[3]	71	11
2859[7]	**Noir Esprit**	(JMCarr) **4-10-9**(3) FLeahy (chsd ldrs: drvn along 7th: wknd appr 3 out)	6	**6**	20/1	66	6
2649[7]	**Recruitment**	(JRTurner) **4-10-12** MBrennan (hld up & bhd: t.o 6th)	18	**7**	50/1	52	—
3031[2]	**Amazing Sail (IRE)**	(MissMKMilligan) **4-10-9**(3) MichaelBrennan (prom tl lost pl 4th: t.o fr 6th)	1¼	**8**	50/1	51	—
2925[8]	**Gulf of Siam**	(JMackie) **4-10-12** TEley (hld up: sme hdwy 7th: sn wknd)	1	**9**	50/1	50	—
2859[8]	**Tagatay**	(MJCamacho) **4-10-12** RichardGuest (stdd s: plld hrd: rapid hdwy to ld 3rd: j.rt 5th: hdd after 7th: sn lost pl)	16	**10**	20/1	37	—
3031[10]	**Port Valenska (IRE)**	(JLHarris) **4-10-12b1** DGallagher (led to 2nd: lost pl 6th: sn t.o: p.u bef 3 out)		**P**	66/1	—	—
					(SP 119.5%)	**11 Rn**	

4m 51.1 (11.10) CSF £17.06 TOTE £2.60: £1.50 £1.70 £1.20 (£10.10) Trio £6.20 OWNER Million In Mind Partnership (6) (WANTAGE) BRED Dermot Ryan and Partners
2805 Disallowed (IRE) buckled down under pressure, despite tending to hang left, to gain the upper hand in the closing stages. She was certainly suited by the extra half-mile. (2/1)
3075 Topaglow (IRE) showed his good Leicester effort was no fluke, and only gave best in the closing stages. (9/1)
2925* Fitzwilliam (USA) proved suited by the step-up in distance, but could not match the first two on the run-in. (6/4)
1370 Precious Island seems to be improving with each outing. (25/1)
2751 Anna Soleil (IRE) is short of pace and may be better suited by three miles. (11/2)

3288 BAWTRY NOVICES' H'CAP CHASE (0-115) (5-Y.O+) (Class D)

4-15 (4-15) **2m 3f 110y (15 fncs)** £3,600.00 (£1,080.00: £520.00: £240.00) GOING: 0.02 sec per fur (G)

Form	Horse	Details	Dist	Pos	SP	RR	SF
3044[2]	**Noyan (110)**	(RAFahey) **7-12-0** PNiven (lw: trckd ldrs: led 10th: clr 3 out)	—	**1**	6/4[1]	129	53
2004[2]	**Kenmore-Speed (100)**	(MrsSJSmith) **10-11-4** RichardGuest (led 2nd to 10th: kpt on fr 4 out: no ch w wnr)	11	**2**	4/1[2]	110	34
2914[3]	**Glamanglitz (82)**	(PTDalton) **7-10-0** BFenton (led to 2nd: chsd ldrs: styd on one pce fr 4 out)	¾	**3**	10/1[3]	91	15
2551[3]	**Key To Moyade (IRE) (95)**	(MJWilkinson) **7-10-13** SMcNeill (hit 1st: wnt prom 9th: hit 4 out: one pce)	1¾	**4**	10/1[3]	103	27
2960*	**Koo's Promise (83)**	(CLPopham) **6-9-12**(3) TDascombe (chsd ldrs: drvn along 8th: outpcd 10th: kpt on fr 4 out: n.d)	3	**5**	12/1	89	13
3097*	**Cover Point (IRE) (95)**	(JGFitzGerald) **6-10-13** RGarritty (hld up: drvn along 8th: sn chsng ldrs: wknd 4 out)	15	**6**	4/1[2]	88	12
2892[4]	**Stage Player (89)**	(MissCJECaroe) **11-10-7** DLeahy (reminders 4th: blnd 7th: sn t.o)	dist	**7**	20/1	—	—
					(SP 110.6%)	**7 Rn**	

4m 53.4 (6.40) CSF £7.02 TOTE £2.10: £1.30 £2.10 (£3.80) OWNER Mr C. H. McGhie (MALTON) BRED Oakgrove Stud
LONG HANDICAP Glamanglitz 9-10
3044 Noyan found this simple, and was out on his own over the last three. He is getting better all the time. (6/4)
2004 Kenmore-Speed jumped soundly but was left behind by the winner. He really needs three miles and easier ground. (4/1)
2914 Glamanglitz, whose jumping was fault-free, could not live with the winner from four out. Three miles will suit him better. (10/1)

2551 Key To Moyade (IRE) could not find the pace to lay up from four out. His jumping was not blemish-free, and he too really needs further. (10/1)
2960* Koo's Promise, a fortunate winner at Wincanton, was in trouble some way from home but, to her credit, stayed on all the way to the line. (12/1)
3097* Cover Point (IRE) suddenly came under pressure at halfway. Never looking to be enjoying himself, he dropped right away in the home straight. He took a weak race at Catterick and is not one to have a lot of faith in. (4/1)

3289 FINNINGLEY H'CAP CHASE (0-110) (5-Y.O+) (Class E)

4-45 (4-45) **2m 3f 110y (15 fncs)** £2,885.00 (£860.00: £410.00: £185.00) GOING: 0.02 sec per fur (G)

				SP	RR	SF
2894^{3}	**Over the Pole (105)** (PRChamings) **10-11-11**(3) MrCBonner (trckd ldrs: styd on to ld between last 2: r.o wl)	—	**1**	7/2^{3}	120	49
3113^{5}	**Jason's Boy (82)** (JMBradley) **7-10-5** BFenton (w ldr: reminders 9th: led next to 3 out: wknd appr last)	9	**2**	2/1^{2}	90	19
3140*	**Dual Image (103)** (JGFitzGerald) **10-11-12** RGarritty (drvn along 7th: wnt prom 9th: rdn to ld 3 out: hdd & wknd between last 2)	¾	**3**	11/8^{1}	110	39
3097^{U}	**Karenastino (77)** (MrsSJSmith) **6-9-7**(7) RWilkinson (mde most tl blnd & hdd 10th: wknd appr 4 out: sn bhd: t.o)	dist	**4**	11/1	—	—
				(SP 106.0%)		**4 Rn**

4m 54.6 (7.60) CSF £9.48 TOTE £5.10 (£7.80) OWNER Pell-Mell Partners (BASINGSTOKE) BRED Mrs C. A. Harnett
LONG HANDICAP Karenastino 9-2
2894 Over the Pole returned to his very best, winning most decisively in the end to give his trainer his first winner as a public trainer. (7/2)
3113 Jason's Boy, who found three miles too far, proved most determined but, possibly still in need of the action, became tired in a couple of strides going to the last. (2/1)
3140* Dual Image, never one to trust, seemed to sulk at halfway. Rousted into the firing line by his determined jockey, he eventually called it a day going to the last. (11/8)
3097 Karenastino, 12lb wrong at the weights, raced too keenly and his jumping was anything but blemish-free. It was no surprise to see him drop right away on the final turn. (11/1)

3290 DONCASTER INTERMEDIATE OPEN N.H. FLAT RACE (4, 5 & 6-Y.O F & M) (Class H)

5-15 (5-15) **2m 110y** £1,035.00 (£285.00: £135.00)

				SP	RR	SF
	Memsahib Ofesteem (SGollings) **6-11-2** KGaule (bit bkwd: led 2f: led ½-wy: styd on wl fnl 2f)	—	**1**	50/1	64 f	—
3006^{2}	**All Done** (SMellor) **4-10-6** NMann (jnd ldrs ½-wy: wnt 2nd 3f out: sn rdn: kpt on: no imp)	3½	**2**	6/4^{1}	61 f	—
2696^{15}	**Rachel Louise** (TKeddy) **5-11-2** SMcNeill (hdwy to chse ldrs ½-wy: one pce fnl 3f)	5	**3**	5/1^{3}	56 f	—
2804*	**Country Orchid** (MrsMReveley) **6-11-9** PNiven (swtg: hld up: hdwy ½-wy: sn chsng ldrs: rdn & hung lft over 2f out: sn wknd)	7	**4**	7/4^{2}	56 f	—
3006^{5}	**Side By Side (IRE)** (CWThornton) **4-9-13**(7) NHorrocks (lw: drvn along & outpcd 7f out: n.d after)	8	**5**	13/2	41 f	—
	What The Devil (JPSmith) **4-10-6** WWorthington (lt-f: hld up: hdwy ½-wy: sn drvn along & bhd)	2½	**6**	66/1	39 f	—
	Islawen Lady (JMBradley) **4-10-6** BFenton (hdwy ½-wy: sn pushed along: lost pl over 4f out)	nk	**7**	40/1	39 f	—
	Lady Boco (FCoton) **4-9-13**(7) CRae (unruly: bhd fnl 4f)	12	**8**	66/1	27 f	—
2904^{16}	**Ceejayell** (NChamberlain) **4-9-13**(7) MissCMetcalfe (plld hrd: led after 2f: sn clr: hdd ½-wy: sn bhd: t.o fnl 4f)	dist	**9**	66/1	—	—
				(SP 115.2%)		**9 Rn**

4m 2.2 CSF £114.70 TOTE £27.00: £6.00 £1.10 £2.20 (£51.90) Trio £41.40 OWNER Mrs R. H. Coole (LOUTH) BRED Mrs P. Birdseye
WEIGHT FOR AGE 4yo-10lb
Memsahib Ofesteem, who looked to be carrying plenty of condition, pulled off a shock but there was no fluke about it. Given a positive ride, she kept up the gallop in relentless fashion all the way up the straight. (50/1)
3006 All Done went in pursuit of the winner, but was never going to find sufficient to get in a blow. (6/4)
1913 Rachel Louise is fully exposed. (5/1)
2804* Country Orchid, a handful beforehand, came off a true line under pressure and, for the time being at least, seems to be going the wrong way. (7/4)
3006 Side By Side (IRE) seems to lack anything in the way of pace. (13/2)

T/Plpt: £35.80 (297.79 Tckts). T/Qdpt: £10.60 (46.13 Tckts) WG

3265-HAYDOCK (L-H) (Good)

Saturday February 22nd

WEATHER: cloudy

3291 SCHLITZ VICTOR LUDORUM LIMITED H'CAP HURDLE (4-Y.O) (Class C)

1-15 (1-15) **2m (8 hdls)** £5,015.50 (£1,519.00: £742.00: £353.50) GOING: Not Established

				SP	RR	SF
2842*	**No More Hassle (IRE) (101)** (MrsMReveley) **4-10-11** PNiven (a gng wl: led 2 out: sn hdd: led flat: edgd lft: drvn out)	—	**1**	9/2^{2}	78	44
3049*	**Globe Runner (101)** (JJO'Neill) **4-10-11** ARoche (lw: hld up: hdwy 3 out: led appr last: hdd flat: not qckn)	1¾	**2**	9/1	76	42
3075*	**Font Romeu (FR) (114)** (MCPipe) **4-11-10** CFSwan (wl bhd 3rd: rdn 5th: gd hdwy 3 out: one pce fr 2 out)	4	**3**	4/1^{1}	85	51
2759^{12}	**Shu Gaa (IRE) (101)** (OSherwood) **4-10-11** JOsborne (led: hit 4th: hdd 5th: rallied to ld appr 2 out: sn hdd & wknd)	5	**4**	4/1^{1}	67	33
3093^{2}	**Meltemison (97)** (MDHammond) **4-10-7** RGarritty (hld up: hdwy 3 out: sn rdn & wknd)	10	**5**	6/1^{3}	53	19
2784*	**Jackson Park (108)** (TDEasterby) **4-11-4** GBradley (prom tl rdn & wknd appr 5th)	14	**6**	8/1	50	16
2615*	**Rossel (USA) (114)** (PMonteith) **4-11-10** ADobbin (prom: led 5th tl wknd appr 2 out)	1¼	**7**	4/1^{1}	55	21
				(SP 113.6%)		**7 Rn**

3m 48.9 (6.90) CSF £37.43 TOTE £4.40: £2.10 £3.40 (£26.80) OWNER The No Hassle Partnership (SALTBURN) BRED Declan MacPartlin
2842* No More Hassle (IRE), racing keenly, defied a 6lb rise in the weights and will now try to become his trainer's first-ever winner at the Festival in the Triumph Hurdle. (9/2)
3049* Globe Runner, looking particularly well, was trying to overcome a 10lb hike in the ratings and should soon regain winning ways. (9/1)
3075* Font Romeu (FR) is probably more effective on softer ground. (4/1)
2060* Shu Gaa (IRE) appeared to fail to stay the extra half-mile last time. (4/1)
3093 Meltemison could only manage a short-lived effort. (6/1)

3292 BLACK DEATH VODKA H'CAP CHASE (0-145) (6-Y.O+) (Class B)

1-45 (1-45) **2m 4f (15 fncs)** £14,332.00 (£4,306.00: £2,078.00: £964.00) GOING: 0.23 sec per fur (G)

	Horse / Trainer / Jockey / Comment	Dist	Pos	SP	RR	SF
2997a^{F}	**The Grey Monk (IRE) (145)** (GRichards) **9-12-0** ADobbin (lw: mde all: rdn appr last: clr flat: eased nr fin)	—	1	8/13^{1}	162+	37
2879^{9}	**Terao (121)** (MCPipe) **11-10-4** CFSwan (lw: hld up: ev ch whn mstke 2 out: rallied flat: nt trble wnr)	1	2	11/1	137	12
2057^{3}	**Major Bell (135)** (ACWhillans) **9-11-4** JOsborne (hld up & bhd: stdy hdwy 10th: ev ch 2 out: r.o one pce flat)	¾	3	7/2^{2}	151	26
1650^{3}	**Uncle Ernie (139)** (JGFitzGerald) **12-11-8** PCarberry (lw: hld up: hdwy 8th: wknd last)	10	4	10/1	147	22
2942^{2}	**Spanish Light (IRE) (120)** (SirJohnBarlowBt) **8-10-3** CMaude (plld hrd: prom tl wknd 4 out)	15	5	8/1^{3}	116	—
2901^{4}	**In Truth (117)** (SGollings) **9-10-0** KGaule (blnd bdly & uns rdr 1st)		U	16/1	—	—

(SP 118.5%) **6 Rn**

5m 12.5 (15.50) CSF £8.21 TOTE £1.60: £1.10 £2.70 (£5.10) OWNER Mr Alistair Duff (PENRITH) BRED James Doran
LONG HANDICAP In Truth 9-11
OFFICIAL EXPLANATION **Spanish Light (IRE): the trainer reported that the gelding was found to have lost his near-fore plate during the race and was cut behind.**

2997a The Grey Monk (IRE) had a nice confidence-booster after his heavy fall in Ireland, and now goes for the Gold Cup with the hope that there is some cut in the ground at Cheltenham. (8/13)
1937 Terao, dropped 6lb, looked much more like his old self here, although flattered by his proximity to the winner. A good effort on ground plenty lively enough for him. (11/1)
2057 Major Bell is not going to get much respite from the Handicapper on the strength of this performance. (7/2)
1650 Uncle Ernie, down 6lb, has only once ever scored beyond two miles. (10/1)
2942 Spanish Light (IRE) lost his near-fore shoe and returned cut behind. (8/1)

3293 STRETTON LEISURE SELECT HURDLE (5-Y.O+) (Class B)

2-15 (2-15) **2m (8 hdls)** £10,065.00 (£3,045.00: £1,485.00: £705.00) GOING: 0.23 sec per fur (G)

	Horse / Trainer / Jockey / Comment	Dist	Pos	SP	RR	SF
3103*	**Juyush (USA)** (JABOld) **5-11-4** JOsborne (lw: led to 3rd: outpcd appr 3 out: rallied 2 out: led last: rdn out)	—	1	5/2^{2}	116	62
3038^{4}	**Mistinguett (IRE) (148)** (NATwiston-Davies) **5-11-7** CMaude (lw: w ldr: led 3rd: qcknd clr appr 3 out: hdd last: hrd rdn: nt qckn)	1¾	2	11/8^{1}	117	63
3038^{8}	**Kissair (IRE) (130)** (NJHenderson) **6-11-4** JRKavanagh (hld up: wl bhd whn rdn 4th: styd on fr 2 out: n.d)	22	3	10/1	92	38
3150^{2}	**Moorish (138)** (NATwiston-Davies) **7-11-0** DWalsh (lw: hld up: hdwy whn hit 5th: mstke 3 out: sn wknd)	6	4	4/1^{3}	82	28
2635^{8}	**Tragic Hero (140)** (MCPipe) **5-11-12b** CFSwan (lw: wl bhd fr 3rd)	3½	5	16/1	91	37
1636^{7}	**Kingsfold Pet (134)** (MJHaynes) **8-11-4** DSkyrme (hld up: sme hdwy appr 3 out: sn wknd: t.o)	18	6	20/1	65	11
3163^{8}	**Marchant Ming (IRE) (125)** (MDHammond) **5-11-4** RGarritty (bhd fr 5th: t.o whn p.u bef last)		P	33/1	—	—

(SP 113.4%) **7 Rn**

3m 46.5 (4.50) CSF £5.87 TOTE £2.80: £1.70 £1.60 (£2.10) OWNER Mr W. E. Sturt (WROUGHTON) BRED Corbin J. Robertson

3103* Juyush (USA) found stamina coming to his aid in the latter stages, having got chopped for speed on this faster ground. (5/2)
3038 Mistinguett (IRE) was able to dominate with no Make a Stand in the field this time, and tried hard to slip the winner early in the home straight. (11/8)
3038 Kissair (IRE) wants softer ground, and could never get near the principals. (10/1)
3150 Moorish found this ground much quicker than the soft at Chepstow last week. (4/1)
2059 Tragic Hero is struggling to recapture the form which saw him end up as one of the leading juveniles last season. (16/1)
Kingsfold Pet requires the mud to be flying. (20/1)

3294 GREENALLS GRAND NATIONAL TRIAL H'CAP CHASE (Gd 3) (5-Y.O+) (Class A)

2-45 (2-45) **3m 4f 110y (22 fncs)** £50,256.00 (£18,456.00: £9,128.00: £4,040.00: £1,920.00) GOING: 0.23 sec per fur (G)

	Horse / Trainer / Jockey / Comment	Dist	Pos	SP	RR	SF
1454^{5}	**Suny Bay (IRE) (144)** (CPEBrooks) **8-10-8** JOsborne (mde all: j.slowly 4th (water): clr appr 2 out: r.o wl)	—	1	7/2^{2}	155	33
2616^{4}	**Into the Red (136)** (MrsMReveley) **13-10-0** ADobbin (hld up: rdn 4 out: chsd wnr fr 2 out: no imp)	19	2	7/1	136	14
2616^{5}	**St Mellion Fairway (IRE) (136)** (DNicholson) **8-10-0** AThornton (hit 1st: chsd wnr fr 6th to 2 out: one pce)	2½	3	12/1	134	12
2848a*	**Couldnt Be Better (160)** (CPEBrooks) **10-11-10** GBradley (lost pl 16th: mstke 17th: rallied appr 3 out: rdn appr 2 out: eased whn btn flat)	10	4	4/1^{3}	152	30
2616^{3}	**Lo Stregone (145)** (TPTate) **11-10-9b** CFSwan (lw: chsd wnr to 6th: lost pl & reminders 13th: t.o fr 4 out)	18	5	4/5^{1}	126	4

(SP 118.0%) **5 Rn**

7m 20.8 (15.80) CSF £23.29 TOTE £4.50: £2.20 £1.60 (£16.90) OWNER Uplands Bloodstock (LAMBOURN) BRED Mrs E. M. Codd
LONG HANDICAP St Mellion Fairway (IRE) 9-7 Into the Red 9-9
OFFICIAL EXPLANATION **Lo Stregone: no explanation offered.**

1454 Suny Bay (IRE) may have been suffering from a virus when breaking a blood-vessel last time. Putting up a near faultless display on ground plenty fast enough for him, his trainer said he will need it to be soft to go for the Gold Cup, and Hills reacted by cutting him from 20/1 to 10/1 for the Grand National. (7/2)
2616 Into the Red could not live with the winner from 5lb out of the handicap. (7/1)
2616 St Mellion Fairway (IRE), 7lb wrong at the weights, is better when ground conditions are more testing. (12/1: op 8/1)
2848a* Couldnt Be Better, raised 9lb, had apparently easily beaten the winner in a recent home gallop. (4/1)
2616 Lo Stregone, with the blinkers refitted, was described by Swan as never travelling and he added that the horse might be sick. (4/5: op 5/4)

3295 SPORTING LIFE MAIDEN HURDLE (4-Y.O+) (Class D)

3-20 (3-21) **2m 6f (12 hdls)** £3,165.00 (£890.00: £435.00) GOING: 0.23 sec per fur (G)

	Horse / Trainer / Jockey / Comment	Dist	Pos	SP	RR	SF
2746^{2}	**Absolutly Equiname (IRE)** (MJHeaton-Ellis) **6-11-7** BPowell (a.p: led appr 7th: clr 2 out: r.o wl)	—	1	3/1^{1}	80	10
2961^{3}	**Barbary Falcon** (PJJones) **7-11-7** GUpton (plld hrd: a.p: one pce fr 3 out)	8	2	16/1	74	4
2959^{2}	**Tremplin (IRE)** (NJHenderson) **6-11-2** JRKavanagh (lw: plld hrd: a.p: one pce fr 3 out)	5	3	7/1^{3}	66	—
3048^{6}	**Love The Blues (91)** (DNicholson) **5-10-13b$^{1(3)}$** RMassey (sn rdn along: hdwy 5th: wknd 3 out)	13	4	9/1	56	—
2958^{2}	**Grosvenor (IRE)** (GRichards) **6-11-7** PCarberry (hld up: hdwy 8th: rdn after 9th: wknd appr 3 out)	21	5	3/1^{1}	46	—
2701^{13}	**Sovereign Pass** (RDEWoodhouse) **5-11-7** CFSwan (t.o fr 6th)	3½	6	50/1	43	—
	Battle Creek (IRE) (JNorton) **7-11-7** WDwan (bit bkwd: t.o fr 7th)	12	7	50/1	35	—
3024^{2}	**Sir Bob (IRE)** (WMcKeown) **5-11-7** ADobbin (rdn 4th: bhd fr 6th: t.o)	4	8	7/2^{2}	32	—
	Docs Boy (OSherwood) **7-11-7** JOsborne (bit bkwd: nvr plcd to chal)	9	9	12/1	25	—
3066^{8}	**Fayette County (IRE)** (JJO'Neill) **6-11-7** AThornton (prom to 8th: t.o)	dist	10	20/1	—	—
2663^{6}	**Supremo (IRE)** (MJWilkinson) **8-11-7** TJO'Sullivan (bhd fr 6th: t.o)	8	11	25/1	—	—

	Horse / details	Dist	Pos	SP	RR	SF
3048[4]	**Stormy Session** (NATwiston-Davies) **7-11-7** DWalsh (prom to 8th: t.o)	1¼	12	20/1	—	—
	Swarf (IRE) (SABrookshaw) **7-11-7** GBradley (led tl appr 7th: wknd qckly: t.o whn p.u bef 9th)		P	16/1	—	—
1640[U]	**Silver Grove** (JJO'Neill) **7-11-0**(7) DJewett (bkwd: t.o whn p.u after 6th)		P	50/1	—	—
	This Time Lucky (NATwiston-Davies) **7-11-7** CMaude (t.o 7th: p.u bef 3 out)		P	12/1	—	—
	Palafico (PRWebber) **7-11-7** RBellamy (plld hrd: prom to 4th: t.o whn p.u bef 8th)		P	33/1	—	—
				(SP 144.1%)	**16 Rn**	

5m 32.8 (22.80) CSF £54.61 TOTE £4.00: £1.80 £5.50 £2.70 (£30.80) Trio £51.30 OWNER Mr F. J. Sainsbury (WROUGHTON) BRED Mrs Brenda Cunningham

2746 Absolutly Equiname (IRE) benefited from having plenty of use made of him, and looks capable of defying a penalty. (3/1)

2961 Barbary Falcon did not settle as well as his rider would have liked, but seems up to taking a similar event. (16/1)

2959 Tremplin (IRE) was another to take a keen hold early on. (7/1)

3048 Love The Blues did not look in love with the game despite the first-time blinkers. (9/1)

2958 Grosvenor (IRE) was most disappointing. (3/1)

Docs Boy has obviously had his training problems, and was given a quiet run on this hurdling debut. (12/1)

This Time Lucky (12/1: op 8/1)

3296 BELLCHARM RENAULT NOVICES' CHASE (5-Y.O+) (Class C)

3-50 (3-51) **2m (12 fncs)** £4,485.75 (£1,356.00: £660.50: £312.75) GOING: 0.23 sec per fur (G)

	Horse / details	Dist	Pos	SP	RR	SF
3167[3]	**Flying Instructor** (PRWebber) **7-11-5** RBellamy (hld up: led 3 out: drvn out)	—	1	6/4[2]	129	45
1386*	**Celibate (IRE) (132)** (CJMann) **6-11-12** JRailton (hld up & bhd: hdwy 3 out: ev ch whn hit last: sn rdn: one pce)	4	2	8/13[1]	132	48
3187[2]	**Heathyards Boy (67)** (DMcCain) **7-11-5b** DWalsh (led 2nd to 6th: led 4th to 3 out: hrd rdn & wknd 2 out)	28	3	50/1	81 t	13
3073[2]	**Frank Knows (68)** (TRGeorge) **7-11-5** PCarberry (led to 2nd: led 6th tl blnd 4 out: wknd 3 out)	12	4	11/1[3]	69 t	1
				(SP 112.2%)	**4 Rn**	

4m 3.5 (8.50) CSF £2.80 TOTE £2.70: (£1.40) OWNER Lady Lyell (BANBURY) BRED Lady Lyell

3167 Flying Instructor now goes for the Arkle having beaten the favourite fair and square. (6/4)

1386* Celibate (IRE), coming back from a mid-season break, lost his unbeaten record over fences, and it is doubtful if going through the top of the last made any difference to the result. (8/13)

3073 Frank Knows (11/1: 16/1-10/1)

3297 TARVIN STANDARD N.H. FLAT RACE (4, 5 & 6-Y.O) (Class H)

4-25 (4-25) **2m** £1,556.50 (£434.00: £209.50)

	Horse / details	Dist	Pos	SP	RR	SF
	Harris Croft Star (IRE) (DNicholson) **6-11-4**(3) RMassey (tall: hld up: rdn over 5f out: hdwy over 3f out: hrd rdn to ld ins fnl f: drvn out)	—	1	3/1[2]	65 f	—
	Shropshire Gale (IRE) (SABrookshaw) **6-11-0**(7) XAizpuru (lengthy: unf: a.p: led over 1f out tl ins fnl f)	2½	2	12/1	63 f	—
2931[5]	**Wise Gunner** (MCPipe) **4-9-13**(7) GSupple (led tl over 1f out: wknd ins fnl f)	5	3	13/8[1]	53 f	—
	Arctic Fox (IRE) (MissHCKnight) **5-11-0**(7) MrAWintle (w'like: leggy: bit bkwd: hmpd s: hdwy 4f out: rdn & edgd lft over 2f out: wknd over 1f out)	1¾	4	5/1	56 f	—
2770[4]	**Portman** (WMcKeown) **5-11-4**(3) PMidgley (chsd ldr tl rdn & wknd over 2f out)	4	5	12/1	52 f	—
	Political Power (WJenks) **6-11-7** MrAMitchell (bit bkwd: hmpd s: rdn & hdwy over 3f out: nt rch ldrs)	3½	6	33/1	48 f	—
3070[4]	**Linwood** (GRichards) **6-11-2** MrRHale (hmpd s: nvr trbld ldrs)	½	7	4/1[3]	43 f	—
	Donnybrook (IRE) (RDEWoodhouse) **4-10-6**(5) BGrattan (bkwd: prom 11f)	3½	8	16/1	44 f	—
	Last Action (JNorton) **4-10-3**(3) GLee (bit bkwd: prom tl wknd over 3f out)	12	9	25/1	27 f	—
	Shawkey (IRE) (DMcCain) **4-10-11** DWalsh (bkwd: hld up: hdwy 10f out: wknd over 3f out)	8	10	33/1	24 f	—
2811[12]	**Bucks Reef** (AJWilson) **5-11-4**(3) DFortt (bkwd: w.r.s: rdn 8f out: a bhd: t.o)	21	11	33/1	3 f	—
2924[12]	**Ferrino Fruits (IRE)** (MGMeagher) **6-11-7** GTormey (lw: bhd: rdn 7f out: sn t.o)	dist	12	50/1	—	—
				(SP 135.7%)	**12 Rn**	

3m 54.0 CSF £39.48 TOTE £4.30: £2.00 £1.70 £1.90 (£23.10) Trio £26.30 OWNER Mr R. F. Nutland (TEMPLE GUITING) BRED Timothy Carey

WEIGHT FOR AGE 4yo-10lb

IN-FOCUS: **A slow early pace allowed horses to quickly recover from a ragged start.**

Harris Croft Star (IRE), a brother to a winner between the flags, continued his stable's fine run in these events and gave the impression that stamina is going to be his forte. (3/1: op 2/1)

Shropshire Gale (IRE) seemed set to score until finding the winner far too strong in the closing stages. (12/1)

2931 Wise Gunner did not set much of a pace early on. (13/8)

Arctic Fox (IRE), supported in the ring, should find this outing putting an edge on him. (5/1)

2770 Portman is a half-brother to a point-to-point winner. (12/1: op 8/1)

T/Plpt: £364.80 (59.16 Tckts). T/Qdpt: £47.80 (18.27 Tckts) KH

3272-KEMPTON (R-H) (Good)

Saturday February 22nd

WEATHER: overcast

3298 DOVECOTE NOVICES' HURDLE (Gd 2) (4-Y.O+) (Class A)

1-55 (1-56) **2m (8 hdls)** £8,792.00 (£3,327.10: £1,628.55: £742.35) GOING: 0.54 sec per fur (GS)

	Horse / details	Dist	Pos	SP	RR	SF
2668*	**Sanmartino (IRE)** (DNicholson) **5-11-10** AMaguire (lw: a gng wl: hld up: led & mstke 2 out: shkn up & qcknd flat: comf)	—	1	2/5[1]	100+	51
2747[4]	**Mister Rm (110)** (NATwiston-Davies) **5-11-3** CLlewellyn (lw: hld up: rdn appr 2 out: chsd wnr appr last: ev ch flat: unable qckn)	2	2	20/1	91	42
2794*	**No Pattern (104)** (GLMoore) **5-11-3** APMcCoy (hdwy 5th: ev ch 3 out: wknd appr last)	7	3	11/1[3]	84	35
3041[3]	**Polydamas** (KCBailey) **5-11-3** DBridgwater (chsd ldr: ev ch 3 out: wknd appr last)	1	4	11/2[2]	83	34
	Classy Lad (NZ) (NJHenderson) **7-11-3** RDunwoody (hdwy appr 2 out: wknd appr last)	3	5	20/1	80	31
3174[F]	**Serenus (USA)** (NJHenderson) **4-11-0** RJohnson (led to 2 out: wknd appr last)	1	6	14/1	86	27

3103[2]	**Glide Path (USA)** (JRJenkins) **8-11-3** NWilliamson (bhd fr 3 out)	23	**7**	40/1	56	7

(SP 113.8%) **7 Rn**

3m 54.9 (12.90) CSF £10.93 TOTE £1.30: £1.10 £6.10 (£7.60) OWNER Mr K. Abdulla (TEMPLE GUITING) BRED Juddmonte Farms
WEIGHT FOR AGE 4yo-10lb

2668* Sanmartino (IRE) maintained his unbeaten record over hurdles. Always travelling supremely well, he had just got to the front when making a mistake two out. He looked in a bit of trouble as he was seriously pressed by the runner-up but, with Maguire waking him up on the run-in, he showed a fine turn of foot to put the issue beyond doubt. A classy Flat performer, he is translating that form to the winter game and has one powerful weapon, acceleration. Connections are still undecided about which race to send him for at the Festival, but thoughts about the Champion Hurdle should be quickly dismissed, as he is not up to that class at this stage in his career. However, he could be a leading player in either of the two novice events with the two miles five furlong Royal SunAlliance Novices' Hurdle likely to reap the better rewards. (2/5)

2747 Mister Rm ran a fine race, and threw down his challenge approaching the last. He looked a serious threat to the winner early on the run-in, but that rival found by far the better turn of foot. (20/1)

2794* No Pattern is not really up to this class, but he was still in contention turning out of the back straight before fading from the penultimate hurdle. (11/1)

3041 Polydamas faced a much stiffer task here, but still had every chance three from home before capitulating in the straight. He can win an ordinary novice event. (11/2)

Classy Lad (NZ), a well-made gelding who won three times on the Flat in New Zealand, two of those coming last year, was certainly thrown in at the deep end on this hurdling debut, his first run in this country. He shaped well, moving into contention turning for home, before tiring from the second last. His trainer obviously thinks quite a bit about him to run him in this company and, with his sights lowered slightly, he can step up on this before long. (20/1)

1935* Serenus (USA) had no easy task under a 7lb penalty, but took the field along until headed two from home. Although he has won a Grade Two event, he was helped by the melee two out on that occasion, and this class does expose his limitations. (14/1: op 8/1)

3299 EMBLEM CHASE (5-Y.O+) (Class B)

2-25 (2-26) **2m (13 fncs)** £7,160.00 (£2,010.00: £980.00) GOING: 0.54 sec per fur (GS)

				SP	RR	SF
2646[4]	**Viking Flagship (170)** (DNicholson) **10-12-0** AMaguire (chsd ldr: mstke 5th: led 7th: qcknd appr last: easily)	—	**1**	8/13[1]	151	53
3037[U]	**Arctic Kinsman (145)** (NATwiston-Davies) **9-12-0** CLlewellyn (lw: led to 7th: ev ch 2 out: rdn appr last: unable qckn)	3	**2**	4/1[3]	148	50
3030[3]	**Marlingford (74)** (MrsJJordan) **10-11-0** LMcGrath (a bhd: t.o fr 7th)	dist	**3**	100/1	—	—
	Martha's Son (164) (CaptTAForster) **10-12-0** NWilliamson (fell 2nd)		**F**	5/2[2]	—	—

(SP 111.5%) **4 Rn**

3m 57.3 (13.30) CSF £3.41 TOTE £1.50 (£2.00) OWNER Roach Foods Ltd (TEMPLE GUITING) BRED Miss E. C. Holdsworth

2646 Viking Flagship, who bruised his foot and had to miss the Game Spirit Chase at Newbury two weeks ago, always starts coming to himself at this time of year, and followed up last season's success in this race with a very impressive display. Not all that fluent at some of his fences early on, he put in a fine leap at the seventh, and from that point his jumping improved markedly. With the situation always in hand in the straight, he quickened up nicely going to the final fence to win with a ton in hand. Connections must have been over the moon with this performance, and once again he is the one they all have to beat in the Queen Mother Chase. (8/13)

3037 Arctic Kinsman ran a fine race but, although still in with every chance jumping the second last, the winner was always laughing at him. (4/1)

3030 Marlingford was completely outclassed, but eventually got round to pick up a decent third prize. (100/1)

Martha's Son had a leg injury following his last racecourse appearance back in November 1995 and had to be fired, resulting in six months' rest in a field. He was due to reappear in the Game Spirit Chase at Newbury two weeks ago, but pulled a muscle in his quarters and had to miss that engagement. Unfortunately, his long-awaited return to action was a far from happy one, as he crashed out of the race at the second fence. Connections must be on the point of having a nervous breakdown over him. (5/2)

3300 PENDIL NOVICES' CHASE (Gd 2) (5-Y.O+) (Class A)

3-00 (3-02) **2m 4f 110y (17 fncs)** £12,159.99 (£4,602.75: £2,253.88: £1,028.38) GOING: 0.54 sec per fur (GS)

				SP	RR	SF
2885[2]	**Land Afar (134)** (PRWebber) **10-11-7** AMaguire (lw: hdwy 11th: chsd ldr fr 4 out: led appr 2 out: rdn out)	—	**1**	4/1[3]	142	68
1981*	**Around The Gale (IRE) (126)** (DRGandolfo) **6-11-3** RDunwoody (chsd ldr: led 2nd to 4th: led 6th tl appr 2 out: unable qckn)	2	**2**	5/2[1]	136	62
2116*	**Greenback (BEL) (126)** (PJHobbs) **6-11-10** JFrost (hld up: 3rd whn mstke 6th: wknd 3 out)	16	**3**	9/1	131	57
2643*	**Fine Thyne (IRE)** (MrsAJPerrett) **8-11-7** NWilliamson (hdwy 13th: wknd appr 3 out)	6	**4**	3/1[2]	123	49
3043[2]	**Guinda (IRE) (111)** (NATwiston-Davies) **7-11-2** CLlewellyn (j.lft 7th: hdwy 11th: wknd appr 3 out)	5	**5**	20/1	114	40
2885*	**Stately Home (IRE) (136)** (PBowen) **6-11-10** RJohnson (lw: led tl blnd bdly & hdd 2nd: led 4th to 6th: rdn 10th: wknd 4 out: p.u bef next)		**P**	4/1[3]	—	—

(SP 108.3%) **6 Rn**

5m 12.2 (11.20) CSF £12.55 TOTE £4.40: £1.90 £1.70 (£5.70) OWNER Mr T. J. Ford (BANBURY) BRED Grange Stud (UK)

IN-FOCUS: This looked an extremely hot novice event on paper but, with Stately Home and Fine Thyne failing to give their running, the edge was taken off it.

2885 Land Afar won his first race over this longer trip and, leading approaching the second last, was ridden along to keep the runner-up at bay. Connections will be well advised to bypass Cheltenham, a course that does not suit him, and bring him out fresh at Aintree where the flat track should be in his favour. (4/1)

1981* Around The Gale (IRE) would have been happier with more cut in the ground, but that did not stop him running a fine race, making most until approaching the second last. Further success awaits him. (5/2)

2116* Greenback (BEL), winner of his last three races, had no easy task under a 7lb penalty, and was left for dead by the front two from the third last. (9/1)

2643* Fine Thyne (IRE) was a major disappointment, and dropped out in the straight. He is much better than this. (3/1)

3043 Guinda (IRE) had called it a day early in the straight. (20/1)

2885* Stately Home (IRE) was a bitter disappointment, for his trademark this season has been his excellent jumping. On this occasion he stood off far too early at the second and landed on top of the fence. How he managed to get over it was a miracle, but from that point he guessed at virtually every obstacle. His earlier antics had taken their toll four out, and he was pulled up early in the straight. He is far better than this, and it is to be hoped that his confidence has not been too badly dented. (4/1)

3301 VOICE NEWSPAPER ADONIS HURDLE (Gd 2) (4-Y.O) (Class A)

3-35 (3-35) **2m (8 hdls)** £8,750.00 (£3,311.00: £1,620.50: £738.50) GOING: 0.54 sec per fur (GS)

				SP	RR	SF
	L'Opera (FR) (DNicholson) **4-10-12** AMaguire (lw: hdwy 3 out: led last: rdn out)	—	**1**	7/2[2]	99+	52

			Pos	SP	RR	SF
3007*	**Kerawi** (NATwiston-Davies) **4-11-2** CLlewellyn (a.p: reminder 3 out: led appr 2 out to last: unable qckn flat)	2½	2	6/4 1	101	54
3007 5	**Summer Spell (USA)** (NJHenderson) **4-11-2** RDunwoody (lw: hdwy 3 out: mstke 2 out: ev ch last: wknd flat)	8	3	6/1	93	46
2865 4	**Chabrol (CAN)** (TTClement) **4-10-12** RJohnson (prom to appr 2 out)	6	4	25/1	83	36
3174*	**Red Raja** (PMitchell) **4-11-6** MRichards (lw: led tl appr 2 out: sn wknd)	2½	5	8/1	88	41
	Fairly Sharp (IRE) (GraemeRoe) **4-10-7** NWilliamson (prom tl appr 2 out)	½	6	33/1	75	28
1935 4	**Ben Bowden (92)** (SWoodman) **4-10-12** DBridgwater (bhd fr 3 out)	26	7	66/1	54	7
1935 5	**Province** (CJMann) **4-10-12** JMagee (a bhd)	3	8	66/1	51	4
2825 2	**Grief (IRE)** (DRCElsworth) **4-10-12** PHolley (bhd fr 3 out)	½	9	5/1 3	50	3
	Allstars Express (KCBailey) **4-10-12** PHide (a bhd)	13	10	33/1	37	—

(SP 117.0%) **10 Rn**

3m 52.3 (10.30) CSF £8.37 TOTE £4.20: £1.50 £1.30 £1.90 (£3.80) Trio £9.00 OWNER Sheikh Ahmed Al Maktoum (TEMPLE GUITING) BRED Darley Stud Management Co Ltd

L'Opera (FR), a useful individual on the Flat for John Oxx in Ireland, where he won three times, was given no easy task on this hurdling debut, but fully justified the confidence put in him. Taking a keen hold early on, he moved into contention three out and, in a tremendous battle with the second and third in the straight, asserted his superiority from the last. His stable has won this race twice before, with the top-class but ill-fated Mysilv in 1994 and last year with Zabadi, and this one is obviously destined for big things with the Triumph Hurdle very much on the agenda. (7/2: 5/2-4/1)

3007* Kerawi did not look to be going very well as his jockey gave him a reminder going to the third last, but he managed to get to the front approaching the penultimate hurdle although was immediately challenged by the winner and third. Collared at the final flight, he then failed to find another gear. (6/4)

3007 Summer Spell (USA) showed his Newbury running to be all wrong, as he had finished nearly thirty-two lengths behind Kerawi on the same terms. Despite being only lightly-made for this game, he had just poked a nostril in front when a mistake at the second last cost him the advantage. He still had every chance jumping the final flight before tiring on the run-in. (6/1)

2865 Chabrol (CAN) was certainly up against it here, but ran quite well, playing an active role until left behind going to the second last. (25/1)

3174* Red Raja looked extremely well beforehand, but had a very stiff task under an 8lb penalty and, after setting the pace, had nothing more to offer once collared approaching the second last. (8/1)

Fairly Sharp (IRE), an ex-Irish filly who was sold at the Goffs November Sales for IR 10,000 guineas, was having her first outing in three-and-a-half months, but was close up until tiring turning into the straight. (33/1)

3302 RACING POST H'CAP CHASE (Gd 3) (5-Y.O+) (Class A)

4-10 (4-12) **3m (19 fncs)** £30,380.00 (£11,399.00: £5,499.50: £2,421.50) GOING: 0.54 sec per fur (GS)

			Pos	SP	RR	SF
3046 2	**Mudahim (125)** (MrsJPitman) **11-10-2** RFarrant (a.p: led 3rd to 4th: led 5th tl appr last: led flat: rdn out)	—	1	14/1	140	65
2782 2	**King Lucifer (IRE) (130)** (DNicholson) **8-10-7** RJohnson (a.p: chsd wnr fr 12th: led appr last tl flat: r.o)	nk	2	6/1 3	145	70
	Percy Smollett (147) (DNicholson) **9-11-10** NWilliamson (mstke 10th: hdwy 13th: wknd 15th: t.o)	dist	3	6/1 3	—	—
3036*	**Call it a Day (IRE) (138)** (DNicholson) **7-11-1** AMaguire (lw: hdwy 13th: wknd 4 out: t.o)	5	4	9/4 1	—	—
	Encore Un Peu (FR) (141) (MCPipe) **10-11-4** APMcCoy (prom tl mstke & wknd 15th: t.o: lame)	3	6	8/1	—	—
2994a 2	**See More Business (IRE) (144)** (PFNicholls) **7-11-7** RDunwoody (lw: hdwy 10th: 4th whn fell 11th)		F	5/2 2	—	—
3147 5	**Sibton Abbey (138)** (GAHubbard) **12-10-12v(3)** PHenley (mstke 5th: bhd fr 10th: bdly hmpd 11th: t.o fr 12th: p.u bef 15th)		P	33/1	—	—
3147 4	**Dextra Dove (140)** (SEarle) **10-11-3** 3x DBridgwater (lw: mstke 5th: prom to 11th: t.o whn p.u bef 15th)		P	16/1	—	—
3039 5	**Forest Sun (125)** (GBBalding) **12-10-2** BClifford (led to 3rd: led 4th to 5th: wknd 9th: bhd whn bdly hmpd 11th: t.o fr 12th: p.u bef 3 out: dismntd)		P	66/1	—	—

(SP 116.0%) **9 Rn**

6m 3.2 (8.20) CSF £87.38 CT £515.37 TOTE £13.50: £1.90 £1.70 £1.90 (£22.50) Trio £60.70 OWNER In Touch Racing Club (UPPER LAMBOURN) BRED Warner Jones and W. Farish

3046 Mudahim caused a real upset, especially considering he did not have the knee-deep mud he loves. There was no fluke about this, as he made a lot of the running until marginally headed by the runner-up approaching the last. Refusing to give way, he battled back to the front on the run-in. (14/1: 10/1-16/1)

2782 King Lucifer (IRE) ran a tremendous race in defeat. In second place from the twelfth, it looked as if he had made a winning move as he edged into a narrow lead approaching the last. He had not bargained on such a tenacious winner, and was worried out of it on the run-in. The softer the ground the better, and the Kim Muir is his Cheltenham objective. (6/1)

Percy Smollett has been ready to run since December, but must have a right-hand track and some give. Tiring five out, he came home a very poor third. (6/1)

3036* Call it a Day (IRE) was very disappointing, and had given best four from home. (9/4)

Encore Un Peu (FR), runner-up in last season's Grand National, has had some niggling problems, but his trainer has reported that he only wanted to give him one run before this year's National. He played an active role until a mistake five out spelt the end. Unfortunately he returned lame, and is reportedly out for the rest of the campaign. (8/1: 6/1-9/1)

2994a See More Business (IRE) was not very convincing at his fences against such experienced rivals. Diving at a number of the obstacles, it was not really a surprise when he took a crashing fall at the eleventh. This is just what connections did not want before Cheltenham. Hopefully, this will not have dented his confidence too much, and he can bounce back in the Royal SunAlliance Chase. (5/2)

3147 Dextra Dove has had a sore mouth and was running in a rubber bit, which may have accounted for this lifeless display. (16/1)

3303 RENDLESHAM LIMITED H'CAP HURDLE (Gd 2) (4-Y.O+) (Class A)

4-40 (4-43) **3m 110y (12 hdls)** £12,034.60 (£4,554.68: £2,229.84: £1,016.88) GOING: 0.54 sec per fur (GS)

			Pos	SP	RR	SF
1936 F	**Pharanear (IRE) (140)** (DNicholson) **7-10-9** AMaguire (swtg: hdwy appr 2 out: led flat: drvn out)	—	1	6/1 3	120	32
2827 F	**Conquering Leader (IRE) (139)** (NJHenderson) **8-10-8** RJohnson (a.p: led appr 2 out tl flat: unable qckn)	2	2	11/2 2	118	30
3017 3	**Escartefigue (FR) (148)** (DNicholson) **5-11-3** DBridgwater (nt clr run on ins & lost pl bnd after 3 out: hdwy appr last: r.o wl flat)	hd	3	6/1 3	127	39
1994 P	**Castlekellyleader (IRE) (142)** (PFNicholls) **8-10-11** PHide (a.p: led 3 out tl appr 2 out: ev ch whn stumbled 2 out: one pce)	3	4	16/1	119	31
2888 5	**Tarrs Bridge (IRE) (138)** (CJMann) **6-10-4b(3)** JMagee (hld up: rdn appr 2 out: one pce)	3	5	8/1	113?	25
2934 4	**Top Spin (138)** (JRJenkins) **8-10-7** NWilliamson (hdwy appr 2 out: sn wknd)	19	6	12/1	100	12
3104 U	**Wee Windy (IRE) (138)** (JTGifford) **8-10-4(3)** LAspell (hld up: rdn 9th: wknd appr 2 out)	21	7	25/1	87	—
2637*	**Ocean Hawk (USA) (152)** (NATwiston-Davies) **5-11-7** CLlewellyn (lw: led to 9th: wknd after 3 out)	13	8	6/4 1	92	4
	Gillan Cove (IRE) (140) (RHAlner) **8-10-9** APMcCoy (w ldr: led 9th to 3 out: sn wknd)	13	9	12/1	72	—

	Horse	Dist	Pos	SP	RR	SF
	Fatack (138) (APJones) **8-10-7** SCurran (bit bkwd: bhd fr 3 out: t.o)	dist	**10**	33/1	—	—
				(SP 123.1%)	**10 Rn**	

6m 7.4 (21.40) CSF £38.01 CT £194.30 TOTE £7.20: £2.60 £1.80 £2.70 (£10.90) OWNER Stainless Threaded Fasteners Ltd (TEMPLE GUITING) BRED Seamus Kennedy
LONG HANDICAP Wee Windy (IRE) 9-11 Tarrs Bridge (IRE) 9-7 Top Spin 10-0 Fatack 9-12
IN-FOCUS: **It was not quite a Frankie Dettori but Adrian Maguire completed a magnificent 355/1 five-timer, a remarkable feat especially considering the high quality of the racing.**
1936 Pharanear (IRE) appreciated the return to the minor obstacles and, getting into top gear in the straight, managed to get on top on the run-in. (6/1)
2827 Conquering Leader (IRE) has not won over fences yet, so connections have decided to put that on hold for the time being and revert back to hurdles. Much happier at this longer trip, she moved to the front approaching the second last, but was unable to cope with the winner on the run-in. She will do even better on softer ground, and the Stayers' Hurdle is her target. (11/2)
3017 Escartefigue (FR) found this huge step-up in trip ideal for him, and must have gone extremely close had he not lost considerable ground and momentum when shuffled back to the rear of the field by the weakening Ocean Hawk turning out of the back straight. Flying from the second last, he finished really well and may have succeeded with a little further to go. At his best in the mud, he could run a big race in the Stayers' Hurdle if the ground comes in his favour. (6/1)
1994 Castlekellyleader (IRE), one of Ireland's leading novice hurdlers last season, had lost his way so far this term, disappointing in his one run over hurdles and failing to complete in two novice chases. He seemed much happier for the return to hurdles and the longer trip, and consequently ran by far and away his best race of the season, having every chance when stumbling at the second last before tapped for toe. (16/1)
2888 Tarrs Bridge (IRE) had no easy task from a stone out of the handicap, and could only struggle on at one pace in the straight. (8/1)
2934 Top Spin, 7lb out of the handicap, is not one to trust, and a brief effort turning for home came to little. (12/1)
2637* Ocean Hawk (USA) has developed into one of the top staying hurdlers in the country this season but, whether because his jockey did not make enough use of him, for he set only a very moderate pace instead of really trying to stretch his field, or whether he just had an off-day, is open to debate. The fact is he ran a lifeless race. This performance is best ignored as he is far better than he showed here, and he can still be a leading player in the Stayers' Hurdle at the Festival. (6/4)

3304 KEMPTON STANDARD OPEN N.H. FLAT RACE (4, 5 & 6-Y.O) (Class H)
5-10 (5-13) **2m** £1,413.00 (£393.00: £189.00)

	Horse	Dist	Pos	SP	RR	SF
2661[6]	**Country Beau** (JSKing) **5-11-3** MRichards (hdwy over 3f out: led over 1f out: rdn out)	—	**1**	50/1	88 f	—
	Arctic Camper (DNicholson) **5-11-10** AMaguire (hdwy over 6f out: chsd ldr over 4f out: led over 2f out tl over 1f out: unable qckn)	2½	**2**	10/11[1]	93 f	—
1986*	**Scoring Pedigree (IRE)** (JWMullins) **5-11-10** SCurran (hdwy 7f out: led 6f out: clr 4f out: hdd over 2f out: wknd fnl f)	4	**3**	13/2[3]	89 f	—
	The Lightmaker (IRE) (SEarle) **4-10-7** DBridgwater (hdwy over 4f out: rdn over 3f out: one pce)	5	**4**	50/1	77 f	—
	Montroe (IRE) (RRowe) **5-11-3** DO'Sullivan (stdy hdwy fnl 2f: nvr nrr)	8	**5**	33/1	69 f	—
2682[6]	**Wisley Warrior** (NATwiston-Davies) **6-11-3** CLlewellyn (prom over 12f)	1¼	**6**	12/1	67 f	—
3021[3]	**Sir Prize (IRE)** (GBBalding) **4-10-7** BClifford (chsd ldr over 8f)	3	**7**	10/1	64 f	—
2938*	**Mister Ermyn** (LMontagueHall) **4-11-0** APMcCoy (plld hrd: hdwy 7f out: wknd 4f out)	4	**8**	9/2[2]	67 f	—
2757[10]	**Aintgotwon** (AHide) **6-10-12** PHide (led 10f)	10	**9**	66/1	45 f	—
	Jet Specials (IRE) (MrsJPitman) **4-10-7** RFarrant (bit bkwd: hdwy over 6f out: wknd 4f out)	1	**10**	9/2[2]	49 f	—
2066[5]	**Ben Eiger (IRE)** (NATwiston-Davies) **5-10-10**(7) MKeighley (lw: prom 7f)	2	**11**	33/1	47 f	—
2911[4]	**Caldebrook (IRE)** (JTGifford) **6-10-10**(7) SLaird (hdwy over 6f out: wknd over 4f out)	5	**12**	33/1	42 f	—
	Gracious Imp (USA) (JRJenkins) **4-9-9**(7) NTEgan (w'like: str: bhd fnl 7f)	2½	**13**	66/1	35 f	—
	Hour Horse (NJHawke) **6-11-3** RGreene (bkwd: prom over 9f)	1¾	**14**	50/1	38 f	—
2911[3]	**Kingswood Imperial** (RJO'Sullivan) **4-10-7** NWilliamson (lw: plld hrd: a bhd: t.o)	dist	**15**	20/1	—	—
2696[22]	**Tupenny Smoke** (GraemeRoe) **5-10-9**(3) PHenley (a bhd: t.o)	26	**16**	66/1	—	—
918[2]	**Woodstock Wanderer (IRE)** (PBowen) **5-11-3** RJohnson (prom 10f: t.o)	dist	**17**	20/1	—	—
				(SP 147.6%)	**17 Rn**	

3m 49.8 CSF £99.82 TOTE £53.60: £7.40 £1.10 £2.60 (£113.30) Trio £195.70 OWNER Mrs J. J. Peppiatt (SWINDON) BRED P. G. Bailey
WEIGHT FOR AGE 4yo-10lb
Country Beau caused a real shock here. Picking up ground turning for home, he got to the front approaching the final furlong, and was ridden along to assert. (50/1)
Arctic Camper, an ex-Irish gelding who was bought privately out of John Kiely's stable after impressively winning a Fairyhouse bumper, probably did too much too soon. Reeling in the clear leader over a quarter of a mile from home, he looked in charge but had not banked on the winner and, collared below the distance, failed to find another gear. He should soon recoup losses. (10/11)
1986* Scoring Pedigree (IRE) suffered his first defeat but he still gave a good account of himself and tried to slip his field turning out of the back straight, quickly stealing a march on his rivals. Collared over a quarter of a mile from home, he grimly tried to hold on, but tired in the final furlong. (13/2: 8/1-12/1)
The Lightmaker (IRE), a well-built gelding, moved up turning for home but could only go up and down in the same place in the straight. (50/1)
Montroe (IRE), a leggy, light-framed gelding, was given a nice educational debut, and was noted making steady headway in the straight under considerate handling. Improvement can be expected. (33/1)
3021 Sir Prize (IRE) (10/1: op 5/1)
Jet Specials (IRE) (9/2: op 8/1)

T/Jkpt: £7,936.20 (0.39 Tckts); £6,818.45 to Newcastle 24/2/97. T/Plpt: £54.10 (494.5 Tckts). T/Qdpt: £23.30 (56.85 Tckts) AK

3091-MUSSELBURGH (R-H) (Good)
Saturday February 22nd
WEATHER: fine

3305 ROYAL BANK OF SCOTLAND MAIDEN HURDLE (I) (4-Y.O+) (Class E)
2-10 (2-10) **2m (9 hdls)** £1,720.00 (£470.00: £220.00) GOING: 0.09 sec per fur (G)

	Horse	Dist	Pos	SP	RR	SF
2953[4]	**Swift Riposte (IRE) (100)** (PMonteith) **6-11-7** RSupple (lw: trckd ldr fr 3rd: blnd 4th: led 3 out: clr whn blnd last)	—	**1**	10/11[1]	62	16

				SP	RR	SF
1687[8]	**Laughing Fontaine (IRE)** (FMurphy) **7-11-7** MFoster (lw: lft in ld 3rd: hdd 3 out: no ch w wnr)	9	**2**	9/2[3]	53	7
2953[11]	**Pearls of Thought (IRE)** (ACWhillans) **4-10-1**(5) STaylor (chsd ldrs: rdn 5th: no imp)	5	**3**	33/1	43	—
1926[10]	**Rasin Standards** (RCraggs) **7-11-7** GCahill (outpcd & no imp fr 4th)	23	**4**	50/1	25	—
3142[17]	**Romaldkirk** (VThompson) **5-11-7** MrMThompson (sn t.o)	28	**5**	66/1	—	—
	Anastasia Windsor (68) (DMoffatt) **6-11-2v** DJMoffatt (disp ld tl carried out 3rd)		**C**	14/1	—	—
2953[P]	**Blood Brother** (JBarclay) **5-11-7** DParker (sn t.o: p.u bef 2 out)		**P**	33/1	—	—
3158[U]	**Jamaican Flight (USA)** (MrsSLamyman) **4-10-8**(3) ECallaghan (plld hrd: disp ld tl ran out 3rd)		**R**	2/1[2]	—	—

(SP 119.9%) **8 Rn**

3m 51.5 (12.50) CSF £5.56 TOTE £1.70: £1.10 £1.30 £3.60 (£2.80) OWNER Mr T. P. Finch (ROSEWELL) BRED Ballylinch Stud Ltd
WEIGHT FOR AGE 4yo-10lb

2953 Swift Riposte (IRE) won this poor event well, but he certainly needs to improve his jumping. (10/11: 4/6-evens)
Laughing Fontaine (IRE), having his second run since coming over from Ireland, took the eye in the paddock but looked pretty slow in the race. (9/2: op 5/2)
Pearls of Thought (IRE), wearing a tongue-strap, ran a deal better than on her debut, but there is plenty more needed. (33/1)
Rasin Standards could never get into this moderate contest. (50/1)
Jamaican Flight (USA) was heavily supported in the market but, for the second week running, he showed he is not one to be trusted. (2/1: op 5/1)

3306 FIONA P. CRAIG NOVICES' H'CAP CHASE (0-105) (5-Y.O+) (Class E)

2-40 (2-40) **3m (18 fncs)** £2,688.00 (£798.00: £378.00: £168.00) GOING: Not Established

				SP	RR	SF
2954[4]	**Mister Trick (IRE) (78)** (LLungo) **7-11-2b**[1] RSupple (lw: a chsng ldrs: led 14th & sn drvn along: hdd last: rallied to ld fnl 80y)	—	**1**	5/2[1]	89	24
2912[4]	**Strongalong (IRE) (68)** (PCheesbrough) **7-10-6** ASSmith (a.p: chal 14th: slt ld last: hdd & nt qckn towards fin)	nk	**2**	9/1	79	14
3067[P]	**Seldom But Severe (IRE) (65)** (EAElliott) **7-9-12**(5) GFRyan (prom tl outpcd fr ½-wy: gd hdwy appr 4 out: one pce fr 2 out)	6	**3**	33/1	72	7
2699[6]	**Master of Troy (79)** (CParker) **9-11-3** DParker (outpcd & lost tch ½-wy: styd on fr 4 out: nrst fin)	6	**4**	12/1	82	17
2789[F]	**Fine Tune (IRE) (62)** (MrsSCBradburne) **7-10-0** MFoster (lw: hld up: hdwy 11th: nvr trbld ldrs)	5	**5**	5/1[2]	62	—
3092[U]	**Most Rich (IRE) (68)** (BEllison) **9-10-6v**[1]ow1 TReed (lw: blnd 5th: sn chsng ldrs: led 11th to 14th: sn lost pl)	7	**6**	10/1	63	—
3094[4]	**Tactix (65)** (MissMKMilligan) **7-10-3** BStorey (blnd 1st: bhd tl hdwy & in tch ½-wy: outpcd fr 12th)	10	**7**	8/1	53	—
3141[P]	**Distillery Hill (IRE) (71)** (VThompson) **9-10-9**[ow4] MrMThompson (led to 11th: wknd 13th)	1½	**8**	33/1	58	—
3067[P]	**Bright Destiny (62)** (JSGoldie) **6-10-0** KJohnson (sn drvn along & a bhd)	7	**9**	33/1	45	—
2799[4]	**Movac (IRE) (86)** (MissLucindaRussell) **8-11-10** MMoloney (chsd ldrs tl wknd fr 11th)	2½	**10**	12/1	67	2
2917[12]	**Master Flashman (73)** (MrsMReveley) **8-10-11** GCahill (blnd 4th: sn bhd: p.u bef 12th)		**P**	7/1[3]	—	—

(SP 112.1%) **11 Rn**

6m 8.8 (15.80) CSF £21.62 CT £527.77 TOTE £2.30: £1.70 £2.30 £7.20 (£11.80) Trio £136.40; £82.65 to Newcastle 24/2/97 OWNER Mr Edward Birkbeck (CARRUTHERSTOWN) BRED M. Parkhill
LONG HANDICAP Bright Destiny 9-12 Fine Tune (IRE) 9-12
OFFICIAL EXPLANATION Most Rich (IRE): swallowed his tongue.

2954 Mister Trick (IRE) had the blinkers on to sharpen him up and looked to have found a poor race here, but this track proved a bit too quick for him at times, and he needed plenty of help from the saddle. (5/2)
2912 Strongalong (IRE) has taken time to get the hang of things, but he does at last seem to be going the right way. (9/1: op 6/1)
Seldom But Severe (IRE), who was warm beforehand, had not previously finished within sight of the leaders, but this was not a very competitive race. (33/1)
Master of Troy showed his first sign of form over fences here, and has the ability to do better when caught in the mood. (12/1)
2176 Fine Tune (IRE) got round safely this time and that should have boosted his confidence. (5/1)
3092 Most Rich (IRE) at last put in a clear round, but appeared to get a sympathetic ride and was later said to have choked. (10/1)
Master Flashman (7/1: op 9/2)

3307 ROYAL BANK OF SCOTLAND E.B.F. 'N.H.' (QUALIFIER) NOVICES' HURDLE (5, 6 & 7-Y.O) (Class D)

3-10 (3-10) **2m 4f (12 hdls)** £3,105.00 (£855.00: £405.00) GOING: 0.09 sec per fur (G)

				SP	RR	SF
2766[4]	**Shanavogh (103)** (GMMoore) **6-11-10** JCallaghan (disp ld tl led 3 out: styd on strly)	—	**1**	4/6[1]	81	24
2917[4]	**Clavering (IRE) (87)** (HowardJohnson) **7-11-0** ASSmith (trckd ldrs: disp ld 6th to 3 out: sn rdn & one pce)	8	**2**	5/2[2]	65	8
2861[9]	**Caught At Last (IRE)** (MrsMReveley) **6-11-0** GCahill (hld up: effrt 4 out: styd on: no imp)	¾	**3**	33/1	64	7
2701[7]	**Antarctic Wind (IRE) (100)** (MDHammond) **7-11-7**(3) ECallaghan (chsd ldrs: outpcd & mstke 4 out: no imp after)	4	**4**	6/1[3]	71	14
2798[7]	**The Sharrow Legend (IRE)** (JSisterson) **5-10-9**(5) STaylor (outpcd 7th: nvr trbld ldrs)	24	**5**	33/1	42	—
2787[P]	**Boris Brook** (RAllan) **6-10-7**(7) SMelrose (disp ld to 5th: outpcd 8th: sn lost tch)	13	**6**	40/1	31	—
3066[4]	**Drakewrath (IRE)** (RABartlett) **7-11-0** DParker (blnd & uns rdr 5th)		**U**	20/1	—	—

(SP 115.9%) **7 Rn**

4m 56.7 (14.70) CSF £2.42 TOTE £1.80: £1.60 £1.40 (£2.40) OWNER Mr Sean Graham (MIDDLEHAM) BRED Brick Kiln Stud Farm

2766 Shanavogh was back to form here after four weeks off, and looks likely to get further. (4/6: 4/5-evens)
2917 Clavering (IRE) travelled equally as well as the winner, but his response off the bridle was disappointing. (5/2)
1827 Caught At Last (IRE) ran reasonably without getting into this, but does seem to be improving. (33/1)
1689 Antarctic Wind (IRE), from an out of form yard, never looked happy on this occasion. (6/1: op 4/1)
1926 The Sharrow Legend (IRE) has proved most disappointing so far over hurdles. (33/1)
2619 Boris Brook looked woefully slow here. (40/1)

3308 SCOTTISH LIFE H'CAP CHASE (0-115) (5-Y.O+) (Class E)

3-45 (3-45) **2m 4f (16 fncs)** £3,200.00 (£950.00: £450.00: £200.00) GOING: 0.09 sec per fur (G)

				SP	RR	SF
3027[2]	**Judicial Field (IRE) (93)** (NTinkler) **8-11-1b** BStorey (lw: prom tl mstke & outpcd 9th: gd hdwy to ld 4 out: drvn out)	—	**1**	7/2[3]	105	31
2765[5]	**Aly Daley (IRE) (97)** (HowardJohnson) **9-11-5** ASSmith (mde most tl hdd 4 out: hit 2 out: rallied last: nt qckn towards fin)	1¼	**2**	8/1	108	34
3094[3]	**Risky Dee (78)** (VThompson) **8-10-0** DBentley (disp ld 7th tl blnd 12th: one pce after)	6	**3**	20/1	84	10
3094[2]	**Buyers Dream (IRE) (89)** (BEllison) **7-10-11v** TReed (mstkes early & sn wl bhd)	12	**4**	3/1[2]	86	12

	Horse	Details	Dist	Pos	SP	RR	SF
2769*	**Montrave (105)**	(PMonteith) **8-11-13** RSupple (trckd ldrs: hit 7th: wknd 4 out)	3	**5**	Evens[1]	99	25
					(SP 113.1%)		**5 Rn**

5m 6.7 (10.70) CSF £24.33 TOTE £4.80: £2.10 £2.60 (£16.50) OWNER Mrs E. E. Newbould (MALTON) BRED Sean Collins
LONG HANDICAP Risky Dee 9-8
OFFICIAL EXPLANATION **Buyers Dream (IRE): the rider reported that the gelding pulled up lame after the race.**
3027 Judicial Field (IRE) never looked particularly happy during the race and occasionally puts in a very slow jump, but he has the speed on the flat and that was enough this time. (7/2)
2765 Aly Daley (IRE) put in a much better effort this time, but found the trip on the short side. (8/1: 6/1-10/1)
3094 Risky Dee again ran quite well, but was short of speed when it mattered. (20/1)
3094 Buyers Dream (IRE) jumped sloppily early on and ran no sort of race. (3/1)
2769* Montrave has always been a bit of a moody customer and was never happy here. This is best ignored. (Evens)

3309 SCOTMID H'CAP HURDLE (0-115) (4-Y.O+) (Class E)

4-20 (4-20) **2m 4f (12 hdls)** £2,560.00 (£760.00: £360.00: £160.00) GOING: 0.09 sec per fur (G)

	Horse	Details	Dist	Pos	SP	RR	SF
3035*	**Here Comes Herbie (87)**	(WStorey) **5-10-0**(5) RMcGrath (hld up: a gng wl: led on bit flat: hrd hld)	—	**1**	2/1[1]	64+	30
3045[4]	**All On (110)**	(JHetherton) **6-11-11**(3) ECallaghan (hld up: smooth hdwy to ld 3 out: hdd flat: r.o: no ch w wnr)	¾	**2**	9/2[2]	86	52
3163[6]	**Old Habits (IRE) (102)**	(JLEyre) **8-10-13**(7) CElliott (in tch: outpcd 4 out: styd on u.p fr 2 out: no imp)	6	**3**	9/2[2]	74	40
3028[8]	**Glenugie (94)**	(GMMoore) **6-10-12** NBentley (cl up: pushed along fr ½-wy: disp ld 3 out: outpcd fr next)	5	**4**	16/1	62	28
1824[3]	**Peggy Gordon (82)**	(MrsDThomson) **6-9-7**(7) CMcCormack (cl up: effrt 3 out: r.o one pce)	8	**5**	14/1[3]	43	9
2802*	**Cheater (IRE) (92)**	(HowardJohnson) **6-10-10b** ASSmith (led tl hdd 3 out: sn rdn & btn)	6	**6**	9/2[2]	48	14
3158[10]	**Toshiba Talk (IRE) (90)**	(BEllison) **5-10-8** TReed (lw: in tch: outpcd 7th: lost tch fr 4 out)	7	**7**	20/1	41	7
	Stingray City (USA) (91)	(RMMcKellar) **8-10-9** DParker (bkwd: cl up to ½-wy: sn t.o: p.u bef 4 out)		**P**	33/1	—	—
805[5]	**Jabaroot (IRE) (82)**	(RMMcKellar) **6-10-0** GCahill (sn t.o: p.u bef 4 out)		**P**	25/1	—	—
					(SP 112.0%)		**9 Rn**

4m 50.0 (8.00) CSF £10.00 CT £31.30 TOTE £2.90: £1.80 £2.30 £1.10 (£8.10) Trio £11.20 OWNER Mr H. S. Hutchinson (CONSETT) BRED H. Hutchinson
LONG HANDICAP Peggy Gordon 9-7 Jabaroot (IRE) 9-12
3035* Here Comes Herbie seems to have got the winning habit, and won this with any amount in hand. (2/1)
3045 All On, who failed to impress on looks, tried hard under top-weight but the winner was always laughing at her. (9/2)
3163 Old Habits (IRE) is slow but sure, and this trip is probably a bit too sharp for him these days. (9/2)
3028 Glenugie ran better on this faster ground. (16/1)
1824 Peggy Gordon ran reasonably after two-and-a-half months off and from 7lb out of the handicap. (14/1)
2802* Cheater (IRE), having his second run in the blinkers, failed to see it out this time. (9/2: op 3/1)

3310 EDINBURGH UNIVERSITY TURF CLUB 'HOLE IN THE WALL' H'CAP HURDLE (0-105) (4-Y.O) (Class E)

4-50 (4-50) **2m (9 hdls)** £2,560.00 (£760.00: £360.00: £160.00) GOING: 0.09 sec per fur (G)

	Horse	Details	Dist	Pos	SP	RR	SF
3093*	**Double Agent (98)**	(HowardJohnson) **4-12-0** ASSmith (trckd ldr: led 3 out: hrd rdn & disp ld whn lft clr last)	—	**1**	11/8[1]	77	19
3066[7]	**Double Dash (IRE) (84)**	(DMoffatt) **4-11-0v[1]** DJMoffatt (in tch: outpcd 6th: styd on fr 2 out: no imp)	10	**2**	10/1	53	—
2615[10]	**Perpetual Light (80)**	(JJQuinn) **4-10-7**(3) ECallaghan (in tch tl outpcd fr 3 out: no ch whn blnd last)	6	**3**	100/30[3]	43	—
2859[15]	**Bridlington Bay (70)**	(BEllison) **4-9-7**(7) CMcCormack (led tl hdd 3 out: sn outpcd)	6	**4**	25/1	27	—
3064[2]	**Joe Shaw (89)**	(MrsMReveley) **4-11-5** GCahill (lw: chsd ldrs: pushed along fr 4th: outpcd & hit 3 out: gd hdwy to disp ld whn fell last)		**F**	2/1[2]	66?	—
					(SP 111.5%)		**5 Rn**

3m 52.4 (13.40) CSF £12.49 TOTE £2.10: £1.20 £2.10 (£4.10) OWNER Hertford Offset Ltd (CROOK) BRED Mrs R. D. Peacock
LONG HANDICAP Bridlington Bay 9-9
3093* Double Agent looked a shade fortunate here, as his only serious rival came to grief at the last when looking to have him in trouble. (11/8)
1700 Double Dash (IRE) was always struggling with the pace here, and may well need either a stiffer track or further. (10/1)
Perpetual Light ran a shade better this time but, apart from the winner, it was not a good event. (100/30)
Bridlington Bay was beaten twenty-two lengths and this is his best effort to date. (25/1)
3064 Joe Shaw always looked as though this trip on this track was too sharp, but he suddenly picked up in the straight, and may well have won but for falling heavily at the last. (2/1)

3311 ROYAL BANK OF SCOTLAND MAIDEN HURDLE (II) (4-Y.O+) (Class E)

5-20 (5-20) **2m (9 hdls)** £1,720.00 (£470.00: £220.00) GOING: 0.09 sec per fur (G)

	Horse	Details	Dist	Pos	SP	RR	SF
3158[4]	**Far Ahead**	(JLEyre) **5-11-7** BStorey (lw: trckd ldr: led appr 3 out: clr whn blnd last: shkn up & styd on)	—	**1**	8/13[1]	67+	10
2806[4]	**Tilaal (USA) (89)**	(MDHammond) **5-11-7** DBentley (hld up: hdwy 5th: chsd wnr fr 2 out: hung rt & nvr able to chal)	3	**2**	2/1[2]	64	7
2804[10]	**Cottstown Boy (IRE)**	(MrsSCBradburne) **6-11-7** MFoster (a.p: effrt 3 out: r.o one pce)	11	**3**	50/1	53	—
3022[5]	**Known Secret (USA)**	(PMonteith) **4-10-11** MMoloney (bit bkwd: hld up & bhd: hdwy 3 out: nvr nr to chal)	10	**4**	25/1	43	—
3098[6]	**Helperby (IRE)**	(HowardJohnson) **5-11-7** ASSmith (chsd ldrs tl wknd fr 3 out)	1¾	**5**	16/1[3]	41	—
3026[6]	**Nordisk Legend**	(MrsDThomson) **5-11-7** TReed (prom tl wknd 3 out)	12	**6**	100/1	29	—
2957[11]	**Rubislaw (50)**	(MrsKMLamb) **5-11-0v**(7) MissSLamb (led tl hdd appr 3 out: btn whn blnd 3 out)	1½	**7**	100/1	28	—
2649[R]	**Coeur Francais (FR)**	(NWaggott) **5-11-0**(7) SHaworth (cl up to 3rd: sn wknd & t.o)	16	**8**	25/1	12	—
					(SP 112.8%)		**8 Rn**

3m 53.0 (14.00) CSF £1.83 TOTE £1.40: £1.00 £2.70 £7.70 (£1.50) OWNER Sunpak Potatoes (HAMBLETON) BRED Sir John Astor
WEIGHT FOR AGE 4yo-10lb
3158 Far Ahead only had to turn up to win this, but he did try to throw it away by blundering at the last. (8/13)
2806 Tilaal (USA) ran reasonably, but when the pressure was on all he wanted to do was hang right. (2/1)
Cottstown Boy (IRE) has been pulling too hard in his bumpers, but did better here and ought to improve with experience. (50/1)
3022 Known Secret (USA) showed nothing on his debut last time, but gave definite signs of encouragement here. (25/1)

T/Plpt: £14.90 (478.93 Tckts). T/Qdpt: £7.50 (48.73 Tckts) AA

3157-NEWCASTLE (L-H) (Good, Good to soft patches)
Monday February 24th
Final fence omitted in all Chases
WEATHER: unsettled & windy

3312 JOHN J. STRAKER CHALLENGE TROPHY H'CAP CHASE (0-125) (5-Y.O+) (Class D)
2-10 (2-10) **2m 4f (15 fncs)** £3,501.25 (£1,060.00: £517.50: £246.25) GOING: 0.49 sec per fur (GS)

				SP	RR	SF
3027^{4}	**Solba (USA) (96)** (CParker) **8-10-10b^{1}** DParker (a.p: chal 8th: led 3 out: styd on wl flat)	—	**1**	11/1	111	27
3069^{2}	**Nicholas Plant (96)** (JSGoldie) **8-10-10** GCahill (led: hit 4th: hdd next: led 8th to 3 out: chal & hit last: no ex)	7	**2**	11/8^{1}	105	21
	Forbidden Time (IRE) (110) (LLungo) **9-11-10** RSupple (chsd ldrs: hit 10th: hrd drvn 4 out: one pce: fin lame)	7	**3**	9/2^{2}	114	30
3027^{3}	**Village Reindeer (NZ) (103)** (PCalver) **10-11-3** LWyer (sn bhd: mstke 7th: sme late hdwy)	6	**4**	5/1^{3}	102	18
11*	**Grouse-N-Heather (94)** (PMonteith) **8-10-8** ADobbin (lw: trckd ldrs: blnd 7th: wknd fr next)	27	**5**	9/2^{2}	71	—
3140^{3}	**Potato Man (90)** (BEllison) **11-10-4v** BStorey (cl up: led 5th to 8th: outpcd fr next)	8	**6**	20/1	61	—
				(SP 108.2%)		**6 Rn**

5m 11.6 (18.60) CSF £23.71 TOTE £9.90: £2.20 £1.10 (£7.50) OWNER Mr & Mrs Raymond Anderson Green (LOCKERBIE) BRED David E. Hager II and Mrs Julian G. Rogers
OFFICIAL EXPLANATION **Forbidden Time (IRE): the trainer reported that the gelding finished lame.**
3027 Solba (USA) had the blinkers on for the first time and they worked the oracle. It will be interesting to see if they have the same effect twice. (11/1)
3069 Nicholas Plant is happier at this trip, but would have preferred a bit more cut in the ground. Nevertheless he ran well, despite taking some fences halfway up. (11/8)
Forbidden Time (IRE), having his first run for over a year, had his chances but a mistake six out had him struggling and, on finishing, he was found to be lame. (9/2: op 3/1)
3027 Village Reindeer (NZ) needs more cut in the ground, and was never going the pace or jumping well enough. (5/1)
11* Grouse-N-Heather looked fit enough for her reappearance here, but she put in a very awkward jump at the seventh and was never happy thereafter. (9/2)
3140 Potato Man would prefer more cut in the ground, and was left behind in the final mile. (20/1)

3313 GREAT NORTH ROAD (S) H'CAP HURDLE (0-95) (4-Y.O+) (Class G)
2-40 (2-40) **2m (9 hdls)** £2,057.00 (£577.00: £281.00) GOING: 0.10 sec per fur (G)

				SP	RR	SF
1971^{4}	**Latin Leader (83)** (CParker) **7-11-8b** DParker (lw: jnd ldr 3rd: led 3 out: r.o)	—	**1**	6/1^{3}	69	18
2862^{4}	**In a Moment (USA) (70)** (CGrant) **6-10-9** RGarritty (bhd tl hdwy 2 out: r.o wl towards fin)	½	**2**	5/1^{2}	56	5
3026^{5}	**Obvious Risk (61)** (EMCaine) **6-9-7**(7) TristanDavidson (blnd 3rd: hdwy 3 out: styd on wl)	5	**3**	16/1	42	—
3091*	**Palace of Gold (85)** (LLungo) **7-11-3**(7) WDowling (led: blnd 2nd: j.slowly 4th: hdd & mstke 3 out: one pce after)	hd	**4**	4/1^{1}	65	14
3064^{P}	**Bill's Pride (75)** (PMonteith) **6-11-0** MMoloney (trckd ldrs: ev ch 3 out: wknd flat)	½	**5**	14/1	55	4
3157^{P}	**Denticulata (70)** (PSpottiswood) **9-10-9** BStorey (bhd & drvn along 3 out: styd on wl towards fin)	1¼	**6**	25/1	49	—
3031^{12}	**Beacon Hill Lady (71)** (BEllison) **4-9-7**(7) NHorrocks (bhd: hdwy 5th: nvr trbld ldrs)	3½	**7**	100/1	46	—
3157^{P}	**Bark'n'bite (81)** (MrsMReveley) **5-11-6** PNiven (prom to 3 out)	3½	**8**	7/1	53	2
2649^{13}	**The Final Spark (75)** (GRichards) **6-11-0** ADobbin (bhd tl sme hdwy u.p fr 3 out)	1¼	**9**	14/1	45	—
2913^{7}	**Charlvic (61)** (WSCunningham) **7-9-7**(7) LMcGrath (n.d)	2½	**10**	12/1	29	—
2958^{6}	**Liam's Loss (IRE) (61)** (JParkes) **8-9-9v^{1}**(5) BGrattan (bhd: hdwy ½-wy: n.d)	½	**11**	100/1	28	—
2505^{4}	**Blue Domain (70)** (RCraggs) **6-10-6**(3) MichaelBrennan (trckd ldrs tl wknd qckly fr 2 out)	14	**12**	9/1	23	—
	The Grey Texan (67) (VThompson) **8-10-6** DBentley (a bhd)	1¾	**13**	50/1	19	—
3284^{12}	**Sharmoor (68)** (MissLCSiddall) **5-10-7** AThornton (prom tl wknd 3 out)	30	**14**	16/1	—	—
1438^{9}	**Promise To Try (IRE) (68)** (MABarnes) **5-10-2**(5) STaylor (mid div & mstke 4th: sn bhd: p.u bef 3 out)		**P**	100/1	—	—
3066^{9}	**Nawtinookey (61)** (MartinTodhunter) **7-9-7b**(7) CMcCormack (prom tl wknd appr 3 out: p.u bef 2 out)		**P**	16/1	—	—
2913^{15}	**Coquet Gold (61)** (FTWalton) **6-10-0** GCahill (a bhd: p.u bef last)		**P**	100/1	—	—
2539^{6}	**Gaelic Charm (IRE) (78)** (JIACharlton) **9-11-3** KJohnson (trckd ldrs tl wknd qckly 3 out: p.u lame bef next)		**P**	8/1	—	—
				(SP 133.0%)		**18 Rn**

4m 5.1 (13.10) CSF £35.50 CT £439.70 TOTE £8.70: £4.10 £1.20 £2.40 £2.00 (£25.50) Trio £96.20 OWNER Mr & Mrs Raymond Anderson Green (LOCKERBIE) BRED Cheveley Park Stud Ltd
LONG HANDICAP Beacon Hill Lady 9-3 Obvious Risk 9-13 Nawtinookey 9-7 Coquet Gold 9-7 Charlvic 9-9
WEIGHT FOR AGE 4yo-10lb
No bid
1971 Latin Leader, happier at this trip, got first run on the runner-up and his rider was always alert to the situation. (6/1)
2862 In a Moment (USA) is difficult to win with but he is in good form just now and, when he decided to run going to the last, he fairly flew, but it was always that stride or two too late. (5/1)
3026 Obvious Risk is a most determined customer, but he spoiled his chances with some moderate jumping. Once he puts that straight, similar events will be found. (16/1)
3091* Palace of Gold did his best but made a few mistakes and, though looking well held from three out, kept plugging gamely away. (4/1)
1666 Bill's Pride went well for a long way, but this stiff track just found her out and she ran out of fuel going to the last. (14/1)
2003 Denticulata was never going the pace until suddenly picking up late on, to show that there is a race to be won again this year. (25/1)
Beacon Hill Lady, who had shown nothing previously, ran a fair race from 11lb out of the handicap. (100/1)
Charlvic (12/1: op 8/1)
2539 Gaelic Charm (IRE) has had plenty of problems over the years, and added to this by pulling up lame here after looking to be going well. (8/1)

3314 GOSFORTH PARK NOVICES' CHASE (5-Y.O+) (Class E)
3-10 (3-11) **2m 4f (15 fncs)** £2,862.75 (£867.00: £423.50: £201.75) GOING: 0.49 sec per fur (GS)

				SP	RR	SF
1296^{6}	**Brighter Shade (IRE)** (MrsMReveley) **7-11-4** PNiven (hld up: hdwy 8th: led 2 out: pushed clr flat)	—	**1**	11/1^{3}	112	22
3068*	**Colonel In Chief (IRE)** (GRichards) **7-11-10** PCarberry (led: clr whn blnd 10th: rdn 3 out: hdd 2 out: no ex: b.b.v)	9	**2**	1/2^{1}	111	21

	Horse	Details	Dist	Pos	SP	RR	SF
1989^{3}	**Shawwell (77)**	(JIACharlton) **10-11-4** BStorey (bhd: hdwy 10th: sn prom: rdn 4 out: sn btn)	16	**3**	25/1	92	2
1968^{4}	**Overwhelm (IRE) (84)**	(VThompson) **9-11-8** MrMThompson (mstkes: nvr wnt pce)	30	**4**	200/1	72	—
3030^{F}	**Childsway**	(SJRobinson) **9-11-1**$^{(3)}$ MichaelBrennan (mstkes: chsd ldrs tl blnd 6th: sn bhd)	9	**5**	100/1	61	—
2653^{4}	**Nijway (73)**	(MABarnes) **7-10-13**$^{(5)}$ STaylor (sn outpcd: no imp whn fell 9th)		**F**	66/1	—	—
2936^{F}	**Brandy Cross (IRE)**	(HowardJohnson) **8-11-4** ADobbin (chsd ldr: rdn fr 7th: blnd 11th: sn wknd: p.u bef 3 out)		**P**	2/1^{2}	—	—
					(SP 115.2%)		**7 Rn**

5m 15.0 (22.00) CSF £17.10 TOTE £9.70: £4.20 £1.10 (£4.50) OWNER Mr D. S. Hall (SALTBURN) BRED N. J. Connors
OFFICIAL EXPLANATION **Brandy Cross (IRE): the trainer reported that the gelding was later found to have a sore back.**
1296 Brighter Shade (IRE), patiently ridden at his first attempt over fences, did the business well, and there would seem to be plenty more to come. (11/1: 8/1-12/1)
3068* Colonel In Chief (IRE) was bowling happily along in front until meeting the open ditch in the back straight on the wrong stride, which seemed to put him off. He made an awful jump at the next and was comfortably picked off. It later transpired that he had broken a blood-vessel. (1/2)
1989 Shawwell looked out of his depth in this company, but still ran well only to weaken over the last three fences. (25/1)
1968 Overwhelm (IRE) was well outclassed throughout. (200/1)
2936 Brandy Cross (IRE) spoiled his chances by trying to take the favourite on and, off the bit by halfway, made mistakes and was wisely pulled up. (2/1)

3315 BRANDLING HOUSE MAIDEN HURDLE (4-Y.O+) (Class E)
3-40 (3-41) **2m (9 hdls)** £2,494.50 (£702.00: £343.50) GOING: 0.10 sec per fur (G)

	Horse	Details	Dist	Pos	SP	RR	SF
3158^{2}	**Nigel's Lad (IRE)**	(PCHaslam) **5-11-8** MFoster (mde all: drew clr fr 3 out: easily)	—	**1**	2/5^{1}	87+	35
2958^{4}	**Supreme Soviet (94)**	(ACWhillans) **7-11-8** ADobbin (chsd ldrs: effrt 4 out: one pce fr next)	10	**2**	6/1^{2}	77	25
2917^{2}	**Dark Phoenix (IRE) (86)**	(OBrennan) **7-11-3v** MBrennan (chsd ldrs: rdn 4 out: one pce fr next)	4	**3**	7/1^{3}	68	16
2785^{U}	**Bold Statement**	(GMMoore) **5-11-8** NBentley (lw: a chsng ldrs: rdn 4 out: btn whn hmpd next)	18	**4**	8/1	55	3
	Mike Stan (IRE)	(LLungo) **6-11-8** RSupple (outpcd & bhd tl styd on fr 3 out)	8	**5**	33/1	47	—
2918^{6}	**Nutty Solera**	(CParker) **7-11-8** BStorey (a.p: rdn ½-wy: no imp after: hmpd 3 out)	¾	**6**	14/1	46	—
3093^{4}	**Falcon's Flame (USA) (90)**	(VThompson) **4-10-12** MrMThompson (plld hrd: nvr trbld ldrs)	3	**7**	33/1	43	—
2920^{P}	**Ottadini (IRE)**	(WGReed) **5-11-3** TReed (t.o fr 3rd)	dist	**8**	200/1	—	—
2861^{13}	**Only A Sioux**	(JRTurner) **5-11-8** DParker (bhd fr 4th: t.o)	10	**9**	100/1	—	—
2953^{P}	**Evening Dusk (IRE)**	(JKMOliver) **5-10-10**$^{(7)}$ SMelrose (prom to 5th: sn wknd & t.o)	10	**10**	200/1	—	—
1692^{21}	**Fly Executive**	(SIPittendrigh) **6-11-8** MrChrisWilson (t.o fr 3rd)	9	**11**	200/1	—	—
2898^{9}	**Royal York**	(GRichards) **5-11-3** PCarberry (trckd ldr: chal 4 out: sn rdn & btn: 4th whn fell 3 out)		**F**	10/1	—	—
	Thornwood (IRE)	(JKMOliver) **5-11-8** AThornton (bhd fr ½-wy: fell 2 out)		**F**	33/1	—	—
2953^{F}	**Solway King**	(MABarnes) **7-11-3**$^{(5)}$ STaylor (plld hrd: prom to 3rd: t.o whn p.u after 4th)		**P**	100/1	—	—
					(SP 137.4%)		**14 Rn**

4m 1.1 (9.10) CSF £4.23 TOTE £1.70: £1.10 £2.00 £1.30 (£6.00) Trio £6.90 OWNER Mr N. C. Dunnington (MIDDLEHAM) BRED Nikita Investments
WEIGHT FOR AGE 4yo-10lb
3158 Nigel's Lad (IRE) did this in some style and looks one to follow. (2/5)
2958 Supreme Soviet did his best, but was never good enough to trouble the very useful winner. (6/1)
2917 Dark Phoenix (IRE) is running consistently well but was never good enough in this company. However, an opportunity will be found. (7/1)
2785 Bold Statement was always in pursuit of the leaders, but he looked very slow when asked a question and may well need either further or easier ground. (8/1)
Mike Stan (IRE) found this trip too sharp, and only got going when it was all over. (33/1)
2918 Nutty Solera was always close enough if good enough, but simply was not. (14/1)
2898 Royal York looked to be travelling as well as the winner for a long way, but she suddenly went to jelly approaching three from home, and was out on her feet when falling very heavily. (10/1: 6/1-12/1)

3316 NORTHERN RACING H'CAP CHASE (0-130) (5-Y.O+) (Class C)
4-10 (4-11) **3m (18 fncs)** £4,279.50 (£1,296.00: £633.00: £301.50) GOING: 0.49 sec per fur (GS)

	Horse	Details	Dist	Pos	SP	RR	SF
3033*	**Act the Wag (IRE) (113)**	(MartinTodhunter) **8-10-11** PCarberry (trckd ldrs: led 4 out: qcknd flat: comf)	—	**1**	7/2^{3}	126+	58
2956^{P}	**Stoney Burke (IRE) (107)**	(MissLucindaRussell) **8-10-5**^{ow5} AThornton (a chsng ldrs: ev ch 2 out: one pce flat)	2½	**2**	50/1	118	45
2542*	**Stormy Coral (IRE) (106)**	(CParker) **7-10-4** BStorey (lw: chsd ldrs: outpcd 12th: styng on whn hit 4 out: no imp after)	10	**3**	5/4^{1}	111	43
2956*	**Davy Blake (111)**	(TNDalgetty) **10-10-9** ADobbin (lw: led tl hdd 4 out: wknd 2 out)	2	**4**	100/30^{2}	114	46
	Strath Royal (130)	(OBrennan) **11-12-0** MBrennan (nvr wnt pce)	dist	**5**	9/2	—	—
3099^{P}	**Johnny Kelly (102)**	(JMCarr) **10-9-11**$^{(3)}$ FLeahy (sn bhd: t.o whn p.u bef 4 out)		**P**	100/1	—	—
					(SP 110.9%)		**6 Rn**

6m 4.0 (12.00) CSF £66.44 TOTE £3.60: £1.80 £3.80 (£57.40) OWNER Mr Robert Ogden (ULVERSTON) BRED J. R. Kidd
LONG HANDICAP Stoney Burke (IRE) 9-12 Johnny Kelly 9-11
3033* Act the Wag (IRE) stays forever and, always travelling within himself here, just needed nudging along to put it beyond doubt. This was a tidy performance. (7/2)
Stoney Burke (IRE) ran a stinker last time but, despite putting up 5lb overweight, left that effort way behind here. He looks one to side with. (50/1)
2542* Stormy Coral (IRE) found the ground had dried out just too much, and was off the bit some way from home, which caused him to make mistakes. He is undoubtedly at his best when things are at their most testing. (5/4)
2956* Davy Blake, looking ultra-fit, tried hard but could never shake off the opposition, and finally cried enough in the home straight. (100/30)
Strath Royal, having his first outing since May 1995, got round safely and that was probably the object of the exercise. (9/2)

3317 ST. MODWEN H'CAP HURDLE (0-130) (4-Y.O+) (Class C)
4-40 (4-40) **3m (13 hdls)** £3,485.00 (£1,055.00: £515.00: £245.00) GOING: 0.49 sec per fur (GS)

	Horse	Details	Dist	Pos	SP	RR	SF
2955*	**Tribune (98)**	(CWThornton) **6-10-10** MFoster (chsd ldrs: shkn up ½-wy: led 7th to 8th: led 4 out: stumbled last: styd on strly)	—	**1**	11/4^{1}	81	21
2922*	**Northern Squire (99)**	(JMJefferson) **9-10-11** ADobbin (lw: mde most to 4 out: sn hrd drvn & outpcd: styd on again appr last)	1½	**2**	7/2^{2}	81	21

3163[5] **Dally Boy (112)** (TDEasterby) **5-11-10** LWyer (cl up: effrt 4 out: wknd appr last) ....3 **3** 9/2[3] 91 32
2787* **Swanbister (IRE) (105)** (LLungo) **7-11-3** RSupple (lw: hld up: mstke 2nd: hdwy 8th: chsng ldrs 4 out: one pce fr next) ....nk **4** 7/2[2] 83 25
2958[3] **Smiddy Lad (95)** (RShiels) **6-10-7** DBentley (hld up: hdwy 8th: prom 4 out: one pce fr next: mstke last) 10 **5** 6/1 63 8
3269[P] **Bang in Trouble (IRE) (104)** (JJO'Neill) **6-10-11**(5) RMcGrath (prom tl outpcd fr 4 out) 5 **6** 12/1 67 14
This Nettle Danger (88) (OBrennan) **13-10-0** MBrennan (hld up & bhd: hdwy on bit appr 4 out: rdn & wknd 3 out) ....17 **7** 100/1 34 —
3157[2] **Flat Top (100)** (MWEasterby) **6-10-12** RGarritty (lw: trckd ldrs: effrt 9th: rdn & btn 4 out: p.u bef 3 out) .... **P** 9/2[3] — —
2698[P] Manor Court (IRE) (101) (DALamb) **9-10-13** JBurke (prom: mstke 7th: wknd qckly 9th: t.o whn p.u bef 3 out) ... **P** 100/1 — —
(SP 131.4%) **9 Rn**

6m 6.0 (24.00) CSF £14.04 CT £42.00 TOTE £5.30: £2.70 £1.50 £1.90 (£9.60) Trio £23.10 OWNER Hexagon Racing (MIDDLEHAM) BRED R. G. Bonson
LONG HANDICAP This Nettle Danger 8-13
2955* Tribune never looks happy but he just gallops forever, and the further they went the better he got. (11/4: 4/1-5/2)
2922* Northern Squire is a real game sort who looked well beaten turning for home, but he would not accept it and battled back after the last. (7/2)
3163 Dally Boy is not all that robust to be carrying big weights, and did well in the circumstances. (9/2)
2787* Swanbister (IRE) likes more cut in the ground and was always short of pace here, despite struggling on. (7/2)
2958 Smiddy Lad ran reasonably and will find a race, especially when the ground is at its most testing. (6/1)
Bang in Trouble (IRE) ran quite well after pulling up only three days previously, and his stable is now in top form. (12/1)
This Nettle Danger, from 15lb out of the handicap, travelled particularly well until suddenly blowing up three out. (100/1)
3157 Flat Top looks to have missed his chances for the time being, as he stopped quickly after four out having been travelling on the bridle. (9/2: 3/1-5/1)

T/Jkpt: Not won; £14,760.14 to Catterick 25/2/97. T/Plpt: £22.60 (789.84 Tckts). T/Qdpt: £8.20 (138.59 Tckts) AA

3057-PLUMPTON (L-H) - Monday February 24th
3318 Abandoned-Waterlogged

3097-CATTERICK (L-H) (Good to soft, Soft patches)
Tuesday February 25th
Race 5: 1 flight omitted.
WEATHER: unsettled and windy

3324 MIDDLEHAM NOVICES' HURDLE (4-Y.O+) (Class E)
1-50 (1-51) **2m (8 hdls)** £2,505.70 (£695.20: £333.10) GOING: 0.80 sec per fur (S)

SP RR SF
2539[2] **Cumbrian Maestro** (TDEasterby) **4-10-7** LWyer (lw: trckd ldrs: shkn up to ld appr 2 out: blnd 2 out: styd on)— **1** 6/1 76 13
3158[7] **Gospel Song (105)** (ACWhillans) **5-11-3** ASSmith (mde most tl hdd appr 2 out: no ex) ....8 **2** 11/4[1] 68 15
3014[6] **Fire on Ice (IRE)** (MrsDHaine) **5-11-3** NWilliamson (trckd ldrs: rdn after 3 out: r.o one pce) ....7 **3** 4/1[3] 61 8
3066[P] **Harfdecent** (MrsMReveley) **6-11-3** GCahill (prom tl lost pl appr 3 out: styd on wl fr 2 out) ....1¼ **4** 40/1 60+ 7
2806[11] **King Rat (IRE) (85)** (JGMO'Shea) **6-11-0v**(3) MichaelBrennan (in tch: effrt 3 out: no imp) 2½ **5** 16/1 57 4
Nasayer (IRE) (NBMason) **7-10-10**(7) SHaworth (mstkes: bhd tl sme late hdwy) ....11 **6** 66/1 46 —
2041[5] **Calder King** (MrsMReveley) **6-11-3** PNiven (bhd: mstke 3rd: n.d) ....1¼ **7** 6/1 45 —
3159[P] **King Fly** (MrsSarahHorner-Harker) **7-11-3** AThornton (chsd ldrs tl wknd qckly appr 2 out) ....2½ **8** 100/1 43 —
Sniper (FPMurtagh) **5-11-3** ADobbin (lw: hmpd 1st: n.d) ....14 **9** 33/1 29 —
2917[19] **Un Poco Loco** (MrsJBrown) **5-11-0**(3) GLee (outpcd & lost tch fr 4th: t.o) ....dist **10** 100/1 — —
3029[12] **Allerbeck** (JLGoulding) **7-10-12** JSupple (mstke 3rd: sn t.o) ....3 **11** 200/1 — —
3007[8] **Full Throttle** (MHTompkins) **4-10-7** DGallagher (disp ld whn fell 1st) .... **F** 100/30[2] — —
2920[P] **Good Venture** (LRLloyd-James) **6-10-12** BStorey (t.o fr 4th: p.u after 5th) .... **P** 100/1 — —
3098[2] **Tawafij (USA) (87)** (MDHammond) **8-11-3** RGarritty (hdwy to trck ldrs whn blnd & uns rdr 5th) .... **U** 7/1 — —
(SP 127.0%) **14 Rn**

4m 5.0 (22.00) CSF £22.44 TOTE £8.30: £1.90 £1.30 £2.80 (£14.00) Trio £7.50 OWNER Cumbrian Industrials Ltd (MALTON) BRED Bearstone Stud
WEIGHT FOR AGE 4yo-10lb
2539 Cumbrian Maestro, after a six-week break, came back here in fine form, and won convincingly despite a terrible jump two out. (6/1)
3158 Gospel Song is a tough little sort and he tried hard, but was off the bit a long way out and was fighting a lost cause from the second last. (11/4)
3014 Fire on Ice (IRE) looks the type to appreciate a more galloping track, and was done for speed from the third last. (4/1)
2005 Harfdecent showed his first real signs of ability over hurdles and finished strongly, suggesting that he is now getting the hang of things. He may need a bit further. (40/1)
2034 King Rat (IRE) had his chances but lacks any change of gear. (16/1)
Nasayer (IRE) last ran over two years ago and was very rusty with his jumping, but he was gradually getting it together at the end. Nevertheless, there is plenty more needed. (66/1)
Full Throttle (100/30: 9/4-7/2)

3325 WENSLEY NOVICES' H'CAP HURDLE (0-95) (4-Y.O+ F & M) (Class F)
2-20 (2-21) **2m (8 hdls)** £2,145.00 (£595.00: £285.00) GOING: 0.80 sec per fur (S)

SP RR SF
1851[U] **First in the Field (68)** (NBMason) **6-9-8**(7) SHaworth (hdwy 4th: chal 3 out: led flat: styd on) ....— **1** 25/1 47 —
2953[2] **Lumback Lady (88)** (BMactaggart) **7-11-7** BStorey (chsd ldrs: led 3 out tl hdd flat: nt qckn) ....2 **2** 6/1[3] 65 15
2787[7] **Decent Penny (IRE) (68)** (MrsRichardArthur) **8-10-1** TEley (lw: w ldrs tl mstke 3 out & lost pl: styd on appr next: nrst fin) ....2 **3** 33/1 43 —
1818[3] **Cliburnel News (IRE) (78)** (ALForbes) **7-10-11** GaryLyons (hdwy 5th: soon in tch & rdn: styd on appr last) ..2½ **4** 12/1 51 1
3026[P] **Alan's Pride (IRE) (68)** (WMcKeown) **6-10-1** GCahill (disp ld to 5th: rdn & r.o one pce) ....2½ **5** 20/1 38 —
2798[2] **Best of All (IRE) (95)** (JBerry) **5-11-7**(7) NHorrocks (lw: prom tl blnd 5th: n.d after) ....6 **6** 5/1[1] 59 9

				SP	RR	SF
3092[F]	**Appearance Money (IRE) (72)** (FMurphy) **6-10-5** PCarberry (lw: hld up & bhd: smooth hdwy to jn ldrs 3 out: rdn & wknd appr next)	1½	**7**	11/2[2]	35	—
2920[4]	**Parson's Lodge (IRE) (77)** (LLungo) **9-10-10** RSupple (lw: rr div: effrt u.p 3 out: sn btn)	½	**8**	6/1[3]	39	—
3098[3]	**Diddy Rymer (75)** (MrsSJSmith) **7-10-8** NWilliamson (prom: rdn after 3 out: sn btn)	9	**9**	6/1[3]	28	—
3029[8]	**Carly-J (69)** (FSJackson) **6-10-2** MrNKent (disp ld tl led 5th: hdd 3 out: sn wknd)	17	**10**	50/1	5	—
2826[7]	**Quinag (89)** (KCBailey) **6-11-8** AThornton (outpcd & lost tch 4th)	3	**11**	14/1	22	—
2898[17]	**Something Speedy (IRE) (70)** (MDHammond) **5-10-3** ADobbin (chsd ldrs to 5th: p.u bef 2 out)		**P**	8/1	—	—
1141[3]	**Kashana (IRE) (70)** (WStorey) **5-10-3v** MMoloney (outpcd whn stumbled bdly 5th & p.u bef next)		**P**	14/1	—	—
2790[7]	**Barefoot Landing (USA) (75)** (CParker) **6-10-8** DParker (hdwy to jn ldrs 4th: wknd appr 3 out: p.u bef 2 out) ...		**P**	9/1	—	—
2806[14]	**Urshi-Jade (70)** (JGMO'Shea) **9-10-0**(3)ow3 MichaelBrennan (sn t.o: p.u after 3 out)		**P**	50/1	—	—
				(SP 132.5%)	**15 Rn**	

4m 7.3 (24.30) CSF £163.08 CT £4,576.60 TOTE £52.00: £8.90 £3.20 £4.30 (£148.70) Trio Not won; £138.11 to Taunton 26/2/97 OWNER Mr N. B. Mason (BRANCEPETH) BRED N. B. Mason

LONG HANDICAP Urshi-Jade 9-12

First in the Field had form a couple of years ago and showed she still retains ability here, staying on most determinedly to gain the upper hand on the run-in. (25/1)

2953 Lumback Lady keeps running well and deserves a change of luck. (6/1: op 4/1)

Decent Penny (IRE) put in a much better effort this time, and a return to longer trips may well help. (33/1)

1818 Cliburnel News (IRE) does not do anything quickly but she does stay, and was gradually making inroads on the leaders. (12/1)

Alan's Pride (IRE) has some ability but is basically short of toe. (20/1)

2798 Best of All (IRE), from a yard whose horses have run moderately of late, made one bad mistake in the back straight which contributed to a poor effort. (5/1)

3092 Appearance Money (IRE) gets more disappointing as time goes on, and again failed to see it out. (11/2)

2920 Parson's Lodge (IRE) is proving most disappointing at present. A return to chasing might help. (6/1: op 4/1)

3326 MALTON NOVICES' CHASE (5-Y.O+) (Class E)

2-50 (2-52) **2m 3f (15 fncs)** £2,894.75 (£863.00: £411.50: £185.75) GOING: 0.80 sec per fur (S)

				SP	RR	SF
2863[3]	**Twin Falls (IRE) (94)** (GMMoore) **6-12-0** JCallaghan (led 5th to 8th: led 11th: clr appr 3 out: eased flat)	—	**1**	8/1	106	19
3030*	**Roberty Lea** (MrsMReveley) **9-11-8** PNiven (mstkes: outpcd & lost tch 8th: styd on strly fr 3 out)	5	**2**	Evens[1]	96	9
2653[F]	**Killbally Boy (IRE) (81)** (HowardJohnson) **7-11-2** AThornton (led to 5th: led 8th tl mstke & hdd 11th: wknd appr 3 out)	13	**3**	8/1	79	—
2914[6]	**Dandy des Plauts (FR)** (MrsSJSmith) **6-11-2** TReed (outpcd & bhd: hit 9th: sme late hdwy)	2½	**4**	66/1	77	—
2957[5]	**Cool Luke (IRE)** (FMurphy) **8-11-2** PCarberry (chsd ldrs: effrt 4 out: sn btn)	8	**5**	4/1[2]	70	—
2954[8]	**Miss Lamplight (69)** (FPMurtagh) **7-10-11** ADobbin (outpcd & lost tch 7th: p.u bef 10th)		**P**	50/1	—	—
2914[2]	**Friendly Knight (81)** (JSHaldane) **7-11-2** ASSmith (ref to s: t.n.p)		**R**	7/1[3]	—	—
				(SP 108.2%)	**7 Rn**	

5m 9.3 (30.30) CSF £14.19 TOTE £9.60: £3.90 £1.40 (£4.00) OWNER Mrs Susan Moore (MIDDLEHAM) BRED Newgate Stud Co

OFFICIAL EXPLANATION **Roberty Lea: jumped too deliberately and was outpaced as a result.**

2863 Twin Falls (IRE) returned here after almost a month off, and was back to something like his old self, but there were so many ifs and buts about the opposition that the form should be treated with caution. (8/1: op 9/2)

3030* Roberty Lea would not have a cut at his fences and got left behind setting out on the final circuit, but he did pick up well at the end and finished full of running. He may well appreciate further yet. (Evens)

1500 Killbally Boy (IRE) had his chances but he looked clumsy at times, and was very tired in the home straight. (8/1)

Dandy des Plauts (FR) is learning but there is still some way to go. (66/1)

2957 Cool Luke (IRE) has disappointed over hurdles, and there was little encouragement at this game. (4/1)

2914 Friendly Knight, in a foul mood, refused point blank to line up at any stage, and the starter had no option but to let them go. Punters had no run for their money. (7/1)

3327 RIPON (S) H'CAP HURDLE (0-90) (4-Y.O+) (Class G)

3-20 (3-22) **2m (8 hdls)** £2,009.80 (£557.80: £267.40) GOING: 0.80 sec per fur (S)

				SP	RR	SF
3098[4]	**Silver Minx (78)** (MrsMReveley) **5-11-2** PNiven (led: hit 5th: hdd appr 2 out: led last: kpt on wl)	—	**1**	9/2[2]	61	30
2629[5]	**Chummy's Saga (73)** (LLungo) **7-10-11b[1]** RSupple (lw: trckd ldrs gng wl: led appr 2 out: hdd & blnd last: sn btn)	4	**2**	7/1	52	21
2862[6]	**Arthur Bee (62)** (BBousfield) **10-10-0** BStorey (hdwy to jn ldrs 4th: one pce fr 3 out)	10	**3**	9/1	31	—
2913[14]	**Storming Lorna (IRE) (62)** (WMcKeown) **7-10-0** GCahill (bhd: hdwy 3 out: nvr rchd ldrs)	1¼	**4**	20/1	30	—
3031[4]	**Robsera (IRE) (90)** (JJQuinn) **6-11-9**(5) RMcGrath (hdwy & prom 3 out: sn rdn & no imp)	3	**5**	8/1	55	24
3031[7]	**Cool Steel (IRE) (70)** (MrsJBrown) **5-10-8** PCarberry (in tch: effrt whn hmpd after 3 out: btn whn blnd last 2)	nk	**6**	11/1	34	3
2913[9]	**Nosmo King (IRE) (64)** (MrsMAKendall) **6-10-2** MrsMKendall (bit bkwd: cl up tl wknd fr 3 out)	2	**7**	20/1	26	—
3091[6]	**Tiotao (IRE) (66)** (CParker) **7-10-4** DParker (chsd ldrs tl wknd after 3 out)	10	**8**	8/1	18	—
2913[5]	**Kierchem (IRE) (71)** (CGrant) **6-10-6**(3) MichaelBrennan (outpcd & mstke 4th: n.d)	9	**9**	7/2[1]	14	—
3076[6]	**Past Master (USA) (77)** (SGollings) **9-11-1** NWilliamson (outpcd fr 3rd: blnd 5th: n.d)	20	**10**	11/2[3]	—	—
3024[8]	**Triona's Hope (IRE) (64)** (EMCaine) **8-9-9**(7)ow2 TristanDavidson (chsd ldrs to 3 out: sn wl bhd)	7	**11**	100/1	—	—
2651[P]	**Eurolink the Rebel (USA) (89)** (SBClark) **5-11-13** RGarritty (in tch tl wknd 3 out: p.u bef next)		**P**	25/1	—	—
3035[F]	**Birthplace (IRE) (72)** (RTate) **7-10-3**(7) NHorrocks (a bhd: p.u bef 2 out)		**P**	9/1	—	—
				(SP 133.2%)	**13 Rn**	

4m 2.9 (19.90) CSF £35.89 CT £265.75 TOTE £3.70: £2.10 £3.70 £4.10 (£21.90) Trio £222.40 OWNER Mrs E. A. Kettlewell (SALTBURN) BRED T. E. Phillips

LONG HANDICAP Triona's Hope (IRE) 9-4

Bt in 3,800 gns

OFFICIAL EXPLANATION **Kierchem (IRE): the trainer reported that the gelding was found to be lame behind the following day.**

3098 Silver Minx, dropped in class, behaved himself this time and proved tougher than the runner-up when the chips were down. (9/2)

2629 Chummy's Saga looked likely to trot up for much of the race but, when it came down to a fight, he was found wanting. (7/1)

2862 Arthur Bee keeps running reasonably on this track, but he was short of speed when it mattered. (9/1)

Storming Lorna (IRE) suddenly decided to run three out, but just when she looked likely to get into at least third place, she decided she had done enough. (20/1)

3031 Robsera (IRE) ran reasonably under top weight, but was making no impression over the last three flights. (8/1)

3031 Cool Steel (IRE) got messed about when staging a run after three out, but then looked very tired and was lucky to get away with two almighty blunders late on. (11/1: 8/1-12/1)

3328 BARTON NOVICES' H'CAP HURDLE (0-100) (4-Y.O+) (Class E)

3-50 (3-51) **3m 1f 110y (11 hdls)** £2,668.10 (£741.60: £356.30) GOING: 0.80 sec per fur (S)

				SP	RR	SF
3102^{2}	**Pilkington (IRE) (84)** (HowardJohnson) **7-11-5** PCarberry (led fr 5th: clr whn hit last: eased flat)	—	**1**	11/4^{1}	68+	18
3032*	**Ruber (80)** (RWThomson) **10-11-1** DParker (a.p: drvn along fr ½-wy: styd on: no ch w wnr)	11	**2**	6/1	57	7
2546^{9}	**Cypress Avenue (IRE) (89)** (MrsVCWard) **5-11-10** NWilliamson (hld up & bhd: hdwy 3 out: nvr rchd ldrs)	17	**3**	20/1	55	5
3096*	**Mr Christie (88)** (MissLCSiddall) **5-11-9** AThornton (racd wd: prom tl outpcd 3 out: n.d after)	17	**4**	9/2^{2}	44	—
2045^{3}	**Corbleu (IRE) (72)** (SBBell) **7-10-7** KJohnson (led to 5th: chsd ldrs tl wknd after 3 out)	nk	**5**	14/1	28	—
3096^{F}	**Cash Box (IRE) (78)** (TJCarr) **9-10-13** NSmith (lw: chsd ldrs tl rdn & btn 4 out)	5	**6**	11/2^{3}	30	—
2800^{14}	**Greenfield Manor (68)** (JSisterson) **10-9-12**(5) STaylor (a bhd: blnd 8th)	½	**7**	25/1	20	—
3029^{6}	**Fro (83)** (HAlexander) **4-10-6** BStorey (wnt prom 7th: rdn 3 out: sn btn)	6	**8**	11/2^{3}	31	—
3097^{U}	**Don't Tell Judy (IRE) (72)** (MissMKMilligan) **9-10-0**(7) NHorrocks (in tch tl wknd fr 8th: t.o)	dist	**9**	25/1	—	—
3096^{P}	**Canonbiebothered (65)** (LLungo) **6-10-0** FPerratt (plld hrd early: prom tl mstke & wknd qckly 8th: t.o)	19	**10**	50/1	—	—
2787^{P}	**Busy Boy (68)** (DALamb) **10-10-3**ow3 JBurke (t.o fr 7th)	dist	**11**	50/1	—	—
2008^{P}	**Escadaro (USA) (77)** (MrsVCWard) **8-10-5v**(7)ow12 MBerry (chsd ldrs tl wknd rapidly & fell 6th: dead)		**F**	150/1	—	—
3180^{2}	**Reluckino (78)** (JGMO'Shea) **7-10-10v**(3) MichaelBrennan (outpcd & lost pl 7th: t.o whn p.u after 3 out)		**P**	9/2^{2}	—	—
				(SP 131.8%)	**13 Rn**	

6m 44.6 (37.60) CSF £19.24 CT £275.44 TOTE £3.50: £1.90 £3.10 £4.10 (£13.80) Trio £67.60 OWNER Mrs Alurie O'Sullivan (CROOK) BRED Thomas Noonan

LONG HANDICAP Busy Boy 9-8 Escadaro (USA) 8-11 Canonbiebothered 9-6

WEIGHT FOR AGE 4yo-12lb

OFFICIAL EXPLANATION **Reluckino: the trainer reported that the gelding may have been feeling the effects of a hard race eight days previous.**

3102 Pilkington (IRE) appreciated this longer trip and was given a fine ride, but he had a look out to his left at the last and lost concentration, making a bad mistake. (11/4)

3032* Ruber, an out-and-out stayer, kept responding to pressure but was no match for the winner. (6/1)

1907 Cypress Avenue (IRE) has been most disappointing since his first run over hurdles, but he showed he has the ability when deciding to run on in the closing stages. (20/1)

3096* Mr Christie raced wide to try and find better ground but that proved against him, as in the end he had quite a detour to make at the by-passed second last, which his rider only realised at the last moment. (9/2)

2045 Corbleu (IRE) returned after two months off, and looked as one-paced as ever. (14/1)

3096 Cash Box (IRE), considering his heavy fall last time, did not run too badly. (11/2)

3180 Reluckino was obviously feeling his hard race of only eight days ago, as he was never happy here. (9/2: 3/1-5/1)

3329 GRETA BRIDGE H'CAP CHASE (0-115) (5-Y.O+) (Class E)

4-20 (4-21) **2m (12 fncs)** £2,842.75 (£847.00: £403.50: £181.75) GOING: 0.80 sec per fur (S)

				SP	RR	SF
3101*	**Weaver George (IRE) (105)** (WStorey) **7-11-9** MMoloney (hdwy 5th: led after 4 out: clr whn hit last)	—	**1**	15/8^{1}	118	51
2914^{F}	**Moss Pageant (82)** (FTWalton) **7-10-0** BStorey (led tl hdd after 4 out: kpt on one pce)	7	**2**	100/1	88	21
1912^{2}	**Newhall Prince (110)** (AStreeter) **9-12-0v** TEley (lw: wnt prom 5th: hit 6th: no imp fr 4 out)	6	**3**	5/1^{3}	110	43
3299^{3}	**Marlingford (82)** (MrsJJordan) **10-9-7**(7) LMcGrath (chsd ldrs: chal & mstke 5th: outpcd 7th: blnd 8th: sn bhd)	11	**4**	6/1	71	4
3140^{2}	**Rebel King (84)** (MABarnes) **7-9-11**(5) STaylor (a outpcd & wl bhd: p.u after 4 out)		**P**	8/1	—	—
3001^{2}	**Jack Doyle (IRE) (100)** (JJO'Neill) **6-11-4** NWilliamson (lw: effrt 5th: lost tch 4 out: p.u bef 2 out)		**P**	9/4^{2}	—	—
				(SP 108.6%)	**6 Rn**	

4m 9.1 (17.10) CSF £48.58 TOTE £3.20: £2.50 £17.60 (£29.30) OWNER Regent Decorators Ltd (CONSETT) BRED G. Cashin

LONG HANDICAP Marlingford 9-6 Moss Pageant 8-6

OFFICIAL EXPLANATION **Jack Doyle (IRE): the jockey reported that the gelding had lost his action but appeared to be sound later.**

3101* Weaver George (IRE) continues in top form despite the ground being softer than he generally prefers. (15/8)

Moss Pageant really attacked his fences and, from 22lb wrong in the handicap, ran out of his skin. It did not appear to be a fluke. (100/1)

1912 Newhall Prince ran reasonably, but this ground was probably softer than he really likes, and he has yet to find his form of last season. (5/1)

3299 Marlingford put in an awkward jump at the water and was never going thereafter. (6/1)

3140 Rebel King never went a yard without being pushed, and was soon well tailed off. (8/1: 5/1-9/1)

3001 Jack Doyle (IRE) looked to have a problem, as he was pulled up when looking very tired after three out. He was reported to have lost his action, but was sound afterwards. (9/4)

3330 AYSGARTH INTERMEDIATE N.H. FLAT RACE (4, 5 & 6-Y.O) (Class H)

4-50 (4-50) **2m** £1,255.50 (£348.00: £166.50)

				SP	RR	SF
	Spirit of Steel (TPTate) **4-10-1**(7) RMcCarthy (trckd ldrs: led 6f out: pushed along 3f out: styd on wl)	—	**1**	7/1	55 f	—
2047^{5}	**First Light** (JJQuinn) **5-11-4** GTormey (lw: in tch: effrt u.p ½-wy: styd on: nt pce of wnr)	4	**2**	11/4^{2}	51 f	—
1926^{8}	**Jennie's Prospect** (JJO'Neill) **6-10-13**(5) RMcGrath (a chsng ldrs: rdn 8f out: one pce)	16	**3**	11/2	35 f	—
	The Gnome (IRE) (FMurphy) **5-11-1**(3) MichaelBrennan (bit bkwd: hdwy ½-wy: wnt prom appr st: no imp after)	16	**4**	7/1	19 f	—
3142^{3}	**Thunderpoint (IRE)** (TDEasterby) **5-11-4** GCahill (lw: prom tl outpcd ½-wy: styd on fnl 3f)	5	**5**	5/2^{1}	14 f	—
3070^{6}	**Cool Kevin** (MrsMAKendall) **4-10-8** MrsMKendall (a wl bhd)	1¼	**6**	33/1	13 f	—
3142^{14}	**Shannon Shoon (IRE)** (HowardJohnson) **5-10-13**(5) GFRyan (hld up: effrt 10f out: no imp)	1¼	**7**	33/1	12 f	—
1781^{6}	**Air Bridge** (RMWhitaker) **5-11-1**(3) EHusband (led tl hdd 6f out: wknd 4f out)	s.h	**8**	20/1	11 f	—
3070^{12}	**Chan Move** (WJSmith) **5-10-13**(5) STaylor (sn wl bhd: t.o)	dist	**9**	200/1	—	—
	Dash On By (SEKettlewell) **4-10-5**(3) GLee (prom to ½-wy: sn wl bhd: t.o)	½	**10**	33/1	—	—
2830^{2}	**Dante's Gold (IRE)** (CREgerton) **6-10-13**(5) SophieMitchell (lw: chsd ldrs tl wknd ½-wy: t.o)	1¼	**11**	5/1^{3}	—	—
2005^{7}	**Brook House** (BBousfield) **6-10-6**(7) CMcCormack (t.o fr ½-wy)	28	**12**	20/1	—	—
				(SP 131.1%)	**12 Rn**	

3m 59.3 CSF £25.39 TOTE £4.30: £2.40 £1.60 £2.50 (£29.00) Trio £126.70; £60.72 to Taunton 26/2/97 OWNER Mr T. P. Tate (TADCASTER) BRED Miss Sara Davies and David Lewis

WEIGHT FOR AGE 4yo-10lb

Spirit of Steel travelled well and did the business in good style, suggesting that hurdle events will be found. (7/1)

2047 First Light is a stayer, and kept plugging away although always in vain. (11/4)
Jennie's Prospect is going to need a real trip over hurdles, as he was off the bit some way out here. (11/2: 3/1-6/1)
The Gnome (IRE) needed this, and after doing a lot of running just after halfway then blew up. (7/1: 7/2-8/1)
3142 Thunderpoint (IRE) looked all at sea on this track. (5/2)

T/Jkpt: Not won; £22,566.56 to Taunton 26/2/97. T/Plpt: £91.80 (155.6 Tckts). T/Qdpt: £14.30 (55.79 Tckts) AA

3071-LEICESTER (R-H) (Good, Soft & heavy patches in front of stands)
Tuesday February 25th
WEATHER: overcast & windy

3331 PICKWELL NOVICES' H'CAP CHASE (0-100) (5-Y.O+) (Class E)
2-10 (2-12) **2m 4f 110y (15 fncs)** £3,315.90 (£991.20: £474.60: £216.30) GOING: 0.54 sec per fur (GS)

	Horse	Dist	Pos	SP	RR	SF
3145[U]	**Red Branch (IRE) (71)** (JSKing) **8-10-0** JCulloty (mde all: clr 2 out: all out)	—	1	4/1[2]	87	12
2679[2]	**Scoresheet (IRE) (95)** (JTGifford) **7-11-10** PHide (hld up: mstke 2nd: hdwy appr 3 out: rdn appr 2 out: r.o wl flat)	s.h	2	3/1[1]	111	36
2795[5]	**Hangover (72)** (RLee) **11-10-1** AMaguire (lw: prom tl wknd appr last)	11	3	9/1	79	4
3138[3]	**Kiltulla (IRE) (71)** (MrsSJSmith) **7-9-7**(7) RWilkinson (plld hrd: a.p: ev ch 4 out: wknd appr 2 out)	3	4	6/1	76	1
3200[6]	**Knockreigh Cross (IRE) (71)** (BSRothwell) **8-10-0** BPowell (mstke 1st: a bhd: t.o whn hmpd 4 out)	dist	5	100/1	—	—
3043[11]	**Mini Fete (FR) (71)** (KRBurke) **8-10-0b** SFox (prom to 7th: t.o)	1¼	6	66/1	—	—
2752[U]	**Smart Casanova (71)** (MJWilkinson) **8-10-0** TJO'Sullivan (a bhd: t.o)	9	7	25/1	—	—
3051[9]	**Bathwick Bobbie (72)** (DLWilliams) **10-9-12**(3) GuyLewis (rdn 5th: a bhd: t.o)	8	8	20/1	—	—
3051[6]	**Eulogy (FR) (79)** (KRBurke) **10-10-8** ALarnach (rdn 3rd: a bhd: t.o)	9	9	14/1	—	—
3001[6]	**Glendoe (IRE) (79)** (AndrewTurnell) **6-10-8** GUpton (lw: hld up: mid div whn fell 8th)		F	6/1	—	—
2915[P]	**Prince Baltasar (71)** (NBycroft) **8-9-7**(7) AScholes (chsd ldrs: 5th & wknd whn fell 4 out)		F	100/1	—	—
3073[5]	**Althrey Aristocrat (IRE) (71)** (FLloyd) **7-10-0** SMcNeill (prom: blnd bdly: rider lost irons 2nd: p.u bef 3rd)		P	100/1	—	—
3188[2]	**Super Ritchart (84)** (BPalling) **9-10-13** RFarrant (blnd & uns rdr 2nd)		U	9/2[3]	—	—
				(SP 121.5%)	**13 Rn**	

5m 22.6 (21.60) CSF £15.26 CT £94.45 TOTE £4.80: £1.60 £1.60 £2.30 (£10.40) Trio £54.00 OWNER Mr E. J. Mangan (SWINDON) BRED Michael Butler
LONG HANDICAP Knockreigh Cross (IRE) 9-3 Smart Casanova 9-3 Red Branch (IRE) 9-12 Prince Baltasar 9-3 Kiltulla (IRE) 9-8 Althrey Aristocrat (IRE) 9-3 Mini Fete (FR) 9-3
2807 Red Branch (IRE), 2lb out of the handicap, had to pull out all the stops after his rider had looked over the wrong shoulder on the run-in, before realising the runner-up was on the other side. (4/1: 5/2-9/2)
2679 Scoresheet (IRE), 9lb higher than when winning at Folkestone, lost no caste in defeat and may now be ready to tackle further. (3/1)
2795 Hangover could not take advantage of a 3lb drop in the ratings. (9/1)
3138 Kiltulla (IRE), 6lb wrong in the handicap, did not help his cause by proving difficult to settle. (6/1)

3332 DRAGON H'CAP CHASE (0-110) (6-Y.O+) (Class E)
2-40 (2-40) **3m (18 fncs)** £3,315.90 (£991.20: £474.60: £216.30) GOING: 0.54 sec per fur (GS)

	Horse	Dist	Pos	SP	RR	SF
3198[5]	**Farney Glen (87)** (JJO'Neill) **10-10-6** AMaguire (hld up: hdwy 14th: led appr last: r.o wl: fin lame)	—	1	3/1[2]	96	22
	Reapers Rock (81) (MrsSJSmith) **10-9-7**(7) RWilkinson (hld up: hdwy 5th: led 13th: rdn & hdd appr last: one pce)	5	2	9/1	87	13
2829*	**Simpson (91)** (JABOld) **12-10-10** GUpton (nt j.w: wl bhd tl styd on fr 4 out: n.d)	15	3	5/4[1]	87	13
3051[10]	**Night Fancy (81)** (MrsAMWoodrow) **9-10-0** JAMcCarthy (prom: led 10th to 13th: wknd appr 3 out)	6	4	40/1	73	—
2660[P]	**Cantoris Frater (101)** (MrsJPitman) **10-11-6** BPowell (led 2nd to 10th: wknd 13th: t.o whn p.u bef 3 out)		P	7/2[3]	—	—
2817[11]	**Far Senior (105)** (PWegmann) **11-11-10** SWynne (bhd fr 5th: t.o 7th: p.u bef 10th)		P	33/1	—	—
2823[11]	**Coasting (81)** (GBBalding) **11-10-0** BClifford (led to 2nd: wknd 9th: t.o 10th: p.u bef 2 out)		P	14/1	—	—
2820[16]	**Lodestone Lad (IRE) (85)** (RDickin) **7-10-4** JCulloty (hld up: hit 10th: sn lost pl: t.o whn p.u bef 4 out)		P	12/1	—	—
				(SP 121.4%)	**8 Rn**	

6m 18.0 (24.00) CSF £28.40 CT £46.28 TOTE £4.20: £1.10 £3.10 £1.10 (£17.60) OWNER Mrs A. Meller (PENRITH) BRED John Purfield
LONG HANDICAP Night Fancy 8-13
3198 Farney Glen, well backed, had the longer trip this time together with Maguire replacing the claimer. Dismounted after the finish, connections were hoping the gelding had only taken a knock. (3/1: op 5/1)
Reapers Rock will have done his confidence the power of good after two falls last season following his novice win. (9/1: op 6/1)
2829* Simpson, raised 4lb, may have preferred softer ground, but this was still a pretty abysmal effort. (5/4: 10/11-11/8)
2620 Lodestone Lad (IRE) (12/1: op 8/1)

3333 SYSTON H'CAP CHASE (0-110) (5-Y.O+) (Class E)
3-10 (3-10) **2m 4f 110y (15 fncs)** £2,906.40 (£865.20: £411.60: £184.80) GOING: 0.54 sec per fur (GS)

	Horse	Dist	Pos	SP	RR	SF
2766[3]	**Lance Armstrong (IRE) (103)** (GMMcCourt) **7-11-11**(3) DFortt (chsd ldr to 5th: rdn 10th: led appr 3 out: r.o wl)	—	1	11/8[1]	114	39
3145[4]	**Juleit Jones (IRE) (87)** (JTGifford) **8-10-9**(3) LAspell (lw: led tl appr 3 out: one pce)	8	2	3/1[2]	92	17
3198[6]	**Dolikos (97)** (THCaldwell) **10-11-8** DWalsh (wl bhd fr 6th: lft poor 3rd 3 out)	dist	3	16/1	—	—
3141[P]	**Royal Paris (IRE) (75)** (MrsSJSmith) **9-9-7**(7) RWilkinson (mstke 3rd: t.o fr 6th: blnd & uns rdr 2 out: rmntd)	dist	4	20/1	—	—
3113[3]	**Jailbreaker (81)** (BRMillman) **10-10-1**(5) DSalter (chsd ldr fr 5th: hit 7th: rdn 10th: ev ch whn fell 3 out)		F	7/2[3]	—	—
2681[7]	**Little-Nipper (95)** (RJSmith) **12-11-6** CMaude (a bhd: t.o whn j.lft 7th: p.u bef 11th)		P	5/1	—	—
553[5]	**Ballad Ruler (75)** (PAPritchard) **11-10-0** RBellamy (t.o 6th: p.u bef 10th)		P	100/1	—	—
				(SP 117.6%)	**7 Rn**	

5m 22.4 (21.40) CSF £6.06 TOTE £2.40: £2.10 £2.60 (£5.70) OWNER Mr G. L. Porter (WANTAGE) BRED Tom Curran
LONG HANDICAP Ballad Ruler 8-13

2766 Lance Armstrong (IRE), in fair form over timber, made a successful return to fences, but his trainer said he is unlikely to take up his entry in the Fulke Walwyn Kim Muir at the Festival. (11/8: Evens-6/4)
3145 Juleit Jones (IRE) again gave the impression that her forcing tactics could pay off over a shorter trip. (3/1)
3113 Jailbreaker, down 5lb, would not have minded more give in the ground, and was arguably not going quite as well as the winner when departing. (7/2)

3334 RUTLAND WATER NOVICES' CHASE (6-Y.O+) (Class D)

3-40 (3-40) **3m (18 fncs)** £4,207.50 (£1,260.00: £605.00: £277.50) GOING: 0.54 sec per fur (GS)

				SP	RR	SF
	Master Toby (NATwiston-Davies) **7-10-12** CLlewellyn (lw: a.p: hrd rdn to ld flat: r.o wl)	—	**1**	8/1	108	31
2776^{3}	**Lively Knight (IRE) (115)** (JTGifford) **8-11-4** PHide (lw: a.p: led 10th: rdn & hdd flat)	1	**2**	$11/4^{1}$	113	36
3044^{3}	**Who Is Equiname (IRE) (100)** (NJHenderson) **7-10-12** JRKavanagh (a.p: hit 10th: ev ch whn hit 4 out: rdn & wknd 2 out)	13	**3**	$11/4^{1}$	99	22
3188^{P}	**Little Gains (60)** (RLee) **8-10-12** JRailton (led tl hit 10th: ev ch 3 out: sn wknd)	dist	**4**	100/1	—	—
3020^{10}	**Major Nova (79)** (NASmith) **8-10-12** JCulloty (hmpd 2nd: a bhd: t.o fr 10th)	10	**5**	25/1	—	—
3155^{9}	**Better Future (IRE)** (TKeddy) **8-10-12** RJohnson (j.slowly 1st: sn rdn & bhd: t.o fr 10th)	11	**6**	25/1	—	—
3020^{P}	**Musical Hit** (PAPritchard) **6-10-12b¹** RBellamy (hld up: hdwy 7th: wknd 9th: t.o)	25	**7**	100/1	—	—
2838^{7}	**Nordic Flight** (RJEckley) **9-10-12** VSlattery (hmpd 2nd: a bhd: t.o fr 10th)	15	**8**	100/1	—	—
	Foxwoods Valley (IRE) (DNicholson) **8-10-12** AMaguire (bit bkwd: fell 2nd)		**F**	$11/2^{3}$	—	—
	Bear Claw (OSherwood) **8-10-12b** JOsborne (fell 1st)		**F**	$3/1^{2}$	—	—
	Strong Glen (IRE) (PWegmann) **9-10-12** SWynne (bkwd: a bhd: t.o whn p.u bef 11th)		**P**	100/1	—	—
2860^{4}	**Dear Jean (60)** (MESowersby) **7-10-4**(3) FLeahy (a bhd: t.o whn p.u bef 10th)		**P**	100/1	—	—
2883^{P}	**Swift Pokey** (DLWilliams) **7-10-12** MClarke (prom tl wknd 9th: j.lft 10th: ref & uns rdr 11th)		**R**	100/1	—	—
				(SP 118.5%)	**13 Rn**	

6m 16.9 (22.90) CSF £27.83 TOTE £8.10: £1.80 £1.80 £1.20 (£14.10) Trio £13.90 OWNER Mr R. D. Russell (CHELTENHAM) BRED C. V. Bravery
IN-FOCUS: **Luckless Adrian Maguire broke an arm in his fall, and will be out for the season.**
Master Toby looked well prepared, having not been seen out since unseating his rider when in command on his fencing debut at Chepstow last May. (8/1)
2776 Lively Knight (IRE) seemed to be getting the better of the argument jumping the final fence, but his penalty began to tell on the run-in. (11/4)
3044 Who Is Equiname (IRE), certainly put in the race this time, was beaten fair and square. (11/4)
Little Gains showed his first sign of ability, but appeared not to stay. (100/1)
Bear Claw sustained a hair-line fracture to a hind leg when making his fencing debut, without his usual blinkers, at Worcester fifteen months ago. (3/1: op 7/4)

3335 GREAT GLEN NOVICES' CHASE (5-Y.O+) (Class E)

4-10 (4-16) **2m 4f 110y (15 fncs)** £3,124.80 (£932.40: £445.20: £201.60) GOING: 0.54 sec per fur (GS)

				SP	RR	SF
2760*	**Wild West Wind (IRE)** (MissHCKnight) **7-11-8** JCulloty (a.p: blnd 2nd: led 8th to 10th: led 2 out: drvn out)	—	**1**	$11/8^{2}$	120	33
3071*	**Macgeorge (IRE) (115)** (RLee) **7-12-0** RJohnson (led tl blnd bdly 2nd: led 7th tl mstke next: led 10th to 2 out: hrd rdn & mstke last: rallied flat)	¾	**2**	$4/6^{1}$	125	38
2841^{6}	**Gemma's Wager (IRE)** (MarkCampion) **7-10-11** LHarvey (hld up: hdwy 5th: wknd 8th: lft poor 3rd 2 out)	dist	**3**	25/1	—	—
	Deep Song (PAPritchard) **7-11-2** RBellamy (plld hrd: lft in ld 2nd: hdd 7th: wknd 8th: sn t.o)	dist	**4**	150/1	—	—
	Craighill (IRE) (NJHenderson) **8-11-2** JRKavanagh (hld up: blnd 4th: j.lft 10th: 3rd & no ch whn mstke 3 out: p.u bef 2 out)		**P**	$20/1^{3}$	—	—
				(SP 111.4%)	**5 Rn**	

5m 22.6 (21.60) CSF £2.53 TOTE £2.50: £1.10 £1.40 (£1.50) OWNER Lord Vestey (WANTAGE) BRED Martin Nestor
2760* Wild West Wind (IRE), apart from the first ditch, jumped better than the favourite. (11/8)
3071* Macgeorge (IRE) was possibly unsettled by making a mess of the first ditch, and did not jump anywhere near so well this time. (4/6)

3336 OAKHAM H'CAP CHASE (0-110) (5-Y.O+) (Class E)

4-40 (4-40) **2m 1f (12 fncs)** £2,933.70 (£873.60: £415.80: £186.90) GOING: 0.54 sec per fur (GS)

				SP	RR	SF
2569^{P}	**Scottish Bambi (105)** (PRWebber) **9-12-0** JOsborne (hld up: lost pl 7th: hdwy appr 3 out: led last: drvn out)	—	**1**	$5/1^{3}$	116	52
3076^{4}	**Chill Wind (87)** (NBycroft) **8-10-10** MFoster (hld up & bhd: hdwy 6th: hrd rdn appr 2 out: styd on flat)	4	**2**	$100/30^{1}$	94	30
3053*	**Thats the Life (77)** (TRGeorge) **12-10-0** RJohnson (led to 5th: led 4 out to last: one pce)	3	**3**	$100/30^{1}$	81	17
2906^{2}	**Dear Do (103)** (NJHenderson) **10-11-12** JRKavanagh (lw: hld up: rdn appr 3 out: no hdwy)	4	**4**	$7/2^{2}$	104	40
3001^{8}	**Cawarra Boy (93)** (CJames) **9-11-2** MrEJames (lw: hld up: rdn 7th: no ch fr 4 out)	5	**5**	9/1	89	25
3053^{5}	**Pegmarine (USA) (77)** (MrsAMWoodrow) **14-10-0** JAMcCarthy (bhd fr 8th)	1¼	**6**	20/1	72	8
3053^{2}	**Dr Rocket (82)** (RDickin) **12-9-12b**(7) XAizpuru (chsd ldr: led 5th to 4 out: hrd rdn & wknd qckly appr 2 out: t.o)	23	**7**	6/1	55	—
3176^{F}	**Churchtown Port (IRE) (99)** (PButler) **7-11-5**(3) LAspell (bhd: blnd 5th: sn t.o: p.u bef 3 out)		**P**	16/1	—	—
				(SP 120.0%)	**8 Rn**	

4m 24.7 (14.70) CSF £21.78 CT £59.03 TOTE £6.20: £1.80 £1.10 £1.50 (£15.80) OWNER Mr William Kelly (BANBURY) BRED Cheveley Park Stud Ltd
2037 Scottish Bambi, who pulled muscles in his quarters last time, was no less than 27lb higher than when beating Poucher at Hereford in November, but that form reads pretty well. (5/1)
3076 Chill Wind, reverting to fences, gave the impression he would not be inconvenienced by a longer trip. (100/30)
3053* Thats the Life, raised 2lb, had beaten Dr Rocket three-and-half lengths at Hereford, but this was a much hotter contest. (100/30)
2906 Dear Do has had his share of chances this season. (7/2)
1860 Cawarra Boy was 5lb lower than when making his chasing debut in a novice handicap earlier in the month. (9/1)

T/Plpt: £9.50 (1,312.59 Tckts). T/Qdpt: £3.50 (181.43 Tckts) KH

3109-TAUNTON (R-H) (Good to soft)
Wednesday February 26th

Race 4: flag start
WEATHER: fine but very windy

3337 TAUNTON 'N.H.' NOVICES' HURDLE (I) (4-Y.O+) (Class D)
1-50 (1-50) **2m 3f 110y (10 hdls)** £2,567.00 (£776.00: £378.00: £179.00) GOING: 0.70 sec per fur (S)

				SP	RR	SF
1938[7]	**Strong Paladin (IRE)** (JTGifford) **6-11-1**(3) LAspell (hld up: hdwy 7th: led flat: all out)	—	**1**	7/2[2]	70	9
2868[5]	**Master Pilgrim** (GBBalding) **5-11-4** APMcCoy (lw: hld up: hdwy 6th: rdn appr 2 out: led appr last: hdd flat: r.o)	hd	**2**	5/2[1]	70	9
2656[2]	**Defendtherealm** (RGFrost) **6-11-4** JFrost (led 3rd to 3 out: ev ch last: nt qckn)	1¼	**3**	6/1[3]	69	8
1450[5]	**Just Jasmine** (KBishop) **5-10-13** RGreene (a.p: led 3 out tl appr last: r.o one pce)	nk	**4**	12/1	64	3
1695[5]	**Moonlight Escapade (IRE)** (RJHodges) **6-11-1**(3) TDascombe (no hdwy fr 3 out)	16	**5**	25/1	56	—
2759[14]	**Connaught's Pride** (PJHobbs) **6-10-13** NWilliamson (mstke 3 out: a bhd)	2½	**6**	25/1	49	—
3109[5]	**Walter's Destiny** (CWMitchell) **5-11-4** SMcNeill (led 2nd to 3rd: wknd appr 3 out)	1¼	**7**	20/1	52	—
3000[8]	**Fred Fuggles** (CFCJackson) **5-10-13**(5) OBurrows (prom tl wknd 7th: t.o)	15	**8**	50/1	40	—
980[4]	**Strike A Light (IRE)** (MissHCKnight) **5-11-4** JCulloty (bhd fr 3 out: p.u bef last)		**P**	7/2[2]	—	—
2677[16]	**Double Achievement (IRE)** (MCPipe) **7-11-4** CMaude (mstke 2nd: a bhd: t.o whn p.u after 3 out)		**P**	33/1	—	—
2872[8]	**Southernhay Boy** (MrsSDWilliams) **6-11-4b[1]** MrIDowrick (led to 2nd: wknd appr 7th: t.o whn p.u after 3 out)		**P**	25/1	—	—
2811[13]	**Grematic** (NJHawke) **6-11-4** JRailton (bhd fr 6th: t.o whn p.u after 3 out)		**P**	50/1	—	—
	Cool Cat (IRE) (JCTuck) **6-11-4** RBellamy (bit bkwd: prom to 5th: t.o fr 7th: p.u after 3 out)		**P**	50/1	—	—
3061[U]	**Orchid House** (NRMitchell) **5-10-13** DSkyrme (bit bkwd: a bhd: t.o whn p.u bef 3 out)		**P**	100/1	—	—
				(SP 121.1%)	**14 Rn**	

4m 59.5 (28.50) CSF £10.71 TOTE £4.60: £1.20 £1.90 £1.90 (£5.30) Trio £5.10 OWNER Mrs Angela Brodie (FINDON) BRED Denis McDonnell

1453 Strong Paladin (IRE) appreciated the step up in distance and gave the impression he would stay further. He will go chasing next season. (7/2)

2868 Master Pilgrim did not seem inconvenienced by this longer trip and looks capable of going one better. (5/2)

2656 Defendtherealm, with not so much an emphasis on stamina this time, pushed the pace and only got tapped for speed on the run-in. (6/1)

1450 Just Jasmine had shown up well in bumpers and made a promising enough start to her hurdling career. (12/1: op 7/1)

3338 PITMINSTER (S) H'CAP HURDLE (0-95) (4-Y.O+) (Class G)
2-20 (2-20) **2m 1f (9 hdls)** £1,931.00 (£541.00: £263.00) GOING: 0.70 sec per fur (S)

				SP	RR	SF
3054[8]	**Blade of Fortune (74)** (VGGreenway) **9-10-6**(7)ow6 MrJTizzard (mde all: clr 3 out: unchal)	—	**1**	10/1	70	15
3234[11]	**Saafi (IRE) (70)** (RJBaker) **6-10-9b** VSlattery (hld up: hdwy 5th: wnt 2nd & blnd 3 out: no ch w wnr)	20	**2**	14/1	47	—
3050[6]	**Almapa (82)** (RJHodges) **5-11-4**(3) TDascombe (hdwy 3 out: rdn appr 2 out: one pce)	6	**3**	7/1[2]	54	5
3110[7]	**Shanakee (73)** (BJLlewellyn) **10-10-12** MrJLLlewellyn (nvr nr to chal)	1	**4**	12/1	44	—
	Pooh Stick (68) (RGFrost) **7-10-7**ow3 JFrost (bit bkwd: nvr nr ldrs)	19	**5**	14/1	21	—
3110[12]	**Mick The Yank (IRE) (63)** (HOliver) **7-10-2v[1]** JacquiOliver (a bhd)	5	**6**	20/1	11	—
2943[10]	**Them Times (IRE) (61)** (FJordan) **8-10-0** SWynne (bit bkwd: chsd wnr: mstke 3rd: wknd 6th)	1½	**7**	16/1	8	—
2815[8]	**Denomination (USA) (84)** (MCPipe) **5-11-2**(7) BMoore (chsd ldrs to 5th)	8	**8**	25/1	23	—
3057[8]	**Minster's Madam (86)** (JNeville) **6-11-6v**(5) ABates (rdn 4th: a bhd)	3	**9**	10/1	22	—
	Va Utu (82) (DMLloyd) **9-11-0**(7) JPrior (bit bkwd: chsd ldrs: wnt 2nd 5th to 3 out: sn wknd: virtually p.u flat)	7	**10**	25/1	12	—
2818[B]	**Red Phantom (IRE) (70)** (SMellor) **5-10-9v** NMann (a bhd: t.o)	16	**11**	14/1	—	—
3206[U]	**Drewitts Dancer (69)** (TPMcGovern) **10-10-8** DBridgwater (bit bkwd: a bhd: t.o whn p.u bef 2 out)		**P**	12/1	—	—
2873[4]	**October Brew (USA) (89)** (MCPipe) **7-12-0b** APMcCoy (reminders after 4th: dropped rr 6th: t.o whn blnd 3 out: p.u bef 2 out)		**P**	8/1[3]	—	—
3207*	**Killing Time (79)** (DBurchell) **6-11-4** 7x DJBurchell (blnd & uns rdr 2nd)		**U**	4/1[1]	—	—
3112[6]	**Alice's Mirror (68)** (KBishop) **8-10-7b** RGreene (blnd & uns rdr 1st)		**U**	9/1	—	—
				(SP 125.5%)	**15 Rn**	

4m 15.3 (22.30) CSF £130.02 CT £962.72 TOTE £11.00: £3.90 £5.60 £1.90 (£135.00) Trio Not won; £154.31 to Ludlow 27/2/97 OWNER Mr V. G. Greenway (TAUNTON) BRED F. H. Lee

LONG HANDICAP Them Times (IRE) 9-12

No bid

Blade of Fortune, twice a runner-up in maiden points, was dropping into a seller after possibly finding the trip too far last time.
At an enquiry into the apparent improvement in form, the trainer told the Stewards that the gelding had travelled badly to Hereford last time. (10/1)

902 Saafi (IRE), dropped 5lb and in a lower grade, caught a tartar on the day in the winner. (14/1: op 33/1)

3050 Almapa, reverting to selling company, really wants the ground on the fast side. (7/1)

Shanakee may be coming to hand. (12/1)

2792 Minster's Madam (10/1: op 6/1)

1446 Alice's Mirror (9/1: 6/1-10/1)

3339 BET WITH THE TOTE (QUALIFIER) NOVICES' CHASE (6-Y.O+) (Class D)
2-50 (2-51) **3m (19 fncs)** £3,712.50 (£1,125.00: £550.00: £262.50) GOING: 0.70 sec per fur (S)

				SP	RR	SF
2947[3]	**Foxtrot Romeo (100)** (CPEBrooks) **7-10-10** GBradley (led 6th to 14th: led 4 out: sn clr)	—	**1**	6/4[1]	92	8
2657[2]	**Mr Playfull (91)** (RGFrost) **7-11-3** JFrost (a.p: led 5th to 6th: outpcd 15th: lft 2nd 3 out: no ch w wnr)	17	**2**	9/1	88	4
3086[3]	**Indian Delight** (MCPipe) **7-10-10** CMaude (hit 8th: sn bhd)	10	**3**	13/2	74	—
3188[P]	**Ekeus (IRE) (60)** (JSKing) **7-10-10** JCulloty (led 2nd to 5th: led 14th to 4 out: sn wknd)	3	**4**	33/1	72	—
3181[5]	**Bells Wood (60)** (AJKDunn) **8-10-10** SMcNeill (bhd fr 13th: t.o)	dist	**5**	50/1	—	—
3059[4]	**Dress Dance (IRE) (72)** (NRMitchell) **7-10-5**(5) SophieMitchell (prom: mstkes 3rd & 6th: 2nd & btn whn fell 3 out)		**F**	33/1	—	—
	Silver Hill (MrsSDWilliams) **7-10-4**(3)ow2 PHenley (bkwd: t.o whn fell 7th)		**F**	66/1	—	—
3173[F]	**Brogeen Lady (IRE) (100)** (DRGandolfo) **7-10-5** APMcCoy (led to 2nd: 2nd whn fell 4th)		**F**	5/1[2]	—	—
	Coralette (IRE) (100) (NJHenderson) **7-10-10** JRKavanagh (lw: bhd fr 13th: t.o whn p.u bef 3 out)		**P**	6/1[3]	—	—
	Rebel Priest (IRE) (CREgerton) **7-10-10** NWilliamson (a bhd: t.o whn p.u bef 3 out)		**P**	20/1	—	—

1426[6] **Strong Tarquin (IRE) (100)** (PFNicholls) **7-11-3** DBridgwater (lw: bhd fr 9th: t.o whn p.u bef 2 out) ... **P** 15/2 — —
2088[5] **Its Grand (63)** (PCRitchens) **8-10-10** SFox (mstke 6th: bhd fr 13th: t.o whn p.u bef 3 out) ... **P** 50/1 — —
2841[P] **Brown Robber (69)** (MrsRGHenderson) **9-10-10** CLlewellyn (hdwy 11th: wknd 13th: t.o whn p.u bef 3 out) ... **P** 33/1 — —
1994[P] **Bullanguero (IRE) (60)** (HSHowe) **8-10-10** GTormey (mstke 3rd: sn bhd: t.o whn p.u bef 13th) ... **P** 100/1 — —
(SP 126.0%) **14 Rn**

6m 31.1 (34.10) CSF £14.78 TOTE £2.50: £1.40 £3.30 £2.60 (£18.80) Trio £14.00 OWNER Lady Cobham (LAMBOURN) BRED Mrs M. Cobham
OFFICIAL EXPLANATION **Indian Delight: gurgled.**
2947 Foxtrot Romeo proved much too good for these rivals and will now be aimed at the final of this series at Uttoxeter next month. (6/4)
2657 Mr Playfull seemed to get three miles and was staying on again when left to play second fiddle to the winner. (9/1: 6/1-11/1)
3086 Indian Delight, supported in the ring, was reported by his rider to have gurgled. (13/2)
2807 Ekeus (IRE) was rather surprisingly trying a longer trip. (33/1)
3059 Dress Dance (IRE), taking a big step up in distance, needs to polish up his fencing. (33/1)
Coralette (IRE) (6/1: 3/1-13/2)
1426 Strong Tarquin (IRE) (15/2: 5/1-8/1)

3340 CROCOMBE NOVICES' HURDLE (4-Y.O+) (Class E)
3-20 (3-22) **3m 110y (12 hdls)** £2,638.40 (£742.40: £363.20) GOING: 0.70 sec per fur (S)

				SP	RR	SF
1191[3]	**Mountain Path** (NJHenderson) **7-11-5** JRKavanagh (hld up: hdwy 8th: led after 3 out: pushed out)	—	**1**	Evens[1]	72+	23
3205*	**Rare Spread (IRE) (76)** (MCPipe) **7-11-11** APMcCoy (hld up: hdwy 8th: r.o one pce fr 2 out)	2½	**2**	7/2[2]	76	27
1874[4]	**Te Amo (IRE)** (MCPipe) **5-11-5** JamieEvans (hld up: stdy hdwy 6th: shkn up appr last: r.o flat)	5	**3**	14/1	67+	18
3154[8]	**Little Jake (IRE)** (NoelChance) **7-11-5** DLeahy (a.p: rdn 3 out: no hdwy)	1¼	**4**	12/1	66	17
3085[3]	**Credo Boy** (KBishop) **8-11-5** RGreene (plld hrd: a.p: led 6th to 7th: led 8th tl after 3 out: ev ch whn mstke 2 out: wknd last)	8	**5**	20/1	61	12
3184[7]	**Look In The Mirror** (NATwiston-Davies) **6-11-5** CLlewellyn (lw: hld up: hdwy 8th: wknd 3 out)	5	**6**	15/2[3]	58	9
3085[P]	**Mr Lovely (IRE)** (JNeville) **6-11-2**(3) TDascombe (hld up: hdwy 8th: wknd 3 out)	13	**7**	25/1	49	—
2794[7]	**Tanglefoot Tipple** (RHAlner) **6-11-5** DBridgwater (mstke 1st: bhd most of wy: t.o)	29	**8**	8/1	30	—
2878[P]	**Rory'm (IRE)** (LWaring) **8-10-12b**[1](7) MGriffiths (nt j.w: prom tl wknd 8th: t.o whn p.u bef 3 out)		**P**	100/1	—	—
3115[11]	**Abbeydoran** (MrsJEHawkins) **6-11-0** RBellamy (plld hrd: prom to 8th: t.o whn p.u bef 2 out)		**P**	100/1	—	—
2875[7]	**Alice Shorelark** (SGKnight) **6-11-0** MrTGreed (led: mstke 2nd: hdd 6th: led 7th to 8th: wknd after 3 out: p.u bef last)		**P**	100/1	—	—
	Miss Gee-Ell (NBThomson) **5-10-11**(3) GuyLewis (bkwd: a bhd: t.o whn p.u bef 6th)		**P**	100/1	—	—

(SP 122.0%) **12 Rn**

6m 23.8 (31.80) CSF £4.17 TOTE £2.40: £1.40 £2.10 £2.90 (£3.60) Trio £7.30 OWNER Mr Anthony Speelman (LAMBOURN) BRED J. Thompson
1191 Mountain Path won with something in hand and is clearly going the right way. (Evens)
3205* Rare Spread (IRE) was penalised for winning a claimer last week. (7/2)
1874 Te Amo (IRE), who made his debut in a seller, did not appear to be given too hard a time over this longer trip. (14/1: 8/1-16/1)
1336 Little Jake (IRE) fared better than on his hurdling debut which was only over two miles. (12/1)
Credo Boy did not last home after pulling for his head. (20/1)
Look In The Mirror appeared to find this distance beyond him. (15/2)
2648 Tanglefoot Tipple (8/1: op 4/1)

3341 MITFORD SLADE CHALLENGE TROPHY HUNTERS' CHASE (6-Y.O+) (Class H)
3-50 (3-51) **4m 2f 110y (27 fncs)** £3,631.25 (£1,100.00: £537.50: £256.25) GOING: 0.70 sec per fur (S)

				SP	RR	SF
3055[3]	**Rusty Bridge** (MrsSMJohnson) **10-12-8**(7) MrRBurton (mde all: pckd 6th: clr 9th: hit 3 out: unchal)	—	**1**	20/1	106	—
3089*	**Vicompt de Valmont** (PFNicholls) **12-12-8**(7) MrJTizzard (lw: wl bhd tl gd hdwy 21st: hit 22nd: styd on fr 2 out: nt rch wnr)	7	**2**	Evens[1]	102	—
3055[U]	**Kettles** (MRDaniell) **10-11-0**(7) MrAPhillips (a chsng ldrs: one pce fr 3 out)	3	**3**	11/2[2]	78	—
2930[3]	**Sirisat** (MissTOBlazey) **13-11-12**(7) MissTBlazey (a.p: chsd wnr fr 22nd tl hit last)	½	**4**	25/1	90	—
	Expressment (MissASRoss) **13-11-12**(7) MrGPenfold (lw: blnd 6th: a bhd: t.o)	dist	**5**	13/2[3]	—	—
	Final Express (MWHoskins) **9-11-0**(7) MissSVickery (a bhd: t.o)	dist	**6**	33/1	—	—
	Golden Mac (RLFanshawe) **10-11-5**(7) MajorOEllwood (prom to 16th: t.o whn blnd last: virtually p.u flat)	dist	**7**	50/1	—	—
	Noisy Welcome (MPJones) **11-11-7**(7)ow2 MrMPJones (last whn fell 4th)		**F**	50/1	—	—
	Lazzaretto (LSaunders) **9-11-5**(7) MrIJohnson (sn t.o: p.u bef 23rd)		**P**	66/1	—	—
2951[P]	**Rising Sap** (JDDownes) **7-11-5**(7) MrADalton (hdwy 11th: chsd wnr 14th to 22nd: wknd qckly 4 out: t.o whn p.u bef 3 out)		**P**	25/1	—	—
	Misty (NZ) (MissCGordon) **10-11-5**(7) MrJMPritchard (prom to 11th: bhd whn j.lft 16th: t.o whn mstke 20th: p.u bef 3 out)		**P**	50/1	—	—
3089[P]	**Major Mac** (DLWilliams) **10-11-5**(7) MrSDurack (prom to 11th: t.o whn p.u bef 3 out)		**P**	50/1	—	—
	Afterkelly (MrsTWhite) **12-11-12**(7) MrIDowrick (a bhd: t.o 12th: p.u bef 21st)		**P**	10/1	—	—
	Nearly Splendid (SRStevens) **12-12-8**(7) MrTGreed (blnd 8th: sn bhd: hmpd 16th: t.o whn p.u bef 2 out)		**P**	11/1	—	—
	Princess Wenllyan (RLBlack) **12-11-0**(7) MrAHoldsworth (bhd whn j.lft 18th: t.o whn p.u bef 3 out)		**P**	66/1	—	—
	Conna Moss (IRE) (DBrace) **8-11-7**(5) MrJJukes (bit bkwd: mid div whn blnd & uns rdr 10th)		**U**	16/1	—	—

(SP 128.2%) **16 Rn**

9m 55.6 (70.60) CSF £38.58 TOTE £22.80: £5.10 £1.10 £2.10 (£14.60) Trio £28.00 OWNER Mr I. K. Johnson (MADLEY) BRED J. I. Johnson
3055 Rusty Bridge had the marathon trip this time and ran his field ragged. (20/1)
3089* Vicompt de Valmont did not mind the extended trip but the ground was nowhere near as testing as at Lingfield last time. (Evens)
Kettles won over four miles at the Heythrop last April. (11/2)
Sirisat scored over three and three-quarter miles at the Heythrop last April. (25/1)
Afterkelly (10/1: op 5/1)
Nearly Splendid (11/1: 8/1-12/1)

3342 TAUNTON 'N.H.' NOVICES' HURDLE (II) (4-Y.O+) (Class D)
4-20 (4-21) **2m 3f 110y (10 hdls)** £2,567.00 (£776.00: £378.00: £179.00) GOING: 0.70 sec per fur (S)

				SP	RR	SF
2053[7]	**Colonel Blazer** (MissHCKnight) **5-11-4** JCulloty (a.p: led & lft clr last)	—	**1**	11/2[2]	82	12

	Horse	Dist	Pos	SP	RR	SF
3115*	**Tristram's Image (NZ)** (NJHenderson) **6-11-6**(5) MrCVigors (lw: hld up: hdwy appr 6th: ev ch 3 out: wknd appr 2 out: lft 2nd last)	13	**2**	7/1[3]	78	8
2875*	**Atavistic (IRE) (99)** (CLPopham) **5-11-8**(3) TDascombe (lw: a.p: rdn & ev ch 3 out: wknd appr 2 out)	3	**3**	11/2[2]	76	6
3085[P]	**Roll Again** (MCPipe) **6-11-4** JamieEvans (prom to 7th)	hd	**4**	25/1	69	—
3143[4]	**Star Mystery** (CREgerton) **6-11-4** NWilliamson (a.p: ev ch 3 out: wknd appr 2 out: hmpd last)	3	**5**	6/4[1]	66	—
2682[11]	**Norlandic (NZ)** (PJHobbs) **5-11-4** GTormey (nvr nr ldrs)	16	**6**	33/1	53	—
2959[P]	**Camillas Legacy** (HTCole) **6-10-13** DGallagher (a bhd)	1¼	**7**	100/1	47	—
3115[5]	**Givry (IRE)** (GMMcCourt) **7-11-4** DBridgwater (led: hit 4th & 5th: sn hdd & wknd)	9	**8**	16/1	45	—
	Clifton Match (BRMillman) **5-10-8**(5) DSalter (hld up: hdwy 6th: wknd appr 3 out)	2	**9**	66/1	38	—
2840[P]	**Out For A Duck (66)** (HEHaynes) **6-10-11**(7) MrSDurack (lw: plld hrd: prom to 6th)	10	**10**	66/1	35	—
2931[16]	**Fine Spirit** (NMLampard) **5-10-6**(7) MrLBaker (lw: a bhd)	13	**11**	66/1	19	—
3233[P]	**Boozys Dream** (NBThomson) **6-11-4** SBurrough (bhd fr 5th: t.o)		**12**	100/1	—	—
549*	**Storm Run (IRE) (98)** (PFNicholls) **7-11-11** APMcCoy (a.p: led after 5th: hdd & fell last)		**F**	11/2[2]	78?	—
2034[P]	**Aqua Amber** (JMBradley) **5-11-1**(3) LAspell (bhd fr 7th: t.o whn hmpd & uns rdr last)		**U**	100/1	—	—

(SP 118.8%) **14 Rn**

4m 58.8 (27.80) CSF £38.13 TOTE £8.00: £2.30 £2.70 £1.50 (£41.00) Trio £31.50 OWNER Exors of the late Mr T H Shrimpton (WANTAGE) BRED F. C. T. Wilson

Colonel Blazer appeared to be getting just the better of Storm Run when presented the race at the final flight. He can score again. (11/2: 4/1-6/1)
3115* Tristram's Image (NZ) found life difficult under his penalty when the real race began. (7/1)
2875* Atavistic (IRE) had more on his plate than when winning over course and distance last month. (11/2)
Roll Again presumably got bogged down over a longer trip in the Lingfield mud last time but could in fact need further. (25/1)
3143 Star Mystery may be more effective over the minimum distance. (6/4)
549* Storm Run (IRE) appeared to be in the process of being mastered by the winner when he may have got half-lengthed at the last. (11/2)

3343 SANNACOTT NOVICES' H'CAP CHASE (0-100) (5-Y.O+) (Class E)

4-50 (4-51) **2m 110y (13 fncs)** £2,913.75 (£882.00: £430.50: £204.75) GOING: 0.70 sec per fur (S)

	Horse	Dist	Pos	SP	RR	SF
3053[P]	**Northern Singer (81)** (RJHodges) **7-11-5**(3) TDascombe (a.p: led 4 out: clr 3 out: r.o wl)	—	**1**	9/1	104	11
	Speedy Snaps Image (72) (PRRodford) **6-10-13** SBurrough (a.p: led 7th to 4 out: one pce)	8	**2**	33/1	87	—
2870[7]	**Rovestar (81)** (JSKing) **6-11-8** CMaude (hld up: hdwy whn hmpd 8th: r.o one pce fr 3 out)	3½	**3**	9/1	93	—
3229[2]	**After The Fox (84)** (NJHawke) **10-11-4**(7) MrJTizzard (bhd whn rdn 7th: n.d)	19	**4**	3/1[1]	77	—
3179[6]	**Full Shilling (USA) (64)** (DLWilliams) **8-10-2b**(3) GuyLewis (prom to 4 out)	4	**5**	33/1	54	—
3001[P]	**Bold Acre (80)** (JMBradley) **7-11-7b** SWynne (bit bkwd: a bhd)	nk	**6**	8/1	69	—
2752[B]	**Master Pangloss (IRE) (62)** (AndrewTurnell) **7-9-10**(7) CRae (mstke 3rd: hdwy 7th: wknd 9th)	5	**7**	33/1	46	—
2873[3]	**Nordic Valley (IRE) (86)** (MCPipe) **6-11-13** APMcCoy (bhd fr 6th)	8	**8**	11/2[2]	63	—
3051[4]	**Olliver Duckett (82)** (CLPopham) **8-11-9** GTormey (prom tl mstke 8th)	3½	**9**	9/1	55	—
3073[C]	**Dannicus (76)** (NMBabbage) **6-11-3** VSlattery (t.o whn mstke 6th)	3	**10**	16/1	46	—
3010[4]	**Flowing River (USA) (72)** (NRMitchell) **11-10-8**(5) SophieMitchell (bhd: blnd 8th: fell 3 out)		**F**	14/1	—	—
	Ketchican (76) (SGKnight) **5-10-8** SCurran (bit bkwd: bhd: mstke 6th: t.o whn p.u bef 3 out)		**P**	33/1	—	—
2926[3]	**Lobster Cottage (87)** (KCBailey) **9-12-0** SMcNeill (led tl hit 7th: blnd 4 out: sn wknd: p.u bef 3 out)		**P**	9/1	—	—
2752[F]	**Relkowen (80)** (AndrewTurnell) **7-11-7** MRichards (bhd fr 6th: t.o whn p.u bef 4 out)		**P**	15/2[3]	—	—

(SP 127.6%) **14 Rn**

4m 25.3 (25.30) CSF £251.72 CT £2,491.56 TOTE £13.20: £4.70 £7.70 £2.30 (£332.00) Trio £550.90; £550.93 to Ludlow 27/2/97 OWNER Mr Joe Panes (SOMERTON) BRED N. J. Dent

WEIGHT FOR AGE 5yo-9lb

3053 Northern Singer, whose trainer could offer the Stewards no explanation for his disappointing performance at Hereford, may have found this ground a shade faster. (9/1: op 5/1)
Speedy Snaps Image, not seen over jumps since winning a juvenile seller in October 1994, showed nothing in two outings on the Flat last summer and this effort was surprising to say the least. (33/1)
1663* Rovestar was making his chasing debut off a mark 2lb lower than when winning a Novices' Handicap hurdle at Warwick in November. (9/1)
3229 After The Fox never gave his supporters much cause for hope. (3/1)
2569 Bold Acre (8/1: 6/1-9/1)
2873 Nordic Valley (IRE) (11/2: 4/1-6/1)
3051 Olliver Duckett (9/1: op 5/1)
2926 Lobster Cottage (9/1: 5/1-10/1)

3344 BLACKDOWN HILLS H'CAP HURDLE (0-105) (4-Y.O+) (Class F)

5-20 (5-20) **2m 1f (9 hdls)** £1,962.50 (£550.00: £267.50) GOING: 0.70 sec per fur (S)

	Horse	Dist	Pos	SP	RR	SF
3056*	**Added Dimension (IRE) (99)** (PWinkworth) **6-11-4**(7) XAizpuru (lw: chsd ldr: led 5th: clr whn hit last: r.o wl)	—	**1**	3/1[1]	88	34
2932[3]	**Handson (90)** (BRMillman) **5-10-11**(5) DSalter (lw: hld up: hdwy after 4th: chsd wnr after 3 out: rdn & hit 2 out: no imp)	8	**2**	3/1[1]	72	18
3110[2]	**D'naan (IRE) (98)** (MCPipe) **4-11-0b** APMcCoy (lw: led tl rdn & hdd 5th: wknd flat)	5	**3**	100/30[2]	75	11
	Runic Symbol (74) (MBlanshard) **6-10-0** DGallagher (bit bkwd: hld up: hdwy after 4th: wknd after 3 out)	½	**4**	16/1	50	—
3234[P]	**Concinnity (USA) (74)** (BScriven) **8-9-7**(7) MrOMcPhail (hld up: hdwy after 4th: rdn & wknd 3 out)	s.h	**5**	100/1	50	—
	Sevso (89) (RJBaker) **8-11-1** VSlattery (bit bkwd: rdn appr 5th: bhd fr 6th: mstke last)	1½	**6**	10/1	64	10
	Persian Mystic (IRE) (98) (DJWintle) **5-11-10** WMarston (a bhd)	13	**7**	12/1	61	7
2870[3]	**Steel Gem (IRE) (74)** (PMRich) **8-9-7**(7) MGriffiths (a bhd: fin lame)	8	**8**	4/1[3]	29	—
885[P]	**Dante's Rubicon (IRE) (75)** (NGAyliffe) **6-10-1**ow1 CMaude (bit bkwd: a bhd: t.o 5th: p.u bef 3 out)		**P**	66/1	—	—

(SP 118.2%) **9 Rn**

4m 13.4 (20.40) CSF £12.00 CT £28.71 TOTE £3.30: £1.40 £1.40 £1.10 (£7.40) Trio £4.20 OWNER Mr N. A. Dunger (DUNSFOLD) BRED Swettenham Stud and Ron Con Limited

LONG HANDICAP Concinnity (USA) 9-2 Runic Symbol 9-10 Dante's Rubicon (IRE) 9-0

WEIGHT FOR AGE 4yo-10lb

3056* Added Dimension (IRE), up a further 6lb, completed the hat-trick but seems to like giving his backers heart-stopping moments at the final flight. (3/1)

2932 Handson, dropping back in trip, was still in with a squeak when rapping the penultimate hurdle. (3/1)
3110 D'naan (IRE), up a further 5lb, was only second in a seller last time. (100/30)
Runic Symbol, 4lb out of the handicap, should be a bit sharper for the run. (16/1)
Concinnity (USA), 10lb wrong at the weights, stepped up considerably on his two previous efforts this season. (100/1)
Sevso (10/1: op 16/1)
Persian Mystic (IRE) (12/1: 6/1-14/1)

T/Jkpt: Not won; £35,968.96 to Ludlow 27/2/97. T/Plpt: £26.90 (534.52 Tckts). T/Qdpt: £5.40 (156.2 Tckts) KH

2898-WETHERBY (L-H) (Ch Heavy, Soft patches, Hdls Soft, Heavy patches)
Wednesday February 26th

One flight omitted all races. One fence omitted all races.
WEATHER: unsettled

3345 HOGARTH NOVICES' HURDLE (4-Y.O+) (Class E)
2-00 (2-22) **2m (8 hdls)** £2,670.00 (£745.00: £360.00) GOING: 1.35 sec per fur (HY)

	Horse	Dist	Pos	SP	RR	SF
2948^{4}	**Carlito Brigante** (PRWebber) **5-11-9** JOsborne (cl up: led 2 out: styd on wl)	—	**1**	5/1^{3}	87	22
2670^{8}	**Fassan (IRE) (103)** (MDHammond) **5-11-4** RGarritty (mde most tl hdd 2 out: kpt on one pce)	4	**2**	5/1^{3}	78	13
2631^{15}	**Mithraic (IRE) (100)** (WSCunningham) **5-11-9** RJohnson (t: a w ldrs: rdn appr 3 out: r.o one pce)	3	**3**	20/1	80	15
	Old Hush Wing (IRE) (PCHaslam) **4-10-8** JCallaghan (hld up: hdwy appr 3 out: styd on flat)	½	**4**	33/1	75	—
	China Castle (PCHaslam) **4-10-8** MFoster (lw: trckd ldrs: rdn to chal 3 out: wknd next)	14	**5**	10/1	61	—
3065^{3}	**Monica's Choice (IRE) (113)** (MrsMReveley) **6-11-9** PNiven (bhd: hmpd 4th: sme hdwy 3 out: n.d)	2	**6**	100/30^{2}	64	—
3159^{11}	**Well Armed (IRE)** (JJO'Neill) **6-10-13**$^{(5)}$ RMcGrath (chsd ldrs tl wknd appr 3 out)	4	**7**	20/1	55	—
1921^{9}	**Rothari** (BSRothwell) **5-11-4** BStorey (bhd: sme hdwy appr 3 out: sn wknd)	7	**8**	20/1	48	—
1652^{5}	**Bold Classic (IRE)** (CGrant) **4-10-9**^{ow1} TReed (cl up: chal after 5th tl wknd appr 3 out)	14	**9**	12/1	35	—
	Windyedge (USA) (MrsAMNaughton) **4-10-8** JSupple (a bhd)	22	**10**	40/1	12	—
2697^{9}	**Petrico** (PBeaumont) **5-11-4** RSupple (in tch tl wknd after 5th)	dist	**11**	50/1	—	—
2917^{13}	**Dan de Man (IRE)** (MissLCSiddall) **6-11-4** AThornton (lw: in tch whn fell 4th)		**F**	50/1	—	—
3026*	**Foresworn (USA)** (DWWhillans) **5-11-9** DBentley (trckd ldrs whn hmpd & p.u lame bef 5th: dead)		**P**	2/1^{1}	—	—
3197^{P}	***O K Kealy*** (MCChapman) **7-11-4** WWorthington (Withdrawn not under Starter's orders: uns rdr & bolted bef s)		**W**	100/1	—	—
				(SP 131.1%)	**13 Rn**	

4m 13.9 (31.90) CSF £28.34 TOTE £6.40: £1.90 £1.50 £5.20 (£14.40) Trio £44.10 OWNER Lady Bamford (BANBURY) BRED Whitsbury Manor Stud
WEIGHT FOR AGE 4yo-10lb
OFFICIAL EXPLANATION **Monica's Choice (IRE): was hampered by a faller and unable to get back into the race thereafter.**
2948 Carlito Brigante has done all his winning on good or fast ground previously but these testing conditions proved no problem and he won in most emphatic style. (5/1)
2041 Fassan (IRE), made plenty of use of in this testing ground, ran well but found the winner too tough when it mattered. (5/1)
1312 Mithraic (IRE), normally happier on faster ground, ran well in the conditions. (20/1)
Old Hush Wing (IRE), a maiden off the Flat, handled this very soft ground really well and showed enough to suggest that there is an opportunity to be found at this game. (33/1)
China Castle has been very busy and successful on the All-Weather but these testing conditions found him out and he tired badly from the third last. (10/1)
3065 Monica's Choice (IRE) got badly hampered by a faller early on and never got into the race but showed enough to suggest that he can do better. (100/30: 9/4-7/2)

3346 ASKHAM BRYAN H'CAP HURDLE (0-110) (4-Y.O+) (Class E)
2-30 (2-55) **2m (8 hdls)** £2,460.00 (£685.00: £330.00) GOING: 1.35 sec per fur (HY)

	Horse	Dist	Pos	SP	RR	SF
3158^{3}	**Durano (100)** (TDEasterby) **6-11-4** LWyer (a.p: led appr 3 out: styd on wl)	—	**1**	100/30^{1}	84	22
2902^{4}	**Ham N'Eggs (110)** (MDHammond) **6-12-0** RGarritty (chsd ldrs fr 5th: ev ch 3 out: nt qckn flat)	1¾	**2**	9/1	92	30
3035^{B}	**Court Joker (IRE) (82)** (HAlexander) **5-10-0** RJohnson (bhd: hdwy & prom appr 3 out: one pce appr last)	4	**3**	20/1	60	—
3065^{4}	**Our Robert (92)** (JGFitzGerald) **5-10-7**$^{(3)}$ FLeahy (bhd: hdwy u.p 3 out: 3rd & styng on whn blnd last: nt rcvr)	5	**4**	10/1	65+	3
3035^{4}	**Innocent George (87)** (MissLCSiddall) **8-10-5** AThornton (bhd tl styd on fr 3 out)	5	**5**	16/1	55	—
3072^{3}	**Tulu (104)** (MrsJRRamsden) **6-11-1**$^{(7)}$ MrABalding (hld up & bhd: effrt 3 out: nvr rchd ldrs)	1¾	**6**	13/2^{3}	71	9
2946^{3}	**Eurotwist (99)** (SEKettlewell) **8-11-0**$^{(3)}$ GLee (lw: prom tl outpcd appr 3 out: sme late hdwy)	¾	**7**	14/1	65	3
1123^{P}	**Muizenberg (83)** (EHOwenjun) **10-9-12**$^{(3)ow1}$ MichaelBrennan (plld hrd: led 2nd to 4th: cl up tl wknd appr 3 out)	4	**8**	100/1	45	—
3137^{7}	**Fox Sparrow (100)** (NTinkler) **7-11-4** ASSmith (chsd ldrs fr 4th tl wknd fr 3 out)	3½	**9**	14/1	58	—
3065^{2}	**Merry Mermaid (96)** (BMactaggart) **7-11-0** ADobbin (mde most tl hdd & wknd qckly appr 3 out)	5	**10**	100/30^{1}	49	—
1027^{4}	**Sea God (83)** (MCChapman) **6-10-1** WWorthington (prom tl wknd after 5th)	1	**11**	20/1	35	—
3136^{2}	**Ajdar (82)** (OBrennan) **6-10-0** MBrennan (a bhd)	3	**12**	16/1	31	—
3137^{3}	**Bend Sable (IRE) (106)** (FSStorey) **7-11-10** BStorey (lw: prom tl rdn & wknd appr 3 out)	1½	**13**	5/1^{2}	54	—
				(SP 130.9%)	**13 Rn**	

4m 13.0 (31.00) CSF £33.68 CT £508.33 TOTE £4.40: £2.30 £2.80 £6.20 (£12.70) Trio £243.50; £140.61 to Ludlow 27/2/97 OWNER Mr C. H. Stevens (MALTON) BRED A. M. Wragg
LONG HANDICAP Muizenberg 9-5 Ajdar 9-12
3158 Durano was winning on ground as soft as this for the first time and he did this in most determined style. (100/30)
2902 Ham N'Eggs has always looked a top of the ground performer in the past and in the conditions this was a useful effort. (9/1)
2509 Court Joker (IRE) obviously likes this soft ground as this was a much-improved effort. (20/1)
3065 Our Robert won at this meeting last year and had a chance of repeating that, but was under strong driving, when he made a hash of things at the last. (10/1)
3035 Innocent George has always looked at his best on fast ground and, in the circumstances, this was not a bad effort. (16/1)
3072 Tulu, who loves the soft ground, was given a lot to do here but failed to make much headway when asked a question in the straight. (13/2)
2946 Eurotwist loves the conditions but seems a bit of a moody customer these days. (14/1)
3065 Merry Mermaid, a mud lover, ran poorly, dropping out tamely when challenged in the straight. (100/30: op 7/1)

3347 SICKLINGHALL NOVICES' CHASE (5-Y.O+) (Class D)

3-00 (3-22) **3m 1f (16 fncs)** £3,574.00 (£1,072.00: £516.00: £238.00) GOING: 1.35 sec per fur (HY)

				SP	RR	SF
3155^{P}	**Credo Is King (IRE) (112)** (PRWebber) **7-11-10** JOsborne (chsd ldrs: reminders 10th & appr 4 out: led appr last: drvn out)	—	1	9/2^{2}	109	—
2919*	**Crown Equerry (IRE)** (GRichards) **7-11-13** PCarberry (led tl hdd appr last: hrd rdn & kpt on wl)	1	2	7/4^{1}	111	—
2915^{P}	**Dorlin Castle (93)** (LLungo) **9-11-4** RSupple (hld up: hdwy 9th: ev ch & mstke 2 out: sn rdn: nt qckn flat)	¾	3	9/1^{3}	102	—
3047^{3}	**What's Your Story (IRE) (112)** (DNicholson) **8-11-4** RJohnson (mstkes: chsd ldrs: 3rd & rdn whn blnd 4 out: sn btn)	15	4	7/4^{1}	92	—
2912^{3}	**Black Brook (IRE)** (MDHammond) **8-11-4** RGarritty (lw: cl up: mstke 9th: wknd 12th: p.u bef 4 out)		P	9/1^{3}	—	—
	Dee Light (GRichards) **8-10-13** ADobbin (prom to 9th: sn t.o: p.u bef 4 out)		P	20/1	—	—
3067^{4}	**Clonroche Lucky (IRE) (67)** (JWade) **7-11-4b^{1}** KJones (lw: outpcd & lost tch ½-wy: t.o whn p.u bef 4 out)		P	100/1	—	—
				(SP 116.7%)	**7 Rn**	

7m 2.6 CSF £12.68 TOTE £5.70: £2.40 £1.50 (£6.00) OWNER Mr G. L. Porter (BANBURY) BRED Robert McCarthy

OFFICIAL EXPLANATION **Credo Is King (IRE): regarding the apparent improvement in form, the trainer reported that the gelding had been tackling much better opposition last time and that the jockey had made too much use of him.**

2883 Credo Is King (IRE), out of his depth last time, found this much more to his liking but it took some strong handling to persuade him. (9/2)

2919* Crown Equerry (IRE), aggressively ridden again, found no problem with the very soft conditions and to his credit he fought back well when looking beaten. (7/4)

1989 Dorlin Castle, given a most patient ride, looked likely to win early in the straight but, once asked to struggle after a poor jump two out, he was never coming up with the goods. He loved the conditions but does like things to go all his way. (9/1)

3047 What's Your Story (IRE) just needs to improve his jumping and, once he does, there are plenty of opportunities to be found. (7/4)

2912 Black Brook (IRE) went quite well until pulling up. (9/1)

3348 HOECHST ROUSSEL PANACUR E.B.F. 'N.H.' (QUALIFIER) NOVICES' HURDLE (5-Y.O+ F & M) (Class D)

3-30 (3-51) **2m 4f 110y (8 hdls)** £2,985.00 (£835.00: £405.00) GOING: 1.35 sec per fur (HY)

				SP	RR	SF
2870^{4}	**Fantasy Line (87)** (PRWebber) **6-10-7** JOsborne (a gng wl: hdwy to ld appr 3 out: sn clr)	—	1	6/1	62+	—
2920^{2}	**Lippy Louise** (MrsMReveley) **5-10-7** PNiven (a.p: mstke 4th: chsd wnr fr 3 out: no imp)	7	2	4/1^{2}	57	—
3066^{5}	**Cherry Dee** (PBeaumont) **6-10-2**(5) BGrattan (chsd ldrs tl outpcd 5th: styd on again fr 2 out)	½	3	12/1	56	—
	Raise A Dollar (PBeaumont) **7-10-7** MrSSwiers (cl up: disp ld after 5th tl grad wknd appr 3 out)	29	4	20/1	34	—
3029^{2}	**Spritzer (IRE) (100)** (JGFitzGerald) **5-11-0** PCarberry (prom tl outpcd after 5th: sme hdwy u.p appr 3 out: sn btn)	9	5	5/6^{1}	34	—
1802^{P}	**Pharrambling (IRE)** (MrsMReveley) **6-10-4**(3) GLee (a bhd)	12	6	33/1	17	—
2920*	**Daisy Days (IRE) (92)** (HowardJohnson) **7-11-7** ASSmith (led tl hdd & wknd appr 3 out)	10	7	9/2^{3}	23	—
				(SP 122.4%)	**7 Rn**	

5m 33.6 (46.60) CSF £29.91 TOTE £7.90: £3.30 £1.70 (£9.30) Trio £35.90 OWNER Mrs P. Starkey (BANBURY) BRED Dunchurch Lodge Stud

OFFICIAL EXPLANATION **Spritzer (IRE): was unable to act on the heavy going.**

2870 Fantasy Line revelled in the conditions here and, always on the bridle, there were never any doubts about the result from three out. (6/1)

2920 Lippy Louise is just a stayer and kept plugging away, although always well second best. (4/1)

3066 Cherry Dee jumped a shade better this time but looks woefully short of pace and is likely to need much longer distances. (12/1)

Raise A Dollar ran a smashing race and was given a most sympathetic ride. Better now looks likely. (20/1)

3029 Spritzer (IRE) was most disappointing, presumably due to the very testing conditions. (5/6)

2920* Daisy Days (IRE), attempting to make all, was found out by this testing ground but will be an interesting prospect when put over the bigger obstacles. (9/2: op 3/1)

3349 EAST KESWICK H'CAP CHASE (0-135) (5-Y.O+) (Class C)

4-00 (4-20) **2m 4f 110y (14 fncs)** £4,402.50 (£1,320.00: £635.00: £292.50) GOING: 1.35 sec per fur (HY)

				SP	RR	SF
3025^{4}	**Beachy Head (115)** (JJO'Neill) **9-10-4**(5) RMcGrath (hld up: mstke 5th: led 4 out: pushed out)	—	1	3/1^{3}	123	56
3198*	**Aljadeer (USA) (114)** (MWEasterby) **8-10-8**^{5x} RGarritty (lw: hld up: mstke 7th: hdwy 10th: chal last: kpt on u.p)	¾	2	11/4^{2}	121	54
3106^{2}	**No Pain No Gain (IRE) (120)** (JTGifford) **9-11-0** PHide (lw: chsd ldrs: led 10th to 4 out: rdn & wknd appr 2 out)	13	3	2/1^{1}	117	50
3071^{2}	**Sailor Jim (106)** (PTDalton) **10-10-0** JOsborne (lw: led to 3rd: chsd ldrs: ev ch 10th: wknd appr 4 out)	dist	4	9/2	—	—
953^{P}	**Master Boston (IRE) (130)** (RDEWoodhouse) **9-11-10** PCarberry (bit bkwd: led fr 3rd: blnd 8th: hdd 10th: wknd qckly & p.u bef 4 out)		P	12/1	—	—
				(SP 110.9%)	**5 Rn**	

5m 35.1 (28.10) CSF £10.76 TOTE £4.30: £1.30 £1.90 (£5.40) OWNER Mr M. Tabor (PENRITH) BRED G. Reed

LONG HANDICAP Sailor Jim 9-12

3025 Beachy Head cannot have the ground soft enough and, although a shade deliberate at some fences, he was always going best and his rider just needed hands and heels to keep him going. (3/1)

3198* Aljadeer (USA), produced with a lovely run in the straight, had his chances but, despite the strongest attentions, he was never quite doing enough. (11/4: 5/4-3/1)

3106 No Pain No Gain (IRE) likes soft ground but, when it came down to a battle, these conditions just found him out. (2/1)

3071 Sailor Jim went really well until suddenly running out of fuel approaching the fourth last, from which point he was certainly not knocked about. (9/2)

Master Boston (IRE), needing this, ran well until stopping as though shot five from home. (12/1: op 8/1)

3350 HELMSLEY NOVICES' H'CAP CHASE (5-Y.O+) (Class C)

4-30 (4-46) **2m (11 fncs)** £4,640.00 (£1,290.00: £620.00) GOING: 1.35 sec per fur (HY)

				SP	RR	SF
3161^{4}	**Crosshot (85)** (RMcDonald) **10-10-0** RJohnson (hld up: mstke 5th: led 3 out: clr whn blnd last: rdr lost iron & sddle slipped)	—	1	7/2^{3}	92	—
3161^{2}	**Bold Boss (109)** (GMMoore) **8-11-10** BStorey (chsd ldrs: outpcd appr 4 out: no imp after)	7	2	11/10^{1}	109	9
2921*	**Marble Man (IRE) (92)** (MDHammond) **7-10-7** RGarritty (led tl hdd & wknd 3 out)	23	3	13/8^{2}	69	—
				(SP 107.9%)	**3 Rn**	

4m 26.5 (34.50) CSF £6.90 TOTE £3.70 (£2.00) OWNER Mr R. McDonald (DUNS) BRED Robert McDonald

LONG HANDICAP Crosshot 9-11
3161 Crosshot got his jumping together this time and was probably suited by the slower pace in these conditions. Once produced in the straight, he always had a bit in hand. (7/2)
3161 Bold Boss was anchored by his weight when the race began in earnest four out but he did keep on well at the end. (11/10)
2921* Marble Man (IRE) was most disappointing, dropping tamely away once tackled three out. (13/8)

3351 MICKLETHWAITE H'CAP HURDLE (0-125) (4-Y.O+) (Class D)

5-00 (5-12) **2m 4f 110y (8 hdls)** £2,792.50 (£780.00: £377.50) GOING: 1.35 sec per fur (HY)

Form	Horse	Dist	Pos	SP	RR	SF
3137^{2}	**Danbys Gorse (90)** (JMJefferson) **5-10-0** LWyer (lw: hld up: hdwy appr 3 out: led last: r.o)	—	1	$9/4^{1}$	72	—
2915^{F}	**Duke of Perth (91)** (HowardJohnson) **6-10-1** ASSmith (hld up: stdy hdwy appr 3 out: led 2 out & sn hrd drvn: hdd last: kpt on)	½	2	11/2	73	—
3309^{2}	**All On (110)** (JHetherton) **6-11-6** DerekByrne (cl up: led 4th tl after next: effrt appr last: r.o)	1½	3	$4/1^{3}$	90	1
2797^{4}	**Claireswan (IRE) (97)** (MHTompkins) **5-10-7** KGaule (chsd ldrs: led 3 out tl hdd next: r.o one pce)	1¼	4	7/1	77	—
3201*	**Boston Man (90)** (RDEWoodhouse) **6-10-0** 6x PCarberry (led tl j.slowly & hdd 4th: led after next to 3 out: wknd 2 out)	20	5	$7/2^{2}$	54	—
2915^{P}	**Moonshine Dancer (95)** (DWBarker) **7-10-5** JCallaghan (prom tl outpcd appr 3 out)	2	6	20/1	57	—
3199^{5}	**Summerhill Special (IRE) (113)** (DWBarker) **6-11-9** RJohnson (hld up: rdn appr 3 out: wknd appr 2 out)	9	7	11/1	68	—
3163^{10}	**Viardot (IRE) (102)** (HAlexander) **8-10-7**(5) RMcGrath (a bhd)	4	8	16/1	54	—

(SP 119.9%) **8 Rn**

5m 33.6 (46.60) CSF £14.82 CT £43.93 TOTE £2.90: £1.30 £1.20 £2.10 (£5.80) Trio £21.70 OWNER Mr D. T. Todd (MALTON) BRED D. T. Todd
3137 Danbys Gorse appreciated the trip in this ground but did seem to idle in front. There would seem to be more to come. (9/4)
2915 Duke of Perth, given a most aggressive ride, kept responding to pressure when looking beaten and deserves a change of luck. (11/2)
3309 All On, having her second run in less than a week, put up another useful performance and was not knocked about. She looks likely to do better. (4/1)
2797 Claireswan (IRE) goes in the ground and stays well and, after looking beaten some way out, kept plugging away. (7/1: 5/1-8/1)
3201* Boston Man showed signs of temperament here when looking to duck out when passing the stands. Losing all concentration, he jumped very slowly at the first hurdle in the back straight. (7/2: op 9/4)
3199 Summerhill Special (IRE) (11/1: 8/1-12/1)

T/Plpt: £1,499.80 (9.8 Tckts). T/Qdpt: £141.00 (5.15 Tckts) AA

3222-HUNTINGDON (R-H) (Good to soft, Soft patches)

Thursday February 27th

WEATHER: overcast

3352 COLESDEN (S) HURDLE (4-Y.O+) (Class G)

2-00 (2-05) **2m 110y (8 hdls)** £2,075.30 (£575.80: £275.90) GOING: 0.34 sec per fur (GS)

Form	Horse	Dist	Pos	SP	RR	SF
2939^{11}	**Mellow Master** (NJHWalker) **4-10-7** RFarrant (a.p: rdn to ld nr fin)	—	1	20/1	65	8
3228^{5}	**Halham Tarn (IRE) (80)** (HJManners) **7-11-1**(7) ADowling (chsd ldr: led appr 4th: sn clr: ct nr fin)	1¼	2	12/1	69	22
3057^{P}	**Battleship Bruce (85)** (TCasey) **5-11-2b** DGallagher (hdwy 5th: rdn appr last: one pce)	1¼	3	$11/2^{3}$	62	15
1449^{5}	**Tenayestelign (85)** (DMarks) **9-11-3** JAMcCarthy (bit bkwd: hld up: hdwy 5th: rdn appr last: fnd nil)	1¼	4	6/1	61	14
2792^{11}	**Lucy Tufty (78)** (JPearce) **6-11-3** NMann (chsd ldrs: rdn appr 2 out: wknd flat)	3	5	14/1	59	12
2705^{6}	**Song For Jess (IRE) (70)** (FJordan) **4-9-13**(3) LAspell (chsd ldrs to 3 out)	22	6	16/1	32	—
3136^{6}	**Thefieldsofathenry (IRE) (98)** (CREgerton) **7-12-0** NWilliamson (lw: hld up: hdwy 5th: rdn & btn next)	4	7	$5/1^{2}$	44	—
3204^{P}	**Patong Beach (64)** (PCRitchens) **7-10-11** SFox (bit bkwd: effrt 5th: nvr rchd ldrs)	2½	8	50/1	25	—
	Jonbel (TTClement) **9-11-2** CMaude (bkwd: a bhd)	17	9	50/1	13	—
	Rafter-J (JohnHarris) **6-11-2** JRailton (bkwd: nvr nr to chal)	10	10	33/1	4	—
	Tigana (MrsLCJewell) **5-10-11** DLeahy (bkwd: a bhd)	½	11	25/1	—	—
3173^{10}	**Convamore Queen (IRE)** (NMBabbage) **8-10-11** VSlattery (prom: blnd 4th: wknd next)	19	12	33/1	—	—
2682^{19}	**X-Ray (IRE)** (JRJenkins) **4-10-0**(7) NTEgan (led: sn clr: rn wd after 3rd: sn hdd & wknd)	dist	13	66/1	—	—
2678*	**Bella Sedona (92)** (LadyHerries) **5-11-3** JOsborne (nvr gng wl: t.o whn p.u bef 5th)		P	$13/8^{1}$	—	—
	Foreign Judgement (USA) (WJMusson) **4-10-7** DFuhrmann (bit bkwd: uns rdr 2nd)		U	40/1	—	—

(SP 127.0%) **15 Rn**

4m 4.2 (16.20) CSF £214.35 TOTE £38.90: £8.30 £3.10 £2.30 (£157.80) Trio Not won; £287.56 to Newbury 28/2/97 OWNER Mr Paul Green (BLEWBURY) BRED Paul Green
WEIGHT FOR AGE 4yo-10lb
No bid
OFFICIAL EXPLANATION **Bella Sedona: the rider reported that the mare made a mistake at the third and then pulled herself up. The vet added that the mare was distressed after the race.**
Mellow Master, taking a big drop in class, was patiently ridden on the heels of the leaders and produced at the right time. This is his trip. (20/1)
3228 Halham Tarn (IRE), dropped in class, had most of these in trouble some way from home and should soon find a similar race. (12/1: 8/1-14/1)
2818 Battleship Bruce looked a danger turning for home but didn't find much at the business end. (11/2: 5/1-8/1)
1449 Tenayestelign cruised up to the leaders on the home turn but didn't find much in the final battle. (6/1)
1861 Lucy Tufty ran a little better than of late and may be set for a return to form. (14/1: 10/1-16/1)
1908 Song For Jess (IRE) didn't appear to stay the trip on ground softer than she is used to. (16/1)
2678* Bella Sedona reverted to type after last time's amazing effort, for she was the first beaten. (13/8)

3353 COLMWORTH HUNTERS' CHASE (5-Y.O+) (Class H)

2-30 (2-30) **3m (19 fncs)** £1,213.50 (£336.00: £160.50) GOING: 0.73 sec per fur (S)

Form	Horse	Dist	Pos	SP	RR	SF
3107*	**Mr Boston** (MrsMReveley) **12-12-5** MrSSwiers (hld up: hdwy 10th: chsd ldr fr next tl led appr 2 out: rdn out flat)	—	1	$8/11^{1}$	110	43
	Granville Guest (PFNicholls) **11-11-7**(7) MrJTizzard (mstke 1st: hdwy 14th: ev ch appr 2 out: rdn & hung lft flat)	5	2	11/1	102	35
3089^{P}	**Colonial Kelly** (MrsDMGrissell) **9-12-4**(3) MrPHacking (chsd ldrs: mstke 13th: one pce fr 3 out)	12	3	12/1	101	34

	Horse	Details	Dist	Pos	SP	RR	SF
3062*	**Loyal Note**	(SRAndrews) **9-12-4**(3) MrSimonAndrews (lw: chsd ldr tl blnd 6th: no imp fr 16th)	1½	**4**	14/1	100	33
	Gay Ruffian	(MrsDJDyson) **11-11-7**(7) MissCDyson (bit bkwd: chsd ldr to 8th: wknd 13th)	27	**5**	40/1	75	8
	Fire and Reign (IRE)	(NeilKing) **9-11-7**(7) MrNKing (bkwd: s.i.s: in tch whn fell 4th)		**F**	100/1	—	—
	Itsgoneoff	(MissCSaunders) **8-11-9**(5) MrBPollock (bit bkwd: led: clr 5th: hdd & p.u appr 2 out: dead)		**P**	3/1 2	—	—
	Richard Hunt	(MrsPRowe) **13-11-7**(7) MissLRowe (lw: bhd fr 5th: rdn 9th: t.o whn p.u bef 3 out)		**P**	9/1 3	—	—

(SP 119.0%) **8 Rn**

6m 27.1 (30.10) CSF £10.08 TOTE £1.60: £1.30 £3.10 £1.70 (£8.10) OWNER Mr M. K. Oldham (SALTBURN) BRED Mrs D. M. Hurndall-Waldron

3107* Mr Boston, back at something approaching his optimum trip, needed reminders on the run-in only because he was taking things easy. He is going to be a tough nut to crack in ordinary Hunter Chases as he stays so well. (8/11: evens-4/6)

Granville Guest has had his problems since being a decent novice in the 93/4 season, and this run was his best in a long time. (11/1: 5/1-14/1)

Colonial Kelly is still capable of the odd bad mistake and it certainly didn't help his chance here. (12/1: 8/1-14/1)

3062* Loyal Note likes to lead, but couldn't get into the same parish as Itsgoneoff, and lost the lead in the chasing group following a mistake after a mile. (14/1: 8/1-16/1)

Gay Ruffian didn't look fit but ran quite well for two miles, although only time will tell if he retains his ability. (40/1)

Itsgoneoff led these a merry dance until breaking down on the home turn. Sadly, the injury was so serious that he had to be destroyed. (3/1)

3354 CHAWSTON H'CAP CHASE (0-100) (5-Y.O+) (Class F)

3-00 (3-00) **3m (19 fncs)** £3,116.50 (£869.00: £419.50) GOING: 0.73 sec per fur (S)

	Horse	Details	Dist	Pos	SP	RR	SF
2947*	**Cariboo Gold (USA) (99)**	(KCBailey) **8-12-0b** JOsborne (hld up: hdwy 11th: hit 2 out: sn led: easily)	—	**1**	10/11 1	116++	32
2940 4	**Bolshie Baron (72)**	(MHWeston) **8-10-1** DGallagher (chsd ldrs: outpcd 11th: styd on fr 3 out: r.o wl flat)	3	**2**	14/1	87	3
3053 3	**Blazer Moriniere (FR) (78)**	(PCRitchens) **8-10-7** SFox (hdwy 11th: led 3 out: rdn & hdd appr last: wknd flat)	1¼	**3**	7/1 3	92	8
3153 10	**Space Cappa (92)**	(MissVAStephens) **9-11-7** MissVStephens (prom tl wknd 4 out)	dist	**4**	16/1	—	—
3181*	**Furry Fox (IRE) (78)**	(RCurtis) **9-10-7** 6x DWalsh (prom: hit 13th: wknd appr 2 out)	hd	**5**	2/1 2	—	—
3185 4	**Pant Llin (80)**	(FJordan) **11-10-6b**(3) LAspell (mstkes: hld up: rdn & lost tch 12th: sn t.o)	dist	**6**	25/1	—	—
3176 P	**King's Courtier (IRE) (71)**	(SMellor) **8-10-0v** NMann (led to 3 out: wknd qckly & p.u bef next)		**P**	50/1	—	—

(SP 116.6%) **7 Rn**

6m 29.2 (32.20) CSF £13.24 TOTE £1.80: £1.40 £4.40 (£10.40) OWNER Mrs Sharon Nelson (UPPER LAMBOURN) BRED Regal Oak Farm & Albert G. Clay

LONG HANDICAP King's Courtier (IRE) 9-10

2947* Cariboo Gold (USA) is still off a mark a couple of stone lower than he won off over hurdles, and won like it, being eased down to a walk near the line. (10/11: 8/11-evens)

2704 Bolshie Baron shaped like a real stayer and could be a different proposition over further. (14/1: 8/1-16/1)

3053 Blazer Moriniere (FR) ran a cracking race, being the only one to give the winner anything to think about, but faded going to the last and possibly doesn't quite get this trip. (7/1: 5/1-8/1)

Space Cappa couldn't dominate, having to play second fiddle to King's Courtier instead, and gave up the ghost in the last half-mile. (16/1)

3181* Furry Fox (IRE) had proven his stamina in the past but stopped quickly in the straight on this occasion. (2/1: op 7/1)

3355 LEVY BOARD 'N.H.' NOVICES' HURDLE (4-Y.O+) (Class E)

3-30 (3-32) **3m 2f (12 hdls)** £2,600.00 (£725.00: £350.00) GOING: Not Established

	Horse	Details	Dist	Pos	SP	RR	SF
2546 2	**Flying Gunner (117)**	(DNicholson) **6-11-7**(3) RMassey (trckd ldrs: led appr 3 out: sn hdd: led 2 out: drvn out: jst hld on)	—	**1**	Evens 1	88	—
3048 3	**Banny Hill Lad**	(CPMorlock) **7-11-1**(3) DFortt (in tch: hdwy 8th: led 3 out to next: r.o flat: jst failed)	hd	**2**	25/1	82	—
2746 3	**Satcotino (IRE)**	(MHTompkins) **6-10-13** NWilliamson (chsd ldrs: rdn appr 2 out: kpt on)	3½	**3**	7/2 2	75	—
2826 4	**Music Master (IRE)**	(CREgerton) **7-11-4b1** JAMcCarthy (hld up & plld hrd)	19	**4**	16/1	68	—
2861 4	**September Breeze (IRE) (84)**	(KAMorgan) **6-10-13** ASSmith (lw: w ldrs: ev ch 9th: rdn & wknd appr next)	8	**5**	16/1	58	—
1938 6	**Wristburn**	(CJMann) **7-11-4** JRailton (hdwy 9th: nvr rchd ldrs)	5	**6**	9/2 3	60	—
2826 6	**Hardy Breeze (IRE)**	(DMGrissell) **6-11-4** DGallagher (bhd tl sme hdwy fr 3 out)	½	**7**	50/1	60	—
3085 6	**Brave Edwin (IRE)**	(JABOld) **7-10-13**(5) SophieMitchell (effrt 8th: nvr nr ldrs)	nk	**8**	12/1	60	—
2759 P	**Madam's Walk**	(NATwiston-Davies) **7-10-13** DWalsh (w.r.s: hdwy 5th: led 9th to appr 3 out: sn wknd)	16	**9**	50/1	45	—
1013 8	**Counter Attack (IRE)**	(MissAEEmbiricos) **6-10-13** KGaule (bhd fr 8th)	dist	**10**	50/1	—	—
3133 5	**Holkham Bay**	(LWordingham) **5-10-11**(7) CRae (pushed along 6th: sn bhd)	4	**11**	50/1	—	—
2759 11	**Jet Files (IRE)**	(MrsJPitman) **6-11-4** RFarrant (plld hrd: prom to 7th: t.o whn p.u bef 2 out)		**P**	14/1	—	—
3190*	**Sammorello (IRE)**	(NATwiston-Davies) **6-11-10** CMaude (led to 4th: led 8th to next: sn wknd: p.u bef last)		**P**	25/1	—	—
3283 U	**Push On Polly (IRE)**	(JParkes) **7-10-13** GCahill (hmpd s: j.slowly & rdn 3rd: t.o fr 8th: p.u bef 2 out)		**P**	50/1	—	—
2812 9	**Ely's Harbour (IRE)**	(OSherwood) **6-11-4** JOsborne (w ldrs: led 4th to 8th: sn wknd: p.u bef 2 out)		**P**	16/1	—	—

(SP 139.9%) **15 Rn**

6m 43.5 (37.50) CSF £38.10 TOTE £2.10: £1.50 £5.00 £1.40 (£29.50) Trio £39.30 OWNER Mrs R. J. Skan (TEMPLE GUITING) BRED Mrs E. A. Prowting

STEWARDS' ENQUIRY Fortt susp. 8 & 10/3/97 (excessive use of whip).

2546 Flying Gunner has finished second in four of his last six runs and this looks no coincidence, for despite his pilot doing everything right he only just lasted home after appearing in total control at the last. (Evens)

3048 Banny Hill Lad stalked the leaders on the outside of the pack, but looked held between the last two. Rallying under strong pressure as the winner idled, he almost snatched the spoils on the line. (25/1)

2746 Satcotino (IRE) ran another sound race and was still staying on at the line. (7/2: 9/2-3/1)

2826 Music Master (IRE) didn't settle in the first-time blinkers and again failed to last home despite a patient ride. (16/1)

2861 September Breeze (IRE) took a good hold and did appear to find this much longer trip too far for her. (16/1)

1938 Wristburn a rangy, attractive gelding, continues to take the eye and is well worth keeping in mind. (9/2)

3356 WYBOSTON NOVICES' CHASE (5-Y.O+) (Class E)

4-00 (4-02) **2m 4f 110y (16 fncs)** £3,023.25 (£906.00: £435.50: £200.25) GOING: 0.73 sec per fur (S)

	Horse	Details	Dist	Pos	SP	RR	SF
2867 F	**Teinein (FR)**	(CaptTAForster) **6-11-2** NWilliamson (hld up: hdwy 9th: mstke 11th: ev ch whn mstke 2 out: led flat: v.easily)	—	**1**	6/5 2	107++	39
3060*	**High Learie**	(AHHarvey) **7-11-8** JAMcCarthy (led tl flat: no ch w wnr)	1¼	**2**	7/1 3	112	44
3145*	**Arfer Mole (IRE) (115)**	(JABOld) **9-12-0** JOsborne (chsd ldr: mstke 12th: blnd next: sn rdn & btn: eased flat)	dist	**3**	11/10 1	—	—
	Corrib Song	(LadyHerries) **8-10-13**(3) LAspell (bit bkwd: prom to 7th: sn wl bhd)	6	**4**	33/1	—	—
3173 P	**Jolis Absent**	(MJRyan) **7-10-11** DGallagher (nt j.w: t.o fr 3rd)	1¾	**5**	20/1	—	—

				SP	RR	SF
3019P	**Benji** (TCasey) **6-10-13**(3) DFortt (chsd ldrs tl blnd & uns rdr 8th)		U	100/1	—	—

(SP 114.3%) **6 Rn**

5m 22.1 (22.10) CSF £8.76 TOTE £1.80: £1.40 £1.70 (£8.90) OWNER Mr Simon Sainsbury (LUDLOW) BRED Tomohiro Wada
1793 Teinein (FR) does not yet impress at his fences but he is a classy horse on this ground. (6/5)
3060* High Learie ran a fine race at this shorter trip but lacks anything like the pace of the winner. (7/1)
3145* Arfer Mole (IRE) lost all chance at the two quick fences down the back. Still only ten lengths down at the last, he was then eased right down. (11/10)
Corrib Song is lightly-raced but has yet to show much ability. (33/1)
1417 Jolis Absent jumped very poorly and has an awful lot of improving to do if she is going to achieve anything over fences. (20/1)

3357 LANGFORD END NOVICES' HUNTERS' CHASE (6-Y.O+) (Class H)
4-30 (4-30) **3m (19 fncs)** £1,262.25 (£378.00: £181.50: £83.25) GOING: 0.73 sec per fur (S)

				SP	RR	SF
954[14]	**Bitofamixup (IRE)** (MJRoberts) **6-12-2**(3) MrPHacking (trckd ldrs: led 15th: wandered appr last: rdn out)	—	1	7/2 1	118+	32
	Ask Antony (IRE) (TDWalford) **7-12-0**(5) MrNWilson (hdwy 13th: ev ch 2 out: hit last: unable qckn flat)	1¼	2	7/2 1	117	31
	Broad Steane (CHenn) **8-12-0**(5) MrASansome (chsd ldr: led appr 13th: hdd 15th: wknd appr 2 out)	15	3	7/2 1	107	21
	Ideal Partner (IRE) (PFNicholls) **8-11-12**(7) MrJTizzard (trckd ldrs to 15th)	dist	4	11/1 3	—	—
3208[2]	**Sands of Gold (IRE)** (CNNimmo) **9-11-12**(7) MrLLay (led tl appr 13th: wknd 4 out)	1	5	11/1 3	—	—
2951[2]	**Lurriga Glitter (IRE)** (RJSmith) **9-11-12**(7) MrSJoynes (hdwy 11th: mstke 14th: wknd next)	3	6	10/1 2	—	—
	Coolvawn Lady (IRE) (WRHalliday) **8-11-7**(7) MrSWalker (in tch tl blnd 13th)	dist	7	20/1	—	—
3173[9]	**Multi Line** (MrsPTownsley) **7-11-7**(7) MissCTownsley (dwlt: sn prom: wknd qckly 4 out)	1¼	8	40/1	—	—
	Dad's Pipe (MrsPSmith) **7-11-12**(7) MrTEGSmith (bkwd: bhd tl fell 3rd)		F	40/1	—	—
	Taura's Rascal (FJBrennan) **8-11-12**(7) MrFBrennan (in tch whn fell 7th)		F	40/1	—	—
	True Steel (JonTrice-Rolph) **11-12-0**(5) MrJTrice-Rolph (a bhd: t.o whn p.u bef 15th)		P	14/1	—	—
3089P	**Amadeus (FR)** (RobertBarr) **9-11-12**(7) MrCWard (t.o fr 8th: p.u bef 13th)		P	40/1	—	—
95[5]	**La Fontainbleau (IRE)** (DHBrown) **9-11-12**(7) MrARebori (a bhd: t.o whn p.u bef 15th)		P	50/1	—	—

(SP 115.6%) **13 Rn**

6m 30.9 (33.90) CSF £12.51 TOTE £4.00: £2.50 £1.80 £1.50 (£9.80) Trio £5.60 OWNER Mr Mike Roberts (HAILSHAM) BRED Mrs Norma G. Cook
Bitofamixup (IRE), a good winner at Higham twelve days ago, did this in fine style despite proving difficult to steer briefly, and looks sure to progress further, particularly when the ground dries up. (7/2: op 9/4)
Ask Antony (IRE) chased the winner hard in the last half-mile and will not always find one so good in a similar race. (7/2)
Broad Steane tried to make his stamina tell but was brushed aside by the two useful recruits on the home turn. (7/2)
Ideal Partner (IRE) travelled quite well until the quickening pace proved beyond him. (11/1: 6/1-12/1)
3208 Sands of Gold (IRE) didn't seem to get home over this longer trip. (11/1: 8/1-12/1)
2951 Lurriga Glitter (IRE) was stopped in his tracks by a mistake at the water. (10/1)

3358 WILDEN H'CAP HURDLE (0-110) (4-Y.O+) (Class E)
5-00 (5-00) **3m 2f (12 hdls)** £2,635.00 (£735.00: £355.00) GOING: 0.34 sec per fur (GS)

				SP	RR	SF
3088[5]	**Red Lighter (77)** (JABOld) **8-10-0** JOsborne (lw: chsd ldrs: led appr 3 out: sn clr: rdn out)	—	1	12/1	59+	3
3016[2]	**Ehtefaal (USA) (95)** (JSKing) **6-11-4** TJMurphy (hld up: hdwy 7th: kpt on fr 2 out)	6	2	9/2 2	73	17
2864*	**Tilty (USA) (101)** (AStreeter) **7-11-10v** TEley (led to 3rd: led 7th: hit 9th: sn hdd: one pce fr next)	3½	3	9/1	77	21
3157*	**Dockmaster (89)** (MissMKMilligan) **6-10-12** NWilliamson (hld up: hdwy 6th: rdn appr 2 out: wknd appr last)	22	4	4/1 1	52	—
3157[6]	**Hudson Bay Trader (USA) (84)** (PBeaumont) **10-10-7** MissPRobson (hdwy 5th: lost pl 8th: kpt on again appr last)	1½	5	8/1	46	—
2915[12]	**Quiet Mistress (79)** (WABethell) **7-10-2b** ASSmith (prom: mstke 3rd: wknd appr 3 out)	10	6	14/1	35	—
2941[4]	**Madame President (IRE) (85)** (CPMorlock) **6-10-5**(3) DFortt (rdn & hdwy 7th: wknd 9th)	5	7	5/1 3	38	—
3200[3]	**Merilena (IRE) (87)** (GAHubbard) **7-10-3**(7) NRossiter (chsd ldrs to 8th)	dist	8	10/1	—	—
3146[4]	**Rosie-B (89)** (NMBabbage) **7-10-9**(3) LAspell (swtg: bhd fr 7th)	8	9	6/1	—	—
3157[7]	**Ansuro Again (81)** (MrsMReveley) **8-10-4** GCahill (sn pushed along: a bhd: t.o whn p.u bef 2 out)		P	12/1	—	—
3180P	**Cunninghams Ford (IRE) (94)** (AHHarvey) **9-11-3b** JAMcCarthy (led 3rd to 7th: wknd qckly: p.u bef 9th)		P	33/1	—	—
3189P	**Milly le Moss (IRE) (77)** (RJEckley) **8-10-0v** VSlattery (nt j.w: a bhd: t.o fr 7th: p.u bef 2 out)		P	33/1	—	—

(SP 127.3%) **12 Rn**

6m 31.3 (25.30) CSF £64.84 CT £482.23 TOTE £20.70: £3.30 £1.50 £3.10 (£29.50) Trio £180.90 OWNER Mrs C. H. Antrobus (WROUGHTON) BRED Ian Bryant
LONG HANDICAP Red Lighter 9-7 Milly le Moss (IRE) 8-9
Red Lighter seems to have been hiding his light under a bushel so far, for this stamina test seemed to suit him and he won quite decisively. (12/1)
3016 Ehtefaal (USA) does stay forever and ran another sound race but is gradually creeping up the handicap. (9/2)
2864* Tilty (USA) set the pace, and stuck on surprisingly well once he lost the advantage. (9/1)
3157* Dockmaster is certainly back to form now but looked to find the last couple of furlongs stretching him. (4/1)
3157 Hudson Bay Trader (USA) again dropped out once things got going only to run on past beaten horses at the death. (8/1)
2008 Quiet Mistress made most when running well over course and distance in November but was unable to get to the front this time. (14/1: 8/1-16/1)

T/Plpt: £67.50 (144.91 Tckts). T/Qdpt: £4.90 (141.46 Tckts) Dk

2939-LUDLOW (R-H) (Good)
Thursday February 27th
WEATHER: overcast

3359 CORVEDALE NOVICES' HURDLE (4-Y.O+) (Class E)
2-10 (2-12) **2m (9 hdls)** £2,654.00 (£744.00: £362.00) GOING minus 0.28 sec per fur (GF)

				SP	RR	SF
2747[3]	**Green Green Desert (FR)** (OSherwood) **6-11-9** DBridgwater (s.s: stdy hdwy fr 5th: led on bit last: easily)	—	1	9/1	91+	39
2939*	**High In The Clouds (IRE)** (CaptTAForster) **5-11-9** SWynne (lw: hld up: hdwy 5th: led 3 out to last: no ch w wnr)	3½	2	6/5 1	88	36
3174[8]	**Fasil (IRE)** (NJHWalker) **4-10-7** TJenks (hld up & bhd: hdwy 6th: r.o flat)	s.h	3	33/1	81	19

	Horse	Dist	Pos	SP	RR	SF
	Midnight Legend (DNicholson) **6-11-3** RJohnson (lw: a.p: wnt 2nd appr 4th: led after 6th to 3 out: 3rd & btn whn mstke last)	5	**4**	5/1 3	76+	24
3093 3	**Formidable Partner** (MrsVCWard) **4-10-7v** JRKavanagh (rdn appr 3 out: no hdwy)	7	**5**	50/1	69	7
2668 3	**Moonax (IRE)** (BWHills) **6-11-3** BPowell (unruly s: bhd tl styd on fr 3 out: nrst fin)	3	**6**	3/1 2	66	14
2060 U	**Sharp Command** (PEccles) **4-10-7** PHolley (no hdwy fr 6th)	10	**7**	100/1	56	—
3231 R	**Florid (USA)** (CPEBrooks) **6-11-3** GBradley (lw: led tl after 6th: rdn & wknd appr 3 out)	3½	**8**	16/1	53	1
3283 4	**Geisway (CAN)** (NJHWalker) **7-11-3** MRichards (nvr nrr)	3	**9**	100/1	50	—
3148 4	**Blaze of Song** (DJWintle) **5-11-3b** LHarvey (w ldr tl wknd appr 4th)	½	**10**	50/1	49	—
1679 3	**Slippery Fin** (WGMTurner) **5-10-5(7)** NWillmington (bhd fr 6th)	6	**11**	66/1	38	—
	Toraja (NoelChance) **5-11-3** SCurran (bit bkwd: a bhd)	5	**12**	50/1	38	—
2939 6	**Glen Garnock (IRE)** (RTJuckes) **5-11-3** GaryLyons (mstkes: bhd fr 5th)	12	**13**	100/1	26	—
3075 13	**Fencer's Quest (IRE)** (CaptTAForster) **4-10-7** AThornton (lw: chsd ldrs to 5th)	1¾	**14**	66/1	25	—
3058 P	**Noblesse Oblige** (KCBailey) **4-10-7** SMcNeill (a bhd)	6	**15**	100/1	19	—
	Safecracker (CPMorlock) **4-10-7** WMcFarland (bhd whn blnd 6th: t.o)	10	**16**	100/1	9	—
	Churchworth (MissHCKnight) **6-11-3** JCulloty (blnd bdly 1st: a wl bhd: t.o)	14	**17**	50/1	—	—
1283 7	**Admiral Bruny (IRE)** (NAGaselee) **6-11-3** CLlewellyn (s.s: a wl bhd: t.o)	21	**18**	100/1	—	—

(SP 122.7%) **18 Rn**

3m 39.0 (2.00) CSF £18.34 TOTE £9.70: £2.20 £1.10 £11.90 (£9.30) Trio £182.90 OWNER Mr Darren Mercer (UPPER LAMBOURN) BRED Gainsborough Stud Management
WEIGHT FOR AGE 4yo-10lb
IN-FOCUS: **This was a hot contest for a class E.**
2747 Green Green Desert (FR), very much the forgotten horse in the betting, went some way to salvaging his reputation in a strongly-run race where his rider never had to move a muscle. He now goes to Aintree. (9/1)
2939* High In The Clouds (IRE), who seemed to start at a ridiculously short price, had his reputation well and truly dented by a horse who had one of those days when he was really on song. (6/5)
Fasil (IRE), a dual winner at Goodwood for John Benstead, stepped up considerably on his hurdling debut. A Triumph Hurdle entry, he deserves to take his chance on the strength of this run. (33/1)
Midnight Legend, a smart performer for Luca Cumani on the Flat, was at his best when forcing the pace and did his bit in a fast-run race. He would have finished closer but for missing out at the last, and holds entries for both novice events at the Festival. (5/1: op 2/1)
3093 Formidable Partner got a strong pace this time but was taking on some useful rivals here. (50/1)
2668 Moonax (IRE), who played up before the start, has been strangely campaigned en route to the Stayers' Hurdle at Cheltenham, having been kept to the minimum trip and run on two of the fastest tracks in the country. (3/1)

3360 E.B.F. TATTERSALLS (IRELAND) (QUALIFIER) NOVICES' CHASE (6-Y.O+ Mares Only) (Class D)

2-40 (2-41) **2m 4f (17 fncs)** £3,501.25 (£1,060.00: £517.50: £246.25) GOING minus 0.28 sec per fur (GF)

	Horse	Dist	Pos	SP	RR	SF
3040 5	**Tellicherry (83)** (MissHCKnight) **8-10-10** JCulloty (lw: a.p: led 2 out: drvn out)	—	**1**	11/8 1	95	—
2746 4	**Coole Hill (IRE)** (DNicholson) **6-10-10** RJohnson (hld up: mstke 5th: hdwy 10th: led 3 out to 2 out: hrd rdn & r.o flat)	nk	**2**	7/4 2	95	—
3043 3	**Jasilu (99)** (KCBailey) **7-11-8b** SMcNeill (led tl wknd 3 out)	13	**3**	3/1 3	96	—
3173 5	**Country Town** (APJones) **7-10-10** PHolley (hld up: 5th whn mstke 9th (water): no hdwy fr 13th: mstke last)	15	**4**	33/1	72	—
3043 8	**Lambrini (IRE)** (DMcCain) **7-10-10** TJenks (no hdwy fr 13th)	hd	**5**	66/1	72	—
2816 9	**Rent Day (64)** (JWMullins) **8-10-10** SCurran (bhd fr 11th: t.o)	dist	**6**	33/1	—	—
3112 F	**Summer Haven** (NMLampard) **8-10-10** MrAKinane (bhd: mstke 7th: sn t.o)	1¾	**7**	25/1	—	—
2576 5	**Eleanora Muse** (PaddyFarrell) **7-10-7(3)** GuyLewis (chsd ldrs tl wknd 13th: poor 5th whn fell 2 out)		**F**	25/1	—	—
2838 P	**Daring Hen (IRE)** (RTJuckes) **7-10-10** GaryLyons (j.bdly: sn t.o: p.u bef 12th)		**P**	66/1	—	—
2576 12	**Tinker's Cuss** (APJones) **6-10-10** LHarvey (t.o 4th: p.u bef 12th)		**P**	66/1	—	—

(SP 121.5%) **10 Rn**

5m 4.4 (12.40) CSF £3.94 TOTE £2.20: £1.10 £1.50 £1.40 (£3.10) Trio £2.90 OWNER Mrs C. Clatworthy (WANTAGE) BRED R. Jenks
2614 Tellicherry found this a lot easier than when running behind Cyborgo at Newbury last time, and now goes for the final of this series at Uttoxeter next month. (11/8)
2746 Coole Hill (IRE), graduating to fences, has been running over three miles over hurdles, and the way she kept battling to the end suggests a return to that trip would not come amiss. (7/4)
3043 Jasilu adopted her usual front-running tactics but was trying to overcome a double penalty. (3/1)

3361 FORBRA GOLD CHALLENGE CUP H'CAP CHASE (0-125) (5-Y.O+) (Class D)

3-10 (3-10) **3m (19 fncs)** £3,777.50 (£1,145.00: £560.00: £267.50) GOING minus 0.28 sec per fur (GF)

	Horse	Dist	Pos	SP	RR	SF
2758 3	**Rectory Garden (IRE) (110)** (CaptTAForster) **8-11-2** AThornton (lw: a.p: mstke 8th: wnt 2nd 12th tl appr 4 out: rallied to ld last: r.o wl)	—	**1**	11/8 1	116	48
3074 2	**Romany Creek (IRE) (117)** (JPearce) **8-11-9v** APMcCoy (lw: led tl pckd last: nt qckn)	1½	**2**	5/2 2	122	54
3074 7	**Dont Tell the Wife (112)** (CREgerton) **11-11-4** JCulloty (hld up: hdwy & ev ch 4 out: wknd last)	7	**3**	16/1	112	44
3175 3	**Royal Saxon (94)** (PBowen) **11-10-0** RJohnson (chsd ldr: reminders after 5th: rdn 9th: lost pl 15th: rallied appr 4 out: sn wknd)	12	**4**	20/1	86	18
3074 3	**Act of Parliament (IRE) (118)** (KCBailey) **9-11-10b** SMcNeill (lw: t.o fr 3rd: blnd 9th)	21	**5**	4/1 3	96	28
3185 2	**Alice Smith (95)** (BJEckley) **10-10-1ow1** WMcFarland (t.o fr 3rd)	3	**6**	9/1	71	2

(SP 111.3%) **6 Rn**

5m 58.5 (-1.50) CSF £4.92 TOTE £2.10: £1.50 £2.20 (£3.30) OWNER Lord Cadogan (LUDLOW) BRED Jeremiah Dunne
LONG HANDICAP Royal Saxon 9-12 Alice Smith 9-5
2758 Rectory Garden (IRE), let down by his jumping when beaten by his stable companion Maamur in this event last season, made amends off a 5lb higher mark. (11/8)
3074 Romany Creek (IRE) was being strongly pressed by the winner when nodding on landing at the final fence, and it is doubtful the outcome was affected. (5/2)
2004 Dont Tell the Wife was 4lb better off with the runner-up than when beating him half a length at Fakenham in December. (16/1)
3175 Royal Saxon, 2lb out of the handicap, looked rather lazy and was inclined to run in snatches. (20/1)
3074 Act of Parliament (IRE) was reported by his rider to be never going. (4/1)

3362 HENLEY HALL GOLD CHALLENGE CUP H'CAP HURDLE (0-110) (4-Y.O+) (Class E)

3-40 (3-40) **2m 5f 110y (11 hdls)** £2,682.00 (£752.00: £366.00) GOING minus 0.28 sec per fur (GF)

				SP	RR	SF
3146^{3}	**Jackson Flint (90)** (TThomsonJones) **9-10-7**$^{(7)}$ XAizpuru (hld up: hdwy 6th: led 2 out: edgd lft flat: rdn out)..	—	**1**	$13/2^{2}$	76	18
3050^{2}	**Operetto (IRE) (78)** (MrsSusanNock) **7-10-2** JRKavanagh (lw: a.p: led appr 2 out: sn hdd: one pce)............	2½	**2**	$13/2^{2}$	62	4
2941^{2}	**First Crack (84)** (FJordan) **12-10-8** SWynne (hld up: hdwy after 8th: hit 3 out: r.o one pce)	3	**3**	$7/1^{3}$	66	8
3114^{3}	**Fawley Flyer (94)** (WGMTurner) **8-10-11**$^{(7)}$ JPower (a.p: ev ch appr 3 out: one pce).......................................	2½	**4**	$13/2^{2}$	74	16
	Blatant Outburst (83) (MissSJWilton) **7-10-4**$^{(3)}$ MichaelBrennan (plld hrd: hdwy 6th: led after 8th tl appr 2 out: sn btn)	1¾	**5**	20/1	62	4
1946^{2}	**Star Performer (IRE) (100)** (AGHobbs) **6-11-3**$^{(7)}$ MrGShenkin (hld up: rdn 7th: hdwy 8th: wknd appr 3 out)..	1½	**6**	14/1	78	20
2838^{3}	**Viscount Tully (77)** (CFCJackson) **12-10-1** MissSJackson (hld up & bhd: hdwy 8th: wknd appr 3 out)..........	1¼	**7**	14/1	54	—
3013^{7}	**Derring Bridge (85)** (MrsSMJohnson) **7-10-9** RJohnson (lw: prom tl wknd appr 3 out)..	½	**8**	20/1	61	3
1718^{2}	**Desert Force (IRE) (92)** (GFierro) **8-11-2** GBradley (hld up: hdwy 3rd: wknd appr 3 out)...............................	nk	**9**	$5/1^{1}$	68	10
2632^{U}	**Bossymoss (IRE) (78)** (AStreeter) **8-10-2**^{ow2} GaryLyons (a bhd: t.o)..	25	**10**	25/1	36	—
3112^{U}	**Miss Marigold (96)** (RJHodges) **8-11-6b** BPowell (s.s: hdwy 3rd: rdn appr 6th: wknd 8th: t.o)	½	**11**	$5/1^{1}$	53	—
3013^{12}	**Better Bythe Glass (IRE) (93)** (NATwiston-Davies) **8-11-3** CLlewellyn (a bhd: t.o)...	6	**12**	16/1	46	—
3269^{10}	**Hoodwinker (IRE) (104)** (WJenks) **8-12-0b**^{1} TJenks (lw: led appr 3rd: hdd & wknd qckly after 8th: p.u bef 3 out)........		**P**	16/1	—	—
3053^{P}	**Monks Jay (IRE) (81)** (GThorner) **8-10-5** JCulloty (lost pl 6th: rallied 8th: sn wknd: p.u bef 3 out)		**P**	25/1	—	—
2882^{15}	**Deep Isle (76)** (BJLlewellyn) **11-10-0** PHolley (led tl appr 3rd: wknd qckly: t.o whn p.u bef 6th).........................		**P**	50/1	—	—

(SP 130.1%) **15 Rn**

5m 7.8 (6.80) CSF £44.82 CT £291.78 TOTE £9.00: £3.20 £2.40 £1.80 (£52.70) Trio £102.20 OWNER Mrs L. G. Turner (UPPER LAMBOURN) BRED James and Dominic Wigan

LONG HANDICAP Bossymoss (IRE) 9-11 Deep Isle 9-7

3146 Jackson Flint, who did not take to fences last season, has looked much more at home over hurdles this term. (13/2)

3050 Operetto (IRE) was stepping up from a novice handicap from a 2lb higher rating. (13/2)

2941 First Crack, dropped 2lb, again flattened a hurdle at a critical stage. (7/1)

3114 Fawley Flyer, still 8lb above the highest mark off which he has won, was already due to go down 2lb. (13/2)

Blatant Outburst, who has changed stables, showed ability and will do better when accepting restraint. (20/1)

1946 Star Performer (IRE), another to have changed stables, had plenty of weight for one beaten in a seller last time. (14/1)

3363 WEATHERBYS HUNTER CHASE RACE PLANNER HUNTERS' CHASE (6-Y.O+) (Class H)

4-10 (4-10) **3m (19 fncs)** £1,563.50 (£436.00: £210.50) GOING minus 0.28 sec per fur (GF)

				SP	RR	SF
3055^{2}	**Cape Cottage** (DJCaro) **13-11-7**$^{(7)}$ MrAPhillips (hld up: pckd 2nd (water): hdwy 13th: led 2 out: rdn out)......	—	**1**	$7/2^{3}$	108	30
	Fox Pointer (MrsLTJEvans) **12-11-9**$^{(5)}$ MrJJukes (lw: a.p: led appr 15th: hdd 2 out: rdn & one pce)	3	**2**	$5/2^{2}$	106	28
3005^{*}	**Inch Maid** (SABrookshaw) **11-11-9**$^{(7)}$ MissHBrookshaw (prom: lost pl 15th: rallied 2 out: styd on wl flat)........	¾	**3**	$10/11^{1}$	108	30
3055^{P}	**J B Lad** (HRTuck) **11-11-7**$^{(7)}$ MissPGundry (prom to 5th: bhd whn mstke 9th: t.o)...	dist	**4**	66/1	—	—
	Welsh Lightning (GCEvans) **9-11-7**$^{(7)}$ CaptRInglesant (mstkes: a bhd: t.o fr 12th)..	dist	**5**	66/1	—	—
	Kingfisher Bay (OALittle) **12-11-7**$^{(7)}$ MrGShenkin (bhd whn blnd 11th (water): sn t.o)...................................	s.h	**6**	66/1	—	—
	Star Oats (MrsRMLampard) **11-11-7**$^{(7)}$ MrAKinane (mstke 3rd: led 5th: clr after 6th: blnd 9th: hdd appr 15th: wknd qckly: p.u bef 4 out: lame)........		**P**	14/1	—	—
3005^{B}	**King of Shadows** (MissCMCarden) **10-12-0**$^{(7)}$ MrSPrior (led to 5th: mstke 11th (water): sn bhd: t.o whn p.u bef 2 out)........		**P**	25/1	—	—

(SP 118.2%) **8 Rn**

6m 8.9 (8.90) CSF £12.23 TOTE £5.30: £1.10 £1.60 £1.10 (£11.80) OWNER Mr D. J. Caro (MALMESBURY) BRED A. T. Smith

3055 Cape Cottage had no Miss Millbrook to contend with on this occasion. (7/2)

Fox Pointer went on to run some sound races after twice unseating his rider here last Spring. (5/2)

3005* Inch Maid did not get much assistance from the saddle, and served as a lesson not to take a short price in these events when an inexperienced rider is aboard. (10/11)

3364 CLEE HILL NOVICES' HURDLE (4-Y.O+) (Class E)

4-40 (4-40) **2m 5f 110y (11 hdls)** £2,556.00 (£716.00: £348.00) GOING minus 0.28 sec per fur (GF)

				SP	RR	SF
2886^{5}	**Ionio (USA) (118)** (MrsVCWard) **6-11-10** JRKavanagh (a.p: wnt 2nd 6th: rdn appr 3 out: led flat: r.o wl)	—	**1**	$5/2^{2}$	79	25
2701^{3}	**Cherokee Chief** (OSherwood) **6-11-4** MRichards (hld up: hdwy 7th: led appr 3 out: rdn appr 2 out: hdd flat)	1¾	**2**	$2/1^{1}$	72	18
3075^{9}	**Ezanak (IRE)** (MissHCKnight) **4-10-7** JCulloty (hld up & bhd: hdwy appr 3 out: n.d)	24	**3**	$7/2^{3}$	54	—
3172^{4}	**Brookhampton Lane (IRE)** (MrsAJBowlby) **6-11-4** BPowell (chsd ldrs tl lost pl 6th: styd on fr 3 out: n.d).....	1¼	**4**	8/1	53	—
872^{10}	**Carlingford Gale (IRE)** (TRGeorge) **6-10-13** SWynne (plld hrd: led appr 3rd: hdd appr 3 out: wknd qckly)....	19	**5**	12/1	34	—
1920^{U}	**High Handed (IRE)** (THCaldwell) **6-11-4** GaryLyons (nvr nr ldrs)	¾	**6**	50/1	38	—
3052^{9}	**Lady of Mine** (PBowen) **7-10-13** RJohnson (prom: lost pl appr 6th: rallied 7th: wknd after 8th)	¾	**7**	100/1	33	—
3054^{9}	**Brownscroft** (MissPMWhittle) **9-10-6**$^{(7)}$ KHibbert (bhd fr 6th: t.o)..	18	**8**	100/1	19	—
3109^{10}	**South West Express (IRE)** (DJWintle) **5-10-11**$^{(7)}$ MrAWintle (a bhd: t.o)..	2	**9**	25/1	23	—
1594^{7}	**Roc Age (68)** (GWDavies) **6-11-0**$^{(7)ow8}$ JTNolan (dropped rr after 5th: t.o)...	3	**10**	66/1	24	—
3041^{12}	**Mister Goodguy (IRE)** (RCurtis) **8-10-13**$^{(5)}$ ABates (led tl appr 3rd: wknd after 8th: t.o)	¾	**11**	33/1	20	—
3054^{2}	**Arioso (60)** (JLNeedham) **9-10-10**$^{(3)}$ MichaelBrennan (swtg: hld up: hdwy 7th: wknd after 8th: t.o)................	14	**12**	10/1	5	—
2566^{9}	**Red Lane** (JDDownes) **7-11-4** MrADalton (a bhd: t.o)	4	**13**	100/1	7	—
3021^{12}	**Seven Four Seven** (MrsLWilliamson) **6-10-13** SMcNeill (a bhd: t.o)...	10	**14**	100/1	—	—
2965^{2}	**Kylami (NZ)** (AGHobbs) **5-11-4** RGreene (fell 2nd)..		**F**	25/1	—	—
3019^{P}	**A Badge Too Far (IRE)** (MrsLWilliamson) **7-10-13** RBellamy (plld hrd: prom tl wknd 5th: t.o whn p.u after 8th).		**P**	100/1	—	—
2746^{12}	**One More Rupee** (CPMorlock) **6-11-4** AThornton (reminders after 3rd: t.o after 4th: p.u bef 3 out)		**P**	100/1	—	—

(SP 132.0%) **17 Rn**

5m 8.3 (7.30) CSF £7.75 TOTE £3.20: £1.40 £1.70 £1.30 (£4.80) Trio £5.90 OWNER Mrs R F Key & Mrs V C Ward (GRANTHAM) BRED Flaxman Holdings Ltd

WEIGHT FOR AGE 4yo-11lb

2886 Ionio (USA), highly tried in his last two outings, was supported in the ring and bounced back to form. (5/2)

2701 Cherokee Chief, could not hold the winner but beat the others easily enough and can take a similar event. (2/1: op 5/4)

Ezanak (IRE), bought for 22,000 guineas at Newmarket Autumn Sales, is a half-brother to Erzadjan. Given a lot to do, it should be noted that he ran his best race on his final outing on the Flat in Ireland wearing first-time blinkers. (7/2: op 2/1)
3172 Brookhampton Lane (IRE), a half-brother to staying chaser Brave Highlander, seems blessed with stamina rather than speed. (8/1:6/1-10/1)
Carlingford Gale (IRE), the winner of a maiden Point in Ireland, was a springer in the market in her bumper, and ran much too freely on this hurdling debut. (12/1: 7/1-14/1)
3054 Arioso (10/1: op 16/1)

3365 BORDER INTERMEDIATE OPEN N.H. FLAT RACE (4, 5 & 6-Y.O) (Class H)
5-10 (5-13) **2m** £1,266.00 (£351.00: £168.00)

	Horse	Details	Dist	Pos	SP	RR	SF
1834[6]	**Benvenuto**	(KCBailey) **6-11-4** SMcNeill (a.p: led over 2f out: clr over 1f out: r.o wl)	—	**1**	9/2[3]	65 f	—
	Good Lord Murphy (IRE)	(PJHobbs) **5-11-4** LHarvey (hdwy over 4f out: styd on fnl f)	10	**2**	8/1	55 f	—
2804[2]	**Es Go**	(RBastiman) **4-10-5**(3) HBastiman (led after 4f: hdd over 2f out: eased whn btn nr fin)	½	**3**	100/30[2]	55 f	—
	Count Karmuski	(WJenks) **5-11-4** TJenks (bhd tl hdwy 5f out: nt rch ldrs)	6	**4**	33/1	49 f	—
2931[6]	**Miss Match**	(LGCottrell) **6-10-8**(5) OBurrows (prom tl rdn & wknd over 2f out)	4	**5**	10/1	40 f	—
3235[2]	**Filscot**	(WGMTurner) **5-10-11**(7) JPower (prom tl wknd over 3f out)	9	**6**	6/1	36 f	—
2844[14]	**Boundtohonour (IRE)**	(HOliver) **5-11-4** JacquiOliver (bhd tl r.o fnl 4f: nvr nrr)	½	**7**	20/1	35 f	—
3006[10]	**Ta-Ra-Abit (IRE)**	(TWall) **4-10-3** BPowell (n.d)	9	**8**	66/1	21 f	—
3235[10]	**Two Lords**	(GAHam) **5-11-4** SBurrough (prom 8f)	10	**9**	50/1	16 f	—
	Gallant Taffy	(MrsLWilliamson) **5-11-4** CLlewellyn (bkwd: wl bhd after 6f)	10	**10**	50/1	6 f	—
	Cariboo (IRE)	(BPreece) **5-10-11**(7) JMogford (bhd fnl 6f)	nk	**11**	50/1	6 f	—
2904[8]	**Strong Magic (IRE)**	(MissCJohnsey) **5-11-1**(3) MichaelBrennan (wl bhd after 6f)	1¼	**12**	20/1	4 f	—
3170[15]	**Celtic Carrot**	(RJPrice) **5-11-4** JRKavanagh (prom 11f)	¾	**13**	50/1	4 f	—
3170[17]	**Haberdasher**	(MissPMWhittle) **6-10-11**(7) KHibbert (a bhd)	8	**14**	50/1	—	—
2844[16]	**Oriental Boy (IRE)**	(RLee) **5-11-4** RJohnson (bhd fnl 8f)	2	**15**	50/1	—	—
	Ask In Time (IRE)	(MissHCKnight) **5-11-4** DBridgwater (hld up: hdwy after 5f: wknd qckly 4f out: eased whn btn)	3	**16**	11/8[1]	—	—
3170[21]	**Ginger Watt (IRE)**	(RJPrice) **5-11-1**(3) TDascombe (a bhd: t.o)	dist	**17**	33/1	—	—
2811[18]	**Miss Mighty**	(JHPeacock) **4-10-3** RBellamy (led 4f: wknd 8f out: t.o)	dist	**18**	100/1	—	—

(SP 147.5%) **18 Rn**

3m 38.5 CSF £41.35 TOTE £5.90: £2.00 £3.40 £2.20 (£58.40) Trio £13.60 OWNER Mrs Lucia Farmer (UPPER LAMBOURN) BRED Mrs K. I. Hayward
WEIGHT FOR AGE 4yo-10lb
STEWARDS' ENQUIRY Bastiman susp. 8 & 10-11/3/97 (failure to ensure best possible placing).
1834 Benvenuto ran out a most convincing winner and is seemingly progressing along the right lines. (9/2)
Good Lord Murphy (IRE) stretched out well in the closing stages to steal second prize. (8/1: 4/1-10/1)
2804 Es Go could not go with the winner, and his rider picked up a three-day ban, when dropping his hands after looking over the wrong shoulder close home. (100/30)
Count Karmuski is a half-brother to a winner of an Irish Point. (33/1)
2931 Miss Match again ran well until failing to last home. (10/1)
3235 Filscot folded up tamely inside the last half-mile. (6/1: op 3/1)
Ask In Time (IRE) did not live up to the market support. (11/8)

T/Jkpt: £33,207.50 (1.56 Tckts). T/Plpt: £5.50 (2,662.2 Tckts). T/Qdpt: £2.80 (212.82 Tckts) KH

3345-WETHERBY (L-H) (Heavy)
Thursday February 27th
One fence & one flight omitted all races.
WEATHER: overcast and raining

3366 REPLACEMENT 'N.H.' NOVICES' HURDLE (4-Y.O+) (Class E)
2-20 (2-20) **2m (8 hdls)** £2,389.50 (£672.00: £328.50) GOING: 1.92 sec per fur (HY)

	Horse	Details	Dist	Pos	SP	RR	SF
3000[2]	**Gods Squad**	(JMackie) **5-11-2** RSupple (chsd ldrs: effrt appr 3 out: rdn to ld flat)	—	**1**	4/1[2]	87	35
3139[3]	**Good Vibes (116)**	(TDEasterby) **5-11-7** LWyer (led fr 2nd: rdn flat: sn hdd & no ex)	1¾	**2**	4/5[1]	90	38
2904[6]	**Banker Count**	(MWEasterby) **5-10-13**(3) PMidgley (lw: hld up: hdwy 3 out: mstke 2 out: styd on)	9	**3**	33/1	76	24
	Lord Fortune (IRE)	(MDHammond) **7-11-2** RGarritty (in tch: hdwy appr 3 out: r.o one pce)	7	**4**	16/1	69	17
2785[2]	**Ardarroch Prince**	(MrsMReveley) **6-11-2** PNiven (lw: a.p: effrt appr 3 out: one pce)	s.h	**5**	5/1[3]	69	17
3019[F]	**Ferrers (85)**	(MrsPSly) **6-11-2** WMarston (hld up: hdwy 3 out: nvr trbld ldrs)	1¼	**6**	10/1	68	16
2627[P]	**Edstone (IRE)**	(JWCurtis) **5-11-2** DerekByrne (led to 2nd: cl up tl wknd appr 3 out)	11	**7**	100/1	57	5
2066[11]	**Strong Mint (IRE)**	(MrsMReveley) **6-10-13**(3) GLee (hld up: shkn up appr 3 out: sn btn)	12	**8**	9/1	45	—
	Second Fiddle (IRE)	(OBrennan) **7-10-11** MBrennan (chsd ldrs: hit 5th: sn lost pl)	14	**9**	16/1	26	—
1362[7]	**Skiddaw Knight (IRE)**	(MrsMReveley) **6-11-2** NSmith (blnd 2nd: sme hdwy after 5th: sn wknd)	3½	**10**	33/1	27	—
	Perky Too (IRE)	(HowardJohnson) **5-11-2** PCarberry (mstke 5th: t.o whn p.u 2 out)		**P**	20/1	—	—

(SP 134.7%) **11 Rn**

4m 18.9 (36.90) CSF £8.08 TOTE £6.60: £1.20 £1.30 £10.70 (£5.10) Trio £71.10 OWNER Mr R. M. Kirkland (CHURCH BROUGHTON) BRED Mrs A. C. Wakeham
3000 Gods Squad handled this ground well, and in particular it was his staying power that won the day, and there are going to be plenty more opportunities for him. Another half-mile would not go amiss. (4/1: 3/1-5/1)
3139 Good Vibes jumped well out in front but, despite wearing his now customary pricker on his off-side, he did tend to edge to his right and didn't find as much as looked likely when ridden. (4/5: op 5/4)
2904 Banker Count put in a decent hurdles debut, and was given a fairly sympathetic ride, and once he gets his jumping together there should be some improvement. (33/1)
Lord Fortune (IRE), running for the first time for over a year, and making his hurdles debut, showed plenty and should now improve. (16/1)
2785 Ardarroch Prince again had his chances, but proved short of toe and perhaps longer trips will bring out the best in him. (5/1)
2010 Ferrers had a nice confidence booster, and should pick up a race in due course. (10/1)
Edstone (IRE), who had shown nothing previously, gave some signs of encouragement here. (100/1)

2066 Strong Mint (IRE) (9/1: 6/1-10/1)

3367 UNDERSTUDY NOVICES' CHASE (5-Y.O+) (Class E)
2-50 (2-50) **2m 4f 110y (14 fncs)** £3,317.50 (£930.00: £452.50) GOING: 1.92 sec per fur (HY)

				SP	RR	SF
3141[2]	**River Unshion (IRE) (98)** (HowardJohnson) **7-11-3** PCarberry (hld up: hdwy to disp ld 7th: led 4 out: sn clr)	—	**1**	4/11[1]	101	46
3099[2]	**Tico Gold (84)** (PCheesbrough) **9-11-8** RSupple (disp ld tl blnd 4 out: no imp after)	13	**2**	5/2[2]	96	41
3097[3]	**Alicat (IRE)** (JWCurtis) **6-11-3** DerekByrne (disp ld: hit 6th: wknd appr next: sn t.o)	dist	**3**	20/1[3]	—	—
				(SP 106.7%)	**3 Rn**	

5m 51.9 (44.90) CSF £1.52 TOTE £1.40: (£1.80) OWNER Mr R. J. Crake (CROOK) BRED Jerry Regan
3141 River Unshion (IRE) went well in these conditions and, when his only serious rival blundered four out, the race was his. (4/11)
3099 Tico Gold, without the blinkers this time, made a race of it until blundering all chances away four from home. (5/2)
3097 Alicat (IRE) looked very moderate. (20/1)

3368 PROXY NOVICES' HURDLE (5-Y.O+) (Class E)
3-20 (3-20) **3m 1f (10 hdls)** £2,337.00 (£657.00: £321.00) GOING: 1.92 sec per fur (HY)

				SP	RR	SF
2880*	**Young Kenny (118)** (PBeaumont) **6-11-7** RSupple (lw: swtg: trckd ldrs: led appr 3 out: clr whn hit 2 out: easily)	—	**1**	13/8[2]	90+	27
2627[2]	**Smart Approach (IRE) (98)** (MrsMReveley) **7-10-12** PNiven (lw: a.p: outpcd after 7th: styd on fr 2 out: no ch w wnr)	16	**2**	8/1	71	8
3066*	**Military Academy (119)** (GRichards) **8-11-3** PCarberry (lw: chsd ldrs: chal & hit 7th: sn rdn & btn)	nk	**3**	11/10[1]	76	13
2900[2]	**Share Options (IRE) (105)** (TDEasterby) **6-11-3** LWyer (led tl hdd appr 3 out: sn wknd: fin tired)	26	**4**	7/1[3]	59	—
2915[7]	**The Other Man (IRE) (66)** (MissLCSiddall) **7-10-12** OPears (bhd: effrt 6th: sn rdn & btn)	13	**5**	50/1	46	—
3100[6]	**La Chance (53)** (MrsHLWalton) **7-10-12v[1]** MrAWalton (cl up to 4th: sn outpcd & t.o)	dist	**6**	100/1	—	—
2917[9]	**Dromore Dream (IRE)** (MrsJBrown) **8-10-12** ADobbin (lw: prom tl mstke 6th: sn wknd: t.o whn p.u bef 3 out)		**P**	25/1	—	—
				(SP 116.1%)	**7 Rn**	

6m 55.2 (62.20) CSF £13.49 TOTE £2.40: £1.10 £2.30 (£9.50) OWNER Mr J. G. Read (BRANDSBY) BRED Mowbray Properties Ltd
2880* Young Kenny got a little stirred up beforehand, but his performance was superb, and these testing conditions really brought out the best in him. (13/8)
2627 Smart Approach (IRE) ran well in this company, staying on determinedly from three out, but the winner was in a different league. (8/1)
3066* Military Academy is from a yard that is in and out of form at the moment, and he was already in trouble when blundering at the seventh, from which point he had no further hopes. (11/10: evens-4/5)
2900 Share Options (IRE) was bowling along in front looking the only one likely to trouble the winner when he suddenly bottomed out on the home turn and, extremely tired, it was all he could do to finish. (7/1)
The Other Man (IRE) was never anything like good enough. (50/1)
2917 Dromore Dream (IRE) is a good-looking sort but proved disappointing, but by sticking to the inner he was always racing in the worst ground. (25/1)

3369 WEATHERBYS INSURANCE SERVICES H'CAP CHASE (0-135) (5-Y.O+) (Class C)
3-50 (3-52) **2m (11 fncs)** £4,571.00 (£1,281.00: £623.00) GOING: 1.92 sec per fur (HY)

				SP	RR	SF
3064[3]	**Political Tower (128)** (RNixon) **10-11-10** ADobbin (lw: hld up: outpcd & hit 4 out: rdn to ld 2 out: hit last: styd on)	—	**1**	6/5[1]	131	68
3225[2]	**Regal Romper (IRE) (111)** (MrsSJSmith) **9-10-7** RichardGuest (led: hit 2nd: qcknd 4 out: hdd 2 out: hit last: no ex)	6	**2**	2/1[2]	108	45
3160[4]	**Cross Cannon (105)** (JWade) **11-10-1** BStorey (lw: chsd ldr: hit 2nd: ev ch 4 out: outpcd fr next)	13	**3**	11/4[3]	89	26
				(SP 105.5%)	**3 Rn**	

4m 23.4 (31.40) CSF £3.37 TOTE £2.10 (£1.10) OWNER Mr G. R. S. Nixon (SELKIRK) BRED R. Nixon
3064 Political Tower was in trouble when the pace increased entering the straight, but he was the one most likely to act in this ground, and that proved to be decisive from the second last. (6/5: evens-5/4)
3225 Regal Romper (IRE), a fast-ground lover, was given an intelligent ride here, but the conditions eventually found him out. (2/1)
3160 Cross Cannon, happier on faster ground and at Sedgefield, ran well to the third last. (11/4)

3370 SUBSTITUTE NOVICES' H'CAP CHASE (0-115) (5-Y.O+) (Class D)
4-20 (4-21) **3m 1f (16 fncs)** £3,566.25 (£1,080.00: £527.50: £251.25) GOING: 1.92 sec per fur (HY)

				SP	RR	SF
2788[3]	**Coverdale Lane (90)** (MrsSJSmith) **10-11-10** RichardGuest (lw: j.w: led fr 3rd: clr fr 12th: wknd flat)	—	**1**	3/1[1]	105	—
3099*	**Gold Pigeon (IRE) (75)** (BSRothwell) **8-10-9** BStorey (prom: chsd wnr fr 12th: kpt on u.p flat: nrst fin)	2½	**2**	8/1[3]	88	—
3141[6]	**Garbo's Boy (79)** (JRTurner) **7-10-13** DParker (wnt prom 6th: outpcd whn blnd 10th: n.d after)	dist	**3**	12/1	—	—
3067[3]	**D'Arblay Street (IRE) (80)** (WTKemp) **8-11-0** PCarberry (chsd ldrs: wnt 2nd 9th: hit 11th: sn btn)	dist	**4**	3/1[1]	—	—
2699[4]	**Be Brave (78)** (TJEtherington) **7-10-12** RRourke (lw: mstkes: chsd ldrs: 5th & rdn whn fell 9th)		**F**	6/1[2]	—	—
3067[F]	**Noosa Sound (IRE) (79)** (LLungo) **7-10-13** RSupple (lw: outpcd 8th: sn lost tch: t.o whn p.u bef 4 out)		**P**	6/1[2]	—	—
3181[3]	**Plassy Boy (IRE) (70)** (KRBurke) **8-10-4** ADobbin (prom to 7th: sn wknd: p.u bef 9th)		**P**	8/1[3]	—	—
3067[F]	**Quixall Crossett (66)** (EMCaine) **12-9-7**(7) TristanDavidson (t.o fr 5th: p.u bef 4 out)		**P**	50/1	—	—
	King of Steel (86) (MDHammond) **11-11-6** RGarritty (led to 3rd: cl up whn blnd & uns rdr 5th)		**U**	16/1	—	—
				(SP 116.3%)	**9 Rn**	

7m 9.3 CSF £25.04 CT £230.35 TOTE £4.90: £1.90 £1.20 £4.90 (£12.00) Trio £136.70 OWNER Mr Jim Pilkington (BINGLEY) BRED Mrs M. J. Cole
LONG HANDICAP Quixall Crossett 9-4
2788 Coverdale Lane, well handled, jumped and galloped her rivals into the ground on the final circuit and, despite tying up on the run-in, was never in any danger. (3/1)
3099* Gold Pigeon (IRE) went in pursuit of the winner five out, but it was only her rider's persistence that got her so close. (8/1: 6/1-9/1)
3141 Garbo's Boy spoiled his chances with a terrible blunder in the back straight, and jumping has always been his problem. (12/1)
3067 D'Arblay Street (IRE) ran pretty well in this ground and should be kept in mind for drier conditions. (3/1)
2699 Be Brave looked clumsy, and was being asked a question when falling at the first fence in the back straight. (6/1)
3067 Noosa Sound (IRE), not surprisingly after his fall last time, was never happy here. (6/1: op 7/2)

3371 SURROGATE NOVICES' H'CAP HURDLE (0-115) (4-Y.O+) (Class D)
4-50 (4-51) **2m 4f 110y (8 hdls)** £2,871.00 (£806.00: £393.00) GOING: 1.92 sec per fur (HY)

Form	Horse		Pos	SP	RR	SF
	Into the West (IRE) (96) (MrsSJSmith) **8-11-10** RichardGuest (lw: hld up: a gng wl: led last: r.o)	—	1	11/2	80+	41
3102*	**Enchanted Cottage (78)** (JMJefferson) **5-10-3**(3) ECallaghan (trckd ldrs: led appr 3 out tl hdd & mstke last: sn btn)	4	2	11/8[1]	59	20
2947[P]	**Bassenhally (89)** (MrsPSly) **7-11-3** WMarston (led tl hdd, rdn & wknd appr 3 out)	dist	3	9/1	—	—
3004[5]	**Dont Forget Curtis (IRE) (87)** (GMMoore) **5-11-1** JCallaghan (prom tl outpcd appr 3 out: n.d after)	2	4	4/1[2]	—	—
3313[3]	**Obvious Risk (72)** (EMCaine) **6-9-7**(7) TristanDavidson (prom to 5th: wknd & sn t.o: virtually p.u flat)	dist	5	14/1	—	—
2898[4]	**Mudlark (90)** (JNorton) **5-11-4** WDwan (prom: mstke 4th: sn outpcd: virtually p.u flat)	10	6	5/1[3]	—	—
3158[12]	**Greenfinch (CAN) (72)** (MrsAMNaughton) **6-10-0v** MFoster (prom early: outpcd & lost tch 5th: p.u bef last)		P	14/1	—	—
				(SP 117.5%)	**7 Rn**	

5m 34.5 (47.50) CSF £13.31 CT £62.34 TOTE £5.20: £2.40 £1.10 (£7.00) Trio £19.70 OWNER Mr J. Mason (BINGLEY) BRED Edward Kearns
LONG HANDICAP Obvious Risk 9-2 Greenfinch (CAN) 9-7

Into the West (IRE), off the track for over two years, was turned out in fine trim. Given a superb ride picking the best ground, he was always traveling best and won nicely. (11/2: 5/1-8/1)

3102* Enchanted Cottage showed he is still in good heart and put up a game performance, but he was getting the worst of the exchanges when the winner cramped him for room when he made a mess of the last. (11/8)

1253* Bassenhally, back to hurdling after an unsuccessful attempt at chasing, ran reasonably to the third last. (9/1: 6/1-10/1)

2662 Dont Forget Curtis (IRE), a weak-looking individual, was stuck in the mud by the home turn. (4/1)

3313 Obvious Risk had his limitations exposed a long way out. (14/1)

2898 Mudlark didn't live up to his name. (5/1)

T/Plpt: £32.70 (250.06 Tckts). T/Qdpt: £15.00 (28.6 Tckts) AA

3372a - 3379a & 3381a : (Irish Racing) - See Computer Raceform

3236a-NAAS (Ireland) (L-H) (Yielding to soft)
Saturday February 22nd

3380a NAS NI RIOGH E.B.F. NOVICES' CHASE (Gd 3) (5-Y.O+)
2-30 (2-31) **2m 4f (13 fncs)** IR £6,850.00 (IR £1,550.00: IR £650.00: IR £350.00) GOING: Not Established

Form	Horse		Pos	SP	RR	SF
	Corket (IRE) (APO'Brien,Ireland) **7-11-9** THorgan (j.w: mde all: drew clr 2 out: styd on wl: easily)	—	1	2/5[1]	120+	46
3255a[2]	**Le Ginno (FR)** (TFoley,Ireland) **10-11-6** TPTreacy (slow 1st: sn chsng ldr: chal & ev ch 2 out: rdn, drifted lft & nt qckn)	15	2	5/1[2]	105	34
	Maid For Dancing (IRE) (JRHFowler,Ireland) **8-10-4**(7) MrRHFowler (cl up early: lost tch 4 out: kpt on flat)	3	3	9/1[3]	94	24
	Shisoma (IRE) (PDay,Ireland) **7-11-2** JPBroderick (hld up: mstke 6th: chsd wnr whn mstke 3 out: one pce)	.nk	4	9/1[3]	98	28
				(SP 108.1%)	**4 Rn**	

5m 52.1 (32.10) OWNER S. J. O'Sullivan (PILTOWN)

Corket (IRE), completing his hat-trick over fences in some style, had nothing to beat and, making all, drew clear between the last two to win unchallenged. He has a choice of three Cheltenham engagements, with the Cathcart favoured at the moment. His jumping is exemplary for a novice. (2/5)

2856a Le Ginno (FR) stayed in touch until approaching two out. (5/1)

Maid For Dancing (IRE), a long way behind five out, stayed on to go third close home. (9/1)

Shisoma (IRE) made his quota of mistakes and dropped away after a blunder three out. (9/1: op 6/1)

3382a JOHNSTOWN E.B.F. NOVICES' HURDLE (Gd 3) (5-Y.O+)
3-30 (3-30) **2m 4f (11 hdls)** IR £9,675.00 (IR £2,775.00: IR £1,275.00: IR £375.00) GOING: Not Established

Form	Horse		Pos	SP	RR	SF
2857a[5]	**Delphi Lodge (IRE)** (TJTaaffe,Ireland) **7-11-3** CO'Dwyer (hld up: hdwy 3 out: chal 2 out: rdn to led flat: styd on)	—	1	8/1	105	49
2995a[6]	**Tarthooth (IRE)** (ALTMoore,Ireland) **6-11-9** FWoods (2nd & disp ld: led 5th: hdd 3 out: disp ld again 2 out: ev ch last: rallied u.p flat)	nk	2	3/1[1]	111	54
3126a[6]	**Difficult Times (IRE)** (GMLyons,Ireland) **5-11-6** SCLyons (cl up early: chsd ldrs whn mstke 3 out: rdn & nt rch ldrs appr last)	2	3	8/1	109	50
	Kings Return (IRE) (WPMullins,Ireland) **6-11-9** DJCasey (hld up: wnt 3rd at 6th: led 3 out: jnd bef 2 out: hdd flat: no ex)	1	4	9/2[2]	108	52
	Cairncross (IRE) (KWoods,Ireland) **6-11-3** JPBroderick (hld up towards rr: trckd ldrs 2 out: nt rch ldrs nr last)	2	5	14/1	101	45
	Gazalani (IRE) (POBrady,Ireland) **5-10-11** TPTreacy (in tch: chsd ldrs whn mstke 3 out: rdn & nt qckn after 2 out)	9	6	7/1[3]	91	34
	Coq Hardi Venture (IRE) (NMeade,Ireland) **6-11-3** RHughes (hld up: hdwy 4 out: 3rd 3 out: rdn & btn bef 2 out)	2½	7	7/1[3]	92	38
	Jodesi (IRE) (WPMullins,Ireland) **7-10-12**(5) PMorris (cl up: led briefly 4th: mstke next & 4 out: sn wknd: t.o)	25	8	11/1	72	22
	Clady Boy (IRE) (SAKirk,Ireland) **6-10-10**(7) RPHogan (plld hrd: disp ld tl appr 4th: mstke & reminders7th: rdn 4 out: lost pl bef next: t.o)	15	9	16/1	60	12
2857a[4]	**Buggy (IRE)** (KFarrelly,Ireland) **8-11-3** TJMitchell (mstke 1st: hld up: hdwy & 5th 4 out: rdn & lost pl bef next: p.u bef 2 out)		P	7/1[3]	—	—
				(SP 123.8%)	**10 Rn**	

5m 6.7 (8.70) OWNER Mark Ferran (STRAFFAN)

2347a Delphi Lodge (IRE) got a very patient ride, being taken back when landing third two out. Making his effort at the last, he stayed on well under pressure on the flat and certainly gets this trip. Soft ground is essential. (8/1: op 5/1)

2995a Tarthooth (IRE) put his moderate effort last time well behind him. Leading and disputing the advantage throughout, he was under strong pressure from the last and just could not produce any more. His rider was given a £200 fine for using his whip with excessive force and frequency. (3/1)

1156 Difficult Times (IRE) blundered three out and lost his place, but came back for more from two out and stayed on well on the flat. (8/1: op 5/1)

Kings Return (IRE) got to the front three out but, joined before the last, looked very one-paced. (9/2: op 5/2)
Cairncross (IRE) looked outclassed in this company on previous form, but came through with plenty of kudos. He just could not quicken from the last. (14/1)
Gazalani (IRE), ridden along to hold his place three out, weakened from the second last. (7/1)

3383a Q.K. COLD STORES NEWLANDS (LISTED) CHASE (5-Y.O+)
4-00 (4-00) **2m 40y (10 fncs)** IR £12,900.00 (IR £3,700.00: IR £1,700.00: IR £500.00) GOING: Not Established

				SP	RR	SF
2741a6	**Opera Hat (IRE)** (JRHFowler,Ireland) **9-11-4** APowell (led tl after 2nd: cl 2nd 4 out: led after 3 out: rdn & styd on flat)	—	1	2/1 1	153	58
3245a*	**Merry Gale (IRE)** (JTRDreaper,Ireland) **9-11-9** CO'Dwyer (hld up in tch: cld after next: led 6th: hdd after 3 out: one pce)	4½	2	5/2 2	154	59
3245a2	**Royal Mountbrowne** (APO'Brien,Ireland) **9-11-9** THorgan (sn led: mstke & hdd next: cl 3rd 3 out: nt qckn 2 out)	3	3	8/1	151	56
2602a*	**Time for a Run** (EJO'Grady,Ireland) **10-11-2** MrPFenton (towards rr: reminders 4th: mstke 4 out: no imp appr 2 out)	8	4	10/1	136	44
2848a5	**The Crazy Bishop (IRE)** (AMullins,Ireland) **9-11-5b** TPTreacy (prom: led after 2nd: mstke 5th: hdd bef next: mod 4th & slow 3 out: no imp appr next)	4	5	6/1 3	135	43
3128a2	**Idiots Venture** (APO'Brien,Ireland) **10-11-5** MrBMCash (hld up: wnt 4th at 5th: hdwy to disp ld whn fell 4 out)		F	7/1	—	—
	Wacko Jacko (IRE) (EPMitchell,Ireland) **8-11-2** JPBroderick (a bhd: slow 3rd & 4th: p.u bef 4 out)		P	100/1	—	—
				(SP 109.9%)		**7 Rn**

4m 29.4 (21.40) OWNER Mrs T. K. Cooper (SUMMERHILL)
2741a Opera Hat (IRE) is a real course specialist, (this was her eighth win here) and she again showed her appreciation for the track. Always close up, she took over just before the straight and went away. (2/1)
3245a* Merry Gale (IRE) jumped to the front five out, but gave away quite tamely to the winner in the straight ,and just isn't the force he was. The ground was no help to him. (5/2)
3245a Royal Mountbrowne was totally outpaced by the first pair from two out but stayed on from the last. (8/1: op 5/1)
2602a* Time for a Run had no chance over the trip or at the weights, but still put in an eyecatching effort, staying on nicely in the straight without ever threatening. Given the right conditions, he can return to winning form. (10/1: op 6/1)

3384a - 3388a & 3390a : (Irish Racing) - See Computer Raceform

2986a-FAIRYHOUSE (Dublin, Ireland) (R-H) (Soft)
Sunday February 23rd

3389a E.B.F. FINAL NOVICES' H'CAP CHASE (Gd 3) (5-Y.O+)
3-45 (3-50) **3m 1f (17 fncs)** IR £9,675.00 (IR £2,775.00: IR £1,275.00: IR £375.00) GOING: 0.00 sec per fur (G)

				SP	RR	SF
3260a2	**Papillon (IRE)** (TMWalsh,Ireland) **6-11-13** NWilliamson (hld up: wnt 3rd bef 4 out: sn led: rdn clr between last 2)	—	1	7/4 1	117+	30
	Coolafinka (IRE) (JABerry,Ireland) **8-10-7** THorgan (led tl hdd 4th: cl up: led 11th: jnd 13th: hdd after 4 out: styd on)	6	2	9/1	93	9
3261aU	**Executive Options (IRE)** (JMcCaghy,Ireland) **8-11-5** PCarberry (hld up & plld hrd: trckd ldrs 4 out: nt qckn u.p after 2 out)	9	3	14/1	99	15
	Royal Rosy (IRE) (APO'Brien,Ireland) **6-11-3** CFSwan (hld up: cld bef 4 out: disp ld briefly bef next: sn rdn: no ex)	4	4	7/1	95	11
2856a2	**Amble Speedy (IRE)** (ALTMoore,Ireland) **7-12-0** FWoods (hld up towards rr: nt j.w: mod 7th whn mstke 3 out: nvr nrr)	½	5	100/30 2	106	21
	Shining Willow (JRHFowler,Ireland) **7-11-1** CO'Dwyer (cl up: led 8th to 10th: cl 2nd whn bad mstke 14th: rdn after 3 out: no imp)	15	6	9/2 3	83	2
	Baile Na Gcloch (IRE) (JPBerry,Ireland) **8-10-9**(3) DPMurphy (prom: led 4th to 7th: chsd wnr whn mstke 3 out: wknd)	25	7	10/1	64	—
1405a5	**Crehelp Express (IRE)** (VBowens,Ireland) **7-10-6**(3) BBowens (in tch: mstke 10th: mod 7th whn pckd bdly 4 out: p.u bef 2 out: b.b.v.)		P	12/1	—	—
				(SP 123.6%)		**8 Rn**

6m 54.2 (23.20) OWNER Mrs Maxwell Moran (KILL)
3260a Papillon (IRE) really appreciated this trip and, going up to dispute the lead four out, was soon in control. He went clear between the last two for an easy win. Upped 7lb for this effort, he might find things more difficult in the future and the value of this form (he beat a mare 7lb out of the handicap) may be questionable. (7/4)
Coolafinka (IRE) had a very stiff task on paper, but acquitted herself quite well. She lost her place four out but stayed on again after the second last. She would be interesting in something like the EBF Tattersalls (Div Ireland) at Uttoxeter on Midlands National day. (9/1)
1758a Executive Options (IRE) must have regained a lot of his confidence here. He jumped up to join the leaders four out, but looked beaten when making a mistake two out and wandered about afterwards. (14/1)
Royal Rosy (IRE) would give the outside to no-one until weakening before the straight. She was going on again at the finish with no chance of getting on terms. (7/1)
2856a Amble Speedy (IRE) was never placed to deliver any sort of challenge. (100/30)
1240a Crehelp Express (IRE) (12/1: op 8/1)

3391a HURLEY RIVER HUNTERS' CHASE (5-Y.O+)
4-45 (4-54) **3m 1f (17 fncs)** IR £3,425.00 (IR £775.00: IR £325.00: IR £175.00) GOING: Not Established

				SP	RR	SF
2998a5	**Stay In Touch (IRE)** (JJCostello,Ireland) **7-11-11**(3) MrDPCostello (mde all: hdd briefly last: rallied: styd on u.p)	—	1	7/4 2	108	27
	Irish Stout (IRE) (AJMartin,Ireland) **6-11-1**(3) MrRWalsh (hld up towards rr: 2nd bef 2 out: chal to ld & mstke last: hdd flat:)	½	2	33/1	98	18
	Bob Treacy (IRE) (MWHickey,Ireland) **8-11-2**(7) MrAGCostello (s.s: hdwy 7th: 3rd & lost tch next)	dist	3	7/1	—	23
	Only One (IRE) (JFBrennan,Ireland) **7-10-11**(7) MrMO'Connor (mstks: 2nd after 2nd tl appr 10th: lost pl: t.o)	dist	4	40/1	—	18

				SP	RR	SF
2998a[4]	**Life of a King (IRE)** (WPMullins,Ireland) **9-11-9** MrJANash (hld up: 4th & chsg ldrs whn fell 15th)		F	11/2[3]	—	—
	Dixon Varner (IRE) (EBolger,Ireland) **7-11-9** MrPFenton (hld up: 2nd fr 13th: chsd wnr 4 out: rdn next: 3rd & btn whn fell 2 out)		F	5/4[1]	—	—
	Upshepops (IRE) (MissSReidy,Ireland) **9-10-7**(7)ow1 MrAnthonyCostello (cl up early: 3rd whn fell 14th)		F	50/1	—	—
	Killmurray Buck (IRE) (AJWhelan,Ireland) **9-11-0**ow1 MrGJHarford (mstkes: sn towards rr: p.u bef 12th)		P	50/1	—	—

(SP 118.0%) **8 Rn**

6m 55.6 (24.60) OWNER Barry Brazier (NEWMARKET-ON-FERGUS)

Stay In Touch (IRE) made virtually all and his jumping was a treat. He is a possible for the Foxhunters but does lack experience. (7/4)

Irish Stout (IRE), beaten in a point-to-point the previous week, came with a wet sail from four out, and but for a mistake at the last, might have caused a major upset. (33/1)

Dixon Varner (IRE), again failed to get round, having dropped back to third when falling two out. (5/4)

3392a - (Irish Racing) - See Computer Raceform

2953-KELSO (L-H) (Good to soft, Soft patches)
Friday February 28th

WEATHER: Fine but cloudy

3393 CYRIL ALEXANDER MEMORIAL MAIDEN CHASE (6-Y.O+) (Class D)

2-20 (2-21) **3m 1f (19 fncs)** £3,598.75 (£1,090.00: £532.50: £253.75) GOING: 0.71 sec per fur (S)

				SP	RR	SF
3141[7]	**Kalajo** (BMactaggart) **7-11-5** BStorey (in tch: jnd ldrs ½-wy: led 14th: lft clr last)	—	1	10/1	90	28
3068[3]	**Desperate Days (IRE) (62)** (FKirby) **8-11-5** WDwan (in tch: hdwy 12th: chal 4 out tl blnd last: nt rcvr)	15	2	12/1	80	18
	Two For One (IRE) (MissLucindaRussell) **8-11-5** TReed (w ldrs to 10th: outpcd 13th: no imp after)	8	3	5/1[2]	75	13
3306[5]	**Fine Tune (IRE) (60)** (MrsSCBradburne) **7-11-5** MFoster (mstkes: lft in ld 3rd: mde most tl hdd 14th: outpcd 3 out: btn whn swvd lft after last)	nk	4	8/1[3]	75	13
1845[8]	**Miss Colette** (MrsDThomson) **9-11-0** DParker (prom tl lost pl 7th: lost tch fr 13th)	1½	5	50/1	69	7
2860[3]	**Millies Image (60)** (FPMurtagh) **6-11-0** ADobbin (prom tl outpcd 13th: btn whn blnd 4 out)	dist	6	25/1	—	—
3138[6]	**Aristodemus (72)** (MrsLMarshall) **8-11-5** KJohnson (bhd whn blnd bdly 11th: t.o after)	dist	7	25/1	—	—
	Safety Factor (IRE) (HowardJohnson) **9-11-5** ASSmith (led tl fell 3rd)		F	16/1	—	—
3159[P]	**Lyford Cay (IRE)** (JRBewley) **7-10-12**(7) SMelrose (bhd: hdwy ½-wy: hit 15th: 5th & btn whn fell 3 out)		F	100/1	—	—
2919[4]	**Call Me Black (IRE)** (MDHammond) **8-11-0** RGarritty (lw: w ldrs tl outpcd 4 out: 3rd & btn whn p.u lame after 2 out: dead)		P	evens[1]	—	—
3066[P]	**Just Eve** (MrsDThomson) **10-11-0** GCahill (mstkes: bhd tl p.u bef 12th)		P	100/1	—	—

(SP 112.1%) **11 Rn**

6m 41.3 (31.30) CSF £95.84 TOTE £13.00: £2.30 £4.70 £2.10 (£90.50) Trio £82.50 OWNER Kelso Members Lowflyers Club (HAWICK) BRED P. J. and G. F. Burman

2803 Kalajo won this poor race really well, and staying looks to be his forte. (10/1: 5/1-12/1)

3068 Desperate Days (IRE) ran much better this time but this was not a very competitive event. (12/1)

Two For One (IRE) has had his tube removed, but he did have his tongue tied down here and was struggling some way out. (5/1)

3306 Fine Tune (IRE) has the ability to win races such as this, but beats himself with indifferent jumping, and he was tending to hang left yet again. (8/1)

1291 Miss Colette was always struggling with the pace in this moderate event. (50/1)

3394 PENNY FARTHING RESTAURANT HURDLE (4-Y.O) (Class D)

2-50 (2-53) **2m 110y (8 hdls)** £2,749.00 (£832.00: £406.00: £193.00) GOING: 0.71 sec per fur (S)

				SP	RR	SF
3022[2]	**Clash of Swords** (PCalver) **4-10-12** LWyer (a.gng wl: led last: easily)	—	1	8/11[1]	70+	—
	Anika's Gem (IRE) (MrsSCBradburne) **4-10-7** MFoster (prom chsng group tl outpcd 5th: hdwy u.p to chse ldrs last: nt pce of wnr)	8	2	33/1	57	—
3022*	**Cry Baby (88)** (ACWhillans) **4-10-13**(5) STaylor (chsd clr ldr to 4th: rdn 3 out: ev ch last: no ex)	hd	3	6/4[2]	68	—
2859[P]	**Principal Boy (IRE)** (TJEtherington) **4-10-12** RRourke (led & sn wl clr: hit 3rd & 2 out: hdd & wknd last)	15	4	16/1	48	—
3093[5]	**Knave** (PMonteith) **4-10-12** ADobbin (outpcd ½-wy: n.d)	25	5	10/1[3]	23	—
3142[16]	**Political Mandate** (RNixon) **4-10-7** BStorey (t.o fr 5th)	5	6	50/1	14	—

(SP 117.8%) **6 Rn**

4m 16.5 (30.50) CSF £21.49 TOTE £1.80: £1.10 £7.80 (£23.80) OWNER Mrs Janis MacPherson (RIPON) BRED Sheikh Mohammed Bin Rashid Al Maktoum

3022 Clash of Swords behaved himself this time and, always going well, fairly trotted up. In this mood he could be quite useful. (8/11)

Anika's Gem (IRE) put in a reasonable first effort, and looks likely to stay further. (33/1)

3022* Cry Baby had his chances but was completely outclassed by the winner on this occasion. (6/4)

Principal Boy (IRE), who takes a strong hold, was allowed to go clear, but his jumping left something to be desired and he was easily picked off. (16/1)

3093 Knave looked very moderate on this occasion. (10/1)

3395 M. & J. BALLANTYNE (HAMILTON MEMORIAL TROPHY) AMATEUR H'CAP CHASE (0-125) (5-Y.O+) (Class E)

3-20 (3-20) **3m 4f (21 fncs)** £3,117.50 (£944.00: £461.00: £219.50) GOING: Not Established

				SP	RR	SF
2956[2]	**Off The Bru (100)** (MrsSCBradburne) **12-10-1**(7)ow8 MrMBradburne (lw: led 3rd to 7th: led 11th to 17th: led 2 out to last: led flat: r.o wl)	—	1	4/1[2]	106	26
3162[U]	**Ceilidh Boy (117)** (MrsJDGoodfellow) **11-11-6v**(5) MrRHale (mstkes: chsd ldrs tl outpcd 4 out: kpt on flat)	9	2	5/1	118	46
3027[P]	**Whaat Fettle (120)** (GRichards) **12-11-7**(7) CaptAOgden (led to 3rd: cl up: led 17th to 2 out: led last: sn hdd & one pce)	hd	3	16/1	121	49
2956[3]	**Seeking Gold (IRE) (92)** (JBarclay) **8-9-9**(5) MissPRobson (sn bhd: wl outpcd fr 15th tl r.o fr 2 out)	4	4	4/1[2]	90	18
2571[6]	**White Diamond (95)** (MissLucindaRussell) **9-9-10**(7)ow3 MrDReid (w ldrs: led 7th to 11th: cl up: outpcd 4 out: wknd last)	½	5	66/1	93	18
3162[P]	**Pink Gin (108)** (MDHammond) **10-10-13**(3) MrCBonner (outpcd & bhd: sme hdwy 15th: sn btn)	15	6	10/1	97	25

3033[2] **Heavenly Citizen (IRE) (93)** (JLGledson) **9-10-1**ow1 MrPCraggs (in tch tl mstke & outpcd fr 15th)................dist **7** 9/2 [3] — —
3067* **Judicious Captain (94)** (MrsJStorey) **10-9-11**(5)ow2 MrCStorey (lw: chsd ldrs tl fell 13th).................................. **F** 7/2 [1] — —
(SP 113.5%) **8 Rn**

7m 27.9 (31.90) CSF £22.09 CT £258.61 TOTE £4.80: £1.70 £2.00 £2.90 (£12.50) OWNER The Fife Steeplechasing Partnership (CUPAR) BRED J. O'Donnell
LONG HANDICAP White Diamond 9-1 Off The Bru 9-9 Judicious Captain 9-10
2956 Off The Bru again put up overweight, and was also out of the handicap, but this grand old performer is in tremendous heart and won in really good style. (4/1)
2765 Ceilidh Boy tends to make mistakes as he slightly backs off some fences, but he gallops forever albeit only slowly. (5/1)
3027 Whaat Fettle loves this track but prefers faster ground. Nevertheless, he ran his best race of the season. (16/1)
2956 Seeking Gold (IRE) got completely outpaced here until finishing with her usual flourish, but this time it was far too late. (4/1)
1138 White Diamond ran a useful race, but when it came down to a fight he was again found wanting. (66/1)
2063* Pink Gin, whose yard is out of form, was never going the pace at any stage. (10/1)

3396 HENNESSY COGNAC SPECIAL SERIES FINAL NOVICES' HURDLE (4-Y.O+) (Class B)
3-50 (3-51) **2m 2f (10 hdls)** £13,745.00 (£4,160.00: £2,030.00: £965.00) GOING: Not Established

SP RR SF

3158* **Marello** (MrsMReveley) **6-10-12** PNiven (lw: hld up: smooth hdwy 4 out: led 2 out: impressive)....................— **1** 1/2 [1] 89++ 37
3065* **Star Selection (104)** (JMackie) **6-11-3** EHusband (lw: j.w: led tl hdd 2 out: kpt on: no ch w wnr)..............................8 **2** 14/1 87 35
3139[2] **Dana Point (IRE) (120)** (MrsSJSmith) **5-11-3** RichardGuest (trckd ldrs: effrt 4 out: one pce fr next)..................7 **3** 4/1 [2] 81 29
2937[5] **Mister Ross (IRE) (108)** (HowardJohnson) **7-11-3** PCarberry (lw: w ldr: mstkes 3rd & 7th: outpcd 4 out: n.d after)..dist **4** 20/1 — —
2596a[P] **Ask The Butler (IRE)** (CRoche,Ireland) **6-11-10** RHughes (lw: trckd ldrs: effrt 4 out: rdn next: sn btn: eased flat)..2 **5** 7/1 [3] — —
2815* **Brambles Way (112)** (MrsMReveley) **8-11-10b** MrSSwiers (in tch tl outpcd appr 4 out: n.d after).......................6 **6** 33/1 — —
2957[7] **Maple Bay (IRE) (95)** (BEllison) **8-11-3** ADobbin (mstke 1st: a bhd: t.o)..dist **7** 100/1 — —
1667[3] **Nick Ross** (RBrewis) **6-11-3** BStorey (wl bhd fr ½-wy: t.o)..2 **8** 100/1 — —
(SP 115.5%) **8 Rn**

4m 31.4 (18.40) CSF £8.20 TOTE £1.50: £1.40 £1.90 £1.10 (£9.20) OWNER Mrs M. Williams (SALTBURN) BRED R. Chugg
3158* Marello has done everything right so far and, well in here, she looked different class. It is going to take something extra special to lower her colours. (1/2)
3065* Star Selection ran without doubt his best race of the season, and the most pleasing thing was his jumping, but the winner was far too good for him. (14/1)
3139 Dana Point (IRE) is a game and consistent sort who again ran his heart out, but was put in his place over the last three flights. (4/1)
2937 Mister Ross (IRE) did not seem to like being taken on here and his hurdling left something to be desired. He was beaten some way out. (20/1)
2596a Ask The Butler (IRE) looked in good trim and had his chances, but once off the bit three from home he was quickly put in his place. (7/1)
2815* Brambles Way has improved all season but was not up to this class. (33/1)

3397 ALBA COUNTRY FOODS HUNTERS' CHASE (6-Y.O+) (Class H)
4-20 (4-20) **3m 1f (19 fncs)** £1,982.00 (£552.00: £266.00) GOING: 0.71 sec per fur (S)

SP RR SF

Jigtime (JWHughes) **8-11-7**(7) MrMBradburne (cl up: led 13th: hit 15th: r.o wl flat)..— **1** 5/2 [1] 111 30
Royal Jester (CStorey) **13-12-7**(5) MrCStorey (a chsng ldrs: pushed along fr 14th: hit 2 out: styd on flat: no ch w wnr)..12 **2** 4/1 115 34
3095* **Howayman** (KAnderson) **7-11-12**(7) MrAParker (lw: in tch: effrt 4 out: blnd 2 out: chsng ldrs whn hmpd last: no ex)..6 **3** 100/30 [3] 105 24
3095[P] **Little Wenlock** (MrsDSCGibson) **13-12-3**(5) MrsVJackson (in tch: effrt 13th: sn chsng ldrs: outpcd 4 out: hdwy & prom 2 out: one pce)..¾ **4** 40/1 107 26
2903[4] **Fordstown (IRE)** (JamieAlexander) **8-12-1**(7) MrJamieAlexander (lw: led to 5th: mstke & lost pl 9th: jnd ldr 14th: wknd fr 2 out)..14 **5** 20/1 98 17
Little General (MrsDMcCormack) **14-12-5**(7) MrTScott (outpcd & bhd fr 12th)..14 **6** 66/1 93 12
Savoy (GRichards) **10-11-12**(7) CaptAOgden (lw: hld up: mstke 6th: hdwy 12th: wnt 2nd 2 out: rdn whn fell last).. **F** 11/4 [2] — —
Buck's Delight (IRE) (MrsRichardArthur) **9-11-9**(3) MrCBonner (lw: cl up: led 5th to 13th: wknd 14th: p.u bef 3 out).. **P** 14/1 — —
(SP 113.7%) **8 Rn**

6m 43.7 (33.70) CSF £11.80 TOTE £4.10: £1.30 £1.30 £1.20 (£5.60) OWNER Mr J. W. Hughes (GALASHIELS) BRED M. H. D. Madden and Partners
Jigtime looks even better this season, although she had her task simplified when her only real serious rival fell at the last. (5/2)
Royal Jester just gallops and stays, but is basically short of speed these days. (4/1)
3095* Howayman is a game sort who had his chances but, after a blunder two out and being knocked sideways by a faller at the last, he had nothing more to give. (100/30)
Little Wenlock is running better and should be able to pick up a race again this season. (40/1)
2903 Fordstown (IRE) ran reasonably until finding this all too much from the penultimate fence. (20/1)
Savoy, given a most patient ride, was stalking the winner but still had plenty on when he fell at the last. (11/4)

3398 SHIP HOTEL, EYEMOUTH H'CAP HURDLE (0-120) (4-Y.O+) (Class D)
4-50 (4-50) **2m 2f (10 hdls)** £2,892.00 (£876.00: £428.00: £204.00) GOING: 0.71 sec per fur (S)

SP RR SF

2957* **Ingletonian (110)** (BMactaggart) **8-11-6** BStorey (mde all: kpt on fr 2 out)..— **1** 9/2 [3] 98 11
3137[5] **Elation (107)** (GRichards) **5-11-3** ADobbin (lw: trckd wnr: chal 3 out: nt qckn appr last)..................................5 **2** 4/1 [2] 91 4
2178[3] **Ifallelsefails (90)** (LLungo) **9-10-0** RSupple (lw: hld up & bhd: styd on fr 3 out: nrst fin)..............................2½ **3** 12/1 71 —
1314[3] **Field of Vision (IRE) (104)** (MrsASwinbank) **7-11-0** JSupple (a chsng ldrs: rdn 4 out: r.o one pce)................1¾ **4** 25/1 84 —
3028[2] **Pariah (IRE) (93)** (MartinTodhunter) **8-10-3** PCarberry (lw: in tch: stdy hdwy whn mstke 4 out: effrt & chsng ldrs whn hit 2 out: sn btn)..nk **5** 5/2 [1] 73 —
Festival Fancy (93) (BMactaggart) **10-10-0**(3) GLee (chsd ldrs tl wknd fr 4 out)..10 **6** 66/1 64 —
3028[3] **Palacegate King (116)** (ACWhillans) **8-11-7**(5) STaylor (lw: in tch tl outpcd appr 4 out: n.d after)......................½ **7** 4/1 [2] 86 —
2617[7] **Aragon Ayr (118)** (PMonteith) **9-11-7**(7) CMcCormack (outpcd fr ½-wy)..7 **8** 6/1 82 —

3065[5]	**Common Sound (IRE) (103)** (JBarclay) **6-10-13** PNiven (hld up: sme hdwy 4 out: sn wknd)	30	**9**	14/1	40	—

(SP 120.7%) **9 Rn**

4m 39.6 (26.60) CSF £22.28 CT £188.80 TOTE £5.50: £1.60 £1.50 £2.70 (£15.00) Trio £49.10 OWNER Mrs Hilary MacTaggart (HAWICK) BRED A. D. Redhead

2957* Ingletonian has found a new lease of life, and is proving a difficult customer to peg back. (9/2)
3137 Elation ran by far his best race of the season and is obviously back on track. (4/1)
2178 Ifallelsefails, dropped back in trip, was finishing strongly without being knocked about, to show yet again that if he can be persuaded there is more ability there. (12/1)
1314 Field of Vision (IRE), having his first run for over three months, ran well in the circumstances. (25/1)
3028 Pariah (IRE) probably found this trip a bit too sharp causing him to make mistakes. (5/2)
Festival Fancy had a nice pipe-opener after a three-year lay-off. (66/1)
3028 Palacegate King was out of sorts here and most likely needs a more aggressive ride. (4/1)
T/Plpt: £140.80 (71.64 Tckts). T/Qdpt: £12.80 (73.05 Tckts) AA

3036-NEWBURY (L-H) (Good to soft, Hdles Soft in bk st)
Friday February 28th

WEATHER: Overcast

3399 ARDINGTON 'N.H.' NOVICES' HURDLE (5-Y.O+) (Class C)

2-00 (2-00) **2m 110y (8 hdls)** £4,068.00 (£1,224.00: £592.00: £276.00) GOING: 0.83 sec per fur (S)

				SP	RR	SF
3143[3]	**Splendid Thyne** (TCasey) **5-11-4** JOsborne (a.p: led 3 out: rdn out)	—	**1**	9/4[1]	93	37
3133[2]	**Clinton (IRE)** (KCBailey) **6-11-0** CO'Dwyer (lw: hld up & bhd: hdwy 4th: ev ch 2 out: one pce)	9	**2**	4/1[3]	80	24
1573[3]	**Strong Tel (IRE)** (MCPipe) **7-11-0** DWalsh (hld up: hdwy 4th: rdn & ev ch 3 out: wknd appr last)	5	**3**	14/1	75	19
3042[8]	**Moon Devil (IRE)** (MarkCampion) **7-11-0** JRailton (plld hrd: hdwy 3rd: led after 5th to 3 out: wknd appr last)	4	**4**	33/1	72	16
3041[6]	**Get Real (IRE)** (NJHenderson) **6-11-0** NWilliamson (lw: hld up: mstke 2nd: hdwy 4th: ev ch 3 out: hrd rdn & wknd after 2 out)	6	**5**	3/1[2]	66	10
1457[4]	**Military Law** (MissHCKnight) **6-11-0** JCulloty (prom to 3 out)	19	**6**	7/1	47	—
	News Flash (IRE) (AndrewTurnell) **5-11-0** SMcNeill (bit bkwd: hld up & bhd: nvr nr to chal)	9	**7**	12/1	39	—
	Catherine's Way (IRE) (AndrewTurnell) **5-11-0** LHarvey (bkwd: nvr nr ldrs)	3½	**8**	12/1	35	—
	Marchies Magic (JTGifford) **7-10-11**(3) LAspell (bkwd: led tl after 5th: sn wknd: t.o)	19	**9**	50/1	17	—
2911[5]	**Hulalea (NZ)** (MissSEdwards) **5-11-0** GTormey (a bhd: t.o fr 4th)	3½	**10**	50/1	13	—
	Relkander (MrsJPitman) **7-11-0** RFarrant (bit bkwd: bhd fr 4th: t.o)	5	**11**	16/1	9	—
2794[P]	**Crampscastle (IRE)** (NoelChance) **7-10-7**(7) PRyan (chsd ldr: pckd 3rd: wknd 5th)	8	**12**	33/1	1	—
	Georgetown (JTGifford) **6-11-0** PHide (a bhd: t.o)	9	**13**	12/1	—	—
	Prestigious Man (IRE) (JRJenkins) **6-10-7**(7) NTEgan (swtg: a bhd: t.o)	dist	**14**	20/1	—	—
1683[11]	**West Bay Breeze** (RHBuckler) **5-10-9** PHolley (bhd whn fell 5th)		**F**	50/1	—	—
3084[5]	**Frys No Fool** (JABOld) **7-11-0** CLlewellyn (blnd & uns rdr 3rd)		**U**	8/1	—	—

(SP 151.5%) **16 Rn**

4m 9.9 (19.90) CSF £12.95 TOTE £3.10: £1.50 £2.00 £2.50 (£6.40) Trio £17.70 OWNER Mr John Galvanoni (DORKING) BRED Mrs S. C. Welch

3143 Splendid Thyne had ground conditions more to his liking, and his trainer would be keen to run in the Royal SunAlliance in the unlikely event that it came up soft at Cheltenham. (9/4)
3133 Clinton (IRE) did not seem to mind the give in the ground, but again had to settle for the runner-up spot. (4/1)
1573 Strong Tel (IRE) made a satisfactory hurdling debut and is bred to need further. (14/1)
Moon Devil (IRE), disappointing in his two bumpers this season, ran too freely on this first outing over timber and is capable of improvement.(33/1)
3041 Get Real (IRE) had been beaten over fifteen lengths by the winner on his bumper debut at this meeting a year ago. (3/1)
1457 Military Law (7/1: 8/1-12/1)
News Flash (IRE) (12/1: 8/1-14/1)
Catherine's Way (IRE) (12/1: op 8/1)
Georgetown (12/1: op 7/1)

3400 HAMPSHIRE NOVICES' H'CAP CHASE (0-115) (5-Y.O+) (Class D)

2-30 (2-31) **3m (18 fncs)** £3,852.00 (£1,161.00: £563.00: £264.00) GOING: 0.83 sec per fur (S)

				SP	RR	SF
2896[4]	**Top Javalin (NZ) (88)** (NJHawke) **10-10-11** RGreene (bhd tl hdwy appr 14th: rdn appr 2 out: led flat: r.o wl)	—	**1**	6/1	100	33
2052[2]	**Majors Legacy (IRE) (83)** (CaptTAForster) **8-10-6** AThornton (chsd ldr: rdn to ld briefly flat: nt qckn)	2½	**2**	6/1	93	26
2883[8]	**Penncaler (IRE) (86)** (PJHobbs) **7-10-9b[1]** CLlewellyn (led: blnd 2 out: hdd flat: one pce)	2	**3**	16/1	95	28
2883[7]	**Kendal Cavalier (92)** (GBBalding) **7-11-1** BFenton (bhd tl rdn & sme hdwy 13th: wknd appr 4 out)	14	**4**	9/2[2]	92	25
3188*	**Cardinal Rule (IRE) (89)** (MissVenetiaWilliams) **8-10-12** 6x NWilliamson (lw: hld up: hit 7th: hdwy 8th: blnd bdly 11th: hit 14th: rdn & wknd 3 out)	20	**5**	9/4[1]	75	8
3176[F]	**Sophie May (89)** (LMontagueHall) **6-10-12b** JFTitley (lw: a bhd: t.o whn p.u bef 2 out)		**P**	11/2[3]	—	—
3279[U]	**Lottery Ticket (IRE) (101)** (TRGeorge) **8-11-10** CO'Dwyer (lost pl 9th: j.slowly 10th: sn bhd: t.o whn p.u bef 4 out)		**P**	13/2	—	—
3086[F]	**Country Keeper (77)** (BJMRyall) **9-10-0** SMcNeill (mstke 1st: hit 3rd: p.u bef 4th)		**P**	16/1	—	—
2795[6]	**Purbeck Rambler (77)** (GBBalding) **6-10-0** JRKavanagh (bhd whn rdn 12th: t.o whn p.u bef 4 out)		**P**	33/1	—	—

(SP 120.9%) **9 Rn**

6m 18.7 (28.70) CSF £40.14 CT £509.34 TOTE £8.10: £2.00 £1.60 £3.30 (£24.80) Trio £97.40 OWNER Mrs Valerie Thum (CHARD) BRED Ainsley Downs No 3 Breeding Partnership

LONG HANDICAP Country Keeper 9-12 Purbeck Rambler 9-2

2896 Top Javalin (NZ), dropped 10lb, relished the give in the ground and handled these big fences well. (6/1)
2052 Majors Legacy (IRE), raised 2lb, could not hold the winner from the elbow around the water jump. (6/1)
Penncaler (IRE), transformed by the blinkers, still looked capable of making all until a bad error at the penultimate fence knocked the stuffing out of him. (16/1)
2072 Kendal Cavalier, could only mount a token gesture of an effort. (9/2: 5/2-5/1)
3188* Cardinal Rule (IRE), 9lb higher than when completing his hat-trick, has gone up 23lb in all, and was due to be raised a further 1lb. Reverting to three miles, his jumping was simply not good enough over these big fences. (9/4)

3401 GEOFFREY GILBEY H'CAP CHASE (0-135) (5-Y.O+) (Class C)

3-00 (3-00) **2m 1f (13 fncs)** £4,429.00 (£1,342.00: £656.00: £313.00) GOING: 0.83 sec per fur (S)

Form	Horse / details	Dist	Pos	SP	RR	SF
2949[2]	**Kings Cherry (IRE) (106)** (JABOld) **9-10-0** CLlewellyn (mde all: clr last: rdn out)	—	1	11/2[3]	112	47
3009[2]	**High Alltitude (IRE) (106)** (MJHeaton-Ellis) **9-10-0** DGallagher (hld up: rdn & hdwy 9th: r.o flat: nt rch wnr)	1½	2	9/4[2]	111	46
3144*	**Mister Oddy (133)** (JSKing) **11-11-10**(3) DFortt (chsd ldr: ev ch 2 out: sn rdn: wknd flat)	11	3	4/5[1]	127	62
3009[P]	**James the First (121)** (PFNicholls) **9-11-1** PHide (hld up: hit 2nd: hdwy whn mstke 6th: rdn appr 3 out: btn whn hung lft appr 2 out)	dist	4	12/1	—	—

(SP 109.4%) **4 Rn**

4m 18.5 (14.50) CSF £16.05 TOTE £4.50 (£5.10) OWNER Mr T. J. Swaffield (WROUGHTON) BRED Miss A. M. and Miss J. R. Baker
LONG HANDICAP High Alltitude (IRE) 9-13 Kings Cherry (IRE) 9-13

2949 Kings Cherry (IRE), just out of the handicap proper, had softer ground this time and sensibly forced the pace over a trip on the short side for him. (11/2)

3009 High Alltitude (IRE), 6lb better off, decisively turned around last month's course and distance form with Mister Oddy, but only got going late in the day. All his hurdling wins came over two and a half miles, and he gave the impression a longer distance would not come amiss. (9/4: op 6/4)

3144* Mister Oddy, a stone higher than when winning this race last season, had beaten the runner-up a length and a quarter here last month on 6lb better terms. (4/5: evens-11/10)

1949* James the First (12/1: 6/1-14/1)

3402 SCOTTISH EQUITABLE/JOCKEYS ASSOCIATION SERIES (QUALIFIER) H'CAP HURDLE (0-125) (5-Y.O+) (Class D)

3-30 (3-30) **2m 5f (11 hdls)** £3,288.00 (£984.00: £472.00: £216.00) GOING: 0.83 sec per fur (S)

Form	Horse / details	Dist	Pos	SP	RR	SF
3136[3]	**Lord Mcmurrough (IRE) (109)** (JNeville) **7-11-2** RFarrant (swtg: hld up & bhd: hdwy on ins after 7th: led on bit 2 out: clr last: drvn out)	—	1	6/1[3]	90	25
3146*	**Oatis Rose (103)** (MSheppard) **7-10-10** NWilliamson (rdn appr 5th: mstke 6th: hdwy appr 3 out: styd on flat)	1¼	2	11/4[1]	83	18
3166[5]	**Hooded Hawk (IRE) (99)** (NJHenderson) **6-10-6** JRKavanagh (hld up: hdwy 7th: hrd rdn & ev ch 2 out: wknd flat)	8	3	11/2[2]	73	8
3013[10]	**The Toiseach (IRE) (110)** (JRFanshawe) **6-11-3** JOsborne (lw: led tl mstke 2nd: led appr 3 out to 2 out: wknd appr last)	2½	4	8/1	82	17
1950[2]	**Lake Kariba (120)** (PFNicholls) **6-11-6**(7) LCummins (s.s: hld up: hdwy appr 5th: stumbled appr 3 out: sn wknd)	14	5	7/1	81	16
1947[8]	**Carmel's Joy (IRE) (102)** (TRGeorge) **8-10-9** RJohnson (led 2nd to 3rd: wknd after 7th)	10	6	7/1	56	—
2950[4]	**Uron V (FR) (115)** (CFWall) **11-11-8** KGaule (led 3rd tl appr 3 out: wknd 2 out)	6	7	8/1	64	—
3156[P]	**The Mexicans Gone (104)** (DPGeraghty) **9-10-11** VSlattery (bit bkwd: bhd fr 8th: t.o)	18	8	20/1	40	—
3164[6]	**Kino's Cross (110)** (AJWilson) **8-11-3** AThornton (hld up: hit 3rd: bhd fr 8th: t.o)	7	9	16/1	40	—
3209[5]	**Monks Soham (IRE) (100)** (GAHubbard) **9-10-7b[1]** BFenton (plld hrd early: dropped rr 6th: p.u bef 7th)		P	20/1	—	—
3180[P]	**Arabian Sultan (107)** (MCPipe) **10-11-0** JamieEvans (a bhd: t.o whn p.u bef 8th)		P	9/1	—	—

(SP 129.0%) **11 Rn**

5m 22.5 (28.50) CSF £23.51 CT £92.07 TOTE £10.60: £2.40 £1.70 £2.30 (£9.80) Trio £46.90 OWNER Mr J. Neville (NEWPORT, GWENT) BRED B. Galvin in Ireland

3136 Lord Mcmurrough (IRE), down 2lb, had softer ground and a longer trip this time, although he gave the impression he did not want to go much further. (6/1: 7/2-13/2)

3146* Oatis Rose, up 7lb, seems to need it even more testing when she does not have an uphill finish to help. (11/4)

3166 Hooded Hawk (IRE), dropped 4lb, fared better after a couple of disappointing runs and possibly failed to get home in this softish ground. (11/2: 3/1-6/1)

2702 The Toiseach (IRE) was 2lb down in the ratings and seems to need to be dropped even further. (8/1)

1950 Lake Kariba seemed to lose his action once in line for home, and soon dropped back beaten. (7/1)

2950 Uron V (FR) (8/1: op 5/1)

Arabian Sultan (9/1: 16/1-8/1)

3403 PETER HAMER MEMORIAL HUNTERS' CHASE (6-Y.O+) (Class H)

4-00 (4-04) **3m (18 fncs)** £1,576.00 (£436.00: £208.00) GOING: Not Established

Form	Horse / details	Dist	Pos	SP	RR	SF
3089[U]	**Holland House** (PRChamings) **11-12-0**(5) MrCVigors (mde all: hit 14th & 4 out: j.rt 2 out: clr whn hit last)	—	1	4/5[1]	123	33
3055*	**Miss Millbrook** (DTGoldsworthy) **9-11-7**(7) MrEWilliams (hld up: hit 3rd: mstke & lost pl 11th: mstke 4 out: lft poor 3rd 3 out: styd on flat)	12	2	7/4[2]	110	20
	Clobracken Lad (MrsJSwaffield) **9-11-2**(7) MrGBaines (chsd wnr to 10th: rdn 13th: wnt 2nd 15th: wknd flat)	28	3	20/1	86	—
	Otter River (OJCarter) **8-11-2**(7) MrEJames (bhd: mstke 4th: hit 7th: t.o 10th: mstkes 12th & 13th: p.u bef last)		P	66/1	—	—
3273[2]	**Mediane (USA)** (MissAnnabelWilson) **12-11-7v[1]**(3)ow1 MrSimonAndrews (unruly s: ref to r)		R	25/1	—	—
3010[2]	**Principle Music (USA)** (MrsPGrainger) **9-11-2**(7) MrAPhillips (hld up: hdwy & hit 9th: chsd wnr 10th to 14th: 3rd & btn whn blnd & uns rdr 3 out)		U	10/1[3]	—	—

(SP 111.1%) **6 Rn**

6m 25.6 (35.60) CSF £2.33 TOTE £1.70: £1.30 £1.30 (£1.60) OWNER Mr E. Knight (BASINGSTOKE) BRED E. Knight

3089 Holland House who just held on to beat Coome Hill at Chepstow last season, did not have much to beat with the runner-up's jumping failing to come up to scratch, although his fencing deteriorated as he began to tire. (4/5: 4/6-11/10)

3055* Miss Millbrook did not jump well enough on this occasion. (7/4)

Clobracken Lad would have preferred better ground and was not disgraced in this company. (20/1)

3404 HIGHCLERE HURDLE (4-Y.O) (Class C)

4-30 (4-31) **2m 110y (8 hdls)** £3,652.00 (£1,096.00: £528.00: £244.00) GOING: 0.83 sec per fur (S)

Form	Horse / details	Dist	Pos	SP	RR	SF
3226[3]	**Takeamemo (IRE)** (OSherwood) **4-10-9** JOsborne (mde all: sn clr: r.o wl fr 2 out)	—	1	9/2[3]	78+	17
3075[2]	**Circus Star** (DNicholson) **4-11-0** RJohnson (lw: hld up: hdwy 4th: lft 2nd last: no imp)	5	2	5/1	78	17
3174[6]	**Salty Girl (IRE)** (JSMoore) **4-10-9** DGallagher (a.p: one pce fr 2 out)	4	3	20/1	69	8

				SP	RR	SF
	Ginger Fox (USA) (MrsJPitman) **4-11-0** RFarrant (bit bkwd: hld up: hdwy 4th: wknd appr last)	1¼	**4**	7/2^{2}	73	12
3109^{7}	**Alpine Joker** (PJHobbs) **4-11-0** GTormey (nvr nr to chal)	20	**5**	33/1	54	—
	Timidjar (IRE) (DRGandolfo) **4-10-11**(3) DFortt (hld up & plld hrd: hdwy 3 out: wknd 2 out: bdly hmpd last)	10	**6**	10/1	44	—
3174^{9}	**Hisar (IRE)** (CPEBrooks) **4-11-0** GBradley (plld hrd in rr: hdwy 3 out: wkng whn mstke 2 out)	12	**7**	8/1	32	—
	Witherkay (PFNicholls) **4-10-9**(5) OBurrows (mstkes 2nd & 3rd: a bhd)	5	**8**	20/1	28	—
2677^{14}	**Zaisan (IRE)** (JTGifford) **4-11-0** PHide (prom to 4th: t.o)	20	**9**	20/1	8	—
	Classic Victory (ICampbell) **4-11-0** KGaule (sme hdwy 3rd: bhd whn mstke 3 out: t.o)	10	**10**	33/1	—	—
3174^{3}	**Infamous (USA)** (RJO'Sullivan) **4-11-0** NWilliamson (chsd wnr fr 3rd: 2nd & btn whn fell last)		**F**	3/1^{1}	79?	—
2925^{4}	**Tiutchev** (MissHCKnight) **4-11-0** JFTitley (hld up & plld hrd: hdwy & mstke 5th: wknd 2 out: 5th & no ch whn fell last)		**F**	11/2	—	—
	Baron Hrabovsky (GThorner) **4-11-0** JCulloty (bhd: rdn 4th: t.o whn p.u bef 2 out)		**P**	33/1	—	—

(SP 140.8%) **13 Rn**

4m 12.6 (22.60) CSF £27.67 TOTE £5.10: £1.60 £2.50 £8.20 (£11.40) Trio £105.70 OWNER Sherwood Partnership Owners Club (UPPER LAMBOURN) BRED Killarkin Stud

3226 Takeamemo (IRE), well ridden, stole several lengths at the start and was given a breather leaving the back straight, which meant she had a bit up her sleeve when the race was really on. (9/2)

3075 Circus Star should be capable of getting off the mark at one of the minor courses. (5/1)

Salty Girl (IRE) stepped up on her debut, and appears to be progressing along the right lines. (20/1)

Ginger Fox (USA), a 75,000 guineas purchase out of Henry Cecil's stable, needed thirteen furlongs to gain a hard fought win in a Chester maiden last September, so he is likely to need further than this over timber. (7/2)

Timidjar (IRE) (10/1: 8/1-12/1)

3174 Infamous (USA) had given a good account of himself until crashing out at the final flight. (3/1)

3405 WHATCOMBE NOVICES' CONDITIONAL H'CAP HURDLE (0-115) (4-Y.O+) (Class E)

5-00 (5-00) **2m 5f (11 hdls)** £2,978.50 (£826.00: £395.50) GOING: 0.83 sec per fur (S)

				SP	RR	SF
2074^{2}	**Stormy Passage (IRE) (103)** (PJHobbs) **7-11-11**(3) GTormey (a.p: led appr 2 out: clr whn mstke last: r.o wl)	—	**1**	9/2^{3}	91	33
3108^{2}	**Lord Khalice (IRE) (79)** (GAHubbard) **6-10-4** MichaelBrennan (led to 3rd: lft in ld 3 out: sn hdd: one pce)	9	**2**	7/2^{1}	60	2
2826^{3}	**Unsinkable Boxer (IRE) (96)** (NJHWalker) **8-10-13**(8) DFinnegan (hld up: hdwy 8th: sn rdn: one pce)	8	**3**	11/2	71	13
2620*	**Captain Jack (103)** (MCPipe) **7-12-0** DWalsh (prom: rdn & wknd appr 3 out: t.o)	dist	**4**	6/1	—	—
2797*	**Flaxley Wood (88)** (RHBuckler) **6-10-10**(3) GSupple (plld hrd: led 3rd tl blnd bdly 3 out: p.u bef 2 out)		**P**	4/1^{2}	—	—
2878^{4}	**Lauren's Treasure (IRE) (80)** (MrsSDWilliams) **6-10-5** LAspell (bhd: rdn 7th: sn t.o: p.u bef 3 out)		**P**	33/1	—	—
3052^{2}	**Moonlighter (78)** (CFCJackson) **7-10-0**(3) OBurrows (a bhd: rdn after 7th: sn t.o: p.u bef 2 out)		**P**	7/2^{1}	—	—

(SP 115.2%) **7 Rn**

5m 23.2 (29.20) CSF £19.33 TOTE £4.90: £2.00 £2.10 (£8.10) OWNER Mr Peter Luff (MINEHEAD) BRED Denis J. Murphy

OFFICIAL EXPLANATION **Moonlighter: hung badly left throughout.**

2074 Stormy Passage (IRE) stays well and seems to relish plenty of give in the ground. (9/2)

3108 Lord Khalice (IRE) was unable to cope with the winner. (7/2)

2826 Unsinkable Boxer (IRE) moved up at the cross-flight, but it proved only to be a token gesture. (11/2: 4/1-6/1)

2620* Captain Jack is fast beginning to look an expensive six-figure purchase. (6/1)

2797* Flaxley Wood, still racing keenly, held the narrowest of advantages when effectively putting himself out of the contest three from home.(4/1)

T/Jkpt: £7,100.00 (0.2 Tckts); £3,873.63 to Newbury 1/3/97. T/Plpt: £103.30 (153.14 Tckts). T/Qdpt: £17.10 (43.16 Tckts) KH

3318-PLUMPTON (L-H) (Soft, Heavy patches)

Friday February 28th

Race 3 flag start

WEATHER: Damp

3406 CROWBOROUGH NOVICES' HURDLE (4-Y.O+) (Class E)

2-10 (2-10) **2m 1f (10 hdls)** £2,284.50 (£642.00: £313.50) GOING: 1.60 sec per fur (HY)

				SP	RR	SF
3154^{5}	**Rhythm And Blues** (RHBuckler) **7-11-2** BPowell (lost pl 3rd: rallied 5th: led appr last: r.o wl)	—	**1**	7/2^{3}	75	—
3019^{3}	**Tonka** (DRGandolfo) **5-11-2** APMcCoy (led: j.slowly 3rd: mstke 3 out: hdd appr last: unable qckn)	6	**2**	7/4^{1}	69	—
3184^{2}	**Into The Web (IRE)** (MrsMerritaJones) **6-11-2** DerekByrne (bit bkwd: a.p: mstke 5th: ev ch 3 out: wknd appr 2 out)	12	**3**	9/4^{2}	58	—
	Welsh Wizzard (JRBest) **5-10-9**(7) MrPO'Keeffe (hdwy 2nd: 3rd whn mstke 3 out: sn wknd)	7	**4**	50/1	52	—
	May Sunset (IRE) (CREgerton) **7-11-2** JAMcCarthy (lw: bhd fr 6th)	12	**5**	7/1	40	—
2840^{12}	**Contract Bridge (IRE)** (PGMurphy) **4-10-3** WMcFarland (a bhd)	10	**6**	16/1	28	—
2939^{10}	**Apollono** (RLee) **5-11-2** WMarston (hdwy 5th: wknd 7th)	s.h	**7**	20/1	31	—
	My Nad Knows (JCPoulton) **4-10-8** TJMurphy (a bhd: t.o whn fell 3 out)		**F**	50/1	—	—

(SP 116.4%) **8 Rn**

4m 38.2 (42.20) CSF £9.54 TOTE £5.60: £1.70 £1.20 £1.10 (£4.60) Trio £2.80 OWNER Mrs Peter Gregson (BRIDPORT) BRED W. G. Spink

WEIGHT FOR AGE 4yo-10lb

3154 Rhythm And Blues, who has been plagued with muscle problems, was in his element in these extremely testing conditions. Nevertheless, he got to the front approaching the last and soon asserted his authority. (7/2: 9/4-4/1)

3019 Tonka is certainly at home in the mud, and took the field along until collared by the winner approaching the last. (7/4)

3184 Into The Web (IRE), still not looking fully fit despite a promising recent run, jumped into a very slender lead three out, but he was soon passed and tired in these very testing conditions. (9/4)

Welsh Wizzard, making his hurdling debut after an absence of two years, ran quite well, playing an active role until tiring out of the back straight. (50/1)

May Sunset (IRE), an ex-Irish gelding who won a bumper at Roscommon back in August in 1994, has been off the course since then but looked very well for this first run for his new stable. Unfortunately his jumping was far from fluent on this hurdling debut and he was left behind on the final circuit. (7/1)

3407 PLUMPTON NOVICES' CHASE (5-Y.O+) (Class E)
2-40 (2-40) **2m (13 fncs)** £2,753.75 (£830.00: £402.50: £188.75) GOING: 1.24 sec per fur (HY)

			SP	RR	SF
3001[7]	**Indian Arrow (NZ) (100)** (MCPipe) **9-11-8** CMaude (led 2nd: clr appr 2 out: easily)——	1	11/8[2]	100+	33
2827[5]	**Court Master (IRE)** (RHBuckler) **9-11-2** BPowell (a.p: chsd wnr fr 5th: rdn appr 3 out: unable qckn) 15	2	11/10[1]	79	12
3187[F]	**Purbeck Cavalier (77)** (RHAlner) **8-11-2** WMcFarland (a.p: chsd wnr 2nd to 5th: rdn appr 3 out: 3rd & btn whn mstke 2 out) 2	3	11/2[3]	77	10
3059[F]	**Eau So Sloe** (JRPoulton) **6-11-2** ADicken (lw: a wl bhd: t.o fr 6th) dist	4	50/1	—	—
	Finnegais (PButler) **10-11-2** TJMurphy (a wl bhd: t.o fr 6th) dist	5	50/1	—	—
	Roadrunner (MrsLRichards) **7-11-2** MRichards (led: j.slowly 1st: j.slowly & hdd 2nd: 4th whn fell 5th)	F	50/1	—	—

(SP 111.0%) **6 Rn**

4m 20.0 (28.00) CSF £3.04 TOTE £2.00: £1.10 £1.20 (£1.80) OWNER Joe & Joanne Richards (WELLINGTON) BRED Mrs M.E. and R.E. Lee

3001 Indian Arrow (NZ) who flopped on good ground last time out, was ideally suited by a return to the mud and, soon at the head of affairs, forged clear to win this extremely bad race without turning a hair. (11/8: op evens)

2827 Court Master (IRE) likes the mud and almost lost his maiden tag under rules at Exeter in similar conditions recently, but he has had countless chances, and yet again his lack of acceleration was savagely exposed. (11/10)

3059 Purbeck Cavalier played an active role, but was already beaten when making a mistake at the second last. He is extremely moderate. (11/2: 7/2-6/1)

3408 WIVELSFIELD NOVICES' H'CAP HURDLE (0-105) (4-Y.O+) (Class E)
3-10 (3-12) **3m 110y (14 hdls)** £2,200.50 (£618.00: £301.50) GOING: 1.60 sec per fur (HY)

			SP	RR	SF
3088[3]	**Roskeen Bridge (IRE) (71)** (CWeedon) **6-10-0** MRichards (chsd ldr: led appr 3 out to last: led flat: rdn out) .—	1	6/1	49	—
3085[2]	**Dancetillyoudrop (IRE) (96)** (PFNicholls) **6-11-11** APMcCoy (lw: hld up: mstke 1st: 4th whn mstke 11th: chsd wnr appr 2 out: led & mstke last: hdd flat: hrd rdn: r.o) ½	2	5/2[1]	74	—
3016[4]	**Mister Blake (89)** (RLee) **7-10-11**(7) XAizpuru (hld up: rdn 3 out: unable qckn) 8	3	7/1	61	—
3019[6]	**Blazing Storm (IRE) (89)** (CREgerton) **5-11-4** JAMcCarthy (lw: a.p: rdn 11th: wknd appr 2 out: t.o) dist	4	100/30[2]	—	—
3209[2]	**Ainsi Soit Il (FR) (99)** (GMMcCourt) **6-12-0b** DBridgwater (led tl appr 3 out: wknd appr 2 out: mod 4th whn p.u bef last)	P	7/2[3]	—	—
3086[P]	**Minor Key (IRE) (92)** (JRJenkins) **7-11-7** BPowell (a bhd: t.o whn p.u bef 10th)	P	20/1	—	—
3063[6]	**Kybo's Revenge (IRE) (73)** (RRowe) **6-10-2**ow2 DO'Sullivan (lw: mstkes 2nd & 4th: a bhd: t.o whn p.u bef 11th)	P	20/1	—	—

(SP 110.2%) **7 Rn**

6m 38.8 CSF £18.47 TOTE £8.50: £2.20 £1.50 (£6.70) OWNER Mr Tony Rooth (CHIDDINGFOLD) BRED G. Verling

LONG HANDICAP Roskeen Bridge (IRE) 9-12 Kybo's Revenge (IRE) 9-7

3088 Roskeen Bridge (IRE) has been running much better since encountering the mud, and moved to the front approaching the third last. He looked set for second place as the runner-up moved to the front at the final flight, but that rival made a mistake there and he was able to get back in front again on the run-in. This is his ground. (6/1)

3085 Dancetillyoudrop (IRE) is well-suited by a searching test of stamina such as this, and moved into second place turning for home. He had just jumped into the lead at the last when making a mistake, and was soon headed by the winner as a result. There is a small race to be found with him in these conditions. (5/2)

3016 Mister Blake seems well-suited by the mud, but he was already held when not very fluent at the penultimate hurdle. (7/1)

3019 Blazing Storm (IRE) failed to stay this longer trip in these very severe conditions, and had come to the end of his tether turning for home. (100/30)

3409 COOKSBRIDGE MAIDEN CHASE (5-Y.O+) (Class F)
3-40 (3-40) **3m 1f 110y (20 fncs)** £2,541.00 (£768.00: £374.00: £177.00) GOING: 1.24 sec per fur (HY)

			SP	RR	SF
3060[3]	**Apatura Hati (80)** (RHAlner) **8-11-0** WMcFarland (hld up: chsd ldr fr 10th: led 16th: lft clr last) —	1	7/1	98	19
2827[3]	**Normarange (IRE)** (DMGrissell) **7-11-5** MRichards (lw: lost pl 9th: rallied 13th: 3rd whn mstke 15th: lft 2nd 4 out: wknd appr 2 out: lft poor 2nd last) dist	2	11/8[1]	—	—
3279[P]	**Fortytwo Dee (IRE)** (NASmith) **7-11-0** TJMurphy (hld up: chsd wnr appr 3 out: cl 2nd whn fell last: rmntd)..dist	3	20/1	—	—
3060[P]	**Nikkis Pet** (JNeville) **10-11-0** WMarston (bhd fr 14th: t.o whn ref last: continued) 26	4	20/1	—	—
3134[2]	**Rolleston Blade (72)** (JRBest) **10-10-12**(7) MrPO'Keeffe (lw: led to 16th: 2nd whn fell 4 out)	F	8/1	—	—
2883[P]	**Dextra (IRE)** (SEarle) **7-11-5** CMaude (lw: bhd whn fell 8th)	F	33/1	—	—
3181[2]	**Jac Del Prince (60)** (PFNicholls) **7-11-5** APMcCoy (lw: bhd whn fell 12th)	F	6/1[2]	—	—
3155[7]	**Clontoura (IRE)** (IPWilliams) **9-11-5** BPowell (mstke 1st: blnd 5th: hdwy 13th: wknd 14th: bhd whn fell 16th) ...	F	13/2[3]	—	—
3086[4]	**Plumbridge** (PRChamings) **9-11-5** TJenks (lw: bhd fr 14th: t.o whn p.u bef 2 out)	P	16/1	—	—

(SP 111.7%) **9 Rn**

7m 7.3 (47.30) CSF £15.37 TOTE £7.80: £1.40 £1.20 £3.70 (£6.50) Trio £74.70 OWNER Mrs R. O. Hutchings (BLANDFORD) BRED Mrs Rita Hutchings

3060 Apatura Hati jumped into the lead five out, and was about a length up when Fortytwo Dee departed at the last, making it plain sailing for her to win this quite appalling novice event. (7/1)

2827 Normarange (IRE), who looked very well in the paddock, was left in second place four out. Soon collared for that position, he was very leg-weary in the straight but was left a very poor second at the final fence. (11/8: 4/5-6/4)

Fortytwo Dee (IRE) is very appropriately named being by the sire Amazing Bust. Moving into second place approaching the water - three out, she was just mounting her challenge at the last when falling. She was remounted for third. Still a maiden at the age of ten, she has obviously got her knockers but this was a pleasing display. (20/1)

3134 Rolleston Blade (8/1: op 5/1)

1854 Clontoura (IRE) (13/2: op 10/1)

3410 CHAILEY H'CAP CHASE (0-115) (5-Y.O+) (Class E)
4-10 (4-10) **2m 5f (16 fncs)** £2,967.50 (£830.00: £402.50) GOING: 1.24 sec per fur (HY)

			SP	RR	SF
2908[U]	**Pavlova (IRE) (87)** (RRowe) **7-10-2**ow2 DO'Sullivan (chsd ldr to 3rd: dropped rr 5th: rallied appr last: led flat: r.o wl) —	1	16/1	93	1
3053[U]	**Winspit (IRE) (87)** (RHAlner) **7-10-2**ow1 WMcFarland (led: clr 10th: mstke 2 out: hdd flat: unable qckn) 3	2	4/1[3]	91	—
2823[9]	**Beau Babillard (113)** (PFNicholls) **10-12-0b** APMcCoy (hld up: lft 2nd 8th: rdn 4 out: eased whn btn flat)......11	3	2/1[2]	108	18

3043[7] **Mammy's Choice (IRE) (95)** (RHAlner) **7-10-10** DBridgwater (chsd ldr fr 3rd tl b.d 8th)	B	15/8[1]	—	—
3179[2] **Golden Opal (85)** (RHBuckler) **12-10-0** BPowell (4th whn b.d 8th)	B	6/1	—	—
		(SP 108.3%)	**5 Rn**	

5m 54.1 (41.10) CSF £64.39 TOTE £12.70: £2.40 £2.60 (£22.20) OWNER Mrs Margaret McGlone (PULBOROUGH) BRED Patrick Ryan
LONG HANDICAP Pavlova (IRE) 9-4 Golden Opal 9-13

2756 Pavlova (IRE), carrying 12lb more than her long handicap weight, had quite a few lengths to make up on the front two entering the straight, but as they began to tire she began to pick them up nicely and managed to get on top on the run-in to gain her just desserts. This is her ground - hence the reason for running - but she is screaming out for three miles according to her trainer. (16/1)
2796 Winspit (IRE), whose three wins to date have come over two miles, stayed this longer trip. Dictating matters from the front, he forged clear early on the final circuit but he began to tire in these very testing conditions and was eventually overhauled on the run-in. (4/1)
1837 Beau Babillard had the ground in his favour, but he is an awkward individual and did not look to be enjoying the experience. Left in second place at the eighth, he held that position until the final fence, and was eased on the run-in when his chance had evaporated. (2/1)

3411 PORTSLADE H'CAP HURDLE (0-100) (4-Y.O+) (Class F)
4-40 (4-40) **2m 4f (12 hdls)** £1,941.50 (£544.00: £264.50) GOING: 1.60 sec per fur (HY)

			SP	RR	SF
3201[F] **Mayb-Mayb (76)** (JNeville) **7-10-4** APMcCoy (lw: chsd ldr: led 6th: hrd rdn appr last: r.o wl) —	1	2/1[1]	56	17
3180[3] **St Ville (88)** (RHBuckler) **11-11-2** BPowell (rdn 8th: hdwy appr 2 out: r.o one pce) 6	2	7/1	63	24
3061* **Bula Vogue (IRE) (95)** (RRowe) **7-11-9** DO'Sullivan (stdy hdwy 9th: chsd wnr appr 3 out: ev ch 2 out: swtchd rt appr last: wknd flat) 5	3	5/2[2]	66	27
3207[10] **Script (74)** (JRJenkins) **6-10-2** TJMurphy (lw: hld up: rdn 8th: wknd appr 2 out) 7	4	12/1	40	1
2680[5] **King's Gold (77)** (MrsLRichards) **7-10-5** MRichards (lw: hld up: rdn 8th: wknd appr 2 out) 4	5	7/1	39	—
Tonys Gift (100) (MCPipe) **5-12-0** CMaude (a bhd: t.o) dist	6	6/1[3]	—	—
2808[5] **Quiet Moments (IRE) (83)** (PGMurphy) **4-10-0** WMarston (lw: led to 6th: wknd 9th: t.o) 9	7	16/1	—	—
		(SP 114.8%)	**7 Rn**	

5m 28.7 (41.70) CSF £14.99 TOTE £2.50: £1.30 £3.70 (£9.50) OWNER Mr J. Neville (NEWPORT, GWENT) BRED Bram Davies and R. J. Holder
LONG HANDICAP Quiet Moments (IRE) 9-9
WEIGHT FOR AGE 4yo-11lb

3201 Mayb-Mayb goes well in this ground and, leading at the sixth, responded to pressure going to the final flight. (2/1)
3180 St Ville needs a real test of stamina and, although the ground certainly helped, he needs three miles for he was doing all his best work in the straight. (7/1: op 4/1)
3061* Bula Vogue (IRE) found this longer trip beyond her in this very testing ground. On level terms with the winner jumping the second last, her jockey switched her over to the stands' side in search of the better ground, but the mare had nothing more to offer on the run-in. A drop in distance should see her soon regain the winning thread. (5/2)
3207 Script is one to avoid and had come to the end of his tether early in the straight. (12/1: 10/1-16/1)
2680 King's Gold chased the leaders until calling it a day approaching the second last. He remains a maiden after eighteen attempts. (7/1)
Tonys Gift (6/1: op 4/1)

T/Plpt: £44.10 (192.41 Tckts). T/Qdpt: £17.20 (23.41 Tckts) AK

3284-DONCASTER (L-H) (Good)
Saturday March 1st
WEATHER: Fine and Windy

3412 LIGHT INFANTRY PLATE H'CAP HURDLE (0-135) (4-Y.O+) (Class C)
12-50 (12-50) **2m 110y (8 hdls)** £3,678.00 (£1,104.00: £532.00: £246.00) GOING: 0.21 sec per fur (G)

			SP	RR	SF
3177* **More Dash Thancash (IRE) (108)** (MrsMerritaJones) **7-10-8** DerekByrne (lw: j.rt: mde all: lft clr last: easily) —	1	15/8[1]	89+	27
2902[8] **Holders Hill (IRE) (103)** (MGMeagher) **5-10-3** PCarberry (chsd ldrs: effrt 3 out: one pce fr next) 5	2	20/1	79	17
3163[9] **Sea Victor (118)** (JLHarris) **5-11-4** DGallagher (lw: w wnr tl outpcd fr 3 out) 5	3	5/1[3]	89	27
2952[2] **Glanmerin (IRE) (118)** (KAMorgan) **6-11-4** ADobbin (lw: chsd ldrs: rdn appr 3 out: r.o one pce) 5	4	9/2[2]	85	23
2779[6] **Charming Girl (USA) (127)** (OSherwood) **6-11-13** JOsborne (hld up & bhd: hdwy appr 3 out: one pce fr 2 out) 6	5	16/1	88	26
2902[P] **Uncle Doug (125)** (MrsMReveley) **6-11-8**(3) GLee (outpcd & bhd fr 4th) 28	6	16/1	59	—
3286[3] **Desert Fighter (110)** (MrsMReveley) **6-10-10** PNiven (hld up: hdwy 5th: chsd wnr fr 2 out: 3l 2nd & btn whn fell last)	F	7/1	87?	—
3164[2] **Thornton Gate (122)** (TDEasterby) **8-11-8** LWyer (hld up: hdwy whn fell 5th: dead)	F	5/1[3]	—	—
		(SP 115.3%)	**8 Rn**	

3m 59.9 (9.90) CSF £32.77 CT £151.21 TOTE £2.50: £1.30 £5.40 £2.10 (£38.90) OWNER Mr F. J. Sainsbury (LAMBOURN) BRED Miss Roseanne Millett & Paul McEnery

3177* More Dash Thancash (IRE) is obviously still improving, but his tendency to jump right was a shade worrying, and he does seem to have some sort of problem as he was kept on the grass whilst in the paddock. (15/8)
1125 Holders Hill (IRE) showed something of his old form here, and has slipped down to a handy mark. (20/1)
3163 Sea Victor still ran a bit flat here and seems to have lost his sparkle for the time being. (5/1)
2952 Glanmerin (IRE) was 13lb better in with the winner on their Huntingdon running, but he ran most disappointingly and gave up once asked a question approaching three out. (9/2)
1510 Charming Girl (USA) seems to have lost her way of late. (16/1)
3286 Desert Fighter was in second place and making no impression on the winner when taking a crashing fall at the last, where not surprisingly he lay for some time. (7/1)

3413 MITSUBISHI SHOGUN TROPHY H'CAP CHASE (0-130) (5-Y.O+) (Class C)
1-25 (1-25) **2m 3f 110y (15 fncs)** £6,840.00 (£2,070.00: £1,010.00: £480.00) GOING: 0.21 sec per fur (G)

			SP	RR	SF
3286[7] **Frickley (110)** (GRichards) **11-10-10** PCarberry (lw: a.p: hrd drvn 4 out: hdwy next: led between last 2: styd on) —	1	9/1	122	39
Destiny Calls (123) (NAGaselee) **7-11-9** PNiven (sn cl up: led after 11th to 3 out: ev ch tl outpcd appr last) 2½	2	2/1[1]	133	50
2879[4] **Conti D'Estruval (FR) (112)** (GBBalding) **7-10-12** BClifford (trckd ldrs: chal 9th: led 3 out tl between last 2: no ex) s.h	3	9/2[3]	122	39

2890[2] **Wee River (IRE) (128)** (GMMoore) **8-12-0** JCallaghan (lw: hld up: hdwy whn hit 10th: hmpd next: sn btn: blnd 2 out) ....18 **4** 9/2[3] 123 40
3292[U] **In Truth (114)** (SGollings) **9-11-0** KGaule (cl up tl outpcd 8th) ....hd **5** 16/1 109 26
3132* **Artic Wings (IRE) (105)** (OBrennan) **9-10-5** MBrennan (hld up: effrt whn blnd 10th: n.d after) ....12 **6** 4/1[2] 90 7
2674[4] **Real Glee (IRE) (106)** (JJQuinn) **8-10-6** AThornton (mstkes: led: blnd 8th: hdd after 11th: sn wknd) ....15 **7** 16/1 79 —
3140[F] **Monnaie Forte (IRE) (100)** (JRAdam) **7-10-0** MMoloney (mstke 1st: hld up & bhd: stdy hdwy to trck ldrs whn fell 11th) .... **F** 20/1 — —
(SP 116.2%) **8 Rn**

4m 56.4 (9.40) CSF £26.53 CT £86.04 TOTE £9.20: £1.80 £1.40 £1.50 (£10.90) OWNER Mr Robert Ogden (PENRITH) BRED Frank Motherway
LONG HANDICAP Monnaie Forte (IRE) 9-4
Frickley last won a chase over three years ago and had to battle to take this, but it was certainly no fluke. (9/1)
Destiny Calls, having his first run of the season, put up a useful effort, and should be all the better for it. (2/1)
2879 Conti D'Estruval (FR), who wears a tongue-strap, was on a useful mark here and had every chance, but has lost his form of last season. (9/2)
2890 Wee River (IRE) was testing his stamina limitations here, and a poor jump six out knocked the stuffing out of him. (9/2)
2901 In Truth got outpaced halfway through the race and may well be happier with more cut in the ground. (16/1)
3132* Artic Wings (IRE) found this trip too sharp and, because of the pace, made mistakes. (4/1)
3140 Monnaie Forte (IRE) was on the bridle when hitting the floor five out. (20/1)

3414 VELKA PARDUBICKA GRIMTHORPE H'CAP CHASE (0-145) (5-Y.O+) (Class B)
2-00 (2-00) **3m 2f (19 fncs)** £10,191.75 (£3,084.00: £1,504.50: £714.75) GOING: 0.21 sec per fur (G)

SP RR SF
3280* **Father Sky (115)** (OSherwood) **6-10-11b** JOsborne (a cl up: led 2 out: styd on u.p) ....— **1** 9/2[2] 131 41
2671[3] **Change the Reign (107)** (MissAEEmbiricos) **10-10-3** PCarberry (led tl hdd 2 out: sn btn) ....14 **2** 12/1[3] 114 24
3025* **Whispering Steel (128)** (GRichards) **11-11-10** ADobbin (trckd ldrs: rdn 4 out: sn btn) ....15 **3** 4/1[1] 126 36
2928* **Musthaveaswig (123)** (DNicholson) **11-11-5** AThornton (chsd ldrs: mstke 9th: rdn 14th: no imp after) ....13 **4** 4/1[1] 113 23
3036[3] **Le Meille (IRE) (109)** (KRBurke) **8-10-5** ALarnach (hld up: effrt 14th: no imp: b.b.v) ....1½ **5** 9/2[2] 98 8
3033[3] **Pims Gunner (IRE) (104)** (MDHammond) **9-10-0** DBentley (in tch tl outpcd fr 12th) ....13 **6** 16/1 85 —
2765[3] **Ali's Alibi (113)** (MrsMReveley) **10-10-9** PNiven (p.u bef 2nd) .... **P** 9/2[2] — —
2782[10] **Merry Master (111)** (GMMoore) **13-10-7b**[ow1] JCallaghan (lw: mstkes: hld up: lost tch fr 12th) .... **P** 33/1 — —
(SP 111.1%) **8 Rn**

6m 34.1 (12.10) CSF £45.40 CT £203.33 TOTE £4.20: £1.70 £3.40 £1.40 (£43.80) OWNER Mr Kenneth Kornfeld (UPPER LAMBOURN) BRED Sheikh Mohammed
LONG HANDICAP Pims Gunner (IRE) 9-10
OFFICIAL EXPLANATION **Le Meille (IRE): the trainer reported that the gelding was found to be bleeding from the nose after the race.**
Ali's Alibi: lost his action.
3280* Father Sky, given a smashing ride, did the job well and seems to be improving. (9/2)
2671 Change the Reign enjoyed himself out in front but, when it came down to a struggle, he lacked any change of gear. (12/1)
3025* Whispering Steel would have preferred easier ground and, once he came off the bit, the response was disappointing. (4/1)
2928* Musthaveaswig was never really happy after a mistake at the water jump. (4/1)
3036 Le Meille (IRE), after looking to be going well, failed to get in a blow, and it later transpired he had broken a blood-vessel. (9/2)
2765 Ali's Alibi was pulled up before the second with his rider thinking he had gone lame, but was later found to be perfectly sound. (9/2)

3415 AIR POWER PRODUCTS H'CAP HURDLE (4-Y.O+) (Class B)
2-30 (2-32) **3m 110y (11 hdls)** £4,711.00 (£1,408.00: £674.00: £307.00) GOING: 0.21 sec per fur (G)

SP RR SF
3013[3] **Ealing Court (101)** (NMBabbage) **8-10-0** JOsborne (a.p: effrt 3 out: styd on gamely flat to ld cl home) ....— **1** 9/2[3] 77 20
2895[2] **Smith Too (IRE) (109)** (MrsJPitman) **9-10-8** AThornton (led: mstke 5th: rdn 2 out: r.o: jst ct) ....s.h **2** 7/2[1] 85 28
2888[10] **Lochnagrain (IRE) (122)** (MrsMReveley) **9-11-7** PNiven (lw: hld up: stdy hdwy 4 out: shkn up 2 out: nvr able to chal) ....6 **3** 4/1[2] 94 37
3156* **Bankhead (IRE) (128)** (JLSpearing) **8-11-6**(7) MissCSpearing (chsd ldrs: mstke 4 out: outpcd fr 3 out) ....½ **4** 4/1[2] 100 43
2888[8] **Fired Earth (IRE) (129)** (JRFanshawe) **9-12-0** PCarberry (hld up: effrt & in tch 3 out: sn rdn & btn) 10 **5** 5/1 94 37
3269[9] **Amillionmemories (101)** (MrsBarbaraWaring) **7-10-0** RGreene (lw: hld up: effrt 4 out: rdn & btn after next) ..30 **6** 20/1 47 —
2900[7] **Jocks Cross (IRE) (114)** (GRichards) **6-10-13** ADobbin (chsd ldrs tl rdn & btn appr 3 out) ....½ **7** 7/1 59 2
(SP 114.3%) **7 Rn**

5m 57.7 (14.70) CSF £19.01 CT £61.23 TOTE £5.30: £2.50 £2.40 (£6.50) OWNER Mr R. S. Brookhouse (CHELTENHAM) BRED Stud-On-The-Chart
LONG HANDICAP Amillionmemories 9-2 Ealing Court 9-12
3013 Ealing Court is a tough sort who stays well. Given a fine ride, he just made it. (9/2)
2895 Smith Too (IRE) was well handicapped and had the ground and the trip he likes, but just met one too good. (7/2)
2545 Lochnagrain (IRE) looked to be going well for much of the trip but then just failed to pick up when it mattered. He looks as well as ever. (4/1)
3156* Bankhead (IRE) would probably have preferred easier ground and was always short of toe from the third last. (4/1: 3/1-9/2)
948* Fired Earth (IRE) has never won at this trip and was in trouble fully three flights out, but is not giving his true running at the moment. (5/1)

3416 PARDUBICE NOVICES' HURDLE (4-Y.O+) (Class E)
3-05 (3-06) **2m 4f (10 hdls)** £2,547.50 (£710.00: £342.50) GOING: 0.21 sec per fur (G)

SP RR SF
3315* **Nigel's Lad (IRE)** (PCHaslam) **5-11-8** MFoster (lw: led to 2nd: w ldr tl led again 6th: r.o strly fr 3 out: pushed out) ....— **1** 2/5[1] 90 53
2953* **Secret Service (IRE)** (CWThornton) **5-11-8** PCarberry (lw: trckd ldrs: ev ch 3 out: wknd last) ....22 **2** 11/4[2] 72 35
2897[3] **Leap in the Dark (IRE) (80)** (MissLCSiddall) **8-11-2** AThornton (in tch: outpcd 4 out: hdwy u.p 3 out: sn btn).10 **3** 20/1[3] 58 21
3004[8] **Rare Occurance (78)** (JGMO'Shea) **7-11-2** KGaule (chsd ldrs: drvn along fr 5th: hit 6th: btn appr 3 out) 17 **4** 33/1 45 8
3305[2] **Laughing Fontaine (IRE)** (FMurphy) **7-11-2** DBentley (hld up: sme hdwy 4 out: n.d) ....1½ **5** 25/1 44+ 7
3305[C] **Anastasia Windsor (68)** (DMoffatt) **6-10-11v** DJMoffatt (led fr 2nd to 6th: wknd appr 3 out) ....15 **6** 66/1 27 —
872[14] **Miss Nonnie** (MissLShally) **5-10-4**(7) MLane (in tch tl outpcd fr 4 out) ....½ **7** 100/1 26 —
The Wasp (IRE) (HowardJohnson) **5-11-2** ADobbin (a bhd: wl t.o) ....dist **8** 25/1 — —
2746[P] **Book of Dreams (IRE) (59)** (JGMO'Shea) **9-11-2** DGallagher (lost tch fr 6th: t.o whn p.u bef 3 out) .... **P** 100/1 — —

				SP	RR	SF
3226[P]	**Bally Wonder** (MrsEHHeath) **5-10-11** JSupple (a bhd: t.o whn p.u bef 3 out)		**P**	100/1	—	—
				(SP 118.0%)		**10 Rn**

4m 48.4 (8.40) CSF £1.53 TOTE £1.40: £1.10 £1.50 £1.40 (£1.50) Trio £3.30 OWNER Mr N. C. Dunnington (MIDDLEHAM) BRED Nikita Investments

STEWARDS' ENQUIRY Murphy fined £1,000 & Bentley susp. 10-15 & 17/3/97 (failure to run horse on its merits). Laughing Fontaine (IRE) banned 3/3-1/4/97.

3315* Nigel's Lad (IRE) left nothing to chance and, getting the trip well, was driven out to show just how good he is. (2/5)
2953* Secret Service (IRE) tried hard to keep tabs on the winner, but was well outclassed by the finish. (11/4)
2897 Leap in the Dark (IRE) found the effort required here too much for his liking. (20/1)
2744 Rare Occurance was never on the bridle and looked slow throughout the final mile. (33/1)
3305 Laughing Fontaine (IRE) failed to get into this and was certainly not knocked about but, as he showed last time, he is not all that good (25/1)

3417 HMS ANDROMEDA NOVICES' CHASE (5-Y.O+) (Class D)

3-40 (3-40) **2m 110y (12 fncs)** £3,526.75 (£1,054.00: £504.50: £229.75) GOING: 0.21 sec per fur (G)

				SP	RR	SF
2783[6]	**Sublime Fellow (IRE) (116)** (NJHenderson) **7-11-12** JOsborne (chsd ldrs: led 8th: clr fr 4 out: drvn out)	—	**1**	2/1[2]	106	44
3073*	**Just Bruce (83)** (MrsEHHeath) **8-11-7** DGallagher (led: mstke 4th: hdd 8th & sn outpcd: kpt on fr 3 out)	3	**2**	16/1	98	36
3045[P]	**Gimme (IRE) (90)** (JGMO'Shea) **7-11-2v** KGaule (mstkes: chsd ldrs: effrt 7th: outpcd appr 4 out: no imp after)	1¼	**3**	16/1	92	30
3001[P]	**Sigma Run (IRE) (81)** (JGMO'Shea) **8-11-7** MFoster (lw: in tch tl outpcd fr 6th)	30	**4**	16/1	68	6
3030[F]	**Great Gable (IRE) (60)** (DMoffatt) **6-11-2** DJMoffatt (lw: a bhd)	25	**5**	66/1	39	—
3167[4]	**Blair Castle (IRE)** (GBBalding) **6-11-2** BClifford (trckd ldrs: mstke 3rd: cl 4th whn blnd & uns rdr 5th)		**F**	5/4[1]	—	—
3030[2]	**Royal Crimson (82)** (MDHammond) **6-11-2** RGarritty (bhd fr 4th: p.u bef 2 out)		**P**	13/2[3]	—	—
				(SP 110.3%)		**7 Rn**

4m 5.0 (10.00) CSF £24.91 TOTE £2.70: £1.90 £3.10 (£18.40) OWNER Mr Rory McGrath (LAMBOURN) BRED John Kent

2116 Sublime Fellow (IRE) was well in command over the last four fences but, after a careful jump at the final obstacle, he needed to be kept up to his work. (2/1)
3073* Just Bruce has a real cut at his fences, and by the way he was keeping on he should get further. (16/1)
208* Gimme (IRE), switching back to chasing, was again let down by some chancy jumping. (16/1)
2745 Sigma Run (IRE) was found out a long way from home. (16/1)
3167 Blair Castle (IRE) was going well enough when he made a bad mistake, giving his rider no chance of staying aboard, at about the halfway point. Once his jumping improves his turn will obviously come. (5/4)

3418 TOWN MOOR STANDARD N.H. FLAT RACE (4, 5 & 6-Y.O) (Class H)

4-10 (4-13) **2m 110y** £1,035.00 (£285.00: £135.00)

				SP	RR	SF
3203[16]	**Landler** (JNorton) **4-10-6**(3) ECallaghan (hld up: hdwy ½-wy: led 2f out: hung lft: r.o)	—	**1**	33/1	63 f	—
	Carlingford Tyke (IRE) (TJCarr) **5-11-3** GCahill (bit bkwd: cl up: chal over 3f out: nt qckn ins fnl f)	1	**2**	33/1	62 f	—
3142[4]	**Generous Streak (FR)** (JNorton) **4-10-4**(5) BGrattan (cl up: disp ld 5f out to 2f out: kpt on one pce)	1	**3**	13/2[3]	61 f	—
2675[9]	**Dig For Gold** (MissSEHall) **4-10-6**(3) FLeahy (lw: hld up: smooth hdwy 6f out: led over 3f out tl wknd 2f out)	7	**4**	12/1	54 f	—
2696[10]	**Pedlar's Cross (IRE)** (GMMcCourt) **5-11-0**(3) DFortt (w ldr: disp ld ½-wy to 5f out: one pce)	4	**5**	20/1	50 f	—
3142[11]	**Lord of The Rings** (FMurphy) **5-10-10**(7) MrTJBarry (bhd: sme hdwy 3f out: n.d)	6	**6**	14/1	45 f	—
3170[8]	**Weapons Free** (TPTate) **6-10-10**(7) RMcCarthy (prom tl wknd fnl 5f)	1½	**7**	7/1	43 f	—
	Nothing To It (CPMorlock) **6-11-0**(3) MrCBonner (bit bkwd: plld hrd: in tch tl outpcd fnl 4f)	6	**8**	33/1	37 f	—
3042[10]	**Sprightley Pip (IRE)** (MissCJohnsey) **6-10-10**(7) JPower (mde most tl hdd 5f out: wknd)	1½	**9**	20/1	36 f	—
	Judicious Charlie (IRE) (JRAdam) **5-10-12**(5) RMcGrath (lw: hld up: hdwy to jn ldrs ½-wy: wknd over 4f out)	29	**10**	9/2[2]	8 f	—
	Aeolus (LRLloyd-James) **4-10-2**(7) NHorrocks (a bhd: t.o fr ½-wy)	5	**11**	33/1	3 f	—
2904[2]	**Wynyard Knight** (MrsMReveley) **5-11-0**(3) GLee (trckng ldrs whn n.m.r & rn out ½-wy)		**R**	8/11[1]	—	—
	Mill Bay Sam (MrsMerritaJones) **6-10-10**(7) MLane (ref to r: t.n.p)		**R**	16/1	—	—
				(SP 143.4%)		**13 Rn**

4m 3.2 CSF £854.82 TOTE £56.80: £12.20 £7.70 £2.30 (£1,008.80) Trio £152.70 OWNER Bradlor Developments Ltd (BARNSLEY) BRED Sheikh Mohammed Bin Rashid Al Maktoum

WEIGHT FOR AGE 4yo-8lb

3203 Landler, who showed nothing on his debut over a shorter trip, showed he really stays, despite edging left towards the finish. (33/1)
Carlingford Tyke (IRE), just needing this, ran well, and will obviously improve. (33/1)
3142 Generous Streak (FR) is a real battler but is short of any turn of foot. (13/2)
Dig For Gold looked fit here and ran pretty well, but failed to see the trip out. (12/1: op 7/1)
Nothing To It was going really well and may well have trotted up, but he ran out halfway through the race. (33/1)
Judicious Charlie (IRE) (9/2: 2/1-6/1)
2904 Wynyard Knight (8/11: evens-5/4)

T/Plpt: £43.20 (518.12 Tckts). T/Qdpt: £11.60 (96.26 Tckts) AA

3399-NEWBURY (L-H) (Good to Soft, Hdles Soft in bk st)

Saturday March 1st

WEATHER: Dull

3419 NORTH SYDMONTON H'CAP CHASE (0-135) (5-Y.O+) (Class C)

1-15 (1-15) **2m 4f (16 fncs)** £4,497.00 (£1,356.00: £658.00: £309.00) GOING: 0.80 sec per fur (S)

				SP	RR	SF
3106*	**Too Plush (113)** (AndrewTurnell) **8-10-6** LHarvey (lw: hld up: chsd ldr fr 12th: led appr last: mstke last: drvn out)	—	**1**	9/2	119	39
3018[3]	**Mely Moss (FR) (135)** (CREgerton) **6-12-0** GBradley (led to 2nd: led 5th tl appr last: ev ch flat: r.o wl)	hd	**2**	11/8[1]	141	61
2707*	**Newlands-General (118)** (PFNicholls) **11-10-11** APMcCoy (hld up: 4th whn mstke 9th: rdn 4 out: wknd appr 2 out)	26	**3**	4/1[3]	103	23
	The Frog Prince (IRE) (125) (NAGaselee) **9-11-4** CLlewellyn (bit bkwd: led 2nd: pckd 3rd: hdd 5th: wknd 12th: t.o)	dist	**4**	100/30[2]	—	—

			SP	RR	SF
3312[6]	**Potato Man (107)** (BEllison) **11-9-9v**(5) DJKavanagh (bhd fr 8th: t.o fr 11th) 27	**5**	66/1	—	—
			(SP 104.9%)		**5 Rn**

5m 15.3 (20.30) CSF £9.59 TOTE £3.90: £2.10 £1.20 (£3.70) OWNER Mrs C. C. Williams (WANTAGE) BRED Miss B. Sykes
LONG HANDICAP Potato Man 8-11

3106* Too Plush has won three soft races on the bounce, but despite the much tougher competition here was not going to be denied. Gaining a narrow advantage approaching the last, he got right under that fence but did not lose much ground. In a tremendous tussle with the runner-up he just managed to prevail. (9/2: 11/4-5/1)

3018 Mely Moss (FR) was back over his optimum trip. A bit hesitant at some of his fences, he nevertheless made the vast majority of the running until collared approaching the last. Refusing to give way, it looked as if he might well get back up again in the closing stages, but he just failed. Compensation should soon be found. (11/8)

2707* Newlands-General has won a couple of soft races this season, but this was much more competitive and he was a spent force going to the second last. He has done most of his winning at two miles. (4/1)

The Frog Prince (IRE), looking just in need of this first run in over a year, ran accordingly, showing up well until tiring entering the straight.(100/30)

3420 BERKSHIRE H'CAP CHASE (0-135) (5-Y.O+) (Class C)

1-45 (1-45) **3m (18 fncs)** £4,627.00 (£1,396.00: £678.00: £319.00) GOING: 0.80 sec per fur (S)

			SP	RR	SF
2782[4]	**Turning Trix (125)** (DNicholson) **10-11-4** JRKavanagh (hld up: jnd ldr 2 out: rdn appr last: led last strides)...—	**1**	11/4[3]	137	57
2839*	**Sister Stephanie (IRE) (123)** (GMMcCourt) **8-11-2** DBridgwater (led 1st to 2nd: mstke 3 out: led 2 out: hrd rdn flat: hdd last strides) ....hd	**2**	9/4[1]	135	55
3036[2]	**River Mandate (123)** (CaptTAForster) **10-11-2b** APMcCoy (led 2nd: clr 7th: rdn 13th: hdd 2 out: ev ch last: swtchd rt flat: r.o) 1	**3**	5/2[2]	134	54
	Hill Trix (119) (KBishop) **11-10-12** BPowell (bit bkwd: led to 1st: bhd fr 3rd: t.o fr 10th) ....dist	**4**	40/1	—	—
	Smith's Band (IRE) (135) (MrsJPitman) **9-12-0** RFarrant (bit bkwd: hld up: 3rd whn mstke 11th: 4th & wkng whn p.u bef 3 out)	**P**	7/2	—	—
			(SP 110.7%)		**5 Rn**

6m 12.1 (22.10) CSF £8.78 TOTE £4.00: £1.80 £1.50 (£3.90) OWNER Mr Mel Davies (TEMPLE GUITING) BRED Robert McCarthy

2782 Turning Trix joined issue with the leader two out and, in a tremendous battle on the run-in, managed to get up in the last few strides. The Grand National is his main objective. (11/4)

2839* Sister Stephanie (IRE), who beat River Mandate by half a length last time out, confirmed that form on 2lb worse terms. Delivering her challenge when making a bad mistake three from home, she nevertheless managed to recover and jump into a narrow lead at the next. Engaged in a tremendous battle with the winner on the run-in, she only just lost out. At her best with some cut, she should soon gain compensation. (9/4)

3036 River Mandate again did little wrong, and set the pace. Collared two from home, he was still in with every chance jumping the final fence and kept on to the line. (5/2)

Smith's Band (IRE), looking as though this first run in fourteen months was needed, was beginning to feel the pinch when nodding slightly at the fourth last and was soon pulled up. At his best with some cut, the Grand National is his target and he is sure to come on a lot for this. (7/2: 5/2-4/1)

3421 EASTLEIGH H'CAP HURDLE (0-130) (4-Y.O+) (Class C)

2-15 (2-15) **2m 110y (8 hdls)** £3,785.00 (£1,130.00: £540.00: £245.00) GOING: 0.80 sec per fur (S)

			SP	RR	SF
3228*	**Sheriffmuir (117)** (MrsLWadham) **8-11-7** JFTitley (hdwy 4th: led last: rdn out) ....—	**1**	4/1[1]	101	51
3012*	**Rangitikei (NZ) (112)** (CJMann) **6-11-2** JRailton (a.p: led 4th to last: unable qckn)....3½	**2**	9/2[2]	93	43
3087*	**Nipper Reed (103)** (THind) **7-10-7** DBridgwater (led to 4th: ev ch 3 out: rdn appr 2 out: one pce) 7	**3**	10/1	77	27
2884[9]	**Slew Man (FR) (117)** (MCPipe) **6-11-7** APMcCoy (a.p: rdn 3 out: wknd appr 2 out) 7	**4**	8/1	84	34
2926[7]	**Moving Out (120)** (MissHCKnight) **9-11-3**(7) MrAWintle (w ldr to 4th: wknd 5th)....3	**5**	40/1	84	34
3164*	**Goldingo (108)** (GMPrice) **10-10-12** JRKavanagh (lw: hdwy 4th: wknd appr 2 out) 5	**6**	10/1	67	17
3177[5]	**Ros Castle (115)** (RJHodges) **6-10-12b**(7) JHarris (hdwy 5th: wknd appr 2 out: fin lame: dead) ....¾	**7**	16/1	74	24
3177[2]	**Shepherds Rest (IRE) (101)** (SMellor) **5-10-5** NMann (lw: hdwy 5th: wknd appr 3 out) 12	**8**	7/1[3]	48	—
	'iggins (IRE) (110) (JTGifford) **7-11-0** PHide (bit bkwd: sme hdwy appr 3 out: wknd appr 2 out) 2	**9**	12/1	55	5
3034[3]	**Centaur Express (117)** (AStreeter) **5-11-7** TEley (bhd fr 5th) 9	**10**	8/1	53	3
3008[3]	**Intermagic (110)** (JCFox) **7-11-0** SFox (mstke 1st: bhd fr 4th)....8	**11**	10/1	39	—
3164[7]	**Saint Ciel (USA) (105)** (FJordan) **9-10-9** RFarrant (bhd fr 5th: t.o)....dist	**12**	33/1	—	—
1567[3]	**Chef Comedien (IRE) (120)** (MJWilkinson) **7-11-10** WMarston (bhd fr 4th: t.o whn p.u bef 5th)	**P**	25/1	—	—
			(SP 123.0%)		**13 Rn**

4m 7.0 (17.00) CSF £20.88 CT £158.83 TOTE £5.50: £2.40 £2.70 £2.80 (£8.20) Trio £20.00 OWNER Mr J. J. W. Wadham (NEWMARKET) BRED Stetchworth Park Stud Ltd

3228* Sheriffmuir completed the hat-trick despite the stiffer opposition and another 5lb rise in the weights, leading at the last and being ridden along to dispose of the runner-up. (4/1)

3012* Rangitikei (NZ) was up against experienced opposition and 8lb higher in the weights, but still ran a fine race. In front at halfway, he appeared to be travelling well in the straight but, collared at the final flight, was then put in his place. He should soon regain the winning thread. (9/2)

3087* Nipper Reed had much more on his plate this time but still gave a good account of himself. In front to halfway, he still had every chance early in the straight before tapped for toe. (10/1)

Slew Man (FR) ran his best race since his lengthy lay-off, he was forced to concede defeat going to the penultimate hurdle. (8/1)

2048 Moving Out, reverting back to hurdles after flopping badly twice over fences, was a spent force turning into the straight. Two and a half miles is really his trip. (40/1)

3164* Goldingo moved up at halfway but had shot his bolt approaching the penultimate hurdle. His last three victories have all come at Warwick. (10/1)

3422 JACK O'NEWBURY NOVICES' CHASE (5-Y.O+) (Class E)

2-45 (2-46) **2m 4f (16 fncs)** £2,927.50 (£880.00: £425.00: £197.50) GOING: 0.80 sec per fur (S)

			SP	RR	SF
2926[2]	**Flight Lieutenant (USA) (105)** (TCasey) **8-11-9** DBridgwater (hdwy 11th: hrd rdn appr 3 out: led appr 2 out: clr appr last: r.o wl) ....—	**1**	4/1[2]	120	26
2660[P]	**Madison County (IRE) (110)** (PJHobbs) **7-11-4v** CLlewellyn (hld up: rdn 12th: sn wknd)....20	**2**	6/1[3]	99	5

3278[3] **Gordon (84)** (PRWebber) **6-11-1b**[1(3)] EHusband (lw: led 4th: mstke 12th: hdd 4 out: lft in ld 3 out: sn hdd & wknd) 5 **3** 14/1 95 1
Spin Echo (IRE) (RWaley-Cohen) **8-11-4** WMarston (lw: bhd fr 7th) ....8 **4** 50/1 89 —
3086[2] **Angelo's Double (IRE)** (RHBuckler) **9-11-4** BPowell (led: j.slowly 3rd: hdd 4th: led 4 out tl fell 3 out) .... **F** Evens[1] — —
Campeche Bay (IRE) (130) (GBBalding) **8-11-4** APMcCoy (Withdrawn not under Starter's orders: spread plate at s) .... **W** 4/1[2] — —
(SP 112.9%) **5 Rn**

5m 23.7 (28.70) CSF £15.22 TOTE £3.40: £1.40 £2.00 (£8.50) OWNER Mrs Laura Pegg (DORKING) BRED Dale Barlage
2926 Flight Lieutenant (USA) can consider himself a very fortunate winner, for Angelo's Double was laughing at the opposition when he came down three out. With his departure Flight Lieutenant had little to beat and, soon in front, forged clear for a decisive victory. (4/1: 5/2-9/2)
1635 Madison County (IRE) has failed to progress since his promising debut over this course and distance back in November, and was in trouble turning into the straight. However with the opposition tiring and Angelo's Double falling he managed to struggle into a very poor second place. (6/1)
3278 Gordon, fitted with blinkers for the first time and racing over a more suitable trip, was soon in front. Collared four out, he was left in front again by the departure of Angelo's Double, but he was very leg-weary and soon tired. (14/1)
3086 Angelo's Double (IRE), always travelling nicely, cruised into the lead four out and had the situation nicely in hand when crumpling on landing at the next. Losses are only lent. (Evens)

3423 SCUDAMORE CLOTHING 0800 301 301 'N.H.' NOVICES' HURDLE (4-Y.O+) (Class D)

3-15 (3-19) **2m 5f (11 hdls)** £3,467.00 (£1,046.00: £508.00: £239.00) GOING: 0.80 sec per fur (S)

SP RR SF

3186* **Spring Double (IRE) (98)** (NATwiston-Davies) **6-11-7** CLlewellyn (hld up: rdn appr 2 out: chsd ldr appr last: led flat: r.o wl) ....— **1** 9/1[3] 89 44
3152[4] **Fiddling The Facts (IRE) (109)** (NJHenderson) **6-11-2** JRKavanagh (lw: a.p: led appr 2 out tl flat: unable qckn) ....2½ **2** 5/6[1] 82 37
3133* **Peace Lord (IRE) (110)** (MrsDHaine) **7-11-7** JFTitley (lw: hld up: ev ch 2 out: wknd appr last) ....27 **3** 7/2[2] 67 22
3108[5] **Allow (IRE) (93)** (BLlewellyn) **6-11-2b**[1(5)] DJKavanagh (a.p: led 6th to 8th: sn wknd) 21 **4** 14/1 51 6
1539[3] **Fashion Maker (IRE) (86)** (MrsIMcKie) **7-11-2** LHarvey (lw: sme hdwy 7th: wknd 8th) ....5 **5** 33/1 42 —
3172[5] **Professor Page (IRE)** (TThomsonJones) **7-11-2** JRailton (bhd fr 6th) ....1¾ **6** 33/1 40 —
3108[6] **Vintage Claret (99)** (JTGifford) **8-11-2** PHide (led to 2nd: led 8th tl appr 2 out: 4th & wkng whn fell ast) .... **F** 9/1[3] — —
2844[7] **Jupiter Probe (IRE)** (RWaley-Cohen) **6-11-2** WMarston (prom to 8th: t.o whn fell last) .... **F** 66/1 — —
Model Tee (IRE) (PRWebber) **8-11-2** DBridgwater (a bhd: t.o whn p.u bef 3 out) .... **P** 33/1 — —
Gratomi (IRE) (PCRitchens) **7-11-2** SFox (a bhd: t.o whn p.u bef 7th) .... **P** 66/1 — —
3052* **Halona (96)** (CPEBrooks) **7-11-2** GBradley (led 2nd: mstke 5th: hdd 6th: wknd 7th: bhd whn p.u bef 8th) .... **P** 9/1[3] — —
3226[14] **Mistress Tudor** (SMellor) **6-10-11** NMann (a bhd: t.o whn p.u bef 3 out) .... **P** 66/1 — —
2042[P] **Toshiba House (IRE)** (BEllison) **6-10-11** KJohnson (a bhd: t.o whn p.u bef last) .... **P** 66/1 — —
(SP 128.2%) **13 Rn**

5m 17.7 (23.70) CSF £16.74 TOTE £7.30: £2.00 £1.20 £1.50 (£5.90) Trio £7.30 OWNER Mrs Lorna Berryman (CHELTENHAM) BRED Mrs Catherine Kenneally
OFFICIAL EXPLANATION **Halona: hung badly.**
3186* Spring Double (IRE) moved into second place approaching the last and managed to overhaul the leader on the run-in. (9/1: op 6/1)
3152 Fiddling The Facts (IRE) moved to the front approaching the second last but, try as she might, was unable to contain the winner on the run-in. She should soon return to the winner's enclosure, especially if the ground remains soft. (5/6)
3133* Peace Lord (IRE) appeared to be travelling well in the straight, but had come to the end of his tether soon after jumping the penultimate hurdle. (7/2: 5/2-4/1)
3108 Allow (IRE), fitted with blinkers for the first time, again disappointed, and was in trouble turning into the straight. (14/1: 8/1-16/1)
3052* Halona (9/1: op 5/1)

3424 LEVY BOARD NOVICES' H'CAP HURDLE (0-110) (4-Y.O+) (Class D)

3-50 (3-51) **2m 110y (8 hdls)** £3,566.25 (£1,080.00: £527.50: £251.25) GOING: 0.80 sec per fur (S)

SP RR SF

2961[8] **The Brewmaster (IRE) (85)** (IPWilliams) **5-10-9** PHide (lw: mde all: lft clr 2 out: r.o wl) ....— **1** 7/1 67 32
1663[3] **Mr Poppleton (76)** (RBrotherton) **8-10-0** LHarvey (lw: chsd wnr to 5th: lft 2nd 2 out: no imp) 8 **2** 12/1 50 15
3054[10] **Noble Colours (84)** (SGGriffiths) **4-9-9**(5) DJKavanagh (hdwy appr 3 out: rdn appr last: one pce) ....hd **3** 33/1 58 15
3234[7] **I Recall (IRE) (76)** (PHayward) **6-10-0v** RFarrant (hld up: rdn appr 3 out: wknd appr last) 7 **4** 12/1 43 8
3084[4] **Rising Dough (IRE) (100)** (GLMoore) **5-11-10** APMcCoy (hld up: mstke 4th: rdn appr 3 out: wknd appr 2 out)21 **5** 100/30[2] 47 12
2771[6] **Palladium Boy (82)** (MrsJGRetter) **7-10-6** GBradley (lw: prom to 5th) ....12 **6** 6/1 17 —
2886[6] **Daunt (88)** (FJordan) **5-10-12** DBridgwater (a bhd) ....1 **7** 5/1[3] 22 —
3309[7] **Toshiba Talk (IRE) (84)** (BEllison) **5-10-8** WMarston (mstke 4th: prom to 5th) ....13 **8** 20/1 6 —
1962[F] **Sweetly Disposed (IRE) (88)** (NJHenderson) **9-10-12** JRKavanagh (lw: bhd fr 4th: t.o whn p.u bef 2 out) .... **P** 33/1 — —
2552[9] **Supreme Genotin (IRE) (95)** (JABOld) **8-11-5** CLlewellyn (hld up: chsd wnr fr 5th: ev ch whn blnd & uns rdr 2 out) .... **U** 11/4[1] — —
(SP 119.2%) **10 Rn**

4m 8.8 (18.80) CSF £76.65 CT £2,344.69 TOTE £9.40: £2.40 £2.50 £6.30 (£40.80) Trio £414.00; £414.06 to Windsor 3/3/97 OWNER Mr John Poynton & Mr Jim Brewer (ALVECHURCH) BRED Angela Bracken
LONG HANDICAP Noble Colours 9-10 Mr Poppleton 9-5
WEIGHT FOR AGE 4yo-8lb
2808 The Brewmaster (IRE), taking a drop in distance, made all the running and was greatly helped by the departure of his main rival two from home. The result could have been different had Supreme Genotin remained in the race. (7/1)
1663 Mr Poppleton, given a three-month break and running from 9lb out of the handicap, was left in second place again two out, but had no hope of reeling in the winner. Still a maiden at the winter game after twenty-one attempts, lack of acceleration is a serious problem. (12/1)
Noble Colours ran his best race to date and only just failed to take second prize. (33/1)
3012 I Recall (IRE) ran better here in a visor, if having nothing more to give soon after the penultimate hurdle. (12/1)
3084 Rising Dough (IRE) was not very fluent at several of his hurdles and could never really get in a telling blow. (100/30)
1995 Supreme Genotin (IRE), back over a more suitable trip, was travelling really strongly and had every chance when very awkward at the second last, getting rid of his rider. His turn is surely not far away. (11/4)

3425 THATCHAM STANDARD OPEN N.H. FLAT RACE (4, 5 & 6-Y.O) (Class H)

4-20 (4-21) **2m 110y** £1,323.60 (£369.60: £178.80)

Form	Horse / details	Dist	Pos	SP	RR	SF
	Red Curate (IRE) (GMMcCourt) **6-11-2** DBridgwater (hdwy over 12f out: led 2f out: r.o wl)	—	**1**	16/1	76 f	—
3170^{3}	**Bold Leap** (PRWebber) **5-11-2** MrASansome (led 11f: led over 2f out: sn hdd: unable qckn)	9	**2**	11/2^{2}	67 f	—
3290^{2}	**All Done** (SMellor) **4-10-3** NMann (a.p: led over 5f out tl over 2f out: one pce)	3	**3**	6/1^{3}	59 f	—
3006^{4}	**Crystal Jewel** (PJHobbs) **5-10-11** APMcCoy (hld up: rdn over 4f out: one pce)	2	**4**	11/2^{2}	57 f	—
2844^{15}	**Embargo (IRE)** (JLDunlop) **5-10-9**(7) MrHDunlop (hdwy over 3f out: nvr nrr)	½	**5**	33/1	62 f	—
	Celtic Season (MissHCKnight) **5-10-9**(7) MrAWintle (nvr nr to chal)	½	**6**	12/1	62 f	—
3090^{3}	**Fin Bec (FR)** (APJones) **4-10-8** SMcNeill (a.p: rdn over 4f out: wknd fnl f)	6	**7**	10/1	56 f	—
	Purple Ace (IRE) (NAGaselee) **5-11-2** CLlewellyn (lw: rdn over 4f out: hdwy over 2f out: wknd fnl f)	4	**8**	16/1	52 f	—
	Conquer The Kilt (JWMullins) **6-11-2** SCurran (hdwy 9f out: wknd wl over 1f out)	nk	**9**	33/1	52 f	—
	Sweep Clean (IRE) (JTGifford) **5-11-2** PHide (hld up: shkn up over 4f out: sn wknd)	3½	**10**	4/1^{1}	48 f	—
	Caras Rose (IRE) (MrsJPitman) **5-11-2** RFarrant (bkwd: bhd fnl 4f)	10	**11**	8/1	38 f	—
	Millers Action (LGCottrell) **4-10-3** MissMCoombe (bhd fnl 5f: t.o)	dist	**12**	33/1	—	—
	Champagne Friend (AJWilson) **6-10-11** LHarvey (bhd fnl 9f: t.o)	¾	**13**	14/1	—	—
3090^{9}	**Monmouth Way (IRE)** (PRChamings) **5-11-2** JRKavanagh (prom 8f: t.o)	2½	**14**	33/1	—	—
3170^{6}	**River Dawn (IRE)** (CPEBrooks) **5-11-2** GBradley (lw: hld up: shkn up over 4f out: sn wknd: t.o)	1¾	**15**	16/1	—	—
2938^{8}	**Yonder Star** (GRSmith) **5-10-9**(7) CHynes (bit bkwd: a bhd: t.o)	dist	**16**	33/1	—	—
				(SP 132.0%)	**16 Rn**	

4m 9.7 CSF £96.15 TOTE £23.40: £4.40 £2.20 £3.00 (£75.10) Trio £226.60 OWNER Mrs M Turner & Mr C White (WANTAGE) BRED F. Maxwell
WEIGHT FOR AGE 4yo-8lb

Red Curate (IRE), a full brother to the useful Morgans Harbour, struck the front a quarter-of-a-mile from home and soon asserted. (16/1)
3170 Bold Leap gave a good account of himself and set the pace. Collared over five furlongs from home, he had just got back in front over a quarter-of-a-mile out when passed by the winner. (11/2: 10/1-5/1)
3290 All Done, runner-up on both her previous starts, went for home over five furlongs out but, collared approaching the final quarter mile, was then tapped for toe. (6/1: op 4/1)
3006 Crystal Jewel chased the leaders but could only go up and down in the same place in the straight. (11/2: 4/1-6/1)
Embargo (IRE) received little assistance from the saddle, but stayed on to be nearest at the line. (33/1)
Celtic Season was certainly fit for this racecourse debut and stayed on without ever posing a threat. (12/1: 8/1-14/1)
3090 Fin Bec (FR) (10/1: 6/1-12/1)
Sweep Clean (IRE) (4/1: 5/2-11/2)
Champagne Friend (14/1: 16/1-33/1)

T/Jkpt: £7,571.20 (0.1 Tckts); £9,597.40 to Windsor 3/3/97. T/Plpt: £120.70 (169.79 Tckts). T/Qdpt: £37.80 (21.18 Tckts) AK

3164-WARWICK (L-H) (Good)

Saturday March 1st

WEATHER: Cloudy and windy

3426 WATERGALL NOVICES' HURDLE (I) (4-Y.O+) (Class E)

1-30 (1-32) **2m 4f 110y (11 hdls)** £2,197.50 (£610.00: £292.50) GOING: 0.16 sec per fur (G)

Form	Horse / details	Dist	Pos	SP	RR	SF
2961^{7}	**Silver Thyne (IRE) (95)** (MrsJPitman) **5-11-2** DLeahy (lw: mde all: clr 4th: hit 3 out: r.o wl fr next)	—	**1**	7/1^{3}	89	18
2865*	**Cheerful Aspect (IRE)** (CaptTAForster) **4-10-13** NWilliamson (sn chsng wnr: effrt 3 out: rdn appr next: btn whn blnd last)	18	**2**	4/7^{1}	81	1
	Vadlawys (FR) (SABrookshaw) **6-11-2** RJohnson (bit bkwd: hdwy 7th: nvr trbld ldrs)	10	**3**	13/2^{2}	67	—
3222^{7}	**Torch Vert (IRE) (86)** (NJHWalker) **5-11-2** CMaude (hdwy 6th: rdn 8th: no imp)	12	**4**	12/1	58	—
1950^{3}	**Raffles Rooster** (AGNewcombe) **5-11-2** PHolley (bhd: hdwy 3 out: r.o flat)	hd	**5**	14/1	58+	—
965^{3}	**Kirov Royale** (MarkCampion) **6-10-11** WMcFarland (mstke 2nd: hdwy 6th: wknd appr 3 out)	5	**6**	66/1	49	—
	Tursal (IRE) (TWDonnelly) **8-11-2** MrRArmson (bkwd: s.i.s: plld hrd: bhd tl sme progress fr 3 out)	8	**7**	100/1	48	—
3029^{10}	**Kaye's Secret** (JLHarris) **4-10-2** RSupple (bhd: j.rt 6th: nvr trbld ldrs)	2½	**8**	66/1	41	—
	Glaisnock Lad (IRE) (RHAlner) **5-11-2** RichardGuest (bit bkwd: j.slowly 3rd: sn bhd)	4	**9**	100/1	43	—
3171^{10}	**Grizzly Bear (IRE)** (RMStronge) **7-11-2** SWynne (prom to 6th: sn wknd)	1	**10**	50/1	42	—
2759^{P}	**Goatsfut (IRE)** (BPreece) **7-11-2** TJenks (prom: reminder after 4th: wknd 7th)	26	**11**	100/1	21	—
2893^{4}	**Elgintorus (IRE)** (CJMann) **7-10-13**(3) JMagee (bhd fr 7th)	s.h	**12**	50/1	21	—
3111^{F}	**Lucky Tanner** (MissHCKnight) **6-11-2** JCulloty (nt j.w: chsd ldrs to 7th)	4	**13**	40/1	18	—
	Gildoran Palace (TTBill) **6-11-2** DWalsh (bkwd: mstke 1st: sn t.o: rdn 5th: p.u bef 7th)		**P**	100/1	—	—
1992^{11}	**My Shenandoah (IRE) (62)** (HOliver) **6-11-2** JacquiOliver (in tch: hdwy after 6th: wknd next: bhd whn blnd & uns rdr 3 out)		**U**	40/1	—	—
				(SP 119.6%)	**15 Rn**	

5m 2.9 (15.90) CSF £10.34 TOTE £6.50: £1.40 £1.10 £2.30 (£2.90) Trio £10.50 OWNER Robert & Elizabeth Hitchins (UPPER LAMBOURN) BRED Shane Garvey
WEIGHT FOR AGE 4yo-9lb

2547 Silver Thyne (IRE), the paddock pick, loved being allowed to bowl along and never looked in serious danger. (7/1: op 4/1)
2865* Cheerful Aspect (IRE) went in pursuit of the winner in the final mile but was very weary by the last. He stayed surprisingly well in bad ground on his debut, but was effective at eight to ten furlongs on the level and is certainly worth a try over shorter. (4/7)
Vadlawys (FR), who beat Sunshack in the Group Two Prix Hocquart in 1994, is a very impressive-looking individual and showed enough to suggest success will come his way at this game. He will certainly have the speed to be effective over shorter. (13/2: 3/1-7/1)
Torch Vert (IRE) is still rather on the small side and, bandaged all round, was forcefully ridden just to get near the leaders. (12/1: 16/1-10/1)
1950 Raffles Rooster has won twice on the All-Weather since his hurdles debut, but could never get near these, despite some promising late running. (14/1)
Kirov Royale tried to close in the back straight but the effort came to little. (66/1)

3427 EXTERIOR PROFILES LTD. NOVICES' H'CAP CHASE (5-Y.O+) (Class C)

2-05 (2-06) **2m 4f 110y (17 fncs)** £7,165.00 (£2,170.00: £1,060.00: £505.00) GOING: 0.16 sec per fur (G)

		Dist	Pos	SP	RR	SF
2926*	**Garnwin (IRE) (106)** (NJHenderson) **7-11-5** NWilliamson (lw: j.w: hld up: hdwy 6th: led 4 out: rdn 2 out: r.o)	—	**1**	3/1[1]	122	55
3001[4]	**Whirly (IRE) (95)** (RHAlner) **8-10-8** SMcNeill (hld up: mstke 2nd: hdwy 10th: chsd wnr fr 3 out: rdn & r.o fr next)	1¾	**2**	10/1	110	43
3044[U]	**Exterior Profiles (IRE) (110)** (NATwiston-Davies) **7-11-9** TJMurphy (prom tl lost pl 10th: rallied 4 out: hit 2 out: one pce flat)	¾	**3**	9/2[3]	124	57
2885[3]	**Amber Valley (USA) (97)** (DLWilliams) **6-10-7**(3) GuyLewis (mstke 1st: hdwy appr 11th: hit 4 out: sn btn)	20	**4**	33/1	95	28
3173[2]	**Strokesaver (IRE) (88)** (CPEBrooks) **7-10-1b** JCulloty (led to 3rd: led 10th tl hdd & mstke 12th: hit 4 out: sn btn)	29	**5**	7/1	64	—
3175[U]	**Plunder Bay (USA) (113)** (NJHenderson) **6-11-7**(5) MrCVigors (led 3rd tl mstke & hdd 10th: hit next: sn bhd)	8	**6**	20/1	83	16
2827*	**The Reverend Bert (IRE) (110)** (GBBalding) **9-11-9** BFenton (hld up: fell 10th)		**F**	4/1[2]	—	—
3176[2]	**Jovial Man (IRE) (95)** (RJO'Sullivan) **8-10-8** PHolley (lw: w ldrs: led 12th to 4 out: 3rd & rdn whn blnd & uns rdr next)		**U**	7/1	—	—
3015[4]	**Dream Ride (IRE) (115)** (DNicholson) **7-12-0** RJohnson (j.slowly: blnd & uns rdr 5th)		**U**	9/1	—	—
				(SP 115.0%)	**9 Rn**	

5m 10.7 (6.70) CSF £29.43 CT £121.19 TOTE £3.90: £1.80 £2.30 £2.40 (£30.40) Trio £231.30; £35.84 to Windsor 3/3/97 OWNER Pioneer Heat-Treatment (LAMBOURN) BRED John Kehoe

2926* Garnwin (IRE) won this with some prodigious leaps, and is the sort to prove hard for the Handicapper as he is bone idle once in front. (3/1)

3001 Whirly (IRE), now fully fit, ran a fine race and kept trying to peg back the winner even when the cause looked lost. He deserves to find an opportunity. (10/1)

3044 Exterior Profiles (IRE) put in a better round of jumping this time but ran rather in snatches. After looking held turning for home, he stayed on well after the last. (9/2)

2885 Amber Valley (USA) had closed right up on the leaders when the mistake four out soon saw him in trouble. (33/1)

3173 Strokesaver (IRE), not able to hold the lead for so long this time, did not run as well. The effect of the blinkers may have been less this time. (7/1)

2814 Plunder Bay (USA) took Strokesaver on up front and his mistakes at ten and eleven were followed by him ballooning over the following fence liked a tired horse. (20/1)

3015 Dream Ride (IRE) (9/1: op 6/1)

3428 CRUDWELL CUP H'CAP CHASE (0-135) (5-Y.O+) (Class C)

2-35 (2-36) **3m 5f (22 fncs)** £7,262.50 (£2,200.00: £1,075.00: £512.50) GOING: 0.16 sec per fur (G)

		Dist	Pos	SP	RR	SF
2869[5]	**Jurassic Classic (112)** (MrsLRichards) **10-10-6** MRichards (led tl after 2nd: led 5th to 7th: led 9th to next: led 12th: hit 3 out: mstke last: rdn & hld on wl flat)	—	**1**	14/1	119	44
3018[4]	**Beaurepaire (IRE) (106)** (RHAlner) **9-10-0** SMcNeill (a.p: mstke 14th: ev ch flat: r.o)	¾	**2**	7/1[3]	113	38
2881[3]	**Full of Oats (119)** (MissHCKnight) **11-10-13** JCulloty (lw: hdwy 15th: hit 3 out: styd on flat)	¾	**3**	100/30[1]	125	50
3162[3]	**Killeshin (130)** (HJManners) **11-11-10** SCurran (bhd: hdwy appr 16th: nt pce to chal)	7	**4**	11/2[2]	132	57
3153[2]	**Rocky Park (106)** (GBBalding) **11-10-0** BFenton (hld up: mstke 4th: hdwy 12th: blnd next: wknd 16th)	9	**5**	10/1	103	28
3182[P]	**Danger Baby (106)** (DLWilliams) **7-9-11**(3) GuyLewis (chsd ldr: blnd 8th: mstke 14th: wknd 17th)	3½	**6**	16/1	100	25
2782[6]	**Sounds Strong (IRE) (126)** (DNicholson) **8-11-6** RJohnson (lw: lost pl & mstke 6th: sn pushed along: p.u & dismntd bef 11th)		**P**	100/30[1]	—	—
3153[P]	**Nazzaro (121)** (WGMTurner) **8-11-1b** NWilliamson (led after 2nd to 5th: led 7th to 9th: led 10th to 12th: rdn & wknd 15th: p.u bef 18th)		**P**	10/1	—	—
3046[P]	**Woodlands Genhire (106)** (PAPritchard) **12-10-0b** RBellamy (a bhd: t.o whn p.u bef 2 out)		**P**	50/1	—	—
				(SP 106.7%)	**9 Rn**	

7m 28.9 (8.90) CSF £85.91 CT £314.62 TOTE £16.10: £3.40 £1.50 £1.50 (£44.40) Trio £62.20 OWNER Brian Seal & Roger Rees (CHICHESTER) BRED C. L. Gilman

LONG HANDICAP Danger Baby 9-11 Rocky Park 9-5 Woodlands Genhire 7-13

OFFICIAL EXPLANATION Sounds Strong (IRE): the trainer reported that the gelding was subsequently found to be wrong behind.

2869 Jurassic Classic may have found the ground a little quick for him, but was helped by the step up in trip and is nothing if not game. (14/1)

3018 Beaurepaire (IRE), second in this race last year, repeated the feat off a pound higher mark. (7/1)

2881 Full of Oats won this last season and could not confirm those placings with Beaurepaire on 10lb worse terms, not allowing for Culloty's claim a year ago. (100/30)

3162 Killeshin found the ground too fast and the trip too short, but did enough to show that he is now in form, and in a soft ground Grand National he would be a live outsider as he loves the fences and loves the trip. (11/2)

3153 Rocky Park has appeared in the Handicapper's grip for some while now and, running from 9lb out of the handicap, little more could have been expected. (10/1: op 6/1)

2821 Danger Baby, as a half-brother to one-time Derby hope Traikey, and being by the Guineas runner-up Bairn, has an odd pedigree for an out-and-out stayer, and has yet to prove that this trip is really what he needs. (16/1)

2782 Sounds Strong (IRE) was never really travelling and pulled up rather feelingly and was dismounted after a circuit. He was found to be wrong behind. (100/30)

3429 EMSCOTT CONDITIONAL H'CAP HURDLE (0-100) (4-Y.O+) (Class F)

3-10 (3-10) **2m (8 hdls)** £2,390.00 (£665.00: £320.00) GOING: Not Established

		Dist	Pos	SP	RR	SF
2805[9]	**Galway Boss (IRE) (68)** (IPWilliams) **5-10-1** TDascombe (hld up & plld hrd: hdwy 5th: r.o to ld nr fin)	—	**1**	10/1	51	23
3186[P]	**Sylvester (IRE) (74)** (MissAEBroyd) **7-10-2**(5) MGriffiths (chsd ldr tl led 4th: mstke last: ct nr fin)	½	**2**	16/1	57	29
3131[2]	**Nagobelia (79)** (JPearce) **9-10-7**(5) JO'Shaughnessy (hdwy appr 3 out: rdn & one pce fr next)	3½	**3**	13/2	58	30
2895[3]	**Cambo (USA) (83)** (MCBanks) **11-10-11**(5) RHobson (in tch: lost pl 5th: styd on wl fr 2 out)	6	**4**	10/1	56	28
2842[3]	**Ambidextrous (IRE) (86)** (EJAlston) **5-11-0**(5) LCummins (lw: hdwy appr 4th: no imp fr 3 out)	½	**5**	3/1[1]	59	31
2882[14]	**Anotherone to Note (67)** (HJManners) **6-9-9**(5) ADowling (hdwy appr 4th: rdn 3 out: sn btn)	1¼	**6**	50/1	38	10
3002[4]	**Shifting Moon (77)** (FJordan) **5-10-10b** LAspell (led to 4th: wknd appr 2 out)	nk	**7**	5/1[3]	48	20
3049[U]	**Out of The Blue (67)** (MWEckley) **5-9-9**(5) XAizpuru (bhd fr 4th: mstke 2 out)	6	**8**	14/1	32	4
2874[6]	**Royal Glint (67)** (HEHaynes) **8-10-0** SophieMitchell (nvr plcd to chal)	13	**9**	25/1	19	—
3030[P]	**Rain-N-Sun (76)** (JLHarris) **11-10-9** ChrisWebb (rdn 3rd: a bhd)	½	**10**	16/1	27	—
2943*	**Tango Man (IRE) (72)** (JGMO'Shea) **5-10-5** MichaelBrennan (hdwy 5th: mstke next: sn wknd)	¾	**11**	9/2[2]	23	—

				SP	RR	SF
3056^{7}	**Erlking (IRE) (85)** (SMellor) **7-10-13v**(5) SHearn (prom to 4th)	1	**12**	20/1	35	7
475^{P}	**Days of Thunder (79)** (MrsSMOdell) **9-10-12** DWalsh (chsd ldr to 4th)	dist	**13**	25/1	—	—
2897^{9}	**Millenium Lass (IRE) (84)** (MissMERowland) **9-11-3** PMidgley (bhd tl p.u bef 2 out)		**P**	33/1	—	—
	Kano Warrior (86) (BPreece) **10-11-0**(5) JMogford (prom: blnd 2nd: sn bhd whn p.u bef 3 out)		**P**	50/1	—	—
	Steve Ford (91) (CPMorlock) **8-11-3**(7) MHandley (bkwd: prom tl blnd & uns rdr 1st)		**U**	25/1	—	—
				(SP 133.0%)	**16 Rn**	

3m 50.3 (8.30) CSF £144.18 CT £1,045.74 TOTE £10.90: £1.40 £4.90 £1.70 £1.90 (£140.50) Trio £231.20 OWNER Mr & Mrs John Poynton (ALVECHURCH) BRED Peter Tonery

LONG HANDICAP Royal Glint 9-9 Anotherone to Note 9-6 Out of The Blue 9-7

STEWARDS' ENQUIRY Cummins susp. 10 & 14/3/97 (failure to ensure best possible placing).

Galway Boss (IRE) had cut little ice in novice hurdles but came into his own off this low mark. (10/1)

3050 Sylvester (IRE), back helping to force the pace, looked to have shaken off his rivals off by the second last but then got tired. (16/1)

3131 Nagobelia again ran well but looked short of gears in the home straight. (13/2)

2895 Cambo (USA) really needs further, and the way he stayed on at the finish suggests he is coming to hand. (10/1)

2842 Ambidextrous (IRE), back over hurdles after a couple of placed efforts on the All-Weather, looked held from two out but would probably have finished fourth had he been ridden out. (3/1)

Anotherone to Note settled a little better this time but his effort at halfway only briefly put him in contention. (50/1)

3002 Shifting Moon (5/1: op 12/1)

3430 BLACKDOWN H'CAP HURDLE (0-135) (4-Y.O+) (Class C)

3-45 (3-46) **2m 4f 110y (11 hdls)** £3,649.00 (£1,102.00: £536.00: £253.00) GOING: 0.16 sec per fur (G)

				SP	RR	SF
2880^{9}	**Edgemoor Prince (104)** (PJHobbs) **6-10-2** GTormey (a.p: led 7th: edgd rt flat: all out)	—	**1**	14/1	82	7
3166^{*}	**Lets Be Frank (108)** (NoelChance) **6-10-6** RJohnson (hld up: hdwy appr 7th: ev ch 2 out: hrd rdn: swtchd lft flat: r.o)	nk	**2**	15/8^{1}	86	11
2670^{12}	**Mim-Lou-and (113)** (MissHCKnight) **5-10-11** JCulloty (hld up & bhd: hdwy 8th: nt rch ldrs)	20	**3**	12/1	75	—
2929^{*}	**Reaganesque (USA) (115)** (PGMurphy) **5-10-10**(3) LAspell (lw: hld up: hit 6th: hdwy appr 7th: rdn & wknd 3 out)	1¼	**4**	9/2^{2}	76	1
3105^{3}	**Can Can Charlie (102)** (JPearce) **7-9-7**(7) JO'Shaughnessy (bhd 6th: n.d after)	8	**5**	16/1	57	—
2780^{3}	**Alltime Dancer (IRE) (117)** (OSherwood) **5-11-1b** JAMcCarthy (led 3rd to 6th: wknd 7th)	6	**6**	7/1	67	—
3150^{9}	**Thinking Twice (USA) (128)** (NJHenderson) **8-11-12** BFenton (led to 3rd: led 6th to 7th: wknd appr 3 out)	14	**7**	20/1	67	—
3177^{8}	**Linden's Lotto (IRE) (107)** (JWhite) **8-9-12**(7)ow5 SParker (a bhd: t.o fr 6th)	22	**8**	66/1	29	—
2069^{4}	**Silver Shred (130)** (MissVenetiaWilliams) **6-12-0** NWilliamson (b.d 4th)		**B**	11/1	—	—
2895^{*}	**Silver Standard (108)** (CaptTAForster) **7-10-6b** SWynne (mstkes 1st & 3rd: fell 4th)		**F**	13/2^{3}	—	—
	So Proud (121) (MrsAJPerrett) **12-11-5** CMaude (bkwd: hmpd & uns rdr 4th)		**U**	33/1	—	—
				(SP 116.6%)	**11 Rn**	

5m 2.3 (15.30) CSF £37.07 CT £309.61 TOTE £16.10: £2.60 £1.30 £2.10 (£19.90) Trio £109.90 OWNER The Racing Hares (MINEHEAD) BRED Mrs A. C. Wakeham

LONG HANDICAP Can Can Charlie 9-11 Linden's Lotto (IRE) 9-11

2576 Edgemoor Prince, who ran too freely when highly-tried over three miles at Chepstow last time, was 8lb higher than when winning at Exeter. (14/1)

3166* Lets Be Frank, raised 4lb for his course and distance win a fortnight ago, has gone up exactly two stone in the ratings this season. (15/8)

1353 Mim-Lou-and, who was reported to have been suffering from a throat infection last time, was give a fair bit to do over this longer trip. (12/1)

2929* Reaganesque (USA), up 4lb, had the decent ground he needs, but this contest was much more competitive than his two previous wins here this season. (9/2)

2069 Silver Shred (11/1: 8/1-16/1)

3431 WATERGALL NOVICES' HURDLE (II) (4-Y.O+) (Class E)

4-15 (4-17) **2m 4f 110y (11 hdls)** £2,197.50 (£610.00: £292.50) GOING: 0.16 sec per fur (G)

				SP	RR	SF
2074^{10}	**Manasis (NZ)** (SABrookshaw) **6-11-2** RJohnson (lw: hld up: hdwy after 6th: led 8th: lft clr 3 out: all out)	—	**1**	16/1^{3}	76	1
2891^{*}	**El Freddie (93)** (JABOld) **7-11-8** NWilliamson (lw: led to 8th: lft 2nd & sltly hmpd 3 out: hrd rdn & rallied flat)	3	**2**	11/8^{2}	80	5
3088^{P}	**Amber Ring (70)** (MissKMGeorge) **4-10-2** BFenton (lw: mstke 3rd: hdwy appr 7th: wknd 8th)	25	**3**	20/1	49	—
3184^{9}	**Cool Harry (USA)** (HEHaynes) **6-10-9**(7) MrSDurack (a bhd: t.o)	dist	**4**	66/1	—	—
3049^{5}	**Alpha Leather (62)** (LPGrassick) **6-11-2** MrJGrassick (prom to 7th: t.o)	2½	**5**	66/1	—	—
	Sille Me (IRE) (GAHubbard) **5-11-2** RichardGuest (bkwd: hld up: hdwy appr 7th: wknd 8th: t.o)	5	**6**	25/1	—	—
	Ri Na Mara (IRE) (BAMcMahon) **6-10-11**(5) SRyan (bkwd: bhd fr 7th: t.o)	dist	**7**	66/1	—	—
26^{7}	**Pot Blackbird (68)** (RLee) **8-10-11** RSupple (b.d 1st)		**B**	33/1	—	—
1085^{P}	**Kirby Moorside (49)** (DJMinty) **6-11-2** VSlattery (s.s: fell 1st)		**F**	100/1	—	—
2868^{4}	**Mr Darcy (100)** (PRWebber) **5-11-2** CMaude (prom: wnt 2nd & fell 3 out)		**F**	6/5^{1}	—	—
	Charlie Bigtime (ICampbell) **7-11-2** JCulloty (bit bkwd: bhd: mstke 2nd: t.o 5th: p.u bef 7th)		**P**	25/1	—	—
1795^{P}	**Lumo (IRE)** (KSBridgwater) **6-10-13**(3) RMassey (broke leg & p.u after 1st: dead)		**P**	50/1	—	—
2656^{P}	**Summit Else** (NATwiston-Davies) **6-10-11** TJenks (a bhd: t.o whn p.u bef 7th)		**P**	25/1	—	—
	Cleric on Broadway (IRE) (JPearce) **9-10-4**(7) JO'Shaughnessy (bit bkwd: prom: 4th & wkng whn blnd & uns rdr 8th)		**U**	66/1	—	—
				(SP 121.6%)	**14 Rn**	

5m 8.1 (21.10) CSF £34.18 TOTE £18.30: £2.70 £1.20 £4.00 (£14.30) Trio £52.40 OWNER Mr Stanley Clarke (SHREWSBURY) BRED Glenlogan Park Syndicate & N. D. Landers

WEIGHT FOR AGE 4yo-9lb

1280 Manasis (NZ), twice a winner on the Flat in New Zealand, made hard work of it in the end and probably benefited from the departure of the favourite. (16/1)

2891* El Freddie seemed to find this trip on the short side on a course as sharp as this. (11/8)

1131 Amber Ring had been pulled up in a Lingfield bog last time. (20/1)

2868 Mr Darcy, stepping up in distance, was about three lengths down when making his exit, and the way things turned out he probably would have prevailed. (6/5)

3432 TOWN OF WARWICK FOXHUNTERS' TROPHY HUNTERS' CHASE (5-Y.O+) (Class H)
4-45 (4-45) **3m 2f (20 fncs)** £1,095.80 (£303.80: £145.40) GOING: Not Established

				SP	RR	SF
2930*	**The Malakarma** (MissCSaunders) **11-12-5**(5) MrBPollock (lw: chsd ldr tl appr 4th: outpcd 11th: hdwy 15th: led 4 out: rdn out)	—	**1**	9/2[2]	100	28
3270*	**Lord Relic (NZ)** (SABrookshaw) **11-12-2**(5) MrRFord (lw: chsd clr ldr appr 4th: led appr 14th: j.slowly 15th: hdd 4 out: rallied appr last: styd on)	1¾	**2**	1/2[1]	96	24
	Ardesee (RJPeake) **17-11-10**(7) MrJGoldstein (bit bkwd: bhd: pckd 7th: hit 12th: hdwy appr 14th: wknd 4 out)	28	**3**	66/1	75	3
3005[P]	**My Young Man** (CPEBrooks) **12-11-10**(7) MrEJames (led: sn clr: hit 12th: wknd & hdd appr 14th: t.o whn p.u bef 2 out)		**P**	16/1	—	—
	Cappajune (IRE) (DLWilliams) **9-11-9**(3) MrMRimell (blnd & uns rdr 3rd)		**U**	6/1[3]	—	—
3270[P]	**Will it Last** (FLMatthews) **11-11-5v**[1](7) MrLBrown (hit 2nd: j.slowly 4th: sn t.o: j.slowly & uns rdr 15th)		**U**	150/1	—	—
				(SP 107.2%)		**6 Rn**

6m 50.0 (25.00) CSF £6.30 TOTE £4.60: £1.70 £1.20 (£2.50) OWNER Mr Charles Dixey (NORTHAMPTON) BRED C. R. Dixey

2930* The Malakarma repeated last month's course and distance win with the help of a race run at a good pace. (9/2: op 3/1)

3270* Lord Relic (NZ) seemed to be taking command when having a long look at the final ditch. Dismounted after the line, he appeared lame, but was later reported sound. (1/2)

3433 EDSTONE INTERMEDIATE OPEN N.H. FLAT RACE (4, 5 & 6-Y.O F & M) (Class H)
5-15 (5-17) **2m** £1,028.00 (£278.00: £128.00)

				SP	RR	SF
2931[2]	**Melody Maid** (NJHenderson) **5-11-4** NWilliamson (a gng wl: led on bit wl over 1f out: easily)	—	**1**	5/4[1]	76 f	—
3297[3]	**Wise Gunner** (MCPipe) **4-10-10** JamieEvans (led tl hdd wl over 1f out: no ch w wnr)	2	**2**	11/2[3]	74 f	—
	Capsoff (IRE) (GAHubbard) **4-10-10** RichardGuest (neat: unf: hld up: hdwy over 4f out: r.o one pce fnl 2f)	5	**3**	33/1	69 f	—
3006*	**Potter Again (IRE)** (DNicholson) **5-11-8**(3) RMassey (lw: a.p: ev ch 3f out: wknd 2f out)	3½	**4**	3/1[2]	73 f	—
3149[9]	**Cinnamon Club** (NAGaselee) **5-11-4** AThornton (hld up: hdwy 9f out: rdn over 2f out: sn wknd)	2½	**5**	33/1	63 f	—
	Dressed In Style (IRE) (MBradstock) **5-11-4** PHolley (neat: hdwy 7f out: rdn 5f out: wknd over 3f out)	7	**6**	33/1	56 f	—
2965[3]	**Golden Lily** (MissGayKelleway) **4-10-7**(3) TDascombe (nvr nrr)	2	**7**	16/1	54 f	—
	Curtis The Second (CRBarwell) **4-10-10** RJohnson (rangy: s.i.s: nvr nr to chal)	1½	**8**	50/1	53 f	—
	Phoebe The Freebee (IRE) (MrsSRichardson) **6-11-4** JCulloty (cmpt: unf: bkwd: hdwy 9f out: wknd over 3f out)	s.h	**9**	33/1	52 f	—
2911[8]	**See Minnow** (MissSWaterman) **4-10-3**(7) NWillmington (bit bkwd: hdwy 9f out: nvr rchd ldrs)	11	**10**	66/1	41 f	—
3090[10]	**Overrunning** (AHHarvey) **5-11-4** MRichards (bit bkwd: plld hrd: prom 11f)	2½	**11**	100/1	39 f	—
3304[13]	**Gracious Imp (USA)** (JRJenkins) **4-10-3**(7) NTEgan (lw: plld hrd: prom 8f)	5	**12**	33/1	34 f	—
1665[5]	**Oxbridge Lady** (NATwiston-Davies) **6-11-4** TJenks (n.d)	1¾	**13**	20/1	32 f	—
2931[9]	**Nearly A Score** (GBBalding) **5-11-4** BFenton (a bhd)	2½	**14**	16/1	30 f	—
	Hill Sprite (JCMcConnochie) **6-11-4** DLeahy (lengthy: a bhd)	1¾	**15**	100/1	28 f	—
2757[8]	**Folesclave (IRE)** (JSKing) **5-11-4** TJMurphy (lw: a bhd)	¾	**16**	33/1	27 f	—
3170[9]	**Proper Primitive** (CJDrewe) **4-10-3**(7) CRae (hdwy 9f out: wknd 5f out)	4	**17**	33/1	23 f	—
2750[9]	**Coromandel** (AHHarvey) **5-11-4** JAMcCarthy (a bhd)	5	**18**	33/1	18 f	—
	Glowing Moon (MissGayKelleway) **4-10-5**(5) ABates (leggy: bit bkwd: chsd ldr 10f)	5	**19**	20/1	13 f	—
	Miss Kilworth (IRE) (KSBridgwater) **6-11-4** RSupple (neat: unf: bit bkwd: plld hrd: a in rr)	6	**20**	66/1	7 f	—
	Newgate Pixie (IRE) (BAMcMahon) **4-10-5**(5) SRyan (leggy: bhd fnl 8f: t.o)	dist	**21**	16/1	—	—
1820[11]	**Hands Off Millie** (CFCJackson) **6-10-13**(5) OBurrows (s.i.s: plld hrd: bhd whn slipped up 6f out)		**S**	100/1	—	—
				(SP 143.4%)		**22 Rn**

3m 48.3 CSF £7.63 TOTE £2.60: £1.40 £3.70 £10.00 (£6.10) Trio £140.30 OWNER Mr R. J. Parish (LAMBOURN) BRED Brian McLean

WEIGHT FOR AGE 4yo-8lb

2931 Melody Maid, with no French raider to contend with this time, made short work of these rivals. (5/4)

3297 Wise Gunner tried her best but the winner was toying with her in the final quarter-mile. (11/2)

Capsoff (IRE), a half-sister to the novice hurdler Ernest William, made a promising enough start to her career. (33/1)

3006* Potter Again (IRE) found this race a good deal hotter than the one she won at Bangor. (3/1: 2/1-7/2)

Cinnamon Club ran better than on her Sandown debut. (33/1)

T/Plpt: £66.90 (193.93 Tckts). T/Qdpt: £36.90 (15.17 Tckts) Dk/KH

3412-DONCASTER (L-H) (Hdles Good to firm, Ch Good to firm, Good patches)
Monday March 3rd
WEATHER: overcast

3434 SPROTBROUGH CLAIMING HURDLE (4-Y.O+) (Class G)
2-00 (2-00) **2m 4f (10 hdls)** £1,639.50 (£452.00: £214.50) GOING minus 0.16 sec per fur (G)

				SP	RR	SF
3269[7]	**Sweet Trentino (IRE) (75)** (MTate) **6-11-2** WMarston (chsd ldrs fr 6th: sn pushed along: disp ld 2 out: hung lft appr last: styd on wl)	—	**1**	16/1	60	17
3201[14]	**Just Supposen (IRE) (75)** (BSRothwell) **6-10-12** BStorey (chsd ldrs fr 5th: led appr 3 out tl hmpd & outpcd 2 out: kpt on flat)	2½	**2**	33/1	54?	11
	Cutthroat Kid (IRE) (119) (MrsMReveley) **7-11-12v** PNiven (lw: hld up: hdwy to chse ldrs 6th: sn pushed along & ev ch fr 3 out: hung rt fr 2 out: one pce flat)	hd	**3**	8/13[1]	68	25
2570[9]	**Westerly Gale (IRE) (85)** (NJHenderson) **7-11-8** JRKavanagh (lw: chsd ldrs tl outpcd fr 3 out)	10	**4**	11/1	56	13
3072[4]	**White Willow (100)** (TWall) **8-11-1b**(3) RMassey (led & sn clr: hdd & wknd appr 3 out)	2	**5**	11/2[2]	50	7
3284[6]	**Dame Prospect (79)** (MissMERowland) **6-10-9v** GaryLyons (chsd ldrs to 4 out: sn outpcd)	7	**6**	9/1[3]	36	—
1249[6]	**Marsh's Law (82)** (GPKelly) **10-11-1**(3) PMidgley (a bhd: t.o fr 4 out)	27	**7**	25/1	23	—
	Coup de Vent (MrsVCWard) **7-10-9**(3) MichaelBrennan (bkwd: a bhd: t.o fr 4 out)	1¾	**8**	50/1	16	—
2012[12]	**Thetwokays** (OBrennan) **6-11-2** MBrennan (t.o whn p.u 4 out)		**P**	33/1	—	—

				SP	RR	SF
2763^{6}	**Tarry (88)** (AStreeter) **4-10-8** TEley (mstke 4th: sn outpcd: p.u bef 2 out: b.b.v)		P	10/1	—	—
				(SP 122.3%)		**10 Rn**

4m 49.5 (9.50) CSF £377.35 TOTE £19.60: £2.60 £5.40 £1.10 (£298.30) Trio £65.40 OWNER Mr R. C. Smith (KIDDERMINSTER) BRED Swettenham Stud

WEIGHT FOR AGE 4yo-9lb

OFFICIAL EXPLANATION **Tarry: the trainer reported that the filly had bled from the nose.**

Sweet Trentino (IRE), dropped in class, at last found the right opportunity, but he had to work hard for it. (16/1)

Just Supposen (IRE), who last won almost two years ago, has been right out of form this season, but this was obviously a much better effort. (33/1)

Cutthroat Kid (IRE) had his chances, but when asked to struggle he showed his true colours, and just wanted to hang right. (8/13)

1041 Westerly Gale (IRE) has been running moderately over fences as well as hurdles, but this was a better effort, although he looked well short of speed when it mattered. (11/1: 8/1-12/1)

1942* White Willow has lost his way since winning a similar event first time out this year. (11/2)

3284 Dame Prospect wears a pricker on her near side and, after running moderately here, finished lame. (9/1)

3435 WADWORTH NOVICES' CHASE (5-Y.O+) (Class E)

2-30 (2-30) **3m (18 fncs)** £3,262.00 (£897.00: £431.00) GOING minus 0.16 sec per fur (G)

				SP	RR	SF
3281^{9}	**Suvla Bay (IRE)** (OBrennan) **9-11-3** MBrennan (trckd ldr: mstkes 2nd & 10th: led last: rdn & r.o)	—	1	$13/2^{3}$	81	—
3201^{15}	**Final Beat (IRE) (78)** (JWCurtis) **8-11-3b** PNiven (lw: trckd ldrs: chal 4 out: led 2 out to last: kpt on)	2	2	$5/1^{2}$	80	—
3173^{3}	**Monicasman (IRE)** (APJarvis) **7-11-3** JFTitley (set slow pce: qcknd fr 12th: hdd 2 out: sn rdn & btn)	7	3	$1/3^{1}$	75	—
				(SP 105.0%)		**3 Rn**

6m 18.6 (24.60) CSF £21.37 TOTE £4.40 (£6.40) OWNER Lady Anne Bentinck (WORKSOP) BRED Patrick Cashman

OFFICIAL EXPLANATION **Monicasman (IRE): no explanation offered.**

Suvla Bay (IRE) had shown nothing for almost two years, and his stable has been out of sorts this season, but he won this very moderate event quite well. (13/2)

2551 Final Beat (IRE) is certainly nothing special, which rather shows this up to be a moderate event. He had every chance until being outpaced on the run-in. (5/1)

3173 Monicasman (IRE) looked as though he only had to stand up to win this, but in the end he proved most disappointing. (1/3)

3436 JOHN BOOTLE MEMORIAL NOVICES' H'CAP CHASE (0-110) (5-Y.O+) (Class D)

3-05 (3-05) **2m 3f 110y (15 fncs)** £4,305.00 (£1,290.00: £620.00: £285.00) GOING minus 0.16 sec per fur (G)

				SP	RR	SF
3202^{4}	**Highbeath (79)** (MrsMReveley) **6-11-5** PNiven (lw: trckd ldrs: disp ld 9th tl led & lft clr 3 out)	—	1	$7/2^{2}$	95+	26
3051^{7}	**Jolly Boat (82)** (FJordan) **10-11-8** PCarberry (chsd ldrs: outpcd 4 out: no ch after)	11	2	7/1	89	20
2799^{3}	**Arctic Sandy (IRE) (85)** (JKMOliver) **7-11-11** BStorey (rr div: effrt 9th: sn rdn & nt pce to chal)	7	3	$9/4^{1}$	86	17
3201^{11}	**Shoofe (USA) (83)** (KAMorgan) **9-11-9** RJohnson (chsd ldrs tl outpcd 11th)	6	4	10/1	79	10
3001^{11}	**Devilry (88)** (AStreeter) **7-12-0** TEley (mstke 5th: wl bhd after)	21	5	12/1	67	—
2672^{P}	**Fair Ally (77)** (MESowersby) **7-11-3** DParker (lw: cl up: disp ld 6th to 9th: sn wknd)	1¼	6	20/1	55	—
3288^{3}	**Glamanglitz (80)** (PTDalton) **7-11-6** RSupple (lw: mde most tl hdd & fell 3 out)		F	$5/1^{3}$	—	—
2877^{4}	**Batty's Island (72)** (BPreece) **8-10-12** TJenks (prom: mstke 8th: sn outpcd: p.u bef 3 out)		P	16/1	—	—
3188^{P}	**Gipsy Rambler (67)** (PJBevan) **12-10-7** WWorthington (p.u bef 6th)		P	16/1	—	—
				(SP 115.5%)		**9 Rn**

4m 55.0 (8.00) CSF £25.85 CT £60.11 TOTE £3.40: £1.50 £1.60 £1.40 (£13.70) Trio £20.60 OWNER Mr A. Sharratt (SALTBURN) BRED Huttons Ambo Stud

2789 Highbeath, after two rehearsals, got his act together here, and was just getting the upper hand when he was left clear. (7/2)

2571 Jolly Boat had his chances, but looked very one-paced when asked a question. (7/1)

2799 Arctic Sandy (IRE), trying a longer trip, again looked woefully short of pace. (9/4)

Shoofe (USA) probably found this ground a bit quick, and ran reasonably until being left struggling in the home straight. (10/1)

2506 Devilry never looked happy. (12/1)

3288 Glamanglitz was probably second best here, as he had just been headed by the winner when he fell three out. (5/1)

3437 E.B.F. 'N.H.' (QUALIFIER) NOVICES' HURDLE (5, 6 & 7-Y.O) (Class E)

3-35 (3-35) **2m 4f (10 hdls)** £2,679.00 (£744.00: £357.00) GOING minus 0.16 sec per fur (G)

				SP	RR	SF
2948^{5}	**Spring Gale (IRE) (111)** (OSherwood) **6-11-10** JOsborne (lw: trckd ldrs: effrt 3 out: styd on to ld fnl 100y)	—	1	Evens ^{1}	82	30
3159^{4}	**Charley Lambert (IRE)** (JMackie) **6-10-11**(3) EHusband (lw: plld hrd: trckd ldrs: led 4 out: rdn & hit 2 out: hdd & nt qckn towards fin)	1¼	2	$11/2^{3}$	71	19
2898^{4}	**Chopwell Drapes (IRE)** (HowardJohnson) **7-11-0** PCarberry (trckd ldrs: effrt 3 out: r.o one pce)	10	3	$7/2^{2}$	63	11
2931^{3}	**Castle Mews (IRE)** (GCBravery) **6-10-9** KGaule (in tch: effrt appr 3 out: styd on: no imp)	8	4	7/1	52	—
1959^{4}	**Smart Lord (86)** (MRBosley) **6-11-0** SMcNeill (hdwy 5th: chsd ldrs fr 4 out tl mstke & wknd 3 out)	15	5	10/1	45	—
3197^{P}	**Florrie Gunner** (JJQuinn) **7-10-6**(3) ECallaghan (hdwy & in tch 4 out: outpcd fr next)	9	6	50/1	32	—
	Belle Baroness (JCMcConnochie) **7-10-9** JRKavanagh (cl up: led 4th to 4 out: sn wknd)	5	7	50/1	28	—
	Barnabe Lad (ALForbes) **7-11-0** GaryLyons (sn t.o: p.u 4 out)		P	50/1	—	—
3102^{P}	**Dougal (72)** (BSRothwell) **6-11-0** BStorey (led to 4th: sn wknd: p.u bef 3 out)		P	33/1	—	—
				(SP 118.0%)		**9 Rn**

4m 47.9 (7.90) CSF £6.65 TOTE £1.90: £1.10 £1.50 £1.70 (£6.00) Trio £3.70 OWNER Crabb, Ead, Moore (UPPER LAMBOURN) BRED T. J. Hurley

2948 Spring Gale (IRE) is an honest sort who stays well, and he certainly needed all his courage to overhaul a very persistent runner-up. (Evens)

3159 Charley Lambert (IRE) put up a tremendous effort. He appreciated this faster ground, and it will surely not be long before he finds a suitable event. (11/2)

2898 Chopwell Drapes (IRE) was always close enough, but he was struggling with the pace in the home straight and may well need either further or more testing ground. (7/2)

2931 Castle Mews (IRE) ran a fair first race here, and the way she was keeping on suggests the name of the game for her will be staying. (7/1)

1959 Smart Lord had his limitations exposed in this event, and he was feeling the pace when a mistake three out finished his hopes. (10/1)

Florrie Gunner got around for the first time, and the experience should have done her good. (50/1)

3438 SOUTH YORKSHIRE NOVICES' H'CAP HURDLE (0-105) (4-Y.O+) (Class E)

4-05 (4-05) **2m 110y (8 hdls)** £2,616.00 (£726.00: £348.00) GOING minus 0.16 sec per fur (G)

Form	Horse	Dist	Pos	SP	RR	SF
3265^{2}	**Silly Money (93)** (TDEasterby) **6-11-4** RGarritty (in tch: effrt 3 out: led flat: all out)	—	1	$11/2^{2}$	72	30
1995^{6}	**Above the Cut (USA) (83)** (CPMorlock) **5-10-8** RJohnson (hdwy 5th: led 2 out tl flat: rallied)	nk	2	16/1	62	20
3166^{2}	**Beaumont (IRE) (98)** (JEBanks) **7-11-9** JRKavanagh (lw: trckd ldrs: chal 3 out: nt qckn towards fin)	1¼	3	$11/4^{1}$	76	34
2953^{7}	**Western General (75)** (MissMKMilligan) **6-9-7**(7) NHorrocks (chsd clr ldr: led after 5th to 2 out: ev ch tl wknd towards fin)	1	4	$10/1^{3}$	52	10
3049^{4}	**Arabian Heights (89)** (JMackie) **4-10-6** TEley (hld up: hdwy appr 3 out: outpcd next: styd on flat)	1¾	5	$11/2^{2}$	64	14
	Daru (USA) (87) (RHollinshead) **8-10-12** JRailton (bhd tl styd on fr 3 out: n.d)	5	6	33/1	57	15
3307^{5}	**The Sharrow Legend (IRE) (75)** (JSisterson) **5-10-0** PCarberry (chsd ldrs tl outpcd fr 3 out)	1¼	7	14/1	43	1
1417^{6}	**Children's Choice (IRE) (75)** (WJMusson) **6-10-0** WMarston (hld up: sme hdwy 3 out: rdn & nvr nr to chal)	3	8	$10/1^{3}$	40	—
2744*	**I'm a Dreamer (IRE) (99)** (MissMERowland) **7-11-10** GaryLyons (chsd ldrs: ev ch appr 3 out: wknd 2 out)	1¾	9	$10/1^{3}$	63	21
3049^{6}	**Nagara Sound (77)** (BPreece) **6-9-9**(7) JMogford (bhd: effrt appr 3 out: n.d)	4	10	20/1	37	—
2939^{8}	**Bright Eclipse (USA) (83)** (JGMO'Shea) **4-9-11**(3) MichaelBrennan (sme hdwy 3 out: sn btn)	s.h	11	25/1	43	—
3204^{8}	**Danny Gale (IRE) (85)** (GMMcCourt) **6-10-10** SMcNeill (prom tl outpcd fr 3 out)	2½	12	14/1	42	—
3019^{10}	**Orchard King (90)** (OBrennan) **7-11-1** MBrennan (hdwy ½-wy: sn w ldrs: wknd fr 3 out)	8	13	16/1	40	—
3049^{F}	**Toulston Lady (IRE) (75)** (JWharton) **5-9-9b**(5) MrRThornton (bhd: hdwy u.p 5th: btn 3 out)	2½	14	14/1	22	—
3158^{11}	**Sioux Warrior (75)** (NTinkler) **5-10-0b** BStorey (mstke 2nd: sn bhd)	dist	15	20/1	—	—
	Blotoft (75) (SGollings) **5-10-0v1** KGaule (plld hrd: led & sn wl clr: wknd & hdd after 5th: sn t.o)	dist	16	33/1	—	—

(SP 135.7%) **16 Rn**

3m 55.3 (5.30) CSF £84.76 CT £279.63 TOTE £4.60: £1.10 £3.60 £1.50 £3.30 (£57.70) Trio £51.90 OWNER Mrs Jean Connew (MALTON) BRED Mrs Joan Pringle

LONG HANDICAP Children's Choice (IRE) 9-11 Bright Eclipse (USA) 9-3 The Sharrow Legend (IRE) 9-13 Western General 9-9 Toulston Lady (IRE) 9-11 Sioux Warrior 9-11 Blotoft 9-11

WEIGHT FOR AGE 4yo-8lb

3265 Silly Money at last got his head in front, but he needed all his rider's considerable strength to do so. (11/2)
1375 Above the Cut (USA) seems to be on a useful handicap mark, and should find a similar event. (16/1)
3166 Beaumont (IRE) had his chances, but was always short of a real turn of foot, and will surely appreciate a bit further. (11/4)
Western General ran a fine race, and kept battling away. He is obviously on good terms with himself. (10/1)
3049 Arabian Heights gives the impression that he has ability, and will improve when he really gets it together. (11/2: 7/2-6/1)
Daru (USA), a noted character, ran pretty well here making late headway, but is never one to trust. (33/1)
3049 Toulston Lady (IRE) (14/1: op 8/1)

3439 HAMBLETON HILLS HUNTERS' CHASE (5-Y.O+) (Class H)

4-40 (4-40) **2m 3f 110y (15 fncs)** £1,177.70 (£327.20: £157.10) GOING: Not Established

Form	Horse	Dist	Pos	SP	RR	SF
3010*	**Slievenamon Mist** (VictorDartnall) **11-11-13**(5) MrJJukes (hdwy 6th: led 9th: r.o strly fr 3 out)	—	1	$11/8^{2}$	114	37
3005^{4}	**Driving Force** (MrsHMobley) **11-12-1b**(7) MrACharles-Jones (a.p: chsng ldrs 4 out: kpt on: no ch w wnr)	20	2	20/1	102	25
	Double Collect (MrsMDRebori) **11-11-11**(7) MrARebori (a chsng ldrs: one pce fr 4 out)	11	3	$12/1^{3}$	89	12
	Tommys Webb (IRE) (CNNimmo) **9-11-7**(7) MrLLay (mstke 3rd: hdwy 8th: nvr trbld ldrs)	6	4	66/1	80	3
2944^{F}	**Al Hashimi** (NTRidout) **13-11-7**(7) MrNRidout (mstke 5th: n.d)	20	5	20/1	63	—
2903^{P}	**No Word** (IBaker) **10-11-7**(7) MrIBaker (led: hit 7th: hdd 9th: sn wknd & t.o)	dist	6	66/1	—	—
	Tipp Down (MsHelenWallis) **14-11-7**(7) MrRThomas (rr div whn fell 8th: dead)		F	50/1	—	—
	The Communicator (MAHill) **11-11-7b**(7) MrMMunrowd (chsd ldr to 8th: wknd qckly: p.u bef 3 out)		P	33/1	—	—
873^{5}	**Dear Emily** (JESwiers) **9-11-9** MrSSwiers (mstkes: sn wl bhd: t.o whn p.u bef 10th)		P	33/1	—	—
	Sheer Jest (WJWarner) **12-12-5**(3) MrAHill (hld up: stdy hdwy 9th: 3rd whn p.u lame after 3 out)		P	$5/4^{1}$	—	—
3095^{3}	**Free Transfer (IRE)** (DJFairbairn) **8-11-11**(3) MrCBonner (hdwy & prom 8th: 2nd whn blnd & uns rdr 11th)		U	$12/1^{3}$	—	—

(SP 122.3%) **11 Rn**

4m 55.4 (8.40) CSF £28.37 TOTE £2.60: £1.10 £4.70 £2.50 (£23.20) Trio £30.30 OWNER Mr Nick Viney (BARNSTAPLE) BRED James Mulcahy

3010* Slievenamon Mist is looking better than ever this season and is worth following. (11/8)
3005 Driving Force had his chances, but was made to look very one-paced by the useful winner. (20/1)
Double Collect likes to be up with the pace, but he was firmly put in his place when the pressure was on in the home straight. (12/1)
Tommys Webb (IRE) was struggling after a mistake early on, but to his credit he kept on at the finish. (66/1)
Sheer Jest likes to come from behind and had just moved into third place, although still with plenty to do, when he broke down three out. (5/4)
3095 Free Transfer (IRE) was in second place, but struggling, when he made a real mess of the fifth last, getting rid of his rider. (12/1)

3440 DONCASTER STANDARD OPEN N.H. FLAT RACE (4, 5 & 6-Y.O F & M) (Class H)

5-10 (5-10) **2m 110y** £1,070.00 (£295.00: £140.00)

Form	Horse	Dist	Pos	SP	RR	SF
2757^{7}	**Ardrom** (PRWebber) **5-11-4** JOsborne (trckd ldrs: outpcd 4f out: hdwy u.p 2f out: led ins fnl f: styd on wl)	—	1	$6/1^{3}$	58 f	—
2675^{4}	**Jessica One (IRE)** (MrsMReveley) **6-11-4** PNiven (hld up & bhd: smooth hdwy ½-wy: led on bit 1½f out: hdd ins fnl f: rdn & fnd nil)	3	2	$6/1^{3}$	55 f	—
3290*	**Memsahib Ofesteem** (SGollings) **6-11-11** KGaule (led: rdn 3f out: hdd 1½f out: kpt on)	1¾	3	$6/1^{3}$	60 f	—
3203^{3}	**Alisande (IRE)** (JAGlover) **5-11-1**(3) MrCBonner (lw: hld up: hdwy 7f out: outpcd 4f out: kpt on fnl f)	4	4	$11/2^{2}$	50 f	—
3070^{9}	**Delightfool** (RNixon) **6-11-4** ADobbin (chsd ldrs: rdn 5f out: outpcd fnl 3½f)	14	5	20/1	36 f	—
	Community Service (IRE) (JNorton) **6-11-1**(3) ECallaghan (narrow: lean: bhd: hdwy u.p 6f out: nvr rchd ldrs)	1¾	6	11/1	34 f	—
	Asked To Leave (JNorton) **5-10-13**(5) BGrattan (hdwy & prom 10f out: wknd 6f out)	5	7	20/1	29 f	—
2931^{7}	**Suilven** (KCBailey) **5-11-4** CO'Dwyer (lw: hld up & bhd: drvn along & hdwy ½-wy: hung lft: wknd fnl 3f)	3½	8	$2/1^{1}$	26 f	—
3142^{6}	**Miss Moneypenny** (MrsAJFindlay) **5-10-11**(7) RBurns (in tch tl outpcd fnl 5f)	½	9	20/1	26 f	—
3149^{6}	**Zephyrelle (IRE)** (NJHenderson) **5-11-4** JRKavanagh (effrt ½-wy: n.d)	1¼	10	$6/1^{3}$	24 f	—
3297^{9}	**Last Action** (JNorton) **4-10-7**(3) GLee (chsd ldrs tl wknd fnl 7f)	11	11	25/1	14 f	—
	Connie Leathart (MsLCPlater) **6-11-4** DBentley (hld up & bhd: n.d)	14	12	33/1	—	—
	Nangeo Brae (IRE) (JLEyre) **6-11-4** OPears (prom tl rdn & wknd 5f out)	¾	13	12/1	—	—

(SP 143.0%) **13 Rn**

3m 54.4 CSF £43.19 TOTE £7.00: £1.90 £2.10 £2.20 (£14.90) Trio £18.40 OWNER Mr F. J. Haggas (BANBURY) BRED F. J. Haggas

WEIGHT FOR AGE 4yo-8lb

1913 Ardrom just stays, and that was all that was needed to gain the upper hand late on. (6/1)
2675 Jessica One (IRE) looked as though she was going to trot up for much of the trip but, when it came down to an effort inside the final furlong, she was caught slightly by surprise and in the end was found wanting. (6/1)
3290* Memsahib Ofesteem just gallops forever and tried to make this a real test, but was done for foot in the closing stages. (6/1)
3203 Alisande (IRE) kept staying on but never looked likely to take a real hand in proceedings. She looks one who will really make her mark when she switches to the National Hunt game proper. (11/2)
2804 Delightfool ran reasonably but is basically short of toe. (20/1)
Suilven did not help her rider by hanging left all the way. (2/1)
3149 Zephyrelle (IRE) (6/1: op 4/1)

T/Plpt: £97.40 (117.82 Tckts). T/Qdpt: £3.10 (310.46 Tckts) AA

3171-WINDSOR (Fig. 8) (Ch Good to firm, Good in st, Hdles Good)
Monday March 3rd
WEATHER: Overcast

3441 BONUSPRINT NOVICES' HURDLE (I) (4-Y.O+) (Class E)
1-50 (1-50) **2m 4f (10 hdls)** £2,022.50 (£560.00: £267.50) GOING: 0.08 sec per fur (G)

				SP	RR	SF
2865[3]	**Pleasureland (IRE) (102)** (RCurtis) **4-10-7** DMorris (a.p: rdn to ld after 7th: sn clr: r.o wl)	—	1	13/8[1]	79	20
727[3]	**Garrynisk (IRE)** (DRGandolfo) **7-10-13**(3) DFortt (led to 7th: rdn appr 3 out: r.o one pce)	4	2	100/30[2]	76	26
1966[7]	**Christchurch (FR)** (SEarle) **7-11-2** CMaude (hdwy 7th: rdn 3 out: lft 2nd 2 out: r.o one pce)	¾	3	16/1	75	25
3000[6]	**Sleazey (70)** (JGO'Neill) **6-11-2b** SCurran (hdwy 7th: wknd appr 3 out: t.o)	dist	4	33/1	—	—
3108[9]	**Farleyer Rose (IRE) (69)** (MrsLRichards) **8-10-11** MRichards (prom to 6th: t.o)	2	5	25/1	—	—
2822[7]	**Maeterlinck (IRE)** (GThorner) **5-10-9**(7) ClareThorner (a.p: led 7th: sn hdd: wknd appr 3 out: t.o)	1¾	6	50/1	—	—
3103[7]	**Modajjaj** (MissLBower) **5-11-2** LHarvey (hdwy & mstke 7th: sn wknd: t.o)	25	7	50/1	—	—
2830[4]	**Mike's Music (IRE)** (DMGrissell) **6-11-2** DGallagher (bhd fr 5th: t.o)	11	8	9/1	—	—
1422[6]	**Dictum (IRE)** (MissHCKnight) **6-11-2** JCulloty (a.p: rdn 3 out: 2nd & btn whn fell 2 out)		F	11/2[3]	—	—
	Delos (NZ) (MrsMerritaJones) **7-11-2** DerekByrne (bit bkwd: mstke 1st: bhd whn jinked & uns rdr appr 3rd)		U	7/1	—	—

(SP 115.6%) **10 Rn**

4m 57.2 (11.20) CSF £6.22 TOTE £2.10: £1.40 £1.40 £2.30 (£5.30) Trio £30.60 OWNER Mrs Sylvia McGarvie (LAMBOURN) BRED Lodge Park Stud
WEIGHT FOR AGE 4yo-9lb
2865 Pleasureland (IRE), well clear on official ratings, had no problems once his jockey had kicked into a clear lead on the long loop and stayed on far too well for the very poor opposition. He stays forever and is sure to find the Triumph Hurdle, his next intended outing, far too classy and quick for him. (13/8)
727 Garrynisk (IRE), having his first run in five months, did not do badly on this hurdling debut, setting the pace to the fourth last. Scrubbed along in the straight, he just won the battle for second prize, but had no hope with the winner. (100/30)
Christchurch (FR) ran much better here. Left in second place two from home, he just lost out in the scrap for the minor honours. (16/1)
2830 Mike's Music (IRE) (9/1: op 6/1)
Dictum (IRE), who has reportedly had a wind operation since flopping on his hurdling debut at Plumpton three-and-a-half months ago, was never far away but was held in second place when falling at the penultimate hurdle. (11/2: op 3/1)
Delos (NZ) (7/1: op 3/1)

3442 FINAL (S) H'CAP HURDLE (0-95) (4-Y.O+) (Class G)
2-20 (2-24) **2m 6f 110y (11 hdls)** £2,300.50 (£643.00: £311.50) GOING: 0.08 sec per fur (G)

				SP	RR	SF
2907[8]	**Noddadante (IRE) (60)** (NRMitchell) **7-9-7**(7) MGriffiths (rdn 6th: hdwy 2 out: str run flat: led nr fin)	—	1	16/1	47	6
3072[8]	**Khazari (USA) (64)** (RBrotherton) **9-10-4** SCurran (hdwy 8th: led appr 2 out: rdn: hdd nr fin)	1¼	2	20/1	50	9
3051[P]	**Hello Me Man (IRE) (79)** (BJLlewellyn) **9-11-5** MrJLLlewellyn (a.p: led 5th tl appr 2 out: one pce flat)	5	3	25/1	62	21
2820[6]	**Jay Em Ess (NZ) (83)** (AGHobbs) **8-11-2**(7) MrGShenkin (lw: hdwy 8th: hrd rdn appr 2 out: one pce flat)	2	4	6/1[1]	64	23
3205[5]	**Ewar Bold (69)** (KOCunningham-Brown) **4-10-0** CLlewellyn (mstkes: nvr nr to chal)	6	5	16/1	46	—
725[P]	**Fox Chapel (83)** (RTJuckes) **10-11-9** GTormey (hdwy fr 3 out: nvr nrr)	hd	6	20/1	60	19
3209[6]	**Lajadhal (FR) (71)** (KBishop) **8-10-11** LHarvey (nvr nrr)	1¼	7	14/1	47	6
2008[P]	**Seminole Wind (61)** (CRBarwell) **6-9-12v**(3)ow1 PHenley (hdwy 8th: wknd 3 out)	2	8	33/1	36	—
3110[5]	**Kashan (IRE) (63)** (PHayward) **9-10-3** NWilliamson (mstke 8th: a mid div)	6	9	6/1[1]	33	—
3209[3]	**Roger's Pal (72)** (PEccles) **10-10-12b** DGallagher (a mid div)	2	10	14/1	41	—
3222[4]	**Katballou (61)** (KGWingrove) **8-9-8**(7) MrOMcPhail (prom to 8th)	¾	11	12/1[3]	29	—
2680[15]	**Murphy's Run (IRE) (60)** (PEccles) **7-9-9**(5) DJKavanagh (bhd fr 5th)	2½	12	33/1	27	—
2943[14]	**Jobber's Fiddle (60)** (DLWilliams) **5-10-0v** MClarke (prom to 8th)	½	13	20/1	26	—
3016[5]	**Whitebonnet (IRE) (84)** (CREgerton) **7-11-5b**(5) SophieMitchell (lw: bhd fr 7th)	5	14	11/1[2]	47	6
2838[5]	**Fortunes Rose (IRE) (61)** (JSKing) **5-10-1** TJMurphy (led to 5th: wknd 8th)	2½	15	16/1	22	—
2820[12]	**Scalp 'em (IRE) (60)** (DrPPritchard) **9-10-0** DrPPritchard (prom to 7th)	11	16	33/1	13	—
3234[14]	**Fane Park (IRE) (78)** (CLPopham) **9-10-11**(7) XAizpuru (bhd fr 7th)	3	17	14/1	29	—
2905[4]	**Raahin (USA) (69)** (SWoodman) **12-10-9** MRichards (a bhd)	20	18	14/1	6	—
2820[17]	**Trehane (70)** (NAGraham) **5-10-10b**[1] PHide (bhd fr 7th: t.o)	29	19	33/1	—	—
2882[9]	**Jonjas Chudleigh (74)** (RGFrost) **10-11-0** JFrost (bhd fr 8th: p.u bef last)		P	11/1[2]	—	—
3205[2]	**Scorpion Bay (61)** (DJSffrenchDavis) **9-9-12**(3) JMagee (t.o whn p.u after 8th)		P	12/1[3]	—	—
1950[P]	**Lees Please (IRE) (60)** (NGAyliffe) **5-10-0** JCulloty (a bhd: t.o whn p.u bef 3 out)		P	33/1	—	—
3205[P]	**Seven Crowns (USA) (72)** (CLPopham) **4-10-0b**(3)ow3 TDascombe (prom to 7th: t.o whn p.u bef 3 out)		P	33/1	—	—
2905[P]	**Kayfaat (USA) (82)** (MCPipe) **9-11-8v** APMcCoy (p.u after 2nd: dismntd)		P	11/1[2]	—	—

(SP 149.0%) **24 Rn**

5m 38.1 (15.10) CSF £301.13 CT £7,089.63 TOTE £28.00: £3.60 £9.10 £9.40 £1.90 (£665.00) Trio Not won; £500.24 to Leicester 4/3/97
OWNER Mr N. R. Mitchell (DORCHESTER) BRED J. and Mrs Harold-Barry
LONG HANDICAP Scalp 'em (IRE) 9-10 Noddadante (IRE) 9-8 Murphy's Run (IRE) 9-13 Ewar Bold 9-10 Lees Please (IRE) 9-10 Seven Crowns (USA) 9-10 Seminole Wind 9-9
WEIGHT FOR AGE 4yo-9lb
Bt in 3,400 gns

Noddadante (IRE), described by his trainer as a nutcase when he first joined the stable, looked anything but the winner as he was being scrubbed along towards the back of the field early on the final circuit. Still only a moderate fifth two out and only fourth jumping the last, he went into overdrive on the run-in and sped past his rivals to grab the initiative near the line. (16/1)
Khazari (USA) bounced back to form and looked to have made a winning move as he went to the front approaching the second last. Grimly trying to fend off his rivals, he appeared to have done so when the late flourish of the winner found him out. (20/1)
1695 Hello Me Man (IRE), pulled up on his last three starts, ran better here and moved to the front with a circuit to go. Collared approaching the second last, he kept on snapping at the leader's heels and was only tapped for toe on the run-in. (25/1)
2820 Jay Em Ess (NZ) was given a far more forceful ride on this occasion. Grimly trying to get into the action in the straight, he was on the leaders' heels jumping the last before lack of acceleration found him out. (6/1)
Ewar Bold stayed on to be nearest at the line. (16/1)
415 Fox Chapel, off the course for five months, stayed on in the straight without posing a threat. He has not won for over two years. (20/1)
3063 Lajadhal (FR) (14/1: op 8/1)
1836* Kayfaat (USA) (11/1: 8/1-12/1)

3443 STORACALL NOVICES' CHASE (5-Y.O+) (Class E)
2-50 (2-53) **2m (12 fncs)** £3,114.25 (£934.00: £449.50: £207.25) GOING: 0.08 sec per fur (G)

			SP	RR	SF
3052[4]	**Quick Quote** (MrsIMcKie) **7-10-10** LHarvey (lw: s.s & wl bhd: poor 3rd whn lft in ld last: r.o wl).....—	1	9/2[2]	78?	—
3172[9]	**Black Statement (IRE)** (JTGifford) **7-10-12**(3) LAspell (rn v.wd bnd after 3rd: bhd fr 4th: t.o whn lft 2nd last).19	2	12/1	64?	—
2926[P]	**Mheanmetoo** (DLWilliams) **6-11-1** PHolley (led: mstke 7th: hdd after 8th: sn wknd: poor 4th whn blnd 2 out).¾	3	33/1	63?	—
1948[7]	**Queens Curate (70)** (MrsEBScott) **10-10-10** DLeahy (a bhd: t.o fr 6th) .....dist	4	40/1	—	—
1452[4]	**Marksman Sparks** (DrDChesney) **7-11-1** SBurrough (bit bkwd: chsd ldr fr 5th: led after 8th tl fell last).....	F	5/1[3]	—	—
	Malwood Castle (IRE) (RHAlner) **7-11-1** AThornton (fell 1st).....	F	11/2	—	—
3229[3]	**Robins Pride (IRE) (95)** (CLPopham) **7-10-12**(3) TDascombe (chsd ldr to 5th: hard rdn appr 3 out: 2nd whn bdly hmpd & uns rdr last).....	U	11/4[1]	—	—
3161[P]	**Mr Bureaucrat (NZ)** (SABrookshaw) **8-11-1** CLlewellyn (blnd 3rd: mod 4th whn j.b rt & uns rdr 6th).....	U	11/4[1]	—	—
			(SP 116.6%)		**8 Rn**

4m 10.5 (20.50) CSF £48.94 TOTE £5.40: £1.30 £2.60 £4.00 (£17.60) Trio £30.40 OWNER Mr M. H. D. Barlow (TWYFORD) BRED J. M. Castle
3052 Quick Quote can be regarded as one of the luckiest winners of the season. Losing considerable ground at the start, she was always well adrift and only plodded around in her own time. At least twenty-five lengths down, she was presented with the race at the last when the front two both came to grief. Luke Harvey is becoming something of a specialist in these disaster-type races and reckons this is about the fifth time it has happened to him and the second this season, Too Plush having been presented a race at Wincanton in December.(9/2)
Black Statement (IRE) can consider himself extremely fortunate to take second place, for he was struggling early on the final circuit and was tailed off when left second at the last. Absolutely nothing should be read into this performance. (12/1: op 8/1)
Mheanmetoo, pulled up on all three of his previous starts to date, set the pace, but he was collared soon after the fifth last and quickly back-pedalled. (33/1)
Marksman Sparks went on soon after the fifth last, and was about a length up on Robins Pride when coming to grief at the final fence. (5/1)
3229 Robins Pride (IRE) kept on snapping at the heels of the leader in the straight, and was only about a length down when badly hampered by that rival at the final fence, causing his rider to fall off. (11/4)

3444 ROBERT WALTERS H'CAP CHASE (0-120) (5-Y.O+) (Class D)
3-25 (3-25) **3m 4f 110y (21 fncs)** £3,933.00 (£1,179.00: £567.00: £261.00) GOING: 0.08 sec per fur (G)

			SP	RR	SF
3132[9]	**Mr Invader (88)** (NAGaselee) **10-10-4** CLlewellyn (in tch: mstke 12th: led 16th: clr 3 out: comf: fin lame)......—	1	11/2[3]	86	—
3175[4]	**Fast Thoughts (99)** (DRGandolfo) **10-11-1** GBradley (in tch: lost pl 16th: rallied 3 out: styd on to go 2nd last).3	2	13/2	95	5
1383[4]	**Vicosa (IRE) (108)** (RHAlner) **8-11-10** AThornton (a.p: mstke 15th: rdn 3 out: one pce).....9	3	9/2[2]	99	9
3182[3]	**Credon (100)** (SWoodman) **9-11-2** MRichards (bhd fr 13th).....11	4	11/2[3]	84	—
3003[5]	**Banntown Bill (IRE) (99)** (MCPipe) **8-11-1v** APMcCoy (led 13th: hdd 16th: wknd 3 out).....16	5	5/2[1]	74	—
	Rio Haina (95) (GFJohnsonHoughton) **12-10-11v**[1] DGallagher (mde most to 13th: wknd 15th: p.u bef 18th).....	P	25/1	—	—
3003[P]	**Celtic Town (104)** (OSherwood) **9-11-6** JAMcCarthy (lost tch 9th: t.o whn p.u bef 17th).....	P	8/1	—	—
3173[6]	**Cruise Control (86)** (RRowe) **11-10-2**ow2 DO'Sullivan (in tch: mstke 17th: wknd appr 4 out: p.u bef 2 out).....	P	14/1	—	—
			(SP 112.5%)		**8 Rn**

7m 27.7 (25.70) CSF £35.71 CT £156.76 TOTE £7.00: £2.00 £1.50 £1.50 (£9.20) Trio £25.00 OWNER Mr M. A. Boddington (LAMBOURN) BRED Dr J. F. Gillespie
LONG HANDICAP Cruise Control 9-8
2821 Mr Invader appreciated this test of stamina and had this contest sewn up turning for home. Unfortunately he finished lame, but if he recovers quickly, he can find another moderate staying handicap. (11/2)
3175 Fast Thoughts ran rather in snatches, but was staying on nicely at the finish. (13/2)
1383 Vicosa (IRE) gave the impression that this extended trip tests his stamina to the full. (9/2)
3182 Credon was no threat in the final mile. (11/2)
3003 Banntown Bill (IRE), not for the first time, did not look very genuine. (5/2)

3445 BONUSPRINT NOVICES' HURDLE (II) (4-Y.O+) (Class E)
3-55 (3-57) **2m 4f (10 hdls)** £2,022.50 (£560.00: £267.50) GOING: 0.08 sec per fur (G)

			SP	RR	SF
3088[2]	**Lord Rooble (IRE) (94)** (JTGifford) **6-11-2** PHide (a.p: led appr 7th: clr last: r.o).....—	1	4/5[1]	65	12
3084[9]	**Cheeky Charlie** (JFfitch-Heyes) **5-10-13**(3) PHenley (hld up: hdwy appr 3 out: chsd wnr 2 out: r.o one pce flat).....3	2	50/1	63	10
2676[P]	**Letmo Warrior (IRE)** (KRBurke) **5-11-2** CMaude (hld up: rdn 3 out: kpt on one pce appr last).....6	3	33/1	58	5
3133[3]	**Super Rapier (IRE)** (GAHubbard) **5-11-2** NWilliamson (chsd ldrs: ev ch 3 out: mstke 2 out: wknd flat).....1½	4	4/1[3]	57	4
	Taarish (IRE) (SMellor) **4-10-7** NMann (in tch tl wknd appr 2 out).....15	5	7/2[2]	45	—
3282[P]	**Risky Tu** (PAKelleway) **6-10-11** APMcCoy (prom: mstke 5th: ev ch 3 out: wknd appr 2 out).....3½	6	12/1	37	—
603[11]	**Bath Times** (BJLlewellyn) **5-10-11** AThornton (in tch tl wknd 7th: t.o).....dist	7	33/1	—	—
	Executive (IRE) (DJSffrenchDavis) **5-10-13**(3) JMagee (bit bkwd: mstkes 1st & 2nd: t.o whn p.u after 3rd).....	P	20/1	—	—
3085[P]	**King's Affair** (PRHedger) **7-11-2** MRichards (led tl appr 7th: sn wknd: t.o whn p.u bef 3 out).....	P	33/1	—	—
			(SP 121.0%)		**9 Rn**

5m 1.9 (15.90) CSF £58.62 TOTE £1.50: £1.20 £4.10 £6.70 (£14.40) Trio £209.40; £126.88 to Leicester 4/3/97 OWNER The Findon Partnership (FINDON) BRED J. and Mrs Liggett
WEIGHT FOR AGE 4yo-9lb

3088 Lord Rooble (IRE), despite fears about the ground, broke his duck here in a moderate event. (4/5)
Cheeky Charlie kept on well in the closing stages but was no threat to the winner. (50/1)
Letmo Warrior (IRE) kept on under pressure in the straight. (33/1)
Risky Tu (12/1: op 8/1)

3446 THAMES VALLEY HUNTERS' CHASE (5-Y.O+) (Class H)

4-25 (4-25) **3m (18 fncs)** £1,287.00 (£357.00: £171.00) GOING: Not Established

				SP	RR	SF
3165[F]	**Capo Castanum** (MissHCKnight) **8-11-7**(7) MrAWintle (t: chsd ldrs: lft 2nd 13th: led appr 3 out: r.o wl)	—	**1**	9/2[2]	106	28
2964[P]	**Jupiter Moon** (MrsCHicks) **8-11-7**(7) MrJMPritchard (hld up: hdwy 4 out: chsd wnr appr 2 out: sn rdn & one pce)	8	**2**	25/1	101	23
3089[P]	**Gambling Royal** (DrPPritchard) **14-11-7**(7) DrPPritchard (swtg: bit bkwd: chsd ldr: lft in ld 13th: hdd appr 3 out: wknd 2 out)	14	**3**	33/1	91	13
	Bollinger (MrsJTGifford) **11-11-7**(7) MrPO'Keeffe (hdwy 4 out: rdn appr next: kpt on one pce)	¾	**4**	13/2	91	13
2964[3]	**Sonofagipsy** (JWDufosee) **13-11-7**(7) MrRNuttall (chsd ldrs: rdn appr 4 out: grad wknd)	12	**5**	5/1[3]	83	5
3062[4]	**Annio Chilone** (RChampion) **11-11-9**(5) MrTMcCarthy (bhd fr ½-wy: t.o)	dist	**6**	12/1	—	—
3089[P]	**Faringo** (MrsDMGrissell) **12-11-11**(7)ow4 MrWGowlett (sn t.o: a bhd)	dist	**7**	25/1	—	—
	Great Simplicity (MichaelAppleby) **10-11-9b**(5) MrASansome (a bhd: t.o whn p.u bef 9th)		**P**	50/1	—	—
3135[U]	**Prinzal** (GMMcCourt) **10-11-7**(7) MrMEmmanuel (uns rdr 1st)		**U**	5/1[3]	—	—
483[8]	**Emerald Moon** (MrsMREagleton) **10-11-7**(7) MrDMaitland (chsd ldrs tl wknd 13th: t.o whn uns rdr 3 out)		**U**	33/1	—	—
	Quiet Confidence (IRE) (MrsSKerley) **7-11-2**(7) MissDStafford (led: 10l clr whn blnd & uns rdr 13th)		**U**	5/2[1]	—	—
				(SP 116.6%)	**11 Rn**	

6m 12.8 (17.80) CSF £96.13 TOTE £5.20: £1.10 £4.20 £8.50 (£148.60) Trio £225.70; £79.49 to Leicester 4/3/97 OWNER Mr D. C. G. Gyle-Thompson (WANTAGE) BRED D. Gyle-Thompson
1068 Capo Castanum jumped soundly and won this going away. (9/2)
Jupiter Moon ran much better than on his seasonal debut, but never looked like getting to the winner. (25/1)
Gambling Royal still looked in need of this and in the circumstances ran quite well. (33/1)
Bollinger made a bit of late headway without threatening the leaders. (13/2)
2964 Sonofagipsy (5/1: op 3/1)
3062 Annio Chilone (12/1: 8/1-14/1)
3135 Prinzal (5/1: 4/1-6/1)
Quiet Confidence (IRE) set a good pace, and was still bowling along in a clear lead when coming to grief six out. (5/2)

3447 MARCH CONDITIONAL H'CAP HURDLE (0-105) (4-Y.O+) (Class F)

5-00 (5-01) **2m (8 hdls)** £2,104.50 (£587.00: £283.50) GOING: 0.08 sec per fur (G)

				SP	RR	SF
3050[P]	**Storm Tiger (IRE) (75)** (SMellor) **6-10-7v** ChrisWebb (hdwy 4th: led next: rdn out)	—	**1**	14/1	57	20
3056[3]	**Fontanays (IRE) (91)** (GMMcCourt) **9-11-9** DFortt (a.p: hrd rdn 2 out: r.o one pce flat)	1¼	**2**	7/2[2]	72	35
3207[5]	**Derisbay (IRE) (71)** (JJBridger) **9-10-0b**(3) MBatchelor (a.p: rdn appr 3 out: mstke 2 out: r.o one pce)	s.h	**3**	20/1	52	15
2666[14]	**Boyfriend (88)** (MrsJPitman) **7-11-6** LAspell (hdwy appr 3 out: hrd rdn appr 2 out: one pce)	7	**4**	12/1	62	25
3234[6]	**Tissisat (USA) (92)** (JKirby) **8-11-10** SophieMitchell (mid div: rdn 5th: kpt on one pce appr last)	nk	**5**	6/1[3]	65	28
3148[3]	**Pedaltothemetal (IRE) (88)** (PMitchell) **5-11-6** GTormey (mid div: rdn 5th: kpt on one pce appr last)	nk	**6**	10/1	61	24
2907[4]	**Night in a Million (80)** (SWoodman) **6-10-9**(3) XAizpuru (prom tl wknd 2 out)	7	**7**	11/1	46	9
3110[10]	**General Shirley (IRE) (79)** (PRHedger) **6-10-8**(3) MClinton (hdwy 5th: wknd appr 2 out)	hd	**8**	16/1	45	8
2828[P]	**Play Games (USA) (88)** (LadyElizaMays-Smith) **9-11-6** DJKavanagh (chsd ldrs tl wknd appr 2 out)	8	**9**	20/1	46	9
2791[10]	**The Bizzo (68)** (JFPanvert) **6-10-0** PHenley (nvr nrr)	5	**10**	66/1	21?	—
3204[4]	**Theme Arena (90)** (MCPipe) **4-11-0** DWalsh (led 4th tl j.slowly next: sn wknd)	2½	**11**	3/1[1]	41	—
831[4]	**Bath Knight (76)** (DJSffrenchDavis) **4-10-0b** JMagee (in tch tl wknd appr 3 out)	8	**12**	16/1	19	—
1768[12]	**Achill Prince (IRE) (68)** (NGAyliffe) **6-10-0** GuyLewis (a bhd)	2	**13**	33/1	9	—
2870[P]	**Braydon Forest (68)** (CJDrewe) **5-10-0b** CRae (mid div tl wknd appr 3 out)	3	**14**	33/1	6	—
3057[7]	**Slightly Special (IRE) (68)** (BAPearce) **5-10-0** SRyan (led tl hdd 4th: sn wknd)	nk	**15**	20/1	5	—
3207[3]	**Precious Wonder (68)** (PButler) **8-10-0** ABates (a bhd)	1½	**16**	20/1	4	—
1207[7]	**Chapel of Barras (IRE) (78)** (MissKMGeorge) **8-10-10** TDascombe (keen hold: bhd fr 3rd)	1½	**17**	33/1	12	—
				(SP 134.4%)	**17 Rn**	

3m 57.1 (9.10) CSF £57.53 CT £957.37 TOTE £13.50: £2.90 £1.50 £3.80 £2.20 (£36.30) Trio £490.10 OWNER W R Partnership (SWINDON) BRED Michael Sinclair
LONG HANDICAP The Bizzo 8-10 Achill Prince (IRE) 9-11 Braydon Forest 9-9 Slightly Special (IRE) 9-4 Precious Wonder 9-8 Bath Knight 9-12
WEIGHT FOR AGE 4yo-8lb
OFFICIAL EXPLANATION **Storm Tiger (IRE): the gelding had been squeezed out last time and could not recover. He had also returned with one shoe missing and another twisted.**
3050 Storm Tiger (IRE) provided his jockey with a winner on his second ride back from a broken leg. It was also the jockey's third successive win in this race. (14/1: op 8/1)
3056 Fontanays (IRE) ran well here on ground that was a shade too lively for him. (7/2)
3207 Derisbay (IRE) ran his best race for some time. (20/1)
Boyfriend was under pressure some way out, and could only keep on at the one speed. (12/1)
3234 Tissisat (USA) appears harshly treated at present. (6/1: 8/1-5/1)
3148 Pedaltothemetal (IRE) finds this trip too short on a sharp track like this. (10/1: 7/1-11/1)
3204 Theme Arena did not look at all keen. (3/1)

T/Jkpt: Not won; £13,859.23 to Leicester 4/3/97. T/Plpt: £1,100.00 (10.92 Tckts). T/Qdpt: £101.80 (8.27 Tckts) SM

3393-KELSO (L-H) (Ch Good, Good to soft ptchs, Hdles Good to soft, Good ptchs)
Tuesday March 4th

Transferred from Sedgefield.
WEATHER: fine

3448 TWEED CONDITIONAL (S) H'CAP HURDLE (0-90) (4-Y.O+) (Class G)
2-00 (2-00) **2m 110y (8 hdls)** £1,866.50 (£519.00: £249.50) GOING: 0.55 sec per fur (S)

Form	Horse	Dist	Pos	SP	RR	SF
2654^{11}	**Cuillin Caper (61)** (TRWatson) **5-10-4b¹** ECallaghan (mde all: drvn out)	—	1	15/2	44	—
3327^{3}	**Arthur Bee (62)** (BBousfield) **10-10-0**(5) CMcCormack (a.p: chsd wnr fr 5th: nt qckn fr 2 out)	3½	2	$5/1^{3}$	42	—
2864^{4}	**Barton Heights (81)** (MrsMReveley) **5-11-5**(5) MHerrington (lw: in tch tl outpcd 4th: styd on fr 2 out: nvr rchd ldrs)	5	3	$3/1^{1}$	56	8
3371^{5}	**Obvious Risk (60)** (EMCaine) **6-9-10**(7) TristanDavidson (in tch: effrt 5th: r.o one pce)	½	4	$9/2^{2}$	34	—
3327^{4}	**Storming Lorna (IRE) (62)** (WMcKeown) **7-10-5** MichaelBrennan (hld up: hdwy 5th: chsng ldrs 2 out: wknd last)	2½	5	$9/2^{2}$	34	—
3031^{9}	**Anorak (USA) (85)** (GMMoore) **7-11-9**(5) THogg (outpcd ½-wy: sn bhd)	24	6	7/1	34	—
3305^{P}	**Blood Brother (57)** (JBarclay) **5-9-11b¹**(3) NHorrocks (chsd wnr fr 5th: sn wknd)	1¾	7	25/1	4	—
3327^{P}	**Birthplace (IRE) (72)** (RTate) **7-11-1** DJKavanagh (outpcd & lost pl fr 3rd: t.o whn p.u bef 2 out)		P	50/1	—	—
				(SP 108.1%)	**8 Rn**	

4m 7.6 (21.60) CSF £36.49 CT £109.60 TOTE £7.20: £1.50 £1.90 £1.10 (£10.90) OWNER Mr R. T. Watson (CRAYKE) BRED W. A. Bromley
LONG HANDICAP Blood Brother 9-12
No bid
Cuillin Caper had blinkers on for the first time and they did the trick. (15/2)
3327 Arthur Bee had his chances again, but looked happy just to follow the winner home. (5/1)
2864 Barton Heights showed something at last, and once he returns to longer trips better looks likely. (3/1)
3371 Obvious Risk was happier on this faster ground, but proved too slow when the pressure was on. (9/2)
3327 Storming Lorna (IRE) looked very dangerous three out but, asked for a real effort going to the next, she again ran out of fuel. (9/2)
2629 Anorak (USA) looked to be in an awkward mood, and would have none of it from the word go. (7/1)

3449 LEVY BOARD 'N.H.' MAIDEN HURDLE (5-Y.O+) (Class F)
2-30 (2-30) **3m 3f (13 hdls)** £2,090.50 (£583.00: £281.50) GOING: Not Established

Form	Horse	Dist	Pos	SP	RR	SF
2919^{P}	**Establish (IRE) (73)** (JPDodds) **9-11-0** AThornton (disp ld tl led 9th: kpt on wl towards fin)	—	1	50/1	60	7
3159^{2}	**Ashgrove Dancer (IRE)** (LLungo) **7-11-5** RSupple (lw: mstkes: hld up: hdwy 8th: ev ch 4 out: disp ld flat: no ex towards fin)	½	2	$1/2^{1}$	65	12
3271^{7}	**Riveaux (IRE)** (GRichards) **7-11-5** PCarberry (lw: hld up: smooth hdwy to disp ld 2 out: rdn flat: fnd nil)	2	3	$5/1^{2}$	64	11
3334^{P}	**Dear Jean** (MESowersby) **7-11-0** DParker (disp ld tl hdd 9th: wknd 4 out: hmpd 3 out)	dist	4	100/1	—	—
1705^{6}	**Hadaway Lad** (HowardJohnson) **5-11-5** ADobbin (chsd ldrs tl wknd fr 4 out)	5	5	11/1	—	—
3328^{11}	**Busy Boy (59)** (DALamb) **10-11-5** JBurke (chsd ldrs tl wknd 7th)	dist	6	100/1	—	—
3066^{6}	**Allerbank** (MrsJStorey) **6-11-5** MrCStorey (prom: outpcd 9th: 6th: rdn & styng on whn fell 3 out)		F	10/1	—	—
2917^{14}	**Grampsawinna** (GROldroyd) **9-11-0** GCahill (outpcd 7th: t.o whn p.u bef 9th: b.b.v)		P	25/1	—	—
3295^{6}	**Sovereign Pass** (RDEWoodhouse) **5-11-5** RGarritty (mstke 1st: p.u lame after 3rd)		P	$8/1^{3}$	—	—
3203^{14}	**Farm Talk** (MESowersby) **5-11-5** BStorey (mstke 6th: sn t.o: p.u after 8th)		P	100/1	—	—
				(SP 120.6%)	**10 Rn**	

6m 56.1 (35.10) CSF £75.54 TOTE £90.20: £5.40 £1.30 £1.30 (£34.90) Trio £35.40 OWNER Mr William Harvey (ALNWICK) BRED Miss Elizabeth Kennedy
OFFICIAL EXPLANATION **Establish (IRE): the mare had lost her confidence over fences and was much happier back hurdling.**
Grampsawinna: the trainer reported that the mare bled form the nose.
Ashgrove Dancer (IRE): the rider reported that the gelding finished distressed.
1968 Establish (IRE) has had a torrid time over fences, but seemed to enjoy this and proved most resilient on the run-in. (50/1)
3159 Ashgrove Dancer (IRE) did not help his chances with some moderate hurdling. On finishing, he was distressed and needed oxygen. (1/2)
Riveaux (IRE), all the better for his recent pipe-opener, looked likely to trot up here but, when it came down to a struggle after the last, his response was disappointing to say the least. (5/1: op 11/4)
2860 Dear Jean, having a rest from chasing, was left way behind over the last four flights. (100/1)
Hadaway Lad, having his first run for three months, showed little. (11/1: 7/1-12/1)

3450 TEVIOT NOVICES' CHASE (5-Y.O+) (Class D)
3-00 (3-01) **2m 1f (12 fncs)** £3,880.00 (£1,080.00: £520.00) GOING: 0.55 sec per fur (S)

Form	Horse	Dist	Pos	SP	RR	SF
3138^{F}	**Real Tonic** (GRichards) **7-11-1** PCarberry (trckd ldrs: led 8th: easily)	—	1	$11/10^{1}$	98+	21
3329^{2}	**Moss Pageant (60)** (FTWalton) **7-11-1** BStorey (led: blnd 6th: hdd 8th: no ch w wnr)	11	2	$9/1^{3}$	88	11
2628^{F}	**Cardinal Sinner (IRE) (56)** (JWade) **8-11-1b** KJones (sn t.o)	dist	3	100/1	—	—
3092^{2}	**Hee's a Dancer (96)** (MissLucindaRussell) **5-10-7** AThornton (chsd ldrs: hit 6th: 2nd whn fell 7th)		F	$5/4^{2}$	—	—
3314^{5}	**Childsway** (SJRobinson) **9-10-12**(3) MichaelBrennan (sn bhd: hdwy 6th: 4th & outpcd whn fell 8th)		F	66/1	—	—
3314^{F}	**Nijway (73)** (MABarnes) **7-10-10**(5) STaylor (chsd ldrs: rdn 6th: hit 3 out: disp 2nd whn blnd bdly & uns rdr 2 out)		U	33/1	—	—
				(SP 107.5%)	**6 Rn**	

4m 26.3 (19.30) CSF £8.67 TOTE £2.00: £1.00 £4.10 (£5.10) OWNER Mr Robert Ogden (PENRITH) BRED Mrs D. A. Whitaker
WEIGHT FOR AGE 5yo-8lb
3138 Real Tonic had a nice confidence-booster here, and never came off the bridle. (11/10)
3329 Moss Pageant ran pretty well again and will obviously pick up a modest event. (9/1)
733 Cardinal Sinner (IRE) managed to get round, which was the only plus point. (100/1)
3092 Hee's a Dancer never looked all that safe, and the downhill section in the back straight had him on the floor. (5/4)
2653 Nijway never looked happy, but did keep responding to pressure and may well have finished second but for blundering away his rider two out. (33/1)

3451 ETTRICK H'CAP CHASE (0-130) (5-Y.O+) (Class C)
3-30 (3-30) **3m 4f (21 fncs)** £6,775.00 (£2,050.00: £1,000.00: £475.00) GOING: 0.55 sec per fur (S)

				SP	RR	SF
2671[2]	**Call the Shots (IRE) (100)** (JWade) **8-10-0** RJohnson (disp ld 4th to 10th: led 13th to 15th: chsd ldrs: r.o u.p flat to ld cl home)	—	1	10/1	111	17
3160[2]	**Fiveleigh Builds (124)** (MissLucindaRussell) **10-11-10** AThornton (lw: mde most to 13th: chal 3 out: lft in ld 2 out: hdd & no ex towards fin)	hd	2	5/2 [2]	135	41
3162[9]	**Parsons Boy (125)** (GRichards) **8-11-11** ADobbin (prom tl outpcd fr 15th: mstke & lost tch 5 out)	24	3	7/2 [3]	122	28
3349[P]	**Master Boston (IRE) (128)** (RDEWoodhouse) **9-12-0** PNiven (a last: mstke 12th: lost tch fr 15th)	dist	4	25/1	—	—
3046[3]	**Court Melody (IRE) (119)** (PFNicholls) **9-11-5b** APMcCoy (lw: a.p: mstke 8th & 13th: led fr 15th: blnd 4 out: disp ld whn blnd & uns rdr 2 out)		U	11/8 [1]	—	—
				(SP 105.8%)		**5 Rn**

7m 24.0 (28.00) CSF £29.56 TOTE £11.00: £5.90 £1.40 (£18.30) OWNER Mr John Wade (MORDON) BRED Jerry Power
LONG HANDICAP Call the Shots (IRE) 9-5

2671 Call the Shots (IRE) has been running really well and gained his just reward here, but he required all his courage and a tremendous ride to make it. (10/1)

3160 Fiveleigh Builds, trying this sort of trip for the first time, got it well, but the weight concession proved just too much in a desperate finish.(5/2)

3162 Parsons Boy was always finding things happening too quickly for his liking on this drying ground, and that caused him to make mistakes. He was left behind on the final circuit. (7/2: op 2/1)

3046 Court Melody (IRE) found the ground drying out too quickly for his liking. Although still at the head of affairs, he never looked all that safe, and a diabolical blunder two out gave his rider no chance of staying aboard. (11/8)

3452 YARROW H'CAP CHASE (0-110) (5-Y.O+) (Class E)
4-00 (4-03) **2m 6f 110y (17 fncs)** £3,418.00 (£1,024.00: £492.00: £226.00) GOING: 0.55 sec per fur (S)

				SP	RR	SF
2900[5]	**Disco des Mottes (FR) (102)** (GRichards) **6-12-0** PCarberry (lw: mde most fr 4th: v.easily)	—	1	6/4 [1]	110++	41
3032[4]	**Last Refuge (IRE) (94)** (TJCarr) **8-11-6** NSmith (led to 4th: cl up tl blnd 10th: sn rdn & lost tch: styd on wl flat)	3½	2	25/1	100	31
1941[5]	**Blazing Dawn (88)** (JSHubbuck) **10-11-0** BStorey (trckd ldrs: chsd wnr fr 10th tl blnd 13th: no imp after)	3	3	25/1	91	22
3289[2]	**Jason's Boy (82)** (JMBradley) **7-10-8** RJohnson (chsd ldrs: hit 9th: hdwy u.p to chse wnr 4 out: wknd fr 2 out: 2nd whn hit last: virtually p.u)	dist	4	9/4 [2]	—	—
2923[4]	**Grand Scenery (IRE) (85)** (HowardJohnson) **9-10-11** ADobbin (hld up: last whn fell 8th)		F	9/2 [3]	—	—
3308[3]	***Risky Dee* (74)** (VThompson) **8-10-0** DBentley (Withdrawn not under Starter's orders: lame at s)		W	9/1	—	—
				(SP 106.6%)		**5 Rn**

5m 55.2 (23.20) CSF £16.82 TOTE £2.10: £1.20 £4.20 (£21.80) OWNER Mr Robert Ogden (PENRITH) BRED Joel Poirier
LONG HANDICAP Risky Dee 9-12

2900 Disco des Mottes (FR) found a poor race here and won with any amount in hand. (6/4: op evens)

3032 Last Refuge (IRE), after getting completely outpaced halfway through the race, struggled on well from the last, but the winner was in a different league. (25/1)

1941 Blazing Dawn breaks blood-vessels, and after two months off this was a reasonable effort. (25/1)

3289 Jason's Boy needed a most determined ride to get into contention four out, and then tired badly soon afterwards. He was virtually pulled up on the run-in. (9/4)

3453 GLEN NOVICES' HURDLE (4-Y.O+) (Class E)
4-30 (4-30) **2m 6f 110y (11 hdls)** £2,320.00 (£645.00: £310.00) GOING: 0.55 sec per fur (S)

				SP	RR	SF
3152[5]	**Lagen Bridge (IRE) (112)** (DMoffatt) **8-12-0** DJMoffatt (lw: led fr 2nd: hit 7th & 2 out: pushed along & r.o)	—	1	2/7 [1]	82	21
1161[8]	**Castle Red (IRE)** (JWade) **6-11-2** KJones (prom: effrt 4 out: styd on: no ch w wnr)	9	2	14/1 [3]	64	3
3100[P]	**Persian Grange (IRE) (50)** (DALamb) **7-11-2** JBurke (trckd ldrs fr 2nd tl rdn & btn appr 2 out)	5	3	100/1	60	—
2861[10]	**Donnegale (IRE)** (TPTate) **5-11-2** RGarritty (lw: chsd ldrs: outpcd 7th: effrt whn hit 3 out: n.d after)	18	4	20/1	47	—
3307[3]	**Caught At Last (IRE)** (MrsMReveley) **6-11-2** PNiven (lw: hld up: effrt ½-wy: outpcd 4 out: n.d after)	15	5	7/2 [2]	37	—
3100[5]	**Houselope Spring** (HowardJohnson) **5-10-11**(5) STaylor (rdn & wknd 3rd: sn wl t.o: p.u after 6th)		P	25/1	—	—
	Absolutely John (IRE) (MartinTodhunter) **9-10-9**(7) CMcCormack (prom 7th: sn outpcd & bhd: p.u bef last)		P	50/1	—	—
2958[P]	**Rye Rum (IRE)** (JWFAynsley) **6-11-2** BStorey (led to 2nd: wknd 6th: p.u 7th)		P	150/1	—	—
				(SP 118.9%)		**8 Rn**

5m 46.1 (29.10) CSF £5.51 TOTE £1.30: £1.10 £4.30 £14.30 (£10.90) Trio £73.50 OWNER Mrs Eileen Milligan (CARTMEL) BRED James Flahavan

3152 Lagen Bridge (IRE) had a simple task here but did not help matters with a couple of poor jumps, and needed to be kept up to his work to make sure of it. (2/7)

Castle Red (IRE) stays well and will surely get further, and a modest race or two can be found. (14/1)

Persian Grange (IRE) looked to be going as well as the winner for a long way, but suddenly ran out of fuel two from home. Nevertheless, this was a much-improved effort. (100/1)

2675 Donnegale (IRE) looked fit but, once off the bit, his jumping left something to be desired, and he failed to make any impression. (20/1)

3307 Caught At Last (IRE) was very disappointing this time, showing little. (7/2)

3454 TILL H'CAP HURDLE (0-120) (4-Y.O+) (Class D)
5-00 (5-00) **3m 3f (13 hdls)** £2,763.00 (£768.00: £369.00) GOING: 0.55 sec per fur (S)

				SP	RR	SF
3368[2]	**Smart Approach (IRE) (98)** (MrsMReveley) **7-11-4** PNiven (trckd ldrs: led after 4 out: sn clr: rdn out)	—	1	5/4 [1]	76	38
2864[2]	**Soloman Springs (USA) (80)** (MrsVCWard) **7-10-0** RJohnson (chsd ldrs: drvn along fr 5th: wl outpcd 4 out: styd on flat)	3½	2	8/1	56	18
1418[7]	**Master of the Rock (104)** (JMackie) **8-11-7v**(3) EHusband (disp ld to 8th: outpcd next: no imp fr 4 out)	22	3	5/1 [3]	67	29
3281[4]	**Pharare (IRE) (97)** (RDEWoodhouse) **7-11-3** PCarberry (mde most tl hdd after 4 out: sn rdn, btn & eased)	dist	4	7/4 [2]	—	—
	Kir (IRE) (82) (VThompson) **9-10-2** DBentley (wl bhd fr 4th: t.o whn p.u after 8th)		P	50/1	—	—
				(SP 110.5%)		**5 Rn**

6m 46.0 (25.00) CSF £9.87 TOTE £1.70: £1.10 £3.10 (£4.70) OWNER Mrs M. B. Thwaites (SALTBURN) BRED Thomas and John Lombard

LONG HANDICAP Soloman Springs (USA) 9-12
3368 Smart Approach (IRE) had the race set up for her but, after going clear three out, she needed driving out to put it beyond doubt. Reportedly, she will now retire to stud. (5/4)
2864 Soloman Springs (USA) was never on the bridle at any stage, but kept struggling on to make sure the winner did not have things all her own way. (8/1)
1418 Master of the Rock had a tussle for the lead which burnt him off four from home. (5/1)
3281 Pharare (IRE) found the ground drying out too much, and had run himself out by the third last. (7/4)

T/Plpt: £63.90 (154.1 Tckts). T/Qdpt: £29.80 (14.27 Tckts) AA

3331-LEICESTER (R-H) (Good, Soft & Heavy patches in front of stands)
Tuesday March 4th
WEATHER: overcast

3455 SQUIRE OSBALDESTON MAIDEN HUNTERS' CHASE (6-Y.O+) (Class H)
2-20 (2-21) **2m 4f 110y (15 fncs)** £2,087.50 (£625.00: £300.00: £137.50) GOING: 0.28 sec per fur (GS)

				SP	RR	SF
	Teeton Mill (MissCSaunders) **8-12-2**(5) MrBPollock (j.w: hld up in tch: led 9th: pushed out flat)	—	1	11/10 1	94+	37
	Cherry Island (IRE) (HWLavis) **9-12-2**(5) MrJJukes (hld up: hdwy 8th: chsd wnr appr last: r.o)	3	2	10/1 3	92	35
1083[4]	**Up For Ransome (IRE)** (MrsAMNaughton) **8-12-0**(7) MrGShenkin (hld up: hdwy 6th: mstke 4 out: one pce appr last)	3½	3	50/1	89	32
	Arctic Chill (IRE) (MrsRAVickery) **7-12-0**(7) MissSVickery (chsd ldrs to 4 out: sn lost tch)	dist	4	9/2 2	—	—
	Count Balios (IRE) (MHWood) **8-12-0**(7) MrPHowse (in tch: blnd 7th: wknd 11th)	3½	5	33/1	—	—
	Dark Rhytham (GACoombe) **8-12-0**(7) MrSMorris (nvr nr ldrs)	2	6	20/1	—	—
3208[P]	**Dashboard Light** (MrsCharlotteCooke) **7-12-4**(3) MrSimonAndrews (prom tl wknd 11th: t.o)	21	7	66/1	—	—
	Diamond Wind (USA) (CountessGoess-Saurau) **9-11-9**(7) MrABeedles (lw: prom tl wknd after 3 out: t.o)	¾	8	16/1	—	—
	Pamela's Lad (GDHanmer) **11-12-0**(7) MrGHanmer (bkwd: a bhd: t.o)	5	9	16/1	—	—
	Pokey Grange (SNBurt) **9-12-0**(7) MajorSJRobinson (bit bkwd: chsd ldrs to 8th: sn lost tch: t.o)	dist	10	40/1	—	—
	Noble Angel (IRE) (PRWhiston) **9-12-0**(7) MrADalton (plld hrd: led 4th tl appr 6th: fell 9th)		F	66/1	—	—
	Judgeroger (TLJones) **11-12-0**(7) MrGLewis (bkwd: a bhd: t.o fr 6th: p.u bef 3 out)		P	20/1	—	—
	Coolgreen (IRE) (MrsSLBates) **9-12-0**(7) MrNBradley (led to 4th: led appr 6th to 9th: wknd & p.u bef 4 out)		P	66/1	—	—
	Samsword (JIPritchard) **8-12-0**(7) MrJIPritchard (lw: a bhd: t.o: p.u bef 2 out)		P	40/1	—	—
	Craftsman (GWPaul) **11-12-0**(7) MissAEmbiricos (lw: blnd & uns rdr 3rd)		U	10/1 3	—	—

(SP 119.5%) **15 Rn**

5m 19.5 (18.50) CSF £10.34 TOTE £2.30: £1.50 £4.20 £13.90 (£13.20) Trio £205.30; £115.69 to Bangor 5/3/97 OWNER Mr C. R. Saunders (NORTHAMPTON) BRED Mrs K. I. Hayward
Teeton Mill, winner of three races between the flags, kicked on at halfway and, making sure there was no let-up in the pace, had the prize in safe-keeping from the penultimate fence. (11/10: evens-5/4)
Cherry Island (IRE) needs a stiffer test of stamina when the ground rides as well as it does round here, and his determined late effort was always being comfortably held. (10/1: 6/1-11/1)
1083 Up For Ransome (IRE), produced very fit after over four months out of action, did his chance no good when missing out at the final ditch, but he gave of his best and is capable of winning at this level. (50/1)
Arctic Chill (IRE) found this trip inadequate, and he was fighting a lost cause from the turn into the straight. (9/2)

3456 LEICESTERSHIRE AND DERBYSHIRE YEOMANRY AMATEUR H'CAP CHASE (0-105) (5-Y.O+) (Class F)
2-50 (2-50) **2m 4f 110y (15 fncs)** £2,846.00 (£848.00: £404.00: £182.00) GOING: 0.28 sec per fur (GS)

				SP	RR	SF
3223[2]	**Eastern River (87)** (CaptTAForster) **11-11-5**(5) MrRThornton (a.p: led 10th: clr 2 out: drvn out)	—	1	4/7 1	84	—
3333[3]	**Dolikos (87)** (THCaldwell) **10-11-5**(5) MrRFord (bhd: hdwy fr 3 out: styd on towards fin)	5	2	25/1	80	—
2910[6]	**Prize Match (72)** (JCTuck) **8-10-2**(7) MrOMcPhail (led to 3rd: w ldrs to 3 out: rdn next: kpt on flat)	hd	3	14/1	65	—
3179[7]	**Salcombe Harbour (NZ) (66)** (DrPPritchard) **13-9-10**(7)ow3 DrPPritchard (led 3rd to 10th: ev ch 3 out: kpt on u.p)	3	4	50/1	57	—
	Stratton Flyer (65) (HSHowe) **7-9-9**(7) MrRWidger (bit bkwd: chsd ldrs tl lost tch 8th: n.d afterwards)	12	5	50/1	46	—
1445[F]	**Ennistymon (IRE) (66)** (JWMullins) **6-9-10**(7)ow2 MrGWeatherley (a bhd: t.o)	15	6	25/1	36	—
3053[U]	**Prudent Peggy (69)** (RGFrost) **10-9-13b**(7) MrAHoldsworth (trckd ldrs to 7th: sn wknd: t.o)	3½	7	11/2 2	36	—
3179*	**Opal's Tenspot (72)** (JMBradley) **10-10-2**(7) MissVRoberts (fell 3rd)		F	8/1 3	—	—
3132[6]	**Glen Mirage (82)** (MJCoombe) **12-10-12**(7) MissMCoombe (a in rr: fell 9th)		F	12/1	—	—

(SP 116.1%) **9 Rn**

5m 29.1 (28.10) CSF £18.20 CT £100.86 TOTE £1.40: £1.10 £3.50 £2.20 (£6.60) Trio £25.60 OWNER Gamston Equine (LUDLOW) BRED Robert Blake
LONG HANDICAP Salcombe Harbour (NZ) 9-7
3223 Eastern River was faced with a very simple task, but he made hard work of it, winning in a very slow time. (4/7)
Dolikos, still one of the backmarkers and tailed-off turning in, did extremely well to gain the runner-up prize, and he has ability when he cares to use it. (25/1)
1865 Prize Match, much more effective at this shorter trip, was tapped for toe early in the straight, but she renewed her effort approaching the last, and is long overdue another success. (14/1)
Salcombe Harbour (NZ) has not won a race for several years, and age is catching up with him, but he did his share of the pacemaking. (50/1)
3132 Glen Mirage (12/1: op 8/1)

3457 MELTON HUNT CLUB HUNTERS' CHASE (6-Y.O+) (Class H)
3-20 (3-22) **2m 4f 110y (15 fncs)** £2,005.00 (£555.00: £265.00) GOING: 0.28 sec per fur (GS)

				SP	RR	SF
3208*	**Trifast Lad** (MJRoberts) **12-11-12**(3) MrPHacking (lw: hld up: hdwy 8th: led 2 out: r.o wl)	—	1	5/1	104+	18
	Minella Express (IRE) (MissCSpearing) **8-11-12**(7) MissCSpearing (j.lft: led to 10th: rdn 2 out: styd on)	2	2	15/8 1	106	20
	Busman (IRE) (KeithPearce) **8-11-8**(7) MrDSJones (a.p: led 10th tl hdd & pckd 2 out: sn btn)	3½	3	4/1 3	100	14
	Kambalda Rambler (MrsHelenHarvey) **13-11-3**(7) MrRArmson (lw: prom: ev ch 3 out: wknd next)	5	4	7/2 2	91	5

	Horse		SP	RR	SF
	Young Nimrod (MrsDMGrissell) **10-11-3**(7) MrGWragg (racd wd: hld up in rr: lost tch 3 out: t.o) 21	5	12/1	74	—
3135[3]	**Pro Bono (IRE)** (AndyMorgan) **7-11-10**(5) MrASansome (prom to 9th: t.o whn p.u bef 2 out)....	P	7/1	—	—

(SP 113.9%) **6 Rn**

5m 23.8 (22.80) CSF £14.36 TOTE £5.70: £2.20 £2.20 (£6.50) OWNER Mr Mike Roberts (HAILSHAM) BRED Wilfred White
3208* Trifast Lad followed up his triumph last month with another readily-gained success. He is on a high at present. (5/1)
Minella Express (IRE), a well-grown, useful-looking individual with winning form in Ireland, gave away valuable ground by jumping to the left, but he made a race of it and there is more success in store. (15/8)
Busman (IRE) landed on his nose at the penultimate obstacle, and lost his pitch, but he was renewing his challenge on the run-in and will return to form when tackling a longer trip. (4/1: op 5/2)
Kambalda Rambler, at his best when the ground is testing over this sort of trip, ran well until finding the quickening tempo too much for him on the run to the second last. (7/2)
Young Nimrod (12/1: 5/1-14/1)
3135 Pro Bono (IRE) (7/1: 7/2-8/1)

3458 ARTHUR CLERKE-BROWN & GRAHAM PIDGEON MEMORIAL HUNTERS' CHASE (6-Y.O+) (Class H)

3-50 (3-51) **3m (18 fncs)** £3,590.00 (£1,070.00: £510.00: £230.00) GOING: 0.28 sec per fur (GS)

	Horse		SP	RR	SF
2903[7]	**Highlandman** (JSHaldane) **11-11-0**(7) MrChrisWilson (a.p: led 9th to 13th: lft in ld 3 out: all out)....—	1	66/1	99	21
2903[6]	**Peajade** (MissJillWormall) **13-11-0**(7) MissJWormall (led to 9th: disp ld fr 2 out: no ex nr fin) ....½	2	25/1	99	21
3270[3]	**Glen Oak** (DGDuggan) **12-11-0**(7) MrMFitzgerald (chsd ldrs: reminders 8th: mstke 12th: hmpd 3 out: styd on u.p) 2½	3	20/1 [3]	97	19
	Corner Boy (CDDawson) **10-11-0**(7) MrsJDawson (lw: hld up: hdwy 4 out: led & j.bdly rt next: sn hdd: nt rcvr) 10	4	7/4 [1]	90	12
	Green Archer (MrsTJHill) **14-11-0**(7) MrsTHill (a in rr) 1¼	5	20/1 [3]	90	12
3270[2]	**Country Tarrogen** (TDWalford) **8-11-2**(5) MrNWilson (hld up: hdwy 9th: led 13th tl hdd & b.d 3 out)....	B	9/4 [2]	—	—
3089[2]	**Avostar** (MissCSaunders) **10-11-2**(5) MrBPollock (lw: lost pl 6th: t.o whn p.u bef 3 out)....	P	9/4 [2]	—	—

(SP 112.8%) **7 Rn**

6m 16.9 (22.90) CSF £839.60 TOTE £48.70: £13.40 £3.70 (£50.80) OWNER Mrs Hugh Fraser (KELSO) BRED Mrs G. MacKean
Highlandman was a very fortunate winner, but the name of the game is jumping and he can certainly do that. (66/1)
Peajade helped force the pace and, was given a second bite at the cherry three out, but strength from the saddle was the deciding factor on the flat. (25/1)
3270 Glen Oak looks to be a hard ride, but he does stick to the task in hand, and had he not been brought to a standstill at the third last, would have gone close to winning. (20/1)
Corner Boy is not an easy ride, and may have won this if his jumping had held together. (7/4)
3270 Country Tarrogen had just been collared when Corner Boy jumped violently right and knocked him over at the third last. He was far from done with when the mishap occurred. (9/4)

3459 GARTHORPE MAIDEN HUNTERS' CHASE (6-Y.O+) (Class H)

4-20 (4-20) **3m (18 fncs)** £2,152.50 (£645.00: £310.00: £142.50) GOING: Not Established

	Horse		SP	RR	SF
	Copper Thistle (IRE) (NJPomfret) **9-11-12**(7) MrRHunnisett (racd wd: a.p: lft in ld 12th: hdd 4 out: led next: sn clr)....—	1	13/2 [3]	91	21
	Elmore (MJRoberts) **10-12-2**(3) MrPHacking (j.w: led to 4th: led 4 out to 3 out: one pce fr next) 11	2	9/4 [1]	84	14
	Mitchells Best (AHollingsworth) **11-12-0**(5) MrJJukes (hdwy 6th: wknd 3 out)....11	3	6/1 [2]	76	6
	Garrylucas (JDLomas) **11-11-12**(7) MrGHanmer (trckd ldrs: j.slowly 9th: lost pl 11th: n.d afterwards)....5	4	10/1	73	3
	Penlet (JIPritchard) **9-11-12**(7) MrJIPritchard (hld up: hdwy & hit 10th: mstke next: wknd appr 3 out) 1¾	5	9/4 [1]	72	2
	The Difference (MGChatterton) **10-11-12**(7) MrMChatterton (j.bdly: a t.o) 6	6	20/1	68	—
	Scale Down (IRE) (MrsJAPickering) **8-12-0**(5) MrASansome (bkwd: led 4th tl fell 12th)....	F	20/1	—	—
	Ollardale (IRE) (WilfredLittleworth) **9-11-12**(7) MrADalton (bkwd: mstkes: rdn ½-wy: t.o whn p.u bef 14th)....	P	20/1	—	—
	Moon Monkey (IRE) (MrsDButler) **9-11-12**(7) MrOMcPhail (prom to 13th: bhd whn blnd & uns rdr 2 out)....	U	50/1	—	—

(SP 114.5%) **9 Rn**

6m 21.0 (27.00) CSF £19.22 TOTE £6.60: £2.80 £1.60 £1.10 (£3.90) Trio £6.00 OWNER Mr R. S. Hunnisett (NORTHAMPTON) BRED Park Enterprises
STEWARDS' ENQUIRY Sansome fined £150 (violent & improper conduct).
Copper Thistle (IRE) won this running away, and it is planned to let him take his chance at Cheltenham next week. (13/2: 3/1-7/1)
Elmore turned in a bold display of fencing, and was the only one able to make a race of it until left in the winner's wake between the last two. (9/4)
Mitchells Best appears to be coming to himself, but the principals proved much too good for him. (6/1)
Garrylucas (10/1: 8/1-12/1)
Penlet made too many jumping errors when he got himself into the action, and he had shot his bolt early in the straight. (9/4)
Scale Down (IRE), winner of a point-to-point in Ireland in 1994, did not look fully wound up for this English debut, but he bowled along in front, and was showing no signs of stopping when overjumping and falling out in the country. (20/1)

3460 THRUSTERS HUNTERS' CHASE (6-Y.O+) (Class H)

4-50 (4-52) **2m 1f (12 fncs)** £2,057.50 (£570.00: £272.50) GOING: Not Established

	Horse		SP	RR	SF
	A Windy Citizen (IRE) (MrsCHicks) **8-11-4**(5) MrASansome (hld up: hdwy appr 3 out: led 2 out: r.o wl)....—	1	5/2 [1]	98	5
	Nowhiski (TimTarratt) **9-11-3**(7) MissCTarratt (a.p: ev ch 2 out: one pce flat)....2	2	8/1	97	4
	Corly Special (MissSJKScott) **10-11-3**(7) MrEJames (hld up: hdwy 8th: rdn 3 out: styd on)....4	3	9/2 [2]	93	—
2944*	**Beau Dandy** (MissCSaunders) **10-12-1**(7) MrTMarks (chsd ldrs: rdn & one pce fr 2 out)....nk	4	5/2 [1]	105	12
	Tumlin Oot (IRE) (JSHaldane) **8-11-3**(7) MrChrisWilson (bit bkwd: hld up: hdwy 8th: hmpd 2 out: nt rcvr) 11	5	40/1	83+	—
	Quarter Marker (IRE) (RLee) **9-11-3**(7) MrJMPritchard (bkwd: in tch to 8th: grad wknd: t.o)....dist	6	50/1	—	—
	Happy Paddy (BRSummers) **14-11-3b**(7) MrMCowley (bkwd: a bhd: t.o fr ½-wy)....dist	7	50/1	—	—
	How Friendly (DGDuggan) **7-11-3**(7) MrMFitzgerald (prom tl fell 8th)....	F	20/1	—	—
	Master Crozina (JCornforth) **9-11-3**(7) MrPCornforth (mstke 3rd: wknd 7th: t.o whn p.u bef 2 out)....	P	25/1	—	—
	Tbilisi (MALloyd) **10-11-3**(7) MrMMunrowd (rel to r: t.o whn p.u 4 out)....	P	66/1	—	—
3432[U]	**Cappajune (IRE)** (DLWilliams) **9-11-2**(3) MrMRimell (s.s: sn chsng ldrs: blnd 4 out: bhd whn p.u bef last)....	P	7/1 [3]	—	—
	Jack the Td (IRE) (JRCornwall) **8-11-3**(7) MrJRCornwall (lw: led tl hdd, blnd & uns rdr 2 out)....	U	14/1	—	—

Michelles Crystal (FLMatthews) **6-11-0**(7)ow2 MrLBrown (bkwd: blnd & uns rdr 2nd).. **U** 100/1 — —
(SP 123.1%) **13 Rn**

4m 30.7 (20.70) CSF £21.51 TOTE £4.60: £2.50 £5.00 £1.20 (£14.80) Trio £39.50 OWNER Mrs J. A. Thomson (CHELTENHAM) BRED Hugh Suffern Bloodstock Ltd

STEWARDS' ENQUIRY Marks susp. 13-15/3/97 (failure to ensure best possible placing).

A Windy Citizen (IRE), a previous winner here, who comes to hand early, took command at the penultimate fence. Galloping on strongly, she won with something to spare. (5/2)

Nowhiski, looking very starey in his coat, ran a fine race in defeat. Once the warmer weather arrives, he should be able to go one better. (8/1: op 9/2)

Corly Special has won at this trip over hurdles, but he was only getting into top gear in the closing stages, and it would seem too sharp for him nowadays. (9/2)

2944* Beau Dandy, poised to challenge from the home turn, failed to pick up when the race began in earnest, and the weight concession could have been the telling factor. (5/2)

Tumlin Oot (IRE) closed on the leaders at the end of the back straight, but was feeling the strain when confronted by a faller at the penultimate fence, and that was the final straw. (40/1)

Cappajune (IRE) (7/1: 4/1-8/1)

Jack the Td (IRE), still to open his account, raced very freely and set the pace, but he been forced to give best when he dived at the second last, and sent his rider into orbit. (14/1)

T/Jkpt: £19,580.10 (0.1 Tckts); £24,819.86 to Bangor 5/3/97. T/Plpt: £1,214.40 (9.33 Tckts). T/Qdpt: £334.60 (1.54 Tckts) IM

3216-SEDGEFIELD (L-H) - Tuesday March 4th

3461- Abandoned - Course Unsafe

3000-BANGOR-ON-DEE (L-H) (Good to soft, Chse Soft patches) Wednesday March 5th

WEATHER: overcast

3468 CHIRK 'N.H.' NOVICES' HURDLE (4-Y.O+) (Class E)

2-10 (2-11) **2m 1f (9 hdls)** £2,379.00 (£669.00: £327.00) GOING: 0.71 sec per fur (S)

	Horse / details	Dist	Pos	SP	RR	SF
3000*	**Darakshan (IRE) (106)** (MissHCKnight) **5-11-8** JCulloty (lw: chsd ldrs: rdn appr last: styd on to ld cl home)	—	**1**	8/11 1	75	38
2677 10	**Zander** (NATwiston-Davies) **5-11-2** CLlewellyn (hld up: hdwy appr 5th: led appr 2 out to last: rdn & r.o)	½	**2**	7/1 3	69	32
3197 3	**Morpheus (99)** (DNicholson) **8-11-2** RJohnson (swtg: lw: hld up: hdwy 6th: slt ld last: hrd rdn & hdd nr fin)	hd	**3**	15/8 2	68	31
3014 7	**Hills Gamble** (PJBevan) **7-11-2** WWorthington (led: sn wl clr: wknd & hdd appr 2 out)	18	**4**	20/1	52	15
	Flutterbud (BJEckley) **5-10-11** JRKavanagh (bit bkwd: nvr plcd to chal: t.o)	22	**5**	100/1	26	—
1665 9	**Gaf** (BRCambidge) **5-11-2** GaryLyons (bkwd: a bhd: t.o)	1½	**6**	100/1	29	—
3295 P	**Palafico** (PRWebber) **7-11-2** AThornton (bkwd: a in rr: t.o)	10	**7**	40/1	20	—
2622 14	**Saucy Dancer** (JCTuck) **4-10-3** SMcNeill (a bhd: t.o)	16	**8**	100/1	—	—
2572 11	**Vita Nuova (IRE)** (WJenks) **6-10-11** RBellamy (bit bkwd: s.s: a bhd: t.o)	25	**9**	66/1	—	—
	Gunny's Girl (FJordan) **6-10-11** RFarrant (chsd ldrs to 6th: wl bhd whn b.d last)		**B**	100/1	—	—
	A Boy Called Rosie (JGMO'Shea) **6-10-13**(3) MichaelBrennan (bkwd: a bhd: t.o: fell last)		**F**	66/1	—	—
	Althrey Mist (IRE) (FLloyd) **5-11-2** TJMurphy (bkwd: lost pl ½-wy: t.o whn p.u bef 6th)		**P**	100/1	—	—
	Mickleover (DMcCain) **7-11-2** DWalsh (bkwd: a in rr: t.o whn p.u bef 2 out)		**P**	100/1	—	—
2668 12	**Worth The Bill (60)** (FJordan) **4-10-8** DerekByrne (chsd ldr to 5th: sn lost tch: t.o whn p.u bef 2 out)		**P**	100/1	—	—

(SP 122.3%) **14 Rn**

4m 14.1 (19.10) CSF £6.70 TOTE £1.60: £1.10 £1.10 £1.50 (£4.50) Trio £1.50 OWNER Mr Michael Watt (WANTAGE) BRED His Highness the Aga Khans Studs S. C.

WEIGHT FOR AGE 4yo-8lb

3000* Darakshan (IRE) looked to be getting the worst of the battle into the last but, with the rail to assist, stayed on doggedly to gain command nearing the line. (8/11)

1665 Zander improved on his first effort over hurdles, and was only tapped for speed in an all-out duel to the finish. He will come into his own when faced with a stiffer test of stamina. (7/1)

3197 Morpheus delivered his challenge and jumped the last in front but, try as he might, he lost out in the battle to remain there. He deserves to find an opening. (15/8)

Hills Gamble attempted to gallop his rivals into the ground, and for most of the way looked sure to do so, but he began to tie up soon after entering the straight, and was legless before reaching the penultimate hurdle. (20/1)

3469 HUGH PEEL CHALLENGE TROPHY HUNTERS' CHASE (5-Y.O+) (Class H)

2-40 (2-41) **3m 110y (18 fncs)** £1,474.00 (£414.00: £202.00) GOING: 1.51 sec per fur (HY)

	Horse / details	Dist	Pos	SP	RR	SF
	Highway Five (IRE) (LadySusanBrooke) **9-12-0**(7) MissEJames (swtg: hdwy 8th: led 11th to 12th: led 4 out to 3 out: hrd rdn to ld post)	—	**1**	20/1	94	19
	Teatrader (MissTOBlazey) **11-11-7**(7) MissTBlazey (lw: j.w: led tl appr 9th: led 3 out: impeded by loose horse & ct cl home)	s.h	**2**	7/1 3	87	12
3363*	**Cape Cottage** (DJCaro) **13-12-0**(7) MrRLawther (lost pl 4th: hdwy 10th: chal last: unable qckn cl home)	1	**3**	5/4 1	93	18
	Orton House (SKelly) **10-11-7**(7) MrRBurton (prom: led appr 9th to 11th: led 12th tl hdd & mstke 4 out: sn btn)	12	**4**	14/1	79	4
	True Fortune (JohnMoore) **7-11-9**(5) MrJJukes (lw: hld up in rr: fell 9th)		**F**	13/8 2	—	—
3055 P	**Corn Exchange** (DGDuggan) **9-11-11**(3) MrMRimell (blnd & uns rdr 4th)		**U**	33/1	—	—

(SP 109.4%) **6 Rn**

7m 0.9 (58.90) CSF £118.59 TOTE £30.30: £7.40 £3.40 (£42.80) OWNER Lady Susan Brooke (BROMYARD) BRED Andrew Magnier

Highway Five (IRE), with a recent outing between the flags to put an edge on him, won this courtesy of his undoubted stamina. (20/1)

Teatrader, a very bold jumper, always appeared to have the measure of his hard-ridden rivals, but he had the company of a loose horse for the majority of the trip and, with that rival drifting across him on the flat, was touched off right on the line. (7/1)

3363* Cape Cottage, sweating and edgy before the start, put in a determined bid at the last, but had to admit his younger rivals too sharp for him on the flat. (5/4)

Orton House (14/1: op 8/1)

3470 CROXTON NOVICES' CHASE (5-Y.O+) (Class D)
3-10 (3-10) **2m 1f 110y (12 fncs)** £3,387.50 (£1,025.00: £500.00: £237.50) GOING: 1.51 sec per fur (HY)

				SP	RR	SF
3229*	**Indian Jockey (117)** (MCPipe) **5-11-5** APMcCoy (mde all: clr fr 3 out: eased flat)	—	**1**	4/9[1]	92++	14
3073F	**The Secret Grey (67)** (DMcCain) **6-11-1** DWalsh (nt j.w: chsd wnr fr 8th: pckd 2 out: no imp)	9	**2**	20/1	72	2
	Santaray (TWDonnelly) **11-11-1** MrRArmson (bkwd: chsd ldrs tl lost pl 8th: styd on again fr 2 out)	hd	**3**	5/1[2]	72	2
477P	**Another Comedy** (RLee) **7-11-1** RJohnson (bit bkwd: mstke 3rd: wknd 8th: t.o)	28	**4**	17/2[3]	46	—
	Althrey Lord (IRE) (FLloyd) **7-11-1** TJMurphy (bkwd: wl bhd fr 3rd: t.o whn p.u bef 6th)		**P**	66/1	—	—
	Jasons Farm (WClay) **7-10-12**(3) GuyLewis (chsd wnr fr 4th tl wknd & blnd 4 out: p.u bef next)		**P**	50/1	—	—
3331P	**Althrey Aristocrat (IRE) (60)** (FLloyd) **7-11-1** SMcNeill (t.o whn p.u bef 7th)		**P**	66/1	—	—
3187[3]	**Relaxed Lad** (JHPeacock) **8-11-1** RBellamy (bit bkwd: blnd & uns rdr 2nd)		**U**	33/1	—	—
				(SP 109.1%)	**8 Rn**	

4m 49.2 (39.20) CSF £10.38 TOTE £1.30: £1.10 £1.80 £1.30 (£7.70) OWNER Mr Stuart Mercer (WELLINGTON) BRED John Hayter
WEIGHT FOR AGE 5yo-8lb

3229* Indian Jockey had much more testing ground to contend with, but his rivals were second class, and he did not need to exert himself to pull them apart. (4/9: 1/4-1/2)

The Secret Grey is a very inept jumper of fences as yet, but he at least got round in one piece this time and the experience can only be beneficial. (20/1)

Santaray is a bit long in the tooth to be making his debut over fences, but he survived, and will be considerably fitter next time he appears. (5/1)

3471 HOLYWELL (S) HURDLE (4-Y.O+) (Class G)
3-40 (3-42) **2m 1f (9 hdls)** £2,337.00 (£657.00: £321.00) GOING: 0.71 sec per fur (S)

				SP	RR	SF
793[5]	**Knight in Side (83)** (MCPipe) **11-12-0** CMaude (led to 2nd: led 4th: clr 3 out: unchal)	—	**1**	10/1	75	48
	Edward Seymour (USA) (74) (WJenks) **10-11-1**(7) MrRBurton (swtg: hld up in tch: hdwy 5th: chsd wnr fr 3 out: no imp)	11	**2**	16/1	59	32
1659[8]	**A S Jim** (OO'Neill) **6-11-2** VSlattery (hld up in rr: styd on fr 3 out: nvr nrr)	13	**3**	20/1	40	13
2874[4]	**Laughing Buccaneer (72)** (DNCarey) **4-10-8** BPowell (hdwy 4th: styd on: nt rch ldrs)	½	**4**	20/1	40	5
3284[15]	**Quixotry** (JMackie) **6-11-2** WMarston (hld up: hdwy 5th: nt rch ldrs)	7	**5**	50/1	33	6
3352[2]	**Halham Tarn (IRE) (78)** (HJManners) **7-11-1**(7) ADowling (led 2nd to 4th: chsd wnr tl wknd appr 3 out)	1	**6**	13/2	38	11
	Verro (USA) (55) (KBishop) **10-11-2** LHarvey (bkwd: prom tl wknd appr 5th: t.o)	29	**7**	50/1	5	—
2806[12]	**Kings Vision (65)** (WJenks) **5-11-2** TJenks (a in rr: t.o)	2¼	**8**	50/1	3	—
3029[5]	**Analogical** (DMcCain) **4-10-3** DWalsh (swtg: prom to 5th: sn lost pl: t.o)	10	**9**	20/1	—	—
2666P	**Ramsdens (IRE) (95)** (NATwiston-Davies) **5-11-8** CLlewellyn (a in rr: t.o)	12	**10**	11/4[1]	—	—
1628[2]	**Ela Man Howa (81)** (ABailey) **6-11-2** DGallagher (hld up: effrt & drvn along 5th: wknd next: t.o)	4	**11**	11/2[3]	—	—
	Bit of Rough (IRE) (WClay) **7-11-2** RJohnson (bit bkwd: a in rr: t.o)	dist	**12**	50/1	—	—
3324[5]	**King Rat (IRE) (85)** (JGMO'Shea) **6-11-2b** APMcCoy (hdwy appr 4th: wknd 6th: no ch whn fell 2 out)		**F**	5/1[2]	—	—
2705[4]	**El Bardador (IRE)** (RJHodges) **4-10-5b**(3) TDascombe (hdwy 4th: wknd 3 out: no ch whn fell next)		**F**	10/1	—	—
1818*	**First Bee (75)** (FJordan) **6-11-3** JOsborne (bkwd: p.u bef 2nd: lame)		**P**	10/1	—	—
3072P	**Backhander (IRE)** (RTPhillips) **5-11-2** DBridgwater (a bhd: t.o whn p.u bef 2 out)		**P**	33/1	—	—
3131[5]	**Emerald Venture (68)** (FCoton) **10-11-7**(7) CRae (a in rr: t.o whn hmpd & uns rdr 2 out)		**U**	33/1	—	—
				(SP 133.2%)	**17 Rn**	

4m 13.2 (18.20) CSF £138.33 TOTE £14.30: £3.10 £11.60 £5.60 (£127.70) Trio £325.50; £412.65 to Wincanton 6/3/97 OWNER Joe & Joanne Richards (WELLINGTON) BRED R. J. Hodges
WEIGHT FOR AGE 4yo-8lb
Bt in 5,250 gns

OFFICIAL EXPLANATION **First Bee: the rider reported that the mare appeared to be lame at the time of pulling up, but subsequently walked out sound.**

Knight in Side has not won a race for five years, and he looked as though he would benefit from the run, but he began to forge clear entering the last half mile, and sauntered home at his leisure. (10/1: 7/1-12/1)

Edward Seymour (USA) went in pursuit of the winner on the approach to the straight but, with the tempo being maintained, could not get near enough to pose a threat. (16/1)

1303 A S Jim did not get going until far too late and, though he is bred for speed, it is more likely that trips in excess of this are what he really needs. (20/1)

2874 Laughing Buccaneer has got some ability and this is his grade, and there could be a small prize or two to be won. (20/1)

3352 Halham Tarn (IRE) helped force the pace, but the winner proved much the stronger, and he called enough before reaching the home straight. (13/2)

1355 Ramsdens (IRE) has only had one outing in the past four months, and paddock inspection would suggest he was still in need of this. (11/4)

3472 CLOY NOVICES' H'CAP CHASE (0-105) (5-Y.O+) (Class E)
4-10 (4-11) **3m 110y (18 fncs)** £3,712.50 (£1,125.00: £550.00: £262.50) GOING: 1.51 sec per fur (HY)

				SP	RR	SF
3354*	**Cariboo Gold (USA) (105)** (KCBailey) **8-12-2b** 6x JOsborne (hld up in tch: led 2 out: comf)	—	**1**	4/5[1]	116+	41
3173[4]	**Calleva Star (IRE) (82)** (RHAlner) **6-10-7** AThornton (chsd ldrs: led 8th to 2 out: kpt on u.p)	3	**2**	9/2[2]	91	16
3176[6]	**Rubins Boy (75)** (NJHWalker) **11-10-0** RFarrant (chsd ldrs to 4 out: sn lost tch)	25	**3**	33/1	68	—
3188[5]	**Burntwood Melody (75)** (PTDalton) **6-10-0b[1]** BFenton (prom tl lost tch 13th: styd on again fr 3 out)	14	**4**	50/1	59	—
3043[6]	**Captiva Bay (75)** (MrsARHewitt) **8-10-0** JRKavanagh (prom to 10th: sn wknd: t.o)	25	**5**	25/1	42	—
3111[5]	**Astral Invasion (USA) (78)** (TWall) **6-10-0b**(3) RMassey (hld up: fell 7th)		**F**	25/1	—	—
2671P	**Ocean Leader (92)** (MrsDHaine) **10-11-3** JFTitley (hld up: hdwy 12th: rdn 4 out: wknd & p.u bef 2 out)		**P**	17/2[3]	—	—
3370P	**Plassy Boy (IRE) (75)** (KRBurke) **8-10-0v[1]** JCulloty (chsd ldrs to 14th: wknd qckly: p.u bef 2 out)		**P**	16/1	—	—
3134[4]	**Milwaukee (IRE) (75)** (OBrennan) **8-10-0** MBrennan (a bhd: t.o whn p.u bef 14th)		**P**	20/1	—	—
2947[7]	**Bonnifer (IRE) (75)** (MJWilkinson) **8-10-0** WMarston (led appr 4th to 6th: led 7th to 8th: wknd 4 out: p.u bef 2 out)		**P**	25/1	—	—
	Canaver (80) (PRWebber) **11-10-5** RBellamy (swtg: led tl appr 4th: led 6th to 7th: wknd 14th: p.u bef 3 out)		**P**	10/1	—	—
3334[8]	**Nordic Flight (75)** (RJEckley) **9-10-0** VSlattery (nt j.w: a bhd: t.o whn p.u bef 12th)		**P**	50/1	—	—
1632P	**Over The Wrekin (78)** (JLNeedham) **10-10-3**ow3 DGallagher (a bhd: t.o whn p.u bef 14th)		**P**	66/1	—	—

			SP	RR	SF
2819^{9}	**Napoleon's Gold (IRE) (87)** (AGFoster) **7-10-5**$^{(7)ow12}$ DCreech (reluctant to r: t.o whn p.u bef 12th)	**P**	100/1	—	—
			(SP 124.9%)	**14 Rn**	

6m 51.2 (49.20) CSF £4.37 CT £69.63 TOTE £1.70: £1.70 £1.50 £10.10 (£4.00) Trio £93.70 OWNER Mrs Sharon Nelson (UPPER LAMBOURN) BRED Regal Oak Farm & Albert G. Clay

LONG HANDICAP Captiva Bay 9-8 Bonnifer (IRE) 9-6 Plassy Boy (IRE) 9-11 Milwaukee (IRE) 8-13 Rubins Boy 9-11 Burntwood Melody 8-13 Nordic Flight 8-13 Over The Wrekin 9-11 Napoleon's Gold (IRE) 8-13

3354* Cariboo Gold (USA) completed his hat-trick within a month with another very smooth success, and the only surprise was that the bookmakers were so generous. (4/5)

3173 Calleva Star (IRE) continues to run well, but luck has not favoured him as yet, though it can only be a matter of time before it does. (9/2)

1372 Rubins Boy does not appear to really stay this trip, and he was going in reverse half-a-mile from home. (33/1)

2671 Ocean Leader moved up smoothly out in the country, and looked sure to take a hand, but he did not find a lot when put under pressure four out, and was well behind when pulled up. He is capable of much better. (17/2: 6/1-9/1)

3473 SANDY LANE NOVICES' H'CAP HURDLE (0-105) (4-Y.O+) (Class E)

4-40 (4-41) **2m 4f (11 hdls)** £2,442.00 (£687.00: £336.00) GOING: 0.71 sec per fur (S)

			SP	RR	SF
3108*	**Lough Tully (IRE) (87)** (FJordan) **7-10-10** JOsborne (mde virtually all: clr whn mstke 3 out: hit last: unchal) .—	**1**	6/4^{1}	75+	21
3049^{8}	**Snowshill Shaker (80)** (NATwiston-Davies) **8-10-3** CLlewellyn (chsd ldrs: wnt 2nd 3 out: no imp) 10	**2**	12/1	60	6
2694^{3}	**Luke Warm (77)** (DRGandolfo) **7-9-9**$^{(5)}$ SophieMitchell (hld up: hdwy 6th: no imp fr 3 out) 3½	**3**	15/2	54	—
3004^{4}	**Lothian Commander (83)** (DMcCain) **5-10-6**^{ow5} DWalsh (prom: pushed along ½-wy: wknd 8th: t.o) 29	**4**	10/1	37	—
3429^{8}	**Out of The Blue (78)** (MWEckley) **5-9-12**$^{(3)ow1}$ MichaelBrennan (chsd ldrs to 4th: sn lost pl: t.o) 6	**5**	50/1	27	—
1953^{6}	**Balmoral Princess (86)** (JHPeacock) **4-10-0b** RBellamy (in tch to 6th: sn lost tch: t.o) 1½	**6**	25/1	34	—
747^{3}	**Ordog Mor (IRE) (103)** (MGMeagher) **8-11-12** DerekByrne (bit bkwd: a bhd: t.o) 20	**7**	16/1	35	—
3344^{3}	**D'naan (IRE) (98)** (MCPipe) **4-10-12b** APMcCoy (prom: rdn 5th: sn wknd: t.o whn p.u bef 2 out)	**P**	7/1^{3}	—	—
2074^{8}	**Rood Music (79)** (MGMeagher) **6-10-2** BPowell (in rr fr ½-wy: t.o whn p.u bef 2 out)	**P**	14/1	—	—
3004^{2}	**Vallingale (IRE) (89)** (MissHCKnight) **6-10-12** JCulloty (hld up in rr: p.u bef 6th)	**P**	9/2^{2}	—	—
2870^{9}	**Kennett Square (IRE) (77)** (LadyElizaMays-Smith) **8-10-0** JAMcCarthy (chsd ldrs to 7th: bhd whn p.u bef 2 out)	**P**	33/1	—	—
1183^{5}	**Alpine Mist (IRE) (95)** (JGMO'Shea) **5-10-11**$^{(7)ow3}$ JTNolan (bkwd: a bhd: t.o whn p.u bef 2 out)	**P**	25/1	—	—
	Montezumas Revenge (IRE) (84) (MJWilkinson) **9-10-7** WMarston (bkwd: prom to 4th: wknd qckly: t.o whn p.u bef 6th)	**P**	33/1	—	—
			(SP 127.3%)	**13 Rn**	

5m 0.1 (24.10) CSF £19.33 CT £107.78 TOTE £2.50: £1.40 £2.20 £1.60 (£43.10) Trio £61.70 OWNER Mr R. A. Hancocks (LEOMINSTER) BRED Seamus Richmond

LONG HANDICAP Kennett Square (IRE) 9-3 Out of The Blue 8-11 Balmoral Princess 9-8

WEIGHT FOR AGE 4yo-9lb

OFFICIAL EXPLANATION Vallingale (IRE): had choked and was unable to handle the soft ground.

3108* Lough Tully (IRE), a different proposition now that he is adopting forcing tactics, had this won a long way out, but there is still room for improvement in his hurdling. (6/4)

Snowshill Shaker gave signs that he is coming back to himself and, if not over-faced, should be able to get off the mark. (12/1: 8/1-14/1)

2694 Luke Warm threatened to take the winner when he wanted, when cruising through to reach a challenging position. However, he does not seem to keep anything in the locker, and his run had come to an end once in line for home. (15/2)

3004 Lothian Commander, nudged along, but remaining in the action, stopped very quickly four out, and this more testing ground appeared to catch him out. (10/1)

Rood Music (14/1: 10/1-16/1)

3004 Vallingale (IRE) (9/2: op 3/1)

T/Jkpt: £17,186.90 (2.25 Tckts). T/Plpt: £394.60 (36.49 Tckts). T/Qdpt: £36.90 (22.31 Tckts) IM

3324-CATTERICK (L-H) (Good)

Wednesday March 5th

WEATHER: overcast

3474 ASKEW DESIGN AND PRINT (S) HURDLE (4-Y.O+) (Class G)

1-55 (1-55) **2m (8 hdls)** £1,952.50 (£540.00: £257.50) GOING: 0.32 sec per fur (GS)

			SP	RR	SF
3031^{5}	**Radmore Brandy (76)** (GRichards) **4-9-12**$^{(3)}$ GLee (lw: trckd ldrs: led 2 out: drvn clr flat) —	**1**	7/1	68	28
3287^{6}	**Noir Esprit (85)** (JMCarr) **4-10-3**$^{(3)}$ FLeahy (lw: chsd ldrs: led 5th to 2 out: nt qckn) 7	**2**	15/8^{1}	66	26
1526^{8}	**Fiasco** (MJCamacho) **4-10-0**$^{(3)ow2}$ ECallaghan (sn bhd: styd on appr 2 out) 18	**3**	14/1	45	3
3305^{4}	**Rasin Standards** (RCraggs) **7-11-0** ADobbin (a in tch: one pce appr 2 out) 2½	**4**	25/1	46	14
3327^{9}	**Kierchem (IRE) (71)** (CGrant) **6-11-0** PNiven (hld up: hdwy 4th: sn prom: wknd appr 2 out) 5	**5**	6/1^{3}	41	9
	I'm Tyson (NZ) (MrsDianneSayer) **9-11-0** MMoloney (bit bkwd: plld hrd: trckd ldrs: ev ch tl rdn & nt run on appr 2 out) 3	**6**	7/1	38	6
3069^{P}	**Emerald Sea (USA) (90)** (JBarclay) **10-11-7** BStorey (hdwy 4th: sn chsng ldrs: wknd qckly appr 2 out: virtually p.u flat: t.o) dist	**7**	10/1	—	—
	Lixos (95) (WStorey) **6-11-2**$^{(5)}$ RMcGrath (lw: nt j.w: bhd & drvn along 3rd: t.o 2 out) 19	**8**	3/1^{2}	—	—
2798^{9}	**Primitive Heart (72)** (HowardJohnson) **5-11-0b**^{1} ALarnach (led to 5th: t.o 2 out) 1½	**9**	20/1	—	—
3313^{13}	**The Grey Texan (67)** (VThompson) **8-11-0** MrMThompson (mstkes: chsd ldrs tl lost pl 4th: t.o 2 out) 3½	**10**	100/1	—	—
	Mr Titch (WMcKeown) **4-10-6** GCahill (fell 1st)	**F**	50/1	—	—
3311^{8}	**Coeur Francais (FR)** (NWaggott) **5-10-7b**$^{1(7)}$ SHaworth (plld hrd: trckd ldrs: blnd & lost pl 4th: mstke & uns rdr next)	**U**	200/1	—	—
			(SP 126.9%)	**12 Rn**	

3m 52.8 (9.80) CSF £20.13 TOTE £9.90: £2.60 £1.10 £7.60 (£8.60) Trio £39.20 OWNER Mr J. R. Salter (PENRITH) BRED W. D. Hockenhull

WEIGHT FOR AGE 4yo-8lb

No bid

3031 Radmore Brandy is not very big, but she seems to be improving with each outing, and she could be named the winner some way from home here. (7/1)

2175 Noir Esprit made the best of his way home, but the winner had far too much toe for him between the last two. On the Flat he was usually fitted with headgear. (15/8)
Fiasco, who lacks substance, was staying on when it was all over. (14/1)
3305 Rasin Standards may be suited by a slight step-up in distance. (25/1)
2913 Kierchem (IRE) ran better here than he did a week ago, but was still well-beaten. (6/1)
I'm Tyson (NZ), well-backed despite looking in need of the outing, wore a tongue-strap. Racing keenly, he moved up on to the heels of the leader rounding the home turn looking as if he could win any time he liked but, suddenly coming under pressure, he carried his head high and looked to have a serious problem. (7/1)
Emerald Sea (USA) (10/1: 14/1-8/1)
Lixos looked well, but was never going at any stage. (3/1)

3475 BEAUFORD PLC NOVICES' HURDLE (4-Y.O+) (Class E)

2-25 (2-26) **2m (8 hdls)** £2,469.00 (£684.00: £327.00) GOING: 0.32 sec per fur (GS)

				SP	RR	SF
3324*	**Cumbrian Maestro** (TDEasterby) **4-10-13** RGarritty (chsd ldrs: led 5th: rdn clr flat)	—	1	4/9[1]	76	20
1652[22]	**Oversman** (JGFitzGerald) **4-10-6** PCarberry (trckd ldrs: hit 4th: chal 2 out: hung lft & nt qckn appr last)	9	2	7/1[3]	60	4
	Undawaterscubadiva (MPBielby) **5-11-0** ADobbin (lw: sn trckng ldrs: nt qckn fr 2 out)	3	3	10/1	57	9
1992*	**Last Try (IRE) (98)** (BSRothwell) **6-11-11**(3) ECallaghan (hdwy 4th: sn prom: outpcd fr 3 out)	7	4	6/1[2]	64	16
3098[8]	**Penny Peppermint** (REBarr) **5-10-9** DParker (chsd ldrs: rdn & outpcd 3 out: grad wknd)	5	5	200/1	40	—
3098[5]	**Milenberg Joys** (PCalver) **5-11-0** TReed (hld up & bhd: plld hrd: hdwy appr 2 out: styd on appr last: nvr nr ldrs)	½	6	33/1	45	—
3271[10]	**Praise Be (FR)** (TPTate) **7-11-0** JCallaghan (a in rr)	16	7	33/1	29	—
	Queen's Counsel (IRE) (MissMKMilligan) **4-10-1** BStorey (plld hrd: sn trckng ldrs: wkng whn blnd 2 out)	½	8	12/1	23	—
	Allerby (JLGoulding) **9-11-0** JSupple (bit bkwd: uns rdr gng to s: bhd fr 4th)	8	9	25/1	20	—
2175[8]	**Respecting** (JAMoore) **4-10-6** NSmith (stdd s: plld hrd: sn trckng ldrs: lost pl 3rd)	7	10	100/1	13	—
	Twablade (IRE) (FMurphy) **9-10-9** MFoster (outpcd & bhd fr 5th: t.o)	23	11	50/1	—	—
2633[12]	**Hunting Slane** (CGrant) **5-11-0** PNiven (plld hrd: w ldrs: led 3rd to 5th: hung bdly rt & lost pl after next: eased: t.o)	¾	12	25/1	—	—
3305[5]	**Romaldkirk** (VThompson) **5-11-0** MrMThompson (led to 3rd: mstkes: w ldrs tl lost pl 5th: blnd next: t.o)	¾	13	500/1	—	—
				(SP 130.0%)	**13 Rn**	

3m 56.9 (13.90) CSF £4.45 TOTE £1.60: £1.30 £1.80 £2.10 (£4.80) Trio £13.60 OWNER Cumbrian Industrials Ltd (MALTON) BRED Bearstone Stud
WEIGHT FOR AGE 4yo-8lb
OFFICIAL EXPLANATION **Hunting Slane: was unrideable because he was hanging badly to the right.**
3324* Cumbrian Maestro took a modest event in most decisive fashion. Though nothing special to look at, he seems to be improving at a rate of knots. (4/9)
Oversman, reappearing after running badly on his debut ninety-five days earlier, was the only one to seriously trouble the winner. (7/1)
Undawaterscubadiva, winner of a low-class handicap on the All-Weather, travelled strongly on the heels of the leaders, but as usual he did not find as much as expected under pressure. (10/1)
1992* Last Try (IRE), having his first outing for seventy-seven days, and with a double penalty, ran as well as could be expected. (6/1)
3098 Milenberg Joys, settled off the pace, took a keen grip. He should get a little better once he learns to settle. (33/1)

3476 PYTCHLEY ECHO NOVICES' HUNTERS' CHASE (5-Y.O+) (Class H)

3-00 (3-00) **3m 1f 110y (19 fncs)** £1,116.00 (£333.00: £159.00: £72.00) GOING: 0.32 sec per fur (GS)

				SP	RR	SF
	Sayin Nowt (KAnderson) **9-11-2**(7) MrAParker (lw: hld up: hdwy 12th: hit next: mstke 3 out: led & hung lft flat: drvn clr)	—	1	5/2[1]	89	—
	Greenmount Lad (IRE) (JCornforth) **9-11-7**(7) MrPCornforth (mstkes: w ldrs: led & blnd 4 out: hdd & nt qckn flat)	3½	2	20/1	92	2
	Admission (IRE) (MrsSarahHorner-Harker) **7-11-7**(7) MissLHorner (lw: mstkes: hld up: hdwy 14th: styd on wl fr 2 out)	2	3	8/1	91	1
	Eastlands Hi-Light (JGStaveley) **8-11-7**(7) MrTMorrison (hdwy 12th: outpcd fr 4 out: blnd 2 out)	9	4	10/1	85	—
	Political Sam (DavidSmith) **8-11-7**(7) MrNFSmith (chsd ldrs: led 12th to 4 out: wkng whn mstke 2 out)	14	5	9/2[3]	76	—
3270[F]	**Mobile Messenger (NZ)** (TRGeorge) **9-11-7**(7) MissSSamworth (lw: ldrs: hit 7th: sn lost pl)	3	6	8/1	74	—
	Bervie House (IRE) (WJWarner) **9-11-9**(5) MrRFord (chsd ldrs to 11th: bhd whn blnd 14th)	12	7	20/1	67	—
	Boulevard Bay (IRE) (TDWalford) **6-11-9**(5) MrNWilson (trckd ldrs: ev ch whn blnd 15th: wknd qckly between last 2: virtually p.u flat)	dist	8	3/1[2]	—	—
	Galzig (MrsDEHTurner) **9-11-7**(7) MrWTellwright (led: blnd 4th: hdd 12th: wknd 15th: bhd whn mstke 3 out: p.u bef next)		P	12/1	—	—
	Sir Harry Rinus (FPMurtagh) **11-11-9**(5) MrRHale (mstkes: trckd ldrs: blnd 3rd & 10th: bhd whn mstke 12th: sn p.u)		P	33/1	—	—
				(SP 123.2%)	**10 Rn**	

6m 52.6 (34.60) CSF £49.57 TOTE £3.20: £1.10 £5.00 £2.30 (£140.20) Trio £158.80 OWNER Mr Dennis Waggott (LOCKERBIE) BRED A. L. Robinson
Sayin Nowt, who is not very big and has had her last four outings in point-to-points spread over four seasons, took time to get the hang of jumping regulation fences. Given a confident ride, she showed a nice turn of foot to lead and go clear on the run-in. (5/2)
Greenmount Lad (IRE), pulled up in a point-to-point eleven days earlier, survived a bad blunder when taking charge four out, but the mare had too much toe for him on the run-in. (20/1)
Admission (IRE), third in this race last year, was taken quietly to post. Settled in at the start, he made mistakes, but the way he was picking up over the last two suggests both horse and rider have improvement in them. (8/1)
Eastlands Hi-Light, runner-up in a maiden hunter chase last season, has been placed twice in points this time, but he could not live with the pace from four out. (10/1)
Boulevard Bay (IRE), unbeaten in two points this time, is an edgy sort and was very keen going to post. After almost coming to grief five out, he stopped to nothing between the last two and was pulled up to a walk on the run-in. Something was clearly amiss. (3/1)

3477 ROBERT FLEMING NOVICES' H'CAP CHASE (0-100) (5-Y.O+) (Class E)

3-30 (3-30) **3m 1f 110y (19 fncs)** £3,102.75 (£927.00: £443.50: £201.75) GOING: 0.32 sec per fur (GS)

	Horse			SP	RR	SF
3289^{4}	**Karenastino (65)** (MrsSJSmith) **6-9-9**$^{(7)}$ RWilkinson (trckd ldrs: hmpd 13th: styd on to ld after last: hld on towards fin)	—	**1**	8/1	77	—
3202^{F}	**Kings Sermon (IRE) (85)** (PBeaumont) **8-11-8** RSupple (mstkes: outpcd 12th: hdwy u.p & hit 4 out: ev ch flat: nt qckn towards fin)	nk	**2**	$3/1^{2}$	97	5
3367^{2}	**Tico Gold (84)** (PCheesbrough) **9-11-7** TReed (hit 6th: outpcd 12th: kpt on one pce fr 4 out)	6	**3**	$9/2^{3}$	92	—
3327^{11}	**Triona's Hope (IRE) (63)** (EMCaine) **8-9-9**$^{(5)}$ STaylor (chsd ldrs: outpcd whn blnd 15th: sn bhd: styd on flat)	4	**4**	200/1	69	—
3138*	**Bold Account (IRE) (87)** (GMMoore) **7-11-10b** ADobbin (trckd ldrs: mstke 11th: lft in clr ld 13th: wknd & hdd after last: fin tired)	nk	**5**	$13/8^{1}$	92	—
3331^{5}	**Knockreigh Cross (IRE) (63)** (BSRothwell) **8-10-0** BStorey (led tl fell 13th)		**F**	50/1	—	—
3100^{3}	**Elliott's Wish (IRE) (81)** (HowardJohnson) **6-11-4** MMoloney (wnt prom 7th: wknd 15th: bhd whn blnd 3 out: p.u bef next)		**P**	11/1	—	—
2540^{9}	**Rathfardon (IRE) (72)** (FMurphy) **9-10-9** PCarberry (lw: mstkes: chsd ldrs: drvn along 8th: t.o 11th: p.u bef next: b.b.v)		**P**	6/1	—	—
				(SP 117.5%)	**8 Rn**	

6m 51.0 (33.00) CSF £31.17 CT £112.94 TOTE £7.50: £2.00 £1.80 £1.40 (£11.30) Trio £13.20 OWNER Miss J. Wood (BINGLEY) BRED Miss J. U. Wood

LONG HANDICAP Knockreigh Cross (IRE) 9-11 Triona's Hope (IRE) 9-11

OFFICIAL EXPLANATION Rathfardon (IRE): the trainer reported that the gelding had bled from the nose.

3289 Karenastino, who had an impossible task this time, jumped better than on some occasions in the past. Relishing the step up to three miles, he did not have an ounce to spare at the line. (8/1)

3202 Kings Sermon (IRE), who had a crashing fall last time, is still not the best of jumpers. Knocked back when hitting four out, he was almost upsides on the run-in, but then could find no more. (3/1)

3367 Tico Gold, who again had the headgear left off, is woefully one-paced. (9/2)

Triona's Hope (IRE), on his chasing debut, was knocked right back by a blunder five out. Picking up ground in his own time at the finish, he will be suited by extreme distances. (200/1)

3138* Bold Account (IRE), left in a commanding lead seven out, began to tire turning for home and was out on his feet after jumping the last. (13/8)

3100 Elliott's Wish (IRE) (11/1: 8/1-12/1)

3478 CONISTON HALL RESTAURANT H'CAP HURDLE (0-100) (4-Y.O+) (Class F)

4-00 (4-02) **2m 3f (10 hdls)** £2,110.00 (£585.00: £280.00) GOING: 0.32 sec per fur (GS)

	Horse			SP	RR	SF
3201^{9}	**Major Yaasi (USA) (82)** (JAGlover) **7-10-13b** ADobbin (chsd ldrs: led 6th: styd on strly fr 2 out)	—	**1**	14/1	66	—
3102^{3}	**Fryup Satellite (83)** (MrsJBrown) **6-11-0** MissPRobson (lw: chsd ldrs: chal appr 2 out: styd on same pce)	5	**2**	$7/1^{2}$	63	—
3234^{5}	**Mrs Jawleyford (USA) (78)** (CSmith) **9-10-9** MRanger (lw: hld up: stdy hdwy 6th: chsd ldrs appr 2 out: one pce)	8	**3**	$7/1^{2}$	51	—
3325*	**First in the Field (74)** (NBMason) **6-9-12**$^{(7)}$ 6x SHaworth (drvn along & blnd 6th: sn bhd: styd on fr 2 out)	nk	**4**	$9/1^{3}$	47	—
2915^{4}	**Aide Memoire (IRE) (76)** (RJohnson) **8-10-7** KJohnson (bhd: hdwy u.p 7th: lost pl appr 2 out: styd on towards fin)	½	**5**	$9/1^{3}$	48	—
2862*	**Yacht Club (75)** (JLEyre) **15-9-13**$^{(7)ow3}$ CElliott (outpcd 6th: kpt on fr 2 out: nvr nr ldrs)	¾	**6**	10/1	47	—
3199^{2}	**Tip it In (90)** (ASmith) **8-11-0**$^{(7)}$ NHorrocks (chsd ldrs: outpcd 3 out: n.d after)	5	**7**	$7/1^{2}$	58	—
892^{3}	**Shelton Abbey (69)** (JWade) **11-10-0b** BStorey (outpcd 6th: sme hdwy 2 out: n.d)	½	**8**	20/1	36	—
1990*	**Tirmizi (USA) (97)** (MrsASwinbank) **6-12-0** JSupple (lw: in tch: rdn & lost pl 5th: sme hdwy 2 out: n.d)	½	**9**	20/1	64	—
2178^{4}	**Helens Bay (IRE) (78)** (VThompson) **7-10-9**^{ow3} MrMThompson (bhd & drvn along 5th: sme late hdwy)	2	**10**	25/1	43	—
3351^{6}	**Moonshine Dancer (95)** (DWBarker) **7-11-9**$^{(3)}$ PMidgley (chsd ldrs tl wknd after 3 out)	1½	**11**	16/1	59	—
3200^{4}	**Auntie Alice (79)** (JGFitzGerald) **7-10-10** PCarberry (hdwy 5th: sn chsng ldrs: rdn 3 out: sn wknd)	1¾	**12**	14/1	41	—
3325^{5}	**Alan's Pride (IRE) (72)** (WMcKeown) **6-10-3**^{ow3} NSmith (unruly s: led to 6th: wknd qckly 3 out: t.o)	dist	**13**	20/1	—	—
3325^{3}	**Decent Penny (IRE) (69)** (MrsRichardArthur) **8-10-0** TEley (lw: bhd fr 5th: t.o 3 out)	9	**14**	12/1	—	—
3346^{3}	**Court Joker (IRE) (82)** (HAlexander) **5-10-8**$^{(5)}$ RMcGrath (hld up & plld hrd: effrt 6th: no rspnse: t.o whn p.u bef 2 out: lame)		**P**	$6/1^{1}$	—	—
3137^{8}	**All Clear (IRE) (81)** (HowardJohnson) **6-10-12** DParker (prom tl wknd qckly 5th: t.o 7th: p.u bef 2 out)		**P**	25/1	—	—
				(SP 129.8%)	**16 Rn**	

4m 47.4 (22.40) CSF £98.16 CT £698.87 TOTE £25.30: £8.30 £1.30 £1.70 £1.60 (£79.00) Trio £323.50; £109.37 to Wincanton 6/3/97 OWNER P and S Partnership (WORKSOP) BRED Gainsborough Farm Inc

LONG HANDICAP Shelton Abbey 9-12 Decent Penny (IRE) 9-13 Alan's Pride (IRE) 9-13

Major Yaasi (USA), who according to his trainer has taken time to get fit, scored in decisive fashion. (14/1)

3102 Fryup Satellite ran another good race and certainly likes it round here. (7/1)

3234 Mrs Jawleyford (USA), who has slipped down the weights and stepped up in distance, looked a real danger on the home turn but, on this ground, found the first two running away from her. She prefers the mud. (7/1)

3325* First in the Field showed that her win here was no fluke. (9/1)

2915 Aide Memoire (IRE), awkward as usual beforehand, swished her tail under pressure. Sticking on at the finish, she will be suited by a step-up to three miles. (9/1)

2862* Yacht Club is a truly remarkable veteran. (10/1)

3346 Court Joker (IRE), very keen, seemed to lose his action setting out onto the final circuit. He was found to be lame afterwards. (6/1)

3479 PETER VAUX MEMORIAL TROPHY NOVICES' CHASE (5-Y.O+) (Class D)

4-30 (4-30) **2m 3f (15 fncs)** £3,557.50 (£1,060.00: £505.00: £227.50) GOING: 0.32 sec per fur (GS)

	Horse			SP	RR	SF
3326^{2}	**Roberty Lea** (MrsMReveley) **9-11-9** PNiven (wnt prom 8th: chal 3 out: hrd drvn to ld fnl 50y)	—	**1**	$4/5^{1}$	91	23
3199^{4}	**Tapatch (IRE)** (MWEasterby) **9-11-2** PCarberry (lw: racd wd: trckd ldrs: led 3 out: hdd & nt qckn towards fin)	¾	**2**	$4/1^{2}$	83	15
	Monkey Wench (IRE) (MrsJDGoodfellow) **6-10-11** BStorey (trckd ldrs: led after 4 out: hdd next: wknd last)	13	**3**	$6/1^{3}$	67	—
3085^{8}	**High Mood** (TRGeorge) **7-11-2** KJohnson (lw: plld hrd: trckd ldrs: led 7th: stumbled next: hdd after 4 out: grad wknd)	6	**4**	33/1	67	—
3306^{6}	**Most Rich (IRE) (67)** (BEllison) **9-11-2v** TReed (lw: led 3rd to 7th: hit 10th: wknd after 4 out)	5	**5**	9/1	63	—

3306[8] **Distillery Hill (IRE) (67)** (VThompson) **9-11-2** MrMThompson (led to 3rd: reminders & lost pl 7th: t.o 4 out) .dist **6** 33/1 — —
1999[10] **Fort Zeddaan (IRE)** (MrsSJSmith) **7-10-9**(7) RWilkinson (last whn fell 6th) .... **F** 16/1 — —
Oaklands Billy (MrsMReveley) **8-11-2** NSmith (mstkes: plld hrd: trckd ldrs: lost pl after 7th: blnd 9th: t.o 4 out: p.u bef last) .... **P** 20/1 — —
(SP 116.4%) **8 Rn**

4m 57.7 (18.70) CSF £4.17 TOTE £1.60: £1.10 £1.60 £1.60 (£4.20) OWNER Wentdale Const Ltd (SALTBURN) BRED Stud-On-The-Chart

3326 Roberty Lea, whose jumping was more fluent, was able to take up a good position with a circuit to go. Responding to pressure, he did just enough. (4/5)

3199 Tapatch (IRE) was taken wide in search of the better ground, but after a good battle had to give best near the line. (4/1)

Monkey Wench (IRE), on her chasing debut, was having her first run for over five-hundred days, having finished lame when she last ran and won over hurdles. She was in need of the outing, tiring in two strides going to the last. (6/1)

High Mood, on his chasing debut, would not settle at all, and gave problems going to the start. He was collared after jumping four out, and it was no surprise to see him drop away. (33/1)

3306 Most Rich (IRE) was already looking unhappy in his work when he hit five out. That persuaded him to call it a day. (9/1)

3480 LANE, CLARK & PEACOCK INTERMEDIATE OPEN N.H. FLAT RACE (4, 5 & 6-Y.O) (Class H)

5-00 (5-00) **2m** £1,175.00 (£325.00: £155.00)

SP RR SF

3070[5] **Easby Blue** (SEKettlewell) **5-11-2** PNiven (lw: hld up & plld hrd: stdy hdwy 6f out: led 2f out: drvn clr fnl f) ...— **1** Evens[1] 61 f —
Going Primitive (JHetherton) **6-11-2** ADobbin (trckd ldrs: led over 2f out: hung lft & nt qckn appr fnl f) ....7 **2** 15/2 54 f —
2924[4] **Eastcliffe (IRE)** (WMcKeown) **5-11-2** NSmith (led tl over 2f out: one pce) ....10 **3** 9/2[2] 44 f —
Keriali (USA) (MDHammond) **4-10-8** RGarritty (prom: outpcd 4f out: grad wknd: sddle slipped) ....11 **4** 7/1[3] 33 f —
Royal Chip (MissMKMilligan) **5-10-9**(7) NHorrocks (stdd s: sn trckng ldrs: rdn & lost pl 4f out) ....18 **5** 12/1 15 f —
Stanwick Hall (MissSWilliamson) **5-11-2** JSupple (bit bkwd: hld up: effrt 5f out: sn lost pl) ....½ **6** 20/1 15 f —
Oh Brother (WRaw) **4-10-8** JCallaghan (sn chsng ldrs: rdn 6f out: sn bhd) ....21 **7** 16/1 — —
Boston Bomber (RDEWoodhouse) **6-11-2** PCarberry (chsd ldrs: rdn 5f out: sn bhd: t.o) ....dist **8** 8/1 — —
Whinholme Lass (IRE) (FKirby) **5-10-11** WDwan (lost pl ½-wy: sn t.o: virtually p.u) ....dist **9** 33/1 — —
(SP 124.8%) **9 Rn**

3m 54.4 CSF £9.66 TOTE £1.60: £1.10 £1.90 £2.50 (£6.20) Trio £43.10 OWNER Mr G. R. Orchard (MIDDLEHAM) BRED Easby Stud and Development Co Ltd

WEIGHT FOR AGE 4yo-8lb

3070 Easby Blue, outstanding in the paddock, took some settling, but scored in decisive fashion in the end. (Evens)

Going Primitive hung left in the home straight, and in the end found the winner much too strong. (15/2)

2924 Eastcliffe (IRE), having his fourth outing, has a pronounced knee action and seems to have nothing in the way of pace. (9/2: 8/1-4/1)

Keriali (USA), from a stable bang out of form, was eased when getting outpaced on the home turn. His saddled slipped and he unseated his rider soon after the line. (7/1: 5/1-8/1)

Royal Chip (12/1: 6/1-14/1)

T/Plpt: £26.40 (364.94 Tckts). T/Qdpt: £11.80 (63.24 Tckts) WG

3191-CARLISLE (R-H) (Heavy, Soft patches, becoming Soft)

Thursday March 6th

WEATHER: Fine

3481 BORDER ESK 'N.H.' NOVICES' H'CAP HURDLE (0-100) (4-Y.O+) (Class E)

2-00 (2-00) **3m 110y (12 hdls)** £2,416.00 (£676.00: £328.00) GOING: 0.90 sec per fur (S)

SP RR SF

3358[P] **Ansuro Again (81)** (MrsMReveley) **8-11-2** PNiven (lw: hld up & bhd: hdwy 8th: chal & hung rt 2 out: hrd rdn flat to ld fnl 50y) ....— **1** 11/1 60 16
3201[8] **Mrs Robinson (IRE) (76)** (JMackie) **6-10-8**(3) EHusband (lw: a.p: chal 3 out: led last: kpt on u.p: jst ct) ....nk **2** 6/1[2] 55 11
3348[6] **Pharrambling (IRE) (78)** (MrsMReveley) **6-10-10**(3) GLee (lw: hld up & bhd: hdwy 8th: chal 3 out: hmpd 2 out: swtchd: mstke last: kpt on wl towards fin) ....½ **3** 14/1 57 13
3325[9] **Diddy Rymer (75)** (MrsSJSmith) **7-10-10** RichardGuest (chsd ldrs: led 7th tl hdd last: wknd) 7 **4** 11/1 49 5
2838* **Parade Racer (78)** (PGMurphy) **6-10-13** WMcFarland (hld up & bhd: hdwy on bit 7th: chsng ldrs & effrt 3 out: one pce) ....3½ **5** 2/1[1] 50 6
2920[P] **Sandrift (80)** (CParker) **8-11-1** DParker (prom tl mstke & outpcd 4 out: no imp after) ....16 **6** 14/1 41 —
1992[10] **Jonaem (IRE) (77)** (MrsESlack) **7-10-12** KJohnson (bhd: wnt prom 6th: outpcd 4 out: n.d after) ....12 **7** 20/1 30 —
3032[P] **Strong Character (70)** (DALamb) **11-10-5**ow5 JBurke (chsd ldrs to 5th: outpcd whn blnd 7th: n.d after) ....19 **8** 100/1 11 —
3032[5] **Black Ice (IRE) (67)** (TPTate) **6-10-2** JCallaghan (in tch: effrt 7th: sn rdn & wknd) ....½ **9** 6/1[2] 8 —
2654[5] **Dashmar (68)** (MsLCPlater) **10-10-3v** DBentley (lw: outpcd & lost tch ½-wy: wl bhd after) ....7 **10** 8/1[3] 4 —
1654[20] **Willie Wannabe (IRE) (65)** (MrsDThomson) **7-10-0** BStorey (led & clr to 4th: hdd 7th: sn t.o: p.u bef 3 out) .... **P** 16/1 — —
3157[11] **Ski Path (65)** (NBycroft) **8-10-0** MFoster (chsd ldrs: led 6th to 7th: sn hrd drvn: wknd 4 out: p.u bef 2 out) .... **P** 100/1 — —
(SP 115.6%) **12 Rn**

6m 22.0 (38.00) CSF £67.23 CT £850.09 TOTE £14.00: £3.30 £1.70 £3.00 (£59.90) Trio £143.50 OWNER Frickley Holdings Ltd (SALTBURN) BRED Frickley Holdings Ltd

LONG HANDICAP Strong Character 9-0 Willie Wannabe (IRE) 9-4 Ski Path 9-13

OFFICIAL EXPLANATION **Ansuro Again: had resented being pushed along when off the bridle last time and was more suited by today's slower-run race and heavier ground.**

3157 Ansuro Again at last showed what he can do, but he certainly takes some riding and almost threw it away by hanging right two out. (11/1: 8/1-14/1)

3004 Mrs Robinson (IRE) appreciated this step up in trip, and this stiff track, and kept battling all the way to the line. (6/1)

Pharrambling (IRE), who had shown nothing previously, looked unlucky here, as she was hampered by her stable companion, and took time to regain her stride. She should make amends in due course. (14/1: 16/1-25/1)

3098 Diddy Rymer, stepping up in trip, put up a decent effort, but this is a very stiff track in these conditions, and her stamina gave out late on. (11/1: op 7/1)

2838* Parade Racer looked to be going particularly well for much of the trip, but when asked a question failed to pick up and looks the type who is at his best when things go all his own way. (2/1)

Sandrift ran a shade better, but there is still a long way to go. (14/1: op 8/1)

3482 DERWENT H'CAP CHASE (0-100) (5-Y.O+) (Class F)

2-30 (2-30) **2m (12 fncs)** £2,696.00 (£756.00: £368.00) GOING: 0.90 sec per fur (S)

Form	Horse	Dist	Pos	SP	RR	SF
3336[2]	**Chill Wind (87)** (NBycroft) **8-11-2** MFoster (trckd ldrs: led 6th to 8th: led 4 out: disp ld next: hld on gamely flat)	—	**1**	5/2[2]	101	22
3398[5]	**Pariah (IRE) (91)** (MartinTodhunter) **8-11-6** PCarberry (lw: trckd ldrs: disp ld on bit 3 out: j.lft & mstke last: rallied towards fin)	nk	**2**	2/1[1]	105	26
3312[5]	**Grouse-N-Heather (94)** (PMonteith) **8-11-9** ADobbin (lw: chsd ldrs: rdn fr 8th: kpt on: no imp)	14	**3**	6/1[3]	94	15
3069[7]	**Super Sandy (72)**(FTWalton) **10-10-1** KJohnson (mde most tl 6th: led 8th tl 4 out: rdn & btn between last 2)	1¾	**4**	6/1[3]	70	—
3329[P]	**Rebel King (84)** (MABarnes) **7-10-8**(5) STaylor (sn pushed along: prom tl outpcd fr 8th)	20	**5**	10/1	62	—
3370[P]	**Quixall Crossett (71)** (EMCaine) **12-10-0b** MMoloney (disp ld to 4th: outpcd & lost tch fr 8th)	3½	**6**	50/1	45	—
3101[3]	**Blazing Trail (IRE) (99)** (MissLucindaRussell) **9-12-0** TReed (lw: nt j.w: lost tch 5th: t.o whn p.u bef 4 out)		**P**	7/1	—	—
				(SP 114.0%)		**7 Rn**

4m 17.7 (23.70) CSF £7.55 TOTE £3.60: £1.60 £1.80 (£4.30) OWNER Mr E. H. Daley (BRANDSBY) BRED Alasdair J. Simpson
LONG HANDICAP Quixall Crossett 8-13
OFFICIAL EXPLANATION **Blazing Trail (IRE): finished distressed.**

3336 Chill Wind, made a bit more use of this time, proved too game for the runner-up. All his wins have been on this track. (5/2)
3398 Pariah (IRE) sat on the leader's heels and it looked a question of when, and how far, but when asked for an effort, he made a hash of the last and could never fully recover. Perhaps more use should be made of him. (2/1)
3312 Grouse-N-Heather stayed on after getting outpaced, and is gradually coming to hand. (6/1)
2544 Super Sandy loves these conditions, and ran her best race of the season here. No doubt if she gets similar ground at her favourite track, Hexham, she will be back in the winner's enclosure. (6/1)
3329 Rebel King was almost off the bridle from leaving the saddling boxes, and was left behind over the last five fences. (10/1)
3101 Blazing Trail (IRE) has lost all confidence at present. (7/1)

3483 GOLDEN PHEASANT, YOUNGERS NOVICES' HURDLE (4-Y.O+) (Class E)

3-00 (3-00) **2m 4f 110y (11 hdls)** £2,584.00 (£724.00: £352.00) GOING: 0.90 sec per fur (S)

Form	Horse	Dist	Pos	SP	RR	SF
3226[2]	**Ardrina** (FMurphy) **6-10-11** ADobbin (lw: chsd ldrs: rdn 4 out: led 2 out: styd on strly)	—	**1**	4/1[2]	72	23
3371*	**Into the West (IRE) (96)** (MrsSJSmith) **8-11-8** RichardGuest (lw: trckd ldrs: chal 3 out: nt qckn appr last)	11	**2**	2/1[1]	74	25
3324[6]	**Nasayer (IRE)** (NBMason) **7-10-9**(7) SHaworth (bhd: hdwy u.p 6th: kpt on wl fr 3 out: nrst fin)	6	**3**	33/1	64	15
3315[5]	**Mike Stan (IRE)** (LLungo) **6-11-2** RSupple (lw: hdwy 6th: chsng ldrs appr 3 out: kpt on one pce: blnd last)	½	**4**	14/1	63	14
3315[4]	**Bold Statement** (GMMoore) **5-11-2** NBentley (lw: hdwy & prom 5th: led after 4 out tl hdd 2 out: wknd)	s.h	**5**	12/1	63	14
3070[2]	**Prime Example (IRE)** (MartinTodhunter) **6-11-2** PCarberry (hld up: hdwy ½-wy: prom & effrt 4 out: btn next)	20	**6**	6/1	48	—
3327[7]	**Nosmo King (IRE) (64)** (MrsMAKendall) **6-11-2** MrsMKendall (prom tl rdn & lost pl appr 6th: n.d after)	7	**7**	100/1	42	—
2787[5]	**The Khoinoa (IRE)** (MrsASwinbank) **7-11-2** JSupple (hld up: hit 4th: sme hdwy 4 out: n.d)	1¾	**8**	14/1	41	—
3330[3]	**Jennie's Prospect** (JJO'Neill) **6-10-11**(5) RMcGrath (nvr trbld ldrs)	1	**9**	33/1	40	—
	Peak A Boo (DWWhillans) **6-10-11** DBentley (in tch tl outpcd fr 4th)	9	**10**	100/1	28	—
3295[8]	**Sir Bob (IRE)** (WMcKeown) **5-11-2** GCahill (prom early: rdn & lost tch ½-wy)	9	**11**	9/2[3]	26	—
2927[3]	**Jayfcee** (MPBielby) **5-11-2** TReed (led & sn clr: hdd after 4 out: sn btn & eased)	17	**12**	16/1	13	—
3066[P]	**Border Image** (FPMurtagh) **6-10-13**(3) ECallaghan (prom tl wknd fr 7th)	9	**13**	200/1	6	—
2917[20]	**Montein** (SJLeadbetter) **6-11-2** NLeach (a bhd: wl t.o)	dist	**14**	500/1	—	—
3024[P]	**Thromedownsometing** (MrsDThomson) **7-10-11** BStorey (a bhd: t.o whn p.u bef 6th)		**P**	100/1	—	—
				(SP 122.3%)		**15 Rn**

5m 19.4 (28.40) CSF £11.59 TOTE £5.10: £2.50 £1.70 £5.80 (£8.00) Trio £180.30; £63.49 to Sandown 7/3/97 OWNER L G M Racing (MIDDLEHAM) BRED P. E. Atkinson

3226 Ardrina at last got the trip, track, and the ground she needs, and did the job really well, looking as though even further will be appreciated. (4/1)
3371* Into the West (IRE) ran another fine race only to find the winner too good. He should continue to pay his way, and looks one to watch when put over fences. (2/1)
3324 Nasayer (IRE) looked a real stayer here, and was making useful progress all the way up the straight. (33/1)
3315 Mike Stan (IRE) is a stayer in the making, but he does need to improve his jumping. (14/1)
3315 Bold Statement looked to have done everything right when cantering into the lead on the home turn, but he then ran out of fuel two from home, and either didn't stay or has a problem. (12/1: op 7/1)
3070 Prime Example (IRE), having his first run over hurdles after a promising effort in a bumper, proved to be disappointing. (6/1)
2787 The Khoinoa (IRE) (14/1: 7/1-20/1)

3484 EDINBURGH WOOLLEN MILL NOVICES' CHASE (5-Y.O+) (Class C)

3-30 (3-30) **2m 4f 110y (16 fncs)** £4,442.60 (£1,344.80: £656.40: £312.20) GOING: 0.90 sec per fur (S)

Form	Horse	Dist	Pos	SP	RR	SF
3288[2]	**Kenmore-Speed (100)** (MrsSJSmith) **10-11-3** RichardGuest (hit 1st: mde all: kpt on wl fr 4 out)	—	**1**	7/4[2]	110	36
2113[2]	**Solomon's Dancer (USA) (129)** (GRichards) **7-11-13** ADobbin (hld up: mstke 4th: chsd wnr fr 11th: rdn after 4 out: sn btn)	13	**2**	4/7[1]	110	36
3450[U]	**Nijway (73)** (MABarnes) **7-10-12**(5) STaylor (prom: hit 9th: outpcd whn blnd 12th: no ch after)	12	**3**	33/1	91	17
3306[4]	**Master of Troy (78)** (CParker) **9-11-3b[1]** DParker (chsd wnr fr 5th to 11th: sn rdn & wl outpcd)	5	**4**	20/1[3]	87	13
				(SP 107.7%)		**4 Rn**

5m 29.6 (26.60) CSF £2.97 TOTE £2.70 (£1.40) OWNER Mr K. M. Dacker (BINGLEY) BRED Mrs Davina Whiteman
OFFICIAL EXPLANATION **Solomon's Dancer (USA): finished distressed.**

3288 Kenmore-Speed has plenty of stamina, and goes in the ground. Making full use of that, he proved too determined for the runner-up. (7/4)
2113 Solomon's Dancer (USA) likes faster ground, and once he came of the bridle early in the straight, he failed to pick up at all. (4/7)
3450 Nijway, having his second run in three days, made his usual mistakes which eventually finished his hopes five out. (33/1)
3306 Master of Troy had blinkers on for the first time, but found this company too hot, and had to accept it some way out. (20/1)

3485 WAVER CONDITIONAL H'CAP HURDLE (0-110) (4-Y.O+) (Class E)

4-00 (4-00) **2m 1f (9 hdls)** £2,374.00 (£664.00: £322.00) GOING: 0.90 sec per fur (S)

Form	Horse	Dist	Pos	SP	RR	SF
3398[3]	**Ifallelsefails (90)** (LLungo) **9-10-6**(8) IJardine (lw: a.p: led 2 out: r.o)	—	**1**	8/1[3]	72	—

3371[2]	**Enchanted Cottage (79)** (JMJefferson) **5-10-0**(3)ow1 ECallaghan (lw: hld up & bhd: stdy hdwy appr 3 out: r.o flat: too much to do)	2	**2**	9/4[1]	59	—
3159[7]	**Pappa Charlie (USA) (82)** (CParker) **6-10-6** GLee (lw: cl up: chal 5th: led appr 3 out: hdd 2 out: no ex)	5	**3**	9/1	57	—
3028[P]	**Kirstenbosch (80)** (LLungo) **10-9-10**(8) WDowling (hld up & bhd: stdy hdwy fr 3 out: fin strly: nvr plcd to chal)	3½	**4**	33/1	52	—
3309[4]	**Glenugie (92)** (GMMoore) **6-10-6**(10) NHannity (a chsng ldrs: rdn 4 out: one pce fr next)	1	**5**	16/1	63	—
3035[9]	**Apollo's Daughter (76)** (JLGoulding) **9-10-0** BGrattan (hld up: effrt 4 out: styd on: no imp)	2	**6**	50/1	45	—
2044[5]	**Highland Way (IRE) (90)** (MartinTodhunter) **9-10-6**(8) CMcCormack (bhd: wnt prom 5th: ev ch 3 out: wknd between last 2)	½	**7**	20/1	59	—
3346[4]	**Our Robert (92)** (JGFitzGerald) **5-10-13**(3) FLeahy (rr div: hdwy appr 3 out: sn btn)	nk	**8**	7/1[2]	61	—
3315[2]	**Supreme Soviet (94)** (ACWhillans) **7-11-4** STaylor (bhd: hdwy & prom 4 out: rdn appr next: sn btn)	5	**9**	7/1[2]	58	—
3096[2]	**Eternal City (88)** (GRichards) **6-10-4**(8) RBurns (chsd ldrs fr 3rd tl rdn & wknd appr 3 out)	28	**10**	7/1[2]	26	—
3346[9]	**Fox Sparrow (100)** (NTinkler) **7-11-7**(3) EHusband (lost tch fr 5th)	5	**11**	25/1	33	—
3346[10]	**Merry Mermaid (96)** (BMactaggart) **7-11-6** SMelrose (led tl hdd & wknd appr 3 out)	4	**12**	8/1[3]	25	—
2786[9]	**See You Always (IRE) (79)** (DMoffatt) **7-9-7**(10)ow3 IPike (cl up to 3rd: sn rdn & bhd)	7	**13**	100/1	1	—
				(SP 120.9%)		**13 Rn**

4m 32.1 (31.10) CSF £23.79 CT £157.87 TOTE £9.00: £2.50 £1.60 £2.80 (£17.10) Trio £55.50 OWNER Mrs Barbara Lungo (CARRUTHERSTOWN) BRED R. Chugg
LONG HANDICAP Apollo's Daughter 9-6 See You Always (IRE) 8-7
3398 Ifallelsefails, put into the race this time, did the job required well. (8/1: 6/1-9/1)
3371 Enchanted Cottage, who is now due to go up 10lb, may well have won this, but his rider overdid the waiting tactics. (9/4)
1687 Pappa Charlie (USA) has really come to himself lookswise, and ran a fair race, but proved short of toe when it mattered. (9/1)
Kirstenbosch, a stable companion of the winner, left the impression that he might well have been in the shake-up with a more vigorous ride. (33/1)
3309 Glenugie is running reasonably, but that final dash isn't quite there at the moment. (16/1)
1249* Apollo's Daughter ran a fair race from 8lb out of the handicap. (50/1)
2044 Highland Way (IRE) looked to be going well here, until suddenly running out of petrol between the final two flights. He certainly has the ability when he gets it together. (20/1)

3486 EDEN H'CAP CHASE (0-120) (5-Y.O+) (Class D)

4-30 (4-30) **3m 2f (19 fncs)** £3,623.10 (£1,096.80: £535.40: £254.70) GOING: 0.90 sec per fur (S)

				SP	RR	SF
3317[2]	**Northern Squire (105)** (JMJefferson) **9-10-12**(3) ECallaghan (lw: hld up: effrt whn mstke 13th: hdwy 4 out: led 2 out: r.o)	—	**1**	7/4[1]	108	6
3395[2]	**Ceilidh Boy (117)** (MrsJDGoodfellow) **11-11-13v** MrRHale (mde most to 14th: mstke 4 out: led 3 out to 2 out: kpt on wl)	1¾	**2**	7/2[3]	119	17
2956[F]	**Acajou III (FR) (110)** (GRichards) **9-11-6** PCarberry (plld hrd: qcknd to ld 14th: hit next: hdd 3 out: rdn & fnd nil)	26	**3**	2/1[2]	96	—
2542[4]	**Ubu Val (FR) (118)** (WABethell) **11-12-0** BStorey (lw: w ldr tl hit 12th: sn outpcd: wknd 4 out)	17	**4**	9/2	94	—
				(SP 110.1%)		**4 Rn**

7m 12.9 (44.90) CSF £7.22 TOTE £2.00 (£3.30) OWNER Mrs M. E. Dixon (MALTON) BRED J. M. Jefferson and Mrs M. E. Dixon
3317 Northern Squire, despite one poor jump, won really well to gain his sixth course victory. (7/4)
3395 Ceilidh Boy had conditions in his favour, but he is prone to mistakes and, despite trying hard, was well held on the run-in. (7/2)
2956 Acajou III (FR) raced very freely for much of the trip, and when an effort was required from four out it was a different matter, and he immediately downed tools. (2/1)
2542 Ubu Val (FR) looked well enough, but didn't show any spark. After some careful jumps, he was left behind in the final mile. (9/2)

3487 LIDDEL WATER INTERMEDIATE OPEN N.H. FLAT RACE (4, 5 & 6-Y.O) (Class H)

5-00 (5-00) **2m 1f** £1,213.50 (£336.00: £160.50)

				SP	RR	SF
3297[7]	**Linwood** (GRichards) **6-10-13** ADobbin (lw: trckd ldrs: led over 2f out: rdn & styd on wl)	—	**1**	11/10[1]	56 f	—
2924*	**Tom's River (IRE)** (MrsMReveley) **5-11-8**(3) GLee (hld up: hdwy ½-wy: chsng ldrs 3f out: kpt on u.p: nt pce of wnr)	9	**2**	2/1[2]	60 f	—
3290[5]	**Side By Side (IRE)** (CWThornton) **4-9-12**(7) NHorrocks (chsd ldr: led 4f out tl over 2f out: one pce)	3	**3**	11/1	45 f	—
3330[6]	**Cool Kevin** (MrsMAKendall) **4-10-10** MrsMKendall (bhd: hdwy fnl 4f: nrst fin)	17	**4**	25/1	34 f	—
2633[14]	**Snooty Eskimo (IRE)** (JSHaldane) **5-11-1**(3) ECallaghan (hdwy ½-wy: wnt prom 4f out: sn outpcd)	2	**5**	25/1	32 f	—
	Smile Pleeze (IRE) (MrsMStirk) **5-11-4** MFoster (prom tl lost pl after 7f: sme late hdwy)	2	**6**	16/1	30 f	—
3070[7]	**Just Ned** (JSHaldane) **6-11-4** BStorey (lw: bhd: sme hdwy 4f out: n.d)	6	**7**	12/1	24 f	—
2924[9]	**Jumbo's Dream** (JEDixon) **6-11-4** FPerratt (led tl hdd & wknd 4f out)	1¼	**8**	66/1	23 f	—
2924[7]	**Superexalt** (JGFitzGerald) **5-11-4** WDwan (prom: rn wd paddock bnd: wknd 6f out)	24	**9**	10/1	1 f	—
2750[15]	**Woodhouse Lane** (NChamberlain) **5-10-11**(7) MissCMetcalfe (a bhd: t.o)	13	**10**	100/1	—	—
3330[9]	**Chan Move** (WJSmith) **5-10-13b**1(5) STaylor (prom tl rdn & wknd 5f out: wl t.o)	dist	**11**	100/1	—	—
2675[11]	**Gymcrak-Gypsy** (GHolmes) **5-10-13** RGarritty (lost tch fr ½-wy: virtually p.u)	dist	**12**	9/1[3]	—	—
				(SP 133.1%)		**12 Rn**

4m 28.2 CSF £3.47 TOTE £2.70: £1.10 £1.10 £3.50 (£2.70) Trio £5.10 OWNER Emral Lakes Partnership (PENRITH) BRED R. F. Broad
WEIGHT FOR AGE 4yo-8lb
3070 Linwood did the job well, and is coming on nicely, but her real future will be over fences. (11/10)
2924* Tom's River (IRE) showed his previous win to be no fluke, but he was never good enough to peg the winner back. (2/1: op 5/4)
3290 Side By Side (IRE) is honest but slow. (11/1: 7/1-12/1)
Cool Kevin has ability, and is one likely to pop up at a big price sometime. (25/1)
Superexalt (10/1: op 11/2)

T/Plpt: £254.30 (38.93 Tckts). T/Qdpt: £29.70 (18.99 Tckts) AA

3014-TOWCESTER (R-H) (Chases Good to soft, Hdles Soft)
Thursday March 6th
WEATHER: Fine

3488 BANQUE ARJIL ESPANA NOVICES' CONDITIONAL H'CAP HURDLE (0-100) (4-Y.O+) (Class E)
2-20 (2-20) **3m (12 hdls)** £2,547.50 (£710.00: £342.50) GOING: 1.03 sec per fur (HY)

	Horse	Dist		SP	RR	SF
3186^{4}	**Winter Rose (72)** (MissPMWhittle) **6-10-6**$^{(5)}$ KHibbert (hdwy 6th: chal 3 out: led next: rdn out)	—	1	10/1	52	—
3020^{5}	**Ardent Love (IRE) (68)** (DNicholson) **8-10-7** RMassey (chsd ldrs: rdn 3 out: styd on fr next)	1½	2	11/4^{1}	47	—
3201^{2}	**Hancock (76)** (JHetherton) **5-10-12**$^{(3)}$ JPower (hdwy appr 8th: led appr 3 out: hdd 2 out: one pce)	7	3	6/1^{2}	50	—
3088^{S}	**Karen's Typhoon (IRE) (72)** (TPMcGovern) **6-10-6**$^{(5)}$ MBatchelor (prom: led 9th tl appr 3 out: sn rdn & btn)	16	4	16/1	36	—
2820^{11}	**Ross Dancer (IRE) (85)** (JSMoore) **5-11-10** JMagee (led to 7th: wknd appr 2 out)	3	5	25/1	47	—
3272^{7}	**Rosehall (82)** (MrsTDPilkington) **6-11-4**$^{(3)}$ LSuthern (nvr nr to chal)	7	6	9/1^{3}	39	—
3338^{U}	**Killing Time (76)** (DBurchell) **6-10-10**$^{(5)}$ JPrior (hmpd 6th: sn bhd)	16	7	14/1	22	—
3189^{2}	**Cardinal Gayle (IRE) (75)** (RHAlner) **7-11-0** DWalsh (in tch: hdwy 9th: wknd appr 2 out)	21	8	14/1	7	—
2570^{10}	**Evezio Rufo (84)** (NPLittmoden) **5-11-9v** DJKavanagh (in tch tl wknd 3 out: bhd whn p.u bef next)		P	16/1	—	—
3189^{4}	**One More Dime (IRE) (70)** (JLNeedham) **7-10-9** ABates (w ldr to 7th: bhd whn p.u bef 2 out)		P	25/1	—	—
3189*	**Fancy Nancy (IRE) (79)** (MissCJohnsey) **6-11-4** MichaelBrennan (w.r.s: hdwy 4th: wknd 8th: bhd whn p.u bef 2 out)		P	6/1^{2}	—	—
3173^{U}	**Mystic Court (IRE) (68)** (AndrewTurnell) **6-10-7** CRae (mstke 1st: hdwy 6th: blnd 8th: sn wknd: bhd whn p.u bef 2 out)		P	10/1	—	—
3189^{5}	**Wickens One (65)** (DPGeraghty) **7-10-4b**^{1} GSupple (in tch to 8th: mid div whn p.u bef 2 out)		P	33/1	—	—
2838^{6}	**Lovelark (61)** (RLee) **8-9-11**$^{(3)}$ XAizpuru (bhd fr 6th: p.u bef 2 out)		P	16/1	—	—
3190^{3}	**Otter Prince (61)** (TRGeorge) **8-9-7b**$^{(7)}$ CHynes (w ldrs: led 7th: hit next: hdd & wknd 9th: bhd whn p.u bef 2 out)		P	33/1	—	—

(SP 128.0%) **15 Rn**

6m 31.1 (51.10) CSF £35.58 CT £173.85 TOTE £11.70: £2.20 £1.30 £2.50 (£18.70) Trio £43.00 OWNER Glass Pig Racing Syndicate (LEDBURY) BRED W. E. and Mrs Donohue

LONG HANDICAP Lovelark 9-12 Otter Prince 9-13

3186 Winter Rose, given a patient ride, certainly seemed to go on this tacky ground, as he could be called the winner a long way from home.(10/1)
3020 Ardent Love (IRE) stayed on to the line on this return to hurdles but is proving hard to place. (11/4)
3201 Hancock again ran well and showed the improved effort last time was no fluke. (6/1: op 3/1)
1762 Karen's Typhoon (IRE) travelled nicely for a long way but didn't seem to get the trip, given the testing track and conditions. (16/1)
1550 Ross Dancer (IRE) looked harshly treated, but was in the thick of things until found out in the last half-mile. (25/1)
2932 Rosehall rather overdid the waiting tactics in an effort to get the trip. (9/1: 5/1-10/1)
3207* Killing Time (14/1: 10/1-16/1)

3489 JOHN WEBBER MEMORIAL NOVICES' CHASE (5-Y.O+) (Class E)
2-50 (2-50) **2m 6f (16 fncs)** £3,483.00 (£1,044.00: £502.00: £231.00) GOING: 0.65 sec per fur (S)

	Horse	Dist		SP	RR	SF
3155^{3}	**Him of Praise (IRE)** (OSherwood) **7-11-3** JOsborne (led: j.lft 5th & 6th: hdd 8th: chal 3 out: hung lft appr last: rdn to ld flat)	—	1	4/5^{1}	97	29
3334^{5}	**Major Nova (79)** (NASmith) **8-11-3** JCulloty (hdwy 11th: led 2 out tl flat: unable qckn)	½	2	20/1	97	29
3155^{8}	**Ballydougan (IRE) (74)** (RMathew) **9-11-3v** DWalsh (a.p: rdn 6th: ev ch 3 out: wknd appr last)	12	3	50/1	88	20
3060^{U}	**Thermal Warrior (78)** (JABOld) **9-11-3** GUpton (nt j.w: hdwy 4 out: nvr nr ldrs)	12	4	12/1	79	11
3339^{F}	**Brogeen Lady (IRE) (100)** (DRGandolfo) **7-10-12** JFTitley (prom: led 10th: hdd & wknd 2 out)	7	5	11/2^{3}	69	1
3165^{4}	**The Booley House (IRE) (92)** (VSoane) **7-11-3** DerekByrne (chsd ldrs tl blnd 4 out)	17	6	10/1	62	—
	Senna Blue (63) (RCPugh) **12-11-3** MSharratt (bhd fr 12th)	dist	7	40/1	—	—
	Ardscud (MBradstock) **10-11-3** WMarston (mstkes 6th & 8th: a bhd)	1½	8	50/1	—	—
1947^{2}	**Country Store (89)** (APJones) **8-10-12** SMcNeill (w ldr: hmpd 6th: led 8th to 10th: hit next: wknd 4 out: bhd whn p.u bef last)		P	7/2^{2}	—	—
3334^{R}	**Swift Pokey** (DLWilliams) **7-11-3** MClarke (blnd 1st & 5th: ref 6th)		R	66/1	—	—
3155^{P}	**Mystic Manna** (AndrewTurnell) **11-11-3** GCrone (mstke 5th: blnd & uns rdr 7th)		U	33/1	—	—
3043^{10}	**Becky's Girl** (RBrotherton) **7-10-9**$^{(3)}$ GuyLewis (in tch whn blnd & uns rdr 4th)		U	66/1	—	—

(SP 127.0%) **12 Rn**

5m 54.4 (25.40) CSF £21.04 TOTE £2.20: £1.30 £2.00 £8.60 (£16.20) Trio £56.70 OWNER Mr M. G. St Quinton (UPPER LAMBOURN) BRED Seamus Kennedy

3155 Him of Praise (IRE) looked to badly need a left-handed track, and could hardly be said to have won convincingly. (4/5)
Major Nova, in form at this time last year, suddenly bounced back to his best and does look capable of winning a novice chase. (20/1)
Ballydougan (IRE), the first off the bridle, didn't look very enthusiastic but only gave up going to the last. (50/1)
2795 Thermal Warrior doesn't inspire much confidence at the obstacles but clearly stays well. (12/1)
2660 Brogeen Lady (IRE) looked to be going best for much of the final circuit but ran out of stamina in the testing ground. (11/2: 4/1-6/1)
3165 The Booley House (IRE) clearly had place claims when his mistake finished him. (10/1)

3490 BANQUE ARJIL ITALIA HUNTERS' CHASE (6-Y.O+) (Class H)
3-20 (3-20) **3m 1f (18 fncs)** £1,563.50 (£436.00: £210.50) GOING: 0.65 sec per fur (S)

	Horse	Dist		SP	RR	SF
3273^{4}	**Teaplanter** (MissCSaunders) **14-12-1**$^{(5)}$ MrBPollock (led to 2nd: led 4th: rdn & wandered appr last: r.o)	—	1	8/13^{1}	108	5
3055^{P}	**Fiddlers Pike** (MrsRGHenderson) **16-11-5**$^{(7)}$ MrsRHenderson (plld hrd: a.p: chal appr 2 out: no ex flat)	3	2	7/1^{2}	98	—
3357^{6}	**Lurriga Glitter (IRE)** (RJSmith) **9-11-5**$^{(7)}$ MrSJoynes (prom: led 2nd to 4th: hit 9th: wknd 4 out)	dist	3	7/1^{2}	—	—
	Direct (TRGeorge) **14-11-11**$^{(7)ow2}$ MrTEdwards (chsd ldrs to 10th: bhd whn mstke 3 out)	21	4	8/1^{3}	—	—
3341^{P}	**Major Mac** (DLWilliams) **10-11-5**$^{(7)}$ MrSDurack (a bhd)	9	5	33/1	—	—
	What a to Do (CJRSweeting) **13-11-13**$^{(7)}$ MissLSweeting (prom: hit 6th: lost pl 8th: rallied 13th: poor 4th whn blnd & uns rdr last)		U	8/1^{3}	—	—
	Solar Gem (JohnMason) **10-11-5**$^{(7)}$ MrsCMcCarthy (mstkes: a bhd: blnd 3 out: uns rdr)		U	33/1	—	—

(SP 115.0%) **7 Rn**

6m 59.0 (44.00) CSF £5.49 TOTE £1.70: £1.10 £1.80 (£3.90) OWNER Mr R. G. Russell (NORTHAMPTON) BRED Oakgrove Stud

3273 Teaplanter looked rather a shadow of his former self but really dug deep and will be retired at the end of the season. Strength from the saddle proved a decisive factor. (8/13)
Fiddlers Pike, who recently returned to winning ways between the flags, ran a tremendous race and lost little in defeat. (7/1)
3357 Lurriga Glitter (IRE) looks to need a trip short of three miles. (7/1: 5/1-8/1)
Direct probably needs the ground even softer than this. (8/1: op 4/1)
What a to Do (8/1: op 5/1)

3491 HOECHST ROUSSEL PANACUR E.B.F. (QUALIFIER) 'N.H.' NOVICES' HURDLE (5-Y.O+ Mares Only) (Class D)

3-50 (3-52) **2m 5f (11 hdls)** £3,247.50 (£975.00: £470.00: £217.50) GOING: 1.03 sec per fur (HY)

Form	Horse / details	Dist	Pos	SP	RR	SF
3186^{2}	**Konvekta Queen (IRE) (95)** (OSherwood) **6-11-0** JOsborne (hld up: hdwy 7th: led 2 out: rdn out)	—	1	5/4^{2}	76	—
3222*	**Lady High Sheriff (IRE) (88)** (CaptTAForster) **7-11-0** NWilliamson (trckd ldrs: led appr 3 out: hdd 2 out: one pce)	5	2	6/5^{1}	72	—
3052^{3}	**Kosheen (IRE)** (MissHCKnight) **6-10-7** JCulloty (hld up: hdwy 6th: rdn & hit 2 out: btn whn blnd last)	8	3	7/1^{3}	59	—
3052^{5}	**Fun While It Lasts** (CaptTAForster) **6-10-7** CLlewellyn (chsd ldrs to 7th: n.d after)	14	4	33/1	48	—
	King's Rainbow (IRE) (MrsDHaine) **8-10-7** JFTitley (w ldrs: led 4th tl appr 3 out: sn wknd)	1½	5	20/1	47	—
3014^{P}	**Red River (IRE)** (CJDrewe) **6-10-2**$^{(5)}$ MrRThornton (w ldrs to 8th: sn wknd)	7	6	50/1	42	—
	Final Rose (RJSmith) **7-10-7** DWalsh (bhd fr 7th: t.o whn p.u bef 2 out)		P	25/1	—	—
3088^{7}	**Miss Mylette (IRE) (58)** (DJWintle) **6-10-7** WMarston (led to 4th: wknd appr 7th: t.o whn p.u bef 2 out)		P	50/1	—	—
	Pinxton Penny (JMackie) **5-10-7** TEley (a bhd: t.o whn p.u bef 7th)		P	50/1	—	—
				(SP 119.8%)	**9 Rn**	

5m 46.4 (44.40) CSF £2.89 TOTE £2.30: £1.00 £1.40 £1.60 (£1.70) Trio £2.30 OWNER Konvekta Ltd (UPPER LAMBOURN) BRED Mrs E. Skelly
3186 Konvekta Queen (IRE), niggled along down the back, got a good run on the runner-up's inside on the home turn and soon had matters in hand. (5/4: 4/5-11/8)
3222* Lady High Sheriff (IRE) crept up King's Rainbow's inside to take the lead but then had the winner doing the same to her. (6/5)
3052 Kosheen (IRE) got very tired in the home straight and her jumping suffered. (7/1: 5/1-8/1)
Fun While It Lasts lost her pitch a mile out, only to run on past beaten horses late in the day. (33/1)
King's Rainbow (IRE), who showed promise in points in 1995, shaped well until a lack of a run found her out. (20/1)
Red River (IRE) raced with the leaders for two miles but the hill found her out. (50/1)

3492 BANQUE ARJIL & COMPAGNIE H'CAP CHASE (0-120) (5-Y.O+) (Class D)

4-20 (4-20) **3m 1f (18 fncs)** £3,643.75 (£1,090.00: £522.50: £238.75) GOING: 0.65 sec per fur (S)

Form	Horse / details	Dist	Pos	SP	RR	SF
2681^{4}	**Carlingford Lakes (IRE) (89)** (TThomsonJones) **9-10-0** JCulloty (led to 11th: led 4 out tl j.slowly next: led 2 out: clr last: jst hld on)	—	1	3/1^{1}	97	—
3332^{3}	**Simpson (91)** (JABOld) **12-10-2** GUpton (prom: blnd 13th: ev ch 2 out: r.o wl flat: jst failed)	s.h	2	7/2^{2}	99	—
3153^{7}	**Holy Sting (IRE) (92)** (NATwiston-Davies) **8-10-3b** CLlewellyn (chsd ldrs tl lost pl 14th: r.o again appr 2 out)	1½	3	7/1	99	—
3153^{9}	**Shamarphil (89)** (RHAlner) **11-10-0** MissSBarraclough (j.slowly & lost tch 10th: gd hdwy appr 3 out: fin wl)	1½	4	33/1	95	—
3153^{12}	**Scribbler (117)** (GMMcCourt) **11-12-0b** JFTitley (prom: led 11th to 4 out: led 3 out to next: wknd flat)	5	5	14/1	120	18
3223^{3}	**Solo Gent (93)** (APJones) **8-10-4** DerekByrne (hld up: hdwy 11th: wknd 4 out)	dist	6	6/1^{3}	—	—
	Taramoss (114) (TRGeorge) **10-11-11** NWilliamson (chsd ldrs tl p.u bef 14th)		P	10/1	—	—
	Primitive Singer (89) (JAPickering) **9-10-0** WMarston (mstkes 1st & 9th: a bhd: t.o whn p.u bef 3 out)		P	33/1	—	—
3223*	**Celtic Barle (102)** (HBHodge) **13-10-13** SMcNeill (hld up: mstke 5th: blnd & uns rdr 11th)		U	7/2^{2}	—	—
				(SP 117.9%)	**9 Rn**	

6m 51.0 (36.00) CSF £13.53 CT £60.39 TOTE £3.60: £1.20 £2.10 £1.70 (£8.30) Trio £27.00 OWNER Mrs L. G. Turner (UPPER LAMBOURN) BRED Robert McCarthy
LONG HANDICAP Carlingford Lakes (IRE) 9-11 Primitive Singer 9-6 Shamarphil 9-8
2681 Carlingford Lakes (IRE) likes this type of ground and would have won with a little more in hand but for being forced to slow at the third last by a loose horse. Clear coming to the last, he was clever enough in putting in an extra stride but it almost cost him the race as his lead was disappearing quickly at the line. (3/1)
3332 Simpson really needs it soft and this patchy ground could have been the reason that he ran in snatches. After looking well held going to the last, he found his stride to such effect that he nearly snatched victory. On soft ground, he remains a very well-handicapped horse over fences. (7/2)
2671 Holy Sting (IRE) really needs further than this but his stamina was coming into play nearing the finish. (7/1)
1983 Shamarphil has only ever won once and is a bit of a madam. She dropped herself right out on the final circuit, only to suddenly take off meeting the rising ground, finishing as well as any. (33/1)
Scribbler, who finished a close third in the Midlands National on heavy ground two years ago off a 14lb higher mark when trained in Ireland, shaped like a horse returning to form. (14/1: 10/1-16/1)
3223 Solo Gent found conditions too testing, after travelling quite well. (6/1)

3493 BANQUE ARJIL POLSKA H'CAP HURDLE (0-120) (4-Y.O+) (Class D)

4-50 (4-50) **2m (8 hdls)** £2,714.00 (£754.00: £362.00) GOING: 1.03 sec per fur (HY)

Form	Horse / details	Dist	Pos	SP	RR	SF
3201^{4}	**Wassl Street (IRE) (100)** (KAMorgan) **5-11-10** NWilliamson (racd wd: a.p: hit 3rd: rdn appr 2 out: led appr last: all out)	—	1	6/4^{2}	80	32
3014^{5}	**Harlequin Chorus (91)** (JABOld) **7-11-1** GUpton (sn w ldr: led 4th: blnd 2 out: sn hdd: ev ch last: unable qckn)	s.h	2	11/8^{1}	71	23
483^{3}	**Simply (IRE) (100)** (TPMcGovern) **8-11-10** JOsborne (led to 4th: rdn appr 3 out: sn btn)	18	3	4/1^{3}	62	14
3056^{F}	**Karline Ka (FR) (90)** (RDickin) **6-10-7**$^{(7)}$ XAizpuru (a bhd: t.o whn mstke 4th)	dist	4	11/1	—	—
				(SP 110.4%)	**4 Rn**	

4m 10.9 (24.90) CSF £3.80 TOTE £2.40 (£2.40) OWNER Mr Rex Norton (MELTON MOWBRAY) BRED Cliveden Stud
3201 Wassl Street (IRE), dropped in trip, tried to look for the better ground for much of the race but was fortunate to have found such a moderate contest. (6/4)
3014 Harlequin Chorus looked just in command when ploughing through the second last and this eventually proved the deciding factor. (11/8: evens-6/4)
330 Simply (IRE) didn't appear to enjoy the tacky and patchy underfoot conditions. (4/1)

Karline Ka (FR) on her third run since a break of over a year and a half, again ran badly. Something appears to be amiss. (11/1: 6/1-12/1)

T/Jkpt: £7,100.00 (0.86 Tckts); £567.73 to Sandown 7/3/97. T/Plpt: £11.00 (1,066.32 Tckts). T/Qdpt: £4.30 (133.42 Tckts) Dk

3229-**WINCANTON (R-H) (Good)**
Thursday March 6th
WEATHER: Fine

3494 SEAVINGTON MAIDEN HURDLE (I) (4-Y.O+) (Class F)
2-10 (2-11) **2m (8 hdls)** £1,917.50 (£530.00: £252.50) GOING: 0.16 sec per fur (G)

				SP	RR	SF
2939[2]	**Talathath (FR)** (DNicholson) **5-11-5** RJohnson (hld up: hdwy 5th: led last: all out)	—	1	2/1[1]	85	41
	Samuel Scott (MCPipe) **4-10-11** APMcCoy (chsd ldrs: led after 3 out: hdd last: hrd rdn: r.o)	¾	2	9/2[2]	84	32
2840[5]	**Nordance Prince (IRE) (105)** (MissGayKelleway) **6-11-5** DBridgwater (hld up: hdwy 6th: ev ch 2 out: sn hung rt: btn whn j.rt last)	7	3	13/2[3]	77	33
2622[3]	**Quality (IRE)** (PJHobbs) **4-10-11** GTormey (lw: hld up: hdwy appr 3 out: hrd rdn appr 2 out: one pce)	3½	4	2/1[1]	74	22
3026[4]	**The Stuffed Puffin (IRE)** (CJMann) **5-11-5** JRailton (hdwy appr 3 out: wknd appr 2 out)	3	5	50/1	71	27
	Regal Splendour (CAN) (RJO'Sullivan) **4-10-11** DO'Sullivan (hdwy appr 3 out: wknd appr 2 out)	17	6	25/1	54	2
	Isis Dawn (AGNewcombe) **5-11-0** AThornton (bit bkwd: nvr nr ldrs)	6	7	66/1	43	—
2925[12]	**Green Bopper (USA)** (CPMorlock) **4-10-11** CMaude (lw: s.s: a bhd)	2	8	50/1	46	—
2805[14]	**Classic Model** (JCTuck) **6-11-5** RBellamy (bit bkwd: chsd ldrs to 5th)	12	9	66/1	34	—
	Alsahib (USA) (WRMuir) **4-10-11** BPowell (bkwd: a bhd: t.o)	dist	10	15/2	—	—
3233[7]	**Zidac** (PJMakin) **5-11-5** JRKavanagh (s.s: a bhd: t.o)	8	11	25/1	—	—
2696[17]	**Stonehenge Sam (IRE)** (JWMullins) **5-11-5** SCurran (lw: fell 1st)		F	66/1	—	—
3115[8]	**Pearl Hart** (RTPhillips) **5-10-11**(3) DFortt (j.b: a bhd: t.o whn p.u bef 2 out)		P	50/1	—	—
3012[5]	**Reverse Thrust (81)** (PRHedger) **6-11-5** MRichards (plld hrd: led tl after 3 out: wknd qckly: p.u bef 2 out)		P	50/1	—	—
	Honeyshan (DJSffrenchDavis) **5-11-0** GBradley (a bhd: t.o whn p.u bef 2 out)		P	66/1	—	—
	Stellar Line (USA) (DRCElsworth) **4-10-11** PHolley (chsd ldr to 5th: wknd qckly: t.o whn p.u bef 2 out)		P	16/1	—	—
3337[P]	**Orchid House** (NRMitchell) **5-11-0** DSkyrme (hmpd & uns rdr 1st)		U	100/1	—	—
				(SP 138.3%)	**17 Rn**	

3m 47.8 (7.80) CSF £11.52 TOTE £3.00: £1.30 £2.20 £2.10 (£10.00) Trio £14.70 OWNER Million In Mind Partnership (6) (TEMPLE GUITING) BRED Gainsborough Stud Management Ltd
WEIGHT FOR AGE 4yo-8lb

2939 Talathath (FR) had no High In The Clouds to contend with this time, but had to pull out all the stops. (2/1)
Samuel Scott, who showed little on the Flat in five runs for Michael Bell, is a half-brother to the hurdler Peter Monamy, and should soon go one better. (9/2: 4/1-6/1)
2840 Nordance Prince (IRE) gave his rider plenty of problems from the penultimate hurdle. (13/2: 4/1-7/1)
2622 Quality (IRE) found disappointingly little coming down the hill to the home straight. (2/1: 6/4-5/2)
3026 The Stuffed Puffin (IRE) had previously been trained in Scotland by Len Lungo. (50/1)
Alsahib (USA) (15/2: 10/1-6/1)

3495 BROADSTONE NOVICES' CHASE (5-Y.O+) (Class D)
2-40 (2-42) **2m 5f (17 fncs)** £3,704.00 (£1,112.00: £536.00: £248.00) GOING: 0.16 sec per fur (G)

				SP	RR	SF
3171[9]	**Full of Bounce (IRE)** (RJHodges) **6-11-1**(3) TDascombe (hld up: hdwy 9th: chsd ldr fr 13th: lft clr last)	—	1	33/1	106	31
3227*	**Frazer Island (IRE) (110)** (RRowe) **8-11-10** DO'Sullivan (nt j.w: hdwy whn mstke 11th: nt rcvr: lft poor 2nd last)	21	2	11/8[1]	96	21
158[9]	**Trust Deed (USA)** (SGKnight) **9-11-4b** MRichards (bhd: blnd 1st: t.o whn mstke 11th: n.d)	3½	3	33/1	87	12
3086[5]	**Reeshloch (90)** (AndrewTurnell) **8-11-4b** LHarvey (prom tl wkng whn mstke 13th)	9	4	8/1[3]	81	6
	Raincheck (MarkCampion) **6-11-4** JRailton (s.i.s: hdwy 4th: wknd 11th: t.o)	20	5	33/1	65	—
3400[P]	**Purbeck Rambler (65)** (GBBalding) **6-11-4v** BFenton (mde most to 10th: wknd after 4 out: lft 2nd & fell last)		F	33/1	—	—
3422[W]	**Campeche Bay (IRE) (130)** (GBBalding) **8-11-4** APMcCoy (a.p: led 10th: 7l clr whn fell last)		F	6/4[2]	—	—
3339[F]	**Dress Dance (IRE) (72)** (NRMitchell) **7-10-13**(5) SophieMitchell (a bhd: t.o whn fell 2 out)		F	12/1	—	—
3154[9]	**Dukes Castle (IRE)** (RGFrost) **6-11-4** JFrost (hld up: 4th whn mstke 10th: sn wknd: t.o whn p.u bef 13th)		P	25/1	—	—
	Le Grand Loup (DMHyde) **8-11-4** AThornton (a bhd: t.o 6th: p.u bef 11th)		P	100/1	—	—
				(SP 117.5%)	**10 Rn**	

5m 21.7 (13.70) CSF £74.06 TOTE £23.80: £3.80 £1.40 £2.80 (£23.10) Trio £238.60; £181.54 to Sandown 7/3/97 OWNER Fieldspring Racing (SOMERTON) BRED The Countess of Mount Charles

Full of Bounce (IRE), who won a maiden Irish point on soft ground at the beginning of last year, was a fortunate winner of his first race over fences. (33/1)
3227* Frazer Island (IRE) was let down by some indifferent jumping, and only finished second because of a couple of casualties at the final fence. (11/8)
Trust Deed (USA) would have finished a well-beaten fifth without the grief at the last. (33/1)
Campeche Bay (IRE) had the race at his mercy when departing but, with Frazer Island well below par, was not going to beat a lot. (6/4)

3496 'WINCANTON LOGISTICS' H'CAP CHASE (0-135) (5-Y.O+) (Class C)
3-10 (3-11) **2m 5f (17 fncs)** £5,410.00 (£1,630.00: £790.00: £370.00) GOING: 0.16 sec per fur (G)

				SP	RR	SF
3169*	**Senor El Betrutti (IRE) (135)** (MrsSusanNock) **8-12-0** GBradley (wnt 2nd 5th: led 12th to 13th: led 3 out: drvn out)	—	1	15/8[2]	144	40
3176*	**Hawaiian Youth (IRE) (107)** (GMMcCourt) **9-10-0** DBridgwater (chsd ldr to 5th: led 11th to 12th: led 13th: rdn & hdd 3 out: ev ch last: r.o)	1¼	2	7/4[1]	115	11
2821[P]	**Fools Errand (IRE) (115)** (GBBalding) **7-10-8** APMcCoy (mstke 2nd: j.slowly 3rd: hit 10th: no hdwy fr 4 out)	13	3	6/1	113	9
3182[P]	**Black Church (107)** (RRowe) **11-10-0** DO'Sullivan (led tl mstke 11th: sn wknd)	14	4	20/1	95	—
3232*	**Maestro Paul (109)** (JTGifford) **11-9-13**(3)ow2 LAspell (nt j.w: t.o fr 9th)	dist	5	9/2[3]	—	—
				(SP 108.4%)	**5 Rn**	

5m 21.7 (13.70) CSF £5.10 TOTE £2.70: £1.70 £1.10 (£3.40) OWNER Mr Gerard Nock (STOW-ON-THE-WOLD) BRED Bretton Blood Stock PLC

LONG HANDICAP Hawaiian Youth (IRE) 9-13 Black Church 9-4 Maestro Paul 9-6
3169* Senor El Betrutti (IRE), upped 6lb, had only to contend with one rival in the handicap proper, and just had the edge over the last three fences. (15/8)
3176* Hawaiian Youth (IRE), raised 7lb for his two victories, was still just out of the handicap, and lost little in a good duel from the third last. (7/4)
2660 Fools Errand (IRE) had softer ground this time, but may need further on a course as easy as this. (6/1)

3497 TOMMY WALLIS H'CAP HURDLE (0-130) (4-Y.O+) (Class C)

3-40 (3-41) **2m (8 hdls)** £3,415.00 (£1,030.00: £500.00: £235.00) GOING: 0.16 sec per fur (G)

				SP	RR	SF
2963*	**Northern Starlight (108)** (MCPipe) **6-11-6** APMcCoy (mde all: rdn appr 2 out: hit last: r.o wl)	—	**1**	11/10[1]	88	46
2932*	**Flying Fiddler (IRE) (99)** (MJRoberts) **6-10-8b**(3) PHenley (bhd: rdn after 3 out: styd on fr 2 out: nt trble wnr)	1¾	**2**	9/4[2]	77	35
2932[6]	**Morstock (112)** (RJHodges) **7-11-7**(3) TDascombe (chsd wnr: rdn & ev ch appr 2 out: wknd flat)	2½	**3**	5/1[3]	88	46
1255[5]	**Mutazz (USA) (102)** (MajorWRHern) **5-11-0** RFarrant (hld up: rdn & wknd appr 2 out)	dist	**4**	13/2	—	—
				(SP 108.4%)	**4 Rn**	

3m 47.0 (7.00) CSF £3.67 TOTE £1.80 (£2.10) OWNER Mr Arthur Souch (WELLINGTON) BRED R. J. Glenn and K. Leadbetter
2963* Northern Starlight, defying a 10lb rise in the weights, may have preferred faster ground, but it rarely gets too soft here. (11/10: 4/5-6/5)
2932* Flying Fiddler (IRE), raised 10lb, was not suited by the shorter trip, especially on an easy course like this. (9/4)
2932 Morstock, dropped 3lb, was back to his best trip, but failed to deliver the goods when the chips were down. (5/1)
1255 Mutazz (USA) seems to have lost his zest for the game. (13/2)

3498 DICK WOODHOUSE HUNTERS' CHASE (5-Y.O+) (Class H)

4-10 (4-11) **3m 1f 110y (21 fncs)** £1,492.00 (£412.00: £196.00) GOING: 0.16 sec per fur (G)

				SP	RR	SF
	Ryming Cuplet (MJTrickey) **12-12-0**(7) MrLJefford (mde virtually all: lft clr 3 out: drvn out)	—	**1**	6/1	113	—
3107[3]	**Wild Illusion** (MissJenniferPidgeon) **13-12-0**(7) MrRLawther (w ldr tl lost pl 15th: lft 2nd 3 out: rallied appr last: nt qckn flat)	1¾	**2**	13/8[1]	112	—
	Young Brave (MrsAYoung) **11-12-0**(7) MrMGMiller (hld up: hdwy 13th: rdn & lost pl after 15th: btn whn mstke 2 out)	3½	**3**	5/2[2]	110	—
	Panda Shandy (JWDufosee) **9-11-2**(7) MrRNuttall (hld up: hmpd 9th: hdwy 12th: wnt 2nd 15th: ev ch whn fell 3 out)		**F**	7/2[3]	—	—
129[P]	**Tom's Gemini Star** (OJCarter) **9-11-7**(7) MrEJames (hld up: pckd 1st: hdwy 8th: w ldrs whn fell 9th)		**F**	50/1	—	—
3403[R]	**Mediane (USA)** (MissAnnabelWilson) **12-11-11v**(3) MrSimonAndrews (unruly s: ref to r)		**R**	25/1	—	—
				(SP 109.0%)	**6 Rn**	

7m 0.2 (41.20) CSF £14.53 TOTE £7.10: £2.90 £1.10 (£5.60) OWNER Mr Gerald Tanner (SOUTH MOLTON) BRED G. Tanner
Ryming Cuplet looked to have a fight on his hands when Panda Shandy departed three from home. (6/1: op 7/2)
3107 Wild Illusion had the right sort of trip this time, and fought back after looking held early in the home straight. (13/8)
Young Brave, a winner over four-and-a-quarter miles at Uttoxeter last season, was not beaten far in the end. (5/2)
Panda Shandy won two of her three points last season, and there is every reason to believe she would have gone very close here. (7/2)

3499 SPARKFORD H'CAP HURDLE (0-100) (4-Y.O+) (Class F)

4-40 (4-40) **2m 6f (11 hdls)** £2,425.00 (£675.00: £325.00) GOING: 0.16 sec per fur (G)

				SP	RR	SF
2891[9]	**Country Tarquin (71)** (RJHodges) **5-9-11**(3) TDascombe (lw: hdwy 8th: led appr 2 out: edgd rt flat: drvn out)	—	**1**	16/1	52	9
1571[P]	**Spring Hebe (90)** (BJMRyall) **7-11-0**(5) SophieMitchell (bhd tl hdwy appr 2 out: styd on wl flat: nt rch wnr)	3	**2**	20/1	69	26
3358[2]	**Ehtefaal (USA) (95)** (JSKing) **6-11-10** TJMurphy (a.p: ev ch whn n.m.r bnd appr 2 out: one pce flat)	½	**3**	11/2[2]	74	31
3180[P]	**Daring King (83)** (MJBolton) **7-10-9**(3) LAspell (hdwy 8th: ev ch appr 2 out: r.o one pce)	¾	**4**	20/1	61	18
3112[2]	**Apachee Flower (74)** (HSHowe) **7-10-3** RJohnson (a.p: led 7th tl appr 2 out: one pce)	1¼	**5**	14/1	51	8
2905*	**Quelque Chose (97)** (BJMeehan) **7-11-12** DGallagher (hld up & bhd: hdwy 5th: ev ch 2 out: wknd flat)	4	**6**	7/2[1]	71	28
2959*	**Galatasori Jane (IRE) (98)** (PFNicholls) **7-11-6**(7) LCummins (lw: a.p: ev ch appr 3 out: wknd appr 2 out)	16	**7**	13/2[3]	61	18
3234[10]	**Imalight (80)** (RGFrost) **8-10-9** JFrost (hdwy 7th: wknd 3 out)	12	**8**	16/1	34	—
792[4]	**Crohane Quay (IRE) (90)** (GBBalding) **8-10-12**(7) MrABalding (nvr nr to chal)	10	**9**	10/1	37	—
3016[6]	**Mountain Reach (89)** (PRWebber) **7-11-4** AThornton (bit bkwd: bhd fr 8th)	¾	**10**	11/1	35	—
3344[5]	**Concinnity (USA) (71)** (BScriven) **8-9-7**(7) MrOMcPhail (mstke 1st: bhd fr 8th)	1¾	**11**	50/1	16	—
3186[7]	**Hanging Grove (IRE) (81)** (PGMurphy) **7-10-10** NMann (a bhd: t.o)		**12**	20/1	—	—
	An Spailpin Fanach (IRE) (90) (DRGandolfo) **8-11-2**(3) DFortt (bhd most of wy: t.o)		**13**	20/1	—	—
3180*	**Paddysway (94)** (RHBuckler) **10-11-9** BPowell (a bhd: t.o)		**14**	8/1	—	—
3269[11]	**Nuns Cone (84)** (REPeacock) **9-10-13** JRKavanagh (bit bkwd: a bhd: t.o)		**15**	33/1	—	—
2959[5]	**Dunnicks Country (74)** (FGTucker) **7-9-10**(7)ow3 MGriffiths (led 3rd to 7th: wknd 8th: t.o)		**16**	50/1	—	—
3063[5]	**Kilcoran Bay (88)** (JWMullins) **5-11-3v** RGreene (nt j.w: a bhd: t.o whn p.u bef 6th)		**P**	33/1	—	—
3234[4]	**Lucayan Cay (IRE) (88)** (MrsAJBowlby) **6-11-3** DLeahy (bhd most of wy: t.o whn p.u bef 2 out)		**P**	10/1	—	—
3016[P]	**Huge Mistake (89)** (NATwiston-Davies) **8-11-4b**[1] DBridgwater (reminders after 1st: sn bhd: t.o whn p.u bef 7th)		**P**	20/1	—	—
1675[P]	**Prove The Point (IRE) (80)** (MrsPNDutfield) **4-10-0** PHolley (led to 3rd: rdn & wknd 7th: t.o whn p.u bef 2 out)		**P**	50/1	—	—
				(SP 142.6%)	**20 Rn**	

5m 24.5 (15.50) CSF £292.28 CT £1,845.51 TOTE £9.10: £1.80 £4.10 £1.60 £4.70 (£136.00) Trio £1,464.00 OWNER Miss C. A. James (SOMERTON) BRED Miss C. A. James
LONG HANDICAP Concinnity (USA) 9-3 Country Tarquin 9-13 Dunnicks Country 9-10 Prove The Point (IRE) 8-9
WEIGHT FOR AGE 4yo-9lb
2642 Country Tarquin, just wrong at the weights on his handicap debut, stayed on for a hard-fought win, and may be even better in a pair of blinkers. (16/1)
Spring Hebe, dropped 10lb, would probably have preferred it even softer, and made up a considerable amount of ground in the home straight. (20/1)
3358 Ehtefaal (USA) really needs a stiffer test of stamina than this. (11/2)
1710 Daring King, hardly a model of consistency, is now 4lb lower than when winning at Fontwell a year ago. (20/1)
3112 Apachee Flower did not throw in the towel when collared, and should be suited by a return to three miles. (14/1)
2905* Quelque Chose has been put up 7lb for winning a seller at Fontwell. (7/2)

3500 SEAVINGTON MAIDEN HURDLE (II) (4-Y.O+) (Class F)

5-10 (5-12) **2m (8 hdls)** £1,900.00 (£525.00: £250.00) GOING: 0.16 sec per fur (G)

Form	Horse	Dist	Pos	SP	RR	SF
3007^{9}	**Muhtadi (IRE)** (LadyHerries) **4-10-11** RJohnson (hld up: hdwy 5th: led appr last: drvn out)	—	**1**	9/1	78	22
	Ring of Vision (IRE) (CJMann) **5-11-5** JRailton (a.p: ev ch last: nt qckn)	2½	**2**	16/1	76	28
	Kedwick (IRE) (PRHedger) **8-11-5** GBradley (hld up & bhd: hdwy 5th: ev ch last: one pce)	1¼	**3**	14/1	74	26
3233^{4}	**Embankment (IRE)** (NJHenderson) **7-11-0**(5) MrCVigors (plld hrd early: a.p: led 2 out: sn hdd: hit last: one pce)	1¾	**4**	5/2[1]	73	25
3205^{P}	**Piper's Rock (IRE)** (GBBalding) **6-10-12**(7) MrABalding (led to 3rd: led appr 2 out: sn hdd: wknd appr last)	4	**5**	33/1	69	21
2669^{9}	**White Plains (IRE)** (MCPipe) **4-10-11** BFenton (a.p: ev ch appr 2 out: wknd last)	s.h	**6**	7/2[2]	68	12
	Little Elliot (IRE) (SEarle) **9-11-5** CMaude (bhd: rdn 5th: nvr trbld ldrs)	15	**7**	20/1	53	5
3233^{12}	**Prototype** (GFJohnsonHoughton) **6-11-5** DGallagher (plld hrd: led 3rd: rdn & hdd appr 2 out: sn wknd)	2	**8**	25/1	51	3
3109^{9}	**Vanborough Lad** (MJBolton) **8-11-2**(3) TDascombe (hld up: bhd fr 3 out)	5	**9**	50/1	46	—
3000^{4}	**Althrey Pilot (IRE)** (AndrewTurnell) **6-11-5** LHarvey (hdwy 5th: wknd 3 out)	10	**10**	7/1	36	—
	Viking Dream (IRE) (JCFox) **5-11-0** SFox (a bhd)	3	**11**	50/1	28	—
3399^{F}	**West Bay Breeze** (RHBuckler) **5-11-0** BPowell (prom to 3 out)	2	**12**	33/1	26	—
	Quiet Arch (IRE) (WRMuir) **4-10-11** MRichards (nt j.w: sme hdwy appr 3 out: sn wknd: t.o)	dist	**13**	8/1	—	—
3109^{P}	**Jobie** (RTPhillips) **7-11-5** DBridgwater (a bhd: t.o)		**14**	50/1	—	—
1289^{17}	**Beweldered** (RGFrost) **5-11-5** JFrost (bit bkwd: a bhd: t.o)		**15**	50/1	—	—
	Genereux (SMellor) **4-10-11** NMann (a bhd: t.o 4th: p.u bef 2 out)		**P**	50/1	—	—
	Cool Virtue (IRE) (CaptTAForster) **6-11-0** AThornton (hld up mid div: mstke 2nd: hdwy whn stumbled & uns rdr 5th)		**U**	11/2[3]	—	—

(SP 136.6%) **17 Rn**

3m 50.4 (10.40) CSF £131.08 TOTE £10.90: £3.40 £3.20 £3.70 (£222.50) Trio £333.70; £376.00 to Sandown 7/3/97 OWNER The C I G S Partnership (LITTLEHAMPTON) BRED Ash Hill Stud

WEIGHT FOR AGE 4yo-8lb

Muhtadi (IRE), who won over ten furlongs at Ripon last April, stepped up on his debut in a hot contest at Newbury. (9/1)

Ring of Vision (IRE), twice a winner at Redcar for Mary Reveley, had apparently been schooling well at home, and can soon find a suitable opening. (16/1)

Kedwick (IRE), not seen out over timber for nearly two years, won over a mile-and-a-quarter at Lingfield in December, and looks capable of making up for lost time. (14/1)

3233 Embankment (IRE) will have to settle better early on if he is going to get the trip. (5/2)

Piper's Rock (IRE), a half-brother to Thumbs Up, appreciated this better ground. (33/1)

2669 White Plains (IRE) needs faster ground, which will also help him get the trip. (7/2)

3000 Althrey Pilot (IRE) (7/1: 5/1-8/1)

Quiet Arch (IRE) (8/1: op 5/1)

Cool Virtue (IRE) (11/2: 4/1-6/1)

T/Plpt: £22.30 (509.85 Tckts). T/Qdpt: £11.50 (40.18 Tckts) KH

3501a - 3502a : (Irish Racing) - See Computer Raceform

1741a-DOWNPATRICK (Ireland) (R-H) (Heavy)
Wednesday February 26th

3503a JAMESON ULSTER NATIONAL E.B.F. H'CAP CHASE (5-Y.O+)

3-30 (3-35) **3m 4f (18 fncs)** IR £7,021.25 (IR £1,588.75: IR £666.25: IR £358.75)

Form	Horse	Dist	Pos	SP	RR	SF
	Teal Bridge (IRE) (AHeffernan,Ireland) **12-10-4** CO'Dwyer (hld up in tch: 2nd after 4 out: led bef next: mstke 2 out: drvn clr flat: styd on wl)	—	**1**	6/1[2]	109	—
	Tout Va Bien (TCarberry,Ireland) **9-9-0**(7) LJFleming (rn 2nd: rdn & chsd wnr fr 3 out: kpt on same pce)	6	**2**	10/1	94	—
	Fairy Mist (IRE) (JPRyan,Ireland) **9-9-2**(7)ow2 RPHogan (towards rr: early mstkes: hdwy 12th: styd on)	9	**3**	10/1	91	—
1291^{F}	**Cabbery Rose (IRE)** (PFGraffin,Ireland) **9-9-1**(7)ow1 AO'Shea (in tch: rdn & chsd ldrs whn slow 3 out: no imp appr next)	2½	**4**	25/1	89	—
$3261a^{F}$	**Fissure Seal** (ALTMoore,Ireland) **11-11-7**(7) MrWEwing (mid div: 3rd, rdn & chsd ldrs 3 out: one pce)	4½	**5**	14/1	120	—
	Pennybridge (IRE) (IRFerguson,Ireland) **8-10-4** LPCusack (led: j.w: hdd bef 3 out: rdn & one pce appr 2 out)	2	**6**	10/1	95	—
	Olympic D'Or (IRE) (MFMorris,Ireland) **9-9-10** DJCasey (mid div: mstkes 10th & 11th: t.o)	dist	**7**	14/1	—	—
	Over The Maine (IRE) (IRFerguson,Ireland) **7-9-8** PatrickMcWilliams (towards rr: mstkes: t.o)	nk	**8**	25/1	—	—
$2848a^{6}$	**Monkey Ago** (MrsSABramall,Ireland) **10-10-5**(3) KWhelan (mid div: n.d fr 12th: t.o)	15	**9**	16/1	—	—
	Diorraing (IRE) (TO'Neill,Ireland) **7-9-0b**(7) JMMaguire (in tch early: mstkes: bad mstke & rdn 12th: wl t.o.)	dist	**10**	25/1	—	—
$3261a^{P}$	**Corymandel (IRE)** (HdeBromhead,Ireland) **8-11-1** TPRudd (rn 3rd: mstke 8th: btn 14th: p.u bef 4 out)		**P**	6/1[2]	—	—
$3255a^{*}$	**Nuaffe** (PAFahy,Ireland) **12-11-13** TJMitchell (towards rr: rdn & t.o 11th: p.u bef 4 out)		**P**	9/1[3]	—	—
$317a^{4}$	**Final Tub** (VTO'Brien,Ireland) **14-10-5** TPTreacy (in tch: wknd 11th: p.u bef 14th)		**P**	14/1	—	—
	Trench Hill Lass (IRE) (GStewart,Ireland) **8-10-8** JShortt (towards rr: trailing & p.u bef 10th)		**P**	6/1[2]	—	—
$2361a^{4}$	**Dee Ell** (ALTMoore,Ireland) **11-10-3** FWoods (hld up in rr: mstke & rdn 13th: no imp after next: p.u flat)		**P**	4/1[1]	—	—

(SP 137.6%) **15 Rn**

7m 42.0 OWNER Mrs M. Heffernan (DUBLIN)

Teal Bridge (IRE), a promoted Hunter Chaser, continues his rate of improvement. He really appreciates heavy ground and a mistake at the second last took nothing out of him. (6/1)

Tout Va Bien was the only threat to the winner from three out and will hardly remain a maiden over fences for long. (10/1)

Fairy Mist (IRE), 27lb out of the handicap and carrying 2lb overweight, was staying on from three out without ever promising to get on terms.(10/1)

8 Cabbery Rose (IRE) was chasing the leaders when blundering three out. (25/1)

2848a Fissure Seal looked desperately one-paced from three out. (14/1)

3255a* Nuaffe is no longer the force he was. (9/1)

3504a - 3522a & 3524a : (Irish Racing) - See Computer Raceform

2993a-LEOPARDSTOWN (Dublin, Ireland) (L-H) (Soft)

Sunday March 2nd

3523a BRANNOCKSTOWN H'CAP HURDLE (0-144) (4-Y.O+)

3-00 (3-01) **2m (8 hdls)** IR £4,110.00 (IR £930.00: IR £390.00: IR £210.00)

Form	Horse	Dist	Pos	SP	RR	SF
1656*	**Space Trucker (IRE)** (MrsJHarrington,Ireland) **6-12-0** JShortt (hld up: led after 2 out: styd on)	—	**1**	9/2 2	143+	78
	Sentosa Star (IRE) (MHourigan,Ireland) **6-10-1** MPHourigan (hld up: hdwy bef 3 out: bad mstke last: styd on)	2	**2**	7/1	114	49
	Ciara's Prince (IRE) (FFlood,Ireland) **6-9-0b**(7) LJFleming (rn 2nd: chsd ldr whn mstke 3 out: led after 3 out: rdn & nt qckn appr last)	4	**3**	11/2 3	102	37
2345a*	**Miltonfield** (JEMulhern,Ireland) **8-10-3** THorgan (hld up towards rr: pushed along bef 2 out: styd on)	12	**4**	9/2 2	100	35
3254a6	**Bolino Star (IRE)** (SJTreacy,Ireland) **6-10-12** TPTreacy (hld up: mstke 3 out: sn rdn: kpt on same pce)	s.h	**5**	7/2 1	109	44
3254a9	**Mayasta (IRE)** (FBerry,Ireland) **7-10-6** CFSwan (towards rr: rdn st: styd on: nvr nrr)	3	**6**	7/1	100	35
	Power Pack (IRE) (JFCMaxwell,Ireland) **9-9-2**(7) RPHogan (led: hdd after 3 out: rdn & nt qckn early st)	s.h	**7**	8/1	89	24
2345a2	**Collon Leader (IRE)** (AJMartin,Ireland) **8-9-7** JRBarry (hld up: no imp early st)	¾	**8**	7/1	86	21
2603a21	**Lady Arpel (IRE)** (PO'Leary,Ireland) **5-10-2**ow2 KFO'Brien (towards rr: n.d)	15	**9**	8/1	82	13
3382aP	**Buggy (IRE)** (KFarrelly,Ireland) **8-9-12**(7) MrAJDempsey (rn mod 3rd to 3 out: rdn & wknd appr next)	2	**10**	12/1	81	16
3254a8	**Anusha** (WJLanigan,Ireland) **7-10-12** LPCusack (mid div early: rdn & no imp appr 2 out)	20	**11**	14/1	68	3
				(SP 148.1%)	**11 Rn**	

4m 0.2 (-0.80) OWNER Mrs E. Queally (IRELAND) BRED John Harrington

1656* Space Trucker (IRE) continues to improve, but the idea that he is just a high-class handicapper is hard to dispel. Going to the front two out, in what looked a strongly-run race, he came wide into the straight for better ground and, despite 'blowing up' after the last, was always in total command. This ground was really too soft for him and he was undoubtedly in front for longer than he appreciates. He has improved 33lb since his second (to Mystical City) in the Galway Hurdle back in August. (9/2)

Sentosa Star (IRE), fit from recent outings on the snow in Saint-Moritz, was in pursuit and making little headway when blundering at the last. That mistake cost him more than the two lengths he was beaten by, but he would never have got past the winner. (7/1)

Ciara's Prince (IRE) helped set the gallop and came back for more after being headed two out. He is on nice mark for the County Hurdle. (11/2)

2345a* Miltonfield was in fifth place and making little headway two out and looked pretty one-paced in the straight, admittedly under a considerate ride. This trip is much too short and he will de better over the longer trips of his Cheltenham engagements. (9/2)

Mayasta (IRE) got herself well behind before staying on in the straight, but this was not encouraging. (7/1)

3525a BALLSBRIDGE HURDLE (4 & 5-Y.O)

4-00 (4-07) **2m (8 hdls)** IR £3,082.50 (IR £697.50: IR £292.50: IR £157.50)

Form	Horse	Dist	Pos	SP	RR	SF
	Stylish Allure (USA) (DKWeld,Ireland) **4-10-13** DTEvans (hld up: hdwy 3 out: chal to ld last: styd on flat)	—	**1**	6/1	86+	34
	Fishin Joella (IRE) (PMatthews,Ireland) **5-11-2**(7) AO'Shea (in tch: disp ld st: led appr last: sn hdd: no ex u.p)	3	**2**	9/2 2	85	41
	Grey Guy (IRE) (ALTMoore,Ireland) **5-12-0** FWoods (led: hdd appr last: one pce)	6	**3**	9/4 1	84	40
2993a3	**Strategic Ploy** (JohnMcKay,Ireland) **4-11-1** TJMitchell (in tch: rdn bef 2 out: styd on)	s.h	**4**	5/1 3	79	27
	Double Colour (IRE) (MissSCollins,Ireland) **5-11-0**(7) APSweeney (cl up: rdn & chsd ldrs after 3 out: nt rch ldrs appr last)	s.h	**5**	50/1	77	33
	Welcome Parade (TJTaaffe,Ireland) **4-11-6** CO'Dwyer (hld up: chsd ldrs 2 out: kpt on same pce)	7	**6**	7/1	77	25
	Rainbow Victor (IRE) (APO'Brien,Ireland) **4-10-13** THorgan (towards rr: nt fluent: no imp whn mstke last)	5	**7**	12/1	65	13
16516	**Murphy's Malt (IRE)** (APO'Brien,Ireland) **5-12-0** CFSwan (cl up: nt fluent: chsd ldrs 2 out: 6th & btn st)	½	**8**	11/2	71	27
	Doubleback (IRE) (MichaelFlynn,Ireland) **4-10-1**(7) KAKelly (towards rr: mod 9th & no imp st)	4½	**9**	33/1	55	3
	Wooden Dance (IRE) (PMcCreery,Ireland) **4-10-1b**1(7) MPCooney (mid div: 4th & 3 out: sn rdn: wknd bef 2 out)	s.h	**10**	25/1	55	3
	Royal Santal (IRE) (MHourigan,Ireland) **5-11-2** MPHourigan (towards rr: lost tch after 3 out: t.o)	25	**11**	50/1	30	—
				(SP 126.2%)	**11 Rn**	

4m 7.3 (6.30) OWNER P. A. Byrnes (CURRAGH)

Stylish Allure (USA), above average on the Flat, (rated 90) made an impressive hurdling debut here. Cruising over his older rivals in the straight, he drew clear on the flat and will have benefited measurably for the experience. Better ground would help and he is a live Triumph Hurdle outsider. (6/1)

Fishin Joella (IRE), ridden with more restraint this time, had every chance but found the winner much too strong on the run-in. (9/2: op 3/1)

Grey Guy (IRE) found this a much tougher task than when landing a gamble at Fairyhouse last time. He went off in front, but could never really dominate and was beaten well before the last. (9/4)

Rainbow Victor (IRE) (12/1: op 8/1)

3526a KILTERNAN H'CAP CHASE (5-Y.O+)

4-30 (4-35) **2m 5f (14 fncs)** IR £6,850.00 (IR £1,550.00: IR £650.00: IR £350.00)

Form	Horse	Dist	Pos	SP	RR	SF
2348a2	**Wylde Hide** (ALTMoore,Ireland) **10-11-9** PCarberry (sn led hdd briefly 3 out: rdn clr flat: eased nr fin)	—	**1**	9/10 1	144+	41
3128a4	**Monalee River (IRE)** (WPMullins,Ireland) **9-10-12** TPTreacy (cl up early: wnt 2nd after 4 out: ev ch last: rdn, edgd lft & no ex flat)	4½	**2**	8/1 3	130	27
	Barnageera Boy (IRE) (JTRDreaper,Ireland) **8-10-0** TJMitchell (hld up towards rr: clsd 2 out: rdn & nt trble ldrs appr last)	7	**3**	33/1	112	9
2741a4	**Belvederian** (MFMorris,Ireland) **10-11-7** CO'Dwyer (led & disp ld: 3rd & rdn after 4 out: no imp u.p st)	15	**4**	10/1	122	19
2348a7	**Feathered Gale** (ALTMoore,Ireland) **10-12-0** FWoods (rn 4th: lost tch bef 4 out: n.d)	4	**5**	2/1 2	126	23
				(SP 109.1%)	**5 Rn**	

5m 47.1 (10.10) OWNER John McManus (NAAS) BRED Paul Ryan

2348a Wylde Hide did not really have ground conditions heavy enough for him and was changing his legs frequently. Despite this, he made all and found enough on the flat to draw away again in the closing stages. The Handicapper has upped him 5lb for this and he is now Aintree-bound. (9/10)

3128a Monalee River (IRE) put two absolutely appalling efforts well behind him here and arrived in the straight cruising on the outside of the winner. Still on the bridle at the last, he found nothing when let down. (8/1)

Barnageera Boy (IRE), trailing for most of the trip, stayed on without threatening. (33/1)

2741a Belvederian was constantly out-jumped by the winner and was sulking after the third last. (10/1)

1649 Feathered Gale was always struggling at the rear and needs better ground. (2/1)

3527a - 3528a : (Irish Racing) - See Computer Raceform

3064-AYR (L-H) (Soft, Good to soft patches)
Friday March 7th

WEATHER: cloudy and windy

3529 LOCH DOON 'N.H.' MAIDEN HURDLE (4-Y.O+) (Class F)

1-50 (1-51) **2m (9 hdls)** £2,335.50 (£648.00: £310.50) GOING: 1.24 sec per fur (HY)

				SP	RR	SF
3024[3]	**Derannie (IRE)** (GRichards) **5-11-8** ADobbin (lw: hld up: hdwy ½-wy: led 3 out: drvn clr)	—	1	5/6[1]	75	41
3282[3]	**Carlisle Bandito's (IRE)** (JBerry) **5-11-8** MMoloney (hld up: hdwy on ins whn hmpd after 5th: hmpd after 4 out: hdwy 3 out: no ch w wnr)	14	2	9/2[3]	61	27
2917[7]	**La Riviera (IRE)** (JIACharlton) **5-11-8** KJohnson (in tch: hdwy to chse ldrs 4 out: one pce fr next)	3	3	25/1	58	24
3325[2]	**Lumback Lady (88)** (BMactaggart) **7-11-3** BStorey (lw: in tch: effrt 4 out: no imp)	7	4	3/1[2]	46	12
3024[P]	**Cream O The Border** (ACWhillans) **5-11-3** FPerratt (prom: outpcd 4 out: no imp after)	7	5	100/1	39	5
1349[5]	**Alnbrook** (ACWhillans) **6-11-8** DParker (lw: prom tl outpcd fr 5th)	½	6	25/1	44	10
3311[3]	**Cottstown Boy (IRE)** (MrsSCBradburne) **6-11-8** MFoster (cl up: led 5th to 3 out: wknd 2 out)	½	7	20/1	43	9
3066[F]	**Meadowleck (56)** (WGYoung) **8-11-3** PCarberry (led: hit 3rd: hdd 5th: sn t.o)	dist	8	66/1	—	—
3142[10]	**One Stop** (MABarnes) **4-10-4**(5) STaylor (prom to 4th: sn bhd: fell last)		F	25/1	—	—
	Craigie Rambler (IRE) (DRobertson) **8-11-3** JBurke (fell 1st)		F	100/1	—	—
	Prince of Thyne (IRE) (MrsJDGoodfellow) **8-11-8** GCahill (bit bkwd: t.o fr 5th: p.u bef 3 out)		P	50/1	—	—

(SP 119.5%) **11 Rn**

4m 2.6 (25.60) CSF £4.35 TOTE £2.00: £1.30 £1.80 £5.10 (£4.30) Trio £34.20 OWNER Mrs Stewart Catherwood (PENRITH) BRED Don Kelly

WEIGHT FOR AGE 4yo-8lb

3024 Derannie (IRE), dropped back in trip, was well suited by this fairly testing ground. Kept up to his work, he won most emphatically. (5/6: evens-4/5)

3282 Carlisle Bandito's (IRE), on ground much softer than he has previously encountered, ran well and, but for finding trouble, would have been a fair bit closer. (9/2: op 3/1)

La Riviera (IRE) ran his best race to date and is obviously improving. (25/1)

3325 Lumback Lady looked a picture but never really showed any real spark in the race and seems to need faster ground. (3/1)

Cream O The Border showed a fair bit of improvement on her first effort. (100/1)

3311 Cottstown Boy (IRE) ran quite well until the testing conditions sapped his stamina dramatically in the home straight. (20/1)

3530 JOHN BROWN MEMORIAL NOVICES' CHASE (5-Y.O+) (Class E)

2-20 (2-20) **2m (12 fncs)** £3,119.00 (£932.00: £446.00: £203.00) GOING: 1.24 sec per fur (HY)

				SP	RR	SF
3092*	**Singing Sand (79)** (PMonteith) **7-11-10** ADobbin (lw: led tl after 3rd: chsd ldrs: led 7th: blnd 4 out: sn clr: eased flat)	—	1	8/1[3]	107+	40
3450*	**Real Tonic** (GRichards) **7-11-10** PCarberry (lw: cl up: mstke 5th: outpcd 8th: no imp after)	27	2	1/2[1]	80	13
2786[7]	**Corston Joker (77)** (LLungo) **7-11-4** JCallaghan (mstkes: outpcd fr 5th)	28	3	25/1	46	—
3092[F]	**Shut Up (60)** (MrsEMoscrop) **8-10-13** KJohnson (t.o fr 5th)	25	4	200/1	16	—
3398[8]	**Aragon Ayr** (PMonteith) **9-11-4** MMoloney (nt j.w: sn drvn along: p.u bef 7th)		P	12/1	—	—
3161[3]	**Nooran** (ACWhillans) **6-11-4** BStorey (led after 3rd to 7th: outpcd 4 out: 2nd & wl btn whn blnd & uns rdr 2 out)		U	4/1[2]	—	—

(SP 109.8%) **6 Rn**

4m 11.6 (26.60) CSF £11.66 TOTE £7.50: £3.50 £3.20 (£4.10) OWNER Hamilton House Ltd (ROSEWELL) BRED Miss H. B. Hamilton

OFFICIAL EXPLANATION Real Tonic: rider reported that the gelding did not act on the ground.

3092* Singing Sand is really getting the hang of this game and won this in fine style. (8/1: op 5/1)

3450* Real Tonic, having his second run of the week, found the testing conditions against him and was going nowhere from the fifth last. (1/2)

Corston Joker looked clumsy and never got into it. (25/1)

2617 Aragon Ayr had shown nothing over hurdles this season and this switch to chasing was certainly not a successful idea, as he was never jumping at all well. (12/1: 6/1-14/1)

3161 Nooran ran a fair race and would probably have been a remote second until a terrible blunder had his rider on the floor two out. (4/1: 9/4-9/2)

3531 JAMES BARCLAY MEMORIAL H'CAP HURDLE (0-125) (4-Y.O+) (Class D)

2-55 (2-55) **3m 110y (12 hdls)** £2,815.25 (£842.00: £403.50: £184.25) GOING: 1.24 sec per fur (HY)

				SP	RR	SF
3317*	**Tribune (104)** (CWThornton) **6-11-6** 6x MFoster (mde all: styd on strly fr 3 out)	—	1	2/1[1]	85	38
2802[7]	**Leading Prospect (97)** (MrsJDGoodfellow) **10-10-6**(7) NHorrocks (a cl up: chsd wnr fr 4 out: nt qckn fr 2 out)	6	2	20/1	74	27
3317[6]	**Bang in Trouble (IRE) (104)** (JJO'Neill) **6-11-1**(5) RMcGrath (hld up: hdwy 8th: wnt 3rd 3 out: sn rdn & no imp)	22	3	9/1	67	20
3066[2]	**Sunny Leith (84)** (PMonteith) **6-10-0** ADobbin (lw: in tch: hdwy to chse ldrs 8th: one pce fr 4 out)	4	4	7/2[2]	44	—
3358[5]	**Hudson Bay Trader (USA) (84)** (PBeaumont) **10-10-0** MissPRobson (cl up tl outpcd 8th: no imp after)	1¼	5	7/1	43	—
3368[3]	**Military Academy (112)** (GRichards) **8-12-0** PCarberry (mstke 3rd: hdwy & prom 6th: rdn & wknd fr 8th)	10	6	6/1[3]	65	18
3398[6]	**Festival Fancy (93)** (BMactaggart) **10-10-6**(3) GLee (outpcd & lost tch fr 7th)	6	7	20/1	42	—
3317[5]	**Smiddy Lad (95)** (RShiels) **6-10-11** DBentley (prom tl outpcd fr 7th: sn btn)	dist	8	8/1	—	—

(SP 113.0%) **8 Rn**

6m 26.2 (40.20) CSF £33.46 CT £265.46 TOTE £3.60: £1.70 £3.60 £2.30 (£32.90) OWNER Hexagon Racing (MIDDLEHAM) BRED R. G. Bonson

LONG HANDICAP Sunny Leith 9-10

3317* Tribune, racing on testing ground for the first time, really enjoyed it and, by the looks of things, the stiffer the test the better he goes. (2/1)

1690 Leading Prospect put in a determined effort and kept trying hard albeit in vain, and a repeat of this will surely find him success. (20/1)

3317 Bang in Trouble (IRE) travels well on the bridle, but didn't seem to find much off it. Nevertheless, he is in quite good form at the moment. (9/1: op 6/1)

3066 Sunny Leith tries hard but he is basically short of any turn of foot in this soft ground. (7/2)

3358 Hudson Bay Trader (USA) runs when in the mood and was not here. (7/1)

3368 Military Academy had plenty on at these weights and was done with some way out. (6/1: op 7/2)
3317 Smiddy Lad was most disappointing, getting stuck in the mud here a mile from home. (8/1: 6/1-9/1)

3532 ARTHUR CHALLENGE CUP H'CAP CHASE (0-120) (5-Y.O+) (Class D)

3-30 (3-30) **2m 4f (17 fncs)** £3,557.50 (£1,060.00: £505.00: £227.50) GOING: 1.24 sec per fur (HY)

				SP	RR	SF
3452^{*}	**Disco des Mottes (FR) (107)** (GRichards) **6-11-12** ^{5x} PCarberry (mde all: drew clr fr 4 out: easily)	—	1	8/13 ^{1}	133+	33
3312^{*}	**Solba (USA) (101)** (CParker) **8-11-6b** ^{5x} DParker (lw: prom tl j.slowly & outpcd 9th: sn lost tch: r.o flat)	23	2	3/1 ^{2}	109	9
3326^{*}	**Twin Falls (IRE) (99)** (GMMoore) **6-11-4** ^{5x} JCallaghan (chsd ldrs tl outpcd 12th: 3rd whn blnd bdly 4 out: no imp)	1	3	9/1	106	6
3308^{5}	**Montrave (105)** (PMonteith) **8-11-10** ADobbin (chsd wnr fr 5th: rdn 13th: wknd fr 3 out)	½	4	7/1 ^{3}	111	11
3027^{U}	**Peter (91)** (DWWhillans) **9-10-10** DBentley (5th & prom whn fell 5th)		F	20/1	—	—
				(SP 114.2%)		**5 Rn**

5m 31.1 (36.10) CSF £3.00 TOTE £1.60: £1.10 £1.80 (£2.60) OWNER Mr Robert Ogden (PENRITH) BRED Joel Poirier
3452* Disco des Mottes (FR) has really taken to this game and scored easily from his rather iffy opponents. (8/13)
3312* Solba (USA), having his second run in the blinkers, was up to his old tricks and looked none too keen until suddenly sprinting up the run-in to snatch second. (3/1)
3326* Twin Falls (IRE) was already finding this beyond him when he almost fell four out. (9/1: op 6/1)
3308 Montrave is good on his day, but needs things to be just right and these conditions were always going to make things too hard for his liking. (7/1)

3533 AYRSHIRE AGRICULTURAL ASSOCIATION CHALLENGE CUP NOVICES' HUNTERS' CHASE (5-Y.O+) (Class H)

4-00 (4-05) **2m 5f 110y (18 fncs)** £1,443.60 (£399.60: £190.80) GOING: 1.24 sec per fur (HY)

			SP	RR	SF
Denim Blue (MissPaulineRobson) **8-11-5**(5) MissPRobson (trckd ldr: led 12th: styd on wl fr 4 out)	—	1	9/4 ^{1}	84	—
Woody Dare (PNeedham) **7-11-3**(7) MrChrisWilson (led tl hdd 12th: blnd bdly 4 out: no ch after)	21	2	11/2 ^{3}	68	—
Frozen Stiff (IRE) (AJBrown) **9-11-5**(5) MrNWilson (mstke 5th: hdwy whn mstke 14th: nvr trbld ldrs)	8	3	5/2 ^{2}	62	—
Planning Gain (MrsJMHollands) **6-11-3**(7) MrMBradburne (lw: w.r.s: j.b: rn in snatches: sme hdwy & 4th whn fell 3 out)		F	6/1	—	—
Canny Chronicle (MissCEJDawson) **9-11-3**(7) MrAParker (trckd ldrs: 3rd whn fell 12th)		F	14/1	—	—
Molly Grey (IRE) (PMonteith) **6-11-0**(5) MrRHale (bit bkwd: nt j.w: blnd 13th: t.o whn p.u bef 4 out)		P	10/1	—	—
Eli Peckanpah (IRE) (MrsJeanMcGregor) **7-11-3**(7) MrARobson (v.unruly bef s: dismntd & t.n.p: deemed to have been a runner)		R	10/1	—	—
			(SP 113.9%)		**7 Rn**

6m 17.5 (65.50) CSF £13.70 TOTE £2.60: £1.20 £3.00 (£10.10) OWNER Mrs L. Walby (CAPHEATON) BRED G. Reed
Denim Blue was the only one in the race who had any idea of how to jump and that was enough to win it. (9/4)
Woody Dare ran reasonably well but was already beaten when almost coming to grief at the fourth last. (11/2)
Frozen Stiff (IRE) looked both slow and clumsy in these testing conditions. (5/2: op 6/4)
Planning Gain has ability but at present either can't or won't jump. (6/1: op 4/1)
Molly Grey (IRE) (10/1: 7/1-12/1)
Eli Peckanpah (IRE) was extremely unruly before the start and, when his rider got off some way from the tape, the starter let the others go, deeming him to have started, which seems a gross injustice to any misguided punter who may have backed him. (10/1)

3534 DOON NOVICES' H'CAP HURDLE (0-110) (4-Y.O+) (Class D)

4-35 (4-42) **2m (9 hdls)** £2,933.00 (£813.00: £389.00) GOING: 1.24 sec per fur (HY)

				SP	RR	SF
3265^{3}	**Phar Echo (IRE) (93)** (LLungo) **6-11-9** MFoster (led fr 3rd: rdn 4 out: kpt on gamely)	—	1	5/2 ^{1}	80	26
3265^{7}	**Jervaulx (IRE) (95)** (GRichards) **6-11-11** PCarberry (chsd ldrs: hrd rdn & chal last: kpt on)	½	2	9/1	82	28
3064^{*}	**Solsgirth (77)** (JBarclay) **6-10-7** BStorey (trckd ldrs: ev ch 3 out: nt qckn appr last)	2	3	7/2 ^{2}	62	8
3028^{5}	**Kemo Sabo (89)** (CParker) **5-11-5b**[1] DParker (led to 3rd: cl up tl outpcd 4 out: hdwy u.p 3 out: nvr able chal)	3	4	9/2 ^{3}	71	17
3139^{5}	**Menaldi (IRE) (73)** (PCheesbrough) **7-10-3** GCahill (in tch: outpcd 5th: sn no ch)	22	5	7/2 ^{2}	33	—
3313^{5}	**Bill's Pride (75)** (PMonteith) **6-9-12**(7) CMcCormack (hld up: stdy hdwy 4 out: rdn appr 3 out: sn btn)	¾	6	14/1	34	—
1344^{4}	**Skane River (IRE) (71)** (GRichards) **6-10-1** ADobbin (uns rdr & bolted full circuit bef s: a bhd: lost tch fr 4 out)	27	7	10/1	3	—
3158^{15}	**On The Off Chance (70)** (LLungo) **5-9-7**(7) IJardine (bhd: sme hdwy & 6th whn fell 4 out)		F	50/1	—	—
				(SP 118.9%)		**8 Rn**

4m 6.1 (29.10) CSF £23.72 CT £73.55 TOTE £3.30: £1.10 £1.50 £1.60 (£13.40) OWNER S H C Racing (CARRUTHERSTOWN) BRED John O'Connor
3265 Phar Echo (IRE), dropping back in trip, found his stamina coming into play in these conditions and, that coupled with determination, he would not be denied. (5/2)
3265 Jervaulx (IRE) kept trying hard but just met one too good. (9/1: op 4/1)
3064* Solsgirth ran a fine race off an 8lb higher mark but was just short of a turn of foot and may do better if more use were made of him. (7/2)
3028 Kemo Sabo had blinkers on for the first time but they had little effect. (9/2)
3139 Menaldi (IRE), racing on soft ground for the first time, proved very disappointing. (7/2)
3313 Bill's Pride again travelled well, but failed to see the trip out in these conditions. (14/1)
1344 Skane River (IRE) (10/1: op 6/1)

T/Plpt: £13.80 (526.88 Tckts). T/Qdpt: £7.30 (62.55 Tckts) AA

2284-EXETER (R-H) (Good to soft)

Friday March 7th

Race 3 - one fence omitted
WEATHER: overcast & slight drizzle

3535 HMS EXETER NOVICES' HURDLE (I) (4-Y.O+) (Class E)

1-45 (2-00) **2m 3f 110y (9 hdls)** £2,008.00 (£563.00: £274.00) GOING: 0.85 sec per fur (S)

				SP	RR	SF
3291[3]	**Font Romeu (FR) (114)** (MCPipe) **4-11-0** APMcCoy (lw: hld up: hdwy 4th: led 2 out: sn clr: comf)	—	1	4/6[1]	82+	30
2010[10]	**Foxies Lad** (DNicholson) **6-11-2** RJohnson (hdwy 6th: outpcd appr 2 out: btn & mstke last)	7	2	10/1[3]	70	26
3233[3]	**Crandon Boulevard** (MrsJPitman) **4-10-8** JOsborne (hdwy to ld 4th: hdd 2 out: sn outpcd)	nk	3	7/2[2]	70	18
3109[4]	**Mystic Hill** (RGFrost) **6-11-2** JFrost (in tch tl wknd 6th)	dist	4	12/1	—	—
3233[5]	**Spread The Word** (LGCottrell) **5-10-11v** MrLJefford (hdwy to chse ldr 4th tl outpcd appr 2 out: wknd)	2	5	10/1[3]	—	—
2927[6]	**Commuter Country** (CRBarwell) **6-10-13**(3) PHenley (bhd: hmpd 4th: hdwy 7th: nvr on terms: t.o)	dist	6	100/1	—	—
3178[P]	**Millcroft Regatta (IRE)** (RHAlner) **5-11-2** AThornton (prom early: lost pl: hdwy 4th: wknd fr 7th: t.o)	7	7	50/1	—	—
3233[10]	**Langtonian** (GFEdwards) **8-10-9**(7) MrTDennis (a bhd: lost tch 5th: t.o)	18	8	100/1	—	—
	Dunnicks Well (FGTucker) **8-10-9**(7) MGriffiths (bit bkwd: led to 4th: wknd fr next: t.o)	dist	9	100/1	—	—
	Nearly All Right (SEarle) **8-11-2** CMaude (bit bkwd: cl 3rd whn fell 4th)		F	100/1	—	—
1685[P]	**Supreme Crusader (IRE)** (WGMcKenzie-Coles) **6-11-2** EByrne (bit bkwd: chsd ldrs tl wknd 5th: t.o whn p.u bef last)		P	100/1	—	—
	Aqua Star (IRE) (AJKDunn) **4-10-8** MrRNuttall (bit bkwd: Withdrawn not under Starter's orders: loose bef s)		W	100/1	—	—

(SP 116.0%) **11 Rn**

4m 56.8 (24.80) CSF £7.83 TOTE £1.50: £1.10 £3.00 £1.10 (£8.90) Trio £5.80 OWNER Pond House Gold (WELLINGTON) BRED Mrs A. Daubin
WEIGHT FOR AGE 4yo-8lb

3291 Font Romeu (FR) justified his market support to win this most convincingly. Holding the advantage two out, he soon showed his superiority over these lesser rivals and can win again in these conditions, though his future lies over the larger obstacles. (4/6: 4/7-10/11)
Foxies Lad put in a decent effort against an impressive winner, and this was an encouraging debut for his new stable, keeping on well for second place close home. (10/1: 6/1-12/1)
3233 Crandon Boulevard, who showed up third behind The Flying Phantom on his debut, was up with the pace throughout here and will surely improve with racing. (7/2)
3109 Mystic Hill (12/1: 5/1-14/1)
3233 Spread The Word (10/1: 5/1-12/1)

3536 HMS EXETER NOVICES' HURDLE (II) (4-Y.O+) (Class E)

2-15 (2-28) **2m 3f 110y (9 hdls)** £2,008.00 (£563.00: £274.00) GOING: 0.85 sec per fur (S)

				SP	RR	SF
3233[2]	**Give And Take** (MCPipe) **4-10-8** APMcCoy (lw: led: sn wl clr: rdn 2 out: unchal)	—	1	11/10[1]	80	21
	Solazzi (FR) (LGCottrell) **5-10-6**(5) OBurrows (hdwy 5th: chsd wnr after 7th: no imp)	14	2	100/1	64	13
3110[4]	**Steer Point (72)** (RGFrost) **6-11-2** JFrost (chsd ldrs: slt mstke 7th: wknd appr 2 out)	16	3	33/1	55	4
3156[10]	**Spirit Level (70)** (JRPayne) **9-11-3**ow6 MrRPayne (bhd: hdwy 5th: nvr nr: lft poor 4th 2 out)	28	4	100/1	33	—
3340[P]	**Rory'm (IRE)** (LWaring) **8-10-9b**(7) MGriffiths (a bhd: t.o)	23	5	100/1	14	—
3364[F]	**Kylami (NZ)** (AGHobbs) **5-11-2** RGreene (a bhd: lost tch 5th: t.o)	½	6	20/1	13	—
3184*	**Avanti Express (IRE) (113)** (CREgerton) **7-11-8** JOsborne (lw: stdy hdwy to chse wnr 5th: btn whn p.u bef 2 out)		P	5/4[2]	—	—
1830[P]	**Talk Back (IRE)** (MissHCKnight) **5-11-2** JFTitley (p.u 6th: in tch to 4th: grad wknd: t.o whn p.u bef 2 out)		P	7/1[3]	—	—
3115[12]	**Rapid Liner** (RJBaker) **4-10-8** VSlattery (chsd wnr tl appr 4th: wknd qckly next: t.o whn p.u bef 2 out)		P	100/1	—	—
2805[16]	**Cuillin** (RJSmith) **5-10-11** SMcNeill (bkwd: a bhd: t.o & p.u bef 7th)		P	100/1	—	—
3340[7]	**Mr Lovely (IRE)** (JNeville) **6-10-13**(3) TDascombe (w.r.s & uns rdr)		U	40/1	—	—

(SP 119.7%) **11 Rn**

4m 57.7 (25.70) CSF £110.62 TOTE £2.50: £1.90 £6.20 £2.00 (£259.30) Trio £152.80 OWNER Nelson, Newman and Moran (WELLINGTON)
BRED The Queen
WEIGHT FOR AGE 4yo-8lb
OFFICIAL EXPLANATION Avanti Express (IRE): rider reported that the gelding never picked up his bit and was never travelling.
Talk Back (IRE): gurgled.

3233 Give And Take handled this step up in distance well, annihilating this field in the process. Making all, he soon went clear and, from then on, there only ever seemed one winner. (11/10)
Solazzi (FR) ran better than her long market-price predicted and was the only contender to have the winner in her sights. Keeping on at the one pace in the straight, it was to no avail, but there can be a race found for her, if she can repeat this performance. (100/1)
3110 Steer Point could give nothing more in the closing stages and settled for a remote third prize. (33/1)
3184* Avanti Express (IRE) (5/4: 4/5-6/4)

3537 DIAMOND EDGE NOVICES' CHASE (5-Y.O+) (Class E)

2-50 (2-52) **2m 7f 110y (16 fncs)** £3,440.00 (£965.00: £470.00) GOING: 0.85 sec per fur (S)

				SP	RR	SF
3334[F]	**Bear Claw** (OSherwood) **8-11-2b** JOsborne (lw: led 3rd: mde rest: j.lft 10th: clr 13th: unchal)	—	1	5/2[2]	94	30
3443[F]	**Malwood Castle (IRE)** (RHAlner) **7-11-2** AThornton (bit bkwd: bhd: hdwy 12th: chsd wnr 14th: wknd 2 out: fin 3rd, 15l & 13l: plcd 2nd)	28	2	20/1	75	11
3339[3]	**Indian Delight** (MCPipe) **7-11-2** CMaude (chsd ldrs tl wknd appr 14th: fin 4th: 1 3/4l: plcd 3rd)	1 3/4	3	8/1[3]	74	10
3274[F]	**Pleasure Shared (IRE)** (PJHobbs) **9-11-8** GTormey (lw: fell 3rd)		F	5/2[2]	—	—
3409[F]	**Dextra (IRE)** (SEarle) **7-11-2** SMcNeill (a bhd: t.o whn p.u bef 10th)		P	66/1	—	—
3108[8]	**Rathkeal (IRE)** (MJHeaton-Ellis) **6-11-2** BPowell (mid div & chsd ldrs 11th: blnd & p.u 14th)		P	100/1	—	—
2704*	**Stormy Sunset (79)** (WWDennis) **10-10-10**(7) MrTDennis (led to 3rd: chsd wnr to 10th: wknd next: p.u bef 12th)		P	20/1	—	—
2883[P]	**Oats N Barley (85)** (PRRodford) **8-11-2** SBurrough (bit bkwd: hdwy to chse wnr 11th: outpcd 13th: t.o whn p.u bef last)		P	33/1	—	—
3339[F]	**Silver Hill** (MrsSDWilliams) **7-10-11** RGreene (bkwd: a bhd: t.o whn p.u bef 9th)		P	100/1	—	—
2819[7]	**Secret Bid (IRE) (100)** (RHAlner) **7-11-2** WMcFarland (prom & 3rd whn blnd & uns rdr 11th)		U	10/1	—	—

				SP	RR	SF
3165*	**Carole's Crusader (113)** (DRGandolfo) **6-11-3** GBradley (bhd: hdwy 11th: chsd wnr 14th: no imp: fin 2nd, 15l: disq)		**D**	9/4[1]	85	21
				(SP 124.1%)	**11 Rn**	

6m 18.2 (31.20) CSF £47.46 TOTE £3.20: £2.00 £19.40 £1.50 (£31.80) Trio £19.70 OWNER Roach Foods Ltd (UPPER LAMBOURN) BRED R. Aston

STEWARDS' ENQUIRY Bradley susp. 17-22 & 24/3/97 (taking wrong crse).

3334 Bear Claw got his jumping act together on this occasion and by doing so, turned the race into something of a procession. He looks a promising chaser in the making, especially if he can learn from this jumping performance. (5/2)

Malwood Castle (IRE), like the winner, fell on his chasing debut but, staying on his feet here, earned himself a promoted second place. (20/1)

3339 Indian Delight has shown promise on his previous form and there can be a small race found for him. (8/1)

3274 Pleasure Shared (IRE) is a frustrating character to say the least. If he could only tidy up his jumping, he would certainly be a force over the larger obstacles. (5/2)

3165* Carole's Crusader finished a remote second but was disqualified for taking the wrong route around a dolled-off fence. Compensation would seem to await her. (9/4)

3538 SITWELL ARMS NOVICES' H'CAP CHASE (0-105) (5-Y.O+) (Class E)

3-25 (3-26) **2m 2f (12 fncs)** £2,981.25 (£900.00: £437.50: £206.25) GOING: 0.85 sec per fur (S)

				SP	RR	SF
2873[5]	**Bishops Castle (IRE) (87)** (RGFrost) **9-11-4** JFrost (lw: hld up mid div: hdwy 6th: led appr last: rdn out)	—	**1**	6/1[3]	93	29
3178[6]	**Alpine Song (69)** (MissVAStephens) **12-10-0** MissVStephens (led 2nd tl hdd 9th: ev ch last: hrd drvn: jst failed)	½	**2**	33/1	75	11
3343[4]	**After The Fox (80)** (NJHawke) **10-10-4**(7) MrJTizzard (lw: hdwy to chse ldr 4th: led 9th: hdd appr last: wknd)	9	**3**	3/1[1]	78	14
2943[6]	**Indian Temple (69)** (KBishop) **6-10-0** RGreene (led: hdd 2nd: in tch to 7th: stdly wknd)	16	**4**	20/1	52	—
3111[P]	**Gemini Mist (69)** (MrsPNDutfield) **6-10-0** AProcter (mid div: wkng & mstke 7th: sn t.o)	30	**5**	50/1	26	—
1274[9]	**Trail Boss (IRE) (88)** (MissHCKnight) **6-11-5** JFTitley (chsd ldrs tl wknd 7th: p.u bef next: b.b.v)		**P**	5/1[2]	—	—
3112[7]	**Colette's Choice (IRE) (72)** (GAHam) **8-10-3**ow2 SBurrough (hmpd & uns rdr 3rd)		**U**	25/1	—	—
2679[3]	**Amber Spark (IRE) (88)** (DRGandolfo) **8-11-5** GBradley (bhd whn hmpd & uns rdr 3rd)		**U**	3/1[1]	—	—
2578[10]	**Chili Heights (73)** (KBishop) **7-9-11b**(7)ow4 MGriffiths (2nd whn blnd & uns rdr 3rd)		**U**	33/1	—	—
3336[5]	**Cawarra Boy (93)** (CJames) **9-11-10** MrEJames (4th whn hmpd & uns rdr 3rd)		**U**	13/2	—	—
				(SP 110.7%)	**10 Rn**	

4m 45.4 (24.40) CSF £149.99 CT £614.44 TOTE £8.70: £2.00 £4.80 £1.50 (£137.30) Trio £86.40; £98.63 to Sandown 7/3/97 OWNER A E C Electric Fencing Ltd (Hotline) (BUCKFASTLEIGH) BRED Mrs Dolors Dinneen

LONG HANDICAP Indian Temple 9-9 Alpine Song 9-5 Chili Heights 9-12 Gemini Mist 9-5

903* Bishops Castle (IRE) may not have found this ground to his liking, but has won here over fences before. Tracking the leaders throughout, he challenged at the second last and ran on well to lead over the final fence, and was kept up to his work on the run-in to hold his closest rival at bay. (6/1)

Alpine Song made most of the running, but lost the advantage in the home straight. In third place over the last, she rallied on the run-in and, though not affecting her chances, drifted left close home. (33/1)

3343 After The Fox, on the heels of the leaders throughout, still had a chance approaching the last, but weakened quickly and settled for third place on the run-in (3/1)

3539 BRITISH RACING CENTRE H'CAP HURDLE (0-120) (4-Y.O+) (Class D)

3-55 (3-55) **2m 3f 110y (9 hdls)** £2,775.00 (£775.00: £375.00) GOING: 0.85 sec per fur (S)

				SP	RR	SF
3019[4]	**Cool Gunner (84)** (JSKing) **7-10-4** CMaude (lw: hld up & bhd: stdy hdwy tl led appr 2 out: sn clr: easily)	—	**1**	13/8[1]	58+	19
3109[2]	**Devon Peasant (95)** (LGCottrell) **5-11-1** MrLJefford (lw: hld up mid div: disp ld 2 out: outpcd appr last)	3	**2**	5/1[3]	67	28
2871[5]	**Friendly House (IRE) (94)** (MCPipe) **8-11-0** APMcCoy (chsd ldrs: in tch tl outpcd appr 2 out)	12	**3**	6/1	56	17
3084[6]	**Trouvaille (IRE) (96)** (AndrewTurnell) **6-11-2** LHarvey (chsd ldr: in tch tl wknd appr 2 out)	6	**4**	7/1	53	14
2759[5]	**The Bargeman (NZ) (95)** (DRGandolfo) **9-10-12**(3) DFortt (led tl hdd appr 2 out: sn wknd)	7	**5**	7/2[2]	46	7
3156[6]	**Pennymoor Prince (104)** (RGFrost) **8-11-10** JFrost (a bhd: lost tch 5th)	dist	**6**	13/2	—	—
				(SP 117.1%)	**6 Rn**	

4m 57.2 (25.20) CSF £9.94 TOTE £2.20: £1.10 £2.80 (£6.90) OWNER Mr Richard Peterson (SWINDON) BRED R. Burton

3019 Cool Gunner is improving with racing and, with conditions to suit, was found a good opportunity here. Held up towards the rear, he made his challenge entering the straight and gradually pulled clear, only needing to be shaken up on the run-in to succeed. (13/8)

3109 Devon Peasant went clear with the winner after entering the straight but was soon outpaced when tackling the final fence. With such a bad case of seconditis, she deserves a change of fortune. (5/1)

2871 Friendly House (IRE) may have finished closer with slightly softer conditions. (6/1)

2759 The Bargeman (NZ) (7/2: 3/1-9/2)

3540 WEATHERBYS BULLETIN MAGAZINE H'CAP CHASE (0-115) (5-Y.O+) (Class E)

4-30 (4-31) **2m 3f 110y (15 fncs)** £3,055.00 (£855.00: £415.00) GOING: 0.85 sec per fur (S)

				SP	RR	SF
3333*	**Lance Armstrong (IRE) (109)** (GMMcCourt) **7-11-6**(3) 6x DFortt (lw: chsd ldrs: in tch: lft in ld 13th: hmpd appr last: hld on gamely u.p)	—	**1**	2/1[1]	114	16
3410[B]	**Mammy's Choice (IRE) (95)** (RHAlner) **7-10-9** AThornton (led tl hdd after 12th: lft 2nd next: ev ch last: no ex flat)	1¼	**2**	7/1[3]	99	1
3074[5]	**Shining Light (IRE) (114)** (DNicholson) **8-12-0** RJohnson (chsng ldrs: mstke 7th: ev ch whn hmpd 13th: rdn & one pce last)	nk	**3**	9/4[2]	118	20
3339[2]	**Mr Playfull (91)** (RGFrost) **7-10-5** JFrost (chsd ldr tl led after 12th: blnd & uns rdr next)		**U**	9/4[2]	—	—
				(SP 107.4%)	**4 Rn**	

5m 16.5 (31.50) CSF £11.60 TOTE £2.40 (£8.70) OWNER Mr G. L. Porter (WANTAGE) BRED Tom Curran

3333* Lance Armstrong (IRE) is on the upgrade, but had his task made slightly easier here by the departure of the leader at the fourth last. Hampered by the loose horse when setting himself up for his final leap, he jumped it safely enough and kept on strongly on the run-in. (2/1)

1812* Mammy's Choice (IRE), in and out of the lead throughout, still had every chance over the last and, although rallying well on the run-in, just could not find enough to challenge the winner. (7/1)

3074 Shining Light (IRE) could only keep on at the same pace over the final fence and, although having to contend with the loose horse on the run-in, it did not affect his placing. (9/4)

3339 Mr Playfull was travelling well and had as good a chance as any when unseating his rider at the fourth last (9/4)

3541 ENJOYMENT OF BEING AN OWNER NOVICES' HURDLE (5-Y.O+) (Class E)

5-00 (5-03) **3m 2f (13 hdls)** £2,452.50 (£690.00: £337.50) GOING: 0.85 sec per fur (S)

				SP	RR	SF
3156^{5}	**Menesonic (IRE) (111)** (RHAlner) **7-10-7**(3) PHenley (lw: a.p: disp ld last: rdn & qckdn clr flat)	—	**1**	$9/4^{2}$	74	29
3156^{2}	**Scotby (BEL) (111)** (RHBuckler) **7-11-8** BPowell (lw: a.p: chsd ldr 11th: led 2 out tl hdd & outpcd flat)	5	**2**	$6/1^{3}$	83	38
3108^{7}	**Spaceage Gold (96)** (JABOld) **8-11-2** GUpton (led tl hdd 2 out: wknd appr last)	2½	**3**	10/1	75	30
3048^{11}	**Coole Cherry** (CRBarwell) **7-10-10** RJohnson (mid div tl wknd 10th: t.o)	dist	**4**	33/1	—	—
3190^{F}	**Blazing Miracle (76)** (MrsRGHenderson) **5-10-0**(5) DSalter (prom: chsd ldr 7th tl 9th: wknd fr next: t.o)	2½	**5**	20/1	—	—
3234^{P}	**Mu-Tadil (65)** (RJBaker) **5-10-10** VSlattery (a bhd: t.o fr 6th)	dist	**6**	66/1	—	—
3057^{P}	**Deceit the Second (49)** (PRRodford) **5-10-10** SBurrough (a bhd: mstke 8th: sn t.o)	23	**7**	100/1	—	—
3265^{4}	**Logical Step (IRE) (96)** (DRGandolfo) **7-10-10** GBradley (bhd 4th: hdwy 7th: wknd 10th: t.o whn p.u bef last)		**P**	10/1	—	—
	Pollerman (JSKing) **7-10-10** CMaude (bit bkwd: w ldrs tl wknd 7th: t.o & p.u bef 2 out)		**P**	33/1	—	—
3181^{P}	**Akiymann (USA) (76)** (MCPipe) **7-10-9b**(7) BMoore (a bhd: t.o 4th: p.u bef 10th)		**P**	33/1	—	—
1998^{7}	**Ginger Maid** (MCPipe) **9-10-0**(5) GSupple (a bhd: t.o whn p.u bef 2 out)		**P**	25/1	—	—
3050^{12}	**Flashman (78)** (BJLlewellyn) **7-10-10** MrJLLlewellyn (a bhd: t.o & p.u bef 11th)		**P**	50/1	—	—
2676*	**Kind Cleric (115)** (PJHobbs) **6-11-2** APMcCoy (chsd ldrs tl wknd 8th: t.o & p.u bef 2 out)		**P**	$7/4^{1}$	—	—
	Han Line (MJCoombe) **9-10-10** MrLJefford (bit bkwd: chsd ldr & in tch tl 9th: wknd & p.u bef 11th)		**P**	66/1	—	—
3052^{P}	**Sula's Dream** (GAHam) **8-10-5** RGreene (bit bkwd: chsd ldr to 5th: wknd next: t.o whn p.u bef 10th)		**P**	100/1	—	—
2550^{10}	**Bank Avenue** (MrsJPitman) **6-10-10** RFarrant (chsd ldr 5th to 11th: wkng 4th whn blnd & uns rdr 2 out)		**U**	10/1	—	—

(SP 133.0%) **16 Rn**

6m 42.2 (32.20) CSF £15.66 TOTE £3.20: £1.50 £2.70 £3.60 (£25.00) Trio £48.00 OWNER Mrs W. H. Walter (BLANDFORD) BRED J. L. Rothwell

OFFICIAL EXPLANATION **Kind Cleric: gurgled at the end of the back straight.**

3156 Menesonic (IRE), who finished second to Yahmi at Newbury in November, sat in behind the leaders. Ridden to challenge entering the straight, he only took the lead over the last and showed good stamina to run on well close home. A decent stayer, he will be tackling the larger obstacles next season. (9/4)

3156 Scotby (BEL) was one of three with a chance in the straight, but was simply out-stayed by a decent rival. (6/1)

1915 Spaceage Gold raced on the rails in the straight and, still with a chance approaching the last, could find little in reserve on the run-in, only keeping on at the one pace. He may appreciate a firmer surface to show his capability. (10/1: 6/1-12/1)

3265 Logical Step (IRE) (10/1: op 6/1)

2676* Kind Cleric (7/4: 5/4-15/8)

T/Plpt: £129.20 (58.63 Tckts). T/Qdpt: £35.50 (9.07 Tckts) T

3197-MARKET RASEN (R-H) (Good, Good to soft patches)

Friday March 7th

WEATHER: cloudy

3542 'FARMERS DAY' (S) H'CAP HURDLE (0-95) (4 & 5-Y.O) (Class G)

1-40 (1-40) **2m 1f 110y (8 hdls)** £1,864.90 (£516.40: £246.70) GOING: 0.23 sec per fur (G)

				SP	RR	SF
2943^{5}	**Spitfire Bridge (IRE) (65)** (GMMcCourt) **5-10-8** DBridgwater (lw: outpcd & drvn along 3rd: hdwy & hrd rdn appr 2 out: led flat: kpt on)	—	**1**	$7/4^{1}$	48	—
3131^{9}	**Summer Villa (67)** (KGWingrove) **5-10-10b** KGaule (led 3rd: sn clr: hdd & nt qckn flat)	1½	**2**	$9/2^{2}$	49	—
3284^{8}	**Oakbury (IRE) (70)** (MissLCSiddall) **5-10-6**(7) TSiddall (chsd ldrs tl lost pl 4th: sn bhd: hdwy between last 2: fin wl)	3½	**3**	$5/1^{3}$	48	—
3327^{P}	**Eurolink the Rebel (USA) (85)** (SBClark) **5-11-7**(7) MissRClark (chsd ldrs: 4th & styng on whn blnd 2 out: one pce)	½	**4**	33/1	63	14
3058*	**Supreme Illusion (AUS) (72)** (JohnBerry) **4-10-7** PHolley (nt j.w: led to 3rd: wknd 3 out)	22	**5**	$5/1^{3}$	30	—
3438^{16}	**Blotoft (72)** (SGollings) **5-11-1** RGarritty (trckd ldrs: chal 3 out: wkng whn mstke 2 out)	s.h	**6**	12/1	30	—
2943^{15}	**Woodlands Lad Too (57)** (PAPritchard) **5-10-0** RBellamy (sn bhd: sme hdwy u.p 5th: sn wknd)	30	**7**	50/1	—	—
3327^{6}	**Cool Steel (IRE) (70)** (MrsJBrown) **5-10-10**(3) ECallaghan (hld up: blnd 3 out: bhd whn fell next: dead)		**F**	13/2	—	—

(SP 113.8%) **8 Rn**

4m 20.6 (17.60) CSF £9.40 CT £29.26 TOTE £2.20: £1.40 £1.90 £1.10 (£5.30) Trio £12.60 OWNER Mercaston Consultants Ltd (WANTAGE) BRED John Harrington

LONG HANDICAP Woodlands Lad Too 9-2

WEIGHT FOR AGE 4yo-8lb

No bid

2943 Spitfire Bridge (IRE), heavily backed, showed a return to form, but his supporters owe a debt of gratitude to his rider's persistence. Hard at work a circuit from home, he looked slightly reluctant, but his rider would have no part of it and forced his head in front inside the last hundred. (7/4: op 3/1)

3057 Summer Villa, allowed to set her own pace, had to give best in the closing stages. (9/2: op 3/1)

3091 Oakbury (IRE) ran a sour sort of race, dropping himself right out setting out on the final circuit, but finished with quite a rattle. (5/1)

Eurolink the Rebel (USA) ran his best race for a long time. (33/1)

3058* Supreme Illusion (AUS) hardly jumped a flight properly, and may be flattered by her Leicester success where she came from off the pace in a strongly-run race. (5/1)

Blotoft, with the blinkers left off, seemed to be short on stamina. (12/1: op 7/1)

3543 BEAUMONTCOTE HUNTERS' CHASE (6-Y.O+) (Class H)

2-10 (2-10) **3m 1f (19 fncs)** £1,329.00 (£369.00: £177.00) GOING: 0.67 sec per fur (S)

				SP	RR	SF
3353*	**Mr Boston** (MrsMReveley) **12-12-12** MrSSwiers (lw: wnt 2nd 10th: shkn up to ld 3 out: clr last: pushed out)	—	**1**	$4/11^{1}$	113	40
	Carly Brrin (MrsJRBuckley) **12-11-12**(7) MrCMulhall (led 3rd to 3 out: wkng whn mstke last)	20	**2**	$7/1^{3}$	93	20
3162^{6}	**Matt Reid** (JPLeigh) **13-12-5**(7) MrWMorgan (nt j.w: nvr gng wl: sn pushed along: outpcd fr 14th)	7	**3**	$4/1^{2}$	96	23
	R N Commander (JRCornwall) **11-11-12**(7) MrJRCornwall (led to 3rd: outpcd 11th: lost tch 14th: t.o)	dist	**4**	33/1	—	—

3095[4] **Fish Quay** (MrsKMLamb) **14-11-12**(7) MissSLamb (blnd 10th: sn bhd: t.o fr 13th: ref 2 out) **R** 66/1 — —
(SP 110.3%) **5 Rn**

6m 44.3 (33.30) CSF £3.42 TOTE £1.20: £1.20 £1.20 (£2.60) OWNER Mr M. K. Oldham (SALTBURN) BRED Mrs D. M. Hurndall-Waldron
3353* Mr Boston had a straightforward task, but he was by no means impressive. (4/11)
Carly Brrin, who won over the point-to-point course here five days earlier, should be able to pick up a novices' Hunter Chase. (7/1)
3162 Matt Reid never runs two races alike, and he was never going here from start to finish. (4/1: op 5/2)

3544 WHEATLEY PACKAGING HURDLE (4-Y.O) (Class D)

2-45 (2-45) **2m 1f 110y (8 hdls)** £2,997.50 (£905.00: £440.00: £207.50) GOING: 0.23 sec per fur (G)

Form	Horse / Details	Dist	Pos	SP	RR	SF
3226[8]	**Belmarita (IRE)** (GAHubbard) **4-10-6**(3) MichaelBrennan (chsd ldrs: hrd rdn & styd on to ld flat)	—	1	11/1	60	37
3301[6]	**Fairly Sharp (IRE) (105)** (GraemeRoe) **4-11-1** RichardGuest (chsd ldrs: led 4th: mstke 2 out: hdd flat: no ex)	¾	2	6/4[1]	65	42
3098*	**Six Clerks (IRE) (92)** (JGFitzGerald) **4-11-3**(3) FLeahy (in tch: effrt 5th: kpt on one pce fr 2 out)	8	3	7/2[2]	63	40
3359[7]	**Sharp Command** (PEccles) **4-11-0** PHolley (led to 4th: wknd appr last)	2	4	9/1[3]	55	32
3305[R]	**Jamaican Flight (USA)** (MrsSLamyman) **4-11-0** JRailton (nt j.w: bhd fr 4th: sme hdwy 3 out: nvr nr ldrs)	7	5	16/1	49	26
589[3]	**Down The Yard** (MCChapman) **4-10-9** WWorthington (prom: rdn 3 out: sn wknd)	10	6	20/1	35	12
3394[4]	**Principal Boy (IRE)** (TJEtherington) **4-11-0** RRourke (trckd ldrs tl wknd 3 out)	3	7	25/1	37	14
3197[P]	**Marigliano (USA)** (KAMorgan) **4-11-0** RGarritty (hld up & plld hrd: nvr nr ldrs)	10	8	11/1	28	5
3158[16]	**African Sun (IRE)** (MCChapman) **4-11-0** KGaule (bhd fr 5th: hmpd 2 out)	12	9	50/1	17	—
3014[P]	**Khalikhoum (IRE)** (SirJohnBarlowBt) **4-11-0** RSupple (prom tl lost pl 5th: blnd 2 out)	2	10	16/1	15	—
3345[10]	**Windyedge (USA)** (MrsAMNaughton) **4-11-0** JSupple (hld up: bhd fr 4th: t.o 3 out)	14	11	33/1	2	—
	Spencer Stallone (GraemeRoe) **4-10-11**(3) RMassey (sn bhd: t.o 3rd)	2	12	50/1	—	—
	Saturiba (USA) (JohnHarris) **4-11-0** PNiven (sn bhd: t.o fr 5th)	15	13	33/1	—	—
	Gold of Arabia (USA) (KAMorgan) **4-10-11**(3) ECallaghan (bit bkwd: bhd: sme hdwy & 9th whn fell 2 out)		F	20/1	—	—
3226[7]	**Summer Princess** (GFierro) **4-10-9** GaryLyons (t.o 5th: p.u bef 2 out)		P	16/1	—	—
3197[7]	**Tonto** (WHTinning) **4-11-0** DerekByrne (p.u lame after 3rd: dead)		P	25/1	—	—
	Alpheton Prince (JohnHarris) **4-11-0** DBridgwater (t.o fr 3rd: p.u bef 2 out)		P	33/1	—	—

(SP 136.5%) **17 Rn**

4m 11.7 (8.70) CSF £26.14 TOTE £13.00: £2.90 £1.50 £1.90 (£11.40) Trio £6.00 OWNER Mr G. A. Hubbard (WOODBRIDGE) BRED Cambremont Ltd Partnership
STEWARDS' ENQUIRY Brennan susp.17-20/3/97 (excessive & improper use of whip).
2889 Belmarita (IRE), who wore a tongue-strap, answered her rider's every call to scrape home. She will be suited by two and a half miles. (11/1: op 7/1)
3301 Fairly Sharp (IRE), knocked back by a blunder two out, had to give best in the closing stages. (6/4)
3098* Six Clerks (IRE), under a 6lb penalty, could never get near the first two. (7/2)
2060 Sharp Command forced the pace but his stride shortened going to the last. (9/1: op 6/1)
3305 Jamaican Flight (USA), kept covered up this time, tended to run about at his hurdles, but showed that he does possess some ability. (16/1)
3197 Marigliano (USA), who bolted off in front last time, was dropped in on this occasion but he never settled. (11/1: 8/1-12/1)

3545 LINCOLNSHIRE AGRICULTURAL SOCIETY H'CAP HURDLE (0-110) (4-Y.O+) (Class E)

3-20 (3-20) **2m 5f 110y (10 hdls)** £2,477.50 (£690.00: £332.50) GOING: 0.23 sec per fur (G)

Form	Horse / Details	Dist	Pos	SP	RR	SF
3201[10]	**Sassiver (USA) (85)** (PAKelleway) **7-10-5** KGaule (chsd ldrs: drvn along 5th: led & hit last: styd on wl)	—	1	11/2[3]	68	—
2545[3]	**Thursday Night (IRE) (108)** (JGFitzGerald) **6-12-0** PNiven (trckd ldrs: chal & blnd 2 out: kpt on same pce appr last)	2½	2	4/1[2]	89	13
3357[P]	**La Fontainbleau (IRE) (85)** (DHBrown) **9-10-5** PHolley (mde most tl appr last: one pce)	3	3	33/1	64	—
2694[P]	**Moobakkr (USA) (82)** (KAMorgan) **6-10-2**ow2 DerekByrne (trckd ldrs: smooth hdwy 3 out: sn rdn: kpt on flat)	nk	4	9/1	61	—
3166[9]	**Needwood Poppy (91)** (BCMorgan) **9-10-11** BClifford (sn outpcd: styd on fr 2 out: nvr nr to chal)	2½	5	16/1	68	—
3166[7]	**No Fiddling (IRE) (90)** (GMMcCourt) **6-10-10b**[1] DBridgwater (plld hrd: trckd ldrs: chal appr 2 out: sn wknd)	1¼	6	5/2[1]	66	—
	Doctor Dunklin (USA) (82) (MrsVCWard) **8-9-13**(3)ow2 MichaelBrennan (w ldrs tl wknd 3 out)	15	7	50/1	47	—
1922[3]	**Dawn Mission (101)** (TDEasterby) **5-11-7** RGarritty (hld up: effrt 3 out: sn rdn & outpcd)	12	8	6/1	57	—
582[4]	**Crazy Horse Dancer (USA) (81)** (FJordan) **9-10-1** RSupple (hld up & bhd: sme hdwy 3 out: sn wknd)	6	9	14/1	32	—
3200[7]	**High Penhowe (80)** (JJQuinn) **9-9-9**(5) MrRThornton (chsd ldrs tl drvn along & lost pl 6th: t.o 2 out)	13	10	20/1	22	—
642*	**What's Secreto (USA) (88)** (HAlexander) **5-10-8v** JRailton (mstkes: w ldrs: blnd 4th: p.u bef 7th: lame)		P	12/1	—	—

(SP 118.1%) **11 Rn**

5m 27.4 (23.40) CSF £25.44 CT £611.03 TOTE £6.20: £2.30 £1.50 £5.40 (£16.80) Trio £202.40; £202.46 to Sandown 8/3/97 OWNER Mr P. A. Kelleway (NEWMARKET) BRED Juddmonte Farms Inc
LONG HANDICAP Doctor Dunklin (USA) 9-0 High Penhowe 9-9
2828 Sassiver (USA), happy to be back over hurdles, was under pressure from halfway, but stuck on in grim fashion to gain the upper-hand on the run-in. (11/2)
2545 Thursday Night (IRE) was full of running when he blundered two out, but on the run-in found the winner too strong. (4/1)
La Fontainbleau (IRE), pulled up in a Hunter Chase and a point-to-point on his last two outings, made a determined attempt to make every post a winning one. (33/1)
2003 Moobakkr (USA), over a stone lower in the weights than when successful here a year and a half ago, tended to run in snatches but at least some of the old ability is there. From this sort of mark, he will surely find another opening in due course. (9/1: 6/1-10/1)
Needwood Poppy, on the comeback trail, stayed on nicely and will be suited by further. (16/1)
No Fiddling (IRE), who has dropped down the weights, raced too freely in first-time blinkers. (5/2)

3546 WHEATLEY PACKAGING NOVICES' CHASE (6-Y.O+) (Class D)

3-50 (3-52) **2m 4f (15 fncs)** £3,678.00 (£1,104.00: £532.00: £246.00) GOING: 0.67 sec per fur (S)

Form	Horse / Details	Dist	Pos	SP	RR	SF
2699[F]	**Gaelic Blue (73)** (MrsSJSmith) **7-10-10** RichardGuest (chsd ldrs: led last: styd on wl)	—	1	6/1[3]	81	14
2899[4]	**Golden Hello (113)** (TDEasterby) **6-11-8** RGarritty (lw: trckd ldrs: hit 9th: led 3 out: blnd & hdd next: nt qckn flat)	3	2	11/10[1]	91	24
64[4]	**Gorby's Myth** (JPLeigh) **7-10-10** KGaule (lw: jnd ldrs 9th: led & hit 2 out: hdd last: nt qckn)	s.h	3	10/1	79	12
3202[P]	**Claverhouse (IRE)** (JGFitzGerald) **8-10-10** PNiven (nt j.w: hit 1st: chsd ldrs: outpcd 11th: sme hdwy 3 out: sn wknd)	13	4	7/2[2]	68	1
3227[4]	**Dream Leader (IRE)** (MJRoberts) **7-10-10** JRailton (lw: led to 3 out: wkng whn blnd next)	1¼	5	9/1	67	—
3179[U]	**Tug Your Forelock (60)** (GFJohnsonHoughton) **6-10-7**(3) MichaelBrennan (bhd & drvn along 9th: n.d)	1	6	50/1	66	—

				SP	RR	SF
1859P	**Captain My Captain (IRE)** (RBrotherton) **9-10-10** SCurran (bhd fr 9th)	3	**7**	50/1	64	—
	Parsons Belle (IRE) (MrsCMBowman) **9-10-5** MSharratt (mstkes: prom: blnd 10th: sn lost pl)	14	**8**	33/1	48	—
	Seabright Saga (MCChapman) **7-10-10** WWorthington (bit bkwd: nt j.w: sn bhd: t.o 10th: p.u bef 3 out)		**P**	50/1	—	—
3073F	**Pleasure Cruise** (JKCresswell) **7-10-3**(7) NTEgan (mstkes: sn bhd & drvn along: t.o whn blnd 4 out: sn p.u)		**P**	50/1	—	—

(SP 114.0%) **10 Rn**

5m 16.9 (25.90) CSF £12.00 TOTE £5.90: £1.50 £1.20 £2.40 (£5.20) Trio £5.40 OWNER Mr Trevor Hemmings (BINGLEY) BRED Michael Lysaght

2699 Gaelic Blue, who had failed to complete the course on his two previous outings, took this in decisive fashion and has further improvement in him. (6/1)

2899 Golden Hello is certainly not happy in his work over fences. Blundering two out, he did not find anything like as much as the winner on the run-in. (11/10: evens-5/4)

64 Gorby's Myth, having his first run for 265 days, having gurgled on that occasion, did not have the tongue-strap fitted that he has worn in the past. On paper he looked to run really well, but in the past has flattered often to deceive. (10/1)

Claverhouse (IRE) did not take the eye in the paddock. His jumping lacked fluency but he did show a little promise. (7/2: op 2/1)

3547 LINPAC GARAGES GROUP H'CAP CHASE (0-110) (5-Y.O+) (Class E)

4-25 (4-25) **2m 1f 110y (13 fncs)** £2,808.75 (£840.00: £402.50: £183.75) GOING: 0.67 sec per fur (S)

				SP	RR	SF
31983	**Netherby Said (105)** (PBeaumont) **7-12-0** RSupple (trckd ldr: led 7th: styd on wl u.p flat)	—	**1**	5/4 1	119	45
32893	**Dual Image (103)** (JGFitzGerald) **10-11-12** RGarritty (trckd ldrs: chal 3 out: rdn last: fnd little)	4	**2**	9/4 2	113	39
32782	**Record Lover (IRE) (77)** (MCChapman) **7-10-0** WWorthington (outpcd & drvn along 6th: styd on fr 3 out: nvr nr to chal)	30	**3**	12/1	60	—
1146*	**Super Sharp (NZ) (90)** (HOliver) **9-10-13** JacquiOliver (led to 7th: hit next: ev ch tl wknd 4 out)	28	**4**	3/1 3	47	—
32065	**Rustic Gent (IRE) (77)** (MrsLCJewell) **9-10-0** DLeahy (drvn along: hit 7th: bhd fr 4 out)	3	**5**	50/1	32	—

(SP 109.9%) **5 Rn**

4m 34.0 (19.00) CSF £4.23 TOTE £2.20: £1.50 £1.40 (£2.70) OWNER Mrs S. Sunter (BRANDSBY) BRED J. Sunter

LONG HANDICAP Record Lover (IRE) 9-6 Rustic Gent (IRE) 9-2

3198 Netherby Said jumped much better this time and showed far too much determination for the runner-up. (5/4)

3289 Dual Image, back over his best trip, challenged on the bridle three out, but when asked to race in earnest at the last, he said no thank you. (9/4)

3278 Record Lover (IRE), 8lb out of the handicap, was racing over a trip short of his best. (12/1)

1146* Super Sharp (NZ), a confirmed top of the ground performer, was having his first outing for 125 days and stopped in two strides four out as if needing the run badly. (3/1)

3548 FARMERS STANDARD OPEN N.H. FLAT RACE (4, 5 & 6-Y.O) (Class H)

4-55 (4-56) **1m 5f 110y** £1,308.00 (£363.00: £174.00)

				SP	RR	SF
18343	**Bessie Browne (IRE)** (GAHubbard) **5-10-13** RichardGuest (chsd ldrs: led 2f out: drvn clr fnl f)	—	**1**	8/1 3	53 f	—
	Classic Jenny (IRE) (ICampbell) **4-10-5** TGMcLaughlin (lw: hld up: hdwy ½-wy: led over 3f out to 2f out: nt qckn appr fnl f)	6	**2**	12/1	41 f	—
263310	**Stonesby (IRE)** (GMMoore) **5-11-4** NBentley (chsd ldrs: hung rt & nt qckn fnl 2f)	2	**3**	8/1 3	49 f	—
	Happy Days Bill (KAMorgan) **5-11-4** GaryLyons (led tl over 3f out: sn outpcd: edgd lft & rallied fnl f)	s.h	**4**	25/1	49 f	—
27703	**Woodfield Vision (IRE)** (MrsMReveley) **6-11-4** PNiven (swtg: hdwy ½-wy: kpt on fnl 3f: nvr nr to chal)	1¼	**5**	7/2 1	47 f	—
	Kota (JWharton) **4-10-7**(3) RMassey (hld up: stdy hdwy 10f out: effrt over 2f out: grad wknd)	2½	**6**	7/1 2	39 f	—
	Dinky Dora (JKCresswell) **4-9-12**(7) NTEgan (small: cmpt: hld up & plld hrd: hdwy 5f out: kpt on fnl 3f: nvr nr ldrs)	3	**7**	33/1	31 f	—
26755	**Juniper Hill** (KAMorgan) **5-10-13**(5) MrRThornton (a chsng ldrs: one pce fnl 3f)	¾	**8**	10/1	40 f	—
290410	**Noble Tom (IRE)** (RCollins) **5-11-4** JSupple (chsd ldrs: wkng whn hmpd over 3f out)	9	**9**	12/1	29 f	—
	Percy's Joy (TDEasterby) **5-11-4** RGarritty (sn bhd: sme late hdwy)	3½	**10**	10/1	25 f	—
	Brandon Bridge (DPGeraghty) **6-11-4** RSupple (hld up & plld hrd: a in rr)	8	**11**	16/1	15 f	—
26828	**Welsh Asset** (KGWingrove) **6-10-11**(7) MrAWintle (sn bhd: t.o 4f out)	nk	**12**	14/1	15 f	—
33304	**The Gnome (IRE)** (FMurphy) **5-11-1**(3) MichaelBrennan (chsd ldrs tl lost pl over 3f out: eased)	26	**13**	7/2 1	—	—
177414	**Surprise City** (AJWilson) **6-11-4** DLeahy (bhd fr ½-wy: t.o 4f out)	6	**14**	20/1	—	—
166514	**Toro Loco (IRE)** (IPWilliams) **5-10-11**(7) FBogle (bhd fr ½-wy: t.o)	5	**15**	20/1	—	—
	Dellen Walker (IRE) (JSWainwright) **4-10-10** DerekByrne (bhd fnl 5f: t.o)	19	**16**	20/1	—	—
	The Chase (DTTodd) **6-10-11**(7) MNewton (bkwd: bhd fnl 6f: t.o 4f out)	20	**17**	33/1	—	—
	Sweepaway (IRE) (MJRoberts) **4-10-5** JRailton (in tch tl lost pl over 3f out: p.u towards fin: lame)		**P**	14/1	—	—

(SP 156.0%) **18 Rn**

3m 15.5 CSF £107.42 TOTE £9.50: £2.40 £2.70 £3.90 (£49.10) Trio £168.60; £125.88 to Sandown 8/3/97 OWNER Mr G. A. Hubbard (WOODBRIDGE) BRED J. R. Weston

WEIGHT FOR AGE 4yo-3lb

1834 Bessie Browne (IRE) took an ordinary bumper in decisive fashion. (8/1: op 5/1)

Classic Jenny (IRE), an expensive yearling, took the lead on the home turn and then was outstayed by the winner. (12/1: 7/1-14/1)

Stonesby (IRE), a springer in the market, hung badly under pressure and gave his rider no help. (8/1)

Happy Days Bill, who lacks size, rallied in the closing stages and will need two and a half miles over hurdles. (25/1)

2770 Woodfield Vision (IRE), sweating and edgy in the paddock, never threatened to take a hand. (7/2)

Kota, who came in for some market support, showed some ability and was by no means knocked about when he tired. (7/1)

2675 Juniper Hill (10/1: 8/1-12/1)

3330 The Gnome (IRE) went backwards after his decent first effort. Dropping out in two strides on the final turn, he was allowed to come home in his own time. (7/2)

T/Plpt: £7.60 (895.48 Tckts). T/Qdpt: £4.50 (77.18 Tckts) WG

3143-SANDOWN (R-H) (Good)

Friday March 7th

WEATHER: overcast

3549 WORCESTER PARK NOVICES' H'CAP HURDLE (0-110) (4-Y.O+) (Class D)

2-00 (2-01) **2m 110y (8 hdls)** £2,885.00 (£810.00: £395.00) GOING: 0.35 sec per fur (GS)

			SP	RR	SF
3222P	**Sir Dante (IRE) (78)** (RRowe) **6-10-0** DO'Sullivan (hdwy 2 out: led flat: rdn out) .... —	**1**	11/2 3	64	14
3204*	**Museum (IRE) (88)** (PWinkworth) **6-10-3**(7) XAizpuru (lw: a.p: led appr 2 out tl flat: unable qckn) 6	**2**	9/2 2	68	18
29328	**Shahrani (105)** (MCPipe) **5-11-13** JamieEvans (chsd ldr: led 4th tl appr 2 out: 2nd whn mstke 2 out: one pce) 2½	**3**	7/1	83	33
	Premier League (IRE) (78) (JELong) **7-10-0** LeesaLong (nt j.w: led to 4th: hrd rdn appr last: one pce) 2	**4**	33/1	54	4
3282*	**Otto E Mezzo (100)** (MJPolglase) **5-11-8** RDunwoody (hld up: hrd rdn appr last: one pce) 1½	**5**	4/1 1	74	24
15052	**Regal Pursuit (IRE) (103)** (NJHenderson) **6-11-4**(7) PMaher (swtg: bit bkwd: a bhd) 18	**6**	9/2 2	60	10
26773	**Jakes Justice (IRE) (93)** (JTGifford) **6-11-1** PHide (swtg: a bhd) 3	**7**	4/1 1	47	—
30584	**Whispering Dawn (88)** (CPEBrooks) **4-10-2** DGallagher (blnd 1st: fell 2nd)	**F**	12/1	—	—
			(SP 114.9%)		**8 Rn**

4m 4.4 (13.40) CSF £28.12 CT £159.45 TOTE £8.10: £1.80 £1.80 £2.60 (£13.40) OWNER Mr Peter Wilby (PULBOROUGH) BRED Martin Molony

LONG HANDICAP Sir Dante (IRE) 9-13 Premier League (IRE) 9-6

WEIGHT FOR AGE 4yo-8lb

1766 Sir Dante (IRE) was only asked to get into the action in the straight and, coming with a nice run, collared the leader on the run-in. His trainer reported that his two recent poor performances were as a result of the soft ground and even this surface was soft enough for him. He needs top of the ground to be seen at his best. (11/2)

3204* Museum (IRE) made his bid for glory approaching the second last but was unable to contain the winner on the run-in. (9/2)

1418 Shahrani is beginning to come down in the weights following three handicap flops and went on at halfway. Collared approaching the second last, he could then only struggle on at one pace. (7/1)

Premier League (IRE), 8lb out of the handicap, had not raced over hurdles since August 1995 and is only a plater on the Flat. Nevertheless, he showed in front to halfway and then kept on at one pace. Yet to win over hurdles, his last victory on the Flat came way back in May 1993. (33/1)

3282* Otto E Mezzo, chased the leaders, but try as he might, could never raise another gear in the straight. (4/1)

1505 Regal Pursuit (IRE), looking as though this first run in three and a half months would do her good, never looked like getting into the action under her inexperienced rider. (9/2: op 9/4)

2815 Whispering Dawn (12/1: op 8/1)

3550 ANITE SYSTEMS NOVICES' H'CAP CHASE (0-110) (5-Y.O+) (Class D)

2-35 (2-36) **3m 110y (22 fncs)** £4,335.00 (£1,065.00) GOING: 0.35 sec per fur (GS)

			SP	RR	SF
2679P	**Parliamentarian (IRE) (82)** (TCasey) **8-10-0** JAMcCarthy (led to 3rd: led 4th to 17th: wknd 4 out: poor 2nd whn lft in ld 2 out: r.o) .... —	**1**	16/1	78	—
33394	**Ekeus (IRE) (82)** (JSKing) **7-10-0** JCulloty (lw: chsd ldr: led 3rd to 4th: wknd 18th: lft poor 2nd 2 out) 16	**2**	9/2 3	68	—
31452	**Eulogy (IRE) (108)** (RRowe) **7-11-9**(3) LAspell (lw: hld up: mstke 14th: chsd ldr fr 16th: led 17th: clr whn fell 2 out)	**F**	10/11 1	—	—
1554*	**Funcheon Gale (95)** (RCurtis) **10-10-13** DMorris (hld up: mstke 15th: rdn 16th: 4th whn p.u bef 18th: b.b.v)	**P**	9/4 2	—	—
31328	**Victory Gate (USA) (83)** (MrsLCJewell) **12-9-10v**(5)ow1 ChrisWebb (bhd fr 3rd: t.o fr 12th: p.u bef 17th)	**P**	66/1	—	—
			(SP 108.7%)		**5 Rn**

6m 44.1 (42.10) CSF £69.53 TOTE £8.50: £2.10 £1.30 (£13.80) OWNER Mr J. G. M. Wates (DORKING) BRED Bobby McCarthy

LONG HANDICAP Ekeus (IRE) 8-6 Victory Gate (USA) 8-6

IN-FOCUS: **This was an appalling race which was completely out of place for Sandown.**

Parliamentarian (IRE) is an absolutely desperate performer but needed to show very little ability other than to stand on his feet to win this. Having cut out the running to the sixth last, he was left for dead by the winner turning out of the back straight, and was only plodding round for second prize when lady luck smiled on him two out, handing him the race on a plate. Nothing should be read into this performance and it will surely be a miracle if he ever wins another race. (16/1)

3339 Ekeus (IRE), 22lb out of the handicap, is a very poor performer and had been seen off five from home. However he did manage to complete and picked up a useful second prize. (9/2: op 8/1)

3145 Eulogy (IRE) could hardly have been found an easier opportunity to open his account, and it all looked plain sailing when he led at the sixth last and was some eighteen lengths clear with the race well and truly in the bag when he fell two from home. (10/11: 8/11-evens)

1554* Funcheon Gale (9/4: 6/4-5/2)

3551 HORSE & HOUND GRAND MILITARY GOLD CUP AMATEUR CHASE (5-Y.O+) (Class E)

3-10 (3-10) **3m 110y (22 fncs)** £4,879.00 (£1,477.00: £721.00: £343.00) GOING: 0.35 sec per fur (GS)

			SP	RR	SF
3316*	**Act the Wag (IRE) (113)** (MartinTodhunter) **8-12-1**(7) CaptAOgden (stdy hdwy 10th: chsd ldr fr 18th: led appr last: eased flat: shkn up nr fin) .... —	**1**	10/11 1	106	14
28092	**Jultara (IRE) (98)** (IPWilliams) **8-11-5**(7) MajorGWheeler (led 5th tl appr last: r.o) .... ½	**2**	8/1 3	96	4
18775	**Maxxum Express (IRE) (80)** (GBBalding) **9-11-5**(7) MajorOEllwood (bit bkwd: a.p: 2nd whn mstke 17th: 4th whn blnd 4 out: one pce) 18	**3**	33/1	84	—
	Cardinal Richelieu (CSporborg) **10-11-5**(7) MrSSporborg (swtg: led to 5th: 4th whn mstke 17th: wknd 4 out: t.o) .... dist	**4**	9/2 2	—	—
31132	**Duhallow Lodge (110)** (CRBarwell) **10-11-10**(7) MrDAlers-Hankey (mstke 8th: hdwy 12th: 6th whn mstke 17th: wkng whn blnd 18th: t.o) 22	**5**	9/2 2	—	—
34004	**Kendal Cavalier (92)** (GBBalding) **7-11-5v**1(7) MrCWardThomas (hdwy 12th: 5th whn fell 18th)	**F**	10/1	—	—
	Gunner Stream (AGSims) **13-11-5**(7) CaptAWood (fell 1st)	**F**	66/1	—	—
2910R	**Icantelya (IRE) (80)** (JWMullins) **8-11-5v**(7) Lt-ColRWebb-Bowen (lw: j.slowly 12th: prom to 13th: t.o whn p.u bef 17th)	**P**	50/1	—	—
	Toddling Inn (RJRSymonds) **10-11-3**(7)ow3 MrCFarr (lw: mstke 2nd: bhd fr 5th: t.o fr 12th: p.u bef 4 out)	**P**	50/1	—	—

				SP	RR	SF
2656P	**Vancouver Lad (IRE)** (AGSims) **8-11-5**(7) MrSGreany (lw: a bhd: blnd 11th: t.o fr 12th: p.u bef 3 out)		P	66/1	—	—

(SP 118.8%) **10 Rn**

6m 34.7 (32.70) CSF £8.47 TOTE £1.90: £1.20 £1.90 £3.50 (£7.30) Trio £34.30 OWNER Mr Robert Ogden (ULVERSTON) BRED J. R. Kidd
STEWARDS' ENQUIRY Farr susp. 17 - 20/3/97 (incorrect use of whip)

3316* Act the Wag (IRE) who missed an engagement at Kelso on Tuesday because of a bruised foot, is in tremendous form at present and was always travelling well. Moving into second place five out, his jockey was extremely confident on him and the combination moved to the front approaching the last. His rider continually looked over his shoulder on the run-in and took things very easy. The combination nearly came a cropper when the runner-up bravely tried to rally, but Ogden managed to shake the reins near the line and keep the gelding in front. He is yet to win on ground worse than good. (10/11: 4/5-evens)

2809 Jultara (IRE) was taking on more experienced rivals but still ran very well and was in front from the fifth. Collared approaching the last, he was firmly held by the winner, but with that rival taking things easy, he nearly caught him napping. (8/1: 6/1-9/1)

1564 Maxxum Express (IRE), carrying condition for this first run in three months, was made to look woefully one-paced in the last half mile. (33/1)

3552 RACAL NOVICES' HURDLE (4-Y.O+) (Class D)

3-45 (3-46) **2m 6f (11 hdls)** £3,022.00 (£916.00: £448.00: £214.00) GOING: 0.35 sec per fur (GS)

				SP	RR	SF
3171*	**Friendship (IRE)** (NJHenderson) **5-11-7** RDunwoody (lw: hdwy 6th: swtchd rt appr 2 out: hrd rdn appr last: led flat: r.o wl)	—	1	11/4[2]	85	45
3272[5]	**Millersford (101)** (NAGaselee) **6-11-7** WMarston (lw: led: hrd rdn appr last: hung bdly lft & hdd flat: unable qckn)	¾	2	14/1	85	45
2948[3]	**Emerald Statement (IRE) (121)** (DMGrissell) **7-11-7** BFenton (lw: a.p: blnd 3rd: rdn 3 out: ev ch flat: one pce)	2½	3	10/11[1]	83	43
3172*	**Jazzman (IRE) (105)** (APJarvis) **5-11-7** NWilliamson (hdwy 3 out: hrd rdn appr last: sn wknd)	7	4	9/1	78	38
	Scenic Waters (NATwiston-Davies) **5-10-11** CLlewellyn (nvr nr to chal)	12	5	16/1	59	19
3222[11]	**Music Class (IRE) (79)** (CPEBrooks) **6-11-2** DGallagher (sme hdwy 6th: wknd 3 out)	18	6	66/1	51	11
2891[4]	**Camera Man** (NJHenderson) **7-11-2** JRKavanagh (lw: prom to 7th)	1	7	25/1	50	10
2822[2]	**Jack Gallagher** (MissBSanders) **6-11-2** MRichards (hld up: rdn 3 out: wknd appr 2 out)	1¾	8	8/1[3]	49	9
3272[10]	**Mister Generosity (IRE)** (CWeedon) **6-11-2** DO'Sullivan (prom to 5th: t.o whn p.u bef 2 out)		P	66/1	—	—

(SP 119.5%) **9 Rn**

5m 27.5 (14.50) CSF £35.88 TOTE £3.70: £1.40 £2.40 £1.20 (£24.10) Trio £13.90 OWNER Mr T Benfield and Mr W Brown (LAMBOURN) BRED G. Merrigan

3171* Friendship (IRE), still a baby according to his trainer, looked extremely well in the preliminaries and appears to have done some work on his jumping. Easing his way into the action on the final circuit, he threw down his challenge in the straight, and, with the leader steering a very erratic course on the run-in, managed to get on top in a tight finish. The EBF Final at Cheltenham next month is his target. (11/4)

3272 Millersford looked an absolute picture in the paddock and ran a tremendous race. Dictating matters from the front, he came under pressure approaching the last as he raced up the stands rail. However that running rail disappears soon after the last and he was in a complete wilderness. As a result, he then drifted badly to his left, ending right up under the stands and losing plenty of ground in the process. Not surprisingly, he lost the advantage and the race. A real stayer who will make a lovely chaser, he can add to his November win at Kempton before long. (14/1: 10/1-16/1)

2948 Emerald Statement (IRE) looked very well in the paddock but he is a real stayer and was rather tapped for toe as the tempo increased towards the end of the back straight. Nevertheless, he rallied to get back into it from the last and was one of three battling for honours before being tapped for toe. He should soon return to the winner's enclosure possible over three miles. (10/11: evens-4/5)

3172* Jazzman (IRE) stylishly moved into the action three form home, but was a spent force approaching the last. He is still very weak according to his trainer. (9/1)

3553 DUKE OF GLOUCESTER MEMORIAL PAST AND PRESENT HUNTERS' CHASE (5-Y.O+) (Class H)

4-15 (4-15) **3m 110y (22 fncs)** £1,348.50 (£408.00: £199.00: £94.50) GOING: 0.35 sec per fur (GS)

				SP	RR	SF
	Brackenfield (RBarber) **11-11-11b**(7) MrDAlers-Hankey (lw: hdwy 3rd: led 4th: mstke 8th: hdd 12th: mstke 13th: led 16th: clr appr 3 out: easily)	—	1	4/5[1]	107	—
	Across the Card (MajorGenCARamsay) **9-12-4**(7) CaptWRamsay (hdwy fr 3 out: r.o one pce)	26	2	14/1	97	—
3089P	**Over the Edge** (CSporborg) **11-12-4**(7) MrSSporborg (lw: no hdwy fr 12th)	13	3	3/1[2]	89	—
3357P	**True Steel** (JonTrice-Rolph) **11-11-13**(5) MrJTrice-Rolph (mstke 9th: hdwy 10th: led 12th: mstke 13th: hdd 16th: wknd appr 3 out)	6	4	7/1[3]	78	—
2951U	**No Joker (IRE)** (NAGaselee) **9-11-11**(7) CaptRHall (bit bkwd: led to 4th: mstke 11th: sn wknd: t.o whn blnd 4 out)	4	5	16/1	75	—
	American Eyre (MrsGMGladders) **12-12-3**(7)ow6 MrRGladders (prom to 8th: t.o whn p.u bef 12th)		P	16/1	—	—
3341[7]	**Golden Mac** (RLFanshawe) **10-11-11**(7) MajorOEllwood (lw: bhd fr 11th: t.o whn blnd & uns rdr 17th)		U	33/1	—	—

(SP 114.4%) **7 Rn**

6m 42.4 (40.40) CSF £11.99 TOTE £1.90: £1.60 £4.70 (£10.80) OWNER Mr R. W. Humphreys (BEAMINSTER) BRED C. Kenneally

Brackenfield, winner of two point-to-point races this season and runner up in the other to Still In Business, looked very well in the paddock. He did make a couple of mistakes but had only True Steel to worry about on the final circuit as the pair pulled well clear. Showing in front again at the water - the sixteenth - he had no problems forging clear turning for home to win with a ton in hand. (4/5)

Across the Card raced at the back of the field, but did plod on past tired rivals to finish a very poor second. (14/1)

Over the Edge, winner of this race last year, was successful in a point-to-point recently, but after going third with a circuit to race was making little impression on the principals. (3/1)

True Steel did not have the ground in his favour but ran considerably better than at Huntingdon eight days ago. The only one to make a race of it with the winner on the final circuit, he was brushed off turning for home and was completely out on his feet by the time he crossed the line. (7/1)

3554 RAYNES PARK H'CAP HURDLE (0-125) (4-Y.O+) (Class D)

4-45 (4-48) **2m 6f (11 hdls)** £3,550.00 (£1,075.00: £525.00: £250.00) GOING: 0.35 sec per fur (GS)

				SP	RR	SF
2694[11]	**Swing Quartet (IRE) (92)** (NATwiston-Davies) **7-10-2** CLlewellyn (a.p: jnd ldr appr 2 out: hrd rdn flat: led last strides)	—	1	14/1	73	35
3114*	**Jefferies (103)** (JABOld) **8-10-13** NWilliamson (hdwy 7th: chsd ldr fr 3 out: led appr 2 out: hrd rdn appr last: hdd last strides)	nk	2	2/1[1]	84	46
2797[6]	**Indian Quest (101)** (NAGaselee) **8-10-11** WMarston (lw: led tl appr 2 out: sn wknd)	15	3	8/1	71	33

				SP	RR	SF
2932[4]	**Smuggler's Point (USA) (102)** (JJBridger) **7-10-7**(5) SophieMitchell (chsd ldr to 3 out: wknd appr 2 out)	1¼	**4**	12/1	71	33
3281[8]	**Fortunes Course (IRE) (107)** (JSKing) **8-11-3** TJMurphy (sme hdwy 3 out: sn wknd)	10	**5**	13/2	69	31
3105[U]	**Court Nap (IRE) (104)** (SMellor) **5-11-0** MrPScott (lw: sme hdwy 3 out: sn wknd)	½	**6**	33/1	65	27
3180[4]	**Mirador (92)** (RCurtis) **6-10-2** DMorris (rdn 6th: a bhd)	8	**7**	11/4[2]	48	10
3277[8]	**Wings Cove (114)** (LadyHerries) **7-11-10** RDunwoody (prom to 6th)	16	**8**	6/1[3]	58	20
				(SP 116.0%)	**8 Rn**	

5m 25.4 (12.40) CSF £40.33 CT £227.44 TOTE £17.00: £2.30 £1.10 £2.50 (£15.90) Trio £73.80 OWNER Mr Gold Blyth (CHELTENHAM) BRED G. Browne

1037 Swing Quartet (IRE), dropped 7lb by the Handicapper since her last run, bounced back to form. Joining the leader, she had a tremendous tussle with that rival and eventually managed to get on top in the last couple of strides. (14/1)

3114* Jefferies only 2lb higher for his recent victory, had no problems with this longer trip and moved to the front approaching the second last. Immediately collared by the winner, he looked to be just holding that rival but was worried out of it in the last couple of strides. (2/1)

2797 Indian Quest took the field along but, collared approaching the second last, was soon left for dead. (8/1)

2932 Smuggler's Point (USA) in second place to the third last, had little more to give in the straight. (12/1)

2568 Fortunes Course (IRE) never really threatened, and a brief effort three from home came to little. (13/2)

3180 Mirador (11/4: 2/1-3/1)

T/Jkpt: £7,100.00 (0.09 Tckts); £6,399.86 to Sandown 8/3/97. T/Plpt: £165.20 (88.49 Tckts). T/Qdpt: £3.40 (339.23 Tckts) AK

3529-AYR (L-H) (Soft, Good to soft patches)
Saturday March 8th

WEATHER: fine

3555 CRAIGIE HURDLE (4-Y.O) (Class E)

1-50 (1-50) **2m (9 hdls)** £2,134.50 (£636.00: £303.00: £136.50) GOING: 1.49 sec per fur (HY)

				SP	RR	SF
2541[F]	**Son of Anshan (105)** (MrsASwinbank) **4-11-4** JSupple (chsd ldr: led after 4th: pushed clr 4 out: styd on)	—	**1**	4/6[1]	84	41
3004[P]	**Crabbie's Pride (78)** (MGMeagher) **4-10-12** RichardGuest (prom: chsd wnr fr 5th: no imp)	19	**2**	20/1	59	16
	Bourbon Dynasty (FR) (GRichards) **4-10-12** ADobbin (mstkes: hld up: rdn & styd on fr 4 out: no imp)	3½	**3**	10/1[3]	56	13
3022[3]	**Phantom Haze** (CParker) **4-10-12** DParker (lw: prom tl outpcd fr 4 out)	1	**4**	3/1[2]	55	12
3310[2]	**Double Dash (IRE) (82)** (DMoffatt) **4-11-4v** DJMoffatt (prom tl outpcd & mstke 4 out: n.d after)	9	**5**	14/1	52	9
3311[4]	**Known Secret (USA)** (PMonteith) **4-10-12** MMoloney (mstkes: effrt 5th: wknd after 4 out: t.o)	dist	**6**	33/1	—	—
3139[P]	**Jungle Fresh** (MrsDThomson) **4-10-12** BStorey (led tl after 4th: t.o 4 out: p.u bef next)		**P**	50/1	—	—
				(SP 110.4%)	**7 Rn**	

4m 6.0 (29.00) CSF £13.72 TOTE £1.80: £1.40 £6.00 (£14.50) OWNER Mr F. J. Sainsbury (RICHMOND) BRED C. J. R. Trotter

2541 Son of Anshan, from a yard that has been under a cloud, left nothing to chance here, and put his stamp on this a long way out. (4/6)

1205 Crabbie's Pride tried to make a race of it, but was well outclassed once the winner turned the heat on from the fourth last. (20/1)

Bourbon Dynasty (FR), a French import, needs to brush up his hurdling. There should be some improvement in the pipeline. (10/1)

3022 Phantom Haze will do better once the ground firms up. (3/1)

3310 Double Dash (IRE) didn't seem to act on this soft ground. (14/1)

3311 Known Secret (USA) was disappointing this time, but he is probably better on faster ground. (33/1)

3556 MAD MARCH HARE NOVICES' CHASE (5-Y.O+) (Class D)

2-20 (2-20) **3m 1f (19 fncs)** £3,152.00 (£872.00: £416.00) GOING: 1.49 sec per fur (HY)

				SP	RR	SF
3393*	**Kalajo (74)** (BMactaggart) **7-11-9** BStorey (a.p: led fr 13th: styd on wl towards fin)	—	**1**	9/1	97	17
3312[2]	**Nicholas Plant (96)** (JSGoldie) **8-11-9** GCahill (chsd ldrs: ev ch whn hit 15th: styd on & ev ch last: no ex)	3½	**2**	2/1[1]	95	15
2912[5]	**Celtic Giant (97)** (LLungo) **7-11-3** RSupple (led to 5th: led 9th to 13th: kpt on one pce)	1¾	**3**	3/1[2]	88	8
	Royal Banker (IRE) (MartinTodhunter) **7-11-3** PNiven (lw: cl up: led 5th to 9th: blnd 10th: sn bhd: fell 13th)		**F**	6/1	—	—
3141[3]	**Majority Major (IRE) (80)** (PCheesbrough) **8-11-9** ADobbin (outpcd & lost tch fr 10th: t.o whn p.u bef 13th)		**P**	11/2[3]	—	—
	Strathmore Lodge (MissLucindaRussell) **8-10-12** MFoster (mstkes: lost tch fr 11th: p.u bef 15th)		**P**	12/1	—	—
				(SP 105.7%)	**6 Rn**	

7m 3.1 (56.10) CSF £22.91 TOTE £13.00: £3.00 £1.20 (£17.00) OWNER Kelso Members Lowflyers Club (HAWICK) BRED P. J. and G. F. Burman

3393* Kalajo loved the conditions and proved game under pressure, and thoroughly deserved this. (9/1)

3312 Nicholas Plant, in the conditions he really does like, tried his best but had to admit he had met one too determined. (2/1)

2912 Celtic Giant goes well in soft ground, and put up a decent show, but he was short of toe when it mattered in the home straight. (3/1)

Royal Banker (IRE) looked fit enough, but a blunder stopped him with a circuit to go, and he was well adrift when coming to grief seven from home. (6/1)

3141 Majority Major (IRE) ran a stinker here, never going at any stage. (11/2)

Strathmore Lodge (12/1: op 8/1)

3557 MASON ORGANISATION NOVICES' H'CAP HURDLE (0-110) (4-Y.O+) (Class D)

2-50 (2-51) **3m 110y (12 hdls)** £3,652.00 (£1,096.00: £528.00: £244.00) GOING: 1.49 sec per fur (HY)

				SP	RR	SF
3348[3]	**Cherry Dee (78)** (PBeaumont) **6-9-12**(5) BGrattan (lw: mde all: styd on gamely fr 3 out)	—	**1**	5/2[2]	59	11
3317[4]	**Swanbister (IRE) (103)** (LLungo) **7-12-0** RSupple (chsd ldrs tl outpcd 7th: hdwy u.p 4 out: ev ch fr next: nt qckn flat)	1½	**2**	9/4[1]	83	35
3157[10]	**Kings Lane (85)** (JMDun) **8-10-10** DParker (lw: effrt 7th: sn outpcd: styd on fr 4 out: no imp)	16	**3**	10/1	55	7
2958[8]	**Stepdaughter (75)** (MrsDThomson) **11-10-0** LO'Hara (outpcd fr ½-wy: n.d after)	13	**4**	100/1	36?	—
3100[2]	**Clever Boy (IRE) (82)** (JWCurtis) **6-10-7** RichardGuest (cl up: chal 6th tl wknd appr 3 out)	2	**5**	4/1[3]	42	—
3066[3]	**Adib (USA) (92)** (GMMoore) **7-11-3b1** NBentley (lw: prom: outpcd 8th: wknd next: sn t.o)	dist	**6**	10/1	—	—
2042[13]	**Crashballoo (IRE) (77)** (PCheesbrough) **6-10-2** GCahill (a bhd: t.o whn p.u bef 3 out)		**P**	25/1	—	—
3032[P]	**Belle Rose (IRE) (87)** (GRichards) **7-10-12** ADobbin (in tch: rdn fr ½-wy: mstke 8th: wknd & p.u bef next)		**P**	12/1	—	—
				(SP 110.1%)	**8 Rn**	

6m 36.2 (50.20) CSF £7.38 CT £36.85 TOTE £3.60: £1.20 £1.70 £3.90 (£8.30) OWNER Mr George Dilger (BRANDSBY) BRED R. Burton

LONG HANDICAP Stepdaughter 9-0

3348 Cherry Dee, given a real chance by the Handicapper, was wisely made a lot of use of, as all she does is stay. (5/2)

3317 Swanbister (IRE) had plenty on with the winner on their previous meeting, but he kept trying hard, only to lose the battle after the last. (9/4)
2915 Kings Lane is a funny customer who runs when in the mood, and it was all too late when he decided to on this occasion. (10/1)
Stepdaughter hasn't much to recommend her, and what form she has previously shown has been on faster ground. (100/1)
3100 Clever Boy (IRE) seems happier on a faster surface. (4/1)
2768 Belle Rose (IRE) (12/1: 8/1-14/1)

3558 HUGH BARCLAY CHALLENGE CUP H'CAP CHASE (0-115) (5-Y.O+) (Class E)
3-25 (3-26) **2m (12 fncs)** £3,492.50 (£1,040.00: £495.00: £222.50) GOING: 1.49 sec per fur (HY)

	Horse	Dist	Pos	SP	RR	SF
3138^{2}	**Coqui Lane (86)** (JMDun) **10-10-4** DParker (lw: mde all: kpt on wl flat)	—	1	7/4^{2}	99	20
3068^{2}	**Mr Knitwit (110)** (PMonteith) **10-12-0** ADobbin (in tch: effrt 8th: chsd wnr fr 3 out: nt qckn flat)	11	2	9/4^{3}	112	33
3350^{2}	**Bold Boss (109)** (GMMoore) **8-11-13** BStorey (lw: w wnr fr 4th tl rdn & btn after 4 out)	10	3	13/8^{1}	101	22
3064^{P}	**Teejay'n'aitch (IRE) (90)** (JSGoldie) **5-10-0** GCahill (cl up to 4th: hit 5th & 7th: sn bhd)	6	4	25/1	76	—
				(SP 109.1%)		**4 Rn**

4m 15.8 (30.80) CSF £5.58 TOTE £2.60 (£3.70) OWNER Mr J. M. Dun (HERIOT) BRED G. R. Hutchinson
LONG HANDICAP Teejay'n'aitch (IRE) 9-4
WEIGHT FOR AGE 5yo-8lb
3138 Coqui Lane treats his fences with plenty of caution, but he looked well-handicapped here, and although this trip was on the short side he was helped by the testing ground. (7/4)
3068 Mr Knitwit looked to have plenty on at these weights, but he ran a smashing race and is obviously still in good heart. (9/4)
3350 Bold Boss tried hard to take the winner on, but in doing this he had run himself into the ground by the fourth last. (13/8)
1911 Teejay'n'aitch (IRE), although well beaten, didn't run too badly on his first attempt over fences here, and was also 10lb out of the handicap. (25/1)

3559 AYRSHIRE YEOMANRY CUP H'CAP HURDLE (0-125) (4-Y.O+) (Class D)
4-00 (4-00) **2m 4f (11 hdls)** £2,924.00 (£872.00: £416.00: £188.00) GOING: 1.49 sec per fur (HY)

	Horse	Dist	Pos	SP	RR	SF
3398*	**Ingletonian (116)** (BMactaggart) **8-11-13** BStorey (led tl hdd last: rallied gamely to ld cl home)	—	1	100/30^{2}	98	49
3269^{8}	**Oat Couture (117)** (LLungo) **9-12-0** RSupple (lw: chsd ldrs: effrt 6th: chal 3 out: slt ld last: hdd & nt qckn towards fin)	nk	2	9/2^{3}	99	50
3398^{4}	**Field of Vision (IRE) (104)** (MrsASwinbank) **7-11-1** JSupple (bhd: outpcd 6th: styd on fr 4 out: n.d)	24	3	11/2	67	18
2044*	**Brumon (IRE) (92)** (DMoffatt) **6-10-3v** DJMoffatt (in tch: hdwy 6th: outpcd fr next)	14	4	11/2	43	—
	Linngate (108) (LLungo) **8-11-5** MFoster (hld up: stdy hdwy 4 out: nvr nr to chal)	8	5	33/1	53	4
693^{3}	**Jubran (USA) (95)** (JPDodds) **11-10-6** RichardGuest (chsd ldrs tl outpcd 6th: n.d after)	10	6	20/1	32	—
3398^{2}	**Elation (108)** (GRichards) **5-11-5** ADobbin (lw: cl up: hit 7th & sn rdn: wknd 4 out)	8	7	3/1^{1}	39	—
3309^{P}	**Stingray City (USA) (89)** (RMMcKellar) **8-10-0** DParker (a bhd)	13	8	100/1	9	—
				(SP 105.7%)		**8 Rn**

5m 17.6 (36.60) CSF £14.40 CT £56.51 TOTE £3.90: £1.70 £1.30 £1.90 (£8.80) OWNER Mrs Hilary MacTaggart (HAWICK) BRED A. D. Redhead
LONG HANDICAP Stingray City (USA) 9-10
3398* Ingletonian is proving to be a revelation this season, and showed tremendous battling qualities to take this. (100/30)
3028* Oat Couture looked magnificent and tried hard, but the winner proved just too tough. (9/2)
3398 Field of Vision (IRE) never looked likely to get into this, but in the circumstances he ran well, and will do better on a sounder surface. (11/2)
2044* Brumon (IRE), off the track for almost three months, and stepping up in trip here, was found out at the end of the back straight. (11/2: 8/1-5/1)
Linngate, having his first run for over two years, ran really well and should now improve. (33/1)
693 Jubran (USA) hasn't been out for over five months, and that, coupled with the soft ground, found him out a long way from home. (20/1)
3398 Elation is better on a firmer surface, and ran poorly here. (3/1)

3560 POLYFLOR H'CAP CHASE (0-115) (5-Y.O+) (Class E)
4-30 (4-31) **3m 1f (19 fncs)** £3,824.00 (£1,064.00: £512.00) GOING: 1.49 sec per fur (HY)

	Horse	Dist	Pos	SP	RR	SF
3162^{5}	**Kilcolgan (104)** (MrsJDGoodfellow) **10-11-8** NBentley (swtg: a.p: led 13th: kpt on u.p fr 4 out)	—	1	5/1^{3}	120	32
3141*	**Ask Me Later (IRE) (86)** (MrsSCBradburne) **8-10-4** MFoster (a chsng ldrs: ev ch fr 14th tl rdn & btn appr last)	5	2	5/4^{1}	99	11
3332*	**Farney Glen (90)** (JJO'Neill) **10-10-8** ADobbin (prom tl rdn & wknd after 13th)	dist	3	7/2^{2}	—	—
3033^{4}	**Dark Oak (110)** (JWCurtis) **11-12-0** RichardGuest (mstke 4th: lost tch 11th: p.u bef 15th)		P	10/1	—	—
2042^{11}	**Barney Rubble (92)** (DWWhillans) **12-10-10** DBentley (mstke 1st: led to 13th: sn wknd: p.u bef 2 out)		P	25/1	—	—
3069^{4}	**Funny Old Game (84)** (DMcCune) **10-9-13**$^{(3)ow2}$ MichaelBrennan (cl up tl wknd & blnd 12th: sn t.o: p.u bef 3 out)		P	20/1	—	—
3312^{4}	**Village Reindeer (NZ) (100)** (PCalver) **10-11-4** TReed (wnt prom 5th: mstkes 11th & 13th: ev ch 4 out: hrd rdn & cl 3rd whn blnd & uns rdr 2 out: dead)		U	10/1	—	—
				(SP 110.1%)		**7 Rn**

6m 57.5 (50.50) CSF £10.38 TOTE £5.90: £3.10 £1.10 (£5.20) OWNER Mr J. D. Goodfellow (EARLSTON) BRED Frank Burke
LONG HANDICAP Funny Old Game 9-4
3162 Kilcolgan gallops for ever and a day, and these testing conditions proved ideal. (5/1)
3141* Ask Me Later (IRE) ran his heart out, but just found the winner too determined. (5/4)
3332* Farney Glen was in trouble once he came off the bit setting out on the final circuit, and is obviously better on slightly faster ground. (7/2: op 9/4)

3561 AYR STANDARD OPEN N.H. FLAT RACE (4, 5 & 6-Y.O) (Class H)
5-00 (5-02) **2m** £1,035.00 (£285.00: £135.00)

	Horse	Dist	Pos	SP	RR	SF
	Castle Clear (IRE) (MrsMReveley) **4-10-10** PNiven (lw: hld up: hdwy on bit 7f out: led 2f out: qcknd)	—	1	7/4^{1}	72 f	—
	Minisioux (CWThornton) **4-10-3**$^{(7)}$ NHorrocks (a cl up: led 5f out to 2f out: one pce)	8	2	15/2	64 f	—
2770*	**Lord Podgski (IRE)** (PMonteith) **6-11-11** ADobbin (lw: hld up: jnd ldrs 7f out: outpcd 4f out: kpt on towards fin)	4	3	2/1^{2}	67 f	—
	Amlwch (JBerry) **4-10-10** MMoloney (hld up: hdwy to jn ldrs ½-wy: disp ld 5f out: nt qckn fnl 2½f)	hd	4	12/1	60 f	—
3142*	**Mac's Supreme (IRE)** (FMurphy) **5-11-8**$^{(3)}$ MichaelBrennan (cl up tl wknd fnl 3f)	2½	5	4/1^{3}	64 f	—

3142[7] **Lord Knows (IRE)** (JIACharlton) **6-11-4** KJohnson (in tch tl outpcd fnl 4f)......6 **6** 20/1 51 f —
Above The Grass (IRE) (DRobertson) **6-10-13** FPerratt (bit,bkwd: bhd fnl 5f)......15 **7** 250/1 31 f —
High Celleste (IRE) (MartinTodhunter) **6-10-6**(7) CMcCormack (outpcd fnl 5f)......1½ **8** 50/1 30 f —
Meggie Scott (JPDodds) **4-10-6**ow1 RichardGuest (set slow pce: hdd 5f out: sn wknd)......4 **9** 150/1 27 f —
(SP 116.9%) **9 Rn**

4m 16.2 CSF £14.37 TOTE £2.40: £1.10 £1.70 £1.10 (£17.60) Trio £16.70 OWNER Mr R. Hilley (SALTBURN) BRED Daniel J. Shirley
WEIGHT FOR AGE 4yo-8lb
Castle Clear (IRE), more a flat race type than a jumper, travelled well and had too much toe for this lot in this slowly-run event. (7/4)
Minisioux ran a fair first race here, and should be better suited by a stronger pace. (15/2)
2770* Lord Podgski (IRE) found the slow pace against him, and in the circumstances ran well. He looks a real National Hunt type. (2/1)
Amlwch ran pretty well, and gave the impression that he should be all the better for it. (12/1: 8/1-14/1)
3142* Mac's Supreme (IRE) had his limitations exposed here, but the ground and the slow pace were probably both against him.(4/1: op 2/1)

T/Plpt: £41.40 (217.79 Tckts). T/Qdpt: £14.70 (31.85 Tckts) AA

3150-CHEPSTOW (L-H) (Good to soft, Soft patches becoming Soft)
Saturday March 8th
WEATHER: rain

3562 'RACING POST FOR CHELTENHAM' H'CAP HURDLE (0-130) (4-Y.O+) (Class C)
1-15 (1-15) **2m 4f 110y (11 hdls)** £5,637.50 (£1,700.00: £825.00: £387.50) GOING: 1.15 sec per fur (HY)

SP RR SF
3231[7] **Potentate (USA) (128)** (MCPipe) **6-11-12** APMcCoy (mde all: clr 7th: mstke 4 out: eased flat)......— **1** 4/1[2] 110 73
3267[3] **Kingdom of Shades (USA) (127)** (AndrewTurnell) **7-11-11** PCarberry (lw: hld up: rdn after 5th: sn lost pl: rallied 3 out: wnt 2nd appr last: no ch w wnr)......3 **2** 4/1[2] 107 70
3269[3] **Selatan (IRE) (111)** (DRGandolfo) **5-10-9** RDunwoody (a.p: chsd wnr fr 6th: rdn appr 4 out: wknd appr last) ...9 **3** 7/2[1] 84 47
3183[2] **Marius (IRE) (118)** (JTGifford) **7-11-2** PHide (lw: hld up: stdy hdwy 6th: wknd appr 2 out)......5 **4** 9/1[3] 87 50
3045[8] **Call My Guest (IRE) (112)** (REPeacock) **7-10-10** NWilliamson (hld up: hdwy after 4th: rdn appr 4 out: sn wknd)......1½ **5** 33/1 80 43
3402[5] **Lake Kariba (119)** (PFNicholls) **6-11-3** RJohnson (bhd fr 6th: t.o)......17 **6** 12/1 73 36
3277[7] **Purple Splash (117)** (PJMakin) **7-11-1v** JRKavanagh (bhd fr 6th: t.o 4 out: p.u bef last)...... **P** 4/1[2] — —
3421[11] **Intermagic (107)** (JCFox) **7-10-5** SFox (nt fluent 1st: prom tl wknd qckly 5th: t.o whn p.u bef 4 out)...... **P** 33/1 — —
(SP 105.8%) **8 Rn**

5m 10.8 (23.80) CSF £15.99 CT £43.52 TOTE £4.10: £2.10 £1.30 £1.50 (£5.90) OWNER Mr Jim Weeden (WELLINGTON) BRED Stelcar Stables Incorporated
3231 Potentate (USA), not inconvenienced by the morning rain, made it five out of five on this course and the extra half-mile proved no problem. (4/1)
3267 Kingdom of Shades (USA) had soft ground this time but is greatly flattered by his proximity to the winner. (4/1)
3269 Selatan (IRE) had ground conditions in his favour, but was 7lb higher than when winning at Towcester a year ago and needs to come down a few pounds. (7/2)
3183 Marius (IRE) had plenty of weight for this sort of company. (9/1: 6/1-10/1)
948 Call My Guest (IRE), 22lb lower than when winning at Wetherby nearly two years ago, had been tried in blinkers last time. (33/1)
3402 Lake Kariba (12/1: op 6/1)

3563 TOTE TEN TO FOLLOW H'CAP CHASE (5-Y.O+) (Class B)
1-45 (1-46) **3m 2f 110y (22 fncs)** £8,431.60 (£2,552.80: £1,246.40: £593.20) GOING: 1.41 sec per fur (HY)

SP RR SF
3153* **Giventime (115)** (AndrewTurnell) **9-10-1** LHarvey (a.p: led 13th: j.rt 3 out: r.o wl)......— **1** 11/4[2] 127 —
2997a[P] **Belmont King (IRE) (142)** (PFNicholls) **9-12-0** APMcCoy (hld up: hdwy 12th: ev ch 4 out: pckd 3 out: no imp) 7 **2** 11/2[3] 150 14
3153[3] **Spuffington (116)** (JTGifford) **9-10-2**ow2 PHide (lw: hld up: hdwy appr 5 out: one pce fr 3 out)......6 **3** 20/1 120 —
3266* **General Wolfe (140)** (CaptTAForster) **8-11-12** RDunwoody (led to 2nd: led 12th tl blnd 13th: sn lost pl: rallied appr 5 out: wknd 4 out: t.o)......dist **4** 5/4[1] — —
763a* **Bishops Hall (142)** (RHAlner) **11-12-0** NWilliamson (bit bkwd: led 2nd to 12th: hit 14th: sn wknd: t.o whn p.u bef 3 out)...... **P** 16/1 — —
Buckboard Bounce (142) (GRichards) **11-12-0** PCarberry (hld up: hdwy after 17th: sn wknd: t.o whn p.u bef 4 out)...... **P** 9/1 — —
3162[8] **See Enough (114)** (RHBuckler) **9-10-0** SMcNeill (prom tl wknd qckly 12th: mstke 13th: p.u bef 15th. b.b.v)...... **P** 20/1 — —
(SP 111.9%) **7 Rn**

7m 30.1 (60.10) CSF £15.88 TOTE £3.50: £1.70 £2.60 (£6.60) OWNER Mr L. G. Kimber (WANTAGE) BRED C. L. Loyd
LONG HANDICAP Spuffington 9-11 See Enough 9-10
3153* Giventime completed the hat-trick off a 4lb higher mark, and may go for next week's Midlands Grand National if it comes up soft. (11/4)
1785* Belmont King (IRE) who did not find the ground testing enough in Ireland last time, was 7lb higher than when winning the Rehearsal Chase here before Christmas. Held up recently by a leg infection, his trainer was satisfied with this effort and he will now go straight to the Grand National where he will want it soft. (11/2)
3153 Spuffington was 3lb better off with the winner than when beaten fifteen lengths over course and distance last month. (20/1)
3266* General Wolfe, up 5lb, was never really travelling after making a mess of the third ditch but his trainer was far from downhearted and stated the gelding was still on course for the Grand National. (5/4)
Buckboard Bounce (9/1: 5/1-10/1)

3564 PETER O'SULLEVAN NOVICES' HURDLE (5-Y.O) (Class B)
2-15 (2-18) **2m 110y (8 hdls)** £13,875.00 (£4,200.00: £2,050.00: £975.00) GOING: 1.15 sec per fur (HY)

SP RR SF
What's the Verdict (IRE) (APO'Brien,Ireland) **5-11-5** CFSwan (lw: hld up in rr: hdwy appr 4 out: led last: lft clr flat)......— **1** 13/8[1] 87 22
2808* **Motoqua** (DNicholson) **5-11-0** RJohnson (a.p: ev ch whn j.lft 2 out: btn whn lft 2nd flat)......8 **2** 8/1 74 9
3271* **Break the Rules (110)** (MCPipe) **5-11-5** APMcCoy (lw: hld up & bhd: hdwy appr 4 out: one pce fr 3 out)......¾ **3** 11/2[3] 79 14
2791[7] **Burn Out** (JPearce) **5-11-5** PCarberry (hld up & bhd: hdwy appr 4 out: wknd appr 3 out)......17 **4** 16/1 62 —
3271[2] **Royal Scimitar (USA)** (MrsAJPerrett) **5-11-5** RDunwoody (led: j.slowly 2nd: hdd 4 out: sn wknd)......8 **5** 5/1[2] 54 —

				SP	RR	SF
3298[3]	**No Pattern (104)** (GLMoore) **5-11-5** DGallagher (a bhd: t.o)	12	**6**	9/1	43	—
2937[7]	**Percy Braithwaite (IRE) (100)** (MissPMWhittle) **5-11-5** CLlewellyn (mstke 1st: a bhd: t.o)	3½	**7**	50/1	39	—
3103[4]	**Absolute Limit** (JTGifford) **5-11-5** PHide (plld hrd early: bhd tl p.u & dismntd bef 4 out)		**P**	33/1	—	—
3366*	**Gods Squad (110)** (JMackie) **5-11-5** NWilliamson (chsd ldr: led 4 out: hdd & mstke last: 2nd & btn whn p.u lame flat: dead)		**P**	11/2[3]	—	—

(SP 117.4%) **9 Rn**

4m 17.9 (28.90) CSF £14.68 TOTE £2.50: £1.40 £1.90 £1.70 (£8.20) Trio £13.60 OWNER Mr S. O'Farrell (PILTOWN) BRED Islanmore Stud

What's the Verdict (IRE), a dual winner on the Flat for Mark Johnston, was confidently ridden to complete the hat-trick, despite the step up in class. In command when left clear after the last, he will now attempt a quick follow up at Cheltenham. (13/8)
2808* Motoqua gave a good account of herself but only finished second because of the unfortunate accident to Gods Squad. (8/1)
3271* Break the Rules deserved to take his chance but proved a little out of his depth in this company. (11/2: 4/1-6/1)
2791 Burn Out may need better ground. (16/1)
3271 Royal Scimitar (USA) had only been beaten a length and half by Break the Rules at Haydock. (5/1)
3366* Gods Squad was second best on merit, but unfortunately severed his off-fore tendon at the final flight. (11/2)

3565 LLANGIBBY NOVICES' CHASE (5,6,7 & 8-Y.O) (Class E)

2-45 (2-55) **2m 3f 110y (16 fncs)** £3,134.00 (£874.00: £422.00) GOING: 1.41 sec per fur (HY)

				SP	RR	SF
3086[F]	**With Impunity (102)** (PFNicholls) **8-11-2** RJohnson (led to 8th: led 10th: r.o wl)	—	**1**	2/1[2]	91+	34
3020[9]	**Mystic Isle (IRE)** (NAGaselee) **7-11-2** CLlewellyn (hld up: hit 2nd: lft 2nd 2 out: mstke last: wknd)	9	**2**	5/1[3]	84	27
3111[4]	**Dunnicks View (71)** (FGTucker) **8-10-9**(7) MGriffiths (hld up: wnt 2nd 6th: led 8th tl mstke 10th: wknd after 11th: t.o)	dist	**3**	20/1	—	—
3331[2]	**Scoresheet (IRE) (95)** (JTGifford) **7-11-9** PHide (hld up: hdwy 11th: 2l 2nd whn fell 2 out)		**F**	11/10[1]	—	—
2870[P]	**Felloo (IRE) (91)** (TRGeorge) **8-11-2** PCarberry (chsd wnr tl wknd 6th: mstke 7th: t.o whn p.u bef 9th)		**P**	14/1	—	—
2039[P]	**Saucy's Wolf** (MrsEMBrooks) **7-11-2** MSharratt (a bhd: t.o 5th: mstke 7th: p.u bef 11th)		**P**	100/1	—	—

(SP 110.0%) **6 Rn**

5m 24.8 (35.80) CSF £10.80 TOTE £2.90: £1.10 £2.10 (£9.70) OWNER Guest Leasing & Bloodstock Co Ltd (SHEPTON MALLET) BRED Guest Leasing and Bloodstock Co

With Impunity likes the soft and never put a foot wrong despite having fallen on his seasonal debut last month. (2/1)
1195 Mystic Isle (IRE) generally jumped better and it was a case of fatigue that caused him to miss out at the last. (5/1)
3331 Scoresheet (IRE) was probably held when coming to grief. (11/10: 4/5-5/4)

3566 TOTE QUADPOT H'CAP HURDLE (4-Y.O) (Class C)

3-20 (3-21) **2m 110y (8 hdls)** £3,488.00 (£1,049.00: £507.00: £236.00) GOING: 1.15 sec per fur (HY)

				SP	RR	SF
3291[4]	**Shu Gaa (IRE) (100)** (OSherwood) **4-11-0** JAMcCarthy (lost pl 3rd: hdwy appr 4 out: led 3 out: rdn & r.o wl flat)	—	**1**	2/1[1]	73	—
3168*	**Influence Pedler (113)** (JABOld) **4-11-13** CLlewellyn (lw: hld up: hdwy 3rd: ev ch last: r.o)	s.h	**2**	9/4[2]	86	8
2784[3]	**Seattle Alley (USA) (97)** (PRWebber) **4-10-11** PCarberry (lw: hld up: hdwy appr 3 out: ev ch 2 out: sn rdn: fnd nil)	3½	**3**	11/4[3]	67	—
2872[5]	**Doctor Green (FR) (114)** (MCPipe) **4-12-0v** JamieEvans (led to 3 out: one pce fr 2 out)	1½	**4**	4/1	82	4
3222[6]	**Come On In (86)** (RDickin) **4-9-9**(5) MrRThornton (prom tl wknd qckly 4 out: t.o)	30	**5**	33/1	25	—

(SP 113.7%) **5 Rn**

4m 23.0 (34.00) CSF £6.71 TOTE £3.10: £2.00 £1.50 (£3.70) OWNER Mr Ali K Al Jafleh (UPPER LAMBOURN) BRED Ali K. Al Jafleh
LONG HANDICAP Come On In 9-2

3291 Shu Gaa (IRE), dropped 4lb, seemed more at home on this testing surface and held on well in the closing stages. (2/1)
3168* Influence Pedler ran a fine race in trying to concede nearly a stone to the winner. (9/4)
2784 Seattle Alley (USA) looked to be travelling like a winner until finding precious little off the bridle. (11/4: 5/1-3/1)
2872 Doctor Green (FR) adopted his usual front-running tactics on what was easily the most testing ground he has encountered to date. (4/1)

3567 COTSWOLD VALE H'CAP CHASE (0-125) (5-Y.O+) (Class D)

3-50 (3-50) **2m 3f 110y (16 fncs)** £3,488.00 (£1,049.00: £507.00: £236.00) GOING: 1.41 sec per fur (HY)

				SP	RR	SF
	Donjuan Collonges (FR) (103) (CaptTAForster) **6-11-4** PCarberry (lw: a gng wl: hit 7th: led 10th: clr 4 out: easily)	—	**1**	6/1[3]	117++	28
3407[2]	**Court Master (IRE) (90)** (RHBuckler) **9-10-5** BPowell (bhd tl hdwy appr 5 out: j.lft 4 out: wnt 2nd 3 out: no ch w wnr)	9	**2**	13/2	97	8
3113[P]	**Benjamin Lancaster (95)** (MAGriffin) **13-10-3**(7) MGriffiths (bhd tl hdwy 5 out: one pce fr 3 out)	6	**3**	25/1	97	8
3407*	**Indian Arrow (NZ) (105)** (MCPipe) **9-11-6** CMaude (w ldr tl wknd 4 out)	14	**4**	11/8[1]	95	6
3401*	**Kings Cherry (IRE) (109)** (JABOld) **9-11-10** CLlewellyn (led to 10th: wknd 4 out)	16	**5**	7/2[2]	86	—
3198[4]	**Jacob's Wife (103)** (PRWebber) **7-11-4** RBellamy (a bhd: t.o whn fell 4 out)		**F**	7/1	—	—
	Persian Sword (92) (DNicholson) **11-10-4**(3) RMassey (a wl bhd: t.o whn hmpd & uns rdr 4 out)		**U**	14/1	—	—

(SP 115.0%) **7 Rn**

5m 26.8 (37.80) CSF £39.39 TOTE £11.50: £3.10 £2.20 (£31.20) OWNER Mr Robert Ogden (LUDLOW) BRED Gaec Delorme Freres

Donjuan Collonges (FR), a winner on soft ground at Auteuil, had been off course since running out at Newcastle a year ago. With his rider looking round for dangers entering the long home straight, he made mincemeat of this opposition. (6/1: op 3/1)
3407 Court Master (IRE) was never going to get near the winner. (13/2)
1570 Benjamin Lancaster is now 3lb lower than when winning over two miles here in November (25/1)
3407* Indian Arrow (NZ), 15lb higher than when scoring on his reappearance, may be better at the minimum trip but this was still rather disappointing. (11/8)
3401* Kings Cherry (IRE) was only 3lb higher than when winning at Newbury. (7/2)
Persian Sword (14/1: op 8/1)

T/Plpt: £104.20 (172.86 Tckts). T/Qdpt: £26.00 (23.59 Tckts) KH

3549-SANDOWN (R-H) (Good, chases Good to firm patches)
Saturday March 8th
WEATHER: dull

3568 DICK MCCREERY HUNTERS' CHASE (5-Y.O+) (Class H)
1-55 (1-55) **2m 4f 110y (17 fncs)** £2,684.00 (£812.00: £396.00: £188.00) GOING: 0.39 sec per fur (GS)

	Horse / details	Dist	Pos	SP	RR	SF
	Archies Oats (JonTrice-Rolph) **8-11-9**(5) MrJTrice-Rolph (hdwy 12th: led last: rdn out)	—	1	11/2 3	91	—
	Mister Main Man (IRE) (CSporborg) **9-11-7**(7) MrSSporborg (lw: blnd 4th: chsd ldr 3rd to 6th: lost pl 7th: rallied 12th: ev ch whn mstke last: unable qckn)	2½	2	10/11 1	89	—
	Berrings Dasher (MrsJRichardson) **10-11-7**(7) MrMWatson (chsd ldr fr 6th: led appr 2 out tl hdd & mstke last: wknd flat)	6	3	5/1 2	84	—
	Electric Committee (IRE) (AWWood) **7-11-7**(7) CaptAWood (led: clr 3rd: hdd appr 2 out: wknd appr last)	17	4	16/1	71	—
2944 4	**Hickelton Lad** (DLWilliams) **13-11-13**(7) MajorSJRobinson (blnd 1st: hdwy 10th: wknd appr 3 out)	1¼	5	12/1	76	—
130 P	**Taurean Tycoon** (DLWilliams) **13-11-7**(7) MajorOEllwood (chsd ldr to 3rd: wknd 6th)	4	6	12/1	67	—

(SP 105.7%) **6 Rn**

5m 29.7 (30.70) CSF £9.35 TOTE £5.60: £1.80 £1.30 (£2.80) OWNER Mr Jon Trice-Rolph (MORETON-IN-MARSH) BRED R. and Mrs Healy-Fenton

Archies Oats, who showed poor form in point-to-points last season, did finish second in a similar event recently and made a winning debut under Rules, coming through to lead at the last and being ridden along to keep his two main rivals at bay. His owner-trainer-rider is very much one to note at this meeting and the Royal Artillery meeting later in the month, where several races are restricted to the Armed Forces, and his experience comes in particularly useful against riders who often look as if they will fall off at any minute. (11/2: 4/1-6/1)

Mister Main Man (IRE) lost his pitch early on the final circuit but managed to get back into it jumping the Railway Fences. One of three in line at the final fence, he was rather untidy there and failed to find another gear up the hill. (10/11: evens-5/4)

Berrings Dasher looked straight for this first run in ten months and was sent to the front approaching the second last. Collared at the final fence where made a mistake, he then had little more to offer. (5/1: 3/1-11/2)

Electric Committee (IRE), who has been pulled up, refused to race and fallen in his three point-to-points this season, tore off in front, but he was collared approaching the second last and had given his all soon after jumping that fence. (16/1)

Hickelton Lad (12/1: 7/1-14/1)

3569 BUSHY PARK 'N.H.' NOVICES' HURDLE (4-Y.O+) (Class D)
2-25 (2-27) **2m 110y (8 hdls)** £2,957.00 (£896.00: £438.00: £209.00) GOING: 0.39 sec per fur (GS)

	Horse / details	Dist	Pos	SP	RR	SF
2771 P	**Sounds Like Fun (94)** (MissHCKnight) **6-11-7** JFTitley (chsd ldr: ev ch whn lft in ld last: hdd flat: hrd rdn: led last strides)	—	1	20/1	84	37
3154 F	**Wise King** (JABOld) **7-11-2** GUpton (led to 2 out: led flat: hrd rdn: hdd last strides)	s.h	2	13/2	79	32
3012 2	**Neat Feat (IRE) (94)** (DRCElsworth) **6-11-2** PHolley (lw: a.p: rdn appr 2 out: sn wknd)	17	3	16/1	63	16
3041 5	**Donnington (IRE) (110)** (OSherwood) **7-11-7** JOsborne (hmpd 3 out: hdwy appr 2 out: r.o one pce)	2	4	4/1 2	66	19
3275 6	**Calm Down (IRE)** (TCasey) **6-11-2** DBridgwater (nvr nr to chal)	1	5	20/1	60	13
3275 8	**Huish (IRE)** (GFHCharles-Jones) **6-11-2** MrACharles-Jones (a bhd)	9	6	100/1	51	4
3041 8	**The Flying Doctor (IRE)** (GBBalding) **7-11-2** BFenton (mid div tl appr 2 out)	½	7	12/1	50	3
3154 6	**Close Harmony** (NJHenderson) **5-10-11** MAFitzgerald (bhd fr 3 out: t.o)	dist	8	10/1	—	—
	Tom Pinch (IRE) (GBBalding) **8-11-2** RGreene (a bhd: t.o)	2	9	20/1	—	—
3143 2	**Lively Encounter (IRE)** (MrsMerritaJones) **6-11-2** DerekByrne (swtg: stdy hdwy 5th: cl 4th whn b.d last)		B	6/1 3	79?	—
2747 2	**Hurricane Lamp (117)** (DNicholson) **6-11-12** AThornton (a.p: led 2 out tl fell last)		F	2/1 1	89?	—
	Knock Star (IRE) (RChampion) **6-11-2** JRailton (bkwd: prom to 5th: t.o whn p.u bef last)		P	50/1	—	—
2947 P	**Starlight Fool** (KCBailey) **8-11-2b** WMcFarland (mstke 3rd: bhd fr 5th: t.o whn p.u bef last)		P	66/1	—	—

(SP 122.3%) **13 Rn**

4m 4.4 (13.40) CSF £128.66 TOTE £33.90: £5.60 £2.40 £2.50 (£104.30) Trio £566.80; £263.46 to 10/3/97 OWNER Mrs H. Brown (WANTAGE) BRED B. King

OFFICIAL EXPLANATION **Sounds Like Fun: had developed sore shins after his previous run when he was pulled up at the second last hurdle.**

2093 Sounds Like Fun, who subsequently developed sore shins after pulling up at Cheltenham at the end of January, bounced back here. Throwing down his challenge in the straight, he was one of three in line when Hurricane Lamp fell at the last. Engaged in a tremendous tussle with the runner-up, he just managed to poke a nostril in front in the last couple of strides. (20/1)

2825 Wise King was much better suited by this ground and ran a tremendous race. Setting the pace, he was marginally collared two out but managed to battle his way back into a slender advantage on the run-in. However, despite giving his all, he was just worried out of it in the last couple of strides. He can pick up a race before long. (13/2)

3012 Neat Feat (IRE) played an active role until calling it a day two from home. However, with two casualties at the last, he was able to collect third prize. His limitations have certainly been exposed this season and he needs to find a less competitive novice event. (16/1)

3041 Donnington (IRE), done no favours at the back of the field at the third last, struggled on in the straight to be nearest at the line. We may already have seen the best of him this season - when beating Wade Road at Uttoxeter in January - and if he does run again this term, he may be worth a step up in distance. (4/1)

3154 Close Harmony (10/1: 5/1-11/1)

3143 Lively Encounter (IRE) crept closer in the back straight and was right on the heels of the front three when brought down by Hurricane Lamp at the last. There is a race to be won with him over hurdles on decent ground and a step up in distance may well help. (6/1)

2747 Hurricane Lamp, with a double penalty to contend with, poked a whisker in front two out and still had a very slender advantage when crashing to the deck at the final flight. Compensation awaits. (2/1)

3570 BARCLAYS BANK AMATEUR H'CAP HURDLE (0-120) (4-Y.O+) (Class E)
2-55 (2-57) **2m 110y (8 hdls)** £4,065.00 (£1,230.00: £600.00: £285.00) GOING: 0.39 sec per fur (GS)

	Horse / details	Dist	Pos	SP	RR	SF
2907*	**Jovie King (IRE) (89)** (RHBuckler) **5-11-3**(7) MrDAlers-Hankey (lw: mde all: clr 3rd: r.o wl)	—	1	7/2 2	72	33
3177 4	**Kelly Mac (89)** (DCO'Brien) **7-11-3**(7) MajorOEllwood (chsd wnr: rdn appr 2 out: unable qckn)	3½	2	9/2 3	69	30
3272 9	**Iron N Gold (90)** (TCasey) **5-11-4**(7) MajorGWheeler (nvr nr to chal)	10	3	11/2	60	21
1058 3	**Desert Calm (IRE) (87)** (PDEvans) **8-11-1**(7)ow2 CaptJFuller (hld up: rdn appr 2 out: sn wknd)	2½	4	10/1	55	14
3228 3	**Bigwheel Bill (IRE) (84)** (JRJenkins) **8-10-12**(7) MissVHaigh (hld up: rdn appr 2 out: sn wknd)	15	5	11/2	37	—

				SP	RR	SF
3177^{3}	**Colossus of Roads (100)** (TThomsonJones) **8-12-7** MrTThomsonJones (mstke 3rd: hdwy & j.lft 3 out: sn wknd: bhd whn p.u bef 2 out)		P	15/8^{1}	—	—
				(SP 115.0%)		**6 Rn**

4m 6.0 (15.00) CSF £18.13 TOTE £4.80: £2.50 £2.30 (£10.90) OWNER Mr M. H. M. Reid (BRIDPORT) BRED John B. Hughes
OFFICIAL EXPLANATION **Colossus of Roads: was later found to have severe muscle damage over its quarters.**
2907* Jovie King (IRE) dictated matters from the front and, with a useful advantage entering the back straight, was not going to be denied. (7/2)
3177 Kelly Mac raced in second place throughout. He grimly tried to get closer to the winner in the home straight but could never find that necessary turn of foot. (9/2)
1709 Iron N Gold never got in a blow at the front two. (11/2)
1058 Desert Calm (IRE), who has had a couple of runs on the All-Weather recently, has yet to shine over hurdles and had been seen off two from home. (10/1: 8/1-12/1)
3228 Bigwheel Bill (IRE) had been hung out to dry early in the straight. His only two wins to date both came back in 1994. (11/2)
3177 Colossus of Roads, whose trainer is a former champion amateur and was having his first ride since 1988, was very disappointing following his pleasing comeback at Windsor three weeks ago. A mistake at the third seemed to un-nerve him and he jumped out to his left at the third last. The writing was soon on the wall and his trainer wisely pulled him up before the next. (15/8)

3571 BURNT OAK & SPECIAL CARGO NOVICES' CHASE (5-Y.O+) (Class C)

3-30 (3-30) **2m (13 fncs)** £4,463.00 (£1,349.00: £657.00: £311.00) GOING: 0.39 sec per fur (GS)

				SP	RR	SF
3417*	**Sublime Fellow (IRE) (116)** (NJHenderson) **7-11-6** MAFitzgerald (chsd ldr fr 4th: led appr 2 out: rdn out)	—	**1**	3/1^{2}	124	47
3333^{2}	**Juleit Jones (IRE) (87)** (JTGifford) **8-10-8**(3) LAspell (led tl appr 2 out: unable qckn)	8	**2**	7/2^{3}	107	30
3336*	**Scottish Bambi (110)** (PRWebber) **9-11-6** JOsborne (hdwy appr 3 out: rdn appr 2 out: one pce)	2½	**3**	2/1^{1}	114	37
3417^{F}	**Blair Castle (IRE)** (GBBalding) **6-11-2** BFenton (lw: chsd ldr to 3rd: mstke & lost pl 4th: mstke 9th: rallied appr 3 out: wknd appr 2 out)	5	**4**	3/1^{2}	105	28
1714^{5}	**Cheeka (76)** (CSmith) **8-11-2** MRanger (bit bkwd: a bhd: t.o fr 6th)	dist	**5**	66/1	—	—
3296^{3}	**Heathyards Boy (67)** (DMcCain) **7-11-2b** DWalsh (bhd fr 7th: t.o)	1¾	**6**	40/1	—	—
				(SP 109.5%)		**6 Rn**

4m 1.8 (10.80) CSF £12.16 TOTE £4.00: £1.80 £1.70 (£6.80) OWNER Mr Rory McGrath (LAMBOURN) BRED John Kent
3417* Sublime Fellow (IRE), who has done all his winning on good ground or faster, had things to suit him here, leading approaching the second last and needing only to be shaken up to have the situation in hand. (3/1)
3333 Juleit Jones (IRE) at last got the return to two miles she has been crying out for. Adopting her usual front-running role, she was eventually collared approaching the second last and, although no match for the winner, held on for second prize. (7/2)
3336* Scottish Bambi has been in good form this season and closed right up going to the Pond Fence. Soon ridden along, he then failed to find another gear. (2/1)
3417 Blair Castle (IRE) is not the best of jumpers and a mistake at the fourth shuffled him back through the pack. He tried to get back into it again going to the Pond Fence, but was soon a spent force. (3/1)

3572 SUNDERLANDS IMPERIAL CUP H'CAP HURDLE (0-150) (4-Y.O+) (Class B)

4-05 (4-08) **2m 110y (8 hdls)** £21,456.00 (£6,498.00: £3,174.00: £1,512.00) GOING: 0.39 sec per fur (GS)

				SP	RR	SF
3345*	**Carlito Brigante (112)** (PRWebber) **5-10-0** JOsborne (lw: hld up: rdn appr 2 out: led flat: r.o wl)	—	**1**	10/1	98	55
3105*	**Doctoor (USA) (122)** (MCPipe) **7-10-10** APMcCoy (hld up: led 2 out tl flat: unable qckn)	2	**2**	3/1^{1}	106	63
3148*	**Express Gift (130)** (MrsMReveley) **8-11-4** NWilliamson (hdwy 3 out: ev ch fr 2 out: one pce flat)	1	**3**	20/1	113	70
3254a^{3}	**Lady Daisy (IRE) (133)** (AMullins,Ireland) **8-11-7** CFSwan (hdwy 5th: rdn appr 2 out: one pce)	1¾	**4**	14/1	114	71
2777*	**Forestal (117)** (SGGriffiths) **5-10-5** TJMurphy (lw: a.p: pckd 3rd: rdn appr 2 out: one pce)	3	**5**	10/1	96	53
3150^{7}	**Kadastrof (FR) (134)** (RDickin) **7-11-1**(7) XAizpuru (led to 2nd: led appr 2 out: sn hdd: wknd appr last)	½	**6**	40/1	112	69
3412*	**More Dash Thancash (IRE) (118)** (MrsMerritaJones) **7-10-6** DerekByrne (swtg: stdy hdwy 3 out: wknd appr 2 out)	4	**7**	13/2^{2}	92	49
3038^{5}	**Silver Groom (IRE) (138)** (RAkehurst) **7-11-7**(5) SRyan (lw: rdn 3 out: nvr nrr)	½	**8**	20/1	112	69
3038^{14}	**Chief's Song (134)** (SDow) **7-11-8** RDunwoody (lw: lost pl 4th: rallied appr 2 out: wknd appr last)	2½	**9**	25/1	105	62
3137*	**Samanid (IRE) (112)** (MissLCSiddall) **5-10-0** OPears (bhd fr 3 out)	3½	**10**	25/1	80	37
3293^{6}	**Kingsfold Pet (130)** (MJHaynes) **8-11-4** DSkyrme (sme hdwy appr 2 out: sn wknd)	3	**11**	50/1	95	52
3041^{2}	**Mr Percy (IRE) (124)** (JTGifford) **6-10-12** SMcNeill (lw: mid div tl appr 2 out)	7	**12**	12/1	82	39
3286*	**Shining Edge (126)** (TDEasterby) **5-11-0** GBradley (swtg: prom to appr 2 out)	3	**13**	12/1	81	38
3231^{6}	**Ground Nut (IRE) (123)** (RHBuckler) **7-10-6**(5) GSupple (led 2nd tl appr 2 out: sn wknd)	nk	**14**	33/1	78	35
2771^{3}	**Danegold (IRE) (112)** (MRChannon) **5-10-0v** RHughes (swtg: bhd fr 3 out)	12	**15**	14/1	55	12
3229^{F}	**Shankar (IRE) (131)** (DNicholson) **6-11-5** WMarston (a bhd: t.o)	dist	**16**	20/1	—	—
2114^{2}	**Chai-Yo (126)** (JABOld) **7-11-0** GUpton (hdwy 3 out: ev ch whn fell 2 out)		F	14/1	—	—
3286^{2}	**Star Rage (IRE) (133)** (JLHarris) **7-11-7** DGallagher (lw: bhd fr 3 out: t.o whn p.u bef last)		P	8/1^{3}	—	—
				(SP 132.3%)		**18 Rn**

3m 56.0 (5.00) CSF £35.76 CT £579.61 TOTE £11.00: £2.40 £1.50 £4.10 £2.20 (£28.20) Trio £547.50 OWNER Lady Bamford (BANBURY) BRED Whitsbury Manor Stud
LONG HANDICAP Samanid (IRE) 9-8 Carlito Brigante 9-12 Danegold (IRE) 9-11
3345* Carlito Brigante is turning into a very progressive youngster and although still a novice gave a good beating to these experienced handicappers. Wound up in the straight, he came through to get on top on the run-in. (10/1)
3105* Doctoor (USA), all the rage in the ante-post betting following his demolition job here recently, has been raised 9lb for that victory. Favourite backers must have been very hopeful as he led at the second last, but he was unable to contain the winner on the run-in.(3/1)
3148* Express Gift, who gained a confidence-boosting victory here in a claimer recently after several poor performances, ran a tremendous race in this very competitive handicap. Battling hard for the advantage in the straight, he may even have got his head in front for a few strides going to the last before tapped for toe on the run-in. (20/1)
3254a Lady Daisy (IRE), who made the journey over from Ireland to contest this race and the County Hurdle at Cheltenham, has won three handicaps this season and has shot up 33lb as a result. Taking closer order halfway down the back straight, she failed to find the necessary turn of foot over the last two hurdles. (14/1)
2777* Forestal, 8lb higher than when successful at Cheltenham, was never far away but could only go up and down in the same place in the straight. (10/1)
2884* Kadastrof (FR) was much happier with the return to two miles, but he is vulnerable to fast finishers and that was the case here, for after struggling into a narrow lead approaching the second last, he was soon headed and beaten. (40/1)
3412* More Dash Thancash (IRE) has won his last three races in tremendous style, but is now 26lb higher than at the beginning of the season. Cruising into the action three form home, he had been seen off turning into the straight. (13/2)

2114 Chai-Yo, given a ten-week break, was just about to jump into the lead when taking a crashing fall at the second last. Compensation awaits. (14/1)

3573 HAMBRO COUNTRYWIDE H'CAP CHASE (0-135) (5-Y.O+) (Class C)

4-40 (4-49) **3m 110y (22 fncs)** £6,872.50 (£2,080.00: £1,015.00: £482.50) GOING: 0.39 sec per fur (GS)

				SP	RR	SF
3046[4]	**Samlee (IRE) (115)** (PJHobbs) **8-10-11** DBridgwater (lw: hdwy 17th: led appr 3 out: drvn out)	—	**1**	4/1[2]	127	10
1997*	**Full of Fire (119)** (KCBailey) **10-11-1** AThornton (stdy hdwy 11th: blnd 13th: rdn appr 3 out: chsd wnr fr 2 out: ev ch flat: r.o)	½	**2**	4/1[2]	131	14
3274[3]	**Aardwolf (128)** (CPEBrooks) **6-11-10** GBradley (lw: led to 18th: lost pl appr 3 out: 4th whn mstke 2 out: rallied appr last: unable qckn)	5	**3**	3/1[1]	136	19
3147*	**Denver Bay (119)** (JTGifford) **10-10-12**(3) LAspell (hld up: led 18th tl appr 3 out: wknd appr last)	16	**4**	4/1[2]	117	—
3153[P]	**Top Brass (IRE) (104)** (KCBailey) **9-10-0** SMcNeill (chsd ldr to 18th: wknd appr 3 out)	5	**5**	33/1	99	—
3151[4]	**Montecot (FR) (120)** (SMellor) **8-11-2** DGallagher (lw: 5th whn blnd 8th: bhd fr 11th: t.o whn p.u bef 13th: b.b.v)		**P**	10/1	—	—
3175*	**Equity Player (107)** (RCurtis) **12-10-3** DMorris (4th whn mstke 16th: sn wknd: t.o whn p.u bef 3 out)		**P**	9/2[3]	—	—
				(SP 115.2%)		**7 Rn**

6m 28.8 (26.80) CSF £19.09 TOTE £5.20: £2.50 £2.20 (£15.00) OWNER White Lion Partnership (MINEHEAD) BRED Mrs. E. Moorhead
LONG HANDICAP Top Brass (IRE) 9-9

3046 Samlee (IRE), put to sleep at the back of the field, worked his way into the action jumping the Railway Fences for the final time and, sent on approaching the Pond Fence, just managed to hold off the very persistent runner-up on the run-in. (4/1)
1997* Full of Fire, given an eleven-week break, moved into second place two from home and threw down a determined challenge jumping the last. It looked as if he might be successful but he had not counted on such a tenacious rival. (4/1)
3274 Aardwolf has yet to recapture the form he showed here in November and December. Setting the pace, he was collared five out and, after looking likely to drop out of it going to the Pond Fence, grimly tried to get back into it going to the last before tapped for toe. (3/1)
3147* Denver Bay went on five from home but he was collared approaching the Pond Fence and was eventually seen off soon after the second last. (4/1)
Top Brass (IRE) manage to complete but had been seen off going to the Pond Fence. (33/1)
2759 Montecot (FR) (10/1: 8/1-14/1)

3574 H.M.S. SANDOWN STANDARD OPEN N.H. FLAT RACE (4, 5 & 6-Y.O) (Class H)

5-15 (5-22) **2m 110y** £1,406.00 (£391.00: £188.00)

				SP	RR	SF
	Billy Box (GMMcCourt) **5-11-4** DBridgwater (hdwy over 7f out: led over 2f out: shkn up over 1f out: comf)	—	**1**	11/4[1]	72 f	—
	Fortunes Flight (IRE) (JSKing) **4-10-10** TJMurphy (a.p: chsd wnr fnl 2f: no imp)	5	**2**	25/1	67 f	—
	Timely Magic (IRE) (JNeville) **5-11-4** APMcCoy (hld up: ev ch over 2f out: one pce)	2½	**3**	8/1	65 f	—
	Golden Eagle (NJHenderson) **5-11-4** MAFitzgerald (nice c: rdn & hdwy over 2f out: r.o)	hd	**4**	4/1[2]	65 f	—
	Desert Way (IRE) (MissHCKnight) **4-10-10** JCulloty (hdwy over 3f out: rdn over 2f out: one pce)	3½	**5**	6/1[3]	61 f	—
	Homme de Fer (KCBailey) **5-10-11**(7) CScudder (leggy: hdwy over 3f out: wknd over 1f out)	2	**6**	14/1	59 f	—
	Kabylie Ouest (FR) (RDickin) **4-9-12**(7) XAizpuru (neat: hdwy fnl 2f: nvr nrr)	3	**7**	33/1	51 f	—
	Satellite Express (IRE) (BSmart) **4-10-10** WMarston (bit bkwd: hdwy over 6f out: wkng whn swvd bdly lft over 1f out)	3	**8**	20/1	54 f	—
	Kapco (IRE) (CPEBrooks) **5-11-4** GBradley (lw: gd hdwy 13f out: led over 7f out tl over 2f out: sn wknd)	2	**9**	16/1	52 f	—
	Eagle Dancer (LadyHerries) **5-11-4** RDunwoody (leggy: bkwd: hdwy over 6f out: wknd over 2f out)	2	**10**	4/1[2]	50 f	—
3304[7]	**Sir Prize (IRE)** (GBBalding) **4-10-10** BClifford (led 9f: wknd over 2f out)	hd	**11**	14/1	50 f	—
3235[6]	**Moonraker's Mirage** (DRCElsworth) **6-11-4** PHolley (nvr nrr)	7	**12**	20/1	43 f	—
	Express Again (MJHaynes) **5-11-4** JRailton (w'like: prom 11f)	nk	**13**	33/1	42 f	—
	Securon Gale (IRE) (NJHenderson) **5-11-4** JRKavanagh (bhd fnl 3f)	7	**14**	20/1	36 f	—
3418[R]	**Mill Bay Sam** (MrsMerritaJones) **6-11-4** DerekByrne (prom 14f)	9	**15**	33/1	27 f	—
	Clare's Spring (IRE) (RJHodges) **4-10-7**(3) TDascombe (lw: a bhd)	2	**16**	16/1	25 f	—
1665[13]	**Tatibag** (RJSmith) **5-10-11**(7) LSuthern (bhd fnl 4f: t.o)	dist	**17**	33/1	—	—
	Plumpton Wood (IRE) (JGSmyth-Osbourne) **5-10-13** NWilliamson (bkwd: bhd fnl 5f: t.o)	dist	**18**	25/1	—	—
	Lift The Latch (IRE) (MrsIMcKie) **5-11-4** LHarvey (bit bkwd: a bhd: t.o)	2	**19**	33/1	—	—
	Lovely Outlook (RMCarson) **5-11-4** DMorris (prom 10f: t.o fnl 4f: p.u ins fnl f)		**P**	25/1	—	—
				(SP 157.7%)		**20 Rn**

4m 5.8 CSF £86.83 TOTE £4.50: £1.90 £15.00 £4.50 (£118.40) Trio £690.00; £485.95 to Taunton 10/3/97 OWNER Mr Alec Tuckerman (WANTAGE) BRED Ulceby Vale Stud Ltd
WEIGHT FOR AGE 4yo-8lb

Billy Box, a stocky individual, made a very impressive racecourse debut, cruising into the lead over a quarter of a mile from home and needing only to be shaken up to pull away for a very decisive victory. He can follow up. (11/4)
Fortunes Flight (IRE) moved into second place two furlongs from home but had no hope with the winner. (25/1)
Timely Magic (IRE), related to several winners, had every chance over a quarter of a mile from home before left for dead. (8/1)
Golden Eagle stayed on up the hill and only just failed to take third prize. (4/1: 3/1-5/1)
Desert Way (IRE), out of a dam who won at middle distances in the French provinces, took closer order early in the straight, but could then only go up and down in the same place. (6/1)
Homme de Fer was scrubbed along to take closer order early in the straight, but had shot his bolt below the distance. (14/1)
Eagle Dancer (4/1: 3/1-5/1)
3021 Sir Prize (IRE) (14/1: op 8/1)

T/Jkpt: Not won; £14,766.18 to Stratford 10/3/97. T/Plpt: £320.50 (94.21 Tckts). T/Qdpt: £62.00 (33.06 Tckts) AK

3406-PLUMPTON (L-H) (Good to soft, soft patches)
Monday March 10th
Race 7 - last flight omitted
WEATHER: fine

3575 ARDINGLEY NOVICES' HURDLE (4-Y.O+) (Class E)
2-10 (2-10) **2m 1f (10 hdls)** £2,553.00 (£708.00: £339.00) GOING: 1.21 sec per fur (HY)

			SP	RR	SF
3024[4]	**Cuthill Hope (IRE)** (MHTompkins) **6-11-2** RichardGuest (a.p: chsd ldr 3 out: led appr last: r.o).....—	1	13/8[1]	73	15
2669[14]	**Suranom (IRE)** (MrsDHaine) **5-11-2** JFTitley (lw: nt fluent: led: hdd appr last: one pce).....5	2	7/2[3]	68	10
3075[7]	**Daydreamer (USA)** (RHBuckler) **4-10-8** BPowell (lw: hld up in tch: hrd rdn appr 3 out: one pce).....12	3	9/4[2]	52	—
3057[4]	**Zadok (65)** (JFfitch-Heyes) **5-11-2b** BFenton (sme hdwy 6th: sn rdn: one pce).....8	4	33/1	45	—
3061[3]	**Kilshey** (JTGifford) **6-10-8**(3) LAspell (a.p: chsd ldr 4th to 3 out: wknd appr next).....26	5	7/1	15	—
3406[4]	**Welsh Wizzard** (JRBest) **5-10-9**(7) MrPO'Keeffe (in tch: rdn 4th: wknd 6th).....2	6	25/1	18	—
3061[B]	**Knot True** (JohnBerry) **7-10-11** PHolley (a bhd).....2	7	50/1	11	—
3406[F]	**My Nad Knows** (JCPoulton) **4-10-8** TJO'Sullivan (chsd ldr to 4th: mstkes 6th & 7th: wknd appr next).....s.h	8	66/1	16	—
	Arcus (IRE) (WRMuir) **4-10-3**(5) ABates (mstke 3rd: a bhd).....12	9	33/1	5	—
	Mega Tid (JRPoulton) **5-11-2** ADicken (in tch tl wknd 7th).....12	10	33/1	—	—
	Civil Law (IRE) (RCurtis) **7-11-2** DMorris (j.poorly: sn bhd: t.o whn p.u after 5th).....	P	50/1	—	—
			(SP 121.7%)	**11 Rn**	

4m 27.8 (31.80) CSF £7.10 TOTE £2.70: £1.20 £1.70 £1.50 (£6.70) Trio £7.40 OWNER Mrs Emma Gilchrist (NEWMARKET) BRED C. McCann
WEIGHT FOR AGE 4yo-8lb
3024 Cuthill Hope (IRE) was given a competent ride by Guest. He took up the running approaching the last and the race was soon in safe-keeping. (13/8)
Suranom (IRE) lost ground at a number of hurdles and did well to get as close as he did. He will find a race as his hurdling improves. (7/2)
Daydreamer (USA) was hard at work some way out, and may need slightly better ground. (9/4: 6/4-5/2)
3057 Zadok plugged on for a modest fourth. (33/1)
3061 Kilshey (7/1: 5/1-8/1)

3576 CORINTHIAN-CASUALS NOVICES' CHASE (5-Y.O+) (Class E)
2-40 (2-40) **2m 5f (16 fncs)** £3,501.40 (£844.60) GOING: 0.93 sec per fur (S)

			SP	RR	SF
3334[2]	**Lively Knight (IRE) (115)** (JTGifford) **8-11-6**(3) LAspell (lw: j.w: led 5th: made rest: clr 3 out: easily).....—	1	13/8[2]	117+	49
3422[F]	**Angelo's Double (IRE)** (RHBuckler) **9-11-2** BPowell (lw: led: hdd 5th: blnd next: rdn appr 3 out: one pce)....23	2	8/15[1]	93	25
3407[4]	**Eau So Sloe** (JRPoulton) **6-11-2** ADicken (rdn 9th: sn wknd: t.o whn fell 11th).....	F	50/1[3]	—	—
			(SP 105.3%)	**3 Rn**	

5m 38.7 (25.70) CSF £2.66 TOTE £2.40 (£1.10) OWNER Mr A. D. Weller (FINDON) BRED Jack Forristal
3334 Lively Knight (IRE) jumped superbly, and had the race in safe-keeping from some way out. (13/8)
3422 Angelo's Double (IRE) did not look a natural fencer, and was comprehensively outjumped by the winner. (8/15)

3577 DON BUTCHERS CHALLENGE TROPHY H'CAP HURDLE (0-100) (4-Y.O+) (Class F)
3-10 (3-11) **2m 4f (12 hdls)** £2,012.40 (£556.40: £265.20) GOING: 1.21 sec per fur (HY)

			SP	RR	SF
3411*	**Mayb-Mayb (82)** (JNeville) **7-11-10** APMcCoy (led to 2nd: styd prom: mstkes 4th & 5th: led appr 9th: clr 2 out: eased nr fin).....—	1	Evens[1]	69+	27
2905[2]	**Do Be Ware (77)** (JFfitch-Heyes) **7-11-5** BFenton (in tch: rdn & outpcd appr 3 out: kpt on again to go 2nd appr last).....12	2	11/1	54	12
3411[4]	**Script (71)** (JRJenkins) **6-10-13** WMarston (led 2nd: hdd 4th: lost pl 5th: rallied appr last: kpt on one pce flat).7	3	11/1	43	1
3442[3]	**Hello Me Man (IRE) (79)** (BJLlewellyn) **9-11-7** MrJLLlewellyn (swtg: keen hold: led 4th: mstke 7th: hdd appr 9th: wknd appr last: fin tired).....2½	4	6/1[3]	49	7
3209[4]	**August Twelfth (81)** (DCO'Brien) **9-11-4**(5) DJKavanagh (prom: rdn 8th: wknd appr next: lame).....14	5	100/30[2]	40	—
3204[9]	**Kentavrus Way (IRE) (69)** (GLMoore) **6-10-4**(7) MBatchelor (ref to r).....	R	12/1	—	—
			(SP 111.7%)	**6 Rn**	

5m 23.3 (36.30) CSF £10.85 TOTE £1.60: £1.40 £2.30 (£5.20) OWNER Mr J. Neville (NEWPORT, GWENT) BRED Bram Davies and R. J. Holder
OFFICIAL EXPLANATION **August Twelfth: trainer reported that the gelding's blood had been wrong after his last run, and that he only ran him here as the race was re-opened. The vet added that the gelding finished lame.**
3411* Mayb-Mayb did not race particularly kindly early on, but the further he went the stronger he got. (Evens)
2905 Do Be Ware was left behind when the tempo increased on the run to three out. Although keeping on for second, there was no catching the winner. (11/1: 8/1-12/1)
3411 Script appeared to lose interest approaching halfway, and only consented to run on again when the race was over. (11/1: 8/1-12/1)
3442 Hello Me Man (IRE) did not help his cause by taking a tug early on, and he was a very tired horse at the finish. (6/1)
3209 August Twelfth lost touch early on the final circuit, and it later transpired that he had finished lame. (100/30)
3204 Kentavrus Way (IRE) (12/1: 8/1-14/1)

3578 PHILIP HALL MEMORIAL H'CAP CHASE (0-110) (5-Y.O+) (Class E)
3-40 (3-40) **2m 5f (16 fncs)** £3,058.60 (£844.60: £401.80) GOING: 0.93 sec per fur (S)

			SP	RR	SF
3059[6]	**Regal Aura (IRE) (64)** (DCO'Brien) **7-10-2** WMarston (led to 3rd: led 8th: clr 3 out: mstke 2 out: easily).....—	1	16/1	92?	—
3410[2]	**Winspit (IRE) (86)** (RHAlner) **7-11-10** WMcFarland (led 7th: hdd next: wknd appr 3 out: wl btn whn blnd next).....dist	2	11/4[2]	—	—
3176[3]	**Key Player (IRE) (77)** (RRowe) **8-11-1** DO'Sullivan (led 3rd: hdd 7th: mstke 11th: sn wknd).....28	3	10/11[1]	—	—
3410[B]	**Golden Opal (79)** (RHBuckler) **12-11-3** BPowell (last whn blnd & uns rdr 4th).....	U	3/1[3]	—	—
			(SP 109.9%)	**4 Rn**	

5m 51.0 (38.00) CSF £49.76 TOTE £15.50 (£20.30) OWNER Mrs V. O'Brien (TONBRIDGE) BRED Upstream Ltd
OFFICIAL EXPLANATION Key Player (IRE): **did not handle the sticky ground.**
Regal Aura (IRE) had not shown much in three previous chases, but had the race in the bag from the third last. (16/1)
3410 Winspit (IRE) had the race between himself and the winner for much of the final circuit, but was quickly left behind from the third last. (11/4)

3176 Key Player (IRE) was never having a cut at his fences, and a mistake at the eleventh finished him off. (10/11: 8/11-evens)

3579 UCKFIELD H'CAP HURDLE (0-110) (4-Y.O+) (Class E)

4-10 (4-10) **2m 1f (10 hdls)** £2,217.00 (£612.00: £291.00) GOING: 1.21 sec per fur (HY)

Form	Horse	Dist	Pos	SP	RR	SF
3447[3]	**Derisbay (IRE) (79)** (JJBridger) **9-9-7b**(7) MBatchelor (chsd ldrs: rdn & outpcd appr 3 out: rallied appr last: led flat: r.o)	—	1	13/2[3]	62	—
3421[3]	**Nipper Reed (103)** (THind) **7-11-10** APMcCoy (led: hdd appr 7th: rallied to ld 2 out: hdd flat: one pce)	3	2	10/11[1]	83	21
3570[2]	**Kelly Mac (89)** (DCO'Brien) **7-10-7**(3) LAspell (lw: led appr 7th: hdd 2 out: ev ch flat: one pce)	hd	3	5/2[2]	69	7
3344[7]	**Persian Mystic (IRE) (90)** (DJWintle) **5-10-11** WMarston (chsd ldr to 5th: rdn next: wknd appr 3 out)	21	4	12/1	50	—
	Doctor Death (IRE) (88) (SDow) **6-10-9v** ADicken (mstke 2nd: bhd fr 5th: t.o whn p.u after 3 out)		P	9/1	—	—
				(SP 112.0%)		**5 Rn**

4m 27.7 (31.70) CSF £12.54 TOTE £8.80: £2.30 £1.20 (£3.50) OWNER Miss Julie Self (LIPHOOK) BRED Kilfrush Stud Ltd in Ireland

LONG HANDICAP Derisbay (IRE) 9-6

3447 Derisbay (IRE), who ran well at Windsor last week, did not look like scoring when coming under strong pressure on the run to three out. However, his stamina came into play approaching the last, and he got on top on the run-in to win going away. (13/2: 9/2-7/1)

3421 Nipper Reed ran another sound race. (10/11)

3570 Kelly Mac only just gets this trip, and his rider would have been better off holding on to him for longer. (5/2)

Persian Mystic (IRE) (12/1: 9/2-14/1)

3580 'CLAPPER' CHALLENGE CUP HUNTERS' CHASE (5-Y.O+) (Class H)

4-40 (4-40) **3m 1f 110y (20 fncs)** £1,492.00 (£412.00: £196.00) GOING: 1.21 sec per fur (HY)

Form	Horse	Dist	Pos	SP	RR	SF
3446[2]	**Jupiter Moon** (MrsCHicks) **8-11-7**(7) MrJMPritchard (a.p: led appr 16th: rdn & edgd lft flat: r.o)	—	1	8/1[3]	100	14
3353[4]	**Loyal Note** (SRAndrews) **9-12-5**(3) MrSimonAndrews (a.p: chsd wnr fr 16th: hrd rdn 2 out: ev ch flat: unable qckn)	1½	2	5/2[2]	107	21
3341[2]	**Vicompt de Valmont** (PFNicholls) **12-12-0b**(5) MrTMitchell (sn bhd & pushed along: hdwy 14th: hrd rdn appr 3 out: one pce)	6	3	5/6[1]	100	14
1088[4]	**Northern Village** (LukeDace) **10-11-7**(7) MrDAlers-Hankey (nt fluent: in tch tl wknd appr 16th: t.o)	dist	4	14/1	—	—
	Ballyandrew (AHBHodge) **12-11-7**(7) MissSGritton (plld hrd: led: hdd 7th: wknd 11th: t.o whn p.u after 14th)		P	25/1	—	—
3107[P]	**Royal Irish** (ACAyres) **13-11-7**(7) MissCTownsley (bhd fr 14th: t.o whn p.u appr 4 out)		P	40/1	—	—
3273[U]	**Fifth Amendment** (CJMann) **12-11-11b**(7)ow4 MrAHales (led 7th: hdd appr 16th: wkng qckly whn ref next)		R	20/1	—	—
				(SP 111.9%)		**7 Rn**

7m 6.4 (46.40) CSF £25.25 TOTE £9.20: £2.60 £1.20 (£4.60) OWNER The Stanton Seven (CHELTENHAM) BRED H. W. and J. G. King

3446 Jupiter Moon put in a sound round of jumping and ran on gamely for pressure on the run-in, despite edging to his left. (8/1: 5/1-9/1)

3353 Loyal Note ran a good race, but found his penalty weighing him down. (5/2)

3341 Vicompt de Valmont is a very one-paced animal and needs a stiffer test of stamina. (5/6)

1088 Northern Village did not impress with his jumping. (14/1)

3581 E.B.F. 'N.H.' (QUALIFIER) NOVICES' HURDLE (5, 6 & 7-Y.O) (Class E)

5-10 (5-10) **2m 4f (12 hdls)** £2,343.00 (£648.00: £309.00) GOING: 1.21 sec per fur (HY)

Form	Horse	Dist	Pos	SP	RR	SF
3405*	**Stormy Passage (IRE) (111)** (PJHobbs) **7-11-3** APMcCoy (led 6th: clr 8th: v.easily)	—	1	1/10[1]	72+	38
3226[5]	**Supreme Troglodyte (IRE)** (CPMorlock) **5-10-2**(5) SophieMitchell (in tch: rdn appr 8th: sn outpcd by wnr: wnt mod 2nd flat)	21	2	12/1[2]	45	11
3090[6]	**Brook Bee** (NAGaselee) **5-10-12** WMarston (led: hdd 6th: outpcd fr 8th: lost mod 2nd flat)	3½	3	25/1[3]	47	13
2073[8]	**Pitarry** (DMGrissell) **7-10-12** BFenton (mstke 5th: bhd fr next: last & losing tch whn fell 7th)		F	25/1[3]	—	—
				(SP 106.3%)		**4 Rn**

5m 18.4 (31.40) CSF £1.87 TOTE £1.10 (£1.60) OWNER Mr Peter Luff (MINEHEAD) BRED Denis J. Murphy

3405* Stormy Passage (IRE) won here as his starting price suggested he would. (1/10)

3226 Supreme Troglodyte (IRE) kept on for a very modest second, but is grossly flattered by the winning distance. (12/1: 5/1-14/1)

Brook Bee is a big gelding, and the best of him will probably be seen when he goes over fences. (25/1)

T/Plpt: £348.90 (21.86 Tckts). T/Qdpt: £92.40 (4.18 Tckts) SM

2892-STRATFORD-ON-AVON (L-H) (Good)

Monday March 10th

WEATHER: Fine

3582 'TIP-TOP TIMEFORM RATINGS' NOVICES' CHASE (5-Y.O+) (Class D)

2-20 (2-21) **2m 4f (15 fncs)** £4,354.00 (£1,312.00: £636.00: £298.00) GOING: 0.15 sec per fur (G)

Form	Horse	Dist	Pos	SP	RR	SF
3356*	**Teinein (FR) (119)** (CaptTAForster) **6-11-7** NWilliamson (hld up: j.slowly 10th: hdwy 4 out: led flat: comf)	—	1	8/11[1]	94++	41
3145[3]	**The Captain's Wish (108)** (DNicholson) **6-11-2** RJohnson (hld up in tch: led appr 2 out: hdd & outpcd flat)	2	2	3/1[2]	87	34
3278[B]	**Dandie Imp (78)** (AWCarroll) **9-11-2** DWalsh (swtg: led: sn clr: rdn & hdd appr 2 out: sn outpcd)	6	3	66/1	83	30
1831[5]	**Total Asset (72)** (ALForbes) **7-11-2** GaryLyons (bkwd: a in rr)	21	4	66/1	66	13
3171[6]	**Chapilliere (FR)** (TThomsonJones) **7-11-2** SMcNeill (lw: prom: mstke 9th: wkng whn blnd 4 out: t.o)	24	5	66/1	47	—
	Go Mary (MissCPhillips) **11-10-11** JRKavanagh (bhd fr 8th: t.o)	13	6	33/1	31	—
1681[3]	**Mr Snaggle (IRE) (89)** (SEarle) **8-11-2** SCurran (bkwd: fell 1st)		F	16/1	—	—
3356[U]	**Benji** (TCasey) **6-11-2** JAMcCarthy (nt j.w: in rr tl fell 6th)		F	100/1	—	—
2880[10]	**Best of Friends (IRE)** (MissHCKnight) **7-11-2** JCulloty (j.w: prom tl lost pl appr 4 out: p.u bef next: lame)		P	6/1[3]	—	—
3173[U]	**My Warrior** (MarkCampion) **9-11-2** LHarvey (bhd tl p.u bef 4th)		P	100/1	—	—
3190[P]	**Ledburian** (MissPMWhittle) **7-10-13**(3) PHenley (a bhd: t.o whn p.u bef 10th)		P	100/1	—	—
				(SP 113.5%)		**11 Rn**

5m 6.6 (10.60) CSF £2.77 TOTE £1.60: £1.10 £1.40 £6.40 (£2.30) Trio £35.50 OWNER Mr Simon Sainsbury (LUDLOW) BRED Tomohiro Wada

3356* Teinein (FR), prepared to wait on the leaders, did not need to get serious to take the measure of the runner-up after the last, and he looks a useful recruit to chasing. (8/11)

3145 The Captain's Wish has really taken to fences, and he threw down the gauntlet on the turn for home but, hard as he tried, could never get away from the useful winner. His turn will come. (3/1)
Dandie Imp, a headstrong individual who is a winner between the flags, did his best to stretch the field, but the principals had a touch of class about them, and he was soon in trouble after being headed. (66/1)
1581 Best of Friends (IRE) jumped really well on this chasing debut, and he would have been the one to beat had he not gone lame approaching the fourth last. His injuries are such that it is doubtful he will race again. (6/1)

3583 RICHARDSON PARKWAY (S) HURDLE (4, 5 & 6-Y.O) (Class G)

2-50 (2-52) **2m 3f (10 hdls)** £2,999.00 (£902.00: £436.00: £203.00) GOING: 0.57 sec per fur (S)

	Horse			SP	RR	SF
3284[3]	**Riverbank Rose (70)** (WClay) **6-10-7v**(3) GuyLewis (mde all: clr 3 out: unchal)	—	**1**	13/2	58	21
1959[3]	**Always Greener (IRE) (82)** (JWMullins) **6-11-8** SCurran (bit bkwd: chsd ldrs: wnt 2nd 3 out: no imp)	10	**2**	9/2[3]	62	25
3362[6]	**Star Performer (IRE) (97)** (AGHobbs) **6-11-2**(5) OBurrows (chsd wnr to 3 out: sn pushed along & btn)	1	**3**	5/2[1]	60	23
3438[12]	**Danny Gale (IRE) (85)** (GMMcCourt) **6-11-7** SMcNeill (lost pl ½-wy: styd on again 2 out)	16	**4**	10/1	46	9
3352[3]	**Battleship Bruce (83)** (TCasey) **5-11-1b** RDunwoody (chsd ldrs to 3 out: sn lost tch)	4	**5**	4/1[2]	37	—
3063[7]	**Yellow Dragon (IRE) (90)** (BAPearce) **4-10-13** KGaule (chsd ldrs tl wknd appr 4 out: t.o)	dist	**6**	11/2	—	—
3364[10]	**Roc Age (68)** (GWDavies) **6-10-10** DLeahy (trckd ldrs to 6th: sn wknd: t.o)	2½	**7**	20/1	—	—
	Stipple (JAPickering) **6-10-10** JCulloty (bkwd: a bhd: t.o)	9	**8**	50/1	—	—
2815[10]	**Irish Kinsman (65)** (GHYardley) **4-10-2**(5) MrRThornton (prom tl wknd appr 6th: t.o)	8	**9**	50/1	—	—
	Eric The King (THind) **6-11-1** PMcLoughlin (bkwd: mid div whn j.v.slowly 6th: sn t.o)	24	**10**	20/1	—	—
	Bold Time Monkey (MTate) **6-10-10** CLlewellyn (t.o fr 4th)	30	**11**	50/1	—	—
360[P]	**Kerrier (IRE)** (HJManners) **5-10-8**(7) ADowling (bhd fr 5th: t.o wh p.u bef 2 out)		**P**	50/1	—	—
	New Regime (IRE) (PTDalton) **4-10-2** JSupple (a bhd: t.o whn blnd 3 out: p.u bef next)		**P**	66/1	—	—
	Ms Jones (IRE) (TPWalshe) **4-9-10**(7)ow1 LSuthern (bkwd: chsd ldrs: j.slowly 2nd: blnd & lost pl next: t.o whn p.u after 6th)		**P**	100/1	—	—

(SP 124.4%) **14 Rn**

4m 38.1 (20.10) CSF £32.40 TOTE £8.40: £1.60 £1.90 £1.50 (£11.90) Trio £8.50 OWNER Mr Don Walker, Mr F E & Mrs J J Brindley (STOKE-ON-TRENT) BRED G. Wheildon
WEIGHT FOR AGE 4yo-8lb
Bt in 4,000 gns
3284 Riverbank Rose made sure the emphasis was on stamina, and her nearest rivals were forced to call enough before reaching the home straight. (13/2)
1959 Always Greener (IRE), never too far away, tried to close the gap from the third last, but the winner kept up the gallop, and she could do nothing about it. (9/2: 4/1-7/1)
3362 Star Performer (IRE) appreciated being given a lead, but he did not find the expected response when let down, and was easily shaken off. (5/2: 7/4-11/4)
859 Danny Gale (IRE) (10/1: 5/1-11/1)
3352 Battleship Bruce did not appear to see out this longer trip, and he was back-pedalling before reaching the third-last flight. (4/1)
2871 Yellow Dragon (IRE) (11/2: 4/1-13/2)

3584 'MAKE YOUR RACING PAY WITH TIMEFORM' H'CAP HURDLE (0-130) (4-Y.O+) (Class C)

3-20 (3-21) **2m 110y (9 hdls)** £4,328.00 (£1,304.00: £632.00: £296.00) GOING: 0.57 sec per fur (S)

	Horse			SP	RR	SF
3007[7]	**Desert Mountain (IRE) (109)** (NACallaghan) **4-10-7** DGallagher (hld up: hdwy on ins appr 3 out: led last: drvn clr)	—	**1**	5/1[3]	93	28
3346*	**Durano (107)** (TDEasterby) **6-10-13** RGarritty (disp ld: led 5th to last: sn rdn: no ex)	2½	**2**	7/2[2]	89	32
3136*	**Kintavi (99)** (TWDonnelly) **7-10-5** PNiven (lw: hld up: hdwy 5th: disp ld fr 3 out tl rdn & one pce appr last)	3	**3**	9/4[1]	78	21
3163*	**Celestial Choir (120)** (JLEyre) **7-11-12** BStorey (hld up: gd hdwy appr 3 out: outpcd appr next)	3	**4**	7/2[2]	96	39
3421[6]	**Goldingo (107)** (GMPrice) **10-10-13** JRKavanagh (hld up: reminders 5th: hrd rdn appr 3 out: no imp)	13	**5**	10/1	70	13
3402[9]	**Kino's Cross (105)** (AJWilson) **8-10-11** RJohnson (prom: wkng whn j.slowly 3 out)	5	**6**	25/1	63	6
3412[2]	**Holders Hill (IRE) (103)** (MGMeagher) **5-10-9** RDunwoody (led to 5th: wknd appr 3 out: t.o)	8	**7**	15/2	54	—
	Ballet Royal (USA) (115) (HJManners) **8-11-0**(7) ADowling (bkwd: a bhd: t.o whn p.u bef 3 out)		**P**	50/1	—	—

(SP 118.5%) **8 Rn**

4m 2.2 (15.20) CSF £22.06 CT £46.11 TOTE £6.00: £1.50 £1.60 £1.40 (£18.90) Trio £23.20 OWNER Easy Monk Partnership (NEWMARKET) BRED Ron Con Ltd
WEIGHT FOR AGE 4yo-8lb
2751* Desert Mountain (IRE), taking on older rivals in his first handicap, won a shade cosily in the end. (5/1)
3346* Durano looked the likely winner for the majority of the trip, before the winner took his measure after the last. (7/2: 5/2-4/1)
3136* Kintavi joined issue three out, but was soon being made to struggle, and he decided enough was enough between the last two. (9/4)
3163* Celestial Choir appeared to be travelling smoothly when closing on the principals half-a-mile out, but top weight took its toll, and she was unable to mount a serious challenge. (7/2)

3585 '50 YEARS OF TIMEFORM' H'CAP CHASE (0-130) (5-Y.O+) (Class C)

3-50 (3-50) **3m (18 fncs)** £5,312.50 (£1,600.00: £775.00: £362.50) GOING: 0.15 sec per fur (G)

	Horse			SP	RR	SF
3046[P]	**Church Law (102)** (MrsLCTaylor) **10-10-1** RSupple (lw: chsd ldr fr 5th: led 2 out: styd on strly)	—	**1**	6/1[3]	111	10
3074*	**Merlins Dream (IRE) (113)** (OSherwood) **8-10-12** JOsborne (led to 2 out: btn whn mstke last)	6	**2**	5/4[1]	118	17
2346a[5]	**Pyr Four (125)** (GMMcCourt) **10-11-10** DBridgwater (a chsng ldrs: one pce fr 2 out)	4	**3**	14/1	127	26
3349[3]	**No Pain No Gain (IRE) (117)** (JTGifford) **9-11-2** PHide (lw: chsd ldrs tl wknd 3 out)	4	**4**	3/1[2]	117	16
2762[P]	**Postman's Path (103)** (CaptTAForster) **11-10-2** NWilliamson (hld up: hdwy 9th: wknd appr 3 out)	8	**5**	25/1	97	—
	Light Veneer (120) (MrsMerritaJones) **12-11-5** DerekByrne (bkwd: dropped rr 6th: t.o fr 13th)	dist	**6**	11/1	—	—
3039[P]	**Around the Horn (129)** (JTGifford) **10-12-0** SMcNeill (hld up in rr: blnd & uns rdr 12th)		**U**	10/1	—	—

(SP 111.7%) **7 Rn**

6m 9.2 (17.20) CSF £12.77 TOTE £6.40: £2.00 £1.50 (£4.60) OWNER Mrs L. C. Taylor (CHIPPING WARDEN) BRED Col Sir John Thomson
1871 Church Law, not inconvenienced by the step down to three miles, took the measure of the favourite turning in and, taking advantage of the pull in the weights, stormed clear to win very easily indeed. (6/1)
3074* Merlins Dream (IRE) decided to force the pace, and for most of the way seemed to be well in control, but the winner gave him no peace for the final mile, and he had already given best when he was down on his nose at the last. (5/4: op evens)

Pyr Four, an ex-Irish gelding attempting a trip for the first time, ran a race full of promise, and a step back to two-and-a-half miles or thereabouts, should see him paying his way again. (14/1: 10/1-16/1)
3349 No Pain No Gain (IRE) did not stay the trip when tried at Lingfield earlier in the season and, even on this easier track, again found it beyond him. (3/1)
Light Veneer (11/1: 7/1-12/1)
2783 Around the Horn sauntering around in the rear, had still not been asked to improve when he got into the bottom of the twelfth, and dislodged his jockey. (10/1)

3586 CREDIT CALL CUP NOVICES' HUNTERS' CHASE (5-Y.O+) (Class H)

4-20 (4-21) **3m (18 fncs)** £1,943.00 (£584.00: £282.00: £131.00) GOING: 0.15 sec per fur (G)

	Horse / details	Dist	Pl	SP	RR	SF
2951*	**Orchestral Suite (IRE)** (MissJenniferPidgeon) **9-11-13**(7) MrFHutsby (lw: swtg: j.w: chsd ldrs: slt ld 4 out: clr last)	—	1	5/2[2]	117+	31
	King's Treasure (USA) (IABalding) **8-12-3**(7) MrABalding (bit bkwd: led 5th to 4 out: wknd appr last)	14	2	Evens[1]	112	26
3357[4]	**Ideal Partner (IRE)** (PFNicholls) **8-11-12b**[1](5) MrRThornton (a.p: rdn appr 3 out: sn btn)	3	3	12/1[3]	103	17
	Royal Segos (MissSEBaxter) **10-11-11**(7)ow1 MrCStockton (led to 5th: wknd 14th)	20	4	16/1	90	3
	Tangle Baron (KCumings) **9-11-10**(7) MissJCumings (prom to 14th: sn lost tch)	1	5	20/1	89	3
3055[4]	**Not My Line (IRE)** (AndyMorgan) **8-11-12**(5) MrASansome (a in rr: t.o fr 14th)	20	6	50/1	75	—
	Rambling Lord (IRE) (GJSmith) **9-11-10**(7) MrGJSmith (a bhd: t.o whn blnd 13th)	3	7	25/1	73	—
3341[P]	**Rising Sap** (JDDownes) **7-11-10**(7) MrADalton (hld up: hdwy 9th: wknd 13th: t.o)	3	8	33/1	71	—
	Freddie Fox (MrsABGarton) **11-11-13**(7) MrTGarton (a bhd: t.o & p.u bef 12th)		P	16/1	—	—
	Babil (MrsCHicks) **12-11-12**(5) MrJTrice-Rolph (bkwd: mid div tl wknd 10th: t.o whn p.u bef 4 out)		P	16/1	—	—
651[B]	**Fantastic Fleet (IRE)** (MrsJWebber) **5-11-0**(7) MrRWakley (lw: hld up in rr: blnd & uns rdr 13th)		U	25/1	—	—
	Tellaporky (THind) **8-11-10**(7) MrAMiddleton (bkwd: nt j.w: in tch whn blnd & uns rdr 11th)		U	66/1	—	—

(SP 122.8%) **12 Rn**

6m 12.3 (20.30) CSF £4.94 TOTE £4.10: £1.70 £1.30 £2.20 (£2.80) Trio £9.40 OWNER Exors of the late Mr G Pidgeon (BRACKLEY) BRED G. Browne
WEIGHT FOR AGE 5yo-10lb
2951* Orchestral Suite (IRE) followed up his success at Huntingdon last month with another very smooth performance. He is thriving this season. (5/2)
King's Treasure (USA) looked as though he would benefit from the run, and he finally called enough approaching the last. (Evens)
3357 Ideal Partner (IRE), much sharper in the blinkers, ran well, and a race of this description is very much within his reach. (12/1: op 8/1)
Royal Segos may have found the ground livelier than is ideal, and though he was picking up again in the latter stages, the principals had gone beyond recall. (16/1)

3587 'BET-COMPELLING TIMEFORM COMMENTARIES' NOVICES' HURDLE (4-Y.O+) (Class D)

4-50 (4-51) **2m 6f 110y (12 hdls)** £3,421.50 (£1,032.00: £501.00: £235.50) GOING: 0.57 sec per fur (S)

	Horse / details	Dist	Pl	SP	RR	SF
3108[4]	**Mahler (94)** (NATwiston-Davies) **7-11-2** DWalsh (chsd ldrs: led appr 4 out: rdn appr 2 out: hld on gamely)	—	1	5/1[3]	69	26
2661[5]	**Dublin Freddy** (MissVenetiaWilliams) **6-11-2** NWilliamson (hld up: hdwy 7th: rdn & pckd 2 out & last: kpt on)	1½	2	9/2[2]	68	25
3222[5]	**Toby Brown (98)** (DNicholson) **4-10-7** RDunwoody (hld up: hdwy to chal appr 2 out: sn rdn: unable qckn)	1½	3	5/4[1]	67	15
1905[7]	**Sun of Spring** (JWhite) **7-11-2** JCulloty (bit bkwd: trckd ldrs: rdn & outpcd appr 4 out)	14	4	33/1	57	14
3265[8]	**Whiter Morn (58)** (CaptJWilson) **7-10-4**(7) MrOMcPhail (lw: nvr nr ldrs)	20	5	66/1	38	—
2812[13]	**Hit The Bid (IRE)** (IPWilliams) **6-11-2** JRKavanagh (hld up: hdwy 8th: mstke & wknd 3 out: t.o)	2	6	66/1	41	—
3340[4]	**Little Jake (IRE)** (NoelChance) **7-11-2** RJohnson (prom tl wknd 8th: t.o)	22	7	5/1[3]	26	—
2696[21]	**Justjim** (NATwiston-Davies) **5-11-2** CLlewellyn (lw: a bhd: t.o)	6	8	20/1	21	—
1810[P]	**Stellar Force (IRE)** (OSherwood) **6-11-2** JAMcCarthy (led appr 3rd tl appr 4 out: wknd & p.u 2 out)		P	25/1	—	—
3052[7]	**Madam Polly** (MissPMWhittle) **5-10-8**(3) PHenley (lost pl 5th: t.o whn p.u bef 3 out)		P	50/1	—	—
1959[9]	**Blue And Royal (IRE) (70)** (VSoane) **5-11-2b** DerekByrne (trckd ldrs tl wknd 4 out: p.u bef 2 out)		P	25/1	—	—
3235[9]	**Act In Time (IRE)** (TRGeorge) **5-11-2** PNiven (led tl appr 3rd: wknd 4 out: t.o whn p.u bef 2 out)		P	20/1	—	—
2926[R]	**Typhoon (IRE)** (MarkCampion) **7-11-2** LHarvey (a bhd: t.o 8th: p.u bef 2 out)		P	66/1	—	—

(SP 122.6%) **13 Rn**

5m 40.2 (24.20) CSF £23.57 TOTE £5.70: £1.70 £1.60 £1.50 (£9.70) Trio £6.70 OWNER English Badminton Partnership (CHELTENHAM) BRED E. Peary
WEIGHT FOR AGE 4yo-9lb
3108 Mahler kicked on from a long way out, and looked to be a sitting duck once in line for home, but he found extra under a very strong ride and simply refused to be beaten. (5/1)
2661 Dublin Freddy could be a useful individual once he gets his act together, but he was very clumsy on this hurdling debut, though he showed enough to suggest he will make the grade. (9/2: 3/1-5/1)
3222 Toby Brown travelled comfortably, and looked to hold all the aces entering the straight, but with the winner in no mood to give best, he was far from foot-perfect over the last two, and had to admit he had met his match. (5/4)

T/Jkpt: £23,825.00 (0.5 Tckts); £16,778.21 to Cheltenham 11/3/97. T/Plpt: £3.40 (4,952.9 Tckts). T/Qdpt: £2.20 (353.39 Tckts) IM

3337-TAUNTON (R-H) (Good, Good to Soft patches)

Monday March 10th

WEATHER: fine

3588 SHEPTON MALLET CONDITIONAL H'CAP CHASE (0-105) (5-Y.O+) (Class F)

2-00 (2-00) **2m 110y (13 fncs)** £2,556.00 (£716.00: £348.00) GOING minus 0.20 sec per fur (G)

	Horse / details	Dist	Pl	SP	RR	SF
3336[7]	**Dr Rocket (77)** (RDickin) **12-9-9v**(8) XAizpuru (hld up: trckd ldr fr 5th: led 3 out: rdn appr last: r.o wl)	—	1	100/30[3]	80	—
2674[8]	**Lasata (102)** (RMCarson) **12-11-9**(5) JPower (hld up: hit 3rd: hdwy 3 out: ev ch whn hit last: rdn & nt qckn)	2	2	9/1	103	9
3188[3]	**Chris's Glen (75)** (JMBradley) **8-10-1v**ow1 MichaelBrennan (chsd ldr: hit 4th: lft in ld 5th: rdn & hdd 3 out: sn wknd)	14	3	11/4[2]	63	—
3342[8]	**Givry (IRE) (80)** (GMMcCourt) **7-9-10**(10) RHobson (led tl fell 5th)		F	6/1	—	—

				SP	RR	SF
3206[2]	**Fenwick (82)** (RJHodges) **10-10-5**(3) TDascombe (lw: hld up: cl 3rd whn blnd & uns rdr 9th)		U	9/4 1	—	—
				(SP 104.8%)		**5 Rn**

4m 12.3 (12.30) CSF £22.29 TOTE £3.40: £1.90 £3.80 (£12.00) OWNER The Rocketeers (STRATFORD) BRED Noel Fenton
LONG HANDICAP Chris's Glen 9-10
3053 Dr Rocket, disappointing last time, came back to form in an uncompetitive race off a 5lb lower mark. (100/30)
1769 Lasata, dropped 5lb, caused a real threat until outjumped at the final fence. (9/1: op 5/1)
3188 Chris's Glen, 4lb out of the handicap, would not have minded faster ground. (11/4)
3115 Givry (IRE) (6/1: op 4/1)
3206 Fenwick, down 3lb, gave his rider no chance of staying aboard. (9/4)

3589 MELODY MAN CHALLENGE CUP H'CAP HURDLE (0-110) (4-Y.O+) (Class E)

2-30 (2-30) **2m 3f 110y (10 hdls)** £2,242.50 (£630.00: £307.50) GOING minus 0.20 sec per fur (G)

				SP	RR	SF
3447[2]	**Fontanays (IRE) (91)** (GMMcCourt) **9-10-3v1**(7) RHobson (sn chsng ldr: led 7th: sn clr: rdn appr last:r.o wl)	—	1	11/4 1	72	23
3362[9]	**Desert Force (IRE) (92)** (GFierro) **8-10-11** RFarrant (lw: hld up: hdwy 7th: chsd wnr after 3 out: no imp)	9	2	11/2 3	66	17
3362[11]	**Miss Marigold (92)** (RJHodges) **8-10-8b**(3) TDascombe (hld up: rdn after 6th: hdwy appr 3 out: wknd appr 2 out)	7	3	5/1 2	60	11
3549[3]	**Shahrani (105)** (MCPipe) **5-11-10b1** JamieEvans (prom: mstke 7th: wknd 3 out)	13	4	11/4 1	62	13
	Frown (97) (PBowen) **7-11-2** MAFitzgerald (hld up: rdn & hdwy appr 7th: wknd 3 out)	5	5	11/2 3	50	1
3499[11]	**Concinnity (USA) (82)** (BScriven) **8-9-8**(7)ow1 MGriffiths (nt j.w: mstke 1st: bhd most of wy)	1½	6	25/1	34	—
1984[7]	**Sheep Stealer (86)** (REPeacock) **9-10-0**(5) ChrisWebb (led: j.slowly 2nd: hdd & mstke 7th: sn wknd: t.o)	18	7	11/1	23	—
				(SP 112.9%)		**7 Rn**

4m 36.3 (5.30) CSF £16.17 TOTE £3.40: £1.40 £2.80 (£6.70) OWNER Mr M. A. Dore (WANTAGE) BRED F. Feeney
LONG HANDICAP Concinnity (USA) 9-1
STEWARDS' ENQUIRY Evans susp. 19-20/3/97 (incorrect use of whip).
3447 Fontanays (IRE), reverting to more positive tactics, turned the race into a procession in the first-time visor. (11/4)
1718 Desert Force (IRE) is 9lb higher than when winning on his seasonal debut. (11/2)
3112 Miss Marigold could only mount a short-lived effort. (5/1)
3549 Shahrani, making a quick reappearance, did not find the fitting of first-time blinkers doing the trick. (11/4)

3590 MARCH (S) HURDLE (4, 5 & 6-Y.O) (Class G)

3-00 (3-01) **2m 1f (9 hdls)** £1,889.00 (£529.00: £257.00) GOING minus 0.20 sec per fur (G)

				SP	RR	SF
3284[10]	**Hawanafa (70)** (MissKMGeorge) **4-10-3** CMaude (a.p: led appr 2 out: drvn out)	—	1	4/1 2	53	—
3471[3]	**A S Jim** (OO'Neill) **6-11-2** VSlattery (led: hrd rdn & hdd appr 2 out: ev ch last: nt qckn)	2½	2	7/2 1	56	6
3338[8]	**Denomination (USA) (80)** (MCPipe) **5-11-9**(7) BMoore (plld hrd: a.p: one pce fr 3 out)	15	3	7/1	56	6
2813[8]	**Paulton (65)** (KBishop) **4-10-8** RGreene (nvr nr to chal)	2½	4	7/1	39	—
3115[10]	**Song of Kenda** (BRMillman) **5-10-6**(5) DSalter (prom to 6th)	½	5	10/1	34	—
2818[F]	**Rose of Glenn** (BPalling) **6-10-11** TJenks (lw: prom: j.slowly 5th: wknd after 3 out)	5	6	5/1 3	29	—
3235[16]	**Mac'smyuncle** (RGFrost) **6-11-2** MrAHoldsworth (rdn appr 6th: a bhd)	2½	7	25/1	32	—
2655[P]	**Miss Night Owl** (RGFrost) **6-10-11** JFrost (hld up & bhd: hdwy on ins after 3 out: 4th whn j.lft 2 out: sn wknd)	8	8	20/1	19	—
	Ndaba (MissKMGeorge) **6-10-13**(3) TDascombe (bit bkwd: hdwy 6th: wknd 3 out)	5	9	20/1	19	—
3115[13]	**Fiery Footsteps** (CLPopham) **5-10-4**(7) TO'Connor (a bhd: t.o)	dist	10	25/1	—	—
2872[12]	**Chalcuchima** (NJHawke) **4-10-8** JRailton (a bhd: t.o whn p.u bef 2 out)		P	20/1	—	—
3431[F]	**Kirby Moorside (49)** (DJMinty) **6-11-2** SBurrough (prom tl wknd qckly after 5th: sn t.o: p.u bef 3 out)		P	33/1	—	—
				(SP 117.9%)		**12 Rn**

4m 2.6 (9.60) CSF £15.00 TOTE £4.50: £1.60 £1.70 £3.00 (£5.60) Trio £13.20 OWNER Mr Geo Taylor (ASTON ROWANT) BRED Mrs D. Hammerson
WEIGHT FOR AGE 4yo-8lb
Bt in 3,200 gns
3058 Hawanafa had changed hands for only 1,100 guineas at Ascot Sales two weeks ago. (4/1: op 5/2)
3471 A S Jim adopted totally different tactics. (7/2)
1425 Denomination (USA) seems more effective on faster ground. (7/1: op 4/1)
2574 Paulton never posed a threat. (7/1: op 4/1)
Song of Kenda was dropped into a seller on only her second run. (10/1)

3591 ROYAL BATH & WEST NOVICES' CHASE (5-Y.O+) (Class D)

3-30 (3-30) **2m 3f (15 fncs)** £3,355.00 (£1,015.00: £495.00: £235.00) GOING minus 0.20 sec per fur (G)

				SP	RR	SF
3538[3]	**After The Fox (80)** (NJHawke) **10-10-9**(7) MrJTizzard (lw: hld up: hdwy 8th: led 4 out: clr whn nt fluent last)	—	1	4/1 3	96	—
3188[U]	**Mozemo (84)** (MCPipe) **10-11-2** JamieEvans (sn chsng ldr: mstke 6th: led 8th to 4 out: sn rdn: one pce)	9	2	15/8 2	88	—
3111[3]	**Lucky Eddie (IRE) (99)** (PJHobbs) **6-11-2b** CMaude (led to 8th: wkng whn mstke 3 out)	29	3	10/11 1	64	—
3111[P]	**Rustic Flight (60)** (LWaring) **10-10-9**(7) MGriffiths (n j.w: sn bhd: t.o fr 5th)	24	4	50/1	44	—
				(SP 109.1%)		**4 Rn**

4m 58.8 (16.80) CSF £10.80 TOTE £4.30 (£4.80) OWNER Mrs Robert Blackburn (CHARD) BRED J. A. G. Meaden
3538 After The Fox finally broke his duck over fences in an uncompetitive event. (4/1)
2876 Mozemo proved no match for the winner from the third last. (15/8)
3111 Lucky Eddie (IRE) looked in trouble as early as the tenth. (10/11: evens-5/6)

3592 BATH & WEST MEMBERS MAIDEN HURDLE (4-Y.O+) (Class F)

4-00 (4-01) **2m 3f 110y (10 hdls)** £2,249.50 (£632.00: £308.50) GOING minus 0.20 sec per fur (G)

				SP	RR	SF
3359[3]	**Fasil (IRE)** (NJHWalker) **4-10-10** TJenks (prom tl lost pl 6th: hdwy 3 out: led appr 2 out: drvn out)	—	1	7/4 1	77	21
3233[8]	**Kinnescash (IRE)** (PBowen) **4-10-10** MAFitzgerald (lw: a.p: ev ch 2 out: hrd rdn & nt qckn flat)	2½	2	12/1	75	19
	Lord Mills (IRE) (NoelChance) **6-11-5** TJMurphy (hld up: hdwy appr 6th: ev ch 2 out: one pce flat)	1¼	3	10/1	75	27
3197[4]	**Country Lover** (MCPipe) **6-11-5b** JamieEvans (prom: ev ch 3 out: wknd appr 2 out)	12	4	7/1 3	65	17
3103[3]	**Keen Bid (IRE)** (MrsLRichards) **6-11-5** MRichards (prom: led 6th tl hdd & wknd qckly appr 2 out)	6	5	10/1	60	12
	The Parsons Fox (CaptTAForster) **5-11-5** SWynne (nvr nr ldrs)	8	6	33/1	54	6

				SP	RR	SF
3431[3]	**Amber Ring (70)** (MissKMGeorge) **4-10-5** CMaude (bhd fr 7th)	5	**7**	40/1	44	—
3365[5]	**Miss Match** (LGCottrell) **6-10-9**(5) DSalter (bhd fr 7th)	2	**8**	33/1	43	—
3500[U]	**Cool Virtue (IRE)** (CaptTAForster) **6-11-0** AThornton (bhd fr 7th)	½	**9**	9/2[2]	42	—
3342[4]	**Roll Again** (MCPipe) **6-11-0**(5) GSupple (lw: bhd fr 7th: t.o)	10	**10**	25/1	39	—
3359[17]	**Churchworth** (MissHCKnight) **6-11-5** JRailton (led to 2nd: wknd qckly 6th: t.o whn p.u bef 7th)		**P**	33/1	—	—
3364[5]	**Carlingford Gale (IRE)** (TRGeorge) **6-11-0** RFarrant (lw: plld hrd: led 2nd: mstke 5th: hdd 6th: wknd qckly: t.o whn p.u bef 2 out)		**P**	10/1	—	—
2661[13]	**St Mabyn Inn Boy** (PRRodford) **5-11-5** SBurrough (a bhd: t.o 6th: p.u bef 2 out)		**P**	100/1	—	—
	Milestone (NGAyliffe) **5-11-2**(3) TDascombe (bhd: rdn after 5th: t.o whn p.u bef 7th)		**P**	150/1	—	—

(SP 118.8%) **14 Rn**

4m 36.7 (5.70) CSF £21.13 TOTE £2.20: £1.80 £2.20 £4.10 (£15.40) Trio £124.20 OWNER Mr Tony Usher (BLEWBURY) BRED Ballyvolane Stud

WEIGHT FOR AGE 4yo-8lb

3359 Fasil (IRE) showed his Ludlow run to be no fluke, but made quite hard work of it over this longer trip. (7/4: evens-15/8)
3109 Kinnescash (IRE) had a longer distance this time, but could not cope with the winner. (12/1)
Lord Mills (IRE) had some reasonable form in bumpers, and made a satisfactory start to his hurdling career. (10/1: 8/1-12/1)
3197 Country Lover did not seem to benefit from this longer distance. (7/1: 5/1-8/1)
3103 Keen Bid (IRE) may need a stiffer test of stamina if his Flat form is anything to go by. (10/1: op 4/1)

3593 SOMERSET HUNTERS' CHASE (6-Y.O+) (Class H)

4-30 (4-30) **3m (19 fncs)** £1,040.00 (£290.00: £140.00) GOING minus 0.20 sec per fur (G)

				SP	RR	SF
	Full Alirt (MissSusanYoung) **9-11-7**(7) MissSYoung (led 5th: r.o wl)	—	**1**	11/2[3]	93	—
3353[2]	**Granville Guest** (PFNicholls) **11-12-5**(7) MrJTizzard (a.p: chsd wnr fr 12th: rdn & ev ch whn hit last: edgd lft: wknd flat)	7	**2**	11/8[1]	100	5
	Ragtime Boy (MissSClarke) **9-12-0**(5) MrAFarrant (bhd tl hdwy 13th: wknd appr 3 out)	17	**3**	3/1[2]	82	—
1063[P]	**Artful Arthur** (LPGrassick) **11-11-12**(7) MrJGrassick (bhd: rdn after 12th: sn t.o)	21	**4**	20/1	68	—
	Prince Nepal (TerryHopkins) **13-12-5**(7) MrGBarfoot-Saunt (lft in ld 1st: hit 2nd: hdd 3rd: hit 6th & 7th: wknd 13th: t.o)	5	**5**	40/1	72	—
	Mo's Chorister (MrsJMarsh) **11-11-12**(7) MissFWilson (led tl fell 1st)		**F**	33/1	—	—
	Great Pokey (MissNellCourtenay) **12-12-5**(7) MissNCourtenay (led 3rd to 5th: wknd after 12th: sn t.o: p.u bef 3 out)		**P**	9/1	—	—
	Doubting Donna (MrsDHughes) **11-12-2**(5) MrJJukes (bhd: reminders appr 11th: hdwy 13th: 4th whn blnd & uns rdr 15th)		**U**	9/1	—	—

(SP 112.6%) **8 Rn**

6m 19.2 (22.20) CSF £12.53 TOTE £9.00: £2.90 £1.10 £1.40 (£6.10) OWNER Mr B. R. J. Young (LISKEARD) BRED B. R. J. and M. C. Young

Full Alirt, four times a winner between the flags, jumped much better than when eventually falling here nearly a year ago. (11/2: op 7/2)
3353 Granville Guest could never really bustle up the winner over the last three fences. (11/8)
Ragtime Boy had won by a distance on his only previous race this season at Lemalla. (3/1)
Doubting Donna was just getting into the race when coming to grief. (9/1)

3594 WIDCOMBE NOVICES' H'CAP HURDLE (0-95) (4-Y.O+) (Class F)

5-00 (5-01) **2m 1f (9 hdls)** £2,123.50 (£596.00: £290.50) GOING minus 0.20 sec per fur (G)

				SP	RR	SF
1675[4]	**Siberian Mystic (79)** (PGMurphy) **4-10-12** CMaude (lw: hld up: hdwy appr 3 out: led appr last: comf)	—	**1**	11/2[1]	64+	20
3359[9]	**Geisway (CAN) (78)** (NJHWalker) **7-11-5** TJenks (lw: a.p: led 3 out tl appr last: one pce)	7	**2**	15/2	56	20
	Dovetto (76) (AEPrice) **8-11-3** SWynne (hld up & bhd: gd hdwy 3 out: one pce fr 2 out)	1¾	**3**	25/1	53	17
3204[2]	**Dissolve (77)** (NMLampard) **5-10-11**(7) MrLBaker (a.p: led 6th to 3 out: ev ch whn hit 2 out: one pce)	nk	**4**	10/1	54	18
3186[5]	**Fastini Gold (75)** (RJPrice) **5-11-2** MAFitzgerald (nvr plcd to chal)	¾	**5**	10/1	51	15
3359[10]	**Blaze of Song (82)** (DJWintle) **5-11-9** MRichards (lw: nvr nr to chal)	4	**6**	7/1[3]	54	18
3338[2]	**Saafi (IRE) (70)** (RJBaker) **6-10-11b** VSlattery (prom: led 5th to 6th: wknd appr 2 out)	2	**7**	16/1	40	4
3186[F]	**Ranger Sloane (81)** (GFierro) **5-11-8** RFarrant (hld up mid div: hung rt 3 out: sn bhd)	2½	**8**	6/1[2]	49	13
3337[5]	**Moonlight Escapade (IRE) (77)** (RJHodges) **6-10-11**(7) JHarris (blnd 1st: a bhd)	10	**9**	11/1	35	—
2925[9]	**Still Here (IRE) (76)** (PBowen) **4-10-6**(3) MichaelBrennan (lw: dropped rr 5th: t.o)	11	**10**	14/1	24	—
3338[*]	**Blade of Fortune (86)** (VGGreenway) **9-11-6**(7) MrJTizzard (lw: led tl after 2nd: wknd 5th: t.o)	2½	**11**	7/1[3]	32	—
3424[7]	**Daunt (84)** (FJordan) **5-11-11** AThornton (led after 2nd to 5th: wknd 6th: t.o)	3½	**12**	12/1	26	—
3233[13]	**Dormy Three (84)** (RJHodges) **7-11-8b**1(3) TDascombe (a bhd: t.o whn p.u bef 2 out)		**P**	16/1	—	—

(SP 122.9%) **13 Rn**

3m 58.5 (5.50) CSF £43.92 CT £887.02 TOTE £8.80: £2.40 £4.30 £18.30 (£45.30) Trio £631.60 OWNER Glenferry And Partners (BRISTOL) BRED Deerfield Farm

WEIGHT FOR AGE 4yo-8lb

1675 Siberian Mystic, coming back after a winter break, scored with a fair bit in hand. (11/2)
3283 Geisway (CAN) ran his best race over timber to date. (15/2)
Dovetto gave a good account of himself having been off-course for nearly eighteen months. (25/1)
3204 Dissolve was 6lb higher than when winning a seller over course and distance last month. (10/1)
3050 Fastini Gold would have preferred faster ground, and appeared to be given a quiet run. (10/1)
3148 Blaze of Song had probably run too freely when tried in blinkers in a hot race at Ludlow last time. (7/1)
918 Moonlight Escapade (IRE) (11/1: 8/1-14/1)
2886 Daunt (12/1: op 7/1)

T/Plpt: £57.60 (149.61 Tckts). T/Qdpt: £14.00 (38.51 Tckts) KH

2771-CHELTENHAM (L-H) (Good)

Tuesday March 11th

WEATHER: fine & warm

3595 CITROEN SUPREME NOVICES' HURDLE (Gd 1) (4-Y.O+) (Class A)

2-00 (2-00) **2m 110y (Old) (8 hdls)** £45,884.60 (£17,131.40: £8,345.70: £3,553.50: £1,556.75: £758.05) GOING:0.10 sec per fur (G)

Form	Horse / Details	Dist	Pos	SP	RR	SF
3041*	**Shadow Leader** (CREgerton) **6-11-8** JOsborne (lw: hld up: hdwy appr 3 out: led 2 out: pushed clr flat)	—	1	5/1 [2]	108+	85
3154*	**Princeful (IRE) (107)** (MrsJPitman) **6-11-8** RFarrant (lw: hld up: hdwy 5th: styd on flat: no ch w wnr)	10	2	25/1	98	75
2573U	**Nordic Breeze (IRE) (102)** (MCPipe) **5-11-8** DWalsh (hld up & bhd: hdwy appr 3 out: rdn & ev ch next: one pce)	½	3	100/1	98?	75
3275*	**Wade Road (IRE) (115)** (MissHCKnight) **6-11-8** JCulloty (chsd ldrs: mstke 3rd: ev ch 2 out: 3rd & btn whn mstke last)	4	4	12/1	94	71
2857a3	**Graphic Equaliser (IRE)** (FJLacy,Ireland) **5-11-8** DTEvans (hdwy to chse ldrs 4th: ev ch 2 out: rdn & wknd appr last)	3½	5	12/1	91	68
2995a4	**Three Scholars** (WPMullins,Ireland) **6-11-8** DJCasey (hld up: hdwy 4th: lft in ld 3 out: hdd next: sn btn)	1¼	6	20/1	89	66
1950*	**Deano's Beeno** (MCPipe) **5-11-8** CMaude (prom tl wknd 3 out)	2	7	14/1	87	64
32984	**Polydamas** (KCBailey) **5-11-8** CO'Dwyer (lw: hdwy whn mstke 4th: n.d after)	5	8	33/1	83	60
3143*	**Queen of Spades (IRE) (120)** (NATwiston-Davies) **7-11-3** CLlewellyn (lw: led after 1st: hdd & hmpd 3 out: bdly hmpd next: nt rcvr)	s.h	9	15/2	78	55
31972	**Whip Hand (IRE)** (JGFitzGerald) **6-11-8** GBradley (lw: plld hrd: prom: blnd 3rd: ev ch 3 out: blnd & hmpd next: sn t.o)	dist	10	14/1	—	—
2995a2	**Finnegan's Hollow (IRE)** (APO'Brien,Ireland) **7-11-8** CFSwan (a.p: led & fell 3 out)		F	2/1 [1]	—	—
3233*	**The Flying Phantom** (MHTompkins) **6-11-8** PNiven (led tl after 1st: fell 2nd)		F	20/1	—	—
32982	**Mister Rm (110)** (NATwiston-Davies) **5-11-8** DBridgwater (lw: hld up: hdwy on ins appr 3 out: ev ch whn fell next)		F	25/1	—	—
32752	**Kailash (USA) (118)** (MCPipe) **6-11-8** APMcCoy (in rr tl fell last)		F	20/1	—	—
	Humbel (USA) (DKWeld,Ireland) **5-11-8b** RDunwoody (lw: chsd ldr tl wknd qckly after 4th: t.o whn p.u bef 3 out)		P	7/1 [3]	—	—
32833	**Smolensk (IRE) (100)** (JBerry) **5-11-8** MAFitzgerald (a bhd: t.o whn p.u bef 2 out)		P	200/1	—	—

(SP 129.4%) **16 Rn**

3m 49.5 (1.10 under best) (-1.50) CSF £120.65 TOTE £5.50: £2.40 £6.50 £25.40 (£69.60) Trio £6,294.60; £4,521.50 to Cheltenham 12/3/97
OWNER Mr James Blackshaw (CHADDLEWORTH) BRED A. J. Sexton

3041* Shadow Leader retained his unbeaten record over hurdles with a very impressive performance, taking more than a second off the track record. If ground conditions remain in his favour, he will attempt a repeat performance at Aintree. (5/1)

3154* Princeful (IRE) handled this step up in class surprisingly well, and though he could not get within striking range of the winner, this was his best effort yet. (25/1)

2573 Nordic Breeze (IRE), brought back to the minimum trip, was almost upsides the winner at the penultimate flight, but was fighting a losing battle despite running on. (100/1)

3275* Wade Road (IRE) had the fast ground he requires, but he made mistakes at a crucial time and a last-flight error probably cost him third prize. (12/1)

2857a Graphic Equaliser (IRE) has not yet raced on such lively ground as this, and he found the quickening tempo too much for him between the last two. (12/1)

2995a Three Scholars, left with a marginal advantage at the third last, was in trouble when the winner took over at the next. (20/1)

3143* Queen of Spades (IRE) was a shade unfortunate not to run into the prizes, for she was extremely lucky not to be brought down at the penultimate hurdle, which put paid to her chances. (15/2)

2995a Finnegan's Hollow (IRE) had the full following of the Irish contingent, and he was in the right place when he departed at the third last. (2/1)

3298 Mister Rm took closer order on the inside approaching the third last and was challenging for the lead when coming a purler at the next.(25/1)

3596 GUINNESS ARKLE CHALLENGE TROPHY NOVICES' CHASE (Gd 1) (5-Y.O+) (Class A)

2-35 (2-35) **2m (Old) (12 fncs)** £53,762.00 (£19,958.00: £9,629.00: £3,995.00: £1,647.50: £708.50) GOING: 0.10 sec per fur (G)

Form	Horse / Details	Dist	Pos	SP	RR	SF
20542	**Or Royal (FR) (135)** (MCPipe) **6-11-8b1** APMcCoy (lw: a.p: mstkes 8th & 2 out: chal last: rdn to ld flat)	—	1	11/2 [2]	143	79
31672	**Squire Silk** (AndrewTurnell) **8-11-8** JOsborne (lw: hdwy 5th: hit 7th: led 2 out tl flat: hrd rdn & no ex)	½	2	11/2 [2]	143	79
32962	**Celibate (IRE) (132)** (CJMann) **6-11-8** JRailton (led tl after 1st: ev ch 3 out: one pce fr next)	6	3	13/2 [3]	137	73
3296*	**Flying Instructor** (PRWebber) **7-11-8** RBellamy (chsd ldrs: rdn & outpcd 8th: styd on fr 2 out)	1¾	4	8/1	135	71
3015*	**Lightening Lad** (JSKing) **9-11-8** CMaude (lw: prom: lft in ld 4 out: hdd & mstke 2 out: sn btn: lame)	1½	5	11/1	133	69
3260aF	**Penndara (IRE)** (APO'Brien,Ireland) **8-11-8** CFSwan (hld up: bhd fr 8th: t.o)	18	6	33/1	115	51
3260aP	**Beakstown (IRE)** (WPMullins,Ireland) **8-11-8** TPTreacy (nt j.w: a bhd: t.o fr ½-wy)	nk	7	33/1	115	51
3167*	**Mulligan (IRE) (150)** (DNicholson) **7-11-8** RDunwoody (swtg: led 2nd tl fell 4 out)		F	11/10 [1]	—	—
33005	**Guinda (IRE) (111)** (NATwiston-Davies) **7-11-3** CLlewellyn (hld up: hdwy on ins 4 out: sn rdn: mstke next: 6th & no ch whn blnd & uns rdr last)		U	66/1	—	—

(SP 118.5%) **9 Rn**

3m 52.5 (-0.50) CSF £33.18 TOTE £7.10: £1.90 £1.80 £1.40 (£21.90) Trio £25.80 OWNER Mr D. A. Johnson (WELLINGTON) BRED Haras du Mezeray S. A.

2054 Or Royal (FR), back on song on this return to two miles and helped in no small way by the re-introduction of blinkers, which he had worn before in France, proved the stronger in an all-out duel to the line. He obviously runs best when fresh. (11/2: 4/1-6/1)

3167 Squire Silk should have found the task much easier once the favourite had departed, and he looked all over the winner at the last, but maybe he made his move too soon and he was worried out of it up the hill. (11/2)

3296 Celibate (IRE) was lucky to find a leg at the final ditch four out, but he worked his way back into the action and was only tapped for toe approaching the last. He will now go on a recovery mission to Aintree. (13/2)

3296* Flying Instructor looked to be feeling the strain when getting left behind five out, but he stayed on well after getting his second wind and there are more races in him. (8/1)

3015* Lightening Lad, much more effective when he can get his toe in, nevertheless gave a good account of himself and he is gaining experience all the time. (11/1)

3167* Mulligan (IRE) set the pace, but could never quite put his stamp on proceedings and he had been joined when he came to grief at the final ditch. (11/10: evens-6/5)

3597 SMURFIT CHAMPION HURDLE CHALLENGE TROPHY(Gd 1) (4-Y.O+) (Class A)

3-15 (3-15) **2m 110y (Old) (8 hdls)** £124,138.00 (£46,342.00: £22,571.00: £9,605.00: £4,202.50: £2,041.50) GOING: 0.10 sec per fur (G)

	Horse / details	Dist	Pos	SP	RR	SF
3038*	**Make a Stand (152)** (MCPipe) **6-12-0** APMcCoy (mde all: clr fr 3rd: unchal)	—	**1**	7/1	147	96
3254a*	**Theatreworld (IRE)** (APO'Brien,Ireland) **5-12-0** NWilliamson (lw: hld up: effrt appr 2 out: styd on flat)	5	**2**	33/1	142	91
3523a*	**Space Trucker (IRE)** (MrsJHarrington,Ireland) **6-12-0** JShortt (lw: hld up: hdwy 4th: chsd wnr fr 3 out: rdn & one pce flat)	¾	**3**	9/2 3	141	90
2857a*	**I'm Supposin (IRE)** (KPrendergast,Ireland) **5-12-0** CFSwan (lw: trckd ldrs: hdwy appr 5th: rdn 2 out: one pce)	2	**4**	13/2	140+	89
2603a10	**Hill Society (IRE)** (NMeade,Ireland) **5-12-0** JFTitley (hld up in rr: hdwy appr 2 out: nvr nr to chal)	3½	**5**	100/1	136?	85
3298*	**Sanmartino (IRE)** (DNicholson) **5-12-0** RDunwoody (lw: hdwy appr 4th: rdn & wknd appr last)	s.h	**6**	9/1	136+	85
27742	**Pridwell (154)** (MCPipe) **7-12-0** CMaude (lw: hld up in rr: sme hdwy fr 3 out: nvr nrr)	¾	**7**	25/1	135	84
32934	**Moorish (138)** (NATwiston-Davies) **7-12-0** DBridgwater (lw: nvr nrr)	2	**8**	100/1	133	82
2740a*	**Cockney Lad (IRE)** (NMeade,Ireland) **8-12-0** JCulloty (a in rr)	4	**9**	33/1	130	79
32932	**Mistinguett (IRE) (148)** (NATwiston-Davies) **5-11-9** CLlewellyn (lw: swtg: chsd wnr to 3 out: sn rdn & wknd)	3	**10**	33/1	122	71
32315	**Zabadi (IRE) (139)** (DNicholson) **5-12-0** RJohnson (lw: bhd: hdwy 5th: wknd 3 out)	3	**11**	100/1	124	73
3254a4	**Dardjini (USA)** (NMeade,Ireland) **7-12-0** CO'Dwyer (hdwy 5th: outpcd 3 out: t.o)	8	**12**	50/1	116	65
26353	**Bimsey (IRE) (150)** (RAkehurst) **7-12-0** MAFitzgerald (lw: chsd ldrs tl rdn & wknd 5th: t.o)	1½	**13**	33/1	115	64
3231*	**Dreams End (129)** (PBowen) **9-12-0** RFarrant (lw: outpcd: t.o)	10	**14**	50/1	105	54
3254a2	**Guest Performance (IRE)** (DTHughes,Ireland) **5-12-0v1** RHughes (lw: chsd ldrs to 4th: bhd whn blnd 2 out: t.o)	1	**15**	100/1	104	53
2774*	**Large Action (IRE) (163)** (OSherwood) **9-12-0** JOsborne (lw: p.u after 2nd: lame)		**P**	7/2 1	—	—
3017*	**Collier Bay (175)** (JABOld) **7-12-0** GBradley (mstkes: dropped rr ½-wy: t.o whn p.u bef 3 out)		**P**	4/1 2	—	—

(SP 119.7%) **17 Rn**

3m 48.4 (1.10 under best) (-2.60) CSF £193.06 TOTE £8.60: £2.90 £6.60 £2.50 (£183.20) Trio £316.60 OWNER Mr P. A. Deal (WELLINGTON) BRED R. M. West

OFFICIAL EXPLANATION **Large Action (IRE): rider reported that the gelding did not appear his usual self at the start. The gelding appeared to lose his action approaching the first and, fearing he had gone lame, his rider pulled him up. The vet reported the horse to be slightly lame. Collier Bay: rider reported that the gelding made a bad mistake at the third and quickly lost interest, and that he was never going on ground too fast for him. The trainer added that the ground was faster than he had anticipated.**

3038* Make a Stand made mincemeat of some highly thought-of rivals with another all-the-way success which lowered the course record in the process. Hardly out of the novice stage, he must have been some certainty in the handicaps he won earlier in the season. (7/1: 5/1-8/1)

3254a* Theatreworld (IRE) made up a lot of ground in the last half-mile, and won the race for the runner-up prize, but was unable to get within striking range of the winner. (33/1)

3523a* Space Trucker (IRE) tried hard not to let the winner get away, but it took its toll and he was galloping on the spot on reaching the flat. (9/2)

2857a* I'm Supposin (IRE) was thrown in at the deep end here, but he is a useful performer on the Flat and had won both his races over hurdles, and could be all the rage if he turns up here in twelve months' time. (13/2)

2461a Hill Society (IRE) has been tackling the best at home, but he seemed to find the pace much too fast and was unable to start picking them up until far too late. (100/1)

3298* Sanmartino (IRE) did not impress to post, but he was close enough to pose a threat coming down the hill until his stride shortened between the last two. (9/1)

2774* Large Action (IRE) attracted a strong following that saw him go off as favourite, but backers soon knew their fate as he was pulled up feelingly after jumping the second. (7/2)

3017* Collier Bay clouted the third flight hard and quickly dropped out of contention and, on ground that was not ideal, his jockey wisely pulled him up. (4/1)

3598 ASTEC BUZZ SHOP NATIONAL HUNT H'CAP CHASE (5-Y.O+) (Class B)

3-55 (3-55) **3m 1f (Old) (19 fncs)** £34,414.00 (£10,312.00: £4,956.00: £2,278.00) GOING: 0.10 sec per fur (G)

	Horse / details	Dist	Pos	SP	RR	SF
3046P	**Flyer's Nap (137)** (RHAlner) **11-11-2** DBridgwater (swtg: hld up & bhd: stdy hdwy appr 3 out: rdn appr last: led flat: r.o)	—	**1**	20/1	145	57
1354*	**Stormtracker (IRE) (121)** (CWeedon) **8-10-0** MRichards (lw: led 2nd to 5th: led 10th to 12th: led 3 out tl after next: led last: hdd & no ex towards fin)	1½	**2**	25/1	128	40
2782*	**General Command (IRE) (137)** (GRichards) **9-11-2** JOsborne (lw: led 5th to 10th: led 12th to 3 out: kpt on u.p: fin lame)	1¾	**3**	9/4 1	143	55
33612	**Romany Creek (IRE) (121)** (JPearce) **8-10-0v** JCulloty (hld up: hdwy 10th: led after 2 out to last: rdn & no ex flat)	½	**4**	25/1	127	39
33024	**Call it a Day (IRE) (138)** (DNicholson) **7-11-3** RJohnson (hld up: hdwy 10th: rdn & ev ch 2 out: one pce flat)	nk	**5**	9/1	143	55
3302*	**Mudahim (129)** (MrsJPitman) **11-10-8** RFarrant (hdwy 6th: mstke 12th: sn lost pl: styd on again flat)	4	**6**	5/1 2	132	44
27753	**Yorkshire Gale (137)** (JTGifford) **11-11-2** NWilliamson (lw: chsd ldrs: ev ch 2 out: rdn & wknd appr last)	1	**7**	11/1	139	51
32305	**Kadi (GER) (138)** (DNicholson) **8-11-3** RDunwoody (hld up: hdwy 13th: mstke 15th: n.d after)	½	**8**	8/1 3	140	52
3302P	**Sibton Abbey (132)** (GAHubbard) **12-10-8**(3) MichaelBrennan (a bhd: t.o)	22	**9**	66/1	120	32
2636P	**Grange Brake (125)** (NATwiston-Davies) **11-10-4b** DWalsh (prom: rdn 12th: wknd 4 out: t.o)	14	**10**	33/1	104	16
13668	**Bavard Dieu (IRE) (135)** (NAGaselee) **9-11-0** CLlewellyn (in rr whn blnd 11th: sn t.o)	1	**11**	33/1	113	25
34203	**River Mandate (123)** (CaptTAForster) **10-10-2b** APMcCoy (lw: hld up in tch: hmpd & fell 12th)		**F**	8/1 3	—	—
31476	**James Pigg (130)** (PFNicholls) **10-10-9** MAFitzgerald (swtg: a bhd: t.o whn p.u bef 8th)		**P**	25/1	—	—
32304	**Maamur (USA) (145)** (CaptTAForster) **9-11-10** AThornton (lw: led to 2nd: prom whn j.rt & cannoned into12th: broke leg & p.u: dead)		**P**	9/1	—	—

(SP 121.7%) **14 Rn**

6m 13.8 (4.80) CSF £363.28 CT £1,432.48 TOTE £35.40: £6.70 £3.00 £1.80 (£211.80) Trio £440.50 OWNER Mr R. J. Tory (BLANDFORD) BRED R. J. and Mrs Tory

LONG HANDICAP Stormtracker (IRE) 9-5 Romany Creek (IRE) 9-10

OFFICIAL EXPLANATION **Flyer's Nap: accounting for the improvement in form, the trainer reported that the gelding's previous run had come too soon.**

2881* Flyer's Nap, winner of the Kim Muir here in 1995, has done all his winning on a much easier surface, but he showed he can handle all types of ground with a strong, late challenge that was timed to perfection. (20/1)

1354* Stormtracker (IRE), 9lb out of the handicap, ran a cracker on this first outing in four months, and he battled so hard all the way that he did not deserve to be beaten. (25/1)
2782* General Command (IRE) finished on three legs after being a leading contender from the start, and it is to be hoped that the injury does not curtail his career. (9/4)
3361 Romany Creek (IRE) made relentless progress and struck the front soon after the second last, but the hill caught him out and he was forced to give best. (25/1)
3302 Call it a Day (IRE), one of several in with every chance at the penultimate fence, kept answering his rider's every call, but found an extra effort beyond him up the final climb. (9/1)
3302* Mudahim ran a fine race on going that did not favour him, and had he not lost ground out in the country, could well have taken a hand in the outcome. (5/1)
2775 Yorkshire Gale has turned in some of his best performances at this track, and he once again gave it his best shot and was only shaken off on the run to the last. He gave the impression that he was feeling the ground. (11/1)
3420 River Mandate (8/1: 6/1-9/1)
3230 Maamur (USA) (9/1: 6/1-10/1)

3599 FULKE WALWYN KIM MUIR CHALLENGE CUP AMATEUR H'CAP CHASE (5-Y.O+) (Class B)

4-30 (4-30) **3m 1f (Old) (19 fncs)** £21,362.50 (£6,400.00: £3,075.00: £1,412.50) GOING: 0.10 sec per fur (G)

				SP	RR	SF
3302[2]	**King Lucifer (IRE) (132)** (DNicholson) **8-11-5**(5) MrRThornton (a.p: led after 4 out: hrd rdn flat: all out)	—	**1**	7/2[2]	145	77
3383a[4]	**Time for a Run (130)** (EJO'Grady,Ireland) **10-11-8** MrPFenton (hld up: hdwy 13th: ev ch fr last: no ex nr fin)	nk	**2**	15/8[1]	143	75
2940*	**Lucky Dollar (IRE) (108)** (KCBailey) **9-9-7**(7) MrOMcPhail (hld up & bhd: rdn 3 out: hdwy next: styd on)	15	**3**	20/1	111	43
3230[6]	**All for Luck (126)** (MCPipe) **12-11-1**(3) MrBRHamilton (hld up: hdwy 4 out: wknd appr last)	5	**4**	16/1	126	58
3428[6]	**Danger Baby (108)** (DLWilliams) **7-9-7v**(7) MrSDurack (chsd ldrs: wkng whn mstke 3 out)	2	**5**	40/1	107	39
3266[4]	**Camelot Knight (117)** (NATwiston-Davies) **11-10-6**(3) MrMRimell (led to 5th: rdn 13th: outpcd 4 out: rallied & ev ch next: sn wknd)	7	**6**	12/1	111	43
3036[P]	**Bradbury Star (129)** (JTGifford) **12-11-0**(7) MrPO'Keeffe (prom tl wknd 13th: t.o)	24	**7**	25/1	108	40
3018[P]	**So Far Bold (IRE) (115)** (IPWilliams) **7-10-2b**(5)ow6 MrTDoumen (mstke 3rd: led 5th: sn clr: j.slowly 4 out: sn hdd: hit next: sn wknd: t.o)	8	**8**	20/1	89	15
2928[U]	**Christmas Gorse (120)** (NAGaselee) **11-10-5**(7) MrPScott (a bhd: t.o)	6	**9**	8/1	90	22
3047[2]	**Lord of the West (IRE) (110)** (JJO'Neill) **8-9-13**(3) MrCBonner (a in rr: fell 12th)		**F**	15/2[3]	—	—
3230[F]	**Cherrynut (130)** (PFNicholls) **8-11-1**(7) MrJTizzard (swtg: a bhd: rdn 11th: t.o whn p.u bef 15th)		**P**	8/1	—	—
				(SP 120.4%)	**11 Rn**	

6m 9.6 (0.60) CSF £9.73 CT £106.09 TOTE £4.20: £1.90 £1.70 £1.90 (£4.40) Trio £15.90 OWNER Mr A. J. Davies (TEMPLE GUITING) BRED P. Downes
LONG HANDICAP Danger Baby 9-9 Lucky Dollar (IRE) 9-5
STEWARDS' ENQUIRY Fenton susp. 20-22 & 24/3/97 (excessive & improper use of whip).
3302 King Lucifer (IRE) had to work really hard to win this, but his heart is in the right place and he was determined to fight to the end. (7/2: 5/2-4/1)
3383a Time for a Run was never really happy on such fast ground, but he stuck to the task in hand and is still a likely contender for the Grand National. (15/8)
2940* Lucky Dollar (IRE) was only 2lb wrong at the weights with his rider's allowance and, staying on inside the last half-mile, did well to make the frame. (20/1)
All for Luck can handle all types of ground, but he was never able to get close enough to cause concern. (16/1)
3428 Danger Baby kept tabs on the leaders, but he was beginning to tire when an untidy mistake at the third last was the final straw. (40/1)
3018 Camelot Knight needs cut to produce his best, but did not fare badly on this occasion and all is not lost yet. (12/1)
2773 Bradbury Star has reportedly been retired after a fine career. (25/1)

3600 HAMLET EXTRA MILD CIGARS GOLD CARD (FINAL) H'CAP HURDLE (4-Y.O+) (Class B)

5-05 (5-06) **3m 2f (Old) (13 hdls)** £27,910.00 (£8,380.00: £4,040.00: £1,870.00) GOING: 0.10 sec per fur (G)

				SP	RR	SF
3303*	**Pharanear (IRE) (145)** (DNicholson) **7-11-9**(5) MrRThornton (hld up: hdwy 6th: led after 2 out to last: rdn to ld & veered lft flat: r.o)	—	**1**	14/1	127	62
2888[2]	**Yahmi (IRE) (130)** (JABOld) **7-10-13** JOsborne (hld up in tch: hdwy to ld last: sn hdd: unable qckn)	2	**2**	7/2[1]	111	46
1353[R]	**Danjing (IRE) (128)** (MCPipe) **5-10-11b** APMcCoy (trckd ldrs: ev ch appr 2 out: one pce)	5	**3**	33/1	106	41
2934*	**Haile Derring (123)** (NATwiston-Davies) **7-10-6** TJenks (chsd ldrs: led 8th tl after 2 out: one pce)	1	**4**	9/1	100	35
3523a[4]	**Miltonfield (128)** (JEMulhern,Ireland) **8-10-11** RDunwoody (hld up & bhd: hdwy 10th: rdn & mstke 2 out: sn wknd)	5	**5**	9/2[2]	102	37
3045[3]	**Freddie Muck (132)** (NATwiston-Davies) **7-11-1** CLlewellyn (a chsng ldrs: rdn & outpcd 2 out: styd on flat)	nk	**6**	10/1	106	41
2950*	**Henrietta Howard (IRE) (121)** (MrsDHaine) **7-10-4** JFTitley (hld up in rr: hdwy 9th: rdn & wknd after 2 out)	3½	**7**	8/1[3]	93	28
3281[2]	**Linton Rocks (123)** (TThomsonJones) **8-9-13**(7) XAizpuru (hld up: hdwy 7th: wknd 3 out)	1	**8**	11/1	94	29
3013[4]	**General Mouktar (117)** (MCPipe) **7-10-0** RHughes (hld up & bhd: hdwy 10th: wknd appr 2 out)	12	**9**	50/1	81	16
3267[8]	**Diwali Dancer (117)** (MCPipe) **7-9-9**(5) GSupple (nvr trbld ldrs)	3½	**10**	40/1	79	14
3408[3]	**Mister Blake (117)** (RLee) **7-10-0** RJohnson (hld up: hdwy 10th: wknd appr 2 out)	1	**11**	66/1	78?	13
3157[3]	**Give Best (117)** (JJO'Neill) **6-10-0** CFSwan (hdwy 8th: wknd appr 3 out)	2	**12**	14/1	77	12
3277[5]	**Tim (IRE) (121)** (JRJenkins) **7-10-4**ow4 MAFitzgerald (a bhd)	3	**13**	50/1	79	10
2960[F]	**Palosanto (IRE) (119)** (MCPipe) **7-9-11**(5) SophieMitchell (mstkes 4th & 6th: a bhd)	4	**14**	33/1	74	9
3551[5]	**Duhallow Lodge (117)** (CRBarwell) **10-10-0** JRKavanagh (a in rr)	nk	**15**	100/1	72	7
3047[5]	**Karar (IRE) (117)** (RRowe) **7-9-9**(5) DJKavanagh (chsd ldrs tl wknd 9th)	5	**16**	50/1	69	4
3402[7]	**Uron V (FR) (117)** (CFWall) **11-10-0** KGaule (lost pl 7th: t.o)	10	**17**	50/1	63	—
3016[3]	**Snow Board (117)** (MrsMerritaJones) **8-10-0** DerekByrne (a bhd: t.o)	9	**18**	66/1	57	—
2888[6]	**Runaway Pete (USA) (123)** (MCPipe) **7-10-6** DWalsh (trckd ldrs to 10th: eased whn btn: t.o)	5	**19**	25/1	59	—
3317[3]	**Dally Boy (117)** (TDEasterby) **5-9-11**(3) MichaelBrennan (w ldr to 8th: wknd appr 3 out: t.o)	4	**20**	33/1	50	—
2625[2]	**Olympian (121)** (JNeville) **10-10-4b** NWilliamson (led: mstke 3rd: hdd 8th: wknd qckly: t.o)	27	**21**	20/1	37	—
1915[2]	**Southern Nights (117)** (KCBailey) **7-10-0** CO'Dwyer (hdwy 8th: rdn 10th: wknd & p.u after 3 out)		**P**	10/1	—	—
3045[7]	**Arithmetic (117)** (MrsJPitman) **7-10-0** RFarrant (in tch tl p.u appr 8th)		**P**	25/1	—	—
2888[4]	**Erzadjan (IRE) (131)** (MrsMReveley) **7-11-0** PNiven (hld up: hdwy & rdn appr 3 out: 5th & btn whn blnd & uns rdr last)		**U**	10/1	107?	—
				SP 146.0%)	**24 Rn**	

6m 24.2 (7.20) CSF £60.13 CT £1,582.81 TOTE £22.00: £4.50 £1.90 £7.00 £2.60 (£38.70) Trio £582.70 OWNER Stainless Threaded Fasteners Ltd (TEMPLE GUITING) BRED Seamus Kennedy

LONG HANDICAP Diwali Dancer 9-9 Tim (IRE) 9-10 General Mouktar 9-2 Karar (IRE) 9-6 Uron V (FR) 9-12 Duhallow Lodge 9-7 Give Best 9-2 Dally Boy 9-9 Snow Board 8-4 Arithmetic 9-13 Southern Nights 9-13 Mister Blake 8-0

3303* Pharanear (IRE), third in this event last year, showed how much he has progressed with a gutsy performance under top weight, and completed a very rewarding day for trainer and jockey. (14/1)

2888 Yahmi (IRE), squeezed for room at the penultimate hurdle, switched right and looked all over the winner when he landed in front at the last, but Pharanear proved more resolute up the final climb. (7/2)

1353 Danjing (IRE) was back on his best behaviour after a complete break from racing and, if he could be relied on, an early success would be a formality. (33/1)

2934* Haile Derring had to settle for second best until past halfway, and he was unable to get away once in control. He was found wanting when collared after negotiating the penultimate hurdle. (9/1)

3523a Miltonfield returned to a more suitable trip, but this lively terrain is not for him and he was already under all the aids when making a hash of the second last. (9/2)

3045 Freddie Muck was at full stretch and struggling to hold on on the approach to the third last. Though he kept plugging away, he was unable to make his presence felt. (10/1)

2950* Henrietta Howard (IRE) seemed not to last out the trip, for she was close enough if good enough at the second last. (8/1)

2888 Erzadjan (IRE), bustled along from some way out, did not appear to be making any progress when he blundered and got rid of his pilot at the last. (10/1)

T/Jkpt: Not won; £69,272.21 to Cheltenham 12/3/97. T/Plpt: £332.80 (575.49 Tckts). T/Qdpt: £23.10 (316.98 Tckts) IM/KH

3178-FONTWELL (Fig. 8) (Good, Good to firm patches)
Tuesday March 11th

WEATHER: fine

3601 BRIGHTON HURDLE (4-Y.O) (Class D)
2-10 (2-12) **2m 2f 110y (9 hdls)** £2,906.00 (£816.00: £398.00) GOING: 0.57 sec per fur (S)

Form	Horse	Details	Dist	Pos	SP	RR	SF
3174[5]	**Ela Agapi Mou (USA)**	(GLMoore) **4-10-10** DGallagher (hdwy 5th: led appr 3 out: rdn out)	—	1	7/1[3]	82	26
3404[F]	**Infamous (USA)**	(RJO'Sullivan) **4-10-10** DO'Sullivan (mstke 3rd: stdy hdwy 6th: ev ch 2 out: unable qckn)	3	2	6/4[1]	79	23
3287[2]	**Topaglow (IRE)**	(PTDalton) **4-10-10** BFenton (lw: hld up: ev ch appr 2 out: 3rd & btn whn mstke 2 out)	6	3	4/1[2]	74	18
548[3]	**Spring Campaign (IRE)**	(MCPipe) **4-10-10** JamieEvans (led to 6th: wknd appr 2 out)	17	4	12/1	60	4
3404[3]	**Salty Girl (IRE)**	(JSMoore) **4-10-5** WMcFarland (hdwy 6th: wknd 3 out: j.b rt last 2)	nk	5	7/1[3]	54	—
	Dubai Dolly (IRE)	(JWMullins) **4-10-5** SCurran (hdwy 6th: wknd after 3 out)	22	6	100/1	35	—
3177[7]	**Hever Golf Diamond (100)**	(JRBest) **4-10-13**(3) PHenley (lw: bhd fr 6th)	8	7	20/1	39	—
3224[5]	**Silvretta (IRE)**	(JTGifford) **4-10-5b** PHide (w ldr: mstke 3rd: led 6th tl appr 3 out: sn wknd)	8	8	14/1	21	—
3404[6]	**Timidjar (IRE)**	(DRGandolfo) **4-10-7**(3) DFortt (a bhd: t.o whn virtually p.u flat)	dist	9	7/1[3]	—	—
3359[16]	**Safecracker**	(CPMorlock) **4-10-10b** BPowell (prom to 4th: t.o whn p.u bef 2 out)		P	33/1	—	—
3058[3]	**Petros Gem**	(MJBolton) **4-9-12**(7) JHarris (bhd fr 6th: t.o whn p.u bef 2 out)		P	66/1	—	—
					(SP 122.0%)	**11 Rn**	

4m 36.4 (18.40) CSF £17.13 TOTE £9.70: £2.30 £1.10 £1.70 (£6.10) Trio £10.30 OWNER Ballard (1834) Ltd (BRIGHTON) BRED Patrick Eddery Ltd and Midcounts Ltd

3174 Ela Agapi Mou (USA), who found two miles on Windsor's flat track far too sharp for him, was beaten nine-and-a-half lengths by today's runner-up on that occasion, but reversed that form over this longer trip. Leading approaching the third last, he had a real tussle with Infamous, but ridden along, proved just too strong for that rival. (7/1: op 12/1)

3404 Infamous (USA) gradually crept into the action on the final circuit, and threw down his challenge turning for home. With every chance jumping the penultimate hurdle, he then found the winner a little bit too good. He should soon find a race. (6/4)

3287 Topaglow (IRE) had every chance turning for home, but was already feeling the pinch when clouting the second last. (4/1: op 7/1)

548 Spring Campaign (IRE), who beat just one home on his hurdling debut six months ago, set a very brisk pace to the fourth last. Not surprisingly he was left for dead turning out of the back straight. (12/1: op 7/1)

3224 Silvretta (IRE) (14/1: op 8/1)

3602 HOUGHTON NOVICES' H'CAP CHASE (0-100) (5-Y.O+) (Class E)
2-45 (2-46) **2m 3f (16 fncs)** £2,916.25 (£880.00: £427.50: £201.25) GOING: 0.57 sec per fur (S)

Form	Horse	Details	Dist	Pos	SP	RR	SF
3331[*]	**Red Branch (IRE) (73)**	(JSKing) **8-10-11** TJMurphy (lw: mde all: clr appr 3 out: easily)	—	1	4/6[1]	86+	19
3339[P]	**Brown Robber (69)**	(MrsRGHenderson) **9-10-7** BFenton (chsd wnr: mstkes 9th & 10th: blnd 11th: mstke 4 out: rdn appr 3 out: sn wknd)	4	2	6/1[3]	79	12
3188[P]	**Colonel Colt (75)**	(RDickin) **6-10-13** DLeahy (no hdwy fr 12th)	7	3	14/1	79	12
3343[8]	**Nordic Valley (IRE) (86)**	(MCPipe) **6-11-10** JamieEvans (lw: 4th whn pckd 11th: sn wknd)	24	4	11/4[2]	70	3
					(SP 107.6%)	**4 Rn**	

5m 0.7 (21.70) CSF £4.39 TOTE £1.80 (£2.90) OWNER Mr E. J. Mangan (SWINDON) BRED Michael Butler

3331* Red Branch (IRE) is certainly much better over fences and, making all the running, forged clear with the minimum of fuss turning for home to win this shocking race. He was eased considerably on the run-in, and the winning distance is certainly no true reflection of his superiority. (4/6)

1875 Brown Robber, pulled up in three of his five outings this season, was much happier for the return to a shorter trip. Racing in second place, his jumping went to pieces on the final circuit. Not surprisingly, he was in trouble turning for home, and is greatly flattered to finish so close. (6/1: op 4/1)

Colonel Colt at least got round on this occasion, but was making little impression on the front two over the last five fences. (14/1: 10/1-16/1)

2873 Nordic Valley (IRE), racing with his tongue tied down, was given a reminder every now and then during the race but, after pecking at the sixth last, was soon in trouble. (11/4)

3603 STORRINGTON MAIDEN HURDLE (5-Y.O+) (Class E)
3-20 (3-20) **3m 2f 110y (13 hdls)** £2,274.00 (£639.00: £312.00) GOING: 0.57 sec per fur (S)

Form	Horse	Details	Dist	Pos	SP	RR	SF
3355[3]	**Satcotino (IRE)**	(MHTompkins) **6-10-2**(3) PHenley (a.p: rdn & chsd wnr fr 10th: ev ch appr 2 out: swtchd lft flat: r.o wl: fin 2nd, hd: awrdd r)	—	1	8/13[1]	75	—

3178[2] **Brackenheath (IRE)** (DMGrissell) **6-10-10** BFenton (lw: chsd ldr: led 9th: mstke last: hung rt flat: drvn out: fin 1st: disq: plcd 2nd)		**2**	4/1[2]	80	—
2959[3] **Win I Did (IRE)** (RHAlner) **7-10-5** BPowell (hdwy 9th: wknd 3 out)	23	**3**	14/1	61	—
3447[7] **Night in a Million (80)** (SWoodman) **6-10-10** DMorris (hld up: rdn 10th: sn wknd: t.o)	dist	**4**	16/1	—	—
3426[4] **Torch Vert (IRE) (86)** (NJHWalker) **5-10-10** DGallagher (hdwy 8th: wknd appr 3 out: t.o whn p.u bef 2 out)		**P**	11/2[3]	—	—
High Burnshot (MrsLCJewell) **10-10-10** DLeahy (led: sn clr: hdd 9th: wknd qckly: t.o fr 10th: p.u bef 2 out)		**P**	33/1	—	—
3426[9] **Glaisnock Lad (IRE)** (RHAlner) **5-10-10** RGreene (lw: a bhd: t.o whn p.u bef 8th)		**P**	40/1	—	—
3416[7] **Miss Nonnie** (MissLShally) **5-9-12**(7) MLane (mstke 1st: bhd fr 6th: t.o whn p.u bef 8th)		**P**	66/1	—	—
3340[P] **Miss Gee-Ell** (NBThomson) **5-9-12**(7) MrEBabington (a bhd: t.o whn p.u bef 10th)		**P**	100/1	—	—

(SP 117.7%) **9 Rn**

6m 55.5 (42.50) CSF £3.24 TOTE £1.70: £1.10 £1.90 £2.50 (£2.70) Trio £5.70 OWNER Grangewood (Sales & Marketing) Ltd (NEWMARKET) BRED Stuart Weld

STEWARDS' ENQUIRY Fenton susp. 20-22 & 24/3/97 (careless riding & excessive use of whip).

3355 Satcotino (IRE), who had to be ridden along every now and then during the race, was done absolutely no favours as Fenton's whip flashed in front of her face on the run-in and, with Brackenheath drifting right across her, she had to be switched as a result. She ran on strongly and, only just failing to get there, was awarded the race in the Stewards' Room. (8/13)

3178 Brackenheath (IRE) appreciated this longer trip. Sent on with a circuit to go, he had a tremendous ding-dong battle with Satcotino in the last half mile. Untidy at the final flight, he then hung right under pressure on the run-in, doing his rival no favours, and it was no surprise that he lost the race in the Stewards' Room. His rider was suspended for two days for careless riding, and another two days for excessive use of the whip. There is certainly a race waiting for Brackenheath, but his trainer may now put him away to keep him for novice events next season. (4/1: op 5/2)

Win I Did (IRE) took closer order with a circuit to race, but was left for dead by the front two three from home. (14/1)

2907 Night in a Million quite simply failed to stay this longer trip, and had shot his bolt going to the third last. (16/1)

3604 NATIONAL SPIRIT H'CAP HURDLE (0-110) (4-Y.O+) (Class E)

3-50 (3-50) **2m 6f 110y (11 hdls)** £2,200.50 (£618.00: £301.50) GOING: 0.57 sec per fur (S)

			SP	RR	SF
3411[2] **St Ville (88)** (RHBuckler) **11-11-8** BPowell (a.p: rdn 8th: led after 3 out: clr appr 2 out: all out)	—	**1**	3/1[2]	63	—
3442[10] **Roger's Pal (70)** (PEccles) **10-10-4** DGallagher (lw: hdwy 7th: hrd rdn 8th: mstke 2 out: r.o wl flat)	s.h	**2**	10/1	45	—
3442[18] **Raahin (USA) (66)** (SWoodman) **12-10-0** DMorris (chsd ldr: led 4th tl after 3 out: wknd appr 2 out)	9	**3**	12/1	35	—
3180[P] **Punch's Hotel (90)** (RRowe) **12-11-3b**(7) AGarrity (led: mstke 3rd: hdd 4th: wknd 6th: t.o fr 8th)	24	**4**	7/2[3]	42	—
2694[4] **Swan Street (NZ) (83)** (CJMann) **6-11-0**(3) JMagee (lw: hld up: ev ch 3 out: sn wknd: t.o)	11	**5**	11/4[1]	27	—
3415[6] **Amillionmemories (89)** (MrsBarbaraWaring) **7-11-9** RGreene (a bhd: t.o fr 8th: p.u bef 2 out)		**P**	4/1	—	—

(SP 110.7%) **6 Rn**

5m 51.4 (35.40) CSF £25.86 TOTE £3.30: £1.70 £3.50 (£10.50) OWNER Melplash Racing (BRIDPORT) BRED David and Mrs Shirley

LONG HANDICAP Raahin (USA) 9-13

3411 St Ville went on soon after the third last, and forged clear for what looked like being a decisive victory in the straight. However, he started to have ideas of his own going to the last and, swishing his tail, started to down tools on the run-in. As a result the runner-up finished with a real flourish, and St Ville held on only by the skin of his teeth. (3/1)

3209 Roger's Pal is just a plater, and looked well held in the straight. However, with the winner deciding to call it a day, he finished with a real flourish, and would certainly have prevailed in another stride. (10/1: 8/1-12/1)

2905 Raahin (USA) ran better here, and went on at the fourth. Collared after the third last, he was soon in trouble. (12/1)

2694 Swan Street (NZ) quite simply failed to stay the trip and, after appearing to be travelling well in the back straight, stopped as if shot turning for home. (11/4)

3605 FONTWELL H'CAP CHASE (0-120) (5-Y.O+) (Class D)

4-20 (4-21) **3m 2f 110y (22 fncs)** £3,403.75 (£1,030.00: £502.50: £238.75) GOING: 0.57 sec per fur (S)

			SP	RR	SF
3444[4] **Credon (100)** (SWoodman) **9-10-8** BFenton (lw: led 3rd to 5th: led 10th to 12th: led 13th: lft clr appr 18th: eased flat)	—	**1**	7/1	94+	15
2758[7] **Harristown Lady (105)** (GBBalding) **10-10-13b** BClifford (3rd whn mstke 16th: lft 2nd appr 18th: unable qckn)	2½	**2**	6/1[3]	98	19
3179[4] **Master Comedy (92)** (MissLBower) **13-10-0b** DGallagher (nvr nr to chal)	2	**3**	14/1	83	4
3428[P] **Nazzaro (120)** (WGMTurner) **8-12-0** TJMurphy (led after 1st: j.slowly 2nd: hdd 3rd: led 5th to 10th: wknd 13th)	18	**4**	6/1[3]	100	21
3444[3] **Vicosa (IRE) (108)** (RHAlner) **8-10-13**(3) PHenley (5th whn fell 14th)		**F**	2/1[1]	—	—
3280[3] **Childhay Chocolate (98)** (PFNicholls) **9-10-6** RGreene (led tl after 1st: mstke 9th: pckd 11th: led 12th to 13th: 2nd whn j.slowly 17th: p.u bef 18th: lame)		**P**	9/4[2]	—	—

(SP 111.8%) **6 Rn**

7m 11.0 (31.00) CSF £40.71 TOTE £9.70: £3.30 £3.90 (£37.40) OWNER Fusilier Racing (CHICHESTER) BRED J. C. Bolam

LONG HANDICAP Master Comedy 8-6

3444 Credon, who made a lot of the running, was left clear going to the fifth, and was some eighteen lengths in front jumping the final fence. With his rider realising there was absolutely no danger, he was eased right down to a walk in the closing stages. (7/1)

2089 Harristown Lady, left in second place going to the fifth last, was well behind the winner jumping the last, but with that rival eased right down, she is considerably flattered to finish to close. (6/1)

3179 Master Comedy, 20lb out of the handicap, is another who is greatly flattered to finish so close. At the back of the field from the start, he plodded on in the straight, and was set to finish a very moderate third, until the winner was eased right down. (14/1)

2616 Nazzaro (6/1: 3/1-7/1)

3280 Childhay Chocolate, whose jumping left something to be desired, was in second place when jumping slowly at the seventeenth, and was soon pulled-up lame. (9/4)

3606 TORTINGTON INTERMEDIATE OPEN N.H. FLAT RACE (4, 5 & 6-Y.O) (Class H)

4-55 (4-58) **2m 2f** £1,255.50 (£348.00: £166.50)

			SP	RR	SF
2811[2] **Spunkie** (RFJohnsonHoughton) **4-10-10** DGallagher (lw: stdy hdwy 6f out: led wl over 1f out: qcknd: easily)	—	**1**	15/8[1]	70 f	—
2572[4] **Certain Shot** (GMMcCourt) **6-11-1**(3) DFortt (a.p: led over 2f out tl wl over 1f out: unable qckn)	6	**2**	15/8[1]	65 f	—
3006[3] **Hot 'n Saucy** (APJones) **5-10-13** MrSBush (hdwy 6f out: one pce fnl 3f)	12	**3**	6/1[2]	49 f	—
3203[4] **Macy (IRE)** (RDickin) **4-11-3** TJMurphy (hld up: led 7f out tl over 2f out: wknd over 1f out)	3	**4**	10/1[3]	58 f	—
Blazing Batman (MrsRGHenderson) **4-10-10** MrWHenderson (w'like: lost pl 14f out: one pce fnl 4f)	17	**5**	40/1	36 f	—

				SP	RR	SF
2811^{16}	**Tingrith Lad** (JABennett) **5-11-4** WMcFarland (hdwy 14f out: wknd 5f out)	22	**6**	50/1	17 f	—
1966^{15}	**Young Manny** (AEJessop) **6-11-1**$^{(3)}$ RMassey (hdwy 9f out: wknd over 4f out)	17	**7**	40/1	2 f	—
3235^{11}	**Arrange** (JCABatchelor) **5-11-4** VSlattery (chsd ldr: led 9f out to 7f out: wknd over 4f out)	10	**8**	20/1	—	—
	Minnie (IRE) (JWMullins) **4-10-5** SCurran (small: hdwy over 6f out: wknd 5f out)	2½	**9**	16/1	—	—
3304^{15}	**Kingswood Imperial** (RJO'Sullivan) **4-10-10** AMcCabe (hld up: rdn over 4f out: sn wknd)	1½	**10**	16/1	—	—
	Royal Member (MrsBarbaraWaring) **4-10-5** RGreene (small: a bhd)	9	**11**	14/1	—	—
3090^{13}	**Hold My Hand** (PRChamings) **6-11-4** BFenton (led 9f: t.o fnl 7f)	dist	**12**	33/1	—	—
	Sissinghurst Flyer (IRE) (RDickin) **5-10-13** DLeahy (neat: bhd fnl 6f: t.o whn virtually p.u fnl f)	dist	**13**	20/1	—	—
				(SP 130.7%)	**13 Rn**	

4m 34.1 CSF £4.50 TOTE £2.50: £1.10 £1.20 £2.20 (£3.90) Trio £9.20 OWNER Mr Jim Short (DIDCOT) BRED Jim Short, Brian Jenkins and Isobel McMillan

WEIGHT FOR AGE 4yo-8lb

2811 Spunkie put up an impressive display. Cruising into the lead early in the final quarter-mile, he then showed an impressive turn of foot to pull right away, and win doing handsprings. (15/8)

2572 Certain Shot, one of three disputing the lead in the straight, was left for dead by the winner from below the distance. He will not always meet one so good. (15/8)

3006 Hot 'n Saucy is not very big, and was only going up and down in the same place in the straight. (6/1)

3203 Macy (IRE) went on seven furlongs from home, but he was collared early in the straight, and was a spent force below the distance. (10/1: op 6/1)

T/Plpt: £44.60 (168.32 Tckts). T/Qdpt: £19.60 (15.41 Tckts) AK

3461-SEDGEFIELD (L-H) (Good to firm, Good patches)
Tuesday March 11th

WEATHER: fine

3607 MONKEY PUZZLE (S) H'CAP HURDLE (0-90) (4-Y.O+) (Class G)

2-20 (2-20) **3m 3f 110y (13 hdls)** £2,080.00 (£580.00: £280.00) GOING minus 0.66 sec per fur (F)

				SP	RR	SF
3328^{7}	**Greenfield Manor (64)** (JSisterson) **10-10-3**$^{(5)}$ STaylor (cl up: mde most fr 5th: kpt on wl)	—	**1**	33/1	48	6
3478^{8}	**Shelton Abbey (67)** (JWade) **11-10-8b**$^{(3)}$ ECallaghan (rr div tl hdwy 3 out: fin wl)	3	**2**	8/1	49	7
3306^{9}	**Bright Destiny (56)** (JSGoldie) **6-10-0v** GCahill (swtg: disp ld to 5th: cl up tl outpcd 3 out: styd on again next)	½	**3**	50/1	38	—
2915^{P}	**Haughton Lad (IRE) (68)** (JParkes) **8-10-12** VSmith (bhd: hdwy & prom 9th: chal 3 out: one pce appr last)	1	**4**	7/1^{3}	49	7
3478^{10}	**Helens Bay (IRE) (72)** (VThompson) **7-11-2** MrMThompson (prom: mstke & outpcd 4 out: kpt on fr 2 out)	2½	**5**	16/1	52	10
3313^{6}	**Denticulata (70)** (PSpottiswood) **9-11-0** BStorey (hdwy & prom 8th: disp ld 3 out: sn rdn: wknd fr next)	¾	**6**	6/1^{2}	49	7
2629^{12}	**Weather Alert (IRE) (73)** (KAMorgan) **6-10-10**$^{(7)}$ NHorrocks (lw: prom tl outpcd fr 3 out)	6	**7**	9/1	49	7
2915^{10}	**Mardood (69)** (SBClark) **12-10-6**$^{(7)}$ MissRClark (nvr bttr than mid div)	3½	**8**	25/1	43	1
3328^{2}	**Ruber (80)** (RWThomson) **10-11-10** DParker (mstkes: sn drvn along: nvr trbld ldrs)	5	**9**	5/2^{1}	51	9
3157^{P}	**Murphaideez (60)** (RAFahey) **10-10-4** RHodge (n.d)	16	**10**	33/1	21	—
3328^{9}	**Don't Tell Judy (IRE) (69)** (MissMKMilligan) **9-10-13** ADobbin (chsd ldrs: rdn 8th: wknd 4 out)	½	**11**	20/1	30	—
3454^{P}	**Kir (IRE) (74)** (VThompson) **9-11-4** KJones (a bhd: t.o fr 8th)	16	**12**	50/1	25	—
3222^{10}	**Our Rainbow (75)** (MrsPSly) **5-11-5v^{1}** MBrennan (led to 5th: cl up tl lost pl 8th: hdwy u.p 3 out: sn wknd: virtually p.u flat)	7	**13**	6/1^{2}	22	—
2958^{7}	**Boyzontoowa (IRE) (62)** (RCollins) **5-10-6** WMarston (prom tl wknd fr 3 out)	nk	**14**	25/1	9	—
2862^{5}	**Ijab (CAN) (78)** (JParkes) **7-11-8** MMoloney (lw: hld up & bhd: t.o)	25	**15**	10/1	10	—
509*	**Playful Juliet (CAN) (82)** (JCHaynes) **9-11-12b** MrCStockton (cl up tl wknd 4 out: p.u bef last)		**P**	11/1	—	—
				(SP 136.3%)	**16 Rn**	

6m 36.1 (1.10) CSF £269.01 CT £11,507.13 TOTE £119.50: £12.30 £1.30 £10.20 £2.60 (£371.10) Trio Not won; £203.82 to Cheltenham 12/3/97 OWNER Mr J. Sisterson (SEATON) BRED L. Chamberlain (Acrum) Ltd

LONG HANDICAP Bright Destiny 9-11

No bid

Haughton Lad (IRE) clmd Mrs J. Webber £6,000

Greenfield Manor had very little to recommend him over the last three years, but this was no fluke and he needed a deal of determination to hold on. (33/1)

892 Shelton Abbey is from a yard that is just coming to hand. This old dodger showed he is in good heart and fairly sprinted up the run-in. (8/1)

2788 Bright Destiny, sweating profusely and 3lb out of the handicap, put up a greatly-improved performance. (50/1)

2654 Haughton Lad (IRE) went really well for a long way but, when a real effort was needed going to the last, he was found wanting yet again. (7/1)

2178 Helens Bay (IRE) stays forever and keeps showing bits of form, and has the ability to pick up a small race. (16/1)

3313 Denticulata looked to be going well three out, but in a few strides he was in trouble, and perhaps this trip was just beyond him. (6/1)

3328 Ruber found the ground and this track too sharp, and was never going. (5/2)

3608 BET WITH THE TOTE NOVICES' CHASE (5-Y.O+) (Class E)

2-55 (2-55) **2m 5f (16 fncs)** £3,023.25 (£906.00: £435.50: £200.25) GOING minus 0.66 sec per fur (F)

				SP	RR	SF
3484^{3}	**Nijway (73)** (MABarnes) **7-10-11**$^{(5)}$ STaylor (led to 9th: disp ld 4 out tl led flat: jst hld on)	—	**1**	5/1^{2}	79	17
3306^{P}	**Master Flashman (73)** (MrsMReveley) **8-10-13**$^{(3)}$ GLee (a cl up: led 11th tl disp ld 4 out: hdd flat: rallied towards fin)	s.h	**2**	8/1^{3}	79	17
2510^{6}	**Fern Leader (IRE)** (MrsASwinbank) **7-11-2** JSupple (blnd 1st: hdwy & prom whn mstke 9th: chsng ldrs & rdn 4 out: no imp)	8	**3**	8/11^{1}	73	11
3479^{F}	**Fort Zeddaan (IRE)** (MrsSJSmith) **7-10-9**$^{(7)}$ RWilkinson (chsd ldrs: hit 10th: one pce fr 4 out)	6	**4**	16/1	68	6
2632^{8}	**Camptosaurus (IRE) (66)** (DSAlder) **8-11-2** BStorey (prom tl outpcd fr 12th)	3	**5**	16/1	66	4
	Arctic Bloom (CIRatcliffe) **11-10-11** MrCMulhall (s.s: hdwy whn hit 6th: chsng ldrs fr 11th tl blnd & wknd 3 out)	7	**6**	25/1	56	—
3477^{4}	**Triona's Hope (IRE) (60)** (EMCaine) **8-11-2** MMoloney (cl up: led 9th to 11th: sn wknd)	12	**7**	20/1	52	—
1688^{P}	**Nobodys Flame (IRE) (84)** (SIPittendrigh) **9-11-2** KJohnson (outpcd fr 8th: wl bhd fr 11th)	14	**8**	16/1	41	—
3393^{F}	**Safety Factor (IRE)** (HowardJohnson) **9-10-11**$^{(5)}$ GFRyan (chsng ldrs whn fell 7th)		**F**	11/1	—	—

3450F **Childsway** (SJRobinson) **9-11-2** KJones (s.s: a t.o: wl t.o whn fell 3 out) ... F 20/1 — —
3314[4] **Overwhelm (IRE) (77)** (VThompson) **9-11-6** MrMThompson (in tch whn hmpd 7th: sn drvn along: t.o fr 11th: p.u bef 2 out) ... P 10/1 — —
2177[8] **Ringrone (IRE)** (VThompson) **8-10-11** NBentley (sn bhd: t.o whn p.u bef 9th) ... P 100/1 — —
(SP 135.1%) **12 Rn**

5m 11.3 (0.30) CSF £44.86 TOTE £4.50: £1.90 £2.30 £1.50 (£16.90) Trio £27.90 OWNER Mr T. A. Barnes (PENRITH) BRED Bacton Stud
3484 Nijway did not make his customary mistakes this time, and that made the difference. (5/1)
Master Flashman put in by far his best effort to date, and another stride would have seen him come out on top. (8/1: op 9/2)
2510 Fern Leader (IRE) almost fell at the first and that seemed to unsettle him, as he was never all that happy thereafter. He will probably do better over further and most likely with some give in the ground. (8/11)
Fort Zeddaan (IRE) showed a little here and is obviously learning. (16/1)
Camptosaurus (IRE) has shown bits of ability in the past and, when the ground really firms up in the spring, there will no doubt be some very moderate races where he will have a chance. (16/1)
Arctic Bloom, a headstrong individual, has ability but is prone to mistakes. (25/1)
Safety Factor (IRE) (11/1: 7/1-12/1)

3609 WIN WITH THE TOTE HUNTERS' CHASE (6-Y.O+) (Class H)

3-30 (3-30) **3m 3f (21 fncs)** £1,140.00 (£315.00: £150.00) GOING minus 0.66 sec per fur (F)

	Horse / details	Dist	Pos	SP	RR	SF
3458[3]	**Glen Oak** (DGDuggan) **12-11-7**(7) MrJMPritchard (chsd ldrs: mstke & outpcd 5 out: styd on appr last: led cl home)	—	1	2/1[2]	96	16
2903[9]	**Kushbaloo** (CParker) **12-12-3**(7) MrAParker (mstke 1st: led 4th to 8th: led 15th: clr fr 3 out tl wknd flat & ct cl home)	1	2	11/10[1]	105	25
3397[5]	**Fordstown (IRE)** (JamieAlexander) **8-12-0**(7) MrJamieAlexander (led to 4th: led 8th tl hdd & mstke 15th: outpcd 3 out: kpt on flat)	nk	3	7/2[3]	102	22
	Tartan Tornado (MrsPLaws) **11-12-2**(5) MrPJohnson (chsd ldrs: mstkes 8th & 15th: outpcd fr 3 out)	4	4	16/1	100	20
	Fast Study (SJRobinson) **12-12-3**(7) MrSimonRobinson (mstke 2nd: in tch tl outpcd fr 12th)	dist	5	16/1	—	—
	Side Brace (NZ) (JSSwindells) **13-11-7**(7) MissSSwindells (outpcd & wl bhd fr ½-wy)	9	6	25/1	—	—
	Polynth (WBrown) **8-11-7**(7) MrGMarkham (mstke 6th: a bhd: blnd 2 out: p.u bef last)		P	20/1	—	—

(SP 123.5%) **7 Rn**

6m 51.4 (5.40) CSF £4.94 TOTE £2.90: £1.90 £1.80 (£2.50) OWNER Mr R. J. Mansell (REDMARLEY) BRED Kitone Ltd
STEWARDS' ENQUIRY Mr A. Parker susp. 20-22 & 24-25/3/97 (failure to ensure best possible placing).
3458 Glen Oak stays well and that won him the day here. (2/1)
1024 Kushbaloo looked to have this sewn up on the final circuit, but he tired late on and that, coupled with a touch of over-confidence from his rider, proved to be his undoing. His rider got a fair amount of abuse from the crowd and the Stewards seemed to be influenced by this and gave him what seems a very harsh five-day suspension. (11/10: evens-5/4)
3397 Fordstown (IRE) gave up the outside to no-one and had his chances, but lacked any change of gear. (7/2)
Tartan Tornado made mistakes and looked one-paced. (16/1)

3610 SCREENCO JUMBOTRON H'CAP CHASE (0-120) (5-Y.O+) (Class D)

4-10 (4-10) **2m 110y (13 fncs)** £3,366.00 (£1,008.00: £484.00: £222.00) GOING minus 0.66 sec per fur (F)

	Horse / details	Dist	Pos	SP	RR	SF
3369[3]	**Cross Cannon (103)** (JWade) **11-11-7** BStorey (lw: j.w: mde all: r.o wl fr 3 out)	—	1	4/1[3]	117	15
3329*	**Weaver George (IRE) (109)** (WStorey) **7-11-13** MMoloney (trckd ldrs: wnt 2nd 7th: hit 3 out & no imp after)	7	2	6/5[1]	116	14
2674[6]	**Reve de Valse (USA) (91)** (RJohnson) **10-10-9** KJohnson (outpcd & bhd fr 5th)	10	3	8/1	89	—
3369[2]	**Regal Romper (IRE) (110)** (MrsSJSmith) **9-12-0** RichardGuest (lw: chsd wnr tl outpcd & hit 8th & 9th: sn btn)	20	4	13/8[2]	88	—

(SP 114.7%) **4 Rn**

3m 59.5 (1.50) CSF £9.16 TOTE £4.90 (£3.20) OWNER Mr John Wade (MORDON) BRED Andrew Murphy
3369 Cross Cannon had the track and the ground and, although the trip was shorter than he really prefers, he won well. (4/1)
3329* Weaver George (IRE) was a shade warm beforehand, and perhaps his busy time of late has caught up with him as, when he was stretched, he blundered his chance away three out. (6/5)
1846 Reve de Valse (USA) was being taken off his legs throughout. (8/1)
3369 Regal Romper (IRE) has been running his heart out all season, but he made uncustomary mistakes here, and ran disappointingly. (13/8)

3611 STANLEY RACING GOLDEN NUMBERS SERIES NOVICES' HURDLE (4-Y.O+ F & M) (Class E)

4-45 (4-52) **2m 5f 110y (10 hdls)** £2,845.00 (£795.00: £385.00) GOING minus 0.66 sec per fur (F)

	Horse / details	Dist	Pos	SP	RR	SF
3032[3]	**Pontevedra (IRE) (83)** (KAMorgan) **4-9-10**(7) NHorrocks (a.p: led 3 out: styd on u.p)	—	1	6/1	64	—
3290[4]	**Country Orchid** (MrsMReveley) **6-10-9**(3) GLee (swtg: mstke 2nd: hdwy ½-wy: ev ch 2 out: kpt on)	¾	2	11/4[2]	63	—
2923[5]	**Wayuphill (87)** (CParker) **10-10-12** BStorey (lw: hld up: hdwy & prom 3 out: nt qckn fr next)	3½	3	5/2[1]	61	—
3006[7]	**Supreme Target (IRE)** (MrsMReveley) **5-10-12** GCahill (prom tl mstke & grad lost pl fr 3 out)	3½	4	8/1	58+	—
3004[7]	**Anglesey Sea View (103)** (ABailey) **8-11-4** TKent (cl up: led 6th to 3 out: sn outpcd)	15	5	3/1[3]	53	—
2920[7]	**Best Friend** (JWCurtis) **5-10-12** JCallaghan (dwlt: wnt prom 3rd: chal 3 out: wknd appr next)	9	6	25/1	40	—
3315[8]	**Ottadini (IRE) (54)** (WGReed) **5-10-12** TReed (a bhd)	2½	7	66/1	39	—
3026[7]	**De-Veers Currie (IRE)** (DMoffatt) **5-10-12** DJMoffatt (plld hrd: bhd: sme hdwy 4 out: sn btn)	hd	8	25/1	38	—
3440[7]	**Asked To Leave** (JNorton) **5-10-9**(3) ECallaghan (wl bhd fr 6th: t.o)	21	9	16/1	23	—
	Shultan (IRE) (JWade) **8-10-12** KJohnson (prom tl wknd 3 out: t.o whn p.u bef last)		P	33/1	—	—
2917[15]	**Henbrig** (GROldroyd) **7-10-5**(7) CMcCormack (led to 6th: sn wknd: p.u bef last)		P	50/1	—	—
3100P	**Kambletree (IRE)** (MESowersby) **6-10-12b**[1] DParker (cl up to 3rd: sn t.o: p.u bef 6th)		P	66/1	—	—
	Moreflash (JSHaldane) **5-10-12** MMoloney (Withdrawn not under Starter's orders: uns rdr on wy to s)		W	66/1	—	—

(SP 128.6%) **12 Rn**

5m 4.1 (4.10) CSF £22.00 TOTE £6.70: £1.70 £1.30 £1.90 (£10.60) Trio £12.40 OWNER Mrs P. A. L. Butler (MELTON MOWBRAY) BRED Sheikh Mohammed bin Rashid al Maktoum
WEIGHT FOR AGE 4yo-9lb
STEWARDS' ENQUIRY Reveley fined £600 under Rule 151 (iii) & Jockey Club Instruction H2. Cahill susp. 20-25/3/97 under Rule 151 (ii).
3032 Pontevedra (IRE) stays well and, given a most positive ride, that proved to be enough in this company. (6/1)
3290 Country Orchid again sweated up, and gave the impression that if she would concentrate on her racing, she would do a deal better. (11/4: 7/2-9/4)

2923 Wayuphill had his chances, but she lacked any turn of foot to take them. (5/2)
2633 Supreme Target (IRE) has been disappointing in bumpers, but there was plenty to like about this, and she was certainly not overpunished. (8/1)
3004 Anglesey Sea View, on this sharp track, found things happening too quickly when the race began in earnest. (3/1)

3612 TOTE PLACEPOT NOVICES' H'CAP HURDLE (0-105) (4-Y.O+) (Class E)
5-20 (5-22) **2m 1f (8 hdls)** £2,442.50 (£680.00: £327.50) GOING minus 0.66 sec per fur (F)

	Horse	Dist	Pos	SP	RR	SF
3345^{8}	**Rothari (82)** (BSRothwell) **5-10-12** RSupple (w ldrs: led 3 out to last: rallied to ld post)	—	**1**	7/1	64	11
3158^{8}	**Diamond Beach (83)** (GMMoore) **4-10-5** NBentley (hdwy 5th: hit 2 out: rdn to ld last: jst ct)	s.h	**2**	14/1	65	4
	Jendorcet (70) (CWFairhurst) **7-10-0** JCallaghan (hdwy ½-wy: ev ch 2 out: kpt on u.p)	s.h	**3**	16/1	52	—
3366^{6}	**Ferrers (85)** (MrsPSly) **6-11-1** WMarston (hld up: effrt 5th: rdn & sn chsng ldrs: styd on: nt pce to chal)	2	**4**	$7/2^{2}$	65	12
2800^{9}	**Pangeran (USA) (85)** (MrsASwinbank) **5-11-1** JSupple (prom: ev ch 3 out: outpcd fr next)	2	**5**	$11/2^{3}$	63	10
2631^{P}	**Beau Matelot (80)** (MissMKMilligan) **5-10-3**(7) NHorrocks (hld up: hdwy to chal 3 out: wknd next)	3	**6**	16/1	55	2
2957^{6}	**Adamatic (IRE) (98)** (RAllan) **6-12-0** BStorey (hld up: gd hdwy to disp ld 3 out: btn next)	1¾	**7**	8/1	72	19
3315^{7}	**Falcon's Flame (USA) (88)** (VThompson) **4-10-10** MrMThompson (prom tl outpcd fr 3 out)	5	**8**	14/1	57	—
3102^{P}	**Ten Past Six (70)** (MartynWane) **5-10-0** LO'Hara (in tch to 3 out)	3	**9**	13/2	36	—
3311^{7}	**Rubislaw (70)** (MrsKMLamb) **5-9-7v**(7) MissSLamb (lost tch 5th: sn wl bhd)	3½	**10**	33/1	33	—
3371^{3}	**Bassenhally (89)** (MrsPSly) **7-11-5** MBrennan (led tl hdd & wknd qckly 3 out)	11	**11**	11/1	42	—
3265^{6}	**Mapleton (87)** (MrsSJSmith) **4-10-9** RichardGuest (lost tch fr 5th)	6	**12**	11/1	34	—
3313^{P}	**Promise To Try (IRE) (70)** (MABarnes) **5-9-9**(5) STaylor (sn t.o)	3½	**13**	33/1	14	—
3307^{2}	**Clavering (IRE) (88)** (HowardJohnson) **7-11-4** ADobbin (chsd ldrs to 5th: wknd & p.u bef last)		**P**	$9/4^{1}$	—	—
				(SP 153.0%)	**14 Rn**	

3m 54.9 (-0.10) CSF £115.78 CT £1,469.35 TOTE £20.00: £4.80 £4.50 £21.70 (£31.30) Trio Not won; £273.02 to Cheltenham 12/3/97
OWNER Mr Michael Saunders (MALTON) BRED Sheikh Mohammed Bin Rashid Al Maktoum
LONG HANDICAP Rubislaw 8-8 Ten Past Six 9-11 Promise To Try (IRE) 9-3
WEIGHT FOR AGE 4yo-8lb

1640 Rothari has taken time to come right, but he showed fine battling qualities here, and there should be some more to come. (7/1)
Diamond Beach proved difficult to win with on the Flat but, by the looks of things, he should break his duck at this game. (14/1)
Jendorcet put in a decent first effort of the season, and will obviously pick up a race or two. (16/1)
3366 Ferrers always seemed to be stuck in behind other runners, and was short of pace to get out of trouble, but to his credit he did keep struggling on. (7/2)
2001 Pangeran (USA), from a stable just coming back to form, was having his first run for six weeks, and in the circumstances it was not a bad effort. (11/2)
Beau Matelot travelled well but, once off the bit, he failed to go through with his effort To give him the benefit, it was his first outing for over seven weeks. (16/1)
1921 Ten Past Six (13/2: 14/1-6/1)

T/Plpt: £2,136.20 (4.07 Tckts). T/Qdpt: £131.30 (3.26 Tckts) AA

3595-CHELTENHAM (L-H) (Good to firm)
Wednesday March 12th
Race 5- 4th last fence omitted.
WEATHER: fine

3613 ROYAL SUNALLIANCE NOVICES' HURDLE (Gd 1) (4-Y.O+) (Class A)
2-00 (2-00) **2m 5f (Old) (10 hdls)** £49,585.00 (£18,535.00: £9,047.50: £3,872.50: £1,716.25: £853.75) GOING: 0.07 sec per fur (G)

	Horse	Dist	Pos	SP	RR	SF
2995a*	**Istabraq (IRE)** (APO'Brien,Ireland) **5-11-7** CFSwan (lw: hld up in rr: hdwy 7th: chal & bmpd 2 out: led appr last: all out)	—	**1**	$6/5^{1}$	101+	73
3152^{2}	**Mighty Moss (IRE) (124)** (DNicholson) **6-11-7** MrFHutsby (led after 4th tl appr last: rallied u.p towards fin)	1	**2**	11/1	100	72
2771^{7}	**Daraydan (IRE) (120)** (MCPipe) **5-11-7** RHughes (prom: ev ch 2 out: styd on u.p flat)	¾	**3**	16/1	100	72
2948^{2}	**Forest Ivory (NZ)** (DNicholson) **6-11-7** RJohnson (chsd ldrs: chal, edgd lft & bmpd 2 out: hrd rdn & one pce)	3	**4**	14/1	97	69
3152^{P}	**Soldat (USA) (114)** (DNicholson) **4-10-12** DBridgwater (nvr nr to chal)	7	**5**	33/1	92	55
3152^{6}	**Harbour Island** (MCPipe) **5-11-7b** NWilliamson (hld up: hdwy & blnd 5th: n.d after)	10	**6**	25/1	84	56
3382a^{3}	**Difficult Times (IRE)** (GMLyons,Ireland) **5-11-7** SCLyons (prom to 7th)	s.h	**7**	33/1	84	56
3152^{3}	**Marching Marquis (IRE)** (NoelChance) **6-11-7** APMcCoy (lw: hld up: hdwy 5th: wknd appr 3 out)	¾	**8**	20/1	84	56
3272*	**Royaltino (IRE)** (FDoumen,France) **5-11-7** AKondrat (swtg: hld up: smooth hdwy 6th: ev ch whn blnd next: wkng whn hit 2 out)	7	**9**	$9/1^{3}$	79	51
2746^{8}	**Hand Woven (120)** (NATwiston-Davies) **5-11-7** CMaude (lw: a in rr)	1½	**10**	66/1	77	49
	Boss Doyle (IRE) (MFMorris) **5-11-7** CO'Dwyer (chsd ldrs: pushed along appr 3 out: sn wknd: t.o)	14	**11**	20/1	67	39
3265*	**The Proms (IRE) (109)** (NATwiston-Davies) **6-11-7** CLlewellyn (lw: a bhd: t.o)	¾	**12**	25/1	66	38
2690^{5}	**Nasone (IRE) (110)** (JTGifford) **6-11-7** PHide (lw: hdwy 5th: jnd ldrs 7th: wknd appr next: t.o)	3	**13**	100/1	64	36
3049^{7}	**Prussia (95)** (WClay) **6-11-7** GuyLewis (rdn appr 6th: a bhd: t.o)	¾	**14**	200/1	63	35
2880^{6}	**Hurdante (IRE) (115)** (GBBalding) **7-11-7** BFenton (led tl after 2nd: wknd appr 7th: t.o)	¾	**15**	50/1	63	35
3272^{4}	**Latahaab (USA)** (JTGifford) **6-11-7** LAspell (led after 2nd tl after 4th: wknd 7th: t.o)	9	**16**	100/1	56	28
2948*	**Agistment (127)** (JGFitzGerald) **6-11-7** RDunwoody (fell 1st: dead)		**F**	$6/1^{2}$	—	—
				(SP 119.7%)	**17 Rn**	

4m 58.2 (0.20) CSF £11.43 TOTE £2.40: £1.50 £2.20 £3.30 (£10.60) Trio £68.70 OWNER Mr J. P. McManus (PILTOWN) BRED Shadwell Estate Company Limited
WEIGHT FOR AGE 4yo-9lb
STEWARDS' ENQUIRY Hughes susp. 21-22 & 24-26/3/97 (excessive use of whip).

2995a* Istabraq (IRE), given a very patient ride over this extended trip, almost got knocked over when joining issue at the second last, but he is a tough individual and powered home for a very popular success. (6/5)
3152 Mighty Moss (IRE) does not know how to run a bad race, and he looks to have a very interesting future ahead of him. (11/1)
2771 Daraydan (IRE), running over a more suitable trip, ran possibly his best race yet over hurdles, and it seemed a tough decision by the Stewards to suspend his jockey for five days for trying too hard. (16/1)

2948 Forest Ivory (NZ) is not short on stamina, but the ground was all against him, and the fact that he was able to perform so well shows what a promising prospect he really is. (14/1)
3152 Harbour Island ruined what chance he had with a bad mistake going out into the country, and had little hope of recovery. (25/1)
3272* Royaltino (IRE) (9/1: 6/1-10/1)

3614 QUEEN MOTHER CHAMPION CHASE (Gd 1) (5-Y.O+) (Class A)

2-35 (2-38) **2m (Old) (12 fncs)** £81,650.00 (£30,350.00: £14,675.00: £6,125.00: £2,562.50: £1,137.50) GOING: 0.07 sec per fur (G)

				SP	RR	SF
3299^{F}	**Martha's Son (164)** (CaptTAForster) **10-12-0** RFarrant (hld up in rr: hdwy appr 3 out: led last: r.o wl)	—	**1**	9/1	169	94
2646*	**Ask Tom (IRE) (160)** (TPTate) **8-12-0** RGarritty (lw: swtg: led appr 2nd to 6th: lft in ld 3 out: hdd after next: ev ch last: unable qckn)	2½	**2**	6/1^{3}	167	92
3299*	**Viking Flagship (170)** (DNicholson) **10-12-0** RDunwoody (hld up: hdwy 4th: led after 2 out to last: rdn & no ex flat)	½	**3**	3/1^{2}	166	91
3128a*	**Klairon Davis (FR) (175)** (ALTMoore,Ireland) **8-12-0** FWoods (hld up: plld hrd: hdwy 6th: outpcd appr 2 out: styd on strly towards fin)	1	**4**	3/1^{2}	165	90
2935*	**Strong Promise (IRE) (160)** (GAHubbard) **6-12-0** NWilliamson (lw: led tl appr 2nd: led 6th tl blnd & hdd 3 out: wknd appr last)	5	**5**	5/2^{1}	160	85
3144^{2}	**Lord Dorcet (IRE) (133)** (JIACharlton) **7-12-0** JOsborne (prom to 8th: sn lost pl)	8	**6**	50/1	145 t	77
3299^{2}	***Arctic Kinsman* (145)** (NATwiston-Davies) **9-12-0** CLlewellyn (Withdrawn not under Starter's orders: b.b.v at s)		**W**	16/1	—	—
				(SP 110.7%)		**6 Rn**

3m 50.1 (-2.90) CSF £45.94 TOTE £11.00: £3.10 £2.00 (£21.10) OWNER Mr P. J. Hartigan (LUDLOW) BRED M. Ward-Thomas
3299 Martha's Son let the leaders cut their own throats and, staying on strongly up the hill after taking command at the last, won going away. He has had a very quiet time of it in the past couple of seasons, but has certainly lost none of his ability. (9/1)
2646* Ask Tom (IRE), a very progressive chaser who is destined for the top, ran a blinder in this very strong line-up, and connections must be over the moon with his progress. (6/1)
3299* Viking Flagship invariably reserves his best for this and, although the fast ground was not in his favour, he was only run out of it up the hill. (3/1)
3128a* Klairon Davis (FR), a real racehorse when he can get his toe in, was fighting a lost cause in his attempt to repeat last year's victory, but he stayed on really well up the final climb, after getting outpaced on the downhill run to the penultimate obstacle. (3/1)
2935* Strong Promise (IRE) has enjoyed a fantastic season, but he had it all to do on this return to the minimum trip against these smart rivals. To his credit, he was still calling the tune when a bad mistake three out took the stuffing out of him. (5/2)

3615 CORAL CUP H'CAP HURDLE (5-Y.O+) (Class B)

3-15 (3-15) **2m 5f (Old) (10 hdls)** £41,486.00 (£12,488.00: £6,044.00: £2,822.00) GOING: 0.07 sec per fur (G)

				SP	RR	SF
3269*	**Big Strand (IRE) (122)** (MCPipe) **8-10-0** JamieEvans (bhd: gd hdwy appr last: str run to ld last stride)	—	**1**	16/1	106	57
3267*	**Allegation (142)** (MCPipe) **7-11-6v** APMcCoy (chsd ldr: led appr 3 out: hrd rdn: ct post)	s.h	**2**	20/1	126	77
2774^{3}	**Castle Sweep (IRE) (150)** (DNicholson) **6-12-0** RJohnson (hld up: hdwy appr 3 out: ev ch whn mstke last: r.o wl nr fin)	hd	**3**	14/1	134+	85
2888*	**Tullymurry Toff (IRE) (135)** (JMJefferson) **6-10-10**(3) ECallaghan (mid div: pushed along ½-wy: outpcd appr 3 out: r.o strly flat)	1	**4**	9/2^{1}	118	69
	Tamarpour (USA) (122) (MCPipe) **10-9-7b**(7) BMoore (hld up & bhd: gd hdwy 3 out: styd on flat)	1	**5**	100/1	104+	55
3150^{5}	**Dr Leunt (IRE) (125)** (PJHobbs) **6-10-3** GTormey (a.p: rdn 2 out: kpt on)	1	**6**	40/1	107	58
	Ballyrihy Boy (IRE) (122) (CaptDGSwan,Ireland) **6-10-0** CFSwan (nvr nrr)	½	**7**	33/1	103	54
	Eton Gale (IRE) (122) (TFoley,Ireland) **8-10-0** RHughes (bhd tl styd on appr 2 out: nrst fin)	hd	**8**	100/1	103	54
1793^{7}	**Mystical City (IRE) (137)** (WPMullins,Ireland) **7-10-12**(3) DJCasey (nvr nrr)	¾	**9**	25/1	118	69
3227^{2}	**Mandys Mantino (144)** (JTGifford) **7-11-8** PHide (hld up: hdwy 6th: wknd appr 2 out)	2½	**10**	20/1	123	74
2603a^{5}	**Metastasio (125)** (DGMcArdle,Ireland) **5-10-3b** HRogers (prom tl wknd appr 3 out)	5	**11**	33/1	100	51
3045*	**Supreme Lady (IRE) (128)** (MissHCKnight) **6-10-6** JCulloty (nvr plcd to chal)	3	**12**	10/1^{2}	101	52
2651*	**Ela Mata (124)** (MrsASwinbank) **5-10-2** JRailton (prom: wkng whn blnd 2 out)	¾	**13**	10/1^{2}	96	47
	Rawy (USA) (126) (CRoche,Ireland) **5-10-4b** CO'Dwyer (prom: rdn 3 out: wknd & eased appr last)	1¾	**14**	12/1^{3}	97	48
3231^{3}	**Blast Freeze (IRE) (126)** (NJHenderson) **8-10-4** MAFitzgerald (nvr trbld ldrs)	2½	**15**	12/1^{3}	95	46
3199*	**Non Vintage (IRE) (126)** (MCChapman) **6-10-4** WWorthington (a bhd)	1¼	**16**	40/1	94	45
2603a^{7}	**Executive Design (132)** (MrsMReveley) **5-10-10** PNiven (a in rr)	nk	**17**	16/1	100	51
3163^{7}	**Nijmegen (125)** (JGFitzGerald) **9-10-3b** DerekByrne (hdwy 6th: wknd appr 3 out)	¾	**18**	33/1	92	43
3150^{6}	**Lying Eyes (122)** (WGMTurner) **6-9-7**(7) JPower (a in rr)	¾	**19**	50/1	88	39
3293^{3}	**Kissair (IRE) (130)** (NJHenderson) **6-10-8** RDunwoody (prom to 7th: sn wknd)	s.h	**20**	25/1	96	47
2551^{F}	**Gysart (IRE) (122)** (MCPipe) **8-10-0b** CMaude (nt j.w: rcd wd: w ldrs tl mstke 7th: t.o)	8	**21**	33/1	82	33
3303^{10}	**Fatack (122)** (PRWebber) **8-10-0** SCurran (in tch to 6th: sn wknd: t.o)	17	**22**	50/1	69	20
3286^{5}	**Sesame Seed (IRE) (122)** (NJHenderson) **9-10-0** JOsborne (prom: wkng whn hmpd 3 out: t.o)	1	**23**	33/1	69	20
3011*	**Copper Boy (126)** (RHBuckler) **8-10-4** BPowell (led tl hdd & blnd 3 out: sn wknd: t.o)	12	**24**	10/1^{2}	63	14
3112^{4}	**Scottish Wedding (122)** (TWall) **7-9-11**(3) RMassey (a bhd: t.o fr 6th)	12	**25**	200/1	50	1
3412^{3}	**Sea Victor (122)** (JLHarris) **5-10-0** DGallagher (a bhd: t.o fr 3 out)	7	**26**	12/1^{3}	45	—
3038^{3}	**Direct Route (IRE) (138)** (HowardJohnson) **6-11-2** NWilliamson (hdwy 6th: hmpd bnd after next: sn bhd: p.u after 2 out: dismntd)		**P**	16/1	—	—
2603a^{4}	**Family Way (127)** (ALTMoore,Ireland) **10-10-5** FWoods (a bhd: t.o: p.u lame bef 3 out: dead)		**P**	16/1	—	—
				(SP 141.9%)		**28 Rn**

4m 57.0 (-1.00) CSF £292.83 CT £4,196.60 TOTE £26.10: £5.40 £4.40 £3.50 £2.10 (£138.10) Trio £761.70 OWNER Mr E. C. Jones (WELLINGTON) BRED M. Parkhill
LONG HANDICAP Lying Eyes 9-13 Eton Gale (IRE) 9-2 Fatack 9-12 Sesame Seed (IRE) 9-11 Ballyrihy Boy (IRE) 9-9 Scottish Wedding 7-3 Sea Victor 9-10 Gysart (IRE) 9-13
IN-FOCUS: A year after he broke a leg at the meeting, Jamie Evans became the first Australian to ride a Festival winner.
3269* Big Strand (IRE) looked to have been set a hopeless task when making stealthy progress on meeting the rising ground, but his jockey knows him well, and the partnership burst through to collar his stablemate right on the line. (16/1)
3267* Allegation ran up to his best on such lively ground, looking all over the winner until touched-off in the final stride. He certainly deserves consolation after such a game effort. (20/1)
2774 Castle Sweep (IRE) came late on the scene, and would have landed in front but for a last-flight mistake. The fact that he was able to renew his effort only goes to prove what an unlucky loser he was. (14/1)

2888* Tullymurry Toff (IRE) never seemed to be enjoying himself, and looked out of it at the second last, but he began to pick up on reaching the rising ground, and was still gaining fast at the finish. It is intended to send him chasing next year. (9/2)
Tamarpour (USA), out of action for 588 days, was pegging back the principals in the latter stages, and this good effort should help put an edge on him. (100/1)
3150 Dr Leunt (IRE) has not won beyond two miles, but he was prepared to push the pace, and it was not lack of stamina that beat him. (40/1)
3045* Supreme Lady (IRE) (10/1: 6/1-11/1)
3011* Copper Boy (10/1: 6/1-11/1)

3616 ROYAL SUNALLIANCE NOVICES' CHASE (Gd 1) (5-Y.O+) (Class A)

3-55 (3-55) **3m 1f (Old) (19 fncs)** £57,282.49 (£21,417.50: £10,458.75: £4,481.25: £1,990.63: £994.38) GOING: 0.07 sec per fur (G)

				SP	RR	SF
3230[3]	**Hanakham (IRE) (118)** (RJHodges) **8-11-4** RDunwoody (lw: hld up gng wl: led 2 out: clr whn mstke last: rdn out)	—	**1**	13/2[3]	150	71
3268*	**Eudipe (FR)** (MCPipe) **5-10-8** APMcCoy (hld up & bhd: hdwy 15th: rdn appr 3 out: styd on flat)	2½	**2**	4/1[2]	148	59
2936*	**Djeddah (FR) (139)** (FDoumen,France) **6-11-4** AKondrat (lw: hld up: hdwy 7th: ev ch 2 out: btn whn mstke last)	5	**3**	100/30[1]	145	66
3274*	**Berude Not to (IRE)** (OSherwood) **8-11-4b** JOsborne (led to 2nd: led 15th to 2 out: rdn & wknd appr last)	2	**4**	15/2	144	65
3380a*	**Corket (IRE)** (APO'Brien,Ireland) **7-11-4** CFSwan (plld hrd: prom to 4 out)	9	**5**	9/1	138	59
3086*	**Glitter Isle (IRE) (119)** (JTGifford) **7-11-4** PHide (hld up: hdwy 9th: wknd 4 out)	6	**6**	16/1	134	55
3104*	**Hawaiian Sam (IRE) (105)** (AndrewTurnell) **7-11-4** GCrone (prom: led 6th to 15th: sn wknd: t.o)	16	**7**	66/1	124	45
2883[3]	**Baronet (IRE) (120)** (DNicholson) **7-11-4** RJohnson (a bhd: t.o)	1½	**8**	25/1	124	45
	Lord Muff (IRE) (LComer,Ireland) **8-11-4** JKKinane (mstkes: a bhd: t.o)	1	**9**	100/1	123	44
3285*	**Bell Staffboy (IRE) (124)** (JGMO'Shea) **8-11-4** MichaelBrennan (mstke 3rd: sn bhd: t.o)	½	**10**	14/1	123	44
2883[2]	**Indian Tracker** (MCPipe) **7-11-4** CMaude (led 2nd: mstke 5th: hdd next: ev ch 3 out: wknd appr next: t.o)	3	**11**	10/1	121	42
3068[P]	**Ballyline (IRE) (88)** (WTKemp) **6-11-4** JRailton (prom: mstke 2nd: wknd 10th: p.u bef 12th)		**P**	150/1	—	—
3155[2]	**Buckhouse Boy (132)** (NATwiston-Davies) **7-11-4** DBridgwater (in rr: mstke 7th: p.u bef 13th)		**P**	11/1	—	—
3160[3]	**The Last Fling (IRE) (124)** (MrsSJSmith) **7-11-4** RichardGuest (nt j.w: hdwy 13th: prom whn blnd & uns rdr 4 out)		**U**	33/1	—	—
				(SP 118.1%)	**14 Rn**	

6m 8.8 (-0.20) CSF £29.38 TOTE £7.40: £2.30 £2.20 £1.90 (£18.70) Trio £19.30 OWNER Mr M. Brereton (SOMERTON) BRED Eamonn McCarthy
WEIGHT FOR AGE 5yo-10lb

3230 Hanakham (IRE), always travelling cosily, took control at the penultimate fence, and was forging clear when he took off a stride too soon at the last, and in the end had to be ridden out to retain his advantage. He looks set to go a long way. (13/2)
3268* Eudipe (FR), having his first try at this longer trip, stayed on stoutly in the closing stages, but he is highly flattered to run the winner so close. (4/1: 5/2-9/2)
2936* Djeddah (FR) failed in his bid to make it a hat-trick in this country, but he was still a live threat at the penultimate obstacle, before the winner left him trailing. (100/30)
3274* Berude Not to (IRE) helped force the pace, and kept the pressure on until finding the demands just too much for him when faced with the hill. (15/2)
3380a* Corket (IRE) has remained unbeaten over fences in Ireland, but he has not raced on this type of ground, and was a spent force soon after jumping the final ditch. (9/1)
3104* Hawaiian Sam (IRE) gave a bold display of jumping out in front, until fading rather quickly approaching the fourth last. He will soon regain form when put back into his own class. (66/1)
3285* Bell Staffboy (IRE) (14/1: 10/1-16/1)

3617 127TH YEAR OF THE NATIONAL HUNT CHALLENGE CUP AMATEUR CHASE (5-Y.O+) (Class B)

4-30 (4-33) **4m (Old) (23 fncs)** £21,525.00 (£6,450.00: £3,100.00: £1,425.00) GOING: GOING: 0.07 sec per fur (G)

				SP	RR	SF
3047[4]	**Flimsy Truth (104)** (MHWeston) **11-12-7** MrMHarris (j.w: mde all: rdn out)	—	**1**	33/1	126	53
2908*	**Vol Par Nuit (USA) (110)** (FDoumen,France) **6-12-4** MrTDoumen (chsd wnr thrght: blnd 20th: r.o wl flat)	1¼	**2**	13/2[2]	122	49
3020[2]	**Robsand (IRE) (83)** (GBBalding) **8-12-0** MrABalding (lw: trckd ldrs tl wknd appr 3 out)	27	**3**	9/1	102	29
	Irish Light (IRE) (MJMcDonagh,Ireland) **9-12-7** MrAnthonyMartin (lw: hld up: hdwy 17th: rdn 3 out: wknd 2 out)	3	**4**	16/1	107	34
2936[2]	**Dromhana (IRE) (110)** (PFNicholls) **7-12-7** MrJTizzard (a chsng ldrs: hit 12th: btn whn mstke 3 out)	1¼	**5**	9/1	107	34
3155[4]	**Parahandy (IRE)** (GBBalding) **7-12-0** MrDO'Brien (hld up: mstke 7th: nvr rchd ldrs)	7	**6**	16/1	95	22
3389a[2]	**Coolafinka (IRE)** (JABerry,Ireland) **8-11-9** MrJBerry (a bhd: t.o)	12	**7**	12/1	83	10
3018[5]	**Ballyea Boy (IRE) (112)** (DNicholson) **7-12-7b**[1] MrRThornton (chsd ldrs: rdn & lost pl 17th: t.o)	6	**8**	14/1	92	19
3185[P]	**Loch Garman Hotel (IRE) (81)** (PTDalton) **8-12-0** MrBPollock (lw: chsd ldrs: wkng whn j.b rt 3 out: sn t.o)	8	**9**	100/1	80	7
2345a[8]	**Young Mrs Kelly (IRE)** (EMcNamara,Ireland) **7-11-9** MrGJHarford (mstkes: bhd tl fell 14th)		**F**	33/1	—	—
3270[U]	**Master Kit (IRE)** (JNRBillinge) **8-12-4** MrJBillinge (mstke 5th: bhd whn fell 16th)		**F**	50/1	—	—
3047*	**General Pongo (105)** (TRGeorge) **8-12-7** MrCVigors (lw: mid div tl wknd 18th: blnd 20th: t.o whn p.u bef 3 out)		**P**	9/1	—	—
	Macaunta (IRE) (AJMcNamara,Ireland) **7-12-7** MrJTMcNamara (lw: a bhd: t.o whn p.u bef 3 out)		**P**	25/1	—	—
	Itsajungleoutthere (IRE) (MFMorris,Ireland) **7-12-4** MrWEwing (bhd: mstke 15th: t.o whn p.u bef 2 out)		**P**	16/1	—	—
3202*	**Random Harvest (IRE) (112)** (MrsMReveley) **8-12-7** MrSSwiers (lw: j.rt 5th: hdwy & hit 16th: wknd 20th: p.u bef 2 out)		**P**	6/1[1]	—	—
3132[4]	**Wixoe Wonder (IRE) (77)** (MBradstock) **7-12-0** MrEJames (chsd ldrs: rdn 16th: wkng whn mstke 19th: bhd whn p.u bef 3 out)		**P**	66/1	—	—
3472[P]	**Plassy Boy (IRE) (72)** (KRBurke) **8-12-0v** MrNWilson (bhd: mstke 13th: bdly hmpd next: t.o whn p.u bef 7th)		**P**	100/1	—	—
3400[5]	**Cardinal Rule (IRE) (90)** (MissVenetiaWilliams) **8-12-7** MrRBurton (a bhd: t.o whn p.u bef 2 out)		**P**	50/1	—	—
3360[3]	**Jasilu (99)** (KCBailey) **7-12-2b** MrOMcPhail (bhd whn mstke 18th: t.o whn p.u bef 3 out)		**P**	50/1	—	—
3073[3]	**Charlie Parrot (IRE)** (MCPipe) **7-12-0** MrAFarrant (sn t.o: p.u bef 16th)		**P**	50/1	—	—
3202[2]	**Slideofhill (IRE)** (JJO'Neill) **8-12-0b**[1] MrPFenton (mstke 5th: a bhd: t.o whn p.u after 20th)		**P**	7/1[3]	—	—
3446*	**Capo Castanum (86)** (MissHCKnight) **8-12-7** MrAWintle (mid div whn blnd & uns rdr 12th)		**U**	33/1	—	—
3047[P]	**Little Martina (IRE) (108)** (DMGrissell) **9-11-13** MrCBonner (prom tl blnd & uns rdr 12th)		**U**	14/1	—	—

				SP	RR	SF
*3003**	*Ceridwen* **(85)** (TRGreathead) **7-12-2** MrJTrice-Rolph (Withdrawn not under Starter's orders: lame)		**W**	33/1	—	—
				(SP 135.7%)	**23 Rn**	

8m 11.09 (1.61 under best) (15.09) CSF £220.29 TOTE £56.60: £11.70 £2.60 £3.90 (£163.10) Trio £333.90 OWNER Mr M. H. Weston (WORCESTER) BRED M. H. Weston

3047 Flimsy Truth, much happier when allowed to bowl along at the head of affairs, jumped these fences for fun and, showing little sign of stopping, ran out a deserved winner. (33/1)

2908* Vol Par Nuit (USA) readily accepted a lead, and looked able to take over at will, but an untidy mistake five out made him work a bit harder. Although he stayed on strongly on the run-in, the winner refused to give best. Only a six-year-old, he looks a promising prospect.(13/2)

3020 Robsand (IRE) kept tabs on the leading pair, until he became very leg-weary and called enough on the downhill run to the third last. (9/1)

Irish Light (IRE) took closer order inside the final mile, but failed to raise his pace approaching the third last, and dropped away tamely at the next. (16/1)

2936 Dromhana (IRE) appeared to be waiting on the leaders, but he began to fade at the top of the hill, and was already labouring when barging his way through the third last. (9/1)

3202* Random Harvest (IRE) found these bigger fences a bit of a problem and, although he did make an effort to get into it, was struggling from a long way out, and was eventually pulled up. (6/1)

3618 47TH YEAR OF THE MILDMAY OF FLETE CHALLENGE CUP H'CAP CHASE (5-Y.O+) (Class B)

5-05 (5-08) **2m 4f 110y (Old) (15 fncs)** £30,044.00 (£9,002.00: £4,326.00: £1,988.00) GOING: 0.07 sec per fur (G)

Form	Horse	Dist	Pos	SP	RR	SF
3292^{2}	**Terao (121)** (MCPipe) **11-10-7** TJMurphy (prom: led 6th to 4 out: led appr last: r.o wl)	—	**1**	20/1	137	63
3160*	**All the Aces (125)** (JJO'Neill) **10-10-11** CFSwan (hld up & bhd: gd hdwy fr 2 out: hmpd bnd appr last: mstke last: fin strly)	1¼	**2**	14/1	140	66
3151*	**Air Shot (135)** (DNicholson) **7-11-7** RJohnson (hld up: hdwy & mstke 4 out: hrd rdn appr last: r.o wl)	hd	**3**	15/2	150	76
3288*	**Noyan (115)** (RAFahey) **7-10-1** ADobbin (swtg: chsd ldrs: rdn 3 out: hit last: styd on)	1¾	**4**	11/2^{2}	129	55
3413^{2}	**Destiny Calls (123)** (NAGaselee) **7-10-9** PNiven (a.p: led 2 out: sn hdd: one pce)	1½	**5**	6/1^{3}	135	61
3279*	**As du Trefle (FR) (114)** (MCPipe) **9-10-0** APMcCoy (led to 6th: led 4 out to 2 out: hung lft & wknd flat)	8	**6**	100/30^{1}	120	46
3169^{2}	**Southampton (120)** (GBBalding) **7-10-6v** BFenton (hld up: pckd 8th: nvr trbld ldrs)	2½	**7**	16/1	124	50
3151^{3}	**Bells Life (IRE) (132)** (PJHobbs) **8-11-4** GTormey (a bhd)	5	**8**	25/1	132	58
2887^{2}	**Northern Hide (127)** (MSalaman) **11-10-13** PHolley (rdn 7th: hdwy 9th: wknd 11th)	3½	**9**	16/1	125	51
3254a^{7}	**New Co (IRE) (136)** (MFMorris,Ireland) **9-11-8** CO'Dwyer (hld up: hdwy 11th: mstkes 4 out & 3 out: sn wknd: t.o)	9	**10**	14/1	127	53
2773^{5}	**Pashto (130)** (NJHenderson) **10-11-2** RDunwoody (prom tl wknd 10th: bhd whn blnd 4 out: t.o)	dist	**11**	16/1	—	—
2901*	**Konvekta King (IRE) (138)** (OSherwood) **9-11-10** JOsborne (a bhd: t.o whn p.u bef 4 out)		**P**	11/1	—	—
3039*	**Golden Spinner (133)** (NJHenderson) **10-11-5** MAFitzgerald (mstke 1st: chsd ldrs to 8th: bhd whn p.u bef 3 out)		**P**	7/1	—	—
				(SP 124.9%)	**13 Rn**	

5m 1.2 (-0.80) CSF £254.85 CT £2,104.22 TOTE £31.40: £6.40 £3.30 £2.50 (£148.90) Trio £152.70 OWNER Mr B. A. Kilpatrick (WELLINGTON) BRED J. F. C. Maxwell

IN-FOCUS: **This was Martin Pipe's fourth winner at the Festival, a post-war record.**

3292 Terao, winning for the first time in thirteen months, gave his younger rivals a lesson in jumping, and stole the prize when gaining a decisive lead into the last. (20/1)

3160* All the Aces, unproven on this ground, did not enjoy the clearest of passages when making rapid progress on the elbow between the last two, and made a horrid mistake when thrown into the last. In the circumstances he did well to rally so strongly nearing the finish. (14/1)

3151* Air Shot ran a fine race in defeat and, but for a mistake at the final ditch, would almost certainly have won. This ground was plenty fast enough for him. (15/2)

3288* Noyan coped reasonably well with these big fences, but he was making hard work of it inside the last half-mile, and was never able to land a blow despite staying on. (11/2)

3413 Destiny Calls looked set to score when gaining a slight lead at the penultimate fence, but the winner took his measure in next to no time, and he found an extra effort beyond him. (6/1)

3279* As du Trefle (FR), subject of heavy support in his first real test over fences, was soon fighting a losing battle after being headed at the second last, and he was a tired horse when he hung off a true line on the run-in. (100/30)

3619 WEATHERBYS CHAMPION BUMPER STANDARD OPEN N.H. FLAT RACE (Gd 1) (4, 5 & 6-Y.O) (Class A)

5-40 (5-45) **2m 110y (Old)** £18,760.00 (£7,068.00: £3,434.00: £1,538.00)

Form	Horse	Dist	Pos	SP	RR	SF
	Florida Pearl (IRE) (WPMullins,Ireland) **5-11-6** RDunwoody (hld up: a.p: led over 3f out: sn clr: readily)	—	**1**	6/1^{2}	99 f	—
3304^{2}	**Arctic Camper** (DNicholson) **5-11-6** RJohnson (lw: hld up: rdn & hdwy 4f out: hung lft & r.o fnl f: no ch w wnr)	5	**2**	16/1	94 f	—
	All The Colours (IRE) (JEMulhern,Ireland) **4-10-12** JOsborne (a.p: rdn & one pce fnl 2f)	2	**3**	10/1	92 f	—
3304^{3}	**Scoring Pedigree (IRE)** (JWMullins) **5-11-6** SCurran (lw: hld up & bhd: gd hdwy over 3f out: rdn 2f out: styd on)	¾	**4**	66/1	92 f	—
3042*	**Mr Markham (IRE)** (JTGifford) **5-11-6** PHide (lw: hld up mid div: styd on fnl 2f: nvr nrr)	1½	**5**	9/1	90 f	—
	French Holly (USA) (FMurphy) **6-11-6** RHughes (prom tl rdn & wknd over 1f out)	s.h	**6**	10/1	90 f	—
3170*	**Samuel Wilderspin** (DNicholson) **5-11-3**(3) RMassey (hld up & bhd: hdwy 5f out: wknd over 1f out)	¾	**7**	7/1^{3}	89 f	—
1966^{2}	**Brownes Hill Lad (IRE)** (RJO'Sullivan) **5-11-6** DBridgwater (lw: prom tl rdn & wknd over 2f out)	¾	**8**	33/1	89 f	—
	Musical Mayhem (IRE) (DKWeld,Ireland) **4-10-12** CO'Dwyer (plld hrd: trckd ldrs tl wknd 2f out)	1¾	**9**	16/1	87 f	—
2931*	**Erintante (IRE)** (FDoumen,France) **4-10-2**(5) MrTDoumen (nvr nr to chal)	1¾	**10**	8/1	80 f	—
1774^{3}	**Bozo (IRE)** (BJMRyall) **6-11-6** BFenton (nvr nr ldrs)	nk	**11**	100/1	85 f	—
3090^{2}	**Curraduff Moll (IRE)** (NATwiston-Davies) **6-11-1** CLlewellyn (nvr nr ldrs)	3	**12**	33/1	77 f	—
3149*	**Dawn Leader (IRE)** (JABOld) **6-11-6** GUpton (lw: hld up & bhd: stdy hdwy 7f out: wknd over 2f out)	3	**13**	4/1^{1}	79 f	—
3042^{5}	**Iranos (FR)** (MCPipe) **5-11-6** APMcCoy (led tl over 3f out: sn rdn & wknd)	7	**14**	33/1	72 f	—
3021^{2}	**King Mole** (JABOld) **6-11-6** MAFitzgerald (lw: a bhd)	s.h	**15**	40/1	72 f	—
3042^{2}	**Dom Beltrano (FR)** (NATwiston-Davies) **5-11-6** CMaude (prom 12f: sn wknd)	s.h	**16**	50/1	72 f	—
	Furnitureville (IRE) (JMCanty,Ireland) **5-11-6** MrDMcGoona (lw: chsd ldrs 12f)	nk	**17**	16/1	72 f	—
	Our Bid (IRE) (KPrendergast,Ireland) **6-11-6** SCraine (hld up: hdwy 6f out: wknd over 3f out)	5	**18**	20/1	67 f	—
2750*	**Mr Lurpak** (MrsMReveley) **5-11-6** PNiven (lw: hld up: hdwy 8f out: wknd 3f out)	½	**19**	10/1	67 f	—
3021*	**Endeavour (FR)** (MJRoberts) **5-11-6** JRailton (lw: prom: rdn ½-wy: sn lost tch)	1	**20**	100/1	66 f	—
2830*	**Top Note (IRE)** (JTGifford) **5-11-3**(3) LAspell (t.o)	10	**21**	50/1	56 f	—
2640^{2}	**Ballad Minstrel (IRE)** (JGFitzGerald) **5-11-6** NWilliamson (bhd fnl 4f: t.o)	9	**22**	40/1	47 f	—

	Horse	Dist	Pos	SP	RR	SF
	Frankie Willow (IRE) (PFGraffin,Ireland) **4-10-12** MrPGraffin (t.o)	2	**23**	50/1	45 f	—
	Fawn Prince (IRE) (APO'Brien,Ireland) **4-10-12** CFSwan (lw: t.o)	21	**24**	12/1	25 f	—
3440[3]	**Memsahib Ofesteem** (SGollings) **6-11-1** JCulloty (t.o)	dist	**25**	100/1	—	—
				(SP 149.3%)	**25 Rn**	

3m 45.1 CSF £98.49 TOTE £5.90: £2.60 £9.40 £3.20 (£137.80) Trio £310.90 OWNER Mrs V. O'Leary (MUINE BEAG) BRED Mrs Patricia Mackean

WEIGHT FOR AGE 4yo-8lb

Florida Pearl (IRE) has been all the rage for this for quite some time and, giving the impression of a Derby horse in a maiden, simply outclassed the opposition and won in a canter. It will be interesting to see if he returns next year in one of the staying hurdles. (6/1: 4/1-7/1)

3304 Arctic Camper, from a stable whose animals appear in fine form, did not seem all that happy on the prevailing ground, but he beat the remainder easily enough, and lost no caste in defeat. (16/1)

All The Colours (IRE), a highly thought-of colt, was caught flat-footed when the winner quickened the tempo, and in this class could need much softer ground. (10/1)

3304 Scoring Pedigree (IRE) came from another county in the final mile, and stayed on doggedly to the end, but never promised to get on terms with the runaway winner. (66/1)

3042* Mr Markham (IRE) lost his unbeaten record but ran his best race yet, although he left his final effort plenty late enough. (9/1)

French Holly (USA) had more use made of him on this belated return to action, and his run had come to an end starting the final climb. This was a run full of promise. (10/1)

3170* Samuel Wilderspin did not quite get home in this better-class race, but he only called enough below the distance and can soon get back to winning ways. (7/1)

3149* Dawn Leader (IRE) made progress soon after halfway, but he was under pressure and in serious trouble approaching the final quarter-mile. (4/1)

2750* Mr Lurpak (10/1: 8/1-12/1)

T/Jkpt: Not won; £129,698.13 to Cheltenham 13/3/97. T/Plpt: £1,259.60 (139.94 Tckts). T/Qdpt: £90.80 (84.44 Tckts) IM

3352-**HUNTINGDON** (R-H) (Good, Good to firm patches, becoming Good to firm)
Wednesday March 12th

WEATHER: fine

3620 KEYSOE (S) H'CAP HURDLE (0-90) (4-Y.O+) (Class G)

1-50 (1-50) **2m 5f 110y (10 hdls)** £1,978.50 (£551.00: £265.50) GOING minus 0.59 sec per fur (F)

	Horse	Dist	Pos	SP	RR	SF
3471[2]	**Edward Seymour (USA) (74)** (WJenks) **10-11-4** TJenks (hld up: hdwy 7th: chal 2 out: led on bit flat: cleverly)	—	**1**	3/1[1]	59+	3
3284[U]	**Code Red (75)** (WRMuir) **4-10-10** MRichards (lw: hld up: mstke 1st: hdwy 6th: rdn appr 2 out: lft in ld 2 out: hdd flat: no ch w wnr)	1½	**2**	6/1[3]	59	—
3313[8]	**Bark'n'bite (80)** (MrsMReveley) **5-11-7**(3) GLee (lw: in tch tl blnd 7th: rallied & hit 3 out: rdn & one pce appr next)	3	**3**	6/1[3]	62	6
3352[6]	**Song For Jess (IRE) (70)** (FJordan) **4-10-5** SWynne (prom: led after 6th: swvd lft & hdd 2 out: sn btn)	1½	**4**	16/1	51	—
3338[6]	**Mick The Yank (IRE) (59)** (HOliver) **7-10-3b** JacquiOliver (chsd ldrs: ev ch 7th tl hmpd 2 out: nt rcvr)	2	**5**	5/1[2]	38	—
3362[7]	**Viscount Tully (74)** (CFCJackson) **12-10-13**(5) OBurrows (hld up: hdwy 7th: ev ch appr 2 out: sn rdn & wknd)	3	**6**	6/1[3]	51	—
3284[9]	**Autumn Flame (IRE) (62)** (OBrennan) **6-10-6** MBrennan (lw: t.o fr 7th)	dist	**7**	14/1	—	—
3447[15]	**Slightly Special (IRE) (58)** (BAPearce) **5-10-2** KGaule (chsd ldr: mstkes 3rd & 6th: wknd next)	2	**8**	14/1	—	—
3429[P]	**Kano Warrior (80)** (BPreece) **10-11-3**(7) JMogford (led: clr 2nd: j.lft 6th: sn hdd & wknd)	5	**9**	33/1	—	—
3338[4]	**Shanakee (73)** (BJLlewellyn) **10-11-3** MrJLLlewellyn (trckd ldrs tl wknd appr 3 out: p.u bef next)		**P**	6/1[3]	—	—
				(SP 121.0%)	**10 Rn**	

5m 5.8 (5.80) CSF £20.71 CT £95.51 TOTE £2.50: £1.30 £1.60 £2.20 (£13.10) Trio £19.00 OWNER Mr W. Jenks (BRIDGNORTH) BRED Equigroup Thoroughbreds

WEIGHT FOR AGE 4yo-9lb

No bid

3471 Edward Seymour (USA) caught a real tartar last time, but met nothing of that standard here and never came off the bridle. (3/1)

3284 Code Red was just moving up to challenge when left in front at the penultimate flight. He kept plugging away, but the winner was just laughing at him on the run-in. (6/1)

Bark'n'bite looked a tricky ride, but would probably have finished second with a better round of jumping. (6/1: 7/2-13/2)

3352 Song For Jess (IRE), back on faster ground, was still just at the head of affairs when swerving away her chance early in the straight. (16/1)

Mick The Yank (IRE) has been a rather disappointing horse this season, but ran better on the faster ground and should have finished closer. (5/1: op 10/1)

2838 Viscount Tully moved up threateningly on the home turn, but failed to sustain the effort for long. (6/1)

3338 Shanakee (6/1: 4/1-7/1)

3621 MELCHBOURNE MAIDEN HURDLE (4-Y.O+) (Class E)

2-25 (2-26) **2m 5f 110y (10 hdls)** £2,635.00 (£735.00: £355.00) GOING minus 0.59 sec per fur (F)

	Horse	Dist	Pos	SP	RR	SF
1800[8]	**Northern Star** (JAPickering) **6-10-12**(7) MissJWormall (bit bkwd: nt j.w: hdwy 7th: qcknd to ld appr 2 out: sn rdn: r.o)	—	**1**	16/1	66	14
3233[9]	**Loch Na Keal** (CPMorlock) **5-10-11**(3) DFortt (plld hrd: chsd ldrs: kpt on fr 2 out)	2	**2**	9/1	60	8
3426[7]	**Tursal (IRE)** (TWDonnelly) **8-11-5** MrRArmson (hdwy 5th: one pce fr 2 out)	3	**3**	66/1	62	10
2800[7]	**Not To Panic (IRE) (63)** (KRBurke) **7-11-0** RSupple (hdwy 7th: one pce appr last)	2	**4**	33/1	56	4
3416[3]	**Leap in the Dark (IRE) (80)** (MissLCSiddall) **8-10-12**(7) TSiddall (lw: prom tl mstke 3 out)	4	**5**	10/1	58	6
3365[7]	**Boundtohonour (IRE)** (HOliver) **5-11-5** JacquiOliver (plld hrd: prom tl wknd appr 3 out)	nk	**6**	20/1	58	6
3437[4]	**Castle Mews (IRE)** (GCBravery) **6-11-0** KGaule (lw: chsd ldrs tl rdn & btn appr 2 out)	s.h	**7**	6/1	53	1
2961[4]	**Dacelo (FR) (95)** (OSherwood) **6-11-5** JAMcCarthy (chsd ldrs tl wknd appr 2 out)	1½	**8**	4/1[3]	56	4
3362[5]	**Blatant Outburst (83)** (MissSJWilton) **7-11-5** GaryLyons (lw: plld hrd: chsd ldrs tl mstke 3 out)	20	**9**	16/1	42	—
3315[3]	**Dark Phoenix (IRE) (86)** (OBrennan) **7-11-0v** MBrennan (prom: led 7th tl appr 2 out: sn btn: virtually p.u flat)	18	**10**	3/1[1]	23	—
	Bright Flame (IRE) (MissSEdwards) **5-11-5** MrTHills (bkwd: mstke 3rd: a bhd)	2½	**11**	66/1	26	—

3205[4]	**Teoroma** (JRJenkins) **7-11-5** MrMGingell (led: hit 3rd: hdd 7th: sn wknd)	8	**12**	25/1	20	—
2805[17]	**Nuns Lucy (56)** (FJordan) **6-11-0** SWynne (lw: w ldrs to 6th: wknd appr 3 out)	2	**13**	50/1	14	—
	Buster (MrsBarbaraWaring) **9-11-5** EByrne (s.i.s: plld hrd: a bhd)	6	**14**	33/1	14	—
2746[P]	**Lilly The Filly** (MrsBarbaraWaring) **6-11-0** RBellamy (bhd: hdwy 6th: wknd appr 3 out)	3½	**15**	66/1	7	—
2010[6]	**Strathminster** (KCBailey) **6-11-5** TJO'Sullivan (lw: a.p: ev ch whn p.u lame appr 2 out: dead)		P	100/30 2	—	—
	Bandit Boy (WJMusson) **4-10-10** TJenks (a bhd: t.o whn p.u bef 3 out)		P	16/1	—	—
				(SP 140.0%)	**17 Rn**	

5m 2.5 (2.50) CSF £150.35 TOTE £54.60: £11.70 £4.10 £21.20 (£194.10) Trio Not won; £319.34 to Cheltenham 13/3/97 OWNER Mrs R. Wormall (HINCKLEY) BRED R. B. Stokes
WEIGHT FOR AGE 4yo-9lb
OFFICIAL EXPLANATION **Dark Phoenix (IRE): the jockey reported that he felt the mare to have gone lame, which caused him to pull her up. The mare was subsequently sound.**
Northern Star did not excel at the hurdles, particularly early on, but swept round the outside of the field to lead on the home turn, and won in the style of a quite useful horse. (16/1)
Loch Na Keal was taking something of a drop in class after contesting two fairly hot hurdles. (9/1: 9/2-10/1)
Tursal (IRE) is tall and has a high knee-action, but handled the fast ground well enough, doing enough to suggest he may find a race. (66/1)
Not To Panic (IRE) made a forward move on the inside rounding the home turn, but lacked the pace to take her chance. (33/1)
3416 Leap in the Dark (IRE) seemed to be travelling well enough when a mistake ended his hopes. (10/1)
24 Boundtohonour (IRE) took too strong a hold, but did enough to show his ability. (20/1)
3437 Castle Mews (IRE) travelled nicely, but was soon in trouble when the winner quickened. (6/1: op 4/1)
2961 Dacelo (FR) (4/1: 3/1-9/2)
3315 Dark Phoenix (IRE) stopped almost as quickly as she had last time she tried the trip, her pilot clearly believing her to be lame after the last. (3/1)

3622 BLETSOE H'CAP CHASE (0-105) (5-Y.O+) (Class F)
3-00 (3-01) **3m (19 fncs)** £2,822.50 (£785.00: £377.50) GOING minus 0.59 sec per fur (F)

				SP	RR	SF
3223[6]	**Sheelin Lad (IRE) (81)** (MrsTJMcInnesSkinner) **9-10-13** TReed (hld up: hit 9th: hdwy to ld 4 out: all out)	—	1	33/1	92	19
3223[4]	**Tim Soldier (FR) (89)** (MFBarraclough) **10-11-7** RSupple (lw: hld up: hdwy 13th: ev ch whn hit last: unable qckn nr fin)	nk	2	11/4 2	100	27
3332[4]	**Night Fancy (68)** (MrsAMWoodrow) **9-10-0** JAMcCarthy (a.p: led 15th to next: one pce appr 2 out)	15	3	20/1	69	—
3332[P]	**Coasting (76)** (GBBalding) **11-10-3**(5) ABates (prom to 4 out: one pce)	4	4	20/1	74	1
3051[F]	**King's Shilling (USA) (79)** (HOliver) **10-10-11** JacquiOliver (chsd ldrs: mstkes 12th, 15th & 16th: no ch after)	16	5	7/1	67	—
2894[7]	**Royal Square (CAN) (91)** (NPLittmoden) **11-11-9** KGaule (chsd ldrs tl wknd 4 out)	10	6	20/1	72	—
3113[6]	**Celtino (92)** (CaptTAForster) **9-11-10** SWynne (in tch tl p.u bef 10th: dead)		P	5/1 3	—	—
3209[P]	**Celtic Laird (80)** (DBurchell) **9-10-12** DJBurchell (mde most to 15th: wknd 3 out: p.u bef next)		P	25/1	—	—
3206[3]	**Retail Runner (87)** (MissSEdwards) **12-11-5** MrTHills (nt j.w: sn bhd: t.o whn p.u bef 3 out)		P	5/1 3	—	—
3333[P]	**Ballad Ruler (68)** (PAPritchard) **11-10-0** RBellamy (prom tl lost pl 6th: t.o whn p.u bef 14th)		P	40/1	—	—
3332[2]	**Reapers Rock (81)** (MrsSJSmith) **10-10-6**(7) RWilkinson (lw: bhd whn blnd & uns rdr 2nd)		U	5/2 1	—	—
				(SP 124.6%)	**11 Rn**	

5m 57.1 (0.10) CSF £113.57 CT £1,797.46 TOTE £58.80: £5.70 £2.40 £5.10 (£32.20) Trio £169.70; £119.58 to Cheltenham 13/3/97 OWNER Mrs T. J. McInnesSkinner (MELTON MOWBRAY) BRED Kenneth Parkhill
LONG HANDICAP Ballad Ruler 9-6 Night Fancy 9-12
OFFICIAL EXPLANATION **Retail Runner: was unsuited by the ground.**
3223 Sheelin Lad (IRE) tried to charge the tapes before the start, but was then taken to the back of the field and missed a couple of lengths at the start. Dropped in off the frantic early pace, this seemed to suit him. He would have won a little more decisively had he not put in a short one at the last, but proved most resolute. (33/1)
3223 Tim Soldier (FR) certainly gets an A for effort and got the trip on this fast ground. (11/4)
Night Fancy, still in with a shout three out, was then left toiling. (20/1)
Coasting has a knee-action which hardly looks suited to such fast ground. (20/1)
3051 King's Shilling (USA) forfeited his chance at the fences, but gave the impression that he would have gone quite close with a clear round. (7/1)
Royal Square (CAN) has shown precious little since leaving the Harwood yard. (20/1)

3623 LADY RIDERS' CHAMPION H'CAP HURDLE (0-110) (4-Y.O+) (Class E)
3-35 (3-36) **2m 110y (8 hdls)** £2,267.50 (£630.00: £302.50) GOING minus 0.59 sec per fur (F)

				SP	RR	SF
3570[3]	**Iron N Gold (90)** (TCasey) **5-11-4**(5) SophieMitchell (chsd ldrs: rdn to ld flat)	—	1	2/1 1	72	38
3102[5]	**Highly Charming (IRE) (78)** (MFBarraclough) **5-10-11** AnnStokell (lw: hld up: hdwy 4th: led after next: hit 3 out: hdd flat: unable qckn)	½	2	9/2 3	60	26
3429[7]	**Shifting Moon (75)** (FJordan) **5-10-8b** JacquiOliver (lw: led 2nd tl after 5th: ev ch 3 out: sn btn: blnd last)	11	3	11/2	46	12
3228[2]	**Alka International (80)** (MrsPTownsley) **5-10-6**(7) MissCTownsley (led to 2nd: rdn 5th: no imp fr next)	s.h	4	4/1 2	51	17
2070[15]	**Veronica Franco (75)** (BAPearce) **4-10-0** LeesaLong (mstkes: nvr nr to chal)	3½	5	14/1	42	—
3429[U]	**Steve Ford (91)** (CPMorlock) **8-11-10** MissPJones (plld hrd: chsd ldrs tl wknd appr 3 out)	s.h	6	25/1	58	24
3053[U]	**Fairy Park (95)** (HOliver) **12-11-7b1**(7) MissCSpearing (trckd ldrs to 5th: sn wknd)	dist	7	12/1	—	—
3234[16]	**Daily Sport Girl (80)** (BJLlewellyn) **8-10-13** MissEJJones (hdwy 3rd: ev ch appr 3 out: sn rdn & wknd: p.u bef last)		P	10/1	—	—
	Highland Flame (67) (AGBlackmore) **8-10-0** MrsFNeedham (bit bkwd: prom tl wknd 4th: t.o whn p.u bef 2 out)		P	33/1	—	—
				(SP 117.1%)	**9 Rn**	

3m 45.2 (-2.80) CSF £11.00 CT £39.11 TOTE £2.30: £1.10 £2.50 £3.20 (£9.00) Trio £15.50 OWNER D C T Partnership (DORKING) BRED M. F. Kentish
LONG HANDICAP Veronica Franco 9-9 Highland Flame 9-10
WEIGHT FOR AGE 4yo-8lb
3570 Iron N Gold got the result due to the pilot's ability to claim her allowance in the race. (2/1: op 7/2)
3102 Highly Charming (IRE), for the jockey/trainer combination that took this a year ago, looked trained to the minute. Appearing in complete control when going on, the combination did not strike decisively for home and could not rally well enough when headed after the last. (9/2: op 5/2)
3002 Shifting Moon tried forcing tactics, but was well beaten by the straight. (11/2)

3228 Alka International looked fully fit this time, but could not go with the leaders in the last half-mile. (4/1: op 5/2)
1712 Veronica Franco jumped alarmingly and to the left on occasions, and probably did well to get so close. (14/1)
Steve Ford took a good hold early in the race and was already looking held when he had little racing room turning for home. (25/1)
1817 Fairy Park (12/1: 8/1-14/1)

3624 THURLEIGH H'CAP HURDLE (0-110) (4-Y.O+) (Class E)

4-05 (4-09) **3m 2f (12 hdls)** £2,285.00 (£635.00: £305.00) GOING minus 0.59 sec per fur (F)

	Horse / details	Dist	Pos	SP	RR	SF
3358[3]	**Tilty (USA) (101)** (AStreeter) **7-11-6v** TEley (led: hit 5th: hdd 2 out: rdn to ld flat)	—	1	7/4[1]	77	17
3317[7]	**This Nettle Danger (81)** (OBrennan) **13-10-0** MBrennan (lw: hld up: hdwy to ld 2 out: rdn flat: sn hdd & no ex)	2½	2	11/2	56	—
2877[3]	**Tiger Claw (USA) (81)** (AGHobbs) **11-9-9**(5) OBurrows (lw: chsd wnr: rdn appr 9th: outpcd appr 2 out: r.o flat)	½	3	8/1	55	—
2941[5]	**Stac-Pollaidh (82)** (KCBailey) **7-9-8**(7) WWalsh (lw: hld up: sme hdwy 9th: btn & eased appr 2 out)	4	4	3/1[3]	54	—
	Johnstons Buck (IRE) (81) (BJCurley) **8-10-0** EMurphy (stdd s: hld up: hdwy 9th: eased whn btn appr 2 out)	26	5	9/4[2]	37	—

(SP 118.6%) **5 Rn**

6m 8.7 (2.70) CSF £11.12 TOTE £2.30: £1.60 £1.90 (£11.80) OWNER Cheadle Racing (UTTOXETER) BRED Mrs Emory A. Hamilton
LONG HANDICAP This Nettle Danger 9-12 Tiger Claw (USA) 9-13 Johnstons Buck (IRE) 9-13
OFFICIAL EXPLANATION **Johnstons Buck (IRE): rider reported that the gelding had been off the track for a year and raced keenly early on, appearing unsuited by the ground. When asked to quicken, he seemed to have blown up. The rider added that the gelding is temperamental, needs kidding and does not respond to vigorous riding. The vet reported that the horse was blowing hard after the race.**
3358 Tilty (USA) proved tenacious and his courage won the day. (7/4: evens-15/8)
3317 This Nettle Danger, cruising for most of the race, found precious little off the bridle. (11/2)
2877 Tiger Claw (USA) seemed the first beaten, but kept battling away and came up the run-in as well as any. (8/1: 6/1-9/1)
2941 Stac-Pollaidh, held up, made a brief, token effort turning out of the back. This trip may be beyond her, but this hardly looked reliable evidence. (3/1: 2/1-100/30)
Johnstons Buck (IRE) was rugged up beforehand despite the pleasant day, preventing paying customers from forming a judgement as to his fitness. He looked to be travelling best for a long way, but the situation changed on the home turn, and the position was accepted. (9/4: 6/4-5/2)

3625 BOLNHURST NOVICES' CHASE (5-Y.O+) (Class E)

4-40 (4-42) **2m 4f 110y (16 fncs)** £3,087.00 (£857.00: £411.00) GOING minus 0.59 sec per fur (F)

	Horse / details	Dist	Pos	SP	RR	SF
2823[3]	**Mr Conductor (IRE) (108)** (RHAlner) **6-11-8** JRKavanagh (mde all: clr 8th: v.easily)	—	1	1/6[1]	98+	—
3442[11]	**Katballou** (KGWingrove) **8-11-2** KGaule (sn pushed along: chsd wnr appr 2 out: no imp)	21	2	6/1[2]	76	—
3335[4]	**Deep Song** (PAPritchard) **7-11-2** RBellamy (chsd wnr: blnd 11th: wknd appr 2 out)	14	3	11/1[3]	65	—

(SP 108.3%) **3 Rn**

5m 8.6 (8.60) CSF £1.64 TOTE £1.10 (£1.40) OWNER Mr P M De Wilde (BLANDFORD) BRED Miss Laura Devitt
2823 Mr Conductor (IRE) had little more than a school round, putting in some spectacular leaps when seeing a stride. (1/6: 1/10-2/11)
3222 Katballou showed the virtue of perseverance, finally passing a rival on the home turn. (6/1)
Deep Song did his best to chase the winner, but dropping his hind-legs in the water, six from home, effectively finished him. (11/1)

3626 SWINESHEAD STANDARD OPEN N.H. FLAT RACE (4, 5 & 6-Y.O) (Class H)

5-15 (5-16) **2m 110y** £1,329.00 (£369.00: £177.00)

	Horse / details	Dist	Pos	SP	RR	SF
2180*	**Lord Lamb** (MrsMReveley) **5-11-11**(3) GLee (bit bkwd: a.p: led over 1f out: rdn & r.o wl)	—	1	4/5[1]	80 f	—
	Dad's Army Two (IRE) (BJCurley) **4-10-10** EMurphy (w'like: trckd ldrs: rdn over 1f out: r.o)	4	2	7/2[2]	66 f	—
	Kandyson (JRJenkins) **6-11-4** RSupple (unf: bit bkwd: prom: led over 2f out tl over 1f out: one pce)	2	3	12/1	64 f	—
2844[17]	**Query Line** (JMCastle) **6-10-6**(7) MissCSpearing (bit bkwd: led over 7f: led 4f out tl over 2f out: wknd over 1f out)	2½	4	33/1	57 f	—
3425[5]	**Embargo (IRE)** (JLDunlop) **5-10-11**(7) MrHDunlop (prom tl wknd 2f out)	nk	5	12/1	62 f	—
	Teejay's Future (IRE) (OBrennan) **6-10-6**(7) WWalsh (plld hrd: hdwy 3f out: r.o)	nk	6	14/1	56 f	—
2080[4]	**Mr Montague (IRE)** (TWDonnelly) **5-11-4** TEley (hld up: hdwy 6f out: wknd over 2f out)	8	7	6/1[3]	53 f	—
	Nirvana Princess (BPreece) **5-10-6**(7) JMogford (lengthy: unf: stdd s: plld hrd: hmpd & almost uns rdr 8f out: nvr nr ldrs)	14	8	20/1	35 f	—
3021[10]	**Denstar (IRE)** (JWhite) **4-10-10** KGaule (lw: hld up: effrt 6f out: nvr able to chal)	8	9	14/1	32 f	—
3090[14]	**Muallaf (IRE)** (MrsAMWoodrow) **5-11-4** JAMcCarthy (lw: stdd s: plld hrd: hdwy to ld 9f out: hdd 4f out: sn wknd)	hd	10	25/1	32 f	—
	Perfect Answer (JNeville) **4-10-2**(3) TDascombe (w'like: hld up: plld hrd: hit rails 9f out: hdwy 7f out: ev ch 5f out: sn wknd)	dist	11	6/1[3]	—	—
1774[2]	***Sunday Venture (NZ)*** (NJHenderson) **5-11-4** JRKavanagh (Withdrawn not under Starter's orders)		W		—	—

(SP 146.6%) **11 Rn**

3m 51.1 CSF £4.75 TOTE £1.40: £1.10 £1.60 £5.00 (£5.70) Trio £26.60 OWNER Mr A Sharratt & Mr J Renton (SALTBURN) BRED Mrs T. Hall
WEIGHT FOR AGE 4yo-8lb
2180* Lord Lamb looked to be feeling the ground when let down, holding his head on one side whilst threatening to hang, but still won in good style. (4/5)
Dad's Army Two (IRE) settled better than most in a race run at an early crawl. A half-brother to the decent miler Belfry Green, he looks the sort who should jump hurdles. (7/2: 5/2-6/1)
Kandyson, a rather unfurnished newcomer who looked to need the race, shaped quite well but it is doubtful if the form amounts to much. (12/1)
Query Line is a half sister to Newlands-General, and this performance represents considerable improvement. (33/1)
3425 Embargo (IRE) again ran below what might have been expected. (12/1: op 9/2)
Teejay's Future (IRE) looked green on the way down but did catch the eye late in the day, and this lengthy half-sister to Killula Chief is worth keeping an eye on. (14/1: 10/1-16/1)
Nirvana Princess was most unruly before the race, and proved impossible to settle. (20/1)
Muallaf (IRE) looks a decent sort but was sold unraced from the Flat, and proved impossible to settle. (25/1)
Perfect Answer (6/1: 7/2-13/2)

T/Plpt: £901.40 (8.6 Tckts). T/Qdpt: £8.70 (71.3 Tckts) Dk

2655-NEWTON ABBOT (L-H) (Heavy)
Wednesday March 12th
WEATHER: sunny intervals

3627 EAST OGWELL MAIDEN CHASE (5-Y.O+) (Class F)
2-10 (2-10) **2m 110y (13 fncs)** £2,346.05 (£709.40: £345.70: £163.85) GOING: 1.59 sec per fur (HY)

	Horse	Dist	Pos	SP	RR	SF
3567^{2}	**Court Master (IRE) (90)** (RHBuckler) **9-11-5** PHolley (lw: led: hdd 4th: led next: mde rest: clr appr 2 out: drvn out flat)	—	1	8/11^{1}	79	38
3166^{11}	**Finnigan Free** (GAHam) **7-10-12**$^{(7)}$ MrMFrith (bit bkwd: hdwy to chse wnr 9th: rdn & outpcd appr 2 out: styd on u.p flat)	1	2	10/1	78	37
3499^{8}	**Imalight** (RGFrost) **8-11-0** JFrost (chsd ldr to 3rd: chsd wnr 7th to 9th: wknd next)	11	3	5/1^{2}	62	21
3186^{P}	**Market Mayhem** (JLSpearing) **7-11-5** AThornton (lw: in tch: wknd 8th: sn t.o)	dist	4	7/1	—	—
	Walk in the Woods (DCTurner) **10-11-0** MrAHoldsworth (bit bkwd: plld hrd: led 4th: hdd next: wknd 7th: sn t.o)	dist	5	16/1	—	—
3470^{2}	**The Secret Grey (67)** (DMcCain) **6-11-5** DWalsh (mstke 1st: a bhd: t.o: p.u bef 9th)		P	6/1^{3}	—	—
3339^{5}	**Bells Wood (60)** (AJKDunn) **8-11-0**$^{(5)}$ DJKavanagh (in tch: mstke 4th: rdn 6th: sn bhd: t.o: p.u bef 9th)		P	10/1	—	—
				(SP 125.4%)	**7 Rn**	

4m 32.7 (32.70) CSF £9.89 TOTE £1.50: £1.20 £8.70 (£18.90) OWNER Adml Sir Vice Fitzroy Talbot (BRIDPORT) BRED John Flanagan

3567 Court Master (IRE) finally broke his duck here under Rules. Holding a good advantage entering the straight, he jumped the final two fences well, but had to be pushed along to hold off the challenge of the runner-up on the flat. (8/11)

Finnigan Free put in a good effort here for his first run over fences. He was closing on the leader steadily in the straight but, although finishing well under pressure, found the line coming too soon. (10/1)

3000 Market Mayhem (7/1: op 4/1)

3470 The Secret Grey (6/1: op 4/1)

3628 TEABOY MAIDEN HURDLE (4-Y.O+) (Class E)
2-40 (2-41) **2m 6f (10 hdls)** £2,284.50 (£642.00: £313.50) GOING: 1.59 sec per fur (HY)

	Horse	Dist	Pos	SP	RR	SF
3337^{3}	**Defendtherealm (93)** (RGFrost) **6-11-5** JFrost (hld up mid div: hdwy 7th: led appr 2 out: clr last: comf)	—	1	11/8^{1}	69+	19
	Armateur (FR) (83) (JCMcConnochie) **9-11-5** DLeahy (bit bkwd: prom: lost pl 8th: styd on to go 2nd last)	7	2	25/1	64	14
	Rich Tycoon (IRE) (PMRich) **8-11-5** WMarston (bit bkwd: led 2nd to 3rd: led 4th tl hdd & wknd appr 2 out)	6	3	33/1	60	10
2772^{6}	**Sally's Twins** (JSMoore) **4-10-4** WMcFarland (hdwy appr 5th: rdn 7th: wknd after next)	7	4	3/1^{2}	49	—
3431^{4}	**Cool Harry (USA)** (HEHaynes) **6-10-12**$^{(7)}$ MrSDurack (led to 2nd: prom to 5th: wknd appr 7th)	2½	5	33/1	53	3
3536^{4}	**Spirit Level (70)** (JRPayne) **9-11-1**^{ow1} MrRPayne (bhd: styd on fr 8th: nvr nrr)	22	6	50/1	33	—
3473^{4}	**Lothian Commander (78)** (DMcCain) **5-11-5** VSlattery (led 3rd to next: chsd ldr tl wknd 7th: t.o)	23	7	9/1	20	—
3085^{P}	**Paprika (IRE) (80)** (AGNewcombe) **8-11-0** AThornton (bit bkwd: prom to 7th: wknd after next: t.o & p.u bef last)		P	7/1	—	—
	Bridie's Pride (66) (GAHam) **6-11-2**$^{(3)}$ PHenley (bit bkwd: in tch tl wknd 5th: t.o & p.u after 8th)		P	25/1	—	—
3184^{4}	**Benfleet (85)** (MCPipe) **6-11-5** DWalsh (hdwy to chse ldrs 7th: wknd qckly: p.u bef 2 out)		P	11/2^{3}	—	—
1950^{P}	**Jackamus (IRE)** (GAHam) **6-10-12**$^{(7)}$ MrMFrith (a bhd: t.o & p.u bef 7th)		P	50/1	—	—
3337^{6}	**Connaught's Pride** (PJHobbs) **6-10-9**$^{(5)}$ DJKavanagh (a bhd: t.o & p.u after 8th)		P	14/1	—	—
3342^{12}	**Boozys Dream** (NBThomson) **6-11-5** SBurrough (bhd whn p.u after 6th)		P	100/1	—	—
				(SP 130.1%)	**13 Rn**	

6m 1.4 (49.40) CSF £43.41 TOTE £2.30: £1.40 £5.50 £6.80 (£56.70) Trio Not won; £143.39 to Cheltenham 13/3/97 OWNER Mr George Standing (BUCKFASTLEIGH) BRED R. G. Frost

WEIGHT FOR AGE 4yo-9lb

3337 Defendtherealm, always tracking the leading group, cruised up alongside the long-time leader turning into the straight and, going clear, only had to be pushed out on the run-in. (11/8)

Armateur (FR) made up some good ground on the final turn and, although staying on well in the straight, was never going to trouble the winner. This was a good effort after such a long absence. (25/1)

Rich Tycoon (IRE), who showed nothing in a bumper on his debut over two years ago, put in a good round here. He was still in front until the home turn, but found very little in the straight. He is sure to come on for this. (33/1)

3473 Lothian Commander (9/1: op 6/1)

Paprika (IRE) (7/1: op 12/1)

3184 Benfleet (11/2: 3/1-6/1)

3629 HORSES FOR COURSES H'CAP CHASE (0-115) (5-Y.O+) (Class E)
3-10 (3-10) **2m 5f 110y (16 fncs)** £2,764.25 (£836.00: £407.50: £193.25) GOING: 1.59 sec per fur (HY)

	Horse	Dist	Pos	SP	RR	SF
3047^{P}	**Orswell Lad (112)** (PJHobbs) **8-11-6**$^{(7)}$ MrSDurack (lw: mde all: qcknd clr 14th: unchal)	—	1	6/4^{1}	123	56
3333^{F}	**Jailbreaker (87)** (BRMillman) **10-9-11**$^{(5)ow2}$ DSalter (in tch tl mstke 10th: lost pl & mstke next: rallied appr 2 out: no imp)	12	2	11/4^{2}	89	20
3044^{5}	**Bit of A Touch (90)** (RGFrost) **11-10-5**^{ow1} JFrost (hld up & bhd: in tch: hdwy & mstke 13th: wknd next)	15	3	4/1	81	13
1949^{4}	**Allo George (113)** (AGNewcombe) **11-12-0** AThornton (chsd wnr tl wknd qckly appr 2 out: fin lame)	dist	4	3/1^{3}	—	—
				(SP 111.7%)	**4 Rn**	

5m 56.7 (39.70) CSF £5.61 TOTE £3.70 (£3.30) OWNER Mr R. M. E. Wright (MINEHEAD) BRED G. Amey

LONG HANDICAP Jailbreaker 9-10

2660* Orswell Lad put in a good round of jumping and never looked in any danger of losing this. This was his promising rider's first winner under Rules. (6/4)

3333 Jailbreaker stayed on well from three out after seemingly struggling in the back straight. (11/4)

835* Bit of A Touch found these conditions too tough and began to weaken a long way out. (4/1: 3/1-9/2)

1949 Allo George was on the heels of the winner and going well for a long way but, outjumped four out, he soon weakened. He reportedly finished lame. (3/1: op 7/4)

3630 LITTLE CLOSE H'CAP HURDLE (0-120) (4-Y.O+) (Class D)
3-45 (3-45) **2m 6f (10 hdls)** £2,695.60 (£756.60: £368.80) GOING: 1.59 sec per fur (HY)

				SP	RR	SF
3229U	**Hold Your Ranks (112)** (RGFrost) **10-12-0** JFrost (lw: hld up & bhd: in tch & hdwy to ld 2 out: styd on u.p flat)	—	1	5/1 3	94	33
3269 5	**Cassio's Boy (88)** (RJEckley) **6-9-11**(7) XAizpuru (lw: hld up: hdwy to chse ldr 6th: led after 8th: hdd 2 out: rallied wl flat: nt get up)	¾	2	2/1 1	70	9
1342 5	**La Menorquina (USA) (95)** (DMarks) **7-10-6**(5) DJKavanagh (chsd ldr to 6th: rallied & ev ch appr 2 out: wknd appr last)	5	3	9/2 2	73	12
1424*	**Ritto (95)** (JNeville) **7-10-11** WMarston (bit bkwd: led: mstke 6th: hdd & wknd qckly after 8th: p.u bef 2 out)		P	2/1 1	—	—
3207 8	**Valianthe (USA) (90)** (MCPipe) **9-10-6b** DWalsh (nt j.w: in tch tl j.slowly 7th: sn bhd: t.o: p.u bef 2 out)		P	7/1	—	—
				(SP 114.0%)		**5 Rn**

5m 59.6 (47.60) CSF £14.77 TOTE £6.20: £3.10 £1.60 (£7.00) OWNER Mrs C. Loze (BUCKFASTLEIGH) BRED R. G. Frost
OFFICIAL EXPLANATION **Ritto: rider reported that the gelding became very tired, started to make a noise and choked.**
Hold Your Ranks has done all his winning here and had conditions to suit. Despite jumping big at some of his hurdles, he was well placed turning into the straight. Taking the lead two out, he stayed on well to keep the persistent runner-up at bay. (5/1: op 3/1)
3269 Cassio's Boy, dropped 3lb, had every chance over the last but just could not overcome the winner on the run-in. (2/1)
1342 La Menorquina (USA) was seen with a chance two out, but seemed one-paced over the last flight. (9/2: op 3/1)
1424* Ritto, stepping up in distance, was hard ridden when leading into the straight but stopped very quickly and was pulled up before the second last. (2/1)

3631 LITTLE TOWN HUNTERS' NOVICES' CHASE (5-Y.O+) (Class H)
4-20 (4-20) **2m 5f 110y (16 fncs)** £1,054.00 (£294.00: £142.00) GOING: 1.59 sec per fur (HY)

				SP	RR	SF
	Herhorse (MissAHoward-Chappell) **10-11-5**(7) MrLJefford (prom: mstke 6th: chsd ldr 9th tl led after 2 out: lft clr last)	—	1	16/1	101	26
	Kaloore (PScholfield) **8-11-10**(7) MrRNuttall (bhd: rdn 9th: hdwy 11th: ev ch next: wkng whn lft poor 2nd last)	12	2	7/4 1	97	22
	Good King Henry (IJWiddicombe) **11-11-10**(7) MrIWiddicombe (in tch to 10th: lft poor 3rd last)	dist	3	9/1 3	—	—
	Cedar Square (IRE) (HWLavis) **6-11-12**(5) MrJJukes (lw: led: blnd 2 out: sn hdd: fell last)		F	7/4 1	—	—
	Baldhu Chance (TLong) **9-11-10**(7) MrJamesYoung (in tch tl wknd 9th: t.o & p.u bef 13th)		P	12/1	—	—
	Seventh Lock (MissLBlackford) **11-11-10**(7) MissLBlackford (prom: mstke 3rd: blnd bdly 6th: wknd next: t.o & p.u bef 13th)		P	10/1	—	—
	Tom's Apache (OJCarter) **8-11-10**(7) MrIDowrick (mstke 1st: a bhd: t.o: p.u bef 10th)		P	25/1	—	—
	Bryn's Story (GDBlagbrough) **10-11-10**(7) MajorGWheeler (a bhd: t.o 3rd: p.u bef 13th)		P	50/1	—	—
	Absent Minds (BRJYoung) **11-11-5**(7) MissSYoung (mid div tl wknd 9th: t.o & p.u bef last)		P	33/1	—	—
	Mecado (FJYardley) **10-11-10v**(7) MrMMunrowd (hdwy 8th: in tch tl rdn & wknd 11th: ref 2 out)		R	20/1	—	—
3498F	**Tom's Gemini Star** (OJCarter) **9-11-10**(7) MrGPenfold (bhd: blnd & uns rdr 6th)		U	8/1 2	—	—
				(SP 130.0%)		**11 Rn**

6m 5.6 (48.60) CSF £45.40 TOTE £32.20: £2.60 £1.50 £2.60 (£22.20) Trio £44.50 OWNER Miss A. Howard-Chappell (TOTNES) BRED G. Cook
Herhorse, a temperamental maiden pointer, has been known to pull herself up in the past, but she seems to have got her act together this season. Always prominent, she went into the lead after the second last and came home for an easy victory, although she may not always be one to trust. (16/1)
Kaloore gave his rider a difficult time here, but was staying on when handed second place at the last. (7/4)
Good King Henry could make no impression on the only other two finishers. (9/1)
Cedar Square (IRE) disputed the lead two out, but soon lost the advantage and was being hard ridden when coming to grief at the final fence.(7/4)
Baldhu Chance (12/1: op 8/1)
Tom's Gemini Star (8/1: op 12/1)

3632 JOKERS H'CAP HURDLE (0-100) (4-Y.O+) (Class F)
4-55 (4-55) **2m 1f (8 hdls)** £1,871.40 (£525.40: £256.20) GOING: 1.59 sec per fur (HY)

				SP	RR	SF
3338U	**Alice's Mirror (68)** (KBishop) **8-10-2b** RGreene (hld up & bhd: rapid hdwy 6th: led appr last: sn clr)	—	1	12/1	48	—
3404 5	**Alpine Joker (82)** (PJHobbs) **4-10-3**(5) DJKavanagh (a.p: led after 6th: hdd appr last: outpcd)	3	2	5/2 1	59	—
3539 3	**Friendly House (IRE) (94)** (MCPipe) **8-12-0** DWalsh (hld up & bhd: hdwy 5th: ev ch next: wknd appr 2 out)	5	3	5/2 1	67	9
2882 5	**Urban Lily (75)** (RJHodges) **7-10-2b**(7) JHarris (hit 1st: chsd ldr tl led 5th: hdd after next: wknd appr 2 out)	16	4	9/2 2	32	—
3207 9	**Aldwick Colonnade (67)** (MDIUsher) **10-10-1**ow1 WMcFarland (prom tl wknd 5th)	16	5	25/1	9	—
3338 5	**Pooh Stick (66)** (RGFrost) **7-10-0** MrAHoldsworth (bhd: hdwy after 4th: ev ch next tl wknd appr 2 out)	nk	6	16/1	8	—
3207P	**Tilt Tech Flyer (78)** (IRJones) **12-10-5**(7) JPrior (led to 5th: wknd qckly next)	1	7	16/1	19	—
3344 4	**Runic Symbol (70)** (MBlanshard) **6-10-4** AThornton (hdwy 5th: wknd after next)	16	8	13/2 3	—	—
3429 9	**Royal Glint (66)** (HEHaynes) **8-9-7**(7) MrLBaker (prom early: in tch tl wknd 5th: t.o whn p.u bef 2 out)		P	20/1	—	—
				(SP 116.7%)		**9 Rn**

4m 34.1 (41.10) CSF £39.86 CT £93.29 TOTE £13.90: £1.70 £1.70 £1.60 (£21.60) Trio £27.70 OWNER A M Partnership (BRIDGWATER) BRED W. A. Wood
LONG HANDICAP Pooh Stick 9-13 Aldwick Colonnade 9-12 Royal Glint 9-10
WEIGHT FOR AGE 4yo-8lb
1446 Alice's Mirror, under a good ride here, was pushed along in the back straight to make some headway. Throwing down her challenge between the final two, she was kept up to her work and ran on very well close home. (12/1: op 7/1)
Alpine Joker held the advantage in the straight, but found the determined challenge of the winner too much over the last. (5/2)
3539 Friendly House (IRE), scrubbed along under pressure turning into the straight, could only run on at the same pace over the last two obstacles. (5/2)

3633 TEMPLERS ROAD H'CAP CHASE (0-105) (5-Y.O+) (Class F)
5-30 (5-30) **3m 2f 110y (20 fncs)** £2,527.90 (£709.40: £345.70) GOING: 1.59 sec per fur (HY)

				SP	RR	SF
2910P	**Silverino (81)** (PRRodford) **11-10-12** SBurrough (hld up mid div: hdwy to chse ldr 11th: led 14th: clr 16th: unchal)	—	1	14/1	90	22

Form	Horse	Dist	Pos	SP	RR	SF
3400*	**Top Javalin (NZ) (93)** (NJHawke) **10-11-3**(7) MrGShenkin (lw: hld up: j.slowly 10th: hdwy 13th: chsd wnr & mstke 17th: sn outpcd)	dist	2	5/4[1]	—	—
3181[4]	**Bournel (76)** (CRBarwell) **9-10-4**(3) PHenley (chsd ldr: mstke 7th: lost pl 11th: rdn & wknd 14th)	1¼	3	6/1[3]	—	—
3003[6]	**Keano (IRE) (92)** (PJHobbs) **8-11-9** WMarston (lw: led to 14th: wknd fr next)	3	4	2/1[2]	—	—
	Bottle Black (81) (THind) **10-10-12** PMcLoughlin (chsd ldrs in tch tl rdn & wknd fr 13th: t.o & p.u bef 16th)		P	25/1	—	—
3354[4]	**Space Cappa (89)** (MissVAStephens) **9-11-6** MissVStephens (bhd & mde mstkes: t.o 11th: p.u bef last)		P	8/1	—	—
				(SP 113.7%)		**6 Rn**

7m 30.6 (56.60) CSF £31.38 TOTE £12.80: £3.40 £1.40 (£7.90) OWNER Mr S. N. Burfield (MARTOCK) BRED Mrs R. Newton

Silverino has shown little of late, but was always at the head of affairs here. He had his closest rival under pressure as early as the back straight, and he soon went clear, with only the fences to beat from then on. (14/1)

3181 Bournel stayed on from the home turn and finished well. (6/1)

Keano (IRE) was keeping tabs on the winner in the back straight, but was soon finding very little. (2/1)

T/Plpt: £55.50 (127.19 Tckts). T/Qdpt: £27.00 (11.52 Tckts) T

3613-CHELTENHAM (L-H) (Good, Good to firm patches)
Thursday March 13th

WEATHER: overcast

3634 ELITE RACING CLUB TRIUMPH HURDLE (Gd 1) (4-Y.O) (Class A)

2-00 (2-01) **2m 1f (New) (8 hdls)** £44,289.60 (£16,526.40: £8,043.20: £3,416.00: £1,488.00: £716.80) GOING: 0.08 sec per fur (G)

Form	Horse	Dist	Pos	SP	RR	SF
3258a*	**Commanche Court (IRE)** (TMWalsh,Ireland) **4-11-0** NWilliamson (lw: hld up: hdwy 3 out: led last: drvn out)	—	1	9/1	101	54
3404[2]	**Circus Star** (DNicholson) **4-11-0** RJohnson (hld up: hdwy 5th: ev ch whn hit last: r.o)	1	2	40/1	100	53
2772*	**Shooting Light (IRE)** (PGMurphy) **4-11-0** RDunwoody (lw: hld up: hdwy 5th: ev ch last: r.o)	1¼	3	7/1[3]	99	52
3301*	**L'Opera (FR)** (DNicholson) **4-11-0** JOsborne (led tl after 1st: led after 2 out: hdd last: one pce)	1¾	4	11/2[2]	97+	50
3174[4]	**Hayaain** (KCBailey) **4-11-0** JRailton (a.p: r.o one pce fr 2 out)	4	5	33/1	94	47
2993a[4]	**Marlonette (IRE)** (WPMullins,Ireland) **4-10-9** DJCasey (hdwy appr 2 out: hrd rdn appr last: r.o flat)	1	6	33/1	88	41
3566[3]	**Seattle Alley (USA) (97)** (PRWebber) **4-11-0** JAMcCarthy (hld up: hdwy appr 3 out: one pce fr 2 out)	3	7	66/1	90	43
3174[7]	**Mr Wild (USA)** (RAkehurst) **4-11-0** JCulloty (bhd: mstke 3rd: hdwy 3 out: one pce fr 2 out)	4	8	50/1	86	39
3007[2]	**White Sea (IRE)** (MCPipe) **4-10-9** CFSwan (led after 1st tl after 2 out: sn wknd: fin lame)	½	9	9/2[1]	81	34
3291*	**No More Hassle (IRE) (101)** (MrsMReveley) **4-11-0** PNiven (prom: mstke 3 out: rdn & wknd 2 out)	1½	10	16/1	84	37
3441*	**Pleasureland (IRE) (102)** (RCurtis) **4-11-0** DMorris (n.d)	¾	11	100/1	83	36
3271[3]	**Mutanassib (IRE)** (MCPipe) **4-11-0** CMaude (no hdwy fr 3 out)	1½	12	50/1	82	35
3301[2]	**Kerawi** (NATwiston-Davies) **4-11-0** CLlewellyn (hdwy 4th: wknd 2 out)	¾	13	10/1	81	34
3298[6]	**Serenus (USA) (115)** (NJHenderson) **4-11-0** MAFitzgerald (lw: prom to 3 out)	5	14	50/1	77	30
3525a*	**Stylish Allure (USA)** (DKWeld,Ireland) **4-11-0** CO'Dwyer (bhd tl hdwy on outside appr 2 out: wknd appr last)	2½	15	12/1	74	27
3234*	**Always Happy (93)** (MissGayKelleway) **4-10-9** TDascombe (lw: bhd fr 3 out)	3½	16	66/1	66	19
3075[15]	**Pomme Secret (FR)** (MCPipe) **4-11-0b**[1] APMcCoy (prom: j.slowly 3rd: wknd appr 2 out)	2	17	25/1	69	22
2993a[5]	**Evriza (IRE)** (APO'Brien,Ireland) **4-10-9b** THorgan (a bhd)	3½	18	50/1	61	14
3174[10]	**Palamon (USA)** (JWhite) **4-11-0** TJMurphy (lw: prom to 4th)	11	19	200/1	55	8
3224[4]	**Exalted (IRE)** (WJenks) **4-11-0** TJenks (lw: bhd fr 5th: t.o)	25	20	100/1	32	—
2939[7]	**Society Girl** (JGMO'Shea) **4-10-9** JRKavanagh (t.o)	1½	21	200/1	25	—
3258a[3]	**Miss Roberto (IRE)** (MBrassil,Ireland) **4-10-9** KFO'Brien (bhd: blnd 4th: sn t.o)	7	22	33/1	19	—
3184[3]	**Merawang (IRE)** (PFNicholls) **4-11-0** PHide (lw: s.s: a bhd: t.o)	nk	23	100/1	24	—
3204[6]	**Warning Reef (76)** (CLPopham) **4-11-0b** WMarston (mstke 1st: a bhd: t.o fr 5th)	3½	24	200/1	20	—
3544*	**Belmarita (IRE)** (GAHubbard) **4-10-9** MichaelBrennan (lw: a bhd: t.o)	1½	25	50/1	14	—
3084*	**Harbet House (FR)** (RJO'Sullivan) **4-11-0** DO'Sullivan (fell 2nd)		F	40/1	—	—
3310*	**Double Agent (98)** (HowardJohnson) **4-11-0** ADobbin (bhd whn fell 3rd)		F	50/1	—	—
3224*	**Kings Witness (USA)** (PFNicholls) **4-11-0** DBridgwater (mstke 1st: blnd bdly 4th: sn bhd: t.o whn p.u bef last)		P	14/1	—	—
				(SP 122.2%)		**28 Rn**

4m 0.2 (3.20) CSF £302.52 CT £2,425.80 TOTE £8.70: £1.90 £7.50 £1.90 £1.50 (£301.70) Trio £577.40 OWNER Mr D. F. Desmond (KILL) BRED Cambremont Ltd Partnership

3258a* Commanche Court (IRE) showed he could handle all types of ground, and that the Irish juvenile form is well up to scratch. (9/1)

3404 Circus Star seems to have put his earlier problems of pulling too hard behind him, and showed a tremendous improvement in form. The faster ground may be the key to him. (40/1)

2772* Shooting Light (IRE) again showed he is a smart juvenile, and is a credit to all concerned. (7/1)

3301* L'Opera (FR) confirmed the promise of his debut, and a lot more will be heard of him. (11/2)

3174 Hayaain did not mind the ground having won on firm on the Flat, and gave the impression he should stay further. (33/1)

2738a Marlonette (IRE) seems to handle all sorts of ground, and finished six lengths closer to the winner than she had done at Leopardstown. (33/1)

3566 Seattle Alley (USA) should have no trouble winning a race on this evidence, but he should still be treated with some caution. (66/1)

2751 Mr Wild (USA) has been disappointing, but should not be hard to place on this form. (50/1)

3007 White Sea (IRE) unfortunately finished lame, and her rider feared it might be quite serious. (9/2)

3635 BONUSPRINT STAYERS' HURDLE (Gd 1) (4-Y.O+) (Class A)

2-35 (2-36) **3m 110y (New) (12 hdls)** £53,440.00 (£19,960.00: £9,730.00: £4,150.00: £1,825.00: £895.00) GOING: 0.08 sec per fur (G)

Form	Horse	Dist	Pos	SP	RR	SF
3011[3]	**Karshi (142)** (MissHCKnight) **7-11-10** JOsborne (a.p: led 5th to 7th: lost pl 3 out: rallied 2 out: led & mstke last: drvn out)	—	1	20/1	126	72
3150[3]	**Anzum (138)** (DNicholson) **6-11-10** RJohnson (hld up mid div: rdn 6th: lost pl 7th: mstke 3 out: rallied appr last: styd on wl flat)	2½	2	25/1	124	70
3038[11]	**Paddy's Return (IRE) (138)** (FMurphy) **5-11-10b** RHughes (hld up: gd hdwy after 6th: led 9th tl after 3 out: led after 2 out to last: one pce)	2	3	20/1	123	69
	Sohrab (IRE) (140) (MCPipe) **9-11-10** CMaude (bit bkwd: hld up & bhd: mstke 9th: hdwy appr 2 out: styd on one pce flat)	1½	4	33/1	122	68

				SP	RR	SF
3303^3	**Escartefigue (FR) (148)** (DNicholson) **5-11-10** DBridgwater (hld up: hdwy 8th: led after 3 out: rdn & hdd after 2 out: one pce)	s.h	**5**	$9/2^1$	122	68
3126a*	**What a Question (IRE)** (MFMorris,Ireland) **9-11-5** CO'Dwyer (hld up: hdwy 7th: j.slowly & lost pl 8th: rallied appr 2 out: nt rch ldrs)	1¾	**6**	$6/1^2$	116	62
2056^2	**Trainglot (148)** (JGFitzGerald) **10-11-10** RDunwoody (nvr trbld ldrs)	10	**7**	$7/1^3$	114	60
3597^7	**Pridwell (154)** (MCPipe) **7-11-10** APMcCoy (hld up: stdy hdwy 9th: wknd after 3 out)	¾	**8**	8/1	114	60
3303^5	**Tarrs Bridge (IRE) (124)** (CJMann) **6-11-10b** JMagee (prom: led 7th to 9th: wknd 3 out: t.o)	20	**9**	40/1	101	47
3126a^3	**Derrymoyle (IRE)** (MCunningham,Ireland) **8-11-10** JPBroderick (hld up: hdwy 6th: wknd after 3 out: t.o)	13	**10**	25/1	92	38
3303^8	**Ocean Hawk (USA) (152)** (NATwiston-Davies) **5-11-10b^1** CLlewellyn (lw: led to 5th: wknd 7th: t.o)	hd	**11**	$7/1^3$	92	38
3415*	**Ealing Court (99)** (NMBabbage) **8-11-10** BFenton (bhd fr 5th: t.o)	hd	**12**	100/1	92	38
3303^6	**Top Spin (131)** (JRJenkins) **8-11-10** TJMurphy (mstke 4th: t.o fr 7th)	hd	**13**	100/1	92	38
3020^3	**Wisley Wonder (IRE) (127)** (NATwiston-Davies) **7-11-10** DWalsh (lw: prom to 8th: t.o)	8	**14**	66/1	87	33
3126a^8	**Urubande (IRE)** (APO'Brien,Ireland) **7-11-10** CFSwan (fell 2nd)		**F**	$6/1^2$	—	—
3303^2	**Conquering Leader (IRE) (139)** (NJHenderson) **8-11-5** MAFitzgerald (hld up: hdwy 6th: fell 7th)		**F**	15/2	—	—
3293^5	**Tragic Hero (140)** (MCPipe) **5-11-10b** NWilliamson (hld up: rn out 6th)		**R**	50/1	—	—

(SP 122.7%) **17 Rn**

5m 43.9 (1.90) CSF £369.73 TOTE £26.90: £6.00 £6.70 £4.40 (£219.60) Trio £1,080.50 OWNER Lord Vestey (WANTAGE) BRED Lord Vestey

STEWARDS' ENQUIRY Hughes susp. 29-31/3 & 1-2/4/97 (improper use of whip).

3011 Karshi, trying a longer trip, likes this ground, and was quite content to let the two leaders slip him at the top of the hill. Swinging off the bridle leaving the last, he gave both his owner and trainer their first ever Festival winner. (20/1)

3150 Anzum stays forever, and softer ground would have brought his stamina even more into play. (25/1)

2059 Paddy's Return (IRE), taking a big step up in distance, likes this type of ground, and ran his best race since winning last year's Triumph Hurdle. (20/1)

Sohrab (IRE) certainly gets three miles on ground as fast as this, although three of his wins have come with it on the soft side. (33/1)

3303 Escartefigue (FR) does seem more effective when the ground is riding soft. (9/2: 3/1-5/1)

3126a* What a Question (IRE) was suited by this surface, but was left with a lot do from the top of the hill. (6/1)

2056 Trainglot (7/1: 5/1-15/2)

3303 Ocean Hawk (USA) (7/1: op 9/2)

3636 TOTE CHELTENHAM GOLD CUP CHASE (Gd 1) (5-Y.O+) (Class A)

3-15 (3-20) **3m 2f 110y (New) (22 fncs)** £134,810.00 (£50,390.00: £24,595.00: £10,525.00: £4,662.50: £2,317.50) GOING: 0.08 sec per fur (G)

				SP	RR	SF
2115^F	**Mr Mulligan (IRE) (158)** (NoelChance) **9-12-0** APMcCoy (a.p: led 13th: hit 4 out: clr 3 out: edgd rt flat: drvn out)	—	**1**	20/1	171	80
2775^2	**Barton Bank (157)** (DNicholson) **11-12-0** DWalsh (a.p: hit 9th: outpcd appr 3 out: hrd rdn & styd on one pce fr 2 out)	9	**2**	33/1	166	75
3245a^F	**Dorans Pride (IRE)** (MHourigan,Ireland) **8-12-0** JPBroderick (hld up: hdwy 14th: hrd rdn & styd on one pce fr 2 out)	½	**3**	10/1	165	74
2887^F	**Go Ballistic (135)** (JGMO'Shea) **8-12-0** ADobbin (nvr nr to chal)	6	**4**	50/1	162	71
2962*	**Challenger du Luc (FR) (150)** (MCPipe) **7-12-0b** CMaude (hld up: hdwy 17th: rdn & one pce fr 3 out)	3	**5**	16/1	160	69
2935^2	**One Man (IRE) (172)** (GRichards) **9-12-0** RDunwoody (hld up in rr: mstke 7th: hdwy 16th: rdn & wnt 2nd appr 2 out: wknd last: fin tired)	16	**6**	$7/1^2$	150	59
3230*	**Coome Hill (IRE) (147)** (WWDennis) **8-12-0** JOsborne (lw: prom to 18th: t.o)	16	**7**	$15/2^3$	141	50
3155*	**Cyborgo (FR)** (MCPipe) **7-12-0** CFSwan (hld up: stdy hdwy 13th: wknd appr 3 out: t.o)	7	**8**	12/1	136	45
2997a*	**Danoli (IRE)** (TFoley,Ireland) **9-12-0** TPTreacy (hld up: hdwy 7th: reminders 12th: wknd 17th: bhd whn fell 2 out)		**F**	$7/1^2$	—	—
3230^2	**Unguided Missile (IRE) (157)** (GRichards) **9-12-0** NWilliamson (bhd tl fell 13th)		**F**	16/1	—	—
3151^2	**Nahthen Lad (IRE) (150)** (MrsJPitman) **8-12-0** RFarrant (lw: reminders after 10th: bhd fr 15th: t.o whn p.u bef 2 out)		**P**	20/1	—	—
2773*	**Dublin Flyer (169)** (CaptTAForster) **11-12-0** BPowell (swtg: led to 13th: rdn & wknd 15th: bhd whn p.u bef 2 out)		**P**	8/1	—	—
	Banjo (FR) (150) (DNicholson) **7-12-0** DBridgwater (bit bkwd: a bhd: hmpd 13th: t.o whn p.u bef 2 out)		**P**	33/1	—	—
2997a^3	**Imperial Call (IRE)** (FSutherland,Ireland) **8-12-0** CO'Dwyer (hld up: lost pl 14th: bhd whn mstke 17th: t.o whn p.u bef 18th)		**P**	$4/1^1$	—	—

(SP 113.8%) **14 Rn**

6m 35.5 (0.50) CSF £448.05 TOTE £21.50: £4.30 £5.60 £4.10 (£296.50) Trio £1,823.40 OWNER Michael And Gerry Worcester (LAMBOURN) BRED J. Rowley

2115 Mr Mulligan (IRE) handles this sort of ground, and pushed the pace on the second circuit. Jumping much better than on some occasions in the past, he stayed on far too well for his pursuers up the final climb. His trainer later admitted that it had been difficult to keep the gelding's legs right, but there is no doubt everything came right on the day. (20/1)

2775 Barton Bank started at a big price compared with One Man given his narrow defeat by the grey last time. He is better than ever this season, which can be put down to the fact that his jumping has greatly improved. (33/1)

3245a Dorans Pride (IRE), justifying the decision to go for the race, jumped well for a novice, and the fast ground probably contributed to his undoing. (10/1: 7/1-11/1)

2887 Go Ballistic had ground conditions in his favour, but this is the Blue Riband of steeplechasing, and it is not run around Ascot. (50/1)

2962* Challenger du Luc (FR) ran a sound race, but this trip with the stiff finish would have stretched his stamina to the limit. (16/1)

2935 One Man (IRE), ridden to get the trip, looked capable of picking up the winner turning for home, but even his greatest fan, his trainer, is now convinced that he simply does not stay. (7/1)

3230* Coome Hill (IRE) disappointed on ground that would not have been all that different to Wincanton last time. (15/2: 9/2-8/1)

3155* Cyborgo (FR) found the ground too lively. (12/1)

2997a* Danoli (IRE) created a lot of hype in Ireland last time, but it seems to have been forgotten that Jodami broke down, and that Imperial Call is a shadow of the horse of last season. (7/1)

2773* Dublin Flyer was again a Gold Cup flop, and can be more aggressively ridden from the front over shorter trips when stamina is not a worry. (8/1: 5/1-9/1)

2997a Imperial Call (IRE), with nothing having gone right this season, had anything but an ideal preparation, and it remains to be seen if, at the tender age of eight, we have already seen the best of him. (4/1)

3637 CHRISTIES FOXHUNTER CHALLENGE CUP CHASE (5-Y.O+) (Class B)

3-55 (3-56) **3m 2f 110y (New) (22 fncs)** £19,867.50 (£5,940.00: £2,845.00: £1,297.50) GOING: 0.08 sec per fur (G)

				SP	RR	SF
	Fantus (RBarber) **10-12-0** MrTMitchell (hld up: hdwy 10th: led 17th: mstke 18th: j.rt 3 out: all out)	—	1	10/1	136	55
3135*	**Cab on Target** (MrsMReveley) **11-12-0** MrSSwiers (hld up: hdwy 12th: ev ch appr last: hrd rdn: nt qckn)	1¾	2	4/1[1]	135	54
2998a*	**What A Hand** (EJO'Grady,Ireland) **9-12-0** MrPFenton (hld up: hdwy 16th: mstke 4 out: one pce fr 2 out)	11	3	6/1[2]	128	47
3055[P]	**Celtic Abbey** (MrsChristineHardinge) **9-12-0** MrDSJones (hld up: hdwy 13th: rdn & wknd appr 2 out)	7	4	16/1	124	43
2964*	**Double Silk** (RCWilkins) **13-12-0** MrRTreloggen (a.p: led 9th to 17th: wknd qckly appr 3 out)	9	5	13/2[3]	119	38
68[4]	**Final Pride** (MrsCHiggon) **11-11-9** MissPJones (led 2nd tl blnd 9th: wknd 4 out)	15	6	100/1	105	24
3273*	**The Jogger** (CLTizzard) **12-12-0** MrJTizzard (prom to 16th: t.o)	18	7	10/1	99	18
	Clonrosh Slave (RTyner,Ireland) **10-12-0** MrSHHadden (a bhd: t.o fr 12th)	2	8	100/1	98	17
3459*	**Copper Thistle (IRE)** (NJPomfret) **9-12-0** MrRHunnisett (bhd: j.rt 5th: sn t.o)	dist	9	33/1	—	—
	Tearaway King (IRE) (EBolger,Ireland) **7-12-0** MrEBolger (hld up & bhd: hdwy 13th: mstke 17th: wknd 4 out: t.o whn p.u bef 2 out)		P	13/2[3]	—	—
3403[2]	**Miss Millbrook** (DTGoldsworthy) **9-11-9** MrEWilliams (prom to 11th: bhd whn blnd 16th: t.o whn p.u bef last)		P	20/1	—	—
	Mr Golightly (MrsSCobden) **10-12-0** MrsSGodfrey (bhd: blnd 1st: mstke 4th: blnd 8th: t.o whn p.u bef 10th)		P	20/1	—	—
3353[3]	**Colonial Kelly** (MrsDMGrissell) **9-12-0** MrPHacking (bhd: reminders 12th: blnd 13th: t.o whn p.u bef 16th)		P	33/1	—	—
3403*	**Holland House** (PRChamings) **11-12-0** MrCVigors (hld up: bhd whn rdn 10th: t.o whn p.u bef 16th)		P	10/1	—	—
3270[4]	**My Nominee** (DENicholls) **9-12-0b** MrRBurton (led to 2nd: wknd 17th: t.o whn p.u bef 2 out)		P	33/1	—	—
3403[3]	**Clobracken Lad** (MrsJSwaffield) **9-12-0** MrGBaines (bhd: blnd 4th: t.o whn p.u bef 15th)		P	100/1	—	—
3432[2]	**Lord Relic (NZ)** (SABrookshaw) **11-12-0** MrRFord (bhd whn rdn 10th: mstke 13th: t.o whn p.u bef 16th)		P	12/1	—	—
	Still In Business (RBarber) **9-12-0** MissPCurling (blnd & uns rdr 1st)		U	9/1	—	—

(SP 133.1%) **18 Rn**

6m 44.6 (9.60) CSF £47.34 TOTE £23.30: £5.20 £2.20 £2.30 (£58.10) Trio £90.40 OWNER Mr J. A. Keighley (BEAMINSTER) BRED Mrs Irene Appelbe

Fantus would have preferred softer ground, which makes the repeat of his win in this event two years ago all the more creditable. (10/1: op 6/1)
3135* Cab on Target acts well on this type of surface, but had to concede he had met one too good in the winner. (4/1: 3/1-9/2)
2998a* What A Hand lost his unbeaten tag when having completed the course, and would have preferred more cut in the ground. (6/1)
3055 Celtic Abbey would not have minded the ground a bit faster. (16/1)
2964* Double Silk won this race in '93 and '94, but is getting a bit long in the tooth. (13/2)

3638 125TH YEAR OF THE CHELTENHAM GRAND ANNUAL CHALLENGE CUP H'CAP CHASE (5-Y.O+) (Class B)

4-30 (4-31) **2m 110y (New) (14 fncs)** £28,679.00 (£8,582.00: £4,116.00: £1,883.00) GOING: 0.08 sec per fur (G)

				SP	RR	SF
3292[4]	**Uncle Ernie (137)** (JGFitzGerald) **12-11-4** GBradley (hld up: hdwy 9th: led last: r.o wl)	—	1	20/1	147	73
3187*	**Elzoba (FR) (135)** (MCPipe) **5-10-8b[1]** APMcCoy (led to 2nd: led 8th to last: nt qckn)	2	2	13/2[2]	143	61
	Perknapp (119) (AMartin) **10-10-0** CFSwan (blnd 1st: bhd tl hdwy 4 out: r.o flat)	1	3	25/1	126	52
2783[3]	**Time Won't Wait (IRE) (134)** (RTPhillips) **8-11-1** JRailton (lw: hld up: hdwy 9th: one pce fr 2 out)	2½	4	8/1[3]	139	65
	Scobie Boy (IRE) (120) (RVShaw) **9-10-1** JPBroderick (hld up: hdwy 9th: rdn appr 2 out: one pce)	3	5	25/1	122	48
3369*	**Political Tower (130)** (RNixon) **10-10-11** 3x ADobbin (bhd: hmpd 10th: hdwy 3 out: one pce fr 2 out)	nk	6	16/1	132	58
2884[4]	**Kibreet (142)** (PJHobbs) **10-11-9** NWilliamson (lw: prom: rdn & wknd 9th: eased whn btn appr 3 out)	7	7	14/1	137	63
3144[F]	**Certainly Strong (IRE) (134)** (DNicholson) **7-11-1** RDunwoody (plld hrd: led 2nd to 4th: hit 7th: wknd appr 2 out)	1¼	8	7/2[1]	128	54
	Cable Beach (IRE) (130) (MCunningham,Ireland) **8-10-11** CO'Dwyer (led 4th tl hit 8th: wknd appr 2 out)	5	9	25/1	119	45
3037[2]	**Dancing Paddy (147)** (KOCunningham-Brown) **9-12-0** DWalsh (lw: blnd 3rd: sn bhd)	4	10	16/1	132	58
3015[2]	**Super Coin (120)** (RLee) **9-10-1** RJohnson (bhd most of wy)	3	11	9/1	102	28
2952[8]	**Storm Falcon (USA) (121)** (SMellor) **7-9-11**(5) ChrisWebb (prom tl wknd qckly 10th)	10	12	20/1	93	19
2942[3]	**Norse Raider (119)** (MCPipe) **7-10-0** CMaude (fell 4th)		F	33/1	—	—
3039[2]	**Easthorpe (136)** (MissHCKnight) **9-11-3** JFTitley (a bhd: t.o whn p.u bef 4 out)		P	8/1[3]	—	—
3111[2]	**Garolo (FR) (119)** (CPEBrooks) **7-10-0b** JOsborne (lw: a bhd: mstke 3 out: t.o whn p.u bef last)		P	10/1	—	—
3401[3]	**Mister Oddy (133)** (JSKing) **11-11-0** JCulloty (lw: prom tl blnd & uns rdr 10th)		U	16/1	—	—

(SP 125.2%) **16 Rn**

4m 0.8 (-0.20) CSF £127.80 CT £3,014.11 TOTE £23.00: £3.20 £2.10 £4.20 £2.60 (£145.70) Trio £1,775.30 OWNER Lady Lloyd Webber (MALTON) BRED Moor Stud

LONG HANDICAP Garolo (FR) 9-12 Perknapp 9-11 Norse Raider 9-7
WEIGHT FOR AGE 5yo-8lb

3292 Uncle Ernie, dropped a further 2lb, was back to the right trip. He now goes to Aintree and his trainer, rather surprisingly after this performance, stated that the intention is to retire him this season. (20/1)
3187* Elzoba (FR), blinkered for the first time in this country, found it a case of the new kid on the block coming up against the grand old man, who had been given a chance by the Handicapper. (13/2)
Perknapp, 3lb out of the handicap, was taught a salutary lesson at the first, and kept on willingly up the final climb. (25/1)
2783 Time Won't Wait (IRE), ridden closer to the pace than usual, was 2lb higher than when fifth in this event last year. (8/1)
Scobie Boy (IRE) has been a model of consistency in Ireland this season, but the Handicapper had him 12lb higher than when he won at Fairyhouse in January. (25/1)
3369* Political Tower could not sustain his run from the penultimate fence. (16/1)
2890* Certainly Strong (IRE) ran too freely, and soon pulled her way to the front having been last to leave the start. (7/2)
3111 Garolo (FR) (10/1: 7/1-11/1)

3639 CATHCART CHALLENGE CUP CHASE (6-Y.O+) (Class B)

5-05 (5-05) **2m 5f (New) (17 fncs)** £32,850.00 (£9,900.00: £4,800.00: £2,250.00) GOING: 0.08 sec per fur (G)

				SP	RR	SF
3023*	**Sparky Gayle (IRE) (133)** (CParker) **7-11-3** BStorey (lw: hld up: stdy hdwy 10th: led 3 out: sn clr: rdn out)	—	1	3/1[1]	152+	83
3292[3]	**Major Bell (134)** (ACWhillans) **9-11-3** ADobbin (chsd ldr to 6th: wnt 2nd 9th: led & hit 4 out: hdd 3 out: r.o one pce)	4	2	5/1[3]	149	80
3596*	**Or Royal (FR) (135)** (MCPipe) **6-11-3b** APMcCoy (hld up: hdwy 8th: hrd rdn appr 2 out: one pce)	2½	3	4/1[2]	147	78
3335*	**Wild West Wind (IRE) (115)** (MissHCKnight) **7-11-0** JFTitley (prom tl wknd 13th)	13	4	10/1	134	65
3266[3]	**Destin d'Estruval (FR) (123)** (DNicholson) **6-11-7** DBridgwater (a bhd)	8	5	20/1	135	66

3300[P] **Stately Home (IRE) (136)** (PBowen) **6-11-3** NWilliamson (lw: led: clr 3rd: hit 12th: hdd & hit 4 out: eased whn btn appr 2 out) 2½ **6** 11/1 129 60
1520[6] **Pimberley Place (IRE) (122)** (NATwiston-Davies) **9-11-3** CLlewellyn (bit bkwd: hld up: hdwy 6th: chsd ldr 7th to 9th: wknd 11th) ....nk **7** 66/1 129 60
3427[F] **The Reverend Bert (IRE) (110)** (GBBalding) **9-11-0** BFenton (a bhd: t.o fr 8th) 12 **8** 40/1 117 48
3037* **Double Symphony (IRE) (148)** (CPEBrooks) **9-11-7** GBradley (hld up: lost pl 8th: hit 13th: t.o whn p.u bef 4 out) .... **P** 4/1[2] — —
2741a* **Manhattan Castle (IRE) (138)** (ALTMoore,Ireland) **8-11-7** FWoods (lw: hld up & bhd: p.u bef 8th) .... **P** 15/2 — —
(SP 119.5%) **10 Rn**

5m 5.3 (-3.70) CSF £17.28 TOTE £3.70: £1.50 £1.90 £2.00 (£8.00) Trio £12.80 OWNER Mr & Mrs Raymond Anderson Green (LOCKERBIE) BRED Thomas Walsh

3023* Sparky Gayle (IRE) retained his unbeaten record over fences, and may now go to Fairyhouse or the Scottish Grand National meeting at Ayr. His trainer is convinced he will eventually stay three miles, and his jockey is hoping he may turn into a Gold Cup contender next year. (3/1)
3292 Major Bell does not seem to know how to run a bad race, and completed a one-two for Scotland. (5/1)
3596* Or Royal (FR) attempting a Festival double, had the edge taken off him by his first-day exertions and was also on ground plenty fast enough for him. (4/1: 7/4-9/2)
3335* Wild West Wind (IRE) is unproven on ground on the fast side of good. (10/1)
3266 Destin d'Estruval (FR) could never land a blow on ground as quick as this. (20/1)
3300 Stately Home (IRE) was highly tried here, but again did not jump as well as he can. (11/1)

3640 VINCENT O'BRIEN COUNTY H'CAP HURDLE (Gd 3) (5-Y.O+) (Class A)

5-40 (5-41) **2m 1f (New) (8 hdls)** £26,614.99 (£10,048.25: £4,899.13: £2,212.63) GOING: 0.08 sec per fur (G)

SP RR SF

3011[4] **Barna Boy (IRE) (130)** (NJHenderson) **9-10-12** RDunwoody (hld up: hdwy 4th: led flat: rdn out) ....— **1** 14/1 116 58
3572* **Carlito Brigante (118)** (PRWebber) **5-10-0** 7x JOsborne (lw: prom: lost pl 3 out: rallied appr last: ev ch flat: r.o) ....1 **2** 13/2[2] 103 45
2603a[3] **Penny a Day (IRE) (140)** (MrsMReveley) **7-11-8** PNiven (prom: mstke & lost pl 5th: gd hdwy appr last: fin wl).3 **3** 15/2 122+ 64
2603a[2] **Black Queen (IRE) (122)** (JEKiely,Ireland) **6-10-4** AJO'Brien (hld up: hdwy whn mstke 2 out: mstke last: r.o)..1 **4** 12/1 103 45
1793[3] **Tidjani (IRE) (118)** (FBerry,Ireland) **5-10-0** CO'Dwyer (a.p: led after 2 out tl flat: wknd nr fin) ....hd **5** 11/2[1] 99 41
3497[3] **Morstock (118)** (RJHodges) **7-9-11**(3) TDascombe (hld up: hdwy 2 out: styd on flat) ....nk **6** 50/1 99? 41
3163[3] **Tom Brodie (128)** (HowardJohnson) **7-10-10** ADobbin (hld up: hdwy 4th: ev ch appr last: one pce) 1 **7** 14/1 108 50
3572[14] **Ground Nut (IRE) (124)** (RHBuckler) **7-10-6** BPowell (lw: plld hrd in rr: rapid late hdwy: nrst fin) ....1 **8** 40/1 103+ 45
2645[6] **Mytton's Choice (IRE) (127)** (DNicholson) **6-10-4**(5) MrRThornton (hld up: hdwy appr 2 out: rdn & wknd appr last) 1 **9** 33/1 105 47
3231[4] **Ambleside (IRE) (118)** (MrsSDWilliams) **6-10-0** DBridgwater (lw: w ldr: ev ch appr 2 out: sn wknd) ....nk **10** 16/1 96 38
2054[4] **Cheryl's Lad (IRE) (136)** (NJHenderson) **7-11-4** MAFitzgerald (no hdwy fr 2 out) 1¼ **11** 14/1 113 55
3572[4] **Lady Daisy (IRE) (133)** (AMullins,Ireland) **8-11-1** GBradley (led 3rd tl tried to run out 2 out: wknd appr last)...¾ **12** 14/1 109 51
3421[4] **Slew Man (FR) (118)** (MCPipe) **6-10-0b**1 DWalsh (lw: prom: ev ch 2 out: wknd appr last) 3½ **13** 16/1 91 33
3038[2] **Hamilton Silk (132)** (MCPipe) **5-11-0** APMcCoy (hld up & bhd: hdwy whn mstke 2 out: wknd appr last) ....nk **14** 7/1[3] 104 46
Toast The Spreece (IRE) (133) (APO'Brien,Ireland) **5-11-1** CFSwan (hld up & bhd: hdwy after 3 out: ev ch whn blnd last: nt rcvr) ....1¾ **15** 12/1 104+ 46
3231[2] **Romancer (IRE) (138)** (NATwiston-Davies) **6-11-6b** CLlewellyn (swtg: s.s: hdwy 3 out: wknd 2 out) 2 **16** 12/1 107 49
3572[P] **Star Rage (IRE) (133)** (JLHarris) **7-11-1** DGallagher (prom: ev ch 2 out: wknd appr last) ....nk **17** 16/1 102 44
Stompin (142) (MissHCKnight) **6-11-10** JCulloty (bkwd: swtg: led to 3rd: wknd appr 3 out) 4 **18** 33/1 107 49
Celtic Lore (118) (DKWeld,Ireland) **5-10-0b** NWilliamson (prom: lft in ld 2 out: sn hdd: eased whn btn appr last) 3½ **19** 8/1 80 22
790[9] **Faustino (118)** (PJHobbs) **5-10-0** RJohnson (mid div: mstke 3rd: wknd appr 2 out) 12 **20** 50/1 68 10
(SP 143.7%) **20 Rn**

3m 58.9 (1.90) CSF £104.97 CT £709.22 TOTE £20.80: £3.20 £2.10 £2.60 £3.00 (£50.30) Trio £214.10 OWNER Mr Lynn Wilson (LAMBOURN) BRED M. Collison
LONG HANDICAP Carlito Brigante 9-6 Tidjani (IRE) 9-11 Morstock 9-8 Slew Man (FR) 9-13 Celtic Lore 9-12 Faustino 9-8

3011 Barna Boy (IRE), supported in the morning exchanges, held on well up the run-in, with his undoubted stamina coming into play. (14/1)
3572* Carlito Brigante, 6lb higher than when winning the Imperial Cup, was due to go up a further 2lb, and only just missed out on the £50,000 bonus. His trainer intimated he may be campaigned with the Arkle Chase in mind next season. (13/2)
2603a Penny a Day (IRE), 10lb higher than when third in the Ladbroke, was knocked back by a mistake, but finished to some effect. (15/2)
2603a Black Queen (IRE), no less than 17lb higher than when narrowly beaten in the Ladbroke, was let down by his jumping at a critical stage. (12/1)
1793 Tidjani (IRE), 3lb out of the handicap, has disappointed on soft ground since his third to Make a Stand at Sandown in December. Very much the Irish getting-out bet, he did not even repay the each-way money in the end. (11/2)
3497 Morstock likes this ground, and ran surprisingly well from 6lb out of the handicap. (50/1)
3163 Tom Brodie remains a model of consistency. (14/1)
3231 Ground Nut (IRE), adopting totally different tactics, fairly flew up the hill. (40/1)
3038 Hamilton Silk was just getting into the picture, when missing out at the penultimate hurdle. (7/1)
Toast The Spreece (IRE) looked to be going as well as any until throwing his chance away at the final flight. (12/1)

T/Jkpt: Not won; £228,233.20 to Folkestone 14/3/97. T/Plpt: £6,227.50 (30.79 Tckts). T/Qdpt: £140.80 (63.11 Tckts) KH

3210-HEXHAM (L-H) (Good, Good to soft patches)

Thursday March 13th

WEATHER: overcast & windy

3641 MEDALLION LAGER CONDITIONAL H'CAP HURDLE (0-110) (4-Y.O+ F & M) (Class E)

2-25 (2-25) **2m (8 hdls)** £2,322.00 (£642.00: £306.00) GOING: 0.55 sec per fur (S)

SP RR SF

3485[6] **Apollo's Daughter (68)** (JLGoulding) **9-10-6** FLeahy (a cl up: led appr 2 out: sn clr: hit last) ....— **1** 5/1[3] 53 10
3481[P] **Ski Path (64)** (NBycroft) **8-10-2** GLee (in tch: effrt 3 out: styd on: no ch w wnr) ....13 **2** 25/1 36 —
3309[5] **Peggy Gordon (76)** (MrsDThomson) **6-10-11**(3) NHorrocks (led tl hdd appr 2 out: sn outpcd) ....11 **3** 4/1[2] 37 —

				SP	RR	SF
2840[14]	**Millers Goldengirl (IRE) (65)** (MrsSJSmith) **6-10-3** GFRyan (chsd ldrs tl outpcd fr 2 out)	4	**4**	12/1	22	—
1855[8]	**Qualitair Pride (88)** (JFBottomley) **5-11-12** ECallaghan (lw: hld up: effrt 5th: sn outpcd & no imp after)	2½	**5**	3/1[1]	43	—
3166[12]	**Mill Thyme (84)** (PBeaumont) **5-11-8** BGrattan (lw: cl up tl lost pl appr 7th: sn t.o)	17	**6**	11/1	22	—
1853[F]	**Amber Holly (75)** (JEDixon) **8-10-8**(5) IJardine (chsd ldr tl rdn & wknd appr 3 out)	19	**7**	11/1	—	—
1822[6]	**Tancred Mischief (78)** (DWBarker) **6-11-2** PMidgley (lw: b.d 1st)		**B**	15/2	—	—
3529[8]	**Meadowleck (62)** (WGYoung) **8-10-0** STaylor (b.d 1st)		**B**	25/1	—	—
	Catch the Pigeon (78) (REBarr) **8-11-2** RMcGrath (fell 1st)		**F**	10/1	—	—
3534[6]	**Bill's Pride (75)** (PMonteith) **6-10-8**(5) CMcCormack (trckd ldrs: 4th & effrt whn blnd & uns rdr 2 out)		**U**	8/1	—	—
				(SP 125.7%)	**11 Rn**	

4m 6.7 (18.70) CSF £110.37 CT £508.39 TOTE £6.30: £1.80 £9.00 £2.00 (£121.10) Trio £120.50 OWNER Mrs M. Goulding (BRIGHAM) BRED Mrs Mary Goulding

LONG HANDICAP Meadowleck 9-8

3485 Apollo's Daughter loves this track, and this tough little mare did the business in good style. (5/1: op 3/1)

Ski Path was placed for the first time here, and by the looks of things a bit further might help her cause. (25/1)

3309 Peggy Gordon again tried her forcing tactics, but she is basically a mare who likes things all to go her own way. (4/1: 9/4-9/2)

Millers Goldengirl (IRE) looked very slow once the race began in earnest. (12/1)

Qualitair Pride is not running well at present, and was beaten fully three flights out. (3/1: op 6/1)

1204 Mill Thyme, after jumping the first almost in front, soon decided it was not for her, and would have none of it from then on.(11/1)

1020 Amber Holly (11/1: 8/1-12/1)

3534 Bill's Pride (8/1: op 5/1)

3642 ANN LEBON NOVICES' CHASE (5-Y.O+) (Class E)

3-00 (3-00) **2m 110y (12 fncs)** £2,961.00 (£882.00: £420.00: £189.00) GOING: 0.55 sec per fur (S)

				SP	RR	SF
3069*	**Rallegio (97)** (PMonteith) **8-11-10** GCahill (mstkes: a.p: led 2 out: styd on u.p)	—	**1**	10/11[1]	95	35
3201[7]	**Exemplar (IRE) (81)** (MrsSJSmith) **9-10-12**(5) GFRyan (chsd clr ldr: hit 4th: lft in ld 8th: hdd 2 out: kpt on same pce)	1¾	**2**	6/1[3]	86	26
3479[2]	**Tapatch (IRE)** (MWEasterby) **9-11-3** RGarritty (a.p: outpcd 2 out: hdwy whn mstke last: rider lost irons: kpt on towards finish)	3	**3**	7/4[2]	83	23
3313[P]	**Nawtinookey** (MartinTodhunter) **7-10-5**(7) CMcCormack (in tch: outpcd whn blnd 3 out: n.d.)	27	**4**	25/1	52	—
3331[F]	**Prince Baltasar (60)** (NBycroft) **8-11-3** MFoster (in tch to 8th: sn wl bhd)	24	**5**	33/1	34	—
3453[P]	**Absolutely John (IRE)** (MartinTodhunter) **9-11-3** MMoloney (outpcd & lost tch whn blnd 8th: t.o whn p.u bef last)		**P**	40/1	—	—
3448[4]	**Obvious Risk** (EMCaine) **6-10-12**(5) STaylor (last whn blnd bdly & uns rdr 6th)		**U**	7/1	—	—
3479[6]	**Distillery Hill (IRE) (67)** (VThompson) **9-11-3** MrMThompson (led & clr tl blnd & uns rdr 8th)		**U**	40/1	—	—
				(SP 127.2%)	**8 Rn**	

4m 14.2 (17.20) CSF £7.51 TOTE £1.50: £1.00 £1.80 £2.70 (£6.10) OWNER Mr Guthrie Robertson (ROSEWELL) BRED Mrs Florence C. McCaw

3069* Rallegio did not jump as well this time, but he kept responding to pressure and won in game style. (10/11: 4/7-evens)

1945 Exemplar (IRE) put in a decent effort over these bigger obstacles this time, and judging from this he should have no difficulty in finding a race or two. (6/1)

3479 Tapatch (IRE) has plenty of ability, but was always finding the effort required beyond him. (7/4)

2045 Nawtinookey, having her first run over fences. showed some ability until a blunder steadied her three out. (25/1)

3448 Obvious Risk (7/1: op 16/1)

1850 Distillery Hill (IRE) showed his first signs of form here, and was still clear when he ploughed through the fifth last, giving his rider no chance of staying aboard. (40/1)

3643 WIN WITH THE TOTE H'CAP CHASE (0-120) (5-Y.O+) (Class D)

3-35 (3-37) **4m (24 fncs)** £4,056.25 (£1,210.00: £577.50: £261.25) GOING: 0.55 sec per fur (S)

				SP	RR	SF
3531[5]	**Hudson Bay Trader (USA) (87)** (PBeaumont) **10-10-3**(5) BGrattan (in tch: hdwy 5 out: led 3 out: styd on strly)	—	**1**	10/1	99	3
3395*	**Off The Bru (92)** (MrsSCBradburne) **12-10-6**(7) MrMBradburne (a chsng ldrs: outpcd 3 out: kpt on flat)	1½	**2**	2/1[1]	103	7
3370[2]	**Gold Pigeon (IRE) (79)** (BSRothwell) **8-10-0** RSupple (cl up: hit 19th: chal appr 3 out: one pce appr last)	3	**3**	5/1[3]	88	—
3395[7]	**Heavenly Citizen (IRE) (91)** (JLGledson) **9-10-12** KJohnson (led tl hdd 3 out: wknd fr next)	11	**4**	9/1	94	—
3477[3]	**Tico Gold (84)** (PCheesbrough) **9-10-5** GCahill (prom: hit 7th: blnd 20th: sn wknd)	dist	**5**	8/1	—	—
3316[2]	**Stoney Burke (IRE) (103)** (MissLucindaRussell) **8-11-10** AThornton (lw: blnd bldy 1st: bhd tl hdwy 16th: blnd 19th: sn t.o: p.u bef 4 out)		**P**	9/2[2]	—	—
3162[7]	**Pennine Pride (96)** (MDHammond) **10-11-3b1** RGarritty (mstkes: prom tl blnd 17th & p.u bef next)		**P**	9/2[2]	—	—
3482[6]	**Quixall Crossett (80)** (EMCaine) **12-9-10**(5)ow1 STaylor (a bhd: t.o whn j.v.slowly 5 out: p.u bef next)		**P**	50/1	—	—
				(SP 118.5%)	**8 Rn**	

8m 42.8 (42.80) CSF £30.00 CT £106.78 TOTE £11.00: £2.70 £1.40 £1.80 (£8.30) OWNER Mr P. C. N. Curtis (BRANDSBY) BRED Ryedale Farm

LONG HANDICAP Gold Pigeon (IRE) 9-12 Quixall Crossett 8-5

OFFICIAL EXPLANATION Tico Gold: finished distressed. Stoney Burke (IRE): was unsuited by the going.

3531 Hudson Bay Trader (USA) goes well on this track, and obviously was suited by this marathon trip. Getting first run on the favourite from three out, he was always doing enough thereafter. (10/1)

3395* Off The Bru doesn't know how to run a bad race these days, but he was just chopped for toe at a vital stage here. (2/1)

3370 Gold Pigeon (IRE) remains in good form, and tried really hard, but was tapped for speed from the second last. (5/1)

3033 Heavenly Citizen (IRE) enjoyed himself out in front but, once collared three out, he had nothing more to give. (9/1: op 6/1)

3477 Tico Gold seems to have lost his way at the moment, and mistakes finally stopped him over the last six fences. (8/1)

3316 Stoney Burke (IRE) made a blunder-and-a-half at the first, and that seemed to put him off altogether and he was never going or jumping thereafter. (9/2)

2542 Pennine Pride, from a yard that can do little right, was never jumping. (9/2)

3644 KEOGHANS NOVICES' HURDLE (4-Y.O+) (Class E)

4-05 (4-06) **3m (12 hdls)** £2,490.00 (£690.00: £330.00) GOING: 0.55 sec per fur (S)

				SP	RR	SF
2770[2]	**Magpie Melody (IRE)** (LLungo) **6-11-3** RSupple (a cl up: led appr last: kpt on wl)	—	**1**	11/4[2]	66	23
2787[F]	**Pebble Beach (IRE) (89)** (GMMoore) **7-11-9** JCallaghan (led tl hdd appr last: kpt on)	2	**2**	8/1	71	28

			SP	RR	SF
2673[4]	**Southern Cross** (MWEasterby) **5-11-0**[(3)] PMidgley (mstkes: hdwy ½-wy: outpcd 3 out: 3rd & styng on whn blnd last: no ex)....3½	**3**	9/4[1]	62	19
2654[7]	**Fenloe Rambler (IRE) (79)** (RJohnson) **6-11-3** KJohnson (chsd ldrs: outpcd appr 2 out: 4th & btn whn blnd last)....3½	**4**	10/1	60	17
3449[F]	**Allerbank** (MrsJStorey) **6-11-3** MrCStorey (in tch: hdwy & ch 3 out: sn rdn: wl outpcd fr next)....11	**5**	12/1	53	10
3328[4]	**Mr Christie (88)** (MissLCSiddall) **5-11-9** AThornton (bhd: sme hdwy 4 out: n.d)....1	**6**	8/1	58	15
2787[3]	**Celtic Duke** (MDHammond) **5-11-3** RGarritty (in tch tl wknd fr 4 out)....2½	**7**	6/1[3]	50	7
3481[4]	**Diddy Rymer (73)** (MrsSJSmith) **7-10-12** RichardGuest (chsd ldrs tl wknd 3 out)....23	**8**	9/1	30	—
3159[10]	**Sutherland Moss (100)** (TPTate) **6-11-9** MFoster (rr div whn fell 7th: dead)....	**F**	7/1	—	—
3449[5]	**Hadaway Lad** (HowardJohnson) **5-11-3** MMoloney (prom to 7th: t.o whn p.u bef 2 out)....	**P**	12/1	—	—
1926[9]	**Tartan Joy (IRE)** (JAMoore) **6-11-3** NSmith (sn bhd: t.o whn p.u bef 3 out)....	**P**	33/1	—	—
3481[P]	**Willie Wannabe (IRE) (55)** (MrsDThomson) **7-11-3** DParker (mstke 2nd: t.o fr 6th: p.u bef 2 out)....	**P**	33/1	—	—
			(SP 146.8%)	**12 Rn**	

6m 7.0 (27.00) CSF £29.95 TOTE £3.40: £2.40 £2.30 £1.70 (£22.00) Trio £27.70 OWNER Mr R. J. Gilbert (CARRUTHERSTOWN) BRED E. Campion

OFFICIAL EXPLANATION **Celtic Duke: rider reported that the gelding gurgled and felt listless, and that many of the yard's horses have been running below-par.**

2770 Magpie Melody (IRE), having his first attempt over hurdles, showed fine determination, and staying is certainly the name of the game with him. (11/4)

2787 Pebble Beach (IRE) put up a good performance but, despite trying hard, always found the winner too strong in the closing stages. (8/1)

2673 Southern Cross jumped moderately, but still had his chances. However, yet another bad mistake at the last finished him. (9/4)

Fenloe Rambler (IRE) put in a reasonable effort here, and seems to be coming to form. (10/1)

3066 Allerbank again looked slow when the pressure was on. (12/1)

3328 Mr Christie was never giving it his best shot. (8/1)

3645 FEDERATION BREWERY H'CAP CHASE (0-100) (5-Y.O+) (Class F)

4-40 (4-40) **2m 4f 110y (15 fncs)** £3,013.20 (£835.20: £399.60) GOING: 0.55 sec per fur (S)

			SP	RR	SF
3141[4]	**Cullane Lake (IRE) (73)** (MissMKMilligan) **7-10-1** RSupple (chsd ldrs: led 11th: styd on wl to go clr fr 2 out).—	**1**	6/1[3]	93	20
2955[3]	**Willie Sparkle (72)** (MrsSCBradburne) **11-10-0** GCahill (lw: in tch: chsd ldrs fr 10th: one pce fr 2 out)....8	**2**	12/1	86	13
3099[P]	**Snook Point (77)** (DALamb) **10-10-5**[ow2] JBurke (a.p: effrt & hit 11th: one pce fr 2 out)....11	**3**	20/1	82	7
3452[W]	**Risky Dee (72)** (VThompson) **8-10-0** KJohnson (rr div: effrt & hit 10th: styd on fr 3 out: nvr rchd ldrs)....6	**4**	14/1	73	—
3452[2]	**Last Refuge (IRE) (94)** (TJCarr) **8-11-8** NSmith (lw: plld hrd: blnd 2nd & 9th: n.d)....1	**5**	8/1	94	21
1823[4]	**Tighter Budget (USA) (100)** (MrsDianneSayer) **10-12-0** MMoloney (cl up: led 5th to 11th: lost pl: rallied 3 out: wknd after next)....12	**6**	6/1[3]	90	17
3452[F]	**Grand Scenery (IRE) (85)** (HowardJohnson) **9-10-13** AThornton (hld up: gd hdwy to chal 11th: wknd 2 out) 1¼	**7**	7/1	74	1
3223[P]	**Supposin (91)** (MrsSJSmith) **9-11-5** RichardGuest (bhd fr ½-wy)....6	**8**	16/1	76	3
3094[P]	**Rusty Blade (90)** (PMonteith) **8-11-4** MrRHale (blnd 5th: sn t.o)....1¾	**9**	25/1	73	—
3482*	**Chill Wind (94)** (NBycroft) **8-11-8**[6x] MFoster (lw: hdwy to trck ldrs whn fell 9th)....	**F**	4/1[2]	—	—
3482[2]	**Pariah (IRE) (91)** (MartinTodhunter) **8-11-5** JCallaghan (lw: hld up & bhd whn blnd & fell 5th)....	**F**	13/8[1]	—	—
	Moss Bee (80) (WGReed) **10-10-8**[ow8] TReed (led to 5th: blnd 7th & sn wknd after)....	**P**	33/1	—	—
			(SP 142.1%)	**12 Rn**	

5m 16.7 (19.70) CSF £78.88 CT £1,311.18 TOTE £11.30: £2.00 £2.70 £8.00 (£21.90) Trio £116.00 OWNER Mrs J. M. L. Milligan (LEYBURN) BRED Thomas Larkin

3141 Cullane Lake (IRE), dropped back in trip, got stronger as the race progressed, and won really well. (6/1)

2955 Willie Sparkle, after a run over hurdles last time, put in a better effort here, but the winner was always too good for him. (12/1)

3099 Snook Point was back to something like his form here, but he looked very slow at the business end. (20/1)

3308 Risky Dee found this trip a bit sharp, and only got going when it was too late. (14/1)

3452 Last Refuge (IRE) raced too freely and made two particularly bad errors. (8/1)

1823 Tighter Budget (USA) obviously needed this after over three months off. (6/1)

3482* Chill Wind looked to be going well when coming to grief at the ninth. (4/1: 3/1-9/2)

3482 Pariah (IRE) was settled out the back when falling early on. (13/8)

3646 BUCHANAN ALE H'CAP HURDLE (0-100) (4-Y.O+) (Class F)

5-15 (5-17) **3m (12 hdls)** £2,284.00 (£634.00: £304.00) GOING: 0.55 sec per fur (S)

			SP	RR	SF
3328[5]	**Corbleu (IRE) (72)** (SBBell) **7-10-0** KJohnson (hld up & bhd: hdwy 4 out: led last: drvn out)....—	**1**	12/1	53	—
2922[4]	**Five Flags (IRE) (88)** (MrsSJSmith) **9-11-2** RichardGuest (a.p: styd on u.p fr 2 out: nrst fin)....1¼	**2**	6/1	68	11
3368[5]	**The Other Man (IRE) (72)** (MissLCSiddall) **7-10-0** OPears (lw: a.p: led appr last: sn hdd & r.o one pce)....nk	**3**	10/1	52	—
3557[3]	**Kings Lane (85)** (JMDun) **8-10-13** DParker (lw: prom tl outpcd 3 out: hdwy appr last: nt qckn flat)....1½	**4**	4/1[3]	64	7
3281[6]	**Rimouski (91)** (BRCambidge) **9-11-5** GaryLyons (bhd: hdwy 3 out: styd on appr last: nrst fin)....¾	**5**	8/1	70	13
2768[3]	**Menshaar (USA) (100)** (LLungo) **5-12-0** RSupple (mstkes: prom tl outpcd appr 2 out: styd on & ev ch last: no ex)....nk	**6**	3/1[1]	78	21
3358[4]	**Dockmaster (87)** (MissMKMilligan) **6-10-8**[(7)] NHorrocks (chsd ldrs: outpcd 3 out: kpt on appr last: no imp)...s.h	**7**	7/2[2]	65	8
3157[B]	**New Charges (92)** (PBeaumont) **10-11-1**[(5)] BGrattan (hld up & bhd: gd hdwy to ld appr 2 out: hdd & wknd appr last)....12	**8**	8/1	62	5
3201[16]	**Grace Card (90)** (BRCambidge) **11-11-4b** MissPRobson (chsd ldrs tl outpcd fr 4 out)....dist	**9**	25/1	—	—
2790[P]	**Kings Minstral (IRE) (76)** (DALamb) **7-10-4**[ow4] JBurke (led tl hdd & wknd qckly appr 2 out)....10	**10**	14/1	—	—
	Kenilworth Lad (93) (WSCunningham) **9-11-0**[(7)] LMcGrath (blnd 4th: lost tch fr 8th: t.o whn p.u bef 2 out)....	**P**	25/1	—	—
			(SP 134.9%)	**11 Rn**	

6m 10.7 (30.70) CSF £86.43 CT £710.82 TOTE £20.30: £4.10 £2.40 £1.70 (£68.80) Trio £143.90; £52.70 to Southwell 14/3/96 OWNER Mr David Woodcock (DRIFFIELD) BRED M. and Mrs Ross

LONG HANDICAP The Other Man (IRE) 9-8 Kings Minstral (IRE) 9-12 Corbleu (IRE) 9-13

3328 Corbleu (IRE), patiently ridden this time, proved determined once in front to hold on from a host of challengers. (12/1)

2922 Five Flags (IRE) just stays and goes on soft ground and, after looking in trouble, he was keeping on best of all at the finish. (6/1)

3368 The Other Man (IRE) put in by far his best performance here, and being 6lb wrong in the handicap probably made all the difference. (10/1: op 5/1)

3557 Kings Lane ran in snatches, and was never doing enough when it mattered. (4/1)

2761 Rimouski ran well enough here to suggest that he still retains some ability. (8/1: op 5/1)

2768 Menshaar (USA) ran well, but the weight finally anchored him on the run-in. (3/1: 4/1-5/2)
3358 Dockmaster (7/2: 5/2-4/1)
3028 New Charges did too much running too quickly here from the third last, and this was not a bad effort in the circumstances. (8/1)

T/Plpt: £409.10 (22.37 Tckts). T/Qdpt: £165.80 (3.41 Tckts) AA

3647a - 3649a : (Irish Racing) - See Computer Raceform

3124a-NAVAN (Ireland) (L-H) (Soft)
Saturday March 8th

3650a I.N.H. STALLION OWNERS E.B.F. NOVICES' H'CAP HURDLE (Gd 3) (5-Y.O+)
3-30 (3-33) **3m (13 hdls)** IR £9,675.00 (IR £2,775.00: IR £1,275.00: IR £375.00)

			SP	RR	SF
3126a[5]	**Blushing Sand (IRE)** (PTLeonard,Ireland) **7-10-1**(7) MrTJBeattie (hld up towards rr: hdwy 4 out: chal whn pckd 2 out: led appr last: styd on u.p) ——	**1**	11/2[2]	82+	40
	Pat Hartigan (IRE) (ALTMoore,Ireland) **7-10-10** FWoods (hld up: hdwy 4 out: sn chal: disp ld last: hdd u.p last 100 yds) ½	**2**	9/2[1]	84	42
1485a[5]	**Hollybank Buck (IRE)** (AJMartin,Ireland) **7-10-8** JShortt (in tch: 3rd 4 out: lost pl: r.o wl fr last) 1	**3**	7/1[3]	81	39
	Bells Bridge (IRE) (APO'Brien,Ireland) **7-10-9** THorgan (in tch early: lost tch 9th: hdwy 3 out: styd on flat) s.h	**4**	7/1[3]	82	40
	Go Now (IRE) (TFoley,Ireland) **7-11-2** TPTreacy (hld up: trckd ldrs 2 out: chal whn bad mstke last: no ex) s.h	**5**	7/1[3]	89	47
3382a[7]	**Coq Hardi Venture (IRE)** (NMeade,Ireland) **6-10-8**(7) BJGeraghty (hld up: rdn & nt trble ldrs 2 out: styd on flat) ½	**6**	12/1	88	46
	Be Home Early (IRE) (AMullins,Ireland) **7-10-9**(7) AO'Shea (cl up: led appr 2 out: rdn & hdd appr last: nt qckn) 9	**7**	8/1	83	41
319a[4]	**Diamond Double (IRE)** (APO'Brien,Ireland) **6-10-4**(3) JButler (mid div: mstke 9th: sn rdn: no imp appr 2 out) 4	**8**	33/1	71	29
	Heavy Hustler (IRE) (ALTMoore,Ireland) **6-10-7** JPBroderick (led & disp ld: slight mstkes 5th & 6th: hdd 2 out: rdn & nt qckn) 1½	**9**	12/1	70	28
	Toureen Gale (IRE) (WPMullins,Ireland) **8-10-2**(5) PMorris (hld up: jnd ldrs 3rd: 2nd briefly 3 out: rdn & wknd appr next) 6	**10**	7/1[3]	66	24
	Brass Band (IRE) (JRHFowler,Ireland) **6-10-0**(7) MrRHFowler (towards rr: rdn after 4 out: no imp appr 2 out) 10	**11**	14/1	59	17
	Pinkpinkfizz (IRE) (TJTaaffe,Ireland) **6-10-0**(7) PGHourigan (hld up towards rr: sme hdwy 8th: sn rdn & btn) 1½	**12**	10/1	58	16
3382a[4]	**Kings Return (IRE)** (WPMullins,Ireland) **6-12-0** DJCasey (led & disp ld: wknd bef 3 out: t.o) 25	**13**	8/1	63	21
			(SP 139.9%)	**13 Rn**	

6m 5.0 (0.00) OWNER Miss D. Leonard (KILCOCK)
Blushing Sand (IRE), looking very well treated on his first run in a handicap, scored narrowly enough. He received rather unorthodox handling from the saddle, but was always going like a winner from two out. He goes up 5lb for this and there is still improvement to come. (11/2)
Pat Hartigan (IRE), also making his debut in handicap company, had a much harder race than the winner, but just could not get in front. The jockey got a seven day holiday for excessive use of the stick. (9/2: op 3/1)
Hollybank Buck (IRE) finished with a real rattle after losing his place three out. (7/1)
Bells Bridge (IRE) was another who got himself detached, but stayed on well at the finish. (7/1: op 4/1)
Go Now (IRE) blundered at the last and it possibly cost him more than he was beaten by, but he was under pressure at that stage. (7/1)
Coq Hardi Venture (IRE) (12/1: op 8/1)
Be Home Early (IRE) (8/1: op 5/1)
Pinkpinkfizz (IRE) (10/1: op 6/1)
3382a Kings Return (IRE) (8/1: op 4/1)

3651a - 3662a : (Irish Racing) - See Computer Raceform

3131-FAKENHAM (L-H) (Good)
Friday March 14th
WEATHER: Fine

3663 WYMONDHAM (S) H'CAP HURDLE (0-90) (4-Y.O+) (Class G)
2-10 (2-11) **2m (9 hdls)** £2,785.00 (£850.00: £420.00: £205.00) GOING: 0.00 sec per fur (G)

			SP	RR	SF
2006[10]	**Antiguan Flyer (65)** (GProdromou) **8-10-2v**[1](3) MichaelBrennan (mde all: sn clr: blnd 2 out: comf) ——	**1**	20/1	55+	1
3447[8]	**General Shirley (IRE) (79)** (PRHedger) **6-10-12**(7) MClinton (hdwy 6th: r.o appr last: no ch w wnr) 11	**2**	8/1	58	4
3284[4]	**Arch Angel (IRE) (76)** (GFHCharles-Jones) **4-10-1**(7) XAizpuru (hdwy appr 2 out: fin wl) 2	**3**	7/1[3]	53	—
3050[9]	**Happy Brave (78)** (PDCundell) **5-11-4** LHarvey (lw: prom: no imp fr 6th) 3	**4**	16/1	52	—
1818[2]	**Caddy's First (84)** (SMellor) **5-11-5**(5) ChrisWebb (lw: prom: chsd wnr 4th tl wknd appr 2 out) 2½	**5**	10/1	56	2
3313[12]	**Blue Domain (68)** (RCraggs) **6-10-8** ADobbin (hdwy 5th: chsd wnr appr 2 out: wknd appr last) 1	**6**	12/1	39	—
3429[3]	**Nagobelia (80)** (JPearce) **9-10-13**(7) JO'Shaughnessy (chsd wnr to 4th) 2½	**7**	4/1[2]	48	—
1027[9]	**Wordsmith (IRE) (79)** (JLHarris) **7-11-2**(3) RMassey (bkwd: nvr nr ldrs) 25	**8**	12/1	22	—
3131*	**Ruth's Gamble (62)** (MrsLCJewell) **9-10-2v** DLeahy (lw: in tch: hit 4th: rdn next: sn btn) 10	**9**	3/1[1]	—	—
2567[3]	**Cosmic Star (64)** (PWinkworth) **7-9-13b**(5) MrRThornton (prom tl rdn & wknd 5th) 3½	**10**	7/1[3]	—	—
3352[10]	**Rafter-J (66)** (JohnHarris) **6-10-6** MBrennan (mstke 4th: a bhd) 7	**11**	33/1	—	—
2114[4]	**Pyrrhic Dance (75)** (MJHaynes) **7-11-1** JRailton (pckd 1st: prom to 6th: t.o whn p.u bef last)	**P**	10/1	—	—
			(SP 128.3%)	**12 Rn**	

3m 55.5 (11.50) CSF £168.81 CT £1,153.53 TOTE £33.50: £7.70 £2.40 £1.80 (£187.50) Trio £240.40 OWNER Mr George Prodromou (EAST HARLING) BRED Crest Stud Ltd
WEIGHT FOR AGE 4yo-8lb
No bid
OFFICIAL EXPLANATION Ruth's Gamble: no explanation offered.

355 Antiguan Flyer ran well fresh early in the season and that, combined with the first-time visor, enabled him to show these a clean pair of heels. (20/1)
22 General Shirley (IRE), dropping in class, was one of a number ridden on the basis that the winner would come back to them. Only in the last half-mile did he really get going. (8/1)
3284 Arch Angel (IRE) was not even in the chasing pack going to two out, but finished to great effect. (7/1: 5/1-8/1)
Happy Brave again took a strong hold and does struggle to last home. (16/1)
1818 Caddy's First was the first to take the winner's bid to make all seriously, but vain pursuit had beaten him by two out. (10/1)
2505 Blue Domain, set alight to go a clear second two out, looked a danger to the winner briefly, but might have done too much too soon as he faded dramatically on the short uphill turn into the straight. (12/1: op 8/1)
648 Wordsmith (IRE) (12/1: op 7/1)
Pyrrhic Dance (10/1: op 6/1)

3664 WILLIAM BULWER-LONG MEMORIAL NOVICES' HUNTERS' CHASE (5-Y.O+) (Class H)
2-40 (2-40) **2m 5f 110y (16 fncs)** £2,382.00 (£726.00: £358.00: £174.00) GOING: 0.00 sec per fur (G)

	Horse / details		SP	RR	SF
	What Chance (IRE) (MrsHMobley) **9-10-11**(7) MrACharles-Jones (hld up: hdwy 3 out: led appr last: rdn out)—	1	7/2 2	81	—
3476P	**Galzig** (MrsDEHTurner) **9-11-4**(7)ow2 MrWTellwright (lw: led 4th: led 8th to 10th: led 4 tl appr last: one pce).3½	2	12/1	85	—
32085	**Gypsy King (IRE)** (GICooper) **9-11-2**(7) MrACoe (chsd ldrs: mstke 12th: hit 2 out: kpt on) 2	3	5/1 3	82	—
3586U	**Tellaporky** (THind) **8-11-2**(7) MrAMiddleton (led 4th tl blnd & hdd 8th: led 10th to 4 out: btn whn blnd & rider lost irons last) 8	4	50/1	76	—
31352	**Arise (IRE)** (AWVarey) **8-11-2**(7) MrNRMitchell (hmpd s: t.o tl hdwy 6th: blnd next: wknd appr 2 out) 9	5	11/10 1	69	—
	Try God (MissLouiseAllan) **10-11-2**(7) MissLAllan (trckd ldrs: pckd 13th: sn btn & t.o) 11	6	14/1	61	—
	Rayman (IRE) (ATredwell) **9-11-2**(7) MrRLawther (swtg: bhd fr 6th) 8	7	50/1	55	—
	Foxbow (IRE) (JMTurner) **7-11-4**(5) MrASansome (fell 3rd)	F	14/1	—	—
	Old Dundalk (NeilKing) **13-11-2b**(7) MrNKing (t.o fr 6th: blnd next: p.u bef last)	P	50/1	—	—
5559	**Gone For Lunch** (JohnWhyte) **6-11-2**(7) MrMGingell (w.r.s: t.o wh j.rt & blnd 5th: p.u bef next)	P	14/1	—	—

(SP 120.1%) **10 Rn**

5m 38.5 (23.50) CSF £40.25 TOTE £4.50: £1.40 £4.00 £1.70 (£24.50) Trio £39.30 OWNER Mrs Helen Mobley (BANBURY) BRED Mrs Edith Mulcahy
What Chance (IRE), who has shown fair form in a couple of ladies' opens between the flags, was ridden with great confidence to win what turned into a poor race. (7/2: op 6/1)
Galzig, fourth in this race last year, jumped soundly and was always in the firing line, but could not quicken with the winner. (12/1: op 6/1)
3208 Gypsy King (IRE), with the favourite effectively out of the way, could have been expected to take this on last season's form, but was again a disappointment. (5/1)
Tellaporky hardly looks the safest conveyance, but showed ability, disputing the lead for most of the trip. He would have finished a little closer but for the last-fence mistake. (50/1)
3135 Arise (IRE), hampered at the start when a rival whipped round in front of him, set off a good twenty lengths behind the others. This eventually took its toll, but his jumping was far from satisfactory with a series of rather hesitant jumps, and he may have struggled in any case. (11/10: 4/5-6/5)
Try God wears a tongue-strap, and his head went up and he stopped to nothing after pecking four out. (14/1: op 25/1)
Foxbow (IRE) (14/1: op 8/1)

3665 JEWSON H'CAP CHASE (0-120) (5-Y.O+) (Class D)
3-10 (3-10) **2m 5f 110y (16 fncs)** £4,335.00 (£1,320.00: £650.00: £315.00) GOING: 0.00 sec per fur (G)

	Horse / details		SP	RR	SF
20465	**Pats Minstrel (100)** (RChampion) **12-11-4** ADobbin (lw: mde all: rdn out) ....—	1	9/1	101	19
34136	**Artic Wings (IRE) (105)** (OBrennan) **9-11-9** MBrennan (hld up: hdwy 8th: ev ch 3 out tl no ex appr last) 2	2	9/4 2	105	23
31322	**Whippers Delight (IRE) (92)** (GFHCharles-Jones) **9-10-3**(7) XAizpuru (chsd ldrs: hit 8th: no imp fr 12th) 20	3	100/30 3	77	—
34962	**Hawaiian Youth (IRE) (106)** (GMMcCourt) **9-11-7**(3) DFortt (lw: trckd wnr tl blnd bdly 11th: btn whn j.slowly 3 out) 1¾	4	Evens 1	89	7
3332P	**Lodestone Lad (IRE) (82)** (RDickin) **7-10-0v1** DLeahy (nt j.w: sn t.o: p.u bef 12th)	P	25/1	—	—

(SP 117.7%) **5 Rn**

5m 29.2 (14.20) CSF £28.73 TOTE £8.60: £3.70 £1.50 (£12.00) OWNER Mr K. J. Hunt (NEWMARKET) BRED J. Fitzpatrick
LONG HANDICAP Lodestone Lad (IRE) 9-12
2046 Pats Minstrel often carries condition, but looked particularly well on this occasion. The trip seemed to suit him, and he proved a tough nut when the heat was on. (9/1)
3413 Artic Wings (IRE) looked likely to score when joining the winner at the third last but, ridden going to the last, she was soon outbattled. She seems to like this place, but the way she moves suggests that a right-handed track would suit her better. (9/4)
3132 Whippers Delight (IRE) was unable to dominate with Pats Minstrel in the field. (100/30)
3496 Hawaiian Youth (IRE) made a spectacular mistake in front of the stands, six from home, from which his pilot made a quite wonderful recovery. However, the combination were no longer travelling best and this run is best forgiven. (Evens)

3666 DOWNHAM MARKET H'CAP HURDLE (0-115) (4-Y.O+) (Class E)
3-40 (3-41) **2m (9 hdls)** £3,696.50 (£1,127.00: £556.00: £270.50) GOING: 0.00 sec per fur (G)

	Horse / details		SP	RR	SF
32864	**Barford Sovereign (109)** (JRFanshawe) **5-12-0** ADobbin (w ldr: led appr 4th to 3 out: rdn to ld cl home) ....—	1	3/1 2	91	31
35843	**Kintavi (99)** (TWDonnelly) **7-11-4** PNiven (lw: trckd ldrs: slt ld 3 out: hit last: hdd & unable qckn cl home) ....hd	2	6/4 1	81	21
334612	**Ajdar (81)** (OBrennan) **6-10-0** MBrennan (bhd: hit 6th: hdwy appr 2 out: r.o) 16	3	8/1	47	—
	Salman (USA) (93) (MrsVCWard) **11-10-7**(5) MrRThornton (bit bkwd: led tl hdd & hit 2nd: rdn 5th: kpt on fr 2 out) 7	4	20/1	52	—
31835	**Isaiah (108)** (MrsJCecil) **8-11-13** TKent (led 2nd tl appr 4th: rdn & wknd appr 2 out) 1	5	9/2 3	66	6
33525	**Lucy Tufty (81)** (JPearce) **6-9-7**(7) JO'Shaughnessy (prom: lost pl & hit 3rd: n.d after) 5	6	7/1	34	—
97P	**Eriny (USA) (93)** (JJQuinn) **8-10-9**(3) ECallaghan (lw: prom: hit 6th: sn btn) 17	7	16/1	29	—
31316	**Stone Island (89)** (JohnWhyte) **4-9-7**(7) MissCTownsley (a bhd: t.o whn blnd & uns rdr 2 out)	U	50/1	—	—

(SP 119.4%) **8 Rn**

3m 53.4 (9.40) CSF £7.85 CT £29.50 TOTE £4.80: £1.70 £1.10 £1.70 (£4.80) Trio £5.70 OWNER Barford Bloodstock (NEWMARKET) BRED Mrs C. Handscombe
LONG HANDICAP Ajdar 9-11 Lucy Tufty 9-12 Stone Island 9-3
WEIGHT FOR AGE 4yo-8lb

3286 Barford Sovereign, always disputing the lead, went head-to-head with Kintavi over the last three flights. Her courage may have been questioned in the past, but she dug deep here without flinching. (3/1)
3584 Kintavi ran another fine race on the track, and lost nothing in defeat other than a decent handicap mark. (6/4)
3136 Ajdar only got going in the last half-mile, and the leaders were long gone. (8/1)
Salman (USA) has been chasing for most of the last two years, and got rather outpaced midway through the race. Not a bad seasonal debut. (20/1)
3183 Isaiah took on the two principals but was the first to crack. (9/2)

3667 CASTLEACRE MAIDEN CHASE (5-Y.O+) (Class D)

4-10 (4-10) **3m 110y (18 fncs)** £3,417.00 (£1,041.00: £513.00: £249.00) GOING: 0.00 sec per fur (G)

				SP	RR	SF
3489[5]	**Brogeen Lady (IRE) (100)** (DRGandolfo) **7-11-0** PNiven (lw: led 4th to 6th: led 9th: clr 13th: hdd appr 3 out: rallied to ld last: r.o)	—	1	6/4[1]	88	—
3436[2]	**Jolly Boat (82)** (FJordan) **10-11-5** SWynne (in tch: mstke 8th: hmpd 12th: hdwy next: led appr 3 out: clr 2 out: wknd & hdd last)	2½	2	4/1[3]	91	—
3134[3]	**Charter Lane (IRE) (63)** (MrsLCJewell) **7-11-5** DLeahy (chsd ldrs tl wknd appr 3 out)	18	3	12/1	80	—
3393[2]	**Desperate Days (IRE) (69)** (FKirby) **8-11-5** WDwan (lw: a bhd)	13	4	11/2	71	—
3208[6]	**Ell Gee** (MrsPTownsley) **7-10-7**(7) MissCTownsley (prom to 11th)	dist	5	50/1	—	—
3546[P]	**Seabright Saga** (MCChapman) **7-11-5** WWorthington (plld hrd: in tch tl fell 7th)		F	50/1	—	—
3020[P]	**Glendine (IRE)** (CJMann) **7-11-5** JRailton (lw: led to 4th: led 6th tl hdd & hit 9th: 2nd whn fell 12th)		F	8/1	—	—
3355[4]	**Music Master (IRE)** (CREgerton) **7-11-5b** ADobbin (prom to 9th: t.o whn p.u bef 2 out)		P	7/2[2]	—	—
				(SP 120.3%)	**8 Rn**	

6m 28.1 (25.10) CSF £8.02 TOTE £3.30: £1.80 £2.20 £2.50 (£8.50) OWNER Starlight Racing (WANTAGE) BRED E. Farrell
3489 Brogeen Lady (IRE) looked well beaten soon after losing the lead going to three out, but got a second wind and came home very much better than the runner-up. (6/4)
3436 Jolly Boat looked all over the winner when clear at the second last, but was caught out by lack of stamina. (4/1)
3134 Charter Lane (IRE) was again easily outpaced in the last half-mile. (12/1: op 8/1)
3393 Desperate Days (IRE), on such a sharp track, never threatened to go the pace. (11/2)

3668 HOLKHAM MAIDEN CONDITIONAL HURDLE (I) (4-Y.O+) (Class E)

4-40 (4-40) **2m (9 hdls)** £1,838.00 (£518.00: £254.00) GOING: 0.00 sec per fur (G)

				SP	RR	SF
3359[8]	**Florid (USA)** (CPEBrooks) **6-11-8** MBerry (lw: led to 2nd: led 4th: clr whn blnd 2 out: easily)	—	1	3/1[2]	92+	10
3445[5]	**Taarish (IRE)** (SMellor) **4-11-0** ChrisWebb (lw: chsd ldrs: lost pl appr 2 out: r.o flat)	22	2	9/2[3]	70	—
3359[5]	**Formidable Partner** (MrsVCWard) **4-11-0v** MichaelBrennan (in tch: chsd wnr appr 2 out: wknd flat)	¾	3	9/4[1]	69	—
3494[5]	**The Stuffed Puffin (IRE)** (CJMann) **5-11-8** JMagee (lw: hld up: hdwy 5th: btn whn pckd 3 out)	7	4	3/1[2]	62	—
	Majra (USA) (MissAEEmbiricos) **5-11-8** DFortt (led 2nd to 4th: wknd 3 out)	19	5	5/1	43	—
	Coven Moon (CRMillington) **7-11-3** ECallaghan (a bhd)	dist	6	33/1	—	—
648[11]	**Shedansar (IRE) (62)** (RCSpicer) **5-11-8** CRae (mstkes: a bhd)	12	7	33/1	—	—
				(SP 121.5%)	**7 Rn**	

3m 46.9 (2.90) CSF £16.84 TOTE £3.80: £2.10 £1.60 (£8.60) OWNER Lord Howard de Walden (LAMBOURN) BRED Lord Howard de Walden
WEIGHT FOR AGE 4yo-8lb
2886 Florid (USA), who went far too fast when taken on last time, had no such problem here, dictating most of the pace to outclass these rivals in a very fast time. When things go his way, he looks very useful at this game. (3/1)
Taarish (IRE) was not able to live with the winner on the final circuit, but his stamina earned him second place near the finish. (9/2)
3359 Formidable Partner had beaten today's winner in the Ludlow race, but this showed just how misleading that form was. Looking booked for second, he stopped to nothing on the run-in. (9/4)
3494 The Stuffed Puffin (IRE) ran well for his new yard at Wincanton, but failed to shine this time, although this would have been a hard race to win. (3/1)
Majra (USA), whose intended jockey ended up near Bury St Edmunds, was disqualified after winning his only previous race on the Flat, at the then Edinburgh two-and-a-half years ago. He raced far too freely and was a spent force by the second last, but he did help to set up the very fast time. (5/1)
Coven Moon could never go the pace. (33/1)

3669 HOLKHAM MAIDEN CONDITIONAL HURDLE (II) (4-Y.O+) (Class E)

5-10 (5-10) **2m (9 hdls)** £1,831.00 (£516.00: £253.00) GOING: 0.00 sec per fur (G)

				SP	RR	SF
	Muhandam (IRE) (MrsDHaine) **4-11-0** PHenley (plld hrd: chsd ldrs: chal & blnd 2 out: led appr last: rdn clr)	—	1	6/1[3]	67	—
3275[5]	**Wentworth (USA)** (GThorner) **5-11-8** ClareThorner (lw: hld up: hdwy 4th: led appr 3 out: hdd appr last)	6	2	2/1[2]	61	—
	Air Commodore (IRE) (DWPArbuthnot) **6-11-8** DJKavanagh (plld hrd: trckd ldrs: mstke 6th: rdn & btn whn hit last: fin lame)	3	3	5/4[1]	58	—
3500[P]	**Genereux** (SMellor) **4-11-0** ChrisWebb (bhd: hdwy 4th: lost pl 3 out: r.o again appr last)	7	4	20/1	51	—
3355[11]	**Holkham Bay** (LWordingham) **5-11-8** DFortt (lw: a bhd)	17	5	8/1	34	—
	Reservation Rock (IRE) (THind) **6-11-8** ABates (led to 3rd: led appr 6th tl appr next: wknd 2 out)	1½	6	20/1	33	—
	Credite Risque (JAGlover) **4-10-9** RMassey (s.s: bhd tl fell 3 out)		F	14/1	—	—
	Acerbus Dulcis (MCChapman) **6-11-8** FLeahy (led 3rd tl appr 6th: sn wknd: p.u bef last)		P	20/1	—	—
				(SP 124.1%)	**8 Rn**	

4m 3.5 (19.50) CSF £18.36 TOTE £7.60: £3.10 £1.00 £1.50 (£10.30) OWNER Mrs Diana Haine (NEWMARKET) BRED Gay O'Callaghan
WEIGHT FOR AGE 4yo-8lb
Muhandam (IRE) has been gelded and has changed yards since his Flat career. A sprinter on the Flat, he took a bit of settling but won well in the end, albeit in a very slow time. (6/1: op 4/1)
3275 Wentworth (USA), only ten lengths behind Wade Road with a more-experienced pilot last time, was well supported, but the winner nipped up his inside on the home turn, and the combination had no more to give. (2/1)
Air Commodore (IRE), a specialist miler on the level, took a strong hold, and despite some sloppy jumping, looked as if he might not have stayed, even on this sharp track. This may not have been the case as, unfortunately, he finished sore. (5/4)
Genereux may not have been suited by such a muddling race as this, for the way he finished suggests that he stays well. (20/1)
3133 Holkham Bay, with his tongue tied down and having shown no ability in four previous runs, becomes Fakenham's entry in the 'strange gamble of the year' contest as supporters must have known their fate with a couple of circuits left. (8/1: op 20/1)

Reservation Rock (IRE) looked fairly fit despite two-and-a-half years off, but certainly did not last home, stopping to nothing. Whether this was lack of fitness or lack of stamina remains to be seen. (20/1)

T/Plpt: £291.00 (44.27 Tckts). T/Qdpt: £18.10 (55.05 Tckts) Dk

3204-FOLKESTONE (R-H) (Good, Good to soft patches hdles crse)
Friday March 14th
WEATHER: Fine

3670 SANDGATE CLAIMING HURDLE (4-Y.O+ F & M) (Class F)
2-00 (2-01) **2m 1f 110y (9 hdls)** £2,092.50 (£580.00: £277.50) GOING: 0.14 sec per fur (G)

				SP	RR	SF
2678^{12}	**Flash In The Pan (IRE) (78)** (JSMoore) **4-10-3** WMcFarland (lw: a.p: chsd ldr fr 2 out: hrd rdn appr last: led flat: r.o wl)	—	1	$11/2^{3}$	60	—
2678^{4}	**Laura Lye (IRE) (75)** (BdeHaan) **7-11-0** JOsborne (a.p: led 5th tl flat: unable qckn)	8	2	6/1	56	—
3447^{6}	**Pedaltothemetal (IRE) (88)** (PMitchell) **5-11-3** GTormey (rdn & hdwy 5th: wknd appr last)	7	3	$9/4^{1}$	52	—
3549^{F}	**Whispering Dawn (88)** (CPEBrooks) **4-10-12** GBradley (stdy hdwy 5th: wknd appr last)	5	4	$9/2^{2}$	51	—
	Uoni (PButler) **4-10-0** TJMurphy (hdwy 5th: wknd appr last)	nk	5	12/1	38	—
2907^{7}	**Olivipet (55)** (FGray) **8-10-5** RFarrant (a bhd)	22	6	25/1	15	—
2907^{11}	**Special Topic** (APJones) **7-9-12**(7) DCarey (prom to 4th)	16	7	33/1	1	—
3338^{9}	**Minster's Madam (82)** (JNeville) **6-10-11v** APMcCoy (chsd ldr: led after 4th tl mstke & hdd 5th: wknd 2 out)	3	8	$9/2^{2}$	4	—
2946^{14}	**Classic Delight (USA)** (ICampbell) **4-10-0** MrRayBarrett (a bhd)	3	9	25/1	—	—
1673^{P}	**Prussian Eagle (IRE)** (MBradstock) **5-11-12b**[1] PHolley (led tl after 4th: sn wknd: t.o whn p.u bef 6th)		P	25/1	—	—
3352^{11}	**Tigana** (MrsLCJewell) **5-10-5** JRKavanagh (bit bkwd: a bhd: t.o whn p.u bef last)		P	33/1	—	—
				(SP 121.9%)	**11 Rn**	

4m 22.5 (16.50) CSF £34.06 TOTE £7.20: £2.30 £1.70 £1.10 (£24.80) Trio £26.00 OWNER Mrs Victoria Goodman (HUNGERFORD) BRED Denis Brosnan
WEIGHT FOR AGE 4yo-8lb

2050 Flash In The Pan (IRE) left her poor run at Lingfield behind. Moving into second place two from home, she responded to pressure and managed to sprint away from the leader on the run-in. (11/2)
2678 Laura Lye (IRE) ran better here. Sent on early on the final circuit, she was left for dead by the winner halfway up the run-in. A small race may soon come her way. (6/1)
3447 Pedaltothemetal (IRE) has been placed on numerous occasions, but her problem is lack of pace and she remains a maiden. Two-and-a-half miles would surely help. (9/4)
2815 Whispering Dawn steadily crept into the action on the final circuit travelling well, but had come to the end of her tether on the long run to the final flight. (9/2)

3671 WHITELAW GOLD CUP NOVICES' CHASE (5-Y.O+) (Class D)
2-30 (2-30) **3m 2f (19 fncs)** £3,773.65 (£1,127.20: £539.10: £245.05) GOING: 0.14 sec per fur (G)

				SP	RR	SF
3134^{*}	**Flippance (98)** (NAGaselee) **7-11-11** CLlewellyn (hdwy 15th: led appr last: comf)	—	1	6/1	117+	19
3356^{2}	**High Learie (94)** (AHHarvey) **7-11-11** JAMcCarthy (led tl appr last: unable qckn)	8	2	$9/4^{2}$	112	14
1784^{P}	**Bond Jnr (IRE) (115)** (PFNicholls) **8-11-11** RJohnson (lw: chsd ldr: mstkes 2nd, 9th & 13th: hrd rdn 3 out: wknd appr last)	16	3	$100/30^{3}$	102	4
3356^{4}	**Corrib Song (63)** (LadyHerries) **8-11-1**(3) LAspell (lw: a bhd: mstke 2nd: t.o fr 13th)	dist	4	25/1	—	—
3360^{7}	**Summer Haven (63)** (NMLampard) **8-10-13** MrAKinane (a bhd: t.o fr 13th: blnd 3 out)	30	5	66/1	—	—
3047^{7}	**Sir Leonard (IRE) (115)** (OSherwood) **7-11-11** JOsborne (nvr gng wl: chsd ldrs: reminder 4th & 6th: j.slowly 10th: poor 4th whn p.u bef 13th)		P	$13/8^{1}$	—	—
3407^{5}	**Finnegais** (PButler) **10-11-4** TJMurphy (a bhd: t.o fr 6th: p.u bef 13th)		P	100/1	—	—
				(SP 112.6%)	**7 Rn**	

6m 43.1 (23.10) CSF £18.10 TOTE £5.10: £2.20 £1.60 (£5.20) OWNER Exors of the late Mr C L Rykens (LAMBOURN) BRED Mrs E. J. Floyd
OFFICIAL EXPLANATION **Sir Leonard (IRE): was never travelling and finished distressed.**

3134* Flippance was far more convincing on this occasion. Gradually creeping closer on the final circuit, he cruised into the lead approaching the last, and had no problems asserting his authority for a comfortable success. (6/1)
3356 High Learie was happier for the return to this longer trip. Setting the pace, he was eventually collared approaching the last and found the winner too good. He should soon return to the winner's enclosure. (9/4)
1784 Bond Jnr (IRE) raced in second place but made several mistakes. Not surprisingly, he had come to the end of his tether approaching the last. (100/30: 9/4-7/2)
2693* Sir Leonard (IRE) was never travelling according to his jockey, who needed to give his mount a reminder as early as the fourth and again at the sixth. Not surprisingly he was pulled up with a circuit to go. (13/8: evens-7/4)

3672 SOMERFIELD COURT NOVICES' HURDLE (4-Y.O+) (Class E)
3-00 (3-00) **2m 1f 110y (9 hdls)** £2,566.60 (£712.60: £341.80) GOING: 0.14 sec per fur (G)

				SP	RR	SF
2624^{2}	**Sharpical (119)** (NJHenderson) **5-11-9** MAFitzgerald (a gng wl: stdy hdwy 3 out: led on bit flat: hrd hld)	—	1	$1/12^{1}$	76++	7
3324^{3}	**Fire on Ice (IRE)** (MrsDHaine) **5-11-2** JFTitley (led to 5th: led 3 out: rdn appr last: hdd flat: unable qckn)	3	2	$14/1^{2}$	66	—
1766^{4}	**Leap Frog** (NAGaselee) **6-11-2** WMarston (bit bkwd: hdwy 5th: rdn appr last: r.o one pce flat)	nk	3	$14/1^{2}$	66	—
2070^{8}	**Hanbitooh (USA) (83)** (MrsAJPerrett) **4-10-8** CMaude (stdy hdwy 3 out: rdn after 2 out: one pce)	4	4	$50/1^{3}$	62	—
1938^{11}	**Hi Marble (IRE)** (MrsMerritaJones) **6-10-11** DerekByrne (chsd ldr tl appr 4th: wknd 2 out)	11	5	$50/1^{3}$	47	—
1921^{7}	**Rising Man (79)** (JTGifford) **6-10-13**(3) LAspell (bkwd: chsd ldr appr 4th: led 5th to 3 out: wknd appr last)	13	6	$50/1^{3}$	40	—
3352^{9}	**Jonbel** (TTClement) **9-11-2** NMann (bit bkwd: bhd fr 5th: t.o)	30	7	100/1	13	—
3426^{6}	**Kirov Royale** (MarkCampion) **6-10-11** WMcFarland (bhd fr 5th: t.o whn p.u bef last: dismntd)		P	$50/1^{3}$	—	—
				(SP 114.5%)	**8 Rn**	

4m 23.8 (17.80) CSF £2.28 TOTE £1.20: £1.00 £2.40 £2.70 (£2.80) Trio £4.40 OWNER Thurloe Thoroughbreds II (LAMBOURN) BRED E. R. W. Stanley and New England Stud Farm Ltd
WEIGHT FOR AGE 4yo-8lb

2624 Sharpical was an even bigger certainty than the Spice Girls having yet another number one, and went off at a virtually unbackable price. He had little more that a schooling session, as he lobbed around on the bridle and treated the opposition with complete contempt. He will now head for the Seagram Top Novices' Hurdle at Aintree in which he should go well. (1/12: op 1/6)
3324 Fire on Ice (IRE) regained the initiative three from home, but the winner was only toying with him in the straight and he was firmly put in his place on the run-in. He is greatly flattered to finish so close. (14/1: 6/1-16/1)
Leap Frog, not looking fully wound-up for this first run in three months, stayed on in the straight and only just failed to take second prize. (14/1: 7/1-16/1)
1706 Hanbitooh (USA) looked big and well for this first run in nearly three months, and after smoothly getting into the action three from home, was made to look very pedestrian from the next. He is well worth trying at two-and-a-half miles. (50/1)
Hi Marble (IRE), off the track for three months, had come to the end of her tether two from home. (50/1)
Rising Man, who has changed stables since his last run three months ago, was carrying plenty of surplus flesh but ran an encouraging race, and was only seen off turning for home. Improvement can be expected. (50/1)

3673 CLIFTONVILLE H'CAP CHASE (0-125) (5-Y.O+) (Class D)

3-30 (3-30) **2m (12 fncs)** £3,759.00 (£1,039.00: £495.00) GOING: 0.14 sec per fur (G)

				SP	RR	SF
3232[5]	**The Carrot Man (100)** (PWinkworth) **9-10-9** PHide (lw: chsd ldrs fr 4th: led 8th: lft clr 3 out)	—	1	7/4[1]	111	46
3059*	**Coolteen Hero (IRE) (93)** (RHAlner) **7-10-2**ow2 WMcFarland (chsd ldr to 4th: mstke & wknd 6th: blnd 4 out: lft poor 2nd 3 out: no imp)	24	2	3/1[3]	80	13
3588[2]	**Lasata (102)** (RMCarson) **12-10-11** DMorris (lw: hld up: 3rd whn mstke 7th: sn wknd: t.o)	dist	3	13/2	—	—
3419[3]	**Newlands-General (115)** (PFNicholls) **11-11-10** APMcCoy (swtg: led to 8th: 2nd & btn whn fell 3 out)		F	2/1[2]	—	—
				(SP 108.0%)	**4 Rn**	

3m 56.7 (4.70) CSF £6.48 TOTE £2.40 (£3.30) OWNER Mrs Jill Winkworth (DUNSFOLD) BRED Swallowbay Ltd
LONG HANDICAP Coolteen Hero (IRE) 9-12
1393 The Carrot Man looked extremely well in the paddock and had conditions to suit. Leading five out, he had mastered Newlands-General when that rival's departure three from home left him with a clear advantage. (7/4)
3059* Coolteen Hero (IRE) was in trouble setting out on the final circuit but, with the departure of Newlands-General, he was left a very poor second three from home. (3/1)
3588 Lasata (13/2: 7/2-7/1)
3419 Newlands-General took the field along to the fifth last, but he was feeling the pinch in second place when taking a crashing fall at the third last. (2/1)

3674 PEASMARSH (S) H'CAP HURDLE (0-90) (4-Y.O+) (Class G)

4-00 (4-08) **2m 1f 110y (9 hdls)** £1,961.50 (£544.00: £260.50) GOING: 0.14 sec per fur (G)

				SP	RR	SF
3054*	**Caracol (68)** (JNeville) **8-10-10**(3) TDascombe (a.p: led after 2 out: rdn out)	—	1	6/1	56	12
3209[P]	**Mullintor (IRE) (80)** (RRowe) **6-11-11** DO'Sullivan (led to 4th: led 3 out tl after 2 out: unable qckn)	3	2	8/1	65	21
3204[5]	**Swinging Sixties (IRE) (75)** (GLMoore) **6-11-6** APMcCoy (hdwy 3 out: rdn appr last: one pce)	3½	3	7/2[2]	57	13
3207[2]	**Parisian (63)** (JABennett) **12-10-1**(7) ALucas (hdwy appr last: nvr nrr)	9	4	14/1	37	—
3172[P]	**Anif (USA) (55)** (JJoseph) **6-10-0** DSkyrme (hdwy 3 out: rdn 2 out: sn wknd)	nk	5	40/1	29	—
2907[6]	**Zesti (75)** (TTClement) **5-11-6** RJohnson (a.p: ev ch appr last: 3rd & btn whn pckd last)	1½	6	10/1	47	3
3547[5]	**Rustic Gent (IRE) (60)** (MrsLCJewell) **9-10-0b1**(5) SophieMitchell (hdwy 5th: wknd 6th)	26	7	40/1	8	—
2838[10]	**Annabel's Baby (IRE) (64)** (DJWintle) **8-10-9** WMarston (a.p: led 4th to 3 out: sn wknd: t.o)	dist	8	9/2[3]	—	—
1703[19]	**Vintage Taittinger (IRE) (63)** (CWeedon) **5-10-8** MRichards (prom tl appr 2 out: t.o)	2½	9	9/1	—	—
	Moynsha House (IRE) (83) (BJCurley) **9-12-0** BFenton (a bhd: t.o whn p.u bef 5th)		P	5/1	—	—
	Mirage of Windsor (IRE) (60) (BJCurley) **9-10-5** EMurphy (a.p: ev ch 2 out: sn wknd: bhd whn p.u bef last)		P	3/1[1]	—	—
3447[16]	**Precious Wonder (62)** (PButler) **8-10-7** TJMurphy (lw: bhd whn p.u bef 5th: b.b.v)		P	20/1	—	—
				(SP 142.9%)	**12 Rn**	

4m 20.1 (14.10) CSF £58.18 CT £189.64 TOTE £8.70: £2.30 £2.60 £2.30 (£25.00) Trio £41.80 OWNER Mr C. G. Bolton (NEWPORT, GWENT)
BRED Mrs David Gordon Lennox
LONG HANDICAP Anif (USA) 9-10
No bid
OFFICIAL EXPLANATION **Precious Wonder: bled from the nose.**
IN-FOCUS: **Both the Barney Curley horses had been off the track for considerable lengths of time, Moynsha House for nearly a year and Mirage of Windsor since March 1993, but both had huge rugs on which were not removed until they started to gallop down to #the start, making it impossible to see how fit or backward they were. This was hardly helpful to punters but presumably that was the intention.**
3054* Caracol followed up his victory at Hereford last month, leading soon after the second last and being rousted along to score. (6/1: op 11/4)
2907 Mullintor (IRE) showed in front for a second time three from home, but he was collared after the second last and, after looking likely to drop away, plodded on for second prize. (8/1: 4/1-10/1)
3204 Swinging Sixties (IRE), taking a drop in class, took closer order three from home, but could only struggle on at one pace in the last half-mile. (7/2)
3207 Parisian stayed on when it was all over. (14/1: 8/1-16/1)
Anif (USA) made an effort three from home, but was done with soon after the next. (40/1)
2907 Zesti was still travelling well and had every chance turning for home, but he was soon feeling the pinch and was held in third place when pecking badly at the final flight. (10/1: 5/1-12/1)
Moynsha House (IRE) (5/1: tchd 8/1)
Mirage of Windsor (IRE) (3/1: 8/1-5/2)

3675 FAIR ROSAMUND H'CAP CHASE (0-105) (5-Y.O+) (Class F)

4-30 (4-38) **3m 2f (19 fncs)** £2,779.30 (£769.80: £367.90) GOING: 0.14 sec per fur (G)

				SP	RR	SF
3361[4]	**Royal Saxon (85)** (PBowen) **11-10-8** RJohnson (a.p: reminder 6th: led 13th: all out)	—	1	5/1[2]	98	13
3492[4]	**Shamarphil (83)** (RHAlner) **11-10-6** MissSBarraclough (lw: hdwy appr 2 out: str run flat: fin wl)	2½	2	13/2	95	10
3223[7]	**Yeoman Warrior (102)** (RRowe) **10-11-11** DO'Sullivan (lw: led to 13th: mstke 2 out: ev ch last: unable qckn)	½	3	11/2[3]	113	28
3472[3]	**Rubins Boy (77)** (NJHWalker) **11-10-0** RFarrant (a.p: rdn 13th: 3rd whn mstke 15th: one pce)	3	4	16/1	86	1
3409*	**Apatura Hati (87)** (RHAlner) **8-10-10** WMcFarland (hld up: rdn 13th: sn wknd)	13	5	5/1[2]	88	3
3176[4]	**Be Surprised (77)** (GLMoore) **11-10-0** BPowell (t.o whn p.u bef 14th)		P	14/1	—	—
2681[6]	**Sugar Hill (IRE) (90)** (JTGifford) **7-10-13** PHide (5th whn blnd 10th: sn wknd: t.o whn blnd bdly 3 out: p.u bef 2 out)		P	5/2[1]	—	—

3409[4] **Nikkis Pet (77)** (JNeville) **10-10-0** WMarston (bhd fr 4th: t.o whn p.u bef 9th) .... **P** 16/1 — —
3134[5] **Joker Jack (78)** (RDean) **12-9-12**(3)ow1 TDascombe (bhd fr 4th: t.o whn p.u bef 13th) .... **P** 33/1 — —
2908[P] **Little Rowley (77)** (MrsLRichards) **8-10-0** MRichards (prom to 13th: t.o whn p.u bef 2 out) .... **P** 50/1 — —
(SP 114.0%) **10 Rn**

6m 39.6 (19.60) CSF £33.73 CT £167.32 TOTE £8.00: £2.60 £1.90 £2.40 (£14.40) Trio £36.20 OWNER Mr G. Morris (HAVERFORDWEST) BRED Paddy Byrne

LONG HANDICAP Be Surprised 9-9 Rubins Boy 9-9 Nikkis Pet 9-2 Joker Jack 8-13 Little Rowley 8-11

OFFICIAL EXPLANATION Nikkis Pet: was unsuited by the going.

3361 Royal Saxon went to the front early on the final circuit, but he was out on his feet by the time they reached the run-in and, with the second absolutely flying, he found the line only just saving him. (5/1)

3492 Shamarphil is a real stayer who has gained her only victory under Rules in thick mud. Out with the washing for the majority of the race, she was still miles behind turning for home, with best prospects of reaching a very moderate third. However with the leaders out on their feet in the closing stages, she finished with a tremendous rattle and would surely have prevailed in another fifty yards. (13/2)

3223 Yeoman Warrior took the field along until headed early on the final circuit. Nevertheless, he kept badgering away at the winner and still had every chance jumping the final fence. However, like that rival he was out of his feet on the run-in, and had absolutely nothing left in reserve. (11/2: 4/1-6/1)

3472 Rubins Boy was never far away, but was made to look very pedestrian over the last four fences. (16/1)

3176 Be Surprised (14/1: 10/1-16/1)

3676 H.B.L.B. FOLKESTONE OPEN MAIDEN N.H. FLAT RACE (4, 5 & 6-Y.O) (Class H)

5-00 (5-07) **2m 1f 110y** £1,329.00 (£369.00: £177.00)

				SP	RR	SF
3626[W]	**Sunday Venture (NZ)** (NJHenderson) **5-11-8** MAFitzgerald (lw: hdwy on bit over 2f out: led 1f out: drvn out)	—	**1**	15/8[1]	68 f	—
3149[3]	**Shebang (IRE)** (JLDunlop) **5-11-1**(7) MrHDunlop (a.p: rdn 2f out: ev ch ins fnl f: r.o)	¾	**2**	4/1[2]	67 f	—
	Silver Sirocco (IRE) (MrsMerritaJones) **5-11-8** DerekByrne (bit bkwd: led 10f: led over 5f out to 1f out: unable qckn)	3½	**3**	14/1	64 f	—
	Cue Call (IRE) (MrsDHaine) **4-10-9** JFTitley (bkwd: hdwy over 2f out: rdn over 1f out: wknd fnl f)	3	**4**	10/1	56 f	—
3425[10]	**Sweep Clean (IRE)** (JTGifford) **5-11-8** PHide (a.p: ev ch over 2f out: sn wknd)	6	**5**	6/1[3]	56 f	—
	Maine Marie (DMGrissell) **5-11-3** JRKavanagh (hdwy 7f out: lost pl over 4f out: one pce fnl 2f)	1½	**6**	25/1	50 f	—
2750[6]	**Polo Ridge (IRE)** (OSherwood) **5-11-8** JOsborne (prom 15f)	3½	**7**	4/1[2]	51 f	—
	Ceeyou At Midnight (WGMTurner) **6-11-1**(7) JPower (plain: hdwy 7f out: wknd over 2f out)	2½	**8**	25/1	49 f	—
3149[10]	**Gower-Slave** (PBowen) **5-11-8** RJohnson (prom 15f)	½	**9**	25/1	49 f	—
	Leggies Legacy (MissAMNewton-Smith) **6-11-8** RFarrant (bit bkwd: hld up: rdn over 2f out: sn wknd)	½	**10**	25/1	48 f	—
1986[8]	**The Croppy Boy** (JNeville) **5-11-5**(3) TDascombe (a bhd)	3	**11**	20/1	45 f	—
3433[7]	**Golden Lily** (MissGayKelleway) **4-10-9** APMcCoy (a.p: led over 7f out tl over 5f out: wknd over 2f out)	4	**12**	16/1	37 f	—
	Pure Swing (JPearce) **4-11-0** NMann (bit bkwd: bhd fnl 5f: t.o)	28	**13**	12/1	16 f	—
	King of Swing (IRE) (VSoane) **5-11-8** JCulloty (bkwd: a bhd: t.o)	13	**14**	25/1	4 f	—
	Smart Guy (MrsLCJewell) **5-11-8** AThornton (a bhd: t.o fnl 6f)	10	**15**	25/1	—	—
	Last Penny (JRinger) **5-11-3b**[1] BPowell (bit bkwd: a bhd: t.o whn p.u ins fnl f: dismntd)		**P**	25/1	—	—

(SP 150.1%) **16 Rn**

4m 17.1 CSF £9.41 TOTE £2.70: £1.20 £1.80 £6.80 (£5.40) Trio £65.00 OWNER Mr F. J. Sainsbury (LAMBOURN) BRED Mrs V. M. and Est Late J. W. Morris

WEIGHT FOR AGE 4yo-8lb

1774 Sunday Venture (NZ) was given a very confident ride. Travelling supremely well, he cruised into the action entering the straight, and gained a slender advantage on the bridle entering the final furlong. However, the runner-up kept battling and, when Fitzgerald let the gelding down, he did not find as much as first looked likely. However, superior riding gained the day and the combination held on. This race was won by Josh Gifford's Boardroom Shuffle last year, and Henderson believes Sunday Venture could be just as good. He will now head for the big bumper at Aintree. (15/8)

3149 Shebang (IRE) was never far away and launched his challenge in the straight. With every chance inside the final furlong, he looked a serious threat to the winner, but Fitzgerald's superior strength in the saddle proved decisive. (4/1)

Silver Sirocco (IRE), winner of an Irish point-to-point in the mud last April, looked as though the run would do him good, but made the majority of the running until collared a furlong from home. (14/1: 12/1-20/1)

Cue Call (IRE), bought out of Dick Hern's stable for 4,500 gns at the Newmarket December Sales, was carrying plenty of condition but moved nicely into the action entering the straight, before lack of fitness took its toll in the final furlong. (10/1: op 5/1)

Sweep Clean (IRE) had every chance entering the straight before tiring. He is going the right way. (6/1: op 4/1)

Maine Marie, who cost just 2,000gns as a yearling, plodded on in the last half-mile. (25/1)

Pure Swing (12/1: op 8/1)

T/Jkpt: £11,083.50 (37.42 Tckts). T/Plpt: £58.00 (689.74 Tckts). T/Qdpt: £11.70 (78.53 Tckts) AK

3184-HEREFORD (R-H) (Good to firm, Good patches)

Saturday March 15th

WEATHER: fine

3677 MARCH NOVICES' (S) HURDLE (4-Y.O+) (Class G)

2-20 (2-25) **2m 1f (9 hdls)** £2,122.00 (£592.00: £286.00) GOING: 0.33 sec per fur (GS)

				SP	RR	SF
3499[12]	**Hanging Grove (IRE) (75)** (PGMurphy) **7-11-1** WMcFarland (lw: a.p: lft in ld 5th: mstke 6th: r.o wl)	—	**1**	15/2[2]	60	22
3284[2]	**Proud Image (86)** (GMMcCourt) **5-11-7** JOsborne (hld up: hdwy appr 5th: ev ch 2 out: rdn appr last: nt qckn)	3½	**2**	8/11[1]	63	25
1390[3]	**Sharp Thrill (68)** (BSmart) **6-11-1** CLlewellyn (hld up: hdwy appr 5th: one pce fr 2 out)	5	**3**	8/1[3]	52	14
3471[F]	**El Bardador (IRE)** (RJHodges) **4-10-4**(3) TDascombe (hld up & bhd: hdwy 3 out: nvr trbld ldrs)	21	**4**	10/1	32	—
3594[10]	**Still Here (IRE) (76)** (PBowen) **4-10-2b**[1](5) MrRThornton (lw: chsd ldr tl led, blnd & hdd 5th: nt rcvr)	hd	**5**	10/1	32	—
3468[9]	**Vita Nuova (IRE)** (WJenks) **6-10-10** VSlattery (prom: hit 6th: rdn & wknd appr 3 out)	1½	**6**	33/1	26	—
	Vital Wonder (JParfitt) **9-10-8**(7) MGriffiths (bit bkwd: nvr nr ldrs)	¾	**7**	66/1	30	—
	Corporate Image (THind) **7-11-1** PMcLoughlin (hld up: hdwy appr 5th: 4th whn blnd bdly 3 out: nt rcvr: mstke 2 out)	10	**8**	100/1	21	—
1964[P]	**Noquita (NZ)** (JCMcConnochie) **10-10-8**(7) XAizpuru (a bhd)	2½	**9**	66/1	18	—

3364[P] **A Badge Too Far (IRE)** (MrsLWilliamson) **7-10-10** RBellamy (hld up: hdwy appr 5th: wknd 6th).......8 **10** 66/1 6 —
Slaney Rasher (BJLlewellyn) **10-11-1** MrJLLlewellyn (bit bkwd: a bhd).......2 **11** 10/1 9 —
Karibu (GER) (JABennett) **6-11-1** LHarvey (led tl hdd & fell 5th: dead)....... **F** 100/1 — —
Boot Jack (IRE) (PMRich) **8-11-1** WMarston (bolted bef s: sn t.o: p.u bef 5th)....... **P** 50/1 — —
Amany (IRE) (DBurchell) **5-10-10** DJBurchell (a bhd: t.o whn p.u bef 6th)....... **P** 16/1 — —
3072[7] **Ernest Aragorn** (MrsSLamyman) **8-10-12v**(3) RMassey (nt j.w: prom tl rdn & wknd appr 5th: t.o whn p.u bef 3 out)....... **P** 50/1 — —
(SP 127.2%) **15 Rn**

4m 7.8 (14.80) CSF £12.94 TOTE £14.90: £2.90 £1.20 £1.80 (£7.10) Trio £13.50 OWNER Mr J. H. Forbes (BRISTOL) BRED William Codd
WEIGHT FOR AGE 4yo-8lb
No bid
Hanging Grove (IRE), appreciating this drop in class, was possibly a shade more resolute than the favourite. (15/2)
3284 Proud Image gave the impression he may not have relished a battle as much as the winner. (8/11: op evens)
1390 Sharp Thrill, given a mid-season break, has probably been waiting for the ground to dry up. (8/1)
2705 El Bardador (IRE) had been tried in blinkers last time. (10/1: 7/1-11/1)
388 Still Here (IRE), dropped in grade, had just taken it up when effectively blundering away his chance. (10/1: 5/1-11/1)
Slaney Rasher (10/1: 7/1-12/1)

3678 NEWENT H'CAP CHASE (0-120) (5-Y.O+) (Class D)

2-55 (2-58) **2m (12 fncs)** £3,387.50 (£1,025.00: £500.00: £237.50) GOING: 0.33 sec per fur (GS)

SP RR SF

3571[3] **Scottish Bambi (110)** (PRWebber) **9-11-10** JOsborne (w ldr: led 6th: rdn out).......— **1** 8/11[1] 110 42
1660[5] **Monday Club (100)** (JCTuck) **13-11-0** RBellamy (hld up: wnt 2nd appr 3 out: ev ch 2 out: one pce flat).......5 **2** 9/1 95 27
3588* **Dr Rocket (86)** (RDickin) **12-9-7v**(7) XAizpuru (hld up: hit 4th: chsd wnr 7th tl appr 3 out: sn wknd).......8 **3** 4/1[2] 73 5
Corpus (88) (RJHodges) **8-9-13**(3)ow2 TDascombe (bkwd: led to 6th: wknd 4 out).......28 **4** 25/1 47 —
1445[6] **Northern Optimist (87)** (BJLlewellyn) **9-9-10**(5) MrRThornton (hld up: blnd bdly 6th (water): nt rcvr).......nk **5** 11/2[3] 46 —
(SP 107.1%) **5 Rn**

4m 2.7 (11.70) CSF £6.35 TOTE £1.50: £1.10 £3.60 (£7.10) OWNER Mr William Kelly (BANBURY) BRED Cheveley Park Stud Ltd
LONG HANDICAP Dr Rocket 9-5 Corpus 9-8
3571 Scottish Bambi, 5lb higher than when winning at Leicester, found this less competitive than Sandown a week ago. (8/11: op evens)
1660 Monday Club, dropped 12lb, confirmed he still retains some ability. (9/1: 6/1-10/1)
3588* Dr Rocket could not follow up his recent Taunton win from 9lb wrong at the weights. (4/1)
1445 Northern Optimist did everything bar unseat her rider at the water, and it needed a miraculous recovery to keep the partnership intact. (11/2)

3679 BOSBURY H'CAP HURDLE (0-120) (4-Y.O+) (Class D)

3-25 (3-26) **2m 1f (9 hdls)** £2,717.00 (£762.00: £371.00) GOING: 0.33 sec per fur (GS)

SP RR SF

3338[10] **Va Utu (83)** (DMLloyd) **9-9-11**(3) SophieMitchell (led: j.slowly 2nd: hdd 3rd: led appr 5th to 6th: led 2 out: r.o wl).......— **1** 16/1 65? 22
3344* **Added Dimension (IRE) (107)** (PWinkworth) **6-11-3**(7) XAizpuru (lw: plld hrd: led 3rd tl appr 5th: led 6th tl hdd & hit 2 out: r.o one pce flat).......1¼ **2** 4/5[1] 88 45
1984[6] **Schnozzle (IRE) (89)** (KSBridgwater) **6-10-3**(3) RMassey (bit bkwd: hld up: hdwy 6th: hit 2 out: sn wknd).......9 **3** 4/1[3] 61 18
3136[5] **Menelave (IRE) (103)** (OSherwood) **7-11-6b**[1] JOsborne (hld up: eased whn btn 3 out).......20 **4** 5/2[2] 57 14
(SP 110.0%) **4 Rn**

4m 4.5 (11.50) CSF £28.37 TOTE £8.70 (£5.90) OWNER Mr D. M. Lloyd (BRIDGEND) BRED J. W. Orbell
LONG HANDICAP Va Utu 9-13
Va Utu did not mind this faster ground, and took advantage of the odds-on favourite running too freely. (16/1)
3344* Added Dimension (IRE) was raised another 8lb, but it was the fact that he refused to settle rather than the weight or the faster ground that beat him. (4/5)
1984 Schnozzle (IRE) will be sharper for this. (4/1)
3136 Menelave (IRE), only 4lb higher than when winning at Huntingdon in October, flopped in the blinkers and seems best left alone for the time being. (5/2)

3680 CHARLIE KNIPE HUNTERS' CHASE (6-Y.O+) (Class H)

4-00 (4-00) **3m 1f 110y (19 fncs)** £1,492.00 (£412.00: £196.00) GOING: 0.33 sec per fur (GS)

SP RR SF

Penlea Lady (MrsSGAddinsell) **10-11-2**(7) MrSLloyd (hld up: hdwy 8th: blnd 10th: bmpd & nearly uns rdr 12th: wnt 2nd 15th: r.o to ld nr fin).......— **1** 7/1 92 13
3055[P] **The Rum Mariner** (MrsJASkelton) **10-11-9**(5) MrRThornton (led: rdn appr last: hdd nr fin).......1¼ **2** 5/1[3] 96 17
Chip'n'run (MsMTeague) **11-11-7**(7) MrJCornes (chsd ldr to 15th: wknd after 3 out).......17 **3** 4/1[2] 86 7
3353[5] **Gay Ruffian** (MrsDJDyson) **11-11-7**(7) MissCDyson (prom tl wknd 13th).......16 **4** 20/1 76 —
First Harvest (PatrickHanly) **10-11-7**(7) MrPHanly (lw: prom: blnd 14th: sn wknd: t.o).......23 **5** 6/1 61 —
Prince of Verona (TDHolland-Martin) **10-11-7**(7) MrRupertSweeting (lw: hld up & bhd: hdwy 10th: wknd 13th: t.o whn p.u bef 15th)....... **P** 7/2[1] — —
3469[2] **Teatrader** (MissTOBlazey) **11-11-7**(7) MissTBlazey (bhd: mstke 6th: t.o 11th: p.u bef 4 out)....... **P** 15/2 — —
3469* **Highway Five (IRE)** (LadySusanBrooke) **9-12-0**(7) MissEJames (bhd: hit 9th: t.o 11th: p.u bef 15th)....... **P** 11/1 — —
3469[4] **Orton House** (SKelly) **10-11-7**(7) MrRBurton (lw: bhd fr 9th: t.o 11th: p.u bef 15th)....... **P** 20/1 — —
3363[6] **Kingfisher Bay** (OALittle) **12-11-7**(7) MrGShenkin (bhd whn rdn 10th: sn t.o: p.u bef 13th)....... **P** 50/1 — —
(SP 117.3%) **10 Rn**

6m 38.9 (28.90) CSF £38.12 TOTE £8.80: £2.50 £1.80 £1.70 (£22.50) Trio £40.10 OWNER Mrs S. G. Addinsell (CLIFFORD) BRED Mrs S. G. Addinsell
Penlea Lady, off course since winning twice at Southwell for Merrita Jones in the spring of 1995, was supported in the ring. Her rider made a remarkable recovery when bumped in mid-air at the third ditch, and the mare finished sore after snatching the race close home. (7/1)
The Rum Mariner, seven times a winner between the flags, had finished second at Llanfrynach a week ago. (5/1)
Chip'n'run had won the men's open at Eyton-on-Severn last Saturday. (4/1)
Prince of Verona (7/2: op 2/1)
3469 Teatrader (15/2: 5/1-8/1)

3469* Highway Five (IRE) (11/1: 6/1-12/1)

3681 TEME H'CAP HURDLE (0-120) (4-Y.O+ F & M) (Class D)

4-30 (4-30) **2m 3f 110y (11 hdls)** £2,703.00 (£758.00: £369.00) GOING: 0.33 sec per fur (GS)

	Horse / details	Dist	Pos	SP	RR	SF
3281[3]	**Kadari (93)** (WClay) **8-10-1v**(3) GuyLewis (a.p: led 7th tl appr 3 out: led 2 out: rdn out)	—	1	7/2[2]	69	5
3554*	**Swing Quartet (IRE) (98)** (NATwiston-Davies) **7-10-9** CLlewellyn (hld up: stdy hdwy appr 7th: blnd bdly & lost pl 8th: rallied appr 2 out: hrd rdn: r.o one pce)	1½	2	11/10[1]	73	9
3344[6]	**Sevso (89)** (RJBaker) **8-10-0** VSlattery (chsd ldr: led appr 3 out to 2 out: wknd last)	8	3	7/1	57	—
1994[7]	**Josifina (115)** (AGFoster) **6-11-7**(5) MrRThornton (hld up: rdn appr 7th: sn bhd: t.o)	24	4	13/2	64	—
3287[4]	**Precious Island (97)** (PTDalton) **4-10-0** WMarston (led to 7th: wknd after 8th: eased whn btn)	16	5	9/2[3]	32	—
				(SP 113.9%)		**5 Rn**

4m 49.9 (18.90) CSF £7.67 TOTE £2.90: £2.70 £1.10 (£2.90) OWNER Mr H. Clewlow (STOKE-ON-TRENT) BRED Lord Rotherwick

LONG HANDICAP Sevso 9-12 Precious Island 9-7

WEIGHT FOR AGE 4yo-8lb

3281 Kadari usually comes to hand at this time of year, but was fortunate to beat the favourite. (7/2: 5/2-4/1)

3554* Swing Quartet (IRE), raised 6lb, was very unlucky and had a hard race in being beaten by far less than the ground she had lost four out. (11/10)

Sevso won a bumper and a novice hurdle for David Nicholson on good to soft ground here at the end of 1994. (7/1)

1677 Josifina (13/2: op 4/1)

3682 MALVERN NOVICES' CHASE (5-Y.O+) (Class E)

5-00 (5-01) **2m (12 fncs)** £2,867.50 (£865.00: £420.00: £197.50) GOING: 0.33 sec per fur (GS)

	Horse / details	Dist	Pos	SP	RR	SF
3443*	**Quick Quote** (MrsIMcKie) **7-11-3** LHarvey (j.lft: led 5th: clr appr last: r.o wl)	—	1	7/2[2]	79	12
3352[4]	**Tenayestelign (79)** (DMarks) **9-10-12**(5) MrRThornton (lw: hld up: hdwy 8th: r.o fr 2 out: no ch w wnr)	6	2	7/2[2]	73	6
3470[U]	**Relaxed Lad** (JHPeacock) **8-11-2** RBellamy (mstkes: no ch fr 6th)	18	3	25/1	54	—
3073[F]	**Whod of Thought It (IRE)** (PRChamings) **6-11-2** VSlattery (prom: hit 5th: mstke 3 out: sn wknd)	11	4	25/1	43	—
2807[4]	**Quick Decision (IRE)** (JKCresswell) **6-10-9**(7) NTEgan (lw: hit 5th: sn bhd: t.o fr 8th)	dist	5	25/1	—	—
3343*	**Northern Singer (88)** (RJHodges) **7-11-11**(3) TDascombe (led 2nd to 5th: disp 2nd & wkng whn fell last)		F	6/5[1]	—	—
3470[P]	**Jasons Farm** (WClay) **7-10-13**(3) GuyLewis (fell 1st)		F	66/1	—	—
3443[4]	**Queens Curate (70)** (MrsEBScott) **10-10-11** BPowell (led to 2nd: bhd whn hit 7th: sn t.o: p.u bef last: lame)		P	16/1[3]	—	—
				(SP 108.8%)		**8 Rn**

4m 8.2 (17.20) CSF £13.25 TOTE £3.40: £1.60 £1.10 £2.90 (£8.30) OWNER Mr M. H. D. Barlow (TWYFORD) BRED J. M. Castle

OFFICIAL EXPLANATION **Queens Curate: returned lame.**

3443* Quick Quote did not need any divine intervention this time, despite regularly jumping out to the left. (7/2: op 2/1)

3352 Tenayestelign was in the process of going second when Northern Singer fell at the last. (7/2)

Relaxed Lad seems likely to return to hurdles, and his rider did well to complete the course. (25/1)

3343* Northern Singer would have finished third. (6/5: 4/5-5/4)

3683 LEVY BOARD NOVICES' H'CAP HURDLE (0-95) (4-Y.O+) (Class F)

5-30 (5-32) **3m 2f (13 hdls)** £2,528.00 (£708.00: £344.00) GOING: 0.33 sec per fur (GS)

	Horse / details	Dist	Pos	SP	RR	SF
1448[10]	**Young Tess (72)** (PBowen) **7-10-0**(5) MrRThornton (lw: prom tl lost pl 8th: rallied appr 9th: led after 2 out: clr last: r.o wl)	—	1	5/1[1]	55	4
3355[P]	**Sammorello (IRE) (73)** (NATwiston-Davies) **6-10-6** CLlewellyn (lw: led to 6th: led 3 out tl after 2 out:one pce)	7	2	7/1	52	1
3048[5]	**Copper Coil (94)** (WGMTurner) **7-11-6**(7) JPower (prom tl lost pl 8th: styd on fr 3 out)	8	3	13/2[3]	68	17
3112[10]	**Brown Wren (67)** (PJHobbs) **6-10-0** GTormey (hld up: hdwy appr 9th: wknd 3 out)	7	4	11/1	37	—
3542*	**Spitfire Bridge (IRE) (71)** (GMMcCourt) **5-9-11**(7) RHobson (hld up: gd hdwy 8th: led 9th to 3 out: wknd qckly)	3	5	6/1[2]	39	—
3364[7]	**Lady of Mine (67)** (PBowen) **7-10-0** WMarston (hld up: hdwy appr 9th: wknd appr 3 out)	3½	6	20/1	33	—
3190[2]	**Cravate (FR) (67)** (PJHobbs) **7-9-7**(7) MMoran (bhd: hit 6th: rdn after 7th: sme hdwy appr 3 out: n.d)	8	7	12/1	28	—
3423[6]	**Professor Page (IRE) (84)** (TThomsonJones) **7-10-10**(7) XAizpuru (bhd whn rdn after 7th: n.d after)	5	8	6/1[2]	42	—
2039[F]	**Lord Nitrogen (USA) (88)** (BJLlewellyn) **7-11-7** MrJLLlewellyn (prom: led 6th tl mstke 9th: wknd 10th)	2½	9	25/1	44	—
957[4]	**Manor Bound (67)** (MrsSDWilliams) **7-9-11**(3) RMassey (a bhd: t.o)	14	10	16/1	14	—
3003[P]	**Pennant Cottage (IRE) (67)** (WJenks) **9-10-0** RBellamy (lw: prom to 8th: t.o)	6	11	50/1	11	—
3541[4]	**Coole Cherry (78)** (CRBarwell) **7-10-11** LHarvey (bhd fr 8th: t.o)	10	12	10/1	16	—
3279[P]	**Kentucky Gold (IRE) (67)** (MrsLWilliamson) **8-10-0b**[1] LO'Hara (a bhd: t.o)	7	13	25/1	—	—
3442[8]	**Seminole Wind (67)** (CRBarwell) **6-10-0v** BPowell (a bhd: t.o)	dist	14	50/1	—	—
3472[P]	**Nordic Flight (67)** (RJEckley) **9-10-0hb** VSlattery (prom to 3rd: t.o whn p.u after 8th)		P	50/1	—	—
3442*	**Noddadante (IRE) (69)** (NRMitchell) **7-9-13**(3) SophieMitchell (hld up & bhd: hdwy appr 9th: mstke 10th: sn wknd: blnd & uns rdr last)		U	5/1[1]	—	—
				(SP 137.1%)		**16 Rn**

6m 29.0 (26.00) CSF £39.02 CT £223.57 TOTE £5.20: £2.40 £3.00 £1.50 £2.70 (£34.10) Trio £71.30 OWNER Mr G. Morris (HAVERFORD-WEST) BRED Hascombe and Valiant Studs

LONG HANDICAP Lady of Mine 9-6 Manor Bound 9-13 Pennant Cottage (IRE) 9-2 Brown Wren 9-11 Kentucky Gold (IRE) 9-4 Seminole Wind 9-1 Nordic Flight 9-5 Cravate (FR) 9-10

Young Tess, bought for 500 guineas at Ascot December Sales, is reported to have recovered from a serious uterus infection and, well backed, she certainly stays well. (5/1: 6/1-4/1)

3190* Sammorello (IRE) could not go with the winner from the penultimate hurdle. (7/1)

3048 Copper Coil was 7lb higher than when scoring at Plumpton in December. (13/2)

2875 Brown Wren, 3lb wrong at the weights, had been dropped 5lb after disappointing last time. (11/1: 8/1-12/1)

3542* Spitfire Bridge (IRE), raised 6lb for a hard-fought win in a seller, found this marathon trip beyond him. (6/1: op 4/1)

2822 Coole Cherry (10/1: 7/1-12/1)

3442* Noddadante (IRE) had been raised 9lb for his Windsor selling win. (5/1)

T/Plpt: £371.40 (27.87 Tckts). T/Qdpt: £320.10 (1.17 Tckts) KH

3084-LINGFIELD (L-H) (Good to Soft, Chse Good ptchs, Hdles Heavy ptchs bk st)
Saturday March 15th
WEATHER: fine

3684 RUBY CONDITIONAL (S) H'CAP CHASE (0-95) (5-Y.O+) (Class G)
2-10 (2-10) **2m 4f 110y (14 fncs)** £2,244.60 (£620.60: £295.80) GOING: 0.99 sec per fur (S)

	Horse		Pos	SP	RR	SF
3331[3]	**Hangover (68)** (RLee) **11-11-6** PHenley (lft in ld 3rd: hdd 5th: lft 2nd 6th: led after 4 out: clr appr last: r.o wl: dismntd)	—	1	5/4[1]	79	—
3188[6]	**Madam Rose (IRE) (60)** (JWMullins) **7-10-5**(7) DavidTurner (led 5th tl after 4 out: ev ch 3 out: 2nd & btn whn bdly hmpd by loose horse 2 out: t.o)	dist	2	50/1	—	—
469[5]	**Fattash (USA) (69)** (PMooney) **5-10-12b** SRyan (bhd fr 8th: t.o whn j.slowly last)	dist	3	14/1	—	—
	Riseupwilliereilly (60) (DFBassett) **11-10-5**(7) WGreatrex (swtg: led: clr 2nd: fell 3rd)		F	13/2[3]	—	—
3456[F]	**Opal's Tenspot (72)** (JMBradley) **10-11-10** LAspell (w ldr whn blnd & p.u 6th: dead)		P	2/1[2]	—	—
3343[5]	**Full Shilling (USA) (60)** (DLWilliams) **8-10-12b** DJKavanagh (w ldr whn bmpd & uns rdr 4th)		U	10/1	—	—

(SP 108.8%) **6 Rn**

5m 40.1 (41.10) CSF £29.05 TOTE £2.20: £1.20 £3.60 (£36.90) OWNER Mr Richard Edwards (PRESTEIGNE) BRED M. A. Doyle
WEIGHT FOR AGE 5yo-9lb
No bid
IN-FOCUS: **This was surely one of the worst races ever staged, featuring horses with very little ability and old-timers.**
3331 Hangover needed to show little ability to win this quite atrocious contest and, leading after the fourth last, soon opened up a commanding advantage. The runner-up managed to get back on terms jumping the next, but Hangover was in control again from the penultimate fence. His trainer reported afterwards that the gelding was very sore. (5/4)
Madam Rose (IRE) is a very bad performer, and the fact that she still had every chance three out shows just what a dire race this was. She was held when badly hampered by a loose horse at the next. (50/1)
Fattash (USA) (14/1: op 8/1)

3685 GUILD VENTURE DIAMOND NOVICES' HURDLE (4-Y.O+) (Class D)
2-40 (2-41) **2m 3f 110y (10 hdls)** £3,400.80 (£943.80: £452.40) GOING: 0.99 sec per fur (S)

	Horse		Pos	SP	RR	SF
3601*	**Ela Agapi Mou (USA)** (GLMoore) **4-10-13** 6x PHolley (chsd ldr fr 2nd: led 6th: wandered 2 out: all out)	—	1	9/2[2]	84	30
3426[2]	**Cheerful Aspect (IRE)** (CaptTAForster) **4-10-13** NWilliamson (a.p: chsd wnr fr 6th: hrd rdn & swtchd lft appr last: ev ch flat: r.o)	½	2	7/4[1]	84	30
3399*	**Splendid Thyne** (TCasey) **5-12-0** MAFitzgerald (hld up: mstke 7th: mod 3rd whn mstke 3 out: sn wknd: t.o)	dist	3	7/4[1]	—	—
3445[2]	**Cheeky Charlie** (JFfitch-Heyes) **5-10-13**(3) PHenley (hld up: rdn 7th: wknd 3 out: t.o)	14	4	14/1	—	—
3359[12]	**Toraja** (NoelChance) **5-11-2** DLeahy (chsd ldr to 2nd: wknd 7th: t.o)	22	5	20/1	—	—
3085[P]	**Charlie's Folly** (BdeHaan) **6-11-2** GUpton (bhd fr 6th: t.o)	8	6	50/1	—	—
3425[3]	**All Done** (SMellor) **4-10-2** NMann (a bhd: t.o)	1	7	10/1[3]	—	—
3535[P]	**Supreme Crusader (IRE)** (WGMcKenzie-Coles) **6-11-2** EByrne (a wl bhd: t.o fr 5th)	28	8	100/1	—	—
	Cool Spot (IRE) (GPEnright) **9-11-2** JRKavanagh (bit bkwd: j.rt: led: clr 2nd: j.bdly rt & hdd 6th: wknd qckly: t.o whn p.u bef 2 out)		P	50/1	—	—

(SP 116.3%) **9 Rn**

5m 1.3 (27.30) CSF £11.93 TOTE £7.10: £1.50 £1.00 £2.00 (£5.50) Trio £3.30 OWNER Ballard (1834) Ltd (BRIGHTON) BRED Patrick Eddery Ltd and Midcounts Ltd
WEIGHT FOR AGE 4yo-8lb
3601* Ela Agapi Mou (USA) followed up Tuesday's victory at Fontwell over this longer trip. Leading at the sixth, he had only the runner-up to worry about from the third last, but had very little left in the locker to repel that rival come the line. (9/2: 5/1-11/1)
3426 Cheerful Aspect (IRE) moved into second place from the sixth and was the only danger to the winner from the third last. However, try as he might, he was unable to overhaul his rival. (7/4)
3399* Splendid Thyne goes well in the mud but, on this occasion, the ground varied a lot at differing parts of the track. Taking a step up in distance and conceding lumps of weight all round, he was already held in third place when making a mistake at the third last. (7/4)
3445 Cheeky Charlie had come to the end of his tether three from home. (14/1: 10/1-16/1)
3425 All Done (10/1: 6/1-12/1)

3686 NORTHERN TRUST SAPPHIRE H'CAP CHASE (0-110) (5-Y.O+) (Class E)
3-10 (3-10) **2m (12 fncs)** £3,052.30 (£909.40: £433.20: £195.10) GOING: 0.99 sec per fur (S)

	Horse		Pos	SP	RR	SF
3206[4]	**Red Bean (86)** (KVincent) **9-11-5** MAFitzgerald (lw: chsd ldr: led 3rd to 4th: lft in ld 2 out: rdn out)	—	1	6/1	95	25
3206*	**Buckland Lad (IRE) (81)** (DMGrissell) **6-11-0** JRKavanagh (hld up: led 4 out tl blnd bdly & hdd 2 out: nt rcvr)	4	2	4/5[1]	86+	16
2752[4]	**River Leven (91)** (DRGandolfo) **8-11-10b** NWilliamson (lw: reluctant to r: led 4th to 4 out: rdn appr 2 out: wknd appr last)	3	3	7/2[2]	93	23
1965[3]	**Fichu (USA) (78)** (MrsLRichards) **9-10-11** MRichards (bit bkwd: led to 3rd: lost pl 7th: rallied appr 3 out: wknd last)	12	4	9/2[3]	68	—

(SP 110.2%) **4 Rn**

4m 17.2 (25.20) CSF £11.00 TOTE £6.60: £5.10 (£3.00) OWNER Mr Kage Vincent (REIGATE) BRED Mrs M. Woolgar
3206 Red Bean, beaten over nineteen lengths by the runner-up at Folkestone last time out, reversed the form on 7lb better terms, helped by his rival all but falling two out and handing him the advantage. (6/1)
3206* Buckland Lad (IRE) was jumping well and put in a fine leap to lead at the fourth last. However, he made his only mistake at the second last and he all but came down. Losses are only lent. (4/5: tchd evens)
2752 River Leven, 10lb higher than when winning at Huntingdon on his reappearance, disappointed last time out but ran better here. Soon in front, he was headed four out and was not beaten off until approaching the last. (7/2: 7/4-4/1)
1965 Fichu (USA) looked as though this first run in three months would do him good and, after getting back into the action entering the straight, tired jumping the final fence. (9/2)

3687 T.J.H. GROUP LINGFIELD GOLD CUP H'CAP HURDLE (0-130) (4-Y.O+) (Class C)
3-45 (3-45) **2m 3f 110y (10 hdls)** £4,441.50 (£1,323.00: £630.00: £283.50) GOING: 0.99 sec per fur (S)

	Horse		Pos	SP	RR	SF
3087[3]	**Tickerty's Gift (109)** (GLMoore) **7-11-6**(7) MBatchelor (lw: a.p: led 7th: clr appr 2 out: r.o wl)	—	1	11/4[2]	91	28

				SP	RR	SF
3277^{4}	**Spring to Glory (100)** (PHayward) **10-11-4** MAFitzgerald (lw: chsd ldr to 7th: chsd wnr appr 2 out: no imp)	5	**2**	9/2^{3}	78	15
3001^{P}	**Rachael's Owen (85)** (CWeedon) **7-10-3** MRichards (hdwy 3 out: wknd 2 out)	16	**3**	11/4^{2}	50	—
3088^{P}	**Equity's Darling (IRE) (82)** (DCO'Brien) **5-10-0b** NWilliamson (bhd fr 5th)	7	**4**	10/1	41	—
2010^{2}	**Sprintfayre (98)** (JELong) **9-10-9**(7) AIrvine (bit bkwd: led to 7th: 2nd whn mstke 3 out: wknd appr 3 out)	11	**5**	5/2^{1}	48	—
				(SP 109.2%)		**5 Rn**

5m 5.5 (31.50) CSF £13.21 TOTE £2.20: £1.30 £2.90 (£8.20) OWNER Mr K. Higson (BRIGHTON) BRED K. Higson

OFFICIAL EXPLANATION **Sprintfayre: the trainer reported that the gelding did not get the trip on this ground.**

3087 Tickerty's Gift loves it round here, and he has yet to win elsewhere. Leading four out, he forged clear entering the straight to gain his sixth course victory. (11/4)

3277 Spring to Glory moved into second place approaching the penultimate hurdle but, try as he might, failed to reel in the winner. (9/2)

1732 Rachael's Owen took closer order three from home, but had shot his bolt jumping the penultimate hurdle. (11/4)

2870* Equity's Darling (IRE) is a temperamental individual and was in trouble from halfway. (10/1: 7/1-12/1)

2010 Sprintfayre, not looking fully wound up for this first run in three months, failed to stay this longer trip and dropped right out of it approaching the second last. (5/2)

3688 OPAL MAIDEN CHASE (5-Y.O+) (Class E)

4-15 (4-18) **2m 4f 110y (14 fncs)** £2,946.75 (£879.00: £419.50: £189.75) GOING: 0.99 sec per fur (S)

				SP	RR	SF
3538^{U}	**Amber Spark (IRE) (88)** (DRGandolfo) **8-11-10** NWilliamson (hdwy 10th: led 3 out: rdn out)	—	**1**	3/1^{3}	101	33
3409^{2}	**Normarange (IRE) (90)** (DMGrissell) **7-11-7**(3) PHenley (lw: led tl after 2nd: rdn 3 out: ev ch 2 out: mstke last: unable qckn)	3½	**2**	11/4^{2}	98	30
	Debonair Dude (IRE) (NJHenderson) **7-11-10** MAFitzgerald (lw: a.p: led 4th to 5th: ev ch whn blnd bdly 3 out: wknd appr last)	18	**3**	6/4^{1}	84+	16
3181^{S}	**Oneofus (69)** (MrsLRichards) **8-11-10** MRichards (led after 2nd to 4th: led 5th: mstke 10th: hdd 3 out: sn wknd: mstke 2 out: t.o whn blnd bdly last)	dist	**4**	16/1	—	—
3409^{P}	**Plumbridge** (PRChamings) **9-11-10** JRKavanagh (lw: bhd fr 7th: t.o)	11	**5**	25/1	—	—
3048^{P}	**The Wayward Bishop (IRE) (69)** (OSherwood) **8-11-10** JAMcCarthy (5th whn fell 4th)		**F**	8/1	—	—
	Romalito (MBlanshard) **7-11-10** PHide (Withdrawn not under Starter's orders: lame at s)		**W**	20/1	—	—
				(SP 117.3%)		**6 Rn**

5m 30.2 (31.20) CSF £10.99 TOTE £3.80: £1.60 £1.80 (£4.00) OWNER Mr R. E. Brinkworth (WANTAGE) BRED Mrs M. Farrell

2679 Amber Spark (IRE) at last came good, leading at the third last and being ridden along to hold off his rivals. (3/1: 2/1-4/1)

3409 Normarange (IRE) once again looked in good shape, and had every chance at the penultimate fence before failing to find another gear. (11/4: 2/1-3/1)

Debonair Dude (IRE), who won an Irish maiden point-to-point last April when racing under the name Debonair Duke, is a nice-looking individual. Travelling well, he was on terms with the winner when making an horrendous mistake at the third last. Not surprisingly this knocked the stuffing out of him and he tired going to the final fence. He can pick up a race before long. (6/4)

3689 HBLB BULL INFORMATION SYSTEMS LTD. NOVICES' H'CAP HURDLE (0-100) (4-Y.O+) (Class E)

4-45 (4-47) **2m 7f (12 hdls)** £2,442.50 (£680.00: £327.50) GOING: 0.99 sec per fur (S)

				SP	RR	SF
	Workingforpeanuts (IRE) (64) (CASmith) **7-10-0** MrsDSmith (hdwy 7th: chsd ldr appr 2 out: led appr last: r.o wl)	—	**1**	5/1^{3}	56+	11
3358*	**Red Lighter (86)** (JABOld) **8-11-8** GUpton (a.p: led 7th tl appr last: unable qckn)	8	**2**	9/4^{1}	72	27
3088^{4}	**Shanagore Warrior (IRE) (85)** (SMellor) **5-11-7** NMann (hdwy 6th: mstke 8th: rdn 3 out: wknd appr 2 out)	17	**3**	13/2	60	15
3408*	**Roskeen Bridge (IRE) (76)** (CWeedon) **6-10-12** MRichards (hdwy 7th: wknd 8th)	3	**4**	3/1^{2}	49	4
3178^{P}	**Nordic Spree (IRE) (83)** (GLMoore) **5-11-5** PHolley (prom to 9th: t.o)	22	**5**	7/1	40	—
3295^{12}	**Stormy Session (85)** (NATwiston-Davies) **7-11-7** CMaude (lw: prom to 6th: t.o whn p.u bef 3 out)		**P**	13/2	—	—
3542^{5}	**Supreme Illusion (AUS) (73)** (JohnBerry) **4-10-0** NWilliamson (hdwy 7th: wknd 8th: t.o whn p.u bef 2 out)		**P**	12/1	—	—
3442^{5}	**Ewar Bold (73)** (KOCunningham-Brown) **4-10-0b** JRKavanagh (a bhd: mstke 1st: t.o fr 7th: p.u bef 9th)		**P**	14/1	—	—
2897^{10}	**That Old Feeling (IRE) (65)** (JWhite) **5-10-1b^{1}** DGallagher (led: mstke 2nd: hdd 7th: wknd 8th: t.o whn p.u bef 2 out)		**P**	20/1	—	—
2806^{9}	**Upham Rascal (64)** (DRGandolfo) **6-10-0** DLeahy (prom to 7th: t.o whn p.u bef 2 out)		**P**	25/1	—	—
				(SP 134.6%)		**10 Rn**

5m 57.4 (34.40) CSF £18.24 CT £75.48 TOTE £6.90: £1.90 £1.40 £2.40 (£19.20) Trio £20.70 OWNER Mrs D. A. Smith (HANLEY SWAN) BRED Dennis Johnson and D. Covette

LONG HANDICAP Supreme Illusion (AUS) 9-11 Ewar Bold 9-9 Workingforpeanuts (IRE) 9-6 Upham Rascal 9-10

WEIGHT FOR AGE 4yo-9lb

Workingforpeanuts (IRE), who won two point-to-points at the end of last season, may have been off the course for eleven months and 8lb out of the handicap, but she was given a fine ride. Quite content to let the leaders tear off in front, she gradually worked her way into the action on the final circuit and, leading approaching the last, soon asserted. (5/1)

3358* Red Lighter, 9lb higher for his recent success, gained control early on the final circuit but, collared approaching the final flight, found the winner too strong. (9/4)

2656 Shanagore Warrior (IRE) moved up with a circuit to race, but was left for dead early in the straight. (13/2: 9/2-7/1)

3408* Roskeen Bridge (IRE) made an effort early on the final circuit, but the writing was soon on the wall. (3/1)

1388 Nordic Spree (IRE) does not stay this trip and had been beaten off four out. (7/1)

3542 Supreme Illusion (AUS) (12/1: 8/1-14/1)

3690 EMERALD INTERMEDIATE OPEN N.H. FLAT RACE (4, 5 & 6-Y.O) (Class H)

5-15 (5-15) **2m 110y** £1,203.00 (£333.00: £159.00)

				SP	RR	SF
2757^{3}	**Quistaquay** (JWMullins) **5-10-8**(3) PHenley (plld hrd: lost pl over 6f out: rallied over 2f out: led ins fnl f: r.o wl)	—	**1**	7/2^{2}	50 f	—
	Country House (JABOld) **6-10-11** GUpton (neat: hld up: led over 1f out tl ins fnl f: unable qckn)	1½	**2**	2/1^{1}	49 f	—
2073^{5}	**Peace Initiative** (KVincent) **5-11-2** MAFitzgerald (bit bkwd: w ldr: led 11f out to 7f out: ev ch over 1f out: hrd rdn: one pce ins fnl f)	1¾	**3**	11/2	52 f	—
	Dunsfold Dolly (PWinkworth) **4-10-0**(3) LAspell (lt-f: bit bkwd: hld up: led 7f out tl over 1f out: ev ch ins fnl f: one pce)	1¾	**4**	7/2^{2}	45 f	—
1801^{8}	**Big Stan's Boy** (CPEBrooks) **6-11-2** DGallagher (plld hrd: hld up: rdn over 3f out: sn wknd)	27	**5**	9/2^{3}	24 f	—
2012^{13}	**Mr Robstee** (AJChamberlain) **6-10-11**(5) OBurrows (bit bkwd: led over 5f: wknd over 6f out)	14	**6**	33/1	10 f	—

3574[13]	**Express Again** (MJHaynes) **5-11-2** NWilliamson (plld hrd: bhd fnl 6f) 23	**7**	6/1	—	—
	Whisky Wilma (RCurtis) **5-10-11** DMorris (neat: bit bkwd: a bhd) 13	**8**	15/2	—	—
			(SP 140.3%)		**8 Rn**

4m 15.0 CSF £12.66 TOTE £6.50: £1.50 £1.20 £2.70 (£6.40) OWNER Mrs Heather Bare (AMESBURY) BRED Mrs H. Bare
WEIGHT FOR AGE 4yo-8lb

2757 Quistaquay got outpaced as the race began in earnest at halfway. Responding to very strong pressure, she managed to close up on the leaders again in the straight and burst through to lead inside the final furlong. (7/2)

Country House, a nippy sort, travelled well during the race and cruised into the lead on the bridle below the distance. Victory looked hers, but she had not bargained on the winner's late burst and she failed to quicken when collared inside the final furlong. (2/1: 5/4-5/2)

Peace Initiative, looking in need of this first run in three months, went to the front early on the final circuit. Collared seven furlongs from home, he remained in the thick of the action and was still challenging for the lead in the straight, only being seen off inside the final furlong. (11/2)

Dunsfold Dolly, a lightly-made individual who looked as though the run would do her good, moved to the front seven furlongs from home. Collared below the distance, she was one of four still battling for honours inside the final furlong before tapped for toe. (7/2)

1013 Big Stan's Boy, off the course for three months, once again quickly back-pedalled. He seems to be having problems staying even the minimum trip. (9/2: 5/2-5/1)

T/Plpt: £140.80 (68.51 Tckts). T/Qdpt: £69.10 (5.4 Tckts) AK

3312-NEWCASTLE (L-H) (Good, Good to firm patches)

Saturday March 15th

All chases: one fence omitted
WEATHER: fine

3691 'WELCOME TO GOSFORTH PARK' NOVICES' HURDLE (4-Y.O+) (Class E)

2-15 (2-15) **2m (9 hdls)** £2,452.50 (£690.00: £337.50) GOING minus 0.53 sec per fur (GF)

			SP	RR	SF
3311*	**Far Ahead (97)** (JLEyre) **5-11-8** BStorey (a.p: led 2 out: styd on wl flat) ....—	**1**	4/1[2]	83	44
3366[3]	**Banker Count** (MWEasterby) **5-10-13**(3) PMidgley (lw: trckd ldrs: chal 2 out: nt qckn towards fin) ....¾	**2**	5/1[3]	76	37
3324[2]	**Gospel Song (100)** (ACWhillans) **5-10-13**(3) GLee (lw: cl up: led 4 out to 2 out: kpt on same pce) 10	**3**	7/2[1]	66	27
3345[3]	**Mithraic (IRE) (100)** (WSCunningham) **5-11-8** MFoster (t: a chsng ldrs: chal 3 out: hit next & one pce after) 5	**4**	4/1[2]	67	28
	Battery Fired (53) (NBMason) **8-10-9**(7) SHaworth (bhd: hdwy 4 out: chsng ldrs 3 out: r.o one pce) ....hd	**5**	100/1	61?	22
3159[13]	**Paparazzo** (GMMoore) **6-11-2b[1]** JCallaghan (in tch: hdwy 4 out: hrd rdn next: nt pce to chal) 9	**6**	33/1	52	13
1921[5]	**Advance East (100)** (MDods) **5-11-8** RSupple (hld up: hdwy 4 out: effrt next: sn btn) 3	**7**	7/1	55	16
3348[4]	**Raise A Dollar** (PBeaumont) **7-10-11** MrSSwiers (chsd ldrs: effrt 4 out: wknd next) 7	**8**	50/1	37	—
3326[3]	**Killbally Boy (IRE) (86)** (HowardJohnson) **7-11-8** MMoloney (cl up: led 4th to 4 out: wknd next) 1¼	**9**	20/1	47	8
1700[5]	**Onyourown (IRE) (86)** (HowardJohnson) **4-10-8** DParker (nvr bttr than mid div) 2	**10**	16/1	39	—
3475[7]	**Praise Be (FR)** (TPTate) **7-11-2** RGarritty (hdwy 4 out: nvr trbld ldrs) ....hd	**11**	50/1	39	—
	Rambling Rajah (MrsSCBradburne) **5-10-9**(7) MrMBradburne (prom tl wknd 4 out) ....hd	**12**	100/1	39	—
3440[5]	**Delightfool** (RNixon) **6-10-11** GCahill (lost tch 3rd: sme late hdwy) 3½	**13**	100/1	30	—
3544[10]	**Khalikhoum (IRE)** (SirJohnBarlowBt) **4-10-8** JSupple (mstke 1st: bhd tl hdwy ½-wy: n.d) 4	**14**	33/1	31	—
	Sharley Cop (MJCamacho) **5-10-11** LWyer (bhd: sme hdwy 4 out: n.d) ....s.h	**15**	20/1	26	—
3324[9]	**Sniper** (FPMurtagh) **5-11-2** ARoche (n.d) 10	**16**	100/1	21	—
3315[10]	**Evening Dusk (IRE)** (JKMOliver) **5-10-4**(7) SMelrose (bhd fr 4 out) 1	**17**	200/1	15	—
3345[11]	**Petrico** (PBeaumont) **5-10-11**(5) BGrattan (bhd fr 4th: t.o) 20	**18**	100/1	—	—
344[P]	**Soccer Ball** (TRWatson) **7-10-13**(3) ECallaghan (led to 4th: sn wknd: t.o) 18	**19**	200/1	—	—
	Inyougoblue (IRE) (HAlexander) **5-10-9**(7) MrTJBarry (lost tch fr ½-wy: p.u bef 3 out)	**P**	100/1	—	—
3315[P]	**Solway King** (MABarnes) **7-10-11**(5) STaylor (t.o fr 4th: p.u bef 3 out)	**P**	200/1	—	—
			(SP 124.0%)		**21 Rn**

3m 49.1 (-2.90) CSF £20.60 TOTE £4.90: £2.20 £2.20 £1.70 (£16.50) Trio £20.50 OWNER Sunpak Potatoes (HAMBLETON) BRED Sir John Astor
WEIGHT FOR AGE 4yo-8lb
OFFICIAL EXPLANATION Sharley Cop: spread a plate.

3311* Far Ahead failed to impress on looks but he jumped better this time and won most convincingly. (4/1: 3/1-9/2)

3366 Banker Count is improving and surely his turn will not be delayed much longer. (5/1)

3324 Gospel Song ran his usual consistent race, but yet again got tapped for toe at the business end. (7/2)

3345 Mithraic (IRE) is running well and looks likely to pick up another race or two this spring. (4/1)

Battery Fired has not been seen for over three years, but this was a really useful effort and he looks well worth keeping an eye on. (100/1)

Paparazzo, tried in blinkers for the first time here, ran a shade better but looked well short of pace when the pressure was applied. (33/1)

1921 Advance East, having his first run for three months, was swinging off the bit as he always does until blowing up in the home straight. (7/1: op 9/2)

3692 GRAINGER TOWN H'CAP CHASE (0-115) (5-Y.O+) (Class E)

2-50 (2-50) **2m 110y (12 fncs)** £2,784.75 (£843.00: £411.50: £195.75) GOING minus 0.14 sec per fur (G)

			SP	RR	SF
3350*	**Crosshot (92)** (RMcDonald) **10-10-5** RSupple (hld up: smooth hdwy 3 out: led last: comf) ....—	**1**	5/2[1]	104	24
3452[3]	**Blazing Dawn (87)** (JSHubbuck) **10-9-11**(3) GLee (led tl hdd & outpcd after 3 out: r.o flat) 1¼	**2**	4/1[3]	98	18
3482[3]	**Grouse-N-Heather (90)** (PMonteith) **8-10-3** GCahill (lw: cl up: led after 3 out & qcknd: hdd last: no ex) 1¼	**3**	5/2[1]	100	20
3547[2]	**Dual Image (102)** (JGFitzGerald) **10-11-1** RGarritty (hld up: mstke 6th & 7th: effrt 3 out: rdn & nt qckn fr next) 1¾	**4**	3/1[2]	110	30
2921[3]	**Timbucktoo (115)** (JKMOliver) **10-12-0** BStorey (chsd ldrs tl rdn & wknd appr 3 out) ....dist	**5**	14/1	—	—
			(SP 108.8%)		**5 Rn**

4m 2.4 (4.40) CSF £11.12 TOTE £3.70: £2.40 £1.80 (£8.20) OWNER Mr R. McDonald (DUNS) BRED Robert McDonald
LONG HANDICAP Blazing Dawn 9-13

3350* Crosshot handled this very fast ground well and, always going best, he had the required speed to settle it after the last. (5/2)

3452 Blazing Dawn likes this fast ground and put up a decent performance. Providing he does not break blood-vessels, he will pick up another race or two. (4/1: op 7/1)

3482 Grouse-N-Heather ran well but was just tapped for toe on the run-in, and her turn will come in due course. (5/2)

3547 Dual Image likes things to go just right, but he had to fight from the third last and the effort required was always too much for his liking. (3/1)
2921 Timbucktoo looked woefully slow on this ground once the heat was turned on from the fourth last. (14/1: 7/1-16/1)

3693 TYNE BRIDGE H'CAP HURDLE (0-130) (4-Y.O+) (Class C)
3-20 (3-20) **3m (13 hdls)** £3,403.75 (£1,030.00: £502.50: £238.75) GOING minus 0.14 sec per fur (G)

				SP	RR	SF
3269[6]	**Purevalue (IRE) (111)** (MWEasterby) **6-11-10** RGarritty (lw: mde most: kpt on wl u.p flat)	—	1	5/2[2]	91	28
	Linlathen (109) (MrsMReveley) **7-11-5**(3) GLee (trckd ldrs: smooth hdwy to chal whn swtchd 3 out: disp ld 2 out: no ex towards fin)	1¾	2	2/1[1]	88	25
2545[9]	**Sudden Spin (98)** (JNorton) **7-10-8**(3) ECallaghan (a.p: effrt 3 out: one pce)	9	3	10/1	71	8
3531[2]	**Leading Prospect (97)** (MrsJDGoodfellow) **10-10-3**(7) NHorrocks (cl up tl outpcd 4 out: fin lame)	9	4	11/4[3]	64	1
3326[5]	**Cool Luke (IRE) (100)** (FMurphy) **8-10-10**(3) MichaelBrennan (lw: in tch tl outpcd appr 4 out: n.d after)	14	5	20/1	58	—
	Kinda Groovy (99) (IPark) **8-10-12** NSmith (prom: effrt 7th: rdn & wknd 4 out)	dist	6	20/1	—	—
				(SP 107.2%)		**6 Rn**

5m 52.8 (10.80) CSF £6.72 TOTE £3.40: £2.10 £1.90 (£3.40) OWNER Mr A. D. Simmons (SHERIFF HUTTON) BRED Limestone Stud
3269 Purevalue (IRE) seems a shade unpredictable these days, but he does enjoy getting his own way out in front and, given a super ride here, held on well. (5/2)
Linlathen looked the likely winner from three out, but this being his first run of the season probably just made the difference. (2/1)
1988 Sudden Spin, trying a longer trip, had his chances but lacked any finishing kick. (10/1)
3531 Leading Prospect was not made enough use of, and was well outpaced in the closing stages. On pulling up, he looked lame. (11/4)
3326 Cool Luke (IRE) did his usual, disappointing once off the bit. (20/1)

3694 NEWCASTLE H'CAP CHASE (0-135) (5-Y.O+) (Class C)
3-55 (3-58) **3m (18 fncs)** £4,279.50 (£1,296.00: £633.00: £301.50) GOING minus 0.14 sec per fur (G)

				SP	RR	SF
3349[2]	**Aljadeer (USA) (114)** (MWEasterby) **8-10-12** RGarritty (hld up: hdwy 4 out: effrt last: rdn to ld cl home)	—	1	7/4[1]	125	31
2765[7]	**Deep Decision (102)** (PCheesbrough) **11-10-0** KJohnson (a.p: effrt 4 out: led last: r.o: jst ct)	½	2	7/2	113	19
3033[F]	**Westwell Boy (105)** (PBeaumont) **11-10-3** RSupple (lw: led: hit 4 out: hdd last: sn outpcd)	11	3	3/1[3]	108	14
3486[2]	**Ceilidh Boy (112)** (MrsJDGoodfellow) **11-10-10** MrRHale (cl up tl outpcd 13th: blnd bdly 14th: sn t.o)	dist	4	11/4[2]	—	—
				(SP 110.3%)		**4 Rn**

5m 58.5 (6.50) CSF £7.23 TOTE £2.20 (£4.80) OWNER Miss V. Foster (SHERIFF HUTTON) BRED Arthur I. Appleton
LONG HANDICAP Deep Decision 9-12
3349 Aljadeer (USA), given a cracking ride, was held up until being produced at the last and then found a turn of foot to snatch it late on. (7/4)
1657 Deep Decision likes fast ground, is off a decent mark and put up a useful effort here after seven weeks off. (7/2)
3033 Westwell Boy, happy to set the pace, jumped better until getting the fourth last all wrong, from which point he was then left struggling. (3/1)
3486 Ceilidh Boy was already finding this ground too fast when he made a diabolical blunder five out. (11/4)

3695 NORTHUMBERLAND NOVICES' CHASE (5-Y.O+) (Class E)
4-25 (4-32) **2m 4f (15 fncs)** £2,849.75 (£863.00: £421.50: £200.75) GOING minus 0.14 sec per fur (G)

				SP	RR	SF
3530[3]	**Corston Joker (72)** (LLungo) **7-11-2** RSupple (mde all: r.o wl flat)	—	1	20/1	90	9
3314*	**Brighter Shade (IRE)** (MrsMReveley) **7-11-8** RGarritty (lw: trckd ldrs: effrt & blnd last: r.o: nt pce to chal)	2½	2	1/2[1]	94	13
3477[5]	**Bold Account (IRE) (87)** (GMMoore) **7-11-8b** BStorey (cl up fr 5th: disp ld 11th tl wknd 2 out)	9	3	100/30[2]	87	6
3393[4]	**Fine Tune (IRE) (60)** (MrsSCBradburne) **7-11-2** MFoster (mstke 1st: lost tch fr 9th)	dist	4	14/1	—	—
3530[4]	**Shut Up (60)** (MrsEMoscrop) **8-10-11** KJohnson (outpcd & lost pl fr 8th)	5	5	50/1	—	—
3608*	**Nijway (73)** (MABarnes) **7-11-3**(5) 6x STaylor (mstkes: chsd ldrs tl blnd & uns rdr 9th)		U	10/1[3]	—	—
				(SP 112.2%)		**6 Rn**

5m 5.9 (12.90) CSF £30.17 TOTE £22.50: £4.60 £1.20 (£11.00) OWNER Mr A. S. Lyburn (CARRUTHERSTOWN) BRED Corston Farms
OFFICIAL EXPLANATION **Brighter Shade (IRE): was in a distressed state.**
3530 Corston Joker was allowed to dictate things at his own steady pace and got his confidence together this time. Getting first run on the favourite, he would not give in. (20/1)
3314* Brighter Shade (IRE) showed signs of temperament before the start. In a slowly-run event, he blundered at the last and could never fully recover. He reportedly finished distressed. (1/2)
3477 Bold Account (IRE), after contesting the lead, was found wanting when the pressure was on from the second last. (100/30)
3393 Fine Tune (IRE) has ability but is his own worst enemy. (14/1: 16/1-25/1)
Shut Up is basically slow. (50/1)
3608* Nijway (10/1: 8/1-12/1)

3696 STUDENT CITY NOVICES' H'CAP HURDLE (4-Y.O+) (Class C)
4-55 (5-02) **2m 4f (11 hdls)** £3,550.00 (£1,075.00: £525.00: £250.00) GOING minus 0.14 sec per fur (G)

				SP	RR	SF
1689[4]	**Stan's Your Man (100)** (MrsJDGoodfellow) **7-11-4** NBentley (lw: cl up: led 5th to 2 out: ½l 2nd & rdn whn lft clr last)	—	1	8/1	74	46
2552*	**Mock Trial (IRE) (98)** (MrsJRRamsden) **4-10-7** RGarritty (lw: hld up: hmpd 5th: stdy hdwy to chse ldrs 4 out: rdn & nt qckn fr next)	21	2	7/2[2]	55	18
3307*	**Shanavogh (106)** (GMMoore) **6-11-10** JCallaghan (chsd ldrs: 4th & outpcd whn hit 3 out)	5	3	4/1[3]	59	31
2787[8]	**Lostris (IRE) (85)** (MDods) **6-10-3** NSmith (cl up: disp ld 7th tl outpcd & hit next: sn wknd)	dist	4	20/1	—	—
3559[6]	**Jubran (USA) (91)** (JPDodds) **11-10-9** BStorey (chsd ldrs: blnd 6th: wknd 4 out)	1½	5	20/1	—	—
3309*	**Here Comes Herbie (97)** (WStorey) **5-10-10**(5) RMcGrath (hld up: hdwy to trck ldrs 4 out: led 2 out: slt ld & gng wl whn fell last)		F	2/1[1]	72?	—
1907[3]	**Tweedswood (IRE) (92)** (PBeaumont) **7-10-10** RSupple (lw: led tl hdd & fell 5th)		F	9/2	—	—
				(SP 114.4%)		**7 Rn**

4m 50.5 (2.50) CSF £33.15 CT £116.55 TOTE £6.50: £2.80 £2.00 (£9.70) OWNER Mrs J. D. Goodfellow (EARLSTON) BRED Mrs J. D. Goodfellow
WEIGHT FOR AGE 4yo-9lb
1689 Stan's Your Man likes fast ground and loves being up with the pace, but he appeared lucky here as he was second best when Here Comes Herbie fell at the last, leaving him with a simple task. (8/1)

2552* Mock Trial (IRE) was almost brought down by a faller early on but recovered well to have his chances only to cry enough three out. (7/2: 3/1-9/2)
3307* Shanavogh failed to impress on looks and ran moderately. (4/1: 3/1-9/2)
2787 Lostris (IRE) is a disappointing individual who stopped quickly once off the bit. (20/1)
3559 Jubran (USA) made an awful blunder halfway through the race which must have affected him. (20/1)
3309* Here Comes Herbie travelled on the bridle as he likes to and was a good half-length in front and still looking to be going well when he misjudged the last and came down. (2/1)
1907 Tweedswood (IRE) took a crashing fall at the fifth. (9/2)

T/Plpt: £34.40 (357.79 Tckts). T/Qdpt: £9.50 (68.34 Tckts) AA

3043-UTTOXETER (L-H) (Good, Good to firm patches hdles crse in st)
Saturday March 15th
WEATHER: overcast

3697 E.B.F. TATTERSALLS (IRELAND) FINAL NOVICES' H'CAP CHASE (6-Y.O+ Mares Only) (Class C)
12-45 (12-51) **2m 5f (16 fncs)** £10,796.25 (£3,270.00: £1,597.50: £761.25) GOING: 0.06 sec per fur (G)

			SP	RR	SF
3360*	**Tellicherry (90)** (MissHCKnight) **8-10-7** JCulloty (hld up in tch: hdwy 12th: led 3 out: rdn & hld on gamely)...—	**1**	6/1[3]	101	28
2947[2]	**Goldenswift (IRE) (94)** (GBBalding) **7-10-11** BFenton (lw: hld up: hdwy 7th: jnd wnr 2 out: hrd rdn flat: r.o)...nk	**2**	3/1[1]	105	32
3288[5]	**Koo's Promise (83)** (CLPopham) **6-10-0** RFarrant (lw: a.p: ev ch 3 out: wknd appr next)..........15	**3**	25/1	82	9
3232[3]	**Harvest View (IRE) (99)** (CPEBrooks) **7-10-9**(7) MBerry (lw: hld up: hdwy 8th: led appr 4 out tl mstke & hdd 3 out: sn btn)..........½	**4**	9/1	98	25
3227[3]	**Second Call (110)** (CaptTAForster) **8-11-13** RDunwoody (hld up in rr: hdwy u.p 12th: nvr nr to chal)..........1	**5**	10/1	108	35
2658[5]	**Miss Diskin (IRE) (100)** (RHBuckler) **8-11-3** BPowell (chsd ldrs tl rdn & btn appr 3 out)..........1¼	**6**	12/1	97	24
	Blaze Of Honour (IRE) (111) (APO'Brien,Ireland) **6-12-0** CFSwan (hld up & bhd: hit 9th: effrt appr 4 out: mstke 2 out: eased whn btn)..........12	**7**	15/2	99	26
3370*	**Coverdale Lane (95)** (MrsSJSmith) **10-10-12** RichardGuest (prom: led after 4th to 6th: wknd 4 out: t.o).......dist	**8**	16/1	—	—
901[3]	**Dubelle (83)** (JSKing) **7-10-0** TJMurphy (plld hrd: led to 2nd: led 6th tl appr 4 out: sn wknd: t.o)..........10	**9**	14/1	—	—
3489[P]	**Country Store (89)** (APJones) **8-10-6** DBridgwater (swtg: lw: led 2nd tl after 4th: prom whn fell 9th)..........	**F**	20/1	—	—
3173*	**Sail by the Stars (107)** (CaptTAForster) **8-11-10** SWynne (hld up: hdwy 12th: 5th & btn whn blnd & uns rdr 2 out)..........	**U**	9/2[2]	—	—
			(SP 117.2%)		**11 Rn**

5m 14.2 (9.20) CSF £22.88 CT £386.07 TOTE £6.50: £2.00 £1.70 £9.00 (£8.90) Trio £188.00 OWNER Mrs C. Clatworthy (WANTAGE) BRED R. Jenks
LONG HANDICAP Dubelle 9-12 Koo's Promise 9-11
3360* Tellicherry, finding top form at the right time, followed up her hard fought first success at the end of last month with another brave performance and there is no reason why she cannot win again. (6/1)
2947 Goldenswift (IRE), taking a step down in distance, looked sure to score when moving upsides the winner at the penultimate fence but, hard as she tried, could never quite poke her head in front. (3/1)
3288 Koo's Promise, always handy, was close enough to pose a threat three out but, once the principals took one another on, she had to admit her measure taken. (25/1)
3232 Harvest View (IRE) had worked her way to the front on the home turn and looked to have plenty in hand but an error at the final ditch took the stuffing out of her and she was soon in trouble. (9/1)
3227 Second Call, probably better over the minimum trip in a true-run race, was off the bridle before reaching the home straight and could not summon the pace to deliver a challenge. (10/1)
2658 Miss Diskin (IRE), who would have been happier with more cut in the ground, remained in the chasing group until finding the quickening tempo too much for her. (12/1: op 8/1)

3698 SCOTTISH EQUITABLE/JOCKEYS ASSOCIATION SERIES (FINAL) H'CAP HURDLE (4-Y.O+) (Class B)
1-15 (1-16) **2m 4f 110y (12 hdls)** £10,065.00 (£3,045.00: £1,485.00: £705.00) GOING: 0.06 sec per fur (G)

			SP	RR	SF
2780[2]	**Domappel (111)** (MrsJCecil) **5-11-7** TKent (hld up & bhd: hdwy appr 9th: led appr 2 out: drvn out)..........—	**1**	7/2[2]	94	21
3545[2]	**Thursday Night (IRE) (109)** (JGFitzGerald) **6-11-5** PNiven (lw: led 3rd tl appr 2 out: sn rdn: no ex flat).........3½	**2**	4/1[3]	89	16
3402*	**Lord Mcmurrough (IRE) (115)** (JNeville) **7-11-11** RFarrant (lw: hld up: hdwy appr 7th: rdn & wknd appr 3 out)..........15	**3**	11/2	84	11
3430*	**Edgemoor Prince (110)** (PJHobbs) **6-11-6** GTormey (chsd ldrs tl rdn & outpcd appr 3 out)..........2½	**4**	3/1[1]	77	4
3183*	**Grouseman (118)** (MissHCKnight) **11-12-0b** JCulloty (led to 3rd: w ldr to 8th: wknd next: p.u bef 3 out)..........	**P**	7/1	—	—
3269[4]	**Topsawyer (95)** (MissSEHall) **9-10-5** APMcCoy (chsd ldrs tl wknd appr 3 out: p.u bef next)..........	**P**	9/2	—	—
			(SP 113.3%)		**6 Rn**

4m 58.2 (14.20) CSF £16.44 TOTE £4.60: £2.50 £1.90 (£10.10) OWNER Mr M. C. Banks (NEWMARKET) BRED Bolton Grange
2780 Domappel sauntered around off the pace and picked up immediately when asked, winning readily in the end. (7/2)
3545 Thursday Night (IRE) had more use made of him and, though he was brushed aside when the winner said go, he kept plugging away and this could be the right way to ride him. (4/1)
3402* Lord Mcmurrough (IRE) took closer order a mile out and promised to make a race of it until getting left behind from the turn for home.(11/2)
3430* Edgemoor Prince was a little bit out of his depth here and he was back-pedalling as soon as he reached the straight. (3/1)
3183* Grouseman helped share the lead but he was always coming off second best in his duel with the runner-up and, with the weight taking its toll, was out of contention when pulled up early in the straight. (7/1)

3699 MARSTONS PEDIGREE MIDLANDS GRAND NATIONAL H'CAP CHASE (Gd 3) (6-Y.O+) (Class A)
1-50 (1-50) **4m 2f (24 fncs)** £30,867.00 (£11,553.00: £5,651.50: £2,432.50: £1,091.25: £554.75) GOING: 0.06 sec per fur (G)

			SP	RR	SF
3162*	**Seven Towers (IRE) (134)** (MrsMReveley) **8-11-4** PNiven (hld up: hdwy 15th: led appr 2 out: styd on strly)..—	**1**	4/1[2]	150	52
3046*	**Lord Gyllene (NZ) (140)** (SABrookshaw) **9-11-10** ADobbin (j.w: led to 16th: led 17th tl appr 2 out: sn btn).......7	**2**	5/2[1]	152	54
3420[2]	**Sister Stephanie (IRE) (124)** (GMMcCourt) **8-10-8** DBridgwater (lw: hld up: stdy hdwy fr 17th: styd on flat)..s.h	**3**	8/1	136	38
3428[4]	**Killeshin (129)** (HJManners) **11-10-13** SCurran (bhd: rdn 10th: styd on fr 4 out: nvr nrr)..........12	**4**	16/1	134	36
3266[2]	**McGregor The Third (125)** (GRichards) **11-10-9** RDunwoody (lw: j.w: chsd ldr: led 16th to 17th: wknd 4 out)23	**5**	9/2[3]	116	18
3153[4]	**Special Account (116)** (CRBarwell) **11-10-0** BFenton (chsd ldrs: lost pl 6th: sn rdn: mstke 11th: t.o)..........17	**6**	100/1	97	—

3428[2]	**Beaurepaire (IRE) (118)** (RHAlner) **9-10-2**ow2 AThornton (prom tl rdn & wknd 18th: t.o) 12	**7**	25/1	91	—
3551*	**Act the Wag (IRE) (119)** (MartinTodhunter) **8-10-3** APMcCoy (lw: swtg: mstke 4th: lost tch 18th: t.o)........6	**8**	11/2	89	—
3492[5]	**Scribbler (116)** (GMMcCourt) **11-10-0b** CFSwan (chsd ldrs tl wknd 18th: bhd whn fell 3 out)	**F**	25/1	—	—
3414[4]	**Musthaveaswig (121)** (DNicholson) **11-10-5** RJohnson (hld up mid div: lost pl 17th: t.o & p.u bef 3 out)........	**P**	14/1	—	—
			(SP 114.5%)	**10 Rn**	

8m 33.7 (0.60 under best) (8.70) CSF £13.21 CT £68.09 TOTE £5.20: £2.10 £1.90 £2.30 (£7.40) Trio £22.60 OWNER Mrs E. A. Murray (SALTBURN) BRED J. Mernagh

LONG HANDICAP Special Account 8-6 Scribbler 9-10 Beaurepaire (IRE) 9-5

STEWARDS' ENQUIRY Bridgwater susp. 24-25/3/97 (improper use of whip). McCourt fined £200 (failure to inform rider of horse's hypersensitive skin).

3162* Seven Towers (IRE) made it four wins on the trot with another dour staying performance and, after taking the measure of the favourite soon after negotiating the last ditch, only needed to keep up the gallop to forge clear. This is some horse. (4/1)

3046* Lord Gyllene (NZ) set the pace but was being hounded all the way and, forced to put in a short one when running into the bottom of the third last, forfeited his lead and all hope of success. He still remains at the head of affairs in the betting for the Grand National, but he looked a bit shouldery in the final mile and would appreciate an easing of the ground. (5/2)

3420 Sister Stephanie (IRE), a heavy-topped mare who needs bottomless ground, ran really well, staying on relentlessly in the final mile and only just failing to grab the runner-up prize. (8/1: 6/1-10/1)

3428 Killeshin did not get going until far too late and in turn was never a factor. (16/1)

3266 McGregor The Third, jumping from fence to fence, gave the favourite no peace, but in the end he was the one to crack and had had enough entering the straight for the final time. (9/2)

3551* Act the Wag (IRE) could never cope with this step up in class and he ran as if he had not fully recovered from his success in the Grand Military Gold Cup eight days earlier. (11/2)

3700 BET WITH THE TOTE (FINAL) NOVICES' H'CAP CHASE (6-Y.O+) (Class C)

2-25 (2-25) **3m 2f (20 fncs)** £14,070.00 (£4,260.00: £2,080.00: £990.00) GOING: 0.06 sec per fur (G)

			SP	RR	SF
3395[F]	**Judicious Captain (92)** (MrsJStorey) **10-10-0** MrCStorey (trckd ldrs: effrt 3 out: 2nd & btn whn lft clr last)....—	**1**	12/1	107	4
3339*	**Foxtrot Romeo (100)** (CPEBrooks) **7-10-8** GBradley (a chsng ldrs: effrt & ev ch 4 out: wknd appr 2 out).......12	**2**	9/4 1	108	5
3113*	**Mr Pickpocket (IRE) (112)** (MissHCKnight) **9-11-6** JFTitley (lw: j.w: led tl appr 2 out: sn rdn & outpcd) 5	**3**	7/2 2	117	14
3410*	**Pavlova (IRE) (93)** (RRowe) **7-10-1**ow1 DO'Sullivan (lw: chsd ldr tl rdn & outpcd 14th) 11	**4**	25/1	91	—
3020[4]	**Kamikaze (116)** (KCBailey) **7-11-10b** CO'Dwyer (nt j.w: hld up: hdwy 14th: led appr 2 out: clr whn fell last).......	**F**	9/2 3	—	—
3285[2]	**Monymoss (IRE) (105)** (MrsSJSmith) **8-10-13** RichardGuest (prom tl wknd 14th: t.o whn p.u bef 2 out)........	**P**	11/2	—	—
2693[7]	**The Shy Padre (IRE) (92)** (MrsJPitman) **8-10-0** RFarrant (lw: hld up: rdn & hdwy 12th: sn wknd: t.o whn p.u bef 16th)........	**P**	10/1	—	—
3489[3]	**Ballydougan (IRE) (92)** (RMathew) **9-10-0v** DWalsh (reluctant to r: in rr tl p.u bef 16th)	**P**	50/1	—	—
			(SP 109.1%)	**8 Rn**	

6m 45.6 (18.60) CSF £33.97 CT £96.37 TOTE £14.30: £3.00 £1.10 £1.70 (£19.10) Trio £19.30 OWNER Mr James Adam (KELSO) BRED Mrs V. Lippiatt

LONG HANDICAP Judicious Captain 9-10 The Shy Padre (IRE) 9-12 Pavlova (IRE) 9-3 Ballydougan (IRE) 8-10

3067* Judicious Captain turned in an almost faultless display of jumping and travelled well for most of the trip but he was only destined for the runner-up prize when left clear at the last. (12/1)

3339* Foxtrot Romeo joined issue four out and did look to have timed his effort just right but stamina appeared to desert him halfway up the straight and he stopped to nothing. (9/4)

3113* Mr Pickpocket (IRE) tried hard to make all but he tied up rather quickly after being collared and this trip could be stretching his stamina to the limit. (7/2)

3410* Pavlova (IRE), in pursuit of the leader, looked to be enjoying herself until getting left behind entering the final mile. This company could be a bit too hot for her. (25/1)

3020 Kamikaze is not a fluent jumper of fences as yet and he had been asking for a fall some time before hitting the deck at the last. There is no doubt he was in complete control at the time and losses will be recovered. (9/2)

3701 DHL WORLDWIDE EXPRESS H'CAP CHASE (0-135) (5-Y.O+) (Class C)

3-00 (3-00) **2m 5f (16 fncs)** £4,508.50 (£1,363.00: £664.00: £314.50) GOING: 0.06 sec per fur (G)

			SP	RR	SF
3532*	**Disco des Mottes (FR) (115)** (GRichards) **6-11-7** RDunwoody (lw: a.p: led 12th: clr fr 3 out: eased flat: impressive)........—	**1**	11/8 1	138++	31
3484*	**Kenmore-Speed (100)** (MrsSJSmith) **10-10-6** RichardGuest (swtg: led: blnd 4th: hdd 12th: sn outpcd)..........12	**2**	13/2 3	114	7
3289*	**Over the Pole (110)** (PRChamings) **10-11-2** AThornton (lw: mstke 1st: chsd ldrs: pushed along ½-wy: one pce fr 4 out)........5	**3**	9/1	120	13
3106[F]	**Garrylough (IRE) (118)** (DRGandolfo) **8-11-7v**1(3) DFortt (prom tl wknd 9th: t.o 4 out) 5	**4**	9/2 2	124	17
3413[3]	**Conti D'Estruval (FR) (112)** (GBBalding) **7-11-4v**1 APMcCoy (lw: hld up & bhd: hdwy 10th: rdn appr 3 out: sn btn) 5	**5**	9/2 2	114	7
1697[P]	**Florida Sky (105)** (CPEBrooks) **10-10-11** GBradley (bit bkwd: wl bhd tl p.u bef 12th)........	**P**	33/1	—	—
2949[4]	**Flapjack Lad (95)** (NATwiston-Davies) **8-10-1** DWalsh (chsd ldr fr 7th: rdn & wknd 11th: t.o: p.u 3 out)	**P**	20/1	—	—
			(SP 109.5%)	**7 Rn**	

5m 17.1 (12.10) CSF £9.09 TOTE £2.20: £1.40 £2.00 (£5.10) OWNER Mr Robert Ogden (PENRITH) BRED Joel Poirier

3532* Disco des Mottes (FR) completed his hat-trick with another effortless display and, though he has been extremely well placed, he has improved out of all recognition and is certainly capable of taking a step up in class. (11/8)

3484* Kenmore-Speed was in a muck sweat by the time he got to post but once again he employed forceful tactics and there was only the useful winner who was capable of getting past him. He will not always come up against one so good. (13/2)

3289* Over the Pole could not get in a blow against the leading pair but he did nothing wrong and will find his way again in his own class. (9/1)

3106 Garrylough (IRE), given a confidence-booster after falling on her previous outing, lost touch soon after halfway and completed in her own time. (9/2)

3413 Conti D'Estruval (FR) seems to have lost the habit of winning and his promising-looking effort a mile out had come to an end early in the straight. (9/2)

3702 WEATHERBYS INSURANCE H'CAP HURDLE (0-135) (5-Y.O+) (Class C)

3-30 (3-30) **2m 6f 110y (12 hdls)** £3,501.25 (£1,060.00: £517.50: £246.25) GOING: 0.06 sec per fur (G)

				SP	RR	SF
	Winn's Pride (IRE) (101) (RHollinshead) **6-10-8** SWynne (bkwd: hld up in rr: hdwy 9th: led 3 out: styd on wl)	—	**1**	25/1	83	43
721^{4}	**Santella Boy (USA) (105)** (CJMann) **5-10-12b** JRailton (lw: hld up: hdwy 7th: ev ch 2 out: unable qckn)	3	**2**	9/2^{3}	85	45
3277^{3}	**Royal Piper (NZ) (107)** (AJWilson) **10-11-0** RGreene (lw: prom tl outpcd after 9th: rallied appr 2 out: one pce flat)	1¾	**3**	9/2^{3}	86	46
3421^{5}	**Moving Out (117)** (MissHCKnight) **9-11-10** RDunwoody (led to 7th: sn rdn & wknd: t.o)	24	**4**	5/2^{2}	79	39
3159*	**Bobby Grant (108)** (CGrant) **6-11-1** PNiven (chsd ldr: led 7th tl hdd & hit 3 out: wknd qckly: t.o)	1½	**5**	11/8^{1}	69	29
				(SP 110.9%)	**5 Rn**	

5m 22.2 (5.20) CSF £111.10 TOTE £15.90: £3.20 £1.90 (£44.70) OWNER Mrs W. L. Bailey (UPPER LONGDON) BRED John Breslin

OFFICIAL EXPLANATION **Bobby Grant: was found to be jarred up in front and to have a bad back.**

Winn's Pride (IRE) only had a single outing last season and he understandably looked burly for this first run in 497 days. Coming from last to first, he won with a bit to spare to cause another big upset. (25/1)

721 Santella Boy (USA) goes well when fresh but he probably found the ground more yielding than he cares for, for he was still on the bridle when mounting a challenge at the second last and yet was well outpointed on the run-in. (9/2)

3277 Royal Piper (NZ) needed a more testing surface to produce his best and, although he was getting back into it at the death, was never going well enough to really threaten danger. (9/2)

3421 Moving Out has not won since May 1995 and this mediocre performance would suggest he has lot the zest for racing. (5/2)

3159* Bobby Grant has won his novices very easily indeed but, in this first handicap, he stopped as if shot when headed soon after turning in and proved most disappointing. (11/8)

3703 PRUE FARMER 17TH BIRTHDAY 'N.H.' NOVICES' HURDLE (4-Y.O+) (Class E)

4-05 (4-05) **2m (10 hdls)** £2,389.50 (£672.00: £328.50) GOING: 0.06 sec per fur (G)

				SP	RR	SF
2690^{4}	**Shekels (IRE)** (CPEBrooks) **6-11-1** GBradley (mde all: drew clr 2 out: unchal)	—	**1**	4/1^{2}	90	32
3421^{2}	**Rangitikei (NZ) (115)** (CJMann) **6-11-8** RDunwoody (lw: a.p: chsd wnr fr 6th: ev ch 3 out: rdn next: sn btn)	10	**2**	8/13^{1}	87	29
3064^{P}	**Fils de Cresson (IRE) (85)** (JRAdam) **7-11-1** JRailton (lw: a chsng ldrs: nvr able to chal)	5	**3**	20/1	75	17
2785^{5}	**Maitre de Musique (FR) (95)** (MartinTodhunter) **6-11-1** APMcCoy (chsd wnr to 6th: wknd 3 out)	4	**4**	10/1	71	13
3271^{5}	**Eurofast Pet (IRE)** (SABrookshaw) **7-11-1** ADobbin (chsd ldrs tl wknd 7th: t.o)	15	**5**	25/1	56	—
3000^{7}	**The Eens** (DMcCain) **5-11-1** TJenks (swtg: a bhd: t.o fr 6th)	1½	**6**	50/1	55	—
	Eager Beaver (MissHCKnight) **5-11-1** JFTitley (bkwd: a bhd: t.o fr 6th)	7	**7**	8/1^{3}	48	—
3203^{9}	**Red Oassis** (HOliver) **6-11-1** JacquiOliver (a bhd: t.o)	dist	**8**	66/1	—	—
	Barty Boy (IRE) (JMackie) **5-11-1** TEley (bkwd: a bhd: t.o)	5	**9**	16/1	—	—
3297^{10}	**Shawkey (IRE)** (DMcCain) **4-10-7** DWalsh (hld up: hdwy whn fell 5th)		**F**	100/1	—	—
3178^{P}	**Lord Love (IRE)** (PRChamings) **5-11-1** AThornton (bkwd: s.u & fell after 1st)		**F**	100/1	—	—
2931^{17}	**Sunsword** (MFBarraclough) **6-10-10** TJMurphy (a bhd: t.o whn p.u bef 3 out)		**P**	50/1	—	—
				(SP 124.0%)	**12 Rn**	

3m 48.4 (7.40) CSF £6.51 TOTE £5.00: £1.80 £1.10 £6.20 (£3.20) Trio £28.50 OWNER Uplands Bloodstock (LAMBOURN) BRED R. Guiry

WEIGHT FOR AGE 4yo-8lb

2690 Shekels (IRE), much wiser for the experience gained on his hurdling debut, gave an exhibition of jumping from the front and proved much too good for the hotpot. This success could be the first of many. (4/1: 3/1-5/1)

3421 Rangitikei (NZ) looked to have found a simple task but, after travelling comfortably for over a mile and a half, quite simply had no answer to the winner's extra pace. (8/13)

2785 Fils de Cresson (IRE) has got the ability to win a race but connections are having problems finding his correct trip and until they do he is best watched. (20/1)

2785 Maitre de Musique (FR) won a two-mile National Hunt Flat race on heavy ground in his first season so he is not short of stamina and this minimum trip has got to be inadequate. (10/1)

Eager Beaver, a plain-looking half-brother to a couple of winning hurdlers, was far too backward to do himself justice on this racecourse debut and may well need even more time. (8/1)

T/Jkpt: Not won; £7,613.19 to Southwell 17/3/97. T/Plpt: £216.70 (168.17 Tckts). T/Qdpt: £50.40 (35.64 Tckts) IM

3542-MARKET RASEN (R-H) (Good)

Monday March 17th

WEATHER: fine

3704 BONUS DAY CLAIMING HURDLE (4-Y.O+) (Class F)

2-10 (2-10) **2m 3f 110y (10 hdls)** £1,994.00 (£559.00: £272.00) GOING: 0.16 sec per fur (G)

				SP	RR	SF
3434^{3}	**Cutthroat Kid (IRE) (115)** (MrsMReveley) **7-11-3v** MAFitzgerald (lw: prom tl mstke & outpcd 4 out: hdwy next: led and pckd 2 out: edgd rt)	—	**1**	8/13^{1}	68	39
3054^{11}	**Eskimo Kiss (IRE)** (GFJohnsonHoughton) **4-10-4** DGallagher (lw: hld up & bhd: hdwy ½-wy: chal appr 2 out: nt pce of wnr flat)	2½	**2**	12/1	61	24
3434^{2}	**Just Supposen (IRE) (80)** (BSRothwell) **6-10-11** RJohnson (lw: a chsng ldrs: one pce fr 2 out)	7	**3**	11/2^{2}	54	25
3327^{2}	**Chummy's Saga (76)** (LLungo) **7-11-1b** RSupple (swtg: prom: outpcd 4 out: rdn & btn appr 2 out)	nk	**4**	6/1^{3}	58	29
2862^{10}	**World Without End (USA) (65)** (MESowersby) **8-10-13b** DParker (a.p: led after 6th to 2 out: wknd)	2½	**5**	25/1	54	25
3592^{P}	**Churchworth** (MissHCKnight) **6-10-13b^{1}** JCulloty (led tl after 1st: 2nd whn fell 3rd)		**F**	12/1	—	—
1781^{5}	**Game Drive (IRE)** (KAMorgan) **5-11-1** WFry (a bhd: t.o whn p.u bef last)		**P**	20/1	—	—
3029^{F}	**Primitive Light** (ASmith) **7-11-3**(3) PMidgley (outpcd & lost pl fr 4 out: t.o whn p.u bef last)		**P**	25/1	—	—
	Man of Wisley (IRE) (SWCampion) **7-10-13** GaryLyons (led after 1st: hit 4th: clr to 6th: sn hdd & wknd qckly: p.u bef last)		**P**	50/1	—	—
				(SP 121.4%)	**9 Rn**	

4m 42.9 (9.90) CSF £8.90 TOTE £1.50: £1.30 £2.60 £1.10 (£7.90) Trio £8.30 OWNER Mr P. D. Savill (SALTBURN) BRED Mrs T. V. Ryan

WEIGHT FOR AGE 4yo-8lb

3434 Cutthroat Kid (IRE), after looking in trouble, was coaxed into action from three out and, despite again showing a tendency to hang right, he did the business this time. (8/13)

2705 Eskimo Kiss (IRE) looked particularly well and had her chances, but she was never doing enough when the pressure was applied and may well need either a visor or blinkers. (12/1: op 8/1)
3434 Just Supposen (IRE) was always close enough if good enough but he failed to pick up when ridden and, on finishing, was found to be lame. (11/2)
3327 Chummy's Saga got very hot and sweaty beforehand, and was not in a co-operative mood. (6/1)
World Without End (USA), who has been showing bits of form on the All-Weather, put up his best performance for a while over hurdles.(25/1)
Churchworth (12/1: op 8/1)

3705 ADDITIONAL MEETING NOVICES' CHASE (5-Y.O+) (Class D)
2-40 (2-40) **2m 6f 110y (15 fncs)** £3,680.00 (£1,030.00: £500.00) GOING: 0.16 sec per fur (G)

			SP	RR	SF
3546[4] **Claverhouse (IRE)** (JGFitzGerald) **8-11-2** RGarritty (lw: hld up: effrt 3 out: rdn to ld flat: r.o)	—	1	11/2	100	23
3314[P] **Brandy Cross (IRE)** (HowardJohnson) **8-11-2** JOsborne (swtg: led tl hdd flat: no ex u.p)	3	2	9/4[2]	98	21
3268[3] **Garethson (IRE) (103)** (MissHCKnight) **6-11-2** DBridgwater (lw: mstkes & j.rt: chsd ldr: hmpd bnd after 4 out: chal 3 out: rdn & blnd next: nt rcvr)	7	3	5/4[1]	93	16
3546[3] **Gorby's Myth (73)** (JPLeigh) **7-11-2** KGaule (lw: hld up: stdy 4 out: effrt & fell 2 out)		F	5/1[3]	—	—
			(SP 107.3%)		**4 Rn**

5m 43.3 (16.30) CSF £15.77 TOTE £8.20 (£15.90) OWNER Mrs Peter Corbett (MALTON) BRED William O'Donnell
3546 Claverhouse (IRE), given a patient ride, jumped much better this time and, produced late on, he did all that was required. (11/2: 7/2-6/1)
3314 Brandy Cross (IRE) got very stirred up beforehand, but then really enjoyed himself out in front before he was tapped for toe from the last. This should have boosted his confidence. (9/4: 6/4-5/2)
3268 Garethson (IRE) seems to have lost confidence with his jumping for the time being and, until he gets it back, he is best left alone. (5/4)
3546 Gorby's Myth spends much of the race on the bridle but, once he comes off it, he is generally disappointing, and was beaten when taking a crashing fall two out. (5/1: op 3/1)

3706 MORE OPPORTUNITIES NOVICES' HURDLE (5-Y.O+) (Class E)
3-10 (3-10) **3m (12 hdls)** £2,305.50 (£648.00: £316.50) GOING: 0.16 sec per fur (G)

			SP	RR	SF
2759[3] **Supreme Flyer (IRE) (100)** (KCBailey) **7-10-10** JOsborne (lw: trckd ldr: led appr 2 out: hit last: pushed out)	—	1	8/11[1]	71	—
2701[11] **Larkshill (IRE)** (JGFitzGerald) **6-10-10** WDwan (hld up: hdwy to chal 2 out: kpt on u.p)	¾	2	5/1[3]	71	—
3355[5] **September Breeze (IRE) (84)** (KAMorgan) **6-9-12**(7) XAizpuru (lw: led to 4th: chsd ldrs: ev ch 2 out: kpt on u.p)	½	3	9/2[2]	65	—
3594[8] **Ranger Sloane (81)** (GFierro) **5-11-2** RFarrant (bhd: hdwy 8th: chsng ldrs appr 2 out: r.o one pce)	4	4	11/1	74	—
3283[5] **Dry Hill Lad (80)** (JNorton) **6-10-10b** DerekByrne (chsd ldrs: led 8th tl apppr 2 out: sn btn)	24	5	20/1	52	—
3355[10] **Counter Attack (IRE)** (MissAEEmbiricos) **6-10-5** RJohnson (cl up: led 4th to 8th: wknd appr 2 out)	1½	6	33/1	46	—
Edge of Night (JPLeigh) **8-10-10** KGaule (bhd: effrt 4 out: wknd appr 2 out)	3½	7	20/1	48	—
Our Laughter (OBrennan) **7-10-5** MBrennan (bhd fr ½-wy: t.o fr 4 out)	dist	8	50/1	—	—
			(SP 115.5%)		**8 Rn**

6m 3.2 (24.20) CSF £4.23 TOTE £1.40: £1.00 £2.00 £1.30 (£3.60) OWNER Mrs E. A. Kellar (UPPER LAMBOURN) BRED Hugh McMahon
2759 Supreme Flyer (IRE) found a moderate race here, but needed some kid-glove treatment to get him home in front after making a hash of the last. (8/11)
1802 Larkshill (IRE) looked ultra-fit, and for the first time had a live chance, but he proved short of toe in the closing stages.(5/1)
3355 September Breeze (IRE) got this trip well enough but, despite struggling on, was always short of a change of gear. (9/2)
3050* Ranger Sloane, trying by far his longest trip to date, was given every chance to get it but he made no further impression from the second last. (11/1)
2860 Dry Hill Lad looked very slow once the pace was really applied from the third last. (20/1)
Counter Attack (IRE) is only small and, on this showing, is not very good. (33/1)

3707 TWO ENCLOSURE DAY H'CAP CHASE (0-115) (5-Y.O+) (Class E)
3-45 (3-45) **2m 4f (15 fncs)** £3,078.75 (£930.00: £452.50: £213.75) GOING: 0.16 sec per fur (G)

			SP	RR	SF
3547* **Netherby Said (108)** (PBeaumont) **7-11-8** RSupple (lw: mde all: sn clr: blnd 9th & 3 out: j.rt last: eased flat)	—	1	15/8[1]	119+	52
3415[3] **Lochnagrain (IRE) (110)** (MrsMReveley) **9-11-10** MAFitzgerald (mstkes: bhd: styd on fr 3 out: nrst fin)	6	2	2/1[2]	116	49
3452[4] **Jason's Boy (86)** (JMBradley) **7-10-0** RJohnson (chsd wnr: rdn 4 out: no imp)	nk	3	3/1[3]	92	25
2769[5] **Juke Box Billy (IRE) (86)** (MrsJBrown) **9-10-0** JCulloty (effrt ½-wy: rdn 4 out & no imp: wl btn whn blnd bdly 2 out)	19	4	5/1	77	10
			(SP 109.8%)		**4 Rn**

4m 59.1 (8.10) CSF £5.61 TOTE £2.60 (£2.70) OWNER Mrs S. Sunter (BRANDSBY) BRED J. Sunter
LONG HANDICAP Jason's Boy 9-10 Juke Box Billy (IRE) 9-9
3547* Netherby Said, despite going off far too freely and taking the odd liberty with his fences, never looked in any danger and won unchallenged. (15/8: 5/4-2/1)
3415 Lochnagrain (IRE) has never really liked chasing, and his jumping left plenty to be desired, but his rider did a great job on him and persuaded him to run late on. (2/1)
3452 Jason's Boy, who ran poorly last time, showed a bit more here but there was never any real spark about his performance. (3/1)
2769 Juke Box Billy (IRE) has been disappointing this season and, returning here after a lay-off, gave little encouragement. (5/1)

3708 ANNUAL BOX HOLDERS NOVICES' H'CAP CHASE (0-105) (5-Y.O+) (Class E)
4-15 (4-15) **3m 1f (19 fncs)** £3,387.50 (£950.00: £462.50) GOING: 0.16 sec per fur (G)

			SP	RR	SF
3546* **Gaelic Blue (79)** (MrsSJSmith) **7-11-5** RichardGuest (led tl hdd 4 out: led 3 out: sn clr)	—	1	15/8[1]	103	14
3472[P] **Milwaukee (IRE) (60)** (OBrennan) **8-10-0v[1]** MBrennan (hld up: hdwy to chal 13th: led 4 out to 3 out: hung rt & wknd)	19	2	20/1	72	—
3547[3] **Record Lover (IRE) (69)** (MCChapman) **7-10-9** WWorthington (hdwy & prom 7th: outpcd fr 13th: blnd 2 out: fin lame)	dist	3	11/2	—	—
3306* **Mister Trick (IRE) (84)** (LLungo) **7-11-10b** RGarritty (lw: bhd & blnd 11th: t.o whn p.u after next)		P	5/2[2]	—	—
2816* **Primitive Penny (82)** (MrsDHaine) **6-11-8** JFTitley (lw: nt j.w: cl up tl wknd appr 13th: p.u bef 14th)		P	3/1[3]	—	—
			(SP 108.5%)		**5 Rn**

6m 34.0 (23.00) CSF £22.26 TOTE £2.10: £2.30 £6.40 (£15.00) OWNER Mr Trevor Hemmings (BINGLEY) BRED Michael Lysaght

OFFICIAL EXPLANATION **Mister Trick (IRE): needs softer ground and jumped poorly. Primitive Penny: trainer reported that the mare hung left, stumbled on the bend after the stands and lost her action thereafter.**
3546* Gaelic Blue stays and jumps and that was all that was needed against this opposition. (15/8)
3134 Milwaukee (IRE) had the visor on for the first time, and ran much better until his stamina gave out in the home straight. (20/1)
3547 Record Lover (IRE) was left behind on the final circuit and, after a terrible blunder two out, he finished very lame. (11/2: 4/1-6/1)
3306* Mister Trick (IRE) found things happening too quickly for his liking, and his jumping was moderate to say the least, so his rider wisely pulled him up with a circuit left. (5/2)
2816* Primitive Penny, who came from behind to win last time, did not seem to like being up with the pace on this occasion, and would not have a cut at her fences. (3/1)

3709 EASTER MONDAY COMES NEXT H'CAP HURDLE (0-110) (4-Y.O+) (Class E)
4-45 (4-46) **2m 5f 110y (10 hdls)** £2,263.50 (£636.00: £310.50) GOING: 0.16 sec per fur (G)

	Horse / details	Dist	Pos	SP	RR	SF
3429[4]	**Cambo (USA) (83)** (MCBanks) **11-10-4** DSkyrme (lw: in tch: outpcd 6th: hdwy appr 2 out: styng on whn lft in ld last)	—	1	11/2[3]	65	12
3589[2]	**Desert Force (IRE) (92)** (GFierro) **8-10-13** RFarrant (in tch: styd on u.p fr 2 out: nvr able chal)	1¾	2	7/1	73	20
3545*	**Sassiver (USA) (90)** (PAKelleway) **7-10-11** KGaule (in tch: drvn along fr ½-wy: styd on: no imp)	3	3	7/1	69	16
680*	**Sujud (IRE) (92)** (MrsJBrown) **5-10-13** RGarritty (chsd ldrs tl outpcd appr 2 out: btn whn hmpd last)	6	4	9/1	66	13
3478*	**Major Yaasi (USA) (91)** (JAGlover) **7-10-12b** JOsborne (led tl blnd & hdd 2 out: btn whn hmpd last)	1½	5	5/1[2]	64	11
2694[6]	**Brancher (90)** (JNorton) **6-10-6**(5) BGrattan (bhd: pushed along fr ½-wy: hdwy 3 out: led 2 out: rdn & 1l clr whn fell last)		F	11/2[3]	—	—
3473[7]	**Ordog Mor (IRE) (103)** (MGMeagher) **8-11-10** DerekByrne (lw: a bhd: wl t.o whn p.u bef 2 out)		P	10/1	—	—
3089[R]	**Castlebay Lad (92)** (RCurtis) **14-10-13**ow13 MrMAppleby (sn bhd: wl t.o whn p.u bef 2 out)		P	100/1	—	—
3545[4]	**Moobakkr (USA) (80)** (KAMorgan) **6-9-8**(7) XAizpuru (chsd ldrs tl sddle slipped & uns rdr after 3 out)		U	7/2[1]	—	—

(SP 114.7%) **9 Rn**

5m 19.2 (15.20) CSF £39.41 CT £247.89 TOTE £7.90: £1.90 £2.10 £2.50 (£35.90) Trio £54.00 OWNER Mr M. C. Banks (SANDY) BRED Juddmonte Farms
LONG HANDICAP Castlebay Lad 7-13
3429 Cambo (USA) looked in tremendous condition and, after taking time to find his stride, he was staying on strongly. He may well have won even if Brancher had remained upright. (11/2)
3589 Desert Force (IRE) again ran well, and finished in determined style to show that he should certainly get further yet. (7/1)
3545* Sassiver (USA) takes a lot of driving to get him going, and he was never doing enough soon enough here. (7/1: op 9/2)
680* Sujud (IRE), having her first run for her new stable, ran reasonably. (9/1)
3478* Major Yaasi (USA) likes things to go his way and, once taken on, he blundered his chance away two out. (5/1: op 5/2)
2694 Brancher, after looking in trouble, suddenly picked up three out and led over the next, but it was far from over when he took a terrible fall at the final flight. (11/2)
3545 Moobakkr (USA) ran pretty well until his saddle slipped and he unshipped his rider on the home turn. (7/2)

T/Plpt: £183.40 (49.3 Tckts). T/Qdpt: £17.20 (28.98 Tckts) AA

3691-NEWCASTLE (L-H) (Good to firm, Good patches)
Monday March 17th
Final fence omitted each circuit all chases. Race 4: fifth-last fence also omitted
WEATHER: overcast

3710 GREAT NORTH ROAD H'CAP CHASE (0-115) (5-Y.O+) (Class E)
2-00 (2-02) **3m (18 fncs)** £2,862.75 (£867.00: £423.50: £201.75) GOING minus 0.28 sec per fur (GF)

	Horse / details	Dist	Pos	SP	RR	SF
3027[5]	**Golden Fiddle (IRE) (93)** (JKMOliver) **9-10-6v1** AThornton (lw: w ldrs: led 8th to 10th: led 4 out: styd on strly fr 2 out)	—	1	10/1	107	18
3486*	**Northern Squire (105)** (JMJefferson) **9-11-1**(3) ECallaghan (nt j.w: hld up: outpcd 11th: styd on wl fr 2 out: nt rch wnr)	3	2	11/4[2]	117	28
136[5]	**Strong Sound (100)** (PCheesbrough) **10-10-8**(5) GFRyan (hld up: stdy hdwy 11th: mstke 14th: ev ch next: one pce fr 2 out)	7	3	14/1	107	18
3198[2]	**Rustic Air (104)** (JGFitzGerald) **10-11-3** PNiven (lw: trckd ldrs: hit 7th: led 14th: hdd next: wknd 2 out)	3	4	9/2[3]	109	20
2916[2]	**Gale Ahead (IRE) (97)** (GMMoore) **7-10-10** BStorey (w ldrs: led 10th: hdd 12th: outpcd 4 out: 5th & btn whn blnd 2 out)	6	5	9/4[1]	98	9
2801[2]	**Vicaridge (93)** (RBrewis) **10-10-6** ADobbin (trckd ldrs: outpcd 13th: wknd after 4 out: eased: fin lame)	dist	6	6/1	—	—
2916[6]	**Over the Stream (115)** (MissMKMilligan) **11-12-0** TJMurphy (led to 8th: lost pl 10th: sn bhd: t.o 4 out)	dist	7	25/1	—	—

(SP 109.5%) **7 Rn**

5m 57.6 (5.60) CSF £32.36 TOTE £7.70: £2.40 £2.30 (£13.70) OWNER Mr Stuart Wilson (HAWICK) BRED Thomas Webb & Gerard Crowley
IN-FOCUS: **The ground looked to be a good deal firmer than the official Good to firm.**
3027 Golden Fiddle (IRE), a frustrating character, was tried in a visor for the first time and, given a more enterprising ride than usual, the tactics paid off. (10/1: op 5/1)
3486* Northern Squire, whose jumping was far from fluent, was held up in a slowly-run race on this fast ground and struggled to go the pace a mile out. Putting in some solid work over the last two, he was never going to get near the winner. More forceful tactics should have been the order of the day. (11/4: 2/1-3/1)
136 Strong Sound, having his first outing for 257 days, looked on the big side. After moving up on the bridle, he clouted five out and was going up and down in the same place two out. The outing will surely bring him on, and he is on a winning mark. (14/1)
3198 Rustic Air, who took a keen grip, dropped out tamely. (9/2: 3/1-5/1)
2916 Gale Ahead (IRE), who likes fast ground, suddenly came under pressure four from home and was well beaten when he clouted the second last. (9/4)
2801 Vicaridge did not settle. Outpaced three-quarters of a mile from home, he was allowed to come home in his own time. (6/1)

3711 TOWN MOOR (S) H'CAP HURDLE (0-95) (4-Y.O+) (Class G)
2-30 (2-34) **2m 4f (11 hdls)** £2,025.50 (£568.00: £276.50) GOING minus 0.28 sec per fur (GF)

	Horse / details	Dist	Pos	SP	RR	SF
2862[2]	**Jalmaid (67)** (HAlexander) **5-9-13**(5) RMcGrath (lw: chsd ldrs: led 3 out: hld on wl flat)	—	1	6/1[1]	47	3

				SP	RR	SF
3159[9]	**Don't Tell Tom (IRE) (80)** (JWade) **7-10-12**(5) STaylor (chsd ldrs: chal 3 out: nt qckn last 50y)	¾	**2**	10/1	59	15
3485[4]	**Kirstenbosch (80)** (LLungo) **10-10-10**(7) WDowling (in tch: drvn along 7th: styd on one pce fr 2 out)	2	**3**	6/1[1]	58	14
3474[3]	**Fiasco (75)** (MJCamacho) **4-10-0**(3) FLeahy (chsd ldrs: rdn 7th: one pce fr 3 out)	12	**4**	16/1	43	—
3371[P]	**Greenfinch (CAN) (65)** (MrsAMNaughton) **6-10-2v** JSupple (hdwy 6th: kpt on fr 3 out: nvr nr to chal)	1¼	**5**	20/1	32	—
3096[7]	**Dalusman (IRE) (68)** (FPMurtagh) **9-10-2**(3) ECallaghan (sn bhd & drvn along: styd on fr 3 out)	hd	**6**	16/1	35	—
3478[6]	**Yacht Club (72)** (JLEyre) **15-10-9** BStorey (jnd ldrs 5th: led next: hdd 3 out: wknd next)	½	**7**	10/1	39	—
3313[2]	**In a Moment (USA) (73)** (CGrant) **6-10-10** AThornton (sn bhd & drvn along: styd on fr 3 out: nvr nr to chal)	¾	**8**	7/1[2]	39	—
3371[4]	**Dont Forget Curtis (IRE) (87)** (GMMoore) **5-11-10** JCallaghan (hld up: mid div: effrt 7th: wknd after next)	1½	**9**	16/1	52	8
3481[10]	**Dashmar (63)** (MsLCPlater) **10-10-0** MMoloney (bhd: rdn along 4th: sme hdwy 7th: sn wknd)	1½	**10**	16/1	27	—
3542[3]	**Oakbury (IRE) (70)** (MissLCSiddall) **5-10-0**(7) TSiddall (sn bhd & drvn along: n.d)	1¾	**11**	8/1[3]	32	—
2913[13]	**Over Stated (IRE) (73)** (PCheesbrough) **7-10-5**(5) GFRyan (hld up: stdy hdwy 6th: sn chsng ldrs: wknd after 4 out)	2	**12**	20/1	34	—
3483[7]	**Nosmo King (IRE) (63)** (MrsMAKendall) **6-10-0** MrsMKendall (led to 4th: lost pl 4 out)	¾	**13**	33/1	23	—
3448[2]	**Arthur Bee (63)** (BBousfield) **10-9-7**(7) CMcCormack (chsd ldrs: rdn 7th: wknd appr 3 out)	6	**14**	16/1	18	—
	Rhyming Thomas (77) (JRAdam) **9-11-0** TReed (plld hrd: trckd ldrs: led 4th to 6th: wknd 4 out)	hd	**15**	25/1	32	—
2802[2]	**Highland Park (89)** (RCraggs) **11-11-12** ADobbin (chsd ldrs: drvn along 5th: wknd 7th)	½	**16**	7/1[2]	44	—
3620[3]	**Bark'n'bite (80)** (MrsMReveley) **5-11-3b[1]** PNiven (bhd: p.u bef 3 out)		**P**	8/1[3]	—	—
3453[3]	**Persian Grange (IRE) (69)** (DALamb) **7-10-6**ow3 JBurke (bhd: t.o whn p.u bef 3 out)		**P**	14/1	—	—
	No Takers (73) (SEKettlewell) **10-10-7**(3) GLee (sn bhd: t.o whn p.u bef 3 out)		**P**	20/1	—	—
1824[7]	**Doon Ridge (63)** (MissLCSiddall) **6-10-0** OPears (chsd ldrs to 5th: sn wknd: bhd whn p.u bef 7th)		**P**	50/1	—	—
				(SP 153.1%)	**20 Rn**	

4m 56.2 (8.20) CSF £67.80 CT £375.91 TOTE £9.60: £3.10 £3.10 £1.30 £3.50 (£74.50) Trio £325.90; £188.23 to Uttoxeter 18/3/97 OWNER Mr R. V. Jackson (LANCHESTER) BRED W. H. F. Carson

LONG HANDICAP Dashmar 9-13 Nosmo King (IRE) 9-13 Arthur Bee 9-13 Doon Ridge 9-9

WEIGHT FOR AGE 4yo-9lb

No bid. Don't Tell Tom (IRE) clmd MrsASwinbank £5,000

2862 Jalmaid, well suited by this stiffer track, did just enough. (6/1)

2701 Don't Tell Tom (IRE), whose best form in the past has been shown on much softer ground, stuck to his guns in willing fashion. (10/1: 7/1-14/1)

3485 Kirstenbosch became outpaced on ground much faster than he really likes but, to his credit, he kept going all the way to the line. (6/1)

3474 Fiasco looked to have been given more than her fair share of weight. (16/1)

Greenfinch (CAN), having his first run in a seller, ran his best race for some time. (20/1)

3 Dalusman (IRE), a failure over fences, gave connections some encouragement. (16/1)

2802 Highland Park (7/1: 5/1-8/1)

3712 NORTHUMBERLAND HUSSARS HUNTERS' CHASE (6-Y.O+) (Class H)

3-00 (3-03) **3m (18 fncs)** £1,108.50 (£225.75: £225.75) GOING minus 0.28 sec per fur (GF)

				SP	RR	SF
	Final Hope (IRE) (RTate) **9-11-3**(7) MrsFNeedham (trckd ldrs: led 14th: jst hld on)	—	**1**	10/1	97	27
3458*	**Highlandman** (JSHaldane) **11-11-6**(7) MrChrisWilson (led to 14th: kpt on fr 2 out: rallied flat)	d.h	**2**	5/1[3]	100	30
3397[4]	**Little Wenlock** (MrsDSCGibson) **13-11-8**(5) MrsVJackson (in tch: styd on wl fr 2 out: ev ch flat: nt qckn towards fin)	½	**2**	9/2[2]	100	30
	Piper O'Drummond (MissPaulineRobson) **10-11-5**(5) MissPRobson (lw: trckd ldrs: effrt 4 out: one pce fr next)	3	**4**	9/2[2]	95	25
3439[U]	**Free Transfer (IRE)** (DJFairbairn) **8-11-5**(5) MrCStorey (in tch: outpcd 13th: hmpd next: sme hdwy u.p 3 out: sn wknd: fin lame)	21	**5**	9/1	81	11
	Washakie (FTWalton) **12-11-5**(5) MrPJohnson (lw: outpcd & drvn along 8th: sn bhd)	21	**6**	2/1[1]	67	—
	Gathering Time (MrsSJSmith) **11-11-3**(7) MrABirch (sn bhd: drvn along 6th)	17	**7**	33/1	55	—
3439[3]	**Double Collect** (MrsMDRebori) **11-11-3**(7) MrARebori (chsd ldrs: 5th & outpcd whn fell 14th)		**F**	9/1	—	—
				(SP 118.4%)	**8 Rn**	

6m 0.3 (8.30) CSF FH&H £27.97 FH&LW £25.93 TOTE £11.30: £1.80 H £2.10 LW £1.90 (FH&H £13.80 FH&LW £12.10) OWNER Mr R. Tate (THIRSK) BRED Ashleigh Stud (USA)

OFFICIAL EXPLANATION **Washakie: no explanation offered.**

Final Hope (IRE), winner of one of his three points this season, hung on in a desperate finish. (10/1)

3458* Highlandman rallied bravely under pressure, and was closing the gap all the way to the line. His rider dismounted, but it was thought the gelding had only suffered a minor back injury. (5/1)

3397 Little Wenlock seems effective on any ground. (9/2)

Piper O'Drummond ran as if he will appreciate extreme distances. (9/2)

3439 Free Transfer (IRE) finished very lame. (9/1)

Washakie, who has a fine record in points, ran no race at all, struggling fully a circuit from home. Connections could offer no excuse. (2/1)

3713 TOWN & COUNTRY NOVICES' HUNTERS' CHASE (5-Y.O+) (Class H)

3-35 (3-36) **2m 4f (14 fncs)** £1,047.75 (£312.00: £148.50: £66.75) GOING minus 0.28 sec per fur (GF)

				SP	RR	SF
3533[2]	**Woody Dare** (PNeedham) **7-12-2**(5) MrRThornton (chsd ldrs: led appr 3 out: hit 2 out: styd on wl)	—	**1**	7/1[3]	75	18
	General Delight (MrsARWood) **10-12-0**(7) MrDWood (sn bhd: hdwy 8th: sn chsng ldrs: ev ch 3 out: nt qckn between last 2)	2	**2**	12/1	73	16
	Pennine View (JJDixon) **10-12-2**(5) MrRFord (chsd ldrs: led after 4 out: sn hdd: kpt on one pce)	½	**3**	9/1	73	16
	Bells Will Ring (IRE) (MrsAHamilton) **7-12-0**(7) MrTScott (mstkes: led: blnd 4 out: sn hdd: wknd appr 2 out)	29	**4**	4/1[2]	50	—
3460[P]	**Master Crozina** (JCornforth) **9-12-0**(7) MrPCornforth (sn trckng ldrs: wknd 11th)	20	**5**	33/1	34	—
3460[5]	**Tumlin Oot (IRE)** (JSHaldane) **8-12-0**(7) MrChrisWilson (in tch: blnd 10th: sn lost pl)	19	**6**	10/1	19	—
	Eilid Anoir (JShearer) **8-12-2**(5) MrRShiels (j.rt: in tch: effrt 11th: sn wknd)	7	**7**	14/1	13	—
	Drumcairn (IRE) (PGForster) **9-12-2**(5) MrPJohnson (blnd 1st: sn bhd: t.o 8th)	5	**8**	20/1	9	—
3455[3]	**Up For Ransome (IRE)** (MrsAMNaughton) **8-12-0**(7) MrGShenkin (fell 1st)		**F**	7/4[1]	—	—
	Count Surveyor (TRBeadle) **10-12-0**(7) MrAParker (p.u lame after 1st)		**P**	20/1	—	—
	Lindon Run (KRobson) **8-12-0**(7) MrRMorgan (lw: hdwy 8th: outpcd whn blnd & uns rdr next)		**U**	10/1	—	—
				(SP 123.9%)	**11 Rn**	

5m 5.5 (12.50) CSF £79.04 TOTE £7.20: £1.60 £3.60 £1.60 (£63.30) Trio £65.00 OWNER Mr P. Needham (DARLINGTON) BRED V. and Mrs Burgass

3533 Woody Dare had the upper hand between the last two. (7/1: op 4/1)
General Delight, an infrequent runner in points, could only stick on at the same pace and was unable to get in a blow. (12/1: op 8/1)
Pennine View, who has been let down by his jumping in the past, did nothing wrong here. (9/1: op 6/1)
Bells Will Ring (IRE), a winner of a confined point two weeks earlier, found difficulty jumping these fences, and his rider did well to survive a bad blunder four out. (4/1)
Eilid Anoir (14/1: op 7/1)
3455 Up For Ransome (IRE) came to grief at the very first fence. (7/4)

3714 NEWCASTLE CITY NOVICES' CLAIMING HURDLE (4-Y.O+) (Class F)

4-05 (4-06) **2m (9 hdls)** £2,039.50 (£572.00: £278.50) GOING minus 0.67 sec per fur (F)

				SP	RR	SF
3396[6]	**Brambles Way (112)** (MrsMReveley) **8-11-8b** PNiven (hld up: led on bit 3 out: hit last: drvn out)	—	1	4/11[1]	72	—
910[4]	**Parklife (IRE)** (PCHaslam) **5-11-4** MFoster (hld up: outpcd after 4 out: chal 2 out: eased whn btn flat)	4	2	11/4[2]	64	—
	Lucker (MrsEMoscrop) **10-11-0** KJohnson (t: led to 3 out: wknd qckly next: mstke last: t.o)	dist	3	16/1[3]	—	—
	Nine Pipes (IRE) (JJBirkett) **6-11-2** LO'Hara (bit bkwd: plld hrd: trckd ldrs tl wknd 4 out: bhd whn fell 2 out)		F	33/1	—	—
				(SP 108.8%)		**4 Rn**

4m 1.0 (9.00) CSF £1.63 TOTE £1.30 (£1.10) OWNER Mr Nigel Jones (SALTBURN) BRED W. P. S. Johnson
3396 Brambles Way, hopelessly out of his class last time, always looked to have this under control. (4/11)
910 Parklife (IRE), a pronounced tail-swisher, was given an easy time when it was clear after the last that the winner was too good. (11/4)

3715 GLENGOYNE HIGHLAND MALT TAMEROSIA SERIES (QUALIFIER) NOVICES' CHASE (5-Y.O+) (Class E)

4-35 (4-35) **3m (18 fncs)** £2,966.75 (£899.00: £439.50: £209.75) GOING minus 0.28 sec per fur (GF)

				SP	RR	SF
3556*	**Kalajo (84)** (BMactaggart) **7-12-2** BStorey (stumbled 2nd: jnd ldr 8th: hit 12th: led 14th: drvn clr between last 2: all out)	—	1	7/4[1]	99	32
3608[3]	**Fern Leader (IRE)** (MrsASwinbank) **7-11-4** JSupple (nt j.w: led: hit 9th: hdd 14th: hit 2 out: kpt on wl flat)	2½	2	15/8[2]	85	18
3306[2]	**Strongalong (IRE) (73)** (PCheesbrough) **7-11-4** ADobbin (chsd ldrs: effrt u.p 4 out: 3rd & btn whn blnd last)	9	3	3/1[3]	79	12
3067[5]	**Abbey Lamp (IRE) (86)** (MissLucindaRussell) **8-11-4** AThornton (chsd ldrs: drvn along 10th: wknd appr 3 out)	26	4	12/1	62	—
3306[3]	**Seldom But Severe (IRE) (67)** (EAElliott) **7-10-13**(5) GFRyan (chsd ldrs: reminders 6th: lost pl 13th: sn bhd)	11	5	20/1	55	—
				(SP 108.6%)		**5 Rn**

6m 0.6 (8.60) CSF £4.99 TOTE £2.10: £1.20 £1.90 (£3.30) OWNER Kelso Members Lowflyers Club (HAWICK) BRED P. J. and G. F. Burman
3556* Kalajo, who wore a tongue-strap, struggled under his big weight in the closing stages, and at the line and there was not an ounce to spare. (7/4)
3608 Fern Leader (IRE) is not yet a fluent jumper but, to his credit, he kept on all the way to the line. All he lacks is experience. (15/8)
3306 Strongalong (IRE) was held when he blundered at the last. (3/1)
Abbey Lamp (IRE) again showed very little. (12/1)

3716 NORTHUMBERLAND INTERMEDIATE N.H. FLAT RACE (4, 5 & 6-Y.O) (Class H)

5-05 (5-05) **2m** £1,215.00 (£340.00: £165.00)

				SP	RR	SF
	Go Native (IRE) (MrsSJSmith) **5-10-11**(7) RWilkinson (w'like, str: hld up & plld hrd: sn trckng ldrs: led 1f out: pushed out)	—	1	12/1	59 f	—
3418[R]	**Wynyard Knight** (MrsMReveley) **5-11-1**(3) GLee (hld up: hdwy ½-wy: chal over 1f out: nt qckn ins fnl f)	1½	2	4/6[1]	58 f	—
3418*	**Landler** (JNorton) **4-10-12**(5) MrRThornton (w ldr: led 3f out to 1f out: kpt on same pce)	2	3	7/1[3]	63 f	—
	Polar King (IRE) (CWThornton) **4-10-3**(7) NHorrocks (narrow sort: led to 3f out: kpt on one pce fnl f)	½	4	8/1	55 f	—
	Salmon Cellar (IRE) (JMJefferson) **4-10-7**(3) ECallaghan (lengthy: trckd ldrs: outpcd 3f out: kpt on wl fnl f)	¾	5	9/2[2]	54 f	—
	Kit Smartie (IRE) (DMForster) **5-10-13**(5) GFRyan (lengthy: bit bkwd: hld up: effrt & outpcd 3f out: kpt on wl fnl f)	nk	6	14/1	54 f	—
	Merry Major (TDBarron) **4-10-5**(5) RMcGrath (unf: bkwd: hld up: pushed along & outpcd over 3f out: grad wknd)	9	7	12/1	45 f	—
	Runhim (JKMOliver) **5-10-11**(7) SMelrose (bit bkwd: trckd ldrs: pushed along 4f out: sn wknd)	13	8	50/1	32 f	—
	Millstone Hill (MABarnes) **5-10-13**(5) STaylor (plain, unf: hld up: pushed along 5f out: sn lost pl)	18	9	100/1	14 f	—
	Rising Mill (RBrewis) **6-11-4** MrARobson (chsng type: bkwd: w ldr: drvn along & outpcd over 3f out: sn bhd: virtually p.u)	20	10	50/1	—	—
				(SP 128.8%)		**10 Rn**

3m 57.5 CSF £20.62 TOTE £20.60: £4.10 £1.10 £2.10 (£19.50) Trio £15.30 OWNER Mr Trevor Hemmings (BINGLEY) BRED Bobby Donworth and Honora Corridan
WEIGHT FOR AGE 4yo-8lb
IN-FOCUS: **This race turned into nothing more than a three-furlong sprint and the form should be treated with caution.**
Go Native (IRE) looked to be walking stiffly in the paddock but, in the race, he travelled well throughout and did it in good style. (12/1)
2904 Wynyard Knight, ridden for foot, did not produce it when asked to go and win his race. He needs more use making of him. (4/6)
3418* Landler, a tail-swisher, did nothing wrong in the race, keeping on grimly. (7/1: op 4/1)
Polar King (IRE) stuck on bravely, but will need a trip over hurdles. (8/1)
Salmon Cellar (IRE), a decent, athletic looking type who showed a nice action going down, ran a pleasing first race and will come on for it. (9/2)
Kit Smartie (IRE), who showed a pronounced knee action, did really well considering he looked one of the most backward in the field. (14/1: tchd 33/1)
Merry Major looks as if he will need more time. (12/1: op 8/1)
Rising Mill showed a lot of knee action going down. (50/1)

T/Plpt: £270.20 (42.75 Tckts). T/Qdpt: £17.60 (40.41 Tckts) WG

3601-FONTWELL (Fig. 8) (Good to firm, Firm patches)
Tuesday March 18th
WEATHER: sunny & windy

3717 'CERTAIN JUSTICE' CHALLENGE CUP NOVICES' H'CAP CHASE (0-100) (5-Y.O+) (Class E)
2-00 (2-00) **2m 2f (15 fncs)** £2,961.00 (£882.00: £420.00: £189.00) GOING: 0.06 sec per fur (G)

Form	Horse	Dist	Pos	SP	RR	SF
3602*	**Red Branch (IRE) (79)** (JSKing) **8-11-4** 6x TJMurphy (lw: mde all: clr appr 3 out: eased flat)	—	1	5/6[1]	95+	8
3343[2]	**Speedy Snaps Image (73)** (PRRodford) **6-10-12** SBurrough (a.p: chsd wnr appr 6th: 2nd & btn whn j.bdly rt last 2)	12	2	5/1[2]	78	—
3588[3]	**Chris's Glen (70)** (JMBradley) **8-10-9v** BFenton (lw: chsd wnr tl appr 6th: 3rd whn blnd 6th: wknd 10th)	4	3	11/2[3]	72	—
3550[P]	**Victory Gate (USA) (61)** (MrsLCJewell) **12-9-11**(3) SophieMitchell (lw: a bhd)	nk	4	40/1	63	—
3343[P]	**Ketchican (76)** (SGKnight) **5-10-7** SAnderson (plld hrd: nt j.w: bhd fr 8th)	8	5	50/1	70	—
3427[5]	**Strokesaver (IRE) (88)** (CPEBrooks) **7-11-13b** DGallagher (a bhd: t.o fr 9th)	20	6	5/1[2]	65	—
				(SP 107.7%)		**6 Rn**

4m 37.7 (15.70) CSF £4.70 TOTE £1.40: £1.20 £1.70 (£3.20) OWNER Mr E. J. Mangan (SWINDON) BRED Michael Butler
LONG HANDICAP Victory Gate (USA) 9-13
WEIGHT FOR AGE 5yo-8lb

3602* Red Branch (IRE) looked very well in the paddock and completed the hat-trick without turning a hair. He was eased down to a walk on the run-in, and was value for at least twenty-five lengths. (5/6: 4/5-evens)
3343 Speedy Snaps Image moved into second place approaching the sixth, but he was left behind turning for home and was very leg-weary when jumping violently right at the last two fences. (5/1)
3588 Chris's Glen, who has yet to win on ground worse than good, was 15lb lower than when last successful, but even that was not enough to help him. (11/2: 4/1-6/1)
3427 Strokesaver (IRE) (5/1: 5/2-11/2)

3718 E.B.F. N.H. (QUALIFIER) NOVICES' HURDLE (5, 6 & 7-Y.O) (Class E)
2-30 (2-30) **2m 2f 110y (9 hdls)** £2,385.00 (£660.00: £315.00) GOING: 0.06 sec per fur (G)

Form	Horse	Dist	Pos	SP	RR	SF
3337*	**Strong Paladin (IRE) (96)** (JTGifford) **6-11-7**(3) LAspell (mde all: edgd rt flat: rdn out)	—	1	100/30[3]	84	11
3569[3]	**Neat Feat (IRE) (94)** (DRCElsworth) **6-11-0** PHolley (lw: hld up: chsd wnr fr 6th: hrd rdn & ev ch last: swtchd lft flat: unable qckn)	1¾	2	15/8[1]	73	—
3406*	**Rhythm And Blues (94)** (RHBuckler) **7-11-5** BPowell (hld up: chsd wnr 4th to 6th: one pce)	7	3	3/1[2]	71	—
2794[8]	**Yarsley Jester** (DMGrissell) **5-10-9** JRKavanagh (prom to 6th)	3	4	66/1	59	—
3569[7]	**The Flying Doctor (IRE)** (GBBalding) **7-11-0** BFenton (hdwy 3 out: sn wknd)	22	5	7/2	45	—
	Woman From Hell (MrsLRichards) **7-10-9** MRichards (bhd fr 6th: t.o whn p.u bef 2 out)		P	66/1	—	—
				(SP 108.1%)		**6 Rn**

4m 34.3 (16.30) CSF £8.67 TOTE £3.50: £1.70 £1.40 (£2.40) OWNER Mrs Angela Brodie (FINDON) BRED Denis McDonnell

3337* Strong Paladin (IRE) was racing on much faster ground and dropping back a furlong in distance but, despite this, he made all the running and proved far more resolute than the runner-up from the penultimate hurdle. (100/30)
3569 Neat Feat (IRE) certainly had the less competitive event he was looking for, and was turned out in great shape. Travelling really well as he cruised into second place four from home he, not for the first time, found little when let down and did not appear to be putting it all in. He is certainly one to have reservations about. (15/8)
3406* Rhythm And Blues found this ground far too lively, and could only struggle on at one pace as the tempo increased from the fourth last. He is at his best in the mud. (3/1)

3719 HEDDY SIMPSON MEMORIAL CHALLENGE TROPHY MAIDEN CHASE (5-Y.O+) (Class E)
3-00 (3-00) **3m 2f 110y (22 fncs)** £3,133.20 (£865.20: £411.60) GOING: 0.06 sec per fur (G)

Form	Horse	Dist	Pos	SP	RR	SF
1763[2]	**The Whole Hog (IRE) (76)** (KCBailey) **8-11-8** AThornton (hld up: chsd ldr fr 17th: led last: pushed out)	—	1	7/4[2]	89	14
3354[2]	**Bolshie Baron (72)** (MHWeston) **8-11-8** MrMHarris (chsd ldr: led 4th to last: unable qckn)	3½	2	Evens[1]	87	12
3444[P]	**Cruise Control (78)** (RRowe) **11-11-8** DO'Sullivan (lw: led to 4th: mstke 10th: wknd 16th: t.o)	dist	3	9/2[3]	—	—
2819[8]	**Bonita Blakeney (60)** (GBBalding) **7-11-3** BFenton (hdwy 9th: chsd ldr 12th to 17th: 3rd whn fell 18th)		F	16/1	—	—
				(SP 110.4%)		**4 Rn**

7m 3.2 (23.20) CSF £3.79 TOTE £2.70 (£1.90) OWNER Mrs Sharon Nelson (UPPER LAMBOURN) BRED Owen O'Leary
IN-FOCUS: **This was an appalling race for extremely slow horses.**

1763 The Whole Hog (IRE) moved into second place six out and, joining the leader in the straight, gained a slender advantage at the last and needed only to be nudged along to secure victory. (7/4: evens-2/1)
3354 Bolshie Baron was soon at the head of affairs, but he was joined by the winner in the straight and, collared at the final fence, failed to find another gear. (Evens)

3720 GRAND SPLENDOUR H'CAP HURDLE (0-115) (4-Y.O+) (Class E)
3-30 (3-30) **2m 6f 110y (11 hdls)** £2,807.00 (£777.00: £371.00) GOING: 0.06 sec per fur (G)

Form	Horse	Dist	Pos	SP	RR	SF
3554[4]	**Smuggler's Point (USA) (101)** (JJBridger) **7-11-6**(3) SophieMitchell (led after 1st tl appr 3 out: led appr last: rdn out)	—	1	5/1[2]	81	27
3423[F]	**Vintage Claret (98)** (JTGifford) **8-11-6** PHide (a.p: rdn 8th: lost pl 3 out: rallied appr last: mstke last: r.o one pce)	5	2	7/2[1]	74	20
3013[9]	**Sorbiere (90)** (NJHenderson) **10-10-12b** MAFitzgerald (led tl after 1st: led appr 3 out tl appr last: nt run on)	hd	3	7/1	66	12
	Gentleman Sid (81) (PGMurphy) **7-10-0**(3)ow3 LAspell (lw: hld up: rdn 3 out: wknd 2 out)	19	4	11/2[3]	44	—
3183[3]	**Walking Tall (IRE) (104)** (TPMcGovern) **6-11-12** DBridgwater (lw: a bhd: t.o whn p.u bef 2 out)		P	7/2[1]	—	—
3183[4]	**Never Forgotten (80)** (GLMoore) **12-10-2** PHolley (lw: p.u bef 2nd: sddle slipped)		P	20/1	—	—
3499[14]	**Paddysway (92)** (RHBuckler) **10-11-0** BPowell (lw: p.u bef 3rd: lame)		P	11/2[3]	—	—
3604[3]	**Raahin (USA) (78)** (SWoodman) **12-10-0** DMorris (lw: a bhd: t.o whn p.u bef 8th)		P	20/1	—	—
				(SP 113.9%)		**8 Rn**

5m 30.5 (14.50) CSF £21.04 CT £109.18 TOTE £6.10: £2.10 £1.60 £1.70 (£19.50) OWNER Mrs V. R. Hoare (LIPHOOK) BRED G. M. Breeding Farms Inc
LONG HANDICAP Gentleman Sid 9-1 Raahin (USA) 9-1

3554 Smuggler's Point (USA) was given a fine ride. Soon at the head of affairs, he was collared approaching the third last and the signs did not look good turning out of the back straight. However, with his jockey beavering away, the gelding managed to get back in front again approaching the final flight and was rousted along to score. (5/1)
Vintage Claret got outpaced as the race began in earnest three from home but he struggled on again going to the final flight and, despite an error there, stayed on to snatch second place. (7/2)
1391 Sorbiere, who has been out of form this season, was taking a drop in class but unfortunately disgraced himself. In front approaching the third last, he appeared to have the race in the bag entering the straight but, having jumped the second last, he decided he had done enough and threw in the towel. Collared approaching the final flight, he refused to give his all. He is certainly not one to trust. (7/1)
Gentleman Sid, off the track since last July and carrying 13lb more than his long handicap mark, did not run badly and only tired as lack of a recent run took its toll two from home. (11/2)

3721 HORSE AND HOUND CHARLTON HUNT CHALLENGE CUP HUNTERS' CHASE (5-Y.O+) (Class H)

4-00 (4-02) **2m 3f (16 fncs)** £1,562.00 (£432.00: £206.00) GOING: 0.06 sec per fur (G)

				SP	RR	SF
3457[3]	**Busman (IRE)** (KeithPearce) **8-11-13**(7) MrDSJones (hdwy 9th: led 12th: clr appr 3 out: r.o wl)	—	**1**	11/4[2]	103	45
3010[5]	**Tea Cee Kay** (COKing) **7-11-9**(5) MrASansome (led 5th to 12th: chsd wnr appr last: unable qckn)	10	**2**	12/1	89	31
	Spitfire Jubilee (MrsLASyckelmoore) **11-11-7**(7) MrRNuttall (led to 5th: dropped rr 10th: r.o one pce flat)	9	**3**	2/1[1]	81	23
	Eagle Bid (IRE) (MrsDHMcCarthy) **9-11-9h**(5) MrTMcCarthy (hdwy 10th: ev ch 4 out: wknd appr last)	1	**4**	7/2[3]	80	22
3460[3]	**Corly Special** (MissSJKScott) **10-11-7**(7) MrEJames (mstke 4th: bhd fr 7th)	1¾	**5**	4/1	79	21
	Miss Magic (FJBrennan) **12-11-2**(7) MrFBrennan (hdwy 7th: mstke 10th: wknd appr 3 out: 4th & no ch whn mstke last)	¾	**6**	50/1	73	15
	Feltham Mistress (DCTucker) **7-11-2**(7) MrEBabington (swtg: bhd fr 4 out: t.o whn p.u bef last)		**P**	66/1	—	—

(SP 113.4%) **7 Rn**

4m 49.7 (10.70) CSF £28.64 TOTE £3.50: £1.80 £3.00 (£10.80) OWNER Mr Keith Pearce (CARMARTHEN) BRED Ballymacoll Stud Farm Ltd
3457 Busman (IRE) proved to be just the ticket, leading at the fifth last and forging clear turning for home for a decisive victory. (11/4)
Tea Cee Kay, who cut out a lot of the running, eventually managed to regain second place approaching the final fence, but had no hope of reeling in the winner. (12/1: 8/1-14/1)
Spitfire Jubilee, the early leader, dropped back to last place setting out on the final circuit and punters knew their fate. However, he did struggle on again on the run-in to snatch third prize. (2/1: op evens)
Eagle Bid (IRE), one of three with every chance jumping the water, four out, then remained in second place until collared for that position approaching the last. (7/2)

3722 R.N.L.I. H'CAP HURDLE (0-110) (4-Y.O+) (Class E)

4-30 (4-30) **2m 2f 110y (9 hdls)** £2,280.00 (£630.00: £300.00) GOING: 0.06 sec per fur (G)

				SP	RR	SF
3351[4]	**Claireswan (IRE) (97)** (MHTompkins) **5-11-1** RichardGuest (lw: hld up: led after 3 out to 2 out: hrd rdn flat: led nr fin)	—	**1**	7/4[1]	77	22
3286[6]	**Decide Yourself (IRE) (100)** (TThomsonJones) **7-11-4** MAFitzgerald (lw: hdwy 3 out: led 2 out: hrd rdn flat: hdd nr fin)	hd	**2**	9/2[3]	80	25
2680[12]	**Topanga (83)** (JABennett) **5-10-1b** CLlewellyn (led to 3rd: hrd rdn appr 2 out: one pce)	6	**3**	7/1	58	3
	Frozen Sea (USA) (110) (GPEnright) **6-11-9**(5) MrRThornton (lw: hld up: ev ch 2 out: wknd appr last)	1¾	**4**	3/1[2]	83	28
2907[5]	**Adilov (88)** (JJBridger) **5-10-3**(3) SophieMitchell (lw: a bhd)	7	**5**	13/2	55	—
	Sea Barn (82) (MJCoombe) **14-9-9**(5) GSupple (chsd ldr: led 3rd tl after 3 out: sn wknd)	2½	**6**	25/1	47	—
1390[P]	**Matamoros (83)** (RRowe) **5-10-1**ow1 DO'Sullivan (bhd fr 2nd: t.o fr 6th: p.u bef 2 out: dismntd)		**P**	12/1	—	—

(SP 116.9%) **7 Rn**

4m 29.3 (11.30) CSF £9.85 TOTE £2.20: £1.50 £3.10 (£4.20) OWNER Claire and Beryl (NEWMARKET) BRED Thomas Bean
LONG HANDICAP Sea Barn 9-2
3351 Claireswan (IRE) went on soon after the third last, but was collared by the runner-up two from home. However, refusing to give way, he battled his heart out and got back on top near the line. (7/4)
51a Decide Yourself (IRE) managed to jump into a narrow lead two from home, but he was unable to shake off the winner and, carrying his head slightly high, was worried out of it near the finish. He was dismounted and led in and his trainer reported him to be wrong behind. (9/2: 4/1-6/1)
1388 Topanga, the early leader, came under pressure turning for home but could only go up and down in the same place. (7/1)
Frozen Sea (USA), one of three in line jumping the second last, had soon come to the end of his tether. (3/1)
2907 Adilov (13/2: 4/1-7/1)
Matamoros (12/1: 5/1-14/1)

T/Plpt: £38.40 (252.43 Tckts). T/Qdpt: £36.00 (11.16 Tckts) AK

3607-SEDGEFIELD (L-H) (Good to firm, Good patches)

Tuesday March 18th

WEATHER: fine

3723 STANLEY RACING SERIES NOVICES' HURDLE (4-Y.O+) (Class E)

2-10 (2-10) **2m 1f (8 hdls)** £2,253.00 (£633.00: £309.00) GOING minus 0.56 sec per fur (F)

				SP	RR	SF
2509[11]	**Stylish Interval (89)** (NWaggott) **5-11-8** RSupple (mde most: hit 5th & last: styd on wl u.p)	—	**1**	5/1[2]	67	—
743[7]	**Suvalu (USA)** (MGMeagher) **5-11-2** DerekByrne (trckd ldrs: effrt 2 out: sn hrd drvn: kpt on: nt pce to chal)	1	**2**	6/1[3]	60	—
3475[3]	**Undawaterscubadiva** (MPBielby) **5-11-2** ADobbin (lw: trckd ldrs: effrt 3 out: sn rdn & one pce)	3	**3**	13/8[1]	57	—
3098[7]	**Tsanga** (GMMoore) **5-11-2** JCallaghan (disp ld to 4th: sn pushed along: one pce fr 3 out)	3½	**4**	33/1	54	—
3474[6]	**I'm Tyson (NZ)** (MrsDianneSayer) **9-11-2** MMoloney (hld up & bhd: hit 5th: styd on fr 3 out: nrst fin)	1½	**5**	12/1	53	—
3098[P]	**Point Duty** (FPMurtagh) **7-11-2** DBentley (chsd ldrs tl rdn & btn appr 2 out)	7	**6**	25/1	46	—
3159[15]	**Whitegates Willie** (HowardJohnson) **5-11-2** DParker (prom tl outpcd fr 5th)	1¾	**7**	100/1	44	—
3000[9]	**Gazanali (IRE)** (GMMoore) **6-11-2** NBentley (hld up: stdy hdwy 5th: rdn & wknd fr 3 out)	1	**8**	13/2	43	—
3474[10]	**The Grey Texan (60)** (VThompson) **8-11-2** MrMThompson (in tch tl outpcd fr 5th)	dist	**9**	66/1	—	—
3418[7]	**Weapons Free** (TPTate) **6-11-2** RGarritty (plld hrd: lost tch fr 5th: p.u bef 2 out)		**P**	7/1	—	—

				SP	RR	SF
3453^{P}	**Rye Rum (IRE)** (JWFAynsley) **6-11-2b^{1}** BStorey (hld up: lost tch fr 5th: p.u bef 2 out)		**P**	100/1	—	—
				(SP 112.8%)		**11 Rn**

4m 1.6 (6.60) CSF £29.70 TOTE £6.60: £2.00 £1.40 £1.20 (£27.20) Trio £21.60 OWNER Mrs J. Waggott (SPENNYMOOR) BRED R. J. Turner

1141* Stylish Interval is a tough sort and, despite getting a shade warm in the preliminaries, he did nothing wrong in the race and refused to give in. (5/1)

Suvalu (USA) went really well for most of the race, but failed to pick up sufficiently when pressure was applied. There are some moderate races from now on, and he should find his mark. (6/1)

3475 Undawaterscubadiva is on the lean side for this game, but he travels quite well, only failing to pick up when it matters. (13/8)

Tsanga, who had shown nothing previously, gave some signs of encouragement here and may well need further. (33/1)

3474 I'm Tyson (NZ), without the tongue-strap and dropped out this time, made some late headway without being knocked about and, if his problems can be sorted out, there is obviously plenty of ability there. (12/1: op 6/1)

3724 STANLEY CASINOS NOVICES' CHASE (5-Y.O+) (Class E)

2-40 (2-41) **3m 3f (21 fncs)** £2,770.00 (£835.00: £405.00: £190.00) GOING minus 0.56 sec per fur (F)

				SP	RR	SF
3393^{5}	**Miss Colette** (MrsDThomson) **9-10-11** MFoster (outpcd 12th: sn drvn along: hdwy 15th: led 3 out: styd on wl)	—	**1**	9/1^{3}	79	—
2954^{5}	**Cool Weather (IRE) (72)** (PCheesbrough) **9-11-2b** RSupple (a.p: ev ch 2 out: wknd last)	6	**2**	6/1^{2}	80	—
3306^{7}	**Tactix (63)** (MissMKMilligan) **7-10-11** BStorey (mstkes: prom: outpcd 5 out: styd on fr 3 out: no imp)	4	**3**	6/1^{2}	73	—
3436^{6}	**Fair Ally (70)** (MESowersby) **7-11-2** DParker (unruly s: s.s: j.rt: hdwy & prom 5 out: one pce fr 3 out)	4	**4**	6/1^{2}	76	—
3479^{P}	**Oaklands Billy** (MrsMReveley) **8-11-2** PNiven (led: hit 5 out: hdd & blnd 3 out: sn wknd)	18	**5**	9/1^{3}	65	—
3642^{U}	**Distillery Hill (IRE) (67)** (VThompson) **9-11-2** MrMThompson (chsd ldrs tl outpcd & lost pl 12th: drvn along & n.d after)	½	**6**	20/1	65	—
3370^{4}	**D'Arblay Street (IRE) (80)** (WTKemp) **8-11-8** RGarritty (chsd ldr tl mstke & stumbled 5 out: wknd qckly: p.u bef 3 out: dismntd: b.b.v)		**P**	6/5^{1}	—	—
				(SP 113.1%)		**7 Rn**

6m 55.5 (9.50) CSF £53.18 TOTE £11.60: £18.00 £7.20 (£21.80) OWNER Mr Robert Drysdale (MILNATHORT) BRED R. Drysdale

OFFICIAL EXPLANATION **D'Arblay Street (IRE): had bled from the nose.**

3393 Miss Colette is slow but sure and, in this moderate event, she won it purely by staying well. (9/1)

2954 Cool Weather (IRE) had his chances here but, when a real effort was required from the second last, he was never doing enough. (6/1)

3094 Tactix has ability but her jumping is iffy to say the least. (6/1)

2000 Fair Ally looks a real handful but, if he would settle down, races such as this could be found. (6/1)

Oaklands Billy looked a tearaway both in the paddock and in the race, and a blunder three out finally stopped him. (9/1)

3370 D'Arblay Street (IRE) (6/5: 5/4-evens)

3725 ROBIN AND JOHN SIMPSON MEMORIAL H'CAP CHASE (0-110) (5-Y.O+) (Class E)

3-10 (3-12) **2m 5f (16 fncs)** £2,967.50 (£830.00: £402.50) GOING minus 0.56 sec per fur (F)

				SP	RR	SF
2956^{P}	**The Toaster (95)** (MissMKMilligan) **10-10-13**$^{(3)}$ ECallaghan (hld up: chsd ldr fr 12th: rdn 4 out: led last: drvn out)	—	**1**	9/2^{3}	104	22
3610*	**Cross Cannon (109)** (JWade) **11-12-2** ^{6x} BStorey (lw: led: j.slowly 2nd & 3rd: rdn 2 out: hdd flat: no ex)	2	**2**	4/5^{1}	117	35
3532^{3}	**Twin Falls (IRE) (99)** (GMMoore) **6-11-6** JCallaghan (chsd ldr: mstke 2nd: outpcd fr 12th)	12	**3**	9/4^{2}	97	15
3645^{4}	***Risky Dee*** **(79)** (VThompson) **8-10-0** RSupple (Withdrawn not under Starter's orders: veterinary advice at s)		**W**	11/1	—	—
				(SP 112.8%)		**3 Rn**

5m 11.7 (0.70) CSF £7.32 TOTE £5.30 (£2.50) OWNER The Aunts (LEYBURN) BRED A. Redmond

LONG HANDICAP Risky Dee 9-7

1991 The Toaster did not impress on looks, but he stuck to his task well and this drop back in trip seemed to suit. (9/2)

3610* Cross Cannon, back at possibly his best trip, went well after two hesitant jumps early on, but his weight just anchored him in the closing stages. (4/5)

3532 Twin Falls (IRE) made the mistake of trying to take the pacemaker on, and was shaken off over the last five fences. (9/4)

3726 MARY REVELEY RACING CLUB NOVICES' CHASE (5-Y.O+) (Class E)

3-40 (3-40) **2m 5f (16 fncs)** £2,753.75 (£830.00: £402.50: £188.75) GOING minus 0.56 sec per fur (F)

				SP	RR	SF
3367*	**River Unshion (IRE) (98)** (HowardJohnson) **7-11-8** ADobbin (hld up: hdwy to ld 9th: blnd 12th: kpt on wl fr 2 out)	—	**1**	2/1^{1}	88	23
3479^{5}	**Most Rich (IRE) (67)** (BEllison) **9-10-13v**$^{(3)}$ ECallaghan (mde most to 9th: drvn along & chsd ldrs: kpt on wl fr 2 out)	2½	**2**	14/1	80	15
2923^{7}	**Dawn Lad (IRE) (77)** (MrsASwinbank) **8-11-8** JSupple (chsd ldrs: chal 12th: hrd rdn & disp 2nd whn hit last)	4	**3**	4/1^{3}	83	18
3138^{4}	**Le Denstan (80)** (MrsDThomson) **10-11-8** DParker (lw: prom tl outpcd 8th: hdwy & 4th whn blnd 11th: no imp after)	5	**4**	4/1^{3}	79	14
3608^{2}	**Master Flashman (73)** (MrsMReveley) **8-11-2** PNiven (w ldr tl mstke 4th: outpcd & blnd 10th: sn bhd)	dist	**5**	11/4^{2}	—	—
3546^{8}	**Parsons Belle (IRE)** (MrsCMBowman) **9-10-11** WFry (outpcd & lost tch 8th: p.u bef 2 out)		**P**	33/1	—	—
3608^{P}	**Ringrone (IRE)** (VThompson) **8-10-11** MrMThompson (hdwy to disp ld 5th: hdd & wknd 9th: p.u bef 4 out)		**P**	100/1	—	—
				(SP 110.6%)		**7 Rn**

5m 13.0 (2.00) CSF £23.55 TOTE £2.20: £1.50 £8.00 (£23.20) OWNER Mr R. J. Crake (CROOK) BRED Jerry Regan

3367* River Unshion (IRE), despite the fast ground and one really bad blunder, did the job in determined style. (2/1)

3479 Most Rich (IRE) seems to be getting it together at last and, although struggling some way out, he kept battling all the way to the line. (14/1)

2923 Dawn Lad (IRE) is coming back to form, but he did tend to jump to his right. (4/1)

3138 Le Denstan ran in snatches and made the odd blunder, and has plenty more ability when he really gets it right. (4/1)

3608 Master Flashman ran as though this might have come too soon, as his jumping left something to be desired. (11/4)

3727 STANLEY RACING GOLDEN NUMBERS SERIES NOVICES' HURDLE (4-Y.O+) (Class E)

4-10 (4-10) **2m 5f 110y (10 hdls)** £2,253.00 (£633.00: £309.00) GOING minus 0.56 sec per fur (F)

				SP	RR	SF
3324^{4}	**Harfdecent** (MrsMReveley) **6-11-2** PNiven (lw: cl up: chal 5th: led 3 out: hld on wl flat)	—	**1**	5/4^{1}	67	—
3324^{8}	**King Fly** (MrsSarahHorner-Harker) **7-11-2** MFoster (w ldr: led 5th to 3 out: chal & hit 2 out: disp ld last: no ex)	¾	**2**	33/1	66	—
2627^{6}	**Erni (FR)** (TPTate) **5-10-9**$^{(7)}$ RMcCarthy (chsd ldrs tl outpcd fr 4 out: kpt on fr 2 out: no imp)	23	**3**	9/2^{3}	49	—

3142[5] **Major Hage (IRE)** (HowardJohnson) **6-11-2** ADobbin (lw: hld up: smooth hdwy 4 out: effrt after 3 out: rdn & fnd nil)....7 **4** 4/1[2] 44 —
3449[6] **Busy Boy (59)** (DALamb) **10-10-9**(7) MissSLamb (mstkes: sn outpcd & bhd: styd on fr 3 out: n.d)....2½ **5** 100/1 42 —
3646[10] **Kings Minstral (IRE) (70)** (DALamb) **7-11-8** JBurke (chsd ldrs tl outpcd fr 4 out)....6 **6** 10/1 44 —
2918[P] **Bunny Buck (IRE)** (HowardJohnson) **7-11-2** MMoloney (sn outpcd & wl bhd: t.o fr 4 out)....dist **7** 50/1 — —
3100[P] **Al Jinn** (MartynWane) **6-11-2** BStorey (sn t.o: p.u bef 4 out).... **P** 33/1 — —
2503[9] **Our Wilma** (MrsDThomson) **8-10-11** OPears (prom tl wknd fr 4 out: p.u bef 2 out).... **P** 50/1 — —
3475[13] **Romaldkirk** (VThompson) **5-11-2** MrMThompson (outpcd & bhd fr ½-wy: p.u bef last).... **P** 100/1 — —
3438[7] **The Sharrow Legend (IRE) (73)** (JSisterson) **5-10-11**(5) STaylor (mde most tl blnd & hdd 5th: wknd 3 out: p.u bef last).... **P** 9/2[3] — —
(SP 121.7%) **11 Rn**

5m 8.7 (8.70) CSF £47.18 TOTE £2.20: £1.10 £5.30 £1.60 (£29.20) Trio £12.50 OWNER Mr A. G. Knowles (SALTBURN) BRED A. G. Knowles
3324 Harfdecent looked tremendously well, appreciated this trip and showed fine courage in a battle. (5/4: op 9/4)
King Fly put up a vastly-improved effort and looked to have the edge going to the last, but found one just too tough. (33/1)
1843 Erni (FR) looked well short of pace at a vital stage. (9/2)
3142 Major Hage (IRE) again travelled well but, once off the bit, his response was most disappointing. (4/1: 3/1-9/2)
Busy Boy looked slow and clumsy until picking up late on. (100/1)

3728 STANLEY RACING H'CAP HURDLE (0-115) (4-Y.O+) (Class E)
4-40 (4-40) **2m 1f (8 hdls)** £2,169.00 (£609.00: £297.00) GOING minus 0.56 sec per fur (F)

SP RR SF
3485[5] **Glenugie (90)** (GMMoore) **6-10-4** NBentley (outpcd & wl bhd ½-wy: hdwy after 3 out: styd on strly to ld flat).— **1** 2/1[1] 67 10
3478[2] **Fryup Satellite (88)** (MrsJBrown) **6-10-2** MissPRobson (lw: chsd ldr: led 5th: wl clr appr 2 out: rdn & hdd flat: no ex)....2½ **2** 3/1[2] 63 6
3199[3] **Our Kris (114)** (MESowersby) **5-12-0b** DParker (lw: led: rdn along appr 4th: hdd next: wknd 3 out)....27 **3** 9/2 63 6
3351[7] **Summerhill Special (IRE) (110)** (DWBarker) **6-11-10** JCallaghan (chsd ldrs tl rdn & btn appr 3 out)....¾ **4** 8/1 59 2
3346[13] **Bend Sable (IRE) (105)** (FSStorey) **7-11-5** BStorey (lw: hld up & bhd: effrt ½-wy: sn btn)....27 **5** 7/2[3] 28 —
(SP 109.8%) **5 Rn**

3m 55.1 (0.10) CSF £7.67 TOTE £2.00: £1.30 £2.10 (£5.40) OWNER Mr Frazer Hines (MIDDLEHAM) BRED F. Hines
3485 Glenugie likes this track and at last found his form, but it looked a hopeless task three out when he was virtually tailed off. He stuck to his task well and thoroughly deserved this. (2/1)
3478 Fryup Satellite looked the winner for a long way and was well clear over the penultimate flight, but the early pace then began to tell and he was picked off on the run-in. (3/1)
3199 Our Kris helped make this a really strong pace, but he had shot his bolt fully three flights out. (9/2)
3199 Summerhill Special (IRE) has disappointed since her first run of the season, and there was nothing to enthuse about here. (8/1)
3137 Bend Sable (IRE) has lost his way for the time being. (7/2)

T/Plpt: £251.40 (33.96 Tckts). T/Qdpt: £26.10 (16.43 Tckts) AA

3697-UTTOXETER (L-H) (Good to firm, Good patches)
Tuesday March 18th
Race 6: one flight omitted
WEATHER: showery

3729 KING STURGE H'CAP CHASE (0-110) (5-Y.O+) (Class E)
2-20 (2-20) **3m 2f (20 fncs)** £2,888.75 (£875.00: £427.50: £203.75) GOING minus 0.16 sec per fur (G)

SP RR SF
3622* **Sheelin Lad (IRE) (87)** (MrsTJMcInnesSkinner) **9-10-7** 6x TReed (hld up: hdwy 13th: mstke 15th: led 3 out: all out)....— **1** 5/1[3] 96 14
3349[4] **Sailor Jim (100)** (PTDalton) **10-11-6** CMaude (lw: j.w: led to 3 out: chal u.p last: unable qckn flat)....1 **2** 11/2 108 26
2665[6] **Lay it Off (IRE) (82)** (JGO'Neill) **8-10-2** SCurran (chsd ldr: ev ch tl wknd appr 2 out)....13 **3** 11/1 82 —
2916[P] **Uranus Collonges (FR) (105)** (JGFitzGerald) **11-11-11** KGaule (hld up: hdwy 8th: rdn 12th: wknd 15th: t.o) .18 **4** 16/1 94 12
Sheephaven (90) (DNicholson) **13-10-10** RJohnson (bkwd: chsd ldrs to 3 out: bhd whn p.u bef last).... **P** 7/2[2] — —
3361[3] **Dont Tell the Wife (108)** (CREgerton) **11-11-7**(7) MBerry (hld up & bhd: mstke 10th: reminders 12th: sn t.o: p.u bef 2 out).... **P** 3/1[1] — —
3573[5] **Top Brass (IRE) (99)** (KCBailey) **9-11-5** CO'Dwyer (prom: reminder 5th: lost pl 10th: bhd whn p.u bef 13th).... **P** 5/1[3] — —
3274[P] **Swiss Tactic (IRE) (80)** (AEJessop) **8-10-0** VSmith (trckd ldrs: lost pl 7th: t.o whn mstke 16th: p.u bef 2 out).... **P** 50/1 — —
(SP 112.1%) **8 Rn**

6m 38.2 (11.20) CSF £28.59 CT £258.66 TOTE £7.30: £2.00 £1.50 £1.80 (£13.30) OWNER Mrs T. J. McInnesSkinner (MELTON MOWBRAY) BRED Kenneth Parkhill
LONG HANDICAP Swiss Tactic (IRE) 8-12
OFFICIAL EXPLANATION Dont Tell the Wife: no explanation offered.
3622* Sheelin Lad (IRE) has found his form with a vengeance in the past few weeks and, though he had to work hard to defy a 6lb penalty, he always looked likely to do so. (5/1)
3349 Sailor Jim, still to succeed at this trip under Rules, gave an impressive display of front-running, and found extra under pressure on the run-in, but the concession of 13lb proved just too much. (11/2)
Lay it Off (IRE) (11/1: 8/1-12/1)
Sheephaven, out of action since May 1995, ran very well for almost three miles before having to admit lack of peak fitness taking its toll. He is certainly capable of winning more races. (7/2)
3361 Dont Tell the Wife, never happy on this lively ground, ran no race at all and is best put away until we get some rain. (3/1)

3730 GEO. HODGES & SON NOVICES' (S) HURDLE (4, 5 & 6-Y.O) (Class G)
2-50 (2-50) **2m (9 hdls)** £1,899.50 (£532.00: £258.50) GOING minus 0.16 sec per fur (G)

SP RR SF
3474* **Radmore Brandy (81)** (GRichards) **4-10-5**(3) GLee (lw: hld up in tch: led on bit 3 out: shkn up flat: comf)....— **1** 7/4[1] 68 4
Distant Storm (BJLlewellyn) **4-10-7** VSlattery (lw: chsd ldrs: ev ch fr 2 out: rdn appr last: rallied cl home)....1 **2** 25/1 66 2
3471[9] **Analogical** (DMcCain) **4-10-2** DWalsh (hld up: gd hdwy 6th: ev ch 3 out: rdn next: one pce flat)....4 **3** 25/1 57 —
3583* **Riverbank Rose (70)** (WClay) **6-10-13v**(3) GuyLewis (w ldr: rdn 2 out: wknd appr last)....4 **4** 4/1[2] 59 3

3542[2]	**Summer Villa (69)** (KGWingrove) **5-10-10b** KGaule (hld up & bhd: effrt appr 3 out: nt rch ldrs) 7	**5**	7/1	46	—
3677[4]	**El Bardador (IRE)** (RJHodges) **4-10-7** WMcFarland (hld up: nvr nr to chal) 3½	**6**	11/1	48	—
2050[3]	**How Could-I (IRE)** (ABailey) **4-10-2** WMarston (mde most tl hdd & mstke 3 out: sn btn) 1½	**7**	9/2 [3]	41	—
3548[12]	**Welsh Asset** (KGWingrove) **6-10-11**(7)ow3 MrAWintle (a in rr) 2½	**8**	16/1	47	—
3404[8]	**Witherkay** (PFNicholls) **4-10-2**(5) OBurrows (hld up: hdwy 5th: stumbled after next: sn lost tch) 1½	**9**	7/1	42	—
3352[U]	**Foreign Judgement (USA)** (WJMusson) **4-10-7** CMaude (a bhd: t.o) 20	**10**	25/1	22	—
3019[11]	**Tudor Falcon** (PBradley) **4-10-7b[1]** SWynne (hld up in rr: t.o fr 3 out) 6	**11**	14/1	16	—
3583[8]	**Stipple** (JAPickering) **6-10-10** JCulloty (bkwd: prom to 6th: sn wknd: t.o) 12	**12**	50/1	—	—
	Toat Chieftain (MissAEEmbiricos) **5-11-1** RJohnson (bkwd: hld up mid div: wknd appr 6th: t.o) 3½	**13**	33/1	1	—

(SP 136.9%) **13 Rn**

3m 49.7 (8.70) CSF £57.62 TOTE £2.60: £1.60 £3.40 £6.90 (£258.00) Trio £192.80; £247.12 to Exeter 19/3/97 OWNER Mr J. R. Salter (PENRITH) BRED W. D. Hockenhull
WEIGHT FOR AGE 4yo-8lb
Bt in 5,600 gns
3474* Radmore Brandy, full of running when nosing ahead three out, looked likely to win on the bridle, but the runner-up delivered a determined late challenge and she had to be kept up to her work in the closing stages. (7/4)
Distant Storm, fit from the Flat, made a very pleasing debut over hurdles, and he will hardly need to improve to pick up a similar event. (25/1)
1980 Analogical closed up going very easily turning in, and was soon poised to challenge, but the winner was always travelling that bit better, and she was fighting a lost cause on the run to the last. (25/1)
3583* Riverbank Rose intended to set the pace, but she was being matched all the way and, off the bridle early in the straight, had shot her bolt approaching the last. (4/1)
3542 Summer Villa, settled off the pace, began to stay on from the turn for home but, with the tempo not slacking, was unable to get to terms. (7/1)
3677 El Bardador (IRE) (11/1: op 7/1)

3731 MONTRACON H'CAP HURDLE (4-Y.O+) (Class B)
3-20 (3-20) **3m 110y (12 hdls)** £4,621.60 (£1,397.80: £681.40: £323.20) GOING minus 0.16 sec per fur (G)

			SP	RR	SF
3415[2]	**Smith Too (IRE) (112)** (MrsJPitman) **9-10-8** RFarrant (lw: mde all: drvn clr appr last: comf) ....—	**1**	10/11 [1]	86+	20
3415[4]	**Bankhead (IRE) (128)** (JLSpearing) **8-11-3**(7) MissCSpearing (chsd wnr most of wy: effrt 2 out: one pce appr last) 2½	**2**	3/1 [3]	100	34
2888[13]	**Lansdowne (120)** (PFNicholls) **9-11-2** APMcCoy (lw: hld up: j.slowly 4th: hdwy 9th: rdn 2 out: sn outpcd) 3½	**3**	5/2 [2]	90	24
3442[6]	**Fox Chapel (104)** (RTJuckes) **10-10-0** WMarston (hld up: rdn appr 8th: sn outpcd: t.o) ....dist	**4**	33/1	—	—

(SP 108.9%) **4 Rn**

5m 49.9 (7.90) CSF £3.73 TOTE £1.70 (£2.10) OWNER Smith Mansfield Meat Co Ltd (UPPER LAMBOURN) BRED Bobby McCarthy
LONG HANDICAP Fox Chapel 8-7
3415 Smith Too (IRE), opening his account for the season, was always calling the tune and only needed to keep up the gallop to win comfortably. (10/11: evens-11/10)
3415 Bankhead (IRE) was unable to turn the tables on the winner on 3lb better terms, but he never stopped trying, and a return to chasing could be the change he needs to get back to winning ways. (3/1)
1571 Lansdowne found the ground faster than he cares for, and the short-lived effort entering the straight came to little, as he was throwing out distress signals between the last two. (5/2)

3732 EXTERIOR PROFILES NOVICES' H'CAP CHASE (0-100) (5-Y.O+) (Class E)
3-50 (3-50) **2m 4f (15 fncs)** £3,018.75 (£915.00: £447.50: £213.75) GOING minus 0.16 sec per fur (G)

			SP	RR	SF
3051[P]	**Quite A Man (83)** (SABrookshaw) **9-11-10** CMaude (trckd ldrs: led after 7th to next: led last: lft clr) ....—	**1**	10/1	92	—
3571[6]	**Heathyards Boy (67)** (DMcCain) **7-10-8b** DWalsh (lw: lft in ld after 1st: hdd 3rd: mstke 5th: led 8th tl hdd & blnd last) 5	**2**	7/1	72	—
3470[4]	**Another Comedy (67)** (RLee) **7-10-8** RJohnson (chsd ldrs: j.b lft 4 out & 3 out: sn outpcd) 22	**3**	12/1	54	—
3472[F]	**Astral Invasion (USA) (78)** (TWall) **6-11-2**(3) RMassey (chsd ldrs: rdn & lost pl 10th: n.d after) 1¼	**4**	16/1	64	—
3408[P]	**Ainsi Soit Il (FR) (73)** (GMMcCourt) **6-10-11b**(3) DFortt (led 3rd tl after 7th: wknd 9th) 2½	**5**	9/2 [2]	57	—
3201[5]	**Alaskan Heir (72)** (AStreeter) **6-10-13** TEley (bhd: mstke 7th: hdwy 11th: wknd appr 3 out) 2½	**6**	10/1	54	—
3582[4]	**Total Asset (72)** (ALForbes) **7-10-13v** GaryLyons (chsd ldrs: mstke 9th: sn rdn: 5th & btn whn fell 4 out)	**F**	11/2 [3]	—	—
3591*	**After The Fox (87)** (NJHawke) **10-11-7**(7) 7x MrJTizzard (hld up in tch: smooth hdwy 11th: chal & fell 3 out)	**F**	3/1 [1]	—	—
2892[U]	**Curragh Peter (72)** (MrsPBickerton) **10-10-10**(3) GuyLewis (led: j.b lft 1st: sn hdd: p.u bef next)	**P**	11/1	—	—
1472[7]	**Sweet Buck (61)** (RCPugh) **8-10-2**ow1 MSharratt (bkwd: bdly hmpd 1st: blnd & uns rdr next)	**U**	50/1	—	—

(SP 113.1%) **10 Rn**

5m 0.1 CSF £69.33 CT £771.88 TOTE £15.20: £4.70 £1.60 £1.90 (£46.90) Trio £155.60 OWNER Mr W. R. J. Everall (SHREWSBURY) BRED R. Everall
OFFICIAL EXPLANATION **Quite A Man: regarding the impovement in form, the trainer reported that the gelding needs good to firm ground.**
1814 Quite A Man, never far away, got the better of his battle with the runner-up at the last and, with that rival all but departing the scene, was able to stretch clear without much difficulty. (10/1: 7/1-11/1)
3187 Heathyards Boy handled the ground surprisingly well and, making the best of his way home, looked to be coming off second best when a last fence blunder all but severed the partnership. (7/1)
359 Another Comedy again gave away considerable ground in the latter stages by jumping violently left, and he was struggling to hold on from the turn for home. (12/1: op 8/1)
3591* After The Fox, waiting on the leaders, moved up effortlessly entering the straight and he was still running away and challenging for the lead when he capsized on landing at the third last. He would have won in a canter and deserves to find consolation.(3/1: op 2/1)

3733 STREBEL BOILERS & RADIATORS NOVICES' CONDITIONAL H'CAP HURDLE (0-100) (4-Y.O+) (Class E)
4-20 (4-20) **2m (9 hdls)** £2,316.00 (£651.00: £318.00) GOING minus 0.16 sec per fur (G)

			SP	RR	SF
3102[7]	**Kildrummy Castle (74)** (JGFitzGerald) **5-10-5** FLeahy (a.p: led on bit 3 out: rdn appr last: hld on) ....—	**1**	20/1	56	9
3186[P]	**Country Minstrel (IRE) (70)** (SADouch) **6-10-1** CRae (hld up: hdwy 6th: outpcd appr last: r.o strly towards fin) ....½	**2**	16/1	52	5
3429*	**Galway Boss (IRE) (75)** (IPWilliams) **5-10-6** TDascombe (hld up: hdwy appr 3 out: rdn & r.o wl cl home) ....¾	**3**	5/1 [3]	56	9
3325[4]	**Cliburnel News (IRE) (78)** (ALForbes) **7-10-9** PHenley (chsd ldrs: rdn 6th: rallied appr last: unable qckn flat)nk	**4**	12/1	58	11
3406[7]	**Apollono (70)** (RLee) **5-10-1** GLee (hld up: hdwy 3 out: rdn appr last: one pce) 1¾	**5**	9/1	49	2

			SP	RR	SF
3283^{2}	**Beechfield Flyer (85)** (WClay) **6-11-2** GuyLewis (w ldr: led 4th to 3 out: rdn & one pce appr last) ....¾	**6**	9/2^{2}	63	16
3158^{6}	**Barton Scamp (93)** (SABrookshaw) **5-11-10** XAizpuru (prom: ev ch appr 2 out: sn rdn & outpcd) 1½	**7**	4/1^{1}	69	22
3429^{P}	**Millenium Lass (IRE) (77)** (MissMERowland) **9-10-8** DJKavanagh (hld up: hdwy 5th: ev ch appr last: wknd flat) 2½	**8**	33/1	51	4
3594^{9}	**Moonlight Escapade (IRE) (77)** (RJHodges) **6-10-4**$^{(4)}$ JHarris (nvr trbld ldrs) 2	**9**	11/1	49	2
3234^{3}	**The Brewer (73)** (JCTuck) **5-10-4** DFortt (led to 4th: wknd 3 out) 3½	**10**	6/1	41	—
3287^{9}	**Gulf of Siam (78)** (JMackie) **4-10-1** EHusband (a bhd: t.o) 12	**11**	11/1	34	—
3473^{5}	**Out of The Blue (69)** (MWEckley) **5-9-10v**$^{(4)}$ JMogford (trckd ldrs to 6th: sn wknd: t.o) ....½	**12**	40/1	25	—
3338^{7}	**Them Times (IRE) (69)** (FJordan) **8-9-7**$^{(7)}$ RHodges (chsd ldrs to 6th: sn rdn & wknd: t.o) 2	**13**	40/1	23	—
3569^{P}	**Starlight Fool (73)** (KCBailey) **8-10-0b**$^{(4)}$ WWalsh (a bhd: t.o) 10	**14**	33/1	17	—
			(SP 124.9%)		**14 Rn**

3m 47.9 (6.90) CSF £271.93 CT £1,695.42 TOTE £20.00: £4.70 £6.20 £2.40 (£268.60) Trio £623.80; £43.93 to Exeter 19/3/97 OWNER The Kildrummy Partnership (MALTON) BRED J. B. H. Stevens
LONG HANDICAP Them Times (IRE) 9-2
WEIGHT FOR AGE 4yo-8lb
OFFICIAL EXPLANATION **Kildrummy Castle: regarding the improvement in form, the trainer reported that the gelding had had a wind operation prior to his last run and the ground appeared to suit him here.**
Kildrummy Castle, taking a step down in distance, travelled like a winner throughout. Once in front from three out, he had to battle but always appeared to hold all the aces. (20/1)
1984 Country Minstrel (IRE) is an in-and-out performer, but this is a step up on what he has achieved so far, and he has got the ability to win a race. (16/1)
3429* Galway Boss (IRE) timed his effort to perfection last time, but he just misjudged it here, though to be fair he was tackling stronger opposition. (5/1)
3325 Cliburnel News (IRE) looked to be in trouble when bustled along at the end of the back straight, but she picked up well once in line for home, and was in pursuit of the winner until running out of puff nearing the finish. (12/1)
Apollono winner of two one-mile events on the Flat but so far struggling to make the frame over hurdles, was within striking range at the last but, failing to respond to pressure, was always being held. (9/1)
3283 Beechfield Flyer, sharing the lead to the third last, kept staying on, but his measure had been taken on the run to the final flight. (9/2)
3158 Barton Scamp ran much better than his finishing position might suggest, and he was only shaken off between the last two. (4/1: op 5/2)

3734 SQ MAGAZINE 'N.H.' NOVICES' HURDLE (4-Y.O+) (Class D)
4-50 (4-50) **2m 4f 110y (9 hdls)** £3,044.00 (£859.00: £422.00) GOING minus 0.16 sec per fur (G)

			SP	RR	SF
3441^{F}	**Dictum (IRE)** (MissHCKnight) **6-11-2** JCulloty (chsd ldrs: chal last: sn led: all out) ....—	**1**	9/1	82?	33
3426*	**Silver Thyne (IRE) (105)** (MrsJPitman) **5-11-9** DLeahy (lw: led & sn clr: blnd last: sn hdd: rallied nr fin) ....nk	**2**	7/4^{1}	89	40
3171^{7}	**Man of The Match** (MrsJPitman) **7-11-2** RFarrant (bit bkwd: prom tl outpcd appr 3 out: kpt on towards fin)...21	**3**	16/1	65	16
2805^{6}	**Pot Black Uk** (PJHobbs) **6-11-2** JFrost (lw: hld up: hdwy appr 3 out: rdn & wknd appr last) 4	**4**	12/1	62	13
3345^{F}	**Dan de Man (IRE)** (MissLCSiddall) **6-11-2** CMaude (hld up: nvr plcd to chal) 6	**5**	50/1	58	9
3042^{9}	**Bellidium** (AEJessop) **5-10-11** TKent (a bhd: t.o) 10	**6**	100/1	45	—
	Sidney (JCMcConnochie) **8-11-2** SWynne (bkwd: a bhd: t.o) 12	**7**	100/1	40	—
3423^{P}	**Mistress Tudor** (SMellor) **6-10-11** NMann (lw: a bhd: t.o fr 3 out) 8	**8**	100/1	29	—
3437^{2}	**Charley Lambert (IRE)** (JMackie) **6-10-13**$^{(3)}$ EHusband (lw: carried out & b.d 1st)	**B**	7/2^{3}	—	—
3399^{3}	**Strong Tel (IRE)** (MCPipe) **7-11-2** APMcCoy (rn out, crashed thro wing & fell 1st)	**F**	3/1^{2}	—	—
3189^{P}	**Kyle David (IRE)** (FJordan) **5-10-13**$^{(3)}$ GuyLewis (prom: rdn & lost pl 5th: t.o whn p.u bef next)	**P**	100/1	—	—
2642^{8}	**Gwithian** (NJHawke) **5-11-2** JRailton (bit bkwd: in rr tl p.u bef 5th)	**P**	100/1	—	—
			(SP 114.1%)		**12 Rn**

4m 49.0 (5.00) CSF £22.89 TOTE £8.00: £2.50 £1.50 £2.60 (£13.20) Trio £37.60 OWNER Mrs R. A. Humphries (WANTAGE) BRED Mrs V. P. Bowen
3441 Dictum (IRE), a drifter in the market, appreciated these more patient tactics and, taking advantage of the favourite's blunder at the last, found the line arriving not a stride too soon. (9/1: op 5/1)
3426* Silver Thyne (IRE) put the emphasis on stamina and always appeared to have the situation under control, but he was fortunate to find a leg after a bad mistake at the last, and the fact that he was only beaten in a photo shows what an unlucky loser he was. (7/4)
Man of The Match, a tall gelding who still looks to have something left to work on, performed with credit and is gradually getting his act together. (16/1)
2805 Pot Black Uk, trying a longer trip and given plenty of time to warm up, looked likely to get himself into contention when making progress early in the straight, but the principals got away from him and he lost out in the battle for the minor places on the run-in. (12/1: op 8/1)
3399 Strong Tel (IRE) had a rival on his outside going into the first, but he made a beeline for the wing and, carrying that rival with him, they both finished up on the floor. (3/1: 5/2-4/1)

T/Jkpt: Not won; £22,291.98 to Exeter 19/3/97. T/Plpt: £1,537.60 (12.63 Tckts). T/Qdpt: £380.80 (2.35 Tckts) IM

3535-EXETER (R-H) (Good to firm, Good in places)
Wednesday March 19th
WEATHER: overcast with sunny intervals

3735 ROBERT WEBB TRAVEL NOVICES' (S) HURDLE (4,5,6 & 7-Y.O) (Class G)
2-20 (2-20) **2m 2f (8 hdls)** £1,940.90 (£537.40: £256.70) GOING: 0.39 sec per fur (GS)

			SP	RR	SF
3050^{8}	**Fleet Cadet (87)** (MCPipe) **6-10-11v**$^{(5)}$ GSupple (lw: hld up & bhd: j.slowly 3rd: rapid hdwy 6th: led after 2 out: clr last: easily) ....—	**1**	8/13^{1}	63+	4
3590^{6}	**Rose of Glenn** (BPalling) **6-10-11** TJenks (prom: chsd ldr 3rd: led after 6th: hdd after 2 out: wknd after last)..8	**2**	6/1^{3}	51	—
3683^{14}	**Seminole Wind (54)** (CRBarwell) **6-11-2v** BPowell (led tl after 6th: wknd appr last) 6	**3**	16/1	51	—
3499^{P}	**Prove The Point (IRE) (60)** (MrsPNDutfield) **4-10-3** PHolley (mid div: hdwy to chse ldr after 6th: wkng & mstke 2 out) 7	**4**	10/1	39	—
	Across the Bow (USA) (64) (AJKDunn) **7-11-2** GTormey (bit bkwd: in tch: rdn 5th: wknd next) ....¾	**5**	14/1	44	—
3536^{P}	**Rapid Liner** (RJBaker) **4-10-8** VSlattery (lost pl 2nd: hdwy 4th: wknd appr 2 out) 2	**6**	33/1	42	—
3541^{7}	**Deceit the Second (49)** (PRRodford) **5-11-2** SBurrough (in tch to 5th: steadily wknd) 5	**7**	50/1	37	—
3442^{P}	**Seven Crowns (USA) (61)** (CLPopham) **4-10-5v**$^{1(3)}$ TDascombe (bit bkwd: in tch to 5th: steadily wknd).......3½	**8**	33/1	34	—

	Horse / details	Dist	Pos	SP	RR	SF
	Tales Of Hearsay (GER) (89) (CFCJackson) **7-10-11**(5) OBurrows (bit bkwd: bhd: hdwy 5th: rdn & wknd appr 2 out)	12	**9**	11/2[2]	24	—
3500[15]	**Beweldered** (RGFrost) **5-11-2** JFrost (chsd ldr to 3rd: wknd 5th: p.u bef 2 out)		**P**	25/1	—	—
3590[P]	**Chalcuchima** (NJHawke) **4-10-8b[1]** JRailton (prom to 5th: wknd after next: bhd whn blnd & uns rdr last)		**U**	50/1	—	—
				(SP 126.9%)	**11 Rn**	

4m 31.6 (21.60) CSF £4.86 TOTE £1.50: £1.20 £1.70 £2.60 (£3.30) Trio £9.90 OWNER Sir John Swaine (WELLINGTON) BRED R. D. Hollingsworth
WEIGHT FOR AGE 4yo-8lb
No bid
2813 Fleet Cadet, disappointing last time out, was back in a favourable grade here. His only two wins have come on a much softer surface, but he took this poor event with ease. (8/13)
2818 Rose of Glenn can find a similar bad seller within her capabilities, but may prefer a softer surface. (6/1)
Seminole Wind ran his best race to date over obstacles, and showing up well for most of the way, just weakened in the closing stages. (16/1)
1413 Prove The Point (IRE) has shown a glimpse of ability in the past. (10/1)
Across the Bow (USA) put in a promising reappearance after being off for over two years. (14/1: op 7/1)

3736 AXWORTHYS' LTD NOVICES' H'CAP CHASE (0-100) (5-Y.O+) (Class E)
2-50 (2-50) **2m 7f 110y (17 fncs)** £4,337.50 (£1,300.00: £625.00: £287.50) GOING: 0.39 sec per fur (GS)

	Horse / details	Dist	Pos	SP	RR	SF
3495[3]	**Trust Deed (USA) (74)** (SGKnight) **9-10-2b**(5) DSalter (lw: a.p: chsd ldr 5th: led 3 out: clr last: comf)	—	**1**	14/1	88+	21
3488[8]	**Cardinal Gayle (IRE) (67)** (RHAlner) **7-10-0** JRKavanagh (bhd: styd on fr 13th: nrst fin)	10	**2**	14/1	74	7
2947[4]	**Claymore Lad (70)** (JSKing) **7-10-3** TJMurphy (lw: led to 12th: ev ch 2 out: sn wknd)	2½	**3**	4/1[1]	76	9
3016[P]	**Mendip Prince (IRE) (82)** (PJHobbs) **7-11-1** GTormey (mstke 2nd: hdwy 13th: nvr nrr)	12	**4**	6/1[3]	79	12
3188[4]	**Winnow (69)** (AndrewTurnell) **7-10-2** CRae (chsd ldrs: in tch tl outpcd 13th)	1	**5**	9/1	66	—
3495[F]	**Purbeck Rambler (67)** (GBBalding) **6-10-0v** BFenton (a mid div: nvr trbld ldrs)	½	**6**	15/2	63	—
3178[P]	**Charlie Bee (67)** (RHBuckler) **8-10-0** BPowell (bit bkwd: in tch tl wknd appr 10th: t.o 14th)	23	**7**	33/1	48	—
3173[7]	**Volleyball (IRE) (72)** (PRHedger) **8-10-5b[1]** MRichards (mid div: hdwy to ld 12th: hdd 3 out: wknd qckly next)	15	**8**	14/1	42	—
3591[2]	**Mozemo (84)** (MCPipe) **10-11-3** CMaude (a bhd: t.o whn p.u bef 14th)		**P**	9/2[2]	—	—
	Philatelic (IRE) (85) (RHAlner) **6-11-4** JRailton (bit bkwd: chsd ldrs tl wknd 12th: p.u bef 2 out)		**P**	14/1	—	—
752[U]	**River Gala (IRE) (68)** (RJHodges) **7-10-1** PHolley (disp ld 1st: prom to 10th: t.o whn p.u bef 14th)		**P**	9/1	—	—
3354[P]	**King's Courtier (IRE) (67)** (SMellor) **8-10-0** NMann (bit bkwd: in tch to 11th: steadily wknd: t.o whn p.u bef 14th)		**P**	33/1	—	—
3495*	**Full of Bounce (IRE) (94)** (RJHodges) **6-11-10**(3) TDascombe (a.p: 3rd whn blnd & uns rdr 12th)		**U**	7/1	—	—
3060[4]	**Dunlir (70)** (PRRodford) **7-10-3**ow[1] SBurrough (hdwy 11th: blnd & uns rdr next)		**U**	33/1	—	—
				(SP 132.2%)	**14 Rn**	

6m 7.6 (20.60) CSF £188.04 CT £863.56 TOTE £13.30: £2.70 £4.20 £2.00 (£72.10) Trio £138.50 OWNER Mr Malcolm Enticott (TAUNTON) BRED Ballymacoll Stud Farm Inc
LONG HANDICAP Cardinal Gayle (IRE) 9-13 Purbeck Rambler 9-12 Charlie Bee 9-12
3495 Trust Deed (USA), a winner four times here over hurdles, has had numerous chances over fences and finally came good in a woeful contest. (14/1)
3189 Cardinal Gayle (IRE), making his chasing debut, stayed on from way back and is not without hope. (14/1)
2947 Claymore Lad, who tried to make all, plugged on at one pace once headed. (4/1)
3188 Winnow (9/1: op 6/1)
2643 Volleyball (IRE), nibbled at in the market, looked set to collect when cruising to the front but weakened very quickly. He might be worth another chance over shorter. (14/1: op 25/1)
3495* Full of Bounce (IRE) (7/1: 5/1-15/2)

3737 AXWORTHYS' COMPUTER SUPPLIES H'CAP HURDLE (0-125) (4-Y.O+) (Class D)
3-20 (3-21) **3m 2f (13 hdls)** £3,034.50 (£842.00: £403.50) GOING: 0.39 sec per fur (GS)

	Horse / details	Dist	Pos	SP	RR	SF
3600[18]	**Snow Board (93)** (MrsMerritaJones) **8-10-9** DerekByrne (lw: hld up: hdwy 11th: led 2 out: hld on gamely flat)	—	**1**	9/2[2]	74	38
3604*	**St Ville (93)** (RHBuckler) **11-10-9** 5x BPowell (lw: prom tl lost pl 11th: rdn & rallied appr 2 out: ev ch last: rdn out: jst failed)	hd	**2**	12/1	74	38
3499[3]	**Ehtefaal (USA) (95)** (JSKing) **6-10-11** TJMurphy (hdwy 7th: in tch & rdn after 7th: ev ch last: wknd flat)	2½	**3**	3/1[1]	74	38
3499[5]	**Apachee Flower (84)** (HSHowe) **7-10-0** GTormey (a.p: ev ch appr last: sn wknd)	11	**4**	16/1	57	21
3112*	**Maid Equal (108)** (MCPipe) **6-11-5**(5) GSupple (bhd: mstke 4th: in tch appr 2 out: one pce)	½	**5**	3/1[1]	80	44
3362[8]	**Derring Bridge (84)** (MrsSMJohnson) **7-9-9**(5) MrRThornton (chsd ldr tl led 5th to 7th: led briefly appr 2 out: sn wknd)	4	**6**	14/1	54	18
3551[F]	**Kendal Cavalier (102)** (GBBalding) **7-11-4v** BFenton (bhd fr 7th)	3½	**7**	12/1	70	34
3566[4]	**Doctor Green (FR) (113)** (MCPipe) **4-11-5v** MRichards (led to 5th: led 7th tl hdd appr 2 out: wknd qckly: p.u flat)		**P**	8/1[3]	—	—
221[5]	**Same Difference (IRE) (97)** (GMMcCourt) **9-10-10**(3) DFortt (bit bkwd: bhd 6th: sn t.o: p.u bef 10th)		**P**	25/1	—	—
3537[U]	**Secret Bid (IRE) (96)** (RHAlner) **7-10-12** JRKavanagh (chsd ldrs tl rdn 11th: sn wknd: p.u flat)		**P**	14/1	—	—
				(SP 117.7%)	**10 Rn**	

6m 27.0 (17.00) CSF £51.72 CT £171.60 TOTE £6.40: £1.70 £2.80 £1.50 (£44.50) Trio £21.80 OWNER Mr F. J. Sainsbury (LAMBOURN) BRED Juddmonte Farms
LONG HANDICAP St Ville 10-9 Derring Bridge 9-12 Apachee Flower 9-3
WEIGHT FOR AGE 4yo-10lb
STEWARDS' ENQUIRY Murphy susp. 29 & 31/3 & 1-2/4/97 (excessive use of whip).
3016 Snow Board was back in an easier grade after his Festival exertions. He has shown good improvement this season and quite a liking for this ground, and connections may give him a summer campaign over the larger obstacles. (9/2)
3604* St Ville is not always in the mood, but is in good heart at present and put in another fine display, only losing out on the run-in. (12/1)
3499 Ehtefaal (USA) deserves to find a similar event on this performance after so many placed efforts. (3/1)
3499 Apachee Flower ran well from out of the handicap, and can find an opportunity in a lower grade. (16/1)
2761 Derring Bridge (14/1: 10/1-16/1)
3400 Kendal Cavalier (12/1: op 8/1)
3566 Doctor Green (FR) (8/1: op 5/1)

3738 HEAVITREE BREWERY CHALLENGE CUP H'CAP CHASE (0-130) (5-Y.O+) (Class C)
3-50 (3-50) **2m 2f (12 fncs)** £4,919.00 (£1,472.00: £706.00: £323.00) GOING: 0.39 sec per fur (GS)

				SP	RR	SF
3225*	**Thumbs Up (127)** (GMMcCourt) **11-11-4**(7) RHobson (hdwy to chse ldr 8th: led 3 out: clr last: easily)	—	1	9/4 2	135	35
20 2	**Polden Pride (113)** (GBBalding) **9-10-11** BFenton (bhd: in tch: wnt 2nd appr last: r.o flat)	1¼	2	5/2 3	120+	20
3538 2	**Alpine Song (102)** (MissVAStephens) **12-10-0** MissVStephens (led to 3rd: led 4th to 8th: one pce 3 out)	5	3	33/1	104	4
2621 2	**Fine Harvest (122)** (JLSpearing) **11-11-6** TJMurphy (lw: chsd ldr tl led 3rd: hdd next: led 8th: hdd 3 out: mstke next: outpcd appr last)	18	4	5/4 1	108	8
				(SP 106.7%)	**4 Rn**	

4m 37.3 (16.30) CSF £7.20 TOTE £3.00 (£2.40) OWNER Mrs B. Taylor (WANTAGE) BRED Peader McCoy
LONG HANDICAP Alpine Song 7-10
STEWARDS' ENQUIRY Fenton susp. 29 & 31/3, 1-5/4 & 7/4/97 (failure to obtain best possible placing).
3225* Thumbs Up is a consistent sort who is in good heart at present. He now goes to Fairyhouse for the Irish National meeting where, if the ground conditions are good, he will take part in the Dan Moore Memorial Chase. (9/4)
20 Polden Pride put in a very good performance after a lengthy lay-off, and may have finished closer if set to work earlier on the run-in. He can certainly go on to find a race on this effort. (5/2)
3538 Alpine Song showed up well in this step-up in class, and would seem to be improving.. (33/1)
2621 Fine Harvest likes to control the race from the front, but was never able to do that here. With a more appropriate track for his front-running style and a clean round of jumping, he can soon make amends. (5/4)

3739 ROBERT WEBB TRAVEL HUNTERS' CHASE (5-Y.O+) (Class H)
4-20 (4-21) **3m 2f (19 fncs)** £1,568.60 (£434.60: £207.80) GOING: 0.39 sec per fur (GS)

				SP	RR	SF
	Tinotops (MrsRAVickery) **7-11-10**(7) MissSVickery (a.p: chsd ldr 11th tl led 14th: clr 3 out: unchal)	—	1	5/2 1	107	37
3341 4	**Sirisat** (MissTOBlazey) **13-11-10**(7) MissTBlazey (lw: chsd ldrs: styd on fr 3 out: nrst fin)	12	2	20/1	100	30
3432*	**The Malakarma** (MissCSaunders) **11-12-5**(5) MrBPollock (lw: a.p: led 11th: hdd 14th: outpcd 3 out)	1	3	100/30 2	106	36
3341*	**Rusty Bridge** (MrsSMJohnson) **10-12-3**(7) MrRBurton (lw: led to 11th: wknd 15th)	14	4	9/1	97	27
	Brabazon (USA) (MrsEScott) **12-11-10**(7) MrJScott (a bhd: lost tch 11th)	21	5	50/1	78	8
	Baron's Heir (RELivermore) **10-11-10**(7) MrSLloyd (bit bkwd: a bhd: wknd 11th: styd on one pce fr 16th)	5	6	20/1	74	4
3490 2	**Fiddlers Pike** (MrsRGHenderson) **16-11-10**(7) MrsRHenderson (b.d 1st)		B	14/1	—	—
3593*	**Full Alirt** (MissSusanYoung) **9-11-12**(7) MissSYoung (chsd ldrs tl wknd 10th: t.o whn p.u bef 16th)		P	6/1	—	—
	Knifeboard (PaulHosgood) **11-11-12**(5) MrAFarrant (lw: a.p: ev ch 13th tl wknd 17th: p.u bef 2 out)		P	25/1	—	—
	Miles More Fun (ERetter) **8-11-5**(7) MrLJefford (lw: in tch tl wknd 15th: p.u bef next)		P	4/1 3	—	—
	More Manners (MissMBragg) **12-11-10**(7) MrJCreighton (bkwd: prom: chsd ldr 10th to 11th: j.slowly next: sn wknd: t.o & p.u after 15th)		P	50/1	—	—
	Silver Age (USA) (MrsCDay) **11-11-10**(7) MissPCooper (blnd & uns rdr 1st)		U	100/1	—	—
				(SP 120.9%)	**12 Rn**	

6m 52.4 (25.40) CSF £50.98 TOTE £4.80: £1.50 £4.70 £1.50 (£51.20) Trio £83.10 OWNER Mr R. H. H. Targett (YEOVIL) BRED F. H. Gilman
Tinotops scored well here on his debut under Rules. He is a good jumper, is improving fast and is certainly one to consider in future events. (5/2)
3341 Sirisat has shown little under Rules, but was staying on well in the closing stages. (20/1)
3432* The Malakarma, a deserved favourite on current form, should not be hard to place for a return to winning ways. (100/30)
3341* Rusty Bridge prefers more cut in the ground than he encountered here, and a greater test of stamina. (9/1: op 6/1)
3490 Fiddlers Pike (14/1: 8/1-16/1)

3740 ROBERT WEBB TRAVEL H'CAP HURDLE (0-115) (4-Y.O+) (Class E)
4-50 (4-50) **2m 2f (8 hdls)** £2,444.80 (£677.80: £324.40) GOING: 0.39 sec per fur (GS)

				SP	RR	SF
3539*	**Cool Gunner (92)** (JSKing) **7-11-10** CMaude (lw: hld up & bhd: stdy hdwy 6th: led appr last: qcknd clr flat)	—	1	7/4 1	77+	17
3344 2	**Handson (90)** (BRMillman) **5-11-3**(5) DSalter (lw: a in tch: lft 2nd 6th: led appr 2 out: hdd appr last: rdn & outpcd flat)	3	2	3/1 3	72	12
299 5	**Commanche Creek (80)** (MissJduPlessis) **7-10-9**(3) SophieMitchell (led after 1st tl hdd appr 2 out: rdn & wknd appr last)	4	3	8/1	59	—
3536 5	**Rory'm (IRE) (68)** (LWaring) **8-9-7b**(7) MGriffiths (chsd ldr tl mstke 4th: wknd next: sn t.o)	dist	4	66/1	—	—
3012 3	**Bietschhorn Bard (90)** (DRGandolfo) **7-11-5b**(3) DFortt (a.p: 2nd & ev ch whn fell 6th)		F	11/4 2	—	—
1993 5	**Borjito (SPA) (80)** (CRBarwell) **6-10-12** BFenton (led tl after 1st: blnd next: p.u bef 3rd)		P	10/1	—	—
3589 6	**Concinnity (USA) (68)** (BScriven) **8-9-9**(5) GSupple (blnd & uns rdr 1st)		U	33/1	—	—
				(SP 112.7%)	**7 Rn**	

4m 30.1 (20.10) CSF £6.79 TOTE £2.50: £2.00 £1.50 (£2.90) OWNER Mr Richard Peterson (SWINDON) BRED R. Burton
LONG HANDICAP Rory'm (IRE) 9-6 Concinnity (USA) 9-12
3539* Cool Gunner seemed to handle this firmer surface well to record a quick repeat course and distance win. He will go over fences next term. (7/4: op evens)
3344 Handson put in a good effort, but met a decent rival in the winner. He can find a race on this performance. (3/1)
75 Commanche Creek probably found this distance stretching him a little after such a lay-off, and should be noted when running over the minimum trip. (8/1)

T/Jkpt: £6,362.00 (5.62 Tckts). T/Plpt: £39.00 (391.99 Tckts). T/Qdpt: £9.90 (69.31 Tckts) T

3359-LUDLOW (R-H) (Good to firm, Good patches)
Wednesday March 19th
WEATHER: fine but overcast

3741 SEIFTON CLAIMING HURDLE (4-Y.O+) (Class F)
2-00 (2-00) **2m (9 hdls)** £2,094.00 (£584.00: £282.00) GOING minus 0.49 sec per fur (GF)

				SP	RR	SF
3184P	**Chief Mouse (105)** (MissHCKnight) **4-11-3** JFTitley (chsd ldr: led after 6th to 2 out: led last: rdn out)	—	1	4/5 1	65	—
2943U	**Night Boat (71)** (WClay) **6-10-13**(3) GuyLewis (hld up: hdwy 5th: led 2 out to last: sn rdn: one pce)	2½	2	5/1 2	54	—
1875P	**Anlace (80)** (SMellor) **8-10-10**(5) ChrisWebb (trckd ldrs: rdn & ev ch whn hit 3 out: sn btn)	3	3	8/1	50	—

				SP	RR	SF
3131[7]	**Dr Dave (IRE) (70)** (PRChamings) **6-11-8** AThornton (plld hrd: chsd ldrs tl wknd appr 2 out)	10	**4**	12/1	47	—
2952[10]	**Re Roi (IRE) (95)** (WGMTurner) **5-10-11**(7) NWillmington (hld up in rr: hdwy after 6th: one pce fr 3 out)	6	**5**	7/1[3]	37	—
3471[8]	**Kings Vision (60)** (WJenks) **5-11-0** DWalsh (t: bhd whn blnd 4th: sn t.o)	dist	**6**	50/1	—	—
3583[11]	**Bold Time Monkey** (MTate) **6-10-9** CLlewellyn (bit bkwd: a bhd: t.o)	8	**7**	50/1	—	—
	Double Vintage (IRE) (MCChapman) **4-10-9** WWorthington (nt j.w: t.o fr 5th)		**8**	66/1	—	—
3677[7]	**Vital Wonder** (JParfitt) **9-10-5**(7) XAizpuru (bit bkwd: plld hrd: led tl after 6th: sn wknd: no ch whn blnd & uns rdr last)		**U**	50/1	—	—
				(SP 110.9%)	**9 Rn**	

3m 43.5 (6.50) CSF £4.29 TOTE £1.50: £1.10 £1.40 £2.10 (£2.20) Trio £6.20 OWNER Lady Vestey (WANTAGE) BRED Lady Vestey
WEIGHT FOR AGE 4yo-8lb
Chief Mouse clmd WTGavin £8,000
OFFICIAL EXPLANATION **Chief Mouse: regarding the improvement in form, the trainer reported that the gelding was suited by today's drop in class and the faster ground.**
2872 Chief Mouse, racing on a more favourable surface, looked to have a fight on his hands in the latter stages, but he quickened up readily on the flat and soon put the issue beyond doubt. (4/5: 10/11-evens)
1118 Night Boat would have gone close to winning with a clear round at this venue last month, and he briefly looked likely to make amends when gaining a slight lead at the penultimate hurdle, but the winner had his measure on the run-in. He is gradually getting it right. (5/1)
Anlace moved into a challenging position turning in and soon had every chance, but she got left behind between the last two as the tempo hotted up. (8/1)
3131 Dr Dave (IRE) took a keen hold and pressed the leaders until feeling the strain and fading on the approach to the straight. (12/1: op 6/1)
2815 Re Roi (IRE) (7/1: op 4/1)

3742 BANKS'S BUSINESS BUILDER H'CAP CHASE (0-115) (5-Y.O+) (Class E)

2-30 (2-30) **3m (19 fncs)** £3,387.50 (£1,025.00: £500.00: £237.50) GOING minus 0.49 sec per fur (GF)

				SP	RR	SF
2089[4]	**Foxgrove (76)** (RJPrice) **11-9-7**(7) XAizpuru (chsd ldr fr 6th: led after 15th: styd on strly)	—	**1**	16/1	86	25
1564[4]	**Trumpet (95)** (JGMO'Shea) **8-11-5** RJohnson (led to 2nd: led 3rd to 11th: ev ch fr 4 out: one pce appr last)	4	**2**	3/1[3]	102	41
3232[2]	**Scotoni (92)** (RJO'Sullivan) **11-11-2** AThornton (lw: led 2nd to 3rd: dropped rr 10th: rdn 13th: sn lost tch)	13	**3**	9/4[2]	91	30
3354[6]	**Pant Llin (76)** (FJordan) **11-10-0b** RSupple (hld up: hdwy to ld 11th: sn clr: rdn & hdd after 15th: sn wknd)	5	**4**	10/1	71	10
3176[5]	**Too Sharp (100)** (MissHCKnight) **9-11-10** JFTitley (hld up: mstke 4th: hdwy 8th: rdn & lost pl 12th: p.u bef next)		**P**	7/4[1]	—	—
				(SP 107.1%)	**5 Rn**	

5m 56.3 (-3.70) CSF £53.23 TOTE £12.30: £2.70 £1.70 (£10.10) OWNER Mrs C. W. Middleton (ULLINGSWICK) BRED Mrs C. W. Richards
LONG HANDICAP Foxgrove 9-7 Pant Llin 9-13
OFFICIAL EXPLANATION **Too Sharp: no explanation offered.**
932 Foxgrove, running for the first time this year, forged ahead at the end of the back straight and, staying on strongly, was well in control some way before reaching the finish. (16/1)
1564 Trumpet just needed this run after being out of action for four months and, after being in the firing line from the start, blew up at the second last. This is his ground and he can soon go one better. (3/1)
3232 Scotoni has yet to prove he stays this trip, but he dropped out of contention far too early to suggest that was the reason for such a mediocre performance. (9/4)
3176 Too Sharp, a very uneasy favourite, was never racing with any zest and was struggling in the rear when pulled up halfway down the back straight. (7/4)

3743 RACING CHANNEL H'CAP HURDLE (0-115) (4-Y.O+) (Class E)

3-00 (3-00) **2m (9 hdls)** £2,584.00 (£724.00: £352.00) GOING minus 0.49 sec per fur (GF)

				SP	RR	SF
3438[2]	**Above the Cut (USA) (87)** (CPMorlock) **5-10-12** CLlewellyn (hld up: hdwy 6th: disp ld fr 3 out: led last: r.o wl)	—	**1**	15/8[1]	62+	11
3346[8]	**Muizenberg (79)** (EHOwenjun) **10-10-4**ow4 AThornton (sn prom: led 5th tl hdd & mstke last)	1¾	**2**	11/1	52	—
3570[4]	**Desert Calm (IRE) (83)** (PDEvans) **8-10-8** DWalsh (lw: hld up: hdwy 3 out: nvr nrr)	18	**3**	7/1	38	—
1567[7]	**Zine Lane (100)** (JGMO'Shea) **5-11-11** RJohnson (chsd ldrs: rdn appr 3 out: sn outpcd)	½	**4**	9/2[2]	55	4
1816[P]	**Britannia Mills (75)** (MCChapman) **6-10-0** WWorthington (a in rr: t.o)	10	**5**	33/1	20	—
	Live Action (99) (MissHCKnight) **10-11-10** JCulloty (bit bkwd: led 4th to 5th: wknd next: sn t.o)	dist	**6**	15/2	—	—
2929[F]	**Vision of Freedom (IRE) (92)** (PBowen) **9-11-3** RFarrant (led to 3rd: prom whn fell next)		**F**	6/1[3]	—	—
3229[F]	**Swahili Run (80)** (JGMO'Shea) **9-10-0**(5) DJKavanagh (w ldrs: led 3rd to 4th: wknd after 6th: t.o & p.u bef 3 out)		**P**	25/1	—	—
				(SP 106.6%)	**8 Rn**	

3m 39.4 (2.40) CSF £17.46 CT £86.98 TOTE £2.30: £1.10 £2.50 £1.50 (£20.70) Trio £49.70 OWNER J P M & J W Cook (WANTAGE) BRED Pendley Farm in USA
LONG HANDICAP Muizenberg 9-12 Britannia Mills 9-11
3438 Above the Cut (USA), finally getting off the mark, looked to be travelling best from some way out and, gaining control at the last, won with quite a bit in hand. (15/8)
Muizenberg, running by far his best race for quite some time, looked to be coming off second best when a last-flight mistake was the final straw. (11/1)
3570 Desert Calm (IRE) stayed on in his own time to run into the places without ever being in a position to cause concern. (7/1)
677 Zine Lane, sharpened up with a run on the Flat last month, has not found his true form since changing stables, and was hard at work and in trouble entering the straight. (9/2)
Live Action (15/2: op 9/2)
1474 Vision of Freedom (IRE) (6/1: op 4/1)

3744 MAGNUS-ALLCROFT MEMORIAL TROPHY HUNTERS' CHASE (6-Y.O+) (Class H)

3-30 (3-32) **2m 4f (17 fncs)** £1,642.00 (£462.00: £226.00) GOING minus 0.49 sec per fur (GF)

				SP	RR	SF
	Blue Cheek (JMahon) **11-11-11**(7) MrNBradley (lw: j.w: mde virtually all: clr appr last)	—	**1**	9/2[2]	117	38
	Landsker Missile (MrsMaryEvans) **8-11-9**(7) MrEWilliams (lw: chsd wnr: blnd 2 out: nt rcvr)	16	**2**	12/1	102	23
3457[2]	**Minella Express (IRE)** (MissCSpearing) **8-12-0**(7) MissCSpearing (a.p: rdn & styd on one pce fr 4 out)	4	**3**	9/4[1]	104	25
13*	**Tuffnut George** (MrsPGrainger) **10-12-0**(7) MrAPhillips (hdwy 8th: mstke 11th: wknd 4 out)	10	**4**	13/2[3]	96	17
	Great Gusto (MissLBlackford) **11-11-11**(7) MissLBlackford (hld up in rr: hdwy 12th: nt rch ldrs)	hd	**5**	9/1	93	14

				SP	RR	SF
	Simply Perfect (JSSwindells) **11-11-7**(7) MissKSwindells (nvr rchd ldrs)	8	**6**	16/1	83	4
3010P	**Ramstar** (MissPollyCurling) **9-12-2**(5) MissPCurling (lw: mstke 5th: chsd ldrs to 11th: sn wknd: t.o)	½	**7**	10/1	89	10
3363P	**King of Shadows** (MissCMCarden) **10-11-11**(7) MrSPrior (chsd ldrs to 12th: sn lost pl: t.o)	3	**8**	33/1	84	5
3005P	**Kino** (AndrewMartin) **10-11-7**(7) MrAndrewMartin (lw: a bhd: t.o)	2½	**9**	66/1	78	—
34395	**Al Hashimi** (NTRidout) **13-11-7**(7) MrNRidout (t: a in rr: t.o)	1¾	**10**	33/1	76	—
	Familiar Friend (SJGilmore) **11-12-0b**(7) MrLLay (mid div tl wknd 13th: t.o)	6	**11**	16/1	79	—
3593P	**Great Pokey** (MissNellCourtenay) **12-11-7**(7) MissNCourtenay (lw: s.s: a t.o)	dist	**12**	25/1	—	—
29442	**Hennerwood Oak** (LadySusanBrooke) **7-11-2**(7) MrMMunrowd (hmpd 2nd: mstke 4th: t.o whn p.u bef 2 out)		**P**	16/1	—	—
3439P	**The Communicator** (MAHill) **11-11-9b**(5) MrCVigors (in rr tl p.u after 9th)		**P**	50/1	—	—
	Winter's Lane (MsKayRees) **13-11-7**(7) MrDAlers-Hankey (bhd: hit 10th: t.o whn p.u bef 12th)		**P**	50/1	—	—
	Stylish Gent (StephenRichardGriffiths) **10-11-7**(7) MrADalton (s.s: blnd & uns rdr 4th)		**U**	66/1	—	—
3270P	**Mhemeanles** (FrankNicholls) **7-11-7**(7) MrAGribbin (chsd ldrs: rdn 9th: blnd & uns rdr 11th)		**U**	66/1	—	—
	Majic Belle (MJJackson) **9-11-2b1**(7) MrAWintle (blnd & uns rdr 2nd)		**U**	66/1	—	—
				(SP 126.3%)	**18 Rn**	

4m 53.6 (1.60) CSF £50.29 TOTE £8.50: £2.50 £2.80 £1.30 (£31.90) Trio £26.60 OWNER Mrs B. Graham (STRATFORD-ON-AVON) BRED M. Dwan

Blue Cheek gained his revenge over the favourite with an impressive all-the-way success and, in this form, ought to be able to follow up. (9/2)

Landsker Missile won her only race on much more testing ground, but she gave a good account of herself here, chasing the winner throughout, although she was treading water when making her only serious mistake at the second last. (12/1)

3457 Minella Express (IRE) did not jump as badly left as he has done on occasions, and was always where he wanted to be but, with the principals making sure there was no hanging about, he was unable to make any impression inside the last half-mile. (9/4)

13* Tuffnut George has enjoyed a long rest since winning on his previous outing in June, and his run had come to an end soon after entering the home straight. (13/2)

Great Gusto began to stay on inside the final mile, but could not muster enough speed to become a serious contender. (9/1)

3745 BANKS'S LEASES AND TENANCIES HURDLE (4-Y.O) (Class F)

4-00 (4-00) **2m** **(9 hdls)** £2,696.00 (£756.00: £368.00) GOING minus 0.49 sec per fur (GF)

				SP	RR	SF
35353	**Crandon Boulevard** (MrsJPitman) **4-10-12** JCulloty (chsd ldr: led appr 3 out: pushed out)	—	**1**	3/1[1]	67	3
32242	**Sulawesi (IRE)** (NATwiston-Davies) **4-10-7** CLlewellyn (prom: outpcd 5th: rallied 3 out: chsng wnr whn hit next: one pce)	3	**2**	100/30[2]	59	—
34243	**Noble Colours (80)** (SGGriffiths) **4-10-7**(5) DJKavanagh (lw: plld hrd: hld up: hdwy 6th: rdn & one pce fr 2 out)	4	**3**	10/1	60	—
3029*	**Meg's Memory (IRE)** (AStreeter) **4-11-0** TEley (chsd ldrs tl outpcd appr 3 out)	13	**4**	3/1[1]	49	—
35446	**Down The Yard** (MCChapman) **4-10-7** WWorthington (lw: a bhd)	8	**5**	16/1	34	—
34948	**Green Bopper (USA)** (CPMorlock) **4-10-12** RJohnson (lw: hld up & bhd: mstke 6th: t.o)	3	**6**	25/1	36	—
35006	**White Plains (IRE)** (MCPipe) **4-10-12** DWalsh (led: clr 4th: hdd appr 3 out: sn btn & eased: t.o)	21	**7**	7/2[3]	15	—
35449	**African Sun (IRE)** (MCChapman) **4-10-12** RSupple (hld up & bhd: t.o fr 5th)	1	**8**	66/1	14	—
				(SP 115.6%)	**8 Rn**	

3m 41.3 (4.30) CSF £12.57 TOTE £3.80: £1.60 £1.30 £1.70 (£4.50) OWNER Stefes Plant Protection Ltd (UPPER LAMBOURN) BRED Maverick Productions Ltd

OFFICIAL EXPLANATION **White Plains (IRE): gurgled.**

3535 Crandon Boulevard, in no hurry to take on the clear leader, took that rival's measure soon after turning in and, from then on, there was only going to be one winner. He can continue to improve. (3/1: op 2/1)

3224 Sulawesi (IRE) did not look particularly happy cantering to post and she seemed to have lost all hope when getting outpaced at half-way. However, she stayed on in fine style in the latter stages and a longer trip looks a must. (100/30: 5/2-4/1)

3424 Noble Colours turned in another promising performance, and there is certainly a race to be won with him. (10/1)

3029* Meg's Memory (IRE) tried hard to keep tabs on the leaders, but she was struggling on the long home turn, and had to admit the task beyond her. (3/1)

3500 White Plains (IRE), soon bowling along in a clear lead, tied up rather quickly on the approach to the straight, and was eased right down once his measure had been taken. (7/2)

3746 ASTON MUNSLOW NOVICES' CHASE (5-Y.O+) (Class D)

4-30 (4-30) **2m 4f** **(17 fncs)** £3,371.25 (£1,020.00: £497.50: £236.25) GOING minus 0.49 sec per fur (GF)

				SP	RR	SF
3582F	**Mr Snaggle (IRE) (89)** (SEarle) **8-11-2** RJohnson (hld up: hdwy 8th: lft clr & hit 2 out)	—	**1**	4/1[2]	94	14
33624	**Fawley Flyer** (WGMTurner) **8-11-2** AThornton (a.p: led 10th to 13th: ev ch whn hit 4 out: j.lft last: sn btn)	6	**2**	11/4[1]	89	9
34563	**Prize Match (68)** (JCTuck) **8-10-11** SMcNeill (chsd ldrs to 13th: sn wknd)	24	**3**	8/1	65	—
15508	**Sporting Fixture (IRE)** (KSBridgwater) **6-10-13**(3) RMassey (mstke 4th: sn bhd: t.o)	5	**4**	40/1	66	—
3200P	**Riverbank Red** (WClay) **6-10-8v1**(3) GuyLewis (mstkes: a in rr: t.o whn fell 2 out)		**F**	33/1	—	—
30327	**Gutteridge (IRE)** (PDEvans) **7-11-2** DWalsh (mstke 2nd: hdwy 4th: led 13th tl fell 2 out)		**F**	5/1[3]	—	—
3538P	**Trail Boss (IRE) (88)** (MissHCKnight) **6-11-2** JFTitley (led to 10th: bhd whn p.u bef 12th: b.b.v)		**P**	11/2	—	—
304810	**Westcote Lad** (WJenks) **8-11-2** CLlewellyn (prom: hit 4th: blnd 12th: sn lost tch: t.o whn p.u bef 2 out)		**P**	6/1	—	—
1947P	**Knowing (69)** (PGWatkins) **10-10-11** MissEJames (a bhd: t.o 13th: p.u bef 2 out)		**P**	50/1	—	—
				(SP 111.5%)	**9 Rn**	

4m 56.2 (4.20) CSF £13.80 TOTE £4.40: £1.80 £1.30 £1.30 (£4.80) Trio £5.10 OWNER The Plum Merchants (STURMINSTER NEWTON) BRED Mrs W. H. Young

OFFICIAL EXPLANATION **Trail Boss (IRE): had bled from the nose.**

1681 Mr Snaggle (IRE), a faller at the first on his chasing debut, made no mistake this time and was closing fast when presented with the prize at the penultimate obstacle. (4/1)

3362 Fawley Flyer, returning to fences, ran well all the way, but he was getting left behind early in the straight and was fortunate to pick up the decent runner-up prize. (11/4: 2/1-3/1)

Gutteridge (IRE), making his chasing debut, survived an early mistake and still held a two-length advantage when hitting the deck at the second last. He appeared to be tying up, but the race was still there for the taking at the time. (5/1)

900 Trail Boss (IRE) once again bled from the nose after setting the pace for a circuit. (11/2: 4/1-6/1)

3747 LUDLOW STANDARD OPEN N.H. FLAT RACE (4, 5 & 6-Y.O) (Class H)
5-00 (5-11) **2m** £1,329.00 (£369.00: £177.00)

	Horse	Dist	Pos	SP	RR	SF
	Mayday Lauren (ABailey) **5-10-13** SWynne (lengthy: unf: a.p: led over 2f out: r.o wl)	—	1	$5/1^{3}$	66 f	—
2811^{15}	**Sandville Lad** (MrsDThomas) **5-11-1**$^{(3)}$ GuyLewis (lt-f: led tl hdd over 2f out: one pce)	4	2	50/1	67 f	—
	Rajadora (LASnook) **5-10-13** AThornton (lt-f: hld up: hdwy 6f out: ev ch 3f out: one pce)	hd	3	16/1	62 f	—
	Mazileo (IPWilliams) **4-10-3**$^{(7)}$ FBogle (w'like: hld up: hdwy 10f out: ev ch whn c wd ent s: kpt on u.p)	hd	4	10/1	67 f	—
	Diamond Hall (KRBurke) **4-10-10** RJohnson (lt-f: hld up: hdwy 5f out: ev ch 3f out: sn rdn: no ex)	1¼	5	$3/1^{2}$	66 f	—
3574^{6}	**Homme de Fer** (KCBailey) **5-10-11**$^{(7)}$ CScudder (leggy: chsd ldrs tl rdn & wknd over 3f out)	12	6	$11/8^{1}$	54 f	—
	Teal Bay (SABrookshaw) **5-10-6**$^{(7)}$ XAizpuru (leggy: hld up: hdwy 8f out: wknd 4f out)	3	7	9/1	46 f	—
3290^{6}	**What The Devil** (JPSmith) **4-10-5** WWorthington (lt-f: unf: chsd ldrs 10f: sn wknd: t.o)	¾	8	50/1	45 f	—
	Commanche Cup (IRE) (APJames) **4-10-10** DWalsh (leggy: unf: unruly bef s: a bhd: t.o)	7	9	20/1	43 f	—
3433^{20}	**Miss Kilworth (IRE)** (KSBridgwater) **6-10-10**$^{(3)}$ RMassey (unf: a in rr: t.o fnl 3f)	14	10	50/1	24 f	—
	Pecan Princess (IRE) (CASmith) **4-10-5** MrsDSmith (lt-f: a bhd: t.o)	6	11	33/1	18 f	—

(SP 122.3%) **11 Rn**

3m 36.6 CSF £222.89 TOTE £7.60: £2.00 £5.60 £3.60 (£127.10) Trio £239.00; £306.41 to Doncaster 20/3/97 OWNER B K Racing (TARPORLEY) BRED K. Benson and R. Kinsey
WEIGHT FOR AGE 4yo-8lb

Mayday Lauren, making her racecourse debut, struck the front early in the straight and stayed on strongly to draw clear. (5/1:7/2-6/1)
Sandville Lad tried to gallop his rivals into submission, but he could not get away, and was tapped for finishing speed when the dash to the post really developed. (50/1)
Rajadora had a chance second to none entering the straight, but she did not find a lot under pressure despite staying on. She should be able to win a race. (16/1)
Mazileo, a half-brother to a winner, delivered his challenge under the stands' rail in the straight, but he could never quicken enough, and may have done better with company. (10/1: 6/1-12/1)
Diamond Hall, the gamble of the race, looked full of running on the home turn but, when pressure was applied, he lacked the pace to go through with his effort. One to bear in mind. (3/1)
3574 Homme de Fer did not fulfil the promise shown on his debut earlier in the month, and he was in deep trouble before reaching the home straight. (11/8: 10/11-6/4)
Teal Bay (9/1: 5/1-10/1)

T/Plpt: £43.10 (267.67 Tckts). T/Qdpt: £3.50 (203.87 Tckts) IM

3488-TOWCESTER (R-H) (Good to firm)
Wednesday March 19th
WEATHER: sunny & windy

3748 GRAFTON AMATEUR (S) HURDLE (4,5,6 & 7-Y.O) (Class G)
2-10 (2-12) **2m (8 hdls)** £1,824.50 (£507.00: £243.50) GOING minus 0.16 sec per fur (G)

	Horse	Dist	Pos	SP	RR	SF
3085^{P}	**Derrybelle** (DLWilliams) **6-10-13**$^{(7)}$ MrSDurack (hld up: hdwy 5th: led 2 out: clr last: pushed out)	—	1	33/1	55?	1
3677^{*}	**Hanging Grove (IRE) (75)** (PGMurphy) **7-11-10**$^{(7)}$ ^{6x} MrMatthewWells (lw: chsd ldrs: hit 4th: pckd 2 out: sn chsng wnr: no imp)	6	2	$11/4^{2}$	60	6
3284^{5}	**Boy Blakeney (78)** (MrsSJSmith) **4-10-10**$^{(7)}$ MrCMulhall (hld up: hdwy 3 out: r.o flat: nvr able chal)	1½	3	$9/4^{1}$	53	—
3228^{7}	**Paula's Boy (IRE) (70)** (DFBassett) **7-11-4**$^{(7)}$ MissKDiMarte (prom: mstke 5th: wknd appr last)	4	4	40/1	49	—
3100^{F}	**Royal Hand (66)** (RJArmson) **7-11-4v**$^{1(7)}$ MrRArmson (chsd ldr: led 4th: clr next: wknd & hdd 2 out)	1½	5	33/1	47	—
3205^{3}	**Sprig Muslin** (DRGandolfo) **5-11-1v**$^{(5)}$ MissPJones (led: sn clr: hdd 4th: wknd appr 3 out)	15	6	$3/1^{3}$	27	—
	Curra Minstral (IRE) (JELong) **7-10-13**$^{(7)}$ MrJRyan (prom: mstke 5th: wknd appr 3 out)	12	7	33/1	15	—
3621^{12}	**Teoroma** (JRJenkins) **7-11-4**$^{(7)}$ MrMGingell (bhd fr 3rd)	30	8	16/1	—	—
1952^{9}	**Web of Steel (65)** (CJHemsley) **7-11-4b**$^{1(7)}$ MissADudley (chsd ldr tl appr 4th: rallied appr 3 out: 6th & btn whn fell last: dead)		F	33/1	—	—
3471^{6}	**Halham Tarn (IRE) (88)** (HJManners) **7-11-10**$^{(7)}$ MrACharles-Jones (prom tl hit 3rd: t.o whn p.u bef 2 out)		P	11/2	—	—
2676^{P}	**Rakaposhi Imp** (CHJones) **7-10-13**$^{(7)}$ MissBSmall (bit bkwd: tried to run out & uns rdr 1st)		U	40/1	—	—

(SP 120.3%) **11 Rn**

3m 58.3 (12.30) CSF £112.56 TOTE £42.90: £5.80 £1.60 £1.40 (£82.00) Trio £160.00; £33.81 to Doncaster 20/3/97 OWNER Miss B. W. Palmer (NEWBURY) BRED Miss B. W. Palmer
WEIGHT FOR AGE 4yo-8lb
No bid

Derrybelle, settled at the back, handled the fast ground as well as she had in bumpers, and benefited from not joining in with the suicidal early pace. (33/1)
3677* Hanging Grove (IRE), reappearing quickly on a very different track, gave his inexperienced pilot a good ride. (11/4)
3284 Boy Blakeney was never travelling particularly well, but found the patient tactics leaving him with enough to pass beaten horses in the last half-mile. (9/4)
Paula's Boy (IRE), whose only previous sign of ability came on fast ground, again showed that the surface suits him. (40/1)
917 Royal Hand has had a torrid time jumping over both hurdles and fences this season, but would have gone close here had he not been dashed into a clear lead off an already fast pace coming up the hill. (33/1)
3205 Sprig Muslin is tiny and has appeared to stay well in the past, but went off far too quickly on this occasion. (3/1)
3471 Halham Tarn (IRE) (11/2: 4/1-6/1)

3749 ALEX LAWRIE NOVICES' CHASE (5-Y.O+) (Class D)
2-40 (2-40) **2m 110y (12 fncs)** £3,465.00 (£1,035.00: £495.00: £225.00) GOING minus 0.16 sec per fur (G)

	Horse	Dist	Pos	SP	RR	SF
2885^{F}	**Grooving (IRE)** (JTGifford) **8-11-9** RDunwoody (lw: led to 2nd: blnd 4th: hit 4 out: led & j.rt 2 out: eased flat)	—	1	$10/11^{1}$	105+	32
3441^{4}	**Sleazey (64)** (JGO'Neill) **6-11-2** SCurran (a.p: led 4 out: rdn next: hdd & sltly hmpd 2 out: sn btn)	12	2	20/1	86	13
3417^{2}	**Just Bruce (88)** (MrsEHHeath) **8-11-9** DGallagher (swtg: j.lft: led 2nd to 4 out: wknd appr 2 out)	4	3	$5/2^{2}$	90	17

3427^{4}	**Amber Valley (USA) (95)** (DLWilliams) **6-10-9**$^{(7)}$ MrSDurack (stdd s: hld up: hit 5th: in tch whn fell 3 out: rmntd) ....dist	4	7/2^{3}	—	—
			(SP 107.9%)	4 Rn		

4m 8.3 (6.30) CSF £10.62 TOTE £1.70 (£9.90) OWNER Mrs T. Brown (FINDON) BRED T. Simmons
2885 Grooving (IRE) was rather unlucky on one occasion, but came into the race having fallen in three of his four chases, and jumped like it, for it took considerable skill on Dunwoody's part to get him round. (10/11: 4/5-evens)
Sleazey, moderate over hurdles, was making his chasing debut and jumped very much better than his three more-experienced rivals. On this evidence his fencing might find him a small race. (20/1)
3417 Just Bruce looked really well, but got warm and on his toes beforehand. He jumped out to his left on many occasions and might have been feeling the ground. (5/2)
3427 Amber Valley (USA) lost many lengths at the start, but had closed to within five lengths of the leader when coming to grief. He was eventually remounted for fourth prize. (7/2)

3750 BRITISH BAKELS H'CAP HURDLE (0-120) (4-Y.O+) (Class D)
3-10 (3-10) **2m 5f (11 hdls)** £2,945.00 (£820.00: £395.00) GOING minus 0.16 sec per fur (G)

			SP	RR	SF
3402^{4}	**The Toiseach (IRE) (109)** (JRFanshawe) **6-11-11v^{1}** JOsborne (mde all: clr 5th: rdn & hit last: r.o) ....—	1	11/4^{1}	86	33
3493^{*}	**Wassl Street (IRE) (102)** (KAMorgan) **5-11-4** RDunwoody (lw: chsd wnr: rdn 8th: btn whn hit last)....7	2	11/4^{1}	74	21
3076^{7}	**Bob's Ploy (86)** (MHTompkins) **5-9-13**$^{(3)ow2}$ PHenley (hdwy 6th: rdn appr 2 out: one pce)....2½	3	7/1^{3}	56	1
3545^{6}	**No Fiddling (IRE) (87)** (GMMcCourt) **6-10-3v^{1}** DBridgwater (in tch: hit 3rd: effrt 3 out: nvr nr ldrs) 9	4	3/1^{2}	50	—
810^{4}	**Cabochon (90)** (JJoseph) **10-10-6** DSkyrme (chsd ldr to 7th: bhd whn blnd 2 out) 18	5	20/1	39	—
3624^{2}	**This Nettle Danger (84)** (OBrennan) **13-10-0** MBrennan (lw: hld up: hdwy 7th: rdn & wknd appr 3 out)....20	6	7/1^{3}	18	—
			(SP 108.1%)	6 Rn	

5m 9.9 (7.90) CSF £9.20 TOTE £3.60: £2.40 £2.50 (£5.60) OWNER T & J Vestey (NEWMARKET) BRED T. Hennessy
LONG HANDICAP Bob's Ploy 9-10 This Nettle Danger 9-9
3402 The Toiseach (IRE), running on going as fast as this for the first time, bounced off the ground in fine style and, given an excellent tactical ride by Osborne who gave him a breather on the stiff climb to two out, never looked in much danger. (11/4)
3493* Wassl Street (IRE), whose last encounter with such fast ground came in a Sandown maiden as a three-year-old, did not run too badly after racing rather wide of the others trying to find ground that had been less poached through the winter. (11/4)
3076 Bob's Ploy was a stayer on the Flat, and these longer distances probably hold the key to him over timber. (7/1: 5/1-8/1)
3545 No Fiddling (IRE) settled better this time, but gives the impression that he needs softer ground. (3/1)
810 Cabochon was a Royal Ascot winner at his peak, but it is now three years since his last victory and he never threatened to improve his record. (20/1)
3624 This Nettle Danger, flat to the boards over this shorter trip, was well beaten by the bottom of the hill. (7/1)

3751 JULIAN BELFRAGE MEMORIAL H'CAP CHASE (0-130) (5-Y.O+) (Class C)
3-40 (3-40) **3m 1f (18 fncs)** £4,435.00 (£1,330.00: £640.00: £295.00) GOING minus 0.16 sec per fur (G)

			SP	RR	SF
3605^{2}	**Harristown Lady (105)** (GBBalding) **10-10-3b** BClifford (prom: mstke 2nd: led 11th: sn clr: easily)....—	1	100/30^{3}	104+	17
3444^{2}	**Fast Thoughts (102)** (DRGandolfo) **10-10-0** JOsborne (mstkes: led to 11th: dropped rr 14th: r.o again appr 2 out)....15	2	11/8^{1}	91	4
3622^{U}	**Reapers Rock (102)** (MrsSJSmith) **10-9-7**$^{(7)}$ RWilkinson (prom: hit 8th: one pce fr 14th) 4	3	10/1	89	2
3316^{5}	**Strath Royal (130)** (OBrennan) **11-12-0** MBrennan (hld up: hit 9th & 13th: btn 4 out: virtually p.u flat)....25	4	2/1^{2}	101	14
			(SP 107.6%)	4 Rn	

6m 23.5 (8.50) CSF £7.71 TOTE £4.50: £5.20 (£4.00) OWNER Mr Roger Spencer (ANDOVER) BRED J. A. Comerford
LONG HANDICAP Fast Thoughts 9-11 Reapers Rock 8-7
3605 Harristown Lady has had plenty of chances in the past, but found ground conditions to her liking and the opposition weak. Kicking clear in a few strides, she won without really having a race. (100/30: 7/4-7/2)
3444 Fast Thoughts, hesitant at some obstacles probably due to the ground, is nothing like the horse he was a couple of years back. (11/8)
3332 Reapers Rock did respectably from so far out of the handicap. (10/1)
3316 Strath Royal looked to be cruising until hitting the ninth. Steadied going down the hill on the final circuit, he was never going thereafter. (2/1)

3752 HARTWELL LAND ROVER NOVICES' H'CAP HURDLE (0-100) (4-Y.O+) (Class E)
4-10 (4-10) **2m (8 hdls)** £2,495.00 (£695.00: £335.00) GOING minus 0.16 sec per fur (G)

			SP	RR	SF
3594^{4}	**Dissolve (77)** (NMLampard) **5-10-6**$^{(7)}$ MrLBaker (chsd ldr: led 2 out: rdn out) ....—	1	7/1	63	22
1959^{10}	**Positivo (72)** (MissCJECaroe) **6-10-8** DLeahy (in tch: hit 3rd: hdwy appr 2 out: r.o flat)....1½	2	10/1	57	16
3424^{2}	**Mr Poppleton (72)** (RBrotherton) **8-10-8** LHarvey (led to 2 out: one pce)....1¾	3	6/1	55	14
3072^{*}	**Apache Park (USA) (96)** (DBurchell) **4-11-10** DJBurchell (lw: trckd ldrs: ev ch 2 out: btn appr last) ....¾	4	5/1^{2}	78	29
3612^{4}	**Ferrers (85)** (MrsPSly) **6-11-7** WMarston (hdwy appr 4th: wkng whn mstke last) 9	5	5/2^{1}	58	17
3641^{4}	**Millers Goldengirl (IRE) (65)** (MrsSJSmith) **6-9-8**$^{(7)}$ RWilkinson (prom tl rdn & wknd 3 out)....11	6	12/1	27	—
2823^{F}	**Romany Blues (66)** (CPEBrooks) **8-10-2** DGallagher (prom: rdn 5th: sn wknd)....5	7	16/1	23	—
3054^{5}	**Fairelaine (78)** (KCBailey) **5-11-0** CO'Dwyer (lw: nvr gng wl: a bhd) 21	8	11/2^{3}	14	—
3416^{P}	**Bally Wonder (64)** (MrsEHHeath) **5-10-0** JSupple (lw: hld up: hdwy appr 3rd: wknd appr next) 14	9	33/1	—	—
			(SP 113.0%)	9 Rn	

3m 52.0 (6.00) CSF £64.87 CT £402.62 TOTE £7.70: £2.50 £3.40 £1.50 (£22.20) Trio £83.80 OWNER Western Solvents Ltd (MARLBOROUGH) BRED Enterprise Bloodstock Ltd
WEIGHT FOR AGE 4yo-8lb
3594 Dissolve is a real trier and that counted for a lot in this contest. (7/1)
1539 Positivo stayed on for second on the run-in, but does not impress with his attitude. (10/1)
3424 Mr Poppleton enjoyed himself in front but failed to respond when challenged in the straight. (6/1)
3072* Apache Park (USA) looked harshly treated and is not very big for carrying top weight, but he did really well, albeit in an ordinary race. (5/1)
3612 Ferrers, from a yard out of sorts at present, did not do nearly so well on his second encounter with fast ground in quick succession. (5/2)
3641 Millers Goldengirl (IRE) did not last long once the tempo increased. (12/1)
3054 Fairelaine looked to be hating the ground on the way to post and ran like it. (11/2)

3753 EMPRESS ELIZABETH OF AUSTRIA OPEN HUNTERS' CHASE (5-Y.O+) (Class H)
4-40 (4-40) **2m 6f (16 fncs)** £1,605.50 (£448.00: £216.50) GOING minus 0.16 sec per fur (G)

				SP	RR	SF
3363P	**Star Oats** (MrsRMLampard) **11-11-7**(7) MrAKinane (hld up & plld hrd: mstkes 5th & 6th: led 2 out: rdn clr flat)	—	1	7/1 3	95	4
35685	**Hickelton Lad** (DLWilliams) **13-11-11**(7) MrSDurack (led 2nd to 6th: ev ch whn hmpd 2 out: hit last: sn btn)	4	2	7/2 2	96	5
34464	**Bollinger** (MrsJTGifford) **11-11-7**(7) MrPO'Keeffe (prom: blnd & dropped rr 10th: sn rdn: rallied appr 3 out: one pce appr last)	1½	3	4/7 1	91	—
3270F	**Charlies Delight (IRE)** (MrsCHicks) **9-11-9**(5) MrASansome (lw: led to 2nd: led 6th to 2 out: sn rdn & wknd)	4	4	8/1	88?	—
				(SP 109.5%)		**4 Rn**

5m 48.3 (19.30) CSF £25.38 TOTE £8.30 (£7.00) OWNER Mr Hayden Phillips (MARLBOROUGH) BRED Mrs L. Meylan

Star Oats, who had completed the course only twice in his last thirteen outings in points and hunter chases, made mistakes but was able to stay in touch because of the sedate pace. When it came down to a sprint, he found a good jump at the last and showed the best speed. (7/1: 10/1-6/1)

Hickelton Lad was slightly unlucky and would have given the winner a race with a good jump at the last. (7/2: 9/4-4/1)

3446 Bollinger probably needs further, and the fast ground and muddling pace were all against him. (4/7)

Charlies Delight (IRE), given a fine ride, did his best to dictate affairs but was outspeeded in the end. (8/1)

3754 LETHEBY & CHRISTOPHER 'N.H.' NOVICES' HURDLE (4-Y.O+) (Class E)
5-10 (5-11) **2m 5f (11 hdls)** £2,722.50 (£760.00: £367.50) GOING minus 0.16 sec per fur (G)

				SP	RR	SF
31727	**Stormyfairweather (IRE)** (NJHenderson) **5-11-2** MAFitzgerald (hld up: chal & hit 2 out: led last: rdn & wnt lft flat)	—	1	2/1 2	—	13
3445*	**Lord Rooble (IRE) (101)** (JTGifford) **6-11-8** PHide (led: rdn 2 out: hdd last: one pce)	1¼	2	5/4 1	—	18
34235	**Fashion Maker (IRE) (86)** (MrsIMcKie) **7-11-2** LHarvey (lw: hdwy appr 7th: rdn & wknd 3 out)	dist	3	5/2 3	—	—
270114	**Corrimulzie (IRE)** (KAMorgan) **6-11-2v1** WFry (bit bkwd: prom tl wknd appr 3 out)	dist	4	33/1	—	—
339914	**Prestigious Man (IRE)** (JRJenkins) **6-11-2** WMarston (chsd ldr to 7th: sn wl bhd)	dist	5	33/1	—	—
	Silver Spinney (PSHewitt) **6-10-11** DGallagher (bit bkwd: sn t.o: p.u bef 3 out)		P	33/1	—	—
				(SP 115.2%)		**6 Rn**

5m 13.5 (11.50) CSF £4.76 TOTE £2.80: £1.70 £1.30 (£2.60) OWNER Mrs Christopher Hanbury (LAMBOURN) BRED P. J. O'Connor

2808 Stormyfairweather (IRE) had already run well on this ground and, given a very confident ride, had taken charge when hanging violently away from the whip in the final hundred yards. (2/1)

3445* Lord Rooble (IRE) tried to make all on the bridle but, once let down, looked ill at ease on the ground. (5/4: op 4/7)

1539 Fashion Maker (IRE), a rangy horse, was probably feeling the ground as he stopped to nothing in the last half-mile. (5/2)

Corrimulzie (IRE) dropped out quickly over the final three flights and finished very tired. (33/1)

T/Plpt: £589.90 (14.91 Tckts). T/Qdpt: £137.70 (3.47 Tckts) Dk

3575-PLUMPTON (L-H) (Good to firm)
Thursday March 20th
WEATHER: sunny

3755 PEASE POTTAGE NOVICES' HURDLE (4-Y.O+) (Class E)
2-25 (2-25) **2m 4f (12 hdls)** £2,826.00 (£786.00: £378.00) GOING minus 0.32 sec per fur (GF)

				SP	RR	SF
30842	**Eau de Cologne** (MrsLRichards) **5-11-2** MRichards (chsd ldr: led 3 out: rdn out)	—	1	2/1 2	78	34
35923	**Lord Mills (IRE)** (NoelChance) **6-11-2** TJMurphy (stdy hdwy 6th: chsd wnr fr 3 out: ev ch 2 out: mstke & stumbled last: unable qckn)	3½	2	Evens 1	75	31
35008	**Prototype** (GFJohnsonHoughton) **6-11-2** DGallagher (lw: hdwy 3 out: rdn appr 2 out: one pce)	7	3	16/1	70	26
30612	**Maylin Magic (83)** (TCasey) **6-10-11** DBridgwater (rdn & hdwy 3 out: one pce)	8	4	7/1 3	58	14
3408P	**Kybo's Revenge (IRE) (64)** (RRowe) **6-11-2** DO'Sullivan (lw: lost pl 2nd: nvr nr to chal)	16	5	20/1	50	6
3084P	**Clock Watchers (68)** (JJBridger) **9-11-2** DMorris (led: clr 5th: blnd bdly & hdd 3 out: sn wknd)	3½	6	66/1	48	4
3582F	**Benji** (TCasey) **6-11-2** JAMcCarthy (hld up: rdn 8th: sn wknd)	9	7	66/1	40	—
	Philisitate (JFfitch-Heyes) **8-10-8**(3) PHenley (lw: a bhd)	1¼	8	66/1	34	—
2751P	**Jamies First (IRE)** (RIngram) **4-10-0**(7) BDove (lw: a bhd)	12	9	66/1	30	—
35757	**Knot True** (JohnBerry) **7-10-11** AMcCabe (mstkes 4th & 8th: a bhd)	3½	10	50/1	22	—
3535F	**Nearly All Right** (SEarle) **8-11-2** SCurran (hld up: rdn 8th: sn wknd)	22	11	66/1	9	—
3445P	**King's Affair** (PRHedger) **7-10-9**(7) MClinton (lw: stumbled after 1st: bhd fr 5th: t.o whn p.u bef 9th)		P	50/1	—	—
				(SP 117.9%)		**12 Rn**

4m 48.8 (1.80) CSF £3.88 TOTE £2.30: £1.10 £1.20 £1.90 (£2.40) Trio £8.00 OWNER D and M Evans (CHICHESTER) BRED G. Reed

WEIGHT FOR AGE 4yo-9lb

3084 Eau de Cologne, who came out in spots before the race, did not let that prevent him from confirming the promise he had shown on his first two outings. Gaining control strides after the third last, he had only the runner-up to worry about from then on. Described as a very nice horse by connections, he does not want it any firmer than this. (2/1: 6/4-9/4)

3592 Lord Mills (IRE) moved into second place a few strides after the third last and was the only danger to the winner. Throwing down a very determined challenge, he made a mistake at the last which unbalanced him, as he then stumbled a few yards after that flight. From that point he was unable to find another gear. His trainer believes he blew up as he has been unable to do anything with him since last week's race, his first run in a year. He should have no problems finding a small race. (Evens)

1275 Prototype ran his best race over hurdles and, after taking closer order three from home, could then only plod on in his own time. (16/1)

3061 Maylin Magic made a forward move three from home but she was then made to look woefully one-paced. (7/1: 5/1-15/2)

3756 CUCKFIELD H'CAP CHASE (0-105) (5-Y.O+) (Class F)
2-55 (2-55) **2m 5f (16 fncs)** £2,887.20 (£799.20: £381.60) GOING minus 0.32 sec per fur (GF)

				SP	RR	SF
3578*	**Regal Aura (IRE) (76)** (DCO'Brien) **7-10-0** 6x WMarston (led to 3rd: led 11th: rdn out)	—	1	5/1 2	89	10
	Suffolk Road (102) (RRowe) **10-11-12** DO'Sullivan (bit bkwd: hld up: rdn appr 3 out: chsd wnr appr last: unable qckn)	6	2	6/1 3	110	31

				SP	RR	SF
3427^{U}	**Jovial Man (IRE) (95)** (RJO'Sullivan) **8-11-5** JOsborne (lw: lost pl 12th: rallied appr last: r.o one pce)	4	**3**	11/8 [1]	100	21
3206^{P}	**Oxford Quill (77)** (RCurtis) **10-10-1** DMorris (lw: hdwy 12th: chsd wnr fr 3 out: mstke 2 out: wknd flat)	5	**4**	12/1	79	—
3550^{*}	**Parliamentarian (IRE) (82)** (TCasey) **8-10-6b** JAMcCarthy (led 3rd: mstke 8th: mstke & hdd 11th: wknd appr 2 out)	10	**5**	10/1	76	—
2796^{P}	**Young Alfie (78)** (JFPanvert) **12-9-13b**(3)ow1 PHenley (a bhd: t.o fr 7th: p.u bef 10th)		**P**	100/1	—	—
3493^{3}	**Simply (IRE) (99)** (TPMcGovern) **8-11-9** DBridgwater (bhd whn p.u bef 11th)		**P**	6/1 [3]	—	—
3456^{4}	**Salcombe Harbour (NZ) (76)** (DrPPritchard) **13-10-0** DrPPritchard (lw: bhd fr 12th: p.u bef last)		**P**	50/1	—	—
				(SP 107.1%)	**8 Rn**	

5m 18.1 (5.10) CSF £27.79 CT £47.61 TOTE £6.80: £1.80 £2.00 £1.10 (£21.60) OWNER Mrs V. O'Brien (TONBRIDGE) BRED Upstream Ltd
LONG HANDICAP Regal Aura (IRE) 9-2 Salcombe Harbour (NZ) 8-8

3578* Regal Aura (IRE), 12lb higher than when winning here last week, showed that run to be no fluke, leading at the sixth last and being ridden along to keep his rivals at bay. The faster the ground the better, according to his trainer. (5/1: 7/2-11/2)

Suffolk Road looked in need of this first run in thirteen months but still gave plenty of encouragement despite this trip being on the short side. Moving into second place approaching the last, he was unable to reel in his rival. He has come down nicely in the weights, and when stepped up in distance should soon make up for lost time. (6/1)

3176 Jovial Man (IRE) got outpaced five from home and looked in real trouble. However, he got his second wind going to the last and stayed on to take third prize. (11/8)

3206 Oxford Quill is not the best of jumpers but moved into second place jumping the water. Untidy at the next, he was collared for the runner-up berth going to the final fence and tired badly on the run-in. (12/1: 8/1-14/1)

3757 MARCH (S) H'CAP HURDLE (0-90) (4-Y.O+) (Class G)

3-25 (3-27) **2m 1f (10 hdls)** £2,111.00 (£586.00: £281.00) GOING minus 0.32 sec per fur (GF)

				SP	RR	SF
3663^{2}	**General Shirley (IRE) (75)** (PRHedger) **6-10-11**(7) MClinton (hdwy 7th: led after 3 out: pushed out)	—	**1**	11/4 [1]	58	—
3442^{16}	**Scalp 'em (IRE) (57)** (DrPPritchard) **9-10-0** DrPPritchard (chsd ldr: ev ch appr 2 out: unable qckn)	5	**2**	25/1	35	—
3500^{9}	**Vanborough Lad (68)** (MJBolton) **8-10-11** JOsborne (hdwy appr 2 out: wknd appr last)	6	**3**	9/1	41	—
3674^{5}	**Anif (USA) (57)** (JJoseph) **6-10-0** DSkyrme (hdwy 7th: wknd appr 2 out)	2½	**4**	12/1	27	—
3583^{5}	**Battleship Bruce (81)** (TCasey) **5-11-5**(5) SRyan (hdwy 3 out: wknd appr 2 out)	4	**5**	7/1 [3]	48	—
3575^{4}	**Zadok (65)** (JFfitch-Heyes) **5-10-5b**(3) PHenley (lw: rdn 6th: nvr nr to chal)	2½	**6**	5/1 [2]	29	—
3603^{P}	**High Burnshot (59)** (MrsLCJewell) **10-10-2** DLeahy (led: clr 2nd: hdd after 3 out: sn wknd)	3	**7**	14/1	20	—
2866^{F}	**Tomal (70)** (RIngram) **5-10-13** DGallagher (lw: rdn 6th: hdwy & mstke 7th: sn wknd: lame)	22	**8**	11/4 [1]	11	—
2868^{8}	**Nishaman (67)** (THind) **6-10-10** PMcLoughlin (4th whn bmpd 4th: wknd 3 out)	4	**9**	16/1	4	—
3670^{P}	**Tigana (57)** (MrsLCJewell) **5-10-0** SCurran (swtg: 3rd whn mstke 4th: bhd fr 7th)	1¾	**10**	50/1	—	—
				(SP 118.5%)	**10 Rn**	

4m 6.6 (10.60) CSF £59.92 CT £509.56 TOTE £3.90: £1.80 £5.80 £1.80 (£64.20) Trio £49.70 OWNER Mr P. R. Hedger (CHICHESTER) BRED Airlie Stud
LONG HANDICAP Scalp 'em (IRE) 9-13 Anif (USA) 9-8 Tigana 9-12
No bid

OFFICIAL EXPLANATION **Tomal: the gelding is a difficult ride, might have been feeling the effects of a bad fall last time and was found to be lame on his off-fore.**

3663 General Shirley (IRE), uneasy in the market, moved to the front soon after the third last and, with a useful advantage going to the final flight, needed only to be nudged along to win this very bad race. (11/4: op 7/4)

1446 Scalp 'em (IRE) is a very poor plater, but nevertheless had every chance turning for home before tapped for toe. (25/1)

Vanborough Lad does appear to have a stamina problem for, after moving up on the home turn appearing to be travelling very well indeed, he found little when popped a serious question in the straight. (9/1: 6/1-10/1)

3674 Anif (USA), 6lb out of the handicap, took closer order in the back straight but had shot his bolt going to the penultimate hurdle. (12/1)

3583 Battleship Bruce has become very disappointing, and a brief effort towards the end of the back straight came to little. (7/1: 4/1-8/1)

3758 WEATHERBYS DATA SERVICES NOVICES' CHASE (5-Y.O+) (Class E)

4-00 (4-04) **2m (13 fncs)** £2,906.40 (£865.20: £411.60: £184.80) GOING minus 0.32 sec per fur (GF)

				SP	RR	SF
3422^{*}	**Flight Lieutenant (USA) (111)** (TCasey) **8-12-0** DBridgwater (lw: chsd ldr: reminder 7th: blnd 4 out: led appr last: rdn out)	—	**1**	1/4 [1]	120	20
3443^{U}	**Robins Pride (IRE) (95)** (CLPopham) **7-10-11**(5) MrRThornton (hld up: mstkes 2nd & 3rd: led 4 out tl appr last: unable qckn)	4	**2**	7/2 [2]	104	4
3443^{3}	**Mheanmetoo** (DLWilliams) **6-10-9**(7) MrSDurack (lw: led: sn clr: hdd 4 out: wknd appr 2 out)	23	**3**	50/1	81?	—
1836^{6}	**Fruit Town (IRE)** (PButler) **8-11-2** TJMurphy (bit bkwd: t.o fr 4th)	dist	**4**	33/1 [3]	—	—
3178^{5}	**Tin Pan Alley** (DMGrissell) **8-10-13**(3) PHenley (in rr tl blnd & uns rdr 3rd)		**U**	33/1 [3]	—	—
				(SP 110.1%)	**5 Rn**	

3m 59.2 (7.20) CSF £1.45 TOTE £1.20: £1.00 £1.70 (£1.50) OWNER Mrs Laura Pegg (DORKING) BRED Dale Barlage

3422* Flight Lieutenant (USA) made very heavy weather of winning this. Far from fluent at his fences, he was given a reminder with fully a circuit still to race. Clouting the fourth last hard, he nevertheless had far too much class for the runner-up and, moving to the front approaching the final fence, was ridden along to score. (1/4)

3443 Robins Pride (IRE) gained the initiative four from home but, collared approaching the last, was soon brushed aside. (7/2)

3759 HAILSHAM H'CAP CHASE (0-100) (5-Y.O+) (Class F)

4-30 (4-30) **3m 1f 110y (20 fncs)** £2,937.60 (£813.60: £388.80) GOING minus 0.32 sec per fur (GF)

				SP	RR	SF
3496^{4}	**Black Church (97)** (RRowe) **11-11-12** DO'Sullivan (lw: a gng wl: hld up: chsd ldr fr 15th: led 16th: hrd hld)	—	**1**	2/5 [1]	103	15
3675^{P}	**Joker Jack (71)** (RDean) **12-10-0** DLeahy (lw: chsd ldr: led 8th to 16th: rdn 4 out: unable qckn)	4	**2**	14/1 [3]	75	—
3060^{P}	**Pinoccio (72)** (DCO'Brien) **10-10-1** WMarston (led to 8th: wknd 16th: t.o)	dist	**3**	7/1 [2]	—	—
3134^{F}	**Sharrow Bay (NZ) (71)** (AGHobbs) **10-10-0** RGreene (lw: bhd fr 8th: t.o fr 14th: blnd 15th: p.u bef 4 out)		**P**	7/1 [2]	—	—
				(SP 103.1%)	**4 Rn**	

6m 33.5 (13.50) CSF £4.54 TOTE £1.50 (£2.50) OWNER Dr B. Alexander (PULBOROUGH) BRED A. E. Hanbidge
LONG HANDICAP Joker Jack 9-5 Sharrow Bay (NZ) 9-3

3182 Black Church is not the most reliable character but, up against three useless rivals, he was on the bridle throughout and, won with a ton in hand. (2/5: op 1/5)

3134 Joker Jack is an extremely poor performer who does nothing more than plod around in his own time, and the fact that he was still on the bridle and in the lead on the final circuit- shows just how desperate this race was. Collared five from home, he was made to look extremely one-paced. (14/1)

3760 LEWES AMATEUR H'CAP HURDLE (0-105) (4-Y.O+) (Class F)
5-00 (5-00) **2m 4f (12 hdls)** £2,193.00 (£608.00: £291.00) GOING minus 0.32 sec per fur (GF)

				SP	RR	SF
3579^{3}	**Kelly Mac (89)** (DCO'Brien) **7-11-5**$^{(5)}$ MrRThornton (lw: a.p: led 9th: hrd rdn appr last: r.o wl)	—	**1**	11/4^{2}	71	28
3583^{2}	**Always Greener (IRE) (82)** (JWMullins) **6-10-10**$^{(7)}$ MrPO'Keeffe (a.p: led after 3rd to 5th: chsd wnr appr 2 out: ev ch last: unable qckn)	2½	**2**	2/1^{1}	62	19
3411^{5}	**King's Gold (73)** (MrsLRichards) **7-10-1**$^{(7)}$ MissSVickery (lw: led tl after 3rd: led 5th to 9th: one pce fr 3 out)	6	**3**	5/1^{3}	48	5
3536^{U}	**Mr Lovely (IRE) (68)** (JNeville) **6-9-10b**$^{1(7)}$ MrOMcPhail (lw: lost pl 9th: one pce)	7	**4**	16/1	38	—
217^{6}	**Prince of Spades (72)** (AGHobbs) **5-10-0**$^{(7)ow6}$ MrGShenkin (lw: hdwy 8th: ev ch appr 2 out: sn wknd)	1½	**5**	9/1	40	—
	Baylord Prince (IRE) (65) (MrsJAEwer) **9-9-7**$^{(7)}$ MrJGoldstein (bkwd: mstke 4th: bhd fr 8th)	10	**6**	33/1	25	—
3012^{8}	**Mazirah (82)** (RCurtis) **6-10-10**$^{(7)ow2}$ MrMAppleby (lw: plld hrd: hdwy 4th: wknd appr 3 out)	1¼	**7**	7/1	41	—
3664^{P}	**Gone For Lunch (88)** (JohnWhyte) **6-11-2**$^{(7)ow3}$ MrMGingell (swtg: bhd fr 8th: t.o whn p.u bef 2 out)		**P**	25/1	—	—

(SP 111.8%) **8 Rn**

4m 52.5 (5.50) CSF £7.76 CT £21.59 TOTE £3.10: £1.20 £1.20 £2.00 (£3.20) OWNER Mrs V. O'Brien (TONBRIDGE) BRED John L. Moore

3579 Kelly Mac, surprisingly moving up in distance, jumped into the lead at the fourth last and, responding to pressure, kept on too well for the runner-up to give his trainer his first double. He would prefer much softer ground according to O'Brien. (11/4)

3583 Always Greener (IRE) moved into second place approaching the second last and threw down a very determined challenge. Still in with every chance jumping the final flight, she found the winner a little too quick. (2/1)

3411 King's Gold made much of the running, but he was collared four from home and could then only plod on in his own time. He remains a maiden at the winter game after nineteen attempts. (5/1)

Mr Lovely (IRE) was outpaced four from home and from that point could only keep on in his own time. (16/1)

Prince of Spades, without a run in eight months, had every chance turning from home before lack of a recent run took its toll. (9/1: 6/1-10/1)

T/Plpt: £4.00 (2,238.29 Tckts). T/Qdpt: £2.80 (139.71 Tckts) AK

3494-WINCANTON (R-H) (Good to firm, Firm patches)
Thursday March 20th
WEATHER: overcast

3761 BRITISH FIELD SPORTS SOCIETY MAIDEN HURDLE (4-Y.O+) (Class F)
2-15 (2-15) **2m (8 hdls)** £2,477.50 (£690.00: £332.50) GOING minus 0.53 sec per fur (GF)

				SP	RR	SF
3359^{4}	**Midnight Legend** (DNicholson) **6-11-2** RJohnson (lw: led to 2nd: led appr 2 out: edgd lft flat: rdn out)	—	**1**	4/7^{1}	86	40
3500^{4}	**Embankment (IRE)** (NJHenderson) **7-11-2** MAFitzgerald (hld up: hdwy 3 out: ev ch 2 out: one pce)	3½	**2**	10/1	83	37
3500^{2}	**Ring of Vision (IRE)** (CJMann) **5-11-2** RDunwoody (a.p: rdn & ev ch appr 2 out: r.o one pce)	nk	**3**	13/2^{2}	82	36
3494^{3}	**Nordance Prince (IRE) (107)** (MissGayKelleway) **6-10-11**$^{(5)}$ ABates (hld up & bhd: stdy hdwy 4th: wknd 2 out)	5	**4**	7/1^{3}	77	31
3500^{5}	**Piper's Rock (IRE)** (GBBalding) **6-10-10**$^{(7)ow1}$ MrABalding (led 2nd tl appr 2 out: sn rdn & wknd)	11	**5**	33/1	67	20
3103^{5}	**He Knows The Rules** (RHBuckler) **5-11-2** BPowell (hld up & bhd: hdwy 5th: wknd appr 2 out: blnd last)	6	**6**	20/1	60	14
3172^{6}	**Over The Water (IRE) (87)** (RHAlner) **5-11-2** AThornton (prom tl wknd appr 2 out)	6	**7**	33/1	54	8
1683^{U}	**Derring Jack** (DNicholson) **6-10-13**$^{(3)}$ RMassey (t: prom: mstke 3rd: wknd after 3 out)	1½	**8**	40/1	53	7
3226^{10}	**Callermine** (MissHDay) **8-10-11** MFoster (prom tl wknd 3 out)	10	**9**	100/1	38	—
3399^{10}	**Hulalea (NZ)** (MissSEdwards) **5-10-13**$^{(3)}$ LAspell (rdn 3 out: a bhd: t.o)	1½	**10**	100/1	41	—
3535^{6}	**Commuter Country** (CRBarwell) **6-11-2** JRKavanagh (a bhd: t.o fr 3 out)	3	**11**	66/1	38	—
3494^{9}	**Classic Model** (JCTuck) **6-11-2** SMcNeill (bhd whn blnd 4th: t.o fr 3 out)	3	**12**	100/1	35	—
3399^{13}	**Georgetown** (JTGifford) **6-11-2** PHide (prom to 5th)	1¼	**13**	33/1	34	—
	Oscilights Gift (MarkCampion) **5-10-11** LHarvey (swvd lft s: t.o whn p.u bef 2 out)		**P**	100/1	—	—

(SP 120.0%) **14 Rn**

3m 36.5 (-3.50) CSF £6.09 TOTE £1.70: £1.40 £2.30 £1.20 (£5.50) Trio £5.20 OWNER Mrs H. J. Clarke (TEMPLE GUITING) BRED Limestone Stud

OFFICIAL EXPLANATION **He Knows The Rules: the trainer reported that the gelding had coughed after the race.**

3359 Midnight Legend really needs a stiffer course than this and was workmanlike rather than impressive. He now goes for the two-mile novice at Aintree and will encounter the same problem with the track there. (4/7)

3500 Embankment (IRE), rated three stone inferior to the winner on the Flat, seems to be going the right way and should soon get off the mark over timber. (10/1)

3500 Ring of Vision (IRE) did not mind fast ground and again ran well, but gave the impression he would be suited by a stiffer course or longer trip. (13/2)

3494 Nordance Prince (IRE) kept straight this time but did not find an awful lot when the chips were down. (7/1: 5/1-8/1)

3762 CORTON DENHAM NOVICES' CHASE (5-Y.O+) (Class E)
2-45 (2-45) **2m 5f (17 fncs)** £3,246.00 (£978.00: £474.00: £222.00) GOING minus 0.53 sec per fur (GF)

				SP	RR	SF
3537^{2}	**Malwood Castle (IRE)** (RHAlner) **7-11-3** AThornton (hld up: hdwy 10th: led 11th to 4 out: rdn to ld last strides)	—	**1**	5/2^{2}	76	—
3495^{5}	**Raincheck (63)** (MarkCampion) **6-11-3** JRailton (j.lft: led to 11th: led 4 out: mstke 3 out: rdn & hdd last strides)	hd	**2**	33/1	76	—
3427^{U}	**Dream Ride (IRE) (115)** (DNicholson) **7-11-10** RJohnson (a.p: ev ch 3 out: btn whn blnd last)	7	**3**	8/11^{1}	78	—
3067^{P}	**Pocaire Gaoithe (IRE) (65)** (CLPopham) **7-11-0**$^{(3)}$ TDascombe (nt j.w: bhd fr 11th: t.o)	dist	**4**	40/1	—	—
2037^{5}	**San Diego Charger (IRE) (67)** (ABarrow) **6-11-3** PHolley (hld up: hdwy 10th: cl 4th whn fell 4 out: dead)		**F**	20/1	—	—
3060^{P}	**Givus a Call (IRE) (93)** (JTGifford) **7-11-0**$^{(3)}$ LAspell (w ldr: bmpd 6th: wknd 11th: hmpd & uns rdr 4 out)		**U**	11/2^{3}	—	—

(SP 112.0%) **6 Rn**

5m 22.4 (14.40) CSF £48.53 TOTE £3.00: £1.40 £5.80 (£15.30) OWNER Mrs U. Wainwright (BLANDFORD) BRED Gerry Doyle

3537 Malwood Castle (IRE) appreciated this faster ground, but this was not a great contest. (5/2)

Raincheck seemed likely to overcome some indifferent fencing until touched off near the line. (33/1)

3015 Dream Ride (IRE) was already booked for third when making a hash of the final fence. (8/11)

3763 STEWART TORY MEMORIAL TROPHY AMATEUR H'CAP CHASE (0-120) (5-Y.O+) (Class D)

3-15 (3-15) **3m 1f 110y (21 fncs)** £4,440.00 (£1,240.00: £600.00) GOING minus 0.53 sec per fur (GF)

				SP	RR	SF
3496[3]	**Fools Errand (IRE) (112)** (GBBalding) **7-10-13v**[1](7) MrABalding (led tl appr 4th: led 11th to 13th: hit 14th: mstke 15th: led 4 out: r.o wl)	—	1	7/4[2]	120	—
3036[P]	**Sunley Bay (120)** (PFNicholls) **11-11-9**(5) MissPCurling (led appr 4th to 6th: led after 8th tl hit 11th: led 13th to 16th: led after 17th tl j.slowly 4 out: hrd rdn appr last: one pce)	4	2	6/4[1]	126	—
3113[P]	**Spring to it (97)** (MCPipe) **11-9-12**(7)ow2 MrMFrith (led 6th tl after 8th: hit 14th: led 16th tl after 17th: wknd appr 3 out)	10	3	5/2[3]	96	—
				(SP 104.9%)		**3 Rn**

6m 39.1 (20.10) CSF £4.08 TOTE £2.70 (£2.10) OWNER Mrs David Russell (ANDOVER) BRED K. E. and Mrs Moeran in Ireland

3496 Fools Errand (IRE), tried in a visor, was not foot-perfect but jumped better than the runner-up. (7/4)

2881 Sunley Bay usually jumps better for Polly Curling, but this was not the case on this occasion, and the fast ground may have been the reason. (6/4: op 10/11)

Spring to it should have been more suited to the prevailing fast ground than the other two. (5/2)

3764 MOTCOMBE NOVICES' HURDLE (4-Y.O+ F & M) (Class E)

3-50 (3-50) **2m 6f (11 hdls)** £2,635.00 (£735.00: £355.00) GOING minus 0.53 sec per fur (GF)

				SP	RR	SF
3564[2]	**Motoqua (108)** (DNicholson) **5-11-6** RJohnson (a gng wl: led on bit appr 2 out: rdn appr last: sn clr: easily)	—	1	1/2[1]	73+	—
2961[10]	**Regal Gem (IRE) (69)** (CRBarwell) **6-11-0** JRKavanagh (hld up: hdwy 7th: one pce fr 2 out)	8	2	20/1	61	—
3552[5]	**Scenic Waters** (NATwiston-Davies) **5-11-0** CLlewellyn (bhd tl hdwy 6th: j.slowly 7th: one pce fr 2 out)	2½	3	9/2[2]	59	—
3234[12]	**Gladys Emmanuel (76)** (REPocock) **10-10-9**(5) DJKavanagh (hld up & bhd: hdwy 6th: ev ch appr 2 out: one pce)	3	4	16/1	57	—
3325[11]	**Quinag (83)** (KCBailey) **6-11-0** SMcNeill (lw: a.p: led 7th tl appr 2 out: sn wknd)	7	5	10/1[3]	52	—
2959[8]	**Castle Lynch (IRE)** (RHAlner) **5-11-0** JCulloty (hld up & bhd: hdwy 6th: wknd appr 2 out)	15	6	25/1	41	—
865[9]	**Gobalino Girl (IRE)** (FGray) **5-10-11**(3) DFortt (hdwy 5th: wknd appr 2 out)	3	7	25/1	39	—
3406[6]	**Contract Bridge (IRE)** (PGMurphy) **4-10-5** WMcFarland (prom to 6th: t.o fr 3 out)	22	8	33/1	23	—
	Areal (IRE) (BPalling) **8-11-0** TJenks (bkwd: hld up & bhd: hdwy 8th: wknd appr 2 out: t.o)	2½	9	66/1	21	—
	Buckbee Flyer (RHAlner) **5-11-0** AThornton (j.slowly 1st: a bhd: t.o whn p.u bef 2 out)		P	16/1	—	—
3340[P]	**Abbeydoran** (MrsJEHawkins) **6-11-0** DWalsh (led tl hdd & mstke 7th: sn wknd: t.o whn p.u bef 2 out)		P	100/1	—	—
912[7]	**Lunar Gris** (AJChamberlain) **4-10-5** BPowell (bkwd: bhd: blnd 7th: sn t.o: p.u bef 2 out)		P	100/1	—	—
2959[P]	**Queen Of The Suir (IRE)** (NRMitchell) **8-10-11**(3) SophieMitchell (plld hrd: prom: mstkes 3rd & 4th: wknd 7th: t.o whn p.u bef 2 out)		P	100/1	—	—
3110[P]	**Bold Reine (FR) (53)** (ABarrow) **8-11-0** PHolley (mid div: blnd bdly 5th: t.o whn p.u bef 7th)		P	100/1	—	—
	Lady Callernish (MissHDay) **7-11-0** MFoster (j.slowly 1st: blnd & uns rdr 2nd)		U	100/1	—	—
				(SP 127.5%)		**15 Rn**

5m 18.3 (9.30) CSF £16.77 TOTE £1.60: £1.10 £3.80 £1.50 (£9.80) Trio £9.70 OWNER Mrs Claire Smith (TEMPLE GUITING) BRED Darley Stud Management Co Ltd

WEIGHT FOR AGE 4yo-9lb

3564 Motoqua was thought by her trainer to have jumped better on this faster ground, and may go novice chasing next season. (1/2)

492 Regal Gem (IRE) found the winner holding all the aces. (20/1)

Scenic Waters won over twelve furlongs in Sweden after disappointing on the Flat for Reg Hollinshead. (9/2)

Gladys Emmanuel, the winner of a couple of two-mile chases in soft ground in March 1995, had come back after a near two-year lay-off here last month. (16/1)

1673 Quinag did not mind this faster ground. (10/1)

3765 SOMERTON NOVICES' HUNTERS' CHASE (6-Y.O+) (Class H)

4-20 (4-20) **2m 5f (17 fncs)** £1,174.50 (£351.00: £168.00: £76.50) GOING minus 0.53 sec per fur (GF)

				SP	RR	SF
3631[U]	**Tom's Gemini Star** (OJCarter) **9-11-7**(7) MrEJames (s.s: hdwy 10th: hmpd 4 out: led 3 out: r.o wl)	—	1	33/1	104	—
	Vital Song (MHDare) **10-11-7**(7) MrGMatthews (plld hrd: a.p: lft in ld 4 out: hdd 3 out: btn whn blnd last)	5	2	7/2[2]	100	—
3580[4]	**Northern Village** (LukeDace) **10-11-7**(7) MrDAlers-Hankey (bhd: mstke 1st: hdwy 10th: one pce fr 13th)	10	3	33/1	93	—
3055[6]	**Some-Toy** (JohnSquire) **11-11-13**(7) MissLBlackford (sme hdwy 8th: mstke 11th: sn bhd)	5	4	14/1	95	—
	Master Donnington (MrsDWilesmith) **9-11-7**(7) MrJMPritchard (hmpd 6th: hdwy 10th: wknd 12th)	3	5	33/1	87	—
3586[2]	**King's Treasure (USA)** (IABalding) **8-11-13**(7) MrABalding (t: hld up: 4th whn fell 6th)		F	5/4[1]	—	—
3627[2]	**Finnigan Free** (GAHam) **7-11-7**(7) MrMFrith (s.s: bhd tl p.u bef 7th)		P	16/1	—	—
	West Quay (TLong) **11-11-7**(7) MrJCreighton (led to 3rd: led 13th tl p.u lame bef 4 out)		P	4/1[3]	—	—
	Salvo (MissMBragg) **6-11-8**(7)ow1 MrIDowrick (plld hrd: led 3rd to 13th: lft in ld, blnd & uns rdr 4 out)		U	12/1	—	—
				(SP 115.7%)		**9 Rn**

5m 19.5 (11.50) CSF £134.84 TOTE £51.50: £5.70 £1.20 £2.60 (£197.00) Trio £144.90; £71.48 to Doncaster 21/3/97 OWNER Mr O. J. Carter (OTTERY ST MARY) BRED T. Staddon

Tom's Gemini Star appeared to benefit from the misfortune of others. (33/1)

Vital Song, three times a winner between the flags, likes to front-run, and certainly proved a handful under restraint. (7/2)

3580 Northern Village had faster ground in his favour this time. (33/1)

Some-Toy (14/1: 10/1-16/1)

West Quay was in the process of taking command when breaking down at the cross fence. (4/1)

Salvo had just been handed back the lead when unshipping his rider at the cross fence. (12/1)

3766 QUANTOCK H'CAP HURDLE (0-120) (4-Y.O+) (Class D)

4-50 (4-50) **2m (8 hdls)** £2,805.00 (£780.00: £375.00) GOING minus 0.53 sec per fur (GF)

				SP	RR	SF
3497*	**Northern Starlight (112)** (MCPipe) **6-11-11** CMaude (mde all: rdn appr 2 out: r.o wl)	—	1	13/8[2]	94	52
2872*	**Easy Listening (USA) (104)** (NJHawke) **5-11-3** JRailton (sn chsng wnr: ev ch 2 out: btn whn mstke last)	12	2	11/8[1]	74	32
3584[6]	**Kino's Cross (105)** (AJWilson) **8-11-4** AThornton (hld up: lost pl 4th: rdn 3 out: n.d after)	18	3	12/1	57	15
3234[8]	**Dontdressfordinner (89)** (RJHodges) **7-9-13**(3) TDascombe (lost pl 3rd: rdn 3 out: sn bhd: virtually p.u flat)	dist	4	7/2[3]	—	—
				(SP 110.1%)		**4 Rn**

3m 35.8 (-4.20) CSF £4.06 TOTE £1.90 (£2.10) OWNER Mr Arthur Souch (WELLINGTON) BRED R. J. Glenn and K. Leadbetter

3497* Northern Starlight, raised another 4lb, completed the hat-trick and could certainly hear his feet rattle this time. (13/8: evens-7/4)
2872* Easy Listening (USA), graduating to handicaps, looked to be travelling better than the winner going to the penultimate flight. (11/8)
3164 Kino's Cross was already due to go down 4lb. (12/1: op 7/1)

3767 LEVY BOARD STANDARD OPEN N.H. FLAT RACE (4, 5 & 6-Y.O) (Class H)
5-20 (5-20) **2m** £1,490.00 (£415.00: £200.00)

			SP	RR	SF
3235*	**Noisy Miner (IRE)** (DNicholson) **5-11-8**(3) RMassey (unf: hld up: hdwy 6f out: led ins fnl f: edgd lft: drvn out)—	1	1/3[1]	59 f	—
	Normania (NZ) (MissSEdwards) **5-11-4** MrTHills (w'like: a.p: rn wd bnd over 3f out: n.m.r & r.o fnl f)1¼	2	33/1	51 f	—
	Sally Scally (AGHobbs) **5-10-13** MrLJefford (small: a.p: led 3f out tl ins fnl f)1	3	14/1[3]	45 f	—
	Tommy Tickle (GMPrice) **5-11-4** JRKavanagh (w'like: hld up mid div: lost pl 8f out: hrd rdn & rallied over 3f out: styd on one pce)11	4	20/1	39 f	—
	Mister River (IRE) (DRCElsworth) **6-11-4** PHolley (w'like: bkwd: hld up: hdwy 4f out: wknd over 2f out)¾	5	9/1[2]	38 f	—
	Longstone Lad (GFEdwards) **5-10-11**(7) MrJTizzard (w'like: hdwy 9f out: wknd over 2f out)1½	6	16/1	37 f	—
	See Prosperity (MissSWaterman) **5-10-11**(7) NWillmington (lt-f: unf: prom tl wknd 3f out)6	7	50/1	31 f	—
	Festival (FR) (APJones) **4-10-10** SMcNeill (leggy: unf: bit bkwd: led 13f: wknd qckly)4	8	14/1[3]	27 f	—
	Five Boys (IRE) (RJHodges) **5-11-1**(3) TDascombe (lt-f: bkwd: nvr nr ldrs)1¼	9	16/1	25 f	—
	Technical Move (IRE) (GAHam) **6-10-13** SBurrough (neat: prom tl hrd rdn & wknd 3f out)12	10	66/1	8 f	—
	Little Beau (MrsJAYoung) **6-11-4** MrACharles-Jones (small: unf: a bhd: t.o fnl 6f)14	11	50/1	—	—
2965[6]	**Splash of Blakeney** (SGKnight) **6-10-13** SAnderson (str: a bhd: t.o fnl 6f)4	12	66/1	—	—
	Dunnicks Dolittle (FGTucker) **4-10-4**(7)ow1 MGriffiths (bkwd: s.s: gd hdwy 10f out: wknd qckly 6f out: t.o)...dist	13	66/1	—	—
	Kellsboro Queen (RHBuckler) **6-10-13** BPowell (lt-f: unf: gd hdwy 10f out: wknd qckly 6f out: t.o whn p.u 3f out)	P	14/1[3]	—	—
			(SP 132.9%)	**14 Rn**	

3m 37.7 CSF £27.66 TOTE £1.30: £1.10 £6.50 £1.90 (£24.30) Trio £184.00 OWNER Mrs R. J. Skan (TEMPLE GUITING) BRED Andrew Kavanagh
WEIGHT FOR AGE 4yo-8lb
STEWARDS' ENQUIRY Massey susp. 29 & 31/3/97 (careless riding).
3235* Noisy Miner (IRE) had to dig deep and, with his rider picking up a two-day ban for careless riding, would have lost this race under the old rules. (1/3)
Normania (NZ) did not help his cause by racing wide into the home straight, and then found the winner cramping him for room against the stands' rails in the closing stages. (33/1)
Sally Scally slipped through on the inside after taking the home turn better than most. (14/1: tchd 33/1)
Tommy Tickle is out of a two-mile hurdle winner. (20/1)
Mister River (IRE) is a half-brother to Flat winners and a winner over hurdles. (9/1: op 4/1)
Longstone Lad is out of a dual hurdle winner. (16/1)
Festival (FR) (14/1: op 7/1)
Kellsboro Queen (14/1: 8/1-16/1)

T/Plpt: £82.70 (105.43 Tckts). T/Qdpt: £42.40 (9.37 Tckts) KH

3768a - 3788a : (Irish Racing) - See Computer Raceform

3448-KELSO (L-H) (Good)
Friday March 21st
WEATHER: fine

3789 PERCY ARMS HURDLE (4-Y.O) (Class D)
1-40 (1-41) **2m 2f (10 hdls)** £2,815.00 (£790.00: £385.00) GOING: 0.03 sec per fur (G)

			SP	RR	SF
3555*	**Son of Anshan (106)** (MrsASwinbank) **4-11-10** JSupple (mde all: sn clr: drvn along 3 out: eased flat)—	1	5/4[1]	88+	18
3345[9]	**Bold Classic (IRE)** (CGrant) **4-10-12** TReed (sn drvn along: in tch: styd on fr 2 out: no ch w wnr)22	2	5/1[2]	56	—
3394*	**Clash of Swords** (PCalver) **4-11-4** LWyer (lw: chsd ldrs: effrt ½-wy: 3rd & btn whn blnd 3 out)½	3	5/1[2]	62	—
3555[3]	**Bourbon Dynasty (FR)** (GRichards) **4-10-12** ADobbin (lw: mid div: sme hdwy whn blnd 3 out: styd on flat: no imp)hd	4	20/1	56	—
3475[2]	**Oversman** (JGFitzGerald) **4-10-12** PNiven (chsd wnr fr 5th: rdn 3 out: sn btn: wknd flat)1	5	7/1[3]	55	—
3555[6]	**Known Secret (USA)** (PMonteith) **4-10-12** MMoloney (hld up & bhd: styd on grad fr 3 out: n.m.r towards fin)1¼	6	50/1	54	—
2669[12]	**Honeyschoice (IRE)** (MDHammond) **4-10-12** RGarritty (hld up: stdy hdwy appr 4 out: hit 3 out: wknd next) .30	7	10/1	27	—
3475[8]	**Queen's Counsel (IRE)** (MissMKMilligan) **4-10-7** BStorey (outpcd & no ch fr ½-wy)7	8	33/1	16	—
3394[2]	**Anika's Gem (IRE)** (MrsSCBradburne) **4-10-7** MFoster (chsd ldrs tl outpcd fr ½-wy)hd	9	33/1	16	—
	Caulker (MABarnes) **4-10-7**(5) STaylor (mstkes: wl bhd fr ½-wy)dist	10	200/1	—	—
3070[10]	**Chief Chippie** (WTKemp) **4-10-12** SMcDougall (t.o fr ½-wy: p.u bef last)	P	200/1	—	—
	Mystical Mind (MartynWane) **4-10-12** ASSmith (t.o fr ½-wy: p.u bef 4 out)	P	200/1	—	—
			(SP 113.5%)	**12 Rn**	

4m 26.6 (13.60) CSF £6.33 TOTE £1.70: £1.10 £2.00 £1.90 (£10.50) Trio £7.80 OWNER Mr F. J. Sainsbury (RICHMOND) BRED C. J. R. Trotter
3555* Son of Anshan, who stays well, again left nothing to chance and had galloped his rivals into the ground by the second last. (5/4)
1652 Bold Classic (IRE), judging from this, needs further yet, as he was never on the bridle at any stage. (5/1)
3394* Clash of Swords had his chances, but when asked to struggle he rooted the third last, and was treading water from then on. (5/1)
3555 Bourbon Dynasty (FR) is likely to improve once he gets his jumping together. (20/1)
3475 Oversman may well have been second best here, but he burnt himself out by chasing the useful winner. (7/1)
3555 Known Secret (USA) went much better on this faster surface, and may well have been placed but for being hampered late on. (50/1)
2669 Honeyschoice (IRE) obviously needed this after a layoff, and this trip was stretching his stamina. (10/1)

3790 TWEEDDALE PRESS NOVICES' CHASE (5-Y.O+) (Class D)
2-15 (2-15) **2m 1f (12 fncs)** £3,947.40 (£1,195.20: £583.60: £277.80) GOING: 0.03 sec per fur (G)

			SP	RR	SF
	American Hero (RAllan) **9-11-2** BStorey (j.w: mde all: sn clr: kpt on u.p flat)—	1	9/1	111	45

				SP	RR	SF
3558[2]	**Mr Knitwit (105)** (PMonteith) **10-11-8** ADobbin (lw: a.p: effrt 6th: mstke 2 out: styd on u.p: nt rch wnr)	5	2	2/1 2	112	46
3530[2]	**Real Tonic** (GRichards) **7-11-8** RDunwoody (lw: mstkes: chsd ldrs: rdn fr 8th: wnt 2nd & hit 4 out: one pce after)	2	3	7/4 1	110	44
3450[2]	**Moss Pageant (74)** (FTWalton) **7-11-2** KJohnson (chsd wnr to 4 out: 4th & btn whn blnd 2 out)	17	4	50/1	88	22
3159[8]	**Malta Man (IRE)** (PCheesbrough) **7-11-2** ASSmith (sn outpcd & bhd: sme late hdwy)	9	5	25/1	80	14
2544[5]	**Jymjam Johnny (IRE) (99)** (JJO'Neill) **8-10-11**(5) RMcGrath (hld up & bhd: mstkes: n.d)	4	6	16/1	76	10
1847[4]	**Music Blitz (73)** (MrsDThomson) **6-11-2** TReed (outpcd whn blnd 6th: sn t.o)	8	7	16/1	69	3
3479[3]	**Monkey Wench (IRE)** (MrsJDGoodfellow) **6-10-11** AThornton (lw: in tch tl outpcd fr 8th)	18	8	8/1 3	47	—
				(SP 108.4%)		**8 Rn**

4m 11.8 (4.80) CSF £23.40 TOTE £6.40: £1.30 £1.80 £1.50 (£20.90) OWNER Mrs R. P. Aggio (CORNHILL-ON-TWEED) BRED Sir Gordon White

OFFICIAL EXPLANATION **Monkey Wench (IRE): the mare was found to be lame on her near-hind stifle after the race.**

American Hero, making his chase debut, is an exciting front-runner who set a scorching pace. Jumping boldly, he never looked likely to be caught. (9/1)

3558 Mr Knitwit just found this trip on this ground too sharp, but he never stopped trying. (2/1)

3530 Real Tonic had his courage tested by the strong pace here, his jumping went to pot, and he was fighting a lost cause from the third last. (7/4)

3450 Moss Pageant ran well again, and in more modest company an opportunity can be found. (50/1)

3159 Malta Man (IRE), making his debut over fences, found things happening far too quickly, but was getting the hang of things at the end. (25/1)

2544 Jymjam Johnny (IRE) likes things to go all his own way, and over this trip that was never likely to happen. (16/1)

3791 LOTHIAN PLUMBING H'CAP HURDLE (0-120) (4-Y.O+) (Class D)

2-45 (2-45) **2m 2f (10 hdls)** £2,827.00 (£856.00: £418.00: £199.00) GOING: 0.03 sec per fur (G)

				SP	RR	SF
3413[F]	**Monnaie Forte (IRE) (94)** (JRAdam) **7-10-2**ow2 JRailton (lw: disp ld to 6th: cl up: disp ld 2 out: slt ld last: r.o u.p)	—	1	7/1	72	—
3559*	**Ingletonian (120)** (BMactaggart) **8-12-0** BStorey (disp ld tl led 6th: hdd last: kpt on wl towards fin)	½	2	4/1 1	98	27
3485[8]	**Our Robert (92)** (JGFitzGerald) **5-9-11**(3) FLeahy (in tch: rdn 4 out: styd on fr 2 out: no imp)	5	3	10/1	65	—
3485[9]	**Supreme Soviet (94)** (ACWhillans) **7-10-2** ADobbin (chsd ldrs: effrt 4 out: one pce fr next)	hd	4	8/1	67	—
3412[6]	**Uncle Doug (120)** (MrsMReveley) **6-12-0** PNiven (chsd ldrs: rdn 3 out: no imp)	½	5	10/1	93	22
3346[2]	**Ham N'Eggs (114)** (MDHammond) **6-11-8** RGarritty (hld up: hdwy 4 out: rdn & outpcd fr next)	12	6	5/1 2	76	5
3559[5]	**Linngate (105)** (LLungo) **8-10-13** RSupple (hld up: mstke 1st: hdwy 4 out: sn rdn: btn whn blnd last)	12	7	5/1 2	56	—
3530[P]	**Aragon Ayr (114)** (PMonteith) **9-11-1**(7) CMcCormack (hld up: rdn 4 out: hit next: a bhd)	30	8	33/1	39	—
3612[7]	**Adamatic (IRE) (98)** (RAllan) **6-10-6** LWyer (bhd: wl outpcd fr 4 out)	13	9	6/1 3	11	—
				(SP 112.4%)		**9 Rn**

4m 26.3 (13.30) CSF £31.44 CT £252.67 TOTE £7.60: £2.00 £1.80 £3.00 (£26.20) Trio £116.50; £19.71 to Doncaster 22/3/97 OWNER Mr James Adam (GORDON) BRED E. Stuart Knape

LONG HANDICAP Our Robert 9-12 Monnaie Forte (IRE) 9-12

3413 Monnaie Forte (IRE) enjoyed this run back over hurdles, and won under a determined drive. (7/1)

3559* Ingletonian is unbelievably game, and after looking beaten jumping the last he kept battling back. He is a credit to all concerned. (4/1: op 5/2)

3346 Our Robert ran well, staying on determinedly on ground faster than he really prefers. (10/1)

3315 Supreme Soviet, whose yard has not been firing, again ran quite well but was never doing enough at the business end. (8/1)

2617 Uncle Doug was off the bit some way out, and does seem to need further yet. (10/1: 7/1-12/1)

3346 Ham N'Eggs, raised 4lb in the weights for a decent effort last time, is from a stable out of form, and ran accordingly. (5/1)

3559 Linngate always found this ground much too fast. (5/1)

3792 KING'S OWN SCOTTISH BORDERERS CHALLENGE CUP H'CAP CHASE (0-125) (5-Y.O+) (Class D)

3-15 (3-15) **3m 1f (19 fncs)** £4,143.00 (£1,254.00: £612.00: £291.00) GOING: 0.03 sec per fur (G)

				SP	RR	SF
2923*	**Son of Iris (109)** (MrsMReveley) **9-11-5** PNiven (lw: hld up: shkn up & hdwy after 13th: led 2 out: drvn out)	—	1	2/1 1	120	48
3558*	**Coqui Lane (93)** (JMDun) **10-10-3** DParker (a cl up: ev ch appr last: styd on u.p)	1	2	4/1 2	103	31
3645[6]	**Tighter Budget (USA) (100)** (MrsDianneSayer) **10-10-10** MMoloney (led tl hdd 2 out: wknd last)	13	3	12/1	102	30
3395[3]	**Whaat Fettle (114)** (GRichards) **12-11-10** ADobbin (cl up: rdn along fr 13th: wknd fr 4 out)	dist	4	2/1 1	—	—
3560*	**Kilcolgan (106)** (MrsJDGoodfellow) **10-11-2** NBentley (mstkes: shkn up & hdwy 9th: ev ch whn blnd & uns rdr 11th)		U	11/2 3	—	—
				(SP 109.7%)		**5 Rn**

6m 17.1 (7.10) CSF £9.25 TOTE £2.20: £1.10 £2.10 (£5.70) OWNER M H G Systems Ltd (SALTBURN) BRED James Roche

2923* Son of Iris did all that was required here, and won the race with one tremendous leap three out, but at the end there was nothing more in the locker. (2/1)

3558* Coqui Lane ran well on ground faster than he really likes, and was sticking on in persistent style at the finish. (4/1)

3645 Tighter Budget (USA) ran much better this time, and is obviously coming back to form. (12/1)

3395 Whaat Fettle could never lead here, and this seemed to disappoint him, as he ran poorly. (2/1)

3560* Kilcolgan was like an accident waiting to happen, and after several mistakes he blundered his rider out of the saddle with over a circuit left. (11/2)

3793 J.RUTHERFORD (EARLSTON) HUNTERS' CHASE (5-Y.O+) (Class H)

3-50 (3-50) **3m 4f (21 fncs)** £2,211.00 (£621.00: £303.00) GOING: 0.03 sec per fur (G)

				SP	RR	SF
3397*	**Jigtime** (JWHughes) **8-11-4**(7) MrMBradburne (trckd ldrs: hdwy 16th: led 3 out: r.o wl flat)	—	1	1/2 1	107	31
3397[2]	**Royal Jester** (CStorey) **13-11-11**(5) MrCStorey (lw: cl up tl outpcd 4 out: styd on flat: no ch w wnr)	7	2	3/1 2	108	32
	Orange Ragusa (SHShirley-Beavan) **11-11-5**(5) MissPRobson (lw: led tl hdd 3 out: hit next: ev ch last: hung rt & no ex flat)	1¼	3	11/2 3	101	25
2903[5]	**Southern Minstrel** (NChamberlain) **14-11-9**(7) MissCMetcalfe (hld up: effrt 15th: outpcd fr next)	2½	4	25/1	106	30
3609[4]	**Tartan Tornado** (MrsPLaws) **11-11-11**(5) MrPJohnson (a last: hit 11th: outpcd & wl bhd fr 16th)	dist	5	33/1	—	—
				(SP 113.8%)		**5 Rn**

7m 13.3 (17.30) CSF £2.50 TOTE £1.50: £1.10 £1.10 (£1.60) OWNER Mr J. W. Hughes (GALASHIELS) BRED M. H. D. Madden and Partners

3397* Jigtime did the job required in good style again, and it is going to take a useful performer to lower her colours. (1/2)

3397 Royal Jester does nothing quickly these days, but he gallops and stays and needs plenty of use made of him. (3/1)

Orange Ragusa jumps for fun, but he is basically short of toe between the fences and spoiled his chances further by hanging right on the flat. (11/2)
2903 Southern Minstrel never looked likely to get into this, but still ran quite well. (25/1)
3609 Tartan Tornado was never jumping or going well enough on this occasion. (33/1)

3794 KELSO ANNUAL MEMBERS 'N.H' NOVICES' HURDLE (I) (5-Y.O+) (Class D)

4-20 (4-20) **2m 6f 110y (11 hdls)** £2,409.00 (£674.00: £327.00) GOING: 0.03 sec per fur (G)

				SP	RR	SF
3328^{6}	**Cash Box (IRE) (76)** (TJCarr) **9-10-12** NSmith (hld up: stdy hdwy appr 4 out: n.m.r appr last: led 1f out: r.o.)	—	**1**	14/1	76	13
2785^{7}	**Major Harris (IRE)** (MDHammond) **5-10-12** RGarritty (wnt prom 4th: led last: hdd 1f out: kpt on)	1¼	**2**	12/1	75	12
3070^{3}	**No Gimmicks (IRE)** (JGFitzGerald) **5-10-12** RDunwoody (lw: a chsng ldrs: mstke 3 out: one pce fr next)	3	**3**	$9/2^{2}$	73	10
3437^{3}	**Chopwell Drapes (IRE) (89)** (HowardJohnson) **7-10-12** MMoloney (a cl up: led 3 out to last: no ex)	6	**4**	$7/1^{3}$	69	6
2539^{5}	**Political Millstar** (RNixon) **5-10-12** BStorey (hld up: hdwy 7th: ev ch 2 out: wknd flat)	hd	**5**	8/1	69	6
3024^{5}	**Monsieur Darcy (IRE)** (JRAdam) **6-10-12** JRailton (led to 3 out: sn outpcd)	8	**6**	12/1	63	—
	Dowshi (LLungo) **6-10-7** RSupple (hld up & bhd: nvr nr to chal)	7	**7**	33/1	53	—
3711^{P}	**Persian Grange (IRE) (66)** (DALamb) **7-10-12** JBurke (wnt prom ½-wy: outpcd fr 4 out)	5	**8**	100/1	54	—
3534^{5}	**Menaldi (IRE) (72)** (PCheesbrough) **7-10-12** ASSmith (cl up tl wknd fr 4 out)	8	**9**	20/1	49	—
3529*	**Derannie (IRE)** (GRichards) **5-11-5** ADobbin (lw: trckd ldrs tl wknd fr 4 out)	7	**10**	$6/5^{1}$	51	—
	Lord Pat (IRE) (MissMKMilligan) **6-10-9**(3) ECallaghan (chsd ldrs & wknd fr 3 out)	5	**11**	33/1	40	—
3449*	**Establish (IRE) (85)** (JPDodds) **9-11-0** AThornton (prom to ½-wy: sn wl bhd)	4	**12**	25/1	39	—
2627^{P}	**Just Polly** (HAlexander) **5-10-2**(5) RMcGrath (prom early: outpcd & wl bhd fr 7th)	1½	**13**	100/1	31	—
2917^{18}	**Rambling Lane** (RAllan) **8-10-5**(7) SMelrose (lost tch fr ½-wy: wl t.o whn p.u bef 3 out)		**P**	100/1	—	—
3611^{W}	**Moreflash** (JSHaldane) **5-10-4**(3) FLeahy (unruly s: mstkes: sn t.o: p.u bef 7th)		**P**	250/1	—	—

(SP 127.2%) **15 Rn**

5m 32.0 (15.00) CSF £152.49 TOTE £18.90: £2.20 £2.90 £2.00 (£47.50) Trio £269.40 OWNER Dr T. A. Wadrop (STANGHOW) BRED Peter Magnier

OFFICIAL EXPLANATION **Cash Box (IRE): regarding the apparent improvement in form, the trainer reported that the gelding had been unsuited by the soft ground and the longer trip last time. Derannie (IRE): was lame on his off-fore. Chopwell Drapes (IRE): was struck into.**

3328 Cash Box (IRE), given a confident ride, was produced to settle it on the run-in, but he decided he had done enough when in front and needed driving out. (14/1)
2785 Major Harris (IRE) is certainly improving, and once his stable comes back to form there are races to be won with him. (12/1: op 8/1)
3070 No Gimmicks (IRE), making his hurdles debut, ran well and was in contention throughout, but he was short of toe when the pressure was on. He may well need either a bit further or more testing ground. (9/2)
3437 Chopwell Drapes (IRE) had his chances, but looked one-paced when put under pressure, althought it later transpired he had struck into himself quite badly. (7/1)
2539 Political Millstar travelled well but failed to see the trip out. (8/1)
3024 Monsieur Darcy (IRE), made plenty of use of, ran better, and chasing will be the name of the game with him. (12/1)
3529* Derannie (IRE) was most disappointing here, dropping out tamely from the fourth last, and was found to be lame. (6/5)

3795 KELSO ANNUAL MEMBERS 'N.H' NOVICES' HURDLE (II) (5-Y.O+) (Class D)

4-50 (4-50) **2m 6f 110y (11 hdls)** £2,395.00 (£670.00: £325.00) GOING: 0.03 sec per fur (G)

				SP	RR	SF
3396^{4}	**Mister Ross (IRE) (108)** (HowardJohnson) **7-11-12** ADobbin (lw: a cl up: led 2 out: rdn & r.o)	—	**1**	$7/4^{1}$	87	16
3000^{P}	**Just One Question (IRE)** (JJO'Neill) **7-10-12** PNiven (lw: led tl hdd 2 out: kpt on same pce)	6	**2**	6/1	69	—
3295^{5}	**Grosvenor (IRE)** (GRichards) **6-10-12** RDunwoody (chsd ldrs: drvn along fr 7th: styd on fr 2 out: nvr able to chal)	5	**3**	$7/2^{3}$	65	—
2785^{10}	**My Mavourneen** (MrsSCBradburne) **5-10-7** MFoster (prom tl mstke & outpcd 7th: styd on fr 2 out)	4	**4**	20/1	57	—
3158^{13}	**Chasing Dreams** (CGrant) **6-10-12** RGarritty (a.p: outpcd 4 out: no imp after)	4	**5**	25/1	60	—
3487^{6}	**Smile Pleeze (IRE)** (MrsMStirk) **5-10-12** MrSSwiers (sn outpcd & wl bhd: styd on u.p fr 3 out: nrst fin)	8	**6**	20/1	54	—
3529^{P}	**Prince of Thyne (IRE)** (MrsJDGoodfellow) **8-10-12** NBentley (wnt prom 6th: sn chsng ldrs: wknd fr 3 out)	3½	**7**	33/1	51	—
3483^{4}	**Mike Stan (IRE)** (LLungo) **6-10-12** RSupple (prom tl wl outpcd fr 7th: sn no ch)	1¼	**8**	$100/30^{2}$	50	—
1139^{8}	**Faster Ron (IRE)** (RAllan) **6-10-5**(7) SMelrose (bhd: hdwy 7th: chsng clr ldrs 3 out: sn wknd)	1½	**9**	100/1	49	—
3481^{7}	**Jonaem (IRE) (74)** (MrsESlack) **7-11-5** KJohnson (lw: mid div: effrt ½-wy: n.d)	1½	**10**	33/1	55	—
3557^{4}	**Stepdaughter (65)** (MrsDThomson) **11-10-7** LO'Hara (outpcd & lost tch ½-wy: sn t.o)	17	**11**	33/1	31	—
2958^{10}	**Weejumpawud** (MrsJStorey) **7-10-7** MrCStorey (outpcd fr ½-wy: t.o)	10	**12**	200/1	24	—
3727^{5}	**Busy Boy (59)** (DALamb) **10-10-12** JBurke (prom tl rdn & lost tch ½-wy: t.o)	3	**13**	100/1	27	—
3487^{10}	**Woodhouse Lane** (NChamberlain) **5-10-5**(7) MissCMetcalfe (a wl bhd: t.o)	4	**14**	200/1	24	—

(SP 121.1%) **14 Rn**

5m 35.2 (18.20) CSF £11.07 TOTE £2.70: £1.40 £2.00 £1.10 (£14.90) Trio £27.40 OWNER Mr Gordon Brown (CROOK) BRED Mrs Kathleen Creedon and Con O'Leary

3396 Mister Ross (IRE) looked particularly well and, despite giving lumps of weight all round, did the business in most determined style. (7/4)
Just One Question (IRE) is a really nice sort who was showing his first signs of form in this country. Whatever he does over hurdles will be a bonus, as he looks every inch a chaser. (6/1)
3295 Grosvenor (IRE) had his chances, but was off the bit some way out and, despite struggling on, was always short of pace. (7/2)
My Mavourneen, stepping up in trip, ran better, and was clawing her way back towards the finish. (20/1)
Chasing Dreams proved well short of toe when the race began in earnest from the fourth last. (25/1)
Smile Pleeze (IRE), clueless early on, was soon virtually tailed off but, kept up to his work, he made a fair amount of late headway. (20/1)
3483 Mike Stan (IRE) found this ground too fast, and was never going the pace. (100/30)

T/Plpt: £28.10 (343.42 Tckts). T/Qdpt: £25.60 (20.58 Tckts) AA

3419-NEWBURY (L-H) (Chases Good to firm, Hdls Good)

Friday March 21st

WEATHER: Sunny

3796 WANTAGE NOVICES' HURDLE (4-Y.O+) (Class D)

1-50 (1-51) **3m 110y (12 hdls)** £3,176.25 (£960.00: £467.50: £221.25) GOING: 0.02 sec per fur (G)

				SP	RR	SF
3272[3]	**Ready Money Creek (IRE) (114)** (OSherwood) **6-11-12** JOsborne (lw: stdy hdwy appr 3 out: led last: hrd rdn: r.o wl)	—	**1**	11/2	86	31
3295*	**Absolutly Equiname (IRE)** (MJHeaton-Ellis) **6-11-12** BPowell (w ldr: ev ch last: unable qckn)	1½	**2**	11/4[1]	85	30
3541*	**Menesonic (IRE) (112)** (RHAlner) **7-11-5**(3) PHenley (swtg: hdwy 4th: hrd rdn appr 2 out: r.o one pce)	½	**3**	7/2[2]	81	26
3178[P]	**Clarkes Gorse (IRE)** (JTGifford) **6-11-4** PHide (led to last: one pce)	2	**4**	20/1	75	20
3295[3]	**Tremplin (IRE) (91)** (NJHenderson) **6-10-13** MAFitzgerald (lw: hld up: 4th & ev ch whn blnd 2 out: nt rcvr)	26	**5**	7/1	53	—
3628[5]	**Cool Harry (USA)** (HEHaynes) **6-10-11**(7) MrSDurack (prom to 9th)	4	**6**	66/1	56	1
3364*	**Ionio (USA) (118)** (MrsVCWard) **6-11-12** JRKavanagh (lw: blnd 4th: bhd fr 5th)	1¼	**7**	4/1[3]	63	8
3441[3]	**Christchurch (FR)** (SEarle) **7-11-4** CMaude (hdwy 3rd: mstke 7th: wknd 8th)	18	**8**	14/1	43	—
	Supreme Rambler (IRE) (BSmart) **8-11-4** WMarston (lw: bhd fr 8th)	12	**9**	33/1	35	—
	Johnymoss (IRE) (SEarle) **8-11-4** WMcFarland (prom to 6th: p.u bef 7th: lame)		**P**	40/1	—	—
3233[11]	**Artistic Plan (IRE)** (RHAlner) **5-10-13**(5) MrRThornton (lw: hdwy 7th: wknd appr 3 out: t.o whn p.u bef last)		**P**	50/1	—	—
1966[13]	**Spirit of Success** (NMLampard) **7-11-4** MrAKinane (bhd fr 2nd: t.o whn p.u after 5th)		**P**	66/1	—	—
3340[6]	**Look In The Mirror** (NATwiston-Davies) **6-11-4** CLlewellyn (t.o whn p.u bef 6th)		**P**	66/1	—	—
3407[F]	**Roadrunner** (MrsLRichards) **7-11-4** MRichards (a bhd: j.slowly 2nd: t.o whn p.u bef 9th)		**P**	66/1	—	—
				(SP 121.5%)	**14 Rn**	

6m 0.6 (14.60) CSF £18.85 TOTE £4.60: £1.30 £1.40 £1.90 (£6.70) Trio £9.50 OWNER Roach Foods Ltd (UPPER LAMBOURN) BRED P. Budds

3272 Ready Money Creek (IRE) relished this longer trip, for he has shown this season that he lacks acceleration but does stay. Adopting more patient tactics, which certainly suited, he cruised into the action in the straight and, jumping into the lead at the last, was given a few reminders to assert. (11/2)

3295* Absolutly Equiname (IRE) disputed the lead from the start and still had every chance jumping the final flight before the winner found a bit extra. He should soon regain the winning thread. (11/4)

3541* Menesonic (IRE) is a real stayer. Soon tucked in behind the leaders, he came under pressure approaching the second last, but kept on well to the finish. He would prefer some cut. (7/2)

2676 Clarkes Gorse (IRE) ran by far and away his best race over hurdles, and took the field along until collared at the final flight. (20/1)

3295 Tremplin (IRE) was just under a length down, with every chance, when a very bad error at the penultimate hurdle knocked the stuffing out of her. (7/1)

3364* Ionio (USA) once again proved he can be an awkward individual for, after a bad error at the fourth, he decided he did not want any more of it. He has plenty of ability, but still looks one to avoid. (4/1)

3797 BETTERTON NOVICES' CHASE (5-Y.O+) (Class D)

2-25 (2-25) **3m (18 fncs)** £3,574.00 (£1,072.00: £516.00: £238.00) GOING minus 0.13 sec per fur (G)

				SP	RR	SF
3600[8]	**Linton Rocks** (TThomsonJones) **8-11-4** BPowell (lw: led 2nd: easily)	—	**1**	6/5[1]	105+	25
3047[P]	**Hatcham Boy (IRE) (114)** (DNicholson) **7-11-12** RJohnson (hld up: chsd wnr 10th tl mstke 11th: chsd wnr 14th tl appr last: chsd wnr flat: r.o one pce)	2	**2**	11/8[2]	112	32
3749[4]	**Amber Valley (USA) (95)** (DLWilliams) **6-10-11**(7) MrSDurack (lw: wl bhd to 12th: hdwy 14th: chsd wnr appr last tl flat: one pce)	2½	**3**	17/2[3]	102	22
2926[F]	**Elite Governor (IRE)** (NMLampard) **8-10-11**(7) MrLBaker (mstke 1st: chsd wnr 3rd to 10th: chsd wnr 11th tl 14th: sn wknd)	18	**4**	16/1	90	10
3537[P]	**Dextra (IRE)** (SEarle) **7-11-4b[1]** CMaude (lw: led to 2nd: wknd 10th: mstke 12th: blnd 13th: t.o whn p.u bef 14th)		**P**	50/1	—	—
				(SP 105.9%)	**5 Rn**	

6m 0.6 (10.60) CSF £2.79 TOTE £2.20: £1.30 £1.20 (£2.20) OWNER The Hon Mrs Townshend (UPPER LAMBOURN) BRED Melbury Park Stud

3281 Linton Rocks made a very pleasing debut over fences. Soon in front, he gave a fine exhibition of jumping and won without turning a hair. (6/5: 4/5-5/4)

2698 Hatcham Boy (IRE) found the concession of 8lb to the winner far too much and, although eventually winning the battle for second prize, had no hope with his rival. (11/8)

3749 Amber Valley (USA), who fell at Towcester on Wednesday, was tackling a much longer trip, and was dropped out some way off the other runners. He gradually edged closer in the last mile, and took second place approaching the last, but he had no chance with the winner, and was collared for the runner-up berth on the flat. It is difficult to say he did not stay, but he may be better over shorter distances. (17/2: 5/1-9/1)

3798 SABIN DU LOIR MAIDEN HURDLE (4-Y.O+) (Class D)

2-55 (3-01) **2m 5f (11 hdls)** £4,102.50 (£1,245.00: £610.00: £292.50) GOING: 0.02 sec per fur (G)

				SP	RR	SF
2676[3]	**Quini Eagle (FR)** (MCPipe) **5-11-9** JamieEvans (chsd ldr fr 4th: led 3 out: blnd 2 out: hrd rdn flat: r.o wl)	—	**1**	8/1[3]	80	39
3569[B]	**Lively Encounter (IRE)** (MrsMerritaJones) **6-11-9** DerekByrne (swtg: stdy hdwy 9th: ev ch appr last: hrd rdn: unable qckn)	2	**2**	15/8[1]	79	38
3535[2]	**Foxies Lad** (DNicholson) **6-11-9** RJohnson (swtg: stdy hdwy 9th: rdn appr 2 out: ev ch appr last: one pce)	hd	**3**	9/1	78	37
3355[9]	**Madam's Walk (85)** (NATwiston-Davies) **7-11-4** CLlewellyn (lw: a.p: rdn appr 2 out: one pce)	8	**4**	33/1	67	26
	High Summer (TThomsonJones) **7-11-9** JCulloty (bit bkwd: a.p: rdn appr 2 out: sn wknd)	15	**5**	16/1	61	20
3564[4]	**Burn Out** (JPearce) **5-11-2**(7) JO'Shaughnessy (nvr nr to chal)	12	**6**	7/1[2]	52	11
3569[9]	**Tom Pinch (IRE)** (GBBalding) **8-11-9** RGreene (hmpd 1st: nvr nrr)	¾	**7**	33/1	51	10
3143[5]	**Father Henry (IRE)** (NJHenderson) **6-11-9** MAFitzgerald (lw: hld up: shkn up appr 3 out: sn wknd)	17	**8**	8/1[3]	38	—
2066[6]	**Breath of Scandal (IRE)** (OSherwood) **6-11-9** JOsborne (led after 1st: clr 2nd: hdd 3 out: sn wknd)	4	**9**	7/1[2]	35	—
1797[P]	**Proud Toby (IRE)** (GBBalding) **7-11-9** JRKavanagh (bkwd: a bhd)	8	**10**	50/1	29	—
	Cockpit (IRE) (GBBalding) **6-11-9** BClifford (bit bkwd: a bhd)	hd	**11**	50/1	29	—
	Happy Henry (IRE) (RHAlner) **7-11-9** TJMurphy (hmpd 1st: bhd fr 7th)	24	**12**	66/1	11	—
2008[P]	**Imperial Honors (IRE)** (NMLampard) **6-11-4**(5) ChrisWebb (a bhd)	2½	**13**	66/1	9	—

1673[8] **Warrio** (MRBosley) **7-11-9** LHarvey (bkwd: hmpd 1st: bhd fr 2nd)	3½ **14**	66/1	6	—
3425[9] **Conquer The Kilt** (JWMullins) **6-11-9** SCurran (fell 1st)	**F**	66/1	—	—
3628[3] **Rich Tycoon (IRE)** (PMRich) **8-11-9** WMarston (led tl after 1st: mid div whn p.u bef 6th)	**P**	33/1	—	—
3304[14] **Hour Horse** (NJHawke) **6-11-9** CMaude (bit bkwd: a bhd: mstke 2nd: t.o whn p.u bef 3 out)	**P**	66/1	—	—
Blazing Dove (AEPrice) **6-11-9** SWynne (bhd fr 5th: t.o whn p.u bef 7th: b.b.v)	**P**	50/1	—	—
Arctic Charmer (USA) (MrsSMOdell) **5-11-9** TJO'Sullivan (bit bkwd: a bhd: t.o whn p.u bef 8th)	**P**	66/1	—	—
		(SP 121.5%)	**19 Rn**	

5m 3.2 (9.20) CSF £19.89 TOTE £8.10: £2.10 £1.40 £3.00 (£12.50) Trio £19.40 OWNER Mr B. A. Kilpatrick (WELLINGTON) BRED Michel le Baron

OFFICIAL EXPLANATION **Blazing Dove: bled from the nose.**

2676 Quini Eagle (FR) would have preferred softer ground, and was only running here because his owner sponsored the race. Nevertheless he led at the third last, only to make a serious error at the next. Strongly tackled on both sides, he responded well to pressure, and proved too strong for his rivals. (8/1)

3569 Lively Encounter (IRE) has looked as though a longer trip would suit, and that is what he got here. Travelling well on the bridle, he looked a serious danger in the straight but, when he came under pressure approaching the last, he started to carry his head rather high, and failed to find another gear. (15/8)

3535 Foxies Lad again ran well, and moved steadily into the action in the straight. One of three with every chance going to the final flight, he was then tapped for toe. His turn is not far away. (9/1: op 5/1)

1090 Madam's Walk was never far away, but failed to quicken over the last three hurdles. (33/1)

High Summer, making his hurdling debut, looked in need of this first run in five months, and played an active role until calling it a day going to the second last. (16/1)

3143 Father Henry (IRE) (8/1: 6/1-10/1)

3799 ALISON ASSOCIATES HUNTERS' CHASE (5-Y.O+) (Class H)

3-25 (3-29) **3m** **(18 fncs)** £2,775.00 (£840.00: £410.00: £195.00) GOING minus 0.13 sec per fur (G)

			SP	RR	SF
3363[2] **Fox Pointer** (MrsLTJEvans) **12-11-13**(5) MrRThornton (lw: mde virtually all: shkn up appr 3 out: clr appr 2 out: easily)	—	**1**	7/4 1	113	45
Ardbrennan (JPorter) **10-11-11**(7) MrEJames (chsd wnr: rdn appr 3 out: unable qckn)	18	**2**	100/30 3	101	33
3498* **Ryming Cuplet** (MJTrickey) **12-12-3**(7) MrLJefford (bhd fr 4th)	21	**3**	2/1 2	93	25
3680[P] **Teatrader** (MissTOBlazey) **11-11-11**(7) MissTBlazey (bhd fr 10th)	s.h	**4**	16/1	87	19
3341[5] **Expressment** (MissASRoss) **13-12-3**(7) MrGPenfold (a bhd)	12	**5**	12/1	85	17
The Bodhran (IRE) (MGillard) **7-11-11**(7) MrSDurack (bhd tl fell 4th)		**F**	33/1	—	—
Alapa (ABCoogan) **10-11-11**(7) MrVCoogan (mstke 1st: hdwy 4th: 3rd & wkng whn mstke 4 out: 3rd & no ch whn blnd & uns rdr 3 out)		**U**	50/1	—	—
			(SP 111.3%)	**7 Rn**	

5m 58.1 (8.10) CSF £7.16 TOTE £2.50: £1.40 £1.50 (£5.40) OWNER Mrs L. T. J. Evans (NARBERTH) BRED Mrs L. T. J. Evans

OFFICIAL EXPLANATION **Ryming Cuplet: was always outpaced and would not let himself down on the good to firm ground.**

3363 Fox Pointer loves this ground and, making virtually all the running, forged clear in the straight to win with a ton in hand. He can win again. (7/4)

Ardbrennan, winner of a point-to-point this season, raced in second place, but was left for dead by the winner in the straight. (100/30)

3498* Ryming Cuplet never threatened to get into it, and his jockey reported afterwards that the gelding would not let himself down on the fast ground. However it is interesting to note that of his five wins under Rules, two have come on good ground and three on fast. (2/1)

Expressment (12/1: op 8/1)

3800 PAUL CROUCHER MEMORIAL TROPHY H'CAP CHASE (0-135) (5-Y.O+) (Class C)

4-00 (4-00) **2m 4f** **(16 fncs)** £4,727.50 (£1,420.00: £685.00: £317.50) GOING minus 0.13 sec per fur (G)

			SP	RR	SF
3618* **Terao (127)** (MCPipe) **11-11-10** 6x TJMurphy (chsd ldr: mstke 1st: led 3rd: j.rt fr 9th: pushed out)	—	**1**	9/4 2	141	67
Change the Act (110) (MissVenetiaWilliams) **12-10-7** RJohnson (hld up: chsd wnr fr 7th: rdn appr last: unable qckn)	2½	**2**	9/2 3	122	48
3401[2] **High Alltitude (IRE) (105)** (MJHeaton-Ellis) **9-10-2** BPowell (lw: hdwy 11th: rdn appr 2 out: wknd appr last)	12	**3**	2/1 1	107	33
3151[P] **Coolree (IRE) (112)** (PFNicholls) **9-10-9** MAFitzgerald (mstke 9th: hdwy 11th: wknd 3 out)	20	**4**	9/2 3	98	24
Mr Jamboree (127) (DRGandolfo) **11-11-7**(3) DFortt (led to 3rd: wknd 11th: t.o)	26	**5**	8/1	93	19
			(SP 111.6%)	**5 Rn**	

4m 53.6 (-1.40) CSF £11.33 TOTE £2.90: £1.60 £2.40 (£6.70) OWNER Mr B. A. Kilpatrick (WELLINGTON) BRED J. F. C. Maxwell

3618* Terao probably found the ground too fast for, after setting the pace and jumping adequately in the first half of the race, he then started to jump out to his right. However, despite this, he needed only to be nudged along to keep his rivals at bay. Most of his winning has come in the mud. (9/4)

Change the Act, off the course for a year, moved into second place early in the back straight for the final time. Close enough if good enough going to the final fence, he then failed to find another gear. This was a good performance, but he is not easy to win with, and has not scored for two and a half years. (9/2)

3401 High Alltitude (IRE) took closer order six out, but had come to the end of his tether soon after the penultimate fence. (2/1)

2942* Coolree (IRE) edged closer six from home, but had shot his bolt three out. (9/2)

3801 NEWBURY RACECOURSE STATION H'CAP HURDLE (0-125) (4-Y.O) (Class D)

4-35 (4-35) **2m 110y** **(8 hdls)** £3,317.50 (£1,000.00: £485.00: £227.50) GOING: 0.02 sec per fur (G)

			SP	RR	SF
3301[5] **Red Raja (118)** (PMitchell) **4-12-0** JOsborne (led to 3rd: hrd rdn appr last: led last: r.o wl)	—	**1**	2/1 2	96	53
3544[2] **Fairly Sharp (IRE) (100)** (GraemeRoe) **4-10-10** RichardGuest (chsd ldr: led 3rd to last: unable qckn)	3½	**2**	13/8 1	75	32
3301[8] **Province (90)** (CJMann) **4-9-11**(3) JMagee (lw: hld up: shkn up appr 2 out: sn wknd)	16	**3**	10/1	49	6
3075[4] **Northern Fleet (106)** (MrsAJPerrett) **4-11-2** MAFitzgerald (lw: bhd fr 2nd)	18	**4**	5/2 3	48	5
			(SP 109.1%)	**4 Rn**	

3m 55.2 (5.20) CSF £5.27 TOTE £2.80 (£1.80) OWNER Mr J. R. Ali (EPSOM) BRED J. Haine

LONG HANDICAP Province 9-11

3301 Red Raja, who did a nice piece of work with the stable's Kentucky Derby entry Running Stag earlier in the week, put up a polished display under his big weight. The early leader, Osborne sat quietly on the gelding in the straight, and then gave him a few reminders going to the last to wake him up. Jumping that flight in front, he soon stamped his authority on the race. (2/1: 6/4-9/4)

3544 Fairly Sharp (IRE) jumped into the lead at the third but, collared by the winner at the final flight, she was then put in her place. (13/8)

1935 Province chased the leaders, but the writing was on the wall going to the second last. (10/1)
3075 Northern Fleet failed to sparkle, and was soon getting left behind. (5/2)

T/Plpt: £17.00 (661.46 Tckts). T/Qdpt: £14.50 (38.93 Tckts) AK

3468-BANGOR-ON-DEE (L-H) (Good, Good to firm patches)
Saturday March 22nd
WEATHER: Fine

3802 STAN CLARKE NOVICES' HURDLE (4-Y.O+) (Class E)
2-10 (2-10) **2m 1f (9 hdls)** £3,186.00 (£896.00: £438.00) GOING minus 0.28 sec per fur (GF)

			SP	RR	SF
3668*	**Florid (USA)** (CPEBrooks) **6-10-9**(7) MBerry (lw: mde virtually all: shkn up 2 out: clr last)——	1	6/4[1]	78+	35
3592[2]	**Kinnescash (IRE) (100)** (PBowen) **4-10-1**(7) LCummins (chsd wnr thrght: rdn appr last: kpt on)3½	2	14/1	75	24
3271[9]	**Jessolle** (GRichards) **5-10-4**(7) RBurns (hld up in rr: hdwy 6th: styd on fr 2 out)5	3	66/1	65	22
3494*	**Talathath (FR) (113)** (DNicholson) **5-11-8** RJohnson (hld up in tch: effrt & rdn 6th: nt rch ldrs)10	4	100/30[2]	67	24
3500*	**Muhtadi (IRE)** (LadyHerries) **4-11-0** PNiven (hld up: hdwy appr 5th: wknd appr 2 out)4	5	5/1[3]	63	12
3431[B]	**Pot Blackbird (68)** (RLee) **8-10-11** WMarston (hld up & rdn 5th: nt rch ldrs)1¾	6	100/1	50	7
	Tabriz (MrsPMAAvison) **4-10-3** OPears (a in rr)3	7	66/1	47	—
	Mr Lowry (LJBarratt) **5-11-2** SWynne (chsd ldrs to 5th: sn wknd: t.o)12	8	66/1	41	—
3500[10]	**Althrey Pilot (IRE)** (AndrewTurnell) **6-11-2** CRae (a bhd: t.o)2½	9	33/1	39	—
3278[F]	**Rinus Major (IRE)** (DMcCain) **6-11-2** DWalsh (bkwd: plld hrd: prom tl wknd 5th: t.o)12	10	100/1	27	—
3426[3]	**Vadlawys (FR)** (SABrookshaw) **6-11-2** ADobbin (bit bkwd: trckd ldrs: effrt & 5th whn fell 3 out)	F	13/2	—	—
2840[11]	**Reach The Clouds (IRE)** (JohnUpson) **5-11-2** RSupple (a bhd: no ch whn fell 2 out)	F	66/1	—	—
3548[11]	**Brandon Bridge** (DPGeraghty) **6-11-2** VSlattery (a bhd: t.o whn p.u bef last)	P	66/1	—	—
2628[3]	**El Crank Senor** (RDEWoodhouse) **5-11-2** RDunwoody (chsd ldrs to 3 out: p.u bef next: lame)	P	14/1	—	—
3468[6]	**Gaf** (BRCambidge) **5-11-2** TEley (a bhd: t.o fr ½-wy: p.u bef 3 out)	P	100/1	—	—
			(SP 119.8%)	**15 Rn**	

3m 56.6 (1.60) CSF £22.83 TOTE £2.40: £1.30 £2.70 £22.10 (£27.90) Trio £279.10 OWNER Lord Howard de Walden (LAMBOURN) BRED Lord Howard de Walden
WEIGHT FOR AGE 4yo-8lb

3668* Florid (USA) again let his class do the talking, and though he was given a reminder soon after entering the straight he always had complete control. (6/4)
3592 Kinnescash (IRE) has taken well to hurdles, but he has been pitted against some useful rivals, and he is sure to find an easier opportunity before long. (14/1)
2924 Jessolle turned in by far her most improved effort yet, and she is beginning to get the hang of things. (66/1)
3494* Talathath (FR) ran most disappointingly, and even allowing for the 6lb penalty he should have figured in the outcome. (100/30)
3500* Muhtadi (IRE) looked to be full of running when moving on to the heels of the leaders three out, but he found absolutely nothing when popped the question, and was beaten in next to no time. (5/1)
Pot Blackbird could not muster the pace to deliver a challenge despite staying on, but she is not without ability. (100/1)
3426 Vadlawys (FR) still looked to have a bit left to work on, but he travelled well throughout, and was within striking range when crash-landing at the third last. (13/2)

3803 CROSS LANES HOTEL CONDITIONAL (S) H'CAP HURDLE (0-95) (4-Y.O+) (Class G)
2-45 (2-45) **2m 1f (9 hdls)** £2,358.00 (£663.00: £324.00) GOING minus 0.28 sec per fur (GF)

			SP	RR	SF
3741[2]	**Night Boat (71)** (WClay) **6-10-10** GuyLewis (hld up: stdy hdwy fr 4th: led appr last: rdn out)——	1	7/2[1]	57	8
3110[9]	**Nord Lys (IRE) (64)** (BJLlewellyn) **6-10-3** MichaelBrennan (hdwy 4th: lft in ld 6th: hdd appr last: one pce)3	2	20/1	47	—
3234[15]	**Never so Blue (IRE) (83)** (PBradley) **6-11-5**(3) RWilkinson (hdwy 4th: rdn 2 out: styd on flat)1½	3	16/1	65	16
3313[4]	**Palace of Gold (85)** (LLungo) **7-11-5**(5) WDowling (chsd ldrs: rdn & one pce fr 2 out)1¼	4	9/2[2]	66	17
3485[10]	**Eternal City (85)** (GRichards) **6-11-5**(5) RBurns (swtg: prom: mstke & lost pl 3rd: hdwy 6th: nt pce to chal)2	5	8/1[3]	64	15
3112[9]	**Strike-a-Pose (68)** (BJLlewellyn) **7-10-7** GLee (lw: hld up: hdwy 6th: nt rch ldrs)s.h	6	8/1[3]	47	—
3091[5]	**Kismetim (61)** (GPKelly) **7-9-9**(5) THogg (stdd s: a bhd)2	7	25/1	38	—
3471[5]	**Quixotry (69)** (JMackie) **6-10-8** EHusband (mstke 5th: a bhd)7	8	25/1	39	—
3091[7]	**Jarrow (61)** (MrsAMNaughton) **6-10-0** GFRyan (chsd ldrs: j.slowly & lost tch 5th: sn rdn: t.o)26	9	25/1	7	—
3677[5]	**Still Here (IRE) (70)** (PBowen) **4-9-10b**(5) LCummins (led to 2nd: wknd 5th: t.o)3	10	11/1	13	—
3091[9]	**Bud's Bet (IRE) (68)** (MissJFCraze) **9-10-4**(3) MNewton (lost tch ½-wy: t.o)¾	11	25/1	10	—
3677[10]	**A Badge Too Far (IRE) (61)** (MrsLWilliamson) **7-9-11**(3) STaylor (a bhd: t.o)8	12	66/1	—	—
	Classic Account (70) (JLEyre) **9-10-4**(5) CElliott (led 2nd: 4l clr whn fell 6th)	F	7/2[1]	—	—
3029[P]	**Regal Jest (61)** (BWMurray) **7-9-9**(5) NHorrocks (a bhd: t.o whn p.u bef 2 out)	P	50/1	—	—
3471[12]	**Bit of Rough (IRE) (61)** (WClay) **7-10-0** DJKavanagh (bkwd: sn bhd & rdn: t.o whn p.u bef 3 out)	P	50/1	—	—
731[3]	**Red March Hare (72)** (JCHaynes) **6-10-6**(5) CMcCormack (bkwd: chsd ldrs to 5th: bhd whn p.u bef 3 out)	P	16/1	—	—
			(SP 130.5%)	**16 Rn**	

4m 1.7 (6.70) CSF £73.12 CT £957.24 TOTE £4.50: £1.60 £4.40 £3.00 £1.50 (£41.10) Trio £233.50; £263.18 to Hexham 24/3/97 OWNER M Bray-Cotton, V Lockley & J Davies (STOKE-ON-TRENT) BRED Chippenham Lodge Stud
LONG HANDICAP A Badge Too Far (IRE) 9-6 Regal Jest 9-7 Bit of Rough (IRE) 9-8 Kismetim 9-13
WEIGHT FOR AGE 4yo-8lb
Bt in 5,750 gns

3741 Night Boat, making a quick reappearance, finally got off the mark with a clear-cut success and was not winning out of turn. (7/2)
357* Nord Lys (IRE) hardly runs two races alike, but he was back on song here only to find the winner much too strong in the battle to the finish. (20/1)
3031 Never so Blue (IRE), returning to selling class, stuck on willingly under pressure in the latter stages and is up to winning another race. (16/1)
3313 Palace of Gold could not dictate on this occasion, but he pushed the pace and remained prominent until tapped for speed from the turn for home. (9/2)
3096 Eternal City could not make his presence felt after making an early mistake, but he did rally inside the last half-mile if lacking the pace to get on terms. (8/1)

2882 Strike-a-Pose, stepping down to the minimum trip, made an effort on the approach to the straight, but could not muster the pace to get serious. (8/1)
Classic Account, fit from the All-Weather, was setting his rivals a merry dance when he came to grief four out, and it is possible he would have remained there. (7/2)

3804 ALTHREY WOODHOUSE H'CAP CHASE (0-130) (5-Y.O+) (Class C)

3-15 (3-15) **2m 4f 110y (15 fncs)** £4,879.00 (£1,477.00: £721.00: £343.00) GOING: 0.07 sec per fur (G)

	Horse	Dist	Pos	SP	RR	SF
3413*	**Frickley (112)** (GRichards) **11-10-10** RDunwoody (sn prom: led appr 7th: drew clr last: eased flat)	—	1	13/8[1]	123+	12
1910*	**Cumbrian Challenge (IRE) (128)** (TDEasterby) **8-11-12** LWyer (hld up: hdwy 10th: chal 2 out: sn outpcd)	5	2	4/1[3]	135	24
3618[7]	**Southampton (115)** (GBBalding) **7-10-13v** RichardGuest (hld up & bhd: hdwy 4th: no imp fr next)	7	3	5/2[2]	117	6
3456[2]	**Dolikos (105)** (THCaldwell) **10-10-0**(3)ow3 MichaelBrennan (prom tl wknd 9th: sn t.o)	17	4	33/1	93	—
3266[5]	**Camitrov (FR) (130)** (TKeddy) **7-12-0** PNiven (bit bkwd: lft in ld 5th: hdd appr 7th: wknd appr 3 out: t.o: b.b.v)	16	5	14/1	106	—
	Andermatt (117) (JMackie) **10-11-1** WMarston (bkwd: hld up in rr: mstke 11th: t.o fr 4 out)	12	6	16/1	84	—
3276*	**General Pershing (130)** (DNicholson) **11-12-0** RJohnson (led: clr whn fell 5th)		F	5/1	—	—
				(SP 118.8%)		**7 Rn**

5m 14.9 (14.90) CSF £8.71 TOTE £2.40: £1.50 £2.80 (£6.50) OWNER Mr Robert Ogden (PENRITH) BRED Frank Motherway
LONG HANDICAP Dolikos 8-9
OFFICIAL EXPLANATION **Camitrov (FR): the trainer reported that the gelding bled from the nose.**
3413* Frickley had more use made of him and looked to have a fight on his hands turning in, but he stepped up the tempo to extend his advantage between the last two, and was able to ease to a walk passing the post. (13/8)
1910* Cumbrian Challenge (IRE) ran extremely well after a break of over three months and, with this outing to put an edge on him, an early return to form is earmarked. (4/1)
3169 Southampton has lost the habit of winning, and his short-lived effort before reaching the straight petered out to nothing. (5/2)
Camitrov (FR), brought back to a more suitable trip, lost touch with the principals before reaching the home straight, and it transpired he had broken a blood-vessel. (14/1)

3805 MILES MACADAM NOVICES' CHASE (5-Y.O+) (Class D)

3-50 (3-51) **3m 110y (18 fncs)** £4,357.50 (£1,320.00: £645.00: £307.50) GOING: 0.07 sec per fur (G)

	Horse	Dist	Pos	SP	RR	SF
1574*	**Chopwell Curtains** (TDEasterby) **7-11-11** LWyer (bit bkwd: chsd ldrs: outpcd 14th: hdwy to ld 2 out: blnd last: all out)	—	1	11/2[2]	121	36
3565[2]	**Mystic Isle (IRE) (85)** (NAGaselee) **7-11-5** WMarston (lw: hld up: hdwy 13th: j.slowly 4 out: rallied u.p appr last: fin wl)	1	2	16/1	114	29
3300[2]	**Around The Gale (IRE) (129)** (DRGandolfo) **6-12-0** RDunwoody (lw: led: mstke 3rd: hdd 14th: led 3 out to 2 out: hrd rdn: kpt on)	1¼	3	1/2[1]	123	38
3700[P]	**Monymoss (IRE) (105)** (MrsSJSmith) **8-11-11** RichardGuest (w ldr: led 14th tl hdd & mstke 3 out: wknd appr next)	18	4	9/1[3]	108	23
3639[8]	**The Reverend Bert (IRE) (110)** (GBBalding) **9-11-11** BClifford (hld up: a in rr)	10	5	10/1	101	16
3426[10]	**Grizzly Bear (IRE)** (RMStronge) **7-11-5** SWynne (bit bkwd: chsd ldrs to 12th: sn wknd: t.o)	28	6	150/1	77	—
3334[F]	**Foxwoods Valley (IRE)** (DNicholson) **8-11-5** RJohnson (bit bkwd: hld up on outside: hdwy 11th: blnd 13th: sn lost pl: no ch whn blnd & uns rdr last)		U	14/1	—	—
				(SP 114.4%)		**7 Rn**

6m 16.4 (14.40) CSF £66.23 TOTE £5.20: £2.10 £2.80 (£29.30) Trio £4.40 OWNER Durham Drapes Ltd (MALTON) BRED Mrs A. C. Wakeham
1574* Chopwell Curtains opened his account over fences on his previous outing in the autumn, but he has performed best when fresh in the past, and he recovered well from a last-fence blunder to run out a very game winner. (11/2)
3565 Mystic Isle (IRE) made more than his fair share of mistakes, and his jockey deserves all the credit for getting him so close at the finish. He is not short on ability and his turn will come. (16/1)
3300 Around The Gale (IRE) was not helped in his quest to get this extended trip by having to contend with a persistent rival to the third last and, though he rallied on the flat, the damage had been done. (1/2: 8/13-6/4)
3285 Monymoss (IRE) decided to take the winner on from the outset, and from time to time outjumped him, but he was getting leg-weary when he ploughed through the third last, and that took what stuffing remained out of him. (9/1: op 5/1)

3806 NORTH WEST RACING CLUB MAIDEN CHASE (5-Y.O+) (Class D)

4-25 (4-30) **2m 4f 110y (15 fncs)** £3,696.25 (£1,120.00: £547.50: £261.25) GOING: 0.07 sec per fur (G)

	Horse	Dist	Pos	SP	RR	SF
3279[3]	**Pearl Epee (81)** (DNicholson) **8-11-2** RJohnson (j.w: led 2nd: drew clr fr 2 out: unchal)	—	1	14/1	94	27
3495[F]	**Campeche Bay (IRE) (130)** (GBBalding) **8-11-7** RDunwoody (chsd wnr fr 2nd: ev ch 3 out: sn rdn & wknd)	21	2	4/7[1]	83	16
3347[P]	**Dee Light** (GRichards) **8-11-2** PNiven (bit bkwd: hld up: hdwy 8th: ev ch 3 out: rdn & wknd appr next)	½	3	25/1	77	10
2659[6]	**Crane Hill** (PJHobbs) **7-11-7b** WMarston (trckd ldrs: rdn 10th: sn lost pl: t.o)	2	4	11/2[2]	81	14
1539[7]	**Little Notice (IRE)** (CaptTAForster) **6-11-7** SWynne (chsd ldrs tl fell 6th)		F	11/1	—	—
3608[4]	**Fort Zeddaan (IRE)** (MrsSJSmith) **7-11-0**(7) RWilkinson (hld up: 4th & rdn whn fell 4 out)		F	25/1	—	—
3052[P]	**Lady Rosebury** (RJPrice) **7-11-2** TJenks (nt j.w: t.o whn p.u bef 6th)		P	66/1	—	—
3546[6]	**Tug Your Forelock (60)** (GFJohnsonHoughton) **6-11-4**(3) MichaelBrennan (sn t.o: p.u bef 9th)		P	66/1	—	—
3582[P]	**Ledburian** (MissPMWhittle) **7-11-4**(3) GuyLewis (prom: rdn 8th: sn wknd: t.o whn p.u bef 2 out)		P	100/1	—	—
3582[3]	**Dandie Imp (78)** (AWCarroll) **9-11-7** DWalsh (led tl rn out 2nd)		R	7/1[3]	—	—
				(SP 118.2%)		**10 Rn**

5m 12.1 (12.10) CSF £21.85 TOTE £8.90: £1.50 £1.30 £2.30 (£6.10) Trio £33.20 OWNER Mrs A. A. Shutes (TEMPLE GUITING) BRED C. Toone
OFFICIAL EXPLANATION **Dandie Imp: the reins broke.**
3279 Pearl Epee adopted more forceful tactics, and produced an almost foot-perfect round of jumping to get off the mark with a runaway success. (14/1: op 8/1)
3495 Campeche Bay (IRE) had the opportunity to make amends for a very unlucky defeat last time, but the winner would not let him take control and, made to struggle turning for home, he had to admit he had met his match. (4/7)
Dee Light, a very lightly-raced mare, turned in a pleasing display under a forceful ride, and she could well be on the upgrade. (25/1)
1938 Crane Hill completed in his own time on this chasing debut, but was never close enough to cause concern, and he will need to improve considerably to make the grade at this game. (11/2: 7/2-6/1)
1085 Little Notice (IRE) (11/1: 8/1-12/1)

3807 LIGHTWOOD GREEN H'CAP HURDLE (0-115) (5-Y.O+) (Class E)

4-55 (4-57) **3m (12 hdls)** £2,957.00 (£896.00: £438.00: £209.00) GOING: 0.07 sec per fur (G)

				SP	RR	SF
3562[3]	**Selatan (IRE) (109)** (DRGandolfo) **5-12-0** RDunwoody (chsd ldrs: rdn appr last: styd on to ld cl home)	—	1	4/1[2]	89	54
3613[14]	**Prussia (95)** (WClay) **6-10-11**(3) GuyLewis (lw: a.p: rdn 3 out: led appr 2 out: sn hdd: led flat: ct nr fin)	nk	2	10/1	75	40
3702*	**Winn's Pride (IRE) (105)** (RHollinshead) **6-11-10** SWynne (hld up: hdwy 6th: led 2 out tl flat: rdn & no ex)	2½	3	4/1[2]	83	48
3317[P]	**Flat Top (98)** (MWEasterby) **6-11-0**(3) PMidgley (hld up: hdwy 8th: rdn appr last: one pce)	s.h	4	11/1	76	41
3157[8]	**Jigginstown (81)** (JJO'Neill) **10-9-7**(7) LCooper (hld up in rr: sme hdwy fr 3 out: nvr nrr)	5	5	20/1	56	21
3545[5]	**Needwood Poppy (88)** (BCMorgan) **9-10-7** BClifford (wl bhd tl styd on fr 2 out)	½	6	11/2[3]	62	27
3534[2]	**Jervaulx (IRE) (99)** (GRichards) **6-11-4** PNiven (lw: chsd ldrs: hdwy & lft in ld 3 out: hdd next: sn btn)	3½	7	7/2[1]	71	36
3442[14]	**Whitebonnet (IRE) (82)** (CREgerton) **7-9-12b**(3) SophieMitchell (chsd ldrs to 8th: sn wknd: t.o)	6	8	25/1	50	15
3434[5]	**White Willow (95)** (TWall) **8-11-0b** TJenks (led & sn clr: wknd & hdd 8th: sn rdn: t.o)	dist	9	16/1	—	—
3554[3]	**Indian Quest (101)** (NAGaselee) **8-11-6** WMarston (chsd ldr: led 8th: fell 3 out)		F	11/1	—	—
3630[2]	**Cassio's Boy (91)** (RJEckley) **6-10-10** RJohnson (hld up in rr: fell 7th)		F	10/1	—	—
2913[11]	**Doolar (USA) (83)** (PTDalton) **10-9-13**(3)ow2 MichaelBrennan (wl bhd whn collapsed & died after 6th)		F	33/1	—	—
3332[P]	**Far Senior (81)** (PWegmann) **11-9-9**(5) DJKavanagh (lost pl 4th: t.o whn p.u after 7th)		P	50/1	—	—
				(SP 131.8%)		**13 Rn**

5m 39.0 (2.50 under best) (0.00) CSF £42.74 CT £165.33 TOTE £6.00: £2.30 £2.90 £2.40 (£33.90) Trio £48.60 OWNER Starlight Racing (WANTAGE) BRED His Highness the Aga Khans Studs S. C.

LONG HANDICAP Jigginstown 9-9 Doolar (USA) 9-9

3562 Selatan (IRE), still to shed his winter coat, found this much easier than the races he had been engaged in most recently, but he still had to work very hard and full credit has to go to the man on board. (4/1)

2074 Prussia saw the trip out well and was only worn down in the dying strides. He should not be long in getting back to winning ways. (10/1)

3702* Winn's Pride (IRE) gave of his best in an attempt to follow up his success at Uttoxeter last week, and he looked all over a winner approaching the last, but this race came too quickly after such a lengthy break and his run had come to an end on the flat. (4/1)

3317 Flat Top had reached a challenging position three out, but he lost out when the tempo picked up between the last two, and may well have found the ground too lively. (11/1)

2915 Jigginstown is slow but he does stay, and now might be the right time for him to return to fences. (20/1)

3534 Jervaulx (IRE) did not appear to see out this longer trip after being presented with a first-class chance at the third last. (7/2)

3554 Indian Quest had never before tackled this trip, but he was a length to the good and still galloping when falling three out. He is lightly-raced and another chance is warranted. (11/1)

3630 Cassio's Boy (10/1: 8/1-12/1)

3808 BANGOR-ON-DEE MAIDEN N.H. FLAT RACE (4, 5 & 6-Y.O) (Class H)

5-25 (5-27) **2m 1f** £1,549.50 (£432.00: £208.50)

				SP	RR	SF
	Go Cahoots (USA) (AndrewTurnell) **4-11-2** CRae (wl grwn: a.p: led 6f out to 2f out: rdn to ld nr fin)	—	1	12/1	50 f	—
3548[7]	**Dinky Dora** (JKCresswell) **4-10-4**(7) NTEgan (small: cmpt: a.p: led 2f out: hrd rdn & ct cl home)	hd	2	16/1	45 f	—
	Galeshan (IRE) (GRichards) **5-11-3**(7) RBurns (w'like: bit bkwd: hld up: hdwy 5f out: nt clr run ent st: styd on strly towards fin)	1¾	3	12/1	48 f	—
	Pennybryn (JLEyre) **4-10-4**(7) CElliott (unf: scope: bit bkwd: hld up mid div: hdwy over 4f out: rdn & wandered 2f out: styd on)	1¼	4	10/1	42 f	—
	Mazzelmo (ABailey) **4-10-4**(7) SMelrose (leggy: unf: bkwd: hld up: hdwy over 4f out: rdn & rn green fnl 2f: nt qckn)	1¼	5	20/1	41 f	—
	Star Adventure (JTEvans) **5-11-10** MissEJames (w'like: bkwd: s.s: hdwy 4f out: styd on appr fnl f)	nk	6	50/1	46 f	—
3006[11]	**Be In Space** (MissPMWhittle) **6-11-2**(3) SophieMitchell (w'like: s.s: sn w ldrs: ev ch whn wknd over 2f out)	3	7	50/1	38 f	—
	Dakota III (FR) (DNicholson) **6-11-3**(7) MrOMcPhail (wl grwn: bkwd: hld up: hdwy 6f out: sn drvn along: grad wknd)	7	8	6/1[2]	36 f	—
3297[2]	**Shropshire Gale (IRE)** (SABrookshaw) **6-11-5**(5) OBurrows (lengthy: unf: hld up: hdwy 5f out: rdn & wknd 3f out)	8	9	9/4[1]	29 f	—
3297[4]	**Arctic Fox (IRE)** (MissHCKnight) **5-11-3**(7) MrAWintle (w'like: leggy: swtg: w.r.s: sn chsng ldrs: rdn & btn 3f out)	5	10	9/4[1]	24 f	—
	Michigan Blue (WJenks) **5-11-10** MrAMitchell (unf: scope: bit bkwd: plld hrd: mde most 11f: rdn & wknd over 3f out)	nk	11	33/1	24 f	—
	See More Angels (APJames) **6-11-2**(3) EHusband (scope: bkwd: hmpd s: pushed along 5f out: no imp)	nk	12	50/1	18 f	—
	Rocky Balboa (MissPMWhittle) **5-11-7**(3) GuyLewis (cmpt: bkwd: chsd ldrs 12f: sn lost tch: t.o)	7	13	50/1	17 f	—
	Outrageous Affair (APJames) **5-11-2**(3) GLee (w'like: str: bkwd: plld hrd: chsd ldrs: wknd over 4f out: t.o)	23	14	33/1	—	—
	Ramillion (IRBrown) **5-11-5** MrABrown (leggy: scope: s.s: hdwy ½-wy: wknd 6f out: t.o)	17	15	50/1	—	—
3626[8]	**Nirvana Princess** (BPreece) **5-10-12**(7) JMogford (lengthy: unf: ref to r: t.n.p)		R	40/1	—	—
3574[10]	**Eagle Dancer** (LadyHerries) **5-11-7**(3) MichaelBrennan (leggy: uns rdr s)		U	8/1[3]	—	—
				(SP 140.2%)		**17 Rn**

4m 5.3 CSF £184.47 TOTE £14.70: £2.80 £8.90 £3.30 (£214.50) Trio Not won; £333.68 to Hexham 24/3/97 OWNER Marisa Bartoli & John Moreton (WANTAGE) BRED Foxfield and Richard Dick

WEIGHT FOR AGE 4yo-8lb

IN-FOCUS: The start of this race was particularly ragged, with one horse unseating the rider, another refusing to start, and several losing considerable ground.

Go Cahoots (USA), quite a well-grown debutant, is certainly not short on stamina and that is what won him the race in the end. He has the size to go chasing. (12/1)

Dinky Dora had the advantage of a run earlier in the month and, having a lot more use made of her, she only just failed to hold on. (16/1)

Galeshan (IRE), who carries the colours of One Man, may have been a shade unlucky on this racecourse debut, and a lot more will be heard of him. (12/1: op 7/1)

Pennybryn, an unfurnished daughter of Teenoso, ran about when staying on inside the distance, but this was all down to greenness, and she should not be hard-pressed to pick up a similar event. (10/1: op 16/1)

Mazzelmo did not look the finished article, but showed plenty of promise and, with this experience under her belt, can only improve. (20/1)

Star Adventure, one of many to lose ground at the start, was staying on well in the closing stages and does look to have some ability. (50/1)

Dakota III (FR) (6/1: op 4/1)

3297 Shropshire Gale (IRE), a very sparely-made Strong Gale gelding who has had previous experience, was finding demands too great for him entering the straight and dropped away tamely. (9/4: op 7/2)

3297 Arctic Fox (IRE) could not improve on his initial outing a month ago, and was fighting a lost cause from some way out. (9/4)
Eagle Dancer (8/1: op 9/2)

T/Plpt: £117.50 (121.93 Tckts). T/Qdpt: £35.10 (18.77 Tckts) IM

3684-LINGFIELD (L-H) (Good to firm, Hdls Good patches in bk st)
Saturday March 22nd
WEATHER: Sunny

3809 NEWLEAF MAIDEN HURDLE (4-Y.O) (Class E)
1-30 (1-30) **2m 110y (8 hdls)** £2,360.80 (£653.80: £312.40) GOING: 0.06 sec per fur (G)

	Horse	Dist	Pos	SP	RR	SF
3634[7]	**Seattle Alley (USA) (97)** (PRWebber) **4-11-0** JAMcCarthy (lw: hdwy 4th: led appr 2 out: rdn out)	—	1	13/8[2]	90	7
	Quakers Field (GLMoore) **4-11-0** DGallagher (lw: hld up: ev ch 2 out: rdn appr last: r.o wl flat)	¾	2	8/11[1]	89+	6
3623[5]	**Veronica Franco (70)** (BAPearce) **4-10-6**(3) PHenley (w ldr: led 3 out tl appr 2 out: 4th & btn whn pckd 2 out)	11	3	66/1	74?	—
3601[8]	**Silvretta (IRE) (80)** (JTGifford) **4-10-6**(3) LAspell (a.p: led 5th to 3 out: ev ch appr 2 out: wknd appr last)	½	4	25/1	73?	—
3404[9]	**Zaisan (IRE)** (JTGifford) **4-11-0** PHide (led to 5th: wknd appr 2 out)	12	5	14/1[3]	67?	—
2751[5]	**Illuminate** (DCO'Brien) **4-11-0** JRKavanagh (lw: plld hrd: prom to 3 out: t.o whn p.u bef last)		P	14/1[3]	—	—
3575[8]	**My Nad Knows** (JCPoulton) **4-11-0** TJO'Sullivan (bhd fr 5th: t.o whn p.u bef 2 out)		P	100/1	—	—
				(SP 115.7%)	**7 Rn**	

3m 58.0 (13.00) CSF £3.04 TOTE £2.90: £1.60 £1.10 (£1.60) OWNER L & P Partnership (BANBURY) BRED Hermitage Farm Inc.
3634 Seattle Alley (USA), who finished seventh in last week's Triumph Hurdle, at last came good. Leading approaching the second last, he managed to keep the runner-up at bay. (13/8)
Quakers Field, a winner of two races and beaten less than two lengths in the Group Three Horris Hill as a juvenile, failed to win as a three-year-old but was beaten under two lengths by St Mawes in the Gordon Stakes at Goodwood. Making his hurdling debut, he was nicely poised turning into the straight but he was hesitant at the last two hurdles as he was trying to make his challenge. Almost three lengths down early on the run-in, he ran on splendidly but was beaten by the line. With cleaner jumping over the last two hurdles he would surely have won this. Compensation awaits. (8/11)
3623 Veronica Franco, who looked rough in the paddock, did not run badly and moved to the front three out. Collared approaching the penultimate hurdle, she was already feeling the pinch when pecking at that flight. (66/1)
3224 Silvretta (IRE) ran her best race to date over hurdles, and still had every chance early in the straight before tiring. (25/1)
Illuminate (14/1: 10/1-16/1)

3810 MALCOLM AND SUE HAVE SAID I DO NOVICES' H'CAP CHASE (0-95) (5-Y.O+) (Class F)
2-05 (2-05) **2m (12 fncs)** £2,467.85 (£735.80: £350.90: £158.45) GOING: 0.06 sec per fur (G)

	Horse	Dist	Pos	SP	RR	SF
3686[2]	**Buckland Lad (IRE) (81)** (DMGrissell) **6-11-10** JRKavanagh (hdwy to chse ldr 4th: led 4 out: lft clr 2 out: eased flat)	—	1	4/11[1]	84+	—
3343[7]	**Master Pangloss (IRE) (60)** (AndrewTurnell) **7-10-3** WMcFarland (lw: w ldr: led 3rd: j.slowly 4th: mstke & hdd 4 out: wknd 3 out: lft mod 2nd & blnd 2 out)	4	2	11/1	59	—
1875[6]	**Nautical George (IRE) (80)** (JohnUpson) **7-11-9** GaryLyons (t: led to 3rd: wknd 8th)	3½	3	6/1[2]	76	—
3576[F]	**Eau So Sloe (60)** (JRPoulton) **6-10-3** ADicken (bhd fr 5th)	nk	4	40/1	55	—
3442[17]	**Fane Park (IRE) (70)** (CLPopham) **9-10-10**(3) PHenley (hdwy 4 out: chsd wnr appr 3 out: 2nd & btn whn fell 2 out: dead)		F	10/1[3]	—	—
	Bright Season (61) (JCPoulton) **9-10-4** TJO'Sullivan (lw: bhd fr 7th: t.o whn p.u bef 3 out)		P	40/1	—	—
				(SP 109.9%)	**6 Rn**	

4m 9.4 (17.40) CSF £4.71 TOTE £1.30: £1.10 £2.60 (£3.70) OWNER Mrs R. M. Hepburn (ROBERTSBRIDGE) BRED Patrick Moore
3686 Buckland Lad (IRE) made up for his bad blunder here last week. Leading at the fourth last, he already had the measure of the ill-fated Fane Park when that rival departed at the penultimate fence. He was eased down considerably on the run-in and was value for at least fifteen lengths. (4/11)
1073 Master Pangloss (IRE) is a poor individual and, after making a lot of the running, was headed four from home. However he was left a moderate second at the penultimate fence, but is greatly flattered to finish so close, as the winner was eased down considerably. (11/1: 7/1-12/1)
1664 Nautical George (IRE), without a run in three-and-a-half months, began to lose touch from the fifth last but, with Fane Park falling and the winner being eased considerably on the run-in, he is greatly flattered to finish so close. He is a very poor performer. (6/1: 4/1-13/2)
Eau So Sloe is very aptly-named. (40/1)

3811 CHELSAM (S) H'CAP HURDLE (0-95) (4-Y.O+) (Class G)
2-40 (2-44) **2m 110y (8 hdls)** £2,024.90 (£561.40: £268.70) GOING: 0.06 sec per fur (G)

	Horse	Dist	Pos	SP	RR	SF
3663[9]	**Ruth's Gamble (60)** (MrsLCJewell) **9-10-3v** JAMcCarthy (a.p: led & bmpd last: rdn out)	—	1	5/1[3]	43	11
3583[6]	**Yellow Dragon (IRE) (80)** (BAPearce) **4-10-12**(3) PHenley (hdwy 4th: led appr last tl mstke & hdd last: unable qckn)	1¾	2	13/2	61	21
3579*	**Derisbay (IRE) (81)** (JJBridger) **9-11-3b**(7) MBatchelor (a.p: led appr 2 out tl appr last: one pce)	½	3	9/2[2]	62	30
3674[3]	**Swinging Sixties (IRE) (75)** (GLMoore) **6-11-4** JRKavanagh (lw: hdwy 5th: rdn appr 2 out: one pce)	6	4	7/4[1]	50	18
3577[3]	**Script (70)** (JRJenkins) **6-10-13** DMorris (lw: led tl appr 2 out: sn wknd)	5	5	10/1	40	8
3632[5]	**Aldwick Colonnade (62)** (MDIUsher) **10-10-5** WMcFarland (bhd fr 5th)	6	6	25/1	26	—
3061[P]	**Tapestry Rose (57)** (JRPoulton) **6-10-0** ADicken (bhd fr 5th)	10	7	50/1	12	—
1322[8]	**Coolegale (65)** (LWells) **11-10-8** PHide (pckd 2nd: prom to 5th)	20	8	25/1	—	—
3063[P]	**Cavo Greco (USA) (64)** (JJoseph) **8-10-7** DSkyrme (bhd tl p.u bef 5th)		P	20/1	—	—
3757[10]	**Tigana (57)** (MrsLCJewell) **5-10-0v[1]** KGaule (bhd fr 5th: t.o whn p.u after 3 out)		P	50/1	—	—
				(SP 110.0%)	**10 Rn**	

3m 54.8 (9.80) CSF £29.38 CT £131.66 TOTE £5.40: £1.50 £2.10 £1.50 (£38.00) Trio £22.40 OWNER Mrs A. Emanuel (SUTTON VALENCE)
BRED D. W. Chapman
LONG HANDICAP Tapestry Rose 9-7 Tigana 9-7
WEIGHT FOR AGE 4yo-8lb
No bid

OFFICIAL EXPLANATION **Ruth's Gamble: regarding the improvement in form, the trainer reported that the gelding had been taken off his legs last time.**
3131* Ruth's Gamble bounced back to form. Mounting his challenge in the straight, he led at the final flight and was ridden along to assert. (5/1)
2871 Yellow Dragon (IRE) threw down his challenge in the straight and poked a nostril in front going to the last. Untidy at that hurdle, losing the advantage, he then failed to find another gear. (13/2)
3579* Derisbay (IRE), who seems at his best with some cut, nevertheless showed in front approaching the second last. Collared going to the final flight, he could only go up and down in the same place. (9/2: 3/1-5/1)
3674 Swinging Sixties (IRE), who reportedly swallowed his tongue at Folkestone, raced with it tied down on this occasion. Taking closer order in the second half of the race, he looked likely to drop away approaching the second last but managed to plod on in his own time. He may now have a wind operation. (7/4)
3577 Script is not one to rely on and, after setting the pace, decided he had done enough when collared approaching the second last. (10/1: 7/1-11/1)

3812 CHRIS PYE 50TH BIRTHDAY NOVICES' CHASE (5-Y.O+) (Class E)
3-10 (3-11) **3m (18 fncs)** £3,316.50 (£919.00: £439.50) GOING: 0.06 sec per fur (G)

				SP	RR	SF
3303[7]	**Wee Windy (IRE) (110)** (JTGifford) **8-11-4** PHide (lw: a.p: w ldr fr 11th: led 3 out: all out)	—	**1**	10/11 1	113	37
3617[U]	**Little Martina (IRE) (108)** (DMGrissell) **9-11-5** JRKavanagh (lw: led to 3 out: ev ch 2 out: r.o wl)	s.h	**2**	10/11 1	114	38
3472[P]	**Napoleon's Gold (IRE) (60)** (AGFoster) **7-11-4b1** DMorris (lw: mstke 2nd: w ldr to 11th: sn wknd: t.o fr 4 out)	dist	**3**	20/1 2	—	—
				(SP 109.5%)		**3 Rn**

6m 5.0 (11.00) CSF £2.02 TOTE £2.20 (£1.10) OWNER Mr W. E. Gale (FINDON) BRED Laurie Allen
2693 Wee Windy (IRE), who looked in tremendous shape beforehand, at last came good over fences, but only by the skin of his teeth after a tremendous scrap with the runner-up in the straight. (10/11: 5/6-evens)
2754 Little Martina (IRE) found this ground too lively and did not appear to be letting herself down properly. Nevertheless she still ran a courageous race, setting the pace to the third last, and then having a tremendous tussle with the winner which failed by a whisker. With a few drops of rain she can soon make it to the winner's enclosure. (10/11: 5/6-evens)

3813 EDEN HUNTERS' CHASE (6-Y.O+) (Class H)
3-45 (3-46) **3m (18 fncs)** £1,285.20 (£310.80) GOING: 0.06 sec per fur (G)

				SP	RR	SF
3637[P]	**Colonial Kelly** (MrsDMGrissell) **9-12-7**(5) MrCVigors (lw: hld up: led 9th: lft clr 2 out)	—	**1**	5/2 2	101?	23
	Run for Free (MrsTJHill) **13-12-2**(3) MrAHill (hung lft fr 5th: bhd fr 10th: t.o fr 13th)	dist	**2**	7/2 3	—	—
	Prince Buck (IRE) (MJRoberts) **7-12-2**(3) MrPHacking (lw: led to 4th: led 7th to 9th: rdn appr 3 out: 2nd whn fell 2 out)		**F**	Evens 1	—	—
	Loyal Gait (NZ) (AMDarlington) **9-11-12**(7) MrAndrewMartin (t: led 4th to 7th: wknd 11th: t.o whn p.u bef 3 out)		**P**	20/1	—	—
3457[P]	**Pro Bono (IRE)** (AndyMorgan) **7-12-5**(7) MrADalton (4th whn blnd & uns rdr 8th)		**U**	11/1	—	—
				(SP 113.9%)		**5 Rn**

6m 17.3 (23.30) CSF £10.87 TOTE £3.00: £1.30 £1.50 (£3.60) OWNER Cockerell Cowing Racing (ROBERTSBRIDGE) BRED E. W. O'F. Wilson
3353 Colonial Kelly, a prolific point-to-point winner, at last got off the mark for the season. Leading at the ninth, he may well have had a fight on his hands with Prince Buck when that rival departed two from home, leaving him miles clear. (5/2)
Run for Free won the Welsh and Scottish Nationals in his heyday, but that was a long time ago and he has gone sour in the meantime. Giving his jockey a nightmare ride, he was almost unsteerable. He is definitely not a suitable ride for an amateur, and should be avoided like the plague. (7/2: op 9/4)
Prince Buck (IRE), winner of both his point-to-points this season, was being pushed along going to the third last, but was just under a length down on the winner, and beginning to mount a challenge, when falling at the second last. (Evens)
3135 Pro Bono (IRE) (11/1: 5/1-12/1)

3814 GUMMER H'CAP HURDLE (0-115) (4-Y.O+) (Class E)
4-20 (4-20) **2m 110y (8 hdls)** £2,343.00 (£648.00: £309.00) GOING: 0.06 sec per fur (G)

				SP	RR	SF
3687*	**Tickerty's Gift (114)** (GLMoore) **7-11-6**(7) MBatchelor (lw: mde all: clr appr 2 out: comf)	—	**1**	11/8 2	92+	50
3562[4]	**Marius (IRE) (115)** (JTGifford) **7-11-7**(7) WGreatrex (lw: chsd wnr fr 2nd: unable qckn fr 3 out)	2½	**2**	5/4 1	91	49
304[4]	**Courageous Knight (88)** (PHayward) **8-9-12**(3)ow1 PHenley (chsd wnr to 2nd: rdn 4th: wknd 3 out)	18	**3**	3/1 3	46	3
				(SP 111.5%)		**3 Rn**

3m 51.2 (6.20) CSF £3.30 TOTE £2.40 (£1.50) OWNER Mr K. Higson (BRIGHTON) BRED K. Higson
LONG HANDICAP Courageous Knight 9-11
3687* Tickerty's Gift did not have the mud he relishes, and was racing off a mark 5lb higher than he has won off before, but he loves Lingfield - he has never won anywhere else. Making it all, he forged clear in the straight to register his seventh course victory. (11/8: 11/10-7/4)
3562 Marius (IRE) does not find much off the bridle and was left behind by the winner from the third last. However, with that rival taking things easy in the closing stages, he is certainly flattered to finish so close. (5/4: 10/11-11/8)
128* Courageous Knight, without a run since August, had been shaken off from the third last. (3/1)

T/Plpt: £30.00 (238.84 Tckts). T/Qdpt: £19.90 (14.27 Tckts) AK

3796-NEWBURY (L-H) (Chases Good to firm, Hdles Good)
Saturday March 22nd
WEATHER: Fine

3815 BROWN CHAMBERLIN H'CAP CHASE (6-Y.O+) (Class B)
1-15 (1-16) **3m (18 fncs)** £6,853.40 (£2,067.20: £1,003.60: £471.80) GOING minus 0.30 sec per fur (GF)

				SP	RR	SF
3496*	**Senor El Betrutti (IRE) (138)** (MrsSusanNock) **8-11-13** JOsborne (mde all: pushed out)	—	**1**	Evens 1	141	42
3585[3]	**Pyr Four (125)** (GMMcCourt) **10-11-0** DBridgwater (hld up: hit 4 out: ev ch whn nt fluent 2 out: rdn & r.o flat: nt trble wnr)	2	**2**	4/1 3	127	28
3160[5]	**Valiant Warrior (129)** (MDHammond) **9-11-4** RGarritty (hld up: wnt 2nd after 8th: hrd rdn & ev ch appr last: nt qckn flat)	1½	**3**	3/1 2	130	31

				SP	RR	SF
3132^{3}	**Darren the Brave (111)** (CPEBrooks) **9-10-0** CLlewellyn (chsd wnr tl after 8th: mstke 12th: wknd 3 out)	12	**4**	9/1	73 t	5
				(SP 105.0%)		**4 Rn**

5m 53.6 (3.60) CSF £4.48 TOTE £1.70 (£2.80) OWNER Mr Gerard Nock (STOW-ON-THE-WOLD) BRED Bretton Blood Stock PLC
LONG HANDICAP Darren the Brave 9-3

3496* Senor El Betrutti (IRE), raised 2lb, was stepping up to three miles and completed a hat-trick with something in hand. He now goes for the John Hughes at Aintree. (Evens)
3585 Pyr Four has been let down by some sloppy jumping in the past, and one could see why when the real race was on. (4/1)
3160 Valiant Warrior, trying a new trip, may be more effective at shorter distances. (3/1: op 7/4)
3132 Darren the Brave, 11lb wrong at the weights, seems to need some give in the ground to show his best. (9/1: 6/1-10/1)

3816 LAMBOURN H'CAP HURDLE (4-Y.O+) (Class B)

1-45 (1-46) **2m 110y (8 hdls)** £4,883.50 (£1,468.00: £709.00: £329.50) GOING minus 0.15 sec per fur (G)

				SP	RR	SF
3572^{6}	**Kadastrof (FR) (133)** (RDickin) **7-11-4**$^{(7)}$ XAizpuru (mde virtually all: qcknd appr 3 out: rdn appr 2 out: hit last: all out)	—	**1**	6/1^{3}	112	15
2645^{F}	**Ashwell Boy (IRE) (132)** (PJHobbs) **6-11-10** DBridgwater (lw: hld up: hdwy 3 out: sltly hmpd 2 out: sn rdn: r.o flat)	¾	**2**	8/1	110	13
3572^{16}	**Shankar (IRE) (128)** (DNicholson) **6-11-1**$^{(5)}$ MrRThornton (hld up & plld hrd: hdwy 3 out: sn rdn: ev ch flat: nt run on)	nk	**3**	11/1	106	9
3430^{3}	**Mim-Lou-and (112)** (MissHCKnight) **5-10-4** JCulloty (hld up: hdwy 4th: wknd 3 out)	12	**4**	7/2^{2}	78	—
2596a^{3}	**Radanpour (IRE) (112)** (HowardJohnson) **5-10-4** ASSmith (bhd: reminder after 4th: outpcd appr 3 out: styd on flat)	s.h	**5**	6/1^{3}	78	—
3571^{4}	**Blair Castle (IRE) (114)** (GBBalding) **6-10-6** MAFitzgerald (lw: prom tl wknd 3 out)	3	**6**	7/1	77	—
3640^{14}	**Hamilton Silk (132)** (MCPipe) **5-11-10** JOsborne (sn chsng wnr: 2l 2nd whn fell 2 out)		**F**	9/4^{1}	—	—
				(SP 113.5%)		**7 Rn**

4m 0.3 (10.30) CSF £45.01 CT £465.87 TOTE £7.60: £2.90 £3.00 (£17.50) OWNER Mr A. P. Paton (STRATFORD) BRED Roland Lepeau in France

3572 Kadastrof (FR), caught broadside at the start, soon got to his favoured front-running position, but had to dig deep in the closing stages on ground plenty fast enough for him. His next run is likely to be at the Fairyhouse Easter meeting. (6/1)
1919 Ashwell Boy (IRE), freshened up by a break, showed signs of recovering the form that saw him just touched off by Silver Shred over an extra half-mile last season. (8/1)
3229 Shankar (IRE), who flopped when put back over hurdles in the Imperial Cup, remains a difficult ride, which is no reflection on his fine amateur partner. (11/1: 8/1-12/1)
3430 Mim-Lou-and, back to two miles, rather lost his position on the outside at the cross-flight and finally gave best at the next. (7/2: 5/2-4/1)
2596a Radanpour (IRE) won a two-and-a-half-mile bumper before completing a two-mile hat-trick over timber for Willie Mullins, but has subsequently campaigned over longer distances and he found two miles too sharp on this good ground. (6/1: op 4/1)
3571 Blair Castle (IRE), who would not have minded faster ground, was reverting to hurdles on what looked a reasonable mark. (7/1)
3640 Hamilton Silk had not been asked a real question when departing, and would probably have scored given the way the winner was forced to struggle. (9/4)

3817 HOECHST ROUSSEL VET PANACUR E.B.F. 'N.H.' (FINAL) NOVICES' H'CAP HURDLE (5-Y.O+ Mares Only) (Class C)

2-15 (2-17) **2m 5f (11 hdls)** £10,502.00 (£3,176.00: £1,548.00: £734.00) GOING minus 0.15 sec per fur (G)

				SP	RR	SF
2961*	**Lucia Forte (102)** (KCBailey) **6-11-8** CO'Dwyer (lw: hld up & bhd: hdwy 8th: led flat: drvn out)	—	**1**	7/2^{1}	84	27
3348*	**Fantasy Line (96)** (PRWebber) **6-11-2** AThornton (a.p: led after 2 out: hit last: hdd flat: r.o)	hd	**2**	12/1	78	21
3423^{2}	**Fiddling The Facts (IRE) (104)** (NJHenderson) **6-11-10** MAFitzgerald (a.p: led 3 out tl after 2 out: one pce flat)	5	**3**	9/2^{2}	82	25
3168^{2}	**Potter's Gale (IRE) (108)** (DNicholson) **6-11-9**$^{(5)}$ MrRThornton (hld up: hdwy 5th: ev ch 3 out: sn wknd)	26	**4**	9/2^{2}	66	9
3411^{3}	**Bula Vogue (IRE) (94)** (RRowe) **7-11-0** DO'Sullivan (led to 4th: mstke & lost pl 6th: n.d after)	4	**5**	20/1	49	—
2941^{7}	**Joy For Life (IRE) (80)** (RMStronge) **6-9-7**$^{(7)}$ XAizpuru (lw: bhd: hit 4th: sn rdn: no ch fr 7th)	8	**6**	50/1	29	—
3348^{7}	**Daisy Days (IRE) (92)** (HowardJohnson) **7-10-12** ASSmith (w ldr: led 4th to 3 out: sn wknd)	4	**7**	20/1	38	—
3491*	**Konvekta Queen (IRE) (102)** (OSherwood) **6-11-8** MRichards (hdwy 6th: rdn after 7th: wknd appr 3 out)	¾	**8**	11/2^{3}	48	—
2746^{5}	**Gaye Fame (92)** (KCBailey) **6-10-12** SMcNeill (bhd: blnd 6th: sn t.o)	dist	**9**	12/1	—	—
3621^{2}	**Loch Na Keal (80)** (CPMorlock) **5-10-0** CLlewellyn (prom tl rdn & wknd 8th: t.o)	15	**10**	8/1	—	—
2822^{3}	**River Bay (IRE) (99)** (MissHCKnight) **6-11-5** JCulloty (bhd fr 7th: p.u bef 3 out)		**P**	12/1	—	—
				(SP 119.6%)		**11 Rn**

5m 2.8 (8.80) CSF £40.40 CT £178.67 TOTE £4.10: £1.60 £3.50 £1.90 (£35.00) Trio £38.90 OWNER Mrs Lucia Farmer (UPPER LAMBOURN) BRED Mrs K. I. Hayward
LONG HANDICAP Joy For Life (IRE) 8-10

2961* Lucia Forte was again produced at just he right time and held on well to the line. She is likely to take up one of her entries at Aintree. (7/2)
3348* Fantasy Line, 9lb higher than when making her handicap debut, showed she needs it soft to be at her best. (12/1)
3423 Fiddling The Facts (IRE) lacked the required finishing speed on this better ground, but was certainly not disgraced. (9/2)
3168 Potter's Gale (IRE) had been raised 10lb since being beaten a length-and-a-half by Boardroom Shuffle at Cheltenham in January. (9/2)
3411 Bula Vogue (IRE) was struggling after being knocked back by a mistake at halfway. (20/1)

3818 FINAL NOVICES' HURDLE (I) (4-Y.O+) (Class D)

2-50 (2-50) **2m 110y (8 hdls)** £3,169.00 (£884.00: £427.00) GOING minus 0.15 sec per fur (G)

				SP	RR	SF
3494^{4}	**Quality (IRE)** (PJHobbs) **4-10-13** GTormey (a.p: wnt 2nd 5th: rdn appr last: led flat: edgd lft: drvn out)	—	**1**	9/4^{1}	82	14
3404^{7}	**Hisar (IRE)** (CPEBrooks) **4-10-13** CO'Dwyer (led: rdn & hdd flat: nt qckn)	1½	**2**	7/1	81	13
	Riparius (USA) (PRWebber) **6-11-7** RBellamy (lw: hld up: hdwy 4th: mstke 5th: one pce fr 3 out)	9	**3**	6/1^{3}	72	12
3399^{5}	**Get Real (IRE)** (NJHenderson) **6-11-7** MAFitzgerald (lw: hld up: stdy hdwy 4th: rdn & one pce fr 3 out)	1	**4**	7/2^{2}	71	11
3424^{4}	**I Recall (IRE) (74)** (PHayward) **6-11-7v** SMcNeill (lw: prom tl wknd 3 out)	20	**5**	33/1	52	—
3103^{U}	**Pealings (IRE)** (GAHubbard) **5-11-2**$^{(5)}$ MrRThornton (bhd tl hdwy appr 3 out: n.d)	2½	**6**	33/1	49	—
2668^{P}	**No Matter (IRE)** (RRowe) **6-11-7** DBridgwater (nvr nr ldrs)	7	**7**	33/1	42	—
	Peers Folly (IRE) (MissHCKnight) **7-11-7** JFTitley (bit bkwd: nvr nr ldrs)	1	**8**	14/1	41	—
2663^{P}	**Don't Mind If I Do (IRE)** (PRWebber) **6-11-7b^{1}** AThornton (prom to 4th)	9	**9**	50/1	33	—
3604^{5}	**Swan Street (NZ) (78)** (CJMann) **6-11-7** JRailton (prom to 4th)	5	**10**	14/1	28	—

				SP	RR	SF
3494[6]	**Regal Splendour (CAN)** (RJO'Sullivan) **4-10-13** DO'Sullivan (prom to 4th: t.o)	14	**11**	16/1	14	—
2898[6]	**Ballyranter** (MDHammond) **8-11-7** RGarritty (nt j.w: bhd fr 5th: t.o)	10	**12**	14/1	4	—
2868[9]	**Bon Luck (IRE)** (JABennett) **5-11-7** LHarvey (blnd 2nd: sn t.o)	2	**13**	33/1	3	—
	Las Animas (USA) (RChampion) **6-11-2b[1]** BPowell (a bhd: t.o)		**14**	33/1	—	—
1651[13]	**Lizium** (JCFox) **5-11-2** SFox (bhd whn p.u bef 3 out)		**P**	33/1	—	—
3536[P]	**Cuillin** (RJSmith) **5-11-2** TJMurphy (a bhd: t.o whn p.u bef 5th)		**P**	66/1	—	—
				(SP 126.8%)	**16 Rn**	

3m 57.9 (7.90) CSF £16.33 TOTE £3.10: £1.60 £2.30 £2.00 (£11.20) Trio £21.70 OWNER Mr D. B. O'Connor (MINEHEAD) BRED Major C.R. Philipson

WEIGHT FOR AGE 4yo-8lb

3494 Quality (IRE) put a slightly disappointing run at Wincanton last time behind him. (9/4)

Hisar (IRE), a ten-furlong winner for John Oxx at Leopardstown last October, had pulled too hard on his two previous outings. Still running a shade freely in the lead this time, he looked to be going better than the winner approaching the last. He will definitely win races when he learns to switch off. (7/1)

Riparius (USA), three times a winner over a mile-and-a-half for Henry Candy on the Flat, lost his way and ended up running in blinkers. Making a promising-enough start to his hurdling career, he will not be inconvenienced by further. (6/1: op 4/1)

3399 Get Real (IRE), already a winner of an Irish point, is probably going to need a longer trip or fences to get off the mark. (7/2)

3819 MARCH NOVICES' H'CAP CHASE (0-110) (5-Y.O+) (Class D)

3-20 (3-20) **2m 4f (16 fncs)** £3,493.00 (£1,054.00: £512.00: £241.00) GOING minus 0.30 sec per fur (GF)

				SP	RR	SF
3717*	**Red Branch (IRE) (85)** (JSKing) **8-11-0** 5x TJMurphy (j.w: mde all: r.o wl)	—	**1**	5/6[1]	100	45
3051[2]	**Boots N All (IRE) (72)** (GBBalding) **7-10-1** RGreene (lw: plld hrd: a.p: hit 12th: ev ch 2 out: one pce flat)	3½	**2**	5/1[2]	84	29
3540[2]	**Mammy's Choice (IRE) (95)** (RHAlner) **7-11-5**(5) MrRThornton (sn chsng ldr: ev ch 4 out: wknd 3 out)	10	**3**	8/1	99	44
3687[2]	**Spring to Glory (95)** (PHayward) **10-11-10** BPowell (hld up: hdwy appr 4 out: btn whn j.lft 2 out)	4	**4**	8/1	96	41
3697[3]	**Koo's Promise (82)** (CLPopham) **6-10-8**(3) TDascombe (trckd ldrs: rdn & wknd appr 4 out)	1¼	**5**	7/1[3]	82	27
3012[9]	**Lagham Lad (77)** (DWPArbuthnot) **8-10-6** SMcNeill (lw: plld hrd: prom: hit 1st: blnd 12th: sn wknd: t.o)	dist	**6**	33/1	—	—
3552[6]	**Music Class (IRE) (80)** (CPEBrooks) **6-10-9** DGallagher (a bhd: t.o fr 6th)	2	**7**	20/1	—	—
				(SP 113.6%)	**7 Rn**	

4m 53.6 (-1.40) CSF £5.31 TOTE £1.80: £1.50 £1.80 (£2.70) OWNER Mr E. J. Mangan (SWINDON) BRED Michael Butler

3717* Red Branch (IRE) has certainly come good over the obstacles, and settled this with the better jump at the final fence. (5/6: op evens)

3051 Boots N All (IRE), raised 2lb, took a strong hold, and was held after being outjumped at the final fence. (5/1: 7/2-11/2)

3540 Mammy's Choice (IRE) would have preferred some give underfoot. (8/1: 6/1-9/1)

3687 Spring to Glory was making a belated chasing debut off a mark 5lb lower than when second over hurdles last time. (8/1: 6/1-9/1)

3697 Koo's Promise got left behind once in the long home straight. (7/1)

3820 FINAL NOVICES' HURDLE (II) (4-Y.O+) (Class D)

3-55 (3-55) **2m 110y (8 hdls)** £3,148.00 (£878.00: £424.00) GOING minus 0.15 sec per fur (G)

				SP	RR	SF
3154[2]	**John Drumm** (PRWebber) **6-11-7** RGarritty (lw: led tl after 1st: led after 3 out: rdn out)	—	**1**	2/1[2]	77	5
3298[5]	**Classy Lad (NZ)** (NJHenderson) **7-11-7** MAFitzgerald (lw: a.p: rdn & ev ch 2 out: one pce flat)	4	**2**	7/4[1]	73	1
3441[6]	**Maeterlinck (IRE) (67)** (GThorner) **5-11-0**(7) ClareThorner (prom: mstke 5th: styd on one pce fr 2 out)	14	**3**	50/1	60	—
	Lucky Archer (PJHobbs) **4-10-13** DBridgwater (bit bkwd: plld hrd in rr: hdwy 5th: 3rd & wkng whn mstke last)	½	**4**	12/1	59	—
	Real Madrid (GPEnright) **6-11-2**(5) MrRThornton (no hdwy fr 5th)	11	**5**	66/1	48	—
3494[P]	**Honeyshan** (DJSffrenchDavis) **5-11-2** SMcNeill (no hdwy fr 5th)	2	**6**	66/1	42	—
	Sadler's Realm (PJHobbs) **4-10-13** GTormey (bhd fr 3 out)	6	**7**	20/1	41	—
3468[7]	**Palafico** (PRWebber) **7-11-7** RBellamy (a bhd: t.o)	dist	**8**	66/1	—	—
	Spectacle Jim (BAPearce) **8-11-0**(7) GordonGallagher (hld up & plld hrd: bhd fr 5th: t.o)	30	**9**	66/1	—	—
3342[10]	**Out For A Duck (62)** (HEHaynes) **6-11-7** CMaude (a bhd: t.o whn p.u bef 3 out: lame)		**P**	66/1	—	—
2696[9]	**Royal Team** (MJWilkinson) **5-11-7** DGallagher (plld hrd: dropped rr & mstke 4th: s.u bnd appr 5th: dead)		**S**	50/1	—	—
3564[P]	**Absolute Limit** (JTGifford) **5-11-4**(3) LAspell (plld hrd: led after 1st tl after 3 out: 4th & btn whn blnd & uns rdr 2 out)		**U**	14/1	—	—
3468[2]	**Zander** (NATwiston-Davies) **5-11-7** CLlewellyn (prom: cl 3rd whn stumbled & uns rdr 3 out)		**U**	4/1[3]	—	—
				(SP 120.2%)	**13 Rn**	

4m 1.8 (11.80) CSF £5.34 TOTE £3.20: £1.50 £1.40 £13.60 (£2.60) Trio £142.20 OWNER Mr Andrew Jenkins (BANBURY) BRED Chesters Stud

WEIGHT FOR AGE 4yo-8lb

3154 John Drumm did not seem to mind this faster surface. (2/1: 6/4-9/4)

3298 Classy Lad (NZ), although always just getting the worse of the argument, would not have to improve much to go one better. (7/4)

Maeterlinck (IRE) did not help his cause by missing out at the cross-hurdle, but one could see why his last two runs have been over an extra half-mile. (50/1)

Lucky Archer, placed five times on the Flat for Clive Brittain, will last longer when he learns to settle. (12/1: op 6/1)

3468 Zander seemed likely to be concerned in the finish when unluckily getting rid of his rider. (4/1)

3821 SPRING STANDARD OPEN N.H. FLAT RACE (4, 5 & 6-Y.O) (Class H)

4-30 (4-31) **2m 110y** £1,320.00 (£370.00: £180.00)

				SP	RR	SF
3304*	**Country Beau** (JSKing) **5-11-11** MRichards (leggy: hld up & bhd: stdy hdwy 6f out: led 2f out: rdn out)	—	**1**	11/4[1]	89 f	—
3574[4]	**Golden Eagle** (NJHenderson) **5-11-4** MAFitzgerald (quite attractive: a.p: ev ch 2f out: r.o ins fnl f)	1	**2**	7/2[2]	81 f	—
3425[2]	**Bold Leap** (PRWebber) **5-11-4** MrASansome (scope: plld hrd: a.p: rdn to ld over 3f out: hdd 2f out: one pce fnl f)	3	**3**	16/1	78 f	—
3548*	**Bessie Browne (IRE)** (GAHubbard) **5-11-1**(5) MrRThornton (lengthy: prom: ev ch 3f out: wknd wl over 1f out)	13	**4**	16/1	68 f	—
	Browjoshy (IRE) (MrsJPitman) **4-10-10** JFTitley (unf: hdwy 3f out: nt rch ldrs)	s.h	**5**	20/1	66 f	—
3149[2]	**Damien's Choice (IRE)** (MrsMerritaJones) **5-11-4** DerekByrne (leggy: lw: hld up: hdwy 5f out: wknd wl over 1f out)	2	**6**	10/1	64 f	—
2572[3]	**Jim's Quest** (PJHobbs) **4-10-10** DBridgwater (neat: plld hrd: led 13f: wknd wl over 1f out)	1¾	**7**	12/1	62 f	—
	Another Rumpus (CPMorlock) **5-11-1**(3) DFortt (neat: unf: hld up: hdwy 6f out: wknd over 2f out)	6	**8**	66/1	56 f	—
	Glevum (NATwiston-Davies) **5-10-13** CLlewellyn (lengthy: nvr nr to chal)	1¾	**9**	16/1	49 f	—

	Ickford Okey (CPMorlock) **5-11-4** DGallagher (tall: unf: nvr nrr) 1	**10**	50/1	53 f	—
	Whistling Rufus (IRE) (NATwiston-Davies) **5-11-4** CMaude (rangy: scope: hdwy 8f out: wknd 5f out) 2	**11**	25/1	51 f	—
3170[4]	War Paint (IRE) (MrsJPitman) **5-10-11**(7) MrGBaines (scope: prom: rdn 4f out: wknd 3f out) ....¾	**12**	8/1	51 f	—
	Keynote (IRE) (GBBalding) **5-11-4** RGreene (cmpt: n.d) 1	**13**	16/1	50 f	—
3574[7]	Kabylie Ouest (FR) (RDickin) **4-9-12**(7) XAizpuru (neat: plld hrd: prom 6f) ....¾	**14**	25/1	44 f	—
	Zabari (IRE) (GThorner) **4-10-10** BPowell (w'like: hdwy 7f out: wknd over 3f out) 1½	**15**	33/1	48 f	—
	Clan Ross (IRE) (DRCElsworth) **6-10-13** PHolley (w'like: lengthy: a bhd) ....nk	**16**	33/1	42 f	—
3235[13]	Cathay (IRE) (MrsJPitman) **5-11-4** DLeahy (w'like: prom: pushed along 8f out: wknd 4f out) 6	**17**	33/1	41 f	—
3297*	Harris Croft Star (IRE) (DNicholson) **6-11-8**(3) RMassey (tall: bhd fnl 6f) ....¾	**18**	11/2[3]	48 f	—
	Silver Treasure (IRE) (MrsMerritaJones) **6-10-11**(7) MLane (rangy: bkwd: prom tl wknd 3f out) 4	**19**	33/1	37 f	—
	Phar Better Off (IRE) (JWMullins) **6-10-13** SCurran (lengthy: unf: bkwd: a bhd) 3½	**20**	33/1	28 f	—
	Just Norman (MissHCKnight) **6-11-4** JCulloty (rangy: bit bkwd: s.s: a bhd) 1½	**21**	25/1	32 f	—
			(SP 150.2%)	**21 Rn**	

3m 56.5 CSF £11.67 TOTE £4.30: £2.20 £2.70 £3.70 (£13.00) Trio £82.40 OWNER Mrs J. J. Peppiatt (SWINDON) BRED P. G. Bailey
WEIGHT FOR AGE 4yo-8lb

3304* Country Beau proved his Kempton win to be no fluke, with the runner-up going on to finish second in the bumper at the Cheltenham Festival. (11/4)
3574 Golden Eagle, out of a half-sister to Brown Chamberlin, is a half-brother to Shimba Hills and looks to have a bright future. (7/2)
3425 Bold Leap again finished in the money despite proving a handful to settle. (16/1)
3548* Bessie Browne (IRE) had to contend with quicker ground under a penalty. (16/1)
Browjoshy (IRE) shaped with promise for the future. (20/1)
3149 Damien's Choice (IRE) had finished second at Sandown to Dawn Leader, who went on to be a disappointing favourite at the Cheltenham Festival. (10/1)
3297* Harris Croft Star (IRE) (11/2: 4/1-6/1)

T/Plpt: £71.10 (269.76 Tckts). T/Qdpt: £4.10 (257.41 Tckts) KH/

3641-HEXHAM (L-H) (Soft)
Monday March 24th

One fence & one flight omitted bk st
WEATHER: unsettled

3822 BUCHANAN ALES CONDITIONAL H'CAP HURDLE (0-110) (4-Y.O+) (Class E)
2-00 (2-00) **2m (6 hdls)** £2,311.50 (£639.00: £304.50) GOING: 0.85 sec per fur (S)

			SP	RR	SF
3612[2]	Diamond Beach (86) (GMMoore) **4-10-6** ECallaghan (hld up & bhd: hdwy on bit to ld last: shkn up & r.o)....—	**1**	7/1	71	7
3485[7]	Highland Way (IRE) (87) (MartinTodhunter) **9-10-10**(5) CMcCormack (lw: hld up & bhd: hdwy & ch last: kpt on: nt pce of wnr) 4	**2**	11/2[3]	68	12
3478[P]	Court Joker (IRE) (83) (HAlexander) **5-10-11** RMcGrath (hld up: hdwy & hit 4th: ch between last 2: r.o one pce) 4	**3**	13/2	60	4
3485*	Ifallelsefails (96) (LLungo) **9-11-5**(5) IJardine (lw: led tl hdd last: no ex) ....s.h	**4**	11/4[1]	73	17
1686[6]	Miss Greenyards (83) (ACWhillans) **6-10-11** STaylor (hld up: effrt 2 out: ev ch last: sn btn) 4	**5**	6/1	56	—
2631[13]	Gallardini (IRE) (82) (BSRothwell) **8-10-3**(7) ACurrie (lw: w ldr tl wknd appr last) 7	**6**	20/1	48	—
3641*	Apollo's Daughter (76) (JLGoulding) **9-10-4** FLeahy (lw: trckd ldrs: chal 2 out: wknd appr last) 2½	**7**	4/1[2]	39	—
	Fiery Sun (86) (REBarr) **12-10-11**(3) NHorrocks (bit bkwd: prom tl wknd between last 2) 10	**8**	25/1	39	—
			(SP 110.8%)	**8 Rn**	

4m 12.2 (24.20) CSF £38.52 CT £227.78 TOTE £5.50: £2.50 £2.30 £2.80 (£26.50) OWNER Valueplace Ltd (MIDDLEHAM) BRED Berkshire Equestrian Services Ltd
WEIGHT FOR AGE 4yo-8lb

3612 Diamond Beach loved this very soft ground and, given a cracking ride, won in fair style and looks to be going the right way. (7/1: op 3/1)
3485 Highland Way (IRE), patiently ridden, was produced, like the winner, late on but was never going as well. His turn will come. (11/2)
3478 Court Joker (IRE) had his chances but when the pressure was on he lacked any turn of foot. (13/2)
3485* Ifallelsefails would ideally like further and was done for toe in the closing stages. (11/4)
1686 Miss Greenyards, after being off the track for almost four months, ran well enough to suggest that she retains her ability. (6/1)
Gallardini (IRE), after two poor efforts earlier this season, gave much more encouragement. (20/1)
3641* Apollo's Daughter is not very big and the 8lb rise in the weights and this better company proved too much late on. (4/1: 3/1-9/2)

3823 E.B.F. 'N.H.' (QUALIFIER) NOVICES' HURDLE (5, 6 & 7-Y.O) (Class E)
2-30 (2-30) **2m (6 hdls)** £2,917.20 (£809.20: £387.60) GOING: 0.85 sec per fur (S)

			SP	RR	SF
3483[5]	Bold Statement (GMMoore) **5-11-0** NBentley (chsd ldrs: led 4th: hld on wl flat) ....—	**1**	5/1[3]	73	25
3644[3]	Southern Cross (MWEasterby) **5-11-0** RGarritty (lw: hld up & bhd: stdy hdwy 4th: ev ch last: hrd rdn & nt qckn) 1¼	**2**	4/1[2]	72	24
3480[3]	Eastcliffe (IRE) (WMcKeown) **5-10-11**(3) MichaelBrennan (swtg: dwlt: hdwy & prom ½-wy: chal after 2 out: wknd appr last) ....dist	**3**	12/1	—	—
3483[6]	Prime Example (IRE) (MartinTodhunter) **6-11-0** PNiven (hld up: hdwy & prom 2 out: one pce appr last) 5	**4**	13/2	—	—
2064[3]	Pentland Squire (95) (JMJefferson) **6-11-0** RichardGuest (lw: hld up & bhd: stdy hdwy ½-wy: chsd ldrs between last 2: btn appr last) 1¼	**5**	3/1[1]	—	—
3802[F]	Reach The Clouds (IRE) (JohnUpson) **5-11-0** JSupple (hld up: hdwy after 2 out: no imp) 7	**6**	33/1	—	—
3529[5]	Cream O The Border (ACWhillans) **5-10-9** FPerratt (led to 4th: wknd fr next) 2½	**7**	25/1	—	—
3283[7]	Over Zealous (IRE) (JohnUpson) **5-11-0** RSupple (hld up: sme hdwy 2 out: n.d) 1¾	**8**	20/1	—	—
3487[7]	Just Ned (JSHaldane) **6-10-11**(3) EHusband (nvr rchd ldrs) ....hd	**9**	25/1	—	—
3453[4]	Donnegale (IRE) (TPTate) **5-11-0** JCallaghan (chsd ldrs tl wknd 4th) ....hd	**10**	20/1	—	—
3396[8]	Nick Ross (67) (RBrewis) **6-11-0** BStorey (chsd ldrs tl wknd 2 out) 10	**11**	10/1	—	—
1152[F]	Hopeful Lord (IRE) (PCheesbrough) **5-11-0** ASSmith (prom tl wknd appr 2 out) 1	**12**	25/1	—	—
3440[12]	Connie Leathart (MsLCPlater) **6-10-9** DBentley (w ldrs tl wknd between last 2) 1	**13**	50/1	—	—
3437[6]	Florrie Gunner (JJQuinn) **7-10-9** LWyer (swtg: rdn ½-wy: a bhd) ....nk	**14**	20/1	—	—
3311[5]	Helperby (IRE) (HowardJohnson) **5-11-0** MMoloney (hdwy u.p 3rd: sn wknd) 20	**15**	25/1	—	—

Form	Horse	Dist	Pos	SP	RR	SF
3691^{19}	**Soccer Ball** (TRWatson) **7-10-11**(3) ECallaghan (lost tch fr 2 out)	6	**16**	50/1	—	—
3097^{P}	**Banner Year (IRE)** (TJCarr) **6-11-0** NSmith (bit bkwd: chsd ldrs tl wknd 2 out: t.o)	dist	**17**	50/1	—	—
3100^{P}	**Beltino** (MrsJStorey) **6-11-0** MrCStorey (bit bkwd: a bhd: blnd 3rd: t.o)	¾	**18**	50/1	—	—
3529^{3}	**La Riviera (IRE)** (JIACharlton) **5-11-0** KJohnson (t.o whn p.u bef last)		**P**	15/2	—	—
3366^{P}	**Perky Too (IRE)** (HowardJohnson) **5-10-7**(7) MrSDurack (bit bkwd: wl t.o whn p.u after 2 out)		**P**	50/1	—	—

(SP 146.0%) **20 Rn**

4m 9.7 (21.70) CSF £24.12 TOTE £7.20: £2.10 £2.00 £4.20 (£8.60) Trio £28.90 OWNER Mr R. I. Graham (MIDDLEHAM) BRED Juddmonte Farms

3483 Bold Statement found this trip to his liking and certainly loves this track, winning convincingly. (5/1)
3644 Southern Cross jumped much better this time but when he had a serious chance at the last he was outbattled. (4/1: 3/1-9/2)
3480 Eastcliffe (IRE) put in a reasonable first effort over hurdles here and a poor start did not help matters. (12/1)
3483 Prime Example (IRE) got into the race on the extended run from the second last, but he proved slow when the pressure was on and this can be counted as disappointing. (13/2)
2064 Pentland Squire has not been out for over three months and, although he looked well enough, to give his the benefit on this occasion he may still have needed it. (3/1)
Reach The Clouds (IRE) showed his first signs of ability here. (33/1)
1667 Nick Ross (10/1: op 6/1)

3824 FEDERATION BREWERY AMATEUR (S) H'CAP CHASE (0-90) (5-Y.O+) (Class G)

3-00 (3-00) **3m 1f (17 fncs)** £2,357.00 (£652.00: £311.00) GOING: 0.85 sec per fur (S)

Form	Horse	Dist	Pos	SP	RR	SF
3607^{3}	**Bright Destiny (60)** (JSGoldie) **6-9-10v**(7) MrOMcPhail (swtg: a cl up: led 9th: clr fr 13th: eased flat)	—	**1**	7/1^{3}	74+	10
	Just For Me (IRE) (60) (JAMoore) **8-9-12**(5) MrCStorey (swtg: hdwy ½-wy: styd on fr 2 out: no ch w wnr)	22	**2**	100/1	60	—
3645^{9}	**Rusty Blade (85)** (PMonteith) **8-11-9**(5) MrRHale (led to 9th: outpcd & lost tch fr 13th)	14	**3**	12/1	76	12
896^{6}	**Upwell (67)** (RJohnson) **13-10-5**(5) MrMHNaughton (chsd ldrs: ev ch & hit 12th: wknd fr next)	1	**4**	25/1	57	—
2956^{5}	**Jendee (IRE) (82)** (BEllison) **9-11-6**(5) MissPRobson (a bhd: blnd 10th)	10	**5**	5/1^{2}	66	2
3347^{P}	**Clonroche Lucky (IRE) (70)** (JWade) **7-10-6**(7)ow3 MrsSGrant (wl t.o fr ½-wy)	dist	**6**	33/1	—	—
3393^{3}	**Two For One (IRE) (67)** (MissLucindaRussell) **8-10-10** MrSSwiers (lw: nvr gng wl: sn t.o: p.u bef 13th)		**P**	11/4^{1}	—	—
3623^{7}	**Fairy Park (84)** (HOliver) **12-11-6v**(7) MrNHOliver (chsd ldrs: outpcd & blnd 10th: wknd 12th: wl t.o whn p.u bef last)		**P**	7/1^{3}	—	—
1653^{9}	**More Joy (73)** (BEllison) **9-10-11**(5)ow1 MrNWilson (a wl bhd: wl t.o whn p.u bef 13th)		**P**	9/1	—	—
1138^{3}	**Donovans Reef (61)** (MrsLMarshall) **11-9-11**(7) MrSDurack (j.slowly: chsd ldrs: wnt 2nd 13th: wknd rapidly & p.u bef last)		**P**	14/1	—	—
3608^{P}	**Overwhelm (IRE) (77)** (VThompson) **9-11-3**(3) MrMThompson (bhd fr 12th: j.slowly 2 out & p.u)		**P**	16/1	—	—
3712^{7}	**Gathering Time (70)** (MrsSJSmith) **11-10-6**(7)ow8 MrABirch (sn drvn along: t.o whn hmpd & uns rdr 2 out)		**U**	16/1	—	—
3643^{P}	**Quixall Crossett (57)** (EMCaine) **12-9-7**(7) MrCRussell (hdwy & in tch whn blnd & uns rdr 11th)		**U**	50/1	—	—

(SP 114.2%) **13 Rn**

6m 47.0 (36.00) CSF £490.72 CT £7,229.41 TOTE £9.60: £2.40 £13.30 £3.40 (£805.70) Trio Not won; £299.71 to Newcastle 25/3/97 OWNER Mr J. S. Goldie (GLASGOW) BRED Jim Goldie
LONG HANDICAP Quixall Crossett 9-13
No bid
OFFICIAL EXPLANATION **Two For One (IRE): did not act in the ground.**
IN-FOCUS: **This was a first win for Ollie McPhail.**

3607 Bright Destiny, very sweaty as usual, really attacked his fences and had galloped his rivals into the ground before the fourth last. He is obviously in good form but it has to be said this was a desperate contest. (7/1)
Just For Me (IRE) had pulled up on his last nine starts and this effort probably shows the quality of this event. (100/1)
Rusty Blade seems to have lost his way at present. (12/1: 8/1-14/1)
785 Upwell likes faster ground and this was a particularly poor effort. (25/1)
2956 Jendee (IRE) has only ever won at Sedgefield. (5/1)
3393 Two For One (IRE) is from a yard that is having a dreadful season and, after jumping two fences, he was in trouble, but he has always had breathing problems. (11/4)
1138 Donovans Reef (14/1: 10/1-16/1)

3825 L.C.L. PILS NOVICES' H'CAP HURDLE (0-100) (4-Y.O+) (Class E)

3-30 (3-30) **2m 4f 110y (8 hdls)** £2,794.50 (£777.00: £373.50) GOING: 0.85 sec per fur (S)

Form	Horse	Dist	Pos	SP	RR	SF
3485^{2}	**Enchanted Cottage (85)** (JMJefferson) **5-11-4**(3) ECallaghan (lw: hld up: stdy hdwy 6th: led appr last: drvn out)	—	**1**	7/2^{1}	69	4
3703^{4}	**Maitre de Musique (FR) (92)** (MartinTodhunter) **6-11-7**(7) CMcCormack (lw: in tch: led between last 2: hdd appr last: kpt on u.p)	1¼	**2**	10/1	75	10
3485^{3}	**Pappa Charlie (USA) (82)** (CParker) **6-11-4** BStorey (lw: hdwy ½-wy: wnt prom 2 out: one pce appr last)	6	**3**	8/1	60	—
2042^{8}	**My Missile (65)** (RGCockburn) **7-10-1** LO'Hara (hld up: gd hdwy 6th: ev ch appr last: sn wknd)	7	**4**	20/1	38	—
3641^{B}	**Meadowleck (64)** (WGYoung) **8-9-9**(5) STaylor (wnt prom 4th: led after 2 out: sn hdd & one pce)	3	**5**	33/1	35	—
3646^{*}	**Corbleu (IRE) (74)** (SBBell) **7-10-10** KJohnson (hdwy 5th: chsng ldrs 2 out: no imp after)	7	**6**	7/1^{2}	39	—
3351^{5}	**Boston Man (89)** (RDEWoodhouse) **6-11-11b**^{1} RichardGuest (chsd ldrs: led 5th tl after 2 out: wknd)	nk	**7**	7/1^{2}	54	—
3483^{3}	**Nasayer (IRE) (84)** (NBMason) **7-10-13**(7) SHaworth (chsd ldrs: outpcd 6th: wknd between last 2)	10	**8**	15/2^{3}	41	—
3534^{7}	**Skane River (IRE) (71)** (GRichards) **6-10-0**(7) RBurns (a bhd)	15	**9**	14/1	16	—
3608^{7}	**Triona's Hope (IRE) (64)** (EMCaine) **8-9-9**(5) MrMHNaughton (prom to 5th)	2½	**10**	33/1	7	—
3645^{5}	**Last Refuge (IRE) (81)** (TJCarr) **8-11-3** NSmith (outpcd & lost pl fr ½-wy)	3	**11**	12/1	22	—
3612^{3}	**Jendorcet (73)** (CWFairhurst) **7-10-9** JCallaghan (a bhd)	1¾	**12**	7/1^{2}	13	—
1776^{5}	**Kingfisher Brave (83)** (MGMeagher) **4-10-10** LWyer (led to 3rd: outpcd & lost tch 6th)	7	**13**	12/1	17	—
3157^{P}	**Mr Sloan (64)** (JSGoldie) **7-9-11**(3) GLee (cl up: led 3rd to 5th: sn wknd)	5	**14**	33/1	—	—
3691^{10}	**Onyourown (IRE) (80)** (HowardJohnson) **4-10-7** ASSmith (stdd s: a bhd)	4	**15**	14/1	7	—
3641^{2}	**Ski Path (67)** (NBycroft) **8-10-3** MFoster (chsd ldrs to 6th: wknd qckly)	hd	**16**	14/1	—	—
3159^{P}	**War Whoop (89)** (MissLucindaRussell) **5-11-11** TReed (prom to 4th: sn t.o: p.u bef last)		**P**	20/1	—	—

(SP 145.4%) **17 Rn**

5m 23.7 (35.70) CSF £40.52 CT £263.98 TOTE £3.70: £1.30 £3.10 £2.00 £6.00 (£24.90) Trio £76.00 OWNER Mrs J. M. Davenport (MALTON) BRED Alan G. Byrne
LONG HANDICAP Triona's Hope (IRE) 9-2 Meadowleck 9-6 Mr Sloan 9-3

WEIGHT FOR AGE 4yo-9lb
3485 Enchanted Cottage got it right this time and was produced to settle it going to the last. (7/2: 5/2-4/1)
3703 Maitre de Musique (FR) got the trip and the ground he needs but just met one too good. (10/1)
3485 Pappa Charlie (USA) again had his chances but looked very one-paced under pressure. (8/1: op 5/1)
2042 My Missile, after three months off, ran well again here and there is a modest race to be found. (20/1)
2768 Meadowleck has only troubled the judge once in thirty-eight attempts and this was one of her better efforts. (33/1)
3646* Corbleu (IRE) found this more testing ground all too much. (7/1)
3351 Boston Man had blinkers on for the first time and they proved no apparent help. (7/1: 5/1-8/1)
3483 Nasayer (IRE) was most disappointing on this occasion. (15/2)
1776 Kingfisher Brave (12/1: op 8/1)

3826 FEDERATION BREWERY NOVICES' CHASE (5-Y.O+) (Class E)
4-00 (4-00) **2m 110y (11 fncs)** £3,140.75 (£938.00: £448.50: £203.75) GOING: 0.85 sec per fur (S)

				SP	RR	SF
3326R	**Friendly Knight (81)** (JSHaldane) **7-11-3** ASSmith (lw: prom tl outpcd & lost pl 7th: hdwy 2 out: styd on wl flat to ld last 75y)	—	**1**	5/1 3	75	—
3642 4	**Nawtinookey** (MartinTodhunter) **7-10-5**(7) CMcCormack (hld up: hdwy 7th: chal & ev ch appr last: kpt on u.p flat)	5	**2**	12/1	65	—
3642 2	**Exemplar (IRE) (86)** (MrsSJSmith) **9-10-12**(5) GFRyan (mstke 1st: sn prom: outpcd 4 out: hit 3 out: styd on appr last)	½	**3**	9/4 1	70	—
3530U	**Nooran (83)** (ACWhillans) **6-11-3** KJohnson (lw: bhd: hdwy ½-wy: led appr last: hdd & wknd towards fin)	nk	**4**	100/30 2	69	—
3608 5	**Camptosaurus (IRE) (66)** (DSAlder) **8-11-3** BStorey (led to 5th: chsd ldrs: outpcd 4 out: kpt on fr next)	1¾	**5**	10/1	68	—
3278 6	**Old Redwood (60)** (MrsLWilliamson) **10-11-3** LO'Hara (cl up: led 5th tl appr last: wknd flat)	5	**6**	12/1	63	—
3138 5	**Robara** (SJLeadbetter) **7-11-3** NLeach (outpcd & hit 6th: sn t.o)	dist	**7**	20/1	—	—
3393 7	**Aristodemus (65)** (MrsLMarshall) **8-10-10**(7) MrSDurack (chsd ldrs tl blnd & lost pl 4th: sn t.o: p.u bef last)		**P**	25/1	—	—
3642 5	**Prince Baltasar (60)** (NBycroft) **8-11-3** MFoster (chsd ldrs fr ½-wy tl blnd & wknd 2 out: p.u bef last)		**P**	25/1	—	—
3695 5	**Shut Up (60)** (MrsEMoscrop) **8-10-9b**(3) EHusband (a.p: effrt 4 out: blnd bdly 2 out & p.u bef last)		**P**	33/1	—	—
3558 4	**Teejay'n'aitch (IRE) (80)** (JSGoldie) **5-10-6**(3) GLee (hdwy whn blnd & uns rdr 7th)		**U**	15/2	—	—
				(SP 122.1%)	**11 Rn**	

4m 27.1 (30.10) CSF £54.48 TOTE £8.10: £2.40 £1.40 £1.80 (£64.00) Trio £41.40 OWNER Mr G. J. Johnston (KELSO) BRED Mrs L. Fenton
WEIGHT FOR AGE 5yo-8lb
3326 Friendly Knight, who refused to race last time, looked in trouble here when suddenly losing touch five from home, but he then decided to run from the second last and settled it emphatically late on. (5/1: 7/2-11/2)
3642 Nawtinookey, from a yard whose horses are just coming right, put in her best effort and deserves to find a race. (12/1)
3642 Exemplar (IRE) prefers faster ground and in the circumstances this was a decent effort. (9/4)
3530 Nooran has yet to win a race, but this little gelding goes in the soft ground and should break his duck in due course. (100/30: 2/1-7/2)
3608 Camptosaurus (IRE) was always struggling with these soft conditions but he did stay on quite well. (10/1)
3695 Shut Up ran much better in this soft ground until a terrible blunder two out stopped her altogether. (33/1)

3827 KEOGHAN H'CAP HURDLE (0-120) (4-Y.O+) (Class D)
4-30 (4-30) **2m 4f 110y (8 hdls)** £2,802.90 (£774.40: £368.70) GOING: 0.85 sec per fur (S)

				SP	RR	SF
3645F	**Pariah (IRE) (92)** (MartinTodhunter) **8-10-13** PNiven (lw: hld up: smooth hdwy 6th: led last: rdn & hung lft: styd on)	—	**1**	4/1 3	72	—
3351 2	**Duke of Perth (94)** (HowardJohnson) **6-11-1** ASSmith (hld up: wnt prom 5th: led after 2 out tl hdd last: kpt on u.p)	1	**2**	7/2 2	73	—
3645F	**Chill Wind (83)** (NBycroft) **8-10-4** MFoster (cl up: led after 5th tl after 2 out: wknd appr last)	23	**3**	9/2	44	—
	Rascally (88) (MissLCSiddall) **7-10-9** RSupple (bit bkwd: chsd ldrs tl rdn & btn appr last)	nk	**4**	8/1	49	—
3351*	**Danbys Gorse (96)** (JMJefferson) **5-11-0**(3) ECallaghan (lw: hld up: hdwy 6th: prom & rdn between last 2: btn appr last)	hd	**5**	5/2 1	57	—
2631 12	**Master Hyde (USA) (103)** (RAllan) **8-11-10** BStorey (hld up: effrt 2 out: wknd appr last)	18	**6**	16/1	50	—
3646P	**Kenilworth Lad (87)** (WSCunningham) **9-10-8**ow1 RichardGuest (bit bkwd: led to 3rd: prom tl rdn & wknd 5th: sn wl bhd)	28	**7**	25/1	12	—
3556P	**Strathmore Lodge (90)** (MissLucindaRussell) **8-10-11**ow5 TReed (led 3rd tl after 5th: wknd next: sn t.o: p.u bef last)		**P**	14/1	—	—
				(SP 116.5%)	**8 Rn**	

5m 25.0 (37.00) CSF £17.48 CT £59.46 TOTE £4.30: £2.00 £1.70 £2.60 (£9.70) Trio £10.90 OWNER Mrs D. Miller (ULVERSTON) BRED James Maher
3645 Pariah (IRE) had the ground he likes and was always going best but he did his utmost to throw it away when in front. (4/1)
3351 Duke of Perth again tried hard and kept fighting back when all looked lost. (7/2)
3645 Chill Wind had his chances until his stamina gave out going to the last. (9/2)
Rascally is happier on slightly faster ground. (8/1)
3351* Danbys Gorse was disappointing this time, running out of fuel on the long run to the last. (5/2)
1852 Master Hyde (USA) has changed stables but as yet not his attitude. (16/1)
Strathmore Lodge (14/1: op 8/1)

3828 LEVY BOARD MAIDEN N.H. FLAT RACE (4, 5 & 6-Y.O) (Class H)
5-00 (5-00) **2m** £1,350.00 (£375.00: £180.00)

				SP	RR	SF
3142 2	**Into The Black (IRE)** (MrsMReveley) **6-11-5**(3) GLee (lw: a.p: rdn to ld over 1f out: styd on strly)	—	**1**	6/4 1	68 f	—
3561 6	**Lord Knows (IRE)** (JIACharlton) **6-11-1**(7) DThomas (led tl hdd over 1f out: r.o one pce)	4	**2**	12/1	64 f	—
2750 3	**The Snow Burn** (TPTate) **4-10-7**(7) RMcCarthy (lw: trckd ldrs: effrt 2f out: nt qckn)	s.h	**3**	6/1 2	64 f	—
3480 2	**Going Primitive** (JHetherton) **6-11-8** MrSSwiers (prom tl lost pl 7f out: hdwy 3f out: chsng ldrs 1f out: nt qckn)	hd	**4**	9/1	64 f	—
	Pepper Pot Boy (IRE) (MrsMReveley) **5-11-1**(7) MHerrington (mid div: hdwy 3f out: styd on wl)	hd	**5**	8/1	64 f	—
	Time Warrior (IRE) (GMMoore) **6-11-1**(7) NHannity (tall: green: bhd & pushed along tl styd on wl fnl 3f)	2½	**6**	12/1	61 f	—
	Open Fairway (MDods) **4-10-9**(5) RMcGrath (lw: sn trckng ldrs: effrt over 1f out: eased whn btn towards fin)	2	**7**	7/1 3	59 f	—
	Mademist Sam (PBeaumont) **5-11-3**(5) BGrattan (lengthy: unf: uns rdr & bolted bef s: hld up & bhd: hdwy 4f out: nvr nr to chal)	10	**8**	20/1	49 f	—

3203[13]	**Sir Boston** (RDEWoodhouse) **4-10-9**(5) DJKavanagh (w ldrs tl wknd over 2f out)	½	**9**	16/1	49 f	—
2804[11]	**Buddleia** (JRTurner) **4-10-2**(7) NHorrocks (bhd: hdwy & prom ½-wy: outpcd fnl 3f)	4	**10**	50/1	40 f	—
2047[12]	**Johnneys Spirit** (RGCockburn) **5-11-8** MrRHale (nvr trbld ldrs)	1	**11**	33/1	44 f	—
3487[5]	**Snooty Eskimo (IRE)** (JSHaldane) **5-11-5**(3) EHusband (lost tch fr ½-wy)	3	**12**	20/1	41 f	—
	Liam's River (IRE) (JWade) **5-11-3**(5) STaylor (rangy: in tch tl wknd 6f out)	2	**13**	12/1	39 f	—
3365[10]	**Gallant Taffy** (MrsLWilliamson) **5-11-1**(7) RBurns (bhd fr ½-wy)	5	**14**	33/1	34 f	—
3561[8]	**High Celleste (IRE)** (MartinTodhunter) **6-10-10**(7) CMcCormack (a bhd)	5	**15**	50/1	24 f	—
	Hey Sam (IRE) (JWade) **4-11-0** MrNWilson (rangy: unf: bit bkwd: a bhd: t.o)	dist	**16**	33/1	—	—
	Nickys Peril (JSHaldane) **5-10-10**(7) SHaworth (bkwd: sn chsng ldrs: wknd 5f out: t.o)	5	**17**	33/1	—	—
	The True Miller (FPMurtagh) **6-11-5**(3) ECallaghan (lengthy: bkwd: mid div: hdwy 6f out: wknd 3f out: t.o)	8	**18**	50/1	—	—
3561[9]	**Meggie Scott** (JPDodds) **4-10-2**(7) SMelrose (prom 10f: wl t.o)	dist	**19**	50/1	—	—
				(SP 146.0%)	**19 Rn**	

4m 22.7 CSF £22.00 TOTE £1.90: £1.20 £7.00 £1.80 (£33.10) Trio £40.40 OWNER Mr J. Huckle (SALTBURN) BRED M. W. Hickey
WEIGHT FOR AGE 4yo-8lb
OFFICIAL EXPLANATION **Open Fairway: lost his action in the ground.**
3142 Into The Black (IRE) had the conditions to suit and this dour stayer was always too strong for this bunch. (6/4)
3142 Lord Knows (IRE) enjoyed himself out in front and kept battling away but always found the winner too good. (12/1: op 8/1)
2750 The Snow Burn ran pretty well but these testing conditions blunted any finishing speed. (6/1: op 3/1)
3480 Going Primitive again showed ability but this stiff finish just found him out. (9/1: 5/1-10/1)
Pepper Pot Boy (IRE), a stable-companion of the winner, ran as though experience will improve him. (8/1)
Time Warrior (IRE) looked a real stayer, responding to driving in the last half-mile to be nearest at the finish. (12/1: 8/1-14/1)
Open Fairway put up a decent first effort and was not knocked about when beaten in the closing stages. (7/1)

T/Jkpt: Not won; £2,555.01 to Newcastle 25/3/97. T/Plpt: £150.60 (101.44 Tckts). T/Qdpt: £26.30 (39.76 Tckts) AA

3741-LUDLOW (R-H) (Good to firm)
Monday March 24th
WEATHER: overcast, then sunshine

3829 OFFICIALS NOVICES' HURDLE (5-Y.O+) (Class E)
2-10 (2-10) **2m (9 hdls)** £2,158.50 (£606.00: £295.50) GOING minus 0.44 sec per fur (GF)

				SP	RR	SF
3575[2]	**Suranom (IRE)** (MrsDHaine) **5-10-12** JFTitley (lw: chsd ldr: led 3 out: drvn clr flat)	—	**1**	8/15[1]	65+	8
3186[6]	**Little Shefford (81)** (MPMuggeridge) **5-11-4** SCurran (lw: led: clr 4th: hdd 3 out: rdn & outpcd flat)	3	**2**	3/1[2]	68?	11
3019[7]	**Worthy Memories** (MrsMerritaJones) **8-10-7** DerekByrne (plld hrd: chsd ldng pair: no imp fr 3 out)	6	**3**	9/1[3]	51	—
3594[7]	**Saafi (IRE) (67)** (RJBaker) **6-10-12b** VSlattery (trckd ldrs: rdn after 6th: sn lost tch)	16	**4**	14/1	40	—
2035[9]	**Eurolink Shadow (83)** (DMcCain) **5-10-12** DWalsh (hld up: hdwy 5th: wknd appr 3 out: t.o)	14	**5**	50/1	26	—
3184[10]	**Lucky Escape** (CaptTAForster) **6-10-12** SWynne (hld up: outpcd 6th: t.o fr 3 out)	dist	**6**	25/1	—	—
3184[P]	**Nanjizal** (KSBridgwater) **5-10-9b**[1](3) RMassey (a t.o)	7	**7**	66/1	—	—
				(SP 114.2%)	**7 Rn**	

3m 40.9 (3.90) CSF £2.27 TOTE £1.50: £1.20 £1.90 (£1.70) OWNER Mrs Ann Leat (NEWMARKET) BRED Yeomanstown Lodge Stud
3575 Suranom (IRE), winner of four races on the Flat in Italy, is still a full horse and it is more than possible that he has needed his previous couple of runs over hurdles. Winning this without having to really get serious, he will have a job to find an easier contest. (8/15)
2897 Little Shefford, stepping back to the minimum trip, had only the winner to contend with from the start but, forced to give best soon after entering the straight, his attempt to rally was always in vain. (3/1: op 7/4)
2794 Worthy Memories, running into the prize money for the first time, ran a bit too freely for her own good in the early stages and once off the bridle, failed to pick up at all. (9/1: 4/1-10/1)
3338 Saafi (IRE) (14/1: op 8/1)

3830 NATIONAL RIDING WEEK NOVICES' CHASE (5-Y.O+) (Class E)
2-40 (2-40) **3m (19 fncs)** £2,771.75 (£839.00: £409.50: £194.75) GOING minus 0.44 sec per fur (GF)

				SP	RR	SF
3472[5]	**Captiva Bay (64)** (MrsARHewitt) **8-10-11** SWynne (j.w: mde all: rdn out)	—	**1**	6/1[3]	86	24
3736[P]	**Philatelic (IRE) (85)** (RHAlner) **6-11-2** JRailton (bkwd: mstke 1st: chsd wnr fr 5th: disp ld 2 out: no ex flat)	1	**2**	11/4[2]	90	28
3746[2]	**Fawley Flyer** (WGMTurner) **8-11-2** AThornton (chsd wnr to 5th: mstke 13th: outpcd 15th: n.d after)	6	**3**	4/6[1]	86	24
3360[5]	**Lambrini (IRE) (67)** (DMcCain) **7-10-11** DWalsh (hld up: lost tch 10th: t.o whn ref 2 out: continued)	dist	**4**	16/1	—	—
	Stormhill Warrior (JCABatchelor) **6-11-2** VSlattery (bkwd: sn t.o: hit 9th: p.u bef 12th)		**P**	25/1	—	—
				(SP 110.7%)	**5 Rn**	

6m 1.4 (1.40) CSF £20.67 TOTE £6.20: £3.50 £1.30 (£4.00) OWNER Miss M A De Quincey (MALPAS) BRED Mrs J. Broad
Captiva Bay decided on forceful tactics in such a mediocre event and, displaying a good round of jumping, finally opened her account. (6/1)
Philatelic (IRE) ran a race full of promise in only his second outing over fences but he found the race coming far too quickly and was being comfortably held on the flat. He should be able to win at this game. (11/4)
3746 Fawley Flyer never really recovered from a mistake halfway down the back straight for the final time, and it would seem he finds this trip half a mile too far. (4/6)

3831 CLIVE PAVILION H'CAP HURDLE (0-115) (4-Y.O+) (Class E)
3-10 (3-10) **2m 5f 110y (11 hdls)** £2,158.50 (£606.00: £295.50) GOING minus 0.44 sec per fur (GF)

				SP	RR	SF
3362[3]	**First Crack (84)** (FJordan) **12-11-1** SWynne (lw: hld up: hdwy 7th: led appr 2 out: clr whn hit last)	—	**1**	6/4[1]	65	—
3178[4]	**Drum Battle (93)** (WGMTurner) **5-11-10** AThornton (hld up: hdwy 5th: led after 8th tl rdn & hdd appr 2 out: sn btn)	9	**2**	7/2[2]	67	—
3488[P]	**One More Dime (IRE) (69)** (JLNeedham) **7-9-9**(5) ABates (hld up in rr: gd hdwy appr 6th: outpcd 4 out: styd on again 2 out)	4	**3**	8/1	40	—
3621[9]	**Blatant Outburst (80)** (MissSJWilton) **7-10-11** RJohnson (led to 3rd: led 5th tl hdd & wknd after 8th: t.o)	dist	**4**	5/1[3]	—	—
2820[3]	**Colwall (89)** (MissPMWhittle) **6-11-1**(5) MrRThornton (lw: led 3rd to 5th: dropped rr next: sn t.o)	5	**5**	7/2[2]	—	—
				(SP 112.2%)	**5 Rn**	

5m 10.9 (9.90) CSF £6.75 TOTE £1.90: £1.50 £2.30 (£2.30) OWNER Mr D. Pugh (LEOMINSTER) BRED J. Wilding
LONG HANDICAP One More Dime (IRE) 9-10

3362 First Crack, faced with a simple task, achieved it with the minimum of fuss and continued her good record at this venue. (6/4: op 5/2)
3178 Drum Battle, a winner here last month, has not yet come in his coat, and the winner left him for dead from the penultimate flight. (7/2: op 2/1)
3189 One More Dime (IRE), still to trouble the judge, was inclined to run her race in snatches, and she will need a much stiffer test of stamina to find an opening. (8/1)

3832 ANNUAL MEMBERS H'CAP CHASE (0-115) (5-Y.O+) (Class E)

3-40 (3-40) **2m (13 fncs)** £2,745.75 (£831.00: £405.50: £192.75) GOING minus 0.44 sec per fur (GF)

				SP	RR	SF
3686[4]	**Fichu (USA) (78)** (MrsLRichards) **9-10-2** MRichards (hld up: hdwy 4 out: blnd next: hrd rdn to ld nr fin)	—	1	7/2[2]	88	—
3673[2]	**Coolteen Hero (IRE) (89)** (RHAlner) **7-10-13** WMcFarland (lw: chsd ldr: led 4 out: blnd last: hrd rdn & hdd cl home)	1¼	2	11/2[3]	98	—
3588[U]	**Fenwick (82)** (RJHodges) **10-10-3**(3) TDascombe (lw: hld up: hdwy 6th: hit 9th: rdn 3 out: one pce)	5	3	7/2[2]	86	—
3547[4]	**Super Sharp (NZ) (88)** (HOliver) **9-10-12** JacquiOliver (j.w: led to 4 out: sn rdn & wknd)	9	4	11/4[1]	83	—
3678[2]	**Monday Club (100)** (JCTuck) **13-11-10** SMcNeill (hld up: hdwy 9th: rdn 3 out: sn btn)	1½	5	7/2[2]	93	—
3460[6]	**Quarter Marker (IRE) (76)** (RLee) **9-10-0** MrsCFord (bkwd: a bhd: t.o fr ½-wy)	24	6	50/1	45	—
3030[5]	**The Fence Shrinker (76)** (DMcCain) **6-10-0** SWynne (lw: chsd ldrs tl wknd appr 4 out: t.o)	6	7	33/1	39	—
				(SP 113.6%)		**7 Rn**

3m 59.7 (7.70) CSF £20.53 TOTE £4.60: £1.90 £1.90 (£19.50) OWNER Mr B. Seal (CHICHESTER) BRED Thomas P. Whitney
LONG HANDICAP Quarter Marker (IRE) 8-12 The Fence Shrinker 8-12
3686 Fichu (USA) has shown a liking for this track in the past, but he almost threw it away when all but losing his rider three out and, in the end, he needed the luck to go his way to score. (7/2)
3673 Coolteen Hero (IRE) jumped well in the main, and looked home and dried when the winner missed out at the final ditch, but he took off a stride too soon at the last and that cost him the race. (11/2: op 7/2)
3588 Fenwick is not quite so effective over the minimum trip when the ground is lively and, after an error at the fifth last, could not summon the pace to deliver a challenge. (7/2: 5/2-4/1)
3547 Super Sharp (NZ) jumped from fence to fence and set a good pace, but he did not find a lot once headed, and faded rather quickly. (11/4)
3678 Monday Club had to admit age catching up with him and his attempt to concede weight all round was just not on. (7/2)

3833 HUGHES CATERERS NOVICES' H'CAP CHASE (0-105) (5-Y.O+) (Class E)

4-10 (4-10) **2m 4f (17 fncs)** £2,758.75 (£835.00: £407.50: £193.75) GOING minus 0.44 sec per fur (GF)

				SP	RR	SF
3732*	**Quite A Man (89)** (SABrookshaw) **9-12-2** 6x CMaude (lw: a.p: hit 12th: chal 4 out: sn led: clr last)	—	1	6/4[2]	99	18
1073[7]	**Ryton Run (81)** (MrsSMOdell) **12-11-8** TJO'Sullivan (bkwd: j.w: led 4th to 3 out: j.lft last 2: sn outpcd)	16	2	16/1	78	—
3675[P]	**Little Rowley (60)** (MrsLRichards) **8-10-1** MRichards (trckd ldrs: reminders 10th: styd on one pce fr 3 out)	2½	3	25/1	55	—
3746[3]	**Prize Match (68)** (JCTuck) **8-10-9** SMcNeill (lw: j.w: led to 4th: disp ld to 13th: wknd next)	1½	4	8/1[3]	62	—
2926[P]	**Aeolian (68)** (MissPMWhittle) **6-10-4**(5) MrRThornton (bhd: t.o whn mstke 9th: hdwy next: btn whn blnd 3 out: p.u bef 2 out)		P	12/1	—	—
3667[2]	**Jolly Boat (82)** (FJordan) **10-11-9** SWynne (p.u after 4th: dismntd: lame)		P	5/4[1]	—	—
				(SP 113.0%)		**6 Rn**

4m 59.8 (7.80) CSF £19.64 TOTE £2.80: £1.60 £2.70 (£20.00) OWNER Mr W. R. J. Everall (SHREWSBURY) BRED R. Everall
OFFICIAL EXPLANATION Jolly Boat: was found to be lame on the near fore.
3732* Quite A Man was able to complete a double within a week, with a very easily-gained success, and he is certainly thriving at the moment. (6/4)
935 Ryton Run, off the track for five months, ran a fine race considering his burly appearance and he was only shaken off at the second last. If he is given time to recover, he could be in for a decent spring. (16/1)
Little Rowley, pulled up on his only previous appearances this season, at least ran much better over this shorter trip without ever getting close enough to pose a threat. (25/1)
3456 Prize Match helped share the lead to the straight but then faded out rather rapidly, and she has still to prove she truly gets this trip. (8/1: 5/1-9/1)

3834 RACEDAY STAFF NOVICES' H'CAP HURDLE (0-105) (4-Y.O+) (Class E)

4-40 (4-40) **3m 2f 110y (13 hdls)** £2,190.00 (£615.00: £300.00) GOING minus 0.44 sec per fur (GF)

				SP	RR	SF
3683[2]	**Sammorello (IRE) (75)** (NATwiston-Davies) **6-10-9** CLlewellyn (lw: mde all: drvn & styd on strly fr 2 out)	—	1	10/11[1]	56	—
3594[5]	**Fastini Gold (75)** (RJPrice) **5-10-2**(7) XAizpuru (hld up: chsd wnr 10th: ev ch 3 out: swtchd rt appr last: unable qckn)	3½	2	6/1[3]	54	—
3683[3]	**Copper Coil (94)** (WGMTurner) **7-11-7**(7) JPower (prom: hrd drvn 10th: sn btn)	12	3	11/4[2]	66	—
2570[6]	**Awestruck (66)** (BPreece) **7-9-7b**(7) JMogford (hld up & wl bhd: styd on appr 3 out: nvr nrr)	nk	4	12/1	38	—
3603[3]	**Win I Did (IRE) (87)** (RHAlner) **7-11-2**(5) MrRThornton (lw: prom tl rdn & wknd appr 8th: sn t.o)	dist	5	8/1	—	—
				(SP 112.1%)		**5 Rn**

6m 21.5 (22.50) CSF £6.36 TOTE £1.70: £1.10 £2.20 (£2.40) OWNER Mrs S. A. MacEchern (CHELTENHAM) BRED Park Enterprises
LONG HANDICAP Awestruck 9-5
3683 Sammorello (IRE) won this courtesy of his undoubted stamina, but he did adopt the right tactics to find out the strength of the opposition. (10/11: evens-4/5)
3594 Fastini Gold appeared to be going much the better when he joined issue three out, but he was stepping into the unknown over such an extended trip and lack of stamina found him out. (6/1)
3683 Copper Coil finished eight lengths behind the winner when they clashed earlier in the month and, on only 2lb better terms, had no chance at all of gaining revenge. (11/4: op 7/4)
1251 Awestruck, tailed off for the majority of the way, did begin to stay on in the last half-mile, but could never quicken up enough to run into the prizes. (12/1: tchd 20/1)
3603 Win I Did (IRE) (8/1: 6/1-10/1)

T/Plpt: £127.00 (70.43 Tckts). T/Qdpt: £16.80 (33.87 Tckts) IM

3568-SANDOWN (R-H) (Good to firm)
Tuesday March 25th

Race 2: 2nd last fence omitted fnl circ
WEATHER: overcast

3835 GUNNER HERITAGE CAMPAIGN NOVICES' CHASE (5-Y.O+) (Class D)
2-15 (2-15) **2m (13 fncs)** £4,030.00 (£1,130.00: £550.00) GOING: 0.17 sec per fur (G)

				SP	RR	SF
3749[3]	**Just Bruce (88)** (MrsEHHeath) **8-11-6** DGallagher (swtg: chsd ldr: led 2 out: drvn out)	—	1	20/1[3]	117?	38
3111*	**Mister Drum (IRE) (125)** (MJWilkinson) **8-11-6** 4x WMarston (led to 2 out: ev ch last: unable qckn)	1¼	2	13/8[2]	116	37
3596[4]	**Flying Instructor (130)** (PRWebber) **7-11-10** RBellamy (hld up: ev ch whn mstke 2 out: nt rcvr)	1	3	4/7[1]	119	40
				(SP 106.5%)		**3 Rn**

4m 0.2 (9.20) CSF £41.28 TOTE £8.00 (£3.60) OWNER Mr A. M. Heath (ROYSTON) BRED A. M. Heath

3749 Just Bruce, 37lb inferior to Mister Drum and 38lb inferior to Flying Instructor on official adjusted ratings, caused an upset here, touching down narrowly in front at the second last and responding to pressure to keep his two rivals at bay. The result would surely have been different had the favourite jumped the second last cleanly. (20/1)

3111* Mister Drum (IRE), given a break since his last outing nearly seven weeks ago, is well suited by a right-handed track and fast ground. Bowling along in front, he was marginally collared at the second last, but was only tapped for toe up the hill. (13/8)

3596 Flying Instructor was travelling really well and was on level terms with his two rivals when a mistake at the second last cost him valuable ground and momentum. His jockey quickly got at the gelding but, try as he might, he failed to get back on terms. Losses are only lent. (4/7)

3836 MOUSETRAP CHALLENGE CUP NOVICES' CHASE (5-Y.O+) (Class D)
2-50 (2-50) **2m 4f 110y (16 fncs)** £4,658.00 (£1,142.00) GOING: 0.17 sec per fur (G)

				SP	RR	SF
160[2]	**Pontoon Bridge (100)** (MrsAJPerrett) **10-11-4** RDunwoody (lw: led 2nd: lft clr 12th: eased flat)	—	1	4/9[1]	87+	—
2007[9]	**Chiappucci (IRE) (87)** (MrsEHHeath) **7-11-0** DGallagher (bkwd: 3rd whn mstkes 8th & 10th: sn wknd: lft poor 2nd 12th: r.o one pce)	3	2	6/1[3]	81	—
3578[3]	**Key Player (IRE) (77)** (RRowe) **8-11-4** DO'Sullivan (lw: led to 2nd: 2nd & ev ch whn fell 12th)		F	7/2[2]	—	—
3667[5]	**Ell Gee** (MrsPTownsley) **7-10-2**(7) MissCTownsley (lw: mstke 3rd: in rr tl fell 5th)		F	40/1	—	—
				(SP 108.2%)		**4 Rn**

5m 28.7 (29.70) CSF £3.28 TOTE £1.40 (£2.10) OWNER Sir Eric Parker (PULBOROUGH) BRED Patrick Cotter

160 Pontoon Bridge looked in good shape for this first run since last July. Jumping well in front, he got under the eleventh - the water - and from that point rather lost his confidence and was more hesitant at his fences. Left well clear by the departure of Key Player at the next, he was allowed to lob home in his own time and was some 25 lengths clear of his only other rival jumping the Pond Fence. Dunwoody took things extremely easily on the run-in and eased the gelding down to a complete walk in the closing stages. He was value for at least twenty lengths. Well suited by fast ground, he can win again. (4/9)

Chiappucci (IRE) looked fat for this first run in over three months, and after a mistake at the tenth was soon done with. He was left a very poor second at the first of the Railway Fences but never had a hope of getting near the winner. However that rival was greatly eased on the run-in and he is extremely flattered to finish so close. Nothing should be read into this at all. (6/1)

3578 Key Player (IRE), 23lb inferior to the winner on official adjusted ratings, was on level terms with that rival when falling at the twelfth. (7/2: op 2/1)

3837 ROYAL ARTILLERY GOLD CUP AMATEUR CHASE (5-Y.O+) (Class E)
3-20 (3-22) **3m 110y (22 fncs)** £3,468.75 (£1,050.00: £512.50: £243.75) GOING: 0.17 sec per fur (G)

				SP	RR	SF
3599[3]	**Lucky Dollar (IRE) (99)** (KCBailey) **9-11-12**(7) MajorSJRobinson (lw: hmpd 6th: hdwy 7th: led 16th: mstke last: rdn out)	—	1	2/1[2]	103	5
3553[5]	**No Joker (IRE)** (NAGaselee) **9-11-3**(7) CaptRHall (led tl mstke & hdd 14th: lost pl 16th: rallied flat: r.o wl)	2	2	25/1	93	—
3446[5]	**Sonofagipsy** (JWDufosee) **13-11-12**(7) MrAWood (hdwy 7th: led 14th tl hdd & mstke 16th: ev ch fr 4 out: blnd last: unable qckn)	nk	3	12/1	102	4
3551[3]	**Maxxum Express (IRE) (80)** (GBBalding) **9-11-12**(7) MrJThatcher (lw: prom to 13th)	17	4	16/1	90	—
3568*	**Archies Oats** (JonTrice-Rolph) **8-12-0**(5) MrJTrice-Rolph (sme hdwy 11th: wknd 12th)	3	5	8/1[3]	88	—
3456[6]	**Ennistymon (IRE) (60)** (JWMullins) **6-10-12**(7) MrGWeatherley (lw: bhd fr 12th)	15	6	66/1	65	—
	New Ghost (GWGiddings) **12-11-7v**[1](7) MajorOEllwood (3rd whn fell 6th)		F	16/1	—	—
3553*	**Brackenfield** (RBarber) **11-12-3b**(7) MrDAlers-Hankey (lw: 4th whn fell 6th)		F	6/5[1]	—	—
3551[P]	**Icantelya (IRE) (80)** (JWMullins) **8-11-3v**(7) MrSGreany (swtg: a bhd: mstke 2nd: blnd 11th: t.o whn fell 18th)		F	66/1	—	—
3490[5]	**Major Mac** (DLWilliams) **10-11-3**(7) CaptEAndrewes (bhd fr 7th: t.o whn p.u bef 2 out)		P	66/1	—	—
3551[P]	**Toddling Inn** (RJRSymonds) **10-11-1**(7)ow3 MrCFarr (bhd fr 9th: t.o whn p.u bef last)		P	66/1	—	—
3568[6]	**Taurean Tycoon** (DLWilliams) **13-11-12**(7) MrBLogan (pckd 5th: bhd whn blnd & uns rdr 7th)		U	66/1	—	—
				(SP 120.7%)		**12 Rn**

6m 32.8 (30.80) CSF £48.28 TOTE £3.30: £1.50 £5.60 £3.50 (£29.50) Trio £202.70 OWNER Major-Gen Burges (UPPER LAMBOURN) BRED Edward Vaughan

3599 Lucky Dollar (IRE), third in the Kim Muir two weeks ago, had a lot less on his plate here, especially after the early departure of the favourite. Leading at the water - the sixteenth - he had a real battle with the third but, despite a mistake at the last, kept on well up the hill to lift this much sought after prize in the armed forces. (2/1)

No Joker (IRE), who has a bad habit of unshipping Captain Hall, ran better here. After leading until giving away the advantage with a mistake at the fourteenth, he soon lost his pitch but he came with a wet sail again from the last and snatched second place in the last couple of strides. (25/1)

2964 Sonofagipsy, very much in the veteran stage, had a real battle with the winner in the last mile. Clouting the last very hard indeed, his jockey's reins were all over the place on the run-in and the combination was not helped by a loose horse running in front of him. However, the gelding failed to find another gear up the hill. (12/1: 8/1-14/1)

3551 Maxxum Express (IRE) was already sending out distress signals entering the back straight for the final time. (16/1)

3838 ALANBROOKE MEMORIAL H'CAP CHASE (0-135) (5-Y.O+) (Class C)
3-55 (3-57) **3m 110y (22 fncs)** £5,873.00 (£1,442.00) GOING: 0.17 sec per fur (G)

Form	Horse	Dist	Pos	SP	RR	SF
3573^{4}	**Denver Bay (116)** (JTGifford) **10-11-7**$^{(3)}$ LAspell (lw: lft 2nd 3rd: led 14th: clr appr 2 out: comf)	—	1	7/4^{1}	124+	—
3605*	**Credon (103)** (SWoodman) **9-10-11** RDunwoody (lw: led to 14th: mstke 17th: rdn appr 3 out: wknd appr 2 out)	19	2	2/1^{2}	100	—
3751*	**Harristown Lady (102)** (GBBalding) **10-10-10b** ^{4x} BClifford (lw: 2nd whn uns rdr 3rd)		U	7/4^{1}	—	—
				(SP 106.1%)		**3 Rn**

6m 33.8 (31.80) CSF £4.66 TOTE £2.40 (£2.10) OWNER Mr Bill Naylor (FINDON) BRED Marston Stud
3573 Denver Bay may have been racing on ground faster than he would have liked but Credon was also unseated by the surface and, leading at the fourteenth, he was bustled clear from the Pond Fence for a comfortable victory. (7/4)
3605* Credon found this ground too lively but set the pace until the fourteenth. Pushed along turning for home, he was left for dead from the Pond Fence. (2/1)

3839 ROYAL STAR AND GARTER HOME H'CAP CHASE (0-125) (5-Y.O+) (Class D)
4-30 (4-30) **2m (13 fncs)** £4,045.50 (£1,224.00: £597.00: £283.50) GOING: 0.17 sec per fur (G)

Form	Horse	Dist	Pos	SP	RR	SF
3686*	**Red Bean (90)** (KVincent) **9-10-2** RJohnson (swtg: a.p: mstke 7th: chsd ldr fr 8th: led 3 out: rdn out)	—	1	5/2^{2}	96	28
3673*	**The Carrot Man (107)** (PWinkworth) **9-11-5** PHide (swtg: a.p: led 8th to 3 out: ev ch last: unable qckn)	1¾	2	10/11^{1}	111	43
3071^{7}	**Count Barachois (USA) (88)** (MrsEHHeath) **9-10-0** DGallagher (swtg: led tl pckd & hdd 8th: wknd 9th)	24	3	16/1	68	—
3638^{F}	**Norse Raider (112)** (MCPipe) **7-11-10** JamieEvans (a bhd)	7	4	4/1^{3}	85	17
3756^{P}	**Young Alfie (88)** (JFPanvert) **12-10-0b** WMarston (bhd fr 5th)	21	5	66/1	40	—
				(SP 108.3%)		**5 Rn**

3m 58.6 (7.60) CSF £4.81 TOTE £3.10: £1.30 £1.20 (£2.10) OWNER Mr Kage Vincent (REIGATE) BRED Mrs M. Woolgar
LONG HANDICAP Count Barachois (USA) 9-4 Young Alfie 9-3
3686* Red Bean coped well with this much faster ground. Touching down narrowly at the Pond Fence, he was travelling better than the runner-up and was ridden along to assert his authority from the last. (5/2)
3673* The Carrot Man, who has been raised 7lb for his recent Folkestone success, loves to hear his feet rattle and went on at the sixth last. Collared at the Pond Fence, he remained alongsides the winner but was not travelling as well as that rival and was tapped for toe from the last. (10/11)
2843 Count Barachois (USA), 10lb out of the handicap, is a poor performer and, after losing the advantage after pecking very badly at the eighth, was soon done with. (16/1)
2942 Norse Raider got round but never threatened at any stage. (4/1: op 2/1)

3840 'UBIQUE' HUNTERS' CHASE (5-Y.O+) (Class H)
5-00 (5-00) **2m 4f 110y (17 fncs)** £1,576.00 (£436.00: £208.00) GOING: 0.17 sec per fur (G)

Form	Horse	Dist	Pos	SP	RR	SF
3568^{4}	**Electric Committee (IRE)** (AWWood) **7-11-5**$^{(7)}$ MrAWood (led 3rd: clr appr 3 out: rdn out)	—	1	9/1	93	—
3744^{12}	**Great Pokey** (MissNellCourtenay) **12-11-5**$^{(7)}$ MissNCourtenay (lw: led to 3rd: rdn appr 3 out: r.o flat)	3	2	20/1	91	—
3439^{2}	**Driving Force** (MrsHMobley) **11-11-13b**$^{(7)}$ MrACharles-Jones (lw: hld up: chsd ldr 13th tl flat: sn wknd)	16	3	7/2^{3}	86	—
3553^{4}	**True Steel** (JonTrice-Rolph) **11-11-3**$^{(5)}$ MrJTrice-Rolph (lw: hdwy 7th: 3rd whn mstke 8th: lost pl 9th: wknd 13th)	9	4	7/4^{1}	67	—
3664^{2}	**Galzig** (MrsDEHTurner) **9-11-1**$^{(7)}$ MrWTellwright (4th whn mstke 13th: sn wknd: wl bhd whn p.u bef 3 out)		P	11/4^{2}	—	—
	The Mill Height (IRE) (KTork) **7-11-1**$^{(7)}$ MrCWardThomas (lw: bhd fr 7th: t.o whn p.u bef 12th)		P	9/1	—	—
				(SP 110.0%)		**6 Rn**

5m 24.0 (25.00) CSF £103.07 TOTE £11.70: £4.90 £2.90 (£45.10) OWNER Mr James Kearsley BRED Brookhill Stud
3568 Electric Committee (IRE) tore off in front at the last meeting here but did give his amateur more of a chance on this occasion. In front from the third, he forged clear turning for home and, rousted along, proved too good for his rivals. (9/1)
Great Pokey, who has given no encouragement so far this season, managed to regain the runner-up berth on the run-in and kept on well to the line. (20/1)
3439 Driving Force, conceding weight all round, moved into second place five out, but he failed to get on terms with the winner and was tired when collared for the runner-up spot on the run-in. (7/2)
3553 True Steel found the ground far too fast and after making an effort early on the final circuit, made a mistake at the first fence in the back straight. This cost him ground he could ill-afford and, although he tried to get back into it, eventually had to concede defeat five from home. (7/4: evens-2/1)

T/Plpt: £4,818.20 (2.28 Tckts). T/Qdpt: £92.10 (8.4 Tckts) AK

3278-SOUTHWELL (L-H) (Turf Good, AWT Standard)
Tuesday March 25th
Race 2: One fence omitted. Race 6: All-Weather course
WEATHER: fine

3841 NEWCASTLE H'CAP CHASE (0-120) (5-Y.O+) (Class D)
2-25 (2-25) **3m 110y (19 fncs)** £4,195.00 (£1,030.00) GOING: 0.19 sec per fur (G)

Form	Horse	Dist	Pos	SP	RR	SF
3414*	**Father Sky (120)** (OSherwood) **6-12-0b** JOsborne (trckd ldr: lft in ld 5 out: sn clr)	—	1	4/5^{1}	131?	31
3175^{P}	**Zambezi Spirit (IRE) (98)** (MrsMerritaJones) **8-10-6** DerekByrne (swtg: hld up: effrt 12th: sn prom: hit 14th: wknd after 4 out: virtually p.u)	dist	2	5/2^{2}	—	—
3742^{2}	**Trumpet (95)** (JGMO'Shea) **8-10-0v**$^{(3)}$ MichaelBrennan (lw: led tl fell 5 out: dead)		F	100/30^{3}	—	—
				(SP 107.2%)		**3 Rn**

6m 27.0 (20.00) CSF £2.77 TOTE £1.30 (£2.30) OWNER Mr Kenneth Kornfeld (UPPER LAMBOURN) BRED Sheikh Mohammed
3414* Father Sky simply had to put in a clear round. (4/5)
3175 Zambezi Spirit (IRE), who has a history of breaking blood-vessels, stopped in two strides after jumping four out and was allowed to come home in his own time. He seemed none the worse pulling up. (5/2)
3742 Trumpet took a fatal fall five from home. (100/30)

3842 BIRMINGHAM NOVICES' CHASE (5-Y.O+) (Class E)
3-00 (3-01) **2m (12 fncs)** £3,095.00 (£935.00: £455.00: £215.00) GOING: 0.19 sec per fur (G)

			SP	RR	SF
3200^{5}	**Chorus Line (IRE) (84)** (PBeaumont) **8-10-11** RSupple (mde virtually all: lft clr appr 3 out: j.rt: unchal) ......—	**1**	$3/1^{2}$	85	13
3682^{2}	**Tenayestelign (79)** (DMarks) **9-10-12**(5) MrRThornton (chsd ldrs: outpcd fr 4 out) 25	**2**	7/1	66	—
3470^{3}	**Santaray** (TWDonnelly) **11-11-2** MrRArmson (in tch: drvn along 7th: one pce) ......½	**3**	6/1	65	—
2674^{P}	**Copper Cable (70)** (CSmith) **10-11-2** MRanger (mstkes: trckd ldrs: hit 7th & 2 out: one pce) 1	**4**	20/1	64	—
3442^{P}	**Jonjas Chudleigh** (RGFrost) **10-11-2** JFrost (sn bhd: t.o 6th) 20	**5**	14/1	44	—
3623^{P}	**Highland Flame** (AGBlackmore) **8-10-13**(3) PHenley (w ldr to 7th: wkng whn fell 4 out)	**F**	40/1	—	—
3733^{8}	**Millenium Lass (IRE)** (MissMERowland) **9-10-11** GaryLyons (gd hdwy to go 2nd 8th: no ch w wnr whn p.u bef 3 out: dead)	**P**	25/1	—	—
3030^{F}	**Dash To The Phone (USA)** (KAMorgan) **5-10-8** ASSmith (blnd & uns rdr 2nd)	**U**	$5/1^{3}$	—	—
3417^{3}	**Gimme (IRE) (83)** (JGMO'Shea) **7-11-2v** AThornton (blnd & uns rdr 1st)	**U**	$2/1^{1}$	—	—
			(SP 119.5%)	**9 Rn**	

4m 6.4 (13.40) CSF £22.39 TOTE £3.90: £1.10 £2.30 £3.10 (£8.00) Trio £20.20 OWNER Mrs A. P. Stead (BRANDSBY) BRED Frank Stewart
WEIGHT FOR AGE 5yo-8lb

3200 Chorus Line (IRE) was left out on her own going to three out. This race was a chapter of disasters. (3/1)
3682 Tenayestelign was left a modest second. (7/1)
3470 Santaray was wearing a tongue-strap and his jumping was not blemish-free. (6/1: op 4/1)
1717 Copper Cable, who had his tongue tied down and who was pulled up last time, clouted at least two fences hard. (20/1)
3030 Dash To The Phone (USA) only got as far as the second. (5/1)
3417 Gimme (IRE) only got as far as the first. (2/1)

3843 LONDON H'CAP CHASE (0-115) (5-Y.O+) (Class E)
3-30 (3-30) **2m 4f 110y (16 fncs)** £3,046.25 (£920.00: £447.50: £211.25) GOING: 0.19 sec per fur (G)

			SP	RR	SF
28^{3}	**Counterbalance (93)** (JCMcConnochie) **10-11-5** SMcNeill (lw: chsd ldrs: lft in ld 12th: sn clr) ......—	**1**	11/2	108	41
3732^{P}	**Curragh Peter (75)** (MrsPBickerton) **10-9-12**(3)ow1 GuyLewis (led to 2nd: outpcd after 9th: wnt 2nd appr 3 out: no imp) 21	**2**	25/1	74	6
3629^{3}	**Bit of A Touch (86)** (RGFrost) **11-10-12** JFrost (outpcd 10th: kpt on fr 4 out: n.d) 11	**3**	$4/1^{2}$	76	9
1957^{5}	**Lake of Loughrea (IRE) (102)** (KCBailey) **7-12-0** CO'Dwyer (nvr gng wl: sn bhd & drvn along: t.o 7th) 12	**4**	$5/1^{3}$	83	16
3742^{P}	**Too Sharp (100)** (MissHCKnight) **9-11-12b[1]** JCulloty (lw: led 2nd: mstke & hdd 11th: wknd qckly 4 out) 6	**5**	$5/1^{3}$	76	9
3354^{3}	**Blazer Moriniere (FR) (78)** (PCRitchens) **8-10-4** SFox (chsd ldrs: led 11th: fell next)	**F**	$7/2^{1}$	—	—
	Peace Officer (95) (ABarrow) **11-11-7** MAFitzgerald (sn bhd: hit 8th: t.o whn p.u bef 10th)	**P**	8/1	—	—
3678^{5}	**Northern Optimist (87)** (BJLlewellyn) **9-10-13** MrJLLlewellyn (blnd & uns rdr 4th)	**U**	8/1	—	—
			(SP 117.0%)	**8 Rn**	

5m 15.4 (11.40) CSF £96.44 CT £556.76 TOTE £6.70: £1.60 £7.80 £1.20 (£71.00) OWNER Derwent Dene Farm (STRATFORD)
LONG HANDICAP Curragh Peter 9-12

Counterbalance, having her first outing for 289 days, was left with the prize at her mercy five out. (11/2)
2778 Curragh Peter, who had failed to complete the course on his two previous outings, stuck on to finish second best in an uncompetitive event. (25/1)
3629 Bit of A Touch failed to go the gallop on the final circuit. (4/1)
1957 Lake of Loughrea (IRE), having his first outing for 99 days, ran no race at all. Taking no interest and soon driven along, he lost touch after only six fences. (5/1)
3742 Too Sharp, who had run badly last time, stopped in two strides after a mistake at the eleventh and from there on her jumping went to pieces. (5/1)
3354 Blazer Moriniere (FR) had just taken charge when he fell five out. He would have proved a real threat to the winner. (7/2)
Peace Officer (8/1: op 14/1)

3844 MANCHESTER 'N.H.' NOVICES' HURDLE (4-Y.O+) (Class E)
4-05 (4-05) **2m 4f 110y (11 hdls)** £2,295.00 (£645.00: £315.00) GOING: 0.66 sec per fur (S)

			SP	RR	SF
3423^{3}	**Peace Lord (IRE) (105)** (MrsDHaine) **7-11-8** JFTitley (trckd ldrs gng wl: led 2 out: easily) ......—	**1**	$4/9^{1}$	71+	17
3186^{P}	**Sioux To Speak (85)** (MissHCKnight) **5-11-2** JCulloty (lw: hld up: hdwy 7th: rdn & hit 2 out: kpt on: no ch w wnr) 7	**2**	$11/2^{2}$	60	6
3446^{U}	**Prinzal** (GMMcCourt) **10-10-9**(7) RHobson (trckd ldrs: led 3 out: hdd next: wknd flat) 2	**3**	$9/1^{3}$	58	4
3325^{10}	**Carly-J (63)** (FSJackson) **6-10-11** MrNKent (chsd ldrs: mstke 4th: outpcd 7th: hdwy u.p 3 out: nvr nr to chal)2½	**4**	40/1	51	—
3706^{5}	**Dry Hill Lad (80)** (JNorton) **6-11-2b** DerekByrne (led 4th to 3 out: sn wknd) 1¾	**5**	25/1	55	1
3621^{3}	**Tursal (IRE) (70)** (TWDonnelly) **8-11-2** MrRArmson (rn in snatches: wnt prom 6th: outpcd 3 out: sn lost pl) 6	**6**	$9/1^{3}$	50	—
3536^{3}	**Steer Point (72)** (RGFrost) **6-11-2** JFrost (led to 4th: chsd ldrs tl lost pl 3 out) 18	**7**	20/1	36	—
	More to Life (MPBielby) **8-10-4**(7) MrOMcPhail (chsd ldrs: outpcd 7th: lost pl 3 out: bhd whn uns rdr next)........	**U**	66/1	—	—
			(SP 117.2%)	**8 Rn**	

5m 14.0 (28.00) CSF £3.12 TOTE £1.40: £1.10 £1.40 £2.70 (£2.30) OWNER Sir Peter & Lady Gibbings (NEWMARKET) BRED Ronald Scanlon

3423 Peace Lord (IRE), much happier on this sounder surface, found this very easy. (4/9)
2878 Sioux To Speak, another who appreciated the better ground, stuck on under pressure after hitting two out but the winner was far too good. (11/2: op 7/2)
3135 Prinzal, who had unseated his rider on his last two outings over fences, took a keen grip. Going on three out, it was soon clear the winner was in a different league. (9/1: op 14/1)
1713 Carly-J, who is only plating class, ran better after four poor efforts. (40/1)
3621 Tursal (IRE) (9/1: 8/1-12/1)

3845 GLASGOW MAIDEN HURDLE (5-Y.O+) (Class F)
4-40 (4-40) **3m 110y (13 hdls)** £2,025.50 (£568.00: £276.50) GOING: 0.66 sec per fur (S)

			SP	RR	SF
3178^{3}	**Persian Elite (IRE)** (CREgerton) **6-11-5** JOsborne (mstkes: mde virtually all: rdn clr between last 2) ......—	**1**	$9/4^{2}$	78	24
2927^{2}	**Ryder Cup (IRE)** (NJHenderson) **5-11-5** MAFitzgerald (sn chsng wnr: rdn to chal 3 out: wknd between last 2) 12	**2**	$9/4^{2}$	70	16
1541^{5}	**Jet Boys (IRE) (93)** (MrsJPitman) **7-11-5b[1]** DLeahy (nvr gng wl: hit 4th: reminders 6th: no rspnse: bhd				

		Dist	Pos	SP	RR	SF
	fr 8th)	14	3	13/8[1]	61	7
3621[5]	**Leap in the Dark (IRE) (80)** (MissLCSiddall) **8-11-5** RSupple (effrt 8th: sn outpcd: wkng whn mstke 3 out)	8	4	9/1[3]	56	2
				(SP 109.6%)	**4 Rn**	

6m 16.5 (30.50) CSF £7.01 TOTE £2.70 (£2.60) OWNER Elite Racing Club (CHADDLEWORTH) BRED Mrs M. E. Farrell
OFFICIAL EXPLANATION **Jet Boys (IRE): finished distressed.**
3178 Persian Elite (IRE), whose jumping was far from error-free, in the end took this weak event in decisive fashion. (9/4)
2927 Ryder Cup (IRE), a point to point winner, moved upsides three out but he never looked happy in his work and he was soon clearly second best. (9/4)
1541 Jet Boys (IRE) was tried in blinkers but they had no effect. He never took hold of his bit and was under pressure and finding nothing with over a circuit left to go. (13/8)
3621 Leap in the Dark (IRE) is still a maiden after twenty attempts. (9/1)

3846 DUBLIN STANDARD OPEN N.H. FLAT RACE (4, 5 & 6-Y.O) (Class H)

5-10 (5-11) **2m (AWT)** £1,131.00 (£316.00: £153.00)

		Dist	Pos	SP	RR	SF
3747*	**Mayday Lauren** (ABailey) **5-11-6** SWynne (mde virtually all: styd on wl appr fnl f)	—	1	9/4[2]	65 f	—
	Miry Leader (MrsJCecil) **4-10-5** TKent (tall: plld hrd: trckd ldrs: chal 2f out: nt qckn appr fnl f)	3	2	13/8[1]	55 f	—
	Ballymacool (CREgerton) **5-11-4** JOsborne (rangy: unf: hld up: stdy hdwy 6f out: 3rd & ev ch whn eased over 2f out: fin lame)	21	3	13/2	39 f	—
3203[5]	**Brother Harry** (JWharton) **5-10-13**(5) MrRThornton (trckd ldrs: drvn along over 4f out: sn lost pl)	4	4	9/1	35 f	—
	Charlie Keay (IRE) (GMMcCourt) **5-11-1**(3) DFortt (gd sort: bit bkwd: bhd & drvn along 9f out: sme hdwy 4f out: n.d)	5	5	9/2[3]	30 f	—
3676[8]	**Ceeyou At Midnight** (WGMTurner) **6-10-11**(7) JPower (chsd ldr: pushed along 6f out: sn lost pl)	28	6	20/1	2 f	—
	One Boy (AHHarvey) **5-10-11**(7) MrRJBarrett (wl grwn: chsd ldrs: drvn along 6f out: sn outpcd & wknd)	3½	7	20/1	—	—
3440[6]	**Community Service (IRE)** (JNorton) **6-10-10**(3) ECallaghan (bhd & rdn 9f out: t.o)	26	8	10/1	—	—
				(SP 129.0%)	**8 Rn**	

3m 58.6 (32.60) CSF £6.70 TOTE £3.70: £1.10 £1.40 £3.30 (£3.80) OWNER B K Racing (TARPORLEY) BRED K. Benson and R. Kinsey
WEIGHT FOR AGE 4yo-8lb
OFFICIAL EXPLANATION **Ballymacool: finished lame**
3747* Mayday Lauren is certainly game and she fought off the runner-up coming to the final furlong. (9/4)
Miry Leader, a tall Flat-type, refused to settle, and the tank was empty with just over a furlong left to run. (13/8: 11/10-2/1)
Ballymacool, a lazy walker, moved up travelling strongly but his rider suddenly eased him with over two furlongs left to go and he pulled up very lame. (13/2: 4/1-7/1)
Brother Harry, a fair sort, suddenly came under pressure on the home turn and soon dropped away. (9/1)
Charlie Keay (IRE) looked as if the outing would be more than needed. (9/2: op 2/1)

T/Plpt: £27.80 (301.88 Tckts). T/Qdpt: £10.30 (42.81 Tckts) WG

2932-ASCOT (R-H) (Good, Good to firm patches)
Wednesday March 26th

WEATHER: unsettled

3847 CITY INDEX SPREAD BETTING NOVICES' HURDLE (4-Y.O+) (Class C)

2-00 (2-00) **2m 4f (11 hdls)** £3,745.00 (£1,135.00: £555.00: £265.00) GOING minus 0.09 sec per fur (G)

		Dist	Pos	SP	RR	SF
3272[6]	**Symphony's Son (IRE)** (DNicholson) **6-11-2** RJohnson (hdwy 4th: led on bit appr 2 out: easily)	—	1	12/1	83+	2
3084[3]	**Ivory Coaster (NZ) (95)** (BdeHaan) **6-11-2** CLlewellyn (hdwy 8th: rdn appr last: r.o: nt rch wnr)	11	2	16/1	74	—
3287*	**Disallowed (IRE) (106)** (MissHCKnight) **4-10-12** MAFitzgerald (w ldr: led 5th to 7th: led 3 out: sn hdd & hrd rdn: 2nd & btn whn hit last)	7	3	100/30[2]	74	—
3613[16]	**Latahaab (USA)** (JTGifford) **6-11-2** PHide (a.p: one pce fr 3 out)	7	4	8/1[3]	63	—
3337[7]	**Walter's Destiny** (CWMitchell) **5-11-2** SMcNeill (lost pl 4th: hrd rdn next: nvr on terms)	13	5	50/1	53	—
3497[2]	**Flying Fiddler (IRE) (101)** (MJRoberts) **6-10-13b**(3) PHenley (chsd ldrs: hrd rdn & wknd 3 out)	3	6	100/30[2]	50	—
3595[F]	**The Flying Phantom** (MHTompkins) **6-11-7** RichardGuest (led to 5th: led 7th to 3 out: wknd qckly 2 out)	5	7	5/2[1]	51	—
3703[F]	**Lord Love (IRE)** (PRChamings) **5-11-2** JCulloty (prom tl wknd 8th)	10	8	100/1	38	—
3298[7]	**Glide Path (USA)** (JRJenkins) **8-11-2** JOsborne (hld up in rr: hdwy 8th: sn wknd: p.u bef last)		P	14/1	—	—
3103[9]	**Zipalong** (MrsPTownsley) **6-11-2** DerekByrne (wl bhd fr 5th: t.o whn p.u bef 8th)		P	66/1	—	—
				(SP 110.5%)	**10 Rn**	

4m 57.2 (15.20) CSF £149.99 TOTE £15.60: £3.20 £3.40 £1.20 (£112.70) Trio £172.50 OWNER Mrs J. Mould (TEMPLE GUITING) BRED E. D. Delany
WEIGHT FOR AGE 4yo-9lb
2663 Symphony's Son (IRE) settled well on this occasion and, apparently well suited by the fast ground, was always in control. He cruised to the front going to the second last hurdle and won with any amount in hand. (12/1: 8/1-14/1)
3084 Ivory Coaster (NZ) was struggling at the back of the field to halfway but stayed on strongly from four hurdles out without troubling the winner. (16/1)
3287* Disallowed (IRE) won the battle for the lead at the third last hurdle but was quickly challenged and easily outpaced by the winner. (100/30)
3272 Latahaab (USA), always chasing the leading trio, could make no headway from the third last flight. (8/1: 6/1-9/1)
Walter's Destiny, struggling throughout, was never on terms. (50/1)
3497 Flying Fiddler (IRE), though in touch, was never travelling particularly well and all chance had gone four hurdles out. (100/30)
3233* The Flying Phantom disputed the lead from the start and was one of three clear at the third last hurdle. He weakened rapidly on the long run to the next. (5/2: op 6/4)
3103 Glide Path (USA) (14/1: 10/1-16/1)

3848 FAIRVIEW NEW HOMES NOVICES' CHASE (5-Y.O+) (Class B)

2-30 (2-32) **3m 110y (20 fncs)** £10,892.00 (£3,296.00: £1,608.00: £764.00) GOING minus 0.09 sec per fur (G)

		Dist	Pos	SP	RR	SF
3551[2]	**Jultara (IRE) (98)** (IPWilliams) **8-11-9** BPowell (chsd ldr: led 7th: lft clr 10th: hld on wl)	—	1	11/4[1]	105	41

3334[3] **Who Is Equiname (IRE) (100)** (NJHenderson) **7-11-9b[1]** MAFitzgerald (hld up: chsd wnr fr 10th: mstke 12th: ev ch flat: r.o) ....¾ **2** 4/1[2] 105 41
3700[P] **Ballydougan (IRE) (74)** (RMathew) **9-11-9v** DWalsh (mstke 3rd: lost tch 10th) ....dist **3** 50/1 — —
3489[2] **Major Nova (79)** (NASmith) **8-11-9** JCulloty (mstkes 13th & 14th: a bhd) ....10 **4** 13/2 — —
3667[F] **Glendine (IRE) (72)** (CJMann) **7-11-9** JRailton (prom to 6th: wl bhd fr 10th) ....25 **5** 20/1 — —
3427[3] **Exterior Profiles (IRE) (114)** (NATwiston-Davies) **7-11-9** TJMurphy (led to 7th: 2nd whn fell 10th) .... **F** 11/4[1] — —
3400[3] **Penncaler (IRE) (87)** (PJHobbs) **7-11-9b** RDunwoody (nvr gng wl: t.o whn p.u bef 11th) .... **P** 11/2[3] — —
3602[2] **Brown Robber (68)** (MrsRGHenderson) **9-11-9** BFenton (mstke 2nd: bhd whn blnd & uns rdr 7th) .... **U** 40/1 — —
(SP 111.2%) **8 Rn**

6m 12.8 (7.80) CSF £12.29 TOTE £3.60: £1.20 £1.40 £8.10 (£6.00) OWNER Mr Alan Elliot (ALVECHURCH)
OFFICIAL EXPLANATION **Penncaler (IRE): was in a distressed state.**
3551 Jultara (IRE), left clear at the tenth fence, was strongly pressed from the third last but kept finding what was required. (11/4)
3334 Who Is Equiname (IRE), blinkered for the first time, jumped adequately for most of the way. Patiently ridden, he joined the winner two hurdles out but after having every chance, could find no extra near the finish. (4/1)
3489 Ballydougan (IRE) struggled on to be a remote third of the five finishers without ever holding out any hope. (50/1)
3427 Exterior Profiles (IRE) went off in front but his jumping did not inspire confidence. It was no surprise when he fell at the tenth fence when in second place. (11/4: 7/4-3/1)

3849 DAILY TELEGRAPH NOVICES' H'CAP CHASE (5-Y.O+) (Class C)

3-05 (3-05) **2m 3f 110y (16 fncs)** £14,070.00 (£4,260.00: £2,080.00: £990.00) GOING minus 0.09 sec per fur (G)

SP RR SF

3427* **Garnwin (IRE) (112)** (NJHenderson) **7-10-10** MAFitzgerald (hld up: jnd ldr 4 out: led 2 out: drvn out) ....— **1** 11/8[1] 122+ 29
3495[2] **Frazer Island (IRE) (110)** (RRowe) **8-10-8** DO'Sullivan (led 7th: mstke & hdd 2 out: ev ch whn hit last: r.o) ....½ **2** 9/1 120 27
3300[3] **Greenback (BEL) (126)** (PJHobbs) **6-11-10** RDunwoody (hld up in rr: hdwy 11th: 3rd & rdn whn mstke 3 out: no ch after) ....26 **3** 7/2[2] 114 21
3334* **Master Toby (114)** (NATwiston-Davies) **7-10-12** CLlewellyn (mstke & lost pl 8th: hrd rdn 4 out: no rspnse) ..3½ **4** 4/1[3] 99 6
1452[2] **Wilde Music (IRE) (115)** (CPEBrooks) **7-10-13** DGallagher (led to 7th: wknd 11th) 1 **5** 8/1 100 7
(SP 105.4%) **5 Rn**

4m 53.3 (6.30) CSF £10.34 TOTE £2.10: £1.50 £1.80 (£5.50) OWNER Pioneer Heat-Treatment (LAMBOURN) BRED John Kehoe
3427* Garnwin (IRE) appeared to be travelling much better than the second from a long way out but had to be put to his best in the closing stages to make sure of it. (11/8)
3495 Frazer Island (IRE) went to the front at the seventh fence and, when losing the lead after a mistake at the second last, looked beaten. Despite another error at the final fence, he battled all the way to the line. (9/1)
3300 Greenback (BEL) appeared held in third place when a mistake three fences out cost him any chance. (7/2: 9/4-75/20)
3334* Master Toby probably finds the trip too short nowadays on this fast ground. He was always struggling to get back into the race after a mistake at the eighth fence. (4/1: 3/1-9/2)

3850 CITY INDEX SPREAD BETTING H'CAP HURDLE (0-135) (4-Y.O+) (Class C)

3-35 (3-36) **2m 110y (9 hdls)** £4,856.25 (£1,470.00: £717.50: £341.25) GOING minus 0.09 sec per fur (G)

SP RR SF

3180[P] **Rosencrantz (IRE) (108)** (MissVenetiaWilliams) **5-10-8** RJohnson (a gng wl: led on bit appr 2 out: easily)....— **1** 100/30[2] 95+ 3
3595[F] **Mister Rm (111)** (NATwiston-Davies) **5-10-11** DBridgwater (rdn 6th: hdwy on ins to ld after 3 out: sn hdd: no ch w wnr) ....7 **2** 6/4[1] 91 —
2777[5] **Fourth in Line (IRE) (124)** (MJWilkinson) **9-11-10** WMarston (lft in ld 3rd: hdd 4th: led 3 out: sn hdd: wknd appr last) 3 **3** 14/1 101 9
3640[8] **Ground Nut (IRE) (122)** (RHBuckler) **7-11-8** BPowell (led 4th to 3 out: sn wknd) ....3½ **4** 9/2[3] 96 4
2963[4] **Keep Me in Mind (IRE) (108)** (NRMitchell) **8-10-8** DSkyrme (hld up: ev ch 3 out: sn wknd) ....5 **5** 16/1 77 —
1470[3] **Chickawicka (IRE) (100)** (BPalling) **6-9-9(5)** MrRThornton (led: sn clr: ref & uns rdr 3rd) .... **R** 11/2 — —
(SP 109.2%) **6 Rn**

4m 0.6 (10.60) CSF £7.79 TOTE £3.50: £1.70 £1.60 (£3.00) OWNER Mr L. J. Fulford (HEREFORD) BRED Sheikh Mohammed bin Rashid al Maktoum
3180 Rosencrantz (IRE), well suited by the shorter trip and faster ground, was always travelling well. He cruised into the lead approaching the second last hurdle and won with a ton in hand. (100/30)
3595 Mister Rm appeared to be struggling when last of the five remaining runners four hurdles out but, energetically ridden, found a way through on the inside to lead momentarily on the home turn. However, he had no chance once the winner was sent on. (6/4: 4/5-13/8)
2777 Fourth in Line (IRE) went with the leaders but, after having every chance on the home turn, was quickly outpaced. (14/1)
3640 Ground Nut (IRE), whose rider tried to settle him at the back, jumped to the front at the fourth hurdle and was quickly outpaced after being headed at the third last. (9/2)
Keep Me in Mind (IRE), having only his second race of the season, was right on terms three hurdles out but weakened on the long run to the next. (16/1)
1470 Chickawicka (IRE) soon set up a clear lead but dug his toes in and refused at the third, ejecting his rider. He has proved somewhat eccentric in the past. (11/2)

3851 ALPINE MEADOW H'CAP HURDLE (0-135) (4-Y.O+) (Class C)

4-10 (4-10) **3m (13 hdls)** £4,924.50 (£1,491.00: £728.00: £346.50) GOING minus 0.09 sec per fur (G)

SP RR SF

3531* **Tribune (111)** (CWThornton) **6-10-10** MFoster (led 7th: drvn out) ....— **1** 100/30[2] 94 4
3600[19] **Runaway Pete (USA) (121)** (MCPipe) **7-11-6** RDunwoody (led to 5th: hrd rdn 9th: ev ch 2 out: r.o) 1¼ **2** 13/2 103 13
3615[5] **Tamarpour (USA) (125)** (MCPipe) **10-11-10b** CMaude (hld up in rr: hdwy 9th: hrd rdn 2 out: r.o one pce)....2½ **3** 4/1[3] 106 16
3600[4] **Haile Derring (124)** (NATwiston-Davies) **7-11-9** CLlewellyn (chsd ldrs: hrd rdn & j.slowly 4 out: one pce fr next) ....7 **4** 11/4[1] 100 10
3541[3] **Spaceage Gold (108)** (JABOld) **8-10-7** GUpton (dropped rr & rdn 7th: sme hdwy 2 out: nvr on terms) ....5 **5** 10/1 81 —
3720* **Smuggler's Point (USA) (105)** (JJBridger) **7-10-1**(3) 4x SophieMitchell (led 5th to 7th: ev ch 4 out: hrd rdn & wknd 3 out) ....8 **6** 14/1 72 —
3600[11] **Mister Blake (101)** (RLee) **7-9-7**(7) XAizpuru (wl bhd fr 8th: t.o) ....24 **7** 9/1 52 —
(SP 108.8%) **7 Rn**

5m 54.8 (15.80) CSF £20.29 TOTE £3.80: £2.10 £2.30 (£9.10) OWNER Hexagon Racing (MIDDLEHAM) BRED R. G. Bonson
LONG HANDICAP Mister Blake 9-2

3531* Tribune, whose rider was determined to make this a real test of stamina, was sent on from halfway. Galloping on gamely, he won decisively. (100/30)
2888 Runaway Pete (USA) made the early running. Hard ridden over a mile from home, he kept staying on and still had every chance at the last hurdle. Near the finish he could do no more. (13/2)
3615 Tamarpour (USA), held up in last place, moved on to the heels of the leaders on the home turn but was soon under maximum pressure and kept on at one pace. (4/1: 11/4-9/2)
3600 Haile Derring likes to make the running but was unable to do so owing to the very strong pace. Driven up to join the leaders approaching the fourth last hurdle, he lost ground with a slow jump and was flat out from that point. (11/4)
3541 Spaceage Gold dropped back to last at halfway and had no chance after. (10/1)

3852 MAHONIA HUNTERS' CHASE (5-Y.O+) (Class H)

4-45 (4-45) **2m 3f 110y (16 fncs)** £2,762.00 (£836.00: £408.00: £194.00) GOING minus 0.09 sec per fur (G)

	Horse	Details	Dist	Pos	SP	RR	SF
3273[3]	**Poors Wood**	(SBreen) **10-11-9**(5) MrTMcCarthy (hdwy 10th: led 4 out: r.o wl)	—	1	5/1[3]	97	22
3446[U]	**Quiet Confidence (IRE)**	(KeithKerley) **7-11-2**(7) MissDStafford (racd wd: led 2nd to 4 out: r.o)	2½	2	15/8[1]	90	15
3446[3]	**Gambling Royal**	(DrPPritchard) **14-11-7**(7) DrPPritchard (a.p: 2nd whn mstke 11th: one pce fr 3 out)	5	3	33/1	91	16
3343[F]	**Flowing River (USA)**	(NRMitchell) **11-11-7**(7) MrNRMitchell (bhd whn mstke 8th: sn hrd rdn: t.o)	26	4	20/1	70	—
	Tom Furze	(MrsDBuckett) **10-11-11**(7) MrMBatters (led to 2nd: wknd 11th: t.o)	19	5	12/1	58	—
3664[4]	**Tellaporky**	(THind) **8-11-7**(7) MrAMiddleton (a bhd: blnd 6th: t.o)	2	6	33/1	52	—
3460*	**A Windy Citizen (IRE)**	(MrsCHicks) **8-11-12**(5) MrASansome (3rd whn fell 9th: dead)		F	9/4[2]	—	—
3753*	**Star Oats**	(MrsRMLampard) **11-12-1**(7) MrAKinane (stdd s: j.b: t.o whn p.u bef 2 out)		P	14/1	—	—
3744[11]	**Familiar Friend**	(SJGilmore) **11-12-3b**(5) MrBPollock (prom tl wknd 11th: t.o whn p.u bef 2 out)		P	20/1	—	—

(SP 112.0%) **9 Rn**

4m 59.9 (12.90) CSF £12.99 TOTE £5.30: £1.70 £1.70 £5.70 (£7.40) Trio £105.70 OWNER Mr F. R. Jackson BRED M. B. Small
3273 Poors Wood owed his success to the strength and skill of his rider. He sneaked up on the inside to lead four fences out and, soon clear, was flat out to the finish. (5/1)
3446 Quiet Confidence (IRE), although leading for much of the way, took mostly a wide course. Headed at the fourth last fence, she still appeared to be going well but her rider was unable to get the best out of her. (15/8)
3446 Gambling Royal was in second place when a mistake six fences out cost him ground and he always appeared likely to be third best thereafter. (33/1)
3010 Flowing River (USA), soon towards the rear, made a bad mistake at the eighth fence and was never in the race with a chance. (20/1)
Tom Furze disputed the early running but weakened a mile from home. (12/1)
3460* A Windy Citizen (IRE) suffered a fatal fall at the ninth fence when in third place. (9/4)
3753* Star Oats jumped off many lengths last and made appalling blunders at three of the first four fences. He was well behind until pulling up before the second last and, on this performance, it is amazing that he managed to win his previous race. (14/1: 10/1-16/1)

3853 FAIRVIEW NEW HOMES STANDARD N.H. FLAT RACE (4, 5 & 6-Y.O) (Class H)

5-15 (5-16) **2m** £1,955.50 (£548.00: £266.50)

	Horse	Details	Dist	Pos	SP	RR	SF
	Gatflax (IRE)	(NATwiston-Davies) **5-11-1**(7) MKeighley (led 1f: led over 2f out: drvn out)	—	1	15/2[3]	75 f	—
	Dragon King	(CRBarwell) **5-11-5**(3) PHenley (hdwy 8f out: ev ch 2f out: no imp)	12	2	16/1	63 f	—
3090[4]	**Royal Pot Black (IRE)**	(PJHobbs) **6-11-1**(7) MMoran (a.p: rdn over 2f out: r.o one pce)	7	3	8/1	56 f	—
3574[9]	**Kapco (IRE)**	(CPEBrooks) **5-11-1**(7) GBrace (led after 1f tl over 2f out: wknd over 1f out)	4	4	8/1	52 f	—
	Cold Feet	(CWMitchell) **6-10-10**(7) JPower (bhd tl gd hdwy 3f out: one pce fnl 2f)	nk	5	50/1	47 f	—
3574[12]	**Moonraker's Mirage**	(DRCElsworth) **6-11-1**(7) MBatchelor (nvr bttr than mid div)	3	6	12/1	49 f	—
2811[10]	**Bulko Boy (NZ)**	(PJHobbs) **5-11-3**(5) DJKavanagh (nvr nr to chal)	1¼	7	14/1	47 f	—
	Mr Bojangles (IRE)	(IPWilliams) **6-11-3**(5) MrRThornton (prom tl wknd 3f out)	1¾	8	7/1[2]	46 f	—
1685[11]	**Nicanjon**	(RDickin) **6-11-1**(7) XAizpuru (wl bhd tl hdwy 3f out: nvr on terms)	4	9	33/1	42 f	—
3606[5]	**Blazing Batman**	(MrsRGHenderson) **4-11-0** MrWHenderson (prom tl rn wd 7f out: hrd rdn & hung lft: styd on fnl 2f)	½	10	50/1	41 f	—
	Born At Kings	(JWhite) **4-10-11**(3) MichaelBrennan (dropped rr after 6f: nvr nr ldrs)	8	11	25/1	33 f	—
	Seymour Who	(KRSupple) **4-10-9**(5) GSupple (a wl bhd)	6	12	25/1	27 f	—
3330*	**Spirit of Steel**	(TPTate) **4-11-0**(7) RMcCarthy (plld hrd: chsd ldrs: ev ch 5f out: wknd qckly 4f out: t.o)	24	13	7/4[1]	10 f	—
3235[4]	**Racketball**	(NATwiston-Davies) **4-10-7**(7) LSuthern (prom tl wknd qckly 4f out: t.o)	22	14	7/1[2]	—	—

(SP 130.1%) **14 Rn**

3m 55.5 CSF £114.04 TOTE £8.90: £2.70 £4.00 £2.50 (£72.30) Trio £582.20; £492.02 to Musselburgh 27/3/97 OWNER Mr Giles Clarke (CHELTENHAM) BRED J. Gahan
WEIGHT FOR AGE 4yo-8lb
OFFICIAL EXPLANATION **Spirit of Steel: got wound up before and pulled hard during the race.**
Gatflax (IRE) was steadied after jumping off in front but was never far behind the leaders. Going strongly, he went to the front over two furlongs out and readily came clear. He was driven right out. (15/2)
Dragon King moved up at halfway but, after having every chance, could make no impression on the winner in the final quarter-mile. (16/1)
3090 Royal Pot Black (IRE) chased the leaders throughout and ran on at one pace when pressure was applied from approaching the straight. (8/1: op 9/2)
Kapco (IRE), in front after a furlong, was quickly beaten when headed early in the straight. (8/1: 5/1-9/1)
Cold Feet made strong headway approaching the straight but, having reached a good position two furlongs out, could make no further progress. (50/1)
3235 Moonraker's Mirage ran a respectable race though never in with a chance. From a good yard, he can improve on this. (12/1: 6/1-14/1)
Bulko Boy (NZ) (14/1: 8/1-16/1)
3330* Spirit of Steel sweated up badly and raced far too freely. Although moving into second place after halfway, she weakened rapidly four furlongs out and was soon tailed off. This is not her form at all. (7/4)
3235 Racketball (7/1: op 9/2)

T/Plpt: £60.50 (447.81 Tckts). T/Qdpt: £13.50 (104.57 Tckts) Hn

3854a - 3881a : (Irish Racing) - See Computer Raceform

3481-**CARLISLE (R-H) (Good to soft)**
Saturday March 29th
WEATHER: fine

3882 BORDER GARDEN CENTRE NOVICES' CHASE (5-Y.O+) (Class E)
2-05 (2-06) **3m (18 fncs)** £3,077.55 (£932.40: £455.70: £217.35) GOING: 0.40 sec per fur (GS)

				SP	RR	SF
3314[2]	**Colonel In Chief (IRE) (114)** (GRichards) **7-11-8** RDunwoody (cl up: led 13th: r.o wl fr 2 out)	—	**1**	5/2[2]	119	—
3537[D]	**Carole's Crusader (113)** (DRGandolfo) **6-11-3** GBradley (a.p: ev ch fr 2 out: r.o: nt pce of wnr)	2	**2**	2/1[1]	113	—
3489[4]	**Thermal Warrior (78)** (JABOld) **9-11-2** CLlewellyn (lw: a chsng ldrs: ev ch fr 14th: nt qckn appr last)	5	**3**	20/1	108	—
3347[3]	**Dorlin Castle (93)** (LLungo) **9-11-2** RSupple (lw: hld up & bhd: hdwy 11th: sn chsng ldrs: one pce fr 4 out)	12	**4**	4/1[3]	100	—
3556[P]	**Majority Major (IRE) (80)** (PCheesbrough) **8-11-8** ASSmith (in tch: effrt 4 out: sn btn)	6	**5**	50/1	102	—
	Harristown (IRE) (MrsMReveley) **9-11-2** PNiven (hld up & bhd: hdwy appr 4 out: sn chsng ldrs: wknd 2 out)	1	**6**	50/1	96	—
3531[7]	**Festival Fancy** (BMactaggart) **10-10-8**(3) GLee (in tch tl outpcd fr 13th)	14	**7**	100/1	81	—
3067[2]	**Naughty Future (93)** (JJO'Neill) **8-11-8** SMcNeill (lw: mstke 1st: hld up & bhd: hdwy 14th: mstke 4 out: sn wknd)	3	**8**	10/1	90	—
3370[U]	**King of Steel (86)** (MDHammond) **11-11-2** RGarritty (in tch tl p.u bef 11th: lame)		**P**	50/1	—	—
3556[F]	**Royal Banker (IRE)** (MartinTodhunter) **7-11-2** LWyer (a bhd: t.o whn p.u bef 4 out)		**P**	66/1	—	—
3683[13]	**Kentucky Gold (IRE) (60)** (MrsLWilliamson) **8-11-2** LO'Hara (in tch: mstke 9th: wknd 13th: p.u bef 3 out)		**P**	300/1	—	—
	Supermarine (BMactaggart) **11-11-2** BStorey (swtg: prom to 10th: sn wknd: p.u bef 13th)		**P**	500/1	—	—
3715[2]	**Fern Leader (IRE)** (MrsASwinbank) **7-11-2** JSupple (lw: led: hit 6th & 11th: blnd & hdd 13th: hit 14th & wknd: blnd & uns rdr 3 out)		**U**	6/1	—	—

(SP 118.9%) **13 Rn**

6m 28.2 (36.20) CSF £7.33 TOTE £3.20: £1.70 £1.60 £2.50 (£2.70) Trio £13.80 OWNER Mr Robert Ogden (PENRITH) BRED John Noonan
3314 Colonel In Chief (IRE) is certainly at his best when he can get his toe in and, although he had to fight to win this, he did it well. (5/2)
3537 Carole's Crusader does not do anything quickly, but does keep galloping and certainly stays. (2/1)
3489 Thermal Warrior put in a better effort this time, and it would seem he is at his best when conditions are at their most testing. (20/1)
3347 Dorlin Castle, who loves cut in the ground, travelled well on the bridle but yet again was disappointing off it. (4/1)
3556 Majority Major (IRE) ran a shade better this time and may be coming back to form. (50/1)
Harristown (IRE) has not been out for over three years but he certainly showed ability here, and should not be written off. (50/1)
3715 Fern Leader (IRE) was let down by some very erratic jumping, and was on the retreat when he finally got rid of his rider three out. (6/1)

3883 BBC RADIO CUMBRIA NOVICES' HURDLE (I) (4-Y.O+) (Class E)
2-35 (2-36) **2m 1f (9 hdls)** £2,136.00 (£596.00: £288.00) GOING: 0.40 sec per fur (GS)

				SP	RR	SF
3396[2]	**Star Selection (116)** (JMackie) **6-11-9**(3) EHusband (lw: j.w: led fr 2nd: clr fr 3 out: easily)	—	**1**	8/11[1]	94+	18
1362[3]	**Ardronan (IRE)** (JJO'Neill) **7-11-0** SMcNeill (lw: lost pl ½-wy: stdy hdwy 3 out: nvr plcd to chal)	12	**2**	14/1	71+	—
3789[4]	**Bourbon Dynasty (FR)** (GRichards) **4-10-8** ADobbin (a in tch: rdn 4 out: styd on: no imp)	½	**3**	16/1	72	—
3345[2]	**Fassan (IRE) (103)** (MDHammond) **5-11-0** RGarritty (chsd wnr most of wy: rdn appr 3 out: grad wknd)	7	**4**	4/1[2]	64	—
3315[F]	**Thornwood (IRE)** (JKMOliver) **5-10-7**(7) SMelrose (chsd ldrs tl rdn & btn appr 3 out)	4	**5**	100/1	60	—
3305*	**Swift Riposte (IRE) (100)** (PMonteith) **6-11-6** RDunwoody (in tch: outpcd 4 out)	4	**6**	7/1[3]	62	—
3475[9]	**Allerby (65)** (JLGoulding) **9-10-9**(5) BGrattan (bit bkwd: bhd tl sme late hdwy)	12	**7**	66/1	45	—
3612*	**Rothari (86)** (BSRothwell) **5-11-6** RSupple (lw: a chsng ldrs: outpcd & disp 2nd whn blnd 3 out: wknd)	4	**8**	10/1	47	—
3714[F]	**Nine Pipes (IRE)** (JJBirkett) **6-11-0** LO'Hara (a bhd)	13	**9**	100/1	29	—
3529[F]	**One Stop** (MABarnes) **4-9-12**(5) STaylor (mstkes: lost tch fr ½-wy)	1¼	**10**	66/1	25	—
	Heads Or Tails (IRE) (BMactaggart) **6-10-9** BStorey (a bhd)	½	**11**	100/1	22	—
3483[10]	**Peak A Boo** (DWWhillans) **6-10-9** DBentley (in tch to 5th: sn wl bhd)	8	**12**	66/1	15	—
3611[P]	**Shultan (IRE)** (JWade) **8-10-9** KJones (lw: led to 2nd: wknd 4th: wl t.o)	dist	**13**	66/1	—	—
3483[8]	**The Khoinoa (IRE)** (MrsASwinbank) **7-11-0** JSupple (lw: effrt ½-wy: no imp: p.u appr 3 out)		**P**	25/1	—	—
3691[16]	**Sniper** (FPMurtagh) **5-11-0** ARoche (bhd fr 4th: p.u bef 3 out)		**P**	100/1	—	—

(SP 125.8%) **15 Rn**

4m 20.8 (19.80) CSF £13.04 TOTE £2.30: £1.10 £2.60 £2.80 (£11.30) Trio £22.00 OWNER Mr R. M. Mitchell (CHURCH BROUGHTON) BRED Stanley Estate and Stud Co
WEIGHT FOR AGE 4yo-8lb
OFFICIAL EXPLANATION **Ardronan (IRE): rider reported that his instructions were to lie handy and allow his mount daylight at his hurdles. He was told not to use his whip but to obtain the best possible placing. He felt the gelding starting to choke turning down the back and felt it prudent to hold him together for as long as possible. The gelding had run through beaten horses in the latter stages.**
3396 Star Selection jumps like a buck and is getting better every time he runs. He won this with a great deal of ease. (8/11)
1362 Ardronan (IRE) put in an eye-catching performance and was given a very easy time. He will appreciate longer trips and better now looks likely. (14/1)
3789 Bourbon Dynasty (FR) is still learning, but he certainly takes time to find his stride and should stay further. (16/1)
3345 Fassan (IRE) had his chances but, once he really had to struggle in the home straight, it soon proved well beyond him. (4/1)
Thornwood (IRE) showed ability, but his limitations were exposed over the last four flights. (100/1)
3305* Swift Riposte (IRE), after five weeks off, ran as though this was needed. (7/1)
Allerby showed a little ability here, making late headway, and gave the impression that he will be all the better for this. (66/1)
3612* Rothari had no chance at these weights and a blunder three out stopped him altogether. (10/1: 7/1-12/1)

3884 QUILTER H'CAP CHASE (0-125) (5-Y.O+) (Class D)
3-05 (3-05) **3m (18 fncs)** £3,485.00 (£1,055.00: £515.00: £245.00) GOING: 0.40 sec per fur (GS)

				SP	RR	SF
3697[8]	**Coverdale Lane (95)** (MrsSJSmith) **10-9-7**(7) RWilkinson (chsd ldr: led 9th: clr fr 12th: comf)	—	**1**	9/1	114+	—
3710[2]	**Northern Squire (105)** (JMJefferson) **9-10-7**(3) ECallaghan (lw: hld up: hdwy to chse wnr 11th: rdn & one pce fr 4 out)	11	**2**	6/4[1]	117	—
3792[U]	**Kilcolgan (106)** (MrsJDGoodfellow) **10-10-11b** NBentley (led tl mstke & hdd 9th: mstke 10th: outpcd 11th: styd on fr 4 out: no imp)	1¼	**3**	6/1[3]	117	—
3699[8]	**Act the Wag (IRE) (119)** (MartinTodhunter) **8-11-10** RDunwoody (in tch: effrt 14th: rdn 4 out: sn btn)	dist	**4**	9/2[2]	—	—
3492[2]	**Simpson (95)** (JABOld) **12-10-0** CLlewellyn (lw: chsd ldrs tl mstke & outpcd 12th: n.d after)	16	**5**	9/2[2]	—	—

			SP	RR	SF
3280[4]	**Really a Rascal (100)** (DRGandolfo) **10-10-5** GBradley (rdn ½-wy: a bhd: p.u bef 2 out)	P	15/2	—	—
			(SP 112.4%)		**6 Rn**

6m 25.4 (33.40) CSF £21.99 TOTE £10.60: £3.10 £1.50 (£14.30) OWNER Mr Jim Pilkington (BINGLEY) BRED Mrs M. J. Cole
LONG HANDICAP Simpson 9-9

3370* Coverdale Lane jumps, stays and loves soft ground and, after finding everything against her last time, had things in her favour here and won in splendid style. (9/1: op 6/1)

3710 Northern Squire, on his favourite track, tried hard, but his jumping was always a shade deliberate, and he found the winner far too good over the last four. (6/4)

3792 Kilcolgan made mistakes again and got outpaced at various stages, but he stays forever and was making ground again at the finish. (6/1)

3699 Act the Wag (IRE), as he showed last time, has lost his way for the time-being. (9/2: op 3/1)

3492 Simpson is a shadow of his former self, and this was a very poor effort. (9/2)

3280 Really a Rascal did not want to know at any stage. (15/2)

3885 CUMMERSDALE H'CAP HURDLE (0-125) (4-Y.O+) (Class D)

3-35 (3-38) **2m 4f 110y (11 hdls)** £2,885.00 (£810.00: £395.00) GOING: 0.40 sec per fur (GS)

			SP	RR	SF
3557[2]	**Swanbister (IRE) (106)** (LLungo) **7-10-9** RSupple (a chsng ldrs: led 2 out: styd on strly) —	1	7/1[2]	88	13
	True Scot (IRE) (97) (PCheesbrough) **7-10-0** ASSmith (bit bkwd: hld up & bhd: hdwy ½-wy: ch last: nt qckn)..5	2	20/1	75	—
3398[7]	**Palacegate King (113)** (ACWhillans) **8-10-9**(7) IJardine (trckd ldrs: ev ch 3 out: nt qckn appr last)....2½	3	16/1	89	14
1981[5]	**Chipped Out (107)** (MartinTodhunter) **7-10-3**(7) CMcCormack (trckd ldrs: chal & hit 3 out: blnd 2 out: one pce after)....1½	4	14/1	82	7
2918*	**Paperising (112)** (GRichards) **5-11-1** ADobbin (lw: trckd ldrs: led 4 out to 2 out: sn btn)....¾	5	11/8[1]	86	11
3309[3]	**Old Habits (IRE) (101)** (JLEyre) **8-10-4** BStorey (led to 4 out: one pce)....5	6	10/1	72	—
3545[8]	**Dawn Mission (98)** (TDEasterby) **5-10-1** LWyer (lw: mid div: effrt 7th: sn outpcd)....5	7	16/1	65	—
3563[P]	**Buckboard Bounce (125)** (GRichards) **11-12-0** RDunwoody (lw: nvr nr to chal)....13	8	16/1	81	6
3478[9]	**Tirmizi (USA) (97)** (MrsASwinbank) **6-10-0** JSupple (sn drvn along & a bhd)....1¼	9	14/1	53	—
3709[2]	**Desert Force (IRE) (97)** (GFierro) **8-10-0** KGaule (lw: outpcd & lost tch ½-wy: sn wl bhd)....16	10	20/1	40	—
3531[3]	**Bang in Trouble (IRE) (100)** (JJO'Neill) **6-10-3** SMcNeill (prom tl wknd fr 7th: p.u lame between last 2: dead) ..	P	12/1	—	—
3028[4]	**Cittadino (104)** (CWThornton) **7-10-7** MFoster (chsd ldrs tl outpcd 4 out: p.u bef last)	P	8/1[3]	—	—
			(SP 123.0%)		**12 Rn**

5m 11.6 (20.60) CSF £125.44 CT £1,964.53 TOTE £6.40: £2.10 £3.30 £5.30 (£100.70) Trio £110.30; £139.85 to Kempton 31/3/97 OWNER Col D. C. Greig (CARRUTHERSTOWN) BRED Ned Sullivan
LONG HANDICAP Desert Force (IRE) 9-9 Tirmizi (USA) 9-11

3557 Swanbister (IRE) is an honest stayer and that should bring him further successes, especially when he goes over fences. (7/1)

True Scot (IRE) looked in need of this and ran a super race, but he needs give in the ground to be at his best. (20/1)

3398 Palacegate King ran his best race for a long time, but this trip probably just found him out. Shorter distances and a more aggressive ride are what he seems to need. (16/1)

1653 Chipped Out goes well on the bridle, but once off it his jumping goes to pot. (14/1)

2918* Paperising was most disappointing here, stopping from the second last, and this excitable sort seems to beat himself. (11/8)

3309 Old Habits (IRE) is running consistently well and should find his mark in due course. (10/1)

Buckboard Bounce, having a pipe-opener for the Grand National, showed a little, when making some late headway, and should be all the sharper for it. (16/1)

3886 SUNDAY CAR BOOT H'CAP CHASE (0-105) (5-Y.O+) (Class F)

4-05 (4-18) **2m 4f 110y (16 fncs)** £3,046.00 (£856.00: £418.00) GOING: 0.40 sec per fur (GS)

			SP	RR	SF
3726[4]	**Le Denstan (77)** (MrsDThomson) **10-10-0** GCahill (lw: hld up: hdwy 12th: led flat: styd on wl) —	1	12/1	92	32
3790[6]	**Jymjam Johnny (IRE) (97)** (JJO'Neill) **8-11-6** SMcNeill (led fr 2nd: hit 10th & 11th: hdd flat: no ex u.p)....5	2	8/1[3]	108	48
3827*	**Pariah (IRE) (91)** (MartinTodhunter) **8-11-0** PNiven (hld up & bhd: blnd 9th: hdwy next: chsng ldrs whn hit 4 out: one pce fr next)....12	3	4/1[1]	93	33
3486[3]	**Acajou III (FR) (105)** (GRichards) **9-12-0** RDunwoody (lw: chsd ldrs: effrt & ev ch whn blnd 3 out: sn btn) ....s.h	4	9/1	107	47
3532[F]	**Peter (91)** (DWWhillans) **9-11-0** KJohnson (bhd tl styd on fr 4 out: nrst fin)....4	5	20/1	90	30
3532[2]	**Solba (USA) (101)** (CParker) **8-11-10b** DParker (in tch tl outpcd 10th: n.d after)....15	6	7/1[2]	88	28
3645[8]	**Supposin (86)** (MrsSJSmith) **9-10-9** RichardGuest (bhd: sme hdwy fr 3 out: n.d)....1	7	16/1	72	12
3329[4]	**Marlingford (77)** (MrsJJordan) **10-9-7**(7) LMcGrath (blnd 3rd: bhd: sme hdwy 4 out: n.d)....½	8	16/1	63	3
	Jaunty Gig (79) (JJBirkett) **11-10-2b** LO'Hara (a rr div)....5	9	66/1	61	1
3645*	**Cullane Lake (IRE) (79)** (MissMKMilligan) **7-10-2** RSupple (lw: mstkes 2nd & 3rd: hdwy & in tch 8th: outpcd fr 10th)....2	10	4/1[1]	59	—
3692[2]	**Blazing Dawn (87)** (JSHubbuck) **10-10-10** BStorey (led to 2nd: chsd ldrs tl wknd 10th)....dist	11	10/1	—	—
2045*	**Precipice Run (89)** (JJBirkett) **12-10-12** MMoloney (outpcd & rr div whn fell 9th)	F	33/1	—	—
3827[3]	**Chill Wind (88)** (NBycroft) **8-10-11** MFoster (a chsng ldrs: blnd & lost pl 11th: hdwy 4 out: cl 3rd & rdn whn fell last)	F	8/1[3]	—	—
3804[4]	**Dolikos (83)** (THCaldwell) **10-10-6** ADobbin (blnd 6th: p.u bef 9th)	P	14/1	—	—
	Overflowing River (IRE) (89) (JWade) **8-10-12** KJones (bkwd: t.o fr 8th: p.u bef 10th)	P	33/1	—	—
3711[6]	**Dalusman (IRE) (77)** (FPMurtagh) **9-10-0** ARoche (chsd ldrs: blnd 7th: sn wknd: t.o whn p.u bef 2 out)....	P	66/1	—	—
			(SP 133.6%)		**16 Rn**

5m 16.1 (13.10) CSF £101.58 CT £429.02 TOTE £28.50: £5.60 £2.70 £1.60 £2.10 (£233.30) Trio £134.20; £113.45 to Kempton 31/3/97 OWNER Mr L. Wright (MILNATHORT) BRED S. Powell
LONG HANDICAP Marlingford 9-11 Le Denstan 9-10 Dalusman (IRE) 9-9

3726 Le Denstan, back to form here against sticky opposition, won really well. (12/1)

3790 Jymjam Johnny (IRE) tried different tactics here and ran much better, but he still left the impression that if he really put his heart into it, there is more to offer. (8/1)

3827* Pariah (IRE) travelled well until an effort was required, and then it all proved too much for him. (4/1)

3486 Acajou III (FR) had his chances this time, but blundered them away three out and looks the type who will continually beat himself. (9/1)

3027 Peter got round for the first time this season and is well worth keeping in mind. (20/1)

3532 Solba (USA) was always finding the effort required here well beyond him. (7/1)

3827 Chill Wind ran well, but his stamina was really being tested when he came down at the last. (8/1)

3887 CARLISLE RACE CLUB MEMBERS NOVICES' H'CAP HURDLE (0-105) (4-Y.O+) (Class E)

4-35 (4-50) **2m 4f 110y (11 hdls)** £3,081.00 (£866.00: £423.00) GOING: 0.40 sec per fur (GS)

Form	Horse / details	Dist	Pos	SP	RR	SF
3557*	**Cherry Dee (84)** (PBeaumont) **6-10-6**(5) BGrattan (lw: led to 6th: w ldr: led flat: styd on wl)	—	**1**	6/1	68	18
3019[8]	**Welsh Silk (73)** (DRGandolfo) **5-10-0** CLlewellyn (bhd: hdwy 3 out: styd on wl appr last: nrst fin)	1¾	**2**	10/1	56	6
3789[2]	**Bold Classic (IRE) (88)** (CGrant) **4-10-6** PNiven (lw: cl up: led 6th tl flat: no ex)	hd	**3**	5/1[2]	71	12
3689*	**Workingforpeanuts (IRE) (75)** (CASmith) **7-10-2** MrsDSmith (lw: lost tch ½-wy: styd on u.p fr 3 out: nrst fin)	4	**4**	11/2[3]	54+	4
2920[5]	**Clairabell (IRE) (75)** (JIACharlton) **6-10-2** KJohnson (chsd ldrs: outpcd 4 out: styng on whn blnd 2 out: no imp)	nk	**5**	25/1	54	4
3691[5]	**Battery Fired (73)** (NBMason) **8-9-7**(7) SHaworth (hdwy 6th: sn chsng ldrs: wknd fr 3 out)	16	**6**	9/1	40	—
3646[4]	**Kings Lane (83)** (JMDun) **8-10-10** DParker (outpcd & drvn along 5th: n.d after)	3	**7**	16/1	47	—
1822*	**Barnstormer (73)** (EAElliott) **11-9-9b**(5) GFRyan (chsd ldrs tl wknd fr 4 out)	14	**8**	50/1	26	—
3706[4]	**Ranger Sloane (81)** (GFierro) **5-10-8** KGaule (hdwy ½-wy: ev ch 4 out: wknd after next)	4	**9**	20/1	31	—
3534*	**Phar Echo (IRE) (98)** (LLungo) **6-11-11** RSupple (chsd ldrs tl wknd fr 4 out)	nk	**10**	8/1	48	—
3394[3]	**Cry Baby (88)** (ACWhillans) **4-10-6** GBradley (in tch tl wknd 4 out)	20	**11**	25/1	23	—
3315[6]	**Nutty Solera (81)** (CParker) **7-10-8** BStorey (in tch to 7th)	6	**12**	25/1	11	—
3328*	**Pilkington (IRE) (93)** (HowardJohnson) **7-11-6** RDunwoody (chsd ldrs tl wknd rapidly 6th: sn t.o)	dist	**13**	3/1[1]	—	—
3696[5]	**Jubran (USA) (85)** (JPDodds) **11-10-12** RichardGuest (hdwy to jn ldrs 6th: wknd next: p.u bef 3 out)		**P**	50/1	—	—
3534[3]	**Solsgirth (79)** (JBarclay) **6-10-6** GCahill (outpcd & lost tch 6th: t.o whn p.u bef 3 out)		**P**	14/1	—	—
2898[11]	**Tremendisto (96)** (CaptJWilson) **7-11-9** ADobbin (cl up tl lost pl & p.u bef 6th)		**P**	33/1	—	—
3143[6]	**Thirty Below (IRE) (77)** (JABOld) **8-10-4** SMcNeill (wknd qckly 6th: p.u bef 4 out)		**P**	14/1	—	—
3557[P]	**Crashballoo (IRE) (73)** (PCheesbrough) **6-10-0** ASSmith (sn t.o: p.u bef 6th)		**P**	100/1	—	—
				(SP 144.9%)	**18 Rn**	

5m 10.8 (19.80) CSF £65.11 CT £317.26 TOTE £6.70: £2.00 £2.80 £1.90 £1.60 (£68.90) Trio Not won; £215.38 to 31/3/97 OWNER Mr George Dilger (BRANDSBY) BRED R. Burton

LONG HANDICAP Welsh Silk 9-12 Crashballoo (IRE) 9-9

WEIGHT FOR AGE 4yo-9lb

OFFICIAL EXPLANATION Pilkington (IRE): no explanation offered.

3557* Cherry Dee, despite dropping back in trip, found the stiff track helped and the further they went the stronger she got. (6/1)

1801 Welsh Silk has been in races where he had little chance so far this season and, off a really useful mark, ran better and his turn should come. (10/1)

3789 Bold Classic (IRE) is happy at this trip, and on this galloping track put up a much better performance. (5/1: 4/1-6/1)

3689* Workingforpeanuts (IRE) finished well after getting left behind, and would seem to need a stiffer test of stamina. (11/2)

2920 Clairabell (IRE) just seems to stay and a blunder here cost her any chance of a place. (25/1)

3691 Battery Fired, having his second run after a very long lay-off, ran well to the second-last. (9/1)

3888 BBC RADIO CUMBRIA NOVICES' HURDLE (II) (4-Y.O+) (Class E)

5-05 (5-22) **2m 1f (9 hdls)** £2,122.00 (£592.00: £286.00) GOING: 0.40 sec per fur (GS)

Form	Horse / details	Dist	Pos	SP	RR	SF
3042[6]	**New Leaf (IRE)** (DRGandolfo) **5-11-0** GBradley (lw: hld up: mstke 5th: hdwy 3 out: led flat: r.o wl)	—	**1**	5/2[1]	78+	—
3559[4]	**Brumon (IRE) (89)** (DMoffatt) **6-11-6v** DJMoffatt (a.p: led between last 2: hdd & one pce flat)	3½	**2**	5/1	72	—
3555[2]	**Crabbie's Pride (80)** (MGMeagher) **4-10-8** RichardGuest (in tch: effrt 3 out: styd on: nt pce to chal)	3	**3**	10/1	58	—
	Swandale Flyer (NBycroft) **5-10-9**(5) BGrattan (lw: hld up: hdwy 5th: ev ch 2 out: sn rdn & btn)	2½	**4**	100/1	72	—
3612[12]	**Mapleton (82)** (MrsSJSmith) **4-10-1**(7) RWilkinson (cl up: led after 4 out tl between last 2: wknd)	2	**5**	20/1	55	—
3474[4]	**Rasin Standards** (RCraggs) **7-11-0** BStorey (bhd: styd on fr 3 out: nrst fin)	s.h	**6**	50/1	61	—
3449[3]	**Riveaux (IRE)** (GRichards) **7-11-0** RDunwoody (chsd ldrs tl wknd fr 3 out)	24	**7**	7/2[2]	45	—
3159[14]	**Bonny Rigg (IRE) (62)** (LLungo) **5-10-9** TReed (led tl hdd & wknd after 4 out)	1¾	**8**	100/1	49	—
3487[3]	**Side By Side (IRE)** (CWThornton) **4-9-10**(7) NHorrocks (a rr div)	nk	**9**	25/1	32	—
3534[4]	**Kemo Sabo (89)** (CParker) **5-11-0b** DParker (chsd ldrs tl wknd 3 out)	18	**10**	9/2[3]	41	—
3789[6]	**Known Secret (USA)** (PMonteith) **4-10-8** ADobbin (prom tl wknd fr 4 out)	7	**11**	10/1	21	—
	Just Whistle (MissMKMilligan) **5-10-9** ASSmith (bit bkwd: a bhd: fell 3 out)		**F**	50/1	—	—
	Jungle Patrol (IRE) (ACWhillans) **5-11-0** MFoster (prom to 4th: sn wknd: p.u bef 2 out)		**P**	25/1	—	—
2953[9]	**Chain Line** (JWFAynsley) **7-11-0** PNiven (t.o fr ½-wy: p.u bef 3 out)		**P**	100/1	—	—
3478[4]	**First in the Field (74)** (NBMason) **6-10-8**(7) SHaworth (in tch: hit 5th: wknd 4 out: p.u bef last)		**P**	20/1	—	—
				(SP 127.9%)	**15 Rn**	

4m 27.1 (26.10) CSF £13.70 TOTE £4.30: £1.90 £2.20 £2.10 (£11.90) Trio £12.90 OWNER Mrs D. J. Hues (WANTAGE) BRED A. E. Smith and C. Dockar-Drysdale

WEIGHT FOR AGE 4yo-8lb

2696 New Leaf (IRE) had a good look at his hurdles, but he did it well and the real future for him will be over the bigger obstacles. (5/2)

3559 Brumon (IRE), dropped back in trip here, had his chances, but when tackled at the last, he put up little resistance. (5/1)

3555 Crabbie's Pride is running consistently well at the moment and deserves to pick up a race. (10/1)

Swandale Flyer put in a fair first effort here, and this may well be the game for him. (100/1)

2785 Mapleton is showing signs of improvement. (20/1)

3474 Rasin Standards appreciated this stiffer track and may well do better over further yet. (50/1)

3449 Riveaux (IRE) is going the wrong way. (7/2)

3789 Known Secret (USA) (10/1: 8/1-12/1)

T/Plpt: £96.90 (113.04 Tckts). T/Qdpt: £46.40 (7.73 Tckts) AA

3627-NEWTON ABBOT (L-H) (Good to firm, Good patches)

Saturday March 29th

WEATHER: Fine

3889 MILE END MAIDEN HURDLE (4-Y.O+ F & M) (Class E)

1-30 (1-30) **2m 1f (8 hdls)** £2,400.00 (£675.00: £330.00) GOING minus 0.44 sec per fur (GF)

Form	Horse / details	Dist	Pos	SP	RR	SF
1444[P]	**Secret Gift** (MrsJPitman) **4-10-8b**[1] DLeahy (lw: chsd ldr tl led appr 5th: sn clr: unchal)	—	**1**	5/1[3]	54	—

	Horse / Details	Dist	Pos	SP	RR	SF
	Powder Monkey (TNeedham) **7-11-0** GTormey (bit bkwd: hld up mid div: gd hdwy 6th: lft 2nd appr last)	9	2	14/1	44	—
3590[5]	**Song of Kenda** (BRMillman) **5-10-9**(5) DSalter (lw: hld up mid div: r.o fr 6th: nvr on terms)	10	3	11/1	34	—
3764[U]	**Lady Callernish** (MissHDay) **7-10-7**(7) MrSDurack (bit bkwd: styd on fr 2 out: nvr nrr)	3	4	100/1	31	—
1857[6]	**Scottish Park** (MCPipe) **8-11-0** JamieEvans (nt j.w: mstke 2nd & bhd: styd on fr 2 out: nvr nrr)	6	5	15/2	26	—
3590[8]	**Miss Night Owl** (RGFrost) **6-11-0** JFrost (bhd & mstke 6th: hdwy & mstke 2 out: wknd)	2½	6	20/1	23	—
1855[10]	**Neptunes Miss** (MJWilkinson) **5-11-0** WMarston (prom early: wknd appr 5th)	3	7	25/1	21	—
	Oyster Delight (IRE) (NoelChance) **6-10-7**(7) PRyan (bit bkwd: nvr trbld ldrs)	1¼	8	4/1[2]	19	—
3433[16]	**Folesclave (IRE)** (JSKing) **5-11-0** DWalsh (prom to 5th: steadily wknd)	10	9	20/1	10	—
3606[9]	**Minnie (IRE)** (JWMullins) **4-10-8** SCurran (in tch tl 5th: sn wknd)	25	10	16/1	—	—
1090[P]	**Lady Noso (89)** (MrsJPitman) **6-11-0** BPowell (led tl hdd appr 5th: 2nd & btn whn p.u bef last: lame)		P	5/2[1]	—	—
3764[P]	**Abbeydoran** (MrsJEHawkins) **6-10-9**(5) DJKavanagh (lw: prom to 5th: steadily wknd & p.u bef 2 out)		P	50/1	—	—
191[12]	**Final Score (IRE)** (PaddyFarrell) **7-10-11**(3) TDascombe (bit bkwd: mid div tl wknd 5th: p.u bef last)		P	33/1	—	—
3606[11]	**Royal Member** (MrsBarbaraWaring) **4-10-8** EByrne (bit bkwd: a bhd: veered rt & uns rdr last)		U	50/1	—	—

(SP 119.1%) **14 Rn**

4m 5.2 (12.20) CSF £59.20 TOTE £7.60: £2.10 £3.20 £2.40 (£61.70) Trio £96.80 OWNER Regal Racing (UPPER LAMBOURN) BRED GAINSBOROUGH STUD MANAGEMENT LTD

WEIGHT FOR AGE 4yo-8lb

Secret Gift got off the mark here on only her second attempt. She may have found the soft conditions against her last time out, but had no problems here against less-than-average opposition. (5/1)

Powder Monkey put in a decent effort here to finish a clear second and, like the winner, may have found this ground to her liking. (14/1)

3590 Song of Kenda had shown little on her only two previous outings, the last coming in a seller, but showed a glimpse of encouragement here. (11/1)

Lady Callernish ran better than her market price predicted. (100/1)

Scottish Park (15/2: 5/1-8/1)

3890 SOUTH WEST RACING CLUB CHALLENGE TROPHY H'CAP HURDLE (0-125) (4-Y.O+) (Class D)

2-00 (2-00) **2m 1f (8 hdls)** £2,849.30 (£794.80: £383.90) GOING minus 0.44 sec per fur (GF)

	Horse / Details	Dist	Pos	SP	RR	SF
3766*	**Northern Starlight (118)** (MCPipe) **6-11-10** CMaude (lw: chsd ldr tl led 3rd: mde rest: hld on wl u.p flat)	—	1	4/9[1]	95	23
3594[11]	**Blade of Fortune (94)** (VGGreenway) **9-9-7**(7) XAizpuru (led to 3rd: ev ch tl slt mstke last: no ex flat)	¾	2	10/1	70	—
3679*	**Va Utu (94)** (DMLloyd) **9-9-11**(3) SophieMitchell (hdwy & in tch 5th: rdn & wknd 2 out)	4	3	5/1[2]	67	—
822[F]	**Verde Luna (94)** (DWPArbuthnot) **5-9-9**(5) DJKavanagh (bhd: hdwy & in tch 5th tl rdn & wknd appr 2 out)	13	4	6/1[3]	54	—
3535[8]	**Langtonian (97)** (GFEdwards) **8-9-12**(5)ow3 DSalter (hdwy & in tch 5th: rdn & wknd next: t.o)	dist	5	50/1	—	—

(SP 111.2%) **5 Rn**

3m 56.3 (3.30) CSF £5.21 TOTE £1.30: £1.10 £2.30 (£3.10) OWNER Mr Arthur Souch (WELLINGTON) BRED R. J. Glenn and K. Leadbetter

LONG HANDICAP Blade of Fortune 9-3 Va Utu 9-5 Verde Luna 9-6 Langtonian 8-8

3766* Northern Starlight, has been a revelation over the obstacles, and has shown a liking for these conditions. He is still progressing. (4/9)

3338* Blade of Fortune, stepping up in grade, put in a promising effort and did well to finish so close. (10/1: 8/1-12/1)

3679* Va Utu, scoring when out of the handicap last time out, could not reproduce that form here. (5/1)

3891 HACCOMBE (S) H'CAP CHASE (0-95) (5-Y.O+) (Class G)

2-30 (2-30) **2m 5f 110y (16 fncs)** £2,390.00 (£670.00: £326.00) GOING minus 0.44 sec per fur (GF)

	Horse / Details	Dist	Pos	SP	RR	SF
	Jay Jay's Voyage (74) (MrsJScrivens) **14-10-4**(3) TDascombe (hdwy to chse ldr 9th: led next: clr 3 out: hld on wl flat)	—	1	25/1	84	19
3578[U]	**Golden Opal (79)** (RHBuckler) **12-10-12** BPowell (a.p: r.o to chse wnr & ev ch 2 out: one pce)	1½	2	9/1[3]	88	23
3763[3]	**Spring to it (92)** (MCPipe) **11-11-11** JamieEvans (led 2nd to 5th: wknd fr 12th)	7	3	5/2[2]	96	31
3132[5]	**Good for a Laugh (80)** (AGHobbs) **13-10-8**(5) OBurrows (hdwy & in tch 9th: rdn 12th: hrd rdn appr 2 out: one pce)	nk	4	2/1[1]	84	19
3155[P]	**Sound Carrier (USA) (85)** (CLPopham) **9-11-4** SWynne (bit bkwd: led to 2nd: led 5th to 9th: ev ch to 13th: wknd appr 2 out)	3½	5	12/1	86	21
2681[F]	**Valnau (FR) (81)** (MCPipe) **10-10-7b**(7) BMoore (bit bkwd: mstke 4th: j.slowly next: sn bhd: t.o 11th)	dist	6	10/1	—	—
3824[P]	**Fairy Park (84)** (HOliver) **12-11-3v** JacquiOliver (a bhd: t.o whn p.u after 9th)		P	10/1	—	—
2704[P]	**Miramare (67)** (RJHodges) **7-9-7**(7) XAizpuru (a bhd: t.o whn p.u bef 11th)		P	20/1	—	—
3565[P]	**Saucy's Wolf (68)** (MrsEMBrooks) **7-10-1**ow1 MSharratt (nt j.w: a bhd: t.o whn rn out & uns rdr on bnd after 9th)		R	66/1	—	—
1993[P]	**Allahrakha (67)** (MHill) **6-10-0** SFox (lw: mid div whn blnd & uns rdr 6th)		U	16/1	—	—

(SP 113.8%) **10 Rn**

5m 18.7 (1.70) CSF £201.77 CT £700.79 TOTE £26.20: £5.00 £2.20 £1.80 (£138.30) Trio £98.90; £72.49 to Kempton 31/3/97 OWNER Mrs J. Scrivens (BAMPTON) BRED Mrs M. Simms

LONG HANDICAP Miramare 9-7 Saucy's Wolf 9-7 Allahrakha 9-12

No bid

Jay Jay's Voyage, dropped in trip after a lengthy absence and a series of disappointing efforts, caused quite a shock. (25/1)

3179 Golden Opal has been highly-tried at this course, and this was a performance of some promise. (9/1)

3763 Spring to it, a decent hurdle campaigner in his youth, has yet to produce similar results over fences. (5/2)

3132 Good for a Laugh has only won on good ground or softer. (2/1: op 3/1)

Sound Carrier (USA) (12/1: op 8/1)

Valnau (FR) (10/1: op 6/1)

3892 ST AUSTELL CLAIMING HURDLE (4-Y.O+) (Class F)

3-00 (3-01) **3m 3f (12 hdls)** £2,071.00 (£581.00: £283.00) GOING minus 0.44 sec per fur (GF)

	Horse / Details	Dist	Pos	SP	RR	SF
3600[14]	**Palosanto (IRE) (116)** (MCPipe) **7-12-0b** JamieEvans (chsd ldr tl led 9th: clr next: hld on wl u.p flat)	—	1	5/2[1]	81	29
3737[2]	**St Ville (96)** (RHBuckler) **11-11-8** BPowell (lw: a.p: chsd wnr after 10th: ev ch last: outpcd flat)	2	2	5/2[1]	74	22
3624[3]	**Tiger Claw (USA) (76)** (AGHobbs) **11-10-12** RGreene (mid div: gd hdwy 10th: sn ev ch: wknd appr last)	3	3	10/1	62	10
3583[3]	**Star Performer (IRE) (97)** (AGHobbs) **6-10-13**(5) OBurrows (mid div: hdwy 9th: wknd appr 2 out)	16	4	8/1[3]	58	6
3339[P]	**Its Grand (70)** (PCRitchens) **8-11-6** SFox (prom tl after 8th: steadily wknd)	1¼	5	33/1	60	8
2008[4]	**Snowy Lane (IRE) (70)** (JNeville) **9-11-2hb** DWalsh (led to 9th: outpcd next: sn wknd)	4	6	14/1	53	1
3541[6]	**Mu-Tadil (65)** (RJBaker) **5-11-4b** VSlattery (a bhd: t.o fr 8th)	23	7	66/1	41	—

				SP		
3751[2]	**Fast Thoughts (99)** (DRGandolfo) **10-11-3b**(3) SophieMitchell (prom tl wknd appr 3 out: p.u bef last)		**P**	5/1[2]	—	—
2708[9]	**Top Skipper (IRE) (80)** (VGGreenway) **5-10-13**(7) MrJTizzard (a bhd: t.o whn p.u bef 2 out)		**P**	12/1	—	—
587[6]	**Bravo Star (USA) (67)** (PaddyFarrell) **12-11-6** WMarston (bit bkwd: a bhd: t.o 8th: p.u bef 2 out)		**P**	25/1	—	—
1528[4]	**Nick the Dreamer (86)** (WGMTurner) **12-10-7**(7) NWillmington (bit bkwd: chsd ldrs in tch tl rdn 8th: t.o whn p.u bef 2 out)		**P**	25/1	—	—
3755[11]	**Nearly All Right** (SEarle) **8-11-2** CMaude (a bhd: t.o whn p.u bef last)		**P**	50/1	—	—
3171[P]	**Ilewinit (IRE)** (PCRitchens) **8-11-4v**[1] GUpton (mid div tl wknd 7th: t.o whn p.u bef 2 out)		**P**	50/1	—	—
3709[P]	**Castlebay Lad (50)** (RCurtis) **14-10-13**ow1 MrMAppleby (bit bkwd: bhd fr 8th: t.o whn p.u bef 2 out)		**P**	100/1	—	—
3736[U]	**Dunlir** (PRRodford) **7-11-4** SBurrough (bhd whn blnd & uns rdr 5th)		**U**	20/1	—	—
				(SP 130.2%)	**15 Rn**	

6m 28.0 (5.00) CSF £7.50 TOTE £3.80: £1.80 £1.50 £2.10 (£6.00) Trio £19.10 OWNER Mr B. A. Kilpatrick (WELLINGTON) BRED W. R. Jackson

2960 Palosanto (IRE), dropped in here after his Cheltenham effort, proved far too good for these. This would seem to be his grade. (5/2)

3737 St Ville, keeping tracks on the leader, could not get to his market rival on the run-in, but is capable of finding a small race. (5/2)

3624 Tiger Claw (USA) may find a change of fortune in a smaller race if repeating this performance. (10/1)

2008 Snowy Lane (IRE) (14/1: op 8/1)

3893 'TOUCH OF SPRING' H'CAP CHASE (0-120) (5-Y.O+) (Class D)

3-35 (3-35) **3m 2f 110y (20 fncs)** £3,680.90 (£1,113.20: £542.60: £257.30) GOING minus 0.44 sec per fur (GF)

				SP	RR	SF
3554[5]	**Fortunes Course (IRE) (95)** (JSKing) **8-11-0** DWalsh (lw: led to 6th: led 10th: drvn out to hold on flat)	—	**1**	Evens[1]	107	37
3185[P]	**Diamond Fort (97)** (JCMcConnochie) **12-11-2** SWynne (hdwy to chse ldr 15th: ev ch 2 out: disp ld last: rdn & no ex nr fin)	½	**2**	11/2[3]	109	39
3633*	**Silverino (89)** (PRRodford) **11-10-8** SBurrough (bhd: in tch tl rdn 11th: wknd 14th)	dist	**3**	5/2[2]	—	—
3701[P]	**Florida Sky (100)** (CPEBrooks) **10-10-12**(7) MBerry (chsd ldr 4th: led 6th to 10th: slt mstke & rdn 14th: wknd next)	dist	**4**	6/1	—	—
				(SP 108.2%)	**4 Rn**	

6m 31.6 (-2.40) CSF £5.78 TOTE £2.10 (£3.30) OWNER Mrs A. J. Garrett (SWINDON) BRED Mrs Patricia Conway

3554 Fortunes Course (IRE) is a brave mare and proved so here, getting the better of her only serious rival on the run-in. Her trainer may have reservations about running her on ground as fast as this again. (Evens)

2063 Diamond Fort put in a good round here but met one too tough in the winner, and would have preferred a little cut in the ground. (11/2: 4/1-6/1)

Florida Sky (6/1: 4/1-13/2)

3894 DARTMOOR NOVICES' CONDITIONAL H'CAP HURDLE (0-100) (4-Y.O+) (Class E)

4-05 (4-05) **2m 6f (10 hdls)** £2,379.00 (£669.00: £327.00) GOING minus 0.44 sec per fur (GF)

				SP	RR	SF
3628[P]	**Connaught's Pride (64)** (PJHobbs) **6-10-2** DJKavanagh (lw: hld up bhd: hdwy 7th: led appr 2 out: sn clr: tried to ref last: rdn out to hld on flat)	—	**1**	4/1[2]	47	1
3500[7]	**Little Elliot (IRE) (72)** (SEarle) **9-10-10** PHenley (lw: led to 2nd: led appr 7th: hdd appr 2 out: sn outpcd)	2	**2**	5/2[1]	54	8
3683[9]	**Lord Nitrogen (USA) (83)** (BJLlewellyn) **7-11-7** MichaelBrennan (hdwy to chse ldr after 6th: ev ch next: rdn & wknd after 8th)	8	**3**	7/1[3]	59	13
	Rising's Lass (IRE) (75) (MJWeeden) **7-10-10**(3) NWillmington (bhd in tch whn hit rail on bnd after 6th: rallied: in tch 8th: wknd appr 2 out)	4	**4**	14/1	48	2
3437[5]	**Smart Lord (86)** (MRBosley) **6-11-10** XAizpuru (lw: in tch tl rdn & wknd 8th: p.u bef 2 out)		**P**	5/2[1]	—	—
	Irish Dominion (62) (AGHobbs) **7-10-0** OBurrows (bit bkwd: led 2nd tl appr 7th: sn wknd: p.u after next)		**P**	20/1	—	—
3752[7]	**Romany Blues (62)** (CPEBrooks) **8-9-7**(7) CRafter (in tch whn blnd & uns rdr 3rd)		**U**	9/1	—	—
				(SP 111.1%)	**7 Rn**	

5m 17.4 (5.40) CSF £12.68 CT £57.32 TOTE £5.50: £3.10 £1.60 (£6.90) OWNER Mrs Angela Tincknell (MINEHEAD) BRED J. L. C. Shedden

LONG HANDICAP Irish Dominion 9-2 Romany Blues 9-12

Connaught's Pride was fortunate to finish here, as she tried to run out at the final obstacle with the race as good as hers. She did, however, keep on well on the run-in for a deserved success. This was her second attempt at course and distance this month, the only difference being the much firmer ground this time. (4/1)

Little Elliot (IRE) was given a slight chance with the antics of the winner at the last, but could not take advantage on the run-in. (5/2)

889 Lord Nitrogen (USA), who has reverted to hurdles after a chasing campaign, was seen with a chance until weakening over the final two obstacles. (7/1)

Rising's Lass (IRE) (14/1: op 7/1)

Irish Dominion apparently broke a blood-vessel, although this did not become apparent until after his next race. (20/1)

2052 Romany Blues (9/1: op 6/1)

3895 DARTMOOR MAIDEN OPEN N.H. FLAT RACE (4, 5 & 6-Y.O) (Class H)

4-35 (4-35) **2m 1f** £1,299.00 (£364.00: £177.00)

				SP	RR	SF
3747[4]	**Mazileo** (IPWilliams) **4-10-7**(7) FBogle (lw: hld up & bhd: hdwy 6f out: led ent fnl f)	—	**1**	9/2[2]	67 f	—
	Abigails Star (PGMurphy) **5-11-6** BPowell (lw: hdwy ½-wy: chsd ldr 4f out: ev ch ins fnl f: outpcd nr fin)	2	**2**	12/1	63 f	—
	Run For Cover (IRE) (MrsPNDutfield) **5-11-1** AProcter (bit bkwd: mid div: hdwy 6f out: str run ins fnl f: nt rch ldrs)	¾	**3**	20/1	57 f	—
1573[10]	**Country Kris** (BJMRyall) **5-11-6** GUpton (a.p: led 7f out tl ent fnl f: hdd & sn wknd)	6	**4**	25/1	57 f	—
3767[6]	**Longstone Lad** (GFEdwards) **5-10-13**(7) MrJTizzard (bhd: hdwy 7f out: sn prom: wknd 2f out)	3½	**5**	10/1	54 f	—
2844[12]	**Bomba Charger** (AGHobbs) **5-11-6** RGreene (bit bkwd: bhd: styd on 4f out: nvr nrr)	s.h	**6**	33/1	53 f	—
2661[15]	**Baby Lancaster** (MAGriffin) **6-10-13**(7) MGriffiths (lw: prom to 6f: wknd 2f out)	7	**7**	50/1	47 f	—
3821[7]	**Jim's Quest** (PJHobbs) **4-11-0** GTormey (lw: prom: led ½-wy to 7f out: wknd 4f out)	18	**8**	3/1[1]	32 f	—
3574[8]	**Satellite Express (IRE)** (BSmart) **4-11-0** WMarston (prom 6f out tl wknd 3f out: hung lft ins fnl f)	21	**9**	5/1[3]	12 f	—
3433[10]	**See Minnow** (MissSWaterman) **4-10-2**(7) NWillmington (nvr trbld ldrs)	8	**10**	50/1	—	—
3203[10]	**Phone The Pipeline** (MCPipe) **4-10-7**(7) BMoore (led to ½-wy: sn wknd)	1	**11**	10/1	4 f	—
	Etta Dove (MissVenetiaWilliams) **6-10-8**(7) MrSDurack (bit bkwd: bhd fr ½-wy: t.o)	dist	**12**	5/1[3]	—	—
3235[12]	**Salix** (NJHawke) **5-11-6** JRailton (bit bkwd: prom 10f: t.o)	dist	**13**	50/1	—	—
3767[9]	**Five Boys (IRE)** (RJHodges) **5-11-3**(3) TDascombe (a bhd: t.o after 7f: p.u ½-wy)		**P**	20/1	—	—

	Horse	Dist	Pos	SP	RR	SF
	Vexford Lucy (VGGreenway) **4-10-2**(7) XAizpuru (bit bkwd: a bhd: t.o whn p.u ½-wy)		P	50/1	—	—
				(SP 126.5%)		**15 Rn**

3m 54.4 (233.40) CSF £50.07 TOTE £7.10: £2.30 £3.20 £4.90 (£54.70) Trio Not won; £140.03 to Kempton 31/3/97 OWNER Mrs H. Parrott (ALVECHURCH) BRED Tedwood Bloodstock Ltd and Partners
WEIGHT FOR AGE 4yo-8lb
IN-FOCUS: **Young Irishman Fergus Bogle rode his first winner.**
3747 Mazileo came on well from his first outing at Ludlow, to take this rather ordinary bumper. (9/2: 3/1-5/1)
Abigails Star showed notable improvement from his Worcester debut last season. (12/1)
Run For Cover (IRE) showed nothing in two similar events last season, but put in a good late effort here to show slight promise for the future. (20/1)
3767 Longstone Lad (10/1: op 4/1)
2572 Jim's Quest (3/1: op 2/1)
Satellite Express (IRE) (5/1: 4/1-6/1)

T/Plpt: £174.90 (47.56 Tckts). T/Qdpt: £25.90 (15.73 Tckts) T

3755-PLUMPTON (L-H) (Good to firm)
Saturday March 29th
WEATHER: fine

3896 AMERICAN EXPRESS FOREIGN EXCHANGE CONDITIONAL (S) H'CAP HURDLE (0-95) (4-Y.O+) (Class G)
2-25 (2-26) **2m 1f (10 hdls)** £2,111.00 (£586.00: £281.00) GOING minus 0.29 sec per fur (GF)

	Horse	Dist	Pos	SP	RR	SF
3811^{3}	**Derisbay (IRE) (82)** (JJBridger) **9-11-6b** LAspell (hld up: hdwy 6th: led 3 out: clr next: pushed out)	—	1	2/1 [1]	71	11
3674^{2}	**Mullintor (IRE) (82)** (RRowe) **6-11-1**(5) AGarrity (a.p: ev ch 3 out: sn rdn: one pce)	6	2	9/4 [2]	65	5
3110^{6}	**Glowing Path (86)** (RJHodges) **7-11-7**(3) JHarris (lw: hld up: hdwy appr 3 out: rdn appr next: one pce)	2½	3	3/1 [3]	67	7
3670^{6}	**Olivipet (62)** (FGray) **8-9-9**(5) NTEgan (rr: mod hdwy fr 3 out: nvr nrr)	15	4	25/1	29	—
3720^{P}	**Never Forgotten (80)** (GLMoore) **12-11-1**(3) MBatchelor (led: hit 4th: hdd 3 out: sn wknd)	11	5	7/1	37	—
2567^{9}	**Against The Clock (63)** (PBowen) **5-10-1**ow1 GuyLewis (prom tl wknd 3 out)	15	6	11/1	5	—
3811^{7}	**Tapestry Rose (62)** (JRPoulton) **6-9-9**(5) MClinton (a bhd: t.o)	20	7	66/1	—	—
2753^{P}	**Saboteuse (70)** (JCPoulton) **5-10-1b**[1](7)ow8 GordonGallagher (keen hold: rdn 5th: sn wknd: t.o)	8	8	50/1	—	—
				(SP 117.2%)		**8 Rn**

4m 4.1 (8.10) CSF £6.68 CT £11.51 TOTE £2.70: £1.20 £1.40 £1.40 (£3.40) OWNER Miss Julie Self (LIPHOOK) BRED Kilfrush Stud Ltd in Ireland
LONG HANDICAP Olivipet 9-7 Against The Clock 9-4 Tapestry Rose 9-1 Saboteuse 9-6
No bid
3811 Derisbay (IRE) is in good heart at present, and was not hard-pressed to score. (2/1)
3674 Mullintor (IRE) had his chance three from home, but was soon put in his place. (9/4)
3110 Glowing Path looked dangerous momentarily three from home, but soon came under pressure, and had little more to give. (3/1: 9/4-4/1)
17 Against The Clock (11/1: 8/1-12/1)

3897 ASHDOWN HOSPITAL H'CAP CHASE (0-110) (5-Y.O+) (Class E)
2-55 (2-57) **2m 2f (14 fncs)** £3,124.80 (£932.40: £445.20: £201.60) GOING minus 0.29 sec per fur (GF)

	Horse	Dist	Pos	SP	RR	SF
3832^{3}	**Fenwick (82)** (RJHodges) **10-11-6** PHolley (lw: a.p: led appr 9th: clr whn hit 2 out: r.o)	—	1	11/8 [1]	91	—
3578^{2}	**Winspit (IRE) (86)** (RHAlner) **7-11-10** JRKavanagh (a.p: pushed along 7th: chsd wnr appr 3 out: hrd rdn appr last: one pce)	5	2	13/8 [2]	91	—
2867^{7}	**Full of Tricks (65)** (JJBridger) **9-10-3**ow3 PHide (led: hdd appr 9th: mstke 10th: wknd appr 2 out)	14	3	25/1	57	—
3429^{13}	**Days of Thunder (85)** (MrsSMOdell) **9-11-9** TJO'Sullivan (prom tl wknd appr 9th)	6	4	8/1	72	—
	Upward Surge (IRE) (62) (RRLedger) **7-10-0** MrsNLedger (in tch tl wknd 4 out)	5	5	5/1 [3]	44	—
				(SP 111.8%)		**5 Rn**

4m 31.6 (13.60) CSF £3.92 TOTE £2.50: £1.40 £1.40 (£2.00) OWNER Major A. W. C. Pearn (SOMERTON) BRED A. E. Bishop
LONG HANDICAP Full of Tricks 9-12
3832 Fenwick asserted starting down the far side for the last time, and only a mistake two from home threatened to stop him scoring. (11/8)
3578 Winspit (IRE) was never travelling particularly well, and it is to his credit that he kept on for second. (13/8)
Full of Tricks made much of the running, but was put in his place over the final three fences. (25/1)
Days of Thunder (8/1: 5/1-9/1)

3898 MELLA HOPKINS HURDLE (4-Y.O) (Class E)
3-30 (3-30) **2m 1f (10 hdls)** £2,490.00 (£690.00: £330.00) GOING minus 0.29 sec per fur (GF)

	Horse	Dist	Pos	SP	RR	SF
3802^{2}	**Kinnescash (IRE) (100)** (PBowen) **4-10-12** MAFitzgerald (led to 2nd: led appr 7th: mstke next: clr appr 2 out: easily)	—	1	4/5 [1]	77+	4
3447^{12}	**Bath Knight (72)** (RCurtis) **4-10-5**(7) MrJGoldstein (led 2nd tl appr 7th: one pce fr next)	26	2	33/1	53	—
3669^{*}	**Muhandam (IRE)** (MrsDHaine) **4-10-12** JFTitley (lw: hld up: effrt 7th: wknd next)	24	3	2/1 [2]	30	—
3809^{P}	**Illuminate** (DCO'Brien) **4-10-12** PHide (bhd fr 7th)	1¾	4	14/1	28	—
3109^{12}	**Master-H** (RHAlner) **4-10-12** AThornton (a in rr: lost tch fr 6th)	4	5	50/1	25	—
	Hever Golf Eagle (TJNaughton) **4-10-12** RJohnson (lw: mstke 2nd: a in rr: lost tch appr 7th)	4	6	6/1 [3]	21	—
				(SP 114.7%)		**6 Rn**

4m 3.9 (7.90) CSF £22.55 TOTE £1.70: £1.20 £3.90 (£17.30) OWNER Mr D. R. James (HAVERFORDWEST) BRED Frank Barry
3802 Kinnescash (IRE) had run well behind Florid at Bangor last time, and outclassed the opposition here. (4/5: evens-11/10)
831 Bath Knight ran well enough, but was no match for the winner from four out. (33/1)
3669* Muhandam (IRE) won a bad race last time, and was in trouble before the third last here. In a truly-run race he struggles to stay. (2/1)
Illuminate (14/1: 8/1-16/1)
Hever Golf Eagle (6/1: 5/1-8/1)

3899 SINGER & FRIEDLANDER H'CAP CHASE (0-105) (5-Y.O+) (Class F)
4-00 (4-00) **3m 1f 110y (20 fncs)** £3,038.40 (£842.40: £403.20) GOING minus 0.29 sec per fur (GF)

	Horse / details	Dist	Pos	SP	RR	SF
3759*	**Black Church (97)** (RRowe) **11-11-10** DO'Sullivan (lw: a gng wl: hld up in tch: chsd ldr after 13th: led appr 4 out: sn clr: v.easily)	—	1	11/10 1	109+	35
3675P	**Be Surprised (73)** (GLMoore) **11-10-0** PHolley (led: hdd appr 4 out: sn outpcd)	12	2	5/1 3	78	4
3675*	**Royal Saxon (87)** (PBowen) **11-11-0** RJohnson (rdn thrght: chsd ldr to 7th: mstke 10th: outpcd fr 15th)	2½	3	11/8 2	90	16
3759 2	**Joker Jack (73)** (RDean) **12-9-7**(7) NTEgan (chsd ldr 7th tl blnd 13th: outpcd fr 15th)	3	4	16/1	74	—

(SP 112.3%) **4 Rn**

6m 25.7 (5.70) CSF £6.17 TOTE £2.10 (£6.10) OWNER Dr B. Alexander (PULBOROUGH) BRED A. E. Hanbidge
LONG HANDICAP Be Surprised 9-13 Joker Jack 9-3
3759* Black Church was always cantering over his rivals, and could have won by a distance. (11/10)
3176 Be Surprised, supported in the ring, ran better than of late, but is very flattered by the winning distance. (5/1: 6/1-12/1)
3675* Royal Saxon was never going well. (11/8)

3900 SEEBOARD NOVICES' CHASE (5-Y.O+) (Class E)
4-30 (4-30) **2m 5f (16 fncs)** £3,368.40 (£932.40: £445.20) GOING minus 0.29 sec per fur (GF)

	Horse / details	Dist	Pos	SP	RR	SF
1472 5	**Stormhill Pilgrim (70)** (MJRoberts) **8-11-2** PHide (lw: led 2nd: mde rest: hrd rdn appr last: r.o)	—	1	9/1 3	85	33
3576*	**Lively Knight (IRE) (120)** (JTGifford) **8-11-11**(3) LAspell (lw: hld up & bhd: pushed along 9th: tk closer order next: chsd wnr 4 out: rdn appr 3 out: unable qckn)	7	2	1/7 1	92	40
3719 3	**Cruise Control (68)** (RRowe) **11-11-2** DO'Sullivan (lw: led to 2nd: chsd wnr to 4 out: rdn appr next: one pce)	12	3	6/1 2	71	19

(SP 111.8%) **3 Rn**

5m 16.0 (3.00) CSF £11.13 TOTE £7.30 (£1.50) OWNER Mr Mike Roberts (HAILSHAM) BRED Mrs A. E. Ratcliff
OFFICIAL EXPLANATION **Lively Knight (IRE): no explanation offered.**
1472 Stormhill Pilgrim led at the second and, with the favourite running below par, made the rest to score. (9/1: 5/1-10/1)
3576* Lively Knight (IRE) was being nudged along some way from home, and ran well below form. He probably found the ground too lively. (1/7)
1965 Cruise Control was beaten three from home. (6/1: 8/1-12/1)

3901 EUROP ASSISTANCE NOVICES' HURDLE (4-Y.O+) (Class E)
5-00 (5-02) **2m 4f (12 hdls)** £2,826.00 (£786.00: £378.00) GOING minus 0.29 sec per fur (GF)

	Horse / details	Dist	Pos	SP	RR	SF
3172 2	**Sparkling Spring (IRE) (108)** (KCBailey) **6-11-9** AThornton (a.p: led appr 3 out: rdn last: r.o)	—	1	4/5 1	78+	45
3755 3	**Prototype** (GFJohnsonHoughton) **6-11-2** MAFitzgerald (hld up: hdwy 9th: chsd wnr appr 2 out: rdn appr last: unable qckn)	1¾	2	7/2 2	70	37
3689 5	**Nordic Spree (IRE) (80)** (GLMoore) **5-11-2v1** PHolley (a.p: led appr 5th: hdd appr 3 out: one pce)	9	3	20/1	62	29
3754 2	**Lord Rooble (IRE) (101)** (JTGifford) **6-11-9** PHide (led: hdd appr 5th: wknd appr 2 out)	11	4	4/1 3	61	28
3722 5	**Adilov (85)** (JJBridger) **5-11-2** DO'Sullivan (keen hold: prom: w ldr 5th to 9th: wknd next)	11	5	20/1	45	12
3284F	**Magical Blues (IRE)** (MissAEEmbiricos) **5-11-2** RJohnson (virtually ref to r: t.o whn p.u after 3rd)		P	12/1	—	—
3587P	**Typhoon (IRE)** (MarkCampion) **7-11-2** WMcFarland (virtually ref to r: a t.o: p.u after 7th)		P	50/1	—	—
	Silly Point (PButler) **5-10-4**(7) MrJGoldstein (lost tch 5th: t.o whn p.u 7th)		P	50/1	—	—

(SP 118.9%) **8 Rn**

4m 48.0 (1.00) CSF £3.71 TOTE £1.60: £1.10 £1.20 £2.20 (£2.40) Trio £16.00 OWNER Mr E. Benfield (UPPER LAMBOURN) BRED Mrs H. McCormick
3172 Sparkling Spring (IRE) won a shade more comfortably than the winning margin suggests. (4/5)
3755 Prototype was supported beforehand and ran well, throwing down a challenge from two out without ever quite looking like pegging back the winner. (7/2)
3689 Nordic Spree (IRE) ran a sound-enough race, but was outpaced from three out. (20/1)
3754 Lord Rooble (IRE) ran as though feeling the ground. (4/1: 5/2-5/1)
3284 Magical Blues (IRE) (12/1: 5/1-14/1)

T/Plpt: £72.50 (89.52 Tckts). T/Qdpt: £56.90 (5.14 Tckts) SM

3748-TOWCESTER (R-H) (Good to firm)
Saturday March 29th
WEATHER: fine & sunny

3902 GRACE NOVICES' HURDLE (4-Y.O+) (Class E)
2-20 (2-20) **3m (12 hdls)** £2,652.50 (£740.00: £357.50) GOING minus 0.16 sec per fur (G)

	Horse / details	Dist	Pos	SP	RR	SF
3634 11	**Pleasureland (IRE) (102)** (RCurtis) **4-11-0** DMorris (lw: hld up: qcknd & led after 7th: sn clr: rdn 2 out: edgd lft flat: all out)	—	1	4/5 1	82	—
3755 4	**Maylin Magic (83)** (TCasey) **6-10-11** DBridgwater (hld up: chsd wnr appr 8th: rdn appr last: r.o: nt rch wnr)	1¼	2	7/2 3	68	—
2826 5	**Kingswood Manor** (MissVenetiaWilliams) **5-10-11**(5) MrRThornton (w ldr: pushed along 5th: lost pl after 7th: styd on again appr 2 out)	10	3	12/1	67	—
3491 5	**King's Rainbow (IRE)** (MrsDHaine) **8-10-11** JOsborne (lw: led tl after 7th: sn btn)	11	4	11/4 2	54	—
3798 13	**Imperial Honors (IRE)** (NMLampard) **6-11-2** MrAKinane (hdwy 5th: ev ch 7th: sn wknd)	dist	5	66/1	—	—

(SP 113.6%) **5 Rn**

6m 8.9 (28.90) CSF £3.98 TOTE £1.80: £1.20 £1.80 (£2.40) OWNER Mrs Sylvia McGarvie (LAMBOURN) BRED Lodge Park Stud
WEIGHT FOR AGE 4yo-10lb
3441* Pleasureland (IRE) kicked hard for home at the bottom of the hill and nearly paid the penalty. He is better than this. (4/5: evens-11/10)
3755 Maylin Magic looked well-suited by the step-up in trip, staying on strongly in the straight to stretch the winner. (7/2: 9/4-4/1)
2826 Kingswood Manor, who was completely taken off his feet when the winner injected some pace with a mile left, stayed on quite well when the cause was lost. (12/1: 6/1-14/1)
3491 King's Rainbow (IRE) looked a lot fitter this time and appeared to like the ground on the way down, but again faded in the closing stages. (11/4)

3903 32ND YEAR OF THE SCHILIZZI 1906 COMMEMORATIVE CHALLENGE CUP H'CAP CHASE (0-130) (5-Y.O+) (Class C)

2-50 (2-50) **2m 6f (16 fncs)** £4,647.75 (£1,392.00: £668.50: £306.75) GOING minus 0.16 sec per fur (G)

				SP	RR	SF
3550[P]	**Funcheon Gale (95)** (RCurtis) **10-11-0** DMorris (lw: trckd ldrs: mstke 4 out: sn outpcd: rallied & hit last: r.o to ld nr fin)	—	**1**	3/1[2]	97	25
3585[5]	**Postman's Path (98)** (CaptTAForster) **11-11-3** JOsborne (lw: j.lft: led tl hdd & unable qckn nr fin)	1	**2**	3/1[2]	99	27
3665[2]	**Artic Wings (IRE) (105)** (OBrennan) **9-11-10** MBrennan (lw: trckd ldr: ev ch 3 out: sn rdn: btn appr last)	5	**3**	10/11[1]	103	31
2821[10]	**Staunch Rival (USA) (105)** (GThorner) **10-11-3b**[(7)] ClareThorner (mstke & rdn 6th: bhd fr 10th)	21	**4**	9/1[3]	87	15
				(SP 112.4%)	**4 Rn**	

5m 37.1 (8.10) CSF £10.90 TOTE £4.10 (£6.30) OWNER Kings Of The Road Partnership (LAMBOURN) BRED Patrick Moakley

1554* Funcheon Gale looked fit and well after breaking a blood-vessel last time. Getting left behind on the climb up the hill, he had let his two rivals cut their own throats, and would have won a shade more cosily but for an untidy jump at the last when closing fast. (3/1)

Postman's Path, who has not won since 1994, looked in magnificent shape and almost put the record straight despite jumping alarmingly left at many fences. (3/1)

3665 Artic Wings (IRE), sensibly taken up the inside of Postman's Path, unlike the winner, again found very little when the chips were down. (10/11: op 11/8)

1876 Staunch Rival (USA) seems to have lost his way and was never really travelling. (9/1: op 4/1)

3904 TURF CLUB H'CAP HURDLE (0-105) (4-Y.O+) (Class F)

3-25 (3-25) **2m (8 hdls)** £2,160.50 (£603.00: £291.50) GOING minus 0.16 sec per fur (G)

				SP	RR	SF
2573[4]	**Euro Singer (92)** (TKeddy) **5-11-2**[(5)] SRyan (lw: a.p: rdn to ld after 3 out: clr & hit next: jst hld on)	—	**1**	14/1	77	33
695[5]	**Bourdonner (89)** (MDHammond) **5-11-1**[(3)] MrCBonner (led 2nd to 4th: chsd wnr 2 out: r.o flat: jst failed)	½	**2**	9/1	74	30
3623[6]	**Steve Ford (88)** (CPMorlock) **8-11-3** JAMcCarthy (in tch: hdwy 3 out: r.o flat)	9	**3**	10/1	64	20
3623*	**Iron N Gold (91)** (TCasey) **5-11-6** DBridgwater (lw: mstkes 1st & 2nd: bhd: hdwy 3 out: one pce flat)	nk	**4**	100/30[1]	66	22
	Northern Charmer (89) (EJAlston) **5-10-11**[(7)] LCummins (hdwy 4th: wknd appr 2 out)	2	**5**	7/1	62	18
3234[9]	**Nashville Star (USA) (95)** (RMathew) **6-11-10v** JOsborne (lw: led to 2nd: led 4th tl after 3 out: 3rd & btn whn blnd last)	¾	**6**	10/1	67	23
3752[2]	**Positivo (75)** (MissCJECaroe) **6-10-1**[(3)ow2] DFortt (in tch: pushed along fr 2nd: no imp fr 3 out)	hd	**7**	9/2[2]	47	1
3741[3]	**Anlace (80)** (SMellor) **8-10-4**[(5)] ChrisWebb (lw: bhd fr 4th)	5	**8**	14/1	47	3
3666[3]	**Ajdar (77)** (OBrennan) **6-10-6** MBrennan (bhd fr 4th)	19	**9**	9/1	25	—
3814[3]	**Courageous Knight (82)** (PHayward) **8-10-11** DGallagher (mstke 3rd: a bhd)	3½	**10**	12/1	27	—
3478[3]	**Mrs Jawleyford (USA) (78)** (CSmith) **9-10-7** MRanger (prom to 5th: t.o whn p.u bef 2 out)		**P**	16/1	—	—
3752*	**Dissolve (80)** (NMLampard) **5-10-2**[(7)] MrLBaker (prom: pckd 4th: wknd appr 3 out: p.u bef next)		**P**	5/1[3]	—	—
				(SP 135.5%)	**12 Rn**	

3m 51.1 (5.10) CSF £138.58 CT £1,242.67 TOTE £18.30: £3.60 £3.00 £3.30 (£138.70) Trio £303.00; £298.83 to Kempton 31/3/97 OWNER BCD Steels Ltd (HANLEY SWAN) BRED Mrs A. Plummer

OFFICIAL EXPLANATION **Dissolve: gurgled.**

1954 Euro Singer, taken down early, loves this fast ground and got a lead almost to the home turn. After looking in total charge, he tied up quite dramatically on the run-in. (14/1: 10/1-20/1)

695 Bourdonner, taking a big drop in trip, could not dominate but found his stamina coming into play over the final two flights. (9/1)

3623 Steve Ford did not pull this time, as he could not lay-up with the very fast pace. (10/1)

3623* Iron N Gold got detached early on and could never get back into the race. A stayer on the Flat, he gives the impression that he would stay further in this grade. (100/30)

Northern Charmer, who had a pipe-opener on the All-Weather a couple of weeks ago, shaped well to two out and should be kept in mind. (7/1)

3002* Nashville Star (USA), at his best when tearing off in front, found another of like mind, but was still a clear third when making a total hash of the final flight. (10/1)

3752 Positivo, having his second taste of fast ground in ten days, was struggling from an early stage and was not knocked about in the last half-mile. (9/2)

3741 Anlace (14/1: 12/1-20/1)

3666 Ajdar (9/1: 12/1-8/1)

3905 36TH YEAR OF THE SCHILIZZI CHALLENGE BOWL H'CAP CHASE (0-125) (5-Y.O+) (Class D)

3-55 (3-55) **2m 110y (12 fncs)** £3,435.75 (£1,026.00: £490.50: £222.75) GOING minus 0.16 sec per fur (G)

				SP	RR	SF
3746*	**Mr Snaggle (IRE) (89)** (SEarle) **8-10-5** JOsborne (hld up: hdwy 8th: led last: drvn out)	—	**1**	11/8[2]	89	21
3756[5]	**Parliamentarian (IRE) (84)** (TCasey) **8-10-0b** DBridgwater (lw: led tl mstke & hdd last: r.o)	½	**2**	13/2[3]	84	16
3276[2]	**Lackendara (105)** (MissHCKnight) **10-11-7** JCulloty (chsd ldr: pckd 5th: rdn 3 out: wknd appr last)	7	**3**	11/10[1]	98	30
3430[8]	**Linden's Lotto (IRE) (108)** (JWhite) **8-11-5**[(5)] MrRThornton (in tch tl j.slowly & dropped rr 7th: n.d after)	5	**4**	9/1	96	28
				(SP 113.1%)	**4 Rn**	

4m 6.8 (4.80) CSF £8.60 TOTE £2.30 (£3.80) OWNER The Plum Merchants (STURMINSTER NEWTON) BRED Mrs W. H. Young

LONG HANDICAP Parliamentarian (IRE) 9-8

3746* Mr Snaggle (IRE) hardly impressed with his head-carriage, but did just enough to scramble home. (11/8)

3550* Parliamentarian (IRE) tries his best, and might have prevailed with a good jump at the last. (13/2)

3276 Lackendara has bled in the past ,and looks a bit of a lost cause if he cannot even win in this grade. (11/10)

2748 Linden's Lotto (IRE) has shown nothing all season. (9/1)

3906 LARRY CONNELL MEMORIAL HUNTERS' CHASE (5-Y.O+) (Class H)

4-25 (4-25) **3m 1f (18 fncs)** £1,150.50 (£318.00: £151.50) GOING minus 0.16 sec per fur (G)

				SP	RR	SF
3765[3]	**Northern Village** (LukeDace) **10-11-7**[(7)] MrDAlers-Hankey (hld up: hit 2nd: hdwy 13th: mstke 4 out: rdn appr last: led nr fin)	—	**1**	10/1	105	26
3458[P]	**Avostar** (MissCSaunders) **10-11-9**[(5)] MrBPollock (led to 7th: led 9th to 12th: led appr 2 out: hdd & unable qckn nr fin)	¾	**2**	100/30[3]	105	26
3458[2]	**Peajade** (MissJillWormall) **13-11-7**[(7)] MissJWormall (lw: prom: led 7th to 9th: led 12th tl appr 2 out: one pce)	5	**3**	4/1	101	22
3357[3]	**Broad Steane** (CHenn) **8-11-9**[(5)] MrASansome (lw: chsd ldrs: mstke 6th: rdn 13th: one pce appr 2 out)	1¼	**4**	5/2[1]	101	22

3609* **Glen Oak** (DGDuggan) **12-11-13**(5) MrRThornton (prom: rdn 13th: hit 2 out: sn btn) ....1½ **5** 11/4[2] 104 25
3593[4] **Artful Arthur** (LPGrassick) **11-11-7**(7) MrJGrassick (a bhd) 17 **6** 33/1 89 10
3799[4] **Teatrader** (MissTOBlazey) **11-11-7**(7) MissTBlazey (lw: prom to 9th) ....½ **7** 14/1 88 9
3490[U] **Solar Gem** (JohnMason) **10-11-7b**[1](7) MrsCMcCarthy (nt j.w: t.o fr 10th tl p.u bef 13th) .... **P** 33/1 — —
(SP 120.0%) **8 Rn**

6m 28.7 (13.70) CSF £42.49 TOTE £13.60: £1.80 £1.60 £1.20 (£18.50) OWNER Mr L. P. Dace (STORRINGTON) BRED Mrs R. Owen-George
STEWARDS' ENQUIRY Pollock susp. 7,9-10,12&14-15/4/97(improper & incorrect use of whip) Grassick susp.7,9-10, 12&14/4/97(excessive & improper use of whip)
3765 Northern Village loved the ground but is still not the best of fencers. Going best from three out, he took some time to get on top once let down. (10/1)
3089 Avostar left his Leicester flop behind him, but could not hold off the winner however hard he tried. (100/30)
3458 Peajade looked magnificent and put in some fine leaps, but has lost some of his speed. (4/1: 3/1-9/2)
3357 Broad Steane was a little disappointing as he was being niggled along by halfway. (5/2)
3609* Glen Oak was just beginning to feel the strain when brought to a standstill by a mistake two from home. (11/4)

3907 HOILE INTERMEDIATE OPEN N.H. FLAT RACE (4, 5 & 6-Y.O) (Class H)
4-55 (4-55) **2m** £1,413.00 (£393.00: £189.00)

SP RR SF

Sir Lunchalot (IRE) (PRWebber) **4-10-12** JOsborne (scope: lw: hld up: hdwy 3f out: shkn up & qcknd to ld ins fnl f: cleverly) ....— **1** 9/4[1] 70 f —
Murchan Tyne (IRE) (EJAlston) **4-10-0**(7) LCummins (lengthy: unf: chsd ldrs: led over 2f out: hdd ins fnl f: r.o) ....1 **2** 10/1 64 f —
3676[3] **Silver Sirocco (IRE)** (MrsMerritaJones) **5-11-4** DerekByrne (rangy: set stdy pce: qcknd over 3f out: hdd over 2f out: r.o fnl f) ....2½ **3** 5/2[2] 65 f —
Misty Class (IRE) (CPEBrooks) **5-11-4** DGallagher (w'like: hld up & plld hrd: hdwy after 6f: ev ch over 2f out: one pce) ....4 **4** 13/2 61 f —
3626[6] **Teejay's Future (IRE)** (OBrennan) **6-10-6**(7) WWalsh (unf: hld up & plld hrd: hdwy 4f out: rdn 2f out: one pce) ....2½ **5** 15/2 53 f —
3418[3] **Generous Streak (FR)** (JNorton) **4-10-7**(5) MrRThornton (w'like: prom: no hdwy fnl 3f) ....3½ **6** 5/1[3] 57 f —
Fresh Rose Mary (IRE) (JSMoore) **5-10-6**(7) JKeenan (cmpt: s.i.s: hdwy 5f out: ev ch 3f out: sn wknd) ....¾ **7** 25/1 49 f —
Wishing William (IRE) (MissHCKnight) **5-11-4** JCulloty (lengthy: prom over 12f) ....¾ **8** 5/1[3] 53 f —
The Millstone (CHJones) **6-10-11**(7) MKeighley (rangy: unf: plld hrd: prom tl wknd qckly 3f out) ....29 **9** 25/1 24 f —
Highland Prince (JWhite) **5-10-13**(5) SRyan (rangy: bkwd: in tch 10f) ....29 **10** 25/1 — —
(SP 138.4%) **10 Rn**

3m 57.3 CSF £28.65 TOTE £3.80: £1.80 £2.50 £1.90 (£19.90) Trio £34.10 OWNER The Random Partnership (BANBURY) BRED Memon Bloodstock
WEIGHT FOR AGE 4yo-8lb
Sir Lunchalot (IRE), by the former Cecil miler Homo Sapien, found the ridiculously slow early pace playing right into his hands. Ridden with supreme confidence, he crept up the inside and quickened impressively when let down. (9/4)
Murchan Tyne (IRE) is not much to look at, but did settle better than most early on. It was no disgrace to get outpaced by a more speedily-bred horse and she has some ability. (10/1: op 6/1)
3676 Silver Sirocco (IRE) set such a slow pace that he did much to contribute to his own defeat, as he was staying on as strongly as any at the line. (5/2)
Misty Class (IRE), a full-brother to Beatson, failed to settle and pulled his way up to the leaders after a few furlongs. Allowing for this he came home quite well and may be a different proposition in a more strongly-run race. (13/2)
3626 Teejay's Future (IRE) pulled hard in rear but, having made her ground on the home turn, failed to respond to some sharp reminders in the straight. (15/2)
3418 Generous Streak (FR), although Flat-bred, is not suited to the sort of sprint this race needed. (5/1: 4/1-6/1)

T/Plpt: £651.60 (11.35 Tckts). T/Qdpt: £282.50 (4.84 Tckts) Dk

3882-CARLISLE (R-H) (Good)
Monday March 31st
WEATHER: cloudy

3908 SOLWAY NOVICES' CLAIMING HURDLE (4-Y.O+ F & M) (Class G)
2-20 (2-21) **2m 1f (9 hdls)** £1,828.00 (£508.00: £244.00) GOING: 0.20 sec per fur (G)

SP RR SF

3284* **Sousse (82)** (MrsMReveley) **4-10-12**(3) GLee (in tch: hdwy 4th: led next: hit 3 out: j.lft next: styd on) ....— **1** 6/4[1] 61 —
3802[7] **Tabriz** (MrsPMAAvison) **4-10-9** OPears (prom: ev ch last: styd on same pce flat) ....2½ **2** 7/1[3] 53 —
3305[3] **Pearls of Thought (IRE)** (ACWhillans) **4-10-2**(3)ow5 ECallaghan (hld up & bhd: hdwy appr 3 out: rdn & one pce fr last) ....1 **3** 12/1 48 —
2505[10] **Simand (71)** (GMMoore) **5-10-6** NBentley (a.p: rdn & one pce fr 2 out) ....4 **4** 8/1 37 —
3481[6] **Sandrift (77)** (CParker) **8-11-1** DParker (in tch: rdn 3 out: no imp fr next) ....3 **5** 12/1 43 —
3823[13] **Connie Leathart** (MsLCPlater) **6-10-9** MMoloney (cl up tl lost pl appr 3 out) ....15 **6** 16/1 23 —
3478[13] **Alan's Pride (IRE) (65)** (WMcKeown) **6-10-12** GCahill (led to 3rd: prom tl wknd 4 out: t.o) ....29 **7** 12/1 — —
3325[P] **Something Speedy (IRE) (68)** (MDHammond) **5-10-6** DBentley (lost pl 6th: sme hdwy fr 3 out: n.d: t.o) ....1¼ **8** 33/1 — —
2614[F] **Game Point** (DALamb) **8-11-7** JBurke (prom to ½-wy: sn t.o) ....3 **9** 100/1 4 —
3641[U] **Bill's Pride (71)** (PMonteith) **6-9-13**(7) CMcCormack (lost tch 6th: t.o) ....1¾ **10** 9/2[2] — —
3313[7] **Beacon Hill Lady (65)** (BEllison) **4-9-7**(7) NHorrocks (j.bdly: a bhd) ....2 **11** 20/1 — —
3611[8] **De-Veers Currie (IRE)** (DMoffatt) **5-11-4** BStorey (led 3rd to 5th: sn lost pl: t.o) ....22 **12** 25/1 — —
1990[P] **Meesonette** (BEllison) **5-10-6** KJohnson (reminders 2nd: sn t.o) ....16 **13** 33/1 — —
(SP 126.2%) **13 Rn**

4m 20.6 (19.60) CSF £11.44 TOTE £2.30: £1.40 £2.00 £2.60 (£6.70) OWNER Wentdale Racing Partnership (SALTBURN) BRED Manor Grange Stud Co Ltd
WEIGHT FOR AGE 4yo-8lb
3284* Sousse, a somewhat temperamental sort, jumped moderately over the final three obstacles, tending to hang left at the second of them, but he is okay in this class. (6/4)

Tabriz stuck on as best he could but lacked finishing speed. (7/1)
3305 Pearls of Thought (IRE) was confidently ridden in a style that suggests that a race of this calibre is within his grasp in the future. (12/1: op 8/1)
3481 Sandrift (12/1: op 8/1)
3534 Bill's Pride (9/2: 3/1-5/1)

3909 BARCLAYS CORPORATE BANKING NOVICES' H'CAP CHASE (0-100) (5-Y.O+) (Class E)

2-50 (2-52) **2m 4f 110y (16 fncs)** £2,957.00 (£896.00: £438.00: £209.00) GOING: 0.20 sec per fur (G)

			SP	RR	SF
2954[3]	**Tough Test (IRE) (80)** (MrsJDGoodfellow) **7-10-8** BStorey (a.p: outpcd 3 out: rallied to ld next: styd on wl) ..—	1	5/1[3]	92	32
3331[4]	**Kiltulla (IRE) (72)** (MrsSJSmith) **7-9-9**(5) GFRyan (chsd ldrs: led 4 out to 2 out: ev ch appr last: no ex) 9	2	11/2	77	17
3695*	**Corston Joker (82)** (LLungo) **7-10-10** JSupple (mde most to 4 out: rdn & one pce fr 2 out) ....s.h	3	11/4[1]	87	27
2919[3]	**Trump (88)** (CParker) **8-11-2** DParker (in tch: outpcd 10th: no imp fr 3 out) 3	4	7/1	91	31
3479*	**Roberty Lea (99)** (MrsMReveley) **9-11-10**(3) GLee (hld up & bhd: nt fluent: hdwy & in tch 10th: btn 3 out)........3	5	4/1[2]	99	39
3795[10]	**Jonaem (IRE) (72)** (MrsESlack) **7-10-0** KJohnson (a bhd) 18	6	25/1	58	—
3790[7]	**Music Blitz (73)** (MrsDThomson) **6-10-1** MFoster (prom: rdn & wknd appr 4 out) 4	7	5/1[3]	56	—
875[6]	**German Legend (80)** (DALamb) **7-10-8** JBurke (chsd ldrs: wknd & hit 11th: sn no ch) 12	8	20/1	54	—
3326[4]	**Dandy des Plauts (FR) (72)** (MrsSJSmith) **6-10-0** DBentley (wl bhd fr ½-wy) 12	9	16/1	36	—
3726[2]	**Most Rich (IRE) (77)** (BEllison) **9-10-2v**(3)ow5 ECallaghan (w ldr tl wknd 11th: p.u bef 4 out)............	P	9/1	—	—
3188[F]	**Mindyerownbusiness (IRE) (72)** (RLee) **8-10-0** OPears (a bhd: t.o whn p.u bef 10th)............	P	25/1	—	—
3326[P]	**Miss Lamplight (72)** (FPMurtagh) **7-10-0** GCahill (a bhd: t.o whn p.u bef 4 out)............	P	66/1	—	—
3711[10]	**Dashmar (72)** (MsLCPlater) **10-10-0** MMoloney (in tch to 8th: sn bhd: p.u bef 2 out)............	P	66/1	—	—
			(SP 139.2%)	**13 Rn**	

5m 14.1 (11.10) CSF £34.16 CT £89.72 TOTE £6.80: £1.90 £2.40 £1.80 (£43.90) OWNER Mr J. D. Goodfellow (EARLSTON) BRED Liam Burke
LONG HANDICAP Jonaem (IRE) 9-11 Kiltulla (IRE) 9-7 Most Rich (IRE) 9-9 Mindyerownbusiness (IRE) 9-8 Miss Lamplight 9-11 Dashmar 9-2
2954 Tough Test (IRE), possibly a shade unlucky, is a decent a novice off this rating. He stuck on bravely and won nicely. (5/1)
3331 Kiltulla (IRE), from a stable very much in form at the moment, was outpointed by the winner but has a similar race within his grasp. (11/2)
3695* Corston Joker was a shade disappointing and it could be down to the ground being a touch faster than he likes. (11/4)
2919 Trump has yet to recapture the form over fences that he showed over hurdles. (7/1)
3479* Roberty Lea was confidently ridden, but wasn't going as well as he might have been and possibly the ground was on the fast side. (4/1)

3910 BORDER TELEVISION NOVICES' HURDLE (4-Y.O+) (Class E)

3-20 (3-25) **2m 4f 110y (11 hdls)** £2,444.00 (£684.00: £332.00) GOING: 0.20 sec per fur (G)

			SP	RR	SF
3483*	**Ardrina** (FMurphy) **6-11-1** MFoster (mde most fr after 5th: styd on wl flat: eased towards fin) ....—	1	2/1[1]	71+	19
3100*	**Meadow Hymn (IRE) (107)** (JGFitzGerald) **6-11-12** WDwan (in tch: disp ld fr 3 out: styd on same pce flat)......2	2	6/1	80	28
3644*	**Magpie Melody (IRE)** (LLungo) **6-11-1**(5) BGrattan (chsd ldrs: rdn & ev ch 3 out: styd on one pce fr next).....11	3	9/2[3]	66	14
3483[2]	**Into the West (IRE) (107)** (MrsSJSmith) **8-11-1**(5) GFRyan (jnd ldrs ½-wy: ev ch 4 out: one pce fr next) 1¼	4	100/30[2]	65	13
3368[P]	**Dromore Dream (IRE)** (MrsJBrown) **8-10-11**(3) MrCBonner (mid div: rdn ½-wy: nvr nrr)............3	5	33/1	57	5
3727[2]	**King Fly** (MrsSarahHorner-Harker) **7-10-7**(7) CMcCormack (in tch: ev ch tl rdn & wknd after 3 out) 18	6	20/1	43	—
	Thorntoun House (IRE) (JSGoldie) **4-10-7** DParker (in tch to 7th: sn bhd) 12	7	100/1	35	—
3066[P]	**Royal Spruce (IRE)** (GMMoore) **6-11-0** NBentley (mid div: rdn & wknd ½-wy)............1¼	8	100/1	32	—
3487[2]	**Tom's River (IRE)** (MrsMReveley) **5-10-11**(3) GLee (hdwy & in tch 4 out: sn wknd)............1¾	9	5/1	31	—
3355[P]	**Push On Polly (IRE)** (JParkes) **7-10-6**(3) ECallaghan (a rr) ....½	10	100/1	25	—
3802[6]	**Pot Blackbird (75)** (RLee) **8-10-9** OPears (n.d) 22	11	33/1	8	—
3644[P]	**Hadaway Lad** (HowardJohnson) **5-11-0** MMoloney (in tch to 6th) 4	12	100/1	10	—
	Another George (MissMKMilligan) **7-11-0** BStorey (lost tch 7th)............16	13	33/1	—	—
3795[13]	**Busy Boy (62)** (DALamb) **10-11-0** JBurke (a bhd)	14	66/1	—	—
2917[17]	**Itsahardlife (IRE)** (MDHammond) **6-11-0** DBentley (wl bhd fr 7th)............	15	100/1	—	—
	Pitsburgh (WMcKeown) **6-11-0** GCahill (sn t.o: p.u 6th)............	P	100/1	—	—
3483[14]	**Montein** (SJLeadbetter) **6-11-0b**[1] NLeach (led tl after 5th: wkn qckly & p.u bef 7th)	P	250/1	—	—
			(SP 127.0%)	**17 Rn**	

5m 7.3 (16.30) CSF £13.53 TOTE £3.40: £1.60 £2.70 £2.00 (£6.00) OWNER L G M Racing (MIDDLEHAM) BRED P. E. Atkinson
WEIGHT FOR AGE 4yo-9lb
3483* Ardrina enjoys dominating in the thick of things. She is on the upgrade and will make a decent mare over fences next season. This ground would be fast enough for her. (2/1)
3100* Meadow Hymn (IRE), with a couple of penalties here, was just outpointed by an above average winner. (6/1: op 4/1)
3644* Magpie Melody (IRE) again had every chance swinging for home, was outspeeded more than anything and more cut would be to his liking. (9/2)
3483 Into the West (IRE) looked a touch one-paced and maybe a longer trip would be to his liking. (100/30)
3487 Tom's River (IRE) (5/1: 8/1-9/2)

3911 JOHN DIXON H'CAP CHASE (0-105) (5-Y.O+) (Class F)

3-50 (3-54) **3m (18 fncs)** £3,355.00 (£1,015.00: £495.00: £235.00) GOING: 0.20 sec per fur (G)

			SP	RR	SF
3695[U]	**Nijway (77)** (MABarnes) **7-10-0** BStorey (hld up: hdwy ½-wy: led 3 out: styd on gamely)............—	1	20/1	91	—
3710[5]	**Gale Ahead (IRE) (95)** (GMMoore) **7-11-4** MFoster (hld up in tch: mstke 4 out: ev ch appr last: styd on).......2½	2	6/1[3]	107	—
3751[3]	**Reapers Rock (81)** (MrsSJSmith) **10-9-13**(5) GFRyan (cl up: led 6th to 11th: led 13th to 3 out: one pce)........14	3	11/2[2]	84	—
3886[6]	**Solba (USA) (101)** (CParker) **8-11-10b** DParker (hld up & bhd: jnd ldrs ½-wy: led 11th to 13th: btn whn blnd 3 out) 15	4	14/1	94	—
3824[P]	**More Joy (77)** (BEllison) **9-9-7**(7) CMcCormack (in tch: ev ch appr 4 out: sn wknd)............15	5	50/1	60	—
3643[4]	**Heavenly Citizen (IRE) (91)** (JLGledson) **9-11-0** KJohnson (led to 3rd: lost pl 9th: sn t.o)............15	6	11/1	64	—
3884[2]	**Northern Squire (105)** (JMJefferson) **9-11-11**(3) ECallaghan (prom: lost pl 9th: sn bhd: p.u bef 4 out)............	P	2/1[1]	—	—
3792[3]	**Tighter Budget (USA) (99)** (MrsDianneSayer) **10-11-8** MMoloney (cl up: led 3rd to 6th: wknd 12th: p.u bef next)	P	7/1	—	—
3643*	**Hudson Bay Trader (USA) (90)** (PBeaumont) **10-10-8**(5) BGrattan (a wl bhd: t.o & p.u bef 4 out)............	P	6/1[3]	—	—
3560[3]	**Farney Glen (88)** (JJO'Neill) **10-10-11** GCahill (bhd whn uns rdr 9th)............	U	6/1[3]	—	—
			(SP 125.8%)	**10 Rn**	

6m 21.6 (29.60) CSF £133.18 CT £707.40 TOTE £13.00: £2.60 £1.70 £2.60 (£39.50) OWNER Mr T. A. Barnes (PENRITH) BRED Bacton Stud

LONG HANDICAP Nijway 9-11 More Joy 9-9
OFFICIAL EXPLANATION Hudson Bay Trader (USA): missed the break and sulked thereafter.
3608* Nijway, who has never scored at this trip, jumped a lot better than he has been in the past and, although he finished a shade tired, he stuck on bravely. (20/1)
3710 Gale Ahead (IRE) shows signs of inconsistency but did little wrong here, although he pecked when making his challenge at the fourth-last and he was sprawled over the last and fairly leg-weary on the run-in. (6/1)
3751 Reapers Rock, who was miles out of the handicap when running last time, ran another good race here and he's shaping as though a slight drop in class will do him good. (11/2)
3884 Northern Squire, very much a course specialist here where he has gained six of his eight career wins, reappeared after finishing runner up just forty-eight hours earlier. He never seemed to be happy and another course win was always a remote possibility. He is always feared round here but perhaps he needs freshening up slightly. (2/1)

3912 BARCLAYS PREMIER BANKING H'CAP HURDLE (0-115) (4-Y.O+) (Class E)

4-20 (4-23) **2m 1f (9 hdls)** £2,213.00 (£618.00: £299.00) GOING: 0.20 sec per fur (G)

				SP	RR	SF
3791*	**Monnaie Forte (IRE) (99)** (JRAdam) **7-11-10** BStorey (mde virtually all: rdn & kpt on wl flat)	—	**1**	11/4[2]	79	2
1577[8]	**Well Appointed (IRE) (94)** (BMactaggart) **8-11-2**(3) GLee (in tch: hdwy ½-wy: ev ch last: styd on)	4	**2**	10/1	70	—
3827[5]	**Danbys Gorse (96)** (JMJefferson) **5-11-4**(3) ECallaghan (hld up & bhd: hdwy 3 out: ev ch last: no ex)	hd	**3**	9/1	72	—
3641[3]	**Peggy Gordon (75)** (MrsDThomson) **6-9-7**(7) NHorrocks (prom tl lost pl 5th: rallied & ev ch 3 out: wknd next)	19	**4**	7/1	33	—
3416[2]	**Secret Service (IRE) (98)** (CWThornton) **5-11-9** MFoster (prom tl wknd appr 2 out)	12	**5**	9/4[1]	45	—
3313*	**Latin Leader (89)** (CParker) **7-11-0b** DParker (in tch tl rdn & outpcd 2 out)	5	**6**	12/1	31	—
3711[8]	**In a Moment (USA) (75)** (CGrant) **6-10-0** GCahill (lost pl 3rd: n.d after)	29	**7**	16/1	—	—
3634[F]	**Double Agent (102)** (HowardJohnson) **4-11-5** MMoloney (cl up tl rdn & wknd qckly)	1	**8**	3/1[3]	16	—

(SP 127.6%) **8 Rn**

4m 20.8 (19.80) CSF £30.29 CT £213.51 TOTE £5.10: £1.70 £2.10 £1.20 (£17.00) OWNER Mr James Adam (GORDON) BRED E. Stuart Knape
LONG HANDICAP Peggy Gordon 9-12 In a Moment (USA) 9-10
WEIGHT FOR AGE 4yo-8lb
3791* Monnaie Forte (IRE) had his confidence restored since returning to hurdles after some crashing consecutive falls over fences. He thoroughly enjoyed himself at the head of affairs here and he could now be stepped up in class. Who would bet against him making it three in a row. (11/4)
1314 Well Appointed (IRE) ran his best race for some time although he just had to be second best on this occasion. (10/1)
3827 Danbys Gorse was confidently ridden. He is almost exclusively raced on an easy surface and perhaps found things a bit quick for him. (9/1)
3416 Secret Service (IRE), who was probably running over his shortest trip, is worth a try over further again. (9/4)

3913 JOHN MCKIE MAIDEN HUNTERS' CHASE (5-Y.O+) (Class H)

4-50 (4-51) **3m 2f (19 fncs)** £1,272.00 (£381.00: £183.00: £84.00) GOING: 0.20 sec per fur (G)

				SP	RR	SF
3397[P]	**Buck's Delight (IRE)** (MrsRichardArthur) **9-12-0**(7) MrMBradburne (a.p: led 4 out: hld on wl flat)	—	**1**	33/1	101	1
3357[2]	**Ask Antony (IRE)** (TDWalford) **7-12-2**(5) MrRFord (led 5th to 4 out: rallied flat: styd on wl)	½	**2**	4/5[1]	101	1
3476[3]	**Admission (IRE)** (MrsSarahHorner-Harker) **7-12-0**(7) MissLHorner (sn in tch: hdwy 14th: one pce fr 3 out)	14	**3**	8/1[3]	92	—
	Roly Prior (MrsAHamilton) **8-11-9**(5) MrsVJackson (bhd: hdwy 14th: styd on same pce fr 2 out)	8	**4**	9/2[2]	80	—
	All Or Nothing (NMLEwart) **9-11-2**(7) MrJEwart (bhd: styd on fr 2 out: n.d)	1½	**5**	50/1	74	—
3713[2]	**General Delight** (MrsARWood) **10-12-0**(7) MrDWood (in tch: outpcd 14th: n.d after)	13	**6**	10/1	78	—
3824[2]	**Just For Me (IRE)** (JAMoore) **8-12-2**(5) MrMHNaughton (prom: wknd 14th)	29	**7**	20/1	60	—
	Rushing Burn (MrsGESnowden) **11-11-9**(7) MissNCSnowden (prom: rdn 13th: wknd next)		**8**	33/1	—	—
	Madame Beck (MichaelSmith) **8-11-10**(7)ow1 MrRMSmith (hdwy & in tch 12th: wknd 4 out: p.u bef last)		**P**	33/1	—	—
	Eostre (KAnderson) **8-12-0** MrPCraggs (led to 5th: lost pl after 11th: bhd whn p.u bef 4 out)		**P**	11/1	—	—
3533[3]	**Frozen Stiff (IRE)** (AJBrown) **9-12-2**(5) MrRShiels (a bhd: p.u bef 5 out)		**P**	10/1	—	—
	Solwaysands (KLittle) **7-11-7**(7) MrBGibson (bhd fr 13th: p.u bef 4 out)		**P**	33/1	—	—
	Green Sheen (IRE) (ErnieFenwick) **9-12-0**(7) MrChrisWilson (prom: wknd 14th: p.u bef 3 out)		**P**	10/1	—	—
3476[P]	**Sir Harry Rinus** (FPMurtagh) **11-12-0**(7) MissFBarnes (in tch: wknd 14th: p.u bef 3 out)		**P**	50/1	—	—

(SP 140.9%) **14 Rn**

7m 4.1 (36.10) CSF £64.51 TOTE £50.10: £13.50 £1.40 £3.60 (£28.30) OWNER Mrs Richard Arthur (HALLINGTON) BRED M. O'Sullivan
Buck's Delight (IRE) made a lot of the running here, jumped well enough, and seems brave when it comes down to a battling finish. (33/1)
3357 Ask Antony (IRE) was up forcing the pace and, judging by his tenacity here, looks sure to win in similar company. (4/5)
3476 Admission (IRE) cast a fair amount of money when changing hands at Doncaster in January. He seems to be gradually getting the hang of things and is shaping up reasonably well. (8/1: op 9/2)
Roly Prior is another who was doing his best work at the finish and who would prefer more cut underfoot. (9/2: 5/2-5/1)
All Or Nothing, a winning pointer, was just getting going when the race was ending. (50/1)
3533 Frozen Stiff (IRE) (10/1: 8/1-12/1)

3914 FINALE INTERMEDIATE N.H. FLAT RACE (4, 5 & 6-Y.O) (Class H)

5-20 (5-24) **2m 1f** £1,035.00 (£285.00: £135.00)

				SP	RR	SF
	Brother of Iris (IRE) (MrsMReveley) **4-10-9**(3) GLee (trckd ldrs: shkn up to ld 1f out: r.o strly)	—	**1**	9/4[1]	65 f	—
	What A Fiddler (IRE) (TPTate) **4-10-5**(7) LCooper (in tch: ev ch 3f out: kpt on fnl f: no ch w wnr)	5	**2**	33/1	60 f	—
3716[6]	**Kit Smartie (IRE)** (DMForster) **5-11-6**ow2 MrRFord (hdwy to ld ½-wy: hdd 1f out)	4	**3**	14/1	57 f	—
2904[4]	**Roman Outlaw** (MDHammond) **5-11-1**(3) MrCBonner (a.p: rdn & no ex fnl f)	2½	**4**	8/1	52 f	—
	China King (IRE) (JGFitzGerald) **6-11-4**(7) MrMBradburne (chsd ldrs: rdn & no ex fnl 2f)	1¾	**5**	4/1[3]	58 f	—
	Ben Doula (MrsMReveley) **5-10-13**(5) MrMHNaughton (hld up: hdwy 5f out: no imp)	3½	**6**	25/1	47 f	—
3716[5]	**Salmon Cellar (IRE)** (JMJefferson) **4-10-9**(3) ECallaghan (led to ½-wy: wknd over 2f out)	13	**7**	5/2[2]	37 f	—
3487[4]	**Cool Kevin** (MrsMAKendall) **4-10-5**(7) IJardine (chsd ldrs to ½-wy)	20	**8**	33/1	18 f	—
3142[12]	**Hollow Palm (IRE)** (LLungo) **6-10-11**(7) WDowling (a in rr)	¾	**9**	50/1	16 f	—
	Mill-Dot (FPMurtagh) **5-10-11**(7) CMcCormack (hld up: hdwy ½-wy: wknd 3f out)	10	**10**	33/1	6 f	—
	Floss The Boss (MrsJBrown) **4-10-0**(7) NHannity (a bhd)	2½	**11**	33/1	1 f	—
3297[6]	**Political Power** (WJenks) **6-11-4** MrAMitchell (prom tl wknd over 4f out)	3	**12**	20/1	1 f	—
3170[14]	**Paypnutsgetmonkeys (IRE)** (CASmith) **4-10-7** MrsDSmith (chsd ldrs tl wknd 6f out)	5	**13**	50/1	—	—

Form	Horse (Trainer) Age-Wt Jockey (Comment)	Dist	Pos	SP	RR	SF
2904^{9}	**Our Carol (IRE)** (JParkes) **5-10-6**(7) TSiddall (mid div tl wknd ½-wy)	7	**14**	66/1	—	—
3808^{5}	**Mazzelmo** (ABailey) **4-10-0**(7) SMelrose (in tch: rdn ½-wy: wknd 6f out)		**15**	9/1	—	—
3828^{8}	**Mademist Sam** (PBeaumont) **5-10-13**(5) BGrattan (hdwy ½-wy: sn wknd)		**16**	12/1	—	—
	Graceland (FMurphy) **5-10-6**(7) NHorrocks (wl bhd fr ½-wy)		**17**	25/1	—	—
3716^{8}	**Runhim** (JKMOliver) **5-10-11**(7) SHaworth (a in rr)		**18**	100/1	—	—
	Elliott The Butler (MrsSJSmith) **5-10-13**(5) GFRyan (in tch to ½-wy)		**19**	50/1	—	—
	Rag Doll (HowardJohnson) **5-10-8**(5) STaylor (w ldr: lost pl ½-wy: sn wl bhd)		**20**	16/1	—	—
				(SP 153.3%)	**20 Rn**	

4m 12.4 CSF £94.90 TOTE £4.80: £3.00 £7.30 £2.90 (£160.20) OWNER M H G Systems Ltd (SALTBURN) BRED J. Perrot
WEIGHT FOR AGE 4yo-8lb
OFFICIAL EXPLANATION **Mademist Sam: the trainer reported that the gelding had gurgled.**
Brother of Iris (IRE) was given a fine ride and was obviously showing plenty at home judging by his support in the market. He is a half-brother to a miler in France and, judging by this eye-catching introduction, looks the sort whose future will eventually be over obstacles. (9/4: 5/4-5/2)
What A Fiddler (IRE) was far from disgraced against what will probably end up to be an above average winner, and he too could be capable of picking up something along these lines. (33/1)
3716 Kit Smartie (IRE) is gradually coming to hand. He battled on well at the head of affairs but had no answer when the first two swept past. (14/1)
Ben Doula, a well-bred sort related to winners both on the Flat and over hurdles, is a stablemate of the winner. He had a nice introduction when coming from quite a bit off the pace and this will no doubt bring him on somewhat. (25/1)
Mademist Sam (12/1: op 7/1)

T/Plpt: £71.60 (66.5 Tckts). T/Qdpt: £24.80 (5.89 Tckts) GB

3562-CHEPSTOW (L-H) (Good, Good to firm patches)
Monday March 31st
WEATHER: Fine, sunny

3915 SPRINGTIME CLAIMING HURDLE (4-Y.O+) (Class F)
2-00 (2-00) **2m 4f 110y (11 hdls)** £2,094.00 (£584.00: £282.00) GOING minus 0.39 sec per fur (GF)

Form	Horse (Trainer) Age-Wt Jockey (Comment)	Dist	Pos	SP	RR	SF
2666^{8}	**Out Ranking (FR) (117)** (MCPipe) **5-11-9** JamieEvans (j.rt: mde all: qcknd 8th: easily)	—	**1**	15/8 1	89	48
827*	**Holy Joe (102)** (DBurchell) **15-11-0** DJBurchell (a.p: one pce fr 3 out)	3	**2**	15/2	78	37
3681*	**Kadari (96)** (WClay) **8-10-13v** JOsborne (a.p: hrd rdn 8th: one pce)	½	**3**	6/1	76	35
3704*	**Cutthroat Kid (IRE) (108)** (MrsMReveley) **7-11-6v** MAFitzgerald (lw: hld up: hrd rdn 8th: one pce)	4	**4**	100/30 2	80	39
3589*	**Fontanays (IRE) (97)** (GMMcCourt) **9-11-1v**(3) DFortt (prom tl wknd 3 out)	9	**5**	11/2 3	71	30
3471^{10}	**Ramsdens (IRE) (95)** (NATwiston-Davies) **5-11-6** CLlewellyn (lw: hdwy 5th: mstke 7th: wknd 8th)	7	**6**	10/1	68	27
	Father O'Brien (97) (JCPoulton) **10-11-8** ADicken (swtg: in tch to 6th: t.o)	dist	**7**	33/1	—	—
3471^{4}	**Laughing Buccaneer (73)** (DNCarey) **4-10-12** BPowell (lw: t.o whn p.u bef 8th: lame)		**P**	25/1	—	—
3429^{12}	**Erlking (IRE) (80)** (SMellor) **7-11-4v** NMann (t.o whn p.u bef 8th)		**P**	33/1	—	—
3632^{7}	**Tilt Tech Flyer (73)** (IRJones) **12-10-7**(7) JPrior (t.o whn p.u after 7th)		**P**	50/1	—	—
				(SP 120.1%)	**10 Rn**	

4m 45.1 (-1.90) CSF £15.46 TOTE £3.10: £1.30 £1.80 £1.40 (£12.60) OWNER Knight Hawks Partnership (WELLINGTON) BRED Jacques Beres
WEIGHT FOR AGE 4yo-9lb
Out Ranking (FR) clmd DLewis £10,000
2666 Out Ranking (FR), again showing a tendency to jump right-handed especially early on, was value for ten lengths at least. (15/8)
827* Holy Joe came back from his winter break with a fine effort but was flattered by the winning margin. (15/2)
3681* Kadari would have been receiving 11lb more from the winner in a handicap. (6/1: 15/1-13/2)
3704* Cutthroat Kid (IRE) did not find much when coming off the bridle entering the home straight. (100/30)

3916 FULKE WALWYN H'CAP CHASE (0-135) (5-Y.O+) (Class C)
2-30 (2-31) **3m (18 fncs)** £4,783.00 (£1,444.00: £702.00: £331.00) GOING: 0.02 sec per fur (G)

Form	Horse (Trainer) Age-Wt Jockey (Comment)	Dist	Pos	SP	RR	SF
2894^{2}	**Seod Rioga (IRE) (110)** (SMellor) **8-10-6** NMann (hld up: led 2 out: rdn out)	—	**1**	3/1 1	119	35
1799*	**Harwell Lad (IRE) (125)** (RHAlner) **8-11-7** MrRNuttall (led to 2nd: led 4th to 2 out: unable qckn flat)	6	**2**	7/2 2	130	46
3039^{F}	**Old Bridge (IRE) (130)** (OSherwood) **9-11-12** JOsborne (a.p: ev ch 3 out: eased whn btn appr last)	26	**3**	3/1 1	118	34
3763*	**Fools Errand (IRE) (115)** (GBBalding) **7-10-11v** MAFitzgerald (blnd 1st: chsd ldr 8th to 11th: wknd 14th: no ch whn blnd 2 out)	3½	**4**	3/1 1	100	16
3598^{11}	**Bavard Dieu (IRE) (132)** (NAGaselee) **9-12-0b1** CLlewellyn (lw: led 2nd to 4th: j.slowly & lost pl 9th: rallied 14th: sn wknd)	2	**5**	13/2 3	116	32
3697^{6}	**Miss Diskin (IRE) (104)** (RHBuckler) **8-10-0** BPowell (in rr whn p.u bef 8th)		**P**	14/1	—	—
				(SP 117.2%)	**6 Rn**	

6m (7.00) CSF £13.54 TOTE £4.20: £1.70 £2.10 (£8.20) OWNER Mr S. P. Tindall (SWINDON) BRED Miss Siobhan Cashman
LONG HANDICAP Miss Diskin (IRE) 9-7
OFFICIAL EXPLANATION **Miss Diskin (IRE): the jockey reported she did not like the ground.**
2894 Seod Rioga (IRE), second in this race last year, won convincingly this time and looks the sort to do well over the next couple of months. (3/1)
1799* Harwell Lad (IRE) was on his best behaviour but simply met one too good. (7/2)
3039 Old Bridge (IRE) has had a disastrous season and has changed stables but he seems out of sorts and did not appear to be moving with great fluency on the run-in. (3/1)
3763* Fools Errand (IRE) found this more competitive than last time . (3/1)
1277 Bavard Dieu (IRE) has not looked very interested in his last few races. (13/2)
3697 Miss Diskin (IRE) was reported not to have liked the ground. (14/1)

3917 WELSH CHAMPION HURDLE (4-Y.O+) (Class B)
3-00 (3-02) **2m 110y (8 hdls)** £6,947.00 (£2,096.00: £1,018.00: £479.00) GOING minus 0.39 sec per fur (GF)

Form	Horse (Trainer) Age-Wt Jockey (Comment)	Dist	Pos	SP	RR	SF
3562*	**Potentate (USA) (135)** (MCPipe) **6-11-6** JamieEvans (mde all: rdn 5th: r.o wl)	—	**1**	100/30 3	110	42
3613^{3}	**Daraydan (IRE) (128)** (MCPipe) **5-11-6** MAFitzgerald (a.p: rdn appr 5th: no imp)	3½	**2**	9/4 2	107	39

3597[10] **Mistinguett (IRE) (146)** (NATwiston-Davies) **5-11-9** CLlewellyn (rdn & lost pl 4th: styd on fr 2 out)................1¼ **3** 11/8[1] 108 40
3007[3] **Noble Lord** (RHBuckler) **4-11-0** BPowell (lw: bhd fr 3 out)................15 **4** 10/1 93 17
Castle Secret (127) (DBurchell) **11-11-6** DJBurchell (a wl bhd: sme late hdwy)................1¼ **5** 20/1 90 22
(SP 109.8%) **5 Rn**

3m 48.2 (-0.80) CSF £10.32 TOTE £3.30: £1.50 £1.90 (£3.40) OWNER Mr Jim Weeden (WELLINGTON) BRED Stelcar Stables Incorporated
WEIGHT FOR AGE 4yo-8lb
3562* Potentate (USA), a relatively fresh horse, had no problems handling the fastish ground. His six wins have all been at Chepstow. (100/30)
3613 Daraydan (IRE), dropping back in trip, completed a one-two for Pipe but was beaten on merit by his stable companion. (9/4: op 6/4)
3293 Mistinguett (IRE) ran as if a longer trip would suit. (11/8)
3007 Noble Lord is useful but found himself a bit out of his depth here when the tempo increased. (10/1)
Castle Secret, off the track for ten months and a remote last for most of the race, finished much closer than ever seemed likely. (20/1)

3918 CASTLE NOVICES' HURDLE (4-Y.O+) (Class E)
3-30 (3-34) **2m 110y (8 hdls)** £2,654.00 (£744.00: £362.00) GOING minus 0.39 sec per fur (GF)

SP RR SF
3820[U] **Zander** (NATwiston-Davies) **5-11-0** CLlewellyn (a.p: hrd rdn flat: led nr fin)................— **1** 9/4[2] 69 18
2865[6] **Major Dundee (IRE)** (MCPipe) **4-10-7** JamieEvans (led: clr 5th: hrd rdn & hung lft flat: hdd nr fin)................1¼ **2** 9/4[2] 69 10
3109[6] **Rumpelstiltskin** (HSHowe) **5-10-11**(3) DFortt (lw: hdwy 5th: 3rd & wkng whn mstke 2 out)................13 **3** 25/1[3] 55 4
3342[U] **Aqua Amber** (JMBradley) **5-10-7**(7) JPower (prom to 3rd)................15 **4** 40/1 41 —
3275[9] **Smart Remark** (THind) **5-11-0** PMcLoughlin (bhd fr 4th)................2½ **5** 33/1 38 —
3404[P] **Baron Hrabovsky** (GThorner) **4-10-7b** BPowell (hdwy 3rd: wknd 5th)................23 **6** 66/1 17 —
Forest Rose (MSheppard) **7-10-2**(7) MMoran (mstke 3rd: t.o fr 4th: blnd last)................dist **7** 66/1 — —
3583[P] **Kerrier (IRE)** (HJManners) **5-10-7**(7) ADowling (lw: prom tl blnd 2nd: t.o whn p.u bef 5th)................ **P** 66/1 — —
3569[4] **Donnington (IRE) (110)** (OSherwood) **7-11-5** JOsborne (lw: prom tl p.u appr 4th)................ **P** 6/4[1] — —
(SP 115.2%) **9 Rn**

3m 52.3 (3.30) CSF £6.91 TOTE £3.10: £1.10 £1.20 £2.10 (£4.50) OWNER Mrs Karen Duggan (CHELTENHAM) BRED G. Burton
WEIGHT FOR AGE 4yo-8lb
OFFICIAL EXPLANATION **Donnington(IRE): the trainer stated that he considered withdrawing the horse before the race because of the fast ground but decided to run. He instructed the jockey that if he did not like the ground he should pull up. The Jockey confirmed these instructions and added that the gelding was not jumping well on this ground and he therefore thought it prudent to pull up.**
3820 Zander got his reward for some good efforts, knuckling down gamely and taking advantage when the runner-up drifted left on the run-in. (9/4)
2865 Major Dundee (IRE) threw it away by hanging badly but, with the running rail to help him, he would be capable of picking up a race. (9/4)
Rumpelstiltskin ran with credit but the first two outclassed him over the last couple of flights. (25/1)
3569 Donnington (IRE), whose trainer had instructed Osborne to pull up if the horse did not like the ground, duly defected from the race around halfway when lying third. Punters must have been tempted to ask for their money back. (6/4: op evens)

3919 EASTER BONNET H'CAP CHASE (0-120) (5-Y.O+) (Class D)
4-00 (4-05) **2m 3f 110y (16 fncs)** £3,670.00 (£1,105.00: £535.00: £250.00) GOING: 0.02 sec per fur (G)

SP RR SF
3401[4] **James the First (117)** (PFNicholls) **9-12-0** MAFitzgerald (lw: hld up: led 11th: easily)................— **1** 4/1[3] 121 39
2949[P] **Pharsilk (IRE) (104)** (THind) **8-11-1** PMcLoughlin (led 4th to 9th: led 10th tl blnd 11th: one pce fr 13th)................5 **2** 10/1 104 22
3762* **Malwood Castle (IRE) (89)** (RHAlner) **7-10-0** NMann (lw: wl bhd to 12th: mstke 13th: nvr nrr)................16 **3** 5/4[1] 76 —
3198[P] **Distinctive (IRE) (109)** (MJWilkinson) **8-11-6** CLlewellyn (led to 4th: led 9th to 10th: wknd appr 12th)................22 **4** 9/4[2] 78 —
3456[F] **Glen Mirage (89)** (RHBuckler) **12-10-0** BPowell (j.slowly: a bhd: rdn 5th: t.o)................1¼ **5** 14/1 57 —
(SP 111.0%) **5 Rn**

4m 59.2 (10.20) CSF £30.70 TOTE £4.20: £1.60 £2.70 (£15.30) OWNER Mr B. L. Blinman (SHEPTON MALLET) BRED Stetchworth Park Stud Ltd
LONG HANDICAP Glen Mirage 9-7
OFFICIAL EXPLANATION **Malwood Castle (IRE): the jockey reported he was never going well on the fast ground.**
1949* James the First could not be faulted on this occasion, jumping with admirable precision and never threatening to stop as he has done in the past. (4/1)
2949 Pharsilk (IRE), the only one to give the winner a race, had some reasonable form in Ireland and is not without hope. (10/1: 6/1-12/1)
3762* Malwood Castle (IRE), whose supporters had no run at all for their money, ambled round very slowly until making some late headway and was reported to have never been going well on the fastish ground. (5/4)
3198 Distinctive (IRE) has run poorly since being raised 6lb by the Handicapper but the new mark does not fully explain his current lack of sparkle. On this occasion he probably went off too fast over the first few fences. (9/4)
3132 Glen Mirage (14/1: op 7/2)

3920 EASTER SURPRISE H'CAP HURDLE (0-125) (4-Y.O+) (Class D)
4-30 (4-34) **2m 4f 110y (11 hdls)** £3,160.00 (£885.00: £430.00) GOING minus 0.39 sec per fur (GF)

SP RR SF
3807[F] **Cassio's Boy (95)** (RJEckley) **6-10-1**ow1 NMann (hdwy 7th: led appr 2 out: rdn out)................— **1** 20/1 78 36
3430[4] **Reaganesque (USA) (114)** (PGMurphy) **5-11-6** MAFitzgerald (lw: a.p: ev ch fr 8th: unable qckn flat)................1¾ **2** 11/2[3] 96 55
3570* **Jovie King (IRE) (94)** (RHBuckler) **5-10-0** BPowell (lw: led to 3rd: led 5th tl after 3 out: 3rd & btn whn mstke 2 out)................11 **3** 5/1[2] 67 26
3615[19] **Lying Eyes (118)** (WGMTurner) **6-11-3**(7) JPower (hdwy 8th: one pce fr 3 out)................2½ **4** 8/1 89 48
3850[5] **Keep Me in Mind (IRE) (108)** (NRMitchell) **8-11-0** MrRNuttall (hld up: hdwy 8th: rdn 2 out: one pce)................1½ **5** 10/1 78 37
Henry Cone (109) (MissVenetiaWilliams) **8-11-1** DJBurchell (hdwy 7th: wknd 8th)................15 **6** 14/1 67 26
Propaganda (94) (PRWebber) **9-10-0** PMcLoughlin (bit bkwd: prom tl mstke 6th: t.o)................dist **7** 25/1 — —
3681[2] **Swing Quartet (IRE) (99)** (NATwiston-Davies) **7-10-5** CLlewellyn (rdn 5th: bhd fr 6th: t.o)................ **8** 9/2[1] — —
3640[13] **Slew Man (FR) (112)** (MCPipe) **6-11-4b** JamieEvans (prom to 6th: t.o)................ **9** 11/2[3] — —
3562[5] **Call My Guest (IRE) (107)** (REPeacock) **7-10-6**(7) MMoran (a.p: 5th whn fell 8th)................ **F** 20/1 — —
3342[3] **Atavistic (IRE) (96)** (CLPopham) **5-9-9**(7) TO'Connor (prom to 7th: wkng whn fell 8th)................ **F** 6/1 — —
3615[22] **Fatack (115)** (PRWebber) **8-11-7** JOsborne (led 3rd to 5th: wknd 7th: bhd whn p.u bef 8th)................ **P** 6/1 — —
(SP 134.4%) **12 Rn**

4m 42.8 (-4.20) CSF £128.30 CT £609.15 TOTE £31.70: £4.90 £2.50 £3.10 (£154.70) OWNER Lyonshall Racing (KINGTON) BRED Mrs E. C. Carberry

LONG HANDICAP Propaganda 9-13 Cassio's Boy 9-11
3630 Cassio's Boy had only ever previously won on ground with cut in it but he looked well at home here and was always travelling like a winner. (20/1)
3430 Reaganesque (USA) should continue to run well particularly if the ground remains fast. (11/2: 4/1-6/1)
3570* Jovie King (IRE), trying a longer trip, attempted to dominate but did not quite get home. (5/1)
3150 Lying Eyes did not run badly and may be running back into form. (8/1: op 5/1)
3850 Keep Me in Mind (IRE), currently on a handy mark, gave the leaders quite a start. (10/1)
3562 Call My Guest (IRE), currently running off a lenient handicap mark, was still in contention when coming down. (20/1)

T/Plpt: £702.60 (9.85 Tckts). T/Qdpt: £81.70 (3.9 Tckts) LMc

3663-FAKENHAM (L-H) (Good)
Monday March 31st
WEATHER: sunny

3921 RAYNHAM (S) H'CAP HURDLE (0-90) (4-Y.O+) (Class G)
2-30 (2-30) **2m (9 hdls)** £3,071.00 (£938.00: £464.00: £227.00) GOING: 0.16 sec per fur (G)

		Dist	Pos	SP	RR	SF
3542^{6}	**Blotoft (67)** (SGollings) **5-11-2** DO'Sullivan (lw: cl up: led between last 2: drvn & all out)	—	1	16/1	52	5
3811*	**Ruth's Gamble (66)** (MrsLCJewell) **9-11-1v**ow1 MrASansome (lw: chsd ldrs: drvn along fr ½-wy: ev ch 2 out: r.o wl u.p flat)	nk	2	7/2 1	51	3
3663^{3}	**Arch Angel (IRE) (76)** (GFHCharles-Jones) **4-10-10**(7) XAizpuru (lw: bhd & pushed along: drvn & styd on fr 2 out: unable to chal)	5	3	7/2 1	56	1
2050^{10}	**Lebedinski (IRE) (74)** (MrsPSly) **4-11-1** VSmith (hdwy 6th: ev ch 2 out: rdn & no ex appr last)	1½	4	25/1	52	—
3757^{2}	**Scalp 'em (IRE) (59)** (DrPPritchard) **9-10-8** DrPPritchard (a chsng ldrs: no imp fr 2 out)	2½	5	6/1 3	35	—
1332^{2}	**Blurred Image (IRE) (65)** (JCPoulton) **6-11-0** LeesaLong (swtg: plld hrd in rr: wnt cl up 5th: wknd appr 2 out)	6	6	9/2 2	35	—
1861^{6}	**Alosaili (70)** (JCullinan) **10-11-5** MrACharles-Jones (led 3rd: hdd between last 2: sn wknd)	¾	7	20/1	39	—
	Wicklow Boy (IRE) (54) (MrsLCJewell) **6-10-3**ow1 WFry (bkwd: bhd: no ch fr 6th)	2½	8	33/1	20	—
3471^{U}	**Emerald Venture (66)** (FCoton) **10-11-1** CRae (sn lost tch: struggled rnd in rr)	½	9	20/1	32	—
3669^{5}	**Holkham Bay (65)** (LWordingham) **5-11-0** RRourke (a bhd)	19	10	12/1	12	—
3757^{9}	**Nishaman (60)** (THind) **6-10-2**(7) AGarrity (led to 3rd: chsd ldr to 6th: wknd rapidly: t.o)	10	11	50/1	—	—
3668^{7}	**Shedansar (IRE) (61)** (RCSpicer) **5-10-10v**1 MSharratt (prom to 5th: wknd rapidly: t.o)	2½	12	50/1	—	—
	Striffolino (65) (MissAEEmbiricos) **5-11-0** TKent (prom tl pushed along 5th: rr whn p.u 2 out)		P	14/1	—	—
3757^{3}	**Vanborough Lad (68)** (MJBolton) **8-11-3** MRichards (rr div: t.o & p.u last)		P	8/1	—	—
3674^{6}	**Zesti (75)** (TTClement) **5-11-3**(7) MrRWakley (hld up: hdwy 3 out: 5th & pressing ldrs whn uns rdr 2 out)		U	14/1	—	—
				(SP 135.2%)	**15 Rn**	

3m 59.5 (15.50) CSF £69.32 CT £236.00 TOTE £24.50: £5.30 £1.70 £1.50 (£40.60) OWNER Mr R. N. Forman (LOUTH) BRED R. N. Forman
WEIGHT FOR AGE 4yo-8lb
No bid
3542 Blotoft tends to pull very hard but was well settled this afternoon and found extra when tackled from the last. (16/1)
3811* Ruth's Gamble, bidding to win for the third time on the track, is a moody individual but put his best foot forward this afternoon. (7/2)
3663 Arch Angel (IRE) is only small. She was flat to the boards a long way out and, as on her previous appearance here, was doing all her best work at the finish. A longer trip would suit. (7/2)
501 Lebedinski (IRE) had every chance and may come on for this run which was her first for some while. (25/1)

3922 ROBERT HOARE MEMORIAL NOVICES' HUNTERS' CHASE (5-Y.O+) (Class H)
3-05 (3-05) **2m 5f 110y (16 fncs)** £2,388.50 (£728.00: £359.00: £174.50) GOING: 0.16 sec per fur (G)

		Dist	Pos	SP	RR	SF
3586^{6}	**Not My Line (IRE)** (AndyMorgan) **8-11-9**(5) MrWWales (lw: cl up: wnt 2nd 4 out: led after 2 out: drvn & hld on gamely cl home)	—	1	20/1	89	13
3713^{F}	**Up For Ransome (IRE)** (MrsAMNaughton) **8-11-7**(7) MrTJBarry (lw: hit 4th: wnt 2nd at 7th: led 12th tl after 2 out: rallied & ev ch flat)	½	2	11/4 2	89	13
3840^{P}	**Galzig** (MrsDEHTurner) **9-11-7**(7) MrWTellwright (mid div: effrt to chse ldng pair fr 4 out: no imp between last 2)	5	3	7/1	85	9
	Reverend Brown (IRE) (JMTurner) **7-11-9**(5) MrASansome (bhd & sn pushed along: nvr gng wl: no ch fr 4 out)	7	4	5/2 1	80	4
	Sperrin View (MrsHMobley) **11-11-2**(7) MrACharles-Jones (lw: nt fluent in rr: rdn 4 out: n.d after)	4	5	5/1	72	—
3721^{2}	**Tea Cee Kay** (COKing) **7-11-7**(7) MrRupertSweeting (dropped rr 7th: poor last 4 out)	20	6	4/1 3	62	—
	Scraptastic (MrsABell) **6-11-7**(7) MrNMBell (bit bkwd: nt fluent: led 3rd to 7th: last whn fell 10th)		F	20/1	—	—
	Cardinal Black (DJHarding-Jones) **11-11-7**(7) MrRWakley (led to 3rd: led 7th to 12th: lost pl qckly: p.u bef last)		P	8/1	—	—
	Sunset Run (MissCatherineTuke) **11-11-7b**1(7) MissCTuke (s.i.s: rel to r & hung rt: t.o & p.u 7th)		P	40/1	—	—
				(SP 127.5%)	**9 Rn**	

5m 37.6 (22.60) CSF £75.85 TOTE £14.90: £3.30 £1.80 £3.20 (£55.50) OWNER Mr P. C. Caudwell (ABINGDON) BRED J. A. Doherty
Not My Line (IRE) was winning for the first time in eighteen attempts under Rules and did not have very much to beat. (20/1)
3713 Up For Ransome (IRE), tongue-tied as usual, has run well in both English completions and deserves a win. He would probably appreciate some cut in the ground. (11/4)
3664 Galzig lacks consistency and proved onepaced in the final half-mile. (7/1: op 9/2)
Reverend Brown (IRE), a disappointing animal for Oliver Sherwood, declined to put his best foot forward and was never taking much interest in proceedings. (5/2)

3923 EVENT CATERERS H'CAP HURDLE (0-100) (4-Y.O+) (Class F)
3-40 (3-40) **2m 4f (11 hdls)** £3,755.00 (£1,145.00: £565.00: £275.00) GOING: 0.16 sec per fur (G)

		Dist	Pos	SP	RR	SF
3549*	**Sir Dante (IRE) (86)** (RRowe) **6-11-6** DO'Sullivan (lw: trckd clr ldr: hdwy to ld 2 out: a gng wl: readily)	—	1	9/4 1	70+	33
3663*	**Antiguan Flyer (78)** (GProdromou) **8-10-5v**(7) XAizpuru (led tl hdd 2 out: kpt on wl: no ch w wnr)	9	2	6/1	55	18
3672^{2}	**Fire on Ice (IRE) (90)** (MrsDHaine) **5-11-3**(7) MrRWakley (hld up mid div: wnt 3rd at 7th: rdn & one pce fr 2 out)	2½	3	5/1 3	65	28

				SP	RR	SF
3709*	**Cambo (USA) (85)** (MCBanks) **11-11-5** TKent (lw: rr div: rdn appr 2 out: no rspnse)	8	**4**	7/2[2]	53	16
3752[4]	**Apache Park (USA) (96)** (DBurchell) **4-11-7** CRae (lw: chsd ldrs tl pushed along fr 7th: sn outpcd: t.o appr 2 out)	21	**5**	6/1	48	2
3612[11]	**Bassenhally (84)** (MrsPSly) **7-11-4** VSmith (bhd fr 6th: t.o fr 3 out)	18	**6**	16/1	21	—
3499[4]	**Daring King (83)** (MJBolton) **7-11-3** MRichards (rel to r & drvn along: sn t.o: p.u 7th)		**P**	7/1	—	—
				(SP 116.6%)		**7 Rn**

4m 57.5 (12.50) CSF £15.28 TOTE £3.50: £2.10 £1.90 (£8.80) OWNER Mr Peter Wilby (PULBOROUGH) BRED Martin Molony
WEIGHT FOR AGE 4yo-9lb
OFFICIAL EXPLANATION Daring King: no explanation offered.
3549* Sir Dante (IRE) looked superb in the paddock. He is clearly suited by a sounder surface and made mincemeat of this opposition. (9/4)
3663* Antiguan Flyer, who had won a seller here last time, made another brave attempt to lead throughout but was no match for the winner. However he kept on well and could score again when dropped in grade. (6/1)
3672 Fire on Ice (IRE) was tongue-tied. He has been consistent but does not find much in the closing stages. (5/1)
3709* Cambo (USA) is not particularly consistent these days and rather got run off his feet on this tight circuit. (7/2)

3924 QUEENS CUP, AN EASTERN COUNTIES HUNTERS' CHASE (5-Y.O+) (Class H)

4-15 (4-15) **3m 110y (18 fncs)** £2,510.00 (£710.00: £350.00) GOING: 0.16 sec per fur (G)

				SP	RR	SF
	Dromin Leader (JMTurner) **12-11-7**(5) MrWWales (lw: led to 2nd: chsd ldr & gng easily tl lft in ld 15th: drvn out flat)	—	**1**	7/4[1]	95	—
	Cherry Chap (JIbbott) **12-11-5**(7) CaptDRParker (lw: hld up & bhd: hdwy & cl up 15th: chsd wnr & ev ch fr 2 out: rallied & kpt on wl cl home)	hd	**2**	20/1	95	—
957[8]	**Saint Bene't (IRE)** (GProdromou) **9-11-5b**(7) MrJGTownson (rr & rdn 5th: nvr gng wl after: mod hdwy fr 3 out)	10	**3**	8/1	88	—
	Romany Ark (MrsABell) **11-11-1**(7) MrNMBell (bhd: hdwy to 4th whn mstke 13th: wknd 15th)	1	**4**	4/1[2]	84	—
3135[4]	**Just Jack** (PJonason) **11-11-5**(7) MrNBloom (chsd ldrs tl outpcd fr 15th)	10	**5**	6/1	81	—
	Lyme Gold (IRE) (JMTurner) **8-11-5**(7) MrDKeane (nt fluent: mstke 9th: ev ch 13th: rdn & no rspnse after next: t.o whn p.u last)		**P**	9/2[3]	—	—
	Tammy's Friend (MrsGMHay) **10-11-5b**(7) MrJFerguson (lw: plld hrd: led 2nd: blnd 6th: uns rdr 15th)		**U**	7/1	—	—
				(SP 117.2%)		**7 Rn**

6m 34.1 (31.10) CSF £30.42 TOTE £3.30: £1.80 £4.40 (£19.80) OWNER Mr J. M. Turner (BURY ST EDMUNDS)
Dromin Leader was recording his second course and distance success but he had to pull out all the stops to hold off the runner-up. (7/4)
Cherry Chap barely gets the trip and was dropped out at the back of the field. He had every chance from the second last and tried bravely to catch the winner on the flat. (20/1)
Saint Bene't (IRE) was being scrubbed along in the early stages and never looked like taking a hand in proceedings. (8/1)
Romany Ark would probably be better on slightly softer ground. (4/1)

3925 BETTY AND HERBERT CASSELL MEMORIAL H'CAP CHASE (0-100) (5-Y.O+) (Class F)

4-50 (4-50) **2m 5f 110y (16 fncs)** £4,712.00 (£1,436.00: £708.00: £344.00) GOING: 0.16 sec per fur (G)

				SP	RR	SF
3622[2]	**Tim Soldier (FR) (91)** (MissAStokell) **10-11-3**(7) MrRWakley (bhd: hdwy & trckd ldrs 12th: styd on wl fr 3 out to ld last: rdn clr)	—	**1**	2/1[1]	101	20
3665[3]	**Whippers Delight (IRE) (90)** (GFHCharles-Jones) **9-11-2**(7) XAizpuru (lw: led & disp ld to 5th: prom & led again 3 out: hdd last: drvn & nt qckn flat)	2	**2**	3/1[2]	99	18
1300[4]	**Call Me Albi (IRE) (78)** (MrsLRichards) **6-10-11** MRichards (lw: hld up: hdwy 12th: led next: hdd 3 out: ev ch last: no ex)	nk	**3**	6/1	86	5
3444[P]	**Rio Haina (95)** (GFJohnsonHoughton) **12-12-0v** TKent (bit bkwd: chsd ldrs: pushed along 9th: rallied & cl up 13th: sn outpcd)	18	**4**	25/1	90	9
3844[3]	**Prinzal (92)** (GMMcCourt) **10-11-11** VSmith (lw: mstkes: plld hrd: a.p: led 5th: clr 9th: hdd appr 4 out: t.o whn p.u bef 2 out)		**P**	7/2[3]	—	—
3633[P]	**Bottle Black (81)** (THind) **10-11-0** CRae (bit bkwd: a last: hit 1st: mstkes 5th & 6th: t.o whn p.u 7th)		**P**	25/1	—	—
3836[F]	**Key Player (IRE) (77)** (RRowe) **8-10-10** DO'Sullivan (lw: chsd ldr fr 7th tl p.u after 11th: lame)		**P**	7/2[3]	—	—
				(SP 124.8%)		**7 Rn**

5m 34.1 (19.10) CSF £9.11 CT £28.65 TOTE £2.80: £1.50 £1.70 (£2.80) OWNER Mr Ken Dale (CLAVERDON) BRED Bernard Geffroy
3622 Tim Soldier (FR), a first winner since Ann Stokell took over the licence from Melvin Barraclough, put up a brave performance and found plenty after being sent to the front at the last. (2/1)
3665 Whippers Delight (IRE) is always a hard horse to catch right but this was one of his better efforts. (3/1)
1300 Call Me Albi (IRE) looked well despite a long lay-off and still had every chance at the last. This was a weak race however and he is always hard to win with. (6/1)
3844 Prinzal gave his rider plenty of frights with some appalling jumping and it was a miracle he got as far as he did. (7/2)

3926 ST JOHN AMBULANCE NOVICES' H'CAP HURDLE (0-100) (4-Y.O+) (Class E)

5-25 (5-25) **2m (9 hdls)** £2,885.00 (£860.00: £410.00: £185.00) GOING: 0.16 sec per fur (G)

				SP	RR	SF
3594[2]	**Geisway (CAN) (81)** (NJHWalker) **7-10-5**(7) XAizpuru (lw: plld hrd: hld up in tch: effrt 2 out: led flat: drvn out)	—	**1**	6/5[1]	62	—
2939[4]	**Music Please (92)** (KCBailey) **5-11-2**(7) MrRWakley (lw: cl up: led last: rdn & ct cl home)	nk	**2**	11/4[2]	73	5
3549[5]	**Otto E Mezzo (97)** (MJPolglase) **5-12-0** VSmith (lw: led: mstke 3 out: hdd last: drvn & nt qckn)	4	**3**	3/1[3]	74	6
3544[7]	**Principal Boy (IRE) (77)** (TJEtherington) **4-10-0** RRourke (cl up: rdn & ev ch after 2 out: no ex)	nk	**4**	6/1	53	—
3666[U]	**Stone Island (77)** (JohnWhyte) **4-10-0** CRae (lw: chsd ldrs tl wknd qckly 2 out)	18	**5**	20/1	35	—
				(SP 116.2%)		**5 Rn**

4m 1.2 (17.20) CSF £4.99 TOTE £2.20: £1.40 £1.80 (£3.20) OWNER Mr Paul Green (BLEWBURY) BRED Michael Byrne
LONG HANDICAP Principal Boy (IRE) 9-12 Stone Island 9-10
WEIGHT FOR AGE 4yo-8lb
3594 Geisway (CAN) was given a peach of a ride by Mr X. Delaying his effort until the last moment, he popped his head in front close home and this is obviously the way to ride him. (6/5: evens-5/4)
2939 Music Please, whose rider was bidding for a quick double, looked to have matters in command on the flat but the jockey reported that the horse threw his head in the air and chucked away the prize close home. (11/4)

3549 Otto E Mezzo is only small and did well considering this big weight would hardly have suited him. (3/1)

T/Plpt: £41.70 (72.3 Tckts). T/Qdpt: £11.90 (28.46 Tckts) Mk

3677-HEREFORD (R-H) (Good to firm)
Monday March 31st
WEATHER: fine, warm & sunny

3927 ROSS-ON-WYE HURDLE (4-Y.O) (Class E)
2-30 (2-30) **2m 1f (9 hdls)** £2,402.00 (£672.00: £326.00) GOING minus 0.22 sec per fur (G)

Form	Horse and details	Dist	Pos	SP	RR	SF
3745[3]	**Noble Colours (86)** (SGGriffiths) **4-10-7**(7) MrAWintle (lw: plld hrd: led: clr 3rd: rdn out)	—	1	7/2[2]	88?	45
3809*	**Seattle Alley (USA) (105)** (PRWebber) **4-11-3**(3) EHusband (hld up: hdwy 5th: chsd wnr next: drvn appr last: no imp)	4	2	4/7[1]	90	47
3601[P]	**Safecracker** (CPMorlock) **4-11-0** SWynne (chsd wnr to 3rd: bhd fr 5th: t.o)	dist	3	25/1[3]	—	—
3544[12]	**Spencer Stallone** (GraemeRoe) **4-10-9**(5) DSalter (mid div: chsd wnr 5th to next: wknd qckly: t.o)	3	4	100/1	—	—
1064[P]	**Startingo** (RLBrown) **4-10-7**(7) NTEgan (bit bkwd: in rr: hdwy 2nd: chsd wnr 3rd to 5th: wkng whn fell 6th)		F	40/1	—	—
3007[11]	**Kutman (USA)** (MCPipe) **4-11-0** GTormey (plld hrd in rr: mstke 2nd: no ch fr 4th: t.o whn p.u bef 2 out: dismntd)		P	7/2[2]	—	—
3468[P]	**Worth The Bill (55)** (FJordan) **4-11-0** JacquiOliver (a bhd: t.o whn p.u bef 3 out)		P	100/1	—	—

(SP 116.3%) **7 Rn**

3m 52.9 (-0.10) CSF £5.80 TOTE £4.90: £1.70 £1.20 (£2.80) OWNER Mr S. G. Griffiths (CARMARTHEN) BRED Ravenstonedale Fold and Bloodstock

3745 Noble Colours, racing with his tongue tied down, was soon in a clear lead and kept up the gallop to score nicely. (7/2)
3809* Seattle Alley (USA) was set a lot to do in the expectation that the leader would come back to them but, not for the first time, found little when let down. (4/7)

3928 JAMES DALY HUNTERS' CHASE (5-Y.O+) (Class H)
3-05 (3-06) **2m 3f (14 fncs)** £1,537.00 (£432.00: £211.00) GOING minus 0.22 sec per fur (G)

Form	Horse and details	Dist	Pos	SP	RR	SF
3744[2]	**Landsker Missile** (MrsMaryEvans) **8-11-2**(7) MrNBradley (a.p: led 7th: drvn clr flat)	—	1	Evens[1]	106	21
3852[P]	**Familiar Friend** (SJGilmore) **11-12-3b**(7) MrPScott (prom: chsd wnr 8th: one pce appr last)	15	2	9/1	108	23
	Bowl of Oats (PGWarner) **11-11-7b**(7) MrARPrice (bhd fr 4th)	30	3	5/1[2]	73	—
	Leeswood (MMAllen) **9-11-7v**(7) MrsCFord (a bhd: t.o)	15	4	14/1	61	—
	Emrys (DavidBond) **14-11-7**(7) MissEJJones (b: prom: mstke 4th: bhd fr 8th: t.o whn p.u bef 2 out)		P	8/1	—	—
	Enchanted Man (MrsJASkelton) **13-11-7**(7) MrAWintle (bit bkwd: bhd fr 4th: t.o whn p.u bef 3 out)		P	8/1	—	—
	Double the Stakes (USA) (MissMBragg) **8-11-7**(7) MrJCreighton (swtg: mstke & reminders 5th: chsd ldrs 7th: wknd next: p.u bef 10th)		P	12/1	—	—
2944[P]	**Pastoral Pride (USA)** (MissPollyCurling) **13-11-9**(5) MissPCurling (led to 7th: wknd qckly after next: p.u bef 10th)		P	7/1[3]	—	—
	Shareef Star (FLMatthews) **9-11-7b[1]**(7) MrSJoynes (t.o fr 3rd: p.u bef 11th)		P	66/1	—	—

(SP 127.2%) **9 Rn**

4m 38.8 (8.80) CSF £11.98 TOTE £2.20: £1.30 £2.10 £1.30 (£7.00) OWNER Mr W. J. Evans (HAVERFORDWEST) BRED Mrs J. K. L. Watts
3744 Landsker Missile won with plenty in hand and can go in again. (Evens)
Familiar Friend could not repeat his victory of twelve months ago. (9/1)
Emrys (8/1: op 9/2)
Pastoral Pride (USA) clearly has physical problems and is not the force he was. (7/1)

3929 NEWTOWN H'CAP CHASE (0-100) (5-Y.O+) (Class F)
3-40 (3-42) **3m 1f 110y (19 fncs)** £3,130.00 (£880.00: £430.00) GOING minus 0.22 sec per fur (G)

Form	Horse and details	Dist	Pos	SP	RR	SF
2947[P]	**Just One Canaletto (71)** (NATwiston-Davies) **9-9-10b[1]**(7) MrJGoldstein (a.p: led 10th to 12th: outpcd 3 out: rallied appr last: str run flat to ld nr fin)	—	1	9/1	79	11
3071[3]	**Howgill (88)** (CaptTAForster) **11-11-6b** SWynne (hld up: hdwy to ld 12th: wnt clr 3 out: rdn appr last: ct nr fin)	½	2	9/2[3]	96	28
3736*	**Trust Deed (USA) (82)** (SGKnight) **9-10-9b**(5) DSalter (lw: hdwy to chse ldrs 9th: mstke 13th: outpcd next: styd on fr 2 out)	6	3	5/2[2]	86	18
3492[6]	**Solo Gent (92)** (APJones) **8-11-10** SBurrough (in tch: mstke 11th: sn wknd: bhd whn p.u bef 2 out)		P	13/2	—	—
3707[3]	**Jason's Boy (79)** (JMBradley) **7-10-4**(7) MKeighley (b: in rr: mstke 6th: lost tch fr 10th: p.u bef 2 out)		P	5/1	—	—
3742[4]	**Pant Llin (72)** (FJordan) **11-10-4b** DWalsh (in tch: hit 10th: sn drvn: bhd fr 12th: p.u bef 15th)		P	16/1	—	—
639*	**Warner's Sports (80)** (PJHobbs) **8-10-12** GTormey (led to 10th: wknd 12th: bhd whn p.u bef 2 out)		P	15/8[1]	—	—

(SP 127.4%) **7 Rn**

6m 18.8 (8.80) CSF £49.70 TOTE £9.50: £2.90 £2.40 (£14.50) OWNER Farmers Racing Partnership (CHELTENHAM)
IN-FOCUS: This was a first winner for Jamie Goldstein, son of Ray.
2665 Just One Canaletto acts very well on this track and is likely to have his ground at the remaining fixtures. (9/1: op 4/1)
3071 Howgill, who looked to have it sewn up two out, was dismounted after the line. (9/2: 3/1-5/1)
3492 Solo Gent (13/2: 5/1-9/1)

3930 HOLIDAY NOVICES' (S) HURDLE (4-Y.O+) (Class G)
4-15 (4-15) **3m 2f (13 hdls)** £2,080.00 (£580.00: £280.00) GOING minus 0.22 sec per fur (G)

Form	Horse and details	Dist	Pos	SP	RR	SF
2088[4]	**Le Baron (70)** (CREgerton) **6-11-2b[1]** GTormey (led: mstke 5th: clr to 8th: drvn 2 out: all out)	—	1	5/2[2]	55	—
3620[4]	**Song For Jess (IRE) (70)** (FJordan) **4-10-3** SWynne (hld up: chsd wnr 9th: rdn appr last: r.o flat)	2½	2	100/30[3]	51	—
3541[P]	**Akiymann (USA) (73)** (MCPipe) **7-11-8b** DWalsh (chsd wnr to 9th: sn rdn & outpcd: kpt on fr 2 out)	3½	3	7/2	57	—
3359[11]	**Slippery Fin** (WGMTurner) **5-10-11** SBurrough (plld hrd early: hld up: hdwy 8th: wknd 3 out: t.o)	dist	4	7/4[1]	—	—

(SP 110.2%) **4 Rn**

6m 24.7 (21.70) CSF £9.65 TOTE £3.80 (£3.80) OWNER Mr Charles Egerton (CHADDLEWORTH) BRED Mrs E. C. York
WEIGHT FOR AGE 4yo-10lb

Bt in 3,200 gns
2088 Le Baron made hard work of landing a rock-bottom seller. (5/2)

3931 MARLBROOK NOVICES' CHASE (5-Y.O+) (Class E)
4-50 (4-51) **2m (12 fncs)** £2,866.00 (£868.00: £424.00: £202.00) GOING minus 0.22 sec per fur (G)

				SP	RR	SF
3842^{2}	**Tenayestelign (79)** (DMarks) **9-11-2** SWynne (hld up: hdwy 8th: led 9th: clr 2 out: hit last: comf)	—	**1**	6/4^{2}	66+	7
3591^{3}	**Lucky Eddie (IRE) (97)** (PJHobbs) **6-11-0** GTormey (lw: cl up: j.lft 6th: chsd wnr 8th: one pce fr 2 out)	6	**2**	4/5^{1}	58	—
3832^{6}	**Quarter Marker (IRE) (60)** (RLee) **9-11-0** SBurrough (lw: led to 9th: one pce fr next)	7	**3**	7/1^{3}	51	—
3746^{P}	**Knowing (67)** (PGWatkins) **10-10-9** MissEJJones (swtg: in tch: wkng whn mstke 2 out)	5	**4**	14/1	41	—
				(SP 114.7%)	**4 Rn**	

4m 0.3 (9.30) CSF £3.17 TOTE £2.30 (£1.40) OWNER Mr G. J. King (UPPER LAMBOURN) BRED Snailwell Stud Co Ltd
3842 Tenayestelign was never threatened once taking it up, which is just as well as she needs to do it all on the bridle. (6/4)
3591 Lucky Eddie (IRE), an uneasy favourite, looked short of pace once again. (4/5: 1/2-10/11)

3932 PETERSTOW NOVICES' H'CAP HURDLE (0-95) (4-Y.O+) (Class F)
5-25 (5-25) **2m 3f 110y (11 hdls)** £2,486.00 (£696.00: £338.00) GOING minus 0.22 sec per fur (G)

				SP	RR	SF
832*	**Kymin (IRE) (84)** (JMBradley) **5-10-11**(7) MrAWintle (trckd ldrs: led appr 3 out: clr 2 out: drvn out)	—	**1**	4/1^{3}	64	35
3188^{F}	**Saxon Mead (66)** (PJHobbs) **7-10-0b** GTormey (led tl appr 3 out: sn rdn: unable qckn)	14	**2**	8/1	35	6
2573^{2}	**Burlington Sam (NZ) (90)** (AGHobbs) **9-11-5**(5) OBurrows (chsd ldrs: rdn 8th: wkng whn blnd 2 out)	3½	**3**	5/2^{2}	56	27
2941^{8}	**Go Frolic (69)** (MissCPhillips) **9-9-12**(5)ow1 DSalter (lw: in tch tl wknd fr 4 out)	4	**4**	9/1	31	1
3204^{P}	**Royrace (66)** (WMBrisbourne) **5-9-7**(7) MrJGoldstein (hld up mid div: outpcd 8th: kpt on fr 2 out: nvr nr to chal)	12	**5**	33/1	19	—
3438^{5}	**Arabian Heights (89)** (JMackie) **4-11-1** DWalsh (hld up: hmpd 6th: hdwy to chse ldrs next: wknd after 8th)	7	**6**	2/1^{1}	36	—
3186^{P}	**Milling Brook (81)** (JMBradley) **5-11-1** SWynne (trckd ldrs tl fell 6th)		**F**	6/1	—	—
	Whatashot (69) (DMcCain) **7-10-3**ow2 SBurrough (cl up: mstke 4th: wknd 7th: mstke next: t.o whn p.u bef 3 out)		**P**	33/1	—	—
3732^{3}	**Another Comedy (68)** (RLee) **7-9-9**(7)ow2 MKeighley (b.off hind: in rr: tried to ref & hmpd 6th: sn t.o: p.u bef 2 out)		**P**	8/1	—	—
				(SP 134.3%)	**9 Rn**	

4m 34.7 (3.70) CSF £38.18 CT £92.69 TOTE £4.10: £1.70 £3.70 £2.40 (£45.20) OWNER Mr Martyn James (CHEPSTOW) BRED Sheikh Mohammed bin Rashid al Maktoum
LONG HANDICAP Royrace 9-8 Saxon Mead 9-10 Another Comedy 9-13
WEIGHT FOR AGE 4yo-8lb
832* Kymin (IRE), having her first run since October, won with plenty to spare. (4/1)
1875 Saxon Mead is capable of finding a little race. (8/1)
Go Frolic (9/1: op 5/1)
3438 Arabian Heights flattered to deceive once again. (2/1)

T/Plpt: £247.50 (9.58 Tckts). T/Qdpt: £77.50 (0.19 Tckts); £84.87 to Uttoxeter 1/4/97 RL

3620-HUNTINGDON (R-H) (Good to firm)
Monday March 31st
WEATHER: fine

3933 ADDENBROOKES DIALYSIS (S) H'CAP HURDLE (0-95) (4-Y.O+) (Class G)
2-00 (2-00) **2m 110y (8 hdls)** £2,090.50 (£583.00: £281.50)

				SP	RR	SF
3488^{P}	**Evezio Rufo (80)** (NPLittmoden) **5-11-10b^{1}** KGaule (led to 1st: led appr 2 out: r.o wl)	—	**1**	12/1	66	—
3677^{3}	**Sharp Thrill (72)** (BSmart) **6-11-2** WMarston (hdwy 5th: chsd wnr & hrd rdn fr 2 out: no imp)	8	**2**	11/4^{1}	50	—
3730^{5}	**Summer Villa (67)** (KGWingrove) **5-10-4b**(7) DYellowlees (a.p: r.o one pce fr 2 out)	2	**3**	10/1	43	—
3663^{7}	**Nagobelia (79)** (JPearce) **9-11-2**(7) JO'Shaughnessy (led 1st tl appr 2 out: hrd rdn: one pce)	¾	**4**	6/1^{3}	55	—
3670^{2}	**Laura Lye (IRE) (76)** (BdeHaan) **7-11-6** SMcNeill (a.p: rdn 3 out: sn wknd)	6	**5**	7/2^{2}	46	—
2943^{4}	**Just for a Reason (73)** (RTJuckes) **5-11-3** LO'Hara (hrd rdn & no hdwy fr 3 out)	3½	**6**	13/2	39	—
	Our Eddie (71) (KGWingrove) **8-11-1b** TJenks (hrd rdn 5th: no rspnse)	8	**7**	14/1	30	—
	Fret (USA) (64) (JSWainwright) **7-10-1**(7) WWalsh (bhd fr 5th)	6	**8**	20/1	17	—
3760^{7}	**Mazirah (76)** (RCurtis) **6-11-6** DMorris (a bhd: t.o fr 5th)	23	**9**	6/1^{3}	7	—
				(SP 119.0%)	**9 Rn**	

No Time Taken CSF £43.37 CT £324.22 TOTE £17.70: £3.50 £1.30 £3.00 (£43.20) OWNER Mr T. Clarke (WOLVERHAMPTON) BRED Lode Moors Farm
No bid
2570 Evezio Rufo, blinkered for the first time, was always close up and shot clear when given the office approaching the second last hurdle. (12/1: 8/1-16/1)
3677 Sharp Thrill made headway three hurdles out but was driven along to do so and could make no impression on the winner from the second last. (11/4)
3730 Summer Villa, close up throughout, ran on again after looking beaten two hurdles out. (10/1)
3429 Nagobelia, soon in the lead, was quickly outpaced when the winner went on approaching the second last hurdle. (6/1)
3670 Laura Lye (IRE) proved very disappointing and, though always close up, was under pressure at halfway, and all chance had gone before the straight. (7/2: 5/2-4/1)

3934 SIDNEY THE KIDNEY NOVICES' CHASE (5-Y.O+) (Class E)
2-30 (2-31) **3m (19 fncs)** £3,046.00 (£913.00: £439.00: £202.00)

				SP	RR	SF
3617^{P}	**Jasilu (95)** (KCBailey) **7-11-9b** SMcNeill (led to 4th: led 8th to 12th: led flat: drvn out)	—	**1**	Evens^{1}	102	—
3739^{6}	**Baron's Heir** (RELivermore) **10-11-2** WMarston (led 4th to 8th: hrd rdn 10th: led 12th to flat: r.o)	1¼	**2**	10/1	94	—
3141^{5}	**Pantara Prince (IRE) (85)** (JIACharlton) **8-11-2** LO'Hara (a.p: ev ch appr 2 out: wknd appr last)	20	**3**	9/4^{2}	81	—
3622^{3}	**Night Fancy (66)** (MrsAMWoodrow) **9-10-9**(7) WWalsh (bhd fr 11th)	11	**4**	8/1^{3}	74	—

	Horse and details	Dist	Pos	SP	RR	SF
3625[2]	**Katballou** (KGWingrove) **8-11-2** KGaule (blnd 5th: wl bhd fr 10th: ref & uns rdr 15th)		**R**	8/1 [3]	—	—

(SP 112.1%) **5 Rn**

No time taken CSF £9.74 TOTE £2.20: £1.60 £2.20 (£4.20) OWNER Mr A. G. Lay (UPPER LAMBOURN) BRED C. L. Loyd
3360 Jasilu had a long battle with the runner-up and, after looking like coming off the worse for much of the way, stayed his rival out of it. (Evens)
Baron's Heir was being hard-ridden with a circuit to go, but a good jump at the fence down the far side gained him the upper hand, which he did not lose until after the last fence. (10/1)
3141 Pantara Prince (IRE), a close third for much of the way, had every chance on the home turn but weakened quickly approaching the last.(9/4)
3622 Night Fancy (8/1: 5/1-9/1)

3935 SHERRIFFS GRAIN H'CAP HURDLE (0-110) (4-Y.O+) (Class E)

3-00 (3-01) **2m 5f 110y (10 hdls)** £2,419.50 (£677.00: £328.50)

	Horse and details	Dist	Pos	SP	RR	SF
3709[3]	**Sassiver (USA) (89)** (PAKelleway) **7-11-4** KGaule (a.p: led 4 out: r.o wl)	—	**1**	15/8 [1]	74	—
12075	**Scud Missile (IRE) (91)** (JWPayne) **6-11-6** MrMArmytage (hld up: hdwy 3 out: ev ch last: nt qckn)	1	**2**	4/1	75	—
3630[3]	**La Menorquina (USA) (95)** (DMarks) **7-11-10** SMcNeill (hld up: effrt & rdn appr 3 out: one pce fr 2 out)	20	**3**	3/1 [2]	64	—
2620[5]	**Wanstead (IRE) (82)** (JRJenkins) **5-10-11b** TJenks (jnd ldrs 4 out: wknd appr 2 out)	2½	**4**	7/2 [3]	50	—
3181[P]	**Ronans Glen (75)** (MJWilkinson) **10-10-4b**[1] WMarston (led: hdd & hrd rdn 4 out: wknd qckly: p.u bef last)		**P**	6/1	—	—

(SP 116.3%) **5 Rn**

No Time Taken CSF £9.37 TOTE £2.80: £1.60 £2.10 (£5.70) OWNER Mr P. A. Kelleway (NEWMARKET) BRED Juddmonte Farms Inc
3709 Sassiver (USA) was going easily when he took up the running four hurdles out. He had to be shaken up in earnest at the last but stayed on strongly. (15/8)
1074 Scud Missile (IRE), going easily behind the leaders for most of the race, moved up to challenge at the last hurdle but, after having every chance, could find no extra. (4/1)
3630 La Menorquina (USA), though in touch, was being pushed along some way from the finish and, though she made some headway on the home turn, quickly found the leading pair drawing away from her. (3/1)

3936 SHERRIFFS GRAIN H'CAP CHASE (0-125) (5-Y.O+) (Class D)

3-30 (3-31) **2m 4f 110y (16 fncs)** £4,563.00 (£1,107.00)

	Horse and details	Dist	Pos	SP	RR	SF
	Raba Riba (122) (JLSpearing) **12-11-11** TJenks (mde all: lft clr 5th: jst hld on)	—	**1**	9/2 [3]	123	—
3625*	**Mr Conductor (IRE) (108)** (RHAlner) **6-10-11** SMcNeill (hdwy 2 out: ev ch flat: r.o)	hd	**2**	11/8 [2]	109	—
3835[2]	**Mister Drum (IRE) (125)** (MJWilkinson) **8-12-0** WMarston (2nd whn uns rdr 5th)		**U**	Evens [1]	—	—

(SP 110.3%) **3 Rn**

No Time Taken CSF £9.60 TOTE £3.90 (£3.20) OWNER Mr J. Spearing (ALCESTER) BRED R. A Beswick
STEWARDS' ENQUIRY Jenks susp. 9-12/4/97 (incorrect use of the whip).
Raba Riba, who unseated his rider at halfway in a Point-to-Point in February, had not run under Rules for almost exactly two years. He made all the running, constantly out-jumping his rivals, and held on under hard driving from the last. (9/2)
3625* Mr Conductor (IRE) was continually out-jumped by the winner and had several lengths to make up for most of the way. He closed rapidly and challenged on the run-in but could not quite force his head in front. (11/8)

3937 HUNTINGDON ASSOCIATION OF TOURISM MAIDEN HURDLE (4-Y.O+) (Class E)

4-05 (4-05) **2m 5f 110y (10 hdls)** £2,867.50 (£805.00: £392.50)

	Horse and details	Dist	Pos	SP	RR	SF
3222[2]	**Seabrook Lad (82)** (MJWilkinson) **6-11-3** WMarston (hdwy 5th: led appr 2 out: r.o wl)	—	**1**	2/1 [1]	67	—
3798[6]	**Burn Out** (JPearce) **5-11-3** LO'Hara (hdwy 6th: ev ch 2 out: nt qckn)	7	**2**	9/4 [2]	62	—
3764[3]	**Scenic Waters** (NATwiston-Davies) **5-10-12b**[1] TJenks (led tl wknd appr 2 out)	6	**3**	100/30 [3]	52	—
3621[7]	**Castle Mews (IRE)** (GCBravery) **6-10-12** MrMArmytage (w ldrs to 5th: same pce & no hdwy fr 4 out)	12	**4**	12/1	43	—
3226[9]	**Derring Floss** (JAPickering) **7-10-5**(7) MissJWormall (w ldrs tl wknd 6th)	12	**5**	20/1	35	—
3706[6]	**Counter Attack (IRE)** (MissAEEmbiricos) **6-10-5**(7) JO'Shaughnessy (a bhd)	16	**6**	25/1	23	—
2949[5]	**Ramstown Lad (IRE)** (KCBailey) **8-11-3** SMcNeill (wl bhd fr 6th)	12	**7**	8/1	19	—
3730[13]	**Toat Chieftain** (MissAEEmbiricos) **5-11-3** KGaule (bhd tl some hdwy 6th: sn wknd: t.o)	dist	**8**	33/1	—	—
2811[14]	**Royal Mist (IRE)** (MrsJPitman) **6-11-3** DMorris (dropped rr after 5th: t.o whn p.u bef 2 out)		**P**	7/1	—	—

(SP 130.0%) **9 Rn**

No Time Taken CSF £7.23 TOTE £3.60: £1.80 £1.40 £1.60 (£6.30) OWNER Seabrook Partners (BANBURY) BRED W. D. Hockenhull
3222 Seabrook Lad moved up at halfway and, after going to the front approaching the second last hurdle, ran on to beat a poor field. (2/1)
3564 Burn Out tracked the leaders, and had every chance but could make no impression on the winner from two hurdles out. (9/4)
3764 Scenic Waters, blinkered for the first time, made the running. Driven along from halfway, she weakened quickly when headed approaching the second last hurdle. (100/30)
3621 Castle Mews (IRE) went with the leaders on the first circuit but was a well beaten fourth from three hurdles out. (12/1)

3938 KIDNEY FOUNDATION NOVICES' CHASE (5-Y.O+) (Class E)

4-35 (4-35) **2m 110y (12 fncs)** £3,258.50 (£906.00: £435.50)

	Horse and details	Dist	Pos	SP	RR	SF
1664[6]	**Odell (IRE) (1)** (KCBailey) **7-11-0** SMcNeill (j.w: mde all: r.o wl)	—	**1**	11/4 [3]	74	—
3682*	**Quick Quote (86)** (MrsIMcKie) **7-11-9** WMarston (chsd wnr: hdwy & hrd rdn 2 out: one pce flat)	4	**2**	Evens [1]	79	—
3325[7]	**Appearance Money (IRE) (81)** (FMurphy) **6-10-9** KGaule (a last: hdwy appr 2 out: wknd appr last)	30	**3**	9/4 [2]	36	—

(SP 107.4%) **3 Rn**

No Time Taken CSF £5.33 TOTE £3.40 (£2.20) OWNER Mrs Christine Davies (UPPER LAMBOURN) BRED Thomas McGuinness
1664 Odell (IRE) gave his rivals a lesson in jumping. He made all, was soon clear and quickly settled the issue when pushed along between the last two fences. (11/4)
3682* Quick Quote closed on the winner from four fences out but was under strong pressure to do so, and had no more to give between the last two. (Evens)
3325 Appearance Money (IRE), though always last, was in touch until weakening on the home turn. (9/4)

3939 EASTERTIDE MAIDEN OPEN N.H. FLAT RACE (4, 5 & 6-Y.O) (Class H)

5-05 (5-06) **2m 110y** £1,539.00 (£429.00: £207.00)

	Horse and details	Dist	Pos	SP	RR	SF
	Mad Harry (KCBailey) **5-11-6** SMcNeill (a.p: led 3f out: r.o wl)	—	**1**	7/4 [1]	61 f	—

				SP	RR	SF
3676[4]	**Cue Call (IRE)** (MrsDHaine) **4-10-9** MissAEmbiricos (a.p: ev ch 3f out: one pce fnl 2f)	4	**2**	9/4[2]	54 f	—
	French County (IRE) (JRJenkins) **5-10-13**(7) DYellowlees (gd hdwy 3f out: nt rch ldrs)	3	**3**	12/1	54 f	—
3418[6]	**Lord of The Rings** (FMurphy) **5-11-6** KGaule (a.p: ev ch 3f out: wknd 2f out)	8	**4**	4/1[3]	47 f	—
2924[8]	**Sabu** (JIACharlton) **5-11-6** LO'Hara (a.p: led 5f out to 3f out: sn wknd)	3½	**5**	11/1	43 f	—
3433[18]	**Coromandel** (AHHarvey) **5-11-1** TJenks (hdwy 5f out: wknd 3f out)	3	**6**	20/1	35 f	—
	Pirate Minstrel (IRE) (RChampion) **5-11-6** MrMArmytage (led 1f: prom tl wknd 5f out)	19	**7**	10/1	22 f	—
	Troystar (TMJones) **6-11-6** DMorris (led after 1f to 5f out: sn wknd)	3	**8**	25/1	19 f	—
2811[17]	**Super Nova** (CJHemsley) **6-10-13**(7) MissADudley (t.o fr ½-wy)	dist	**9**	25/1	—	—
3676[14]	**King of Swing (IRE)** (VSoane) **5-11-6** WMarston (t.o fnl 7f)	12	**10**	20/1	—	—
				(SP 129.5%)	**10 Rn**	

No Time Taken CSF £5.71 TOTE £2.40: £1.30 £1.70 £2.60 (£3.20) OWNER Mr W. J. Ives (UPPER LAMBOURN) BRED E. J. B. Maude
WEIGHT FOR AGE 4yo-8lb
Mad Harry, always going well, took up the running three furlongs out, and readily drew clear when required. (7/4)
3676 Cue Call (IRE), patiently ridden, moved up with the winner on the home turn but was comfortably outpaced from two furlongs out. (9/4)
French County (IRE), a long way behind for much of the way, made good headway to take third place halfway up the straight, but could not reach the leading pair. (12/1)
Lord of The Rings tracked the leaders going well but, after having every chance three furlongs out, was ridden and beaten soon afterwards. (4/1)
Sabu led momentarily five furlongs out, but was quickly beaten when headed approaching the straight. (11/1)
Pirate Minstrel (IRE) (10/1: op 20/1)

T/Plpt: £327.80 (8.31 Tckts). T/Qdpt: £119.60 (0.96 Tckts); £6.47 to Uttoxeter 1/4/97 Hn

3704-MARKET RASEN (R-H) (Good to firm, Good patches)
Monday March 31st
WEATHER: fine & sunny

3940 'PAY AND PLAY GOLF' (S) HURDLE (4, 5 & 6-Y.O) (Class G)
2-15 (2-15) **2m 1f 110y (8 hdls)** £1,716.00 (£476.00: £228.00) GOING minus 0.23 sec per fur (G)

				SP	RR	SF
3791[3]	**Our Robert (90)** (JGFitzGerald) **5-11-4**(3) FLeahy (trckd ldrs: chal & hit 2 out: led & blnd last: sn hdd: rallied to ld again towards fin: all out)	—	**1**	5/2[2]	69	32
3447[11]	**Theme Arena (88)** (MCPipe) **4-10-10** RJohnson (mde most tl jnd 2 out: hdd last: sn led again: hdd & no extra towards fin)	hd	**2**	7/4[1]	66	21
2918[P]	**Dantes Amour (IRE)** (MDHammond) **6-11-0** RGarritty (chsd ldrs: hdwy after 3 out: ev ch 2 out: one pce appr last)	4	**3**	25/1	58	21
3803[3]	**Never so Blue (IRE) (84)** (PBradley) **6-11-0**(7) RWilkinson (chsd ldrs: rdn appr 2 out: one pce appr last)	2	**4**	5/1[3]	63	26
3666[6]	**Lucy Tufty (76)** (JPearce) **6-11-2** MBrennan (hld up: stdy hdwy 3 out: chasd ldrs 2 out: wknd appr last)	½	**5**	12/1	58	21
2915[14]	**Grandman (IRE) (79)** (DMoffatt) **6-11-7** DJMoffatt (in tch: rdn 3 out: sn outpcd)	4	**6**	14/1	59	22
3730[3]	**Analogical** (DMcCain) **4-10-3** RSupple (hld up & plld hrd: btn 3 out)	16	**7**	8/1	35	—
3371[6]	**Mudlark (89)** (JNorton) **5-10-7v**(7) MNewton (hld up & bhd: effrt ½-wy: btn appr 3 out)	2	**8**	10/1	36	—
3098[F]	**Parry** (SBBell) **5-10-9** NSmith (bhd: lost tch ½-wy: t.o)	dist	**9**	33/1	—	—
3548[4]	**Happy Days Bill** (KAMorgan) **5-11-0** ASSmith (cl up: led 2nd to 3rd: lost pl next: sn bhd: t.o)	4	**10**	8/1	—	—
3741[8]	**Double Vintage (IRE)** (MCChapman) **4-10-8b** WWorthington (sn bhd: drvn along: t.o fr 4)	dist	**11**	66/1	—	—
				(SP 135.6%)	**11 Rn**	

4m 7.5 (4.50) CSF £8.04 TOTE £3.10: £1.40 £1.60 £4.30 (£3.00) OWNER Mr Tony Fawcett (MALTON) BRED C. L. Loyd
WEIGHT FOR AGE 4yo-8lb
Bt in 3,000 gns
3791 Our Robert, dropped in class, won with not an ounce to spare after ploughing through the last. (5/2)
3447 Theme Arena made a bold bid to lead all the way and did not go down without a fight. (7/4: op 11/4)
2180 Dantes Amour (IRE), dropped in class, ran better and held every chance until tapped for finishing speed. (25/1)
3803 Never so Blue (IRE) was unable to match the pace of the principals from the second last. (5/1)
3352 Lucy Tufty looked dangerous approaching the home straight but, once in contention, could do no more. (12/1)

3941 GEOFFREY BOOTH MEMORIAL NOVICES' CHASE (5-Y.O+) (Class D)
2-45 (2-47) **2m 4f (15 fncs)** £3,773.75 (£1,130.00: £542.50: £248.75) GOING: 0.03 sec per fur (G)

				SP	RR	SF
1714[2]	**Formal Invitation (IRE)** (DNicholson) **8-11-2** RJohnson (hld up gng wl: stdy hdwy to chse ldr 4 out: ev ch fr next: rdn to ld & lft wl clr last)	—	**1**	4/7[1]	103?	30
3049[9]	**Bowles Patrol (IRE) (70)** (JohnUpson) **5-10-8** RSupple (hld up: mstke 8th: outpcd 10th: hdwy appr 3 out: styd on: lft 2nd at last)	dist	**2**	33/1	—	—
1702[F]	**Desert Brave (IRE) (77)** (MrsSJSmith) **7-10-9**(7) RWilkinson (chsd ldrs: lost pl 10th: kpt on one pce fr 3 out)	4	**3**	6/1[3]	—	—
3732[2]	**Heathyards Boy (63)** (DMcCain) **7-11-2b** ASSmith (cl up tl rdn & wknd appr 4 out: sn btn)	13	**4**	7/2[2]	—	—
3402[P]	**Monks Soham (IRE)** (GAHubbard) **9-10-13**(3) MichaelBrennan (led: jnd & rdn fr 3 out: jst hdd & ev ch whn fell last)		**F**	10/1	—	—
3227[P]	**Bucket of Gold** (OBrennan) **7-11-2** MBrennan (chsd ldrs: hit 6th: bhd fr 10th: t.o whn p.u bef 3 out)		**P**	8/1	—	—
3035[P]	**Queen Buzzard** (EWeymes) **9-10-8**(3) FLeahy (mstke 3rd: sn t.o: p.u bef 3 out)		**P**	33/1	—	—
				(SP 126.2%)	**7 Rn**	

5m 1.0 (10.00) CSF £20.58 TOTE £1.60: £1.40 £6.50 (£20.80) OWNER The Plough Partnership (TEMPLE GUITING) BRED Patrick Eddery Ltd
WEIGHT FOR AGE 5yo-9lb
1714 Formal Invitation (IRE), who pulled some muscles in his quarters in his comeback race at Southwell, was just beginning to get on top here when he was left clear at the last. He would otherwise have had to work hard for victory. (4/7)
Bowles Patrol (IRE) took time to warm up but began to get the hang of things late on and showed some promise. (33/1)
1702 Desert Brave (IRE) may have needed this race after an absence of 117 days. (6/1: op 4/1)
3732 Heathyards Boy faded quickly leaving the back straight having raced up with the pace. (7/2)
3209 Monks Soham (IRE), a chasing debutant, made a spirited effort to make all and, although just headed when he fell at the last, was certainly not done for. He deserves to find compensation. (10/1)
3015 Bucket of Gold (8/1: op 5/1)

3942 CARAVAN & CAMPING SITE H'CAP HURDLE (0-120) (4-Y.O+) (Class D)
3-20 (3-21) **2m 3f 110y (10 hdls)** £3,043.00 (£848.00: £409.00) GOING minus 0.23 sec per fur (G)

				SP	RR	SF
3197*	**My Cheeky Man (110)** (DNicholson) **6-11-12** RJohnson (hld up: outpcd & lost tch after 6th: sn hrd drvn: hdwy fr 3 out: styd on to ld last: sn clr)	—	**1**	11/10 [1]	93	39
2651[4]	**Keen To The Last (FR) (97)** (MDHammond) **5-10-13v** RGarritty (chsd ldrs: effrt & hdwy after 3 out: chal 2 out: no ex flat)	6	**2**	9/1	75	21
3728[3]	**Our Kris (110)** (MESowersby) **5-11-12b** ASSmith (chsd ldrs: led 3 out: jnd & rdn 2 out: hdd last & no ex flat)	2½	**3**	10/1	86	32
3709[5]	**Major Yaasi (USA) (92)** (JAGlover) **7-10-8b** RSupple (led: hit 3rd: hdd 3 out: one pce fr next)	3	**4**	9/2 [2]	66	12
3103[8]	**Go With The Wind (95)** (CWeedon) **4-10-3** DJMoffatt (sn prom: rdn after 3 out: wknd fr 2 out)	10	**5**	10/1	60	—
3600[10]	**Diwali Dancer (112)** (MCPipe) **7-12-0** MBrennan (chsd ldr: pushed along & mstke 4 out: sn wknd: eased whn btn)	15	**6**	5/1 [3]	65	11
582[P]	**Rudi's Pride (IRE) (97)** (SBBell) **6-10-13** NSmith (a bhd: lost tch 4 out: t.o)	dist	**7**	16/1	—	—
3445[4]	***Super Rapier (IRE) (86)*** (GAHubbard) **5-9-13**(3)ow2 MichaelBrennan (Withdrawn not under Starter's orders: Jockey unfit to ride)		**W**	10/1	—	—
				(SP 125.6%)		**7 Rn**

4m 37.4 (4.40) CSF £12.53 CT £70.64 TOTE £2.00: £2.00 £2.60 (£7.00) OWNER Mrs A. A. Shutes (TEMPLE GUITING) BRED Mrs Diana Shutes

WEIGHT FOR AGE 4yo-8lb

3197* My Cheeky Man, badly outpaced a mile from home, owed this to a never-say-die ride from Johnson who refused to accept defeat. (11/10)

2651 Keen To The Last (FR), after a ten-week break and from a stable out of form at present, ran well, only to find the winner too good after the last. (9/1)

3728 Our Kris looked the most likely winner entering the home straight but came to the end of his tether at the final flight. (10/1)

3709 Major Yaasi (USA) found little once headed and could only stay on at the same speed. (9/2)

2889 Go With The Wind found things a bit hot in the closing stages after racing up with the pace. (10/1)

2625 Diwali Dancer was eased when beaten with his rider looking slightly ill at ease in the home straight, but something may be amiss. (5/1)

3943 VICTOR LUCAS MEMORIAL H'CAP CHASE (0-120) (5-Y.O+) (Class D)
3-55 (3-55) **2m 1f 110y (12 fncs)** £3,878.50 (£1,076.00: £515.50) GOING: 0.03 sec per fur (G)

				SP	RR	SF
3707*	**Netherby Said (114)** (PBeaumont) **7-12-0** RSupple (mde all: sn clr: j.rt & blnd bdly 3 out: j.rt last: unchal)	—	**1**	1/2 [1]	122+	21
2914[4]	**Daring Past (100)** (MDHammond) **7-11-0** RGarritty (chsd wnr fr 5th: blnd 4 out: no imp after)	22	**2**	7/2 [3]	88	—
3329[3]	**Newhall Prince (108)** (AStreeter) **9-11-8v** TEley (chsd wnr to 5th: drvn along 7th: sn t.o)	26	**3**	3/1 [2]	72	—
				(SP 113.9%)		**3 Rn**

4m 28.8 (13.80) CSF £2.57 TOTE £1.50 (£1.80) OWNER Mrs S. Sunter (BRANDSBY) BRED J. Sunter

3707* Netherby Said notched his fifth course win and never looked likely to be denied despite giving his supporters near heart failure with a terrible blunder three from home. (1/2)

2914 Daring Past, coming back after a two-month lay-off, never looked likely to make a race of it with the winner. (7/2)

3329 Newhall Prince seems to be out of sorts at present. (3/1)

3944 EASTER MONDAY 'N.H.' NOVICES' HURDLE (5-Y.O+) (Class D)
4-30 (4-32) **2m 3f 110y (10 hdls)** £3,260.00 (£910.00: £440.00) GOING minus 0.23 sec per fur (G)

				SP	RR	SF
2904*	**Phar Smoother (IRE)** (JGFitzGerald) **5-10-11**(3) FLeahy (trckd ldr: led 3 out: rdn between last 2: hit last: r.o strly)	—	**1**	11/10 [2]	74+	13
3468[3]	**Morpheus (99)** (DNicholson) **8-11-0** RJohnson (hld up & plld hrd: hdwy to chse wnr after 3 out: sn ev ch: rdn & edgd rt between last 2: no ex flat)	7	**2**	10/11 [1]	68	7
3691[8]	**Raise A Dollar** (PBeaumont) **7-10-9** RSupple (led tl hdd 3 out: styd on one pce)	3	**3**	12/1	61	—
3818[6]	**Pealings (IRE)** (GAHubbard) **5-11-0** ASSmith (hld up & bhd: stdy hdwy appr 3 out: no imp fr 2 out)	3½	**4**	10/1 [3]	63	2
3667[F]	**Seabright Saga** (MCChapman) **7-11-0b[1]** WWorthington (chsd ldrs tl wknd 3 out: sn bhd: t.o)	dist	**5**	50/1	—	—
				(SP 118.7%)		**5 Rn**

4m 41.4 (8.40) CSF £2.60 TOTE £2.00: £1.20 £1.40 (£1.50) OWNER John Smith's Ltd (MALTON) BRED J. J. Harty

2904* Phar Smoother (IRE), making his hurdles debut, jumped well apart from a mistake at the last and won in good style. He looks to have a bright future. (11/10)

3468 Morpheus proved his own worst enemy, pulling far too hard for too long and leaving himself with nothing in reserve when the chips were down. (10/11: evens-4/5)

3348 Raise A Dollar did the donkey work and kept on quite well in the closing stages. (12/1)

Pealings (IRE), a headstrong individual, looked as though he might run quite well leaving the back straight but he then failed to pick up. (10/1)

3945 WEST LINDSEY EASTER CUP NOVICES' H'CAP CHASE (0-100) (5-Y.O+) (Class E)
5-00 (5-02) **3m 1f (19 fncs)** £3,103.00 (£934.00: £452.00: £211.00) GOING: 0.03 sec per fur (G)

				SP	RR	SF
3472[P]	**Ocean Leader (92)** (MrsDHaine) **10-11-10** RJohnson (bhd: hdwy & in tch 12th: ev ch fr 3 out: styd on u.p flat to ld post)	—	**1**	15/2	100	33
3477*	**Karenastino (70)** (MrsSJSmith) **6-9-9**(7) RWilkinson (a.p: jnd ldrs 9th: led 14th: rdn appr last: wnt rt flat: hdd post)	½	**2**	3/1 [2]	78	11
3732[6]	**Alaskan Heir (68)** (AStreeter) **6-10-0v[1]** TEley (led: mde most to 14th: rdn & btn appr 3 out)	dist	**3**	14/1	—	—
3435*	**Suvla Bay (IRE) (80)** (OBrennan) **9-10-12** MBrennan (chsd ldrs: hit 6th: led briefly 13th: ev ch tl wknd qckly fr 4 out)	18	**4**	3/1 [2]	—	—
3436[4]	**Shoofe (USA) (77)** (KAMorgan) **9-10-9** ASSmith (cl up tl wknd bef 15th: sn t.o)	nk	**5**	7/1 [3]	—	—
896[2]	**The Gallopin'major (IRE) (90)** (MrsMReveley) **7-11-8b** NSmith (hld up in tch: trckd ldrs fr 12th: gng wl whn fell 4 out: dead)		**F**	5/4 [1]	—	—
3724[4]	**Fair Ally (71)** (MESowersby) **7-10-0**(3)ow1 FLeahy (a in rr: lost tch 10th: t.o whn p.u bef 13th)		**P**	12/1	—	—
3181[P]	**The Millmaster (IRE) (69)** (JohnUpson) **6-10-1** RSupple (sn bhd: t.o whn p.u bef 13th)		**P**	33/1	—	—
				(SP 136.0%)		**8 Rn**

6m 25.5 (14.50) CSF £33.86 CT £308.87 TOTE £11.20: £2.30 £1.10 £5.80 (£24.90) OWNER Sir Peter Gibbings (NEWMARKET) BRED W. Lombard

LONG HANDICAP Alaskan Heir 9-11
OFFICIAL EXPLANATION Ocean Leader: the gelding was better suited by the faster ground and was wearing a tongue strap for the first time.
3472 Ocean Leader came back to form thanks to a superb ride and the fitting of a tongue-strap for the first time. He reportedly gurgled at Bangor the previous time he ran. (15/2: 5/1-8/1)
3477* Karenastino made a gallant attempt but hung right on the flat and was just worried out of it towards the finish. He looks in particularly good heart at present. (3/1)
3201 Alaskan Heir raced too freely in a first-time visor and was out on his feet from the fourth last. (14/1)
3435* Suvla Bay (IRE) dueled for the lead along the back straight but stopped to a virtual walk going to the third last. (3/1)
896 The Gallopin'major (IRE), a useful money-spinner, tragically broke a leg when falling. (5/4)

3946 MARKET RASEN STANDARD N.H. FLAT RACE (4, 5 & 6-Y.O) (Class H)
5-30 (5-33) **1m 5f 110y** £1,318.50 (£366.00: £175.50)

	Horse	Dist	Pos	SP	RR	SF
	Laredo (IRE) (NoelChance) **4-10-5**(7) CScudder (mid div: hdwy 5f out: led & edgd rt 2f out: drvn clr)	—	1	8/1	71 f	—
	Sawaab (USA) (CPMorlock) **5-10-11**(7) MNewton (rr div: gd hdwy 6f out: led wl over 2f out: sn hdd: kpt on one pce)	5	2	10/1	68 f	—
	Double Star (JLHarris) **6-11-4** MrCWatson (bhd: effrt 4f out: kpt on fnl 2f: nrst fin)	2½	3	20/1	65 f	—
3548^{8}	**Juniper Hill** (KAMorgan) **5-10-11**(7) LSuthern (led tl hdd wl over 2f out: one pce)	¾	4	10/1	64 f	—
	Totem Fole (MrsMReveley) **4-10-5**(7) MHerrington (bhd: styd on fnl 3f: nvr nrr: fin 6th plcd 5th)	2¼	5	$9/2^{3}$	58 f	—
2931^{10}	**Night Escapade (IRE)** (CWeedon) **5-10-6**(7) RWilkinson (in tch tl wknd fnl 3f)	½	6	10/1	56 f	—
	Westerly (IRE) (JGFitzGerald) **6-11-1**(3) FLeahy (keen hold early: trckd ldrs tl rdn & wknd fr over 2f out: fin 8th plcd 7th)	3½	7	$4/1^{2}$	57 f	—
	Molonys Dram (JLHarris) **6-10-11**(7) DWebb (mid div: effrt ½-wy: sn outpcd: fin 9th plcd 8th)	2½	8	10/1	54 f	—
3418^{4}	**Dig For Gold** (MissSEHall) **4-10-5**(7) RBurns (cl up tl wknd over 2f out: fin 10th plcd 9th)	3½	9	$Evens^{1}$	47 f	—
	Lislaughtin Abbey (OBrennan) **5-10-11**(7) WWalsh (chsd ldrs: effrt on outside appr st: sn btn: fin 11th plcd 10th)	10	10	10/1	38 f	—
3433^{3}	**Capsoff (IRE)** (GAHubbard) **4-10-10**ow3 MrJWeymes (chsd ldrs: rdn on outside appr st: sn wknd: fin 12th plcd 11th)	2½	11	$4/1^{2}$	30 f	—
	West Lutton (MWEasterby) **5-11-1**(3) PMidgley (outpcd & rdn along in rr 6f out: sn btn: fin 13th plcd 12th)	1	12	16/1	34 f	—
3574^{18}	**Plumpton Wood (IRE)** (JGSmyth-Osbourne) **5-10-13** MrABrown (t.o: fin 14th plcd 13th)	dist	13	14/1	—	—
	A Day On The Dub (TPTate) **4-10-5**(7) RMcCarthy (in tch: effrt & gd hdwy 3f out: sn ev ch: 3rd whn rdn & tk wrong crse over 1f out: fin 5th btn 8½l: disq)		D	15/2	61 f	—
				(SP 193.8%)	**14 Rn**	

3m 6.8 CSF £126.39 TOTE £9.60: £2.50 £7.70 £6.00 (£206.20) OWNER Michael And Gerry Worcester (LAMBOURN) BRED Frank Lacy
WEIGHT FOR AGE 4yo-3lb
STEWARDS' ENQUIRY McCarthy susp. 9-10&12/4/97 (took wrong course).
Laredo (IRE), making his racecourse debut, created a useful impression and sprinted clear in the final furlong. (8/1: op 5/1)
Sawaab (USA) shaped well on his debut only to find the winner carrying too many guns in the closing stages. (10/1)
Double Star kept on stoutly in the home straight to be nearest at the finish. A stiffer test of stamina will probably suit him. (20/1)
2675 Juniper Hill raced freely at the head of affairs and could do no more when the chips were down. (10/1)
Totem Fole, in the rear for much of the race, stayed on in the straight to be nearest at the finish. (9/2)
872 Night Escapade (IRE) raced in touch with the leaders but could do no more in the final quarter-mile. (10/1)
Westerly (IRE) raced quite freely just behind the leaders and faded in the home straight. He may just have needed this. (4/1: op 9/4)
3418 Dig For Gold raced rather keenly in the front rank and had nothing more to offer in the home straight. (Evens)
3433 Capsoff (IRE) (4/1: op 9/4)
A Day On The Dub shaped with promise, holding every chance early in the straight only to go on the wrong side of a hurdle over a furlong out which meant he took the wrong course. He was inevitably disqualified. (15/2: 5/1-8/1)

T/Plpt: £15.90 (175.18 Tckts). T/Qdpt: £25.60 (3.47 Tckts) O'R

3889-NEWTON ABBOT (L-H) (Firm, Good to firm patches)
Monday March 31st
WEATHER: sunny

3947 FRENCH CONNECTION HURDLE (4-Y.O) (Class D)
2-15 (2-15) **2m 1f (8 hdls)** £2,871.00 (£806.00: £393.00) GOING minus 0.62 sec per fur (F)

	Horse	Dist	Pos	SP	RR	SF
2872^{7}	**Melt The Clouds (CAN)** (MCPipe) **4-10-12b1** CMaude (lw: plld hrd: hld up tl chsd ldr after 2nd: hdwy to ld 2 out: sn clr: unchal)	—	1	$4/7^{1}$	75	—
3745^{7}	**White Plains (IRE)** (MCPipe) **4-10-5**(7) BMoore (led tl hdd 2 out & sn outpcd)	7	2	$9/4^{2}$	68	—
3669^{4}	**Genereux** (SMellor) **4-10-7**(5) ChrisWebb (chsd ldr tl after 2nd: in tch tl wknd 5th)	20	3	$9/2^{3}$	50	—
				(SP 112.6%)	**3 Rn**	

4m 0.9 (7.90) CSF £2.18 TOTE £1.80 (£1.40) OWNER Promo-Sherring Ltd (WELLINGTON) BRED Huntingdon Stud Farm Inc
2751 Melt The Clouds (CAN), a maiden on the Flat, had no problem in getting off the mark here, and can find a similar event within his capabilities. (4/7)
3745 White Plains (IRE) appreciates this surface. Leading for most of the way, he was headed with two obstacles left and could do little about the winner. (9/4)
3669 Genereux may improve with time and possibly a little further. (9/2)

3948 HILL BREEZE NOVICES' CHASE (5-Y.O+) (Class E)
2-50 (2-50) **2m 5f 110y (16 fncs)** £3,182.50 (£895.00: £437.50) GOING minus 0.62 sec per fur (F)

	Horse	Dist	Pos	SP	RR	SF
2878^{2}	**Decyborg (FR) (95)** (MCPipe) **6-11-8** CMaude (lw: led: mstke 3rd: qcknd clr next: unchal: eased flat)	—	1	$2/5^{1}$	103?	12
3400^{P}	**Country Keeper (75)** (BJMRyall) **9-11-2** JFrost (j.slowly: mstke 2nd: chsd wnr 9th: nvr nrr)	dist	2	$9/4^{2}$	—	—

3591[4] **Rustic Flight (60)** (LWaring) **10-10-9**(7) MGriffiths (j.rt: chsd wnr: j.slowly 6th: lost pl 9th: wknd appr next: b.b.v.)....dist **3** 9/1[3] — —
(SP 112.2%) **3 Rn**

5m 21.5 (4.50) CSF £1.72 TOTE £1.40 (£1.40) OWNER Mr Terry Neill (WELLINGTON) BRED Bernard Touillon
OFFICIAL EXPLANATION **Rustic Flight: the gelding had bled from the nose.**
2878 Decyborg (FR) was found a good opportunity here to get off the mark and could not have won any more convincingly. Improvement seems inevitable. (2/5: 1/2-1/3)
2657 Country Keeper knows this track well and only had to put in a clear round to pick up a share of the prize-money. (9/4: 6/4-5/2)
Rustic Flight (9/1: 8/1-14/1)

3949 TERRACE RESTAURANT (S) H'CAP HURDLE (0-95) (4-Y.O+) (Class G)

3-25 (3-26) **2m 6f (10 hdls)** £1,932.70 (£542.20: £264.10) GOING minus 0.62 sec per fur (F)

				SP	RR	SF
1946P	**Bowden Surprise (60)** (RJBaker) **7-10-0** VSlattery (bit bkwd: a in tch: rdn to chse ldr 8th: led 2 out: styd on u.p flat)	—	**1**	16/1	44	—
413[4]	**Sukaab (75)** (BJMRyall) **12-10-10**(5) ChrisWebb (bit bkwd: hld up bhd: hdwy 8th: disp ld 2 out: one pce appr last)	2	**2**	4/1[3]	58	6
3442[4]	**Jay Em Ess (NZ) (83)** (AGHobbs) **8-11-9** RGreene (lw: hld up bhd: hdwy 7th: wknd after next)	6	**3**	11/8[1]	61	9
3338P	**October Brew (USA) (84)** (MCPipe) **7-11-3b**(7) BMoore (mstke 1st: slt mstke 4th: stdy hdwy to ld 7th: sn clr: hdd 2 out: wknd)	2	**4**	15/2	61	9
3892P	**Castlebay Lad (60)** (RCurtis) **14-9-7**(7) JParkhouse (led 2nd to 3rd: led 4th: hdd 7th: wknd next)	7	**5**	33/1	32	—
3722[6]	**Sea Barn (70)** (MJCoombe) **14-10-10** MissMCoombe (bit bkwd: racd wd: led 3rd to 4th: in tch tl wknd 8th)	½	**6**	100/30[2]	41	—
3740U	**Concinnity (USA) (67)** (BScriven) **8-10-0b**1(7)ow1 CRWeaver (chsd ldrs tl wknd 7th)	6	**7**	14/1	34	—
3594P	**Dormy Three (81)** (RJHodges) **7-11-7** CMaude (led to 2nd: wknd fr 7th)	1½	**8**	5/1	47	—
3740[4]	**Rory'm (IRE) (60)** (LWaring) **8-9-7b**(7) MGriffiths (a bhd: t.o fr 4th)	23	**9**	25/1	9	—
				(SP 132.9%)		**9 Rn**

5m 15.9 (3.90) CSF £83.48 CT £141.33 TOTE £21.80: £3.00 £1.70 £1.60 (£97.20) OWNER Mr R. J. Baker (TIVERTON) BRED Mrs J. Heywood
LONG HANDICAP Bowden Surprise 9-11 Castlebay Lad 9-4 Rory'm (IRE) 9-12
No bid
Bowden Surprise, who pulled up on his last outing here over course and distance, was meeting ground as fast as this for the first time. (16/1)
Sukaab, has been lightly raced in recent years, but showed up well here and there may still be a race for him. (4/1: op 8/1)
3442 Jay Em Ess (NZ) was a disappointing market leader and is becoming hard to place. (11/8)
October Brew (USA) (15/2: 5/1-8/1)
3344 Concinnity (USA) (14/1: op 9/1)
3115 Dormy Three (5/1: 4/1-7/1)

3950 MANICOU RESTAURANT H'CAP CHASE (0-105) (5-Y.O+ Mares Only) (Class F)

4-00 (4-01) **2m 110y (13 fncs)** £2,916.20 (£719.00) GOING minus 0.62 sec per fur (F)

				SP	RR	SF
2657P	**Mistress Rosie (69)** (MHill) **10-10-7**(5) ChrisWebb (lw: chsd ldrs tl led 6th: mde rest: clr appr 2 out: unchal)	—	**1**	9/2[3]	72	11
3627[5]	**Walk in the Woods (72)** (DCTurner) **10-11-1** RGreene (led to 6th: chsd ldr: in tch tl wknd 3 out)	14	**2**	9/4[2]	61	—
3697[9]	**Dubelle (81)** (JSKing) **7-11-10** CMaude (lw: chsd ldr to 6th: lost pl: blnd 8th & p.u)		**P**	4/9[1]	—	—
				(SP 118.2%)		**3 Rn**

4m 1.1 (1.10) CSF £12.16 TOTE £5.50 (£4.80) OWNER Mr Martin Hill (TOTNES) BRED V. N. F. Tjolle
OFFICIAL EXPLANATION **Dubelle: the jockey reported that the mare changed her legs and felt wrong.**
Mistress Rosie, the outsider of three, was never in any danger of losing this and only had the fences to beat from some way out. (9/2: 6/1-9/1)
Walk in the Woods has had three of her four runs here but has yet to succeed. Putting up a slight challenge to the winner, she was soon left a clear second to complete for a share of the money. (9/4)
901 Dubelle had conditions to suit but could not run up to her market price. (4/9)

3951 BANK HOLIDAY MONDAY NOVICES' H'CAP HURDLE (0-100) (4-Y.O+) (Class E)

4-35 (4-35) **2m 1f (8 hdls)** £2,431.50 (£684.00: £334.50) GOING minus 0.62 sec per fur (F)

				SP	RR	SF
3352*	**Mellow Master (85)** (NJHWalker) **4-11-10** CMaude (lw: chsd ldr tl led 6th: clr 2 out: j.lft last: eased)	—	**1**	15/8[2]	65+	—
3733[10]	**The Brewer (72)** (JCTuck) **5-11-0**(5) ChrisWebb (hdwy to ld appr 5th: hdd next: rdn & outpcd appr 2 out)	2½	**2**	5/1	50	—
3733[9]	**Moonlight Escapade (IRE) (73)** (RJHodges) **6-11-6** VSlattery (drvn along to stay in tch 5th: wknd appr 2 out)	4	**3**	4/1[3]	47	—
3760[5]	**Prince of Spades (66)** (AGHobbs) **5-10-13** RGreene (chsd ldrs tl wknd appr 2 out)	3½	**4**	6/4[1]	37	—
3745[6]	**Green Bopper (USA) (75)** (CPMorlock) **4-11-0** JFrost (bhd: in tch to 5th: wknd next: p.u bef 2 out)		**P**	13/2	—	—
3447[13]	**Achill Prince (IRE) (62)** (NGAyliffe) **6-10-2**(7) MGriffiths (lw: plld hrd: led: sn clr: hdd appr 5th: wknd qckly & p.u bef next)		**P**	12/1	—	—
				(SP 132.5%)		**6 Rn**

4m 2.6 (9.60) CSF £13.02 TOTE £3.60: £1.80 £2.80 (£7.20) OWNER Mr Paul Green (BLEWBURY) BRED Paul Green
WEIGHT FOR AGE 4yo-8lb
OFFICIAL EXPLANATION **Achill Prince (IRE): had bled from the nose.**
3352* Mellow Master stepped up on his winning debut in a seller last time out, to take this more easily than the winning margin suggests. (15/8)
3234 The Brewer has shown a glimpse of ability in the past, but showed up well here to run his best race to date. There can be a small race found for him. (5/1: op 3/1)
918 Moonlight Escapade (IRE) has been busier than his rivals, but has yet to encounter success. (4/1: tchd 6/1)
3760 Prince of Spades looked to have been found a good opportunity here but proved a shade disappointing. (6/4)
Green Bopper (USA) (13/2: op 3/1)

3952 TEIGN SUITE H'CAP HURDLE (0-125) (4-Y.O+) (Class D)

5-10 (-) **2m 6f (10 hdls)** £4,190.00 GOING minus 0.62 sec per fur (F)

				SP	RR	SF
2807F	**Holdimclose (115)** (RGFrost) **7-11-11** JFrost (Walked over)		**1**		—	—
						1 Rn

OWNER Mrs C. Loze (BUCKFASTLEIGH) BRED R. G. Frost

T/Plpt: £189.50 (10.19 Tckts). T/Qdpt: £90.00 (0.86 Tckts); £17.04 to Uttoxeter 1/4/97 T

3896-PLUMPTON (L-H) (Good to firm)

Monday March 31st

Race 4: no time taken

WEATHER: fine

3953 JEVINGTON H'CAP HURDLE (0-100) (4-Y.O) (Class E)

2-30 (2-31) **2m 4f (12 hdls)** £2,364.00 (£654.00: £312.00) GOING minus 0.20 sec per fur (G)

	Horse / details	Dist	Pos	SP	RR	SF
3287^{5}	**Anna Soleil (IRE) (100)** (OSherwood) **4-11-7**$^{(7)}$ DThomas (a.p: led 9th: hrd rdn appr last: r.o)	—	1	9/2^{3}	72	35
3634^{19}	**Palamon (USA) (85)** (JWhite) **4-10-13** JRKavanagh (hld up: hdwy 9th: chsd wnr appr 2 out: hrd rdn appr last: r.o)	½	2	4/1^{2}	57	20
3301^{7}	**Ben Bowden (92)** (SWoodman) **4-11-3**$^{(3)}$ LAspell (lw: led: hdd 9th: wknd appr 2 out)	13	3	4/1^{2}	53	16
2865^{8}	**Bigwig (IRE) (73)** (GLMoore) **4-9-8v**$^{1(7)}$ MBatchelor (chsd ldrs tl wknd appr 2 out)	20	4	20/1	18	—
3809^{3}	**Veronica Franco (75)** (BAPearce) **4-10-0**$^{(3)}$ SophieMitchell (prom tl wknd 9th)	11	5	20/1	11	—
3730^{6}	**El Bardador (IRE) (72)** (RJHodges) **4-10-0b** PHolley (mstke 3rd: in tch tl wknd 9th)	6	6	16/1	4	—
3704^{2}	**Eskimo Kiss (IRE) (79)** (GFJohnsonHoughton) **4-10-7v** DGallagher (a bhd: t.o whn p.u appr 2 out)		P	11/4^{1}	—	—
3811^{2}	**Yellow Dragon (IRE) (82)** (BAPearce) **4-10-10** ALarnach (ref to r)		R	4/1^{2}	—	—
				(SP 120.3%)	**8 Rn**	

4m 54.1 (7.10) CSF £22.32 CT £70.56 TOTE £6.80: £2.10 £1.90 £1.80 (£18.30) OWNER Mr M. G. St Quinton (UPPER LAMBOURN) BRED Seamus MacKenna

OFFICIAL EXPLANATION **Eskimo Kiss (IRE): the jockey reported that the filly did not handle the visors and jumped right throughout. The trainer reported that on returning to the yard the following day, the filly was found to be lame behind.**

3287 Anna Soleil (IRE) responded gamely to repel the runner-up's challenge on the flat. (9/2: 7/2-11/2)

2925 Palamon (USA) looked very dangerous approaching two out but could never quite get his head in front. He appears well suited by a sound surface and can also be a useful animal for the summer jumping. (4/1)

1935 Ben Bowden made a lot of the running but was left behind from three out. (4/1: 3/1-9/2)

3704 Eskimo Kiss (IRE) was never travelling and her rider reported her unsuited to the first-time visor. (11/4)

3954 EASTER (S) H'CAP CHASE (0-90) (5-Y.O+) (Class G)

3-00 (3-00) **2m (13 fncs)** £2,385.00 (£660.00: £315.00) GOING minus 0.20 sec per fur (G)

	Horse / details	Dist	Pos	SP	RR	SF
3674^{7}	**Rustic Gent (IRE) (65)** (MrsLCJewell) **9-10-6** JRKavanagh (a.p: led after 3 out: mstke & lft clr next: easily)	—	1	10/1	76+	1
3278^{7}	**Mr Bean (87)** (KRBurke) **7-12-0** ALarnach (chsd ldrs: mstke 3rd: lft 2nd 2 out: one pce)	12	2	7/4^{2}	86	11
1965^{6}	**Dawn Chance (77)** (RJHodges) **11-11-4** PHolley (lw: prom: nt fluent: mstkes 6th & 9th: wknd appr 3 out: lft 3rd 2 out)	4	3	6/4^{1}	72	—
3810^{P}	**Bright Season (67)** (JCPoulton) **9-10-1b**$^{1(7)ow6}$ GordonGallagher (fell 1st)		F	50/1	—	—
3684^{3}	**Fattash (USA) (71)** (PMooney) **5-10-1b**$^{(3)ow3}$ LAspell (nt fluent: a bhd: t.o whn p.u bef 9th)		P	8/1	—	—
3684^{F}	**Riseupwilliereilly (60)** (DFBassett) **11-9-8**$^{(7)}$ CRafter (led: hdd after 3 out: 2nd & ev ch whn blnd & uns rdr 2 out)		U	7/2^{3}	—	—
				(SP 120.7%)	**6 Rn**	

4m 1.0 (9.00) CSF £28.60 TOTE £8.30: £2.80 £1.80 (£10.10) OWNER Mrs A. Emanuel (SUTTON VALENCE) BRED John and Mrs McNamara

WEIGHT FOR AGE 5yo-8lb

No bid

Rustic Gent (IRE) jumped quite well apart from a mistake two out. His only serious rival capsized at this fence but he would probably have prevailed anyway. (10/1)

2752 Mr Bean was outpaced from three out and was lucky to get second. (7/4)

1421* Dawn Chance jumped poorly. (6/4)

Fattash (USA) (8/1: 6/1-9/1)

Riseupwilliereilly jumped well until falling two out. He still had every chance here but would probably have been second. (7/2)

3955 ALFRISTON NOVICES' HURDLE (5-Y.O+) (Class E)

3-30 (3-31) **2m 1f (10 hdls)** £2,742.00 (£762.00: £366.00) GOING minus 0.20 sec per fur (G)

	Horse / details	Dist	Pos	SP	RR	SF
3494^{P}	**Reverse Thrust (76)** (PRHedger) **6-10-7**$^{(7)}$ MClinton (hld up in rr: hdwy appr 3 out: led last: r.o)	—	1	14/1	63	—
3623^{4}	**Alka International (77)** (MrsPTownsley) **5-10-11**$^{(3)}$ LAspell (lw: led 7th: hdd last: rallied flat: r.o)	s.h	2	7/2^{2}	63	—
3820^{5}	**Real Madrid** (GPEnright) **6-10-7**$^{(7)}$ MBatchelor (a.p: w ldr to 2 out: rdn appr last: one pce)	5	3	6/1	58	—
3755^{6}	**Clock Watchers (67)** (JJBridger) **9-10-11**$^{(3)}$ SophieMitchell (led 2nd: sn hdd: led after 5th: hdd 7th: rdn appr 2 out: one pce)	¾	4	16/1	58	—
3587^{4}	**Sun of Spring** (JWhite) **7-11-0** JRKavanagh (hld up: rdn appr 3 out: wknd appr 2 out)	7	5	7/4^{1}	51	—
3061^{5}	**Ilandra (IRE)** (GLMoore) **5-10-9** DGallagher (prom tl wknd 3 out)	15	6	9/2^{3}	32	—
3494^{P}	**Pearl Hart** (RTPhillips) **5-10-2**$^{(7)}$ MartinSmith (a bhd: t.o)	16	7	33/1	17	—
	Blasted (85) (DRGandolfo) **5-11-0** PHolley (rr: effrt 6th: sn btn: t.o)	14	8	10/1	9	—
3575^{6}	**Welsh Wizzard** (JRBest) **5-10-7**$^{(7)}$ MrPO'Keeffe (led to 2nd: wknd 5th: t.o)	1½	9	33/1	7	—
3820^{9}	**Spectacle Jim** (BAPearce) **8-11-0** ALarnach (a bhd: t.o fr 7th)	20	10	33/1	—	—
	Global Dancer (LWells) **6-10-7**$^{(7)}$ WGreatrex (plld hrd: led appr 3rd: hdd after 5th: sn wknd: p.u after 6th)		P	14/1	—	—
				(SP 128.2%)	**11 Rn**	

4m 9.4 (13.40) CSF £62.59 TOTE £21.50: £4.30 £1.60 £2.20 (£59.70) OWNER Mrs M. N. Tufnell (CHICHESTER) BRED Mrs M. N. Tufnell

OFFICIAL EXPLANATION **Global Dancer: the jockey thought the gelding to be lame, but this was not the case.**

2690 Reverse Thrust was suited by the pace and tactics employed here. (14/1)

3623 Alka International led four out and, after fighting off the challenge of the third, tried valiantly to repel the winner and only just failed. (7/2: op 2/1)

Real Madrid looked dangerous turning for home but could find no more from two out. (6/1)

Sun of Spring dropped away disappointingly from the home turn. (7/4)

Blasted (10/1: op 6/1)

Global Dancer (14/1: 10/1-16/1)

3956 ABERGAVENNY CHALLENGE CUP NOVICES' H'CAP CHASE (0-95) (5-Y.O+) (Class F)
4-00 (4-00) **3m 1f 110y (20 fncs)** £3,189.60 (£885.60: £424.80) GOING minus 0.20 sec per fur (G)

			SP	RR	SF
3546[5]	**Dream Leader (IRE) (72)** (MJRoberts) **7-11-3** DGallagher (lw: hld up in tch: mstke 12th: led 16th: clr 2 out: easily) ——	1	9/4[2]	90+	—
3207[11]	**Side Bar (60)** (PMooney) **7-10-2v**(3) LAspell (led 3rd: hdd 16th: wknd appr 2 out) 28	2	14/1	60	—
3759[3]	**Pinoccio (62)** (DCO'Brien) **10-10-4**(3) SophieMitchell (led to 3rd: mstke 13th: wknd 15th: mod 3rd 17th) 16	3	7/1	52	—
3113[4]	**Call Me River (IRE) (79)** (PRHedger) **9-11-10** JRKavanagh (lw: hld up in tch: 4th whn fell 9th)	F	4/5[1]	—	—
3810[3]	**Nautical George (IRE) (77)** (JohnUpson) **7-11-8** PHolley (in tch: wknd 15th: mod 3rd whn blnd & uns rdr 17th)	U	6/1[3]	—	—
			(SP 119.8%)		**5 Rn**

No Time Taken CSF £23.61 TOTE £3.40: £1.60 £4.20 (£32.10) OWNER Mr Mike Roberts (HAILSHAM) BRED Frank Barry
3227 Dream Leader (IRE) was always going well and, apart from a couple of untidy jumps, looked sure to win throughout the final circuit. (9/4)
Side Bar cut out a lot of the running but was put in his place by the winner over the final three fences. (14/1: 20/1-33/1)
Pinoccio ran alright but was a tired horse over the final four fences. (7/1: op 12/1)
3113 Call Me River (IRE) was close up when falling at halfway. (4/5)
3810 Nautical George (IRE) (6/1: op 11/4)

3957 HOLIDAY MAIDEN CHASE (5-Y.O+) (Class F)
4-30 (4-30) **2m 2f (14 fncs)** £3,304.80 (£799.20) GOING minus 0.20 sec per fur (G)

			SP	RR	SF
3688[2]	**Normarange (IRE) (86)** (DMGrissell) **7-11-7** JRKavanagh (led to 2nd: lft 2nd 10th: led 3 out: hrd rdn appr next: r.o) ——	1	1/2[1]	79	—
3736[P]	**River Gala (IRE) (68)** (RJHodges) **7-11-7** PHolley (hld up: in tch: lft in ld 10th: hdd 3 out: sn rdn: unable qckn) 4	2	7/2[2]	75	—
	Shanagore Hill (IRE) (JCPoulton) **7-11-7** ALarnach (led 2nd: mstke 9th: fell 10th)	F	9/2[3]	—	—
3758[4]	**Fruit Town (IRE)** (PButler) **8-11-4**(3) LAspell (last but in tch whn fell 8th)	F	14/1	—	—
			(SP 113.7%)		**4 Rn**

4m 33.5 (15.50) CSF £2.78 TOTE £1.60 (£2.30) OWNER Mr D. Curtis (ROBERTSBRIDGE) BRED John O'Mahony
3688 Normarange (IRE) had to be driven out to win this poor race. (1/2)
752 River Gala (IRE) ensured the winner had to fight for his money. (7/2)
Shanagore Hill (IRE) made most of the running and was still two lengths clear when falling. (9/2: op 3/1)
Fruit Town (IRE) (14/1: 12/1-20/1)

3958 'MANHATTAN BOY' H'CAP HURDLE (0-110) (5-Y.O+) (Class E)
5-00 (5-01) **2m 4f (12 hdls)** £2,637.00 (£732.00: £351.00) GOING minus 0.20 sec per fur (G)

			SP	RR	SF
3603[4]	**Night in a Million (81)** (SWoodman) **6-9-13**(3)ow2 LAspell (chsd ldr: led 7th: hrd rdn flat: r.o wl) ——	1	7/1	66	12
2797[8]	**Bon Voyage (USA) (92)** (DMGrissell) **5-10-13b** JRKavanagh (lw: hld up: hdwy 8th: jnd wnr appr 2 out: ev ch flat: unable qckn) 2½	2	4/1[3]	75	23
3851[6]	**Smuggler's Point (USA) (107)** (JJBridger) **7-12-0** PHolley (lw: led: hdd 7th: hrd rdn appr 2 out: one pce) 10	3	7/2[2]	82	30
3499[13]	**An Spailpin Fanach (IRE) (86)** (DRGandolfo) **8-10-4b**[1](3) SophieMitchell (chsd ldrs: wknd appr 2 out) 4	4	9/1	58	6
3488[4]	**Karen's Typhoon (IRE) (79)** (TPMcGovern) **6-9-7**(7) MBatchelor (in tch tl wknd 8th) 9	5	7/1	44	—
3760*	**Kelly Mac (93)** (DCO'Brien) **7-11-0** DGallagher (hld up: rdn 9th: wknd 3 out) ¾	6	11/8[1]	57	5
3760[6]	**Baylord Prince (IRE) (79)** (MrsJAEwer) **9-10-0** MrKGoble (bhd fr 5th) 6	7	50/1	38?	—
			(SP 121.3%)		**7 Rn**

4m 53.8 (6.80) CSF £34.35 TOTE £7.50: £2.20 £2.80 (£14.70) OWNER Leith Hill Chasers (CHICHESTER) BRED Biddestone Stud
LONG HANDICAP Night in a Million 9-10 Karen's Typhoon (IRE) 9-7 Baylord Prince (IRE) 8-8
3603 Night in a Million won this in very game fashion. (7/1)
1045 Bon Voyage (USA) looked sure to win when joining the winner on the run to two out but found his rival too tough a nut to crack. (4/1: tchd 6/1)
3720* Smuggler's Point (USA) was outpaced for much of the final circuit. (7/2: 3/1-9/2)
3760* Kelly Mac dropped away tamely over the final three flights. (11/8)

T/Plpt: £131.80 (26.3 Tckts). T/Qdpt: £42.00 (4.28 Tckts) SM

3902-TOWCESTER (R-H) (Good to firm, Firm patches)
Monday March 31st
WEATHER: fine & sunny

3959 LISA HOLMAN 18TH BIRTHDAY (S) H'CAP HURDLE (0-95) (4-Y.O+) (Class G)
2-15 (2-16) **2m (8 hdls)** £2,034.50 (£567.00: £273.50) GOING minus 0.42 sec per fur (GF)

			SP	RR	SF
3757[4]	**Anif (USA) (58)** (JJoseph) **6-10-1**ow1 DSkyrme (chsd ldrs: rdn & hit last: r.o to ld nr fin) ——	1	5/1	50	—
3590[4]	**Paulton (65)** (KBishop) **4-9-9b**[1](5) SRyan (lw: hdwy 5th: led appr 2 out: veered lft & hdd nr fin) s.h	2	9/2[3]	57	—
2006[11]	**Captain Tandy (IRE) (70)** (CSmith) **8-10-13** TReed (chsd clr ldr: led appr 3 out: hdd appr next: sn btn) 8	3	10/1	54	2
3748*	**Derrybelle (81)** (DLWilliams) **6-11-3**(7) MrSDurack (hld up: hdwy 4th: blnd 3 out: sn wknd) 20	4	3/1[2]	45	—
950[7]	**Timely Example (USA) (68)** (BRCambidge) **6-10-11b** GaryLyons (bhd tl sme hdwy appr 2 out) hd	5	10/1	32	—
3670*	**Flash In The Pan (IRE) (87)** (JSMoore) **4-11-8** WMcFarland (lw: nvr trbld ldrs) 3	6	9/4[1]	48	—
2088[8]	**Catwalker (IRE) (57)** (HJMWebb) **6-10-0** SCurran (lw: bhd fr 4th) 20	7	8/1	—	—
3677[P]	**Ernest Aragorn (57)** (MrsSLamyman) **8-10-0v** MRanger (led: sn clr: blnd 5th: wknd & hdd appr next: t.o whn p.u bef 2 out)	P	25/1	—	—
			(SP 123.8%)		**8 Rn**

3m 51.0 (5.00) CSF £27.74 CT £205.17 TOTE £7.10: £1.70 £1.60 £2.20 (£18.70) OWNER Mr Jack Joseph (AMERSHAM) BRED Dick, Elia, Cooper & Freeman Betz
LONG HANDICAP Anif (USA) 9-11 Catwalker (IRE) 9-13 Ernest Aragorn 9-10
WEIGHT FOR AGE 4yo-8lb
No bid

3757 Anif (USA) plugged on straight and true, and this won him the race in the last fifty yards. (5/1)
3590 Paulton should have won, but seemed intent on throwing the race away by diving for the stands' rails in the straight. (9/2)
Captain Tandy (IRE) seemed to be travelling well enough until, headed coming up the hill, he faded rather tamely. He won three times in the summer of 1995, but this was his first prominent showing for some time. (10/1)
3748* Derrybelle repeated the tactics that were successful at the last meeting, and may have gone close, but a terrible blunder three out ended all hope. (3/1)
950 Timely Example (USA) tried to close in the straight, but to little effect. (10/1: 7/1-11/1)
3670* Flash In The Pan (IRE) tried to close on the climb to the straight, but got nowhere. She had been well beaten at Doncaster since her Folkestone win. (9/4)

3960 HARTWELL LANDROVER NOVICES' H'CAP CHASE (0-100) (5-Y.O+) (Class E)
2-45 (2-46) **2m 110y (12 fncs)** £3,137.00 (£941.00: £453.00: £209.00) GOING minus 0.42 sec per fur (GF)

				SP	RR	SF
3749[2]	**Sleazey (72)** (JGO'Neill) **6-11-10** SCurran (led to 2nd: led 5th to 2 out: sn rdn: led again flat)	—	1	4/5[1]	83	31
3684[U]	**Full Shilling (USA) (60)** (DLWilliams) **8-10-5b**(7) MrSDurack (lw: led 2nd to 5th: rdn to ld 2 out: hdd & unable qckn flat)	1	2	5/2[2]	70	18
3842[4]	**Copper Cable (70)** (CSmith) **10-11-8** MRanger (sn chsng ldrs: hit 6th: no imp fr 4 out: eased flat)	dist	3	4/1[3]	—	—
3842[F]	**Highland Flame (60)** (AGBlackmore) **8-10-12** BClifford (j.slowly 3rd: sn wl bhd)	dist	4	9/1	—	—
				(SP 114.1%)		**4 Rn**

4m 4.5 (2.50) CSF £3.26 TOTE £1.80 (£2.20) OWNER Mr J. G. O'Neill (BICESTER) BRED Finbar O'Neill
3749 Sleazey again jumped soundly, but had to pull out all the stops to win a poor event. (4/5: evens-11/10)
Full Shilling (USA) put in a good round of jumping, and gave the winner a real race, coming as close as he has ever done to breaking his duck. (5/2: op 4/1)
3842 Copper Cable put in a better, although somewhat deliberate, round of jumping. He would have been beaten about fifteen lengths but for being eased. (4/1: op 9/4)
Highland Flame, who fell less than a week ago, was never travelling. (9/1: 5/1-10/1)

3961 PHILIP BRANGWYN MEMORIAL H'CAP CHASE (0-115) (5-Y.O+) (Class E)
3-15 (3-16) **3m 1f (18 fncs)** £3,455.50 (£1,039.00: £502.00: £233.50) GOING minus 0.42 sec per fur (GF)

				SP	RR	SF
3585[2]	**Merlins Dream (IRE) (114)** (OSherwood) **8-12-0** JAMcCarthy (lw: w ldr: led appr 3 out: clr appr next: rdn out)	—	1	7/2[2]	125	41
3729[3]	**Lay it Off (IRE) (86)** (JGO'Neill) **8-10-0** SCurran (lw: j.w: led tl appr 3 out: styd on wl appr last)	3	2	6/1	95	11
3599[5]	**Danger Baby (98)** (DLWilliams) **7-10-5v**(7) MrSDurack (chsd ldrs: mstke 12th: one pce fr 3 out)	1½	3	5/1[3]	106	22
3729*	**Sheelin Lad (IRE) (92)** (MrsTJMcInnesSkinner) **9-10-6**ow4 TReed (hld up: hit 3rd: hdwy 11th: rdn 14th: wnt 2nd appr 2 out: wknd appr last)	4	4	3/1[1]	98	10
2876[5]	**Steeple Jack (86)** (KBishop) **10-9-9b**1(5) SRyan (mstke 2nd: chsd ldrs tl rdn & btn 13th: n.d after)	9	5	33/1	86	2
3616[7]	**Hawaiian Sam (IRE) (105)** (AndrewTurnell) **7-11-5** GCrone (lw: hld up: mstkes 5th & 6th: hdwy 11th: wknd 14th)	15	6	7/2[2]	95	11
3428[P]	**Woodlands Genhire (89)** (PAPritchard) **12-10-3v**ow3 WMcFarland (bhd fr 9th)	14	7	33/1	70	—
3838[U]	**Harristown Lady (103)** (GBBalding) **10-11-3b** BClifford (in tch tl j.slowly 9th: sn bhd)	30	8	7/2[2]	65	—
				(SP 128.5%)		**8 Rn**

6m 16.6 (1.60) CSF £25.64 CT £100.35 TOTE £5.00: £1.70 £1.70 £1.90 (£24.30) OWNER Mr W. S. Watt (UPPER LAMBOURN) BRED Neville Bourke
LONG HANDICAP Lay it Off (IRE) 9-5 Woodlands Genhire 9-5 Steeple Jack 9-4
OFFICIAL EXPLANATION Harristown Lady: the rider reported that the mare finished distressed.
3585 Merlins Dream (IRE) looked in fine shape and put in his best performance yet. He is thriving since his mid-season break. (7/2)
Lay it Off (IRE) did nearly enough to win this with an excellent round of jumping, but being nine pounds out of the handicap proved too much in the end. (6/1: op 14/1)
3599 Danger Baby, at last given a chance by the Handicapper, looked short of pace on such fast ground. (5/1)
3729* Sheelin Lad (IRE) was asked for his effort on the climb to the straight and, like so many over the years, paid the penalty. In mitigation, the pilot is hardly a regular here, and the combination may have not finished winning yet. (3/1: 9/4-7/2)
Steeple Jack, was not even rejuvenated by first-time blinkers and his favourite track, although he stayed on in the last half-mile after losing his place. (33/1)
3616 Hawaiian Sam (IRE) adopted very different tactics from those that brought improvement at Cheltenham, and the writing was on the wall almost a mile from home. (7/2)

3962 PENRHYN H'CAP HURDLE (0-105) (4-Y.O+) (Class F)
3-50 (3-51) **3m (12 hdls)** £2,372.50 (£660.00: £317.50) GOING minus 0.42 sec per fur (GF)

				SP	RR	SF
3488[5]	**Ross Dancer (IRE) (85)** (JSMoore) **5-11-3**(3) JMagee (lw: led to 2nd: led 5th: hit last: all out)	—	1	7/1	65	—
3624[4]	**Stac-Pollaidh (77)** (KCBailey) **7-10-12** WMcFarland (lw: hld up: hdwy appr 8th: ev ch 2 out: unable qckn nr fin)	nk	2	9/4[1]	57	—
3750[5]	**Cabochon (85)** (JJoseph) **10-11-6** DSkyrme (chsd ldrs: ev ch whn hit 2 out: one pce)	1¼	3	8/1	64	—
3737[6]	**Derring Bridge (80)** (MrsSMJohnson) **7-11-1** JAMcCarthy (lw: w ldrs: outpcd 3 out: r.o flat)	2	4	9/2[3]	58	—
3075[12]	**Sterling Fellow (80)** (DLWilliams) **4-9-12v**(7) MrSDurack (hld up: hit 1st: hdwy next: no imp appr 2 out)	½	5	6/1	57	—
1819[P]	**Crown Ivory (NZ) (74)** (PCRitchens) **9-10-9** SFox (bhd fr 8th)	5	6	12/1	48	—
3646[5]	**Rimouski (89)** (BRCambidge) **9-11-10** GaryLyons (dropped rr 4th: hdwy 7th: wknd appr 3 out)	22	7	100/30[2]	48	—
3671[5]	**Summer Haven (69)** (NMLampard) **8-9-11**(7) MrLBaker (led 2nd to 5th: wknd 7th: t.o whn p.u bef 3 out)		P	16/1	—	—
				(SP 123.5%)		**8 Rn**

6m 0.5 (20.50) CSF £23.51 CT £124.27 TOTE £10.00: £2.50 £1.20 £1.70 (£12.20) OWNER Mr Gerard O'Loughlin (HUNGERFORD) BRED Kilnamoragh Stud
WEIGHT FOR AGE 4yo-10lb
3488 Ross Dancer (IRE) lasted home gamely on this much faster ground. (7/1)
3624 Stac-Pollaidh loves fast ground but, after appearing to be going best, was just worried out of it in a tight finish. She should find an opportunity before long. (9/4)
3750 Cabochon got the trip well, and handled the ground. He looked set to go even closer when kicking the second last out of the ground. (8/1: 4/1-9/1)
2761 Derring Bridge, caught-out when the steady pace quickened with half-a-mile left, was coming back for more at the finish. (9/2: op 5/2)

2070 Sterling Fellow, ridden to get the trip, was getting nowhere in the straight after creeping up to the leaders three out. He hit the downhill flight on both circuits. (6/1)
978* Crown Ivory (NZ), held up towards the rear, failed to close at all as the pace quickened. (12/1)
3646 Rimouski (100/30: 7/1-3/1)

3963 SCHILIZZI 1906 SIXTY YEARS COMMEMORATIVE CHALLENGE CUP HUNTERS' CHASE (5-Y.O+) (Class H)

4-25 (4-25) **2m 6f (16 fncs)** £1,059.00 (£294.00: £141.00) GOING minus 0.42 sec per fur (GF)

				SP	RR	SF
3490*	**Teaplanter** (MissCSaunders) **14-12-0**(5) MrBPollock (lw: led to 7th: led & blnd 3 out: sn hdd: led again next: sn clr: rdn out)	—	**1**	4/9[1]	119	23
3744[4]	**Tuffnut George** (MrsPGrainger) **10-11-7**(7) MrAPhillips (trckd wnr: led 7th to 3 out: sn led again: hdd 2 out: sn rdn & btn)	19	**2**	5/2[2]	100	4
3753[2]	**Hickelton Lad** (DLWilliams) **13-11-7**(7) MrSDurack (lost tch fr 7th)	dist	**3**	7/1[3]	—	—
				(SP 110.3%)		**3 Rn**

5m 37.8 (8.80) CSF £1.89 TOTE £1.50 (£1.30) OWNER Mr R. G. Russell (NORTHAMPTON) BRED Oakgrove Stud
3490* Teaplanter, gaining his ninth course win, finds the job harder these days but, after an uncharacteristic blunder three from home, he showed great powers of recovery to take charge by the next. (4/9: 1/2-1/3)
3744 Tuffnut George showed enough speed to get the favourite in trouble on the final circuit, but his stamina failed him on this stiff track. (5/2)
3753 Hickelton Lad, in a race over ten seconds faster than the one he contested at the previous meeting, was never going well. (7/1: 4/1-8/1)

3964 DUNCOTE MAIDEN HURDLE (4-Y.O+) (Class F)

4-55 (4-57) **2m (8 hdls)** £2,706.50 (£759.00: £369.50) GOING minus 0.42 sec per fur (GF)

				SP	RR	SF
3761[3]	**Ring of Vision (IRE)** (CJMann) **5-11-2**(3) JMagee (hdwy 5th: led appr last: rdn clr flat)	—	**1**	9/4[2]	76	11
3544[5]	**Jamaican Flight (USA)** (MrsSLamyman) **4-10-13** MRanger (lw: hld up: hdwy 3 out: r.o flat)	1¾	**2**	25/1	76	3
3424[5]	**Rising Dough (IRE) (97)** (GLMoore) **5-11-5** WMcFarland (lw: hld up: hdwy appr 2 out: hit last: r.o)	4	**3**	3/1[3]	70	5
	Gipsy Geof (IRE) (GAHubbard) **6-11-5** TReed (bit bkwd: hld up: hdwy 5th: led appr 2 out: rdn & hdd appr last: sn btn)	hd	**4**	16/1	70	5
1523[2]	**Aradia's Diamond** (TKeddy) **6-10-9**(5) SRyan (chsd ldrs tl appr 2 out)	18	**5**	6/1	47	—
3431[F]	**Mr Darcy (99)** (PRWebber) **5-11-5** JAMcCarthy (lw: chsd ldrs: led 3rd to 5th: rdn & btn appr 2 out)	1¾	**6**	2/1[1]	50	—
3007[P]	**Sassy Street (IRE)** (RFJohnsonHoughton) **4-10-13** BClifford (led to 3rd: wknd appr 2 out)	8	**7**	12/1	44	—
	Red Viper (NMLampard) **5-11-5** MrAKinane (plld hrd: prom: led 5th: hdd & wknd appr 2 out)	6	**8**	25/1	36	—
3489[R]	**Swift Pokey** (DLWilliams) **7-10-12**(7) MrSDurack (w ldrs to 4th: sn bhd)	6	**9**	50/1	30	—
3287[P]	**Port Valenska (IRE)** (MrsJConway) **4-10-13b** MissLAllan (prom to 4th)	dist	**10**	66/1	—	—
				(SP 128.1%)		**10 Rn**

3m 51.5 (5.50) CSF £55.31 TOTE £3.60: £1.10 £4.40 £1.60 (£27.00) OWNER Mr Harold Bray (UPPER LAMBOURN) BRED Amberush Investments
WEIGHT FOR AGE 4yo-8lb
3761 Ring of Vision (IRE) took to the track well, staying on very strongly after the last. This was a well-above average novice hurdle for the time of year, and he should have no difficulty finding further races. (9/4)
3544 Jamaican Flight (USA) stayed well on the Flat, and the early kinks in his jumping look to have been sorted out by adopting waiting tactics. He will stay further, and should not be hard to place. (25/1)
3424 Rising Dough (IRE), put in his place from the last, goes on the ground, and there will be plenty of easier chances. (3/1)
Gipsy Geof (IRE), a half-brother to Imperial Call by the sire of Falmouth Bay and Well Briefed, has always looked the sort to make a chaser, and has done well physically during a twelve-month absence. Not fully wound-up, he showed fine speed to lead coming up the hill before the effort took its toll. There is time for him yet. (16/1)
1523 Aradia's Diamond could not live with these from the home turn. (6/1)
3431 Mr Darcy probably wants the ground a little easier, but was unlucky to find such a warm race at this time of year. (2/1)

T/Plpt: £78.90 (38.65 Tckts). T/Qdpt: £28.50 (3.13 Tckts) Dk

3729-UTTOXETER (L-H) (Good to firm, Good in places)
Monday March 31st

WEATHER: fine & sunny

3965 JENKINSONS CATERERS NOVICES' HURDLE (4-Y.O) (Class E)

2-15 (2-15) **2m 4f 110y (10 hdls)** £2,200.50 (£618.00: £301.50) GOING minus 0.12 sec per fur (G)

				SP	RR	SF
3634[5]	**Hayaain (122)** (KCBailey) **4-11-4** TJO'Sullivan (lw: hld up: chsd ldrs fr 7th: led 3 out: hit last: drvn out)	—	**1**	2/5[1]	66	18
1900[8]	**Arrogant Heir** (DHBrown) **4-10-12** DerekByrne (hld up bhd: hdwy appr 3 out: rdn to chse wnr fr 2 out: kpt on u.p: no ex cl home)	nk	**2**	16/1	60	12
3364[3]	**Ezanak (IRE)** (MissHCKnight) **4-10-12** JCulloty (led tl appr 2nd: chsd ldrs to 7th: rdn appr 2 out: styd on flat)	2½	**3**	7/2[2]	58	10
3668[3]	**Formidable Partner** (MrsVCWard) **4-10-7v**(5) MrRThornton (led appr 2nd tl rdn & hdd 3 out: wknd appr last)	20	**4**	5/1[3]	42	—
				(SP 116.2%)		**4 Rn**

4m 54.6 (10.60) CSF £6.78 TOTE £1.40 (£7.80) OWNER Quicksilver Racing Partnership (UPPER LAMBOURN) BRED Shadwell Estate Company Limited
IN-FOCUS: **Irishman Timmy O'Sullivan rode his first winner since coming to Britain.**
3634 Hayaain looked a certainly for this modest event after his great effort in the Triumph but already had a fight on his hands when clouting the final flight and won this with nothing to spare. (2/5)
906 Arrogant Heir took a keen hold going to post and, far and away his best run to date, the form of this slowly-run race should be treated with caution. (16/1)
3364 Ezanak (IRE) briefly lost his pitch when coming under pressure two from home but was closing again all the way up the run-in. A step up in trip should help. (7/2)
3668 Formidable Partner once again stopped quickly in the closing stages. (5/1)

3966 1152 XTRA AM (S) H'CAP CHASE (0-90) (5-Y.O+) (Class G)
2-50 (2-50) **2m 5f (16 fncs)** £2,358.00 (£663.00: £324.00) GOING minus 0.12 sec per fur (G)

				SP	RR	SF
3891[4]	**Good for a Laugh (80)** (AGHobbs) **13-11-2**(5) OBurrows (lw: a.p: led 3 out: clr last: comf)	—	1	7/2[2]	92	24
3732[4]	**Astral Invasion (USA) (71)** (TWall) **6-10-7**(5) MrRThornton (lw: disp ld to 7th: mstke & hdd 3 out: rdn & wknd appr last)	15	2	12/1	72	4
3891[P]	**Fairy Park (84)** (HOliver) **12-11-11v** MrMMunrowd (in tch: rdn & one pce fr 3 out)	5	3	11/1	81	13
3278[5]	**Saymore (83)** (WClay) **11-11-7**(3) GuyLewis (mid div: hdwy appr 4 out: rdn & kpt on one pce fr 3 out)	nk	4	4/1[3]	80	12
3472[4]	**Burntwood Melody (60)** (PTDalton) **6-9-8b**(7) THagger (mid div: kpt on fr 4 out: n.d)	1½	5	6/1	55	—
3622[6]	**Royal Square (CAN) (84)** (NPLittmoden) **11-11-11** DLeahy (chsd ldrs to 12th: sn wknd)	7	6	20/1	74	6
833[2]	**Turpin's Green (71)** (JSKing) **14-10-12** JCulloty (lw: mde most to 7th: wknd appr 4 out)	9	7	11/4[1]	54	—
3830[4]	**Lambrini (IRE) (67)** (DMcCain) **7-10-8b**[1] FPerratt (lw: mid div: lost pl 10th: t.o)	27	8	16/1	30	—
3227[5]	**Pandora's Prize (72)** (JLSpearing) **11-10-6**(7)ow12 SLycett (a bhd: t.o)	2½	9	14/1	33	—
3833[2]	**Ryton Run (81)** (MrsSMOdell) **12-11-8** TJO'Sullivan (in tch to 6th: wknd 8th: t.o whn p.u bef 12th)		P	7/1	—	—
3339[P]	**Rebel Priest (IRE) (62)** (CREgerton) **7-10-3**ow2 GUpton (bit bkwd: bhd fr 4th: t.o & p.u bef 10th)		P	9/1	—	—
2038[9]	**Applianceofscience (74)** (KOWarner) **10-11-1** DerekByrne (bit bkwd: sn bhd: t.o whn p.u bef 4th)		P	20/1	—	—

(SP 143.8%) **12 Rn**

5m 15.4 (10.40) CSF £50.35 CT £420.22 TOTE £3.90: £1.50 £3.20 £9.10 (£26.70) OWNER Mr Derek Walker (KINGSBRIDGE) BRED Mrs E. C. York
No bid
3891 Good for a Laugh made the most of his favourable mark to land his first victory for over three years in most emphatic fashion. (7/2)
2567 Astral Invasion (USA), just headed when untidy three from home, found the winner much too strong. (12/1)
1817 Fairy Park, slipping down the handicap, put in a reasonable effort but was well outpointed in the home straight. (11/1: op 6/1)
3001* Saymore (4/1: op 5/2)
833 Turpin's Green, well supported to maintain his yard's good form, was a spent force a long way out. (11/4: op 5/1)
Rebel Priest (IRE) (9/1: op 6/1)

3967 JOHN PARTRIDGE ENGLISH CLOTHING NOVICES' H'CAP HURDLE (0-100) (5-Y.O+) (Class E)
3-25 (3-25) **3m 110y (12 hdls)** £2,568.00 (£723.00: £354.00) GOING minus 0.12 sec per fur (G)

				SP	RR	SF
3431[2]	**El Freddie (93)** (JABOld) **7-11-10** GUpton (mde all: jnd 2 out: rdn & r.o flat)	—	1	5/2[1]	77	22
3733[6]	**Beechfield Flyer (85)** (WClay) **6-10-13**(3) GuyLewis (hld up: hdwy appr 9th: chsd wnr fr 3 out: ev ch fr 2 out: rdn & no ex cl home)	nk	2	12/1	69	14
3733[4]	**Cliburnel News (IRE) (79)** (ALForbes) **7-10-3**(7) EGreehy (hld up: stdy hdwy appr 3 out: rdn appr last: wknd flat)	8	3	8/1	58	3
3488[3]	**Hancock (77)** (JHetherton) **5-10-8** FPerratt (hld up: hdwy appr 4 out: rdn & wknd 2 out)	nk	4	7/2[2]	55	—
3644[6]	**Mr Christie (86)** (MissLCSiddall) **5-10-10**(7) SLycett (bhd: pushed along fr 8th: kpt on fr 3 out: n.d)	s.h	5	12/1	64	9
3628[7]	**Lothian Commander (75)** (DMcCain) **5-10-6v**[1] JCulloty (mid div: reminders 6th: lost tch 8th: t.o)	dist	6	20/1	—	—
3473[P]	**Rood Music (71)** (MGMeagher) **6-9-9**(7) JMogford (chsd wnr tl appr 3 out: sn rdn & wknd)	4	7	25/1	—	—
3483[12]	**Jayfcee (84)** (MPBielby) **5-11-1** DLeahy (in tch tl wknd 8th: t.o)	6	8	14/1	—	—
3328[3]	**Cypress Avenue (IRE) (89)** (MrsVCWard) **5-11-1b**(5) MrRThornton (bhd fr ½-wy: t.o)	4	9	10/1	—	—
3831[3]	**One More Dime (IRE) (69)** (JLNeedham) **7-9-7**(7) THagger (mid div tl wknd 8th: t.o)	s.h	10	25/1	—	—
3557[5]	**Clever Boy (IRE) (81)** (JWCurtis) **6-10-12** DerekByrne (hld up bhd: t.o whn p.u bef 3 out)		P	7/1	—	—
2945[2]	**Tantara Lodge (IRE) (77)** (KCBailey) **6-10-8** TJO'Sullivan (chsd ldrs tl wknd 8th: t.o whn p.u bef 3 out)		P	9/2[3]	—	—

(SP 136.2%) **12 Rn**

5m 55.5 (13.50) CSF £34.60 CT £211.91 TOTE £4.20: £1.90 £3.10 £3.40 (£19.70) OWNER Mr Martin Lovatt (WROUGHTON) BRED Mrs J. Bugg
LONG HANDICAP One More Dime (IRE) 9-10
3431 El Freddie put in a real gutsy display of front-running, seeing off a persistent runner-up in the final fifty yards. (5/2)
3733 Beechfield Flyer seemed well suited by the step up in trip and really made the consistent winner pull out all the stops. (12/1)
3733 Cliburnel News (IRE) looked to be going best of all turning for home but had come to the end of her tether approaching the final flight. A slight step back in distance might do the trick. (8/1)
3488 Hancock put in his third consecutive good run since being stepped up in distance and should be able to land a similar contest. (7/2)
3644 Mr Christie, under pressure at the back of the field with a circuit to go, just plugged on without ever being able to land a blow. (12/1: op 6/1)
3328 Cypress Avenue (IRE) (10/1: op 6/1)

3968 WELLMAN PLC NOVICES' CHASE (5-Y.O+) (Class E)
4-00 (4-01) **3m 2f (20 fncs)** £3,144.00 (£884.00: £432.00) GOING minus 0.12 sec per fur (G)

				SP	RR	SF
3805[6]	**Grizzly Bear (IRE)** (RMStronge) **7-11-2** JCulloty (a.p: chsd ldr appr 4 out: chal 2 out: hrd rdn to ld nr fin)	—	1	14/1	90	—
3617[9]	**Loch Garman Hotel (IRE) (81)** (PTDalton) **8-10-11**(5) MrRThornton (lw: led tl appr 9th: led 14th: rdn & jnd 2 out: slt ld tl hdd & no ex cl home)	2	2	7/4[2]	89	—
3435[2]	**Final Beat (IRE) (78)** (JWCurtis) **8-11-2b** FPerratt (hld up: chsd ldrs fr 12th: wknd 3 out)	22	3	13/8[1]	75	—
3731[4]	**Fox Chapel** (RTJuckes) **10-10-13**(3) GuyLewis (in tch whn p.u bef 13th)		P	4/1[3]	—	—
3582[5]	**Chapilliere (FR)** (TThomsonJones) **7-11-2** GUpton (chsd ldrs: led appr 9th: hdd 14th: j.slowly 16th: sn wknd: t.o: p.u bef 3 out)		P	7/1	—	—
3334[7]	**Musical Hit** (PAPritchard) **6-11-2b** TJO'Sullivan (lost tch 12th: t.o whn p.u bef 2 out)		P	20/1	—	—
3732[U]	**Sweet Buck (60)** (RCPugh) **8-11-2** DLeahy (a bhd: j.lft fr 9th: t.o whn p.u bef 15th)		P	33/1	—	—

(SP 121.3%) **7 Rn**

6m 48.1 (21.10) CSF £39.75 TOTE £12.50: £3.50 £1.60 (£19.40) OWNER Mr G. B. Barlow (NEWBURY) BRED Michael Ryan
Grizzly Bear (IRE), showing marked improvement on his first three runs, stayed on stoutly to lead in the final fifty yards. (14/1)
3003 Loch Garman Hotel (IRE) looked a picture and seemed set to open his account when he appeared to be just holding his rival up the run-in but he had no more to give in the last few strides. He deserves compensation. (7/4)
3435 Final Beat (IRE) got on to the heels of the leaders turning for home but looked very one-paced after that. (13/8)
3442 Fox Chapel (4/1: op 5/2)

3969 HOUGHTON VAUGHAN H'CAP CHASE (0-125) (5-Y.O+) (Class D)

4-35 (4-35) **3m (19 fncs)** £3,790.00 (£1,065.00: £520.00) GOING minus 0.12 sec per fur (G)

	Horse / details	Dist	Pos	SP	RR	SF
3492*	**Carlingford Lakes (IRE) (96)** (TThomsonJones) **9-10-2**ow2 GUpton (chsd ldrs: wknd 13th: 3rd & btn whn lft clr 3 out)	—	1	3/1[3]	102	—
3617[8]	**Ballyea Boy (IRE) (110)** (DNicholson) **7-10-11**(5) MrRThornton (chsd ldr 7th to 11th: sn drvn along: lft mod 2nd & hmpd 3 out)	16	2	11/4[2]	105	—
3560[P]	**Dark Oak (110)** (JWCurtis) **11-10-13**(3) GuyLewis (dropped rr 10th: sn t.o: lft poor 3rd 3 out)	8	3	5/1	100	—
2776[4]	**Imperial Vintage (IRE) (118)** (MissVenetiaWilliams) **7-11-10** JCulloty (led tl blnd & uns rdr 3 out)		U	7/4[1]	—	—
3332[P]	**Cantoris Frater (101)** (MrsJPitman) **10-10-7** DLeahy (hld up in tch: chsd ldr fr 11th: 3l 2nd whn blnd & uns rdr 3 out)		U	6/1	—	—
				(SP 119.0%)		5 Rn

6m 17.2 CSF £11.58 TOTE £4.30: £1.80 £1.40 (£6.60) OWNER Mrs Solna ThomsonJones (UPPER LAMBOURN) BRED Robert McCarthy

LONG HANDICAP Carlingford Lakes (IRE) 9-9

3492* Carlingford Lakes (IRE), 5lb out of the handicap and racing on ground much quicker that she would prefer, was on the retreat and booked for third place when the two leaders came to grief three from home. A very lucky winner but jumping is the name of the game. (3/1: op 2/1)

3018 Ballyea Boy (IRE), bustled along to hold his place a long way from home, was a distant fourth approaching three out and a fortunate second a short while later. His rider did very well to skip round one of the casualties. (11/4)

3033 Dark Oak trailed the field for the final mile. (5/1: op 3/1)

2776 Imperial Vintage (IRE) was all set for his ninth win of the season when he catapulted his pilot off at the third last when holding a three-length lead. He can gain compensation. (7/4)

Cantoris Frater, although held when coming to grief, had put up a much-improved run. (6/1: op 4/1)

3970 LLOYD HOPKINSON NOVICES' HURDLE (5-Y.O+ Mares Only) (Class E)

5-10 (5-10) **2m 4f 110y (10 hdls)** £2,473.50 (£696.00: £340.50) GOING minus 0.12 sec per fur (G)

	Horse / details	Dist	Pos	SP	RR	SF
3764*	**Motoqua (108)** (DNicholson) **5-11-1**(5) MrRThornton (a.p: chsd ldr fr 5th: rdn & outpcd appr 2 out: lft clr last)	—	1	6/4[2]	74	14
	Kaytu's Carousel (MissVenetiaWilliams) **8-10-10** GUpton (in tch: rdn & btn whn nt fluent 2 out: lft 2nd last)	6	2	16/1	59	—
3730[4]	**Riverbank Rose (82)** (WClay) **6-10-13v**(3) GuyLewis (led tl appr 4 out: rdn & wknd 3 out: lft 3rd last)	1¼	3	10/1	64	4
3491[3]	**Kosheen (IRE)** (MissHCKnight) **6-10-10** JCulloty (mid div: wknd 7th)	5	4	4/1[3]	54	—
3468[5]	**Flutterbud** (BJEckley) **5-10-3**(7) THagger (bhd: effrt 5th: btn 7th: t.o)	24	5	33/1	36	—
3844[U]	**More to Life** (MPBielby) **8-10-10** DLeahy (bit bkwd: dropped rr 5th: t.o fr next)	dist	6	33/1	—	—
3817[2]	**Fantasy Line (103)** (PRWebber) **6-10-13**(3) EHusband (lw: chsd ldrs: led appr 7th: clr appr 2 out: 10l ld whn fell last)		F	11/8[1]	78?	—
3491[P]	**Final Rose** (RJSmith) **7-10-6**(7)ow3 SLycett (plld hrd: chsd ldr to 4th: wknd qckly appr 6th: t.o: p.u bef 3 out)		P	25/1	—	—
	Shabo Shabo (MrsSMOdell) **5-10-10** TJO'Sullivan (bit bkwd: a bhd: t.o fr 3rd: p.u bef 4 out)		P	40/1	—	—
				(SP 129.2%)		9 Rn

4m 56.2 (12.20) CSF £23.82 TOTE £2.70: £1.60 £4.00 £1.50 (£39.20) OWNER Mrs Claire Smith (TEMPLE GUITING) BRED Darley Stud Management Co Ltd

3764* Motoqua found herself comprehensively outpointed two from home but was presented with the race when the favourite came a cropper at the last. (6/4)

Kaytu's Carousel made a promising effort in her first run for well over a year. (16/1)

3730 Riverbank Rose once again tried to stretch her field but found a few of these too good. (10/1)

3817 Fantasy Line took command four from home and had forged clear by the second last. She held a ten-length lead when taking a crashing fall at the final flight. She certainly has the ability to resume winning ways but this fall may take some getting over. (11/8)

T/Plpt: £183.40 (21.74 Tckts). T/Qdpt: £109.70 (1.19 Tckts) J

3366-WETHERBY (L-H) (Good, Good to firm patches)

Monday March 31st

WEATHER: fine

3971 WHARFEDALE (S) H'CAP HURDLE (0-100) (4-Y.O+) (Class G)

2-15 (2-15) **2m 7f (12 hdls)** £2,250.00 (£625.00: £300.00) GOING minus 0.03 sec per fur (G)

	Horse / details	Dist	Pos	SP	RR	SF
3448[3]	**Barton Heights (80)** (MrsMReveley) **5-11-5** PNiven (lw: trckd ldrs: chal 4 out: led appr last: drvn out)	—	1	5/2[1]	64	—
3711*	**Jalmaid (71)** (HAlexander) **5-10-5**(5) RMcGrath (lw: w ldrs: led 5th tl appr last: styd on wl)	¾	2	11/4[2]	55	—
3607[8]	**Mardood (65)** (SBClark) **12-9-11**(7) MissRClark (drvn along & outpcd 6th: wnt prom 4 out: one pce fr next)	7	3	33/1	44	—
3646[2]	**Five Flags (IRE) (88)** (MrsSJSmith) **9-11-13** RichardGuest (in tch: reminders 4th: rdn & outpcd fr 4 out)	5	4	5/2[1]	63	—
805[F]	**Valiant Dash (86)** (JSGoldie) **11-11-11** JCallaghan (lw: led to 5th: rdn 8th: sn wknd)	22	5	5/1[3]	46	—
3313[10]	**Charlvic (61)** (WSCunningham) **7-9-7b**1(7) LMcGrath (drvn along 6th: hdwy to chse ldrs 4 out: sn wknd: mstke 3 out)	1¼	6	33/1	20	—
3825[14]	**Mr Sloan (61)** (JSGoldie) **7-9-7**(7) MrOMcPhail (chsd ldrs: rdn 8th: sn lost pl)	6	7	50/1	16	—
	Owes the Till (61) (RSWood) **7-10-0** MissPRobson (bit bkwd: bhd fr 7th: t.o whn p.u bef 3 out)		P	33/1	—	—
3711[4]	**Fiasco (74)** (MJCamacho) **4-10-4** LWyer (trckd ldrs: hit 7th: wknd next: p.u bef 3 out)		P	8/1	—	—
				(SP 122.4%)		9 Rn

5m 41.4 CSF £9.64 CT £170.66 TOTE £3.50: £1.40 £1.30 £7.30 (£6.60) OWNER Miss C. J. Raines (SALTBURN) BRED Mrs S. Raines

LONG HANDICAP Mr Sloan 9-6 Charlvic 9-8

WEIGHT FOR AGE 4yo-9lb

No bid

3448 Barton Heights, who has slipped down the weights, looked to be travelling the better some way from home but in front he did very little and had to be driven right out near the line. (5/2)

3711* Jalmaid, from a 4lb higher mark, battled on gamely. (11/4)

1562 Mardood, on this ground, was left behind by the first two from three out. (33/1)

3646 Five Flags (IRE) never looked happy on this fast ground. (5/2)

3972 HUDDERSFIELD NOVICES' CHASE (5-Y.O+) (Class D)

2-45 (2-46) **2m 4f 110y (15 fncs)** £3,652.00 (£1,096.00: £528.00: £244.00) GOING minus 0.03 sec per fur (G)

Form	Horse	Dist	Pos	SP	RR	SF
3695^{2}	**Brighter Shade (IRE)** (MrsMReveley) **7-11-8** PNiven (lw: trckd ldrs: blnd 7th: chal 10th: led 3 out: drvn out flat)	—	1	10/11^{1}	103	44
3616^{P}	**Ballyline (IRE) (88)** (WTKemp) **6-11-8** JCallaghan (lw: led to 3 out: rallied flat: r.o)	3	2	5/1^{3}	101	42
3546^{2}	**Golden Hello (110)** (TDEasterby) **6-12-0** LWyer (lw: j.rt: trckd ldrs: ev ch and rdn whn blnd 3 out)	12	3	13/8^{2}	97	38
	Evening Rush (JWade) **11-11-6** RichardGuest (chasd ldrs tl wknd 7th: t.o 4 out)	dist	4	12/1	—	—
				(SP 114.8%)		**4 Rn**

5m 13.8 (6.80) CSF £5.49 TOTE £1.90 (£3.00) OWNER Mr D. S. Hall (SALTBURN) BRED N. J. Connors

3695 Brighter Shade (IRE), much more composed beforehand this time, survived a bad blunder at the seventh. Running lazily in front, he had to be kept right up to his work. Stamina is his strong suit and he will be an even better horse next season. (10/11: evens-11/10)

3068 Ballyline (IRE) made the running and proved very willing under pressure, putting his last two poor efforts behind him. (5/1)

3546 Golden Hello continually lost ground jumping right. He was only a length down but under pressure when he ploughed through the third last. Whether he would have done enough to trouble the first two is doubtful. (13/8)

3973 MALTON RACING ASSOCIATION NOVICES' HURDLE (5-Y.O+) (Class D)

3-15 (3-16) **2m (9 hdls)** £2,985.00 (£835.00: £405.00) GOING minus 0.03 sec per fur (G)

Form	Horse	Dist	Pos	SP	RR	SF
3366^{2}	**Good Vibes (115)** (TDEasterby) **5-11-2** LWyer (lw: mde all: hung rt: clr 2 out: rdn out)	—	1	4/11^{1}	86	19
3366^{5}	**Ardarroch Prince** (MrsMReveley) **6-10-10** PNiven (lw: nt j.w: trckd wnr: hit last: kpt on wl)	3	2	3/1^{2}	77	10
	Starlin Sam (JSisterson) **8-10-3**(7) MrOMcPhail (bit bkwd: chsd ldrs tl wknd appr 3 out)	25	3	33/1	52	—
	M-I-Five (IRE) (RonaldThompson) **6-10-10** RichardGuest (trckd ldrs to 4 out: sn wknd: blnd last)	5	4	15/2^{3}	47	—
	Thomas Rand (MDods) **8-10-5**(5) RMcGrath (nt j.w: sn wl bhd: sme hdwy 2 out)	13	5	33/1	34	—
3487^{9}	**Superexalt** (JGFitzGerald) **5-10-10** MissPRobson (bhd fr 5th)	4	6	33/1	30	—
	Red Hot Prince (MrsJJordan) **6-10-3**(7) LMcGrath (nt.j.w: t.o fr 4th)	dist	7	50/1	—	—
3475^{12}	**Hunting Slane** (CGrant) **5-10-10** JCallaghan (hung bdly rt: plld v.hrd: trckd ldrs tl eased & lost pl 5th: t.o whn p.u bef 3 out)		P	33/1	—	—
				(SP 123.8%)		**8 Rn**

3m 51.2 (9.20) CSF £1.93 TOTE £1.60: £1.20 £1.10 £4.50 (£1.40) OWNER Mr G. E. Shouler (MALTON) BRED Mrs Trisha Dunbar

3366 Good Vibes looked to have been found a simple task but he again showed a marked tendency to hang right. Clear two out, he was kept right up to his work and was far from impressive. (4/11)

3366 Ardarroch Prince travelled strongly but did not jump fluently. After being left behind he stuck to his guns and should have no difficulty finding an opening. (3/1)

Starlin Sam, third in a point-to-point on his final outing last term, looked burly and ran like it, travelling nicely until stopping in a few strides going to three out. (33/1)

M-I-Five (IRE), having his first outing for 479 days, weakened quickly on the long run to three out. He presumably needed this more than his paddock appearance suggested. (15/2)

3974 WETHERBY H'CAP CHASE (0-140) (5-Y.O+) (Class B)

3-45 (3-47) **3m 1f (18 fncs)** £7,140.50 (£2,008.00: £966.50) GOING minus 0.03 sec per fur (G)

Form	Horse	Dist	Pos	SP	RR	SF
3701^{2}	**Kenmore-Speed (107)** (MrsSJSmith) **10-10-3**ow3 RichardGuest (mde all: lft clr 4 out: eased flat)	—	1	5/1	119+	—
3694^{2}	**Deep Decision (104)** (PCheesbrough) **11-9-9**(5) RMcGrath (lw: hld up: effrt 13th: rdn & outpcd next: kpt on appr last)	17	2	7/1	105	—
1266^{2}	**Royal Vacation (114)** (GMMoore) **8-10-10** JCallaghan (chsd ldrs: outpcd 12th: wkng whn hit 3 out: 2nd & tired whn blnd last)	4	3	4/1^{3}	113	—
1048^{6}	**Toogood to Be True (128)** (TDEasterby) **9-11-10** LWyer (lw: lost pl 10th: sn bhd: t.o whn p.u bef 5 out)		P	3/1^{2}	—	—
3617^{P}	**Random Harvest (IRE) (112)** (MrsMReveley) **8-10-8** PNiven (trckd wnr: ev ch & rdn whn blnd & uns rdr 4 out)		U	5/4^{1}	—	—
				(SP 118.6%)		**5 Rn**

6m 23.9 CSF £32.32 TOTE £5.70: £2.00 £2.20 (£15.30) OWNER Mr K. M. Dacker (BINGLEY) BRED Mrs Davina Whiteman

LONG HANDICAP Kenmore-Speed 9-10 Deep Decision 9-10

OFFICIAL EXPLANATION **Toogood to Be True: the trainer reported that the gelding had suffered from a respiratory problem.**

3701 Kenmore-Speed paid a big compliment to Disco des Mottes who defeated him in such smooth style at Uttoxeter. 4lb out of the handicap and carrying 3lb overweight, he looked to be holding the upper hand when left clear when Random Harvest went four out. (5/1)

3694 Deep Decision, 4lb out of the handicap, was left behind on the home turn but stuck on to take second place after the last. He certainly seems to stay this trip alright. (7/1)

1266 Royal Vacation, having his first outing for 142 days, was leg-weary when he hit three out. He was still just second when he ploughed through the last and he looked to finish tired. (4/1)

1048 Toogood to Be True, having his first outing for 155 days, has apparently undergone a wind operation. Looking very fit, he never looked happy in his work and his rider wisely called it a day. The trainer reported that the gelding had suffered from a respiratory problem. (3/1)

3617 Random Harvest (IRE) was on the heels of the winner but under pressure when he ploughed through the fourth last, giving his rider no chance. He would only have finished second in any case. (5/4: tchd evens)

3975 LEEDS NOVICES' H'CAP CHASE (0-110) (5-Y.O+) (Class D)

4-15 (4-18) **3m 1f (18 fncs)** £3,964.00 (£1,104.00: £532.00) GOING minus 0.03 sec per fur (G)

Form	Horse	Dist	Pos	SP	RR	SF
3477^{2}	**Kings Sermon (IRE) (89)** (PBeaumont) **8-11-10** LWyer (lw: led: blnd 10th: hdd 13th: blnd 3 out: lft clr last)	—	1	9/2^{2}	103	—
3643^{5}	**Tico Gold (82)** (PCheesbrough) **9-10-12**(5) RMcGrath (hit 8th: outpcd 10th: kpt on fr 4 out)	11	2	7/1	89	—
3724^{2}	**Cool Weather (IRE) (72)** (PCheesbrough) **9-10-7b** MissPRobson (outpcd 9th: hdwy 5 out: prom whn hmpd next: one pce)	1½	3	11/2^{3}	78	—
3708*	**Gaelic Blue (85)** (MrsSJSmith) **7-11-6** RichardGuest (trckd ldrs: lft in ld 4 out: 6l clr whn fell last)		F	Evens^{1}	—	—
3824*	**Bright Destiny (66)** (JSGoldie) **6-9-8v**(7) 6x MrOMcPhail (w ldr: led 13th: rdn whn fell 4 out)		F	11/2^{3}	—	—
3724^{P}	**D'Arblay Street (IRE) (80)** (WTKemp) **8-11-1** JCallaghan (chsd ldrs: lost pl 7th: t.o whn p.u after 9th: b.b.v)		P	10/1	—	—
				(SP 120.5%)		**6 Rn**

6m 29.9 CSF £32.10 TOTE £5.10: £2.10 £3.40 (£29.00) OWNER Mrs P. A. H. Hartley (BRANDSBY) BRED Nicholas Morrissey

OFFICIAL EXPLANATION **D'Arblay Street (IRE): bled from the nose.**
3477 Kings Sermon (IRE) certainly had luck on his side and but for two departing at the last four fences, would probably have only finished third. A heavy-topped gelding, the ground here was probably on the fast side for him. (9/2)
3643 Tico Gold seems to lack anything in the way of pace. (7/1)
3724 Cool Weather (IRE) was getting into the argument when hampered by a faller four out. Like the runner-up, he seems to lack anything in the way of finishing speed. (11/2)
3708* Gaelic Blue, happy to let the two leaders set a strong pace, was six lengths clear and still on the bridle when he unluckily fell at the last. (Evens)
3824* Bright Destiny helped force the pace but his lead was only a narrow one and he was under pressure when he fell four out. Had they both stood up, he would definitely not have beaten Gaelic Blue. (11/2)

3976 WILSTROP AMATEUR H'CAP HURDLE (0-100) (4-Y.O+) (Class F)

4-45 (4-49) **2m (9 hdls)** £2,477.50 (£690.00: £332.50) GOING minus 0.03 sec per fur (G)

				SP	RR	SF
3474[5]	**Kierchem (IRE) (73)** (CGrant) **6-10-1**(7)ow2 MrsSGrant (trckd ldrs: styd on u.p fr 2 out: led last 50y)	—	1	8/1	55	5
3826[U]	**Teejay'n'aitch (IRE) (77)** (JSGoldie) **5-10-5**(7) MrOMcPhail (lw: mde most: clr 3 out: hdd nr fin)	1¼	2	7/1[3]	58	10
1911[2]	**Faithful Hand (89)** (MrsSJSmith) **7-11-3**(7) CaptAOgden (w ldrs: one pce fr 2 out)	12	3	3/1[2]	58	10
3542[4]	**Eurolink the Rebel (USA) (85)** (SBClark) **5-10-13**(7) MissRClark (in tch: rdn & outpcd fr 3 out)	3½	4	7/1[3]	50	2
3728[2]	**Fryup Satellite (89)** (MrsJBrown) **6-11-5**(5) MissPRobson (lw: trckd ldrs: effrt 3 out: sn rdn & grad wknd)	10	5	evens[1]	44	—
3691[18]	**Petrico (65)** (PBeaumont) **5-9-7**(7) MissAArmitage (sn bhd: t.o 4 out: sme hdwy 2 out: n.d)	9	6	20/1	11	—
784[8]	**Swank Gilbert (65)** (TAKCuthbert) **11-9-7**(7) MissHCuthbert (a in rr: t.o 4 out)	10	7	33/1	1	—
3434[7]	**Marsh's Law (75)** (GPKelly) **10-10-3b**(7)ow1 MrABirch (chsd ldrs: drvn along & outpcd 5th: sn bhd)	hd	8	12/1	11	—
3612[10]	**Rubislaw (65)** (MrsKMLamb) **5-9-7v**(7) MissSLamb (chsd ldrs: rdn 4 out: sn lost pl)	1½	9	33/1	—	—
	Dancing Holly (82) (RSWood) **10-10-10**(7) MrMBennison (bit bkwd: sn bhd: p.u lame bef last)		P	33/1	—	—

(SP 132.4%) **10 Rn**

3m 52.7 (10.70) CSF £61.53 CT £194.28 TOTE £10.30: £2.50 £1.80 £1.50 (£40.50) OWNER Mrs M. Hunter (BILLINGHAM) BRED T. Coughlan
LONG HANDICAP Rubislaw 8-13 Swank Gilbert 9-10
3474 Kierchem (IRE) answered his rider's vigorous calls to get up near the line. This was Sue Grant's first winner under Rules but she has twenty-five point winners to her credit. (8/1)
3558 Teejay'n'aitch (IRE), who unseated his rider over fences last time, wore a tongue-strap. He looked to have stolen it when jumping the third last four lengths clear but was collared near the line. (7/1)
1911 Faithful Hand, having his first outing for 108 days, ran as if just in need of it. (3/1)
3542 Eurolink the Rebel (USA) was left flat-footed from three out. (7/1)
3728 Fryup Satellite ran a rather stale race and, under pressure three out, never posed a threat. (evens)
Marsh's Law (12/1: op 8/1)

T/Plpt: £190.00 (21.83 Tckts). T/Qdpt: £29.50 (4.22 Tckts) WG

3761-WINCANTON (R-H) (Firm)

Monday March 31st

WEATHER: sunny

3977 NINE HOLE 'N.H.' NOVICES' HURDLE (4-Y.O+) (Class E)

2-00 (2-00) **2m (8 hdls)** £2,232.50 (£620.00: £297.50) GOING minus 0.86 sec per fur (HD)

				SP	RR	SF
3226[4]	**Mrs Em** (PFNicholls) **5-10-2**(7) LCummins (a.p: chal 2 out: led appr last: drvn out)	—	1	2/1[1]	69	25
2868[7]	**Royal Ruler (IRE)** (JTGifford) **6-10-9** PHide (chsd ldr: led 5th to last: ev ch flat: drvn & unable qckn)	1½	2	14/1	68	24
3718[2]	**Neat Feat (IRE) (94)** (DRCElsworth) **6-10-11**(3) TDascombe (hld up: hdwy 6th: ev ch 2 out: one pce)	1¾	3	2/1[1]	71	27
3761[5]	**Piper's Rock (IRE)** (GBBalding) **6-10-9**(5) ABates (led 1st to 5th: rdn 2 out: one pce)	¾	4	9/2[2]	70	26
2874[5]	**Lonicera (85)** (RHAlner) **7-10-6**(3) PHenley (prom to 2 out)	¾	5	8/1[3]	64	20
2690[15]	**Tidal Force (IRE)** (PJHobbs) **6-10-9**(5) DJKavanagh (hdwy 4th: nvr nr to chal)	hd	6	14/1	69	25
3494[U]	**Orchid House** (NRMitchell) **5-10-4**(5) GSupple (bhd fr 6th)	dist	7	66/1	—	—
3628[P]	**Boozys Dream** (NBThomson) **6-10-7b[1]**(7) MrEBabington (bhd fr 6th)	3	8	50/1	—	—
3747[2]	**Sandville Lad** (MrsDThomas) **5-10-7**(7) MrJTizzard (led tl pckd 1st: hit 3 out: t.o fr 5th: p.u bef 2 out)		P	14/1	—	—

(SP 119.4%) **9 Rn**

3m 33.0 (-7.00) CSF £31.88 TOTE £3.10: £1.20 £3.20 £1.40 (£13.70) OWNER Mr G. Z. Mizel (SHEPTON MALLET) BRED Guest Leasing and Bloodstock Co
3226 Mrs Em raced prominently. Joining issue two out, she led at the last but had to be driven out to ensure victory. (2/1)
1555 Royal Ruler (IRE) looked well and ran creditably. Leading from the fifth, she responded when the winner challenged and kept on bravely despite an untidy jump at the last. Compensation awaits. (14/1: op 8/1)
3718 Neat Feat (IRE) was held up until being launched into the argument at the second last. He failed to quicken thereafter. (2/1)
3500 Piper's Rock (IRE) helped to set the pace early on but could do no more from the penultimate flight. (9/2)
2874 Lonicera (8/1: op 5/1)

3978 GARDENS NIGHT CLUB NOVICES' CHASE (5-Y.O+) (Class E)

2-30 (2-30) **3m 1f 110y (21 fncs)** £3,976.00 (£964.00) GOING minus 0.86 sec per fur (HD)

				SP	RR	SF
3717[6]	**Strokesaver (IRE) (86)** (CPEBrooks) **7-10-9b**(7) MBerry (j.w: prom: lft in ld 13th: comf)	—	1	5/1[3]	97+	—
3617[5]	**Dromhana (IRE) (110)** (PFNicholls) **7-11-7**(7) MrJTizzard (prom: chsd wnr fr 14th: rdn 17th: one pce)	20	2	4/7[1]	97	—
3495[P]	**Le Grand Loup** (DMHyde) **8-10-11**(5) ABates (led 2nd to 4th: wknd 13th: t.o whn fell 19th)		F	50/1	—	—
3178[P]	**Country Style** (RHAlner) **8-10-8**(3) PHenley (bhd fr 7th: p.u bef 12th)		P	20/1	—	—
3683[7]	**Cravate (FR)** (PJHobbs) **7-10-6**(5) DJKavanagh (mstke 1st: j.slowly: bhd fr 6th: p.u bef 12th)		P	12/1	—	—
3736[U]	**Full of Bounce (IRE) (94)** (RJHodges) **6-11-5**(3) TDascombe (led to 2nd: led 4th tl uns rdr 13th)		U	3/1[2]	—	—

(SP 119.7%) **6 Rn**

6m 34.6 (15.60) CSF £8.70 TOTE £6.40: £2.30 £1.50 (£2.80) OWNER The Bow Lane Partnership (LAMBOURN) BRED Edward Power
3427 Strokesaver (IRE), looking on good terms with himself, fenced well and led from the fourteenth. He soon had the race in safe keeping. (5/1)
3617 Dromhana (IRE) seemed unhappy on this lively ground. He chased the winner from five out but never threatened to catch him. (4/7)

3190 Cravate (FR) met the first fence wrong and things got progressively worse until his jockey called it a day with a circuit to go. This was an unfortunate introduction to chasing. (12/1)
3495* Full of Bounce (IRE) made most of the running until blundering and getting rid of his pilot at the second water jump. (3/1)

3979 GOLF COURSE CONDITIONAL CLAIMING HURDLE (4, 5 & 6-Y.O) (Class F)
3-00 (3-00) **2m (8 hdls)** £1,970.00 (£545.00: £260.00) GOING minus 0.86 sec per fur (HD)

				SP	RR	SF
3677[2]	**Proud Image (86)** (GMMcCourt) **5-10-12**(4) RHobson (hdwy 6th: led last: rdn out)	—	**1**	2/1[2]	63	32
3050[11]	**Ath Cheannaithe (FR) (81)** (JNeville) **5-11-2v[1]** PHenley (plld hrd: hit 2nd: led to last: drvn & one pce)	5	**2**	5/1	58	27
3338[3]	**Almapa (82)** (RJHodges) **5-11-4** TDascombe (chsd ldr to 6th: btn whn hit last)	10	**3**	3/1[3]	50	19
3735*	**Fleet Cadet (87)** (MCPipe) **6-11-8v** GSupple (hld up: j.slowly 4th & 5th: rdn 6th: n.d)	6	**4**	6/4[1]	48	17
3741[5]	**Re Roi (IRE) (88)** (WGMTurner) **5-10-8**(4) NWillmington (chsd ldr to 6th: t.o fr 2 out)	dist	**5**	8/1	—	—

(SP 126.1%) **5 Rn**

3m 32.8 (-7.20) CSF £12.51 TOTE £2.40: £1.40 £2.30 (£11.60) OWNER Town and Country Tyre Services Ltd (WANTAGE) BRED Miss S. E. Jarvis
3677 Proud Image made ground from three out. Leading at the last, he won cosily. (2/1)
2578 Ath Cheannaithe (FR) pulled hard and made mistakes in the lead. He had little in reserve when the winner collared him. (5/1)
3338 Almapa chased the runaway leader but found little from the sixth. (3/1)
2815 Re Roi (IRE) (8/1: op 5/1)

3980 GARDENS NIGHT CLUB H'CAP HURDLE (0-115) (4-Y.O+) (Class E)
3-30 (3-30) **2m 6f (11 hdls)** £2,385.00 (£660.00: £315.00) GOING minus 0.86 sec per fur (HD)

				SP	RR	SF
3681[3]	**Sevso (86)** (RJBaker) **8-10-4**(3) PHenley (j.w: chsd ldr: led 8th: drvn out)	—	**1**	11/2	67	15
3589[3]	**Miss Marigold (89)** (RJHodges) **8-10-7b**(3) TDascombe (prom: rdn 2 out: r.o flat)	2	**2**	4/1[3]	69	17
3720[2]	**Vintage Claret (99)** (JTGifford) **8-11-6** PHide (led to 8th: rdn 8th: rdn & wkng whn hit 9th)	dist	**3**	2/1[2]	—	—
3702[2]	**Santella Boy (USA) (106)** (CJMann) **5-11-13b** JRailton (hld up: ev ch & fell 2 out)		**F**	6/5[1]	—	—

(SP 114.2%) **4 Rn**

5m 2.2 (0.30 under best) (-6.80) CSF £22.57 TOTE £8.30 (£13.50) OWNER Mr G. K. Hullett (TIVERTON) BRED Lord Northampton
3681 Sevso looked well and was always prominent. Leading four out, she kept on stoutly from the last. (11/2: op 7/2)
3589 Miss Marigold was being rousted along from two out but rallied on the flat to push the winner to the limit. (4/1)
3720 Vintage Claret led to the eighth but things soon turned sour. (2/1)
3702 Santella Boy (USA), well supported in the ring, was still going nicely when tipping up two out. (6/5)

3981 DICK HUNT 80TH BIRTHDAY H'CAP CHASE (0-125) (5-Y.O+) (Class D)
4-00 (4-01) **2m (13 fncs)** £4,248.00 (£1,032.00) GOING minus 0.86 sec per fur (HD)

				SP	RR	SF
3678[4]	**Corpus (87)** (RJHodges) **8-9-9**(5) DJKavanagh (hdwy 9th: lft in ld 2 out: r.o wl)	—	**1**	12/1	93	—
3343[9]	**Olliver Duckett (88)** (CLPopham) **8-9-12**(3)ow1 PHenley (nvr nr to chal)	25	**2**	11/2[3]	69	—
3682[F]	**Northern Singer (88)** (RJHodges) **7-9-12**(3) TDascombe (prom tl hit 7th: t.o whn p.u bef 2 out: lame)		**P**	13/8[1]	—	—
3673[F]	**Newlands-General (115)** (PFNicholls) **11-11-7**(7) MrJTizzard (led tl uns rdr 2 out)		**U**	7/4[2]	—	—
190[5]	**Evening Rain (89)** (RJHodges) **11-9-9**(7)ow2 RHobson (s.s: a in rr: uns rdr 9th)		**U**	11/2[3]	—	—

(SP 112.9%) **5 Rn**

3m 52.0 (-1.00) CSF £61.79 TOTE £11.80: £3.20 £2.30 (£19.30) OWNER Mr J. Newsome (SOMERTON) BRED D. R. and Mrs Fairbairn
LONG HANDICAP Corpus 9-7 Evening Rain 9-7 Olliver Duckett 9-9
OFFICIAL EXPLANATION Northern Singer: was lame.
Corpus got into contention from five out and looked to be travelling marginally better than the leader when handed the race on a plate two out. (12/1: 8/1-14/1)
3051 Olliver Duckett never went the pace and was lucky to take second prize. (11/2)
3673 Newlands-General set a good pace and still just led when blundering two out, and ejecting his jockey. (7/4: op evens)

3982 PAY AND PLAY 'N.H.' NOVICES' HURDLE (4-Y.O+) (Class E)
4-30 (4-30) **2m 6f (11 hdls)** £2,425.00 (£675.00: £325.00) GOING minus 0.86 sec per fur (HD)

				SP	RR	SF
3146[5]	**Kilmington (IRE) (106)** (JTGifford) **8-11-7** PHide (led to 3rd: led 5th: clr 9th: hit last: easily)	—	**1**	9/4[2]	80+	15
3337[P]	**Southernhay Boy** (MrsSDWilliams) **6-10-9**(5) DJKavanagh (hld up: hdwy 9th: rdn 2 out: unable qckn)	15	**2**	16/1	62	—
3764[2]	**Regal Gem (IRE) (69)** (CRBarwell) **6-10-6**(3) PHenley (prom: rdn 2 out: one pce)	3½	**3**	7/2[3]	55	—
3281*	**Mr Strong Gale (IRE) (101)** (PFNicholls) **6-11-0**(7) MrJTizzard (hld up: nvr nr to chal)	4	**4**	evens[1]	64	—
3426[12]	**Elgintorus (IRE)** (CJMann) **7-11-0** JRailton (a mid div)	1¼	**5**	25/1	56	—
3798[11]	**Cockpit (IRE)** (GBBalding) **6-10-9**(5) ABates (prom to 9th)	2½	**6**	20/1	54	—
3764[6]	**Castle Lynch (IRE)** (RHAlner) **5-10-6**(3) TDascombe (reminders 5th: hit 6th: t.o fr 9th)	dist	**7**	14/1	—	—
3798[12]	**Happy Henry (IRE)** (RHAlner) **7-10-9**(5) GSupple (s.s: led 3rd to 5th: wknd 6th: t.o whn hit last)	dist	**8**	12/1	—	—

(SP 131.8%) **8 Rn**

5m 6.1 (-2.90) CSF £37.43 TOTE £3.30: £1.50 £4.50 £1.10 (£46.30) OWNER Mr H. T. Pelham (FINDON)
3146 Kilmington (IRE) repeated his course and distance win in style. He lengthened his stride from three out to score impressively, and may stay even further. (9/4)
Southernhay Boy was held up, then chased the winner from the ninth, but to no avail. (16/1)
3764 Regal Gem (IRE) looked and ran well. Though unable to find an extra gear from two out, she kept on bravely. (7/2)
3281* Mr Strong Gale (IRE) never threatened to figure in the shake-up. He may require a longer trip. (evens)
Castle Lynch (IRE) (14/1: op 7/1)

T/Plpt: £566.00 (4.89 Tckts). T/Qdpt: Not won; £85.30 to Uttoxeter 1/4/97 AH

3965-UTTOXETER (L-H) (Good To Firm)
Tuesday April 1st
WEATHER: Fine and sunny

3983 CENTRAL TELECOM/SDX NOVICES' H'CAP HURDLE (0-105) (4-Y.O+) (Class E)
2-10 (2-14) **2m (9 hdls)** £2,536.50 (£714.00: £349.50) GOING minus 0.23 sec per fur (G)

				SP	RR	SF
	Erin's Lad (72) (RDickin) **6-10-0** JCulloty (bit bkwd: hld up: stdy hdwy fr 6th: led appr 2 out: sn clr)	—	**1**	33/1	60	19
3733*	**Kildrummy Castle (78)** (JGFitzGerald) **5-10-3**(3) FLeahy (a.p: kpt on u.p fr 2 out: no ch w wnr)	10	**2**	11/2[1]	56	15
3359[14]	**Fencer's Quest (IRE) (78)** (CaptTAForster) **4-10-0** SWynne (trckd ldrs: rdn & outpcd whn hit 2 out)	1	**3**	25/1	55	8
3803*	**Night Boat (78)** (WClay) **6-10-3**(3) GuyLewis (hld up & bhd: hdwy 3 out: nrst fin)	nk	**4**	8/1[3]	55	14
3829[3]	**Worthy Memories (72)** (MrsMerritaJones) **8-10-0** DBridgwater (j.rt: led tl appr 2 out: sn rdn & outpcd)	1½	**5**	8/1[3]	47	6
3050[4]	**O My Love (78)** (MissHCKnight) **6-10-6** JOsborne (hld up: effrt appr 3 out: nt rch ldrs)	8	**6**	6/1[2]	45	4
3723*	**Stylish Interval (90)** (NWaggott) **5-10-13**(5) MrRThornton (swtg: prom: rdn 3 out: sn lost tch)	2½	**7**	12/1	55	14
3438[9]	**I'm a Dreamer (IRE) (99)** (MissMERowland) **7-11-13** GaryLyons (lw: a in rr: t.o)	7	**8**	11/1	57	16
2541[5]	**Golf Land (IRE) (82)** (LLungo) **5-10-10** MFoster (in rr: rdn 6th: t.o)	¾	**9**	16/1	39	—
2961[9]	**Cyphratis (IRE) (89)** (MrsJPitman) **6-11-3** DLeahy (lw: s.s: a bhd: t.o)	2	**10**	10/1	44	3
3743[3]	**Desert Calm (IRE) (80)** (PDEvans) **8-10-8b** DWalsh (chsd ldrs: drvn along 6th: wknd qckly next: t.o)	2	**11**	16/1	33	—
3733[2]	**Country Minstrel (IRE) (72)** (SADouch) **6-10-0** CRae (in tch to 6th: grad wknd: t.o)	1½	**12**	8/1[3]	23	—
3473[P]	**Alpine Mist (IRE) (91)** (JGMO'Shea) **5-11-5v** MAFitzgerald (prom tl wknd appr 3 out: t.o)	24	**13**	25/1	18	—
3621[10]	**Dark Phoenix (IRE) (82)** (OBrennan) **7-10-10** MBrennan (a bhd: m wd appr 5th: t.o)	nk	**14**	8/1[3]	9	—
3733[5]	***Apollono (72)*** (RLee) **5-10-0** RJohnson (Withdrawn not under Starters' orders: kicked at s)		**W**	9/1	—	—
				(SP 131.6%)	**14 Rn**	

3m 43.5 (2.50) CSF £171.53 CT £3,176.99 TOTE £125.60: £17.10 £1.50 £8.70 (£228.00) Trio £255.40; £179.89 to Worcester 2/4/97 OWNER Mr Anthony Smith (STRATFORD) BRED J. K. Dancer
LONG HANDICAP Worthy Memories 9-12 Fencer's Quest (IRE) 9-10 Erin's Lad 9-7 Apollono 9-12
WEIGHT FOR AGE 4yo-6lb

Erin's Lad had not seen a racecourse since September 1995, and looked to have little chance from 7lb out of the handicap, but he defied his burly looks with a runaway success that could be the first of many. (33/1)
3733* Kildrummy Castle, unable to get to the front, kept on under pressure but the winner proved to be in a class of his own. (11/2: 4/1-6/1)
2655 Fencer's Quest (IRE) produced his best effort yet, and he could now be getting the hang of the game. (25/1)
3803* Night Boat was not quite up to this better class, but he was certainly not disgraced in finishing a staying-on fourth, and there should be another race to be won with him. (8/1)
3829 Worthy Memories adopted more forceful tactics and set the pace, but she was inclined to jump to the right and had her goose was cooked once the winner took command. (8/1)
3050 O My Love was unable to go the pace on this much faster ground, and her final position was as close as she could get. (6/1: op 4/1)
3723* Stylish Interval (12/1: op 8/1)
2744* I'm a Dreamer (IRE) (11/1: 8/1-12/1)

3984 MOUNT ARGUS HUNTERS' CHASE (5-Y.O+) (Class H)
2-40 (2-40) **2m 7f (16 fncs)** £1,584.50 (£442.00: £213.50) GOING minus 0.23 sec per fur (G)

				SP	RR	SF
3135[5]	**Idiotic** (PRChamings) **9-11-12**(5) MrCVigors (hld up: hdwy 12th: led 3 out tl hdd & hit next: rallied to ld nr fin)	—	**1**	4/1[2]	110	49
3637[P]	**My Nominee** (DENicholls) **9-11-10b**(7) MrRBurton (a.p: led 2 out tl hdd & no ex cl home)	nk	**2**	5/4[1]	110	49
3813[U]	**Pro Bono (IRE)** (AndyMorgan) **7-11-12**(5) MrASansome (chsd ldrs: hdwy 8th: mstke 11th: wknd appr 2 out)	17	**3**	9/1	98	37
3744[8]	**King of Shadows** (MissCMCarden) **10-11-10**(7) MrSPrior (led to 5th: wknd 10th: mstke 12th: t.o)	dist	**4**	12/1	—	—
3586[8]	**Rising Sap** (JDDownes) **7-11-10**(7) MrMMunrowd (hld up: hdwy 6th: blnd 8th: bhd whn j.bdly fr 3 out: p.u bef last)		**P**	40/1	—	—
	Frank Be Lucky (MsBarbaraAshby-Jones) **11-11-12**(5) MrRThornton (bkwd: w ldr: led 5th to 3 out: wknd qckly: bhd whn p.u bef last)		**P**	9/2[3]	—	—
3586[P]	**Babil** (MrsCHicks) **12-11-12**(5) MrJTrice-Rolph (bit bkwd: prom to 7th: t.o whn p.u bef 10th)		**P**	25/1	—	—
	Idiomatic (MrsSMShone) **8-11-10**(7) MrDSherlock (lw: in rr whn pckd 1st: sn t.o: p.u bef 11th)		**P**	66/1	—	—
3712[F]	**Double Collect** (MrsMDRebori) **11-11-10**(7) MrNFSmith (lw: hld up in rr: blnd & uns rdr 7th)		**U**	9/1	—	—
				(SP 118.1%)	**9 Rn**	

5m 39.9 (3.90) CSF £9.15 TOTE £5.50: £2.00 £1.10 £2.10 (£4.70) Trio £8.20 OWNER Mr E. Knight (BASINGSTOKE) BRED E. Knight

3135 Idiotic took advantage of a very patient ride to regain the lead on the run-in, after a mistake at the penultimate obstacle looked to have cost him his chance. (4/1)
3270 My Nominee appeared well in command when Idiotic made an error two out, but he slowed up to negotiate the final fence and, losing his momentum, was run out of it close home. (5/4)
3135 Pro Bono (IRE) moved up smoothly entering the straight and briefly looked to be travelling best but, once off the bridle, he found very little and was brushed aside with ease. (9/1)
King of Shadows (12/1: op 20/1)

3985 MARSTON'S FREE TRADE (S) H'CAP HURDLE (0-95) (4-Y.O+) (Class G)
3-10 (3-11) **2m 4f 110y (10 hdls)** £1,857.50 (£520.00: £252.50) GOING minus 0.23 sec per fur (G)

				SP	RR	SF
2838[8]	**Polo Pony (IRE) (63)** (JohnUpson) **5-10-0** JSupple (lw: in rr: pushed along ½-wy: styd on fr 2 out to ld cl home)	—	**1**	20/1	42	—
3620*	**Edward Seymour (USA) (82)** (WJenks) **10-11-5** TJenks (swtg: hld up & bhd: hdwy appr 7th: led appr last: hrd rdn & hdd cl home)	1¼	**2**	5/2[1]	60	18
3411[7]	**Quiet Moments (IRE) (73)** (PGMurphy) **4-10-3** WMcFarland (hld up & bhd: hdwy 7th: styd on u.p flat)	1½	**3**	8/1	50	1
3072[9]	**Bites (73)** (TTBill) **4-10-3**ow3 JRailton (a.p: led 2 out: sn hdd: rdn & unable qckn flat)	½	**4**	50/1	50	—
3072[F]	**Sheecky (72)** (BAMcMahon) **6-10-9** DBridgwater (a.p: led 3 out to 2 out: rdn & btn appr last)	3	**5**	11/1	46	4
3545[9]	**Crazy Horse Dancer (USA) (78)** (FJordan) **9-10-12**(3) LAspell (hld up in tch: no hdwy fr 3 out)	½	**6**	7/1[3]	52	10
3072[12]	**Admiral's Guest (IRE) (65)** (WClay) **5-9-13**(3)ow1 GuyLewis (hdwy 5th: wknd appr 3 out)	5	**7**	25/1	35	—
3807[9]	**White Willow (91)** (TWall) **8-12-0b** RJohnson (led & sn clr: wknd & hdd 3 out: t.o)	10	**8**	12/1	53	11
3284[11]	**Bluntswood Hall (87)** (RHollinshead) **4-11-3** GaryLyons (a bhd: t.o)	7	**9**	14/1	44	—

3711[11] **Oakbury (IRE) (67)** (MissLCSiddall) **5-10-4** CMaude (mid div tl hrd rdn & wknd appr 2 out: t.o) 6	**10**	8/1	19	—
1814[3] **Saltis (IRE) (75)** (ALForbes) **5-10-9**(3) PHenley (prom tl wknd after 7th: t.o) 26	**11**	6/1[2]	7	—
3283[P] **Captain Navar (IRE) (71)** (JGMO'Shea) **7-10-8** MAFitzgerald (hld up in tch: wknd 6th: t.o & p.u bef 2 out)	**P**	6/1[2]	—	—
3663[8] **Wordsmith (IRE) (77)** (JLHarris) **7-11-0b[1]** DGallagher (sn t.o: p.u bef 3 out)	**P**	14/1	—	—
		(SP 131.8%)	**13 Rn**	

4m 52.9 (8.90) CSF £70.31 CT £432.57 TOTE £26.50: £5.80 £1.50 £3.40 (£49.40) Trio £262.00 OWNER Mr T. S. Palin (TOWCESTER) BRED Mrs G. Kavanagh
LONG HANDICAP Bites 9-8
WEIGHT FOR AGE 4yo-7lb
Bt in 3,600 gns

2006 Polo Pony (IRE), ridden along from halfway, took an age to pick up and was several lengths adrift at the last, but he produced a stunning burst of speed to collar the favourite nearing the line. (20/1)
3620* Edward Seymour (USA) really needs more cut than he had here, but he picked up his rivals with ease and had the race won at the last, only to tie up and lose out in the dying strides. (5/2)
Quiet Moments (IRE) performed much better on this step down to selling company, and he should be able to find a race at this level. (8/1)
Bites had far more use made of her over this longer trip and, running her best race yet over hurdles, showed she has the ability to win a small contest. (50/1)
2813 Sheecky appeared not to see out the trip, for he was already held when she fluffed the last. (11/1)
582 Crazy Horse Dancer (USA), in more or less the same place throughout, failed to pick up when asked to quicken early in the straight, and he could do little more than plug on at the one pace. (7/1)

3986 CJ PEARCE H'CAP CHASE (0-135) (5-Y.O+) (Class C)
3-40 (3-40) **2m 4f (15 fncs)** £4,856.00 (£1,366.00: £668.00) GOING minus 0.23 sec per fur (G)

		SP	RR	SF
3427[6] **Plunder Bay (USA) (109)** (NJHenderson) **6-10-3**ow1 MAFitzgerald (lw: j.w: chsd ldr fr 4th: led appr 3 out: all out) .... —	**1**	5/2[2]	118	—
3286[8] **Callisoe Bay (IRE) (130)** (OSherwood) **8-11-10** JOsborne (j.w: led & sn clr: hdd appr 3 out: rallied u.p flat: jst failed) ....nk	**2**	13/8[1]	139	—
2962[2] **Beatson (IRE) (112)** (RHBuckler) **8-10-6** BPowell (lw: mstke 1st: outpcd 9th: t.o appr 4 out) ....dist	**3**	13/8[1]	—	—
		(SP 104.8%)	**3 Rn**	

4m 53.8 CSF £5.76 TOTE £3.70 (£1.90) OWNER W V & Mrs E S Robins (LAMBOURN) BRED Marion G. Montanari
3427 Plunder Bay (USA) never put a foot wrong and looked set to win comfortably between the last two, but the favourite found top gear again on the flat and, in the end, he was all out to score. (5/2)
2783 Callisoe Bay (IRE) has never won beyond the minimum trip, but he was prepared to bowl along in the lead and, rallying in spirited fashion nearing the finish, almost worried the winner out of it. This was a promising run considering the weight he was conceding. (13/8)
2962 Beatson (IRE) moved to post as though he was jarred up and, losing touch from halfway, got round in his own time. (13/8)

3987 MOBILEFONE GROUP H'CAP HURDLE (0-140) (4-Y.O+) (Class B)
4-10 (4-10) **2m (9 hdls)** £4,756.15 (£1,439.20: £702.10: £333.55) GOING minus 0.23 sec per fur (G)

		SP	RR	SF
1831[7] **Serious (107)** (KCBailey) **7-10-0** SMcNeill (hld up: hdwy appr 3 out: led appr 2 out: rdn & edgd lft flat: r.o) ...—	**1**	11/4[1]	87	9
2779[F] **Tejano Gold (USA) (119)** (PBradley) **7-10-12** SWynne (lw: led tl appr 2 out: rdn & n.m.r flat: nt rcvr) 2	**2**	11/4[1]	97	19
3640[17] **Star Rage (IRE) (132)** (JLHarris) **7-11-11** DGallagher (lw: prom tl rdn & outpcd appr 3 out: sn btn) 11	**3**	11/4[1]	99	21
3443[U] **Mr Bureaucrat (NZ) (114)** (SABrookshaw) **8-10-7** CMaude (prom: ev ch 3 out: outpcd fr next) 4	**4**	12/1[3]	77	—
3412[5] **Charming Girl (USA) (124)** (OSherwood) **6-11-3** JOsborne (swtg: a.p: ev ch whn fell 3 out)	**F**	5/1[2]	—	—
Test Match (109) (WClay) **10-9-13**(3)ow2 GuyLewis (bkwd: sn t.o: p.u bef 5th)	**P**	16/1	—	—
		(SP 110.2%)	**6 Rn**	

3m 45.9 (4.90) CSF £9.60 TOTE £3.90: £1.90 £1.80 (£5.50) OWNER Tony and Dee Lousada (UPPER LAMBOURN) BRED Wretham Stud
LONG HANDICAP Serious 9-7 Test Match 9-7
1831 Serious, taking on handicappers on this return to hurdles, kept up his stable's good recent run with a success that would have been far easier had he not blown up on the run-in. (11/4)
2048* Tejano Gold (USA) ran well on ground plenty fast enough for him and, at this stage of the season, it is doubtful if conditions will get any easier in the short time that remains. (11/4: 2/1-3/1)
3286 Star Rage (IRE) was conceding weight all round, but he was the class act of the field, and this very much below par performance would suggest that he has had enough for the time being. (11/4)
3161 Mr Bureaucrat (NZ) did not take to fences, but he gave it his best shot on this return to hurdles which, in the circumstances, was just not good enough. (12/1: op 8/1)
3412 Charming Girl (USA), breathing down the necks of the leaders from the start, was travelling as well as any when she bit the dust at the third last. (5/1)

3988 CJ PEARCE NOVICES' CHASE (5-Y.O+) (Class D)
4-40 (4-40) **2m 5f (16 fncs)** £3,550.00 (£1,075.00: £525.00: £250.00) GOING minus 0.23 sec per fur (G)

		SP	RR	SF
3833* **Quite A Man (84)** (SABrookshaw) **9-12-0** CMaude (lw: a.p: blnd 9th: led appr 2 out: rdn & drifted lft flat: r.o).—	**1**	15/8[2]	106	38
3806* **Pearl Epee (90)** (DNicholson) **8-11-3** RJohnson (led: hit 1st: hdd next: led 12th to 4 out: ev ch 2 out: one pce) 2½	**2**	11/8[1]	93	25
3436[F] **Glamanglitz (80)** (PTDalton) **7-10-11**(5) MrRThornton (j.w: led 2nd to 12th: led 4 out tl appr 2 out: sn outpcd)..6	**3**	9/2[3]	88	20
3416[4] **Rare Occurance** (JGMO'Shea) **7-10-9**(7) JTNolan (hld up: hdwy 10th: outpcd fr 12th: t.o) 14	**4**	14/1	77	9
3842[3] **Santaray (67)** (TWDonnelly) **11-11-2** MrRArmson (a bhd: t.o fr 11th) 7	**5**	16/1	72	4
3732[F] **Total Asset (72)** (ALForbes) **7-11-2** GaryLyons (hdwy 6th: hit 8th: rdn & wknd 11th: t.o) 12	**6**	20/1	62	—
		(SP 112.4%)	**6 Rn**	

5m 10.8 (5.80) CSF £4.68 TOTE £2.40: £1.40 £1.50 (£1.70) OWNER Mr W. R. J. Everall (SHREWSBURY) BRED R. Everall
3833* Quite A Man completed his hat-trick with a very deserved victory and, if the ground remains lively, there could still be more to follow. (15/8)
3806* Pearl Epee did nothing wrong and never once stopped trying, but she had to admit the winner too good for her on this ground. (11/8)
3436 Glamanglitz jumped boldly in the lead for most of the way, but he was getting the worst of the battle on the approach to the second last, and this trip could be testing his stamina to the full. (9/2)

3989 JENKINSONS CATERERS MAIDEN HURDLE (4-Y.O+) (Class E)
5-10 (5-10) **2m (9 hdls)** £2,432.25 (£738.00: £361.50: £173.25) GOING minus 0.23 sec per fur (G)

	Horse	Dist	Pos	SP	RR	SF
2697P	**King of Sparta** (OSherwood) **4-11-0** DBridgwater (bit bkwd: a.p: led last: drvn out: edgd lft nr fin)	—	1	5/1 3	68	13
3802F	**Vadlawys (FR)** (SABrookshaw) **6-11-6** CMaude (hld up: hdwy 6th: chal last: ev ch flat: btn whn nt clr run & snatched up cl home)	1¼	2	11/8 1	67	18
	Sicarian (MrsMerritaJones) **5-11-6** DerekByrne (bit bkwd: hld up in rr: stdy hdwy fr 3 out: fin wl)	1½	3	25/1	65	16
25479	**Laburnum Gold (IRE) (95)** (MrsJPitman) **6-11-6** DLeahy (lw: a.p: led 6th: rdn, hdd & mstke last: nt rcvr)	4	4	3/1 2	61	12
34315	**Alpha Leather (62)** (LPGrassick) **6-11-6** MrJGrassick (hld up: hdwy appr 3 out: nt rch ldrs)	6	5	50/1	55	6
	If Only (RHollinshead) **7-11-6** GaryLyons (bit bkwd: hdwy 5th: rdn & btn appr 3 out)	9	6	50/1	46	—
37232	**Suvalu (USA)** (MGMeagher) **5-11-6** MAFitzgerald (prom tl outpcd appr 3 out)	9	7	6/1	37	—
28933	**Freno (IRE)** (KCBailey) **6-11-6** SMcNeill (lw: hld up: in tch to 5th: sn lost pl: t.o)	13	8	11/1	24	—
	Polar Wind (NWaggott) **8-11-6** MFoster (bkwd: plld hrd: led to 6th: sn wknd: t.o)	18	9	50/1	6	—
3682F	**Jasons Farm** (WClay) **7-11-3**(3) GuyLewis (chsd ldrs to 6th: sn outpcd: t.o)	15	10	100/1	—	—
3569P	**Knock Star (IRE)** (RChampion) **6-11-6** BPowell (bkwd: a bhd: t.o fr 6th)	18	11	50/1	—	—

(SP 119.1%) **11 Rn**

3m 47.9 (6.90) CSF £11.45 TOTE £5.60: £1.60 £1.40 £4.40 (£5.30) Trio £79.30 OWNER Mr Darren Mercer (UPPER LAMBOURN) BRED Sheikh Mohammed bin Rashid al Maktoum
WEIGHT FOR AGE 4yo-6lb
STEWARDS' ENQUIRY Obj. to King of Sparta by Maude overruled.

2697 King of Sparta, pulled up on his only previous outing over hurdles, looked to need this, but he showed his full battling qualities under a very polished ride and won a shade easier than the margin would suggest. He should only improve on this and he does look useful. (5/1)
3802 Vadlawys (FR) may well be better suited to a stiffer test of stamina, for he was produced to win his race at the last, only to find the winner much too good for him in the duel to the finish. (11/8)
Sicarian made a very promising start to his hurdling career and, with this run and the experience under his belt, he could be set to go places in the long-term. (25/1)
1375 Laburnum Gold (IRE) is being given plenty of time to recover from his races and he ran well here, but his measure had been taken when he missed out at the last and it is possible he blew up. (3/1)
Alpha Leather has little form to his name so far, but it could be a different matter if he was allowed to take his chance in a seller. (50/1)
2893 Freno (IRE) (11/1: 7/1-12/1)

T/Jkpt: £50,838.90 (0.3 Tckts); £50,122.95 to Worcester 2/4/97. T/Plpt: £93.50 (187.51 Tckts). T/Qdpt: £34.10 (30.71 Tckts) IM

3971-WETHERBY (L-H) (Good to firm)
Tuesday April 1st
WEATHER: fine

3990 W. CLIFFORD WATTS LTD. NOVICES' HURDLE (4-Y.O+) (Class D)
2-20 (2-20) **2m 4f 110y (10 hdls)** £3,265.00 (£915.00: £445.00) GOING: 0.01 sec per fur (G)

	Horse	Dist	Pos	SP	RR	SF
37942	**Major Harris (IRE)** (MDHammond) **5-11-0** RGarritty (hld up: stdy hdwy 4 out: chal 3 out: rdn to ld nr fin)	—	1	11/2	75	34
289819	**The Road West (IRE)** (JLEyre) **8-11-0** BStorey (a.p: led 3 out: edgd rt: r.o: jst ct)	s.h	2	20/1	75	34
38232	**Southern Cross** (MWEasterby) **5-11-0** PNiven (lw: prom: reminder 6th: chsng ldr 3 out: one pce)	3	3	7/2 2	73	32
3611*	**Pontevedra (IRE) (92)** (KAMorgan) **4-10-1**(7) NHorrocks (lw: outpcd ½-wy: styd on u.p fr 3 out: no imp)	8	4	14/1	67	19
33485	**Spritzer (IRE) (100)** (JGFitzGerald) **5-11-1** WDwan (lw: hld up: effrt appr 3 out: sn prom: rdn & btn 2 out)	4	5	100/30 1	64	23
348313	**Border Image** (FPMurtagh) **6-11-0** ADobbin (chsd ldrs tl outpcd fr 3 out)	6	6	50/1	59	18
3696F	**Tweedswood (IRE) (92)** (PBeaumont) **7-11-0** RSupple (led to 5th: cl up tl rdn & wknd 3 out: eased whn btn)	12	7	13/2	49	8
10814	**Rule Out The Rest (90)** (MrsSarahHorner-Harker) **6-11-6** AThornton (mstke 2nd: lost tch ½-wy: fell 3 out)		F	16/1	—	—
369111	**Praise Be (FR)** (TPTate) **7-11-0** JCallaghan (prom to 5th: lost tch 4 out: p.u bef 3 out)		P	33/1	—	—
3734B	**Charley Lambert (IRE)** (JMackie) **6-10-11**(3) EHusband (lw: w ldr: slt ld 5th: hdd & hmpd 3 out: disp 3rd & btn whn stumbled bdly & p.u bef 2 out)		P	4/1 3	—	—
3621*	**Northern Star** (JAPickering) **6-10-13**(7) MissJWormall (tried to run out & uns rdr 1st)		U	16/1	—	—

(SP 122.1%) **11 Rn**

4m 54.7 (7.70) CSF £96.92 TOTE £6.70: £1.60 £6.30 £1.50 (£139.30) Trio £155.60; £92.07 to Worcester 2/4/97 OWNER Mr H. G. Owen (MIDDLEHAM) BRED T. Simmons
WEIGHT FOR AGE 4yo-7lb

3794 Major Harris (IRE) is a tough sort who stays well. His determination won the day and he gave his stable their first win for over six weeks. (11/2)
The Road West (IRE) had form in Irish bumpers but this was his first decent effort over hurdles, and it should not be long before he finds a suitable opening. (20/1)
3823 Southern Cross ran in snatches, and gave the impression that a pair of blinkers might make the difference. (7/2)
3611* Pontevedra (IRE) found this company too hot and, despite struggling on, was always short of toe. (14/1)
3348 Spritzer (IRE) has been off the track for almost five weeks and, although she looked well enough, ran as though this was needed. (100/30)
Border Image, having his first run on fast ground, put in a better effort. (50/1)
3696 Tweedswood (IRE) looked very slow when the pace was on, and his real future is over fences. (13/2)
3437 Charley Lambert (IRE), unlucky last time, found things against him again and was wisely pulled up after stumbling very badly two from home, which may well have caused an injury. (4/1)

3991 FERDY MURPHY'S OWNERS H'CAP CHASE (0-115) (5-Y.O+) (Class E)
2-50 (2-52) **2m (12 fncs)** £3,171.00 (£948.00: £454.00: £207.00) GOING: 0.01 sec per fur (G)

	Horse	Dist	Pos	SP	RR	SF
36923	**Grouse-N-Heather (89)** (PMonteith) **8-10-3** ADobbin (lw: chsd ldrs: shkn up to ld 4 out: styd on strly)	—	1	6/5 1	107	19
34825	**Rebel King (86)** (MABarnes) **7-10-0** BStorey (cl up: led 8th to 4 out: rdn & one pce)	8	2	8/1	96	8
36104	**Regal Romper (IRE) (104)** (MrsSJSmith) **9-11-4** RichardGuest (led to 8th: sn rdn & btn)	10	3	15/8 2	104	16

	Horse / details	Dist	Pos	SP	RR	SF
1070F	**De Jordaan (114)** (WSCunningham) **10-12-0** NSmith (bit bkwd: lost tch 4th: sn wl bhd)	dist	4	4/1 3	—	—
				(SP 111.3%)		**4 Rn**

3m 59.4 (7.40) CSF £8.52 TOTE £2.20 (£5.90) OWNER Mr D. J. Fairbairn (ROSEWELL) BRED R. A. Cameron
LONG HANDICAP Rebel King 9-7
3692 Grouse-N-Heather had nothing much to beat here and, once she got her head in front four out, she galloped resolutely on. (6/5)
3482 Rebel King ran better this time, holding every chance until finding things too much from the fourth last. (8/1)
3610 Regal Romper (IRE) has lost form for the time being. (15/8)
1070 De Jordaan needed this and showed little. (4/1: 3/1-9/2)

3992 LAMBSON H'CAP HURDLE (0-135) (4-Y.O+) (Class C)
3-20 (3-20) **2m 4f 110y (10 hdls)** £3,731.50 (£1,117.00: £536.00: £245.50) GOING: 0.01 sec per fur (G)

	Horse / details	Dist	Pos	SP	RR	SF
3584 4	**Celestial Choir (120)** (JLEyre) **7-11-4** BStorey (lost pl ½-wy: hdwy 4 out: led 3 out: pushed clr: eased flat)	—	1	15/8 1	107	43
3415 5	**Fired Earth (IRE) (127)** (JRFanshawe) **9-11-11** ADobbin (chsd ldrs: effrt 4 out: outpcd next: kpt on flat)	6	2	5/1 3	109	45
3698*	**Domappel (118)** (MrsJCecil) **5-11-2** TKent (hld up: stdy hdwy to ld after 4 out: hdd 3 out: rdn & no ex)	½	3	11/4 2	100	36
3850 3	**Fourth in Line (IRE) (120)** (MJWilkinson) **9-11-4** WMarston (prom tl outpcd 4 out: kpt on fr next: no imp)	3½	4	10/1	99	35
3698 2	**Thursday Night (IRE) (111)** (JGFitzGerald) **6-10-9** AThornton (lw: chsd ldrs: hit 4 out: rdn & btn appr next)	25	5	11/2	71	7
3693 6	**Kinda Groovy (102)** (IPark) **8-10-0b** NSmith (led tl hdd & wknd after 4 out)	7	6	25/1	56	—
2701 4	**Suas Leat (IRE) (102)** (JMJefferson) **7-9-7**(7) MNewton (prom tl rdn & wknd 4 out)	¾	7	9/1	56	—
				(SP 116.4%)		**7 Rn**

4m 53.4 (6.40) CSF £11.28 CT £23.04 TOTE £2.50: £1.70 £2.50 (£6.10) Trio £4.50 OWNER Mrs Carole Sykes (HAMBLETON) BRED J. L. Eyre
LONG HANDICAP Kinda Groovy 9-10
3584 Celestial Choir seems to need this trip these days and, the further they went the stronger she got and, in the end, won pulling up. (15/8)
3415 Fired Earth (IRE) does not do anything quickly, but he responded to pressure without having a hope against the winner. (5/1)
3698* Domappel went well for much of the trip but, when an effort was required from the third last, his response was disappointing. (11/4)
3850 Fourth in Line (IRE) found this ground too lively and was always struggling with the pace. (10/1)
3698 Thursday Night (IRE) has been running consistently well, but this fast ground seemed to find him out. (11/2)
Kinda Groovy likes fast ground but found this company too hot. (25/1)

3993 SEBEL HOUSE GROUP 'NATIONAL' NOVICES' H'CAP CHASE (5-Y.O+) (Class C)
3-50 (3-51) **3m 5f (21 fncs)** £5,078.00 (£1,408.00: £674.00) GOING: 0.01 sec per fur (G)

	Horse / details	Dist	Pos	SP	RR	SF
3708P	**Mister Trick (IRE) (96)** (LLungo) **7-10-0b** RSupple (mde most to 13th: rdn to ld between last 2 out: styd on wl)	—	1	16/1 3	93	7
3719*	**The Whole Hog (IRE) (96)** (KCBailey) **8-10-0** AThornton (chsd ldrs: effrt u.p 4 out: led 2 out: sn hdd & one pce)	6	2	6/1 2	89	3
3841*	**Father Sky (124)** (OSherwood) **6-12-0b** 4x JAMcCarthy (lw: led to 2nd: chsd ldr: led 13th to 2 out: no ex)	10	3	5/4 1	111	25
3162 2	**Ivy House (IRE) (106)** (JJO'Neill) **9-10-5**(5) RMcGrath (lw: hld up & bhd: hit 14th: p.u after 5 out)		P	5/4 1	—	—
				(SP 109.1%)		**4 Rn**

7m 23.4 (17.40) CSF £72.74 TOTE £12.70 (£12.80) OWNER Mr Edward Birkbeck (CARRUTHERSTOWN) BRED M. Parkhill
LONG HANDICAP The Whole Hog (IRE) 8-8 Mister Trick (IRE) 9-2
OFFICIAL EXPLANATION Ivy House (IRE): was unable to act on the ground.
3708 Mister Trick (IRE), although 12lb out of the handicap, is a funny customer who is obviously suited by this longer trip and, to give him credit, he responded to pressure in the closing stages. (16/1)
3719* The Whole Hog (IRE) was 20lb wrong in the handicap, but was still heavily supported in this moderate event, and had his chances until getting out-battled late on. (6/1)
3841* Father Sky ran well here under top-weight, but really beat himself by jumping deliberately when in front. That sapped all his reserves and he weakened two out. (5/4)
3162 Ivy House (IRE) likes softer ground and, never really happy, was pulled up on the home turn. (5/4: op evens)

3994 HOWARD BROWN MEMORIAL NOVICES' HUNTERS' CHASE (5-Y.O+) (Class H)
4-20 (4-21) **3m 1f (18 fncs)** £1,155.00 (£345.00: £165.00: £75.00) GOING: 0.01 sec per fur (G)

	Horse / details	Dist	Pos	SP	RR	SF
3533*	**Denim Blue** (MissPaulineRobson) **8-11-7**(5) MissPRobson (chsd ldrs: outpcd appr 4 out: styd on u.p to chal 3 out: led flat: all out)	—	1	4/11 1	84	—
	Sovereigns Match (IanNichol) **9-11-7**(5) MrNWilson (led: clr whn j.slowly 4 out: hdd flat: rallied towards fin)	½	2	11/2 2	84	—
	Syrus P Turntable (MissPFitton) **11-11-5**(7) MrJSaville (chsd ldrs: hit 10th: sn rdn along: outpcd fr 14th)	dist	3	33/1	—	—
2903 8	**Tom Log** (WMBurnell) **10-11-5**(7) MrWBurnell (mstkes 6th & 7th: sn bhd)	18	4	13/2 3	—	—
3543 4	**R N Commander** (JRCornwall) **11-11-5**(7) MrJRCornwall (prom tl outpcd appr 10th: sn bhd)	dist	5	12/1	—	—
				(SP 112.7%)		**5 Rn**

6m 30.0 CSF £2.99 TOTE £1.40: £1.10 £3.30 (£2.70) OWNER Mrs L. Walby (CAPHEATON) BRED G. Reed
3533* Denim Blue, after looking in trouble four out, responded gamely to pressure and just made it. (4/11)
Sovereigns Match, given a fine ride, put up a decent performance and was battling back at the end. (11/2)
Syrus P Turntable had his limitations exposed from the fifth-last. (33/1)
Tom Log made mistakes early on and soon lost all interest. (13/2)
R N Commander (12/1: 8/1-14/1)

3995 HENDERSON INSURANCE BROKERS LTD. H'CAP HURDLE (0-125) (4-Y.O+) (Class D)
4-50 (4-50) **2m (9 hdls)** £2,880.00 (£805.00: £390.00) GOING: 0.01 sec per fur (G)

	Horse / details	Dist	Pos	SP	RR	SF
3412F	**Desert Fighter (110)** (MrsMReveley) **6-11-10** PNiven (a.p: led appr 3 out: qcknd 2 out: comf)	—	1	9/4 1	98	52
2952 5	**Anabranch (109)** (JMJefferson) **6-11-6**(3) ECallaghan (lw: hld up: stdy hdwy appr 3 out: effrt 2 out: nt pce of wnr)	3	2	11/1	94	48
3475 4	**Last Try (IRE) (95)** (BSRothwell) **6-10-9** ASSmith (chsd ldrs: effrt appr 3 out: r.o one pce)	8	3	7/1	72	26
3572 10	**Samanid (IRE) (106)** (MissLCSiddall) **5-11-6** OPears (rn in snatches: ch 3 out: btn whn hit next)	1¼	4	3/1 2	82	36
1163 3	**Bures (IRE) (110)** (MrsJBrown) **6-11-5**(5) BGrattan (led tl hdd & wknd appr 3 out)	10	5	14/1	76	30
3485 11	**Fox Sparrow (95)** (NTinkler) **7-10-9b1** ADobbin (prom tl lost pl 4 out)	30	6	25/1	31	—
3584 7	**Holders Hill (IRE) (102)** (MGMeagher) **5-11-2** RichardGuest (lw: bhd fr 4th: fell last)		F	14/1	—	—

				SP	RR	SF
3002^{3}	**Russian Rascal (IRE) (102)** (TDEasterby) **4-10-10** LWyer (mstke 1st: sn t.o & nt j.w: p.u after 5th: b.b.v.)		P	4/1^{3}	—	—
2955^{P}	**Ralitsa (IRE) (104)** (MDHammond) **5-11-4** RGarritty (lw: ref to s: t.n.p.)		R	16/1	—	—
				(SP 119.7%)		**9 Rn**

3m 46.3 (4.30) CSF £25.71 CT £141.92 TOTE £3.00: £1.30 £2.60 £2.30 (£13.70) Trio £57.60 OWNER Mr A. Frame (SALTBURN) BRED P. D. and Mrs Player
WEIGHT FOR AGE 4yo-6lb
OFFICIAL EXPLANATION **Russian Rascal (IRE): had bled from the nose.**
3412 Desert Fighter likes this track and he is useful on his day, and this was certainly one of them. (9/4)
2952 Anabranch improved on the bridle three out, and it looked a question of how far but, when she was asked a question, she failed to come up with the goods. Nevertheless, this was not a bad effort and she looks in good trim. (11/1)
3475 Last Try (IRE), an edgy individual, ran well until being made to look one-paced in the home straight. (7/1)
3137* Samanid (IRE) did not impress on looks and never seemed all that happy in the race. He was beaten after the third last. (3/1)
1163 Bures (IRE) probably needed this, his first run for five months. (14/1)
3002 Russian Rascal (IRE) made a mess of the first and seemed to hurt himself, for he was never happy thereafter and was pulled-up. (4/1)

T/Plpt: £495.20 (22.96 Tckts). T/Qdpt: £69.10 (8.29 Tckts) AA

3735-**EXETER** (R-H) (Firm)
Wednesday April 2nd

Race 2: last flight omitted fnl circ
WEATHER: Fine and sunny

3996 ALL WOOL AXMINSTER 100 HURDLE (4-Y.O) (Class E)
2-20 (2-20) **2m 2f (8 hdls)** £2,248.50 (£621.00: £295.50) GOING minus 0.40 sec per fur (GF)

				SP	RR	SF
3745^{2}	**Sulawesi (IRE)** (NATwiston-Davies) **4-10-0**$^{(7)}$ MrJGoldstein (lw: mde virtually all: clr appr last: easily)	—	**1**	9/4^{2}	71?	19
3536*	**Give And Take (106)** (MCPipe) **4-11-4** CMaude (lw: chsd wnr: led briefly 2nd: mstke 3rd: sn rdn: in tch tl wknd 2 out)	5	**2**	8/13^{1}	78?	26
3601^{9}	**Timidjar (IRE)** (DRGandolfo) **4-10-9**$^{(3)}$ DFortt (hdwy & in tch 3rd: outpcd fr next)	12	**3**	13/2^{3}	61?	9
				(SP 106.0%)		**3 Rn**

4m 11.6 (1.60) CSF £3.74 TOTE £2.60 (£1.10) OWNER Mr Jack Joseph (CHELTENHAM) BRED P. D. Player and Darley Stud Management
3745 Sulawesi (IRE) at last got off the mark after some good placed efforts. She outstayed her closest rival in the closing stages, and may be set for a summer campaign. (9/4)
3536* Give And Take, successful here last month on ground softer than this, had his chances, but put in a not-so-fluent round of jumping and was simply outpaced by an improving rival. (8/13)
Timidjar (IRE) has yet to show anything worth noting, and did not change that here. (13/2)

3997 MOORLAND AXMINSTER 100 (S) H'CAP HURDLE (0-100) (4-Y.O+ F & M) (Class G)
2-50 (2-51) **2m 2f (7 hdls)** £1,895.20 (£532.20: £259.60) GOING minus 0.40 sec per fur (GF)

				SP	RR	SF
546^{P}	**On My Toes (56)** (RGFrost) **6-10-6**^{ow2} JFrost (lw: mde all: hld on wl u.p flat)	—	**1**	14/1	42	2
2753^{4}	**Quaker Waltz (74)** (JCTuck) **7-11-3**$^{(7)}$ MrAWintle (hld up: hdwy 5th: ev ch last: rdn & no ex nr fin)	¾	**2**	5/1^{3}	59	21
3735^{4}	**Prove The Point (IRE) (59)** (MrsPNDutfield) **4-10-3** AProcter (chsd ldrs to 6th: sn rdn & wknd)	6	**3**	6/1	39	—
3488^{P}	**Lovelark (55)** (RLee) **8-10-5** RJohnson (chsd wnr: rdn 6th: grad wknd)	11	**4**	11/4^{2}	25	—
3628^{6}	**Spirit Level (66)** (JRPayne) **9-11-2** MrRPayne (in tch to 5th: wknd next)	5	**5**	14/1	32	—
3735^{2}	**Rose of Glenn (70)** (BPalling) **6-11-6** TJenks (hmpd 1st: bhd: hdwy 4th: in tch tl rdn & wknd fr 6th)	2½	**6**	5/2^{1}	34	—
3352^{8}	**Patong Beach (59)** (PCRitchens) **7-10-9** CMaude (bit bkwd: a bhd: rdn & wknd fr 6th)	14	**7**	12/1	10	—
3733^{13}	**Them Times (IRE) (57)** (FJordan) **8-10-4**$^{(3)}$ LAspell (fell 1st)		**F**	10/1	—	—
				(SP 116.3%)		**8 Rn**

4m 15.6 (5.60) CSF £76.17 CT £431.21 TOTE £13.30: £2.60 £1.40 £1.80 (£42.20) OWNER Mr G. Chambers (BUCKFASTLEIGH) BRED G. Chambers
WEIGHT FOR AGE 4yo-6lb
No bid
STEWARDS' ENQUIRY Obj. to On My Toes by Wintle overruled.
On My Toes, returning after an absence of over two hundred days took, it has to be said, quite a poor event. A considerable drifter in the market, she made all and kept on well in the home straight to keep her only serious rival at bay. (14/1: op 9/2)
2753 Quaker Waltz tracked the leaders throughout, and looked to be going the best of them all on the turn into the straight. However, once put to work, she found little and could not overhaul the long-time leader on the run-in. (5/1)
3735 Prove The Point (IRE), chasing the leaders throughout, could only keep on at the one pace in the straight. (6/1)
3735 Rose of Glenn took a very keen hold going to post, and never really got into contention. (5/2)
2567 Them Times (IRE) (10/1: 8/1-12/1)

3998 ROYAL SEATON AXMINSTER 100 NOVICES' CHASE (5-Y.O+) (Class D)
3-20 (3-21) **2m 3f 110y (14 fncs)** £3,629.50 (£1,096.00: £533.00: £251.50) GOING minus 0.40 sec per fur (GF)

				SP	RR	SF
	Sorciere (GBBalding) **6-10-11** BClifford (chsd ldr 5th tl led 11th: j.lft next: hld on strly flat)	—	**1**	3/1^{3}	77	—
3736^{P}	**Mozemo (81)** (MCPipe) **10-11-2** CMaude (hdwy & in tch 9th: ev ch last: no ex flat)	3½	**2**	2/1^{2}	79	—
3842^{5}	**Jonjas Chudleigh (65)** (RGFrost) **10-11-2** JFrost (chsd ldr tl lft in ld 5th: hdd 11th: one pce)	6	**3**	12/1	74	—
3538^{5}	**Gemini Mist (60)** (MrsPNDutfield) **6-10-11** AProcter (j.lft: in tch tl wknd 8th)	dist	**4**	25/1	—	—
3166^{3}	**First Class** (GNAlford) **7-11-2** RGreene (lw: led tl fell 5th)		**F**	6/4^{1}	—	—
				(SP 109.9%)		**5 Rn**

4m 54.7 (9.70) CSF £8.80 TOTE £3.00: £1.70 £1.40 (£4.30) OWNER Mr M. Henriques (ANDOVER) BRED M. Henriques
Sorciere, who attracted support in the market, had her cause made a lot easier by the early departure of the favourite. One of three with a chance turning into the straight, she made an erratic jump to the left at the second last, but did enough from then on to secure success. (3/1)
3591 Mozemo was held up behind the leaders for most of the way, until set to work in the straight. He stayed on well and had every chance over the final obstacle, but found little on the run-in and had just met one too good in the winner. (2/1: 6/4-9/4)
1390 Jonjas Chudleigh led the way after the departure of the favourite, but was swallowed up by his pursuers soon after entering the straight. (12/1)

Gemini Mist was always at the rear, and did himself no favours by jumping out to his left throughout. (25/1)

3999 TORBAY AXMINSTER 100 H'CAP HURDLE (0-120) (4-Y.O+) (Class D)
3-50 (3-50) **2m 3f 110y (9 hdls)** £2,862.50 (£860.00: £415.00: £192.50) GOING minus 0.40 sec per fur (GF)

				SP	RR	SF
3905*	**Mr Snaggle (IRE) (90)** (SEarle) **8-10-0** CMaude (chsd ldrs: in tch 5th: rdn to ld appr last: drvn out to hold on flat)	—	1	2/1[2]	71	13
	Kiwi Crystal (NZ) (90) (AGHobbs) **8-10-0** RGreene (bit bkwd: bhd: wl bhd 4th: rdn & str run fr 2 out to chse wnr flat: nt get up)	nk	2	7/1	71	13
3589[4]	**Shahrani (104)** (MCPipe) **5-10-7b**(7) BMoore (lw: led to 3rd: rdn to disp ld 5th: lost pl appr 2 out: rallied & ev ch last: wknd flat)	2	3	3/1[3]	83	25
2890[F]	**Super Tactics (IRE) (115)** (RHAlner) **9-11-6**(5) MrRThornton (swtg: chsd ldr: led 3rd tl hdd appr last: wknd flat)	5	4	7/4[1]	90	32
				(SP 107.2%)	**4 Rn**	

4m 33.6 (1.60) CSF £11.72 TOTE £2.10 (£9.00) OWNER The Plum Merchants (STURMINSTER NEWTON) BRED Mrs W. H. Young
LONG HANDICAP Kiwi Crystal (NZ) 9-12
3905* Mr Snaggle (IRE) has a liking for the fast ground and seems a versatile individual. Always going well, he was kept under a tight hold on the heels of the leaders, and was sent about his work in the straight. After going on, he was challenged by the fast-finishing runner-up, and only just held on at the line. (2/1: 6/4-9/4)
Kiwi Crystal (NZ), who has not been out since pulling up lame over a year and a half ago, was always well behind and seemingly out of it from some way out. She did, however, make up a lot of ground after jumping the second last, and came with a late run on the flat, but found the line coming too soon. She will come on a lot for this effort. (7/1)
3589 Shahrani appreciates this ground and, always holding a prominent position, found little on the run-in. (3/1)
2621* Super Tactics (IRE), successful over fences, was possibly using this as a confidence booster after falling last time out. (7/4)

4000 ROYAL DARTMOUTH AXMINSTER 100 H'CAP CHASE (0-125) (5-Y.O+) (Class D)
4-20 (4-20) **2m 2f (13 fncs)** £3,798.50 (£1,148.00: £559.00: £264.50) GOING minus 0.40 sec per fur (GF)

				SP	RR	SF
3362[P]	**Monks Jay (IRE) (89)** (GThorner) **8-10-0** CMaude (chsd ldr tl led 5th: mde rest: qcknd clr flat)	—	1	12/1	100	32
3738[2]	**Polden Pride (113)** (GBBalding) **9-11-10** BClifford (hld up in tch: chsd wnr 10th: ev ch 2 out: one pce appr last)	5	2	Evens[1]	120	52
1598[4]	**Herbert Buchanan (IRE) (101)** (PFNicholls) **7-10-12** RJohnson (bit bkwd: hdwy to chse wnr 6th: ev ch & mstke 10th: wkng & mstke 2 out)	4	3	4/1[3]	104	36
3538*	**Bishops Castle (IRE) (94)** (RGFrost) **9-10-5**ow4 JFrost (led to 5th: in tch tl wknd 9th)	3	4	9/4[2]	94	22
				(SP 108.5%)	**4 Rn**	

4m 17.9 (-3.10) CSF £23.17 TOTE £11.90 (£8.80) OWNER Mr J. A. Cover (WANTAGE) BRED Jeremy Hill
LONG HANDICAP Monks Jay (IRE) 9-13
1769 Monks Jay (IRE) has been disappointing of late, but caused quite an upset here against some in-form rivals. Taking up the lead some way out, he was challenged entering the straight but, on 24lb better terms with the runner-up, held that rival at bay and found another gear on the flat. (12/1: 8/1-14/1)
3738 Polden Pride, sitting just off the leaders, made an effort to challenge turning into the straight. He was still close up over the last fence but, under top-weight, was outspeeded on the run-in. (Evens)
3538* Bishops Castle (IRE) (9/4: 6/4-5/2)

4001 TAMAR AXMINSTER 100 NOVICES' AMATEUR HURDLE (5-Y.O+) (Class E)
4-50 (4-50) **2m 3f 110y (9 hdls)** £2,830.50 (£788.00: £379.50) GOING minus 0.40 sec per fur (GF)

				SP	RR	SF
3592[4]	**Country Lover (95)** (MCPipe) **6-11-3v**(5)ow1 MrAFarrant (lw: hld up in tch: led after 7th: clr appr last: easily)	—	1	11/4[2]	64+	32
3798[3]	**Foxies Lad (102)** (DNicholson) **6-11-2**(5) MrRThornton (lw: hdwy to ld 6th: hdd after next: ev ch 2 out: wknd)	8	2	Evens[1]	56	25
3051[8]	**Castleconner (IRE) (70)** (RGFrost) **6-11-0b**(7) MrAHoldsworth (prom: lost pl 4th: rdn & rallied appr 2 out: one pce appr last)	2½	3	25/1	54	23
	Mon Amie (AGHobbs) **7-11-0**(7) MrGShenkin (bit bkwd: bhd: styd on appr 2 out: nrst fin)	2	4	25/1	53	22
3683[U]	**Noddadante (IRE) (67)** (NRMitchell) **7-11-6**(7) MrNRMitchell (lw: bhd: styd on appr 2 out: nvr nrr)	3	5	25/1	56	25
3748[4]	**Paula's Boy (IRE) (71)** (DFBassett) **7-11-0**(7) MissKDiMarte (bit bkwd: led 2nd: clr tl hdd 6th: sn wknd: t.o)	dist	6	66/1	—	—
3413[7]	**Real Glee (IRE)** (JJQuinn) **8-11-0**(7) MrAWintle (chsd ldrs tl wknd appr 2 out: p.u bef last)		P	9/2[3]	—	—
3208[F]	**Joctor Don (IRE)** (GBBalding) **5-11-0**(7) MrEBabington (bit bkwd: led to 2nd: bhd 4th: t.o whn p.u bef 2 out)		P	33/1	—	—
	Sharp Thyne (IRE) (PJHobbs) **7-11-0**(7) MrSMulcaire (prom to 2nd: bhd & mstke next: t.o whn p.u bef 2 out)		P	25/1	—	—
	Rogerson (SGKnight) **9-11-0**(7) MrLJefford (bhd: sme hdwy after 3rd: sn wknd: t.o whn p.u bef 2 out)		P	66/1	—	—
				(SP 116.2%)	**10 Rn**	

4m 33.9 (1.90) CSF £5.15 TOTE £3.00: £1.80 £1.10 £3.70 (£2.80) Trio £11.50 OWNER Pond House Gold (WELLINGTON) BRED Sir Gordon Brunton
3592 Country Lover had only one rival to contend with from some way out, as the race turned into something of a match. He took the initiative at the second last, and was clear approaching the final flight. Although not fluent over it, it did not hinder his chance and he went on to score well. (11/4)
3798 Foxies Lad, close to the winner turning into the straight, was only keeping on at the one pace over the last two flights. (Evens)
2068 Castleconner (IRE) seemed to lose his place and was going backwards at halfway, but he struggled on at one pace in the closing stages. (25/1)

T/Plpt: £1,137.50 (8.04 Tckts). T/Qdpt: £130.70 (5.42 Tckts) T

1679-WORCESTER (L-H) (Good, Gd to frm ptchs, Frm ptchs grandstand bend)
Wednesday April 2nd
WEATHER: Overcast

4002 ROUNDHEAD (S) HURDLE (4-Y.O+) (Class G)
2-00 (2-00) **2m (8 hdls)** £2,048.50 (£571.00: £275.50) GOING: 0.45 sec per fur (GS)

				SP	RR	SF
3590[2]	**A S Jim** (OO'Neill) **6-11-0** VSlattery (hld up & bhd: hdwy 5th: led appr 2 out: drvn clr)	—	1	11/4[2]	56	21

				SP	RR	SF
	Brave Spy (DBurchell) **6-11-0** DJBurchell (bit bkwd: hld up: hdwy 4th: wandered 3 out: disp ld next: wknd flat)	7	**2**	16/1	49	14
3803^{6}	**Strike-a-Pose (67)** (BJLlewellyn) **7-11-2** MrJLLlewellyn (lw: a.p: ev ch 3 out: wknd next)	7	**3**	6/1	44	9
2959^{6}	**Daydream Believer** (MSalaman) **5-10-9** PHolley (hld up & bhd: hdwy 5th: wknd appr 2 out)	7	**4**	14/1	30	—
3050^{P}	**Glenmavis (75)** (DrPPritchard) **10-11-0** DrPPritchard (nt j.w: prom: led after 5th: hdd & wknd appr 2 out)	1½	**5**	33/1	34	—
3677^{8}	**Corporate Image** (THind) **7-11-0** PMcLoughlin (chsd ldrs: hmpd & mstke 3rd: wknd appr 3 out)	7	**6**	16/1	27	—
3803^{12}	**A Badge Too Far (IRE) (52)** (MrsLWilliamson) **7-10-9b^{1}** RBellamy (swtg: led to 2nd: led 5th: sn hdd & wknd: t.o)	dist	**7**	50/1	—	—
	Westcoast (MTate) **6-11-0** WMarston (bkwd: led 2nd to 5th: sn wknd: t.o)	12	**8**	25/1	—	—
3748^{U}	**Rakaposhi Imp** (CHJones) **7-10-2**$^{(7)}$ MKeighley (sddle slipped & p.u after 2nd)		**P**	50/1	—	—
3207^{4}	**Ilewin Janine (IRE) (78)** (PCRitchens) **6-10-9** DGallagher (bhd: hdwy 3rd: stumbled & sddle slipped next: p.u bef 5th)		**P**	5/2^{1}	—	—
3748^{6}	**Sprig Muslin** (DRGandolfo) **5-10-6**$^{(3)}$ SophieMitchell (sn t.o: p.u bef 2 out)		**P**	11/2^{3}	—	—
3677^{6}	**Vita Nuova (IRE)** (WJenks) **6-10-9** MrAMitchell (swvd rt & uns rdr 1st)		**U**	20/1	—	—
2690^{P}	**Just Andy** (BPreece) **6-10-7v^{1}**$^{(7)}$ JMogford (sn bhd: sme hdwy 5th: no ch whn uns rdr 2 out)		**U**	50/1	—	—
				(SP 120.8%)	**13 Rn**	

3m 55.8 (15.80) CSF £37.84 TOTE £3.10: £1.50 £3.40 £1.50 (£30.70) Trio £30.50 OWNER Mr Owen O'Neill (CHELTENHAM) BRED T. J. Atkin

Bt in 4,200 gns

OFFICIAL EXPLANATION **Ilewin Janine: the rider reported the saddle had slipped after the fifth hurdle forcing him to pull up.**

Rakaposhi Imp: the rider reported the saddle had slipped after the second hurdle forcing him to pull up.

3590 A S Jim has been knocking at the door for quite some time now, and this runaway success was certainly not coming out of turn. (11/4: 2/1-3/1)

Brave Spy, winner of a fourteen-furlong event on the All-Weather in July 1995, was making his hurdling debut. Not relishing this fast ground, he showed he could be better than a selling plater on an easier surface. (16/1)

3803 Strike-a-Pose, always poised to challenge, got left behind when the winner kicked for home, and supporters soon knew their fate. (6/1)

Daydream Believer has been competing over longer trips and, though she had reached the heels of the principals turning in, was left struggling once the battle to the line got underway. (14/1: 10/1-16/1)

3207 Ilewin Janine (IRE), taking closer order when stumbling and all but departing the scene at the fourth, caused her jockey to lose his irons and, with the saddle slipping as well, he had no option but to pull up. (5/2)

3748 Sprig Muslin (11/2: 7/2-6/1)

4003 LEVY BOARD NOVICES' HURDLE (4-Y.O+) (Class E)

2-30 (2-30) **2m (8 hdls)** £2,880.00 (£805.00: £390.00) GOING: 0.45 sec per fur (GS)

				SP	RR	SF
3818^{3}	**Riparius (USA)** (PRWebber) **6-11-0** JOsborne (lw: a.p: slt ld 2 out: pushed clr flat)	—	**1**	13/8^{1}	79	19
	Mischief Star (NJHenderson) **4-10-3** MAFitzgerald (lw: led to 2 out: sn rdn: unable qckn flat)	3	**2**	9/1	71	5
3399^{4}	**Moon Devil (IRE)** (MarkCampion) **7-11-0** JRailton (hdwy 4th: rdn appr 2 out: kpt on one pce)	4	**3**	10/1	72	12
3601^{4}	**Spring Campaign (IRE)** (MCPipe) **4-10-8** JamieEvans (chsd ldrs: ev ch 3 out: sn rdn: wknd appr last)	1¼	**4**	9/1	71	5
3672^{3}	**Leap Frog** (NAGaselee) **6-11-0** WMarston (swtg: hld up: hdwy 4th: wknd appr 3 out)	9	**5**	7/1	62	2
2655^{8}	**Kevasingo (84)** (JLSpearing) **5-11-0** DBridgwater (w ldr early: wknd 3 out: t.o)	7	**6**	14/1	55	—
3592^{5}	**Keen Bid (IRE)** (MrsLRichards) **6-11-0** MRichards (chsd ldrs tl rdn & outpcd after 5th: t.o)	2	**7**	6/1^{3}	53	—
3718^{5}	**The Flying Doctor (IRE) (87)** (GBBalding) **7-11-0v^{1}** JRKavanagh (lost tch 5th: t.o)	s.h	**8**	20/1	53	—
	Fearless Hussar (CFCJackson) **7-11-0** PHolley (bit bkwd: a bhd: t.o)	1½	**9**	50/1	51	—
	Mordros (MrsJScrivens) **7-10-11**$^{(3)}$ TDascombe (bkwd: in tch tl wknd after 5th: t.o)	13	**10**	100/1	38	—
	Rough Diamond (IRE) (MSheppard) **5-11-0** BPowell (nt j.w: a bhd: t.o)	30	**11**	66/1	8	—
2931^{14}	**Artic Meadow** (AEJessop) **6-10-9** TKent (bit bkwd: mstkes 1st & 2nd: sddle slipped: p.u appr 3rd)		**P**	100/1	—	—
3404^{F}	**Tiutchev** (MissHCKnight) **4-10-8** JCulloty (bhd tl blnd & uns rdr 3rd)		**U**	11/2^{2}	—	—
				(SP 126.2%)	**13 Rn**	

3m 56.4 (16.40) CSF £16.81 TOTE £2.40: £1.40 £3.10 £2.40 (£13.00) Trio £95.90 OWNER Mrs David Blackburn (BANBURY) BRED Rogers Trust

WEIGHT FOR AGE 4yo-6lb

OFFICIAL EXPLANATION **Artic Meadow: the rider reported the saddle had slipped after the second hurdle forcing him to pull up.**

3818 Riparius (USA) looked to have found quite a simple task, and so it proved in the end. He has really taken to jumping hurdles. (13/8)

Mischief Star was well tuned-up for this debut over hurdles, and she did her best to make it a true test of stamina. However, the winner was merely delaying his challenge, and she had no answer when he was let loose. Successful over two miles on the Flat, she will go one better when tackling extended trips. (9/1)

3399 Moon Devil (IRE), short on experience at this game, performed with credit and he will also benefit when faced with a stiffer test of stamina. (10/1)

3601 Spring Campaign (IRE) seems to be having problems getting even this minimum trip, for she was travelling as well as any at the penultimate flight, only to drop in a heap before reaching the last. (9/1: op 5/1)

3672 Leap Frog may well benefit from a much longer trip in time, as his effort to get himself into the action on the home turn was destined for failure once the tempo increased. (7/1: 5/1-15/2)

2035 Kevasingo (14/1: op 25/1)

4004 BROMYARD NOVICES' CHASE (5-Y.O+) (Class D)

3-00 (3-00) **2m 7f 110y (18 fncs)** £5,643.00 (£1,377.00) GOING: 0.45 sec per fur (GS)

				SP	RR	SF
2896*	**Domaine de Pron (FR) (97)** (MrsLCTaylor) **6-11-8** RBellamy (a.p: led 11th to 12th: led appr 3 out: sn clr)	—	**1**	7/2^{3}	117?	31
3671^{2}	**High Learie (94)** (AHHarvey) **7-11-8** JAMcCarthy (lw: led to 11th: led 12th: j.rt next 2: hdd appr 3 out: sn btn)	dist	**2**	13/8^{1}	—	—
2672^{P}	**Halkopous** (MissVenetiaWilliams) **11-11-2** NWilliamson (hld up: hdwy 7th: disp ld whn fell 3 out)		**F**	11/4^{2}	—	—
3422^{4}	**Spin Echo (IRE)** (RWaley-Cohen) **8-11-2** WMarston (lw: hld up: j.rt & fell 8th)		**F**	16/1	—	—
2947^{6}	**Pavi's Brother (88)** (PRHedger) **9-11-8** MRichards (prom: wkng whn hit 9th: t.o whn p.u bef 12th: b.b.v)		**P**	9/2	—	—
3736^{7}	**Charlie Bee (65)** (RHBuckler) **8-11-2** BPowell (j.b: a bhd: t.o whn p.u bef 12th)		**P**	50/1	—	—
	Hazle Wand (TTBill) **10-11-2** MrRArmson (bkwd: prom: mstke 10th: blnd & uns rdr 13th)		**U**	50/1	—	—
3806^{P}	**Ledburian** (MissPMWhittle) **7-10-13b^{1}**$^{(3)}$ GuyLewis (chsd ldrs: blnd & uns rdr 6th)		**U**	66/1	—	—
				(SP 116.5%)	**8 Rn**	

6m 8.2 CSF £9.38 TOTE £4.20: £1.70 £1.80 (£3.00) Trio £2.00 OWNER Mrs L. C. Taylor (CHIPPING WARDEN) BRED Jacques Cypres

OFFICIAL EXPLANATION **Pavi's Brother: had bled from the nose.**

2896* Domaine de Pron (FR) stays this trip extremely well, and had just regained the advantage when his nearest pursuer fell three out. From then on it was no contest. (7/2)
3671 High Learie needs more cut in the ground to produce his best, but he still held the call entering the straight, only to stop to a walk after being headed approaching the third last. (13/8)
2672 Halkopous has been very lightly-raced in recent years and he still looked to have plenty left to work on here. However, he travelled and jumped extremely well, and was obviously the one to beat when he capsized on landing three out. It looked quite an easy fall and he should have little trouble making the grade over fences. (11/4: 2/1-3/1)

4005 EVESHAM H'CAP HURDLE (0-135) (4-Y.O+) (Class C)

3-30 (3-30) **3m (12 hdls)** £3,955.75 (£1,186.00: £570.50: £262.75) GOING: 0.45 sec per fur (GS)

Form	Horse	Dist	Pos	SP	RR	SF
3702[3]	**Royal Piper (NZ) (106)** (AJWilson) **10-10-4** LHarvey (hld up & bhd: gd hdwy 9th: chal last: led flat: rdn out)	—	1	14/1	86	16
3666*	**Barford Sovereign (112)** (JRFanshawe) **5-10-10** ADobbin (lw: chsd ldrs: led 9th tl flat: hrd rdn & rallied)	½	2	13/2[3]	92	22
3402[2]	**Oatis Rose (105)** (MSheppard) **7-10-3** NWilliamson (reminders 5th: lost pl 7th: mstke 9th: rallied appr 3 out: styd on u.p)	1½	3	6/1[2]	84	14
3731[2]	**Bankhead (IRE) (127)** (JLSpearing) **8-11-4**(7) MissCSpearing (lost pl 5th: hdwy 7th: outpcd 9th: sn rdn: styd on strly flat)	1¼	4	9/2[1]	105	35
3541[2]	**Scotby (BEL) (112)** (RHBuckler) **7-10-10** BPowell (chsd ldrs: outpcd & rdn after 9th: styd on appr last)	1¼	5	9/1	89	19
3013[P]	**Uluru (IRE) (104)** (CPMorlock) **9-10-2** JAMcCarthy (trckd ldrs: outpcd 9th: swtchd lft & styd on flat)	2	6	10/1	80	10
3600[9]	**General Mouktar (110)** (MCPipe) **7-10-8** JamieEvans (hld up & bhd: effrt appr 2 out: sn rdn: nt pce to chal)	s.h	7	13/2[3]	86	16
3635[14]	**Wisley Wonder (IRE) (125)** (NATwiston-Davies) **7-11-9** CLlewellyn (lw: led: j.slowly 7th: hdd 9th: rdn & wknd 2 out)	3½	8	6/1[2]	98	28
	Jimbalou (102) (RGBrazington) **14-10-0** DGallagher (bkwd: sn wl bhd: sme late hdwy: nvr nrr)	nk	9	100/1	75	5
3281[7]	**Nick the Beak (IRE) (107)** (JohnUpson) **8-10-5** RSupple (lw: hld up: hdwy 6th: rdn & wknd 2 out: t.o)	14	10	14/1	71	1
3603[2]	**Brackenheath (IRE) (105)** (DMGrissell) **6-10-3** JRKavanagh (w ldr: rdn 8th: wknd appr 3 out: t.o)	3½	11	9/1	66	—

(SP 116.8%) **11 Rn**

5m 58.6 (22.60) CSF £93.11 CT £558.64 TOTE £13.60: £3.70 £2.10 £2.40 (£40.30) Trio £155.60 OWNER Mr A. M. Darlington (CHELTENHAM) BRED Estate of the Late J. L. Macky
LONG HANDICAP Jimbalou 8-6
3702 Royal Piper (NZ) has never won on ground as fast as this and, for most of the way, he was keeping the back-markers company. Nevertheless, once he began to stay on, he went right through with his effort and was always the master after striking the front. (14/1)
3666* Barford Sovereign travelled well and promised to win her first race away from home, but the winner saw the trip out better and her determined last-gasp effort was always in vain. (13/2)
3402 Oatis Rose is not short on ability but she has a mind of her own and, inclined to run her race in snatches, had given herself just too much to do. (6/1)
3731 Bankhead (IRE) struggled with the pace on this unsuitable ground, and was never going well enough to pose a serious threat. However, he is an out-and-out stayer, and he was pegging the principals back on this lengthy run-in. (9/2)
3541 Scotby (BEL) held his pitch in the chasing group, but always seemed to be at full stretch and, with the pace being maintained, could never get in a blow. (9/1)
2117 Uluru (IRE) stays further than this, and was only just finding top gear when the race was over. (10/1)

4006 COMMANDERY AMATEUR H'CAP HURDLE (0-115) (4-Y.O+) (Class E)

4-00 (4-00) **2m 2f (9 hdls)** £2,635.00 (£735.00: £355.00) GOING: 0.45 sec per fur (GS)

Form	Horse	Dist	Pos	SP	RR	SF
2797[11]	**Handy Lass (95)** (JSSmith) **8-10-2**(7) MrOMcPhail (chsd ldrs: led after 2 out: drvn out)	—	1	10/1	77	45
2946[4]	**Peter Monamy (100)** (MCPipe) **5-10-11b**(3) MrMRimell (a.p: ev ch appr 2 out: hrd rdn: r.o one pce)	3	2	11/2[3]	79	47
3766[3]	**Kino's Cross (100)** (AJWilson) **8-10-9**(5) MrJJukes (hld up & bhd: hdwy 6th: hrd rdn 2 out: one pce)	10	3	16/1	70	38
3733[7]	**Barton Scamp (94)** (SABrookshaw) **5-10-1**(7)ow1 MrRWakley (led tl after 2 out: sn rdn: hung rt & wknd)	2	4	9/2[2]	63	30
3743*	**Above the Cut (USA) (94)** (CPMorlock) **5-10-1**(7)ow5 MrPScott (hld up: hdwy 4th: ev ch 3 out: fnd nil)	6	5	3/1[1]	57	20
3919[5]	**Glen Mirage (86)** (RHBuckler) **12-9-7**(7) MissMCoombe (prom: lost pl 4th: n.d after)	¾	6	20/1	49	17
3748[P]	**Halham Tarn (IRE) (88)** (HJManners) **7-9-9**(7) MissADudley (hmpd 4th: nvr nr ldrs)	2½	7	20/1	48	16
3623[P]	**Daily Sport Girl (86)** (BJLlewellyn) **8-9-7**(7) MissEJJones (lw: hld up: hdwy 5th: rdn 3 out: sn wknd)	8	8	33/1	39	7
3748[2]	**Hanging Grove (IRE) (86)** (PGMurphy) **7-9-7**(7) MrMatthewWells (lw: prom tl m wd & wknd appr 3 out)	7	9	12/1	33	1
3584[P]	**Ballet Royal (USA) (114)** (HJManners) **8-11-7**(7) MrACharles-Jones (a bhd)	1½	10	33/1	60	28
3717[3]	**Chris's Glen (89)** (JMBradley) **8-9-10v**(7)ow1 MissVRoberts (prom tl rdn & wknd 6th: t.o)	10	11	16/1	26	—
3500[12]	**West Bay Breeze (86)** (RHBuckler) **5-9-7**(7) MrSDurack (a bhd: t.o)	s.h	12	33/1	23	—
3343[P]	**Relkowen (88)** (AndrewTurnell) **7-9-9**(7)ow2 MrJRees (prom tl rdn & wknd 5th: t.o)	16	13	14/1	11	—
3234[2]	**Classic Pal (USA) (86)** (NRMitchell) **6-9-9**(5) MissPJones (trckd ldrs tl fell 4th)		F	12/1	—	—
3176[P]	**The Caumrue (IRE) (110)** (GBBalding) **9-11-3**(7) MrJThatcher (swtg: a bhd: t.o 5th: p.u bef 3 out)		P	20/1	—	—

(SP 124.6%) **15 Rn**

4m 20.9 (10.90) CSF £55.31 CT £807.61 TOTE £13.00: £2.50 £2.30 £5.30 (£37.30) Trio £114.80 OWNER Mr G. W. Hackling (TIRLEY) BRED John Rose
LONG HANDICAP Glen Mirage 9-10 Hanging Grove (IRE) 9-11 West Bay Breeze 9-0 Relkowen 9-13 Classic Pal (USA) 9-6 Daily Sport Girl 9-3
2666 Handy Lass, given a break after disappointing last time, did not mind this faster ground. (10/1)
2946 Peter Monamy, freshened up for the spring campaign, likes this fast surface and was his usual consistent self. (11/2)
3766 Kino's Cross, having come down a stone in the ratings, ran his best race since returning to hurdles on ground plenty lively enough for him. (16/1)
3733 Barton Scamp gave the impression he wanted to head for the paddock exit going to the final flight. (9/2)
3743* Above the Cut (USA), raised only 2lb, looked to be going like a winner when possibly taking a fractional advantage at the third last, but folded up in a matter of strides. (3/1)
3748 Hanging Grove (IRE) (12/1: op 7/1)

4007 RESTORATION NOVICES' H'CAP CHASE (0-100) (5-Y.O+) (Class E)

4-30 (4-30) **2m 4f 110y (15 fncs)** £3,910.50 (£1,179.00: £572.00: £268.50) GOING: 0.45 sec per fur (GS)

Form	Horse	Dist	Pos	SP	RR	SF
3750[4]	**No Fiddling (IRE) (79)** (GMMcCourt) **6-10-9** DBridgwater (gd hdwy fr 3 out: styd on to ld nr fin)	—	1	10/1	95	24
3736[5]	**Winnow (70)** (AndrewTurnell) **7-10-0** CRae (hld up: hdwy 7th: outpcd 10th: rallied 2 out: styd on flat)	½	2	16/1	86	15
3343[P]	**Lobster Cottage (87)** (KCBailey) **9-11-3** SMcNeill (lw: chsd ldr: led 10th: clr whn hit 2 out: wknd & hdd nr fin)	1	3	14/1	102	31
3806[R]	**Dandie Imp (78)** (AWCarroll) **9-10-8** DWalsh (led to 10th: wknd appr last)	13	4	8/1[3]	83	12

3819[2]	**Boots N All (IRE) (77)** (GBBalding) **7-10-7** ADobbin (prom: 3rd whn hit 2 out: sn wknd) 2½	**5**	11/4[1]	80	9
3355[7]	**Hardy Breeze (IRE) (80)** (DMGrissell) **6-10-7**(3) PHenley (hdwy 5th: outpcd 10th: wknd appr 4 out) 4	**6**	33/1	80	9
3819[4]	**Spring to Glory (93)** (PHayward) **10-11-9** AThornton (prom: j.slowly 8th: wknd 10th) ....nk	**7**	14/1	92	21
3627*	**Court Master (IRE) (88)** (RHBuckler) **9-11-4** BPowell (lw: a bhd: t.o) 17	**8**	9/1	74	3
2891[3]	**Riding Crop (IRE) (88)** (NJHenderson) **7-11-4** JRKavanagh (dropped rr 6th: t.o whn p.u bef 4 out)	**P**	7/1[2]	—	—
3756[3]	**Jovial Man (IRE) (94)** (RJO'Sullivan) **8-11-10** PHolley (bhd fr 7th: t.o whn p.u bef 4 out)	**P**	11/1	—	—
3762[2]	**Raincheck (75)** (MarkCampion) **6-10-5** LHarvey (blnd 5th: sn bhd: t.o whn p.u bef 4 out)	**P**	16/1	—	—
3622[5]	**King's Shilling (USA) (75)** (HOliver) **10-10-5** JacquiOliver (bhd: mstke 5th: t.o whn p.u bef 4 out)	**P**	16/1	—	—
3495[F]	**Dress Dance (IRE) (72)** (NRMitchell) **7-10-2** GUpton (bhd: blnd 8th: t.o whn p.u bef 4 out)	**P**	20/1	—	—
	Stamp Duty (74) (NJHenderson) **10-10-4**ow3 MAFitzgerald (bkwd: mstkes: bhd fr 7th: t.o whn p.u bef 4 out)	**P**	14/1	—	—
3472[P]	**Bonnifer (IRE) (70)** (MJWilkinson) **8-10-0** WMarston (swtg: bhd: blnd 11th: t.o whn p.u bef 4 out)	**P**	33/1	—	—
3588[F]	**Givry (IRE) (80)** (GMMcCourt) **7-10-7**(3) SophieMitchell (a bhd: t.o whn p.u bef 4 out)	**P**	20/1	—	—
3165[P]	**Top it All (70)** (PRHarriss) **9-10-0** CLlewellyn (bkwd: rdn & lost pl after 6th: t.o whn p.u bef 4 out)	**P**	50/1	—	—
			(SP 132.7%)	**17 Rn**	

5m 19.9 (18.90) CSF £145.73 CT £2,082.63 TOTE £12.60: £3.20 £3.80 £2.20 £2.20 (£168.70) Trio £1,028.80; £869.47 to Aintree 3/4/97
OWNER Mr Malcolm Batchelor (WANTAGE) BRED Duncan A. McGregor
LONG HANDICAP Bonnifer (IRE) 9-11 Winnow 9-11 Top it All 9-13
3750 No Fiddling (IRE), without the headgear tried on his last two starts, needed every yard of this trip on this return to fences. (10/1)
3188 Winnow, 3lb out of the handicap, seemed to find this trip the bare minimum and deserves a change of luck. (16/1)
2926 Lobster Cottage is more effective at shorter distances when ridden as aggressively as this. (14/1)
3582 Dandie Imp may have a better chance of his forcing tactics paying off over two miles. (8/1)
3819 Boots N All (IRE) had been put up a total of 7lb for finishing runner-up in his last two starts. (11/4)
Hardy Breeze (IRE), graduating to fences, had completed only once in four outings in Irish Points. (33/1)
3756 Jovial Man (IRE) (11/1: 8/1-12/1)

4008 WORCESTER STANDARD OPEN N.H. FLAT RACE (I) (4, 5 & 6-Y.O) (Class H)

5-00 (5-02) **2m** £1,399.20 (£391.20: £189.60)

			SP	RR	SF
	Rupert Blues (JSKing) **5-11-4** MRichards (leggy: lt-f: hld up: hdwy 8f out: led over 2f out: drvn out) ....—	**1**	16/1	68 f	—
3808[6]	**Star Adventure** (JTEvans) **5-11-4** MissEJames (w'like: hld up: hdwy 5f out: carried rt 3f out: r.o ins fnl f)....¾	**2**	12/1	67 f	—
3606[2]	**Certain Shot** (GMMcCourt) **6-11-4** DBridgwater (lt-f: a.p: led 3f out: sn hdd: r.o) ....nk	**3**	5/1[3]	67 f	—
3821[6]	**Damien's Choice (IRE)** (MrsMerritaJones) **5-11-4** DerekByrne (lt-f: tk keen hold: hdwy 8f out: r.o one pce fnl 2f) 2½	**4**	4/1[1]	64 f	—
	Duty Free (AHHarvey) **4-10-12** JAMcCarthy (w'like: bit bkwd: hld up: hdwy 5f out: c wd st: r.o fnl f)....3½	**5**	50/1	61 f	—
3304[5]	**Montroe (IRE)** (RRowe) **5-11-4** DO'Sullivan (lt-f: unf: hld up & bhd: hdwy 5f out: c wd st: one pce fnl 2f) ....nk	**6**	9/2[2]	61 f	—
	Windle Brook (KCBailey) **5-11-4** SMcNeill (w'like: unf: bkwd: nvr plcd to chal) ....nk	**7**	16/1	60 f	—
	Jazz Duke (RJO'Sullivan) **4-10-12** AMcCabe (lt-f: unf: hld up: hdwy 8f out: hung rt 3f out: sn wknd) 1½	**8**	20/1	59 f	—
	Knightsbridge Girl (IRE) (PJHobbs) **6-10-13** NWilliamson (lengthy: bit bkwd: hdwy 9f out: wknd 4f out) 10	**9**	8/1	44 f	—
	Emerald Lamp (IRE) (OO'Neill) **6-11-4** VSlattery (w'like: str: bkwd: nvr nrr) 3½	**10**	33/1	45 f	—
3808[9]	**Shropshire Gale (IRE)** (SABrookshaw) **6-10-11**(7) XAizpuru (lengthy: unf: plld hrd: chsd ldr: led 6f out to 3f out: sn wknd) 3	**11**	9/1	42 f	—
3821[10]	**Ickford Okey** (CPMorlock) **5-11-4** DGallagher (leggy: prom 10f) 1	**12**	16/1	41 f	—
	Twelve Club (KCBailey) **4-10-12** AThornton (lengthy: unf: hld up: hdwy over 4f out: wknd 3f out) 1½	**13**	10/1	40 f	—
	Bertie Bavard (RFJohnsonHoughton) **5-11-4** MissEJohnsonHoughton (lt-f: unf: a bhd) ....s.h	**14**	16/1	40 f	—
	Jolson (CRBarwell) **6-11-1**(3) PHenley (unf: bkwd: a bhd) 3	**15**	25/1	37 f	—
	Miner's Rose (IRE) (MrsJGRetter) **6-10-13** MAFitzgerald (str: bkwd: a bhd) 2	**16**	50/1	30 f	—
	Avoncliff (JSKing) **4-10-7** WMarston (scope: bkwd: bhd fnl 5f: t.o) 12	**17**	14/1	18 f	—
1820[6]	**Ballina** (JGMO'Shea) **5-10-11**(7) JTNolan (small: unf: hdwy 9f out: wknd over 4f out: t.o) 10	**18**	25/1	13 f	—
	Chatter Box (JohnUpson) **5-10-13** RSupple (cmpt: bkwd: a bhd: t.o) ....hd	**19**	33/1	8 f	—
	Hotel Casino (NZ) (AJKDunn) **5-11-4** GTormey (w'like: a bhd: t.o) 9	**20**	33/1	4 f	—
	So Welcome (NPLittmoden) **5-10-13** TGMcLaughlin (lt-f: led: sn clr: hdd 10f out: wknd qckly: p.u 7f out)	**P**	50/1	—	—
			(SP 150.1%)	**21 Rn**	

3m 56.2 CSF £196.63 TOTE £24.20: £5.90 £5.30 £1.90 (£174.20) Trio Not won; £216.11 to Aintree 3/4/97 OWNER Mr Robert Skillen (SWINDON) BRED Mrs D. B. Mulley
WEIGHT FOR AGE 4yo-6lb
Rupert Blues, a full-brother to Thrower, and half-brother to Laughing Buccaneer, seems likely to turn out much better than those two maidens. (16/1)
3808 Star Adventure, a half-brother to Martha's Son, certainly seems to be going the right way. (12/1: op 5/1)
3606 Certain Shot should do even better when put over timber. (5/1: op 5/2)
3821 Damien's Choice (IRE) is another who now seems ready to tackle hurdles. (4/1: 3/1-9/2)
Duty Free showed promise for the future. (50/1)
3304 Montroe (IRE) was a shade disappointing after his promising debut. (9/2: op 5/2)
Windle Brook appeared to be given a pipe-opener, having looked in need of the run. (16/1)
Knightsbridge Girl (IRE) (8/1: op 5/1)
3808 Shropshire Gale (IRE) (9/1: 5/1-10/1)
Twelve Club (10/1: op 4/1)
Avoncliff (14/1: 8/1-16/1)

4009 WORCESTER STANDARD OPEN N.H. FLAT RACE (II) (4, 5 & 6-Y.O) (Class H)

5-30 (5-35) **2m** £1,399.20 (£391.20: £189.60)

			SP	RR	SF
3433*	**Melody Maid** (NJHenderson) **5-11-6** MAFitzgerald (lt-f: unf: hld up: hdwy 10f out: led 2f out: r.o wl) ....—	**1**	2/1[1]	74 f	—
3021[5]	**Coble Lane** (IPWilliams) **5-11-4** JOsborne (leggy: lt-f: led: sn wl clr: wknd & hdd 2f out: fin tired) 10	**2**	16/1	62 f	—
	Brush With Fame (IRE) (PJHobbs) **5-11-4** GTormey (lt-f: unf: bhd: hdwy over 3f out: rdn over 1f out: r.o) 2	**3**	16/1	60 f	—
	Quabmatic (KBishop) **4-10-7**(5) GSupple (lt-f: chsd ldr 12f: one pce) 2½	**4**	50/1	58 f	—
	Regal Spring (IRE) (KCBailey) **5-11-4** AThornton (w'like: leggy: bit bkwd: hld up & bhd: hdwy 5f out: rdn over 2f out: one pce) 1	**5**	9/1	57 f	—
1966[16]	**Saras Delight** (DNicholson) **5-11-1**(3) RMassey (leggy: lt-f: unf: nvr nrr) 16	**6**	14/1	41 f	—
3574[2]	**Fortunes Flight (IRE)** (JSKing) **4-10-12** MRichards (lt-f: prom: btn whn hung lft over 2f out) 3	**7**	9/2[2]	38 f	—

				SP	RR	SF
	Miss Blues Singer (AJChamberlain) **4-10-7** BPowell (lt-f: bit bkwd: nvr nr ldrs)	6	**8**	66/1	27 f	—
	Lightening Steel (DJCaro) **6-11-4** MrAPhillips (leggy: nvr nr ldrs)	hd	**9**	50/1	31 f	—
	Our Man Flin (IRE) (DrDChesney) **4-10-12** SBurrough (w'like: bkwd: n.d)	¾	**10**	25/1	31 f	—
	Dande Dove (KCBailey) **6-11-4** SMcNeill (w'like: scope: bkwd: n.d)	2½	**11**	6/1[3]	28 f	—
	Longshore (MrsPSly) **4-10-12** MBrennan (w'like: bkwd: prom 10f)	10	**12**	66/1	18 f	—
3821[19]	**Silver Treasure (IRE)** (MrsMerritaJones) **6-11-4** DerekByrne (w'like: bit bkwd: hdwy 8f out: wknd 5f out)	s.h	**13**	33/1	18 f	—
	Rosglinn (IRE) (HMKavanagh) **5-10-13** JacquiOliver (small: lt-f: prom 8f: t.o)	13	**14**	66/1	— f	—
	Roxy Hicks (RJPrice) **5-10-6**(7) MrOMcPhail (small: lt-f: chsd ldrs tl wknd 5f out: t.o)	2½	**15**	66/1	—	—
	National Fiasco (CLPopham) **4-10-12** SWynne (w'like: bit bkwd: a bhd: t.o fnl 8f)	13	**16**	33/1	—	—
	Lucys Red Slipper (PJJones) **5-10-6**(7) MrLBaker (small: lengthy: prom 8f: t.o)	23	**17**	66/1	—	—
3433[8]	**Curtis The Second** (CRBarwell) **4-10-4**(3) PHenley (lt-f: unf: a bhd: t.o)	16	**18**	50/1	—	—
	Hey Zoe (CHJones) **4-10-0**(7) MKeighley (small: bkwd: swtg: a bhd: t.o 8f out: p.u over 1f out)		**P**	66/1	—	—
3574[5]	**Desert Way (IRE)** (MissHCKnight) **4-10-12** NWilliamson (w'like: leggy: t.o whn p.u over 4f out)		**P**	7/1	—	—
				(SP 131.3%)	**20 Rn**	

3m 51.1 CSF £35.03 TOTE £3.00: £1.70 £2.20 £4.30 (£20.70) Trio £53.30 OWNER Mr R. J. Parish (LAMBOURN) BRED Brian McLean
WEIGHT FOR AGE 4yo-6lb

IN-FOCUS: A strongly-run race which was five seconds quicker than the first division.

3433* Melody Maid gained another impressive victory and looks a useful prospect. (2/1: op 4/5)

3021 Coble Lane tried to run this field into the ground, but the winner found little difficulty reeling him in. (16/1)

Brush With Fame (IRE), bought for 19,000 guineas as a four-year-old, put in some good work in the home straight but could not catch the runner-up, let alone bother the smart winner. (16/1)

Quabmatic, in pursuit of the clear leader, kept on after the winner deprived him of second place with half-a-mile to go. (50/1)

Regal Spring (IRE), who cost 6,000 guineas as a four-year-old, should come on for the outing. (9/1: 5/1-10/1)

T/Jkpt: Not won; £72,366.75 to Aintree 3/4/97. T/Plpt: £505.80 (39.44 Tckts). T/Qdpt: £103.10 (9.57 Tckts) IM/KH

1511-AINTREE (L-H) (Good)
Thursday April 3rd

WEATHER: fine

4010 SEAGRAM TOP NOVICES' HURDLE (Gd 2) (4-Y.O+) (Class A)

2-00 (2-00) **2m 110y (9 hdls)** £16,730.00 (£6,351.50: £3,125.75: £1,442.75) GOING: 0.07 sec per fur (G)

				SP	RR	SF
3761*	**Midnight Legend** (DNicholson) **6-11-0** RJohnson (lw: chsd ldr: hit 5th: led 3 out: hung lft flat: rdn & r.o wl)	—	**1**	11/2	100+	57
3672*	**Sharpical (119)** (NJHenderson) **5-11-0** MAFitzgerald (trckd ldrs: hdwy on bit to chal last: rdn & no ex)	2	**2**	100/30[1]	98	55
3359[2]	**High In The Clouds (IRE) (120)** (CaptTAForster) **5-11-0** SWynne (trckd ldrs: smooth hdwy appr 3 out: ev ch 2 out: rdn & nt qckn)	3	**3**	9/1	95	52
3850[2]	**Mister Rm (111)** (NATwiston-Davies) **5-11-0** CLlewellyn (lw: in tch: effrt 4 out: sn hrd rdn & nvr trbld ldrs)	10	**4**	11/1	86	43
3416*	**Nigel's Lad (IRE)** (PCHaslam) **5-11-0** MFoster (lw: led tl hdd 3 out: outpcd fr next)	2	**5**	9/2[3]	84	41
3359*	**Green Green Desert (FR) (125)** (OSherwood) **6-11-0** DBridgwater (stdd s: mstkes 4th & 5th: effrt 4 out: btn & eased fr 3 out)	dist	**6**	4/1[2]	—	—
3595[3]	**Nordic Breeze (IRE) (102)** (MCPipe) **5-11-0b** DWalsh (hld up: pushed along fr 4th: btn 4 out)	25	**7**	9/1	—	—
3745*	**Crandon Boulevard** (MrsJPitman) **4-10-8** JOsborne (lw: chsd ldrs: hit 5th: sn rdn & btn: p.u bef 2 out)		**P**	20/1	—	—
3564[6]	**No Pattern (104)** (GLMoore) **5-11-0v** LWyer (mstke 1st: sn bhd: t.o whn p.u bef 2 out)		**P**	25/1	—	—
				(SP 113.6%)	**9 Rn**	

3m 56.1 (2.10) CSF £22.10 TOTE £7.20: £2.50 £1.70 £2.30 (£10.10) Trio £42.30 OWNER Mrs H. J. Clarke (TEMPLE GUITING) BRED Limestone Stud
WEIGHT FOR AGE 4yo-6lb

3761* Midnight Legend likes to be up with the pace and, once he got his head in front three out, his class carried him through. There is more to come as his hurdling improves. (11/2: 7/2-6/1)

3672* Sharpical loves it when on the bridle, but does not find much off it and, once asked to struggle at the last, he showed his true colours. (100/30)

3359 High In The Clouds (IRE) travelled well for much of the race, but was found out when the pace was really on from the second last. He gave the impression that easier ground will bring the best out in him. (9/1: op 6/1)

3850 Mister Rm was never on the bridle, but he kept responding to pressure and is likely to appreciate stiffer tests. (11/1: 8/1-12/1)

3416* Nigel's Lad (IRE), as usual, tried to gallop the opposition into the ground but, in doing so, he set the race up and was comfortably picked off. (9/2)

3359* Green Green Desert (FR) was in one of his non co-operative moods and never had a chance. (4/1: op 5/2)

3595 Nordic Breeze (IRE) (9/1: op 5/1)

4011 MARTELL CUP CHASE (Gd 2) (5-Y.O+) (Class A)

2-35 (2-35) **3m 1f (Mildmay) (19 fncs)** £39,156.00 (£13,636.00: £6,618.00: £2,790.00) GOING: 0.16 sec per fur (G)

				SP	RR	SF
3636[2]	**Barton Bank (157)** (DNicholson) **11-11-5** DWalsh (lw: hit 1st: led tl hdd 4 out: hit 3 out: rallied to ld between last 2: styd on wl)	—	**1**	100/30[2]	161	54
3383a[2]	**Merry Gale (IRE)** (JTRDreaper,Ireland) **9-11-5** CO'Dwyer (lw: trckd ldr: hit 11th: led 4 out tl hdd & wknd between last 2)	9	**2**	11/2	155	48
	Rouyan (134) (MrsJPitman) **11-11-5** JFTitley (bkwd: chsd ldrs: outpcd 4 out: no imp after)	1½	**3**	20/1	154	47
3636[5]	**Challenger du Luc (FR) (150)** (MCPipe) **7-11-5b** CMaude (hld up & bhd: blnd 15th: sn rdn & btn)	2	**4**	7/2[3]	153	46
3636[6]	**One Man (IRE) (172)** (GRichards) **9-11-13** RDunwoody (lw: hld up: p.u bef 11th: b.b.v)		**P**	6/4[1]	—	—
				(SP 105.4%)	**5 Rn**	

6m 25.9 (8.90) CSF £16.67 TOTE £4.10: £2.00 £1.40 (£7.60) OWNER Mrs J. Mould (TEMPLE GUITING) BRED Miss P. Hutton

OFFICIAL EXPLANATION One Man (IRE): had bled from the nose.

3636 Barton Bank jumps and stays and, once the favourite pulled up, that was all he needed to gain the victory he thoroughly deserved. (100/30)

3383a Merry Gale (IRE) looked to be going best, but he committed himself too soon and his stamina gave out at the second last. (11/2)

Rouyan, considering he had not run for well over a year, produced a sound effort. (20/1)

3636 Challenger du Luc (FR) has yet to win over three miles, but stamina was not the problem this time, as he ran no sort of race. (7/2)

3636 One Man (IRE) (6/4: op evens)

4012 SANDEMAN MAGHULL NOVICES' CHASE (Gd 1) (5-Y.O+) (Class A)

3-10 (3-10) **2m (Mildmay) (12 fncs)** £28,850.00 (£10,905.00: £5,327.50: £2,417.50) GOING: 0.16 sec per fur (G)

	Horse / details	Dist	Pos	SP	RR	SF
3596[2]	**Squire Silk** (AndrewTurnell) **8-11-4** JOsborne (hld up: mstkes 4th & 5th: hdwy 8th: bdly hmpd & lft clr 2 out: blnd bdly last)	—	1	2/1[2]	142	75
2054[3]	**Oh So Risky** (DRCElsworth) **10-11-4** PHolley (lw: in tch: effrt 4 out: sn outpcd)	15	2	11/1	127	60
3571*	**Sublime Fellow (IRE) (116)** (NJHenderson) **7-11-4** MAFitzgerald (chsd ldrs: blnd 7th: sn lost tch)	16	3	16/1	111	44
2933*	**Amancio (USA) (129)** (MrsAJPerrett) **6-11-4** CMaude (led to 6th: chsd ldrs tl wknd fr 4 out)	12	4	15/2[3]	99	32
3596[F]	**Mulligan (IRE) (150)** (DNicholson) **7-11-4** RDunwoody (lw: cl up: led fr 6th: 3l clr whn fell 2 out)		F	11/8[1]	—	—
3835[3]	**Flying Instructor (127)** (PRWebber) **7-11-4** NWilliamson (lw: hld up: hdwy ½-wy: chal & rdn whn fell 3 out)		F	8/1	—	—
				(SP 112.5%)		**6 Rn**

3m 58.5 (0.50) CSF £19.50 TOTE £3.10: £1.60 £2.70 (£13.60) OWNER Mr Robert Ogden (WANTAGE) BRED R. Ogden

3596 Squire Silk was clumsy at various stages, but he remained upright as the opposition bit the dust, and that was all that was required in the end, as he was possibly third best on merit. (2/1: 6/4-9/4)

2054 Oh So Risky looked a picture and was close enough four out, but the effort required was always beyond this old character. (11/1)

3571* Sublime Fellow (IRE) went well until blundering at the seventh, from which point he seemed to lose all interest. (16/1)

2933* Amancio (USA) is good when things go his way, but it was always going to be tough here and, once asked to struggle, he was quickly found out in the back straight. (15/2)

3596 Mulligan (IRE), going well, was in front from halfway, and had the race apparently sewn up when he completely misjudged the open ditch two out and came to grief. (11/8)

3835 Flying Instructor put up a fair performance here, and had just moved up to take the favourite on, although not appearing to be going quite as well, when he fell three out. (8/1)

4013 JOHN HUGHES TROPHY H'CAP CHASE (0-145) (5-Y.O+) (Class B)

3-45 (3-45) **2m 6f (National) (18 fncs)** £23,577.00 (£7,116.00: £3,458.00: £1,629.00) GOING: 0.16 sec per fur (G)

	Horse / details	Dist	Pos	SP	RR	SF
3618[8]	**Bells Life (IRE) (130)** (PJHobbs) **8-11-4** GTormey (in tch: hdwy 11th: led 4 out: clr whn bdly hmpd elbow: kpt on wl)	—	1	14/1	141	50
3675[3]	**Yeoman Warrior (115)** (RRowe) **10-10-3**[ow3] DO'Sullivan (in tch: hdwy 3 out: sn chsng wnr: nt qckn fnl f)	3	2	33/1	124	30
3598[8]	**Kadi (GER) (135)** (DNicholson) **8-11-9** RJohnson (lw: in tch: hdwy u.p 4 out: one pce fr 2 out)	5	3	8/1[1]	140	49
3308[2]	**Aly Daley (IRE) (112)** (HowardJohnson) **9-9-11**(3) MrCBonner (lw: mstkes: chsd ldrs: outpcd 12th (Canal Turn): kpt on fr 2 out)	1¼	4	33/1	116	25
3585[4]	**No Pain No Gain (IRE) (116)** (JTGifford) **9-10-4** PHide (a chsng ldrs: one pce fr 4 out)	4	5	14/1	117	26
3815*	**Senor El Betrutti (IRE) (140)** (MrsSusanNock) **8-12-0** GBradley (lw: in tch tl outpcd fr 8th: sme hdwy u.p 3 out: n.d)	18	6	8/1[1]	128	37
3482[4]	**Super Sandy (112)** (FTWalton) **10-10-0** KJohnson (chsd ldrs to ½-wy: sn bhd)	11	7	150/1	92	1
3729[2]	**Sailor Jim (112)** (PTDalton) **10-10-0** NWilliamson (lw: cl up: lft in ld & mstke 10th (Becher's): hdd 4 out: wknd)	3½	8	20/1	90	—
3618[P]	**Golden Spinner (133)** (NJHenderson) **10-11-7** MAFitzgerald (chsd ldrs tl wknd fr 9th)	4	9	8/1[1]	108	17
3414[2]	**Change the Reign (112)** (MissAEEmbiricos) **10-9-9**(5) MrRThornton (b.d 1st)		B	20/1	—	—
3617*	**Flimsy Truth (121)** (MHWeston) **11-10-9**[ow7] MrMHarris (rr div whn fell 9th)		F	12/1	—	—
3280[6]	**Cropredy Lad (114)** (PRWebber) **10-10-2**[ow2] AThornton (fell 1st)		F	50/1	—	—
3567[5]	**Kings Cherry (IRE) (112)** (JABOld) **9-10-0** CLlewellyn (bhd whn fell 1st)		F	20/1	—	—
3419*	**Too Plush (115)** (AndrewTurnell) **8-10-3** LHarvey (lw: rr div whn fell 3rd (Chair))		F	10/1[3]	—	—
3598[4]	**Romany Creek (IRE) (117)** (JPearce) **8-10-5v** JCulloty (mstkes: sn bhd: p.u bef 9th: lame)		P	8/1[1]	—	—
	Coonawara (137) (CaptTAForster) **11-11-11** RDunwoody (led tl blnd & p.u 10th (Becher's): dead)		P	9/1[2]	—	—
3419[4]	**The Frog Prince (IRE) (125)** (NAGaselee) **9-10-13** JOsborne (lw: p.u lame bef 7th)		P	9/1[2]	—	—
3451[4]	**Master Boston (IRE) (125)** (RDEWoodhouse) **9-10-13** RichardGuest (mstke & uns rdr 2nd)		U	20/1	—	—
3223[5]	**Griffins Bar (112)** (MrsPSly) **9-10-0** WMarston (chsd ldrs: 3rd whn mstke & uns rdr 12th (Canal Turn))		U	100/1	—	—
409[P]	**Pond House (IRE) (112)** (MCPipe) **8-10-0** JamieEvans (blnd & uns rdr 1st)		U	20/1	—	—
				(SP 127.9%)		**20 Rn**

5m 38.7 (8.70) CSF £378.77 CT £3,584.37 TOTE £20.50: £4.20 £12.80 £2.80 £7.00 (£369.80) Trio £3,300.50 OWNER Mr R. Gibbs (MINEHEAD) BRED Dr Welby Henry

LONG HANDICAP Change the Reign 9-9 Cropredy Lad 8-1 Sailor Jim 9-2 Aly Daley (IRE) 8-13 Kings Cherry (IRE) 9-8 Yeoman Warrior 9-2 Super Sandy 6-11 Griffins Bar 8-0 Pond House (IRE) 8-13

3151 Bells Life (IRE) really enjoyed these fences and, once he struck the front four out, he was not going to stop. The only danger was two loose horses on the run-in that did their best to carry him out. (14/1)

3675 Yeoman Warrior, with some decent fences to jump, improved dramatically in that department but, in the end, was well short of pace. (33/1)

3230 Kadi (GER) always seems better when there is more cut in the ground, and was made to look very one-paced here. (8/1)

3308 Aly Daley (IRE) ran amazingly well considering how many mistakes he made. (33/1)

3585 No Pain No Gain (IRE) was always up with the pace, but he is probably better on easier ground, and found the struggle beyond him from four out. (14/1)

3815* Senor El Betrutti (IRE) did not seem to like the hustle and bustle of this type of event, and ran no race at all. (8/1)

3482 Super Sandy ran as well as could be expected from over two stone out of the handicap. (150/1)

3729 Sailor Jim ran out of fuel so fast from the fourth last, that something must have gone amiss. (20/1)

3617* Flimsy Truth (12/1: op 8/1)

3419* Too Plush (10/1: op 6/1)

3419 The Frog Prince (IRE) (9/1: 6/1-10/1)

4014 GLENLIVET ANNIVERSARY HURDLE (Gd 2) (4-Y.O) (Class A)

4-20 (4-21) **2m 110y (9 hdls)** £26,234.00 (£9,902.20: £4,826.10: £2,177.70) GOING: 0.07 sec per fur (G)

	Horse / details	Dist	Pos	SP	RR	SF
3809[2]	**Quakers Field** (GLMoore) **4-11-0** DGallagher (lw: rr div: hit 5th: gd hdwy appr 3 out: led flat: hung lft: r.o wl)	—	1	8/1	104+	49
3174[2]	**Far Dawn (USA) (116)** (MrsAJPerrett) **4-11-0** CMaude (a chsng ldrs: led appr 3 out tl hdd flat: nt qckn)	5	2	14/1	99	44
3634[2]	**Circus Star (133)** (DNicholson) **4-11-0** RJohnson (hld up: hdwy 4 out: ev ch fr 3 out: nt qckn appr last)	5	3	6/1[2]	94	39
3301[3]	**Summer Spell (USA)** (NJHenderson) **4-11-0** MAFitzgerald (lw: hld up & bhd: hdwy whn nt clr run appr 3 out: one pce fr 2 out)	1	4	7/1	93	38
3634[8]	**Mr Wild (USA)** (RAkehurst) **4-11-0** RDunwoody (chsd ldrs tl rdn & wknd fr 3 out: hit last)	4	5	16/1	90	35

				SP	RR	SF
3818*	**Quality (IRE)** (PJHobbs) **4-11-0** NWilliamson (chsd ldrs: hit 4 out: n.m.r appr 3 out: grad wknd)	2	**6**	14/1	88	33
3634[6]	**Marlonette (IRE)** (WPMullins,Ireland) **4-10-9** DJCasey (bhd: hdwy on outside 4 out: sn chsng ldrs: wknd bef 3 out)	11	**7**	10/1	72	17
2840[P]	**Balladur (USA)** (MrsJPitman) **4-11-0** JFTitley (lw: bhd: hit 4th & 4 out: n.d)	2	**8**	25/1	75	20
3917[4]	**Noble Lord** (RHBuckler) **4-11-0** BPowell (led to 2nd: chsd ldrs tl wknd appr 3 out)	17	**9**	20/1	58	3
2993a[2]	**Hard News (USA)** (DPKelly,Ireland) **4-11-0** CO'Dwyer (led 2nd tl appr 3 out: wknd)	½	**10**	13/2[3]	58	3
3634[4]	**L'Opera (FR)** (DNicholson) **4-11-0** JOsborne (lw: hld up: effrt whn nt clr run after 4 out & appr 3 out: hdwy & prom whn fell 2 out)		**F**	5/2[1]	—	—
3404[4]	**Ginger Fox (USA)** (MrsJPitman) **4-11-0** JCulloty (mid div: hmpd bnd after 4 out: sn wknd: p.u bef 2 out)		**P**	12/1	—	—
				(SP 124.4%)	**12 Rn**	

3m 58.0 (4.00) CSF £107.54 TOTE £10.20: £2.50 £4.80 £2.50 (£141.40) Trio £262.20 OWNER Mr K. Higson (BRIGHTON) BRED Summertree Stud

OFFICIAL EXPLANATION **Hard News (USA): had pulled a muscle in his back.**

3809 Quakers Field, after looking in trouble halfway down the back straight, suddenly picked up and won well despite hanging left, and will obviously improve further with experience. (8/1)

3174 Far Dawn (USA) helped force the pace, but was tapped for speed late on and may well need even more use made of him. (14/1)

3634 Circus Star, in a messy race, had his chances but again failed to pick up when ridden. (6/1: 4/1-13/2)

3301 Summer Spell (USA) found trouble in running as the field bunched up on the home turn, and basically lacked the speed to compensate for this. (7/1)

3634 Mr Wild (USA) had his chances but, when the pace was really on in the home straight, he proved disappointing. (16/1)

3818* Quality (IRE), happy to track the leaders, got involved in some scrimmaging on the turn for home and was then short of pace thereafter. (14/1)

3634 Marlonette (IRE) who prefers softer ground, had to do a lot of running around the outside of the field to find a clear passage, and probably did too much too quickly and can be forgiven this. (10/1)

3634 L'Opera (FR), held up in this messy event, got into all sorts of trouble on the turn for home, but had improved nicely and certainly had a chance when falling two out. (5/2)

4015 CUVEE NAPA NOVICES' HUNTERS' CHASE (5-Y.O+) (Class B)

4-50 (4-50) **3m 1f (Mildmay) (19 fncs)** £7,107.50 (£2,135.00: £1,030.00: £477.50) GOING: 0.16 sec per fur (G)

				SP	RR	SF
3357*	**Bitofamixup (IRE)** (MJRoberts) **6-12-0** MrPHacking (hld up: hdwy ½-wy: wnt 2nd 13th: led after 4 out: sn clr)	—	**1**	9/4[2]	123++	43
3397[3]	**Howayman** (KAnderson) **7-12-0** MrAParker (chsd ldr: effrt 14th: outpcd next: hdwy u.p 4 out: styd on: no ch w wnr)	dist	**2**	7/1[3]	—	—
3799[2]	**Ardbrennan** (JPorter) **10-12-0** MrEJames (led fr 2nd: hit 10th: hdd after 4 out: sn outpcd)	1	**3**	8/1	—	—
3357[5]	**Sands of Gold (IRE)** (CNNimmo) **9-12-0** MrLLay (lw: led to 2nd: chsd ldrs: rdn 11th: blnd next: sn t.o)	11	**4**	20/1	—	—
3490[3]	**Lurriga Glitter (IRE)** (RJSmith) **9-12-0** MrRWakley (sn bhd: t.o fr 9th)	3½	**5**	20/1	—	—
3586[5]	**Tangle Baron** (KCumings) **9-12-0** MissJCumings (chsd ldrs tl wknd 13th: t.o)	4	**6**	33/1	—	—
3586*	**Orchestral Suite (IRE)** (MissJenniferPidgeon) **9-12-0** MrFHutsby (lw: fell 3rd)		**F**	7/4[1]	—	—
3765*	**Tom's Gemini Star** (OJCarter) **9-12-0** MrMHarris (fell 3rd)		**F**	9/1	—	—
	Johnny The Fox (IRE) (JPorter) **9-12-0** MrRLawther (w ldrs whn blnd & uns rdr 1st)		**U**	16/1	—	—
				(SP 119.1%)	**9 Rn**	

6m 33.2 (16.20) CSF £17.03 TOTE £3.00: £1.50 £1.70 £2.80 (£6.20) Trio £9.10 OWNER Mr Mike Roberts (HAILSHAM) BRED Mrs Norma G. Cook

3357* Bitofamixup (IRE) proved different class to this lot and won in tremendous style. (9/4)

3397 Howayman is honest and kept responding to pressure, but the winner was in a different league. (7/1)

3799 Ardbrennan has had his problems in getting round under Rules, but that proved no problem here. However, his limitations were well-exposed when the pressure was on from the fourth last. (8/1: 6/1-9/1)

3357 Sands of Gold (IRE) had his limitations well exposed once the pace was really on in the final mile. (20/1)

4016 BARTON & GUESTIER H'CAP HURDLE (5-Y.O+) (Class B)

5-20 (5-20) **3m 110y (13 hdls)** £11,088.75 (£3,360.00: £1,642.50: £783.75) GOING: 0.07 sec per fur (G)

				SP	RR	SF
3635[5]	**Escartefigue (FR) (151)** (DNicholson) **5-11-10** RDunwoody (hld up: hdwy on bit 4 out: led last: edgd lft & styd on u.p)	—	**1**	6/1[1]	134	50
3615*	**Big Strand (IRE) (129)** (MCPipe) **8-10-2** CMaude (hld up: hdwy 9th: n.m.r between last 2: ev ch last: kpt on one pce)	3	**2**	8/1	110	26
3600[6]	**Freddie Muck (132)** (NATwiston-Davies) **7-10-5** TJenks (a cl up: rdn appr 3 out: styd on & ev ch last: no ex)	5	**3**	10/1	110	26
3635[6]	**What a Question (IRE) (143)** (MFMorris,Ireland) **9-11-2** CO'Dwyer (chsd ldrs fr 4th: led 2 out to last: no ex)	1	**4**	15/2[3]	120	36
3615[6]	**Dr Leunt (IRE) (127)** (PJHobbs) **6-10-0** GTormey (a chsng ldrs: effrt appr 3 out: sn hrd drvn: n.m.r appr last: one pce)	3½	**5**	14/1	102	18
1363*	**Victor Bravo (NZ) (127)** (NAGaselee) **10-10-0b** WMarston (led tl hdd 2 out: wknd last)	hd	**6**	25/1	102?	18
3600[U]	**Erzadjan (IRE) (130)** (MrsMReveley) **7-10-3b** PNiven (in tch: effrt 9th: sn rdn & no imp)	12	**7**	13/2[2]	97	13
3851[3]	**Tamarpour (USA) (127)** (MCPipe) **10-9-7b**(7) BMoore (mstkes & bhd: sme late hdwy)	1¼	**8**	14/1	93	9
3562[2]	**Kingdom of Shades (USA) (127)** (AndrewTurnell) **7-10-0** JOsborne (lw: trckd ldrs tl rdn & wknd appr 3 out)	21	**9**	14/1	79	—
3150*	**Brave Tornado (130)** (GBBalding) **6-10-3** BClifford (a bhd: t.o fr 9th)	9	**10**	12/1	77	—
3731*	**Smith Too (IRE) (127)** (MrsJPitman) **9-10-0** BPowell (lw: cl up tl outpcd 6th: sn wknd)	2½	**11**	14/1	72	—
3600[3]	**Danjing (IRE) (129)** (MCPipe) **5-10-2b** DWalsh (in tch: pushed along fr 7th: wknd 4 out: t.o)	16	**12**	11/1	63	—
3635[13]	**Top Spin (130)** (JRJenkins) **8-10-3** RSupple (a wl bhd: t.o fr 9th)	25	**13**	20/1	48	—
3267[P]	**Better Times Ahead (138)** (GRichards) **11-10-11** ADobbin (lost tch 4th: t.o whn p.u bef 9th)		**P**	33/1	—	—
3430[B]	**Silver Shred (130)** (MissVenetiaWilliams) **6-10-3** NWilliamson (mid div whn p.u lame bef 8th: dead)		**P**	14/1	—	—
3045[2]	**House Captain (127)** (JGFitzGerald) **8-10-0** RJohnson (lw: p.u bef 5th)		**P**	12/1	—	—
2910[5]	**Rose King (130)** (MissSEdwards) **10-10-3**ow3 PHide (mstke 2nd: chsd ldrs to 7th: sn wknd: p.u bef 9th)		**P**	100/1	—	—
				(SP 129.2%)	**17 Rn**	

6m 0.1 (9.10) CSF £49.62 CT £449.56 TOTE £6.50: £2.40 £2.40 £2.70 £1.70 (£36.40) Trio £190.40 OWNER Mr Darren Mercer (TEMPLE GUITING) BRED Mrs A. Daubin and Mrs Jean-Francois Daubin

LONG HANDICAP Victor Bravo (NZ) 9-3 Kingdom of Shades (USA) 9-13 Tamarpour (USA) 9-12 Dr Leunt (IRE) 9-12 House Captain 9-11 Smith Too (IRE) 9-4 Rose King 8-0

STEWARDS' ENQUIRY Jenks susp. 15-17/4/97 (incorrect use of whip).

3635 Escartefigue (FR), given a superb ride, was brought through on the bridle to lead at the last and, although not doing a lot when in front, he was not allowed to stop. (6/1: 9/2-13/12)
3615* Big Strand (IRE), with a change of jockey this time, got there a lot sooner but found the winner too strong. (8/1)
3600 Freddie Muck looked in trouble some way out, but this tough sort refused to give in and just kept battling away. (10/1: 8/1-12/1)
3635 What a Question (IRE) does not seem to know how to run a bad race, especially in this event but, after trying hard, she got tapped for speed from the last. (15/2)
3615 Dr Leunt (IRE) is running well at the moment, but does seem short of a real turn of foot and this extra distance appeared no problem. (14/1)
1363* Victor Bravo (NZ), after well over four months off, ran really well here from 11lb out of the handicap. (25/1)

T/Jkpt: £102,882.20 (0.2 Tckts); £115,923.70 to Aintree 4/4/97. T/Plpt: £520.10 (120.29 Tckts). T/Qdpt: £85.70 (40.9 Tckts) AA

3588-TAUNTON (R-H) (Firm)
Thursday April 3rd
WEATHER: fine but cloudy

4017 ORCHARD FM TIM MANNS MAIDEN HURDLE (4-Y.O+) (Class F)
2-15 (2-16) **2m 1f (9 hdls)** £2,039.50 (£572.00: £278.50) GOING minus 1.08 sec per fur (HD)

				SP	RR	SF
3535[4]	**Mystic Hill (84)** (RGFrost) **6-11-5** JFrost (led to 5th: led on bit last: v.easily)	—	1	1/6[1]	42+	—
1149[12]	**Kai's Lady (IRE) (62)** (CLPopham) **4-10-5**(3) TDascombe (chsd ldr: led 5th to last: no ch w wnr)	2½	2	5/1[2]	35	—
3603[P]	**Miss Gee-Ell** (NBThomson) **5-10-7**(7) MrEBabington (hld up: reminder after 4th: rdn 6th: no rspnse)	12	3	20/1[3]	23	—
3761[P]	**Oscilights Gift** (MarkCampion) **5-11-0** WMcFarland (plld hrd: rn wd bnd appr 3rd: lost tch fr 5th)	nk	4	25/1	23	—
				(SP 111.0%)		**4 Rn**

4m 7.9 (14.90) CSF £1.56 TOTE £1.20 (£1.70) OWNER Mr Jack Joseph (BUCKFASTLEIGH) BRED Hascombe and Valiant Studs
WEIGHT FOR AGE 4yo-6lb
3109 Mystic Hill had 22lb in hand over the runner-up on official ratings and it showed. (1/6)
874 Kai's Lady (IRE) changed hands for 600 guineas at Ascot December Sales, having already been well beaten in selling company. (5/1)

4018 MARCH HARE CONDITIONAL (S) H'CAP HURDLE (0-95) (4-Y.O+) (Class G)
2-45 (2-47) **3m 110y (12 hdls)** £1,880.50 (£523.00: £251.50) GOING minus 1.08 sec per fur (HD)

				SP	RR	SF
	Co-Tack (66) (RELivermore) **12-10-2** ChrisWebb (lw: chsd clr ldr fr 3rd: led appr 9th: sn clr)	—	1	13/2[2]	53	—
3448[6]	**Anorak (USA) (80)** (RMStronge) **7-11-2** XAizpuru (hld up & plld hrd: lost pl appr 8th: rdn to chse wnr 9th: no imp)	20	2	6/4[1]	54	—
2905[F]	**Master Goodenough (IRE) (70)** (AGFoster) **6-10-1**(5)ow5 DCreech (led: clr after 2nd: wkng whn mstke 8th: sn hdd: 3rd & btn whn mstke 3 out)	dist	3	13/2[2]	—	—
	Prince Equiname (92) (RSimpson) **5-11-7**(7) NRossiter (plld hrd: chsd ldr to 3rd: bhd fr 7th: t.o whn mstke 3 out)	2½	4	6/4[1]	—	—
				(SP 106.7%)		**4 Rn**

5m 47.3 (-4.70) CSF £14.93 TOTE £8.60 (£5.00) OWNER Mrs J. L. Livermore (USK) BRED C. W. Rogers
No bid
Co-Tack, who won a selling hurdle on hard ground in 1989, had not been seen under Rules for seven years, although he did win a members' point-to-point three years ago. (13/2)
3448 Anorak (USA), who has changed stables, began to swish his tail when coming under pressure. (6/4)
Prince Equiname (6/4: op evens)

4019 WSM MERCEDES BENZ ACTROS H'CAP CHASE (0-125) (5-Y.O+) (Class D)
3-20 (3-20) **3m (19 fncs)** £4,155.00 (£1,020.00) GOING minus 1.08 sec per fur (HD)

				SP	RR	SF
3166[8]	**Doualago (FR) (117)** (MCPipe) **7-11-9b**(5) GSupple (lw: led tl after 8th: lft in ld 9th: rdn 15th: r.o wl)	—	1	4/7[1]	121	—
4000[3]	**Herbert Buchanan (IRE) (101)** (PFNicholls) **7-10-5**(7) MrJTizzard (plld hrd: led after 8th tl blnd 9th: mstke 12th (water): no imp fr 3 out)	11	2	6/4[2]	98	—
				(SP 103.6%)		**2 Rn**

5m 57.7 (0.70) TOTE £1.30 OWNER Martin Pipe Racing Club (WELLINGTON) BRED Monsieur et Madame Bernard le Douarin
Doualago (FR) found better jumping helping him dispose of a doubtful stayer. (4/7)
1598 Herbert Buchanan (IRE) did not help his chances of getting the trip with two jumping errors after proving difficult to settle. (6/4)

4020 ORCHARD FM BOB MCCREADIE H'CAP HURDLE (0-115) (4-Y.O+) (Class E)
3-55 (3-55) **2m 1f (9 hdls)** £2,200.50 (£618.00: £301.50) GOING minus 1.08 sec per fur (HD)

				SP	RR	SF
3623[3]	**Shifting Moon (72)** (FJordan) **5-10-6** DerekByrne (lw: hld up: wnt 2nd after 4th: led appr 6th: r.o wl)	—	1	7/4[2]	53	11
798[4]	**Layham Low (IRE) (90)** (OSherwood) **6-11-10** JAMcCarthy (lw: chsd ldr tl after 4th: wnt 2nd 3 out: sn rdn: no imp)	7	2	7/2[3]	64	22
3829[2]	**Little Shefford (81)** (MPMuggeridge) **5-11-1** SCurran (led: hit 3rd: hdd appr 6th: 3rd whn fell 3 out: rmntd)	dist	3	11/10[1]	—	—
				(SP 106.2%)		**3 Rn**

3m 43.9 (-9.10) CSF £5.98 TOTE £2.10 (£3.00) OWNER Mrs K. Roberts-Hindle (LEOMINSTER) BRED Pinfold Stud and Farms Ltd
3623 Shifting Moon, dropped 3lb, showed a tendency to go left-handed but proved too good for his solitary remaining opponent. (7/4)
798 Layham Low (IRE), dropped 5lb, has had an operation to help his breathing since he last ran, and he should be treated with caution for the time being. (7/2)
3829 Little Shefford did not appear to be going anywhere when coming to grief. (11/10: 4/5-6/5)

4021 WSM MERCEDES BENZ SPRINTER NOVICES' CHASE (5-Y.O+) (Class E)
4-30 (4-30) **2m 110y (13 fncs)** £3,317.50 (£930.00: £452.50) GOING minus 1.08 sec per fur (HD)

				SP	RR	SF
3981[P]	**Northern Singer (88)** (RJHodges) **7-11-11**(3) TDascombe (hld up: wnt 2nd 3rd: led appr 3 out: r.o wl)	—	1	Evens[1]	89	—
3717[5]	**Ketchican (69)** (SGKnight) **5-10-7** SAnderson (plld hrd: led 2nd: mstke 8th: hdd appr 3 out: btn whn hit 2 out)	7	2	4/1[3]	68	—

				SP	RR	SF
3538[4]	**Indian Temple (64)** (KBishop) **6-11-0** RGreene (led to 2nd: hit 9th: sn bhd: r.o flat)	1¾	**3**	7/4[2]	67	—
				(SP 106.4%)		**3 Rn**

4m 6.8 (6.80) CSF £4.08 TOTE £1.90 (£1.80) OWNER Mr Joe Panes (SOMERTON) BRED N. J. Dent
WEIGHT FOR AGE 5yo-7lb
3682 Northern Singer was apparently never going after clouting a ditch at Wincanton three days earlier. (Evens)
Ketchican could not cope with the winner in the home straight. (4/1)
2943 Indian Temple appeared likely to be beaten a long way until running on at the death. (7/4)

4022 WSM MERCEDES BENZ VITO HUNTERS' CHASE (5-Y.O+) (Class H)
5-00 (5-00) **3m (19 fncs)** £1,145.00 (£320.00: £155.00) GOING minus 1.08 sec per fur (HD)

				SP	RR	SF
957[P]	**L'Uomo Piu** (ABarrow) **13-12-0**(7) MrOMcPhail (mde all: mstke 12th (water): r.o wl)	—	**1**	10/1	95	18
3739[4]	**Rusty Bridge** (MrsSMJohnson) **10-12-0**(7) MrRBurton (lw: chsd wnr: mstke 4th (water): hit 2 out: rdn & edgd lft flat: styd on)	1¾	**2**	2/1[1]	94	17
3363[4]	**J B Lad** (HRTuck) **11-11-7**(7) MissPGundry (hld up: hdwy 14th: hit 15th: rdn & styng on wl whn carried lft flat)	hd	**3**	25/1	87	10
	Arctic Baron (MissMRaymond) **12-12-0**(7) MissLBlackford (lw: hdwy 9th: wknd 15th: blnd 4 out)	12	**4**	5/1	86	9
3631[3]	**Good King Henry** (IJWiddicombe) **11-11-7**(7) MrIWiddicombe (j.slowly 5th: t.o 14th: p.u bef 2 out)		**P**	100/30[3]	—	—
	Departure (MissMBragg) **10-11-2**(7) MrJCreighton (sn t.o: p.u bef 14th)		**P**	11/4[2]	—	—
	Cleasby Hill (MrsFJWalker) **12-11-7**(7) MrDAlers-Hankey (rdn 10th: t.o 13th: p.u after 4 out)		**P**	14/1	—	—
				(SP 119.3%)		**7 Rn**

5m 53.2 (-3.80) CSF £30.46 TOTE £16.60: £2.60 £1.30 (£9.20) OWNER Mr A. Barrow (BRIDGWATER) BRED T. O'Brien
658 L'Uomo Piu had shown nothing between the flags this season, but ran out when in the lead at Kingston St Mary on Monday. (10/1)
3739 Rusty Bridge found this trip too short on this fast ground. He only kept second place because of the new rules, with his pilot picking up a caution as to his future riding. (2/1: 11/10-9/4)
J B Lad, whose rider adopted a safety first policy in the home straight, was only let down on the short run-in. Unlucky not to finish second, one could not help feeling he really should have won. (25/1)
Departure (11/4: 2/1-3/1)

T/Plpt: £308.20 (23.6 Tckts). T/Qdpt: £30.20 (7.88 Tckts) KH

4023a - 4047a (Irish Racing) - See Computer Raceform

4010-AINTREE (L-H) (Good)
Friday April 4th
WEATHER: overcast

4048 MARTELL MERSEY NOVICES' HURDLE (Gd 2) (4-Y.O+) (Class A)
2-00 (2-00) **2m 4f (11 hdls)** £14,582.00 (£5,528.10: £2,714.05: £1,245.85) GOING: 0.52 sec per fur (GS)

				SP	RR	SF
3597[6]	**Sanmartino (IRE)** (DNicholson) **5-11-5** RDunwoody (lw: hld up & bhd: hdwy 8th: chal last: shkn up to ld flat: r.o)	—	**1**	8/11[1]	100	57
2937*	**Courbaril (124)** (MCPipe) **5-11-1b** NWilliamson (chsd ldrs: outpcd appr 3 out: styd on u.p flat)	1¼	**2**	10/1	95	52
3613[15]	**Hurdante (IRE) (115)** (GBBalding) **7-11-1** MAFitzgerald (hld up & bhd: gd hdwy to ld 3 out: hrd rdn & hdd flat: no ex)	1½	**3**	20/1	94	51
3691*	**Far Ahead (97)** (JLEyre) **5-11-1** BStorey (hld up: hdwy appr 3 out: rdn & one pce flat)	s.h	**4**	12/1	94	51
3595[7]	**Deano's Beeno** (MCPipe) **5-11-1** CMaude (led 2nd to 4th: hrd rdn appr last: one pce)	2½	**5**	7/1[2]	92	49
2995a[7]	**Liss De Paor (IRE)** (APO'Brien,Ireland) **6-11-0** CFSwan (lw: hld up in tch: led 7th to 3 out: wknd appr last)	½	**6**	9/1[3]	90	47
	Nicola Marie (IRE) (MsMFlynn,Ireland) **8-10-10** WMarston (prom: hrd rdn & wknd 8th: t.o)	dist	**7**	50/1	—	—
3566[2]	**Influence Pedler (116)** (JABOld) **4-10-12** CLlewellyn (lost pl 5th: sn t.o)	26	**8**	12/1	—	—
3820*	**John Drumm** (PRWebber) **6-11-1** JOsborne (led to 2nd: wknd appr 3 out: t.o)	2½	**9**	11/1	—	—
3766[2]	**Easy Listening (USA) (104)** (NJHawke) **5-11-1** JRailton (plld hrd: led 4th to 7th: wknd qckly: p.u bef 3 out)		**P**	20/1	—	—
				(SP 124.7%)		**10 Rn**

4m 54.7 (12.70) CSF £9.18 TOTE £1.80: £1.30 £1.90 £5.30 (£6.10) Trio £76.80 OWNER Mr K. Abdulla (TEMPLE GUITING) BRED Juddmonte Farms
WEIGHT FOR AGE 4yo-7lb
3597 Sanmartino (IRE), with the longer trip that he has been crying out for, should have brushed aside these rivals with ease, but he made hard work of it, and could still have been feeling the effects of a hard race in the Champion Hurdle. (8/11: 4/5-evens)
2937* Courbaril, looked out of it when getting left behind on the home turn, but he renewed his effort into the last, and is retaining his form remarkably well. (10/1)
2880 Hurdante (IRE) loomed up as a major threat going to the third last, and did not go down without a fight. Connections are looking forward to campaigning him over fences. (20/1)
3691* Far Ahead has trained up very light, and did not stride out to post. However, he turned in a very pleasing display on his first attempt at the trip. (12/1)
1950* Deano's Beeno was finding difficulty in holding his pitch on the approach to the third last, but he is not short on stamina, and was plugging on right to the end. (7/1: 5/1-15/2)
2596a* Liss De Paor (IRE) has more than paid her way in Ireland, and she did her best to make a race of it here. She was unable to increase her pace when the field bunched approaching the last two. (9/1: 6/1-10/1)
3820* John Drumm (11/1: 7/1-12/1)

4049 MUMM MELLING CHASE (Gd 1) (5-Y.O+) (Class A)
2-35 (2-37) **2m 4f (Mildmay) (16 fncs)** £47,460.00 (£17,915.50: £8,732.75: £3,941.75) GOING: 0.22 sec per fur (G)

				SP	RR	SF
3614*	**Martha's Son (164)** (CaptTAForster) **10-11-10** CLlewellyn (blnd 1st: hld up & bhd: hdwy appr 3 out: led appr last: sn clr)	—	**1**	5/2[2]	173	89
3614[5]	**Strong Promise (IRE) (160)** (GAHubbard) **6-11-10** NWilliamson (lw: j.w: a.p: led 2 out: sn hdd: nt pce of wnr)	5	**2**	9/4[1]	169	85
3614[3]	**Viking Flagship (166)** (DNicholson) **10-11-10** RDunwoody (swtg: chsd ldng pair: outpcd 4 out: blnd next: sn btn)	3½	**3**	11/4[3]	166	82

				SP	RR	SF
3614[2]	**Ask Tom (IRE) (160)** (TPTate) **8-11-10** RGarritty (lw: j.w: led: rn wd bnd after 8th: hdd 2 out: sn wknd)	20	**4**	4/1	150	66
				(SP 106.0%)		**4 Rn**

4m 58.7 (0.70) CSF £7.38 TOTE £3.30: (£4.70) OWNER Mr P. J. Hartigan (LUDLOW) BRED M. Ward-Thomas

3614* Martha's Son confirmed his superiority over this extra half-mile after all-but departing the scene at the first. He really is something else. (5/2)

3614 Strong Promise (IRE) had the leader covered a long way out, and was still on the bridle when leading at the penultimate fence. However, when it developed into a sprint, he was found wanting. There was certainly no disgrace in this defeat and, if he can continue his progress next year, he will win his share of the major prizes. (9/4)

3614 Viking Flagship, attempting to win this event for the third successive year, was struggling to keep tabs on the leading pair turning in, and a bad mistake three out put paid to what chance he held. (11/4)

3614 Ask Tom (IRE) was not afraid to force the pace on his first attempt at the trip, but he was flat to the boards when collared at the second last, and then stopped as if shot. (4/1)

4050 MUMM MILDMAY NOVICES' CHASE (Gd 2) (5-Y.O+) (Class A)

3-10 (3-10) **3m 1f (Mildmay) (19 fncs)** £25,567.70 (£8,848.20: £4,324.10) GOING: 0.22 sec per fur (G)

				SP	RR	SF
3636[8]	**Cyborgo (FR)** (MCPipe) **7-11-4** RDunwoody (a.p: led 9th to 10th: led after 11th: hrd rdn appr last: r.o)	—	**1**	13/8[1]	136	68
3616[U]	**The Last Fling (IRE) (124)** (MrsSJSmith) **7-11-7** RichardGuest (hld up: hdwy 10th: disp ld whn stumbled 4 out: rdn & ev ch whn hit last: nt rcvr)	3½	**2**	11/2[3]	137	69
3700*	**Judicious Captain (97)** (MrsJStorey) **10-11-7** MrCStorey (outpcd: a t.o)	dist	**3**	33/1	—	—
3616[P]	**Buckhouse Boy (132)** (NATwiston-Davies) **7-11-4** CMaude (chsd ldrs: ev ch whn fell 12th)		**F**	6/1	—	—
3347[2]	**Crown Equerry (IRE)** (GRichards) **7-11-4** PCarberry (prom: led 10th tl after next: rdn whn hit 14th: sn wknd: blnd 4 out: p.u bef next)		**P**	11/1	—	—
3805*	**Chopwell Curtains** (TDEasterby) **7-11-4** LWyer (j.slowly early: sn outpcd: t.o whn p.u bef 15th)		**P**	6/1	—	—
3537*	**Bear Claw** (OSherwood) **8-11-4b** JOsborne (led to 9th: blnd 11th: wknd 14th: 3rd & btn whn blnd & uns rdr 3 out)		**U**	9/2[2]	—	—
				(SP 111.5%)		**7 Rn**

6m 23.2 (6.20) CSF £9.65 TOTE £2.30: £1.70 £2.30 (£5.70) OWNER County Stores (Somerset) Holdings Ltd (WELLINGTON) BRED Francois Cottin and Alfred Lefevre

3636 Cyborgo (FR) has in the past needed to get his toe in, but he handled this watered ground, and stayed on far too strongly for the persistent runner-up. (13/8)

3160 The Last Fling (IRE) almost bit the dust on landing four out, but he renewed his effort and was certainly not out of it, despite being under pressure, when a last-fence error was the final straw. (11/2)

3155 Buckhouse Boy has twice been runner-up to the winner this spring, and he was travelling well within himself when coming down out in the country. (6/1)

3537* Bear Claw never recovered from a bad mistake at the last fence first-time around, and was trailing in third place when getting rid of his jockey at the third last. (9/2)

4051 MARTELL FOX HUNTERS' CHASE (6-Y.O+) (Class B)

3-45 (3-45) **2m 6f (National) (18 fncs)** £14,070.00 (£4,260.00: £2,080.00: £990.00) GOING: 0.22 sec per fur (G)

				SP	RR	SF
3744*	**Blue Cheek** (JMahon) **11-12-0** MrRThornton (lw: chsd ldrs: outpcd 4 out: styd on to ld last: sn clr)	—	**1**	9/2[2]	110	39
3712[2]	**Highlandman** (JSHaldane) **11-12-0** MrChrisWilson (hld up: outpcd 4 out: styd on u.p flat)	17	**2**	20/1	98	27
158[F]	**Abbotsham** (OJCarter) **12-12-0** MrEJames (hld up: hdwy & mstke 11th: blnd next: styd on u.p fr 3 out)	1	**3**	33/1	97	26
1063[5]	**K C'S Dancer** (RDickin) **12-12-0** MrJMPritchard (bhd: hdwy 4 out: styd on u.p flat)	1¾	**4**	66/1	96	25
3457[5]	**Young Nimrod** (MrsDMGrissell) **10-12-0** MrGWragg (lw: prom: chsd ldr fr 14th: ev ch whn lft in ld 2 out: hdd last: fin tired)	3½	**5**	14/1	93	22
3457*	**Trifast Lad** (MJRoberts) **12-12-0** MrPHacking (lw: a bhd: t.o fr 8th)	18	**6**	6/1	80	9
3840[2]	**Great Pokey** (MissNellCourtenay) **12-12-0** MissNCourtenay (lw: led after 4th: wknd appr 10th: t.o)	28	**7**	100/1	60	—
3609[3]	**Fordstown (IRE)** (JamieAlexander) **8-12-0** MrJamieAlexander (lost tch 6th: sn t.o)	7	**8**	100/1	55	—
3446[7]	**Faringo** (MrsDMGrissell) **12-12-0** MrWGowlett (lw: hld up in rr: t.o fr 7th)	1¼	**9**	100/1	54	—
	Chilipour (VictorDartnall) **10-12-0** MrJJukes (lw: fell 1st)		**F**	5/1[3]	—	—
3543*	**Mr Boston** (MrsMReveley) **12-12-0** MrSSwiers (led after 4th: fell 2 out)		**F**	15/8[1]	—	—
3458[B]	**Country Tarrogen** (TDWalford) **8-12-0** MrNWilson (fell 1st)		**F**	7/1	—	—
3680[P]	**Highway Five (IRE)** (LadySusanBrooke) **9-12-0** MrMPJones (fell 1st)		**F**	40/1	—	—
3543[3]	**Matt Reid** (JPLeigh) **13-12-0b** MrWMorgan (fell 1st)		**F**	20/1	—	—
				(SP 122.5%)		**14 Rn**

5m 48.2 (18.20) CSF £79.82 TOTE £5.40: £1.90 £3.70 £16.50 (£51.00) Trio £1,284.10 OWNER Mrs B. Graham (STRATFORD-ON-AVON) BRED M. Dwan

3744* Blue Cheek jumps for fun and, making relentless progress on the long run to the penultimate fence, landed in front at the last, and soon put daylight between himself and his toiling rivals. (9/2)

3712 Highlandman looked to have lost touch with the leaders soon after Valentine's, but he stays well, and this enabled him to gain the runner-up prize on the flat. (20/1)

130 Abbotsham, thought to be a gallop short, would have gone very close with a clear round. He chanced his luck at the fences, but lives to tell the tale. (33/1)

823 K C'S Dancer hunted round in his own time and, despite staying on strongly, his final position was as close as he could manage. (66/1)

Young Nimrod travelled well, and was just about to take the measure of the favourite when that rival fell. He may have got there too soon, for he was legless when forced to give best at the last. In future more patient tactics may bring their reward. (14/1)

3543* Mr Boston, unbeaten this term, made the majority of the running. He was there to be shot at when he crumpled on landing two out. (15/8: 5/4-2/1)

4052 BELLE EPOQUE SEFTON NOVICES' HURDLE (Gd 1) (4-Y.O+) (Class A)

4-20 (4-20) **3m 110y (13 hdls)** £21,532.00 (£8,130.60: £3,965.30: £1,792.10) GOING: 0.52 sec per fur (GS)

				SP	RR	SF
3613[4]	**Forest Ivory (NZ)** (DNicholson) **6-11-4** RJohnson (hld up: hdwy 8th: led 2 out: hrd rdn flat: hld on gamely)	—	**1**	11/2[3]	97	54
	Private Peace (IRE) (APO'Brien,Ireland) **7-11-4** CFSwan (hld up & bhd: hdwy appr 3 out: swtchd lft appr 2 out: str chal flat: r.o)	s.h	**2**	11/2[3]	97	54
3048*	**Mentmore Towers (IRE)** (MrsJPitman) **5-11-4** BPowell (chsd ldrs: led 9th to 2 out: outpcd appr last)	5	**3**	5/1[2]	94	51

				SP	RR	SF
3600[2]	**Yahmi (IRE) (130)** (JABOld) **7-11-4** NWilliamson (lost pl ½-wy: hdwy 10th: rdn whn hmpd appr 2 out: sn btn)	14	**4**	100/30[1]	85	42
3355*	**Flying Gunner (117)** (DNicholson) **6-11-4** MrRThornton (hld up: hdwy 10th: rdn & wknd appr 2 out)	28	**5**	25/1	66	23
2961[2]	**Lady Peta (IRE) (112)** (NJHenderson) **7-11-4** JRKavanagh (lw: hld up & bhd: effrt 8th: nvr plcd to chal: t.o)	14	**6**	16/1	57	14
3613[10]	**Hand Woven (120)** (NATwiston-Davies) **5-11-4** CLlewellyn (lw: chsd ldrs tl rdn & wknd appr 8th: t.o)	4	**7**	33/1	55	12
3581*	**Stormy Passage (IRE) (111)** (PJHobbs) **7-11-4** RDunwoody (lw: hld up: a in rr: t.o)	11	**8**	14/1	47	4
2746*	**Salmon Breeze (IRE) (107)** (NJHenderson) **6-11-4** MAFitzgerald (lw: chsd ldrs to 8th: sn rdn & wknd: t.o whn p.u bef 3 out)		**P**	10/1	—	—
3734[2]	**Silver Thyne (IRE) (105)** (MrsJPitman) **5-11-4** JFTitley (lw: j.rt: led: mstke 2nd: hdd after 7th: t.o whn p.u bef 2 out)		**P**	16/1	—	—
3423*	**Spring Double (IRE) (110)** (NATwiston-Davies) **6-11-4** CMaude (hld up in tch: ev ch whn blnd 10th: sn lost pl: p.u bef next)		**P**	14/1	—	—
3635[9]	**Tarrs Bridge (IRE) (124)** (CJMann) **6-11-4b** JRailton (prom: led after 7th to 9th: hmpd & uns rdr next)		**U**	10/1	—	—

(SP 120.6%) **12 Rn**

6m 7.4 (16.40) CSF £33.72 TOTE £7.50: £2.60 £1.70 £1.80 (£15.50) Trio £29.90 OWNER The Old Foresters Partnership (TEMPLE GUITING) BRED P. S. and Mrs C. Nelson

3613 Forest Ivory (NZ) kept up his stable's fantastic run at this meeting with his most important success on his first attempt at the trip. He should prove a useful recruit to fences next term. (11/2: op 7/2)

Private Peace (IRE) has been making a name for himself in Ireland, and may well have won here had he had the soft ground that seems to bring out the best in him. (11/2)

3048* Mentmore Towers (IRE), facing his first big test, ran up to his best and, with time on his side, could be a more mature individual next season. (5/1)

3600 Yahmi (IRE) ran his race in snatches, but seemed set to pick them up entering the straight, but he was hard at work when forced to switch approaching the second last, and dropped away in a matter of strides. He has had some hard races this season, and may have gone over the top. (100/30)

3423* Spring Double (IRE), waiting on the leaders, had moved into the action when he made a very bad mistake four out which put paid to him. He can soon make amends. (14/1)

3303 Tarrs Bridge (IRE) (10/1: 8/1-12/1)

4053 ODDBINS H'CAP HURDLE (4-Y.O+) (Class B)

4-50 (4-56) **2m 4f (11 hdls)** £12,653.00 (£3,824.00: £1,862.00: £881.00) GOING: 0.52 sec per fur (GS)

				SP	RR	SF
3150[4]	**Cadougold (FR) (131)** (MCPipe) **6-10-4** CFSwan (hld up: hdwy 8th: led last: qcknd clr: readily)	—	**1**	8/1	115	62
3421*	**Sheriffmuir (127)** (MrsLWadham) **8-9-9**(5) MrRThornton (lw: hld up & bhd: mstke 6th: hdwy whn hmpd 3 out: ev ch last: kpt on u.p)	4	**2**	10/1	108	55
3640[10]	**Ambleside (IRE) (127)** (MrsSDWilliams) **6-10-0** DBridgwater (hld up: hdwy & hit 3 out: ev ch last: unable qckn)	¾	**3**	16/1	107	54
3267[4]	**Outset (IRE) (127)** (MDHammond) **7-9-11**(3) MrCBonner (chsd ldrs: mstke 7th: led 3 out to last: rdn & no ex flat)	1¼	**4**	9/1	106	53
3615[2]	**Allegation (148)** (MCPipe) **7-11-7v** CLlewellyn (prom: led 7th to 8th: rdn & wknd appr 3 out)	14	**5**	8/1	116	63
3816[2]	**Ashwell Boy (IRE) (133)** (PJHobbs) **6-10-6** MAFitzgerald (hld up mid div: hmpd 8th: hdwy & ch 3 out: wknd next)	6	**6**	7/1	96	43
3635[R]	**Tragic Hero (136)** (MCPipe) **5-10-9b** CMaude (lw: hld up: hdwy 5th: led 8th to 3 out: wknd qckly: t.o)	17	**7**	33/1	86	33
3804*	**Frickley (128)** (GRichards) **11-10-1** PCarberry (chsd ldrs: hit 5th: wknd appr 8th: t.o)	14	**8**	8/1	66	13
2890[3]	**Gales Cavalier (IRE) (133)** (DRGandolfo) **9-10-6** RDunwoody (trckd ldrs to 8th: sn lost tch: t.o)	1½	**9**	5/1[2]	70	17
2950[8]	**Lucky Blue (127)** (SEarle) **10-10-0** NWilliamson (lw: led to 7th: wknd after next: t.o)	23	**10**	33/1	46	—
3615[3]	**Castle Sweep (IRE) (155)** (DNicholson) **6-12-0** RJohnson (hld up: hit 6th: b.d 8th)		**B**	6/1[3]	—	—
3640[3]	**Penny a Day (IRE) (141)** (MrsMReveley) **7-11-0** PNiven (lw: hld up in tch: fell 8th: dead)		**F**	4/1[1]	—	—

(SP 127.6%) **12 Rn**

4m 49.5 (7.50) CSF £83.57 CT £1,161.70 TOTE £11.00: £2.80 £3.30 £4.90 (£52.70) Trio £419.70 OWNER Mr D. A. Johnson (WELLINGTON) BRED Jacques Seror

LONG HANDICAP Ambleside (IRE) 9-5 Lucky Blue 9-9 Sheriffmuir 9-11

3150 Cadougold (FR) began to take closer order at the end of the back straight, and was still full of running when leading at the last, quickly putting the issue beyond doubt. He is fresher than most at this late stage of the season. (8/1)

3421* Sheriffmuir is at the top of his form this year, and confirmed that with possibly his best performance yet. He shows a lot of knee action, and is no doubt better with more cut in the ground. (10/1)

3231 Ambleside (IRE), 9lb out of the handicap, gave his connections possibly their biggest surprise yet with a very determined effort, and he is another who is destined for the bigger obstacles next season. (16/1)

3267 Outset (IRE) tried hard to follow up his success in this race twelve months ago, and he did not fail for the want of trying. However, an extra turn of speed was missing when it was most needed. If he runs again, he deserves to make amends. (9/1)

3615 Allegation had a punishing race when touched off at the Cheltenham Festival, and he performed as if not fully recovered. (8/1)

3816 Ashwell Boy (IRE), lucky not to be brought down four out, came back to challenge for the lead at the next, but the exertions caught up with him, and he gradually faded. He can make amends next time. (7/1)

3640 Penny a Day (IRE) was settled in behind the leaders, and had not been popped the question when turning a somersault at the fourth last. Sadly he had to be put down after breaking a leg. (4/1)

4054 PERRIER JOUET H'CAP CHASE (5-Y.O+) (Class B)

5-20 (5-26) **3m 1f (Mildmay) (19 fncs)** £10,269.75 (£3,108.00: £1,516.50: £720.75) GOING: 0.22 sec per fur (G)

				SP	RR	SF
3636[F]	**Unguided Missile (IRE) (157)** (GRichards) **9-12-0** RDunwoody (j.w: mde all: r.o wl)	—	**1**	7/2[2]	167	61
3637[2]	**Cab on Target (130)** (MrsMReveley) **11-10-1** NWilliamson (prom: blnd & lost pl 7th: hdwy 11th: chsd wnr fr 2 out: kpt on)	1¾	**2**	100/30[1]	139	33
1917[4]	**Bertone (IRE) (130)** (KCBailey) **8-10-1** CO'Dwyer (hld up & bhd: hdwy 15th: ev ch 3 out: sn rdn: one pce)	3	**3**	5/1[3]	137	31
3598[5]	**Call it a Day (IRE) (138)** (DNicholson) **7-10-9** RJohnson (hld up: hdwy 10th: rdn 14th: one pce fr 3 out)	1¼	**4**	7/2[2]	144	38
3451[2]	**Fiveleigh Builds (129)** (MissLucindaRussell) **10-10-0** AThornton (mstke 1st: chsd wnr to 4 out: rdn & hit next: sn wknd)	3	**5**	9/1	133	27
3599[4]	**All for Luck (129)** (MCPipe) **12-10-0** CFSwan (lw: a bhd: t.o fr 6th)	7	**6**	6/1	129	23
	Wudimp (129) (MrsJStorey) **8-10-0** MrCStorey (prom tl wknd appr 3 out: p.u bef last)		**P**	33/1	—	—

(SP 111.4%) **7 Rn**

6m 29.2 (12.20) CSF £13.81 CT £49.78 TOTE £3.20: £2.10 £1.80 (£4.50) OWNER Mr D. E. Harrison (PENRITH) BRED Samac and Potomac Ltd

LONG HANDICAP Fiveleigh Builds 9-8 All for Luck 9-10 Wudimp 8-9
3230 Unguided Missile (IRE) made up for his fall at Cheltenham with an impressive all-the-way success and, never putting a foot wrong, always had too much pace for his closest pursuers. (7/2)
3637 Cab on Target tried to take the seventh by the roots, and did extremely well to recover. He was far from foot-perfect on several occasions, and in the circumstances did well to get so close. (100/30)
1917 Bertone (IRE) runs best when fresh, and looked set to score when cruising up to the winner three out. However, with that rival refusing to give in, he was in trouble at the next. (5/1)
3598 Call it a Day (IRE) was close enough to cause concern in the final mile, but he is not the most fluent of jumpers when the pressure is on, and was fighting a lost cause from the third last. (7/2)
3451 Fiveleigh Builds, in pursuit of the winner, was being tapped for toe when hitting the third last, and his measure was soon taken. From 6lb out of the handicap, this was not a bad effort. (9/1)

T/Jkpt: £5,919.40 (27.78 Tckts). T/Plpt: £609.40 (117.6 Tckts). T/Qdpt: £68.90 (50.51 Tckts) AA

3723-SEDGEFIELD (L-H) (Good to firm)
Friday April 4th
WEATHER: raining

4055 STONEGRAVE AGGREGATES NOVICES' (S) H'CAP HURDLE (0-95) (4-Y.O+) (Class G)
2-10 (2-11) **2m 5f 110y (10 hdls)** £2,076.50 (£579.00: £279.50) GOING minus 0.48 sec per fur (GF)

				SP	RR	SF
3287^{8}	**Amazing Sail (IRE) (83)** (MissMKMilligan) **4-11-4** ASSmith (lw: trckd ldrs: led 7th: lft clr 2 out: pushed out)	—	**1**	8/1	72	23
	Nite Sprite (58) (REBarr) **7-9-7**(7) NHorrocks (bit bkwd: bhd: hdwy 3 out: styd on between last 2: no ch w wnr)	9	**2**	50/1	40	—
2505^{3}	**Catton Lady (58)** (RCraggs) **7-9-11**(3) GLee (bhd: hdwy 5th: kpt on fr 2 out)	1½	**3**	6/1^{3}	39	—
3748^{5}	**Royal Hand (66)** (RJArmson) **7-10-8v** MrRArmson (wnt prom 5th: one pce fr 3 out)	4	**4**	16/1	44	2
3620^{5}	**Mick The Yank (IRE) (59)** (HOliver) **7-10-1b** JacquiOliver (trckd ldrs: effrt appr 2 out: grad wknd)	2	**5**	3/1^{1}	36	—
3711^{5}	**Greenfinch (CAN) (64)** (MrsAMNaughton) **6-10-6v** MFoster (chsd ldrs: outpcd after 3 out: n.d)	s.h	**6**	11/2^{2}	41	—
2803^{P}	**Broomhill Duker (IRE) (58)** (HowardJohnson) **7-10-0b¹** ADobbin (led to 7th: wknd after 3 out)	3	**7**	20/1	33	—
	Whitegatesprincess (IRE) (60) (BEllison) **6-9-9**(7) CMcCormack (bhd: hdwy 3 out: 4th & styng on whn bdly hmpd next)	2	**8**	20/1	33	—
3908^{11}	**Beacon Hill Lady (65)** (BEllison) **4-10-0** DParker (hdwy 6th: rdn & blnd 3 out: n.d)	hd	**9**	25/1	38	—
3825^{5}	**Meadowleck (58)** (WGYoung) **8-9-9**(5) STaylor (bhd: drvn along 5th: n.d)	1¾	**10**	20/1	30	—
3711^{9}	**Dont Forget Curtis (IRE) (84)** (MrsKMLamb) **5-11-5**(7) MissSLamb (a bhd)	14	**11**	10/1	45	3
3711^{13}	**Nosmo King (IRE) (58)** (MrsMAKendall) **6-10-0** KJohnson (chsd ldrs: 4l 2nd whn fell 2 out)		**F**	25/1	—	—
2838^{P}	**Dugort Strand (IRE) (69)** (KAMorgan) **6-10-4**(7) XAizpuru (lw: w ldrs tl wknd 5th: sn bhd: t.o whn p.u bef 3 out)		**P**	12/1	—	—
3711^{14}	**Arthur Bee (61)** (BBousfield) **10-10-3** MMoloney (prom: reminder 6th: lost pl 3 out: p.u lame between last 2)		**P**	17/2	—	—
	Rostino (IRE) (58) (JWade) **8-10-0** GCahill (bit bkwd: in tch tl lost pl 6th: t.o whn p.u bef 2 out)		**P**	12/1	—	—
				(SP 130.6%)	**15 Rn**	

5m 2.3 (2.30) CSF £348.00 CT £2,374.91 TOTE £10.70: £4.00 £89.30 £2.70 (£264.90) Trio Not won; £152.02 to Aintree 5/4/97 OWNER Maritime (LEYBURN)
LONG HANDICAP Catton Lady 9-13 Nite Sprite 9-7 Meadowleck 9-12 Broomhill Duker (IRE) 9-10
WEIGHT FOR AGE 4yo-7lb
Bt in 9,400 gns
3031 Amazing Sail (IRE) stood out in condition in the paddock. Left clear two out, he scored with plenty in hand, but connections were pushed all the way at the auction. (8/1)
Nite Sprite, who looked on the burly side and was racing from 7lb out of the handicap, stayed on really well up the hill. (50/1)
2505 Catton Lady certainly stayed this extended trip. (6/1)
3748 Royal Hand, with the visor back on, could not go the gallop from three out. (16/1)
3620 Mick The Yank (IRE), suited by fast ground, travelled strongly but found disappointingly little under pressure. (3/1)
Dugort Strand (IRE) (12/1: 6/1-14/1)

4056 STANLEY RACING GOLDEN NUMBERS SERIES NOVICES' HURDLE (4-Y.O+) (Class E)
2-45 (2-46) **2m 1f (8 hdls)** £2,547.50 (£710.00: £342.50) GOING minus 0.48 sec per fur (GF)

				SP	RR	SF
3327*	**Silver Minx (86)** (MrsMReveley) **5-11-3**(3) GLee (j.bdly lft thrght: led to 3 out: sn led again: drvn out)	—	**1**	6/1	75	31
3822*	**Diamond Beach (86)** (GMMoore) **4-10-5**(3) ECallaghan (hld up: stdy hdwy 3 out: hmpd & blnd last: kpt on)	3	**2**	2/1^{1}	66	16
3544^{3}	**Six Clerks (IRE) (93)** (JGFitzGerald) **4-10-11**(3) FLeahy (lw: trckd ldrs: led 3 out: sn hdd: nt qckn fr next)	1¼	**3**	5/2^{2}	71	21
1843^{8}	**The Mickletonian** (JIACharlton) **6-11-0** KJohnson (hdwy 5th: kpt on fr 2 out: nvr rchd ldrs)	3	**4**	66/1	62	18
3475^{6}	**Milenberg Joys** (WHTinning) **5-11-0** TReed (hdwy 5th: sn prom: wknd 3 out)	7	**5**	20/1	56	12
1159*	**Silent Guest (IRE) (88)** (MDHammond) **4-11-0** DBentley (lw: chsd ldrs: rdn 3 out: wknd appr next)	2	**6**	6/1	60	10
3396^{7}	**Maple Bay (IRE) (94)** (BEllison) **8-11-6** ADobbin (chsd ldrs: rdn 3 out: sn wknd)	14	**7**	11/2^{3}	47	3
3789^{8}	**Queen's Counsel (IRE)** (MissMKMilligan) **4-10-3** ASSmith (hdwy 4th: sn trckng ldrs: wkng whn hit 2 out: eased)	1¼	**8**	33/1	34	—
3711^{12}	**Over Stated (IRE) (69)** (JWade) **7-11-0** KJones (chsd ldrs tl lost pl after 5th)	7	**9**	33/1	33	—
	Topup (MABarnes) **4-10-3**(5) STaylor (bdly hmpd & carried out after 1st)		**C**	100/1	—	—
3475^{5}	**Penny Peppermint (64)** (REBarr) **5-10-9** DParker (bdly hmpd & carried out after 1st)		**C**	33/1	—	—
	Believe It (NWaggott) **8-11-0** RSupple (sn bhd: t.o 5th: fell 2 out)		**F**	100/1	—	—
	Lucky Hoof (KAMorgan) **4-9-10**(7) XAizpuru (sn bhd: t.o whn tried to ref 4th: sn p.u)		**P**	16/1	—	—
				(SP 128.8%)	**13 Rn**	

3m 55.1 (0.10) CSF £17.98 TOTE £6.30: £2.00 £1.50 £2.00 (£10.30) Trio £12.00 OWNER Mrs E. A. Kettlewell (SALTBURN) BRED T. E. Phillips
WEIGHT FOR AGE 4yo-6lb
3327* Silver Minx jumped badly left throughout and even managed to put two opponents out of the race at the first flight. He certainly does not lack ability though and in the end won going away. (6/1)
3822* Diamond Beach was given a patient ride. It was surprising to see his jockey elect to deliver his challenge on the winner's inside going to the last, as Silver Minx had jumped badly left throughout. Unsighted, Diamond Beach hit the hurdle hard and lost what outside chance he had. (2/1)
3544 Six Clerks (IRE) is possibly better on easier ground. (5/2: op 6/4)

The Mickletonian is nothing to look at. Ducking about going to two out, he kept on in pleasing fashion and might improve a bit yet. (66/1)
1159* Silent Guest (IRE), from a stable struggling to regain form, ran as if just needing the outing, his first for 151 days. (6/1)

4057 WASHINGTON HOSPITAL NOVICES' CHASE (5-Y.O+) (Class D)
3-20 (3-20) **2m 110y (13 fncs)** £3,574.00 (£1,072.00: £516.00: £238.00) GOING minus 0.81 sec per fur (F)

			SP	RR	SF
3642[3]	**Tapatch (IRE) (85)** (MWEasterby) **9-11-0** ADobbin (lw: chsd ldrs: blnd 4th: led after 4 out: jst hld on)......—	**1**	9/4[1]	94	—
3723[7]	**Whitegates Willie** (HowardJohnson) **5-10-7** ASSmith (hld up: gd hdwy 6th: chal 3 out: nt qckn towards fin) .nk	**2**	33/1	94	—
3825[10]	**Triona's Hope (IRE) (60)** (EMCaine) **8-10-9**(5) MrMHNaughton (hdwy 7th: one pce fr 3 out)......8	**3**	50/1	86	—
3826[2]	**Nawtinookey (74)** (MartinTodhunter) **7-10-2**(7) CMcCormack (hld up & bhd: hdwy 4 out: nvr nr ldrs)......10	**4**	5/1	71	—
3450[F]	**Hee's a Dancer (96)** (MissLucindaRussell) **5-10-7** MFoster (mde most to 9th: led next: sn hdd: wknd 3 out)....4	**5**	5/2[2]	72	—
3725[3]	**Twin Falls (IRE) (96)** (GMMoore) **6-11-12** JCallaghan (mstkes: chsd ldrs to 7th: sn lost pl)......hd	**6**	3/1[3]	84	—
3724[6]	**Distillery Hill (IRE) (60)** (VThompson) **9-11-0** MrMThompson (chsd ldrs: blnd 5th: bhd fr 9th: t.o 2 out)......20	**7**	25/1	53	—
3826[P]	**Aristodemus (65)** (MrsLMarshall) **8-11-0** KJohnson (sn bhd: t.o 2 out)......¾	**8**	100/1	52	—
3608[8]	**Nobodys Flame (IRE) (84)** (SIPittendrigh) **9-10-7**(7) MrTJBarry (jnd ldrs 5th: led 9th: blnd & hdd next: sn wknd)......1	**9**	50/1	51	—
2628[P]	**Gone Ashore (IRE) (60)** (MABarnes) **6-11-0** JBurke (mstkes: wnt prom 5th: lost pl 8th: t.o 2 out)......2	**10**	33/1	49	—
	Its a Deal (SGChadwick) **11-11-0** GCahill (blnd 1st: sn bhd: t.o whn p.u bef 7th)......	**P**	66/1	—	—
			(SP 117.1%)		**11 Rn**

4m 3.0 (5.00) CSF £62.28 TOTE £2.90: £1.10 £4.20 £6.10 (£33.10) Trio £169.80; £217.64 to Aintree 5/4/97 OWNER Miss V. Foster (SHERIFF HUTTON) BRED London T'bred Services & M. McCalmont in Ireland
WEIGHT FOR AGE 5yo-7lb
3642 Tapatch (IRE), who has not been in the winner's enclosure since November 1994, was persuaded to do just enough. (9/4)
Whitegates Willie ran really well on his debut over fences. Moving upsides three out, he gave his all in a tight finish. (33/1)
3477 Triona's Hope (IRE) could never summon the pace to get in a blow at the first two, and will be better suited by longer distances. (50/1)
3826 Nawtinookey was given a patient ride on ground that was probably too fast for her. (5/1)
3450 Hee's a Dancer stopped in two strides three out. The stable seems to be off the boil at present. (5/2)
3725 Twin Falls (IRE) could not dominate and as a result his jumping suffered. (3/1: op 2/1)

4058 REG AND RIDLEY LAMB MEMORIAL H'CAP CHASE (0-115) (5-Y.O+) (Class E)
3-55 (3-56) **2m 5f (16 fncs)** £3,496.00 (£1,048.00: £504.00: £232.00) GOING minus 0.81 sec per fur (F)

			SP	RR	SF
3710[4]	**Rustic Air (102)** (JGFitzGerald) **10-11-10** WDwan (trckd ldr fr 3rd: led 4 out: drvn out flat)......—	**1**	9/4[2]	114	18
3725*	**The Toaster (96)** (MissMKMilligan) **10-11-1**(3) ECallaghan (lw: wnt prom 10th: effrt 2 out: kpt on same pce).2½	**2**	2/1[1]	106	10
3610[3]	**Reve de Valse (USA) (86)** (RJohnson) **10-10-8** KJohnson (led to 4 out: one pce)......7	**3**	7/2[3]	91	—
3645[7]	**Grand Scenery (IRE) (80)** (HowardJohnson) **9-10-2b1** ASSmith (hld up & plld hrd: hit 9th: sn lost tch)......30	**4**	7/2[3]	62	—
3824[U]	**Quixall Crossett (78)** (EMCaine) **12-9-9**(5) MrMHNaughton (j.slowly: chsd ldr: blnd 2nd: bhd fr 9th)......nk	**5**	50/1	60	—
			(SP 110.5%)		**5 Rn**

5m 10.7 (-0.30) CSF £6.79 TOTE £2.90: £1.30 £1.20 (£2.80) OWNER Mrs G. M. Sturges (MALTON) BRED Mrs A. M. Kenny
LONG HANDICAP Quixall Crossett 8-6
3710 Rustic Air is ideally suited by this sort of trip and decent ground. (9/4)
3725* The Toaster, from just a 1lb higher mark, was always giving the winner first run. Sticking on from two out, he was never going to get on level terms. (2/1: 11/10-9/4)
3610 Reve de Valse (USA), who wore a tongue-strap, usually gives a good account of himself round here. (7/2)
2923 Grand Scenery (IRE), tried in blinkers, would not settle. (7/2)
1566 Quixall Crossett, who lost ground in the air, is still a maiden after fifty-two attempts. (50/1)

4059 STANLEY THOMPSON MEMORIAL HUNTERS' CHASE (5-Y.O+) (Class H)
4-30 (4-30) **3m 3f (21 fncs)** £1,604.00 (£444.00: £212.00) GOING minus 0.81 sec per fur (F)

			SP	RR	SF
3476[2]	**Greenmount Lad (IRE)** (JCornforth) **9-11-2**(7) MrPCornforth (chsd ldr: led 16th: shkn up & styd on strly flat)—	**1**	10/11[1]	67+	7
	La Maja (IRE) (NWilson) **8-10-11**(7) MrCMulhall (lw: j.rt: wnt prom 15th: hit last: unable qckn)......6	**2**	12/1	58	—
3824[4]	**Upwell** (RJohnson) **13-11-4**(5) MrPJohnson (led: hdd 16th: outpcd fr 3 out)......9	**3**	3/1[3]	58	—
	Boreen Owen (DavidAlanHarrison) **13-11-2**(7) MrAParker (chsd ldrs: rdn & outpcd 13th: sn bhd)......7	**4**	11/4[2]	54	—
3543[R]	**Fish Quay** (MrsKMLamb) **14-11-2**(7) MissSLamb (bhd fr 14th: t.o 17th: p.u bef last)......	**P**	50/1	—	—
			(SP 113.7%)		**5 Rn**

6m 50.7 (4.70) CSF £10.44 TOTE £1.80: £1.90 £1.40 (£11.50) OWNER Mr J. Cornforth (WETHERBY) BRED James Brown-Kerr
3476 Greenmount Lad (IRE) looked to have a battle on his hands going to the last but, when shaken up, stayed on in most determined fashion to score decisively in the end. (10/11)
La Maja (IRE), a keen-going sort, continually lost ground by jumping out to her right. Challenging when she hit the last, the winner then proved much too strong. She is probably still learning. (12/1)
3824 Upwell, better suited by this much faster ground, set out to make every post a winning one, but this veteran was left behind from three out. (3/1)
Boreen Owen, placed on his last two outings in point-to-points, wore a tongue-strap and, getting long in the tooth, was unable to go the pace on the final circuit. (11/4)

4060 JOHN JOYCE H'CAP HURDLE (0-115) (4-Y.O+) (Class E)
5-00 (5-00) **2m 1f (8 hdls)** £2,320.00 (£645.00: £310.00) GOING minus 0.48 sec per fur (GF)

			SP	RR	SF
3728*	**Glenugie (97)** (GMMoore) **6-11-8** NBentley (trckd ldrs: led after 3 out: pushed out flat)......—	**1**	5/2[1]	76	17
3137[6]	**Skiddaw Samba (80)** (MrsMReveley) **8-10-2**(3) GLee (hld up: jnd ldrs 3 out: nt qckn flat)......1¼	**2**	9/1	58	—
3822[2]	**Highland Way (IRE) (87)** (MartinTodhunter) **9-10-5**(7) CMcCormack (lw: sn trckng ldrs: one pce fr 2 out)......10	**3**	5/1[3]	55	—
3666[7]	**Eriny (USA) (88)** (JJQuinn) **8-10-10**(3) ECallaghan (lw: hld up: hdwy appr 2 out: kpt on: nvr nr to chal)......3½	**4**	10/1	53	—
3559[3]	**Field of Vision (IRE) (101)** (MrsASwinbank) **7-11-12** JSupple (chsd ldrs: drvn along & outpcd after 5th: n.d after)......½	**5**	3/1[2]	66	7
3641[F]	**Catch the Pigeon (78)** (REBarr) **8-10-3** NSmith (j.lft: lost pl 2nd: n.d after)......1¼	**6**	14/1	42	—
1047[4]	**Red Jam Jar (94)** (SBBell) **12-11-5** KJohnson (plld hrd: led tl hdd & hmpd after 3 out: sn wknd)......¾	**7**	10/1	57	—
731[5]	**Stags Fell (75)** (TAKCuthbert) **12-10-0** CarolCuthbert (chsd ldrs tl lost pl appr 2 out)......10	**8**	25/1	28	—

				SP	RR	SF
3478[5]	**Aide Memoire (IRE) (76)** (RJohnson) **8-9-10**(5) MrMHNaughton (hld up & plld hrd: blnd 1st: effrt 3 out: sn wknd)	2½	**9**	12/1	27	—
3723[5]	**I'm Tyson (NZ) (75)** (MrsDianneSayer) **9-10-0** MMoloney (hld up & plld hrd: effrt on ins whn n.m.r 3 out: sn wknd: blnd & uns rdr last)		**U**	11/2	—	—
				(SP 132.0%)	**10 Rn**	

3m 58.9 (3.90) CSF £27.03 CT £105.94 TOTE £3.40: £1.40 £2.40 £2.10 (£15.20) Trio £67.40 OWNER Mr Frazer Hines (MIDDLEHAM) BRED F. Hines

LONG HANDICAP Stags Fell 9-4

3728* Glenugie, from a 6lb higher mark, showed his liking for this track and scored in rather comfortable fashion. (5/2)

1686 Skiddaw Samba ran her best race over hurdles for a long time. (9/1)

3822 Highland Way (IRE), as usual, found little under pressure. (5/1)

Eriny (USA), who looked in particularly good shape, was by no means knocked about. Now on a fair mark, he relishes fast ground and should find a race before much longer. (10/1)

3559 Field of Vision (IRE) ran another lifeless race. (3/1)

3723 I'm Tyson (NZ) (11/2: 6/1-10/1)

T/Plpt: £66.40 (149.74 Tckts). T/Qdpt: £10.50 (63.08 Tckts) WG

4048-AINTREE (L-H) (Good)
Saturday April 5th

Meeting Abandoned after Race 3: course evacuated due to security alert. Grand National run 7/4/97.
WEATHER: overcast

4061 CORDON BLEU H'CAP HURDLE (5-Y.O+) (Class B)

1-45 (1-46) **2m 110y (9 hdls)** £19,870.00 (£6,010.00: £2,930.00: £1,390.00) GOING: 0.53 sec per fur (GS)

				SP	RR	SF
3816[3]	**Shankar (IRE) (128)** (DNicholson) **6-10-7**(5) MrRThornton (hld up: hdwy appr 3 out: led last: r.o wl)	—	**1**	25/1	114	72
3615[P]	**Direct Route (IRE) (138)** (HowardJohnson) **6-11-8** ADobbin (trckd ldrs: chal 3 out: led 2 out to last: kpt on wl)	2½	**2**	16/1	122	80
3597[14]	**Dreams End (140)** (PBowen) **9-11-7**(3) LAspell (hdwy 4 out: r.o wl fr last: nrst fin)	nk	**3**	12/1	123	81
3038[P]	**Clifton Beat (USA) (139)** (PJHobbs) **6-11-9** CFSwan (lw: mid div: hdwy 5th: kpt on fr 3 out: nvr able chal)	3½	**4**	16/1	119	77
3597[11]	**Zabadi (IRE) (138)** (DNicholson) **5-11-8** RJohnson (lw: hld up: hdwy 4 out: rdn next: styd on one pce)	3½	**5**	14/1	115	73
2952[3]	**Prizefighter (116)** (JLEyre) **6-10-0** BStorey (lw: chsd ldr: led 3 out to 2 out: grad wknd)	1½	**6**	20/1	91	49
3572[5]	**Forestal (117)** (SGGriffiths) **5-10-1** TJMurphy (chsd ldrs tl wknd after 4 out)	8	**7**	14/1	84	42
3722[4]	**Frozen Sea (USA) (116)** (GPEnright) **6-10-0** JRKavanagh (in tch: effrt appr 3 out: btn whn hit last)	hd	**8**	33/1	83	41
456[3]	**Amlah (USA) (116)** (PJHobbs) **5-10-0b[1]** BPowell (bit bkwd: led tl hdd & wknd 3 out)	s.h	**9**	40/1	83	41
3850*	**Rosencrantz (IRE) (116)** (MissVenetiaWilliams) **5-10-0** 7x NWilliamson (trckd ldrs: hit 4 out: wknd fr 3 out)	1¾	**10**	11/2[2]	81	39
3987[2]	**Tejano Gold (USA) (119)** (PBradley) **7-10-3** SWynne (chsd ldrs: effrt appr 3 out: wknd 2 out)	s.h	**11**	20/1	84	42
2624*	**Secret Spring (FR) (125)** (PRHedger) **5-10-9** MRichards (lw: hld up & bhd: effrt 3 out: nvr plcd to chal)	¾	**12**	3/1[1]	90	48
3816[F]	**Hamilton Silk (132)** (MCPipe) **5-11-2** JOsborne (mstkes: a rr div)	1½	**13**	8/1[3]	95	53
2777[8]	**Most Equal (116)** (MCPipe) **7-9-9**(5) GSupple (bhd & pushed along 4th: n.d)	2½	**14**	25/1	77	35
3816[6]	**Blair Castle (IRE) (116)** (GBBalding) **6-10-0** BFenton (nvr trbld ldrs)	1½	**15**	50/1	75	33
3640[18]	**Stompin (140)** (MissHCKnight) **6-11-10** JCulloty (bit bkwd: chsd ldrs tl wknd appr 3 out)	2½	**16**	9/1	97	55
3572[13]	**Shining Edge (125)** (TDEasterby) **5-10-9** LWyer (in tch to 4 out)	nk	**17**	16/1	82	40
3267[2]	**Kaitak (IRE) (118)** (JMCarr) **6-9-13**(3) FLeahy (chsd ldrs: rdn 5th: sn wknd)	½	**18**	25/1	74	32
				(SP 128.6%)	**18 Rn**	

3m 59.9 (5.90) CSF £330.64 CT £4,558.11 TOTE £22.80: £3.80 £2.70 £3.40 £6.20 (£204.40) Trio £1,125.00 OWNER International Plywood Plc (TEMPLE GUITING) BRED J. M. Valerio

LONG HANDICAP Rosencrantz (IRE) 9-6 Most Equal 9-13 Blair Castle (IRE) 9-10 Prizefighter 9-13 Frozen Sea (USA) 9-8 Amlah (USA) 9-10

3816 Shankar (IRE), is not an easy ride but, put to sleep early by his talented young rider, he came with a smooth run to lead at the last, and stayed on far too strongly for his rivals. (25/1)

3038 Direct Route (IRE) ran yet another good race, holding every chance between the last two flights until passed by the winner on the run-in. Apart from the unfortunate blip at Cheltenham last time, he has been wonderfully consistent this season and fully deserves further successes. (16/1)

3231* Dreams End, who had run on the Flat just five days earlier, stayed on very late to snatch third prize. This was a good effort under top weight, and he should be noted if going to Haydock for the Swinton Hurdle in May, a race he won three years ago. (12/1)

Clifton Beat (USA) was runner-up in this race last year, and again ran a good race here. This was only his second start since a wind operation last summer and, judging by this effort, he ought to find a race before the season is out. (16/1)

3231 Zabadi (IRE) ran by far his best race since winning at Newbury in November. If he can reproduce his best juvenile form, then he looks well-handicapped. (14/1)

2952 Prizefighter looked a little out of his depth beforehand, but nonetheless ran well until fading after jumping the second last. He will win more races when the ground rides fast. (20/1)

2624* Secret Spring (FR) was held up at the back of the field. An effort approaching the third last proved short-lived, and he never managed to threaten the leaders. At the subsequent enquiry, connections told the stewards that the horse seemed 'flat'. (3/1)

4062 MARTELL RED RUM LIMITED H'CAP CHASE (Gd 2) (5-Y.O+) (Class A)

2-20 (2-21) **2m (Mildmay) (12 fncs)** £25,780.00 (£9,759.00: £4,779.50: £2,181.50) GOING: 0.21 sec per fur (G)

				SP	RR	SF
2901[3]	**Down the Fell (122)** (HowardJohnson) **8-10-7** NWilliamson (swtg: chsd ldr: lft in ld 5th: kpt on wl flat)	—	**1**	20/1	137	69
3614[6]	**Lord Dorcet (IRE) (133)** (JIACharlton) **7-11-4** JOsborne (in tch: hdwy 3 out: chsd wnr fr 2 out: ch last: nt qckn)	7	**2**	13/2	141	73
3413[4]	**Wee River (IRE) (125)** (GMMoore) **8-10-10** JCallaghan (trckd ldrs: swtchd & effrt appr 2 out: one pce appr last)	6	**3**	14/1	127	59
3638[U]	**Mister Oddy (128)** (JSKing) **11-10-13** JCulloty (lw: chsd ldrs tl wknd appr 3 out)	11	**4**	16/1	119	51
3614[W]	**Arctic Kinsman (143)** (NATwiston-Davies) **9-12-0** CLlewellyn (lw: chsd ldrs: chal 7th: cl 2nd & rdn whn fell 2 out)		**F**	5/1[2]	—	—
3596[3]	**Celibate (IRE) (132)** (CJMann) **6-11-3** RDunwoody (hld up: fell 5th)		**F**	7/2[1]	—	—
3638[2]	**Elzoba (FR) (138)** (MCPipe) **5-11-2b** CMaude (lw: led tl fell 5th: dead)		**F**	11/2[3]	—	—

3638[6]	**Political Tower (127)** (RNixon) **10-10-12** ADobbin (lw: outpcd whn fell 6th)	F	12/1	—	—
2933[2]	**Jathib (CAN) (128)** (MrsMerritaJones) **6-10-13** DerekByrne (nt j.w: t.o fr 6th: p.u bef 4 out)	P	12/1	—	—
3638[4]	**Time Won't Wait (IRE) (133)** (RTPhillips) **8-11-4** DBridgwater (lw: hld up: bdly hmpd & uns rdr 5th)	U	11/2[3]	—	—
			(SP 115.7%)	**10 Rn**	

3m 58.2 (0.20) CSF £131.17 CT £1,723.97 TOTE £36.90: £5.80 £2.30 £3.70 (£92.00) Trio £410.80 OWNER Mrs S. Johnson (CROOK) BRED J. R. Raine
LONG HANDICAP Down the Fell 10-5
WEIGHT FOR AGE 5yo-7lb

2901 Down the Fell, who has shown his liking for this track before, took over in front when Elzoba crashed out at the fifth. He was sent clear, and showed real determination to keep the runner-up at bay after jumping the last. (20/1)
3144 Lord Dorcet (IRE) looked the one most likely to benefit from the grief going on around him, especially as he closed in on the winner approaching the last. However, he found that his rival was in no mood to surrender. (13/2)
3413 Wee River (IRE) could never seriously threaten the two principals in the closing stages, but plugged on for third prize. (14/1)
3401 Mister Oddy could never get to the front, and was a spent force before the third last. (16/1)
3299 Arctic Kinsman was still in with a chance when crashing out at the second last. He has so much talent but his jumping is a major concern. He has completed only once in his last four outings. (5/1)
3638 Elzoba (FR) was bowling along in front when taking a fatal fall at the fifth. (11/2)

4063 MARTELL AINTREE HURDLE (Gd 1) (4-Y.O+) (Class A)
2-55 (2-55) **2m 4f (11 hdls)** £40,750.00 (£15,405.00: £7,527.50: £3,417.50) GOING: 0.53 sec per fur (GS)

				SP	RR	SF
3597[13]	**Bimsey (IRE) (150)** (RAkehurst) **7-11-7** MAFitzgerald (trckd ldr: led appr 3 out: all out)	—	1	14/1	136	73
3635[8]	**Pridwell (150)** (MCPipe) **7-11-7** RDunwoody (hld up: hdwy gng wl 4 out: effrt next: hung lft & styd on: nvr able to chal)	1½	2	12/1	135	72
3597*	**Make a Stand (165)** (MCPipe) **6-11-7** CMaude (led tl hdd appr 3 out: sn rdn & btn)	16	3	7/4[1]	122	59
3597[3]	**Space Trucker (IRE)** (MrsJHarrington,Ireland) **6-11-7** JShortt (hld up: stdy hdwy 4 out: rdn next: sn btn)	2	4	5/1[3]	120	57
3635[F]	**Urubande (IRE)** (APO'Brien,Ireland) **7-11-7** CFSwan (trckd ldrs: effrt appr 3 out: sn wknd)	dist	5	13/2	—	—
3597[P]	**Large Action (IRE) (165)** (OSherwood) **9-11-7** JOsborne (bhd: pushed along fr 6th: sn wknd: t.o whn p.u bef 4 out)		P	3/1[2]	—	—
3639[P]	**Double Symphony (IRE) (130)** (CPEBrooks) **9-11-2b** GBradley (outpcd & lost tch after 5th: wl t.o whn p.u bef 3 out)		P	25/1	—	—
				(SP 109.6%)	**7 Rn**	

4m 51.0 (9.00) CSF £126.31 TOTE £15.40: £4.00 £2.70 (£48.40) OWNER Mr Aidan Ryan (EPSOM) BRED Golden Vale Stud

2635 Bimsey (IRE), who has won here before, never let Make a Stand get away from him and, taking over approaching the third last, gamely held off the runner-up in the closing stages. He seemed to relish the longer trip, and it is now planned for him to run on the Flat, with a possible crack at the Ebor. (14/1)
2774 Pridwell, put to sleep at the back of the field, crept closer at the fourth last and looked a real danger coming to the next. However, he started to hang and could never quite get to grips with the winner. It is now well over two years since he won a race. (12/1)
3597* Make a Stand, could never get away from his rivals here and, after a couple of clumsy jumps running down the far side, found himself being taken on from both sides. The writing was on the wall soon after turning into the straight. It is unlikely that the trip was the problem as he has won over nineteen furlongs, albeit against modest opposition. It is more likely that he has just had enough for now. (7/4)
3597 Space Trucker (IRE) looked to have a real chance after jumping the fourth last, but found nothing under pressure. This trip looked to be stretching his stamina. (5/1)
3126a Urubande (IRE), the winner of this race last year, looked likely to take a hand in the finish approaching three out but stopped to nothing soon after. His jockey reported that the gelding had made a noise. (13/2)
3597 Large Action (IRE) got a little further than he had done at Cheltenham before being pulled up, but this was still a major disappointment. He was later reported to be 'not right' in front. (3/1)

4064 MARTELL GRAND NATIONAL H'CAP CHASE (Gd 3) (7-Y.O+) (Class A)
- Abandoned -Course evacuated-security alert

4065 CHIVAS REGAL AMATEUR NOVICES' H'CAP CHASE (5-Y.O+) (Class C)
- Abandoned -Course evacuated-security alert

4066 MARTELL CHAMPION STANDARD N.H. FLAT RACE (Gd 2) (Class A)
- Abandoned -Course evacuated-security alert

T/Jkpt: Not won; £15,307.29 to Southwell 7/4/97. T/Plpt: £333.00 (292.41 Tckts). T/Qdpt: £13.50 (415.88 Tckts) AA

3927-HEREFORD (R-H) (Good to firm)
Saturday April 5th
WEATHER: cloudy

4067 KILPECK MAIDEN HURDLE (5-Y.O+) (Class E)
1-35 (1-36) **2m 1f (9 hdls)** £2,332.00 (£652.00: £316.00) GOING minus 0.28 sec per fur (GF)

				SP	RR	SF
1537[6]	**Nautical Jewel** (KGWingrove) **5-10-12**(7) JPower (hld up: hdwy appr 3 out: led last: r.o wl)	—	1	7/2[3]	31	—
418[8]	**Pridewood Fuggle** (RJPrice) **7-11-5** WMcFarland (lw: nt j.w: hld up: hdwy 5th: chsd clr ldr after 5th: lft in ld 2 out: hdd & mstke last)	6	2	Evens[1]	25	—
3741[7]	**Bold Time Monkey** (MTate) **6-11-0** WMarston (chsd clr ldr tl after 6th: sn wknd: mstke last)	13	3	8/1	8	—
3189[P]	**Woldsman** (NATwiston-Davies) **7-10-12**(7) MrJGoldstein (led: sn clr: hung lft 3 out: rn out 2 out)		R	2/1[2]	—	—
				(SP 116.7%)	**4 Rn**	

4m 17.8 (24.80) CSF £7.57 TOTE £3.70: (£2.00) OWNER Mrs A. Squires (NEWMARKET) BRED J. M. and Mrs Jeyes

1537 Nautical Jewel, who changed hands for 1,100 guineas in February, may well have had his work cut out had Woldsman stayed in the race. (7/2)
191 Pridewood Fuggle found the winner galloping all over him going to the final flight. (Evens)
Bold Time Monkey (8/1: 5/1-10/1)

3189 Woldsman had a handy lead when making his exit and his rider subsequently told the Stewards that his mount had hung progressively worse left-handed throughout the race. (2/1: 5/4-9/4)

4068 CUSOP H'CAP CHASE (0-110) (5-Y.O+) (Class E)
2-10 (-) **3m 1f 110y** £4,560.00

				SP	RR	SF
3899[3]	**Royal Saxon (86)** (PBowen) **11-11-10b** WMarston (Walked over)	—	1	—	—	

OWNER Mr G. Morris (HAVERFORDWEST) BRED Paddy Byrne/Paddy Byrne

4069 BREDWARDINE NOVICES' (S) HURDLE (4-Y.O+) (Class G)
2-40 (2-41) **2m 1f (9 hdls)** £2,010.00 (£560.00: £270.00) GOING minus 0.28 sec per fur (GF)

				SP	RR	SF
3764[8]	**Contract Bridge (IRE) (62)** (PGMurphy) **4-10-3** WMcFarland (hld up: hdwy 5th: led on bit after 3 out: qcknd clr after 2 out: all out)	—	1	2/1[1]	43	—
3901[P]	**Magical Blues (IRE)** (MissAEEmbiricos) **5-11-0** KGaule (hld up: stdy hdwy 5th: rdn & r.o flat: too much to do)	½	2	8/1	48+	11
3979[3]	**Almapa (82)** (RJHodges) **5-11-3**(3) TDascombe (prom tl stdd appr 3rd: hdwy appr 5th: ev ch 3 out: rdn & wknd after 2 out)	24	3	2/1[1]	31	—
3359[13]	**Glen Garnock (IRE) (75)** (RTJuckes) **5-11-0** GaryLyons (prom: mstke 3rd: led 5th tl after 3 out: wknd appr 2 out)	6	4	7/1[3]	19	—
	Lady Eclat (KGWingrove) **4-9-12**(5) SRyan (a bhd: t.o)	dist	5	16/1	—	—
3574[17]	**Tatibag** (RJSmith) **5-10-7**(7) MrJGoldstein (swtg: a bhd: t.o)	4	6	40/1	—	—
3735[6]	**Rapid Liner (60)** (RJBaker) **4-10-8b[1]** VSlattery (nt j.w: mde most to 5th: wknd 6th: t.o)	1¾	7	20/1	—	—
555[7]	**More Bills (IRE) (74)** (JNeville) **5-11-0** DJBurchell (prom: rdn appr 5th: led 3 out: sn hdd: wknd after 2 out: fell last)		F	5/1[2]	—	—
3677[P]	**Boot Jack (IRE)** (PMRich) **8-10-7**(7) MGriffiths (bhd: mstke 2nd: t.o whn p.u bef 2 out)		P	33/1	—	—
1700[11]	**Northern Diamond (IRE)** (MissMERowland) **4-10-5**(3) PHenley (bit bkwd: prom tl wknd 6th: t.o whn p.u bef 2 out)		P	40/1	—	—
	Mummy's Mole (GraemeRoe) **6-10-9**(5) DSalter (bkwd: prom to 5th: t.o whn p.u bef 2 out)		P	50/1	—	—

(SP 127.4%) **11 Rn**

4m 1.6 (8.60) CSF £19.22 TOTE £2.70: £1.10 £2.80 £1.30 (£16.40) Trio £51.00 OWNER LM Racing (BRISTOL) BRED E. O'Leary
WEIGHT FOR AGE 4yo-6lb
Bt in 4,600 gns

Contract Bridge (IRE) was well backed on this drop in class. It was just as well McFarland caught the rider of the second napping when he stole it on the home turn. (2/1: op 4/1)
3284 Magical Blues (IRE), on his best behaviour this time, would have won this had Gaule not been caught out by the winner setting sail for home on the last bend. (8/1: op 5/1)
3979 Almapa was disappointingly left for dead from the penultimate hurdle. (2/1: 6/4-9/4)
2939 Glen Garnock (IRE) was reverting to selling company. (7/1: op 4/1)
More Bills (IRE) (5/1: 4/1-6/1)

4070 GARWAY NOVICES' HUNTERS' CHASE (5-Y.O+) (Class H)
3-10 (3-15) **2m (12 fncs)** £1,095.00 (£330.00: £160.00: £75.00) GOING: 0.08 sec per fur (G)

				SP	RR	SF
	Nectanebo (IRE) (NParker) **9-11-7**(7) MrMFrith (lw: hld up & bhd: hdwy 6th: led after 2 out: clr last: r.o wl)	—	1	25/1	91	24
3631[P]	**Tom's Apache** (OJCarter) **8-11-7**(7) MrEJames (led: sn clr: hdd after 2 out: one pce)	6	2	13/2[3]	85	18
1041[2]	**Dalametre** (MJMEvans) **10-11-7**(7) MrMMunrowd (rdn 6th: hdwy 9th: wknd 2 out)	16	3	6/5[1]	69	2
1065[5]	**Chan The Man** (DBurchell) **6-11-7**(7) MrMHarris (a.p: mstke 8th: chsd wnr 4 out tl hit 2 out: 3rd & btn whn blnd last)	2½	4	10/1	67	—
	Ann's Ambition (MrsCHussey) **10-11-7**(7) MrCHeard (lw: nt j.w: a bhd)	12	5	3/1[2]	55	—
3744[P]	**The Communicator** (MAHill) **11-11-9b**(5) MrBPollock (lw: chsd clr ldr tl hit 4 out: sn wknd)	2½	6	10/1	52	—
191[4]	**Oats For Notes** (MrsRFKnipe) **7-11-2**(7) MrRBurton (a bhd: t.o whn mstke 3 out)	14	7	7/1	33	—
3460[7]	**Happy Paddy** (BRSummers) **14-11-7**(7) MrMCowley (mstke 5th: bhd whn mstke 7th: sn t.o)	dist	8	20/1	—	—
3721[P]	**Feltham Mistress** (DCTucker) **7-11-2**(7) MrEBabington (hld up: 4th whn fell 7th)		F	33/1	—	—
3460[U]	**Michelles Crystal** (FLMatthews) **6-11-2**(7) MrJGoldstein (s.s: mstkes 1st & 2nd: fell 3rd)		F	33/1	—	—
	Space Molly (MrsNLay) **8-11-2b[1]**(7) MrPCowley (a bhd: t.o whn p.u bef 3 out)		P	33/1	—	—

(SP 131.9%) **11 Rn**

4m 4.1 (13.10) CSF £171.61 TOTE £55.80: £7.40 £1.50 £1.50 (£56.40) Trio £29.90 OWNER Mrs R. E. Parker (YEOVIL) BRED Newtownbarry House Stud

Nectanebo (IRE) took the eye in the paddock despite not having run in a point for two years. (25/1)
Tom's Apache, appreciating this faster ground, was supported in the ring and gave his backers a good run for their money. (13/2)
1041 Dalametre, the winner of a men's open at Garnons last month, is normally a front-runner, but could never get to the head of affairs over this shorter trip. (6/5)
Chan The Man, graduating to fences, was just beginning to feel the pace when he clouted the penultimate fence. (10/1)
Ann's Ambition, second in his last two points, had trouble handling these bigger fences. (3/1)

4071 RACING CHANNEL H'CAP HURDLE (0-105) (4-Y.O+) (Class F)
4-25 (4-25) **2m 1f (9 hdls)** £2,794.00 (£784.00: £382.00) GOING minus 0.28 sec per fur (GF)

				SP	RR	SF
3904*	**Euro Singer (98)** (TKeddy) **5-11-5**(5) SRyan (a.p: wnt 2nd appr 4th: rdn whn lft clr 2 out: r.o wl)	—	1	9/4[1]	87	10
3890[3]	**Va Utu (85)** (DMLloyd) **9-10-8**(3) SophieMitchell (w ldr: led 3rd tl after 6th: one pce fr 3 out)	8	2	9/2[2]	67	—
3904[P]	**Dissolve (80)** (NMLampard) **5-9-13**(7) MrLBaker (hdwy appr 5th: rdn 6th: one pce fr 3 out)	2½	3	9/2[2]	59	—
1995[7]	**Tap Shoes (IRE) (74)** (RJBaker) **7-10-0** VSlattery (bkwd: hld up: hdwy appr 5th: wknd appr 3 out)	6	4	14/1	48	—
3766[4]	**Dontdressfordinner (89)** (RJHodges) **7-10-12**(3) TDascombe (lw: hld up: hdwy appr 5th: wknd 3 out)	13	5	6/1[3]	50	—
1763[8]	**Jewel Thief (83)** (GBBalding) **7-10-2v**(7) MrEBabington (bhd: pushed along after 3rd: t.o appr 5th)	26	6	14/1	20	—
210[P]	**Noble Society (92)** (KGWingrove) **9-10-11**(7) JPower (bit bkwd: a bhd: t.o fr 5th)	26	7	10/1	4	—

3904[10] **Courageous Knight (78)** (PHayward) **8-10-4** WMarston (led to 3rd: led after 6th: hrd rdn after 3 out: 1l clr whn rn out & crashed thro wing 2 out)........ **R** 7/1 — —
(SP 116.3%) **8 Rn**

4m 2.4 (9.40) CSF £12.25 CT £38.11 TOTE £3.30: £1.50 £1.10 £2.80 (£5.00) OWNER BCD Steels Ltd (HANLEY SWAN) BRED Mrs A. Plummer
LONG HANDICAP Tap Shoes (IRE) 9-6
3904* Euro Singer, raised 6lb, again went down early and was effectively presented the race two out. (9/4)
3890 Va Utu was effectively 2lb higher than when winning here last month. (9/2)
3752* Dissolve was 3lb higher than when successful at Towcester, having pulled up behind the winner on the same course a week ago. (9/2)
1693 Tap Shoes (IRE) ran respectably considering he was 8lb wrong at the weights. (14/1)
3814 Courageous Knight, last of ten finishers behind the winner last week, may even have beaten his rival this time had he not disgraced himself at the penultimate hurdle. (7/1)

4072 PANDY NOVICES' CHASE (5-Y.O+) (Class E)

4-55 (4-55) **2m 3f (14 fncs)** £2,918.00 (£884.00: £432.00: £206.00) GOING: 0.08 sec per fur (G)

			SP	RR	SF
886[P]	**Duke of Dreams (82)** (RJBaker) **7-11-6** VSlattery (hld up: led 9th: hit 10th: clr appr 3 out: easily)........—	**1**	15/8[2]	64+	—
3966[9]	**Pandora's Prize (60)** (TWall) **11-10-9** TEley (chsd ldr: lft in ld 4th: hdd 9th: hit 10th: btn whn blnd last)........10	**2**	10/1	45	—
	Something Catchy (IRE) (ABarrow) **7-10-9** WMarston (lw: prom: rdn after 4 out: 3rd & btn whn mstke 2 out)........¾	**3**	15/2[3]	44	—
	Diamond Light (VRBishop) **10-11-0** MrSLloyd (hit 6th: bhd fr 8th: sn t.o)........dist	**4**	20/1	—	—
2544[P]	**Another Venture (IRE) (87)** (FMurphy) **7-11-0** MFoster (lw: led tl fell 4th)........	**F**	4/5[1]	—	—
1174[P]	**Freeline Lustre (IRE) (60)** (PGMurphy) **7-11-0** WMcFarland (lw: mstke & lost pl 3rd: hmpd 4th: sn t.o: p.u bef 7th)........	**P**	20/1	—	—

(SP 120.7%) **6 Rn**

4m 56.9 (26.90) CSF £18.70 TOTE £3.20: £1.40 £2.00 (£12.10) OWNER Mrs V. W. Jones (TIVERTON) BRED H. D. and M. J. Gee
547 Duke of Dreams has presumably been kept for a spring campaign, having been off-course since pulling up at Newton Abbot in mid-October. (15/8)
Pandora's Prize ran her best race over fences, which says a lot for this contest. (10/1)
Something Catchy (IRE) scored once from six attempts in Irish points two years ago. (15/2)
1831 Another Venture (IRE) had been let down by his jumping in the past. (4/5)

4073 BROAD OAK NOVICES' CONDITIONAL H'CAP HURDLE (0-100) (4-Y.O+) (Class F)

5-25 (5-26) **3m 2f (13 hdls)** £2,248.00 (£628.00: £304.00) GOING minus 0.28 sec per fur (GF)

			SP	RR	SF
2627[7]	**Clongour (IRE) (78)** (FMurphy) **7-11-1b[1]** DJKavanagh (hld up: hdwy 8th: led 3 out: clr whn hit last: styd on)—	**1**	6/1	64	—
3902[3]	**Kingswood Manor (81)** (MissVenetiaWilliams) **5-11-4** PHenley (a.p: mstke 6th: led 9th to 3 out: styd on one pce)........2½	**2**	4/1[3]	66	—
3672[5]	**Hi Marble (IRE) (68)** (MrsMerritaJones) **6-10-0(5)** MLane (hld up: hdwy 5th: wknd 3 out: hit 2 out)........23	**3**	7/4[1]	38	—
3683[6]	**Lady of Mine (63)** (PBowen) **7-9-11(3)** LCummins (a.p: mstke 2nd: led appr 8th to 9th: wknd qckly 3 out)........¾	**4**	8/1	33	—
3834[3]	**Copper Coil (90)** (WGMTurner) **7-11-10(3)** JPower (hmpd bnd after 1st: reminders after 7th: sn bhd: t.o whn p.u bef 2 out)........	**P**	100/30[2]	—	—
3819[7]	**Music Class (IRE) (75)** (CPEBrooks) **6-10-9(3)** MBerry (a.p: led 6th tl appr 8th: wknd qckly appr 3 out: p.u bef 2 out)........	**P**	13/2	—	—
3621[13]	**Nuns Lucy (63)** (FJordan) **6-10-0** GuyLewis (led to 6th: bhd fr 8th: t.o whn p.u bef 9th)........	**P**	50/1	—	—

(SP 120.1%) **7 Rn**

6m 31.7 (28.70) CSF £29.35 TOTE £7.90: £2.90 £3.00 (£14.40) OWNER Mr Liam Mulryan (MIDDLEHAM) BRED Billy Phelan
LONG HANDICAP Lady of Mine 9-13 Nuns Lucy 9-7
Clongour (IRE) found the combination of a switch to a handicap and first-time blinkers doing the trick. (6/1: 7/2-7/1)
3902 Kingswood Manor was getting the worse of the argument when rather awkward at the final flight. (4/1)
3672 Hi Marble (IRE), taking a big step-up in distance, did not live up to the market support. (7/4: 5/2-6/4)
Lady of Mine, who fell in two points in 1995, has yet to prove she stays this sort of trip. (8/1)
3834 Copper Coil (100/30: 2/1-7/2)

T/Plpt: £22.70 (315.99 Tckts). T/Qdpt: £3.70 (170.74 Tckts) KH

4061-AINTREE (L-H) (Good, Good to firm patches)

Monday April 7th

Race rescheduled from 5/4/97
WEATHER: fine

4074 MARTELL GRAND NATIONAL H'CAP CHASE (Gd 3) (7-Y.O+) (Class A)

5-00 (5-01) **4m 4f (National) (30 fncs)** £178,146.00 (£67,014.00: £33,057.00: £14,535.00: £6,817.50: £3,730.50) GOING: 0.14 sec per fur (G)

			SP	RR	SF
3699[2]	**Lord Gyllene (NZ) (141)** (SABrookshaw) **9-10-0** ADobbin (j.w: mde virtually all: bdly hmpd & hdd briefly 16th (water): sn led again: drew clr appr 2 out)........—	**1**	14/1	157+	76
3294*	**Suny Bay (IRE) (144)** (CPEBrooks) **8-10-3** JOsborne (chsd wnr: ev ch whn blnd 4 out: outpd fr 2 out)........25	**2**	8/1[2]	145	70
3599[6]	**Camelot Knight (141)** (NATwiston-Davies) **11-10-0** CLlewellyn (hld up: hdwy 25th (Valentine's): styd on fr 2 out: mstke last)........2	**3**	100/1	141	67
3885[8]	**Buckboard Bounce (142)** (GRichards) **11-10-1** PCarberry (hld up: hdwy appr 13th: drvn 3 out: styd on: nvr nrr)........1¾	**4**	40/1	141	67
3261a[P]	**Master Oats (165)** (KCBailey) **11-11-10** NWilliamson (lw: hmpd 11th: hdwy 19th: ev ch 4 out: wknd appr 2 out)........1¾	**5**	25/1	163	88
2887[U]	**Avro Anson (144)** (MJCamacho) **9-10-3ow1** PNiven (lw: mstke 1st: hld up: hdwy 16th: hmpd 23rd (Foinavon): ev ch 25th (Valentine's): mstke 4 out: wknd next)........8	**6**	12/1	137	66
3699[4]	**Killeshin (141)** (HJManners) **11-10-0** SCurran (swtg: in rr: lost tch 22nd: styd on fr 3 out)........7	**7**	33/1	130	60
3153[11]	**Dakyns Boy (141)** (NATwiston-Davies) **12-10-0** TJMurphy (lw: in tch to ½-wy: wl bhd 22nd: sme late hdwy)...9	**8**	100/1	124	57

3636P **Nahthen Lad (IRE) (150)** (MrsJPitman) **8-10-9** JFTitley (lw: prom: mstke 10th: blnd 22nd: wkng whn mstke 26th) 1¼ **9** 14/1 133 65

38153 **Valiant Warrior (144)** (MDHammond) **9-10-3**ow3 RGarritty (mid div: hdwy to chse ldrs ½-wy: rdn appr 3 out: sn wknd) 8 **10** 50/1 122 57

3261a* **Antonin (FR) (141)** (MrsSABramall,Ireland) **9-10-0** CO'Dwyer (nt j.w: nvr nr ldrs) 12 **11** 14/1 112 50

36189 **Northern Hide (142)** (MSalaman) **11-10-1**ow1 PHolley (prom: mstke 9th (Valentine's): lost pl 22nd: blnd 25th (Valentine's): n.d after) 3 **12** 66/1 111 50

3420* **Turning Trix (141)** (DNicholson) **10-10-0** JRKavanagh (in rr: hmpd 1st & 11th: lost tch 22nd: t.o) 22 **13** 25/1 97 42

33956 **Pink Gin (141)** (MDHammond) **10-10-0** MrCBonner (mstke 6th (Becher's): a bhd: t.o) 13 **14** 100/1 89 37

361810 **New Co (IRE) (141)** (MFMorris,Ireland) **9-10-0** DJCasey (b: nt j.w: mstke 6th (Becher's): hmpd 13th: t.o) 6 **15** 40/1 85 35

35634 **General Wolfe (141)** (CaptTAForster) **8-10-0** LWyer (nvr gng wl: a in rr: mstke 6th (Becher's): lost tch 23rd: t.o) 6 **16** 16/1 82 33

25752 **Evangelica (USA) (141)** (MCPipe) **7-10-0** RSupple (in tch tl lost pl 7th (Foinavon): bhd fr 19th: t.o) ....dist **17** 33/1 — —

2848a7 **Back Bar (IRE) (141)** (ALTMoore,Ireland) **9-10-0** TPTreacy (fell 7th (Foinavon)) .... **F** 100/1 — —

3503aP **Nuaffe (141)** (PAFahy,Ireland) **12-10-0b** TMitchell (lw: pckd 1st: hdwy to chse ldrs 8th (Canal Turn): 4th whn fell 11th) .... **F** 100/1 — —

3420P **Smith's Band (IRE) (143)** (MrsJPitman) **9-10-2**ow2 RDunwoody (prom: mstke 3rd: led briefly 16th (Water): disp 2nd whn fell 20th: dead) .... **F** 12/1 — —

1513U **Straight Talk (144)** (PFNicholls) **10-10-3**ow3 MrJTizzard (in rr: fell 14th: dead) .... **F** 50/1 — —

Don't Light Up (141) (MissVenetiaWilliams) **11-10-0b** MrRThornton (mstkes 5th & 6th (Becher's): bhd whn fell 13th) .... **F** 100/1 — —

34283 **Full of Oats (141)** (MissHCKnight) **11-10-0** JCulloty (fell 1st) .... **F** 33/1 — —

3526a5 **Feathered Gale (144)** (ALTMoore,Ireland) **10-10-3** FWoods (a bhd: t.o: p.u bef 4 out) .... **P** 16/1 — —

3563P **Bishops Hall (142)** (RHAlner) **11-10-1** MRichards (mid div: effrt to chse ldrs 25th (Valentine's): wknd appr 3 out: bhd whn p.u bef 2 out) .... **P** 50/1 — —

32805 **Mugoni Beach (141)** (MCPipe) **12-10-0b** GTormey (lw: prom tl hit 13th: reminders 17th: bhd whn p.u bef 21st) .... **P** 100/1 — —

3699F **Scribbler (143)** (GMMcCourt) **11-10-2**ow2 DFortt (a bhd: mstke 9th (Valentine's): blnd 17th: t.o whn p.u bef 21st) .... **P** 100/1 — —

36364 **Go Ballistic (144)** (JGMO'Shea) **8-10-3**ow3 MAFitzgerald (in rr: effrt u.p 19th: blnd bdly 25th (Valentine's): nt rcvr: t.o whn p.u bef 2 out) .... **P** 7/1 1 — —

3302P **Dextra Dove (141)** (SEarle) **10-10-0** CMaude (mstke 4th: rdn & wkng whn mstke 20th: bhd whn p.u bef 4 out) . **P** 33/1 — —

3598F **River Mandate (142)** (CaptTAForster) **10-10-1v**1ow1 AThornton (reminders after 2nd: hmpd 7th: in rr tl p.u bef 21st) .... **P** 50/1 — —

32945 **Lo Stregone (145)** (TPTate) **11-10-4** GBradley (mstke 1st: in rr: pckd 22nd (Becher's): sn lost tch: p.u bef 4 out) .... **P** 14/1 — —

359810 **Grange Brake (145)** (NATwiston-Davies) **11-10-4**ow4 DWalsh (mid div to ½-wy: lost tch 22nd: ref 4 out) .... **R** 100/1 — —

19042 **Glemot (IRE) (141)** (KCBailey) **9-10-0** SMcNeill (hmpd & uns rdr 7th) .... **U** 50/1 — —

3526a* **Wylde Hide (141)** (ALTMoore,Ireland) **10-10-0** CFSwan (lw: chsd ldrs tl blnd bdly & lost pl 13th: blnd & uns rdr 22nd (Becher's)) .... **U** 11/1 3 — —

36374 **Celtic Abbey (141)** (MissVenetiaWilliams) **9-10-0** RJohnson (in tch tl blnd & uns rder 15th (Chair)) .... **U** 66/1 — —

35633 **Spuffington (143)** (JTGifford) **9-10-2**ow2 PHide (lw: cl up tl mstke 8th (Canal Turn): j.lft 20th: wkng whn blnd & uns rdr 22nd (Becher's)) .... **U** 100/1 — —

(SP 132.8%) **36 Rn**

9m 5.8 (3.80) CSF £97.64 CT £9,503.36 TOTE £13.20: £3.40 £3.60 £24.10 £9.50 (£48.40) Trio £20,732.50; £6,716.17 to Nottingham 8/4/97

OWNER Mr Stanley Clarke (SHREWSBURY) BRED Mrs N. M. Taylor

LONG HANDICAP Dakyns Boy 8-9 Lord Gyllene (NZ) 9-13 Antonin (FR) 9-13 Camelot Knight 8-6 Turning Trix 8-12 Pink Gin 8-0 New Co (IRE) 9-9 Killeshin 9-3 Evangelica (USA) 8-10 Back Bar (IRE) 8-10 Nuaffe 9-2 Full of Oats 8-6 Straight Talk 9-2 Smith's Band (IRE) 9-10 Don't Light Up 8-2 Dextra Dove 9-13 General Wolfe 9-8 Mugoni Beach 8-4 Scribbler 8-8 Go Ballistic 9-8 Valiant Warrior 9-6 River Mandate 8-12 Northern Hide 9-0 Grange Brake 8-12 Glemot (IRE) 9-7 Wylde Hide 9-13 Celtic Abbey 8-7 Spuffington 8-0

3699 Lord Gyllene (NZ), with only joint bottom weight to carry, must have thought he was running loose and, doing what he likes to do best, galloped and jumped his rivals into the ground and won going away. (14/1)

3294* Suny Bay (IRE) took the winner on and briefly looked to be travelling best when he made a dreadful mistake four out and, with the pace never dropping, had to admit he had met one too good. He is comparatively lightly-raced for an eight-year-old and this race will no doubt be his target in twelve months' time. (8/1)

3599 Camelot Knight, who has done all his winning on much softer ground, was taken off his legs in the early stages, but he stayed on really strongly inside the final mile, and ran the race of his life. (100/1)

3885 Buckboard Bounce has had an interrupted training programme, but he gave his young jockey the thrill of a lifetime and was still galloping on at the finish, and with not many miles on the clock, he does deserve to pick up another good prize. (40/1)

3261a Master Oats had the misfortune to be kicked at the start, but he ran a blinder from the top of the handicap and finished a couple of places closer than he did two years ago. If he gets the testing ground that suits him, he could still be up there with the best of them. (25/1)

2636 Avro Anson gave the impression that he did not see the trip out, but his jockey reported the gelding had received a kick in the head on the first circuit and could have been suffering from semi-concussion, so this performance was probably much better than his finishing position might suggest. (12/1)

3699 Killeshin was always finding the tempo too hot to handle but he does stay and he was beginning to find his feet when the race was all but over. (33/1)

2881 Dakyns Boy was beginning to feel the strain at the Canal Turn and he was very leg-weary before reaching the penultimate fence. (100/1)

3151 Nahthen Lad (IRE) had far more than his fair share of weight, but pushed the pace for almost four miles before calling enough. (14/1)

3261a* Antonin (FR) again succeeded in completing the course but his jumping was a bit sketchy and he was unable to make his presence felt. (14/1)

2887 Northern Hide kept tabs on the leaders and jumped boldly, until gradually fading out of contention soon after the Canal Turn. (66/1)

3420 Smith's Band (IRE), trained with this race in mind, was giving a very good account of himself and was disputing second place when falling with fatal consequences at the twentieth. (12/1)

3636 Go Ballistic ran a bit flat after such a good effort in last month's Gold Cup and, trailing when he made a mess of Valentine's second time around, he was pulled up before the penultimate fence. (7/1)

3526a* Wylde Hide has not enjoyed the best of fortune round here for he was still in with a shout when his rider got knocked out of the saddle at the Canal Turn last year, and this time round he was still hunting up the leaders when he overdid it at Becher's second time and sent his jockey into orbit. (11/1)
IM

3789-KELSO (L-H) (Good to firm)
Monday April 7th
WEATHER: fine

4075 CHEVIOT RENTALS (MODULAR MARQUEES) 'N.H.' NOVICES' HURDLE (4-Y.O+) (Class D)
2-00 (2-15) **2m 110y (8 hdls)** £2,871.00 (£806.00: £393.00) GOING minus 0.60 sec per fur (F)

Form	Horse	Dist	Pos	SP	RR	SF
3802[3]	**Jessolle** (GRichards) **5-10-2**(7) RBurns (lw: hld up: smooth hdwy 3 out: led last: qcknd)	—	**1**	6/5[1]	65	—
3823[11]	**Nick Ross (67)** (RBrewis) **6-11-0** ASSmith (lw: cl up: led 2 out to last: nt qckn)	1¾	**2**	11/1	68	3
3159[12]	**Pentlands Flyer (IRE)** (HowardJohnson) **6-10-7**(7) CMcCormack (lw: plld hrd: trckd ldrs: disp ld & hit last: no ex)	4	**3**	16/1	64	—
3823[3]	**Eastcliffe (IRE)** (WMcKeown) **5-11-0** GCahill (plld hrd: bhd: hdwy 3 out: nrst fin)	2½	**4**	8/1	62	—
3823[5]	**Pentland Squire (95)** (JMJefferson) **6-11-0** NSmith (hld up: mstke 4th: hdwy & prom 3 out: one pce appr last)	2	**5**	4/1[2]	60	—
3940[3]	**Dantes Amour (IRE)** (MDHammond) **6-11-0** DBentley (in tch: effrt 5th: sn rdn & one pce)	7	**6**	12/1	53	—
3641[7]	**Amber Holly (71)** (JEDixon) **8-10-9** FPerratt (cl up: led 4th to 2 out: wknd)	8	**7**	100/1	41	—
3436[3]	**Arctic Sandy (IRE)** (JKMOliver) **7-11-0** BStorey (in tch tl outpcd fr 3 out)	7	**8**	11/2[3]	39	—
3394[6]	**Political Mandate** (RNixon) **4-10-0**(3) FLeahy (led to 4th: outpcd fr 3 out)	1	**9**	100/1	33	—
3789[10]	**Caulker** (MABarnes) **4-10-3**(5) STaylor (plld hrd: cl up tl mstke & wknd 5th)	1½	**10**	200/1	36	—
3098[9]	**Salem Beach** (MartinTodhunter) **5-10-9** JCallaghan (hld up: effrt ½-wy: sn btn)	7	**11**	50/1	25	—
3888[P]	**Chain Line** (JWFAynsley) **7-11-0** TReed (hld up: wnt prom 3rd: wknd 5th: sn t.o)	30	**12**	66/1	—	—
	Kings Adventure (BMactaggart) **5-10-11**(3) GLee (in tch tl mstke & wknd 3 out: t.o)	3	**13**	25/1	—	—
				(SP 123.6%)	**13 Rn**	

3m 49.5 (3.50) CSF £15.67 TOTE £2.40: £1.20 £2.10 £4.20 (£14.00) Trio £108.20 OWNER Mr C. R. Fleet (PENRITH) BRED Mrs I. H. Lowe
WEIGHT FOR AGE 4yo-6lb

3802 Jessolle won a moderate contest here and the only anxious moment was when she was short of room on the home turn. (6/5)
1667 Nick Ross likes this fast ground and ran his best race for a while and should stay further. (11/1: 14/1-25/1)
2918 Pentlands Flyer (IRE), yet again, did not help his chances by pulling hard, but he did show enough to suggest that a race can be found. (16/1)
3823 Eastcliffe (IRE) is learning to settle and finished well here suggesting that his turn will come. (8/1: 6/1-9/1)
3823 Pentland Squire is liable to make mistakes but he has an engine if he should fully get it together. (4/1)
3940 Dantes Amour (IRE), from a yard that is just coming back to form, ran reasonably until stopping two out. (12/1)

4076 HOLLAND & HOLLAND BUCCLEUCH CUP MAIDEN HUNTERS' CHASE (5-Y.O+) (Class H)
2-30 (2-38) **3m 1f (19 fncs)** £2,081.25 (£630.00: £307.50: £146.25) GOING minus 0.60 sec per fur (F)

Form	Horse	Dist	Pos	SP	RR	SF
	Gallants Delight (MrsCJohnston) **7-11-3**(7)ow1 MrARobson (chsd ldrs: hdwy 4 out: led last: r.o wl)	—	**1**	9/2[2]	87	19
	Ensign Ewart (IRE) (CStorey) **6-11-9**(5) MrCStorey (bhd: effrt 13th: wnt prom 3 out: one pce appr last)	8	**2**	9/4[1]	86	19
3713[3]	**Pennine View** (JJDixon) **10-11-9**(5) MrRFord (cl up: led fr 6th tl hdd & mstke last: wknd)	5	**3**	10/1	83	16
	Cool Yule (IRE) (RWThomson) **9-11-7**(7) MrBGibson (sn wl bhd: sme hdwy 4th: n.d)	19	**4**	10/1	71	4
	Lothian Commodore (GRichards) **7-11-7**(7) CaptAOgden (mid div: effrt 13th: hit 4 out: n.d)	3½	**5**	11/2	68	1
	Storm Alive (IRE) (MrsRichardArthur) **6-11-7**(7) MrTScott (outpcd & wl bhd fr 13th)	dist	**6**	20/1	—	—
	Hula (MissFrancesWilson) **9-11-7**(7) MrMBradburne (mid div: effrt 14th: outpcd & 5th whn b.d 3 out)		**B**	100/1	—	—
	Seymour Fiddles (JPSeymour) **6-11-2**(7) MrMJRuddy (j.rt & mstkes: bhd tl fell 11th)		**F**	66/1	—	—
	Leannes Man (IRE) (WGReed) **8-11-7**(7) MrChrisWilson (led to 6th: chsd ldr: blnd 9th, 13th & 14th: disp 3rd & rdn whn fell 3 out)		**F**	5/1[3]	—	—
3713[U]	**Lindon Run** (KRobson) **8-11-7**(7) MrRMorgan (in tch: outpcd & hmpd 3 out: wl bhd whn fell last)		**F**	9/1	—	—
3713[6]	**Tumlin Oot (IRE)** (JSHaldane) **8-11-9**(5) MrNWilson (prom tl outpcd 14th: p.u bef 2 out)		**P**	33/1	—	—
	Canister Castle (MissZAGreen) **9-11-9**(5) MrRShiels (chsd ldrs: outpcd whn hit 16th & 4 out: sn wknd & p.u bef 3 out)		**P**	16/1	—	—
				(SP 125.3%)	**12 Rn**	

6m 14.4 (4.40) CSF £14.84 TOTE £8.10: £2.50 £1.10 £2.30 (£8.50) Trio £8.40 OWNER Mrs C. Johnston (PENRITH) BRED Mrs C. Johnston

Gallants Delight has done well in Points this year and looks to be on the upgrade, as she won this in really good style. (9/2)
Ensign Ewart (IRE) had to work to get into this and, once he did, he then always found the winner too strong. (9/4)
3713 Pennine View really attacked his fences and tried to gallop his rivals into the ground, but he ran out of fuel and hitting the last made no difference to the result. (10/1)
Cool Yule (IRE) looked slow but he was keeping on reasonably well at the end. (10/1)
Lothian Commodore, having his first run for over a year, had no sparkle at all. (11/2)

4077 GLENGOYNE HIGHLAND MALT (TAMEROSIA SERIES QUALIFIER) NOVICES' CHASE (5-Y.O+) (Class D)
3-00 (3-05) **3m 1f (19 fncs)** £4,111.20 (£1,245.60: £608.80: £290.40) GOING minus 0.60 sec per fur (F)

Form	Horse	Dist	Pos	SP	RR	SF
3790[3]	**Real Tonic (97)** (GRichards) **7-11-8** CaptAOgden (hdwy & prom 12th: led 2 out: lft clr last & eased)	—	**1**	5/2[2]	105+	16
1988[F]	**Tall Measure** (DGSwindlehurst) **11-11-2** BStorey (chsd ldrs: effrt 4 out: r.o one pce)	9	**2**	14/1	93	4
3909[8]	**German Legend (80)** (DALamb) **7-11-8** JBurke (prom tl outpcd fr 12th: n.d after)	20	**3**	16/1	86	—
3975[3]	**Cool Weather (IRE) (72)** (PCheesbrough) **9-11-2b** ASSmith (hld up: stdy hdwy 12th: effrt 14th: sn rdn: btn 3 out)	nk	**4**	25/1	80	—
3724*	**Miss Colette (73)** (MrsDThomson) **9-11-3** MFoster (lw: disp ld to 10th: cl up tl outpcd fr 15th)	1¼	**5**	14/1	80	—
3695[4]	**Fine Tune (IRE) (60)** (MrsSCBradburne) **7-10-9**(7) MrMBradburne (chsd ldrs tl outpcd fr 13th: wl btn whn blnd 2 out)	dist	**6**	33/1	—	—
2919[P]	**Mamica (80)** (MDods) **7-11-2** NSmith (a bhd: blnd 4 out)	dist	**7**	10/1[3]	—	—
3792[2]	**Coqui Lane (97)** (JMDun) **10-11-8** DParker (lw: mde most tl hdd 2 out: 4l 2nd & rdn whn fell last)		**F**	10/11[1]	—	—
				(SP 116.0%)	**8 Rn**	

6m 15.1 (5.10) CSF £31.88 TOTE £3.10: £1.60 £3.10 £2.10 (£28.10) OWNER Mr Robert Ogden (PENRITH) BRED Mrs D. A. Whitaker

3790 Real Tonic, well handled, sailed into the lead two out and looked in command when his task was simplified as his nearest rival fell at the last. (5/2)
1344 Tall Measure put up a fair first effort over fences here, but he never had a hope with the winner. (14/1)
802 German Legend is basically moderate but is the type to pick up a race or two this time of year, when they become less competitive. (16/1)
3975 Cool Weather (IRE) has ability but doesn't always put it to full use. (25/1)
3724* Miss Colette is slow but sure and was left wanting for speed over the last six fences. (14/1: 10/1-16/1)
2788 Mamica (10/1: 8/1-12/1)
3792 Coqui Lane was the only one good enough to make a race of it with the winner, but he looked held in second when falling at the last. (10/11)

4078 PAT DE CLERMONT H'CAP CHASE (0-110) (5-Y.O+) (Class E)
3-30 (3-35) **3m 1f (19 fncs)** £3,217.60 (£974.80: £476.40: £227.20) GOING minus 0.60 sec per fur (F)

				SP	RR	SF
3560[2]	**Ask Me Later (IRE) (85)** (MrsSCBradburne) **8-10-3** GCahill (in tch: outpcd 12th: hdwy 4 out: led last: styd on strly)	—	1	3/1[1]	99	—
3911*	**Nijway (82)** (MABarnes) **7-10-0** 5x BStorey (a chsng ldrs: hrd rdn 3 out: kpt on: nt pce to chal)	4	2	9/2[3]	93	—
3094P	**Hurricane Andrew (IRE) (86)** (JAMoore) **9-10-4** NSmith (lw: mde most tl hdd last: no ex)	1¼	3	20/1	97	—
3094[5]	**Forward Glen (82)** (PCheesbrough) **10-10-0b** ASSmith (outpcd 13th: styd on fr last: n.d)	nk	4	14/1	92	—
3911[2]	**Gale Ahead (IRE) (95)** (GMMoore) **7-10-13** MFoster (w ldrs: effrt 3 out: wknd appr last)	6	5	7/2[2]	102	—
3444[5]	**Banntown Bill (IRE) (99)** (MCPipe) **8-11-3v** TReed (chsd ldrs: drvn along fr 12th: wknd 4 out)	3½	6	5/1	103	—
3792[4]	**Whaat Fettle (110)** (GRichards) **12-12-0** MMoloney (w ldr tl wknd 3 out)	29	7	13/2	96	—
3882[7]	**Festival Fancy (82)** (BMactaggart) **10-9-11**(3) GLee (a bhd: fell 4 out)		F	33/1	—	—
3645[3]	**Snook Point (86)** (DALamb) **10-10-4**ow4 JCallaghan (lw: prom tl p.u bef 9th: b.b.v)		P	33/1	—	—

(SP 112.7%) **9 Rn**

6m 18.7 (8.70) CSF £15.01 CT £200.52 TOTE £3.60: £1.10 £2.30 £6.00 (£9.70) Trio £57.50 OWNER Mr Timothy Hardie (CUPAR) BRED Andrew Conway
LONG HANDICAP Forward Glen 9-5 Nijway 9-6 Festival Fancy 8-12 Snook Point 9-7
OFFICIAL EXPLANATION **Snook Point: bled from the nose.**
3560 Ask Me Later (IRE) found the pace on this ground a bit too quick with a circuit to go but he is honest and, sticking to the task, won going away. (3/1)
3911* Nijway always seems to do things the hard way but, to his credit, he does respond to pressure and was keeping on really well at the end. (9/2)
2179* Hurricane Andrew (IRE), after almost two months off, was turned out looking superb here and ran well, suggesting that there is another race to be picked up. (20/1)
3094 Forward Glen is a moody customer who was never giving it his best shot here. (14/1)
3911 Gale Ahead (IRE) had his chances but he cracked going to the last when things became too competitive. (7/2)
3444 Banntown Bill (IRE) was off the bit with a circuit to go and soon decided it was not for him. (5/1)
3792 Whaat Fettle has lost his sparkle at the moment and was wisely not knocked about here and should benefit from it. (13/2: 9/2-7/1)

4079 E. SCARTH & SON H'CAP HURDLE (0-125) (4-Y.O+) (Class D)
4-00 (4-04) **2m 110y (8 hdls)** £2,788.00 (£844.00: £412.00: £196.00) GOING minus 0.60 sec per fur (F)

				SP	RR	SF
3912[2]	**Well Appointed (IRE) (94)** (BMactaggart) **8-9-12**(3) GLee (chsd clr ldrs: hdwy 5th: led flat: rdn & r.o)	—	1	2/1[2]	78	11
3691[9]	**Killbally Boy (IRE) (93)** (HowardJohnson) **7-9-7**(7) CMcCormack (lw: led & sn clr: hdd flat: rdn & nt qckn)	2	2	7/1	75?	8
1852[5]	**Done Well (USA) (118)** (PMonteith) **5-11-11** BStorey (hld up: effrt 2 out: eased whn btn flat)	17	3	11/10[1]	84	17
	Astraleon (IRE) (106) (RAllan) **9-10-6**(7) SMelrose (hld up: hdwy 5th: wknd 2 out)	30	4	9/2[3]	43	—

(SP 111.6%) **4 Rn**

3m 44.5 (-1.50) CSF £12.14 TOTE £2.40: (£9.10) OWNER Drumlanrig Racing (HAWICK) BRED Oldtown Bloodstock Holdings Ltd
LONG HANDICAP Killbally Boy (IRE) 9-1
3912 Well Appointed (IRE), off a decent mark here, this fast ground specialist took this fairly uncompetitive event in determined style at the last. (2/1)
3326 Killbally Boy (IRE) looked tremendously well and enjoyed himself out in front, and considering he was 13lb out of the handicap this was a reasonable effort. (7/1: 5/1-8/1)
1852 Done Well (USA) was bathed in sweat during the race and was most disappointing. (11/10: 11/8-evens)
Astraleon (IRE), having his first run for fourteen months, obviously needed it. (9/2: 3/1-5/1)

4080 STEFES CHAMPION HUNTERS' CHASE (5-Y.O+) (Class H)
4-30 (4-30) **3m 1f (19 fncs)** £2,736.00 (£828.00: £404.00: £192.00) GOING minus 0.60 sec per fur (F)

				SP	RR	SF
	Now Young Man (IRE) (MrsASwinbank) **8-11-7**(7) MrChrisWilson (chsd ldrs: hit 7th: outpcd whn hmpd after 9th: lost tch 14th: hdwy 2 out: r.o wl to ld fnl 50y)	—	1	13/2	112	3
3793[2]	**Royal Jester** (CStorey) **13-11-9**(5) MrCStorey (chsd ldr: outpcd 3 out: styd on appr last: ev ch fnl f: kpt on)	½	2	13/8[1]	112	3
3609[2]	**Kushbaloo** (CParker) **12-12-0**(7) MrAParker (led: blnd 2 out: ct fnl 50y)	2½	3	5/2[2]	117	8
	Dark Dawn (MrsJMNewitt) **13-12-0**(7) MissLornaFoxton (hld up: hdwy & prom 10th: ev ch 2 out: wknd last)	19	4	4/1[3]	105	—
3712[2]	**Little Wenlock** (MrsDSCGibson) **13-11-9**(5) MrsVJackson (prom tl p.u lame after 9th: dead)		P	8/1	—	—

(SP 111.1%) **5 Rn**

6m 22.5 (12.50) CSF £16.64 TOTE £9.30: £6.10 £1.00 (£11.30) OWNER Mr Grant Mitchell (RICHMOND) BRED Richard Fitzgerald
Now Young Man (IRE) has been off the track for well over a year. After being hampered and getting completely detached, he proved determined to get up late on but in doing so did have a hard race. (13/2)
3793 Royal Jester always has a chance but he lacks any turn of foot and needs to be forcing the pace throughout. (13/8)
Dark Dawn was stretching his stamina here and, when it came down to a struggle from the last, he was found wanting. (4/1)
3712 Little Wenlock (8/1: 5/1-9/1)

4081 CROALL BRYSON H'CAP HURDLE (0-120) (4-Y.O+) (Class D)
5-20 (5-23) **2m 6f 110y (11 hdls)** £2,840.00 (£860.00: £420.00: £200.00) GOING minus 0.60 sec per fur (F)

				SP	RR	SF
3827[4]	**Rascally (87)** (MissLCSiddall) **7-10-10** MFoster (led fr 4th: hld on wl flat)	—	1	8/1	67	14
3646[7]	**Dockmaster (85)** (MissMKMilligan) **6-10-8** ASSmith (a chsng ldrs: ev ch fr 2 out: kpt on wl)	¾	2	7/1	65	12
3794*	**Cash Box (IRE) (87)** (TJCarr) **9-10-10** NSmith (hld up: hdwy 4 out: ev ch flat: kpt on)	½	3	3/1[1]	66	13
3885[6]	**Old Habits (IRE) (100)** (JLEyre) **8-11-2**(7) CElliott (a chsng ldrs: ev ch last: r.o one pce)	2	4	9/2[2]	78	25

	Horse / details	Dist	Pos	SP	RR	SF
3484[4]	**Master of Troy (99)** (CParker) **9-11-8** DParker (bhd: outpcd ½-wy: styd on fr 3 out: nrst fin)	2½	**5**	20/1	75	22
3883[7]	**Allerby (77)** (JLGoulding) **9-9-9**(5) BGrattan (lw: bhd: hit 3rd: n.d)	26	**6**	25/1	34	—
1704[P]	**Mullingar (IRE) (86)** (MissZAGreen) **8-10-9** KJohnson (led to 4th: chsd ldrs tl outpcd 7th: n.d after)	¾	**7**	100/1	43	—
3825[2]	**Maitre de Musique (FR) (94)** (MartinTodhunter) **6-10-10**(7) CMcCormack (trckd ldrs: ev ch 2 out: sn rdn & wknd)	5	**8**	9/2 2	47	—
3827[6]	**Master Hyde (USA) (101)** (RAllan) **8-11-10** BStorey (stdy hdwy 4 out: chsng ldrs whn fell 2 out)		**F**	5/1 3	—	—

(SP 111.2%) **9 Rn**

5m 17.3 (0.30) CSF £53.15 CT £181.96 TOTE £8.10: £2.20 £1.90 £1.20 (£20.40) Trio £37.50 OWNER Mr J. Townson (TADCASTER) BRED G. Edwards

LONG HANDICAP Allerby 9-12

3827 Rascally came good at this time of year last season and, on the ground she loves, proved very resolute. (8/1)

3358 Dockmaster is running well and kept battling away, and will obviously find another race or two. (7/1)

3794* Cash Box (IRE), up 9lb for his win last time, put in a sound effort and kept responding to pressure. (3/1: 9/4-7/2)

3885 Old Habits (IRE), always up with the pace, kept plugging away but he lacked a change of gear and was tending to hang in the closing stages. (9/2)

3484 Master of Troy, back to hurdling after an unsuccessful spell over fences, ran with a touch more enthusiasm. (20/1)

3825 Maitre de Musique (FR) had his chances only to run out of fuel in dramatic fashion from the second last. (9/2: op 3/1)

T/Plpt: £83.00 (167.37 Tckts). T/Qdpt: £25.60 (23.62 Tckts) AA

3915-CHEPSTOW (L-H) (Firm)
Wednesday April 9th

WEATHER: fine

4082 BEAGLES NOVICES' HURDLE (4-Y.O+) (Class E)
2-00 (2-01) **2m 110y (8 hdls)** £2,808.00 (£788.00: £384.00) GOING minus 0.59 sec per fur (F)

	Horse / details	Dist	Pos	SP	RR	SF
3898*	**Kinnescash (IRE) (105)** (PBowen) **4-11-0** MAFitzgerald (lw: mde all: rdn appr 2 out: r.o wl)	—	**1**	6/4 2	75	30
3564[3]	**Break the Rules (112)** (MCPipe) **5-11-12** APMcCoy (lw: hld up & bhd: hdwy 4th: ev ch whn hit 3 out: rdn appr last: no imp)	2	**2**	Evens 1	79	40
	Ami Bleu (FR) (PMooney) **5-11-12** JFTitley (bit bkwd: tk keen hold: hdwy 3rd: ev ch 4 out: wknd appr 2 out)	13	**3**	13/2 3	67	28
3955[P]	**Global Dancer** (LWells) **6-11-0** MRichards (bkwd: hld up: hdwy appr 4th: nt trble ldrs)	12	**4**	50/1	43	4
3601[7]	**Hever Golf Diamond (95)** (JRBest) **4-10-7**(7) MrPO'Keeffe (chsd wnr appr 4 out: sn rdn & wknd)	2½	**5**	20/1	46	1
3927[F]	**Startingo** (RLBrown) **4-10-8** MrACharles-Jones (plld hrd: wnt prom appr 2nd: wknd appr 4 out: t.o)	dist	**6**	100/1	—	—
	Margier (DJWintle) **7-10-9** WMarston (a bhd: t.o fr 4th)	22	**7**	100/1	—	—
3918[7]	**Forest Rose** (MSheppard) **7-10-2**(7) MMoran (mstke 1st: a bhd: t.o fr 4th)	dist	**8**	100/1	—	—
	Bache Dingle (MrsSMJohnson) **6-11-0** AThornton (bit bkwd: nt j.w: lost pl 3rd: t.o whn p.u after 4th)		**P**	100/1	—	—

(SP 114.0%) **9 Rn**

3m 46.2 (-2.80) CSF £3.07 TOTE £2.60: £2.10 £1.00 £3.00 (£1.60) Trio £2.10 OWNER Mr D. R. James (HAVERFORDWEST) BRED Frank Barry

WEIGHT FOR AGE 4yo-6lb

3898* Kinnescash (IRE) was effectively 9lb better off with the favourite than when beaten nearly five lengths on his hurdling debut. (6/4)

3564 Break the Rules, who won the Ladies' Handicap at the Doncaster Lincoln meeting, was 9lb worse off with the winner than when beating him when ridden by a claimer at Taunton in February. (Evens)

Ami Bleu (FR), three times a winner in the French Provinces, had not run since scoring on soft ground last October and will come on for the outing. (13/2)

4083 ANVIL NOVICES' H'CAP CHASE (0-100) (5-Y.O+) (Class E)
2-30 (2-31) **2m 3f 110y (16 fncs)** £3,161.50 (£952.00: £461.00: £215.50) GOING minus 0.59 sec per fur (F)

	Horse / details	Dist	Pos	SP	RR	SF
1763[5]	**Jhal Frezi (67)** (ABarrow) **9-10-10** AThornton (mde virtually all: r.o wl fr 3 out)	—	**1**	7/2 3	84	16
3960[2]	**Full Shilling (USA) (60)** (DLWilliams) **8-9-10**(7) MrSDurack (lw: jnd wnr 3rd: ev ch 4 out: one pce fr 3 out)	8	**2**	100/30 2	70	2
3998[2]	**Mozemo (81)** (MCPipe) **10-11-10b** APMcCoy (hld up: hdwy 10th: 3rd & wkng whn blnd bdly 2 out)	29	**3**	9/4 1	68	—
3852[4]	**Flowing River (USA) (72)** (NRMitchell) **11-11-1** KGaule (lw: hld up: rdn 11th: bhd whn hmpd 4 out: t.o)	7	**4**	7/1	53	—
	Eden Stream (73) (MissLShally) **10-11-2** DLeahy (bkwd: hld up: hit 4th: sme hdwy after 11th: 5th & btn whn fell 4 out)		**F**	20/1	—	—
3934[4]	**Night Fancy (66)** (MrsAMWoodrow) **9-10-9** JAMcCarthy (lw: prom: hit 8th: rdn after 11th: sn bhd: p.u bef 4 out: b.b.v)		**P**	6/1	—	—
3954[P]	**Fattash (USA) (69)** (PMooney) **5-9-12b**(7)ow1 FQuinlan (prom tl wknd 4 out: poor 4th whn blnd & uns rdr last)		**U**	25/1	—	—

(SP 111.5%) **7 Rn**

4m 49.2 (0.20) CSF £13.82 TOTE £6.00: £1.60 £1.90 (£5.70) OWNER Mrs R. T. H. Heeley (BRIDGWATER) BRED R. J. Lyles

WEIGHT FOR AGE 5yo-7lb

OFFICIAL EXPLANATION Night Fancy: bled from the nose.

1763 Jhal Frezi, freshened up by a break, finally lost his maiden tag over hurdles and fences at the eighteenth attempt. He was lame behind on pulling up. (7/2: 5/2-4/1)

3960 Full Shilling (USA) seems more effective at two miles. (100/30)

3998 Mozemo would have finished a more respectable third had he not done the splits at the penultimate fence. (9/4: 6/4-5/2)

4084 FARRIER H'CAP HURDLE (0-135) (4-Y.O+) (Class C)
3-00 (3-02) **2m 4f 110y (11 hdls)** £3,533.50 (£1,063.00: £514.00: £239.50) GOING minus 0.59 sec per fur (F)

	Horse / details	Dist	Pos	SP	RR	SF
2771[P]	**El Don (105)** (MJRyan) **5-11-8** KGaule (plld hrd: a gng wl: led after 7th: clr whn mstke 3 out: easily)	—	**1**	5/2 2	91+	51
3156[3]	**Glengarrif Girl (IRE) (107)** (MCPipe) **7-11-10v** APMcCoy (led 2nd: rdn & hdd after 7th: no imp fr 3 out)	6	**2**	6/5 1	88	48
3962*	**Ross Dancer (IRE) (90)** (JSMoore) **5-10-4**(3) 5x JMagee (led to 2nd: dropped rr 5th: rallied appr 4 out: hrd rdn 3 out: one pce)	8	**3**	4/1 3	65	25
3920[F]	**Call My Guest (IRE) (106)** (REPeacock) **7-11-9** MAFitzgerald (hld up: rdn appr 4 out: wknd 3 out)	7	**4**	11/2	76	36

(SP 109.4%) **4 Rn**

4m 39.9 (-7.10) CSF £5.60 TOTE £2.90 (£2.20) OWNER Mr Don Morris (NEWMARKET) BRED Ian Hunter

1791 El Don, rested after disappointing last time, found no problems with this longer trip. (5/2)
3156 Glengarrif Girl (IRE) needs three miles and could never get the winner off the bridle. (6/5: evens-6/4)
3962* Ross Dancer (IRE) was another dropping back from three miles. (4/1)

4085 OSTLER H'CAP CHASE (0-120) (5-Y.O+) (Class D)

3-30 (3-30) **3m (18 fncs)** £4,175.50 (£1,168.00: £566.50) GOING minus 0.59 sec per fur (F)

	Horse	Dist	Pos	SP	RR	SF
3899*	**Black Church (104)** (RRowe) **11-11-10** DO'Sullivan (hld up & plld hrd: hdwy 8th: led on bit 5 out: pushed out)	—	1	6/4[1]	114	3
3961[3]	**Danger Baby (98)** (DLWilliams) **7-10-11**(7) MrSDurack (chsd ldr: led 9th to 5 out: rdn & ev ch 2 out: r.o one pce)	2	2	7/4[2]	107	—
3797[4]	**Elite Governor (IRE) (82)** (NMLampard) **8-9-11**(5)ow1 ChrisWebb (led to 9th: wknd 12th: lft poor 3rd 2 out)	dist	3	11/2	—	—
3905[4]	**Linden's Lotto (IRE) (98)** (JWhite) **8-11-4** JRKavanagh (lw: hld up & plld hrd: hdwy 8th: rdn appr 3 out: cl 3rd whn fell 2 out)		F	9/2[3]	—	—
				(SP 109.9%)	**4 Rn**	

6m 2.4 (9.40) CSF £4.30 TOTE £1.90 (£1.60) OWNER Dr B. Alexander (PULBOROUGH) BRED A. E. Hanbidge
3899* Black Church completed a hat-trick in four-runner affairs despite being 7lb higher this time. (6/4)
3961 Danger Baby was playing second fiddle to the winner all the way up the long home straight. (7/4)
3905 Linden's Lotto (IRE), dropped 6lb, would definitely not have beaten the winner. (9/2)

4086 COURT (S) HURDLE (4,5,6 & 7-Y.O) (Class G)

4-00 (4-00) **2m 110y (8 hdls)** £2,038.00 (£568.00: £274.00) GOING minus 0.59 sec per fur (F)

	Horse	Dist	Pos	SP	RR	SF
3985[5]	**Sheecky (72)** (BAMcMahon) **6-10-9**(5) SRyan (a.p: led 3 out: drvn out)	—	1	12/1	67?	33
3940[2]	**Theme Arena (88)** (MCPipe) **4-10-8** APMcCoy (lw: led to 3 out: sn swtchd rt: rallied after 2 out: ev ch whn wnt lft & nt fluent last: r.o)	1	2	10/11[1]	66	26
3997[2]	**Quaker Waltz (74)** (JCTuck) **7-10-9** RBellamy (lw: prom: outpcd appr 4 out: styd on fr 2 out)	9	3	5/1[3]	52	18
4006[7]	**Halham Tarn (IRE) (88)** (HJManners) **7-11-5** SCurran (prom tl rdn & wknd appr 3 out)	4	4	16/1	58	24
3933*	**Evezio Rufo (80)** (NPLittmoden) **5-11-5b** KGaule (lw: hld up & bhd: rdn & hdwy appr 4 out: n.d)	3	5	7/2[2]	56	22
3959[4]	**Derrybelle (81)** (DLWilliams) **6-10-7**(7) MrSDurack (a bhd: rdn 4 out: t.o)	dist	6	7/1	—	—
3538[U]	**Chili Heights (72)** (KBishop) **7-11-0v** GTormey (bhd fr 4th: t.o)	4	7	33/1	—	—
1980[P]	**Persian Dawn** (RTPhillips) **4-10-3** AThornton (prom: hit 3rd: wknd appr 4 out: t.o)	28	8	33/1	—	—
3889[P]	**Abbeydoran** (MrsJEHawkins) **6-10-4b**[1](5) DJKavanagh (j.slowly & lost pl 2nd: t.o whn p.u after 4th)		P	25/1	—	—
3818[P]	**Cuillin (65)** (RJSmith) **5-10-9** CMaude (sn bhd: t.o whn p.u bef 4 out)		P	33/1	—	—
				(SP 130.0%)	**10 Rn**	

3m 45.6 (-3.40) CSF £24.16 TOTE £13.30: £2.50 £1.30 £1.20 (£11.40) Trio £14.50 OWNER Mrs Angela Beard (TAMWORTH) BRED Mrs A. J. Beard
WEIGHT FOR AGE 4yo-6lb
Sld APBrady 6,800 gns
3985 Sheecky would have been 16lb better off with the runner-up on official ratings had this been a handicap. (12/1: 8/1-14/1)
3940 Theme Arena found landing flat-footed at the final flight putting paid to her fight-back. (10/11: evens-5/4)
3997 Quaker Waltz did not appear suited to this slightly shorter trip. (5/1: 7/2-11/2)
3933* Evezio Rufo (7/2: 5/2-4/1)
3959 Derrybelle (7/1: 5/1-8/1)

4087 EARTHSTOPPERS HUNTERS' CHASE (6-Y.O+) (Class H)

4-30 (4-30) **3m (18 fncs)** £1,702.00 (£472.00: £226.00) GOING minus 0.59 sec per fur (F)

	Horse	Dist	Pos	SP	RR	SF
3765[4]	**Some-Toy** (JohnSquire) **11-11-8**(7) MissLBlackford (lw: hld up: hdwy 11th: led after 5 out: shkn up flat: r.o wl)	—	1	5/1	106	14
4022[2]	**Rusty Bridge** (MrsSMJohnson) **10-11-11**(7) MrOMcPhail (lw: led to 10th: outpcd appr 5 out: rallying whn hit 4 out: one pce flat)	4	2	5/2[1]	106	14
3852[3]	**Gambling Royal** (DrPPritchard) **14-11-5**(7) DrPPritchard (tk keen hold: wnt 2nd 4th: led 10th tl after 5 out: wknd appr 2 out)	22	3	4/1[3]	86	—
3490[U]	**What a to Do** (CJRSweeting) **13-11-8**(7) MissLSweeting (prom to 7th: wl bhd fr 9th)	9	4	13/2	83	—
	Catch the Cross (MrsMandyHand) **11-11-5b**(7) MrsAHand (hld up: stdy hdwy appr 8th: effrt appr 5 out: wknd 4 out)	½	5	12/1	79	—
3837[3]	**Sonofagipsy** (JWDufosee) **13-11-5b**[1](7) MrNRMitchell (pushed along 5th: t.o fr 8th)	7	6	3/1[2]	75	—
				(SP 111.3%)	**6 Rn**	

6m (7.00) CSF £16.43 TOTE £9.10: £2.70 £2.20 (£9.20) OWNER Mr John Squire (TORRINGTON) BRED Miss J. Ludwell
Some-Toy came back to his best with a pretty convincing win. (5/1)
4022 Rusty Bridge had the familiar problem of trying to overcome an inadequate trip. (5/2: 7/4-11/4)
3852 Gambling Royal appeared to pull up a little short but seemed alright afterwards. (4/1)

4088 WHIPPERS IN STANDARD OPEN N.H. FLAT RACE (4, 5 & 6-Y.O) (Class H)

5-00 (5-01) **2m 110y** £1,686.00 (£471.00: £228.00)

	Horse	Dist	Pos	SP	RR	SF
3747[5]	**Diamond Hall** (KRBurke) **4-10-12** APMcCoy (hld up & bhd: stdy hdwy 6f out: led on bit 2f out: rdn & r.o wl ins fnl f)	—	1	100/30[2]	55 f	—
3626[10]	**Muallaf (IRE)** (MrsAMWoodrow) **5-11-4** JAMcCarthy (str: w'like: lw: plld hrd: led tl hdd 2f out: rdn & swished tail ins fnl f: no ch w wnr)	6	2	50/1	49 f	—
	Shimmy Dancing (JohnBerry) **4-10-7** KGaule (unf: hld up: hdwy 6f out: one pce fnl 3f)	6	3	5/1	38 f	—
3853[11]	**Born At Kings** (JWhite) **4-10-12** BFenton (w'like: hld up & bhd: hdwy 4f out: nt rch ldrs)	½	4	20/1	43 f	—
	Little Time (BJEckley) **5-10-13** MSharratt (unf: rn v.wd bnd after 3f: hdwy 12f out: one pce fnl 3f)	d.h	4	14/1	38 f	—
	Dancing In Rio (IRE) (TPWalshe) **5-10-6**(7) LSuthern (neat: hdwy 10f out: wknd over 3f out)	5	6	40/1	33 f	—
2012[14]	**Benjamin Jones** (CJHemsley) **5-10-11**(7) MissADudley (lt-f: unf: a bhd)	11	7	33/1	27 f	—
3235[14]	**General Killiney (IRE)** (DJCaro) **5-11-4** JFTitley (unf: plld hrd early: prom over 12f)	¾	8	33/1	27 f	—
3767[4]	**Tommy Tickle** (GMPrice) **5-11-4** JRKavanagh (rn wd bnd after 3f: hdwy 10f out: wknd 5f out)	8	9	9/2[3]	19 f	—
	Ogulla (MissLShally) **5-10-13** DLeahy (lt-f: unf: hdwy 11f out: wknd 6f out)	3	10	33/1	11 f	—
3330[10]	**Dash On By** (MissAStokell) **4-10-12b**[1] GTormey (unf: chsd ldr tl wknd 4f out)	½	11	50/1	16 f	—

				SP		
3808[2]	**Dinky Dora** (JKCresswell) **4-10-7** MAFitzgerald (prom: ev ch over 3f out: sn rdn: 3rd & btn whn wnt lame & virtually p.u over 1f out)	dist	**12**	2/1[1]	—	—

(SP 117.9%) **12 Rn**

3m 48.0 CSF £153.31 TOTE £3.40: £1.70 £14.40 £2.00 (£147.90) Trio £200.70; £115.95 to Hamilton 10/4/97 OWNER Mr R. D. Tudor (WANTAGE) BRED Robert Derek Tudor
WEIGHT FOR AGE 4yo-6lb
3747 Diamond Hall showed why he had been a springer in the market on his debut. (100/30)
3626 Muallaf (IRE) found the winner laughing at him when the chips were down. (50/1)
Shimmy Dancing only finished third because the favourite went wrong. (5/1)
Little Time (14/1: op 6/1)
3767 Tommy Tickle (9/2: op 5/2)
3808 Dinky Dora had already found the winner holding all the aces when she went wrong behind approaching the final furlong. (2/1: 6/4-9/4)

T/Plpt: £49.90 (215.46 Tckts). T/Qdpt: £21.20 (27.59 Tckts) KH

3829-LUDLOW (R-H) (Good to firm, Firm patches, Firm after 2nd race) Wednesday April 9th

WEATHER: fine & sunny

4089 CAYNHAM (S) H'CAP HURDLE (0-90) (4-Y.O+) (Class G)

2-20 (2-20) **2m (9 hdls)** £2,024.00 (£564.00: £272.00) GOING minus 0.65 sec per fur (F)

				SP	RR	SF
2943[9]	**Kalzari (USA) (75)** (AWCarroll) **12-11-1**(7) MrAWintle (bit bkwd: hld up & bhd: hdwy appr 3 out: led last: drvn out)	—	**1**	12/1	59	11
3959[3]	**Captain Tandy (IRE) (70)** (CSmith) **8-11-3** PMcLoughlin (swtg: hld up: hdwy appr 3 out: styd on u.p flat)	1½	**2**	12/1	53	5
3896[6]	**Against The Clock (53)** (PBowen) **5-10-0** RJohnson (led to 3rd: led 4th to last: rdn & no ex flat)	½	**3**	20/1	35	—
3921*	**Blotoft (74)** (SGollings) **5-11-7** 7x NWilliamson (lw: a.p: ev ch 2 out: rdn appr last: one pce)	4	**4**	11/2[2]	52	4
3985[P]	**Wordsmith (IRE) (77)** (JLHarris) **7-11-10** RSupple (led 3rd to next: rdn & outpcd appr 3 out: n.d afterwards)	2	**5**	20/1	53	5
3743[5]	**Britannia Mills (70)** (MCChapman) **6-11-3** WWorthington (chsd ldrs: outpcd ½-wy: rallied appr 3 out: nt rch ldrs)	1¼	**6**	16/1	45	—
2882[12]	**Tee Tee Too (IRE) (70)** (AWCarroll) **5-11-3** DWalsh (hld up: hdwy 4th: rdn 3 out: sn btn)	1	**7**	16/1	44	—
3205[6]	**Ecu de France (IRE) (58)** (PCRitchens) **7-10-5v** SFox (swtg: prom tl wknd appr 3 out)	¾	**8**	16/1	31	—
1857[5]	**Fenian Court (IRE) (75)** (PDEvans) **6-11-8** TJMurphy (hld up: hdwy 6th: rdn & wknd appr 2 out: t.o)	6	**9**	3/1[1]	42	—
2664[7]	**Bold Charlie (53)** (SMellor) **5-10-0b**[1] NMann (a bhd: t.o)	4	**10**	33/1	16	—
3921[2]	**Ruth's Gamble (71)** (MrsLCJewell) **9-10-11v**(7) XAizpuru (prom tl wknd appr 6th: t.o)	½	**11**	3/1[1]	34	—
4002[5]	**Glenmavis (75)** (DrPPritchard) **10-11-8** DrPPritchard (hld up: effrt appr 3 out: wknd 2 out: t.o)	1½	**12**	50/1	36	—
3829[4]	**Saafi (IRE) (67)** (RJBaker) **6-11-0b** VSlattery (swtg: a bhd: t.o: b.b.v)	3½	**13**	10/1[3]	25	—

(SP 121.9%) **13 Rn**

3m 39.0 (2.00) CSF £129.69 CT £2,605.54 TOTE £15.30: £3.90 £3.50 £3.20 (£60.40) Trio £217.90; £15.35 to Hamilton 10/4/97 OWNER Mr Dennis Deacon (WORCESTER) BRED H. H. Aga Khan
LONG HANDICAP Against The Clock 9-13 Bold Charlie 9-11
No bid
OFFICIAL EXPLANATION **Saafi (IRE): bled from the nose.**
1060 Kalzari (USA), winner of his only previous race in the 1991/92 season, belied his somewhat burly looks after a two-month break and showed his younger rivals the way home after taking command at the last. (12/1: op 8/1)
3959 Captain Tandy (IRE), well suited to fast ground, responded willingly to a more patient ride and, with a stiffer test of stamina, may well have made it. (12/1: op 8/1)
17 Against The Clock, who has trained up very light and looked to be feeling the ground, tried his best to gallop his rivals into submission but the principals proved too strong for him on the flat. (20/1)
3921* Blotoft, attempting to follow up after opening his account at the end of last month, travelled well in behind the leaders until feeling the strain and dropping away between the last two. (11/2: 4/1-6/1)
648 Wordsmith (IRE) is a law unto himself and looked out of it when losing his pitch on the approach to the straight. He decided to run on again once in line for home and he has got the ability to win when the mood takes him. (20/1)
Britannia Mills is only small and dropped towards the rear down the back straight, but she rallied on the home turn if unable to go through with her run. (16/1)
1857 Fenian Court (IRE) was ill at ease on this lively ground and that, plus the lack a recent run, was beginning to tell early in the home straight. (3/1)
3921 Ruth's Gamble has had some hardish races recently and the way he dropped out of contention at the end of the back straight would suggest he needs a break. (3/1)

4090 BUNDY (UK) H'CAP CHASE (0-125) (5-Y.O+) (Class D)

2-50 (2-50) **2m 4f (17 fncs)** £3,387.50 (£1,025.00: £500.00: £237.50) GOING minus 0.65 sec per fur (F)

				SP	RR	SF
3969[U]	**Imperial Vintage (IRE) (118)** (MissVenetiaWilliams) **7-11-10** NWilliamson (swtg: j.w: chsd ldr: led 8th tl appr 10th: led 11th: drew clr appr 2 out)	—	**1**	10/11[1]	123+	38
3936*	**Raba Riba (128)** (JLSpearing) **12-12-6** 6x VSlattery (j.w: led to 8th: led appr 10th to 11th: rdn appr 4 out: wknd 2 out)	13	**2**	2/1[2]	123	38
3897*	**Fenwick (94)** (RJHodges) **10-10-0** TDascombe (lw: outpcd: poor 3rd fr 4th: no imp)	dist	**3**	4/1[3]	—	—
4072[2]	**Pandora's Prize (94)** (TWall) **11-10-0** TEley (outpcd: a t.o)	dist	**4**	33/1	—	—

(SP 108.7%) **4 Rn**

4m 48.3 (0.10 under best) (-3.70) CSF £2.94 TOTE £1.70 (£2.40) OWNER Mr David Williams (HEREFORD) BRED W. J. Mernagh
LONG HANDICAP Fenwick 9-5 Pandora's Prize 7-8
3969 Imperial Vintage (IRE) got back to winning ways with his ninth success of the season and it came as no surprise that he shaved the track record in the process. (10/11: 4/5-evens)
3936* Raba Riba had a head to head with the winner after a pace more suitable to hurdles and, feeling the strain on the home turn, eventually called enough at the second last. He is in fine form and there are more prizes to be gained before the season ends. (2/1)

4091 D.J. PROFILES NOVICES' CONDITIONAL H'CAP HURDLE (0-100) (4-Y.O+) (Class E)

3-20 (3-21) **2m 5f 110y (11 hdls)** £2,528.00 (£708.00: £344.00) GOING minus 0.65 sec per fur (F)

				SP	RR	SF
3977^{4}	**Piper's Rock (IRE) (76)** (GBBalding) **6-11-2** ABates (a.p: led appr 3 out: hit next: rdn & styd on strly)	—	1	3/1^{1}	52+	22
3932*	**Kymin (IRE) (91)** (JMBradley) **5-12-3** 7x LAspell (hld up in rr: rdn appr 8th: hdwy to chse wnr 3 out: rdn & one pce appr last)	4	2	4/1^{3}	64	34
3985^{11}	**Saltis (IRE) (75)** (ALForbes) **5-10-8**(7) EGreehy (hld up: hdwy 8th: nt rchd ldrs)	6	3	16/1	44	14
1814^{7}	**Shannon Lad (IRE) (74)** (AWCarroll) **7-11-0** DFortt (hld up: lost pl 6th: hdwy appr 3 out: nrst fin)	3	4	16/1	40	10
4073^{4}	**Lady of Mine (61)** (PBowen) **7-9-12**(3) LCummins (led tl appr 3 out: sn rdn: one pce)	½	5	14/1	27	—
3891^{P}	**Miramare (60)** (RJHodges) **7-9-8**(6) JHarris (mstke 1st: prom tl wknd appr 3 out)	5	6	50/1	22	—
3834^{2}	**Fastini Gold (75)** (RJPrice) **5-10-12**(3) XAizpuru (hld up & bhd: t.o ½-wy: sme late hdwy: n.d)	1½	7	7/2^{2}	36	6
3997^{4}	**Lovelark (60)** (RLee) **8-9-11**(3) MGriffiths (trckd ldrs to 8th: wknd appr 3 out)	3	8	20/1	19	—
3345^{7}	**Well Armed (IRE) (84)** (JJO'Neill) **6-11-4**(6) RMcGrath (hld up: effrt 8th: sn no imp: t.o)	9	9	11/2	36	6
157^{P}	**Credit Call (IRE) (60)** (RGBrazington) **9-10-0** RMassey (lost tch 7th: t.o)	18	10	66/1	—	—
3473^{6}	**Balmoral Princess (80)** (JHPeacock) **4-10-10b**(3) OBurrows (a bhd: rdn 5th: t.o & p.u bef 7th)		P	33/1	—	—
				(SP 112.2%)	**11 Rn**	

4m 59.0 (-2.00) CSF £13.08 CT £143.94 TOTE £3.60: £2.10 £2.40 £5.30 (£9.60) Trio £43.80 OWNER Mrs G. B. Balding (ANDOVER) BRED Peader McCoy

LONG HANDICAP Lovelark 9-9 Credit Call (IRE) 9-9

WEIGHT FOR AGE 4yo-7lb

3977 Piper's Rock (IRE) came good at the first time of asking over this more suitable trip with a very comfortable success, and this could just be the start. (3/1)

3932* Kymin (IRE) made relentless progress and, with the winner, began to draw away from the rest entering the straight but the weight concession proved just too much and her measure had been taken approaching the last. (4/1: 3/1-9/2)

1814 Saltis (IRE) was never able to get close enough to cause concern but he did stay on and there could be a small race in him. (16/1)

1065 Shannon Lad (IRE), returning after a four-month break, ran in snatches but he did stay on well in the latter stages and, with his stable striking form, he is certainly capable of adding to the score. (16/1)

4073 Lady of Mine, who has been running over extended trips, did her best to make this a true test of stamina but her run had come to an end early in the straight. (14/1)

3834 Fastini Gold (7/2: op 11/2)

Well Armed (IRE) ran no race at all and it could be that such fast ground is not for him. (11/2: op 3/1)

4092 BUNDY (EUROPE) NOVICES' CHASE (5-Y.O+) (Class E)

3-50 (3-50) **2m (13 fncs)** £2,851.25 (£860.00: £417.50: £196.25) GOING minus 0.65 sec per fur (F)

				SP	RR	SF
2940^{3}	**Inch Emperor (IRE)** (AWCarroll) **7-11-7** TJMurphy (j.lft: led & sn clr: hdd 3 out: led last: jst hld on)	—	1	13/8^{1}	87	—
3278^{4}	**Snowy Petrel (IRE) (84)** (KCBailey) **5-10-7b** SMcNeill (lw: a.p: slt ld 3 out: hdd last: swtchd rt & str run flat: jst failed)	hd	2	2/1^{2}	80	—
3931*	**Tenayestelign (79)** (DMarks) **9-11-9** SWynne (hld up: hdwy 9th: rdn & one pce fr 3 out)	8	3	4/1^{3}	81	—
3682^{4}	**Whod of Thought It (IRE)** (PRChamings) **6-11-0** VSlattery (lw: chsd ldrs: j.slowly 7th: rdn & wknd appr 4 out: t.o)	dist	4	12/1	—	—
3833^{P}	**Aeolian (63)** (MissPMWhittle) **6-11-0** DWalsh (lw: a bhd: t.o fr 8th)	10	5	40/1	—	—
3931^{3}	**Quarter Marker (IRE) (60)** (RLee) **9-11-0** RJohnson (mstke 1st: a.p: ev ch 3 out: rdn & fell next)		F	16/1	—	—
				(SP 107.4%)	**6 Rn**	

3m 57.6 (5.60) CSF £4.51 TOTE £2.20: £1.40 £1.90 (£2.30) OWNER Mr T. V. Cullen (WORCESTER) BRED Catherine O'Brien

WEIGHT FOR AGE 5yo-7lb

2940 Inch Emperor (IRE), taking a big step down in distance, adopted his favourite front-running tactics but was being worn down with every stride on the run in and the line just arrived just in time. (13/8)

3278 Snowy Petrel (IRE), still to get off the mark, may well have done so here had the run-in not been dolled off so far across the track nearing the finish, for he was gaining with every stride when he ran out of room close home. (2/1)

3931* Tenayestelign moved to post like a crab but she got better as she warmed up, only having to admit the leading pair too smart for her from the third last. (4/1)

Quarter Marker (IRE), always in the firing line, disputed the lead three out and he was still a lively contender when falling at the next. (16/1)

4093 SARA HAMILTON-RUSSELL MEMORIAL TROPHY H'CAP HURDLE (0-120) (4-Y.O+) (Class D)

4-20 (4-20) **2m 5f 110y (11 hdls)** £2,723.00 (£824.00: £402.00: £191.00) GOING minus 0.65 sec per fur (F)

				SP	RR	SF
3996*	**Sulawesi (IRE) (101)** (NATwiston-Davies) **4-11-8**(7) 6x MrJGoldstein (lw: mde all: r.o strly fr 2 out)	—	1	3/1^{2}	82	39
3831*	**First Crack (88)** (FJordan) **12-11-9** SWynne (swtg: hld up in rr: smooth hdwy appr 3 out: rdn appr last: nt pce of wnr)	2½	2	5/2^{1}	67	31
3709^{U}	**Moobakkr (USA) (80)** (KAMorgan) **6-11-1** WFry (lw: a.p: chsd wnr fr 8th: rdn & hung rt flat: unable qckn)	nk	3	100/30^{3}	59	23
3980^{2}	**Miss Marigold (89)** (RJHodges) **8-11-10b** TDascombe (lw: hld up: hdwy appr 3 out: rdn & wknd 2 out)	15	4	8/1	57	21
3949^{5}	**Castlebay Lad (65)** (RCurtis) **14-10-0** DMorris (chsd wnr: rdn 6th: wknd appr 3 out: t.o)	dist	5	66/1	—	—
3615^{25}	**Scottish Wedding (83)** (TWall) **7-11-1**(3) RMassey (dropped rr 4th: sn t.o: p.u bef 3 out)		P	4/1	—	—
				(SP 109.3%)	**6 Rn**	

4m 57.6 (-3.40) CSF £9.61 TOTE £3.70: £2.40 £1.80 (£2.80) OWNER Mr Jack Joseph (CHELTENHAM) BRED P. D. Player and Darley Stud Management

LONG HANDICAP Castlebay Lad 8-13

WEIGHT FOR AGE 4yo-7lb

3996* Sulawesi (IRE) had the choice of three engagements today and connections must be congratulated on making the right decision. Again dictating from the front, she had too much pace for her nearest pursuers and won readily. She was well handled. (3/1)

3831* First Crack loomed up as a live threat turning in but she does not find a lot off the bridle and was throwing out distress signals before reaching the last. (5/2)

3709 Moobakkr (USA) showed definite signs of a return to form and may well have gained the runner-up prize had he not hung into the whip on the run-in. (100/30)

3980 Miss Marigold was close enough if good enough entering the straight but, on ground as fast as this, she was struggling to hold her pitch from the penultimate flight. (8/1)

4094 CHASE MEREDITH MEMORIAL TROPHY HUNTERS' CHASE (5-Y.O+) (Class H)
4-50 (4-50) **3m (19 fncs)** £1,481.00 (£416.00: £203.00) GOING minus 0.65 sec per fur (F)

Form	Horse	Dist	Pos	SP	RR	SF
3984[2]	**My Nominee** (DENicholls) **9-11-12b**(7) MrRBurton (j.w: led to 2nd: led 3rd to 3 out: rdn to ld last: all out)	—	1	11/4[2]	110	41
3469[3]	**Cape Cottage** (DJCaro) **13-11-12**(7) MrAPhillips (chsd ldrs: led 3 out to last: rallied nr fin)	hd	2	9/1[3]	110	41
3799*	**Fox Pointer** (MrsLTJEvans) **12-12-0**(5) MrJJukes (lw: a.p: 2nd whn blnd 7th: outpcd appr 2 out)	12	3	7/4[1]	102	33
	Candle Glow (PHutchinson) **9-11-7**(7) MrSMorris (bit bkwd: led 2nd to 3rd: wknd appr 15th)	5	4	10/1	94?	25
3498[2]	**Wild Illusion** (MissJenniferPidgeon) **13-11-12**(7) MrFHutsby (lw: sn wl bhd: hdwy appr 12th: wknd 15th: p.u & dsmntd 4 out)		P	11/4[2]	—	—
3055[P]	**Judy Line** (GWLewis) **8-11-2**(7) MrSShinton (sn outpcd: t.o fr ½-wy: p.u bef 4 out)		P	33/1	—	—

(SP 111.7%) **6 Rn**

5m 57.6 (-2.40) CSF £22.30 TOTE £3.90: £1.90 £2.40 (£17.00) OWNER Mr D. E. Nicholls (WREXHAM) BRED Dr O. Zawawi

3984 My Nominee won this courtesy of a fine ride with strength from the saddle the deciding factor close home. (11/4)

3469 Cape Cottage has won his only race under Rules over this course and distance and he did appear to be travelling best between the last two. In an all out battle to the post, he was always going to come out second best. (9/1)

3799* Fox Pointer could never get his own way and, though he was always a threat, he was found wanting when the race really developed. (7/4)

Candle Glow was another who needs to dictate but she was denied that role here and gave up the fight at the end of the back straight. (10/1)

3498 Wild Illusion (11/4: 2/1-3/1)

4095 BURWARTON NOVICES' HURDLE (4-Y.O+) (Class E)
5-20 (5-20) **2m (9 hdls)** £2,248.00 (£628.00: £304.00) GOING minus 0.65 sec per fur (F)

Form	Horse	Dist	Pos	SP	RR	SF
3564[7]	**Percy Braithwaite (IRE) (100)** (MissPMWhittle) **5-10-13**(7) MrJGoldstein (a.p: led 6th: rdn & r.o wl)	—	1	7/2[2]	72	14
3075[6]	**Name of Our Father (USA) (100)** (PBowen) **4-11-0** RJohnson (a.p: ev ch appr 3 out: rdn & one pce appr last)	3½	2	2/1[1]	69	5
3820[4]	**Lucky Archer** (PJHobbs) **4-10-8** NWilliamson (bit bkwd: hld up: hdwy appr 6th: rdn 2 out: one pce)	3½	3	2/1[1]	59	—
3951[3]	**Moonlight Escapade (IRE) (73)** (RJHodges) **6-11-0** VSlattery (led to 6th: rdn & outpcd appr 3 out)	15	4	14/1	44	—
1781[3]	**Poppy's Dream** (JWharton) **7-10-6**(3) MrRThornton (bit bkwd: trckd ldrs tl outpcd 5th: n.d after)	1	5	9/1[3]	38	—
3918[6]	**Baron Hrabovsky** (GThorner) **4-10-8b** BPowell (hld up & bhd: t.o fr 6th)	20	6	66/1	23	—
3946[8]	**Molonys Dram** (JLHarris) **6-11-0** RSupple (mstkes: lost pl 4th: sn t.o)	25	7	50/1	—	—

(SP 109.0%) **7 Rn**

3m 37.9 (0.90) CSF £9.27 TOTE £4.70: £2.40 £2.20 (£3.30) OWNER Glass Pig Racing Syndicate (LEDBURY) BRED J. G. O'Brien in Ireland
WEIGHT FOR AGE 4yo-6lb

2566* Percy Braithwaite (IRE) scored his second success over course and distance this year with a very easily gained win and this useful winner on the Flat has taken well to hurdles. (7/2)

3075 Name of Our Father (USA), poised to challenge on the approach to the third-last flight, lacked a turn of speed when let down and from then on the winner always had his measure. (2/1)

3820 Lucky Archer, still with a bit left to work on, did not stride out with any freedom but he moved easily into contention entering the straight and was only shaken off approaching the last. He should be able to win races but it is doubtful if he will get suitable ground at this late stage of the season. (2/1: op 5/4)

3951 Moonlight Escapade (IRE) adopted more forceful tactics on this occasion but he probably did too much too soon for he was in trouble on the long home turn. (14/1)

1781 Poppy's Dream, on her hurdling debut, lost her place halfway down the back straight. She did stay on again in the latter stages but was never a threat and a much longer trip is what this bumper winner needs. (9/1)

T/Plpt: £289.00 (34.33 Tckts). T/Qdpt: £13.50 (62.11 Tckts) IM

3717-FONTWELL (Fig. 8) (Good to firm, Firm patches)
Thursday April 10th
Race 1: 2nd last flight omitted.
WEATHER: sunny & warm

4096 FONTWELL PARK (S) H'CAP HURDLE (0-95) (4-Y.O+) (Class G)
2-10 (2-11) **2m 6f 110y (10 hdls)** £1,941.60 (£537.60: £256.80) GOING minus 0.22 sec per fur (G)

Form	Horse	Dist	Pos	SP	RR	SF
3811[6]	**Aldwick Colonnade (60)** (MDIUsher) **10-10-2**ow2 WMcFarland (hdwy appr 2 out: led appr last: r.o wl)	—	1	14/1	40	—
3958[7]	**Baylord Prince (IRE) (59)** (MrsJAEwer) **9-9-12**(3) SophieMitchell (lw: rdn appr 2 out: hdwy appr last: r.o wl flat)	1	2	8/1	38	—
3892[5]	**Its Grand (70)** (PCRitchens) **8-10-12** SFox (led to 3 out: lost pl 2 out: r.o one pce flat)	1½	3	9/2[2]	48	—
3892[P]	**Nick the Dreamer (78)** (WGMTurner) **12-11-6** RDunwoody (lw: w ldr: led 3 out tl appr last: one pce)	3	4	11/1	54	—
3806[P]	**Tug Your Forelock (62)** (GFJohnsonHoughton) **6-10-4** AThornton (hdwy 7th: ev ch appr last: sn wknd)	5	5	9/1	35	—
3604[2]	**Roger's Pal (75)** (PEccles) **10-11-3** DGallagher (a bhd)	7	6	5/1[3]	43	—
3617[P]	**Charlie Parrot (IRE) (82)** (MCPipe) **7-11-10** APMcCoy (hdwy 5th: 3rd whn p.u bef 6th: dead)		P	100/30[1]	—	—
3735[5]	**Across the Bow (USA) (64)** (AJKDunn) **7-10-6** GTormey (hld up: rdn 2 out: sn wknd: p.u bef last: lame)		P	12/1	—	—
3085[P]	**Fashion Leader (IRE) (58)** (CWeedon) **6-10-0** MRichards (a bhd: t.o whn p.u bef 8th)		P	33/1	—	—
	Inchydoney Boy (IRE) (58) (TPMcGovern) **8-9-7**(7) MBatchelor (uns rdr bef s: 3rd whn blnd & uns rdr 2nd)		U	20/1	—	—

(SP 109.4%) **10 Rn**

5m 32.0 (16.00) CSF £101.47 CT £494.69 TOTE £14.40: £3.20 £1.80 £1.70 (£24.60) Trio £47.50 OWNER Midweek Racing (WANTAGE) BRED Home Stud Ltd
LONG HANDICAP Aldwick Colonnade 9-13 Fashion Leader (IRE) 9-7 Inchydoney Boy (IRE) 9-6
No bid

Aldwick Colonnade is getting on in years and appreciated the longer trip which made up for losing some of her speed. Moving into the lead approaching the final flight, she kept on well and was not going to be caught in time. (14/1: 10/1-16/1)

Baylord Prince (IRE) ran his best race for a very long time but, despite running on strongly in the straight, found the line always coming too soon. (8/1)

2088 Its Grand, who may well not have stayed last time out, decided to set the pace over this shorter trip. Collared at the first hurdle in the back straight, he got out-paced turning for home but did stay on again from the last to take third prize. (9/2)

1528 Nick the Dreamer has been very disappointing this season and consequently has been dropped 19lb since his last handicap run back in November. Looking in tremendous shape in the paddock, he ran much better in this very bad race and, disputing the lead from the start, showed with a definite advantage in the back straight for the final time. Collared approaching the final flight, he could then only plod on at one pace. (11/1: 6/1-12/1)
1814 Tug Your Forelock, reverting back to hurdles, appeared to be going well and had every chance early in the straight before tiring. (9/1)
3735 Across the Bow (USA) (12/1: 8/1-14/1)

4097 KYBO MAIDEN HURDLE (I) (4-Y.O+) (Class F)

2-40 (2-42) **2m 2f 110y (9 hdls)** £1,824.80 (£502.80: £238.40) GOING minus 0.22 sec per fur (G)

				SP	RR	SF
3918^{2}	**Major Dundee (IRE)** (MCPipe) **4-11-0** APMcCoy (w ldr: stumbled bdly bnd after 3rd: reminders after 4th: led 5th: clr next: easily)	—	1	4/9^{1}	66+	14
3955^{4}	**Clock Watchers (67)** (JJBridger) **9-11-6** DMorris (led to 5th: rdn 6th: unable qckn)	9	2	25/1	58	12
3847^{8}	**Lord Love (IRE)** (PRChamings) **5-11-6** AThornton (lw: hld up: rdn 3 out: one pce)	½	3	50/1	58	12
99^{9}	**Robert Samuel** (NJHenderson) **6-11-6** MAFitzgerald (a bhd: t.o fr 3rd)	dist	4	10/1	—	—
3575^{5}	**Kilshey** (JTGifford) **6-10-8**(7) SLaird (hld up: rdn 6th: sn wknd: t.o)	6	5	8/1^{3}	—	—
3955^{2}	**Alka International (77)** (MrsPTownsley) **5-11-6** DerekByrne (a bhd: t.o whn p.u bef 3 out: dismntd)		P	6/1^{2}	—	—
	Danucha (JCPoulton) **5-11-1** TJMurphy (a bhd: t.o fr 3rd: p.u bef 6th)		P	33/1	—	—
2624^{P}	**Itani** (MJWilkinson) **5-11-6** WMarston (lw: prom to 5th: t.o whn p.u bef 3 out)		P	33/1	—	—
	Granstown Lake (IRE) (TCasey) **6-11-6** RDunwoody (a bhd: blnd 4th: t.o whn p.u bef 6th)		P	9/1	—	—
				(SP 125.4%)	**9 Rn**	

4m 25.8 (7.80) CSF £19.12 TOTE £1.50: £1.10 £3.50 £9.40 (£15.80) Trio £210.80; £95.03 to Nottingham 11/4/97 OWNER Mr Michael Jaye (WELLINGTON) BRED Brittas House Stud
WEIGHT FOR AGE 4yo-6lb
3918 Major Dundee (IRE), who managed just one win on the Flat (and that was due to Willie Carson dropping his hands on the runner-up), was given a fine ride by McCoy who was not going to be messed around on the gelding who was far superior to his rivals on the book. Given a couple of reminders with over a circuit to race, he soon moved to the front and forged clear to win with a ton in hand. (4/9: op 8/11)
2791 Clock Watchers has shown himself to be a very moderate novice and, after setting the pace until past halfway, was made to look extremely pedestrian by the winner on the final circuit. (25/1)
Lord Love (IRE), who has shown little to date, ran better here if made to look very one-paced over the last four hurdles. (50/1)
3061 Kilshey (8/1: 4/1-9/1)
Granstown Lake (IRE) (9/1: 4/1-10/1)

4098 GEORGE GALE & CO. H'CAP CHASE (0-115) (5-Y.O+) (Class E)

3-10 (3-10) **3m 2f 110y (22 fncs)** £3,343.20 (£999.60: £478.80: £218.40) GOING minus 0.22 sec per fur (G)

				SP	RR	SF
3838^{2}	**Credon (100)** (SWoodman) **9-11-4** BFenton (lw: a.p: rdn 18th: led 2 out: r.o wl)	—	1	4/1^{2}	107	28
3675^{P}	**Sugar Hill (IRE) (90)** (JTGifford) **7-10-8** PHide (led tl mstke & hdd 2 out: unable qckn)	2	2	4/1^{2}	96	17
3605^{3}	**Master Comedy (82)** (MissLBower) **13-10-0b** NWilliamson (hdwy 6th: hrd rdn appr 3 out: r.o wl flat)	2	3	10/1	87	8
3700^{4}	**Pavlova (IRE) (84)** (RRowe) **7-10-2**ow2 DO'Sullivan (lw: nvr nr to chal)	18	4	5/1^{3}	78	—
3739^{B}	**Fiddlers Pike (88)** (MrsRGHenderson) **16-10-6** MrsRHenderson (lw: bhd fr 9th: mstke 10th: t.o)	20	5	14/1	70	—
	Native Venture (IRE) (100) (TCasey) **9-11-4** AThornton (prom to 4 out: t.o)	25	6	12/1	67	—
4013^{B}	**Change the Reign (107)** (MissAEEmbiricos) **10-11-8**(3) MrRThornton (lw: nvr gng wl: hdwy 8th: wknd 16th: t.o whn p.u bef 3 out)		P	2/1^{1}	—	—
				(SP 113.4%)	**7 Rn**	

6m 48.7 (8.70) CSF £18.49 CT £133.39 TOTE £3.60: £2.30 £2.60 (£8.90) OWNER Fusilier Racing (CHICHESTER) BRED J. C. Bolam
LONG HANDICAP Master Comedy 9-4 Pavlova (IRE) 9-13
OFFICIAL EXPLANATION **Change the Reign: no explanation offered.**
3838 Credon certainly did not have the ground in his favour but he looked extremely well in the paddock and, with his jockey bustling away at him for the last three-quarters of a mile, the combination managed to get to the front two out and powered their way home. (4/1)
2681 Sugar Hill (IRE) set the pace and appeared to be travelling much better than the winner five from home. A mistake at the second last cost him the advantage, and although his jockey desperately tried to get him back on terms, the gelding just failed to find that vital turn of toe. (4/1: 3/1-9/2)
3605 Master Comedy, 10lb out of the handicap, knows this course so well he could probably go round it blindfolded. Despite being winnerless for three years and made to look woefully exposed on numerous occasions, he actually ran well this time and was certainly closing on the front two on the run-in. (10/1)
3700 Pavlova (IRE) found this ground far too lively and never looked like getting in it. She needs plenty of rain. (5/1)
Native Venture (IRE) (12/1: 8/1-14/1)
3414 Change the Reign (2/1: 5/2-11/)

4099 TUSCAN NOVICES' HURDLE (4-Y.O+) (Class E)

3-40 (3-40) **3m 3f (13 hdls)** £2,448.00 (£678.00: £324.00) GOING minus 0.22 sec per fur (G)

				SP	RR	SF
1840^{4}	**Honey Mount (90)** (NJHWalker) **6-11-6** NWilliamson (lw: a gng wl: hld up: led 2 out: v.easily)	—	1	7/4^{2}	58+	—
3755^{5}	**Kybo's Revenge (IRE) (64)** (RRowe) **6-11-0** DO'Sullivan (lw: hld up: ev ch 2 out: unable qckn)	3	2	8/1^{3}	50	—
3848^{5}	**Glendine (IRE)** (CJMann) **7-11-0** JRailton (lw: chsd ldr to 2nd: chsd ldr 6th tl blnd 7th: led after 9th to 2 out: sn wknd)	11	3	12/1	44	—
3902^{2}	**Maylin Magic (84)** (TCasey) **6-10-9** RDunwoody (lw: chsd ldr 2nd to 6th: chsd ldr fr 7th: ev ch 3 out: sn wknd)	21	4	11/10^{1}	26	—
3937^{6}	**Counter Attack (IRE)** (MissAEEmbiricos) **6-10-9** KGaule (led tl after 9th: sn wknd: blnd 10th: t.o)	dist	5	40/1	—	—
				(SP 105.2%)	**5 Rn**	

6m 34.1 CSF £11.89 TOTE £2.20: £1.10 £2.80 (£7.50) OWNER Mr Paul Green (BLEWBURY) BRED Cliveden Stud
1840 Honey Mount looked in good shape for this first run in four months and thoroughly enjoyed this very fast ground. Always travelling supremely well, he cruised into the lead two from home, and with his jockey slightly moving his arms the gelding forged clear to win pulling the proverbial bus. He looks one to follow on this fast surface and will be sent chasing in the summer. (7/4: 5/4-2/1)
3063 Kybo's Revenge (IRE) was much happier on this fast surface and appeared to see out this longer trip. On level terms with the winner two from home, he was then firmly put in his place. (8/1: op 5/1)

2704 Glendine (IRE), racing with his tongue tied down, is a poor performer over fences. Making his hurdling debut, he got to the front with a circuit to race but, collared two from home, was soon a spent force. (12/1: 7/1-14/1)
3902 Maylin Magic was disappointing for after having every chance three from home, she then tamely dropped away. (11/10: 6/4-evens)

4100 SILVER SHADOW NOVICES' CHASE (5-Y.O+) (Class E)

4-10 (4-10) **2m 3f (16 fncs)** £3,097.50 (£924.00: £441.00: £199.50) GOING minus 0.22 sec per fur (G)

				SP	RR	SF
3900[3]	**Cruise Control (68)** (RRowe) **11-11-2** DO'Sullivan (lw: hld up: mstke 9th: rdn appr last: led flat: r.o wl)	—	1	4/1[2]	75	8
3848[U]	**Brown Robber (68)** (MrsRGHenderson) **9-11-2** BFenton (hdwy 9th: led 11th tl flat: unable qckn: lame)	1¾	2	7/2[1]	74	7
3627[P]	**Bells Wood (60)** (AJKDunn) **8-11-2** SMcNeill (led to 2nd: ev ch 2 out: wknd appr last)	11	3	11/1	64	—
3447[17]	**Chapel of Barras (IRE)** (MissKMGeorge) **8-11-2** PHide (t: hld up: 3rd whn blnd 3 out: sn wknd: t.o: b.b.v)	dist	4	13/2	—	—
3897[3]	**Full of Tricks (60)** (JJBridger) **9-11-2** DMorris (led 2nd: mstke next: hdd 11th: wknd 4 out: fell 3 out)		F	7/1	—	—
3836[F]	**Ell Gee** (MrsPTownsley) **7-10-11** DerekByrne (lw: a bhd: t.o whn p.u bef 3rd)		P	25/1	—	—
3954[F]	**Bright Season (61)** (JCPoulton) **9-11-2b** TJMurphy (pckd 1st: blnd next: blnd bdly 4th: bhd whn p.u bef 5th)		P	33/1	—	—
3837[F]	**Icantelya (IRE) (80)** (JWMullins) **8-11-2v** SCurran (a bhd: t.o whn blnd 10th: ref 11th)		R	11/2[3]	—	—
1042[P]	**Gunner John** (TCasey) **6-11-2** AThornton (lw: chsd ldr 4th tl blnd & uns rdr 7th)		U	10/1	—	—

(SP 107.7%) **9 Rn**

4m 50.1 (11.10) CSF £15.28 TOTE £3.00: £1.30 £1.50 £3.50 (£5.20) Trio £30.10 OWNER Mr N. Blair (PULBOROUGH) BRED A. L. Holland
OFFICIAL EXPLANATION **Chapel Of Barras (IRE): bled from the nose.**
3900 Cruise Control at long last gained his first ever victory at the ripe old age of eleven in this truly atrocious race, eventually managing to get on top on the run-in. (4/1)
3602 Brown Robber went to the front six out but was eventually mastered on the run-in. He unfortunately finished lame. (7/2: 5/2-4/1)
3181 Bells Wood is a very bad novice but this fast ground seemed to suit and he still had every chance two from home before tiring. (11/1: 8/1-12/1)
Chapel of Barras (IRE), who has been tubed since his last outing when he was found to have gurgled, was making his chasing debut. In third place, although beginning to feel the pinch when making a bad error three from home that proved the undoing of him. Unfortunately he broke a blood vessel. Connections feel he may be best on a right-handed track. (13/2)
964 Icantelya (IRE) (11/2: 7/2-6/1)

4101 COMEDY OF ERRORS H'CAP HURDLE (0-110) (4-Y.O+) (Class E)

4-40 (4-41) **2m 2f 110y (9 hdls)** £2,574.00 (£714.00: £342.00) GOING minus 0.22 sec per fur (G)

				SP	RR	SF
1911*	**Out on a Promise (IRE) (100)** (NJHWalker) **5-11-9** NWilliamson (hdwy 3 out: led 2 out: r.o wl)	—	1	2/1[1]	83	33
3579[4]	**Persian Mystic (IRE) (83)** (DJWintle) **5-10-6** WMarston (lw: rdn 3 out: hdwy appr last: r.o)	4	2	16/1	63	13
3958*	**Night in a Million (81)** (SWoodman) **6-10-1**(3) 6x LAspell (led tl after 1st: led 6th to 2 out: unable qckn)	½	3	7/1	60	10
3105[4]	**Mazzini (IRE) (96)** (RRowe) **6-10-12**(7) MrPO'Keeffe (hld up: rdn 3 out: hmpd 2 out: r.o flat)	hd	4	10/1	75	25
3904[4]	**Iron N Gold (91)** (TCasey) **5-11-0v[1]** RDunwoody (lw: hld up: ev ch appr 2 out: wknd appr last)	6	5	7/2[2]	65	15
601[8]	**Stapleford Lady (86)** (JSMoore) **9-10-9** WMcFarland (lw: sme hdwy appr 2 out: sn wknd)	5	6	10/1	56	6
3896*	**Derisbay (IRE) (88)** (JJBridger) **9-10-8b**(3) SophieMitchell (led 2nd to 3rd: wknd 3 out)	29	7	13/2[3]	32	—
3962[3]	**Cabochon (85)** (JJoseph) **10-10-8** DSkyrme (led 3rd to 6th: ev ch whn fell 2 out)		F	16/1	—	—
3743[6]	**Live Action (96)** (MissHCKnight) **10-11-5** JCulloty (led after 1st to 2nd: mstke 5th: sn wknd: p.u bef 6th)		P	14/1	—	—
3953[R]	**Yellow Dragon (IRE) (87)** (BAPearce) **4-10-1b[1]**(3) PHenley (ref to r: t.n.p)		R	20/1	—	—

(SP 122.8%) **10 Rn**

4m 23.2 (5.20) CSF £32.76 CT £183.94 TOTE £3.20: £1.70 £4.30 £2.00 (£23.30) Trio £46.20 OWNER Mr Paul Green (BLEWBURY) BRED H. H. and Mrs Morriss
WEIGHT FOR AGE 4yo-6lb
1911* Out on a Promise (IRE), who disappointed on the All-Weather at the beginning of the year, has been off the course since. However, he returned in fine form and, leading two from home, quickly asserted. He loves this ground, comes from a stable in form and can win again. (2/1)
Persian Mystic (IRE) raced at the back of the field until running on nicely in the last two furlongs, although by then, it was far too late. He probably needs further. (16/1)
3958* Night in a Million showed in front early on the final circuit but, collared two from home, could then only go up and down in the same place. (7/1: 5/1-15/2)
3105 Mazzini (IRE) got hampered by Cabochon two from home which certainly did his cause no good. He would not have troubled the winner but he ran on creditably on the run-in and could possibly have finished second but for the interference. (10/1: 8/1-12/1)
3904 Iron N Gold poked a whisker in front for a few strides turning out of the back straight but he was soon in trouble, and was a spent force once in line for home. (7/2)
3962 Cabochon, who has done most of his winning with some cut in the ground, had every chance when taking a crashing fall two from home. (16/1)

4102 KYBO MAIDEN HURDLE (II) (4-Y.O+) (Class F)

5-10 (5-10) **2m 2f 110y (9 hdls)** £1,806.60 (£497.60: £235.80) GOING minus 0.22 sec per fur (G)

				SP	RR	SF
3820[U]	**Absolute Limit** (JTGifford) **5-11-6** PHide (hdwy 2nd: led appr 2 out: rdn out)	—	1	2/1[1]	67	18
3896[2]	**Mullintor (IRE) (82)** (RRowe) **6-11-6** DO'Sullivan (a.p: ev ch last: unable qckn)	2	2	4/1	65	16
3953[5]	**Veronica Franco (75)** (BAPearce) **4-10-6**(3) PHenley (hld up: ev ch 2 out: one pce)	2	3	20/1	59	4
3955[3]	**Real Madrid** (GPEnright) **6-11-3**(3) MrRThornton (hdwy appr 2 out: one pce)	3	4	7/2[3]	61	12
3755[7]	**Benji** (TCasey) **6-11-6b[1]** JAMcCarthy (led tl appr 2 out: sn wknd)	20	5	40/1	44	—
4017[3]	**Miss Gee-Ell** (NBThomson) **5-10-8**(7) MrEBabington (a bhd)	8	6	50/1	32	—
3808[10]	**Arctic Fox (IRE)** (MissHCKnight) **5-11-6** JFTitley (hld up: mstke 3rd: pckd 6th: wknd 3 out)	9	7	3/1[2]	29	—
3818[14]	**Las Animas (USA)** (RChampion) **6-11-1b** BPowell (lw: virtually ref to r: ref 1st)		R	20/1	—	—

(SP 114.5%) **8 Rn**

4m 26.2 (8.20) CSF £9.16 TOTE £3.10: £1.30 £1.20 £3.00 (£6.50) Trio £24.60 OWNER Mr B. M. Wootton (FINDON) BRED Chippenham Lodge Stud
WEIGHT FOR AGE 4yo-6lb
3103 Absolute Limit appreciated the drop in class and, leading approaching the second last, was ridden along to score. (2/1)
3896 Mullintor (IRE) once again had to settle for being the bridesmaid for, after throwing down his challenge in the straight, he was tapped for toe from the last. (4/1)

3809 Veronica Franco, a poor performer, looked dreadful in the paddock but had every chance two from home before lack of acceleration proved her undoing. She returned with a cut on her near-fore leg as a result of an over-reach sustained during the race, but the injury was no more than superficial according to connections. (20/1)
3955 Real Madrid tried to get into the action approaching the second last but could then only go up and down in the same place. (7/2:4/1- 9/2)
3808 Arctic Fox (IRE) (3/1: 2/1-7/2)

T/Plpt: £79.50 (150.37 Tckts). T/Qdpt: £13.00 (53.76 Tckts) AK

4103a - 4108a : (Irish Racing) - See Computer Raceform

3386a-FAIRYHOUSE (Dublin, Ireland) (R-H) (Good)
Monday March 31st
Race 2: 3rd last & 2nd last fence omitted

4109a JAMESON GOLD CUP NOVICES' HURDLE (Gd 2) (5-Y.O+)
3-15 (3-15) **2m (10 hdls)** IR £13,000.00 (IR £3,800.00: IR £1,800.00: IR £600.00)

Form	Horse	Dist	Pos	SP	RR	SF
3382a[6]	**Gazalani (IRE)** (POBrady,Ireland) **5-11-3** TPTreacy (hld up: 4th 3 out: chsd ldr bef 2 out: clsd appr last: styd on flat: led nr fin)	—	1	33/1	101	36
3595[P]	**Humbel (USA)** (DKWeld,Ireland) **5-11-6b** RDunwoody (led: clr 2nd tl appr 3 out: clr again after 3 out tl between last 2: mstke last: kpt on u.p: hdd nr fin)	1½	2	6/1[3]	103	38
3525a[3]	**Grey Guy (IRE)** (ALTMoore,Ireland) **5-11-6** FWoods (rn 2nd: clsd bef 3 out: chsd ldr: rdn & nt trble wnr after 2 out: 3rd & one pce appr last: no imp)	14	3	14/1	89	24
3523a[2]	**Sentosa Star (IRE)** (MHourigan,Ireland) **6-11-11** JPBroderick (hld up towards rr: mod 5th 3 out: sn rdn: no imp 2 out: kpt on same pce)	6	4	7/1	86	23
3595[F]	**Finnegan's Hollow (IRE)** (APO'Brien,Ireland) **7-11-8** CFSwan (hld up towards rr: hdwy 4 out: pushed along bef next: slt mstke: sn rdn: btn bef 2 out: lame)	s.h	5	4/7[1]	82	19
	Native-Darrig (IRE) (WPMullins,Ireland) **6-11-8** DJCasey (rn 4th: mod 6th 4 out: n.d fr 3 out: kpt on)	2	6	14/1	80	17
3595[2]	**Princeful (IRE)** (MrsJPitman) **6-11-8** JFTitley (rn 3rd early: mstkes: towards rr whn mstkes 4th & 5th: dropped bhd: sn p.u)		P	3/1[2]	—	—
				(SP 131.7%)	**7 Rn**	

3m 43.8 (-1.20) OWNER Miss Rita Shah (CASTLEBLANEY)
3382a Gazalani (IRE) finally came good. He had the ground to suit and, from well before the last, always looked like catching the runner-up. (33/1)
Humbel (USA) ran along in front and was clear until he began to tie-up after the second last. He made a mistake at the final flight and, not showing a lot of enthusiasm from there on, was headed close home. (6/1)
3525a Grey Guy (IRE), in second place, was unable to get on terms from the turn in and just looked one-paced in third place from the last. (14/1: op 8/1)
3523a Sentosa Star (IRE) showed little sparkle and this was a below par effort. (7/1)
3595 Finnegan's Hollow (IRE), held up at the back, made some headway to go third four out but the alarm bells were ringing before he made a slight mistake at the next, and he was beaten early in the straight. Subsequently, it was disclosed that he was lame behind. (4/7)
Native-Darrig (IRE) (14/1: op 8/1)
3595 Princeful (IRE) made early mistakes and had got himself well behind when pulled up after the fifth. (3/1)

4110a JAMESON IRISH GRAND NATIONAL H'CAP CHASE (Gd 1) (4-Y.O+)
3-55 (3-59) **3m 5f (21 fncs)** IR £62,700.00 (IR £19,300.00: IR £9,300.00: IR £3,300.00)

Form	Horse	Dist	Pos	SP	RR	SF
3598[6]	**Mudahim** (MrsJPitman) **11-10-3** JFTitley (mid div: hdwy whn mstke 8th: led after 20th: rdn appr st: jnd last: hdd flat: rallied u.p: led again last stride)	—	1	13/2[3]	140	35
3389a[5]	**Amble Speedy (IRE)** (ALTMoore,Ireland) **7-10-0** FWoods (hld up towards rr: hdwy 19th: wnt 2nd appr st: chsd ldr: chal & ev ch whn mstke last: led flat tl last stride)	s.h	2	14/1	135	32
3292*	**The Grey Monk (IRE)** (GRichards) **9-12-0** ADobbin (in tch: wnt 3rd at 20th: 3rd u.p st: edgd lft early st: styd on: nt trble ldrs)	11	3	9/2[1]	156	53
3389a*	**Papillon (IRE)** (TMWalsh,Ireland) **6-10-4** CFSwan (hld up towards rr: hdwy 16th: rdn 20th: 4th u.p & nt trble ldrs early st: kpt on same pce)	2	4	6/1[2]	131	28
3294[3]	**St Mellion Fairway (IRE)** (DNicholson) **8-10-4**ow1 AThornton (cl up: 3rd whn mstkes 11th & 14th: 4th & rdn after 20th: 5th, one pce & no imp st)	25	5	20/1	116	12
2348a[12]	**Lord Singapore (IRE)** (JJWalsh,Ireland) **9-10-10** DJCasey (hld up: mstke 6th: 5th & chsd ldrs 19th: 6th, rdn & no imp st: one pce)	3	6	14/1	120	17
2348a[8]	**Heist** (NMeade,Ireland) **8-10-1**ow1 KFO'Brien (a towards rr: n.d: kpt on)	6	7	20/1	108	4
3503a[5]	**Fissure Seal** (ALTMoore,Ireland) **11-10-3** TPTreacy (mid div: mstke 9th: hmpd next: n.d fr 19th)	20	8	20/1	98	—
3503a[P]	**Corymandel (IRE)** (HdeBromhead,Ireland) **8-10-0** TPRudd (led: mstke 6th: hdd after 20th: rdn & wknd: dist 7th & n.d st)	5	9	33/1	92	—
3585*	**Church Law** (MrsLCTaylor) **10-10-0** RBellamy (mid div: 9th at 11th: n.d fr 18th)	7	10	50/1	88	—
	Flashy Lad (IRE) (TJTaaffe,Ireland) **6-10-0** JPBroderick (cl up: 4th at 13th: wkng 5th whn mstke 17th: mod 7th at 19th: sn n.d)	3½	11	33/1	86	—
	Coq Hardi Affair (IRE) (NMeade,Ireland) **9-10-1** MrBMCash (mid div early: 7th whn fell 9th: dead)		F	20/1	—	—
3503a*	**Teal Bridge (IRE)** (AHeffernan,Ireland) **12-10-0** TJMitchell (towards rr: fell 13th)		F	20/1	—	—
	The Latvian Lark (IRE) (NMeade,Ireland) **9-10-0** CO'Dwyer (hld up in tch whn fell 10th: dead)		F	14/1	—	—
3573[3]	**Aardwolf** (CPEBrooks) **6-10-3b**1ow2 GBradley (in tch whn fell 2nd)		F	16/1	—	—
3503a[P]	**Trench Hill Lass (IRE)** (GStewart,Ireland) **8-10-3**ow3 3x LPCusack (sn in tch: 4th at 10th: 9th at 14th: lost pl: p.u 18th)		P	50/1	—	—
	Consharon (IRE) (APO'Brien,Ireland) **9-10-3** THorgan (sn towards rr: trailing 12th: bhd & p.u bef 14th)		P	33/1	—	—
3302[3]	**Percy Smollett** (DNicholson) **9-11-5** RDunwoody (hld up: towards rr: hdwy to 7th at 11th: reminders 14th: lost pl & p.u 17th)		P	14/1	—	—
3563*	**Giventime** (AndrewTurnell) **9-10-0** LHarvey (mid div early: dropped bhd & p.u bef 12th)		P	10/1	—	—

				SP	RR	SF
3699[3]	**Sister Stephanie (IRE)** (GMMcCourt) **8-10-0** DBridgwater (ref to race)		R	10/1	—	—
				(SP 133.1%)		**20 Rn**

7m 28.6 (-4.40) OWNER In Touch Racing Club (UPPER LAMBOURN) BRED Warner Jones and W. Farish
3598 Mudahim, on which the jockey weighed in at 10st 5lb, put up a tremendously game performance. Second from halfway, he jumped what was to be the second last in front and, joined at the last, showed real courage in rallying under pressure to lead again in the last stride. (13/2)
3389a Amble Speedy (IRE) started to creep into it from four out. He went second before the straight and chased the leader hard. He was on terms when blundering at the last, but rallied strongly to lead on the flat. He edged slightly left close home and that cost him the photo, although he was originally declared the winner in error. (14/1)
3292* The Grey Monk (IRE), in fourth place from seven out, went third with two to jump but, under pressure in the straight, could never get on terms with the two principals. (9/2)
3389a* Papillon (IRE) had plenty to do in the last mile, but swung into the straight under pressure in fourth place. He just kept on at one pace and will be more battle-hardened next season. (6/1)
3294 St Mellion Fairway (IRE) made some mistakes, but held a prominent position until dropping away after the second last. In fifth place going into the straight, he gradually lost touch. (20/1)
1495a* Lord Singapore (IRE) made headway to chase the leaders three out, but was left struggling before turning into the straight. (14/1)
1495a Heist never got into it. (20/1)
3585* Church Law, in mid-division at halfway, was not a threat over the last four. (50/1)
3573 Aardwolf came down at the second. (16/1)
3302 Percy Smollett made a bit of headway at halfway, but was under the stick with a mile to race and eventually pulled up before four out. (14/1)
3563* Giventime ran in mid-division early, but was well behind when pulling up before the twelfth. (10/1)
3699 Sister Stephanie (IRE) got a bit worked up in the melee at the start and eventually refused to race. (10/1)

4111a - 4115a : (Irish Racing) - See Computer Raceform

4107a-FAIRYHOUSE (Dublin, Ireland) (R-H) (Good)
Tuesday April 1st

4116a POWER GOLD CUP NOVICES' CHASE (Gd 1) (5-Y.O+)
3-15 (3-15) **2m 4f (15 fncs)** IR £24,265.00 (IR £6,650.00: IR £3,150.00)

				SP	RR	SF
3636[3]	**Dorans Pride (IRE)** (MHourigan,Ireland) **8-11-7** RDunwoody (cl up: disp ld fr 2nd: slt mstke 4 out: led on ins after 3 out: rdn clr flat: styd on wl)	—	1	4/7[1]	130+	21
3260a*	**Jeffell** (ALTMoore,Ireland) **7-11-7** FWoods (led & disp ld: hdd after 3 out: ev ch next: rdn & no ex appr last: kpt on same pce flat)	5	2	3/1[2]	126	17
4110a[P]	**Consharon (IRE)** (APO'Brien,Ireland) **9-11-2** THorgan (cl up early: mod 4th at 9th: lost tch: n.d 4 out)	dist	3	20/1	—	—
	Stroll Home (IRE) (JJMangan,Ireland) **7-11-7** MDMurphy (hld up: 5th & in tch whn fell 8th)		F	33/1	—	—
3616[10]	**Bell Staffboy (IRE)** (JGMO'Shea) **8-11-7** CO'Dwyer (hld up: disp ld briefly 10th: cl 4th & rdn 4 out: losing tch whn fell 3 out)		F	10/1	—	—
3596[6]	**Penndara (IRE)** (APO'Brien,Ireland) **8-11-7** CFSwan (in tch: 4th at 8th: lost tch next: sn n.d: p.u bef 4 out: b.b.v.)		P	9/1[3]	—	—
				(SP 115.4%)		**6 Rn**

4m 56.1 (-4.90) OWNER T. J. Doran (PATRICKSWELL) BRED Hugh Suffern Bloodstock Ltd
3636 Dorans Pride (IRE) allowed Jeffell to do the donkey work. He touched down in front briefly at the tenth, but was taken back again and, after a slight mistake four out, was allowed to take the initiative after the next. With the inside easily gained, he was in total command afterwards and was ridden clear on the flat for an impressive win. (4/7: op 1/3)
3260a* Jeffell made the running but, headed after three out, was fighting a losing battle from then on. (3/1)
Consharon (IRE) never got into contention. (20/1)
3285* Bell Staffboy (IRE) went up to dispute the lead at the tenth and stayed on well until ridden along four out. He had dropped away when falling at the next. (10/1)
3260a Penndara (IRE) lost touch at the ninth and was pulled up a bit before four out having broken a blood vessel. (9/1)

4117a BISQUIT COGNAC H'CAP HURDLE (Gd 2) (4-Y.O+)
3-50 (3-52) **2m (10 hdls)** IR £13,000.00 (IR £3,800.00: IR £1,800.00: IR £600.00) GOING: 0.00 sec per fur (G)

				SP	RR	SF
2603a[6]	**Khayrawani (IRE)** (CRoche,Ireland) **5-10-5** CO'Dwyer (cl up: mstke 3rd: rdn to jn ldrs appr 3 out: disp ld st: led 2 out: rdn clr flat: eased nr fin)	—	1	6/4[1]	124+	—
2995a[3]	**Palette (IRE)** (WPMullins,Ireland) **5-9-8** DJCasey (hld up in tch: 4th 3 out: 2nd & chal appr last: rdn & nt rch wnr flat: kpt on)	1	2	10/1	112	—
3615[9]	**Mystical City (IRE)** (WPMullins,Ireland) **7-10-11** RDunwoody (in tch: 5th & rdn 3 out: effrt u.p between last 2: 3rd over last: styd on: nt rch wnr)	½	3	13/2[3]	128	5
1485a[3]	**Saving Bond (IRE)** (NMeade,Ireland) **5-9-0**(7) BJGeraghty (prom early: hld up: 5th & chsd ldrs 2 out: rdn & effrt appr last: 4th & no ex flat: kpt on)	½	4	9/1	110	—
3597[2]	**Theatreworld (IRE)** (APO'Brien,Ireland) **5-12-0** CFSwan (dwlt: hld up: 7th & pushed along 4th: 6th & chsd ldrs 2 out: nt rch ldrs last: styd on)	hd	5	6/1[2]	145	21
3816*	**Kadastrof (FR)** (RDickin) **7-10-1**(7) 2x XAizpuru (led: hdd 6th: disp ld again next tl hdd & mstke 2 out: rdn & one pce appr last: no imp flat)	6	6	8/1	118	—
	Valley Erne (IRE) (MCunningham,Ireland) **6-9-7** FWoods (mstke 1st: rn 2nd: led briefly 6th & appr 3 out: 3rd 3 out: rdn & wknd bef st: no imp)	6	7	14/1	97	—
	Bank Statement (IRE) (TJTaaffe,Ireland) **6-9-0**(7) PGHourigan (hld up towards rr: sme hdwy 3 out: no imp next)	5	8	25/1	92	—
3595[6]	**Three Scholars** (WPMullins,Ireland) **6-9-11** TPTreacy (towards rr: n.d)	4½	9	12/1	91	—
				(SP 116.0%)		**9 Rn**

3m 41.4 (-3.60) OWNER John McManus
2603a Khayrawani (IRE) was the only one punters were interested in and he landed a considerable gamble. He had to be ridden along on the outside before three out but had gained command at the next and, ridden clear on the flat, he was eased down close home, but still goes up 5lb. (6/4: op 9/4)
2995a Palette (IRE) challenged over the last but could not get to the winner on the flat. (10/1)

1365 Mystical City (IRE), under pressure over the last two, landed third over the last but despite running on strongly, was never going to trouble the winner. (13/2: op 4/1)
Saving Bond (IRE) ran well for a novice but failed to find anything extra on the flat. (9/1)
3597 Theatreworld (IRE) never held out any hope but, in sixth place over the second last, was allowed to run on to be nearest at the line. (6/1: op 5/2)
3816* Kadastrof (FR) ran along in front until headed after a mistake two out. (8/1)
Valley Erne (IRE) got an extraordinary ride for a horse which needs to be held up. (14/1)
3595 Three Scholars (12/1: op 8/1)

4118a GOFFS LAND ROVER BUMPER N.H. FLAT RACE (4 & 5-Y.O)
4-25 (4-27) **2m** IR £29,500.00 (IR £9,500.00: IR £5,500.00: IR £1,500.00)

	Horse	Dist	Pos	SP	RR	SF
	The Oozler (IRE) (MFMorris,Ireland) **4-11-3** MrAJMartin (hld up towards rr: hdwy on ins 4f out: str chal over 1f out: edgd rt early fnl f: rdn to ld nr fin)	—	1	14/1	85 f	—
	Native Estates (IRE) (NMeade,Ireland) **5-11-10** MrGJHarford (hld up in tch: 5th & trckd ldrs st: sn chal: led over 1f out: hdd u.p nr fin: kpt on)	hd	2	7/1^{3}	85 f	—
	Do Ye Know Wha (IRE) (SJTreacy,Ireland) **5-12-6** MrJPMcNamara (in tch: rdn & chsd ldrs st: 6th u.p & nt rch ldrs over 1f out: styd on wl fnl f)	2½	3	8/1	92 f	—
	Minella Hotel (IRE) (WPMullins,Ireland) **5-11-10** MrJANash (hld up mid div: hmpd after 4f: hdwy 4f out: 10th over 2f out: styd on ins last: nrst fin)	2½	4	8/1	80 f	—
	Templemary Lad (IRE) (MHalford,Ireland) **5-11-10** MrJPDempsey (towards rr: hdwy 4f out: 9th & swtchd 2f out: rdn & clsd: styd on wl fnl f: nrst fin)	s.h	5	12/1	80 f	—
	Air Force One (IRE) (WPMullins,Ireland) **5-11-10** MrACCoyle (in tch: 4th 6f out: disp ld over 3f out: led 2f out: hdd u.p over 1f out: kpt on same pce)	1½	6	16/1	78 f	—
	Men Of Ninetyeight (IRE) (PHughes,Ireland) **5-11-10** MrDMarnane (prom: 3rd 6f out: disp ld 4f out: led briefly early st: ev ch, rdn & no ex over 1f out: kpt on same pce)	½	7	6/1^{2}	78 f	—
	Mykon Gold (IRE) (WPMullins,Ireland) **4-11-3** MrRWalsh (hld up towards rr early: hdwy to track ldrs 5f out: rdn & effrt early st: no ex u.p 1½f out: one pce)	9	8	4/1^{1}	69 f	—
	Homeville (IRE) (APO'Brien,Ireland) **5-11-10** MrPMKelly (mid div: 11th ½-wy: chsd ldrs over 4f out: no imp early st: kpt on)	nk	9	20/1	69 f	—
	Toscanini (IRE) (NMeade,Ireland) **4-11-3** MrGElliott (towards rr: kpt on in st: nvr nrr)	1	10	20/1	68 f	—
	Alotawanna (IRE) (TJTaaffe,Ireland) **4-11-3** MrJABerry (led & disp ld: ev ch st: 5th u.p & one pce over 1f out)	½	11	12/1	67 f	—
3606^{4}	**Macy (IRE)** (RDickin) **4-11-10** MrFHutsby (in tch: 8th 6f out: chsd ldrs: nt trble ldrs 1½f out: kpt on same pce)	½	12	14/1	74 f	—
	Kazaran (IRE) (MMLynch,Ireland) **4-11-10** MrPFGraffin (hld up: mid div: 9th & chsd ldrs over 3f out: rdn & nt trble ldrs 2f out: one pce)	½	13	10/1	73 f	—
	Total Success (IRE) (TMWalsh,Ireland) **5-11-10** MrEBolger (towards rr: hld up: hdwy 5f out: nt trble ledrs early st: kpt on same pce)	1	14	14/1	65 f	—
	Get Even (IRE) (APO'Brien,Ireland) **5-11-10** MrBRHamilton (mid div: rdn & no imp 3f out: kpt on)	½	15	14/1	65 f	—
	Mister Audi (IRE) (AJMcNamara,Ireland) **5-11-10b^{1}** MrJTMcNamara (led & disp ld: hdd early st: wknd fr 2f out)	1	16	20/1	64 f	—
	Ashwell April (IRE) (CAMcBratney,Ireland) **5-11-5** MrEdgarByrne (nvr bttr than mid div)	s.h	17	50/1	56 f	—
	Candy Gale (IRE) (JGGroome,Ireland) **5-11-5** MrPEnglish (mid div best: no imp fr 3f out)	3	18	50/1	56 f	—
3235^{5}	**Gorman (IRE)** (MissHCKnight) **5-11-10** MrARCoonan (in tch: 10th ½-wy: rdn & wknd appr st: no imp)	3	19	14/1	58 f	—
	Mega Gale (IRE) (APO'Brien,Ireland) **5-11-10** MrHFCleary (mid div: rdn & chsd ldrs 6f out: no imp u.p st)	s.h	20	16/1	57 f	—
	Paula Jane (IRE) (MButler,Ireland) **4-10-12** MrCAMurphy (n.d)	½	21	33/1	52 f	—
	Dockline (IRE) (APO'Brien,Ireland) **5-11-10** MrMPhillips (mid div best: no imp 3f out)	1½	22	20/1	55 f	—
	Dante's Battle (IRE) (MrsJHarrington,Ireland) **5-11-10** MrPJHealy (mid div early: jnd ldrs after 5f: 5th 4f out: rdn appr st: wknd: n.d 2f out)	¾	23	25/1	55 f	—
	Michelles Gold (IRE) (EJCreighton,Ireland) **5-11-5** MrMO'Connor (mid div: no imp fr 4f out)	10	24	50/1	40 f	—
	Datem (IRE) (TMWalsh,Ireland) **5-11-10** MrAJDempsey (never a danger)	1	25	25/1	44 f	—
	Roses Niece (IRE) (THogan,Ireland) **4-10-12** MrRonaldFlavin (towards rr: never a danger: t.o)	dist	26	50/1	—	—
	Smiling Always (IRE) (EJO'Grady,Ireland) **4-10-12** MrPFenton (in tch: lost pl qckly after ½-wy: p.u 6f out)		P	8/1	—	—
3090^{7}	**Crackon Jake (IRE)** (JSMoore) **4-11-3** MrEJames (mid div whn hmpd & rn out through rail after 3½f)		R	20/1	—	—
				(SP 192.0%)	**28 Rn**	

3m 40.8 OWNER The Birdie Racing Club (FETHARD)
The Oozler (IRE) challenged from over a furlong out and, despite edging right, stayed on to lead close home. (14/1)
Native Estates (IRE) got through the pack to lead over a furlong out until headed close home. (7/1)
Do Ye Know Wha (IRE), sixth and under pressure over a furlong out, stayed on well. (8/1)
Minella Hotel (IRE) didn't enjoy the best of runs, but stayed on well late to be closest at the finish. (8/1)
Men Of Ninetyeight (IRE) (6/1: op 4/1)
3606 Macy (IRE) chased the leaders throughout the last half-mile but wasn't a threat from a furlong and a half out. (14/1)
Total Success (IRE) (14/1: op 8/1)
Get Even (IRE) (14/1: op 8/1)
3235 Gorman (IRE) never progressed much further than mid-division and had dropped away before the straight. (14/1)
2844 Crackon Jake (IRE) ran out through the inside rail after three and a half furlongs. (20/1)

4119a - 4122a : (Irish Racing) - See Computer Raceform

4114a-FAIRYHOUSE (Dublin, Ireland) (R-H) (Good to firm)
Wednesday April 2nd

4123a OLIVER FREANEY & CO. DAN MOORE (LISTED) H'CAP CHASE (4-Y.O+)
2-45 (2-46) **2m (12 fncs)** IR £13,000.00 (IR £3,800.00: IR £1,800.00: IR £600.00) GOING: 0.00 sec per fur (G)

	Horse	Dist	Pos	SP	RR	SF
3383a^{F}	**Idiots Venture** (APO'Brien,Ireland) **10-10-11** CFSwan (hld up: wnt 3rd at 8th: 2nd bef st: chal fr 2 out: led nr last: rdn & styd on flat)	—	1	100/30^{3}	130	33

3638^{9} **Cable Beach (IRE)** (MCunningham,Ireland) **8-10-11** RDunwoody (led & disp ld: hit 4th: hdd briefly 4 out: hdd nr last: slt mstke: rdn & no ex flat: kpt on) ....1½ **2** 2/1^{1} 129 32
Oh So Grumpy (MrsJHarrington,Ireland) **9-10-11** JShortt (2nd fr 2nd: disp ld 7th: led briefly 4 out: 3rd u.p bef st: no imp after 2 out) 11 **3** 6/1 118 21
3596^{7} **Beakstown (IRE)** (PMullins,Ireland) **8-10-11** TPTreacy (hld up: 3rd whn mstke 5th: 4th & rdn whn mstke 3 out: no imp 2 out) ....s.h **4** 3/1^{2} 117 20
2741a^{2} **Arctic Weather (IRE)** (MJPO'Brien,Ireland) **8-10-11** TPRudd (hld up towards rr: cld 4 out: rdn bef next: lost tch after 3 out: no imp) ....dist **5** 6/1 — —
(SP 110.0%) **5 Rn**

3m 52.3 (-5.70) OWNER Blackwater Racing Syndicate (PILTOWN)
3128a Idiots Venture, with the defection of Klairon Davis (coughing), had an easy task here on paper, rated 15lb and upwards superior to these and allowed to meet them at levels. Going second before the straight, he picked off Cable Beach before the last and went on to win snugly. (100/30: op 2/1)
Cable Beach (IRE) went off in front and, despite mistakes, stayed there until the run to the last. He made a slight mistake there and didn't find much on the flat. (2/1: op 3/1)
Oh So Grumpy has been point-to-pointing and, although making no impression in the straight, was not disgraced. (6/1)
3260a Beakstown (IRE) made mistakes and held out no hope over the last two. (3/1)
2741a Arctic Weather (IRE) dropped away from the third last. (6/1)

4124a O DEA CROP FLEX NUTRITION FESTIVAL NOVICES' HURDLE (Gd 3) (5-Y.O+)
3-15 (3-18) **2m 4f (12 hdls)** IR £6,850.00 (IR £1,550.00: IR £650.00: IR £350.00)

SP RR SF

Moscow Express (IRE) (APO'Brien,Ireland) **5-11-12** CFSwan (hld up: nt fluent: trckd ldrs 3 out: chal 2 out: narrow ld between last 2: mstke & hdd: rallied to ld cl home) ....— **1** 5/2^{2} 105 35
Liver Bird (IRE) (JABerry,Ireland) **7-11-10** CO'Dwyer (mstke 2nd: led bef 8th: mstke 3 out, jnd 2 out: hdd between last 2: led again early flat: hdd cl home: rdn & kpt on) ....½ **2** 6/4^{1} 102 33
3650a* **Blushing Sand (IRE)** (PTLeonard,Ireland) **7-11-0**(7) MrTJBeattie (towards rr: rdn 8th: rdn 4 out: chsd ldrs: 3rd u.p & nt trble ldrs between last 2: kpt on same pce) 7 **3** 9/1 93 24
Lancastrian Pride (IRE) (WPMullins,Ireland) **7-11-10** DJCasey (led & disp ld: hdd bef 8th: rdn bef 3 out: 3rd, rdn & nt qckn bef st: rallied u.p appr last: nt rch ldrs flat) 1 **4** 7/1 95 26
Step On Eyre (IRE) (WPMullins,Ireland) **7-11-7** RDunwoody (rn 4th: mstkes 5th & 7th: chsd ldrs 3 out: 5th & no imp 2 out: one pce) ....4 **5** 13/2^{3} 89 20
4117a^{9} **Three Scholars** (WPMullins,Ireland) **6-11-10** TPTreacy (towards rr: 5th at 8th: lost tch bef 3 out: n.d) 25 **6** 8/1 72 3
(SP 115.5%) **6 Rn**

4m 44.7 (-5.30) OWNER T. Conroy (PILTOWN)
Moscow Express (IRE) wasn't particularly fluent, but gained the advantage between the last two. Headed after a mistake at the last, he rallied well to regain the lead close home. (5/2)
Liver Bird (IRE) wasn't foot perfect either. He blundered three out, was joined at the next and looked like playing second fiddle until gaining the advantage early on the flat, before being unable to find anything extra close home. (6/4)
3650a* Blushing Sand (IRE) was not in a position to trouble the leaders between the last two, but kept on well and this would be his best run to date. (9/1)
Lancastrian Pride (IRE) led and disputed the lead, but was beaten between the last two. (7/1: op 4/1)
Step On Eyre (IRE) was making little impression from two out but will come on for this. (13/2: op 4/1)
3595 Three Scholars (8/1: op 5/1)

4125a - 4128a : (Irish Racing) - See Computer Raceform

0326a-LES LANDES (Jersey) (L-H) (Good)
Monday March 31st

4129a SUPPORTERS H'CAP HURDLE (4-Y.O+)
2-30 (2-30) **2m** £900.00 (£375.00)

SP RR SF

822^{3} **Wollboll** (JSOArthur,Jersey) **7-12-0** DSEvans ....— **1** 85? —
3689^{P} **Supreme Illusion (AUS)** (JohnBerry) **4-9-7** MrCJMcEntee ....4 **2** 54? —
2 Rn

4m 8.0 TOTE £2.60 OWNER Mr M. J. Weaver BRED Henry Saunders and M. Weaver

3847-ASCOT (R-H) (Good to Firm)
Saturday April 12th
WEATHER: Sunny

4130 PEREGRINE H'CAP HURDLE (4-Y.O+) (Class B)
2-00 (2-00) **2m 110y (9 hdls)** £5,409.60 (£1,636.80: £798.40: £379.20) GOING minus 0.15 sec per fur (G)

SP RR SF

3983^{8} **I'm a Dreamer (IRE) (109)** (MissMERowland) **7-9-11**(3) MrRThornton (stdy hdwy 5th: led 2 out: rdn out) ....— **1** 50/1 95? 33
3640^{20} **Faustino (110)** (PJHobbs) **5-10-1** NWilliamson (stdy hdwy 6th: ev ch last: unable qckn) ....1¾ **2** 6/1^{3} 94 32
3177^{6} **Albemine (USA) (122)** (MrsJCecil) **8-10-13b^{1}** TKent (a.p: bmpd & led appr 2 out: sn hdd: one pce) ....6 **3** 6/1^{3} 101 39
3638^{10} **Dancing Paddy (137)** (KOCunningham-Brown) **9-12-0** RDunwoody (lw: hld up: hrd rdn 5th: one pce fr 3 out) .2 **4** 10/1 114 52
3430^{6} **Alltime Dancer (IRE) (116)** (OSherwood) **5-10-7b** JOsborne (lw: w ldr: led 3rd to 3 out: sn wknd) 1½ **5** 9/1 91 29
3904^{6} **Nashville Star (USA) (109)** (RMathew) **6-10-0v** CLlewellyn (lw: led to 3rd: led 3 out tl bmpd & hdd appr 2 out: sn wknd) ....2½ **6** 50/1 82? 20
2691^{3} **Crack On (130)** (PJHobbs) **7-11-7** APMcCoy (lw: stdy hdwy 5th: mstke 3 out: wknd appr 2 out) ....5 **7** 11/4^{2} 98 36
3987* **Serious (113)** (KCBailey) **7-10-4** CO'Dwyer (lw: stdy hdwy 6th: fell 3 out) .... **F** 5/2^{1} — —

2569[6]	**Holy Wanderer (USA) (120)** (TRGeorge) **8-10-11** MAFitzgerald (bit bkwd: a wl bhd: t.o fr 5th: p.u bef 2 out).....		P	16/1	—	—
				(SP 112.7%)	**9 Rn**	

3m 50.9 (0.90) CSF £290.77 CT £1,893.98 TOTE £34.00: £5.80 £1.90 £1.50 (£94.10) Trio £437.80 OWNER Miss M. E. Rowland (LOWER BLIDWORTH) BRED A. Watkins

LONG HANDICAP I'm a Dreamer (IRE) 9-1 Nashville Star (USA) 8-13

2744* I'm a Dreamer (IRE), still carrying 10lb more than his long handicap despite his rider's claim, caused a real shock. He crept closer in Swinley Bottom and, leading at the second last, was ridden along to secure victory. (50/1)

459* Faustino, at his best on this ground, bounced back to form. Swinging off the bridle entering the straight, his jockey seemed very keen not to get to the front too soon, and he was quite happy that the winner went by. With every chance jumping the final flight, he failed to quicken on the run-in. (6/1)

3177 Albemine (USA), tried in blinkers, loves this ground and pushed his way to the front turning for home. Collared a few strides before the second last, he could then only go up and down in the same place. (6/1)

3037 Dancing Paddy, prone to making bad mistakes over fences, was reverting back to hurdles for the first time since 1994, but found that over the minor obstacles his speed has been blunted and was unable to find another gear when the race began in earnest. Although he has won on this ground, it is probably too lively for him and a few drops of rain would be appreciated. (10/1: 8/1-12/1)

2780 Alltime Dancer (IRE), a useful juvenile last season, has been very disappointing this term apart from his first run in blinkers at Doncaster in January. They have failed to work since and, after disputing the lead to the third last, he soon capitulated. (9/1)

3904 Nashville Star (USA), 15lb out of the handicap, disputed the lead but was collared turning for home and was soon done with. (50/1)

2691 Crack On, given an eleven-week break, was reverting back to hurdles after just one run over fences. Unfortunately he proved very disappointing and, having crept closer from Swinley Bottom, a mistake three out spelt the beginning of the end. So impressive in his first two victories this season, he has failed to reproduce that since and should be put away until next term. (11/4)

3987* Serious had edged closer but was still at the back of a tightly-knit pack, having not yet been asked any sort of question, when departing three from home. (5/2: 6/4-11/4)

4131 KYLE STEWART H'CAP CHASE (5-Y.O+) (Class B)

2-35 (2-36) **2m 3f 110y (16 fncs)** £8,122.20 (£2,457.60: £1,198.80: £569.40) GOING minus 0.15 sec per fur (G)

				SP	RR	SF
4054[3]	**Bertone (IRE) (130)** (KCBailey) **8-10-4** CO'Dwyer (lw: hld up: jnd ldr appr last: led flat: easily)	—	1	11/8 [1]	139+	35
3999[4]	**Super Tactics (IRE) (135)** (RHAlner) **9-10-9** RDunwoody (lw: hld up: led 2 out tl flat: unable qckn)	1½	2	100/30 [3]	143	39
	Amtrak Express (145) (NJHenderson) **10-11-5** MAFitzgerald (lw: led 6th to 2 out: eased whn btn appr last)	9	3	11/2	145	41
2646[6]	**Storm Alert (154)** (DNicholson) **11-12-0** RJohnson (lw: led 2nd to 6th: rdn 3 out: wknd appr 2 out: t.o)	dist	4	3/1 [2]	—	—
3839[5]	**Young Alfie (126)** (JFPanvert) **12-10-0b** CLlewellyn (led to 2nd: wknd 7th: mstke 8th: t.o fr 10th)	dist	5	66/1	—	—
				(SP 107.1%)	**5 Rn**	

4m 48.7 (1.70) CSF £5.55 TOTE £2.30: £1.50 £1.70 (£3.30) OWNER Mrs Harry Duffey (UPPER LAMBOURN) BRED Mrs Marie Behan

LONG HANDICAP Young Alfie 6-2

4054 Bertone (IRE) seemed more than happy with the drop back in distance and, on ground he loves, bolted up. He is yet to win beyond two miles five and a half furlongs. (11/8)

3999 Super Tactics (IRE), who started the season on 116, has had a tremendous campaign but has risen to a mark of 135 as a result. Despite that, he jumped into the lead at the second last but the winner was always toying with him and, collared on the run-in, he was firmly put in his place. He is a real credit to his trainer. (100/30)

Amtrak Express, off the track since finishing third in last year's Whitbread, is an athletic individual who gives the impression he does not take much getting fit. Looking in very good shape following his lengthy break, he was given very tender handling over a trip which is surely short of his best these days. Leading at the sixth, he was collared two from home and his jockey was very quick to accept the situation. Sure to be sharper for this, he is once again being targeted at the Sandown showpiece and will go into that race considerably fresher than many of his rivals who will have had long, hard seasons. A big run can be expected. (11/2: 4/1-6/1)

2646 Storm Alert loves this track, but once again demonstrated he does not get this trip and was in trouble turning for home. He has had a very rewarding season but he is certainly at his best in the autumn - seven of his fourteen victories have come in October and November - and has won just once after February. (3/1)

4132 LETHEBY & CHRISTOPHER LONG DISTANCE HURDLE (Gd 2) (4-Y.O+) (Class A)

3-10 (3-11) **3m (13 hdls)** £18,750.00 (£7,095.00: £3,472.50: £1,582.50) GOING minus 0.15 sec per fur (G)

				SP	RR	SF
3635[7]	**Trainglot (145)** (JGFitzGerald) **10-11-10** RDunwoody (hld up: mstke 6th: rdn appr 2 out: led appr last: r.o wl)	—	1	1/2 [1]	108	16
3902*	**Pleasureland (IRE) (105)** (RCurtis) **4-10-9** DMorris (lw: hld up: led appr 3 out tl appr last: wknd flat)	4	2	7/1 [3]	98?	—
3935*	**Sassiver (USA) (92)** (PAKelleway) **7-11-3** KGaule (hld up: ev ch appr 2 out: one pce)	nk	3	16/1	98?	6
3600[21]	**Olympian (118)** (JNeville) **10-11-3b** MAFitzgerald (lw: led 2nd tl appr 3 out: rdn: one pce)	s.h	4	9/2 [2]	98	6
4005[3]	**Oatis Rose (105)** (MSheppard) **7-10-12** SophieMitchell (led to 2nd: rdn 6th: wknd 9th)	11	5	12/1	86?	—
				(SP 110.9%)	**5 Rn**	

5m 53.7 (14.70) CSF £4.34 TOTE £1.50: £1.20 £1.60 (£2.80) OWNER Marquesa de Moratalla (MALTON) BRED Marquesa de Moratalla

WEIGHT FOR AGE 4yo-8lb

2056 Trainglot was making his last racecourse appearance and bowed out on a winning note in this valuable event, which had unfortunately produced a poor turnout. Woken up entering the straight, he managed to get on top going to the final flight and bounded clear on the run-in. He has been a grand servant over the years amassing £200,000 in prize money, winning the Coral Cup at Cheltenham in 1996 andthe valuable Tote Bookmakers Handicap Hurdle at Sandown in 1993 and 1996, as well as lifting the 1990 Cesarewitch on the Flat. He will be missed, but richly deserves his retirement. (1/2)

3902* Pleasureland (IRE) may be only a novice but he ran extremely well against experienced rivals. Making his bid for glory approaching the third last, it looked as if he had got the odds-on favourite in some trouble going to the penultimate hurdle, but he was collared going to the final flight and tied up on the run-in. With the summer to strengthen up, he should see out three miles better next season. (7/1: 5/1-8/1)

3935* Sassiver (USA) had every chance turning for home before tapped for toe. He is yet to win beyond two miles five and a half furlongs. (16/1)

2625 Olympian goes well on this ground and was soon at the head of affairs. Collared approaching the third last, he could only keep on in his own time. (9/2)

4005 Oatis Rose is a very hard ride and her jockey must have been exhausted at the end of the race, for she was scrubbing the ears off the mare for the majority of the final circuit. Unfortunately, it all proved to be to no avail for she was getting left behind in Swinley Bottom. (12/1: 7/1-14/1)

4133 KESTREL NOVICES' CHASE (5-Y.O+) (Class C)

3-40 (3-42) **2m 3f 110y (16 fncs)** £6,092.00 (£1,712.00: £836.00) GOING minus 0.15 sec per fur (G)

				SP	RR	SF
3849[3]	**Greenback (BEL) (125)** (PJHobbs) **6-11-12** NWilliamson (lw: j.lft: hdwy 10th: lft in ld 4 out: all out)	—	1	11/4[3]	131	44
3849*	**Garnwin (IRE) (120)** (NJHenderson) **7-11-12** MAFitzgerald (j.lft: hld up: chsd wnr appr 2 out: ev ch last: hrd rdn: r.o wl)	s.h	2	13/8[1]	131	44
3835*	**Just Bruce (96)** (MrsEHHeath) **8-11-12** DGallagher (lw: chsd ldr: mstke 11th: wknd appr 2 out)	23	3	8/1	112	25
3849[2]	**Frazer Island (IRE) (115)** (RRowe) **8-11-9** DO'Sullivan (led tl blnd & uns rdr 4 out)		U	5/2[2]	—	—
				(SP 104.4%)	**4 Rn**	

4m 51.9 (4.90) CSF £6.60 TOTE £3.30 (£2.50) OWNER Mr Jack Joseph (MINEHEAD) BRED Patrick Madelein

3849 Greenback (BEL) is a model of consistency and once again demonstrated what a real fighter he is. Left in front four out, he seemed to be going much worse than the runner-up but, jumping the last really well, he held on in a tremendous struggle. He has an excellent strike-rate, winning half of his twenty-four races on ground varying from heavy to good-to-firm, and is a real credit to his trainer. (11/4)

3849* Garnwin (IRE) has been in terrific form this season, but he has shown that he does idle once in front and that is surely why Fitzgerald kept a very tight rein on him until as late as possible. Laughing at Greenback as he drew alongside in the straight, he jumped the last big whilst his rival got away from it more quickly. Fitzgerald quickly got down to work and the combination would surely have got up in another stride. Compensation should soon be found. (13/8)

3835* Just Bruce found this longer trip too much for him, and was being left behind turning for home. (8/1)

3849 Frazer Island (IRE) set the pace and still had the call when a bad error got rid of his rider four from home. (5/2)

4134 'PARTNERSHIP PARADE' NOVICES' HURDLE (4-Y.O+) (Class C)

4-20 (4-20) **2m 4f (11 hdls)** £3,728.75 (£1,130.00: £552.50: £263.75) GOING minus 0.15 sec per fur (G)

				SP	RR	SF
3917[2]	**Daraydan (IRE) (131)** (MCPipe) **5-11-10** APMcCoy (mde all: sn clr: unchal)	—	1	1/4[1]	94+	34
	Over The Way (IRE) (NJHenderson) **7-11-2** MAFitzgerald (stdy hdwy to chse wnr fr 2 out: no imp)	20	2	10/1[2]	70	10
3798[5]	**High Summer** (TThomsonJones) **7-11-2** JCulloty (lw: chsd wnr to 7th: chsd wnr 8th to 2 out: wknd flat)	7	3	10/1[2]	64	4
3944[4]	**Pealings (IRE)** (GAHubbard) **5-11-2** RJohnson (hld up: mstke 5th: chsd wnr 7th tl mstke 8th: wknd appr 2 out)	1¼	4	33/1	63	3
3669[2]	**Wentworth (USA)** (GThorner) **5-11-2** BPowell (a bhd: t.o)	dist	5	16/1[3]	—	—
3818[8]	**Peers Folly (IRE)** (MissHCKnight) **7-11-2** JFTitley (lw: bhd tl p.u bef 6th: b.b.v)		P	33/1	—	—
3364[11]	**Mister Goodguy (IRE)** (RCurtis) **8-11-2** DMorris (a bhd: t.o whn p.u bef 2 out)		P	66/1	—	—
				(SP 111.4%)	**7 Rn**	

4m 49.0 (7.00) CSF £3.11 TOTE £1.40: £1.10 £2.00 (£3.10) OWNER Mr D. A. Johnson (WELLINGTON) BRED His Highness the Aga Khans Studs S. C.

OFFICIAL EXPLANATION **Peers Folly (IRE): bled from the nose.**

3917 Daraydan (IRE) was in a completely different league to these rivals and had nothing more than an afternoon stroll. (1/4)

Over The Way (IRE), who won an Irish point-to-point last year, was given a nice educational ride on this debut under Rules. Although not having the vaguest hope against the winner, he took second place two out and beat the rest quite decisively. Sure to have learnt a lot from this, he should pick up a race in due course. (10/1: 6/1-11/1)

3798 High Summer gave vain chase to the winner for the majority of the race, but he was collared for that pitch two from home and had nothing more to offer. (10/1: 7/1-11/1)

3944 Pealings (IRE), who showed in second place briefly in Swinley Bottom, was at the end of his tether early in the straight. (33/1)

4135 'MERLIN' NOVICES' HUNTERS' CHASE (5-Y.O+) (Class H)

5-00 (5-00) **3m 110y (20 fncs)** £2,879.00 (£872.00: £426.00: £203.00) GOING minus 0.15 sec per fur (G)

				SP	RR	SF
	Struggles Glory (IRE) (DCRobinson) **6-12-0**(7)ow7 MrDCRobinson (lw: j.w: chsd ldr fr 3rd: led 10th: r.o wl)	—	1	3/1[1]	112+	36
4015[5]	**Lurriga Glitter (IRE)** (RJSmith) **9-11-7b[1]**(7) MrRWakley (lw: lost pl 11th: blnd 12th: rallied 4 out: chsd wnr appr last: mstke last: unable qckn)	5	2	25/1	102	33
3617[U]	**Capo Castanum** (MissHCKnight) **8-12-7**(7) MrAWintle (t: swtg: a.p: chsd wnr 11th tl appr last: sn wknd)	9	3	8/1[3]	110	41
	Balasani (FR) (JGO'Neill) **11-11-9**(5) MrASansome (bit bkwd: mstke 1st: nvr nr to chal)	11	4	10/1	89	20
3568[3]	**Berrings Dasher** (MrsJRichardson) **10-11-7**(7) MrMWatson (prom to 3 out)	1½	5	33/1	88	19
3906*	**Northern Village** (LukeDace) **10-12-0**(7) MrDAlers-Hankey (lw: mid div whn mstke 11th: 5th whn blnd 15th: sn wknd)	2	6	9/1	93	24
	Apatura King (MrsSAlner) **7-12-0**(5)ow5 MrTMitchell (lw: a bhd)	3	7	5/1[2]	89	15
	Bilbo Baggins (IRE) (MrsPATetley) **9-11-7**(7) MrMGorman (bhd fr 3rd: t.o)	dist	8	33/1	—	—
3852*	**Poors Wood** (SBreen) **10-12-2**(5) MrTMcCarthy (bhd whn p.u bef 10th: dismntd)		P	10/1	—	—
	Making Time (MFLoggin) **10-11-2**(7) MrAndrewMartin (hdwy 10th: mstke 11th: blnd 12th: wknd 13th: t.o whn p.u bef 3 out)		P	25/1	—	—
3459[2]	**Elmore** (MJRoberts) **10-11-11**(3) MrPHacking (lw: bhd fr 15th: t.o whn p.u bef 3 out)		P	8/1[3]	—	—
3357[P]	**Amadeus (FR)** (RobertBarr) **9-11-7**(7) MrMGingell (swtg: led to 10th: wknd 14th: t.o whn p.u bef last)		P	33/1	—	—
3813[P]	**Loyal Gait (NZ)** (AMDarlington) **9-11-9**(5) MrJTrice-Rolph (t: mid div whn blnd bdly 4th: bhd fr 11th: t.o whn p.u bef 15th)		P	33/1	—	—
4015[F]	**Tom's Gemini Star** (OJCarter) **9-12-0**(7) MrEJames (hdwy 9th: rdn 15th: 4th & no ch whn blnd & uns rdr 2 out)		U	12/1	—	—
				(SP 119.2%)	**14 Rn**	

6m 17.2 (12.20) CSF £77.95 TOTE £3.80: £1.60 £5.40 £3.80 (£88.30) Trio £734.90 OWNER Mr D. C. Robinson (LEWES) BRED Philip Gould

Struggles Glory (IRE), unbeaten in three point-to-points in this country, demonstrated on this debut under Rules that he could be a leading force in Hunter Chases in the coming years. With his fifty-five-year-old pilot riding so long his feet were nearly touching the ground, he gave a fine exhibition of jumping and, leading at the tenth, kept up the gallop in tremendous style. At the age of just six he has got plenty of improvement in him, and he looks an exciting prospect for next season. (3/1)

3490 Lurriga Glitter (IRE) ran much better in first-time blinkers. Moving into second place approaching the last, a mistake at that fence sealed his fate. (25/1)

3446* Capo Castanum moved into second place setting out on the final circuit, but he failed to reel in the winner and was collared for that pitch going to the last. (8/1: 6/1-10/1)

Balasani (FR), a one-time high-class hurdler for Martin Pipe, looked in need of this first run in just over a year and, although plodding on for fourth prize, never had a hope of troubling the principals. (10/1: 6/1-12/1)

3568 Berrings Dasher played an active role until coming to the end of his tether three from home. (33/1)

3906* Northern Village had the ground to suit but he is not the best of jumpers, and that was demonstrated here. He was in fifth place when a bad error six out sealed his fate. (9/1)
3852* Poors Wood (10/1: 8/1-12/1)
3459 Elmore (8/1: op 4/1)
3765* Tom's Gemini Star (12/1: 6/1-14/1)

4136 'ROYAL ASCOT CRICKET CLUB' NOVICES' H'CAP HURDLE (4-Y.O+) (Class C)

5-35 (5-35) **2m 110y (9 hdls)** £5,402.25 (£1,638.00: £801.50: £383.25) GOING minus 0.15 sec per fur (G)

				SP	RR	SF
4048^{9}	**John Drumm (108)** (PRWebber) **6-11-10** JOsborne (lw: w ldr: led 2nd: rdn out)	—	**1**	9/2^{3}	87	47
3801^{2}	**Fairly Sharp (IRE) (100)** (GraemeRoe) **4-10-10** NWilliamson (led to 2nd: ev ch appr 2 out: unable qckn)	2½	**2**	5/2^{2}	77	31
3942^{W}	**Super Rapier (IRE) (84)** (GAHubbard) **5-10-0** RJohnson (hld up: rdn appr 2 out: one pce)	3½	**3**	20/1	57	17
3592*	**Fasil (IRE) (112)** (NJHWalker) **4-11-8** APMcCoy (lw: mstkes 3rd & 6th: nvr nr to chal)	2½	**4**	13/8^{1}	83	37
3820^{3}	**Maeterlinck (IRE) (87)** (GThorner) **5-9-10**(7)ow3 ClareThorner (hld up: 5th whn mstke 3 out: sn wknd)	hd	**5**	10/1	58	15
3549^{6}	**Regal Pursuit (IRE) (100)** (NJHenderson) **6-11-2** MAFitzgerald (swtg: bhd fr 3rd)	3½	**6**	11/1	67	27
3901^{5}	**Adilov (84)** (JJBridger) **5-9-11**(3) SophieMitchell (lw: hld up: rdn appr 2 out: sn wknd)	1	**7**	25/1	50	10
				(SP 110.9%)		**7 Rn**

3m 52.9 (2.90) CSF £14.16 TOTE £5.00: £2.80 £1.50 (£6.50) OWNER Mr Andrew Jenkins (BANBURY) BRED Chesters Stud
LONG HANDICAP Maeterlinck (IRE) 9-8 Adilov 9-13
WEIGHT FOR AGE 4yo-6lb
3820* John Drumm appreciated the drop in class and return to two miles and, making the vast majority of the running, was ridden along to keep the runner-up at bay. (9/2: 3/1-5/1)
3801 Fairly Sharp (IRE) gave chase for the majority of the race, and had every chance entering the straight before tapped for toe. (5/2)
3133 Super Rapier (IRE) moved into third place turning for home but failed to find another gear. (20/1)
3592* Fasil (IRE) ruined any hopes he may have had with poor jumping. Awkward at the first and untidy at the third, he was just about to edge closer when a mistake four out put the lid on him. (13/8)
3820 Maeterlinck (IRE) chased the leaders, but a mistake three from home sealed his fate. (10/1)
3549 Regal Pursuit (IRE) does not look an easy ride and, carrying her head rather high, was at the back of the field for the final circuit. (11/1: 6/1-12/1)

T/Plpt: £92.30 (313.88 Tckts). T/Qdpt: £15.50 (69.4 Tckts) AK

3947-NEWTON ABBOT (L-H) (Firm)

Saturday April 12th

Water Jump omitted in all chases
WEATHER: Sunny

4137 HAPPY BIRTHDAY PARTYFARE NOVICES' H'CAP HURDLE (0-105) (4-Y.O) (Class E)

2-10 (2-10) **2m 1f (8 hdls)** £2,169.00 (£609.00: £297.00) GOING minus 0.25 sec per fur (GF)

				SP	RR	SF
3927^{3}	**Safecracker (72)** (CPMorlock) **4-10-4** DerekByrne (lw: led to 1st: reminders after 4th: disp ld 2 out: led appr last: drvn out)	—	**1**	8/1^{3}	53	5
3898^{2}	**Bath Knight (72)** (RCurtis) **4-9-11**(7) MrJGoldstein (nt fluent: led 1st: rdn 2 out: hdd appr last: no ex flat)	½	**2**	9/4^{2}	53	5
4069^{7}	**Rapid Liner (68)** (RJBaker) **4-10-0** VSlattery (a bhd: t.o 5th)	dist	**3**	20/1	—	—
3468^{8}	**Saucy Dancer (68)** (JCTuck) **4-10-0** SMcNeill (bhd after 2nd: hdwy 5th: in tch next tl wknd appr 2 out)	hd	**4**	25/1	—	—
4017^{2}	**Kai's Lady (IRE) (68)** (CLPopham) **4-10-0** TDascombe (bhd fr 4th: lost tch next: t.o)	10	**5**	14/1	—	—
3951*	**Mellow Master (92)** (NJHWalker) **4-11-3**(7) XAizpuru (lw: chsd ldrs in tch tl mstke 6th: lost pl: p.u bef 2 out: lame)		**P**	4/6^{1}	—	—
				(SP 117.2%)		**6 Rn**

3m 59.6 (6.60) CSF £25.71 TOTE £11.10: £4.20 £1.10 (£31.50) OWNER West Lancs Antiques Export Racing (WANTAGE) BRED L. H. J. Ward
LONG HANDICAP Saucy Dancer 9-11 Kai's Lady (IRE) 9-8 Rapid Liner 9-5
OFFICIAL EXPLANATION **Mellow Master: was found to be lame behind after the race.**
Safecracker appreciated the firm ground and gained the upper hand between the last two flights. While the current dry conditions prevail he can win again. (8/1)
3898 Bath Knight, the long-time leader, had no answer to the winner's challenge on the flat. A similar contest should soon come his way. (9/4: 3/1-2/1)
3951* Mellow Master, seeking a hat-trick and with his stable in fine form, was surprisingly being pushed along with a full circuit to go. He was eventually pulled up after reportedly pulling muscles in his back. (4/6)

4138 ADDISONS QUALITY MEATS NOVICES' CHASE (6-Y.O+) (Class E)

2-45 (2-45) **3m 2f 110y (17 fncs)** £3,507.80 (£861.20) GOING minus 0.25 sec per fur (GF)

				SP	RR	SF
3948^{3}	**Rustic Flight (60)** (LWaring) **10-10-3**(7) MGriffiths (led to 2nd: lft in ld 3rd: tk wrong crse appr next: fin 1st: disq)		**1D**	16/1	—	—
3993^{2}	**The Whole Hog (IRE) (76)** (KCBailey) **8-11-3** SMcNeill (lw: lft 2nd at 3rd: sn tk wrong crse: retraced & tk correct crse: fin 2nd; dist: awrdd race)	—	**1**	4/11^{1}	—	—
3892^{U}	**Dunlir (69)** (PRRodford) **7-10-10** MSharratt (tk wrong crse after 3rd: retraced & tk correct crse: fin 3rd; dist & dist: plcd 2nd)	dist	**2**	7/1^{3}	—	—
3978^{P}	**Cravate (FR)** (PJHobbs) **7-10-5b^{1}** GTormey (lw: j.slowly 1st: led 2nd: blnd bdly & uns rdr 3rd)		**U**	5/1^{2}	—	—
				(SP 108.4%)		**4 Rn**

7m 23.6 (49.60) CSF £3.16 TOTE £1.30 (£3.10) OWNER Mrs Sharon Nelson (UPPER LAMBOURN) BRED Owen O'Leary
STEWARDS' ENQUIRY Griffiths susp. 21-26 & 29/04/97 (continuing after taking wrong course).
IN-FOCUS: **Chaos ensued when Griffiths, on Rustic Flight, was left in front by the departure of Cravate at the third. What would have been the next fence, the water, was dolled off, and Griffiths made the error of switching to the hurdles track immediately after taking the third, rather than waiting until just before the water, the correct route. He compounded his error by taking the wrong route on the next two circuits aswell. The Whole Hog and Dunlir were initially carried onto the wrong course by the loose horse, but quickly retraced, The Whole Hog being awarded the race after finishing more than a minute behind Rustic Flight.**

Rustic Flight carried on after taking the wrong course after the open ditch on the first circuit, and was later disqualified. (16/1)
3993 The Whole Hog (IRE), the clear form choice, was awarded the race after the disqualification of Rustic Flight. (4/11: 1/4-2/5)

4139 SQUIRES RECRUITMENT CONDITIONAL H'CAP HURDLE (0-125) (4-Y.O+) (Class E)
3-15 (3-15) **2m 6f (10 hdls)** £2,210.70 (£620.20: £302.10) GOING minus 0.25 sec per fur (GF)

				SP	RR	SF
3932[3]	**Burlington Sam (NZ) (89)** (AGHobbs) **9-11-10** OBurrows (lw: hld up: hdwy to chse ldr 8th: rdn & disp ld 2 out: led appr last: drvn out)	—	**1**	11/10[1]	67	22
4071[3]	**Dissolve (77)** (NMLampard) **5-10-12** ChrisWebb (led 2nd: briefly hdd appr 7th: hdd appr last: wknd flat)	3½	**2**	11/8[2]	53	8
3891[U]	**Allahrakha (70)** (MHill) **6-10-5** TDascombe (led to 2nd: qcknd to ld briefly appr 2nd: sn rdn: wknd fr next)	dist	**3**	9/2[3]	—	—
				(SP 107.9%)		**3 Rn**

5m 21.3 (9.30) CSF £2.74 TOTE £2.10 (£1.50) OWNER Mrs Jackie Reip (KINGSBRIDGE) BRED G. H. L. Broughton
2573 Burlington Sam (NZ), in fine form in the early part of the season, got back to winning ways here with a gutsy display. (11/10: op evens)
4071 Dissolve did not seem to quite get home over this longer trip. (11/8)

4140 PAIGNTON AND DARTMOUTH STEAM RAILWAY H'CAP CHASE (0-125) (5-Y.O+) (Class D)
3-45 (3-45) **2m 5f 110y (14 fncs)** £3,533.75 (£1,070.00: £522.50: £248.75) GOING minus 0.25 sec per fur (GF)

				SP	RR	SF
4000[2]	**Polden Pride (113)** (GBBalding) **9-11-5** BClifford (lw: hld up: hdwy to chse ldr 11th: led next: sn clr: easily)	—	**1**	4/5[1]	116+	46
4090[3]	**Fenwick (94)** (RJHodges) **10-10-0** TDascombe (bhd 7th: sn outpcd: stdy hdwy 11th: chsd wnr appr 2 out: no imp)	8	**2**	9/1	91	21
4019*	**Doualago (FR) (122)** (MCPipe) **7-11-9b**(5) GSupple (lw: j.w: led tl hdd 12th: wknd steadily)	3½	**3**	9/4[2]	116	46
3410[3]	**Beau Babillard (110)** (PFNicholls) **10-11-2b** BFenton (chsd ldr: in tch: j.slowly 10th: sn lost pl: wknd 12th)	16	**4**	8/1[3]	93	23
3966[P]	**Ryton Run (94)** (MrsSMOdell) **12-10-0** TJO'Sullivan (a bhd: wkng & p.u bef 8th)		**P**	40/1	—	—
				(SP 109.9%)		**5 Rn**

5m 17.8 (0.80) CSF £7.30 TOTE £1.90: £1.10 £3.20 (£3.70) OWNER Lockyer,C Parry,G Balding (ANDOVER) BRED G. B. Balding
LONG HANDICAP Fenwick 9-5 Ryton Run 9-1
OFFICIAL EXPLANATION Ryton Run: hung badly and lost a front shoe.
4000 Polden Pride, a real fast-ground performer, relished the extra three furlongs and won very easily in the hands of Brian Clifford. He will be kept going right through the summer and, over this sort of trip, this victory could be the start of a sequence. (4/5: op 5/4)
3897* Fenwick ran well from out of the handicap, and this consistent sort should soon regain the winning thread. (9/1)
4019* Doualago (FR), raised 5lb for winning a poor match last time, seems too high in the weights at the moment (9/4: op 5/4)

4141 WILLIAM HILL H'CAP HURDLE (0-125) (4-Y.O+) (Class D)
4-15 (4-15) **2m 1f (8 hdls)** £2,735.50 (£768.00: £374.50) GOING minus 0.25 sec per fur (GF)

				SP	RR	SF
2963[3]	**Hay Dance (109)** (PJHobbs) **6-11-3** GTormey (lw: hld up: hdwy to chse ldr appr 5th: led appr 2 out: clr last: unchal)	—	**1**	7/4[2]	95+	44
3471*	**Knight in Side (96)** (MCPipe) **11-10-4** CMaude (led: sn clr: hdd appr 2 out: rdn & outpcd appr last: dead)	7	**2**	5/4[1]	75	24
3915*	**Out Ranking (FR) (117)** (JNeville) **5-11-4**(7) XAizpuru (lw: chsd ldr to 3rd: sn outpcd & bhd: styd on wl 2 out)	5	**3**	5/1[3]	92	41
3890[4]	**Verde Luna (92)** (DWPArbuthnot) **5-10-0** SMcNeill (bhd: some hdwy 6th: nvr on terms)	2½	**4**	14/1	64	13
3896[3]	**Glowing Path (92)** (RJHodges) **7-9-7**(7) JHarris (hdwy to chse ldr 3rd: lost pl appr 5th & wknd)	3½	**5**	16/1	61	10
				(SP 110.0%)		**5 Rn**

3m 53.4 (0.40) CSF £4.09 TOTE £2.10: £1.30 £1.20 (£2.50) OWNER Wessex Go Racing Partnership (MINEHEAD) BRED Limestone Stud
LONG HANDICAP Verde Luna 9-7 Glowing Path 9-7
2963 Hay Dance has been in excellent form this season, and returned fresh here to win in a canter. Small fields and fast ground are what he relishes and, in this sort of mood, he has not stopped winning yet. (7/4)
3471* Knight in Side unfortunately collapsed and died in the unsaddling enclosure. (5/4: op 2/1)
3915* Out Ranking (FR) having her first run since being claimed out of Martin Pipe's stable, dropped behind rather early in the race, but stayed on again to some effect. Her shrewd connections will no doubt find a suitable race for her in the coming weeks. (5/1: op 5/2)

4142 WILF TOWNSEND MEMORIAL H'CAP CHASE (0-105) (5-Y.O+) (Class F)
4-45 (4-45) **2m 110y (11 fncs)** £2,641.30 (£741.80: £361.90) GOING minus 0.25 sec per fur (GF)

				SP	RR	SF
3981[U]	**Evening Rain (80)** (RJHodges) **11-10-11** TDascombe (chsd ldr tl led appr 2 out: hld on wl flat)	—	**1**	8/1	90	12
793[7]	**Toomuch Toosoon (IRE) (88)** (PFNicholls) **9-11-5** BFenton (lw: mid div: hdwy to chse wnr appr 2 out: btn & mstke last)	2	**2**	9/2[2]	96	18
3950*	**Mistress Rosie (72)** (MHill) **10-10-3** SFox (mstke 3rd: lost pl: rallied 5th: styd on 2 out: no imp)	8	**3**	5/1[3]	72	—
3891*	**Jay Jay's Voyage (76)** (MrsJScrivens) **14-10-4**(3) GuyLewis (chsd ldrs tl wknd 7th: styd on 2 out: nvr nrr)	2½	**4**	7/1	74	—
2092[3]	**Spinning Steel (92)** (PRRodford) **10-11-9** SBurrough (lw: led tl hdd appr 2 out: wknd)	2½	**5**	5/2[1]	88	10
3832[5]	**Monday Club (93)** (JCTuck) **13-11-10** RBellamy (hdwy to chse ldrs 8th: wknd appr 2 out)	7	**6**	11/2	82	4
3897[4]	**Days of Thunder (82)** (MrsSMOdell) **9-10-13** TJO'Sullivan (lw: a bhd: wknd 7th)	2	**7**	16/1	69	—
3954[3]	**Dawn Chance (77)** (RJHodges) **11-10-8** PHolley (a bhd: wknd 6th: t.o & p.u bef 9th)		**P**	10/1	—	—
				(SP 117.4%)		**8 Rn**

4m 6.8 (6.80) CSF £41.45 CT £183.50 TOTE £8.70: £2.10 £1.70 £1.70 (£15.10) Trio £35.50 OWNER The Gardens Entertainments Ltd (SOMERTON) BRED Universal Stables
190 Evening Rain, without a win in four years, was given a fine ride by Dascombe and bravely held the runner-up at bay. Connections stated the winner handles the ground really well and will continue right through the summer months. (8/1: op 5/1)
361 Toomuch Toosoon (IRE), off the course for five months and running out of Paul Nicholls' yard for the first time, made a very pleasing debut. Had he not pecked at the last fence it would have been a tight finish. With this run under his belt he can soon go one better. (9/2)
3950* Mistress Rosie ran well on this step up in class, and stayed on really well without posing a serious threat. A step up in trip should pose no problems. (5/1)
3891* Jay Jay's Voyage, a winner over three miles, found this trip on the sharp side. A step up in distance is essential to regain the winning thread. (7/1)
2092 Spinning Steel, off the course for four months, presumably needed this. He set a furious pace and was very tired by the time he reached the second last. With this run under his belt he will be a different proposition next time, and will be the one they all have to catch. (5/2)
3954 Dawn Chance (10/1: op 7/12)

4143 SAPPHIRE AND DIAMONDS INTERMEDIATE OPEN N.H. FLAT RACE (4, 5 & 6-Y.O) (Class H)
5-15 (5-15) **2m 1f** £1,278.00 (£358.00: £174.00)

	Horse / details	Dist	Pos	SP	RR	SF
3365[6]	**Filscot** (WGMTurner) **5-10-11**(7) JPower (lw: chsd ldr tl led 7f out: clr 3f out: unchal)	—	1	5/2[2]	66 f	—
3895[4]	**Country Kris** (BJMRyall) **5-11-4** GUpton (mid div: chsd ldrs 6f: rdn to chse wnr 2f out: no imp)	21	2	2/1[1]	46 f	—
	Brother Nero (NZ) (AGHobbs) **5-11-4** RGreene (hld up & bhd: hdwy to chse wnr 7f out: outpcd 4f out: rdn & lost pl 2f out)	2	3	7/2[3]	44 f	—
3767[7]	**See Prosperity** (MissSWaterman) **5-10-11**(7) NWillmington (bit bkwd: bhd after 3f: t.o ½-wy)	dist	4	8/1	—	—
3895[11]	**Phone The Pipeline** (MCPipe) **4-10-5b**[1](7) BMoore (led: sn wl clr: hdd 7f out: wknd qckly: t.o)	1¼	5	7/1	—	—

(SP 107.7%) **5 Rn**

3m 52.6 (231.60) CSF £6.86 TOTE £2.50: £1.30 £1.10 (£2.50) OWNER Mr G. F. Beazley (SHERBORNE) BRED G. F. Beazley
WEIGHT FOR AGE 4yo-6lb
3365 Filscot won this very easily after a couple of decent efforts, and looks to be going the right way. (5/2)
Country Kris tried hard to peg back the winner but he proved no match. (2/1)
Brother Nero (NZ) was struggling to keep up half-a-mile from home. (7/2: 9/4-4/1)
See Prosperity (8/1: 6/1-9/1)
Phone The Pipeline (7/1: op 4/1)

T/Plpt: £57.80 (122.05 Tckts). T/Qdpt: £13.90 (27.71 Tckts) T

4055-SEDGEFIELD (L-H) (Good to firm)
Saturday April 12th
Race 1: flight number 6 bypassed, jockey injured. Race 5 Flag Start.
WEATHER: Fine

4144 J.R. TILES MAIDEN HURDLE (4-Y.O+) (Class E)
1-45 (1-45) **2m 5f 110y (9 hdls)** £2,740.00 (£765.00: £370.00)GOING minus 0.80 sec per fur (F)

	Horse / details	Dist	Pos	SP	RR	SF
3544[4]	**Sharp Command (85)** (PEccles) **4-10-12** RichardGuest (trckd ldrs: led after 4 out: clr next: unchal)	—	1	9/4[1]	58+	20
4060[6]	**Catch the Pigeon (78)** (REBarr) **8-11-0** NSmith (in tch: effrt 4 out: wnt 2nd appr 2 out: no imp)	15	2	9/1	42	11
3453[5]	**Caught At Last (IRE)** (MrsMReveley) **6-11-5** GCahill (lw: in tch: hdwy to chse wnr 3 out: no imp)	13	3	7/2[2]	37	6
2802[6]	**Carnmoney (IRE) (75)** (JSisterson) **9-11-5** BStorey (prom tl lost pl ½-wy: styd on again fr 3 out)	6	4	20/1	33	2
3910[6]	**King Fly (91)** (MrsSarahHorner-Harker) **7-11-5** AThornton (lw: led to 5th: wknd 3 out)	6	5	7/2[2]	28	—
4075[11]	**Salem Beach** (MartinTodhunter) **5-11-0** JCallaghan (a bhd)	22	6	16/1	7	—
3946[12]	**West Lutton** (MWEasterby) **5-11-2**(3) PMidgley (prom to 4 out)	5	7	20/1	8	—
3794[P]	**Moreflash** (JSHaldane) **5-11-0** TReed (in tch tl wknd 3 out)	6	8	100/1	—	—
3823[17]	**Banner Year (IRE)** (TJCarr) **6-11-5** PNiven (bhd fr ½-wy)	dist	9	100/1	—	—
3795[6]	**Smile Pleeze (IRE)** (MrsMStirk) **5-11-5** MrSSwiers (nt j.w: a outpcd: bhd whn fell last)		F	8/1[3]	—	—
3644[P]	**Tartan Joy (IRE)** (JAMoore) **6-11-0**(5) MrMHNaughton (mstkes: t.o whn p.u bef 5th: sddle slipped)		P	50/1	—	—
3418[11]	**Aeolus** (LRLloyd-James) **4-10-9**(3) ECallaghan (bit bkwd: sn t.o: p.u bef last)		P	66/1	—	—
3723[6]	**Point Duty (60)** (FPMurtagh) **7-11-5b**[1] ADobbin (cl up: led 5th: blnd 4 out: sn hdd: wknd qckly & p.u bef 2 out)		P	33/1	—	—
3474[9]	**Primitive Heart (69)** (HowardJohnson) **5-11-5** ASSmith (sn bhd: t.o whn p.u bef 2 out)		P	33/1	—	—
2918[P]	**Matachon** (MSmith) **7-11-5** RSupple (bit bkwd: in tch: drvn along fr 3rd: wknd fr 4 out: s.u appr 2 out)		S	100/1	—	—
3803[P]	**Regal Jest** (BWMurray) **7-11-0** WDwan (blnd & uns rdr 1st)		U	100/1	—	—

(SP 125.0%) **16 Rn**

4m 54.5 (-5.50) CSF £21.13 TOTE £3.10: £1.40 £1.90 £1.80 (£16.50) Trio £11.40 OWNER Mr A. P. Holland (LAMBOURN) BRED Coral'S Farm and Stud
WEIGHT FOR AGE 4yo-7lb
OFFICIAL EXPLANATION **Tartan Joy (IRE): saddle slipped.**
IN-FOCUS: **This meeting produced a series of fast times.**
3544 Sharp Command beat some moderate rivals here, but did it in some style. (9/4)
Catch the Pigeon got the trip well enough but, despite staying on, never had a chance with the winner. (9/1)
3453 Caught At Last (IRE) has always been a bit of a handful and needed two lads in the paddock, but once he came off the bit he was disappointing. (7/2: 9/4-4/1)
2802 Carnmoney (IRE) is basically well short of speed. (20/1)
3727 King Fly has ability but does not produce it often. (7/2)

4145 TRADE WINDOWS UK LTD. H'CAP CHASE (0-115) (5-Y.O+) (Class E)
2-15 (2-16) **2m 110y (13 fncs)** £3,119.00 (£932.00: £446.00: £203.00) GOING minus 0.80 sec per fur (F)

	Horse / details	Dist	Pos	SP	RR	SF
3991*	**Grouse-N-Heather (92)** (PMonteith) **8-11-10** ADobbin (chsd ldrs: mstke & pushed along 7th: hdwy to ld after 4 out: sn clr: styd on)	—	1	10/11[1]	108	6
2569[4]	**Uk Hygiene (IRE) (80)** (MDHammond) **7-10-12** RGarritty (lw: led tl hdd after 4 out: kpt on u.p: no ch w wnr)	5	2	4/1[2]	91	—
3991[2]	**Rebel King (79)** (MABarnes) **7-10-6**(5) STaylor (cl up: drvn along fr 5th: outpcd fr 4 out)	2	3	4/1[2]	88	—
4058[3]	**Reve de Valse (USA) (85)** (RJohnson) **10-11-3** KJohnson (sn outpcd & bhd: sme hdwy 2 out: sn btn)	3	4	11/2[3]	91	—

(SP 107.8%) **4 Rn**

4m (2.00) CSF £4.38 TOTE £1.70 (£3.10) OWNER Mr D. J. Fairbairn (ROSEWELL) BRED R. A. Cameron
3991* Grouse-N-Heather never looks to be going that well, but she gets stronger as the race goes on and can win again. (10/11)
2569 Uk Hygiene (IRE) put up a really good performance after almost three months off, and looks likely to be back on the winning trail before long. (4/1)
3991 Rebel King is running reasonably well at present but he is basically one-paced. (4/1)
4058 Reve de Valse (USA) found this company too quick. (11/2: 4/1-6/1)

4146 STANLEY RACING GOLDEN NUMBERS SERIES FINAL NOVICES' H'CAP HURDLE (4-Y.O+) (Class C)
2-50 (2-51) **2m 5f 110y (10 hdls)** £10,503.75 (£3,180.00: £1,552.50: £738.75) GOING minus 0.80 sec per fur (F)

	Horse / details	Dist	Pos	SP	RR	SF
3910[2]	**Meadow Hymn (IRE) (114)** (JGFitzGerald) **6-12-0** PCarberry (lw: a.p: styd on u.p to ld cl home)	—	1	3/1[1]	92	31

3983⁷	**Stylish Interval (89)** (NWaggott) **5-10-3** ADobbin (swtg: chsd ldrs: led 2 out: sn rdn: hdd & no ex towards fin)nk	**2**	14/1	67	6
3714*	**Brambles Way (112)** (MrsMReveley) **8-11-12b** PNiven (lw: bhd: effrt ½-wy: chal 2 out: hung lft: nt qckn towards fin) nk	**3**	3/1 1	90	29
4056⁶	**Silent Guest (IRE) (93)** (MDHammond) **4-10-0** DBentley (cl up: led after 3 out to 2 out: sn btn) 22	**4**	11/1	54	—
3990F	**Rule Out The Rest (89)** (MrsSarahHorner-Harker) **6-10-3** AThornton (prom tl outpcd fr 4 out) nk	**5**	10/1	50	—
536*	**Good Hand (USA) (92)** (SEKettlewell) **11-10-6** RGarritty (bhd: effrt ½-wy: no imp) ¾	**6**	4/1 2	52	—
450⁵	**Longcroft (86)** (SEKettlewell) **5-9-7(7)** NHorrocks (lost pl ½-wy: some hdwy u.p 4 out: sn btn) 6	**7**	16/1	42	—
4060U	**I'm Tyson (NZ) (86)** (MrsDianneSayer) **9-10-0** BStorey (hld up: effrt 4 out: sn btn) 2½	**8**	25/1	40	—
4056*	**Silver Minx (99)** (MrsMReveley) **5-10-13** GLee (led tl hdd after 3 out: 4th whn fell 2 out)	**F**	5/1 3	—	—
4057²	**Whitegates Willie (86)** (HowardJohnson) **5-9-7(7)** CMcCormack (bhd fr ½-wy: t.o whn p.u bef last)	**P**	20/1	—	—
			(SP 125.2%)		**10 Rn**

4m 55.4 (-4.60) CSF £43.12 CT £130.55 TOTE £4.40: £1.80 £4.00 £1.80 (£92.70) Trio £74.30 OWNER Mrs M. Nowell (MALTON) BRED Dermot O'Mahony

LONG HANDICAP Longcroft 9-12 I'm Tyson (NZ) 9-1 Silent Guest (IRE) 9-8 Whitegates Willie 9-4

WEIGHT FOR AGE 4yo-7lb

3910 Meadow Hymn (IRE) certainly stays and is game as they come, and that won him the day. (3/1)

3723* Stylish Interval did not impress on looks, but this tough sort ran his heart out only to be just touched off. (14/1)

3714* Brambles Way looks superb, but in the race he was on and off the bit at various stages. He was always tending to hang left which proved his undoing in the fight from the last. (3/1)

4056 Silent Guest (IRE), 6lb out of the weights, ran well to the second last. (11/1)

1081 Rule Out The Rest, who fell last time, never showed any spark here. (10/1)

536* Good Hand (USA), after a winter's rest, did not look quite right. He ran no sort of race and this was obviously needed. (4/1: op 6/1)

4056* Silver Minx again went to the left at his hurdles, but his measure had been taken when he fell heavily two out. (5/1)

4147 EDEN ARMS SWALLOW HOTEL CONDITIONAL H'CAP HURDLE (0-105) (4-Y.O+) (Class F)

3-25 (3-25) **3m 3f 110y (13 hdls)** £2,547.50 (£710.00: £342.50) GOING minus 0.80 sec per fur (F)

			SP	RR	SF
3887⁷	**Kings Lane (82)** (JMDun) **8-10-10** EHusband (sn pushed along: mid div: hdwy 4 out: led appr 2 out: sn clr) .—	**1**	12/1	64	16
1844*	**Troodos (100)** (MrsASwinbank) **11-12-0** BGrattan (lw: bhd: hdwy 8th: chsd wnr fr 2 out: no imp) 6	**2**	7/2 1	78	30
3096⁶	**Blooming Spring (IRE) (72)** (MrsDThomson) **8-10-0** DThomas (lw: hld up & bhd: gd hdwy to jn ldrs 8th: rdn 4 out: outpcd 2 out: kpt on flat) 6	**3**	20/1	47	—
3157F	**Scarba (100)** (JMJefferson) **9-12-0** ECallaghan (lw: hld up: hdwy 4 out: one pce fr 2 out) nk	**4**	5/1 2	75	27
3309⁶	**Cheater (IRE) (90)** (HowardJohnson) **6-11-4b** CMcCormack (w ldr: led 4 out tl appr 2 out: btn whn mstke 2 out) 2	**5**	8/1	63	15
3887⁸	**Barnstormer (72)** (EAElliott) **11-10-0b** GFRyan (trckd ldrs tl rdn & wknd 2 out) 3½	**6**	20/1	43	—
2787¹⁰	**Movie Man (73)** (JRTurner) **5-10-1** RBurns (hld up: rdn 9th: no imp) ¾	**7**	20/1	44	—
3100⁴	**Chill Factor (82)** (MrsMReveley) **7-10-10** GLee (lw: stdd s: pushed along fr 7th: no imp) 16	**8**	11/2 3	43	—
3454²	**Soloman Springs (USA) (78)** (MrsVCWard) **7-10-6** PHenley (prom: pushed along fr 4th: wknd fr 9th) 12	**9**	9/1	32	—
3589⁵	**Frown (95)** (PBowen) **7-11-9** LCummins (chsd ldrs tl rdn & wknd qckly 4 out: t.o) dist	**10**	16/1	—	—
4073*	**Clongour (IRE) (85)** (FMurphy) **7-10-13b** DJKavanagh (hld up: hdwy whn b.d 3 out)	**B**	5/1 2	—	—
3822⁸	**Fiery Sun (76)** (REBarr) **12-10-4** NHorrocks (mde most to 4 out: wkng whn fell next)	**F**	33/1	—	—
3795¹¹	**Stepdaughter (72)** (MrsDThomson) **11-10-0** RMcGrath (sn bhd: wl t.o whn p.u bef 3 out)	**P**	50/1	—	—
3481⁸	**Strong Character (72)** (DALamb) **11-9-9(5)** NHannity (shkn up after s: sn chsng ldrs: wknd qckly 8th: t.o whn p.u bef 3 out)	**P**	66/1	—	—
			(SP 126.3%)		**14 Rn**

6m 29.0 (1.50 under best) (-6.00) CSF £48.70 CT £797.98 TOTE £9.80: £2.50 £1.90 £4.30 (£25.90) Trio £219.20 OWNER Mr J. M. Dun (HERIOT) BRED G. R. Hutchinson

LONG HANDICAP Blooming Spring (IRE) 9-12 Barnstormer 9-13 Stepdaughter 9-2 Strong Character 8-12

OFFICIAL EXPLANATION **Clongour (IRE): bled from the nose.**

3646 Kings Lane, in a co-operative mood this time, made the race his going to the second last, but he is never one to fully rely on. (12/1)

1844* Troodos, returning here after four months off, put up a fair performance and will obviously be all the sharper for it. (7/2)

536 Blooming Spring (IRE) is obviously in good heart and can pick up a race. (20/1)

3157 Scarba is normally happier on easier ground, but this was a sound effort after almost two months off. (5/1)

3309 Cheater (IRE) likes things to go his way and this proved far too competitive in the closing stages. (8/1)

1822* Barnstormer travelled well for a long way but proved slow when asked a question. (20/1)

3100 Chill Factor looked none too keen here when asked for an effort with over a circuit to go. (11/2)

4148 MCEWAN'S DURHAM NATIONAL H'CAP CHASE (0-130) (5-Y.O+) (Class C)

3-55 (3-55) **3m 4f (22 fncs)** £7,132.50 (£2,160.00: £1,055.00: £502.50) GOING minus 0.80 sec per fur (F)

			SP	RR	SF
3884⁴	**Act the Wag (IRE) (117)** (MartinTodhunter) **8-11-11b¹** PCarberry (hld up: wnt prom 12th: chal 18th: lft clr 2 out: eased flat) —	**1**	5/1 3	132+	46
4068*	**Royal Saxon (92)** (PBowen) **11-10-0** WMarston (lw: chsd ldrs: led 8th to 10th: drvn along fr 13th: kpt on fr 3 out: no ch wnr) 1½	**2**	8/1	106	20
3694³	**Westwell Boy (100)** (PBeaumont) **11-10-8** ADobbin (lw: chsd ldrs: hmpd & lost pl after 15th: hdwy 5 out: one pce fr 3 out) 3	**3**	7/2 2	112	26
3837*	**Lucky Dollar (IRE) (99)** (KCBailey) **9-10-7** AThornton (lw: mstke 2nd: bhd: effrt 15th: styd on: nvr rchd ldrs) 1¾	**4**	11/8 1	110	24
3729P	**Dont Tell the Wife (108)** (CREgerton) **11-11-2** JAMcCarthy (bhd: mstke 4th & 10th: hdwy & prom 15th: wknd 5 out) 30	**5**	9/1	101	15
4059³	**Upwell (92)** (RJohnson) **13-10-0** KJohnson (led to 8th: hit next: sn wknd: t.o fr 16th) 2½	**6**	50/1	84	—
3710⁷	**Over the Stream (96)** (MissMKMilligan) **11-10-4** ASSmith (prom: led 14th tl disp ld & fell 2 out)	**F**	16/1	—	—
3729⁴	**Uranus Collonges (FR) (100)** (JGFitzGerald) **11-10-8b** LWyer (chsd ldrs: led 10th to 14th: wknd qckly 16th: p.u after 4 out)	**P**	14/1	—	—
4057³	**Triona's Hope (IRE) (92)** (EMCaine) **8-9-9(5)** MrMHNaughton (hdwy & prom 15th: wknd 6 out: sn t.o: p.u bef last)	**P**	66/1	—	—
3886⁹	**Jaunty Gig (92)** (JJBirkett) **11-10-0b** LO'Hara (hld up: hdwy 15th: 3rd & rdn whn bdly hmpd & uns rdr 2 out)	**U**	33/1	—	—
			(SP 121.0%)		**10 Rn**

6m 53.2 (18.40 under best) (-11.80) CSF £41.44 CT £146.84 TOTE £6.00: £1.40 £2.10 £1.80 (£17.50) Trio £32.90 OWNER Mr Robert Ogden (ULVERSTON) BRED J. R. Kidd

LONG HANDICAP Upwell 7-12 Royal Saxon 9-8 Triona's Hope (IRE) 7-13 Jaunty Gig 9-1
3884 Act the Wag (IRE) had blinkers on for the first time and they certainly worked, but the issue was still in doubt until Over the Stream fell. (5/1)
3899 Royal Saxon is a hard ride and needs plenty of driving but he does respond, although it was always in vain here. (8/1)
3694 Westwell Boy did not have much luck in running but did jump better this time. (7/2)
3837* Lucky Dollar (IRE) had no problems with the extra distance but he found the pace too strong and, despite struggling on, could never land a blow. (11/8)
3729 Dont Tell the Wife is not a reliable character and had his limitations exposed over the last five fences. (9/1)
Over the Stream, who missed the Grand National after getting upset by all the fuss on the Saturday, ran a cracker here and may have well made the winner fight but for coming to grief two out. (16/1)
Jaunty Gig showed signs of coming back to form here, and looks worth keeping in mind. (33/1)

4149 KEITH THOMAS ASSOCIATES NOVICES' CHASE (5-Y.O+) (Class E)

4-25 (4-25) **3m 3f (21 fncs)** £3,345.00 (£1,005.00: £485.00: £225.00) GOING minus 0.80 sec per fur (F)

	Horse	Dist	Pos	SP	RR	SF
3812[2]	**Little Martina (IRE) (108)** (DMGrissell) **9-11-4** JRKavanagh (lw: mde most tl hdd flat: rallied to ld cl home)	—	1	4/7[1]	91	28
4072[F]	**Another Venture (IRE) (87)** (FMurphy) **7-11-2** PCarberry (hld up: hdwy 15th: wnt 2nd after 4 out: chal 2 out: slt ld flat: no ex towards fin)	nk	2	7/1[3]	89	26
3724[3]	**Tactix (63)** (MissMKMilligan) **7-10-11** BStorey (bhd: hdwy & prom 13th: outpcd & lost tch fr 16th)	dist	3	16/1	—	—
3367[3]	**Alicat (IRE)** (JWCurtis) **6-11-2** MFoster (chsd ldrs: wkng whn blnd 4 out & 3 out)	nk	4	50/1	—	—
3824[P]	**Donovans Reef (61)** (MrsLMarshall) **11-11-6** KJohnson (hld up: effrt 14th: sn rdn & no imp)	1¾	5	50/1	—	—
3911[5]	**More Joy (72)** (BEllison) **9-10-9**(7) CMcCormack (disp ld 4th to 12th: cl up tl wknd 4 out)	8	6	25/1	—	—
3477[P]	**Elliott's Wish (IRE) (79)** (HowardJohnson) **6-11-2**(7) MrTJBarry (mstkes 4th & 6th: chsd ldrs fr 9th tl wknd 5 out)	1¾	7	16/1	—	—
3393[F]	**Lyford Cay (IRE)** (JRBewley) **7-10-9**(7) SMelrose (fell 1st)		F	66/1	—	—
4077[3]	**German Legend (80)** (DALamb) **7-11-9** JBurke (lw: bdly hmpd 1st: t.o tl p.u bef 12th)		P	12/1	—	—
3268[5]	**Gone Away (IRE) (64)** (MDHammond) **8-11-2** DBentley (lw: outpcd & lost tch fr 13th: blnd 15th: t.o whn p.u bef 5 out)		P	25/1	—	—
3726[5]	**Master Flashman (73)** (MrsMReveley) **8-11-2** GLee (prom: mstke 7th & 8th: sn rdn along: wknd 14th: t.o whn p.u bef 4 out)		P	11/2[2]	—	—
				(SP 124.1%)	**11 Rn**	

6m 39.1 (0.80 under best) (-6.90) CSF £5.18 TOTE £1.80: £1.90 £2.90 £1.50 (£4.80) Trio £25.60 OWNER Mr Christopher Newport (ROBERTSBRIDGE) BRED Michael Hickey
3812 Little Martina (IRE) had to really fight to win this and, in doing so, put up a record time. (4/7)
4072 Another Venture (IRE) obviously appreciated this trip and jumped much better, putting up his best performance for a long time. (7/1)
3724 Tactix was made to look very one-paced on the final circuit. (16/1)
3367 Alicat (IRE) ran a shade better this time but spoiled any chances late on with some moderate jumps. (50/1)
3726 Master Flashman, unsuited by the strong pace, made mistakes and decided he had had enough with a full circuit to go. (11/2)

4150 SEDGEFIELD STANDARD OPEN N.H. FLAT RACE (4, 5 & 6-Y.O) (Class H)

4-55 (4-55) **2m 1f** £1,437.50 (£400.00: £192.50)

	Horse	Dist	Pos	SP	RR	SF
	Just Nip (JRTurner) **4-10-1**(7) RBurns (tall & narrow: hdwy ½-wy: led over 2f out: hld on wl)	—	1	20/1	57 f	—
3716[3]	**Landler** (JNorton) **4-10-12**(3) ECallaghan (unf: scratchy action: bhd: effrt 5f out: hdwy 2f out: carried lft & r.o wl towards fin: fin 3rd; ½l & nk: plcd 2nd)	½	2	9/2[2]	63 f	—
3828[4]	**Going Primitive** (JHetherton) **6-11-0** MrSSwiers (trckd ldrs: effrt 2f out: hung lft: styd on towards fin: fin 2nd; ½l: disq & plcd 3rd)	nk	3	5/1[3]	57 f	—
	Old Bombay (IRE) (TDBarron) **5-11-0** AThornton (sturdy type: effrt ½-wy: gd hdwy 2f out: sn chsng ldrs: nt qckn ins fnl f)	2	4	13/2	54 f	—
3716[4]	**Polar King (IRE)** (CWThornton) **4-10-1**(7) NHorrocks (medium sized: quite attractive: lw: led after 3f to ½-wy: led 5f out tl over 2f out: one pce)	1½	5	6/4[1]	53 f	—
	Happy Blake (MrsJStorey) **6-11-0** BStorey (rangy chasing type: bhd: styd on fnl 4f: nrst fin)	5	6	33/1	48 f	—
	Gikongoro (PCHaslam) **4-10-8** MFoster (cl cpld bkwd type: very kn: bkwd: hld up: nvr trbld ldrs)	¾	7	7/1	48 f	—
2804[8]	**Chief of Khorassan (FR)** (SEKettlewell) **5-11-0** GLee (tall: unf: chsd ldrs tl rdn & btn 5f out)	6	8	11/1	42 f	—
3548[10]	**Percy's Joy** (TDEasterby) **5-11-0** LWyer (tall: chasing type: led 3f: prom tl wknd 3f out)	2	9	10/1	40 f	—
	Swiftly Supreme (IRE) (EMCaine) **4-9-10**(7) TristanDavidson (medium sized: narrow: outpcd fr ½-wy)	3	10	66/1	32 f	—
	No Time To Wait (WWHaigh) **6-11-0** OPears (tall: hdwy to ld ½-wy: hdd 5f out: sn wknd)	2	11	10/1	35 f	—
	Toejam (REBarr) **4-10-8** NSmith (rangy: unf: very poor mover: hld up: n.d)	4	12	25/1	32 f	—
3142[15]	**Jo Lightning (IRE)** (BEllison) **4-10-8** KJohnson (plain: a bhd)	5	13	50/1	27 f	—
3203[18]	**Frugal** (BWMurray) **4-10-5**(3) EHusband (medium sized: poor mover: lost tch fnl 6f)	7	14	33/1	20 f	—
				(SP 145.1%)	**14 Rn**	

3m 53.7 CSF £112.59 TOTE £56.70: £10.50 £2.20 £2.00 (£105.00) Trio Not won; £147.79 to Musselburgh 14/4/97 OWNER Mr J. R. Turner (HELPERBY) BRED J. R. and T. Turner
WEIGHT FOR AGE 4yo-6lb
Just Nip pinched this by getting first run early in the straight. (20/1)
3716 Landler, given a lot to do, took time to respond to pressure and then did remarkably well to finish so close. (9/2)
3828 Going Primitive looked the likely winner for a long way but, when asked for an effort, all he wanted to do was hang left. (5/1)
Old Bombay (IRE) ran a fair first race and gave the impression he should be all the better for it. (13/2)
3716 Polar King (IRE) had his chances but looked far too slow when pressure was applied. (6/4)
Happy Blake showed a little ability, picking up steady ground late on. (33/1)
Gikongoro (7/1: op 4/1)

T/Plpt: £24.00 (467.49 Tckts). T/Qdpt: £11.90 (64.5 Tckts) AA

3822-HEXHAM (L-H) (Firm)
Monday April 14th
WEATHER: fine

4151 FEDERATION BREWERY NOVICES' CHASE (5-Y.O+) (Class E)
2-10 (2-10) **2m 110y (12 fncs)** £3,206.75 (£959.00: £459.50: £209.75) GOING minus 0.45 sec per fur (GF)

	Horse	Dist	Pos	SP	RR	SF
4057^{10}	**Gone Ashore (IRE) (60)** (MABarnes) **6-11-0** ADobbin (mde all: clr 3 out: drvn out)	—	**1**	13/2	69	2
3478^{P}	**All Clear (IRE)** (HowardJohnson) **6-10-11**(3) MrCBonner (chsd ldrs: wnt 2nd 3 out: no imp)	6	**2**	7/1	63	—
3909^{6}	**Jonaem (IRE) (68)** (MrsESlack) **7-11-0** KJohnson (hld up: hdwy 6th: sn outpcd: styd on appr last)	5	**3**	$9/4^{1}$	58	—
3882^{P}	**Supermarine** (BMactaggart) **11-11-0** BStorey (mstkes: chsd wnr to 9th: sn wknd)	15	**4**	25/1	44	—
4058^{5}	**Quixall Crossett (56)** (EMCaine) **12-10-7**(7) MrTJBarry (reminders 5th: sn bhd: t.o 8th)	18	**5**	33/1	26	—
3908^{13}	**Meesonette** (BEllison) **5-9-9**(7) CMcCormack (chsd ldrs: outpcd whn fell 7th)		**F**	33/1	—	—
3945^{P}	**Fair Ally (63)** (MESowersby) **7-11-0** DParker (fell 2nd)		**F**	$5/1^{3}$	—	—
694^{P}	**Speaker's House (USA) (86)** (MissLucindaRussell) **8-11-7** TReed (hld up: bdly hmpd 2nd & p.u)		**P**	$5/2^{2}$	—	—
				(SP 111.6%)	**8 Rn**	

4m 3.5 (6.50) CSF £42.39 TOTE £6.70: £2.20 £3.00 £1.40 (£15.20) OWNER Armstrong/Greenwell/Smithson (PENRITH) BRED Joe Crowe
WEIGHT FOR AGE 5yo-7lb

2506 Gone Ashore (IRE), who jumped and ran poorly on his two most recent outings, was given a most positive ride and had this in the bag three from home. (13/2)
All Clear (IRE), pulled up last time, went in pursuit of the winner three out but was never going to get anywhere near him. (7/1)
1081 Jonaem (IRE), tapped for foot at halfway, stuck on going to the last and will be better suited by two and a half miles. (9/4)
Supermarine, pulled up on his reappearance, still looked burly and after making mistakes he was leg-weary three from home. (25/1)
694 Speaker's House (USA), having his first outing for two hundred and one days, was almost brought down by a faller at the second and was immediately pulled up. (5/2: op 6/4)

4152 BUCHANAN ALES NOVICES' HURDLE (4-Y.O+) (Class E)
2-40 (2-41) **2m 4f 110y (10 hdls)** £2,857.50 (£795.00: £382.50) GOING minus 0.45 sec per fur (GF)

	Horse	Dist	Pos	SP	RR	SF
4075^{4}	**Eastcliffe (IRE)** (WMcKeown) **5-11-0** GCahill (lw: j.w: hld up & plld hrd: led after 2nd: styd on strly appr last: readily)	—	**1**	$7/4^{1}$	64+	19
3825^{3}	**Pappa Charlie (USA) (82)** (CParker) **6-11-0** BStorey (lw: sn prom: wnt 2nd 9th: rdn appr last: no imp)	5	**2**	$3/1^{2}$	60	15
3944^{3}	**Raise A Dollar** (PBeaumont) **7-10-9** MrSSwiers (lw: chsd ldrs: one pce fr 7th)	11	**3**	$4/1^{3}$	47	2
4055^{11}	**Dont Forget Curtis (IRE) (79)** (MrsKMLamb) **5-10-7**(7) MissSLamb (sn bhd: kpt on fr 7th: nvr nr ldrs)	10	**4**	20/1	44	—
3727^{6}	**Kings Minstral (IRE) (69)** (DALamb) **7-11-6** JBurke (nt j.w: sn bhd: sme hdwy 3 out: sn wknd)	13	**5**	16/1	40	—
4075^{7}	**Amber Holly (71)** (JEDixon) **8-10-9** FPerratt (bit bkwd: chsd ldrs to 7th: sn wknd)	nk	**6**	20/1	28	—
3611^{7}	**Ottadini (IRE) (54)** (WGReed) **5-10-11**ow2 TReed (hld up & plld hrd: lost pl 4th: n.d)	7	**7**	40/1	25	—
3789^{P}	**Chief Chippie** (WTKemp) **4-10-7** SMcDougall (chsd ldrs to 4th: t.o 7th)	dist	**8**	50/1	—	—
2041^{7}	**Posted Abroad (IRE)** (HowardJohnson) **5-10-9**(5) STaylor (hld up: wnt prom 6th: wknd after next: t.o: fin lame)	18	**9**	16/1	—	—
4081^{6}	**Allerby (75)** (JLGoulding) **9-11-0** ADobbin (led tl after 2nd: outpcd whn fell 6th)		**F**	6/1	—	—
2504^{8}	**Jed Abbey** (RShiels) **5-10-9** DBentley (unruly gng to s: nt j.w: prom to 6th: t.o whn p.u after 3 out)		**P**	50/1	—	—
	Margot's Boy (DMcCune) **6-11-0** KJohnson (sn bhd: t.o 6th: p.u between last 2)		**P**	66/1	—	—
				(SP 124.8%)	**12 Rn**	

4m 50.7 (2.70) CSF £6.49 TOTE £4.30: £1.10 £1.70 £2.10 (£6.30) Trio £4.00 OWNER Mrs L. E. McKeown (NEWCASTLE-UPON-TYNE) BRED J. and Mrs Liggett
WEIGHT FOR AGE 4yo-7lb

4075 Eastcliffe (IRE), a keen-going type, settled down well once in front. Jumping particularly well, he proved much too good for this lot. (7/4)
3825 Pappa Charlie (USA), an excitable type, finished clear second best in what was probably a poor race. (3/1)
3944 Raise A Dollar seems to lack anything in the way of foot and is a prospective chaser. (4/1)
3371 Dont Forget Curtis (IRE), well beaten in selling handicaps, ran his best race by far since switching stables. (20/1)
1825 Kings Minstral (IRE) is not a fluent jumper. (16/1)

4153 LCL PILS H'CAP CHASE (0-105) (5-Y.O+) (Class F)
3-10 (3-11) **2m 4f 110y (15 fncs)** £3,083.50 (£856.00: £410.50) GOING minus 0.45 sec per fur (GF)

	Horse	Dist	Pos	SP	RR	SF
2923^{8}	**Bishopdale (75)** (SGChadwick) **16-10-9** FPerratt (led 2nd: drew clr appr last)	—	**1**	$6/1^{3}$	78	1
3314^{3}	**Shawwell (77)** (JIACharlton) **10-10-11** BStorey (w ldrs: rdn 3 out: one pce)	18	**2**	Evens ^{1}	66	—
4057^{8}	**Aristodemus (66)** (MrsLMarshall) **8-10-0b1** KJohnson (mstkes: sn trckng ldrs: hit 8th & 11th: chal 3 out: wknd between last 2)	2	**3**	12/1	53	—
3911^{P}	**Hudson Bay Trader (USA) (90)** (PBeaumont) **10-11-10** LWyer (lw: led to 2nd: reminders & lost pl 5th: j.bdly rt 9th: sn t.o)	17	**4**	$7/4^{2}$	64	—
				(SP 108.3%)	**4 Rn**	

5m 4.2 (7.20) CSF £11.80 TOTE £5.80: (£2.70) OWNER Mr S. Chadwick (HAYTON) BRED Thomas Horgan
LONG HANDICAP Aristodemus 9-13

1846 Bishopdale, racing with the zest and enthusiasm of one half his age, galloped right away up the final hill. (6/1)
3314 Shawwell, suited by fast ground, was having his first outing for forty-nine days and possibly just needed it. (Evens)
Aristodemus, with the blinkers on for the first time, hardly jumped a fence properly. (12/1)
3643* Hudson Bay Trader (USA) did not want to know anything about the job on this occasion. (7/4)

4154 LCL LAGER H'CAP HURDLE (0-115) (4-Y.O+) (Class E)
3-40 (3-40) **2m (8 hdls)** £2,395.50 (£663.00: £316.50) GOING minus 0.45 sec per fur (GF)

	Horse	Dist	Pos	SP	RR	SF
4060*	**Glenugie (104)** (GMMoore) **6-11-10** NBentley (lw: w ldr: rdn 2 out: led appr last: r.o strly)	—	**1**	Evens ^{1}	84	—
4060^{4}	**Eriny (USA) (87)** (JJQuinn) **8-10-4**(3) ECallaghan (lw: trckd ldrs: plld hrd: led 2 out: hdd appr last: hit last: unable qckn)	1¼	**2**	$15/8^{2}$	66	—
4060^{3}	**Highland Way (IRE) (89)** (MartinTodhunter) **9-10-2**(7) CMcCormack (hld up: hdwy & ev ch 2 out: edgd lft & nt qckn flat)	s.h	**3**	$7/2^{3}$	68	—

				SP	RR	SF
	Son of Tempo (IRE) (80) (MrsKMLamb) **8-9-7**(7) MissSLamb (set mod pce to 2 out: wknd qckly: sn t.o)	dist	**4**	40/1	—	—
				(SP 109.4%)	**4 Rn**	

4m (12.00) CSF £3.09 TOTE £2.10: (£2.00) OWNER Mr Frazer Hines (MIDDLEHAM) BRED F. Hines
LONG HANDICAP Son of Tempo (IRE) 8-13
IN-FOCUS: **This was just a sprint from the second-last flight.**
4060* Glenugie seems better than ever and, seizing the initiative going to the last, was always doing enough. (Evens)
4060 Eriny (USA), bidding to repeat last year's victory in this race, wouldn't settle in what was a sprint over the last two. After taking it up, he failed to press home the advantage and a clumsy jump at the last handed the winner the advantage. (15/8: 5/4-2/1)
4060 Highland Way (IRE) as usual travelled strongly, but under pressure edged left and was never giving it his all. (7/2)

4155 CHEVY CHASE MAIDEN HUNTERS' CHASE (5-Y.O+) (Class H)

4-10 (4-10) **3m 1f (19 fncs)** £1,058.85 (£316.80: £151.90: £69.45) GOING minus 0.45 sec per fur (GF)

				SP	RR	SF
	Secret Bay (CPDennis) **8-12-7** MrSSwiers (lw: led to 4 out: led 2 out: styd on strly appr last: pushed clr)	—	**1**	4/5[1]	98+	5
3922[2]	**Up For Ransome (IRE)** (MrsAMNaughton) **8-12-0**(7) MrTJBarry (w ldr: led 4 out to 2 out: no ch w wnr)	14	**2**	9/4[2]	89	—
4076[4]	**Cool Yule (IRE)** (RWThomson) **9-12-2**(5) MissPRobson (hld up: mstke 9th: sn outpcd & drvn along: kpt on appr last: n.d)	19	**3**	9/1	77	—
	Park Drift (GThornton) **11-12-0**(7) MrRTate (trckd ldrs: ev ch whn hit 4 out: rdn next: sn wknd)	3	**4**	6/1[3]	75	—
3913[5]	**All Or Nothing** (NMLEwart) **9-11-9**(7) MrJEwart (uns rdr 3rd)		**U**	20/1	—	—
				(SP 115.4%)	**5 Rn**	

6m 27.7 (16.70) CSF £3.08 TOTE £1.90: £2.20 £1.00 (£1.70) OWNER Mr Stuart Dent (DARLINGTON) BRED Mrs T. Cunningham-Jardine
Secret Bay, a robust sort and an ex-eventer, came here on the back of three point-to-point wins, including a Restricted by twenty lengths and a walkover last time. Jumping particularly well when sent about his business, he soon pulled right away. (4/5)
3922 Up For Ransome (IRE) wore a tongue-strap. After taking it up he soon found the winner much too strong. (9/4)
4076 Cool Yule (IRE), struggling after a mistake at the ninth, looks an out-and-out stayer. (9/1)
Park Drift has always looked short of stamina and this stiff uphill finish certainly found him out. (6/1: op 7/2)

4156 KEOGHANS MAIDEN OPEN N.H. FLAT RACE (4, 5 & 6-Y.O) (Class H)

4-40 (4-40) **2m** £1,486.50 (£414.00: £199.50)

				SP	RR	SF
	Lunar Dancer (JIACharlton) **5-11-6** KJohnson (unf: hld up: hdwy to jn ldrs 4f out: led 3f out: sn drvn clr)	—	**1**	11/1	61 f	—
2750[13]	**Connel's Croft** (JMackie) **5-11-6** TEley (cmpt: attractive: hld up & bhd: hdwy 6f out: effrt over 3f out: kpt on: no ch w wnr)	20	**2**	6/1	41 f	—
	Master Bradan (ABMulholland) **4-11-0** DBentley (lt-f: unf: hld up: hdwy ½-wy: drvn along & outpcd 4f out: styd on appr fnl f)	1½	**3**	14/1	40 f	—
	Buckley House (JIACharlton) **5-11-6** TReed (lt-f: unf: bkwd: plld hrd: w ldr: led over 3f out: sn hdd & wknd: eased fnl f)	8	**4**	5/1[3]	32 f	—
3330[12]	**Brook House** (BBousfield) **6-11-1** BStorey (swtg: leggy: unf: mde most tl over 3f out: grad wknd)	nk	**5**	12/1	26 f	—
	Gilsan Star (CWFairhurst) **4-10-9** LWyer (lengthy: unf: in tch: effrt over 4f out: sn wknd)	2½	**6**	7/2[2]	24 f	—
	Dunnellie (MABarnes) **4-10-4**(5) STaylor (v.bkwd: trckd ldrs tl lost pl 6f out: sn bhd)	9	**7**	10/1	15 f	—
3828[17]	**Nickys Peril** (JSHaldane) **5-10-8**(7) SHaworth (in tch: drvn along 5f out: sn lost pl)	¾	**8**	33/1	14 f	—
	Satpura (SEKettlewell) **5-11-6** GLee (narrow: unf: trckd ldrs tl lost pl over 3f out: sn bhd)	25	**9**	7/4[1]	—	—
				(SP 124.3%)	**9 Rn**	

3m 51.2 CSF £73.78 TOTE £12.40: £2.70 £1.40 £3.30 (£41.60) Trio Not won; £114.40 to Newmarket 15/4/97 OWNER Mr J. W. Robson (STOCKSFIELD) BRED J. W. Robson
WEIGHT FOR AGE 4yo-6lb
Lunar Dancer, an angular, narrow type, was driven well clear of some poor rivals. This was by no means a good bumper. (11/1: 8/1-14/1)
Connel's Croft, a medium, quite attractive sort, is bred to be a sprinter not a stayer. Dropped in at the start, he stuck on to take second place but this was a very ordinary National Hunt Flat Race at best. (6/1: op 3/1)
Master Bradan, who lacks substance, was out-paced when the race began in earnest but was sticking on at the finish. (14/1: op 8/1)
Buckley House took a keen grip going to post. A very keen sort, he was allowed to coast home when all chance had gone. (5/1)
Brook House, sweating beforehand, took a keen grip. (12/1: 8/1-14/1)
Dunnellie (10/1: op 5/1)
Satpura, a narrow type, dropped right away in the final half-mile and finished a remote last. (7/4)

T/Plpt: £276.90 (29.11 Tckts). T/Qdpt: £86.60 (6.79 Tckts) WG

3841-SOUTHWELL (L-H) (Good, Good to firm patches)

Monday April 14th

Race 5: last flight omitted fnl 2 circ
WEATHER: cloudy & overcast

4157 NORFOLK CONDITIONAL H'CAP CHASE (0-100) (5-Y.O+) (Class F)

2-00 (2-00) **2m (13 fncs)** £2,962.80 (£820.80: £392.40) GOING minus 0.06 sec per fur (G)

				SP	RR	SF
3678[3]	**Dr Rocket (77)** (RDickin) **12-10-10v**(3) XAizpuru (lw: trckd ldrs: rdn 4 out: jnd ldr next: led last: drvn out)	—	**1**	11/2	91	24
3960*	**Sleazey (73)** (JGO'Neill) **6-10-9** MBerry (j.w: hdwy 6th: led 9th to last: rdn & no ex flat)	1½	**2**	3/1[1]	86	19
4007*	**No Fiddling (IRE) (82)** (GMMcCourt) **6-11-4** DFortt (bhd: pushed along ½-wy: lost tch 4 out: n.d afterwards)	9	**3**	7/2[2]	86	19
3839[3]	**Count Barachois (USA) (78)** (MrsEHHeath) **9-11-0** JMagee (lw: led 3rd to 8th: rdn & wknd 3 out)	4	**4**	12/1	78	11
3981*	**Corpus (87)** (RJHodges) **8-11-9** DJKavanagh (swtg: led to 3rd: led 8th to 9th: wkng whn fell 3 out)		**F**	8/1	—	—
3960[4]	**Highland Flame (67)** (AGBlackmore) **8-10-3**ow3 PHenley (prom: blnd bdly 4th: rider lost irons: p.u bef next)		**P**	33/1	—	—
1696[P]	**Chain Shot (68)** (JHPeacock) **12-10-4** OBurrows (bkwd: bhd whn p.u bef 3rd)		**P**	33/1	—	—
	Bali Tender (64) (JWharton) **6-10-0** FLeahy (bkwd: hld up: hdwy 5th: j.slowly & lost tch 7th: bhd whn p.u bef 4 out)		**P**	20/1	—	—
3842*	**Chorus Line (IRE) (90)** (PBeaumont) **8-11-9**(3) BGrattan (lw: hld up: effrt & rdn 3 out: btn 3rd whn blnd & uns rdr 2 out)		**U**	9/2[3]	—	—
3684[2]	**Madam Rose (IRE) (64)** (JWMullins) **7-9-4v**1(10) DavidTurner (lw: a bhd: t.o fr 7th: uns rdr 2 out)		**U**	33/1	—	—

Form	Horse	Dist	Pos	SP	RR	SF
3826[P]	**Shut Up (64)** (MrsEMoscrop) **8-10-0b** EHusband (blnd & uns rdr 4th)		**U**	25/1	—	—
				(SP 117.0%)		**11 Rn**

4m 0.4 (7.40) CSF £19.67 CT £58.72 TOTE £5.20: £1.40 £1.30 £1.70 (£10.40) Trio £12.60 OWNER The Rocketeers (STRATFORD) BRED Noel Fenton

LONG HANDICAP Highland Flame 9-10 Madam Rose (IRE) 9-10 Shut Up 9-10

3678 Dr Rocket has been around a long time but he always pays his way, though this success was gained on ground that could have been plenty lively enough. (11/2)

3960* Sleazey jumped these big fences well and stuck on gamely under strong pressure, but the winner, who was winning races the year he was born, brought his experience into good use and took his measure from the last. (3/1)

4007* No Fiddling (IRE) has not got the pace to win at this trip on such a flat track and he was never able to get himself into the action. (7/2)

3839 Count Barachois (USA) made his share of the pacemaking, but he was hard at work soon after entering the straight and was brushed aside with ease. (12/1)

3842* Chorus Line (IRE), always struggling in an attempt to reach the leaders, was staying on but a well-beaten third when blundering and getting rid of her pilot at the penultimate fence. (9/2)

4158 DALY NOVICES' CHASE (5-Y.O+) (Class E)

2-30 (2-30) **3m 110y (19 fncs)** £3,050.75 (£911.00: £435.50: £197.75) GOING minus 0.06 sec per fur (G)

Form	Horse	Dist	Pos	SP	RR	SF
3762[3]	**Dream Ride (IRE) (110)** (DNicholson) **7-11-8** RJohnson (a.p: jnd ldr 15th: mstke 4 out: led appr next: drvn out)	—	**1**	13/8[1]	106	32
3900*	**Stormhill Pilgrim (75)** (MJRoberts) **8-11-8** PHide (lw: j.w: led: clr 10th: hdd appr 3 out: btn appr last)	6	**2**	3/1[2]	102	28
2704[F]	**Fortria Rosie Dawn** (MissVenetiaWilliams) **7-10-11** NWilliamson (bkwd: blnd 2nd: hdwy 12th: wnt 3rd whn bd mstke 14th: nt rcvr)	2½	**3**	16/1	89	15
4055[5]	**Mick The Yank (IRE)** (HOliver) **7-11-2v** MrMMunrowd (a bhd: t.o fr 14th)	dist	**4**	20/1	—	—
3971[4]	**Five Flags (IRE)** (MrsSJSmith) **9-10-11**(5) GFRyan (a bhd: t.o fr ½-wy)	23	**5**	8/1	—	—
3830*	**Captiva Bay (74)** (MrsARHewitt) **8-11-3** SWynne (chsd ldr tl appr 13th: sn rdn & wknd: t.o)	3½	**6**	11/2[3]	—	—
3836[2]	**Chiappucci (IRE) (87)** (MrsEHHeath) **7-11-2** DGallagher (a bhd: t.o & p.u bef 13th)		**P**	15/2	—	—
3545[7]	**Doctor Dunklin (USA)** (MrsVCWard) **8-11-2** JRKavanagh (bit bkwd: a bhd: rdn 12th: t.o p.u bef 4 out)		**P**	33/1	—	—
4004[U]	**Ledburian** (MissPMWhittle) **7-11-2b** DWalsh (sn t.o: p.u bef 10th)		**P**	50/1	—	—
3968[P]	**Sweet Buck (60)** (RCPugh) **8-11-2** VSlattery (nt j.w: lost tch 10th: t.o whn p.u bef 4 out)		**P**	50/1	—	—
				(SP 118.9%)		**10 Rn**

6m 18.6 (11.60) CSF £6.23 TOTE £2.20: £1.50 £1.40 £2.20 (£5.10) Trio £43.50 OWNER C G Clarke and G C Mordaunt (TEMPLE GUITING) BRED Mrs Concepta Dormer-Lewis

3762 Dream Ride (IRE) succeeding in winning at the first attempt at this extended trip but he needed to work hard to get the better of a very game runner-up. (13/8: op evens)

3900* Stormhill Pilgrim is proven at the trip and he did his best to make it a true test of stamina, but the winner always had him in his sights and out-gunned him when the chips were down. (3/1)

Fortria Rosie Dawn lacks experience and did not look fully wound up for this first run in almost three months, but if she had not almost departed the scene with a bad mistake six out, she would have gone very close to winning. (16/1)

3830* Captiva Bay (11/2: 7/2-6/1)

3836 Chiappucci (IRE) (15/2: 5/1-8/1)

4159 HARRY BISSILL MEMORIAL CHALLENGE TROPHY H'CAP CHASE (0-115) (5-Y.O+) (Class E)

3-00 (3-00) **2m 4f 110y (16 fncs)** £4,077.50 (£1,220.00: £585.00: £267.50) GOING minus 0.06 sec per fur (G)

Form	Horse	Dist	Pos	SP	RR	SF
3200*	**Chadwick's Ginger (95)** (WHTinning) **9-10-12** DerekByrne (a.p: led after 4 out: styd on strly)	—	**1**	5/1[3]	102	17
3571[5]	**Cheeka (83)** (CSmith) **8-10-0** MRanger (hld up: hdwy 9th: chsd wnr appr 2 out: no imp)	3½	**2**	33/1	87	2
	Peruvian Gale (IRE) (91) (MrsSJSmith) **8-10-8** RichardGuest (hld up in tch: effrt appr 3 out: rdn & styd on towards fin)	nk	**3**	8/1	95	10
3988[2]	**Pearl Epee (90)** (DNicholson) **8-10-7** RJohnson (mstkes: led: blnd 3rd: clr 8th: blnd & hdd 4 out: mstke next: nt rcvr)	½	**4**	13/8[1]	94	9
3665[4]	**Hawaiian Youth (IRE) (108)** (GMMcCourt) **9-11-8**(3) DFortt (hdwy 6th: hrd rdn 3 out: kpt on same pce)	1¼	**5**	9/2[2]	111	26
3756[4]	**Oxford Quill (83)** (RCurtis) **10-10-0** DMorris (lw: nt j.w: a in rr: t.o fr 4 out)	24	**6**	14/1	67	—
3966[3]	**Fairy Park (83)** (HOliver) **12-9-9v**(5) GSupple (hld up: hdwy 11th: rdn 4 out: sn lost tch: t.o)	¾	**7**	20/1	66	—
3132[7]	**Call Me Early (83)** (DShaw) **12-10-0** MBrennan (dropped rr 7th: j.bdly rt 4 out: sn t.o)	1	**8**	50/1	66	—
3991[4]	**De Jordaan (110)** (WSCunningham) **10-11-13** NSmith (swtg: lost pl 8th: sn t.o)	9	**9**	8/1	86	1
2548[6]	**River Red (83)** (KFrost) **11-10-0** PMcLoughlin (bkwd: a bhd: t.o fr 9th)	6	**10**	33/1	54	—
3200[P]	**Morcat (83)** (CIRatcliffe) **8-9-11**(3) FLeahy (sn bhd: j.slowly 4th: t.o whn p.u bef 4 out)		**P**	20/1	—	—
				(SP 119.2%)		**11 Rn**

5m 15.4 (11.40) CSF £139.80 CT £1,193.78 TOTE £5.90: £2.20 £11.70 £2.50 (£144.30) Trio £227.40; £99.32 to Newmarket 15/4/97 OWNER Mr W. H. Tinning (THORNTON-LE-CLAY) BRED Ian Hunter and A. Knight

LONG HANDICAP Cheeka 9-7 Fairy Park 9-8 Call Me Early 9-10 Oxford Quill 9-5 River Red 8-12 Morcat 9-1

3200* Chadwick's Ginger, three times a winner here over hurdles, again showed a liking for the track with quite a comfortably-gained success and, now that she is in the winning mood, she can be followed right to the end of the season. (5/1)

Cheeka showed something of a return to form with a much-improved performance, and he is capable of finding a race when he puts his mind to it. (33/1)

Peruvian Gale (IRE) will need a stiffer test of stamina to produce his best, but there was a lot to like about this very belated seasonal reappearance, and he should soon be paying his way again. (8/1)

3988 Pearl Epee makes hard work of jumping these fences, and a particularly bad mistake at the end of the back straight more or less put paid to her chance. (13/8)

3665 Hawaiian Youth (IRE) looked to be waiting to pounce turning out of the back straight, but he did not find a lot when shown the whip and he was always being comfortably held. (9/2)

4160 JACK RUSSELL NOVICES' HUNTERS' CHASE (5-Y.O+) (Class H)

3-30 (3-30) **3m 110y (19 fncs)** £1,084.20 (£324.60: £155.80: £71.40) GOING minus 0.06 sec per fur (G)

Form	Horse	Dist	Pos	SP	RR	SF
	Mister Horatio (WDLewis) **7-11-7**(7) MrMLewis (lw: chsd ldrs: led after 4 out: clr 2 out: v.easily)	—	**1**	7/2[1]	91+	25
4059*	**Greenmount Lad (IRE)** (JCornforth) **9-12-0**(7) MrPCornforth (bhd: hdwy 9th: hrd rdn 2 out: styd on)	10	**2**	9/2[2]	92	26

				SP	RR	SF
	Wolver's Pet (IRE) (RWJWillcox) **9-11-7**(7) MrDSJones (trckd ldrs: mstke 8th: chsd wnr whn pckd 2 out: sn btn)	1¼	**3**	6/1[3]	84	18
3922*	**Not My Line (IRE)** (AndyMorgan) **8-12-2**(5) MrASansome (lw: a.p: led 15th tl after next: wknd appr 2 out)	2½	**4**	8/1	89	23
	Back The Road (IRE) (PaulJones) **9-11-9**(7)ow2 MrGHanmer (t: a bhd: t.o)	dist	**5**	12/1	—	—
	Andretti's Heir (TSSharpe) **11-11-13**(7)ow6 MrABonson (lw: hld up: hdwy 11th: ev ch 4 out: wkng whn fell next)		**F**	25/1	—	—
	The Point Is (PSHewitt) **10-11-7**(7) MrPHewitt (mde most to 15th: wknd qckly & p.u bef 2 out)		**P**	7/2[1]	—	—
	Ryders Wells (MrsMMorris) **10-11-7**(7) MrSWalker (hld up & bhd: mstke 6th: t.o: p.u bef 12th)		**P**	14/1	—	—
3455[P]	**Judgeroger** (TLJones) **11-11-7**(7) MrGLewis (lost pl 9th: t.o: p.u bef 4 out)		**P**	14/1	—	—
	Gonalston Percy (RJJackson) **9-11-7b[1]**(7) MrNKent (sn t.o: p.u bef 10th)		**P**	100/1	—	—
	Gunner Boon (DBrace) **7-11-9**(5) MissPJones (hld up in tch: hdwy 12th: mstke next: blnd & uns rdr 14th)		**U**	7/1	—	—
				(SP 126.4%)	**11 Rn**	

6m 23.4 (16.40) CSF £19.60 TOTE £6.70: £2.10 £1.40 £2.30 (£12.10) Trio £29.60 OWNER Mr W. D. Lewis (CLYNDERWEN) BRED G. J. Phillips

OFFICIAL EXPLANATION **The Point Is: no explanation offered.**

Mister Horatio, winning his first race under Rules, was always travelling like a winner and he is obviously useful on his day. (7/2)

4059* Greenmount Lad (IRE) did just enough to win a hard fought duel for the runner-up prize without being able to get anywhere near the winner. (9/2)

Wolver's Pet (IRE) may well have made a race of it with a trouble-free round, but he found these regulation fences a bigger test than those between the flags, and he will need a bit more practice. (6/1)

3922* Not My Line (IRE) had more use made of him this time and it was beginning to take its toll on the approach to the straight. (8/1)

The Point Is, successful three times on the Point-to-Point course here, again tried to gallop his rivals into the ground but he faded quickly after being collared turning out of the back straight, and was eventually pulled up. (7/2: 5/2-4/1)

4161 BLACK AND TAN 'N.H.' NOVICES' HURDLE (4-Y.O+) (Class E)

4-00 (4-00) **2m 4f 110y (9 hdls)** £2,679.00 (£744.00: £357.00) GOING: 0.26 sec per fur (GS)

				SP	RR	SF
2844[9]	**Forbidden Waters (IRE)** (MissVenetiaWilliams) **6-11-0** NWilliamson (hld up: hdwy 5th: rdn to ld 2 out: all out)	—	**1**	7/2[2]	58	1
3989[6]	**If Only** (RHollinshead) **7-11-0** GaryLyons (a.p: hrd rdn & ev ch 2 out: one pce flat)	2	**2**	3/1[1]	56	—
1689[P]	**General Parker** (MissMKMilligan) **6-11-0** ASSmith (w ldrs: led 8th to 2 out: ev ch flat: unable qckn)	s.h	**3**	16/1	56	—
3703[6]	**The Eens** (DMcCain) **5-11-0** DWalsh (lw: chsd ldrs: ev ch whn n.m.r 2 out: sn rdn: one pce)	1½	**4**	5/1[3]	55	—
	Singh Song (KAMorgan) **7-10-9** WFry (bkwd: prom tl rdn & wknd after 3 out: t.o)	17	**5**	14/1	37	—
	Bet Wiltshire (MrsNMacauley) **5-11-0** SWynne (bkwd: hld up in tch: hrd rdn & wknd appr 2 out: t.o)	1¾	**6**	10/1	41	—
2080[11]	**The Bug** (KAMorgan) **7-11-0** AThornton (bkwd: mde most to 8th: wknd qckly: t.o)	17	**7**	8/1	27	—
3703[8]	**Red Oassis** (HOliver) **6-11-0** JacquiOliver (swtg: fell 1st)		**F**	16/1	—	—
3494[F]	**Stonehenge Sam (IRE)** (JWMullins) **5-11-0** SCurran (w ldrs: pckd 2nd: prom whn fell 5th)		**F**	33/1	—	—
3365[14]	**Haberdasher** (MissPMWhittle) **6-10-7**(7) MrJGoldstein (fell 3rd)		**F**	33/1	—	—
	Sutton Boy (LadyAnnBowlby) **8-10-7**(7) THogg (prom to 5th: bhd whn p.u bef 7th)		**P**	25/1	—	—
3170[22]	**Honest George** (KSBridgwater) **6-10-7**(7) MGriffiths (hld up: hdwy 6th: wknd 3 out: p.u bef next)		**P**	20/1	—	—
	Runwell Hall (THind) **5-10-9** PMcLoughlin (bkwd: bdly hmpd 1st: sn t.o: p.u bef 2 out)		**P**	20/1	—	—
				(SP 121.8%)	**13 Rn**	

5m 8.4 (22.40) CSF £12.68 TOTE £4.20: £2.00 £1.40 £4.20 (£4.40) Trio £83.20 OWNER Mrs Maureen Russell (HEREFORD) BRED Thomas Hatton

Forbidden Waters (IRE) succeeded in making a winning debut over hurdles but he had a hard race where strength from the saddle was the deciding factor. (7/2: 5/2-4/1)

If Only performed much better over this more suitable trip, and there is no reason why he would not benefit from another half-mile. (3/1)

General Parker ran so much better than he did on his early debut and was only shaken off nearing the finish. There is certainly a race to be won with him. (16/1)

The Eens improved on his previous outing over hurdles on this step up in distance and there is a race waiting to be picked up. (5/1)

Bet Wiltshire (10/1: op 4/1)

4162 FOX (S) HURDLE (4-Y.O+) (Class G)

4-30 (4-39) **2m (9 hdls)** £2,077.40 (£576.40: £276.20) GOING: 0.26 sec per fur (GS)

				SP	RR	SF
1821*	**Kilnamartyra Girl (87)** (JParkes) **7-11-1** AThornton (a.p: led 2 out: sn drvn clr)	—	**1**	15/2	76	30
3915[5]	**Fontanays (IRE) (97)** (GMMcCourt) **9-10-13b[1]**(7) RHobson (hld up in tch: hdwy appr 3 out: ev ch next: sn rdn & outpcd)	9	**2**	100/30[1]	72	26
2943[7]	**Follow de Call (66)** (DMcCain) **7-11-0** DWalsh (hdwy 4th: rdn appr 2 out: r.o one pce)	3	**3**	33/1	63?	17
3666[4]	**Salman (USA) (88)** (MrsVCWard) **11-11-3**(3) MrRThornton (swtg: hld up: hdwy 6th: rdn appr 2 out: btn whn hit last)	2½	**4**	13/2	67	21
3976[3]	**Faithful Hand (88)** (MrsSJSmith) **7-11-0** RichardGuest (chsd ldrs: mstke 7th: led after 3 out to 2 out: sn wknd)	5	**5**	9/2[3]	56	10
	Bodantree (NMBabbage) **6-11-6** NWilliamson (bkwd: hld up: hdwy appr 3 out: nt rch ldrs)	1½	**6**	4/1[2]	60	14
3189[3]	**Gi Moss (68)** (PRHarriss) **10-10-9** WMarston (a in rr: rdn 6th: no rspnse)	6	**7**	33/1	43	—
3474[2]	**Noir Esprit (82)** (JMCarr) **4-10-5**(3) FLeahy (a in rr)	1½	**8**	9/2[3]	47	—
3933[5]	**Laura Lye (IRE) (74)** (BdeHaan) **7-10-9b[1]** CLlewellyn (lw: led appr 3rd: mstke 3 out: sn hdd & wknd: t.o)	dist	**9**	12/1	—	—
4002[6]	**Corporate Image** (THind) **7-11-0** PMcLoughlin (chsd ldrs to 5th: sn lost tch: t.o)	15	**10**	33/1	—	—
3583[P]	**New Regime (IRE)** (PTDalton) **4-10-3** BFenton (a bhd: t.o 5th)	dist	**11**	50/1	—	—
3989[9]	**Polar Wind** (NWaggott) **8-11-0** MFoster (a in rr: t.o whn p.u bef 2 out)		**P**	33/1	—	—
3714[3]	**Lucker** (MrsEMoscrop) **10-10-11**(3) EHusband (bit bkwd: led tl appr 3rd: sn rdn & lost pl: j.slowly 5th: t.o & p.u bef next)		**P**	33/1	—	—
3921[9]	**Emerald Venture (63)** (FCoton) **10-11-0** DGallagher (sn t.o: p.u bef 2 out)		**P**	33/1	—	—
				(SP 131.8%)	**14 Rn**	

3m 53.1 (11.10) CSF £31.82 TOTE £7.30: £3.30 £1.60 £12.50 (£8.30) Trio £444.70; £501.09 to Newmarket 15/4/97 OWNER Mr P. J. Cronin (MALTON) BRED F. R. Colley

WEIGHT FOR AGE 4yo-6lb

Bt in 3,400 gns

1821* Kilnamartyra Girl, fit from the Flat, found this step down to selling company ideal and, finding a good turn of speed when leading at the penultimate flight, stormed clear in a matter of strides. (15/2: 4/1-8/1)
3589* Fontanays (IRE) did pose a serious danger at the second last but, when the winner was let loose, he must have wondered what had hit him. (100/30: 5/2-4/1)
636 Follow de Call, on the heels of the leaders turning in, could only keep on at the one pace when pressure was applied, but he is progressing and will get it right one day. (33/1)
3666 Salman (USA), taking a big step down in class, showed his age when a turn of finishing speed was called for early in the straight, but now that he is performing with credit, it might be wise to let him return to fences. (13/2)
3976 Faithful Hand, still struggling to get off the mark, only got left behind from the penultimate hurdle, and he is surely better than this. (9/2)
Bodantree won on his hurdling debut in July 1995 and has not been heard of since. Understandably looking burly, he was given the kid glove treatment once the task was hopeless and he will be worth watching from now on. (4/1)
3933 Laura Lye (IRE) (12/1: 8/1-14/1)

4163 BORDER H'CAP HURDLE (0-105) (4-Y.O+ F & M) (Class F)

5-00 (5-04) **2m (9 hdls)** £2,162.50 (£600.00: £287.50) GOING: 0.26 sec per fur (GS)

				SP	RR	SF
4006[8]	**Daily Sport Girl (75)** (BJLlewellyn) **8-11-10** MrJLLlewellyn (hld up: hdwy 6th: rdn to chal last: led flat: all out)	—	**1**	8/1	58	13
345[4]	**Cromaboo Crown (71)** (PJBevan) **6-11-6** WWorthington (led: lft clr 2 out: rdn & hdd flat)	2	**2**	9/1	52	7
	Stylish Rose (IRE) (70) (PCheesbrough) **7-11-5** ASSmith (chsd ldrs: drvn along & outpcd appr 2 out: styd on again towards fin)	3	**3**	10/1	48	3
3608[6]	**Arctic Bloom (59)** (ClRatcliffe) **11-10-5**(3) FLeahy (hdwy 4th: wknd 3 out)	15	**4**	20/1	22	—
3825[12]	**Jendorcet (73)** (CWFairhurst) **7-11-8** JCallaghan (hld up & bhd: hit 4th: blnd next: sn btn)	5	**5**	4/1[1]	31	—
206[2]	**Saxon Magic (70)** (JABennett) **7-11-5** LHarvey (bkwd: prom to 5th: sn wknd: t.o)	8	**6**	5/1[3]	20	—
3752[9]	**Bally Wonder (56)** (MrsEHHeath) **5-10-5** JSupple (swtg: a bhd: t.o)	13	**7**	33/1	—	—
4055[3]	**Catton Lady (57)** (RCraggs) **7-10-6** RJohnson (trckd ldrs tl wknd appr 3 out: t.o)	hd	**8**	9/2[2]	—	—
3752[6]	**Millers Goldengirl (IRE) (59)** (MrsSJSmith) **6-10-3**(5) GFRyan (prom tl wknd qckly 6th: t.o)	26	**9**	14/1	—	—
3904[P]	**Mrs Jawleyford (USA) (75)** (CSmith) **9-11-10** MRanger (hld up: hdwy 5th: jnd ldr whn fell 2 out)		**F**	11/2	—	—
881[9]	**Water Music Melody (65)** (TRGreathead) **4-10-3**(5) ABates (prom to 5th: bhd whn p.u bef 2 out)		**P**	16/1	—	—
				(SP 120.7%)		**11 Rn**

3m 58.8 (16.80) CSF £72.66 CT £672.62 TOTE £10.00: £3.80 £4.10 £3.10 (£32.30) Trio £252.40; £188.44 to Newmarket 15/4/97 OWNER Mr B. J. Llewellyn (BARGOED) BRED Roldvale Ltd
WEIGHT FOR AGE 4yo-6lb
2871 Daily Sport Girl has not won a race for twelve months but usually comes good at this time of year, so this hard fought success could signal a change of fortune. (8/1)
345 Cromaboo Crown was running over longer trips when she last appeared on the racecourse eight months ago, but she was prepared to force the pace and only the winner proved too strong in the battle to the line. This was a very praiseworthy effort. (9/1)
Stylish Rose (IRE), returning after being on the sidelines for eleven months, ran a race full of promise and, if there is any improvement to come, she ought to be able to find an opening. (10/1)
3612 Jendorcet never seems to run two races alike and a couple of mistakes down the back straight left her with far too much to do. (4/1: op 5/2)
206 Saxon Magic, off the track since being narrowly beaten over fences last summer, blew up after pressing the leaders until past halfway, but she will be fresher than most if she does appear again this term. (5/1)

T/Jkpt: Not won; £2,965.11 to Newmarket 15/4/97. T/Plpt: £35.10 (385.75 Tckts). T/Qdpt: £24.90 (28.34 Tckts) IM

3634-CHELTENHAM (L-H) (Good to firm)

Tuesday April 15th

WEATHER: fine

4164 MITIE GROUP HURDLE (4-Y.O+) (Class B)

2-20 (2-20) **2m 4f (New) (10 hdls)** £6,216.00 (£1,524.00) GOING minus 0.12 sec per fur (G)

				SP	RR	SF
4063[2]	**Pridwell (157)** (MCPipe) **7-11-8** RDunwoody (lw: mde all: clr appr last: easily)	—	**1**	1/8[1]	116+	10
4006*	**Handy Lass (101)** (JSSmith) **8-10-9** TJMurphy (hld up: rdn after 2 out: no imp: eased flat)	30	**2**	6/1[2]	79	—
				(SP 103.2%)		**2 Rn**

4m 53.7 (13.70) TOTE £1.10: OWNER Jones, Berstock and Fleet Partnership (WELLINGTON) BRED Hascombe and Valiant Studs
4063 Pridwell proved a different class to his solitary opponent. (1/8)
4006* Handy Lass, a bit keen in the first half of the race, found the winner in a totally different league. (6/1)

4165 FAUCETS FOR MIRA RADA SHOWERS SILVER TROPHY CHASE (Gd 2) (5-Y.O+) (Class A)

2-55 (2-55) **2m 5f (New) (17 fncs)** £18,840.00 (£7,129.50: £3,489.75: £1,590.75) GOING minus 0.12 sec per fur (G)

				SP	RR	SF
4049[2]	**Strong Promise (IRE) (165)** (GAHubbard) **6-11-7** NWilliamson (lw: a gng wl: led appr 13th: clr appr 2 out: easily)	—	**1**	4/5[1]	171	85
4053[9]	**Gales Cavalier (IRE) (155)** (DRGandolfo) **9-11-4** RDunwoody (lw: led tl appr 13th: ev ch 3 out: sn rdn & outpcd)	21	**2**	5/1[3]	152	66
4049[3]	**Viking Flagship (163)** (DNicholson) **10-11-4** RJohnson (chsd ldr to 5th: rdn 4 out: wknd appr 2 out)	17	**3**	2/1[2]	139	53
3622[P]	**Celtic Laird (74)** (DBurchell) **9-11-0** DJBurchell (nt j.w: a t.o)	dist	**4**	100/1	—	—
				(SP 106.5%)		**4 Rn**

5m 1.9 (-7.10) CSF £4.45 TOTE £1.90: (£2.50) OWNER Mr G. A. Hubbard (WOODBRIDGE) BRED William McCarthy
4049 Strong Promise (IRE) really bounced off this fast ground and will now be put away until next season, when his first main target will be the King George. (4/5: tchd evens)
2890 Gales Cavalier (IRE) has not scored since winning this race last season and was well out-pointed by the winner. (5/1)
4049 Viking Flagship will also be stepped up to three miles and aimed at the King George next term but, unlike the winner, he does not have age on his side. (2/1)

4166 E.B.F. 'N.H' FINAL NOVICES' H'CAP HURDLE (Gd 3) (5, 6 & 7-Y.O) (Class A)

3-30 (3-30) **2m 4f (New) (10 hdls)** £16,200.00 (£6,117.50: £2,983.75: £1,348.75) GOING minus 0.12 sec per fur (G)

				SP	RR	SF
3923*	**Sir Dante (IRE) (94)** (RRowe) **6-10-4** DO'Sullivan (hld up & plld hrd: hdwy 3rd: wnt 2nd 4th: led on bit after 2 out: shkn up & qcknd clr: easily)	—	1	5/1[1]	83+	25
4052[P]	**Silver Thyne (IRE) (105)** (MrsJPitman) **5-11-1b[1]** DLeahy (lw: plld hrd: led after 1st: hrd rdn & hdd after 2 out: no ch w wnr)	14	2	6/1[2]	83	25
3973*	**Good Vibes (115)** (TDEasterby) **5-11-11** LWyer (hld up & bhd: gd hdwy 3 out: blnd 2 out: nt rcvr)	3½	3	7/1[3]	90	32
3937*	**Seabrook Lad (90)** (MJWilkinson) **6-10-0** WMarston (lw: hld up & bhd: hdwy 5th: one pce fr 2 out)	1	4	5/1[1]	64	6
3718[3]	**Rhythm And Blues (93)** (RHBuckler) **7-10-3** SMcNeill (lw: no hdwy fr 3 out)	6	5	20/1	62	4
3540*	**Lance Armstrong (IRE) (106)** (GMMcCourt) **7-10-13v[1](3)** DFortt (chsd ldr to 4th: rdn after 3 out: wknd 2 out)	3½	6	12/1	73	15
3970[F]	**Fantasy Line (108)** (PRWebber) **6-11-4** AThornton (lw: hld up: hdwy 3 out: 4th & btn whn fell last: dead)		F	5/1[1]	—	—
3552*	**Friendship (IRE) (111)** (NJHenderson) **5-11-7** MAFitzgerald (hld up: hdwy 6th: prom whn fell 2 out)		F	5/1[1]	—	—
3437*	**Spring Gale (IRE) (116)** (OSherwood) **6-11-12** JOsborne (lw: led tl after 1st: mstke 6th: sn wknd: t.o whn p.u bef 2 out)		P	12/1	—	—

(SP 113.6%) **9 Rn**

4m 44.9 (4.90) CSF £31.52 CT £189.67 TOTE £5.20: £1.80 £1.70 £2.00 (£17.10) Trio £52.90 OWNER Mr Peter Wilby (PULBOROUGH) BRED Martin Molony

LONG HANDICAP Seabrook Lad 9-8

3923* Sir Dante (IRE), still considered well-handicapped by his trainer, effortlessly completed a hat-trick despite already having being raised a total of 16lb. He was certainly a different animal on fast ground. (5/1)

3734 Silver Thyne (IRE) likes to dominate and certainly ran freely in the first-time blinkers. (6/1)

3973* Good Vibes, stepping up in distance, did not help his cause with a bad mistake at a crucial stage, but probably had an impossible task in trying to concede so much weight to the winner. (7/1)

3937* Seabrook Lad was supported in the offices despite being 6lb out of the handicap. (5/1)

3718 Rhythm And Blues again had to contend with fast ground. (20/1)

3540* Lance Armstrong (IRE) was visored for this return to the smaller obstacles. (12/1)

4167 LARKSHILL ENGINEERING GOLDEN MILLER H'CAP CHASE (0-135) (5-Y.O+) (Class C)

4-00 (4-01) **3m 2f 110y (New) (22 fncs)** £4,879.00 (£1,477.00: £721.00: £343.00) GOING minus 0.12 sec per fur (G)

				SP	RR	SF
3414[5]	**Le Meille (IRE) (107)** (KRBurke) **8-10-9** NWilliamson (lw: hld up & bhd: stdy hdwy 14th: led 2 out: drvn out)	—	1	7/1[3]	119	22
3047[P]	**God Speed You (IRE) (108)** (CPMorlock) **8-10-10b** JRKavanagh (led 3rd to 2 out: mstke last: r.o)	1¼	2	8/1	119	22
2758[10]	**Copper Mine (117)** (OSherwood) **11-11-5** JOsborne (lw: a.p: r.o one pce fr 2 out)	3	3	9/1	126	29
3699[P]	**Musthaveaswig (121)** (DNicholson) **11-11-9** RJohnson (mstkes: hld up mid div: hdwy 15th: hrd rdn & wknd appr 2 out)	11	4	13/2[2]	124	27
3598[P]	**James Pigg (125)** (PFNicholls) **10-11-13** RDunwoody (bhd: reminders 10th: hdwy 17th: wknd appr 3 out)	12	5	16/1	121	24
3742*	**Foxgrove (98)** (RJPrice) **11-9-11(3)** MrRThornton (lw: bhd: rdn 11th: mstke 12th: t.o fr 17th)	nk	6	50/1	93	—
3974[3]	**Royal Vacation (114)** (GMMoore) **8-11-2** JCallaghan (lw: hdwy 8th: wknd 3 out: t.o)	18	7	5/1[1]	99	2
3838*	**Denver Bay (119)** (JTGifford) **10-11-4(3)** LAspell (lw: a bhd: t.o whn p.u bef 4 out)		P	5/1[1]	—	—
3756[2]	**Suffolk Road (104)** (RRowe) **10-10-6** DO'Sullivan (led to 2nd: bhd whn mstke 13th: t.o whn p.u & dismntd bef 3 out)		P	13/2[2]	—	—
4013[F]	**Flimsy Truth (114)** (MHWeston) **11-11-2** MrMHarris (lw: led 2nd to 3rd: wkng whn blnd 18th: p.u bef 4 out)		P	5/1[1]	—	—

(SP 118.1%) **10 Rn**

6m 45.1 (10.10) CSF £56.85 CT £467.74 TOTE £5.80: £1.40 £3.60 £3.30 (£58.70) Trio £283.10 OWNER Mr N. J. Mitchell (WANTAGE) BRED E. McCormack

LONG HANDICAP Foxgrove 8-8

3414 Le Meille (IRE), dropped 2lb, bounced back to form off a 5lb lower mark than when runner up to Proud Sun in this race last year. (7/1)

3047 God Speed You (IRE), 7lb higher than when successful at Doncaster, had been given a rest since disappointing next time. (8/1)

1558 Copper Mine, returning after a break, showed he is no back number yet. (9/1)

3414 Musthaveaswig was let down by some slipshod jumping. (13/2)

4168 CIRENCESTER NOVICES' H'CAP CHASE (0-115) (5-Y.O+) (Class D)

4-35 (4-35) **2m 5f (New) (17 fncs)** £4,279.50 (£1,296.00: £633.00: £301.50) GOING minus 0.12 sec per fur (G)

				SP	RR	SF
4007[5]	**Boots N All (IRE) (76)** (GBBalding) **7-10-0** BFenton (hld up: led after 3 out: clr whn mstke 2 out: rdn out)	—	1	9/2[3]	88	25
3948*	**Decyborg (FR) (100)** (MCPipe) **6-11-10** RDunwoody (led 2nd tl after 3 out: btn whn hit last)	7	2	100/30[2]	107	44
3288[4]	**Key To Moyade (IRE) (93)** (MJWilkinson) **7-11-3** WMarston (mstkes 3rd & 4th: hdwy 8th: rdn 12th: lost pl 4 out: styd on fr 2 out)	3	3	10/1	97	34
3756*	**Regal Aura (IRE) (80)** (DCO'Brien) **7-10-4** PHide (led to 2nd: wknd 4 out: t.o)	dist	4	11/4[1]	—	—
3617[P]	**Plassy Boy (IRE) (76)** (KRBurke) **8-10-0v** NWilliamson (lw: bhd: mstke 3rd: reminders 5th: hdwy 12th: cl 3rd whn p.u lame bef 4 out)		P	25/1	—	—
3988[3]	**Glamanglitz (80)** (PTDalton) **7-10-1(3)** MrRThornton (lw: uns rdr after 1st)		U	5/1	—	—
3957*	**Normarange (IRE) (86)** (DMGrissell) **7-10-10** JRKavanagh (last whn blnd & uns rdr 10th)		U	11/2	—	—

(SP 112.9%) **7 Rn**

5m 13.4 (4.40) CSF £18.05 TOTE £5.10: £2.50 £2.20 (£6.40) OWNER Mrs Toni Tipper (ANDOVER) BRED Megan and Karl Strecker

LONG HANDICAP Plassy Boy (IRE) 9-10 Boots N All (IRE) 9-10

4007 Boots N All (IRE), although 4lb wrong at the weights, would have scored even more convincingly had he not met the penultimate fence all wrong. (9/2)

3948* Decyborg (FR) could not cope with the winner at these weights. (100/30)

3288 Key To Moyade (IRE) needs to return to three miles. (10/1)

3756* Regal Aura (IRE), raised a further 4lb, handled the fast ground last time but this might have been once too often. (11/4)

4169 STOKE ORCHARD H'CAP HURDLE (4-Y.O) (Class C)
5-10 (5-10) **2m 4f (New) (10 hdls)** £4,788.00 (£1,449.00: £707.00: £336.00) GOING minus 0.12 sec per fur (G)

				SP	RR	SF
3741*	**Chief Mouse (100)** (FJordan) **4-11-4** PCarberry (hld up: hdwy appr 2 out: hrd rdn & w ldr whn lft clr last: eased)	—	1	7/2 3	76+	17
3962 5	**Sterling Fellow (82)** (DLWilliams) **4-9-7**(7) MrSDurack (bhd tl hdwy appr last: r.o wl flat: nt trble wnr)	1¼	2	12/1	57	—
3965 2	**Arrogant Heir (87)** (DHBrown) **4-10-5** DerekByrne (bhd: mstke 3 out: no ch whn j.lft & mstke last)	17	3	3/1 1	48	—
3996 2	**Give And Take (106)** (MCPipe) **4-11-10** DWalsh (lw: led to 2nd: rdn 7th: wknd appr 2 out)	30	4	100/30 2	43	—
3927*	**Noble Colours (95)** (SGGriffiths) **4-10-6**(7) MrAWintle (lw: plld hrd: led 2nd: clr appr 2 out: rdn & slt ld whn fell last)		F	7/2 3	—	—
3007 10	**Squire's Occasion (CAN) (100)** (RCurtis) **4-10-11**(7) JParkhouse (hld up: 5th & btn whn blnd & uns rdr 2 out)	..	U	7/1	—	—
				(SP 112.7%)	**6 Rn**	

4m 50.7 (10.70) CSF £34.83 TOTE £3.10: £1.40 £4.30 (£24.20) OWNER Mr Bill Gavan (LEOMINSTER) BRED Lady Vestey
LONG HANDICAP Sterling Fellow 9-10

3741* Chief Mouse, ridden to get the trip, was presented the race at the last when the outcome was hanging in the balance. (7/2)
3962 Sterling Fellow, although flattered by his proximity to the winner, certainly showed how well he stays. (12/1)
3965 Arrogant Heir was never a factor. (3/1: op 5/1)
3996 Give And Take (100/30: 5/2-4/1)
3927* Noble Colours, although strongly pressed, had it all to play for when coming down at the final flight. (7/2)
2781 Squire's Occasion (CAN) (7/1: op 4/1)

T/Plpt: £123.30 (138.98 Tckts). T/Qdpt: £129.00 (8.56 Tckts) KH

3996-EXETER (R-H) (Firm)
Tuesday April 15th
WEATHER: fine

4170 BUZZARD HURDLE (4-Y.O) (Class E)
2-10 (2-10) **2m 2f (8 hdls)** £2,332.50 (£645.00: £307.50) GOING minus 0.78 sec per fur (F)

				SP	RR	SF
4097*	**Major Dundee (IRE)** (MCPipe) **4-11-4v1** APMcCoy (lw: mde all: mstke 5th: shkn up appr next: rdn out: styd on flat)	—	1	4/5 1	74	35
3953*	**Anna Soleil (IRE) (108)** (OSherwood) **4-11-4** DThomas (lw: chsd ldr: in tch 3rd: rdn appr 2 out: rallied last: in tch tl one pce flat)	2	2	11/10 2	72	33
3889U	**Royal Member** (MrsBarbaraWaring) **4-10-7** EByrne (bhd: t.o 2nd: wnt poor 3rd last)	dist	3	66/1	—	—
3927 4	**Spencer Stallone** (GraemeRoe) **4-10-7**(5) DSalter (chsng ldrs whn mstkes 1st & 2nd: sn t.o: lost pl last)	7	4	33/1 3	—	—
				(SP 107.6%)	**4 Rn**	

4m 3.2 (5.60 under best) (-6.80) CSF £1.86 TOTE £1.70: (£1.10) OWNER Mr Michael Jaye (WELLINGTON) BRED Brittas House Stud
4097* Major Dundee (IRE) had conditions to suit here and put up a resolute display to keep his market rival at bay. (4/5)
3953* Anna Soleil (IRE) was the only other runner good enough to make a race of it and did not let the winner have it all his own way. (11/10)

4171 PAULINE TRUNDLE NOVICES' CHASE (5-Y.O+) (Class E)
2-45 (2-45) **2m 7f 110y (17 fncs)** £2,948.75 (£890.00: £432.50: £203.75) GOING minus 0.78 sec per fur (F)

				SP	RR	SF
3891 3	**Spring to it (90)** (MCPipe) **11-11-2** APMcCoy (mde all: reminder 7th: clr 9th: rdn & hld on wl flat)	—	1	Evens 1	93	18
3998 3	**Jonjas Chudleigh (65)** (RGFrost) **10-11-2** JFrost (lw: hld up: hdwy to chse wnr 9th: disp ld 2 out: one pce & hung sltly lft flat)	9	2	8/1 3	87	12
3929 3	**Trust Deed (USA) (82)** (SGKnight) **9-11-8b** GUpton (chsd ldrs: in tch to 8th: rdn & grad wknd 11th)	22	3	7/4 2	78	3
4085 3	**Elite Governor (IRE) (81)** (NMLampard) **8-10-9**(7) MrLBaker (disp ld 3rd to 5th: outpcd 9th: wkng & mstke 12th)	12	4	8/1 3	64	—
				(SP 108.6%)	**4 Rn**	

5m 44.0 (-3.00) CSF £7.24 TOTE £1.70: (£5.10) OWNER Mr M. C. Pipe (WELLINGTON) BRED R. Pitman
3891 Spring to it only needed a few reminders to be kept up to his work entering the straight. He jumped well but had relatively little to beat. (Evens)
3998 Jonjas Chudleigh tried to make a race of it with the winner but, having every chance two out, was slightly one-paced on the run-in. (8/1: op 9/2)
3736* Trust Deed (USA) was a beaten force turning into the home straight. (7/4)
1909 Elite Governor (IRE) (8/1: 9/2-9/1)

4172 TOTE CREDIT H'CAP HURDLE (0-130) (4-Y.O+) (Class C)
3-20 (3-21) **2m 3f 110y (9 hdls)** £4,448.50 (£1,348.00: £659.00: £314.50) GOING minus 0.78 sec per fur (F)

				SP	RR	SF
3890*	**Northern Starlight (118)** (MCPipe) **6-12-0** APMcCoy (lw: mde all: clr appr 2 out: eased flat)	—	1	6/4 1	103+	47
3999 2	**Kiwi Crystal (NZ) (90)** (AGHobbs) **8-10-0** RGreene (chsd ldrs tl lost tch appr 3rd: rdn & rallied appr 2 out: styd on flat: no imp)	5	2	11/4 2	71	15
3980*	**Sevso (90)** (RJBaker) **8-10-0** VSlattery (in tch & hdwy to chse wnr 6th: outpcd appr 2 out: lost pl & wknd flat)	½	3	4/1	71	15
4001 3	**Castleconner (IRE) (90)** (RGFrost) **6-10-0b** MrAHoldsworth (bhd: t.o 4th: rdn & styd on fr 2 out)	19	4	20/1	55	—
936*	**Born to Please (IRE) (98)** (PJHobbs) **5-10-8** GTormey (chsd wnr: in tch tl rdn 4th: lost pl 6th: wknd next)	1¼	5	7/2 3	62	6
				(SP 113.7%)	**5 Rn**	

4m 24.0 (6.10 under best) (-8.00) CSF £5.87 TOTE £1.90: £1.10 £1.60 (£3.40) OWNER Mr Arthur Souch (WELLINGTON) BRED R. J. Glenn and K. Leadbetter
LONG HANDICAP Sevso 9-12 Castleconner (IRE) 9-4
3890* Northern Starlight continued his one hundred per-cent record so far this season, with all five wins coming on good ground or firmer. (6/4)
3999 Kiwi Crystal (NZ) battled on to win the only prize left on offer and a small race can be found for her. (11/4)
3980* Sevso, dropped in trip since her recent Wincanton success, just lost out in the battle on the run-in. (4/1)

4173 PETER OWEN FAREWELL NOVICES' HURDLE (5-Y.O+) (Class E)

3-50 (3-54) **2m 3f 110y (9 hdls)** £2,521.50 (£699.00: £334.50) GOING minus 0.78 sec per fur (F)

				SP	RR	SF
4001*	**Country Lover (103)** (MCPipe) **6-11-6v** APMcCoy (hld up & bhd: hdwy & ev ch appr 2 out: led flat: cheekily)	—	**1**	1/10^{1}	53+	—
	Tommy Cooper (MrsBarbaraWaring) **6-11-0** EByrne (bit bkwd: led: rdn appr 2 out: hld on u.p tl hdd flat: no ex)	½	**2**	9/1^{2}	47	—
218^{7}	**Carnival Clown** (KBishop) **5-11-0** RGreene (bit bkwd: chsd ldr: in tch tl rdn & wknd appr 2 out)	13	**3**	33/1^{3}	36	—
3735^{7}	**Deceit the Second (49)** (PRRodford) **5-11-0** SBurrough (a bhd: lost tch 7th)	15	**4**	100/1	24	—
2875^{10}	**Moreceva (IRE)** (PaddyFarrell) **7-11-0** TDascombe (chsd ldrs: in tch tl wknd 7th)	10	**5**	40/1	15	—
				(SP 107.3%)	**5 Rn**	

4m 35.6 (3.60) CSF £1.36 TOTE £1.10: £1.20 £1.10 (£1.80) OWNER Pond House Gold (WELLINGTON) BRED Sir Gordon Brunton

4001* Country Lover took this much more easily than the winning margin suggests, but was up against very little in the way of competition. He is in good heart at present and his jockey stated that this success, his one hundred and fiftieth, was his 'easiest winner of the season.' (1/10)

Tommy Cooper will appreciate this outing after a lengthy lay-off. Under pressure when in front on the flat, he had no chance when the winner decided to take the initiative and is flattered by his close proximity to the winner. (9/1)

4174 TOTE BOOKMAKERS H'CAP CHASE (0-125) (5-Y.O+) (Class D)

4-25 (4-25) **2m 3f 110y (15 fncs)** £3,629.50 (£1,096.00: £533.00: £251.50) GOING minus 0.78 sec per fur (F)

				SP	RR	SF
3832^{2}	**Coolteen Hero (IRE) (89)** (RHAlner) **7-11-2** PHolley (lw: chsd ldr tl mstke 9th: in tch & mstke 12th: rdn: rallied to disp ld last: r.o wl to ld flat)	—	**1**	8/1	100	36
851a^{3}	**Henley Regatta (93)** (PRRodford) **9-11-6** SBurrough (hld up & bhd: hdwy to chse ldr 10th: led 12th: hdd flat: no ex)	3	**2**	9/1	102	38
3540^{U}	**Mr Playfull (91)** (RGFrost) **7-11-4** JFrost (hdwy to chse ldrs 8th: lost pl 10th: rallied appr last: nrst fin)	12	**3**	3/1^{2}	90	26
4013^{U}	**Pond House (IRE) (97)** (MCPipe) **8-11-10** APMcCoy (led tl hdd 12th: mstke next: sn wknd & blnd last)	3	**4**	2/1^{1}	93	29
903^{5}	**Tango's Delight (73)** (RJBaker) **9-10-0** VSlattery (bit bkwd: chsd ldrs tl wknd 10th: bhd whn fell last)		**F**	25/1	—	—
1445^{P}	**Millies Own (93)** (HSHowe) **10-11-6** GTormey (bit bkwd: chsd ldrs tl wknd 8th: t.o whn p.u bef 10th)		**P**	12/1	—	—
3966*	**Good for a Laugh (82)** (AGHobbs) **13-10-2**$^{(7)}$ MrGShenkin (a bhd: lost tch 7th: t.o whn p.u bef 11th)		**P**	9/2^{3}	—	—
3819^{3}	**Mammy's Choice (IRE) (94)** (RHAlner) **7-11-7** JCulloty (in tch early: bhd 7th: p.u bef next)		**P**	8/1	—	—
				(SP 120.3%)	**8 Rn**	

4m 37.2 (-7.80) CSF £70.20 CT £244.90 TOTE £7.50: £1.80 £2.80 £1.10 (£17.30) Trio £32.50 OWNER J P M & J W Cook (BLANDFORD) BRED T. Simmons

LONG HANDICAP Tango's Delight 9-11

3832 Coolteen Hero (IRE) relished this step up in distance, staying on well in the straight and taking the lead on the run-in. He is prone to the odd jumping mistake, but has put up some good recent efforts and a similar event can be found for him on this form. (8/1: op 5/1)

851a Henley Regatta looked the winner when taking it up from the long-time leader in the home straight but had little in reserve when tackled for the lead after the last. (9/1: 6/1-12/1)

3540 Mr Playfull looked beaten in the straight before the home turn, but stayed on close home to take advantage of the last-fence blunder of Pond House. (3/1)

409 Pond House (IRE) ended the Pipe-McCoy attempt of going through the card and was disappointing in the process. He went off at a scorching pace and his early exertions took their toll in the straight, with a last-fence blunder ending any hopes of him filling a place. (2/1)

3819 Mammy's Choice (IRE) (8/1: op 5/1)

4175 KESTREL CONDITIONAL H'CAP HURDLE (0-105) (4-Y.O+) (Class F)

5-00 (5-00) **2m 2f (8 hdls)** £2,031.30 (£561.80: £267.90) GOING minus 0.78 sec per fur (F)

				SP	RR	SF
3977*	**Mrs Em (92)** (PFNicholls) **5-11-5**$^{(5)}$ LCummins (lw: hld up mid div: hdwy to chse ldr after 7th: led appr last: sn clr)	—	**1**	9/4^{2}	82	26
2806^{5}	**Time Leader (72)** (RDickin) **5-10-1**$^{(3)}$ XAizpuru (lw: hdwy to ld 4th: hdd appr last: wknd)	8	**2**	100/30^{3}	55	—
3740^{3}	**Commanche Creek (75)** (MissJduPlessis) **7-10-7** SophieMitchell (led to 3rd: prom tl outpcd appr last)	4	**3**	2/1^{1}	54	—
4086^{7}	**Chili Heights (72)** (KBishop) **7-9-13v**$^{(5)}$ MGriffiths (chsd ldr tl led 3rd: hdd next: ev ch tl rdn & wknd appr 2 out)	nk	**4**	50/1	51	—
3590^{3}	**Denomination (USA) (80)** (MCPipe) **5-10-7**$^{(5)}$ BMoore (chsd ldrs tl rdn & wknd after 7th)	16	**5**	13/2	45	—
1763^{P}	**Up the Tempo (IRE) (68)** (PaddyFarrell) **8-10-0** TDascombe (in tch tl wknd after 7th)	7	**6**	20/1	27	—
27^{9}	**Station Express (IRE) (68)** (CLPopham) **9-10-0** GuyLewis (bit bkwd: a bhd: wknd 6th: t.o)	1¼	**7**	50/1	26	—
4001^{P}	**Rogerson (68)** (SGKnight) **9-10-0** DSalter (bit bkwd: a bhd: lost tch 6th: t.o)	17	**8**	66/1	10	—
				(SP 110.7%)	**8 Rn**	

4m 6.8 (2.00 under best) (-3.20) CSF £8.69 CT £13.76 TOTE £2.30: £1.40 £1.40 £1.00 (£3.70) OWNER Mr G. Z. Mizel (SHEPTON MALLET) BRED Guest Leasing and Bloodstock Co

LONG HANDICAP Up the Tempo (IRE) 9-7 Station Express (IRE) 9-0 Rogerson 9-6

OFFICIAL EXPLANATION **Commanche Creek: the rider reported that the gelding appeared to her to go lame on the run in. Subsequently, the gelding walked out sound.**

3977* Mrs Em had shown good form in this grade previously and is capable of stepping up on this effort. (9/4: 6/4-5/2)

2806 Time Leader was seen off by the winner over the last, but will come on for this run after a slight lay-off. (100/30)

3740 Commanche Creek, placed here over course and distance last time out, was expected to put up a better performance being 5lb better off today. He may still appreciate a drop in trip. (2/1)

T/Plpt: £13.80 (574.06 Tckts). T/Qdpt: £3.00 (140.23 Tckts) T

4164-CHELTENHAM (L-H) (Good to firm, Firm patches)
Wednesday April 16th
WEATHER: Fine

4176 NEW BARN LANE NOVICES' HURDLE (4-Y.O+) (Class D)
2-20 (2-20) **2m 1f (New) (8 hdls)** £2,957.00 (£896.00: £438.00: £209.00) GOING minus 0.34 sec per fur (GF)

	Horse / details	Dist	Pos	SP	RR	SF
3802⁴	**Talathath (FR) (111)** (DNicholson) **5-11-5** RJohnson (a.p: chal whn n.m.r appr last: led flat: r.o wl)	—	1	5/4 2	85	28
3989*	**King of Sparta** (OSherwood) **4-10-13** JOsborne (lw: led to 2 out: led appr last: hdd flat: wknd)	12	2	Evens 1	74	11
3730²	**Distant Storm** (BJLlewellyn) **4-10-8** VSlattery (hld up: reminders 3rd: rdn & hdwy 3 out: wknd after 2 out)	4	3	9/1 3	65	2
3601⁶	**Dubai Dolly (IRE)** (JWMullins) **4-10-3** SCurran (hld up: hdwy after 3 out: led 2 out: rdn & hdd appr last: sn wknd)	1½	4	66/1	59?	—
	Allez Cyrano (IRE) (OO'Neill) **6-11-0** DLeahy (swtg: hld up & plld hrd: chsd ldrs fr 2nd tl appr 3 out: wknd appr 2 out: t.o)	22	5	33/1	43	—

(SP 108.9%) **5 Rn**

4m (3.00) CSF £2.62 TOTE £2.10: £1.20 £1.30 (£1.30) OWNER Million In Mind Partnership (6) (TEMPLE GUITING) BRED Gainsborough Stud Management Ltd
WEIGHT FOR AGE 4yo-6lb
3802 Talathath (FR) apparently broke a blood vessel when below par last time, and bounced back to form here. (5/4: evens-11/8)
3989* King of Sparta, who did a fair amount of tail swishing, suffers from a breathing problem and is likely to be operated on it if an Australian noseband does not work next time. (Evens)
3730 Distant Storm was stepping up from selling company. (9/1: 5/1-10/1)
Dubai Dolly (IRE) did not achieve much on the Flat in Ireland but showed she possesses some ability. (66/1)

4177 HOLMAN CUP H'CAP CHASE (0-130) (5-Y.O+) (Class C)
2-55 (2-59) **2m 110y (New) (14 fncs)** £5,121.00 (£1,548.00: £754.00: £357.00) GOING minus 0.60 sec per fur (F)

	Horse / details	Dist	Pos	SP	RR	SF
2879²	**Seek The Faith (USA) (107)** (MSheppard) **8-11-2** RDunwoody (lw: hld up: hdwy 8th: led last: drvn out)	—	1	2/1 1	116	48
3981ᵁ	**Newlands-General (115)** (PFNicholls) **11-11-10** PHide (led: sn clr: mstke & hdd last: r.o)	1½	2	9/2 3	123	55
3839*	**Red Bean (95)** (KVincent) **9-10-4** RJohnson (lw: chsd clr ldr appr 3rd: ev ch 3 out: sn rdn: one pce)	6	3	11/4 2	97	29
3639⁷	**Pimberley Place (IRE) (115)** (NATwiston-Davies) **9-11-10** CLlewellyn (reminders & s.s: hdwy 4th: lost pl 9th: rallied appr 4 out: one pce fr 3 out)	1½	4	11/2	115	47
3954*	**Rustic Gent (IRE) (91)** (DBurchell) **9-10-0** DJBurchell (chsd ldr tl appr 3rd: lost tch fr 7th: t.o)	20	5	25/1	72	4
3843ᵁ	**Northern Optimist (91)** (BJLlewellyn) **9-10-0** NWilliamson (t.o fr 5th)	10	6	8/1	62	—

(SP 108.5%) **6 Rn**

4m 0.9 (-6.10) CSF £9.72 TOTE £2.60: £1.70 £2.40 (£6.10) OWNER Mr R. H. F. Matthews (LEDBURY) BRED Nicholas M. Lotz and Liam Gannon
LONG HANDICAP Rustic Gent (IRE) 8-4 Northern Optimist 9-10
2879 Seek The Faith (USA), patiently ridden, had his task made easier when the runner-up missed out at the final fence. (2/1)
3981 Newlands-General adopted his usual front-running tactics and was being strongly pressed when his recent jumping problems reared their head at the last. (9/2: 3/1-5/1)
3839* Red Bean defied a 4lb rise in the weights at Sandown, but was up a further 5lb this time. (11/4)
1520 Pimberley Place (IRE), rather reluctant to jump off at the start, has certainly not lived up to his incredible run on his seasonal reappearance. (11/2: 4/1-6/1)

4178 LYNX EXPRESS H'CAP HURDLE (5-Y.O+) (Class B)
3-30 (3-30) **2m 5f 110y (New) (10 hdls)** £5,141.80 (£1,554.40: £757.20: £358.60) GOING minus 0.34 sec per fur (GF)

	Horse / details	Dist	Pos	SP	RR	SF
4048²	**Courbaril (124)** (MCPipe) **5-11-10b** APMcCoy (chsd clr ldrs to 3 out: rdn 2 out: led flat: all out)	—	1	11/4 1	95	36
3750*	**The Toiseach (IRE) (114)** (JRFanshawe) **6-11-0v** JOsborne (led: sn clr: hit 3rd & 4th: mstke 3 out: hdd flat)	2	2	11/2	84	25
4084*	**El Don (110)** (MJRyan) **5-10-10** 5x KGaule (hld up & bhd: hdwy 5th: wnt 2nd 3 out: rdn 2 out: ev ch flat: nt qckn)	hd	3	3/1 2	79	20
3980ᶠ	**Santella Boy (USA) (106)** (CJMann) **5-10-6b** JRailton (lw: hld up: hdwy 6th: wknd appr 2 out)	8	4	7/1	70	11
3915²	**Holy Joe (102)** (DBurchell) **15-10-2** DJBurchell (bhd fr 7th)	13	5	14/1	56	—
3920⁸	**Swing Quartet (IRE) (100)** (NATwiston-Davies) **7-10-0** CLlewellyn (lw: bhd fr 6th)	3	6	12/1	52	—
1957⁷	**Nickle Joe (100)** (MTate) **11-9-7**(7) MrOMcPhail (prom to 4th: t.o)	dist	7	66/1	—	—
3600⁷	**Henrietta Howard (IRE) (121)** (MrsDHaine) **7-11-7** JFTitley (bhd tl p.u bef 5th)		P	4/1 3	—	—
3430ᵁ	**So Proud (120)** (MrsAJPerrett) **12-11-6** CMaude (bhd fr 6th: t.o whn p.u bef last)		P	20/1	—	—

(SP 120.2%) **9 Rn**

5m 2.8 (2.80) CSF £17.81 CT £44.87 TOTE £3.10: £1.50 £1.60 £1.60 (£5.40) Trio £14.20 OWNER Richard Green (Fine Paintings) (WELLINGTON) BRED George & Mrs Steinberg
LONG HANDICAP Nickle Joe 9-9 Swing Quartet (IRE) 9-12
OFFICIAL EXPLANATION **Henrietta Howard (IRE): rider reported that the mare was never travelling on the ground.**
4048 Courbaril, 4lb higher than when last in a handicap, lived up to his good effort behind Sanmartino at Aintree. (11/4)
3750* The Toiseach (IRE), raised 5lb, showed his win in the first-time visor to be no flash in the pan. (11/2)
4084* El Don could have found this trip with the stiff uphill finish stretching his stamina to the limit. (3/1)
3980 Santella Boy (USA) had ground conditions in his favour but was safely held once in line for home. (7/1: 5/1-8/1)
3681 Swing Quartet (IRE) (12/1: op 8/1)

4179 HOWARD E. PERRY HUNTERS' CHASE (6-Y.O+) (Class H)
4-00 (4-00) **3m 2f 110y (New) (22 fncs)** £2,801.00 (£848.00: £414.00: £197.00) GOING minus 0.60 sec per fur (F)

	Horse / details	Dist	Pos	SP	RR	SF
3637⁵	**Double Silk** (RCWilkins) **13-12-0**(7) MrEWilliams (lw: j.w: led 3rd: clr 14th: r.o wl fr 3 out)	—	1	15/8 1	124	16
4087*	**Some-Toy** (JohnSquire) **11-11-10**(7) MissLBlackford (lw: hdwy 9th: wnt 2nd appr 11th: hit 3 out: sn rdn: no imp)	11	2	13/2	113	5
4087²	**Rusty Bridge** (MrsSMJohnson) **10-11-10**(7) MrRBurton (lw: led to 3rd: rdn 11th: sn lost pl: styd on flat)	11	3	14/1	107	—
3984*	**Idiotic** (PRChamings) **9-11-12**(5) MrCVigors (hdwy 7th: hit 10th: j.slowly 18th: hit 3 out: fin tired)	3	4	7/2 2	105	—
3498³	**Young Brave** (MrsAYoung) **11-12-0**(7) MrMGMiller (lw: hdwy 16th: btn whn mstke 3 out)	1¾	5	13/2	108	—

3739[3] **The Malakarma** (MissCSaunders) **11-11-12**(5) MrBPollock (hdwy 7th: dropped rr 11th: wl bhd fr 13th: t.o)....22 **6** 5/1[3] 91 —
4022* **L'Uomo Piu** (ABarrow) **13-11-7**(7) MrOMcPhail (prom tl wknd qckly after 12th: sn t.o: p.u bef 4 out)................. **P** 25/1 — —
3580* **Jupiter Moon** (MrsCHicks) **8-11-7**(7) MrJMPritchard (lw: hld up: blnd & uns rdr 5th).. **U** 16/1 — —
(SP 116.7%) **8 Rn**

6m 45.6 (10.60) CSF £13.91 TOTE £2.40: £1.30 £2.40 £2.00 (£15.90) OWNER Mr R. C. Wilkins (BATH) BRED Mrs P. M. Eyre
3637 Double Silk, gaining his seventh course win, may not be the force of old but proved plenty good enough against these rivals. (15/8)
4087* Some-Toy did not see out the trip as well as the winner and may be better at three miles. (13/2)
4087 Rusty Bridge was 3lb better off than when beaten only four lengths by the runner-up at Chepstow a week ago. (14/1: 10/1-16/1)
3984* Idiotic seemed to find this extended distance beyond him. (7/2)
3498 Young Brave has yet to recapture last season's form. (13/2: 9/2-7/1)

4180 BIRDLIP NOVICES' CHASE (5-Y.O+) (Class D)

4-35 (4-35) **2m 5f (New) (17 fncs)** £3,397.00 (£1,021.00: £493.00: £229.00) GOING minus 0.60 sec per fur (F)

SP RR SF

3941* **Formal Invitation (IRE) (100)** (DNicholson) **8-11-8** RJohnson (lw: tk keen hold: wnt 2nd 5th: led last: rdn & r.o wl)..— **1** 5/2[2] 116 11
3812* **Wee Windy (IRE) (110)** (JTGifford) **8-11-8** PHide (led 3rd to last: one pce)..9 **2** 3/1[3] 109 4
4133* **Greenback (BEL) (125)** (PJHobbs) **6-11-12** NWilliamson (hld up: hdwy 11th: hit 13th & 4 out: ev ch 3 out: rdn 2 out: sn wknd)..6 **3** 5/6[1] 109 4
3956[3] **Pinoccio (60)** (DCO'Brien) **10-11-2** WMarston (led to 3rd: mstke 7th: t.o fr 8th)..dist **4** 50/1 — —
(SP 110.1%) **4 Rn**

5m 14.9 (5.90) CSF £9.07 TOTE £3.60 (£3.60) OWNER The Plough Partnership (TEMPLE GUITING) BRED Patrick Eddery Ltd
3941* Formal Invitation (IRE) is progressing into a useful type on this sort of ground. (5/2)
3812* Wee Windy (IRE) forced the pace over a trip short of his best but had no answer to the winner. (3/1)
4133* Greenback (BEL) could easily have found this coming too soon after his hard race at Ascot. (5/6)

4181 CHELTENHAM SPONSORSHIP CLUB NOVICES' H'CAP HURDLE (0-105) (4-Y.O+) (Class E)

5-10 (5-10) **2m 5f 110y (New) (10 hdls)** £2,996.00 (£908.00: £444.00: £212.00) GOING minus 0.34 sec per fur (GF)

SP RR SF

3754* **Stormyfairweather (IRE) (97)** (NJHenderson) **5-11-8** MAFitzgerald (a.p: wnt 2nd 5th: led after 2 out: rdn out)— **1** 9/2[2] 71 29
4017* **Mystic Hill (84)** (RGFrost) **6-10-9** JFrost (hld up: hdwy 4th: ev ch whn forced wd bnd appr last: r.o flat)........1½ **2** 7/2[1] 57 15
1174[10] **Plinth (79)** (RHAlner) **6-10-4** NWilliamson (hld up: hdwy 7th: ev ch appr last: one pce)..........................3½ **3** 14/1 49 7
3999[3] **Shahrani (103)** (MCPipe) **5-12-0v[1]** APMcCoy (chsd ldr: j.slowly 2nd: led 4th: rdn & hdd after 2 out: wkng whn n.m.r bnd appr last)..10 **4** 7/1 66 24
3488[7] **Killing Time (75)** (DBurchell) **6-10-0** DJBurchell (wl bhd 6th: hdwy appr 2 out: nt trble ldrs)..........................11 **5** 16/1 30 —
3932[4] **Go Frolic (75)** (MissCPhillips) **9-10-0** RJohnson (bhd fr 6th)..1¼ **6** 16/1 29 —
3967[5] **Mr Christie (85)** (MissLCSiddall) **5-10-10** CMaude (bhd fr 6th)..1½ **7** 9/1 38 —
3687[4] **Equity's Darling (IRE) (82)** (DCO'Brien) **5-10-7b** PHide (a bhd: t.o fr 6th)..12 **8** 33/1 26 —
3937[3] **Scenic Waters (75)** (NATwiston-Davies) **5-10-0** CLlewellyn (prom to 7th: t.o)..10 **9** 5/1[3] 11 —
1384[5] **Hylters Chance (IRE) (77)** (PJHobbs) **6-10-2** LHarvey (led to 4th: wknd 7th: t.o)..5 **10** 9/1 10 —
2708[11] **Glistening Dawn (85)** (TKeddy) **7-10-10b** SMcNeill (prom to 7th: t.o whn p.u bef 2 out).......................... **P** 20/1 — —
3761[12] **Classic Model (75)** (JCTuck) **6-10-0** RBellamy (p.u after 3rd: sddle slipped).. **P** 50/1 — —
3831[5] **Colwall (86)** (MissPMWhittle) **6-10-4**(7) MrJGoldstein (hld up: mstke 5th: sn bhd: t.o whn blnd & uns rdr last) .... **U** 20/1 — —
(SP 122.4%) **13 Rn**

5m 4.5 (4.50) CSF £18.83 CT £192.58 TOTE £4.20: £1.80 £2.10 £3.10 (£8.10) Trio £51.80 OWNER Mrs Christopher Hanbury (LAMBOURN)
BRED P. J. O'Connor
LONG HANDICAP Killing Time 9-13 Classic Model 9-6 Go Frolic 9-6
3754* Stormyfairweather (IRE) had the advantage of the inside and missed the trouble rounding the home turn. (9/2)
4017* Mystic Hill looked dangerous when forced right taking it up for home, and could not peg back the winner. (7/2)
641 Plinth was involved in the bunching between the last two hurdles but had no excuses. (14/1)
3999 Shahrani was already feeling the pinch when squeezed out after being headed. (7/1)

T/Plpt: £54.40 (289.56 Tckts). T/Qdpt: £20.70 (37.56 Tckts) KH

3555-AYR (L-H) (Good)

Thursday April 17th

Race 5: 1 fence omitted, & 2nd last bypassed fnl circ
WEATHER: fine

4182 'BREATH OF FRESH AYR' 'N.H' NOVICES' HURDLE (I) (4-Y.O+) (Class D)

2-20 (2-20) **3m 110y (12 hdls)** £2,632.00 (£796.00: £388.00: £184.00) GOING minus 0.06 sec per fur (G)

SP RR SF

3817[3] **Fiddling The Facts (IRE) (110)** (NJHenderson) **6-11-2** MAFitzgerald (trckd ldrs: led after 4 out: rdn & hld on wl flat)..— **1** 11/10[1] 79 12
4052[P] **Spring Double (IRE) (115)** (NATwiston-Davies) **6-11-12** CLlewellyn (hld up: hdwy whn hmpd after 4 out: sn chsng wnr: ev ch flat: nt qckn)..½ **2** 2/1[2] 89 22
3817[P] **River Bay (IRE) (98)** (MissHCKnight) **6-11-2** JCulloty (lw: trckd ldrs: effrt 4 out: one pce)..........................12 **3** 9/1 71 4
3795[4] **My Mavourneen** (MrsSCBradburne) **5-10-4**(7) MrMBradburne (cl up: led 6th tl after 4 out: sn outpcd).............2 **4** 33/1 65? —
3621[11] **Bright Flame (IRE)** (MissSEdwards) **5-11-2** MrTHills (hld up: effrt 4 out: nvr trbld ldrs)..........................4 **5** 300/1 67? —
3910[3] **Magpie Melody (IRE) (100)** (LLungo) **6-11-2**(5) BGrattan (lw: led to 6th: cl up tl wknd appr 3 out)..................1¼ **6** 8/1[3] 71 4
3171[5] **Shariakandi (FR)** (JSKing) **5-11-2** TJMurphy (prom: hit 8th: btn next)..dist **7** 16/1 — —
Gentleman Jim (RCurtis) **7-11-2** DMorris (hld up: hdwy 7th: wnt prom 4 out: sn wknd: no ch whn fell 2 out)..... **F** 100/1 — —
3794[7] **Dowshi** (LLungo) **6-10-4**(7) IJardine (mstkes: t.o fr 6th: p.u bef 3 out).. **P** 66/1 — —
2746[P] **Nautilus The Third (IRE)** (MDHammond) **6-11-2** RGarritty (p.u lame bef 5th).. **P** 100/1 — —
Springlea Tower (RNixon) **4-10-8** BStorey (bit bkwd: mstkes 7th & sn t.o: p.u bef 3 out).. **P** 200/1 — —
(SP 115.2%) **11 Rn**

6m 2.0 (16.00) CSF £3.13 TOTE £1.90: £1.20 £1.50 £1.60 (£2.10) Trio £3.70 OWNER Mrs E. Roberts (LAMBOURN) BRED E. Hamilton
WEIGHT FOR AGE 4yo-8lb

3817 Fiddling The Facts (IRE) certainly appreciated this step up in distance and proved to be a tough sort under pressure. (11/10)
4052 Spring Double (IRE) stays really well but did not help himself when getting hampered on the home turn. However, he still had every chance but just found the winner too tough late on. (2/1)
2822 River Bay (IRE) looked and travelled well but proved to be well short of speed when the chips were down and would seem to need more testing ground. (9/1)
3795 My Mavourneen ran her best race so far and is obviously improving. (33/1)
Bright Flame (IRE) ran reasonably but looked very onepaced over the last four flights. (300/1)
3910 Magpie Melody (IRE) was most disappointing here, dropping tamely away in the home straight, and this is obviously not his true form. (8/1)

4183 ROYAL HIGHLAND FUSILIERS NOVICES' CHASE (5-Y.O+) (Class D)

2-50 (2-50) **2m (12 fncs)** £3,629.50 (£1,096.00: £533.00: £251.50) GOING minus 0.06 sec per fur (G)

	Horse / Running details	Dist	Pos	SP	RR	SF
3790*	**American Hero** (RAllan) **9-11-6** BStorey (lw: mde all: clr whn blnd last: styd on)	—	1	11/4 1	113	46
3530*	**Singing Sand (89)** (PMonteith) **7-11-12** RDunwoody (lw: a chsng wnr: effrt whn blnd 3 out: nt qckn)	2	2	5/1 3	117	50
3523a7	**Power Pack (IRE)** (JFCMaxwell,Ireland) **9-11-6** MrBRHamilton (sn prom: effrt 6th: one pce & no imp fr 8th)	10	3	3/1 2	101	34
37033	**Fils de Cresson (IRE)** (JRAdam) **7-11-0** TReed (bhd: hdwy 5th: nvr able rch ldrs)	4	4	20/1	91	24
39432	**Daring Past (97)** (MDHammond) **7-11-6** RGarritty (outpcd & no imp fr ½-wy)	14	5	14/1	83	16
39413	**Desert Brave (IRE) (77)** (MrsSJSmith) **7-11-0** RichardGuest (outpcd & bhd fr 5th)	12	6	33/1	65	—
3086P	**Sound Statement (IRE)** (MissSEdwards) **8-10-11**(3) LAspell (lw: outpcd & no ch fr ½-wy)	16	7	100/1	49	—
3638P	**Garolo (FR) (117)** (CPEBrooks) **7-11-6b** GBradley (mstkes: chsd ldrs: 3rd whn blnd 4 out: sn btn: 5th whn fell last)		F	3/1 2	—	—
	Smart in Silk (MissLucindaRussell) **8-10-9** MFoster (a bhd: t.o whn p.u bef 4 out)		P	200/1	—	—
				(SP 109.2%)	**9 Rn**	

3m 48.7 (3.70) CSF £13.97 TOTE £3.00: £1.40 £1.10 £1.20 (£3.60) Trio £4.40 OWNER Mrs R. P. Aggio (CORNHILL-ON-TWEED) BRED Sir Gordon White

3790* American Hero gave his opponents a lesson in jumping and then almost blew it with a blunder at the last. (11/4)
3530* Singing Sand ran another fine race but a blunder three out cost him any chance of really troubling the winner. (5/1)
Power Pack (IRE) was always in pursuit of the leaders but the frenetic pace was just beyond him and he never offered a serious threat. (3/1)
3703 Fils de Cresson (IRE) ran well in this fast-run event and also at his first attempt over fences, and a bit further might well see improvement. (20/1)
3943 Daring Past is showing slight signs of coming back to form but he was never able to get into this fast-run event. (14/1)
3111 Garolo (FR) was never jumping with any confidence and got worse as the race progressed. He was a well beaten fifth when coming down at the last. (3/1)

4184 FRIENDLY HOTELS NOVICES' HURDLE (4-Y.O+) (Class D)

3-20 (3-20) **2m 4f (11 hdls)** £3,386.00 (£1,028.00: £504.00: £242.00) GOING minus 0.06 sec per fur (G)

	Horse / Running details	Dist	Pos	SP	RR	SF
3918*	**Zander (103)** (NATwiston-Davies) **5-11-7** CLlewellyn (lw: a.p: led 3 out to 2 out: rallied flat: r.o wl to ld nr fin)	—	1	8/1 2	88	35
2812*	**Red Blazer (133)** (MissHCKnight) **6-11-12** JOsborne (trckd ldrs: smooth hdwy to ld 2 out: rdn flat: hdd & nt qckn towards fin)	hd	2	4/7 1	93	40
	Shortstaff (IRE) (MissLAPerratt) **8-11-2** PCarberry (a.p: ev ch 2 out: kpt on wl)	2	3	100/1	81?	28
26907	**Cherrymore (IRE)** (MrsJPitman) **6-11-2** APMcCoy (hdwy 7th: in tch appr 3 out: 4th & no imp whn blnd last)	6	4	9/1 3	77+	24
39732	**Ardarroch Prince** (MrsMReveley) **6-11-2** PNiven (lw: hld up: effrt 7th: hit 3 out: nvr rchd ldrs)	6	5	12/1	72	19
3634F	**Harbet House (FR)** (RJO'Sullivan) **4-11-0** NWilliamson (chsd ldrs: led 6th to 3 out: wkng whn hit 2 out)	6	6	8/1 2	72	12
	Regal Eagle (MDHammond) **4-10-9** RDunwoody (hld up: effrt 4 out: sn rdn & no imp)	6	7	66/1	62	2
38888	**Bonny Rigg (IRE) (62)** (LLungo) **5-10-11** TReed (led tl after 1st: prom tl rdn & wknd 4 out)	13	8	200/1	47	—
39107	**Thorntoun House (IRE)** (JSGoldie) **4-10-9** DParker (nvr trbld ldrs)	1½	9	200/1	51	—
40089	**Knightsbridge Girl (IRE)** (PJHobbs) **6-10-11** RJohnson (lw: lost tch fr ½-wy)	13	10	33/1	35	—
27845	**Apache Len (USA)** (MDHammond) **4-10-9** RGarritty (prom to 6th: wknd qckly)	4	11	66/1	37	—
20418	**Star Master (58)** (PMonteith) **6-11-2** LWyer (a rr div)	¾	12	50/1	36	—
	Boxgrove Man (IRE) (JABOld) **7-11-2** MAFitzgerald (mstkes: hld up: effrt 6th: wknd appr 4 out: p.u bef 3 out)		P	14/1	—	—
	Minnies Turn (WTKemp) **6-10-11** SMcDougall (plld hrd: led after 1st & sn clr: hdd & wknd rapidly 6th: p.u bef 4 out)		P	100/1	—	—
13439	**Smart In Socks** (MissLucindaRussell) **6-11-2** BStorey (t.o fr 6th: p.u bef 4 out)		P	500/1	—	—
				(SP 121.3%)	**15 Rn**	

4m 48.7 (7.70) CSF £12.25 TOTE £11.30: £2.00 £1.10 £9.70 (£4.70) Trio £72.20 OWNER Mrs Karen Duggan (CHELTENHAM) BRED G. Burton
WEIGHT FOR AGE 4yo-7lb

3918* Zander, trying his longest trip to date, needed every yard of it and proved to be a very game individual to make it. (8/1: op 5/1)
2812* Red Blazer has been waiting for some decent ground and looked likely to win this nicely, but after two and a half months off he probably just needed it and was found out late on. He was later reported to be lame. (4/7)
Shortstaff (IRE), having his first run in this country, ran a cracker and it should not be long before he finds a suitable race. (100/1)
2690 Cherrymore (IRE), off the track for almost three months, ran much better here but never got into it seriously. Nevertheless, he should benefit from it. (9/1: 6/1-10/1)
3973 Ardarroch Prince, patiently ridden, was never good enough to get into it in this company. (12/1: 8/1-14/1)
3084* Harbet House (FR), who seems at his best when the ground is at its most testing, was found out in the home straight here. (8/1: op 5/1)
Regal Eagle looks the type to do well at this game but was a shade disappointing here and this may have come a bit too quick after his effort on the Flat recently. (66/1)

4185 GEORGE GRAHAM MEMORIAL H'CAP CHASE (0-135) (5-Y.O+) (Class C)

3-50 (3-50) **3m 1f (19 fncs)** £5,117.50 (£1,540.00: £745.00: £347.50) GOING minus 0.06 sec per fur (G)

	Horse / Running details	Dist	Pos	SP	RR	SF
3974*	**Kenmore-Speed (106)** (MrsSJSmith) **10-10-4**ow1 RichardGuest (chsd ldrs: led 11th: hld on wl fr 2 out)	—	1	7/1 3	120	38
3567*	**Donjuan Collonges (FR) (110)** (CaptTAForster) **6-10-8** PCarberry (lw: wnt prom 6th: cl up whn blnd bdly & lost pl 13th: hit next: gd hdwy 4 out: ev ch 2 out: kpt on u.p flat)	½	2	7/4 1	124+	43
3472*	**Cariboo Gold (USA) (115)** (KCBailey) **8-10-13b** JOsborne (hld up: hdwy 13th: ev ch 2 out: rdn & no ex)	5	3	13/2 2	126	45
38154	**Darren the Brave (102)** (CPEBrooks) **9-10-0** DGallagher (mstke & lost pl 2nd: hdwy ½-wy: effrt 4 out: styd on: no imp)	7	4	20/1	108	27
33163	**Stormy Coral (IRE) (106)** (CParker) **7-10-4** BStorey (bhd: hdwy whn hit 11th: styd on: no imp)	2	5	12/1	111	30

3884[3] **Kilcolgan (105)** (MrsJDGoodfellow) **10-10-3b** NBentley (mstkes: outpcd tl styd on fr 4 out: n.d)....................1¼ **6** 20/1 109 28
3414[3] **Whispering Steel (127)** (GRichards) **11-11-11** RDunwoody (hld up: hdwy 10th: sn prom: wknd 4 out).............6 **7** 14/1 127 46
4054[P] **Wudimp (110)** (MrsJStorey) **8-10-8** MrCStorey (hdwy & prom 10th: outpcd fr 14th)..15 **8** 25/1 101 20
3804[6] **Andermatt (113)** (JMackie) **10-10-11** NWilliamson (lw: a rr div: t.o fr 14th) 26 **9** 50/1 87 6
3916* **Seod Rioga (IRE) (116)** (SMellor) **8-11-0** NMann (trckd ldrs: 3rd whn fell 4 out) .... **F** 8/1 — —
3804[F] **General Pershing (130)** (DNicholson) **11-12-0** RJohnson (cl up: led 6th to 11th: p.u lame bef 13th).................. **P** 12/1 — —
3911[P] **Northern Squire (106)** (JMJefferson) **9-10-1**(3)ow1 ECallaghan (blnd 4th & 5th: sn t.o: p.u after 10th)................ **P** 33/1 — —
Easter Oats (102) (RHGoldie) **10-10-0** GCahill (sn bhd: p.u bef 12th).. **P** 100/1 — —
3428[5] **Rocky Park (102)** (GBBalding) **11-10-0** BFenton (led to 6th: 3rd whn blnd & uns rdr 12th).................................. **U** 20/1 — —
(SP 119.4%) **14 Rn**

6m 10.4 (3.40) CSF £16.96 CT £79.39 TOTE £6.90: £1.90 £1.90 £2.30 (£13.90) Trio £8.00 OWNER Mr K. M. Dacker (BINGLEY) BRED Mrs Davina Whiteman

LONG HANDICAP Easter Oats 9-1 Darren the Brave 9-12 Rocky Park 9-7

3974* Kenmore-Speed is a grand, consistent sort who runs and jumps for fun and thoroughly deserved this. (7/1)

3567* Donjuan Collonges (FR) should have won this but managed to beat himself with some clumsy jumps and it was only a brilliant ride that got him so close. (7/4)

3472* Cariboo Gold (USA) moved up looking dangerous entering the straight but when it came down to a struggle he was found wanting from the second last. (13/2)

3815 Darren the Brave looks the type who likes things to go his way and that was never likely in this competitive event. (20/1)

3316 Stormy Coral (IRE), after nearly two months off, ran as though he will be all the sharper for this. (12/1)

3884 Kilcolgan found things happening far too quickly for his liking and made mistakes, but this dour stayer was making ground at the end. (20/1)

3414 Whispering Steel travelled well until an effort was required approaching four out from which point he soon packed it in. (14/1)

3916* Seod Rioga (IRE) went well and was certainly not out of it when falling four out. (8/1)

4186 EAGLE TAVERN'S NOVICES' H'CAP CHASE (0-110) (5-Y.O+) (Class D)

4-25 (4-26) **2m 5f 110y (15 fncs)** £4,432.00 (£1,336.00: £648.00: £304.00) GOING minus 0.06 sec per fur (G)

SP RR SF

3975[F] **Gaelic Blue (86)** (MrsSJSmith) **7-10-4**ow1 RichardGuest (in tch: effrt 3 out: styd on strly appr last: r.o to ld nr fin) ....— **1** 9/2[2] 103 32
3556[2] **Nicholas Plant (95)** (JSGoldie) **8-10-13** GCahill (chsd ldrs: led 11th: r.o wl fr 2 out: jst ct).................................hd **2** 10/1[3] 112 42
3975* **Kings Sermon (IRE) (89)** (PBeaumont) **8-10-7** LWyer (a in tch: kpt on wl fr 3 out: nt pce to chal).......................4 **3** 16/1 103 33
3972[2] **Ballyline (IRE) (88)** (WTKemp) **6-10-6** JCallaghan (led 2nd to 5th: led 9th to 11th: ev ch tl wknd fr last 2).........1 **4** 11/1 101 31
3819* **Red Branch (IRE) (90)** (JSKing) **8-10-8** TJMurphy (lw: led to 2nd: led 5th to 9th: outpcd 3 out: wknd next) ....15 **5** 3/1[1] 92 22
3886* **Le Denstan (84)** (MrsDThomson) **10-10-2** RJohnson (lw: unruly s: nvr trbld ldrs) 1 **6** 14/1 85 15
4077* **Real Tonic (103)** (GRichards) **7-11-7** 6x PCarberry (hdwy ½-wy: chsng ldrs whn blnd 11th: sn rcvrd: rdn & wknd appr 2 out) ....7 **7** 9/2[2] 99 29
3805[5] **The Reverend Bert (IRE) (110)** (GBBalding) **9-11-9**(5) ABates (s.s: blnd bdly 7th: n.d)...2 **8** 20/1 105 35
3068[P] **Lien de Famille (IRE) (102)** (JJQuinn) **7-11-6** PNiven (a rr div)..16 **9** 50/1 85 15
2916[3] **Slotamatique (IRE) (100)** (GRichards) **8-11-4** RDunwoody (lost tch fr ½-wy)...3½ **10** 12/1 80 10
4077[F] **Coqui Lane (97)** (JMDun) **10-11-1** DParker (lw: unruly s: sn bhd: t.o fr 8th: p.u bef 11th).. **P** 12/1 — —
3909[3] **Corston Joker (82)** (LLungo) **7-10-0** JSupple (lw: unruly s: mstkes & a bhd: t.o whn p.u bef last)............................ **P** 16/1 — —
Bob Nelson (82) (PBeaumont) **10-10-0** CLlewellyn (prom tl wknd & blnd 11th: p.u bef 2 out) .... **P** 100/1 — —
(SP 120.3%) **13 Rn**

5m 16.9 (9.00 under best) (4.90) CSF £44.56 CT £612.60 TOTE £4.80: £2.00 £3.40 £4.00 (£31.10) Trio £102.70 OWNER Mr Trevor Hemmings (BINGLEY) BRED Michael Lysaght

LONG HANDICAP Bob Nelson 9-0

3975 Gaelic Blue is an improving type who needed every yard of this trip and he can really make his mark in staying handicaps next season. (9/2)

3556 Nicholas Plant, suited by this trip, ran his socks off only to be touched off, but this good sort will find plenty of other opportunities. (10/1)

3975* Kings Sermon (IRE) is running well and seems to be gradually improving. He was keeping on most determinedly at the end, suggesting that further is needed. (16/1)

3972 Ballyline (IRE) ran a fair race and probably just found this trip beyond his best. (11/1)

3819* Red Branch (IRE) has risen 19lb since his winning run started and this seems to have found him out here. (3/1)

3886* Le Denstan always found this too competitive for his liking. (14/1)

4077* Real Tonic likes it when things go his way and that was never on in this useful event and, after making mistakes, he dropped tamely away in the straight. (9/2)

4077 Coqui Lane (12/1: op 8/1)

4187 ROYAL BURGH OF AYR CONDITIONAL H'CAP HURDLE (0-110) (4-Y.O+) (Class E)

4-55 (4-55) **2m (9 hdls)** £3,291.50 (£992.00: £481.00: £225.50) GOING minus 0.06 sec per fur (G)

SP RR SF

3976[2] **Teejay'n'aitch (IRE) (78)** (JSGoldie) **5-10-0** STaylor (mde most: clr appr 3 out: kpt on wl) ....— **1** 6/1[2] 69 14
3325[8] **Parson's Lodge (IRE) (78)** (LLungo) **9-9-9**(5) WDowling (bhd & pushed along: hdwy 4 out: styd on strly fr 2 out: nrst fin) 3½ **2** 14/1 66 11
3912[6] **Latin Leader (86)** (CParker) **7-10-8b** FLeahy (a.p: effrt 4 out: one pce fr next) 5 **3** 14/1 69 14
3687[3] **Rachael's Owen (85)** (CWeedon) **7-10-7** RMcGrath (lw: chsd ldrs: rdn appr 3 out: sn btn) ....2 **4** 6/1[2] 66 11
3822[6] **Gallardini (IRE) (78)** (BSRothwell) **8-9-7**(7) ACurrie (prom: effrt 4 out: outpcd appr next)..................................1½ **5** 14/1 57 2
2001* **Fen Terrier (103)** (FPMurtagh) **5-11-11** ECallaghan (hdwy 4th: sn in tch: rdn & no impr fr 4 out) ....¾ **6** 7/1[3] 81 26
3995[4] **Samanid (IRE) (105)** (MissLCSiddall) **5-11-13** DJKavanagh (hld up: effrt 5th: rdn & btn after 4 out)......................5 **7** 15/2 78 23
4060[2] **Skiddaw Samba (84)** (MrsMReveley) **8-10-6** GLee (hit 4th: effrt next: btn after 4 out)...3 **8** 5/1[1] 54 —
4130[6] **Nashville Star (USA) (94)** (RMathew) **6-11-2v** RMassey (disp ld to 3rd: chsd ldr tl wknd 4 out)............................8 **9** 6/1[2] 56 1
2177[P] **Jaunty General (82)** (CParker) **6-9-13**(5) CMcCormack (in tch: effrt 4 out: sn wknd) ....s.h **10** 16/1 44 —
3885[P] **Cittadino (102)** (CWThornton) **7-11-7**(3) NHorrocks (bhd: effrt 5th: n.d)...1¾ **11** 10/1 62 7
3421[12] **Saint Ciel (USA) (104)** (FJordan) **9-11-12** LAspell (lw: hld up & bhd: n.d) 1¼ **12** 20/1 63 8
High Mind (FR) (102) (MissLCSiddall) **8-11-10** EHusband (a bhd) ....s.h **13** 16/1 61 6
3904[8] **Anlace (78)** (SMellor) **8-10-0** ChrisWebb (lw: bhd fr 5th)..9 **14** 20/1 28 —
(SP 134.2%) **14 Rn**

3m 43.2 (6.20) CSF £88.26 CT £1,062.24 TOTE £8.30: £2.00 £3.70 £5.50 (£62.90) Trio £265.90; £265.99 to Newbury 18/4/97 OWNER Mr Andrew Paterson (GLASGOW) BRED David Hyland

LONG HANDICAP Parson's Lodge (IRE) 9-12

3976 Teejay'n'aitch (IRE) has reportedly had wind problems but he is in tremendous form at present and had this sewn up early in the straight to gain his first ever win. (6/1)
3325 Parson's Lodge (IRE) is a funny customer who runs when in the mood. He certainly put his best foot forward here from the third last to finish fast, but always too late. (14/1)
3313* Latin Leader went well for much of the trip but, once he came off the bit turning for home, he found little. (14/1)
3687 Rachael's Owen was always close enough if good enough but proved very onepaced when ridden. (6/1)
3822 Gallardini (IRE) ran reasonably but, once asked for a serious effort four out, he was soon treading water. (14/1)
2001* Fen Terrier, after four months off, ran quite well to the fourth last. (7/1)
3995 Samanid (IRE) (15/2: 5/1-8/1)

4188 'BREATH OF FRESH AYR' 'N.H' NOVICES' HURDLE (II) (4-Y.O+) (Class D)
5-25 (5-25) **3m 110y (12 hdls)** £2,619.00 (£792.00: £386.00: £183.00) GOING minus 0.06 sec per fur (G)

				SP	RR	SF
3887[5]	**Clairabell (IRE) (75)** (JIACharlton) **6-10-11** BStorey (in tch: hdwy 4 out: slt ld last: styd on u.p)	—	**1**	14/1	69	6
3847[2]	**Ivory Coaster (NZ) (101)** (BdeHaan) **6-11-2** JOsborne (lw: trckd ldrs: led 4 out tl mstke & hdd last: kpt on u.p)	½	**2**	2/1[1]	74	11
4075[2]	**Nick Ross (67)** (RBrewis) **6-11-2** ASSmith (hld up: hdwy 7th: chsng ldrs 4 out: kpt on: nt pce to chal)	2½	**3**	7/1[3]	72	9
3825[7]	**Boston Man (88)** (RDEWoodhouse) **6-11-7b** PCarberry (chsd ldrs: led 8th to 4 out: sn rdn & btn)	16	**4**	12/1	67	4
3481[2]	**Mrs Robinson (IRE) (79)** (JMackie) **6-10-8**(3) EHusband (lw: in tch: rdn 4 out: sn outpcd & n.d after)	2½	**5**	12/1	55	—
3406[5]	**May Sunset (IRE)** (CREgerton) **7-11-2b[1]** NWilliamson (hld up: chal on bit 4 out: rdn next: wknd qckly)	1	**6**	20/1	59	—
	Birkdale (IRE) (LLungo) **6-11-2** JSupple (bit bkwd: pushed along & bhd: sme hdwy 8th: sn wknd)	8	**7**	16/1	54	—
2634[12]	**La Mon Dere (IRE)** (PJHobbs) **6-11-2** RDunwoody (lw: outpcd ½-wy: lost tch 4 out: t.o)	dist	**8**	12/1	—	—
4102[7]	**Arctic Fox (IRE)** (MissHCKnight) **5-11-2** JFTitley (swtg: chsd ldrs tl wknd 4 out: wl t.o)	dist	**9**	16/1	—	—
3887*	**Cherry Dee (92)** (PBeaumont) **6-11-2**(5) BGrattan (lw: chsd ldrs tl rdn & wknd fr 7th: p.u bef 2 out)		**P**	5/2[2]	—	—
	Soldier-B (RCurtis) **7-10-11**(5) ABates (led & sn clr: hdd 8th: sn wknd: p.u bef 2 out)		**P**	33/1	—	—
				(SP 123.6%)	**11 Rn**	

6m 2.5 (16.50) CSF £41.49 TOTE £15.90: £2.40 £1.50 £2.00 (£26.90) Trio £54.80 OWNER Mr W. F. Trueman (STOCKSFIELD) BRED Denis McDonnell
STEWARDS' ENQUIRY Osborne susp. 26&29/4/97 (excessive use of whip).
3887 Clairabell (IRE) needed the trip and, getting her nose in font at the last, she proved game under pressure. (14/1: 10/1-16/1)
3847 Ivory Coaster (NZ), trying his longest trip to date, got it well enough but was just outbattled. He deserves a change of luck. (2/1)
4075 Nick Ross is running particularly well at the moment and certainly stayed well enough. He will surely break his duck before long. (7/1)
3825 Boston Man was given a most positive ride but he found it all too much over the last four flights. (12/1: op 8/1)
3481 Mrs Robinson (IRE) was made to look very onepaced here and was going nowhere from the fifth last. (12/1)
3406 May Sunset (IRE), in blinkers for the first time, came there cantering four out but then folded up in two strides when asked a question over the next. He is obviously a very funny customer. (20/1)
3887* Cherry Dee was most disappointing, dropping tamely away on the final circuit, and was pulled up when well beaten. Something was obviously wrong. (5/2)

T/Plpt: £93.60 (177.34 Tckts). T/Qdpt: £70.80 (10.24 Tckts) AA

4189a - 4202a : (Irish Racing) - See Computer Raceform

4182-AYR (L-H) (Good)
Friday April 18th
Other race under Rules of Flat racing.
WEATHER: Fine

4203 HAMILTON CAMPBELL ILPH NOVICES' CHASE (5-Y.O+) (Class D)
2-00 (2-01) **3m 1f (19 fncs)** £5,478.00 (£1,644.00: £792.00: £366.00) GOING: 0.09 sec per fur (G)

				SP	RR	SF
4050[P]	**Chopwell Curtains** (TDEasterby) **7-11-12b[1]** LWyer (lw: rn in snatches: a in tch: hdwy to ld 4 out: r.o u.p flat)	—	**1**	11/2[3]	113	48
3484[2]	**Solomon's Dancer (USA) (129)** (GRichards) **7-11-12** RDunwoody (lw: trckd ldrs: effrt 3 out: ev ch last: no ex u.p)	2½	**2**	Evens[1]	111	46
4050[U]	**Bear Claw** (OSherwood) **8-11-7b** JOsborne (j.slowly 2nd: a in tch: effrt & mstke 15th: one pce fr 3 out)	4	**3**	7/2[2]	104	39
1989*	**Gems Lad (86)** (MrsSJSmith) **10-11-12** RichardGuest (mstke 1st: chsd ldr: led 12th tl mstke & hdd 4 out: sn wknd)	16	**4**	25/1	99	34
3848[3]	**Ballydougan (IRE) (74)** (RMathew) **9-11-2v** TJMurphy (sn outpcd & bhd: hrd rdn 13th: n.d)	8	**5**	100/1	84	19
3975[F]	**Bright Destiny (67)** (JSGoldie) **6-11-7** GCahill (a outpcd & bhd)	½	**6**	100/1	88	23
3617[P]	**Slideofhill (IRE)** (JJO'Neill) **8-11-2** APMcCoy (nvr gng wl: drvn along & lost tch 11th)	6	**7**	16/1	79	14
3826*	**Friendly Knight (84)** (JSHaldane) **7-11-7** ASSmith (ref to r: t.n.p)		**R**	50/1	—	—
3279[4]	**Easy Breezy (85)** (CJMann) **7-11-2** JRailton (lw: led tl hdd, mstke & uns rdr 12th)		**U**	33/1	—	—
				(SP 104.2%)	**9 Rn**	

6m 17.7 (10.70) CSF £9.04 TOTE £6.40: £2.10 £1.10 £1.40 (£4.70) Trio £3.60 OWNER Durham Drapes Ltd (MALTON) BRED Mrs A. C. Wakeham
OFFICIAL EXPLANATION **Chopwell Curtains: regarding the improved form, the trainer reported that the track had been too sharp last time, and that blinkers had improved the gelding's concentration.**
3805* Chopwell Curtains, after a dismal effort at Aintree, had blinkers for the first time and they certainly made a difference, and he saw the trip out particularly well. (11/2)
3484 Solomon's Dancer (USA) seemed to stay well enough but, when it came down to a fight, he was just found wanting. (Evens)
4050 Bear Claw has plenty of ability, but he seems to have lost confidence with his jumping at the moment, and was never doing enough to seriously to get into this. (7/2)
1989* Gems Lad, having his first run for four months and taking a big step up in class, ran particularly well in the circumstances. (25/1)
3202 Slideofhill (IRE) looked woefully slow and was flat out soon after the start. (16/1)
3279 Easy Breezy looked particularly well, and ran a useful race until he had a disagreement with his jockey about when to take off at the twelfth. (33/1)

4204 EVELYN MATTHEWS MEMORIAL NOVICES' H'CAP HURDLE (4-Y.O+) (Class C)

2-30 (2-31) **2m 4f** **(11 hdls)** £3,220.00 (£970.00: £470.00: £220.00) GOING: 0.09 sec per fur (G)

				SP	RR	SF
3587*	**Mahler (99)** (NATwiston-Davies) **7-9-12**(7) MrJGoldstein (chsd ldrs: led 4 out: hld on wl)	—	**1**	14/1	69	42
3944[2]	**Morpheus (99)** (DNicholson) **8-10-5** RJohnson (hld up: stdy hdwy whn blnd 4 out: ev ch 2 out: kpt on)	1	**2**	16/1	68	41
3727*	**Harfdecent (94)** (MrsMReveley) **6-10-0** JOsborne (s.s: hdwy 4 out: styd on strly fr 2 out: nrst fin)	¾	**3**	16/1	63	36
3226*	**Nishamira (IRE) (95)** (TDBarron) **5-9-12**(3) MrRThornton (mstkes: a cl up: chal 4 out: sn rdn: wknd last)	1¾	**4**	11/2[1]	62	35
3168[3]	**King Pin (118)** (PBeaumont) **5-11-5**(5) BGrattan (lw: hld up & bhd: hdwy 7th: chsd ldrs fr 3 out: hung lft & one pce flat)	1¼	**5**	12/1	84	57
4048[4]	**Far Ahead (118)** (JLEyre) **5-11-10** BStorey (mid div: drvn along fr 7th: styd on wl fr 2 out: nrst fin)	½	**6**	6/1[2]	84	57
3539[5]	**The Bargeman (NZ) (94)** (DRGandolfo) **9-9-11**(3) SophieMitchell (effrt 7th: nvr trbld ldrs)	4	**7**	33/1	57	30
3990[P]	**Charley Lambert (IRE) (98)** (JMackie) **6-10-4** NWilliamson (hld up: hdwy 7th: rdn & btn whn blnd 3 out)	9	**8**	16/1	53	26
3740*	**Cool Gunner (100)** (JSKing) **7-10-6** CMaude (nvr trbld ldrs)	8	**9**	8/1	49	22
3807[7]	**Jervaulx (IRE) (98)** (GRichards) **6-10-4** PCarberry (prom tl wknd fr 4 out)	8	**10**	14/1	41	14
3992[7]	**Suas Leat (IRE) (100)** (JMJefferson) **7-9-13**(7) MNewton (in tch tl wknd fr 4 out)	5	**11**	50/1	39	12
3105[2]	**Royal Event (104)** (DRGandolfo) **6-10-10** RDunwoody (led to 4 out: sn lost pl)	29	**12**	10/1	19	—
3613[13]	**Nasone (IRE) (106)** (JTGifford) **6-10-12** PHide (lw: chsd ldrs to 4 out: sn rdn & wknd: t.o)	dist	**13**	12/1	—	—
3368[4]	**Share Options (IRE) (105)** (TDEasterby) **6-10-11** LWyer (a bhd: p.u bef 7th)		**P**	20/1	—	—
2790[8]	**Kasirama (IRE) (94)** (MDHammond) **6-9-7**(7) NHorrocks (prom to ½-wy: t.o whn p.u bef 3 out)		**P**	100/1	—	—
3342*	**Colonel Blazer (102)** (MissHCKnight) **5-10-8** JFTitley (lw: prom tl wknd 7th: p.u bef 3 out)		**P**	13/2[3]	—	—
3887[10]	**Phar Echo (IRE) (98)** (LLungo) **6-10-4** MFoster (chsd ldrs tl rdn & wknd 6th: p.u bef 3 out)		**P**	14/1	—	—
3453*	**Lagen Bridge (IRE) (112)** (DMoffatt) **8-11-4** DJMoffatt (hld up: hdwy whn hmpd, mstke & uns rdr 6th)		**U**	16/1	—	—
				(SP 132.8%)	**18 Rn**	

4m 45.9 (4.90) CSF £209.24 CT £3,321.85 TOTE £19.90: £3.50 £2.80 £7.00 £2.30 (£111.70) Trio £510.40; £503.22 to Newbury 19/4/97
OWNER English Badminton Partnership (CHELTENHAM) BRED E. Peary
LONG HANDICAP The Bargeman (NZ) 9-12 Kasirama (IRE) 8-12
STEWARDS' ENQUIRY Johnson susp. 29-30/4/ & 2-3/5/97 (excessive use of whip)
OFFICIAL EXPLANATION Colonel Blazer: no explanation offered.

3587* Mahler, a real tough sort, is certainly useful and he will be a real prospect when put over fences. (14/1)

3944 Morpheus raced keenly as usual but did not help his chances with a mistake four out, but he still ran well and will find opportunities. (16/1)

3727* Harfdecent is obviously on the upgrade, as he might well have won this had he jumped off on terms. (16/1)

3226* Nishamira (IRE) looked well in, but spoilt her chances with some very novicey jumping. (11/2)

3168 King Pin did not help matters with some moderate hurdling, and he also again hung left when put under pressure. He may well have had enough for the time being. (12/1)

4048 Far Ahead is a genuine sort who stays well, and was keeping on most determinedly at the end. (6/1)

4205 ROYAL BANK OF SCOTLAND 'N.H.' NOVICES' HURDLE (4-Y.O+) (Class C)

3-00 (3-02) **2m** **(9 hdls)** £4,718.00 (£1,424.00: £692.00: £326.00) GOING: 0.09 sec per fur (G)

				SP	RR	SF
3396*	**Marello** (MrsMReveley) **6-11-10** PNiven (trckd ldr fr 4th: disp ld 3 out: led flat: hung lft: rdn & r.o)	—	**1**	1/8[1]	86	43
3918[P]	**Donnington (IRE) (105)** (OSherwood) **7-11-5** JOsborne (led tl hdd flat: kpt on wl)	1¼	**2**	9/1[2]	80	37
3166[4]	**Penrose Lad (NZ) (97)** (DNicholson) **7-11-0** RJohnson (lw: chsd ldrs tl grad wknd appr 3 out)	15	**3**	10/1[3]	60	17
3529[7]	**Cottstown Boy (IRE)** (MrsSCBradburne) **6-11-0** MFoster (prom tl outpcd fr 4 out)	13	**4**	50/1	47	4
3823[12]	**Hopeful Lord (IRE)** (PCheesbrough) **5-11-0** ASSmith (hld up: hdwy 4 out: lost pl fr next)	½	**5**	100/1	46	3
	Scally Beau (LLungo) **6-11-0** JSupple (hld up & bhd: lost tch 4th)	dist	**6**	200/1	—	—
1726[8]	**Second Step (IRE) (85)** (DRGandolfo) **6-11-0** RDunwoody (fell 4th)		**F**	20/1	—	—
	Master Rupert (RMMcKellar) **5-11-0** DParker (bit bkwd: sn outpcd & wl bhd: p.u 4th)		**P**	200/1	—	—
				(SP 116.7%)	**8 Rn**	

3m 44.2 (7.20) CSF £2.15 TOTE £1.20: £1.10 £1.60 £1.10 (£2.50) OWNER Mrs M. Williams (SALTBURN) BRED R. Chugg

3396* Marello looked to have an easy task here, but she made heavy weather of it and was also hanging quite badly late on. This is obviously not her true form. (1/8)

3918 Donnington (IRE) put in a useful effort and really made the favourite stretch, and he seems to be getting his act together. (9/1: op 5/1)

3166 Penrose Lad (NZ) ran reasonably and was not over-punished when obviously beaten. (10/1)

3529 Cottstown Boy (IRE) is showing enough to suggest that there is a moderate race to be picked up. (50/1)

Hopeful Lord (IRE), who had not shown anything previously, showed signs of ability here and was given an easy time when beaten. (100/1)

4206 HILLHOUSE QUARRY H'CAP CHASE (5-Y.O+) (Class B)

3-30 (3-30) **2m 4f** **(17 fncs)** £7,390.25 (£2,222.00: £1,073.50: £499.25) GOING: 0.09 sec per fur (G)

				SP	RR	SF
3639[5]	**Destin d'Estruval (FR) (121)** (DNicholson) **6-10-0** RJohnson (lw: trckd ldrs: rdn to chal 4 out: 2nd & hrd rdn whn lft clr last)	—	**1**	7/1[3]	135	45
3618[5]	**Destiny Calls (123)** (NAGaselee) **7-10-2**ow1 RDunwoody (prom tl outpcd 10th: hdwy u.p & chsng ldrs appr 4 out: kpt on: no imp)	11	**2**	3/1[1]	128	37
	Leotard (135) (MissVenetiaWilliams) **10-11-0** NWilliamson (hld up: stdy hdwy to trck ldrs 11th: outpcd fr 2 out)	nk	**3**	12/1	140	50
4053[8]	**Frickley (121)** (GRichards) **11-10-0** PCarberry (prom: hit 13th: rdn & no imp after)	8	**4**	9/1	120	30
3804[2]	**Cumbrian Challenge (IRE) (128)** (TDEasterby) **8-10-7** LWyer (lw: in tch: effrt 12th: chsng ldrs whn mstke 4 out: sn btn)	1¼	**5**	8/1	126	36
3636[P]	**Banjo (FR) (145)** (DNicholson) **7-11-7**(3) MrRThornton (chsd ldrs tl rdn & wl outpcd fr 9th: sn bhd)	hd	**6**	11/1	143	53
4074[U]	**Glemot (IRE) (134)** (KCBailey) **9-10-13** CO'Dwyer (cl up: lft in ld 8th: hdd & mstke 10th: sn wknd)	16	**7**	8/1	119	29
3916[3]	**Old Bridge (IRE) (130)** (OSherwood) **9-10-9** JOsborne (lw: a.p: led 10th: 2l clr & rdn whn fell last)		**F**	14/1	—	—
4011[3]	**Rouyan (134)** (MrsJPitman) **11-10-13** JFTitley (led tl blnd bdly & hdd 8th: p.u bef next)		**P**	4/1[2]	—	—
				(SP 112.4%)	**9 Rn**	

4m 57.8 (2.80) CSF £25.84 CT £224.04 TOTE £13.60: £3.50 £1.60 £3.20 (£14.10) Trio £249.50 OWNER Mr Darren Mercer (TEMPLE GUITING) BRED Bernard Le Gentil
LONG HANDICAP Destin d'Estruval (FR) 9-12 Frickley 9-12

3639 Destin d'Estruval (FR) went well for most of the trip, but he did not find quite as much as looked likely when ridden, and appeared a rather fortunate winner. (7/1)
3618 Destiny Calls never looked particularly happy, but he kept staying on under pressure although he was not good enough to make his presence felt. (3/1)
Leotard put in a smashing effort after missing all last season, and appeared to blow up in the home straight. (12/1)
3804* Frickley had his chances, but he found the effort required too much for his liking when the race really began in the final mile. (9/1)
3804 Cumbrian Challenge (IRE) was never really firing here, and a mistake four out finished him. (8/1)
3916 Old Bridge (IRE) came back to form here, and looked to have it won although he was all out when he fell at the last. (14/1)

4207 LICKLEYHEAD CASTLE H'CAP HURDLE (0-145) (4-Y.O+) (Class B)
4-00 (4-00) **3m 2f 110y (14 hdls)** £4,500.00 (£1,350.00: £650.00: £300.00) GOING: 0.09 sec per fur (G)

			SP	RR	SF
2659[P]	**Meditator (106)** (BdeHaan) **13-10-0b** SCurran (lw: hld up: hdwy ½-wy: led appr 3 out tl hdd & blnd last: rallied to ld cl home) ....—	**1**	100/1	85	10
495*	**Nirvana Prince (118)** (BPreece) **8-10-12** MAFitzgerald (lw: hld up: effrt appr 3 out: rdn to ld last: no ex & hdd towards fin) ....¾	**2**	16/1	97	22
4016[7]	**Erzadjan (IRE) (127)** (MrsMReveley) **7-11-7** PNiven (bhd: hdwy u.p 10th: styd on & ev ch 2 out: no ex flat).....5	**3**	10/1	103	28
3851*	**Tribune (116)** (CWThornton) **6-10-10** MFoster (lw: chsd ldrs: led fr 9th to 3 out: r.o one pce).......nk	**4**	9/2[2]	91	16
3624*	**Tilty (USA) (106)** (AStreeter) **7-10-0v** TEley (led: drvn along fr 6th: hdd 9th: sn outpcd: styd on again fr 4 out) 9	**5**	16/1	76	1
4016[6]	**Victor Bravo (NZ) (120)** (NAGaselee) **10-11-0b** CLlewellyn (bhd: styd on fr 4 out: nvr rchd ldrs).......1¼	**6**	5/1[3]	89	14
3347[4]	**What's Your Story (IRE) (116)** (DNicholson) **8-10-10** RJohnson (lw: a chsng ldrs: rdn 4 out: wknd fr next)...3½	**7**	14/1	83	8
3368*	**Young Kenny (122)** (PBeaumont) **6-11-2** NWilliamson (in tch: drvn along fr 9th: sme hdwy 4 out: sn wknd) ..26	**8**	7/2[1]	73	—
2900[3]	**Campaign (111)** (MDHammond) **6-10-5**ow1 RGarritty (lw: in tch: hit 7th & reminders: outpcd fr 10th).......2½	**9**	11/1	61	—
3885*	**Swanbister (IRE) (112)** (LLungo) **7-10-6** APMcCoy (cl up tl wknd fr 4 out).......½	**10**	6/1	62	—
4016[P]	**Better Times Ahead (130)** (GRichards) **11-11-10** PCarberry (chsd ldr tl wknd fr 9th).......12	**11**	50/1	72	—
3550[F]	**Eulogy (IRE) (109)** (RRowe) **7-10-3**ow1 RDunwoody (trckd ldrs tl rdn & wknd after 4 out: t.o).......dist	**12**	10/1	—	—
1632[P]	**Island Jewel (124)** (MRBosley) **9-11-4** CMaude (prom: hit 3rd: bhd fr ½-wy: p.u 4 out)	**P**	50/1	—	—
			(SP 121.2%)	**13 Rn**	

6m 27.1 (0.40 under best) (16.10) CSF £1,159.60 CT £14,712.16 TOTE £113.70: £11.30 £3.90 £3.60 (£1,300.40) Trio £602.10; £440.98 to Newbury 19/4/97 OWNER Miss Jacqueline Doyle (LAMBOURN) BRED Lord Rotherwick
LONG HANDICAP Meditator 9-7 Tilty (USA) 9-10
Meditator has changed stables and seems to have found a new lease of life, and there was certainly no fluke about this. (100/1)
495* Nirvana Prince, travelled well and then, responding to pressure, looked to have it won when taking it up at the last, but this marathon trip just found him out. (16/1)
3600 Erzadjan (IRE) never looked all that happy, but he kept responding to pressure. In the end his weight anchored him from the last. (10/1: 8/1-12/1)
3851* Tribune ran his usual game race but could never get away from his rivals, and was tapped for toe in the closing stages. (9/2)
3624* Tilty (USA) was off the bridle and seemingly going nowhere a long way out but, to his credit, he did struggle on at the end, although he does look a funny customer. (16/1)
4016 Victor Bravo (NZ) was a shade disappointing, never looking likely to get in a blow. (5/1)

4208 ROYAL SCOTS DRAGOON GUARDS CUP HUNTERS' CHASE (6-Y.O+) (Class H)
4-30 (4-30) **3m 3f 110y (21 fncs)** £3,688.00 (£1,114.00: £542.00: £256.00) GOING: 0.09 sec per fur (G)

			SP	RR	SF
3793*	**Jigtime** (JWHughes) **8-11-2**(7) MrMBradburne (lw: cl up: led fr 10th: kpt on wl fr 4 out: pushed out).......—	**1**	4/7[1]	111	26
4080[2]	**Royal Jester** (CStorey) **13-11-9**(5) MrCStorey (lw: chsd ldrs: wnt 2nd 14th: styd on wl fr 2 out: nrst fin) 2½	**2**	11/2[3]	115	30
3793[4]	**Southern Minstrel** (NChamberlain) **14-11-7**(7) MissCMetcalfe (bhd: hdwy 13th: chsng ldrs 5 out: one pce fr next) 12	**3**	25/1	107	22
4080*	**Now Young Man (IRE)** (MrsASwinbank) **8-11-7**(7) MrChrisWilson (in tch: outpcd fr 13th: n.d after).......6	**4**	11/4[2]	104	19
	Green Times (MajorGenCARamsay) **12-11-7**(7) MajorGWheeler (chsd ldrs tl wknd 15th: sn t.o) ....dist	**5**	50/1	—	—
	I'm Toby (MrsRMLampard) **10-11-7**(7) MrAKinane (bhd tl fell 15th)	**F**	100/1	—	—
3432[3]	**Ardesee** (RJPeake) **17-11-7**(7) MrAWintle (led to 10th: prom tl p.u lame bef 15th)	**P**	100/1	—	—
			(SP 113.5%)	**7 Rn**	

7m 2.6 (19.60) CSF £3.97 TOTE £1.60: £1.10 £1.70 (£2.50) OWNER Mr J. W. Hughes (GALASHIELS) BRED M. H. D. Madden and Partners
3793* Jigtime got a shade warm beforehand, but there was nothing wrong with her performance, and she was always in command. (4/7)
4080 Royal Jester did his usual and put in his best work at the end, but there does not seem to be a trip far enough for him. (11/2)
3793 Southern Minstrel ran a sound race, but was never good enough to make any real impression over the last five fences. (25/1)
4080* Now Young Man (IRE) had his limitations well exposed here. (11/4)

T/Plpt: £130.60 (143.09 Tckts). T/Qdpt: £61.10 (15.27 Tckts) AA

0721-AYR (L-H) (Good)
Saturday April 19th
WEATHER: fine

4209 ALBERT BARTLETT AND SONS NOVICES' H'CAP HURDLE (4-Y.O) (Class C)
1-55 (1-55) **2m (9 hdls)** £4,402.50 (£1,320.00: £635.00: £292.50) GOING: 0.11 sec per fur (G)

			SP	RR	SF
3566*	**Shu Gaa (IRE) (105)** (OSherwood) **4-11-5b[1]** JOsborne (lw: led to 2nd: trckd ldrs tl lost pl appr 3 out: hdwy 2 out: hit last: sn led & styd on wl) ....—	**1**	3/1[1]	85	44
3291[5]	**Meltemison (97)** (MDHammond) **4-10-11** RGarritty (led fr 2nd: rdn clr 3 out: hrd drvn 2 out: hdd flat: no ex)....2	**2**	10/1	75	34
3789[3]	**Clash of Swords (94)** (PCalver) **4-10-8** LWyer (hld up: effrt appr 3 out: sn rdn & nvr able chal).......3	**3**	12/1	69	28
3908*	**Sousse (87)** (MrsMReveley) **4-10-1** GLee (chsd ldrs: rdn 3 out: wknd next).......3	**4**	7/2[2]	59	18
3291[7]	**Rossel (USA) (114)** (PMonteith) **4-12-0** RDunwoody (lw: chsd ldrs: effrt appr 3 out: sn outpcd: wknd 2 out) 8	**5**	5/1[3]	78	37
3802[5]	**Muhtadi (IRE) (100)** (LadyHerries) **4-11-0** RJohnson (hld up: effrt 4 out: btn appr next) 11	**6**	8/1	53	12
3632[2]	**Alpine Joker (86)** (PJHobbs) **4-10-0** GTormey (mstke 4th & sn drvn along: hdwy u.p 4 out: wknd next).......5	**7**	11/2	34	—
			(SP 107.2%)	**7 Rn**	

3m 43.3 (6.30) CSF £24.63 TOTE £3.00: £1.80 £3.60 (£25.20) OWNER Mr Ali K Al Jafleh (UPPER LAMBOURN) BRED Ali K. Al Jafleh

LONG HANDICAP Alpine Joker 9-12
3566* Shu Gaa (IRE) travelled well until losing his place on the home turn, with his rider looking down concerned that something may be amiss. However, all was well in the end, and he stayed on strongly with the blinkers first time no doubt helping. (3/1)
3291 Meltemison showed his stable is on the way back after a spell in the doldrums due to the virus. He was kicked for home swinging into the straight, and in future could easily go one better. (10/1: 8/1-12/1)
3789 Clash of Swords, with the blinkers left off, came through from the back three out but never quite got on terms. (12/1)
3908* Sousse was in there at the third last, but weakened rather disappointingly. (7/2)
2615* Rossel (USA) was perhaps feeling the effects of a long, hard season over hurdles, and he has also been campaigned on the Flat. (5/1)
3802 Muhtadi (IRE) (8/1: 6/1-9/1)

4210 HAMLET EXTRA MILD CIGARS GOLD CARD H'CAP HURDLE (4-Y.O+) (Class B)

2-25 (2-25) **2m 6f (12 hdls)** £8,870.00 (£2,660.00: £1,280.00: £590.00) GOING: 0.11 sec per fur (G)

			SP	RR	SF
4016[P]	**House Captain (123)** (JGFitzGerald) **8-10-4** PCarberry (lw: a gng wl: led between last 2 & qckknd: rdn out)...—	**1**	20/1	105	38
4053[2]	**Sheriffmuir (128)** (MrsLWadham) **8-10-9** JFTitley (a.p: disp ld 8th tl between last 2: kpt on)....3½	**2**	7/1[2]	108	41
3615[4]	**Tullymurry Toff (IRE) (138)** (JMJefferson) **6-11-2**(3) ECallaghan (a.p: hdwy 4 out: disp ld 2 out: nt qckn appr last)....3	**3**	11/4[1]	115	48
3615[12]	**Supreme Lady (IRE) (127)** (MissHCKnight) **6-10-8** JCulloty (hld up: hdwy 8th: chsng ldrs 3 out: rdn & styd on one pce)....¾	**4**	9/1[3]	104	37
3615[17]	**Executive Design (130)** (MrsMReveley) **5-10-11** PNiven (bhd: effrt 7th: kpt on: no imp)....17	**5**	12/1	94	27
4053[4]	**Outset (IRE) (127)** (MDHammond) **7-10-5**(3) MrCBonner (cl up: led 5th to 7th: outpcd fr 4 out)....½	**6**	12/1	91	24
4016[5]	**Dr Leunt (IRE) (125)** (PJHobbs) **6-10-6** GTormey (chsd ldrs: disp ld 8th tl mstke & wknd 3 out)....½	**7**	12/1	89	22
3992*	**Celestial Choir (126)** (JLEyre) **7-10-7** BStorey (lw: outpcd ½-wy: hrd rdn & n.d after)....20	**8**	11/4[1]	75	8
4016[3]	**Freddie Muck (132)** (NATwiston-Davies) **7-10-13** CLlewellyn (rdn & wknd 7th: sn bhd)....22	**9**	7/1[2]	65	—
3911[4]	**Solba (USA) (119)** (CParker) **8-10-0b** DParker (a bhd: t.o fr ½-wy)....10	**10**	66/1	45	—
3303[4]	**Castlekellyleader (IRE) (143)** (PFNicholls) **8-11-10** PHide (led to 5th: led 7th tl blnd & hdd next: hrd rdn & wknd 4 out: p.u bef 3 out)....	**P**	14/1	—	—
			(SP 124.3%)		**11 Rn**

5m 17.7 (6.70) CSF £148.00 CT £473.80 TOTE £34.20: £5.00 £1.70 £1.80 (£59.60) Trio £81.30 OWNER Mr & Mrs G Middlebrook (MALTON) BRED Michael Lysaght
LONG HANDICAP Solba (USA) 9-12
STEWARDS' ENQUIRY FitzGerald fined £200 (failure to inform stewards of reason for horse's poor run last time).
OFFICIAL EXPLANATION **House Captain: regarding the improved form, the gelding had found the going too firm and the track too sharp last time. Celestial Choir: finished distressed.**
3045 House Captain came there on the bridle pulling double. He quickened away nicely, but in the end was punched out to make sure of it. (20/1)
4053 Sheriffmuir ran his usual honest race, but was never going as well as the winner. (7/1)
3615 Tullymurry Toff (IRE), aiming to put his Cheltenham defeat behind him, had every chance at the second last, but perhaps he is just too high in the handicap. The plan apparently is to go novice chasing next season, and he would certainly be an interesting prospect at that. (11/4)
3045* Supreme Lady (IRE) is another one with plenty of weight at the moment, and she did the best that she could to finish a reasonable fourth. (9/1)

4211 EDINBURGH WOOLLEN MILL'S FUTURE CHAMPION NOVICES' CHASE (Gd 2) (5-Y.O+) (Class A)

2-55 (2-56) **2m 4f (17 fncs)** £14,490.00 (£5,462.00: £2,656.00: £1,192.00) GOING: 0.11 sec per fur (G)

			SP	RR	SF
3639*	**Sparky Gayle (IRE) (142)** (CParker) **7-11-10** BStorey (lw: trckd ldrs: led appr 3 out: rdn & r.o wl)....—	**1**	8/15[1]	134	66
3335[2]	**Macgeorge (IRE) (120)** (RLee) **7-11-3** RDunwoody (lw: chsd ldrs: blnd 11th & lost pl: hdwy whn hmpd appr 4 out: styd on: blnd 2 out)....2½	**2**	8/1[3]	125	57
3639[6]	**Stately Home (IRE) (135)** (PBowen) **6-11-10** RJohnson (mde most tl hdd appr 3 out: no ex)....¾	**3**	8/1[3]	131	63
3161*	**Chief Minister (IRE)** (MDHammond) **8-11-3** RGarritty (lw: a in tch: effrt 4 out: styd on u.p: nt pce to chal)....nk	**4**	7/1[2]	124	56
4186[8]	**The Reverend Bert (IRE) (110)** (GBBalding) **9-11-3** BFenton (trckd ldrs: led appr 4 out: blnd bdly 4 out: sn hdd & wknd)....30	**5**	66/1	100	32
4050[P]	**Crown Equerry (IRE)** (GRichards) **7-11-3** PCarberry (lw: blnd 8th: hrd rdn & wl bhd after)....26	**6**	12/1	79	11
3565*	**With Impunity (105)** (PFNicholls) **8-11-3** APMcCoy (lw: mstkes: wl outpcd & bhd fr 9th)....4	**7**	20/1	76	8
3596[U]	**Guinda (IRE) (111)** (NATwiston-Davies) **7-10-12** CLlewellyn (lw: unruly s: s.s: p.u after 1st)....	**P**	20/1	—	—
			(SP 118.6%)		**8 Rn**

4m 58.6 (3.60) CSF £5.51 TOTE £1.60: £1.30 £1.10 £2.80 (£3.50) Trio £15.10 OWNER Mr & Mrs Raymond Anderson Green (LOCKERBIE) BRED Thomas Walsh
3639* Sparky Gayle (IRE) extended his unbeaten sequence over fences to six. Soaring into the lead three out, he was never likely to be caught. The plan for the Cathcart hero is to reappear after a summer holiday either back here or in the Murphy's Gold Cup. He could be even better on softer ground and over three miles. (8/15)
3335 Macgeorge (IRE) ran one of his best races to finish second to a decent animal, and is well worth a chance in lesser company. (8/1)
3639 Stately Home (IRE) cut out the donkey work, and is a real honest sort who ran right up to his best. (8/1)
3161* Chief Minister (IRE), with much less experience than several of his rivals, was far from disgraced. He enjoys this firmish ground and could well get his nose in front again before a summer break. (7/1)

4212 SAMSUNG ELECTRONICS SCOTTISH CHAMPION LIMITED H'CAP HURDLE (Gd 2) (4-Y.O+) (Class A)

3-25 (3-26) **2m (9 hdls)** £16,416.00 (£6,200.30: £3,025.15: £1,368.55) GOING: 0.11 sec per fur (G)

			SP	RR	SF
3595*	**Shadow Leader (136)** (CREgerton) **6-10-5** JOsborne (lw: hld up: smooth hdwy to ld between last 2: qckknd: impressive)....—	**1**	Evens[1]	126+	56
4061[5]	**Zabadi (IRE) (137)** (DNicholson) **5-10-6** RJohnson (lw: a.p: led 2 out: sn hdd & no ch w wnr)....3	**2**	14/1	124	54
3038[6]	**Edelweis du Moulin (FR) (135)** (GRichards) **5-10-4** PCarberry (hld up: hdwy u.p 2 out: sn chsng ldrs: nt qckn appr last)....5	**3**	10/1	117	47
3791[2]	**Ingletonian (135)** (BMactaggart) **8-10-4** BStorey (cl up tl outpcd after 4 out: styd on wl after last)....2½	**4**	66/1	115?	45
4061[3]	**Dreams End (142)** (PBowen) **9-10-11** APMcCoy (lw: cl up: dispng ld 4th tl led 4 out: hdd 2 out: sn outpcd)....2	**5**	7/1[3]	120	50
4117a[6]	**Kadastrof (FR) (135)** (RDickin) **7-9-13**(5) XAizpuru (lw: mde most to 4 out: one pce fr 3 out)....s.h	**6**	25/1	112	42
3597[4]	**I'm Supposin (IRE) (152)** (RRowe) **5-11-7** RDunwoody (prom tl wknd appr 3 out)....1	**7**	7/2[2]	128	58
3150[8]	**Home Counties (IRE) (135)** (DMoffatt) **8-10-4** DJMoffatt (chsd ldrs tl outpcd 4 out)....2	**8**	33/1	109	39

				SP	RR	SF
2645[7]	**Master Beveled (139)** (PDEvans) **7-10-5**(3) MrRThornton (outpcd 4th: n.d after)	1¼	**9**	12/1	112	42
4061[4]	**Clifton Beat (USA) (139)** (PJHobbs) **6-10-8** CFSwan (prom tl rdn & btn after 4 out)	1	**10**	10/1	111	41
3572[3]	**Express Gift (135)** (MrsMReveley) **8-10-4** NWilliamson (hit 5th: outpcd & bhd after)	3	**11**	14/1	104	34

(SP 132.2%) **11 Rn**

3m 38.3 (1.30) CSF £17.78 CT £106.65 TOTE £2.00: £1.30 £3.80 £2.20 (£26.90) Trio £54.00 OWNER Mr James Blackshaw (CHADDLEWORTH) BRED A. J. Sexton

LONG HANDICAP Home Counties (IRE) 10-3 Ingletonian 9-6 Express Gift 10-2

3595* Shadow Leader, perhaps the most impressive winner of the entire meeting, showed he had recovered from the effects of his Supreme Novice Hurdle victory. He was never in the slightest danger and is going to be a real force to be reckoned with in the best of company next season. He needs more cut underfoot as he apparently had arthritis in his knees, but he can already be considered a long-term candidate for the Smurfit Champion Hurdle. (Evens)

4061 Zabadi (IRE) seemed to be going as well as anything when moving into the lead two out but, once the winner sped past, that was the end of his winning aspirations. He is certainly worth an interest if he appears before the end of the campaign. (14/1)

3038 Edelweis du Moulin (FR) has not quite fulfilled high expectations. He travels well for most of the race, but does not find a great deal when let down. (10/1)

3791 Ingletonian has given his connections plenty of fun throughout the season, but had a real tough task here and was perhaps running right up to his best to finish fourth. (66/1)

4061 Dreams End seemed to be suited by the flat track. He is useful on his day, but despite taking the eye in the parade, he was quickly put in his place when headed two out. (7/1)

3597 I'm Supposin (IRE) was fancied to run a big race, but was under pressure on the turn. Giving weight away all round may have been his undoing. (7/2)

2645 Master Beveled (12/1: op 8/1)

4213 STAKIS CASINOS SCOTTISH GRAND NATIONAL H'CAP CHASE (Gd 3) (5-Y.O+) (Class A)

4-05 (4-06) **4m 1f (27 fncs)** £41,316.00 (£15,560.30: £7,555.15: £3,378.55) GOING: 0.11 sec per fur (G)

				SP	RR	SF
3563[2]	**Belmont King (IRE) (142)** (PFNicholls) **9-11-10** APMcCoy (lw: mde all: blnd 20th & last: kpt on gamely)	—	**1**	16/1	156	38
3573*	**Samlee (IRE) (118)** (PJHobbs) **8-10-0** NWilliamson (lw: trckd ldrs: blnd bdly 12th & 21st: ev ch 4 out: hrd rdn & kpt on)	1½	**2**	8/1	131	13
3616[8]	**Baronet (IRE) (120)** (DNicholson) **7-10-2** RJohnson (mid div: effrt 18th: outpcd next: styd on strly fr 2 out: gng on fin)	2	**3**	11/1	132	14
4148*	**Act the Wag (IRE) (119)** (MartinTodhunter) **8-10-1b** PCarberry (hld up: hdwy 18th: chsng ldrs 5 out: outpcd next: kpt on appr last)	hd	**4**	15/2[3]	131	13
3451[U]	**Court Melody (IRE) (119)** (PFNicholls) **9-9-12b**(3) MrRThornton (lw: a chsng ldrs: ev ch 5 out: one pce fr 4 out)	nk	**5**	14/1	131	13
4074[8]	**Dakyns Boy (118)** (NATwiston-Davies) **12-10-0** CLlewellyn (mid div: rdn along fr 19th: styd on fr 4 out: no imp)	5	**6**	25/1	127	9
4054[5]	**Fiveleigh Builds (123)** (MissLucindaRussell) **10-10-5** AThornton (chsd ldrs tl outpcd fr 6 out)	2½	**7**	16/1	130	12
3700[F]	**Kamikaze (120)** (KCBailey) **7-10-2b** CO'Dwyer (blnd 9th & sn bhd: hdwy 19th: chsng ldrs whn blnd 5 out: 4th whn blnd 4 out: wknd)	4	**8**	8/1	125	7
4050[F]	**Buckhouse Boy (132)** (NATwiston-Davies) **7-11-0b[1]** CMaude (lw: hld up: hdwy & prom 18th: effrt 6 out: wknd appr 4 out)	2½	**9**	14/1	135	17
4074[7]	**Killeshin (127)** (HJManners) **11-10-9v[1]** SCurran (lw: nvr gng wl: a bhd: t.o)	dist	**10**	14/1	—	—
4074[4]	**Buckboard Bounce (139)** (GRichards) **11-11-7** CaptAOgden (lw: unruly s: s.s: a bhd: t.o whn p.u bef 13th)		**P**	14/1	—	—
	Parsons Brig (118) (JSHaldane) **11-10-0** ASSmith (a bhd: t.o whn p.u bef 19th)		**P**	100/1	—	—
4054[2]	**Cab on Target (130)** (MrsMReveley) **11-10-12** PNiven (a bhd: p.u bef 21st)		**P**	15/2[3]	—	—
4074[U]	**Spuffington (120)** (JTGifford) **9-10-2**ow2 PHide (chsd ldrs tl wknd fr 21st: p.u bef 2 out)		**P**	33/1	—	—
4051[2]	**Highlandman (119)** (JSHaldane) **11-10-1**ow1 MrChrisWilson (prom to 19th: sn lost pl: p.u bef 5 out)		**P**	100/1	—	—
3598[2]	**Stormtracker (IRE) (121)** (CWeedon) **8-10-3** MRichards (lw: chsd ldrs tl wknd fr 19th: p.u bef 4 out)		**P**	7/1[2]	—	—
4110a[R]	**Sister Stephanie (IRE) (124)** (GMMcCourt) **8-10-6** RDunwoody (lw: unruly s: s.s: blnd & uns rdr 5th)		**U**	4/1[1]	—	—

(SP 133.8%) **17 Rn**

8m 24.8 (18.80) CSF £136.80 CT £1,381.06 TOTE £17.70: £3.30 £2.10 £2.80 £2.30 (£58.70) Trio £258.30 OWNER Mrs Billie Bond (SHEPTON MALLET) BRED Simon Lambert

LONG HANDICAP Spuffington 9-7 Parsons Brig 9-5 Highlandman 8-0

STEWARDS' ENQUIRY Carberry susp. 29-30/4, 2-3/5 & 5/5/97 (failure to ensure best possible placing).

3563 Belmont King (IRE) looked absolutely magnificent and, despite the ground being a shade faster than he really likes, his courage carried him through and he thoroughly deserved this. (16/1)

3573* Samlee (IRE) worked a miracle to remain upright after two horrendous blunders at the open ditch on the back straight. His jockey deserves a medal for sticking with him, and he surely would have won but for this. (8/1)

2883 Baronet (IRE) showed here he just stays, and after getting completely outpaced he finished fast as the leaders tired, but the effort was far too late. (11/1)

4148* Act the Wag (IRE), having his second run in the blinkers, acquitted himself really well, but he never looked likely to make it and was caught napping for third. (15/2)

3451 Court Melody (IRE), who would have preferred softer ground, nevertheless ran a cracker and was only run out of it over the last four fences. (14/1)

4074 Dakyns Boy has not won a race for over four years and needs softer ground, but he was picking up well at the end. (25/1)

4054 Fiveleigh Builds, from a stable out of form, has been running consistently well most of the season, and this was a sound effort. (16/1)

3700 Kamikaze has so much ability but is a character and a half, and blundered all chances away here. (8/1)

4110a Sister Stephanie (IRE) refused to race last time and gave problems galore here. Eventually jumping off many lengths adrift, she then completely missed out the fifth fence, giving her rider no chance. (4/1)

4214 CLIENT ENTERTAINMENT SERVICES H'CAP CHASE (0-135) (5-Y.O+) (Class C)

4-40 (4-41) **2m (12 fncs)** £5,182.50 (£1,560.00: £755.00: £352.50) GOING: 0.11 sec per fur (G)

				SP	RR	SF
2700[3]	**Monyman (IRE) (105)** (MDHammond) **7-10-2** NWilliamson (lw: hld up: smooth hdwy to chal 4 out: led 2 out: r.o wl: b.b.v)	—	**1**	11/2[2]	122	47
4062[4]	**Mister Oddy (127)** (JSKing) **11-11-10** TJMurphy (led to 2nd: sn lost pl: hdwy to ld 8th: hdd 2 out: one pce)	8	**2**	7/1[3]	136	61
3610[2]	**Weaver George (IRE) (109)** (WStorey) **7-10-6** MMoloney (lw: in tch: hdwy 7th: 3rd & no imp whn hit 3 out)	5	**3**	11/2[2]	113	38
3972[3]	**Golden Hello (105)** (TDEasterby) **6-10-2** LWyer (outpcd: j.rt & lost tch 5th: styd on fr 4 out: n.d)	1½	**4**	9/1	108	33

				SP	RR	SF
3642*	**Rallegio (103)** (PMonteith) **8-9-11**(3) MrRThornton (outpcd: hdwy u.p 7th: chsng ldrs 4 out: sn rdn & btn)	2½	**5**	7/1[3]	103	28
4062[F]	**Political Tower (127)** (RNixon) **10-11-10** BStorey (outpcd: sme hdwy 8th: sn btn: b.b.v)	3½	**6**	11/2[2]	124	49
3638[12]	**Storm Falcon (USA) (115)** (SMellor) **7-10-7**(5) ChrisWebb (t: chsd ldr: led 4th to 8th: blnd 4 out & wknd qckly)	3½	**7**	11/1	108	33
4013[5]	**No Pain No Gain (IRE) (115)** (JTGifford) **9-10-12b[1]** PHide (lw: led fr 2nd to 4th: w ldr: blnd 7th: wknd qckly after next)	21	**8**	5/1[1]	87	12
2948[8]	**Edredon Bleu (FR) (133)** (MissHCKnight) **5-11-9** RDunwoody (effrt ½-wy: outpcd 8th: t.o whn p.u bef 2 out)		**P**	10/1	—	—
				(SP 115.2%)	**9 Rn**	

3m 47.5 (2.50) CSF £39.60 CT £201.87 TOTE £5.60: £2.00 £2.60 £1.50 (£24.20) Trio £31.40 OWNER Mr Trevor Hemmings (MIDDLEHAM) BRED Lady Naylor Leyland
LONG HANDICAP Rallegio 9-8
WEIGHT FOR AGE 5yo-7lb

2700 Monyman (IRE) came back to top form here after three months off and did it in style, looking one to follow. (11/2)
4062 Mister Oddy would ideally have preferred more cut in the ground, but he still ran a sound race, although he was comprehensively outspeeded from the second last. (7/1)
3610 Weaver George (IRE) ran a fair race here after slightly disappointing last time. It would seem that after almost six weeks off he is coming back to form. (11/2)
3972 Golden Hello, as he has shown in the past, has the ability but he is his own worst enemy. (9/1)
3642* Rallegio found the ground and the company too fast and, although always struggling, finally decided it was all too much four out. (7/1)
3638 Political Tower ran no sort of race and was later said to have broken a blood-vessel. (11/2)
2952 Storm Falcon (USA), who is now tubed, seems to be getting slightly better with each outing. (11/1: 8/1-12/1)
4013 No Pain No Gain (IRE) went far too fast for his own good. (5/1)
2948 Edredon Bleu (FR) (10/1: 8/1-12/1)

4215 GLENMUIR FUTURE CHAMPION STANDARD OPEN N.H. FLAT RACE (I) (4, 5 & 6-Y.O) (Class H)
5-10 (5-10) **2m** £1,710.50 (£478.00: £231.50)

				SP	RR	SF
	Kings Measure (IRE) (JMJefferson) **4-10-9**(3) ECallaghan (a.p: hdwy u.p 3f out: led appr fnl f: rn green: styd on wl towards fin)	—	**1**	25/1	84 f	—
	Siren Song (IRE) (CJMann) **6-12-0** RDunwoody (cl up: led on bit 2f out: hdd over 1f out: rdn & nt pce of wnr)	1½	**2**	9/1	93 f	—
	Simons Castle (IRE) (RJO'Sullivan) **4-11-5** RJohnson (hld up: stdy hdwy to trck ldrs 7f out: effrt 3f out: kpt on: nt pce to chal)	1¼	**3**	7/1	88 f	—
3425*	**Red Curate (IRE)** (GMMcCourt) **6-11-11** APMcCoy (cl up: led ½-wy tl hdd 2f out: one pce)	7	**4**	5/1[3]	81 f	—
	Lord Of The River (IRE) (OSherwood) **5-11-4** JOsborne (hdwy 7f out: styd on fnl 3f: nrst fin)	¾	**5**	4/1[2]	74 f	—
3619[7]	**Samuel Wilderspin** (DNicholson) **5-11-8**(3) RMassey (lw: trckd ldrs: ev ch over 3f out: sn rdn & nt qckn)	1¼	**6**	6/4[1]	79 f	—
	Oh So Cosy (IRE) (CParker) **4-10-12** BStorey (bhd tl stdy hdwy fnl 4f: nrst fin)	3½	**7**	20/1	69 f	—
3297[8]	**Donnybrook (IRE)** (RDEWoodhouse) **4-10-7**(5) BGrattan (lw: styd on u.p fnl 3f: nrst fin)	1	**8**	100/1	68 f	—
	Bala Pyjama (RAFahey) **4-10-12** LWyer (bit bkwd: nvr nr to chal)	2½	**9**	100/1	65 f	—
	Really Useful (IRE) (MissSEHall) **5-11-4** PCarberry (cl up: led 10f out to 8f out: ev ch tl outpcd fnl 3f)	hd	**10**	12/1	65 f	—
	The Operator (IRE) (GRichards) **6-11-4** LO'Hara (wnt prom ½-wy: rn v.green fnl 4f: grad wknd)	1¾	**11**	50/1	63 f	—
	River Mulligan (IRE) (PJHobbs) **5-11-4** CFSwan (lw: hdwy ½-wy: sn pushed along: no ch fnl 4f)	nk	**12**	12/1	63 f	—
	Jowoody (MrsDThomson) **4-10-7** DParker (nvr trbld ldrs)	1½	**13**	200/1	57 f	—
2661[7]	**Heidiqueenofclubs (IRE)** (NATwiston-Davies) **6-10-13** CMaude (led tl hdd 10f out: sn rdn & lost pl)	2	**14**	50/1	55 f	—
2965*	**Society Times (USA)** (DANolan) **4-11-5** NWilliamson (chsd ldrs tl wknd fnl 4f)	1¼	**15**	12/1	65 f	—
	Blake's Oemin (GRichards) **5-10-11**(7) RBurns (pushed along ½-wy: a bhd)	½	**16**	50/1	58 f	—
	Perryman (IRE) (KCBailey) **6-11-4** CO'Dwyer (lw: bhd fnl 6f)	nk	**17**	25/1	58 f	—
	Buabhall Mor (MartinTodhunter) **4-10-5**(7) CMcCormack (a bhd)	3½	**18**	100/1	54 f	—
	Bingley Bank (IRE) (NATwiston-Davies) **5-11-4** CLlewellyn (lw: bhd fnl 6f: t.o)	13	**19**	33/1	41 f	—
	Radical Storm (IRE) (JIACharlton) **6-11-4** KJohnson (bit bkwd: chsd ldrs tl wknd 7f out: t.o)	3½	**20**	50/1	38 f	—
				(SP 148.9%)	**20 Rn**	

3m 39.1 CSF £241.47 TOTE £51.90: £6.10 £3.00 £3.10 (£680.00) Trio Not won; £355.60 to 21/4/97 OWNER Mr John Wilson (MALTON) BRED Miss Mary O'Sullivan
WEIGHT FOR AGE 4yo-6lb

Kings Measure (IRE), a real National Hunt type, showed definite signs of inexperience but did the job well in the end, and the future looks very bright. (25/1)
Siren Song (IRE) spent most of the race on the bridle, but on this occasion his normally brilliant jockey was certainly not at his best and, after the winner got first run on him, he was always second best. (9/1)
Simons Castle (IRE) looked to be going well for most of the trip but, when it came down to a fight, he was lacking in speed. (7/1)
3425* Red Curate (IRE) gave the impression that he will be better suited by more testing conditions. (5/1)
Lord Of The River (IRE) was noted making useful progress all the way up the straight, and more will be heard of him once he faces some obstacles. (4/1)
3619 Samuel Wilderspin looked to be going well entering the straight but, when the tap was turned on, his lack of speed counted against him. (6/4)
Oh So Cosy (IRE), a real chasing type, ran with promise and is certainly one to note for the long-term future. (20/1)
Really Useful (IRE) (12/1: op 7/1)
River Mulligan (IRE) (12/1: op 8/1)

4216 GLENMUIR FUTURE CHAMPION STANDARD OPEN N.H. FLAT RACE (II) (4, 5 & 6-Y.O) (Class H)
5-40 (5-43) **2m** £1,710.50 (£478.00: £231.50)

				SP	RR	SF
	Decoupage (CREgerton) **5-11-4** NWilliamson (a gng wl: smooth hdwy to ld 1f out: shkn up & r.o wl)	—	**1**	3/1[1]	81 f	—
3716*	**Go Native (IRE)** (MrsSJSmith) **5-11-6**(5) RWilkinson (trckd ldrs: led 3f out to 1f out: r.o wl)	1¼	**2**	6/1	87 f	—
	Valhalla (IRE) (MartinTodhunter) **4-10-12** APMcCoy (scope: hld up: smooth hdwy to chal 2f out: sn rdn & no ex)	2½	**3**	12/1	77 f	—
	The Village Way (IRE) (DNicholson) **6-11-4** RJohnson (plld hrd: trckd ldrs: effrt 3f out: nt qckn fnl 2f)	3	**4**	10/1	74 f	—
3548[5]	**Woodfield Vision (IRE)** (MrsMReveley) **6-11-4** PNiven (hdwy ½-wy: sn chsng ldrs: nt qckn fnl 2½f)	3½	**5**	14/1	71 f	—
3821[9]	**Glevum** (NATwiston-Davies) **5-10-13** CLlewellyn (cl up tl wknd fnl 2½f)	7	**6**	33/1	59 f	—
3418[2]	**Carlingford Tyke (IRE)** (TJCarr) **5-11-4** GCahill (in tch: rdn 4f out: styd on one pce)	s.h	**7**	16/1	64 f	—

	Horse	Dist	Pos	SP	RR	SF
	Skillwise (TDEasterby) **5-11-4** LWyer (tall: nvr rchd ldrs)	½	**8**	25/1	63 f	—
	Chocolate Drum (IRE) (JJBirkett) **6-11-4** MMoloney (bhd: styd on fnl 3f: n.d)	nk	**9**	100/1	63 f	—
3767^{2}	**Normania (NZ)** (MissSEdwards) **5-11-4** MrTHills (lw: led tl hdd 3f out: grad wknd)	2½	**10**	12/1	60 f	—
3828^{7}	**Open Fairway** (MDods) **4-10-7**(5) RMcGrath (bit bkwd: hld up: hdwy 5f out: outpcd fnl 3f)	1¼	**11**	33/1	59 f	—
	Hack On (PJHobbs) **5-10-13** GTormey (tall: lengthy: outpcd & lost tch 6f out: sme late hdwy)	1½	**12**	10/1	53 f	—
	William of Orange (GRichards) **5-11-4** LO'Hara (hld up: hdwy 7f out: sn in tch & drvn along: wknd fnl 3f)	nk	**13**	33/1	57 f	—
	Kimdaloo (IRE) (CParker) **5-11-4** BStorey (hld up & bhd: nvr nr to chal)	½	**14**	25/1	57 f	—
	Tied For Time (IRE) (MissHCKnight) **5-11-4** JCulloty (n.d)	1½	**15**	12/1	55 f	—
	Needle Thread (GRichards) **5-10-6**(7) RBurns (trckd ldrs: effrt 4f out: sn wknd)	6	**16**	33/1	44 f	—
	Steals Yer Thunder (IRE) (MrsAJBowlby) **5-11-4** AThornton (bit bkwd: chsd ldrs tl wknd 5f out: t.o)	dist	**17**	66/1	—	—
3090*	**Rasak** (LadyHerries) **5-11-11** RDunwoody (trckd ldrs fr ½-wy tl wknd over 3f out: eased considerably & t.o: dead)	2	**18**	$7/2^{2}$	—	—
	Gem of Holly (RSWood) **4-10-4**(3) MrRThornton (bit bkwd: cl up tl wknd qckly 7f out: sn t.o)	20	**19**	100/1	—	—
3365*	**Benvenuto** (KCBailey) **6-11-11** CO'Dwyer (trckd ldrs: effrt on ins over 3f out: sn p.u)		**P**	$5/1^{3}$	—	—
				(SP 154.9%)	**20 Rn**	

3m 38.7 CSF £23.10 TOTE £5.00: £2.20 £2.60 £4.60 (£19.30) Trio £144.80 OWNER Mr J. F. Dean (CHADDLEWORTH) BRED E. Stuart Knape
WEIGHT FOR AGE 4yo-6lb

Decoupage came here with a real reputation and justified it in some style. (3/1)

3716* Go Native (IRE) ran his heart out despite always looking second best, and is going to really make his mark once put over hurdles and fences. (6/1)

Valhalla (IRE) travelled really well, but just failed to see it out and will obviously be better for the run. (12/1)

The Village Way (IRE) raced too freely, but obviously has plenty of ability and this should have taught him plenty (10/1)

3548 Woodfield Vision (IRE) ran well in this useful race, and seems to be getting his act together. (14/1)

Glevum ran much better than on his debut, and seems to be improving. (33/1)

3090* Rasak, connections reported that he was struck into and severed a tendon on the bend into the straight, but proved impossible to pull up. Regrettably his injuries proved so severe that he had to be put down. (7/2)

T/Plpt: £44.00 (796.13 Tckts). T/Qdpt: £8.80 (216.49 Tckts) AA

3802-BANGOR-ON-DEE (L-H) (Good)
Saturday April 19th

WEATHER: overcast & cold

4217 CREWE NOVICES' HURDLE (4-Y.O+) (Class E)

2-10 (2-10) **2m 4f (11 hdls)** £2,948.00 (£828.00: £404.00) GOING minus 0.09 sec per fur (G)

	Horse	Dist	Pos	SP	RR	SF
3108^{10}	**Special Beat (92)** (NJHenderson) **5-10-10**(5) MrCVigors (lw: chsd ldrs: hdwy to ld & lft clr 3 out: comf)	—	**1**	11/1	80+	27
3364^{2}	**Cherokee Chief** (OSherwood) **6-11-0** JAMcCarthy (lw: hld up: hdwy appr 6th: rdn appr 2 out: sn btn)	9	**2**	$11/10^{1}$	72	19
3964*	**Ring of Vision (IRE) (100)** (CJMann) **5-11-6** JRailton (a chsng ldrs: rdn & one pce fr 3 out)	3½	**3**	$7/2^{2}$	75	22
3691^{14}	**Khalikhoum (IRE)** (SirJohnBarlowBt) **4-10-2**(5) DJKavanagh (hdwy 5th: rdn whn hmpd 3 out: sn lost pl)	14	**4**	50/1	58	—
3676^{9}	**Gower-Slave** (PBowen) **5-11-0** WMarston (chsd ldrs: hit 7th: wknd appr 3 out)	15	**5**	50/1	46	—
	The Naughty Vicar (GRichards) **7-11-0** RichardGuest (bkwd: a in rr: t.o)	2½	**6**	33/1	44	—
3990^{U}	**Northern Star (88)** (JAPickering) **6-10-13**(7) MissJWormall (a in rr: t.o)	6	**7**	16/1	45	—
	Western Sun (JLNeedham) **7-10-9**(5) ABates (bkwd: a t.o)	dist	**8**	66/1	—	—
	Ask Me In (IRE) (TWall) **6-10-9** MFoster (bkwd: chsd ldr tl wknd qckly 6th: sn t.o)	dist	**9**	25/1	—	—
	Pharmony (IRE) (MrsSJSmith) **7-10-9**(5) GFRyan (bkwd: a bhd: t.o fr ½-wy)	dist	**10**	50/1	—	—
2673^{7}	**The Crooked Oak** (NATwiston-Davies) **5-11-0** DWalsh (lw: chsd ldrs to 6th: bhd whn p.u bef 2 out)		**P**	20/1	—	—
600^{8}	**Orinoco Venture (IRE) (65)** (ABailey) **6-11-0** TKent (mstke 1st: chsd ldrs to 6th: bhd whn p.u bef next)		**P**	50/1	—	—
3846^{7}	**One Boy** (AHHarvey) **5-11-0** PHolley (sn bhd: t.o whn p.u bef 7th)		**P**	66/1	—	—
3170^{7}	**Jemaro (IRE)** (WJenks) **6-11-0** TJenks (bkwd: a bhd: t.o whn p.u bef 2 out)		**P**	66/1	—	—
3337^{P}	**Cool Cat (IRE)** (JCTuck) **6-11-0** VSlattery (bkwd: a bhd: t.o whn p.u bef 7th)		**P**	66/1	—	—
	Dunston Knight (BPreece) **4-10-0**(7) JMogford (bkwd: a bhd: t.o whn p.u bef 3 out)		**P**	66/1	—	—
1842^{7}	**Soundpost** (MrsLWilliamson) **5-11-0** CaptAWood (bkwd: t.o fr 5th: p.u bef 3 out)		**P**	66/1	—	—
3845*	**Persian Elite (IRE) (95)** (CREgerton) **6-11-6b** JRKavanagh (lw: led: sn wl clr: hdd whn blnd & uns rdr 3 out)		**U**	$5/1^{3}$	—	—
				(SP 129.1%)	**18 Rn**	

4m 43.8 (7.80) CSF £21.57 TOTE £14.90: £3.30 £1.40 £1.20 (£14.10) Trio £11.60 OWNER Mr C. Marner (LAMBOURN) BRED Christian Marner
WEIGHT FOR AGE 4yo-7lb

2663* Special Beat returned to form on this step down in class with a very comfortably-gained success and, if she is not aimed too high, should be able to go on paying her way. (11/1: 8/1-12/1)

3364 Cherokee Chief was making hard work of it in the last half-mile, and we will probably not see the best of him until his attentions are switched to fences. (11/10)

3964* Ring of Vision (IRE) should have been ideally suited by this extra half-mile but, after travelling well for most of the way, was struggling to hold on before reaching the straight and was easily brushed aside. (7/2)

2697 Khalikhoum (IRE), a winner on the Flat in Ireland, is not yet getting it together over hurdles. (50/1)

3845* Persian Elite (IRE) set a very strong pace on this return to a shorter trip, but he had just been collared when he made a mistake three out and got rid of his pilot. (5/1)

4218 ROBERT JONES 21ST OPEN HUNTERS' CHASE (6-Y.O+) (Class H)

2-40 (2-41) **2m 4f 110y (15 fncs)** £1,689.50 (£472.00: £228.50) GOING: 0.09 sec per fur (G)

	Horse	Dist	Pos	SP	RR	SF
4094*	**My Nominee** (DENicholls) **9-12-0b**(7) MrRBurton (j.w: mde all: clr 4 out: unchal)	—	**1**	$8/13^{1}$	110	40
4070^{3}	**Dalametre** (MJMEvans) **10-11-7**(7) MrMMunrowd (hdwy 5th: chsd wnr fr 7th: lost tch 4 out)	22	**2**	$8/1^{2}$	86	16
	Saahi (USA) (JSSwindells) **8-11-7**(7) MissSSwindells (bhd tl styd on fr 4 out: nvr nrr)	2	**3**	25/1	84	14
3922^{3}	**Galzig** (MrsDEHTurner) **9-11-7**(7) MrWTellwright (hdwy 6th: wknd 10th: t.o)	8	**4**	$9/1^{3}$	78	8
	Nadiad (DMcCain) **11-11-7**(7) MrAWintle (bkwd: hdwy whn hmpd 7th: wknd 10th: t.o)	14	**5**	10/1	67	—
	Thornhill (FLMatthews) **7-11-2**(7) CaptAWood (sn wl bhd: t.o whn p.u bef 3 out)		**P**	66/1	—	—
3984^{4}	**King of Shadows** (MissCMCarden) **10-12-0**(7) MrSPrior (hdwy 6th: wknd 8th: t.o whn p.u bef 2 out)		**P**	16/1	—	—
	Press for Action (SHShirley-Beavan) **12-11-9**(5) MrRFord (lw: prom: j.rt & lost pl 7th: t.o whn p.u bef 4 out)		**P**	12/1	—	—

				SP	RR	SF
20[P]	**Rather Sharp** (SDWatson) **11-12-2**(5) MrBPollock (outpcd: t.o whn p.u bef 10th)		P	50/1	—	—
3753[4]	**Charlies Delight (IRE)** (MrsCHicks) **9-11-9**(5) MrCVigors (in rr whn blnd & uns rdr 5th)		U	25/1	—	—
3744[6]	**Simply Perfect** (JSSwindells) **11-11-7**(7) MissKSwindells (blnd & uns rdr 1st)		U	14/1	—	—

(SP 123.5%) **11 Rn**

5m 13.8 (13.80) CSF £6.20 TOTE £1.60: £1.30 £2.20 £6.30 (£5.10) Trio £115.30 OWNER Mr D. E. Nicholls (WREXHAM) BRED Dr O. Zawawi

4094* My Nominee, successful in this event last year, won very much as he pleased and has been successful four times at this track. (8/13)

4070 Dalametre has only ever won at three miles and on more testing ground, so it came as no surprise that he could not get the winner off the bridle. (8/1)

Saahi (USA) still to succeed over fences under any rules, stayed on in the last half-mile without ever threatening to reach the winner. (25/1)

Simply Perfect (14/1: 10/1-16/1)

4219 HALLIWELL LANDAU NOVICES' CHASE (5-Y.O+) (Class D)

3-10 (3-10) **2m 1f 110y (12 fncs)** £4,201.50 (£1,272.00: £621.00: £295.50) GOING: 0.09 sec per fur (G)

				SP	RR	SF
3470*	**Indian Jockey (117)** (MCPipe) **5-11-11** DWalsh (mde all: j.rt 6th: clr fr 3 out)	—	1	2/5 1	107	20
3826[3]	**Exemplar (IRE) (81)** (MrsSJSmith) **9-10-9**(5) GFRyan (lw: j.w: hld up & bhd: hdwy whn hmpd 4 out: j.rt 2 out: styd on to go 2nd nr fin)	5	2	4/1 2	84	4
3627[P]	**The Secret Grey (67)** (DMcCain) **6-11-0** TJenks (lw: chsd wnr: rdn 3 out: btn whn mstke last)	2½	3	20/1	82	2
3829[5]	**Eurolink Shadow** (DMcCain) **5-10-7** VSlattery (hld up: effrt whn blnd 4 out: sn lost tch)	14	4	33/1	69?	—
3806[3]	**Dee Light** (GRichards) **8-10-9** RichardGuest (lw: prom: rdn & outpcd 3 out: 3rd whn fell last)		F	6/1 3	—	—

(SP 113.4%) **5 Rn**

4m 24.1 (14.10) CSF £2.57 TOTE £1.30: £2.10 £1.10 (£1.80) OWNER Mr Stuart Mercer (WELLINGTON) BRED John Hayter

WEIGHT FOR AGE 5yo-7lb

3470* Indian Jockey looked to have a fight on his hands out in the country, but his nearest pursuer soon began to feel the strain, and in the end he was allowed to saunter home at his leisure. (2/5)

3826 Exemplar (IRE) finds this minimum trip inadequate and, though he did run on well after being impeded at the last open ditch four out, he could not get within striking range of the winner. (4/1)

3470 The Secret Grey finished runner-up to the winner here last month, and adopted more forceful tactics in an attempt to find any weaknesses. The outcome was more or less the same, though a last-fence mistake may have cost him second prize. (20/1)

3806 Dee Light, continuing to step down in distance, was unable to prevent the leading pair from going away from her three out, and looked to be passed for the minor prize when she capsized at the last. (6/1: 5/1-8/1)

4220 SOTHEBY'S H'CAP HURDLE (0-120) (4-Y.O+) (Class D)

3-45 (3-45) **3m (12 hdls)** £3,647.50 (£1,105.00: £540.00: £257.50) GOING minus 0.09 sec per fur (G)

				SP	RR	SF
4093[2]	**First Crack (88)** (FJordan) **12-10-3** TEley (lw: hld up: hdwy appr 8th: rdn appr 2 out: slt ld last: all out)	—	1	6/1 2	67	31
3962[4]	**Derring Bridge (85)** (MrsSMJohnson) **7-10-0** WMarston (hld up: hdwy 4th: led appr 9th to last: rallied u.p)	hd	2	25/1	64	28
3402[3]	**Hooded Hawk (IRE) (99)** (NJHenderson) **6-11-0** JRKavanagh (hld up: hdwy 9th: rdn appr 2 out: nt rch ldrs)	19	3	6/1 2	65	29
4144*	**Sharp Command (97)** (PEccles) **4-10-4**ow2 RichardGuest (lw: hld up: hdwy 7th: hrd rdn appr 2 out: nt rch ldrs)	3	4	2/1 1	61	15
3048[9]	**Old Cavalier (85)** (JJO'Neill) **6-10-0** JCallaghan (chsd ldrs to 9th: sn outpcd)	10	5	25/1	43	7
3454[4]	**Pharare (IRE) (96)** (RDEWoodhouse) **7-10-6**(5) DJKavanagh (chsd ldr to 8th: sn wknd)	7	6	14/1 3	49	13
4020[2]	**Layham Low (IRE) (88)** (OSherwood) **6-10-3** JAMcCarthy (lw: hld up: hdwy 7th: wknd 3 out)	2½	7	14/1 3	39	3
3807[2]	**Prussia (99)** (WClay) **6-10-11**(3) GuyLewis (chsd ldrs tl wknd appr 3 out)	6	8	6/1 2	46	10
3750[6]	**This Nettle Danger (85)** (OBrennan) **13-10-0** MBrennan (a in rr)	2	9	33/1	31	—
3915[4]	**Cutthroat Kid (IRE) (103)** (TRGreathead) **7-11-4** PHolley (a bhd: t.o)	5	10	14/1 3	46	10
3620[9]	**Kano Warrior (85)** (BPreece) **10-9-7**(7) JMogford (bhd fr 7th: t.o)	6	11	50/1	24	—
	Fed on Oats (98) (MissVenetiaWilliams) **9-10-13** JRailton (bit bkwd: hld up: hdwy 8th: chal & hit 2 out: p.u bef last)		P	33/1	—	—
3641[6]	**Mill Thyme (85)** (PBeaumont) **5-10-0** MFoster (led tl appr 9th: wknd qckly: p.u bef 2 out)		P	33/1	—	—
3892[3]	**Tiger Claw (USA) (90)** (AGHobbs) **11-9-12**(7)ow5 MrGShenkin (chsd ldrs: rdn & lost pl after 6th: t.o whn p.u bef 9th)		P	14/1 3	—	—
	Prime Display (USA) (109) (AHHarvey) **11-11-10** TJenks (bkwd: prom tl wknd appr 8th: bhd whn p.u bef 2 out)		P	100/1	—	—
3362[12]	**Better Bythe Glass (IRE) (89)** (NATwiston-Davies) **8-10-4** DWalsh (trckd ldrs tl stumbled & uns rdr appr 7th)		U	14/1 3	—	—

(SP 129.0%) **16 Rn**

5m 43.4 (1.40 under best) (4.40) CSF £140.88 CT £881.88 TOTE £6.40: £1.70 £3.60 £1.50 £1.40 (£50.40) Trio £125.70 OWNER Mr D. Pugh (LEOMINSTER) BRED J. Wilding

LONG HANDICAP This Nettle Danger 9-6 Derring Bridge 9-7 Mill Thyme 9-9 Tiger Claw (USA) 9-10 Old Cavalier 9-5 Kano Warrior 9-3

WEIGHT FOR AGE 4yo-8lb

4093 First Crack, given reminders entering the straight, responded and clung on to the narrow advantage she had gained at the last, but she was all out to hold on at the finish. (6/1)

3962 Derring Bridge tried to slip his rivals on the approach to the third last, but he was unable to get away, though he did show his true battling qualities and was only narrowly denied. (25/1)

3402 Hooded Hawk (IRE), under all the aids turning in, could do little more than gallop on the spot, and he is finding it hard to make much impact in his races so far this term. (6/1)

4144* Sharp Command, heavily supported in the offices in the morning, was at full stretch when trying to get into contention inside the final mile, and the task proved beyond him. (2/1)

2042 Old Cavalier did not fare badly from 9lb out of the handicap, but he was in trouble from some way out and, as he has won between the flags, his future probably lies over fences. (25/1)

4020 Layham Low (IRE) (14/1: 10/1-16/1)

3915 Cutthroat Kid (IRE) (14/1: op 8/1)

Fed on Oats, just needing the run after being off the track for twelve months, looked a likely winner when joining issue at the penultimate flight but he clouted it hard and, losing his momentum, was pulled up. Thought to have gone lame, he was sound on returning and compensation awaits. (33/1)

4221 BROOKES BELL NOVICES' H'CAP CHASE (0-110) (5-Y.O+) (Class D)

4-15 (4-15) **2m 4f 110y (15 fncs)** £3,598.75 (£1,090.00: £532.50: £253.75) GOING: 0.09 sec per fur (G)

Form	Horse	Dist	Pos	SP	RR	SF
3988*	**Quite A Man (104)** (SABrookshaw) **9-11-7**(7) MrRBurton (hld up in tch: shkn up to ld & edgd lft appr last: sn clr)	—	1	3/1^{1}	111	43
3945^{3}	**Alaskan Heir (76)** (AStreeter) **6-10-0v** TEley (led 2nd to 4th: rdn 7th: styd on appr last)	3½	2	25/1	80	12
3909^{2}	**Kiltulla (IRE) (76)** (MrsSJSmith) **7-9-9**(5) GFRyan (chsd ldrs: led 11th to 3 out: led 2 out: hdd & n.m.r appr last: no ex)	nk	3	11/2^{2}	80	12
3843^{2}	**Curragh Peter (79)** (MrsPBickerton) **10-10-0**(3)ow3 GuyLewis (led to 2nd: led 4th to 11th: led 3 out to 2 out: wknd qckly)	4	4	25/1	80	9
1875*	**Frontier Flight (USA) (80)** (MissLCSiddall) **7-10-1**(3) EHusband (bit bkwd: hld up: hdwy 11th: wknd 2 out)	4	5	10/1	78	10
3086^{F}	**Althrey Blue (IRE) (76)** (AndrewTurnell) **8-10-0** MFoster (bkwd: blnd 3rd: a bhd: t.o)	12	6	50/1	64	—
4007^{2}	**Winnow (76)** (AndrewTurnell) **7-10-0** CRae (lw: nt j.w: a bhd: t.o)	1¾	7	11/2^{2}	63	—
3941^{4}	**Heathyards Boy (78)** (DMcCain) **7-10-2b**ow2 DWalsh (s.s: sn chsng ldrs: ev ch whn fell 9th)		F	9/1^{3}	—	—
3004^{P}	**Libertarian (IRE) (78)** (OSherwood) **7-10-2** JAMcCarthy (bkwd: chsd ldrs tl wknd qckly 4 out: p.u bef next)		P	25/1	—	—
3697^{4}	**Harvest View (IRE) (97)** (CPEBrooks) **7-11-0**(7) MBerry (lost pl 4th: rdn 8th: t.o whn p.u bef 10th)		P	3/1^{1}	—	—

(SP 113.4%) **10 Rn**

5m 10.9 (10.90) CSF £64.99 CT £356.99 TOTE £2.80: £1.70 £9.10 £1.10 (£49.90) Trio £76.90; £97.52 to 21/4/97 OWNER Mr W. R. J. Everall (SHREWSBURY) BRED R. Everall

LONG HANDICAP Kiltulla (IRE) 9-10 Alaskan Heir 9-3 Althrey Blue (IRE) 8-12 Heathyards Boy 9-1 Curragh Peter 9-10 Winnow 9-10

3988* Quite A Man jumped much better than he had in the past and, though he gave concern by drifting left when leading into the last, he was full of running and won going away. (3/1)

3945 Alaskan Heir dropped out of contention going into the country, but he found fresh reserves in the latter stages, and stayed on strongly to gain the runner-up prize on the flat. (25/1)

3909 Kiltulla (IRE), an unlucky sort who keeps promising to get off the mark, was battling away but appeared held when the winner took his ground approaching the last. If he had finished second there were certainly grounds for an objection. (11/2)

3843 Curragh Peter turned in a bold display of jumping and made the majority of the running, but he had run himself into the ground between the last two. (25/1)

1875* Frontier Flight (USA), given a break of over four months, crept closer in the final mile but lack of peak fitness took its toll, and he had shot his bolt once in line for home. There is still time for him to regain his form. (10/1)

3697 Harvest View (IRE) took no interest at all and, given reminders going out into the country, failed to respond and, tailed off, was eventually pulled up. (3/1)

4222 JANE MCALPINE MEMORIAL HUNTERS' CHASE (6-Y.O+) (Class H)

4-45 (4-46) **3m 110y (18 fncs)** £1,616.00 (£451.00: £218.00) GOING: 0.09 sec per fur (G)

Form	Horse	Dist	Pos	SP	RR	SF
	Nodform Wonder (RJBevis) **10-11-7**(7) MrRBevis (led to 4th: led 12th: clr 2 out: v.easily)	—	1	5/2^{1}	107+	27
	Mr Busker (IRE) (PHMorris) **8-11-7**(7) MrCJBBarlow (hld up: hdwy 9th: chsd wnr 3 out: one pce fr next)	5	2	14/1	104	24
4179^{U}	**Jupiter Moon** (MrsCHicks) **8-11-13**(5) MrCVigors (lw: hld up: hdwy 9th: nt rch ldrs)	16	3	8/1	97	17
3680^{P}	**Orton House** (SKelly) **10-11-7**(7) MrRBurton (lw: prom early: sn lost pl: n.d after)	hd	4	33/1	93	13
3793^{3}	**Orange Ragusa** (SHShirley-Beavan) **11-11-9**(5) MrRFord (led 4th to 7th: led 8th to 12th: wkng whn hit 3 out)	2½	5	11/4^{2}	92	12
3906^{2}	**Avostar** (MissCSaunders) **10-11-13**(5) MrBPollock (lw: outpcd: sn t.o: no ch whn fell last)		F	7/2^{3}	—	—
	Fair Crossing (MrsTJHill) **11-12-0**(7) MrMEmmanuel (prom: led 7th to 8th: rdn 10th: sn wknd: t.o whn p.u bef 3 out)		P	10/1	—	—
	Fibreguide Tech (TRKinsey) **14-11-7**(7) MrRThomas (a in rr: t.o whn p.u bef 2 out)		P	14/1	—	—
4051^{F}	**Highway Five (IRE)** (LadySusanBrooke) **9-12-0**(7) MissEJames (sn t.o: p.u bef 13th)		P	33/1	—	—

(SP 116.9%) **9 Rn**

6m 21.0 (19.00) CSF £33.58 TOTE £3.10: £1.70 £2.50 £1.50 (£19.90) Trio £96.00; £44.66 to 21/4/97 OWNER Mr D. A. Malam (MALPAS) BRED Miss P. Freaney

OFFICIAL EXPLANATION **Avostar: had a nasal discharge of blood.**

Nodform Wonder, winner of his last two outings between the flags, helped forced the pace and, forging clear entering the straight, simply outclassed this opposition. (5/2)

Mr Busker (IRE) made relentless progress in the final mile but, once the winner stepped on the gas, he had to admit he had met his match. (14/1)

3580* Jupiter Moon, who unseated his rider at Cheltenham three days earlier, was never able to get himself close enough to give the principals any cause for concern. (8/1)

Orton House got round in his own time, but was never going the pace of the leaders. (33/1)

3793 Orange Ragusa took the winner on and looked the only danger in the final mile, but he was feeling the strain when he met the third last all wrong and that was the end of him. (11/4)

Fair Crossing (10/1: 7/1-11/1)

Fibreguide Tech (14/1: 10/1-16/1)

4223 EMRAL H'CAP HURDLE (0-100) (4-Y.O+) (Class F)

5-15 (5-16) **2m 1f (9 hdls)** £2,853.00 (£864.00: £422.00: £201.00) GOING minus 0.09 sec per fur (G)

Form	Horse	Dist	Pos	SP	RR	SF
3674*	**Caracol (76)** (JNeville) **8-10-8** TDascombe (a.p: led 6th: rdn last: r.o wl)	—	1	11/2^{2}	59	17
3951^{2}	**The Brewer (73)** (JCTuck) **5-10-5** WMarston (chsd ldrs: kpt on fr 2 out: no ch w wnr)	2½	2	10/1	54	12
3976*	**Kierchem (IRE) (75)** (CGrant) **6-10-7** JCallaghan (chsd ldrs: chal 2 out: rdn & one pce appr last)	1¼	3	11/2^{2}	55	13
3904^{9}	**Ajdar (74)** (OBrennan) **6-10-6** MBrennan (lw: hld up: styd on appr 2 out: nvr nrr)	5	4	20/1	49	7
4086^{5}	**Evezio Rufo (84)** (NPLittmoden) **5-11-2b** VSlattery (prom: led 4th: sn clr: hdd 6th: rdn & wknd 2 out)	2½	5	12/1	56	14
3940^{4}	**Never so Blue (IRE) (84)** (PBradley) **6-10-11**(5) DJKavanagh (prom tl wknd appr 3 out: t.o)	19	6	12/1	39	—
1007*	**Hamadryad (IRE) (96)** (MrsVCWard) **9-12-0** JRKavanagh (bkwd: hld up: hdwy appr 3 out: nt rch ldrs: t.o)	2½	7	10/1	48	6
2578^{4}	**Shift Again (IRE) (83)** (OSherwood) **5-10-12b**(3) SophieMitchell (mstke 4th: a bhd: t.o)	5	8	8/1^{3}	31	—
3943^{3}	**Newhall Prince (88)** (AStreeter) **9-11-6** TEley (lw: led to 4th: wknd appr 6th: t.o)	5	9	9/1	31	—
3346^{5}	**Innocent George (85)** (MissLCSiddall) **8-11-3** MFoster (a bhd: t.o fr ½-wy)	11	10	8/1^{3}	17	—
3926^{4}	**Principal Boy (IRE) (75)** (TJEtherington) **4-10-1** RRourke (prom to 5th: sn wknd: t.o)	1½	11	20/1	6	—
3438^{10}	**Nagara Sound (72)** (BPreece) **6-10-4** GaryLyons (a bhd: t.o)	3	12	25/1	—	—
3888^{5}	**Mapleton (78)** (MrsSJSmith) **4-10-4** RichardGuest (hld up: hdwy 4th: wknd 6th: t.o whn p.u bef 2 out)		P	5/1^{1}	—	—

3733^{12}	**Out of The Blue (68)** (MWEckley) **5-9-7b**(7) JMogford (racd wd: lost pl 4th: t.o whn p.u bef 2 out)	P	50/1	—	—
			(SP 128.6%)	**14 Rn**	

4m 2.3 (7.30) CSF £55.55 CT £300.98 TOTE £6.70: £2.90 £2.20 £2.70 (£21.70) Trio £58.50 OWNER Mr C. G. Bolton (NEWPORT, GWENT) BRED Mrs David Gordon Lennox
LONG HANDICAP Out of The Blue 9-9
WEIGHT FOR AGE 4yo-6lb
3674* Caracol is a very versatile performer, and he showed his battling qualities after looking to be fighting a losing battle from the penultimate flight. (11/2)
3951 The Brewer needs a stiffer test of stamina and answered his rider's every call in the latter stages but, despite staying on to claim the runner-up prize on the flat, a turn of foot was sadly lacking. (10/1)
3976* Kierchem (IRE) moved up menacingly before reaching the straight and put in his bid at the second last, but the winner was game for a fight and he was the one to crack. (11/2: op 7/2)
3666 Ajdar waiting on the leaders, took time to pick up when given the office and, though he did stay on, could not get himself into it. (20/1)
3933* Evezio Rufo was in the firing iine and holding every chance until tapped for toe from the penultimate flight. (12/1: op 7/1)
3943 Newhall Prince (9/1: op 5/1)
3346 Innocent George (8/1: 7/1-12/1)
3888 Mapleton looks to need more cut in the ground to produce his best, and his short-lived effort had come to an end four out. He was tailed off and pulled up early in the straight. (5/1)

T/Plpt: £7.40 (1142.13 Tckts). T/Qdpt: £4.90 (60.88 Tckts) IM

3582-STRATFORD-ON-AVON (L-H) (Good, Good to firm patches)
Saturday April 19th
WEATHER: fine

4224 JENKINSONS NOVICES' HURDLE (I) (4-Y.O+) (Class E)
2-35 (2-35) **2m 6f 110y (12 hdls)** £1,744.00 (£484.00: £232.00) GOING: 0.52 sec per fur (GS)

				SP	RR	SF
3494^{7}	**Isis Dawn** (AGNewcombe) **5-10-4**(3) PHenley (plld hrd: prom: lost pl 8th: rallied 3 out: led & pckd next: rdn out)	—	1	16/1^{3}	79	32
3703*	**Shekels (IRE)** (CPEBrooks) **6-11-4** GBradley (led to 2 out: hit last: r.o)	2	2	4/9^{1}	89	42
	Occold (IRE) (GAHubbard) **6-10-12** DGallagher (bit bkwd: plld hrd: chsd ldrs: ev ch appr 2 out: one pce flat)	1	3	16/1^{3}	82	35
	Beck and Call (IRE) (MissVenetiaWilliams) **8-10-12** GUpton (chsd ldr: ev ch 9th: wkng whn hmpd appr 2 out)	18	4	11/2^{2}	69	22
2073^{4}	**Irish Delight** (RCurtis) **5-10-12** DMorris (bhd: hit 4th & 5th: hdwy 8th: wkng whn mstke 3 out)	10	5	16/1^{3}	62	15
3734^{7}	**Sidney** (JCMcConnochie) **8-10-12** SWynne (prom tl rdn & wknd 8th)	1¼	6	66/1	61	14
3284^{7}	**Green King** (APJones) **5-10-5**(7) DCarey (lw: mstke 3 out: nvr trbld ldrs)	25	7	20/1	43	—
3574^{15}	**Mill Bay Sam** (MrsMerritaJones) **6-10-12** DerekByrne (lw: nt j.w: bhd fr 8th)	dist	8	33/1	—	—
3970^{P}	**Final Rose** (RJSmith) **7-10-0**(7) MrJGoldstein (bhd fr 7th)	1	9	66/1	—	—
	Marlies Gohr (TTClement) **5-10-4**(3) LAspell (bit bkwd: blnd 1st: hdwy 4th: sn wknd: t.o whn p.u bef 8th)		P	66/1	—	—
3233^{14}	**Freeline Fontaine (IRE)** (NJHenderson) **5-10-12** MAFitzgerald (trckd ldrs tl hmpd & uns rdr 2 out)		U	16/1^{3}	—	—
				(SP 120.3%)	**11 Rn**	

5m 34.6 (18.60) CSF £22.50 TOTE £18.20: £2.20 £1.50 £2.40 (£7.70) Trio £20.40 OWNER Major Bob Darell (BARNSTAPLE) BRED J. Thompson
Isis Dawn took a bit of settling early on, but seemed suited by this longer trip, as it was only in the last half-mile that she began to look a contender. (16/1)
3703* Shekels (IRE) settled well in front but set a pretty sedate pace, understandably given the big step up in trip. However, this probably proved his undoing as he failed to quicken quite as well as the winner in the straight. (4/9)
Occold (IRE), a leggy newcomer who looked well in his coat but in need of the race, travelled keenly on the heels of the leaders until challenging on the home turn. His effort was beginning to peter out when he did not jump the final flight quite as quickly as the first two. (16/1)
Beck and Call (IRE) looked fit despite two years off, but was looking held when hampered starting the home turn, which ended all hope. (11/2)
1685 Irish Delight, making his hurdles debut, is going to have to learn to jump to fulfil his potential at this level. (16/1)
Sidney showed a little more this time, but has some way to go to trouble the judge. (66/1)
Freeline Fontaine (IRE) was still travelling strongly on the heels of the leaders when tightened up on the inside after the third last, causing him to stumble and unseat his rider. This was bad luck and he deserves the chance to atone. (16/1)

4225 LAURENT-PERRIER H'CAP CHASE (0-135) (5-Y.O+) (Class C)
3-05 (3-05) **2m 4f (15 fncs)** £4,133.00 (£1,244.00: £602.00: £281.00) GOING: 0.27 sec per fur (GS)

				SP	RR	SF
2942^{F}	**Philip's Woody (112)** (NJHenderson) **9-10-6** MAFitzgerald (chsd ldrs: led 4 out: clr 2 out: easily)	—	1	7/1	122+	55
3638^{11}	**Super Coin (117)** (RLee) **9-10-8**(3) PHenley (chsd ldrs tl blnd & lost pl 3rd: rallied 4 out: r.o flat)	6	2	8/1	122	55
2894^{5}	**Merry Panto (IRE) (106)** (CPEBrooks) **8-9-7**(7) CRafter (w ldrs: led 4th: sn clr: j.slowly & hdd 4 out: sn btn)	6	3	16/1	106	39
4140*	**Polden Pride (115)** (GBBalding) **9-10-9** BClifford (hld up: blnd 9th: hdwy 11th: wknd appr 2 out)	s.h	4	4/1^{2}	115	48
3986^{2}	**Callisoe Bay (IRE) (130)** (OSherwood) **8-11-10** GBradley (led tl blnd & hdd 4th: wknd 9th)	18	5	9/2^{3}	116	49
1016^{U}	**Boro Vacation (IRE) (125)** (PFNicholls) **8-11-5** KGaule (hld up & plld hrd: hdwy 5th: wknd 4 out)	1	6	14/1	110	43
3701^{3}	**Over the Pole (111)** (PRChamings) **10-10-2**(3)ow4 DFortt (lw: w ldrs: blnd 1st: 3rd whn fell 3rd)		F	7/2^{1}	—	—
3585^{U}	**Around the Horn (129)** (JTGifford) **10-11-9** SMcNeill (chsd ldrs to 10th: wkng whn j.slowly 4 out: p.u bef next)		P	10/1	—	—
3800^{3}	**High Alltitude (IRE) (106)** (MJHeaton-Ellis) **9-10-0** DGallagher (lw: sn bhd: t.o whn p.u bef 9th)		P	8/1	—	—
				(SP 116.8%)	**9 Rn**	

5m 1.3 (5.30) CSF £55.95 CT £790.48 TOTE £5.30: £1.80 £2.20 £4.30 (£20.40) Trio £101.50; £78.70 to 21/4/97 OWNER Mr K. G. Knox (LAMBOURN) BRED Conkwell Grange Stud Ltd
LONG HANDICAP Merry Panto (IRE) 9-6 High Alltitude (IRE) 9-11
2942 Philip's Woody, given his reputation for being hard to win with, has an enviable record of six wins in nine attempts after a break of forty-six days or more in recent years. How relevant that was on this occasion is open to debate, as his lack of finishing speed was offset by the way the race was run, so fast that it was as much the last one conscious wins as anything else. (7/1)
3015 Super Coin hopelessly outpaced after an early mistake, found his stamina coming into play in the last half-mile. (8/1)
2894 Merry Panto (IRE) got away from his pilot, taking on Callisoe Bay from the start and having a clear lead after the first mile. In the circumstances, he did well to finish as close as he did. (16/1)

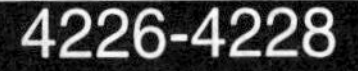

4140* Polden Pride may have been the unlucky horse of the race, for he was just beginning a forward move when a mistake seven from home halted him. Despite this, he managed to get into contention briefly jumping four out, before the effort took its toll. (4/1)
3986 Callisoe Bay (IRE) seems to have two gears, break-neck and slow, and spent the second half of the race in the latter. (9/2)
1016 Boro Vacation (IRE) pulled his way into a prominent position within the first mile, and ended up paying the penalty. (14/1: 10/1-16/1)
3701 Over the Pole, almost on the floor when Callisoe Bay flew past him at the first, was trying to stick with the tearaway leaders when taking a heavy fall at the third. (7/2)
3585 Around the Horn (10/1: 6/1-12/1)

4226 RICHARDSONS PARKWAY NOVICES' H'CAP HURDLE (0-100) (4-Y.O+) (Class E)

3-35 (3-36) **2m 110y (9 hdls)** £2,360.00 (£660.00: £320.00) GOING: 0.52 sec per fur (GS)

				SP	RR	SF
3473[2]	**Snowshill Shaker (80)** (NATwiston-Davies) **8-11-0** RBellamy (lw: chsd ldrs: led 6th: sn clr: blnd last: pushed out)	—	**1**	11/2[1]	70+	28
3955*	**Reverse Thrust (78)** (PRHedger) **6-10-5**(7) MClinton (lw: hld up: hdwy 5th: chsd wnr fr 3 out: no imp)	10	**2**	8/1	58	16
	Nahla (80) (BdeHaan) **7-11-0** SMcNeill (lw: led to 6th: kpt on fr 3 out)	½	**3**	14/1	60	18
3983[3]	**Fencer's Quest (IRE) (78)** (CaptTAForster) **4-10-6** SWynne (chsd ldrs: one pce appr 2 out)	½	**4**	13/2[2]	57	9
3989[5]	**Alpha Leather (66)** (LPGrassick) **6-10-0** MrJGrassick (hld up & plld hrd: hdwy 6th: nvr able chal)	2	**5**	8/1	43	1
2821[9]	**Bally Parson (82)** (RDickin) **11-11-2** DLeahy (chsd ldrs: no hdwy fr 3 out)	¾	**6**	16/1	59	17
3959*	**Anif (USA) (66)** (JJoseph) **6-9-7**(7) MrJGoldstein (in tch: effrt 5th: wknd next)	15	**7**	12/1	28	—
3932[P]	**Another Comedy (73)** (RLee) **7-10-7**[ow7] GUpton (hit 1st: nvr trbld ldrs)	1½	**8**	25/1	34	—
4021[2]	**Ketchican (72)** (SGKnight) **5-10-6** SAnderson (in tch: mstke 5th: wknd 3 out)	23	**9**	14/1	10	—
3424[6]	**Palladium Boy (79)** (MrsJGRetter) **7-10-13** MAFitzgerald (prom to 6th: virtually p.u flat)	dist	**10**	8/1	—	—
3630[P]	**Ritto (93)** (JNeville) **7-11-13** NMann (fell 3rd)		**F**	9/1	—	—
3679[3]	**Schnozzle (IRE) (87)** (KSBridgwater) **6-11-7** GBradley (bhd whn hmpd 3rd: p.u bef 5th)		**P**	7/1[3]	—	—
3932[F]	**Milling Brook (81)** (JMBradley) **5-11-1** DGallagher (bhd whn p.u bef 2 out)		**P**	11/1	—	—
4002[4]	**Daydream Believer (66)** (MSalaman) **5-10-0** BClifford (t.o fr 6th: p.u bef 3 out)		**P**	16/1	—	—
3921[U]	**Zesti (75)** (TTClement) **5-10-6**(3) LAspell (lw: bhd whn p.u bef 3 out)		**P**	14/1	—	—
3918[4]	**Aqua Amber (66)** (JMBradley) **5-10-0** WMcFarland (bhd whn p.u bef 5th)		**P**	33/1	—	—
3205[P]	**Serious Option (IRE) (66)** (RCurtis) **6-10-0** DMorris (in tch to 5th: bhd whn p.u bef 2 out)		**P**	33/1	—	—
				(SP 142.1%)	**17 Rn**	

4m 2.9 (15.90) CSF £51.38 CT £573.05 TOTE £5.50: £1.80 £2.20 £2.40 £2.30 (£40.80) Trio £170.20; £119.92 to 21/4/97 OWNER Mr Austin Knight (CHELTENHAM) BRED Ian Hunter and A. Knight
LONG HANDICAP Anif (USA) 9-8 Another Comedy 9-13 Daydream Believer 9-13 Alpha Leather 9-10 Aqua Amber 9-13 Serious Option (IRE) 9-13
WEIGHT FOR AGE 4yo-6lb
OFFICIAL EXPLANATION **Daydream Believer: the rider reported that the mare had swallowed her tongue.**
3473 Snowshill Shaker looked suited by this return to the minimum trip, and he showed plenty of foot to establish a clear lead in a few strides once sent for home. (11/2: 4/1-6/1)
3955* Reverse Thrust was travelling like he had more in the tank than he found when the winner kicked, although to his credit he kept plugging away. (8/1: 5/1-9/1)
Nahla looked fit despite a year off, and stayed on well enough after trying to make all. (14/1)
3983 Fencer's Quest (IRE) again did quite well, finding a sharp two miles on fastish ground offsetting his lack of stamina. (13/2)
3989 Alpha Leather got going too late to mount a challenge. (8/1)
2621 Bally Parson is arguably very well handicapped over hurdles, but found this far too fast for him and needs more of a test of stamina. (16/1)

4227 STRATFORD-ON-AVON NOVICES' CHASE (6-Y.O+) (Class D)

4-05 (4-05) **3m (18 fncs)** £4,419.00 (£1,332.00: £646.00: £303.00) GOING: 0.27 sec per fur (GS)

				SP	RR	SF
2896[5]	**Big Archie (74)** (MrsAJBowlby) **7-10-12** DLeahy (led 4th to 7th: led 9th to 3 out: led 2 out tl flat: rallied to ld nr fin)	—	**1**	33/1	112?	39
4004*	**Domaine de Pron (FR) (104)** (MrsLCTaylor) **6-11-3** RBellamy (a.p: led 7th: sn hdd: led 3 out tl next: led flat: hdd & no ex nr fin)	nk	**2**	9/2[3]	117?	44
3060[P]	**Melnik** (MrsAJPerrett) **6-11-3** GUpton (led to 4th: led appr 8th to 9th: wknd 12th)	dist	**3**	8/1	—	—
3817[6]	**Joy For Life (IRE)** (RMStronge) **6-10-7** SWynne (mstke 7th: a bhd)	2	**4**	33/1	—	—
3993[3]	**Father Sky (124)** (OSherwood) **6-11-8b** GBradley (lw: chsd ldrs: rdn 10th: mstke 14th: sn wknd)	10	**5**	2/1[1]	—	—
	Hi Hedley (IRE) (GAHubbard) **7-10-12** DGallagher (a bhd: t.o whn p.u bef 3 out)		**P**	10/1	—	—
3894[2]	**Little Elliot (IRE)** (SEarle) **9-10-9**(3) LAspell (bit bkwd: prom: mstke & rdn 11th: 4th & wkng whn blnd 4 out: p.u bef next)		**P**	20/1	—	—
3688[3]	**Debonair Dude (IRE)** (NJHenderson) **7-10-12** MAFitzgerald (lw: in tch tl blnd 8th: t.o whn p.u bef 3 out)		**P**	13/2	—	—
3849[4]	**Master Toby (110)** (NATwiston-Davies) **7-10-10**(7) MrJGoldstein (lw: prom tl blnd & uns rdr 5th)		**U**	100/30[2]	—	—
				(SP 118.8%)	**9 Rn**	

6m 5.3 (13.30) CSF £163.86 TOTE £58.80: £6.80 £1.60 £3.00 (£94.60) Trio £70.70 OWNER Mr Cliff Basson (WANTAGE) BRED C. R. Basson
IN-FOCUS: **This was the first winner under Rules for Mandy Bowlby, sister of Jenny Pitman.**
2896 Big Archie can hardly be said to have been foot-perfect in the past, this being only his third completion in seven attempts if his points are included, but did nothing wrong on this occasion, causing a real upset in the process. (33/1)
4004* Domaine de Pron (FR) took the winner on from the fourth last and they pulled further and further clear but, after looking to take control at the last, he lost the lead nearing the line. (9/2)
3060 Melnik at least managed to complete this time, but does look to have a mind of his own. (8/1: op 9/2)
1958 Joy For Life (IRE) never got remotely into the race on this chasing debut. (33/1)
3993 Father Sky was running miles below his best even before his mistake five from home, and seems to have had enough for the moment. (2/1)

4228 RICHARDSONS STAR SITE HUNTERS' CHASE (6-Y.O+) (Class H)

4-35 (4-41) **2m 5f 110y (16 fncs)** £2,038.00 (£568.00: £274.00) GOING: 0.27 sec per fur (GS)

				SP	RR	SF
	Mankind (JATdeGiles) **6-11-7**(7) MrLBaker (prom: led 5th to 8th: led 2 out: rdn out)	—	**1**	66/1	107	31
3984[3]	**Pro Bono (IRE)** (AndyMorgan) **7-11-9**(5) MrASansome (a.p: led 8th to 2 out: unable qckn flat)	1½	**2**	10/1	106	30
	Eastern Pleasure (IanEmmerson) **10-11-7**(7) MrTJBarry (in tch: kpt on fr 4 out: nvr able to chal)	dist	**3**	20/1	—	—
4094[3]	**Fox Pointer** (MrsLTJEvans) **12-12-0**(7) MrOMcPhail (lw: led 3rd to 5th: wknd 4 out)	2	**4**	7/4[1]	—	—
	Tudor Fable (IRE) (CJRSweeting) **9-12-3**(7) MrRupertSweeting (lw: a bhd)	13	**5**	14/1	—	—
3852[6]	**Tellaporky** (THind) **8-11-7**(7) MrAMiddleton (a bhd)	11	**6**	33/1	—	—

587[11] **Erlemo** (MissSarahGeorge) **8-11-7b**(7) DrPPritchard (lw: blnd 13th: a bhd)........5 **7** 33/1 — —
3963[2] **Tuffnut George** (MrsPGrainger) **10-12-3**(7) MrAPhillips (in tch to 11th: t.o whn p.u bef 3 out)........ **P** 6/1[2] — —
3852[P] **Star Oats** (MrsRMLampard) **11-11-7**(7) MrAKinane (w ldrs whn mstkes 10th, 11th & 12th: p.u bef next)........ **P** 14/1 — —
Emerald Ruler (ADPeachey) **10-11-10**(5)ow1 MrJTrice-Rolph (bkwd: blnd 3rd: sn bhd: p.u bef 11th)........ **P** 20/1 — —
4094[4] **Candle Glow** (PHutchinson) **9-11-2**(7) MrPHutchinson (prom: rdn 8th: sn wknd: p.u bef 10th)........ **P** 7/1 — —
3925[P] **Prinzal** (GMMcCourt) **10-12-0** MrMArmytage (lw: bhd: effrt & mstke 8th: wknd 11th: p.u bef 3 out)........ **P** 9/1 — —
3984[P] **Frank Be Lucky** (MsBarbaraAshby-Jones) **11-11-7**(7) MrRWakley (lw: led to 3rd: blnd 5th: 5th whn blnd 11th: sn wknd: p.u bef 2 out)........ **P** 13/2[3] — —
128[P] **Secret Castle** (MrsLALove) **9-11-7**(7) MrLBrown (bhd: blnd 8th: p.u lame bef next)........ **P** 100/1 — —
Lord Kilton (MrsDCowley) **9-11-7b[1]**(7) MrMCowley (Withdrawn not under Starter's orders: jockey injured & horse bolted bef s)........ **W** 100/1 — —
(SP 127.8%) **14 Rn**

5m 30.9 (18.90) CSF £572.88 TOTE £108.80: £41.00 £3.10 £3.20 (£956.20) Trio £161.80; £125.40 to 21/4/97 OWNER Mr J A T de Giles (SWINDON) BRED J. R. Fenlon

Mankind, pulled up after blundering away his chance in a maiden point-to-point at the start of March, was raised very markedly in class but passed the test in fine style, jumping fluently and proving gallant when asked to battle. (66/1)
3984 Pro Bono (IRE) had shaken off all bar the winner by four from home, but had to admit defeat after the last. This seems his ideal trip. (10/1: 8/1-12/1)
Eastern Pleasure, a former selling hurdler who has won between the flags, tried hard and stayed on to the end but was no match for these. (20/1)
4094 Fox Pointer looks a different horse when he is able to dominate. (7/4)
Tudor Fable (IRE), formerly a quite useful chaser who seemed best at two miles although he did win over half-a-mile further, was soon well in arrears and has yet to show he retains much ability. (14/1)
3963 Tuffnut George (6/1: 3/1-7/1)
3925 Prinzal (9/1: 6/1-10/1)
Frank Be Lucky, formerly with Jim Dreaper in Ireland, showed here that he has the ability to win this type of race if he can learn to jump British fences. (13/2)

4229 RICHARDSONS MERLIN PARK H'CAP HURDLE (0-120) (4-Y.O+ F & M) (Class D)

5-05 (5-05) **2m 110y (9 hdls)** £2,034.00 (£612.00: £296.00: £138.00) GOING: 0.52 sec per fur (GS)

SP RR SF

4005[2] **Barford Sovereign (114)** (JRFanshawe) **5-12-0** MAFitzgerald (led tl appr 3rd: led appr 3 out: hdd last: rallied to ld nr fin)........— **1** 3/1[2] 92 40
4164[2] **Handy Lass (101)** (JSSmith) **8-10-8**(7) MrOMcPhail (hld up: hdwy 5th: led last: hdd & unable qckn nr fin)......hd **2** 9/2[3] 79 27
3594* **Siberian Mystic (92)** (PGMurphy) **4-10-0** WMcFarland (hld up: mstke 4th: hdwy appr 3 out: ev ch whn hit 2 out: one pce)........5 **3** 9/4[1] 65 7
4101[6] **Stapleford Lady (86)** (JSMoore) **9-10-0** SMcNeill (prom to 3 out)........16 **4** 10/1 44 —
3889* **Secret Gift (92)** (MrsJPitman) **4-10-0b** DLeahy (led appr 3rd: pckd 6th: hdd appr next: sn wknd)........21 **5** 9/4[1] 29 —
(SP 113.8%) **5 Rn**

4m 3.1 (16.10) CSF £15.06 TOTE £3.40: £1.80 £1.90 (£7.60) OWNER Barford Bloodstock (NEWMARKET) BRED Mrs C. Handscombe
LONG HANDICAP Siberian Mystic 9-12 Secret Gift 9-10
WEIGHT FOR AGE 4yo-6lb
OFFICIAL EXPLANATION **Secret Gift: the rider reported that the mare was never travelling well.**

4005 Barford Sovereign, dropping back in trip, again won this on courage after appearing held jumping the last. (3/1)
4164 Handy Lass, produced to lead with a quick jump at the last, looked sure to win but was collared on the line. This was no disgrace and she should soon return to winning ways. (9/2)
3594* Siberian Mystic swung for home going best with the steady pace having aided her suspect stamina, but a mistake at the penultimate flight soon put her in trouble. (9/4)
472 Stapleford Lady is still finding her feet after a spell over fences. (10/1)
3889* Secret Gift won a dreadful race last time, and could not handle the big step-up in class. (9/4)

4230 JENKINSONS NOVICES' HURDLE (II) (4-Y.O+) (Class E)

5-35 (5-36) **2m 6f 110y (12 hdls)** £1,744.00 (£484.00: £232.00) GOING: 0.52 sec per fur (GS)

SP RR SF

3706* **Supreme Flyer (IRE) (100)** (KCBailey) **7-10-11**(7) MrRWakley (lw: hld up: hdwy & hit 5th: led last: rdn & qcknd)........— **1** 6/4[1] 76+ 37
3340* **Mountain Path (92)** (NJHenderson) **7-11-4** MAFitzgerald (plld hrd: led 2nd: hit 4th: hdd last: one pce)........2½ **2** 7/4[2] 74 35
Pat Buckley (NATwiston-Davies) **6-10-5**(7) MrJGoldstein (hld up: hit 7th: hdwy next: kpt on wl fr 2 out)........7 **3** 12/1 63 24
3085[4] **Willows Roulette** (AGHobbs) **5-10-12** RGreene (bhd tl r.o fr 9th: nvr rchd ldrs)........9 **4** 20/1 57 18
Sky Burst (MissVenetiaWilliams) **7-10-7** GUpton (hdwy 5th: wknd appr 2 out)........3½ **5** 8/1[3] 49 10
Lord Cool (IRE) (CPEBrooks) **6-10-12** GBradley (bkwd: hld up: hdwy 3rd: chsd ldrs 8th tl wknd appr 2 out).19 **6** 12/1 41 2
3628[2] **Armateur (FR) (82)** (JCMcConnochie) **9-10-12** DLeahy (lw: in tch tl lost pl 5th: n.d afterwards)........22 **7** 11/1 25 —
Fools Future (MrsJGRetter) **8-10-12** DGallagher (plld hrd: w ldrs tl 7th: sn wknd)........22 **8** 40/1 10 —
4003[9] **Fearless Hussar** (CFCJackson) **7-10-12** NMann (mstke 6th: a bhd: t.o whn p.u bef 9th)........ **P** 33/1 — —
Cloudy House (NMLampard) **8-10-1**(7)ow1 MrLBaker (bkwd: in tch: blnd 8th: wknd next: p.u bef 3 out)........ **P** 66/1 — —
Above The Clouds (MissAMNewton-Smith) **6-10-9**(3) PHenley (bkwd: led to 2nd: wknd 6th: t.o whn p.u bef 9th)........ **P** 66/1 — —
(SP 124.3%) **11 Rn**

5m 36.3 (20.30) CSF £4.18 TOTE £2.80: £1.30 £1.60 £2.30 (£2.10) Trio £13.70 OWNER Mrs E. A. Kellar (UPPER LAMBOURN) BRED Hugh McMahon

3706* Supreme Flyer (IRE) hardly looks entirely co-operative, but was given a peach of a ride and only began to hang fire when already three lengths up. (6/4)
3340* Mountain Path takes a good hold, but was made to look pedestrian by the winner when the chips were down. (7/4)
Pat Buckley, a stocky, quite attractive gelding, looked to have done plenty of work, but is a very poor mover in his slower paces. He stayed on strongly in the closing stages and shaped well but, although his action suggests he needs the ground softer, his sire required a firmer surface. (12/1: 9/1-14/1)
1071 Willows Roulette made some progress over the last half-mile to show that an extended trip is likely to bring the best from him. (20/1)
Sky Burst looked suited by a trip just short of two-and-a-half miles when last seen over hurdles two years ago, and it appeared lack of stamina rather than fitness found her out. She certainly has the ability to find a small race. (8/1)

Lord Cool (IRE), a lengthy sort who still has a lot of filling out to do, did not look ready but has a good action and showed plenty of promise in running well for so long. (12/1)

T/Plpt: £1,585.20 (5.68 Tckts). T/Qdpt: £336.30 (1.47 Tckts) Dk

3959-TOWCESTER (R-H) (Good to firm)
Monday April 21st
WEATHER: fine

4231 ROADE NOVICES' (S) HURDLE (4-Y.O+) (Class G)
2-20 (2-21) **2m (8 hdls)** £1,950.50 (£543.00: £261.50) GOING minus 0.29 sec per fur (GF)

				SP	RR	SF
4067*	**Nautical Jewel** (KGWingrove) **5-11-0**(7) JPower (hld up: hdwy appr 3 out: led appr last: sn clr: comf)	—	1	12/1	70+	10
3933[7]	**Our Eddie (66)** (KGWingrove) **8-11-0b** KGaule (lost pl 4th: rallied 3 out: r.o flat: sddle slipped)	6	2	20/1	57+	—
3959[2]	**Paulton (66)** (KBishop) **4-10-8b** APMcCoy (lw: chsd ldrs: lft in ld 2 out: sn hdd: rdn & wknd flat)	nk	3	3/1 [2]	57	—
3748[3]	**Boy Blakeney (76)** (MrsSJSmith) **4-10-8** RichardGuest (hdwy appr 3 out: nrst fin)	s.h	4	5/2 [1]	57	—
4096[U]	**Inchydoney Boy (IRE) (50)** (TPMcGovern) **8-11-0** JFTitley (prom: led 4th tl j.lft, mstke & hdd 2 out: no ch afterwards)	9	5	33/1	48	—
	Inishmann (IRE) (APJones) **6-11-0** CLlewellyn (plld hrd: prom tl lost pl 4th)	14	6	20/1	34	—
3621[14]	**Buster (59)** (MrsBarbaraWaring) **9-11-0** EByrne (bit bkwd: bhd fr 5th)	6	7	10/1	28	—
3758[3]	**Mheanmetoo** (DLWilliams) **6-10-7**(7) MrSDurack (led to 4th: eased whn btn 2 out)	3½	8	12/1	24	—
4096[5]	**Tug Your Forelock (60)** (GFJohnsonHoughton) **6-11-0** AThornton (lw: prom: ev ch 5th: wknd after next)	2½	9	7/1	22	—
3054[3]	**Nicky Wilde** (CPEBrooks) **7-11-0** GBradley (t: bit bkwd: in tch: pushed along 4th: wknd qckly 3 out: p.u bef last: b.b.v)		P	7/2 [3]	—	—
3932[P]	**Whatashot (65)** (DMcCain) **7-11-0** DWalsh (bit bkwd: mstke 1st: a bhd: p.u bef last)		P	20/1	—	—
4069[6]	**Tatibag** (RJSmith) **5-10-7**(7) MrJGoldstein (mstkes: a bhd: p.u bef last)		P	33/1	—	—
3677[9]	**Noquita (NZ)** (JCMcConnochie) **10-10-9b**[1](5) XAizpuru (prom to 3rd: rdn & wknd appr 3 out: p.u bef last)		P	33/1	—	—
				(SP 135.9%)	**13 Rn**	

3m 54.2 (8.20) CSF £216.84 TOTE £13.50: £5.50 £6.00 £1.50 (£106.30) Trio £192.80; £95.04 to Folkestone 22/4/97 OWNER Mrs A. Squires (NEWMARKET) BRED J. M. and Mrs Jeyes
WEIGHT FOR AGE 4yo-6lb
No bid

4067* Nautical Jewel won a very poor non-seller last time but this is his grade. A poor mover in his slower paces, he was always travelling sweetly in the race and looked the likely winner long before he hit the front. (12/1: op 7/1)
Our Eddie ran on well despite a slipping saddle to give the yard a notable one-two. He would surely have gone very close had his pilot been able to give him a proper ride. (20/1)
3959 Paulton at least stayed straight this time but, presented with the lead after the penultimate flight, slowed dramatically from the last. (3/1)
3748 Boy Blakeney again did plenty of running in the closing stages and is worth a try over a little further. (5/2)
Inchydoney Boy (IRE), taken down early, is rather headstrong and got very tired in the home straight after landing in a heap at the second last. (33/1)
Inishmann (IRE) ran too freely on this belated hurdles debut. (20/1)
3443 Mheanmetoo (12/1: op 8/1)
3054 Nicky Wilde is tubed and clearly has his share of problems, for he stopped alarmingly having broken a blood vessel. (7/2)

4232 MILTON NOVICES' CHASE (5-Y.O+) (Class E)
2-50 (2-50) **2m 6f (18 fncs)** £2,560.25 (£767.00: £368.50: £169.25) GOING minus 0.29 sec per fur (GF)

				SP	RR	SF
3848[2]	**Who Is Equiname (IRE) (104)** (NJHenderson) **7-11-2b** MAFitzgerald (lw: prom: led 8th: clr appr 2 out: rdn appr last: eased nr fin)	—	1	4/11 [1]	94+	17
3736[8]	**Volleyball (IRE) (67)** (PRHedger) **8-11-2** MRichards (hld up: stdy hdwy 12th: rdn appr last: no imp)	8	2	16/1	88	11
3173[P]	**Derrys Prerogative** (AWCarroll) **7-11-2** DWalsh (bit bkwd: prom: ev ch 4 out: wknd appr 2 out)	11	3	66/1	80	3
4158[P]	**Chiappucci (IRE) (87)** (MrsEHHeath) **7-11-2** DGallagher (lw: rdn 7th: mstkes 8th & next: nvr trbld ldrs)	11	4	20/1	72	—
3998*	**Sorciere** (GBBalding) **6-11-4** BClifford (led tl hdd & blnd 8th: hit 11th: wknd 3 out)	12	5	9/2 [2]	66	—
3331[7]	**Smart Casanova (60)** (MJWilkinson) **8-11-2** WMarston (mstkes 4th & 11th: rdn 7th: a bhd)	20	6	50/1	49	—
4083[2]	**Full Shilling (USA) (60)** (DLWilliams) **8-10-9**(7) MrSDurack (lw: chsd ldrs to 4 out: 6th & btn whn p.u bef last)		P	12/1 [3]	—	—
3956[2]	**Side Bar (60)** (PMooney) **7-10-11v**(5) DJKavanagh (rdn 7th: sn t.o: p.u bef next)		P	25/1	—	—
3114[P]	**Sausalito Boy (72)** (RJSmith) **9-11-2** CMaude (ref to r: t.n.p)		R	50/1	—	—
				(SP 119.1%)	**9 Rn**	

5m 37.5 (8.50) CSF £6.94 TOTE £1.40: £1.10 £2.60 £10.10 (£10.20) Trio £153.10 OWNER Mr Lynn Wilson (LAMBOURN) BRED Martyn J. McEnery

3848 Who Is Equiname (IRE), best ridden up with the pace, jumped soundly and took command from three out, being able to ease down in the last fifty yards. (4/11)
3736 Volleyball (IRE) looks a tricky ride, for he was held up some way off the pace apparently travelling well but, having cruised into second place, his pilot finally asked for a response and none was forthcoming. (16/1)
Derrys Prerogative, who looked particularly well in his coat despite appearing to just need the race, did much better than on his chasing debut, showing his first signs of promise in the process. (66/1)
3836 Chiappucci (IRE) did not impress with his jumping and looked a hard ride. (20/1)
3998* Sorciere, a rangy chasing type, made a bad mistake when losing the lead to the winner and stopped to nothing in the last half mile. (9/2)
Smart Casanova is out of a good racemare in I'm Smart, but unfortunately he appears to have inherited none of her ability. (50/1)
4083 Full Shilling (USA) (12/1: op 6/1)

4233 FLORE NOVICES' H'CAP HURDLE (0-100) (4-Y.O+) (Class E)
3-20 (3-25) **2m 5f (11 hdls)** £2,132.50 (£595.00: £287.50) GOING minus 0.29 sec per fur (GF)

				SP	RR	SF
4220[4]	**Sharp Command (95)** (PEccles) **4-11-9**(5) XAizpuru (hld up: hdwy 7th: led appr 3 out: pushed out)	—	1	5/1 [2]	83	18
3967[4]	**Hancock (77)** (JHetherton) **5-11-3** APMcCoy (hld up: hdwy 6th: chsd wnr fr 3 out: hit next: no imp)	10	2	3/1 [1]	57	—
4089[8]	**Ecu de France (IRE) (60)** (PCRitchens) **7-10-0v** SFox (wl bhd tl r.o fr 3 out)	30	3	33/1	18	—
3750[3]	**Bob's Ploy (82)** (MHTompkins) **5-11-8** RichardGuest (stdd s: hdwy 7th: wknd 3 out)	15	4	11/2 [3]	28	—

Form	Horse (details)	Dist	Pos	SP	RR	SF
3949*	**Bowden Surprise (65)** (RJBaker) **7-10-5** VSlattery (s.s: nvr nr ldrs)	8	5	10/1	5	—
4163[9]	**Millers Goldengirl (IRE) (60)** (MrsSJSmith) **6-9-9**(5) GFRyan (bhd fr 7th)	dist	6	33/1	—	—
3844[4]	**Carly-J (67)** (FSJackson) **6-10-7b[1]** MrNKent (lw: plld hrd: prom to 7th: sn wknd: p.u bef 2 out)		P	20/1	—	—
3985*	**Polo Pony (IRE) (67)** (JohnUpson) **5-10-7** JSupple (lw: sn rdn along: a bhd: p.u bef 2 out)		P	13/2	—	—
3295[11]	**Supremo (IRE) (68)** (MJWilkinson) **8-10-8** WMarston (lw: hld up: rdn & hdwy 5th: wknd 8th: p.u bef 2 out)		P	20/1	—	—
3958[4]	**An Spailpin Fanach (IRE) (81)** (DRGandolfo) **8-11-7b** RDunwoody (prom to 5th: wknd qckly: p.u bef 7th)		P	9/1	—	—
4102[5]	**Benji (60)** (TCasey) **6-10-0b** JAMcCarthy (lw: chsd ldrs to 6th: bhd whn p.u bef 2 out)		P	25/1	—	—
3983[5]	**Worthy Memories (70)** (MrsMerritaJones) **8-10-10** DerekByrne (led: hit 3rd: hdd appr 3 out: wknd appr next: p.u bef last)		P	10/1	—	—
3964[9]	**Swift Pokey (60)** (DLWilliams) **7-9-7**(7) MrSDurack (lw: prom to 4th: sn bhd: t.o whn p.u bef 2 out)		P	33/1	—	—
				(SP 120.8%)	**13 Rn**	

5m 12.6 (10.60) CSF £17.41 CT £403.94 TOTE £5.70: £2.40 £1.30 £13.00 (£7.60) Trio £275.80 OWNER Mr A. P. Holland (LAMBOURN) BRED Coral'S Farm and Stud

LONG HANDICAP Ecu de France (IRE) 9-7 Benji 9-8 Millers Goldengirl (IRE) 9-13 Swift Pokey 9-6

WEIGHT FOR AGE 4yo-7lb

4220 Sharp Command, who apparently gurgled when beaten two days earlier, proved an impressive winner with his tongue tied down. (5/1: op 5/2)

3967 Hancock was the only one to give the winner any sort of a race but was getting nowhere when jumping two out in the manner of a tired horse. He certainly has the ability to win in this grade. (3/1)

2036 Ecu de France (IRE) once again just stayed on better than beaten horses. (33/1)

3750 Bob's Ploy was a real disappointment as he was close enough and still going well at the bottom of the hill but ground to a halt on the climb. (11/2)

3949* Bowden Surprise lost at least ten lengths at the start and never looked like progressing from the rear. (10/1: op 5/1)

An Spailpin Fanach (IRE) (9/1: op 6/1)

3983 Worthy Memories (10/1: 12/1-8/1)

4234 TORT H'CAP CHASE (0-115) (5-Y.O+) (Class E)

3-50 (3-54) **3m 1f (18 fncs)** £3,137.00 (£941.00: £453.00: £209.00) GOING minus 0.29 sec per fur (GF)

Form	Horse (details)	Dist	Pos	SP	RR	SF
3886[7]	**Supposin (85)** (MrsSJSmith) **9-10-10** RichardGuest (hdwy 6th: led appr last: rdn clr)	—	1	10/1	100	15
3961[2]	**Lay it Off (IRE) (82)** (JGO'Neill) **8-10-7** SCurran (lw: led: blnd 7th: hdd appr 2 out: kpt on)	8	2	7/2[2]	92	7
3354[5]	**Furry Fox (IRE) (78)** (RCurtis) **9-10-3** DMorris (hld up: hdwy 11th: kpt on appr 2 out)	4	3	6/1	85	—
3956*	**Dream Leader (IRE) (79)** (MJRoberts) **7-10-4** JRailton (lw: prom: hit 5th & 13th: led appr 2 out: wknd & hdd appr last)	4	4	6/1	84	—
3911[3]	**Reapers Rock (79)** (MrsSJSmith) **10-9-13**(5) GFRyan (mstkes 2nd & 7th: sn rdn: a bhd)	25	5	13/2	68	—
	Mischievous Girl (75) (RTate) **9-10-0** MrsFNeedham (bit bkwd: chsd ldrs: mstke 5th: wknd 14th)	dist	6	33/1	—	—
3961[7]	**Woodlands Genhire (77)** (PAPritchard) **12-10-2b** CLlewellyn (prom: rdn 9th: wknd next: t.o whn p.u bef last)		P	25/1	—	—
4148[2]	**Royal Saxon (92)** (PBowen) **11-11-3** RJohnson (lw: prom to 7th: sn wknd: p.u bef 11th: lame)		P	5/1[3]	—	—
3903[2]	**Postman's Path (98)** (CaptTAForster) **11-11-9** JOsborne (prom to 10th: p.u bef 3 out: b.b.v)		P	100/30[1]	—	—
1209[3]	**Jim Valentine (99)** (DJWintle) **11-11-10** WMarston (hld up: hdwy 9th: 5th whn blnd & uns rdr 2 out)		U	7/1	—	—
				(SP 132.2%)	**10 Rn**	

6m 23.3 (8.30) CSF £47.91 CT £223.87 TOTE £14.70: £3.60 £1.90 £3.10 (£34.60) Trio £202.90 OWNER Mr J. Kemp (BINGLEY) BRED Mrs E. M. Gauvain

LONG HANDICAP Mischievous Girl 9-9

2652 Supposin is not consistent but stiff tracks and fast ground appear to bring out the best in him. (10/1: 8/1-12/1)

3961 Lay it Off (IRE) was stretching the field in the first mile before a dreadful mistake brought her back to the pack. It might have been a different story without that mistake. (7/2)

3354 Furry Fox (IRE), patiently ridden, kept on trying to the line but without finding the necessary speed. (6/1)

3956* Dream Leader (IRE) made the mistake of kicking for home where the climb is at its steepest and paid the penalty going to the last. There are races to be won with him off this sort of mark. (6/1: op 4/1)

3911 Reapers Rock was never going after a dreadful early mistake. (13/2)

3903 Postman's Path may not have been suited by the ground, which seemed looser on top than at the previous meeting, but eventually pulled up with a broken blood-vessel. (100/30)

4235 DUSTON H'CAP CHASE (0-115) (5-Y.O+) (Class E)

4-20 (4-22) **2m 110y (12 fncs)** £3,000.50 (£899.00: £432.00: £198.50) GOING minus 0.29 sec per fur (GF)

Form	Horse (details)	Dist	Pos	SP	RR	SF
3999*	**Mr Snaggle (IRE) (89)** (SEarle) **8-10-10** RJohnson (hld up: hdwy 4 out: led flat: rdn clr nr fin)	—	1	9/2[1]	98	31
1465[P]	**Crackling Frost (IRE) (83)** (MrsDHaine) **9-9-11**(7)ow4 MrRWakley (prom: led 7th tl flat: unable qckn)	2	2	12/1	90	19
4000*	**Monks Jay (IRE) (93)** (GThorner) **8-11-0** CMaude (chsd ldrs tl blnd & lost pl 4 out: r.o wl appr last)	6	3	11/2[2]	94	27
3839[2]	**The Carrot Man (107)** (PWinkworth) **9-12-0** PHide (lw: chsd ldrs: no hdwy fr 3 out)	1¼	4	9/2[1]	107	40
4157[4]	**Count Barachois (USA) (79)** (MrsEHHeath) **9-10-0** DGallagher (led 3rd to 7th: ev ch 3 out: wknd next)	2½	5	14/1	77	10
72*	**Nadjati (USA) (102)** (DRGandolfo) **8-11-9b** RDunwoody (a bhd)	dist	6	9/2[1]	—	—
3903[3]	**Artic Wings (IRE) (105)** (OBrennan) **9-11-12** MBrennan (lw: fell 4th: dead)		F	6/1[3]	—	—
3905[2]	**Parliamentarian (IRE) (79)** (TCasey) **8-10-0b** JOsborne (chsd ldrs: hit 2nd: mstke 3 out: sn wknd: p.u bef last)		P	6/1[3]	—	—
4131[5]	**Young Alfie (79)** (JFPanvert) **12-10-0b** CLlewellyn (lw: led to 3rd: bhd fr 7th: p.u bef 3 out)		P	33/1	—	—
2664[P]	**Hugh Daniels (79)** (CJHemsley) **9-10-0** SCurran (blnd 4 out: t.o whn p.u bef 2 out)		P	50/1	—	—
3956[U]	**Nautical George (IRE) (79)** (JohnUpson) **7-10-0** JSupple (bhd tl blnd & uns rdr 5th)		U	16/1	—	—
				(SP 123.6%)	**11 Rn**	

4m 3.5 (1.50) CSF £54.16 CT £284.88 TOTE £5.00: £2.00 £2.70 £2.60 (£51.10) Trio £87.10 OWNER The Plum Merchants (STURMINSTER NEWTON) BRED Mrs W. H. Young

LONG HANDICAP Count Barachois (USA) 9-13 Crackling Frost (IRE) 9-12 Young Alfie 9-7 Hugh Daniels 9-0 Nautical George (IRE) 9-12

3999* Mr Snaggle (IRE), off the same mark as when winning here last time he ran over fences was, nevertheless, worse off with the runner-up that day, Parliamentarian. He is not an easy horse for the handicapper as he needs to be held on to as long as possible and won this with something to spare. (9/2)

1012 Crackling Frost (IRE) caught the eye with some fine leaps but could not quicken with the winner. (12/1)

4000* Monks Jay (IRE) was fractionally outpaced when ploughing through the fourth last but the way he finished suggests he would have gone close but for the mistake. (11/2)

3839 The Carrot Man has been consistently beaten off this sort of mark and could make little impact. (9/2)

4157 Count Barachois (USA), unable to dominate, finally gave up on the rise to the second last. (14/1)

4236 NOBOTTLE H'CAP HURDLE (0-105) (4-Y.O+) (Class F)

4-50 (4-50) **2m (8 hdls)** £2,034.50 (£567.00: £273.50) GOING minus 0.29 sec per fur (GF)

				SP	RR	SF
3923²	**Antiguan Flyer (78)** (GProdromou) **8-10-10v** APMcCoy (mde all: sn clr: hit 2 out: hld on wl appr last)	—	1	3/1 ¹	61	28
3904³	**Steve Ford (88)** (CPMorlock) **8-11-6** JAMcCarthy (hld up: hdwy 5th: sn chsng wnr: rdn & no imp appr last)	7	2	7/2 ³	64	31
3904⁷	**Positivo (73)** (MissCJECaroe) **6-10-5** DLeahy (bhd: hdwy 3 out: nvr nr ldrs)	20	3	7/1	29	—
4071²	**Va Utu (84)** (DMLloyd) **9-10-13**(3) SophieMitchell (prom to 5th)	13	4	7/1	27	—
3829*	**Suranom (IRE) (92)** (MrsDHaine) **5-11-10** JFTitley (lw: chsd wnr tl lost pl appr 5th: no ch after)	20	5	100/30 ²	15	—
3448P	**Birthplace (IRE) (68)** (RTate) **7-9-9**(5) DJKavanagh (lw: nvr nr to chal)	8	6	25/1	—	—
3976⁴	**Eurolink the Rebel (USA) (80)** (SBClark) **5-10-5**(7) MissRClark (hdwy appr 4th: wknd 3 out)	1½	7	12/1	—	—
4163⁷	**Bally Wonder (68)** (MrsEHHeath) **5-10-0** JSupple (prom to 4th)	½	8	33/1	—	—
4071⁶	**Jewel Thief (74)** (GBBalding) **7-9-13v**(7) MrEBabington (t.o fr 5th)	dist	9	16/1	—	—
1825R	**Antartictern (USA) (71)** (GROldroyd) **7-10-3v** GCahill (lw: bhd tl swvd lft & uns rdr 4th)		U	16/1	—	—

(SP 121.5%) **10 Rn**

3m 47.8 (1.80) CSF £13.70 CT £63.63 TOTE £4.00: £2.00 £1.50 £1.20 (£7.50) Trio £24.80 OWNER Mr George Prodromou (EAST HARLING) BRED Crest Stud Ltd

LONG HANDICAP Bally Wonder 9-2 Birthplace (IRE) 9-6

3923 Antiguan Flyer, whose latest effort at Fakenham looks much better since Sir Dante's win in the E.B.F Final, tore off in front and the only time the runner-up got close was when McCoy gave him a breather. He can win again as this track is surely stiffer than would be ideal. (3/1: op 9/2)

3904 Steve Ford looked a danger turning into the straight, but had been allowed to get so close on sufferance. He will not always be meeting a rival in such good form. (7/2)

3904 Positivo might have been improved by this well-watered ground but stayed on past stragglers when the race was over. (7/1: op 12/1)

4071 Va Utu is in good form at present and the fact that he was beaten so far, says much for the first two. (7/1: op 9/2)

3829* Suranom (IRE) stopped dramatically at halfway as if something was amiss, the situation being accepted. Shaken up again late in the day, he came home with a flourish. (100/30)

3976 Eurolink the Rebel (USA) (12/1: op 9/2)

T/Plpt: £231.90 (54.81 Tckts). T/Qdpt: £35.50 (28.62 Tckts) Dk

4082-CHEPSTOW (L-H) (Good to firm, Firm ptchs)

Tuesday April 22nd

WEATHER: fine

4237 REYNARD NOVICES' CHASE (5-Y.O+) (Class E)

2-40 (2-41) **2m 3f 110y (16 fncs)** £3,041.00 (£856.00: £413.00) GOING minus 0.56 sec per fur (F)

				SP	RR	SF
	Plan-A (IRE) (RHAlner) **7-11-0** PHolley (lw: hld up: hdwy 5 out: hit 2 out: mstke last: hrd rdn to ld flat: r.o)	—	1	3/1 ³	71	15
3602⁴	**Nordic Valley (IRE) (85)** (MCPipe) **6-11-12** APMcCoy (hld up: mstke 1st: hdwy appr 6th: mstke 9th (water): hit 2 out: chal whn blnd last: r.o)	1	2	13/8 ¹	82	26
2704P	**Golden Drum (IRE) (69)** (TRGeorge) **7-11-0b** TJMurphy (pckd 1st: sn chsng ldr: rdn 4 out: led 3 out: hit 2 out: hdd flat)	1¾	3	12/1	69	13
3891⁵	**Sound Carrier (USA) (80)** (CLPopham) **9-11-0** SWynne (swtg: led tl mstke 3 out: 4th & wkng whn fell 2 out: dead)		F	2/1 ²	—	—
4072⁴	**Diamond Light** (VRBishop) **10-11-0** MrSLloyd (hit 2nd: wl bhd 5th: t.o whn blnd & uns rdr 4 out)		U	40/1	—	—

(SP 106.6%) **5 Rn**

4m 51.3 (2.30) CSF £7.34 TOTE £4.60: £2.30 £1.10 (£3.30) OWNER Mr R. J. Bullock (BLANDFORD) BRED Matthew James Commins

Plan-A (IRE), who has run out in his last three point-to-points, won the time before and was described by his trainer as being a bit quirky. He was thought to have benefited from going left-handed with professional handling. (3/1)

3602 Nordic Valley (IRE), led in at the start, did not help his cause by some indifferent jumping, particularly at the final fence. (13/8: 4/5-7/4)

1252 Golden Drum (IRE), a brother to Amtrak Express, was run out of it despite making by far the best jump of the three leaders at the last. (12/1: 6/1-14/1)

4238 BETTY'S 90TH BIRTHDAY NOVICES' HURDLE (4, 5 & 6-Y.O F & M) (Class E)

3-10 (3-12) **2m 110y (8 hdls)** £2,262.00 (£632.00: £306.00) GOING minus 0.56 sec per fur (F)

				SP	RR	SF
4175*	**Mrs Em (92)** (PFNicholls) **5-10-13**(7) LCummins (lw: a gng wl: led 4 out: easily)	—	1	1/7 ¹	67+	19
4002P	**Ilewin Janine (IRE) (78)** (PCRitchens) **6-11-0** CMaude (plld hrd: chsd ldr 2nd to 4th: wnt 2nd appr 3 out: no imp)	4	2	9/1 ²	57	9
	Nell Valley (CPEBrooks) **6-11-0** GBradley (tk keen hold: led: sn clr: hdd 4 out: sn wknd)	19	3	9/1 ²	39	—
3764P	**Lunar Gris** (AJChamberlain) **4-10-8** MrJJukes (lost tch fr 2nd: t.o)	dist	4	50/1 ³	—	—

(SP 109.5%) **4 Rn**

3m 50.6 (1.60) CSF £2.15 TOTE £1.10 (£1.80) OWNER Mr G. Z. Mizel (SHEPTON MALLET) BRED Guest Leasing and Bloodstock Co

WEIGHT FOR AGE 4yo-6lb

4175* Mrs Em gave those who had taken the long odds-on no cause for concern during the race. (1/7)

4002 Ilewin Janine (IRE) had been in sellers on her last two outings. (9/1)

4239 WEATHERBYS SPONSORSHIP IN RACING H'CAP CHASE (0-120) (5-Y.O+) (Class D)

3-40 (3-40) **3m 2f 110y (22 fncs)** £3,533.50 (£1,063.00: £514.00: £239.50) GOING minus 0.56 sec per fur (F)

				SP	RR	SF
1983²	**Glenfinn Princess (96)** (PBowen) **9-10-4** WMarston (j.w: tk keen hold: led 6th: sn clr: 10l clr whn eased flat)	—	1	5/2 ²	107+	—
2706P	**Frozen Drop (100)** (PCRitchens) **10-10-8** CMaude (led to 6th: rdn appr 5 out: outpcd appr 3 out: rallied flat: no ch w wnr)	¾	2	100/30 ³	111	—
4054⁶	**All for Luck (120)** (MCPipe) **12-12-0** APMcCoy (lw: j.slowly 1st: hdwy 12th: j.slowly 13th: rallied 17th: sn chsng wnr: btn whn j.rt 2 out & last)	¾	3	2/1 ¹	130	—

			SP	RR	SF
3153P	**Have to Think (119)** (PFNicholls) **9-11-6**(7) MrJTizzard (lw: hld up: hdwy appr 5 out: wknd appr 4 out)...........11	4	7/2	123	—
			(SP 107.2%)		4 Rn

6m 45.3 (15.30) CSF £9.37 TOTE £2.50 (£4.50) OWNER Mr Patrick McGinty (HAVERFORDWEST) BRED H. C. and K. A. James
1983 Glenfinn Princess, who has changed stables, had been breaking blood-vessels but, with the help of Peter Bowen's vet and a haematologist, it appears her blood has been sorted out. (5/2)
2575 Frozen Drop, coming back after a break, is greatly flattered by his margin of defeat. (100/30)
3599 All for Luck, dropped 9lb, is another greatly flattered by his proximity to the winner. (2/1)

4240 HANCOCKS H.B. H'CAP HURDLE (5-Y.O+) (Class B)
4-10 (4-10) **2m 110y (8 hdls)** £4,674.65 (£1,407.20: £681.10: £318.05) GOING minus 0.56 sec per fur (F)

			SP	RR	SF
4053 6	**Ashwell Boy (IRE) (133)** (PJHobbs) **6-10-7** WMarston (lw: hld up: hdwy 4th: hit 4 out: sn outpcd: rallied to ld 2 out: r.o wl)...........—	1	11/8 1	110	31
4164*	**Pridwell (160)** (MCPipe) **7-12-6** 6x APMcCoy (lw: a.p: led 4th to 3 out: wandered appr last: rallied flat)..........1½	2	6/4 2	136	57
4061 15	**Blair Castle (IRE) (126)** (GBBalding) **6-9-9**(5) ABates (hld up: led 3 out to 2 out: one pce)..........2	3	16/1	100?	21
4061 7	**Forestal (126)** (SGGriffiths) **5-10-0** TJMurphy (led to 4th: wknd 3 out: eased whn btn)..........21	4	7/2 3	79	—
			(SP 110.2%)		4 Rn

3m 45.1 (-3.90) CSF £3.66 TOTE £2.30 (£1.90) OWNER A B S Racing (MINEHEAD) BRED William Mangan
LONG HANDICAP Blair Castle (IRE) 9-0 Forestal 9-5
4053 Ashwell Boy (IRE), down 3lb, looked in trouble when the pace quickened, but soon bounced back and now goes for the Swinton Hurdle at Haydock. (11/8)
4164* Pridwell, inclined to shirk the issue between the last two, was trying to concede a lot of weight over a shorter trip. (6/4: evens-13/8)
3816 Blair Castle (IRE), a stone wrong at the weights, showed definite signs of a return of form. (16/1)

4241 DUNRAVEN WINDOWS SOUTH AND WEST WALES POINT-TO-POINT CHAMPIONSHIP HUNTERS' CHASE (6-Y.O+) (Class H)
4-40 (4-40) **3m (18 fncs)** £3,649.00 (£1,102.00: £536.00: £253.00) GOING minus 0.56 sec per fur (F)

			SP	RR	SF
3637 6	**Final Pride** (MrsCHiggon) **11-11-10**(5) MissPJones (lw: mde all: clr 3rd: unchal)..........—	1	2/1 1	108	26
3637P	**Miss Millbrook** (DTGoldsworthy) **9-11-12**(7) MrEWilliams (bhd tl stdy hdwy 8th: wnt 2nd & hit 2 out: no ch w wnr)..........15	2	3/1 2	102	20
3721*	**Busman (IRE)** (KeithPearce) **8-12-3**(7) MrDSJones (hdwy 8th: chsd wnr 12th tl wknd 2 out)..........6	3	6/1 3	103	21
457P	**Wake Up Luv** (RWilliams) **12-11-13**(7) MissPCooper (a.p: hit 5 out: one pce)..........1	4	25/1	98	16
901 7	**The Last Mistress** (AJCook) **10-11-5**(7) MrSShinton (styd on fr 3 out: n.d)..........¾	5	25/1	90	8
	Beinn Mohr (DGWilliams) **10-11-8**(7) MrNRMitchell (hit 2nd: sn bhd: t.o)..........dist	6	16/1	—	—
3680P	**Kingfisher Bay** (OALittle) **12-12-1**(7) MrJJPrice (a bhd: t.o fr 11th)..........dist	7	33/1	—	—
	Plas-Hendy (PMRich) **11-11-10**(7) MrGLewis (chsd wnr to 12th: sn wknd: t.o)..........dist	8	9/1	—	—
	Royal Oats (MissDHarries) **12-11-9**(3) MrMRimell (bhd tl fell 6th)..........	F	33/1	—	—
3593U	**Doubting Donna** (MrsDHughes) **11-11-7**(5) MrJJukes (a bhd: t.o whn p.u bef last)..........	P	10/1	—	—
	Culpeppers Dish (MrsLAParker) **6-11-5**(7) MrAPrice (plld hrd: prom to 5th: t.o whn tried to ref 9th: p.u bef 10th)..........	P	33/1	—	—
			(SP 114.1%)		11 Rn

5m 56.7 (3.70) CSF £6.76 TOTE £3.90: £1.20 £2.20 £1.70 (£6.30) Trio £4.10 OWNER Mr Grahame Barrett (HAVERFORDWEST) BRED J. G. and Mrs Thomas
68 Final Pride, the winner of a ladies' open last time, ran this field ragged under an enterprising ride. (2/1)
3403 Miss Millbrook ideally needs some give in the ground, and found the winner well beyond recall. (3/1)
3721* Busman (IRE) was another who would not have minded some cut in the ground. (6/1)
335 Wake Up Luv had been beaten a distance by the winner at Llanvapley last month. (25/1)
Plas-Hendy (9/1: 12/1-8/1)

4242 SAPLING NOVICES' HURDLE (4, 5 & 6-Y.O) (Class E)
5-10 (5-10) **2m 4f 110y (11 hdls)** £2,234.00 (£624.00: £302.00) GOING minus 0.56 sec per fur (F)

			SP	RR	SF
4173*	**Country Lover (103)** (MCPipe) **6-11-12v** APMcCoy (hld up: chal on bit appr last: shkn up & qcknd to ld flat: cleverly)..........—	1	4/5 1	83+	31
4095 2	**Name of Our Father (USA) (99)** (PBowen) **4-10-13** DWalsh (led to flat: nt qckn)..........¾	2	5/4 2	76	17
3818 9	**Don't Mind If I Do (IRE)** (PRWebber) **6-11-0b** CMaude (w ldr: ev ch 4 out: wknd appr 2 out)..........11	3	14/1 3	62	10
	Westfield (AJChamberlain) **5-11-0** DLeahy (hld up: mstke 2nd: hdwy 4 out: wknd 3 out)..........13	4	50/1	52	—
3690 6	**Mr Robstee** (AJChamberlain) **6-11-0** LHarvey (plld hrd: lost tch fr 5th: t.o)..........dist	5	66/1	—	—
			(SP 110.1%)		5 Rn

4m 47.0 (0.00) CSF £1.98 TOTE £1.60: £1.20 £1.10 (£1.10) OWNER Pond House Gold (WELLINGTON) BRED Sir Gordon Brunton
WEIGHT FOR AGE 4yo-7lb
4173* Country Lover was given a peach of a ride and hardly knew he had been in a race. (4/5)
4095 Name of Our Father (USA) was decisively beaten for toe on the run-in. (5/4: op evens)
Don't Mind If I Do (IRE) (14/1: op 6/1)

T/Plpt: £23.20 (417.24 Tckts). T/Qdpt: £8.70 (53.67 Tckts) KH

0699-PERTH (R-H) (Good)
Wednesday April 23rd
WEATHER: overcast & showers

4243 PARTY HAS STARTED MOET & CHANDON MAIDEN HURDLE (I) (4-Y.O+) (Class E)
2-20 (2-21) **2m 4f 110y (10 hdls)** £2,080.00 (£580.00: £280.00) GOING: 0.08 sec per fur (G)

			SP	RR	SF
4075 3	**Pentlands Flyer (IRE)** (HowardJohnson) **6-11-7** PCarberry (cl up: led fr 6th: hit 3 out: easily)..........—	1	7/4 1	64+	10
3794 9	**Menaldi (IRE) (72)** (PCheesbrough) **7-11-7** ASSmith (chsd ldrs fr 5th: ev ch 3 out: sn hrd drvn & one pce)......5	2	12/1	60	6
3932 2	**Saxon Mead (66)** (PJHobbs) **7-11-7b** GTormey (mstkes: led to 6th: sn rdn & one pce)..........6	3	11/2 3	55	1

			Pos	SP	RR	SF
1854[6]	**Raining Stairs (IRE)** (GRichards) **6-11-7** LO'Hara (chsd ldrs: effrt 4 out: rdn & one pce)	2½	**4**	9/4[2]	54	—
3794[11]	**Lord Pat (IRE)** (MissMKMilligan) **6-11-7** RGarritty (mid div: effrt 3 out: no imp)	22	**5**	33/1	36	—
3691[12]	**Rambling Rajah** (MrsSCBradburne) **5-11-0**(7) MrMBradburne (fell 1st)		**F**	10/1	—	—
2954[P]	**Corporal Kirkwood (IRE)** (MartinTodhunter) **7-11-0**(7) CMcCormack (in tch to ½-wy: t.o whn p.u bef 2 out)		**P**	20/1	—	—
3691[13]	**Delightfool** (RNixon) **6-11-2** NBentley (t.o fr 6th: p.u bef 2 out)		**P**	25/1	—	—
	Zoot Money (BMactaggart) **5-11-2** DParker (t.o fr 6th: p.u bef 2 out)		**P**	33/1	—	—
2041[P]	**Guile Point** (DALamb) **6-11-2** JBurke (t.o fr 6th: p.u bef 2 out)		**P**	50/1	—	—
3826[P]	**Prince Baltasar (53)** (NBycroft) **8-11-2**(5) BGrattan (hmpd 1st: a bhd: t.o fr 6th: p.u bef 2 out)		**P**	100/1	—	—
3973[7]	**Red Hot Prince** (MrsJJordan) **6-11-0**(7) LMcGrath (in tch to 5th: sn rdn & t.o: p.u bef 2 out)		**P**	100/1	—	—

(SP 117.7%) **12 Rn**

5m 6.1 (18.10) CSF £20.27 TOTE £2.60: £1.40 £2.80 £1.40 (£17.60) Trio £16.70 OWNER Mrs M. W. Bird (CROOK) BRED Margaret Coakley

4075 Pentlands Flyer (IRE) settled immediately for Carberry and, always on the bridle, won pulling up. (7/4)

3534 Menaldi (IRE) ran well but, try as he might, was never a match for the winner. This was still an improved effort. (12/1: 8/1-14/1)

3932 Saxon Mead has had problems jumping fences, and his hurdling left something to be desired. (11/2)

1854 Raining Stairs (IRE), off the track for well over four months, ran as though this was needed. (9/4)

Rambling Rajah (10/1: 12/1-8/1)

4244 WINIFRED ROYAL MEMORIAL NOVICES' HURDLE (5-Y.O+) (Class E)

2-50 (2-50) **2m 110y (8 hdls)** £2,878.00 (£808.00: £394.00) GOING: 0.08 sec per fur (G)

			Pos	SP	RR	SF
3324[U]	**Tawafij (USA) (87)** (MDHammond) **8-10-12** RGarritty (lw: hld up: hdwy ½-wy: led 2 out: clr & hit last: drvn out)	—	**1**	7/1	68	34
3823*	**Bold Statement (101)** (GMMoore) **5-11-5** NBentley (lw: mde most to 2 out: kpt on u.p flat)	1¾	**2**	3/1[1]	73	39
3888[4]	**Swandale Flyer** (NBycroft) **5-10-7**(5) BGrattan (hld up: hdwy 5th: sn chsng ldrs: kpt on flat)	1¼	**3**	14/1	65	31
3438[4]	**Western General (76)** (MissMKMilligan) **6-10-12** ASSmith (lw: cl up: disp ld 4th to 3 out: one pce fr 2 out)	3	**4**	7/1	62	28
186[9]	**Hand of Straw (IRE)** (MissZAGreen) **5-10-12** KJohnson (bhd: hdwy 5th: styd on: nrst fin)	4	**5**	33/1	58	24
3311[6]	**Nordisk Legend** (MrsDThomson) **5-10-12** TReed (bhd: hdwy 5th: nvr rchd ldrs)	12	**6**	100/1	47	13
3668[4]	**The Stuffed Puffin (IRE) (95)** (CJMann) **5-10-12** JRailton (chsd ldrs tl wknd appr 2 out)	3½	**7**	6/1[2]	43	9
3937[7]	**Ramstown Lad (IRE)** (KCBailey) **8-10-12** SMcNeill (in tch: effrt 5th: sn outpcd)	4	**8**	33/1	39	5
3990[6]	**Border Image** (FPMurtagh) **6-10-9**(3) ECallaghan (nvr bttr than mid div)	3	**9**	25/1	37	3
4056[7]	**Maple Bay (IRE) (90)** (BEllison) **8-10-12**(7) CMcCormack (in tch to 5th)	3	**10**	16/1	41	7
3888[F]	**Just Whistle** (MissMKMilligan) **5-10-7** FPerratt (prom to 5th)	17	**11**	150/1	12	—
3883[6]	**Swift Riposte (IRE) (100)** (PMonteith) **6-11-5** TJenks (blnd 2nd: hrd drvn 5th: no ch whn hit 3 out)	20	**12**	13/2[3]	5	—
3529[4]	**Lumback Lady (90)** (BMactaggart) **7-10-7** BStorey (chsd ldrs to 5th: sn lost pl)	5	**13**	6/1[2]	—	—
3973[P]	**Hunting Slane** (CGrant) **5-10-12b**[1] JCallaghan (a rr div)	½	**14**	100/1	—	—
4184[P]	**Minnies Turn** (WTKemp) **6-10-7** SMcDougall (cl up to 5th: sn wknd)	19	**15**	200/1	—	—
3828[15]	**High Celleste (IRE)** (MartinTodhunter) **6-10-7** MMoloney (rdn & wknd 4th: p.u bef 3 out)		**P**	100/1	—	—
1579[11]	**Chinook's Daughter (IRE)** (GRichards) **5-10-7** LO'Hara (prom tl rdn & wknd 5th: p.u bef 3 out)		**P**	50/1	—	—

(SP 120.3%) **17 Rn**

3m 53.0 (7.00) CSF £24.83 TOTE £5.50: £1.70 £1.70 £2.90 (£6.40) Trio £57.70 OWNER Mr Stephen Laidlaw (MIDDLEHAM) BRED Oxford Stable

OFFICIAL EXPLANATION **Lumback Lady: had injured her hind legs.**

3098 Tawafij (USA), well suited by this sharp track, did just enough when in front. (7/1)

3823* Bold Statement was always struggling to lead on this sharper track and, to give him credit, after looking well beaten he battled back. (3/1)

3888 Swandale Flyer is showing a liking for this game and is worth keeping in mind. (14/1)

3438 Western General is running consistently well at the moment. (7/1: 5/1-8/1)

Hand of Straw (IRE), who ran well in a Flat race last week, showed he is on good terms with himself again here. (33/1)

Nordisk Legend had shown nothing previously but there were signs of hope here. (100/1)

3668 The Stuffed Puffin (IRE) travels well but is disappointing once off the bridle. (6/1)

3883 Swift Riposte (IRE) almost fell at the second and was never happy thereafter. This is best ignored. (13/2)

4245 GLENGOYNE HIGHLAND MALT TAMEROSIA SERIES FINAL NOVICES' CHASE (5-Y.O+) (Class B)

3-20 (3-20) **3m (18 fncs)** £7,064.00 (£2,132.00: £1,036.00: £488.00) GOING: 0.08 sec per fur (G)

			Pos	SP	RR	SF
3882*	**Colonel In Chief (IRE) (120)** (GRichards) **7-11-12** PCarberry (unruly in paddock: mstke 2nd: a chsng ldrs: chal 14th: led 3 out: styd on u.p)	—	**1**	15/8[1]	106	43
4078*	**Ask Me Later (IRE) (87)** (MrsSCBradburne) **8-11-12** MFoster (in tch: hdwy 12th: sn ev ch: outpcd 3 out: kpt on wl flat)	¾	**2**	11/1[2]	106	43
3726*	**River Unshion (IRE) (98)** (HowardJohnson) **7-11-12** ASSmith (lw: hld up: hdwy & prom 11th: ch & effrt 4 out: styd on one pce)	1½	**3**	12/1[3]	105	42
4186[3]	**Kings Sermon (IRE) (89)** (PBeaumont) **8-11-12** RSupple (in tch: outpcd 4 out: hit 3 out & 2 out: styd on flat: nrst fin)	1¾	**4**	14/1	103	40
3409[F]	**Jac Del Prince (64)** (PFNicholls) **7-11-5** PHide (mde most to 3 out: wknd)	13	**5**	66/1	88	25
4203*	**Chopwell Curtains (115)** (TDEasterby) **7-11-12b** LWyer (lw: in tch: j.slowly 7th: fell 12th)		**F**	15/8[1]	—	—
3909*	**Tough Test (IRE) (86)** (MrsJDGoodfellow) **7-11-9** GCahill (cl up: disp ld 10th to 12th: wkng whn hit 14th: p.u bef 3 out)		**P**	16/1	—	—
4078[2]	**Nijway (80)** (MABarnes) **7-11-12** PNiven (lw: in tch to 12th: sn wknd: p.u bef 3 out)		**P**	25/1	—	—
3715*	**Kalajo (95)** (BMactaggart) **7-11-12** BStorey (lw: a bhd: outpcd ½-wy: t.o whn p.u bef 3 out)		**P**	12/1[3]	—	—
938[F]	**Kincardine Bridge (USA)** (MrsSCBradburne) **8-11-5** MrMBradburne (cl up to 12th: wknd qckly: p.u bef 14th)		**P**	100/1	—	—
3824[P]	**Two For One (IRE) (67)** (MissLucindaRussell) **8-11-5** TReed (sn bhd: drvn along ½-wy: t.o whn p.u bef 2 out)		**P**	100/1	—	—

(SP 113.2%) **11 Rn**

6m 10.2 (12.20) CSF £21.21 TOTE £3.00: £1.10 £2.10 £3.50 (£12.00) Trio £64.80 OWNER Mr Robert Ogden (PENRITH) BRED John Noonan

3882* Colonel In Chief (IRE), happy with the rain that fell during the afternoon, was given a most positive ride and was always doing just enough. (15/8)

4078* Ask Me Later (IRE) gave the impression that the stiffer the test the better he will like it. (11/1)

3726* River Unshion (IRE) was facing his stiffest task to date here and ran well. This was probably his best-ever performance. (12/1)

4186 Kings Sermon (IRE) was always finding this track on the sharp side, but he kept on most determinedly in the closing stages. (14/1)

3181 Jac Del Prince runs his best races out in front, but his limitations were well exposed from the third last. (66/1)

4203* Chopwell Curtains had a long look at one fence, but was still going well enough when falling at the first fence on the final circuit. (15/8)

4246 BALLATHIE HOUSE HOTEL H'CAP HURDLE (0-120) (4-Y.O+) (Class D)

3-50 (3-50) **2m 110y (8 hdls)** £3,785.00 (£1,130.00: £540.00: £245.00) GOING: 0.08 sec per fur (G)

Form	Horse	Dist	Pos	SP	RR	SF
4061^{9}	**Amlah (USA) (110)** (PJHobbs) **5-11-6** BPowell (lw: cl up: led 3 out: styd on wl)	—	1	$5/1^{2}$	92	45
3584^{2}	**Durano (110)** (TDEasterby) **6-11-6** LWyer (lw: chsd ldrs: outpcd 5th: kpt on wl fr 2 out)	2	2	$100/30^{1}$	90	43
4187^{4}	**Rachael's Owen (90)** (CWeedon) **7-9-9**(5) RMcGrath (lw: in tch: hdwy 3 out: kpt on u.p: nt pce to chal)	hd	3	20/1	70	23
2764*	**Stash the Cash (IRE) (118)** (MDHammond) **6-12-0** RGarritty (in tch: effrt 3 out: sn chsng ldrs: one pce fr next)	6	4	$5/1^{2}$	92	45
3995^{2}	**Anabranch (110)** (JMJefferson) **6-11-3**(3) ECallaghan (chsd ldrs: wnt 2nd 3 out: wknd between last 2)	4	5	$6/1^{3}$	80	33
1502^{3}	**Sarmatian (USA) (112)** (MDHammond) **6-11-1**(7) NHorrocks (in tch: effrt 3 out: wknd next)	dist	6	9/1	—	—
3995^{5}	**Bures (IRE) (107)** (MrsJBrown) **6-11-3** PCarberry (led to 3 out: sn wknd & eased: t.o)	dist	7	11/1	—	—
3816^{5}	**Radanpour (IRE) (111)** (HowardJohnson) **5-11-7** ASSmith (a rr div: t.o)	½	8	12/1	—	—
4079^{4}	**Astraleon (IRE) (103)** (RAllan) **9-10-6**(7) SMelrose (a bhd: t.o whn p.u bef last)		P	14/1	—	—
3398^{9}	**Common Sound (IRE) (94)** (JBarclay) **6-10-4** BStorey (lost tch fr 5th: t.o whn p.u bef 2 out)		P	20/1	—	—

(SP 112.9%) **10 Rn**

3m 52.1 (6.10) CSF £19.81 CT £272.57 TOTE £6.00: £1.30 £1.70 £2.40 (£23.10) Trio £141.40; £101.58 to Beverley 24/4/97 OWNER In Touch Racing Club (MINEHEAD) BRED Barbara Hunter

LONG HANDICAP Rachael's Owen 9-9

OFFICIAL EXPLANATION **Common Sound (IRE): was coughing after the race.**

456 Amlah (USA) ran well in a good race last time and, finding this much more to his liking, won authoritatively. (5/1)

3584 Durano ran as though this trip on this track was on the sharp side, but he was really sticking on in good style at the end. (100/30)

4187 Rachael's Owen is running well at the moment, and this was not a bad effort from 5lb wrong. (20/1)

2764* Stash the Cash (IRE), from a yard that is just coming back to form, ran well considering this was his first outing for three months. (5/1)

3995 Anabranch showed up well but seems to have stiffish tasks at present. (6/1)

3995 Bures (IRE) (11/1: 8/1-12/1)

3816 Radanpour (IRE) (12/1: op 7/1)

4247 SHEPHERD & WEDDERBURN H'CAP CHASE (0-125) (5-Y.O+) (Class D)

4-20 (4-20) **2m 4f 110y (15 fncs)** £4,890.00 (£1,470.00: £710.00: £330.00) GOING: 0.08 sec per fur (G)

Form	Horse	Dist	Pos	SP	RR	SF
3886^{4}	**Acajou III (FR) (105)** (GRichards) **9-10-13** PCarberry (mstkes: mde all: eased flat)	—	1	$11/2^{3}$	123+	32
4186^{2}	**Nicholas Plant (95)** (JSGoldie) **8-10-3** GCahill (lw: a.p: ev ch 4 out: blnd 3 out: no imp after)	5	2	$7/4^{1}$	109	18
4185^{F}	**Seod Rioga (IRE) (116)** (SMellor) **8-11-5**(5) ChrisWebb (lw: hld up: hdwy & prom 9th: blnd 11th: sn wknd)	21	3	$5/2^{2}$	114	23
3974^{2}	**Deep Decision (97)** (PCheesbrough) **11-10-5** ASSmith (chsd ldrs: drvn along 10th: wl outpcd fr 4 out)	5	4	6/1	91	—
3886^{F}	**Chill Wind (92)** (NBycroft) **8-10-0** MFoster (chsd ldrs: outpcd 10th: blnd next: sn wknd)	18	5	7/1	72	—
4145^{3}	**Rebel King (92)** (MABarnes) **7-9-9**(5) STaylor (drvn along & lost tch 8th: sn wl bhd)	8	6	50/1	66	—

(SP 109.1%) **6 Rn**

5m 9.0 (10.00) CSF £13.95 TOTE £6.70: £3.00 £1.10 (£12.00) OWNER Mr Robert Ogden (PENRITH) BRED Philippe Achard

LONG HANDICAP Chill Wind 9-10 Rebel King 8-13

3886 Acajou III (FR), particularly well handled, made plenty of mistakes but he kept going as his rivals blundered their chances away. (11/2)

4186 Nicholas Plant is getting into the habit of finishing second and, after looking very dangerous, he made a terrible blunder three out which put paid to him. (7/4)

4185 Seod Rioga (IRE) had just moved up to look a real threat when he blundered at the fifth last, and that stopped him in his tracks. (5/2)

3974 Deep Decision has not won for over a year and put up little fight on this occasion. (6/1)

3886 Chill Wind seems to save his best for Carlisle and ran poorly this time. (7/1)

4248 NEWMILN COUNTRY ESTATE AMATEUR H'CAP HURDLE (0-115) (4-Y.O+) (Class E)

4-50 (4-50) **3m 110y (12 hdls)** £3,408.50 (£1,028.00: £499.00: £234.50) GOING: 0.08 sec per fur (G)

Form	Horse	Dist	Pos	SP	RR	SF
3912^{4}	**Peggy Gordon (85)** (MrsDThomson) **6-9-9**(5) MissPRobson (hdwy ½-wy: led between last 2: r.o wl)	—	1	25/1	69?	—
3795^{3}	**Grosvenor (IRE) (95)** (GRichards) **6-10-3**(7)ow3 MrJTizzard (lw: a.p: styd on fr 2 out: nt pce of wnr)	3½	2	$8/1^{2}$	77	5
3697^{F}	**Country Store (95)** (APJones) **8-10-3**(7)ow9 MrEJames (led to 4th: led 3 out tl between last 2: no ex)	4	3	16/1	74	—
3971^{5}	**Valiant Dash (85)** (JSGoldie) **11-9-7**(7) MrOMcPhail (cl up: led 6th to 4 out: one pce fr 2 out)	¾	4	12/1	64	—
4081^{4}	**Old Habits (IRE) (98)** (JLEyre) **8-10-8**(5) MrMHNaughton (lw: cl up: led 4 out to 3 out: wknd next)	8	5	12/1	71	2
3825*	**Enchanted Cottage (93)** (JMJefferson) **5-10-1**(7)ow3 MrMBradburne (hdwy & prom ½-wy: one pce fr 2 out)	3½	6	$5/1^{1}$	64	—
3882^{4}	**Dorlin Castle (88)** (LLungo) **9-9-10**(7) MrBGibson (a in tch: effrt 3 out: one pce)	6	7	$8/1^{2}$	55	—
3886^{3}	**Pariah (IRE) (96)** (MartinTodhunter) **8-10-6**(5) MrRHale (lw: hld up & bhd: hdwy & in tch 3 out: sn btn)	12	8	$8/1^{2}$	55	—
1866^{4}	**Able Player (USA) (94)** (KJDrewry) **10-10-2**(7)ow8 MrKDrewry (outpcd & lost tch ½-wy: n.d after)	10	9	16/1	47	—
3962^{2}	**Stac-Pollaidh (85)** (KCBailey) **7-9-7**(7) MrRForristal (prom tl wknd fr 4 out)	1¼	10	$10/1^{3}$	37	—
3915^{7}	**Father O'Brien (90)** (JCPoulton) **10-9-12**(7) MrJGoldstein (nvr trbld ldrs)	9	11	16/1	36	—
3096^{8}	**Frisky Thyne (IRE) (86)** (MDHammond) **8-9-12**(3)ow1 MrCBonner (lost tch fr 4 out)	nk	12	33/1	32	—
3698^{3}	**Lord Mcmurrough (IRE) (113)** (JNeville) **7-11-7**(7) MrEWilliams (hdwy ½-wy: sn prom: wknd qckly 3 out)	2	13	$8/1^{2}$	58	—
4147^{3}	**Blooming Spring (IRE) (86)** (MrsDThomson) **8-9-8**(7)ow1 MrsJeanMcGregor (a bhd)	3½	14	25/1	28	—
3157^{P}	**Dig Deeper (89)** (RAllan) **10-9-11**(7) MrMJRuddy (cl up: led 4th to 6th: wknd 8th)	5	15	16/1	28	—
4078^{F}	**Festival Fancy (85)** (BMactaggart) **10-9-7**(7) MrDRMcLeod (a bhd)	¾	16	33/1	24	—
3910^{14}	**Busy Boy (85)** (DALamb) **10-9-7**(7) MissSLamb (sn bhd)	17	17	100/1	13	—
3395^{5}	**White Diamond (105)** (MissLucindaRussell) **9-10-13**(7)ow20 MrTScott (sn bhd: t.o)	dist	18	33/1	—	—
3646^{8}	**New Charges (93)** (PBeaumont) **10-10-1**(7)ow4 MrTJBarry (lost tch fr ½-wy: t.o whn p.u bef 2 out)		P	12/1	—	—
	Persian View (IRE) (98) (KCBailey) **7-10-6**(7) MrRWakley (ref to r: t.n.p)		R	16/1	—	—

(SP 140.2%) **20 Rn**

6m 4.3 (18.30) CSF £209.37 CT £3,081.50 TOTE £23.40: £3.30 £2.60 £5.20 £3.10 (£51.20) Trio Not won; £368.12 to Beverley 24/4/97 OWNER Frank Flynn and Richard Madden (MILNATHORT) BRED Mrs M. D. Young

LONG HANDICAP Frisky Thyne (IRE) 9-10 Peggy Gordon 8-13 Stac-Pollaidh 9-7 Festival Fancy 9-13 Busy Boy 8-5 White Diamond 9-13 Blooming Spring (IRE) 9-0 Valiant Dash 9-12

3641 Peggy Gordon likes this track and, despite being 15lb out of the handicap, won in useful style. (25/1)

3795 Grosvenor (IRE) seems to stay well enough but is short of a turn of foot. (8/1)

1947 Country Store, back to hurdling after failing to complete over fences recently, ran a fair race but was just outstayed. (16/1)

805 Valiant Dash stays forever, but has been lightly raced this season and may just have needed this. (12/1)

4081 Old Habits (IRE) was not helped by the rain during the afternoon, and failed to last the trip out. (12/1: op 8/1)
3825* Enchanted Cottage has risen 15lb so far this season and, coupled with the extra distance here, he was found out. (5/1)

4249 PARTY HAS STARTED MOET & CHANDON MAIDEN HURDLE (II) (4-Y.O+) (Class E)

5-20 (5-20) **2m 4f 110y (10 hdls)** £2,080.00 (£580.00: £280.00) GOING: 0.08 sec per fur (G)

	Horse	Details	Dist	Pos	SP	RR	SF
3315F	**Royal York**	(GRichards) **5-11-2** PCarberry (lw: hld up: stdy hdwy fr ½-wy: led 2 out: rdn & r.o)	—	**1**	11/10 1	65	5
41887	**Birkdale (IRE)**	(LLungo) **6-11-7** RSupple (in tch: effrt 3 out: ev ch next: nt qckn flat)	1¾	**2**	10/1	69	9
36126	**Beau Matelot (78)**	(MissMKMilligan) **5-11-7** ASSmith (lw: hdwy ½-wy: sn chsng ldrs: nt qckn fr 2 out)	17	**3**	8/1 3	55	—
3048P	**Granham Pride (IRE)**	(KCBailey) **7-11-7** SMcNeill (prom: effrt 4 out: one pce fr next)	½	**4**	7/2 2	55	—
42054	**Cottstown Boy (IRE)**	(MrsSCBradburne) **6-11-7** MFoster (chsd ldrs: led 4 out to 2 out: sn outpcd)	6	**5**	8/1 3	50	—
168310	**Careysville (IRE) (59)**	(TRGeorge) **6-11-7** PNiven (chsd ldr: led 6th to 4 out: wknd fr next: t.o)	dist	**6**	16/1	—	—
379512	**Weejumpawud**	(MrsJStorey) **7-11-2** MrCStorey (in tch tl outpcd fr 6th: t.o)	16	**7**	66/1	—	—
	Hydropic	(MABarnes) **10-11-2**(5) STaylor (bit bkwd: led: mstke 2nd: hdd 6th: sn wknd: wl t.o)	dist	**8**	100/1	—	—
4184P	**Smart In Socks**	(MissLucindaRussell) **6-11-7** TReed (lost tch ½-wy: wl t.o)	2	**9**	66/1	—	—
19675	**Super Guy**	(JBarclay) **5-11-7** GCahill (bhd fr ½-wy: t.o whn p.u bef 3 out)		**P**	25/1	—	—
	Bold Echo	(MsLCPlater) **5-11-2** DBentley (j.b: p.u bef 4th)		**P**	100/1	—	—

(SP 115.8%) **11 Rn**

5m 6.2 (18.20) CSF £12.01 TOTE £2.10: £1.30 £2.80 £2.00 (£6.60) Trio £9.70 OWNER Mr Robert Ogden (PENRITH) BRED Robert Ogden
3315 Royal York, after almost two months off, was patiently ridden and, although there was nothing left at the end, she was always doing just enough. (11/10)
Birkdale (IRE) had obviously come on a ton for his first run last week, and showed enough here to suggest that there is a race to be picked up, but chasing will be his game. (10/1)
3612 Beau Matelot is both looking and running well at the moment, but his attitude may be the problem. (8/1)
Granham Pride (IRE) looks as though he is going to need much stiffer tests of stamina. (7/2)
4205 Cottstown Boy (IRE) ran as though this trip may have been stretching him stamina. (8/1)

T/Plpt: £92.90 (136.45 Tckts). T/Qdpt: £63.40 (10.69 Tckts) AA

4096-FONTWELL (Fig. 8) (Good to firm)

Thursday April 24th

WEATHER: fair

4250 RAPIDE MORTGAGE SERVICES AND FINBAR NOVICES' HURDLE (4-Y.O+) (Class E)

2-20 (2-20) **2m 6f 110y (11 hdls)** £2,363.60 (£654.60: £312.80) GOING minus 0.17 sec per fur (G)

	Horse	Details	Dist	Pos	SP	RR	SF
34997	**Galatasori Jane (IRE) (98)**	(PFNicholls) **7-11-0**(7) LCummins (a.p: led 6th: clr appr 2 out: r.o wl)	—	**1**	Evens 1	75	16
38312	**Drum Battle (91)**	(WGMTurner) **5-10-13**(7) JPower (lw: led to 2nd: chsd wnr fr 8th: ev ch 3 out: unable qckn)	10	**2**	11/4 2	67	8
39013	**Nordic Spree (IRE) (83)**	(GLMoore) **5-11-0v** PHolley (lw: a.p: rdn 8th: sn wknd)	8	**3**	100/30 3	55	—
3689P	**Ewar Bold (63)**	(KOCunningham-Brown) **4-10-0b**(7) DSlattery (5th whn j.slowly 4th: reminder 7th: wknd 8th)	2½	**4**	33/1	53	—
4188P	**Soldier-B**	(RCurtis) **7-11-0** DMorris (hdwy to ld 2nd: mstke & hdd 6th: sn wknd: t.o fr 8th)	30	**5**	33/1	32	—
39482	**Country Keeper**	(BJMRyall) **9-11-0** GUpton (lw: 5th whn j.slowly 1st: bhd fr 2nd: t.o fr 5th: j.b lft & p.u 2 out)		**P**	25/1	—	—
3581F	**Pitarry**	(DMGrissell) **7-11-0** JRKavanagh (lw: a bhd: t.o fr 5th: p.u bef 7th)		**P**	50/1	—	—
26429	**Honest Dave (57)**	(BAPearce) **7-11-0** KGaule (bhd fr 6th: t.o whn p.u bef 8th)		**P**	50/1	—	—

(SP 113.4%) **8 Rn**

5m 28.1 (12.10) CSF £3.53 TOTE £1.90: £1.10 £1.60 £1.20 (£2.70) OWNER Mr B. L. Blinman (SHEPTON MALLET) BRED Donal O'Keeffe
WEIGHT FOR AGE 4yo-7lb
2959* Galatasori Jane (IRE), whose two previous wins this season have come over this distance, on this ground and in this company, has run up very light but that did not stop her from winning this race in decisive style. Gaining a narrow advantage at the sixth, she forged clear turning into the straight but, with the race well and truly in the bag, her jockey gave her two pointless reminders going to the final flight. (Evens)
3831 Drum Battle was on level terms with the winner three from home but was left for dead by that rival in the straight. (11/4: 2/1-3/1)
3901 Nordic Spree (IRE) played an active role until left behind by the front two approaching the third last. (100/30)

4251 RAPIDE MORTGAGE SERVICES NOVICES' CHASE (5-Y.O+) (Class E)

2-50 (2-50) **3m 2f 110y (22 fncs)** £3,058.60 (£844.60: £401.80) GOING minus 0.17 sec per fur (G)

	Horse	Details	Dist	Pos	SP	RR	SF
41682	**Decyborg (FR) (100)**	(MCPipe) **6-12-0** CMaude (lw: mde all: rdn out)	—	**1**	8/13 1	101	37
3185P	**Keep it Zipped (IRE) (99)**	(OSherwood) **7-11-8b** JAMcCarthy (chsd wnr: rdn appr 3 out: nt run on)	2	**2**	9/4 2	94	30
37362	**Cardinal Gayle (IRE) (68)**	(RHAlner) **7-11-2** JRKavanagh (lw: a wl bhd: t.o fr 5th)	dist	**3**	6/1 3	—	—

(SP 107.0%) **3 Rn**

6m 50.2 (10.20) CSF £2.14 TOTE £1.40: (£1.50) OWNER Mr Terry Neill (WELLINGTON) BRED Bernard Touillon
4168 Decyborg (FR) had nothing to beat as he sauntered around in front with the runner-up throwing in the towel and the third soon tailed off. (8/13)
2908 Keep it Zipped (IRE) once again showed why he is not one to trust. Having closed the gap on the winner entering the straight, he proved very unco-operative and, when asked for a big effort at the last, he proved very awkward. On the run-in, he certainly chucked in the towel. (9/4)

4252 STREBEL BOILERS AND RADIATORS SERIES (QUALIFIER) H'CAP HURDLE (0-110) (4-Y.O+) (Class E)

3-20 (3-20) **2m 6f 110y (11 hdls)** £2,322.00 (£642.00: £306.00) GOING minus 0.17 sec per fur (G)

	Horse	Details	Dist	Pos	SP	RR	SF
39352	**Scud Missile (IRE) (91)**	(JWPayne) **6-11-5** RichardGuest (lw: hld up: chsd ldr fr 3 out: rdn appr last: led flat: r.o wl)	—	**1**	5/4 1	75	—
41367	**Adilov (78)**	(JJBridger) **5-10-3**(3) LAspell (lw: hld up: led 3 out: blnd last: hdd flat: unable qckn)	2½	**2**	13/2	60	—
38303	**Fawley Flyer (92)**	(WGMTurner) **8-10-13**(7) JPower (lw: led to 4th: led 5th to 3 out: sn wknd: lame)	17	**3**	3/1 3	62	—
41725	**Born to Please (IRE) (96)**	(PJHobbs) **5-11-10** MAFitzgerald (lw: chsd ldr: led 4th to 5th: wknd 3 out: t.o)	dist	**4**	11/4 2	—	—

(SP 109.4%) **4 Rn**

5m 33.0 (17.00) CSF £7.77 TOTE £2.30: (£8.50) OWNER Mr J. P. Power (NEWMARKET) BRED Tullamaine Castle Stud and Partners

OFFICIAL EXPLANATION **Fawley Flyer: finished lame.**

3935 Scud Missile (IRE) confirmed the promise shown at Huntingdon recently after a lay-off. Moving into second place three from home, he was greatly helped by the leader making a complete hash of the last and managed to get on top on the run-in. (5/4)

2907 Adilov made a bold bid for glory as he moved to the front three from home and looked to have the winner in some sort of trouble in the straight. However, he made a very bad error at the last which did his cause no good and he was overhauled on the run in. (13/2: 4/1-7/1)

3830 Fawley Flyer, reverting back to hurdles, loves to hear his feet rattle and took the field along but, collared three from home, was soon done with. He returned lame. (3/1)

936* Born to Please (IRE), who finished last at Exeter last week on his first run for six months, raced in second place but was left for dead three from home. He has done all his winning on a fast surface. (11/4)

4253 RAPIDE MORTGAGE SERVICES & CORNHILL LIFE H'CAP HURDLE (0-130) (5-Y.O+) (Class C)

3-50 (3-50) **3m 3f (13 hdls)** £3,655.00 (£1,090.00: £520.00: £235.00) GOING: 0.00 sec per fur (G)

				SP	RR	SF
3892[2]	**St Ville (99)** (RHBuckler) **11-10-0** BPowell (a.p: led 10th: clr appr last: comf)	—	**1**	100/30[3]	84+	—
3851[2]	**Runaway Pete (USA) (123)** (MCPipe) **7-11-10** DWalsh (lw: a.p: rdn 5th: led 9th to 10th: ev ch appr 2 out: wknd appr last)	14	**2**	9/2	100	—
3762[U]	**Givus a Call (IRE) (106)** (JTGifford) **7-10-4**(3) LAspell (lw: stdy hdwy 9th: 3rd whn mstke 10th: wknd appr 2 out)	1½	**3**	14/1	82	—
4005[6]	**Uluru (IRE) (101)** (CPMorlock) **9-10-2** JRKavanagh (hld up: hrd rdn 9th: sn wknd: t.o)	dist	**4**	3/1[2]	—	—
4096[4]	**Nick the Dreamer (101)** (WGMTurner) **12-9-9**(7)ow2 NWillmington (lw: led to 9th: sn wknd: t.o)	2½	**5**	50/1	—	—
597[P]	**Morning Blush (IRE) (100)** (PFNicholls) **7-10-1** BFenton (lw: prom to 10th: t.o whn p.u bef last)		**P**	10/1	—	—
3737*	**Snow Board (101)** (MrsMerritaJones) **8-10-2**ow2 DerekByrne (a bhd: rdn 5th: t.o whn p.u bef 10th)		**P**	2/1[1]	—	—
				(SP 117.3%)	**7 Rn**	

6m 30.3 CSF £17.86 CT £169.31 TOTE £4.10: £2.20 £1.90 (£5.50) OWNER Melplash Racing (BRIDPORT) BRED David and Mrs Shirley

LONG HANDICAP Nick the Dreamer 8-6 Snow Board 9-12

OFFICIAL EXPLANATION **Snow Board: no explanation offered.**

3892 St Ville was on his best behaviour on this occasion and, leading four from home, pulled clear from the second last to win without knowing he had had a race. (100/30)

3851 Runaway Pete (USA), who has never won beyond two miles five and a half furlongs, found this trip beyond him and, after being on level terms with the winner turning for home, had run out of gas going to the last. (9/2: 11/4-5/1)

1963 Givus a Call (IRE), reverting back to hurdles having failed to complete on his last three outings over fences, was left for dead by the front two turning for home. Both his wins to date have come with some cut in the ground. (14/1)

3737* Snow Board, winner of four races this season, ran an absolute stinker and his jockey was already at work with fully two circuits to go. Not surprisingly, he was pulled up early on the final circuit. (2/1)

4254 GEORGE GALE & CO H'CAP CHASE (0-115) (5-Y.O+) (Class E)

4-20 (4-22) **2m 2f (15 fncs)** £3,042.90 (£907.20: £432.60: £195.30) GOING minus 0.17 sec per fur (G)

				SP	RR	SF
3843[F]	**Blazer Moriniere (FR) (78)** (PCRitchens) **8-10-2** SFox (hld up: led 9th: r.o wl)	—	**1**	9/4[1]	94	4
1557[5]	**Mill O'The Rags (IRE) (100)** (MrsDHaine) **8-11-10** JFTitley (bit bkwd: a.p: chsd wnr fr 10th: rdn appr 2 out: unable qckn)	10	**2**	100/30[3]	107	17
3832*	**Fichu (USA) (82)** (MrsLRichards) **9-10-6** MRichards (bhd fr 6th)	20	**3**	9/2	71	—
3897[5]	**Upward Surge (IRE) (76)** (RRLedger) **7-10-0** MrsNLedger (lw: led after 1st tl blnd & hdd 9th: sn wknd)	8	**4**	50/1	58	—
	Beach Bum (79) (MrsJAYoung) **11-10-3** GUpton (lw: led tl after 1st: 2nd whn p.u bef 4th: dismntd)		**P**	10/1	—	—
4142[2]	**Toomuch Toosoon (IRE) (91)** (PFNicholls) **9-11-1** BFenton (lw: hld up: mstke 10th: p.u bef 11th: lame)		**P**	11/4[2]	—	—
				(SP 109.7%)	**6 Rn**	

4m 30.8 (8.80) CSF £9.04 TOTE £3.40: £1.60 £2.10 (£5.20) OWNER Mr John Pearl (TIDWORTH) BRED Robert Jeffroy

LONG HANDICAP Upward Surge (IRE) 9-0

3843 Blazer Moriniere (FR) jumped into the lead at the ninth and kept on too strongly for the runner-up to gain his first victory in this country. (9/4)

1557 Mill O'The Rags (IRE), off the course since flopping at Cheltenham in November, looked in need of this but nevertheless moved into second place six from home. Pushed along approaching the penultimate fence, he then had little more to offer. At his best on a fast surface, he should soon find a small race. (100/30)

3832* Fichu (USA) showed little and three of his four wins have come at Ludlow. (9/2: op 5/2)

4255 RMS AND TCR MAIDEN HURDLE (4-Y.O+) (Class E)

4-50 (4-52) **2m 2f 110y (9 hdls)** £2,485.40 (£689.40: £330.20) GOING minus 0.17 sec per fur (G)

				SP	RR	SF
4102[2]	**Mullintor (IRE) (83)** (RRowe) **6-11-6** DO'Sullivan (led tl after 1st: led appr 3 out: drvn out)	—	**1**	5/2[2]	65	29
3761[6]	**He Knows The Rules (81)** (RHBuckler) **5-11-6** BPowell (hdwy 6th: chsd wnr fr 3 out: ev ch whn j.path flat: nt rcvr)	1½	**2**	13/8[1]	64	28
4082[4]	**Global Dancer** (LWells) **6-11-6** MRichards (hdwy 6th: wknd appr 2 out)	28	**3**	6/1[3]	40	4
3818[10]	**Swan Street (NZ) (76)** (CJMann) **6-11-3**(3) JMagee (hdwy 6th: sn wknd)	4	**4**	9/1	36	—
4102[3]	**Veronica Franco (74)** (BAPearce) **4-10-6**(3) PHenley (hld up: rdn 6th: wknd appr 2 out: blnd last)	4	**5**	10/1	28	—
1388[10]	**Indian Crown (66)** (NBThomson) **7-11-1b** SBurrough (plld hrd: hdwy 2nd: wknd 6th: t.o)	dist	**6**	100/1	—	—
4100[F]	**Full of Tricks (60)** (JJBridger) **9-11-6** DMorris (led after 1st tl appr 3 out: sn wknd: t.o)	16	**7**	50/1	—	—
4097[3]	**Lord Love (IRE) (70)** (PRChamings) **5-11-6** JCulloty (lw: a.p: ev ch 3 out: 4th & wkng whn b.d 2 out)		**B**	14/1	—	—
3304[12]	**Caldebrook (IRE)** (JTGifford) **6-11-3**(3) LAspell (lw: mstke 6th: hdwy appr 2 out: 3rd whn fell 2 out)		**F**	14/1	—	—
4017[4]	**Oscilights Gift** (MarkCampion) **5-11-1** WMcFarland (a bhd: t.o whn p.u bef 2 out)		**P**	50/1	—	—
3052[P]	**Elly's Dream** (PCRitchens) **6-11-1** SFox (a bhd: t.o fr 3rd: p.u bef 6th)		**P**	66/1	—	—
3718[P]	**Woman From Hell** (MrsLRichards) **7-11-1** CMaude (bhd fr 4th: t.o whn p.u bef 2 out)		**P**	50/1	—	—
				(SP 121.7%)	**12 Rn**	

4m 24.3 (6.30) CSF £6.67 TOTE £3.70: £1.90 £1.10 £2.90 (£3.20) Trio £13.00 OWNER Mr Thomas Thompson (PULBOROUGH) BRED Bernadette Whelan

WEIGHT FOR AGE 4yo-6lb

4102 Mullintor (IRE) at last came good after a string of seconds. Gaining the initiative approaching the third last, he had a real set-to with the runner-up in the straight and just held on in a driving finish. (5/2)

3103 He Knows The Rules, who reportedly coughed after his last run, moved into second place three from home. Throwing down his challenge in the straight, he was about a length and a half down early on the run-in but had got back on level terms when jumping a path in the last half-furlong. He lost his momentum slightly as a result and this could have made all the difference. (13/8: 11/10-7/4)

Global Dancer took closer order setting out on the final circuit but had shot his bolt turning for home. (6/1: 8/1-9/2)
3604 Swan Street (NZ) took closer order setting out on the final circuit but it proved short-lived and he was beaten early in the back straight. (9/1: 6/1-10/1)
4102 Veronica Franco (10/1: 6/1-11/1)
2911 Caldebrook (IRE), whose dam is a half-sister to Night Nurse, was making his hurdling debut. A mistake at the fourth last cost him ground he could ill afford, but he began to pick up ground turning for home and was desperately trying to stay on in third place when taking a crashing fall two from home. (14/1: 7/1-16/1)

T/Plpt: £34.80 (277.25 Tckts). T/Qdpt: £25.50 (18.89 Tckts) AK

4243-PERTH (R-H) (Good)
Thursday April 24th

Race 1: 9th, 10th & 17th fences bypassed due to inj jockeys
WEATHER: fine

4256 PERTH HUNT BALNAKEILLY CHALLENGE CUP HUNTERS' CHASE (5-Y.O+) (Class H)

2-00 (2-01) **3m (15 fncs)** £2,388.00 (£668.00: £324.00) GOING: 0.50 sec per fur (GS)

	Horse	Details		SP	RR	SF
4076[2]	**Ensign Ewart (IRE)**	(CStorey) **6-11-9**(5) MrCStorey (lw: bhd: hdwy ½-wy: chsng ldrs 4 out: led flat: all out)..—	**1**	11/2[2]	112	42
4015[2]	**Howayman**	(KAnderson) **7-11-12**(7) MrAParker (lw: a chsng ldrs: led 13th: hdd flat: rallied) ....nk	**2**	3/1[1]	117	47
3913[3]	**Admission (IRE)**	(MrsSarahHorner-Harker) **7-11-7**(7) MissLHorner (a chsng ldrs: one pce fr 3 out)....18	**3**	12/1	100	30
4051[8]	**Fordstown (IRE)**	(JamieAlexander) **8-11-8**(7)ow1 MrJamieAlexander (led to 6th: chsd ldrs tl outpcd fr 4 out) ...3	**4**	16/1	99	28
4080[4]	**Dark Dawn**	(MrsJMNewitt) **13-11-12**(7) MissLornaFoxton (lw: hld up & bhd: hdwy appr 4 out: sn rdn & n.d)..2½	**5**	8/1	101	31
	Bow Handy Man	(MsLCPlater) **15-11-7**(7) MissSLaidlaw (lw: bhd: sme hdwy ½-wy: n.d) 12	**6**	33/1	88	18
3553[2]	**Across the Card**	(MajorGenCARamsay) **9-11-12**(7) MrMBradburne (a bhd) 25	**7**	9/1	77	7
3617[F]	**Master Kit (IRE)**	(JNRBillinge) **8-11-12**(7) MrJBillinge (lw: hld up: hdwy to ld 6th: sn clr: hdd 13th: wknd qckly 4 out: sn t.o) ....dist	**8**	7/1[3]	—	—
3994*	**Denim Blue**	(MissPaulineRobson) **8-12-3**(5) MissPRobson (lw: fell 2nd)	**F**	9/1	—	—
3824[3]	**Rusty Blade**	(PMonteith) **8-11-9**(5) MrRHale (lost tch 6th: t.o whn p.u bef 3 out)	**P**	20/1	—	—
3580[R]	**Fifth Amendment**	(CJMann) **12-11-7b**(7) MrAHales (sn bhd: wl t.o whn p.u bef 13th)	**P**	33/1	—	—
3490[4]	**Direct**	(TRGeorge) **14-11-12**(7) MrTEdwards (a bhd: t.o whn p.u bef 4 out)	**P**	20/1	—	—
	Thank U Jim	(MrsGSunter) **9-11-7**(7) MissTJackson (blnd & uns rdr 1st)	**U**	20/1	—	—
	Border Glory	(ACWhillans) **6-11-7**(7) MrMJRuddy (lw: lost tch fr ½-wy: blnd & uns rdr 4 out)	**U**	50/1	—	—

(SP 119.7%) **14 Rn**

6m 21.4 (23.40) CSF £18.98 TOTE £4.70: £1.50 £1.80 £4.40 (£7.20) Trio £34.50 OWNER Major M. W. Sample (KELSO) BRED James D. Leahy
4076 Ensign Ewart (IRE) stays well and is honest and that won him the day. (11/2: 7/2-6/1)
4015 Howayman ran his heart out as usual and kept fighting back in the closing stages when all looked lost. (3/1)
3913 Admission (IRE) was always well-enough placed but lacked any change of gear when the pressure was on. (12/1)
3609 Fordstown (IRE) is slow but sure and was left wanting for speed from the fourth last. (16/1)
4080 Dark Dawn struggled to truly get this trip. (8/1)
3994* Denim Blue (9/1: 6/1-10/1)

4257 NELSON MORRISON UNDERWRITING AGENCY LTD FUTURE CHAMPIONS 'N.H.' NOVICES' HURDLE (5-Y.O+) (Class C)

2-30 (2-30) **3m 110y (12 hdls)** £4,695.00 (£1,410.00: £680.00: £315.00) GOING: 0.50 sec per fur (GS)

	Horse	Details		SP	RR	SF
4204[U]	**Lagen Bridge (IRE) (112)**	(DMoffatt) **8-11-8** DJMoffatt (lw: hld up: hdwy 3 out: led 2 out: drvn out)....—	**1**	9/1	93	53
4146*	**Meadow Hymn (IRE) (118)**	(JGFitzGerald) **6-11-8** PCarberry (lw: hld up: hdwy ½-wy: disp ld 3 out: hdd next: rallied & chal last: nt qckn) 1¾	**2**	9/4[1]	92	52
4207[8]	**Young Kenny (122)**	(PBeaumont) **6-11-8** RSupple (prom: effrt 4 out: outpcd fr next) 22	**3**	7/2[2]	78	38
3990*	**Major Harris (IRE) (102)**	(MDHammond) **5-11-4** RGarritty (a chsng ldrs: ev ch 3 out: sn rdn & one pce) ....¾	**4**	10/1	73	33
3400[P]	**Lottery Ticket (IRE) (104)**	(TRGeorge) **8-10-12** TJMurphy (hit 4 out: sn rdn & one pce) 1¼	**5**	20/1	66	26
3901*	**Sparkling Spring (IRE) (108)**	(KCBailey) **6-11-8** SMcNeill (cl up: led 8th tl appr 3 out: sn outpcd) 1¾	**6**	7/1[3]	75	35
3644[2]	**Pebble Beach (IRE) (94)**	(GMMoore) **7-11-4** JCallaghan (swtg: chsd ldrs tl rdn & wknd 8th: t.o) ....dist	**7**	25/1	—	—
3823[8]	**Over Zealous (IRE)**	(JohnUpson) **5-10-12** JSupple (sn drvn along & a bhd: t.o) 15	**8**	66/1	—	—
3885[5]	**Paperising (112)**	(GRichards) **5-11-8** PNiven (trckd ldrs: led appr 3 out: hdd 2 out: sn wknd: p.u flat)....	**P**	7/1[3]	—	—
3569[6]	**Huish (IRE)**	(GFHCharles-Jones) **6-10-12** MrACharles-Jones (plld hrd: led 5th to 8th: rdn & wknd qckly: t.o whn p.u bef 2 out)	**P**	33/1	—	—
4147[5]	**Cheater (IRE) (90)**	(HowardJohnson) **6-11-4b** ASSmith (led to 5th: chsd ldrs tl rdn & wknd 8th: t.o whn p.u bef 2 out)	**P**	20/1	—	—
3794[8]	**Persian Grange (IRE) (61)**	(DALamb) **7-10-12b**[1] JBurke (sn bhd: p.u bef 8th)	**P**	200/1	—	—
4144[8]	**Moreflash**	(JSHaldane) **5-10-7** TReed (a bhd: t.o whn p.u bef 2 out)....	**P**	500/1	—	—

(SP 115.6%) **13 Rn**

6m 3.7 (17.70) CSF £25.33 TOTE £9.30: £2.50 £1.30 £2.30 (£16.90) Trio £19.80 OWNER Mrs Eileen Milligan (CARTMEL) BRED James Flahavan
3453* Lagen Bridge (IRE) has really got his act together now. After travelling well, he showed a useful turn of speed and then fought on well under pressure to get the trip in good style. (9/1)
4146* Meadow Hymn (IRE) is a tough sort who doesn't know how to run a bad race but, after a busy season, he was just out-pointed here. (9/4)
3368* Young Kenny, not entirely suited by this sharp track, ran quite well but he was comprehensively outpaced over the last three flights. (7/2)
3990* Major Harris (IRE) raced with every chance until his limitations were well exposed over the last three flights. (10/1)
3279 Lottery Ticket (IRE) has been disappointing over fences lately and looked a shade clumsy here at times. (20/1)
3901* Sparkling Spring (IRE) had his chances until finding this company too hot once the pace was really on from the third last. (7/1)

4258 R M C CATHERWOOD LTD 'LITTLE BAY' H'CAP CHASE (0-145) (5-Y.O+) (Class B)

3-00 (3-00) **2m (12 fncs)** £6,720.80 (£2,026.40: £983.20: £461.60) GOING: 0.50 sec per fur (GS)

	Horse	Details		SP	RR	SF
4145*	**Grouse-N-Heather (100)**	(PMonteith) **8-10-0** PCarberry (hld up: effrt 3 out: rdn to ld flat: r.o wl) ....—	**1**	7/2[2]	109	42
4214[7]	**Storm Falcon (USA) (115)**	(SMellor) **7-10-10**(5) ChrisWebb (t: lw: stdd s: hdwy to ld 7th: hdd & no ex flat)....3½	**2**	14/1	121	54

				SP	RR	SF
4214[6]	**Political Tower (127)** (RNixon) **10-11-13** BStorey (prom: outpcd 4 out: kpt on appr last)	3	**3**	9/1	130	63
4214*	**Monyman (IRE) (111)** (MDHammond) **7-10-11** 6x RGarritty (hld up: hmpd 8th: rdn to chal 2 out: wknd flat)	hd	**4**	Evens[1]	113	46
3943*	**Netherby Said (121)** (PBeaumont) **7-11-7** RSupple (lw: led to 7th: sn drvn along: wknd 3 out)	dist	**5**	9/2[3]	—	—
2769[7]	**Cardenden (IRE) (100)** (JBarclay) **9-10-0** GCahill (chsd ldrs to 6th: sn outpcd & bhd)	8	**6**	200/1	—	—
				(SP 107.6%)	**6 Rn**	

4m 0.5 (9.50) CSF £34.25 TOTE £3.40: £1.40 £3.30 (£11.40) OWNER Mr D. J. Fairbairn (ROSEWELL) BRED R. A. Cameron
LONG HANDICAP Grouse-N-Heather 9-11 Cardenden (IRE) 7-11

4145* Grouse-N-Heather is in tremendous form and, as usual, got stronger as the race progressed to keep her 100% record on this track. (7/2)

4214 Storm Falcon (USA) is improving fast and, well-handicapped, will surely find a race before long. (14/1)

4214 Political Tower, who broke a blood vessel last time, ran well here. (9/1)

4214* Monyman (IRE) was most disappointing and this probably came too quickly for him after his impressive Ayr victory only five days earlier. (Evens)

3943* Netherby Said never showed any sparkle this time, and stopped quickly three out. He has probably gone over the top for the season. (9/2)

1972* Cardenden (IRE), from 31lb out of the handicap, was not surprisingly far too slow for this company. (200/1)

4259 MURRAYSHALL HOTEL (S) HURDLE (4-Y.O+) (Class G)

3-30 (3-30) **2m 110y (8 hdls)** £2,906.00 (£816.00: £398.00) GOING: 0.50 sec per fur (GS)

				SP	RR	SF
1853[B]	**Charlistiona (62)** (JPDodds) **6-10-2**(7) SMelrose (in tch: hdwy u.p 3 out: led 2 out: drvn clr)	—	**1**	25/1	58	21
	Suselja (IRE) (JMJefferson) **6-10-6**(3) ECallaghan (bit bkwd: mstke & reminders 4th: hdwy next: styd on u.p fr 2 out: nrst fin)	10	**2**	25/1	48	11
1832[8]	**Eden Dancer (102)** (MrsMReveley) **5-12-0** PNiven (led fr 2nd to 2 out: sn btn)	3½	**3**	7/2[1]	64	27
4187[14]	**Anlace (78)** (SMellor) **8-10-11v**[1](5) ChrisWebb (lw: bhd: hdwy 3 out: styd on: nvr rchd ldrs)	2½	**4**	12/1[3]	50	13
3790[8]	**Monkey Wench (IRE)** (MrsJDGoodfellow) **6-11-2** BStorey (lw: in tch: effrt appr 3 out: styd on one pce)	6	**5**	8/1[2]	44	7
3921[P]	**Vanborough Lad (60)** (MJBolton) **8-11-0** PCarberry (hdwy 4th: sn prom: one pce fr 2 out)	½	**6**	16/1	41	4
	Media Express (MrsLStubbs) **5-11-0** RGarritty (chsd ldrs tl rdn & btn appr 2 out)	10	**7**	12/1[3]	32	—
	Maggies Lad (PCalver) **9-11-7** LWyer (in tch tl outpcd fr 5th)	8	**8**	33/1	31	—
3070[8]	**Young Semele** (JRAdam) **5-10-9** JRailton (bit bkwd: nvr nr to chal)	2	**9**	16/1	17	—
1942[6]	**Nonios (IRE) (97)** (GMMoore) **6-11-7** JCallaghan (cl up: hmpd 3rd: rdn & wknd 3 out)	1¼	**10**	7/2[1]	28	—
3908[12]	**De-Veers Currie (IRE)** (DMoffatt) **5-10-9** DJMoffatt (bhd fr 4th)	hd	**11**	100/1	16	—
3883[9]	**Nine Pipes (IRE)** (JJBirkett) **6-11-0** LO'Hara (outpcd fr ½-wy)	¾	**12**	12/1[3]	20	—
1969[7]	**Dark Midnight (IRE) (55)** (DALamb) **8-11-0** JBurke (a bhd: t.o)	16	**13**	100/1	4	—
3908[10]	**Bill's Pride (68)** (PMonteith) **6-10-9** TJenks (trckd ldrs tl wknd qckly appr 2 out)	3	**14**	20/1	—	—
3896[8]	**Saboteuse (50)** (JCPoulton) **5-10-9b** TJMurphy (wl t.o)	dist	**15**	100/1	—	—
4097[P]	**Danucha** (JCPoulton) **5-10-9** LeesaLong (bit bkwd: prom whn fell 5th: dead)		**F**	100/1	—	—
3091[10]	**Seconds Away (53)** (JSGoldie) **6-11-0** GCahill (led to 2nd: wknd 5th: p.u bef 2 out)		**P**	25/1	—	—
	Ballochan Linn (CParker) **5-11-0** DParker (t.o fr ½-wy: p.u bef 2 out)		**P**	100/1	—	—
3908[6]	**Connie Leathart** (MsLCPlater) **6-10-9** DBentley (p.u after 3rd)		**P**	33/1	—	—
2957[10]	**Going Public (88)** (PCheesbrough) **10-12-0** ASSmith (a bhd: t.o whn p.u bef 2 out)		**P**	12/1[3]	—	—
2044[P]	**Tashreef (72)** (JJBirkett) **7-12-0b** MMoloney (ref to r after 100y)		**R**	33/1	—	—
				(SP 128.2%)	**21 Rn**	

4m 2.0 (16.00) CSF £483.15 TOTE £66.00: £15.60 £10.50 £1.90 (£1,495.80) Trio £277.00; £351.14 to Sandown 25/4/97 OWNER Mr J. P. Dodds (ALNWICK) BRED D. and Mrs Scullion
Bt in 3,700 gns

5 Charlistiona, who had shown little previously, responded to pressure and won this well suggesting that stiffer tests of stamina will also suit.(25/1)

Suselja (IRE), off the track for eighteen months, ran well and kept staying on, albeit in vain. (25/1)

1144 Eden Dancer likes to be out in front and was well suited by this right-handed track but the lack of a recent run probably just made the difference. (7/2)

3741 Anlace last won a race eighteen months ago and, even with the visor on here, she was never giving any signs of hope despite staying on. (12/1)

3479 Monkey Wench (IRE) ran as though this trip on this track was on the sharp side. (8/1)

Media Express (12/1: op 8/1)

Nine Pipes (IRE) (12/1: 33/1-10/1)

Going Public (12/1: op 8/1)

4260 TOTE CREDIT MAIDEN CHASE (5-Y.O+) (Class D)

4-00 (4-00) **2m (12 fncs)** £3,655.00 (£1,090.00: £520.00: £235.00) GOING: 0.50 sec per fur (GS)

				SP	RR	SF
2927[5]	**Tidebrook** (KCBailey) **7-11-7** SMcNeill (lw: blnd 4th: a.p: led 2 out: hit last & lft wl clr)	—	**1**	7/2[2]	90?	27
4077[4]	**Cool Weather (IRE) (70)** (PCheesbrough) **9-11-7b** ASSmith (cl up: led 5th to 7th: wl outpcd fr 4 out)	dist	**2**	10/1	—	—
3826[4]	**Nooran (80)** (ACWhillans) **6-11-7** BStorey (hmpd 1st: hdwy 6th: blnd 8th: rdn & j.slowly 4 out: sn t.o)	dist	**3**	6/4[1]	—	—
1667[P]	**Regal Domain (IRE)** (MrsLMarshall) **6-11-7** KJohnson (lw: bdly hmpd 1st: a t.o)	12	**4**	50/1	—	—
4057[4]	**Nawtinookey (74)** (MartinTodhunter) **7-10-9**(7) CMcCormack (cl up: led 7th to 2 out: 3l 2nd whn fell last: remntd)	dist	**5**	9/2[3]	—	—
4183[P]	**Smart in Silk** (MissLucindaRussell) **8-11-2** TReed (fell 1st)		**F**	66/1	—	—
2766[P]	**Apollo Colosso** (JRAdam) **7-11-7** JRailton (sn outpcd & wl bhd: p.u bef 6th)		**P**	20/1	—	—
3479[4]	**High Mood (69)** (TRGeorge) **7-11-7** TJMurphy (blnd & uns rdr 3rd)		**U**	12/1	—	—
3882[P]	**Royal Banker (IRE)** (MartinTodhunter) **7-11-7b**[1] PCarberry (lw: led to 5th: sn drvn along: 3rd & btn whn blnd & uns rdr 3 out)		**U**	14/1	—	—
				(SP 112.1%)	**9 Rn**	

4m 8.1 (17.10) CSF £31.84 TOTE £3.00: £1.60 £1.40 £1.40 (£9.20) Trio £13.80 OWNER Mr Richard Williams (UPPER LAMBOURN) BRED Mrs G. E. Jones

2927 Tidebrook, making his debut over fences here, found a bad race and has plenty to learn jumping-wise but he does stay well. (7/2: op 9/4)

4077 Cool Weather (IRE) had his chances throughout but he has never liked a struggle and cried enough four out. (10/1)

3826 Nooran got hampered at the first and was never really happy thereafter, blundering any hopes away five out. (6/4)

3479 High Mood (12/1: 8/1-14/1)

3556 Royal Banker (IRE) had blinkers on the first time but he was not looking too enthusiastic and was in third place when blundering his rider out of the saddle three out. (14/1)

4261 NELSON MORRISON H'CAP HURDLE (0-125) (4-Y.O+) (Class D)

4-30 (4-31) **2m 4f 110y (10 hdls)** £3,647.50 (£1,105.00: £540.00: £257.50) GOING: 0.50 sec per fur (GS)

	Horse	Dist		SP	RR	SF
3904[2]	**Bourdonner (93)** (MDHammond) **5-10-1**(3) MrCBonner (mde all: kpt on wl fr 3 out)	—	1	9/2[3]	85	41
3559[7]	**Elation (108)** (GRichards) **5-11-5** RGarritty (lw: chsd ldrs: ev ch 3 out: nt qckn fr next)	12	2	20/1	91	47
4081[5]	**Master of Troy (96)** (CParker) **9-10-7** DParker (outpcd & bhd ½-wy: styd on fr 3 out: nrst fin)	5	3	16/1	75	31
3693[2]	**Linlathen (113)** (MrsMReveley) **7-11-10** PNiven (lw: chsd ldrs: hit 4 out: sn rdn & btn)	5	4	2/1[1]	88	44
4187[6]	**Fen Terrier (103)** (FPMurtagh) **5-11-0** BStorey (bhd: hdwy ½-wy: chsng ldrs 4 out: wkng whn hit 2 out)	½	5	20/1	77	33
3992[5]	**Thursday Night (IRE) (109)** (JGFitzGerald) **6-11-3**(3) FLeahy (lw: prom: drvn along 4 out: sn btn)	27	6	14/1	62	18
3912[3]	**Danbys Gorse (96)** (JMJefferson) **5-10-4**(3) ECallaghan (lw: a rr div)	3½	7	14/1	47	3
3886[2]	**Jymjam Johnny (IRE) (105)** (JJO'Neill) **8-10-11**(5) RMcGrath (prom tl rdn & wknd 6th)	6	8	10/1	51	7
3795*	**Mister Ross (IRE) (108)** (HowardJohnson) **7-11-5** PCarberry (prom tl rdn & btn appr 3 out)	dist	9	4/1[2]	—	—
3885[4]	**Chipped Out (106)** (MartinTodhunter) **7-10-10**(7) CMcCormack (prom: blnd 2nd: rdn & wknd 4 out: p.u bef 2 out)		P	10/1	—	—
	Moreof a Gunner (101) (JMJefferson) **7-10-12** LWyer (bit bkwd: a bhd: p.u bef 2 out)		P	50/1	—	—
	Fair and Fancy (FR) (107) (MissMKMilligan) **6-11-4** ASSmith (a outpcd & bhd: p.u bef 3 out)		P	33/1	—	—
				(SP 123.3%)	**12 Rn**	

5m 1.3 (13.30) CSF £85.92 CT £1,232.07 TOTE £5.30: £1.80 £2.40 £7.00 (£38.60) Trio £105.20 OWNER Mr Cornelius Lysaght (MIDDLEHAM) BRED The Overbury Stud

3904 Bourdonner has got his hurdling together now and, well ridden, had his own way out in front and won most convincingly. (9/2)
3559 Elation, back to something like his old self here, ran quite well but was never a match for the winner over the last two. (20/1)
4081 Master of Troy was without any headgear here and never showed any real enthusiasm until staying on when it was all over. (16/1)
3693 Linlathen travelled quite well until a blunder four out finished him. (2/1)
4187 Fen Terrier, trying a longer trip here, ran out of fuel two from home. (20/1)
3912 Danbys Gorse (14/1: 10/1-16/1)
3886 Jymjam Johnny (IRE) (10/1: 8/1-12/1)

T/Plpt: £70.10 (198.49 Tckts). T/Qdpt: £16.70 (34.95 Tckts) AA

4262a - 4269a : (Irish Racing) - See Computer Raceform

4130-ASCOT (R-H) (Good to firm, Good patches becoming Good)
Friday April 25th

WEATHER: unsettled

4270 BET WITH THE TOTE AMATEUR H'CAP CHASE (0-125) (5-Y.O+) (Class E)

5-30 (5-30) **3m 110y (20 fncs)** £4,279.50 (£1,296.00: £633.00: £301.50) GOING: 0.33 sec per fur (GS)

	Horse	Dist		SP	RR	SF
3701[4]	**Garrylough (IRE) (115)** (DRGandolfo) **8-11-6**(3) MrCBonner (led to 2nd: remained prom: led 3 out: r.o wl)	—	1	6/1	127	49
1338[4]	**Drumcullen (IRE) (99)** (KCBailey) **8-10-0**(7) MrRWakley (led 2nd to 3 out: ev ch last: nt qckn)	2	2	10/1	110	32
3961[8]	**Harristown Lady (103)** (GBBalding) **10-10-4b**(7) MrLJefford (hdwy 10th: styd on fr 2 out: nvr nrr)	5	3	20/1	110	32
4085[2]	**Danger Baby (93)** (DLWilliams) **7-9-8**(7) MrSDurack (mstkes: nrst fin)	1¾	4	11/2[3]	99	21
3961*	**Merlins Dream (IRE) (117)** (OSherwood) **8-11-8**(3) MrRThornton (hdwy 8th: ev ch whn mstke 4 out: wknd appr last)	¾	5	11/4[1]	123	45
3893[2]	**Diamond Fort (103)** (JCMcConnochie) **12-10-4**(7)ow6 MrPScott (hdwy 12th: ev ch 5 out: wknd 3 out)	4	6	14/1	106	22
	Auto Pilot (NZ) (112) (NJHenderson) **9-11-1**(5) MrCVigors (hdwy 9th: mstke 11th: wknd 3 out)	7	7	5/1[2]	111	33
3175[2]	**Big Ben Dun (105)** (CPEBrooks) **11-10-6**(7) MrEJames (blnd 6th: a bhd)	11	8	12/1	96	18
	Fight to Win (USA) (92) (LPGrassick) **9-9-7**(7) MrJGrassick (prom tl wknd 15th: t.o)	22	9	66/1	69	—
4148[5]	**Dont Tell the Wife (105)** (CREgerton) **11-10-6**(7) MrJGoldstein (fell 2nd)		F	16/1	—	—
3837[F]	**New Ghost (99)** (GWGiddings) **12-10-0v**(7)ow7 MajorOEllwood (prom tl wknd qckly 10th: t.o fr 14th: p.u bef 3 out)		P	66/1	—	—
				(SP 110.1%)	**11 Rn**	

6m 20.4 (15.40) CSF £53.38 CT £953.57 TOTE £6.50: £1.70 £2.20 £5.40 (£24.60) Trio £105.30 OWNER Mr T. J. Whitley (WANTAGE) BRED John Clarke

LONG HANDICAP Fight to Win (USA) 9-2 New Ghost 9-2

3701 Garrylough (IRE) has two ways of running, but was on her best behaviour here. She was never going to be beaten after regaining the upper hand three fences out. (6/1)
1338 Drumcullen (IRE), off the course since November, looked fit and well. Soon in the lead, he had all but the winner in trouble a long way out. (10/1)
3751* Harristown Lady stayed on to take third place without troubling the leading pair. (20/1)
4085 Danger Baby jumped indifferently and, though staying on at the finish, was never in the race with a chance. (11/2: op 7/2)
3961* Merlins Dream (IRE) stalked the leaders from halfway, but a mistake four fences out did not help. (11/4)
Auto Pilot (NZ) (5/1: 7/2-6/1)
3175 Big Ben Dun (12/1: op 8/1)

4271 WOODROW WYATT H'CAP HURDLE (0-140) (4-Y.O+) (Class B)

6-00 (6-01) **2m 110y (9 hdls)** £5,622.80 (£1,702.40: £831.20: £395.60) GOING: 0.33 sec per fur (GS)

	Horse	Dist		SP	RR	SF
3912*	**Monnaie Forte (IRE) (109)** (JRAdam) **7-9-13**(3)ow2 LAspell (w ldr: led after 3 out: wnt lft last: r.o)	—	1	8/1	87	39
3468*	**Darakshan (IRE) (107)** (MissHCKnight) **5-10-0** JCulloty (gd hdwy fr 2 out: nrst fin)	1¼	2	4/1[2]	84	38
3814[2]	**Marius (IRE) (114)** (JTGifford) **7-10-7** PHide (a.p: ev ch 2 out: r.o one pce)	hd	3	12/1	91	45
4130[4]	**Dancing Paddy (135)** (KOCunningham-Brown) **9-12-0** BPowell (hdwy 6th: ev ch last: wknd nr fin)	2½	4	25/1	109	63
4130*	**I'm a Dreamer (IRE) (110)** (MissMERowland) **7-10-0**(3) MrRThornton (nvr nr to chal)	8	5	15/2[3]	77	31
4136*	**John Drumm (114)** (PRWebber) **6-10-7** JOsborne (led tl wknd after 3 out)	7	6	4/1[2]	74	28
4130[3]	**Albemine (USA) (120)** (MrsJCecil) **8-10-13** TKent (prom tl wknd 3 out)	2½	7	14/1	77	31
4130[F]	**Serious (113)** (KCBailey) **7-10-6** NWilliamson (hld up in rr: rdn 3 out: no response: t.o)	dist	8	5/2[1]	—	—

651[F] **Suivez (125)** (MrsNMacauley) **7-11-4** MAFitzgerald (wl bhd fr 6th: t.o whn p.u bef 2 out)	**P**	16/1	—	—
		(SP 115.5%)		**9 Rn**

3m 57.9 (7.90) CSF £37.06 CT £351.07 TOTE £8.40: £2.10 £2.10 £2.50 (£29.80) Trio £58.20 OWNER Mr James Adam (GORDON) BRED E. Stuart Knape
LONG HANDICAP Monnaie Forte (IRE) 9-11
OFFICIAL EXPLANATION **Serious: was never going on this ground.**
3912* Monnaie Forte (IRE) is in tremendous form at present and put up his best performance to date, staying on well after leading two hurdles out. (8/1)
3468* Darakshan (IRE), well enough placed early on, was outpaced in the middle of the race but was running on well at the finish. (4/1)
3814 Marius (IRE), with the leaders all the way, had every chance but could not quicken in the closing stages. (12/1)
4130 Dancing Paddy ran as if a hurdle race is well within his compass. He moved up to challenge two hurdles out, and it was only in the last one-hundred-and-fifty yards that his big weight told. (25/1)
4130* I'm a Dreamer (IRE) never promised to repeat his surprise recent win here. (15/2)
4130 Albemine (USA) (14/1: 10/1-16/1)
4130 Serious, probably inconvenienced by the afternoon rain, was held up in last place but was in trouble fully half-a-mile from home and finished tailed off. He probably needs really fast ground. (5/2)

4272 TOTE DIRECT NOVICES' H'CAP CHASE (0-110) (5-Y.O+) (Class D)

6-30 (6-30) **2m 3f 110y (16 fncs)** £4,192.50 (£1,180.00: £577.50) GOING: 0.33 sec per fur (GS)

			SP	RR	SF
4168* **Boots N All (IRE) (76)** (GBBalding) **7-10-1** 4x BFenton (j.w: led 2nd: comf)	—	**1**	11/10[1]	90+	19
3617[P] **Cardinal Rule (IRE) (90)** (MissVenetiaWilliams) **8-11-1** NWilliamson (led to 2nd: chsd wnr after: hrd rdn & ev ch whn hit 3 out: wknd next: j.b lft last)	7	**2**	11/2[2]	98	27
4007[7] **Spring to Glory (88)** (PHayward) **10-10-13** MAFitzgerald (hdwy 10th: one pce fr 3 out)	4	**3**	7/1	93	22
4157[2] **Sleazey (75)** (JGO'Neill) **6-10-0** SCurran (hit 6th: hdwy 10th: 4th & wkng whn mstke 12th: bhd whn fell 2 out)		**F**	11/2[2]	—	—
964* **Prerogative (99)** (GLMoore) **7-11-10** APMcCoy (t.o fr 8th: p.u bef 3 out)		**P**	6/1[3]	—	—
4140[P] **Ryton Run (81)** (MrsSMOdell) **12-10-6** DGallagher (blnd 1st: t.o whn p.u bef 4th)		**P**	40/1	—	—
3810[4] **Eau So Sloe (75)** (JRPoulton) **6-10-0** DMorris (hdwy 10th: wknd 12th: bhd whn p.u bef 2 out)		**P**	100/1	—	—
			(SP 108.6%)		**7 Rn**

5m 1.8 (14.80) CSF £6.43 TOTE £2.20: £1.70 £2.50 (£4.20) OWNER Mrs Toni Tipper (ANDOVER) BRED Megan and Karl Strecker
LONG HANDICAP Sleazey 9-12 Eau So Sloe 8-13
4168* Boots N All (IRE) won in the style of a fast-improving horse. He jumped brilliantly throughout, a big leap at the second taking him to the front. He never looked in trouble thereafter. (11/10: evens-6/5)
3400 Cardinal Rule (IRE) was the only one to ever have any hope of catching the winner. He was already under strong pressure when he made a mistake three fences out, and all chance had gone when he jumped violently to the left at the last. (11/2: 4/1-6/1)
3819 Spring to Glory trailed in a distant third without ever threatening to trouble the leading pair. (7/1)
4157 Sleazey (11/2: 4/1-6/1)
964* Prerogative ran appallingly and was tailed off before halfway, finally pulling up before the third-last fence. (6/1)

4273 TOTE MOBILE TERMINAL NOVICES' HURDLE (4-Y.O+) (Class C)

7-05 (7-05) **2m 4f (11 hdls)** £3,485.00 (£1,055.00: £515.00: £245.00) GOING: 0.33 sec per fur (GS)

			SP	RR	SF
4014[4] **Summer Spell (USA) (123)** (NJHenderson) **4-10-12** MAFitzgerald (a gng wl: led on bit last: easily)	—	**1**	Evens[1]	83+	16
3755* **Eau de Cologne (103)** (MrsLRichards) **5-11-5** MRichards (chsd ldr: led appr 2 out: hdd last: no ch w wnr)	6	**2**	4/1[3]	78	18
4048[8] **Influence Pedler (116)** (JABOld) **4-10-12** CLlewellyn (led tl wknd appr 2 out)	dist	**3**	2/1[2]	—	—
Bay Lough (IRE) (RRowe) **6-10-4**(7)ow2 MrJLuck (a bhd)	16	**4**	50/1	—	—
1261[P] **Jaime's Joy (49)** (GraemeRoe) **7-10-2**(7) MartinSmith (a t.o)	dist	**5**	100/1	—	—
3154[7] **Hightech Touch** (LPGrassick) **7-11-0** MrJGrassick (prom tl wknd appr 4 out: t.o whn fell 2 out)		**F**	66/1	—	—
Masrur (USA) (JMCastle) **8-11-0** LHarvey (prom tl wknd qckly 5th: t.o whn p.u bef 2 out)		**P**	100/1	—	—
			(SP 108.8%)		**7 Rn**

5m 0.7 (18.70) CSF £4.55 TOTE £1.90: £1.40 £1.80 (£3.40) OWNER W V M W & Mrs E S Robins (LAMBOURN) BRED Jim Robinson, Pam Robinson and Walmac Internationa
WEIGHT FOR AGE 4yo-7lb
4014 Summer Spell (USA) proved much too good for these, toying with the opposition from a long way out and leading on the bit at the final hurdle. (Evens)
3755* Eau de Cologne raced in second place and was always travelling better than the leader, but the winner was sitting waiting to pounce behind them. (4/1)
3566 Influence Pedler faded quickly after leading until approaching the second-last hurdle. (2/1)

4274 TOTE BOOKMAKERS NOVICES' CHASE (5-Y.O+) (Class C)

7-35 (7-35) **2m (12 fncs)** £5,036.50 (£1,414.00: £689.50) GOING: 0.33 sec per fur (GS)

			SP	RR	SF
4219* **Indian Jockey (117)** (MCPipe) **5-11-3** APMcCoy (led: rdn 5th: mstke & hdd last: sn led again: r.o)	—	**1**	11/8[2]	125	51
4012[3] **Sublime Fellow (IRE) (116)** (NJHenderson) **7-11-10** MAFitzgerald (chsd wnr: led last: sn hdd: fnd nil)	1¾	**2**	4/6[1]	123	56
4232[P] **Full Shilling (USA) (60)** (DLWilliams) **8-10-9**(7) MrSDurack (mstkes: a t.o)	dist	**3**	33/1[3]	—	—
			(SP 105.0%)		**3 Rn**

3m 59.3 (8.30) CSF £2.44 TOTE £2.00: (£1.10) OWNER Mr Stuart Mercer (WELLINGTON) BRED John Hayter
WEIGHT FOR AGE 5yo-7lb
4219* Indian Jockey set off in front, but was under pressure early in the race as usual. He appeared to have given it away when making a mistake at the last, but he battled on well, in stark contrast to the runner-up. (11/8)
4012 Sublime Fellow (IRE), apparently always cantering over his rival, as usual found nothing when the chips were down. (4/6)
4083 Full Shilling (USA) was tailed off before the first. (33/1)

4275 TOTE CREDIT NOVICES' H'CAP HURDLE (5-Y.O+) (Class C)

8-05 (8-05) **2m 110y (9 hdls)** £5,061.00 (£1,533.00: £749.00: £357.00) GOING: 0.33 sec per fur (GS)

			SP	RR	SF
3569* **Sounds Like Fun (112)** (MissHCKnight) **6-11-1** JFTitley (a.p: hit 3 out: led 2 out: r.o wl)	—	**1**	11/2[3]	93	11
3920[3] **Jovie King (IRE) (97)** (RHBuckler) **5-10-0** BPowell (led to 5th: led appr 2 out: sn hdd: nt qckn)	6	**2**	15/2	72	—
4001[2] **Foxies Lad (102)** (DNicholson) **6-10-5** RJohnson (effrt & rdn 3 out: one pce fr 2 out: nvr on terms)	7	**3**	5/2[2]	70	—

				SP	RR	SF
4010P	**No Pattern (102)** (GLMoore) **5-10-5** DGallagher (prom tl wknd 3 out) 10	**4**	6/1	61	—
3447 10	**The Bizzo (100)** (JFPanvert) **6-10-0**(3)ow3 PHenley (t.o fr 4th) ....dist	**5**	100/1	—	—
4061 12	**Secret Spring (FR) (125)** (PRHedger) **5-11-7**(7) MClinton (in rr tl plld hrd & hdwy 3rd: led 5th: hit 6th: hdd appr 2 out: 4th & no ch whn fell last)	**F**	9/4 1	—	—
4102*	**Absolute Limit (99)** (JTGifford) **5-10-2**ow2 PHide (hmpd & s.u after 1st)	**S**	12/1	—	—

(SP 109.5%) **7 Rn**

4m 7.1 (17.10) CSF £36.80 CT £106.12 TOTE £5.30: £1.90 £3.40 (£19.50) Trio £9.50 OWNER Mrs H. Brown (WANTAGE) BRED B. King

LONG HANDICAP Jovie King (IRE) 9-11 The Bizzo 7-0 Absolute Limit 9-7

3569* Sounds Like Fun, close up throughout, was carried wide into the straight, but led at the second last hurdle and stayed on strongly. (11/2)

3920 Jovie King (IRE) led to halfway and, after gaining the advantage momentarily on the home turn, was quickly beaten off by the winner. (15/2)

4001 Foxies Lad, dropped in distance, seemed to be struggling from four out. Though staying on under hard driving, he lacked a turn of foot. (5/2)

3298 No Pattern ran disappointingly, and faded after being close-up until three hurdles out. (6/1: 4/1-13/2)

4061 Secret Spring (FR), settled in last place, suddenly took off going into Swinley Bottom and jumped to the front at the fifth. He hit the next and faded quickly in the straight, falling when in fourth at the last. This running can be completely ignored. (9/4)

4102* Absolute Limit was hampered after the first hurdle, lost his footing and slipped up. (12/1)

T/Plpt: £254.30 (69.59 Tckts). T/Qdpt: £28.30 (32.06 Tckts) Hn

4089-**LUDLOW** (R-H) (Good to firm)
Friday April 25th

WEATHER: raining

4276 LOWE & OLIVER NOVICES' (S) HURDLE (4, 5 & 6-Y.O) (Class G)

5-45 (5-46) **2m (9 hdls)** £1,794.00 (£494.00: £234.00) GOING: 0.15 sec per fur (G)

			SP	RR	SF
4086 2	**Theme Arena (88)** (MCPipe) **4-10-9v1** DWalsh (mde virtually all: hit 3rd: clr fr 6th: pushed out) ....—	**1**	8/15 1	52+	7
4226P	**Daydream Believer (65)** (MSalaman) **5-10-9** PHolley (lw: hld up: hdwy 5th: chsd wnr appr 3 out: no imp) 6	**2**	20/1	40	1
3730 9	**Witherkay** (PFNicholls) **4-10-3**(5) OBurrows (lw: chsd ldrs: effrt appr 3 out: no imp fr next) 3	**3**	7/1 2	42	—
4089 7	**Tee Tee Too (IRE) (65)** (AWCarroll) **5-10-8**(7)ow1 MrAWintle (bhd: effrt 6th: nt rch ldrs) 13	**4**	7/1 2	30	—
4069 4	**Glen Garnock (IRE) (70)** (RTJuckes) **5-11-0** GaryLyons (w wnr: slt ld 3rd: sn hdd: wknd appr 3 out) 3	**5**	10/1 3	26	—
4002U	**Vita Nuova (IRE)** (WJenks) **6-10-9** RBellamy (a in rr: t.o) 16	**6**	40/1	5	—
3959 5	**Timely Example (USA) (65)** (BRCambidge) **6-11-0b** SWynne (a bhd: t.o) 10	**7**	20/1	—	—
4067 3	**Bold Time Monkey** (MTate) **6-10-9** WMarston (a bhd: t.o fr 5th) 17	**8**	33/1	—	—
4009 15	**Roxy Hicks** (RJPrice) **5-10-9** JRKavanagh (plld hrd: hit 3rd: t.o whn p.u bef 3 out)	**P**	40/1	—	—
2873F	**Baxworthy Lord (60)** (CLPopham) **6-11-0** SMcNeill (t: outpcd: t.o fr ½-wy: p.u bef 3 out)	**P**	66/1	—	—
4002U	**Just Andy** (BPreece) **6-11-0b1** TJenks (stmbld bdly & lost tch 4th: sn t.o: p.u bef 3 out)	**P**	100/1	—	—

(SP 119.1%) **11 Rn**

3m 49.9 (12.90) CSF £15.57 TOTE £1.40: £1.20 £4.30 £1.70 (£13.70) Trio £25.50 OWNER Mr Antony Sofroniou (WELLINGTON) BRED Halevale Ltd

WEIGHT FOR AGE 4yo-6lb

No bid

4086 Theme Arena, faced with a simple task, hardly needed to come off the bridle for a very comfortable return to form. (8/15)

4002 Daydream Believer, a small mare of little account, at long-last ran into the prizes without threatening to trouble the winner. (20/1)

Witherkay should have the ability to win a race of this description, but he is taking time to strike form, and as yet does not appear to stay this trip. (7/1: op 9/2)

2567 Tee Tee Too (IRE) (7/1: op 12/1)

4069 Glen Garnock (IRE) (10/1: op 6/1)

4277 BROMFIELD SAND AND GRAVEL H'CAP CHASE (0-120) (5-Y.O+) (Class D)

6-15 (6-15) **2m 4f (17 fncs)** £3,450.00 (£950.00: £450.00) GOING: 0.15 sec per fur (G)

			SP	RR	SF
4221*	**Quite A Man (110)** (SABrookshaw) **9-12-2** 6x CMaude (hld up in rr: j.slowly 11th: wnt 2nd next: led 3 out: sn clr) ....—	**1**	4/6 1	122	34
4019 2	**Herbert Buchanan (IRE) (99)** (PFNicholls) **7-11-5** WMarston (lw: led 5th to 8th: led appr 10th tl hdd & mstke 3 out: sn btn) 16	**2**	6/4 2	98	10
3002 7	**Houghton (95)** (WJenks) **11-10-8**(7)ow1 MrRBurton (bit bkwd: led to 5th: led 8th tl appr 10th: wknd 12th: t.o) .25	**3**	9/1 3	74	—
3966P	**Applianceofscience (80)** (KOWarner) **10-10-0** SWynne (chsd ldrs to 13th: wknd whn mstke 4 out: t.o whn fell 2 out)	**F**	25/1	—	—

(SP 113.8%) **4 Rn**

5m 6.9 (14.90) CSF £2.12 TOTE £1.40: (£1.10) OWNER Mr W. R. J. Everall (SHREWSBURY) BRED R. Everall

LONG HANDICAP Applianceofscience 9-1

4221* Quite A Man has beaten nothing of note in a fabulous spring campaign, and a lot of the credit must to go the way he has been placed by his trainer. (4/6)

4019 Herbert Buchanan (IRE) has lost the habit of winning, and was made to look very ordinary once the winner took his measure early in the straight. (6/4)

4278 ROBERT HOLDEN H'CAP HURDLE (0-115) (4-Y.O+) (Class E)

6-45 (6-45) **2m (9 hdls)** £2,560.00 (£760.00: £360.00: £160.00) GOING: 0.15 sec per fur (G)

			SP	RR	SF
2579 4	**Yubralee (USA) (113)** (MCPipe) **5-12-0** DWalsh (mde virtually all: clr 6th: canter) ....—	**1**	7/2 2	107+	40
4130 2	**Faustino (110)** (PJHobbs) **5-11-11** WMarston (lw: bhd & outpcd: hdwy u.p appr 3 out: styd on: no ch w wnr) 10	**2**	7/4 1	94	27
2871 4	**Zingibar (85)** (JMBradley) **5-10-0** SWynne (chsd ldrs: rdn 4th: wnt 2nd appr 3 out: sn wknd) 6	**3**	8/1	63	—
4020 3	**Little Shefford (85)** (MPMuggeridge) **5-10-0** ILawrence (lw: chsd wnr: slt ld appr 4th: sn hdd: rdn & wknd 3 out) 3½	**4**	12/1	60	—
4141 4	**Verde Luna (85)** (DWPArbuthnot) **5-10-0** SMcNeill (lw: bhd: hdwy 6th: nvr rchd ldrs) 3	**5**	11/1	57	—
4154 2	**Eriny (USA) (87)** (JJQuinn) **8-10-2** CMaude (chsd ldng pair tl wknd appr 3 out: t.o) 16	**6**	9/2 3	43	—

4089* **Kalzari (USA) (85)** (AWCarroll) **12-9-9**(5) OBurrows (a bhd: t.o: p.u bef 3 out)........ P 14/1 — —
(SP 110.6%) **7 Rn**

3m 46.6 (9.60) CSF £8.81 TOTE £5.80: £2.40 £1.50 (£6.30) OWNER Mr D. A. Johnson (WELLINGTON) BRED Gainsborough Farm Inc
LONG HANDICAP Little Shefford 9-12 Kalzari (USA) 9-8

2579 Yubralee (USA), fresh and well after a break of over three months, made short work of this opposition and in this form could run up a sequence. (7/2)
4130 Faustino turned in a very disappointing display on this rain-softened ground, and was never within striking range of the winner. (7/4)
2871 Zingibar, stepping back to the minimum trip, briefly moved into second place on the approach to the straight, but was easily brushed aside. (8/1)
4020 Little Shefford continues to run well, but he was a bit out of his depth here and was in trouble from the turn for home. (12/1)
723 Verde Luna could not summon-up the pace to cause concern, and this below par performance was probably due to the rain-softened ground. (11/1)
4154 Eriny (USA), a raider from the North, has won on similar ground but he ran very flat here, and looking for an excuse could prove expensive. (9/2)

4279 DOWNTON HALL STABLES NOVICES' H'CAP CHASE (0-110) (5-Y.O+) (Class D)
7-15 (7-15) **3m (19 fncs)** £3,200.00 (£950.00: £450.00: £200.00) GOING: 0.15 sec per fur (G)

				SP	RR	SF
3934*	**Jasilu (99)** (KCBailey) **7-11-10b** SMcNeill (lw: chsd ldr: rdn 13th: led after 15th: clr appr last)........ —	1	11/8[1]	98	43
1635P	**Blasket Hero (90)** (MrsSDWilliams) **9-11-1b** WMarston (bit bkwd: hld up: hdwy 15th: jnd wnr 4 out: j.b lft fr next: sn rdn & btn)........ 14	2	2/1[2]	80	25
4092*	**Inch Emperor (IRE) (92)** (AWCarroll) **7-11-3** TJMurphy (swtg: j.w: led tl after 15th: wknd qckly: t.o)........ 30	3	9/4[3]	62	7
4090[4]	**Pandora's Prize (75)** (TWall) **11-9-11**(3) RMassey (lw: rdn 9th: lost tch 12th: sn t.o)........ s.h	4	25/1	45	—
			(SP 110.1%)		**4 Rn**

6m 13.1 (13.10) CSF £4.28 TOTE £3.00: (£1.70) OWNER Mr A. G. Lay (UPPER LAMBOURN) BRED C. L. Loyd
LONG HANDICAP Pandora's Prize 9-3

3934* Jasilu carries plenty of condition, but she can jump and was able to follow up her win at the end of last month with another clear-cut success. (11/8)
1376* Blasket Hero looked to be travelling best when joining the winner four out, but he began to jump out to the left as lack of peak condition took its toll, and he was legless between the last two. This run should at least put an edge on him. (2/1)
4092* Inch Emperor (IRE) has won at this trip between the flags but, against this stiffer opposition, he failed to last home after turning in a bold display of fencing. (9/4: op 6/4)

4280 LANE FOX AND BALFOUR & COOKE HUNTERS' CHASE (5-Y.O+) (Class H)
7-45 (7-46) **2m 4f (17 fncs)** £1,725.00 (£475.00: £225.00) GOING: 0.15 sec per fur (G)

				SP	RR	SF
3744[5]	**Great Gusto** (MissLBlackford) **11-12-0**(7) MissLBlackford (j.w: a.p: led after 9th: sn wl clr: r.o wl)........ —	1	4/6[1]	111	10
4094[2]	**Cape Cottage** (DJCaro) **13-12-0**(7) MrAPhillips (hld up: hdwy 9th: chsd wnr appr 4 out: styd on)........ 3	2	2/1[2]	109	8
3744U	**Stylish Gent** (StephenRichardGriffiths) **10-11-7**(7) MrADalton (a in rr: t.o fr 10th)........ dist	3	25/1	—	—
	Emerald Charm (IRE) (GCEvans) **9-11-6**(3) MrMRimell (sn chsng ldrs: wkng whn hit 12th: sn t.o: p.u bef 4 out)........	P	11/2[3]	—	—
	Ballad Song (MrsCarolineChadney) **14-11-7**(7) MrMMunrowd (lw: led & sn clr: hdd after 9th: 2nd whn blnd 13th: sn wknd: t.o whn p.u bef 2 out)........	P	50/1	—	—
			(SP 114.5%)		**5 Rn**

5m 15.4 (23.40) CSF £2.45 TOTE £1.50: £1.10 £1.10 (£2.30) OWNER R C H Racing (TIVERTON) BRED R. M. West

3744 Great Gusto took over with a circuit to race and soon had his rivals off the bit. Though he was beginning to tire in the latter stages, he was always in complete control. (4/6: op 11/10)
4094 Cape Cottage needs all of three miles to produce his best and, though he stayed on relentlessly in the closing stages, the line was always going to arrive too soon. (2/1: op evens)
Ballad Song, reaching the veteran stage now, is at his best over this sort of trip and, though he looked to have shot his bolt, he was still a clear second when a bad mistake at the fifth last all but severed the partnership. (50/1)

4281 I.T.T. LONDON & EDINBURGH NOVICES' HURDLE (4-Y.O+) (Class E)
8-15 (8-15) **3m 2f 110y (13 hdls)** £2,070.00 (£570.00: £270.00) GOING: 0.15 sec per fur (G)

				SP	RR	SF
3834[4]	**Awestruck (57)** (BPreece) **7-10-7b**(7) JMogford (outpcd 9th: hdwy to ld appr 3 out: rdn whn lft clr next)........ —	1	16/1	47?	—
3990[4]	**Pontevedra (IRE) (92)** (KAMorgan) **4-10-7** SMcNeill (led tl hdd & wknd appr 3 out)........ 26	2	4/5[1]	32?	—
3930[2]	**Song For Jess (IRE) (71)** (FJordan) **4-10-1** SWynne (hld up: blnd 6th: sn t.o)........ dist	3	6/1[3]	—	—
3340[2]	**Rare Spread (IRE) (83)** (MCPipe) **7-11-6** DWalsh (plld hrd: a.p: ev ch whn broke leg & fell 2 out: dead)........	F	6/4[2]	—	—
			(SP 115.7%)		**4 Rn**

6m 42.6 (43.60) CSF £29.65 TOTE £11.00: (£5.50) OWNER The Wroxeter Race Club (TELFORD) BRED Cheveley Park Stud Ltd
WEIGHT FOR AGE 4yo-8lb

3834 Awestruck, opening his account over hurdles, was a most fortunate winner, for he was hard at work and about to be overtaken when left with a clear advantage at the penultimate flight. (16/1)
3990 Pontevedra (IRE), forced to make the running, failed to see out the trip and she stopped to nothing after being headed. (4/5)
3620 Song For Jess (IRE), content to be given a lead, was still bowling along happily when she misjudged the sixth flight and all but paid the penalty. Unable to recover, this performance should be ignored. (6/1)
3340 Rare Spread (IRE), always running away on the heels of the leaders, was poised to challenge going by far the best when he broke a foreleg and fell in the wings of the penultimate hurdle. (6/4)

T/Plpt: £123.20 (49.37 Tckts). T/Qdpt: £63.60 (4.26 Tckts) IM

4256-**PERTH (R-H) (Good)**
Friday April 25th
WEATHER: fine

4282 BUSINESS TAX CENTRE NOVICES' HURDLE (4-Y.O) (Class D)
2-10 (2-10) **2m 110y (8 hdls)** £2,804.00 (£842.00: £406.00: £188.00) GOING: 0.28 sec per fur (GS)

Form	Horse	Dist	Pos	SP	RR	SF
2925^{6}	**Brecon** (WRMuir) **4-10-12** PNiven (lw: hld up: hdwy to chal 5th: led & hit last: r.o)	—	**1**	$7/4^{1}$	72+	9
3820^{7}	**Sadler's Realm** (PJHobbs) **4-10-12** GTormey (cl up: led 3 out to last: no ex)	4	**2**	$4/1^{3}$	68	5
3912^{8}	**Double Agent (102)** (HowardJohnson) **4-11-7** PCarberry (lw: cl up tl outpcd 5th: hdwy u.p 2 out: nvr able to chal)	s.h	**3**	$3/1^{2}$	77	14
2859^{5}	**Priddy Fair (87)** (DWBarker) **4-10-13** RichardGuest (lw: trckd ldrs: stdy hdwy & ch 2 out: sn rdn & btn)	12	**4**	15/2	57	—
4184^{9}	**Thorntoun House (IRE)** (JSGoldie) **4-10-12** DParker (led to 3 out: sn wknd)	5	**5**	50/1	52	—
4075^{9}	**Political Mandate** (RNixon) **4-10-7** BStorey (in tch tl outpcd 5th: n.d after)	5	**6**	50/1	42	—
3544^{F}	**Gold of Arabia (USA)** (KAMorgan) **4-10-12** RDunwoody (swtg: jnd ldrs 3rd: rdn & wknd appr 2 out)	dist	**7**	13/2	—	—

(SP 110.4%) **7 Rn**

4m 1.8 (15.80) CSF £7.82 TOTE £2.40: £1.90 £2.80 (£6.40) OWNER The Four Willies Partnership (LAMBOURN) BRED D. J. and Mrs Deer
Brecon, after almost three months off, was turned out looking a picture and won well, suggesting that further success can follow. (7/4)
Sadler's Realm showed enough to suggest that a modest race or two is on the cards. (4/1)
3310* Double Agent needs Carberry on board to make him jump, but this trip on this track was too sharp. (3/1: op 2/1)
2859 Priddy Fair went well for a long way, but her limitations were exposed once ridden going to the last. (15/2)
Thorntoun House (IRE) had shown nothing previously, but there were signs of encouragement here. (50/1)
Political Mandate will need longer trips. (50/1)

4283 SCOTTISH NEWS OF THE WORLD CONDITIONAL (S) H'CAP HURDLE (0-95) (4-Y.O+) (Class G)
2-45 (2-45) **2m 4f 110y (10 hdls)** £3,004.00 (£844.00: £412.00) GOING: 0.28 sec per fur (GS)

Form	Horse	Dist	Pos	SP	RR	SF
3822^{4}	**Ifallelsefails (95)** (LLungo) **9-11-6**(8) WDowling (jnd ldrs 5th: led 3 out: drvn out)	—	**1**	$7/2^{1}$	81	44
3908^{5}	**Sandrift (75)** (CParker) **8-10-8** FLeahy (led tl after 1st: cl up: led 4 out to 3 out: ev ch tl outpcd appr last)	3	**2**	10/1	59	22
3825^{9}	**Skane River (IRE) (67)** (GRichards) **6-9-6**(8) RBurns (lw: hld up: hdwy ½-wy: hmpd appr 3 out: styd on: nvr able to chal)	1¾	**3**	20/1	49	12
3803^{5}	**Eternal City (84)** (GRichards) **6-11-3** GLee (chsd ldrs: effrt 3 out: r.o one pce)	10	**4**	$6/1^{2}$	59	22
1857^{3}	**Parish Walk (IRE) (78)** (KJDrewry) **6-10-11** BGrattan (prom: effrt 4 out: one pce fr next)	½	**5**	12/1	52	15
2913^{16}	**Fanadiyr (IRE) (67)** (JSGoldie) **5-9-11**(3) SMelrose (hdwy 4 out: sn chsng ldrs: one pce appr 2 out)	8	**6**	$13/2^{3}$	35	—
4147^{6}	**Barnstormer (70)** (EAElliott) **11-10-3b** GFRyan (a chsng ldrs: outpcd appr 3 out: no imp after)	14	**7**	20/1	27	—
4248^{11}	**Father O'Brien (90)** (JCPoulton) **10-11-2**(7) NHannity (prom tl outpcd fr 4 out)	4	**8**	33/1	44	7
3909^{P}	**Dashmar (67)** (MsLCPlater) **10-9-11b**(3) RWilkinson (wl bhd tl sme late hdwy)	9	**9**	33/1	14	—
4157^{U}	**Shut Up (67)** (MrsEMoscrop) **8-10-0** EHusband (a rr div)	1½	**10**	40/1	13	—
3886^{F}	**Precipice Run (89)** (JJBirkett) **12-11-8** STaylor (n.d)	2	**11**	14/1	33	—
4055^{8}	**Whitegatesprincess (IRE) (67)** (BEllison) **6-10-0** RMcGrath (swtg: a bhd)	1½	**12**	10/1	10	—
4055^{10}	**Meadowleck (67)** (WGYoung) **8-9-9**(5) IJardine (lw: in tch to 4 out)	8	**13**	100/1	4	—
3607^{P}	**Playful Juliet (CAN) (82)** (JCHaynes) **9-11-1b** ECallaghan (lw: a bhd)	6	**14**	16/1	14	—
1842^{8}	**Akito Racing (IRE) (67)** (MartinTodhunter) **6-9-6**(8) CMcCormack (lost tch fr 6th)	2½	**15**	100/1	—	—
4149^{F}	**Lyford Cay (IRE) (67)** (JRBewley) **7-9-9v1**(5) TSiddall (mstkes: nvr gng wl: t.o)	dist	**16**	100/1	—	—
3827^{P}	**Strathmore Lodge (82)** (MissLucindaRussell) **8-11-1** PMidgley (cl up to ½-wy: t.o whn p.u bef 2 out)		**P**	16/1	—	—
3607^{7}	**Weather Alert (IRE) (72)** (KAMorgan) **6-10-2v**(3) MNewton (led after 1st: blnd 4th: hdd & wknd 4 out: p.u bef 2 out)		**P**	12/1	—	—
3607^{11}	**Don't Tell Judy (IRE) (67)** (MissMKMilligan) **9-9-9**(5) NHorrocks (lost tch fr ½-wy: p.u bef 2 out)		**P**	16/1	—	—

(SP 128.5%) **19 Rn**

5m 2.1 (14.10) CSF £33.93 CT £585.19 TOTE £4.20: £2.20 £3.30 £4.50 £2.20 (£29.30) Trio £53.80 OWNER Mrs Barbara Lungo (CARRUTHERSTOWN) BRED R. Chugg
LONG HANDICAP Shut Up 8-12 Skane River (IRE) 9-13 Meadowleck 9-1 Fanadiyr (IRE) 9-8 Akito Racing (IRE) 9-5 Lyford Cay (IRE) 8-11 Whitegatesprincess (IRE) 9-7 Dashmar 9-7 Don't Tell Judy (IRE) 9-11
No bid
3822 Ifallelsefails appreciated the trip, and showed fine determination when ridden. (7/2)
3481 Sandrift, dropped in class, ran her best race for a while, but found the winner too tough. (10/1)
1344 Skane River (IRE) took the eye in the paddock, and looked a shade unlucky, as he was stopped when trying to improve three out losing him valuable ground at a vital stage. (20/1)
3803 Eternal City had his chance, but looked very one-paced when they started to race in earnest. (6/1: op 4/1)
1857 Parish Walk (IRE), returning after over four months off, ran well in the circumstances. (12/1)
Fanadiyr (IRE) (13/2: 12/1-6/1)
Whitegatesprincess (IRE) (10/1: op 16/1)
1775 Weather Alert (IRE) (12/1: op 8/1)

4284 SUN LIFE OF CANADA H'CAP CHASE (5-Y.O+) (Class B)
3-15 (3-15) **3m (18 fncs)** £8,586.00 (£2,424.00: £1,182.00) GOING: 0.28 sec per fur (GS)

Form	Horse	Dist	Pos	SP	RR	SF
4054*	**Unguided Missile (IRE) (158)** (GRichards) **9-12-0** RDunwoody (lw: mde all: drvn out)	—	**1**	$1/5^{1}$	150	64
3361*	**Rectory Garden (IRE) (130)** (CaptTAForster) **8-10-0** PCarberry (chsd wnr fr ½-wy: chal 3 out: rdn & hit last: styd on towards fin)	1¼	**2**	$5/1^{2}$	121	35
1082^{F}	**Temple Garth (130)** (PBeaumont) **8-10-0** RSupple (cl up tl outpcd fr 12th)	dist	**3**	$14/1^{3}$	—	—
4078^{P}	**Snook Point (133)** (DALamb) **10-10-3**ow3 JBurke (sn t.o: p.u bef 11th: b.b.v)		**P**	100/1	—	—

(SP 107.7%) **4 Rn**

6m 8.6 (10.60) CSF £1.63 TOTE £1.20: (£1.40) OWNER Mr D. E. Harrison (PENRITH) BRED Samac Ltd and Potomac Ltd
LONG HANDICAP Rectory Garden (IRE) 8-9 Temple Garth 8-0 Snook Point 6-1
OFFICIAL EXPLANATION Snook Point: bled from the nose.
4054* Unguided Missile (IRE) won this despite being below his best. His exertions at Aintree have obviously taken the edge off him. (1/5)

3361* Rectory Garden (IRE) gave the winner a real shock from 19lb out of the handicap and, but for a mistake at the last, may well have won. (5/1)
1082 Temple Garth was 24lb wrong, and was well outclassed. (14/1)

4285 SCOTTISH SUN MADE IN SCOTLAND FOR SCOTLAND NOVICES' H'CAP HURDLE (0-110) (4-Y.O+) (Class D)

3-50 (3-50) **2m 110y (8 hdls)** £3,824.50 (£1,156.00: £563.00: £266.50) GOING: 0.28 sec per fur (GS)

Form	Horse	Dist	Pos	SP	RR	SF
4187*	**Teejay'n'aitch (IRE) (78)** (JSGoldie) **5-10-2**(5) STaylor (mde most: hld on wl)	—	1	5/1[2]	69	17
3752[8]	**Fairelaine (75)** (KCBailey) **5-10-4b[1]** CO'Dwyer (lw: prom: hdwy to chal appr last: slt ld flat: nt qckn towards fin)	s.h	2	25/1	66	14
3823[6]	**Reach The Clouds (IRE) (71)** (JohnUpson) **5-10-0** RSupple (hdwy ½-wy: hit 3 out: styd on u.p fr next: nrst fin)	1¾	3	20/1	60	8
4187[2]	**Parson's Lodge (IRE) (76)** (LLungo) **9-9-12**(7) WDowling (lw: drvn along 4th: styd on fr 2 out: nt pce to chal)	1¾	4	12/1	64	12
3983[2]	**Kildrummy Castle (78)** (JGFitzGerald) **5-10-4**(3) FLeahy (chsd ldrs: rdn 3 out: r.o one pce)	3½	5	8/1	62	10
4184[12]	**Star Master (71)** (PMonteith) **6-10-0** GLee (chsd ldrs tl rdn & btn between last 2)	nk	6	10/1	55	3
3888[2]	**Brumon (IRE) (89)** (DMoffatt) **6-11-4v** DJMoffatt (hdwy fr 3 out: nvr nr to chal)	4	7	6/1[3]	69	17
3691[6]	**Paparazzo (80)** (GMMoore) **6-10-9** LWyer (bhd tl sme late hdwy)	6	8	14/1	54	2
4056[3]	**Six Clerks (IRE) (92)** (JGFitzGerald) **4-11-1** PCarberry (prom: rdn appr 4th: wl outpcd fr 3 out)	14	9	9/2[1]	53	—
2798[5]	**Shinerolla (82)** (CParker) **5-10-11** DParker (prom: drvn along appr 4th: wknd 3 out)	15	10	5/1[2]	28	—
3995[3]	**Last Try (IRE) (93)** (BSRothwell) **6-11-8** ASSmith (cl up to 5th: wknd)	8	11	14/1	31	—
4244[10]	**Maple Bay (IRE) (90)** (BEllison) **8-11-5v[1]** GCahill (outpcd & bhd ½-wy: n.d after)	10	12	33/1	19	—
4075*	**Jessolle (95)** (GRichards) **5-11-10** RDunwoody (chsd ldrs tl rdn & wknd after 3 out: p.u bef 2 out)		P	6/1[3]	—	—
4244[7]	**The Stuffed Puffin (IRE) (95)** (CJMann) **5-11-10** RichardGuest (prom tl wknd qckly 5th: p.u bef 2 out)		P	33/1	—	—
				(SP 135.8%)	**14 Rn**	

3m 58.9 (12.90) CSF £125.16 CT £2,176.31 TOTE £7.00: £2.50 £5.70 £9.70 (£211.50) Trio Not won; £597.39 to Leicester 26/4/97 OWNER Mr Andrew Paterson (GLASGOW) BRED David Hyland
LONG HANDICAP Reach The Clouds (IRE) 9-8 Star Master 9-1
WEIGHT FOR AGE 4yo-6lb
OFFICIAL EXPLANATION Jessolle: lost her action.
4187* Teejay'n'aitch (IRE) has taken an age to get his head in front, but now seems to have the winning habit. (5/1)
3752 Fairelaine looked particularly well, and ran her best race for some time but, after looking likely to win, she was outbattled. (25/1)
3823 Reach The Clouds (IRE) is gradually getting his act together, and may well appreciate further. (20/1)
4187 Parson's Lodge (IRE) is running consistently just now, but this trip proved too sharp. (12/1)
3983 Kildrummy Castle ran reasonably, but proved short of pace on this sharp track. (8/1)
Star Master showed his first signs of encouragement, despite being 13lb out of the handicap. (10/1: op 16/1)
4056 Six Clerks (IRE) did not look in love with the game. (9/2)
3995 Last Try (IRE) (14/1: 10/1-16/1)

4286 ERNST & YOUNG NOVICES' CHASE (5-Y.O+) (Class C)

4-20 (4-20) **2m 4f 110y (15 fncs)** £6,285.00 (£1,760.00: £855.00) GOING: 0.28 sec per fur (GS)

Form	Horse	Dist	Pos	SP	RR	SF
3790[5]	**Malta Man (IRE)** (PCheesbrough) **7-11-3** ASSmith (wnt 2nd 7th: disp ld 10th: slt ld last: styd on wl)	—	1	7/1[2]	110	1
4203[2]	**Solomon's Dancer (USA) (129)** (GRichards) **7-11-11** RDunwoody (led fr 2nd: blnd 3rd & 3 out: hdd last: nt qckn u.p)	2½	2	2/9[1]	116	7
2077[P]	**Walls Court (71)** (JJBirkett) **10-11-3** LO'Hara (outpcd & bhd fr ½-wy)	dist	3	66/1	—	—
4077[2]	**Tall Measure** (DGSwindlehurst) **11-11-3** BStorey (led to 2nd: blnd 3rd: lost tch 9th: p.u lame bef 2 out)		P	8/1[3]	—	—
				(SP 106.9%)	**4 Rn**	

5m 23.4 (24.40) CSF £8.86 TOTE £5.70: (£2.00) OWNER Mr J. A. Stephenson (BISHOP AUCKLAND) BRED Lt-Col and Mrs J. A. Dene
3790 Malta Man (IRE) appreciated this trip and jumped well, suggesting he has a bright future. (7/1)
4203 Solomon's Dancer (USA) made a couple of poor jumps, and basically beat himself. He was probably unsuited by being out in front. (2/9)
Walls Court was, not surprisingly, completely outclassed. (66/1)

4287 PARTY IS NEARLY OVER STANDARD OPEN N.H. FLAT RACE (I) (4, 5 & 6-Y.O) (Class H)

4-55 (4-55) **2m 110y** £2,052.00 (£572.00: £276.00)

Form	Horse	Dist	Pos	SP	RR	SF
3561[3]	**Lord Podgski (IRE)** (PMonteith) **6-11-11** GCahill (lw: disp ld tl led 3f out: styd on strly)	—	1	3/1[1]	71 f	—
3828[6]	**Time Warrior (IRE)** (GMMoore) **6-10-11**(7) NHannity (chsd ldrs: effrt 4f out: kpt on: no ch w wnr)	3	2	14/1	61 f	—
2770[6]	**Wellswood (IRE)** (JMJefferson) **4-10-9**(3) ECallaghan (styd on fnl 4f: nrst fin)	2½	3	16/1	59 f	—
2757*	**Tara Gale (IRE)** (JNeville) **5-11-6** PCarberry (lw: hld up & bhd: hdwy 6f out: chsng ldrs & outpcd 3f out: n.d after)	3	4	9/2[3]	58 f	—
	Trouble Ahead (IRE) (KCBailey) **6-11-4** CO'Dwyer (tall: scope: bit bkwd: trckd ldrs: effrt & ch over 3f out: wknd fnl 2f)	5	5	4/1[2]	51 f	—
	Ballymana Boy (IRE) (FMurphy) **4-10-12** MFoster (in tch: outpcd 5f out: n.d after)	hd	6	20/1	51 f	—
3425[4]	**Crystal Jewel** (PJHobbs) **5-10-13** RDunwoody (disp ld tl wknd fnl 3f)	7	7	4/1[2]	39 f	—
3946[4]	**Juniper Hill** (KAMorgan) **5-11-4** WFry (prom tl wknd fnl 5f)	23	8	25/1	22 f	—
1834[13]	**Run For The Mill** (JMJefferson) **5-11-4** LWyer (outpcd & lost tch ½-wy: t.o)	dist	9	14/1	—	—
3828[19]	**Meggie Scott** (JPDodds) **4-10-7** RichardGuest (prom 10f: wknd: t.o)	4	10	100/1	—	—
3828[18]	**The True Miller** (FPMurtagh) **6-11-4** BStorey (bhd fr ½-wy: t.o)	9	11	100/1	—	—
	Non Non Joesephine (MissZAGreen) **6-10-13** MrTMorrison (bhd fr ½-wy: t.o)	17	12	200/1	—	—
	General Manager (USA) (MrsASwinbank) **5-11-4** JSupple (a bhd: wl t.o)	dist	13	10/1	—	—
				(SP 122.6%)	**13 Rn**	

3m 57.3 CSF £44.00 TOTE £4.30: £2.00 £4.00 £4.70 (£83.50) Trio £209.30 OWNER Mrs G. Smyth (ROSEWELL) BRED Gerald Smyth
WEIGHT FOR AGE 4yo-6lb
3561 Lord Podgski (IRE), given the aggressive ride he needs, won this well, and plenty more will be heard of him. (3/1: 9/2-5/2)
3828 Time Warrior (IRE) just stays, and is going to need long distances once put over hurdles. (14/1)
2770 Wellswood (IRE) took the eye, staying on nicely in the latter stages, and looks a real jumping type. (16/1)
2757* Tara Gale (IRE), a winner on soft ground three months ago, will probably need those conditions to show her best. (9/2)
Trouble Ahead (IRE), a real chasing type, showed enough to suggest that, in time, he can do a deal better. (4/1)

4288 PARTY IS NEARLY OVER STANDARD OPEN N.H. FLAT RACE (II) (4, 5 & 6-Y.O) (Class H)

5-25 (5-25) **2m 110y** £2,052.00 (£572.00: £276.00)

	Horse	Details	Dist	Pos	SP	RR	SF
3170^{2}	**Light The Fuse (IRE)**	(KCBailey) **5-11-4** CO'Dwyer (lw: hld up: hdwy ½-wy: led 3f out: r.o: eased ins fnl f)	—	**1**	5/4^{1}	59 f	—
3914^{5}	**China King (IRE)**	(JGFitzGerald) **6-11-11** PCarberry (lw: cl up: led 7f out to 3f out: kpt on)	7	**2**	5/1^{3}	59 f	—
3480*	**Easby Blue**	(SEKettlewell) **5-11-11** PNiven (a.p: effrt 4f out: ev ch 3f out: r.o one pce)	2½	**3**	5/2^{2}	57 f	—
	Toby	(GRichards) **4-10-5**(7) RBurns (bit bkwd: bhd: hdwy 3f out: styd on wl towards fin)	3	**4**	33/1	47 f	—
3939^{5}	**Sabu**	(JIACharlton) **5-11-4** BStorey (bhd tl styd on fnl 4f: nrst fin)	4	**5**	33/1	43 f	—
	Calling The Tune	(BMactaggart) **6-11-4** DBentley (chsd ldrs tl outpcd fnl 4f)	20	**6**	100/1	24 f	—
	Geegee Emmarr	(JJO'Neill) **4-10-2**(5) RMcGrath (prom tl grad wknd fnl 4f)	2	**7**	10/1	17 f	—
4150^{13}	**Jo Lightning (IRE)**	(BEllison) **4-10-12** KJohnson (lw: chsd ldrs 10f: sn rdn & wknd)	½	**8**	100/1	21 f	—
	Hansel's Streak	(TAKCuthbert) **5-11-4** LO'Hara (bit bkwd: nvr trbld ldrs)	6	**9**	100/1	15 f	—
3548^{17}	**The Chase**	(JMJefferson) **6-11-1**(3) ECallaghan (hdwy 6f out: sn chsng ldrs: wknd fnl 2½f)	½	**10**	25/1	15 f	—
2633^{17}	**Tidal Race (IRE)**	(JSHaldane) **5-11-4** ASSmith (led to 7f out: lost tch fnl 6f: t.o)	dist	**11**	100/1	—	—
	Toberlone	(JPDodds) **4-10-12** RichardGuest (t.o fr ½-wy)	dist	**12**	33/1	—	—

(SP 115.4%) **12 Rn**

3m 59.9 CSF £6.63 TOTE £2.10: £1.10 £2.00 £1.40 (£3.70) Trio £1.50 OWNER Mr A. F. Lousada (UPPER LAMBOURN) BRED J. P. N. Parker

WEIGHT FOR AGE 4yo-6lb

3170 Light The Fuse (IRE), a really nice sort, won this well and should make his mark when put over hurdles and fences. (5/4: op evens)

China King (IRE), with long gaps between his three previous races, he seems to have had his problems. He looks the type to take well to hurdling. (5/1)

3480* Easby Blue had his chances, but never really fired. (5/2)

Toby looks a little on the weak side, but he showed plenty of promise, making useful late headway. (33/1)

3939 Sabu tried different tactics, and was picking up really well at the end. (33/1)

Geegee Emmarr (10/1: tchd 16/1)

T/Plpt: £2,545.90 (3.44 Tckts). T/Qdpt: £503.30 (0.57 Tckts); £292.48 to Sandown 26/4/97 AA

4017-TAUNTON (R-H) (Firm, Good to firm patches)

Friday April 25th

WEATHER: cloudy

4289 ASPEN CATERING NOVICES' AMATEUR H'CAP HURDLE (0-100) (4-Y.O+) (Class G)

5-35 (5-35) **2m 3f 110y (10 hdls)** £1,773.50 (£496.00: £240.50) GOING minus 0.78 sec per fur (F)

	Horse	Details	Dist	Pos	SP	RR	SF
3979^{2}	**Ath Cheannaithe (FR) (83)**	(JNeville) **5-11-5v**(5) MrJJukes (mde all: clr 3 out: r.o wl)	—	**1**	4/6^{1}	73+	24
4162^{7}	**Gi Moss (68)**	(PRHarriss) **10-10-2b**(7) MrOMcPhail (chsd wnr: no imp fr 7th)	11	**2**	7/1^{3}	49	—
3894^{P}	**Irish Dominion (64)**	(AGHobbs) **7-9-12**(7)ow5 MrGShenkin (plld hrd in rr: sme hdwy fr 3 out: n.d)	13	**3**	14/1	34	—
4055^{4}	**Royal Hand (75)**	(RJArmson) **7-10-9v**(7)ow11 MrRArmson (mstke 3rd: wl bhd fr 7th: t.o)	21	**4**	3/1^{2}	28	—
4102^{6}	**Miss Gee-Ell (60)**	(NBThomson) **5-9-8**(7) MrEBabington (bhd: reminders 5th: hit 7th: sn t.o)	5	**5**	25/1	9	—

(SP 108.0%) **5 Rn**

4m 28.2 (-2.80) CSF £5.08 TOTE £1.40: £1.30 £2.60 (£3.40) OWNER Mr J. Neville (NEWPORT, GWENT) BRED Russlson and Campbell Stud

LONG HANDICAP Irish Dominion 9-5

STEWARDS' ENQUIRY Hobbs fined £200 under Rule H14 (not reporting horse bleeding from nose).

OFFICIAL EXPLANATION **Irish Dominion: rider reported that his instructions were to switch the gelding off in the rear and get him home, but the gelding had pulled hard and he had needed to keep a good hold of his head. The trainer added that the gelding had a history of breaking blood-vessels.**

3979 Ath Cheannaithe (FR) had finished tailed-off on the Sand since pulling too hard in a first-time visor at Wincanton. (4/6)

3189 Gi Moss, beaten in a two-mile seller last time, had finished third over three-and-a-quarter miles the time before. (7/1)

3894 Irish Dominion was the subject of a Stewards' enquiry into his running and riding. The explanations were accepted but, during the course of the enquiry, it became apparent that the trainer had not reported that the gelding had bled from the nose in his previous race. They therefore fined him £200. (14/1)

4290 TAUNTON RACECOURSE CONFERENCE CENTRE (S) H'CAP HURDLE (0-90) (4, 5 & 6-Y.O) (Class G)

6-05 (6-05) **2m 3f 110y (10 hdls)** £1,763.00 (£493.00: £239.00) GOING minus 0.78 sec per fur (F)

	Horse	Details	Dist	Pos	SP	RR	SF
3979^{4}	**Fleet Cadet (86)**	(MCPipe) **6-11-9v**(5) GSupple (hld up: hdwy 7th: led on bit 2 out: sn clr: easily)	—	**1**	3/1^{1}	71+	19
3933^{6}	**Just for a Reason (71)**	(RTJuckes) **5-10-13v^{1}** JRailton (lw: hld up: hdwy 6th: rdn 7th: r.o flat: no ch w wnr)	7	**2**	6/1	50	—
4089^{3}	**Against The Clock (58)**	(PBowen) **5-9-7**(7) LCummins (lw: chsd ldr: led 7th to 2 out: sn btn)	½	**3**	7/2^{2}	37	—
1707^{7}	**Griffin's Girl (68)**	(NGAyliffe) **5-10-7**(3) GuyLewis (lw: hld up: hdwy 5th: wknd appr last)	4	**4**	12/1	44	—
4137^{3}	**Rapid Liner (64)**	(RJBaker) **4-10-0** VSlattery (nt j.w: a bhd: rdn appr 6th: t.o fr 7th)	10	**5**	33/1	31	—
4137^{5}	**Kai's Lady (IRE) (64)**	(CLPopham) **4-9-7**(7) MrOMcPhail (prom to 5th: t.o fr 7th)	dist	**6**	33/1	—	—
879^{12}	**Night Time (71)**	(AGHobbs) **5-10-6**(7) MrGShenkin (lw: a bhd: t.o whn p.u after 5th: b.b.v)		**P**	6/1	—	—
4018^{4}	**Prince Equiname (80)**	(RSimpson) **5-11-8b^{1}** BClifford (mstke 2nd: sn bhd: t.o whn p.u bef 6th)		**P**	8/1	—	—
4069^{F}	**More Bills (IRE) (72)**	(JNeville) **5-11-0v** TDascombe (lw: led tl mstke 7th: rdn & wknd after 3 out: t.o whn p.u bef last)		**P**	5/1^{3}	—	—

(SP 117.1%) **9 Rn**

4m 30.4 (-0.60) CSF £20.08 CT £58.74 TOTE £3.10: £1.50 £2.20 £1.80 (£10.60) Trio £8.20 OWNER Sir John Swaine (WELLINGTON) BRED R. D. Hollingsworth

LONG HANDICAP Rapid Liner 9-9 Against The Clock 9-9 Kai's Lady (IRE) 9-10

WEIGHT FOR AGE 4yo-6lb

No bid

OFFICIAL EXPLANATION **Night Time: bled from the nose.**

3735* Fleet Cadet has now been well placed to win four sellers this season, and made this one look pretty simple. (3/1)

2943 Just for a Reason, tried in a visor over this longer trip, kept on to secure second place close home. (6/1)

4089 Against The Clock, 5lb out of the handicap, was quickly brushed aside by the winner. (7/2)

Prince Equiname (8/1: 6/1-12/1)

4291 PETER & SYBIL BLACKBURN MEMORIAL CHALLENGE TROPHY NOVICES' CHASE (5-Y.O+) (Class D)

6-35 (6-37) **2m 3f (15 fncs)** £3,420.00 (£1,035.00: £505.00: £240.00) GOING minus 0.78 sec per fur (F)

	Horse	Dist	Pos	SP	RR	SF
3732^{F}	**After The Fox (83)** (NJHawke) **10-11-0**(7) MrJTizzard (hld up: hdwy 7th: led 9th: clr whn veered lft flat: shkn up: comf)	—	1	5/4^{1}	84+	16
4172^{4}	**Castleconner (IRE) (77)** (RGFrost) **6-11-7b** JFrost (led tl j.slowly 2nd: led 7th to 9th: hit 2 out: r.o one pce flat)	2	2	8/1	82	14
4083^{3}	**Mozemo (81)** (MCPipe) **10-10-9v1**(5) GSupple (hld up: wknd 11th)	22	3	5/1^{3}	57	—
	Run With Joy (IRE) (AGHobbs) **6-11-0** RGreene (bit bkwd: bhd fr 9th)	1¼	4	33/1	56	—
4142^{3}	**Mistress Rosie (71)** (MHill) **10-10-11**(5) ChrisWebb (led 2nd to 7th: wknd 9th: t.o)	17	5	10/1	43	—
4072*	**Duke of Dreams (89)** (RJBaker) **7-12-0** VSlattery (hld up & bhd: blnd bdly 8th (water): sn p.u: dead)		P	7/2^{2}	—	—
	Bally Cruise (KCBailey) **10-10-9** TJO'Sullivan (Withdrawn not under Starter's orders: bolted bef s)		W	20/1	—	—
				(SP 111.2%)		**6 Rn**

4m 41.4 (-0.60) CSF £9.53 TOTE £2.00: £1.60 £2.10 (£5.40) OWNER Mrs Robert Blackburn (CHARD) BRED J. A. G. Meaden
3732 After The Fox was well in command when heading towards the paddock exit after the last. (5/4)
4001 Castleconner (IRE), reverting to the larger obstacles, had only won a selling chase at Exeter in December. (8/1: op 5/1)
4083 Mozemo, 7lb better off than when beaten nine lengths by the winner over course-and-distance last month, did not find the first-time visor doing the trick. (5/1: 7/2-11/2)
4142 Mistress Rosie (10/1: 7/1-11/1)

4292 BARNARDOS CENTENARY 'N.H' NOVICES' HURDLE (4-Y.O+) (Class E)

7-10 (7-10) **2m 1f (9 hdls)** £2,169.00 (£609.00: £297.00) GOING minus 0.78 sec per fur (F)

	Horse	Dist	Pos	SP	RR	SF
4162^{9}	**Laura Lye (IRE) (74)** (BdeHaan) **7-10-9** GUpton (lw: hld up: hdwy after 4th: led last: shkn up flat: cleverly)	—	1	8/1	63+	7
1713^{3}	**Red Tel (IRE)** (MCPipe) **5-10-9**(5) GSupple (lw: led: rdn & hit 2 out: hdd last: nt qckn)	1¼	2	5/4^{1}	67	11
3004^{10}	**Bayerd (IRE) (94)** (CREgerton) **6-11-7b** JAMcCarthy (hld up: hdwy 5th: rdn & mstke 2 out: one pce)	1¼	3	5/2^{2}	73	17
2576^{10}	**Piccolina** (RTPhillips) **5-10-9** JRailton (chsd ldr tl after 4th: wknd appr 6th: t.o)	dist	4	25/1	—	—
2878^{3}	**Miss Foxy (85)** (RGFrost) **7-11-2** JFrost (hld up: hdwy after 4th: wknd 5th: sn t.o: p.u nr fin: lame)		P	11/4^{3}	—	—
				(SP 114.6%)		**5 Rn**

3m 51.2 (-1.80) CSF £18.19 TOTE £5.90: £2.20 £1.50 (£4.90) OWNER Charlie Productions (LAMBOURN) BRED Maurice and Jeremiah Sheahan
OFFICIAL EXPLANATION **Laura Lye (IRE): regarding the improvement in form, the mare had run too freely in blinkers last time and settled better on this occasion.**
3933 Laura Lye (IRE) had finished tailed off in a Southwell seller when tried in blinkers last time. (8/1)
1713 Red Tel (IRE) found the winner toying with him in the closing stages. (5/4: op 4/5)
1165* Bayerd (IRE), dropping back in trip, found these conditions totally different to when winning at Plumpton on November. (5/2)

4293 SOMERSET NUFFIELD HOSPITAL H'CAP CHASE (0-120) (5-Y.O+) (Class D)

7-40 (7-40) **3m (19 fncs)** £3,436.25 (£1,040.00: £507.50: £241.25) GOING minus 0.78 sec per fur (F)

	Horse	Dist	Pos	SP	RR	SF
4142^{5}	**Spinning Steel (94)** (PRRodford) **10-10-5**ow4 SBurrough (lw: chsd ldr fr 5th: led 13th: wl clr 4 out: easily)	—	1	15/2	104+	11
3903^{4}	**Staunch Rival (USA) (97)** (GThorner) **10-10-1b**(7) ClareThorner (hit 3rd: sn wl bhd: styd on fr 3 out: no ch w wnr)	12	2	7/2^{3}	99	10
4179^{P}	**L'Uomo Piu (89)** (ABarrow) **13-9-7**(7) MrOMcPhail (led to 13th: outpcd 15th: wknd appr last)	10	3	5/1	84	—
4167^{6}	**Foxgrove (89)** (RJPrice) **11-9-9**(5) XAizpuru (chsd ldr to 5th: lost pl 7th: rallied 12th: hit 13th: mstke 15th: sn bhd)	3	4	5/2^{1}	82	—
4074^{P}	**Mugoni Beach (113)** (MCPipe) **12-11-5b**(5) GSupple (hld up & bhd: hdwy 10th: 3rd & btn whn blnd 3 out)	12	5	11/4^{2}	98	9
				(SP 105.9%)		**5 Rn**

5m 52.8 (-4.20) CSF £27.37 TOTE £5.30: £2.90 £2.20 (£16.80) OWNER Mrs C. A. Lewis-Jones (MARTOCK) BRED R. G. Ellis
LONG HANDICAP L'Uomo Piu 9-2 Foxgrove 9-3
4142 Spinning Steel found no problem with the step-up to three miles. (15/2: 5/1-8/1)
3903 Staunch Rival (USA) only got going late in the day. (7/2)
4022* L'Uomo Piu attracted support in the market, despite being 12lb out of the handicap. (5/1)
3742* Foxgrove (5/2: op 4/1)
3280 Mugoni Beach (11/4: 5/4-3/1)

4294 RED CROSS & ST JOHN H'CAP HURDLE (0-100) (4-Y.O+) (Class F)

8-10 (8-11) **2m 1f (9 hdls)** £1,987.00 (£557.00: £271.00) GOING minus 0.78 sec per fur (F)

	Horse	Dist	Pos	SP	RR	SF
4069*	**Contract Bridge (IRE) (80)** (PGMurphy) **4-11-3** WMcFarland (hld up: hit 6th: wnt 2nd 3 out: rdn whn lft in ld 2 out: lft clr last)	—	1	11/8^{1}	57?	—
4226^{9}	**Ketchican (72)** (SGKnight) **5-11-1** GUpton (lw: plld hrd: set slow pce to 4th: btn whn lft 2nd last)	5	2	9/1	44?	—
975^{5}	**Gabish (57)** (BScriven) **12-9-9**(5) GSupple (chsd ldr tl wknd 3 out)	5	3	25/1	25?	—
4020*	**Shifting Moon (75)** (FJordan) **5-11-4** DerekByrne (lw: plld hrd: led 4th tl fell 2 out)		F	13/8^{2}	—	—
3949^{4}	**October Brew (USA) (81)** (MCPipe) **7-11-3b**(7) BMoore (hld up: hdwy 3 out: hmpd 2 out: 2nd whn rn out & crashed thro wing last)		R	4/1^{3}	—	—
				(SP 114.0%)		**5 Rn**

4m 5.7 (12.70) CSF £11.98 TOTE £2.30: £1.40 £3.00 (£19.00) OWNER LM Racing (BRISTOL) BRED E. O'Leary
LONG HANDICAP Gabish 9-7
WEIGHT FOR AGE 4yo-6lb
4069* Contract Bridge (IRE) would not have beaten Shifting Moon had the latter stood up. (11/8)
4021 Ketchican only finished runner-up because of the misfortune of others. (9/1)
4020* Shifting Moon was looking all over the winner when coming to grief. (13/8)
October Brew (USA) was not travelling anything like as well as Shifting Moon when forced left-handed two out, and that may not have helped his concentration at the last. (4/1: 2/1-9/2)

T/Plpt: £39.50 (138.4 Tckts). T/Qdpt: £29.40 (11.93 Tckts) KH

3940-MARKET RASEN (R-H) (Good)
Saturday April 26th
WEATHER: raining & misty

4295 APRIL (S) H'CAP HURDLE (0-95) (4 & 5-Y.O) (Class G)
2-10 (2-10) **2m 1f 110y (8 hdls)** £1,936.50 (£539.00: £259.50) GOING minus 0.01 sec per fur (G)

Form	Horse	Dist	Pos	SP	RR	SF
4236[7]	**Eurolink the Rebel (USA) (80)** (SBClark) **5-10-9**(7) MissRClark (chsd ldrs: led 3rd: kpt on fr 2 out: all out)	—	**1**	20/1	64	29
3933[3]	**Summer Villa (66)** (KGWingrove) **5-10-2b** WMarston (a chsng ldrs: styd on u.p flat)	1	**2**	11/1	49	14
3723[4]	**Tsanga (68)** (GMMoore) **5-10-4**ow3 NBentley (hdwy 4th: sn chsng ldrs: one pce fr 2 out)	7	**3**	8/1[3]	45	7
3921[4]	**Lebedinski (IRE) (74)** (MrsPSly) **4-10-4** VSmith (bhd: styd on wl fr 2 out: nt rch ldrs)	1½	**4**	16/1	49	8
	Turrill House (64) (WJMusson) **5-10-0** BPowell (lw: stdd s: hld up & bhd: stdy hdwy 2 out: nvr plcd to chal)	nk	**5**	11/1	39+	4
2541[4]	**Mr Gold (IRE) (78)** (JParkes) **4-10-8** KJohnson (hdwy 5th: sn chsng ldrs: blnd 2 out: one pce)	2½	**6**	10/1	51	10
3908[4]	**Simand (71)** (GMMoore) **5-10-7** JCallaghan (chsd ldrs tl rdn & lost pl 5th: sme hdwy 2 out: n.d)	1½	**7**	10/1	42	7
4056[8]	**Queen's Counsel (IRE) (70)** (MissMKMilligan) **4-10-0** ASSmith (hld up: gd hdwy 5th: 4th whn blnd 2 out)	hd	**8**	16/1	41	—
3745[8]	**African Sun (IRE) (70)** (MCChapman) **4-10-0** WWorthington (chsd ldrs tl wknd appr 2 out)	½	**9**	33/1	41	—
4223[5]	**Evezio Rufo (84)** (NPLittmoden) **5-11-6b** KGaule (in tch: reminder 2nd: lost pl after 3 out)	2½	**10**	9/1	53	18
3964[10]	**Port Valenska (IRE) (70)** (MrsJConway) **4-9-9**(5) STaylor (a bhd)	3	**11**	50/1	36	—
743[4]	**Irie Mon (IRE) (79)** (MPBielby) **5-10-8**(7) MrAWintle (hld up: a bhd)	2½	**12**	14/1	43	8
3976[6]	**Petrico (64)** (PBeaumont) **5-9-9**(5) BGrattan (a bhd)	2	**13**	33/1	26	—
3983[9]	**Golf Land (IRE) (78)** (LLungo) **5-11-0** RSupple (nt j.w: plld hrd: led to 3rd: wkng whn blnd 3 out: t.o)	dist	**14**	7/1[2]	—	—
4162[8]	**Noir Esprit (79)** (JMCarr) **4-10-9v** NSmith (reminders 3rd: lost pl & hit next: t.o whn p.u bef 2 out)		**P**	12/1	—	—
3940*	**Our Robert (92)** (JGFitzGerald) **5-11-11**(3) FLeahy (lw: rdn & lost pl 4th: bhd whn p.u bef 2 out)		**P**	9/4[1]	—	—

(SP 138.0%) **16 Rn**

4m 11.0 (8.00) CSF £223.95 CT £1,783.39 TOTE £21.90: £4.50 £2.20 £2.10 £5.20 (£190.10) Trio £181.40; £230.07 to Pontefract 28/4/97
OWNER Mr S. B. Clark (SUTTON-ON-THE-FOREST) BRED Joseph Bryan Jnr
LONG HANDICAP Queen's Counsel (IRE) 9-9 Petrico 9-10 Turrill House 9-8 African Sun (IRE) 9-9 Port Valenska (IRE) 9-9
WEIGHT FOR AGE 4yo-6lb
Bt in 3,800 gns

OFFICIAL EXPLANATION **Eurolink the Rebel (USA): regarding the improved form, the rider reported that the gelding had been unsuited by the stiffer track last time. Our Robert: trainer reported that the gelding lost his action on the paddock bend and was never going thereafter.**

3976 Eurolink the Rebel (USA) appreciated this much easier track, and was given every assistance from the saddle. His twenty-year-old rider was breaking her duck under National Hunt Rules, but she has seventeen point-to-point and nine Flat wins to her credit. (20/1)
3933 Summer Villa, much-improved since blinkers were fitted, never gave up trying. (11/1)
3723 Tsanga appreciated the drop in class. (8/1)
3921 Lebedinski (IRE) stayed on when it was all over and will be suited by either a stiffer track or a longer trip. (16/1)
Turrill House, having her first outing over hurdles for 414 days having failed to complete on her final two runs last term, was racing from 6lb out of the handicap. Looking fit and well, she was dropped in at the start and never put in the race. Picking up ground on the bridle over the final two flights, the impression was that she is capable of much better. (11/1: 8/1-12/1)
4223 Evezio Rufo (9/1: 6/1-10/1)
3940* Our Robert dropped himself out on the paddock bend and looked anything but enthusiastic. (9/4)

4296 'GET AWAY FROM THE ELECTION CAMPAIGN' H'CAP HURDLE (0-105) (4-Y.O+) (Class F)
2-45 (2-46) **2m 5f 110y (10 hdls)** £2,272.50 (£635.00: £307.50) GOING minus 0.01 sec per fur (G)

Form	Horse	Dist	Pos	SP	RR	SF
4233[2]	**Hancock (78)** (JHetherton) **5-10-9** WMarston (gd hdwy 7th: led 2 out: drvn out)	—	**1**	7/2[1]	66	17
4055*	**Amazing Sail (IRE) (88)** (MissMKMilligan) **4-10-12** ASSmith (lw: led to 2 out: nt qckn)	5	**2**	7/1[3]	72	16
4223[4]	**Ajdar (74)** (OBrennan) **6-10-5** MBrennan (plld hrd: trckd ldrs: one pce fr 3 out)	12	**3**	16/1	49	—
4075[6]	**Dantes Amour (IRE) (81)** (MDHammond) **6-10-12** RGarritty (lw: hdwy 6th: one pce fr 3 out)	¾	**4**	16/1	56	7
4081[3]	**Cash Box (IRE) (88)** (TJCarr) **9-11-5** NSmith (lw: hld up & bhd: hit 4th: hdwy 3 out: nvr nr ldrs)	8	**5**	7/1[3]	57	8
3607[2]	**Shelton Abbey (70)** (JWade) **11-10-1b** BStorey (lw: lost pl 6th: n.d)	22	**6**	20/1	23	—
3434[8]	**Coup de Vent (72)** (MrsVCWard) **7-10-0**(3)ow3 PHenley (bit bkwd: swtg: chsd ldrs: rdn 6th: lost pl next)	½	**7**	50/1	24	—
3594[3]	**Dovetto (79)** (AEPrice) **8-10-7**(3) MrRThornton (chsd ldrs to 3 out: grad wknd)	5	**8**	9/1	27	—
3478[7]	**Tip it In (89)** (ASmith) **8-11-3**(3) PMidgley (in tch: drvn along 3 out: sn wknd)	3	**9**	11/1	35	—
3976[8]	**Marsh's Law (69)** (GPKelly) **10-9-7b**(7) LMcGrath (s.i.s: a wl bhd)	3	**10**	25/1	13	—
3992[6]	**Kinda Groovy (93)** (IPark) **8-11-10b** JCallaghan (lw: mid div: drvn along 5th: sn bhd)	9	**11**	25/1	30	—
3173[F]	**The Weatherman (73)** (AEJessop) **9-10-4**ow4 TKent (a wl bhd)	1	**12**	50/1	10	—
3976[9]	**Rubislaw (69)** (MrsKMLamb) **5-9-7v**(7) MissSLamb (chsd ldrs: drvn along 5th: lost pl 7th)	5	**13**	66/1	2	—
3885[10]	**Desert Force (IRE) (90)** (GFierro) **8-11-2**(5) XAizpuru (sn wl bhd: t.o whn p.u bef 3 out)		**P**	10/1	—	—
3923[4]	**Cambo (USA) (85)** (MCBanks) **11-11-2** DSkyrme (chsd ldrs to 4th: sn bhd: t.o whn p.u bef 2 out)		**P**	11/1	—	—
4093[3]	**Moobakkr (USA) (79)** (KAMorgan) **6-10-10** BPowell (lw: chsd ldr: rdn whn blnd & uns rdr 3 out)		**U**	9/2[2]	—	—

(SP 130.8%) **16 Rn**

5m 15.5 (11.50) CSF £26.20 CT £339.00 TOTE £4.80: £1.60 £1.70 £2.60 £3.60 (£16.00) Trio £269.70; £83.59 to Pontefract 28/4/97 OWNER Mr N. Hetherton (MALTON) BRED N. Hetherton
LONG HANDICAP The Weatherman 9-1 Rubislaw 8-9 Marsh's Law 9-12 Coup de Vent 8-10
WEIGHT FOR AGE 4yo-7lb

4233 Hancock appreciated this drop back in distance and the easier track, where he has run well in the past. He broke his duck in most decisive fashion, though to be honest this handicap was little better than a seller. (7/2)
4055* Amazing Sail (IRE), raised 5lb, showed that connections were justified in going up to 9,500 guineas to retain him at Sedgefield. He attacked from the front but, in the end, the winner proved much too good. (7/1)
4223 Ajdar would not settle and this step up in trip did not really suit him. (16/1)
4075 Dantes Amour (IRE) seemed to appreciate attempting an extended trip. (16/1)
4081 Cash Box (IRE) raced keenly but seemed to be given a fair bit to do. (7/1)
4093 Moobakkr (USA) was about six lengths second, but under strong pressure, when he went out of the contest three from home. (9/2)

4297 UK HYGIENE NOVICES' H'CAP CHASE (0-105) (5-Y.O+) (Class E)

3-15 (3-15) **2m 1f 110y (13 fncs)** £3,208.50 (£963.00: £464.00: £214.50) GOING: 0.29 sec per fur (GS)

Form	Horse	Dist	Pos	SP	RR	SF
4183[5]	**Daring Past (90)** (MDHammond) **7-11-10** RGarritty (trckd ldrs: led after 4 out: clr 2 out: drvn out flat)	—	1	3/1[2]	101	17
4157[P]	**Bali Tender (66)** (JWharton) **6-9-11**(3) FLeahy (hld up: stdy hdwy 8th: effrt 2 out: kpt on flat)	4	2	20/1	73	—
4057*	**Tapatch (IRE) (88)** (MWEasterby) **9-11-5b**(3) MrRThornton (led after 2nd to 6th: led 8th tl after 4 out: wknd next)	20	3	9/4[1]	77	—
3960[3]	**Copper Cable (67)** (CSmith) **10-10-1** MRanger (sn outpcd: sme hdwy 4 out: n.d)	3	4	16/1	53	—
3842[U]	**Dash To The Phone (USA) (73)** (KAMorgan) **5-10-0** WMarston (hld up: nt j.w: sn bhd)	5	5	4/1[3]	55	—
4145[4]	**Reve de Valse (USA) (80)** (RJohnson) **10-11-0** KJohnson (led tl after 2nd: led 6th to 8th: wkng whn blnd 4 out: sn bhd)	15	6	4/1[3]	48	—
1252[P]	**Karlovac (70)** (SGChadwick) **11-10-4** FPerratt (sn bhd: t.o 7th: blnd 9th)	dist	7	14/1	—	—
				(SP 113.1%)		**7 Rn**

4m 33.6 (18.60) CSF £43.18 TOTE £4.00: £1.80 £4.20 (£52.40) OWNER Mr John Petty (MIDDLEHAM) BRED P. and Mrs Venner
LONG HANDICAP Bali Tender 9-12
WEIGHT FOR AGE 5yo-7lb

4183 Daring Past continued his stable's revival. Jumping particularly well, he took this with something to spare and, still about 20lb below his best handicap mark over hurdles, he should enjoy further success. (3/1)
Bali Tender, a headstrong sort, ran easily his best race ever and, if reproducing this effort, can surely find an opening. (20/1)
4057* Tapatch (IRE), not for the first time, did not look in love with the game. (9/4)
3960 Copper Cable got in a tangle with Karlovac on the turn into the back straight. (16/1)
3842 Dash To The Phone (USA) lacked any confidence jumping-wise. (4/1)

4298 EUROBALE NOVICES' CHASE (5-Y.O+) (Class D)

3-50 (3-50) **2m 4f (15 fncs)** £3,910.25 (£1,172.00: £563.50: £259.25) GOING: 0.29 sec per fur (GS)

Form	Horse	Dist	Pos	SP	RR	SF
3941[F]	**Monks Soham (IRE)** (GAHubbard) **9-10-13**(3) PHenley (trckd ldrs: styd on fr 3 out: led flat: drvn out)	—	1	9/1[3]	103 t	35
3941[2]	**Bowles Patrol (IRE) (70)** (JohnUpson) **5-10-8** RSupple (trckd ldrs: hit 10th: ev ch whn hit 3 out: rallied last: r.o)	1¼	2	25/1	102 t	26
4090*	**Imperial Vintage (IRE) (124)** (MissVenetiaWilliams) **7-11-9**(3) MrRThornton (led: hit 11th: rdn 2 out: blnd last: sn hdd & nt qckn)	3	3	11/8[2]	110 t	42
3936[U]	**Mister Drum (IRE) (124)** (MJWilkinson) **8-11-12** WMarston (mstkes: chsd ldrs: hit 5th & 6th: rdn 11th: wknd next: eased)	dist	4	11/10[1]	—	—
4232[4]	**Chiappucci (IRE) (87)** (MrsEHHeath) **7-10-13b**(3) JMagee (mstkes: chsd ldrs: rdn & outpcd 11th: sn bhd: t.o)	dist	5	25/1	—	—
3450[3]	**Cardinal Sinner (IRE) (56)** (JWade) **8-11-2** BStorey (sn t.o: p.u bef 3 out)		P	50/1	—	—
				(SP 109.4%)		**6 Rn**

5m 4.8 (13.80) CSF £106.05 TOTE £10.30: £2.50 £3.80 (£30.60) OWNER Mr G. A. Hubbard (WOODBRIDGE) BRED P. J. Reynolds
WEIGHT FOR AGE 5yo-8lb
OFFICIAL EXPLANATION **Mister Drum (IRE): was found to have lost his off-fore shoe.**

3941 Monks Soham (IRE), who was still in contention when falling at the last here last time, seems to be improving with age. Travelling strongly throughout, in the end he had to be driven right out. The runner-up had looked a very poor performer recently and the form of this race must be treated with caution. (9/1: 5/1-10/1)
3941 Bowles Patrol (IRE), a five-year-old running over fences, would have been beaten a long way had Monks Soham stood up last time. (25/1)
4090* Imperial Vintage (IRE), bidding for his tenth steeplechase win this season, looked to have it in the bag when driven four lengths clear two out, but he began to tread water after the last. It remains to be seen if he will bounce back this time. (11/8)
3835 Mister Drum (IRE) lost a shoe, and his jumping seemed to suffer after mistakes at the fifth and sixth fences. He would not have a cut at his fences, and with all chance gone on the home turn was eased right up. This is best overlooked. (11/10: evens-5/4)

4299 SANDERSON TELEPORTERS NOVICES' HURDLE (4-Y.O+) (Class D)

4-25 (4-25) **2m 3f 110y (10 hdls)** £3,156.50 (£947.00: £456.00: £210.50) GOING minus 0.01 sec per fur (G)

Form	Horse	Dist	Pos	SP	RR	SF
4176*	**Talathath (FR) (111)** (DNicholson) **5-11-9**(3) MrRThornton (lw: trckd ldrs: led 2 out: drvn out)	—	1	6/4[1]	89	10
2772[4]	**Mazamet (USA)** (OO'Neill) **4-10-7** VSlattery (gd hdwy 6th: sn rdn: led appr 2 out: sn hdd: nt qckn flat)	1	2	9/4[2]	75	—
3964[4]	**Gipsy Geof (IRE)** (GAHubbard) **6-10-11**(3) LAspell (hdwy 6th: sn chsng ldrs: ev ch last: kpt on same pce)	3	3	8/1	74	—
4095[5]	**Poppy's Dream** (JWharton) **7-10-9** ASSmith (stdd s: hld up & bhd: stdy hdwy 6th: kpt on wl fr 2 out: nvr nr to chal)	4	4	16/1	65+	—
4152[3]	**Raise A Dollar** (PBeaumont) **7-10-9** RSupple (w ldrs: led 7th tl appr 2 out: one pce)	6	5	16/1	61	—
3823[10]	**Donnegale (IRE) (70)** (TPTate) **5-11-0** JCallaghan (led to 7th: wknd appr 2 out)	12	6	40/1	56	—
3973[4]	**M-I-Five (IRE)** (RonaldThompson) **6-11-0** OPears (hld up & bhd: sme hdwy 2 out: n.d)	8	7	14/1	49	—
3907[5]	**Teejay's Future (IRE)** (OBrennan) **6-10-9** MBrennan (hdwy 4th: ev ch tl wknd appr 2 out)	¾	8	20/1	44	—
3544[P]	**Alpheton Prince** (JohnHarris) **4-10-7** JSupple (chsd ldrs to 7th: sn lost pl)	6	9	66/1	43	—
3706[2]	**Larkshill (IRE) (92)** (JGFitzGerald) **6-10-11**(3) FLeahy (lw: chsd ldrs: sn drvn along: wknd 3 out)	5	10	7/1[3]	40	—
	Can She Can Can (CSmith) **5-10-9** MRanger (w ldrs tl wknd 6th: sn bhd)	4	11	50/1	31	—
2550[P]	**Moor Dance Man** (NPLittmoden) **7-11-0** DVerco (bit bkwd: s.s: rapid hdwy to go prom 5th: rdn next: wknd 7th)	2	12	66/1	35	—
	Springfield Rhyme (SGollings) **6-10-9** KGaule (mstkes: bhd fr 7th: t.o)	dist	13	66/1	—	—
3734[6]	**Bellidium** (AEJessop) **5-10-9** TKent (sn trckng ldrs: lost pl 6th: t.o whn p.u bef 2 out)		P	66/1	—	—
4184[11]	**Apache Len (USA)** (MDHammond) **4-10-7** RGarritty (lw: prom to 5th: t.o whn p.u bef 2 out)		P	33/1	—	—
3282[4]	**Nebaal (USA)** (GBarnett) **7-10-9**(5) XAizpuru (drvn along & t.o fr 6th: p.u bef 3 out)		P	66/1	—	—
				(SP 132.4%)		**16 Rn**

4m 49.5 (16.50) CSF £4.69 TOTE £2.10: £1.70 £2.00 £1.80 (£3.70) Trio £6.30 OWNER Million In Mind Partnership (6) (TEMPLE GUITING)
BRED Gainsborough Stud Management Ltd
WEIGHT FOR AGE 4yo-6lb

4176* Talathath (FR) found this step up to two-and-a-half miles no problem. Doing very little in front, he had to be driven right out but, in truth, always looked to have it under control. (6/4)
2772 Mazamet (USA), having his first run for ninety-one days, was flat out early on the second circuit. Sticking to his guns, this outing will have done him good and either a stiffer track or a longer trip will suit him. (9/4)

3964 Gipsy Geof (IRE), a half-brother to the Gold Cup winner Imperial Call, looks to be improving. Three miles will not be a problem for him. (8/1: 6/1-9/1)
4095 Poppy's Dream was not knocked about at any stage, and this bumper winner looks sure to win a mares' novice hurdle at least. (16/1)
4152 Raise A Dollar seems to have nothing in the way of speed. A step up to three miles is called for and, runner-up in a maiden point, she is sure to handle fences in due course. (16/1)
3706 Larkshill (IRE) (7/1: op 14/1)

4300 TONY EDWARDS & GEOFF HUNTER H'CAP CHASE (0-115) (5-Y.O+) (Class E)

5-00 (5-00) **2m 4f (15 fncs)** £3,299.50 (£991.00: £478.00: £221.50) GOING: 0.29 sec per fur (GS)

	Horse		Pos	SP	RR	SF
3436*	**Highbeath (87)** (MrsMReveley) **6-10-0** LWyer (wnt prom 9th: shkn up to ld after 3 out: drvn out)	—	1	5/2[1]	98	26
4058*	**Rustic Air (104)** (JGFitzGerald) **10-11-3** RGarritty (chsd ldrs: blnd 10th: sn lost pl: hdwy 3 out: styd on wl flat)	4	2	5/1[3]	112	40
4225[3]	**Merry Panto (IRE) (98)** (CPEBrooks) **8-10-4**(7) MBerry (a chsng ldrs: led 3 out: sn hdd: kpt on same pce)	¾	3	8/1	105	33
4159[2]	**Cheeka (87)** (CSmith) **8-10-0** MRanger (s.s: hdwy 6th: sn prom: hit 9th: led 4 out: hdd next: one pce)	4	4	16/1	91	19
4226[6]	**Bally Parson (102)** (RDickin) **11-10-10**(5) XAizpuru (lw: led & sn clr: hit 10th: hdd 4 out: one pce)	¾	5	9/1	105	33
	Allimac Nomis (88) (MDHammond) **8-10-1** DBentley (plld hrd: trckd ldrs: stdd 4 out: effrt 2 out: fnd nil)	4	6	20/1	88	16
3725[2]	**Cross Cannon (107)** (JWade) **11-11-6** BStorey (chsd ldrs to 7th: lost pl 9th: n.d)	11	7	7/1	98	26
3707[4]	**Juke Box Billy (IRE) (87)** (MrsJBrown) **9-10-0** ASSmith (blnd 2nd: sn bhd)	25	8	20/1	58	—
3540[3]	**Shining Light (IRE) (114)** (DNicholson) **8-11-10**(3) MrRThornton (blnd 3rd: sn drvn along: lost pl 7th: t.o 10th: p.u bef 3 out)		P	100/30[2]	—	—
4159[8]	**Call Me Early (87)** (DShaw) **12-10-0** MBrennan (blnd 3rd: t.o 10th: p.u bef 3 out)		P	50/1	—	—
				(SP 119.3%)	**10 Rn**	

5m 3.2 (12.20) CSF £14.56 CT £81.17 TOTE £2.90: £1.20 £2.10 £2.30 (£7.00) Trio £26.80 OWNER Mr A. Sharratt (SALTBURN) BRED Huttons Ambo Stud
LONG HANDICAP Highbeath 9-13 Juke Box Billy (IRE) 9-5 Cheeka 9-10 Call Me Early 8-13
OFFICIAL EXPLANATION Shining Light: no explanation offered.
3436* Highbeath made light of a fifty-four day absence. Though tending to run about, he always looked in charge. Still on a lower mark than that from which he was successful over hurdles, he looks ideal summer jumping material. (5/2)
4058* Rustic Air tends to make at least one bad mistake every time. Rousted along, he came back up the straight, and is still on a mark from which he is capable of winning. (5/1)
4225 Merry Panto (IRE) is running up to his best at present. (8/1)
4159 Cheeka, still a maiden after twenty-eight starts over fences, to his credit has run up to his best on his last two outings. (16/1)
4226 Bally Parson, back over fences, set a strong gallop and kept on surprisingly well. (9/1)
Allimac Nomis, making a belated reappearance, travelled really strongly on the heels of the leaders but, when called on for an effort, pulled out very little. He is probably much better suited by two miles. (20/1)

4301 SPRING STANDARD N.H. FLAT RACE (4, 5 & 6-Y.O) (Class H)

5-30 (5-30) **1m 5f 110y** £1,402.50 (£390.00: £187.50)

	Horse		Pos	SP	RR	SF
	Route One (IRE) (CPEBrooks) **4-10-5**(7) MBerry (w'like: trckd ldrs: shkn up to ld over 1f out: qcknd clr: drvn out)	—	1	8/1[3]	68 f	—
3946[3]	**Double Star** (JLHarris) **6-11-1**(3) MrRThornton (mde most tl over 2f out: ev ch over 1f out: kpt on wl)	5	2	6/1[2]	67 f	—
4215[2]	**Siren Song (IRE)** (CJMann) **6-11-11**(3) JMagee (trckd ldrs: rdn over 2f out: kpt on same pce)	3	3	5/4[1]	74 f	—
3946[11]	**Capsoff (IRE)** (GAHubbard) **4-10-4**(3) LAspell (hdwy 4f out: led over 2f out tl over 1f out: one pce)	2½	4	8/1[3]	51 f	—
	Royal Mint (TThomsonJones) **4-10-7**(5) XAizpuru (tall: mid div: styd on fnl 2f: nvr nr to chal)	6	5	8/1[3]	48 f	—
	Miss Mouse (PMooney) **5-10-10**(3) MrCBonner (leggy: unf: cl up: chal 3f out: wknd 2f out)	2	6	20/1	46 f	—
	Maddie (WWHaigh) **5-10-6**(7) MNewton (rangy: hld up: stdy hdwy 6f out: shkn up over 2f out: grad wknd)	1	7	25/1	45 f	—
	Ailsae (MrsJBrown) **4-10-4**(3) ECallaghan (bkwd: bhd: sme hdwy 3f out: nvr nr ldrs)	1	8	33/1	39 f	—
	Spanish Secret (IRE) (NPLittmoden) **5-10-13**(5) ChrisWebb (leggy: unf: plld hrd: trckd ldrs tl lost pl 3f out)	3	9	20/1	45 f	—
	Cahermone Lady (IRE) (RMWhitaker) **6-10-13** MrNKent (w'like: unf: prom to 5f out: sn outpcd)	2½	10	20/1	37 f	—
	Sweet Little Briar (IRE) (GCBravery) **6-10-13** GLee (leggy: unf: bit bkwd: trckd ldrs: rdn & wknd over 2f out)	nk	11	25/1	37 f	—
	Bred For Pleasure (WSCunningham) **4-10-0**(7) LMcGrath (a in rr)	12	12	33/1	18 f	—
	Derring Dove (AEPrice) **5-11-1**(3) FLeahy (lengthy: a in rr)	2	13	25/1	25 f	—
	Angry Native (IRE) (JWade) **5-10-13**(5) STaylor (tall: unf: chsd ldrs 6f: bhd fnl 5f)	9	14	33/1	15 f	—
	New Ross (IRE) (OO'Neill) **5-10-11**(7) LSuthern (leggy: unf: bkwd: a bhd)	4	15	20/1	10 f	—
	Packitin Parky (DMcCain) **4-10-7**(5) OBurrows (bkwd: bhd fnl 4f)	2½	16	33/1	2 f	—
	The Bombers Moon (MrsEHHeath) **4-10-7**(5) BGrattan (rangy: str: bkwd: rn green: bhd fr ½-wy: t.o)	28	17	33/1	—	—
	Lake Aria (MrsAMNaughton) **4-10-0**(7) MrTJBarry (unf: in tch tl lost pl 5f out: sn wl bhd: t.o)	dist	18	25/1	—	—
	Honeysuckle Rose (LRLloyd-James) **4-10-4**(3) RMassey (leggy: w ldrs tl lost pl 4f out: t.o)	24	19	25/1	—	—
				(SP 145.0%)	**19 Rn**	

3m 11.3 CSF £48.67 TOTE £10.90: £2.60 £2.30 £1.60 (£20.40) Trio £10.00 OWNER Uplands Bloodstock (LAMBOURN) BRED Mrs B. M. Browne
WEIGHT FOR AGE 4yo-1lb
OFFICIAL EXPLANATION Honeysuckle Rose: swallowed her tongue.
IN-FOCUS: This race devloped into a three furlong sprint from the home turn.
Route One (IRE), who is bred for speed on his dam's side, took this in impressive fashion and showed a real turn of foot to shoot clear. He looks a very interesting prospect. (8/1: op 5/1)
3946 Double Star waited in front and kicked on off the bend but, in the end, he could not match the winner's turn of foot. (6/1)
4215 Siren Song (IRE) ran a flat race. His trainer thought it was a combination of the weight, the going and the race coming too soon after Ayr just a week ago. A dual bumper winner in Ireland, he looks sure to make a mark over hurdles next term. (5/4: evens-11/8)
3433 Capsoff (IRE) was probably not suited by the way this developed into a sprint. (8/1: op 5/1)
Royal Mint, who looks as though he has needed plenty of time, ran a pleasing first race. There should be improvement to come. (8/1: 5/1-10/1)

T/Plpt: £1,747.30 (6.45 Tckts). T/Qdpt: £163.80 (4.05 Tckts) WG

3835-SANDOWN (R-H) (Good tofirm)

Saturday April 26th

Races hand-timed, other races under Flat Rules
WEATHER: overcast & damp WIND: almost nil

4302 BREWERS FAYRE NOVICES' H'CAP CHASE (5-Y.O+) (Class C)

2-50 (2-52) **2m 4f 110y (17 fncs)** £13,705.00 (£4,165.00: £2,045.00: £985.00) GOING: 0.85 sec per fur (S)

	Horse / details	Dist	Pos	SP	RR	SF
4185*	**Kenmore-Speed (110)** (MrsSJSmith) **10-10-3** RichardGuest (led to 3rd: led 11th to 4 out: led appr 2 out: rdn out)	—	1	7/2 1	117	49
4211 3	**Stately Home (IRE) (135)** (PBowen) **6-12-0** RJohnson (lw: chsd ldr: led 3rd to 11th: led 4 out tl appr 2 out: ev ch whn mstke last: unable qckn)	1½	2	7/1	141	73
3978 U	**Full of Bounce (IRE) (107)** (RJHodges) **6-10-0** TDascombe (lw: bmpd 2nd: mstkes 9th & 4 out: hdwy appr 3 out: hrd rdn appr 2 out: one pce)	8	3	33/1	107	39
3697 2	**Goldenswift (IRE) (107)** (GBBalding) **7-10-0** BFenton (lw: hdwy appr 3 out: rdn appr 2 out: 3rd & btn whn mstke last)	s.h	4	6/1 2	107	39
4133 2	**Garnwin (IRE) (125)** (NJHenderson) **7-11-4** MAFitzgerald (lw: bhd fr 7th)	25	5	7/2 1	105	37
3300 4	**Fine Thyne (IRE) (120)** (MrsAJPerrett) **8-10-13** RDunwoody (3rd whn fell 7th)		F	7/2 1	—	—
3986*	**Plunder Bay (USA) (110)** (NJHenderson) **6-10-3** NWilliamson (lw: 6th whn fell 7th)		F	13/2 3	—	—
4070 2	**Tom's Apache (107)** (OJCarter) **8-10-0** DGallagher (a bhd: t.o fr 7th: p.u bef 11th)		P	100/1	—	—
				(SP 110.7%)	**8 Rn**	

5m 17.0 (18.00) CSF £23.79 CT £588.92 TOTE £4.10: £1.60 £2.20 £3.50 (£24.20) OWNER Mr K. M. Dacker (BINGLEY) BRED Mrs Davina Whiteman

LONG HANDICAP Full of Bounce (IRE) 9-1 Goldenswift (IRE) 9-8 Tom's Apache 8-5

4185* Kenmore-Speed coped well with the drop back in distance. Together with the runner-up, they both really turned on the gas entering the back straight for the final time and forged clear of their rivals. The gelding showed decisively in front approaching the second last and, ridden along, asserted his authority on the run-in. He has been a model of consistency this season and is a real credit to his trainer. (7/2)

4211 Stately Home (IRE) loves it round here where good, clean jumping is paramount. Despite being 15lb higher than when last seen in a handicap, and having been on the go since last June, he still ran a first-class race, cutting out the majority of the running. Collared approaching the second-last, he still had every chance when an untidy jump at the final fence sealed his fate. He loves this ground and a tenth victory of the campaign looks on the cards. (7/1)

3978 Full of Bounce (IRE), 13lb out of the handicap, nevertheless ran well. Closing up approaching the Pond Fence, he came under pressure approaching the second last, but could only go up and down in the same place. (33/1)

3697 Goldenswift (IRE), who has been leniently handicapped this season, had far more on her plate this time and, with a drop in distance that was against her, failed to quicken from the Pond Fence. (6/1)

4133 Garnwin (IRE), 13lb higher than when last seen in a handicap, has been in sparkling form this season but ran a lifeless race here on ground that should have suited. (7/2)

4303 41ST WHITBREAD GOLD CUP H'CAP CHASE (Gd 3) (5-Y.O+) (Class A)

3-30 (3-31) **3m 5f 110y (24 fncs)** £58,300.00 (£21,400.00: £10,400.00: £4,400.00: £1,900.00) GOING: 0.85 sec per fur (S)

	Horse / details	Dist	Pos	SP	RR	SF
3916 2	**Harwell Lad (IRE) (133)** (RHAlner) **8-10-0** MrRNuttall (hld up: mstke 4th: lft in ld 3 out: rdn out)	—	1	14/1	141	60
3598*	**Flyer's Nap (140)** (RHAlner) **11-10-7** APMcCoy (lw: hld up: ev ch 3 out: 2nd whn blnd last: unable qckn)	4	2	4/1 1	146	65
3699 5	**McGregor The Third (134)** (GRichards) **11-10-1**ow1 RDunwoody (a.p: ev ch 3 out: one pce)	4	3	13/2 3	137	55
4074 P	**Feathered Gale (138)** (ALTMoore,Ireland) **10-10-5** PCarberry (led to 2nd: bhd fr 13th: t.o fr 19th)	dist	4	9/1	—	—
4074 6	**Avro Anson (143)** (MJCamacho) **9-10-10** PNiven (led 2nd to 9th: led 11th to 13th: led 14th to 16th: wknd 17th: t.o)	8	5	5/1 2	—	—
4011*	**Barton Bank (157)** (DNicholson) **11-11-10** DWalsh (lw: 4th whn fell 18th)		F	4/1 1	—	—
3598 7	**Yorkshire Gale (135)** (JTGifford) **11-10-2** NWilliamson (lw: a.p: led 9th to 11th: led 13th to 14th: led 16th tl fell 3 out)		F	13/2 3	—	—
4074 P	**Bishops Hall (139)** (RHAlner) **11-10-6** CFSwan (a bhd: t.o fr 14th: p.u bef 17th)		P	15/2	—	—
4135 U	**Tom's Gemini Star (133)** (OJCarter) **9-10-0** DGallagher (lw: a bhd: mstke 10th: t.o fr 14th: p.u bef 17th)		P	150/1	—	—
				(SP 112.4%)	**9 Rn**	

7m 35.5 (20.50) CSF £62.62 CT £366.77 TOTE £16.10: £2.70 £2.30 £1.30 (£33.60) Trio £34.60 OWNER Mr H. Wellstead (BLANDFORD) BRED N. J. Connors

LONG HANDICAP Harwell Lad (IRE) 9-6 McGregor The Third 9-6 Tom's Gemini Star 6-13

IN-FOCUS: **Robert Alner gained his first Sandown winner in some style, with two out of his three runners filling the first two places in the Whitbread.**

3916 Harwell Lad (IRE) can be a tricky customer and was racing from 8lb out of the handicap, but he was on his best behaviour when it mattered most on this big occasion. Despite being 13lb higher than when last successful, he was left in front at the Pond Fence and, ridden along, proved too strong for his stable companion. (14/1)

3598* Flyer's Nap, whose trainer must have been delighted with the overnight rain which must have taken some of the sting out of the ground, travelled well throughout the race and was one of four in line at the Pond Fence. Only about a length down at the final fence, he made a bad error which brought him to a standstill and sealed his fate. (4/1)

3699 McGregor The Third, carrying 9lb more than his long handicap weight, ran a first-class race. One of four in line at the Pond Fence, he then failed to find another gear. (13/2)

3526a Feathered Gale, who has disappointed since his seasonal debut back in October, again failed to shine. (9/1)

4074 Avro Anson was quite obviously feeling the effects of his hard race in the Grand National for, after cutting out the majority of the running to the sixteenth, he was soon in trouble. (5/1: 3/1-11/2)

4011* Barton Bank, who was not brilliant at several fences, was very awkward at the water and slithered to the ground. (4/1)

3598 Yorkshire Gale goes well round this course, having won here four times. Showing in front at the ninth, he made the vast majority of the running from that point and was still in front when crashing out of the race at the Pond Fence, three out. (13/2)

T/Jkpt: Not won; £10,160.32 to 28/4/97. T/Plpt: £515.20 (97.08 Tckts). T/Qdpt: £47.40 (65.09 Tckts) AK

4002-WORCESTER (L-H) (Soft)

Saturday April 26th

Race 3 & 5: 1 fence omitted

WEATHER: raining

4304 HENWICK NOVICES' HURDLE (4-Y.O+ F & M) (Class E)

5-45 (5-45) **2m (8 hdls)** £2,600.00 (£725.00: £350.00) GOING: 1.29 sec per fur (HY)

				SP	RR	SF
3226[6]	**Ring For Rosie** (CaptTAForster) **6-10-12** BFenton (hld up & bhd: gd hdwy appr 3 out: hrd rdn to ld nr fin)	—	**1**	10/1	63	23
2927[4]	**Maid For Adventure (IRE) (100)** (MissHCKnight) **6-11-5** JCulloty (lw: a.p: led 3 out tl hdd nr fin)	hd	**2**	3/1[1]	70	30
3491[4]	**Fun While It Lasts** (CaptTAForster) **6-10-12** SWynne (a.p: ev ch 2 out: r.o flat)	½	**3**	12/1	62	22
4136[6]	**Regal Pursuit (IRE) (95)** (NJHenderson) **6-11-5b** MAFitzgerald (led tl after 2nd: ev ch 2 out: one pce)	2½	**4**	7/2[3]	67	27
3798[4]	**Madam's Walk (85)** (NATwiston-Davies) **7-10-12** CLlewellyn (w ldr: led 3rd to 4th: led 5th to 3 out: wknd appr last)	18	**5**	100/30[2]	42	2
3592[P]	**Carlingford Gale (IRE)** (TRGeorge) **6-10-12** RJohnson (nvr trbld ldrs)	1¼	**6**	20/1	41	1
3764[4]	**Gladys Emmanuel (76)** (REPocock) **10-10-7**(5) DJKavanagh (hld up: hdwy 4th: wknd 3 out)	4	**7**	6/1	37	—
3226[15]	**Mollie Silvers** (JKCresswell) **5-10-12** WMcFarland (dropped rr 4th: sn wl bhd)	6	**8**	100/1	31	—
3226[11]	**Lucrative Perk (IRE)** (MissCJECaroe) **5-10-12** DLeahy (hdwy 4th: wknd after 5th: t.o)	16	**9**	50/1	15	—
4002[7]	**A Badge Too Far (IRE) (52)** (MrsLWilliamson) **7-10-12b** RBellamy (prom tl lost pl & blnd 3rd: bhd fr 5th: t.o)	3½	**10**	100/1	11	—
3275[10]	**Blue Havana** (GraemeRoe) **5-10-12** PHide (a.p: led 4th to 5th: wknd 3 out: t.o)	25	**11**	100/1	—	—
	Heathyards Jade (AStreeter) **4-10-6** TEley (bkwd: a bhd: t.o)	17	**12**	50/1	—	—
3606[13]	**Sissinghurst Flyer (IRE)** (RDickin) **5-10-12** CMaude (a bhd: t.o whn fell last)		**F**	50/1	—	—
	Madam Cora (RDickin) **5-10-12** BPowell (bkwd: bhd tl gd hdwy appr 3 out: wkng whn p.u lame bef last: dead)		**P**	50/1	—	—
4230[P]	**Cloudy House** (NMLampard) **8-10-5**(7) MrLBaker (prom: led after 2nd to 3rd: wknd 5th: t.o whn p.u bef 2 out)		**P**	100/1	—	—
3767[10]	**Technical Move (IRE)** (GAHam) **6-10-12** SBurrough (prom to 3rd: t.o whn p.u bef 3 out)		**P**	50/1	—	—
	The Flying Fiddle (SNCole) **5-10-12** TDascombe (bit bkwd: bhd: mstke 3rd: t.o whn p.u bef 2 out)		**P**	100/1	—	—
4170[3]	**Royal Member** (MrsBarbaraWaring) **4-10-6** EByrne (bhd fr 4th: t.o whn p.u bef 3 out)		**P**	100/1	—	—
3184[P]	**T'Niel** (GFierro) **6-10-6**(7)ow1 SLycett (ref to r: tk no part)		**R**	100/1	—	—
				(SP 122.9%)	**19 Rn**	

4m 8.5 (28.50) CSF £35.57 TOTE £11.80: £2.40 £2.30 £2.80 (£16.10) Trio £31.00 OWNER Mr T. F. F. Nixon (LUDLOW) BRED Simon Sainsbury

WEIGHT FOR AGE 4yo-6lb

IN-FOCUS: Well over an inch of rain in the preceding thirty-six hours transformed the already watered ground into a quagmire.

3226 Ring For Rosie seemed to be suited by the big change in the ground, which put much more of an emphasis on stamina. (10/1)

2927 Maid For Adventure (IRE) has had a soft-palate operation since gurgling at Warwick in February. Encountering testing ground for the first time, she should soon be back to winning ways. (3/1: 7/4-7/2)

3491 Fun While It Lasts, one of the very few to have raced in the mud before, found her stamina coming into play in the closing stages. (12/1: op 8/1)

4136 Regal Pursuit (IRE), tried in blinkers, had finished runner-up on this sort of going over an extra half-mile at Plumpton last season. (7/2: 3/1-9/2)

3798 Madam's Walk has been running over further, but did not get home on this rain-sodden surface. (100/30)

4305 WEST MALVERN NOVICES' CHASE (5-Y.O+) (Class E)

6-15 (6-15) **2m (12 fncs)** £2,841.25 (£850.00: £407.50: £186.25) GOING: 1.29 sec per fur (HY)

				SP	RR	SF
3931[2]	**Lucky Eddie (IRE) (90)** (PJHobbs) **6-11-0** CMaude (a.p: hmpd 2nd: led appr 4 out: clr 3 out: r.o wl)	—	**1**	7/4[1]	76+	—
4237[U]	**Diamond Light** (VRBishop) **10-11-0** MrSLloyd (lost pl & hit 7th: sn bhd: rallied appr last: styd on flat: no ch w wnr)	12	**2**	33/1[3]	64	—
3826[6]	**Old Redwood (60)** (MrsLWilliamson) **10-11-0b[1]** LO'Hara (led: pckd 1st: blnd & hdd 2nd: reminders 7th: ev ch 4 out: sn wknd)	1½	**3**	5/2[2]	63	—
3806[P]	**Lady Rosebury** (RJPrice) **7-10-9** TJMurphy (mstke 1st: hdwy appr 4th: ev ch after 8th: blnd bdly 4 out: btn whn blnd 3 out)	6	**4**	33/1[3]	52	—
4092[3]	**Tenayestelign (79)** (DMarks) **9-11-9** SWynne (hld up: last whn fell 4th)		**F**	7/4[1]	—	—
	Steel Gold (TRKinsey) **7-10-7**(7) MrRBurton (lft in ld 2nd: hdd & wknd appr 4 out: blnd 3 out: p.u bef 2 out)		**P**	33/1[3]	—	—
				(SP 110.1%)	**6 Rn**	

4m 28.6 (37.60) CSF £34.50 TOTE £2.60: £1.60 £3.30 (£13.30) OWNER Mr I. L. Shaw (MINEHEAD) BRED John O. Browne

3931 Lucky Eddie (IRE) handled the rain-drenched ground for a bloodless win. (7/4)

Diamond Light, despite the testing ground, seemed to find this trip too short. (33/1)

3015 Old Redwood, blinkered for the first time, again had to contend with soft ground. (5/2)

4306 NICK HALLIGAN AND PETER HIGGS H'CAP CHASE (0-135) (5-Y.O+) (Class C)

6-45 (6-45) **2m 7f 110y (16 fncs)** £4,731.00 (£1,428.00: £694.00: £327.00) GOING: 1.29 sec per fur (HY)

				SP	RR	SF
4159[5]	**Hawaiian Youth (IRE) (107)** (GMMcCourt) **9-10-2** RDunwoody (led to 2nd: led 8th: clr appr last: r.o wl)	—	**1**	15/8[2]	116	41
1961*	**Bally Clover (111)** (MissVenetiaWilliams) **10-10-6** NWilliamson (blnd 1st: mstke 6th: hdwy 9th: ev ch whn mstke 3 out: sn btn)	10	**2**	7/4[1]	113	38
3916[5]	**Bavard Dieu (IRE) (129)** (NAGaselee) **9-11-10** CLlewellyn (hld up: rdn & lost pl 10th: rallied after 13th: wknd 3 out)	9	**3**	13/2	125	50
4074[P]	**Scribbler (112)** (GMMcCourt) **11-10-4b**(3) DFortt (prom: j.slowly 2nd: led 4th to 8th: lost pl 9th: wkng whn mstke 12th: t.o)	dist	**4**	100/30[3]	—	—
3729[P]	**Top Brass (IRE) (105)** (KCBailey) **9-10-0** SMcNeill (led 2nd to 4th: wknd 10th: t.o whn p.u bef 2 out)		**P**	12/1	—	—
				(SP 115.2%)	**5 Rn**	

6m 18.3 CSF £5.61 TOTE £2.70: £1.50 £1.30 (£2.90) OWNER Mr G. Redford (WANTAGE) BRED Owen Farrell

LONG HANDICAP Top Brass (IRE) 9-8

4159 Hawaiian Youth (IRE), stepping up in distance, did not mind the conditions having scored on heavy ground at Lingfield in his hurdling days. (15/8)

1961* Bally Clover, up 4lb, was suited by conditions underfoot but his jumping did not come up to scratch. (7/4)

3916 Bavard Dieu (IRE), without the headgear this time, was back to the mark off which he had won this race last season. (13/2)

4307 THREE COUNTIES H'CAP HURDLE (0-125) (4-Y.O+) (Class D)

7-15 (7-17) **2m (8 hdls)** £3,092.00 (£862.00: £416.00) GOING: 1.29 sec per fur (HY)

	Horse	Dist	Pos	SP	RR	SF
4006[3]	**Kino's Cross (99)** (AJWilson) **8-10-4** LHarvey (a.p: hrd rdn to ld flat: drvn out)	—	**1**	5/1[1]	72	32
3720[P]	**Walking Tall (IRE) (98)** (TPMcGovern) **6-10-3b[1]** RJohnson (led: sn clr: hdd & nt qckn flat)	1½	**2**	16/1	70	30
4061[11]	**Tejano Gold (USA) (119)** (PBradley) **7-11-10** RDunwoody (plld hrd: chsd ldr appr 3rd tl appr 2 out: hrd rdn: r.o one pce)	½	**3**	5/1[1]	90	50
1123[3]	**Cooley's Valve (IRE) (98)** (MrsSDWilliams) **9-10-3** CFSwan (bhd tl r.o fr 3 out: nvr nrr)	10	**4**	9/1	59	19
4071*	**Euro Singer (104)** (TKeddy) **5-10-4**(5) SRyan (hld up: hdwy appr 3 out: one pce fr 2 out)	3½	**5**	7/1[2]	62	22
299[2]	**Roca Murada (IRE) (100)** (PJHobbs) **8-10-5** NWilliamson (hld up: hdwy appr 3 out: wknd appr 2 out)	6	**6**	14/1	52	12
4048[P]	**Easy Listening (USA) (104)** (NJHawke) **5-10-9** JRailton (s.s: nvr nr ldrs)	¾	**7**	7/1[2]	55	15
3920[5]	**Keep Me in Mind (IRE) (104)** (NRMitchell) **8-10-9** CMaude (hld up mid div: wknd appr 3 out)	1	**8**	8/1[3]	54	14
4141[3]	**Out Ranking (FR) (114)** (JNeville) **5-11-5** TDascombe (a bhd)	5	**9**	11/1	59	19
1664[U]	**Tight Fist (IRE) (111)** (MissHCKnight) **7-11-2** JFTitley (bhd fr 5th: t.o)	18	**10**	10/1	38	—
4187[12]	**Saint Ciel (USA) (102)** (FJordan) **9-10-7** SWynne (hld up: hdwy after 5th: prom whn blnd bdly 3 out: nt rcvr: sn eased)	8	**11**	12/1	21	—
	Caribbean Prince (95) (GMMcCourt) **9-10-0b** SMcNeill (bhd fr 4th: t.o)	10	**12**	33/1	4	—
	Your Risk (IRE) (98) (TCasey) **7-10-3** JAMcCarthy (s.s: a bhd: t.o)	5	**13**	16/1	2	—
4095*	**Percy Braithwaite (IRE) (103)** (MissPMWhittle) **5-10-1**(7) MrJGoldstein (chsd ldr tl appr 3rd: ev ch whn mstke & uns rdr last)		**U**	8/1[3]	76?	—

(SP 137.0%) **14 Rn**

4m 4.8 (24.80) CSF £86.86 CT £407.80 TOTE £5.90: £1.90 £7.70 £1.90 (£143.30) Trio £217.20; £168.31 to Pontefract 28/4/97 OWNER Mr N. V. Harvey (CHELTENHAM) BRED Mrs T. D. Pilkington

LONG HANDICAP Caribbean Prince 9-8

4006 Kino's Cross, 10lb lower than the second of his victories last term, found the big change in the going just what the doctor ordered. (5/1: 8/1-9/2)

3183 Walking Tall (IRE), down 6lb, was sharpened up by the blinkers and did not seem to mind the rain-softened ground. Strongly pressed when Percy Braithwaite exited at the final flight, he could not hold the winner. (16/1)

3987 Tejano Gold (USA), like the winner was helped by the transformation in the ground, but he was 8lb higher than when winning in December. (5/1)

1123 Cooley's Valve (IRE), coming back after a winter break, could not have anticipated running into ground like this and will be sharpened up by the outing. (9/1)

4071* Euro Singer, up a further 6lb, had to contend with totally different going. (7/1)

299 Roca Murada (IRE) (14/1: 10/1-16/1)

3920 Keep Me in Mind (IRE) (8/1: 6/1-10/1)

4141 Out Ranking (FR) (11/1: 8/1-12/1)

Tight Fist (IRE) (10/1: op 5/1)

4095* Percy Braithwaite (IRE), making his handicap debut, acted on the soft ground and looked like going very close when a relatively minor error got rid of his rider. (8/1)

4308 UPTON UPON SEVERN NOVICES' HUNTERS' CHASE (5-Y.O+) (Class H)

7-45 (7-45) **2m 7f 110y (16 fncs)** £1,210.20 (£337.20: £162.60) GOING: 1.29 sec per fur (HY)

	Horse	Dist	Pos	SP	RR	SF
	Phar Too Touchy (VictorDartnall) **10-11-2**(7) MrNHarris (chsd ldr: led 6th: clr 10th: hit 12th & 2 out: unchal)	—	**1**	5/4[1]	91?	35
3922[6]	**Tea Cee Kay** (COKing) **7-11-7**(7) MrRupertSweeting (led to 6th: lost pl 8th: wnt poor 2nd 3 out)	dist	**2**	14/1	—	—
4070[5]	**Ann's Ambition** (MrsCHussey) **10-11-7**(7) MrMFrith (a.p: chsd wnr fr 8th: blnd 10th: nt rcvr: wknd 3 out: lft poor 3rd last)	dist	**3**	10/1	—	—
	Ballyhamage (IRE) (JTEvans) **9-11-7**(7) MrMMunrowd (fell 1st)		**F**	20/1	—	—
4015[U]	**Johnny The Fox (IRE)** (JPorter) **9-11-7**(7) MrRLawther (j.slowly 1st: bhd fr 6th: t.o whn p.u bef 10th)		**P**	7/1	—	—
	Pete's Sake (AMEnnever) **12-11-9**(5) MrCVigors (bhd: hit 6th: sn t.o: p.u bef 13th)		**P**	9/1	—	—
	Call-Me-Dinky (CAFuller) **13-11-2**(7) MissCThomas (bhd whn p.u lame bef 4th)		**P**	25/1	—	—
3837[2]	**No Joker (IRE)** (NAGaselee) **9-11-7**(7) MrPScott (prom: hit 5th: sn bhd: t.o whn p.u bef 3 out)		**P**	11/2[3]	—	—
	Who's Your Man (IRE) (MrsNSharpe) **7-11-7**(7) MrRBurton (bhd whn blnd 7th: sn t.o: p.u bef 9th)		**P**	25/1	—	—
	Sultan's Son (ShanCuthbert) **11-11-7**(7) MrGLewis (bhd fr 8th: wnt poor 3rd 3 out: blnd & uns rdr last)		**U**	9/2[2]	—	—

(SP 128.7%) **10 Rn**

6m 27.0 CSF £20.84 TOTE £2.60: £1.10 £3.30 £3.20 (£33.60) Trio £72.00; £71.02 to Pontefract 28/4/97 OWNER Miss R. A. Francis (BARNSTAPLE) BRED Mrs L. Spuffard

Phar Too Touchy, a prolific winner between the flags and at up to four miles, handles all types of ground and ran this field ragged. (5/4)

3721 Tea Cee Kay would probably have preferred faster ground. (14/1: op 7/1)

4070 Ann's Ambition could not go with the winner after making a mess of the ditch in the back straight. (10/1: 7/1-12/1)

Pete's Sake (9/1: 8/1-12/1)

3837 No Joker (IRE) (11/2: 4/1-6/1)

Sultan's Son (9/2: 3/1-5/1)

4309 POWICK NOVICES' H'CAP HURDLE (0-100) (4-Y.O+) (Class E)

8-15 (8-15) **3m (12 hdls)** £2,775.00 (£775.00: £375.00) GOING: 1.29 sec per fur (HY)

	Horse	Dist	Pos	SP	RR	SF
3577*	**Mayb-Mayb (90)** (JNeville) **7-11-10** APMcCoy (a.p: led appr 7th: drvn out)	—	**1**	4/1[1]	72	25
4181[7]	**Mr Christie (83)** (MissLCSiddall) **5-11-3** RDunwoody (hld up: hdwy 9th: styd on wl flat)	1¼	**2**	12/1	64	17
3481[5]	**Parade Racer (78)** (PGMurphy) **6-10-12** WMcFarland (hld up: hdwy appr 3 out: styd on flat: no ex nr fin)	3	**3**	6/1[2]	57	10
3577[4]	**Hello Me Man (IRE) (77)** (BJLlewellyn) **9-10-11** MrJLLlewellyn (hld up: gd hdwy 7th: ev ch 3 out: sn hrd rdn: wknd flat)	7	**4**	20/1	52	5
3834*	**Sammorello (IRE) (80)** (NATwiston-Davies) **6-11-0** CLlewellyn (wl bhd 6th: styd on fr 3 out: nvr nrr)	8	**5**	7/1[3]	49	2
3689[P]	**Stormy Session (79)** (NATwiston-Davies) **7-10-13** DWalsh (hld up: hdwy appr 7th: ev ch appr 3 out: sn hrd rdn & wknd)	2	**6**	25/1	47	—
3473[P]	**Vallingale (IRE) (87)** (MissHCKnight) **6-11-7** JCulloty (nvr nr ldrs)	1¼	**7**	12/1	54	7
3583[4]	**Danny Gale (IRE) (80)** (GMMcCourt) **6-11-0** SMcNeill (s.s: a bhd: t.o)	30	**8**	20/1	27	—
3552[7]	**Camera Man (89)** (NJHenderson) **7-11-9** MAFitzgerald (prom tl wknd appr 3 out: t.o)	17	**9**	11/1	25	—

3364[4]	**Brookhampton Lane (IRE) (75)** (MrsAJBowlby) **6-10-9** BPowell (bhd fr 6th: t.o fr 8th) ....dist	**10**	6/1[2]	—	—
2945[6]	**Loughdoo (IRE) (76)** (RLee) **9-10-10** BFenton (prom tl wknd appr 3 out: t.o) 7	**11**	25/1	—	—
1961[P]	**Vicar of Bray (79)** (LWells) **10-10-13** MRichards (bhd fr 6th: t.o) 19	**12**	25/1	—	—
3807[5]	**Jigginstown (80)** (JJO'Neill) **10-10-7**(7) LCooper (prom to 6th: t.o) ....dist	**13**	10/1	—	—
3048[8]	**Jobsagoodun (88)** (NJHenderson) **6-11-8** JRKavanagh (bhd fr 6th: t.o whn p.u bef 3 out)	**P**	11/1	—	—
4173[2]	**Tommy Cooper (80)** (MrsBarbaraWaring) **6-11-0** EByrne (led tl appr 7th: wknd qckly 8th: p.u bef 9th)	**P**	16/1	—	—
3851[7]	**Mister Blake (89)** (RLee) **7-11-9** RJohnson (bhd fr 6th: t.o whn p.u bef 3 out)	**P**	7/1[3]	—	—

(SP 141.7%) **16 Rn**

6m 21.8 (45.80) CSF £52.04 CT £279.03 TOTE £3.80: £1.40 £2.90 £2.10 £6.60 (£10.40) Trio £91.90 OWNER Mr J. Neville (NEWPORT, GWENT) BRED Bram Davies and R. J. Holder

3577* Mayb-Mayb, stepping up in distance, loves these testing conditions and defied a 22lb hike in the ratings for his hat-track on completed starts. (4/1)

3967 Mr Christie does not suffer from a lack of stamina, but could not peg back the winner. (12/1)

3481 Parade Racer was 8lb higher than when landing a touch on similar ground in a Towcester seller. (6/1)

3577 Hello Me Man (IRE) registered his only win on soft ground in a Navan bumper in his younger days, but did not quite get the three miles in ground as testing as this. (20/1)

3834* Sammorello (IRE), up 5lb, came from a long way back to reach his finishing position. (7/1)

3048 Stormy Session has yet to prove he stays three miles, especially on ground like this. (25/1)

3004 Vallingale (IRE) (12/1: 7/1-14/1)

2891 Camera Man (11/1: 8/1-12/1)

2546 Jobsagoodun (11/1: 8/1-12/1)

T/Plpt: £37.60 (263.19 Tckts). T/Qdpt: £10.70 (66.59 Tckts) KH

4270-ASCOT (R-H) (Good to firm, Good patches)
Tuesday April 29th

WEATHER: fine

4310 MITSUBISHI DIAMOND VISION H'CAP HURDLE (4-Y.O+) (Class B)

5-30 (5-30) **3m (13 hdls)** £4,756.15 (£1,439.20: £702.10: £333.55) GOING: 0.09 sec per fur (G)

			SP	RR	SF
3967*	**El Freddie (102)** (JABOld) **7-10-8** GUpton (led to 3rd: led 5th: all out) ....—	**1**	11/4[1]	80	11
4207*	**Meditator (112)** (BdeHaan) **13-11-4b** SCurran (lw: 3rd whn pckd 3rd: chsd wnr fr 9th: ev ch fr 3 out: r.o wl)..s.h	**2**	6/1	90	21
3600[16]	**Karar (IRE) (109)** (RRowe) **7-11-1** DO'Sullivan (swtg: bhd: hdwy fr 2 out: nvr nrr) 27	**3**	6/1	69	—
3920*	**Cassio's Boy (99)** (RJEckley) **6-10-5** APMcCoy (lw: 4th whn mstke 10th: wknd appr 2 out) 2	**4**	5/1[3]	58	—
4132[4]	**Olympian (117)** (JNeville) **10-11-9b** MAFitzgerald (hdwy 3rd: mstke 7th: sn wknd) 4	**5**	100/30[2]	73	4
3737[4]	**Apachee Flower (94)** (HSHowe) **7-10-0** BPowell (lw: chsd ldr: led 3rd to 5th: wknd 10th) 10	**6**	40/1	43	—
	Lyphantastic (USA) (118) (CJMann) **8-11-10** JRailton (bhd fr 7th: t.o whn p.u bef 2 out)	**P**	9/1	—	—

(SP 107.4%) **7 Rn**

5m 55.9 (16.90) CSF £15.49 TOTE £3.00: £1.70 £3.20 (£8.70) OWNER Mr Martin Lovatt (WROUGHTON) BRED Mrs J. Bugg

LONG HANDICAP Apachee Flower 9-0

3967* El Freddie continues in fine form. Making the vast majority of the running, he had only the runner-up top beat from the third last and, engaged in a tremendous tussle with that rival, held on by the skin of his teeth with little left to spare. (11/4)

4207* Meditator, who has never won on ground this fast, ran extremely well. The only danger to the winner over the last three hurdles, he gave his all and failed by only a whisker. He is a winner without a penalty. (6/1)

3047 Karar (IRE), well off the pace for the final circuit, struggled on from the second last to finish a very moderate third. (6/1)

3920* Cassio's Boy made a mistake four out and was back-peddling from the next. This trip seems beyond him. (5/1)

4132 Olympian as disappointing and, after a mistake at the seventh, was soon in trouble. (100/30)

Lyphantastic (USA) (9/1: 6/1-10/1)

4311 MICHAEL PAGE GROUP H'CAP CHASE (5-Y.O+) (Class B)

6-00 (6-00) **2m (12 fncs)** £10,230.75 (£3,096.00: £1,510.50: £717.75) GOING: 0.09 sec per fur (G)

			SP	RR	SF
4206[5]	**Cumbrian Challenge (IRE) (125)** (TDEasterby) **8-10-2** LWyer (a.p: rdn appr last: led flat: r.o wl) ....—	**1**	10/1	136	51
3738*	**Thumbs Up (127)** (GMMcCourt) **11-10-4** RDunwoody (chsd ldr: led 7th tl flat: unable qckn) 2½	**2**	7/1	136	51
4214[2]	**Mister Oddy (127)** (JSKing) **11-10-4** TJMurphy (lw: led to 7th: ev ch appr last: one pce) ....nk	**3**	7/1	135	50
4062[U]	**Time Won't Wait (IRE) (133)** (RTPhillips) **8-10-10** JRailton (lw: hld up: cl 5th whn blnd bdly 3 out: swtchd lft appr last: r.o wl flat) ....hd	**4**	3/1[2]	141	56
2824[7]	**Society Guest (123)** (AndrewTurnell) **11-10-0** LHarvey (lost pl 6th: rallied appr 2 out: one pce) 6	**5**	25/1	125	40
4131*	**Bertone (IRE) (133)** (KCBailey) **8-10-10** CO'Dwyer (lw: hld up: mstke 4th: wknd 2 out) 9	**6**	5/2[1]	126	41
2935[4]	**Big Matt (IRE) (144)** (NJHenderson) **9-11-7** MAFitzgerald (lw: rdn 4th: mstke 7th: bhd fr 8th: mstke 4 out: t.o) ....dist	**7**	4/1[3]	—	—

(SP 111.5%) **7 Rn**

3m 52.4 (1.40) CSF £63.89 CT £467.33 TOTE £10.30: £3.20 £1.80 (£31.80) OWNER Cumbrian Industrials Ltd (MALTON) BRED Major V. McCalmont

LONG HANDICAP Society Guest 9-11

4206 Cumbrian Challenge (IRE) coped with the drop back in distance. Never far away, he managed to get to the front on the run-in. (10/1)

3738* Thumbs Up moved to the front six out but, despite giving his all, found the winner too strong on the flat. (7/1)

4214 Mister Oddy is a model of consistency and ran another first class race on ground plenty fast enough for him. In front to the six last, he was still battling for honours going to the final fence, before tapped for toe on the run-in. He has done most of his winning with some cut. (7/1: 5/1-8/1)

Society Guest, 3lb out of the handicap, lost his pitch in Swinley Bottom but he got back into it turning for home, if then tapped for toe. (25/1)

4131* Bertone (IRE) found this drop in distance against him and was left for dead from the second last. Two and a half miles is his trip. (5/2)

4349a Big Matt (IRE) never looked really happy and the writing was on the wall running out of Swinley Bottom. (4/1: 3/1-9/2)

4312 JOHN MOWLEM NOVICES' H'CAP CHASE (6-Y.O+) (Class C)

6-30 (6-31) **3m 110y (20 fncs)** £7,230.00 (£2,190.00: £1,070.00: £510.00) GOING: 0.09 sec per fur (G)

				SP	RR	SF
3848*	**Jultara (IRE) (105)** (IPWilliams) **8-11-5** APMcCoy (lw: led 2nd to 3rd: led 5th: clr 13th: easily)	—	1	4/1 2	126+	61
4186*	**Gaelic Blue (92)** (MrsSJSmith) **7-10-6** RichardGuest (stdy hdwy 13th: chsd wnr fr 16th: no imp)	14	2	11/4 1	104	39
4227 2	**Domaine de Pron (FR) (101)** (MrsLCTaylor) **6-11-1** RBellamy (lw: 5th whn blnd 15th: hdwy fr 2 out: nvr nrr)	2½	3	13/2	111	46
3700 3	**Mr Pickpocket (IRE) (110)** (MissHCKnight) **9-11-10** JFTitley (hdwy 3rd: chsd wnr 11th to 16th: sn wknd)	9	4	14/1	114	49
4168 3	**Key To Moyade (IRE) (87)** (MJWilkinson) **7-10-1** NWilliamson (stdy hdwy 13th: wknd 4 out)	9	5	8/1	86	21
4203 5	**Ballydougan (IRE) (86)** (RMathew) **9-10-0v** TJMurphy (sme hdwy appr 11th: sn wknd)	14	6	66/1	75	10
4239*	**Glenfinn Princess (100)** (PBowen) **9-11-0** 4x WMarston (lw: led 3rd to 5th: 3rd whn blnd 12th: sn wknd: t.o whn p.u bef 2 out)		P	9/2 3	—	—
4180 2	**Wee Windy (IRE) (108)** (JTGifford) **8-11-8** PHide (lw: led to 2nd: wknd 10th: t.o whn p.u bef 2 out)		P	7/1	—	—
3968*	**Grizzly Bear (IRE) (86)** (RMStronge) **7-10-0** JCulloty (bhd fr 13th: t.o whn p.u bef 2 out)		P	16/1	—	—

(SP 115.8%) **9 Rn**

6m 9.0 (4.00) CSF £14.69 CT £63.21 TOTE £4.60: £1.90 £1.50 £2.80 (£6.00) Trio £20.90 OWNER Mr Roger Barby (ALVECHURCH)
LONG HANDICAP Ballydougan (IRE) 9-2
STEWARDS' ENQUIRY Murphy susp. 9-10 & 12-15/05/97 (Rule H9 - improper riding - using the whip forcedly on a horse he knew would be likely to injure).

3848* Jultara (IRE) followed up his win here last month in tremendous style. Making the vast majority of the running, he surged clear in the last mile to win with a ton in hand. (4/1)
4186* Gaelic Blue moved into second place five out but had no hope of reeling in the winner. (11/4)
4227 Domaine de Pron (FR), who made a bad error six out, struggled on over the last two fences without ever posing a threat. (13/2)
3700 Mr Pickpocket (IRE), conceding weight all round, moved into second place setting out on the final circuit but he was collared for that position five out, and soon had bellows to mend. Three of his four victories to date have come in the mud. (14/1: 10/1-16/1)

4313 ERNEST IRELAND NOVICES' H'CAP HURDLE (0-110) (4 & 5-Y.O) (Class D)

7-05 (7-05) **2m 110y (9 hdls)** £3,420.00 (£1,035.00: £505.00: £240.00) GOING: 0.09 sec per fur (G)

				SP	RR	SF
4169*	**Chief Mouse (100)** (FJordan) **4-11-10** APMcCoy (lw: hdwy 3 out: led 2 out: all out)	—	1	11/4 1	83	38
4006 5	**Above the Cut (USA) (90)** (CPMorlock) **5-11-6** CLlewellyn (hdwy appr 2 out: chsd wnr appr last: hrd rdn & ev ch flat: r.o wl)	hd	2	6/1 3	73	34
3429 5	**Ambidextrous (IRE) (86)** (EJAlston) **5-10-9**(7) LCummins (lw: hdwy 3 out: ev ch appr 2 out: one pce)	7	3	9/2 2	62	23
1663 4	**Colour Counsellor (81)** (RMFlower) **4-10-5** RSupple (led: mstke 3 out: hdd 2 out: wknd flat)	3	4	12/1	54	9
3979*	**Proud Image (88)** (GMMcCourt) **5-11-4** RDunwoody (lw: hld up: rdn 3 out: wknd appr 2 out)	1½	5	9/2 2	60	21
3204 7	**Flow Back (70)** (GPEnright) **5-10-0** JRKavanagh (prom to 6th)	10	6	50/1	32	—
4136 5	**Maeterlinck (IRE) (83)** (GThorner) **5-10-6**(7) ClareThorner (lw: prom tl mstke & wknd 3 out)	1½	7	14/1	44	5
4137 2	**Bath Knight (76)** (RCurtis) **4-10-0** DMorris (mstke 4th: sme hdwy 5th: wknd 3 out)	2	8	12/1	35	—
3935 4	**Wanstead (IRE) (78)** (JRJenkins) **5-10-8b** NWilliamson (chsd ldr tl appr 2 out: sn wknd)	6	9	12/1	31	—
4082 5	**Hever Golf Diamond (90)** (JRBest) **4-11-0** MAFitzgerald (lw: bhd whn blnd 5th: t.o whn p.u bef 6th)		P	25/1	—	—

(SP 112.9%) **10 Rn**

3m 58.8 (8.80) CSF £17.56 CT £63.92 TOTE £3.00: £1.50 £3.10 £1.60 (£8.90) Trio £28.40 OWNER Mr Bill Gavan (LEOMINSTER) BRED Lady Vestey
LONG HANDICAP Bath Knight 9-11
WEIGHT FOR AGE 4yo-6lb

4169* Chief Mouse completed the hat-trick. Jumping into the lead at the second last, his rider had to throw everything at him to keep him in front on the run-in. (11/4)
4006 Above the Cut (USA) threw down a dangerous looking challenge on the run-in but, despite giving his all, just failed to get on top. (6/1)
3429 Ambidextrous (IRE), 11lb higher than when last successful, appeared to be going best of all entering the straight, but he was soon being rousted along and could only keep on at one pace. (9/2)
1663 Colour Counsellor attempted to make all the running. Collared two from home, he gamely tried to hold on but tired on the run-in. (12/1: 8/1-14/1)
3979* Proud Image chased the leaders but had given his all approaching the second last. (9/2)
4136 Maeterlinck (IRE) (14/1: 10/1-16/1)
4137 Bath Knight (12/1: 8/1-14/1)
2620 Wanstead (IRE) (12/1: 7/1-14/1)

4314 MICHAEL PAGE NOVICES' CHASE (6-Y.O+) (Class C)

7-35 (7-36) **2m 3f 110y (16 fncs)** £4,394.75 (£1,328.00: £646.50: £305.75) GOING: 0.09 sec per fur (G)

				SP	RR	SF
	Sea Patrol (SGGriffiths) **10-11-5b** MAFitzgerald (lw: mstke 7th: hdwy 10th: led 3 out: all out)	—	1	6/1 3	67	16
3040 P	**Uncle Algy (85)** (MissHCKnight) **8-11-5** JCulloty (hdwy 10th: hrd rdn appr 2 out: r.o wl flat)	nk	2	100/30 2	67	16
254 4	**Bit of A Dream (IRE) (62)** (MrsSJSmith) **7-11-5** RichardGuest (hdwy 8th: led 12th to 3 out: hrd rdn appr last: unable qckn)	4	3	8/1	64	13
3688 4	**Oneofus (69)** (MrsLRichards) **8-11-5** MRichards (lw: hld up: led 10th to 12th: wknd 2 out)	17	4	14/1	50	—
4291 3	**Mozemo (81)** (MCPipe) **10-11-5b** APMcCoy (led to 5th: reminders 6th: led 8th to 10th: sn wknd: t.o)	dist	5	3/1 1	—	—
4158 3	**Fortria Rosie Dawn** (MissVenetiaWilliams) **7-11-0** NWilliamson (a bhd: mstke 6th: fell 9th)		F	3/1 1	—	—
4157 P	**Highland Flame (60)** (AGBlackmore) **8-11-2**(3) PHenley (lw: led 5th to 8th: wknd 12th: t.o whn p.u bef last)		P	33/1	—	—
4100 3	**Bells Wood (62)** (AJKDunn) **8-11-5** SMcNeill (bhd fr 9th: blnd & uns rdr 4 out)		U	16/1	—	—

(SP 114.0%) **8 Rn**

5m 2.8 (15.80) CSF £24.50 TOTE £8.40: £2.30 £1.90 £1.80 (£15.10) Trio £30.40 OWNER Mr S. G. Griffiths (CARMARTHEN) BRED R. D. Hollingsworth
IN-FOCUS: **This was a dreadful novice chase and completely out of place at this prestige course.**

Sea Patrol gained a slender advantage three out and, with his jockey having to get very serious on him, held on with little to spare in this awful contest. (6/1)
2667 Uncle Algy pulled up on three of his four starts this season, was under pressure approaching the second last but he found his second wind on the run-in and, running on really strongly, would surely have prevailed with a little further to go. (100/30)
188 Bit of A Dream (IRE) jumped into the lead five out but he was collared three from home and tapped for toe from the penultimate fence. (8/1)

Oneofus moved to the front going into Swinley Bottom, but he was collared five from home and eventually had to concede defeat jumping the penultimate fence. (14/1)
4291 Mozemo, making a quick reappearance, held a narrow advantage to the fifth but, having marginally lost the advantage, was then given a couple of reminders. He did regain the lead again early on the final circuit but he tamely dropped out of it going to Swinley Bottom. He looks one to have reservations about. (3/1)

4315 MERIDIAN TONIGHT NOVICES' HURDLE (5-Y.O+) (Class C)

8-05 (8-08) **2m 4f (11 hdls)** £3,501.25 (£1,060.00: £517.50: £246.25) GOING: 0.09 sec per fur (G)

				SP	RR	SF
4242*	**Country Lover (103)** (MCPipe) **6-11-0v** APMcCoy (lw: hdwy 7th: hrd rdn to ld flat: r.o wl)	—	**1**	4/5[1]	77	6
4187[7]	**Samanid (IRE) (104)** (MissLCSiddall) **5-11-5** OPears (hdwy to ld 2 out: hdd flat: r.o wl)	nk	**2**	10/1	82	11
3108[3]	**Physical Fun (97)** (AGBlackmore) **6-11-0** RDunwoody (lw: a.p: ev ch 3 out: unable qckn)	8	**3**	11/2[2]	70	—
4003[5]	**Leap Frog (92)** (NAGaselee) **6-11-0** WMarston (swtg: a.p: led 7th tl appr 2 out: one pce)	hd	**4**	16/1	70	—
4134[2]	**Over The Way (IRE)** (NJHenderson) **7-11-0** MAFitzgerald (led: mstke 3rd: hdd 7th: led appr 2 out: sn hdd: one pce)	s.h	**5**	6/1[3]	70	—
3493[2]	**Harlequin Chorus (92)** (JABOld) **7-11-0** GUpton (hld up: shkn up 3 out: eased whn btn appr 2 out)	12	**6**	14/1	61	—
	Eden Roc (GLMoore) **7-11-0** DGallagher (hdwy 8th: sn wknd: t.o)	25	**7**	33/1	41	—
4230[3]	**Pat Buckley** (NATwiston-Davies) **6-11-0** CLlewellyn (lw: bhd fr 8th: t.o)	dist	**8**	12/1	—	—
3149[12]	**The Phantom Farmer (IRE)** (NJHenderson) **6-11-0** JRKavanagh (lw: bhd whn mstke 6th: t.o)		**9**	33/1	—	—
				(SP 120.4%)	**9 Rn**	

4m 59.1 (17.10) CSF £10.02 TOTE £2.00: £1.10 £2.80 £1.40 (£9.00) Trio £10.30 OWNER Pond House Gold (WELLINGTON) BRED Sir Gordon Brunton
4242* Country Lover, pushed along in the straight, produced a strong run under stern riding to get up in the last seventy-five yards, and complete the four-timer. (4/5)
3995 Samanid (IRE) jumped into the lead at the second last but, despite giving his all, found the winner just too strong on the run-in (10/1: 8/1-12/1)
3108 Physical Fun had every chance three from home but then failed to find another gear. (11/2: 4/1-6/1)
4003 Leap Frog moved to the front going into Swinley Bottom, but he was collared approaching the second last and then got out-paced. he struggle on again on the run-in and may have taken third prize with a little further to go. (16/1)
4134 Over The Way (IRE), who caught the eye on his debut here, was given a far more forceful ride on this occasion and set the pace. Headed going into Swinley Bottom, he regained the advantage soon after the third last but he was collared jumping the penultimate hurdle, and could then only go up and down in the same place. (6/1: op 4/1)
3493 Harlequin Chorus was given considerate handling and his jockey was not hard on him from the third last. (14/1: 10/1-16/1)
4230 Pat Buckley (12/1: op 8/1)
T/Plpt: £165.00 (170 Tckts). T/Qdpt: £11.30 (153.94 Tckts) AK

3933-HUNTINGDON (R-H) (Good, Good to firm patches)

Tuesday April 29th

WEATHER: fine

4316 ROBERT LENTON MEMORIAL HUNTERS' CHASE (5-Y.O+) (Class H)

5-15 (5-15) **3m (19 fncs)** £1,147.20 (£319.20: £153.60) GOING minus 0.24 sec per fur (G)

				SP	RR	SF
4080[3]	**Kushbaloo** (CParker) **12-11-7**(7) MrAParker (a.p: led after 8th: shkn up flat: edgd rt: r.o)	—	**1**	13/8[1]	106	30
4179[4]	**Idiotic** (PRChamings) **9-12-2**(5) MrCVigors (hld up: mstke 10th: hdwy 13th: rdn appr last: hung lft & nt qckn flat)	2	**2**	13/8[1]	112	36
3924*	**Dromin Leader** (JMTurner) **12-12-2**(5) MrASansome (w ldrs: rdn 3 out: btn whn hit next)	25	**3**	6/1[2]	95	19
3744[9]	**Kino** (AndrewMartin) **10-11-7**(7) MrAndrewMartin (lw: hit 3rd: dropped rr 8th: rallied & hit 13th: wkng whn blnd 4 out)	16	**4**	10/1[3]	77	1
	Woody Will (MrsEmmaCoveney) **11-11-7**(7) MrsECoveney (bhd fr 15th)	dist	**5**	20/1	—	—
3924[U]	**Tammy's Friend** (MrsGMHay) **10-11-7b**(7) MrJFerguson (lw: led: j.slowly 2nd: hdd after 8th: blnd & uns rdr 12th)		**U**	16/1	—	—
				(SP 110.2%)	**6 Rn**	

6m 6.8 (9.80) CSF £4.14 TOTE £2.20: £1.60 £1.70 (£1.90) OWNER Mr & Mrs Raymond Anderson Green (LOCKERBIE) BRED Andrew Murphy
3609 Kushbaloo jumped better than the runner-up and was always on top, despite finding little as pressure was applied. (13/8)
4179 Idiotic can hardly be described as a fluent jumper but still had a chance when hanging badly after the last. His pilot switched his whip and then dropped it, but the outcome was already decided. (13/8)
3924* Dromin Leader ran as well as could be expected under a penalty. (6/1: 4/1-13/2)
Kino, fit after a surprise win in a Garthorpe Open, didn't jump well enough to give himself hope. (10/1: op 5/1)
Woody Will, in winning form between the flags, found this step up in class much too steep. (20/1)

4317 GEOFFREY BEVAN MEMORIAL NOVICES' HUNTERS' CHASE (5-Y.O+) (Class H)

5-45 (5-45) **3m (19 fncs)** £1,220.40 (£367.20: £177.60: £82.80) GOING minus 0.24 sec per fur (G)

				SP	RR	SF
4155*	**Secret Bay** (CPDennis) **8-12-7** MrSSwiers (lw: j.w: led tl stdd 3rd: led 15th: qcknd clr 3 out: easily)	—	**1**	2/5[1]	110++	41
	Cool Bandit (IRE) (MrsDMGrissell) **7-11-7**(7) MrTHills (bkwd: plld hrd: led 6th: j.rt fr 10th: mstke & hdd 15th: sn outpcd)	dist	**2**	16/1	—	—
	Tau (MissFelicityMcLachlan) **12-11-7**(7) MrAWarr (bhd: hdwy 13th: r.o flat)	3	**3**	40/1	—	—
	Notary-Nowell (MrsRichardPilkington) **11-11-7b**(7) MrRJBarrett (lw: chsd ldrs: no imp fr 15th: lost 3rd pl flat)	3	**4**	50/1	—	—
	Smart Pal (BKnox) **12-11-7**(7) MrsFNeedham (prom to 9th: t.o fr 4 out)	dist	**5**	50/1	—	—
4070[P]	**Space Molly** (MrsNLay) **8-11-2b**(7) MrPCowley (prom: wkng whn blnd 7th: fell 12th)		**F**	25/1	—	—
	Billion Dollarbill (MrsPATetley) **9-11-7**(7) MrMGorman (chsd ldrs to 9th: t.o whn p.u bef 3 out)		**P**	4/1[2]	—	—
	Cardinal Red (JMTurner) **10-12-2b**(5) MrASansome (led 3rd to 6th: wknd 10th: j.slowly 14th: p.u bef next)		**P**	11/1[3]	—	—
	Mr Pinball (MrsDCowley) **10-11-7b[1]**(7) MrMCowley (bkwd: nt j.w: sn t.o: p.u bef 4 out)		**P**	50/1	—	—
4135[P]	**Loyal Gait (NZ)** (AMDarlington) **9-11-7**(7) MrAndrewMartin (bhd fr 8th: t.o whn p.u bef 4 out)		**P**	25/1	—	—
				(SP 121.7%)	**10 Rn**	

6m 5.1 (8.10) CSF £7.60 TOTE £1.30: £1.10 £3.30 £9.30 (£9.90) Trio £123.50 OWNER Mr Stuart Dent (DARLINGTON) BRED Mrs T. Cunningham-Jardine

4155* Secret Bay again impressed with his jumping and, once given his head, shot clear of this field and sauntered home in a very fast time. He sets the pulse racing and could be anything. (2/5)
Cool Bandit (IRE), who ran in Ireland as a five-year-old, took a fearful hold and was one of those who ensured this race was so truly run. He jumped quite alarmingly right as he got tired and going right-handed may prove essential. He did well to cling on to second place and time may show that he was a non-league team taking on Manchester United. (16/1)
Tau got a long way behind due to the fast early pace, but was staying on at the finish. (40/1)
Notary-Nowell looked in great shape, but hasn't won for five years and got very tired in the last half-mile. (50/1)
Smart Pal tried to live with the fast pace and this took its toll on the final circuit. (50/1)
Billion Dollarbill (4/1: 3/1-9/2)

4318 SPS ADVERTISING NOVICES' AMATEUR HURDLE (4-Y.O+) (Class E)
6-15 (6-18) **2m 110y (8 hdls)** £2,250.00 (£625.00: £300.00) GOING minus 0.58 sec per fur (F)

				SP	RR	SF
4102[4]	**Real Madrid** (GPEnright) **6-11-1**(5) MrJJukes (trckd ldrs: led appr 2 out: sn clr: comf)	—	**1**	13/2	71+	34
4275[S]	**Absolute Limit (90)** (JTGifford) **5-11-6**(7) MrRWakley (led: sn clr: wknd & hdd apr 2 out: sn no ch)	11	**2**	11/8[1]	67	30
3723[3]	**Undawaterscubadiva** (MPBielby) **5-10-13**(7) MrAWintle (in tch: efrrt & 3rd whn hit 2 out: kpt on)	9	**3**	9/2[3]	52	15
3272[P]	**Greg's Profiles** (NATwiston-Davies) **6-11-3**(3) MrMRimell (chsd ldrs to after 3rd: chsd ldr 5th to next: sn btn)	4	**4**	16/1	48	11
3331[8]	**Bathwick Bobbie** (MJBolton) **10-11-3**(7)ow4 DrJNaylor (in tch to 4th: n.d afterwards)	5	**5**	50/1	47	6
3431[U]	**Cleric on Broadway (IRE)** (JPearce) **9-10-12**(3) MrCBonner (a bhd)	5	**6**	20/1	33	—
4289[2]	**Gi Moss (68)** (PRHarriss) **10-10-12b**(7)ow4 MrBHarriss (lw: s.s: a bhd)	hd	**7**	33/1	37	—
4238[3]	**Nell Valley** (CPEBrooks) **6-10-8**(7) MrEJames (lw: s.i.s: wl bhd fr 4th)	4	**8**	16/1	29	—
3847[P]	**Glide Path (USA)** (JRJenkins) **8-10-13**(7) DrMMannish (s.s: hdwy 3rd: sn chsng ldr: rdn 5th: sn wknd)	4	**9**	7/2[2]	30	—
				(SP 117.3%)	**9 Rn**	

3m 45.8 (-2.20) CSF £14.95 TOTE £6.70: £3.20 £1.10 £1.30 (£7.70) Trio £5.20 OWNER Mr Chris Wall (LEWES) BRED Chris Wall
4102 Real Madrid, given a sensible ride, was going much the best long before he hit the front turning into the straight to reverse Fontwell form with the runner-up. (13/2: 9/2-7/1)
4275 Absolute Limit took advantage of a particularly ragged start to establish a clear lead, but probably went off too fast as he became more and more weary over the last four flights. (11/8)
3723 Undawaterscubadiva, a stayer on the Flat, could never go the pace but promises to stay further. (9/2)
Greg's Profiles looks highly strung and was taken to post without irons. Taking a good hold, he failed to last home. (16/1)
Bathwick Bobbie has had a poor season over fences and doesn't appear to have the speed for this game anymore. (50/1)
4289 Gi Moss lost all chance at the start, as his pilot over-did the waiting tactics. (33/1)
Nell Valley, who all but bolted last time, failed to respond to exaggerated waiting tactics. (16/1)
3103 Glide Path (USA) lost a lot of ground at the start and, with it, all realistic chance. In the circumstances, it may have been a fair effort to briefly get into contention. (7/2: op 2/1)

4319 HUNTINGDON RESTRICTED SERIES (FINAL) NOVICES' HUNTERS' CHASE (5-Y.O+) (Class H)
6-50 (6-50) **3m (19 fncs)** £1,548.25 (£466.00: £225.50: £105.25) GOING minus 0.24 sec per fur (G)

				SP	RR	SF
4135*	**Struggles Glory (IRE)** (DCRobinson) **6-12-0**(7) MrDCRobinson (led to 2nd: led 9th: pckd 15th: lft clr last: easily)	—	**1**	8/13[1]	113+	39
	Mister Spectator (IRE) (MrsAHickman) **8-12-1**(3) MrSimonAndrews (lw: led 2nd to 9th: mstke 12th: 2nd & btn whn blnd last)	20	**2**	2/1[2]	97	23
3357[F]	**Taura's Rascal** (FJBrennan) **8-11-7**(7) MrFBrennan (chsd ldrs: hit 4th & 12th: wknd 2 out)	3	**3**	12/1[3]	91	17
1[3]	**Ballyallia Castle (IRE)** (MrsJulieRead) **8-11-7**(7) MrNBloom (in tch tl blnd 12th: kpt on again fr 3 out)	5	**4**	20/1	87	13
	Greybury Star (IRE) (MrsDBASilk) **9-11-7**(7) MrPBull (lw: hdwy & hit 12th: wknd 14th)	9	**5**	50/1	81	7
	Grassington (IRE) (ScottQuirk) **8-11-7**(7) MrScottQuirk (nvr trbld ldrs)	4	**6**	50/1	79	5
	Tarry Awhile (CHenn) **11-11-10**(7)ow3 MrJConnell (sn pushed along: nvr nr ldrs)	29	**7**	25/1	62	—
	Some Tourist (IRE) (NigelBenstead) **9-11-7**(7) MrNBenstead (lw: a bhd: t.o whn p.u bef 3 out)		**P**	50/1	—	—
	Current Attraction (HHill) **11-11-2**(7) MissCTuke (a bhd: t.o whn p.u bef 2 out)		**P**	50/1	—	—
	Give it a Bash (IRE) (MrsAClover) **9-11-2**(7) MrTMoore (lw: prom tl mstke 11th: bhd whn p.u bef 2 out)		**P**	50/1	—	—
				(SP 121.3%)	**10 Rn**	

6m 5.8 (8.80) CSF £2.00 TOTE £1.60: £1.20 £1.40 £1.80 (£2.10) Trio £3.20 OWNER Mr D. C. Robinson (LEWES) BRED Philip Gould
4135* Struggles Glory (IRE) gets low on occasions and how much assistance his veteran pilot could offer him when the time comes is open to conjecture, but this tall, attractive gelding remains an exciting prospect for the years ahead. With his main rivals getting very tired in the straight, those from fourth place down are flattered in the extreme to have finished so close to him. (8/13: 2/5-4/6)
Mister Spectator (IRE) completed an impressive front-running hat-trick at Cottenham, which is not dissimilar to Huntingdon, but could never get clear and had to play second fiddle to the winner for much of the final circuit. Down on his nose at the last, his pilot did wonderfully to keep the partnership intact. (2/1)
Taura's Rascal, up against two of the rising stars of the pointing world, fought his corner well and was the only one with a chance of most of the final circuit. Landing awkwardly at the second last, he then got very tired. (12/1)
1 Ballyallia Castle (IRE), beaten on firm ground last time at Higham, was hopelessly outclassed on the final circuit, but kept staying on to the line. (20/1)
Greybury Star (IRE) led the group chasing the three principals as they went clear for much of the final circuit. (50/1)
Grassington (IRE) stayed on from a long way back, and is probably flattered to have finished so close as he was well beaten in points recently. (50/1)

4320 DR. WAKES-MILLER 60TH BIRTHDAY HUNTERS' CHASE (5-Y.O+) (Class H)
7-20 (7-22) **2m 4f 110y (16 fncs)** £1,239.60 (£345.60: £166.80) GOING minus 0.24 sec per fur (G)

				SP	RR	SF
3439*	**Slievenamon Mist** (VictorDartnall) **11-12-2**(5) MrJJukes (lw: hld up: hdwy 8th: led after 3 out: blnd next: rdn out)	—	**1**	4/11[1]	125	57
	Counterbid (JMTurner) **10-11-9b**(5) MrASansome (a.p: ev ch appr 2 out: rdn & one pce appr last)	9	**2**	10/1[3]	111	43
3432[P]	**My Young Man** (CPEBrooks) **12-11-7**(7) MrEJames (lw: led: sn clr: hdd & wknd appr 2 out)	13	**3**	12/1	101	33
3457[4]	**Kambalda Rambler** (MrsHelenHarvey) **13-11-7**(7) MrRArmson (bhd: r.o fr 4 out: nvr able to chal)	8	**4**	6/1[2]	95	27
4160[4]	**Not My Line (IRE)** (AndyMorgan) **8-12-0**(5) MrWWales (chsd ldrs to 12th)	12	**5**	25/1	90	22
4228[P]	**Candle Glow** (PHutchinson) **9-11-7**(7) MrPHutchinson (mstke 1st: prom to 9th)	4	**6**	16/1	82	14
4228[5]	**Tudor Fable (IRE)** (CJRSweeting) **9-11-12**(7) MrRupertSweeting (lw: in tch to 11th)	2	**7**	25/1	86	18
395[P]	**The Lorryman (IRE)** (NickyMitchell) **9-11-7**(7) MrNRMitchell (mstkes: chsd ldrs to 10th)	17	**8**	33/1	67	—

	Killimor Lad (MrsDCSamworth) **10-11-7**(7) MissSSamworth (j.slowly 11th: a bhd) ....¾	**9**	50/1	67	—
4059P	**Fish Quay** (MrsKMLamb) **14-11-7**(7) MissSLamb (a bhd)........5	**10**	50/1	63	—
4135P	**Making Time** (MFLoggin) **10-11-2**(7) MissTHabgood (blnd 9th: bhd tl p.u bef 13th)........	**P**	33/1	—	—
	Basher Bill (KDGiles) **14-11-7**(7) MrsECoveney (lw: pckd 8th: bhd tl blnd & p.u 11th)........	**P**	50/1	—	—
4254[4]	**Upward Surge (IRE)** (RRLedger) **7-11-7**(7) MrsNLedger (chsd ldrs to 11th: t.o whn p.u bef 2 out)	**P**	50/1	—	—
	Lucky Landing (IRE) (AndrewMartin) **8-11-7**(7) MrAndrewMartin (chsd ldrs to 8th: t.o whn p.u bef 12th)........	**P**	50/1	—	—
			(SP 133.7%)	**14 Rn**	

5m 1.8 (1.80) CSF £5.33 TOTE £1.50: £1.20 £1.90 £2.80 (£4.30) Trio £34.70 OWNER Mr Nick Viney (BARNSTAPLE) BRED James Mulcahy
3439* Slievenamon Mist, despite a brief reminder in the back straight, looked in control once My Young Man began to tie up, but must have given odds-on layers palpitations when deciding to bring most of the second last home with him. (4/11)
Counterbid has been called a few names in the past, but a recent win at Horseheath probably did wonders for his confidence, as he battled on really well. (10/1)
My Young Man, a crack two-mile chaser on his day, looked a little more like his old self, but never got this trip at his best. (12/1)
3457 Kambalda Rambler, who gave trouble at the start, could never get competitive on this ground. (6/1: op 3/1)
4160 Not My Line (IRE) was outclassed but ran well enough to suggest he remains in form in his own grade. (25/1)
4094 Candle Glow, a surprise winner on this card last year, never threatened a repeat. (16/1)

4321 EAST ANGLIAN DAILY TIMES AMATEUR H'CAP HURDLE (0-115) (4-Y.O+) (Class E)

7-50 (7-50) **2m 5f 110y (10 hdls)** £2,337.50 (£650.00: £312.50) GOING minus 0.58 sec per fur (F)

			SP	RR	SF
4248[9]	**Able Player (USA) (86)** (KJDrewry) **10-10-10**(7) MrKDrewry (lw: hdwy 5th: led appr 2 out: rdn clr flat) ....—	**1**	4/1[2]	67	20
4226*	**Snowshill Shaker (91)** (NATwiston-Davies) **8-11-5**(3) MrMRimell (lw: plld hrd: trckd ldrs: rdn appr 2 out: ev ch whn hit last: one pce flat)........2½	**2**	4/6[1]	70	23
4248R	**Persian View (IRE) (97)** (KCBailey) **7-11-7**(7) MrRWakley (led 4th tl appr 2 out: ev ch last: wknd flat)........3	**3**	8/1	74	27
4007P	**King's Shilling (USA) (83)** (HOliver) **10-10-7**(7) MrNHOliver (hld up: hit 1st: hdwy 6th: wknd appr 2 out)........9	**4**	12/1	53	6
3811[5]	**Script (70)** (JRJenkins) **6-9-12**(3)ow1 MrCBonner (in tch: pushed along 5th: bhd fr 7th)........8	**5**	9/2[3]	34	—
4220P	**Prime Display (USA) (96)** (AHHarvey) **11-11-6**(7) MrSSporborg (bit bkwd: led to 4th: t.o fr 7th) ....dist	**6**	33/1	—	—
			(SP 119.9%)	**6 Rn**	

5m 0.6 (0.60) CSF £7.31 TOTE £6.00: £2.30 £1.10 (£2.60) OWNER Mr K. J. Drewry (ISLE OF MAN) BRED Angus M. MacLean and Winfield Farm
LONG HANDICAP Script 9-13
1866 Able Player (USA), on a 9lb lower mark than well beaten in this race last year, has often flattered to deceive in the past but was going so well on the home turn that he could hardly help but win. (4/1: 3/1-9/2)
4226* Snowshill Shaker, back over further, took a very strong hold and his pilot had done well to get him into a challenging position at the last, only for an awkward jump to seal his fate. (4/6: 1/2-evens)
Persian View (IRE) did nothing wrong this time but was easily outpaced from the last. (8/1: op 5/1)
3622 King's Shilling (USA), back from fences, clattered the first hurdle and was never going well enough to hold out much hope. (12/1: op 7/1)
3811 Script settled on the heels of the leaders, was soon niggled along and in trouble once the pace quickened. (9/2)

T/Plpt: £2.40 (3,128.79 Tckts). T/Qdpt: £1.60 (278.4 Tckts) Dk

4176-CHELTENHAM (L-H) (Good to firm, Good patches)
Wednesday April 30th

WEATHER: fine

4322 EVESHAM MAIDEN HUNTERS' CHASE (5-Y.O+) (Class H)

5-25 (5-25) **2m 5f (New) (17 fncs)** £1,873.25 (£566.00: £275.50: £130.25) GOING minus 0.08 sec per fur (G)

			SP	RR	SF
3765[2]	**Vital Song** (MHDare) **10-11-7**(7) MrGMatthews (lw: mde all: r.o wl fr 2 out) ....—	**1**	11/2[2]	104	36
4015[3]	**Ardbrennan** (JPorter) **10-11-7**(7) MrEJames (hld up & bhd: hdwy 9th: lft 2nd 13th: one pce fr 2 out)........4	**2**	7/1	101	33
3637P	**Clobracken Lad** (MrsJSwaffield) **9-11-7**(7) MrGBaines (rdn & lost pl appr 8th: bhd whn mstke 12th: styd on fr 2 out)........6	**3**	20/1	96	28
	Double Thriller (RCWilkins) **7-11-11**(3) MrRTreloggen (hld up: hdwy 9th: wknd appr 3 out) 2	**4**	6/5[1]	95	27
4222[4]	**Orton House** (SKelly) **10-11-7**(7) MrRBurton (chsd ldr to 6th: wknd 9th: bhd whn mstkes 11th & 12th: t.o)...dist	**5**	33/1	—	—
	Very Daring (JulianHunt) **7-11-7**(7) MissSSharratt (a bhd: t.o fr 9th)........dist	**6**	50/1	—	—
	Well Bank (MrsCHicks) **10-11-7**(7) MrEWalker (lw: prom tl wknd 9th: mstke 11th: bhd whn fell 4 out)	**F**	66/1	—	—
3906[4]	**Broad Steane** (CHenn) **8-11-9**(5) MrASansome (lw: prom: 2nd whn fell 13th)	**F**	6/1[3]	—	—
4135[5]	**Berrings Dasher** (MrsJRichardson) **10-11-7**(7) MrMWatson (a bhd: t.o 4 out: p.u & dismntd flat)	**P**	25/1	—	—
	Trevveethan (IRE) (GilesSmyly) **8-11-11**(3) MrMRimell (swtg: hld up & bhd: hdwy 10th: in tch whn hmpd & uns rdr 13th)........	**U**	20/1	—	—
			(SP 107.4%)	**10 Rn**	

5m 18.7 (9.70) CSF £31.27 TOTE £5.40: £1.60 £2.00 £4.10 (£18.10) Trio £52.30 OWNER Mr G. Matthews (YEOVIL) BRED Major R. P. Thorman
3765 Vital Song, looking tremendously well, was allowed to lead this time. (11/2)
4015 Ardbrennan had been highly-tried in his two previous hunter chases this season. (7/1)
3403 Clobracken Lad found this trip inadequate. (20/1)
Double Thriller, four times a winner between the flags, was successful in the recent Lady Dudley Cup, so this has to be considered a disappointing start to his hunter-chase career. (6/5)

4323 COLIN NASH MEMORIAL UNITED HUNTS' CHALLENGE CUP HUNTERS' CHASE (6-Y.O+) (Class H)

6-00 (6-00) **3m 1f 110y (New) (21 fncs)** £2,232.00 (£627.00: £306.00) GOING minus 0.08 sec per fur (G)

			SP	RR	SF
4241[2]	**Miss Millbrook** (DTGoldsworthy) **9-11-5**(7) MrEWilliams (hld up: mstke 2nd: hdwy 6th: led 12th to 14th: mstkes 15th & 4 out: led 2 out: hrd rdn: r.o wl)........—	**1**	11/10[1]	101	16
3906[5]	**Glen Oak** (DGDuggan) **12-11-10**(7) MrJMPritchard (hld up: lost pl 11th: hdwy 12th: outpcd appr 2 out: rallied appr last: styd on flat)........3	**2**	11/2[3]	104	19
	Hill Island (CRRSweeting) **10-11-10**(7) MrRupertSweeting (lw: prom: led 7th to 12th: led 14th to 2 out: one pce) 2½	**3**	15/8[2]	103	18

			SP	RR	SF
	Cavalero (HJManners) **8-11-10**(7) MrACharles-Jones (hld up: blnd 2nd: hdwy appr 12th: mstke 3 out: sn wknd: t.o) 30	**4**	20/1	84?	—
3906[7]	**Teatrader** (MissTOBlazey) **11-11-10**(7) MissTBlazey (led to 3rd: wknd qckly 12th: sn t.o: p.u bef 3 out)	**P**	25/1	—	—
4022[3]	**J B Lad** (HRTuck) **11-11-10**(7) MissPGundry (lw: nt j.w: led 3rd to 7th: lost pl & mstke 12th: blnd 14th: sn t.o: p.u bef 17th)	**P**	33/1	—	—
			(SP 109.3%)		**6 Rn**

6m 40.1 (19.10) CSF £6.40 TOTE £1.90: £1.30 £2.20 (£3.80) OWNER Mr D. T. Goldsworthy (BRIDGEND) BRED C. Parker
4241 Miss Millbrook had a little easier ground this time, and was ridden much closer to the pace. (11/10)
3906 Glen Oak again showed how well he stays, and came back for more after seemingly having his measure taken. (11/2)
Hill Island, making his hunter-chase debut, is the winner of no less than nine points, and beat Run for Free ten lengths on Saturday. (15/8)

4324 WRAGGE & CO HUNTERS' CHASE (5-Y.O+) (Class H)
6-35 (6-35) **4m 1f (New) (27 fncs)** £4,260.00 (£1,290.00: £630.00: £300.00) GOING minus 0.08 sec per fur (G)

			SP	RR	SF
4179[3]	**Rusty Bridge** (MrsSMJohnson) **10-11-11**(7) MrRBurton (led to 20th: hrd rdn 4 out: swtchd lft & led last: drvn out) ....—	**1**	4/1[1]	111	18
4179[6]	**The Malakarma** (MissCSaunders) **11-11-13**(5) MrBPollock (chsd ldr to 12th: regained 2nd 18th: led 20th: hrd rdn: edgd rt & hdd last: r.o) 1¼	**2**	5/1[2]	110	17
4179[5]	**Young Brave** (MrsAYoung) **11-12-0**(7) MrMGMiller (lw: hld up: hdwy appr 18th: wknd 3 out) 13	**3**	5/1[2]	105	12
3580[2]	**Loyal Note** (SRAndrews) **9-12-1**(3) MrSimonAndrews (lw: prom: lost pl 19th: 5th & btn whn blnd 22nd)....12	**4**	6/1[3]	95	2
3906[6]	**Artful Arthur** (LPGrassick) **11-11-7**(7) MrJGrassick (a bhd: t.o fr 19th) 5	**5**	50/1	88	—
4135[2]	**Lurriga Glitter (IRE)** (RJSmith) **9-11-7b**(7) MrRWakley (bhd tl hdwy appr 18th: wknd 19th)....2½	**6**	7/1	87	—
3341[3]	**Kettles** (MRDaniell) **10-11-2**(7) MrAPhillips (lw: bhd tl rdn & sme hdwy whn hit 16th: wknd 18th)....8	**7**	4/1[1]	77	—
3924[3]	**Saint Bene't (IRE)** (GProdromou) **9-11-7v**(7) MrACoe (a bhd: t.o 18th: p.u bef 3 out)	**P**	20/1	—	—
3476[6]	**Mobile Messenger (NZ)** (TRGeorge) **9-11-7**(7) MissSSamworth (a bhd: t.o fr 19th: p.u & dismntd flat)	**P**	33/1	—	—
4051[4]	**K C'S Dancer** (RDickin) **12-11-7**(7) MrJMPritchard (prom: chsd ldr 12th to 18th: wknd 22nd: t.o whn p.u bef 2 out)	**P**	9/1	—	—
			(SP 119.8%)		**10 Rn**

8m 37.5 (0.10 under best) (26.50) CSF £22.68 TOTE £3.50: £1.90 £1.80 £2.40 (£5.40) Trio £7.00 OWNER Mr I. K. Johnson (MADLEY) BRED J. I. Johnson
4179 Rusty Bridge stays longer than the mother-in-law, and must have his connections wishing there were more of these marathons on the hunter-chase calendar. (4/1)
3739 The Malakarma, another who stays all day, put a disappointing effort last time behind him. (5/1)
4179 Young Brave, although not beaten for lack of stamina, appeared more like his old self here. (5/1)
3580 Loyal Note probably found this ground too lively. (6/1: op 7/2)

4325 CHELTENHAM CHAMPION HUNTERS' CHASE (5-Y.O+) (Class H)
7-10 (7-10) **3m 2f 110y (New) (22 fncs)** £4,026.00 (£1,218.00: £594.00: £282.00) GOING minus 0.08 sec per fur (G)

			SP	RR	SF
4074[U]	**Celtic Abbey** (MissVenetiaWilliams) **9-11-7**(7) MrDSJones (chsd ldr fr 3rd: led 15th: clr appr 2 out: easily)...—	**1**	11/8[2]	128	43
4179*	**Double Silk** (RCWilkins) **13-12-3**(3) MrRTreloggen (lw: led 2nd to 15th: sn rdn: wknd appr 2 out) 30	**2**	5/4[1]	116	31
3799[3]	**Ryming Cuplet** (MJTrickey) **12-11-10**(7) MrLJefford (hld up: mstke 15th: rdn 13th: sn t.o)....14	**3**	8/1	104	19
4179[2]	**Some-Toy** (JohnSquire) **11-11-10**(7) MissLBlackford (lw: led to 2nd: hit 9th: lost tch fr 12th: sn t.o: mstke 17th: hit 2 out)....2½	**4**	15/2[3]	103	18
			(SP 109.4%)		**4 Rn**

6m 45.0 (10.00) CSF £3.34 TOTE £2.40 (£1.80) OWNER Mr G. J. Powell (HEREFORD) BRED J. P. Powell
3637 Celtic Abbey, 6lb better off than when finishing nine lengths in front of Double Silk in the Foxhunters' at the Festival, will attempt to go one better than last season in the Horse and Hound Cup. (11/8)
4179* Double Silk, nine lengths behind the winner at level weights in the Cheltenham Foxhunters', had a tough task against a younger rival. (5/4)
3799 Ryming Cuplet (8/1: op 7/2)

4326 GOLDEN HARVEST HUNTERS' CHASE (5-Y.O+) (Class H)
7-45 (7-45) **2m 5f (New) (17 fncs)** £2,274.00 (£639.00: £312.00) GOING minus 0.08 sec per fur (G)

			SP	RR	SF
3739*	**Tinotops** (MrsRAVickery) **7-11-7**(7) MissSVickery (lw: a.p: hrd rdn to ld appr 2 out: all out) ....—	**1**	7/4[2]	106	31
3739[P]	**Knifeboard** (PaulHosgood) **11-11-7**(7) MrJMPritchard (lw: hld up: hdwy whn pckd 4 out: hrd rdn appr last: edgd lft flat: r.o) 2	**2**	14/1[3]	105	30
4218*	**My Nominee** (DENicholls) **9-12-0b**(7) MrRBurton (j.rt: led tl appr 2 out: r.o one pce) 1¼	**3**	10/11[1]	111	36
	Greenwine (USA) (MJTrickey) **11-11-7**(7) MissLBlackford (hdwy 6th: mstke 4 out: wknd appr 2 out) 9	**4**	20/1	97	22
4270[9]	**Fight to Win (USA)** (LPGrassick) **9-11-7**(7) MrJGrassick (lw: a.p: no hdwy fr 3 out) 4	**5**	33/1	94	19
4228[P]	**Frank Be Lucky** (MsBarbaraAshby-Jones) **11-11-11**(3) MrRThornton (lw: prom tl wknd 4 out) 9	**6**	14/1[3]	87	12
	Tara Boy (RTeague) **12-11-7**(7) MrRCambray (lw: a bhd) 2½	**7**	33/1	85	10
4218[U]	**Simply Perfect** (JSSwindells) **11-11-7**(7) MissKSwindells (lw: prom: mstke 6th: wknd 8th) 2½	**8**	25/1	83	8
4083[4]	**Flowing River (USA)** (NRMitchell) **11-11-7**(7) MrNRMitchell (chsd ldrs: rdn 11th: wknd 13th)....s.h	**9**	50/1	83	8
4051[7]	**Great Pokey** (MissNellCourtenay) **12-11-7**(7) MissNCourtenay (lw: bhd fr 8th: t.o)....30	**10**	25/1	60	—
	Leigh Boy (USA) (DGDuggan) **11-11-7**(7) MrNHOliver (a bhd: t.o whn p.u bef 2 out)	**P**	33/1	—	—
3010[7]	**Orujo (IRE)** (MissCGordon) **9-11-11**(3) MrAHill (a bhd: t.o whn p.u bef 2 out)	**P**	25/1	—	—
			(SP 129.2%)		**12 Rn**

5m 20.3 (11.30) CSF £21.82 TOTE £2.80: £1.70 £2.40 £1.40 (£14.80) Trio £13.80 OWNER Mr R. H. H. Targett (YEOVIL) BRED F. H. Gilman
3739* Tinotops certainly had to dig deep over this shorter distance. (7/4: 5/4-15/8)
Knifeboard was having his first run for the best part of three years when pulled up behind the winner at Exeter. (14/1)
4218* My Nominee did not assist his cause by tending to jump right-handed. (10/11)

4327 OVERBURY HUNTERS' CHASE (5-Y.O+) (Class H)
8-20 (8-20) **2m 110y (New) (14 fncs)** £2,190.00 (£615.00: £300.00) GOING minus 0.08 sec per fur (G)

			SP	RR	SF
4228[2]	**Pro Bono (IRE)** (AndyMorgan) **7-11-13**(5) MrASansome (hld up & plld hrd: hit 5th: led 3 out: drvn out).....—	**1**	6/4[1]	86	12
	Master Crusader (DLWilliams) **11-11-7**(7) MrSDurack (hld up: hdwy 5th: hit 8th: sn lost pl: rallied & ev ch 3 out: hrd rdn & wandered flat: styd on) 1½	**2**	20/1	81	7

3586[U]	**Fantastic Fleet (IRE)** (MrsJWebber) **5-11-5**(3) MrRThornton (lw: led 3rd to 7th: mstke 4 out: one pce fr 3 out) 6	3	5/2[2]	76	—
3928[2]	**Familiar Friend** (SJGilmore) **11-12-0b**(7) MrLLay (led to 3rd: led 7th to 3 out: wknd flat) 2½	4	6/1	79	5
4070*	**Nectanebo (IRE)** (NParker) **9-11-11**(7) MrMFrith (hld up & plld hrd: blnd & uns rdr 7th)	U	100/30[3]	—	—

(SP 110.7%) **5 Rn**

4m 21.9 (14.90) CSF £19.61 TOTE £2.50: £1.60 £3.90 (£39.50) OWNER Mr P. C. Caudwell (ABINGDON) BRED Mrs Una Heffernan
WEIGHT FOR AGE 5yo-7lb
IN-FOCUS: **Unusually for this event, this race was run at a slow pace.**
4228 Pro Bono (IRE) did not mind the drop back to two miles on a course as stiff as this. (6/4)
Master Crusader, having his first run this side of the Irish Sea, looked well capable of causing an upset three from home. (20/1)
Fantastic Fleet (IRE) won a three-horse affair and then walked over in his last two appearances in points. (5/2)
3928 Familiar Friend faded out of third place in the closing stages. (6/1: 7/2-13/2)
4070* Nectanebo (IRE) (100/30: 2/1-7/2)

T/Plpt: £40.00 (237.01 Tckts). T/Qdpt: £13.60 (52.95 Tckts) KH

4170-EXETER (R-H) (Good to firm)
Wednesday April 30th
Water jump omitted all Chases
WEATHER: fine & sunny

4328 PORTMAN FIXED INTEREST BOND NOVICES' (S) HURDLE (4,5,6 & 7-Y.O) (Class G)
2-20 (2-20) **2m 2f (8 hdls)** £1,767.80 (£495.80: £241.40) GOING minus 0.86 sec per fur (HD)

			SP	RR	SF
4181[5]	**Killing Time (73)** (DBurchell) **6-12-0** DJBurchell (lw: hld up: stdy hdwy to ld 2 out: clr last: easily) —	1	11/8[1]	59+	23
4091[6]	**Miramare (57)** (RJHodges) **7-10-7**(7) JHarris (lw: chsd ldr tl led 3rd: rdn & hdd 2 out: wknd appr last) 7	2	6/1	39	3
4175[4]	**Chili Heights (66)** (KBishop) **7-10-7v**(7) MGriffiths (led to 3rd: in tch tl wknd appr 2 out) 24	3	100/30[2]	17	—
3233[15]	**Moor Dutch** (RGFrost) **6-11-0** JFrost (swvd bdly lft s: racd wl bhd tl fell 4th)	F	14/1	—	—
2965[4]	**Country Cousin** (PFNicholls) **5-10-7**(7) LCummins (bit bkwd: reluctant to r: racd wl bhd tl p.u bef 6th: dismntd)	P	7/2[3]	—	—

(SP 108.4%) **5 Rn**

4m 7.0 (1.80 under best) (-3.00) CSF £8.64 TOTE £2.20: £1.60 £2.80 (£5.60) OWNER Mr Simon Lewis (EBBW VALE) BRED L. H. J. Ward
No bid
3207* Killing Time, dropped in trip from his previous two efforts, took this very poor contest with ease, despite carrying at least a stone more in penalties than his rivals. (11/8)
1419 Miramare is still a maiden after twenty-four attempts, but showed up prominently until weakening over the final two flights. (6/1)
2965 Country Cousin was expected to do a lot better here. (7/2: op 9/4)

4329 ROYAL NAVY 'N.H.' NOVICES' HURDLE (5-Y.O+) (Class E)
2-55 (2-55) **2m 2f (8 hdls)** £2,367.50 (£665.00: £324.50) GOING minus 0.86 sec per fur (HD)

			SP	RR	SF
4204[P]	**Colonel Blazer (99)** (MissHCKnight) **5-11-7** JFTitley (lw: hld up mid div: led appr 2 out: styd on wl flat) —	1	2/5[1]	82	—
2572[6]	**Blowing Rock (IRE)** (MissHCKnight) **5-11-0** JCulloty (chsd ldr tl led 4th: hdd appr 2 out: wknd appr last) 6	2	7/1[3]	70?	—
4230[8]	**Fools Future** (MrsJGRetter) **8-11-0** MAFitzgerald (led: tried to run out 1st & 2nd & j.rt: hdd 4th: lost pl 3 out: rdn: rallied 2 out: wknd appr last) 7	3	12/1	63?	—
	Mr Celebration (NAGaselee) **6-11-0** CLlewellyn (bit bkwd: a bhd: lost tch 4th: sn t.o) dist	4	6/1[2]	—	—
3154[10]	**Lizzys First** (BRMillman) **5-10-9**(5) DSalter (bit bkwd: chsd ldrs: in tch to 3rd: wknd & p.u bef 3 out)	P	25/1	—	—

(SP 109.8%) **5 Rn**

4m 11.6 (1.60) CSF £3.53 TOTE £1.20: £1.10 £1.70 (£2.00) OWNER Exors of the late Mr T H Shrimpton (WANTAGE) BRED F. C. T. Wilson
3342* Colonel Blazer, on ground not totally ideal, had little to beat. He is set to go chasing next season. (2/5)
2080 Blowing Rock (IRE) could do little more than follow his stable-companion home once headed. By Strong Gale, he will do better in time and would have appreciated this workout. (7/1: 5/1-8/1)
Fools Future was not up to this company, but has shown a slight glimpse of ability. (12/1: 9/1-14/1)
Mr Celebration (6/1: op 3/1)

4330 PORTMAN FINANCIAL PLANNERS NOVICES' CHASE (5-Y.O+) (Class D)
3-30 (3-30) **2m 7f 110y (16 fncs)** £4,117.00 (£1,246.00: £608.00: £289.00) GOING minus 0.86 sec per fur (HD)

			SP	RR	SF
2908[F]	**Thunder Road (IRE) (75)** (MissHCKnight) **6-11-2** JCulloty (mid div: lft 3rd 11th: rdn & hdwy 13th: in tch 2 out: drvn to ld last: r.o flat) —	1	5/2[2]	80	8
3488[P]	**Otter Prince** (TRGeorge) **8-10-13**(3) MrRThornton (hdwy to chse ldr 10th: lft in clr ld next: mstke 14th: hdd last: no ex flat) 4	2	14/1	77?	5
1300[6]	**Seachest** (MissVAStephens) **8-10-11** SBurrough (led to 1st: chsd ldr to 10th: lft 2nd 11th: in tch 14th tl rdn & wknd 2 out) 6	3	16/1	68?	—
4138[D]	**Rustic Flight (60)** (LWaring) **10-10-9**(7) MGriffiths (a bhd: lost tch 7th: sn t.o) dist	4	20/1	—	—
4072[3]	**Something Catchy (IRE)** (ABarrow) **7-10-11** WMarston (chsd ldrs: in tch tl appr 9th: grad wknd: t.o whn p.u bef 13th)	P	7/1[3]	—	—
4138[2]	**Dunlir (69)** (PRRodford) **7-11-2** MSharratt (blnd & uns rdr 2nd)	U	20/1	—	—
4171*	**Spring to it (90)** (MCPipe) **11-11-8** DWalsh (led 1st: slt mstke 8th: blnd & uns rdr 11th)	U	11/10[1]	—	—

(SP 110.8%) **7 Rn**

5m 45.8 (-1.20) CSF £27.94 TOTE £2.70: £1.30 £6.70 (£43.30) OWNER Mrs Peter Andrews (WANTAGE) BRED Thomas O'Neill
Thunder Road (IRE) took a slight drop in trip and made a successful winning debut for his new yard. If he steers clear of his previous back trouble, he can go on from this. (5/2)
3190 Otter Prince, holding the advantage in the home straight, was only headed at the last and found little resistance on the run-in. He has been disappointing to say the least over hurdles, but put up a promising show here on his debut over the larger obstacles, and a race can be found for him judged on this effort. (14/1)
Seachest, a rather ordinary maiden pointer last season, has not been out for nearly six months and would have appreciated this opportunity. (16/1)
4171* Spring to it, an uneasy favourite, made a couple of mistakes and paid the penalty. (11/10: op 8/11)

4331 PORTMAN INSTANT ACCESS H'CAP CHASE (0-125) (5-Y.O+) (Class D)
4-00 (4-00) **2m 3f 110y (14 fncs)** £3,844.00 (£1,162.00: £566.00: £268.00) GOING minus 0.86 sec per fur (HD)

				SP	RR	SF
4174^{2}	**Henley Regatta (94)** (PRRodford) **9-10-10** SBurrough (lw: hld up: hdwy 10th: led next: clr whn mstkes 2 out & last)	—	1	7/2 ^{3}	105	25
4000^{4}	**Bishops Castle (IRE) (90)** (RGFrost) **9-10-6** JFrost (a.p: disp ld 9th: outpcd & slt mstke 12th: sn one pce)	12	2	3/1 ^{2}	91	11
3936^{2}	**Mr Conductor (IRE) (108)** (RHAlner) **6-11-10** MAFitzgerald (led to 4th: in tch tl wknd 8th: styd on fr 2 out)	2	3	2/1 ^{1}	108	28
3905^{3}	**Lackendara (100)** (MissHCKnight) **10-11-2** JCulloty (chsd ldr tl led 4th: hdd 11th: rdn & wknd next: b.b.v)	7	4	3/1 ^{2}	94	14
4177^{5}	**Rustic Gent (IRE) (84)** (DBurchell) **9-10-0** DJBurchell (bhd: hdwy 7th: chsd ldr next: mstke 10th: nt rcvr)	dist	5	12/1	—	—
				(SP 113.2%)		**5 Rn**

4m 37.4 (-7.60) CSF £13.38 TOTE £5.50: £1.50 £2.40 (£6.10) OWNER Mr E. T. Wey (MARTOCK) BRED British Thoroughbred Racing and Breeding P L C

LONG HANDICAP Rustic Gent (IRE) 8-11

OFFICIAL EXPLANATION **Lackendara: bled from the nose.**

4174 Henley Regatta, a consistent sort, is rarely successful but was recording his third course win. Despite clouting the last two, he stayed on well, but the misfortunes of two market leaders may have played a part. (7/2)

3538* Bishops Castle (IRE), a consistent sort, still has improvement in him and may show it in a summer campaign. (3/1)

3936 Mr Conductor (IRE) stayed on well in the straight after showing a brief sign of temperament. (2/1)

3905 Lackendara (3/1: op 2/1)

4332 PORTMAN FIXED RATE MORTGAGE H'CAP HURDLE (0-110) (4-Y.O+) (Class E)
4-30 (4-30) **2m 3f 110y (9 hdls)** £2,528.20 (£710.20: £346.60) GOING minus 0.86 sec per fur (HD)

				SP	RR	SF
4181^{2}	**Mystic Hill (90)** (RGFrost) **6-11-3** JFrost (lw: chsd ldr: disp ld last: hrd rdn: led fnl strides)	—	1	1/3 ^{1}	69	14
3589^{7}	**Sheep Stealer (80)** (REPeacock) **9-10-7** MAFitzgerald (led tl rdn & hdd fnl strides)	¾	2	6/1 ^{2}	58	3
546^{2}	**Miss Souter (73)** (HSHowe) **8-9-11**(3) MrRThornton (lw: chsd ldrs: in tch tl wknd 6th)	6	3	12/1 ^{3}	47	—
3620^{6}	**Viscount Tully (77)** (CFCJackson) **12-10-4**ow4 MissSJackson (a bhd: lost tch 5th: t.o)	22	4	14/1	32	—
	Persistent Gunner (78) (RJHodges) **7-10-5** TDascombe (hdwy 4th: in tch tl outpcd appr 2 out: sn wknd)	hd	5	14/1	33	—
				(SP 110.3%)		**5 Rn**

4m 28.6 (1.50 under best) (-3.40) CSF £2.84 TOTE £1.10: £1.10 £1.40 (£2.00) OWNER Mr Jack Joseph (BUCKFASTLEIGH) BRED Hascombe and Valiant Studs

LONG HANDICAP Miss Souter 9-9 Viscount Tully 9-13

4181 Mystic Hill, wandering about approaching the last, finds little when in front and had odds-on backers in a cold sweat on the run-in. To be fair, he stuck his neck out and kept on well to the line, and can find another race of this quality. (1/3: op 1/2)

Sheep Stealer nearly caused the upset of the day and, if he can repeat this performance, may go one step better next time. (6/1)

546 Miss Souter is very ordinary to say the least and this puts a question-mark over the form of the first two. (12/1: op 7/1)

3620 Viscount Tully (14/1: op 6/1)

Persistent Gunner (14/1: 8/1-16/1)

4333 ROYAL MARINES NOVICES' CONDITIONAL H'CAP HURDLE (0-100) (4-Y.O+) (Class F)
5-00 (5-00) **2m 2f (8 hdls)** £1,906.10 (£534.60: £260.30) GOING minus 0.86 sec per fur (HD)

				SP	RR	SF
3926*	**Geisway (CAN) (84)** (NJHWalker) **7-11-7** XAizpuru (lw: hld up mid div: hdwy 6th: chsd ldr 2 out: led last: qckmd clr flat)	—	1	9/4 ^{2}	66	11
4137*	**Safecracker (75)** (CPMorlock) **4-10-6** PHenley (a.p: led appr 2 out: rdn & hdd last: one pce flat)	5	2	6/1	53	—
4091*	**Piper's Rock (IRE) (87)** (GBBalding) **6-11-10** ABates (lw: led to 6th: wknd appr 2 out)	4	3	13/8 ^{1}	61	6
2036^{6}	**Lyphard's Fable (USA) (64)** (TRGeorge) **6-10-1** TDascombe (chsd ldr to 4th: hdwy to ld 6th: hdd appr 2 out: rdn & sn wknd)	3½	4	5/1 ^{3}	35	—
4294*	**Contract Bridge (IRE) (87)** (PGMurphy) **4-11-4** 7x SophieMitchell (chsd ldrs: mstke 4th: in tch tl wknd after next)	1¾	5	13/2	56	—
3949^{9}	**Rory'm (IRE) (63)** (LWaring) **8-10-0v¹** MGriffiths (j.slowly: a bhd: t.o after 2nd: p.u after 6th)		P	100/1	—	—
				(SP 114.1%)		**6 Rn**

4m 8.4 (0.40 under best) (-1.60) CSF £14.67 TOTE £2.70: £1.80 £1.40 (£4.50) OWNER Mr Paul Green (BLEWBURY) BRED Michael Byrne

LONG HANDICAP Rory'm (IRE) 9-2

WEIGHT FOR AGE 4yo-6lb

3926* Geisway (CAN) cannot hit the front too soon and, with Aizpuru holding him together well, he kicked on over the last and soon went clear on the flat. He has at last come to hand over hurdles and is capable of stepping up from this. (9/4)

4137* Safecracker simply met one too good here, and can go on to score again. (6/1: op 7/2)

4091* Piper's Rock (IRE), a half-brother to Thumbs Up, was found out for speed and would have preferred further. (13/8)

4294* Contract Bridge (IRE) (13/2: 4/1-7/1)

T/Plpt: £68.90 (84.06 Tckts). T/Qdpt: £14.10 (27.24 Tckts) T.

4075-KELSO (L-H) (Good to firm)
Wednesday April 30th
WEATHER: fine

4334 SUNLAWS MOET & CHANDON NOVICES' CHASE (5-Y.O+) (Class D)
5-45 (5-48) **2m 1f (12 fncs)** £3,420.00 (£1,035.00: £505.00: £240.00) GOING minus 0.55 sec per fur (F)

				SP	RR	SF
4183*	**American Hero** (RAllan) **9-11-10** BStorey (lw: j.w: mde all: eased flat)	—	1	4/6 ^{1}	122+	36
4183^{2}	**Singing Sand (99)** (PMonteith) **7-11-10** RDunwoody (lw: chsd wnr: hit 7th: hdwy & ch 3 out: eased whn btn flat)	14	2	11/8 ^{2}	109	23
3695^{3}	**Bold Account (IRE) (86)** (GMMoore) **7-11-5** MFoster (outpcd: wnt 3rd 4 out: sn btn)	25	3	14/1 ^{3}	80	—
4057^{9}	**Nobodys Flame (IRE) (74)** (SIPittendrigh) **9-11-0** GCahill (j.slowly 1st: a outpcd & wl bhd)	dist	4	125/1	—	—
4151^{4}	**Supermarine** (BMactaggart) **11-11-0** GLee (chsd ldr: outpcd fr 3rd: wknd 7th: no ch whn blnd & uns rdr 2 out)		U	100/1	—	—

				SP	RR	SF
4245[P]	**Kincardine Bridge (USA)** (MrsSCBradburne) **8-10-7**(7) MrMBradburne (hdwy & 3rd whn blnd & uns rdr 8th) ...		**U**	150/1	—	—
				(SP 111.2%)		**6 Rn**

4m 5.9 (-1.10) CSF £1.80 TOTE £1.80: £1.00 £1.90 (£1.10) OWNER Mrs R. P. Aggio (CORNHILL-ON-TWEED) BRED Sir Gordon White

4183* American Hero put in some superb leaps and looks to have got better with every run. (4/6)

4183 Singing Sand looked really well and was 6lb better off with the winner for a two-length beating, but this time he was well and truly put in his place. (11/8)

3695 Bold Account (IRE), without the blinkers this time, always found the pace here too fast for him and he was not knocked about. (14/1: 8/1-16/1)

704 Kincardine Bridge (USA), dropping back dramatically in trip, had just moved into third but was struggling when he gave his rider no chance of staying aboard at the fifth last. (150/1)

4335 SCOTSMAN MAIDEN HURDLE (4-Y.O+) (Class D)

6-15 (6-18) **2m 110y (8 hdls)** £2,899.00 (£814.00: £397.00) GOING minus 0.55 sec per fur (F)

				SP	RR	SF
3529[2]	**Carlisle Bandito's (IRE)** (JBerry) **5-11-5** DParker (lw: trckd ldrs: led last: rdn & r.o)	—	**1**	Evens[1]	67	27
4144[3]	**Caught At Last (IRE)** (MrsMReveley) **6-11-5** GCahill (lw: cl up: led after 3 out to last: swvd lft & r.o one pce)	3½	**2**	7/1[3]	64	24
4244[5]	**Hand of Straw (IRE)** (MissZAGreen) **5-11-5** KJohnson (lw: in tch: effrt 5th: chsng ldrs 2 out: nt qckn)	6	**3**	11/2[2]	58	18
4244[13]	**Lumback Lady (90)** (BMactaggart) **7-11-0** BStorey (hld up: hdwy & prom 5th: rdn appr 2 out: nt qckn)	3½	**4**	9/1	49	9
4187[10]	**Jaunty General (79)** (CParker) **6-11-5** RSupple (rr div: styd on fr 3 out: hit 2 out: nrst fin)	8	**5**	20/1	47	7
2675[8]	**Lost In The Post (IRE)** (CWThornton) **4-11-0** MFoster (bhd tl styd on wl fr 2 out)	6	**6**	20/1	42	—
4152[6]	**Amber Holly (68)** (JEDixon) **8-11-0** FPerratt (chsd ldrs tl wknd 2 out: hit last)	2½	**7**	25/1	33	—
4152[4]	**Dont Forget Curtis (IRE) (74)** (MrsKMLamb) **5-10-12**(7) MissSLamb (nvr trbld ldrs)	2½	**8**	33/1	36	—
4146[8]	**I'm Tyson (NZ) (73)** (MrsDianneSayer) **9-11-0**(5) RMcGrath (mde most tl hdd & wknd after 3 out)	3	**9**	12/1	33	—
1263[8]	**Teddy Edward** (MrsAMNaughton) **7-10-12**(7) MrTJBarry (chsd ldrs tl wknd appr 2 out)	14	**10**	50/1	20	—
4056[C]	**Topup** (MABarnes) **4-10-9**(5) STaylor (mstkes: a bhd)	dist	**11**	100/1	—	—
3475[10]	**Respecting** (JAMoore) **4-11-0** NSmith (stdd s: plld hrd: n.d)	2½	**12**	100/1	—	—
4156[7]	**Dunnellie** (MABarnes) **4-10-9** TReed (nt j.w: a wl bhd)	21	**13**	66/1	—	—
				(SP 117.3%)		**13 Rn**

3m 45.4 (-0.60) CSF £6.64 TOTE £2.00: £1.10 £1.70 £2.10 (£4.10) Trio £6.90 OWNER Mr Chris Deuters (COCKERHAM) BRED Brendan and Sheila Powell

WEIGHT FOR AGE 4yo-6lb

STEWARDS' ENQUIRY Reveley fined £80 under Rule 145 (incorrect saddling).

3529 Carlisle Bandito's (IRE) looked the part and was always going to win this, but it was never all that easy and his real future lies over fences. (Evens)

4144 Caught At Last (IRE) put up a reasonable performance on his first attempt at the minimum trip, but again showed signs of temperament when swerving left under pressure at the last. (7/1: 5/1-8/1)

4244 Hand of Straw (IRE) is running consistently well just now, but this would seem to be as good as he is. (11/2: 4/1-6/1)

3529 Lumback Lady, after a dismal effort last time, ran much better and she has more ability if she gets it fully together. (9/1)

1345 Jaunty General does not do anything quickly and is a shade clumsy, but he was keeping on well at the end. (20/1)

Lost In The Post (IRE), at his first attempt over hurdles, finished quite well suggesting that longer trips should bring improvement. (20/1)

4336 MASON ORGANISATION CENTRE ATTRACTION H'CAP CHASE (0-120) (5-Y.O+) (Class D)

6-50 (6-51) **3m 1f (19 fncs)** £3,986.75 (£1,208.00: £590.50: £281.75) GOING minus 0.55 sec per fur (F)

				SP	RR	SF
4245[P]	**Nijway (85)** (MABarnes) **7-10-0** BStorey (chsd ldrs: led 4 out: hld on wl)	—	**1**	6/1	101	4
4078[7]	**Whaat Fettle (100)** (GRichards) **12-11-1** RDunwoody (a chsng ldrs: ev ch last: kpt on)	2	**2**	5/1[2]	115	18
4148[3]	**Westwell Boy (100)** (PBeaumont) **11-11-1** RSupple (led to 3rd: chsd ldrs: rdn 3 out: nt qckn appr last)	10	**3**	9/2[1]	108	11
4167[7]	**Royal Vacation (113)** (GMMoore) **8-12-0** JCallaghan (lw: mstke 4th: outpcd & bhd: styd on fr 4 out: nrst fin)	1½	**4**	6/1	120	23
4078[3]	**Hurricane Andrew (IRE) (86)** (JAMoore) **9-10-1** NSmith (lw: chsd ldrs: effrt 4 out: wknd fr 2 out)	2½	**5**	11/2[3]	92	—
4078[4]	**Forward Glen (87)** (PCheesbrough) **10-10-2b**ow2 MrRBevis (in tch: hdwy 14th: wknd 4 out)	8	**6**	20/1	88	—
2956[P]	**Side of Hill (91)** (BMactaggart) **12-10-6** GLee (j.rt: led fr 3rd to 4 out: wknd next)	2	**7**	50/1	90	—
3825[11]	**Last Refuge (IRE) (91)** (TJCarr) **8-10-6**ow4 TReed (effrt 12th: nvr rchd ldrs)	3	**8**	20/1	88	—
4148[U]	**Jaunty Gig (85)** (JJBirkett) **11-10-0b** LO'Hara (prom tl outpcd 13th: bhd & hit 15th: n.d after)	15	**9**	13/2	73	—
4078[5]	**Gale Ahead (IRE) (95)** (GMMoore) **7-10-10b**[1] MFoster (lost tch 8th: bhd & rdn whn fell 15th)		**F**	8/1	—	—
3645[2]	**Willie Sparkle (85)** (MrsSCBradburne) **11-10-0** GCahill (bit bkwd: rr div tl p.u lame after 4 out)		**P**	33/1	—	—
				(SP 117.7%)		**11 Rn**

6m 12.4 (2.40) CSF £32.01 CT £136.04 TOTE £10.00: £2.20 £1.70 £2.50 (£17.00) Trio £28.10 OWNER Mr T. A. Barnes (PENRITH) BRED Bacton Stud

LONG HANDICAP Forward Glen 9-2 Jaunty Gig 9-8 Nijway 9-9 Willie Sparkle 9-1

4078 Nijway stays well and is game as they come and, given a fine ride, battled on splendidly after the last. (6/1)

4078 Whaat Fettle has plummeted down the handicap this season and this was his best effort for a while, and should he regain a glimmer of his old form he is certainly well-in. (5/1: op 8/1)

4148 Westwell Boy had his chances two out but looked well short of pace at the business end. (9/2)

3974 Royal Vacation was at his best on this track in early season, and showed definite signs of coming back to form here. (6/1)

4078 Hurricane Andrew (IRE) could never dominate, and was finally outpaced over the last four fences. (11/2)

4078 Gale Ahead (IRE) tried in blinkers here, did not take to them at all. (8/1)

4337 ROYAL BANK OF SCOTLAND H'CAP HURDLE (0-125) (4-Y.O+) (Class D)

7-25 (7-25) **2m 110y (8 hdls)** £4,788.00 (£1,449.00: £707.00: £336.00) GOING minus 0.55 sec per fur (F)

				SP	RR	SF
4246[4]	**Stash the Cash (IRE) (118)** (MDHammond) **6-12-0** RGarritty (hld up: stdy hdwy ½-wy: chal & blnd last: sn rcvrd & rdn to ld fnl 100y)	—	**1**	9/4[1]	101	54
4079[2]	**Killbally Boy (IRE) (90)** (HowardJohnson) **7-9-7**(7) CMcCormack (lw: led: pushed along fr 4th: hit 5th: hdd flat: kpt on wl)	2	**2**	100/30[3]	71	24
4154*	**Glenugie (107)** (GMMoore) **6-11-3** NBentley (lw: chsd ldrs: pushed along 5th: styd on fr 2 out: no imp)	4	**3**	4/1	84	37
4079*	**Well Appointed (IRE) (96)** (BMactaggart) **8-10-6** GLee (lw: prom: effrt 5th: outpcd 3 out: kpt on fr next)	½	**4**	3/1[2]	73	26
3474[8]	**Lixos (94)** (WStorey) **6-10-4** MMoloney (chsd ldr tl outpcd fr 2 out: eased whn btn flat)	10	**5**	50/1	61	14

				SP	RR	SF
1451[3]	**Ragamuffin Romeo (90)** (SIPittendrigh) **8-10-0** GCahill (sn outpcd & bhd)	dist	**6**	33/1	—	—
4246[P]	**Astraleon (IRE) (103)** (RAllan) **9-10-13** BStorey (a bhd: hit 2nd & 2 out)	12	**7**	11/1	—	—
				(SP 112.1%)	**7 Rn**	

3m 41.5 (-4.50) CSF £9.13 TOTE £2.40: £1.90 £2.30 (£7.90) OWNER Mr G. Shiel (MIDDLEHAM) BRED Airlie Stud in Ireland
LONG HANDICAP Killbally Boy (IRE) 9-12 Ragamuffin Romeo 9-8
4246 Stash the Cash (IRE) was always going much the best, but he did his utmost to throw it away with a blunder at the last. (9/4)
4079 Killbally Boy (IRE) is running well and battled on under pressure, and he deserves a change of luck. (100/30)
4154* Glenugie was being stretched fully four from home this time, and was fighting a lost cause thereafter. (4/1)
4079* Well Appointed (IRE), in this fast-run event, was found out some way from home. (3/1)
3474 Lixos, having his second run for his new stable, ran a deal better and was given an easy time once beaten. (50/1)

4338 CHARLIE BROWN UNITED BORDER HUNTERS' CHASE (5-Y.O+) (Class H)

8-00 (8-00) **3m 1f (19 fncs)** £1,469.00 (£409.00: £197.00) GOING minus 0.55 sec per fur (F)

				SP	RR	SF
3712[6]	**Washakie** (FTWalton) **12-11-12** MrJWalton (sn outpcd: rdn & hdwy 12th: styd on wl fr 3 out to ld last: drvn out)	—	**1**	2/1[1]	92	16
4256[7]	**Across the Card** (MajorGenCARamsay) **9-11-11**(7) MrMBradburne (outpcd & bhd: hdwy appr last: styd on wl towards fin)	1¼	**2**	11/4[2]	97	21
4256[P]	**Rusty Blade** (PMonteith) **8-11-7**(5) MrRHale (lw: chsd ldr tl mstke 9th: hdwy & ch 14th: outpcd 3 out: styd on appr last: one pce flat)	3½	**3**	12/1	89	13
4208[5]	**Green Times** (MajorGenCARamsay) **12-11-7**(5) MrCStorey (lw: prom tl outpcd 7th: sn bhd)	18	**4**	14/1	77	1
3994[2]	**Sovereigns Match** (IanNichol) **9-11-7**(5) MrNWilson (led tl wknd & hdd last)	3½	**5**	11/4[2]	75	—
	Shine A Light (AllanDickman) **7-11-5**(7) CaptAOgden (plld hrd: chsd ldrs: hit 8th: wknd fr 13th: p.u bef last)		**P**	9/1[3]	—	—
				(SP 111.0%)	**6 Rn**	

6m 16.7 (6.70) CSF £7.25 TOTE £2.00: £1.10 £1.80 (£4.30) OWNER Mrs F. T. Walton (MORPETH) BRED Mrs F. T. Walton
3712 Washakie was being taken off his legs for much of the trip, but he does stay and that proved to be the deciding factor. (2/1)
3553 Across the Card needs extreme distances to be at his best, and was completely outpaced until finishing with a tremendous flourish. (11/4)
3824 Rusty Blade has been right out of form so far this season, but he looked particularly well and ran his best race, and seems to be coming to hand. (12/1)
Green Times is too slow for this company on this ground. (14/1)
3994 Sovereigns Match galloped his rivals into the ground for much of the trip, but he had done too much too soon and stopped as though shot going to the last. (11/4)
Shine A Light just needs to learn to settle and he can do better. (9/1)

4339 LOTHIAN PLUMBING H'CAP HURDLE (0-125) (4-Y.O+) (Class D)

8-30 (8-30) **2m 6f 110y (11 hdls)** £2,745.00 (£770.00: £375.00) GOING minus 0.55 sec per fur (F)

				SP	RR	SF
1852[3]	**Colorful Ambition (102)** (MrsASwinbank) **7-10-12** JSupple (lw: hld up & bhd: effrt 3 out: hung rt: styd on wl fr last to ld cl home)	—	**1**	5/1[3]	84	29
2802[3]	**Supertop (111)** (LLungo) **9-11-0**(7) WDowling (lw: trckd ldrs: led 5th: sn clr: rdn flat: hdd & no ex towards fin)	nk	**2**	5/4[1]	93	38
4186[P]	**Coqui Lane (117)** (JMDun) **10-11-13** DParker (led to 5th: chsd ldrs rdn 4 out: no imp after)	12	**3**	13/2	90	35
	Very Evident (IRE) (90) (ACWhillans) **8-9-9**(5) STaylor (in tch tl outpcd 4 out: styd on appr last: n.d)	1	**4**	6/1	63	8
4146[2]	**Stylish Interval (92)** (NWaggott) **5-10-2** RSupple (prom: chsd ldr fr 7th: outpcd 3 out: wknd last)	2½	**5**	3/1[2]	63	8
4213[P]	**Parsons Brig (118)** (JSHaldane) **11-12-0** MissSForster (lost tch fr ½-wy: t.o fr 4 out)	dist	**6**	33/1	—	—
				(SP 116.7%)	**6 Rn**	

5m 14.1 (-2.90) CSF £11.63 TOTE £4.70: £2.40 £1.10 (£4.90) OWNER Mr F. J. Sainsbury (RICHMOND) BRED Meon Valley Stud
1852 Colorful Ambition, given a most patient ride, was coaxed into action from the third last and did just enough to get up. (5/1)
2802 Supertop, normally at his best when held up, made it this time because there was no real pace on in the early stages, and he looked to have it won until getting outbattled late on. (5/4)
4077 Coqui Lane was again a shade awkward at the start and he seems to be getting his own ideas about the game. (13/2)
Very Evident (IRE) has been point-to-pointing but was never going well enough to make an impression here. (6/1)
4146 Stylish Interval had a hard race last time and was certainly not at his best on this occasion. (3/1)

T/Plpt: £8.00 (1,216.57 Tckts). T/Qdpt: £7.40 (59.7 Tckts) AA

3953-PLUMPTON (L-H) (Good to firm, Firm patches Ch crse)
Wednesday April 30th

Race 5 - one flight omitted twice
WEATHER: fine

4340 APRIL CLAIMING HURDLE (4-Y.O+) (Class F)

2-10 (2-10) **2m 4f (12 hdls)** £1,935.00 (£535.00: £255.00) GOING minus 0.55 sec per fur (F)

				SP	RR	SF
2946[7]	**Circus Colours (93)** (JRJenkins) **7-11-2** SFox (hld up in tch: led appr 3 out: hrd rdn appr last: r.o)	—	**1**	8/1[3]	72	13
4006[2]	**Peter Monamy (103)** (MCPipe) **5-11-10b** APMcCoy (lw: hld up in tch: chsd wnr appr 3 out: hrd rdn appr last: unable qckn)	1½	**2**	10/11[1]	79	20
4250[4]	**Ewar Bold (63)** (KOCunningham-Brown) **4-10-1b**(7) DSlattery (led 7th: hdd appr 3 out: grad wknd)	14	**3**	20/1	59	—
3442[15]	**Fortunes Rose (IRE) (58)** (JSKing) **5-10-7** TJMurphy (prom tl wknd 3 out)	8	**4**	25/1	44	—
	Sheyl Seymour (MrsJAEwer) **6-10-11** BFenton (a bhd: t.o fr 7th: p.u appr 2 out)		**P**	40/1	—	—
4093[5]	**Castlebay Lad (50)** (RCurtis) **14-11-4v**[1] MrMAppleby (a bhd: brief effrt 8th: wknd next: t.o whn p.u appr last)		**P**	100/1	—	—
651[F]	**Jenzsoph (IRE) (105)** (PJHobbs) **6-10-10**(5) DJKavanagh (led: mstke 4th: hdd 7th: outpcd 3 out: 4th whn blnd & uns rdr 2 out)		**U**	13/8[2]	—	—
				(SP 113.6%)	**7 Rn**	

4m 50.2 (3.20) CSF £14.81 TOTE £6.10: £2.70 £3.90 (£4.80) OWNER Mr S. A. Barningham (ROYSTON) BRED Sir Robin McAlpine
WEIGHT FOR AGE 4yo-7lb
No bid
2755 Circus Colours took the race by the scruff of the neck three out, but saw off the favourite's challenge by the last. (8/1)

4006 Peter Monamy loomed up threateningly three from home and soon had every chance but he could not find the pace to reel in the winner. (10/11: evens-4/5)
3442 Ewar Bold took it up with a circuit to run but had no more to offer over the final three flights. (20/1)
502 Jenzsoph (IRE) didn't jump particularly fluently and a blunder two from home finally saw her part company with her jockey. (13/8)

4341 COOKSBRIDGE NOVICES' H'CAP HURDLE (0-100) (4-Y.O+) (Class E)
2-45 (2-45) **2m 4f (12 hdls)** £2,343.30 (£648.80: £309.90) GOING minus 0.55 sec per fur (F)

				SP	RR	SF
4217U	**Persian Elite (IRE) (97)** (CREgerton) **6-12-0** JOsborne (a.p: chal & pckd 2 out: sn led: r.o wl)	—	1	6/4 1	79	39
42503	**Nordic Spree (IRE) (83)** (GLMoore) **5-11-0v** PHolley (chsd ldr to 5th: led appr 9th: hdd 3 out: hrd rdn appr next: kpt on one pce flat)	4	2	8/1	62	22
39533	**Ben Bowden (90)** (SWoodman) **4-10-11(3)** LAspell (hld up: hdwy 6th: led 3 out: hdd after 2 out: one pce)	½	3	11/2 3	68	21
322212	**Red Light (70)** (JRJenkins) **5-10-1v** TJMurphy (hld up in tch: rdn appr 3 out: kpt on one pce fr next)	½	4	7/1	48	8
39626	**Crown Ivory (NZ) (71)** (PCRitchens) **9-10-2** SFox (a bhd)	16	5	13/2	36	—
40972	**Clock Watchers (71)** (JJBridger) **9-10-2** DMorris (led: hdd appr 9th: wknd appr 3 out: lame)	15	6	9/2 2	24	—
				(SP 110.5%)	**6 Rn**	

4m 45.9 (-1.10) CSF £11.83 TOTE £1.80: £1.30 £3.90 (£7.50) OWNER Elite Racing Club (CHADDLEWORTH) BRED Mrs M. E. Farrell
WEIGHT FOR AGE 4yo-7lb
OFFICIAL EXPLANATION **Clock Watchers: pulled up lame.**
4217 Persian Elite (IRE) had less use made of him today and obviously appreciated it. (6/4)
4250 Nordic Spree (IRE) kept on gamely for second having been under pressure for some time. (8/1: 9/2-9/1)
3953 Ben Bowden took it up three out but could never get away and was worn down before the last. (11/2)
2692 Red Light (7/1: 5/1-8/1)

4342 OFFHAM NOVICES' CHASE (5-Y.O+) (Class E)
3-20 (3-20) **3m 1f 110y (20 fncs)** £3,176.50 (£879.00: £419.50) GOING minus 0.55 sec per fur (F)

				SP	RR	SF
4133U	**Frazer Island (IRE) (115)** (RRowe) **8-11-8** DO'Sullivan (lw: hld up in tch: chsd ldr 16th: led 3 out: comf)	—	1	2/5 1	105+	—
39193	**Malwood Castle (IRE) (89)** (RHAlner) **7-11-8** PHolley (lw: led to 2nd: led 4th: hdd 3 out: one pce)	8	2	7/2 2	100	—
42344	**Dream Leader (IRE) (79)** (MJRoberts) **7-11-8** JRailton (led 2nd: hdd 4th: w ldr tl 15th: blnd 16th & next: wknd qckly)	dist	3	9/2 3	—	—
				(SP 111.8%)	**3 Rn**	

6m 33.4 (13.40) CSF £2.16 TOTE £1.30 (£2.00) OWNER Dr B. Alexander (PULBOROUGH) BRED John Thompson
4133 Frazer Island (IRE) outclassed his rivals here. (2/5)
3919 Malwood Castle (IRE) ran and jumped well but had no chance once the winner went on. (7/2)
4234 Dream Leader (IRE) was already beaten when blundering five out and at the next. (9/2)

4343 HOVE NOVICE HURDLE (4-Y.O F) (Class E)
3-50 (3-54) **2m 1f (10 hdls)** £2,180.90 (£602.40: £286.70) GOING minus 0.55 sec per fur (F)

				SP	RR	SF
4276*	**Theme Arena (88)** (MCPipe) **4-11-7v** APMcCoy (lw: mde all: sn clr: blnd 6th: drvn out)	—	1	6/4 2	66	—
40868	**Persian Dawn** (RTPhillips) **4-10-7** JRailton (chsd clr ldr: closed appr 2 out: 3l bhd & styng on whn mstke last: unable qckn)	3	2	50/1	49?	—
	Salsian (PWinkworth) **4-10-7** TJMurphy (hld up: rdn appr 3 out: sn btn)	dist	3	33/1	—	—
	Fortuitious (IRE) (JRJenkins) **4-10-7** SFox (j.b: a bhd: t.o fr 3rd: p.u bef last)		P	25/1 3	—	—
3226F	**Threesocks** (BSmart) **4-10-7** ILawrence (nt fluent: hrd rdn 5th: sn lost tch: t.o whn p.u appr 3 out: lame)		P	4/7 1	—	—
				(SP 112.4%)	**5 Rn**	

4m 7.5 (11.50) CSF £36.39 TOTE £2.10: £1.90 £24.00 (£20.90) OWNER Mr Antony Sofroniou (WELLINGTON) BRED Halevale Ltd
4276* Theme Arena was soon well in command. Her stride shortened from the second last and she was helped by the runner-up hitting the final flight, but would probably have held on anyway. (6/4)
Persian Dawn chased the clear winner throughout. She began to close from the second last and would have been closer but for hitting the final obstacle. (50/1)
3226 Threesocks was never jumping or travelling well and was well in arrears when pulled up. She was later found to have badly struck into herself. (4/7)

4344 WIVELSFIELD GREEN H'CAP CHASE (0-115) (5-Y.O+) (Class E)
4-20 (4-20) **2m 5f (14 fncs)** £2,946.75 (£879.00: £419.50: £189.75) GOING minus 0.55 sec per fur (F)

				SP	RR	SF
4085F	**Linden's Lotto (IRE) (98)** (JWhite) **8-11-2** JRKavanagh (hld up: hdwy appr 4 out: led 2 out: r.o wl)	—	1	4/1	110	43
4174*	**Coolteen Hero (IRE) (94)** (RHAlner) **7-10-12** PHolley (lw: a.p: led 4 out: hdd 2 out: one pce)	8	2	11/4 2	100	33
20633	**Paper Star (92)** (MPMuggeridge) **10-10-10** BPowell (led: j.slowly 5th & 6th: hdd 4 out: grad wknd)	6	3	7/2 3	93	26
39667	**Turpin's Green (82)** (JSKing) **14-10-0** TJMurphy (prom tl wknd after 8th)	10	4	25/1	76	9
38992	**Be Surprised (82)** (GLMoore) **11-9-7(7)** MBatchelor (chsd ldrs tl wknd appr 3 out)	24	5	14/1	57	—
23P	**Merivel (110)** (RRowe) **10-12-0** DO'Sullivan (a bhd)	5	6	16/1	82	15
41582	**Stormhill Pilgrim (82)** (MJRoberts) **8-10-0** DGallagher (fell 2nd)		F	9/4 1	—	—
				(SP 116.1%)	**7 Rn**	

5m 7.7 (1.40 under best) (-5.30) CSF £14.97 CT £37.99 TOTE £4.80: £2.70 £2.00 (£6.00) OWNER Crocketts Racing Club (ASTON ROWANT) BRED Tom Mulhall
LONG HANDICAP Turpin's Green 9-3 Be Surprised 9-4 Stormhill Pilgrim 9-12
4085 Linden's Lotto (IRE) was always travelling well and ,after leading at the final water jump, was not hard-pressed to come clear. (4/1)
4174* Coolteen Hero (IRE) is very consistent and ran well again, but was beaten for speed from the second last. (11/4)
2063 Paper Star set out to make all, but was not particularly fluent and was left behind once headed. (7/2)
3899 Be Surprised (14/1: 10/1-16/1)
4158 Stormhill Pilgrim took a crashing fall at the second. (9/4)

4345 LADBROKE H'CAP HURDLE (0-115) (4-Y.O+) (Class E)
4-50 (4-54) **2m 4f (12 hdls)** £2,241.80 (£619.80: £295.40) GOING minus 0.55 sec per fur (F)

				SP	RR	SF
41305	**Alltime Dancer (IRE) (113)** (OSherwood) **5-12-0b** JOsborne (hld up: hdwy 3 out: led last: comf)	—	1	5/4 1	92	48

4101[3]	**Night in a Million (88)** (SWoodman) **6-10-0**(3)ow3 LAspell (lw: led: hdd last: unable qckn)	1¼	**2**	9/4[2]	66	19
3570[5]	**Bigwheel Bill (IRE) (85)** (JRJenkins) **8-10-0** TJMurphy (chsd ldr: outpcd appr 3 out: rallied appr next: sn hrd rdn: one pce)	8	**3**	7/1	57	13
4252[2]	**Adilov (85)** (JJBridger) **5-10-0** DMorris (prom tl wknd appr 2 out)	5	**4**	7/2[3]	53	9
				(SP 109.9%)		**4 Rn**

4m 43.4 (-3.60) CSF £4.18 TOTE £1.80 (£2.00) OWNER Mr H. M. Heyman (UPPER LAMBOURN) BRED K. and Mrs Prendergast
LONG HANDICAP Night in a Million 9-12 Bigwheel Bill (IRE) 9-11 Adilov 9-7
4130 Alltime Dancer (IRE) was given a patient ride by Osborne here and, produced at the last, won in cosy fashion. (5/4)
4101 Night in a Million made a brave attempt to make all, but was flattered to finish quite as close to the winner as he did. (9/4: op 6/4)
3570 Bigwheel Bill (IRE) was outpaced on the run to the third last and, although rallying approaching the next, the damage was done. (7/1: 5/1-15/2)
4252 Adilov raced prominently until dropping away before the second from home. (7/2)

T/Plpt: £28.10 (230.11 Tckts). T/Qdpt: £29.30 (10.54 Tckts) SM

4346a - 4347a : (Irish Racing) - See Computer Raceform

3258a-PUNCHESTOWN (Naas, Ireland) (R-H) (Good)
Tuesday April 22nd

4348a COUNTRY PRIDE CHAMPION NOVICES' HURDLE (Gd 2) (5-Y.O+)
3-15 (3-15) **2m (8 hdls)** IR £24,800.00 (IR £7,600.00: IR £3,600.00: IR £1,200.00)

				SP	RR	SF
4010*	**Midnight Legend** (DNicholson) **6-12-0** RJohnson (led & disp ld: led early st: rdn & styd on flat)	—	**1**	7/4[1]	100	—
3564*	**What's the Verdict (IRE)** (APO'Brien,Ireland) **5-11-13** PCarberry (rn freely: hld up: hdwy 2 out: chal u.p appr last: kpt on)	2½	**2**	9/1	98	—
4109a*	**Gazalani (IRE)** (POBrady,Ireland) **5-11-13** TPTreacy (in tch: 2nd & effrt st: kpt on flat)	4½	**3**	14/1	93	—
3640[15]	**Toast The Spreece (IRE)** (APO'Brien,Ireland) **5-11-13** CFSwan (hld up in tch: rdn early st: no ex appr last)	½	**4**	4/1[2]	93	—
	Colm's Rock (IRE) (APO'Brien,Ireland) **6-12-0** THorgan (hld up: effrt early st: rdn & no ex appr last)	½	**5**	25/1	92	—
	Dromineer (IRE) (TJTaaffe,Ireland) **6-12-0** NWilliamson (hld up towards rr: rdn & chsd ldrs after 2 out: no imp appr last)	7	**6**	8/1	85	—
	Bukhari (IRE) (CRoche,Ireland) **5-11-13** CO'Dwyer (rn 3rd: disp ld bef 3 out: rdn after 2 out: wknd bef st)	5	**7**	9/2[3]	80	—
4117a[2]	**Palette (IRE)** (WPMullins,Ireland) **5-11-8** DJCasey (2nd & disp ld: mstke & lost pl 5th: rdn & no imp after 2 out)	2	**8**	14/1	73	—
4010[2]	**Sharpical** (NJHenderson) **5-11-13** MAFitzgerald (hld up towards rr: in tch whn fell 3 out)		**F**	7/1	—	—
				(SP 125.3%)		**9 Rn**

3m 48.7 OWNER Mrs H. J. Clarke (TEMPLE GUITING) BRED Limestone Stud
4010* Midnight Legend, well backed, quickened nicely early in the straight and was in total command at the last. He had looked a bit vulnerable at the second last flight, but once in line for home, had asserted himself again. (7/4)
3564* What's the Verdict (IRE) went second on the outside before the last, but a mistake did not help his cause and he was never going to be a match for the winner. (9/1: op 6/1)
4109a* Gazalani (IRE) was tapped for toe early in the straight but stayed on again on the flat. (14/1)
3640 Toast The Spreece (IRE) flattered when going second before the straight, but was beaten before the last. A stronger pace might have suited him. (4/1: op 5/2)
Colm's Rock (IRE) closed up before two out and stayed on without ever threatening. He looks well primed now for a handicap success. (25/1)
Dromineer (IRE) was never near enough to challenge. (8/1)
Bukhari (IRE) did not appear to relish the ground and dropped right out from the second last. (9/2)
4117a Palette (IRE) made plenty of mistakes. (14/1)
4010 Sharpical, after being held up, was getting into contention when coming down three out. (7/1)

4349a B.M.W. H'CAP CHASE (Gd 1) (4-Y.O+)
3-45 (3-45) **2m (11 fncs)** IR £31,200.00 (IR £9,500.00: IR £4,500.00: IR £1,500.00)

				SP	RR	SF
3614[4]	**Klairon Davis (FR)** (ALTMoore,Ireland) **8-12-0** FWoods (disp ld: led 3rd: clr after 4 out: rdn & styd on stongly flat)	—	**1**	11/10[1]	165	63
2935[4]	**Big Matt (IRE)** (NJHenderson) **9-10-11** MAFitzgerald (hld up towards rr: mstke 4 out: rdn & no imp between last 2)	8	**2**	7/1[3]	140	38
4123a*	**Idiots Venture** (APO'Brien,Ireland) **10-10-11** CFSwan (hld up in tch: mstke & lost pl 5th: hdwy & chsd wnr bef 2 out: no imp u.p appr last:)	s.h	**3**	8/1	140	38
4062[2]	**Lord Dorcet (IRE)** (JIACharlton) **7-10-11** JOsborne (hld up: 2nd bef 3 out: rdn 2 out: kpt on same pce)	s.h	**4**	12/1	140	38
3383a*	**Opera Hat (IRE)** (JRHFowler,Ireland) **9-10-11** PCarberry (led & disp ld to 3rd: mstke 7th: rdn 3 out: no ex)	12	**5**	7/1[3]	128	26
4062[F]	**Arctic Kinsman** (NATwiston-Davies) **9-10-11** CLlewellyn (in tch: mstks 7th & 3 out: btn 2 out)	8	**6**	7/2[2]	120	18
4123a[2]	**Cable Beach (IRE)** (MCunningham,Ireland) **8-10-11** CO'Dwyer (cl up: mstke 3rd: wknd 4 out)	20	**7**	14/1	100	—
				(SP 120.3%)		**7 Rn**

4m 0.1 (-8.90) OWNER C. Jones (NAAS) BRED M. C. Quellier in France
3614 Klairon Davis (FR), given every chance by the handicapper here, - allowed to run off a mark 2lb below his official rating - was impressive. He jumped superbly and pulled right away from the third last. (11/10)
2935 Big Matt (IRE), 6lb wrong in the weights, was going nowhere three out, but stayed on from the last to snatch second place on the line. (7/1)
4123a* Idiots Venture made mistakes but was the only one in pursuit from three out. He was well held when blundering at the last. (8/1)
4062 Lord Dorcet (IRE), 17lb wrong, was not making any impression after the third last and just plugged on at the one pace on the flat. (12/1: op 8/1)
4062 Arctic Kinsman was finished with when blundering three out. (7/2)

4350a BRADSTOCK INSURANCE (LISTED) CHASE (5-Y.O+)
4-15 (4-15) **2m 4f (14 fncs)** IR £12,900.00 (IR £3,700.00: IR £1,700.00: IR £500.00)

				SP	RR	SF
3797*	**Linton Rocks** (TThomsonJones) **8-11-8** RDunwoody (lft in ld 1st: mde rest: rdn & styd on flat)	—	**1**	7/4[1]	105	30

	Horse	Dist	Pos	SP	RR	SF
2739a[5]	**Headbanger** (MMLynch,Ireland) **10-11-8** DHO'Connor (hld up: trckd ldrs 4 out: effrt appr last: rdn & one pce flat)	4	**2**	13/2[3]	102	27
1936[2]	**Stay Lucky (NZ)** (NJHenderson) **8-11-8b[1]** MAFitzgerald (cl up: chsd wnr fr 10th: rdn & no imp between last 2)	8	**3**	5/1[2]	95	20
4007[8]	**Court Master (IRE)** (RHBuckler) **9-11-8** BPowell (cl up: rdn & chsd ldrs whn slow 3 out: one pce next)	11	**4**	16/1	87	12
	Bangabunny (MrsSABramall,Ireland) **7-11-3** PCarberry (hmpd 1st: chsd ledrs 4 out: no imp after 2 out)	3½	**5**	20/1	79	4
	Father Rector (IRE) (PFennelly,Ireland) **8-11-8** THorgan (hld up: mstke 5th: chsd ldrs bef 4 out: no imp fr next)	13	**6**	13/2[3]	73	—
	Penny Bride (IRE) (TO'Callaghan,Ireland) **8-10-12** AO'Shea (mid div: rdn after 10th: no imp next)	4	**7**	20/1	60	—
1240a[2]	**The Subbie (IRE)** (TFoley,Ireland) **8-11-8** TPTreacy (bdly hmpd 1st: mstke 5th: trailing 7th: n.d)	9	**8**	12/1	63	—
	Macnamarasband (IRE) (RVShaw,Ireland) **8-11-3** JOsborne (in tch: mstke 10th: n.d next)	10	**9**	20/1	50	—
	Always in Trouble (MJPO'Brien,Ireland) **10-11-8** TPRudd (disp ld whn fell 1st)		**F**	10/1	—	—
	Royal Oasis (IRE) (PHeffernan,Ireland) **6-11-8** NWilliamson (cl up: 2nd whn fell 6th)		**F**	14/1	—	—
	Moon-Frog (IRE) (PatrickJohnMurphy,Ireland) **10-11-3** JKKinane (towards rr: hmpd 6th: mstke next: trailing whn p.u 9th)		**P**	100/1	—	—
	Owenduff (USA) (ALTMoore,Ireland) **7-11-3** FWoods (towards rr: hld up: bdly hmpd & u.r 6th)		**U**	8/1	—	—
3260a[P]	**Rocketts Castle (IRE)** (MrsSABramall,Ireland) **7-11-3** CLlewellyn (mid div: blnd & u.r next)		**U**	20/1	—	—

(SP 140.2%) **14 Rn**

5m 10.9 (-2.10) OWNER The Hon Mrs Townshend (UPPER LAMBOURN) BRED Melbury Park Stud
3797* Linton Rocks again underlined the difference between ordinary English Novices and their Irish counterparts. He made all and will certainly need further, while his jumping was very sound. (7/4)
2335a Headbanger was always finding the winner too strong. (13/2: op 4/1)
1936 Stay Lucky (NZ), struggling from three out, just kept on at the one pace. (5/1)
3627* Court Master (IRE) could only keep on at the one pace at the finish. (16/1)
1240a The Subbie (IRE) (12/1: op 8/1)
Always in Trouble (10/1: op 6/1)
Owenduff (USA) (8/1: op 5/1)

4351a BALLYMORE PROPERTIES H'CAP CHASE (4-Y.O+)
4-45 (4-48) **3m 1f (18 fncs)** IR £8,220.00 (IR £1,860.00: IR £780.00: IR £420.00)

	Horse	Dist	Pos	SP	RR	SF
	Triptodicks (IRE) (DAKiely,Ireland) **7-9-4**(3) GCotter (towards rr: hdwy 3 out: chal next: led between last 2: r.o u.p flat)	—	**1**	9/2[1]	95	—
3916[P]	**Miss Diskin (IRE)** (RHBuckler) **8-10-7** BPowell (led 1st: cl up: mstke 9th: rdn 2 out: styd on u.p)	s.h	**2**	12/1	109	14
	All In The Game (IRE) (JBrassil,Ireland) **9-9-10**(7) MDMurphy (in tch: led appr 3 out: hdd after 2 out: rdn & one pce)	15	**3**	9/1	95	—
3503a[4]	**Cabbery Rose (IRE)** (PFGraffin,Ireland) **9-9-11**(5) AO'Shea (disp ld 2nd tl 7th: led again 12th: hdd appr 3 out: one pce bef next)	15	**4**	16/1	85	—
	Lucky Bust (IRE) (WHarney,Ireland) **7-11-1** CFSwan (hld up: chsd ldrs 5 out: mstke next: wknd)	dist	**5**	11/2[3]	—	—
314a[10]	**Loftus Lad (IRE)** (EMO'Sullivan,Ireland) **9-10-6b[1]** NWilliamson (in tch: mstke 4th: no imp appr 3 out)	5	**6**	13/2	—	—
	Matts Dilemma (IRE) (PJPDoyle,Ireland) **9-11-9** DHO'Connor (hld up: bad mstke & lost pl 11th: p.u bef next)		**P**	12/1	—	—
	Paradise Road (ALTMoore,Ireland) **8-10-4** FWoods (towards rr: v. slow 12th: t.o 5 out: p.u bef 4 out)		**P**	7/1	—	—
2362a[6]	**Macallister (IRE)** (VBowens,Ireland) **7-11-7** CO'Dwyer (in tch: wkng whn mstke 5 out: p.u bef next)		**P**	5/1[2]	—	—
	Field Of Destiny (IRE) (MKiernan,Ireland) **8-9-9**(3)ow1 KWhelan (sn towards rr: t.o 8th: p.u 4 out)		**P**	33/1	—	—
3503a[9]	**Monkey Ago** (MrsSABramall,Ireland) **10-11-4** PCarberry (mid div: n.d fr 12th: p.u bef 4 out)		**P**	20/1	—	—
3503a[10]	**Diorraing (IRE)** (TO'Neill,Ireland) **7-10-2b** DJCasey (in tch: blnd & u.r 7th)		**U**	25/1	—	—
	Inniscein (IRE) (JohnJosephMurphy,Ireland) **9-9-12** THorgan (disp ld: led 7th tl 12th: 2nd whn mstke & u.r next)		**U**	16/1	—	—

(SP 124.8%) **13 Rn**

6m 33.5 (3.50) OWNER M. G. O'Huallachain (DUNGARVAN)
Triptodicks (IRE) relishes this ground and got the better of a hard-fought battle from the last. (9/2: op 3/1)
3916 Miss Diskin (IRE) nearly pulled off a surprise on ground thought not to be in her favour, rallying well on the flat and only just going under. (12/1)
Matts Dilemma (IRE) (12/1: op 8/1)
Paradise Road (7/1: op 4/1)

4352a BALCAS H'CAP HURDLE (0-123) (4-Y.O+)
5-15 (5-21) **2m 4f (12 hdls)** IR £4,110.00 (IR £930.00: IR £390.00: IR £210.00)

	Horse	Dist	Pos	SP	RR	SF
4117a[7]	**Valley Erne (IRE)** (MCunningham,Ireland) **6-11-1** RDunwoody (hld up hdwy 5th: trckd ldrs 3 out: chal st: led nr last: styd on)	—	**1**	10/1	97	29
	Thai Electric (IRE) (SByrne,Ireland) **6-9-13** TJMitchell (towards rr: hdwy 6th: chsd ldrs st: styd on flat)	5	**2**	12/1	77	9
3650a[7]	**Be Home Early (IRE)** (AMullins,Ireland) **7-11-3** CFSwan (hld up hdwy 3 out: rdn & nt rch ldrs appr last)	2	**3**	11/2[2]	93	25
4109a[6]	**Native-Darrig (IRE)** (WPMullins,Ireland) **6-10-9** DJCasey (hld up in tch: disp ld appr 2 out: rdn st: hdd nr last: one pce u.p flat)	s.h	**4**	5/1[1]	85	17
	Glenfields Castle (IRE) (IADuncan,Ireland) **7-9-7**(7) PGHourigan (cl up: led after 9th: rdn & hdd st: one pce)	3	**5**	16/1	74	6
	Mariners Reef (IRE) (MMcCullagh,Ireland) **6-9-0**(7) DMcCullagh (mid div early: disp ld 2 out tl st: rdn & nt qckn appr last)	2½	**6**	10/1	65	—
	Fiddlers Bow VI (IRE) (NMeade,Ireland) **9-11-0** PCarberry (hld up: hdwy 4 out: rdn after 2 out: kpt on)	2	**7**	6/1[3]	84	16
	Malacca King (IRE) (WPMullins,Ireland) **6-10-12**(5) PMorris (towards rr: hdwy 8th: chsd ldrs after 2 out: no imp appr last)	3	**8**	25/1	85	17
3396[5]	**Ask The Butler (IRE)** (CRoche,Ireland) **6-11-7**(7) MrPaulMoloney (in tch early: no imp after 2 out)	8	**9**	8/1	90	22
	Native Fleck (IRE) (MKiernan,Ireland) **7-10-7** NWilliamson (hld up: hdwy after 9th: no imp st)	4	**10**	14/1	65	—
	The Wise Knight (IRE) (AJMcNamara,Ireland) **6-9-6**(7) MDMurphy (towards rr: hdwy 4 out: no imp)	½	**11**	33/1	57	—
	Innovative (IRE) (JO'Haire,Ireland) **6-9-4**(3) GCotter (towards rr: hdwy after 4 out: kpt on same pce)	s.h	**12**	25/1	51	—
318a[10]	**West On Bridge St (IRE)** (VTO'Brien,Ireland) **7-10-6** CO'Dwyer (hld up: mstke 9th: lost tch bef 3 out)	12	**13**	14/1	54	—
	Kaselectric (IRE) (EMcNamara,Ireland) **6-10-11** THorgan (in tch early: lost pl: towards rr & rdn 4 out: n.d)	3½	**14**	8/1	57	—
	Merry People (IRE) (JQueally,Ireland) **9-11-4** JShortt (sn mid div: hdwy bef 3 out: no imp appr next)	5	**15**	33/1	60	—
	Siberian Tale (IRE) (PCasey,Ireland) **7-10-8**(3) MrPJCasey (cl up tl wknd bef 3 out)	1	**16**	16/1	52	—

				SP	RR	SF
319a[5]	**Glenreef Boy (IRE)** (CPDonoghue,Ireland) **8-9-5**(5) AO'Shea (hld up: rdn after 4 out: wknd bef next)	3½	**17**	50/1	34	—
	Frau Dante (IRE) (AFenton,Ireland) **7-10-0**ow1 PARoche (hld up: 3rd after 8th: wknd 3 out)	3	**18**	20/1	36	—
	Sleepy River (IRE) (ALTMoore,Ireland) **6-10-9** FWoods (towards rr: n.d)	12	**19**	7/1	35	—
	Mister Chippy (IRE) (SO'Farrell,Ireland) **5-10-12** TPTreacy (in tch: n.d fr 4 out)	¾	**20**	33/1	38	—
3850[4]	**Ground Nut (IRE)** (RHBuckler) **7-11-5** BPowell (led: hdd after 7th: mstke next: sn wknd)	4	**21**	10/1	41	—
	Ferrycarrig Hotel (IRE) (VBowens,Ireland) **8-10-9** CNBowens (prom: led after 7th: hdd after 4 out: wknd bef next)	20	**22**	33/1	15	—
				(SP 167.3%)	**22 Rn**	

4m 54.2 (-4.80) OWNER S A M Syndicate (NAVAN)
4117a Valley Erne (IRE) getting a much more intelligent ride this time, had no trouble in regaining his best from. (10/1)
3850 Ground Nut (IRE), taking a strong hold early, was in front until being headed before five out. He dropped away very quickly from that point on. (10/1)

4353a - 4354a : (Irish Racing) - See Computer Raceform

4346a-PUNCHESTOWN (Naas, Ireland) (R-H) (Good)
Wednesday April 23rd

4355a STANLEY COOKER CHAMPION NOVICES' HURDLE (Gd 1) (4-Y.O+)
2-40 (2-41) **2m 4f (12 hdls)** IR £18,600.00 (IR £5,700.00: IR £2,700.00: IR £900.00)

				SP	RR	SF
3613*	**Istabraq (IRE)** (APO'Brien,Ireland) **5-11-13** CFSwan (cl up: mstkes 4 out & 3 out: disp ld 2 out: sn clr: easily)	—	**1**	4/11 [1]	93++	24
3613[5]	**Soldat (USA)** (DNicholson) **4-11-4** RDunwoody (hld up: hdwy 8th: rdn & nt qckn after 2 out)	9	**2**	13/2 [2]	86	8
	Boro Bow (IRE) (PMullins,Ireland) **6-11-9** TPTreacy (sn led: hdd after 2 out: rdn & nt qckn)	½	**3**	16/1	80	12
3910*	**Ardrina** (FMurphy) **6-11-9** NWilliamson (mstks 1st & 7th: styd on fr 2 out)	10	**4**	20/1	72	4
4124a[2]	**Liver Bird (IRE)** (JABerry,Ireland) **7-12-0** CO'Dwyer (3rd at 4th: rdn 4 out: no imp appr next)	10	**5**	8/1 [3]	69	1
	Glebe Lad (IRE) (MJPO'Brien,Ireland) **5-11-13** TPRudd (hld up: rdn after 4 out: n.d)	20	**6**	20/1	53	—
316a*	**Clonagam (IRE)** (MrsJHarrington,Ireland) **8-12-0** JShortt (hld up towards rr: rdn & btn after 3 out)	3½	**7**	25/1	51	—
4048[6]	**Liss De Paor (IRE)** (APO'Brien,Ireland) **6-11-9** THorgan (led briefly early: rn 2nd to 4th: wknd 8th: p.u bef last)		**P**	10/1	—	—
				(SP 126.1%)	**8 Rn**	

4m 58.7 (-0.30) OWNER John McManus (PILTOWN) BRED Shadwell Estate Company Limited
3613* Istabraq (IRE) confirmed his top-novice status, completing his five-timer in the process. A mistake four out was a bit alarming, but he got to the front two out with the minimum of fuss and sailed clear. He certainly looks Champion Hurdle material, but there must be a temptation to go for something on the Flat with him this season. (4/11)
3007 Soldat (USA) was never a serious threat, being under pressure before two out and just staying on at the one pace. (13/2)
Boro Bow (IRE) did a good job up front but was totally outclassed once headed by the winner, and only relinquished second place late on the flat. (16/1)
3910* Ardrina, well behind from the fifth, plugged on at the one pace. (20/1)
4124a Liver Bird (IRE) travelled well enough in the race until fading from two out. (8/1)

4356a HEINEKEN GOLD CUP NOVICES' H'CAP CHASE (4-Y.O+)
3-15 (3-15) **3m 1f (18 fncs)** IR £37,200.00 (IR £11,400.00: IR £5,400.00: IR £1,800.00)

				SP	RR	SF
3618[4]	**Noyan** (RAFahey) **7-11-1** NWilliamson (mid div: 2nd at 12th: rdn 4 out: led u.p between last 2: lft clr last)	—	**1**	13/2 [2]	114	16
1486a[2]	**Bobbyjo (IRE)** (TCarberry,Ireland) **7-11-2** GCotter (mid div: hdwy 10th: rdn & chsd ldrs next: no imp)	15	**2**	20/1	105	7
2341a[3]	**Woodville Star (IRE)** (WJBurke,Ireland) **8-11-8** CO'Dwyer (sn disp ld: mstke 3 out: hdd & nt qckn appr next)	6	**3**	7/1 [3]	108	10
2345a[4]	**Tell The Nipper (IRE)** (MHourigan,Ireland) **6-10-10b**ow1 KFO'Brien (towards rr: hdwy 10th: mstke 4 out: no imp 2 out)	3	**4**	12/1	94	—
3882[2]	**Carole's Crusader** (DRGandolfo) **6-10-8** RDunwoody (in tch: no imp 2 out)	nk	**5**	10/1	91	—
4110a[4]	**Papillon (IRE)** (TMWalsh,Ireland) **6-11-12** CFSwan (hmpd 2nd: towards rr: n.d 2 out)	1	**6**	4/1 [1]	109	11
	Livin It Up (IRE) (ALTMoore,Ireland) **7-10-11** APMcCoy (jnd ldrs 5th: slight mstke 4 out: no imp fr next)	13	**7**	14/1	86	—
2848a[P]	**The Outback Way (IRE)** (JJO'Connor,Ireland) **7-11-5b** DHO'Connor (towards rr: n.d)	¾	**8**	25/1	93	—
3389a[6]	**Shining Willow** (JRHFowler,Ireland) **7-10-8**ow1 JOsborne (cl up: no imp fr 3 out)	1	**9**	14/1	81	—
4110a[2]	**Amble Speedy (IRE)** (ALTMoore,Ireland) **7-11-12** FWoods (hld up towards rr: n.d)	12	**10**	8/1	92	—
4116a[F]	**Stroll Home (IRE)** (JJMangan,Ireland) **7-10-9** MrEGallagher (mid div: mstke 4 out: sn no imp)	3½	**11**	25/1	72	—
	Prate Box (IRE) (PHughes,Ireland) **7-11-0** GBradley (fell 2nd)		**F**	14/1	—	—
3616[9]	**Lord Muff (IRE)** (LComer,Ireland) **8-10-7** JKKinane (fell 2nd)		**F**	100/1	—	—
3616[5]	**Corket (IRE)** (APO'Brien,Ireland) **7-12-0** THorgan (cl up: led bef 3 out: hdd after 2 out: rdn & rallied: 2nd whn fell last)		**F**	14/1	—	—
3389a[4]	**Royal Rosy (IRE)** (APO'Brien,Ireland) **6-10-8** TJMitchell (towards rr: p.u bef 3 out)		**P**	16/1	—	—
	Ballymacrevan (IRE) (IADuncan,Ireland) **7-10-9** TPTreacy (led early: cl up to 7th: bhd 14th: p.u bef 3 out)		**P**	25/1	—	—
3617[P]	**General Pongo** (TRGeorge) **8-10-7** MAFitzgerald (in tch early: mstke 11th: p.u next)		**P**	20/1	—	—
	The Gopher (IRE) (TFLacy,Ireland) **8-10-7** LPCusack (towards rr: mstkes: bhd 14th: p.u bef 2 out)		**P**	20/1	—	—
				(SP 133.1%)	**18 Rn**	

6m 29.9 (-0.10) OWNER C. H. McGhie (MALTON) BRED Oakgrove Stud
3618 Noyan looked to have taken Corket's measure when that one fell at the last, and was left to win unchallenged. (13/2)
1486a Bobbyjo (IRE) was left struggling after the second last before being presented with the runner-up spot at the final fence. (20/1)
2341a Woodville Star (IRE) jumped well in front but weakened quickly after a slight mistake three out, before staying on again. She would appreciate softer ground. (7/1)
2345a Tell The Nipper (IRE) ran well until mistake four out. (12/1: op 7/1)
3882 Carole's Crusader was looking pretty one paced before four out, but she kept on going and might have finished fourth but for being hampered by a last-fence faller. (10/1)
4110a Papillon (IRE) was possibly showing the effects of his Fairyhouse race and his chance was not helped when hampered by fallers at the second fence. (4/1)
4110a Amble Speedy (IRE) (8/1: op 5/1)
3616 Corket (IRE) (14/1: op 8/1)

3047* General Pongo made a mistake at the sixth and had dropped away when pulled up seven out. (20/1)

4357a PADDY POWER H'CAP HURDLE (Gd 1) (4-Y.O+)

3-45 (3-47) **2m (8 hdls)** IR £21,700.00 (IR £6,650.00: IR £3,150.00: IR £1,050.00)

	Horse / details	Dist	Pos	SP	RR	SF
3640[12]	**Lady Daisy (IRE)** (AMullins,Ireland) **8-10-6**(5) AO'Shea (rn 2nd to 4th: cl up: rdn 2 out: chal u.p last: sn led: styd on)	—	**1**	12/1	128	—
4061*	**Shankar (IRE)** (DNicholson) **6-10-8**(3) MrRThornton (hld up in tch: effrt 3 out: disp ld 2 out: led bef st: rdn clr: jnd last: sn hdd: no ex)	4	**2**	5/2[1]	124	—
4063[4]	**Space Trucker (IRE)** (MrsJHarrington,Ireland) **6-12-0** JShortt (hld up: chsd ldrs 3 out: rdn appr last: kpt on)	4	**3**	5/1[3]	137	—
4117a[3]	**Mystical City (IRE)** (WPMullins,Ireland) **7-10-12** DJCasey (mid div: rdn & chsd ldrs appr 2 out: styd on flat)	1½	**4**	7/1	120	—
3597[5]	**Hill Society (IRE)** (NMeade,Ireland) **5-10-11** RDunwoody (hld up: chsd ldrs: rdn appr last: one pce)	s.h	**5**	7/1	119	—
4117a*	**Khayrawani (IRE)** (CRoche,Ireland) **5-10-11b[1]** CO'Dwyer (cl up: disp ld 3 out: u.p 2 out: no ex appr last)	9	**6**	9/2[2]	110	—
1365[F]	**Just Little** (APO'Brien,Ireland) **5-10-11** CFSwan (hld up towards rr: hdwy 3 out: kpt on flat)	hd	**7**	8/1	110	—
3254a[5]	**Magical Lady (IRE)** (DPKelly,Ireland) **5-10-11** APMcCoy (led: mstke 6th: sn rdn: hdd after 2 out: wknd early st)	4	**8**	16/1	106	—
1793[9]	**Embellished (IRE)** (NMeade,Ireland) **5-10-11** NWilliamson (hld up towards rr: chsd ldrs st: sn no imp)	2½	**9**	9/1	104	—
3640[11]	**Cheryl's Lad (IRE)** (NJHenderson) **7-10-11** MAFitzgerald (hld up in tch: mstke 5th: rdn & no imp appr 2 out: virtually p.u flat)	25	**10**	12/1	78	—

(SP 130.8%) **10 Rn**

3m 45.3 OWNER Patrick Kehoe (GOWRAN)

3572 Lady Daisy (IRE) has maintained her form tremendously well. She started winning in November at Clonmel off a mark of 100 and, after this, is 35lb higher. The Italian Champion Hurdle may be her next target. (12/1)
4061* Shankar (IRE) went to the front two out and looked all over the winner but had no answer to Lady Daisy's challenge. (5/2: op 4/1)
4063 Space Trucker (IRE) ran well under top-weight but had a tremendous amount in his plate. (5/1)
4117a Mystical City (IRE) was going on again at the end. (7/1)
3597 Hill Society (IRE) again demonstrated that his Champion Hurdle run was not to be taken too seriously. (7/1)
4117a* Khayrawani (IRE), equipped with blinkers for the first time, had his chance before the second last but dropped out in the straight. (9/2: op 3/1)
1365 Just Little, held up and far from fluent at some of her flights, wasn't a threat from four out. She had not run since November, but was going on again at the finish in a style which suggests a possible return to form. (8/1)
2054 Cheryl's Lad (IRE) was being driven along five out and dropped right away from the next. (12/1: op 8/1)

4360a DONCASTER BLOODSTOCK SALES JACK WHITE MEMORIAL CHAMPION AMATEUR N.H. FLAT RACE (Gd 1) (4-Y.O+ F & G)

5-15 (5-15) **2m** IR £12,900.00 (IR £3,700.00: IR £1,700.00: IR £500.00)

	Horse / details	Dist	Pos	SP	RR	SF
3619[2]	**Arctic Camper** (DNicholson) **5-12-0** MrRThornton (hld up: hdwy 4f out: chal early st: led over 1f out: rdn clr)	—	**1**	11/4[1]	90f+	—
	Cloone Bridge (IRE) (APO'Brien,Ireland) **5-12-3** MrJABerry (cl up: 3rd ½-wy: led 3f out: rdn, hdd & no ex over 1f out)	5½	**2**	16/1	88 f	—
3619[6]	**French Holly (USA)** (FMurphy) **6-12-4** MrPFenton (hld up: trckd ldrs 5f out: effrt 2f out: nt qckn over 1f out)	1½	**3**	3/1[2]	86 f	—
3626*	**Lord Lamb** (MrsMReveley) **5-12-6** MrSSwiers (hld up towards rr: hdwy after ½-wy: effrt on ins over 1f out: n.m.r ins last: r.o)	½	**4**	16/1	89 f	—
	Garrys Lock (IRE) (TFoley,Ireland) **8-12-3**ow-1 MrPEnglish (hld up towards rr: hdwy over 6f out: nt qckn 1½f out)	2	**5**	14/1	83 f	—
4009*	**Melody Maid** (NJHenderson) **5-11-12** MrCVigors (mid div: hdwy ½-wy: 4th & no ex 1½f out)	7	**6**	12/1	72 f	—
	Promalee (IRE) (APO'Brien,Ireland) **5-12-6** MrBMCash (cl up: chsd ldrs 4f out: no imp 2f out)	1	**7**	8/1[3]	79 f	—
4118a[3]	**Do Ye Know Wha (IRE)** (SJTreacy,Ireland) **5-12-3** MrJPMcNamara (towards rr: sme hdwy 6f out: rdn bef st: kpt on)	1	**8**	12/1	75 f	—
	Aboriginal (IRE) (PMullins,Ireland) **5-12-3** MrACCoyle (towards rr: hdwy 6f out: rdn bef st: no imp)	½	**9**	8/1[3]	74 f	—
	Dr King (IRE) (SDonohoe,Ireland) **5-12-3** MrGElliott (hld up: rdn & chsd ldrs bef st: one pce)	2	**10**	14/1	72 f	—
	Sarah Supreme (IRE) (GTHourigan,Ireland) **6-11-10** MrDMarnane (led to 3f out: rdn bef st: one pce)	4½	**11**	20/1	60 f	—
	Solvang (IRE) (DAKiely,Ireland) **5-12-0** MrWMO'Sullivan (in tch: rdn & no imp over 2f out)	3	**12**	16/1	62 f	—
	Andrea Cova (IRE) (VBowens,Ireland) **5-11-12** MrAJDempsey (cl up: rdn 4f out: wknd appr st)	1	**13**	20/1	59 f	—
3619[4]	**Scoring Pedigree (IRE)** (JWMullins) **5-12-0** MrRWalsh (towards rr: no imp over 3f out)	2	**14**	14/1	59 f	—
	Mr Moylan (APO'Brien,Ireland) **5-11-10** MrEBolger (towards rr: n.d)	5½	**15**	16/1	49 f	—
	Fine De Claire (JRHFowler,Ireland) **4-11-2** MrARCoonan (in tch: no imp last 4f)	1	**16**	20/1	47 f	—
	Cinq Frank (IRE) (DKinsella,Ireland) **7-11-11** MrGJHarford (in tch: rdn 5f out: wknd over 4f out)	15	**17**	100/1	33 f	—
	Cotton Eyed Jimmy (IRE) (MJGilhooly,Ireland) **6-11-11** MrMJGilhooly (nvr bttr than mid div)	¾	**18**	100/1	32 f	—
	Barrington (IRE) (CRoche,Ireland) **4-11-3** MrPaulMoloney (towards rr: n.d)	15	**19**	10/1	17 f	—
	Clay And Wattles (IRE) (PO'Leary,Ireland) **6-12-4** MrAJMartin (mid div best: no imp last 4f)	1½	**20**	20/1	23 f	—
	Cailin Supreme (IRE) (PMullins,Ireland) **6-12-2** MrTMullins (mid div: rdn bef ½-wy: eased & dropped bhd: p.u)		**P**	14/1	—	—

(SP 169.6%) **21 Rn**

3m 41.2 OWNER Lady Harris (TEMPLE GUITING)

3619 Arctic Camper led over a furlong and a half out and absolutely trotted up. (11/4)
Cloone Bridge (IRE) got to the front with three furlongs to race but was totally outpaced when headed. (16/1)
3619 French Holly (USA), second in this race last year, found the winner's Cheltenham superiority confirmed once again. (3/1)
3626* Lord Lamb did not find much room on the inside with a furlong to run, and in the circumstances ran a good race. (16/1)
4009* Melody Maid, second turning into the straight, was soon done with. (12/1)
3619 Scoring Pedigree (IRE) was not a threat in the last half-mile. (14/1)

4361a KEVIN MCMANUS CHAMPION HUNTERS' CHASE (5-Y.O+)

5-45 (5-45) **3m 1f (18 fncs)** IR £13,000.00 (IR £3,800.00: IR £1,800.00: IR £600.00)

	Horse / details	Dist	Pos	SP	RR	SF
3391a[F]	**Dixon Varner (IRE)** (EBolger,Ireland) **7-12-0** MrRWalsh (in tch early: hmpd 5th: 6th at 10th: 2nd bef 3 out: led appr last: sn clr)	—	**1**	6/1	107	—
3391a*	**Stay In Touch (IRE)** (JJCostello,Ireland) **7-12-0** MrDPCostello (lft in led 6th: clr 14th to 3 out: hdd last: rdn & no ex)	3½	**2**	100/30[2]	105	—

				SP	RR	SF
	Bree Hill (IRE) (MCullen,Ireland) **9-12-0** MrGElliott (in tch: mstkes 10th & 11th: chsd ldr 3 out: rdn & one pce)	9	**3**	20/1	99	—
4051[F]	**Mr Boston** (MrsMReveley) **12-12-0** MrSSwiers (cl up: lft 2nd at 6th: lost tch 3 out)	8	**4**	7/4[1]	94	—
	Captain Brandy (ColinMcKeever,Ireland) **12-12-0** MrDMChristie (towards rr early: no imp whn mstke 4 out)	15	**5**	20/1	84	—
	Mack a Day (MCondon,Ireland) **10-12-0** MrKevinO'Sullivan (hld up: lost pl after 14th)	3½	**6**	25/1	82	—
3391a[P]	**Killmurray Buck (IRE)** (AJWhelan,Ireland) **9-11-9** MrJPMcNamara (in tch early: mid div whn b.d 5th)		**B**	50/1	—	—
	Hi Jamie (IRE) (AJMartin,Ireland) **5-11-7** MrGJHarford (towards rr: mstks: n.d whn fell 2 out)		**F**	16/1	—	—
3637[3]	**What A Hand** (EJO'Grady,Ireland) **9-12-0** MrPFenton (in led whn fell 1st)		**F**	7/2[3]	—	—
	Celtic Buck (IRE) (MrsHelenO'KeeffeDaly,Ireland) **11-12-0** MrPO'Keeffe (in tch tl fell 5th)		**F**	33/1	—	—
	Lottover (IRE) (DHassett,Ireland) **8-11-9** MrBrianHassett (cl up whn mstke & u.r 1st)		**U**	20/1	—	—
	Denfield (IRE) (CAMcBratney,Ireland) **6-12-0** MrIBuchanan (lft in led 1st tl u.r 6th)		**U**	16/1	—	—
				(SP 130.7%)		**12 Rn**

6m 44.9 (14.90) OWNER Mrs John Magnier
3391a Dixon Varner (IRE) had everything in his sights and was absolutely cruising from three out. He picked off the runner-up before the last and went clear on the flat. (6/1: op 3/1)
3391a* Stay In Touch (IRE) found himself totally outpaced by the winner this time. (100/30: op 2/1)
4051 Mr Boston was a surprise favourite but this veteran was struggling from three out. (7/4)

4358a - 4361a : (Irish Racing) - See Computer Raceform

4354a-PUNCHESTOWN (Naas, Ireland) (R-H) (Good)
Thursday April 24th

4362a CASTLEMARTIN STUD PAT TAAFFE H'CAP CHASE (5-Y.O+)
2-10 (2-10) **3m 1f (18 fncs)** IR £16,250.00 (IR £4,750.00: IR £2,250.00: IR £750.00)

				SP	RR	SF
	Indestructible (IRE) (ALeahy,Ireland) **9-10-0** CFSwan (hld up: chal to ld nr last: j. rt: rdn & styd on flat)	—	**1**	100/30[2]	111+	31
4110a[7]	**Heist** (NMeade,Ireland) **8-10-10** RDunwoody (disp ld to 13th: disp ld again bef 3 out: hdd 2 out: rallied to ld between last 2: hdd nr last: r.o)	2	**2**	3/1[1]	120	40
3128a[3]	**Shanagarry (IRE)** (PHeffernan,Ireland) **8-11-8** NWilliamson (hld up: disp ld 3 out: led after 2 out: sn rdn & hdd no ex)	7	**3**	7/1	127	47
4074[F]	**Back Bar (IRE)** (ALTMoore,Ireland) **9-10-10** APMcCoy (disp ld tl appr 3 out: rdn & lost tch appr 2 out)	25	**4**	4/1[3]	99	19
4110a[F]	**Teal Bridge (IRE)** (AHeffernan,Ireland) **12-10-3** CO'Dwyer (hld up: mstks: chsd ldrs 4 out: rdn & no imp next)	3½	**5**	11/2	90	10
4110a[8]	**Fissure Seal** (ALTMoore,Ireland) **11-11-3** TPTreacy (rn 3rd early: mstks: lost tch 14th: n.d)	¾	**6**	14/1	104	24
4074[F]	**Nuaffe** (PAFahy,Ireland) **12-11-2b** TJMitchell (in tch: mstke 10th: wknd & p.u bef next)		**P**	16/1	—	—
				(SP 108.5%)		**7 Rn**

6m 24.2 (-5.80) OWNER John Quane (KILMALLOCK)
Indestructible (IRE), a rather enigmatic character even at his best, took this with some ease. There won't be many easier £25,000 Grade Two opportunities in the future. (100/30)
4110a Heist did everything right here but could not quicken on the flat. (3/1)
3128a Shanagarry (IRE), on his favourite course, had the advantage two out but faded between the last two. (7/1)

4364a MURPHYS IRISH STOUT CHAMPION HURDLE (Gd 1) (4-Y.O)
3-15 (3-15) **2m (8 hdls)** IR £31,000.00 (IR £9,500.00: IR £4,500.00: IR £1,500.00)

				SP	RR	SF
3258a[2]	**Grimes** (CRoche,Ireland) **4-11-1**ow1 CO'Dwyer (hld up in tch: trckd ldrs bef 2 out: led early st: rdn clr appr last: r.o.)	—	**1**	5/2[2]	104+	30
2738a[4]	**Snow Falcon** (TJTaaffe,Ireland) **4-11-0** NWilliamson (towards rr early: hld up: led after 3 out: hdd early st: rdn & nt trble wnr appr last)	5	**2**	33/1	98	25
4014[3]	**Circus Star** (Trained) **4-11-0** RJohnson (hld up: hdwy after 5th: rdn & effrt st: no ex whn mstke last)	4	**3**	8/1	94	21
3634[15]	**Stylish Allure (USA)** (DKWeld,Ireland) **4-11-0** RDunwoody (hld up: chsd ldrs 2 out: sn rdn: kpt on same pce)	7	**4**	11/2[3]	87	14
4014*	**Quakers Field** (GLMoore) **4-11-0** APMcCoy (hld up: nt fluent: rdn & hdwy 6th: no imp appr last)	3	**5**	5/4[1]	84	11
3258a[4]	**Spirit Dancer (IRE)** (GMLyons,Ireland) **4-11-0** SCLyons (rn 3rd to 5th: mstke next: sn wknd)	15	**6**	33/1	69	—
4014[10]	**Hard News (USA)** (DPKelly,Ireland) **4-11-0** FWoods (led: hdd after 3 out: wknd appr next)	3	**7**	16/1	66	—
2738a[2]	**Afarka (IRE)** (SJTreacy,Ireland) **4-10-9** TPTreacy (rn 2nd: mstks 5th & 6th: rdn & wknd appr 3 out)	nk	**8**	20/1	61	—
3801*	**Red Raja** (Trained) **4-11-0** JOsborne (mstke 1st: in tch: rdn 3 out: no imp)	2½	**9**	12/1	63	—
3525a[4]	**Strategic Ploy** (DPKelly,Ireland) **4-10-9** CFSwan (mid div: rdn & chsd ldrs bef 3 out: no imp)	nk	**10**	25/1	58	—
	Royal Midyan (JFBaileyJun,Ireland) **4-11-0** DTEvans (towards rr: n.d)	4	**11**	16/1	59	—
3634[13]	**Kerawi** (Trained) **4-11-0** CLlewellyn (sn towards rr: mstke 4th: no imp 3 out)	12	**12**	11/1	47	—
3525a[7]	**Rainbow Victor (IRE)** (APO'Brien,Ireland) **4-11-0** KFO'Brien (mid div early: towards rr whn mstke 4th: n.d)	15	**13**	25/1	32	—
				(SP 145.6%)		**13 Rn**

3m 37.4 OWNER John McManus
3258a Grimes, heavily-backed, was hugely impressive, leading on the bit before the last and drawing clear on the flat. He went up 7lb for this to 120 and it would seem that one such as Commanche Court would always be vulnerable to him on this sort of ground. (5/2: op 4/1)
2738a Snow Falcon, still a maiden, put up a vastly improved performance, but the winner was much too strong. (33/1)
4014 Circus Star was in third place and making no impression when blundering at the last. (8/1)
3525a* Stylish Allure (USA) stayed on inside the straight without holding out any hope. (11/2)
4014* Quakers Field had to be driven into fifth with three to jump and, never for one moment, looked like running up to his Aintree form. (5/4)
3801* Red Raja was no threat after the fourth last. (12/1)
3301 Kerawi never got into contention. (11/1)

4365a I.A.W.S. CENTENARY YEAR CHAMPION STAYERS' HURDLE (Gd 1) (4-Y.O+)
3-45 (3-46) **3m (13 hdls)** IR £21,700.00 (IR £6,650.00: IR £3,150.00: IR £1,050.00)

				SP	RR	SF
3635[3]	**Paddy's Return (IRE)** (FMurphy) **5-11-12b** NWilliamson (hld up in tch: led early st: rdn clr appr last: styd on wl)	—	**1**	100/30[3]	125+	28

				SP	RR	SF
4016*	**Escartefigue (FR)** (DNicholson) **5-11-9** RDunwoody (hld up: trckd ldrs 3 out: rdn & chal appr last: no ex u.p)	2	**2**	6/4[1]	121	24
3635[10]	**Derrymoyle (IRE)** (MCunningham,Ireland) **8-12-0** APMcCoy (hld up towards rr: trckd ldrs 3 out: rdn & no imp appr last)	12	**3**	16/1	116	21
4117a[5]	**Theatreworld (IRE)** (APO'Brien,Ireland) **5-11-9** CFSwan (hld up: trckd ldrs: rdn & one pce early st)	1½	**4**	3/1[2]	112	15
4016[4]	**What a Question (IRE)** (MFMorris,Ireland) **9-11-6** CO'Dwyer (wnt 2nd at 5th: lft in ld 7th: hdd & one pce early st)	1½	**5**	9/1	106	11
3126a[2]	**Antapoura (IRE)** (APO'Brien,Ireland) **5-11-4** TPTreacy (rn 3rd: lft 2nd at 7th to 10th: rdn next: wknd)	20	**6**	16/1	92	—
4052[2]	**Private Peace (IRE)** (APO'Brien,Ireland) **7-11-8** JOsborne (rn 2nd tl fell 4th)		**F**	7/1	—	—
	Windy Bee (IRE) (BrianNolan,Ireland) **6-11-3** ANolan (led: mstke 4th: p.u 7th)		**P**	20/1	—	—
				(SP 127.1%)		**8 Rn**

5m 43.4 OWNER P. O'Donnell (MIDDLEHAM) BRED C. Foy

3635 Paddy's Return (IRE), travelling supremely well from three out, led before the last and stayed on without being unduly punished. (100/30)
4016* Escartefigue (FR) was travelling well when moving into third place after the second last. There was not a lot forthcoming when an effort was asked for in the straight, and he was well held from the last. (6/4: op Evens)
3126a Derrymoyle (IRE) was only a moderate fourth over the last but stayed on well. (16/1)
4117a Theatreworld (IRE) looked to be going as well as anything before the turn in, but this trip is beyond him. (3/1)
4016 What a Question (IRE), in front from the seventh, dropped away very quickly when headed in the straight. (9/1: op 6/1)

4366a TRIPLEPRINT NOVICES' CHASE (Gd 2) (5-Y.O+)

4-15 (4-16) **2m (11 fncs)** IR £18,600.00 (IR £5,700.00: IR £2,700.00: IR £900.00)

				SP	RR	SF
4116a[2]	**Jeffell** (ALTMoore,Ireland) **7-12-0** FWoods (led & disp ld: j.w: rdn after 2 out: styd on u.p)	—	**1**	11/8[1]	128+	40
4062[F]	**Celibate (IRE)** (CJMann) **6-12-0** RDunwoody (rn 4th: reminders 6th: rdn 2 out: styd on u.p)	1½	**2**	100/30[3]	127	39
4012[F]	**Flying Instructor** (PRWebber) **7-11-8** NWilliamson (hld up: 2nd bef 3 out: rdn & no ex appr last)	1½	**3**	3/1[2]	119	31
4123a[4]	**Beakstown (IRE)** (PMullins,Ireland) **8-12-0** TPTreacy (disp ld tl after 4 out: 3rd & btn between last 2)	15	**4**	16/1	110	22
3260a[3]	**Kharasar (IRE)** (AMullins,Ireland) **7-11-8** CFSwan (hld up towards rr: n.d 2 out)	1	**5**	13/2	103	15
	Geallainnban (IRE) (TJTaaffe,Ireland) **7-11-8b** CO'Dwyer (prom: bad mstke & lost pl 3rd: lost tch 6th: t.o)	dist	**6**	50/1	—	—
				(SP 111.4%)		**6 Rn**

4m 4.4 (-4.60) OWNER Thomas Bailey (NAAS)

4116a Jeffell jumped immaculately and is much better value than the official margin suggests. (11/8)
3596 Celibate (IRE) was not a serious threat from three out but stayed on from the last to be nearest at the finish. (100/30)
4012 Flying Instructor took the winner on from three out, but wasn't going anywhere on the run to the last. (3/1)
4123a Beakstown (IRE) was beaten three out. (16/1)
3260a Kharasar (IRE) flattered briefly four out but was soon done with. (13/2)

4367a - 4375a : (Irish Racing) - See Computer Raceform

4217-BANGOR-ON-DEE (L-H) (Good)

Friday May 2nd

WEATHER: fine

4376 J. SCOTT FURNISHERS NOVICES' HURDLE (4-Y.O+) (Class E)

6-00 (6-01) **3m (12 hdls)** £3,032.00 (£852.00: £416.00) GOING minus 0.15 sec per fur (G)

				SP	RR	SF
4001[P]	**Sharp Thyne (IRE)** (PJHobbs) **7-11-0** GTormey (lw: mstke 3rd: rdn & hdwy 9th: led 2 out: drvn out)	—	**1**	40/1	71	27
4230*	**Supreme Flyer (IRE) (102)** (KCBailey) **7-11-12** JOsborne (lw: hld up & bhd: stdy hdwy 5th: rdn appr 2 out: r.o one pce)	4	**2**	7/4[1]	80	36
4217[5]	**Gower-Slave** (PBowen) **5-11-0** BFenton (a.p: led 3 out to 2 out: one pce)	nk	**3**	33/1	68	24
4275[3]	**Foxies Lad (102)** (DNicholson) **6-10-11**(3) MrRThornton (hld up: hdwy 7th: hrd rdn & wknd appr last)	4	**4**	7/4[1]	66	22
3970[3]	**Riverbank Rose (82)** (WClay) **6-10-12v**(3) GuyLewis (chsd ldr: hit 6th: led 7th to 3 out: wknd appr last)	s.h	**5**	20/1[3]	66	22
4217[6]	**The Naughty Vicar** (GRichards) **7-11-0b[1]** RichardGuest (hld up: hdwy 5th: wknd qckly 3 out)	19	**6**	33/1	53	9
4309[P]	**Tommy Cooper (80)** (MrsBarbaraWaring) **6-11-0b[1]** EByrne (nt j.w: bhd whn blnd 6th: nvr nr ldrs)	½	**7**	25/1	52	8
2945[5]	**Danzante (IRE) (62)** (RMStronge) **5-11-0** DGallagher (a bhd)	5	**8**	33/1	49	5
3491[P]	**Pinxton Penny** (JMackie) **5-10-6**(3) EHusband (nt j.w: a bhd)	8	**9**	100/1	39	—
3555[5]	**Double Dash (IRE) (80)** (DMoffatt) **4-10-13** DJMoffatt (bhd fr 5th: t.o)	12	**10**	20/1[3]	42	—
1640[12]	**Seven Potato More (IRE)** (SirJohnBarlowBt) **7-10-9**(5) DJKavanagh (dwlt: a bhd: t.o)	9	**11**	33/1	30	—
4217[P]	**Dunston Knight** (BPreece) **4-10-7** GaryLyons (prom to 7th: t.o)	23	**12**	100/1	14	—
	Itsgonnashine (PBowen) **8-10-9** DWalsh (bhd fr 8th: t.o)	½	**13**	100/1	9	—
	Mosephine (IRE) (THCaldwell) **7-10-9** MSharratt (a bhd: t.o fr 8th)	dist	**14**	100/1	—	—
3459[F]	**Scale Down (IRE)** (JAPickering) **8-11-0** WMarston (s.i.s: plld hrd: sn prom: wknd qckly & p.u after 6th)		**P**	33/1	—	—
3690[5]	**Big Stan's Boy** (CPEBrooks) **6-11-0** GBradley (lw: hdwy 4th: wknd qckly 7th: t.o whn p.u bef 3 out)		**P**	20/1[3]	—	—
	Tilty (USA) (103) (AStreeter) **7-11-12v** TEley (lw: led to 7th: wknd 8th: t.o whn p.u bef last: lame)		**P**	9/2[2]	—	—
				(SP 130.1%)		**17 Rn**

5m 46.6 (7.60) CSF £99.90 TOTE £94.90: £14.10 £1.50 £6.10 (£264.10) Trio £256.30 OWNER Mrs D. R. Rusher (MINEHEAD) BRED J. Tyrrell
WEIGHT FOR AGE 4yo-7lb

OFFICIAL EXPLANATION **Sharp Thyne (IRE): regarding the improvement in form, the trainer's representative stated that the race at Exeter last time was run on fast ground, at a strong pace and the gelding hung left throughout, which he is inclined to do at home. He added that he was evidently suited by today's left-handed track and the extra half-mile.**

Sharp Thyne (IRE) was the subject of an enquiry into his improved form. The Stewards were told that the gelding had hung left-handed at Exeter, and that he was suited by the extra half-mile, better ground, and today's left-handed track. The explanations were accepted. (40/1)
4230* Supreme Flyer (IRE) was trying to defy a double penalty for beating nothing special. (7/4)
2911 Gower-Slave seems blessed with stamina rather than speed. (33/1)
4275 Foxies Lad, stepping-up to three miles, did not find a lot when coming off the bridle. (7/4)
3970 Riverbank Rose, trying a longer trip, is basically only a selling plater. (20/1)

4377 JONES PECKOVER NOVICES' H'CAP CHASE (0-100) (5-Y.O+) (Class E)

6-30 (6-30) **2m 1f 110y (12 fncs)** £3,468.75 (£1,050.00: £512.50: £243.75) GOING minus 0.15 sec per fur (G)

				SP	RR	SF
4174[4]	**Pond House (IRE) (97)** (MCPipe) **8-12-0** DWalsh (lw: mde all: drvn out)	—	1	7/4[2]	108	33
4219[3]	**The Secret Grey (71)** (DMcCain) **6-10-2**ow2 TJenks (hld up: wnt 2nd appr 3 out: pckd 2 out: hrd rdn & r.o flat)	1¼	2	11/2	81	4
4183[6]	**Desert Brave (IRE) (77)** (MrsSJSmith) **7-10-8** RichardGuest (hld up: rdn 4 out: one pce)	8	3	5/1[3]	80	5
4007[4]	**Dandie Imp (73)** (AWCarroll) **9-10-4** RDunwoody (lw: chsd wnr: blnd 4th: rdn 3 out: sn wknd)	1	4	11/8[1]	75	—
*3684**	**Hangover (69)** (RLee) **11-10-0** CLlewellyn (Withdrawn not under Starters' orders)		W		—	—
				(SP 110.5%)		**4 Rn**

4m 17.5 (7.50) CSF £9.35 TOTE £2.50: £2.30 (£5.70) OWNER Mr C. R. Fleet (WELLINGTON) BRED S. Banville
LONG HANDICAP The Secret Grey 9-12 Hangover 9-13
4174 Pond House (IRE) was suited by having things his own way in this small field. (7/4)
4219 The Secret Grey, carrying 4lb more than his long handicap mark, did not find nodding on landing at the penultimate fence coming at the ideal time. (11/2)
4007 Dandie Imp had another front-runner to contend with. (11/8)

4378 CRYSTAL BALLGAZERS (S) H'CAP HURDLE (0-95) (4-Y.O+) (Class G)

7-00 (7-00) **2m 4f (11 hdls)** £2,130.50 (£598.00: £291.50) GOING minus 0.15 sec per fur (G)

				SP	RR	SF
4283[3]	**Skane River (IRE) (66)** (GRichards) **6-10-9** RDunwoody (hld up: wnt 2nd 3 out: sn hrd rdn: led after 2 out: hit last: r.o wl)	—	1	9/4[1]	47	—
3985[2]	**Edward Seymour (USA) (84)** (WJenks) **10-11-13** TJenks (hld up & bhd: stdy hdwy 5th: r.o one pce fr 2 out)	6	2	7/2[2]	60	12
	Squealing Jeanie (57) (JMBradley) **8-10-0** BFenton (lw: s.s: sn prom: led 8th tl after 2 out: btn whn hit last)	1¾	3	33/1	32	—
2751[F]	**Aavasaksa (FR) (65)** (AGNewcombe) **4-9-13**(3) MrRThornton (hdwy 5th: mstke 3 out: one pce)	2	4	14/1	38	—
71[10]	**Sweet Noble (IRE) (80)** (KJDrewry) **8-11-9** MSharratt (hld up: hdwy 5th: led 7th to 8th: wknd appr 2 out)	5	5	25/1	49	1
3940[6]	**Grandman (IRE) (79)** (DMoffatt) **6-11-8** DJMoffatt (hld up & bhd: hdwy 7th: one pce fr 3 out)	½	6	8/1	48	—
3971[3]	**Mardood (64)** (SBClark) **12-10-2**(5) BGrattan (no hdwy fr 8th)	1¾	7	16/1	31	—
4187[5]	**Gallardini (IRE) (77)** (BSRothwell) **8-11-6** DGallagher (hdwy appr 4th: wknd 8th)	2½	8	10/1	42	—
4096[3]	**Its Grand (70)** (PCRitchens) **8-10-13v[1]** CMaude (w ldr: rdn & wknd appr 7th)	14	9	6/1[3]	24	—
4290[3]	**Against The Clock (57)** (PBowen) **5-9-7**(7) LCummins (lw: led: hrd rdn & hdd 7th: sn wknd)	23	10	12/1	—	—
3807[8]	**Whitebonnet (IRE) (79)** (CREgerton) **7-11-8b** JOsborne (lw: a bhd: eased whn no ch appr 2 out)	7	11	8/1	9	—
27[11]	**Lady Lois (57)** (BPreece) **6-9-7**(7) JMogford (a bhd: t.o)	4	12	25/1	—	—
4231[7]	**Buster (58)** (MrsBarbaraWaring) **9-10-1** EByrne (a bhd: t.o fr 6th)	13	13	20/1	—	—
				(SP 134.2%)		**13 Rn**

4m 48.8 (12.80) CSF £10.71 CT £210.89 TOTE £3.50: £1.90 £1.30 £12.10 (£4.10) Trio Not won; £279.09 to Newmarket 4/5/97 OWNER Mr W. J. Peacock (PENRITH) BRED Jim Hanrahan
LONG HANDICAP Squealing Jeanie 9-9 Lady Lois 9-11 Against The Clock 9-10
WEIGHT FOR AGE 4yo-6lb
No bid
4283 Skane River (IRE) was 1lb lower here than when unlucky at Perth a week ago. (9/4)
3985 Edward Seymour (USA), raised 2lb, was 10lb higher than when scoring at Huntingdon. (7/2)
Squealing Jeanie, 5lb out of the handicap, ran her best race to date over a trip that may prove beyond her optimum. (33/1)
Aavasaksa (FR), nibbled at in the market, showed his first signs of ability. (14/1)
4096 Its Grand (6/1: 4/1-13/2)
3016 Whitebonnet (IRE) (8/1: op 5/1)

4379 WYNNSTAY HUNT SUPPORTERS CLUB H'CAP CHASE (0-120) (5-Y.O+) (Class D)

7-30 (7-30) **2m 4f 110y (15 fncs)** £4,182.00 (£1,266.00: £618.00: £294.00) GOING minus 0.15 sec per fur (G)

				SP	RR	SF
3567[F]	**Jacob's Wife (100)** (PRWebber) **7-10-8** JOsborne (a.p: wnt 2nd 8th: slight ld whn lft clr last)	—	1	8/1	111	26
3800[2]	**Change the Act (109)** (MissVenetiaWilliams) **12-11-0**(3) MrRThornton (lw: chsd ldr to 3rd: outpcd 8th: rallied appr 2 out: btn whn lft 2nd last)	12	2	11/4[2]	111	26
4206[4]	**Frickley (119)** (GRichards) **11-11-13** RDunwoody (lw: hld up: blnd & lost pl 9th: rdn after 10th: no respnse)	19	3	15/8[1]	106	21
3919*	**James the First (120)** (PFNicholls) **9-12-0** CMaude (hld up: hdwy 9th: wknd 4 out)	5	4	6/1[3]	103	18
689[3]	**Maggots Green (98)** (JMBradley) **10-10-6** BFenton (led tl mstke 4 out: wknd qckly: t.o)	dist	5	9/1	—	—
4225[F]	**Over the Pole (107)** (PRChamings) **10-10-12**(3) MrCBonner (lw: hld up: hdwy 11th: led 4 out: hdd & fell last)		F	7/1	—	—
4306[P]	**Top Brass (IRE) (99)** (KCBailey) **9-10-7b[1]** SMcNeill (plld hrd: chsd ldr 3rd to 8th: wknd 10th: bhd whn p.u after 3 out)		P	20/1	—	—
				(SP 114.1%)		**7 Rn**

5m 5.5 (5.50) CSF £28.23 CT £53.31 TOTE £9.40: £4.00 £1.50 (£27.50) Trio £10.30 OWNER The Black Sheep Flock (BANBURY) BRED Mrs P. S. M. Taylor
3198 Jacob's Wife, who has been slipping down the ratings, bounced back to form on this sounder surface. (8/1)
3800 Change the Act was only third best on merit. (11/4)
4206 Frickley, dropped 2lb, never recovered from a bad error at the second ditch. (15/8)
3919* James the First (6/1: op 4/1)
4225 Over the Pole was probably in the process of having his measure taken when coming to grief. (7/1)

4380 EASTERN DESTINY (FOR THE JAMES GRIFFITH MEMORIAL TROPHY) NOVICES' HUNTERS' CHASE (5-Y.O+) (Class H)

8-00 (8-00) **3m 110y (18 fncs)** £1,548.25 (£466.00: £225.50: £105.25) GOING minus 0.15 sec per fur (G)

				SP	RR	SF
4015*	**Bitofamixup (IRE)** (MJRoberts) **6-12-4**(3) MrPHacking (lw: a.p: led 14th: clr appr 2 out: r.o wl)	—	1	1/4[1]	113	3
4160*	**Mister Horatio** (WDLewis) **7-11-11**(7) MrMLewis (prom: j.slowly 3rd: lost pl 5th: rallied 12th: mstke 14th: wnt 2nd 3 out: tired whn mstke last)	25	2	9/2[2]	94	—
4218[5]	**Nadiad** (DMcCain) **11-11-7**(7) MrAWintle (hld up & plld hrd: hdwy appr 8th: wknd 14th: no ch whn pckd 2 out)	4	3	20/1	87	—

	Horse	Dist	Pos	SP	RR	SF
	Desmond Gold (IRE) (KeithPearce) **9-11-7**(7) MrDSJones (set slow pce: j.slowly 3rd: qcknd appr 12th: hdd & hit 14th: wknd 3 out)	dist	4	16/1 3	—	—
				(SP 108.8%)	**4 Rn**	

6m 26.2 (24.20) CSF £1.81 TOTE £1.20 (£1.20) OWNER Mr Mike Roberts (HAILSHAM) BRED Mrs Norma G. Cook
4015* Bitofamixup (IRE) made this look straightforward, and now heads for the John Corbet Cup at Stratford. (1/4)
4160* Mister Horatio was taking on an exciting prospect in the winner. (9/2)

4381 LLANDUDNO H'CAP HURDLE (0-105) (4-Y.O+) (Class F)

8-30 (8-30) **2m 1f (9 hdls)** £2,905.00 (£880.00: £430.00: £205.00) GOING minus 0.15 sec per fur (G)

	Horse	Dist	Pos	SP	RR	SF
3087 5	**Winsford Hill (84)** (PJHobbs) **6-10-12** GTormey (lw: hld up: hdwy 5th: led 2 out: mstke last: rdn & r.o wl)	—	1	12/1	63	28
3743 2	**Muizenberg (80)** (EHOwenjun) **10-10-8** DGallagher (plld hrd: led 3rd to 2 out: one pce)	4	2	7/1 3	55	20
4187 9	**Nashville Star (USA) (94)** (RMathew) **6-11-8v** CLlewellyn (led to 3rd: hrd rdn appr 2 out: one pce)	1½	3	10/1	68	33
4163*	**Daily Sport Girl (82)** (BJLlewellyn) **8-10-10** MrJLLlewellyn (hld up: hdwy 4th: ev ch appr 2 out: wknd appr last)	10	4	8/1	46	11
912*	**Cointosser (IRE) (105)** (MCPipe) **4-12-0** SWynne (hld up & bhd: hdwy after 3 out: wknd 2 out)	½	5	15/8 1	69	29
4006 11	**Chris's Glen (83)** (JMBradley) **8-10-11v** BFenton (prom: rdn 6th: wknd appr 2 out)	2½	6	20/1	45	10
677 6	**No Light (99)** (MrsIMcKie) **10-11-13** LHarvey (plld hrd: a in rr)	7	7	9/1	54	19
208 3	**Lawful Love (IRE) (78)** (TWDonnelly) **7-10-3**(3) MrRThornton (hld up: rdn appr 3 out: sn bhd)	4	8	11/2 2	29	—
4295*	**Eurolink the Rebel (USA) (86)** (SBClark) **5-10-9**(5) 6x BGrattan (prom to 5th: t.o)	26	9	9/1	13	—
3802 8	**Mr Lowry (80)** (LJBarratt) **5-10-8** DerekByrne (plld hrd: dropped rr 5th: p.u bef 6th)		P	14/1	—	—
				(SP 122.0%)	**10 Rn**	

3m 59.6 (4.60) CSF £88.83 CT £810.58 TOTE £11.40: £2.60 £2.70 £3.10 (£33.70) Trio £183.30 OWNER Six Horse Power (MINEHEAD) BRED A. L. Hobbs
WEIGHT FOR AGE 4yo-5lb
2842 Winsford Hill, dropped 5lb, took the eye in the paddock and appreciated this better ground. (12/1)
3743 Muizenberg confirmed his return to form, but could not cope with the winner. (7/1)
4130 Nashville Star (USA) was 2lb higher than when winning over course and distance in February. (10/1: 7/1-12/1)
4163* Daily Sport Girl had been put up 7lb for her hard fought Southwell win. (8/1: 6/1-9/1)
912* Cointosser (IRE) had plenty of weight on her handicap debut. (15/8)
677 No Light (9/1: op 6/1)
Mr Lowry (14/1: op 8/1)

T/Plpt: £375.10 (29.67 Tckts). T/Qdpt: £55.50 (13.7 Tckts) KH

4137-NEWTON ABBOT (L-H) (Good to firm)

Friday May 2nd

WEATHER: sunny

4382 THEAKSTONS REAL ALE STAKES MAIDEN HURDLE (4-Y.O+) (Class E)

1-50 (1-50) **2m 1f (8 hdls)** £2,505.00 (£705.00: £345.00) GOING minus 0.36 sec per fur (GF)

	Horse	Dist	Pos	SP	RR	SF
3761 4	**Nordance Prince (IRE) (103)** (MissVenetiaWilliams) **6-11-0** APMcCoy (hld up mid div: hdwy to chse ldr 5th: led next: mde rest: clr flat)	—	1	Evens 1	80+	6
3301 10	**Allstars Express** (KCBailey) **4-10-2**(7) MrRWakley (a.p: led 4th to 6th: ev ch 2 out: wknd flat)	4	2	10/1	76	—
3012 6	**Henrys Port (95)** (MartynMeade) **7-11-0** MRichards (lw: hld up: hdwy 5th: ev ch 2 out: btn & mstke last)	5	3	10/1	72	—
3290 3	**Rachel Louise** (TKeddy) **5-10-9** SMcNeill (lw: prom: ev ch appr 2 out: one pce)	6	4	25/1	61	—
4255 2	**He Knows The Rules (81)** (RHBuckler) **5-11-0** BPowell (lw: a.p: ev ch appr 2 out: wknd)	¾	5	11/2 3	65	—
4294 2	**Ketchican (69)** (SGKnight) **5-11-0** GUpton (a bhd: sme hdwy 6th: nvr nrr)	6	6	40/1	60	—
	Irene's Pet (JCFox) **7-11-0** SFox (prom to 5th: grad wknd)	13	7	25/1	47	—
3590 7	**Mac'smyuncle** (RGFrost) **6-11-0** JFrost (a bhd)	17	8	100/1	31	—
	Calgary Girl (RHBuckler) **5-10-9** PHolley (bhd fr 5th)	6	9	33/1	21	—
	That Big Baby (IRE) (DFBassett) **7-11-0** MissLBlackford (wl bhd fr 2nd: t.o)	14	10	200/1	13	—
	Sunrise Special (IRE) (SNCole) **4-10-9** JFTitley (bit bkwd: mstkes 1st & 2nd: a bhd: t.o)	22	11	100/1	—	—
4231 P	**Noquita (NZ)** (JCMcConnochie) **10-10-9b**(5) XAizpuru (led to 4th: wknd next: p.u bef 2 out)		P	200/1	—	—
4095 3	**Lucky Archer** (PJHobbs) **4-10-9** MAFitzgerald (hmpd & uns rdr 1st)		U	5/1 2	—	—
3997 5	**Spirit Level (63)** (JRPayne) **9-10-2**(7) MrSDurack (blnd & uns rdr 1st)		U	100/1	—	—
				(SP 117.3%)	**14 Rn**	

3m 59.6 (6.60) CSF £10.28 TOTE £2.30: £1.20 £3.70 £2.70 (£22.80) Trio £36.00 OWNER Pinks Gym (HEREFORD) BRED James Doherty
WEIGHT FOR AGE 4yo-5lb
3761 Nordance Prince (IRE), having his first run for Venetia Williams since arriving from Gay Kelleway, finally got off the mark after several good efforts in better company. The opposition was nothing special, but his confidence is bound to have been boosted by this, and he can go on from here. (Evens)
Allstars Express was a little unfortunate to come up against quite a talented rival, but showed that this is more his level than the company he faced on his Kempton debut. He held every chance until being left for dead by the winner on the run-in, and he can land a similar event. (10/1: op 6/1)
2690 Henrys Port may have finished second had he not made a complete hash of the last, but was never going to get to grips with the winner. He has ability, and may well be suited by longer trip. (10/1: op 6/1)
3290 Rachel Louise, making her hurdling debut after showing some ability in bumpers, looked in the closing stages as if she would be suited by more of a stamina test than this. (25/1)
4255 He Knows The Rules had his chance two out, but threw in the towel soon afterwards. He is beginning to look disappointing. (11/2)

4383 BEAMISH RED IRISH ALE RACE NOVICES' CHASE (5-Y.O+) (Class D)

2-25 (2-25) **2m 5f 110y (16 fncs)** £3,436.25 (£1,040.00: £507.50: £241.25) GOING minus 0.36 sec per fur (GF)

	Horse	Dist	Pos	SP	RR	SF
3925 3	**Call Me Albi (IRE) (77)** (MrsLRichards) **6-11-0v** MRichards (mid div: rdn 9th: led after 13th: rdn & sn clr: drvn out flat)	—	1	100/30 2	93	26

				SP	RR	SF
4279[2]	**Blasket Hero (90)** (MrsSDWilliams) **9-11-6b** APMcCoy (hld up bhd: rdn 9th: hdwy to chse wnr appr 2 out: one pce)	2	**2**	5/4[1]	98	31
3051[P]	**Mel (IRE) (71)** (RHBuckler) **7-11-0** BPowell (led to 2nd: chsng ldr & mstke 12th: wknd next)	13	**3**	9/1	82	15
4245[5]	**Jac Del Prince (64)** (PFNicholls) **7-11-0** PHide (chsd ldr 3rd: led briefly 5th: wknd 12th)	13	**4**	7/2[3]	72	5
3950[2]	**Walk in the Woods (70)** (DCTurner) **10-10-9** MrAHoldsworth (led 2nd to 5th: led 6th tl after 13th: wknd qckly: virtually p.u flat)	dist	**5**	25/1	—	—
	Toms Choice (IRE) (JCTuck) **8-11-0** SMcNeill (bhd: hdwy 13th: wkng: wnt lame appr last: virtually p.u flat)	2½	**6**	11/1	—	—

(SP 111.9%) **6 Rn**

5m 20.3 (3.30) CSF £7.57 TOTE £4.30: £2.20 £1.70 (£2.90) OWNER Mr Tony Rooth (CHICHESTER) BRED David Magnier
3925 Call Me Albi (IRE) never appeared to be going all that well, and was being nudged along with a circuit left. Seizing the initiative at the fourth-last, he was urged into a clear lead soon afterwards, and had enough left to hold on over the last two. Richards deserves a medal for this ride. (100/30)
4279 Blasket Hero was detached and being pushed along with a circuit left. He stayed on from the second last, but never looked like getting on terms with the winner. He looks a difficult ride. (5/4)
Mel (IRE) was prominent until being left behind after jumping the fourth-last. (9/1)
4245 Jac Del Prince (7/2: 5/2-4/1)

4384 COURAGE BEST - BRISTOL TRADITION RACE CONDITIONAL (S) H'CAP HURDLE (0-95) (4-Y.O+) (Class G)

2-55 (2-55) **2m 1f (8 hdls)** £1,751.30 (£491.80: £239.90) GOING minus 0.36 sec per fur (GF)

				SP	RR	SF
4328[2]	**Miramare (60)** (RJHodges) **7-9-11**(3) JHarris (hld up mid div: hdwy 6th: sn prom: led appr 2 out: hld on wl)	—	**1**	9/1	41	—
3997*	**On My Toes (63)** (RGFrost) **6-9-12**(5) BMoore (led tl hdd appr 2 out: one pce appr last)	2½	**2**	6/1	42	—
3951[4]	**Prince of Spades (64)** (AGHobbs) **5-10-4** OBurrows (chsd ldrs: in tch tl wknd appr 2 out)	15	**3**	4/1[2]	29	—
4294[R]	**October Brew (USA) (81)** (MCPipe) **7-11-7b** GSupple (lw: hld up & bhd: hdwy 5th: wknd appr 2 out)	2½	**4**	9/4[1]	43	—
2878[5]	**Landsker Star (60)** (FGHollis) **7-10-0** DSalter (chsd ldrs: in tch tl wknd appr 2 out)	16	**5**	20/1	7	—
4294[3]	**Gabish (60)** (BScriven) **12-10-0** LAspell (a bhd: t.o 6th)	25	**6**	25/1	—	—
	Galaxy High (79) (MrsJGRetter) **10-11-5** MichaelBrennan (a bhd: rdn & t.o appr 5th)	27	**7**	10/1	—	—
4162[6]	**Bodantree (88)** (NMBabbage) **6-11-9**(5) MKeighley (prom: ev ch whn fell 6th)		**F**	9/2[3]	—	—
4290[P]	**More Bills (IRE) (70)** (JNeville) **5-10-7v**(3) MBatchelor (chsd ldr: in tch: ev ch 6th: wkng & mstke 2 out: sddle slipped: p.u bef last)		**P**	12/1	—	—

(SP 118.6%) **9 Rn**

4m 0.9 (7.90) CSF £58.08 CT £231.72 TOTE £10.90: £1.80 £1.40 £2.00 (£15.20) Trio £22.50 OWNER Mrs Jonathan Bennett (SOMERTON) BRED Major R. P. Thorman
LONG HANDICAP Miramare 9-11 Gabish 9-4
Sld MSwift 3,500gns
4328 Miramare took up the running coming to the second-last, and stayed on well to win. This was his first win on his twenty-fifth attempt over hurdles or fences, which puts the quality of this race into perspective. (9/1)
3997* On My Toes tried to make all, and only the winner was able to get by her. Being raised 7lb for her previous win probably made all the difference. (6/1)
3951 Prince of Spades was unable to take advantage of the drop in class, and was left behind from the second-last. (4/1: 3/1-5/1)
4294 October Brew (USA) never looked like justifying the support in the market. (9/4)
4162 Bodantree (9/2: op 3/1)
More Bills (IRE) (12/1: 7/1-14/1)

4385 MILLER TIME CLASSIC H'CAP CHASE (0-115) (5-Y.O+) (Class E)

3-30 (3-30) **2m 5f 110y (16 fncs)** £2,900.75 (£878.00: £428.50: £203.75) GOING minus 0.36 sec per fur (GF)

				SP	RR	SF
4186[5]	**Red Branch (IRE) (90)** (JSKing) **8-11-1** TJMurphy (lw: j.w: a in tch: led after 9th: clr 14th: unchal)	—	**1**	Evens[1]	100	31
3843[3]	**Bit of A Touch (83)** (RGFrost) **11-10-8** JFrost (lw: bhd: stdy hdwy 11th: chsd wnr last: one pce)	1¼	**2**	11/2[2]	92	23
4272[3]	**Spring to Glory (88)** (PHayward) **10-10-13v[1]** MAFitzgerald (prom: chsd ldrs 11th: outpcd 14th)	1¼	**3**	7/1	96	27
3843[4]	**Lake of Loughrea (IRE) (99)** (KCBailey) **7-11-3**(7) MrRWakley (bhd: hdwy 14th: one pce fr next)	8	**4**	10/1	101	32
3742[3]	**Scotoni (90)** (RJO'Sullivan) **11-11-1** SCurran (led tl hdd after 9th: wknd next: t.o)	30	**5**	11/1	70	1
1057[4]	**Distant Memory (97)** (PJHobbs) **8-11-8b** APMcCoy (chsd ldr: slt mstke 7th: mstke 9th: rdn next: wkng & mstke 11th)	10	**6**	6/1[3]	69	—
3891[2]	**Golden Opal (79)** (RHBuckler) **12-10-4** BPowell (bhd 9th: sn rdn: t.o fr next)	18	**7**	20/1	38	—

(SP 114.4%) **7 Rn**

5m 18.9 (1.90) CSF £6.77 CT £22.81 TOTE £1.60: £1.30 £3.30 (£5.90) OWNER Mr E. J. Mangan (SWINDON) BRED Michael Butler
4186 Red Branch (IRE), jumping beautifully, was going to win this from some way out. He has had a brilliant season and is a credit to his trainer. (Evens)
3843 Bit of A Touch ran well, though he never looked like overhauling the winner. He looks as if he could win a race before too long. (11/2)
4272 Spring to Glory, visored for the first time, was left behind from the third last. (7/1: op 4/1)
3742 Scotoni (11/1: op 6/1)
1057 Distant Memory (6/1: op 4/1)

4386 HOLSTEN PILS - GET REAL CLASSIC H'CAP HURDLE (0-125) (4-Y.O+) (Class D)

4-05 (4-05) **2m 1f (8 hdls)** £2,735.50 (£768.00: £374.50) GOING minus 0.36 sec per fur (GF)

				SP	RR	SF
4278*	**Yubralee (USA) (118)** (MCPipe) **5-12-1** [5x] APMcCoy (led: sn clr: rdn appr 2 out: clr appr last: eased flat)	—	**1**	Evens[1]	96+	48
4101*	**Out on a Promise (IRE) (107)** (NJHWalker) **5-11-4** MAFitzgerald (chsd wnr thrght: hdwy & in tch 4th: lost pl next: rallied appr 2 out: rdn & wkng whn mstke last)	2	**2**	15/8[2]	83	35
3740[2]	**Handson (91)** (BRMillman) **5-9-11**(5)ow1 DSalter (chsd ldrs: in tch tl appr 6th: grad wknd)	dist	**3**	11/2[3]	—	—
3562[P]	**Intermagic (100)** (JCFox) **7-10-11** SFox (bhd 4th: sn rdn: wknd next: t.o)	dist	**4**	11/1	—	—

(SP 108.5%) **4 Rn**

3m 53.0 (Equals Standard) CSF £3.05 TOTE £1.50 (£1.50) OWNER Mr D. A. Johnson (WELLINGTON) BRED Gainsborough Farm Inc
4278* Yubralee (USA) had the runner-up breathing down his neck approaching the second-last, but jumped the flight better than his rival, and soon went away for a clear cut success. Sharp tracks like this suit him best. (Evens)
4101* Out on a Promise (IRE) chased the winner throughout, and had every chance approaching the second-last. However, he did not jump that flight as well as the winner, and soon found himself adrift. There was no way back from then on. (15/8)
3008 Intermagic (11/1: 6/1-12/1)

4387 FOSTERS OVAL RACE H'CAP CHASE (0-125) (5-Y.O+) (Class D)

4-40 (4-40) **3m 2f 110y (20 fncs)** £3,468.75 (£1,050.00: £512.50: £243.75) GOING minus 0.36 sec per fur (GF)

				SP	RR	SF
4167[2]	**God Speed You (IRE) (109)** (CPMorlock) **8-11-4b** JRKavanagh (led 2nd: drvn out flat)	—	1	11/10[1]	119	40
4078[6]	**Banntown Bill (IRE) (97)** (MCPipe) **8-10-6v** APMcCoy (led to 2nd: chsd wnr thrght: rdn & in tch 18th: no ex appr last)	1½	2	11/1	106	27
4270[6]	**Diamond Fort (97)** (JCMcConnochie) **12-10-6** MAFitzgerald (lw: hdwy 15th: in tch 18th: rdn & one pce 2 out)	3	3	6/1[3]	104	25
3361[5]	**Act of Parliament (IRE) (117)** (KCBailey) **9-11-5b**(7) MrRWakley (nt fluent: bhd: rdn 7th: hdwy 14th: nvr on terms)	21	4	3/1[2]	112	33
1877[F]	**Rainbow Castle (105)** (PFNicholls) **10-11-0** PHide (chsd ldrs in tch: j.slowly 14th: wknd: t.o)	dist	5	6/1[3]	—	—
				(SP 109.5%)		**5 Rn**

6m 33.9 (-0.10) CSF £10.62 TOTE £1.50: £1.40 £1.70 (£6.70) OWNER Wallop (WANTAGE) BRED Mrs Vincent O'Brien

4167 God Speed You (IRE) was able to dominate this field after leading at the second, and kept responding to his rider's urgings to repel all challengers. He is a bit of a character, but possesses plenty of ability. (11/10)

4078 Banntown Bill (IRE) got as close as he did due to his rider's urgings, but was always being well held by the winner. (11/1: op 6/1)

3893 Diamond Fort was settled at the back of the field until making progress on the final circuit. He had a chance approaching the second-last, but was then outpaced. He needs a stiffer track and easier ground. (6/1: 4/1-7/1)

3361 Act of Parliament (IRE) looks to have lost his appetite for the game for the time being. (3/1)

1473 Rainbow Castle (6/1: op 7/2)

4388 ITS NOT ALL OVER YET INTERMEDIATE OPEN N.H. FLAT RACE (4, 5 & 6-Y.O) (Class H)

5-10 (5-11) **2m 1f** £1,264.00 (£354.00: £172.00)

				SP	RR	SF
	Easter Ross (NJHenderson) **4-10-13** MAFitzgerald (lw: hld up in tch: led 2f out: r.o wl)	—	1	6/1	74 f	—
	Vague Hope (IRE) (JCMcConnochie) **5-10-11**(7) MrOMcPhail (chsd ldrs: led 3f out to 2f out: one pce)	1¾	2	12/1	72 f	—
3619[11]	**Bozo (IRE)** (BJMRyall) **6-11-4** GUpton (lw: prom: ev ch 3f out: sn wknd)	10	3	7/4[1]	63 f	—
3767[3]	**Sally Scally** (AGHobbs) **5-10-13** MrLJefford (led after 2f tl hdd 3f out: sn wknd)	hd	4	4/1[2]	58 f	—
3895[3]	**Run For Cover (IRE)** (MrsPNDutfield) **5-10-13** AProcter (mid div: hdwy ½-wy: one pce 2f out)	¾	5	5/1[3]	57 f	—
4008[13]	**Twelve Club** (KCBailey) **4-10-6**(7) MrRWakley (bhd: hdwy 6f out: one pce 3f out)	6	6	16/1	57 f	—
	Katy-Belle (AGHobbs) **5-10-13** RGreene (bit bkwd: plld hrd: bhd: hdwy 6f out: nvr nrr)	9	7	33/1	43 f	—
4009[16]	**National Fiasco** (CLPopham) **4-10-13** TDascombe (prom to ½-wy: t.o)	23	8	100/1	26 f	—
	Arctic Venture (SGKnight) **5-10-13** MRichards (bit bkwd: mid div: wknd ½-wy: t.o)	4	9	100/1	18 f	—
3895[7]	**Baby Lancaster** (MAGriffin) **6-10-11**(7) MGriffiths (lw: led 2f: prom tl wknd 4½f out: t.o)	9	10	100/1	14 f	—
	Eskleybrook (TKeddy) **4-10-8**(5) SRyan (s.s: a bhd: t.o)	2½	11	100/1	12 f	—
2572[5]	**King of The Blues** (JSKing) **5-11-4** TJMurphy (prom to 4f out: t.o)	12	12	10/1	1 f	—
	Rustic Miss (RHBuckler) **6-10-13** BPowell (s.s: a bhd: t.o)	10	13	20/1	—	—
	Fabbl Approved (DCTurner) **5-11-4** MrAHoldsworth (bkwd: a bhd: t.o ½-wy)	dist	14	100/1	—	—
				(SP 122.6%)		**14 Rn**

3m 55.8 (234.80) CSF £68.53 TOTE £3.90: £3.00 £1.20 £1.70 (£49.00) Trio £9.90 OWNER Queen Elizabeth (LAMBOURN) BRED Queen Elizabeth

WEIGHT FOR AGE 4yo-5lb

Easter Ross was always travelling well behind the leaders, and was sent to the front turning into the straight. Once there, he jumped an imaginary flight of hurdles, a path which runs across the track, and also ran very green. His owner may have wondered if she now owns a reincarnation of Devon Loch! (6/1: 3/1-13/2)

Vague Hope (IRE) ran a fine race, and was the only one able to keep tabs on the winner in the closing stages. His future looks bright. (12/1)

1774 Bozo (IRE) found disappointingly little after holding every chance turning into the straight. His good effort in the Festival Bumper may well have flattered him. (7/4: evens-2/1)

3767 Sally Scally ran another sound race here. (4/1)

T/Plpt: £24.10 (306.4 Tckts). T/Qdpt: £14.20 (31.56 Tckts) T

4144-SEDGEFIELD (L-H) (Good to firm, Firm patches)

Friday May 2nd

Race 1-fourth last flght omitted. Race 2-third last omitted.

WEATHER: fine & sunny

4389 LCL PILS JOHN WADE HAULAGE (S) H'CAP HURDLE (0-95) (4-Y.O+) (Class G)

5-45 (5-46) **2m 5f 110y (9 hdls)** £1,992.50 (£555.00: £267.50) GOING minus 0.77 sec per fur (F)

				SP	RR	SF
1027[3]	**Flintlock (IRE) (68)** (HAlexander) **7-10-4** JRailton (trckd ldrs: led appr 2 out: styd on u.p flat)	—	1	12/1	48	8
3971*	**Barton Heights (85)** (MrsMReveley) **5-11-7** PNiven (hdwy u.p 6th: ev ch flat: nt qckn)	1¼	2	6/4[1]	64	24
3607[15]	**Ijab (CAN) (72)** (JParkes) **7-10-8** AThornton (lw: jnd ldrs 6th: sn drvn along: ev ch whn hmpd appr 2 out: 3rd & one pce whn hmpd last)	6	3	11/1	47	7
4295[8]	**Queen's Counsel (IRE) (71)** (MissMKMilligan) **4-10-1**ow1 ASSmith (hld up: gd hdwy 6th: led on bit appr 3 out: hmpd & hdd appr 2 out: wknd between last 2)	6	4	10/1	41	—
4283[7]	**Barnstormer (70)** (EAElliott) **11-10-6b** DParker (outpcd fr 6th: kpt on fr 2 out: n.d)	1¾	5	20/1	39	—
4295[7]	**Simand (71)** (GMMoore) **5-10-7** JCallaghan (trckd ldr: led 3rd tl appr 3 out: sn wknd)	7	6	10/1	35	—
3886[P]	**Dalusman (IRE) (67)** (FPMurtagh) **9-10-3** BStorey (w ldrs tl wknd after 6th)	2½	7	20/1	29	—
	King of the Horse (IRE) (80) (WStorey) **6-10-11**(5) RMcGrath (bhd fr 5th)	1¼	8	13/2[2]	41	1
4055[P]	**Rostino (IRE) (64)** (JWade) **8-9-9**(5) STaylor (chsd ldrs: reminders 6th: sn lost pl)	18	9	25/1	11	—
1942[8]	**Fly to the End (USA) (72)** (JJQuinn) **7-10-8** LWyer (hld up: bhd fr 6th: fin lame)	7	10	16/1	14	—
	Sharp to Oblige (64) (RMWhitaker) **10-10-0** OPears (bhd whn reminders 3rd: b.d bnd bef next)		B	25/1	—	—
	Friendly Society (65) (WStorey) **11-10-1** MMoloney (fell 2nd)		F	100/1	—	—
4147[F]	**Fiery Sun (73)** (REBarr) **12-10-9** NSmith (led to 3rd: reminders 6th: sn wknd: bhd whn p.u bef 2 out)		P	9/1[3]	—	—
3693[5]	**Cool Luke (IRE) (92)** (FMurphy) **8-11-7**(7) NHorrocks (s.s: hld up: s.u bnd bef 4th)		S	10/1	—	—
				(SP 130.7%)		**14 Rn**

4m 56.5 (-3.50) CSF £29.13 CT £211.97 TOTE £9.40: £2.00 £1.40 £4.20 (£12.40) Trio £141.70; £159.66 to Newmarket 4/5/97 OWNER Mrs J. Watters (GARROWBY) BRED Dene Investments N V

LONG HANDICAP Rostino (IRE) 9-3 Queen's Counsel (IRE) 9-9 Sharp to Oblige 9-7
WEIGHT FOR AGE 4yo-6lb
No bid
1027 Flintlock (IRE), absent since October, made the most of the opportunity when the third and fourth were taken wide by a loose horse going to the second last flight. He would almost certainly have won in any case. (12/1)
3971* Barton Heights, from a 5lb higher mark, was flat-out to improve with a circuit to go. He had every chance after the last, but lacked the speed to take it. (6/4)
2862 Ijab (CAN), as usual, was flat-out some way from home. He was staying on when taken wide by a loose horse going to two out, and would have finished within three lengths of the second but for being hampered again by the loose horse after the last. (11/1: 8/1-12/1)
Queen's Counsel (IRE) took it up running away going to three out. Taken wide by a loose horse on the run-in two out, her stamina gave out between the last two. She has the ability to win a similar event over a shorter trip. (10/1: 7/1-11/1)
1992 Simand (10/1: 7/1-11/1)
Fiery Sun (9/1: op 5/1)

4390 FEDERATION SPECIAL NOVICES' CONDITIONAL HURDLE (4-Y.O+) (Class E)
6-15 (6-17) **2m 1f (7 hdls)** £2,320.00 (£645.00: £310.00) GOING minus 0.77 sec per fur (F)

			SP	RR	SF
801[2]	**Fatehalkhair (IRE) (86)** (BEllison) **5-10-9**(5) CMcCormack (j.w: mde all: clr 2nd: styd on wl appr last)........—	**1**	11/4[2]	71	22
3611[2]	**Country Orchid** (MrsMReveley) **6-10-9** GLee (hmpd 1st: hdwy 5th: wnt 2nd appr 2 out: no imp)..................12	**2**	11/10[1]	55	6
893[8]	**Salkeld King (IRE) (70)** (MABarnes) **5-11-0** STaylor (chsd wnr: mstke 4th: wknd 2 out: 4th whn hmpd last) 4	**3**	33/1	56	7
4163[5]	**Jendorcet (72)** (CWFairhurst) **7-10-9v** RMcGrath (hld up & plld hrd: hdwy 5th: wknd appr 2 out: 3rd whn j.lft & mstke last)........1¼	**4**	7/1	50	1
4056[2]	**Diamond Beach (93)** (GMMoore) **4-11-2** ECallaghan (hmpd 1st: sn bhd: drvn along 5th: n.d: eased between last 2)........18	**5**	3/1[3]	45	—
3828[10]	**Buddleia** (JRTurner) **4-9-13**(5) RBurns (chsd ldrs tl wknd 5th: t.o 2 out)........21	**6**	33/1	13	—
3723[P]	**Weapons Free** (TPTate) **6-10-9**(5) RMcCarthy (b.d. 1st)........	**B**	20/1	—	—
4244[11]	**Just Whistle** (MissMKMilligan) **5-10-9** FLeahy (w ldrs whn fell 1st)........	**F**	50/1	—	—
5[7]	**Pats Cross (IRE)** (JHetherton) **8-11-0** MNewton (chsd ldrs tl wknd 5th: t.o whn p.u bef 2 out: fin lame)........	**P**	20/1	—	—
			(SP 129.2%)		**9 Rn**

3m 50.9 (-4.10) CSF £6.34 TOTE £4.10: £1.10 £1.20 £7.30 (£4.40) Trio £74.10 OWNER Mrs Gwen Smith (LANCHESTER) BRED Shadwell Estate Company Limited
WEIGHT FOR AGE 4yo-5lb
801 Fatehalkhair (IRE) bounced off this fast ground jumping particularly well, and stayed on strongly to go clear on the run to the final flight. (11/4)
3611 Country Orchid was almost brought to a stand-still by a faller at the first. Sent in pursuit of the winner going to two out, she found him running right away from her going to the last. (11/10)
Salkeld King (IRE) ran possibly his best race so far, but that is not saying a lot. (33/1)
4163 Jendorcet, tried in a visor, ran too keen for her own good. (7/1)
4056 Diamond Beach, like Country Orchid, was hampered by a faller at the first flight. Knocked right back, he tried to improve setting out on the final circuit, but could never recover the lost ground. (3/1: op 2/1)

4391 KELLYS LAGER NOVICES' CHASE (5-Y.O+) (Class E)
6-45 (6-45) **3m 3f (21 fncs)** £3,059.00 (£917.00: £441.00: £203.00) GOING minus 0.77 sec per fur (F)

			SP	RR	SF
4138*	**The Whole Hog (IRE) (76)** (KCBailey) **8-11-12** AThornton (chsd ldrs: hit 16th: styd on u.p to ld nr fin)........—	**1**	4/5[1]	89	30
4077[5]	**Miss Colette (73)** (MrsDThomson) **9-11-3** MFoster (j.rt: led: kpt on u.p fr 2 out: hdd nr fin)........nk	**2**	100/30[2]	80	21
4149[P]	**German Legend (80)** (DALamb) **7-11-8** JBurke (trckd ldrs: hit 11th: ev ch tl wknd between last 2)........14	**3**	100/30[2]	76	17
3972[4]	**Evening Rush (77)** (JWade) **11-11-6** KJones (bit bkwd: a last: hit 11th: outpcd 14th: t.o 2 out: fin lame) ......dist	**4**	14/1[3]	—	—
			(SP 108.4%)		**4 Rn**

6m 41.9 (-4.10) CSF £3.55 TOTE £1.70 (£1.60) OWNER Mrs Sharon Nelson (UPPER LAMBOURN) BRED Owen O'Leary
4138* The Whole Hog (IRE) is an out-and-out stayer who handles this fast ground and, well ridden, stayed on just the better near the line. (4/5)
4077 Miss Colette set a strong pace. She jumped right throughout, but kept on willingly and was only just worn down. (100/30)
4077 German Legend took a keen grip. It was surprising to see his rider persist in making his effort on the outside of Miss Colette, who jumped right at every fence. Not for the first time he flattered to deceive, and found very little under pressure. (100/30)
Evening Rush lost touch early on the final circuit. He was the final ride for his thirty-four-year-old jockey who retires with over a hundred and twenty winners to his credit. (14/1)

4392 FEDERATION BREWERY H'CAP CHASE (0-125) (5-Y.O+) (Class D)
7-15 (7-15) **2m 5f (16 fncs)** £4,118.00 (£1,148.00: £554.00) GOING minus 0.77 sec per fur (F)

			SP	RR	SF
4214[3]	**Weaver George (IRE) (108)** (WStorey) **7-11-9**(5) RMcGrath (hld up: wnt prom 11th: led between last 2: drvn out)........—	**1**	11/4[2]	122	54
3886[11]	**Blazing Dawn (86)** (JSHubbuck) **10-10-6** TReed (jnd ldrs 7th: outpcd 2 out: styd on wl flat) 1	**2**	13/2	99	31
4247[6]	**Rebel King (80)** (MABarnes) **7-9-9**(5) STaylor (chsd ldrs: led 9th to 4 out: one pce fr 2 out)........2	**3**	10/1	92	24
4013[4]	**Aly Daley (IRE) (97)** (HowardJohnson) **9-11-3** ASSmith (led: reminders & hdd 9th: rdn & outpcd 4 out: 5th & staying on whn b.d last)........	**B**	7/4[1]	—	—
4300[7]	**Cross Cannon (107)** (JWade) **11-11-13** BStorey (lw: trckd ldr: led 4 out tl between last 2: 4th & wkng whn fell last)........	**F**	100/30[3]	—	—
	Wait You There (USA) (87) (HAlexander) **12-10-7** MrSSwiers (lost tch 7th: t.o 9th: p.u after 11th)........	**P**	14/1	—	—
			(SP 115.2%)		**6 Rn**

5m 0.9 (2.00 under best) (-10.10) CSF £18.67 CT £141.16 TOTE £3.20: £1.70 £2.20 (£19.40) OWNER Regent Decorators Ltd (CONSETT) BRED G. Cashin
LONG HANDICAP Rebel King 9-11
4214 Weaver George (IRE) has held his form really well this term, and this was his fifth win from his last eight starts. Held up to get the trip, he quickened to go three lengths clear between the last two, but was coming to the end of his tether at the line. (11/4)
3692 Blazing Dawn, who has a history of breaking blood-vessels, stuck on strongly up the run-in after getting outpaced two out. Three miles really suits him better. (13/2)
4145 Rebel King, 3lb out of the handicap, ran well but is finding it hard to get his head in front this time. (10/1)

4013 Aly Daley (IRE) really needs further. Forcing the pace, he was tapped for foot four out but was staying on, and would probably have finished fourth but for being brought down at the last. (7/4)
3725 Cross Cannon has yet to prove his stamina over this trip. After going on four out, his stamina gave out between the last two, and he was beaten when he fell heavily at the last. (100/30)

4393 BUCHANAN NOVICES' HURDLE (4-Y.O+) (Class E)

7-45 (7-45) **2m 5f 110y (10 hdls)** £2,460.00 (£685.00: £330.00) GOING minus 0.77 sec per fur (F)

				SP	RR	SF
4144[2]	**Catch the Pigeon (81)** (REBarr) **8-10-9** NSmith (jnd ldrs 4th: led 2 out: shkn up & wnt clr appr last)	—	**1**	11/4[2]	61	8
4217[7]	**Northern Star (88)** (JAPickering) **6-11-0**(7) MissJWormall (racd wd: chsd ldrs: led 6th: hit next: hdd 3 out: kpt on one pce fr 2 out)	9	**2**	6/1[3]	66	13
2957[2]	**Flyaway Blues (100)** (MrsMReveley) **5-11-7** PNiven (hld up: mstke 3rd: effrt 3 out: rdn between last 2: found nil)	¾	**3**	4/7[1]	66	13
4147[7]	**Movie Man (71)** (JRTurner) **5-10-7**(7) RBurns (chsd ldrs: led 3 out: hdd & mstke next: wknd appr last)	3½	**4**	16/1	56	3
1030[11]	**Lady Swift** (KWHogg) **6-10-9** MFoster (hld up & plld hrd: jnd ldrs 5th: wknd 3 out)	dist	**5**	25/1	—	—
3795[14]	**Woodhouse Lane** (NChamberlain) **5-10-7**(7) MissCMetcalfe (outpcd & lost tch 7th)	½	**6**	100/1	—	—
4147[P]	**Strong Character (56)** (DALamb) **11-11-0** JBurke (led: mstke 4th: hdd 6th: sn lost pl: t.o 3 out)	dist	**7**	100/1	—	—
3727[3]	***Erni (FR) (80)*** (TPTate) **5-11-0** JCallaghan (Withdrawn not under Starter's orders: state of going)		**W**		—	—
				(SP 116.3%)	**7 Rn**	

4m 57.7 (-2.30) CSF £17.67 TOTE £3.10: £1.30 £2.60 (£11.20) OWNER Mrs R. E. Barr (MIDDLESBROUGH) BRED Mrs R. E. Barr and I. G. Thompson
OFFICIAL EXPLANATION **Flyaway Blues: rider reported that the gelding has a mind of his own and tends not to give of his best.**
4144 Catch the Pigeon has appreciated the step-up in distance, and he soon quickened clear when given the office between the last two. (11/4)
3621* Northern Star raced wide throughout. He kept on under pressure to regain second place on the run-in, but the winner had flown. (6/1)
2957 Flyaway Blues ran a stale race after two recent outings on the Flat. Perhaps this trip is beyond him. (4/7)
2654 Movie Man was already in trouble when he made a mess of the penultimate flight. (16/1)

4394 KEOGHANS H'CAP HURDLE (0-105) (4-Y.O+ F & M) (Class F)

8-15 (8-15) **2m 5f 110y (10 hdls)** £2,092.50 (£580.00: £277.50) GOING minus 0.77 sec per fur (F)

				SP	RR	SF
4283[12]	**Whitegatesprincess (IRE) (66)** (BEllison) **6-9-7v**(7) CMcCormack (trckd ldrs: led 2 out: r.o u.p flat)	—	**1**	12/1	53	—
4299[5]	**Raise A Dollar (75)** (PBeaumont) **7-10-9** MrSSwiers (racd wd: lft in ld bef 4th: hdd 2 out: rallied flat: fin lame)	1¼	**2**	5/2[2]	61	—
4248*	**Peggy Gordon (77)** (MrsDThomson) **6-10-11** 7x MissPRobson (lw: trckd ldrs: kpt on one pce 2 out)	3½	**3**	9/4[1]	61	—
4060[9]	**Aide Memoire (IRE) (73)** (RJohnson) **8-10-7** KJohnson (hld up: trckd ldrs fr 6th: outpcd fr 2 out)	1¼	**4**	15/2	56	—
4055[2]	**Nite Sprite (66)** (REBarr) **7-9-9**(5) STaylor (chsd ldrs: rdn 3 out: outpcd appr next)	1½	**5**	15/2	47	—
3817[7]	**Daisy Days (IRE) (90)** (HowardJohnson) **7-11-10** ASSmith (led tl p.u lame bef 4th)		**P**	4/1[3]	—	—
				(SP 110.6%)	**6 Rn**	

5m 6.2 (6.20) CSF £37.72 TOTE £15.30: £2.70 £1.50 (£29.10) OWNER Red Onion (LANCHESTER) BRED R. W. L. Bowden
LONG HANDICAP Whitegatesprincess (IRE) 9-8 Nite Sprite 9-5
OFFICIAL EXPLANATION **Whitegatesprincess (IRE): regarding the improvement in form, her trainer reported that she did not give her best at Perth last time out, and the visor worn today for the first time had concentrated the mare's mind.**
Whitegatesprincess (IRE), in a visor for the first time, improved considerably on her two previous outings. Relishing the trip and the fast ground, she stayed on with plenty of gusto. (12/1)
4299 Raise A Dollar is a big, heavy sort to run on a tight track on ground as firm as this. Well as she ran, she appeared to finish very lame indeed. (5/2)
4248* Peggy Gordon looked to have an excellent chance here on paper, as her task was 8lb easier than when winning at Perth. However, over this trip and on this fast ground, in what was not a strongly-run race, she was tapped for foot from three out. (9/4: op 11/8)
3478 Aide Memoire (IRE), as usual, travelled strongly, only to flatter to deceive at the business end. (15/2)
4055 Nite Sprite ran as well as could be expected considering she was 9lb out of the handicap. (15/2)

T/Plpt: £385.70 (26.98 Tckts). T/Qdpt: £157.60 (3.65 Tckts) WG

3291-HAYDOCK (L-H) (Good becoming Good to firm after race 2)

Saturday May 3rd

Race 3 - one flight omitted. Hurdles were placed on Flat course.
WEATHER: fine

4395 CROWTHER HOMES HELL NOOK H'CAP HURDLE (4-Y.O) (Class C)

1-10 (1-11) **2m (8 hdls)** £8,862.75 (£2,682.00: £1,308.50: £621.75) GOING minus 0.10 sec per fur (G)

				SP	RR	SF
3927[2]	**Seattle Alley (USA) (105)** (PRWebber) **4-11-3** JAMcCarthy (hld up: hdwy appr 3 out: led last: hrd drvn: jst hld on)	—	**1**	7/1[3]	82	44
4136[2]	**Fairly Sharp (IRE) (103)** (GraemeRoe) **4-11-1** RDunwoody (chsd ldrs: hdwy 3 out: led between last 2: hdd last: jst hld on)	s.h	**2**	8/1	80	42
4209*	**Shu Gaa (IRE) (112)** (OSherwood) **4-11-10b** JOsborne (hld up in tch: sltly outpcd 4 out: hdwy u.p next: chsd ldrs & styd on u.p fr 2 out)	3½	**3**	5/1[2]	85	47
4082*	**Kinnescash (IRE) (108)** (PBowen) **4-11-6** MAFitzgerald (w ldr: led 3 out: drvn & hdd between last 2: one pce)	2½	**4**	9/2[1]	79	41
4282[3]	**Double Agent (102)** (HowardJohnson) **4-11-0** ASSmith (hld up: drvn bef 3 out: n.d)	6	**5**	20/1	67	29
3947*	**Melt The Clouds (CAN) (113)** (MCPipe) **4-11-11b** APMcCoy (hld up in rr: hdwy 3 out: chsng ldrs whn mstke next: wknd bef last)	1½	**6**	8/1	76	38
4209[3]	**Clash of Swords (94)** (PCalver) **4-10-6** LWyer (hld up: rdn 3 out: wknd bef next)	4	**7**	11/1	53	15
3942[5]	**Go With The Wind (90)** (CWeedon) **4-10-2** DJMoffatt (in rr: u.p 3 out: n.d)	1	**8**	25/1	48	10
4169[F]	**Noble Colours (95)** (SGGriffiths) **4-10-4**(3) MrRThornton (led to 3 out: sn wknd: t.o)	dist	**9**	9/2[1]	—	—

				SP	RR	SF
4003[U]	**Tiutchev (93)** (MissHCKnight) **4-10-5** JCulloty (mstke & uns rdr 1st)		**U**	14/1	—	—

(SP 111.4%) **10 Rn**

3m 44.8 (2.80) CSF £53.54 CT £270.03 TOTE £8.30: £2.10 £2.10 £2.10 (£32.60) Trio £29.50 OWNER L & P Partnership (BANBURY) BRED Hermitage Farm Inc.

OFFICIAL EXPLANATION **Noble Colours: The trainer reported that the gelding was found to be in discomfort on its journey home.**

3927 Seattle Alley (USA) made up for his shock Hereford defeat last time out over hurdles with a gutsy effort here. His trainer reports he may go for a race in France now, or have an outing on the level. (7/1)

4136 Fairly Sharp (IRE), an ex-Irish filly, battled on gamely to the line, and looks booked for future success. (8/1)

4209* Shu Gaa (IRE) failed to land a serious blow at the leading pair after being tapped for toe at the end of the back stretch. (5/1)

4082* Kinnescash (IRE) was up in the van throughout on his return from a recent Flat race victory. It has to be said he is still not the most natural of hurdlers. (9/2)

4282 Double Agent was evidently out of his depth but, considering he stayed well on the Flat, it would be reasonable enough to think a step-up in trip may be required over timber. (20/1)

3947* Melt The Clouds (CAN) was anchored by a welter burden. (8/1: op 5/1)

4169 Noble Colours was the subject of an enquiry after fading tamely turning for home. He was keen to get on with things in the race, but his jockey reported that the gelding failed to respond when challenged. (9/2)

4396 CROWTHER HOMES LONG DISTANCE HURDLE (5-Y.O+) (Class B)

1-40 (1-40) **2m 7f 110y (12 hdls)** £8,524.75 (£2,578.00: £1,256.50: £595.75) GOING minus 0.10 sec per fur (G)

				SP	RR	SF
4240[2]	**Pridwell (157)** (MCPipe) **7-11-0** APMcCoy (hld up: hdwy on bit 3 out: led next: cheekily)	—	**1**	5/4[1]	112+	5
4052[4]	**Yahmi (IRE) (132)** (JABOld) **7-11-0** JOsborne (led to 2 out: sn drvn: no ch w wnr)	1¾	**2**	11/4[3]	111	4
3640[16]	**Romancer (IRE) (137)** (NATwiston-Davies) **6-11-0** CLlewellyn (chsd ldrs: pckd 2nd: blnd 4 out: sn bhd)	17	**3**	9/1	99	—
3635[F]	**Conquering Leader (IRE) (143)** (NJHenderson) **8-10-9** MAFitzgerald (chsd ldr: chal 4 out: wknd 2 out: sn eased: virtually p.u flat)	dist	**4**	9/4[2]	—	—

(SP 111.9%) **4 Rn**

5m 48.1 (16.10) CSF £4.78 TOTE £2.20 (£2.50) OWNER Jones, Berstock and Fleet Partnership (WELLINGTON) BRED Hascombe and Valiant Studs

4240 Pridwell, one of the great characters of the game, was certainly the cheeky chappy today, winning over this trip for the first time. His jockey was not required to move a muscle in what was no more than a hack-canter victory. This son of Sadler's Wells has jumped fences, but has decided that the larger obstacles are not for him. (5/4)

4052 Yahmi (IRE) was forced to make the running but, once the winner loomed upsides with a smile on his face, the writing was on the wall. (11/4)

3231 Romancer (IRE) was stepping-up in trip, but appeared not to stay and his jumping was none too perfect. (9/1)

3303 Conquering Leader (IRE) mounted a serious challenge turning out of the back straight, but was a spent force two from home. She was eased in the straight and pulled up rather sore. (9/4)

4397 CROWTHER HOMES SWINTON H'CAP HURDLE (Gd 3) (4-Y.O+) (Class A)

2-10 (2-11) **2m (7 hdls)** £23,197.99 (£8,784.65: £4,304.83: £1,967.53) GOING minus 0.10 sec per fur (G)

				SP	RR	SF
4212[5]	**Dreams End (142)** (PBowen) **9-11-11**(3) LAspell (hld up: hdwy 3 out: sn chal: led flat: r.o)	—	**1**	14/1	130	76
4010[4]	**Mister Rm (114)** (NATwiston-Davies) **5-10-0** CLlewellyn (hld up: rdn & hdwy appr 3 out: lft in ld whn hmpd last: hdd flat: kpt on u.p)	¾	**2**	16/1	101	47
4357a[2]	**Shankar (IRE) (137)** (DNicholson) **6-11-6**(3) MrRThornton (hld up: smooth hdwy 3 out & ch: styd on u.p cl home)	2½	**3**	8/1	122	68
3640*	**Barna Boy (IRE) (135)** (NJHenderson) **9-11-7** MAFitzgerald (hld up in mid div: hmpd 1st: hdwy 4 out: chal appr last: unable qckn flat)	3½	**4**	14/1	116	62
3883*	**Star Selection (122)** (JMackie) **6-10-5**(3) EHusband (prom: rdn & hmpd last: one pce)	nk	**5**	7/1[3]	103	49
4053[7]	**Tragic Hero (134)** (MCPipe) **5-11-6b** RSupple (in tch: effrt 3 out: no imp on ldrs)	5	**6**	25/1	110	56
4212[4]	**Ingletonian (129)** (BMactaggart) **8-11-1** BStorey (bhd: hmpd 2nd: sme late hdwy: nvr nrr)	3½	**7**	12/1	101	47
4212[11]	**Express Gift (133)** (MrsMReveley) **8-11-5** PNiven (hld up: sme hdwy 3 out: n.d)	nk	**8**	20/1	105	51
4212[3]	**Edelweis du Moulin (FR) (135)** (GRichards) **5-11-7** RDunwoody (mid div: hdwy 3 out: sn drvn: wknd bef last)	1½	**9**	6/1[1]	106	52
4010[6]	**Green Green Desert (FR) (125)** (OSherwood) **6-10-11** JOsborne (hld up: hdwy u.p 3 out: nt trble ldrs)	¾	**10**	12/1	95	41
4061[16]	**Stompin (139)** (MissHCKnight) **6-11-11b[1]** JCulloty (prom tl wknd after 3 out)	15	**11**	20/1	94	40
4212[6]	**Kadastrof (FR) (135)** (RDickin) **7-11-2**(5) XAizpuru (cl up: rdn 4 out: wknd qckly)	¾	**12**	25/1	89	35
4212[9]	**Master Beveled (138)** (PDEvans) **7-11-10** RGarritty (in tch: blnd 4th: sn lost pl & bhd)	nk	**13**	20/1	92	38
3640[7]	**Tom Brodie (127)** (HowardJohnson) **7-10-13** ASSmith (mid div: hmpd 2nd: hdwy 4 out: drvn & wknd appr last)	4	**14**	20/1	77	23
4172*	**Northern Starlight (124)** (MCPipe) **6-10-10** APMcCoy (led: rdn appr 3 out: fell last)		**F**	13/2[2]	—	—
4010[7]	**Nordic Breeze (IRE) (120)** (MCPipe) **5-10-6** CMaude (fell 1st)		**F**	16/1	—	—
4061[18]	**Kaitak (IRE) (116)** (JMCarr) **6-10-2** LWyer (prom whn fell 2nd)		**F**	25/1	—	—
4240*	**Ashwell Boy (IRE) (134)** (PJHobbs) **6-11-6** BPowell (a bhd: lost tch 4 out: t.o whn p.u bef last)		**P**	14/1	—	—
4271*	**Monnaie Forte (IRE) (114)** (JRAdam) **7-9-9**(5) RMcGrath (in tch to 4th: sn bhd: t.o whn p.u bef last)		**P**	10/1	—	—

(SP 138.1%) **19 Rn**

3m 40.2 (-1.80) CSF £199.74 CT £1,772.28 TOTE £14.80: £2.70 £2.70 £2.90 £4.40 (£51.60) Trio £579.00 OWNER Mr T. G. Price (HAVERFORDWEST) BRED Hascombe and Valiant Studs

LONG HANDICAP Mister Rm 9-13

4212 Dreams End did it the way he likes today, coming from off the pace. This nine-year-old entire ran on nicely in what can be regarded as his favourite race, having scored in 1994 and finishing second last year. He may now go back to the Flat, however his midsummer objective is Ireland's Galway Hurdle. (14/1)

4010 Mister Rm boxed on gamely to take second, having been interfered with by a faller at the last. Even without the knock at the final flight, it is doubtful he would have been able to repel the efforts of the winner. There may be a good handicap waiting for this novice next term. (16/1)

4357a Shankar (IRE), having been quite busy of late, put in another good effort here despite a great rise in the handicap. (8/1)

3640* Barna Boy (IRE), raised 5lb for his last victory, still returned with credit today. This may have been on the sharp side for him. (14/1)

3883* Star Selection was under pressure but still in the firing line when hampered at the final flight. However, he may pick up a nice race over timber one day. (7/1)

3293 Tragic Hero, last year's winner, never looked like repeating that performance. However this was about his best performance this term. (25/1)

4212 Edelweis du Moulin (FR) was a spent force before the final flight. (6/1)

4172* Northern Starlight, stepping-up in class after a major hike in the handicap this term, came to grief at the last after trying to make all the running. He seemed to be hard-pressed at the time, so it is doubtful it cost him any glory. (13/2)

4398 CROWTHER HOMES NEW FLORIDA H'CAP HURDLE (0-140) (4-Y.O+) (Class B)
2-45 (2-45) **2m 4f (10 hdls)** £5,047.35 (£1,528.80: £746.90: £355.95) GOING minus 0.10 sec per fur (G)

				SP	RR	SF
3942[6]	**Diwali Dancer (107)** (MCPipe) **7-10-1** BPowell (mde all: rdn appr last: edgd lft cl home)	—	**1**	9/1	86	10
4210[2]	**Sheriffmuir (130)** (MrsLWadham) **8-11-10** JOsborne (a.p: rdn 4 out: chal flat: carried sltly lft cl home: no ex)	¾	**2**	3/1[1]	108	32
4261[2]	**Elation (108)** (GRichards) **5-10-2b** RDunwoody (trckd ldr: chal on bit 3 out: drvn appr last: nt keen flat: one pce)	½	**3**	11/2[3]	86	10
4212[8]	**Home Counties (IRE) (132)** (DMoffatt) **8-11-12** DJMoffatt (hld up in rr: effrt 3 out: no imp)	16	**4**	12/1	97	21
4271[P]	**Suivez (122)** (MrsNMacauley) **7-11-2** MAFitzgerald (hld up: brief effrt 4 out: n.d)	¾	**5**	16/1	87	11
3702[4]	**Moving Out (112)** (MissHCKnight) **9-10-6** JCulloty (in tch: rdn after 4 out: wknd fr next)	21	**6**	12/1	60	—
4246[2]	**Durano (113)** (TDEasterby) **6-10-7** RGarritty (cl up: drvn appr 2 out: sn wknd: eased whn btn bef last)	1¼	**7**	11/2[3]	60	—
2644*	**Storm Dust (114)** (MissHCKnight) **8-10-5**(3) MrRThornton (in tch: lost pl qckly 6th: drvn 4 out: sn bhd)	1½	**8**	5/1[2]	60	—
4246[8]	**Radanpour (IRE) (107)** (HowardJohnson) **5-10-1** ASSmith (a bhd: blnd 5th: t.o)	dist	**9**	14/1	—	—
				(SP 110.4%)	**9 Rn**	

4m 45.6 (8.60) CSF £31.44 CT £140.54 TOTE £11.20: £2.10 £1.30 £1.50 (£25.00) Trio £17.20 OWNER Mr B. E. Case (WELLINGTON) BRED Thoroughbred Stock Investors Ltd

3942 Diwali Dancer bounced back to form with this game, front-running effort. (9/1: op 11/2)
4210 Sheriffmuir was being ridden from a long way out, but managed to reach the winner's quarters when carried slightly left towards the finish. It is doubtful this affected the final outcome. (3/1)
4261 Elation, fitted with blinkers for the first time, seemed none too keen once force was applied. It later transpired that the gelding pulled up lame. (11/2)
2617 Home Counties (IRE) never looked like landing a serious challenge. (12/1)
4246 Durano was eased after weakening two from home. He probably failed to see out the trip. (11/2)

4399 CROWTHER HOMES EDGE GREEN NOVICES' CLAIMING HURDLE (4-Y.O+) (Class F)
3-15 (3-15) **2m 4f (10 hdls)** £2,015.00 (£565.00: £275.00) GOING minus 0.10 sec per fur (G)

				SP	RR	SF
4285[P]	**Jessolle (95)** (GRichards) **5-10-10** RDunwoody (trckd ldrs: improved to ld 2 out: r.o wl)	—	**1**	9/4[2]	65	—
4209[4]	**Sousse (87)** (MrsMReveley) **4-10-5** GLee (led tl after 1st: regained ld appr 3rd: hdd 2 out: one pce)	3	**2**	4/1[3]	64	—
3287[7]	**Recruitment** (JRTurner) **4-10-8** RSupple (led after 1st: hdd appr 3rd: outpcd fr ½-wy: no ch whn blnd 3 out)	23	**3**	25/1	48	—
3189[7]	**Tudor Town (68)** (KBishop) **9-11-2** SBurrough (in rr: mstke 3rd: n.d)	9	**4**	25/1	43	—
4315*	**Country Lover (108)** (MCPipe) **6-12-0v** APMcCoy (hld up in rr: p.u appr 2nd: dead)		**P**	11/10[1]	—	—
	Ten More Singhas (AStreeter) **7-10-12** TEley (a bhd: lost tch 5th: t.o whn p.u bef last)		**P**	33/1	—	—
				(SP 109.0%)	**6 Rn**	

4m 57.0 (20.00) CSF £9.69 TOTE £2.70: £1.40 £1.60 (£4.60) OWNER Mr C. R. Fleet (PENRITH) BRED Mrs I. H. Lowe
WEIGHT FOR AGE 4yo-6lb

4075* Jessolle appreciated this step-up in distance, and is still not finished for the season. (9/4)
4209 Sousse, like the winner, is another one who appreciated the trip. (4/1)
4315* Country Lover shattered a pastern before the second hurdle. (11/10: evens-5/4)

4400 CROWTHER HOMES DOCK LANE NOVICES' HURDLE (4-Y.O+) (Class D)
3-50 (3-51) **2m (8 hdls)** £3,004.00 (£844.00: £412.00) GOING minus 0.10 sec per fur (G)

				SP	RR	SF
3595[P]	**Smolensk (IRE) (98)** (JBerry) **5-11-4** RDunwoody (trckd ldrs: chsd ldr appr 3 out: led last: rdn out)	—	**1**	6/1[3]	80	38
4348a[F]	**Sharpical (125)** (NJHenderson) **5-11-7** MAFitzgerald (hld up in rr: hdwy 3 out: ev ch last: nt qckn flat)	2	**2**	4/11[1]	81	39
4003[3]	**Moon Devil (IRE)** (MarkCampion) **7-11-0** BPowell (led tl hdd last: one pce flat)	2½	**3**	14/1	72	30
4003*	**Riparius (USA) (108)** (PRWebber) **6-11-7** JOsborne (prom: n.m.r on bnd appr 3 out: ev ch 2 out: wknd bef last: eased flat: t.o)	dist	**4**	4/1[2]	—	—
				(SP 114.3%)	**4 Rn**	

3m 46.3 (4.30) CSF £8.91 TOTE £4.00 (£3.20) OWNER Mrs Chris Deuters (COCKERHAM) BRED Miss B. Galway-Greer

3283 Smolensk (IRE), stepping-up in class, outpointed the odds-on favourite here. He may have another run over timber, but a chasing career beckons. (6/1)
4348a Sharpical may not have been over-keen to go through with his effort here, however connections were far from happy about the going, as they felt it was fairly firm. (4/11)
4003 Moon Devil (IRE) ran a sound race in his bid to break away from maiden status. A minor race awaits him. (14/1: op 8/1)
4003* Riparius (USA) was quite disappointing here on the fast surface. (4/1)

T/Plpt: £2,210.30 (8.43 Tckts). T/Qdpt: £134.10 (5.78 Tckts) DO

4067-HEREFORD (R-H) (Good)
Saturday May 3rd
WEATHER: overcast

4401 GREIG MIDDLETON (S) H'CAP HURDLE (0-95) (4-Y.O+) (Class G)
2-25 (2-26) **2m 1f (9 hdls)** £1,725.00 (£475.00: £225.00) GOING: 0.11 sec per fur (G)

				SP	RR	SF
4295[5]	**Turrill House (65)** (WJMusson) **5-10-1** MRichards (s.s: hld up: gd hdwy fr 6th: led appr 2 out: clr appr last: easily)	—	**1**	11/4[1]	55+	26
2838[12]	**Honeybed Wood (64)** (MSheppard) **9-10-0** DGallagher (mstke 2nd: sn wl bhd: gd hdwy fr 3 out: fin wl)	12	**2**	11/2[3]	43	14
3921[5]	**Scalp 'em (IRE) (64)** (DrPPritchard) **9-10-0** DrPPritchard (lw: prom: lost pl 3 out: styd on wl flat)	2	**3**	16/1	41	12
3448*	**Cuillin Caper (70)** (TRWatson) **5-10-6b** AThornton (lw: led 2nd: clr 6th: hdd appr 2 out: wknd appr last)	3	**4**	11/2[3]	44	15
751[5]	**Harlequin Walk (IRE) (81)** (RJO'Sullivan) **6-11-3** DO'Sullivan (hld up: hdwy appr 5th: ev ch appr 2 out: wknd appr last)	1½	**5**	5/1[2]	54	25
4175[3]	**Commanche Creek (75)** (MissJduPlessis) **7-10-8**(3) SophieMitchell (bhd fr 5th)	8	**6**	5/1[2]	40	11
3743[F]	**Vision of Freedom (IRE) (92)** (PBowen) **9-11-7**(7) JPower (prom tl wknd 3 out)	nk	**7**	7/1	57	28
4236[9]	**Jewel Thief (68)** (GBBalding) **7-10-4v** BFenton (led to 2nd: rdn after 4th: wknd 6th: t.o)	14	**8**	11/1	20	—
3741[U]	**Vital Wonder (64)** (JParfitt) **9-9-7**(7) MGriffiths (s.s: blnd 3rd: a bhd: t.o)	1¼	**9**	20/1	14	—

3997[7] **Patong Beach (64)** (PCRitchens) **7-10-0** SFox (plld hrd: prom to 5th: t.o)....3 **10** 25/1 12 —
(SP 126.1%) **10 Rn**

4m 0.2 (7.20) CSF £18.71 CT £198.01 TOTE £4.20: £2.20 £1.90 £2.30 (£12.90) Trio £72.20 OWNER Mr J. R. Hawksley (NEWMARKET) BRED J. R. Hawksley and C. H. Pettigrew
LONG HANDICAP Honeybed Wood 9-11 Scalp 'em (IRE) 9-9 Vital Wonder 9-7 Patong Beach 9-2
Bt in 5,400 gns
OFFICIAL EXPLANATION **Honeybed Wood: The mare was having her first run for the yard, was badly hampered early and stayed on past beaten horses. She needs further than two miles.**
IN-FOCUS: **The heavily-watered ground was very wet on top.**
4295 Turrill House made mince-meat of the opposition, and with the explanation having been recorded at Market Rasen a week ago, was again the subject of a Stewards' Enquiry. The matter was referred to Portman Square for further investigation, because last week's video was not available together with the fact her trainer was absent. (11/4: 7/4-3/1)
Honeybed Wood, dropping back in trip, was another to keep the Stewards busy, but the explanations, which included she needed a longer trip, were accepted. (11/2)
3757 Scalp 'em (IRE) needs a return to further on this evidence. (16/1)
3448* Cuillin Caper failed to overcome a 9lb hike in the ratings. (11/2: op 3/1)
Harlequin Walk (IRE), down a stone this season, was descending to selling company and may have lasted longer on true fast ground.(5/1: op 3/1)
1474 Vision of Freedom (IRE) (7/1: 4/1-8/1)
972 Jewel Thief (11/1: 6/1-12/1)

4402 MERCURY ASSET MANAGEMENT NOVICES' CHASE (5-Y.O+) (Class E)
2-55 (2-56) **2m 3f (14 fncs)** £2,690.00 (£800.00: £380.00: £170.00) GOING: 0.11 sec per fur (G)

				SP	RR	SF
3950[P]	**Dubelle (81)** (JSKing) **7-11-1** TJMurphy (mde all: clr appr 2 out: r.o wl)	—	**1**	5/1[3]	92	5
16*	**Eid (USA)** (MrsSJSmith) **8-11-0** RichardGuest (hld up: hdwy appr 3 out: rdn & wnt 2nd 2 out: no imp)	8	**2**	11/8[1]	84	—
3998[F]	**First Class (78)** (GNAlford) **7-11-0** RGreene (nt fluent: plld hrd: hdwy 3rd: chsd wnr 4 out to 2 out: wknd appr last)	5	**3**	7/2[2]	80	—
4021[3]	**Indian Temple (64)** (KBishop) **6-10-9**(5) GSupple (chsd wnr: rdn after 8th: hit 10th: wknd after 4 out)	17	**4**	12/1	66	—
3966[2]	**Astral Invasion (USA) (66)** (TWall) **6-10-11**(3) RMassey (swtg: prom: hit 5th: wknd 7th: t.o whn p.u bef 2 out)		**P**	7/1	—	—
3015[P]	**Dodgy Dealer (IRE)** (MrsSusanNock) **7-11-0** MrEJames (a bhd: t.o fr 6th: p.u bef 2 out)		**P**	20/1	—	—
4305[2]	**Diamond Light** (VRBishop) **10-11-0** MrSLloyd (bhd: hit 6th: sn t.o: blnd & uns rdr 3 out)		**U**	14/1	—	—

(SP 112.6%) **7 Rn**

4m 47.3 (17.30) CSF £11.45 TOTE £8.10: £3.20 £1.40 (£6.30) OWNER Mr W. J. Lee (SWINDON) BRED W. J. and Mrs Lee
3950 Dubelle, with the ground nowhere near so fast this time, put some disappointing runs behind her. (5/1)
16* Eid (USA) was graduating to fences on this comeback. (11/8)
3166 First Class had got no further than the fifth when favourite on his chasing debut. (7/2: 5/2-4/1)
4021 Indian Temple (12/1: op 8/1)
4305 Diamond Light (14/1: op 8/1)

4403 GREAT BRAMPTON HOUSE ANTIQUES NOVICES' HURDLE (4-Y.O+) (Class E)
3-25 (3-27) **2m 3f 110y (11 hdls)** £2,070.00 (£570.00: £270.00) GOING: 0.11 sec per fur (G)

				SP	RR	SF
4273[2]	**Eau de Cologne (111)** (MrsLRichards) **5-11-6** MRichards (swtg: hld up: hdwy 8th: sn rdn: led appr 2 out: clr appr last: r.o wl)	—	**1**	11/10[1]	78	22
2961[6]	**Supreme Charm (IRE)** (KCBailey) **5-10-7**(7) MrRWakley (a.p: led 8th tl appr 2 out: one pce)	11	**2**	8/1[3]	63	7
3337[4]	**Just Jasmine** (KBishop) **5-10-9** RGreene (prom tl wknd appr 2 out)	¾	**3**	12/1	57	1
4134[3]	**High Summer** (TThomsonJones) **7-11-0** GUpton (prom: mstke 6th: lost pl appr 3 out: styd on appr last)	3	**4**	10/1	60	4
3581[3]	**Brook Bee** (NAGaselee) **5-11-0** WMarston (j.slowly 1st: led after 2nd: hdd 8th: wknd appr 3 out)	23	**5**	33/1	41	—
	Rushaway (MissCJohnsey) **6-11-0** DGallagher (led tl after 2nd: wknd qckly 3 out: sn eased)	1¾	**6**	14/1	40	—
1855[5]	**Bay Fair** (MRBosley) **5-10-9** ILawrence (rdn appr 6th: hdwy appr 7th: wknd 8th)	½	**7**	14/1	34	—
3989[3]	**Sicarian** (MrsMerritaJones) **5-11-0** DerekByrne (s.s: hdwy appr 7th: wknd 8th: t.o)	18	**8**	5/1[2]	24	—
3362[2]	**Operetto (IRE) (82)** (MrsSusanNock) **7-11-0** MrEJames (prom to 7th: t.o)	4	**9**	10/1	21	—
4217[8]	**Western Sun** (JLNeedham) **7-10-9**(5) ABates (rdn after 5th: bhd fr 7th: t.o)	4	**10**	100/1	18	—
	Pearla Dubh (IRE) (87) (RJBaker) **8-11-0** VSlattery (bkwd: bhd fr 5th: t.o whn blnd 7th: p.u bef 8th)		**P**	33/1	—	—
3977[P]	**Sandville Lad** (MrsDThomas) **5-10-7**(7) MrAWintle (t.o fr 5th: p.u bef 3 out)		**P**	66/1	—	—
	Marlies Gohr (TTClement) **5-10-9** TDascombe (a bhd: t.o 6th: p.u bef 3 out)		**P**	100/1	—	—
1581[P]	**Ali's Delight** (AJWilson) **6-11-0** AThornton (s.s: a bhd: t.o whn p.u after 6th)		**P**	100/1	—	—
	King Curan (USA) (PBowen) **6-11-0b** RichardGuest (bhd fr 6th: t.o whn p.u bef 7th)		**P**	10/1	—	—
4230[P]	**Fearless Hussar** (CFCJackson) **7-11-0** PHolley (uns rdr s)		**U**	100/1	—	—

(SP 135.0%) **16 Rn**

4m 45.1 (14.10) CSF £11.18 TOTE £1.80: £1.10 £2.60 £4.00 (£16.40) Trio £76.20 OWNER D and M Evans (CHICHESTER) BRED G. Reed
4273 Eau de Cologne, with nothing of the calibre of Summer Spell to contend with this time, regained the sweet smell of success. (11/10: evens-5/4)
2961 Supreme Charm (IRE) appreciated this well-watered ground, but was unable to go with the winner. (8/1)
3337 Just Jasmine seems worth a try over a longer distance. (12/1: op 7/1)
4134 High Summer is another who needs further. (10/1)
1855 Bay Fair (14/1: 8/1-16/1)
3362 Operetto (IRE) (10/1: 6/1-11/1)
King Curan (USA) (10/1: op 6/1)

4404 KIDSONS IMPEY H'CAP CHASE (0-105) (5-Y.O+) (Class F)
4-00 (4-04) **3m 1f 110y (19 fncs)** £2,560.00 (£760.00: £360.00: £160.00) GOING: 0.11 sec per fur (G)

				SP	RR	SF
	Nova Champ (81) (MrsSJSmith) **9-9-13**(5) GFRyan (a gng wl: led 3 out: clr appr last: pushed out)	—	**1**	12/1	95	15
3444*	**Mr Invader (93)** (NAGaselee) **10-11-2** WMarston (a.p: led 4 out to 3 out: hrd rdn: one pce)	13	**2**	11/2[2]	99	19
3929*	**Just One Canaletto (77)** (NATwiston-Davies) **9-9-7b**(7) MrJGoldstein (hdwy 13th: ev ch 3 out: one pce)	nk	**3**	5/1[1]	83	3
4312[6]	**Ballydougan (IRE) (77)** (RMathew) **9-10-0v** TJMurphy (bhd: rdn 10th: styd on appr 3 out: nt rch ldrs)	½	**4**	20/1	82	2
726[6]	**Boxing Match (77)** (JMBradley) **10-10-0** TDascombe (led 2nd to 4 out: sn wknd: t.o)	27	**5**	20/1	65	—
4234*	**Supposin (91)** (MrsSJSmith) **9-11-0** RichardGuest (bhd: hit 10th: hdwy 14th: wknd appr 3 out: t.o)	11	**6**	5/1[1]	73	—

			SP	RR	SF
3837[4]	**Maxxum Express (IRE) (80)** (GBBalding) **9-9-12**(5) ABates (bhd fr 6th: t.o) 8	7	10/1	57	—
4185[U]	**Rocky Park (95)** (GBBalding) **11-11-4** BFenton (lost pl 5th: t.o whn fell 14th)	F	11/2 2	—	—
3925[P]	**Bottle Black (80)** (THind) **10-10-3** PMcLoughlin (hld up: rdn after 10th: bhd whn fell 14th)	F	25/1	—	—
4270[F]	**Dont Tell the Wife (105)** (CREgerton) **11-12-0** AThornton (led to 2nd: wkng whn mstke 14th: t.o whn p.u bef 3 out)	P	12/1	—	—
4234[3]	**Furry Fox (IRE) (78)** (RCurtis) **9-10-1** DMorris (hdwy 7th: mstke 11th: wknd qckly: p.u bef 12th)	P	6/1 3	—	—
4135[3]	**Capo Castanum (92)** (MissHCKnight) **8-10-8**(7) MrAWintle (gd hdwy 3rd: wknd appr 14th: t.o whn p.u bef 3 out)	P	5/1 1	—	—
4177[6]	**Northern Optimist (87)** (BJLlewellyn) **9-10-10** MrJLLlewellyn (bhd fr 13th: t.o whn p.u bef 4 out)	P	20/1	—	—

(SP 137.7%) **13 Rn**

6m 26.3 (16.30) CSF £77.78 CT £361.86 TOTE £28.80: £6.90 £2.70 £1.90 (£94.10) Trio £119.90; £152.07 to Newmarket 4/5/97 OWNER Mrs C. E. Van Praagh (BINGLEY) BRED Mrs J. H. Cobden

LONG HANDICAP Ballydougan (IRE) 9-11 Boxing Match 9-8 Just One Canaletto 9-12

OFFICIAL EXPLANATION Furry Fox (IRE): lame.

Nova Champ, off-course since winning at Catterick in March last year, found no problem in defying a 5lb higher mark and can score again. (12/1: op 8/1)

3444* Mr Invader proved no match for the winner off a 5lb higher mark. (11/2)

3929* Just One Canaletto was still just out of the handicap despite a 6lb rise in the ratings. (5/1)

3848 Ballydougan (IRE) got going far too late in the day. (20/1)

4234* Supposin (5/1: op 3/1)

4405 HEREFORD AUTOMATICS JACKPOT NOVICES' H'CAP HURDLE (0-100) (4-Y.O+) (Class E)

4-30 (4-35) **2m 1f (9 hdls)** £2,070.00 (£570.00: £270.00) GOING: 0.11 sec per fur (G)

			SP	RR	SF
4069[2]	**Magical Blues (IRE) (85)** (MissAEEmbiricos) **5-11-4** KGaule (rel to r: hdwy 4th: led 6th: rdn & r.o wl) ....—	1	5/1 3	67	34
4226[3]	**Nahla (80)** (BdeHaan) **7-10-13** SCurran (a.p: led 5th to 6th: ev ch 2 out: one pce) 2½	2	9/2 2	60	27
4223[2]	**The Brewer (77)** (JCTuck) **5-10-10** RBellamy (hld up: hdwy 5th: r.o one pce fr 3 out) 3	3	4/1 1	54	21
3364[12]	**Arioso (67)** (JLNeedham) **9-9-9**(5) ABates (bhd tl hdwy 3 out: nt rch ldrs) 3	4	13/2	41	8
4226[4]	**Fencer's Quest (IRE) (78)** (CaptTAForster) **4-10-6** SWynne (prom to 6th) 7	5	9/2 2	45	7
3340[5]	**Credo Boy (71)** (KBishop) **8-10-4** RGreene (no hdwy fr 6th) 1	6	14/1	38	5
3823[16]	**Soccer Ball (67)** (TRWatson) **7-9-9**(5) DJKavanagh (hld up: hdwy 6th: wknd 3 out) 2½	7	33/1	31	—
1782[6]	**Kumari King (IRE) (72)** (AWCarroll) **7-10-5** DMorris (bhd tl hdwy appr 5th: wknd appr 3 out) 12	8	16/1	25	—
3632[P]	**Royal Glint (67)** (HEHaynes) **8-10-0** BFenton (mstke 1st: a bhd) 4	9	20/1	16	—
4285[2]	**Fairelaine (79)** (KCBailey) **5-10-12b** CO'Dwyer (prom to 5th: no ch whn mstke 2 out) 14	10	4/1 1	15	—
4217[9]	**Ask Me In (IRE) (87)** (TWall) **6-11-3**(3) RMassey (led to 5th: wknd 6th: fell 3 out)	F	20/1	—	—
4226[F]	**Ritto (93)** (JNeville) **7-11-12** TDascombe (hld up: hdwy appr 5th: mstke 6th: sn wknd: p.u after 2 out)	P	8/1	—	—
4226[P]	**Aqua Amber (71)** (JMBradley) **5-9-11**(7)ow4 JPower (chsd ldr: pckd 2nd: wknd 5th: t.o whn p.u bef 2 out)	P	25/1	—	—

(SP 146.3%) **13 Rn**

4m 1.9 (8.90) CSF £30.77 CT £101.31 TOTE £6.60: £2.40 £1.70 £1.70 (£21.60) Trio £94.60; £66.64 to Newmarket 4/5/97 OWNER Miss A. Embiricos (NEWMARKET) BRED John Breslin

LONG HANDICAP Royal Glint 9-7 Arioso 9-7 Aqua Amber 9-6 Soccer Ball 9-7

WEIGHT FOR AGE 4yo-5lb

4069 Magical Blues (IRE), who looks a very tricky individual, made amends for a rather unlucky defeat in a seller here last time. (5/1)

4226 Nahla did not mind this well-watered ground. (9/2)

4223 The Brewer had been raised 4lb for his second at Bangor. (4/1)

3054 Arioso, 7lb out of the handicap, appeared to find this shorter trip inadequate. (13/2: 4/1-7/1)

4226 Fencer's Quest (IRE) (9/2: op 3/1)

4406 JAIL-BREAK HUNTERS' CHASE (5-Y.O+) (Class H)

5-05 (5-06) **2m 3f (14 fncs)** £1,380.00 (£380.00: £180.00) GOING: 0.11 sec per fur (G)

			SP	RR	SF
	Yquem (IRE) (AWVarey) **7-11-7**(7) MrRWakley (hdwy 6th: led 3 out: lft clr last) ....—	1	7/1	108	—
4327[4]	**Familiar Friend** (SJGilmore) **11-12-0b**(7) MrLLay (hld up & bhd: hdwy 9th: wknd appr 3 out: lft 2nd last) 15	2	10/1	102	—
3928*	**Landsker Missile** (MrsMaryEvans) **8-11-9**(7) MrNBradley (prom: rdn 4 out: sn wknd) ....¾	3	7/4 1	97	—
4228[6]	**Tellaporky** (THind) **8-11-7b**1(7) MrAMiddleton (s.s: mstkes: t.o fr 6th) ....dist	4	33/1	—	—
4218[P]	**Thornhill** (FLMatthews) **7-11-2**(7) CaptAWood (s:s bhd tl fell 5th)	F	50/1	—	—
4228*	**Mankind** (JATdeGiles) **6-11-11**(7) MrLBaker (prom to 8th: t.o whn p.u bef 3 out)	P	7/2 2	—	—
	Sudanor (IRE) (JRudge) **8-11-7**(7) MrMMunrowd (blnd 8th: sn bhd: t.o whn p.u bef 4 out)	P	20/1	—	—
4228[P]	**Tuffnut George** (MrsPGrainger) **10-12-0**(7) MrAPhillips (lw: led to 2nd: wknd 9th: t.o whn p.u & dsmntd bef 2 out)	P	8/1	—	—
	Roo's Leap (IRE) (JRudge) **9-11-2**(7) MrOMcPhail (bhd fr 7th: t.o whn p.u bef 9th)	P	33/1	—	—
	Twist 'n' Scu (MissLucySmith) **9-11-7**(7) MrRLawther (j.slowly 5th: t.o whn p.u bef 10th)	P	33/1	—	—
4320[3]	**My Young Man** (CPEBrooks) **12-12-0**(7) MrEJames (led 2nd: rdn & hdd 3 out: ev ch whn mstke & uns rdr last)	U	4/1 3	—	—

(SP 126.8%) **11 Rn**

4m 52.7 (22.70) CSF £65.77 TOTE £6.20: £2.00 £2.80 £1.10 (£58.00) Trio £24.90 OWNER Mr J. J. Boulter (MARLBOROUGH) BRED Michael Heskin

Yquem (IRE), lightly-raced between the flags, won on good to soft just over a year ago so acted on this ground. With a narrow advantage when presented the race at the last, he had been going best for some time. (7/1)

3963 Tuffnut George (8/1: op 5/1)

4320 My Young Man appeared to be getting the worst of the argument when getting rid of his rider. (4/1)

4407 ST. MICHAEL'S HOSPICE STANDARD AMATR & COND N.H. FLAT RACE (4, 5 & 6-Y.O F & M) (Class H)

5-35 (5-36) **2m 1f** £1,028.00 (£278.00: £128.00)

			SP	RR	SF
	Dawn Spinner (NJHenderson) **5-10-7**(7) THagger (plld hrd: a.p: led over 1f out tl ins fnl f: led last strides) ....—	1	8/1 3	65 f	—
	Vicar's Vase (KCBailey) **4-10-2**(7) MrRWakley (bit bkwd: hld up & bhd: gd hdwy 4f out: led ins fnl f: hdd last strides) ....hd	2	10/1	65 f	—
	Be My Romany (IRE) (JLNeedham) **5-10-9**(5) ABates (led tl hdd over 1f out: one pce) 3½	3	20/1	62 f	—

		Dist	Pos	SP	RR	SF
	Floral Reef (NJHenderson) **6-10-7**(7) MrMWCarroll (bit bkwd: hld up mid div: hdwy 4f out: ev ch 2f out: one pce)	2	**4**	20/1	60 f	—
4287[4]	**Tara Gale (IRE)** (JNeville) **5-11-0**(7) MrAWintle (hld up: hdwy 8f out: ev ch 3f out: one pce fnl 2f)	nk	**5**	5/2[1]	66 f	—
3690[4]	**Dunsfold Dolly** (PWinkworth) **4-10-6**(3) LAspell (lw: a.p: ev ch 3f out: wknd over 1f out)	1¼	**6**	5/1[2]	58 f	—
	Absolute Proof (WGMTurner) **4-10-2**(7) JPower (lw: hdwy over 3f out: one pce fnl 2f)	3	**7**	12/1	55 f	—
	The Lady Scores (IRE) (KCBailey) **5-10-7**(7) CScudder (lw: hld up & bhd: hdwy 6f out: wknd over 2f out)	s.h	**8**	8/1[3]	55 f	—
	Bossa Nova (LGCottrell) **4-10-4**(5) OBurrows (bkwd: plld hrd: hdwy after 6f: wknd over 3f out)	15	**9**	12/1	41 f	—
4088[3]	**Shimmy Dancing** (JohnBerry) **4-10-9** MissAEmbiricos (prom 12f)	9	**10**	10/1	33 f	—
	Flossie Hands (IRE) (JGMO'Shea) **5-11-3**(7)ow10 JTNolan (lw: plld hrd: prom 13f)	4	**11**	20/1	39 f	—
	Seymours Secret (DRGandolfo) **5-10-11**(3) SophieMitchell (a bhd)	1¼	**12**	20/1	28 f	—
3235[3]	**Redgrave Wolf** (KBishop) **4-10-4**(5) GSupple (prom 12f)	5	**13**	5/1[2]	23 f	—
	After Time (NJHenderson) **5-10-7**(7) PMaher (bkwd: a bhd: t.o)	16	**14**	8/1[3]	8 f	—
	Brunida (PGMurphy) **5-11-0** TDascombe (bkwd: hld up: hdwy 8f out: wknd 5f out: t.o)	6	**15**	8/1[3]	3 f	—
	Albertina (MrsSusanNock) **5-11-0** MrEJames (s.s: t.o after 6f)	dist	**16**	20/1	—	—
	Princess Helen (IRE) (MRBosley) **4-10-2**(7) MLane (lw: t.o)	dist	**17**	10/1	—	—

(SP 172.8%) **17 Rn**

3m 58.3 CSF £102.50 TOTE £15.20: £3.60 £3.80 £9.60 (£36.80) Trio Not won; £149.17 to Newmarket 4/5/97 OWNER Sir Peter Miller (LAMBOURN) BRED Mrs Hugh Maitland-Jones
WEIGHT FOR AGE 4yo-5lb
Dawn Spinner is a half-sister to amongst others The Tsarevich and Golden Spinner. (8/1: op 5/1)
Vicar's Vase, given quite a lot to do, will come on for the outing. (10/1: op 6/1)
Be My Romany (IRE) is out of a half-sister to Romany King. (20/1)
Floral Reef, a half-sister to bumper and hurdle winner Give Me An Answer, will be sharper for the run. (20/1)
4287 Tara Gale (IRE) had the ground a bit more like that when successful on her debut. (5/2)
3690 Dunsfold Dolly (5/1: op 3/1)
Absolute Proof (12/1: op 7/1)
The Lady Scores (IRE) (8/1: op 5/1)
Bossa Nova (12/1: 10/1-16/1)
3235 Redgrave Wolf (5/1: 7/2-6/1)

T/Plpt: £50.40 (133.91 Tckts). T/Qdpt: £11.90 (32.23 Tckts) KH

4151-HEXHAM (L-H) (Firm)
Saturday May 3rd

Comments restricted and no time taken races 2 & 4 due to poor visibility
WEATHER: overcast

4408 CHESTERS STUD NOVICES' H'CAP CHASE (0-100) (5-Y.O+) (Class E)

6-00 (6-00) **2m 4f 110y (15 fncs)** £3,440.75 (£1,031.00: £495.50: £227.75) GOING minus 0.54 sec per fur (GF)

		Dist	Pos	SP	RR	SF
4245[P]	**Tough Test (IRE) (86)** (MrsJDGoodfellow) **7-11-2** BStorey (chsd ldrs: led 4 out: wnt clr fr 2 out: easily)	—	**1**	15/8[1]	99+	6
4153[2]	**Shawwell (76)** (JIACharlton) **10-10-6** TReed (led tl hdd 8th: lft in ld next: hdd 4 out: rdn & mstke 2 out: one pce)	11	**2**	6/1[3]	80	—
4144[9]	**Banner Year (IRE) (70)** (TJCarr) **6-10-0** GCahill (a chsng ldrs: hmpd 9th: rdn & no imp fr 3 out)	23	**3**	66/1	57	—
4149[6]	**More Joy (70)** (BEllison) **9-9-7**(7) CMcCormack (chsd ldrs: effrt bef 3 out: btn appr 2 out)	6	**4**	7/1	52	—
4152[5]	**Kings Minstral (IRE) (74)** (DALamb) **7-10-4**ow4 JBurke (bhd whn mstke 7th: nvr nrr)	5	**5**	20/1	52	—
4151[5]	**Quixall Crossett (70)** (EMCaine) **12-9-9**(5) MrMHNaughton (a in rr)	8	**6**	66/1	42	—
4149[P]	**Master Flashman (73)** (MrsMReveley) **8-10-3b**[1] GLee (a bhd)	3	**7**	11/2[2]	42	—
4297[7]	**Karlovac (70)** (SGChadwick) **11-10-0b** FPerratt (in tch: rdn & outpcd ½-wy: sn bhd: t.o)	24	**8**	20/1	21	—
4057[6]	**Twin Falls (IRE) (94)** (GMMoore) **6-11-10b**[1] JCallaghan (fell 1st)		**F**	6/1[3]	—	—
4151[3]	**Jonaem (IRE) (70)** (MrsDianneSayer) **7-10-0** KJohnson (prom: led 8th: fell next)		**F**	8/1	—	—
2954[P]	**Classic Crest (IRE) (70)** (MissLucindaRussell) **6-10-0v** MFoster (a rr div: p.u after 2 out)		**P**	20/1	—	—

(SP 119.6%) **11 Rn**

5m 2.5 (5.50) CSF £12.05 CT £505.17 TOTE £2.80: £1.40 £1.40 £24.00 (£5.70) Trio Not won; £148.30 to 5/5/97 OWNER Mr J. D. Goodfellow (EARLSTON) BRED Liam Burke
LONG HANDICAP Banner Year (IRE) 9-4 Quixall Crossett 9-0 More Joy 9-10 Karlovac 9-12 Jonaem (IRE) 9-12 Kings Minstral (IRE) 9-8 Classic Crest (IRE) 9-13
3909* Tough Test (IRE), back at his right level, won easily. (15/8)
4153 Shawwell extended his creditable if somewhat exasperating sequence of placed efforts. (6/1)
Banner Year (IRE), an ex point-to-pointer, and 10lb out of the handicap, was no danger to the first two when the chips were down. (66/1)
1246 More Joy beat a retreat from the third last. (7/1: op 20/1)
4152 Kings Minstral (IRE), on his chasing debut, was never a factor carrying 6lb more than his handicap rating, plus a further 4lb overweight. (20/1)

4409 DENNIS WAGGOTT BUILDER (S) H'CAP HURDLE (0-95) (4-Y.O+) (Class G)

6-30 (6-31) **2m (8 hdls)** £2,008.10 (£556.60: £266.30) GOING minus 0.54 sec per fur (GF)

		Dist	Pos	SP	RR	SF
4295[3]	**Tsanga (69)** (GMMoore) **5-10-10** NBentley (chsd ldrs: led appr 2 out: clr last: comf)	—	**1**	100/30[1]	52+	—
4259*	**Charlistiona (77)** (JPDodds) **6-10-11**(7) SMelrose (chsd ldrs: effrt 3 out: styd on one pce fr 2 out)	2½	**2**	4/1[3]	58	—
4187[8]	**Skiddaw Samba (83)** (MrsMReveley) **8-11-10** GLee (a.p: effrt 3 out: no ex between last 2)	3	**3**	7/2[2]	61	—
4259[5]	**Monkey Wench (IRE) (82)** (MrsJDGoodfellow) **6-11-9** BStorey (prom: lost pl ½-wy: hdwy 3 out: one pce fr 2 out)	2½	**4**	8/1	57	—
3933[8]	**Fret (USA) (59)** (JSWainwright) **7-10-0** MFoster (cl up: led 5th: hdd appr 2 out: sn wknd)	13	**5**	20/1	21	—
4060[8]	**Stags Fell (64)** (TAKCuthbert) **12-10-5** CarolCuthbert (chsd ldrs to 3 out: sn btn)	4	**6**	20/1	22	—
4259[13]	**Dark Midnight (IRE) (64)** (DALamb) **8-10-5**ow5 JBurke (nvr rchd ldrs)	2½	**7**	50/1	20	—
3912[7]	**In a Moment (USA) (70)** (CGrant) **6-10-11** RGarritty (in tch to 3rd: sn lost pl & bhd)	5	**8**	6/1	21	—
3448[7]	**Blood Brother (59)** (JBarclay) **5-9-7**(7) CMcCormack (led to 5th: sn lost pl & bhd: t.o)	11	**9**	25/1	—	—
4056[9]	**Over Stated (IRE) (67)** (JWade) **7-10-3**(5) STaylor (b.d 1st)		**B**	16/1	—	—

3327[8] Tiotao (IRE) (63) (CParker) 7-10-4 DParker (b.d 1st)	B	10/1	—	—
4236[6] Birthplace (IRE) (60) (RTate) 7-10-1 KJohnson (fell 1st)	F	25/1	—	—
4249[P] Super Guy (60) (JBarclay) 5-10-1ow1 GCahill (a bhd: t.o whn p.u bef last)	P	50/1	—	—
4283[10] Shut Up (62) (MrsEMoscrop) 8-10-0(3)ow3 EHusband (a in rr: t.o whn sddle slipped & uns rdr after 2 out)	U	50/1	—	—
		(SP 128.8%) 14 Rn		

Time Not Taken CSF £15.80 CT £47.36 TOTE £4.40: £1.60 £2.60 £1.60 (£11.90) Trio £11.00 OWNER Mr J. P. Paternoster (MIDDLEHAM) BRED Garry E. West
LONG HANDICAP Blood Brother 9-6 Dark Midnight (IRE) 9-6 Fret (USA) 9-12 Super Guy 9-5 Shut Up 9-6
No bid
4295 Tsanga fulfilled the promise of his latest outing, and was in no danger from the final flight. (100/30)
4259* Charlistiona ran creditably, but was unable to supplement her shock Perth victory. (4/1)
4060 Skiddaw Samba ran a respectable race off top-weight. (7/2)
4259 Monkey Wench (IRE) lacked the finishing speed of the principals when the chips were down. (8/1)
Fret (USA), having only his second start of the season, ran well until weakening from the second last. He will have benefited from this. (20/1)

4410 GILESGATE SUBARU AND SSANGYONG TANT PIS H'CAP CHASE (0-100) (5-Y.O+) (Class F)
7-00 (7-00) **2m 110y** £2,887.50 (£800.00: £382.50) GOING minus 0.54 sec per fur (GF)

			SP	RR	SF
4151[P] **Speaker's House (USA) (86)** (MissLucindaRussell) **8-11-3** TReed (chsd ldrs: led 4 out: r.o strly: clr fr 2 out) —	1	9/2[3]	94	—
4258[6] **Cardenden (IRE) (69)** (JBarclay) **9-10-0** BStorey (led tl hdd 4 out: kpt on u.p fr 2 out: no ch w wnr) 4	2	7/2[1]	73	—
4153* **Bishopdale (80)** (SGChadwick) **16-10-11** FPerratt (prom tl rdn & outpcd bef 3 out: kpt on fr 2 out) 6	3	7/2[1]	78	—
North Pride (USA) (69) (MABarnes) **12-10-0** GCahill (in tch: hit 6th: mstke 3 out: sn outpcd) 18	4	16/1	50	—
Mils Mij (97) (TAKCuthbert) **12-12-0** RSupple (bhd: sme hdwy 3 out: no imp after) 2½	5	4/1[2]	75	—
Wild Brook (IRE) (72) (BEllison) **7-9-10**(7) CMcCormack (blnd bdly 1st: nvr rchd ldrs) 24	6	7/1	27	—
895[P] **Anthony Bell (90)** (TJCarr) **11-11-7** NSmith (rr div: lost tch & p.u bef 3 out)	P	8/1	—	—
		(SP 112.1%)	7 Rn	

4m 1.0 (4.00) CSF £18.39 TOTE £5.80: £2.70 £1.70 (£5.30) OWNER Mrs C. G. Greig (KINROSS) BRED Wakefield Farm
4151 Speaker's House (USA) bounced back to form with a fluent performance, and had the prize in safe-keeping a fair way out. (9/2)
4258 Cardenden (IRE) did the donkey-work for the winner, and stuck to his task solidly, even when getting the worst of the argument. (7/2)
4153* Bishopdale, winner of this race last year, was outpaced as the winner went for home, and could only plug on at the same speed thereafter. (7/2)
North Pride (USA) was making a belated a seasonal debut and seemed to need the race. (16/1)
Mils Mij returning from an eleven-month absence, will have benefited from this outing. (4/1)
Wild Brook (IRE) failed to recover from a bad blunder at the first. (7/1)

4411 GILESGATE SUBARU AND SSANGYONG 10TH ANNIVERSARY HEART OF ALL ENGLAND MAIDEN HUNTERS' CHASE (5-Y.O+) (Class H)
7-30 (7-30) **3m 1f** £2,388.00 (£714.00: £342.00: £156.00) GOING minus 0.54 sec per fur (GF)

			SP	RR	SF
Cumberland Blues (IRE) (MrsALockwood) **8-11-7**(7) MissADeniel (mde all: styd on strly fr 3 out) —	1	4/1[2]	89	—
3357[7] **Coolvawn Lady (IRE)** (WRHalliday) **8-11-2**(7) MrSWalker (sn chsng ldrs: effrt & ev ch appr 2 out: kpt on one pce fr last) 4	2	4/1[2]	81	—
Will Travel (IRE) (AndrewDickman) **8-11-7**(7) MrARobson (chsd wnr tl rdn & one pce appr 2 out) 7	3	5/2[1]	82	—
4155[3] **Cool Yule (IRE)** (RWThomson) **9-11-9**(5) MissPRobson (bhd: kpt on one pce fr 2 out: no ch w ldrs) 22	4	9/2[3]	68	—
Emu Park (MrsRLElliot) **9-11-7**(7) MrJThompson (in tch tl wknd fr 10th: t.o) dist	5	12/1	—	—
Tod Law (MrsRLElliot) **9-11-4**(5) MrCStorey (a in rr: wl t.o) 20	6	12/1	—	—
Fast Fun (KRobson) **9-11-7**(7) MrRMorgan (chsd ldrs tl lost pl & bhd 7th: sn t.o: p.u bef 3 out)	P	14/1	—	—
Donside (GFWhite) **9-12-0** MrJWalton (chsd ldrs tl s.u after 4th)	S	16/1	—	—
		(SP 114.7%)	8 Rn	

Time Not Taken CSF £19.10 TOTE £3.80: £1.70 £1.40 £1.40 (£9.70) OWNER Mr John Holdroyd (MALTON) BRED P. Browne
Cumberland Blues (IRE), twice a winner between the flags this season, led from pillar to post here, and saw his race out in great style. (4/1)
Coolvawn Lady (IRE), in with every chance from the third last, made a determined bid, but was always finding the winner just toostrong. (4/1)
Will Travel (IRE), on his hunter-chase debut, ran well until being outpaced from the penultimate fence. (5/2)
Tod Law (12/1: op 8/1)

4412 ROOSTER COMPUTERS 10TH ANNIVERSARY MAIDEN HURDLE (4-Y.O+) (Class F)
- Abandoned -Poor visibility- Fog

4413 DR MICHAEL REYNOLDS MEMORIAL CONDITIONAL H'CAP HURDLE (0-100) (4-Y.O+) (Class G)
- Abandoned -Poor visibility - Fog

T/Plpt: £6.60 (1492.72 Tckts). T/Qdpt: £3.10 (156.99 Tckts) O'R

3983-UTTOXETER (L-H) (Good)
Saturday May 3rd
WEATHER: fine & sunny

4414 STREBEL BOILERS & RADIATORS NOVICES' HURDLE (4-Y.O) (Class E)
2-10 (2-10) **2m (9 hdls)** £2,232.00 (£627.00: £306.00) GOING minus 0.16 sec per fur (G)

			SP	RR	SF
4014[6] **Quality (IRE) (116)** (PJHobbs) **4-11-5** NWilliamson (prom: wnt 2nd at 6th: ev ch whn blnd 3 out: rdn appr last: r.o to ld flat) —	1	11/8[1]	89	42
3818[2] **Hisar (IRE) (113)** (CPEBrooks) **4-10-12** GBradley (led: sn clr: jnd 3 out: hdd & unable qckn flat) 1½	2	5/2[3]	81	34
3634[P] **Kings Witness (USA) (108)** (PFNicholls) **4-11-5** PHide (trckd ldrs: rdn 3 out: sn chsng ldr: wknd appr last) 8	3	9/4[2]	80	33
3634[21] **Society Girl** (JGMO'Shea) **4-10-4**(3) MichaelBrennan (lw: chsd ldr to 6th: rdn & btn next) 8	4	33/1	60	13
Ambrosia (IRE) (GAHubbard) **4-10-4**(3) PHenley (bkwd: a bhd: t.o fr 3 out) dist	5	16/1	—	—

3703F Shawkey (IRE) (DMcCain) **4-10-12** DWalsh (bit bkwd: t.o fr 6th: p.u bef 2 out) .... P 50/1 — —
(SP 112.2%) **6 Rn**

3m 43.5 (2.50) CSF £4.86 TOTE £2.60: £1.10 £2.40 (£2.90) OWNER Mr D. B. O'Connor (MINEHEAD) BRED Major C.R. Philipson
4014 Quality (IRE) looks to be still on the up, and did well to recover from a bad mistake three from home, which looked to have cost him a winning chance. Wisely, Williamson did not panic, but allowed his mount time to get back on an even keel. (11/8)
3818 Hisar (IRE) could not reverse Newbury form with the winner on 7lb better terms, despite a similar forcing display. (5/2)
3224* Kings Witness (USA), not very fluent early on, did eventually jump rather better than he had in the past. (9/4)
Society Girl, a miler on the level, by a miler, gives the impression that getting the trip is her main problem. (33/1)
Ambrosia (IRE), a rangy but unfurnished newcomer, looked much in need of the run and showed very little. (16/1)

4415 STANTON PLC H'CAP HURDLE (0-125) (4-Y.O+) (Class D)

2-40 (2-40) **2m 4f 110y (10 hdls)** £2,913.00 (£818.00: £399.00) GOING minus 0.16 sec per fur (G)

				SP	RR	SF
4236²	**Steve Ford (92)** (CPMorlock) **8-10-4** JRKavanagh (lw: hld up: hdwy 7th: led 2 out: rdn out)	—	1	3/1²	69	10
3722*	**Claireswan (IRE) (102)** (MHTompkins) **5-11-0v¹** JRailton (a.p: rdn appr 2 out: kpt on flat)	3	2	2/1¹	77	18
	Drummond Warrior (IRE) (95) (TThomsonJones) **8-10-7** NWilliamson (bkwd: plld hrd: led 2nd: hdd 2 out: sn rdn: one pce)	1¼	3	3/1²	69	10
4223¹⁰	**Innocent George (88)** (MissLCSiddall) **8-9-7**(7) TSiddall (lw: led to 2nd: rdn & wknd 7th)	18	4	12/1	48	—
2079³	**Rolfe (NZ) (112)** (SABrookshaw) **7-11-10b** DWalsh (chsd ldrs tl rdn & wknd appr 3 out: p.u bef next)		P	4/1³	—	—
				(SP 111.0%)		**5 Rn**

4m 52.4 (8.40) CSF £8.85 TOTE £4.20: £1.60 £1.40 (£4.50) OWNER Mr P. J. Morgan (WANTAGE) BRED Hever Castle Stud Ltd
LONG HANDICAP Innocent George 9-8
4236 Steve Ford is hardly bred for stamina and does take a keen hold, but dealt with this trip well, although looking rather at the end of his tether from the last. (3/1)
3722* Claireswan (IRE) looked short of pace from the home turn, but simply sticking to his task was getting him back into the race at the finish. (2/1)
Drummond Warrior (IRE) had been off for nineteen months, and looked like it in the paddock despite having a bright coat. Rather fresh and soon in front, he gave the impression he would probably have won but for blowing up in the home straight. (3/1)
3346 Innocent George had appeared to stay this sort of trip in the past, but was going backwards in the last half mile on this occasion. (12/1: 9/1-14/1)

4416 WATERAID H'CAP CHASE (5-Y.O+) (Class B)

3-10 (3-10) **3m 2f (20 fncs)** £6,781.50 (£2,052.00: £1,001.00: £475.50) GOING minus 0.16 sec per fur (G)

				SP	RR	SF
4213⁵	**Court Melody (IRE) (119)** (PFNicholls) **9-11-4b** PHide (lw: trckd ldrs tl dropped rr 15th: rallied to ld appr 4 out: pushed out)	—	1	4/1³	130	19
4167*	**Le Meille (IRE) (112)** (KRBurke) **8-10-11** NWilliamson (lw: hld up & plld hrd: hdwy 13th: chsd wnr appr 4 out: no imp fr 2 out)	4	2	11/10¹	121	10
3598⁹	**Sibton Abbey (125)** (GAHubbard) **12-11-7**(3) MichaelBrennan (bit bkwd: led to 5th: dropped rr 14th: rdn & rallied to ld 16th: hdd appr next: one pce)	10	3	20/1	127	16
3637P	**Lord Relic (NZ) (114)** (SABrookshaw) **11-10-13** DWalsh (led after 8th to 10th: wknd 4 out)	26	4	7/1	100	—
1354²	**Factor Ten (IRE) (123)** (MissHCKnight) **9-11-8** JFTitley (led 5th tl after 8th: led 10th to 16th: wknd qckly & p.u bef next)		P	7/2²	—	—
				(SP 107.1%)		**5 Rn**

6m 40.3 (13.30) CSF £8.02 TOTE £4.80: £2.20 £1.20 (£3.10) OWNER J W Aplin, P K Barber & Mick Coburn (SHEPTON MALLET) BRED Miss E. Charlton
OFFICIAL EXPLANATION **Factor Ten (IRE): finished distressed.**
4213 Court Melody (IRE), third to Lord Gyllene here, in what, with hindsight, was the handicap of the season, was made to work quite hard, but this ground is not really soft enough to be ideal. (4/1: op 5/2)
4167* Le Meille (IRE) was beginning to get warm beforehand and does seem to live on his nerves, as he takes a good hold, and is rather unconvincing at the fences. He met a well-handicapped winner here, and cannot be written off yet as he has had a light season. (11/10: 6/4-evens)
3147 Sibton Abbey looks a light of former days, but the Handicapper is dropping him fast, and he may find a small race if this kindness continues. (20/1)
3432 Lord Relic (NZ), dropped considerably by the Handicapper after not taking the hunter-chase world by storm, again finished very weakly. (7/1: 9/2-8/1)

4417 PETER J. DOUGLAS ENGINEERING LORD GYLLENE NOVICES' H'CAP CHASE (0-105) (5-Y.O+ Mares Only) (Class E)

3-45 (3-45) **2m 5f (16 fncs)** £3,468.75 (£1,050.00: £512.50: £243.75) GOING minus 0.16 sec per fur (G)

				SP	RR	SF
3335³	**Gemma's Wager (IRE) (79)** (MarkCampion) **7-10-2**ow2 WMcFarland (hld up: mstke 4th: hdwy 12th: led 2 out: sn rdn: clr)	—	1	25/1	89	22
3886¹⁰	**Cullane Lake (IRE) (78)** (MissMKMilligan) **7-10-1** NWilliamson (swtg: a.p: led 3 out tl next: btn whn blnd last)	13	2	7/2²	78	13
3966⁸	**Lambrini (IRE) (80)** (DMcCain) **7-10-0b**(3)ow3 PHenley (prom: led 4 out tl next: 3rd & btn whn pckd 2 out)	7	3	66/1	75	7
3915³	**Kadari (91)** (WClay) **8-10-11v**(3) GuyLewis (in tch: rdn 10th: sn btn)	24	4	15/2	68	3
3043⁵	**Wonderfull Polly (IRE) (81)** (PFNicholls) **9-10-4** PHide (bit bkwd: nt j.w: blnd 8th: sn bhd)	19	5	9/2³	43	—
3938²	**Quick Quote (86)** (MrsIMcKie) **7-10-9** LHarvey (w ldr tl led after 8th: hdd 4 out: sn wknd)	1¾	6	7/2²	47	—
4279*	**Jasilu (105)** (KCBailey) **7-12-0b** SMcNeill (bhd whn p.u bef 4 out)		P	3/1¹	—	—
3909P	**Mindyerownbusiness (IRE) (82)** (RLee) **8-10-5**ow5 JRailton (led tl after 8th: in tch whn p.u bef 12th)		P	50/1	—	—
4227⁴	**Joy For Life (IRE) (77)** (RMStronge) **6-10-0** GTormey (mstke 5th: sn bhd: p.u bef 4 out)		P	20/1	—	—
				(SP 111.5%)		**9 Rn**

5m 10.1 (5.10) CSF £97.55 CT £5,077.10 TOTE £20.10: £3.30 £1.60 £10.70 (£34.90) Trio £153.80; £93.16 to Newmarket 4/5/97 OWNER Mr & Mrs Barry Noakes (BASINGSTOKE) BRED Mrs Norah O'Connor
LONG HANDICAP Lambrini (IRE) 8-11 Gemma's Wager (IRE) 9-9 Mindyerownbusiness (IRE) 9-3 Joy For Life (IRE) 9-4
OFFICIAL EXPLANATION **Jasilu: lost her action**
1536 Gemma's Wager (IRE) had shown precious little before, but came good in a very poor race. (25/1)
3645* Cullane Lake (IRE) got very warm beforehand and may have boiled over, for she got tired over a trip she looked guaranteed to get. (7/2)

Lambrini (IRE), achieving her best-ever placing, tried hard, but took a dislike to the penultimate fence, pecking slightly on the first circuit, but much more notably on the second. (66/1)
3915 Kadari looked well-in on her hurdles form, but has had an awful lot of runs over timber to be switching to fences, and it showed. (15/2)
3043 Wonderfull Polly (IRE) will need to jump better than this to win over fences. (9/2)
3938 Quick Quote, whose form figures flatter her, did not appreciate the step-up in trip. (7/2)
4279* Jasilu (3/1: tchd 7/1)

4418 SEDGWICK UK RISK SERVICES H'CAP HURDLE (0-125) (4-Y.O+) (Class D)

4-20 (4-21) **3m 110y (12 hdls)** £2,927.00 (£822.00: £401.00) GOING minus 0.16 sec per fur (G)

				SP	RR	SF
4227^{P}	**Hi Hedley (IRE) (96)** (GAHubbard) **7-9-13**(3)ow2 PHenley (led to 3rd: hld on wl flat)	—	**1**	33/1	68	34
4220^{2}	**Derring Bridge (94)** (MrsSMJohnson) **7-10-0** NWilliamson (lw: hdwy 8th: ev ch 3 out: pckd next: unable qckn nr fin)	½	**2**	7/1	66	34
4016^{11}	**Smith Too (IRE) (117)** (MrsJPitman) **9-11-2**(7) RGarrard (a.p: one pce appr 2 out)	3½	**3**	$9/2^{3}$	86	54
3807^{6}	**Needwood Poppy (94)** (BCMorgan) **9-10-0** BClifford (in tch: no imp fr 3 out)	10	**4**	12/1	57	25
3604^{P}	**Amillionmemories (94)** (MrsBarbaraWaring) **7-10-0** EByrne (hld up: hdwy 9th: wknd after next)	14	**5**	33/1	48	16
4253^{4}	**Uluru (IRE) (98)** (CPMorlock) **9-10-4** JRKavanagh (lw: trckd ldrs: pckd 2nd: rdn & wknd appr 3 out)	4	**6**	9/1	49	17
4207^{6}	**Victor Bravo (NZ) (117)** (NAGaselee) **10-11-9b** CLlewellyn (prom tl wknd 3 out: fin lame)	12	**7**	$100/30^{1}$	60	28
4132^{5}	**Oatis Rose (104)** (MSheppard) **7-10-5**(5) XAizpuru (sn rdn along: a bhd)	22	**8**	$7/2^{2}$	33	1
4204^{P}	**Share Options (IRE) (103)** (TDEasterby) **6-10-9** GBradley (led to 3rd: wknd qckly: p.u bef 8th)		**P**	6/1	—	—

(SP 113.8%) **9 Rn**

5m 43.4 (1.40) CSF £221.19 CT £1,137.25 TOTE £32.70: £5.30 £2.10 £1.50 (£88.20) Trio £95.90 OWNER Mr G. A. Hubbard (WOODBRIDGE) BRED Oliver Burke
LONG HANDICAP Hi Hedley (IRE) 9-9 Derring Bridge 9-7 Amillionmemories 9-2 Needwood Poppy 9-7
OFFICIAL EXPLANATION Oatis Rose: no explanation offered.
Hi Hedley (IRE), who made a belated and rather abortive debut over fences last time, looks the part for that game, but is not the easiest horse to keep sound. His courage cannot be questioned after this front-running effort. (33/1)
4220 Derring Bridge tries hard, but is one-paced and has been having a frustrating time of late. This may well continue as he looks sure to go up in the handicap after this effort from out of the weights. (7/1)
3731* Smith Too (IRE) did not try to lead which may have been a mistake, as he looked to be travelling best on the home turn, only to fail to pick up. (9/2: 7/2-11/2)
3545 Needwood Poppy, a poor mover, showed enough to suggest that she would have a chance off her proper mark. (12/1)
2929 Amillionmemories, with his tongue tied down, began to get closer on the home turn before tiring once asked for his effort. Twelve pounds wrong here, he is beginning to look very well-handicapped if he can return to form. (33/1)
4005 Uluru (IRE) looked well and moved well to post, but his performance off a handicap mark well within his scope at his best, suggests something remains amiss. (9/1)

4419 BIFFA WASTE NOVICES' CHASE (5-Y.O+) (Class E)

4-55 (4-56) **2m (12 fncs)** £2,866.00 (£868.00: £424.00: £202.00) GOING minus 0.16 sec per fur (G)

				SP	RR	SF
4260*	**Tidebrook** (KCBailey) **7-11-6** NWilliamson (led tl hdd & blnd 2nd: led after 8th: lft clr next: mstke 2 out: easily)	—	**1**	$4/6^{1}$	95+	21
3092^{4}	**Spectre Brown (66)** (FJestin) **7-10-7**(7) MrTJBarry (mstke 1st: w ldr tl wknd after 8th: lft mod 2nd next)	23	**2**	40/1	66	—
4163^{4}	**Arctic Bloom (60)** (CIRatcliffe) **11-10-9** MrCMulhall (in tch tl 7th: sn lost pl: 3rd & styng on whn j.rt & blnd 2 out)	24	**3**	9/1	37	—
3832^{7}	**The Fence Shrinker (60)** (DMcCain) **6-11-0** PHide (lw: led 3rd tl after 8th: sn wknd)	3	**4**	25/1	39	—
3743^{4}	**Zine Lane** (JGMO'Shea) **5-10-5**(3) MichaelBrennan (led 2nd to 3rd: ev ch whn fell 4 out)		**F**	$11/4^{2}$	—	—
3983^{4}	**Night Boat** (WClay) **6-10-11**(3) GuyLewis (lw: in tch: blnd 3rd: blnd & uns rdr 7th)		**U**	$11/2^{3}$	—	—

(SP 118.3%) **6 Rn**

3m 57.7 (7.70) CSF £20.40 TOTE £1.70: £1.10 £5.20 (£16.50) OWNER Mr Richard Williams (UPPER LAMBOURN) BRED Mrs G. E. Jones
WEIGHT FOR AGE 5yo-6lb
4260* Tidebrook has taken to fences like a camel takes to needlepoint, but despite a few total guesses at the fences, most spectacularly the second, he managed a completion, and that was all that was needed to slaughter some very poor rivals. (4/6)
Spectre Brown took such a hold that he almost put himself on the floor by jumping into the back of a rival at the first. Not surprisingly, he got very tired in the last half-mile. (40/1)
3608 Arctic Bloom wears a cross noseband, and wanted to gallop once mounted in the paddock. Despite all his antics, he was able to keep up with a modest pace and only stayed on in the straight. (9/1)
3743 Zine Lane, rather lightly-built for fences, would have beaten these over timber and was upsides the winner, going every bit as well, when crumpling on landing at the first in the home straight. (11/4: 7/4-3/1)

4420 HOUGHTON VAUGHAN OPEN MAIDEN N.H. FLAT RACE (I) (4, 5 & 6-Y.O) (Class H)

5-25 (5-25) **2m** £1,609.00 (£449.00: £217.00)

				SP	RR	SF
4216^{3}	**Valhalla (IRE)** (MartinTodhunter) **4-11-0** APMcCoy (hld up & plld hrd: hdwy 5f out: led over 1f out: comf)	—	**1**	$11/8^{1}$	73 f	—
1685^{10}	**Otago Heights (NZ)** (MrsJPitman) **5-11-5** DLeahy (a.p: led 4f out tl over 1f out: unable qckn)	4	**2**	12/1	69 f	—
3946^{5}	**Totem Fole** (MrsMReveley) **4-11-0** PNiven (bit bkwd: bhd: hdwy 5f out: rdn 2f out: kpt on wl fnl f)	3	**3**	$6/1^{2}$	66 f	—
4215^{8}	**Donnybrook (IRE)** (RDEWoodhouse) **4-10-9**(5) BGrattan (plld hrd: hdwy 4f out: sn rdn: one pce fnl 2f)	½	**4**	20/1	66 f	—
3365^{4}	**Count Karmuski** (WJenks) **5-11-5** TJenks (chsd ldrs: rdn 4f out: one pce fnl 2f)	1	**5**	14/1	65 f	—
3747^{6}	**Homme de Fer** (KCBailey) **5-11-5** SMcNeill (bhd: hdwy 3f out: nvr rchd ldrs)	½	**6**	10/1	64 f	—
4216^{8}	**Skillwise** (TDEasterby) **5-11-5** JFTitley (nvr nrr)	12	**7**	10/1	52 f	—
4216^{9}	**Chocolate Drum (IRE)** (JJBirkett) **6-11-5** LO'Hara (bit bkwd: in tch 12f)	2	**8**	16/1	50 f	—
3939^{3}	**French County (IRE)** (JRJenkins) **5-11-5** NWilliamson (nvr trbld ldrs)	½	**9**	$8/1^{3}$	50 f	—
4156^{4}	**Buckley House** (JIACharlton) **5-11-5** PHide (led after 2f to 4f out: sn wknd)	5	**10**	20/1	45 f	—
4156^{6}	**Gilsan Star** (CWFairhurst) **4-10-9** GBradley (prom 12f)	3	**11**	25/1	37 f	—
3808^{R}	**Nirvana Princess** (BPreece) **5-10-7**(7) JMogford (hld up & plld hrd: hdwy after 4f: wknd 6f out)	26	**12**	33/1	11 f	—
2904^{15}	**Coquettish** (JHetherton) **4-10-9** OPears (lw: bhd fnl 8f)	4	**13**	50/1	7 f	—
3821^{8}	**Another Rumpus** (CPMorlock) **5-11-2**(3) DFortt (swtg: led 2f: wknd 5f out)	5	**14**	20/1	7 f	—

3170[18] **Tabbitts Hill** (PRWebber) **5-11-0** MrPScott (bhd whn virtually p.u fnl 3f) ....dist **15** 33/1 — —
(SP 131.9%) **15 Rn**

3m 44.1 CSF £17.86 TOTE £2.20: £1.10 £2.20 £1.90 (£9.60) Trio £15.20 OWNER Great Head House Estates Ltd (ULVERSTON) BRED Martin Joyce
WEIGHT FOR AGE 4yo-5lb
4216 Valhalla (IRE), clearly well-suited by forcing tactics, made no mistake this time. (11/8: evens-6/4)
Otago Heights (NZ), five months after his debut, ran a much better second race, although no match for the winner. (12/1)
3946 Totem Fole gives the impression that there is something left to work on, and that he will stay very well. (6/1)
Donnybrook (IRE), soundly beaten in a hot bumper at Ayr, did slightly better in this easier race. (20/1)
3365 Count Karmuski shaped like a stayer as he battled on for pressure in the straight. (14/1)
3747 Homme de Fer made his move on the home turn, although he lacked the pace to land a blow. (10/1)
4156 Buckley House is not lasting home in bumpers, but was not knocked about, and may do better over hurdles. (20/1)

4421 HOUGHTON VAUGHAN OPEN MAIDEN N.H. FLAT RACE (II) (4, 5 & 6-Y.O) (Class H)
5-55 (6-00) **2m** £1,598.50 (£446.00: £215.50)

	Horse / details	Dist	Pos	SP	RR	SF
3907[2]	**Murchan Tyne (IRE)** (EJAlston) **4-10-2**(7) LCummins (hld up: hdwy 6f out: led over 1f out: rdn out)	—	**1**	7/2 [1]	64 f	—
2830[3]	**Squaddie** (JWPayne) **5-11-5** APMcCoy (a.p: led over 2f out: hdd over 1f out: unable qckn)	4	**2**	9/2 [2]	65 f	—
4287[5]	**Trouble Ahead (IRE)** (KCBailey) **6-11-5** SMcNeill (lw: a.p: led 6f out tl over 2f out: one pce)	1	**3**	8/1 [3]	64 f	—
3914[7]	**Salmon Cellar (IRE)** (JMJefferson) **4-11-0** DLeahy (bhd: hdwy 5f out: one pce fnl 2f)	4	**4**	9/1	60 f	—
3914[15]	**Mazzelmo** (ABailey) **4-10-2**(7) TSiddall (bit bkwd: chsd ldrs 13f)	12	**5**	16/1	43 f	—
3170[10]	**Good Time Dancer** (PRWebber) **5-11-0** MrASansome (chsd ldrs: no hdwy fnl 4f)	2	**6**	33/1	41 f	—
	Win The Toss (CREgerton) **5-11-5** NWilliamson (hdwy 5f out: nvr rchd ldrs)	3	**7**	7/2 [1]	43 f	—
3747[8]	**What The Devil** (JPSmith) **4-10-9** WWorthington (in tch: rdn 6f out: no imp)	½	**8**	50/1	38 f	—
4216[12]	**Hack On** (PJHobbs) **5-11-0** GTormey (nvr trbld ldrs)	1½	**9**	10/1	36 f	—
1834[8]	**Trymyply** (HJMWebb) **5-11-2**(3) DFortt (bhd fnl 6f)	1¼	**10**	33/1	40 f	—
3548[13]	**The Gnome (IRE)** (GMMoore) **5-10-12**(7) NHannity (bit bkwd: in tch 10f)	3	**11**	16/1	37 f	—
4150[11]	**No Time To Wait** (WWHaigh) **6-11-5** OPears (led 10f)	5	**12**	33/1	32 f	—
3203[7]	**Pause For Thought** (MrsMReveley) **4-11-0** PNiven (in tch: shkn up 4f out: sn wknd)	3	**13**	8/1 [3]	29 f	—
3808[14]	**Outrageous Affair** (APJames) **5-11-0** CLlewellyn (bit bkwd: a bhd)	2½	**14**	50/1	21 f	—
3808[11]	**Michigan Blue** (WJenks) **5-11-5** TJenks (bit bkwd: a bhd)	13	**15**	50/1	13 f	—
4009[P]	**Desert Way (IRE)** (MissHCKnight) **4-11-0** JFTitley (chsd ldrs 10f: bhd whn p.u 2f out)		**P**	11/1	—	—
				(SP 138.7%)		**16 Rn**

3m 40.8 CSF £18.93 TOTE £3.90: £1.70 £1.70 £3.70 (£4.10) Trio £12.20 OWNER Harrington-Worrall Racing (PRESTON) BRED Mrs Chris Harrington
WEIGHT FOR AGE 4yo-5lb
3907 Murchan Tyne (IRE) confirmed the promise of her debut with a hard-fought success. (7/2)
2830 Squaddie, a moderate mover, off for three months since his debut, didn't go down without a fight. (9/2: 3/1-5/1)
4287 Trouble Ahead (IRE) has been given time to grow into his considerable frame, and gives the impression that connections may not regret it, as he again showed promise. (8/1)
3716 Salmon Cellar (IRE) didn't seem suited by forcing the pace last time and, after delaying the start by throwing and injuring his intended pilot in the parade ring, ran a much better race. (9/1)
3808 Mazzelmo, another who disappointed in the Carlisle bumper at the end of last month, did much better back on an easier track. (16/1)
Good Time Dancer moved down well, and this effort is quite an improvement. (33/1)
Win The Toss (7/2: op 6/1)
No Time To Wait, whose damsire was a front runner, looks far too keen to get the trip in bumpers, but might be harder to peg back over hurdles if he jumps. (33/1)
3574 Desert Way (IRE) (11/1: 7/1-12/1)

T/Plpt: £71.30 (95.61 Tckts). T/Qdpt: £15.70 (17.88 Tckts) Dk

3426-WARWICK (L-H) (Good to firm, Firm patches)
Saturday May 3rd
WEATHER: warm

4422 WILLOUGHBY DE BROKE CHALLENGE TROPHY NOVICES' HUNTERS' CHASE (5-Y.O+) (Class H)
5-45 (5-45) **2m 4f 110y (17 fncs)** £1,178.80 (£288.20) GOING minus 0.59 sec per fur (F)

	Horse / details	Dist	Pos	SP	RR	SF
4228[W]	**Lord Kilton** (MrsDCowley) **9-11-7**(7) MrMCowley (lw: plld hrd: chsd ldr: mstke 3rd: lost pl 10th: rallied appr last: str run to ld flat: eased last strides)	—	**1**		64?	—
3852[5]	**Tom Furze** (MrsDBuckett) **10-11-12**(7) MrMBatters (led: clr 10th: eased fr 2 out: hdd flat: r.o wl)	nk	**2**		69+	—
						2 Rn

5m 37.0 (33.00) TOTE £3.80 OWNER Mrs D. Cowley (LEAMINGTON SPA) BRED Mrs D. B. Cowley
STEWARDS' ENQUIRY Batters susp. 12-18, 21-24, 26-28/5/97 (failing to ride out for first pl).
IN-FOCUS: **There were no SPs returned on this race.**
Lord Kilton is an extremely bad performer, and was an exceptionally lucky winner, but full marks must go to his jockey, who saw that the red-hot favourite was taking things far too easily in the straight, and seized the opportunity. Galvanising his mount into action from the second last, the combination came with a whirlwind rattle to seize the advantage on the run-in.
3852 Tom Furze should have won this by a distance, and the blame lies entirely with his jockey. 1/16 at the last show, although no SPs were returned due to not one single straight bet being laid with the bookmakers on him because of his short price, he bowled along in front and was a good thirty lengths clear turning for home. However, his jockey then decided he had done enough, and let his mount coast in. The combination was still ten lengths to the good jumping the final fence, and Mr Batters was surprised to say the least when Lord Kilton rushed by on the run-in. Panicking, and bustling his mount along, the combination failed by only a neck to get back up. This was a dreadful piece of riding from Batters, and the Stewards threw the book at him - imposing the maximum sentence of 14 days for failing to ride out.

4423 BARFORD (S) HURDLE (4, 5 & 6-Y.O) (Class G)

6-15 (6-15) **2m (8 hdls)** £1,642.50 (£455.00: £217.50) GOING minus 0.59 sec per fur (F)

Form	Horse / details	Dist	Pos	SP	RR	SF
4089^{9}	**Fenian Court (IRE) (72)** (PDEvans) **6-10-9** MAFitzgerald (lw: hld up: jnd ldr appr 2 out: hrd rdn appr last: led nr fin)	—	1	3/1 ^{2}	49	15
4295^{2}	**Summer Villa (72)** (KGWingrove) **5-10-9b** WMarston (a.p: led appr 2 out: hrd rdn appr last: hdd nr fin)	s.h	2	11/4 ^{1}	49	15
	Northern Grey (DrJDScargill) **5-11-0** NMann (hdwy appr 2 out: 4th & no ch whn blnd 2 out)	8	3	12/1	46	12
4223^{6}	**Never so Blue (IRE) (82)** (PBradley) **6-11-0b**[1] RDunwoody (led to 3rd: led appr 4th tl appr 2 out: sn wknd)	8	4	100/30 ^{3}	38	4
3284^{17}	**Reno's Treasure (USA)** (JohnHarris) **4-10-4** JSupple (4th whn slipped bnd after 3rd: nt rcvr)	28	5	50/1	5	—
	Frans Lad (BPJBaugh) **5-11-0** GaryLyons (bhd fr 3 out)	2	6	50/1	8	—
4299^{8}	**Teejay's Future (IRE)** (OBrennan) **6-10-9** MBrennan (a bhd: t.o whn p.u bef 2 out)		P	6/1	—	—
3590^{9}	**Ndaba** (MissKMGeorge) **6-11-0** JRKavanagh (plld hrd: hdwy 2nd: led 3rd tl appr 4th: sn wknd: t.o whn p.u bef 2 out)		P	20/1	—	—
	Minnisam (AGHobbs) **4-10-9** RGreene (bhd fr 4th: t.o whn p.u bef 3 out)		P	6/1	—	—
4304^{R}	**T'Niel** (GFierro) **6-10-6**(7)ow4 SLycett (ref to r: t.n.p)		R	66/1	—	—
	Highland Spin (KGWingrove) **6-10-7**(7) MrSDurack (bhd tl s.u bnd after 3rd)		S	20/1	—	—

3m 41.7 (-0.30) CSF £11.33 TOTE £6.90: £1.70 £1.10 £2.70 (£8.90) Trio £55.40 OWNER Mr John Pugh (WELSHPOOL) BRED Patrick Hughes (SP 125.9%) **11 Rn**

WEIGHT FOR AGE 4yo-5lb

No bid

OFFICIAL EXPLANATION **Minnisam: the jockey felt it prudent to pull him up as he did not feel right, and had suffered leg problems on the Flat.**

4089 Fenian Court (IRE) at long-last broke her duck over hurdles at the twenty-first attempt. Joining issue appearing to be travelling well, turning into the straight, she came under strong pressure going to the last and, in a driving finish, just managed to get up in the closing stages. (3/1: op 5/1)

4295 Summer Villa has certainly improved with the blinkers, and ran another sound race. Gaining a narrow advantage approaching the second-last, she shared a tremendous battle-royal with the winner, and lost out by only a whisker. (11/4)

Northern Grey, making his hurdling debut in this lowly event, was having his first run in over four months. Waited with well off the pace, he made some progress turning for home, but had no chance of getting near the principals when making a bad error two from home. (12/1: op 8/1)

3940 Never so Blue (IRE), tried with blinkers, made the vast majority of the running, until dropping away approaching the second last. (100/30)

Minnisam (6/1: op 4/1)

4424 VETERANS CHASE (9-Y-O+) (Class D)

6-45 (6-45) **3m 2f (20 fncs)** £4,314.00 (£1,204.00: £582.00) GOING minus 0.59 sec per fur (F)

Form	Horse / details	Dist	Pos	SP	RR	SF
4167^{3}	**Copper Mine (117)** (OSherwood) **11-11-2** JOsborne (lw: mde all: clr 3 out: rdn out)	—	1	Evens ^{1}	120	4
4270^{3}	**Harristown Lady (103)** (GBBalding) **10-10-7b** BClifford (lw: hld up: chsd wnr fr 7th: rdn 3 out: r.o)	1½	2	5/2 ^{2}	110	—
4309^{12}	**Vicar of Bray (87)** (LWells) **10-11-2v** MRichards (lw: j.slowly 3rd: bhd fr 5th: t.o fr 14th: tried to ref 3 out)	dist	3	33/1 ^{3}	—	—
4167^{4}	**Musthaveaswig (119)** (DNicholson) **11-11-7**(3) MrRThornton (lw: chsd wnr tl j.slowly 7th: p.u bef 8th: lame)		P	5/2 ^{2}	—	—

6m 32.0 (7.00) CSF £3.69 TOTE £1.80 (£2.10) OWNER Mr J. Dougall (UPPER LAMBOURN) BRED Michael Purcell (SP 110.1%) **4 Rn**

4167 Copper Mine goes well on this ground, and was able to dictate matters. Forging clear three from home, he did not look over-enthusiastic in the straight, but ridden along, managed to keep the runner-up at bay. (Evens)

4270 Harristown Lady, in second place from the seventh, got rather outpaced three from home, but to her credit, she stuck on well over the last two fences, if unable to master the winner. (5/2)

4425 MINTEX H'CAP HURDLE (0-135) (4-Y.O+) (Class C)

7-15 (7-15) **2m (8 hdls)** £3,492.50 (£1,040.00: £495.00: £222.50) GOING minus 0.59 sec per fur (F)

Form	Horse / details	Dist	Pos	SP	RR	SF
4246*	**Amlah (USA) (115)** (PJHobbs) **5-11-3** BPowell (a.p: led 4th to last: hrd rdn & carried lft flat: led nr fin)	—	1	11/8 ^{1}	91	52
4229*	**Barford Sovereign (116)** (JRFanshawe) **5-11-4** MAFitzgerald (swtg: a.p: chsd wnr fr 3 out: hrd rdn appr last: led last: hung lft flat: hdd nr fin)	½	2	2/1 ^{2}	92	53
3681^{4}	**Josifina (110)** (AGFoster) **6-10-12** AThornton (lw: hld up: rdn 4th: wknd 3 out)	14	3	14/1	72	33
4307^{3}	**Tejano Gold (USA) (122)** (PBradley) **7-11-10** RDunwoody (lw: led to 4th: wknd 3 out)	3½	4	11/4 ^{3}	80	41

3m 35.3 (-6.70) CSF £4.19 TOTE £2.10 (£1.90) OWNER In Touch Racing Club (MINEHEAD) BRED Barbara Hunter (SP 108.8%) **4 Rn**

4246* Amlah (USA) goes well on this surface, and followed up his recent Perth victory, although he had far more of a fight on his hands this time. In front from halfway, he had a tremendous battle-royal with the runner-up in the straight but, despite being carried left by that rival on the run-in, managed to get up near the line. (11/8)

4229* Barford Sovereign has been a model of consistency this season, and ran another first-class race. Engaged in a tremendous ding-dong battle with the winner in the straight, she hung left under pressure on the run-in, and was worried out of it near the line. (2/1)

1677 Josifina has lost her way this season, after an attempt at chasing, and a return to hurdles does not seem to have helped. (14/1: op 8/1)

4307 Tejano Gold (USA) did not have things in his favour - he was 10lb higher than he has ever won off before, and is better-suited by some cut in the ground - and was a spent force three from home. (11/4)

4426 ALDERMINSTER NOVICES' CHASE (5-Y.O+) (Class E)

7-45 (7-45) **2m 4f 110y (17 fncs)** £2,900.00 (£875.00: £425.00: £200.00) GOING minus 0.59 sec per fur (F)

Form	Horse / details	Dist	Pos	SP	RR	SF
4286^{3}	**Walls Court (71)** (JJBirkett) **10-11-2** LO'Hara (lw: chsd ldr: led & mstke 4 out: all out)	—	1	5/1 ^{3}	81	1
4237*	**Plan-A (IRE)** (RHAlner) **7-11-9** PHolley (hld up: 3rd whn mstkes 13th & 4 out: chsd wnr after 3 out: j.slowly 2 out: blnd bdly last: r.o wl)	s.h	2	10/11 ^{1}	88	8
4272^{P}	**Ryton Run (81)** (MrsSMOdell) **12-11-6** BFenton (lw: led to 4 out: wknd appr 2 out: t.o)	dist	3	11/1	—	—
3968^{P}	**Chapilliere (FR) (60)** (TThomsonJones) **7-11-2** GUpton (swtg: bhd fr 3rd: mstke 6th: t.o fr 11th)	dist	4	7/2 ^{2}	—	—
	Cotswold Castle (JGMO'Shea) **11-10-13**(3) MichaelBrennan (a bhd: j.slowly 2nd & 3rd: t.o whn p.u bef 11th)		P	8/1	—	—

5m 10.7 (6.70) CSF £9.73 TOTE £3.90: £2.00 £1.50 (£2.50) OWNER The Claret and Blue Partnership (WORKINGTON) BRED Noel Henley (SP 110.7%) **5 Rn**

STEWARDS' ENQUIRY Holley susp. 12-17/5/97 (improper riding - Rule H9, using whip with excessive force).

4286 Walls Court, who has shown nothing so far this season, grabbed the lead after making a mistake four from home. He was all out on the run-in, and found the line only just saving him. (5/1)
4237* Plan-A (IRE) has shown in point-to-points this season that he has plenty of ability, but is not one to trust - he ran out three times on the trot - and that was once again demonstrated here. Having jumped adequately for much of the race, his fencing went to pieces at the crucial part of the contest, and he looked none-too-keen about jumping the second last, but did manage to clamber over it. However, he made an almighty blunder at the last, and his jockey did wonders to stay in the plate. Giving his mount eight very hard reminders, the gelding sprouted wings, and would have prevailed in another stride. The vet reported that Plan-A had been injured as a result of his jockey's use of the whip, and Holley was given a six-day suspension for excessive force. (10/11: 4/6-6/5)
3833 Ryton Run (11/1: 6/1-12/1)

4427 WASPERTON HILL NOVICES' H'CAP HURDLE (0-100) (4-Y.O+) (Class E)
8-15 (8-15) **2m 4f 110y (11 hdls)** £2,731.50 (£759.00: £364.50) GOING minus 0.59 sec per fur (F)

			SP	RR	SF
3817[10] **Loch Na Keal (75)** (CPMorlock) **5-11-1** CLlewellyn (lw: hld up: led appr 2 out: clr appr last: r.o wl)	—	1	5/2[1]	60	—
3133[4] **Arctic Triumph (78)** (MBradstock) **6-11-4b[1]** PHolley (plld hrd: led 3rd: clr 4th: hdd appr 2 out: unable qckn)	4	2	7/1	60	—
4231* **Nautical Jewel (82)** (KGWingrove) **5-11-1**(7) JPower (nvr nr to chal)	5	3	4/1[3]	60	—
4309[10] **Brookhampton Lane (IRE) (70)** (MrsAJBowlby) **6-10-10b[1]** BPowell (plld hrd: led to 3rd: wknd appr 2 out: 3rd & no ch whn fell last)		F	7/2[2]	—	—
3983[14] **Dark Phoenix (IRE) (78)** (OBrennan) **7-11-4v** MBrennan (a bhd: t.o fr 7th: p.u bef last)		P	9/1	—	—
3796[6] **Cool Harry (USA) (65)** (HEHaynes) **6-9-12**(7) MrSDurack (bhd fr 7th: jinked & uns rdr flat)		U	4/1[3]	—	—
			(SP 113.3%)		**6 Rn**

4m 55.1 (8.10) CSF £17.86 TOTE £2.70: £1.60 £3.20 (£17.10) OWNER Mr S. Kimber (WANTAGE) BRED M. Holley
3621 Loch Na Keal, who may well have found his Newbury race coming too soon after her good second at Huntingdon ten days earlier, has had a seven-week break since then. Moving to the front approaching the second-last, she soon asserted for a cosy success. (5/2)
3133 Arctic Triumph ran his best race so far this season. Taking a very keen hold, he soon forced his way to the front, and set a tremendously fast pace. Collared approaching the second-last, he still managed to hold on to second prize. (7/1: op 4/1)
4231* Nautical Jewel had more on his plate this time, and was tackling a longer trip. No doubt hoping the tearaway leaders would come back to him, as he was held up well off the pace, he did close in the last half-mile, but never threatened to get near the principals. (4/1: op 5/2)
3621 Dark Phoenix (IRE) (9/1: op 5/1)
Cool Harry (USA) (4/1: op 8/1)

T/Plpt: £478.60 (14.76 Tckts). T/Qdpt: £13.70 (49.74 Tckts) AK

4328-EXETER (R-H) (Good, Good to firm patches)
Monday May 5th
Water jump omitted each chase
WEATHER: showers

4428 STEVE BROWNING GOOD ENGLISH NOVICES' HURDLE (4-Y.O+ F & M) (Class E)
2-00 (2-00) **2m 2f (8 hdls)** £2,218.60 (£624.60: £305.80) GOING minus 0.33 sec per fur (GF)

			SP	RR	SF
3847[3] **Disallowed (IRE) (108)** (MissHCKnight) **4-11-3** APMcCoy (lw: mde all: clr 3rd: unchal: eased flat)	—	1	1/12[1]	82+	1
4382[4] **Rachel Louise** (TKeddy) **5-10-10** DGallagher (j.slowly 1st: hdwy to chse wnr appr 3rd: rdn after 6th: in tch appr 2 out: sn outpcd)	10	2	10/1[2]	61	—
4175[6] **Up the Tempo (IRE) (59)** (PaddyFarrell) **8-10-10** TDascombe (chsd wnr tl appr 3rd: bhd 6th: rdn out to go 3rd last)	5	3	33/1[3]	57?	—
Ellen Gail (IRE) (RHAlner) **5-10-10** JFrost (bkwd: bhd to 6th: wknd 2 out)	7	4	10/1[2]	50?	—
			(SP 113.4%)		**4 Rn**

4m 19.8 (9.80) CSF £2.13 TOTE £1.20: (£1.60) OWNER Million In Mind Partnership (6) (WANTAGE) BRED Dermot Ryan and Partners
WEIGHT FOR AGE 4yo-5lb
3847 Disallowed (IRE), looked to have a simple task before the race, and so it proved. In front from the start, this proved to be no more than an exercise canter. (1/12: op 1/4)
4382 Rachel Louise tried hard to make a race of it with the winner when closing up approaching two out, before being left for dead. She looks as if she is going to need much further than this. (10/1: op 4/1)
Ellen Gail (IRE) (10/1: op 6/1)

4429 GEMINI RADIO H'CAP CHASE (0-115) (5-Y.O+) (Class E)
2-30 (2-30) **2m 7f 110y (16 fncs)** £2,881.70 (£811.20: £397.10) GOING minus 0.33 sec per fur (GF)

			SP	RR	SF
4171[3] **Trust Deed (USA) (82)** (SGKnight) **9-10-1b**(5) DSalter (bhd: hdwy 12th: r.o under str pressure to get up fnl strides)	—	1	10/1	91	24
4174[3] **Mr Playfull (91)** (RGFrost) **7-11-1** JFrost (mstke 4th: pckd 6th: mstke 9th: r.o after 12th: chsd ldr next: led 14th tl rdn & hdd fnl strides)	1¼	2	9/4[2]	99	32
4251* **Decyborg (FR) (100)** (MCPipe) **6-11-10** APMcCoy (lw: led to 14th: ev ch 2 out: wknd appr last)	12	3	8/11[1]	100	33
4331* **Henley Regatta (100)** (PRRodford) **9-11-10** 6x SBurrough (lw: hld up bhd: hdwy to chse ldr 9th: wknd 14th)	5	4	6/1[3]	97	30
3622[4] **Coasting (76)** (HEHaynes) **11-10-0** LHarvey (in tch to 7th: wl bhd next: t.o)	dist	5	33/1	—	—
3892[P] **Bravo Star (USA) (77)** (PaddyFarrell) **12-10-1**ow1 TDascombe (in tch tl rdn & wknd fr 8th: t.o)	dist	6	33/1	—	—
			(SP 117.9%)		**6 Rn**

5m 49.4 (2.40) CSF £32.37 TOTE £6.50: £2.50 £1.40 (£10.70) OWNER Mr Malcolm Enticott (TAUNTON) BRED Ballymacoll Stud Farm Inc
LONG HANDICAP Coasting 9-10
OFFICIAL EXPLANATION **Trust Deed (USA): regarding the improved form, trainer reported that the gelding has a mind of his own.**
4171 Trust Deed (USA), held up in the early stages, made headway after jumping six out. He came to challenge on the run-in and, with his jockey throwing everything at him, wore down Mr Playfull in the closing stages to record his sixth course win. (10/1: 8/1-12/1)
4174 Mr Playfull, whose jumping was far from fluent, chased the leader from five out until taking over at the next. He tried to hold on but found the winner too determined in the final strides. (9/4)
4251* Decyborg (FR) made all the running until being headed jumping the fourth last, and remained in touch until crying enough approaching the final fence. His two previous wins in this country were both extremely weak three-runner affairs. (8/11: evens-11/10)

4331* Henley Regatta, held up in the early stages, moved closer jumping the ninth, but he had no more to give after jumping four out. This was his first attempt at a trip as far as this, and he appeared not to stay. (6/1: 4/1-13/2)

4430 AWARD WINNING GEMINI NEWS H'CAP HURDLE (0-115) (4-Y.O+) (Class E)

3-00 (3-01) **2m 2f (8 hdls)** £2,361.50 (£664.00: £324.50) GOING minus 0.33 sec per fur (GF)

				SP	RR	SF
4289*	**Ath Cheannaithe (FR) (86)** (JNeville) **5-10-0v** TDascombe (led: sn clr: styd on wl u.p flat)	—	1	6/4[2]	73+	—
4240[3]	**Blair Castle (IRE) (114)** (GBBalding) **6-12-0** APMcCoy (lw: chsd wnr 3rd: ev ch 2 out tl no ex flat)	4	2	5/4[1]	97	23
4384[6]	**Gabish (86)** (BScriven) **12-10-0** LHarvey (chsd wnr to 3rd: bhd next: sn t.o)	dist	3	50/1	—	—
3199[6]	**Robert's Toy (IRE) (113)** (MCPipe) **6-11-6**(7) BMoore (bhd: in tch whn fell 2nd)		F	3/1[3]	—	—
				(SP 111.4%)	**4 Rn**	

4m 16.3 (6.30) CSF £3.67 TOTE £2.20: (£1.80) OWNER Mr J. Neville (NEWPORT, GWENT) BRED Russlson and Campbell Stud

LONG HANDICAP Gabish 7-6

4289* Ath Cheannaithe (FR) again made all the running, and had enough in reserve to hold off the runner-up over the final two flights. (6/4)

4240 Blair Castle (IRE), dropped in class, chased the winner from the third, but found the concession of 28lb to an in-form rival beyond him. (5/4: evens-6/4)

4431 TOP RATING GEMINI FM NOVICES' H'CAP CHASE (0-100) (5-Y.O+) (Class E)

3-30 (3-35) **2m 3f 110y (14 fncs)** £2,544.00 (£771.00: £377.00: £180.00) GOING minus 0.33 sec per fur (GF)

				SP	RR	SF
3617[P]	**Wixoe Wonder (IRE) (77)** (MBradstock) **7-11-10b[1]** APMcCoy (lw: mde all: mstke 8th: unchal)	—	1	9/4[1]	90	16
4171[2]	**Jonjas Chudleigh (70)** (RGFrost) **10-11-3** JFrost (wl bhd 7th: styd on: mstke 2 out: chsd wnr last: no imp)	16	2	9/4[1]	70	—
2926[8]	**Wot No Gin (65)** (AJWilson) **8-10-12** LHarvey (chsd wnr 4th tl mstke 10th: wknd next)	13	3	3/1[2]	54	—
2816[F]	**Rolled Gold (64)** (MissVenetiaWilliams) **8-10-11** JFTitley (hdwy to chse wnr 10th: not on terms: wkng & j.lft 11th & 12th)	7	4	4/1[3]	48	—
4291[5]	**Mistress Rosie (71)** (MHill) **10-11-4** DGallagher (chsd wnr to 4th: j.lft next: wknd fr 6th: t.o: p.u bef 11th)		P	7/1	—	—
				(SP 119.0%)	**5 Rn**	

4m 53.9 (8.90) CSF £7.93 TOTE £3.20: £1.60 £1.20 (£3.10) OWNER Mr P. J. D. Pottinger (WANTAGE) BRED Egmont Stud

3132 Wixoe Wonder (IRE), whose previous run was at the Cheltenham Festival, found this opposition rather more to his liking. Making all, he was never in any danger apart from a mistake at the eighth fence. The fact that he was able to gain his first ever win so easily, and give weight away in the process, speaks volumes about the quality of the opposition. (9/4)

4171 Jonjas Chudleigh, well behind at halfway, he stayed on into second place without ever looking likely to threaten the winner. His only previous win came in Ireland six years ago. (9/4)

1771 Wot No Gin chased the winner from the fourth until a mistake six out finished him off. (3/1: op 2/1)

4142 Mistress Rosie (7/1: 5/1-8/1)

4432 WEST OF ENGLAND OPEN HUNTERS' CHASE (6-Y.O+) (Class H)

4-00 (4-01) **2m 7f 110y (16 fncs)** £1,138.00 (£318.00: £154.00) GOING minus 0.33 sec per fur (GF)

				SP	RR	SF
4051[F]	**Chilipour** (VictorDartnall) **10-10-13**(7) MrLBaker (lw: a in tch: mstke 5th: hdwy to ld 10th: rdn out to hold on flat)	—	1	4/6[1]	103	5
	Mighty Falcon (MissEmmaTory) **12-11-1**(7)ow2 MissETory (chsd ldrs tl led 9th: hdd next: lost pl 12th: rallied to chse wnr 14th: ev ch 2 out tl rdn & no ex nr fin)	nk	2	7/1[3]	105	5
4051[3]	**Abbotsham** (OJCarter) **12-10-13**(7) MrEJames (hld up & bhd: hdwy 8th: chsd wnr 12th tl wknd 14th)	8	3	11/2[2]	97	—
	Anjubi (MissMBragg) **12-10-13**(7) MrRWidger (prom tl lost pl 12th: rallied to chse ldrs last: rdn & wknd flat)	2½	4	12/1	96	—
3721[3]	**Spitfire Jubilee** (MrsLASyckelmoore) **11-10-13**(7) MrRNuttall (led to 9th: in tch tl wknd 13th)	12	5	8/1	88	—
	Indian Knight (CAGreen) **12-11-4**(7)ow5 MrMGMiller (chsd ldr to 9th: lost pl: chsd wnr 11th: ev ch tl wknd 14th)	dist	6	16/1	—	—
	Try it Alone (MBiddick) **15-10-13**(7) MrGShenkin (in tch tl wknd 8th: t.o & p.u bef 13th)		P	33/1	—	—
	Killelan Lad (MissKDiMarte) **15-10-13**(7) MissKDiMarte (a bhd: t.o & p.u bef 13th)		P	50/1	—	—
				(SP 117.5%)	**8 Rn**	

6m 0.6 (13.60) CSF £6.07 TOTE £1.80: £1.40 £1.10 £1.80 (£5.00) OWNER Mr Nick Viney (BARNSTAPLE) BRED Airlie Stud

Chilipour, who won this race last year, did not have things all his own way here. Always close up, he led soon after halfway and made the best of his way home. However, he faced a strong challenge from the runner-up over the final two fences, and was all-out to hold on in the closing stages. (4/6)

Mighty Falcon was in touch early on, and went into the lead at halfway. Headed soon after, he seemed to lose his place and dropped out of contention. However, he came back to chase the favourite from four out, and mounted a strong challenge jumping the second last. Try as he might, he just found his rival too strong in the closing stages, but this was a fine effort nonetheless. (7/1)

4051 Abbotsham, behind in the early stages, he made headway to get into contention soon after halfway. However, he was soon left behind after jumping four out. (11/2: 4/1-6/1)

Anjubi seemed to be out of contention when losing his prominent position after jumping the twelfth. He worked his way back into a challenging position approaching the last, but had shot his bolt on reaching the run-in. (12/1)

3721 Spitfire Jubilee, in front to halfway, he stayed in touch until crying enough after five out. (8/1)

4433 KEVIN KANE MAIDEN OPEN N.H. FLAT RACE (4, 5 & 6-Y.O) (Class H)

4-30 (4-34) **2m 2f** £1,413.00 (£393.00: £189.00)

				SP	RR	SF
	Bramshaw Wood (IRE) (RHAlner) **5-11-5** JFrost (hld up bhd: hdwy 7f out: styd on u.p to ld fnl strides)	—	1	20/1	51 f	—
	Storm Forecast (IRE) (MissHCKnight) **5-11-5** JFTitley (hld up: hdwy ½-wy: led 4f out to 3f out: rallied to ld ins fnl f: hdd last stride)	nk	2	11/8[1]	51 f	—
	My Micky (KBishop) **6-11-5** LHarvey (a in tch: chsd ldr 4f out tl wknd fnl f)	7	3	20/1	45 f	—
4143[3]	**Brother Nero (NZ)** (AGHobbs) **5-11-5** RGreene (led 6f: prom tl wknd 2f out)	¾	4	20/1	44 f	—
	Hill's Electric (IRE) (TKeddy) **5-11-5** DGallagher (w.r.s sn prom: led 3f out: hdd & wknd ins fnl f)	4	5	20/1	40 f	—
3895[8]	**Jim's Quest** (PJHobbs) **4-11-0** APMcCoy (bhd: r.o strly 7f out: ev ch fnl f: wknd qckly)	1¾	6	5/1[2]	39 f	—
	Cool Norman (NZ) (BdeHaan) **5-10-12**(7) MBerry (bit bkwd: in tch tl wknd 7f out)	1	7	7/1	38 f	—
	Ardent Step (IRE) (PFNicholls) **4-10-4**(5) OBurrows (bit bkwd: a bhd)	18	8	11/2[3]	17 f	—
	Dungannon Lad (WGMTurner) **6-10-12**(7) NWillmington (bit bkwd: chsd ldr tl led after 6f: hdd 4f out: sn wknd)	2½	9	20/1	20 f	—
4143[4]	**See Prosperity** (MissSWaterman) **5-10-12**(7) LCummins (in tch tl wknd ½-wy)	23	10	50/1	—	—

				SP	RR	SF
	Buddy Diver (CLPopham) **4-11-0** TDascombe (bit bkwd: in tch: wknd ½-wy: sn t.o)	dist	**11**	33/1	—	—
	In Harmony (BRMillman) **5-10-9**(5) DSalter (bit bkwd: in tch to ½-wy: sn t.o)	2	**12**	14/1	—	—

(SP 122.0%) **12 Rn**

4m 16.3 CSF £41.61 TOTE £22.00: £4.30 £1.20 £6.40 (£15.50) OWNER Mrs U. Wainwright (BLANDFORD) BRED John Kenneally
WEIGHT FOR AGE 4yo-5lb

Bramshaw Wood (IRE), held up in the early stages, he made progress soon after halfway, and stayed dourly to wear down the favourite in the shadow of the post. He obviously has a future, and looks as if he will appreciate a test of stamina. (20/1)
Storm Forecast (IRE) did everything right, but was just denied in the closing stages. He will win races. (11/8: evens-4/5)
My Micky, who had been off the course for well over a year, was unable to keep tabs on the first two in the closing stages. (20/1)
4143 Brother Nero (NZ) had failed to complete in three point-to-points before being beaten out of sight in a Newton Abbot bumper, ran better here, if unable to trouble the principals in the last two furlongs. (20/1)
Hill's Electric (IRE), after leading three furlongs out, did not seem to quite get home. He will have benefited from the run, and a similar race on an easier track over the minimum trip may prove within his capabilities. (20/1)
2572 Jim's Quest again did not quite get home, and may benefit from being sent over hurdles on a sharp track. (5/1)
Ardent Step (IRE) (11/2: 4/1-6/1)

T/Plpt: £80.80 (22.59 Tckts). T/Qdpt: £6.00 (14.71 Tckts) T.

4250-FONTWELL (Fig. 8) (Good to firm)
Monday May 5th
WEATHER: fair

4434 BRACKLESHAM NOVICES' HURDLE (4-Y.O) (Class E)
2-00 (2-01) **2m 2f 110y (9 hdls)** £2,302.70 (£637.20: £304.10) GOING minus 0.10 sec per fur (G)

				SP	RR	SF
3685*	**Ela Agapi Mou (USA) (117)** (GLMoore) **4-11-10** PHolley (lw: chsd ldrs: led last: drvn out)	—	**1**	6/4 1	84	31
4169 2	**Sterling Fellow (78)** (DLWilliams) **4-10-5**(7) MrSDurack (lw: rdn & hdwy 2 out: nt qckn flat)	2½	**2**	20/1	70?	17
4170 2	**Anna Soleil (IRE) (108)** (OSherwood) **4-11-4** JOsborne (a.p: lft in ld 3 out: hdd & wknd last)	11	**3**	11/4 2	66	13
3953 4	**Bigwig (IRE) (68)** (GLMoore) **4-10-5v**(7) MBatchelor (nvr gng wl: wl bhd fr 6th)	10	**4**	40/1	52	—
2889 P	**Heart** (MissHCKnight) **4-10-7** JCulloty (prom to 6th: wknd 7th)	6	**5**	5/1	42	—
4242 2	**Name of Our Father (USA) (99)** (PBowen) **4-11-4** RJohnson (lw: led: 1l clr whn fell 3 out)		**F**	7/2 3	—	—

(SP 112.8%) **6 Rn**

4m 26.2 (8.20) CSF £25.38 TOTE £2.70: £1.70 £3.90 (£14.70) OWNER Ballard (1834) Ltd (BRIGHTON) BRED Patrick Eddery Ltd and Midcounts Ltd

3685* Ela Agapi Mou (USA) was not going that well entering the last circuit but he kept staying on and gamely conceded the weight in the end. (6/4)
4169 Sterling Fellow had twenty lengths to make up at the fourth last and may have won had he not let the leaders get away from him at that point. (20/1)
4170 Anna Soleil (IRE), presented with a winning chance when the leader fell three out, was unable to take advantage. (11/4: 9/4-7/2)
2889 Heart (5/1: op 9/4)
4242 Name of Our Father (USA) took a heavy fall but is well up to winning a similar event if he suffers no ill effects. (7/2)

4435 BEAUMONT CHALLENGE CUP NOVICES' CHASE (6-Y.O+) (Class E)
2-30 (2-30) **3m 2f 110y (22 fncs)** £3,666.20 (£893.80) GOING minus 0.10 sec per fur (G)

				SP	RR	SF
4251 2	**Keep it Zipped (IRE) (93)** (OSherwood) **7-11-5b** JOsborne (mde all: easily)	—	**1**	8/11 1	94+	26
4327 2	**Master Crusader** (DLWilliams) **11-10-5**(7) MrSDurack (lw: chsd wnr fr 11th: wknd 3 out)	10	**2**	3/1 2	81	13
	Page Royale (FR) (CJMann) **7-11-11**(3) JMagee (chsd wnr to 11th: wknd 14th: t.o whn p.u after 18th)		**P**	7/2 3	—	—
658 4	**Hizal (72)** (HJManners) **8-10-12**(7) ADowling (nt j.w: t.o tl p.u bef 13th)		**P**	16/1	—	—

(SP 111.0%) **4 Rn**

6m 53.1 (13.10) CSF £3.21 TOTE £1.50: (£1.70) OWNER Mrs Luisa Stewart-Brown (UPPER LAMBOURN) BRED J. Fogarty

4251 Keep it Zipped (IRE) does not always look that willing but his sole remaining rival was unable to seriously test him from the third last. (8/11)
4327 Master Crusader has now run two respectable races since arriving from Ireland. (3/1)
Page Royale (FR), a French import, stopped quickly after two circuits. (7/2)

4436 FITTLEWORTH CLAIMING HURDLE (4-Y.O+) (Class F)
3-00 (3-01) **2m 2f 110y (9 hdls)** £2,057.50 (£570.00: £272.50) GOING minus 0.10 sec per fur (G)

				SP	RR	SF
4340 U	**Jenzsoph (IRE) (105)** (PJHobbs) **6-11-0b1** GTormey (mde all: unchal)	—	**1**	9/4 2	81	38
4340 2	**Peter Monamy (103)** (MCPipe) **5-12-0b** NWilliamson (chsd wnr: mstke 3 out: wknd 2 out)	19	**2**	8/13 1	79	36
3723 9	**The Grey Texan (60)** (RRowe) **8-10-13** DO'Sullivan (wl bhd tl hdwy 3 out: nvr nr to chal)	3	**3**	33/1	61	18
3896 4	**Olivipet (55)** (FGray) **8-9-12**(7) MClinton (t.o fr 6th)	dist	**4**	25/1	—	—
4224 7	**Green King** (APJones) **5-11-2** SMcNeill (lw: mod 3rd whn ran v. wd bnd appr 6th: nt rcvr: t.o)	dist	**5**	9/1 3	—	—
	Friar's Oak (PButler) **5-11-2** JCulloty (mstke 3rd: t.o 5th: p.u bef 2 out)		**P**	25/1	—	—

(SP 113.3%) **6 Rn**

4m 22.0 (4.00) CSF £3.80 TOTE £3.30: £1.50 £1.30 (£2.00) OWNER Mr A. Stevens (MINEHEAD) BRED A. T. Robinson

4340 Jenzsoph (IRE), wearing blinkers for the first time, was not let down by her jumping on this occasion and, in this mood, a repeat could be on the cards. (9/4)
4340 Peter Monamy ran into an opponent in top form, and a mistake three out probably made little difference. (8/13)
The Grey Texan, having his first run for his new stable, has shown little form to date but, on this evidence, is capable of better. (33/1)
Green King was eased after trying to run out entering the final circuit. (9/1)

4437 MADEHURST MAIDEN CHASE (5-Y.O+) (Class F)
3-30 (3-32) **2m 2f (15 fncs)** £2,635.50 (£728.00: £346.50) GOING minus 0.10 sec per fur (G)

				SP	RR	SF
4255 7	**Full of Tricks (60)** (JJBridger) **9-11-2**(3) LAspell (led to 2nd: led 7th: rdn 2 out: r.o)	—	**1**	10/1 3	58	—
4272 P	**Eau So Sloe (60)** (JRPoulton) **6-11-2**(3) JMagee (chsd wnr fr 8th: ev ch 12th: one pce fr 2 out)	5	**2**	20/1	54	—
4233 P	**Swift Pokey** (DLWilliams) **7-10-12**(7) MrSDurack (led 2nd to 7th: wknd 9th: 3rd & no ch whn ref 2 out: cont)	dist	**3**	50/1	—	—

				SP	RR	SF
4092[2]	**Snowy Petrel (IRE) (84)** (KCBailey) **5-10-13b** SMcNeill (mstke & uns rdr 1st)		U	1/3 [1]	—	—
4226[8]	***Another Comedy (60)*** (RLee) **7-11-5** RJohnson (Withdrawn not under Starter's orders: veterinary advice)		W	4/1 [2]	—	—
				(SP 110.8%)	**4 Rn**	

4m 44.5 (22.50) CSF £49.60 TOTE £6.90: £2.90 (£17.30) OWNER Mr Brian White (LIPHOOK) BRED B. J. White
WEIGHT FOR AGE 5yo-6lb
3897 Full of Tricks was winning at the twentieth attempt having been placed only twice during his career, but it took a bad race to get him off the mark. (10/1: 6/1-12/1)
3810 Eau So Sloe may never have a better opportunity. (20/1)
Swift Pokey refused for the third time this season, unseating his rider, but popped over the last two fences after being remounted. (50/1)
4092 Snowy Petrel (IRE) fluffed a golden opportunity to break his duck. (1/3)

4438 DIANE OUGHTON MEMORIAL CHALLENGE TROPHY H'CAP CHASE (0-125) (5-Y.O+) (Class D)

4-00 (4-01) **2m 3f (16 fncs)** £3,827.55 (£1,142.40: £545.70: £247.35) GOING minus 0.10 sec per fur (G)

				SP	RR	SF
4254*	**Blazer Moriniere (FR) (90)** (PCRitchens) **8-10-1**ow1 SFox (a.p: led 10th: hrd rdn appr last: r.o wl)	—	1	3/1 [2]	101	32
3749*	**Grooving (IRE) (103)** (JTGifford) **8-11-0** NWilliamson (hld up: chsd wnr 12th: ev ch flat: eased whn btn nr fin)	3	2	11/8 [1]	112	44
4225[4]	**Polden Pride (113)** (GBBalding) **9-11-10** BClifford (rdn 8th: hdwy 13th: nvr nrr)	10	3	9/2 [3]	113	45
3744[7]	**Ramstar (100)** (PJHobbs) **9-10-11** GTormey (led to 10th: wknd appr 3 out)	26	4	14/1	78	10
4098[3]	**Master Comedy (89)** (MissLBower) **13-10-0b** JCulloty (a wl bhd)	5	5	25/1	63	—
2879[P]	**Bo Knows Best (IRE) (110)** (GLMoore) **8-11-7v[1]** PHolley (bhd fr 9th: p.u bef 3 out)		P	10/1	—	—
656*	**Manamour (89)** (RLee) **10-10-0** CLlewellyn (prom to 10th: 4th & no ch whn p.u bef 3 out)		P	7/1	—	—
	Brimpton Bertie (91) (MajorDNChappell) **8-10-2**ow2 GUpton (prom to 10th: t.o whn p.u bef 2 out)		P	25/1	—	—
				(SP 121.2%)	**8 Rn**	

4m 41.7 (2.70) CSF £7.75 CT £16.03 TOTE £4.40: £1.80 £1.60 £1.70 (£4.90) OWNER Mr John Pearl (TIDWORTH) BRED Robert Jeffroy
LONG HANDICAP Master Comedy 8-11 Blazer Moriniere (FR) 9-9 Manamour 9-10 Brimpton Bertie 9-11
4254* Blazer Moriniere (FR), who goes well round here, put in a good round of jumping and gamely found extra when challenged. He may notch up the hat-trick. (3/1)
3749* Grooving (IRE) ran well and would have been beaten only a length or so had he not been eased. He should win plenty more races. (11/8: 7/4-11/4)
4225 Polden Pride was never able to lay up and may be better over a longer trip nowadays. (9/2: 3/1-5/1)
1076 Ramstar is not yet back in the form he showed last Autumn. (14/1)
4098 Master Comedy found these useful types going too fast for him over this trip. (25/1)
656* Manamour (7/1: 5/1-8/1)

4439 FONTWELL H'CAP HURDLE (0-110) (5-Y.O+) (Class E)

4-30 (4-30) **2m 6f 110y (11 hdls)** £2,465.10 (£683.60: £327.30) GOING minus 0.10 sec per fur (G)

				SP	RR	SF
4253*	**St Ville (104)** (RHBuckler) **11-11-5**(5) GSupple (a.p: led 8th: clr appr 2 out: all out)	—	1	9/2 [3]	85	9
4252*	**Scud Missile (IRE) (95)** (JWPayne) **6-11-1** AThornton (lw: rdn & hdwy appr 2 out: r.o wl flat)	1½	2	11/2	75	—
3362*	**Jackson Flint (98)** (TThomsonJones) **9-11-4** JCulloty (hdwy 8th: r.o one pce fr 2 out)	1½	3	9/2 [3]	77	1
4233[3]	**Ecu de France (IRE) (80)** (PCRitchens) **7-9-7**(7) MClinton (hdwy 3 out: nvr nr to chal)	4	4	50/1	56	—
3958[3]	**Smuggler's Point (USA) (103)** (JJBridger) **7-11-6**(3) SophieMitchell (led to 8th: wknd 9th)	14	5	10/1	69	—
4253[3]	**Givus a Call (IRE) (102)** (JTGifford) **7-11-5**(3) LAspell (lw: bhd fr 3 out)	6	6	4/1 [2]	64	—
4086[6]	**Derrybelle (80)** (DLWilliams) **6-9-7**(7) MrSDurack (prom to 8th)	dist	7	33/1	—	—
4220[7]	**Layham Low (IRE) (84)** (OSherwood) **6-10-4** JOsborne (prom to 8th)	6	8	14/1	—	—
4181[3]	**Plinth (82)** (RHAlner) **6-10-2** NWilliamson (hld up: mstke 8th: ev ch 9th: wkng whn blnd last)	dist	9	100/30 [1]	—	—
3958[5]	**Karen's Typhoon (IRE) (80)** (TPMcGovern) **6-9-7**(7) MBatchelor (s.u bnd after 1st)		S	25/1	—	—
				(SP 119.3%)	**10 Rn**	

5m 32.9 (16.90) CSF £27.38 CT £108.96 TOTE £5.20: £1.80 £1.80 £1.90 (£6.30) OWNER Melplash Racing (BRIDPORT) BRED David and Mrs Shirley
LONG HANDICAP Derrybelle 9-9 Ecu de France (IRE) 8-4 Karen's Typhoon (IRE) 9-6
4253* St Ville is in good heart at present, though he frightened his supporters by nearly tying up on the run-in. (9/2)
4252* Scud Missile (IRE) began to run on too late, but for which he might have won. (11/2)
3362* Jackson Flint, off the track for two months, could pick up another race on this evidence. (9/2)
4233 Ecu de France (IRE) still had a bit to do on the home turn, but he is not an easy horse to win with. (50/1)
3958 Smuggler's Point (USA) (10/1: op 6/1)
4020 Layham Low (IRE) (14/1: 8/1-16/1)
4181 Plinth, well supported in the ring and confidently ridden, ran well for a long way. (100/30: 7/1-3/1)

T/Plpt: £429.90 (8.34 Tckts). T/Qdpt: £35.90 (4.66 Tckts) LMc

4276-LUDLOW (R-H) (Good to firm, Good patches)

Monday May 5th

WEATHER: raining

4440 TOTE PLACEPOT CONDITIONAL (S) HURDLE (4-Y.O+) (Class G)

2-30 (2-31) **2m (9 hdls)** £1,861.00 (£521.00: £253.00) GOING minus 0.27 sec per fur (GF)

				SP	RR	SF
3438[11]	**Bright Eclipse (USA) (70)** (JGMO'Shea) **4-10-4**(3) MGriffiths (trckd ldrs: led 5th: hit 2 out: sn hdd: lft clr last)	—	1	11/2 [3]	61	—
4226[P]	**Serious Option (IRE) (58)** (RCurtis) **6-10-5v[1]**(7) JParkhouse (hdwy to trck ldrs 5th: hrd rdn appr 3 out: one pce)	19	2	25/1	42	—
	Flash Chick (IRE) (TMorton) **8-10-0**(7) JMogford (bit bkwd: led to 1st: lost pl 4th: styng on whn blnd 3 out)	8	3	66/1	29	—
4002[P]	**Rakaposhi Imp** (CHJones) **7-10-4b[1]**(3) LSuthern (plld hrd early: blnd 1st: bhd fr 5th: t.o)	dist	4	66/1	—	—
4259[4]	**Anlace (75)** (SMellor) **8-10-7v** ChrisWebb (hld up in rr: stdy hdwy 4th: led after 2 out tl fell last)		F	3/1 [2]	57?	—
	Royal Ag Nag (99) (PJHobbs) **7-11-0** DJKavanagh (led 1st tl mstke 5th: rdn next: wknd qckly: t.o whn p.u bef 3 out)		P	8/11 [1]	—	—

				SP	RR	SF
4069^{P}	**Northern Diamond (IRE)** (MissMERowland) **4-10-4**(3) JPower (t: hld up: lost tch 5th: t.o whn p.u bef 3 out)......		P	16/1	—	—
				(SP 111.0%)		**7 Rn**

3m 48.9 (11.90) CSF £73.14 TOTE £10.40: £2.10 £3.60 (£26.10) OWNER Allfor (WESTBURY-ON-SEVERN) BRED McCombs & Jones Partnership & Robert S. Folsom
WEIGHT FOR AGE 4yo-5lb
No bid
OFFICIAL EXPLANATION **Royal Ag Nag: lost her action at the end of the back straight.**
IN-FOCUS: Steady rain throughout the afternoon turned the ground progressively softer, although the official description was unchanged.
402 Bright Eclipse (USA) was a fortunate winner. (11/2)
4259 Anlace looked sure to win when taking a heavy fall at the last. (3/1)
Royal Ag Nag (8/11: evens-8/13)

4441 RED CROSS NOVICES' HURDLE (4-Y.O+) (Class E)

3-05 (3-07) **2m (9 hdls)** £2,075.00 (£575.00: £275.00) GOING minus 0.27 sec per fur (GF)

				SP	RR	SF
3761^{2}	**Embankment (IRE) (100)** (NJHenderson) **7-11-0** MAFitzgerald (lw: lft in ld after 3rd: pushed out flat)	—	1	2/5^{1}	77+	—
3061^{6}	**Floosy** (TRGeorge) **6-10-9** SWynne (in tch: hdwy to chse ldrs after 6th: ch whn mstke 2 out: kpt on flat)	2	2	12/1^{3}	70	—
3926^{2}	**Music Please (94)** (KCBailey) **5-10-7**(7) MrRWakley (hdwy to trck ldrs 5th: ev ch 2 out: one pce)	2½	3	4/1^{2}	73	—
3964^{8}	**Red Viper** (NMLampard) **5-11-0** MrAKinane (hld up: hdwy after 6th: rdn appr 2 out: one pce)........................	10	4	16/1	63	—
4301^{15}	**New Ross (IRE)** (OO'Neill) **5-11-0** VSlattery (led tl tried to run out bnd after 3rd: styd prom: hrd drvn 6th: one pce fr next)	4	5	50/1	59	—
4082^{P}	**Bache Dingle** (MrsSMJohnson) **6-11-0** WMarston (in tch: hmpd bnd after 3rd: drvn 6th: sn bhd: t.o)	dist	6	100/1	—	—
4301^{16}	**Packitin Parky** (DMcCain) **4-10-9** DWalsh (bit bkwd: bhd fr 5th: t.o)	5	7	100/1	—	—
	Sapphire Son (IRE) (PCClarke) **5-11-0** BFenton (j.b: hld up & a bhd: t.o)	3	8	20/1	—	—
865^{17}	**Just Because (IRE)** (GEJones) **5-10-9**(5) DJKavanagh (hmpd & lost pl bnd after 3rd: bhd fr 5th: t.o)...............	8	9	100/1	—	—
4088^{10}	**Ogulla** (MissLShally) **5-10-9** DLeahy (prom tl mstke 3rd: sn bhd: t.o whn p.u bef 3 out)........		P	100/1	—	—
3365^{18}	**Miss Mighty** (JHPeacock) **4-10-4** RBellamy (in tch: mstke 5th: sn wknd: t.o whn p.u bef 3 out)		P	100/1	—	—
				(SP 116.7%)		**11 Rn**

3m 49.4 (12.40) CSF £6.05 TOTE £1.50: £1.20 £1.50 £1.30 (£4.90) OWNER Lady Tennant (LAMBOURN) BRED Rathasker Stud
WEIGHT FOR AGE 4yo-5lb
3761 Embankment (IRE) won cosily and looks set to do well during the summer jumping campaign. (2/5)
1820 Floosy did nothing wrong but is flattered by the winning margin. (12/1)
3926 Music Please does not quite get two miles. (4/1: 5/2-9/2)

4442 OLDFIELD NOVICES' H'CAP CHASE (0-100) (5-Y.O+) (Class E)

3-35 (3-36) **3m (19 fncs)** £3,061.00 (£928.00: £454.00: £217.00) GOING minus 0.27 sec per fur (GF)

				SP	RR	SF
4237^{2}	**Nordic Valley (IRE) (85)** (MCPipe) **6-11-10** DWalsh (chsd ldrs: rdn 14th: led 2 out: rdn out)	—	1	11/4^{2}	95	40
4404^{P}	**Furry Fox (IRE) (78)** (RCurtis) **9-11-3** DMorris (hld up in tch: drvn 4 out: led next to 2 out: unable qckn)	3	2	4/1^{3}	86	31
4298^{2}	**Bowles Patrol (IRE) (80)** (JohnUpson) **5-10-11** MAFitzgerald (mstke 2nd: hdwy to chse ldrs 5th: led appr 4 out to 3 out: one pce)	10	3	7/4^{1}	81	18
4279^{4}	**Pandora's Prize (64)** (TWall) **11-10-3** SWynne (trckd ldr: led after 15th: hdd appr next: one pce).....................	6	4	20/1	61	6
4232^{P}	**Side Bar (61)** (PMooney) **7-10-0v** BFenton (led tl after 15th: sn rdn & wknd: t.o)........	dist	5	20/1	—	—
3934^{2}	**Baron's Heir (85)** (RELivermore) **10-11-10** WMarston (chsd ldrs tl blnd bdly & lost pl 13th: t.o)	13	6	4/1^{3}	—	—
4083^{U}	**Fattash (USA) (76)** (PMooney) **5-10-0b**(7)ow7 FQuinlan (bhd fr 7th: t.o whn p.u bef 15th)........		P	50/1	—	—
3625^{3}	**Deep Song (61)** (PAPritchard) **7-10-0** RBellamy (in rr fr 4th: t.o whn p.u bef 2 out)........		P	33/1	—	—
4092^{5}	**Aeolian (63)** (MissPMWhittle) **6-9-9**(7) MrJGoldstein (in rr: hdwy 10th: ch whn blnd 3 out: btn whn blnd & uns rdr next)		U	40/1	—	—
				(SP 119.9%)		**9 Rn**

6m 4.1 (4.10) CSF £12.77 CT £22.28 TOTE £3.00: £1.70 £1.70 £1.70 (£10.60) OWNER Pond House Racing (WELLINGTON) BRED David Shubotham
LONG HANDICAP Side Bar 9-13 Deep Song 9-13 Fattash (USA) 9-13
WEIGHT FOR AGE 5yo-8lb
OFFICIAL EXPLANATION **Furry Fox (IRE): bled from the nose.**
4237 Nordic Valley (IRE) won a moderate event in gritty fashion. (11/4)
4234 Furry Fox (IRE), reportedly lame when pulled up two days earlier, was driven to join issue on the home turn. He landed in front three out but was soon grabbed by the winner. (4/1)
4298 Bowles Patrol (IRE) had every chance but was not fluent when the chips were down. (7/4)

4443 BET WITH THE TOTE H'CAP HURDLE (0-115) (4-Y.O+) (Class E)

4-05 (4-05) **2m (9 hdls)** £3,061.00 (£928.00: £454.00: £217.00) GOING minus 0.27 sec per fur (GF)

				SP	RR	SF
4071^{R}	**Courageous Knight (82)** (PHayward) **8-10-5** BFenton (hld up: hdwy after 6th: slt ld 3 out: edgd rt & drvn out flat)	—	1	6/1^{3}	63	—
4307^{U}	**Percy Braithwaite (IRE) (105)** (MissPMWhittle) **5-11-7**(7) MrJGoldstein (chsd ldr: led appr 3 out: sn hdd: ev ch tl no ex nr fin)........	½	2	2/1^{1}	86	7
3429^{11}	**Tango Man (IRE) (77)** (JGMO'Shea) **5-10-0** SWynne (in tch: hdwy 6th: ev ch fr 3 out tl rdn & unable qckn flat)	2	3	6/1^{3}	56	—
	Fraser Carey (IRE) (99) (TRGeorge) **5-11-8b** MAFitzgerald (chsd ldrs: wnt 2nd appr 3 out: one pce fr 2 out)	12	4	7/1	66	—
4162^{3}	**Follow de Call (81)** (DMcCain) **7-10-4**ow4 DWalsh (in tch tl wknd appr 3 out)	11	5	14/1	37	—
3743^{P}	**Swahili Run (77)** (JGMO'Shea) **9-9-7**(7) MGriffiths (led: clr 3rd to 6th: hdd appr 3 out: sn wknd)	5	6	33/1	28	—
4307^{6}	**Roca Murada (IRE) (97)** (PJHobbs) **8-11-1v**(5) DJKavanagh (hld up in rr: rdn 5th: sn no ch)............................	3	7	11/4^{2}	45	—
				(SP 110.7%)		**7 Rn**

3m 47.6 (10.60) CSF £16.16 TOTE £8.00: £3.80 £1.70 (£6.70) OWNER Mr L. Kirkwood (NETHERAVON) BRED C. A. Blackwell
LONG HANDICAP Tango Man (IRE) 9-9 Follow de Call 9-10 Swahili Run 9-9
4071 Courageous Knight, patiently ridden, nosed ahead at the third last. Driven out on the flat, he drifted right but was allowed to keep the race as Fenton had his whip in his correct hand. (6/1: op 4/1)
4307 Percy Braithwaite (IRE) was just losing the battle when carried right close home. (2/1)
2943* Tango Man (IRE) was one of three in line up the straight until outpaced on the run-in. (6/1)

Fraser Carey (IRE) (7/1: op 9/2)
4162 Follow de Call (14/1: op 8/1)

4444 LUDLOW GOLF CLUB NOVICES' CHASE (5-Y.O+) (Class E)

4-35 (4-36) **2m (13 fncs)** £3,116.00 (£876.00: £428.00) GOING minus 0.27 sec per fur (GF)

			SP	RR	SF
3417[4]	**Sigma Run (IRE) (81)** (JGMO'Shea) **8-11-7** MAFitzgerald (led to 9th: pckd 3 out: 5l 2nd whn lft clr last) .... —	1	13/8[1]	84	—
4219[4]	**Eurolink Shadow** (DMcCain) **5-10-8** DWalsh (mstkes: chsd ldrs to 9th: sn wknd: lft poor 2nd last) 25	2	5/1[3]	52	—
4235[P]	**Hugh Daniels (65)** (CJHemsley) **9-10-7**(7) MissADudley (chsd ldrs to 8th: t.o) 6	3	33/1	46	—
2579[F]	**Pridewood Picker** (RJPrice) **10-11-0** BFenton (tk keen hld in rr: hdwy 6th: led 9th: 5l clr whn slipped & fell last)	F	7/4[2]	—	—
4092[F]	**Quarter Marker (IRE) (60)** (RLee) **9-11-0** WMarston (lw: mstke 1st: bhd fr 7th: t.o whn p.u bef 4 out)	P	11/2	—	—
4073[P]	**Nuns Lucy** (FJordan) **6-10-9** DLeahy (bhd fr 4th: t.o whn p.u bef 4 out)	P	50/1	—	—
			(SP 111.4%)		**6 Rn**

4m 8.7 (16.70) CSF £9.23 TOTE £2.70: £1.70 £2.40 (£4.40) OWNER K W Bell & Son Ltd (WESTBURY-ON-SEVERN) BRED David Fenton
WEIGHT FOR AGE 5yo-6lb
3417 Sigma Run (IRE) completed a very fortunate double for his trainer. (13/8)
1954 Pridewood Picker, twice a winner here over hurdles, hit the front sooner than his jockey may have liked. Clear at the last, he did not touch a twig but lost his footing a couple of strides after the obstacle. He should win races over fences. (7/4)

4445 ST JOHNS' NOVICES' H'CAP HURDLE (0-100) (4-Y.O+) (Class E)

5-05 (5-08) **2m 5f 110y (11 hdls)** £2,075.00 (£575.00: £275.00) GOING minus 0.27 sec per fur (GF)

			SP	RR	SF
3967[10]	**One More Dime (IRE) (62)** (JLNeedham) **7-10-0** BFenton (hdwy to ld 6th: hdd 8th: chsd ldr: no imp 3 out: rallied flat to ld nr fin) .... —	1	10/1	50	—
4161[4]	**The Eens (67)** (DMcCain) **5-10-5** DWalsh (led 3rd to 6th: led 8th: rdn appr 2 out: wknd flat: ct nr fin)..............½	2	8/1	55	—
3947[3]	**Genereux (82)** (SMellor) **4-10-9**(5) ChrisWebb (s.v.s & wl bhd: styd on fr 8th: no imp fr 2 out) 19	3	12/1	56	—
4309[7]	**Vallingale (IRE) (86)** (MissHCKnight) **6-11-3**(7) MrAWintle (lw: chsd ldrs to 6th: sn lost tch) 6	4	7/1[3]	55	—
3683[8]	**Professor Page (IRE) (74)** (TThomsonJones) **7-10-12v[1]** MAFitzgerald (mid div: lost tch fr 6th: t.o) ....dist	5	9/1	—	—
3902[5]	**Imperial Honors (IRE) (62)** (NMLampard) **6-10-0** MrAKinane (s.v.s: a bhd: t.o) 8	6	50/1	—	—
4083[F]	**Eden Stream (63)** (MissLShally) **10-10-1** DLeahy (lost tch fr 6th: t.o) 21	7	33/1	—	—
4250[5]	**Soldier-B (62)** (RCurtis) **7-10-0** DMorris (led to 3rd: mstke 5th: bhd fr 7th: t.o) ....nk	8	25/1	—	—
4276[6]	**Vita Nuova (IRE) (62)** (WJenks) **6-10-0** VSlattery (chsd ldrs: hrd drvn 7th: sn wknd: t.o) ....s.h	9	33/1	—	—
4296*	**Hancock (85)** (JHetherton) **5-11-9** WMarston (lw: hld up: rdn 6th: no imp: t.o whn p.u bef 2 out)	P	15/8[1]	—	—
3894*	**Connaught's Pride (70)** (PJHobbs) **6-10-3b[1]**(5) DJKavanagh (chsd ldrs: lost tch fr 7th: t.o whn p.u bef 3 out) ...	P	4/1[2]	—	—
			(SP 116.9%)		**11 Rn**

5m 17.6 (16.60) CSF £75.85 CT £889.48 TOTE £18.90: £2.50 £2.40 £2.50 (£75.60) OWNER Mr J. L. Needham (LUDLOW) BRED Godfrey Deacon
LONG HANDICAP Soldier-B 9-9 Vita Nuova (IRE) 9-13 Imperial Honors (IRE) 9-12
WEIGHT FOR AGE 4yo-6lb
3831 One More Dime (IRE) looked beaten at the third last, but came with a renewed effort to get back up close home. (10/1: op 16/1)
4161 The Eens looked to have it in the bag at the third last but began to flounder in the rain-sodden ground, and was very tired when collared near the line. (8/1)
3947 Genereux (12/1: op 8/1)
3004 Vallingale (IRE) (7/1: op 4/1)
4296* Hancock was never going and may have found conditions too testing. (15/8)

T/Plpt: £380.90 (7.8 Tckts). T/Qdpt: £49.23 (3.6 Tckts) RL

4157-SOUTHWELL (L-H) (Good becoming Good to soft becoming Soft)

Monday May 5th

WEATHER: raining

4446 CLOWN WORKSHOP & BOUNCY CASTLE NOVICES' H'CAP CHASE (0-95) (5-Y.O+) (Class F)

2-30 (2-30) **2m (13 fncs)** £3,262.00 (£976.00: £468.00: £214.00) GOING: 0.85 sec per fur (S)

			SP	RR	SF
3938[3]	**Appearance Money (IRE) (72)** (FMurphy) **6-10-6** MFoster (hld up & bhd: hdwy appr 3 out: styd on to chse ldr after 2 out: 6l 2nd whn lft clr last) .... —	1	6/1	81	—
4260[2]	**Cool Weather (IRE) (70)** (PCheesbrough) **9-10-4b** ASSmith (a.p: effrt & ev ch 4 out: one pce fr 3 out) 9	2	11/2[3]	70	—
4297[2]	**Bali Tender (66)** (JWharton) **6-9-11**(3) MrRThornton (hld up & plld hrd: trckd ldr fr 6th: ev ch 4 out: rdn & hit 3 out: wknd) 5	3	11/2[3]	61	—
4007[P]	**Givry (IRE) (80)** (GMMcCourt) **7-10-11**(3) DFortt (in tch tl lost pl & bhd after 6th: n.d after) 10	4	20/1	65	—
4314[3]	**Bit of A Dream (IRE) (66)** (MrsSJSmith) **7-9-9**(5) GFRyan (trckd ldrs: rdn after 4 out: btn whn hit 3 out) 3	5	2/1[1]	48	—
3288[7]	**Stage Player (82)** (MissCJECaroe) **11-11-2** ILawrence (sn bhd: t.o fr ½-wy) 19	6	10/1	45	—
	Phargold (IRE) (80) (JohnHarris) **8-11-0** JSupple (plld hrd: led after 1st: mstkes: sn clr: hdd 7th: sn wknd: t.o whn p.u bef last)	P	33/1	—	—
4157[U]	**Chorus Line (IRE) (90)** (PBeaumont) **8-11-10** RSupple (led tl after 1st: a.p: led 7th: wnt clr fr 3 out: 6l clr whn blnd bdly & uns rdr last)	U	5/1[2]	—	—
			(SP 111.8%)		**8 Rn**

4m 19.2 (26.20) CSF £33.90 CT £171.68 TOTE £6.90: £1.70 £1.50 £1.60 (£22.90) OWNER Irish Festival Racing Club (MIDDLEHAM) BRED FlyingBolt Syndicate
LONG HANDICAP Bit of A Dream (IRE) 9-10 Bali Tender 9-12
OFFICIAL EXPLANATION Bit of A Dream (IRE): no explanation offered.
3938 Appearance Money (IRE), given a patient ride, had luck on her side when the clear leader departed at the last. (6/1)
4260 Cool Weather (IRE) again illustrated his lack of pace at the minimum distance. (11/2)
4297 Bali Tender, who raced up quite freely, failed to get home and was very weary in the home straight. (11/2: op 3/1)
4314 Bit of A Dream (IRE) may have found this coming too soon after Ascot, for he became a spent force very quickly when the chips when down. (2/1)

4157 Chorus Line (IRE) looked to have this in safe keeping when she made a terrible hash of the last, giving her rider no chance of staying on board. (5/1: 7/1-9/2)

4447 SOUTHWELL RACECOURSE FAMILY FUNDAY NOVICES' CHASE (5-Y.O+) (Class E)

3-00 (3-00) **3m 110y (19 fncs)** £3,507.00 (£1,050.00: £504.00: £231.00) GOING: 0.85 sec per fur (S)

			SP	RR	SF
3813[F]	**Prince Buck (IRE)** (MJRoberts) **7-11-2** JRailton (chsd ldr: led 3rd to 9th: jnd ldr 13th: led 15th: clr fr 3 out: hit last)......—	**1**	13/2[3]	99	17
4221[2]	**Alaskan Heir (72)** (AStreeter) **6-11-2v** TEley (led to 3rd: chsd ldr: led 9th: jnd 13th: hdd 15th: one pce fr 3 out)......20	**2**	14/1	86	4
3882[U]	**Fern Leader (IRE) (79)** (MrsASwinbank) **7-11-2** JSupple (hld up & bhd: nt j.w: hdwy after 4 out: styd on: nvr nr ldrs)......3	**3**	8/1	84	2
3882[5]	**Majority Major (IRE) (80)** (PCheesbrough) **8-11-8** ASSmith (a chsng ldrs: rdn 15th: btn appr 3 out)......6	**4**	14/1	86	4
	Glenbricken (MissAEEmbiricos) **11-11-2** RichardGuest (in tch to 9th: sn outpcd & bhd: sme hdwy 15th: no imp fr 3 out)......hd	**5**	9/1	80	—
4211[6]	**Crown Equerry (IRE)** (GRichards) **7-12-0** RDunwoody (hld up in tch: mstke 3rd: fell 8th)......	**F**	10/11[1]	—	—
3279[P]	**Damcada (IRE) (67)** (AWCarroll) **9-10-9**(7) MrOMcPhail (chsd ldrs tl wknd 12th: sn t.o: p.u after 4 out)......	**P**	33/1	—	—
4158[P]	**Doctor Dunklin (USA)** (MrsVCWard) **8-10-13**(3) MichaelBrennan (sn bhd: t.o whn p.u bef 9th)......	**P**	50/1	—	—
4219[2]	**Exemplar (IRE) (81)** (MrsSJSmith) **9-10-11**(5) GFRyan (mstke 1st: blnd & uns rdr 2nd)......	**U**	6/1[2]	—	—
			(SP 119.3%)	**9 Rn**	

6m 44.3 (37.30) CSF £80.92 TOTE £7.70: £1.80 £2.20 £2.30 (£38.40) OWNER Mr Mike Roberts (HAILSHAM) BRED Frank Stewart

3813 Prince Buck (IRE), twice a winner between the flags, turned in a solid display here and looks a horse with a bright future. (13/2)

4221 Alaskan Heir had no chance with the winner when the chips were down. (14/1)

3882 Fern Leader (IRE), a very chancy jumper, was schooled around at the rear until staying on late in the day. (8/1)

3882 Majority Major (IRE) was struggling from a long way out. (14/1: op 8/1)

3347 Crown Equerry (IRE) was lobbing along in touch with the leaders when he turned a somersault, from which he was lucky to gallop away. (10/11: op 6/4)

4219 Exemplar (IRE) (6/1: op 4/1)

4448 MALCOLM FISHER 50TH BIRTHDAY H'CAP CHASE (0-115) (5-Y.O+) (Class E)

3-30 (3-30) **2m 4f 110y (16 fncs)** £4,883.50 (£1,459.00: £698.00: £317.50) GOING: 0.85 sec per fur (S)

			SP	RR	SF
3966[6]	**Royal Square (CAN) (83)** (NPLittmoden) **11-9-11**(3) MrRThornton (trckd ldr: led appr 3 out: rdn clr fr 2 out: drvn out)......—	**1**	16/1	95	27
4159[3]	**Peruvian Gale (IRE) (91)** (MrsSJSmith) **8-10-8** RichardGuest (hld up in tch: lost pl 9th: hit 11th: kpt on fr 3 out: no ch w wnr)......10	**2**	5/2[2]	95	27
4247*	**Acajou III (FR) (111)** (GRichards) **9-12-0** RDunwoody (led: hit 10th: hdd appr 3 out: btn whn blnd 2 out: wknd qckly & eased flat)......20	**3**	11/10[1]	100	32
4159*	**Chadwick's Ginger (100)** (WHTinning) **9-11-3** DerekByrne (bhd: hdwy to chse ldrs 6th: mstke & lost pl 10th: sn t.o)......dist	**4**	11/4[3]	—	—
4277[F]	**Applianceofscience (87)** (KOWarner) **10-10-1**(3)ow4 MichaelBrennan (bhd: mstke 4th: p.u after 6th)......	**P**	25/1	—	—
			(SP 112.6%)	**5 Rn**	

5m 27.6 (23.60) CSF £51.33 TOTE £12.60: £3.00 £1.30 (£20.10) OWNER R A M Racecourses Ltd (WOLVERHAMPTON) BRED Nassar Abdullah Lootah in Canada

LONG HANDICAP Royal Square (CAN) 9-8 Applianceofscience 8-12

OFFICIAL EXPLANATION **Chadwick's Ginger: was unsuited by the good to soft going. Royal Square (CAN): regarding the improvement in form, his trainer reported that he has shown a tendency to be ungenuine in the past, but enjoyed being able to dominate in a small field today.**

3622 Royal Square (CAN) bounced back to winning form from 6lb out of the handicap, and did so in determined style. He can score again in similar company. (16/1)

4159 Peruvian Gale (IRE) got left behind down the back straight but, although keeping on from three out, never held out much hope of reaching the winner. (5/2)

4247* Acajou III (FR) found next too nothing when let down, and was very weary indeed from the second last. (11/10)

4159* Chadwick's Ginger, on her favourite course, ran no sort of race on ground considered by connections to be too soft for her. (11/4)

4449 DOUBLE DECKER FUN BUS HUNTERS' CHASE (6-Y.O+) (Class H)

4-00 (4-01) **3m 110y (19 fncs)** £2,211.00 (£621.00: £303.00) GOING: 0.85 sec per fur (S)

			SP	RR	SF
4051[6]	**Trifast Lad** (MJRoberts) **12-12-0**(3) MrPHacking (a.p: chsd clr ldr fr 8th: hit 14th: led after 3 out: styd on gamely)......—	**1**	11/10[1]	98	—
4320[4]	**Kambalda Rambler** (MrsHelenHarvey) **13-11-7**(7) MrRArmson (bhd: hdwy fr 4 out: wnt 2nd 2 out: ev ch last: kpt on)......½	**2**	4/1[2]	95	—
4256[P]	**Fifth Amendment** (CJMann) **12-11-11b**(3) MrRThornton (led & sn clr: rdn 15th: hdd after 3 out: sn btn)......25	**3**	12/1	78	—
4208[3]	**Southern Minstrel** (NChamberlain) **14-11-7**(7) MissCMetcalfe (a chsng ldrs: rdn & btn 4 out: sn wl bhd)......8	**4**	4/1[2]	73	—
	Ship the Builder (PeterMaddison) **8-11-0**(7) MrTWhitaker (chsd clr ldr tl hit 7th: 3rd whn fell 11th)......	**F**	20/1	—	—
	Shining Penny (SDWatson) **10-11-0**(7) MrKGreen (a bhd: t.o whn p.u after 12th)......	**P**	33/1	—	—
1009[P]	**Ishma (IRE)** (DarrenPage) **6-11-0**(7) MrDPage (nt j.w: ref 9th)......	**R**	8/1[3]	—	—
			(SP 114.1%)	**7 Rn**	

6m 56.5 (49.50) CSF £5.60 TOTE £2.10: £1.30 £2.90 (£5.30) OWNER Mr Mike Roberts (HAILSHAM) BRED Wilfred White

3457* Trifast Lad did not relish the ground but is nothing if not game. (11/10: 4/5-5/4)

4320 Kambalda Rambler looked a likely winner at the last but was just run out of it. (4/1)

Fifth Amendment, a moody customer, made a dramatic assault to lead all the way but, after holding a clear advantage, was soon cut down to size in the home straight. (12/1)

4208 Southern Minstrel found this very hard work on the rain-softened ground. (4/1)

Ishma (IRE) (8/1: op 12/1)

4450 MARTIN ORANGE 21ST BIRTHDAY 'N.H.' NOVICES' HURDLE (4-Y.O+) (Class E)

4-30 (4-32) **2m 2f (10 hdls)** £2,658.00 (£738.00: £354.00) GOING: 1.49 sec per fur (HY)

			SP	RR	SF
4204[10]	**Jervaulx (IRE) (96)** (GRichards) **6-11-6** RDunwoody (trckd ldrs: led 6th: rdn 2 out: kpt on wl)........................—	**1**	2/1[1]	71	12
3170[11]	**Silent Cracker** (RDickin) **5-11-0** DerekByrne (hld up in tch: hdwy appr 3 out: chsd wnr 2 out: rdn & one pce flat)........................2½	**2**	12/1	63	4
4161[3]	**General Parker** (MissMKMilligan) **6-11-0** ASSmith (led to 6th: chsd wnr tl wknd fr 2 out)........................11	**3**	11/2[3]	53	—
4299[4]	**Poppy's Dream** (JWharton) **7-10-6(3)** MrRThornton (hld up & bhd: hdwy appr 3 out: no imp after)........................4	**4**	3/1[2]	44	—
	Chariot Man (IRE) (MrsSJSmith) **5-11-0** RichardGuest (hld up in mid div: hdwy 4 out: wknd fr 3 out)........................18	**5**	16/1	33	—
2904[13]	**Blaster Watson** (CSmith) **6-11-0** MRanger (j.slowly 1st: mstkes: chsd ldrs: rdn & btn bef 3 out)........................20	**6**	25/1	16	—
4299[12]	**Moor Dance Man** (NPLittmoden) **7-11-0** GaryLyons (nvr bttr than mid div: lost tch: t.o 3 out)........................14	**7**	25/1	3	—
4285[P]	**The Stuffed Puffin (IRE) (87)** (CJMann) **5-11-0** JRailton (a in rr: t.o whn p.u bef 2 out)........................	**P**	10/1	—	—
	Methodius (IRE) (JRJenkins) **5-11-0** RSupple (in tch tl wknd bef 4 out: bhd whn p.u bef 2 out)........................	**P**	20/1	—	—
3021[8]	**Ludo's Orchestra (IRE)** (MarkCampion) **6-11-0** PNiven (a bhd: t.o whn p.u bef 2 out)........................	**P**	20/1	—	—
1505[6]	**Chief Gale (IRE)** (JGMO'Shea) **5-10-11(3)** MichaelBrennan (chsd ldrs tl wknd after 4 out: t.o whn p.u bef 2 out)........................	**P**	8/1	—	—
	Derring Well (JWPayne) **7-10-9** ILawrence (a bhd: t.o whn p.u after 2 out)........................	**P**	25/1	—	—
	Dellone (TRGeorge) **5-11-0** MFoster (nt j.w: t.o whn ref 4th)........................	**R**	25/1	—	—
4161[P]	**Sutton Boy** (LadyAnnBowlby) **8-11-0** NBentley (blnd & uns rdr 1st)........................	**U**	25/1	—	—
			(SP 136.2%)	**14 Rn**	

4m 51.4 (40.40) CSF £26.64 TOTE £3.70: £2.40 £3.30 £2.50 (£41.90) OWNER Mr Robert Ogden (PENRITH) BRED Vincent Byrne

3807 Jervaulx (IRE) provided Richard Dunwoody with his one hundredth winner of the season, the eighth consecutive time he has achieved a ton which is a record under National Hunt Rules. This horse will go novice chasing next season and has the size and scope to make a success of his new role. (2/1)

2811 Silent Cracker threw down a determined challenge between the last two but was never quite finding enough. (12/1)

4161 General Parker was found wanting when the tempo increased in the final half-mile. (11/2)

4299 Poppy's Dream could never get into the race with a serious chance. (3/1)

Chariot Man (IRE), a likeable newcomer, shaped well and looks to possess some ability. Experience should improve him. (16/1)

4244 The Stuffed Puffin (IRE) was reported to have burst a blood vessel. (10/1)

4451 PUNCH & JUDY AND JAZZ BAND (S) HURDLE (4,5,6 & 7-Y.O) (Class G)

5-00 (5-01) **2m (9 hdls)** £2,077.40 (£576.40: £276.20) GOING: 1.49 sec per fur (HY)

			SP	RR	SF
4261[P]	**Fair and Fancy (FR) (99)** (MissMKMilligan) **6-11-0** ASSmith (prom: led 5th: wnt clr next: j.b rt last 2: rdn out)—	**1**	2/1[1]	65	28
4295[12]	**Irie Mon (IRE) (77)** (MPBielby) **5-11-7** JRailton (bhd: effrt 3 out: kpt on u.p fr 2 out: no ch w wnr)........................12	**2**	9/2[2]	60	23
	Craigary (MrsASwinbank) **6-11-0** JSupple (hdwy to chse ldrs 5th: rdn 3 out: one pce fr 2 out)........................7	**3**	9/2[2]	46	9
4313[P]	**Hever Golf Diamond (90)** (JRBest) **4-10-9(7)** MrPO'Keeffe (a bhd: t.o)........................dist	**4**	9/2[2]	—	—
	Lordan Velvet (IRE) (MrsWBAllen,Norway) **5-11-7** RichardGuest (chsd ldrs: led 4th to next: outpcd 3 out: 4th & btn whn fell last)........................	**F**	5/1[3]	—	—
4299[11]	**Can She Can Can** (CSmith) **5-10-9** MRanger (chsd ldrs: wknd 5th: t.o whn p.u bef last)........................	**P**	9/1	—	—
2678[P]	**Sullamell** (PRHarriss) **6-10-7(7)** MrOMcPhail (led to 4th: wknd qckly: sn t.o: p.u after 3 out)........................	**P**	25/1	—	—
			(SP 118.4%)	**7 Rn**	

4m 13.1 (31.10) CSF £11.08 TOTE £2.90: £1.90 £2.20 (£4.10) OWNER The F And F Partnership (LEYBURN) BRED Alec Head

WEIGHT FOR AGE 4yo-5lb

No bid

Fair and Fancy (FR), a one-time smart handicapper, will not find many worse races than this. (2/1)

743 Irie Mon (IRE) never looked like winning. (9/2)

Craigary, an Irish recruit, looks pretty moderate on the evidence of this performance. (9/2)

1158 Hever Golf Diamond, soon struggling, was never at the races. (9/2)

4452 BET WITH THE TOTE H'CAP HURDLE (0-115) (4-Y.O+) (Class E)

5-30 (5-30) **3m 110y (13 hdls)** £2,616.00 (£726.00: £348.00) GOING: 1.49 sec per fur (HY)

			SP	RR	SF
4081[2]	**Dockmaster (87)** (MissMKMilligan) **6-10-11** ASSmith (prom: led 7th: wnt clr appr 9th: unchal)........................—	**1**	7/2[2]	77	8
4147[9]	**Soloman Springs (USA) (76)** (MrsVCWard) **7-9-11(3)** MrRThornton (prom tl lost pl bef 4th: hdwy appr 4 out: chsd wnr fr next: no imp)........................15	**2**	9/1	56	—
4220[6]	**Pharare (IRE) (92)** (RDEWoodhouse) **7-11-2** PNiven (led tl hdd 7th: rdn & outpcd fr 9th: no imp after).........dist	**3**	4/1[3]	—	—
3894[3]	**Lord Nitrogen (USA) (80)** (BJLlewellyn) **7-10-4** ILawrence (in tch: hdwy to chse ldrs appr 7th: rdn along fr 9th: btn 3 out)........................1¾	**4**	10/1	—	—
4318[7]	**Gi Moss (76)** (PRHarriss) **10-9-7b(7)** MrOMcPhail (prom tl wknd fr 9th: sn bhd: t.o)........................20	**5**	20/1	—	—
1778[R]	**Arrange A Game (76)** (MissJBower) **10-10-0** TEley (in tch to 6th: sn bhd: t.o whn p.u bef 9th)........................	**P**	33/1	—	—
4248[2]	**Grosvenor (IRE) (97)** (GRichards) **6-11-7** RDunwoody (prom tl lost pl qckly 3rd: bhd whn p.u after 6th)........................	**P**	11/4[1]	—	—
3925*	**Tim Soldier (FR) (76)** (MissAStokell) **10-10-0** RSupple (a in rr: t.o whn p.u bef 9th)........................	**P**	7/2[2]	—	—
3842[U]	***Gimme* (IRE) (100)** (JGMO'Shea) **7-11-7(3)** MichaelBrennan (Withdrawn not under Starter's orders)........................	**W**		—	—
			(SP 117.9%)	**8 Rn**	

6m 39.6 (53.60) CSF £32.01 CT £120.70 TOTE £4.80: £1.10 £2.20 £1.60 (£18.80) OWNER Mr J. D. Gordon (LEYBURN) BRED Cleaboy Farms Co

LONG HANDICAP Gi Moss 9-3 Soloman Springs (USA) 9-13 Tim Soldier (FR) 9-12 Arrange A Game 9-2

OFFICIAL EXPLANATION Tim Soldier (FR): was unsuited by the soft going. Grosvenor (IRE): no explanation offered.

4081 Dockmaster turned this into a procession and was never in the slightest danger throughout the final circuit. He can win again.(7/2)

3454 Soloman Springs (USA) ran in snatches and was never in the same parish as the winner. (9/1)

3454 Pharare (IRE) did the donkey work but was out on his feet in the final mile. (4/1)

3894 Lord Nitrogen (USA) was unable to raise his game from the third last. (10/1: op 6/1)

4248 Grosvenor (IRE) ran as though something was clearly amiss, though no explanation could be offered by connections. (11/4)

T/Plpt: £227.20 (14.38 Tckts). T/Qdpt: £29.40 (3.72 Tckts) O'R

4231-TOWCESTER (R-H) (Good)

Monday May 5th

WEATHER: mostly fine with scattered showers

4453 MILTON KEYNES JAIPUR RESTAURANT NOVICES' (S) HURDLE (4-Y.O+) (Class G)

2-20 (2-21) **2m (8 hdls)** £1,950.50 (£543.00: £261.50) GOING: 0.25 sec per fur (GS)

Form	Horse / details	Dist	Pos	SP	RR	SF
4003[8]	**The Flying Doctor (IRE) (87)** (GBBalding) **7-10-12** WMcFarland (hld up: hdwy 5th: chal 2 out: sn led: rdn out)	—	**1**	5/2[1]	62	11
4292[3]	**Bayerd (IRE) (87)** (CREgerton) **6-11-5b** JAMcCarthy (lw: prom: led appr 2 out: hdd & one pce appr last)	4	**2**	7/2[3]	65	14
4231[2]	**Our Eddie (70)** (KGWingrove) **8-10-12b** KGaule (hld up & plld hrd: hdwy 5th: rdn & no imp appr last)	¾	**3**	3/1[2]	57	6
3663[5]	**Caddy's First (83)** (SMellor) **5-10-12v** TJMurphy (lw: chsd ldrs: ev ch appr 2 out: sn wknd)	15	**4**	5/1	42	—
	Master Showman (IRE) (DJWintle) **6-10-12b[1]** TJenks (bit bkwd: led: hit 3 out: sn hdd & wknd qckly)	dist	**5**	16/1	—	—
3926[5]	**Stone Island (70)** (JohnWhyte) **4-10-7**(7) WWalsh (mstke 2nd: bhd fr 4th)	18	**6**	16/1	—	—
3575[10]	**Mega Tid** (JRPoulton) **5-10-9**(3) PHenley (in tch to 5th)	½	**7**	33/1	—	—
3566[5]	**Come On In (74)** (RDickin) **4-10-2**(5) XAizpuru (fell 3rd)		**F**	7/1	—	—
4304[10]	**A Badge Too Far (IRE) (52)** (MrsLWilliamson) **7-10-7b** LO'Hara (lw: bhd fr 5th: p.u bef last)		**P**	33/1	—	—

(SP 122.6%) **9 Rn**

4m 0.8 (14.80) CSF £11.54 TOTE £5.00: £2.10 £1.80 £1.10 (£10.50) OWNER The Rumble Racing Club (ANDOVER) BRED E. Finn
WEIGHT FOR AGE 4yo-5lb
Bt in 3,400 gns

The Flying Doctor (IRE) would have been on worse terms with the rest in a handicap and, having moved down well, could be called the winner before he hit the front. (5/2)
4292 Bayerd (IRE) did his best but could not pick up at all when challenged by the winner. (7/2: 3/1-9/2)
4231 Our Eddie was found wanting for stamina as the ground was slightly more testing than last time. (3/1: op 5/1)
3663 Caddy's First again tended to drift under pressure, this time to the left as this stiff track found out his stamina. (5/1)
Master Showman (IRE), who had a pipe-opener on the All-Weather last week, still looked to need the race and got very tired. (16/1)
Mega Tid, bred to stay all day, does not on this evidence. (33/1)
3222 Come On In (7/1: 5/1-8/1)

4454 DOVE NAISH CHARTERED ACCOUNTANTS NOVICES' CHASE (5-Y.O+) (Class E)

2-50 (2-50) **2m 110y (12 fncs)** £3,013.50 (£836.00: £400.50) GOING: 0.25 sec per fur (GS)

Form	Horse / details	Dist	Pos	SP	RR	SF
3044[4]	**Khalidi (IRE) (107)** (DRGandolfo) **8-11-7** GBradley (led to 8th: led appr 3 out: rdn appr last: r.o)	—	**1**	1/3[1]	94	21
4229[4]	**Stapleford Lady (78)** (JSMoore) **9-11-2** WMcFarland (lw: hld up: hdwy 3 out: ev ch whn mstke last: one pce)	5	**2**	3/1[2]	84	11
4305[3]	**Old Redwood (60)** (MrsLWilliamson) **10-11-0** LO'Hara (trckd ldr: mstke 6th: led 8th tl appr 3 out: sn wknd)	dist	**3**	7/1[3]	—	—

(SP 112.5%) **3 Rn**

4m 17.3 (15.30) CSF £1.80 TOTE £1.40: (£1.40) OWNER Mr T. J. Whitley (WANTAGE) BRED H. H. Aga Khan in Ireland

3044 Khalidi (IRE) looked straight enough after three months off but was forced to struggle in what looked a weak race. (1/3)
4229 Stapleford Lady, back over fences after a couple of hurdle runs, was a bit hesitant at some of the fences but would have gone close but for ballooning the last. (3/1)
4305 Old Redwood seems incapable of lasting home these days. (7/1: 4/1-8/1)

4455 LIFE EDUCATION CENTRE FOR NORTHAMPTON H'CAP HURDLE (0-125) (4-Y.O+) (Class D)

3-20 (3-20) **2m 5f (11 hdls)** £2,819.00 (£784.00: £377.00) GOING: 0.25 sec per fur (GS)

Form	Horse / details	Dist	Pos	SP	RR	SF
3737[3]	**Ehtefaal (USA) (95)** (JSKing) **6-11-7** TJMurphy (lw: mde virtually all: clr appr 2 out: eased flat)	—	**1**	15/8[1]	78+	10
4321*	**Able Player (USA) (92)** (KJDrewry) **10-11-4** 6x MSharratt (hld up: hit 5th & 7th: hdwy 3 out: wnt 2nd appr last: no ch w wnr)	10	**2**	9/4[2]	67	—
4296[P]	**Cambo (USA) (82)** (MCBanks) **11-10-1**(7) RStudholme (lw: w wnr to 8th: sn btn)	hd	**3**	11/2	57	—
4220[P]	**Fed on Oats (98)** (MissVenetiaWilliams) **9-11-10** JRKavanagh (trckd ldrs: ev ch 3 out: wkng qckly whn fell next)		**F**	5/2[3]	—	—

(SP 109.5%) **4 Rn**

5m 24.4 (22.40) CSF £5.94 TOTE £2.60: (£1.90) OWNER Mrs Marygold O'Kelly (SWINDON) BRED Shadwell Farm Inc

3737 Ehtefaal (USA) has been knocking at the door in more competitive races and deserved this confidence-boosting win. (15/8: 6/4-9/4)
4321* Able Player (USA), third in this race last year, got detached and found the winner long gone by the time he began to make progress. (9/4)
3923 Cambo (USA), beaten in a photo in this race a year ago, ran poorly last time and folded quickly coming up the hill. (11/2)

4456 TANSWELL H'CAP CHASE (0-115) (5-Y.O+) (Class E)

3-50 (3-50) **2m 110y (12 fncs)** £3,000.50 (£899.00: £432.00: £198.50) GOING: 0.25 sec per fur (GS)

Form	Horse / details	Dist	Pos	SP	RR	SF
4235[2]	**Crackling Frost (IRE) (79)** (MrsDHaine) **9-10-3**(3) PHenley (lw: j.w: mde all: hld on wl flat)	—	**1**	4/5[1]	90	23
2797[P]	**Mine's an Ace (NZ) (95)** (MissVenetiaWilliams) **10-11-8** JRKavanagh (chsd ldrs: lft 2nd 7th: ev ch 2 out: unable qckn flat)	½	**2**	7/1	106	39
4247[5]	**Chill Wind (88)** (NBycroft) **8-11-1** GBradley (prom: hit 4 out: sn btn)	25	**3**	7/2[2]	74	7
4235[P]	**Young Alfie (73)** (JFPanvert) **12-10-0b** TJMurphy (lw: a bhd: t.o fr 3 out: fin lame)	dist	**4**	33/1	—	—
4300[5]	**Bally Parson (97)** (RDickin) **11-11-5**(5) XAizpuru (lw: chsd wnr tl blnd & uns rdr 7th)		**U**	4/1[3]	—	—

(SP 113.2%) **5 Rn**

4m 13.5 (11.50) CSF £6.47 TOTE £1.80: £1.10 £2.60 (£4.30) OWNER The Unlucky For Some Partnership (NEWMARKET) BRED James A. Slattery
LONG HANDICAP Young Alfie 9-13

4235 Crackling Frost (IRE) jumped beautifully and looked in total charge but, joined between the last two, found nothing like as much as he looked likely to find once let down. (4/5: evens-11/10)
959 Mine's an Ace (NZ) ran a cracker after his layoff and made the hotpot pull out all the stops. (7/1)
4247 Chill Wind, on his toes beforehand, had a problematic journey to the course. He didn't tun too badly, but the mistakes knocked the stuffing out of him. (7/2)
Young Alfie looked well, but was never going and finished sore after shedding a plate just after the finish. (33/1)
4300 Bally Parson could not get to the front because of the winner, and was outjumped on a couple of occasions before taking a liberty and losing his pilot. (4/1: 3/1-9/2)

4457 IRONSIDES SOLICITORS NOVICES' HUNTERS' CHASE (5-Y.O+) (Class H)

4-20 (4-20) **2m 6f (16 fncs)** £1,013.70 (£303.60: £145.80: £66.90) GOING: 0.25 sec per fur (GS)

	Runner	Dist	Pos	SP	RR	SF
	Severn Invader (MissHGosling) **12-11-7**(7) MissHGosling (lw: hld up: hdwy 3 out: led appr last: sn clr: comf)	—	1	9/4^{1}	93+	19
4308^{2}	**Tea Cee Kay** (COKing) **7-11-9**(5) MrASansome (j.w: led tl appr 5th: led 7th tl appr last: sn btn)	10	2	4/1	86	12
3637^{9}	**Copper Thistle (IRE)** (NJPomfret) **9-12-0**(7) MrRHunnisett (lw: chsd ldrs tl pushed along & lost pl 6th: n.d after)	3	3	3/1^{2}	91	17
4319^{3}	**Taura's Rascal** (FJBrennan) **8-11-7**(7) MrFBrennan (prom: mstke 7th: ev ch whn hit 3 out: wkng whn blnd next)	30	4	100/30^{3}	62	—
3928^{P}	**Shareef Star** (FLMatthews) **9-11-7v**(7) CaptAWood (blnd 1st: t.o whn fell 4th)		F	50/1	—	—
	Roaming Shadow (JDHankinson) **10-11-7**(7) MrJBarnes (hdwy 2nd: led appr 5th to 7th: wknd qckly: t.o whn p.u bef 2 out)		P	8/1	—	—
	Barichste (IMMason) **9-11-7b^{1}**(7) MrMWatson (nt j.w: bhd fr 6th: t.o whn p.u bef last)		P	20/1	—	—

(SP 116.7%) **7 Rn**

5m 52.2 (23.20) CSF £11.36 TOTE £2.80: £1.70 £1.80 (£4.20) OWNER Mrs Miles Gosling BRED G. Johansen

Severn Invader, in good form between the Flags, was given a confident waiting ride and came with a wet sail in the straight. (9/4)

4308 Tea Cee Kay seems to go well for his pilot and certainly jumped well for him until getting tired. (4/1)

3459* Copper Thistle (IRE) got detached from the leaders early on and was always being nudged along to get in touch. Prolific in points, he really needs further. (3/1)

4319 Taura's Rascal had a very hard race just six days ago and this probably came too soon. (100/30)

4458 BUTTERCUP NOVICES' CONDITIONAL H'CAP HURDLE (0-100) (4-Y.O+ F & M) (Class F)

4-50 (4-50) **3m (12 hdls)** £1,992.50 (£555.00: £267.50) GOING: 0.25 sec per fur (GS)

	Runner	Dist	Pos	SP	RR	SF
3488^{2}	**Ardent Love (IRE) (73)** (DNicholson) **8-10-12** RMassey (lw: a.p: led 2 out: rdn out)	—	1	6/4^{1}	60	—
4304^{5}	**Madam's Walk (85)** (NATwiston-Davies) **7-11-3**(7) MKeighley (w ldr: led 6th to 2 out: wknd flat)	7	2	5/1^{3}	67	—
3764^{5}	**Quinag (83)** (KCBailey) **6-11-1**(7) WWalsh (hld up: lost pl 8th: kpt on appr 2 out)	14	3	8/1	56	—
3226^{16}	**Annie Ruth (IRE) (65)** (MrsJPitman) **6-9-11**(7) RGarrard (in tch tl lost pl 8th: rdn & kpt on appr last)	8	4	25/1	33	—
3937^{4}	**Castle Mews (IRE) (72)** (GCBravery) **6-10-11** SRyan (chsd ldrs tl wknd appr 2 out)	21	5	7/1	26	—
4273^{5}	**Jaime's Joy (61)** (GraemeRoe) **7-10-0v^{1}** MartinSmith (lw: in tch to 3 out: wknd qckly)	dist	6	50/1	—	—
4314^{F}	**Fortria Rosie Dawn (68)** (MissVenetiaWilliams) **7-10-7** XAizpuru (lw: set stdy pce to 6th: wknd 8th: t.o whn p.u bef 2 out)		P	9/2^{2}	—	—
4304^{6}	**Carlingford Gale (IRE) (77)** (TRGeorge) **6-11-2** PHenley (lw: t.o whn p.u bef 3 out)		P	5/1^{3}	—	—

(SP 120.9%) **8 Rn**

6m 13.1 (33.10) CSF £9.70 CT £43.69 TOTE £1.80: £1.10 £1.90 £2.90 (£3.90) OWNER Mrs Claire Smith (TEMPLE GUITING) BRED Blue Bear Stud Co Ltd

LONG HANDICAP Jaime's Joy 9-2

3488 Ardent Love (IRE) showed promise early in her career, but has taken six races to finally break her duck. She stays forever but is onepaced, and finally found a race where she was the last one running. (6/4)

4304 Madam's Walk has been tried over all sorts of trip, but her best would be just short of this judged on the way she ran. (5/1)

3764 Quinag was held up to get this trip, but didn't get going as quickly as the leaders when the field finally began racing. (8/1: op 5/1)

Annie Ruth (IRE) was staying on at the finish under a rather enthusiastic ride as, with fourth place secure and no chance of improvement, she was still under pressure in the shadow of the post. (25/1)

3937 Castle Mews (IRE) didn't appear to stay this longer trip. (7/1)

4158 Fortria Rosie Dawn (9/2: 3/1-5/1)

T/Plpt: £9.70 (227.14 Tckts). T/Qdpt: £4.70 (18.96 Tckts) Dk

3977-WINCANTON (R-H) (Firm)

Tuesday May 6th

WEATHER: overcast

4459 WHITSBURY 'N.H.' NOVICES' HURDLE (4-Y.O+) (Class E)

5-45 (5-46) **2m (8 hdls)** £1,952.50 (£540.00: £257.50) GOING minus 0.87 sec per fur (HD)

	Runner	Dist	Pos	SP	RR	SF
4238*	**Mrs Em (100)** (PFNicholls) **5-11-1**(7) LCummins (lw: led tl appr 3rd: led appr 2 out: easily)	—	1	3/10^{1}	78+	30
4292^{2}	**Red Tel (IRE)** (MCPipe) **5-10-13** APMcCoy (chsd wnr after 2nd: wnt 2nd & hit 2 out: no imp)	1¾	2	3/1^{2}	67	19
3359^{18}	**Admiral Bruny (IRE)** (NAGaselee) **6-10-13** CLlewellyn (plld hrd: led appr 3rd: hit 3 out: hdd appr 2 out: sn wknd)	8	3	20/1^{3}	59	11

(SP 106.7%) **3 Rn**

3m 34.3 (-5.70) CSF £1.45 TOTE £1.30: (£1.10) OWNER Mr G. Z. Mizel (SHEPTON MALLET) BRED Guest Leasing and Bloodstock Co

4238* Mrs Em had another facile victory and could have won by a much wider margin. (3/10)

4292 Red Tel (IRE) is flattered by the margin of defeat. (3/1)

Admiral Bruny (IRE) needs to learn to settle. (20/1)

4460 FONTHILL NOVICES' H'CAP CHASE (0-100) (5-Y.O+) (Class E)

6-15 (6-15) **2m 5f (17 fncs)** £3,120.00 (£870.00: £420.00) GOING minus 0.87 sec per fur (HD)

	Runner	Dist	Pos	SP	RR	SF
3833^{3}	**Little Rowley (60)** (MrsLRichards) **8-10-4** MRichards (led to 2nd: led 6th to 9th: mstke 12th: led 2 out: rdn out: fin lame)	—	1	5/1^{3}	65	—
752^{F}	**Miners Rest (76)** (PJHobbs) **9-10-13**(7) MrRWidger (lw: led 2nd to 6th: led 9th: pckd 3 out: hdd 2 out: nt qckn flat)	¾	2	2/1^{2}	80	—
4221^{5}	**Frontier Flight (USA) (80)** (MissLCSiddall) **7-11-7**(3) EHusband (hld up: blnd bdly 2nd: rdn 11th: btn whn mstke 3 out)	dist	3	5/6^{1}	—	—

(SP 104.5%) **3 Rn**

5m 23.4 (15.40) CSF £11.76 TOTE £4.70: (£2.90) OWNER Mr J. A. Judd (CHICHESTER)

OFFICIAL EXPLANATION **Frontier Flight: did not act on the firm ground.**

3833 Little Rowley has certainly improved for the drop back to this sort of trip. (5/1)
752 Miners Rest was 3lb lower than when winning a three-runner race at Perth last August. (2/1)
4221 Frontier Flight (USA) was reported by his jockey not to have acted on the firm ground. (5/6)

4461 HAYNES PUBLISHING 'N.H.' NOVICES' HURDLE (4-Y.O+) (Class E)
6-45 (6-45) **2m 6f (11 hdls)** £2,442.50 (£680.00: £327.50) GOING minus 0.87 sec per fur (HD)

			SP	RR	SF
3982[4]	**Mr Strong Gale (IRE) (101)** (PFNicholls) **6-11-7b[1]** RJohnson (mde all: mstke 8th: clr whn mstke last: comf) —	1	3/10 [1]	65+	—
4230[4]	**Willows Roulette** (AGHobbs) **5-11-0** RGreene (chsd wnr: ev ch 3 out: sn rdn: btn whn hit 2 out & last) 2	2	7/2 [2]	57	—
4173[3]	**Carnival Clown** (KBishop) **5-10-9**(5) GSupple (hld up: ev ch 3 out: sn rdn: eased whn btn appr 2 out) 16	3	10/1 [3]	45	—
			(SP 108.2%)		**3 Rn**

5m 11.2 (2.20) CSF £1.64 TOTE £1.30: (£1.10) OWNER Mr T. G. A. Chappell (SHEPTON MALLET) BRED Thomas F. Bourke
3982 Mr Strong Gale (IRE) won a weak race in first-time blinkers. (3/10: 1/5-1/3)
4230 Willows Roulette could not bustle-up the winner in the home straight. (7/2)
25 Carnival Clown (10/1: op 6/1)

4462 R.K. HARRISON INSURANCE BROKERS NOVICES' HUNTERS' CHASE (6-Y.O+) (Class H)
7-15 (7-15) **2m 5f (17 fncs)** £1,713.75 (£510.00: £242.50: £108.75) GOING minus 0.87 sec per fur (HD)

			SP	RR	SF
4322[3]	**Clobracken Lad** (MrsJSwaffield) **9-11-7**(7) MrGBaines (mde all: hit 3 out: drvn out) —	1	15/8 [1]	96?	—
	Link Copper (MrsEJTaplin) **8-11-7**(7) MissLBlackford (lw: chsd wnr: rdn 13th: ev ch 4 out: one pce fr 3 out) 2	2	11/4 [2]	95?	—
	Chism (IRE) (MrsSAlner) **6-11-7**(7) MrMGMiller (lw: hld up: hdwy 11th: lost pl 4 out: rallied 3 out: one pce fr 2 out) 3	3	15/8 [1]	92?	—
	Barrow Street (CLTizzard) **7-11-7**(7) MrJTizzard (bhd fr 9th: j.lft 4 out: sn t.o) 27	4	9/1 [3]	72?	—
			(SP 106.2%)		**4 Rn**

5m 15.2 (7.20) CSF £6.38 TOTE £2.60: (£6.00) OWNER Mr T. J. Swaffield (WEYMOUTH) BRED W. D. Thomas
STEWARDS' ENQUIRY Blackford susp. 15-16/5/97 (incorrect use of whip).
4322 Clobracken Lad, again running at less than three miles, sensibly forced the pace this time. (15/8)
Link Copper was inclined to swish his tail and his rider picked up a two-day ban for using the whip in the forehand position. (11/4)
Chism (IRE), successful in three points, had beaten the winner one-and-three-quarter lengths on 5lb better terms at Milborne St. Andrew in February. (15/8: 11/10-2/1)
Barrow Street (9/1: op 6/1)

4463 CHEDINGTON H'CAP CHASE (0-120) (5-Y.O+) (Class D)
7-45 (7-45) **3m 1f 110y (21 fncs)** £3,522.00 (£1,056.00: £508.00: £234.00) GOING minus 0.87 sec per fur (HD)

			SP	RR	SF
4140[3]	**Doualago (FR) (119)** (MCPipe) **7-12-0b** APMcCoy (lw: led to 5th: led 12th: rdn 16th: r.o wl) —	1	5/1 [3]	123	39
4167[5]	**James Pigg (118)** (PFNicholls) **10-11-13** RJohnson (lw: a.p: chsd wnr appr 3 out: r.o one pce flat) 1¾	2	13/2	121	37
4239[2]	**Frozen Drop (100)** (PCRitchens) **10-10-9** SFox (hld up: reminders after 8th: sn t.o: lft poor 3rd 2 out) dist	3	13/2	—	—
4234[P]	**Woodlands Genhire (91)** (PAPritchard) **12-10-0b** CLlewellyn (t.o fr 5th) dist	4	50/1	—	—
4293*	**Spinning Steel (96)** (PRRodford) **10-10-5** SBurrough (lw: plld hrd: 4th tl p.u & dsmntd bef 11th)	P	7/2 [2]	—	—
4293[4]	**Foxgrove (91)** (RJPrice) **11-9-9**(5) XAizpuru (t.o fr 5th: p.u after 12th)	P	16/1	—	—
4270[2]	**Drumcullen (IRE) (100)** (KCBailey) **8-10-9** NWilliamson (led 5th to 12th: hit 4 out: 3rd & wkng whn p.u bef 2 out)	P	13/8 [1]	—	—
			(SP 111.5%)		**7 Rn**

6m 10.0 (5.00 under best) (-9.00) CSF £31.21 TOTE £4.90: £2.60 £2.70 (£10.00) OWNER Martin Pipe Racing Club (WELLINGTON) BRED Monsieur et Madame Bernard le Douarin
LONG HANDICAP Foxgrove 9-1 Woodlands Genhire 9-0
4140 Doualago (FR), dropped 3lb, was reverting to a longer distance. (5/1)
James Pigg, down 7lb, can find a suitable opportunity before long on this evidence. (13/2)
4270 Drumcullen (IRE) appeared to trot away sound enough after being unsaddled. (13/8)

4464 ROCKBOURNE H'CAP HURDLE (0-115) (4-Y.O+) (Class E)
8-15 (8-15) **2m 6f (11 hdls)** £2,095.50 (£624.00: £297.00: £133.50) GOING minus 0.87 sec per fur (HD)

			SP	RR	SF
4250*	**Galatasori Jane (IRE) (99)** (PFNicholls) **7-11-3**(7) LCummins (chsd ldr: hrd rdn appr 3 out: led flat: all out) —	1	8/11 [1]	83	16
4172[3]	**Sevso (87)** (RJBaker) **8-10-9**(3) PHenley (plld hrd: led: hrd rdn appr 2 out: hdd flat: r.o) nk	2	5/4 [2]	71	4
1569[7]	**China Mail (IRE) (76)** (JABennett) **5-10-1** TJMurphy (hld up: rdn 3 out: no rspnse) 16	3	11/1 [3]	48	—
4175[7]	**Station Express (IRE) (75)** (GAHam) **9-9-7**(7) MGriffiths (bhd fr 3 out) 9	4	50/1	41	—
			(SP 112.6%)		**4 Rn**

5m 6.4 (-2.60) CSF £2.01 TOTE £1.80: (£1.50) OWNER Mr B. L. Blinman (SHEPTON MALLET) BRED Donal O'Keeffe
LONG HANDICAP Station Express (IRE) 8-7
4250* Galatasori Jane (IRE), reported to have coughed after making her handicap debut here in March, made hard work of this off a pound higher mark. (8/11)
4172 Sevso, dropped 3lb, was only a 1lb higher than when winning a similar event here on Easter Monday. (5/4)
813 China Mail (IRE) (11/1: 5/1-12/1)

T/Plpt: £655.30 (15.79 Tckts). T/Qdpt: £17.60 (31.76 Tckts) KH

4237-CHEPSTOW (L-H) (Good)
Wednesday May 7th
WEATHER: raining

4465 BALMORAL MAIDEN HURDLE (4-Y.O) (Class E)
2-25 (2-26) **2m 110y (8 hdls)** £2,248.00 (£628.00: £304.00) GOING minus 0.22 sec per fur (G)

			SP	RR	SF
	Song Of The Sword (JABOld) **4-11-0** MAFitzgerald (lw: mde all: qcknd 4 out: clr whn mstke last: comf) —	1	10/11 [1]	74+	—
3996[3]	**Timidjar (IRE) (92)** (DRGandolfo) **4-11-0b** RDunwoody (lw: hld up & bhd: hdwy 4th: ev ch appr 2 out: no imp) 3	2	11/2 [3]	71	—

4003[4] **Spring Campaign (IRE) (97)** (MCPipe) **4-11-0** APMcCoy (lw: hld up & bhd: sme hdwy 4 out: btn whn lft 3rd 2 out) ....24 **3** 4/1[2] 48 —
4170[4] **Spencer Stallone** (GraemeRoe) **4-11-0** WMarston (prom tl wknd appr 4 out: t.o) ....dist **4** 66/1 — —
3964[7] **Sassy Street (IRE)** (RFJohnsonHoughton) **4-11-0** DGallagher (mstke & lost pl 2nd: bhd fr 4 out: t.o) ....1½ **5** 14/1 — —
4176[4] **Dubai Dolly (IRE)** (JWMullins) **4-10-9** SCurran (hld up & bhd: hdwy after 4th: 4th & btn whn b.d 2 out) .... **B** 7/1 — —
Santella Cape (NJHawke) **4-11-0** JRailton (bit bkwd: chsd wnr to 4 out: 3rd & btn whn fell 2 out) .... **F** 25/1 — —
Romantic Warrior (KSBridgwater) **4-10-11**(3) RMassey (hld up & bhd: mstke 3 out: no ch whn hmpd & uns rdr 2 out) .... **U** 50/1 — —
(SP 114.2%) **8 Rn**

3m 59.8 (10.80) CSF £5.89 TOTE £2.20: £1.50 £1.70 £1.10 (£4.60) OWNER Lady Lloyd Webber (WROUGHTON) BRED Sheikh Mohammed Bin Rashid Al Maktoum

Song Of The Sword, a dual winner on the Flat in Ireland, was bought out of Michael Kauntze's yard at Newmarket Autumn Sales for 35,000 guineas. Sharpened up by a couple of runs on the Flat, he is well regarded by his trainer and can defy a penalty. (10/11: 4/6-evens)
3996 Timidjar (IRE), twice successful on the Flat in Ireland for John Oxx, was fitted with blinkers for the second of those wins. (11/2)
4003 Spring Campaign (IRE) was held up this time. (4/1: op 5/2)
Sassy Street (IRE) (14/1: 8/1-16/1)
4176 Dubai Dolly (IRE) was a springer in the market. (7/1: op 20/1)
Santella Cape, bought for 5,000 guineas nearly a year ago, had previously shown nothing in two outings for Richard Hannon. (25/1)

4466 BUCKINGHAM NOVICES' H'CAP HURDLE (0-100) (5-Y.O+) (Class E)

2-55 (2-55) **2m 110y (8 hdls)** £2,262.00 (£632.00: £306.00) GOING minus 0.22 sec per fur (G)

SP RR SF

2874[3] **Ultimate Smoothie (95)** (MCPipe) **5-12-0** APMcCoy (lw: hld up & bhd: mstke 3rd: stdy hdwy appr 4 out: led on bit appr last: easily) ....— **1** 11/2[2] 83+ 29
4226[5] **Alpha Leather (67)** (LPGrassick) **6-9-7**(7) MrOMcPhail (lw: a.p: hrd rdn appr 3 out: r.o flat: no ch w wnr) ....3 **2** 7/1[3] 52 —
3752[3] **Mr Poppleton (72)** (RBrotherton) **8-10-5** LHarvey (chsd ldr: led after 4th: hdd appr last: one pce) 1¾ **3** 10/1 55 1
4333* **Geisway (CAN) (84)** (NJHWalker) **7-10-12**(5) XAizpuru (lw: hld up: rdn & hdwy appr 4 out: wknd appr last)....15 **4** Evens[1] 53 —
3890[2] **Blade of Fortune (86)** (VGGreenway) **9-10-12**(7) MrJTizzard (led tl after 4th: wknd 3 out)....3½ **5** 7/1[3] 52 —
4276[2] **Daydream Believer (68)** (MSalaman) **5-10-1**ow1 PHolley (a bhd) ....9 **6** 16/1 25 —
546[P] **Mutley (67)** (NJHawke) **7-10-0** RGreene (bkwd: plld hrd: a bhd) ....2 **7** 50/1 22 —
3977[2] **Royal Ruler (IRE) (90)** (JTGifford) **6-11-9** RDunwoody (chsd ldrs tl wknd appr 4 out: t.o) ....21 **8** 15/2 24 —
(SP 119.1%) **8 Rn**

3m 55.4 (6.40) CSF £40.76 CT £346.59 TOTE £6.10: £1.60 £3.80 £1.40 (£67.60) OWNER Isca Bloodstock (WELLINGTON) BRED Fares Stables Ltd
LONG HANDICAP Daydream Believer 9-13 Mutley 9-7 Alpha Leather 9-13
OFFICIAL EXPLANATION **Geisway (CAN): was never travelling.**

2874 Ultimate Smoothie, coming back after a rest, scored most impressively off a 2lb lower mark. He will be kept going through the summer, and more success is in store. (11/2: 3/1-6/1)
4226 Alpha Leather may have been getting lumps of weight from the winner but it was simply not a contest. (7/1)
3752 Mr Poppleton, a model of consistency, found the winner galloping all over him. (10/1: 6/1-11/1)
4333* Geisway (CAN) was running off the same mark as when winning last time. His trainer reported to the Stewards that the gelding was never travelling. (Evens)
3890 Blade of Fortune (7/1: op 9/2)

4467 HIGHGROVE H'CAP CHASE (0-130) (5-Y.O+) (Class C)

3-25 (3-25) **3m (18 fncs)** £4,601.00 (£1,388.00: £674.00: £317.00) GOING minus 0.22 sec per fur (G)

SP RR SF

3903* **Funcheon Gale (98)** (RCurtis) **10-10-7** DMorris (hld up: hdwy appr 5 out: led appr 3 out: clr appr last: asily).— **1** 7/2[2] 110+ 17
4387[2] **Banntown Bill (IRE) (97)** (MCPipe) **8-10-6v** APMcCoy (led 2nd tl appr 3rd: led 5 out tl appr 3 out: one pce) .10 **2** 7/2[2] 102 9
4085* **Black Church (110)** (RRowe) **11-11-5** DO'Sullivan (hld up & bhd: hdwy 10th: hit 13th: wknd appr 5 out) ....20 **3** 7/4[1] 102 9
4074[F] **Don't Light Up (115)** (MissVenetiaWilliams) **11-11-7b**(3) MrRThornton (led to 2nd: bhd fr 8th: t.o fr 12th) 5 **4** 10/1 104 11
4177[4] **Pimberley Place (IRE) (110)** (NATwiston-Davies) **9-11-5** CLlewellyn (rel to r: plld hrd: led appr 3rd: hdd 5 out: sn wknd: t.o) ....2½ **5** 6/1[3] 97 4
4178[7] **Nickle Joe (95)** (MTate) **11-9-11**(7) MrOMcPhail (4th whn blnd & uns rdr 3rd) .... **U** 16/1 — —
(SP 110.1%) **6 Rn**

6m 0.9 (7.90) CSF £14.22 TOTE £5.00: £1.90 £1.60 (£7.60) OWNER Kings Of The Road Partnership (LAMBOURN) BRED Patrick Moakley

3903* Funcheon Gale, up 3lb, is considered by his trainer to have enough speed to win at two-and-a-half miles, but this sort of trip puts less pressure on his jumping. (7/2)
4387 Banntown Bill (IRE) found the winner far too much of a handful. (7/2: 5/2-4/1)
4085* Black Church, raised a further 6lb, found this a good bit more competitive. (7/4: op 11/10)

4468 SANDRINGHAM (S) H'CAP HURDLE (0-95) (4-Y.O+) (Class G)

3-55 (3-56) **2m 4f 110y (11 hdls)** £2,080.00 (£580.00: £280.00) GOING minus 0.22 sec per fur (G)

SP RR SF

4309[4] **Hello Me Man (IRE) (78)** (BJLlewellyn) **9-11-0** MrJLLlewellyn (hld up & bhd: hdwy 7th: led 4 out: rdn out).....— **1** 9/2[2] 62 32
3892[4] **Star Performer (IRE) (92)** (AGHobbs) **6-11-7**(7) MrGShenkin (lw: hld up: hdwy appr 5th: ev ch whn hit last: hrd rdn: r.o) ....½ **2** 10/1 76 46
3442[2] **Khazari (USA) (68)** (RBrotherton) **9-10-4** LHarvey (hld up & bhd: hdwy 6th: one pce fr 3 out)....12 **3** 10/1 42 12
3796[P] **Look In The Mirror (71)** (NATwiston-Davies) **6-10-7** CLlewellyn (a.p: ev ch 4 out: hrd rdn 3 out: sn wknd) ....½ **4** 12/1 45 15
3889[2] **Powder Monkey (78)** (TNeedham) **7-11-0** GTormey (lw: plld hrd: hdwy 4th: wknd appr 2 out: mstke last)....1 **5** 10/1 51 21
4290* **Fleet Cadet (91)** (MCPipe) **6-11-13v** APMcCoy (lw: hld up & bhd: hdwy 7th: hmpd appr 4 out: nt rcvr)....12 **6** 5/2[1] 55+ 25
4328* **Killing Time (80)** (DBurchell) **6-11-2** 7x DJBurchell (lw: prom tl wknd 7th) ....s.h **7** 5/1[3] 44 14
3583[7] **Roc Age (68)** (GWDavies) **6-10-1**(3)ow1 MichaelBrennan (led to 4 out: wknd 3 out)....1¾ **8** 25/1 30 —
1562[6] **Provence (64)** (AWCarroll) **10-9-7**(7) MrJGoldstein (lw: prom tl wknd 4 out) ....nk **9** 14/1 26 —
3959[7] **Catwalker (IRE) (64)** (HJMWebb) **6-9-11**(3) SophieMitchell (lw: a bhd)....6 **10** 50/1 21 —
4002[3] **Strike-a-Pose (68)** (BJLlewellyn) **7-10-1**(3) GuyLewis (lw: chsd ldrs tl wknd 7th: eased whn no ch 3 out)....15 **11** 10/1 14 —
4002[8] **Westcoast (64)** (MTate) **6-9-7**(7) MrOMcPhail (lw: bhd fr 6th) ....5 **12** 33/1 6 —
3833[4] **Prize Match (71)** (JCTuck) **8-10-7** SMcNeill (lw: bhd fr 7th: t.o) ....18 **13** 14/1 — —
65[P] **Astrolabe (64)** (JMBradley) **5-10-0** BFenton (prom tl rdn & wknd 6th: t.o) ....7 **14** 16/1 — —

4235U **Nautical George (IRE) (88)** (JohnUpson) **7-11-5**(5) GSupple (sn bhd: t.o)....3 **15** 20/1 8 —
4157U **Madam Rose (IRE) (64)** (JWMullins) **7-10-0b1** SCurran (mstke 5th: sn rdn & bhd: t.o)....10 **16** 33/1 — —
4089[13] **Saafi (IRE) (67)** (RJBaker) **6-10-3b** VSlattery (hdwy 6th: 6th whn s.u appr 4 out).... **S** 25/1 — —
(SP 147.0%) **17 Rn**

4m 50.8 (3.80) CSF £50.99 CT £431.10 TOTE £10.00: £1.60 £1.90 £3.00 £2.80 (£36.00) Trio £46.00 OWNER Lodge Cross Partnership (BARGOED) BRED Mrs E. J. Hogan
LONG HANDICAP Provence 9-10 Astrolabe 9-8 Catwalker (IRE) 9-0 Madam Rose (IRE) 9-5 Westcoast 9-7
Bt in 5,000 gns
4309 Hello Me Man (IRE) found the combination of this shorter distance and a return to selling company doing the trick. (9/2)
3583 Star Performer (IRE), 8lb lower than when last in a handicap, dragged his hind legs through the final flight and found the winner had the edge. He can take a similar event. (10/1)
3442 Khazari (USA) had been raised 4lb for his second at Windsor. (10/1)
3340 Look In The Mirror, dropping back in distance, was descending to selling company for this handicap debut. (12/1)
3889 Powder Monkey will have to settle better to get this sort of trip. (10/1)
4290* Fleet Cadet, up 5lb, was just beginning to work his way into the picture when unfortunately stopped in his tracks. (5/2)
3338 Saafi (IRE) was considered to have brushed against Powder Monkey and tripped over. (25/1)

4469 JORROCKS NOVICES' HUNTERS' CHASE (5-Y.O+) (Class H)

4-30 (4-30) **3m (18 fncs)** £1,067.25 (£318.00: £151.50: £68.25) GOING minus 0.22 sec per fur (G)

			SP	RR	SF
4308*	**Phar Too Touchy** (VictorDartnall) **10-11-7**(7) MrNHarris (mde all: shkn up flat: r.o wl) ....—	**1**	8/11 1	95	14
3397F	**Savoy** (GRichards) **10-11-7**(7) CaptAOgden (hld up: hdwy 8th: chsd wnr fr 9th: rdn appr 2 out: one pce flat)...4	**2**	6/4 2	92	11
	Archer (IRE) (MrsJSLewis) **9-11-7**(7) MrMHarris (chsd wnr tl rdn 9th: wknd 11th) 19	**3**	12/1 3	80	—
4308U	**Sultan's Son** (MrsSCuthbert) **11-11-7**(7) MrGLewis (prom to 8th: t.o fr 11th)....17	**4**	16/1	68	—

(SP 111.5%) **4 Rn**

6m 8.6 (15.60) CSF £2.17 TOTE £1.60 (£1.40) OWNER Miss R. A. Francis (BARNSTAPLE) BRED Mrs L. Spuffard
4308* Phar Too Touchy handled these stiffer fences well until inclined to brush through the top in the later stages. (8/11)
3397 Savoy was forced to accept defeat in the final one hundred yards. (6/4)
Archer (IRE) was all out to win a match at Howick this season. (12/1: 6/1-14/1)

4470 SOUTH WEST AMATEUR H'CAP HURDLE (0-115) (5-Y.O+) (Class E)

5-00 (5-00) **3m (12 hdls)** £2,360.00 (£660.00: £320.00) GOING minus 0.22 sec per fur (G)

			SP	RR	SF
1849 2	**Ballindoo (83)** (RJArmson) **8-11-0**(7) MrRArmson (bkwd: hld up: hdwy appr 4 out: led flat: rdn out)....—	**1**	11/2 3	63	—
4310 6	**Apachee Flower (80)** (HSHowe) **7-10-11**(7) MrRWidger (led tl after 1st: led 7th tl flat: nt qckn)....¾	**2**	9/2 2	60	—
4248 10	**Stac-Pollaidh (78)** (KCBailey) **7-10-9**(7) MrRWakley (s.s: hdwy appr 4 out: sn rdn: styd on flat)....1	**3**	11/2 3	57	—
4278 3	**Zingibar (83)** (JMBradley) **5-11-0**(7) MrOMcPhail (prom: rdn appr 4 out: wknd 3 out)....12	**4**	11/2 3	54	—
4248 3	**Country Store (96)** (APJones) **8-11-13**(7) MrEJames (led 3rd to 7th: hrd rdn appr 4 out: wknd 2 out)....1¾	**5**	100/30 1	66	—
4100R	**Icantelya (IRE) (81)** (JWMullins) **8-10-12**(7) MrGWeatherley (hld up & plld hrd: j.slowly 6th: bhd fr 8th)....11	**6**	33/1	43	—
4220U	**Better Bythe Glass (IRE) (89)** (NATwiston-Davies) **8-11-10**(3) MrMRimell (lw: hld up: rdn after 7th: wknd appr 4 out)....2	**7**	11/2 3	50	—
4181U	**Colwall (81)** (MissPMWhittle) **6-10-12**(7) MrJGoldstein (plld hrd: led after 1st to 3rd: wknd appr 4 out)....3	**8**	8/1	40	—

(SP 116.8%) **8 Rn**

6m 0.5 (20.50) CSF £28.62 CT £130.81 TOTE £4.80: £1.40 £1.60 £2.00 (£19.00) Trio £13.30 OWNER Mr R. J. Armson (LEICESTER) BRED Niland Construction co Ltd.
1849 Ballindoo, hardly winning out of turn, belied his burly appearance in the paddock. (11/2)
3737 Apachee Flower, not foot-perfect at the penultimate hurdle, could not hold the winner on the short run-in. (9/2)
3962 Stac-Pollaidh, who would not have minded faster ground, stays well but is not over-burdened with speed. (11/2)
4278 Zingibar, back to the rating of the second of his wins this season, found this distance beyond him. (11/2: 4/1-6/)
4248 Country Store, 1lb higher than when third at Perth, may be finding three miles beyond her best. (100/30: op 2/1)

T/Plpt: £84.60 (139.92 Tckts). T/Qdpt: £24.10 (28.8 Tckts) KH

4414-UTTOXETER (L-H) (Good to soft)
Wednesday May 7th

WEATHER: showers

4471 MOBILEFONE GROUP NOVICES' HUNTERS' CHASE (5-Y.O+) (Class H)

5-50 (5-51) **3m 2f (20 fncs)** £1,558.00 (£438.00: £214.00) GOING: 0.48 sec per fur (GS)

			SP	RR	SF
	Front Cover (SPike) **7-11-2**(7) MissSVickery (lw: hld up: hdwy 7th: rdn appr 4 out: led 3 out: sn clr: easily) ..—	**1**	5/2 1	93+	12
3586 4	**Royal Segos** (MissSEBaxter) **10-11-7**(7) MrCStockton (led to 3 out: one pce)....13	**2**	14/1	90	9
	Gillie's Fountain (JDCallow) **6-11-7**(7) MrADalton (lw: in tch to 16th) ....dist	**3**	16/1	—	—
4322 6	**Very Daring** (JulianHunt) **7-11-7**(7) MissSSharratt (hld up: b.d 8th)....	**B**	50/1	—	—
	Just Marmalade (MrsDWilliams) **8-11-7**(7) MrRBurton (lw: b.d by loose horse 8th)....	**B**	16/1	—	—
4135 4	**Balasani (FR)** (JGO'Neill) **11-11-9**(5) MrASansome (lw: in tch: mstke 3rd: b.d 8th)....	**B**	5/1 2	—	—
	Domino Night (IRE) (EHaddock) **7-11-7**(7) MrGHanmer (lw: w ldr: mstke 11th: 3rd & wkng whn fell 2 out: dead)....	**F**	10/1 3	—	—
4160P	**Ryders Wells** (MrsMMorris) **10-11-7**(7) MrSWalker (swvd in air & uns rdr 2nd)	**U**	16/1	—	—
	Ita's Fellow (IRE) (ORPrince) **9-11-7**(7) MrsCFord (hmpd & uns rdr 8th)	**U**	5/2 1	—	—
	Fiscal Policy (ARTrotter) **9-11-7**(7) MrRTrotter (blnd & uns rdr 1st)	**U**	12/1	—	—

(SP 116.9%) **10 Rn**

7m 1.6 (34.60) CSF £35.65 TOTE £4.00: £1.60 £3.00 £3.30 (£34.00) Trio £145.70; £127.30 to 9/5/97 OWNER Mr Stewart Pike (SIDMOUTH) BRED S. Pike
Front Cover, a neatly-made half-sister to Proud Sun, looked briefly in trouble on the home turn, but ended up winning with plenty in hand. (5/2)
3586 Royal Segos was in the safest place the way things turned out, in trying to make all. (14/1: 10/1-16/1)
Gillie's Fountain was never out of last place, but only lost touch as he tired in the last half-mile. (16/1)

Ryders Wells, having shed his pilot early on, caused mayhem when loose, bringing down four rivals, and seemed to be lying in wait for the remainder on the final circuit. (16/1)
Fiscal Policy (12/1: op 7/1)

4472 HOUGHTON VAUGHAN (S) H'CAP HURDLE (0-95) (4-Y.O+) (Class G)

6-20 (6-20) **2m (9 hdls)** £1,878.50 (£526.00: £255.50) GOING: 0.48 sec per fur (GS)

	Horse	Details	Dist	Pos	SP	RR	SF
4089^{4}	**Blotoft (73)**	(SGollings) **5-11-3** MAFitzgerald (hld up: hdwy 5th: led appr 2 out: sn clr: comf)	—	**1**	$11/4^{2}$	62+	20
3631^{R}	**Mecado (78)**	(FJYardley) **10-11-3v**$^{(5)}$ XAizpuru (lw: chsd ldrs: rdn 5th: kpt on fr 3 out: no ch w wnr)	7	**2**	12/1	60	18
4283^{14}	**Playful Juliet (CAN) (76)**	(JCHaynes) **9-11-6b** SWynne (led 2nd to 4th: wnt 2nd 2 out: no imp)	hd	**3**	$4/1^{3}$	58	16
1446^{6}	**Bresil (USA) (56)**	(JJBridger) **8-9-7**$^{(7)}$ MarkBrown (lw: dropped rr 5th: styd on fr next)	13	**4**	12/1	25	—
3741^{6}	**Kings Vision (60)**	(WJenks) **5-10-4** TJenks (t: chsd ldrs to 5th: sn rdn & btn)	3	**5**	14/1	26	—
4089^{5}	**Wordsmith (IRE) (70)**	(JLHarris) **7-11-0** JSupple (lw: dropped rr & rdn 5th: n.d afterwards)	1¾	**6**	$9/4^{1}$	34	—
4217^{P}	**Orinoco Venture (IRE) (62)**	(ABailey) **6-10-6b** GaryLyons (lw: led to 2nd: led 4th: clr next: wknd & hdd appr 2 out)	3	**7**	12/1	23	—
3315^{9}	**Only A Sioux (59)**	(JRTurner) **5-10-3**^{ow3} WFry (chsd ldrs to 6th)	10	**8**	25/1	10	—
4142^{7}	**Days of Thunder (74)**	(MrsSMOdell) **9-11-1**$^{(3)}$ EHusband (chsd ldrs: j.rt 3rd: wknd 5th)	hd	**9**	9/1	25	—

(SP 121.0%) **9 Rn**

3m 58.3 (17.30) CSF £33.48 CT £123.79 TOTE £2.50: £1.40 £2.60 £1.90 (£16.50) Trio £69.10 OWNER Mr R. N. Forman (LOUTH) BRED R. N. Forman
LONG HANDICAP Only A Sioux 9-6 Bresil (USA) 9-10
Bt in 3,000 gns
4089 Blotoft appreciated being dropped out, and came there on the home turn absolutely running away. In this mood, he should win again. (11/4)
Mecado, who had pulled up in a point since his most recent run under Rules, was never travelling particularly well, but kept plugging away and would be better-suited by further. (12/1: op 8/1)
509* Playful Juliet (CAN) took a good hold early, but was staying on at the end and clearly is better over further. (4/1: 3/1-9/2)
Bresil (USA), a winning stayer on the Flat, doesn't seem to have taken to hurdles but, if he is to get competitive over hurdles, it will be over a longer trip. (12/1)
Kings Vision, tubed since his two-year-old days, must have been inconvenienced on such a wild, windy night. (14/1)
4089 Wordsmith (IRE) was less than enthusiastic setting out on the final circuit, losing his place and, with it, all chance. (9/4)

4473 BRADSHAW (BROS.) OPEN HUNTERS' CHASE (5-Y.O+) (Class H)

6-50 (6-50) **4m 2f (24 fncs)** £1,840.00 (£515.00: £250.00) GOING: 0.48 sec per fur (GS)

	Horse	Details	Dist	Pos	SP	RR	SF
4324^{2}	**The Malakarma**	(MissCSaunders) **11-12-0b**$^{1(5)}$ MrBPollock (lw: a.p: led 20th: rdn out)	—	**1**	$11/2^{3}$	117	38
4325^{3}	**Ryming Cuplet**	(MJTrickey) **12-11-12**$^{(7)}$ MrLJefford (hit 4th: hdwy 8th: chsd ldr fr 11th: one pce fr 3 out)	7	**2**	12/1	113	34
4324*	**Rusty Bridge**	(MrsSMJohnson) **10-12-2**$^{(3)}$ MrRThornton (led to 7th: rdn & lost pl 15th: rallied 19th: no ch whn hit 3 out)	17	**3**	$9/2^{2}$	103	24
4208^{2}	**Royal Jester**	(CStorey) **13-12-2**$^{(5)}$ MrCStorey (rdn 17th: a bhd)	dist	**4**	13/2	—	—
3637^{P}	**Holland House**	(PRChamings) **11-12-4**$^{(3)}$ MrCBonner (led 7th: hit next: rdn 18th: hdd & mstke 20th: blnd 3 out: 4th & wkng whn fell last)		**F**	$11/10^{1}$	—	—
3593^{2}	**Granville Guest**	(PFNicholls) **11-11-7**$^{(7)}$ MrJTizzard (lw: trckd ldrs: hmpd appr 11th: pckd 14th: wknd 19th: p.u bef 4 out)		**P**	11/1	—	—
3906^{3}	**Peajade**	(MissJillWormall) **13-11-7**$^{(7)}$ MissJWormall (in tch tl blnd & dropped rr 6th: j.slowly 10th: bhd whn p.u bef 19th)		**P**	20/1	—	—

(SP 115.3%) **7 Rn**

9m 1.3 (36.30) CSF £55.79 TOTE £7.50: £2.50 £7.10 (£69.00) OWNER Mr Charles Dixey (NORTHAMPTON) BRED C. R. Dixey
4324 The Malakarma loves this trip and was always travelling well, and repeated his success of two years ago. (11/2)
3799 Ryming Cuplet has done his winning under Rules on faster ground and over shorter trips, but ran on gallantly in the straight although no match for the winner. (12/1)
4324* Rusty Bridge had farmed the marathon hunter chases so far this season, but could not complete the hat-trick after wins at Taunton and Cheltenham. (9/2)
4208 Royal Jester facing his stiffest task in a long time on a rare sortie outside Scotland, was never travelling well. (13/2: op 4/1)
3403* Holland House, off since the Cheltenham Foxhunters', looked in charge until the whip was drawn going out on the final circuit. He got very tired in the closing stages, all but collapsing over the last. (11/10)
3593 Granville Guest (11/1: 8/1-12/1)

4474 COUTTS & CO. H'CAP HURDLE (0-125) (4-Y.O+) (Class D)

7-20 (7-20) **2m (9 hdls)** £2,717.00 (£762.00: £371.00) GOING: 0.48 sec per fur (GS)

	Horse	Details	Dist	Pos	SP	RR	SF
3992^{4}	**Fourth in Line (IRE) (116)**	(MJWilkinson) **9-12-0** WMarston (led 4th: clr 3 out: pushed out)	—	**1**	$7/2^{3}$	93	59
3569^{2}	**Wise King (106)**	(JABOld) **7-11-4** CLlewellyn (led to 4th: chsd wnr after: one pce appr 3 out)	4	**2**	$2/1^{1}$	79	45
4271^{2}	**Darakshan (IRE) (110)**	(MissHCKnight) **5-11-8** JCulloty (hld up: hdwy appr 3 out: no imp fr next)	6	**3**	$5/2^{2}$	77	43
4307^{11}	**Saint Ciel (USA) (102)**	(FJordan) **9-11-0** APMcCoy (hld up: hdwy 6th: rdn & btn next)	12	**4**	4/1	57	23
4229^{2}	**Handy Lass (102)**	(JSSmith) **8-11-0** MAFitzgerald (lw: chsd ldrs: rdn appr 3 out: sn wknd)	29	**5**	5/1	28	—

(SP 120.8%) **5 Rn**

3m 52.1 (11.10) CSF £11.20 TOTE £4.80: £1.70 £2.30 (£8.50) OWNER John Nicholls (Banbury) Ltd (BANBURY) BRED Golden Vale Stud in Ireland
3992 Fourth in Line (IRE) was brought wide in the home straight, and the manoeuvre did nothing to harm his chance. This was the first time he had had the ground in his favour since slipping to a reasonable mark. (7/2)
3569 Wise King, still a novice, was running in a handicap for the first time and was not disgraced, staying on so well that he ought to stay further. (2/1)
4271 Darakshan (IRE), still looks well handicapped on bits of his novice hurdle form, but failed to run a race and may have had enough for now. (5/2: 6/4-11/4)
2048 Saint Ciel (USA) has been out of form, and ran poorly in conditions that should have suited. (4/1: op 6/1)
4229 Handy Lass seemed unsuited by the fact that this race turned into something of a slog. (5/1)

4475 LUCIA FARMER H'CAP CHASE (0-125) (5-Y.O+) (Class D)

7-50 (7-50) **2m 4f (15 fncs)** £3,517.50 (£1,065.00: £520.00: £247.50) GOING: 0.48 sec per fur (GS)

Form	Horse	Dist	Pos	SP	RR	SF
4180*	**Formal Invitation (IRE) (110)** (DNicholson) **8-11-7**$^{(3)}$ MrRThornton (trckd ldr: led appr 3 out: rdn out)	—	1	7/4^{1}	122+	—
4185^{9}	**Andermatt (108)** (JMackie) **10-11-5**$^{(3)}$ EHusband (lw: hld up: blnd 2nd: hdwy 11th: chal appr 3 out: one pce appr next)	3	2	14/1	118	—
4013^{8}	**Sailor Jim (100)** (PTDalton) **10-11-0** APMcCoy (j.w: led tl appr 3 out: sn wknd)	25	3	7/4^{1}	90	—
4302^{F}	**Plunder Bay (USA) (110)** (NJHenderson) **6-11-10** MAFitzgerald (lw: chsd ldrs to 4 out)	15	4	100/30^{2}	88	—
4185^{8}	**Wudimp (105)** (MrsJStorey) **8-11-5** MrCStorey (lw: mskte 1st: rdn 9th: a bhd)	2	5	7/1^{3}	81	—
				(SP 115.0%)		**5 Rn**

5m 6.2 CSF £18.66 TOTE £2.30: £1.90 £2.60 (£20.50) OWNER The Plough Partnership (TEMPLE GUITING) BRED Patrick Eddery Ltd

4180* Formal Invitation (IRE) seemed just as effective on this slower ground, is lightly-raced and remains ahead of the Handicapper. (7/4)

Andermatt, racing with his tongue tied down, bounced back to form and is on a winning mark, so was a little unfortunate to run into such a well-handicapped rival. (14/1)

4013 Sailor Jim again stopped alarmingly quickly after giving a bold display of jumping from the front. (7/4)

3986* Plunder Bay (USA) looked to be travelling well until dropping away in a few strides entering the straight. This ground seems to find him out these days. (100/30)

Wudimp made a mess of the first and was never going well thereafter. (7/1)

4476 A W STOKES DRUMS NOVICES' HURDLE (4-Y.O+) (Class E)

8-20 (8-21) **3m 110y (12 hdls)** £2,410.50 (£678.00: £331.50) GOING: 0.48 sec per fur (GS)

Form	Horse	Dist	Pos	SP	RR	SF
4309^{2}	**Mr Christie (88)** (MissLCSiddall) **5-11-7** AThornton (hld up: hdwy appr 3 out: edgd lft & led last: rdn clr)	—	1	5/1^{3}	72	40
3967^{2}	**Beechfield Flyer (92)** (WClay) **6-11-0** GTormey (a.p: led 3 out tl hdd & hit last: nt pce of wnr)	6	2	4/1^{2}	61	29
4257^{5}	**Lottery Ticket (IRE) (101)** (TRGeorge) **8-11-0** MAFitzgerald (in tch: hdwy 9th: r.o one pce appr last)	1	3	4/1^{2}	60	28
3967^{9}	**Cypress Avenue (IRE) (83)** (MrsVCWard) **5-10-11**$^{(3)}$ MrRThornton (lw: chsd ldrs: one pce fr 3 out)	1	4	16/1	60	28
3355^{2}	**Banny Hill Lad (108)** (CPMorlock) **7-11-0** JRKavanagh (chsd ldrs: led 9th to next: one pce appr last)	½	5	15/8^{1}	59	27
3902^{4}	**King's Rainbow (IRE)** (MrsDHaine) **8-10-9** JFTitley (hld up: hdwy 7th: ev ch 2 out: n.m.r & swtchd appr last: sn btn)	1½	6	16/1	54	22
4224^{6}	**Sidney** (JCMcConnochie) **8-11-0** SWynne (in tch to 9th)	dist	7	66/1	—	—
3910^{10}	**Push On Polly (IRE)** (JParkes) **7-10-9** JSupple (in tch tl mstke 7th)	½	8	66/1	—	—
2826^{P}	**Upham Surprise** (JABOld) **9-11-0** GUpton (bit bkwd: led to 3rd: led after 8th to next: wknd qckly 3 out)	dist	9	8/1	—	—
	Trentside Major (CSmith) **5-11-0** MRanger (bit bkwd: rdn 5th: bhd tl p.u after 8th)		P	33/1	—	—
	Moor Hall Prince (NMBabbage) **7-11-0** BFenton (plld hrd: sn prom: wknd appr 7th: t.o whn p.u bef 9th)		P	50/1	—	—
4404^{F}	**Bottle Black** (THind) **10-11-0** PMcLoughlin (in tch: rdn 8th: sn wknd: t.o whn p.u bef 2 out)		P	66/1	—	—
	Steel Chimes (IRE) (BRCambidge) **8-11-0** GaryLyons (bkwd: blnd 5th: a bhd: t.o whn p.u bef 3 out)		P	66/1	—	—
4376^{P}	**Scale Down (IRE)** (JAPickering) **8-11-0** WMarston (led 3rd: blnd 8th: sn hdd & wknd: p.u bef next)		P	50/1	—	—
	Three Jays (DTThom) **10-11-0** KGaule (bit bkwd: mstke 4th: bhd tl p.u bef 8th)		P	33/1	—	—
				(SP 130.1%)		**15 Rn**

6m 2.9 (20.90) CSF £24.60 TOTE £9.00: £2.50 £2.00 £1.60 (£11.60) Trio £18.90 OWNER David Mann Partnership (TADCASTER) BRED Hesmonds Stud Ltd

4309 Mr Christie, another to adopt the 'wide outside in the home straight' policy with success, came with a terrific run to lead at the last. He has had a long season, but has been pretty consistent. (5/1: 7/2-11/2)

3967 Beechfield Flyer, who couldn't confirm earlier form with the winner on better terms, had just been headed when getting a slight bump in the air from the winner, rapping the final flight. (4/1)

4257 Lottery Ticket (IRE) lacked the pace at a vital time and all he seems to do is stay. (4/1)

3328 Cypress Avenue (IRE) is another who lacks any change of gear. (16/1)

3355 Banny Hill Lad had been off for ten weeks and it probably made all the difference in very testing conditions. (15/8)

3902 King's Rainbow (IRE), ridden with more restraint, ran a much better race, but failed to last home on the sticky ground. (16/1)

T/Plpt: £213.20 (58.82 Tckts). T/Qdpt: £36.90 (21.41 Tckts) Dk

3990-WETHERBY (L-H) (Good to Soft)

Wednesday May 7th

WEATHER: raining

4477 WASHDALE NOVICES' CONDITIONAL HURDLE (4-Y.O) (Class E)

6-05 (6-05) **2m (9 hdls)** £2,232.50 (£620.00: £297.50) GOING: 0.42 sec per fur (GS)

Form	Horse	Dist	Pos	SP	RR	SF
3789^{5}	**Oversman** (JGFitzGerald) **4-10-12** FLeahy (lw: trckd ldrs: chal & lft in ld 3 out: lft wl clr next: rdn out flat)	—	1	2/1^{1}	62	—
4282^{6}	**Political Mandate** (RNixon) **4-10-2**$^{(5)}$ CMcCormack (trckd ldrs: rdn 6th: wknd next: lft poor 2nd 2 out)	15	2	25/1	42	—
	Mr Bruno (MABarnes) **4-10-12** STaylor (hmpd 3rd: sn wl bhd: t.o whn blnd 6th)	dist	3	50/1	—	—
3940^{11}	**Double Vintage (IRE)** (MCChapman) **4-10-12** GLee (sn bhd: reminders 2nd: t.o 6th)	1½	4	50/1	—	—
4296^{2}	**Amazing Sail (IRE) (90)** (MissMKMilligan) **4-11-5** ECallaghan (led tl fell 3 out)		F	2/1^{1}	—	—
4184^{7}	**Regal Eagle** (MDHammond) **4-10-12** LAspell (lw: trckd ldrs: 4th whn fell 3rd)		F	9/4^{2}	—	—
	Irish Oasis (IRE) (BSRothwell) **4-10-12** BGrattan (trckd ldrs: wkng whn sltly hmpd 3 out: 8l 2nd & wl btn whn fell next)		F	20/1^{3}	—	—
				(SP 110.0%)		**7 Rn**

4m 1.9 (19.90) CSF £35.80 TOTE £2.90: £1.90 £5.40 (£20.10) OWNER Marquesa de Moratalla (MALTON) BRED Addison Racing and Peter V. McCalmont

3789 Oversman wore a tongue-strap. Kept slightly wide and out of trouble, he already had his race won when left in a commanding lead at the penultimate flight. Tying up on the run-in, he had to be kept right up to his work and looked to finish tired. Presumably he has some sort of wind problem. (2/1)

4282 Political Mandate raced keenly, but suddenly came under pressure and found nothing at all turning for home. (25/1)

Mr Bruno, an excitable sort, soon lost touch. (50/1)

Double Vintage (IRE) was under the whip as early as the second flight. (50/1)

4296 Amazing Sail (IRE) was just about to be headed when he fell three out. Perhaps he did not appreciate this ground. (2/1)

4184 Regal Eagle, the pick of the paddock, came to grief at the third flight. (9/4: op 6/4)
Irish Oasis (IRE) raced keenly, but had just come off the bit and was finding nothing when he was slightly hampered by the fall of Amazing Sail. He was still in second spot but legless, when he appeared to slip on landing and fall two out. (20/1)

4478 CHURCH FENTON H'CAP CHASE (0-135) (5-Y.O+) (Class C)

6-35 (6-35) **2m (12 fncs)** £4,532.50 (£1,360.00: £655.00: £302.50) GOING: 0.42 sec per fur (GS)

				SP	RR	SF
4258[3]	**Political Tower (125)** (RNixon) **10-11-4** BStorey (pushed along 8th: outpcd next: hdwy u.p 2 out: led appr last: r.o wl)	—	**1**	4/1	134	58
4311[3]	**Mister Oddy (127)** (JSKing) **11-11-6** TJMurphy (lw: mde most tl appr last: unable qckn)	3	**2**	2/1[1]	133	57
4206[3]	**Leotard (135)** (MissVenetiaWilliams) **10-12-0** NWilliamson (w ldr: ev ch & rdn whn mstke 2 out: kpt on same pce)	1¼	**3**	9/4[2]	140	64
4311*	**Cumbrian Challenge (IRE) (131)** (TDEasterby) **8-11-10** 6x RGarritty (trckd ldrs: hit 7th: drvn along next: wknd after 3 out: eased)	16	**4**	5/2[3]	120	44
				(SP 112.7%)		**4 Rn**

4m 0.3 (8.30) CSF £11.50 TOTE £4.90 (£3.60) OWNER Mr G. R. S. Nixon (SELKIRK) BRED R. Nixon
4258 Political Tower, who took a crashing fall at Aintree and then broke a blood-vessel at Ayr, bounced back to take this race for the second year running. Outpaced and under pressure four out, he would not accept defeat. (4/1)
4311 Mister Oddy, 6lb better off with Cumbrian Challenge for a three-length beating at Ascot, tried hard to make all but, in the end, met an even more determined opponent. (2/1)
4206 Leotard ran another creditable race. (9/4)
4311* Cumbrian Challenge (IRE), under a 6lb penalty, was struggling on this easy ground after hitting the seventh and his rider gave up two out. (5/2)

4479 RACING CHANNEL NOVICES' HURDLE (4-Y.O+) (Class D)

7-05 (7-06) **2m 4f 110y (10 hdls)** £2,880.00 (£805.00: £390.00) GOING: 0.42 sec per fur (GS)

				SP	RR	SF
3644[8]	**Diddy Rymer (74)** (MrsSJSmith) **7-10-9** RichardGuest (jnd ldrs 6th: led appr 3 out: clr next: drvn out)	—	**1**	10/1	61?	12
4188[4]	**Boston Man (88)** (RDEWoodhouse) **6-11-6b** RDunwoody (chsd ldrs: rdn & lost pl 6th: styd on fr 3 out: no ch w wnr)	3½	**2**	7/1	69	20
3888[7]	**Riveaux (IRE) (79)** (GRichards) **7-11-0** PCarberry (hld up & plld hrd: jnd ldrs 2nd: blnd 5th: one pce fr 3 out)	10	**3**	7/1	56	7
4224[4]	**Beck and Call (IRE)** (MissVenetiaWilliams) **8-11-0** NWilliamson (chsd ldrs: reminders 3rd: lost pl 6th: t.o fr 3 out: kpt on fr next)	1½	**4**	7/2[2]	54	5
4146[4]	**Silent Guest (IRE) (87)** (MDHammond) **4-11-0** RGarritty (jnd ldrs 3rd: outpcd 6th: wknd appr 3 out)	14	**5**	13/2	49	—
3990[P]	**Praise Be (FR) (73)** (TPTate) **7-11-0b**[1] PNiven (mde most tl appr 3 out: sn wknd)	hd	**6**	33/1	43	—
4243[5]	**Lord Pat (IRE)** (MissMKMilligan) **6-11-0** ASSmith (plld hrd: chsd ldrs to 6th: sn outpcd)	7	**7**	33/1	38	—
4288[2]	**China King (IRE)** (JGFitzGerald) **6-11-0** BStorey (jnd ldrs 5th: 3rd & wkng whn hit 3 out: 4th whn blnd next: eased)	3½	**8**	3/1[1]	35	—
4056[5]	**Milenberg Joys** (WHTinning) **5-11-0** DParker (wnt prom 5th: rdn 7th: wknd next)	9	**9**	16/1	28	—
2012[7]	**Jolly Heart (IRE)** (OBrennan) **7-11-0** MBrennan (plld hrd: drvn along & lost pl 4th: t.o 7th: p.u bef next)		**P**	16/1	—	—
	Moonlight Venture (MartynWane) **5-11-0** NSmith (sn bhd: t.o 7th: p.u bef 2 out)		**P**	50/1	—	—
3990[7]	**Tweedswood (IRE) (90)** (PBeaumont) **7-11-0** RSupple (bhd & drvn along 4th: blnd & uns rdr next)		**U**	5/1[3]	—	—
				(SP 130.9%)		**12 Rn**

5m 8.1 (21.10) CSF £78.25 TOTE £15.00: £2.30 £2.70 £3.00 (£34.90) Trio £76.80 OWNER Brampton Royal Oak (BINGLEY) BRED G. G. A. Gregson
WEIGHT FOR AGE 4yo-6lb
3481 Diddy Rymer proved well suited by the good gallop and the softish ground. Despite not being fluent at the last two, she was never in any danger. (10/1: 8/1-12/1)
4188 Boston Man seemed to sulk and drop himself out halfway through the race. His rider was in no mood to let him get away with it though and, keeping him right up to his work over the last three, he was closing the gap at the line. There is no doubt he has his fair share of ability, but he is not one to rely upon. (7/1)
3888 Riveaux (IRE), who showed a good action going down, raced keenly but found nothing under pressure from three out. He is proving a disappointment. (7/1)
4224 Beck and Call (IRE), who ran well last time after a long absence, ran a strange race. Given some sharp reminders at the third, he was tailed off three out but decided to stay on. It is possible he needs three miles and very soft ground. (7/2)
4288 China King (IRE) wore a tongue-strap. Moving up full of running after halfway, he was already weakening when he hit three out and was legless when he blundered at the next. (3/1)

4480 HEADINGLEY H'CAP CHASE (0-130) (5-Y.O+) (Class C)

7-35 (7-37) **2m 4f 110y** £4,532.50 (£1,360.00: £655.00: £302.50) GOING: 0.42 sec per fur (GS)

				SP	RR	SF
4247[2]	**Nicholas Plant (99)** (JSGoldie) **8-10-0** GCahill (led: mstke 7th: drvn along 10th: hdd next: led 2 out: r.o wl)	—	**1**	3/1[3]	112	47
4206*	**Destin d'Estruval (FR) (123)** (DNicholson) **6-11-10** RJohnson (lw: w ldrs: led 11th: hit 3 out: hdd next: nt qckn)	4	**2**	9/4[2]	133	68
3972*	**Brighter Shade (IRE) (105)** (MrsMReveley) **7-10-6** PNiven (hit 1st: jnd ldrs 10th: effrt & hit 4 out: wknd appr 2 out)	12	**3**	2/1[1]	106	41
4247[4]	**Deep Decision (99)** (PCheesbrough) **11-10-0** ASSmith (w ldrs: outpcd 11th: rdn & wknd appr 3 out)	4	**4**	14/1	96	31
4214[4]	**Golden Hello (103)** (TDEasterby) **6-10-4** NWilliamson (lw: hld up: mstke 9th (water): fell next)		**F**	7/1	—	—
				(SP 108.3%)		**5 Rn**

5m 16.0 (9.00) CSF £9.14 TOTE £3.30: £1.60 £2.10 (£4.00) OWNER Mrs M. F. Paterson (GLASGOW) BRED Mrs J. A. Armstrong
LONG HANDICAP Nicholas Plant 9-11 Deep Decision 9-10
4247 Nicholas Plant, runner-up on his five outings since his last win, was certainly not winning out of turn and he showed commendable zest and enthusiasm to regain the advantage. (3/1)
4206* Destin d'Estruval (FR), from a 2lb higher mark and unsuited by the evening rain, was in front when he hit three out. That made up his mind for him and he soon found the winner too strong. (9/4)
3972* Brighter Shade (IRE) has run-up a shade light. After hitting the first, he was being driven along to keep up when he hit four out and was asked to do just enough from there on to secure third spot. He will be an interesting proposition in similar events next term after a summer at grass. (2/1)
4247 Deep Decision saw the ground turn against him. (14/1)

4481 CATTAL NOVICES' CHASE (5-Y.O+) (Class D)
8-05 (8-07) **3m 1f (18 fncs)** £3,496.00 (£1,048.00: £504.00: £232.00) GOING: 0.42 sec per fur (GS)

				SP	RR	SF
4245*	**Colonel In Chief (IRE) (120)** (GRichards) **7-12-6** PCarberry (led to 3rd: led on bit between last 2: easily)	—	1	Evens 1	111+	—
4221 3	**Kiltulla (IRE) (72)** (MrsSJSmith) **7-11-2** RichardGuest (led 3rd tl between last 2: no ch w wnr)	5	2	15/2	90	—
	Dragons Bay (IRE) (MrsMReveley) **8-11-2** PNiven (bhd: sme hdwy 10th: sn wl outpcd)	dist	3	12/1	—	—
3945 2	**Karenastino (72)** (MrsSJSmith) **6-11-3**(5) RWilkinson (chsd ldrs: rdn 14th: wknd fr 4 out)	16	4	7/1 3	—	—
4408 6	**Quixall Crossett (56)** (EMCaine) **12-10-11**(5) MrMHNaughton (outpcd 5th: bhd whn hit 10th: sn t.o)	dist	5	66/1	—	—
3909 4	**Trump (85)** (CParker) **8-11-2** DParker (nt j.w: hit 2nd: hdwy 10th: mstke & wknd 12th: bhd whn p.u after 4 out)		P	4/1 2	—	—
3715 3	**Strongalong (IRE) (73)** (PCheesbrough) **7-11-2** ASSmith (w ldrs: mstke 6th: rdn & lost pl 8th: t.o 12th: p.u bef 4 out)		P	12/1	—	—
				(SP 111.1%)		**7 Rn**

6m 45.3 CSF £7.99 TOTE £2.00: £1.30 £2.50 (£9.70) OWNER Mr Robert Ogden (PENRITH) BRED John Noonan
OFFICIAL EXPLANATION **Trump: was unsuited by the ground, and gurgled in the closing stages.**

4245* Colonel In Chief (IRE) was never out of second gear and this will have done his confidence a power of good after Perth. A grand type with any amount of potential, there is no doubt he is capable of picking up a big handicap next term. (Evens)

4221 Kiltulla (IRE) never gave up trying, but he was banging his head against a brick wall. He would have been receiving 30lb from the winner in a handicap. (15/2)

Dragons Bay (IRE), making a belated racecourse debut, has been entered in hunter chases. He took time to get his eye in but showed some encouragement for the future. (12/1)

3945 Karenastino, who had plenty on his plate, chased the first two but, under pressure a long way from home, dropped right away over the last four furlongs. (7/1)

4482 HUNSINGORE H'CAP HURDLE (0-120) (4-Y.O+) (Class D)
8-35 (8-38) **2m (9 hdls)** £2,705.00 (£755.00: £365.00) GOING: 0.42 sec per fur (GS)

				SP	RR	SF
4285*	**Teejay'n'aitch (IRE) (85)** (JSGoldie) **5-9-12**(5) STaylor (mde all: r.o strly between last 2: drvn out)	—	1	11/4 1	63	7
4223 3	**Kierchem (IRE) (82)** (CGrant) **6-10-0** NWilliamson (hld up: wnt prom 6th: kpt on fr 2 out: no imp)	5	2	11/4 1	55	—
4154 3	**Highland Way (IRE) (89)** (MartinTodhunter) **9-10-0**(7) CMcCormack (hld up: stdy hdwy 6th: one pce fr 2 out)	9	3	3/1 2	53	—
3995 6	**Fox Sparrow (90)** (NTinkler) **7-10-8b** RDunwoody (trckd ldrs: drvn along 6th: wknd after next)	1	4	5/1 3	53	—
4246 6	**Sarmatian (USA) (110)** (MDHammond) **6-12-0** RGarritty (hld up: hdwy 6th: rdn & wknd after next)	20	5	8/1	53	—
4259 P	**Going Public (82)** (PCheesbrough) **10-10-0** ASSmith (w ldrs: mstke 4th: wknd after 6th)	30	6	20/1	—	—
				(SP 110.9%)		**6 Rn**

3m 58.3 (16.30) CSF £9.72 TOTE £2.70: £1.50 £2.70 (£4.60) OWNER Mr Andrew Paterson (GLASGOW) BRED David Hyland
LONG HANDICAP Kierchem (IRE) 9-10 Going Public 9-13

4285* Teejay'n'aitch (IRE), from a 7lb higher mark, made light of the conditions and, jumping particularly well, took this in good style. (11/4: 2/1-3/1)

4223 Kierchem (IRE), 4lb out of the handicap, looked held by the winner on course and distance running in March, and so it proved. (11/4)

4154 Highland Way (IRE), as usual, travelled strongly, but when popped the question found next to nothing. (3/1: 9/4-7/2)

Fox Sparrow, with the blinkers on again, looked anything but enthusiastic. (5/1)

1502 Sarmatian (USA) found the ground against him after heavy rain for most of the evening. (8/1: op 4/1)

T/Plpt: £398.30 (31.25 Tckts). T/Qdpt: £29.90 (31.14 Tckts) WG

4483a - 4499a : (Irish Racing) - See Computer Raceform

4389-SEDGEFIELD (L-H) (Good to firm, Good patches)
Friday May 9th
WEATHER: fine

4500 ALPHAMERIC NOVICES' HURDLE (4-Y.O+) (Class E)
2-00 (2-00) **2m 5f 110y (10 hdls)** £2,355.00 (£655.00: £315.00) GOING minus 0.40 sec per fur (GF)

				SP	RR	SF
3424 8	**Toshiba Talk (IRE) (77)** (BEllison) **5-10-7**(7) CMcCormack (hld up: gd hdwy 7th: led after 3 out: sn clr: r.o)	—	1	16/1	70	14
4393*	**Catch the Pigeon (81)** (REBarr) **8-11-2** NSmith (chsd ldrs: drvn along 3 out: styd on same pce between last 2)	5	2	5/2 2	68	12
4249*	**Royal York (100)** (GRichards) **5-11-2** PCarberry (hld up: effrt after 3 out: rdn between last 2: one pce)	5	3	11/10 1	65	9
58 2	**Muzrak (CAN) (101)** (MDHammond) **6-11-7** RGarritty (bit bkwd: trckd ldrs: shkn up & outpcd 3 out: kpt on same pce)	hd	4	8/1 3	70	14
4393 W	**Erni (FR) (80)** (TPTate) **5-10-7**(7) RMcCarthy (nt j.w: led to 7th: wknd appr 2 out)	5	5	12/1	59	3
4296 13	**Rubislaw (50)** (MrsKMLamb) **5-10-7v**(7) MissSLamb (trckd ldrs: led 7th tl after next: sn wknd)	24	6	100/1	41	—
4393 7	**Strong Character (56)** (DALamb) **11-11-0** JBurke (bhd fr 3 out)	8	7	200/1	35	—
3910 13	**Another George** (MissMKMilligan) **7-11-0** ASSmith (w ldrs tl lost pl after 7th: sn bhd: t.o)	dist	8	12/1	—	—
				(SP 110.1%)		**8 Rn**

5m 5.4 (5.40) CSF £48.52 TOTE £11.60: £2.30 £1.20 £1.00 (£19.00) OWNER Toshiba (UK) Ltd (LANCHESTER) BRED Dr F. J. Healy

Toshiba Talk (IRE) bounced back to the useful form he showed at one stage last season and it was no surprise to his trainer who thought he had come right. Dashed clear after three out, he was never in danger of being caught. (16/1)

4393* Catch the Pigeon, driven along three out, kept on in pursuit but lacked the pace to get in a blow. (5/2: 3/1-2/1)

4249* Royal York, who has run up very light, took a keen grip. Caught slightly unawares when the winner made his dash for home, under pressure between the last two she pulled out very little. (11/10: evens-11/8)

58 Muzrak (CAN), absent for 329 days, looked in need of the outing and ran like it. (8/1: op 7/2)

3727 Erni (FR) did not treat his hurdles with any respect and might be seen to better advantage over fences next term. (12/1)

Another George (12/1: op 20/1)

4501 JOHN WADE GROUP OF COMPANIES SERIES FINAL (S) H'CAP HURDLE (4-Y.O+) (Class G)

2-30 (2-30) **2m 5f 110y (10 hdls)** £6,775.00 (£2,050.00: £1,000.00: £475.00) GOING minus 0.40 sec per fur (GF)

				SP	RR	SF
4296[6]	**Shelton Abbey (68)** (JWade) **11-10-3b** PCarberry (lw: dropped rr & reminders 6th: hdwy u.p 3 out: hrd rdn & styd on flat: led towards fin)	—	1	12/1	49	—
4389[2]	**Barton Heights (85)** (MrsMReveley) **5-11-6** PNiven (lw: chsd ldrs: drvn along 5th: led 3 out: sn hrd rdn: jst ct)	nk	2	11/8[1]	66	16
4289[4]	**Royal Hand (72)** (RJArmson) **7-10-7v**[ow7] MrRArmson (a chsng ldrs: styd on one pce fr 2 out)	2	3	20/1	51	—
4389*	**Flintlock (IRE) (73)** (HAlexander) **7-10-3**(5) 5x RMcGrath (lw: hld up: jnd ldrs 7th: ev ch 2 out: one pce appr last)	1	4	9/2[2]	52	2
4394[5]	**Nite Sprite (65)** (REBarr) **7-9-9**(5) STaylor (chsd ldrs: mstke 2nd: drvn along & outpcd 6th: one pce fr 3 out)	3½	5	12/1	41	—
3892[6]	**Snowy Lane (IRE) (71)** (JNeville) **9-10-6hb**[ow1] RGarritty (chsd ldrs tl lost pl after 7th: n.d)	2	6	10/1	46	—
4060[7]	**Red Jam Jar (93)** (SBBell) **12-12-0** KJohnson (led to 3 out: wknd appr next)	3	7	11/2[3]	65	15
4163[8]	**Catton Lady (65)** (RCraggs) **7-9-9b[1]**(5) BGrattan (sn bhd: t.o 3 out)	17	8	33/1	25	—
3642[U]	**Obvious Risk (65)** (EMCaine) **6-9-7**(7) CMcCormack (sn drvn along: chsd ldrs tl lost pl 7th: t.o whn p.u bef 2 out: lame)		P	14/1	—	—
				(SP 114.5%)	**9 Rn**	

5m 7.0 (7.00) CSF £27.00 CT £310.73 TOTE £9.40: £1.90 £1.10 £13.30 (£11.60) Trio £55.70 OWNER Mr John Wade (MORDON) BRED Mrs A. T. Grantham

LONG HANDICAP Nite Sprite 9-6 Royal Hand 9-10 Catton Lady 8-13 Obvious Risk 9-8

No bid

3607 Shelton Abbey did everything he could to get out of this, dropping himself right out with a circuit to go. His brilliant jockey would have none of it. Making fifteen lengths up from the third last and six lengths from the last, he struck his mount six times with the whip on the run-in to make his mind up for him and they caught the flagging second in the shadow of the post. Surely no other jump jockey born could have won on this one. (12/1)

4389 Barton Heights, flat out a circuit from home, made the best of his way home three out but, treading water on the run-in, was caught almost on the line. (11/8)

4055 Royal Hand, hard at work some way from home, kept on willingly but at the one pace.The 7lb overweight could not have helped. (20/1)

4389* Flintlock (IRE), under a 5lb penalty, did not find a lot under pressure. (9/2: op 5/2)

4502 DUDLEY DUKES ANTIQUE FAIR NOVICES' CHASE (5-Y.O+) (Class E)

3-00 (3-06) **2m 110y (13 fncs)** £3,127.25 (£938.00: £451.50: £208.25) GOING minus 0.40 sec per fur (GF)

				SP	RR	SF
3030[B]	**Lepton (IRE) (60)** (JWCurtis) **6-11-0b** RGarritty (bhd tl gd hdwy 4 out: hrd rdn & styd on to ld flat)	—	1	33/1	99	1
4057[5]	**Hee's a Dancer (96)** (MissLucindaRussell) **5-10-8** AThornton (w ldrs: led 4 out tl hdd & no ex flat: fin lame)	2½	2	5/2[2]	97	—
	Sunkala Shine (SBClark) **9-10-7**(7) MissRClark (bhd: gd hdwy u.p 9th: one pce fr 3 out)	9	3	50/1	88	—
1138[2]	**Mr Reiner (IRE) (80)** (JWade) **9-11-0** PCarberry (lw: in tch: effrt u.p 4 out: outpcd fr 2 out)	¾	4	5/1[3]	87	—
3790[4]	**Moss Pageant (74)** (FTWalton) **7-11-0** BStorey (led to 4 out: wknd after next)	27	5	9/4[1]	61	—
4153[3]	**Aristodemus (65)** (MrsLMarshall) **8-11-0b** KJohnson (sn bhd: reminders 4th)	2½	6	33/1	59	—
4151[F]	**Meesonette** (BEllison) **5-10-3** DParker (bhd & drvn along 7th: sn t.o)	dist	7	100/1	—	—
4151*	**Gone Ashore (IRE) (70)** (MABarnes) **6-11-7** GCahill (chsd ldrs: hit 8th: wknd appr 2 out: p.u bef last)		P	5/1[3]	—	—
3608[F]	**Childsway** (SJRobinson) **9-11-0** NSmith (nt j.w: sn bhd: t.o whn p.u bef 6th)		P	66/1	—	—
4410[6]	**Wild Brook (IRE) (72)** (BEllison) **7-10-7**(7) CMcCormack (in tch tl outpcd 9th: bhd whn p.u lame bef last)		P	20/1	—	—
4334[4]	**Nobodys Flame (IRE) (74)** (SIPittendrigh) **9-11-0** ASSmith (hit 1st: sn bhd: t.o 8th: p. u bef 2 out)		P	100/1	—	—
				(SP 108.8%)	**11 Rn**	

4m 5.6 (7.60) CSF £98.78 TOTE £45.00: £9.10 £1.20 £6.20 (£95.70) Trio £281.70 OWNER Mr J. W. P. Curtis (DRIFFIELD) BRED J. Boylson

WEIGHT FOR AGE 5yo-6lb

OFFICIAL EXPLANATION Wild Brook (IRE): had struck into himself.

1033 Lepton (IRE), who had failed to complete the course on his five previous outings, was given a fine ride and pulled off a shock victory. (33/1)

4057 Hee's a Dancer looked set for victory when taking it up but he began to tread water after the last and was run out of it up the hill. He was lame afterwards. (5/2)

Sunkala Shine, placed second from three outings in point-to-points, was left behind from three out. (50/1)

1138 Mr Reiner (IRE), having his first outing for 188 days, has recorded all his six victories over hurdles here. Tapped for foot, he needs further than this. (5/1)

3790 Moss Pageant made the running but found very little. (9/4)

4503 GEORGE CARPENTER MEMORIAL H'CAP CHASE (0-110) (5-Y.O+) (Class E)

3-30 (3-32) **3m 3f (21 fncs)** £3,574.00 (£1,072.00: £516.00: £238.00) GOING minus 0.40 sec per fur (GF)

				SP	RR	SF
256[8]	**Jimmy O'Dea (90)** (JMackie) **10-10-5v**(3) EHusband (j.rt: chsd ldrs: led 6th: mde rest: clr 3 out)	—	1	25/1	106+	31
4336[9]	**Jaunty Gig (82)** (JJBirkett) **11-10-0b** LO'Hara (chsd ldrs: drvn along 10th: 3rd whn mstke last: kpt on wl)	5	2	14/1	95	20
3824[5]	**Jendee (IRE) (82)** (BEllison) **9-9-7**(7) CMcCormack (reminders 8th: wnt prom 13th: lost pl 17th: kpt on fr 2 out)	7	3	12/1	91	16
4284[3]	**Temple Garth (102)** (PBeaumont) **8-11-6** RSupple (led to 9th: outpcd fr 4 out)	3	4	6/1[3]	109	34
1778[U]	**Scrabo View (IRE) (95)** (PBeaumont) **9-10-8**(5) BGrattan (nt j.w: sn bhd: sme hdwy 3 out: n.d)	3	5	12/1	100	25
4203[6]	**Bright Destiny (82)** (JSGoldie) **6-9-7v**(7) MrOMcPhail (trckd ldrs: wknd 4 out)	5	6	14/1	84	9
4447[F]	**Crown Equerry (IRE) (114)** (GRichards) **7-12-4** PCarberry (reminder s: racd wd: jnd ldrs 5th: drvn along 14th: lost pl 17th: p.u bef 3 out)		P	3/1[1]	—	—
4148[F]	**Over the Stream (96)** (MissMKMilligan) **11-11-0** ASSmith (prom tl reminders & lost pl 13th: bhd whn blnd 15th: p.u bef next)		P	3/1[1]	—	—
4392[2]	**Blazing Dawn (88)** (JSHubbuck) **10-10-6**[ow2] TReed (lw: hld up & plld hrd: wnt prom 15th: wknd 17th: bhd whn p.u bef last)		P	5/1[2]	—	—
4234[6]	**Mischievous Girl (82)** (RTate) **9-10-0** MrsFNeedham (in tch whn mstke 13th: blnd & lost pl 15th: bhd whn p.u bef 2 out)		P	50/1	—	—
				(SP 115.5%)	**10 Rn**	

6m 45.1 (-0.90) CSF £286.33 CT £3,968.03 TOTE £29.10: £6.20 £3.40 £1.40 (£57.10) Trio £46.20 OWNER Mr J. S. Harlow (CHURCH BROUGHTON) BRED Michael Purcell

LONG HANDICAP Jaunty Gig 9-11 Bright Destiny 8-13 Mischievous Girl 9-2

OFFICIAL EXPLANATION **Blazing Dawn: lost a shoe during the race. Over the Stream: briefly lost his action. Crown Equerry (IRE): was reluctant to race.**
94 Jimmy O'Dea, having his first run for his new trainer, continually lost ground by jumping to his right but had his race won three from home. (25/1)
4148 Jaunty Gig ran much better and stuck on in spirited fashion after clouting the last. (14/1)
3824 Jendee (IRE), from a stable in top form, usually gives a good account of himself round here. (12/1)
4284 Temple Garth ran as if still in need of the outing. (6/1)
1307 Scrabo View (IRE) was having his first run for 154 days and turned in a rusty performance. (12/1)
4447 Crown Equerry (IRE), having his second outing in four days, was not in a good mood at the start and looked most reluctant. (3/1: op 2/1)
4148 Over the Stream seemed to lose his action and dropped right out setting out on to the final circuit. (3/1)

4504 GUY CUNARD HUNTERS' CHASE (5-Y.O+) (Class H)
4-00 (4-00) **2m 5f (16 fncs)** £1,842.00 (£512.00: £246.00) GOING minus 0.40 sec per fur (GF)

Form	Horse	Dist	Pos	SP	RR	SF
4160^{2}	**Greenmount Lad (IRE)** (JCornforth) **9-12-3**(7) MrPCornforth (wnt prom 5th: led between last 2: hdd & mstke last: styd on wl to ld flat: drvn out)	—	1	5/2^{3}	100	33
3664*	**What Chance (IRE)** (MrsHMobley) **9-11-12**(7) MrACharles-Jones (wnt prom 6th: mstke 10th: slt ld last: hdd & nt qckn flat)	¾	2	9/4^{2}	94	27
	Knowe Head (MissCABlakeborough) **13-12-9**(5) MrNWilson (lw: led tl hdd & wknd between last 2)	19	3	13/8^{1}	89	22
179^{P}	**Buckaneer Bay** (SIPittendrigh) **10-12-2**(5) MrRHale (sn bhd: t.o 9th: kpt on fr 2 out)	12	4	33/1	73	6
4218^{P}	**Press for Action** (SHShirley-Beavan) **12-12-5**(5) MissPRobson (chsd ldrs tl wknd after 4 out)	11	5	14/1	67	—
4411^{S}	**Donside** (GFWhite) **9-12-7** MrJWalton (sn bhd: t.o 9th)	dist	6	12/1	—	—

(SP 114.7%) **6 Rn**

5m 18.1 (7.10) CSF £8.39 TOTE £2.50: £1.80 £1.80 (£2.20) OWNER Mr J. Cornforth (WETHERBY) BRED James Brown-Kerr
4160 Greenmount Lad (IRE), whose previous victory under Rules was here over three miles three furlongs, recovered well after a mistake at the last. (5/2)
3664* What Chance (IRE), who is only small, was having her first outing for eight weeks. She looked to have been presented it when the winner hit the last but, up the hill, she was edged out of it. (9/4)
Knowe Head, who looked particularly well, wore a tongue-strap. A fine second in a point-to-point two weeks earlier, he made the running jumping boldly but stopped in a few strides between the last two. (13/8)
Press for Action, on this fast ground, was left behind from four out. (14/1)

4505 FEDERATION BREWERY H'CAP HURDLE (0-100) (5-Y.O+) (Class F)
4-30 (4-30) **2m 1f (8 hdls)** £2,248.00 (£628.00: £304.00) GOING minus 0.40 sec per fur (GF)

Form	Horse	Dist	Pos	SP	RR	SF
4390*	**Fatehalkhair (IRE) (86)** (BEllison) **5-10-8**(7) CMcCormack (lw: trckd ldr: led after 3 out: hit 2 out: styd on u.p flat)	—	1	5/4^{1}	76	22
4259^{3}	**Eden Dancer (95)** (MrsMReveley) **5-11-10** PNiven (lw: j.rt: led tl after 3 out: ev ch between last 2: nt qckn towards fin)	nk	2	7/2^{2}	85	31
4390^{4}	**Jendorcet (72)** (CWFairhurst) **7-10-1** FPerratt (trckd ldrs: mstke 3rd: outpcd fr 3 out)	13	3	7/1^{3}	50	—
4249^{3}	**Beau Matelot (80)** (MissMKMilligan) **5-10-9** ASSmith (chsd ldrs: rdn & outpcd 3 out)	7	4	8/1	51	—
744^{3}	**Sharp Sensation (99)** (GAHarker) **7-12-0** RGarritty (bhd fr 3 out: t.o)	dist	5	16/1	—	—
	Imperial Bid (FR) (95) (FMurphy) **9-11-10** MFoster (pushed along & outpcd 5th: bhd fr next: t.o)	nk	6	20/1	—	—
4278^{6}	**Eriny (USA) (86)** (JJQuinn) **8-11-1** RSupple (plld v.hrd: trckd ldrs tl lost pl 3 out: p.u bef next)		P	7/1^{3}	—	—

(SP 113.4%) **7 Rn**

3m 57.5 (2.50) CSF £5.69 TOTE £1.90: £1.20 £2.70 (£3.10) OWNER Mrs Gwen Smith (LANCHESTER) BRED Shadwell Estate Company Limited
4390* Fatehalkhair (IRE), in this tougher contest, did not jump as well, but he showed the right sort of spirit when the runner-up renewed his challenge. (5/4: evens-11/8)
4259 Eden Dancer must have needed it last time, his first outing for four months. Racing keenly and giving away ground by jumping right, he rallied to renew his effort between the last two and in the end was only just held at bay. (7/2)
4390 Jendorcet settled better with the visor left off. (7/1)
4249 Beau Matelot (8/1: 6/1-9/1)

T/Plpt: £261.60 (36.52 Tckts). T/Qdpt: £278.70 (2.5 Tckts) WG

4224-STRATFORD-ON-AVON (L-H) (Good, Good to soft patches)
Friday May 9th
WEATHER: unsettled

4506 PRAGNELL TROPHY NOVICES' HURDLE (I) (4-Y.O+) (Class E)
5-40 (5-40) **2m 6f 110y (12 hdls)** £2,010.00 (£560.00: £270.00) GOING: 0.57 sec per fur (S)

Form	Horse	Dist	Pos	SP	RR	SF
4304^{2}	**Maid For Adventure (IRE) (99)** (MissHCKnight) **6-11-1** JCulloty (lw: hld up: hdwy 8th: led 2 out: all out)	—	1	10/11^{1}	67	7
3982^{3}	**Regal Gem (IRE) (75)** (CRBarwell) **6-10-9** BFenton (hld up & bhd: stdy hdwy 8th: ev ch last: hrd rdn: nt qckn)	¾	2	10/1	61	1
4304^{9}	**Lucrative Perk (IRE)** (MissCJECaroe) **5-10-9** DLeahy (prom: hmpd 2nd: jnd ldr 7th: led 9th to 2 out: wknd flat)	4	3	100/1	58?	—
3295^{9}	**Docs Boy** (OSherwood) **7-11-0** JOsborne (dwlt: hdwy appr 7th: lost pl 3 out: n.d after)	8	4	8/1^{3}	57	—
4224^{U}	**Freeline Fontaine (IRE)** (NJHenderson) **5-11-0** MAFitzgerald (lw: prom: hmpd 2nd: led 6th to 9th: wknd 3 out)	hd	5	7/2^{2}	57	—
3853^{9}	**Nicanjon** (RDickin) **6-10-9**(5) XAizpuru (led tl fell 2nd)		F	50/1	—	—
	Safwan (PJHobbs) **5-11-0** NWilliamson (hit 2nd: bhd fr 8th: t.o whn mstke 9th: p.u bef 2 out)		P	16/1	—	—
3149^{13}	**Thunderbird** (AHHarvey) **5-10-9** JAMcCarthy (bit bkwd: lft in ld 2nd: hdd 6th: wknd qckly after 8th: sn t.o: p.u bef 2 out)		P	66/1	—	—
4067^{R}	**Woldsman** (NATwiston-Davies) **7-11-0** CLlewellyn (mstke 2nd: sn bhd: rdn after 7th: sn t.o: p.u bef 2 out)		P	9/1	—	—
4069^{P}	**Mummy's Mole (49)** (GraemeRoe) **6-11-0** WMarston (prom: mstke 2nd: rdn after 7th: wkng whn mstke 8th: sn t.o: p.u bef 3 out)		P	100/1	—	—

(SP 116.1%) **10 Rn**

5m 46.1 (30.10) CSF £10.54 TOTE £1.90: £1.40 £1.10 £21.00 (£4.10) Trio £86.10 OWNER Mr Chris Brasher (WANTAGE) BREDMrs M. Crean

4304 Maid For Adventure (IRE), reverting to a longer trip, had to dig deep in this dead ground. (10/11: 4/5-evens)
3982 Regal Gem (IRE) probably ran her best race to date over timber and forced the winner to pull out all the stops. (10/1: 7/1-11/1)
Lucrative Perk (IRE) showed her first sign of ability, having been beaten out of sight last time when the winner finished second at Worcester. (100/1)
3295 Docs Boy may need better ground. (8/1: 3/1-9/1)
4224 Freeline Fontaine (IRE) did not get home in this softish ground. (7/2)
4067 Woldsman (9/1: 6/1-10/1)

4507 RICHARDSON DEVELOPMENTS (FOR THE SHELDON BOSLEY MEMORIAL TROPHY) NOVICES' CHASE (6-Y.O+) (Class D)

6-10 (6-11) **2m 5f 110y (16 fncs)** £3,652.00 (£1,096.00: £528.00: £244.00) GOING: 0.32 sec per fur (GS)

	Horse / Details	Dist	Pos	SP	RR	SF
4298*	**Monks Soham (IRE)** (GAHubbard) **9-11-1**(3) PHenley (lw: a.p: chsd ldr appr 12th: hit 4 out: hrd rdn appr 2 out: led last 50y)	—	1	6/1 3	114	60
4302 2	**Stately Home (IRE) (135)** (PBowen) **6-11-8** RJohnson (led appr 2nd: clr 4 out: hrd rdn appr 2 out: hdd last 50y)	1¼	2	4/6 1	117	63
3334 4	**Little Gains (69)** (RLee) **8-10-12** BFenton (led tl appr 2nd: wknd appr 4 out)	21	3	66/1	91	37
3765 P	**Finnigan Free** (GAHam) **7-10-8**(7)ow3 MrMFrith (hit 2nd: mstke 10th: sn bhd: t.o)	22	4	50/1	78	21
4180 3	**Greenback (BEL) (126)** (PJHobbs) **6-11-8** NWilliamson (lw: nt j.w: hld up: hit 2nd: blnd 5th: rdn after 8th: sn wl bhd: t.o)	13	5	9/4 2	75	21
				(SP 108.5%)		**5 Rn**

5m 20.5 (8.50) CSF £9.91 TOTE £5.90: £2.70 £1.40 (£3.90) OWNER Mr G. A. Hubbard (WOODBRIDGE) BRED P. J. Reynolds
4298* Monks Soham (IRE) is on the upgrade and gave the impression he should stay three miles. (6/1: 4/1-7/1)
4302 Stately Home (IRE) may have found this trip on quite searching ground beyond his best. (4/6)
4180 Greenback (BEL), who has only won once on a left-handed course, is probably better suited to some bounce in the ground. (9/4)

4508 PRAGNELL TROPHY NOVICES' HURDLE (II) (4-Y.O+) (Class E)

6-35 (6-36) **2m 6f 110y (12 hdls)** £1,996.00 (£556.00: £268.00) GOING: 0.57 sec per fur (S)

	Horse / Details	Dist	Pos	SP	RR	SF
4376 3	**Gower-Slave** (PBowen) **5-11-0** RJohnson (a.p: pushed along appr 3rd: lft in ld 2 out: sn clr: all out)	—	1	9/2 2	68	—
4182 F	**Gentleman Jim** (RCurtis) **7-11-0** DMorris (hld up: hdwy 8th: rdn appr 3 out: wknd appr last: fin tired)	10	2	16/1	61	—
3844 2	**Sioux To Speak (85)** (MissHCKnight) **5-11-0** JFTitley (plld hrd early: a.p: hit 7th: qcknd appr last: fin tired)	¾	3	11/2 3	60	—
3006 9	**Saucy Nun (IRE)** (IPWilliams) **5-10-9** BPowell (hdwy 4th: mstke 9th: sn wknd)	15	4	11/1	45	—
	Mariners Memory (RGBrazington) **9-10-11**(3) RMassey (hld up: led after 8th: 12l clr whn fell 2 out)		F	66/1	—	—
3431 P	**Summit Else** (NATwiston-Davies) **6-10-9** CLlewellyn (plld hrd: prom tl mstke 5th: sn t.o: p.u bef 2 out)		P	25/1	—	—
4233*	**Sharp Command (107)** (PEccles) **4-11-5** APMcCoy (led: rdn & hdd after 8th: wknd 9th: p.u bef 3 out)		P	4/6 1	—	—
3748 7	**Curra Minstral (IRE)** (JELong) **7-10-9** LeesaLong (a bhd: t.o whn p.u bef 8th)		P	100/1	—	—
2791 9	**Murray's Million** (JSSmith) **5-11-0** WMarston (plld hrd early: rdn & lost tch after 7th: p.u bef 8th)		P	100/1	—	—
				(SP 115.1%)		**9 Rn**

5m 52.5 (36.50) CSF £56.74 TOTE £5.40: £1.30 £1.80 £1.60 (£18.50) Trio £28.60 OWNER Mr Bob Bevan (HAVERFORDWEST) BRED D. L. Morgan
WEIGHT FOR AGE 4yo-6lb
OFFICIAL EXPLANATION **Sharp Command: choked and lost his action.**
4376 Gower-Slave, despite the yielding going putting the emphasis on stamina, was a very lucky winner. (9/2)
Gentleman Jim travelled well for a long way but did not get the trip in this quite searching ground. (16/1)
3844 Sioux To Speak appears better suited to a sounder surface. (11/2)
Mariners Memory, who has obviously been difficult to train, was all set to spring a surprise on his comeback. (66/1)
4233* Sharp Command was reported by his jockey to have choked and lost his action. (4/6)

4509 HARTSHORNE MOTOR SERVICES LTD. (WALSALL) (FOR THE RODDY BAKER GOLD CUP) H'CAP CHASE (0-140) (5-Y.O+) (Class B)

7-05 (7-05) **2m 5f 110y (16 fncs)** £6,787.50 (£2,040.00: £985.00: £457.50) GOING: 0.32 sec per fur (GS)

	Horse / Details	Dist	Pos	SP	RR	SF
4225*	**Philip's Woody (115)** (NJHenderson) **9-10-4** MAFitzgerald (nt fluent: hld up: stdy hdwy 12th: str run to ld flat: all out)	—	1	10/1	130	40
3701*	**Disco des Mottes (FR) (125)** (GRichards) **6-11-0** PCarberry (lw: led: mstke 10th: rdn 2 out: hdd flat: r.o)	½	2	11/10 1	140	50
3618 3	**Air Shot (135)** (DNicholson) **7-11-10** RJohnson (swtg: a.p: hit 4 out: hrd rdn 3 out: ev ch whn hit 2 out: r.o flat)	½	3	7/4 2	149	59
4206 2	**Destiny Calls (122)** (NAGaselee) **7-10-11** RDunwoody (swtg: chsd ldr: ev ch last: one pce)	1½	4	7/1 3	135	45
2647 5	**Strong Medicine (131)** (KCBailey) **10-11-6** CO'Dwyer (swtg: bhd: j.slowly 3rd: j.rt 9th: sn t.o)	dist	5	16/1	—	—
				(SP 111.5%)		**5 Rn**

5m 22.5 (10.50) CSF £20.92 TOTE £7.00: £2.40 £2.00 (£7.10) OWNER Mr K. G. Knox (LAMBOURN) BRED Conkwell Grange Stud Ltd
4225* Philip's Woody, raised 3lb, was only fourth over the final fence and then appeared to have thought he had done enough once striking the front. (10/1: op 6/1)
3701* Disco des Mottes (FR), up 10lb, has gone up 23lb in all and could not withstand the winner's late burst. (11/10: evens-13/8)
3618 Air Shot has softer ground this time but his jumping was a little untidy when the race began in earnest. (7/4)
4206 Destiny Calls ran a sound race on ground softer than he likes and his turn is near. (7/1)

4510 NEEDHAM & JAMES H'CAP HURDLE (0-120) (4-Y.O+) (Class D)

7-35 (7-35) **2m 110y (9 hdls)** £2,861.00 (£796.00: £383.00) GOING: 0.57 sec per fur (S)

	Horse / Details	Dist	Pos	SP	RR	SF
4061 14	**Most Equal (112)** (MCPipe) **7-11-13** APMcCoy (lw: hld up & bhd: hdwy fr 3 out: qcknd to ld flat: r.o)	—	1	7/2 2	95	44
4386 2	**Out on a Promise (IRE) (107)** (NJHWalker) **5-11-8** NWilliamson (lw: hld up & bhd: hdwy after 5th: led 2 out tl flat)	1	2	11/4 1	89	38
2952 F	**Severn Gale (102)** (JAllen) **7-10-12**(5) XAizpuru (prom: led 4th to 2 out: sn wknd)	13	3	9/1	71	20
4381 3	**Nashville Star (USA) (94)** (RMathew) **6-10-9v** CLlewellyn (prom: pushed along after 4th: wknd appr 2 out)	11	4	12/1	53	2
	Gunner Be Good (85) (JKCresswell) **7-10-0** TEley (led to 4th: wknd 3 out)	½	5	40/1	43	—
1866 6	**Pair of Jacks (IRE) (91)** (PJHobbs) **7-10-6** RDunwoody (hld up: hdwy after 5th: wknd after 3 out)	3½	6	15/2	46	—

		Dist	Pos	SP	RR	SF
4307[8]	**Keep Me in Mind (IRE) (101)** (NRMitchell) **8-11-2b[1]** JFTitley (hld up & plld hrd: hdwy after 5th: hmpd 6th: sn wknd: t.o)	28	**7**	7/1[3]	29	—
4307[9]	**Out Ranking (FR) (112)** (JNeville) **5-11-13** TDascombe (bhd: hit 4th: sn t.o: fell 2 out)		**F**	14/1	—	—
3666[5]	**Isaiah (105)** (MrsJCecil) **8-11-6** TKent (prom: cl 4th whn fell 6th)		**F**	9/1	—	—

(SP 110.0%) **9 Rn**

4m 3.0 (16.00) CSF £11.65 CT £64.37 TOTE £4.30: £1.40 £2.30 £2.10 (£9.80) Trio £41.90 OWNER Mr Heeru Kirpalani (WELLINGTON) BRED H. L. Kirpalani

LONG HANDICAP Gunner Be Good 9-7

2048 Most Equal, back to a mark only 2lb higher than when making a successful seasonal reappearance, did not mind this yielding going. Given a peach of a ride, he scored a shade cleverly in the end. (7/2)

4386 Out on a Promise (IRE), raised 15lb for his two earlier victories, was already due to go down 1lb and lost nothing in defeat on ground softer than ideal. (11/4)

2779 Severn Gale could not live with the two main protagonists once tackled. (9/1)

4381 Nashville Star (USA), due to go up 1lb, could never reach his favourite position at the head of affairs. (12/1: op 7/1)

1866 Pair of Jacks (IRE) needs faster ground. (15/2)

4141 Out Ranking (FR) (14/1: op 7/1)

3666 Isaiah (9/1: op 5/1)

4511 JOHN AND NIGEL THORNE MEMORIAL CUP HUNTERS' CHASE (5-Y.O+) (Class H)

8-05 (8-05) **3m (18 fncs)** £2,108.00 (£588.00: £284.00) GOING: 0.32 sec per fur (GS)

		Dist	Pos	SP	RR	SF
4316[4]	**Kino** (AndrewMartin) **10-11-7**(7) MrAndrewMartin (nt fluent 6th & 7th: hdwy appr 11th: lost pl 14th: lft in ld last)	—	**1**	10/1	85	—
4326[7]	**Tara Boy** (RTeague) **12-11-7**(7) MrRCambray (lost pl 13th: styd on fr 3 out: lft 2nd & bdly hmpd 2 out: nt rcvr)	8	**2**	20/1	80	—
4051[9]	**Faringo** (MrsDMGrissell) **12-11-7**(7) MissCGrissell (bhd fr 5th: rdn after 11th: sn t.o)	5	**3**	50/1	76	—
3270[P]	**The Major General** (GRichards) **10-12-3**(7) CaptAOgden (hld up: wnt 2nd 4 out: lft clr & hit 2 out: mstke & uns rdr last: rmntd)	5	**4**	5/2[2]	83++	—
	Stilltodo (CRWilson) **10-11-2**(7) MrChrisWilson (led 2nd to 14th: wknd appr 3 out: t.o)	dist	**5**	11/2[3]	—	—
4323[3]	**Hill Island** (CJRSweeting) **10-11-7**(7) MrRupertSweeting (lw: led to 2nd: led 14th: slt ld whn fell 2 out)		**F**	Evens[1]	—	—

(SP 109.8%) **6 Rn**

6m 26.2 (34.20) CSF £113.24 TOTE £9.10: £3.30 £4.00 (£33.00) OWNER Mr Andrew Martin (CHIPPING NORTON) BRED Dayspring Co Ltd

4316 Kino, greatly benefiting from the demise of the two market leaders in the home straight, may not have even beaten the runner-up had that rival not been brought to a standstill. (10/1: 7/1-11/1)

Tara Boy looked set to finish in front of the eventual winner in third place until the grief at the last two fences. (20/1)

The Major General looked to be travelling the better when apparently presented the race at the penultimate fence. (5/2: 7/4-11/4)

4323 Hill Island, strongly pressed, was not going quite as well as The Major General when making his exit. (Evens)

4512 A.H.P. TRAILERS WOMBOURNE NOVICES' H'CAP HURDLE (0-100) (4-Y.O+) (Class E)

8-35 (8-37) **2m 110y (9 hdls)** £2,444.00 (£684.00: £332.00) GOING: 0.57 sec per fur (S)

		Dist	Pos	SP	RR	SF
4321[2]	**Snowshill Shaker (91)** (NATwiston-Davies) **8-11-10** CLlewellyn (a.p: led 2 out: r.o wl)	—	**1**	4/1[2]	74+	11
4405[2]	**Nahla (80)** (BdeHaan) **7-10-13** SCurran (lw: a.p: blnd 3 out: sn led: hdd 2 out: one pce)	3	**2**	3/1[1]	60	—
4236[3]	**Positivo (70)** (MissCJECaroe) **6-10-3** DLeahy (a.p: r.o one pce fr 2 out)	hd	**3**	14/1	50	—
3438[13]	**Orchard King (83)** (OBrennan) **7-11-2** MBrennan (lw: hld up: hdwy 6th: one pce fr 2 out)	3	**4**	14/1	60	—
2050*	**Stonecutter (92)** (MRChannon) **4-11-6v** AThornton (lw: a.p: led after 6th tl after 3 out: wknd appr last)	1	**5**	14/1	68	—
2949[3]	**The Lancer (IRE) (87)** (DRGandolfo) **8-11-6** RDunwoody (lw: led tl after 6th: wknd appr 2 out)	2½	**6**	9/1	61	—
912[5]	**Andsome Boy (84)** (CRBarwell) **4-10-12** BFenton (swtg: tk keen hold in rr: nvr nr ldrs)	1	**7**	25/1	57	—
4296[8]	**Dovetto (77)** (AEPrice) **8-10-10** SWynne (hdwy 4th: hrd rdn & wknd appr 2 out)	¾	**8**	12/1	49	—
4405[8]	**Kumari King (IRE) (72)** (AWCarroll) **7-10-5** DMorris (bhd fr 4th: t.o)	25	**9**	33/1	20	—
4229[3]	**Siberian Mystic (90)** (PGMurphy) **4-11-4** MAFitzgerald (lw: hld up mid div: mstke 4th: in tch whn blnd 6th: nt rcvr: t.o)	7	**10**	6/1[3]	31	—
4405[10]	**Fairelaine (79)** (KCBailey) **5-10-12** CO'Dwyer (bhd: rdn appr 5th: bdly hmpd 6th: t.o)	16	**11**	20/1	4	—
3542[7]	**Woodlands Lad Too (67)** (PAPritchard) **5-10-0** RBellamy (a bhd: t.o)	4	**12**	100/1	—	—
4299[3]	**Gipsy Geof (IRE) (95)** (GAHubbard) **6-12-0** NWilliamson (lw: hld up: stdy hdwy whn fell 6th)		**F**	13/2	—	—

(SP 122.9%) **13 Rn**

4m 9.8 (22.80) CSF £15.21 CT £144.75 TOTE £6.10: £2.50 £1.10 £3.00 (£10.80) Trio £35.20 OWNER Mr Austin Knight (CHELTENHAM) BRED Ian Hunter and A. Knight

LONG HANDICAP Woodlands Lad Too 8-6

WEIGHT FOR AGE 4yo-5lb

4321 Snowshill Shaker, back to two miles, was 11lb higher than when winning over course and distance last month. Already due to go up a further 2lb, he scored with something in hand despite being messed about a little on the home turn. (4/1: 3/1-9/2)

4405 Nahla, again had some give underfoot and was already set to go up 3lb for his second at Hereford. (3/1)

4236 Positivo, down 3lb, has become something of a regular at Towcester and appears to need further on a course as easy as this. (14/1)

Orchard King, dropped 7lb, showed definite signs of a return to form. (14/1: 16/1-25/1)

2050* Stonecutter, fit from the Flat, seemed to have plenty of weight for only winning a juvenile seller. (14/1: 8/1-16/1)

2949 The Lancer (IRE) was reverting to hurdles for this return after a break. (9/1)

736 Andsome Boy, off course for six months, appeared to be being taught to settle. (25/1)

3594 Dovetto (12/1: op 8/1)

4229 Siberian Mystic (6/1: op 4/1)

4299 Gipsy Geof (IRE), reverting to two miles, was going strongly when departing. (13/2: op 7/2)

T/Plpt: £332.60 (38.2 Tckts). T/Qdpt: £134.20 (5.48 Tckts) KH

4408-HEXHAM (L-H) (Good to firm)
Saturday May 10th
WEATHER: heavy rain

4513 PENSHER SECURITY DOORS LTD NOVICES' CONDITIONAL HURDLE (4-Y.O+) (Class E)
2-20 (2-20) **3m (12 hdls)** £2,363.60 (£654.60: £312.80) GOING minus 0.18 sec per fur (G)

Form	Horse	Dist	Pos	SP	RR	SF
4152[2]	**Pappa Charlie (USA) (85)** (CParker) **6-11-0** FLeahy (lw: chsd ldrs: rdn to ld whn lft clr 2 out: blnd last: all out)	—	1	4/1[3]	60	28
3993*	**Mister Trick (IRE) (84)** (LLungo) **7-10-9b**(5) WDowling (lw: chsd ldrs: blnd 7th: styd on one pce fr 2 out)	8	2	3/1[2]	55	23
4283[4]	**Eternal City (84)** (GRichards) **6-11-2**(5) RBurns (hld up: hdwy 8th: outpcd 2 out: kpt on u.p)	1½	3	15/2	61	29
4144[4]	**Carnmoney (IRE) (75)** (JSisterson) **9-11-0** STaylor (chsd ldrs: outpcd 3 out: sn lost pl: hrd rdn & kpt on flat)	21	4	20/1	40	8
2800[4]	**Thorntoun Estate (IRE) (74)** (MartinTodhunter) **4-10-2v[1]**(5) CMcCormack (chsd ldrs: lft mod 2nd 2 out: sn wknd: fin lame)	6	5	6/1	36	—
4147[8]	**Chill Factor (79)** (MrsMReveley) **7-11-0** GLee (lw: reminders 6th: sn lost tch: t.o 9th)	20	6	6/1	22	—
4152*	**Eastcliffe (IRE) (90)** (WMcKeown) **5-11-4**(3) DThomas (lw: led: sn clr: hdd & fell 2 out: lame)		F	5/2[1]	—	—
4389[F]	**Friendly Society (60)** (WStorey) **11-11-0** RMcGrath (sn bhd: t.o whn p.u after 8th)		P	50/1	—	—
4144[P]	**Tartan Joy (IRE)** (JAMoore) **6-10-11**(3) RWilkinson (bhd & drvn along 7th: t.o whn p.u bef last)		P	50/1	—	—
4283[13]	**Meadowleck (54)** (WGYoung) **8-10-4**(5) IJardine (bhd fr 7th: t.o whn p.u bef last)		P	100/1	—	—
3723[P]	**Rye Rum (IRE)** (JWFAynsley) **6-10-11**(3) BGrattan (sn bhd: t.o whn p.u after 8th)		P	100/1	—	—
				(SP 124.6%)	**11 Rn**	

5m 46.7 (6.70) CSF £16.01 TOTE £4.30: £1.50 £1.30 £2.40 (£8.50) Trio £29.00 OWNER Mr Raymond Anderson Green (LOCKERBIE) BRED W. S. Farish and W. S. Kilroy
WEIGHT FOR AGE 4yo-7lb
OFFICIAL EXPLANATION **Thorntoun Estate (IRE): was found to be lame.**

4152 Pappa Charlie (USA) had just poked his head in front when left in a commanding lead at the penultimate flight. Falling through the last, he had to be kept right up to his work, and there was not an ounce to spare at the line. (4/1)
3993* Mister Trick (IRE), reverting to hurdles, was left for dead by the two leaders going to two out, but he rallied going to the last to take second spot. All he does is stay. (3/1)
4283 Eternal City, beaten in selling company on his two previous outings, travelled strongly but, when called on for an effort, he did not find much. (15/2)
4144 Carnmoney (IRE) only finished so close because of his rider's persistent use of the whip. (20/1)
2800 Thorntoun Estate (IRE) was left second two out, but weakened badly going to the last and was found to be lame. (6/1)
4147 Chill Factor (6/1: tchd 9/1)
4152* Eastcliffe (IRE) had just been headed by the winner when he took a crashing fall two out which left him lame. The way the winner tied up, the issue must still have been in doubt at the time of his departure. (5/2)

4514 PENSHER SECURITY DOORS LTD 'N.H.' NOVICES' HURDLE (4-Y.O+) (Class E)
2-50 (2-50) **2m (8 hdls)** £2,607.20 (£724.20: £347.60) GOING minus 0.18 sec per fur (G)

Form	Horse	Dist	Pos	SP	RR	SF
4244[2]	**Bold Statement (98)** (GMMoore) **5-11-6** NBentley (chsd ldrs: led appr 2 out: shkn up & wnt clr between last 2: eased towards fin)	—	1	10/11[1]	73+	39
4146[F]	**Silver Minx (99)** (MrsMReveley) **5-11-12** PNiven (led tl appr 2 out: wknd between last 2)	20	2	15/8[2]	59	25
4335[7]	**Amber Holly (68)** (JEDixon) **8-10-9** BStorey (bhd: hdwy 5th: one pce fr 2 out)	9	3	20/1	33	—
4420[10]	**Buckley House** (JIACharlton) **5-11-0** TReed (stdd s: bhd tl hdwy 2 out: edgd lft & kpt on u.p flat)	2½	4	20/1	36	2
4390[B]	**Weapons Free** (TPTate) **6-11-0** RGarritty (hld up: gd hdwy 5th: wknd 2 out)	s.h	5	33/1	35	1
3366[7]	**Edstone (IRE)** (JWCurtis) **5-11-0** MFoster (sn bhd)	13	6	33/1	22	—
4144[6]	**Salem Beach (69)** (MartinTodhunter) **5-10-2**(7) CMcCormack (chsd ldrs tl wknd 3 out)	11	7	40/1	6	—
3973[3]	**Starlin Sam** (JSisterson) **8-11-0** PCarberry (chsd ldrs: reminders 5th: sn lost pl)	15	8	8/1[3]	—	—
4244[14]	**Hunting Slane** (CGrant) **5-11-0** RSupple (plld hrd: trckd ldrs: 3rd & rdn 3 out: wknd qckly appr next)	1½	9	100/1	—	—
4450[5]	**Chariot Man (IRE)** (MrsSJSmith) **5-10-9**(5) RWilkinson (rr div whn fell 3rd)		F	14/1	—	—
	Waver Lane (MABarnes) **4-9-13**(5) STaylor (bit bkwd: blnd 1st: t.o 3 out: p.u bef next)		P	50/1	—	—
3914[19]	**Elliott The Butler** (MrsSJSmith) **5-11-0** ASSmith (hmpd, blnd & uns rdr 1st)		U	33/1	—	—
				(SP 128.7%)	**12 Rn**	

3m 51.2 (3.20) CSF £2.62 TOTE £1.60: £1.50 £1.40 £2.40 (£1.90) Trio £13.80 OWNER Mr R. I. Graham (MIDDLEHAM) BRED Juddmonte Farms
WEIGHT FOR AGE 4yo-5lb

4244 Bold Statement has now won all his three races here, one a bumper. He proved much too good for this lot and will have one more run this time, at Cartmel. (10/11: 4/5-evens)
4146 Silver Minx, a headstrong sort, had little chance of getting the trip round here with the stiff uphill climb to the final flight. (15/8)
1020 Amber Holly possibly ran her best race yet to finish third, but that is not saying a lot. (20/1)
4420 Buckley House was dropped right out at the start and is clearly a headstrong sort. (20/1)

4515 BISHOPS SKINNER LTD NOVICES' CHASE (5-Y.O+) (Class E)
3-20 (3-20) **3m 1f (19 fncs)** £3,232.75 (£967.00: £463.50: £211.75) GOING minus 0.18 sec per fur (G)

Form	Horse	Dist	Pos	SP	RR	SF
4186[7]	**Real Tonic (103)** (GRichards) **7-12-2** PCarberry (hld up: mstke 5th: jnd ldrs 14th: rdn to ld flat: hld on wl)	—	1	11/10[1]	102	27
1844[6]	**Plumbob (IRE) (84)** (LLungo) **8-11-2** RSupple (lw: led: hit 2 out: hdd flat: r.o u.p)	nk	2	7/1	88	13
4447[U]	**Exemplar (IRE) (81)** (MrsSJSmith) **9-10-11**(5) RWilkinson (lw: chsd ldrs: effrt & blnd 3 out: one pce between last 2)	6	3	4/1[2]	84	9
4055[7]	**Broomhill Duker (IRE) (72)** (HowardJohnson) **7-11-2** DParker (w ldrs tl wknd 4 out)	15	4	33/1	74	—
4149[3]	**Tactix (63)** (MissMKMilligan) **7-10-11** ASSmith (blnd bdly 4th: hit 13th: hdwy next: wknd 3 out)	4	5	20/1	67	—
3913[7]	**Just For Me (IRE) (60)** (JAMoore) **8-10-11**(5) MrMHNaughton (blnd & lost pl 10th: bhd fr 14th)	13	6	33/1	64	—
4248[16]	**Festival Fancy (66)** (BMactaggart) **10-10-11** GLee (blnd 7th: sn bhd)	¾	7	25/1	58	—
3934[3]	**Pantara Prince (IRE) (83)** (JIACharlton) **8-11-2** BStorey (chsd ldrs: hit 14th: hdwy 4 out: sn wknd)	13	8	9/2[3]	55	—
4149[4]	**Alicat (IRE)** (JWCurtis) **6-11-2** MFoster (chsd ldrs: wkng whn blnd 10th: t.o whn p.u between last 2)		P	33/1	—	—

			SP	RR	SF
4257P	**Persian Grange (IRE)** (DALamb) **7-11-2** JBurke (bhd whn blnd bdly & p.u 11th)	P	50/1	—	—
			(SP 117.7%)		**10 Rn**

6m 24.2 (13.20) CSF £7.91 TOTE £2.10: £1.50 £2.30 £1.40 (£8.30) Trio £10.30 OWNER Mr Robert Ogden (PENRITH) BRED Mrs D. A. Whitaker

4186 Real Tonic, who has had a soft palate operation since he last ran, took time to get his eye in. Looming up on the bridle going to the last, he did just enough. (11/10: 4/5-5/4)
1844 Plumbob (IRE), reverting from hurdles, gave a sound exhibition of jumping in front. Getting the second last wrong, he did not go under without a real battle. He deserves to go one better. (7/1)
4219 Exemplar (IRE) possibly found his stamina stretched to the limit on this stiff track. (4/1)
1691 Broomhill Duker (IRE), who wore blinkers in selling company last time, had them dispensed with here, but raced with a tongue-strap. (33/1)
3934 Pantara Prince (IRE) (9/2: 6/1-7/2)

4516 LORD'S TAVERNERS (S) HURDLE (4,5,6 & 7-Y.O) (Class G)

3-50 (3-51) **2m (8 hdls)** £1,800.50 (£498.00: £237.50) GOING minus 0.18 sec per fur (G)

				SP	RR	SF
3803[4]	**Palace of Gold (85)** (LLungo) **7-11-0** RSupple (led to 5th: led 2 out: drvn out)	—	1	11/8[1]	66	4
4295P	**Noir Esprit (75)** (JMCarr) **4-10-6**(3) FLeahy (hdwy to chse ldrs 4th: wnt 2nd 2 out: no imp)	4	2	7/1	62	—
4259[2]	**Suselja (IRE)** (JMJefferson) **6-10-9** ASSmith (nt j.w: hit 2nd: hdwy 4th: outpcd fr 2 out)	7	3	9/2[3]	50	—
4409B	**Tiotao (IRE) (63)** (CParker) **7-11-0** DParker (hld up: stdy hdwy 5th: effrt after next: sn wknd)	10	4	14/1	45	—
4259[10]	**Nonios (IRE) (92)** (GMMoore) **6-10-7b**(7) THogg (hld up: jnd ldrs 3rd: led 5th: hdd 2 out: sn wknd)	3½	5	7/2[2]	42	—
4409B	**Over Stated (IRE) (67)** (JWade) **7-10-9**(5) STaylor (chsd ldrs tl wknd after 5th)	5	6	25/1	37	—
4409[8]	**In a Moment (USA) (66)** (CGrant) **6-11-7** PNiven (reminders 2nd: dropped rr 4th: nt r.o: t.o 3 out)	dist	7	12/1	—	—
4204P	**Kasirama (IRE) (78)** (MDHammond) **6-11-0** RGarritty (sme hdwy 4th: wknd after next: t.o whn p.u bef last)		P	9/1	—	—
4335[10]	**Teddy Edward** (MrsAMNaughton) **7-10-7**(7) MrTJBarry (bolted bef s: stdd s: bhd: t.o 5th: p.u bef 2 out)		P	33/1	—	—
				(SP 126.2%)		**9 Rn**

3m 58.1 (10.10) CSF £12.46 TOTE £2.20: £1.10 £2.30 £1.90 (£16.80) Trio £24.70 OWNER Mrs Barbara Lungo (CARRUTHERSTOWN) BRED Cheveley Park Stud Ltd

WEIGHT FOR AGE 4yo-5lb No bid

3803 Palace of Gold looked to have been found a good opportunity and, kept up to his work, made no mistake. (11/8)
3474 Noir Esprit never gave up trying, but his cause was always a lost one. (7/1)
4259 Suselja (IRE) was let down by her hurdling. (9/2)
3091 Tiotao (IRE), who had an impossible task at the weights, found nothing at all when called on for an effort. (14/1)
1942 Nonios (IRE), 7lb best in on official figures, took a keen grip in blinkers. As soon as he was tackled two out, he ran up the white flag.(7/2)

4517 IAN STRAKER MEMORIAL TROPHY H'CAP CHASE (0-105) (5-Y.O+) (Class F)

4-20 (4-20) **2m 110y (12 fncs)** £2,898.00 (£864.00: £412.00: £186.00) GOING minus 0.18 sec per fur (G)

				SP	RR	SF
4297[3]	**Tapatch (IRE) (86)** (MWEasterby) **9-11-0** PCarberry (lw: reminders 4th: hit next: hdwy 6th: hrd rdn to ld last 75y)	—	1	5/2[1]	97	5
4013[7]	**Super Sandy (72)** (FTWalton) **10-10-0** KJohnson (led to 4 out: led appr last: hdd & nt qckn flat)	2	2	13/2	81	—
4410[2]	**Cardenden (IRE) (72)** (JBarclay) **9-10-0** BStorey (w ldr: led 4 out tl appr last: sn wknd)	8	3	3/1[2]	73	—
4336[2]	**Whaat Fettle (100)** (GRichards) **12-12-0** PNiven (chsd ldrs: outpcd 6th: sn lost pl: t.o 4 out: kpt on flat)	28	4	5/2[1]	74	—
4334U	**Supermarine (72)** (BMactaggart) **11-10-0** GLee (chsd ldrs: hit 4th: wknd 4 out)	1¼	5	33/1	45	—
4408F	**Twin Falls (IRE) (94)** (GMMoore) **6-11-8b** NBentley (nvr gng wl: bhd & reminders 4th: t.o 4 out)	16	6	6/1[3]	51	—
				(SP 112.7%)		**6 Rn**

4m 7.2 (10.20) CSF £16.70 TOTE £2.90: £2.00 £2.40 (£12.70) OWNER Miss V. Foster (SHERIFF HUTTON) BRED London T'bred Services & M. McCalmont in Ireland

LONG HANDICAP Super Sandy 9-9 Supermarine 9-3 Cardenden (IRE) 9-11

4297 Tapatch (IRE) jumped stickily and looked reluctant in the early stages, but his brilliant rider was in no mood to let him shirk the issue. Pulled wide of the two leaders at the last, he was persuaded to do enough to put his head in front in the last seventy-five yards. Has there ever been a better jump jockey than Paul Carberry? (5/2)
4013 Super Sandy, whose three previous wins have been over this course, ran right up to her best. (13/2)
4410 Cardenden (IRE) helped force the pace, but his stride shortened dramatically after jumping the final fence. (3/1)
4336 Whaat Fettle found this trip much too short and was run off his feet by the sixth fence. (5/2)

4518 BISHOPS SKINNER LTD H'CAP HURDLE (0-115) (4-Y.O+) (Class E)

4-50 (4-50) **2m 4f 110y (10 hdls)** £2,404.20 (£666.20: £318.60) GOING minus 0.18 sec per fur (G)

				SP	RR	SF
4296[11]	**Kinda Groovy (86)** (IPark) **8-11-1b** NSmith (jnd ldr 4th: reminders next: led between last 2: hrd rdn & styd on flat)	—	1	9/1	66	7
4482[3]	**Highland Way (IRE) (89)** (MartinTodhunter) **9-10-11**(7) CMcCormack (lw: hld up: stdy hdwy 7th: chal on bit whn hit last: rdn & fnd nil)	1¼	2	9/2[2]	68	9
1025[6]	**Jumbo Star (80)** (JEDixon) **7-10-9** BStorey (chsd ldr: led 3 out tl between last 2: one pce)	18	3	12/1	45	—
4335[8]	**Dont Forget Curtis (IRE) (72)** (MrsKMLamb) **5-9-8**(7) MissSLamb (prom tl outpcd 6th: sn lost pl: styd on fr 2 out)	1½	4	10/1	36	—
4081*	**Rascally (91)** (MissLCSiddall) **7-11-6** MFoster (chsd ldrs: drvn along 5th: chal 3 out: sn wl outpcd & lost pl)	7	5	8/11[1]	49	—
4261P	**Moreof a Gunner (95)** (JMJefferson) **7-11-10** RGarritty (mde most: hit 6th: hdd 3 out: sn wknd & eased)	8	6	8/1[3]	47	—
				(SP 114.0%)		**6 Rn**

5m (12.00) CSF £44.15 TOTE £7.90: £2.50 £1.80 (£27.70) OWNER Mr Ian Park (STOCKTON-ON-TEES) BRED Beaufort Bloodstock Ltd

STEWARDS' ENQUIRY Smith susp. 21-24/5/97 (improper use of whip).

3992 Kinda Groovy, nibbled at in the betting, ran much better than on his three previous outings this time. Under strong pressure, he showed far more resolution than the runner-up. (9/1: 12/1-5/1)
4482 Highland Way (IRE) came there cruising but, after hitting the final flight when still on the bridle, he soon decided this was not the game for him. (9/2)
Jumbo Star ran much better than on his only previous outing, but his stamina seemed to give out between the last two. (12/1)
4152 Dont Forget Curtis (IRE) was badly tapped for toe a mile from home. (10/1: 8/1-12/1)
4081* Rascally, up 4lb, ran a sour sort of race. (8/11: 4/5-evens)
Moreof a Gunner, who pulled because of the slow pace, dropped right out and looks a shadow of his former self. (8/1)
T/Plpt: £25.50 (393.25 Tckts). T/Qdpt: £8.60 (43.24 Tckts) WG

4382-NEWTON ABBOT (L-H) (Good, Good to soft patches)
Saturday May 10th

Race 3: one flight by-passed twice
WEATHER: sunny

4519 NEWTON ABBOT RACECOURSE CORPORATE CLUB NOVICES' HURDLE (4-Y.O+) (Class D)

6-05 (6-05) **2m 1f (8 hdls)** £2,933.60 (£824.60: £402.80) GOING minus 0.02 sec per fur (G)

	Horse		Pos	SP	RR	SF
4441*	**Embankment (IRE) (100)** (NJHenderson) **7-11-6** MAFitzgerald (lw: hld up: chsd ldr 4th: led 2 out: clr appr last: easily)	—	1	1/4[1]	73++	—
	Tarragon (IRE) (OSherwood) **7-11-0** JAMcCarthy (led 1st: hdd 2 out: outpcd appr last)	8	2	6/1[2]	60?	—
3889[P]	**Final Score (IRE)** (PaddyFarrell) **7-10-9** TDascombe (lw: in tch tl wknd appr 2 out: lft poor 3rd last)	25	3	40/1	31	—
	Press Again (PHayward) **5-10-9** BFenton (led to 1st: prom tl wknd 5th: sn t.o)	24	4	66/1	8	—
3433[14]	**Nearly A Score** (GBBalding) **5-10-9** JFTitley (bhd 4th: wknd appr next: t.o & hmpd appr 2 out)	7	5	9/1[3]	2	—
1873[P]	**Western Playboy** (RJBaker) **5-11-0** VSlattery (chsd ldrs: in tch tl wknd appr 2 out: fell last)		F	33/1	—	—
				(SP 111.2%)	**6 Rn**	

4m 13.9 (20.90) CSF £2.10 TOTE £1.20: £1.00 £3.20 (£1.60) OWNER Lady Tennant (LAMBOURN) BRED Rathasker Stud
4441* Embankment (IRE) had an easy task here and, running true to his market price, won this very easily. (1/4)
Tarragon (IRE), a half-brother to several Flat winners, made an encouraging start to his hurdling career. (6/1: op 7/2)
Nearly A Score (9/1: 6/1-10/1)

4520 HORSES AWAY RACING CLUB H'CAP CHASE (0-115) (5-Y.O+) (Class E)

6-35 (6-35) **2m 110y (13 fncs)** £2,832.50 (£857.00: £418.00: £198.50) GOING minus 0.02 sec per fur (G)

	Horse		Pos	SP	RR	SF
4142*	**Evening Rain (86)** (RJHodges) **11-10-3** TDascombe (led to 5th: chsd ldr tl led appr last: hld on gamely u.p flat)	—	1	5/1	90	28
3336[3]	**Thats the Life (83)** (TRGeorge) **12-10-0** BFenton (mstke 2nd: a.p: led 5th: hdd appr last: drvn out & nt get up flat)	1¼	2	4/1[3]	86	24
4304[7]	**Gladys Emmanuel (83)** (REPocock) **10-9-9**(5) DJKavanagh (lw: chsd ldrs: hdwy 10th: one pce appr 2 out)	4	3	7/2[2]	82	20
4174[F]	**Tango's Delight (83)** (RJBaker) **9-10-0** VSlattery (bhd: in tch to 7th: styd on fr 2 out: nr nr)	13	4	33/1	69	7
4140[4]	**Beau Babillard (107)** (PFNicholls) **10-11-10b** MAFitzgerald (chsd ldrs: in tch to 8th: wknd fr 10th)	4	5	5/1	89	27
4331[2]	**Bishops Castle (IRE) (90)** (RGFrost) **9-10-7** JFrost (lw: mstke 3rd: a bhd: lost tch 10th)	4	6	2/1[1]	69	7
				(SP 111.8%)	**6 Rn**	

4m 5.0 (5.00) CSF £22.53 TOTE £4.20: £1.70 £3.50 (£7.20) OWNER The Gardens Entertainments Ltd (SOMERTON) BRED Universal Stables
LONG HANDICAP Tango's Delight 9-1 Thats the Life 9-8 Gladys Emmanuel 9-12
4142* Evening Rain, 6lb higher than when winning here last month, continues to progress in his summer campaign, and would seem in good heart at present. (5/1)
3336 Thats the Life, 6lb out of the handicap, put up a decent challenge to the winner and a small race can be found for him. (4/1)
3764 Gladys Emmanuel, returning to these larger obstacles after a spell over hurdles, has shown ability over fences in the past. She would have appreciated this re-introduction and will be better for the experience. (7/2)
3410 Beau Babillard (5/1: op 5/2)
4331 Bishops Castle (IRE) would have appreciated the recent rain, but seemed to lose interest after a mistake at the third obstacle. (2/1)

4521 CARL NEKOLA MEMORIAL H'CAP HURDLE (0-130) (4-Y.O+) (Class C)

7-05 (7-05) **2m 6f (8 hdls)** £3,597.50 (£1,010.00: £492.50) GOING minus 0.02 sec per fur (G)

	Horse		Pos	SP	RR	SF
4016[10]	**Brave Tornado (130)** (GBBalding) **6-12-0** BFenton (hld up: hdwy 6th: led after next: clr appr last)	—	1	7/4[1]	116	50
4398[6]	**Moving Out (109)** (MissHCKnight) **9-10-7** JFTitley (led to 6th: in tch tl outpcd appr last)	7	2	5/1	90	24
3499*	**Country Tarquin (102)** (RJHodges) **5-10-0** TDascombe (hdwy to chse ldr 3rd: led 6th: hdd after next: wknd 2 out)	9	3	8/1	76	10
904[4]	**Echo de Janser (FR) (130)** (AGHobbs) **5-12-0** RGreene (fell 2nd: broke leg: dead)		F	50/1	—	—
4383[2]	**Blasket Hero (106)** (MrsSDWilliams) **9-10-4b** GTormey (lw: hld up: bhd: hmpd 4th: rdn after next: t.o & mstke 7th: p.u broke leg: dead)		P	3/1[2]	—	—
4376[7]	**Tommy Cooper (102)** (MrsBarbaraWaring) **6-10-0b** EByrne (prom tl wknd qckly appr 7th: p.u)		P	50/1	—	—
4166[5]	**Rhythm And Blues (102)** (RHBuckler) **7-9-9**(5) GSupple (lw: bhd: in tch whn blnd & uns rdr 4th)		U	9/2[3]	—	—
				(SP 111.2%)	**7 Rn**	

5m 19.1 (7.10) CSF £9.58 TOTE £3.10: £1.90 £1.90 (£10.10) OWNER Miss B. Swire (ANDOVER) BRED Miss B. Swire
LONG HANDICAP Echo de Janser (FR) 74-1 Tommy Cooper 8-4 Country Tarquin 8-5 Rhythm And Blues 9-2
3150* Brave Tornado, scoring over his furthest distance to date, was the only contender with proven ability in this softish ground. With conditions in his favour, he can score again. (7/4)
3702 Moving Out, dropped in class and weight, ran his best race for some time but met one too good in the winner. (5/1)
3499* Country Tarquin was 23lb out of the handicap, but put in a clear round for his share of the prizemoney. Improvement is likely. (8/1)

4522 TOTNES AND BRIDGETOWN NOVICES' HUNTERS' CHASE (5-Y.O+) (Class H)

7-35 (7-35) **2m 5f 110y (16 fncs)** £1,030.00 (£310.00: £150.00: £70.00) GOING minus 0.02 sec per fur (G)

	Horse		Pos	SP	RR	SF
	King Torus (IRE) (VictorDartnall) **7-11-9**(5) MrJJukes (led 5th to 8th: led 10th: rdn 2 out: hld on)	—	1	11/8[1]	103	35
	Ticket To The Moon (MrsJanitaScott) **7-11-2**(7) MrJMPritchard (a.p: chsd wnr 12th: one pce appr last)	1¾	2	9/2[2]	97	29
3739[P]	**Full Alirt** (MissSusanYoung) **9-11-9**(7) MissSYoung (hld up & bhd: hdwy appr 9th: styd on wl)	9	3	14/1	97	29
4380[2]	**Mister Horatio** (WDLewis) **7-12-0**(7) MrMLewis (hld up: hdwy 9th: sn prom: wknd appr 2 out)	nk	4	11/2[3]	102	34
3631*	**Herhorse** (MissAHoward-Chappell) **10-11-9**(7) MrLJefford (hld up: hdwy & mstke 12th: wkng & mstke 14th)	4	5	11/1	94	26
	Myhamet (MrsPaulineGeering) **10-11-7**(7) MrNHarris (hdwy 11th: nvr on terms)	nk	6	8/1	92	24
	Newski Express (JohnLister) **12-11-2**(7) MrGShenkin (fell 2nd)		F	25/1	—	—
4303[P]	**Tom's Gemini Star** (OJCarter) **9-12-0**(7) MrTDennis (bhd: hdwy 10th: mstke 13th: p.u bef next)		P	10/1	—	—
	Fellow Sioux (STRStevens) **10-11-7**(7) MrIDowrick (plld hrd: prom tl wknd 10th: p.u bef 2 out)		P	14/1	—	—
4326[9]	**Flowing River (USA)** (NRMitchell) **11-11-7b[1]**(7) MrNRMitchell (prom: led 8th to 10th: wknd qckly: p.u bef 2 out)		P	33/1	—	—
	Friendly Viking (MrsJHolden-White) **7-11-7**(7) MrRDarke (a bhd: t.o: p.u after 9th)		P	50/1	—	—

	Horse		Pos	SP	RR	SF
4308[3]	**Ann's Ambition** (MrsCHussey) **10-11-7**(7) MrMFrith (a bhd: t.o & p.u bef 2 out)		P	50/1	—	—
4462[4]	**Barrow Street** (CLTizzard) **7-11-7v1**(7) MrJTizzard (led to 5th: in tch tl wknd appr 9th: p.u bef 2 out)		P	50/1	—	—
	Comedy Gayle (MsSueWillcock) **10-11-7**(7) MrIWiddicombe (a bhd: t.o: p.u after 9th)		P	50/1	—	—
				(SP 132.2%)	**14 Rn**	

5m 28.6 (11.60) CSF £7.58 TOTE £2.40: £1.20 £2.00 £4.90 (£6.10) Trio £107.50 OWNER Mr Nick Viney (BARNSTAPLE) BRED Mrs M. McCullagh

King Torus (IRE), a progressive pointer, made a successful transition to hunter-chasing, and looks to have a future at this game. (11/8)
Ticket To The Moon, making her debut under Rules, ran almost to the pound with the winner compared with their previous meeting, but would have preferred further. (9/2)
3593* Full Alirt, a winner at Taunton in March, finished strongly and appreciated the give in the ground. (14/1)
4380 Mister Horatio, well behind Bitofamixup last time, had every chance before tying up in the straight. (11/2)
3631* Herhorse may have preferred it even softer. (11/1)

4523 HAPPY 50TH BIRTHDAY RICHARD BRINSLEY NOVICES' CHASE (5-Y.O+) (Class D)

8-05 (8-05) **2m 110y (13 fncs)** £3,403.75 (£1,030.00: £502.50: £238.75) GOING minus 0.02 sec per fur (G)

	Horse	Dist	Pos	SP	RR	SF
4307[10]	**Tight Fist (IRE)** (MissHCKnight) **7-11-0** JFTitley (lw: chsd ldr tl lft in ld after 6th: hdd 10th: led appr 2 out: styd on u.p)	—	1	13/8[2]	68	12
3456[5]	**Stratton Flyer (60)** (HSHowe) **7-10-2**(7) MrRWidger (lft 2nd 6th: outpcd 11th: styd on strly flat)	1¼	2	40/1	62	6
4291[4]	**Run With Joy (IRE)** (AGHobbs) **6-11-0** RGreene (lft 3rd 6th: led 10th: hdd appr 2 out: wknd flat)	hd	3	33/1	67	11
3844[7]	**Steer Point** (RGFrost) **6-11-0** JFrost (gd hdwy 9th: rdn & wknd appr last)	5	4	9/1	62	6
4305*	**Lucky Eddie (IRE) (90)** (PJHobbs) **6-11-6** GTormey (in tch tl wknd appr 11th)	22	5	6/4[1]	47	—
4330[4]	**Rustic Flight (60)** (LWaring) **10-10-7**(7) MGriffiths (bhd: j.slowly 7th: sn t.o)	dist	6	50/1	—	—
4302[P]	**Tom's Apache (84)** (OJCarter) **8-11-0** MissSVickery (plld hrd: led: sn clr: p.u after 6th: lame)		P	4/1[3]	—	—
				(SP 115.4%)	**7 Rn**	

4m 11.4 (11.40) CSF £43.56 TOTE £2.50: £1.70 £16.10 (£119.90) OWNER Mrs A. M. Davis (WANTAGE) BRED Brownstown Stud Farm

Tight Fist (IRE) made an encouraging fencing debut in the autumn before suffering a hairline fracture. He fulfilled that promise in this moderate event. (13/8: evens-7/4)
Stratton Flyer showed her first real sign of ability, finishing well. (40/1)
Run With Joy (IRE) had shown little in points last spring, so this was a revelation. (33/1)
3536 Steer Point showed promise on this chasing debut. (9/1)

4524 BLAZE OF GLORY H'CAP HURDLE (0-105) (5-Y.O+) (Class F)

8-35 (8-35) **3m 3f (12 hdls)** £1,944.20 (£546.20: £266.60) GOING minus 0.02 sec per fur (G)

	Horse	Dist	Pos	SP	RR	SF
4470[2]	**Apachee Flower (80)** (HSHowe) **7-10-7** MAFitzgerald (a.p: led appr last: styd on wl u.p flat)	—	1	9/4[1]	62	2
4418[5]	**Amillionmemories (82)** (MrsBarbaraWaring) **7-10-9** EByrne (hld up & bhd: hdwy 9th: ev ch 2 out: led briefly after 2 out: no ex nr fin)	1¼	2	4/1[2]	63	3
4220[P]	**Tiger Claw (USA) (75)** (AGHobbs) **11-10-2** RGreene (hld up & bhd: hdwy 10th: styd on wl fr 2 out)	2	3	10/1	55	—
4309[11]	**Loughdoo (IRE) (73)** (RLee) **9-10-0** BFenton (chsd ldrs tl led 10th: hdd after 2 out: wknd)	1	4	8/1	52	—
4321[3]	**Persian View (IRE) (97)** (KCBailey) **7-11-3**(7) MrRWakley (s.s: in tch 4th: hdwy 7th: wknd appr 10th)	8	5	6/1[3]	72	12
4378[11]	**Whitebonnet (IRE) (75)** (CREgerton) **7-9-13b**(3) SophieMitchell (chsd ldr to 10th: wknd)	8	6	10/1	45	—
3894[4]	**Rising's Lass (IRE) (73)** (MJWeeden) **7-10-0** TDascombe (in tch to 9th: grad wknd)	7	7	9/1	39	—
4096[2]	**Baylord Prince (IRE) (73)** (MrsJAEwer) **9-10-0** GTormey (a bhd: drvn along 8th: not on terms)	5	8	20/1	36	—
	Purbeck Polly (73) (NRMitchell) **7-9-7**(7) MGriffiths (bit bkwd: in tch to 9th: wknd)	9	9	20/1	30	—
4253[5]	**Nick the Dreamer (77)** (WGMTurner) **12-9-11**(7) NWillmington (led tl hdd 10th: sn wknd)	dist	10	16/1	—	—
4399[4]	**Tudor Town (77)** (KBishop) **9-10-4**ow4 SBurrough (plld hrd: in tch & mstke 4th: wknd 9th: t.o & p.u bef last)		P	20/1	—	—
				(SP 124.5%)	**11 Rn**	

6m 42.3 (19.30) CSF £11.30 CT £66.52 TOTE £3.20: £1.30 £1.60 £2.50 (£10.20) Trio £30.30 OWNER Mr John Tackley (TIVERTON) BRED Balding and Howe (Bloodstock) Ltd

LONG HANDICAP Loughdoo (IRE) 9-11 Baylord Prince (IRE) 9-3 Purbeck Polly 9-1 Rising's Lass (IRE) 9-12 Tudor Town 9-9

4470 Apachee Flower, whose stable is in good form, appreciated this extended trip and justified support. (9/4)
4418 Amillionmemories, at his best during the summer months, showed his turn is not far away. (4/1: op 6/1)
3892 Tiger Claw (USA) needs this extended trip to show his best. (10/1: op 5/1)
Loughdoo (IRE), a former Irish pointer, showed his first sign of form in this country, and can win a small race. (8/1: 4/1-9/1)
4321 Persian View (IRE) last a lot of ground at the start, but got back into the race and was close enough until fading from the home turn. (6/1: 7/2-7/1)

T/Plpt: £83.00 (166.3 Tckts). T/Qdpt: £13.20 (47.75 Tckts) T.

4422-WARWICK (L-H) (Good)

Saturday May 10th

WEATHER: raining

4525 FUSILIER H'CAP HURDLE (0-115) (4-Y.O+) (Class E)

5-20 (5-20) **2m (8 hdls)** £2,363.60 (£654.60: £312.80) GOING: 0.05 sec per fur (G)

	Horse	Dist	Pos	SP	RR	SF
4381[2]	**Muizenberg (82)** (EHOwenjun) **10-10-4** AThornton (lw: mde all: sn clr: drvn out)	—	1	7/2[2]	69+	25
4313[2]	**Above the Cut (USA) (95)** (CPMorlock) **5-11-3** CLlewellyn (chsd wnr most of wy: hrd rdn appr 2 out: no imp)	9	2	11/4[1]	73	29
4226[P]	**Schnozzle (IRE) (87)** (KSBridgwater) **6-10-9** GBradley (hld up & bhd: hdwy 3 out: nt fluent next: sn rdn & btn)	1¼	3	8/1	64	20
4384[F]	**Bodantree (88)** (NMBabbage) **6-10-10** JCulloty (trckd ldrs tl rdn & lost pl 5th: n.d afterwards)	2½	4	7/1[3]	62	18
4474[4]	**Saint Ciel (USA) (102)** (FJordan) **9-11-10** DerekByrne (lw: hld up: hdwy appr 4th: chsd wnr next: rdn & btn 2 out)	7	5	7/1[3]	69	25
4382[U]	**Lucky Archer (92)** (PJHobbs) **4-10-9** WMarston (mstke 1st: sn chsng ldrs: wknd after 3 out)	nk	6	11/4[1]	59	10
				(SP 111.7%)	**6 Rn**	

3m 48.7 (6.70) CSF £12.41 TOTE £4.80: £1.10 £3.00 (£3.80) OWNER Mrs Julia Owen (DENBIGH) BRED Tally Ho Stud Co Ltd

WEIGHT FOR AGE 4yo-5lb

4381 Muizenberg gained his revenge over the runner-up on these more advantageous terms, and won with any amount in hand. (7/2)
4313 Above the Cut (USA), at his best when you can hear his feet rattle, tried his best to keep tabs on the winner, but he was always going a gear too fast. (11/4)
3679 Schnozzle (IRE) has been lightly-raced. He ran promisingly here and may have gained second pace had he not landed awkwardly at the penultimate flight. (8/1: op 12/1)
4162 Bodantree dropped to the rear at halfway and, though he did make some late progress, was never a factor. (7/1)
4474 Saint Ciel (USA), at his best when brought late, got there far too soon on this occasion and he was beaten turning in. (7/1)
4095 Lucky Archer, taking on handicappers for the first time, ran a bit too free after making a mistake at the first and he had run himself out at the end of the back straight. (11/4)

4526 FLYING HACKLE NOVICES' CHASE (5-Y.O+) (Class E)

5-50 (5-50) **2m (12 fncs)** £2,770.00 (£835.00: £405.00: £190.00) GOING: 0.05 sec per fur (G)

				SP	RR	SF
3983[13]	**Alpine Mist (IRE)** (JGMO'Shea) **5-10-5**(3) MichaelBrennan (hld up wl bhd: hdwy 7th: rdn 2 out: led last: all out)	—	**1**	6/1[3]	83	18
4278[5]	**Verde Luna** (DWPArbuthnot) **5-10-8** SMcNeill (j.w: chsd ldr: led 6th to last: hrd rdn: r.o)	1½	**2**	7/2[2]	82	17
3921[7]	**Alosaili** (JCullinan) **10-11-0** GBradley (a.p: pushed along 4 out: wkng whn mstke 2 out)	5	**3**	14/1	77	18
4437[U]	**Snowy Petrel (IRE) (84)** (KCBailey) **5-10-8b** AThornton (lw: chsd ldrs: mstke 6th: wkng whn hit 4 out: sn bhd)	15	**4**	11/8[1]	62	—
4454[3]	**Old Redwood (60)** (MrsLWilliamson) **10-11-0** CLlewellyn (lw: swtg: led tl hdd & hit 6th: rdn whn mstke 4 out: sn bhd)	9	**5**	6/1[3]	53	—
4444[3]	**Hugh Daniels (65)** (CJHemsley) **9-10-7**(7) MissADudley (lw: chsd ldrs to 6th: sn wknd: t.o)	23	**6**	20/1	30	—
3283[P]	**Cumberland Youth** (MissCJECaroe) **6-11-0** ILawrence (bkwd: t.o fr ½-wy: p.u bef 4 out)		**P**	50/1	—	—
4305[4]	**Lady Rosebury** (RJPrice) **7-10-9** WMarston (j.b: sn t.o: ref 4th)		**R**	20/1	—	—
4092[4]	**Whod of Thought It (IRE) (60)** (PRChamings) **6-10-11**(3) MrCBonner (hld up: in tch whn blnd & uns rdr 7th)		**U**	25/1	—	—
				(SP 114.9%)	**9 Rn**	

4m 3.4 (9.40) CSF £24.05 TOTE £7.90: £2.10 £2.20 £1.90 (£26.00) Trio £48.60 OWNER Catch-42 (WESTBURY-ON-SEVERN) BRED J. G. O'Brien
WEIGHT FOR AGE 5yo-6lb

1183 Alpine Mist (IRE), given plenty of time to get the hang of things on this chasing debut, touched down with a narrow lead at the last, and was always finding enough to withstand the renewed challenge of the runner-up. (6/1)
4278 Verde Luna had more use made of him on this debut over the bigger obstacles. Jumping boldly, he was always the one to beat and may well benefit from another half-mile at this game. (7/2)
1861 Alosaili seems to have lost the habit of winning, but he performed with credit on this first outing over fences and his interest may just be rekindled. (14/1: op 33/1)
4437 Snowy Petrel (IRE) is taking time to adapt to fences, and at times he looks a bit gutless. (11/8: 1/2-6/4)
4454 Old Redwood (6/1: op 10/1)

4527 6TH OF FOOT H'CAP HURDLE (0-115) (4-Y.O+) (Class E)

6-20 (6-20) **2m 4f 110y (11 hdls)** £2,352.70 (£652.20: £312.10) GOING: 0.05 sec per fur (G)

				SP	RR	SF
4248[13]	**Lord Mcmurrough (IRE) (110)** (JNeville) **7-11-12** APMcCoy (lw: mde all: sn clr: wknd & wnt lft fnl 2: hrd rdn flat: jst hld on)	—	**1**	9/4[1]	90	7
4296[P]	**Desert Force (IRE) (88)** (GFierro) **8-10-4b**ow1 GBradley (chsd wnr fr 3rd: rdn appr 2 out: str run flat: jst failed)	s.h	**2**	12/1	68	—
4136[3]	**Super Rapier (IRE) (84)** (GAHubbard) **5-10-0** RJohnson (hdwy 5th: outpcd 8th: styd on again appr 2 out)	3	**3**	5/1[2]	62	—
1451[4]	**Prime of Life (IRE) (89)** (JMPEustace) **7-10-5** SMcNeill (bkwd: chsd ldng pair fr 6th: wknd appr 3 out: t.o)	27	**4**	9/1	46	—
4313*	**Chief Mouse (106)** (FJordan) **4-11-2** JOsborne (lost tch 6th: t.o)	18	**5**	9/4[1]	49	—
4340*	**Circus Colours (98)** (JRJenkins) **7-11-0** SFox (a in rr: t.o fr 8th)	4	**6**	7/1[3]	37	—
				(SP 108.4%)	**6 Rn**	

5m 6.5 (19.50) CSF £21.69 TOTE £3.00: £1.50 £2.90 (£11.20) OWNER Mr J. Neville (NEWPORT, GWENT) BRED B. Galvin in Ireland
WEIGHT FOR AGE 4yo-6lb

3698 Lord Mcmurrough (IRE) took off at a rate of knots and was soon well clear, but a combination of weight and the ever-softening ground began to take its toll, and he only held on by the skin of his teeth. (9/4)
3709 Desert Force (IRE) tracked the winner at a respectable distance and for most of the way failed to make any impression but, given half a chance once in line for home, he answered his rider's every call and was less than half-a-stride down at the line. (12/1: op 6/1)
4136 Super Rapier (IRE), still to open his account, seems to be progressing and needs all of this trip. (5/1)
1451 Prime of Life (IRE), very much in need of this first run in six months, had reached the end of his tether turning out of the back straight. (9/1)
4313* Chief Mouse has done all his winning on firm, and just could not handle the rain-softened ground. (9/4)
4340* Circus Colours is at his best on firm ground and could not handle this going. (7/1: op 4/1)

4528 BLUE MACAW 'N.H.' NOVICES' HURDLE (4-Y.O+) (Class E)

6-50 (6-52) **2m 4f 110y (11 hdls)** £2,761.20 (£768.20: £369.60) GOING: 0.05 sec per fur (G)

				SP	RR	SF
	Albermarle (IRE) (CaptTAForster) **6-11-0** JOsborne (bit bkwd: nt j.w: hld up: hdwy appr 7th: led after 3 out: clr fr next)	—	**1**	6/1	79	12
3423[P]	**Gratomi (IRE)** (PCRitchens) **7-11-0** SFox (hld up: hdwy 8th: chsd wnr appr 2 out: no imp)	7	**2**	33/1	74	7
4224*	**Isis Dawn** (AGNewcombe) **5-10-12**(3) PHenley (hld up: hdwy 6th: lft poor 3rd at last)	28	**3**	11/4[1]	53	—
3581[2]	**Supreme Troglodyte (IRE) (82)** (CPMorlock) **5-10-9** JRKavanagh (led to 4th: wknd appr 3 out)	2½	**4**	14/1	45	—
	Gamay (NRMitchell) **7-11-0** CLlewellyn (nvr nr to chal)	15	**5**	20/1	38	—
1774[6]	**Crocknamohill (IRE)** (KSBridgwater) **6-11-0** WMarston (bkwd: prom to 7th: sn wknd)	¾	**6**	16/1	37	—
3937[5]	**Derring Floss** (JAPickering) **7-10-2**(7) MissJWormall (lost pl ½-wy: t.o)	20	**7**	33/1	17	—
2510*	**Edge Ahead (IRE)** (TThomsonJones) **7-11-0** RDunwoody (bkwd: chsd ldrs to 7th: sn lost tch: t.o)	11	**8**	9/2[2]	13	—
4134[4]	**Pealings (IRE) (79)** (GAHubbard) **5-11-0** RJohnson (prom: hit 5th: wknd 7th: t.o)	6	**9**	14/1	9	—
2690[17]	**Tullow Lady (IRE)** (OBrennan) **6-10-9** MBrennan (bkwd: prom tl wknd appr 7th: t.o)	30	**10**	20/1	—	—
3989[4]	**Laburnum Gold (IRE) (93)** (MrsJPitman) **6-11-0** DLeahy (lw: led 4th: sn clr: wknd & hdd after 3 out: 3rd & btn whn fell last)		**F**	5/1[3]	—	—
4329[2]	**Blowing Rock (IRE)** (MissHCKnight) **5-11-0** JCulloty (chsd ldrs to 6th: sn wknd: t.o: p.u bef 2 out)		**P**	7/1	—	—

4161[6] **Bet Wiltshire** (MrsNMacauley) **5-11-0** SWynne (a bhd: t.o: p.u bef 7th) .... P 20/1 — —
3798[P] **Blazing Dove** (AEPrice) **6-11-0** AThornton (bkwd: bhd whn p.u after 5th: b.b.v) .... P 25/1 — —
3892[P] **Ilewinit (IRE) (55)** (PCRitchens) **8-11-0** GUpton (t.o fr 5th: p.u bef 7th) .... P 50/1 — —
3853[8] **Mr Bojangles (IRE)** (IPWilliams) **6-11-0** BPowell (mid div to 8th: bhd whn p.u bef 2 out) .... P 10/1 — —
Harington Hundreds (GBBalding) **7-11-0** APMcCoy (swtg: t.o: p.u bef 7th) .... P 20/1 — —
3548[14] ***Surprise City*** (AJWilson) **6-10-9**(5) ChrisWebb (Withdrawn not under Starter's orders: uns rdr gng to post) ...... W 10/1 — —
(SP 156.4%) **17 Rn**

5m 1.9 (14.90) CSF £194.81 TOTE £9.20: £2.80 £10.70 £2.00 (£246.60) Trio Not won; £293.53 to Redcar 12/5/97 OWNER Mr Robert Ogden (LUDLOW) BRED E. Campion
OFFICIAL EXPLANATION **Blazing Dove: bled from the nose.**
Albermarle (IRE), reappearing after fifteen months out of action, is a big, chasing type who looked decidedly burly, but he obviously has a bit of class about him and, once he does learn to pick his feet up, could prove useful. (6/1)
Gratomi (IRE), a winner between the flags in the spring of 1995, showed his first signs of ability under Rules with a running-on performance that was never going to succeed. (33/1)
4224* Isis Dawn did not get going until far too late, and all she does is stay. (11/4)
3581 Supreme Troglodyte (IRE) continues to run well but she is very short of pace, and her future could lie over fences. (14/1)
2510* Edge Ahead (IRE) (9/2: 3/1-5/1)
4134 Pealings (IRE) (14/1: op 8/1)
3989 Laburnum Gold (IRE) raced far too freely over this longer trip and, collared turning out of the back straight, was very leg-weary but assured of third prize when he capsized at the last. He has got ability and we have not seen the best of him yet. (5/1)
4329 Blowing Rock (IRE) (7/1: 5/1-8/1)
Mr Bojangles (IRE) (10/1: op 16/1)

4529 WILLSFORD H'CAP CHASE (0-135) (5-Y.O+) (Class C)

7-20 (7-21) **3m 2f (20 fncs)** £4,597.50 (£1,380.00: £665.00: £307.50) GOING: 0.05 sec per fur (G)

				SP	RR	SF
4351a[2]	**Miss Diskin (IRE) (100)** (RHBuckler) **8-10-2** BPowell (j.w: led to 4th: led 7th to 2 out: rallied gamely to ld cl home)	—	1	100/30 2	112	21
3428[P]	**Sounds Strong (IRE) (126)** (DNicholson) **8-12-0** RJohnson (hld up & bhd: hdwy 10th: led 2 out: hrd rdn & hdd nr fin)	s.h	2	11/2	138	47
4424[2]	**Harristown Lady (103)** (GBBalding) **10-10-5b** APMcCoy (lw: chsd ldrs tl lost pl 10th: styd on again fr 3 out)	dist	3	9/2 3	—	—
3629[4]	**Allo George (110)** (AGNewcombe) **11-10-12** AThornton (trckd ldrs: disp ld 14th & 15th: wknd 3 out)	2½	4	8/1	—	—
4300[3]	**Merry Panto (IRE) (98)** (CPEBrooks) **8-10-0** SMcNeill (hld up: hdwy 10th: mstke 15th: wknd 4 out)	6	5	11/1	—	—
4270*	**Garrylough (IRE) (118)** (DRGandolfo) **8-11-6** RDunwoody (w ldr: led 4th to 7th: wknd 16th: t.o)	19	6	5/2 1	—	—
4270[8]	**Big Ben Dun (102)** (CPEBrooks) **11-10-4**ow1 GBradley (prom: rdn 13th: wknd next: t.o)	3	7	10/1	—	—

(SP 113.8%) **7 Rn**

6m 37.2 (12.20) CSF £19.66 CT £74.36 TOTE £3.60: £2.30 £2.80 (£13.50) OWNER Mr Martyn Forrester (BRIDPORT) BRED John Neary
4351a Miss Diskin (IRE), a very courageous mare who was narrowly beaten at Punchestown on her most recent outing, made amends here with a last gasp effort that proved just sufficient. (100/30)
3428 Sounds Strong (IRE) worked hard to land in front at the penultimate fence and he never once stopped trying, but the concession of 26lb proved just too much of a burden on the run-in. (11/2)
4424 Harristown Lady lost her pitch with a circuit still to go and, though she did stay on to run into the prizes, was never a serious factor. (9/2)
3629 Allo George travelled extremely well for most of the way but, when the leading pair quickened things up at the end of the back straight, he was unable to respond. (8/1)
4300 Merry Panto (IRE) (11/1: 8/1-12/1)
4270* Garrylough (IRE) had one of her non-going days, and she was out of contention for the final mile. (5/2)

4530 NORMANDY NOVICES' HUNTERS' CHASE (5-Y.O+) (Class H)

7-50 (7-50) **3m 2f (20 fncs)** £991.25 (£296.00: £141.50: £64.25) GOING: 0.05 sec per fur (G)

				SP	RR	SF
4447*	**Prince Buck (IRE)** (MJRoberts) **7-12-4**(3) MrPHacking (lw: j.w: mde all: comf)	—	1	4/6 1	106+	24
3469[F]	**True Fortune** (JohnMoore) **7-11-7**(7) MrDSJones (trckd ldrs: wnt 2nd 13th: rallied appr 2 out: eased whn btn flat)	19	2	7/2 2	87	5
	Darton Ri (MrsSMaxse) **14-11-7**(7) MrJMaxse (sn wl bhd: rdn 10th: styng on whn snatched up flat: fin 4th, 3l: plcd 3rd)	dist	3	6/1 3	—	—
4471[B]	**Very Daring** (JulianHunt) **7-11-7**(7) MissSSharratt (prom tl wknd qckly after 13th: rdn & edgd lft flat: fin 3rd, dist: disq: plcd 4th)	3	4	20/1	—	—
	Damers Treasure (BRSummers) **11-11-7b**1(7) MrMHarris (lw: dropped rr 4th: t.o fr 12th)	20	5	16/1	—	—
	Bentley Manor (MALloyd) **8-11-7**(7) MrGHanmer (bhd & rdn 10th: sn t.o: p.u bef 4 out)		P	16/1	—	—
	Polydeuces (CaptRJInglesant) **11-11-7**(7) CaptRInglesant (lw: sn chsng ldrs: wknd 13th: t.o: p.u bef next)		P	33/1	—	—
	Kellytino (PRWebber) **8-11-2**(7) MrPScott (bkwd: hld up: hdwy 9th: blnd & uns rdr 12th)		U	20/1	—	—

(SP 120.7%) **8 Rn**

6m 47.9 (22.90) CSF £3.43 TOTE £1.90: £1.20 £1.10 £1.10 (£2.60) OWNER Mr Mike Roberts (HAILSHAM) BRED Frank Stewart
4447* Prince Buck (IRE) gave an exhibition of jumping from the front and, with only True Fortune to contend with in the final mile, was always calling the tune. (4/6)
True Fortune has never won over regulation fences but he did little wrong here, despite finding the winner much too smart for him. (7/2)

4531 ARTHUR HUTT VC MEMORIAL STANDARD N.H. FLAT RACE (4, 5 & 6-Y.O) (Class H)

8-20 (8-20) **2m** £1,028.00 (£278.00: £128.00)

			SP	RR	SF
Andsuephi (IRE) (CPEBrooks) **5-10-11**(7) GBrace (chsd ldrs: rdn 2 out: str run to ld cl home)	—	1	16/1	58 f	—
Lucy Glitters (CaptTAForster) **5-10-8**(5) ABates (hdwy 7f out: led 2f out: hrd rdn: ct nr fin)	nk	2	10/1	53 f	—
Winston Run (IPWilliams) **5-10-11**(7) FBogle (hld up: hdwy 4f out: styd on wl towards fin)	2½	3	16/1	55 f	—
Oi Mother (IRE) (DNicholson) **5-10-10**(3) RMassey (hld up: hdwy 9f out: ev ch ent fnl f: unable qckn)	1¾	4	11/10 1	48 f	—
Ruby Rosa (CaptTAForster) **5-10-6**(7) JMogford (hld up: hdwy ½-wy: slt ld 4f out: hdd & wknd 2f out)	5	5	20/1	43 f	—
Dark Horse (IRE) (CPEBrooks) **5-10-11**(7) MBerry (trckd ldrs: no hdwy fnl 2f)	4	6	14/1	44 f	—
Melton Made (IRE) (GAHubbard) **4-10-10**(3) MichaelBrennan (hld up: hdwy to ld 6f out: hdd 4f out: wknd fnl 2f)	2	7	10/1	42 f	—

	Horse / details	Dist	Pos	SP	RR	SF
	Truthfully (SGollings) **4-10-3**(5) XAizpuru (nvr nrr)	4	**8**	20/1	33 f	—
	Sumo (OBrennan) **4-10-10**(3) EHusband (w bhd tl hdwy 7f out: nt rch ldrs)	¾	**9**	25/1	38 f	—
	Beacon Lane (IRE) (OO'Neill) **4-10-6**(7) SO'Shea (bhd: hdwy 9f out: wknd over 3f out)	3½	**10**	25/1	34 f	—
	High In The Sky (JRJenkins) **4-10-6**(7) DYellowlees (nvr trbld ldrs)	1½	**11**	20/1	33 f	—
	Doug Eng (IRE) (MrsJPitman) **4-10-10**(3) DFortt (nvr nr to chal)	4	**12**	5/1[2]	29 f	—
3304[17]	**Woodstock Wanderer (IRE)** (PBowen) **5-10-11**(7) LCummins (led 11f: wknd 4f out)	8	**13**	8/1[3]	21 f	—
	Storm Home (OO'Neill) **5-11-4** MrAMitchell (prom tl wknd over 6f out)	1½	**14**	33/1	19 f	—
	Cedric Tudor (PMitchell) **4-10-13** MrTMcCarthy (prom tl wknd 4f out)	nk	**15**	20/1	19 f	—
	Stardante (IRE) (RLee) **5-11-1**(3) PHenley (a bhd: t.o)	14	**16**	14/1	5 f	—
	My Friend Billy (IRE) (TTBill) **5-11-1**(3) LAspell (effrt ½-wy: wknd 4f out: t.o)	5	**17**	33/1	—	—
	Dunston Slick (BPreece) **4-10-6**(7) MissLBoswell (prom: led 9f out to 6f out: wknd qckly: t.o)	13	**18**	33/1	—	—
	Postlip Royale (LPGrassick) **4-10-1**(7) MrOMcPhail (bhd fnl 6f: t.o)	20	**19**	50/1	—	—
	Bristol Gold (PSFelgate) **4-10-6**(7) LSuthern (chsd ldr to ½-wy: grad wknd: t.o)	½	**20**	25/1	—	—
2844[13]	**Old Man of Ramas** (MissJFCraze) **5-11-1**(3) PMidgley (trckd ldrs 10f: sn wknd: t.o)	6	**21**	20/1	—	—

(SP 164.8%) **21 Rn**

3m 48.3 CSF £172.55 TOTE £44.10: £11.90 £2.60 £7.80 (£157.30) Trio Not won; £254.09 to Redcar 12/5/97 OWNER Mrs J. A. Cohen (LAMBOURN) BRED Martin Cullinane

WEIGHT FOR AGE 4yo-5lb

Andsuephi (IRE), an attractive individual, looked to be fighting a lost cause turning in, but he stayed on strongly once straightened up, and had his head in front when it mattered. (16/1)

Lucy Glitters, a half-sister to the useful Sail by the Stars, can be made fitter, but she forced the winner to fight to shade her on the post, and her future looks bright. (10/1)

Winston Run, patiently ridden, was getting down to some serious work in the latter stages and should not be too hard to place. (16/1)

Oi Mother (IRE), a workmanlike mare with plenty about her, looked as though she would benefit from the run. Produced to deliver a determined challenge one furlong out, she just lacked that bit extra this time but she will be all the wiser for the run and should win her share of races. (11/10: op evens)

Ruby Rosa, a lightly-made debutante, ran well and with this experience under her belt, can only improve. (20/1)

Dark Horse (IRE), a stablemate of the winner with plenty left to work on, could not muster the pace to mount a challenge, but he kept staying on and should be able to win races. (14/1)

Melton Made (IRE), a tall gelding who needs time to fill to his frame, ran much better than his finishing position suggests and he is definitely one for the future. (10/1)

Doug Eng (IRE) (5/1: 4/1-6/1)

Stardante (IRE) (14/1: 10/1-16/1)

T/Plpt: £265.90 (39.36 Tckts). T/Qdpt: £43.30 (18.47 Tckts) IM

4304-WORCESTER (L-H) (Good to soft)

Saturday May 10th

WEATHER: showers and sunny spells

4532 HOLLY GREEN HURDLE (4-Y.O) (Class E)

2-10 (2-10) **2m (8 hdls)** £2,302.50 (£640.00: £307.50) GOING: 1.35 sec per fur (HY)

	Horse / details	Dist	Pos	SP	RR	SF
4395[4]	**Kinnescash (IRE) (108)** (PBowen) **4-11-12** MAFitzgerald (mde all: clr appr last: r.o wl)	—	**1**	6/4[2]	82	41
4395[U]	**Tiutchev (93)** (MissHCKnight) **4-10-12** JCulloty (hld up: stdy hdwy 5th: r.o one pce flat: no ch w wnr)	5	**2**	5/1[3]	63	22
4273[3]	**Influence Pedler (116)** (JABOld) **4-11-5** CLlewellyn (w wnr: ev ch 3 out: sn rdn: wknd appr last)	3	**3**	10/11[1]	67	26
4465[U]	**Romantic Warrior** (KSBridgwater) **4-10-12** BPowell (hld up: rdn & wknd appr 3 out)	20	**4**	66/1	40	—
3544[P]	**Summer Princess** (GFierro) **4-10-7** GBradley (hld up: rdn appr 3 out: sn bhd: t.o)	dist	**5**	40/1	—	—

(SP 113.0%) **5 Rn**

4m 8.4 (28.40) CSF £8.64 TOTE £2.90: £1.20 £1.90 (£4.10) OWNER Mr D. R. James (HAVERFORDWEST) BRED Frank Barry

4395 Kinnescash (IRE) had cut in the ground for his recent win on the Flat at Leicester, so it was rather surprising that he did not start favourite for this event. (6/4: evens-13/8)

2925 Tiutchev managed to get round in one piece this time. (5/1: 7/2-6/1)

4273 Influence Pedler was presumably expected to outstay the winner in this ground by those who backed him down to odds-on. (10/11)

4533 GREAT MALVERN NOVICES' CHASE (5-Y.O+) (Class E)

2-40 (2-41) **2m 4f 110y (15 fncs)** £2,977.75 (£892.00: £428.50: £196.75) GOING: 0.91 sec per fur (S)

	Horse / details	Dist	Pos	SP	RR	SF
1550[5]	**Who Am I (IRE) (84)** (RHAlner) **7-11-0** AThornton (hld up: hdwy 6th: mstke 8th: chal whn pckd 3 out: led 2 out: drvn out)	—	**1**	16/1	98	30
4211[7]	**With Impunity (105)** (PFNicholls) **8-11-7** RJohnson (lw: hdwy 5th: rdn 9th: led 11th: blnd 3 out: hdd 2 out: rallied flat)	1½	**2**	7/4[1]	104	36
4204[7]	**The Bargeman (NZ)** (DRGandolfo) **9-11-0** RDunwoody (lw: hld up: hdwy 7th: hit 4 out: wknd 3 out)	12	**3**	7/2[2]	88	20
3806[4]	**Crane Hill (89)** (PJHobbs) **7-11-0b** WMarston (mstke 2nd: a bhd)	9	**4**	11/1	80	12
4377[3]	**Desert Brave (IRE) (74)** (MrsSJSmith) **7-11-0** RichardGuest (hld up: hdwy 7th: wknd appr 4 out: no ch whn mskte last)	¾	**5**	16/1	80	12
4402[P]	**Astral Invasion (USA) (66)** (TWall) **6-11-0** SWynne (lw: chsd ldr: led 4th: hit 8th: hdd 11th: 5th & wkng whn fell 2 out)		**F**	33/1	—	—
4377[W]	**Hangover (68)** (RLee) **11-11-0** CLlewellyn (bhd fr 9th: t.o whn p.u bef 2 out)		**P**	10/1	—	—
	Rich Life (IRE) (CWeedon) **7-11-7** MRichards (bkwd: bhd fr 7th: t.o whn p.u bef 11th)		**P**	6/1[3]	—	—
4318[8]	**Nell Valley** (CPEBrooks) **6-10-9** GBradley (led to 4th: wknd qckly after 6th: p.u bef 7th)		**P**	33/1	—	—
4305[P]	**Steel Gold** (TRKinsey) **7-10-10**(7)ow3 MrRBurton (lw: bhd: mstke 2nd: rdn after 6th: sn t.o: p.u bef 2 out)		**P**	66/1	—	—

(SP 109.4%) **10 Rn**

5m 28.8 (27.80) CSF £38.93 TOTE £17.60: £3.90 £1.70 £1.30 (£14.70) Trio £40.60 OWNER Mr H. Wellstead (BLANDFORD) BRED Michael O'Shea

1550 Who Am I (IRE) fulfilled the promise of his only previous outing over fences here back in November. (16/1)

3565* With Impunity, highly-tried last time, looked much more at home back on this softer ground. (7/4)

2759 The Bargeman (NZ) made a satisfactory start to his chasing career, and is probably better-suited to good ground. (7/2)

3806 Crane Hill (11/1: 7/1-12/1)
3684* Hangover (10/1: 8/1-12/1)
Rich Life (IRE) (6/1: 7/2-13/2)

4534 HORSERACE BETTING LEVY BOARD H'CAP HURDLE (0-105) (4-Y.O+) (Class F)

3-10 (3-12) **2m (8 hdls)** £2,372.50 (£660.00: £317.50) GOING: 1.35 sec per fur (HY)

				SP	RR	SF
1715*	**Stay With Me (FR) (98)** (CREgerton) **7-11-10** JOsborne (a.p: led 2 out: lft clr last: eased flat)	—	1	9/2[2]	79+	37
4295[P]	**Our Robert (92)** (AStreeter) **5-11-4v[1]** TEley (hld up: rdn 4th: hdwy after 5th: bdly hmpd last: r.o wl flat)	4	2	10/1	69	27
4006[F]	**Classic Pal (USA) (78)** (NRMitchell) **6-10-4** DSkyrme (hld up: hdwy appr 3 out: r.o one pce flat)	s.h	3	6/1[3]	55	13
4162[2]	**Fontanays (IRE) (94)** (GMMcCourt) **9-10-13v(7)** RHobson (prom: rdn 5th: sn lost pl: rallied 2 out: btn whn lft 2nd last)	½	4	6/1[3]	70	28
4304[8]	**Mollie Silvers (76)** (JKCresswell) **5-10-2**ow2 WMcFarland (nvr nr to chal)	1½	5	50/1	51	7
3923[5]	**Apache Park (USA) (90)** (DBurchell) **4-10-11b** DJBurchell (led 3rd: hdd & mstke 3 out: wknd 2 out)	6	6	100/30[1]	59	12
4307[5]	**Euro Singer (102)** (TKeddy) **5-11-9(5)** SRyan (lw: hdwy 3rd: led 3 out to 2 out: sn hrd rdn: 2nd & btn whn fell last)		F	13/2	74?	—
4381[P]	**Mr Lowry (74)** (LJBarratt) **5-10-0** SWynne (sme hdwy appr 3 out: wknd & p.u bef 2 out)		P	20/1	—	—
4415[4]	**Innocent George (82)** (MissLCSiddall) **8-10-8** RDunwoody (led to 3rd: wknd qckly after 5th: p.u & dismntd bef 3 out)		P	9/1	—	—
4381[4]	**Daily Sport Girl (82)** (BJLlewellyn) **8-10-8** MrJLLlewellyn (hld up: hdwy appr 3 out: styng on wl lft 2nd: hmpd & uns rdr last)		U	11/1	—	—

(SP 117.3%) **10 Rn**

4m 8.7 (28.70) CSF £44.42 CT £249.69 TOTE £4.00: £2.00 £2.40 £1.40 (£37.10) Trio £40.50 OWNER Mrs Sandra Roe (CHADDLEWORTH) BRED Mr and Mrs Henri Rossi and Gerard Desnoues
LONG HANDICAP Mr Lowry 9-13 Mollie Silvers 9-5
WEIGHT FOR AGE 4yo-5lb

1715* Stay With Me (FR), raised 4lb, was returning after a six-month break, and already had matters under control when left clear at the final flight. (9/2)
4295 Our Robert, tried in a visor, was stepping-up from selling company and, although benefiting from the departure of two rivals at the last, did well to recover to snatch second. (10/1)
3234 Classic Pal (USA), 4lb higher than when second at Wincanton, missed the trouble at the final flight and is flattered by his proximity to the winner. (6/1)
4162 Fontanays (IRE), who had switched to blinkers last time, was 3lb higher than when winning at Taunton, and could not hold on to second place in the closing stages. (6/1)
3752 Apache Park (USA) (100/30: op 8/1)
4307 Euro Singer, dropped 2lb, again had the ground on the soft side for him. (13/2: op 7/2)
4381 Daily Sport Girl was closing on Euro Singer, but would not have beaten the winner. (11/1: 8/1-12/1)

4535 LITTLE MALVERN CONDITIONAL H'CAP CHASE (0-105) (5-Y.O+) (Class F)

3-40 (3-41) **2m 7f 110y (18 fncs)** £2,827.50 (£790.00: £382.50) GOING: 0.91 sec per fur (S)

				SP	RR	SF
4234[2]	**Lay it Off (IRE) (83)** (JGO'Neill) **8-10-6** LAspell (hdwy 9th: led & pckd 10th: hdd 12th: led 13th: lft clr last)	—	1	8/1[3]	99	16
	Martell Boy (NZ) (96) (MissVenetiaWilliams) **10-11-5** PHenley (a.p: ev ch whn pckd 3 out: blnd bdly last: nt recover)	10	2	9/1	105	22
3911[U]	**Farney Glen (88)** (JJO'Neill) **10-10-4(7)** DJewett (hld up & bhd: hdwy 11th: wknd after 14th)	13	3	14/1	88	5
4350a[4]	**Court Master (IRE) (90)** (RHBuckler) **9-10-13** RMassey (lw: a.p: j.slowly 2nd: led 12th to 13th: wknd appr 4 out: fin tired)	13	4	8/1[3]	82	—
4404*	**Nova Champ (87)** (MrsSJSmith) **9-10-10** GFRyan (prom tl rdn & wknd appr 4 out)	4	5	5/2[1]	76	—
4174[P]	**Good for a Laugh (82)** (AGHobbs) **13-10-5** OBurrows (prom to 13th: t.o)	21	6	20/1	57	—
4404[5]	**Boxing Match (77)** (JMBradley) **10-10-0** JPower (prom: led 7th to 10th: fell 11th)		F	40/1	—	—
4157[3]	**No Fiddling (IRE) (82)** (GMMcCourt) **6-10-5** DFortt (bhd tl fell 14th)		F	4/1[2]	—	—
4404[P]	**Dont Tell the Wife (105)** (CREgerton) **11-12-0b** MBerry (bhd fr 10th: t.o whn p.u bef 2 out)		P	25/1	—	—
4429*	**Trust Deed (USA) (88)** (SGKnight) **9-10-11b** 6x XAizpuru (a bhd: t.o whn p.u bef last)		P	16/1	—	—
3333[P]	**Little-Nipper (95)** (RJSmith) **12-11-4** JMagee (mstkes: prom tl blnd 6th: bhd whn p.u bef 10th)		P	40/1	—	—
3185[3]	**Nevada Gold (98)** (FJYardley) **11-11-7** MichaelBrennan (led to 7th: wknd qckly after 9th: p.u bef 10th)		P	20/1	—	—
3629[2]	**Jailbreaker (81)** (BRMillman) **10-10-4** DSalter (bhd whn mstke 14th: t.o whn p.u bef 4 out)		P	14/1	—	—
4385[7]	**Golden Opal (83)** (RHBuckler) **12-9-13(7)**ow6 JMcDermott (nt j.w: hdwy 9th: wkng whn mstke 13th: t.o whn mstke 4 out: p.u bef 3 out)		P	33/1	—	—
3686[3]	**River Leven (88)** (DRGandolfo) **8-10-11b** SophieMitchell (a bhd: t.o whn p.u bef last)		P	16/1	—	—

(SP 127.1%) **15 Rn**

6m 19.2 CSF £68.57 CT £924.88 TOTE £8.70: £2.60 £4.30 £5.30 (£56.30) Trio £314.40; £141.74 to Beverley 11/5/97 OWNER Mr J. G. O'Neill (BICESTER) BRED Finbar O'Neill
LONG HANDICAP Golden Opal 9-11 Boxing Match 9-8

4234 Lay it Off (IRE) seemed in control when effectively presented with the race at the final fence. (8/1)
Martell Boy (NZ), looking big and well, has changed stables and had ground conditions in his favour for this comeback. Looking tired when making mess of the last, normal improvement should see him go one better. (9/1)
3560 Farney Glen struggles to get three miles in ground worse than good. (14/1: op 8/1)
4350a Court Master (IRE) did not see out this longer trip in this rain-softened ground. (8/1: op 9/2)
4404* Nova Champ, up 6lb, could either have found this coming too soon or the ground softer than at Hereford. (5/2)

4536 INA BEARING COMPANY H'CAP HURDLE (0-125) (4-Y.O+) (Class D)

4-10 (4-10) **3m (12 hdls)** £2,903.00 (£808.00: £389.00) GOING: 1.35 sec per fur (HY)

				SP	RR	SF
4178[2]	**The Toiseach (IRE) (117)** (JRFanshawe) **6-12-0v** JOsborne (lw: mde all: clr most of wy: r.o wl fr 2 out)	—	1	2/1[1]	100	33
4418[2]	**Derring Bridge (94)** (MrsSMJohnson) **7-10-5** RJohnson (hld up: wnt 2nd appr 8th: rdn appr 2 out: no imp)	6	2	11/4[2]	73	6
4005[7]	**General Mouktar (107)** (MCPipe) **7-11-4** APMcCoy (hld up in rr: hdwy appr 3 out: r.o flat)	s.h	3	3/1[3]	86	19
4418[4]	**Needwood Poppy (89)** (BCMorgan) **9-10-0** BClifford (nvr nr to chal)	6	4	11/2	64	—
	Bullens Bay (IRE) (101) (BJLlewellyn) **8-10-12** BPowell (bhd fr 8th: t.o)	dist	5	16/1	—	—

				SP	RR	SF
4178[P]	**So Proud (111)** (MrsAJPerrett) **12-11-8** RDunwoody (chsd wnr tl appr 8th: sn wknd: t.o)	29	**6**	20/1	—	—
				(SP 111.0%)		**6 Rn**

6m 21.9 (45.90) CSF £7.24 TOTE £2.90: £2.00 £1.20 (£2.90) OWNER T & J Vestey (NEWMARKET) BRED T. Hennessy
LONG HANDICAP Needwood Poppy 9-12
4178 The Toiseach (IRE), raised a further 3lb, was sensibly given a breather over this longer trip with a circuit to go. (2/1: 6/4-9/4)
4418 Derring Bridge, racing off the same mark as when out of the handicap last time, just held on to second place. (11/4)
3013 General Mouktar was back to a mark only 4lb higher than when completing a hat-trick earlier in the season. (3/1)

4537 SUCKLEY NOVICES' CHASE (5-Y.O+) (Class E)

4-40 (4-41) **2m 7f 110y (18 fncs)** £3,455.50 (£1,039.00: £502.00: £233.50) GOING: 0.91 sec per fur (S)

				SP	RR	SF
4211[2]	**Macgeorge (IRE) (129)** (RLee) **7-12-0** RDunwoody (led 2nd to 12th: led 4 out: all out)	—	**1**	13/8[1]	115	41
4158*	**Dream Ride (IRE) (110)** (DNicholson) **7-12-0** RJohnson (hld up: hdwy 8th: hrd rdn & ev ch appr last: r.o)	nk	**2**	8/1	115	41
4186[9]	**Lien de Famille (IRE) (97)** (JJQuinn) **7-11-8** JRKavanagh (lw: sn prom: led 12th: mstke 14th: hdd 4 out: wknd 3 out)	19	**3**	33/1	96	22
4213[8]	**Kamikaze (120)** (KCBailey) **7-11-8b** JOsborne (prom: hit 7th & 4 out: sn wknd)	24	**4**	9/4[2]	80	6
4249[6]	**Careysville (IRE)** (TRGeorge) **6-11-2** SWynne (bhd fr 13th)	3½	**5**	66/1	71	—
3334[6]	**Better Future (IRE)** (TKeddy) **8-11-2b[1]** DGallagher (bit bkwd: led to 2nd: bhd fr 9th: t.o)	dist	**6**	33/1	—	—
4084[2]	**Glengarrif Girl (IRE)** (MCPipe) **7-10-11v** APMcCoy (mstkes: a bhd: t.o whn p.u bef 10th)		**P**	11/2[3]	—	—
4158[5]	**Five Flags (IRE)** (MrsSJSmith) **9-11-2** RichardGuest (nt j.w: bhd whn mstke 7th: t.o whn p.u bef 4 out)		**P**	33/1	—	—
3181[P]	**Gerry's Pride (IRE) (65)** (JWMullins) **6-11-2** SCurran (bit bkwd: bhd: mstke 10th: t.o whn p.u bef 4 out)		**P**	66/1	—	—
4227[3]	**Melnik** (MrsAJPerrett) **6-11-8** GUpton (a bhd: t.o whn p.u bef 14th)		**P**	16/1	—	—
3112[8]	**Stray Harmony** (RJSmith) **7-10-11** DWalsh (blnd & uns rdr 2nd)		**U**	66/1	—	—
				(SP 114.5%)		**11 Rn**

6m 17.4 CSF £12.91 TOTE £3.00: £1.50 £1.60 £5.70 (£5.50) Trio £66.40 OWNER Mr J. H. Watson (PRESTEIGNE) BRED Mrs B. Brady
4211 Macgeorge (IRE) had won in the mud over two-and-three-quarter miles over hurdles, but had to give his all to keep the runner-up at bay here. (13/8)
4158* Dream Ride (IRE) lost no caste in defeat, and it should be remembered that the winner has some useful form. (8/1: 4/1-9/1)
3068 Lien de Famille (IRE) could not live with a couple of above-average sorts for this time of the season. (33/1)

4538 LONGDON INTERMEDIATE N.H. FLAT RACE (I) (4, 5 & 6-Y.O) (Class H)

5-10 (5-12) **2m** £1,413.00 (£393.00: £189.00)

				SP	RR	SF
	Conchobor (IRE) (KCBailey) **5-10-11**(7) WWalsh (gd sort: lw: hld up: gd hdwy 5f out: led over 3f out: sn clr: rdn out)	—	**1**	6/1[2]	74 f	—
	Roker Joker (REPeacock) **6-10-13**(5) ChrisWebb (w'like: leggy: plld hrd: a.p: chsd wnr fnl 3f: no imp)	22	**2**	33/1	52 f	—
	Whistling Jake (IRE) (CaptTAForster) **6-11-4** MrRBevis (str: bit bkwd: hld up: hdwy over 4f out: r.o one pce fnl 3f)	11	**3**	10/1	41 f	—
	Scally Blue (BPreece) **6-11-5**ow1 MrAHCrow (w'like: bkwd: led over 12f: sn wknd)	6	**4**	16/1	36 f	—
	Deputy Leader (IRE) (NJHenderson) **5-11-4** TCMurphy (w'like: scope: hdwy 9f out: wknd 4f out)	½	**5**	4/1[1]	35 f	—
	Dunabrattin (DTThom) **4-10-8**(5) SRyan (w'like: bkwd: plld hrd: prom: hmpd & lost pl 7f out: rallied over 5f out: wknd over 4f out)	15	**6**	8/1	20 f	—
	Zeny The Nesta (PEccles) **5-10-10**(3) DFortt (lengthy: nvr nr ldrs)	¾	**7**	33/1	14 f	—
	Barton Lil (SABrookshaw) **5-10-8**(5) XAizpuru (w'like: nvr trbld ldrs)	14	**8**	8/1	—	—
	Castle of Light (JTEvans) **6-11-4** MrMMunrowd (w'like: bit bkwd: bhd fnl 4f)	3½	**9**	33/1	1 f	—
	Rare Gift (USA) (DNicholson) **6-11-1**(3) RMassey (w'like: prom over 10f)	3½	**10**	13/2[3]	—	—
4421[14]	**Outrageous Affair** (APJames) **5-10-10**(3) JMagee (w'like: a bhd)	8	**11**	50/1	—	—
	Right Ron Run (FMurphy) **5-11-1**(3) LAspell (unf: bhd fnl 6f)	1¾	**12**	11/1	—	—
	Bernera (JMackie) **5-11-1**(3) EHusband (cmpt: a bhd)	nk	**13**	20/1	—	—
	Babbling Brook (IRE) (SABrookshaw) **5-10-11**(7) MrRBurton (cmpt: prom 10f)	2	**14**	16/1	—	—
	Cloudy Bill (MissHCKnight) **5-10-11**(7) MrAWintle (unf: lw: a bhd)	2½	**15**	6/1[2]	—	—
	Be Broadminded (MissPMWhittle) **5-10-11**(7) MrJGoldstein (w'like: bkwd: prom 8f: wknd qckly: t.o whn p.u 4f out)		**P**	25/1	—	—
				(SP 132.7%)		**16 Rn**

4m 3.7 CSF £194.80 TOTE £8.80: £3.00 £6.10 £3.80 (£162.20) Trio £135.70; £174.00 to Beverley 11/5/97 OWNER Scott Hardy Partnership (UPPER LAMBOURN) BRED P. Dennison
WEIGHT FOR AGE 4yo-5lb
Conchobor (IRE), out of a winner between the flags, took the eye in the paddock and turned the race into a procession in a time much faster than the other division. (6/1: 4/1-7/1)
Roker Joker is out of a winner of two hurdles. (33/1)
Whistling Jake (IRE) does not look short of stamina. (10/1: 7/1-12/1)
Deputy Leader (IRE), a brother to Highlandman, will last longer on better ground. (4/1)
Dunabrattin (8/1: 6/1-9/1)
Barton Lil (8/1: 5/1-10/1)
Rare Gift (USA) (13/2: 4/1-7/1)
Right Ron Run (11/1: 8/1-12/1)
Cloudy Bill (6/1: op 4/1)

4539 LONGDON INTERMEDIATE N.H. FLAT RACE (II) (4, 5 & 6-Y.O) (Class H)

5-40 (5-44) **2m** £1,402.50 (£390.00: £187.50)

				SP	RR	SF
	Holloa Away (IRE) (CaptTAForster) **5-10-13**(5) ABates (unf: hld up: hdwy 3f out: hrd rdn to ld ins fnl f: edgd lft nr fin: r.o)	—	**1**	14/1	65 f	—
3690[2]	**Country House** (JABOld) **6-10-10**(3) SophieMitchell (hld up: hdwy 8f out: lost pl 4f out: rallied over 2f out: r.o ins fnl f)	1½	**2**	11/8[1]	59 f	—
4150[3]	**Going Primitive** (JHetherton) **6-11-1**(3) DFortt (a.p: led 3f out tl ins fnl f)	¾	**3**	11/2[2]	63 f	—
4301[11]	**Sweet Little Briar (IRE)** (GCBravery) **6-10-8**(5) SRyan (hld up: hdwy over 4f out: ev ch 3f out: wknd over 1f out)	6	**4**	25/1	52 f	—
4009[9]	**Lightening Steel** (DJCaro) **6-11-4** MrAPhillips (prom: lost pl 8f out: styd on fnl 2f)	2	**5**	33/1	55 f	—

	Horse	Dist	Pos	SP	RR	SF
	Pamalyn (SABrookshaw) **5-10-8**(5) XAizpuru (lengthy: prom over 12f)	2	**6**	10/1[3]	48 f	—
	Lucky Touch (WRMuir) **4-10-10**(3) LAspell (unf: prom: led over 4f out to 3f out: eased whn btn over 1f out)	1¾	**7**	10/1[3]	51 f	—
	A Verse To Order (MissPMWhittle) **6-10-11**(7) MrJGoldstein (str: nvr nr ldrs)	10	**8**	50/1	41 f	—
	The Kerry Ledgend (IRE) (NoelChance) **4-10-6**(7) CScudder (w'like: hld up: hdwy 5f out: ev ch 3f out: sn wknd & wandered)	2½	**9**	11/1	39 f	—
	Jo's Wedding (BRMillman) **6-10-13**(5) DSalter (str: scope: plld hrd: a bhd)	15	**10**	33/1	24 f	—
3290[8]	**Lady Boco** (FCoton) **4-10-8** CRae (plld hrd: bhd fnl 8f)	1¾	**11**	50/1	17 f	—
3690[8]	**Whisky Wilma** (RCurtis) **5-10-6**(7) JParkhouse (a bhd)	2	**12**	33/1	15 f	—
3090[11]	**Paperprince (NZ)** (AGHobbs) **5-10-13**(5) OBurrows (prom tl wknd 3f out)	4	**13**	33/1	16 f	—
4407[7]	**Absolute Proof** (WGMTurner) **4-10-1**(7) JPower (led over 11f: wknd qckly: t.o)	16	**14**	16/1	—	—
4088[6]	**Dancing In Rio (IRE)** (TPWalshe) **5-10-6**(7) LSuthern (prom 10f: t.o)	6	**15**	20/1	—	—
	Obsidian (MissKMGeorge) **5-11-1**(3) RMassey (bhd fnl 8f: t.o)		**16**	33/1	—	—
	Turf Scorcher (NEBerry) **6-11-1**(3) JMagee (w'like: t.o)		**17**	25/1	—	—

(SP 127.6%) **17 Rn**

4m 10.4 CSF £28.64 TOTE £14.70: £5.30 £1.10 £2.30 (£25.70) Trio £75.90 OWNER Mr W. F. Reid (LUDLOW) BRED G. W. Robinson
WEIGHT FOR AGE 4yo-5lb
Holloa Away (IRE), a full-brother to seven-furlong and mile winner Pytchley Night, stayed on dourly to win what paddock inspection and the watch suggests was the weaker of the two divisions. (14/1: op 9/2)
3690 Country House, out of a two-and-a-half mile chase winner, is blessed with stamina rather than speed. (11/8)
4150 Going Primitive is nothing if not consistent. (11/2: 3/1-13/2)
Sweet Little Briar (IRE) stepped up on her debut. (25/1)
Pamalyn (10/1: 12/1-7/1)
Lucky Touch (10/1: op 5/1)
The Kerry Ledgend (IRE) (11/1: 6/1-12/1)

T/Plpt: £86.30 (129.34 Tckts). T/Qdpt: £18.10 (34.43 Tckts) KH

2150-**WOLVERHAMPTON** (L-H) (Good, Good to Soft patches)

Sunday May 11th

WEATHER: sunny intervals WIND: slt half bhd
Remaining races run under Rules of Flat Racing

4540 WOLVERHAMPTON'S JUMPING AGAIN NOVICES' CHASE (5-Y.O+) (Class D)

3-10 (3-13) **2m (12 fncs)** £4,962.00 (£1,218.00) GOING: 0.00 sec per fur (G)

	Horse	Dist	Pos	SP	RR	SF
4274[2]	**Sublime Fellow (IRE) (116)** (NJHenderson) **7-11-12** MAFitzgerald (lw: mde all: sn wl clr: mstke 8th: canter)	—	**1**	4/7[1]	111+	—
4419[4]	**The Fence Shrinker (60)** (DMcCain) **6-11-0** DWalsh (chsd wnr 3rd to 7th: rdn & lost tch 4 out: t.o whn lft 2nd 3 out)	dist	**2**	20/1[3]	—	—
4297*	**Daring Past (95)** (MDHammond) **7-11-8** RGarritty (mstke 2nd: sn lost pl: rdn 6th: hdwy next: chsng wnr 4l down whn fell 3 out)		**F**	13/8[2]	—	—
4450[7]	**Moor Dance Man** (NPLittmoden) **7-11-0** GaryLyons (hld up: blnd & uns rdr 4th)		**U**	25/1	—	—

(SP 110.3%) **4 Rn**

4m 16.5 CSF £8.09 TOTE £1.50: (£12.10) OWNER Mr Rory McGrath (LAMBOURN) BRED John Kent
4274 Sublime Fellow (IRE), in what proved a very disappointing turnout for a race with added sweepstakes of £6,000, had little more than a good workout, and he never had to come off the bridle. (4/7)
4297* Daring Past gave a disappointing display of jumping, but had closed on the winner and may have proved a threat had he not departed the scene at the third last. (13/8)

4541 NEW CHASE COURSE H'CAP CHASE (5-Y.O+) (Class B)

3-40 (3-44) **3m 1f (18 fncs)** £17,348.00 (£5,234.00: £2,542.00: £1,196.00) GOING: 0.00 sec per fur (G)

	Horse	Dist	Pos	SP	RR	SF
4185[3]	**Cariboo Gold (USA) (114)** (KCBailey) **8-10-3b** JOsborne (lw: swtg: hld up & bhd: hdwy 12th: led appr 2 out: sn clr)	—	**1**	100/30[3]	131	—
4302*	**Kenmore-Speed (113)** (MrsSJSmith) **10-10-2**ow1 RichardGuest (j.w: chsd ldr: led 14th tl appr 2 out: sn btn)	18	**2**	9/4[1]	119	—
4416*	**Court Melody (IRE) (121)** (PFNicholls) **9-10-10b** APMcCoy (lw: hld up in tch: wknd 14th)	22	**3**	3/1[2]	112	—
4306*	**Hawaiian Youth (IRE) (111)** (GMMcCourt) **9-10-0** DGallagher (nt j.w: sn lost pl: t.o fr 10th)	21	**4**	7/1	89	—
4507[2]	**Stately Home (IRE) (135)** (PBowen) **6-11-10** RJohnson (led: clr 4th: hdd 14th: 3rd & btn whn fell 3 out)		**F**	13/2	—	—
4206[7]	**Glemot (IRE) (130)** (KCBailey) **9-11-5** GBradley (lw: hld up: outpcd 13th: t.o & p.u bef 3 out)		**P**	12/1	—	—

(SP 112.4%) **6 Rn**

6m 41.6 (36.60) CSF £10.66 CT £21.22 TOTE £3.70: £2.00 £1.10 (£4.60) Trio £3.00 OWNER Mrs Sharon Nelson (UPPER LAMBOURN) BRED Regal Oak Farm & Albert G. Clay
4185 Cariboo Gold (USA) did not have much trouble turning the tables on the runner-up on 6lb better terms, and it is doubtful if he will again find a valuable race that proves such easy pickings. (100/30)
4302* Kenmore-Speed, a very fluent jumper of fences, travelled like a winner for most of the way but, once Cariboo Gold appeared on the scene, the writing was on the wall. (9/4)
4507 Stately Home (IRE) never has an easy race because he always forces the pace, and that was where he remained for two-and-a-half miles before gradually fading. He was held in third place when he made a rare error and paid the penalty three out. (13/2: 9/2-7/1)
1904 Glemot (IRE) (12/1: op 8/1)

T/Plpt: £128.80 (68.23 Tckts). T/Qdpt: £6.80 (58.35 Tckts) IM

4453-TOWCESTER (R-H) (Chases Good to soft, Soft patches, Hdles Soft)
Monday May 12th
WEATHER: fine & sunny

4542 CHRISTIE & CO. SURVEYORS, VALUERS AND AGENTS (S) HURDLE (4,5,6 & 7-Y.O) (Class G)
5-45 (5-45) **2m (8 hdls)** £1,810.50 (£503.00: £241.50) GOING: 0.90 sec per fur (S)

			SP	RR	SF
4453*	**The Flying Doctor (IRE) (87)** (GBBalding) **7-11-6** WMcFarland (chsd ldr fr 4th: hit 3 out: led appr next: sn rdn clr) ......—	1	15/8 1	74	31
4434 2	**Sterling Fellow (78)** (DLWilliams) **4-10-2**(7) MrSDurack (hld up: hdwy 5th: ev ch 2 out: sn rdn & btn) 11	2	15/8 1	57	9
4423 2	**Summer Villa (76)** (KGWingrove) **5-10-9b** WMarston (lft in ld 3rd: hdd & wknd appr 2 out) 15	3	4/1 2	37	—
	Ultimate Warrior (MrsLRichards) **7-11-0** MRichards (bit bkwd: j.rt 1st: prom tl wknd appr 2 out) 1½	4	6/1 3	41	—
4423 5	**Reno's Treasure (USA)** (JohnHarris) **4-10-4** JSupple (led tl appr 3rd: wknd 4th) 8	5	66/1	28	—
4436 5	**Green King** (APJones) **5-11-0b1** SMcNeill (lw: w.r.s: t.o tl hdwy 2nd: wknd appr 3 out: p.u bef next)	P	16/1	—	—
3072 F	**Espla** (JSMoore) **6-10-11**(3) JMagee (lw: prom: led & rn out 3rd)	R	20/1	—	—

(SP 116.0%) **7 Rn**

4m 8.3 (22.30) CSF £5.29 TOTE £2.60: £1.60 £1.50 (£3.10) OWNER The Rumble Racing Club (ANDOVER) BRED E. Finn
WEIGHT FOR AGE 4yo-5lb
Bt in 5,200 gns

4453* The Flying Doctor (IRE) handled the softer ground well, striding right away from the last. (15/8: 11/10-2/1)
4434 Sterling Fellow, dropping in trip and trying much softer ground, could not reproduce his recent effort as he got stuck in the mud when asked to quicken. (15/8: op 3/1)
4423 Summer Villa did not last home on this softer ground. (4/1: 3/1-9/2)
Ultimate Warrior, a modest Flat performer without a run in eight months, shaped with some promise until blowing up on the home turn. (6/1)

4543 HARTWELL LAND ROVER HUNTERS' CHASE (5-Y.O+) (Class H)
6-15 (6-17) **2m 110y (12 fncs)** £1,674.00 (£464.00: £222.00) GOING: 0.47 sec per fur (GS)

			SP	RR	SF
4320 5	**Not My Line (IRE)** (AndyMorgan) **8-11-11**(5) MrASansome (led to 5th: led 7th: rdn 2 out: r.o wl) ......—	1	14/1	109	37
4406 U	**My Young Man** (CPEBrooks) **12-11-6**(7) MrEJames (lw: prom: led 5th to 7th: ev ch whn blnd 3 out: rdn next: one pce) 8	2	11/4 2	98	26
4327 U	**Nectanebo (IRE)** (NParker) **9-11-9**(7) MrMFrith (lw: mstkes 1st & 4th: hdwy 3 out: btn appr last) 10	3	8/1 3	92	20
4070 F	**Feltham Mistress** (DCTucker) **7-11-1**(7) MrEBabington (hdwy 8th: rdn appr 2 out: no imp) ......¾	4	66/1	83	11
4406*	**Yquem (IRE)** (AWVarey) **7-11-9**(7) MrNRMitchell (lw: a.p: j.slowly 4 out: rdn & btn 2 out) 2	5	2/1 1	89	17
3744 10	**Al Hashimi** (NTRidout) **13-11-6**(7) MrNRidout (t: bhd tl r.o fr 3 out) 4	6	25/1	82	10
4228 P	**Emerald Ruler** (ADPeachey) **10-11-6**(7) MrPCowley (in tch: rdn 9th: sn bhd) 1	7	20/1	81	9
4320 9	**Killimor Lad** (MrsDCSamworth) **10-11-6**(7) MissSSamworth (lw: a bhd) 7	8	50/1	74	2
	Shuil Saor (MissPFitton) **10-11-6**(7) MrJSaville (lw: sn rdn & bhd) 12	9	66/1	63	—
3439 6	**No Word** (IBaker) **10-11-6**(7) MrIBaker (a t.o) 15	10	66/1	48	—
4218 P	**King of Shadows** (MissCMCarden) **10-11-6**(7) MrSPrior (prom to 5th: t.o whn p.u bef 3 out)	P	33/1	—	—
3840 3	**Driving Force** (MrsHMobley) **11-11-6b**(7) MrACharles-Jones (chsd ldrs to 6th: t.o whn p.u bef last)	P	9/1	—	—
4320 P	**Lucky Landing (IRE)** (AndrewMartin) **8-11-6**(7) MrAndrewMartin (bhd whn mstke 3 out: p.u bef last)	P	50/1	—	—
4406 2	**Familiar Friend** (SJGilmore) **11-11-6b**(7) MrLLay (lw: chsd ldrs tl wknd appr 2 out: p.u bef last)	P	9/1	—	—
4218 2	**Dalametre** (MJMEvans) **10-11-6**(7) MrMMunrowd (prom to 6th: t.o whn p.u bef last)	P	10/1	—	—
3963 3	**Hickelton Lad** (DLWilliams) **13-11-6**(7) MrSDurack (bhd tl p.u bef 2 out)	P	12/1	—	—

(SP 134.5%) **16 Rn**

4m 19.0 (17.00) CSF £52.16 TOTE £24.10: £4.50 £1.70 £3.90 (£70.00) Trio £70.50 OWNER Mr P. C. Caudwell (ABINGDON) BRED J. A. Doherty

4320 Not My Line (IRE) caused an upset, as forcing tactics and a drop in trip brought about considerable improvement. (14/1: 10/1-16/1)
4406 My Young Man finally found a hunter-chase over his best trip and, although the ground was plenty testing enough, he may well have prevailed but for a dreadful blunder at a vital stage. (11/4)
4070* Nectanebo (IRE) took a good hold in the rear and was anything but fluent early on, but did a lot of late running. He does not look an easy ride. (8/1: 5/1-9/1)
Feltham Mistress showed her first sign of talent, doing a fair bit of running in the second half of the race. (66/1)
4406* Yquem (IRE) had been off for over a year before his win nine days ago and, despite looking a picture of health, ran as if this race came too soon. (2/1)
Al Hashimi does not stay three miles in points, and is struggling under Rules, having not won for over three years. (25/1)
3963 Hickelton Lad (12/1: 9/1-14/1)

4544 SHOOSMITHS SPRING H'CAP HURDLE (0-105) (4-Y.O+) (Class F)
6-45 (6-46) **2m 5f (11 hdls)** £2,407.50 (£670.00: £322.50) GOING: 0.90 sec per fur (S)

			SP	RR	SF
4341 2	**Nordic Spree (IRE) (83)** (GLMoore) **5-10-10v** APMcCoy (led to 3rd: led & qcknd appr 6th: rdn 8th: kpt on wl fr 2 out) ......—	1	3/1 2	70	—
3473 3	**Luke Warm (76)** (DRGandolfo) **7-10-0**(3) SophieMitchell (trckd ldrs: hit 5th: ev ch 3 out: one pce appr next) 6	2	7/1	58	—
4455 3	**Cambo (USA) (82)** (MCBanks) **11-10-9** MRichards (lw: led 3rd tl appr 6th: wknd appr 2 out) ......¾	3	7/2 3	64	—
4002*	**A S Jim (74)** (OO'Neill) **6-10-1** VSlattery (hld up: hdwy 3 out: rdn & wknd appr last) ......s.h	4	7/2 3	56	—
4230 2	**Mountain Path (98)** (NJHenderson) **7-11-11** MAFitzgerald (lw: trckd ldrs tl rdn & wknd appr 3 out) 29	5	9/4 1	58	—

(SP 112.7%) **5 Rn**

5m 42.5 (40.50) CSF £19.79 TOTE £3.30: £2.00 £2.60 (£13.30) OWNER Mr Roger John Jones (BRIGHTON) BRED Liscannor Stud Ltd

4341 Nordic Spree (IRE) did not seem in love with the ground, and got very tired despite having set a slow pace early on, but was given a great ride and had no chance to quit when ahead. (3/1)
3473 Luke Warm looked a threat when going upsides the winner climbing into the straight but, once the chips were down, he was gradually left behind. (7/1: op 4/1)
4455 Cambo (USA) looks in fine shape, but continues to run a little below his best. (7/2)
4002* A S Jim, stepping up in trip, was found wanting for stamina after making his move on the stiffest part of the track. (7/2: op 9/4)
4230 Mountain Path travelled sweetly but, as the pace increased, he stopped suddenly as if something was amiss. (9/4)

4545 LAND ROVER GENTLEMANS CHAMPIONSHIP HUNTERS' CHASE (5-Y.O+) (Class H)

7-15 (7-15) **3m 1f (18 fncs)** £4,162.50 (£1,260.00: £615.00: £292.50) GOING: 0.47 sec per fur (GS)

Form	Horse	Dist	Pos	SP	RR	SF
	Magnolia Man (MsDCole) **11-11-2**$^{(7)}$ MrNHarris (hld up: hit 7th: hdwy 10th: led appr 2 out: rdn clr flat)	—	1	9/4^{2}	98	13
	Lucky Christopher (GJTarry) **12-11-9**$^{(5)}$ MrGTarry (prom: mstke 12th: effrt on ins & hmpd appr 2 out: sn rdn & ev ch: one pce flat)	5	2	7/4^{1}	100	15
	Lupy Minstrel (MissPaulineRobson) **12-11-11**$^{(7)}$ MrAParker (j.w: led to 4th: led appr 9th: hdd & one pce appr 2 out)	6	3	8/1^{3}	100	15
	The General's Drum (MrsRFell) **10-11-7**$^{(7)}$ MrKHeard (lw: hld up: hdwy 11th: wknd 3 out)	30	4	9/4^{2}	77	—
3994^{3}	**Syrus P Turntable** (MissPFitton) **11-11-2**$^{(7)}$ MrJSaville (lw: prom to 10th: sn wknd: t.o fr 14th: p.u bef last)		P	33/1	—	—
	Secret Truth (AndrewMartin) **8-10-11**$^{(7)}$ MrAndrewMartin (plld hrd: led 4th tl appr 9th: wkng whn blnd next: p.u bef 11th)		P	33/1	—	—

(SP 114.9%) **6 Rn**

6m 47.7 (32.70) CSF £6.56 TOTE £3.30: £1.70 £1.20 (£3.10) OWNER Mrs D. B. Lunt (SOUTH MOLTON) BRED T. C. Le Grice

Magnolia Man, in terrific form between the flags this spring with four wins and two seconds in six efforts to his name, was second to Coome Hill at Wincanton a couple of years back, and won well although he seems to find regulation fences on the big side. (9/4: 6/4-5/2)

Lucky Christopher, who had won his last eight completions, might have made it nine but for going for a gap on the inside that a whippet would have struggled to get through. (7/4)

Lupy Minstrel, very experienced under Rules, gave his rivals a jumping lesson but has become very one-paced in his old age. (8/1: op 4/1)

The General's Drum was given a patient ride, but got a little detached in the first-half of the race. Having made his ground, he looked found-out by the trip, and would be better-suited by half-a-mile less under Rules. (9/4)

4546 MULBERRY INSURANCE NOVICES' CHASE (5-Y.O+) (Class E)

7-45 (7-45) **3m 1f (18 fncs)** £3,104.50 (£931.00: £448.00: £206.50) GOING: 0.47 sec per fur (GS)

Form	Horse	Dist	Pos	SP	RR	SF
4404^{4}	**Ballydougan (IRE) (74)** (RMathew) **9-11-1v** DWalsh (s.v.s: sn rdn along: hdwy 7th: blnd 4 out: led last: ducked lft flat: r.o again cl home)	—	1	14/1	89	22
3667*	**Brogeen Lady (IRE) (100)** (DRGandolfo) **7-11-2** RDunwoody (lw: led: hit 5th: hdd 10th: led 11th to last: ev ch nr fin: outpcd)	nk	2	7/2^{3}	90	23
4312^{P}	**Grizzly Bear (IRE) (85)** (RMStronge) **7-11-7** JCulloty (chsd ldrs: ev ch after 2 out: swtchd lft after last: n.m.r nr fin)	1¾	3	14/1	94	27
4312^{4}	**Mr Pickpocket (IRE) (108)** (MissHCKnight) **9-11-7** JFTitley (w ldr: led 10th to next: ev ch 2 out: sn wknd)	8	4	7/4^{1}	89	22
4227^{P}	**Debonair Dude (IRE)** (NJHenderson) **7-11-1** MAFitzgerald (in tch: hit 9th: tried to ref 13th: p.u bef next)		P	12/1	—	—
4227^{U}	**Master Toby (110)** (NATwiston-Davies) **7-11-7** CLlewellyn (plld hrd: chsd ldrs: 5th & hld whn p.u bef 3 out: lame)		P	9/4^{2}	—	—
4232^{3}	**Derrys Prerogative** (AWCarroll) **7-11-1** RJohnson (lw: hit 1st: prom tl blnd 13th: sn wknd: p.u bef 2 out)		P	16/1	—	—
3968^{P}	**Musical Hit (60)** (PAPritchard) **6-11-1b** RBellamy (j.b: t.o fr 9th: p.u bef last)		P	66/1	—	—

(SP 117.8%) **8 Rn**

6m 41.6 (26.60) CSF £59.96 TOTE £15.40: £2.10 £1.40 £4.30 (£19.00) OWNER Mrs Robin Mathew (BURFORD) BRED J. Wilmott

STEWARDS' ENQUIRY Obj. to Ballydougan & Brogeen Lady by Culloty & to Ballydougan by Dunwoody overruled.

OFFICIAL EXPLANATION **Master Toby: was lame.**

4404 Ballydougan (IRE) has a mind of his own and is quite capable of changing it mid-race, but every dog has his day as he showed here. Having declined to jump off with the others, he looked reluctant and was ridden along until suddenly coming on to the bridle when getting in the race in the final mile. Having hit the front at the last, he put the brakes on and dived for the rails but somehow got going again and was rapidly increasing his advantage at the line. He clearly stays and, were he genuine, would have a future as the ability is definitely there. (14/1)

3667* Brogeen Lady (IRE) got very leg-weary, and could not take her chance after the winner did his best to throw it in her direction. (7/2)

3968* Grizzly Bear (IRE), a tall, scopey, lightly-raced horse, may have been a shade unfortunate as he had to switch around the runner-up after the last to assume the stands' rail berth, only for the winner to duck across to the rail and virtually pull up in front of him soon afterwards. (14/1)

4312 Mr Pickpocket (IRE) remains an enigma, and is one to be wary of. (7/4)

3688 Debonair Dude (IRE) (12/1: 8/1-14/1)

4547 GIBBS AND DANDY 'N.H.' NOVICES' HURDLE (4-Y.O+) (Class D)

8-15 (8-19) **2m (8 hdls)** £2,966.00 (£826.00: £398.00) GOING: 0.90 sec per fur (S)

Form	Horse	Dist	Pos	SP	RR	SF
4181*	**Stormyfairweather (IRE) (105)** (NJHenderson) **5-12-0** MAFitzgerald (sn trckng ldrs: led on bit appr last: rdn clr flat)	—	1	3/1^{1}	95+	52
	Rythm Rock (IRE) (94) (DRGandolfo) **8-11-0** RDunwoody (a.p: led 3 out tl appr last: one pce)	6	2	5/1^{2}	75	32
4315^{3}	**Physical Fun (99)** (AGBlackmore) **6-10-11**$^{(3)}$ PHenley (lw: a.p: hit 3rd: ev ch appr 2 out: sn btn)	5	3	3/1^{1}	70	27
3019^{5}	**Captain Walter (IRE)** (JABOld) **7-11-0** JOsborne (lw: in tch: mstke 5th: kpt on fr 2 out)	14	4	5/1^{2}	56	13
	Belarus (IRE) (MrsIMcKie) **5-11-0** WMcFarland (wl bhd: hdwy 3 out: nvr nr ldrs)	1	5	33/1	55	12
4275^{5}	**The Bizzo (55)** (JFPanvert) **6-10-9** WMarston (in tch: lost pl 4th: n.d after)	3½	6	33/1	47	4
	Ur Only Young Once (MrsDHaine) **7-10-9** JFTitley (prom tl wknd appr 2 out)	14	7	12/1	33	—
	High Pitch (NAGaselee) **5-11-0** CLlewellyn (sn pushed along: a wl bhd)	30	8	33/1	8	—
	Over and Under (IRE) (MrsIMcKie) **4-10-9** LHarvey (a bhd)	18	9	50/1	—	—
4009^{11}	**Dande Dove** (KCBailey) **6-11-0** SMcNeill (pushed along 4th: bhd tl p.u bef 2 out)		P	20/1	—	—
2677^{P}	**Single Sourcing (IRE)** (MissHCKnight) **6-11-0** JCulloty (led tl hung lft & hdd appr 5th: t.o whn p.u bef 2 out)		P	13/2^{3}	—	—
4184^{P}	**Boxgrove Man (IRE)** (JABOld) **7-11-0** GBradley (hld up: hdwy appr 4th: wknd 5th: t.o whn p.u bef last)		P	12/1	—	—
1774^{10}	**Camp Head (IRE)** (OSherwood) **6-11-0** JAMcCarthy (prom: hung lft appr 4th: led 5th tl rn out next: bit slipped)		R	14/1	—	—

(SP 134.3%) **13 Rn**

4m 5.4 (19.40) CSF £18.10 TOTE £4.40: £2.60 £1.40 £1.20 (£5.90) Trio £3.20 OWNER Mrs Christopher Hanbury (LAMBOURN) BRED P. J. O'Connor

WEIGHT FOR AGE 4yo-5lb

4181* Stormyfairweather (IRE), dropped in trip, found the much-more testing ground than of late making full use of his stamina, and won well. (3/1: op 6/4)

Rythm Rock (IRE), making his debut in this country, had looked one-paced in Ireland and confirmed that impression, although he was up against a useful rival for this type of race. (5/1)

4315 Physical Fun, who has been racing over further, was gradually left behind in the home straight. (3/1)
3019 Captain Walter (IRE), knocked back by a mistake four from home, did enough to suggest he may improve over a longer trip. (5/1: 4/1-6/1)
Belarus (IRE), an attractive newcomer, got a long way behind but shaped like a horse that will stay well in time. (33/1)
Single Sourcing (IRE) (13/2: op 7/2)
Boxgrove Man (IRE) (12/1: 8/1-14/1)
Camp Head (IRE) tried to run out turning into the back straight, but had hit the front when succeeding at the third last. The bit had slipped through his mouth, and he is worth another chance. (14/1: 12/1-25/1)

T/Plpt: £93.40 (140.7 Tckts). T/Qdpt: £14.50 (60.64 Tckts) Dk

4465-CHEPSTOW (L-H) (Good to soft)
Tuesday May 13th
WEATHER: raining

4548 STIRRUP CUP NOVICES' CLAIMING HURDLE (4-Y.O+) (Class F)
1-50 (1-55) **2m 110y (8 hdls)** £2,108.00 (£588.00: £284.00) GOING: 0.49 sec per fur (GS)

				SP	RR	SF
4466[5]	**Blade of Fortune (86)** (VGGreenway) **9-10-6**(7) MrJTizzard (mde all: r.o wl)	—	**1**	9/2[2]	70	28
4534[6]	**Apache Park (USA) (90)** (DBurchell) **4-10-8** DJBurchell (hdwy 3rd: chsd wnr after 4th tl hit 2 out: r.o flat)	2	**2**	7/2[1]	68	21
4276[3]	**Witherkay (74)** (PFNicholls) **4-10-8** RJohnson (lw: lft 2nd appr 2nd: hung lft after 2 out: mstke last: hung lft flat: one pce)	nk	**3**	20/1	68?	21
4333[5]	**Contract Bridge (IRE) (81)** (PGMurphy) **4-10-6** WMcFarland (hld up: hdwy appr 4 out: sn rdn: wknd appr 3 out)	14	**4**	9/2[2]	52	5
4292*	**Laura Lye (IRE) (78)** (BdeHaan) **7-11-0** GUpton (hld up & bhd: stdy hdwy 3rd: wknd appr 3 out)	½	**5**	8/1	55	13
4441[4]	**Red Viper** (NMLampard) **5-10-9**(7) MrLBaker (lw: hld up: hdwy 4th: wknd appr 3 out)	8	**6**	25/1	49	7
4289[3]	**Irish Dominion (55)** (AGHobbs) **7-10-6**(7) MrGShenkin (blnd bdly 2nd: a bhd: t.o)	17	**7**	50/1	30	—
4423[P]	**Minnisam** (AGHobbs) **4-10-5b** RGreene (prom tl rdn & wknd appr 4 out: t.o)	6	**8**	16/1	21	—
	Swiss Account (AGNewcombe) **8-10-4**(7) NRossiter (s.i.s: a bhd: t.o)	25	**9**	66/1	—	—
3820[6]	**Honeyshan** (DJSffrenchDavis) **5-11-9** SMcNeill (bhd fr 4th: t.o)	3	**10**	20/1	7	—
4405[P]	**Ritto (93)** (JNeville) **7-11-8** APMcCoy (hdwy 3rd: wknd appr 3 out: p.u bef last)		**P**	6/1[3]	—	—
3889[5]	**Scottish Park** (MCPipe) **8-10-5** DWalsh (bhd: mstke 3rd: t.o whn p.u bef 4 out)		**P**	14/1	—	—
4173[5]	**Moreceva (IRE) (51)** (PaddyFarrell) **7-11-2** TDascombe (swtg: bhd fr 3rd: t.o whn p.u bef last)		**P**	66/1	—	—
4230[P]	**Above The Clouds** (MissAMNewton-Smith) **6-10-4**(7)ow1 MrPO'Keeffe (swtg: plld hrd: chsd ldr: j.lft 1st: p.u bef 2nd: sddle slipped)		**P**	100/1	—	—

(SP 115.8%) **14 Rn**

4m 4.4 (15.40) CSF £17.17 TOTE £6.60: £2.60 £1.80 £4.20 (£6.40) Trio £108.80 OWNER Mr V. G. Greenway (TAUNTON) BRED F. H. Lee
WEIGHT FOR AGE 4yo-5lb
3890 Blade of Fortune did not mind the give in the ground, and took advantage of a drop into a claimer. (9/2)
3752 Apache Park (USA), without the blinkers this time, rallied to regain second place on the run-in. (7/2)
4276 Witherkay contributed to his own downfall in the battle for the runner-up spot. (20/1)
4294* Contract Bridge (IRE) probably wants faster ground. (9/2)
4292* Laura Lye (IRE) had only won a poor novice event at Taunton. (8/1)
3630 Ritto (6/1: op 4/1)

4549 WELSH BREWERS NOVICES' H'CAP CHASE (0-110) (5-Y.O+) (Class D)
2-20 (2-25) **3m (18 fncs)** £3,715.50 (£1,119.00: £542.00: £253.50) GOING: 0.49 sec per fur (GS)

				SP	RR	SF
4342[2]	**Malwood Castle (IRE) (89)** (RHAlner) **7-11-0** AThornton (hld up: hdwy 8th: rdn appr 3 out: led & lft clr 2 out)	—	**1**	5/1[3]	107	40
3882[3]	**Thermal Warrior (81)** (JABOld) **9-10-6** CLlewellyn (a.p: hit 5 out: btn whn lft 2nd 2 out)	26	**2**	2/1[1]	82	15
4442*	**Nordic Valley (IRE) (92)** (MCPipe) **6-11-3** 7x APMcCoy (hld up: hdwy 11th: rdn 5 out: wknd appr 3 out)	10	**3**	7/1	86	19
4310[3]	**Karar (IRE) (97)** (RRowe) **7-11-8** DO'Sullivan (swtg: bhd: mstke 10th: sn t.o)	1	**4**	9/2[2]	90	23
4314*	**Sea Patrol (80)** (SGGriffiths) **10-10-5b** MAFitzgerald (hld up & bhd: sme hdwy 13th: sn wknd: t.o)	dist	**5**	12/1	—	—
4272[P]	**Prerogative (99)** (GLMoore) **7-11-7v**(3) GuyLewis (prom: j.slowly 1st: chsd ldr after 7th tl wknd 11th: t.o)	17	**6**	20/1	—	—
4298[5]	**Chiappucci (IRE) (80)** (MrsEHHeath) **7-10-5** DGallagher (plld hrd early: led to 2nd: wkng whn mstke 12th: t.o)	30	**7**	33/1	—	—
4431*	**Wixoe Wonder (IRE) (84)** (MBradstock) **7-10-9b** 7x GBradley (led 2nd: rdn & hdd whn fell 2 out)		**F**	13/2	—	—
4232[6]	**Smart Casanova (75)** (MJWilkinson) **8-10-0** WMarston (mstke 5th: dropped rr 7th: mstke 8th: p.u bef 9th)		**P**	66/1	—	—

(SP 110.9%) **9 Rn**

6m 12.1 (19.10) CSF £13.75 CT £59.36 TOTE £6.10: £1.60 £1.30 £1.50 (£5.70) Trio £14.70 OWNER Mrs U. Wainwright (BLANDFORD) BRED Gerry Doyle
LONG HANDICAP Smart Casanova 8-13
4342 Malwood Castle (IRE) was already in the process of taking command when presented the race at the penultimate fence. (5/1)
3882 Thermal Warrior found the pace too hot after clouting the first in the straight. (2/1)
4442* Nordic Valley (IRE) did not seem to stay three miles in this softer ground. (7/1)
4310 Karar (IRE) (9/2: op 3/1)
4431* Wixoe Wonder (IRE) appeared to be beginning to get the worst of the argument when coming to grief. (13/2)

4550 MAY H'CAP HURDLE (0-130) (4-Y.O+) (Class C)
2-55 (2-57) **2m 4f 110y (11 hdls)** £3,488.00 (£1,049.00: £507.00: £236.00) GOING: 0.49 sec per fur (GS)

				SP	RR	SF
4398*	**Diwali Dancer (113)** (MCPipe) **7-10-11** APMcCoy (mde all: mstke 5th: clr 2 out: eased flat)	—	**1**	5/2[1]	92+	39
4455*	**Ehtefaal (USA) (102)** (JSKing) **6-10-0** 7x RJohnson (nt j.w: chsd wnr to 3 out: r.o one pce)	4	**2**	9/2[3]	78	25
4527*	**Lord Mcmurrough (IRE) (117)** (JNeville) **7-10-12**(3) 7x MrRThornton (a.p: hit 2nd: rdn appr 4 out: wnt 2nd 3 out: one pce)	nk	**3**	5/1	93	40
4006[10]	**Ballet Royal (USA) (105)** (HJManners) **8-9-10**(7) ADowling (hld up: mstke 3rd: hdwy after 7th: wknd 3 out)	5	**4**	20/1	77	24
4178[3]	**El Don (112)** (MJRyan) **5-10-10** JRyan (prom: hit 7th: wknd appr 4 out: t.o)	dist	**5**	4/1[2]	—	—
3156[8]	**Hebridean (129)** (PRWebber) **10-11-13** MAFitzgerald (hld up & bhd: rdn appr 4 out: sn t.o)	8	**6**	10/1	—	—

				SP	RR	SF
3816[4]	**Mim-Lou-and (109)** (MissHCKnight) **5-10-7** JCulloty (hld up in rr: rdn & sme hdwy appr 4 out: sn t.o)	8	**7**	9/2[3]	—	—
				(SP 115.5%)		**7 Rn**

5m 2.5 (15.50) CSF £13.37 TOTE £2.80: £2.20 £1.90 (£8.70) OWNER Mr B. E. Case (WELLINGTON) BRED Thoroughbred Stock Investors Ltd
4398* Diwali Dancer found no difficulty defying a 6lb rise in the weights. (5/2)
4455* Ehtefaal (USA) did not jump as well as one would have liked on this softer going. (9/2)
4527* Lord Mcmurrough (IRE), attempting a quick follow-up, could not hold on to second place let alone bother the winner. (5/1)
Ballet Royal (USA) gave his first indication that he retains some of his old ability. (20/1)
4178 El Don failed to handle the give underfoot. (4/1: 3/1-9/2)

4551 GREIG MIDDLETON LADIES CHAMPIONSHIP HUNTERS' CHASE (5-Y.O+) (Class H)
3-25 (3-27) **3m (18 fncs)** £3,434.50 (£1,036.00: £503.00: £236.50) GOING: 0.49 sec per fur (GS)

				SP	RR	SF
	Earthmover (IRE) (RBarber) **6-11-2**(7) MissPGundry (hld up: stdy hdwy 4th: wnt 2nd appr 8th: led appr 5 out: hit 2 out: rdn & qcknd clr flat)	—	**1**	1/2[1]	107++	18
	Sams Heritage (RTBaimbridge) **13-11-9**(5) MissADare (hld up: hdwy 9th: ev ch 5 out: rdn appr last: outpcd & eased flat)	9	**2**	8/1[3]	106	17
3458[4]	**Corner Boy** (CDDawson) **10-11-11**(7) MrsJDawson (plld hrd: chsd ldr appr 2nd tl appr 8th: hit 10th & 12th: wknd after 13th: no ch whn blnd 3 out)	dist	**3**	4/1[2]	—	—
	Lonesome Traveller (NZ) (MrsMandyHand) **8-11-2**(7) MrsAHand (hld up: pckd 10th: t.o fr 13th)	26	**4**	66/1	—	—
4411*	**Cumberland Blues (IRE)** (MrsALockwood) **8-11-11**(7) MissADeniel (j.rt: led: clr 3rd: hdd appr 5 out: wknd qckly: p.u bef 3 out)		**P**	14/1	—	—
	Mister Gebo (MrsDJDyson) **12-11-7**(7) MissCDyson (hld up: bhd fr 8th: t.o whn p.u bef 2 out)		**P**	33/1	—	—
	False Economy (MrsDDScott) **12-11-11**(7) MissKScorgie (chsd ldr tl after 2nd: wknd appr 8th: t.o whn ref 4 out)		**R**	100/1	—	—
				(SP 109.9%)		**7 Rn**

6m 22.7 (29.70) CSF £4.43 TOTE £1.50: £1.10 £1.70 (£3.70) OWNER Mr R. M. Penny (BEAMINSTER) BRED Brian McSweeney
STEWARDS' ENQUIRY Scorgie susp. 22-23/5/97 (improper riding).
Earthmover (IRE), unbeaten in five point-to-points this season, is probably at his best with some cut in the ground. (1/2)
Sams Heritage, 5lb worse off than when beaten fifteen lengths by the winner at Woodford last time, tried his best but was eventually forced to admit defeat. (8/1)
3458 Corner Boy appears to find things a lot more difficult over regulation fences. (4/1: op 5/2)
4411* Cumberland Blues (IRE) (14/1: op 8/1)

4552 BARGAIN-BUY (S) H'CAP HURDLE (0-90) (4-Y.O+) (Class G)
3-55 (3-59) **2m 110y (8 hdls)** £1,996.00 (£556.00: £268.00) GOING: 0.49 sec per fur (GS)

				SP	RR	SF
4401[2]	**Honeybed Wood (64)** (MSheppard) **9-10-2** RJohnson (hld up: hdwy 3rd: led appr 4 out tl appr 3 out: sn rdn: led appr last: nt fluent: drvn out)	—	**1**	7/2[2]	49	7
4401[4]	**Cuillin Caper (70)** (TRWatson) **5-10-8** MAFitzgerald (hld up: hdwy 4th: led on bit appr 3 out: rdn & hdd appr last: fnd nil)	4	**2**	10/1	51	9
4382[U]	**Spirit Level (63)** (JRPayne) **9-9-8**(7) MrSDurack (a.p: r.o one pce fr 4 out)	12	**3**	20/1	33	—
4472[4]	**Bresil (USA) (62)** (JJBridger) **8-9-7**(7) MBatchelor (tk keen hold: led 3rd tl appr 4 out: wknd appr 3 out)	13	**4**	25/1	19	—
4468[5]	**Powder Monkey (78)** (TNeedham) **7-11-2** GTormey (prom tl rdn & wknd appr 4 out)	1¼	**5**	11/2[3]	34	—
4472[2]	**Mecado (78)** (FJYardley) **10-10-11v**(5) XAizpuru (bhd fr 4th)	12	**6**	7/1	22	—
2862[11]	**Ilewin (88)** (PCRitchens) **10-11-12** MAhern (a bhd)	3	**7**	16/1	29	—
	Sallow Glen (62) (DrPPritchard) **11-10-0** DrPPritchard (prom to 4th)	4	**8**	50/1	—	—
4382[9]	**Calgary Girl (62)** (RHBuckler) **5-10-0** BPowell (plld hrd: prom: j.slowly 1st: wknd after 4th)	10	**9**	8/1	—	—
3577[2]	**Do Be Ware (77)** (JFfitch-Heyes) **7-11-1** BFenton (hld up & bhd: hdwy appr 4th: wknd appr 4 out: t.o)	16	**10**	7/1	—	—
4384[P]	**More Bills (IRE) (65)** (JNeville) **5-10-3v** DJBurchell (bhd most of wy: t.o)		**11**	33/1	—	—
4459[2]	**Red Tel (IRE) (80)** (MCPipe) **5-11-4b**[1] APMcCoy (led: reminders after 2nd: hdd 3rd: wknd qckly: t.o whn p.u bef 4 out)		**P**	100/30[1]	—	—
				(SP 125.3%)		**12 Rn**

4m 6.7 (17.70) CSF £35.58 CT £581.99 TOTE £5.40: £1.70 £3.90 £5.40 (£33.40) Trio £253.40; £74.96 to York 14/5/97 OWNER R Herbert, T Doxsey and M Drake (LEDBURY) BRED J. M. F. Dibben
LONG HANDICAP Sallow Glen 9-0 Bresil (USA) 9-4 Calgary Girl 9-7
No bid
4401 Honeybed Wood reached a good position before halfway this time. (7/2)
4401 Cuillin Caper, without the blinkers this time, looked all set to score until finding precious little when let down. (10/1: 7/1-11/1)
Spirit Level kept plodding on, and one could see why she has run over longer trips in the past. (20/1)
4459 Red Tel (IRE), dropped into a seller, appeared to resent the fitting of blinkers. (100/30)

4553 HUE AND CRY H'CAP CHASE (0-120) (5-Y.O+) (Class D)
4-25 (4-33) **2m 3f 110y (16 fncs)** £3,488.00 (£1,049.00: £507.00: £236.00) GOING: 0.49 sec per fur (GS)

				SP	RR	SF
4385*	**Red Branch (IRE) (95)** (JSKing) **8-10-3** JCulloty (lw: a.p: wnt 2nd 8th: led 4 out: clr last: r.o wl)	—	**1**	11/10[1]	108	20
4235[4]	**The Carrot Man (105)** (PWinkworth) **9-10-10**(3) LAspell (swtg: hld up: led 7th to 4 out: btn whn blnd bdly last)	12	**2**	11/2[3]	108	20
4177*	**Seek The Faith (USA) (110)** (MSheppard) **8-11-4** BPowell (lw: tk keen hold in rr: hdwy 9th: rdn appr 2 out: one pce)	4	**3**	5/2[2]	110	22
4379[4]	**James the First (120)** (PFNicholls) **9-12-0** MAFitzgerald (lw: hld up: hdwy appr 5 out: wknd appr 3 out)	21	**4**	8/1	103	15
4379[5]	**Maggots Green (98)** (JMBradley) **10-10-6** RJohnson (led to 4th: wknd 10th: t.o)	dist	**5**	16/1	—	—
4225[6]	**Boro Vacation (IRE) (120)** (PFNicholls) **8-11-7**(7) MrJTizzard (bolted bef s: plld hrd: led 4th to 7th: j.slowly 8th: sn wknd: t.o whn p.u bef 4 out)		**P**	16/1	—	—
				(SP 114.5%)		**6 Rn**

5m 7.3 (18.30) CSF £7.40 TOTE £2.10: £1.30 £2.60 (£5.20) OWNER Mr E. J. Mangan (SWINDON) BRED Michael Butler
4385* Red Branch (IRE), raised 5lb, has now gone up 19lb in all and produced a fine leap to lead at the last ditch. (11/10)
4235 The Carrot Man did well to retain second place after a bad error at the final fence. (11/2)
4177* Seek The Faith (USA), up 3lb, could not even overhaul the runner-up after his horrendous blunder at the last. (5/2)

4554 END OF SEASON INTERMEDIATE OPEN N.H. FLAT RACE (4, 5 & 6-Y.O) (Class H)
4-55 (5-00) **2m 110y** £1,297.50 (£360.00: £172.50)

				SP	RR	SF
4216^{4}	**The Village Way (IRE)** (DNicholson) **6-11-4** RJohnson (tk keen hold: led on bit over 4f out: rdn & rn green 1f out: r.o wl)	—	**1**	$4/7^{1}$	68 f	—
4008^{*}	**Rupert Blues** (JSKing) **5-11-4**(7) MrOMcPhail (lw: prom: rdn 5f out: chsd wnr fnl 2f: no imp)	8	**2**	$2/1^{2}$	67 f	—
	Amothebambo (IRE) (AGHobbs) **4-10-6**(7) MrGShenkin (w'like: scope: hld up: hrd rdn & hdwy 3f out: one pce fnl f)	2½	**3**	20/1	58 f	—
	Odda's Chapel (MSheppard) **4-10-13** BPowell (unf: hdwy 10f out: one pce fnl 3f)	3½	**4**	16/1	54 f	—
	Minibelle (DLWilliams) **5-10-13** MClarke (w'like: no hdwy fnl 5f)	4	**5**	50/1	46 f	—
2830^{6}	**Just Bayard (IRE)** (BdeHaan) **5-11-4** CLlewellyn (plld hrd: led 7f out tl over 4f out: wknd over 2f out)	4	**6**	$11/1^{3}$	47 f	—
4008^{18}	**Ballina** (JGMO'Shea) **5-11-1**(3) MichaelBrennan (lw: w ldr: led 11f out to 7f out: sn wknd)	8	**7**	50/1	39 f	—
	Irish Mist (OO'Neill) **5-11-4** VSlattery (w'like: leggy: hld up: sme hdwy over 5f out: sn wknd)	9	**8**	25/1	30 f	—
4301^{17}	**The Bombers Moon** (MrsEHHeath) **4-10-13** DGallagher (led over 5f: wknd qckly 6f out: t.o)	24	**9**	50/1	7 f	—

(SP 125.7%) **9 Rn**

4m 10.8 CSF £1.89 TOTE £1.80: £1.30 £1.10 £2.90 (£1.90) Trio £16.20 OWNER St Mellion Estates Ltd (TEMPLE GUITING) BRED Paul Kwok
WEIGHT FOR AGE 4yo-5lb

4216 The Village Way (IRE), a point-to-point winner in Ireland, proved too sharp for these rivals in a slowly-run race. (4/7: 2/5-8/13)
4008* Rupert Blues was unable to go with the winner. (2/1)
Amothebambo (IRE), a half-brother to mile and ten furlong winner Bailiwick Frontier, responded to pressure and may have preferred a truer-run race. (20/1)

T/Plpt: £44.40 (303.8 Tckts). T/Qdpt: £34.60 (21.23 Tckts) KH

4401-HEREFORD (R-H) (Good)
Wednesday May 14th
WEATHER: Fine but cloudy

4555 WEOBLEY HURDLE (4-Y.O) (Class E)
1-55 (1-56) **2m 1f (9 hdls)** £2,262.00 (£632.00: £306.00) GOING minus 0.07 sec per fur (G)

				SP	RR	SF
4465^{*}	**Song Of The Sword (95)** (JABOld) **4-11-5** MAFitzgerald (a.p: rdn to ld after 2 out: r.o wl)	—	**1**	$4/7^{1}$	80+	26
4395^{6}	**Melt The Clouds (CAN) (111)** (MCPipe) **4-11-5b** RJohnson (chsd ldr: led 6th: rdn & hdd after 2 out: btn whn hit last)	4	**2**	$9/4^{2}$	76	22
4395^{9}	**Noble Colours (100)** (SGGriffiths) **4-10-12**(7) MrAWintle (led to 6th: sn wknd)	14	**3**	$6/1^{3}$	63	9
4082^{6}	**Startingo** (RLBrown) **4-10-12** MrACharles-Jones (no hdwy fr 6th)	14	**4**	100/1	43	—
1712^{P}	**Red Rusty (USA)** (PRHedger) **4-10-5**(7) MClinton (hld up: 4th & btn whn mstke 6th)	16	**5**	50/1	28	—
	Morning Sir (AStreeter) **4-10-12** TEley (a bhd: t.o fr 5th)	3½	**6**	66/1	25	—

(SP 113.1%) **6 Rn**

4m 1.0 (8.00) CSF £2.11 TOTE £1.50: £1.10 £1.20 (£1.50) OWNER Lady Lloyd Webber (WROUGHTON) BRED Sheikh Mohammed Bin Rashid Al Maktoum

4465* Song Of The Sword slipped through on the inside to lead on the home turn, but his trainer thinks he is better-suited to more galloping courses. (4/7)
4395 Melt The Clouds (CAN) committed the cardinal sin on this course, of allowing the winner up his inside on the final bend. (9/4)
4395 Noble Colours had received 18lb from the runner-up when disappointing in a handicap last time. (6/1: op 4/1)

4556 HOLMER (S) HURDLE (4,5,6 & 7-Y.O) (Class G)
2-25 (2-25) **2m 3f 110y (11 hdls)** £1,842.00 (£512.00: £246.00) GOING minus 0.07 sec per fur (G)

				SP	RR	SF
4468^{6}	**Fleet Cadet (91)** (MCPipe) **6-11-7v**(5) GSupple (lw: hld up: led appr 3 out: sn clr: easily)	—	**1**	$2/5^{1}$	75+	2
4468^{4}	**Look In The Mirror (71)** (NATwiston-Davies) **6-11-0** CLlewellyn (chsd ldr to 3rd: led after 8th: sn hdd: no imp)	7	**2**	$7/2^{2}$	57	—
4290^{2}	**Just for a Reason (68)** (RTJuckes) **5-11-0b¹** JRailton (lw: led: sn clr: hit 5th & 8th: sn hdd: wknd)	9	**3**	$8/1^{3}$	50	—
4453^{5}	**Master Showman (IRE)** (DJWintle) **6-10-7**(7) MrAWintle (lw: hld up: chsd ldr appr 6th: ev ch appr 3 out: sn wknd)	9	**4**	40/1	43	—
4458^{6}	**Jaime's Joy (49)** (GraemeRoe) **7-10-2v**(7) MartinSmith (a bhd: t.o fr 4th)	dist	**5**	66/1	—	—
4161^{F}	**Haberdasher** (MissPMWhittle) **6-11-0** WMarston (bhd: j.slowly 4th: sn t.o: p.u bef 3 out)		**P**	66/1	—	—
4440^{4}	**Rakaposhi Imp** (CHJones) **7-10-2**(7) LSuthern (chsd ldr 3rd tl wknd qckly appr 6th: t.o whn blnd 8th: p.u bef 3 out)		**P**	66/1	—	—

(SP 111.7%) **7 Rn**

4m 48.5 (17.50) CSF £1.90 TOTE £1.40: £1.10 £1.90 (£1.90) OWNER Sir John Swaine (WELLINGTON) BRED R. D. Hollingsworth
Bt in 6,200 gns

4468 Fleet Cadet would have had much more to do had this been a handicap, and made amends for last week's unlucky run. (2/5)
4468 Look In The Mirror was 8lb worse off with the winner than in the handicap at Chepstow a week ago. (7/2)
4290 Just for a Reason, switching to a visor instead of blinkers, had been beaten seven lengths by the winner at Taunton on slightly worse terms. (8/1: op 5/1)

4557 CANON PYON H'CAP CHASE (0-115) (5-Y.O+) (Class E)
3-00 (3-00) **3m 1f 110y (19 fncs)** £2,802.50 (£845.00: £410.00: £192.50) GOING minus 0.07 sec per fur (G)

				SP	RR	SF
4306^{2}	**Bally Clover (111)** (MissVenetiaWilliams) **10-12-0** NWilliamson (chsd ldr: mstke 10th: led 14th: clr appr last: jst hld on)	—	**1**	$15/8^{1}$	118	17
4429^{5}	**Coasting (83)** (HEHaynes) **11-9-7**(7) MrSDurack (hld up: hdwy 12th: ev ch appr 3 out: hrd rdn & mstke 2 out: rallied flat)	hd	**2**	20/1	90	—
4387^{3}	**Diamond Fort (95)** (JCMcConnochie) **12-10-12** MAFitzgerald (hld up: reminders after 11th: hdwy 3 out: r.o one pce fr 2 out)	1¾	**3**	$9/4^{2}$	101	—

				SP	RR	SF
4385[6]	**Distant Memory (97)** (PJHobbs) **8-11-0b** GTormey (prom: mstke 11th: sn hrd rdn: lost pl 15th: rallied 3 out: wknd last)	6	4	7/1	99	—
4344[3]	**Paper Star (92)** (MPMuggeridge) **10-10-9** BPowell (lw: led to 14th: rdn 4 out: sn wknd: t.o)	22	5	100/30[3]	80	—

(SP 105.9%) **5 Rn**

6m 29.1 (19.10) CSF £21.33 TOTE £2.10: £2.10 £7.10 (£16.50) OWNER Mr James Williams (HEREFORD) BRED Peter Magnier
LONG HANDICAP Coasting 9-3
4306 Bally Clover seemed to have this well sewn up going to the final fence, but tied up in the closing stages. (15/8)
3622 Coasting, 11lb out of the handicap, seemed to have accepted defeat between the last two, but very nearly pulled it out of the fire. (20/1)
4387 Diamond Fort, now down to a mark 9lb lower than when he last won, would have found softer ground putting more of an emphasis on stamina. (9/4)
1057 Distant Memory would have preferred faster ground. (7/1: op 7/2)

4558 ST RICHARDS SCHOOL NOVICES' CONDITIONAL H'CAP HURDLE (0-100) (4-Y.O+) (Class E)

3-30 (3-31) **2m 1f (9 hdls)** £2,332.00 (£652.00: £316.00) GOING minus 0.07 sec per fur (G)

				SP	RR	SF
3204[3]	**Tathmin (70)** (MRBosley) **4-10-7v**(3) XAizpuru (hld up: hdwy 5th: led after 3 out: lft clr 2 out: r.o)	—	1	13/2[3]	53	18
4313[6]	**Flow Back (70)** (GPEnright) **5-11-1** LAspell (hld up & bhd: hdwy 6th: lft 2nd 2 out: one pce)	4	2	7/1	49	19
4276[4]	**Tee Tee Too (IRE) (65)** (AWCarroll) **5-10-5**(5) RStudholme (bhd: mstke 5th: rdn & hdwy appr 3 out: nt rch ldrs)	¾	3	14/1	44	14
4512[8]	**Dovetto (77)** (AEPrice) **8-11-8** DJKavanagh (hld up & plld hrd: hdwy 4th: wknd appr 3 out)	24	4	5/1[2]	33	3
3932[5]	**Royrace (60)** (WMBrisbourne) **5-10-5** RMassey (bhd fr 3rd)	1½	5	14/1	15	—
4468[8]	**Roc Age (67)** (GWDavies) **6-10-12** MichaelBrennan (led to 5th: ev ch 3 out: 3rd & wkng whn blnd bdly 2 out: blnd last)	1¼	6	8/1	20	—
3989[8]	**Freno (IRE) (70)** (KCBailey) **6-10-7**(8) WWalsh (hdwy 4th: mstke 6th: sn wknd)	4	7	13/2[3]	20	—
4401[9]	**Vital Wonder (55)** (JParfitt) **9-9-11**(3) OBurrows (prom to 5th)	6	8	50/1	—	—
2806[15]	**Sober Island (60)** (MrsDThomas) **8-10-5** GuyLewis (prom to 5th)	2½	9	50/1	2	—
4226[2]	**Reverse Thrust (79)** (PRHedger) **6-11-2**(8) MClinton (hld up & plld hrd: hdwy 4th: led 5th tl after 3 out: 2nd whn fell 2 out)		F	6/4[1]	—	—

(SP 124.2%) **10 Rn**

4m 0.8 (7.80) CSF £50.12 CT £573.83 TOTE £7.90: £2.60 £2.60 £3.50 (£20.60) Trio £116.40; £70.55 to York 15/5/97 OWNER Miss J. M. Bodycote (WANTAGE) BRED Doverlodge Stud
LONG HANDICAP Vital Wonder 9-9
WEIGHT FOR AGE 4yo-5lb
IN-FOCUS: Former jockey Martin Bosley was sending out his first winner.
3204 Tathmin, coming back from a break, was in control when left to win a race which was little more than a seller. (13/2)
2909 Flow Back had finished a long way behind the winner on heavy ground at Folkestone in February. (7/1: 4/1-8/1)
2567 Tee Tee Too (IRE) has been running in sellers. (14/1)
3594 Dovetto (5/1: op 3/1)
2893 Freno (IRE) (13/2: 9/2-7/1)
4226 Reverse Thrust did not settle as well as his rider would have liked, and looked held when coming to grief. (6/4)

4559 TILLINGTON NOVICES' HURDLE (5-Y.O+) (Class E)

4-00 (4-01) **2m 3f 110y (11 hdls)** £2,332.00 (£652.00: £316.00) GOING minus 0.07 sec per fur (G)

				SP	RR	SF
4217*	**Special Beat (107)** (NJHenderson) **5-11-2**(5) MrCVigors (hld up: hdwy 5th: led 7th: clr 3 out: v.easily)	—	1	8/13[1]	80+	24
4403[6]	**Rushaway** (MissCJohnsey) **6-11-0** DGallagher (nt j.w: led to 3rd: wknd 7th: wnt poor 2nd last)	dist	2	12/1	—	—
3170[5]	**Lord Foley (NZ)** (JGMO'Shea) **5-10-11**(3) MichaelBrennan (hld up: hdwy after 6th: wknd 7th: t.o)	23	3	9/1[3]	—	—
1840[P]	**Fairies Farewell (77)** (OSherwood) **7-10-9** JAMcCarthy (led 3rd tl appr 7th: sn wknd: t.o)	20	4	20/1	—	—
4082[3]	**Ami Bleu (FR)** (PMooney) **5-11-12** JFTitley (a.p: led appr 7th: sn hdd: wknd 3 out: 3rd whn fell last: dead)		F	100/30[2]	—	—
4403[5]	**Brook Bee** (NAGaselee) **5-11-0** WMarston (a bhd: t.o whn p.u bef 7th)		P	20/1	—	—
	Haydown (IRE) (MRBosley) **5-10-7**(7) MrPPhillips (a bhd: t.o whn p.u after 8th)		P	66/1	—	—
4403[P]	**Sandville Lad** (MrsDThomas) **5-10-11**(3) GuyLewis (dropped rr 5th: t.o whn p.u bef 6th)		P	66/1	—	—

(SP 115.2%) **8 Rn**

4m 41.1 (10.10) CSF £8.20 TOTE £1.60: £1.10 £1.70 £2.10 (£8.20) OWNER Mr C. Marner (LAMBOURN) BRED Christian Marner
4217* Special Beat proved a different class to these rivals. (8/13)
Rushaway found the winner in a different league. (12/1: 8/1-14/1)
4082 Ami Bleu (FR) paid the ultimate price for trying to make a race of it with the winner. (100/30)

4560 BROCKHAMPTON HUNTERS' CHASE (5-Y.O+) (Class H)

4-30 (4-32) **3m 1f 110y (19 fncs)** £1,194.00 (£334.00: £162.00) GOING minus 0.07 sec per fur (G)

				SP	RR	SF
4323*	**Miss Millbrook** (DTGoldsworthy) **9-11-9**(7) MrEWilliams (hld up: hdwy 9th: j.slowly 10th: led 14th: rdn out)	—	1	2/1[1]	110	26
4449*	**Trifast Lad** (MJRoberts) **12-12-4**(3) MrPHacking (hld up: hdwy 10th: chsd wnr fr 3 out: r.o one pce flat)	3½	2	6/1	113	29
4473[3]	**Rusty Bridge** (MrsSMJohnson) **10-12-0**(7) MrOMcPhail (led tl after 1st: rdn & lost pl after 11th: styd on fr 3 out)	21	3	12/1	100	16
	Jack Sound (MrsMaryEvans) **11-11-7**(7) MrDSJones (chsd ldr: 2nd & btn whn mstke 3 out)	1¾	4	10/1	92	8
4322*	**Vital Song** (MHDare) **10-12-0**(7) MrGMatthews (lw: led after 1st: hdd 14th: wknd 4 out)	2	5	9/2[3]	97	13
4323[P]	**J B Lad** (HRTuck) **11-11-7**(7) MissPGundry (bhd: j.slowly 6th: hdwy 12th: wknd 15th)	¾	6	50/1	90	6
	Layston d'Or (ChristopherHooley) **8-11-7**(7) MrACharles-Jones (a bhd: t.o)	18	7	50/1	79	—
4326[3]	**My Nominee** (DENicholls) **9-12-0b**(7) MrRBurton (hdwy 11th: wknd 14th: t.o)	22	8	7/2[2]	72	—
4432[P]	**Killelan Lad** (MissKDiMarte) **15-11-7**(7) MissKDiMarte (s.s: t.o 5th: p.u bef 8th)		P	66/1	—	—
	Al Billal (RWilliams) **9-11-7**(7) MissPCooper (lw: nt j.w: a bhd: t.o whn p.u bef 12th)		P	100/1	—	—
	No Panic (CRJohnson) **13-11-7**(7) MrGLewis (bhd whn mstke 11th: sn t.o: blnd & uns rdr 4 out)		U	66/1	—	—

(SP 112.7%) **11 Rn**

6m 26.5 (16.50) CSF £12.61 TOTE £2.50: £1.50 £3.20 £1.60 (£8.00) Trio £28.60 OWNER Mr D. T. Goldsworthy (BRIDGEND) BRED C. Parker
4323* Miss Millbrook had some cut in the ground this time and seemed to jump better for it. (2/1)
4449* Trifast Lad never gave up the pursuit, but the winner was not stopping. (6/1)
4473 Rusty Bridge, a bit disappointing last week, did not have a marathon trip in his favour here. (12/1)
Jack Sound was already feeling the pace when missing out at the third last. (10/1)

4322* Vital Song seems more effective forcing the pace over shorter distances. (9/2)
4326 My Nominee (7/2: op 9/4)

4561 MARDEN STANDARD OPEN N.H. FLAT RACE (4, 5 & 6-Y.O) (Class H)
5-00 (5-01) **2m 1f** £1,030.00 (£280.00: £130.00)

				SP	RR	SF
	Castle Owen (IRE) (DNicholson) **5-11-1**(3) MrRThornton (w'like: lw: hld up: hdwy 5f out: led over 2f out: comf)	—	1	4/5 1	71 f	—
3433^{5}	**Cinnamon Club** (NAGaselee) **5-10-13** AThornton (a.p: led over 3f out tl over 2f out: sn outpcd)	12	2	5/2 2	55 f	—
3808^{7}	**Be In Space** (MissPMWhittle) **6-10-6**(7) MrOMcPhail (hld up: hdwy over 3f out: nt rch ldrs)	9	3	12/1	46 f	—
2682^{12}	**Frankie Muck** (NATwiston-Davies) **5-10-11**(7) MrJGoldstein (prom: rdn 6f out: ev ch 3f out: sn wknd)	½	4	12/1	51 f	—
2757^{5}	**Hurricane Jane (IRE)** (MJRoberts) **5-10-13** JRailton (nvr nr to chal)	3½	5	14/1	43 f	—
	Regal Bluff (JCMcConnochie) **5-11-4** SWynne (set slow pce 4f: ev ch 3f out: sn wknd)	5	6	33/1	43 f	—
4407^{9}	**Bossa Nova** (LGCottrell) **4-10-3**(5) OBurrows (hld up: hdwy 9f out: led 4f out: sn hdd & wknd)	1¾	7	20/1	36 f	—
	Pride of Pennker (IRE) (PGMurphy) **4-10-5**(3) LAspell (w'like: prom 10f)	13	8	10/1 3	24 f	—
4301^{6}	**Miss Mouse** (PMooney) **5-10-10**(3) RMassey (plld hrd: w ldr: led after 4f: hdd 4f out: sn wknd)	2	9	14/1	22 f	—
4538^{13}	**Bernera** (JMackie) **5-11-4** TEley (prom 12f: t.o)	12	10	33/1	16 f	—

(SP 132.6%) **10 Rn**

4m 6.2 CSF £3.10 TOTE £1.60: £1.10 £1.20 £5.10 (£2.80) Trio £22.90 OWNER Lord Vestey (TEMPLE GUITING) BRED Joseph O'Dwyer
WEIGHT FOR AGE 4yo-5lb
Castle Owen (IRE) looked the part in the paddock, and produced enough speed in a slowly-run race. (4/5)
3433 Cinnamon Club proved no match for the winner. (5/2)
Be In Space, staying on past beaten rivals, would probably have preferred a truer-run race. (12/1: op 8/1)
Frankie Muck appreciated this better ground. (12/1: op 8/1)
Pride of Pennker (IRE) (10/1: 5/1-11/1)

T/Plpt: £24.00 (299.17 Tckts). T/Qdpt: £15.40 (23.31 Tckts) KH

4316-HUNTINGDON (R-H) (Good to firm, Firm patches)
Wednesday May 14th
WEATHER: sunny

4562 LADIES EVENING (S) H'CAP HURDLE (0-95) (4-Y.O+) (Class G)
6-05 (6-05) **2m 5f 110y (10 hdls)** £1,891.00 (£526.00: £253.00) GOING minus 0.99 sec per fur (HD)

				SP	RR	SF
2570^{2}	**Brindley House (92)** (RCurtis) **10-12-0** DMorris (mde all: rdn clr fr 2 out: eased cl home)	—	1	5/1 3	77+	37
4427^{3}	**Nautical Jewel (80)** (KGWingrove) **5-10-9**(7) MrAWintle (lw: in tch: r.o fr 3 out: nt trble wnr)	9	2	7/2 2	58	18
4321^{5}	**Script (66)** (JRJenkins) **6-10-2** KGaule (chsd ldrs: lft 2nd 3 out: no imp: wknd flat)	7	3	14/1	39	—
4283^{P}	**Weather Alert (IRE) (67)** (KAMorgan) **6-10-3v** RJohnson (prom: rdn appr 3 out: sn btn)	2	4	14/1	39	—
4318^{6}	**Cleric on Broadway (IRE) (64)** (JPearce) **9-10-0** JCulloty (mstkes: in tch: lost pl 6th: n.d after)	3	5	25/1	33	—
4409^{5}	**Fret (USA) (64)** (JSWainwright) **7-10-0** BFenton (lw: bhd fr 5th)	2	6	14/1	32	—
4452^{5}	**Gi Moss (65)** (PRHarriss) **10-10-1b** SMcNeill (plld hrd: prom to 6th)	19	7	25/1	19	—
1007^{7}	**Ben Connan (IRE) (68)** (JohnWhyte) **7-9-11**(7)ow4 MrRWakley (lw: t.o whn fell 6th)		F	50/1	—	—
3683^{5}	**Spitfire Bridge (IRE) (68)** (GMMcCourt) **5-10-4** NWilliamson (chsd ldrs: mstke 2nd: rdn 5th: hit next: wknd appr 3 out: p.u bef 2 out: lame)		P	3/1 1	—	—
4470^{7}	**Better Bythe Glass (IRE) (89)** (NATwiston-Davies) **8-11-11** CLlewellyn (nt j.w: t.o whn p.u bef 6th)		P	8/1	—	—
4439^{4}	**Ecu de France (IRE) (64)** (PCRitchens) **7-9-7**(7) NWillmington (chsd ldrs: 2nd whn blnd & uns rdr 3 out)		U	11/2	—	—

(SP 120.0%) **11 Rn**

4m 49.6 (-10.40) CSF £21.36 CT £214.37 TOTE £8.10: £2.40 £2.10 £3.80 (£23.10) Trio £110.10 OWNER Mr S. B. Glazer (LAMBOURN) BRED Basil Brindley
LONG HANDICAP Ben Connan (IRE) 9-0 Fret (USA) 9-5 Cleric on Broadway (IRE) 9-6 Ecu de France (IRE) 9-6
No bid. Nautical Jewel clmd MPerkins £5,000
2570 Brindley House did not seem to be enjoying this fast ground, but is certainly appreciating being put back over timber and was a class apart from these. (5/1)
4427 Nautical Jewel, with his tongue tied down, came from the back of the main group in the last half-mile, but the leader was not for catching. He looked sore, but it is hoped that the injury is not too serious. (7/2)
4321 Script did not find much once let down, and is proving difficult to win with. (14/1)
1775 Weather Alert (IRE) seems to finish weakly whatever the trip. (14/1)
Cleric on Broadway (IRE), a poor mover on the firm surface, did not seem to relish jumping on it. (25/1)
4409 Fret (USA) won on joining the stable in November 1994, but has yet to score again in twenty-four attempts. (14/1)
725* Better Bythe Glass (IRE) (8/1: op 5/1)

4563 HEALTH SPA WATER NOVICES' H'CAP HURDLE (0-100) (4-Y.O+) (Class E)
6-35 (6-35) **3m 2f (12 hdls)** £2,407.50 (£670.00: £322.50) GOING minus 0.99 sec per fur (HD)

				SP	RR	SF
4458*	**Ardent Love (IRE) (73)** (DNicholson) **8-10-9** RJohnson (lw: a.p: pushed along 7th: led flat: drvn out)	—	1	7/4 1	58	9
4309^{6}	**Stormy Session (78)** (NATwiston-Davies) **7-11-0** TJenks (led after 2nd: hit 3 out: hdd flat: unable qckn)	nk	2	16/1	63	14
4161*	**Forbidden Waters (IRE) (73)** (MissVenetiaWilliams) **6-10-9** NWilliamson (hdwy 4th: ev ch appr 2 out: sn rdn & no ex)	10	3	100/30 2	52	3
4393^{2}	**Northern Star (88)** (JAPickering) **6-11-3**(7) MissJWormall (j.slowly 1st: effrt 7th: nvr trbld ldrs)	1¾	4	9/1	66	17
4452^{P}	**Arrange A Game (64)** (MissJBower) **10-9-9**(5) RWilkinson (lw: nt j.w: in tch to 8th)	16	5	33/1	32	—
4341^{5}	**Crown Ivory (NZ) (65)** (PCRitchens) **9-10-1** SFox (lw: bhd fr 7th)	2	6	10/1	32	—
4445^{7}	**Eden Stream (64)** (MissLShally) **10-10-0** DLeahy (chsd ldrs tl wknd appr 3 out)	6	7	33/1	27	—
4439^{S}	**Karen's Typhoon (IRE) (72)** (TPMcGovern) **6-10-8** MAFitzgerald (hdwy 7th: wknd 3 out: bhd whn fell last)		F	20/1	—	—

4309[5] **Sammorello (IRE) (80)** (NATwiston-Davies) **6-11-2** CLlewellyn (led tl after 2nd: mstke & wknd 9th: t.o whn p.u bef 2 out) ... **P** 7/2[3] — —
(SP 117.3%) **9 Rn**

5m 57.5 (6.60 under best) (-8.50) CSF £25.67 CT £79.25 TOTE £2.50: £1.50 £3.50 £1.60 (£28.40) Trio £11.60 OWNER Mrs Claire Smith (TEMPLE GUITING) BRED Blue Bear Stud Co Ltd
LONG HANDICAP Eden Stream 9-13
4458* Ardent Love (IRE), unpenalised for last week's success, was made to struggle and had to lower the course record to prevail. (7/4)
4309 Stormy Session, trying new tactics, was well inside the old course record and was unfortunate to come up against a well-handicapped rival. He can find a similar race. (16/1)
4161* Forbidden Waters (IRE), in his first handicap after winning a poor race at Southwell, gave the impression that he was travelling well enough to win until folding in a few strides on the home turn. Either the trip or the firm ground found him out. (100/30)
4393 Northern Star, stepping out of novice company and up in trip, never looked a threat. (9/1)
1357 Arrange A Game, who won off a higher mark over course and distance earlier in the season, ruined his chance by jumping deplorably. (33/1)

4564 DELOITTE & TOUCHE CHARTERED ACCOUNTANTS NOVICES' CHASE (5-Y.O+) (Class E)

7-05 (7-05) **2m 110y (12 fncs)** £2,886.75 (£864.00: £414.50: £189.75) GOING minus 0.56 sec per fur (F)

			SP	RR	SF
4452[W]	**Gimme (IRE) (83)** (JGMO'Shea) **7-10-11v**(3) MichaelBrennan (lw: hld up: hit 1st & 2nd: hdwy 5th: led 4 out: rdn clr fr 2 out) ... —	**1**	15/8[2]	100	26
3225[P]	**Lowawatha (97)** (MrsEHHeath) **9-11-7** DGallagher (bit bkwd: led to 4 out: rdn & hit 2 out: sn btn) ... 14	**2**	3/1[3]	93	19
752[2]	**Telmar Systems (60)** (JWhite) **8-11-0** JRKavanagh (lft 2nd 4th: hit 4 out: sn wknd) ... 21	**3**	12/1	66	—
4526[P]	**Cumberland Youth** (MissCJECaroe) **6-11-0** ILawrence (rdn 4th: sn t.o) ... dist	**4**	40/1	—	—
4415[3]	**Drummond Warrior (IRE)** (TThomsonJones) **8-11-0** MAFitzgerald (chsd ldrs tl fell 4th) ...	**F**	5/4[1]	—	—

(SP 114.4%) **5 Rn**

4m 0.1 (-1.90) CSF £7.66 TOTE £3.20: £1.50 £2.30 (£4.00) OWNER Mr Brian O'Kane (WESTBURY-ON-SEVERN) BRED J. Griffin
3842 Gimme (IRE) appears to have scant respect for fences, but has ability, taking this in fine style. (15/8)
862 Lowawatha, off for twelve weeks, looked to just need the race and his attempt to establish a clear lead only lasted to halfway. (3/1)
752 Telmar Systems has been well placed to find some easy opportunities for place money. (12/1: 8/1-14/1)
4415 Drummond Warrior (IRE), making his chasing debut, overjumped at the first ditch and paid the penalty. (5/4: tchd evens)

4565 HARTLEY'S JAM QUANTUM LEAP H'CAP HURDLE (0-120) (4-Y.O+) (Class D)

7-35 (7-35) **2m 110y (8 hdls)** £2,756.00 (£766.00: £368.00) GOING minus 0.99 sec per fur (HD)

			SP	RR	SF
4236*	**Antiguan Flyer (90)** (GProdromou) **8-10-1v**(3) MichaelBrennan (mde all: sn clr: rdn & hld on wl flat) ... —	**1**	11/4[3]	69	33
4061[6]	**Prizefighter (114)** (JLEyre) **6-12-0** DGallagher (chsd clr ldr: hit 3 out: sn rdn: ev ch flat: unable qckn nr fin) ... 1	**2**	Evens[1]	92	56
4311[4]	**Time Won't Wait (IRE) (110)** (RTPhillips) **8-11-10** NWilliamson (hld up: rdn 5th: btn whn hit next) ... dist	**3**	9/4[2]	—	—

(SP 107.4%) **3 Rn**

3m 35.8 (-12.20) CSF £5.33 TOTE £2.90 (£1.70) OWNER Mr George Prodromou (EAST HARLING) BRED Crest Stud Ltd
4236* Antiguan Flyer, up no less than 25lb since winning at Fakenham in March, was in against two rivals who need waiting with and was able to establish a clear lead. Although his advantage was whittled away from the home turn, he responded gamely to hold on. (11/4)
4061 Prizefighter did not get the cover that might have been hoped for, and had to give sole chase to the winner. In the circumstances, he lost little against an in-form rival. (Evens)
3638 Time Won't Wait (IRE), reverting to hurdles off a seemingly advantageous mark, was hard-pressed to stay in touch in such a fast-run race, and failed to do himself justice. (9/4)

4566 Q103 FM NOVICES' H'CAP CHASE (0-100) (5-Y.O+) (Class E)

8-05 (8-06) **2m 4f 110y (16 fncs)** £2,886.75 (£864.00: £414.50: £189.75) GOING minus 0.56 sec per fur (F)

			SP	RR	SF
4134[P]	**Mister Goodguy (IRE) (72)** (RCurtis) **8-10-0** DMorris (hit 3rd: hdwy & hit 8th: rdn to ld appr last: r.o) ... —	**1**	6/1[3]	86	12
4254[2]	**Mill O'The Rags (IRE) (100)** (MrsDHaine) **8-12-0** JFTitley (lw: led 2nd tl appr last: one pce) ... 4	**2**	4/6[1]	111	37
4431[3]	**Wot No Gin (72)** (AJWilson) **8-10-0** LHarvey (plld hrd: led to 2nd: dropped rr 5th: rdn & kpt on fr 3 out) ... 10	**3**	9/2[2]	75	1
2896[6]	**George Ashford (IRE) (86)** (PRJohnson) **7-11-0b**[1] MSharratt (swtg: hdwy 5th: ev ch 4 out: wknd appr 2 out) ... 1¾	**4**	16/1	88	14
4446[6]	**Stage Player (82)** (MissCJECaroe) **11-10-10** ILawrence (lw: hit 1st & 10th: in tch to 12th) ... 12	**5**	10/1	74	—
4297[4]	**Copper Cable (72)** (CSmith) **10-10-0** MRanger (in tch: dropped rr 10th: rallied 3 out: wkng whn blnd next) ... 1¼	**6**	12/1	63	—
4272[2]	**Cardinal Rule (IRE) (90)** (MissVenetiaWilliams) **8-11-4** NWilliamson (Withdrawn not under Starter's orders: State of ground) ...	**W**		—	—

(SP 115.1%) **6 Rn**

4m 59.2 (-0.80) CSF £10.51 TOTE £6.90: £2.80 £1.30 (£2.90) OWNER Mr M. O'Brien (LAMBOURN) BRED Tom Gaffney and David Magnier
LONG HANDICAP Wot No Gin 9-7 Copper Cable 9-5 Mister Goodguy (IRE) 9-2
Mister Goodguy (IRE), a winning pointer, got his lowly handicap mark when well beaten in decent novice hurdles. Despite being 12lb out of the weights, he landed a touch in good style. (6/1)
4254 Mill O'The Rags (IRE), with the trip and ground ideal, looked to have found an easy race but caught a tartar. (4/6)
4431 Wot No Gin took a while to settle, and only stayed on past beaten rivals. (9/2)
581 George Ashford (IRE), dropped in trip, folded tamely on the home turn. (16/1)
2068* Stage Player has shown precious little in four runs since his win. (10/1: 6/1-12/1)
4297 Copper Cable, on his toes and with his tongue tied down, found his effort petering out on the home turn. (12/1: 7/1-14/1)

4567 YELLING NOVICES' HURDLE (4-Y.O+) (Class E)

8-35 (8-35) **2m 110y (8 hdls)** £2,355.00 (£655.00: £315.00) GOING minus 0.99 sec per fur (HD)

			SP	RR	SF
4382*	**Nordance Prince (IRE) (108)** (MissVenetiaWilliams) **6-11-6** NWilliamson (lw: prom: led 5th: qckndappr 2 out: comf) ... —	**1**	4/7[1]	73+	18
4318*	**Real Madrid** (GPEnright) **6-11-6** RJohnson (prom: chsd wnr fr appr 3 out: rdn & no imp flat) ... 3½	**2**	3/1[2]	70	15
4318[3]	**Undawaterscubadiva** (MPBielby) **5-11-0** MAFitzgerald (lw: hdwy appr 4th: one pce fr 2 out: mstke last) ... 7	**3**	8/1[3]	57	2
4441[8]	**Sapphire Son (IRE)** (PCClarke) **5-11-0** BFenton (hld up: hdwy 5th: nvr plcd to chal) ... 6	**4**	50/1	51	—
4453[3]	**Our Eddie (70)** (KGWingrove) **8-11-0b** KGaule (plld hrd: led after 3rd: hdd 5th: sn btn) ... 2	**5**	20/1	41	—
1388[7]	**Kaifoon (USA) (70)** (PCRitchens) **8-11-0** SFox (led 2nd tl after 3rd: j.slowly next: sn btn) ... 8	**6**	50/1	43	—
4420[9]	**French County (IRE)** (JRJenkins) **5-11-0** GBradley (plld hrd: in tch to 4th) ... 3½	**7**	10/1	38	—

	Horse	Dist	Pos	SP	RR	SF
	Duffertoes (MJRyan) **5-11-0** JRyan (led to 2nd: wknd 5th)	10	**8**	25/1	28	—
4441[P]	**Ogulla** (MissLShally) **5-10-9** DLeahy (mstke 4th: sn wl bhd)	15	**9**	66/1	9	—
1818[5]	**Nashaat (USA) (80)** (KRBurke) **9-11-0** ALarnach (swtg: plld hrd: mstke & uns rdr 3rd)		**U**	16/1	—	—
				(SP 128.7%)		**10 Rn**

3m 42.7 (-5.30) CSF £2.69 TOTE £1.70: £1.40 £1.40 £1.60 (£2.20) Trio £4.50 OWNER Pinks Gym (HEREFORD) BRED James Doherty

OFFICIAL EXPLANATION **Sapphire Son (IRE): the gelding is not an easy ride, needs settling, has one burst of speed and is novicey at his hurdles.**

4382* Nordance Prince (IRE) seemed to enjoy this fast ground, and won without having to pull out all the stops. (4/7)

4318* Real Madrid tried hard to give the winner a race, but was already getting the worse of things when tending to edge towards the centre of the track on the run-in. (3/1)

4318 Undawaterscubadiva got closer to the runner-up than he had here last month, but he still looks short of speed at this trip. (8/1)

Sapphire Son (IRE), ridden to settle and get the trip, caught the eyes of the Stewards and was certainly not knocked about. (50/1)

4453 Our Eddie raced too keenly ,and did not give himself a chance of lasting home. (20/1)

Kaifoon (USA), having only his second run in twenty-one months, showed no signs of recapturing his form. (50/1)

T/Plpt: £22.70 (435.85 Tckts). T/Qdpt: £4.90 (87.36 Tckts) Dk

4282-PERTH (R-H) (Good to soft)
Wednesday May 14th

WEATHER: fine

4568 CAMERON MOTORS MAIDEN HURDLE (4-Y.O+) (Class E)

6-20 (6-20) **2m 4f 110y (10 hdls)** £2,747.00 (£772.00: £377.00) GOING: 0.48 sec per fur (GS)

	Horse	Dist	Pos	SP	RR	SF
3791[4]	**Supreme Soviet (94)** (ACWhillans) **7-11-5** BStorey (cl up: disp ld 4 out tl lft clr appr 2 out: all out)	—	**1**	6/4[1]	59	—
4335[3]	**Hand of Straw (IRE)** (MissZAGreen) **5-11-5** KJohnson (prom: outpcd appr 3 out: styd on fr 2 out: nt qckn towards fin)	1	**2**	7/1[3]	58	—
4248[12]	**Frisky Thyne (IRE) (81)** (MDHammond) **8-11-5** RGarritty (lw: in tch: effrt 4 out: one pce fr next)	11	**3**	10/1	50	—
1827[3]	**Lord of The Loch (IRE)** (LLungo) **6-11-5** RSupple (in tch: effrt 4 out: outpcd fr next)	8	**4**	3/1[2]	43	—
4244[6]	**Nordisk Legend** (MrsDThomson) **5-11-5** TReed (hld up & bhd: effrt appr 4 out: n.d)	29	**5**	20/1	21	—
4182[P]	**Springlea Tower** (RNixon) **4-10-13** PNiven (prom to 4th: sn t.o)	6	**6**	33/1	16	—
506[7]	**Ihtimaam (FR)** (MrsASwinbank) **5-11-5** JSupple (bhd: effrt 4 out: sn wknd: t.o)	dist	**7**	16/1	—	—
	Gold Bits (IRE) (GRichards) **6-11-5** RDunwoody (lw: nt j.w: chsd ldrs: wknd 4 out: fell 3 out)		**F**	10/1	—	—
4243[F]	**Rambling Rajah** (MrsSCBradburne) **5-10-12**(7) MrMBradburne (mde most tl p.u appr 2 out)		**P**	16/1	—	—
4288[6]	**Calling The Tune** (BMactaggart) **6-11-5** DBentley (prom to 4th: sn wknd: t.o whn p.u after 3 out)		**P**	50/1	—	—
				(SP 117.1%)		**10 Rn**

5m 23.4 (35.40) CSF £11.53 TOTE £2.30: £1.70 £1.10 £3.40 (£6.60) Trio £37.60 OWNER Mr I. Campbell (HAWICK) BRED B. Minty

WEIGHT FOR AGE 4yo-6lb

3791 Supreme Soviet at last broke his duck, but he needed all the luck going and was far from convincing. (6/4)

4335 Hand of Straw (IRE) keeps running consistently and ought to pick up a modest race. (7/1)

Frisky Thyne (IRE) had shown nothing in two runs previously in this country, and this was slightly more encouraging, but this was a poor race. (10/1)

1827 Lord of The Loch (IRE) had reasonable form in bumpers, but looked very one-paced on his first attempt over hurdles. (3/1)

Gold Bits (IRE) (10/1: 6/1-11/1)

Rambling Rajah really gave the winner a race, and he was still upsides when he lost his action and pulled up going to the second last. He was later found to be okay. (16/1)

4569 BREAK THROUGH BREAST CANCER NOVICES' CHASE (5-Y.O+) (Class D)

6-50 (6-50) **3m (18 fncs)** £3,517.50 (£1,065.00: £520.00: £247.50) GOING: 0.48 sec per fur (GS)

	Horse	Dist	Pos	SP	RR	SF
4186[10]	**Slotamatique (IRE) (98)** (GRichards) **8-11-7b[1]** RDunwoody (a.p: wnt 2nd 4 out: sn rdn: styd on to ld fnl 100y)	—	**1**	7/4[1]	103	36
4447[3]	**Fern Leader (IRE) (79)** (MrsASwinbank) **7-11-1b[1]** MrChrisWilson (led: mstke 1st: sn clr: hit 14th: wknd & hdd flat)	2½	**2**	6/1	95	28
4417[2]	**Cullane Lake (IRE) (78)** (MissMKMilligan) **7-11-2** RSupple (a in tch: effrt u.p 4 out: no imp)	30	**3**	4/1[2]	76	9
4260[U]	**Royal Banker (IRE)** (MartinTodhunter) **7-11-1b** PCarberry (chsd ldrs tl wknd 4 out: sn bhd: blnd 2 out)	28	**4**	10/1	57	—
4481[3]	**Dragons Bay (IRE)** (MrsMReveley) **8-11-1** PNiven (lw: prom: effrt & blnd 14th: wknd 3 out: p.u bef next)		**P**	9/2[3]	—	—
4515[7]	**Festival Fancy (66)** (BMactaggart) **10-10-10** GLee (sn wl bhd: t.o whn p.u bef 14th)		**P**	16/1	—	—
	Another Meadow (JEDixon) **9-11-1** BStorey (sn outpcd & bhd: t.o whn p.u bef 13th)		**P**	33/1	—	—
1968[5]	**The Energiser (67)** (DALamb) **11-11-1** JBurke (mstkes: sn t.o: p.u bef 12th)		**P**	50/1	—	—
				(SP 108.7%)		**8 Rn**

6m 20.6 (22.60) CSF £10.55 TOTE £2.20: £1.20 £1.60 £1.50 (£5.20) Trio £8.60 OWNER Slotamatics (Bolton) Ltd (PENRITH) BRED Stackallan Stud

2916 Slotamatique (IRE) has been disappointing at this game, and had the blinkers on for the first time, and needed all Dunwoody's assistance to gain him the day in this modest event. (7/4)

4447 Fern Leader (IRE) had the blinkers on for the first time and went for this from the word go, but his jumping still left something to be desired and, after looking in command, he ran out of fuel on the flat. (6/1: op 4/1)

4417 Cullane Lake (IRE) was always well enough placed, but proved far too slow when asked a question. (4/1)

4260 Royal Banker (IRE) was given a most promising ride, but he was found out fully four from home. (10/1)

4570 MACALLAN 10 Y.O. SINGLE MALT HURDLE (4-Y.O) (Class E)

7-20 (7-20) **2m 110y (8 hdls)** £2,528.00 (£708.00: £344.00) GOING: 0.48 sec per fur (GS)

	Horse	Dist	Pos	SP	RR	SF
	Breydon (PMonteith) **4-10-12** GCahill (lw: trckd ldrs: wnt 2nd & mstke 3 out: c wd & led 2 out: j.rt last: all out)	—	**1**	13/8[1]	43?	—
	Sheemore (IRE) (MDHammond) **4-10-12** RGarritty (mde most tl hdd 2 out: hung lft: ev ch flat: kpt on)	nk	**2**	5/2[3]	43?	—
3789[9]	**Anika's Gem (IRE)** (MrsSCBradburne) **4-10-7** MFoster (disp ld to 4th: outpcd appr 3 out: btn 2 out)	22	**3**	9/4[2]	16	—

4477[3] **Mr Bruno** (MABarnes) **4-10-7**(5) STaylor (blnd 4th: sn t.o) 7	4	12/1	15	—
		(SP 105.1%)		**4 Rn**

4m 11.5 (25.50) CSF £5.15 TOTE £2.50 (£2.80) OWNER The Dregs Of Humanity (ROSEWELL) BRED Langham Hall Stud
STEWARDS' ENQUIRY Cahill susp. 23-24 & 26-28/5/97 (excessive use of whip).
Breydon looked magnificent, but it took a deal of help from the saddle for him to win this very moderate race. (13/8)
Sheemore (IRE) looked to be his own worst enemy here, as he was continually swishing his tail and hanging, but he still almost won it. (5/2: 7/4-11/4)
3394 Anika's Gem (IRE) ran moderately, coming under pressure approaching three out and being soon well beaten. (9/4)
4477 Mr Bruno looks extremely moderate as he was never able to get into this very poor race. (12/1: op 8/1)

4571 FAMOUS GROUSE H'CAP CHASE (0-125) (5-Y.O+) (Class D)
7-50 (7-50) **2m 4f 110y (15 fncs)** £3,436.25 (£1,040.00: £507.50: £241.25) GOING: 0.48 sec per fur (GS)

		SP	RR	SF
4392* **Weaver George (IRE) (109)** (WStorey) **7-10-7**(5) RMcGrath (in tch: hdwy 9th: ev ch 3 out: sn outpcd: styd on u.p flat to lead post)....—	1	5/2[1]	122	50
4408* **Tough Test (IRE) (97)** (MrsJDGoodfellow) **7-10-0** BStorey (prom: effrt whn blnd bdly & lost pl 10th: hdwy 4 out: led flat: jst ct) ....s.h	2	4/1[2]	110	38
4480* **Nicholas Plant (102)** (JSGoldie) **8-10-5** 6x GCahill (lw: blnd 1st: led: rdn 3 out: hdd flat: sn btn)....7	3	5/2[1]	110	38
4448[3] **Acajou III (FR) (111)** (GRichards) **9-11-0** PCarberry (mstkes: chsd ldr tl wknd fr 4 out) 13	4	5/2[1]	108	36
877* **Wise Advice (IRE) (98)** (MDHammond) **7-10-1** DBentley (lw: prom to 10th: sn wknd)....20	5	12/1[3]	80	8
		(SP 113.4%)		**5 Rn**

5m 11.6 (12.60) CSF £11.76 TOTE £4.10: £1.80 £1.90 (£7.20) OWNER Regent Decorators Ltd (CONSETT) BRED G. Cashin
LONG HANDICAP Tough Test (IRE) 9-9
4392* Weaver George (IRE) is happier on slightly faster ground, but he is game and that won him the day. (5/2)
4408* Tough Test (IRE) would surely have won this but for a diabolical blunder at the tenth, and did well in the circumstances. (4/1)
4480* Nicholas Plant was always being taken on in the lead, and that had sapped all reserves when he was tackled again at the last. (5/2)
4448 Acajou III (FR) is never one to trust as his jumping was chancey to say the least, but his rider has the courage and that kept him in contention for a long way. (5/2)
877* Wise Advice (IRE), having his first run for over seven months, showed a little and is better on faster ground. (12/1)

4572 BUNNAHABHAIN 12 Y.O. SINGLE MALT (S) H'CAP HURDLE (0-100) (4-Y.O+) (Class G)
8-20 (8-20) **3m 110y (12 hdls)** £2,775.00 (£775.00: £375.00) GOING: 0.48 sec per fur (GS)

		SP	RR	SF
3711[3] **Kirstenbosch (80)** (LLungo) **10-11-0**(7) WDowling (hld up: hdwy & prom 8th: rdn to ld after 3 out: clr whn tried to run out last: styd on)....—	1	9/2[2]	67	13
4378[7] **Mardood (61)** (SBClark) **12-9-9**(7)ow1 MissRClark (in tch: mstke 3rd: hdwy & ev ch 3 out: one pce fr next)....12	2	16/1	40	—
4283[11] **Precipice Run (83)** (JJBirkett) **12-11-10** LO'Hara (in tch: effrt 4 out: styd on u.p: nvr able to chal) 2	3	16/1	61	7
4378* **Skane River (IRE) (72)** (GRichards) **6-10-13** RDunwoody (lw: trckd ldrs: led 4 out tl after next: sn outpcd) ....¾	4	7/4[1]	49	—
4283[P] **Don't Tell Judy (IRE) (59)** (MissMKMilligan) **9-9-9**(5) STaylor (chsd ldrs: outpcd 8th: hdwy u.p appr 3 out: sn btn)....12	5	16/1	29	—
4409[4] **Monkey Wench (IRE) (80)** (MrsJDGoodfellow) **6-11-7** BStorey (lw: hdwy ½-wy: sn prom: rdn appr 3 out)....1	6	9/1	49	—
3607[9] **Ruber (80)** (RWThomson) **10-11-7** DParker (lw: chsd ldrs: led after 8th to 4 out: sn outpcd) ....nk	7	9/2[2]	49	—
4394* **Whitegatesprincess (IRE) (67)** (BEllison) **6-10-1v**(7) CMcCormack (bhd: hdwy & in tch 8th: rdn & wknd next)dist	8	7/1[3]	—	—
4472[3] **Playful Juliet (CAN) (76)** (JCHaynes) **9-10-12b**(5) RMcGrath (lw: led & sn clr: hdd & wknd after 8th: t.o whn p.u bef 2 out)	P	12/1	—	—
4513[P] **Meadowleck (60)** (WGYoung) **8-9-8**(7)ow1 IJardine (chsd ldr to 8th: sn t.o: p.u bef 2 out)....	P	33/1	—	—
4248[17] **Busy Boy (63)** (DALamb) **10-10-4**ow1 JBurke (lw: n.m.r & rn out 1st)	R	33/1	—	—
		(SP 126.4%)		**11 Rn**

6m 16.3 (30.30) CSF £70.72 CT £988.13 TOTE £5.60: £1.80 £3.30 £3.90 (£104.20) Trio £180.70 OWNER Mrs Barbara Lungo (CARRUTHERSTOWN) BRED Brownstown Stud and Partners
LONG HANDICAP Meadowleck 9-9 Don't Tell Judy (IRE) 9-10
No bid
3711 Kirstenbosch quickly made this his when sent on approaching two out, but his rider got him unbalanced going to the last and he almost ducked out. (9/2)
3971 Mardood stays well but in his own time, and looked very one-paced. (16/1)
2045* Precipice Run seems happier over hurdles than fences these days, but he does not do anything quickly. (16/1)
4378* Skane River (IRE) always gives the impression that he is better on faster ground. (7/4)
4472 Playful Juliet (CAN) (12/1: op 8/1)

4573 HIGHLAND PARK 12 Y.O. SINGLE MALT CONDITIONAL H'CAP HURDLE (0-115) (4-Y.O+) (Class E)
8-50 (8-50) **2m 110y (8 hdls)** £2,640.00 (£740.00: £360.00) GOING: 0.48 sec per fur (GS)

		SP	RR	SF
4246[3] **Rachael's Owen (90)** (JSGoldie) **7-11-10** RMcGrath (outpcd & bhd: gd hdwy 3 out: rdn to ld 2 out: hmpd last & flat: all out) ....—	1	7/4[1]	72	29
4248[8] **Pariah (IRE) (93)** (MartinTodhunter) **8-11-10**(3) CMcCormack (hld up: smooth hdwy to ld appr 2 out: sn hdd: hung lft u.p: nt qckn towards fin) ....¾	2	3/1[2]	74	31
4409[3] **Skiddaw Samba (82)** (MrsMReveley) **8-11-2** GLee (in tch: hdwy 3 out: rdn appr next: one pce) 8	3	11/2[3]	56	13
3072[5] **High Low (USA) (91)** (MDHammond) **9-11-4**(7) AEde (led tl hdd & wknd appr 2 out)....7	4	14/1	58	15
French Project (IRE) (72) (MrsSCBradburne) **5-10-6** GFRyan (prom tl mskte & wknd 5th)....24	5	33/1	16	—
3485[12] **Merry Mermaid (92)** (PMonteith) **7-11-12** SMelrose (chsd ldrs: rdn appr 3 out: sn outpcd)....18	6	6/1	18	—
4482[4] **Fox Sparrow (90)** (NTinkler) **7-11-10b** EHusband (prom tl outpcd ½-wy: sn wl bhd) 5	7	9/1	11	—
		(SP 110.6%)		**7 Rn**

4m 3.0 (17.00) CSF £6.51 TOTE £2.30: £1.50 £1.80 (£3.80) OWNER Die-Hard Racing Club (GLASGOW) BRED T. Dyer
STEWARDS' ENQUIRY McCormack susp. 23-24/5/97 (careless riding).
4246 Rachael's Owen found the frenetic early pace too much, but he responded to pressure well and, despite the runner-up continually leaning into him from the second last, he always had the edge. (7/4)
3886 Pariah (IRE) looked likely to win this on the bridle, but yet again was disappointing off it and, with his rider's whip continually in his right hand, all he did was lean onto the winner. Had he won it, he would probably have been disqualified. (3/1)
4409 Skiddaw Samba looked likely to get into it three from home but, soon asked for a serious effort, she was most disappointing. (11/2)

3072 High Low (USA) went off at breakneck speed, and had shot his bolt two from home. (14/1)
3346 Merry Mermaid, who has changed stables, tried to keep up with the very fast pace but, probably needing this, her first run for over two months, she stopped quickly from the third last. (6/1)

T/Plpt: £160.30 (64.44 Tckts). T/Qdpt: £65.60 (5.84 Tckts) AA

4568-PERTH (R-H) (Good to Soft)
Thursday May 15th
WEATHER: fine

4574 PIMMS CHARITY POLO TOURNAMENT NOVICES' CHASE (5-Y.O+) (Class E)
1-55 (1-55) **2m (12 fncs)** £3,111.25 (£940.00: £457.50: £216.25) GOING: 0.38 sec per fur (GS)

Form	Horse / Details	Dist	Pos	SP	RR	SF
3092[3]	**Know-No-No (IRE) (74)** (MDHammond) **8-11-0** RGarritty (lw: trckd ldrs: led after 3 out: sn clr)	—	1	9/2[2]	90	22
4334[U]	**Kincardine Bridge (USA)** (MrsSCBradburne) **8-10-7**(7) MrMBradburne (led to 2nd: cl up: led 8th: blnd 3 out: sn hdd & btn)	17	2	25/1	73	5
4151[2]	**All Clear (IRE) (68)** (HowardJohnson) **6-11-0** NWilliamson (chsd ldrs: led 7th to 8th: outpcd fr 3 out)	10	3	9/1[3]	63	—
4214[5]	**Rallegio (97)** (PMonteith) **8-11-12** GCahill (lw: in tch: pushed along fr ½-wy: mstke 4 out: sn btn)	16	4	4/7[1]	59	—
4419[2]	**Spectre Brown (66)** (FJestin) **7-10-7**(7) MrTJBarry (plld hrd: led fr 2nd to 7th: wknd)	11	5	16/1	36	—
4260[4]	**Regal Domain (IRE)** (MrsLMarshall) **6-11-0** KJohnson (mstkes & a bhd)	4	6	33/1	32	—
4502[3]	**Sunkala Shine** (SBClark) **9-10-7**(7) MissRClark (in tch whn fell 4th)		F	12/1	—	—
4283[15]	**Akito Racing (IRE)** (MartinTodhunter) **6-10-2**(7) CMcCormack (prom: 3rd whn fell 8th)		F	50/1	—	—
				(SP 114.1%)	**8 Rn**	

4m 5.9 (14.90) CSF £76.25 TOTE £5.20: £1.10 £2.70 £1.60 (£98.90) Trio £132.40; £85.82 to Thirsk 16/5/97 OWNER Mrs A. Kane (MIDDLEHAM) BRED Paddy Byrne
OFFICIAL EXPLANATION **Rallegio: was unsuited by the ground.**
3092 Know-No-No (IRE) came back looking superb after three months off and won this particularly well, suggesting that further success is likely. (9/2)
4334 Kincardine Bridge (USA) ran his best race to date but he was very tired after a particularly bad blunder three out. (25/1)
4151 All Clear (IRE) is running better over fences than he did over hurdles this season but there is still a lot more needed. (9/1: op 6/1)
4214 Rallegio had a hard race last time and that seems to have knocked the edge off him for the time being as he was never going here. (4/7)
4502 Sunkala Shine (12/1: 8/1-14/1)
Akito Racing (IRE), having her first run over fences, was running a lot better when she got it all wrong at the fifth last and came down. (50/1)

4575 MACDONALDS SOLICITORS QUICK RANSOM NOVICES' HURDLE (4-Y.O+) (Class E)
2-25 (2-27) **3m 110y (12 hdls)** £2,276.00 (£636.00: £308.00) GOING: 0.38 sec per fur (GS)

Form	Horse / Details	Dist	Pos	SP	RR	SF
3531[6]	**Military Academy (110)** (GRichards) **8-11-12** PCarberry (lw: uns rdr & bolted one circuit bef s: trckd ldrs gng wl: led 8th: easily)	—	1	5/4[1]	72+	8
4243*	**Pentlands Flyer (IRE)** (HowardJohnson) **6-11-6** NWilliamson (hld up: chsd wnr fr 4 out: mstke 3 out: no imp)	3½	2	5/4[1]	64	—
4248[14]	**Blooming Spring (IRE) (71)** (MrsDThomson) **8-11-1** LO'Hara (lw: in tch: effrt 4 out: styd on one pce)	12	3	16/1	51	—
4309[13]	**Jigginstown (73)** (JJO'Neill) **10-10-7**(7) LCooper (chsd ldrs: rdn appr 3 out: one pce)	2½	4	10/1[2]	48	—
4481[P]	**Strongalong (IRE)** (PCheesbrough) **7-11-0** ASSmith (chsd ldrs: effrt 4 out: wknd appr 2 out)	½	5	11/1[3]	48	—
4205[6]	**Scally Beau** (LLungo) **6-11-0** RSupple (a bhd: t.o whn blnd last)	dist	6	25/1	—	—
4152[7]	**Ottadini (IRE) (54)** (WGReed) **5-10-9** TReed (lw: led tl hdd & blnd 8th: sn t.o: p.u bef 2 out)		P	33/1	—	—
4243[P]	**Guile Point** (DALamb) **6-10-9** JBurke (chsd ldrs tl blnd & wknd 8th: p.u bef next)		P	40/1	—	—
				(SP 121.4%)	**8 Rn**	

6m 17.5 (31.50) CSF £2.87 TOTE £2.50: £1.10 £1.10 £1.60 (£1.80) Trio £8.90 OWNER Mr Robert Ogden (PENRITH) BRED P. M. Prior-Wandesforde
3531 Military Academy, whose exertions before the race did not bother him at all, was given a typical Carberry ride and hardly knew he had been in a race. (5/4: op 4/6)
4243* Pentlands Flyer (IRE) took his customary strong hold and, in the end, either did not stay or was completely outclassed. (5/4: op 9/4)
4147 Blooming Spring (IRE) looks magnificent just now and ran quite well considering the company. (16/1)
3807 Jigginstown again looked very one-paced once the tempo increased three out. (10/1: 8/1-12/1)
3715 Strongalong (IRE), having a confidence booster after pulling up over fences last time, ran reasonably. (11/1)

4576 RHONE-POULENC SEED PROTECTION H'CAP CHASE (0-110) (5-Y.O+) (Class E)
3-00 (3-00) **3m (18 fncs)** £3,590.50 (£1,084.00: £527.00: £248.50) GOING: 0.38 sec per fur (GS)

Form	Horse / Details	Dist	Pos	SP	RR	SF
1833*	**East Houston (101)** (JJO'Neill) **8-11-5**(5) RMcGrath (trckd ldrs: hmpd after 4 out: led 2 out: shkn up and r.o flat)	—	1	7/1	115	33
4338[3]	**Rusty Blade (80)** (PMonteith) **8-10-3** GCahill (lw: in tch: drvn along fr ½-wy: styd on u.p fr 4 out: nt pce to chal)	2	2	10/1	93	11
4336*	**Nijway (87)** (MABarnes) **7-10-10** BStorey (lw: disp ld tl led 13th: hdd 2 out: one pce)	2½	3	9/4[1]	98	16
4503[6]	**Bright Destiny (77)** (JSGoldie) **6-9-7**(7) MrOMcPhail (prom: hit 13th & sn outpcd: styd on wl fr 3 out)	½	4	10/1	88	6
3643[3]	**Gold Pigeon (IRE) (77)** (BSRothwell) **8-10-0** RSupple (disp ld 4th to 13th: ev ch tl wknd 2 out)	5	5	11/2[3]	84	2
4245[P]	**Kalajo (95)** (BMactaggart) **7-11-4** GLee (hld up: hdwy 12th: sn chsng ldrs: wknd 2 out: eased & virtually p.u flat)	dist	6	9/2[2]	—	—
4447[4]	**Majority Major (IRE) (80)** (PCheesbrough) **8-10-3** ASSmith (mde most to 13th: sn rdn & wknd)	s.h	7	9/1	—	—
4057[P]	**Its a Deal (77)** (SGChadwick) **11-10-0** FPerratt (disp ld to 5th: sn lost pl: t.o whn p.u bef 13th)		P	33/1	—	—
				(SP 108.0%)	**8 Rn**	

6m 20.3 (22.30) CSF £57.21 CT £164.80 TOTE £8.50: £2.10 £1.70 £1.10 (£25.50) Trio £25.90 OWNER Highgreen Partnership (PENRITH) BRED J. R. Mitchell
LONG HANDICAP Bright Destiny 9-4 Its a Deal 8-11
1833* East Houston, returning after five months off, was confidently ridden and did the business nicely but he is never one to trust fully. (7/1: 4/1-8/1)
4338 Rusty Blade is really coming to hand just now but is certainly a hard ride although, to his credit, he does keep responding. (10/1: 8/1-12/1)

4336* Nijway is an honest sort who generally gives his best but, on this occasion he was tapped for toe from the second last. (9/4)
3975 Bright Destiny was rather warm beforehand as he often is, but this was still not a bad effort from 10lb out of the handicap. (10/1: 6/1-11/1)
3643 Gold Pigeon (IRE), after two months off, ran a fair race until running out of steam two out. (11/2)
3715* Kalajo has lost his dash for the time being and was eased considerably once beaten. (9/2: op 3/1)
4447 Majority Major (IRE) (9/1: 5/1-10/1)

4577 BELL & SIME H'CAP HURDLE (0-120) (4-Y.O+) (Class D)
3-30 (3-31) **2m 4f 110y (10 hdls)** £2,818.75 (£850.00: £412.50: £193.75) GOING: 0.38 sec per fur (GS)

				SP	RR	SF
4261[4]	**Linlathen (111)** (MrsMReveley) **7-12-0** PNiven (mde all: qcknd 6th: hung lft fr 2 out: kpt on u.p)	—	**1**	5/4[1]	95	22
4456[3]	**Chill Wind (83)** (NBycroft) **8-10-0** RSupple (a.p: rdn 3 out: ev ch 2 out: sltly hmpd & swtchd appr last: no ex)	4	**2**	11/1	64	—
3827[2]	**Duke of Perth (95)** (HowardJohnson) **6-10-12** NWilliamson (trckd wnr: hit 4 out: outpcd appr 2 out: no imp after)	4	**3**	11/4[3]	73	—
4573[2]	**Pariah (IRE) (93)** (MartinTodhunter) **8-10-10** RDunwoody (hld up: effrt appr 2 out: sn rdn & btn)	13	**4**	9/4[2]	61	—
				(SP 110.2%)		**4 Rn**

5m 10.6 (22.60) CSF £10.42 TOTE £1.70: (£9.90) OWNER Mrs J. A. Niven (SALTBURN) BRED Mrs J. A. Niven
4261 Linlathen was happy to dictate things here and, despite tending to hang left when ridden, he was always doing just enough. (5/4)
4456 Chill Wind, back to hurdling for a change, ran really well, responding to pressure in game style, but was second best when the winner gave him problems by hanging into him. (11/1: op 7/1)
3827 Duke of Perth had his chances, but when it came down to a battle from the third last, his limitations were there for all to see. (11/4)
4573 Pariah (IRE) had a hard race the previous night and this iffy character was not going to get involved in a struggle again. (9/4)

4578 REEVES & NEYLAN NOVICES' H'CAP HURDLE (0-105) (4-Y.O+) (Class E)
4-00 (4-00) **2m 110y (8 hdls)** £2,710.00 (£760.00: £370.00) GOING: 0.38 sec per fur (GS)

				SP	RR	SF
4482*	**Teejay'n'aitch (IRE) (92)** (JSGoldie) **5-11-5**(5) 7x STaylor (mde all: blnd 4th: kpt on wl fr 2 out)	—	**1**	11/4[2]	74	17
4205[5]	**Hopeful Lord (IRE) (78)** (PCheesbrough) **5-10-10** ASSmith (hld up: effrt appr 2 out: styd on: nvr able to chal)	1¼	**2**	8/1	59	2
4409[2]	**Charlistiona (77)** (JPDodds) **6-10-2**(7) SMelrose (lw: drvn along & hdwy 4th: sn chsng ldrs: outpcd appr 2 out: kpt on wl flat)	hd	**3**	7/2	58	1
4244*	**Tawafij (USA) (92)** (MDHammond) **8-11-10** RGarritty (lw: hld up: effrt 3 out: disp 2nd whn rdn last: wknd flat)	6	**4**	3/1[3]	67	10
4285[9]	**Six Clerks (IRE) (90)** (JGFitzGerald) **4-11-3b** PCarberry (trckd ldrs: qcknd to disp ld after 3 out: rdn next: fnd nil)	15	**5**	5/2[1]	50	—
4243[P]	**Prince Baltasar (68)** (NBycroft) **8-10-0** RSupple (cl up: rdn fr 5th: wknd after 3 out)	14	**6**	50/1	15	—
				(SP 115.5%)		**6 Rn**

4m 4.2 (18.20) CSF £21.83 TOTE £2.80: £1.10 £4.30 (£13.30) OWNER Mr Andrew Paterson (GLASGOW) BRED David Hyland
LONG HANDICAP Prince Baltasar 8-12
WEIGHT FOR AGE 4yo-5lb
4482* Teejay'n'aitch (IRE) is incredible now he has found his form and won this with a bit in hand. (11/4)
4205 Hopeful Lord (IRE) is certainly improving and this was the first time he has been asked a serious question. It should have taught him plenty. (8/1: 6/1-9/1)
4409 Charlistiona again ran well and left a distinct impression that, over further, there is better to come. (7/2)
4244* Tawafij (USA) looked particularly well but when it came down to a struggle, his lack of stamina was well exposed. (3/1)
4285 Six Clerks (IRE) had the blinkers on for the first time and travelled well but, once an effort was required, he quickly showed his true colours and would have none of it. (5/2)

4579 LINLITHGOW & STIRLINGSHIRE HUNT NOVICES' HUNTERS' CHASE (5-Y.O+) (Class H)
4-30 (4-30) **2m 4f 110y (15 fncs)** £1,839.00 (£552.00: £266.00: £123.00) GOING: 0.38 sec per fur (GS)

				SP	RR	SF
4469[2]	**Savoy** (GRichards) **10-11-7**(7) CaptAOgden (a.p: effrt 3 out: r.o wl flat to ld cl home)	—	**1**	11/8[1]	112	46
4256[2]	**Howayman** (KAnderson) **7-11-12**(7) MrAParker (chsd ldrs: led 9th to 11th: led 3 out: hdd & no ex towards fin)	nk	**2**	2/1[2]	117	51
4256[8]	**Master Kit (IRE)** (JNRBillinge) **8-11-12**(7) MrJBillinge (chsd ldrs tl wknd fr 3 out)	18	**3**	8/1	103	37
4411[3]	**Will Travel (IRE)** (AndrewDickman) **8-11-7**(7) MrARobson (t: led to 8th: wknd 11th: sn t.o)	21	**4**	14/1	81	15
	Reed (MrsLyalProvan) **12-11-7**(7) MrOMcPhail (chsd ldrs: led 8th to 9th: led 11th to 3 out: 4th & btn whn blnd 2 out)	3	**5**	50/1	79	13
	Harden Glen (CStorey) **6-11-7**(7) MissSLaidlaw (mstkes: lost tch 11th: sn t.o)	dist	**6**	25/1	—	—
	King Spring (MissCEJDawson) **12-11-9**(5) MrsVJackson (s.s: t.o tl p.u bef 4 out)		**P**	33/1	—	—
4256[F]	**Denim Blue** (MissPaulineRobson) **8-12-3**(5) MissPRobson (lw: hmpd s: sddle slipped & p.u 1st)		**P**	15/2[3]	—	—
				(SP 113.7%)		**8 Rn**

5m 15.1 (16.10) CSF £4.10 TOTE £1.80: £1.70 £1.10 £1.30 (£1.80) OWNER Mr Robert Ogden (PENRITH) BRED Mrs Frank Warren
STEWARDS' ENQUIRY Parker susp. 24 & 26-28/5/97 (excessive use of whip).
4469 Savoy, given a really good ride despite his rider dropping his whip at the last, was produced with a good run to settle it late on. (11/8)
4256 Howayman is a grand, consistent sort, and tried his heart out here, but was just done for toe in the last few strides. (2/1)
3095 Master Kit (IRE) ran his best race of the season and may at last be getting his act together after his dreadful fall at Musselburgh first time out. (8/1)

4580 PERTH MAIDEN N.H. FLAT RACE (4, 5 & 6-Y.O) (Class H)
5-00 (5-00) **2m 110y** £1,020.00 (£270.00: £120.00)

				SP	RR	SF
	Queensway (IRE) (JGFitzGerald) **5-11-7**(3) FLeahy (hld up: stdy hdwy ½-wy: led over 1f out: rdn & r.o wl)	—	**1**	7/1[3]	71 f	—
	Young Tomo (IRE) (HowardJohnson) **5-11-3**(7) MrOMcPhail (trckd ldrs: led 3f out tl appr fnl f: kpt on same pce)	6	**2**	20/1	65 f	—
4150[4]	**Old Bombay (IRE)** (TDBarron) **5-11-3**(7) CMcCormack (led tl hdd 3f out: no ex)	9	**3**	4/1[2]	57 f	—
3548[9]	**Noble Tom (IRE)** (RCollins) **5-11-5**(5) STaylor (lw: chsd ldrs after 6f: rdn 4f out: r.o one pce)	10	**4**	14/1	47 f	—
	Wotstheproblem (MrsMReveley) **5-11-10** GLee (in tch tl wl outpcd 6f out: styd on fnl 3f)	1½	**5**	9/4[1]	45 f	—
3914[6]	**Ben Doula** (MrsMReveley) **5-11-3**(7) MHerrington (chsd ldrs: outpcd 5f out: no imp after)	5	**6**	10/1	41 f	—
	Innovate (IRE) (MissLucindaRussell) **5-11-2**(3) PMidgley (bit bkwd: prom tl outpcd fnl 4f)	nk	**7**	25/1	35 f	—
	Rising Dawn (IRE) (MrsASwinbank) **5-11-10** MrChrisWilson (bkwd: hld up: sme hdwy ½-wy: wknd fnl 4f)	8	**8**	14/1	32 f	—

	Horse / details	Dist	Pos	SP	RR	SF
4288[9]	**Hansel's Streak** (TAKCuthbert) **5-11-3**(7) SMelrose (bhd: rdn 10f out: n.d)	12	**9**	50/1	21 f	—
3487[11]	**Chan Move** (WJSmith) **5-11-3b**(7) MrTJBarry (bhd: effrt ½-wy: sn btn)	1¾	**10**	50/1	19 f	—
6797	**Paperwork Pete (IRE)** (WStorey) **5-11-5**(5) RMcGrath (drvn along ½-wy: sn bhd: t.o)	20	**11**	8/1	—	—
	She's All Heart (CParker) **4-11-0** MrAParker (a bhd: t.o)	10	**12**	14/1	—	—
	Yeenoso (IRE) (MrsDThomson) **5-11-5** DThomas (chsd ldrs to ½-wy: sn wknd: t.o)	2	**13**	33/1	—	—
	The Keek (IRE) (HowardJohnson) **5-11-2**(3) GFRyan (plld hrd: jnd ldr after 4f: wknd qckly ½-wy: sn wl t.o)	dist	**14**	14/1	—	—

(SP 125.6%) **14 Rn**

3m 57.6 CSF £136.53 TOTE £5.60: £2.80 £5.30 £2.00 (£108.90) Trio £121.10; £71.69 to Thirsk 16/5/97 OWNER Mr J. G. FitzGerald (MALTON) BRED Dermot and Meta Cantillon
WEIGHT FOR AGE 4yo-5lb

Queensway (IRE) looks a useful type at this game and, given a patient ride, won authoritatively. Over hurdles, he should really make his mark. (7/1)
Young Tomo (IRE) has a good engine and really travels but just found the winner too strong in the closing stages. (20/1)
4150 Old Bombay (IRE) stayed well and was made plenty of use of, but is short of a change of gear. (4/1: tchd 6/1)
2675 Noble Tom (IRE) seems to have trouble in getting home at this trip but should be alright when trying the minimum distance over hurdles. (14/1)
Wotstheproblem looks a dour stayer and will certainly need a test of stamina when he goes hurdling. (9/4)
3914 Ben Doula (10/1: op 6/1)
The Keek (IRE) (14/1: op 8/1)

T/Plpt: £38.80 (266.07 Tckts). T/Qdpt: £11.70 (66.34 Tckts) AA

4581a - 4606a (Irish Racing) - See Computer Raceform

4074-AINTREE (L-H) (Good, Good to firm patches)
Friday May 16th
WEATHER: Cloudy

4607 AINTREE NOVICES' HUNTERS' CHASE (5-Y.O+) (Class H)
5-45 (5-45) **3m 1f (Mildmay) (19 fncs)** £1,738.75 (£526.00: £256.50: £121.75) GOING minus 0.03 sec per fur (G)

	Horse / details	Dist	Pos	SP	RR	SF
4471*	**Front Cover** (SPike) **7-11-7**(7) MissSVickery (lw: chsd ldr fr 7th: led 14th: reminders: clr fr 4 out: unchal)	—	**1**	4/9 1	103+	28
3680[2]	**The Rum Mariner** (MrsJASkelton) **10-11-7**(7) MrDSJones (j.rt: led: mstke 12th: hdd 14th: grad wknd)	dist	**2**	7/2 2	—	—
4530[4]	**Very Daring** (JulianHunt) **7-11-7**(7) MissSSharratt (lost tch 5th: sn t.o)	dist	**3**	33/1	—	—
	San Remo (MrsDCSamworth) **10-11-7b[1]**(7) MissSSamworth (lw: bhd fr 8th: t.o)	3	**4**	25/1	—	—
4449[F]	**Ship the Builder** (PeterMaddison) **8-11-7**(7) MrTWhitaker (lw: wl bhd tl sme hdwy 12th: poor 3rd whn blnd & uns rdr next)		**U**	20/1	—	—
3913[P]	**Frozen Stiff (IRE)** (AJBrown) **9-11-7b[1]**(7) MrTJBarry (blnd 1st: in rr whn blnd & uns rdr 4th)		**U**	9/1 3	—	—

(SP 113.0%) **6 Rn**

6m 33.3 (16.30) CSF £2.28 TOTE £1.60: £1.20 £1.70 (£2.00) OWNER Mr Stewart Pike (SIDMOUTH) BRED S. Pike
4471* Front Cover followed up her success at Uttoxeter nine days ago with another effortless win, and she will begin to think this game is easy. (4/9)
3680 The Rum Mariner was the only one able to make the winner know she had been in a race, but he jumps to the right, and continually loses ground this way round, and he had met his match at the end of the back straight. (7/2)

4608 AUGHTON NOVICES' HURDLE (4-Y.O+) (Class D)
6-15 (6-15) **2m 4f (Mildmay) (11 hdls)** £2,788.00 (£844.00: £412.00: £196.00) GOING minus 0.03 sec per fur (G)

	Horse / details	Dist	Pos	SP	RR	SF
4010[5]	**Nigel's Lad (IRE)** (PCHaslam) **5-11-12** MFoster (lw: mde all: drew clr fr 3 out: canter)	—	**1**	8/15 1	90?	—
4315[2]	**Samanid (IRE) (110)** (MissLCSiddall) **5-11-12** RDunwoody (lw: hld up: hdwy to chse wnr 7th: reminder next: no imp & eased fr 3 out)	dist	**2**	4/1 2	—	—
4169[4]	**Give And Take (103)** (MCPipe) **4-11-0b[1]** APMcCoy (nt j.w: w wnr rdn 4th: wknd 8th: t.o)	14	**3**	9/2 3	—	—
4479[U]	**Tweedswood (IRE) (90)** (PBeaumont) **7-11-0** RSupple (chsd ldrs: j.slowly 3rd: drvn along 5th: t.o fr 7th)	13	**4**	33/1	—	—
3887[P]	**Tremendisto (91)** (DMcCain) **7-11-6** TJenks (lw: a bhd: t.o fr ½-wy)	dist	**5**	20/1	—	—

(SP 111.1%) **5 Rn**

5m 1.6 (19.60) CSF £2.96 TOTE £1.70: £1.80 £1.10 (£1.90) OWNER Mr N. C. Dunnington (MIDDLEHAM) BRED Nikita Investments
WEIGHT FOR AGE 4yo-6lb
4010 Nigel's Lad (IRE) never needed to come off the bridle to win this egg-and-spoon contest, and he has done really well since his attentions were switched to hurdling. (8/15: op 4/5)
4315 Samanid (IRE) could have been fancied to make a race of it judging on his most recent effort, but the winner was always going much too well for him, and he gave up the fight from the turn for home. (4/1)

4609 CEDRIC CROSTON H'CAP CHASE (0-125) (5-Y.O+) (Class D)
6-45 (6-45) **3m 1f (Mildmay) (19 fncs)** £3,639.00 (£1,101.00: £537.00: £255.00) GOING minus 0.03 sec per fur (G)

	Horse / details	Dist	Pos	SP	RR	SF
4463*	**Doualago (FR) (125)** (MCPipe) **7-12-0b** 6x APMcCoy (chsd ldr fr 4th: rdn after 11th: pckd 12th: swtchd lft appr 2 out: styd on to ld flat: all out)	—	**1**	9/4 1	132	47
2821[3]	**Bas de Laine (FR) (124)** (MDHammond) **11-11-13v** RGarritty (bkwd: j.w: led: rdn 2 out: hdd flat)	1¼	**2**	3/1 3	130	45
4448[2]	**Peruvian Gale (IRE) (97)** (MrsSJSmith) **8-9-11**(3) GFRyan (hld up: blnd 3rd: hdwy to go 3rd at 11th: wknd 15th)	27	**3**	7/1	86	1
4247[3]	**Seod Rioga (IRE) (115)** (SMellor) **8-10-13**(5) ChrisWebb (lw: hld up & bhd: blnd 8th: hdwy 12th: wknd 14th: t.o)	26	**4**	11/4 2	87	2
4503[4]	**Temple Garth (102)** (PBeaumont) **8-10-5** RSupple (prom tl outpcd 8th: rdn 11th: t.o: p.u bef 4 out)		**P**	8/1	—	—

(SP 106.0%) **5 Rn**

6m 26.4 (9.40) CSF £7.96 TOTE £2.70: £1.30 £1.40 (£3.30) OWNER Martin Pipe Racing Club (WELLINGTON) BRED Monsieur et Madame Bernard le Douarin
LONG HANDICAP Peruvian Gale (IRE) 9-8

4463* Doualago (FR), denied his front-running role, had to work very hard indeed to win this, and it was only his proven stamina, and race-fitness, that enabled him to do so in the end. (9/4)
2821 Bas de Laine (FR) always performs best when fresh and, giving a bold display of jumping, would have won this very much as he pleased, had he not blown up at the second last. There is still time for him to make amends. (3/1)

4610 WEATHERBYS INSURANCE SERVICES H'CAP HURDLE (0-135) (4-Y.O+) (Class C)

7-20 (7-22) **2m 110y (Mildmay) (9 hdls)** £3,801.60 (£1,067.60: £520.80) GOING minus 0.03 sec per fur (G)

				SP	RR	SF
4386*	**Yubralee (USA) (122)** (MCPipe) **5-11-1** APMcCoy (set str pace: mde all: drew wl clr appr 3 out: eased flat)	—	1	8/13 1	103+	11
4271 4	**Dancing Paddy (135)** (KOCunningham-Brown) **9-12-0** RDunwoody (chsd wnr to 6th: sn rdn: regained 2nd pl 3 out: no ch w wnr)	20	2	100/30 2	97	5
4357a 10	**Cheryl's Lad (IRE) (132)** (DNicholson) **7-11-8**(3) MrRThornton (hld up: hdwy whn hit 4th: rdn after 6th: no imp)	16	3	9/1	78?	—
4397 6	**Tragic Hero (132)** (MCPipe) **5-11-11b** GBradley (lw: hld up: chsd wnr fr 6th: wkng whn fell 3 out)		F	11/2 3	—	—
				(SP 110.4%)		**4 Rn**

4m 5.4 (11.40) CSF £2.97 TOTE £1.60 (£2.00) OWNER Mr D. A. Johnson (WELLINGTON) BRED Gainsborough Farm Inc
4386* Yubralee (USA) completed his hat-trick with another catch-me-if-you-can performance, and he won so easily that he had been pulled up to a walk passing the post. (8/13)
4271 Dancing Paddy, always being taken along faster than he wished, could never get within striking range of the winner, and it is possible he would benefit from easier ground. (100/30)
4357a Cheryl's Lad (IRE) (9/1: 6/1-10/1)

4611 LIVERPOOL ECHO 'WOMAN EXTRA' NOVICES' CHASE (5-Y.O+) (Class E)

7-50 (7-50) **2m 4f (Mildmay) (16 fncs)** £2,951.10 (£892.80: £435.40: £206.70) GOING minus 0.03 sec per fur (G)

				SP	RR	SF
2619 3	**Mythical Approach (IRE)** (DNicholson) **7-10-11**(3) MrRThornton (swtg: bit bkwd: j.w: hld up gng wl: led 2 out: sn clr: readily)	—	1	6/4 1	90+	22
4402 2	**Eid (USA)** (MrsSJSmith) **8-11-0** RichardGuest (j.rt: led after 4th to 4 out: led next: hdd & hit 2 out: sn btn)	12	2	9/4 2	80	12
4338 5	**Sovereigns Match** (BMactaggart) **9-11-0** BStorey (lw: led tl after 4th: slt ld 4 out: hdd next: sn wknd)	17	3	8/1	67	—
4481 5	**Quixall Crossett (56)** (EMCaine) **12-10-7**(7) MrTJBarry (mstke 2nd: hdwy 7th: wknd appr 3 out)	2½	4	66/1	65	—
4235 6	**Nadjati (USA) (97)** (DRGandolfo) **8-11-6b** RDunwoody (lw: hld up: mstke 9th: rdn 12th: effrt 3 out: j.slowly next: sn btn)	3	5	4/1 3	68	—
4300 4	**Cheeka (83)** (CSmith) **8-11-0** MRanger (lost pl 7th: rallied 11th: wknd after next: bhd whn p.u bef 2 out)		P	10/1	—	—
				(SP 112.5%)		**6 Rn**

5m 8.7 (10.70) CSF £5.03 TOTE £3.10: £2.00 £1.30 (£3.10) OWNER Lady Harris (TEMPLE GUITING) BRED N. J. Connors
2619 Mythical Approach (IRE), a winner between the flags in Ireland, but making his debut over regulation fences, turned in a very impressive display to score with the minimum of fuss, and he certainly looks a very useful addition to the ranks. (6/4)
4402 Eid (USA) has a tendency to drift right at his fences, but he races very keenly, and certainly gave a good account of himself against a rival who looks set to go a long way. (9/4)
4338 Sovereigns Match, the paddock pick, has been competing over longer trips, and though he was in and out of the lead until approaching the third last, the quickening tempo soon found him out. (8/1: op 12/1)

4612 SUNDAY BEST COUTURE H'CAP CHASE (0-125) (5-Y.O+) (Class D)

8-20 (8-20) **2m (Mildmay) (12 fncs)** £5,445.00 (£1,335.00) GOING minus 0.03 sec per fur (G)

				SP	RR	SF
4377*	**Pond House (IRE) (102)** (MCPipe) **8-10-12** APMcCoy (lw: mde all: wl clr fr 7th: blnd last)	—	1	11/10 2	112	37
4258 2	**Storm Falcon (USA) (114)** (SMellor) **7-11-5**(5) ChrisWebb (lw: blnd 2nd: lost tch 7th: t.o)	dist	2	4/5 1	—	—
				(SP 103.2%)		**2 Rn**

4m 2.8 (4.80) TOTE £1.70 OWNER Mr C. R. Fleet (WELLINGTON) BRED S. Banville
4377* Pond House (IRE) completed a rewarding night for his trainer and jockey with a very easily-gained victory, and his only semblance of a mistake was when his concentration lapsed at the last. (11/10: tchd evens)
4258 Storm Falcon (USA) recovered his confidence after a very bad mistake at the second, but the winner was always going a gear too fast, and he realised he was fighting a lost cause soon after halfway. (4/5)

4613 CAROL TOWNER SPIRIT OF MERSEYSIDE 'N.H.' NOVICES' HURDLE (4-Y.O+) (Class D)

8-50 (8-50) **2m 110y (Mildmay) (9 hdls)** £3,012.00 (£852.00: £416.00) GOING minus 0.03 sec per fur (G)

				SP	RR	SF
4216 2	**Go Native (IRE)** (MrsSJSmith) **5-11-0** RichardGuest (lw: chsd ldr fr 4th: hit 2 out: led flat & r.o wl)	—	1	11/10 2	72+	—
4459*	**Mrs Em (100)** (PFNicholls) **5-11-6**(7) LCummins (lw: led tl flat: sn rdn: nt pce of wnr)	3	2	4/5 1	82	2
4450 6	**Blaster Watson** (CSmith) **6-11-0** MRanger (bit bkwd: plld hrd: rn wd paddock bend after 3rd: outpcd 6th: sn t.o)	18	3	20/1 3	52?	—
				(SP 107.9%)		**3 Rn**

4m 9.6 (15.60) CSF £2.22 TOTE £2.10 (£1.10) OWNER Mr Trevor Hemmings (BINGLEY) BRED Bobby Donworth and Honora Corridan
4216 Go Native (IRE) made the odd novicey mistake on this hurdling debut, mainly when putting in his bid at the penultimate flight, but he has got a bit of class about him, and he proved the stronger in a duel to the line. A longer trip will suit him better at this game. (11/10)
4459* Mrs Em has been on a roll, but the concession of weight to one who looks decidedly useful was just not on. She gave as good as she got on the run-in, and there is plenty more success to come. (4/5: op 2/5)

T/Plpt: £7.40 (1,221.33 Tckts). T/Qdpt: £5.50 (74.92 Tckts) IM

3670-FOLKESTONE (R-H) (Good)
Friday May 16th
One fence omitted race 3, one fence omitted three times race 4.
WEATHER: Fine

4614 NIGEL COLLISON FUELS NOVICES' HUNTERS' CHASE (5-Y.O+) (Class H)
5-50 (5-51) **3m 2f (19 fncs)** £1,990.00 (£595.00: £285.00: £130.00) GOING minus 0.05 sec per fur (G)

	Horse / details	Dist	Pos	SP	RR	SF
3568[2]	**Mister Main Man (IRE)** (CSporborg) **9-12-0**(7) MrSSporborg (lw: led: mstke 15th: hdd 3 out: led 2 out: drvn out)	—	1	13/8 1	95	28
4308[P]	**No Joker (IRE)** (NAGaselee) **9-12-0**(7) MrPScott (a.p: led 3 out: hdd 2 out: mstke last: rallied flat: r.o)	½	2	7/1	95	28
	Polar Ana (IRE) (MrsGMGladders) **8-11-9**(7) MissSGladders (prom: ev ch 3 out: wknd appr next)	13	3	9/2 2	82	15
	Kates Castle (RParker) **10-11-9**(7) MrJVanPraagh (lw: prom: mstke 3 out: sn wknd)	14	4	13/2 3	73	6
3208[7]	**Centre Stage** (MrsSWarr) **11-12-0**(7) MrAWarr (bhd fr 5th: t.o)	dist	5	40/1	—	—
4319[4]	**Ballyallia Castle (IRE)** (MrsJulieRead) **8-12-0**(7) MrNBloom (5th & in tch whn fell 7th)		F	9/2 2	—	—
	Rustic Ramble (MrsDMGrissell) **11-12-4**(3) MrPHacking (bhd fr 6th: t.o whn p.u bef 13th)		P	9/1	—	—
	Linger Balinda (MrsSHaydon) **11-11-9b**1(7) MrPBull (chsd ldrs: wknd 12th: t.o whn p.u bef 3 out)		P	50/1	—	—
	Bright Hour (MissJaneGoddard) **12-12-0**(7) MissJGrant (bhd fr 10th: t.o whn p.u bef 3 out)		P	66/1	—	—
	Serious Money (USA) (MrsAngusCampbell) **12-12-0**(7) MissCSavell (j.bdly: a wl bhd: ref 13th)		R	100/1	—	—

(SP 117.2%) **10 Rn**

6m 38.5 (18.50) CSF £12.70 TOTE £2.70: £1.40 £1.70 £1.40 (£7.40) Trio £8.60 OWNER Sir Chippendale Keswick (WARE) BRED M. Curran
3568 Mister Main Man (IRE) jumped well apart from a mistake five out and saw it out well. (13/8)
3837 No Joker (IRE) must have gone close had he jumped the last fluently. (7/1: op 4/1)
Polar Ana (IRE) ran well until tiring on the home turn. (9/2)
Kates Castle (13/2: op 4/1)

4615 KENT AND SURREY BLOODHOUNDS CHALLENGE CUP MAIDEN HUNTERS' CHASE (5-Y.O+) (Class H)
6-25 (6-25) **2m 5f (15 fncs)** £1,600.00 (£475.00: £225.00: £100.00) GOING minus 0.05 sec per fur (G)

	Horse / details	Dist	Pos	SP	RR	SF
	Storming Lady (MJRoberts) **7-11-13**(3) MrPHacking (lw: a.p: led after 11th: clr after 3 out: easliy)	—	1	2/1 2	94++	58
	Wednesdays Auction (IRE) (MrsMRigg) **9-12-2**(5) MrTMcCarthy (wl bhd tl styd on appr 2 out: wnt mod 2nd flat)	dist	2	50/1	—	—
	Barn Elms (MrsSJHickman) **10-12-0**(7) MrAHickman (prom: wknd after 3 out: lft 2nd 2 out: fin tired)	7	3	20/1	—	—
	Supreme Dealer (MrsSWarr) **12-12-0**(7) MrAWarr (chsd ldr to 7th: wkng whn mstke 9th: sn lost tch)	14	4	20/1	—	—
581[P]	**Mr Oriental** (GiuseppeGigantesco) **7-12-0**(7) MrGGigantesco (a bhd: mstke 2nd: fell 9th)		F	100/1	—	—
4319[2]	**Mister Spectator (IRE)** (MrsAHickman) **8-12-4**(3) MrSimonAndrews (nvr gng wl: blnd 6th: p.u bef next: fin lame)		P	4/5 1	—	—
	Roscolvin (IRE) (MrsJulieRead) **5-11-7**(7) MrPBull (bhd: brief effrt 8th: t.o whn p.u bef 2 out)		P	12/1	—	—
	Kumada (SHMarriage) **10-12-0**(7) MissSGritton (sn bhd: t.o whn p.u after 3 out)		P	25/1	—	—
4317[2]	**Cool Bandit (IRE)** (MrsDMGrissell) **7-12-0**(7) MrTHills (led: clr to 8th: hdd after 11th: 2nd & btn whn blnd & uns rdr 2 out)		U	8/1 3	—	—
	Your Opinion (MarkWalters) **11-12-0**(7) MrMWalters (cl 4th whn blnd & uns rdr 10th)		U	50/1	—	—

(SP 126.0%) **10 Rn**

5m 12.4 (4.40) CSF £92.10 TOTE £3.80: £1.10 £9.70 £2.50 (£52.10) Trio £78.30 OWNER Mr Mike Roberts (HAILSHAM) BRED F. J. Haggas
WEIGHT FOR AGE 5yo-7lb
Storming Lady was the night's most impressive winner and recorded a good time here, jumping really well and putting up an impressive performance. She looks a most promising young hunter. (2/1)
Wednesdays Auction (IRE) was miles behind until staying on late. (50/1)
Barn Elms finished very tired indeed. (20/1)
4319 Mister Spectator (IRE) was never going or jumping and was later found to be lame. (4/5)
Roscolvin (IRE) (12/1: 7/1-14/1)

4616 IBS APPEAL OPEN HUNTERS' CHASE (5-Y.O+) (Class H)
6-55 (6-58) **3m 2f (18 fncs)** £1,900.00 (£525.00: £250.00) GOING minus 0.05 sec per fur (G)

	Horse / details	Dist	Pos	SP	RR	SF
	Viridian (DGDuggan) **12-12-4**(3) MrMRimell (chsd ldr 11th: chal & gng best whn lft clr 2 out: eased flat)	—	1	6/4 1	108+	29
4511[3]	**Faringo** (MrsDMGrissell) **12-12-0b**1(7) MissCGrissell (led: hdd 5th: wknd 13th: lft poor 2nd 2 out)	19	2	40/1	96	17
4323[P]	**Teatrader** (MissTOBlazey) **11-11-8**(7)ow1 MissTBlazey (bhd fr 3rd: slightly hmpd 7th: lft poor 3rd 2 out)	7	3	14/1	86	6
4280[2]	**Cape Cottage** (DJCaro) **13-12-7**(7) MrAPhillips (in tch whn b.d 7th)		B	5/1 3	—	—
3664[F]	**Foxbow (IRE)** (JMTurner) **7-11-9b**1(5) MrASansome (led 5th: strly pressed whn fell 2 out)		F	11/1	—	—
4319[6]	**Grassington (IRE)** (ScottQuirk) **8-11-7v**1(7) MrScottQuirk (4th whn fell 7th: dead)		F	50/1	—	—
3551[4]	**Cardinal Richelieu** (CSporborg) **10-11-7**(7) MrSSporborg (dwlt: a bhd: p.u bef 12th: dismntd)		P	7/4 2	—	—

(SP 112.4%) **7 Rn**

6m 38.0 (18.00) CSF £36.77 TOTE £2.60: £2.00 £6.40 (£28.40) OWNER Mr Denis Hine (REDMARLEY) BRED Patrick Moore
Viridian was left clear two out but looked the winner anyway. (6/4)
Faringo dropped away on the final circuit and was lucky to be left in second place. (40/1)
3469 Teatrader had no chance through the final two miles. (14/1: 10/1-16/1)
Foxbow (IRE) made much of the running and still had every chance, but looked to be getting the worst of the argument, when falling two out. (11/1: op 6/1)
Cardinal Richelieu started slowly and never held out a prayer. (7/4)

4617 SHEPHERD NEAME UNITED HUNTS OPEN HUNTERS' CHASE (6-Y.O+) (Class H)
7-30 (7-41) **3m 7f (19 fncs)** £2,831.50 (£784.00: £374.50) GOING minus 0.05 sec per fur (G)

	Horse / details	Dist	Pos	SP	RR	SF
4323[2]	**Glen Oak** (DGDuggan) **12-11-10**(7) MrJMPritchard (hld up in tch: hit 12th: chsd ldr after 14th: led after 2 out: pushed clr flat)	—	1	4/6 1	104	26
3739[2]	**Sirisat** (MissTOBlazey) **13-11-7**(7) MissTBlazey (led: hdd after 2 out: wknd flat)	12	2	7/2 2	94	16
4317[3]	**Tau** (MissFelicityMcLachlan) **12-11-7**(7) MrAWarr (chsd ldr tl 13th: wknd next)	24	3	50/1	79	1

3553P **American Eyre** (MrsGMGladders) **12-11-7**(7) MissSGladders (in tch tl wknd appr 4 out) 1½ **4** 12/1 79 1
Early Man (MrsDMGrissell) **10-11-11**(3) MrPHacking (lw: chsd ldr 13th tl after next: mstkes 5 out & 4 out: p.u bef 3 out) .... **P** 4/1 3 — —
(SP 111.9%) **5 Rn**

7m 58.1 CSF £3.38 TOTE £1.60: £1.10 £2.00 (£2.40) OWNER Mr R. J. Mansell (REDMARLEY) BRED Kitone Ltd
4323 Glen Oak is a dour stayer and, after a struggle with the runner-up over the final four fences, he was the one that proved the stronger. (4/6: evens-8/13)
3739 Sirisat made a brave effort to make all, but in the end the favourite was too strong. (7/2: 2/1-4/1)
American Eyre (12/1: 5/1-14/1)

4618 GRANT'S CHERRY BRANDY SOUTH EAST CHAMPION FINAL NOVICES' HUNTERS' CHASE (5-Y.O+) (Class H)

8-00 (8-09) **2m 5f (15 fncs)** £1,800.00 (£540.00: £260.00: £120.00) GOING minus 0.05 sec per fur (G)

SP RR SF

Muskerry Moya (IRE) (JWDufosee) **8-11-9**(7) MissAGoschen (mde all: rdn out) ....— **1** 8/1 90 22
3922 4 **Reverend Brown (IRE)** (JMTurner) **7-12-2**(5) MrASansome (chsd wnr: mstke 9th: rdn to chal 2 out: faltered appr last: fin lame) 29 **2** 13/8 1 73 5
343P **Mutual Memories** (SRAndrews) **9-12-4**(3) MrSimonAndrews (in tch: mstke 9th: sn wknd) ....18 **3** 10/1 59 —
Red Channel (IRE) (MrsSJHickman) **7-12-0**(7) MrAHickman (keen hold: in tch: mstkes 5 out & 3 out: sn wknd) ....1¼ **4** 5/2 2 58 —
Bishops Tale (MrsRichardPilkington) **7-12-0**(7) MrRJBarrett (v.s.a: a bhd) ....23 **5** 6/1 3 41 —
Scarra Darragh (IRE) (MrsCHicks) **7-11-9**(7) MrACharles-Jones (j.slowly 2nd: sn bhd) ....11 **6** 33/1 27 —
30 6 **And Why Not** (RParker) **9-12-0**(7) MrJVanPraagh (fell 1st) .... **F** 9/1 — —
4449R **Ishma (IRE)** (DarrenPage) **6-12-0**(7) MrDPage (bhd fr 4th: t.o whn p.u bef 9th) .... **P** 50/1 — —
(SP 116.1%) **8 Rn**

5m 23.2 (15.20) CSF £20.84 TOTE £8.60: £1.60 £1.10 £1.60 (£8.10) OWNER Mr N. W. Rimington (GILLINGHAM) BRED Barry O'Driscoll
Muskerry Moya (IRE) made all under a fine ride, and ran on strongly from the penultimate fence. (8/1: 5/1-9/1)
3922 Reverend Brown (IRE) was challenging when appearing to go lame on the run to the last, and his rider rather foolishly still jumped the final obstacle. (13/8)
Mutual Memories (10/1: op 5/1)
Bishops Tale (6/1: op 4/1)
And Why Not (9/1: 5/1-10/1)

4619 PETT FARM EQUESTRIAN SERVICES UNITED HUNTS OPEN CHALLENGE CUP HUNTERS' CHASE (5-Y.O+) (Class H)

8-30 (8-33) **2m 5f (15 fncs)** £2,005.00 (£555.00: £265.00) GOING minus 0.05 sec per fur (G)

SP RR SF

4320* **Slievenamon Mist** (VictorDartnall) **11-12-9**(5) MrJJukes (lw: hld up: hdwy 9th: chsd ldr appr 5 out: led appr 2 out: clr last: easily) ....— **1** 4/11 1 120+ 52
4320 2 **Counterbid** (JMTurner) **10-12-2b**(5) MrASansome (led: hdd after 1st: led 4th: hdd appr 2 out: one pce) 6 **2** 15/2 3 108 40
No Inhibitions (MrsSWarr) **10-12-0**(7) MrAWarr (prom tl wknd appr 3 out:) 22 **3** 50/1 92 24
3924 5 **Just Jack** (PJonason) **11-12-4**(3) MrSimonAndrews (prom: mstke 2nd & 5th: chsd ldr after 8th tl appr 5 out: wknd appr 4 out) 13 **4** 20/1 82 14
Sure Pride (USA) (AGRussell) **9-12-0**(7) MrPGHall (bhd fr 4th) ....d.h **5** 50/1 82 14
3446U **Emerald Moon** (MrsMREagleton) **10-12-0**(7) MrTHills (in tch tl wknd 10th) ....nk **5** 40/1 82 14
Boll Weevil (MrsSBowman) **11-12-0**(7) MissJGrant (plld hrd: led after 1st: hdd 4th: chsd ldr tl after 8th: wknd 10th: t.o whn p.u bef 2 out) .... **P** 25/1 — —
4051 5 **Young Nimrod** (MrsDMGrissell) **10-12-0**(7) MrGWragg (6th whn blnd & uns rdr 5th) .... **U** 4/1 2 — —
(SP 120.1%) **8 Rn**

5m 17.4 (9.40) CSF £3.70 TOTE £1.30: £1.10 £1.10 £3.10 (£2.50) Trio £28.70 OWNER Mr Nick Viney (BARNSTAPLE) BRED James Mulcahy
4320* Slievenamon Mist,won at Huntingdon last time despite connections reporting he had corns and wasn't seen at his best there. He ran out a very easy winner, and next stop is the Horse and Hound Cup. (4/11)
4320 Counterbid made much of the running but was no match for the winner. (15/2: 5/1-9/1)

T/Plpt: £54.60 (125.61 Tckts). T/Qdpt: £4.70 (92.82 Tckts) SM

4506-STRATFORD-ON-AVON (L-H) (Good)

Friday May 16th

visibility for race 6 - Dark.
WEATHER: Thundery showers

4620 RICHARDSONS PARKWAY NOVICES' (S) HURDLE (4-Y.O+ F & M) (Class G)

6-00 (6-00) **2m 110y (9 hdls)** £2,090.50 (£583.00: £281.50) GOING: 0.48 sec per fur (GS)

SP RR SF

2943 12 **Persian Butterfly (53)** (RMStronge) **5-10-10** JCulloty (a.p: led appr last: drvn out) ....— **1** 14/1 48 6
3761 9 **Callermine (70)** (MissHDay) **8-10-3**(7) MrSDurack (led tl appr 2 out: r.o one pce flat) 4 **2** 14/1 44 2
4423* **Fenian Court (IRE) (77)** (PDEvans) **6-11-3v**1 MAFitzgerald (chsd ldr: led appr 2 out tl appr last: one pce) 2 **3** 5/2 1 49 7
4276 8 **Bold Time Monkey** (MTate) **6-10-10** CLlewellyn (hld up & bhd: stdy hdwy 6th: nvr plcd to chal) ....10 **4** 33/1 33 —
3940 7 **Analogical** (DMcCain) **4-10-5** VSlattery (prom: mstke 3rd: hrd rdn appr 3 out: sn wknd) ....2½ **5** 10/1 30 —
4343 2 **Persian Dawn (70)** (RTPhillips) **4-10-5** NWilliamson (lw: hld up & bhd: hdwy 6th: nt rch ldrs) ....1¼ **6** 11/2 3 29 —
3730 7 **How Could-I (IRE) (71)** (PRChamings) **4-10-5** AThornton (nvr nr to chal) ....hd **7** 8/1 29 —
2892P **Woodlands Energy (48)** (PAPritchard) **6-10-10** RBellamy (lw: bhd: sme hdwy 5th: nvr nr ldrs) ....1 **8** 66/1 28 —
3670 3 **Pedaltothemetal (IRE) (84)** (RTJuckes) **5-10-10** WMarston (bhd fr 5th) ....2½ **9** 4/1 2 25 —
3818P **Lizium** (JCFox) **5-10-10** SFox (prom to 6th) ....7 **10** 33/1 19 —
872 13 **Gabrielle Gerard** (MDHammond) **5-10-10** DBentley (lw: mstkes: bhd fr 5th) ....7 **11** 10/1 12 —
4009 14 **Rosglinn (IRE)** (HMKavanagh) **5-10-10** MRichards (bit bkwd: a bhd: t.o) ....24 **12** 33/1 — —
4343 3 **Salsian** (PWinkworth) **4-10-5b** TJMurphy (hld up mid div: bhd fr 3 out: t.o) ....9 **13** 50/1 — —
2931 20 **Glendronach** (BRCambidge) **5-10-10** GaryLyons (bit bkwd: mstke 5th: sn bhd: t.o fr 6th) ....7 **14** 66/1 — —

			SP		
4304[12]	**Heathyards Jade** (AStreeter) **4-10-3**(3)ow1 LAspell (swtg: a bhd: t.o whn p.u bef 3 out)	P	33/1	—	—

(SP 123.3%) **15 Rn**

4m 6.5 (19.50) CSF £169.89 TOTE £21.40: £4.60 £5.40 £2.30 (£130.40) Trio Not won; £203.85 to Newbury 18/5/97 OWNER Mr David Hallums (NEWBURY) BRED Theakston Stud

WEIGHT FOR AGE 4yo-5lb

No bid

2818 Persian Butterfly, freshened up following a disappointing effort last time, won a poor event. (14/1)

Callermine, the first foal of a sister to Bonanza Boy, appreciated this drop in class, and fought back to retake second place on the run-in. (14/1: op 25/1)

4423* Fenian Court (IRE), tried in a visor after scrambling home at Warwick, could not defy a penalty. (5/2)

Bold Time Monkey was never put into the race, and this was the first indication that she might be capable of getting the trip. (33/1)

3670 Pedaltothemetal (IRE) (4/1: op 9/4)

4621 FRANCIS GRAVES LTD NOVICES' CHASE (5-Y.O+) (Class D)

6-35 (6-35) **2m 5f 110y (16 fncs)** £3,548.00 (£1,064.00: £512.00: £236.00) GOING: 0.13 sec per fur (G)

				SP	RR	SF
4475*	**Formal Invitation (IRE) (110)** (DNicholson) **8-11-10** RJohnson (hld up: hit 3rd & 5th: wnt 2nd 9th: led after 3 out: lft clr 2 out)	—	1	8/11[1]	115	40
2947[5]	**Bayline Star (IRE) (96)** (MissHCKnight) **7-11-0** JCulloty (hld up: hdwy after 5th: lft 2nd after 2 out: no ch w wnr)	4	2	5/1[3]	102	27
4298[3]	**Imperial Vintage (IRE) (124)** (MissVenetiaWilliams) **7-11-10** NWilliamson (led: mstke 3 out: sn hdd: btn whn stumbled bdly 2 out: nt rcvr)	11	3	2/1[2]	104	29
4227[P]	**Little Elliot (IRE)** (SEarle) **9-10-11**(3) LAspell (chsd ldr to 9th: wknd appr 12th: mstke 4 out: t.o)	dist	4	33/1	—	—

(SP 110.8%) **4 Rn**

5m 24.1 (12.10) CSF £4.42 TOTE £1.70 (£1.90) OWNER The Plough Partnership (TEMPLE GUITING) BRED Patrick Eddery Ltd

4475* Formal Invitation (IRE), taking his trainer through the million pound barrier for the season, had just assumed control when Imperial Vintage lost his hind legs on landing over the second last. (8/11: evens-11/10)

2947 Bayline Star (IRE) took advantage of Imperial Vintage's misfortune at the penultimate fence. (5/1: 11/4-11/2)

4298 Imperial Vintage (IRE) had just had his measure taken by the winner when slipping and losing his hind legs on landing at the penultimate fence. (2/1: 6/4-9/4)

4622 BIRSE CONSTRUCTION H'CAP HURDLE (0-115) (4-Y.O+) (Class E)

7-05 (7-05) **3m 3f (14 hdls)** £2,332.00 (£652.00: £316.00) GOING: 0.48 sec per fur (GS)

				SP	RR	SF
4005[9]	**Jimbalou (80)** (RGBrazington) **14-9-12**(3) RMassey (hld up: hdwy appr 11th: led appr 2 out: easily)	—	1	5/1[3]	60+	11
4476[3]	**Lottery Ticket (IRE) (93)** (TRGeorge) **8-11-0** MAFitzgerald (hld up: hdwy after 9th: led appr 11th: hdd appr 2 out: one pce)	6	2	7/2[1]	69	20
4439*	**St Ville (110)** (RHBuckler) **11-12-3** 6x BPowell (prom: led 6th to 8th: wknd appr 3 out)	3	3	4/1[2]	85	36
4376*	**Sharp Thyne (IRE) (100)** (PJHobbs) **7-11-7** GTormey (lw: prom: rdn appr 11th: wknd appr 3 out)	nk	4	7/2[1]	74	25
4283[8]	**Father O'Brien (83)** (JCPoulton) **10-10-4** AThornton (led to 6th: rdn appr 8th: wknd after 9th: t.o)	dist	5	16/1	—	—
3209*	**Millmount (IRE) (92)** (TPMcGovern) **7-10-13b** RJohnson (hld up: rdn 10th: sn wknd: t.o whn p.u bef last)		P	5/1[3]	—	—
4524[6]	**Whitebonnet (IRE) (79)** (CREgerton) **7-9-11b**(3) SophieMitchell (prom: led 8th tl hdd & wknd appr 11th: bhd whn p.u bef 3 out)		P	20/1	—	—
4417[P]	**Joy For Life (IRE) (79)** (RMStronge) **6-10-0** JCulloty (bhd whn mstke 5th: p.u bef 6th)		P	33/1	—	—
4340[P]	**Castlebay Lad (80)** (RCurtis) **14-9-8**(7)ow1 JParkhouse (hld up: mstke 2nd: rdn after 10th: sn bhd: p.u after 11th)		P	100/1	—	—

(SP 112.4%) **9 Rn**

6m 46.1 (27.10) CSF £20.27 CT £68.40 TOTE £5.60: £1.60 £1.50 £1.90 (£11.60) Trio £16.40 OWNER Mr R. G. Brazington (REDMARLEY) BRED R. G. Brazington

LONG HANDICAP Whitebonnet (IRE) 9-10 Joy For Life (IRE) 9-7 Castlebay Lad 7-13

Jimbalou was 22lb out of the handicap when running a rather strange race on his belated seasonal debut. Fitter this time, he proved something of a revelation and apparently did not go unbacked. (5/1)

4476 Lottery Ticket (IRE) got comprehensively rolled over by the old timer. (7/2)

4439* St Ville was 11lb higher than the first of his two recent Fontwell wins. (4/1: 3/1-9/2)

4376* Sharp Thyne (IRE) must have been difficult for the Handicapper to assess, given he only had one out-of-the-blue win last time to go on. (7/2)

4623 INTERLINK EXPRESS RESTRICTED POINT-TO-POINT FINAL NOVICES' HUNTERS' CHASE (5-Y.O+) (Class H)

7-35 (7-35) **3m (18 fncs)** £2,976.00 (£888.00: £424.00: £192.00) GOING: 0.13 sec per fur (G)

				SP	RR	SF
	Aller Moor (IRE) (MrsSAlner) **6-11-7**(7) MrJTizzard (hld up: hdwy 14th: wnt 2nd after 4 out: rdn to ld 2 out: all out)	—	1	9/4[2]	90	36
	Swansea Gold (IRE) (MrsHENorth) **6-11-2**(7) MrDAlers-Hankey (plld hrd: led to 4th: led 8th: clr 14th: hdd 2 out: rallied flat)	½	2	12/1	85	31
	Barneys Gold (IRE) (AJBealby) **8-11-7**(7) MrABealby (lost pl 8th: styd on 4 out: lft poor 3rd last)	18	3	25/1	78	24
	Brown Baby (GRKerr) **11-11-3**(7)ow1 MrGKerr (plld hrd: led 4th to 8th: wknd 4 out: t.o)	21	4	25/1	60	5
	Mr Bobbit (IRE) (PEMills) **7-11-7**(7) MrRBurton (hit 6th: bhd fr 12th: t.o whn p.u bef 3 out)		P	16/1	—	—
	First Command (NZ) (MarkWellings) **10-11-7**(7) MrADalton (chsd ldrs to 12th: t.o whn p.u bef 3 out)		P	33/1	—	—
	Nearly At Sea (CJDown) **8-11-2**(7) MrLJefford (nt j.w: a bhd: t.o whn p.u after 11th)		P	6/1[3]	—	—
	Mamnoon (USA) (RobWoods) **6-11-7**(7) MrRArmson (bhd: rdn after 10th: p.u after 11th)		P	33/1	—	—
4076*	**Gallants Delight** (MrsCJohnston) **7-11-7**(7) MrARobson (hld up: sme hdwy whn mstke 10th: mstke 12th: rallied 3 out: 3rd & btn whn blnd & uns rdr last)		U	7/4[1]	—	—
	Bit Of A Citizen (IRE) (GLlewellyn) **6-11-2**(7) MrEWilliams (hdwy 11th: 3rd whn blnd & uns rdr 4 out)		U	11/1	—	—

(SP 116.9%) **10 Rn**

6m 8.1 (16.10) CSF £24.51 TOTE £3.00: £1.50 £1.80 £2.30 (£13.20) Trio £128.60 OWNER Mr G. Keirle (BLANDFORD) BRED Alan Dunlop

Aller Moor (IRE), the winner of his last three points, seemed to think he had done enough after the final fence. (9/4)

Swansea Gold (IRE), the winner of two of his three points, had been beaten just over twenty-five lengths by the winner in the other one. (12/1)

Barneys Gold (IRE), twice a winner between the flags, only finished third because of the demise of Gallants Delight. (25/1)

4076* Gallants Delight, whose jumping had not impressed when winning one of her two points this year, was booked for the minor berth when getting rid of her rider at the last. (7/4)

4624 ROM LTD. H'CAP CHASE (0-135) (5-Y.O+) (Class C)

8-10 (8-10) **3m (18 fncs)** £4,576.50 (£1,377.00: £666.00: £310.50) GOING: 0.13 sec per fur (G)

Form	Horse / Details	Dist	Pos	SP	RR	SF
4306^{3}	**Bavard Dieu (IRE) (125)** (NAGaselee) **9-11-10** CLlewellyn (led to 3rd: outpcd 3 out: rallied appr last: hrd rdn to ld last strides)	—	**1**	11/2	132	26
4416^{P}	**Factor Ten (IRE) (123)** (MissHCKnight) **9-11-8** JFTitley (a.p: led 12th to 4 out: cl 2nd whn hmpd bnd appr 2 out: rallied to ld last: ct last strides)	nk	**2**	4/1^{3}	130	24
4225^{2}	**Super Coin (114)** (RLee) **9-10-13** RJohnson (hld up: mstke 5th: hit 10th: led 4 out: mstke 2 out: hdd last: wknd)	5	**3**	6/4^{1}	118	12
3618^{11}	**Pashto (125)** (NJHenderson) **10-11-10** MAFitzgerald (led 3rd to 12th: rdn & wknd appr 3 out: t.o)	dist	**4**	2/1^{2}	—	—
				(SP 108.7%)		**4 Rn**

6m 10.3 (18.30) CSF £21.58 TOTE £7.20 (£13.40) OWNER Saguaro Stables (LAMBOURN) BRED Noel McGrady

4306 Bavard Dieu (IRE), dropped a further 4lb, really pulled this one out of the fire. (11/2)

1354 Factor Ten (IRE), back on song here, was probably a shade unlucky because he lost more ground when his rider was forced to snatch up on the home turn than the narrow margin of defeat. (4/1)

4225 Super Coin, dropped 3lb, will need to jump better than this if he is going to stay three miles. (6/4)

2773 Pashto, down 5lb, seems to have completely lost his form. (2/1)

4625 HAMER FORD 'N.H.' NOVICES' HURDLE (4-Y.O+) (Class D)

8-40 (8-40) **2m 6f 110y (12 hdls)** £3,090.00 (£865.00: £420.00) GOING: 0.48 sec per fur (GS)

Form	Horse / Details	Dist	Pos	SP	RR	SF
4001^{4}	**Mon Amie** (AGHobbs) **7-10-7**$^{(7)}$ MrGShenkin (hld up & plld hrd: hit 8th: hdwy 9th: led 2 out: drvn out)	—	**1**	14/1	65	20
4309^{9}	**Camera Man (85)** (NJHenderson) **7-11-0** MAFitzgerald (a.p: led 8th to 2 out: r.o one pce)	1½	**2**	12/1^{3}	64	19
3086^{U}	**Lucky Call (NZ)** (AGHobbs) **6-11-0** RGreene (lw: hld up & bhd: mstke 5th: hdwy 9th: styd on flat)	s.h	**3**	33/1	64	19
4427^{U}	**Cool Harry (USA) (61)** (HEHaynes) **6-10-7**$^{(7)}$ MrSDurack (a.p: mstke 8th: ev ch appr 2 out: one pce)	2	**4**	33/1	63	18
4204^{2}	**Morpheus (103)** (DNicholson) **8-11-0** RJohnson (hld up & plld hrd: hdwy 7th: ev ch 2 out: wknd flat)	½	**5**	4/6^{1}	62	17
4521^{U}	**Rhythm And Blues (90)** (RHBuckler) **7-11-6** BPowell (hld up: hdwy appr 5th: one pce fr 3 out)	3	**6**	100/30^{2}	66	21
4224^{5}	**Irish Delight** (RCurtis) **5-11-0** DMorris (bhd tl gd hdwy 9th: wknd appr 2 out)	¾	**7**	20/1	60	15
4506^{F}	**Nicanjon** (RDickin) **6-10-9**$^{(5)}$ XAizpuru (mstke 2nd: bhd fr 8th)	18	**8**	100/1	47	2
4382^{7}	**Irene's Pet** (JCFox) **7-11-0** SFox (hdwy 6th: hit 7th: wknd appr 3 out)	9	**9**	33/1	40	—
3052^{P}	**Faithlegg (IRE)** (NJHenderson) **6-10-9** JRKavanagh (mstke 3rd: bhd fr 8th)	9	**10**	20/1	29	—
4508^{4}	**Saucy Nun (IRE)** (IPWilliams) **5-10-9b^{1}** NWilliamson (bhd fr 8th)	3½	**11**	20/1	26	—
4441^{5}	**New Ross (IRE)** (OO'Neill) **5-11-0b^{1}** VSlattery (rdn 6th: a bhd: t.o)	22	**12**	33/1	16	—
2034^{P}	**Amazon Heights (59)** (LPGrassick) **5-10-9** MrJGrassick (prom: j.slowly 4th: wknd 8th: t.o)	dist	**13**	100/1	—	—
4181^{6}	**Go Frolic (67)** (MissCPhillips) **9-10-9** AThornton (led to 8th: wknd qckly: t.o whn p.u bef 3 out)		**P**	33/1	—	—
				(SP 128.4%)		**14 Rn**

5m 39.7 (23.70) CSF £140.87 TOTE £14.70: £2.50 £3.10 £20.50 (£75.30) Trio Not won; £304.70 to Newbury 18/5/97 OWNER Mr John Lister (KINGSBRIDGE) BRED K. J. Palmer

Mon Amie appreciated this longer trip, and stayed on to win a race in the gathering gloom. (14/1)

2891 Camera Man, all at sea on the soft last time, not surprisingly got the best of the photo for second. (12/1: 8/1-14/1)

Lucky Call (NZ), who finished second in his final point last season, was reverting to hurdles, and very nearly made it a one-two for his stable. (33/1)

Cool Harry (USA) ran his best races over hurdles to date. (33/1)

4204 Morpheus again proved a handful to settle, and as a result this longer trip eventually found him out. (4/6)

T/Plpt: £1,629.30 (6.09 Tckts). T/Qdpt: £351.40 (1.78 Tckts) KH

4376-BANGOR-ON-DEE (L-H) (Good)

Saturday May 17th

WEATHER: Overcast

4626 PENYCAE MAIDEN HURDLE (4-Y.O+) (Class D)

11-50 (11-53) **2m 1f (9 hdls)** £2,970.00 (£900.00: £440.00: £210.00) GOING: 0.33 sec per fur (GS)

Form	Horse / Details	Dist	Pos	SP	RR	SF
4534^{P}	**Mr Lowry (73)** (LJBarratt) **5-11-5** SWynne (swtg: chsd ldrs: led after 3 out: sn hrd rdn: hld on gamely)	—	**1**	33/1	65	9
4282^{2}	**Sadler's Realm** (PJHobbs) **4-11-0** GTormey (hld up in tch: hdwy 6th: jnd wnr 2 out: ev ch last: hrd rdn & one pce)	1¼	**2**	5/2^{1}	64	3
4244^{4}	**Western General (78)** (MissMKMilligan) **6-11-5** APMcCoy (hld up: hdwy appr 6th: kpt on u.p fr 2 out)	2½	**3**	4/1^{3}	62	6
4299^{6}	**Donnegale (IRE) (70)** (TPTate) **5-11-5** BPowell (lw: a.p: led appr 6th tl after 3 out: sn rdn: wknd next)	8	**4**	20/1	54	—
3228^{4}	**Biya (IRE) (67)** (DMcCain) **5-11-5** TJenks (lw: hdwy 4th: rdn whn mstke 2 out: sn btn)	13	**5**	25/1	42	—
4450^{2}	**Silent Cracker** (RDickin) **5-11-5** JCulloty (in tch tl wknd 3 out)	8	**6**	100/30^{2}	34	—
4403^{P}	**King Curan (USA)** (PBowen) **6-11-5** NWilliamson (bit bkwd: hld up: effrt 6th: wknd after next)	2	**7**	16/1	32	—
4215^{11}	**The Operator (IRE)** (GRichards) **6-11-5** JOsborne (hld up: nvr plcd to chal)	16	**8**	12/1	17	—
4531^{13}	**Woodstock Wanderer (IRE)** (PBowen) **5-11-5** RJohnson (rel to r: a wl bhd)	2½	**9**	20/1	15	—
4441^{9}	**Just Because (IRE)** (GEJones) **5-11-0**$^{(5)}$ DJKavanagh (a in rr: t.o)	1¼	**10**	66/1	14	—
4423^{6}	**Frans Lad** (BPJBaugh) **5-11-5** GaryLyons (a bhd: t.o)	3	**11**	66/1	11	—
4526^{R}	**Lady Rosebury** (RJPrice) **7-11-0** TJMurphy (a bhd: t.o)	2½	**12**	66/1	4	—
4441^{2}	**Floosy** (TRGeorge) **6-11-0** MAFitzgerald (bhd fr 5th: t.o)	20	**13**	11/2	—	—
4531^{14}	**Storm Home** (OO'Neill) **5-11-5** VSlattery (sn bhd & rdn along: a t.o)	20	**14**	66/1	—	—
4259^{12}	**Nine Pipes (IRE)** (JJBirkett) **6-11-5** JRKavanagh (trckd ldrs to 5th: sn lost pl: t.o whn p.u bef 2 out)		**P**	50/1	—	—
2539^{P}	**Hiltons Travel (IRE)** (EJAlston) **6-10-12**$^{(7)}$ LCummins (bkwd: chsd ldr to 5th: wknd qckly: t.o p.u bef 2 out)		**P**	50/1	—	—
4441^{6}	**Bache Dingle** (MrsSMJohnson) **6-11-5** WMarston (chsd ldrs to 5th: p.u bef 3 out)		**P**	100/1	—	—

			SP	RR	SF
4162P	**Polar Wind** (NWaggott) **8-11-5** AThornton (plld hrd: led tl appr 6th: wknd qckly: t.o whn p.u bef 2 out)	P	100/1	—	—
			(SP 128.8%)	**18 Rn**	

4m 13.9 (18.90) CSF £105.77 TOTE £19.50: £3.10 £1.80 £1.90 (£75.40) Trio £174.70; £98.46 to Newbury 18/5/97 OWNER Mr Doug Brereton (OSWESTRY) BRED R. H. James

WEIGHT FOR AGE 4yo-5lb

OFFICIAL EXPLANATION: Mr Lowry benefited from better ground and a tongue-strap.

Mr Lowry, lowered in grade and fitted with a tongue-strap, caused quite an upset in getting off the mark. (33/1)

4282 Sadler's Realm looking dull in his coat, once again found one too good. He may have trouble finding a race even at this late stage of the season. (5/2)

4244 Western General has failed to progress from two promising runs in recent months, and there appeared to be no excuse this time. (4/1)

3453 Donnegale (IRE), still struggling to find a correct trip, was unable to hold his pitch when the pressure was on soon after entering the straight, and he faded rather tamely. (20/1)

3228 Biya (IRE), close enough to have every chance turning in, was hard at work and held when he made an untidy mistake two out. (25/1)

4450 Silent Cracker seems to find this minimum trip inadequate, for he travelled well until the increasing tempo caught him out. (100/30)

The Operator (IRE) (12/1: op 8/1)

4627 MAY NOVICES' CHASE (5-Y.O+) (Class D)

12-20 (12-20) **2m 1f 110y (12 fncs)** £3,355.00 (£1,015.00: £495.00: £235.00) GOING: 0.33 sec per fur (GS)

				SP	RR	SF
4366a3	**Flying Instructor (130)** (PRWebber) **7-11-7** NWilliamson (hld up: chsd ldr fr 5th: led on bit 3 out: comf)	—	1	2/11 1	93+	31
43774	**Dandie Imp (73)** (AWCarroll) **9-11-0** BPowell (led to 3 out: kpt on: no ch w wnr)	3	2	7/1 2	83	21
44455	**Professor Page (IRE)** (TThomsonJones) **7-11-0** MAFitzgerald (trckd ldrs: hit 3rd: outpcd fr 8th)	26	3	14/1 3	60	—
36823	**Relaxed Lad** (JHPeacock) **8-11-0** RBellamy (hld up: hdwy 7th: wknd 4 out)	16	4	50/1	45	—
4476P	**Steel Chimes (IRE)** (BRCambidge) **8-11-0** GaryLyons (sn pushed along: rdn 6th: a bhd: t.o)	dist	5	150/1	—	—
45265	**Old Redwood (60)** (MrsLWilliamson) **10-11-0v1** CLlewellyn (chsd ldr to 5th: hit 7th: sn wknd: t.o)	4	6	20/1	—	—
				(SP 111.2%)	**6 Rn**	

4m 24.7 (14.70) CSF £1.98 TOTE £1.30: £1.20 £1.70 (£2.30) OWNER Lady Lyell (BANBURY) BRED Lady Lyell

4366a Flying Instructor had little more than a school round to succeed, and would not know he had been in a race. (2/11)

4377 Dandie Imp gave the winner the lead he needed and then did his best to make a race of it, but he was only there on sufferance.(7/1)

4628 TOTE CREDIT CLUB NOVICES' H'CAP HURDLE (0-105) (4-Y.O+) (Class E)

12-50 (12-50) **2m 4f (11 hdls)** £2,738.00 (£768.00: £374.00) GOING: 0.33 sec per fur (GS)

				SP	RR	SF
4399*	**Jessolle (95)** (GRichards) **5-10-13**(7) RBurns (hld up & bhd: hdwy 6th: chal 2 out: sn led: very easily)	—	1	5/1 2	81+	10
4434F	**Name of Our Father (USA) (99)** (PBowen) **4-11-4** RJohnson (a.p: led 8th tl appr last: kpt on same pce)	7	2	8/1	79	2
43395	**Stylish Interval (87)** (NWaggott) **5-10-12** PCarberry (swtg: hld up in tch: effrt u.p appr 2 out: styd on)	½	3	12/1	67	—
45284	**Supreme Troglodyte (IRE) (80)** (CPMorlock) **5-10-5** JRKavanagh (a.p: rdn appr 2 out: r.o one pce)	2	4	20/1	58	—
37454	**Meg's Memory (IRE) (93)** (AStreeter) **4-10-12** NWilliamson (lw: hld up & bhd: hdwy 7th: rdn & wknd appr 2 out)	5	5	12/1	67	—
44452	**The Eens (75)** (DMcCain) **5-10-0** SWynne (led to 8th: wknd qckly: t.o)	28	6	10/1	27	—
4466*	**Ultimate Smoothie (103)** (MCPipe) **5-12-0** APMcCoy (hld up & bhd: hdwy appr 7th: rdn 3 out: no imp)	4	7	6/5 1	52	—
446812	**Westcoast (75)** (MTate) **6-10-0** CLlewellyn (swtg: bit bkwd: dropped rr 6th: sn t.o)	21	8	66/1	7	—
4007P	**Bonnifer (IRE) (76)** (MJWilkinson) **8-10-1b1** WMarston (prom: hit 5th: sn lost tch: t.o)	15	9	33/1	—	—
4479*	**Diddy Rymer (85)** (MrsSJSmith) **7-10-10** RichardGuest (swtg: hld up: hdwy 7th: rdn next: mstke 3 out: p.u)		P	7/1 3	—	—
				(SP 119.4%)	**10 Rn**	

4m 58.1 (22.10) CSF £40.65 CT £420.96 TOTE £5.30: £2.00 £1.90 £6.20 (£25.70) Trio £29.30 OWNER Mr C. R. Fleet (PENRITH) BRED Mrs I. H. Lowe

LONG HANDICAP Westcoast 8-8 The Eens 9-12

WEIGHT FOR AGE 4yo-6lb

OFFICIAL EXPLANATION: Ultimate Smoothie was never travelling or jumping well.

4399* Jessolle, given a very confident ride, had the prize sewn up from some way out and she hardly needed to exert herself. (5/1)

4434 Name of Our Father (USA), an unlucky loser on his previous outing, remained in the firing line all the way, but the winner was galloping all over him in the closing stages. (8/1: op 5/1)

4339 Stylish Interval has only ever won at seventeen furlongs, but he seemed to stay this trip well enough if lacking the speed to match strides with the winner. (12/1: op 8/1)

4528 Supreme Troglodyte (IRE) is finding it increasingly difficult to win a race, but she nearly always gives a good account of herself, and her luck will change one of these days. (20/1)

3745 Meg's Memory (IRE) tried hard to get herself into the action on the approach to the straight, but lack of stamina soon took its toll and she was soon in trouble. (12/1: op 8/1)

4445 The Eens (10/1: 8/1-12/1)

4466* Ultimate Smoothie, tackling an extra half-mile, made only the briefest effort out in the country which came to nothing, and this was a very much below-par performance. (6/5: 7/4-11/10)

4479* Diddy Rymer (7/1: 4/1-15/2)

4629 MARBURY H'CAP CHASE (0-115) (5-Y.O+) (Class E)

1-20 (1-20) **2m 4f 110y (15 fncs)** £3,517.50 (£1,065.00: £520.00: £247.50) GOING: 0.33 sec per fur (GS)

				SP	RR	SF
41594	**Pearl Epee (90)** (DNicholson) **8-10-3** RJohnson (led tl mstke & hdd 8th (water): rallied appr 2 out: hrd rdn to ld last stride)	—	1	9/2 3	101	27
44752	**Andermatt (108)** (JMackie) **10-11-4**(3) EHusband (hld up: hdwy 10th: led appr last: j.lft: hrd rdn: ct post)	nk	2	2/1 1	119	45
4448*	**Royal Square (CAN) (87)** (NPLittmoden) **11-9-11**(3) MrRThornton (a.p: pushed along 5th: led 3 out tl appr last: rdn & no ex flat)	1¾	3	7/1	96	22
4517*	**Tapatch (IRE) (88)** (MWEasterby) **9-10-1b** PCarberry (swtg: hld up in tch: effrt 4 out: rdn next: grad wknd)	8	4	7/1	91	17
4379*	**Jacob's Wife (103)** (PRWebber) **7-11-2** JOsborne (hld up: hdwy 8th: rdn & wknd appr 2 out)	5	5	100/30 2	102	28

1941[3] **Earlymorning Light (IRE) (115)** (GRichards) **8-12-0** APMcCoy (bkwd: hld up: lft in ld 8th: hdd 3 out: wknd next: virtually p.u flat)...dist **6** 7/1 — —
4467[U] **Nickle Joe (95)** (MTate) **11-10-8** WMarston (prom tl wknd 10th: sn t.o)... **7** 25/1 — —
(SP 115.9%) **7 Rn**

5m 13.7 (13.70) CSF £13.65 CT £56.27 TOTE £5.20: £2.40 £1.70 (£8.30) OWNER Mrs A. A. Shutes (TEMPLE GUITING) BRED C. Toone
LONG HANDICAP Royal Square (CAN) 9-11
4159 Pearl Epee, given time to recover from a very bad mistake at the water, showed what she is really made of with a determined late rally that got her to the front a stride form the line. (9/2)
4475 Andermatt, winner of this race twelve months ago, looked sure to increase his score to four over course and distance when taking a definite advantage into the last, but the winner, in receipt of 15lb, had the legs of him in the shadow of the post. (2/1)
4448* Royal Square (CAN) may well benefit from a slightly longer trip now, but he showed a return to some of his old form with a pleasing performance, and the change of scenery does look to have had its effect. (7/1)
4517* Tapatch (IRE) did not appear to see out this longer trip, and he was galloping on the spot in the last half-mile. (7/1)
4379* Jacob's Wife obviously has two ways of running and this was one of her off days. (100/30)
1941 Earlymorning Light (IRE) had a five-month break to overcome, and though he only lost the advantage three out, he was legless before reaching the last and crawled past the post in his own time. (7/1: 4/1-8/1)

4630 WIN WITH THE TOTE H'CAP HURDLE (0-120) (4-Y.O+) (Class D)
1-50 (1-51) **2m 1f (9 hdls)** £3,485.00 (£1,055.00: £515.00: £245.00) GOING: 0.33 sec per fur (GS)

SP RR SF

4400[4] **Riparius (USA) (107)** (PRWebber) **6-11-2** JOsborne (lw: trckd ldrs: drvn along 2 out: swtchd rt & led last: r.o wl)...— **1** 15/2 85 32
4534[2] **Our Robert (93)** (AStreeter) **5-10-2v** NWilliamson (lw: hld up & bhd: hdwy 5th: rdn to ld 2 out: hdd last: no ch w wnr)...2½ **2** 13/2 69 16
4532* **Kinnescash (IRE) (110)** (PBowen) **4-11-0** MAFitzgerald (mde most to 2 out: rdn & one pce appr last)...4 **3** 11/10[1] 82 24
4307* **Kino's Cross (106)** (AJWilson) **8-11-1** LHarvey (chsd ldrs: rdn appr 2 out: sn outpcd)...26 **4** 6/1[3] 53 —
2780[6] **Albertito (FR) (92)** (RHollinshead) **10-10-1** SWynne (bkwd: prom tl wknd 6th: t.o)...2 **5** 33/1 38 —
4425[4] **Tejano Gold (USA) (119)** (PBradley) **7-12-0** APMcCoy (prom: rdn appr 5th: wknd qckly next: t.o)...17 **6** 9/2[2] 49 —
This Is My Life (IRE) (100) (CPEBrooks) **8-10-9** GBradley (bkwd: stdd s: plld hrd: sn trckng ldrs: mstke & wknd 6th: t.o)...1½ **7** 14/1 28 —
(SP 114.8%) **7 Rn**

4m 7.7 (12.70) CSF £48.92 TOTE £5.70: £2.60 £1.90 (£12.00) OWNER Mrs David Blackburn (BANBURY) BRED Rogers Trust
WEIGHT FOR AGE 4yo-5lb
4400 Riparius (USA), stepping up to handicap company, won going away in the end but he did make hard work of it before eventually putting his stamp on proceedings. (15/2)
4534 Our Robert, responding to pressure to nose ahead at the penultimate flight, did not go down without a fight but the winner proved much too good for him on the flat. (13/2)
4532* Kinnescash (IRE) has had plenty of experience over hurdles, but he is far from fluent with his jumping, and an untidy effort when being challenged two out ruined whatever chance remained. (11/10)
4307* Kino's Cross did not have the testing ground he relishes and, off the bridle on the home turn, had no answer at all when the leading pair quickened things up. (6/1)
This Is My Life (IRE) (14/1: op 8/1)

4631 NORTH WESTERN AREA POINT-TO-POINT CHAMPIONSHIP FINAL HUNTERS' CHASE (5-Y.O+) (Class H)
2-20 (2-22) **3m 110y (18 fncs)** £2,788.00 (£844.00: £412.00: £196.00) GOING: 0.33 sec per fur (GS)

SP RR SF

4222* **Nodform Wonder** (RJBevis) **10-12-0**(7) MrRBevis (swtg: led tl after 3rd: led 5th: clr whn mstke 10th: unchal)...— **1** 5/4[1] 116+ 35
Nothing Ventured (CountessGoess-Saurau) **8-11-10**(7) MrABeedles (lw: hld up: chsd wnr fr 9th: no imp)...23 **2** 100/30[2] 97 16
3455[9] **Pamela's Lad** (GDHanmer) **11-11-10**(7) MrGHanmer (swtg: hld up: hdwy 13th: rdn & styd on fr 3 out: nvr nrr)...12 **3** 25/1 89 8
4471[U] **Ita's Fellow (IRE)** (ORPrince) **9-11-10**(7) MrsCFord (swtg: hld up: hdwy 13th: nt rch ldrs)...9 **4** 7/2[3] 83 2
4326[8] **Simply Perfect** (JSSwindells) **11-11-10**(7) MissSSwindells (chsd ldrs tl grad wknd fr 4 out)...6 **5** 40/1 79 —
4511[2] **Tara Boy** (RTeague) **12-11-10**(7) MrRCambray (lw: lost pl 7th: n.d after)...10 **6** 25/1 73 —
Glenrowan (IRE) (RichardFord) **9-11-12**(5) MrRFord (a wl bhd)...3 **7** 10/1 71 —
3005[U] **Spy's Delight** (HNWRayner) **11-11-10**(7) MrHRayner (lw: trckd ldrs to 11th: sn lost tch: t.o)...30 **8** 33/1 51 —
4222[P] **Fibreguide Tech** (TRKinsey) **14-11-10**(7) MrRThomas (hdwy 5th: chsng ldrs whn fell 10th)... **F** 33/1 — —
3455[F] **Noble Angel (IRE)** (PRWhiston) **9-11-10**(7) MrSPrior (led after 3rd to 5th: wknd 9th: t.o whn p.u bef 12th)... **P** 33/1 — —
No More the Fool (RWCrank) **11-11-10**(7) MrLBrennan (s.s: mstke 1st: t.o whn p.u bef 13th)... **P** 50/1 — —
Ultrason IV (FR) (MrsAmandaBryan) **11-11-10**(7) MrRBurton (chsd wnr to 9th: wknd 12th: t.o whn p.u bef last) **P** 50/1 — —
(SP 121.7%) **12 Rn**

6m 26.1 (24.10) CSF £4.95 TOTE £2.10: £1.50 £1.60 £5.60 (£4.50) Trio £59.20 OWNER Mr D. A. Malam (MALPAS) BRED Miss P. Freaney
4222* Nodform Wonder again annihilated the opposition, and in this kind of form he is in a class of his own in this area. (5/4)
Nothing Ventured moved into second place going out on the final circuit, but he was unable to make the slightest impression despite finishing some way clear of the remainder. (100/30)
Pamela's Lad began to stay on inside the final mile, but with the pace being maintained was unable to get within striking range. (25/1)

4632 ERDDIG STANDARD OPEN N.H. FLAT RACE (4, 5 & 6-Y.O F & M) (Class H)
2-50 (2-50) **2m 1f** £1,287.00 (£357.00: £171.00)

SP RR SF

Sea Tarth (PBowen) **6-11-1** NWilliamson (hld up: hdwy ½-wy: led 5f out: styd on strly)...— **1** 33/1 61 f —
4421* **Murchan Tyne (IRE)** (EJAlston) **4-10-10**(7) LCummins (hld up: hdwy 7f out: ev ch wl over 2f out: nt pce to chal)...3½ **2** 3/1[2] 65 f —
Orange Imp (JGFitzGerald) **4-10-10** WDwan (bit bkwd: hld up & bhd: hdwy 6f out: chal over 2f out: wknd appr fnl f)...6 **3** 8/1[3] 52 f —
Deep C Diva (IRE) (JABOld) **5-11-1** JOsborne (hld up in rr: hdwy 4f out: rdn 2f out: nvr able to chal)...4 **4** 9/4[1] 48 f —
Achill Rambler (DNicholson) **4-10-10** RJohnson (hld up: hdwy ½-wy: ev ch 3f out: wknd wl over 1f out)...2½ **5** 9/4[1] 46 f —
4301[8] **Ailsae** (MrsJBrown) **4-10-10** AThornton (hld up: hdwy 5f out: no imp fnl 3f)...7 **6** 20/1 39 f —
4531[8] **Truthfully** (SGollings) **4-10-10** APMcCoy (trckd ldrs: rdn along 3f out: sn btn)...7 **7** 12/1 33 f —

	Greatest Friend (IRE) (IPWilliams) **4-10-3**(7) FBogle (prom tl rdn & wknd over 2f out)	1¼	**8**	33/1	32 f	—
	Dee Dee (OO'Neill) **5-11-1** VSlattery (nvr nrr)	3½	**9**	20/1	28 f	—
4538[7]	**Zeny The Nesta** (PEccles) **5-11-1** MAFitzgerald (prom: jnd ldrs ½-wy: wknd over 3f out)	7	**10**	33/1	22 f	—
4301[10]	**Cahermone Lady (IRE)** (RMWhitaker) **6-11-1** MrNKent (mde most tl hdd 5f out: wknd over 3f out: t.o)	9	**11**	50/1	13 f	—
3846[8]	**Community Service (IRE)** (JNorton) **6-10-10**(5) BGrattan (swtg: chsd ldrs 13f: sn wknd: t.o)	22	**12**	33/1	—	—
	Splicethemainbrace (JGMO'Shea) **5-10-12**(3) MichaelBrennan (prom tl wknd over 4f out: t.o)	21	**13**	25/1	—	—
4420[12]	**Nirvana Princess** (BPreece) **5-10-8**(7) JMogford (prom 10f: sn lost pl: t.o)	½	**14**	50/1	—	—
3170[16]	**Miss Foley** (JHPeacock) **4-10-10** RBellamy (a in rr: t.o)	26	**15**	50/1	—	—
	Miss Matchmaker (MrsAMNaughton) **5-10-8**(7) MrTJBarry (mid div tl wknd 5f out: t.o)	18	**16**	20/1	—	—
				(SP 141.1%)	**16 Rn**	

4m 12.0 CSF £125.12 TOTE £38.60: £6.50 £2.30 £2.50 (£60.10) OWNER Mr F. P. Luff (HAVERFORDWEST) BRED J. W. Barton
WEIGHT FOR AGE 4yo-5lb

Sea Tarth, making her debut under Rules after failing to complete the course in four point-to-points, struck the front five furlongs out and, though she was always being pressurized, she got stronger the further they went and was well on top at the finish. (33/1)

4421* Murchan Tyne (IRE) made relentless progress and put herself in with a live chance soon after straightening up, but the winner kept up the gallop and she was unable to get to terms. (3/1)

Orange Imp, a daughter of a useful staying hurdler, mounted a challenge on the approach to the straight, but lack of peak condition soon began to tell and she could do little more than stay on at the one pace. Sure to strip fitter for the run, she looks up to winning races. (8/1: 5/1-10/1)

Deep C Diva (IRE) making a belated racecourse debut and given a very tender ride, improved stealthily over half-a-mile out and looked sure to be concerned in the outcome, but she appeared to blow up entering the final quarter-mile and failed to make any further progress. She should at least come on for the run. (9/4)

Achill Rambler, from a yard that do extremely well in this type of race, was poised to challenge three furlongs out, but with the pace never slackening she began to feel the strain and the position had to be accepted. (9/4)

T/Plpt: £93.10 (97.68 Tckts). T/Qdpt: £75.90 (8.13 Tckts) IM

3921-FAKENHAM (L-H) (Good)
Sunday May 18th
WEATHER: overcast

4633 SUPER SUNDAY (S) H'CAP HURDLE (0-95) (4-Y.O+) (Class G)
2-20 (2-20) **2m (9 hdls)** £2,746.00 (£838.00: £414.00: £202.00) GOING minus 0.28 sec per fur (GF)

				SP	RR	SF
4451[4]	**Hever Golf Diamond (77)** (JRBest) **4-10-11b**[1](7) MrPO'Keeffe (mde all: rdn & r.o wl appr last)	—	**1**	25/1	63	6
4089[2]	**Captain Tandy (IRE) (70)** (CSmith) **8-11-2** PMcLoughlin (hld up: hit 4th: hdwy next: ev ch 2 out: rdn & r.o flat)	2	**2**	7/1[3]	54	2
4472*	**Blotoft (78)** (SGollings) **5-11-10** MAFitzgerald (lw: hld up: hdwy appr 3 out: ev ch 2 out: one pce appr last)	s.h	**3**	3/1[1]	62	10
3131[3]	**Captain Marmalade (75)** (DTThom) **8-11-7** KGaule (lw: chsd ldrs: no hdwy appr 2 out)	hd	**4**	7/1[3]	59	7
4296[3]	**Ajdar (73)** (OBrennan) **6-11-5** MBrennan (lw: chsd ldrs to 3 out)	2½	**5**	3/1[1]	54	2
4552[10]	**Do Be Ware (77)** (JFfitch-Heyes) **7-11-9b** BFenton (chsd wnr to 3 out)	3	**6**	14/1	55	3
4231[9]	**Tug Your Forelock (59)** (GFJohnsonHoughton) **6-10-5** JCulloty (plld hrd: chsd ldrs to 6th)	3½	**7**	14/1	34	—
4295[4]	**Lebedinski (IRE) (80)** (MrsPSly) **4-11-7** VSmith (bhd: effrt 5th: wknd 3 out)	1½	**8**	16/1	53	—
4162[P]	**Emerald Venture (56)** (FCoton) **10-10-2** CRae (prom to 6th)	¾	**9**	33/1	29	—
3281[10]	**We're in the Money (60)** (RCSpicer) **13-10-6** MSharratt (rdn 5th: a bhd)	12	**10**	33/1	21	—
3933[4]	**Nagobelia (78)** (JPearce) **9-11-10** APMcCoy (hld up: hdwy 6th: wknd 3 out)	2½	**11**	9/2[2]	36	—
				(SP 122.1%)	**11 Rn**	

3m 52.5 (8.50) CSF £178.12 CT £630.49 TOTE £11.60: £4.80 £2.30 £1.80 (£85.30) Trio £174.90; £86.25 to Bath 19/5/97 OWNER Mr H. J. Jarvis (MAIDSTONE) BRED Mrs L. Popely
WEIGHT FOR AGE 4yo-5lb
No bid

IN-FOCUS: This was John Best's first winner under Rules.

4451 Hever Golf Diamond, below form in five efforts for his new trainer, returned to form with a bang in first-time blinkers. (25/1)

4089 Captain Tandy (IRE) was slightly outpaced from the second last, until responding to pressure late on to take second. He likes this fast ground and may get a little further. (7/1)

4472* Blotoft, up 5lb for his latest success, was taken very quietly to post. Moving forward on the final circuit, he disappointed once asked for everything and could only plug on at one speed. (3/1)

3131 Captain Marmalade, raised for his defeat here on his most recent hurdles run, is fit from the Flat, but never looked beating the Handicapper. (7/1)

4296 Ajdar, dropped in class, never looked like taking a hand. (3/1)

3577 Do Be Ware stays further than this, but did not have the speed once the chips were down. (14/1)

4634 HOOD, VORES AND ALLWOOD HUNTERS' CHASE (5-Y.O+) (Class H)
2-55 (2-55) **3m 110y (18 fncs)** £2,594.00 (£734.00: £362.00) GOING minus 0.28 sec per fur (GF)

				SP	RR	SF
4316[3]	**Dromin Leader** (JMTurner) **12-11-13**(5) MrASansome (lw: led 2nd: qcknd & lft clr 3 out: rdn out)	—	**1**	6/1[3]	110	28
	Sandybraes (HHutsby) **12-11-5**(7) MrFHutsby (led to 2nd: w wnr whn blnd 13th: rdn & mstke 3 out: rallied appr last: no imp flat)	5	**2**	9/1	101	19
70[7]	**Cracking Idea (IRE)** (MrsRuthHayter) **9-11-11**(7) MrCWardThomas (hld up: hdwy 8th: one pce fr 4 out)	½	**3**	8/1	106	24
4316[U]	**Tammy's Friend** (MrsGMHay) **10-11-5b**(7) MrRWakley (plld hrd: chsd ldrs: rdn 14th: btn appr last)	1¼	**4**	20/1	100	18
4432[3]	**Abbotsham** (OJCarter) **12-11-5**(7) MissPGundry (lw: chsd ldrs to 10th: bhd whn mstke 4 out)	12	**5**	4/1[2]	92	10
4432*	**Chilipour** (VictorDartnall) **10-12-3**(5) MrJJukes (plld hrd: chsd ldrs: pushed along & hit 13th: sn btn)	2	**6**	4/5[1]	100	18
3924[P]	**Lyme Gold (IRE)** (JMTurner) **8-11-11b**(7) MrDKeane (mstke 7th: sn bhd)	dist	**7**	50/1	—	—
4317[P]	**Cardinal Red** (NeilKing) **10-11-11**(7) MrNKing (lw: nt j.w: bhd whn tried to ref 10th: p.u bef next)		**P**	33/1	—	—
	Skerry Meadow (OJCarter) **13-11-5**(7) MissVRoberts (bhd: blnd 6th: p.u bef 11th)		**P**	66/1	—	—
				(SP 122.1%)	**9 Rn**	

6m 13.8 (10.80) CSF £50.67 TOTE £6.80: £1.60 £1.90 £1.90 (£28.50) Trio £34.90 OWNER Mr J. M. Turner (BURY ST EDMUNDS) BRED John Lett

4316 Dromin Leader, well-ridden and keeping to the inside, was able to dictate and had taken control when left six lengths clear three from home. Gaining his third course win under Rules, he has never been better. (6/1)
Sandybraes ran respectably in a point-to-point recently after a near two-year absence, and would have given the winner more to do but for losing six to eight lengths with a dreadful blunder three from home. (9/1: op 6/1)
Cracking Idea (IRE), in fine form between the flags in the last couple of months, stuck on well on the final circuit and is certainly capable of finding a race under Rules. (8/1: 6/1-9/1)
Tammy's Friend ran much his best race this season and looked more like his old self. (20/1)
4432 Abbotsham has a rather long stride for this track, which suits the handy type of horse, and was found wanting for speed on the final circuit. (4/1)
4432* Chilipour, in great form before his fall in the Aintree Foxhunters', where he got the reins tangled around his legs, has not looked the same horse since. (4/5: op 5/4)

4635 PRINCE OF WALES CUP H'CAP CHASE (0-110) (5-Y.O+) (Class E)

3-30 (3-30) **2m 5f 110y (16 fncs)** £4,405.00 (£1,345.00: £665.00: £325.00) GOING minus 0.28 sec per fur (GF)

				SP	RR	SF
1716^{U}	**Manor Mieo (83)** (GProdromou) **11-9-12v^{1}**(3) MichaelBrennan (led 3rd to 4th: led 6th: clr 3 out: mstke last: wknd flat: all out)	—	1	7/2^{2}	93	17
3925^{2}	**Whippers Delight (IRE) (90)** (GFHCharles-Jones) **9-10-3**(5) XAizpuru (lw: led 2nd to 3rd: led 4th to 6th: outpcd 3 out: r.o wl flat: nt rch wnr)	½	2	9/2^{3}	100	24
4456^{U}	**Bally Parson (97)** (RDickin) **11-11-1** JCulloty (a.p: one pce fr 4 out)	3	3	15/2	104	28
4452^{P}	**Tim Soldier (FR) (94)** (MissAStokell) **10-10-12** RSupple (led to 2nd: chsd ldrs tl wknd 4 out: fin lame)	5	4	11/2	98	22
4344*	**Linden's Lotto (IRE) (104)** (JWhite) **8-11-8** JRKavanagh (in tch: j.slowly 9th: rallied 11th: wknd 4 out)	17	5	100/30^{1}	95	19
4320^{10}	**Fish Quay (82)** (MrsKMLamb) **14-9-7**(7) MissSLamb (mstke 2nd: a bhd: t.o fr 4 out)	dist	6	100/1	—	—
4507*	**Monks Soham (IRE) (119)** (GAHubbard) **9-12-6**(3) PHenley (lw: hit 2nd: p.u bef 4th)		P	7/2^{2}	—	—
4460^{3}	**Frontier Flight (USA) (82)** (MissLCSiddall) **7-9-11**(3) EHusband (mstke 5th: blnd next: sn t.o: mstke & p.u after 11th)		P	12/1	—	—
				(SP 121.5%)	**8 Rn**	

5m 18.7 (3.70) CSF £19.55 CT £104.39 TOTE £5.10: £1.40 £1.10 £2.90 (£11.70) OWNER Mr George Prodromou (EAST HARLING) BRED C. R. Franks
LONG HANDICAP Fish Quay 8-6 Frontier Flight (USA) 9-12
1716 Manor Mieo, most disappointing earlier in the season after looking a high-class hunter at the end of last term, was brought back looking big and well. Well-supported, he would have won by much further but for clouting the last and, repeating his previous winning antics here, digging his toes in after the last. He gives the impression that he would prefer to jump the fences right after the winning post and go round again. (7/2: op 8/1)
3925 Whippers Delight (IRE) is rather one-paced but does not give up if there is even a sniff of hope, and these attributes would have snatched a most unlikely victory in another couple of strides. (9/2)
4456 Bally Parson looked well-held for most of the final circuit but, with the winner stopping after the last, he ended up not being beaten far. (15/2)
3925* Tim Soldier (FR) looked in trouble half-a-mile from home, but kept trying to the line and, with those in front stopping, was closing again at the finish. He stays further but, unfortunately, he appeared to finish a little sore. (11/2)
4344* Linden's Lotto (IRE), who jumped slowly at halfway, was not in a going mood. (100/30)
4507* Monks Soham (IRE) was pulled up early on, his pilot mistakenly believing him to have gone lame. (7/2: op 9/4)

4636 KING'S LYNN NOVICES' H'CAP HURDLE (0-100) (4-Y.O+) (Class E)

4-00 (4-00) **2m 7f 110y (13 hdls)** £3,243.00 (£921.60: £454.80) GOING minus 0.28 sec per fur (GF)

				SP	RR	SF
4453^{6}	**Stone Island (69)** (JohnWhyte) **4-10-12**(7) MrRWakley (lw: dropped rr 6th: hdwy 9th: stdd & shkn up next: wl clr after: hit 2 out: unchal)	—	1	11/2	38?	—
4453^{F}	**Come On In (74)** (RDickin) **4-11-5**(5) XAizpuru (hld up: hdwy 7th: rdn & no imp after 9th: virtually p.u bef next: continued)	dist	2	85/40^{2}	—	—
3921^{10}	**Holkham Bay (61)** (LWordingham) **5-11-0b^{1}**(3) MichaelBrennan (lw: led: sn clr: hrd rdn 8th: still wl clr whn p.u after 9th: eventually completed)	dist	3	5/1^{3}	—	—
4501^{3}	**Royal Hand (68)** (RJArmson) **7-11-10v** MrRArmson (swtg: chsd ldr to 6th: 3rd whn fell next)		F	11/10^{1}	—	—
				(SP 111.7%)	**4 Rn**	

5m 56.3 (25.30) CSF £15.86 TOTE £6.30: (£6.10) OWNER Mr John Whyte (BECCLES) BRED C. A. and R. M. Cyzer
WEIGHT FOR AGE 4yo-6lb
STEWARDS' ENQUIRY Brennan susp. 26-31/5 & 5-7, 11, 13-14 & 18-19/6/97 (failure to acquaint himself w crse & to ensure best possible placing).
IN-FOCUS: This must be one of very few races that requires the field to negotiate the same obstacle, in this case the hurdle in the home straight, four times during the course of a race.
3131 Stone Island looked unlikely to ever find another winning opportunity, and needed a scenario more appropriate to a "Carry On" film (or in this case a not carry on) than a racecourse to produce this victory. His pilot deserves credit for doing such a good job keeping him going on the final circuit. (11/2)
3222 Come On In followed Holkham Bay's lead and pulled up a circuit too soon. By the time Aizpuru realised his mistake, the winner was well clear and, rather than go in serious pursuit, he hunted round for second prize. Exactly what rules Brennan broke that Aizpuru did not are not entirely clear. (85/40)
3669 Holkham Bay set off at a two-mile pace in a three-mile race, and it became obvious why when he pulled up with a circuit to go. His pilot returned to a chorus of boos and a lengthy ban. (5/1)
4501 Royal Hand (11/10: evens-11/8)

4637 WEST NORFOLK MAIDEN HUNTERS' CHASE (5-Y.O+) (Class H)

4-35 (4-35) **2m 5f 110y (16 fncs)** £2,726.50 (£832.00: £411.00: £200.50) GOING minus 0.28 sec per fur (GF)

				SP	RR	SF
	Rough Edge (DAWales) **9-12-2**(5) MrWWales (hdwy 9th: led last: rdn clr)	—	1	5/2^{1}	90	18
4411^{2}	**Coolvawn Lady (IRE)** (WRHalliday) **8-11-9**(7) MrSWalker (w ldr: led 9th to last: one pce)	6	2	3/1^{2}	81	9
4406^{4}	**Tellaporky** (THind) **8-12-0**(7) MrAMiddleton (lw: in tch: rdn 7th: hit next & 12th: styd on fr 3 out)	7	3	20/1	80	8
	Beech Brook (GVergette) **8-12-0**(7) MrTLane (swtg: a.p: hit 10th & 13th: wkng whn blnd last)	12	4	9/2^{3}	71	—
158^{3}	**Menature (IRE)** (NJPomfret) **8-12-2**(5) MrASansome (bhd tl sme hdwy fr 3 out)	22	5	20/1	55	—
	Raki Crazy (OJCarter) **6-12-0**(7) MissPGundry (hdwy 8th: wknd 4 out)	s.h	6	16/1	55	—
	Mccartney (RGreen) **11-12-0**(7) MrKGreen (lw: chsd ldrs tl hit 8th: bhd whn mstke 11th)	28	7	25/1	34	—
	Chester Ben (MrsPABarthorpe) **8-12-4**(3) MrSimonAndrews (led to 9th: wknd 12th)	2½	8	7/1	32	—

	Al Jawwal (MrsJulieRead) **7-12-0**(7) MrRWakley (lw: bhd whn blnd 4th: p.u bef next)		**P**	10/1	—	—
3455[6]	**Dark Rhytham** (GACoombe) **8-12-0**(7) MrSMorris (lw: prom: rdn 9th: wknd 11th: bhd whn p.u bef 4 out)		**P**	6/1	—	—
3799[U]	**Alapa** (ABCoogan) **10-12-0**(7) MrVCoogan (blnd & uns rdr 2nd)		**U**	33/1	—	—
				(SP 129.8%)		**11 Rn**

5m 28.4 (13.40) CSF £10.31 TOTE £3.90: £1.20 £2.10 £3.90 (£8.50) Trio £86.00 OWNER Mr David Wales (KING'S LYNN) BRED D. A. Wales

Rough Edge, a winner here between the flags, gradually got better and better as the race went on, finally taking it up with a fine leap at the last. (5/2)

4411 Coolvawn Lady (IRE) ran another sound race, and jumped well apart from a slight mistake at the seventh, but simply found one too good. (3/1)

3664 Tellaporky ran well here four outings ago and this was much his best effort since. (20/1)

Beech Brook ruined his chance with a string of poor jumps. (9/2)

158 Menature (IRE), kept up to his work to the line, is probably flattered to have got even this close. (20/1)

Raki Crazy, an unfurnished youngster whose only previous appearance had been when pulled up in a point, ran well for a long way and has some ability. (16/1)

Dark Rhytham (6/1: 8/1-12/1)

4638 GEORGINA AND PAUL'S FIRST ANNIVERSARY NOVICES' HURDLE (4-Y.O+) (Class D)

5-10 (5-10) **2m 4f (11 hdls)** £2,700.50 (£824.00: £407.00: £198.50) GOING minus 0.28 sec per fur (GF)

				SP	RR	SF
4341*	**Persian Elite (IRE) (101)** (CREgerton) **6-12-0** JOsborne (mde all: pushed clr appr last)	—	**1**	4/9[1]	79+	41
4341[4]	**Red Light (69)** (JRJenkins) **5-11-0b** APMcCoy (in tch: hdwy 8th: rdn & chsd wnr appr 2 out: no imp appr last)	4	**2**	11/2[2]	62	24
4528[9]	**Pealings (IRE) (77)** (GAHubbard) **5-10-11**(3) MichaelBrennan (chsd ldrs: 3rd whn hit 2 out: one pce)	8	**3**	7/1[3]	55	17
4451[P]	**Can She Can Can** (CSmith) **5-10-9** MRanger (chsd wnr to 5th: chsd wnr 7th tl rdn & btn appr 2 out)	2½	**4**	25/1	48	10
4518[4]	**Dont Forget Curtis (IRE) (69)** (MrsKMLamb) **5-10-7**(7) MissSLamb (bhd tl styd on fr 3 out)	2½	**5**	12/1	51	13
4423[P]	**Teejay's Future (IRE)** (OBrennan) **6-10-9** MBrennan (lw: chsd ldrs tl appr 2 out)	3½	**6**	14/1	44	6
4450[P]	**Derring Well** (JWPayne) **7-10-9** KGaule (hit 5th: a bhd)	15	**7**	33/1	32	—
	Harvest Reaper (JLHarris) **5-11-0** RSupple (chsd wnr fr 5th tl hit 7th: sn wknd)	20	**8**	12/1	21	—
3755[8]	**Philisitate** (JFfitch-Heyes) **8-10-9** BFenton (lw: prom to 4th: bhd fr 7th)	10	**9**	33/1	8	—
				(SP 128.9%)		**9 Rn**

4m 48.7 (3.70) CSF £3.96 TOTE £1.50: £1.30 £1.50 £1.30 (£2.80) Trio £4.40 OWNER Elite Racing Club (CHADDLEWORTH) BRED Mrs M. E. Farrell

4341* Persian Elite (IRE), 13lb better off with the runner-up for having beaten him five lengths last time, was able to dictate matters from the start and won pretty much as he liked. (4/9)

2692 Red Light did everything he could to stretch the winner from two out, but was unable to do so. (11/2)

4134 Pealings (IRE) had two handlers in the paddock and was keen on the way down, but settles reasonably in a race, and may well have finished second but for a late mistake. (7/1)

Can She Can Can got slightly warm and is quite a keen sort. She may well be suited by such a tight track as it settles her, and appeared to show a lot of improvement of her previous efforts. (25/1)

4518 Dont Forget Curtis (IRE) got a long way behind until staying on when the race was over. A stiffer test is surely required. (12/1)

3907 Teejay's Future (IRE) is only lightly-made, but looks as though she will stay further than this. (14/1)

T/Plpt: £196.20 (50.04 Tckts). T/Qdpt: £29.10 (23.1 Tckts) Dk

4519-NEWTON ABBOT (L-H) (Good to soft)

Wednesday May 21st

WEATHER: cloudy

4639 J C MILTON ELECTRICALS H'CAP HURDLE (0-125) (4-Y.O+) (Class D)

6-10 (6-10) **2m 6f (10 hdls)** £2,669.00 (£749.00: £365.00) GOING minus 0.19 sec per fur (G)

				SP	RR	SF
4436*	**Jenzsoph (IRE) (103)** (PJHobbs) **6-11-2b** GTormey (led: hrd rdn & hdd after 3 out: rallied to ld last: all out)	—	**1**	9/4[2]	79	43
4436[2]	**Peter Monamy (103)** (MCPipe) **5-11-2v[1]** APMcCoy (chsd wnr: mstke 5th: hrd rdn after 6th: led after 3 out to last: rallied)	nk	**2**	5/2[3]	79	43
3628*	**Defendthereaim (96)** (RGFrost) **6-10-9** JFrost (hld up: bhd fr 8th: t.o)	dist	**3**	6/4[1]	—	—
4130[P]	**Holy Wanderer (USA) (112)** (TRGeorge) **8-11-4**(7) MrRMorgan (hld up in rr: rdn appr 7th: sn t.o: fell last)		**F**	12/1	—	—
				(SP 107.0%)		**4 Rn**

5m 13.9 (1.90) CSF £7.23 TOTE £3.20 (£3.00) OWNER Mr A. Stevens (MINEHEAD) BRED A. T. Robinson

4436* Jenzsoph (IRE) was a stone worse off with the runner-up than when beating him nineteen lengths over a half-a-mile shorter at Fontwell. She got the better of a duel between a couple of somewhat half-hearted heroes. (9/4)

4436 Peter Monamy, a stone better in than when well-beaten by the winner last time, was stepping up in trip. Driven along for most of the final circuit, he seemed in control until apparently faltering going to the final flight, but ran on again once headed. (5/2)

3628* Defendthereaim presumably needs the ground softer than he encountered here. (6/4: 11/10-evens)

2569 Holy Wanderer (USA) (12/1: 8/1-14/1)

4640 MIKE HOWARD & DICK SPENCER MEMORIAL HUNTERS' CHASE (5-Y.O+) (Class H)

6-40 (6-40) **3m 2f 110y (20 fncs)** £1,152.00 (£322.00: £156.00) GOING minus 0.19 sec per fur (G)

				SP	RR	SF
	Buzz O'The Crowd (MissAVHandel) **10-11-0**(7) MrDAlers-Hankey (lw: a.p: led 16th: sn clr: r.o wl)	—	**1**	14/1	115?	42
4326[5]	**Fight to Win (USA)** (LPGrassick) **9-11-0**(7) MrJGrassick (lw: hld up: hdwy 13th: lost pl appr 15th: wnt poor 2nd 2 out)	dist	**2**	50/1	—	—
4522[P]	**Tom's Gemini Star** (OJCarter) **9-11-7**(7) MissVRoberts (hld up: mstke 13th: sn wl bhd: styd on fr 3 out: n.d)	11	**3**	25/1	—	—
4326[2]	**Knifeboard** (PaulHosgood) **11-11-0**(7) MrEWilliams (lw: hdwy 8th: wknd appr 15th: t.o)	4	**4**	6/1[2]	—	—
4469*	**Phar Too Touchy** (VictorDartnall) **10-11-5**(7) MrNHarris (lw: hdwy 5th: led 7th to 16th: sn wknd: fin tired)	4	**5**	1/3[1]	—	—
	Just Ben (KCumings) **9-11-0**(7) MissJCumings (lw: prom tl wknd 12th)	13	**6**	16/1	—	—
3799[5]	**Expressment** (MissASRoss) **13-11-7**(7) MrGPenfold (bhd: reminders after 5th: t.o fr 8th)	23	**7**	33/1	—	—
4325[4]	**Some-Toy** (JohnSquire) **11-11-10**(7) MissLBlackford (wl bhd 8th: sme hdwy 12th: sn wknd: t.o whn p.u bef 4 out)		**P**	12/1[3]	—	—

				SP	RR	SF
4511*	**Kino** (AndrewMartin) **10-11-10**(7) MrAndrewMartin (led to 7th: wkng whn mstke 15th: t.o whn blnd bdly 3 out: p.u bef 2 out)		P	25/1	—	—
	Alpha One (DFBassett) **12-11-0**(7) MissKDiMarte (a bhd: t.o whn mstke 8th: p.u bef 14th)		P	66/1	—	—
4560[6]	**J B Lad** (HRTuck) **11-11-0**(7) MrSShinton (lw: j.slowly 4th: bhd fr 11th: t.o whn mstke 16th: blnd & uns rdr 4 out)		U	50/1	—	—

(SP 125.6%) **11 Rn**

6m 39.0 (5.00) CSF £465.63 TOTE £13.70: £1.60 £5.40 £5.30 (£109.30) Trio £225.60; £158.93 to 23/5/97 OWNER Mr B. J. Williams (ILMINSTER) BRED Mrs C. Handel

Buzz O'The Crowd, a winner between the flags in 1994, finished a well-beaten third in a novice chase at Exeter just over a year ago. (14/1: 10/1-16/1)

Fight to Win (USA) won three novice chases for Ian Balding back in 1993. (50/1)

3765* Tom's Gemini Star came from the next parish to finish a remote third. (25/1)

4326 Knifeboard (6/1: op 4/1)

4469* Phar Too Touchy was reported by her trainer to have finished distressed. (1/3: op 1/2)

4179 Some-Toy (12/1: 8/1-14/1)

4641 COME RACING AT NEWTON ABBOT NOVICES' HURDLE (4-Y.O+) (Class D)

7-10 (7-11) **2m 1f (8 hdls)** £2,855.20 (£802.20: £391.60) GOING minus 0.19 sec per fur (G)

				SP	RR	SF
4397[F]	**Nordic Breeze (IRE) (120)** (MCPipe) **5-11-7** APMcCoy (hld up: mstke 5th: hdwy to ld on bit after 3 out: hrd hld)	—	1	2/11[1]	55++	—
2959[7]	**Sparkling Buck** (NGAyliffe) **5-10-6**(3) GuyLewis (hld up: hdwy 3 out: sn rdn to chal: no ch w wnr)	1¼	2	10/1[3]	42	—
4304[P]	**Technical Move (IRE)** (GAHam) **6-10-9** SBurrough (chsd clr ldr to 3 out: sn wknd: mstke 2 out)	21	3	100/1	22	—
4003[10]	**Mordros** (MrsJScrivens) **7-11-0** TDascombe (hld up & plld hrd: no ch whn mstke 3 out)	1¼	4	25/1	26	—
	With Intent (LGCottrell) **5-11-0** MrLJefford (plld hrd: led: sn clr: wkng whn hit 3 out: sn hdd & btn)	1¼	5	8/1[2]	25	—
4519[3]	**Final Score (IRE)** (PaddyFarrell) **7-10-4**(5) OBurrows (hld up: rdn 5th: sn t.o)	dist	6	25/1	—	—

(SP 113.5%) **6 Rn**

4m 16.4 (23.40) CSF £2.82 TOTE £1.30: £1.20 £1.60 (£2.70) OWNER Mr Malcolm Jones (WELLINGTON) BRED P. F. N. Fanning

3595 Nordic Breeze (IRE) took his trainer to the double century for the season with a facile win. (2/11)

1594 Sparkling Buck is greatly flattered by her proximity to the winner. (10/1: op 6/1)

4642 SPA-TRANS AND CHAGFORD FOOTBALL CLUB H'CAP CHASE (0-135) (5-Y.O+) (Class C)

7-40 (7-40) **2m 5f 110y (16 fncs)** £4,585.00 (£1,295.00: £630.00) GOING minus 0.19 sec per fur (G)

				SP	RR	SF
4438[3]	**Polden Pride (113)** (GBBalding) **9-10-6** APMcCoy (lw: hld up: mstke 7th: sn rdn: wnt 2nd 2 out: led last: rdn out)	—	1	2/1[2]	124	9
4529[4]	**Allo George (107)** (AGNewcombe) **11-10-0** AThornton (j.rt: led to last: one pce)	3	2	100/30[3]	116	1
4509*	**Philip's Woody (116)** (NJHenderson) **9-10-9** MAFitzgerald (tk keen hold: trckd ldr: rdn 12th: wknd appr last: eased flat)	17	3	10/11[1]	112	—

(SP 108.8%) **3 Rn**

5m 26.8 (9.80) CSF £6.66 TOTE £3.10 (£5.00) OWNER Lockyer,C Parry,G Balding (ANDOVER) BRED G. B. Balding

4438 Polden Pride would probably have preferred the ground a bit faster, but proved good enough off the same mark as when successful over course and distance last month. (2/1)

4529 Allo George was inclined to jump right-handed, and one could not help thinking he may have been feeling something. (100/30)

4509* Philip's Woody disappointed off a mark only 1lb higher than at Stratford. (10/11: 4/5-5/4)

4643 FLORIDA NOVICES' CHASE (5-Y.O+) (Class E)

8-10 (8-13) **2m 110y (13 fncs)** £2,836.75 (£859.00: £419.50: £199.75) GOING minus 0.19 sec per fur (G)

				SP	RR	SF
4430[F]	**Robert's Toy (IRE) (113)** (MCPipe) **6-11-12b** APMcCoy (mde all: sn clr: hit 3 out: eased flat)	—	1	3/1[1]	98+	35
4507[4]	**Finnigan Free** (GAHam) **7-10-7**(7) MrMFrith (sn chsng wnr: rdn 4 out: no ch w wnr)	1½	2	6/1	85	22
1036[10]	**Another Hubblick** (RJBaker) **6-11-0** VSlattery (lw: bhd: hit 4th: hdwy 8th: lft 3rd appr 9th: r.o one pce fr 3 out)	2½	3	66/1	82	19
3952[0]	**Holdimclose** (RGFrost) **7-11-0** JFrost (prom to 7th)	26	4	7/2[2]	57	—
4523[2]	**Stratton Flyer (65)** (HSHowe) **7-10-2**(7) MrRWidger (bhd fr 7th)	1¾	5	12/1	50	—
4458[P]	**Carlingford Gale (IRE)** (TRGeorge) **6-10-9** LHarvey (hit 1st: hdwy 6th: wknd 7th: t.o)	9	6	7/1	42	—
4523[3]	**Run With Joy (IRE)** (AGHobbs) **6-11-0** RGreene (prom: rdn 6th: wknd 8th: blnd 4 out: t.o)	11	7	14/1	36	—
4443[7]	**Roca Murada (IRE)** (PJHobbs) **8-11-0** NWilliamson (hld up & bhd: hdwy on ins 7th: 3rd whn p.u bef 9th)		P	4/1[3]	—	—
4401[10]	**Patong Beach** (PCRitchens) **7-10-9** MAhern (a bhd: t.o 8th: p.u bef 2 out)		P	66/1	—	—

(SP 111.4%) **9 Rn**

4m 5.7 (5.70) CSF £18.74 TOTE £3.60: £1.80 £1.90 £8.90 (£15.90) Trio £44.10 OWNER Mr Clive Smith (WELLINGTON) BRED M. Conaghan

3199 Robert's Toy (IRE) had the blinkers refitted for this return to fences. (3/1)

3627 Finnigan Free, the only one to try and make a race of it on the final circuit, did nothing wrong but is greatly flattered by the margin of defeat. (6/1: tchd 10/1)

Another Hubblick was making his debut over regulation fences, having shown no sign of ability over hurdles or in points. (66/1)

1429 Holdimclose had been an early casualty on his only other run over fences in January. (7/2: op 9/4)

4644 FINAL FLING H'CAP HURDLE (0-105) (4-Y.O+) (Class F)

8-40 (8-40) **2m 1f (8 hdls)** £1,971.50 (£554.00: £270.50) GOING minus 0.19 sec per fur (G)

				SP	RR	SF
4548*	**Blade of Fortune (90)** (VGGreenway) **9-10-9**(7) 7x MrJTizzard (mde all: qcknd & mstke 2 out: r.o wl)	—	1	15/8[2]	71	9
4307[4]	**Cooley's Valve (IRE) (98)** (MrsSDWilliams) **9-11-7**(3) MrRThornton (hld up: wnt 2nd 5th: ev ch last: nt qckn)	1¼	2	7/2[3]	78	16
4332[3]	**Miss Souter (74)** (HSHowe) **8-10-0** BPowell (hld up: rdn after 4th: wknd after 3 out)	17	3	10/1	38	—
4332*	**Mystic Hill (91)** (RGFrost) **6-11-3** JFrost (nt j.w: chsd wnr to 5th: rdn after 3 out: btn whn hit 2 out)	7	4	11/8[1]	48	—

(SP 108.2%) **4 Rn**

4m 2.2 (9.20) CSF £7.54 TOTE £2.60: (£5.70) OWNER Mr V. G. Greenway (TAUNTON) BRED F. H. Lee

LONG HANDICAP Miss Souter 9-8

4548* Blade of Fortune would not have given the runner-up a chance had he jumped the penultimate hurdle properly. (15/8)

4307 Cooley's Valve (IRE) could not take advantage of the winner's error two out. (7/2)

4332 Miss Souter (10/1: 8/1-12/1)
4332* Mystic Hill did not hurdle as fluently as his supporters would have liked. (11/8)

T/Plpt: £3,040.50 (3.62 Tckts). T/Qdpt: £30.20 (17.95 Tckts) KH

4471-UTTOXETER (L-H) (Good to Soft)
Wednesday May 21st
WEATHER: overcast

4645 CARLING BLACK LABEL MAIDEN HURDLE (4-Y.O+) (Class E)
6-25 (6-26) **2m (9 hdls)** £2,389.50 (£672.00: £328.50) GOING: 0.15 sec per fur (G)

	Horse		Pos	SP	RR	SF
4547[P]	**Single Sourcing (IRE)**	(MissHCKnight) **6-11-5** JCulloty (mde all: lft clr last: drvn out)——	1	6/1[2]	65+	23
4238[2]	**Ilewin Janine (IRE) (78)**	(PCRitchens) **6-11-0** CMaude (lw: hld up: hdwy 6th: ev ch whn hit 2 out: styd on same pce flat) 3½	2	6/1[2]	57	15
4465[2]	**Timidjar (IRE) (95)**	(DRGandolfo) **4-11-0b** RDunwoody (wnt prom 5th: pushed along next: rdn & nt r.o appr 2 out) 7	3	4/6[1]	55	8
4567[4]	**Sapphire Son (IRE)**	(PCClarke) **5-11-5** BFenton (plld hrd: sn trckng ldrs: wkng whn mstke 3 out) dist	4	7/1[3]	—	—
4512[12]	**Woodlands Lad Too (45)**	(PAPritchard) **5-11-5** RBellamy (in tch: rdn & outpcd 5th: t.o 3 out) 12	5	66/1	—	—
4476[P]	**Trentside Major**	(CSmith) **5-11-5** MRanger (bit bkwd: prom to 5th: t.o 3 out) nk	6	50/1	—	—
	China Lal	(ABailey) **5-11-0** OPears (nt j.w: lost pl 4th: sn t.o) 5	7	33/1	—	—
3685[5]	**Toraja**	(NoelChance) **5-11-5** DLeahy (trckd wnr: chal 3 out: ev ch whn fell last)	F	10/1	65?	—
	Dunston Queen	(BPreece) **4-10-9** GaryLyons (t.o 6th: p.u bef last)	P	50/1	—	—

(SP 118.5%) **9 Rn**

3m 52.7 (11.70) CSF £37.63 TOTE £7.30: £1.80 £1.30 £1.10 (£24.40) Trio £12.30 OWNER Mr V. J. Adams (WANTAGE) BRED Aidan Furlong
WEIGHT FOR AGE 4yo-5lb

Single Sourcing (IRE), a bumper winner over this course two seasons ago, had been pulled up on his two previous outings this time, breaking a blood vessel first time and then being unable to handle the right-handed track at Towcester. He looked to just have the upper hand when left clear at the last. The Handicapper can surely not rate him too highly because of the proximity of the second and, still in need of more experience before he goes chasing, he could be an interesting proposition in novice handicaps next term. (6/1: op 3/1)
4238 Ilewin Janine (IRE), a very modest performer, showed a poor action going down. (6/1)
4465 Timidjar (IRE) continually swished his tail in the paddock, and when his jockey got serious he looked anything but keen on the task. (4/6)
4567 Sapphire Son (IRE) took a fierce hold going to post, and had run himself to a standstill when he hit the third last. (7/1)
Toraja, a fair stayer on the Flat, is a well-made sort. Moving upsides three out, he was still bang level and the issue was still very much in doubt when he fell at the final flight. (10/1)

4646 DRAUGHT BASS NOVICES' H'CAP HURDLE (0-105) (5-Y.O+) (Class E)
6-55 (6-55) **3m 110y (12 hdls)** £2,326.50 (£654.00: £319.50) GOING: 0.15 sec per fur (G)

	Horse		Pos	SP	RR	SF
4516*	**Palace of Gold (85)**	(LLungo) **7-11-3** RSupple (lw: chsd ldrs: led after 8th: hrd rdn & styd on flat: all out)——	1	9/1	66	37
4476*	**Mr Christie (96)**	(MissLCSiddall) **5-12-0** RDunwoody (lw: chsd ldrs: rdn appr 2 out: rallied flat: swtchd lft: nt qckn nr fin) 1½	2	2/1[1]	76	47
4277*	**Quite A Man (79)**	(SABrookshaw) **9-10-11** CMaude (lw: hdwy 8th: chal & blnd last: nt rcvr) 9	3	100/30[2]	53	24
4558[5]	**Royrace (68)**	(WMBrisbourne) **5-9-11**(3) RMassey (hdwy u.p 7th: sn chsng ldrs & drvn along: wknd 3 out) 10	4	33/1	36	7
4512[2]	**Nahla (83)**	(BdeHaan) **7-11-1** SCurran (hld up: hdwy 9th: sn chsng ldrs: wknd appr next) 9	5	4/1[3]	45	16
4513[6]	**Chill Factor (75)**	(MrsMReveley) **7-10-7b[1]** PNiven (chsd ldr: led 5th: reminders 7th: hdd after next: nt r.o: t.o) dist	6	8/1	—	—
911[3]	**Little Tincture (IRE) (70)**	(MrsTJMcInnesSkinner) **7-10-2** GUpton (swtg: led to 5th: lost pl 7th: sn t.o) 3	7	12/1	—	—
3934[R]	**Katballou (68)**	(KGWingrove) **8-9-7**(7) MrSDurack (wnt prom 7th: drvn along & lost pl after next: t.o whn p.u bef 3 out)	P	14/1	—	—

(SP 114.8%) **8 Rn**

5m 54.7 (12.70) CSF £25.83 CT £67.23 TOTE £5.30: £1.60 £1.50 £1.70 (£10.00) OWNER Mr Andrew Duncan (CARRUTHERSTOWN) BRED Cheveley Park Stud Ltd
LONG HANDICAP Royrace 9-6 Katballou 9-5

4516* Palace of Gold, a son of Slip Anchor, proved well-suited by the step-up in trip, and responded to his rider's vigorous urgings. (9/1: 8/1-12/1)
4476* Mr Christie was 13lb higher in the weights than when runner-up in a similar event at Worcester two outings ago. He never gave up trying but the winner always just had the edge. (2/1)
4277* Quite A Man reverted to hurdling after winning his previous five outings over fences, the latest from a mark of 110. Racing off 79 here, he was upsides when he blundered at the last. It appeared to completely knock the stuffing out of him, but there must be a suspicion that his stamina gave out on the run-in. (100/30)
Royrace ran as well as could be expected considering he was 8lb out of the handicap. (33/1)
4512 Nahla, who wore a crossed-noseband, ran out of stamina turning for home. (4/1)

4647 CAFFREYS IRISH ALE (FRED DIXON TROPHY) H'CAP CHASE (0-130) (5-Y.O+) (Class C)
7-25 (7-25) **3m 2f (20 fncs)** £4,260.00 (£1,290.00: £630.00: £300.00) GOING: 0.15 sec per fur (G)

	Horse		Pos	SP	RR	SF
4546[2]	**Brogeen Lady (IRE) (100)**	(DRGandolfo) **7-10-3** RDunwoody (lw: j.w: led 3rd: styd on strly between last 2: eased towards fin)——	1	15/8[1]	92+	—
4361a[4]	**Mr Boston (125)**	(MrsMReveley) **12-12-0** PNiven (lw: shkn up 12th: sn w wnr: drvn along 5 out: nt qckn between last 2) 6	2	9/4[2]	113	16
4549[2]	**Thermal Warrior (97)**	(JABOld) **9-10-0** CLlewellyn (chsd ldrs: drvn along 14th: rdn & outpcd fr 5 out) 26	3	5/1	69	—
4463[2]	**James Pigg (118)**	(PFNicholls) **10-11-7** RJohnson (led tl blnd & hdd 3rd: drvn along 14th: wkng whn mstke next: sn bhd) 20	4	5/2[3]	78	—

(SP 110.8%) **4 Rn**

6m 52.3 (25.30) CSF £6.04 TOTE £2.80 (£3.40) OWNER Starlight Racing (WANTAGE) BRED E. Farrell
LONG HANDICAP Thermal Warrior 8-12

4546 Brogeen Lady (IRE) turned in an exhibition round and, pushed clear between the last two, would have had ten lengths to spare but for being eased up. She seems to have at last got the hang of jumping regulation fences, and proved well-suited by the trip. (15/8)
4361a Mr Boston, an out-and-out stayer, ran his heart out but the concession of almost two stone was beyond him. (9/4)
4549 Thermal Warrior was 16lb out of the handicap. (5/1: 4/1-6/1)
4463 James Pigg is not one to rely on these days but, in mitigation, the ground was probably on the easy side for him. (5/2: op 13/8)

4648 HOOPER'S HOOCH CONDITIONAL (S) H'CAP HURDLE (0-95) (4-Y.O+) (Class G)

7-55 (7-55) **2m (9 hdls)** £1,868.00 (£523.00: £254.00) GOING: 0.15 sec per fur (G)

				SP	RR	SF
4468^{11}	**Strike-a-Pose (65)** (BJLlewellyn) **7-10-9** MichaelBrennan (hld up & bhd: gd hdwy 6th: led between last 2: r.o wl)	—	**1**	6/1^{3}	54	12
3940^{8}	**Mudlark (76)** (JNorton) **5-11-3**(3) BGrattan (bhd: gd hdwy 6th: styd on flat: no ch w wnr)	6	**2**	12/1	59	17
4548^{3}	**Witherkay (74)** (PFNicholls) **4-10-10**(3) LCummins (chsd ldrs: mstke 4th: one pce fr 2 out)	3½	**3**	7/4^{1}	54	7
4443^{5}	**Follow de Call (72)** (DMcCain) **7-10-11**(5) AEgan (prom: led 3 out: rdn & wnt bdly rt next: sn hdd: grad wknd)	5	**4**	12/1	47	5
4567^{5}	**Our Eddie (77)** (KGWingrove) **8-11-7v** SRyan (hld up: hdwy 6th: one pce fr 3 out)	1¾	**5**	7/1	50	8
4423^{4}	**Never so Blue (IRE) (78)** (PBradley) **6-11-5**(3) RWilkinson (in tch to 5th: sn lost pl: sme hdwy 3 out: nvr nr to chal)	3½	**6**	8/1	47	5
3831^{4}	**Blatant Outburst (74)** (MissSJWilton) **7-11-4v^{1}** SophieMitchell (lw: trckd ldrs: led appr 6th: hdd 3 out: sn wknd)	2	**7**	11/2^{2}	41	—
3471^{7}	**Verro (USA) (56)** (KBishop) **10-9-9**(5) MGriffiths (plld hrd: led to 4th: wknd 6th)	hd	**8**	50/1	23	—
4405^{7}	**Soccer Ball (60)** (TRWatson) **7-10-4** DJKavanagh (hld up: a in rr)	2	**9**	16/1	25	—
	Premier Star (56) (KGWingrove) **7-9-9**(5) JPower (hld up: mstkes 3rd & 5th: n.d)	14	**10**	33/1	7	—
4378^{12}	**Lady Lois (56)** (BPreece) **6-9-9**(5) JMogford (wl bhd fr 5th)	18	**11**	33/1	—	—
4472^{7}	**Orinoco Venture (IRE) (57)** (ABailey) **6-9-12b**(3) XAizpuru (chsd ldrs tl wknd appr 3 out)	10	**12**	12/1	—	—
4299^{P}	**Nebaal (USA) (56)** (GBarnett) **7-10-0b^{1}** RMassey (w ldrs: led 4th tl appr 6th: sn wknd: t.o whn p.u bef last)		**P**	25/1	—	—
				(SP 130.3%)	**13 Rn**	

3m 53.0 (12.00) CSF £72.33 CT £168.45 TOTE £7.70: £1.90 £3.20 £1.20 (£31.80) Trio £56.20 OWNER Mr B. J. Llewellyn (BARGOED) BRED Mrs R. D. Peacock
LONG HANDICAP Verro (USA) 9-13 Premier Star 9-13 Lady Lois 9-8 Nebaal (USA) 9-8
WEIGHT FOR AGE 4yo-5lb
No bid
STEWARDS' ENQUIRY Ryan susp. 30-31/5/97 (improper use of whip).
4002 Strike-a-Pose landed her first win for three years but, judging by the market support, it was not unexpected. Held up off the pace, when sent about her business there was only going to be one winner. (6/1: op 12/1)
3371 Mudlark, an in-and-out sort, ran one of his better races. (12/1)
4548 Witherkay was racing off his old mark, but he has been hoisted 13lb in the weights after his Chepstow effort. Unless the Handicapper relents, he will be banging his head against a brick wall. (7/4)
4162 Follow de Call went on travelling strongly but, once in front and ridden by an inexperienced rider, he dived badly right and, but for that, might have finished second. (12/1)
4567 Our Eddie wore a cross-noseband. Despite being held, his young rider would not put down his stick, and he was suspended for two days. (7/1)

4649 CARLING PREMIER NOVICES' CHASE (5-Y.O+) (Class D)

8-25 (8-26) **2m 5f (16 fncs)** £3,468.75 (£1,050.00: £512.50: £243.75) GOING: 0.15 sec per fur (G)

				SP	RR	SF
4515^{2}	**Plumbob (IRE) (84)** (LLungo) **8-11-0** RSupple (lw: chsd ldrs: drvn along 12th: chal last: styd on wl to ld nr fin)	—	**1**	11/4^{2}	101	15
4480^{3}	**Brighter Shade (IRE) (102)** (MrsMReveley) **7-11-12** PNiven (unruly s: hld up: jnd ldr 8th: led 4 out: hdd nr fin)	hd	**2**	11/4^{2}	113	27
4533^{2}	**With Impunity (105)** (PFNicholls) **8-11-6** RJohnson (led to 4 out: wknd next)	15	**3**	9/4^{1}	96	10
4435^{2}	**Master Crusader (73)** (DLWilliams) **11-10-7**(7) MrSDurack (drvn along & lost tch 9th: t.o 12th: sme hdwy fr 3 out)	12	**4**	14/1	80	—
4533^{F}	**Astral Invasion (USA) (66)** (TWall) **6-11-0b** SWynne (prom: drvn along 9th: sn lost pl)	15	**5**	25/1	69	—
	Mighty Merc (MrsBKBroad) **9-11-0** KJohnson (plld hrd: sn w ldrs: hit 8th: lost pl next: t.o 12th)	dist	**6**	33/1	—	—
2577^{5}	**Bridepark Rose (IRE) (82)** (PCRitchens) **9-10-9** SFox (sn trckng ldrs: wknd 4 out: poor 4th whn blnd & uns rdr last)		**U**	5/1^{3}	—	—
				(SP 114.2%)	**7 Rn**	

5m 22.1 (17.10) CSF £10.18 TOTE £3.80: £1.80 £2.30 (£4.60) OWNER Mr Andrew Duncan (CARRUTHERSTOWN)
4515 Plumbob (IRE), who did not jump as well as at Hexham, found this trip on the sharp side but responded to strong pressure to get up near the finish. (11/4)
4480 Brighter Shade (IRE) was reluctant to line-up at the start. Jumping soundly, he only gave best near the line. Still gaining valuable experience, he looks one to keep on the right side in handicap company next term. (11/4: 7/4-3/1)
4533 With Impunity, who looked very fit, set the pace but was left toiling up the straight. He probably wants softer ground and further. (9/4)
4435 Master Crusader was tailed off a mile from home. (14/1)

4650 WORTHINGTON DRAUGHT BITTER NOVICES' HURDLE (4-Y.O+) (Class D)

8-55 (8-55) **2m 4f 110y (10 hdls)** £2,899.00 (£814.00: £397.00) GOING: 0.15 sec per fur (G)

				SP	RR	SF
4625^{5}	**Morpheus (103)** (DNicholson) **8-11-0** RJohnson (hld up: hdwy after 6th: styd on to ld last 100y)	—	**1**	2/1^{2}	68	—
4536^{5}	**Bullens Bay (IRE) (93)** (BJLlewellyn) **8-11-0** MrJLLlewellyn (chsd ldrs: reminders 7th: rdn & hung lft 2 out: styd on wl flat)	1½	**2**	14/1	67	—
4547^{2}	**Rythm Rock (IRE) (94)** (DRGandolfo) **8-11-0** RDunwoody (hld up: gd hdwy after 6th: led 2 out: mstke last: hdd & no ex flat)	1¾	**3**	13/8^{1}	66	—
4528^{5}	**Gamay** (NRMitchell) **7-11-0** CLlewellyn (chsd ldrs: outpcd appr 3 out: styd on flat)	1¼	**4**	20/1	65	—
4547^{R}	**Camp Head (IRE)** (OSherwood) **6-11-0** JAMcCarthy (jnd ldrs 5th: led 7th to 2 out: sn outpcd: styd on flat)	1¼	**5**	4/1^{3}	64	—
4539^{6}	**Pamalyn** (SABrookshaw) **5-10-9** CMaude (in tch: outpcd after 7th: n.d)	8	**6**	10/1	59	—
4532^{4}	**Romantic Warrior** (KSBridgwater) **4-10-5**(3) RMassey (w ldrs: outpcd 7th: kpt on between last 2)	d.h	**6**	33/1	57	—
4528^{6}	**Crocknamohill (IRE)** (KSBridgwater) **6-11-0** WMarston (led 2nd to 7th: wknd next:)	11	**8**	20/1	49	—
4476^{P}	**Moor Hall Prince** (NMBabbage) **7-11-0** BFenton (hld up & bhd: mstke 2nd: n.d)	4	**9**	50/1	46	—

4506P **Safwan** (PJHobbs) **5-11-0** MRichards (prom tl wknd appr 3 out: sn bhd: t.o) ....dist	**10**	20/1	—	—
4376[12] **Dunston Knight** (BPreece) **4-10-8** GaryLyons (led to 2nd: rdn 6th: wknd next: sn bhd: t.o) ....¾	**11**	100/1	—	—
		(SP 127.4%)	**11 Rn**	

5m 10.5 (26.50) CSF £25.41 TOTE £3.00: £1.30 £3.50 £1.10 (£15.00) Trio £7.40 OWNER Mrs M. A. Powis (TEMPLE GUITING)
WEIGHT FOR AGE 4yo-6lb

4625 Morpheus, who looked very hard-trained, is a strong-pulling type. He finally came good on this his eighth outing but, at the line, the tank was empty. (2/1)
Bullens Bay (IRE), whose first four outings this time came in point-to-points, gave his rider problems by persisting in hanging left but, to his credit, he stayed on under pressure on the run-in and was closing the gap at the line. He will be suited by three miles. (14/1)
4547 Rythm Rock (IRE), who walked stiff behind in the paddock, came through smartly to show ahead at the second last but, after flattening the final flight, he could find no extra. (13/8)
Gamay, a point-to-point winner, was tapped for toe but was staying on again at the finish. He will be suited by a step-up to three miles. (20/1)
4547 Camp Head (IRE), a chasing type, ran out last time when his bit slipped. After kicking for home, he was badly outpaced between the last two but, to his credit, was sticking on at the finish. Three miles will suit him much better. (4/1)

T/Plpt: £7.50 (1,884.9 Tckts). T/Qdpt: £6.90 (88.95 Tckts) WG

4532-WORCESTER (L-H) (Soft)
Wednesday May 21st

Race 7 no extended distances - camera failure.
WEATHER: overcast with showers

4651 EARLS CROOME HURDLE (4-Y.O) (Class E)
2-20 (2-20) **2m (8 hdls)** £2,250.00 (£625.00: £300.00) GOING: 1.07 sec per fur (HY)

		SP	RR	SF
4555[2] **Melt The Clouds (CAN) (111)** (MCPipe) **4-11-5b** APMcCoy (mde all: drvn clr whn blnd last: rdn out) ....—	**1**	11/8[1]	77	40
4299[2] **Mazamet (USA)** (OO'Neill) **4-10-12v[1]** VSlattery (b.nr hind: a.p: rdn 3 out: styd on flat) 1¾	**2**	15/8[2]	68	31
4465F **Santella Cape** (NJHawke) **4-10-12** JRailton (bkwd: hld up & bhd: hdwy to chse wnr 3 out: wknd next) 6	**3**	16/1	62	25
3590* **Hawanafa (71)** (MissKMGeorge) **4-11-0** DGallagher (lw: trckd ldrs tl lost tch 5th: t.o) ....dist	**4**	10/1	—	—
4434[5] **Heart** (MissHCKnight) **4-10-7** JCulloty (prom tl wknd qckly after 5th: t.o whn p.u bef 2 out)	**P**	6/1[3]	—	—
		(SP 106.1%)	**5 Rn**	

4m 2.6 (22.60) CSF £3.64 TOTE £1.40: £1.20 £1.10 (£1.10) OWNER Promo-Sherring Ltd (WELLINGTON) BRED Huntingdon Stud Farm Inc

4555 Melt The Clouds (CAN) had no problem handling this much more testing ground, but a careless mistake at the last almost threw the prize away. (11/8)
4299 Mazamet (USA), visored for the first time and wearing a large bandage on his near hind, looked in trouble when put under pressure soon after entering the straight, but the winner gave him a second bite at the cherry at the final flight and, on a sounder surface, he might have been able to take it. (15/8)
4465 Santella Cape, a faller on his hurdling debut, still looked very much in need of the run, but he showed promise and should be able to go on improving. (16/1)
3590* Hawanafa (10/1: op 4/1)

4652 RIPPLE NOVICES' H'CAP HURDLE (0-100) (4-Y.O+) (Class E)
2-50 (2-50) **2m 4f (10 hdls)** £2,460.00 (£685.00: £330.00) GOING: 1.07 sec per fur (HY)

		SP	RR	SF
4468* **Hello Me Man (IRE) (81)** (BJLlewellyn) **9-11-4** MrJLLlewellyn (lw: swtg: hld up & bhd: hdwy 7th: led 3 out: hrd rdn flat: all out) ....—	**1**	4/1[2]	62	4
4333[4] **Lyphard's Fable (USA) (63)** (TRGeorge) **6-10-0** RJohnson (led to 3rd: jnd wnr 3 out: rider lost whip: no ex nr fin) ....¾	**2**	9/1	43	—
4527[4] **Prime of Life (IRE) (87)** (JMPEustace) **7-11-10** SMcNeill (chsd ldrs tl lost tch 7th: styd on again fr 2 out) 16	**3**	9/1	55	—
3949[3] **Jay Em Ess (NZ) (78)** (AGHobbs) **8-11-1** RGreene (hld up: a in rr) 13	**4**	11/2	35	—
4544[4] **A S Jim (74)** (OO'Neill) **6-10-11** VSlattery (hld up: hdwy 5th: led after 7th to 3 out: wknd qckly) 3½	**5**	5/1[3]	28	—
3760[4] **Mr Lovely (IRE) (63)** (JNeville) **6-10-0** TDascombe (bkwd: prom: hit 6th: b.d by broken hurdle 3 out)	**B**	12/1	—	—
4512[3] **Positivo (72)** (MissCJECaroe) **6-10-9** DLeahy (swtg: chsd ldrs to 5th: wl bhd whn fell 3 out)	**F**	11/2	—	—
3500[11] **Viking Dream (IRE) (71)** (JCFox) **5-10-8** SFox (chsd ldrs: ev ch whn blnd & p.u 7th)	**P**	7/2[1]	—	—
4466[7] **Mutley (64)** (NJHawke) **7-10-1**ow1 CMaude (led 3rd: clr 5th: hdd after 7th: wknd qckly: p.u flat)	**P**	20/1	—	—
4472[5] **Kings Vision (67)** (WJenks) **5-10-4**ow4 TJenks (t: a bhd: t.o fr ½-wy: p.u bef 3 out)	**P**	25/1	—	—
		(SP 126.0%)	**10 Rn**	

5m 16.1 (38.10) CSF £39.36 CT £291.19 TOTE £4.10: £1.60 £3.20 £4.90 (£13.50) Trio £48.20 OWNER Lodge Cross Partnership (BARGOED) BRED Mrs E. J. Hogan
LONG HANDICAP Lyphard's Fable (USA) 9-13 Mutley 9-11 Kings Vision 9-6

4468* Hello Me Man (IRE) only began to get into the action turning out of the back straight but, after striking the front three out, he had to show his true colours to hold off a very persistent rival. (4/1: 3/1-9/2)
Lyphard's Fable (USA) seemed to be a very unfortunate loser, for his jockey dropped his whip soon after the third last and, when a crack was needed on the run-in, it could not be provided. (9/1)
4527 Prime of Life (IRE) is just not firing on his return to hurdling and, though he began to stay on again in the latter stages, the leading pair had long gone. (9/1)
3949 Jay Em Ess (NZ) (11/2: 7/2-6/1)
4544 A S Jim (5/1: 7/2-11/2)
4512 Positivo (11/2: 7/2-6/1)
Viking Dream (IRE), an ex-Irish mare thought to need an extended trip, pressed the leaders and still held a live chance when a bad mistake four out stopped her in her tracks and she was pulled up immediately. She must have shown something at home to be supported down to favourite and, providing she has suffered no ill-effects, she could soon be on a recovery mission. (7/2)

4653 BREWERY TRADERS H'CAP CHASE (0-125) (5-Y.O+) (Class D)
3-20 (3-20) **2m 4f 110y (15 fncs)** £3,614.50 (£1,081.00: £518.00: £236.50) GOING: 1.07 sec per fur (HY)

		SP	RR	SF
4480[2] **Destin d'Estruval (FR) (122)** (DNicholson) **6-12-0** RJohnson (lw: hit 2nd: hld up gng wl: led on bit appr last: canter) ....—	**1**	8/13[1]	128+	40

Form	Horse	Dist	Pos	SP	RR	SF
4454*	**Khalidi (IRE) (107)** (DRGandolfo) **8-10-13** RDunwoody (led to 2nd: dropped rr & drvn along 4th: led after 11th: rdn & hdd appr last: sn btn)	11	**2**	6/4[2]	104	16
4535[P]	**Little-Nipper (95)** (RJSmith) **12-10-1b[1]** CMaude (led 2nd tl after 11th: lost tch 4 out)	20	**3**	20/1[3]	77	—
4438[P]	**Bo Knows Best (IRE) (110)** (GLMoore) **8-11-2v** PHolley (lw: prom: rdn 8th: wknd 10th: t.o)	dist	**4**	20/1[3]	—	—
				(SP 111.4%)		**4 Rn**

5m 32.9 (31.90) CSF £1.91 TOTE £1.40 (£1.10) OWNER Mr Darren Mercer (TEMPLE GUITING) BRED Bernard Le Gentil

4480 Destin d'Estruval (FR), after surviving a mistake at the second, was always travelling like a winner and, when he cruised upsides the runner-up three out, it was just a matter of how far. (8/13)

4454* Khalidi (IRE) is not so effective on such testing ground and, though he has won at this trip, he is better over two miles, and his supporters knew their fate from a long way out. (6/4)

Little-Nipper ran much better in these first-time blinkers and also jumped more fluently, but he was searching for gears on the long home turn and his measure had been taken. (20/1)

4654 BREWERY TRADERS 90TH ANNIVERSARY H'CAP HURDLE (0-105) (4-Y.O+) (Class F)

3-50 (3-50) **2m (8 hdls)** £2,040.00 (£565.00: £270.00) GOING: 1.07 sec per fur (HY)

Form	Horse	Dist	Pos	SP	RR	SF
4534*	**Stay With Me (FR) (104)** (CREgerton) **7-12-0** JOsborne (a.p: led appr 3 out: clr last: comf)	—	**1**	6/5[1]	86+	50
4534[3]	**Classic Pal (USA) (79)** (NRMitchell) **6-10-3**ow[1] DSkyrme (hld up & bhd: effrt 3 out: sn rdn: kpt on: no ch w wnr)	6	**2**	5/1	55	18
4534[U]	**Daily Sport Girl (82)** (BJLlewellyn) **8-10-6** MrJLLlewellyn (chsd ldrs: ev ch 3 out: rdn & one pce appr last)	¾	**3**	7/2[2]	57	21
4443*	**Courageous Knight (86)** (PHayward) **8-10-10** BFenton (lw: lost pl 3rd: rdn & t.o 5th: styd on fr 2 out)	3	**4**	4/1[3]	58	22
3177[9]	**Green Lane (USA) (98)** (JJoseph) **9-11-8** CLlewellyn (bit bkwd: led tl hdd appr 3 out: sn btn)	¾	**5**	25/1	70	34
				(SP 108.2%)		**5 Rn**

4m 2.3 (22.30) CSF £6.60 TOTE £1.80: £1.10 £2.10 (£2.80) OWNER Mrs Sandra Roe (CHADDLEWORTH) BRED Mr and Mrs Henri Rossi and Gerard Desnoues

4534* Stay With Me (FR) is on a roll and, after ploughing a lone furrow on the inside up the straight, galloped on strongly for a very comfortable success. (6/5: 5/4-evens)

4534 Classic Pal (USA) was unable to turn the tables on the winner on 5lb better terms, but he did travel well for the majority of the race, and there is a small event to be won. (5/1: op 3/1)

4534 Daily Sport Girl, who had an outing on the Flat two days ago, moved upsides three out and briefly looked likely to make a race of it, but the winner had a bit more to give and he left her struggling between the last two. (7/2)

4443* Courageous Knight has only ever won on fast ground and, though he did stay on in the closing stages, was never going to be concerned in the finish. (4/1)

4655 HANDLEY CASTLE NOVICES' CHASE (5-Y.O+) (Class E)

4-20 (4-20) **2m 7f 110y (18 fncs)** £4,810.00 GOING: 1.07 sec per fur (HY)

Form	Horse	Dist	Pos	SP	RR	SF
4537[U]	**Stray Harmony** (RJSmith) **7-10-9** TJMurphy (bkwd: hdwy 4th: wknd 11th: t.o whn lft alone 2 out)	—	**1**	66/1	49?	—
4537[2]	**Dream Ride (IRE) (110)** (DNicholson) **7-12-0** RJohnson (a.p: blnd 3 out: 3rd & btn whn b.d next)		**B**	4/5[1]	—	—
4232*	**Who Is Equiname (IRE) (104)** (NJHenderson) **7-11-7b** MAFitzgerald (lw: led tl fell 2 out)		**F**	6/4[2]	—	—
4537[5]	**Careysville (IRE)** (TRGeorge) **6-10-11**(3) MrRThornton (a.p: blnd 14th: 2nd & rdn whn fell 2 out)		**F**	50/1	—	—
4471[B]	**Balasani (FR)** (JGO'Neill) **11-10-11**(3) LAspell (swtg: j.slowly early: bhd whn blnd 11th: sn t.o: p.u bef 4 out)		**P**	14/1[3]	—	—
	Mr Campus (IRE) (PGMurphy) **6-11-0** JRKavanagh (bkwd: a bhd: t.o whn p.u bef 11th)		**P**	66/1	—	—
4564[4]	**Cumberland Youth** (MissCJECaroe) **6-11-0** ILawrence (bhd: blnd 8th: t.o whn p.u after next)		**P**	100/1	—	—
4530[U]	**Kellytino** (PRWebber) **8-10-9** RBellamy (bkwd: a bhd: t.o 12th: p.u 4 out: continued: ref 2 out)		**R**	33/1	—	—
				(SP 111.1%)		**8 Rn**

6m 40.8 CSF £60.97 TOTE £88.10: £20.30 (£18.40) Trio £5.40 OWNER Winwood Connell Partnership (NORTHLEACH) BRED Mrs M. Connell and Mrs S. Winwood

STEWARDS' ENQUIRY Bellamy susp. 30-31/5 & 5- 6/6/97 (improper riding).

Stray Harmony rekindled memories of the Foinavon episode at Aintree many years ago. She was booked to finish a tailed-off fourth three out, only for the picture to change completely. She provided her trainer with an unforgettable first winner. (66/1)

4537 Dream Ride (IRE) appeared to be waiting on the leaders when he blundered badly three out and, with the stuffing taken out of him, he seemed destined for place money only when he was confronted by the fallen Who Is Equiname at the next, and he too was brought to earth. (4/5)

4232* Who Is Equiname (IRE) gave an exhibition of jumping from the front and, though he probably was beginning to get leg-weary, he was three lengths to the good, looking to have the prize in safe-keeping when he turned a somersault at the second last. (6/4)

Careysville (IRE) has shown very little sign of ability in the past, but he was intent on making the leader pull out all the stops when he capsized independently at the penultimate fence. (50/1)

4135 Balasani (FR) (14/1: 16/1-25/1)

4656 SHRAWLEY STANDARD OPEN N.H. FLAT RACE (I) (4, 5 & 6-Y.O) (Class H)

4-55 (4-57) **2m** £1,255.50 (£348.00: £166.50)

Form	Horse	Dist	Pos	SP	RR	SF
	Lewesdon Manor (PRWebber) **6-11-4** JOsborne (str: hld up: hdwy 5f out: styd on to ld wl ins fnl f)	—	**1**	9/1	68 f	—
4554*	**The Village Way (IRE)** (DNicholson) **6-11-11** RJohnson (hld up: hdwy 4f out: led over 2f out tl wl ins fnl f)	1	**2**	8/11[1]	74 f	—
	Kerry's Oats (PRHedger) **5-10-6**(7) MClinton (trckd ldrs: hrd drvn 3f out: r.o one pce)	5	**3**	20/1	57 f	—
	Royal Toast (IRE) (NJHenderson) **5-11-4** JRKavanagh (hld up: hdwy ½-wy: rdn & one pce fnl 2f)	2½	**4**	12/1	60 f	—
4301[2]	**Double Star** (JLHarris) **6-11-1**(3) MrRThornton (led after 2f tl over 2f out: sn rdn & btn)	1½	**5**	7/1[2]	58 f	—
	Esperanza IV (FR) (MJRoberts) **5-10-13** JRailton (trckd ldrs: rdn 3f out: sn wknd)	7	**6**	25/1	46 f	—
4433[5]	**Hill's Electric (IRE)** (TKeddy) **5-11-4** DGallagher (hld up: hdwy 7f out: rdn & wknd fnl 2f)	5	**7**	14/1	46 f	—
4561[4]	**Frankie Muck** (NATwiston-Davies) **5-11-4** CLlewellyn (hld up: hdwy 7f out: rdn over 3f out: sn wknd)	¾	**8**	20/1	45 f	—
4008[2]	**Star Adventure** (JTEvans) **5-11-4** MissEJames (chsd ldrs tl wknd 3f out)	s.h	**9**	8/1[3]	45 f	—
	Arctic Affair (IRE) (KAMorgan) **4-10-8** BPowell (a in rr: t.o)	8	**10**	20/1	32 f	—
4433[9]	**Dungannon Lad** (WGMTurner) **6-10-11**(7) LCummins (led 2f: chsd ldr tl wknd qckly 5f out: t.o)	dist	**11**	50/1	—	—
4539[8]	**A Verse To Order** (MissPMWhittle) **6-10-11**(7) MrOMcPhail (prom 10f: sn wknd: t.o)		**12**	25/1	—	—
4531[20]	**Bristol Gold** (PSFelgate) **4-10-6**(7) LSuthern (a bhd: t.o)		**13**	50/1	—	—
				(SP 131.8%)		**13 Rn**

4m 11.9 CSF £14.81 TOTE £10.60: £1.90 £1.50 £6.60 (£7.30) Trio £140.60; £87.15 to Goodwood 22/5/97 OWNER Mr J. G. Phillips (BANBURY) BRED T. R. Beadle

WEIGHT FOR AGE 4yo-5lb

Lewesdon Manor, a big, strapping individual with a gut to match, timed his run to perfection and made a winning debut. (9/1)
4554* The Village Way (IRE), far more settled on this occasion, set sail for home after leading entering the last quarter-mile, but the 7lb penalty took its toll and he was forced to give best in a thrilling duel to the line. (8/11)
Kerry's Oats was being made to work on the home turn but, to her credit, she kept battling away and, with this experience under her belt, ought to be able to win races. (20/1)
Royal Toast (IRE), a very lightly-made debutant who did not impress in his coat, may well benefit from a sounder surface and he could be worth waiting for. (12/1: 5/1-14/1)
4301 Double Star, trying his longest trip to date, dictated at a sedate pace and held the call until getting tapped for finishing speed inside the distance. (7/1: 4/1-8/1)
Esperanza IV (FR) could have been mistaken for a mare in foal on this racecourse debut, but she hunted up the leaders until calling enough early in the straight. (25/1)
4008 Star Adventure did not relish this soft ground, and was struggling to hold on once the battle to the finish really developed. (8/1: op 5/1)

4657 SHRAWLEY STANDARD OPEN N.H. FLAT RACE (II) (4, 5 & 6-Y.O) (Class H)

5-25 (5-27) **2m** £1,255.50 (£348.00: £166.50)

	Horse / details	Dist	Pos	SP	RR	SF
4531*	**Andsuephi (IRE)** (CPEBrooks) **5-11-4**(7) GBrace (hld up: hmpd & lost pl ent st: hdwy 3f out: led wl over 1f out: r.o wl)	—	1	5/2 1	58 f	—
	Stormhill Stag (PBowen) **5-10-11**(7) LCummins (a.p: chal 2f out: rdn & one pce ins fnl f)	3	2	8/1 3	48 f	—
1801 9	**Never In Debt** (AGHobbs) **5-11-4**(7) MrGShenkin (hld up: hdwy over 3f out: ev ch whn hung rt 1f out: one pce)	1¾	3	11/2 2	53 f	—
4421 10	**Trymyply** (HJMWebb) **5-11-4** SMcNeill (hld up: hdwy 4f out: styd on)		4	33/1	—	—
4531 10	**Beacon Lane (IRE)** (OO'Neill) **4-10-13** VSlattery (chsd ldr: rdn 3f out: r.o one pce)		5	8/1 3	—	—
4554 5	**Minibelle** (DLWilliams) **5-10-13** MClarke (led: clr ½-wy: wknd & hdd wl over 1f out)		6	14/1	—	—
	Blazer (NJHenderson) **4-10-13** JRKavanagh (hld up: stdy hdwy fr ½-wy: wknd 3f out)		7	5/2 1	—	—
	Mossy Buck (IRE) (MJRoberts) **5-11-4** JRailton (reluctant to r: a in rr)		8	25/1	—	—
	How To Run (IRE) (DJWintle) **4-10-13** WMarston (nvr trbld ldrs)		9	25/1	—	—
4539 11	**Lady Boco** (FCoton) **4-10-8** CRae (hld up in rr: effrt 5f out: nt rch ldrs)		10	33/1	—	—
4009 8	**Miss Blues Singer** (AJChamberlain) **4-10-8** BPowell (mid div: effrt ½-wy: wknd 4f out)		11	33/1	—	—
3021 U	**Coolest By Phar (IRE)** (MissPMWhittle) **5-10-11**(7) MrOMcPhail (chsd ldrs 9f: grad wknd: t.o)		12	25/1	—	—
4531 16	**Stardante (IRE)** (RLee) **5-11-4** LHarvey (mid div tl wknd 6f out: t.o)		13	25/1	—	—
				(SP 125.6%)	**13 Rn**	

4m 9.1 CSF £21.36 TOTE £4.20: £1.40 £1.70 £2.20 (£26.70) Trio £36.70 OWNER Mrs J. A. Cohen (LAMBOURN) BRED Martin Cullinane
WEIGHT FOR AGE 4yo-5lb

4531* Andsuephi (IRE) looked done for when he was forced towards the rear after being impeded on the home turn but, under a most competent ride, renewed his challenge to gain command below the distance, and from then on the prize was his. (5/2: 4/5-11/4)
Stormhill Stag gave notice of better things to come with a very encouraging first appearance on the racecourse, and he should not be hard to place. (8/1)
1431 Never In Debt, a winner at the first time of asking in the Autumn but off the track since disappointing in December, came with a promising-looking bid approaching the final furlong, but he hung badly right towards the paddock entrance and gave away a golden opportunity. (11/2)
Trymyply has had more experience than most and, doing all his best work inside the last half-mile, was unable to cause concern. (33/1)
Beacon Lane (IRE) is improving with experience, but he may have done too much too soon this time, and he was in trouble halfway up the straight. (8/1)
Minibelle may have found this race coming plenty soon enough, but she set a telling gallop until headed and fading inside the distance. If she can improve on this, there are races to be won with her. (14/1: 10/1-16/1)
Blazer, a weak-looking newcomer who will fare much better when conditions are in his favour, was at the end of his tether three furlongs out and the position was accepted. (5/2)

T/Plpt: £8,041.10 (0.3 Tckts); £7,710.71 to Goodwood 22/5/97. T/Qdpt: Not won; £448.21 to Goodwood 22/5/97. IM

4428-EXETER (R-H) (Good, Good to firm patches)
Thursday May 22nd

No times taken last 2 races: visibility v.poor
WEATHER: v.misty

4658 SIMPKINS EDWARDS BRANCH OFFICES (S) HURDLE (4,5,6 & 7-Y.O) (Class G)

2-20 (2-21) **2m 2f (8 hdls)** £1,818.50 (£511.00: £249.50) GOING minus 0.37 sec per fur (GF)

	Horse / details	Dist	Pos	SP	RR	SF
4231 3	**Paulton (71)** (KBishop) **4-10-9b** RDunwoody (a.p: reminders after 3 out: led last: drvn out)	—	1	7/1 3	67	—
4384*	**Miramare (61)** (AGHobbs) **7-10-7**(7) MrGShenkin (lw: a.p: led 4th tl after 3 out: led appr 2 out to last: edgd lft flat: nt qckn)	2	2	9/1	65	—
4453 2	**Bayerd (IRE) (87)** (CREgerton) **6-11-6b** NWilliamson (hld up & plld hrd: hdwy 5th: btn whn nt clr run & swtchd rt flat)	1	3	4/1 1	70	—
4552 5	**Powder Monkey (77)** (TNeedham) **7-10-2**(7) MrJTizzard (rdn 3rd: hdwy 5th: one pce fr 2 out)	4	4	6/1 2	56	—
4384 4	**October Brew (USA) (77)** (MCPipe) **7-10-9v1**(5) GSupple (a.p: one pce fr 2 out)	hd	5	10/1	61	—
4401 8	**Jewel Thief (62)** (GBBalding) **7-11-0v** APMcCoy (hld up & bhd: hrd rdn after 3 out: nvr nr to chal)	2	6	10/1	59	—
4340 3	**Ewar Bold (63)** (KOCunningham-Brown) **4-10-9b** MAFitzgerald (lw: led to 4th: led after 3 out: sn hdd & wknd: mstke last)	1	7	11/1	58	—
4552 P	**Red Tel (IRE) (80)** (MCPipe) **5-11-0** CMaude (hld up & bhd: hrd rdn after 3 out: no rspnse)	¾	8	8/1	57	—
4290 4	**Griffin's Girl (65)** (NGAyliffe) **5-10-6**(3) GuyLewis (prom tl wknd appr 2 out)	8	9	14/1	45	—
3889 4	**Lady Callernish** (MissHDay) **7-10-2**(7) MrSDurack (bhd: rdn 4th: t.o whn fell 2 out)		F	10/1	—	—
1333 P	**Minneola** (KBishop) **5-10-9** LHarvey (bkwd: a bhd: t.o whn p.u bef last)		P	66/1	—	—
4548 8	**Minnisam** (AGHobbs) **4-10-9** RGreene (prom: rdn 5th: wkng whn mstke 2 out: blnd & uns rdr last)		U	25/1	—	—
				(SP 115.5%)	**12 Rn**	

4m 19.7 (9.70) CSF £60.95 TOTE £8.00: £1.90 £2.70 £1.50 (£34.80) Trio £17.30 OWNER Business Forms Express (BRIDGWATER) BRED P. Trant

WEIGHT FOR AGE 4yo-5lb
No bid
4231 Paulton had been knocking at the door in this sort of company. (7/1)
4384* Miramare made a good effort of trying to defy a penalty for his new connections. (9/1)
4453 Bayerd (IRE) would have benefited for settling better on a course as stiff as this. (4/1)
4384 October Brew (USA), 21lb better off with the runner-up than when beaten twenty lengths last time, could not reverse the form in the first-time visor. (10/1)
4552 Red Tel (IRE) (8/1: op 5/1)

4659 CORPORATE SERVICES GROUP H'CAP CHASE (0-105) (5-Y.O+) (Class F)

2-50 (2-50) **2m 3f 110y (15 fncs)** £3,249.50 (£986.00: £483.00: £231.50) GOING minus 0.37 sec per fur (GF)

	Horse	Dist	Pos	SP	RR	SF
4429^{2}	**Mr Playfull (91)** (RGFrost) **7-11-7** JFrost (hld up & bhd: hdwy after 11th: hit 4 out: lft 2nd last: r.o wl to ld nr fin)	—	**1**	12/1	100	33
4438*	**Blazer Moriniere (FR) (93)** (PCRitchens) **8-11-9** SFox (a.p: led & lft clr last: ct nr fin)	nk	**2**	$4/1^{2}$	102	35
4535^{4}	**Court Master (IRE) (90)** (RHBuckler) **9-11-6** BPowell (hld up mid div: hdwy appr 4 out: one pce fr 3 out)	8	**3**	14/1	92	25
4272*	**Boots N All (IRE) (84)** (GBBalding) **7-11-0** BFenton (hld up & bhd: hdwy appr 8th: rdn 4 out: 3rd & btn whn mstke 2 out)	6	**4**	$7/4^{1}$	81	14
4535^{P}	**Jailbreaker (81)** (BRMillman) **10-10-11** MAFitzgerald (bhd fr 11th)	15	**5**	20/1	66	—
1731^{4}	**Wilkins (82)** (RJO'Sullivan) **8-10-12** NWilliamson (prom to 10th)	¾	**6**	14/1	66	—
4438^{P}	**Brimpton Bertie (86)** (MajorDNChappell) **8-11-2** GUpton (a bhd: t.o fr 11th)	22	**7**	40/1	52	—
	Desert Run (IRE) (94) (PRRodford) **9-11-10** SBurrough (a bhd: t.o fr 8th)	dist	**8**	50/1	—	—
4344^{2}	**Coolteen Hero (IRE) (94)** (RHAlner) **7-11-10** PHolley (led to 4th: blnd 9th: led after 11th: hdd & fell last)		**F**	14/1	—	—
4549^{F}	**Wixoe Wonder (IRE) (83)** (MBradstock) **7-10-13b** APMcCoy (led 4th: clr 8th: hdd after 11th: wknd qckly 4 out: p.u bef last)		**P**	$5/1^{3}$	—	—
4520^{4}	**Tango's Delight (70)** (RJBaker) **9-10-0** VSlattery (bhd: rdn 10th: t.o whn p.u bef last)		**P**	50/1	—	—
4520^{3}	**Gladys Emmanuel (77)** (REPocock) **10-10-2**(5) DJKavanagh (rdn 8th: sn bhd: t.o whn ref 11th)		**R**	14/1	—	—

(SP 118.5%) **12 Rn**

4m 47.5 (2.50) CSF £54.31 CT £630.00 TOTE £14.40: £2.10 £2.50 £5.00 (£32.60) Trio £170.00 OWNER Mr P. A. Tylor (BUCKFASTLEIGH) BRED P. A. Tylor
4429 Mr Playfull was reverting back to this shorter trip and needed every yard of it to prevail. (12/1: 8/1-14/1)
4438* Blazer Moriniere (FR) defied a 12lb hike in the ratings last time, but was up a further 3lb here. (4/1)
4535 Court Master (IRE) is not living up to his Punchestown effort. (14/1: op 8/1)
4272* Boots N All (IRE) found an 8lb rise in the weights too much. (7/4)
1731 Wilkins (14/1: 8/1-16/1)
4344 Coolteen Hero (IRE) was 5lb worse off with the winner than when beating him fifteen lengths on firm ground over course and distance last month. (14/1: op 8/1)
4549 Wixoe Wonder (IRE) (5/1: 6/1-13/)

4660 PUTTING YOUR BUSINESS FIRST H'CAP HURDLE (0-120) (4-Y.O+) (Class D)

3-20 (3-20) **2m 3f 110y (9 hdls)** £2,676.50 (£754.00: £369.50) GOING minus 0.37 sec per fur (GF)

	Horse	Dist	Pos	SP	RR	SF
4398^{8}	**Storm Dust (113)** (MissHCKnight) **8-11-10** JCulloty (hld up: hdwy whn stumbled appr 2 out: sn rdn: led nr fin: all out)	—	**1**	9/2	94	6
4139*	**Burlington Sam (NZ) (91)** (AGHobbs) **9-9-11**(5) OBurrows (chsd ldr: led appr 2 out: hrd rdn & hdd nr fin)	nk	**2**	4/1	72	—
4468^{2}	**Star Performer (IRE) (97)** (AGHobbs) **6-10-1**(7) MrGShenkin (hld up & plld hrd: hdwy 4th: blnd 3 out: sn hrd rdn: rallied appr last: styd on flat)	2½	**3**	$7/2^{3}$	76	—
4278^{2}	**Faustino (109)** (PJHobbs) **5-11-6** NWilliamson (hld up: wnt 2nd 2 out: wknd last)	2½	**4**	$11/4^{1}$	86	—
4430*	**Ath Cheannaithe (FR) (91)** (JNeville) **5-10-2v** TDascombe (led tl appr 2 out: sn wknd)	28	**5**	$3/1^{2}$	45	—

(SP 112.1%) **5 Rn**

4m 42.3 (10.30) CSF £20.05 TOTE £5.80: £2.00 £2.20 (£22.50) OWNER Mr Sunley Tice (WANTAGE) BRED Sunley Stud
2644* Storm Dust, 6lb higher than when scoring at Kempton in January, put a disappointing comeback run at Haydock last time behind him. (9/2)
4139* Burlington Sam (NZ), raised 2lb, has been a real stalwart for his first-season trainer. (4/1)
4468 Star Performer (IRE), up 5lb, did not settle in this small field and could not overcome a bad error three out. (7/2)
4278 Faustino did not seem to get home over this longer trip on a testing course. (11/4)

4661 ES LITIGATION SUPPORT SERVICES NOVICES' CHASE (5-Y.O+) (Class D)

3-50 (3-50) **2m 7f 110y (17 fncs)** £3,550.00 (£1,075.00: £525.00: £250.00) GOING minus 0.37 sec per fur (GF)

	Horse	Dist	Pos	SP	RR	SF
4178^{4}	**Santella Boy (USA)** (CJMann) **5-10-7b** RDunwoody (a gng wl: led 2 out: sn clr: eased flat)	—	**1**	$11/4^{3}$	96+	—
4213^{P}	**Stormtracker (IRE) (121)** (CWeedon) **8-12-0** MRichards (led to 11th: hrd rdn to ld 4 out: hdd 2 out: no ch w wnr)	8	**2**	$7/4^{1}$	105	16
4172^{2}	**Kiwi Crystal (NZ)** (AGHobbs) **8-10-9** RGreene (blnd 2nd: sn prom: btn whn mstke 2 out)	1½	**3**	12/1	85	—
2908^{R}	**Withycombe Hill** (PJHobbs) **7-10-7**(7) MrRWidger (hld up: hdwy to ld 11th: hdd & hit 4 out: sn wknd)	6	**4**	50/1	85	—
4330^{U}	**Dunlir (69)** (PRRodford) **7-11-0** MSharratt (a bhd: t.o fr 5th)	28	**5**	100/1	66	—
4431^{2}	**Jonjas Chudleigh (70)** (RGFrost) **10-11-0** JFrost (a bhd: t.o fr 5th)	18	**6**	20/1	54	—
4537^{P}	**Glengarrif Girl (IRE)** (MCPipe) **7-10-9v** APMcCoy (j.lft: prom: mstke 6th: wknd 12th: t.o whn p.u bef 4 out)		**P**	11/1	—	—
4004^{F}	**Halkopous** (MissVenetiaWilliams) **11-11-0** NWilliamson (hld up: mstke 5th: t.o whn p.u after 4 out)		**P**	$5/2^{2}$	—	—

(SP 115.3%) **8 Rn**

5m 57.0 (10.00) CSF £7.64 TOTE £4.10: £1.30 £1.60 £1.50 (£5.30) Trio £12.10 OWNER The Link Leasing Partnership (UPPER LAMBOURN) BRED Galbreaph - Phillips Racing Partnership
WEIGHT FOR AGE 5yo-7lb
4178 Santella Boy (USA) always seemed to be travelling well on this fencing debut when in view on the television pictures. (11/4)
3598 Stormtracker (IRE) proved no match for the youngster at these weights. (7/4)
4172 Kiwi Crystal (NZ) made at least two jumping errors on this chasing debut. (12/1)
4084 Glengarrif Girl (IRE) (11/1: 8/1-12/1)

4662 BUSINESS DEVELOPMENT GROUP NOVICES' H'CAP HURDLE (0-100) (4-Y.O+) (Class E)
4-20 (4-21) **3m 2f (13 hdls)** £2,547.00 (£717.00: £351.00) GOING minus 0.37 sec per fur (GF)

				SP	RR	SF
4384^{2}	**On My Toes (65)** (RGFrost) **6-10-6**^{ow2} JFrost (led appr 3rd: clr appr 2 out: eased flat)	—	**1**	11/1	50+	—
4333^{3}	**Piper's Rock (IRE) (87)** (GBBalding) **6-12-0** BFenton (led tl appr 3rd: btn appr 2 out)	4	**2**	4/1 ^{2}	70	—
4552^{3}	**Spirit Level (63)** (JRPayne) **9-9-11**$^{(7)}$ MrSDurack (nvr nrr)	14	**3**	10/1	37	—
4309^{P}	**Jobsagoodun (81)** (NJHenderson) **6-11-8** MAFitzgerald (mid div: bhd fr 3 out)	s.h	**4**	8/1	55	—
4458^{4}	**Annie Ruth (IRE) (63)** (MrsJPitman) **6-9-11**$^{(7)}$ RGarrard (a bhd)	13	**5**	11/1	29	—
4562^{U}	**Ecu de France (IRE) (65)** (PCRitchens) **7-10-6** CMaude (mid div: sn bhd)	1	**6**	7/2 ^{1}	30	—
4464^{3}	**China Mail (IRE) (70)** (JABennett) **5-10-11** TJMurphy (hld up: hdwy 10th: wknd appr 2 out)	1¼	**7**	25/1	35	—
4073^{2}	**Kingswood Manor (82)** (MissVenetiaWilliams) **5-11-9** NWilliamson (prom: reminder after 4th: t.o fr 3 out)	dist	**8**	9/2 ^{3}	—	—
100^{6}	**Hidden Flower (61)** (HSHowe) **8-9-9**$^{(7)ow2}$ MrRWidger (t.o)	9	**9**	33/1	—	—
4445^{4}	**Vallingale (IRE) (84)** (MissHCKnight) **6-11-4**$^{(7)}$ MrAWintle (bhd whn p.u bef last)		**P**	8/1	—	—
4073^{P}	**Music Class (IRE) (71)** (RJBaker) **6-10-12** VSlattery (t.o whn p.u bef 2 out)		**P**	33/1	—	—
4548^{P}	**Moreceva (IRE) (59)** (PaddyFarrell) **7-9-9b**$^{1(5)}$ OBurrows (bhd whn pu bef 2 out)		**P**	50/1	—	—

(SP 120.1%) **12 Rn**

No Time Taken CSF £49.90 CT £426.20 TOTE £5.20: £1.30 £3.50 £5.50 (£18.80) Trio £115.00 OWNER Mr G. Chambers (BUCKFASTLEIGH) BRED G. Chambers

LONG HANDICAP Hidden Flower 9-5 Moreceva (IRE) 9-6

4384 On My Toes is clearly on the upgrade and, stepping up from selling company, ran out a convincing winner of a race where very little could be seen on the television sets, let alone from the stands. (11/1: 8/1-12/1)

4333 Piper's Rock (IRE), 11lb higher than when successful at Ludlow, had a real stamina test here but could not go with the progressive winner at these weights. (4/1: 3/1-9/2)

2546 Jobsagoodun (8/1: op 5/1)

4458 Annie Ruth (IRE) (11/1: 8/1-12/1)

3004 Vallingale (IRE) (8/1: 6/1-10/1)

4663 SELF ASSESSMENT NOVICES' H'CAP HURDLE (0-100) (4-Y.O+) (Class E)
4-55 (5-04) **2m 3f 110y (9 hdls)** £2,295.00 (£645.00: £315.00) GOING minus 0.37 sec per fur (GF)

				SP	RR	SF
4452^{4}	**Lord Nitrogen (USA) (76)** (BJLlewellyn) **7-11-1** MrJLLlewellyn (prom: lft in ld 5th: clr 2 out: eased flat)	—	**1**	6/1	59	—
4428^{3}	**Up the Tempo (IRE) (61)** (PaddyFarrell) **8-10-0** TDascombe (bhd tl hdwy 2 out: r.o flat: nt trble wnr)	3½	**2**	8/1	41	—
4445^{3}	**Genereux (82)** (SMellor) **4-10-11**$^{(5)}$ ChrisWebb (lw: outpcd 3 out: mstke 2 out: styd on wl flat)	hd	**3**	8/1	62	—
4468^{S}	**Saafi (IRE) (67)** (RJBaker) **6-10-6b** VSlattery (hdwy appr 2 out: nvr nr to chal)	3	**4**	15/2	45	—
4445^{P}	**Connaught's Pride (68)** (PJHobbs) **6-10-7b** NWilliamson (hrd rdn & wnt 2nd appr 2 out: sn wknd)	8	**5**	5/1 ^{3}	39	—
4333^{2}	**Safecracker (75)** (CPMorlock) **4-10-9** DGallagher (led early: wknd appr 2 out)	1¼	**6**	100/30 ^{2}	45	—
4461^{3}	**Carnival Clown (68)** (KBishop) **5-10-7** RGreene (bhd whn p.u bef 3 out)		**P**	12/1	—	—
4506^{2}	**Regal Gem (IRE) (82)** (CRBarwell) **6-11-7** BFenton (in ld 4th: blnd & uns rdr 5th)		**U**	5/2 ^{1}	—	—
4508^{3}	***Sioux To Speak (85)*** (MissHCKnight) **5-11-3**$^{(7)}$ MrAWintle (Withdrawn not under Starter's orders: uns rdr & bolted bef s)		**W**	15/2	—	—
4524^{P}	***Tudor Town (63)*** (KBishop) **9-9-9**$^{(7)}$ MGriffiths (Withdrawn not under Starter's orders: jockey inj)		**W**	20/1	—	—

(SP 140.8%) **8 Rn**

No Time Taken CSF £51.07 CT £362.71 TOTE £7.80: £2.80 £2.20 £2.10 (£56.60) Trio £35.10 OWNER Mr B. J. Llewellyn (BARGOED) BRED R. B. Trussell, J. A. Philpott Jnr & H. Wynne

LONG HANDICAP Up the Tempo (IRE) 9-12

WEIGHT FOR AGE 4yo-5lb

4452 Lord Nitrogen (USA), down 4lb, had this won two out, piecing together the glimpses of shapes from the television pictures. (6/1)

360 Up the Tempo (IRE) seemed to show an improvement in form from just out of the handicap. (8/1)

3947 Genereux, who missed an engagement at Worcester yesterday presumably because of soft ground, would have finished second according to his jockey but for an error two out. (8/1)

4468 Saafi (IRE) (15/2: 8/1-20/1)

T/Plpt: £2,329.30 (4.87 Tckts). T/Qdpt: £245.10 (2.84 Tckts) KH

4664a - 4695a (Irish Racing) - See Computer Raceform

4542-TOWCESTER (R-H) (Good)
Friday May 23rd
WEATHER: fine but cloudy

4696 YARDLEY GRAPHICS NOVICES' HURDLE (4-Y.O+) (Class E)
6-20 (6-21) **2m (8 hdls)** £2,407.50 (£670.00: £322.50) GOING minus 0.10 sec per fur (G)

				SP	RR	SF
3964^{2}	**Jamaican Flight (USA)** (MrsSLamyman) **4-10-9** JRailton (lw: j.w: mde all: r.o wl fr 2 out)	—	**1**	6/1 ^{3}	76	36
4567^{*}	**Nordance Prince (IRE) (108)** (MissVenetiaWilliams) **6-12-0** NWilliamson (hld up & bhd: hdwy 4th: ev ch 2 out: sn rdn: one pce)	4	**2**	7/2 ^{2}	86	51
4474^{2}	**Wise King (109)** (JABOld) **7-11-0** CLlewellyn (lw: chsd wnr: ev ch 3 out: sn rdn & wknd)	11	**3**	8/11 ^{1}	61	26
4652^{F}	**Positivo (72)** (MissCJECaroe) **6-11-0** DLeahy (bhd tl r.o fr 3 out: n.d)	9	**4**	20/1	52	17
4512^{4}	**Orchard King (83)** (OBrennan) **7-11-0** MBrennan (lw: hld up & plld hrd: hdwy appr 4th: 4th whn blnd 5th: nt rcvr)	nk	**5**	8/1	52	17
4547^{7}	**Ur Only Young Once** (MrsDHaine) **7-10-9** APMcCoy (prom: mstke 1st: ev ch 3 out: sn wknd)	15	**6**	12/1	32	—
4547^{5}	**Belarus (IRE)** (MrsIMcKie) **5-11-0** WMcFarland (bhd fr 4th)	13	**7**	20/1	24	—
4538^{10}	**Rare Gift (USA)** (DNicholson) **6-11-0** RJohnson (lw: sn bhd)	¾	**8**	16/1	23	—
4547^{6}	**The Bizzo (55)** (JFPanvert) **6-10-9** WMarston (lost tch fr 4th: t.o)	14	**9**	33/1	4	—
4514^{F}	**Chariot Man (IRE)** (MrsSJSmith) **5-11-0** RichardGuest (a bhd: t.o)	½	**10**	33/1	8	—
4436^{P}	**Friar's Oak** (PButler) **5-10-7**$^{(7)}$ MrOMcPhail (prom to 3rd: t.o)	4	**11**	66/1	4	—

				SP	RR	SF
4547[9]	**Over and Under (IRE)** (MrsIMcKie) **4-10-9** LHarvey (t.o 4th: p.u bef 3 out)		**P**	33/1	—	—
				(SP 138.9%)		**12 Rn**

3m 48.9 (2.90) CSF £28.13 TOTE £9.60: £2.40 £1.60 £1.10 (£16.00) Trio £3.30 OWNER Mr P. Lamyman (LINCOLN) BRED Foxfield
WEIGHT FOR AGE 4yo-5lb
3964 Jamaican Flight (USA) used to front-run on the Flat and made sure the emphasis would be on stamina. He can score again. (6/1)
4567* Nordance Prince (IRE) probably had a tough task in trying to concede so much weight to the winner on a course as stiff as this. (7/2)
4474 Wise King could not go with the runner-up from the third last, let alone the winner. (8/11: 10/11-evens)

4697 NATIONAL LETTERBOX MARKETING H'CAP CHASE (0-110) (5-Y.O+) (Class E)
6-45 (6-48) **3m 1f (18 fncs)** £3,137.00 (£941.00: £453.00: £209.00) GOING minus 0.10 sec per fur (G)

				SP	RR	SF
4535[2]	**Martell Boy (NZ) (96)** (MissVenetiaWilliams) **10-11-5** NWilliamson (w ldr: led 5th: clr 10th: rdn appr 2 out: hit last: unchal)	—	**1**	3/1[2]	114	32
4529[3]	**Harristown Lady (102)** (GBBalding) **10-11-11b** APMcCoy (hld up: hdwy 11th: sn chsng wnr: rdn appr 2 out: no imp)	19	**2**	4/1[3]	108	26
3893*	**Fortunes Course (IRE) (97)** (JSKing) **8-11-6** TJMurphy (led to 5th: wknd 4 out: blnd 3 out)	10	**3**	4/1[3]	96	14
4467*	**Funcheon Gale (104)** (RCurtis) **10-11-13** DMorris (hld up & bhd: hdwy appr 12th: rdn & wknd 3 out)	25	**4**	11/4[1]	87	5
4234[U]	**Jim Valentine (99)** (DJWintle) **11-11-8** WMarston (bhd: rdn 8th: blnd 9th: sn t.o: p.u bef 2 out)		**P**	4/1[3]	—	—
4424[3]	**Vicar of Bray (87)** (LWells) **10-10-10v** MRichards (bhd whn mstkes 10th & 11th: t.o whn p.u bef 14th)		**P**	40/1	—	—
4476[P]	**Bottle Black (80)** (THind) **10-10-3b[1]** CLlewellyn (sn prom: 4th whn blnd & uns rdr 11th)		**U**	66/1	—	—
				(SP 115.6%)		**7 Rn**

6m 24.8 (9.80) CSF £14.67 CT £43.55 TOTE £3.10: £2.00 £2.00 (£3.90) OWNER Mr David Jones (HEREFORD) BRED M. P. Kuklinski
4535 Martell Boy (NZ) did not have so much give underfoot this time, but fulfilled the promise of his reappearance and may still be ahead of the handicapper next time. (3/1)
4529 Harristown Lady proved no match for the winner in the home straight. (4/1)
3893* Fortunes Course (IRE), a runner-up on the Flat twelve days ago, had been raised 2lb for winning a weak event at Newton Abbot. (4/1)
4467* Funcheon Gale was a further 6lb higher here. (11/4)

4698 WHITSUN NOVICES' HURDLE (4-Y.O+) (Class D)
7-15 (7-16) **3m (12 hdls)** £2,951.75 (£884.00: £424.50: £194.75) GOING minus 0.10 sec per fur (G)

				SP	RR	SF
4052[P]	**Salmon Breeze (IRE) (107)** (NJHenderson) **6-11-12** MAFitzgerald (lw: a.p: hit 7th: led 9th: clr 2 out: r.o wl)	—	**1**	4/5[1]	81+	—
4500[5]	**Erni (FR) (80)** (TPTate) **5-11-0** RGarritty (a.p: ev ch 3 out: sn hrd rdn: no imp)	5	**2**	10/1	66	—
3185[P]	**Tirley Missile** (JSSmith) **11-10-7**(7) MrOMcPhail (hld up: hdwy 8th: rdn & wnt 2nd briefly 2 out: sn wknd)	3	**3**	25/1	64	—
4528[10]	**Tullow Lady (IRE)** (OBrennan) **6-10-9** MBrennan (swtg: lost tch fr 7th: t.o)	dist	**4**	33/1	—	—
4315[4]	**Leap Frog (96)** (NAGaselee) **6-11-0** WMarston (chsd ldr: hit 6th: led 8th to 9th: wknd appr 3 out: t.o)	dist	**5**	11/4[2]	—	—
4544*	**Nordic Spree (IRE) (83)** (GLMoore) **5-11-6v** PHolley (led tl rdn & mstke 8th: wknd after 9th: t.o whn p.u bef 2 out)		**P**	9/2[3]	—	—
4231[6]	**Inishmann (IRE)** (APJones) **6-10-7**(7) PRyan (lw: a bhd: t.o 7th: p.u bef 2 out)		**P**	50/1	—	—
3798[P]	**Arctic Charmer (USA)** (MrsSMOdell) **5-10-7**(7) MrJGoldstein (a bhd: t.o 7th: p.u bef 9th)		**P**	50/1	—	—
				(SP 120.2%)		**8 Rn**

6m 4.2 (24.20) CSF £9.74 TOTE £1.80: £1.20 £1.50 £4.70 (£5.70) OWNER The Salmon Racing Partnership (LAMBOURN) BRED William Kavanagh
2746* Salmon Breeze (IRE), disappointing when highly tried at Aintree, found this a different kettle of fish. (4/5)
4500 Erni (FR), ridden by a claimer in his previous runs, ran his best race to date. (10/1)
Tirley Missile has obviously been difficult to train and was reverting to hurdles. (25/1)

4699 BROADWAYS STAMPINGS NOVICES' H'CAP CHASE (0-100) (5-Y.O+) (Class E)
7-45 (7-47) **2m 6f (16 fncs)** £3,182.50 (£955.00: £460.00: £212.50) GOING minus 0.10 sec per fur (G)

				SP	RR	SF
4566[W]	**Cardinal Rule (IRE) (90)** (MissVenetiaWilliams) **8-11-10** NWilliamson (lw: a.p: led on bit appr 2 out: rdn ut)	—	**1**	9/2[3]	110	40
4203[4]	**Gems Lad (86)** (MrsSJSmith) **10-11-6** RichardGuest (a.p: led 6th to 7th: lft in ld 8th: rdn & hdd appr 2 out: one pce)	11	**2**	7/2[1]	98	28
4470[5]	**Country Store (88)** (APJones) **8-11-8** SMcNeill (prom tl wknd 4 out)	25	**3**	9/1	82	12
4537[P]	**Gerry's Pride (IRE) (66)** (JWMullins) **6-10-0** SCurran (prom: hrd rdn 11th: sn wknd)	1	**4**	50/1	59	—
4546[P]	**Musical Hit (66)** (PAPritchard) **6-10-0b** RSupple (mstke 7th: sn bhd: no ch whn carried wd by loose horse bnd appr 2 out: styd on)	1	**5**	50/1	58	—
4476[6]	**King's Rainbow (IRE) (72)** (MrsDHaine) **8-10-3**(3) PHenley (prom tl wknd 4 out)	4	**6**	7/1	62	—
4447[5]	**Glenbricken (71)** (MissAEEmbiricos) **11-10-5** RJohnson (mstke 5th: a bhd)	2	**7**	12/1	59	—
4524[5]	**Persian View (IRE) (90)** (KCBailey) **7-11-10** AThornton (w.r.s: bhd whn hit 6th: t.o)	10	**8**	14/1	71	1
3358[9]	**Rosie-B (76)** (NMBabbage) **7-10-10** VSlattery (swtg: bhd: mstke 4th: t.o fr 11th)	8	**9**	10/1	51	—
4330*	**Thunder Road (IRE) (75)** (MissHCKnight) **6-10-9** JCulloty (blnd 6th: sn bhd: t.o whn p.u bef 3 out)		**P**	4/1[2]	—	—
4537[6]	**Better Future (IRE) (67)** (TKeddy) **8-10-1** DGallagher (mstke 3rd: sn t.o: p.u bef 9th)		**P**	14/1	—	—
4566[5]	**Stage Player (79)** (MissCJECaroe) **11-10-13** ILawrence (lw: nt j.w: a bhd: t.o whn p.u bef 2 out)		**P**	25/1	—	—
4237[3]	**Golden Drum (IRE) (69)** (TRGeorge) **7-10-3b** TJMurphy (led to 6th: led 7th tl blnd & uns rdr 8th)		**U**	14/1	—	—
				(SP 127.5%)		**13 Rn**

5m 36.6 (7.60) CSF £20.63 CT £130.52 TOTE £6.10: £1.90 £1.80 £3.50 (£8.30) Trio £41.00 OWNER Mr Peter Burch (HEREFORD) BRED Mrs Patricia Mackean
LONG HANDICAP Gerry's Pride (IRE) 9-13 Musical Hit 9-8
4272 Cardinal Rule (IRE) was thought to have been suffering from a virus when disappointing in two runs prior to finishing second last time. (9/2)
4203 Gems Lad found the winner too much of a handful on the stiff climb to the finish. (7/2)
4470 Country Store would have preferred softer ground for this return to fences. (9/1)

4700 TOWCESTER H'CAP CHASE (0-125) (5-Y.O+) (Class D)
8-15 (8-16) **2m 110y (12 fncs)** £3,468.25 (£1,036.00: £495.50: £225.25) GOING minus 0.10 sec per fur (G)

				SP	RR	SF
4456[2]	**Mine's an Ace (NZ) (98)** (MissVenetiaWilliams) **10-10-3** RGreene (rdn 7th: mstke 8th: hdwy to ld 3 out: sn clr: r.o wl)	—	**1**	9/4[2]	105	22
4566[2]	**Mill O'The Rags (IRE) (100)** (MrsDHaine) **8-10-2**(3) PHenley (lw: chsd ldr: rdn 4 out: ev ch 3 out: one pce)	6	**2**	13/8[1]	101	18

4090[2] **Raba Riba (123)** (JLSpearing) **12-12-0** VSlattery (led to 3 out: sn rdn & outpcd: rallied flat)........s.h **3** 4/1 124 41
4311[5] **Society Guest (120)** (AndrewTurnell) **11-11-11** LHarvey (plld hrd early: hit 1st: j.lft & mstke 3rd: ev ch 3 out: sn wknd)........6 **4** 3/1[3] 115 32
(SP 113.9%) **4 Rn**

4m 7.1 (5.10) CSF £6.19 TOTE £3.30: (£2.30) OWNER Mr Michael Knight (HEREFORD) BRED Clearwood Thoroughbred Stud Ltd
4456 Mine's an Ace (NZ), up 3lb, was never travelling particularly well, but the picture suddenly changed three out and he completed a first treble for his trainer. (9/4)
4566 Mill O'The Rags (IRE) was dropping back to an admittedly stiff two miles. (13/8)
4090 Raba Riba has never won over shorter than nineteen furlongs and his rider should have forced the pace more. (4/1: 3/1-9/2)
4311 Society Guest has yet to hit form this season. (3/1)

4701 ON CUE DESIGN H'CAP HURDLE (0-125) (4-Y.O+) (Class D)

8-45 (8-45) **2m (8 hdls)** £2,840.00 (£790.00: £380.00) GOING minus 0.10 sec per fur (G)

SP RR SF

4525[2] **Above the Cut (USA) (95)** (CPMorlock) **5-10-2**(7) MHandley (led 2nd: clr appr last: r.o wl)........— **1** 6/1[3] 78 36
4299* **Talathath (FR) (114)** (DNicholson) **5-11-11**(3) MrRThornton (hld up: hdwy appr 3 out: chsd wnr fr 2 out: no imp)........8 **2** 11/4[1] 89 47
4550[4] **Ballet Royal (USA) (105)** (HJManners) **8-10-12**(7) ADowling (hld up & bhd: hdwy appr 3 out: one pce fr 2 out)........hd **3** 12/1 80 38
4271[6] **John Drumm (113)** (PRWebber) **6-11-13** JOsborne (led to 2nd: wknd appr last)........6 **4** 11/4[1] 82 40
4534[4] **Fontanays (IRE) (94)** (GMMcCourt) **9-10-1v**(7) RStudholme (prom: rdn after 5th: wkng whn mstke 2 out).....3½ **5** 11/1 59 17
4381[7] **No Light (97)** (MrsIMcKie) **10-10-11** LHarvey (hld up & plld hrd: hdwy 5th: wknd 3 out)........4 **6** 10/1 58 16
4434* **Ela Agapi Mou (USA) (117)** (GLMoore) **4-11-5**(7) MBatchelor (bhd fr 5th)........6 **7** 11/2[2] 72 25
4549[6] **Prerogative (104)** (GLMoore) **7-11-4** APMcCoy (prom: rdn appr 4th: sn wknd: t.o)........15 **8** 16/1 44 2
4425[3] **Josifina (108)** (AGFoster) **6-11-8** AThornton (hld up: a bhd: t.o)........½ **9** 11/1 48 6
(SP 122.3%) **9 Rn**

3m 48.9 (2.90) CSF £22.71 CT £182.33 TOTE £8.20: £2.10 £1.70 £2.90 (£9.00) Trio £184.10 OWNER J P M & J W Cook (WANTAGE) BRED Pendley Farm in USA
WEIGHT FOR AGE 4yo-5lb
4525 Above the Cut (USA), 8lb higher than when scoring at Ludlow in March, has held his form well and gave his rider his first winner. (6/1)
4299* Talathath (FR) was attempting to concede a lot of weight to the winner on this handicap debut. (11/4)
4550 Ballet Royal (USA), due to go down 2lb in future handicaps, did not seem to be given too hard a time in the home straight. (12/1: op 7/1)
4136* John Drumm was 5lb higher than when scoring two outings ago. (11/4)
4534 Fontanays (IRE) (11/1: op 7/1)

T/Plpt: £35.40 (474.83 Tckts). T/Qdpt: £18.40 (37.19 Tckts) KH

0462-CARTMEL (L-H) (Good becoming Good to firm)

Saturday May 24th

Race 4: one flight omitted
WEATHER: fine and sunny

4702 MOORGATE RACING H'CAP HURDLE (0-115) (4-Y.O+) (Class E)

2-10 (2-11) **2m 1f 110y (8 hdls)** £2,430.00 (£680.00: £330.00) GOING minus 0.52 sec per fur (GF)

SP RR SF

4274* **Indian Jockey (103)** (MCPipe) **5-11-9** APMcCoy (mde all: rdn 2 out: styd on u.p)........— **1** 11/8[1] 86 44
4482[5] **Sarmatian (USA) (108)** (MDHammond) **6-11-11**(3) MrCBonner (lw: a in tch: chsd wnr between last 2: nt qckn towards fin)........¾ **2** 20/1 90 48
4573[4] **High Low (USA) (87)** (MDHammond) **9-10-0**(7) NHorrocks (w wnr: rdn 3 out: one pce flat)........4 **3** 14/1 66 24
4573* **Rachael's Owen (95)** (JSGoldie) **7-10-10**(5) RMcGrath (chsd ldrs: rdn 5th: one pce fr 2 out)........2 **4** 8/1 72 30
4335* **Carlisle Bandito's (IRE) (93)** (JBerry) **5-10-13** DParker (lw: hld up: effrt 5th: kpt on fr 2 out: nvr nr to chal)...1½ **5** 9/2[3] 69 27
4568* **Supreme Soviet (94)** (ACWhillans) **7-11-0** KJohnson (lw: sn bhd: drvn along 5th: n.d)........11 **6** 14/1 59 17
4337[3] **Glenugie (107)** (GMMoore) **6-11-13** NBentley (bhd: mstke 2nd: sn drvn along: hdwy 5th: wknd appr 2 out)....½ **7** 9/1 72 30
4246[7] **Bures (IRE) (103)** (MrsJBrown) **6-11-4**(5) BGrattan (chsd ldrs: rdn 5th: wknd appr 2 out)........3 **8** 20/1 65 23
253[2] **Karinska (96)** (MCChapman) **7-11-2** WWorthington (a in rr)........s.h **9** 14/1 58 16
4505* **Fatehalkhair (IRE) (94)** (BEllison) **5-11-0** RDunwoody (chsd ldrs tl wknd after 3 out)........1¾ **10** 4/1[2] 55 13
(SP 130.9%) **10 Rn**

3m 57.9 (-3.10) CSF £31.04 CT £284.76 TOTE £2.70: £1.50 £6.30 £2.60 (£33.80) Trio £159.70 OWNER Mr Stuart Mercer (WELLINGTON) BRED John Hayter
4274* Indian Jockey, reverting to hurdles on the back of five straight victories over fences, took the plum inside rail and, making all the running, was always doing enough. He will revert to fences here next week, and attempt to make it nine wins this season. (11/8)
4482 Sarmatian (USA) was tightened up for room on the inside of High Low after two out. Driven almost upsides a hundred yards from home, he was just held at bay. (20/1)
4573 High Low (USA) took on the winner all the way, and stuck to his guns surprisingly well. (14/1)
4573* Rachael's Owen, from a 6lb higher mark, was flat out to keep up from halfway but, to his credit, stayed on all the way to the line. (8/1)
4335* Carlisle Bandito's (IRE) probably found this track too sharp, and only stayed on late on in the day. (9/2)

4703 MARTEN JULIAN NOVICES' H'CAP CHASE (0-100) (5-Y.O+) (Class E)

2-40 (2-41) **2m 1f 110y (12 fncs)** £2,940.75 (£891.00: £435.50: £207.75) GOING minus 0.52 sec per fur (GF)

SP RR SF

4540[F] **Daring Past (95)** (MDHammond) **7-11-12v** RDunwoody (trckd ldrs: chal 2 out: led on bit flat: sn clr: eased towards fin)........— **1** 8/11[1] 97+ 12
4574[3] **All Clear (IRE) (69)** (HowardJohnson) **6-9-9**(5) RMcGrath (chsd ldrs: led 7th: hdd flat: no ch w wnr)........3 **2** 7/2[3] 68 —
4408[8] **Karlovac (69)** (SGChadwick) **11-10-0b** FPerratt (sn bhd & drvn along: hdwy u.p 7th: one pce fr 4 out)........25 **3** 25/1 45 —
4540[2] **The Fence Shrinker (72)** (DMcCain) **6-10-3**ow3 TJenks (led: blnd 2nd: hdd 7th: one pce fr 3 out)........5 **4** 20/1 44 —
4007[P] **Top it All (69)** (PRHarriss) **9-10-0b** WMarston (w ldrs tl wknd 8th)........2½ **5** 33/1 39 —
4574[6] **Regal Domain (IRE) (69)** (MrsLMarshall) **6-10-0** KJohnson (stdd s: mstkes: a bhd: t.o 8th)........dist **6** 50/1 — —

4446* **Appearance Money (IRE) (72)** (FMurphy) **6-10-3** MFoster (lw: hld up: stdy hdwy 8th: 3rd & prom whn fell 3 out) ..... F 5/2 2 — —
(SP 122.2%) **7 Rn**

4m 16.9 (5.90) CSF £3.87 TOTE £1.70: £1.10 £2.00 (£3.10) OWNER Mr John Petty (MIDDLEHAM) BRED P. and Mrs Venner
LONG HANDICAP All Clear (IRE) 9-9 Karlovac 9-13 Regal Domain (IRE) 9-5 The Fence Shrinker 9-5
4540 Daring Past, in a visor to sharpen up his jumping, took this with plenty to spare. (8/11)
4574 All Clear (IRE) made the best of his way home, but it was obvious the winner was simply toying with him. (7/2)
935* Karlovac is a lazy sort and his rider wore spurs. Soon driven along, he was never in contention. (25/1)
The Fence Shrinker, who raced keenly, nearly went at the second. (20/1)
4446* Appearance Money (IRE) as usual travelled strongly. She was third and poised to challenge when she fell three out. She does not always find much off the bridle, and it was too far from home to be dogmatic about how she would have fared. (5/2)

4704 DODSON & HORRELL MAIDEN HUNTERS' CHASE (5-Y.O+) (Class H)

3-15 (3-15) **3m 2f (18 fncs)** £1,852.00 (£556.00: £268.00: £124.00) GOING minus 0.52 sec per fur (GF)

	Horse / details	Dist	Pos	SP	RR	SF
4015 4	**Sands of Gold (IRE)** (CNNimmo) **9-11-7**(7) MrLLay (chsd ldrs: blnd 3 out: hrd rdn & led flat: styd on)	—	1	5/1 3	89	22
	Jayandoubleu (IRE) (WACrozier) **8-11-7**(7) MrTScott (led to 12th: outpcd 2 out: styd on & ev ch flat: kpt on)	2½	2	4/1 2	88	21
	Worleston Farrier (GDHanmer) **9-11-7**(7) MrGHanmer (t: chsd ldrs: led 12th tl flat: nt qckn)	hd	3	14/1	87	20
4411 4	**Cool Yule (IRE)** (RWThomson) **9-11-9**(5) MissPRobson (sn bhd: gd hdwy after last: styd on wl towards fin)	2½	4	10/1	86	19
4515 6	**Just For Me (IRE)** (JAMoore) **8-11-9**(5) MrMHNaughton (mstke 7th: sn pushed along: hdwy 12th: kpt on flat)	1¾	5	25/1	85	18
	Wang How (MissJMFurness) **9-11-7**(7) MrARobson (hdwy 7th: prom 13th: sn wknd)	19	6	33/1	73	6
4411 5	**Emu Park** (MrsRLElliot) **9-11-7**(7) MrJThompson (bhd: sme hdwy 14th: sn wknd)	9	7	33/1	68	1
4322 5	**Orton House** (SKelly) **10-11-7**(7) MrRBurton (lw: sn bhd: t.o 7th)	4	8	7/1	65	—
3913 8	**Rushing Burn** (MrsGESnowden) **11-11-2**(7) MissNCSnowden (sn bhd)	20	9	33/1	48	—
4076 P	**Canister Castle** (MissZAGreen) **9-11-7**(7) MrDRMcLeod (sn bhd: t.o fr 12th)	dist	10	20/1	—	—
4530 2	**True Fortune** (JohnMoore) **7-11-9**(5) MrJJukes (trckd ldrs: fell 11th)		F	5/4 1	—	—
4579 P	**King Spring** (MissCEJDawson) **12-11-9**(5) MrsVJackson (sn bhd: t.o whn p.u after 14th)		P	20/1	—	—
4155 U	**All Or Nothing** (NMLEwart) **9-11-2**(7) MrJEwart (sn bhd: mstke 10th: wnt prom 13th: 5th & wkng whn blnd & uns rdr 3 out)		U	20/1	—	—
	Bunny Hare (IRE) (JJBirkett) **9-11-7**(7) MrRForristal (blnd & uns rdr 2nd)		U	50/1	—	—

(SP 138.3%) **14 Rn**

6m 30.3 (6.30) CSF £24.96 TOTE £6.50: £1.80 £1.40 £5.90 (£11.20) Trio £31.40 OWNER Mr Brett Badham (DAVENTRY) BRED Mrs H. J. Ponsonby
STEWARDS ENQUIRY Lay susp 5-6/6/97 (excessive use of whip)
4015 Sands of Gold (IRE), who presumably needed it at Aintree after a seven-week absence, survived a blunder three out and, under severe pressure, poked his head in front on the run-in. (5/1)
Jayandoubleu (IRE), who fell at the last obstacle when clear in a point-to-point last time, was tapped for foot two out, but stuck to his guns on the run-in. (4/1)
Worleston Farrier, who is tubed, went on a mile from home but was run out of it from the elbow. (14/1)
4155 Cool Yule (IRE) only got going late in the day. Clearly something of a character, he will be suited by extreme distances. (10/1)
3824 Just For Me (IRE), hitherto has looked very moderate, and his proximity at the finish underlines the low class of this event. (25/1)
4530 True Fortune was on the heels of the leaders and full of running when he came down at the halfway mark. (5/4: op 2/1)

4705 WORTHINGTON BEST BITTER NOVICES' H'CAP HURDLE (0-95) (4-Y.O+) (Class F)

3-45 (3-48) **2m 6f (10 hdls)** £2,542.00 (£712.00: £346.00) GOING minus 0.52 sec per fur (GF)

	Horse / details	Dist	Pos	SP	RR	SF
4628 3	**Stylish Interval (87)** (NWaggott) **5-11-6** APMcCoy (lw: trckd ldrs: blnd 2nd: led 3 out: hrd rdn & styd on to ld flat: all out)	—	1	4/1 3	67	13
4500*	**Toshiba Talk (IRE) (95)** (BEllison) **5-12-0** RDunwoody (lw: hld up: stdy hdwy 6th: rdn to ld last: hdd flat: nt qckn towards fin)	1¼	2	7/2 2	74	20
4445*	**One More Dime (IRE) (67)** (JLNeedham) **7-10-0** BFenton (led to 3 out: styd on same pce)	6	3	8/1	42	—
3825 4	**My Missile (67)** (RGCockburn) **7-10-0** LO'Hara (chsd ldrs tl wknd appr 2 out)	16	4	9/1	30	—
4408 F	**Jonaem (IRE) (74)** (MrsDianneSayer) **7-10-7** KJohnson (chsd ldrs tl wknd 3 out)	5	5	10/1	34	—
4513 P	**Tartan Joy (IRE) (67)** (JAMoore) **6-9-9v1**(5) MrMHNaughton (bhd fr 6th)	10	6	25/1	19	—
4628 P	**Diddy Rymer (82)** (MrsSJSmith) **7-10-10**(5) RWilkinson (b.d 3rd)		B	8/1	—	—
4376 10	**Double Dash (IRE) (78)** (DMoffatt) **4-10-5v** DJMoffatt (b.d 3rd)		B	12/1	—	—
4477 F	**Amazing Sail (IRE) (90)** (MissMKMilligan) **4-11-3** ASSmith (cl up whn fell 3rd)		F	5/2 1	—	—
4572 4	**Skane River (IRE) (71)** (GRichards) **6-9-13**(5) RMcGrath (in tch: bdly hmpd after 6th: sn bhd: t.o whn p.u bef last)		P	6/1	—	—
4477 4	**Double Vintage (IRE) (73)** (MCChapman) **4-10-0** WWorthington (sn t.o: p.u bef 2 out)		P	33/1	—	—
4500 7	**Strong Character (76)** (DALamb) **11-10-9**ow9 JBurke (sn bhd: t.o 8th: p.u bef 3 out)		P	33/1	—	—

(SP 143.8%) **12 Rn**

5m 16.1 (0.20 under best) (5.10) CSF £21.00 CT £110.66 TOTE £5.20: £1.90 £2.40 £2.50 (£6.90) Trio £14.90 OWNER Mrs J. Waggott (SPENNYMOOR) BRED R. J. Turner
LONG HANDICAP My Missile 9-11 Tartan Joy (IRE) 8-13 Double Vintage (IRE) 9-1 Strong Character 9-0
WEIGHT FOR AGE 4yo-6lb
4628 Stylish Interval, who loves this fast ground, gave his all to get the better of a rare head to head on the run-in. (4/1)
4500* Toshiba Talk (IRE), done no favours by the Handicapper, looked to be going slightly the better when sent to the front at the final flight, but he is not very big to be carrying such a welter weight, and the winner proved too strong in the closing stages. (7/2)
4445* One More Dime (IRE), a confirmed front-runner, was racing from a 5lb higher mark. (8/1)
3825 My Missile, having his first outing for sixty-one days, tired from two out. (9/1)
4477 Amazing Sail (IRE) came to grief at the third, bringing down two of his rivals. (5/2)

4706 LAURENT-PERRIER CHAMPAGNE NOVICES' CHASE (5-Y.O+) (Class E)

4-20 (4-21) **3m 2f (18 fncs)** £3,061.50 (£859.00: £418.50) GOING minus 0.52 sec per fur (GF)

	Horse / details	Dist	Pos	SP	RR	SF
4569*	**Slotamatique (IRE) (98)** (GRichards) **8-12-0v1** RDunwoody (mde all: lft wl clr 4 out: virtually p.u nr fin)	—	1	5/6 1	108?	22
4575 5	**Strongalong (IRE) (73)** (PCheesbrough) **7-11-2** APMcCoy (mstkes: sn drvn along: lost tch 12th: wnt poor 2nd 2 out)	dist	2	8/1 3	—	—

				SP	RR	SF
4533P	**Steel Gold** (TRKinsey) **7-10-10**(7)ow1 MrRBurton (chsd ldrs tl wknd 12th: 2nd & tired whn blnd 2 out: virtually p.u)	dist	3	50/1	—	—
4481 2	**Kiltulla (IRE) (72)** (MrsSJSmith) **7-10-11**(5) RWilkinson (w ldrs: 2nd & wkng whn fell 2 out)		F	7/4 2	—	—
4417 3	**Lambrini (IRE) (62)** (DMcCain) **7-10-8b**(3) PHenley (mstkes: chsd ldrs tl wknd 12th: poor 4th whn fell next)		F	10/1	—	—
4408 5	**Kings Minstral (IRE) (64)** (DALamb) **7-11-2** JBurke (ref to r: t.n.p)		R	25/1	—	—
				(SP 116.9%)	**6 Rn**	

6m 30.3 (6.30) CSF £8.15 TOTE £1.60: £1.10 £3.40 (£5.90) OWNER Slotamatics (Bolton) Ltd (PENRITH) BRED Stackallan Stud
4569* Slotamatique (IRE) in a visor this time, was left virtually alone four out and passed the line almost at a walk. (5/6)
4575 Strongalong (IRE) made mistakes and was never going at any stage. (8/1)
Steel Gold pulled up on his previous two outings, was leg-weary when he almost fell two out and all his rider could do was to pop him over the last. (50/1)
4481 Kiltulla (IRE) tried to keep tabs on the winner, but was struggling when he came to grief four out, the water. (7/4)

4707 STICKY TOFFEE PUDDING NOVICES' HURDLE (4-Y.O+) (Class E)
4-50 (4-54) **2m 1f 110y (8 hdls)** £3,072.50 (£860.00: £417.50) GOING minus 0.52 sec per fur (GF)

				SP	RR	SF
4514*	**Bold Statement (105)** (GMMoore) **5-11-12** NBentley (led 1st: mde rest: styd on strly u.p flat)	—	1	9/4 2	85	32
3691 7	**Advance East (97)** (MDods) **5-11-6** APMcCoy (nt j.w: hld up: stdy hdwy 5th: chal after last: kpt on same pce)	2½	2	4/1 3	77	24
4400*	**Smolensk (IRE) (109)** (JBerry) **5-11-12** RDunwoody (sn trckng ldrs: chal last: sn rdn: kpt on same pce)	3½	3	5/4 1	80	27
3825 13	**Kingfisher Brave (80)** (MGMeagher) **4-10-9** BFenton (chsd ldrs: sn drvn along one pce fr 3 out)	5	4	10/1	63	5
1370 7	**Another Quarter (IRE) (71)** (MCChapman) **4-10-4** WWorthington (led to 1st: cl up tl wknd last)	2½	5	25/1	56	—
4568 2	**Hand of Straw (IRE) (90)** (MissZAGreen) **5-11-0** KJohnson (nt j.w: sn bhd: sme hdwy 5th: nvr nr to chal)	nk	6	8/1	60	7
3828 11	**Johnneys Spirit** (RGCockburn) **5-11-0** LO'Hara (in tch to 3rd: bhd fr 5th)	23	7	33/1	39	—
	Dramatic Pass (IRE) (MCChapman) **8-11-0** DJMoffatt (sn bhd: fell 5th)		F	50/1	—	—
4451P	**Sullamell** (PRHarriss) **6-11-0** WMarston (unruly s: plld hrd: sn trckng ldrs: lost pl 4th: bhd whn s.u after 2 out)		S	50/1	—	—
				(SP 126.1%)	**9 Rn**	

4m 1.3 (0.30) CSF £11.84 TOTE £2.90: £1.40 £1.10 £1.20 (£6.10) OWNER Mr R. I. Graham (MIDDLEHAM) BRED Juddmonte Farms
WEIGHT FOR AGE 4yo-5lb
4514* Bold Statement ensured there was no hanging about, and he stayed on in most resolute fashion to gain the upper-hand on the run-in, winning tidily in the end. (9/4)
3691 Advance East, who had an outing on the Flat twelve days ago, did not jump fluently. Driven up onto the quarters of the winner after the last, on this occasion you could not say he shirked the issue. (4/1)
4400* Smolensk (IRE) travelled strongly. Produced on the bridle to challenge at the last, he found the winner a tough nut to crack.(5/4: op 2/1)
1776 Kingfisher Brave, having his first outing for sixty-one days, was soon being driven along and proved woefully one-paced. (10/1)
291 Another Quarter (IRE), taken to post early, seems to struggle to stay two miles even on a sharp track and fast ground. (25/1)

T/Plpt: £38.10 (210.67 Tckts). T/Qdpt: £9.70 (28.92 Tckts) WG

4513-HEXHAM (L-H) (Good to firm)
Saturday May 24th
WEATHER: fine

4708 CO-OPERATIVE BANK NOVICES' HURDLE (4-Y.O+) (Class E)
2-15 (2-15) **2m 4f 110y (10 hdls)** £1,632.00 (£452.00: £216.00) GOING minus 0.14 sec per fur (G)

				SP	RR	SF
4571 4	**Acajou III (FR) (105)** (GRichards) **9-11-0** PCarberry (lw: mde all: easily)	—	1	5/2 2	71+	18
4500 4	**Muzrak (CAN) (101)** (MDHammond) **6-11-8** RGarritty (w ldrs: rdn & ev ch appr last: nt pce of wnr)	3½	2	11/8 1	76	23
4479 2	**Boston Man (88)** (RDEWoodhouse) **6-11-8b** MAFitzgerald (a.p: rdn & one pce fr 2 out)	7	3	3/1 3	71	18
4500 6	**Rubislaw (57)** (MrsKMLamb) **5-10-7**(7) MissSLamb (prom: rdn ½-wy: sn no ch)	28	4	100/1	41	—
4479P	**Moonlight Venture** (MartynWane) **5-11-0** PNiven (chsd ldrs: rdn & wknd 3 out)	2	5	40/1	39	—
4152F	**Allerby (70)** (JLGoulding) **9-11-0** JSupple (no ch fr ½-wy)	17	6	16/1	26	—
	Mintulyar (WTKemp) **6-11-0** LWyer (lost tch ½-wy)	14	7	33/1	15	—
4580 10	**Chan Move** (WJSmith) **5-10-7**(7) MrTJBarry (bhd whn fell 5th)		F	66/1	—	—
	Split The Wind (RNixon) **11-10-6**(3) FLeahy (bhd whn fell 5th)		F	66/1	—	—
	Gardenia's Song (GAHarker) **6-11-0** RSupple (wl t.o whn p.u bef last)		P	66/1	—	—
4570 4	**Mr Bruno** (MABarnes) **4-10-8** BStorey (lw: blnd & uns rdr 2nd)		U	50/1	—	—
				(SP 114.4%)	**11 Rn**	

4m 57.2 (9.20) CSF £5.62 TOTE £4.20: £1.30 £1.10 £1.10 (£3.90) Trio £1.70 OWNER Mr Robert Ogden (PENRITH) BRED Philippe Achard
WEIGHT FOR AGE 4yo-6lb
4571 Acajou III (FR) reverted to hurdling for a confidence-booster, and it worked a treat. He can win again over the smaller obstacles, although he will be back chasing next term. He could continue during the summer jumps. (5/2)
4500 Muzrak (CAN), backed as if defeat was out of the question, could not find the foot of the winner. He should not be discarded just yet. (11/8)
4479 Boston Man was the first of the leading trio to come under pressure. (3/1)
3883 Allerby seems to always run well here, but was out of his depth. (16/1)

4709 THOMPSONS OF PRUDHOE LTD NOVICES' CHASE (5-Y.O+) (Class E)
2-45 (2-46) **2m 110y (12 fncs)** £2,193.00 (£654.00: £312.00: £141.00) GOING minus 0.14 sec per fur (G)

				SP	RR	SF
4574*	**Know-No-No (IRE) (83)** (MDHammond) **8-11-7** RGarritty (lw: hld up: hdwy ½-wy: led appr last: rdn out)	—	1	evens 1	100	37
4337 7	**Astraleon (IRE)** (RAllan) **9-11-0** BStorey (lw: a.p: led 3 out: hdd appr last: kpt on same pce)	9	2	6/1	84	21
4611 3	**Sovereigns Match** (BMactaggart) **9-11-0** PCarberry (led to 2nd: rdn & outpcd 3 out: styd on same pce flat)	9	3	4/1 2	76	13
4502 5	**Moss Pageant (70)** (FTWalton) **7-11-0** TReed (cl up: led 2nd: clr to 8th: hdd 3 out: sn btn)	16	4	9/2 3	60	—
4574 2	**Kincardine Bridge (USA)** (MrsSCBradburne) **8-10-7**(7) MrMBradburne (prom: rdn & wknd 3 out: p.u bef last)		P	10/1	—	—
	Herbalist (JWade) **8-11-0** RichardGuest (wl bhd whn p.u after 8th)		P	20/1	—	—
3825P	**War Whoop** (MissLucindaRussell) **5-10-8** AThornton (cl up early: wl bhd fr ½-wy: p.u after 8th)		P	20/1	—	—

Form	Horse	Dist	Pos	SP	RR	SF
4574[F]	**Akito Racing (IRE)** (MartinTodhunter) **6-10-9** PNiven (a wl in rr: p.u bef 4 out)		P	25/1	—	—
4574[5]	**Spectre Brown (63)** (FJestin) **7-10-7**(7) MrTJBarry (in tch: wl bhd fr ½-wy: p.u bef 3 out)		P	33/1	—	—
				(SP 127.9%)	**9 Rn**	

4m 1.7 (4.70) CSF £7.85 TOTE £1.90: £1.10 £1.70 £1.70 (£9.10) Trio £13.80 OWNER Mrs A. Kane (MIDDLEHAM) BRED Paddy Byrne
WEIGHT FOR AGE 5yo-6lb

4574* Know-No-No (IRE) made hard work of following up his Perth victory, but seems to be going in the right direction. He is set to continue during the summer providing the ground does not firm up too much. (evens)

4079 Astraleon (IRE) ran a cracker on his chasing debut, and kept the winner up to his work on the run-in. He is well capable of going one better. (6/1)

4611 Sovereigns Match was tried over a shorter distance here, and a moderate novice chase is within his grasp. (4/1)

4502 Moss Pageant made them go a real lick, but the fast pace was probably his undoing and he was a spent force once headed. (9/2)

4710 CLAREMONT GARMENTS PLC H'CAP CHASE (0-115) (5-Y.O+) (Class E)

3-15 (3-17) **3m 1f (19 fncs)** £2,406.00 (£666.00: £318.00) GOING minus 0.14 sec per fur (G)

Form	Horse	Dist	Pos	SP	RR	SF
4576[3]	**Nijway (86)** (MABarnes) **7-10-1** AThornton (chsd ldrs: outpcd 3 out: styd on appr last to ld fnl stride)	—	1	11/2[3]	102	23
4404[6]	**Supposin (91)** (MrsSJSmith) **9-10-6** RichardGuest (lw: bhd: stdy hdwy 4 out: chal 2 out tl led flat: hdd fnl stride)	s.h	2	12/1	107	28
4576[2]	**Rusty Blade (85)** (PMonteith) **8-10-0** RJohnson (prom: rdn 14th: led after 3 out: hdd flat: kpt on wl towards fin)	nk	3	6/1	101	22
4517[4]	**Whaat Fettle (100)** (GRichards) **12-11-1** PNiven (led: hdd after 3 out: sn btn)	19	4	5/1[2]	104	25
4503[5]	**Scrabo View (IRE) (94)** (PBeaumont) **9-10-9** RSupple (mid div: in tch & rdn 4 out: outpcd after next)	5	5	14/1	94	15
4576[4]	**Bright Destiny (85)** (JSGoldie) **6-9-7**(7) MrOMcPhail (w ldrs: ev ch 3 out: wknd qckly)	1½	6	20/1	85	6
4336[4]	**Royal Vacation (113)** (GMMoore) **8-12-0** JCallaghan (hld up & bhd: blnd 13th: nvr trbld ldrs)	5	7	7/1	109	30
4503[P]	**Mischievous Girl (85)** (RTate) **9-10-0** MrsFNeedham (hit 8th: lost pl 12th: sn wl bhd: t.o)	30	8	50/1	62	—
4502[4]	**Mr Reiner (IRE) (85)** (JWade) **9-10-0** PCarberry (mid div tl wknd 15th: t.o)	22	9	12/1	48	—
4571[2]	**Tough Test (IRE) (96)** (MrsJDGoodfellow) **7-10-11** BStorey (lw: hld up & bhd: stumbled & uns rdr 10th)		U	9/4[1]	—	—
				(SP 118.4%)	**10 Rn**	

6m 17.1 (6.10) CSF £62.17 CT £376.39 TOTE £6.00: £1.60 £3.70 £2.00 (£55.60) Trio £30.00 OWNER Mr T. A. Barnes (PENRITH) BRED Bacton Stud
LONG HANDICAP Rusty Blade 9-9 Bright Destiny 8-13 Mischievous Girl 8-13 Mr Reiner (IRE) 9-9
STEWARDS' ENQUIRY Monteith fined £230 (failure to inform rdr of horse's hypersensitive skin).

4576 Nijway who found the ground too soft when beaten last time, stayed on to lead close home after getting outpaced in the dip. That may be him for the season but, when conditions are to his liking, he is clearly useful and is still on a handy mark. (11/2)

4234* Supposin is an in-and-out performer but, when he is right, he is worth catching. He looked to have scored his third course win only to be nailed right on the line. (12/1)

4576 Rusty Blade is another who likes things his own way, and afterwards this thin-skinned sort cost his trainer a £230 fine, as he failed to inform the jockey that he would mark easily. He would appear to be well-handicapped at the moment, and is definitely due to win soon. (6/1)

4517 Whaat Fettle, a grand old campaigner, could well be retired during the summer. A course specialist at Kelso where he won eight times, it would be nice if he could bow out on a winning note. (5/1)

4336 Royal Vacation was behind when making an almighty blunder, and it more or less stopped him in his tracks. (7/1)

4571 Tough Test (IRE) was in really good form beforehand according to connections, but he got no further than the water when standing so far off he barely made the other side. He stumbled on the water's edge and his jockey had no chance of staying on board. There are more wins to come from him. (9/4)

4711 S.C.S. THE UPHOLSTERY SPECIALISTS H'CAP HURDLE (0-115) (4-Y.O+ F & M) (Class E)

3-45 (3-46) **2m (8 hdls)** £1,548.00 (£428.00: £204.00) GOING minus 0.14 sec per fur (G)

Form	Horse	Dist	Pos	SP	RR	SF
4500[3]	**Royal York (90)** (GRichards) **5-11-10** PCarberry (lw: a trckng ldrs: led 2 out: sn clr: easily)	—	1	5/2[1]	73	20
4285[4]	**Parson's Lodge (IRE) (80)** (LLungo) **9-11-0** RSupple (lw: prom: rdn 3 out: styd on one pce appr last)	3	2	5/2[1]	60	7
3730*	**Radmore Brandy (90)** (GRichards) **4-10-12**(7) RBurns (hld up: hdwy appr 3 out: styd on same pce appr last)	2	3	4/1[2]	68	10
4573[5]	**French Project (IRE) (67)** (MrsSCBradburne) **5-9-12**(3) GFRyan (chsd ldrs: outpcd 2 out: n.d after)	8	4	25/1	37	—
4573[3]	**Skiddaw Samba (80)** (MrsMReveley) **8-11-0** GLee (mid div: hdwy appr 2 out: no imp)	2½	5	6/1[3]	48	—
3325[6]	**Best of All (IRE) (94)** (JBerry) **5-12-0** PNiven (lw: led tl hdd 2 out: sn wknd)	½	6	6/1[3]	61	8
4572[8]	**Whitegatesprincess (IRE) (66)** (BEllison) **6-10-0v** BStorey (wl bhd fr 5th)	10	7	14/1	23	—
4572[P]	**Meadowleck (66)** (WGYoung) **8-9-9**(5) STaylor (a bhd: t.o fr 5th)	3½	8	50/1	20	—
3711[P]	**No Takers (66)** (SEKettlewell) **10-9-7**(7) JO'Leary (cl up tl wknd qckly 5th: t.o)	dist	9	25/1	—	—
				(SP 122.0%)	**9 Rn**	

3m 57.0 (9.00) CSF £9.09 CT £22.70 TOTE £4.30: £1.60 £1.10 £2.50 (£8.20) Trio £9.10 OWNER Mr Robert Ogden (PENRITH) BRED Robert Ogden
LONG HANDICAP Meadowleck 8-13 No Takers 9-13
WEIGHT FOR AGE 4yo-5lb

4500 Royal York is possibly on the upgrade and won this turning handsprings. She should be kept on the right side. (5/2)

4285 Parson's Lodge (IRE) stayed on without having any chance with the winner, but definitely has a similar event within her grasp.(5/2)

3730* Radmore Brandy, a stablemate of the winner, probably ran up to her best, and a step back to plating grade should see her regain the winning thread. (4/1)

3325 Best of All (IRE) forced the pace but, once headed, there was nothing left. (6/1)

4712 ST. OSWALDS HOSPICE H'CAP HURDLE (0-110) (4-Y.O+) (Class E)

4-15 (4-15) **2m 4f 110y (10 hdls)** £2,075.00 (£575.00: £275.00) GOING minus 0.14 sec per fur (G)

Form	Horse	Dist	Pos	SP	RR	SF
4339*	**Colorful Ambition (104)** (MrsASwinbank) **7-11-13** JSupple (lw: hld up & bhd: stdy hdwy fr 3 out: led appr last: styd on wl)	—	1	15/8[1]	86	23
4518[2]	**Highland Way (IRE) (89)** (MartinTodhunter) **9-10-12** MAFitzgerald (lw: hld up: in tch: led 2 out: hdd appr last: nt qckn)	4	2	7/2[2]	68	5
4501*	**Shelton Abbey (77)** (JWade) **11-10-0b** PCarberry (hld up: mstke 6th: sn rdn along: styd on between last 2: n.d)	4	3	7/1	53	—
4505[5]	**Sharp Sensation (93)** (GAHarker) **7-11-2** PNiven (bhd: hdwy 2 out: styd on one pce flat)	2	4	12/1	67	4

				SP	RR	SF
4638[5]	**Dont Forget Curtis (IRE) (77)** (MrsKMLamb) **5-9-7**(7) MissSLamb (in tch: rdn 3 out: wknd appr next)	¾	**5**	25/1	51	—
4518*	**Kinda Groovy (89)** (IPark) **8-10-12b** JCallaghan (lw: led: hdd 2 out: wknd qckly)	½	**6**	9/2[3]	62	—
4146[7]	**Longcroft (81)** (SEKettlewell) **5-10-4** RJohnson (prom: rdn 3 out: sn wknd)	13	**7**	9/1	44	—
4518[3]	**Jumbo Star (78)** (JEDixon) **7-10-1** BStorey (cl up: wknd qckly 3 out)	2	**8**	14/1	40	—
	Recluse (77) (WTKemp) **6-10-0b** LWyer (cl up tl lost pl qckly 4th: n.d after)	3½	**9**	33/1	36	—

(SP 118.8%) **9 Rn**

4m 59.3 (11.30) CSF £8.74 CT £34.66 TOTE £2.80: £1.20 £1.40 £2.20 (£6.10) Trio £9.10 OWNER Mr F. J. Sainsbury (RICHMOND) BRED Meon Valley Stud

LONG HANDICAP Dont Forget Curtis (IRE) 9-6 Shelton Abbey 9-7

4339* Colorful Ambition, on the sort of ground he needs, has the scope to make a chaser although another hurdle is well within his capabilities. Apparently he is a sulky sort during the cold winter months and will probably be campaigned in the autumn and spring. (15/8)

4518 Highland Way (IRE) is a real dodgy sort who finds nothing once off the bridle. (7/2)

4501* Shelton Abbey, under pressure from a long way out, needs to travel more strongly on the bit if he is to get anywhere near troubling the judge. (7/1)

744 Sharp Sensation (12/1: op 6/1)

4518* Kinda Groovy, who landed a touch over course and distance last time, tried to make every post a winning one. (9/2)

4713 FLYING ACE HUNTERS' CHASE (5-Y.O+) (Class H)

4-50 (4-51) **2m 4f 110y (15 fncs)** £1,316.80 (£364.80: £174.40) GOING minus 0.14 sec per fur (G)

				SP	RR	SF
4579[2]	**Howayman** (KAnderson) **7-12-2**(5) MrRFord (hld up: prom fr ½-wy: qcknd to ld appr last: r.o strly)	—	**1**	10/11[1]	117	36
4551[P]	**Cumberland Blues (IRE)** (MrsALockwood) **8-12-0**(7) MissADeniel (lw: a.p: disp ld fr ½-wy: lft in ld & hmpd 3 out: hdd next: one pce)	12	**2**	10/1	108	27
4579[3]	**Master Kit (IRE)** (JNRBillinge) **8-12-0**(7) MrMBradburne (lw: a in tch: led 2 out: sn hdd & wknd)	10	**3**	4/1[2]	100	19
4579[5]	**Reed** (MrsLyalProvan) **12-11-7**(7) MrOMcPhail (mid div: lost pl & wl bhd 11th: n.d after)	22	**4**	33/1	76	—
4256[U]	**Thank U Jim** (MrsGSunter) **9-11-7**(7) MissTJackson (chsd ldrs: led 8th tl fell 3 out)		**F**	15/2	—	—
4607[U]	**Frozen Stiff (IRE)** (AJBrown) **9-11-9**(5) MrNWilson (t.o whn p.u bef 9th)		**P**	20/1	—	—
4504[4]	**Buckaneer Bay** (SIPittendrigh) **10-11-9**(5) MrRHale (blnd 8th: p.u bef next)		**P**	33/1	—	—
4504[3]	**Knowe Head** (MissCABlakeborough) **13-12-0**(7) MrSBrisby (in tch: hit 7th: wl bhd fr 4 out: t.o whn p.u bef last)		**P**	6/1[3]	—	—
	Kings Token (FTWalton) **7-12-0** MrJWalton (wl bhd whn p.u bef 9th)		**P**	40/1	—	—
	Percy Pit (MrsDMcCormack) **8-11-9**(5) MrPJohnson (led to 8th: sn lost pl: p.u bef 10th)		**P**	50/1	—	—

(SP 122.6%) **10 Rn**

5m 7.2 (10.20) CSF £10.32 TOTE £1.60: £1.10 £2.30 £1.90 (£7.60) Trio £28.00 OWNER Mr Dennis Waggott (LOCKERBIE) BRED Rockhouse Farms Ltd

4579 Howayman is a model of consistency and is very rarely out of the first two. He stormed to the line most convincingly, and he is finished now until the turn of the year. He is a grand, strapping sort who has a shade more improvement left in him. (10/11: evens-4/5)

4411* Cumberland Blues (IRE) was quite badly impeded when left in front after the fall of the leader three out. The defeat could not be put down to that, but he may not have done with winning yet. (10/1: 7/1-12/1)

4579 Master Kit (IRE) had his confidence shattered early in the season by some horrendous falls and this was his best effort to date. It is a shame for him that the season is ending imminently. (4/1: op 6/1)

Thank U Jim (15/2: 12/1-7/1)

4504 Knowe Head (6/1: 4/1-13/2)

T/Plpt: £5.90 (1412.58 Tckts). T/Qdpt: £4.20 (72.09 Tckts) GB

4702-CARTMEL (L-H) (Good to firm)
Monday May 26th

WEATHER: fine

4714 BURLINGTON SLATE (S) H'CAP HURDLE (0-90) (4-Y.O+) (Class G)

2-00 (2-01) **2m 1f 110y (8 hdls)** £2,402.00 (£672.00: £326.00) GOING minus 0.51 sec per fur (GF)

				SP	RR	SF
2088[P]	**Hacketts Cross (IRE) (83)** (PEccles) **9-11-7** RichardGuest (lw: chsd ldrs: led last: drvn clr)	—	**1**	11/2	71	14
3887[6]	**Battery Fired (72)** (NBMason) **8-10-10** JCallaghan (led: hit 4th & 3 out: hdd last: nt qckn)	5	**2**	9/2[2]	55	—
4283[6]	**Fanadiyr (IRE) (64)** (JSGoldie) **5-10-2** BStorey (hld up: hdwy 5th: one pce fr 2 out)	14	**3**	5/1[3]	35	—
4299[P]	**Apache Len (USA) (70)** (MDHammond) **4-9-10v**(7) NHorrocks (chsd ldrs: reminders & lost pl 3rd: hdwy 3 out: one pce)	nk	**4**	9/2[2]	40	—
4516[7]	**In a Moment (USA) (66)** (CGrant) **6-10-4b** RSupple (sn drvn along & bhd: n.d)	7	**5**	12/1	30	—
4446[P]	**Phargold (IRE) (63)** (JohnHarris) **8-10-1** KJohnson (chsd ldrs tl wknd appr 2 out)	19	**6**	20/1	10	—
4056[F]	**Believe It (65)** (NWaggott) **8-10-3**ow3 FPerratt (chsd ldrs tl lost pl 4th: sn bhd)	2½	**7**	50/1	9	—
4409[F]	**Birthplace (IRE) (62)** (RTate) **7-9-9**(5) BGrattan (hit 2nd: sn bhd: t.o 5th: fell last)		**F**	33/1	—	—
	Simply George (90) (JWhite) **8-12-0** PCarberry (hdwy 4th: sn pushed along: 5th whn p.u bef 2 out: lame)		**P**	2/1[1]	—	—
4648[6]	**Never so Blue (IRE) (78)** (PBradley) **6-10-11b**(5) RWilkinson (chsd ldrs: 2nd whn uns rdr 4th)		**U**	6/1	—	—

(SP 133.4%) **10 Rn**

4m 4.9 (3.90) CSF £31.98 CT £129.15 TOTE £6.30: £1.80 £2.00 £2.40 (£9.60) OWNER Mr G. W. Briscoe (LAMBOURN) BRED Lawrence Rowan

LONG HANDICAP Birthplace (IRE) 9-12 Believe It 9-2

WEIGHT FOR AGE 4yo-5lb

No bid

1466 Hacketts Cross (IRE), absent for one hundred and fifty-four days since being pulled up at Ludlow, looked in good trim beforehand and, after jumping to the front at the last, was soon clear with his race won. (11/2)

3887 Battery Fired made the running but never looked happy on this sharp track and his jumping suffered. In the end he was out-speeded by the winner on the run-in. (9/2)

Fanadiyr (IRE) moved up soon after halfway but was left well behind from two out. (5/1)

2784 Apache Len (USA) was tried in a visor but to little effect. (9/2: op 8/1)

Simply George was pulled up very lame. (2/1)

4715 VICTORIA TRADING (FRUIT IMPORTERS) LTD NOVICES' CHASE (5-Y.O+) (Class E)
2-35 (2-36) **2m 5f 110y (14 fncs)** £3,118.20 (£875.20: £426.60) GOING minus 0.51 sec per fur (GF)

			SP	RR	SF
4446[5]	**Bit of A Dream (IRE) (66)** (MrsSJSmith) **7-11-0** RichardGuest (trckd ldrs: chal & lft wl clr last) —-	1	7/2 2	74	7
4569[4]	**Royal Banker (IRE)** (MartinTodhunter) **7-11-0** PCarberry (lw: nt j.w: chsd ldrs: reminders & lost pl after 8th: sn bhd) 23	2	12/1	57	—
4515[P]	**Persian Grange (IRE)** (DALamb) **7-11-0** JBurke (chsd ldrs: mstke 8th: blnd bdly & lost pl next: sn bhd) 2½	3	33/1	55	—
4380[3]	**Nadiad** (DMcCain) **11-11-0v** BStorey (led tl hdd & wknd 4 out: 3rd & wkng whn fell 2 out)	F	11/2 3	—	—
4649*	**Plumbob (IRE) (84)** (LLungo) **8-11-6** RSupple (lw: chsd ldrs: mstke & led 4 out: ½l in front & rdn whn blnd bdly & uns rdr last)	U	1/2 1	—	—
			(SP 114.9%)		**5 Rn**

5m 17.8 (5.80) CSF £30.83 TOTE £3.60: £1.30 £2.30 (£15.20) OWNER The Cartmel Syndicate (BINGLEY) BRED Tom Curran
4446 Bit of A Dream (IRE) was challenging and apparently going the better when he was left clear at the last, rather luckily avoiding being brought down. (7/2)
4569 Royal Banker (IRE) was never jumping or showing any enthusiasm. (12/1: op 5/1)
3453 Persian Grange (IRE), pulled up on his two previous outings, all but fell at the ninth and that put him out of contention. (33/1)
4649* Plumbob (IRE) did not jump as well as he can. Making a mistake when taking it up at the water four out, he was just in front but under pressure when he blundered badly and gave his rider no chance at the last. The winner looked to be going the better at the time but Plumbob just stays and, with the long run-in to negotiate, the outcome must have been in some doubt. (1/2)

4716 BURLINGTON SLATE AMATEUR H'CAP CHASE (0-125) (5-Y.O+) (Class E)
3-10 (3-10) **2m 5f 110y (14 fncs)** £3,048.00 (£924.00: £452.00: £216.00) GOING minus 0.51 sec per fur (GF)

			SP	RR	SF
4213[7]	**Fiveleigh Builds (122)** (MissLucindaRussell) **10-11-6**(7) MrMBradburne (mstkes: lost pl 4th: hdwy 10th: led after last: sn drvn clr: eased fin) —-	1	6/4 2	132	24
4336[5]	**Hurricane Andrew (IRE) (95)** (JAMoore) **9-9-9**(5) MrMHNaughton (nt j.w: hit 1st: chsd ldr: outpcd 8th: ev ch whn hit last: kpt on same pce) 3	2	6/1	103	—
4503[P]	**Blazing Dawn (95)** (JSHubbuck) **10-9-9**(5) MissPRobson (plld hrd: led: clr 8th: wknd 2 out: blnd last: sn hdd) 6	3	5/1 3	98	—
	Sarona Smith (119) (FTWalton) **10-11-10**ow24 MrJWalton (sn bhd: t.o 8th) dist	4	25/1	—	—
4609[2]	**Bas de Laine (FR) (123)** (MDHammond) **11-11-11v**(3) MrCBonner (lw: blnd & uns rdr 2nd)	U	11/10 1	—	—
	Black Spur (104) (JRTurner) **15-10-2**(7)ow9 MrWBurnell (chsd ldrs: 3rd & wkng whn blnd bdly & uns rdr 9th)	U	33/1	—	—
			(SP 125.4%)		**6 Rn**

5m 16.0 (4.00) CSF £11.46 TOTE £2.90: £1.70 £1.90 (£10.50) OWNER Miss Lucinda Russell (KINROSS) BRED Peter Magnier
LONG HANDICAP Blazing Dawn 9-5 Sarona Smith 7-7 Hurricane Andrew (IRE) 9-5 Black Spur 8-5
4213 Fiveleigh Builds, having his first outing since the Scottish National, was taken off his legs and his jumping suffered. Given time to recover, he moved up to take it up at the last and was clear with his race won in a matter of strides. (6/4)
4336 Hurricane Andrew (IRE), 9lb out of the handicap, struggled with the strong pace and his jumping was not fluent. Upsides the winner when hitting the last, he was soon outpaced. (6/1)
4392 Blazing Dawn, 9lb out of the handicap, took a fierce grip and soon had the field strung out. Treading water two out, he fell through the last and lost the advantage in a matter of strides. (5/1)
Sarona Smith, successful in a Point-to-Point nine days earlier, carried 24lb overweight and was tailed off from halfway. (25/1)
4609 Bas de Laine (FR) made a hash of the second and gave his rider no chance. (11/10: op evens)

4717 STANLEY LEISURE H'CAP HURDLE (0-120) (4-Y.O+) (Class D)
3-45 (3-45) **3m 2f (12 hdls)** £2,710.00 (£820.00: £400.00: £190.00) GOING minus 0.51 sec per fur (GF)

			SP	RR	SF
4537[P]	**Five Flags (IRE) (86)** (MrsSJSmith) **9-11-6** RichardGuest (chsd ldr: reminders 4th & 8th: hrd rdn to ld 3 out: styd on wl flat: all out) —-	1	9/4 2	68	15
4321[6]	**Prime Display (USA) (84)** (AHHarvey) **11-11-4** RSupple (chsd ldrs: drvn along 4 out: rallied & ev ch flat: kpt on) 1½	2	14/1	65	12
4248[4]	**Valiant Dash (81)** (JSGoldie) **11-10-10**(5) STaylor (led: mstke & hdd 3 out: rallied & ev ch flat: styd on) nk	3	6/4 1	62	9
4572[7]	**Ruber (78)** (RWThomson) **10-10-5**(7) NHorrocks (prom: hit 6th: effrt 4 out: outpcd between last 2: styd on wl last 100y) 1¼	4	4/1 3	58	5
4705[P]	**Double Vintage (IRE) (73)** (MCChapman) **4-10-0** WWorthington (sn drvn along: wl bhd fr 8th: t.o 3 out) dist	5	33/1	—	—
1849[6]	**Gymcrak Cyrano (IRE) (90)** (NChamberlain) **8-11-3**(7) MissCMetcalfe (lw: stdd s: mstke & uns rdr 3rd)	U	5/1	—	—
			(SP 117.0%)		**6 Rn**

6m 12.3 (5.30) CSF £27.04 TOTE £3.10: £1.60 £3.90 (£17.00) OWNER Mrs S. Smith (BINGLEY) BRED Red Sox Investments in Ireland
LONG HANDICAP Double Vintage (IRE) 9-1
WEIGHT FOR AGE 4yo-7lb
3971 Five Flags (IRE), back over hurdles after being pulled up last time, owed this to his rider's strength and determination. Given some sharp reminders as early as the fourth flight, he had everything but the kitchen sink thrown at him on the run-in and, to his credit, did enough. (9/4)
Prime Display (USA), tailed off last time, ran much better and put in a strong challenge on the run-in. (14/1)
4248 Valiant Dash set a strong pace and stuck on willingly when headed. (6/4)
3607 Ruber, making his effort under pressure four out, was tapped for foot between the last two but, at the line, was staying on best of all. All he does is stay. (4/1)

4718 CROWTHER HOMES HURDLE (4-Y.O) (Class E)
4-20 (4-20) **2m 1f 110y (8 hdls)** £2,654.00 (£744.00: £362.00) GOING minus 0.51 sec per fur (GF)

			SP	RR	SF
4395[8]	**Go With The Wind (86)** (JSGoldie) **4-10-12** DJMoffatt (lw: trckd ldrs: led 3 out: drvn clr flat) —-	1	7/4 1	68	—
3745[5]	**Down The Yard** (MCChapman) **4-10-7** WWorthington (hit 4th: wnt prom next: hrd rdn & kpt on same pce flat) 7	2	6/1	57	—
4707[5]	**Another Quarter (IRE) (71)** (MCChapman) **4-10-7** KJohnson (hld up: hdwy 5th: 2nd & ev ch whn blnd 3 out: sn wknd) 10	3	10/1	48	—
4570[2]	**Sheemore (IRE)** (MDHammond) **4-10-5**(7) NHorrocks (trckd ldrs: rdn 3 out: nt run on) 19	4	9/4 2	35	—
4295[11]	**Port Valenska (IRE) (61)** (MrsJConway) **4-10-7**(5) STaylor (lw: bhd & reminders 5th) 3	5	33/1	32	—
807[P]	**Orange Order (IRE)** (JWhite) **4-10-12** PCarberry (plld hrd: nt j.w: led to 3 out: sn wknd) 8	6	5/1 3	25	—

				SP	RR	SF
4477^{2}	**Political Mandate** (RNixon) **4-10-0**$^{(7)}$ CMcCormack (in tch: rdn & outpcd 5th: sn lost pl & bhd)	24	**7**	8/1	—	—
				(SP 121.2%)	**7 Rn**	

4m 6.8 (5.80) CSF £12.94 TOTE £2.60: £1.80 £2.70 (£6.40) OWNER Mr Alf Chadwick (GLASGOW) BRED B. Long

3942 Go With The Wind was always travelling best in this poor event and, when pushed along after the last, soon settled the issue. (7/4)

589 Down The Yard had stamina to take her into second place between the last two. (6/1)

4707 Another Quarter (IRE), having her second outing in three days, was bang on terms when she blundered two out but her stamina soon gave out. (10/1)

4570 Sheemore (IRE) flashed his tail under pressure and looked far from keen. (9/4)

Port Valenska (IRE) was struggling badly soon after halfway. (33/1)

589 Orange Order (IRE) would not settle and, as a result, his hurdling suffered. Headed three out, he went out like a pricked balloon. (5/1)

4477 Political Mandate was never travelling and, driven along at the fifth, was soon left trailing. (8/1)

4719 SWAN HOTEL AT NEWBY BRIDGE MAIDEN HURDLE (4-Y.O+) (Class E)

4-55 (4-56) **2m 6f (11 hdls)** £2,447.60 (£683.60: £330.80) GOING minus 0.51 sec per fur (GF)

				SP	RR	SF
2633^{6}	**Nosam** (NBMason) **7-11-5** RichardGuest (s.s: hdwy & prom 7th: shkn up to ld after last: sn clr)	—	**1**	7/1^{3}	72+	—
4452^{P}	**Grosvenor (IRE) (94)** (GRichards) **6-11-5b^{1}** PCarberry (lw: trckd ldr: led 8th: fnd nil & hdd flat: eased towards fin)	9	**2**	4/5^{1}	66	—
4707^{6}	**Hand of Straw (IRE) (90)** (MissZAGreen) **5-11-5** KJohnson (chsd ldrs: reminder 6th: one pce fr 2 out)	8	**3**	5/2^{2}	60	—
1581^{P}	**Barrie Stir** (JWhite) **5-11-5** JCallaghan (nt j.w: plld hrd: bhd: sme hdwy 8th: nvr nr ldrs)	9	**4**	11/1	53	—
4259^{11}	**De-Veers Currie (IRE)** (DMoffatt) **5-11-0** DJMoffatt (led: hit 2nd: hdd & blnd 8th: wknd: t.o)	dist	**5**	20/1	—	—
	Noble Norman (MrsASwinbank) **6-10-12**$^{(7)}$ MrJDavies (stumbled bend after 2nd: wnt prom 7th: wknd after next: t.o)	20	**6**	16/1	—	—
4707^{F}	**Dramatic Pass (IRE)** (MCChapman) **8-11-5** WWorthington (sn bhd: t.o whn p.u bef 2 out)		**P**	25/1	—	—
4542^{5}	**Reno's Treasure (USA)** (JohnHarris) **4-10-8** RSupple (chsd ldrs tl lost pl 3rd: t.o whn p.u bef 3 out)		**P**	33/1	—	—
				(SP 122.4%)	**8 Rn**	

5m 21.8 (10.80) CSF £13.08 TOTE £7.40: £1.40 £1.30 £1.40 (£4.60) OWNER Mr N. B. Mason (BRANCEPETH) BRED R. Howe

WEIGHT FOR AGE 4yo-6lb

IN-FOCUS: **This completed a first ever four-timer for Richard Guest at the rewarding odds of 759/1.**

2633 Nosam, whose two previous outings were National Hunt Flat races, wore a cross-noseband and had his tongue tied down. Giving away many lengths at the start, he was given time to recover and, shaken up to lead on the run-in, soon shot clear. (7/1)

4452 Grosvenor (IRE), tried in blinkers, looked to have it in the bag when going on four out but, when tackled on the run-in, he quickly ran up the white flag and his rider soon called it a day. (4/5: op 2/5)

4568 Hand of Straw (IRE) was having his second race in three days. (5/2)

Barrie Stir, pulled up last time, gave his rider problems. He would not settle and, as a result, his hurdling suffered. (11/1)

T/Plpt: £146.50 (37.15 Tckts). T/Qdpt: £22.70 (11.37 Tckts) WG

4434-FONTWELL (Fig. 8) (Good to firm, Good patches)

Monday May 26th

WEATHER: sunny

4720 SOUTH COAST RADIO HURDLE (4-Y.O) (Class E)

2-00 (2-01) **2m 2f 110y (9 hdls)** £2,262.10 (£625.60: £298.30) GOING minus 0.54 sec per fur (GF)

				SP	RR	SF
4170*	**Major Dundee (IRE) (109)** (MCPipe) **4-11-10v** CMaude (lw: mde all: drvn out)	—	**1**	11/10^{1}	90?	42
4014^{9}	**Noble Lord (114)** (RHBuckler) **4-12-2** BPowell (lw: a.p: rdn 2 out: unable qckn flat)	4	**2**	15/8^{2}	93	45
4434^{3}	**Anna Soleil (IRE) (106)** (OSherwood) **4-11-4** JAMcCarthy (prom tl hrd rdn & wknd appr last)	16	**3**	7/2^{3}	67	19
4465^{B}	**Dubai Dolly (IRE)** (JWMullins) **4-10-7** SCurran (bhd fr 5th)	10	**4**	16/1	47	—
	P Grayco Choice (PCClarke) **4-10-7** BFenton (bit bkwd: a bhd: t.o fr 4th)	dist	**5**	100/1	—	—
				(SP 111.5%)	**5 Rn**	

4m 15.2 (-2.80) CSF £3.35 TOTE £2.10: £1.40 £1.60 (£2.30) OWNER Mr Michael Jaye (WELLINGTON) BRED Brittas House Stud

4170* Major Dundee (IRE) threatened to go left-handed in the home straight as he has done before, but Maude was very strong and deserves much of the credit. (11/10)

3917 Noble Lord, dropped in class, looked a picture and ran well too without quite managing to concede the weight. (15/8)

4434 Anna Soleil (IRE) did not reproduce her running with the winner at Exeter last month, and may need a stiffer test of stamina on a track as sharp as this. (7/2)

4721 FONTWELL (S) H'CAP CHASE (0-95) (5-Y.O+) (Class G)

2-30 (2-30) **2m 2f (15 fncs)** £2,366.40 (£655.40: £313.20) GOING minus 0.54 sec per fur (GF)

				SP	RR	SF
4430^{3}	**Gabish (67)** (BScriven) **12-10-0** SFox (led 6th: mstke 8th: drvn out)	—	**1**	33/1	82	—
1088^{8}	**Shikaree (IRE) (87)** (MCPipe) **6-11-6b** CMaude (lw: reminders 3rd: hdwy 6th: ev ch flat: hrd rdn: r.o)	1½	**2**	6/1^{3}	101	10
4552^{7}	**Ilewin (82)** (PCRitchens) **10-11-1** MAhern (a.p: ev ch appr 3 out: one pce)	6	**3**	16/1	90	—
4522^{P}	**Flowing River (USA) (67)** (NRMitchell) **11-9-9b**$^{(5)}$ ABates (hdwy 10th: 4th whn mstke 2 out: hrd rdn: one pce)	2½	**4**	20/1	73	—
4331^{5}	**Rustic Gent (IRE) (67)** (DBurchell) **9-10-0** DJBurchell (rdn 3 out: nvr nrr)	13	**5**	8/1	62	—
4442^{5}	**Side Bar (67)** (PMooney) **7-10-0v** SCurran (hmpd bnd after 1st: nt rcvr)	7	**6**	8/1	55	—
4535^{F}	**Boxing Match (71)** (JMBradley) **10-10-4** BFenton (hdwy 9th: wknd appr 12th)	¾	**7**	12/1	59	—
4320^{P}	**Upward Surge (IRE) (67)** (RRLedger) **7-10-0** MrsNLedger (bhd fr 9th: t.o)	dist	**8**	40/1	—	—
4520*	**Evening Rain (86)** (RJHodges) **11-11-5** TDascombe (prom tl fell 10th)		**F**	2/1^{1}	—	—
3843^{P}	**Peace Officer (95)** (ABarrow) **11-11-7**$^{(7)}$ MrOMcPhail (a bhd: t.o whn p.u bef last)		**P**	16/1	—	—
4472^{9}	**Days of Thunder (74)** (MrsSMOdell) **9-10-7** TJMurphy (lw: bhd fr 8th: p.u bef 11th)		**P**	33/1	—	—
4535^{P}	**Golden Opal (74)** (RHBuckler) **12-10-7** BPowell (a bhd: p.u after 8th: dismntd)		**P**	14/1	—	—
4517^{3}	**Cardenden (IRE) (69)** (JBarclay) **9-10-2** WMcFarland (led to 6th: cl 4th whn blnd & uns rdr 11th)		**U**	7/2^{2}	—	—
				(SP 131.3%)	**13 Rn**	

4m 27.2 (5.20) CSF £216.81 CT £3,069.96 TOTE £39.80: £6.30 £2.30 £3.70 (£126.10) OWNER Mr B. Scriven (TAUNTON) BRED Derrinstown Stud Ltd

LONG HANDICAP Upward Surge (IRE) 9-7 Gabish 9-4 Flowing River (USA) 9-7 Side Bar 9-7
No bid
750 Gabish, gaining only the third win of his career and his first since 1992, seemed to appreciate the switch back to fences and won gamely. (33/1)
791 Shikaree (IRE) needed plenty of encouragement but, to his credit, he kept battling away. (6/1)
783* Ilewin, a winner twice at Fontwell in the past, made a satisfactory return to steeplechasing. (16/1)
3852 Flowing River (USA) has not won for three seasons. (20/1)
597 Boxing Match (12/1: 8/1-14/1)
4520* Evening Rain was still in contention when he came down six fences from home. (2/1)
3891 Golden Opal (14/1: 10/1-16/1)
4517 Cardenden (IRE) threatened to make the long journey worthwhile until losing his rider five from home. (7/2)

4722 THORNFIELD H'CAP CHASE (0-115) (5-Y.O+) (Class E)
3-00 (3-01) **3m 2f 110y (22 fncs)** £2,943.80 (£877.40: £418.20: £188.60) GOING minus 0.54 sec per fur (GF)

				SP	RR	SF
4553*	**Red Branch (IRE) (102)** (JSKing) **8-11-10** TJMurphy (chsd ldr fr 18th: led last: drvn out)	—	**1**	6/4 1	115	50
4463P	**Drumcullen (IRE) (100)** (KCBailey) **8-11-8** WMcFarland (led to last: hrd rdn: unable qckn)	4	**2**	11/2 3	111	46
44672	**Banntown Bill (IRE) (97)** (MCPipe) **8-11-5v** CMaude (chsd ldr: ev ch 18th: wknd 19th)	17	**3**	4/1 2	97	32
45494	**Karar (IRE) (95)** (RRowe) **7-11-3** DO'Sullivan (lw: mstke 2nd: no hdwy fr 17th)	10	**4**	11/2 3	89	24
44385	**Master Comedy (78)** (MissLBower) **13-10-0b** BPowell (bhd fr 16th)	6	**5**	12/1	69	4
1906	**Father Dowling (81)** (GBBalding) **10-10-3v** BFenton (a bhd: t.o fr 6th: p.u bef 10th)		**P**	14/1	—	—
44633	**Frozen Drop (100)** (PCRitchens) **10-11-8** SFox (lw: rdn & lost pl 8th: t.o whn p.u bef 19th)		**P**	10/1	—	—
4535P	**Trust Deed (USA) (84)** (SGKnight) **9-10-6b** TDascombe (hdwy 5th: 2nd & ev ch whn mstke & uns rdr 17th)		**U**	11/1	—	—
				(SP 122.6%)	**8 Rn**	

6m 33.6 (-6.40) CSF £10.70 CT £27.29 TOTE £2.80: £1.70 £1.70 £1.40 (£9.40) OWNER Mr E. J. Mangan (SWINDON) BRED Michael Butler
LONG HANDICAP Master Comedy 9-8
4553* Red Branch (IRE), winning his seventh race since February, put in a performance which was hard to fault. (6/4)
4463 Drumcullen (IRE) had a brave crack at making all but was unlucky to run into a rival in top form. (11/2)
4467 Banntown Bill (IRE) is inconsistent and, on this occasion, he found little under pressure from the home turn. (4/1: 3/1-5/1)
4239 Frozen Drop (10/1: 6/1-11/1)
4429* Trust Deed (USA), having a good season, was bang there when his rider came off six from home. (11/1: 7/1-12/1)

4723 STREBEL BOILERS AND RADIATORS (QUALIFIER) H'CAP HURDLE (0-105) (4-Y.O+) (Class F)
3-30 (3-32) **2m 6f 110y (11 hdls)** £2,048.80 (£566.80: £270.40) GOING minus 0.54 sec per fur (GF)

				SP	RR	SF
44704	**Zingibar (81)** (JMBradley) **5-10-9** BFenton (chsd ldr fr 7th: led 2 out: drvn out)	—	**1**	7/1 3	63	11
4562*	**Brindley House (100)** (RCurtis) **10-11-7**(7) JParkhouse (led to 2 out: r.o one pce)	3½	**2**	3/1 1	80	28
39218	**Wicklow Boy (IRE) (72)** (RIngram) **6-10-0** TJMurphy (chsd ldr to 7th: one pce fr 3 out)	2½	**3**	50/1	50	—
46603	**Star Performer (IRE) (97)** (AGHobbs) **6-11-4**(7) MrGShenkin (lw: rdn 7th: bhd fr 8th: t.o)	dist	**4**	7/2 2	—	—
4542*	**The Flying Doctor (IRE) (97)** (GBBalding) **7-11-11** WMcFarland (fell 6th)		**F**	7/2 2	—	—
45482	**Apache Park (USA) (88)** (DBurchell) **4-10-10** DJBurchell (fell 7th)		**F**	7/1 3	—	—
45443	**Cambo (USA) (80)** (MCBanks) **11-10-8** DSkyrme (prom to 6th: bhd whn p.u bef 2 out: dismntd)		**P**	8/1	—	—
44363	**The Grey Texan (76)** (RRowe) **8-10-4**ow4 DO'Sullivan (wl bhd whn p.u & dismntd after 5th)		**P**	10/1	—	—
				(SP 116.6%)	**8 Rn**	

5m 18.0 (2.00) CSF £26.89 CT £896.10 TOTE £8.30: £1.90 £1.80 £6.60 (£21.00) OWNER Mr D. Holpin (CHEPSTOW) BRED Charlton Down Stud
LONG HANDICAP Wicklow Boy (IRE) 8-9 The Grey Texan 9-2
WEIGHT FOR AGE 4yo-6lb
4470 Zingibar found the trip ideal and seems to go particularly well on a sharp track like this. (7/1)
4562* Brindley House forced a testing gallop and stayed on gamely on the run-in, showing an admirable attitude. (3/1)
Wicklow Boy (IRE) has refused to race in three of his last four races on the Flat, but he did little wrong here and looks best kept to hurdling. (50/1)
4542* The Flying Doctor (IRE), in touch but being held up towards the rear, departed at halfway. (7/2)
4548 Apache Park (USA) (7/1: 5/1-15/2)

4724 FONTWELL PARK HUNTERS' CHASE (5-Y.O+) (Class H)
4-00 (4-00) **3m 2f 110y (22 fncs)** £1,203.00 (£333.00: £159.00) GOING minus 0.54 sec per fur (GF)

				SP	RR	SF
44322	**Mighty Falcon** (MissEmmaTory) **12-11-0**(7) MissETory (led 3rd: mstke & hdd 10th: lost pl 13th: rallied & led last: pushed out)	—	**1**	9/2 3	104	20
	Heathview (MrsPChamings) **10-11-7**(7) MrMPortman (hdwy 9th: led 12th to 15th: mstke 16th: led appr 3 out to last: unable qckn)	13	**2**	16/1	103	19
42564	**Fordstown (IRE)** (JamieAlexander) **8-11-7**(7) MrJamieAlexander (led to 3rd: mstke 16th: rallied & r.o flat)	3	**3**	16/1	101	17
45602	**Trifast Lad** (MJRoberts) **12-12-4**(3) MrPHacking (rdn 14th: hdwy & ev ch 2 out: wknd last)	nk	**4**	6/4 1	108	24
46344	**Tammy's Friend** (MrsLMKemble) **10-11-0b**(7) MrAWintle (led 10th to 12th: wknd appr last)	2½	**5**	15/2	93	9
	Howaryadoon (MrsPACave) **11-11-0**(7) MissTCave (blnd 3rd: bhd fr 5th: p.u bef 3 out)		**P**	14/1	—	—
3813*	**Colonial Kelly** (MrsDMGrissell) **9-12-2**(5) MrCVigors (led 15th tl appr 3 out: wknd 2 out: p.u flat: lame)		**P**	5/2 2	—	—
46174	**American Eyre** (MrsGMGladders) **12-11-0**(7) MissSGladders (a bhd: t.o whn p.u bef 19th)		**P**	33/1	—	—
46193	**No Inhibitions** (MrsSWarr) **10-11-7**(7) MrAWarr (prom to 19th: bhd whn p.u bef last)		**P**	33/1	—	—
4615F	**Mr Oriental** (GiuseppeGigantesco) **7-11-0**(7) MrGGigantesco (bhd whn uns rdr after 3rd: bridle slipped)		**U**	66/1	—	—
				(SP 124.3%)	**10 Rn**	

6m 44.3 (4.30) CSF £64.70 TOTE £4.80: £1.60 £3.50 £3.70 (£34.60) OWNER Miss Emma Tory (BLANDFORD) BRED R. J. and Mrs Tory
4432 Mighty Falcon, with only one of the remaining eight behind him going into the home turn, appeared to have no chance at that point but the race changed rapidly in the straight. (9/2)
Heathview, in good form between the flags earlier this year, had been off for six weeks but he acquitted himself well until the winner stormed past. (16/1)
4256 Fordstown (IRE) stayed on after getting outpaced in mid-race, but only snatched third because Trifast Lad was easing down. (16/1)
4560 Trifast Lad weakened badly after looking dangerous between the last two fences. His rider thought he had gone lame and eased him out of third place near the finish. (6/4)

4634 Tammy's Friend has run well in his last two races without managing to pick up any prizemoney. (15/2: 5/1-8/1)
Howaryadoon (14/1: op 8/1)

4725 TED TRIGGS MEMORIAL H'CAP HURDLE (0-110) (4-Y.O+) (Class E)
4-30 (4-30) **2m 2f 110y (9 hdls)** £2,241.80 (£619.80: £295.40) GOING minus 0.54 sec per fur (GF)

				SP	RR	SF
3063[4]	**Chieftain's Crown (USA) (87)** (THind) **6-10-8** PMcLoughlin (jnd ldr 3 out: led 2 out: drvn out)	—	1	6/1[3]	67	18
4255[B]	**Lord Love (IRE) (79)** (PRChamings) **5-10-0** TJMurphy (led to 2 out: rdn: r.o)	1¾	2	9/1	58	9
4654[2]	**Classic Pal (USA) (80)** (NRMitchell) **6-10-1**ow1 DSkyrme (hld up: gd hdwy fr 2 out: nvr nrr)	3	3	2/1[2]	56	6
4275[2]	**Jovie King (IRE) (95)** (RHBuckler) **5-11-2** BPowell (a.p: ev ch 3 out: 3rd & btn whn mstke last)	nk	4	11/10[1]	71	22
4633[6]	**Do Be Ware (79)** (JFfitch-Heyes) **7-10-0b** BFenton (prom tl wknd 3 out)	16	5	9/1	41	—
				(SP 115.2%)		**5 Rn**

4m 17.4 (-0.60) CSF £44.17 TOTE £9.20: £2.60 £2.50 (£32.40) OWNER Miss J. Rumford (WENDOVER) BRED Ronald K. Kirk
LONG HANDICAP Lord Love (IRE) 9-5 Classic Pal (USA) 9-13 Do Be Ware 9-9
STEWARDS' ENQUIRY Skyrme susp. 5-7 & 11/6/97 (failure to ensure best possible placing).
3063 Chieftain's Crown (USA), whose previous three wins were all at Plumpton, returned to form on his favoured fast ground, despite showing a tendency to flash his tail when hard-ridden. (6/1: 4/1-6/1)
4097 Lord Love (IRE) set a steady early pace and his attempt to slip the field three out did not come to much, but he rallied gamely on the run-in and can make his mark at this level. (9/1)
4654 Classic Pal (USA), set an impossible task, was only shaken up after the last at which point he flew. He ought to have won this, and Skyrme was banned for four days for riding an ill-judged race. (2/1)
4275 Jovie King (IRE) was conceding weight all-round but his response was still a shade disappointing when the pace quickened after jumping three out. (11/10: evens-6/5)

T/Plpt: £4,049.50 (1.11 Tckts). T/Qdpt: Not won; £310.18 to Redcar 27/5/97 LMc

4555-HEREFORD (R-H) (Good, Good to firm patches, becoming Good to firm)
Monday May 26th
WEATHER: hot & sunny

4726 MADLEY NOVICES' HURDLE (4-Y.O+) (Class E)
2-30 (2-32) **2m 1f (9 hdls)** £2,514.00 (£704.00: £342.00) GOING minus 0.27 sec per fur (GF)

				SP	RR	SF
4555*	**Song Of The Sword** (JABOld) **4-11-7** MAFitzgerald (lw: cl up: led appr 4th: drew clr appr last: comf)	—	1	2/11[1]	85+	33
4528[P]	**Blowing Rock (IRE)** (MissHCKnight) **5-11-0** JCulloty (lw: chsd ldrs: hrd rdn & hdwy 3 out: r.o one pce)	3	2	15/2[3]	70	23
4443[4]	**Fraser Carey (IRE) (95)** (TRGeorge) **5-11-3b**(3) MrRThornton (slt ld tl appr 4th: chsd wnr: one pce appr last)	12	3	6/1[2]	65	18
4552[8]	**Sallow Glen (48)** (DrPPritchard) **11-11-0** DrPPritchard (in rr: lost tch 5th: styd on fr 3 out: r.o flat)	nk	4	66/1	59	12
4450[P]	**Ludo's Orchestra (IRE)** (MarkCampion) **6-11-0** MRichards (a bhd: t.o fr 6th)	17	5	50/1	43	—
4626[10]	**Just Because (IRE)** (GEJones) **5-11-0** MrDSJones (chsd ldrs: mstke 5th: 4th & wkng whn fell next)		F	100/1	—	—
	Roger de Mowbray (RBrotherton) **7-11-0** LHarvey (lost tch 5th: t.o whn p.u after 2 out: dismntd)		P	50/1	—	—
	Ameer Alfayaafi (IRE) (DMLloyd) **4-10-6**(3) SophieMitchell (s.s: wl bhd whn rn out bef 3rd)		R	50/1	—	—
3425[16]	**Yonder Star** (GRSmith) **5-11-0** RGreene (bkwd: s.s: wl bhd whn j.slowly & uns rdr 2nd)		U	100/1	—	—
				(SP 120.0%)		**9 Rn**

3m 56.3 (3.30) CSF £2.51 TOTE £1.50: £1.00 £1.50 £1.70 (£2.30) OWNER Lady Lloyd Webber (WROUGHTON) BRED Sheikh Mohammed Bin Rashid Al Maktoum
WEIGHT FOR AGE 4yo-5lb
OFFICIAL EXPLANATION Ameer Alfayaafi (IRE) cocked his jaw and ran out.
4555* Song Of The Sword completed the hat-trick with a smooth success and can go on to much better things next season when he will still have novice status. (2/11)
4329 Blowing Rock (IRE) ought to be suited by two and a half miles in time. (15/2)
Fraser Carey (IRE), a winner in Ireland, can pick up a small race on fast ground. (6/1: 4/1-13/2)

4727 ORCOP (S) H'CAP HURDLE (0-95) (4-Y.O+) (Class G)
3-00 (3-01) **3m 2f (13 hdls)** £2,038.00 (£568.00: £274.00) GOING minus 0.27 sec per fur (GF)

				SP	RR	SF
4572[2]	**Mardood (66)** (SBClark) **12-9-8**(7)ow1 MissRClark (chsd ldrs: led appr 2 out: rdn out)	—	1	10/1	44	—
4468[9]	**Provence (65)** (AWCarroll) **10-10-0v** MRichards (a.p: led 8th to 3 out: kpt on one pce)	1¾	2	12/1	42	—
4524[8]	**Baylord Prince (IRE) (65)** (MrsJAEwer) **9-9-11**(3) SophieMitchell (in rr: styd on fr 2 out: fin wl)	½	3	20/1	42	—
3442[9]	**Kashan (IRE) (65)** (PHayward) **9-10-0** ILawrence (chsd ldrs: lost pl 10th: styd on fr 2 out)	2	4	10/1	40	—
4281[3]	**Song For Jess (IRE) (75)** (FJordan) **4-10-0**(3)ow3 LAspell (hld up in tch: hdwy 8th: led 3 out: sn hdd: wkng whn hit last)	2½	5	10/1	49	—
4524[3]	**Tiger Claw (USA) (75)** (AGHobbs) **11-10-10** RGreene (sn in rr: rdn 5th: nvr rchd ldrs)	8	6	5/1[2]	44	—
4281*	**Awestruck (65)** (BPreece) **7-9-7b**(7) JMogford (a bhd: sme late hdwy)	s.h	7	6/1[3]	34	—
394[F]	**Jennyellen (IRE) (93)** (PBowen) **8-12-0** MAFitzgerald (hld up in rr: hdwy 6th: ch 3 out: wknd qckly next)	4	8	8/1	59	2
4442[4]	**Pandora's Prize (65)** (TWall) **11-10-0** JCulloty (led to 4th: in tch tl wknd 9th)	14	9	16/1	23	—
4663[2]	**Up the Tempo (IRE) (65)** (PaddyFarrell) **8-9-9**(5) OBurrows (a in rr)	10	10	10/1	17	—
4556[2]	**Look In The Mirror (70)** (NATwiston-Davies) **6-10-5** CLlewellyn (led 4th to 6th: led 7th to 8th: wknd 10th: bhd whn p.u bef 3 out)		P	3/1[1]	—	—
4439[7]	**Derrybelle (73)** (DLWilliams) **6-10-1**(7) MrSDurack (bhd fr 5th: t.o whn p.u bef 10th)		P	20/1	—	—
4378[3]	**Squealing Jeanie (65)** (JMBradley) **8-10-0** KGaule (lw: stdy hdwy 7th: rdn & wknd 10th: p.u bef next)		P	9/1	—	—
4468[3]	**Khazari (USA) (68)** (RBrotherton) **9-10-3** LHarvey (a in rr: t.o whn p.u after 8th)		P	7/1	—	—
4220[11]	**Kano Warrior (67)** (BPreece) **10-10-2b**[1] VSlattery (prom: led 6th to 7th: sn wknd: p.u after 8th)		P	20/1	—	—
4563[5]	**Arrange A Game (66)** (MissJBower) **10-9-8**(7)ow1 MHandley (mstke 4th: sn dropped rr: t.o whn p.u bef 3 out)		P	16/1	—	—
				(SP 159.7%)		**16 Rn**

6m 19.1 (16.10) CSF £143.08 CT £2,244.14 TOTE £19.30: £3.80 £3.90 £6.50 £4.50 (£143.80) OWNER Mr S. B. Clark (SUTTON-ON-THE-FOREST) BRED Mrs D. Davison
LONG HANDICAP Mardood 9-9 Baylord Prince (IRE) 9-11 Pandora's Prize 9-10 Kashan (IRE) 9-10 Provence 9-9 Squealing Jeanie 9-5 Arrange A Game 9-10 Song For Jess (IRE) 9-13 Up the Tempo (IRE) 9-8 Awestruck 9-11

WEIGHT FOR AGE 4yo-7lb
No bid
OFFICIAL EXPLANATION Up The Tempo (IRE): the trainer reported that the mare had bled from the nose.
4572 Mardood was winning for the first time for four years but this was a poor contest. (10/1)
1562 Provence ran a good race in a first-time visor. (12/1: 7/1-14/1)
4096 Baylord Prince (IRE), who often gets behind, was flying at the finish and might have got closer but for being slightly hampered at the last. (20/1)
4281 Song For Jess (IRE) (10/1: 8/1-12/1)

4728 CRASWELL NOVICES' CHASE (5-Y.O+) (Class E)

3-30 (3-30) **2m 3f (14 fncs)** £3,130.00 (£880.00: £430.00) GOING minus 0.27 sec per fur (GF)

				SP	RR	SF
4070[4]	**Chan The Man** (DBurchell) **6-10-11**(3) GuyLewis (trckd ldr tl led 8th: mstke & hdd next: led 11th: clr 3 out: hit last)	—	1	11/2[3]	77	—
	Wesshaun (PGMurphy) **7-10-6**(3) LAspell (led to 8th: led next tl mstke 11th: one pce fr next)	22	2	12/1	54	—
4643[7]	**Run With Joy (IRE)** (AGHobbs) **6-11-0** RGreene (chsd ldrs: mstke 10th: sn rdn & one pce)	1¾	3	3/1[2]	57	—
4232[5]	**Sorciere (81)** (GBBalding) **6-11-1** BClifford (hld up: stdy hdwy to chse wnr 3 out: no imp fr next: broke leg & p.u appr last: dead)		P	10/11[1]	—	—
4402[U]	**Diamond Light** (VRBishop) **10-11-0** MRichards (outpcd & lost tch 5th: p.u bef 7th)		P	6/1	—	—
				(SP 114.7%)		**5 Rn**

4m 45.3 (15.30) CSF £46.14 TOTE £5.70: £1.40 £3.50 (£23.00) OWNER Mrs Sandra Worthington (EBBW VALE) BRED D. E. Williams
4070 Chan The Man, who has reportedly suffered from a wind problem, was already well in command when left a long way clear approaching the last. (11/2: 8/1-5/1)
Wesshaun is a very modest performer between the flags. (12/1)
4232 Sorciere (10/11: 4/5-evens)
4305 Diamond Light (6/1: op 7/2)

4729 MICHAELCHURCH H'CAP HURDLE (0-120) (4-Y.O+) (Class D)

4-00 (4-01) **2m 3f 110y (11 hdls)** £2,864.00 (£804.00: £392.00) GOING minus 0.27 sec per fur (GF)

				SP	RR	SF
4630[3]	**Kinnescash (IRE) (110)** (PBowen) **4-11-6** MAFitzgerald (trckd ldr: mstke 7th: lft clr 3 out: j.lft last)	—	1	10/11[1]	82	8
4381[9]	**Eurolink the Rebel (USA) (92)** (SBClark) **5-10-0**(7) MissRClark (hld up in 3rd: dropped rr 8th: styd on again fr 2 out)	12	2	10/1	54	—
	Polish Rider (USA) (86) (BJLlewellyn) **9-10-1** CLlewellyn (hld up in tch: hdwy & rdn 8th: wknd fr 2 out)	7	3	11/2[3]	42	—
4510[3]	**Severn Gale (100)** (JAllen) **7-10-12**(3) MrRThornton (led: mstke 6th: fell 3 out)		F	13/8[2]	—	—
				(SP 115.0%)		**4 Rn**

4m 41.4 (10.40) CSF £8.18 TOTE £1.80: (£4.00) OWNER Mr D. R. James (HAVERFORDWEST) BRED Frank Barry
WEIGHT FOR AGE 4yo-5lb
4630 Kinnescash (IRE), who did not hurdle fluently, was poised to take over when left clear at the third from home. (10/11)
4510 Severn Gale showed a tendency to dive at her hurdles and hit was to cost her dear at the third last although Kinnescash was breathing down her neck at the time. (13/8: 6/4-9/4)

4730 CLIVE MAIDEN HUNTERS' CHASE (5-Y.O+) (Class H)

4-35 (4-37) **3m 1f 110y (19 fncs)** £1,160.00 (£350.00: £170.00: £80.00) GOING minus 0.27 sec per fur (GF)

				SP	RR	SF
4614[2]	**No Joker (IRE)** (NAGaselee) **9-11-10**(7) MrPScott (chsd ldrs: lost tch 11th: hdwy 4 out: styd on to ld appr last: r.o)	—	1	7/2[1]	98	11
4432[4]	**Anjubi** (MissMBragg) **12-11-10**(7) MrSMulcaire (chsd ldrs: w ldr 8th tl led 15th: hdd next: rallied to ld briefly after 2 out: sn hdd & no ex)	3	2	8/1	96	9
4522[P]	**Ann's Ambition** (MrsCHussey) **10-11-10**(7) MrMFrith (hld up in tch: hdwy 10th: led 4 out: hit 2 out: sn hdd & no ex)	4	3	25/1	94	7
4607[2]	**The Rum Mariner** (MrsJASkelton) **10-11-10**(7) MrDSJones (led 3rd: jnd 8th: hdd 15th: sn rdn & wknd)	22	4	13/2	80	—
4616[3]	**Teatrader** (MissTOBlazey) **11-11-10**(7) MrSDurack (led to 3rd: lost tch 13th: t.o)	26	5	8/1	64	—
4462[2]	**Link Copper** (MrsEJTaplin) **8-12-0**(3) MrRTreloggen (mstkes 1st & 3rd: lost tch 10th: t.o whn p.u bef 4 out)		P	5/1[2]	—	—
	Watchit Lad (MrsAPrice) **7-11-12**(7)ow2 MrMPJones (swtg: wl bhd fr 8th: t.o whn p.u bef 3 out)		P	50/1	—	—
4324[6]	**Lurriga Glitter (IRE)** (RJSmith) **9-11-12b**(5) MrRFord (in rr: mstke 8th: lost tch fr 10th: t.o whn p.u bef 2 out)		P	7/1	—	—
	Salmon Poutcher (MrsJLPhelps) **8-11-7**(5) MrJTrice-Rolph (bhd fr 5th: t.o whn p.u bef 13th)		P	33/1	—	—
3469[U]	**Corn Exchange** (DGDuggan) **9-12-0**(3) MrMRimell (lw: lost tch 13th: poor 5th whn blnd 3 out: blnd next & p.u: dismntd)		P	11/2[3]	—	—
	Prime Course (IRE) (MrsAFarrant) **8-11-10**(7) MrPBull (mstke 3rd: bhd fr 10th: t.o whn p.u bef 14th)		P	33/1	—	—
	Majestic Ride (RobWoods) **13-11-10**(7) MrRArmson (a bhd: t.o whn p.u bef 14th)		P	50/1	—	—
4432[6]	**Indian Knight** (CAGreen) **12-11-10**(7) MrEJames (in tch to 12th: bhd whn mstke & uns rdr 15th)		U	20/1	—	—
	Andalucian Sun (IRE) (AWitcomb) **9-11-10**(7) MrPGMoloney (sddle slipped: sn bhd & j.b: t.o whn tried to ref & uns rdr 5th)		U	15/2	—	—
				(SP 132.5%)		**14 Rn**

6m 27.2 (17.20) CSF £30.58 TOTE £4.70: £1.80 £2.90 £6.80 (£19.00) OWNER Brig R. W. S. Hall (LAMBOURN) BRED Mrs P. F. N. Fanning
4614 No Joker (IRE), one of the few with hunter chase form, stayed on from well back to collar rivals who could barely raise a gallop. (7/2)
4432 Anjubi stays well but lacks anything in the way of pace. (8/1: 5/1-9/1)
4607 The Rum Mariner, prominent for a long way, faded rather disappointingly. At least there was no repeat of the drama of his previous visit here when he inadvertently kicked to death a Jack Russell which had strayed on to the course. (13/2)
4616 Teatrader (8/1: 6/1-9/1)
Corn Exchange (11/2: 4/1-6/1)

4731 CAREY NOVICES' H'CAP HURDLE (0-100) (4-Y.O+) (Class E)

5-05 (5-10) **2m 3f 110y (11 hdls)** £2,472.00 (£692.00: £336.00) GOING minus 0.27 sec per fur (GF)

				SP	RR	SF
4405*	**Magical Blues (IRE) (90)** (MissAEEmbiricos) **5-11-10** KGaule (hld up in rr: stdy hdwy 7th: jnd ldrs 3 out: led last: rdn out)	—	1	4/1[1]	68	32

4470[8]	**Colwall (77)** (MissPMWhittle) **6-10-11** MAFitzgerald (mid div: hdwy 8th: led appr 2 out to last: unable qckn)....2	**2**	12/1	53	17
4548[7]	**Irish Dominion (66)** (AGHobbs) **7-9-9**(5) OBurrows (lw: chsd ldrs: led appr 3 out tl appr 2 out: btn whn mstke last).....10	**3**	14/1	34	—
4663[W]	**Sioux To Speak (85)** (MissHCKnight) **5-11-5** JCulloty (chsd ldrs: rdn & one pce fr 8th).....14	**4**	4/1 [1]	42	6
4620[2]	**Callermine (73)** (MissHDay) **8-10-4**(3) SophieMitchell (chsd ldrs tl wknd fr 3 out).....½	**5**	14/1	29	—
4542[2]	**Sterling Fellow (85)** (DLWilliams) **4-10-7v**(7) MrSDurack (s.s: a wl bhd).....6	**6**	5/1 [2]	36	—
4652[2]	**Lyphard's Fable (USA) (66)** (TRGeorge) **6-10-0** MRichards (mid div whn fell 5th).....	**F**	4/1 [1]	—	—
4459[3]	**Admiral Bruny (IRE) (75)** (NAGaselee) **6-10-9** CLlewellyn (led tl appr 3 out: wknd qckly: p.u bef 2 out).....	**P**	7/1 [3]	—	—
157[4]	**Little Court (66)** (EGBevan) **6-10-0** VSlattery (lost tch 6th: t.o whn p.u bef 3 out).....	**P**	14/1	—	—
4440[3]	**Flash Chick (IRE) (66)** (TMorton) **8-9-7**(7) JMogford (b.hind: sn wl bhd: t.o whn p.u bef 2 out).....	**P**	25/1	—	—
4558[9]	**Sober Island (68)** (MrsDThomas) **8-9-13**(3)ow2 GuyLewis (prom to 6th: sn lost tch: t.o whn p.u bef 3 out).....	**P**	40/1	—	—

(SP 123.1%) **11 Rn**

4m 35.8 (4.80) CSF £48.94 CT £574.42 TOTE £5.50: £2.00 £2.70 £5.90 (£18.60) OWNER Miss A. Embiricos (NEWMARKET) BRED John Breslin
LONG HANDICAP Lyphard's Fable (USA) 9-10 Irish Dominion 9-3 Little Court 9-10 Flash Chick (IRE) 9-3 Sober Island 8-12
WEIGHT FOR AGE 4yo-5lb
4405* Magical Blues (IRE) did not give away as much ground at the start as he had last time. (4/1)
2820 Colwall was returning to form after some poor efforts. (12/1: op 8/1)
4289 Irish Dominion would have chances in a seller. (14/1)
4620 Callermine (14/1: op 6/1)
77* Little Court (14/1: op 7/1)

T/Plpt: £821.10 (4.1 Tckts). T/Qdpt: £60.10 (2.4 Tckts) RL

4562-HUNTINGDON (R-H) (Good to firm, Firm patches)
Monday May 26th

WEATHER: warm & sunny

4732 WILLMOTT DIXON CONDITIONAL (S) H'CAP HURDLE (0-95) (4-Y.O+) (Class G)
2-00 (2-00) **2m 110y (8 hdls)** £1,880.50 (£523.00: £251.50) GOING minus 1.05 sec per fur (HD)

			SP	RR	SF
4633[5]	**Ajdar (72)** (OBrennan) **6-10-5** RMassey (lw: hdwy 5th: led appr 2 out: clr whn hit last: jst hld on).....—	**1**	9/2 [1]	54	14
	Major's Law (IRE) (84) (THind) **8-11-3** XAizpuru (bit bkwd: hdwy 5th: ev ch whn hit 2 out: r.o wl flat).....hd	**2**	12/1	66	26
4558[3]	**Tee Tee Too (IRE) (67)** (AWCarroll) **5-9-9**(5) RStudholme (in tch: rdn & hdwy 2 out: r.o flat).....4	**3**	11/1	45	5
4259[8]	**Maggies Lad (80)** (PCalver) **9-10-13** PHenley (lw: chsd ldr to 3rd: rdn appr 2 out: one pce).....2	**4**	12/1	56	16
4542[3]	**Summer Villa (76)** (KGWingrove) **5-10-6b**(3) JPower (plld hrd: prom: led 3 out: sn hdd & btn).....1¾	**5**	6/1 [2]	50	10
2859[9]	**Angus McCoatup (IRE) (85)** (MDHammond) **4-10-13** FLeahy (pushed along appr 4th: hdwy 8th: rdn & wknd appr 2 out).....2½	**6**	6/1 [2]	57	12
4453[4]	**Caddy's First (76)** (SMellor) **5-10-6v**(3) ChrisWebb (lw: prom: led appr 3 out: sn hdd: wknd appr last).....5	**7**	7/1 [3]	43	3
4527[6]	**Circus Colours (95)** (JRJenkins) **7-11-4**(10) DYellowlees (lw: sn pushed along: a bhd).....4	**8**	9/2 [1]	58	18
4278[P]	**Kalzari (USA) (79)** (AWCarroll) **12-10-12** JMagee (in tch to 3 out).....16	**9**	7/1 [3]	27	—
4443[6]	**Swahili Run (68)** (JGMO'Shea) **9-9-12v**[1](3) MGriffiths (led: clr 3rd: pckd 5th: wknd qckly & hdd appr next: p.u bef 2 out).....	**P**	20/1	—	—

(SP 118.4%) **10 Rn**

3m 39.3 (-8.70) CSF £52.13 CT £515.26 TOTE £5.90: £2.20 £2.90 £2.80 (£25.70) OWNER Mrs Sue Catt (WORKSOP) BRED Floors Farming
WEIGHT FOR AGE 4yo-5lb
No bid
4633 Ajdar, outpaced until the field bunched four out, took heart from this and kept on under pressure to break a long losing sequence. (9/2: op 3/1)
Major's Law (IRE) didn't look fully wound up for this first run in over a year, but the handicapper has given him a chance, and he looked the probable winner until blowing up after two out. Dismounted on his return, there are races for him off this sort of mark if the injury is not too serious. (12/1: 5/1-14/1)
4558 Tee Tee Too (IRE) again finished with a flourish and is worth a try over further. (11/1: 7/1-12/1)
Maggies Lad, on his second race back after two and a half years off, ran well but looks short of speed these days. His hope appears to be staying further than this. (12/1: 7/1-12/1)
4542 Summer Villa (6/1: 4/1-13/2)

4733 SWYNFORD PADDOCKS HOTEL H'CAP CHASE (0-115) (5-Y.O+) (Class E)
2-30 (2-30) **2m 110y (12 fncs)** £3,137.50 (£875.00: £422.50) GOING minus 0.62 sec per fur (F)

			SP	RR	SF
4456*	**Crackling Frost (IRE) (83)** (MrsDHaine) **9-10-9** RDunwoody (prom: chsd ldr fr 4 out: rdn & ev ch whn lft clr last: eased).....—	**1**	5/4 [1]	96+	26
4157*	**Dr Rocket (82)** (RDickin) **12-10-3v**(5) XAizpuru (lw: hld up: hdwy 4th: j.slowly & outpcd 7th: lft poor 2nd last).12	**2**	6/1	83	13
4300[6]	**Allimac Nomis (88)** (MDHammond) **8-11-0** RGarritty (nvr trbld ldrs: lft 3rd last: fin lame: dead).....6	**3**	11/2 [3]	84	14
	Come on Dancer (IRE) (83) (JWhite) **9-10-9** JRKavanagh (bit bkwd: a bhd).....9	**4**	25/1	70	—
4543[2]	**My Young Man (100)** (CPEBrooks) **12-11-12** GBradley (chsd ldr: hit 1st & 6th: wknd fr 4 out).....1¾	**5**	6/1	85	15
4612*	**Pond House (IRE) (102)** (MCPipe) **8-12-0** JFTitley (mstkes: led tl fell last).....	**F**	3/1 [2]	—	—
4564[2]	**Lowawatha (93)** (MrsEHHeath) **9-11-5** DGallagher (lw: t.o fr 3rd: p.u bef 8th).....	**P**	12/1	—	—

(SP 124.9%) **7 Rn**

3m 59.1 (-2.90) CSF £10.01 TOTE £2.60: £1.60 £2.40 (£5.50) OWNER The Unlucky For Some Partnership (NEWMARKET) BRED James A. Slattery
OFFICIAL EXPLANATION My Young Man: the rider reported that the gelding was never travelling on the firmish ground and felt it prudent to hold him together in the closing stages, rather than subject him to further pressure.
4456* Crackling Frost (IRE), not able to dominate this time, had made hard work of closing on the leader when presented with the race at the last. It would have been close had Pond House stood up. (5/4: op 9/4)
4157* Dr Rocket, with so many front-runners in the race, could never go the pace. (6/1)
4300 Allimac Nomis was out of the battle for the lead by the second and, unfortunately, finished so lame he had to be put down. (11/2)

4543 My Young Man brought back from hunter chases, was on a 53lb lower mark than when winning the 1992 Grand Annual. A natural front-runner, he needs to dominate and couldn't here. (6/1: op 4/1)
4612* Pond House (IRE) set off at a rate of knots, but was galloping into the bottom of his fences making many mistakes. It was when he went for a long one at the last, that he came to grief. (3/1)
4564 Lowawatha likes making the running but, with all the other early pace in the race, did not want to know. (12/1: op 8/1)

4734 QUALITAIR GROUP H'CAP HURDLE (0-120) (4-Y.O+) (Class D)

3-05 (3-05) **2m 5f 110y (10 hdls)** £2,924.00 (£814.00: £392.00) GOING minus 1.05 sec per fur (HD)

				SP	RR	SF
4550*	**Diwali Dancer (119)** (MCPipe) **7-11-13** RDunwoody (mde all: drvn out)	—	1	10/11[1]	98	25
4439[2]	**Scud Missile (IRE) (97)** (JWPayne) **6-10-5** AThornton (lw: hld up: hdwy 6th: chsd wnr fr 3 out: unable qckn flat)	2	2	7/2[3]	75	2
1859[P]	**Royal Citizen (IRE) (99)** (JFBottomley) **8-10-7**[ow7] DerekByrne (lw: hld up: hdwy 7th: hit next: shkn up flat: nvr plcd to chal)	8	3	16/1	71	—
4577*	**Linlathen (116)** (MrsMReveley) **7-11-10** PNiven (chsd wnr: hit 4th: wknd 3 out)	2	4	5/2[2]	86	13
4296[U]	**Moobakkr (USA) (92)** (KAMorgan) **6-9-9**(5) XAizpuru (chsd ldrs to 5th)	8	5	8/1	56	—
4224[2]	***Shekels (IRE) (106)*** (CPEBrooks) **6-11-0** GBradley (Withdrawn not under Starter's orders: state of ground)		W		—	—
				(SP 120.2%)	**5 Rn**	

4m 51.5 (-8.50) CSF £4.88 TOTE £2.00: £1.40 £1.60 (£2.50) OWNER Mr B. E. Case (WELLINGTON) BRED Thoroughbred Stock Investors Ltd
LONG HANDICAP Moobakkr (USA) 9-7 Royal Citizen (IRE) 9-8
4550* Diwali Dancer was up in the weights but this company represented a drop in class, ensuring a workmanlike success. (10/11: 4/5-evens)
4439 Scud Missile (IRE) jumped into second place at the third last and kept trying to peg back the winner from then on, only admitting defeat in the final stages. (7/2)
Royal Citizen (IRE), fit from the All-Weather, may have been feeling the fast ground, for his pilot seemed unwilling to go for everything after travelling well into the straight. (16/1)
4577* Linlathen, unable to dictate, had had enough of playing second fiddle to the winner in the last half-mile. (5/2)
4296 Moobakkr (USA) (8/1: 5/1-10/1)

4735 AIRFOYLE NOVICES' H'CAP CHASE (0-100) (5-Y.O+) (Class E)

3-35 (3-35) **3m (19 fncs)** £3,068.75 (£920.00: £442.50: £203.75) GOING minus 0.62 sec per fur (F)

				SP	RR	SF
4566*	**Mister Goodguy (IRE) (76)** (RCurtis) **8-10-8** DMorris (trckd ldrs: pckd 12th: led 2 out: rdn out)	—	1	5/2[2]	85	8
3602[3]	**Colonel Colt (72)** (RDickin) **6-9-13**(5)[ow4] ChrisWebb (lw: in tch: hdwy to ld 3 out: hdd next: one pce)	3	2	16/1	79	—
4627[3]	**Professor Page (IRE) (70)** (TThomsonJones) **7-10-2**[ow2] AThornton (prom: outpcd appr 2 out: r.o flat)	2½	3	12/1	75	—
4314[5]	**Mozemo (68)** (MCPipe) **10-9-11**(3) RMassey (hld up: hdwy 12th: 3rd & btn whn j.rt last)	2	4	10/1	72	—
4324[P]	**Saint Bene't (IRE) (68)** (GProdromou) **9-9-9b**(5) XAizpuru (chsd ldrs to 3 out)	1½	5	9/2[3]	71	—
4549*	**Malwood Castle (IRE) (96)** (RHAlner) **7-11-7**(7) MrJTizzard (lw: hit 12th: sn rdn & bhd)	dist	6	2/1[1]	—	—
4447[P]	**Damcada (IRE) (68)** (AWCarroll) **9-10-0b[1]** DGallagher (led: mstke 10th & next: hdd & wknd 3 out)	8	7	25/1	—	—
4404[3]	**Just One Canaletto (75)** (NATwiston-Davies) **9-10-0b**(7) MrJGoldstein (lw: mstke 12th: sn bhd: p.u bef 3 out)		P	6/1	—	—
4408[4]	**More Joy (68)** (BEllison) **9-10-0** JRKavanagh (lw: t.o fr 10th: p.u bef 2 out)		P	25/1	—	—
4426[P]	**Cotswold Castle (68)** (JGMO'Shea) **11-9-7v**(7) MGriffiths (lw: sn rdn along: j.slowly: t.o fr 10th: p.u bef 3 out)		P	33/1	—	—
				(SP 127.7%)	**10 Rn**	

5m 58.7 (1.70) CSF £38.82 CT £398.17 TOTE £4.40: £1.80 £4.60 £3.30 (£53.00) OWNER Mr M. O'Brien (LAMBOURN) BRED Tom Gaffney and David Magnier
LONG HANDICAP Colonel Colt 9-13 Saint Bene't (IRE) 9-9 Damcada (IRE) 9-13 Professor Page (IRE) 9-10 More Joy 9-12 Cotswold Castle 9-9
OFFICIAL EXPLANATION **Just One Canaletto, pulled up lame. Malwood Castle (IRE), was unsuited by the firm going.**
4566* Mister Goodguy (IRE) is probably nothing special but continues to laugh at the handicapper. (5/2: 2/1-3/1)
3602 Colonel Colt coped well with the step up in trip and must surely break his duck over fences soon. (16/1)
3172 Professor Page (IRE), stepping up to a more suitable trip for his second chase run, gives the impression that he will stay further. (12/1: op 8/1)
4314 Mozemo is a very difficult ride in that he needs to be dropped right out, and he is testing even the Pipe powers. (10/1:6/1-12/1)
3924 Saint Bene't (IRE) (9/2: 6/1-7/2)
4549* Malwood Castle (IRE) looks a different horse with more cut in the ground. (2/1)
4404 Just One Canaletto (6/1: op 4/1)

4736 EDWARD WOOTTON NOVICES' CHASE (5-Y.O+) (Class E)

4-05 (4-05) **2m 4f 110y (16 fncs)** £3,209.50 (£892.00: £428.50) GOING minus 0.62 sec per fur (F)

				SP	RR	SF
4298[4]	**Mister Drum (IRE) (124)** (MJWilkinson) **8-12-7** RDunwoody (chsd ldr: led & lft clr 9th: v.easily)	—	1	2/5[1]	122?	30
4444*	**Sigma Run (IRE) (81)** (JGMO'Shea) **8-12-0** JRKavanagh (lw: plld hrd: hit 7th: lft 2nd 9th: sn no ch)	dist	2	3/1[2]	—	—
	Bugsy Moran (IRE) (CRMillington) **7-11-0** GBradley (t.o fr 8th: blnd 11th)	dist	3	8/1[3]	—	—
4549[7]	**Chiappucci (IRE) (76)** (MrsEHHeath) **7-11-0b** DGallagher (led: j.lft 5th: hdd & fell 9th)		F	10/1	—	—
4450[P]	**Methodius (IRE)** (JRJenkins) **5-10-7** DMorris (lw: mstkes 1st & 3rd: bhd whn blnd & uns rdr 8th)		U	33/1	—	—
				(SP 119.6%)	**5 Rn**	

5m 2.1 (2.10) CSF £2.37 TOTE £1.50: £1.30 £1.50 (£1.80) OWNER Mr Malcolm Batchelor (BANBURY) BRED David Mooney
WEIGHT FOR AGE 5yo-7lb
4298 Mister Drum (IRE), left a long way clear at halfway, had a solo for most of the final circuit. (2/5: 2/7-4/9)
4444* Sigma Run (IRE) was left toiling in the final mile. (3/1)
Bugsy Moran (IRE), who hasn't been getting the trip between the flags, was wisely allowed to complete in his own time after a dreadful mistake at the water, six from home. (8/1: 12/1-7/1)
4232 Chiappucci (IRE) (10/1: 12/1-8/1)

4737 HUNTINGDONSHIRE MENCAP SUPPORT ASSOCIATION MAIDEN HURDLE (4-Y.O+) (Class E)

4-35 (4-40) **2m 110y (8 hdls)** £2,687.50 (£750.00: £362.50) GOING minus 1.05 sec per fur (HD)

				SP	RR	SF
	Flic Royal (FR) (SMellor) **4-10-9**(5) ChrisWebb (hld up: hdwy 4th: led 2 out: rdn & edgd lft flat: r.o)	—	1	6/1	69	27
4390[2]	**Country Orchid** (MrsMReveley) **6-11-0** PNiven (swtg: trckd ldrs: led appr 2 out: sn hdd: unable qckn flat)	1¼	2	11/8[1]	63	26
3641[5]	**Qualitair Pride (85)** (JFBottomley) **5-11-0** DerekByrne (led tl appr 2 out: sn outpcd)	11	3	8/1	52	15
4613[3]	**Blaster Watson** (CSmith) **6-11-5** MRanger (chsd ldrs: mstke 3 out: one pce appr next: blnd last)	½	4	20/1	57	20

				SP	RR	SF
4567U	**Nashaat (USA) (80)** (KRBurke) **9-11-5** JFTitley (dwlt: hld up: hit 4th: effrt next: nvr rchd ldrs)	7	**5**	10/1	50	13
	Dublin River (USA) (JGMO'Shea) **4-11-0** JRKavanagh (lw: nt j.w: chsd ldrs tl blnd 3 out)	20	**6**	5/1 3	31	—
46388	**Harvest Reaper** (JLHarris) **5-11-2**(3) RMassey (plld hrd: w ldrs to 4th)	4	**7**	33/1	27	—
4382P	**Noquita (NZ)** (JCMcConnochie) **10-11-0b**(5) XAizpuru (nvr nr ldrs: blnd last)	8	**8**	33/1	19	—
44284	**Ellen Gail (IRE)** (RHAlner) **5-11-0** AThornton (lw: n.d)	2½	**9**	25/1	11	—
	Alicia Lea (IRE) (RCurtis) **5-11-0** DMorris (hld up: nvr nr to chal)	12	**10**	25/1	—	—
29117	**Tedross** (JRPoulton) **6-11-2**(3) JMagee (a bhd)	22	**11**	33/1	—	—
45192	**Tarragon (IRE)** (OSherwood) **7-11-5** RDunwoody (plld hrd: trckd ldrs tl wknd qckly bef 4th: t.o whn p.u bef 3 out)		**P**	3/1 2	—	—
				(SP 139.5%)	**12 Rn**	

3m 38.4 (-9.60) CSF £15.40 TOTE £7.70: £1.50 £1.10 £2.60 (£7.50) OWNER Ken Jaffa, John Lewis & David Shalson (SWINDON) BRED Scea Haras du Fougeray
WEIGHT FOR AGE 4yo-5lb

Flic Royal (FR), a lengthy French import, was dropped right out at the start and made a useful-looking winning debut in this country. (6/1: tchd 10/1)
4390 Country Orchid got warm as usual but did little wrong this time, simply meeting one too good. (11/8: op 9/4)
3641 Qualitair Pride looks a much better horse when she is allowed to bowl along and ought to find a small hurdle event on this showing. (8/1)
Blaster Watson is going to have to learn to jump better to take a hand. (20/1)
1818 Nashaat (USA) (10/1: 8/1-12/1)
Dublin River (USA), making his hurdles debut, was knocked back by a mistake three out but is not a guaranteed stayer. (5/1)
4519 Tarragon (IRE) took a fearsome hold on the way to post and in the first mile of the race. However, once he stopped pulling he stopped as if shot and was pulled up in a distressed state. (3/1: 6/4-7/2)

T/Plpt: £70.80 (58.3 Tckts). T/Qdpt: £20.70 (7.9 Tckts) Dk

4645-**UTTOXETER** (L-H) (Good to firm, Good patches)
Monday May 26th
WEATHER: fine

4738 MOBILEFONE GROUP MAIDEN CHASE (5-Y.O+) (Class E)
2-30 (2-30) **2m 7f (16 fncs)** £2,914.75 (£883.00: £431.50: £205.75) GOING minus 0.29 sec per fur (GF)

				SP	RR	SF
4168U	**Glamanglitz (80)** (PTDalton) **7-11-2** APMcCoy (lw: mde all: clr 9th: unchal)	—	**1**	2/1 1	97	32
45073	**Little Gains (69)** (RLee) **8-11-2** JRailton (chsd wnr to 9th: sn outpcd: styd on u.p fr 3 out: no ch w wnr)	9	**2**	9/2	91	26
3188P	**Dara's Course (IRE) (69)** (MissPMWhittle) **8-10-11** SBurrough (bhd: hdwy 6th: mstke 9th: chsd wnr fr 11th tl wknd appr last)	12	**3**	25/1	77	12
46275	**Steel Chimes (IRE)** (BRCambidge) **8-11-2** GaryLyons (bhd fr 6th: t.o)	dist	**4**	33/1	—	—
43833	**Mel (IRE) (71)** (RHBuckler) **7-11-2** SMcNeill (chsd ldrs: pckd 10th: sn lost tch: t.o)	2	**5**	15/2	—	—
44426	**Baron's Heir (85)** (RELivermore) **10-11-2** WMarston (lw: j.slowly 1st: sn drvn along: t.o fr 3rd: p.u bef 8th: lame)		**P**	7/2 2	—	—
	Fill The Boot (IRE) (MrsIMcKie) **7-11-2** GTormey (lost tch & drvn 8th: t.o whn p.u bef 10th)		**P**	4/1 3	—	—
				(SP 112.3%)	**7 Rn**	

5m 39.4 (3.40) CSF £10.24 TOTE £2.90: £1.90 £2.50 (£8.40) OWNER Mrs Julie Martin (BURTON-ON-TRENT) BRED E. and H. Pelham Farms
3988 Glamanglitz finally got off the mark under Rules, having the race sewn up a long way from home. (2/1)
3334 Little Gains found the winner far too quick up the back straight but he kept going until he claimed second place. (9/2)
Dara's Course (IRE) was very onepaced and had to surrender the runner-up spot on the run to the last. (25/1)
4383 Mel (IRE) (15/2: 5/1-8/1)

4739 JOHN STUBBS MEMORIAL (S) H'CAP HURDLE (0-95) (4-Y.O+) (Class G)
3-00 (3-00) **2m 4f 110y (10 hdls)** £1,899.50 (£532.00: £258.50) GOING minus 0.29 sec per fur (GF)

				SP	RR	SF
4648*	**Strike-a-Pose (65)** (BJLlewellyn) **7-10-3** APMcCoy (lw: trckd ldrs: led after 6th: drvn clr 7th: hit last: rdn out)	—	**1**	7/4 1	54	4
45254	**Bodantree (86)** (NMBabbage) **6-11-10** NWilliamson (towards rr: hdwy 6th: rdn to chse wnr appr 3 out: no imp fr next)	3½	**2**	4/1 3	72	22
46339	**Emerald Venture (62)** (FCoton) **10-10-0** CRae (hdwy 5th: hrd rdn appr 2 out: one pce)	3½	**3**	25/1	46	—
43782	**Edward Seymour (USA) (84)** (WJenks) **10-11-8** TJenks (hld up & bhd: hdwy 5th: cl up tl wknd qckly after 3 out: t.o)	dist	**4**	9/4 2	—	—
45529	**Calgary Girl (62)** (RHBuckler) **5-9-7**(7) JMcDermott (lw: a bhd: t.o)	12	**5**	20/1	—	—
44644	**Station Express (IRE) (62)** (GAHam) **9-9-9**(5) DJKavanagh (bhd fr 6th: t.o)	7	**6**	20/1	—	—
45485	**Laura Lye (IRE) (78)** (BdeHaan) **7-11-2** GUpton (prom after 5th: rdn & wknd 3 out: t.o)	2½	**7**	13/2	—	—
45526	**Mecado (73)** (FJYardley) **10-10-11v** WMarston (chsd ldr: led 6th: sn hdd: bhd whn p.u bef 3 out)		**P**	12/1	—	—
129P	**Orchestral Designs (IRE) (65)** (RHarris) **6-10-3**ow3 TKent (led to 6th: wknd qckly: sn t.o: p.u bef 2 out)		**P**	50/1	—	—
				(SP 123.5%)	**9 Rn**	

4m 51.2 (7.20) CSF £8.94 CT £124.71 TOTE £2.30: £1.10 £1.70 £5.10 (£5.90) OWNER Mr B. J. Llewellyn (BARGOED) BRED Mrs R. D. Peacock
LONG HANDICAP Calgary Girl 9-7 Station Express (IRE) 9-6 Emerald Venture 9-3 Orchestral Designs (IRE) 9-2
Bt in 3,500gns

4648* Strike-a-Pose was rousted several lengths clear leaving the back straight. The race was already in safe-keeping when she clouted the final flight. (7/4)
4525 Bodantree was under maximum pressure to go in pursuit of the winner turning for home but he never looked like pegging him back.(4/1)
3131 Emerald Venture has not won for over two and a half years and did not look like ending that sequence here. (25/1)
4378 Edward Seymour (USA), patiently ridden to get on the heels of the leaders turning for home, was beaten soon after. (9/4)
4472 Mecado (12/1: op 7/1)

4740 NEVILLE LUMB & CO. H'CAP CHASE (0-125) (5-Y.O+) (Class D)

3-30 (3-30) **3m 2f (20 fncs)** £3,517.50 (£1,065.00: £520.00: £247.50) GOING minus 0.29 sec per fur (GF)

	Horse	Dist	Pos	SP	RR	SF
4609*	**Doualago (FR) (125)** (MCPipe) **7-12-0b** APMcCoy (disp ld tl led 5th: hdd 8th: drvn appr 4 out: led 3 out: sn clr: eased flat)	—	1	2/1[1]	140+	34
4503*	**Jimmy O'Dea (97)** (JMackie) **10-9-11v**(3) EHusband (mde most to 5th: led 8th: clr 10th: wkng whn blnd & hdd 3 out: one pce)	9	2	5/1[3]	107	1
4424*	**Copper Mine (117)** (OSherwood) **11-11-6** JOsborne (chsd ldrs: outpcd fr 14th)	15	3	2/1[1]	117	11
4452[2]	**Soloman Springs (USA) (97)** (MrsVCWard) **7-10-0** RBellamy (a bhd: t.o fr 8th)	4	4	25/1	95	—
4535[P]	**Nevada Gold (98)** (FJYardley) **11-9-10**(5) DJKavanagh (lost tch & reminders 6th: t.o whn p.u bef 16th)		P	16/1	—	—
4621[3]	**Imperial Vintage (IRE) (121)** (MissVenetiaWilliams) **7-11-10** NWilliamson (prom tl wknd 15th: t.o whn p.u bef 3 out)		P	7/2[2]	—	—
				(SP 115.3%)		**6 Rn**

6m 34.8 (7.80) CSF £11.72 TOTE £2.60: £1.70 £2.20 (£4.70) OWNER Martin Pipe Racing Club (WELLINGTON) BRED Monsieur et Madame Bernard le Douarin

LONG HANDICAP Soloman Springs (USA) 9-1 Jimmy O'Dea 9-12

4609* Doualago (FR) had a ding-dong battle with the runner-up throughout and looked to be getting the worst of it on the run to four out. He was about to gain the upper hand when his rival's blunder at the next put the issue beyond doubt. (2/1)

4503* Jimmy O'Dea ran a fine race in defeat and, although still holding a two-length lead when making a hash of the third last, he was coming to the end of his tether and already looked booked for second place. (5/1)

4424* Copper Mine was never able to get to the front on this occasion and was left behind six from home. (2/1)

4621 Imperial Vintage (IRE) (7/2: 5/2-4/1)

4741 BACK A WINNER BY TRAIN H'CAP HURDLE (0-135) (4-Y.O+) (Class C)

4-00 (4-00) **2m (10 hdls)** £3,436.25 (£1,040.00: £507.50: £241.25) GOING minus 0.29 sec per fur (GF)

	Horse	Dist	Pos	SP	RR	SF
4397[F]	**Northern Starlight (124)** (MCPipe) **6-11-10** APMcCoy (mde all: clr 3 out: comf)	—	1	5/4[1]	103+	36
4443[2]	**Percy Braithwaite (IRE) (107)** (MissPMWhittle) **5-10-7** JOsborne (bhd: hdwy appr 3 out: sn rdn: kpt on: no ch w wnr)	6	2	5/1[3]	80	13
4425*	**Amlah (USA) (118)** (PJHobbs) **5-11-4** GTormey (a.p: drvn along 5th: r.o one pce)	10	3	5/2[2]	81	14
4271[8]	**Serious (113)** (KCBailey) **7-10-13** NWilliamson (hdwy 4th: chsd wnr fr 6th: rdn appr 3 out: wknd next)	5	4	13/2	71	4
4271[7]	**Albemine (USA) (117)** (MrsJCecil) **8-11-3v[1]** TKent (w ldr to 5th: reminders next: sn lost tch: t.o)	dist	5	6/1	—	—
				(SP 117.3%)		**5 Rn**

3m 43.8 (2.80) CSF £7.76 TOTE £2.10: £1.30 £1.90 (£3.50) OWNER Mr Arthur Souch (WELLINGTON) BRED R. J. Glenn and K. Leadbetter

4397 Northern Starlight had everything in trouble by the fifth and was able to land his sixth win of the season without turning a hair. (5/4)

4443 Percy Braithwaite (IRE) stuck on gamely to claim second place but never held out any hope of troubling the winner. (5/1)

4425* Amlah (USA), unable to lie up with the two leaders early on, was flat to the boards a long way out. (5/2)

4271 Serious got to within four lengths of the winner four from home but that was as close as he managed and he was on the retreat by the second last. (13/2)

4130 Albemine (USA) was a big disappointment, and it seemed that having tried to make the running and failed, he decided that was it and dropped tamely away. (6/1)

4742 WELLMAN PLC NOVICES' H'CAP CHASE (0-100) (5-Y.O+) (Class E)

4-30 (4-30) **2m 5f (16 fncs)** £2,927.75 (£887.00: £433.50: £206.75) GOING minus 0.29 sec per fur (GF)

	Horse	Dist	Pos	SP	RR	SF
4566[3]	**Wot No Gin (64)** (AJWilson) **8-10-6** NWilliamson (led 2nd to 10th: mstke 12th: rdn appr 3 out: led appr 2 out: drvn clr last)	—	1	9/2[3]	87	—
4535[F]	**No Fiddling (IRE) (82)** (GMMcCourt) **6-11-7**(3) DFortt (lw: bhd: kpt on fr 4 out: no ch w wnr)	27	2	7/2[2]	84	—
4460[2]	**Miners Rest (76)** (PJHobbs) **9-10-11**(7) MrRWidger (prom: outpcd appr 12th)	3	3	7/2[2]	76	—
4533[P]	**Hangover (68)** (RLee) **11-10-10** APMcCoy (led to 2nd: reminders after 8th: led 10th: rdn & hdd appr 2 out: btn whn blnd last: fin lame)	nk	4	9/2[3]	68	—
4447[2]	**Alaskan Heir (72)** (AStreeter) **6-11-0v** TEley (chsd ldrs: reminders 7th & 9th: sn wknd: t.o)	6	5	5/2[1]	67	—
4635[P]	**Frontier Flight (USA) (80)** (MissLCSiddall) **7-11-5b**(3) EHusband (bhd fr 9th: t.o)	15	6	16/1	64	—
				(SP 115.3%)		**6 Rn**

5m 18.9 (13.90) CSF £19.43 TOTE £5.60: £1.80 £2.90 (£11.10) OWNER The Up and Running Partnership (CHELTENHAM) BRED Malcolm Armitage Penney

4566 Wot No Gin got off the mark at the twelfth attempt and, never out of the first two, had the race won before the last. (9/2)

4157 No Fiddling (IRE) just kept plugging on and took second place on the run-in. (7/2)

4460 Miners Rest was made to look very onepaced. (7/2)

3684* Hangover vied for the lead with the eventual winner but his measure had been taken when he made a real mess of the last and stopped to a walk. He finished lame. (9/2)

4447 Alaskan Heir was struggling before halfway and tailed off with over half a mile to run. (5/2)

4743 TWYFORDS BATHROOMS NOVICES' HURDLE (4-Y.O+) (Class E)

5-00 (5-00) **2m (10 hdls)** £2,389.50 (£672.00: £328.50) GOING minus 0.29 sec per fur (GF)

	Horse	Dist	Pos	SP	RR	SF
4641*	**Nordic Breeze (IRE) (120)** (MCPipe) **5-12-0** APMcCoy (lw: hld up & bhd: gd hdwy appr 3 out: led appr 2 out: v.easily)	—	1	2/5[1]	78++	18
4299[P]	**Bellidium** (AEJessop) **5-10-9** TKent (a.p: wnt 2nd 2 out: no ch w wnr)	4	2	100/1	55	—
4217[4]	**Khalikhoum (IRE)** (SirJohnBarlowBt) **4-10-4**(5) DJKavanagh (lw: chsd ldr: led 5th: rdn & hdd appr 2 out: one pce)	2	3	16/1	58	—
4626*	**Mr Lowry (87)** (LJBarratt) **5-11-7** SWynne (prom: rdn 6th: kpt on one pce fr 3 out)	4	4	9/1[3]	61	1
	Fancytalkintinker (IRE) (JNDalton) **7-11-0** TJenks (hld up: effrt 3 out: rdn & btn next)	12	5	50/1	42	—
4625[13]	**Amazon Heights (54)** (LPGrassick) **5-10-9** MrJGrassick (bhd fr 5th: t.o)	dist	6	100/1	—	—
1870[4]	**Supermodel (98)** (MrsNMacauley) **5-11-2** NWilliamson (led tl reminders & hdd 5th: sn wknd: t.o whn p.u bef last: lame)		P	3/1[2]	—	—
				(SP 116.3%)		**7 Rn**

3m 48.5 (7.50) CSF £44.14 TOTE £1.40: £1.10 £11.00 (£51.20) OWNER Mr Malcolm Jones (WELLINGTON) BRED P. F. N. Fanning

WEIGHT FOR AGE 4yo-5lb
4641* Nordic Breeze (IRE) outclassed his rivals and won in a canter to give his pilot his fifth winner of the day. (2/5)
1665 Bellidium, even though greatly flattered by her proximity to the winner, ran by far her best race to date. (100/1)
4217 Khalikhoum (IRE) showed enough to suggest he can win a race in the future. (16/1)
4626* Mr Lowry, chased along from some way out, was left trailing in the closing stages. (9/1)

T/Plpt: £20.70 (224.09 Tckts). T/Qdpt: £5.00 (40.53 Tckts) J

4477-**WETHERBY** (L-H) (Good to firm)
Monday May 26th
WEATHER: fine

4744 SANDBECK MOTORS CLAIMING HURDLE (4-Y.O+) (Class F)
2-15 (2-15) **2m 4f 110y (10 hdls)** £2,425.00 (£675.00: £325.00) GOING minus 0.26 sec per fur (GF)

	Horse	Dist	Pos	SP	RR	SF
4572*	**Kirstenbosch (87)** (LLungo) **10-10-5**$^{(7)}$ WDowling (hld up: stdy hdwy 4 out: chsd ldr 3 out: chal after next: led appr last: qcknd clr flat)	—	1	5/1^{3}	75	19
4399^{2}	**Sousse (90)** (MrsMReveley) **4-10-8** GLee (lw: nt j.w: led: jnd & rdn after 2 out: hdd appr last: one pce flat)	6	2	9/4^{1}	72	10
4417^{4}	**Kadari (96)** (WClay) **8-10-7v** RJohnson (chsd ldrs: drvn along after 4 out: one pce fr 3 out)	6	3	5/2^{2}	61	5
4261^{3}	**Master of Troy (95)** (CParker) **9-11-0** DParker (in tch: rdn appr 3 out: btn appr 2 out)	2½	4	11/2	66	10
4451*	**Fair and Fancy (FR) (99)** (MissMKMilligan) **6-11-0** MrSSwiers (chsd ldrs tl rdn & wknd appr 2 out)	¾	5	13/2	65	9
4562^{6}	**Fret (USA) (55)** (JSWainwright) **7-10-10** MrKGreen (in tch tl mstke & lost pl 6th: sn bhd: t.o)	20	6	25/1	46	—
4389^{P}	**Fiery Sun (67)** (REBarr) **12-10-10** NSmith (in tch tl wknd after 4 out: sn lost tch: t.o)	2½	7	20/1	44	—
4399^{3}	**Recruitment** (JRTurner) **4-10-11** TReed (hld up in rr & plld hrd: smooth hdwy 4 out: trckd ldrs 3 out: sn rdn & wknd: btn whn fell last)		F	33/1	—	—
2918^{5}	**Cool Game** (DWBarker) **7-10-11**$^{(3)}$ PMidgley (sn in tch: hit 5th: sn lost tch: no ch whn hmpd & fell last)		F	33/1	—	—
462^{3}	**Manoy** (JHetherton) **4-10-5** LWyer (mid div: hit 3rd & lost pl: hit 6th: hdwy after 4 out: p.u lame bef 3 out)		P	8/1	—	—
				(SP 130.3%)	**10 Rn**	

4m 53.0 (6.00) CSF £17.00 TOTE £6.60: £1.70 £1.20 £1.60 (£6.40) OWNER Mrs Barbara Lungo (CARRUTHERSTOWN) BRED Brownstown Stud and Partners
WEIGHT FOR AGE 4yo-6lb
4572* Kirstenbosch showed a fine turn of foot to settle this beyond any doubt after the last. (5/1)
4399 Sousse failed to jump fluently and had no answer to the winner when the chips were down. (9/4)
4417 Kadari was off the bridle some way out and was never doing enough. (5/2)
4261 Master of Troy is proving hard to win with this season. (11/2)
4451* Fair and Fancy (FR) found this much tougher than last time and was found wanting in the home straight. (13/2)

4745 MOORSIDE LANDROVER CENTRE NOVICES' CHASE (5-Y.O+) (Class D)
2-45 (2-46) **3m 1f (18 fncs)** £3,415.00 (£1,030.00: £500.00: £235.00) GOING minus 0.26 sec per fur (GF)

	Horse	Dist	Pos	SP	RR	SF
4502*	**Lepton (IRE) (72)** (JWCurtis) **6-11-8b** RJohnson (hld up: hit 7th: hdwy gng wl fr 10th: led on bit appr 2 out: rdn out flat)	—	1	7/1	99	—
4393^{4}	**Movie Man** (JRTurner) **5-10-8** TReed (hdwy & in tch fr ½-wy: prom & effrt 4 out: kpt on u.p fr 2 out: nt pce of wnr)	4	2	16/1	90	—
4533^{5}	**Desert Brave (IRE) (74)** (MrsSJSmith) **7-10-13**$^{(3)}$ GFRyan (lw: a in tch: chsd ldrs & rdn 4 out: hit next: one pce)	2	3	8/1	89	—
4706^{F}	**Kiltulla (IRE) (72)** (MrsSJSmith) **7-11-2** LWyer (j.w: led 5th tl appr 2 out: no ex)	1½	4	3/1^{3}	88	—
3989^{11}	**Knock Star (IRE)** (RChampion) **6-11-2** LO'Hara (chsd ldrs: effrt & blnd 4 out: sn btn)	dist	5	33/1	—	—
4208^{4}	**Now Young Man (IRE)** (MrsASwinbank) **8-11-8** JSupple (nt fluent: rr div: sme hdwy ½-wy: rdn & lost pl 13th: t.o)	¾	6	5/2^{2}	—	—
4391^{4}	**Evening Rush (70)** (JWade) **11-11-6** DParker (led to 5th: lost pl fr 10th: t.o fr 13th)	dist	7	33/1	—	—
4286*	**Malta Man (IRE)** (PCheesbrough) **7-11-3**$^{(5)}$ RMcGrath (in tch: hit 2nd & 3rd: sn chsng ldrs: wknd 14th: p.u after 4 out)		P	2/1^{1}	—	—
4611^{4}	**Quixall Crossett (56)** (EMCaine) **12-10-9**$^{(7)}$ MrTJBarry (prom to 9th: lost pl & bhd whn blnd & uns rdr 11th)		U	50/1	—	—
				(SP 124.2%)	**9 Rn**	

6m 16.4 CSF £93.46 TOTE £11.30: £2.80 £2.50 £2.10 (£80.40) OWNER Mr J. W. P. Curtis (DRIFFIELD) BRED J. Boylson
WEIGHT FOR AGE 5yo-8lb
OFFICIAL EXPLANATION Malta Man was not suited by the good to firm going.
4502* Lepton (IRE) proved his Sedgefield win was no fluke and is clearly in great heart at present. He can complete a hat-trick. (7/1)
4393 Movie Man ran a respectable race on his chasing debut but was no match for the winner. (16/1)
3941 Desert Brave (IRE) did not help his chances by clouting the third last. (8/1)
4706 Kiltulla (IRE), making his second appearance in three days, turned in an exhibition of jumping until tapped for toe from the second last. (3/1)
4286* Malta Man (IRE) failed to jump fluently early on and never looked all that happy. (2/1)

4746 'LA FEMME' LADIES' H'CAP HURDLE (0-120) (4-Y.O+) (Class D)
3-15 (3-16) **2m (8 hdls)** £2,600.00 (£725.00: £350.00) GOING minus 0.26 sec per fur (GF)

	Horse	Dist	Pos	SP	RR	SF
4578*	**Teejay'n'aitch (IRE) (96)** (JSGoldie) **5-10-10** MissADeniel (cl up: led 5th: wnt clr appr 3 out: r.o strly)	—	1	7/4^{1}	67+	37
4482^{2}	**Kierchem (IRE) (86)** (CGrant) **6-10-0** MrsSGrant (chsd ldrs: hdwy to chse wnr appr 3 out: hit 2 out: kpt on u.p fr last)	2	2	3/1^{2}	55	25
3076^{5}	**Mr Moriarty (IRE) (96)** (SRBowring) **6-10-10** MrsMMorris (led to 5th: prom tl wknd appr 3 out)	5	3	11/2^{3}	60	30
1305^{2}	**Contrafire (IRE) (108)** (MrsASwinbank) **5-11-8** MrsFNeedham (in tch: hdwy after 4 out: wknd bef 2 out: btn whn blnd last)	8	4	3/1^{2}	64	34
215^{7}	**Nordic Sun (IRE) (114)** (MrsJBrown) **9-11-7**$^{(7)}$ MissJWormall (prom to 4th: sn lost pl: n.d after)	6	5	8/1	64	34
4409^{6}	**Stags Fell (87)** (TAKCuthbert) **12-10-1**^{ow1} CarolCuthbert (a bhd & outpcd fr ½-wy: t.o)	dist	6	33/1	—	—
				(SP 115.8%)	**6 Rn**	

3m 42.3 (0.30) CSF £7.31 TOTE £2.50: £1.60 £1.50 (£3.40) OWNER Mr Andrew Paterson (GLASGOW) BRED David Hyland

LONG HANDICAP Kierchem (IRE) 9-8 Stags Fell 8-2
4578* Teejay'n'aitch (IRE) continues in tremendous form, despite having climbed 18lb in the handicap for his previous four wins. He is not done with yet. (7/4)
4482 Kierchem (IRE) lacked the foot to trouble the winner but ran well all the same from 6lb out of the handicap. (3/1)
2631* Mr Moriarty (IRE), reappearing after an absence of more than three months, should have benefited from this race. (11/2)
1305 Contrafire (IRE) looked dangerous turning into the home straight but, disappointingly, failed to pull out any extra when the chips were down. (3/1)

4747 GODFREY LONG H'CAP CHASE (0-135) (5-Y.O+) (Class C)

3-45 (3-46) **3m 1f (18 fncs)** £5,410.00 (£1,330.00) GOING minus 0.26 sec per fur (GF)

				SP	RR	SF
4541[P]	**Glemot (IRE) (130)** (KCBailey) **9-11-2**(7) MrRWakley (j.w: mde all: rdn & r.o strly fr 2 out)	—	1	15/8 [2]	139	—
4529[2]	**Sounds Strong (IRE) (125)** (DNicholson) **8-11-4** RJohnson (trckd wnr: hit 3 out: sn rdn: kpt on flat)	1¾	2	4/9 [1]	133	—
				(SP 104.0%)		**2 Rn**

6m 15.8 TOTE £2.20 OWNER Mr Dennis Yardy (UPPER LAMBOURN) BRED A. Murphy
1904 Glemot (IRE), allowed to dictate, saw his race out well to notch his first victory over this distance. (15/8)
4529 Sounds Strong (IRE) stalked the winner throughout but spoiled his chance of winning by blundering at the third-last fence. (4/9)

4748 GUY CUNARD HUNTERS' CHASE (5-Y.O+) (Class H)

4-15 (4-17) **2m 4f 110y (15 fncs)** £1,308.00 (£363.00: £174.00) GOING minus 0.26 sec per fur (GF)

				SP	RR	SF
4560[8]	**My Nominee** (DENicholls) **9-12-0b**(7) MrRBurton (lw: cl up: led after 7th: rdn & hit 3 out: kpt on u.p flat)	—	1	4/1 [2]	106	—
4543[9]	**Shuil Saor** (MissPFitton) **10-11-2**(7) MrCMulhall (hld up: stdy hdwy appr 5 out: prom next: styd on same pce fr 2 out)	1¼	2	33/1	93	—
4631[5]	**Simply Perfect** (JSSwindells) **11-11-7**(7) MissKSwindells (a chsng ldrs: effrt 3 out: nt qckn fr 2 out: hit last)	2	3	20/1	97	—
4543*	**Not My Line (IRE)** (AndyMorgan) **8-12-2**(5) MrWWales (led to 3rd: chsd ldrs: rdn 3 out: blnd last: kpt on)	1	4	7/1	103	—
	Caman (JAVDuell) **10-11-2**(7) MrsSGrant (in tch: outpcd 5 out: hdwy 3 out: styd on: nt rch ldrs)	1	5	14/1	90	—
	Indie Rock (RTate) **7-11-2**(7) MrsFNeedham (mid div: rdn 10th: outpcd fr 4 out)	11	6	5/1 [3]	81	—
4280*	**Great Gusto** (MissLBlackford) **11-11-11**(7) MissLBlackford (lw: chsd ldrs: prom 7th: hit 10th: sn rdn: wknd appr 3 out)	1¼	7	2/1 [1]	89	—
4640[P]	**Alpha One** (DFBassett) **12-11-7**(7) MissKDiMarte (rr div: effrt bef 10th: no imp)	7	8	33/1	80	—
	Goodheavens Mrtony (MrsALockwood) **10-11-2**(7) MissADeniel (mid div: outpcd & reminders after 6th: n.d after)	13	9	33/1	65	—
4545[P]	**Syrus P Turntable** (MissPFitton) **11-11-2**(7) MrJSaville (a bhd: t.o)	10	10	33/1	57	—
4228[3]	**Eastern Pleasure** (IanEmmerson) **10-11-2**(7) MrTJBarry (prom: led briefly 7th: effrt 4 out: 6th & btn whn fell 2 out)		F	20/1	—	—
	Gaelic Warrior (MrsEClark) **10-11-9** MrSSwiers (mid div: hdwy & in tch appr 5 out: p.u after 4 out)		P	7/1	—	—
4543[10]	**No Word** (IBaker) **10-11-7**(7) MrIBaker (led 3rd to 7th: prom tl lost pl bef 10th: p.u lame bef 2 out)		P	33/1	—	—
4634[2]	**Sandybraes** (HHutsby) **12-11-7**(7) MrFHutsby (sn bhd: t.o whn p.u bef 7th)		P	13/2	—	—
	Japodene (MrsSarahDent) **9-10-11**(7) MrMHaigh (a in rr: t.o whn p.u bef 4 out)		P	33/1	—	—
				(SP 142.2%)		**15 Rn**

5m 40.3 (33.30) CSF £130.56 TOTE £5.80: £2.00 £33.70 £5.70 (£346.50) OWNER Mr D. E. Nicholls (WREXHAM) BRED Dr O. Zawawi
OFFICIAL EXPLANATION **My Nominee, was unable to dominate and failed to stay on his last outing.**
4326 My Nominee, beaten sixty-nine lengths at Hereford last time, bounced back to winning form here. It was explained to the Stewards afterwards that he got kicked at the start at Hereford and then was unable to dominate in the race and failed to stay the extended three miles. (4/1: op 5/2)
Shuil Saor, who had shown little in Point-to-Points this season, ran an absolute blinder here. (33/1)
Simply Perfect, over his best distance and on his favourite ground, ran right up to scratch. (20/1)
4543* Not My Line (IRE), in the van throughout, lacked the finishing pace to take advantage. (7/1: 5/1-8/1)
Caman did some sterling work in the last half-mile but probably found this trip a bit sharp. (14/1)
4280* Great Gusto blundered badly at the tenth fence when vying for the lead and was soon in trouble. (2/1: op 4/1)

4749 HOLIDAY NOVICES' HURDLE (4-Y.O+) (Class D)

4-45 (4-45) **2m (8 hdls)** £2,757.50 (£770.00: £372.50) GOING minus 0.26 sec per fur (GF)

				SP	RR	SF
1575[6]	**Lagan (100)** (KAMorgan) **4-11-2** RJohnson (mde all: j.w: qcknd clr 3 out: unchal)	—	1	9/2 [3]	78	33
4539[3]	**Going Primitive** (JHetherton) **6-11-0** DParker (lw: chsd wnr: outpcd & n.m.r on bnd appr 3 out: kpt on one pce: no ch w wnr)	12	2	7/1	59	19
	Sailormaite (SRBowring) **6-11-0** JSupple (hld up & plld hrd: jnd ldr 4th: effrt appr 2 out: no ex)	4	3	14/1	55	15
1666[F]	**In Good Faith (98)** (JJQuinn) **5-11-0** LWyer (hld up in tch: stdy hdwy appr 3 out: rdn appr 2 out: sn btn)	nk	4	15/8 [1]	55	15
4578[2]	**Hopeful Lord (IRE) (80)** (PCheesbrough) **5-10-9**(5) RMcGrath (chsd ldrs: hit 4 out: btn after 3 out)	1¼	5	3/1 [2]	53	13
4626[3]	**Western General (82)** (MissMKMilligan) **6-11-0** MrSSwiers (hld up & bhd: hdwy after 4 out: btn after 3 out)	1¼	6	9/2 [3]	52	12
4580[9]	**Hansel's Streak** (TAKCuthbert) **5-11-0** LO'Hara (in tch: blnd 5th: lost tch next: t.o)	dist	7	40/1	—	—
4301[19]	**Honeysuckle Rose** (LRLloyd-James) **4-10-4** MrKGreen (chsd ldrs: hit 4th: sn t.o: p.u after 4 out)		P	33/1	—	—
				(SP 120.7%)		**8 Rn**

3m 44.4 (2.40) CSF £34.18 TOTE £4.70: £1.60 £1.60 £2.20 (£15.30) OWNER Wild Racing (MELTON MOWBRAY) BRED Saeed Manana
WEIGHT FOR AGE 4yo-5lb
1575 Lagan, back after a lengthy break, made this look easy and won unchallenged. He can score again. (9/2)
4539 Going Primitive shaped well on his hurdling debut but was no match for the winner. (7/1)
Sailormaite, a useful handicap sprinter on his day who has shown a fair bit of temperament of late on the Flat, pulled hard here on his hurdling debut but he ran surprisingly well until lack of stamina began to take its toll in the final half-mile. (14/1)
794 In Good Faith, fit from the Flat, proved disappointing here. The ground may have been a shade too fast for him. (15/8)

T/Plpt: £3,533.70 (1.35 Tckts). T/Qdpt: £177.30 (1.04 Tckts) O'R

4708-HEXHAM (L-H) (Good to firm, Firm patches)
Tuesday May 27th
WEATHER: fine and sunny

4750 BUCHANAN HIGH LEVEL BROWN ALE 'N.H.' NOVICES' HURDLE (5-Y.O+) (Class E)
6-35 (6-35) **2m 4f 110y (10 hdls)** £2,444.80 (£677.80: £324.40) GOING minus 0.48 sec per fur (GF)

	Horse / Details		SP	RR	SF
4513*	**Pappa Charlie (USA) (86)** (CParker) **6-11-0** BStorey (trckd ldrs: shkn up to ld appr last: styd on wl)..........—	1	5/4 1	60	14
	Emperor's Magic (IRE) (NBMason) **6-11-0** RichardGuest (trckd ldrs: chal 3 out: led next: hdd & nt qckn appr last)..........7	2	6/1 3	55	9
4450*	**Jervaulx (IRE) (97)** (GRichards) **6-11-12** PCarberry (lw: led to 2 out: wknd qckly: blnd last)..........dist	3	6/4 2	—	—
4514⁵	**Weapons Free** (TPTate) **6-11-0** RGarritty (hld up: hdwy 7th: outpcd: sn wknd)..........13	4	25/1	—	—
4514⁴	**Buckley House** (JIACharlton) **5-11-0** TReed (hld up & plld hrd: effrt & ran wd bnd appr 7th: wknd qckly 2 out: t.o whn p.u bef last)..........	P	8/1	—	—
	With Respect (FTWalton) **6-11-0** KJohnson (chsd ldrs: hit 4th: outpcd 6th: sn bhd: t.o 3 out: p.u bef last)..........	P	100/1	—	—

(SP 114.7%) **6 Rn**

4m 51.5 (3.50) CSF £8.95 TOTE £2.00: £1.10 £6.40 (£11.60) OWNER Mr Raymond Anderson Green (LOCKERBIE) BRED W. S. Farish and W. S. Kilroy

4513* Pappa Charlie (USA), always travelling best, did it nicely and looks sure to make a chaser next term. (5/4)
Emperor's Magic (IRE), making a belated reappearance, looked very fit. Showing a pronounced knee action going down, he went on travelling almost as well as the winner but, in the end, proved no match. (6/1)
4450* Jervaulx (IRE) made the running, but found absolutely nothing under pressure and was legless when he fell through the last. (6/4)

4751 KELLYS LAGER MAIDEN CHASE (5-Y.O+) (Class F)
7-05 (7-07) **2m 4f 110y (15 fncs)** £2,733.05 (£817.40: £391.70: £178.85) GOING minus 0.48 sec per fur (GF)

	Horse / Details		SP	RR	SF
3806F	**Fort Zeddaan (IRE)** (MrsSJSmith) **7-11-3** RichardGuest (led to 7th: blnd 9th: led 2 out: clr last: jst hld on)...—	1	11/2 2	75	—
4245P	**Two For One (IRE) (67)** (MissLucindaRussell) **8-11-3** AThornton (chsd ldrs: rdn & outpcd 9th: styd on fr 3 out: r.o u.p flat: jst failed)..........hd	2	9/1	75	—
4408³	**Banner Year (IRE) (60)** (TJCarr) **6-11-3** PNiven (chsd ldrs: ev ch tl wknd between last 2)..........8	3	20/1	69	—
4389⁹	**Rostino (IRE)** (JWade) **8-11-3** PCarberry (sn bhd: mstke 3rd: sme hdwy 11th: nvr nr ldrs)..........11	4	25/1	60	—
4502⁷	**Meesonette** (BEllison) **5-10-5** DParker (sn bhd: sme hdwy 3 out: n.d)..........1¾	5	33/1	54	—
4709³	**Sovereigns Match (79)** (BMactaggart) **9-11-3** BStorey (lw: trckd ldrs: led 11th tl hdd & wknd qckly 2 out)........6	6	11/4 1	54	—
4502⁶	**Aristodemus (65)** (MrsLMarshall) **8-11-3b** KJohnson (chsd ldrs: led 7th to 11th: wknd 3 out)..........3½	7	25/1	51	—
4515⁵	**Tactix (63)** (MissMKMilligan) **7-10-12** JCallaghan (sn bhd: hit 4th)..........24	8	13/2 3	28	—
4161⁵	**Singh Song** (KAMorgan) **7-10-12** DBentley (chsd ldrs: wkng whn blnd 8th: t.o 3 out)..........dist	9	12/1	—	—
2800¹⁰	**The Next Waltz (IRE)** (LLungo) **6-11-3** RSupple (lw: hdwy 9th: 4th & prom whn blnd bdly 11th: nt rcvr: p.u bef 3 out)..........	P	11/4 1	—	—
	Billy Buoyant (FTWalton) **8-11-3** TReed (bkwd: sn bhd: t.o whn p.u bef 4 out)..........	P	20/1	—	—
4569P	**The Energiser (67)** (DALamb) **11-11-3b¹** JBurke (sn bhd: t.o whn p.u after 9th)..........	P	33/1	—	—
4502P	**Childsway** (SJRobinson) **9-11-3** MrCMulhall (sn bhd: t.o whn p.u bef last)..........	P	33/1	—	—
4517⁵	**Supermarine (61)** (BMactaggart) **11-11-3** GLee (prom whn blnd & uns rdr 3rd)..........	U	25/1	—	—
3971⁶	**Charlvic** (WSCunningham) **7-10-10(7)** LMcGrath (mid div whn blnd & uns rdr 7th)..........	U	33/1	—	—

(SP 132.6%) **15 Rn**

5m 8.2 (11.20) CSF £46.66 TOTE £6.30: £2.10 £3.30 £5.80 (£52.30) Trio £111.90 OWNER Mrs S. Smith (BINGLEY) BRED Mrs. Wendy Reynolds

WEIGHT FOR AGE 5yo-7lb

3608 Fort Zeddaan (IRE), who has enjoyed no luck previously over fences, did well to survive a blunder at the ninth. Eight lengths clear jumping the last, the post came just in time. His jockey is riding out of his skin at present. (11/2: 7/2-6/1)
3824 Two For One (IRE), who at one time was tubed, rallied on the run-in but needed three more strides. (9/1)
4408 Banner Year (IRE) was legless between the last two. (20/1)
Rostino (IRE), making his chasing debut, got a long way behind. (25/1)
1672 The Next Waltz (IRE), making his chasing debut, made an odd minor mistake but was bang on terms until he blundered badly at the eleventh, and was eventually pulled up. (11/4)

4752 KEOGHANS NOVICES' HURDLE (4-Y.O+) (Class E)
7-35 (7-35) **2m (8 hdls)** £2,363.60 (£654.60: £312.80) GOING minus 0.48 sec per fur (GF)

	Horse / Details		SP	RR	SF
4711*	**Royal York (90)** (GRichards) **5-11-11** 8x PCarberry (mde most: eased flat: cleverly)..........—	1	5/6 1	75+	28
4479⁸	**China King (IRE)** (JGFitzGerald) **6-11-0** BStorey (nt j.w: hld up: stdy hdwy 5th: shkn up appr last: kpt on).....½	2	5/1 3	64	17
4409*	**Tsanga (75)** (GMMoore) **5-11-8** NBentley (jnd wnr 3rd: rdn & wl outpcd 2 out: sn btn)..........12	3	10/1	60	13
4335²	**Caught At Last (IRE) (89)** (MrsMReveley) **6-11-0** PNiven (chsd ldrs: drvn along 5th: wl outpcd fr 2 out).......1¼	4	2/1 2	50	3

(SP 113.6%) **4 Rn**

3m 49.9 (1.90) CSF £5.17 TOTE £1.50: (£2.40) OWNER Mr Robert Ogden (PENRITH) BRED Robert Ogden

4711* Royal York scored in very cheeky fashion. (5/6)
4479 China King (IRE), who did not wear a tongue-strap this time, tended to land flat-footed. Shaken up going to the last, he kept on but the margin flatters him considerably. (5/1)
4409* Tsanga, with a lot more to do, was left behind from two out. (10/1)
4335 Caught At Last (IRE), pushed along at halfway, could not live with the first two over the final two flights. (2/1)

4753 LCL PILS H'CAP CHASE (0-105) (5-Y.O+) (Class F)
8-05 (8-05) **2m 4f 110y (15 fncs)** £2,755.50 (£763.00: £364.50) GOING minus 0.48 sec per fur (GF)

	Horse / Details		SP	RR	SF
4515³	**Exemplar (IRE) (81)** (MrsSJSmith) **9-10-11** RichardGuest (chsd ldrs: led last: hrd rdn: all out)..........—	1	3/1 1	96	2
4392³	**Rebel King (77)** (MABarnes) **7-10-7** BStorey (wnt prom 9th: led 11th to last: styd on u.p)..........½	2	6/1	92	—
4058²	**The Toaster (96)** (MissMKMilligan) **10-11-7(5)** RMcGrath (jnd ldrs 5th: ev ch tl wknd appr last)..........8	3	7/2 2	104	10
4336⁸	**Last Refuge (IRE) (85)** (TJCarr) **8-11-1** TReed (lost pl 5th: sn bhd & drvn along: t.o 9th: hdwy 3 out: nvr nr to chal)..........2½	4	16/1	91	—

				SP	RR	SF
696[3]	**Bitacrack (77)** (JJBirkett) **10-10-7** LO'Hara (chsd ldrs: led 10th: hdd next: wkng whn hit 2 out)	6	**5**	14/1	79	—
4408[2]	**Shawwell (76)** (JIACharlton) **10-10-6** PCarberry (led: blnd 8th: hdd 10th: wknd 3 out)	15	**6**	7/2 [2]	66	—
4410[5]	**Mils Mij (95)** (TAKCuthbert) **12-11-11** PNiven (bhd whn mstke 7th: t.o 9th)	10	**7**	5/1 [3]	77	—
4297[6]	**Reve de Valse (USA) (77)** (RJohnson) **10-10-7** KJohnson (in tch: outpcd 6th: sn bhd)	6	**8**	14/1	55	—
				(SP 119.6%)	**8 Rn**	

5m 3.8 (6.80) CSF £20.62 CT £60.90 TOTE £3.80: £2.20 £2.00 £3.10 (£19.00) OWNER Mrs S. Smith (BINGLEY) BRED Mrs R. Stewart

STEWARDS' ENQUIRY Guest susp. 5-7/6/97 (excessive & incorrect use of whip).

4515 Exemplar (IRE), who stays really well, took this but the credit must go to his jockey. Really galvanised at the last, he landed fractionally in front and, under severe pressure, did just enough. (3/1)

4392 Rebel King went into the last almost two lengths up, but his rider did not ride him into it and he lost the advantage. Hard as he tried on the run-in, he could not get his head back in front. (6/1: op 4/1)

4058 The Toaster had every chance until his stamina gave out on this stiff track going to the last. (7/2)

3645 Last Refuge (IRE), who wore a tongue-strap, ran a moody race, dropping himself out after five fences, but consented to stay on again in the closing stages. (16/1)

4754 FEDERATION BREWERY H'CAP HURDLE (0-105) (4-Y.O+) (Class F)

8-35 (8-35) **3m (12 hdls)** £2,385.00 (£660.00: £315.00) GOING minus 0.48 sec per fur (GF)

				SP	RR	SF
4501[5]	**Nite Sprite (66)** (REBarr) **7-9-9**(5) STaylor (trckd ldrs: outpcd 3 out: hdwy between last 2: led flat: drvn out)	—	**1**	12/1	45	—
4470*	**Ballindoo (90)** (RJArmson) **8-11-10** MrRArmson (hld up: hdwy 8th: led next tl flat: nt qckn)	2	**2**	11/8 [2]	68	6
4712[5]	**Dont Forget Curtis (IRE) (69)** (MrsKMLamb) **5-9-10**(7) MissSLamb (trckd ldrs: chal 3 out: one pce flat)	5	**3**	6/1 [3]	43	—
4501[2]	**Barton Heights (86)** (MrsMReveley) **5-11-6** PNiven (reminders 4th: outpcd 7th: lost pl 9th: sme hdwy 2 out: nt rch ldrs: virtually p.u nr fin)	20	**4**	6/5 [1]	47	—
4409[U]	**Shut Up (68)** (MrsEMoscrop) **8-9-13b**(3)ow2 EHusband (led to 9th: sn wknd: t.o 2 out)	dist	**5**	40/1	—	—
				(SP 112.0%)	**5 Rn**	

5m 50.6 (10.60) CSF £27.71 TOTE £17.70: £2.80 £1.10 (£15.40) OWNER Mr R. E. Barr (MIDDLESBROUGH) BRED R. E. Barr

LONG HANDICAP Nite Sprite 9-8 Shut Up 8-13

STEWARDS' ENQUIRY Guest susp.5-6-7/6/97 (incorrect use of whip)

4394 Nite Sprite, who was 6lb out of the handicap, put two poor efforts behind her. This was a selling handicap in all but name. (12/1)

4470* Ballindoo, from a 7lb higher mark, came off just second best on the run-in. (11/8)

4638 Dont Forget Curtis (IRE), who has been slipping down the weights, returned to his best. (6/1)

4501 Barton Heights, who showed a very poor action going down, was given some sharp reminders as early as the fourth flight. Losing his place completely a mile from home, he stuck on under strong pressure two out but, when it was clear that fourth was the most he could hope for, his rider called it a day on the run-in. (6/5: op 4/5)

4755 JACK FAWCUS MEMORIAL CHALLENGE CUP NOVICES' AMATEUR H'CAP HURDLE (0-95) (4-Y.O+) (Class G)

9-05 (9-05) **2m (8 hdls)** £2,042.00 (£567.00: £272.00) GOING minus 0.48 sec per fur (GF)

				SP	RR	SF
1652[8]	**Cottage Prince (IRE) (87)** (JJQuinn) **4-11-3**(7) MrAWintle (hld up: hdwy 4th: nt clr run appr last: qcknd to ld flat: r.o)	—	**1**	Evens [1]	68	2
4505[4]	**Beau Matelot (77)** (MissMKMilligan) **5-11-0**(5) MissPRobson (hld up: wnt prom 5th: ev ch last: styd on towards fin)	1	**2**	7/2 [2]	57	—
4337[6]	**Ragamuffin Romeo (80)** (SIPittendrigh) **8-11-3**(5) MrRHale (chsd ldr: led after 3 out tl flat: r.o same pce)	s.h	**3**	7/1	60	—
4711[7]	**Whitegatesprincess (IRE) (66)** (BEllison) **6-10-3**(5) MrMHNaughton (led tl after 3 out: one pce appr last)	7	**4**	11/2 [3]	39	—
4708[4]	**Rubislaw (58)** (MrsKMLamb) **5-9-7**(7) MissSLamb (a chsng ldrs: one pce between last 2)	½	**5**	25/1	30	—
4562[7]	**Gi Moss (75)** (PRHarriss) **10-10-10b**(7)ow17 MrBHarriss (sn bhd: sme hdwy 2 out: n.d)	11	**6**	10/1	36	—
3976[7]	**Swank Gilbert (58)** (TAKCuthbert) **11-9-7**(7) MissHCuthbert (prom: outpcd after 3 out: n.d)	7	**7**	33/1	12	—
288[5]	**Noted Strain (IRE) (62)** (DFBassett) **9-9-11**(7) MissKDiMarte (unruly: w ldrs: mstke 2nd: wknd after 3 out)	3½	**8**	20/1	13	—
	Doc Spot (67) (SJRobinson) **7-10-2**(7) MrsDWilkinson (hld up & plld hrd: bhd fr 5th: sn t.o)	12	**9**	33/1	6	—
				(SP 123.7%)	**9 Rn**	

3m 55.9 (7.90) CSF £5.00 CT £15.43 TOTE £1.70: £1.10 £1.60 £2.00 (£3.30) Trio £5.00 OWNER Mrs Kay Thomas (MALTON) BRED Owen Bourke

LONG HANDICAP Swank Gilbert 9-13 Rubislaw 9-13 Gi Moss 9-13

WEIGHT FOR AGE 4yo-5lb

1011* Cottage Prince (IRE), who won on the Flat a fortnight earlier, was given a confident ride. Short of room between the last two, he quickened to lead on the run-in, but had to be driven right out. (Evens)

4249 Beau Matelot stuck on strongly under pressure and was hauling in the winner at the line. Unfortunately he does not always run two races alike. (7/2)

1451 Ragamuffin Romeo made the best of his way home and jumped the last two lengths up, but the winner cut him down for speed on the run-in. (7/1)

4394* Whitegatesprincess (IRE), without the visor and dropped back in distance, tried to make her stamina tell, but she was tapped for toe going to the last. (11/2)

1825 Rubislaw seemed to run his best race for some time. (25/1)

T/Plpt: £115.10 (110.41 Tckts). T/Qdpt: £11.80 (73.2 Tckts) WG

4714-CARTMEL (L-H) (Good to firm, Firm patches)

Wednesday May 28th

WEATHER: Fine and sunny

4756 JENNINGS BITTER NOVICES' (S) HURDLE (4-Y.O+ F & M) (Class G)

2-00 (2-02) **2m 1f 110y (8 hdls)** £2,276.00 (£636.00: £308.00) GOING minus 0.36 sec per fur (GF)

				SP	RR	SF
	Palace River (IRE) (DMoffatt) **9-10-10** DJMoffatt (lw: trckd ldrs: effrt appr last: hung bdly lft: led last 75y: styd on wl)	—	**1**	3/1 [2]	55	—
4532[5]	**Summer Princess** (GFierro) **4-10-5** GaryLyons (trckd ldrs: chal 5th: led after last: hdd & nt qckn flat)	2	**2**	11/1	53	—

Form	Horse	Dist	Pos	SP	RR	SF
4389^{4}	**Queen's Counsel (IRE) (70)** (MissMKMilligan) **4-10-5** BStorey (lw: trckd ldrs: led 3 out tl after last: rallied & nt qckn last 100y)	1½	**3**	6/4^{1}	52	—
4453^{P}	**A Badge Too Far (IRE) (59)** (MrsLWilliamson) **7-10-10b** LO'Hara (chsd ldrs: one pce fr 2 out)	6	**4**	40/1	46	—
4528^{7}	**Derring Floss** (JAPickering) **7-10-3**$^{(7)}$ MissJWormall (chsd ldrs: outpcd fr 2 out)	1¾	**5**	8/1	45	—
4620^{11}	**Gabrielle Gerard** (MDHammond) **5-10-3**$^{(7)}$ NHorrocks (v.unruly: hld up & bhd: sme hdwy 5th: nvr nr ldrs)	4	**6**	14/1	41	—
4711^{9}	**No Takers (65)** (SEKettlewell) **10-10-10** PNiven (led to 3 out: sn wknd)	8	**7**	25/1	34	—
	Tolepa (IRE) (JJO'Neill) **4-10-0**$^{(5)}$ RMcGrath (lw: hld up & plld hrd: sme hdwy 5th: wknd next)	3	**8**	14/1	31	—
4711^{8}	**Meadowleck (51)** (WGYoung) **8-10-5**$^{(5)}$ STaylor (outpcd 5th: sn bhd)	1¼	**9**	40/1	30	—
4620^{5}	**Analogical** (DMcCain) **4-10-5** TJenks (hld up: fell 3rd)		**F**	13/2^{3}	—	—

(SP 119.8%) **10 Rn**

4m 9.8 (8.80) CSF £32.61 TOTE £3.20: £1.20 £3.10 £1.50 (£23.10) Trio £8.10 OWNER Mr G. R. Parrington (CARTMEL) BRED A. A. Brown
WEIGHT FOR AGE 4yo-5lb
No bid
Palace River (IRE), absent with leg trouble since finishing runner-up in this event a year ago, hung badly when asked for an effort on the run-in but, in the end, scored decisively. (3/1)
3226 Summer Princess, dropped in class, showed ahead after the last but found the winner too strong in the closing stages. (11/1:8/1-12/1)
4389 Queen's Counsel (IRE), dropped in trip and suited by this track, never gave up trying. (6/4)
A Badge Too Far (IRE), pulled up on his previous outing, could not match the principals over the last two flights. (40/1)
504 Gabrielle Gerard (14/1: op 8/1)

4757 STELLA ARTOIS H'CAP CHASE (0-125) (5-Y.O+) (Class D)

2-30 (2-30) **2m 1f 110y (12 fncs)** £3,481.05 (£1,052.40: £512.70: £242.85) GOING minus 0.36 sec per fur (GF)

Form	Horse	Dist	Pos	SP	RR	SF
4702*	**Indian Jockey (117)** (MCPipe) **5-12-0** APMcCoy (lw: mde all: clr 6th: eased flat)	—	**1**	4/6^{1}	134+	33
4716^{3}	**Blazing Dawn (86)** (JSHubbuck) **10-10-3** BStorey (lw: chsd ldr fr 7th: kpt on flat: no ch w wnr)	5	**2**	7/2^{2}	98	3
4721^{U}	**Cardenden (IRE) (83)** (JBarclay) **9-10-0** PCarberry (chsd ldr to 7th: one pce fr 4 out)	8	**3**	20/1	55 t	—
4410*	**Speaker's House (USA) (92)** (MissLucindaRussell) **8-10-9** AThornton (mstke 2nd: wl bhd fr 6th: t.o)	dist	**4**	4/1^{3}	—	—

(SP 107.0%) **4 Rn**

4m 14.7 (3.70) CSF £3.09 TOTE £1.60 (£1.70) OWNER Mr Stuart Mercer (WELLINGTON) BRED John Hayter
LONG HANDICAP Cardenden (IRE) 9-0
WEIGHT FOR AGE 5yo-6lb
OFFICIAL EXPLANATION **Speaker's House (USA): was unable to go the fast early pace and did not jump as well as usual.**
4702* Indian Jockey again wore a tongue-strap. 14lb higher in the ratings compared with his win here four days earlier, he set much too fast a pace for his opponents, was out on his own from halfway, and won easing right up. He has now won nine times this jumps season. (4/6)
4716 Blazing Dawn, suited by the drop back in distance, chased the winner from halfway but was never going to get anywhere near him.(7/2)
4721 Cardenden (IRE) ran as well as could be expected from a stone out of the handicap. (20/1)
4410* Speaker's House (USA) was taken off his legs and, as a result, his jumping suffered. He lost touch at halfway. (4/1)

4758 JENNINGS CUMBERLAND ALE HUNTERS' CHASE (5-Y.O+) (Class H)

3-00 (3-00) **3m 2f (18 fncs)** £2,253.00 (£633.00: £309.00) GOING minus 0.36 sec per fur (GF)

Form	Horse	Dist	Pos	SP	RR	SF
	Hornblower (RichardFord) **10-11-7v**$^{(7)}$ MrsCFord (trckd ldrs: led 14th: clr last: rdn out)	—	**1**	11/8^{1}	101	18
4724^{3}	**Fordstown (IRE)** (JamieAlexander) **8-11-11**$^{(7)}$ MrJamieAlexander (w ldr: led 6th to 14th: kpt on flat)	6	**2**	14/1	101	18
4338^{2}	**Across the Card** (MajorGenCARamsay) **9-11-11**$^{(7)}$ MrMBradburne (lw: hld up & bhd: effrt 4 out: mstke 2 out: styd on strly flat)	3½	**3**	4/1^{3}	99	16
4449^{4}	**Southern Minstrel** (NChamberlain) **14-12-0**$^{(7)}$ MissCMetcalfe (sn bhd: hdwy 12th: one pce fr 4 out)	12	**4**	10/1	95	12
4545^{3}	**Lupy Minstrel** (MissPaulineRobson) **12-12-2**$^{(5)}$ MissPRobson (in tch: hit 10th: outpcd 12th: 6th & wkng whn mstke 2 out)	7	**5**	7/2^{2}	91	8
	Priory Piper (MrsJLMoule) **8-11-7**$^{(7)}$ MrGHanmer (stdd s: hld up & bhd: sme hdwy 4 out: n.d)	3½	**6**	33/1	81	—
4579^{4}	**Will Travel (IRE)** (AndrewDickman) **8-11-7**$^{(7)}$ MrARobson (t: chsd ldrs: poor 3rd last: wknd flat)	hd	**7**	8/1	81	—
3713^{8}	**Drumcairn (IRE)** (PGForster) **9-11-7b**$^{1(7)}$ MrMJRuddy (mstkes: chsd ldrs: 4th & wkng whn blnd bdly 14th: p.u bef next)		**P**	33/1	—	—
4748^{8}	**Alpha One** (DFBassett) **12-12-0**$^{(7)}$ MissKDiMarte (mstkes: sn bhd: t.o 11th: blnd 13th: p.u after next)		**P**	33/1	—	—
	Rallying Cry (IRE) (MrsJSeymour) **9-11-7b**$^{1(7)}$ MrDRMcLeod (bhd whn blnd 4th: sn t.o: p.u lame after 8th: dead)		**P**	50/1	—	—

(SP 122.0%) **10 Rn**

6m 35.7 (11.70) CSF £20.67 TOTE £2.30: £1.50 £1.90 £1.10 (£13.20) Trio £16.40 OWNER Mr N. J. Barrowclough (TARPORLEY) BRED Mrs H. George
Hornblower, who won a novice hurdle for Peter Easterby, has won his last five outings in point-to-points. Well clear jumping the last, he ran lazily in front and had to be kept up to his work. (11/8)
4724 Fordstown (IRE), having his second outing in three days, proved no match but finished clear second best. (14/1)
4338 Across the Card, whose rider seemed in no hurry to join issue, was only fifth when making a mistake two out and he finished with quite a flourish. Stamina is obviously his strong suit and he is suited by extreme distances. (4/1)
4449 Southern Minstrel jumped soundly but, at fourteen, has lost most of his speed. (10/1)
4411 Will Travel (IRE), who is tubed, was clear third jumping the last but he got very tired on the long run-in. (8/1)

4759 DRY BLACKTHORN CIDER MAIDEN HURDLE (5-Y.O+) (Class E)

3-35 (3-35) **2m 1f 110y (8 hdls)** £2,318.00 (£648.00: £314.00) GOING minus 0.36 sec per fur (GF)

Form	Horse	Dist	Pos	SP	RR	SF
4749^{4}	**In Good Faith (98)** (JJQuinn) **5-10-12**$^{(7)}$ CMcCormack (lw: trckd ldrs gng wl: hit 2 out: led appr last: easily)	—	**1**	7/4^{1}	63+	13
4390^{3}	**Salkeld King (IRE) (75)** (MABarnes) **5-11-5** BStorey (sn bhd: mstke 3rd: hdwy between last 2: styd on flat: no ch w wnr)	8	**2**	7/1	56	6
4296^{4}	**Dantes Amour (IRE) (81)** (MDHammond) **6-11-5** RGarritty (mstkes: bhd: hdwy 4th: one pce fr 3 out)	6	**3**	9/4^{2}	50	—
4479^{6}	**Praise Be (FR) (75)** (TPTate) **7-11-5v**^{1} PNiven (mde most tl hdd appr last: wknd flat)	3	**4**	16/1	48	—
467^{6}	**Stone Cross (IRE)** (MartinTodhunter) **5-11-5** PCarberry (hld up & plld hrd: stdy hdwy 5th: shkn up after next: sn wknd)	10	**5**	14/1	38	—
4514^{8}	**Starlin Sam** (JSisterson) **8-11-5** RichardGuest (chsd ldrs: rdn & hit 5th: wknd qckly: t.o whn p.u bef last)		**P**	10/1	—	—
4628^{6}	**The Eens (70)** (DMcCain) **5-11-5** TJenks (chsd ldr: rdn 3 out: sn wknd: bhd whn p.u bef last)		**P**	5/1^{3}	—	—

				SP	RR	SF
4409[7]	**Dark Midnight (IRE) (55)** (DALamb) **8-11-5b** JBurke (chsd ldrs tl lost pl after 5th: sn bhd: t.o whn p.u bef last)		**P**	25/1	—	—
				(SP 121.8%)		**8 Rn**

4m 7.2 (6.20) CSF £14.77 TOTE £2.90: £1.10 £1.40 £1.70 (£7.50) OWNER Mr Richard Dawson (MALTON) BRED C. W. Rogers
4749 In Good Faith, who apparently found the going too firm when a disappointing fourth at Wetherby two days earlier, made no mistake in this company and won very easily indeed. (7/4: 5/4-15/8)
4390 Salkeld King (IRE) stayed on late in the day to take second spot on the run-in, but the winner was totally different class. (7/1)
4296 Dantes Amour (IRE) hardly jumped a flight properly. (9/4)
Praise Be (FR), tried in a visor, made the running but found next to nothing when tackled. (16/1)
Stone Cross (IRE), a headstrong sort, stopped in two strides when called on for an effort three out. (14/1)

4760 JENNINGS SNECK LIFTER NOVICES' HURDLE (4-Y.O+) (Class E)
4-05 (4-05) **3m 2f (12 hdls)** £2,350.70 (£655.20: £316.10) GOING minus 0.36 sec per fur (GF)

				SP	RR	SF
4146[6]	**Good Hand (USA) (90)** (SEKettlewell) **11-11-12** PNiven (lw: led 5th: styd on wl u.p fr 2 out)	—	**1**	3/1[2]	76	34
4628*	**Jessolle (102)** (GRichards) **5-11-13** RDunwoody (lw: hld up: stdy hdwy 6th: chal 2 out: rdn & no ex flat)	5	**2**	1/2[1]	74	32
4572[5]	**Don't Tell Judy (IRE) (55)** (MissMKMilligan) **9-10-7b[1]**(7) CMcCormack (trckd ldrs: plld hrd: rdn 3 out: one pce)	10	**3**	33/1	55	13
4563[4]	**Northern Star (88)** (JAPickering) **6-10-13**(7) MissJWormall (chsd ldrs: drvn along 7th: outpcd fr 3 out)	8	**4**	13/2[3]	56	14
4393[6]	**Woodhouse Lane** (NChamberlain) **5-10-7**(7) MissCMetcalfe (nt j.w: sn bhd: hdwy 7th: styd on flat)	4	**5**	100/1	47	5
4389[5]	**Barnstormer (66)** (EAElliott) **11-11-0b** DParker (chsd ldrs: mstke 3rd: rdn appr 3 out: sn wl outpcd)	½	**6**	20/1	47	5
4575[3]	**Blooming Spring (IRE) (71)** (MrsDThomson) **8-11-1** LO'Hara (bhd: hdwy 7th: lost pl next)	12	**7**	14/1	41	—
4646[4]	**Royrace (57)** (WMBrisbourne) **5-11-0** RGarritty (bhd: hdwy 6th: lost pl 9th: bhd whn p.u bef 2 out)		**P**	50/1	—	—
4572[R]	**Busy Boy (62)** (DALamb) **10-11-0** JBurke (t: led to 5th: sn drvn along: t.o whn p.u after 8th)		**P**	100/1	—	—
				(SP 123.3%)		**9 Rn**

6m 11.2 (4.20) CSF £4.88 TOTE £3.90: £1.10 £1.30 £3.90 (£1.70) Trio £10.20 OWNER Uncle Jacks Pub (MIDDLEHAM) BRED Tauner Dunlap, Jr. and Brereton C. Jones
4146 Good Hand (USA), who presumably needed the outing at Sedgefield after a six-month lay-off, made sure this was a true test of stamina and he stuck on bravely to see off the favourite on the run-in. He will probably now revert to the Flat and run in a claimer. (3/1)
4628* Jessolle, who had 11lb in hand of the winner on official ratings, was ridden to get the trip. Challenging on the bridle two out, she came under pressure on the run-in and was outstayed. She looked to finish very sore. (1/2)
Don't Tell Judy (IRE) would have been 23lb better off with the winner in a handicap. (33/1)
4563 Northern Star likes the ground but was being driven along from halfway. (13/2)
Woodhouse Lane showed his first glimmer of ability. Novicey at his hurdles, he was in arrears until picking up ground on the long run-in. (100/1)

4761 PIONEER FOODS H'CAP HURDLE (0-120) (4-Y.O+) (Class D)
4-35 (4-36) **2m 6f (11 hdls)** £2,815.00 (£790.00: £385.00) GOING minus 0.36 sec per fur (GF)

				SP	RR	SF
4712[2]	**Highland Way (IRE) (91)** (MartinTodhunter) **9-10-0** PCarberry (lw: hld up & plld hrd: stdy hdwy 3 out: led after last: hld on cl home)	—	**1**	4/1[3]	74	—
4257*	**Lagen Bridge (IRE) (119)** (DMoffatt) **8-12-0** DJMoffatt (lw: trckd ldrs: effrt & hit 2 out: sn led: hdd after last: nt qckn towards fin)	½	**2**	6/5[1]	102	3
4339[2]	**Supertop (111)** (LLungo) **9-11-6** RSupple (lw: trckd ldrs: n.m.r between last 2: kpt on wl last 100 yards)	½	**3**	2/1[2]	93	—
4717[U]	**Gymcrak Cyrano (IRE) (91)** (NChamberlain) **8-9-7**(7) MissCMetcalfe (j.rt: hld up & plld hrd: effrt 2 out: sn chsng ldrs: outpcd appr last: kpt on towards fin)	4	**4**	16/1	70	—
4394[3]	**Peggy Gordon (91)** (MrsDThomson) **6-9-7**(7) NHorrocks (w ldr: led 3 out tl between last 2: sn wl outpcd)	5	**5**	10/1	67?	—
4712[8]	**Jumbo Star (91)** (JEDixon) **7-10-0** BStorey (led to 3 out: wknd between last 2)	5	**6**	33/1	63?	—
				(SP 116.7%)		**6 Rn**

5m 25.8 (14.80) CSF £9.20 CT £10.93 TOTE £4.40: £1.50 £1.70 (£5.00) OWNER Mr J. D. Gordon (ULVERSTON) BRED Jeremiah Dunne
LONG HANDICAP Highland Way (IRE) 9-12 Gymcrak Cyrano (IRE) 9-13 Peggy Gordon 9-8 Jumbo Star 9-1
4712 Highland Way (IRE) was given a peach of a ride by Paul Carberry who has no peer on this type of animal. Taking a keen grip, he was produced to lead after the last and, without his rider picking up his whip, was persuaded to do just enough. (4/1)
4257* Lagen Bridge (IRE) battled back bravely but, hard as he tried, he could not quite worry the winner out of it. (6/5)
4339 Supertop travelled smoothly. Short of room between the last two, he kept on towards the finish. (2/1)
1849 Gymcrak Cyrano (IRE), an early casualty here two days earlier, continually lost ground jumping to the right. After taking a keen grip, he was outpaced between the last two but was sticking on again at the finish. (16/1)
4394 Peggy Gordon, who is only small, was racing from 6lb out of the handicap. After setting sail for home she was left trailing going to the last. (10/1)

T/Plpt: £4.70 (1910.84 Tckts). T/Qdpt: £2.50 (195.97 Tckts) WG

4726-HEREFORD (R-H) (Good to firm)
Wednesday May 28th
Race 2: one fence omitted 2nd circ
WEATHER: fine

4762 BUTTAS NOVICES' HURDLE (4-Y.O+) (Class E)
6-30 (6-30) **2m 3f 110y (11 hdls)** £2,472.00 (£692.00: £336.00) GOING: 0.03 sec per fur (G)

				SP	RR	SF
4628[2]	**Name of Our Father (USA) (99)** (PBowen) **4-11-1** RJohnson (lw: chsd ldr: led 5th: clr 2 out: drvn out)	—	**1**	4/5[1]	79	4
4620[9]	**Pedaltothemetal (IRE) (70)** (RTJuckes) **5-10-9** GaryLyons (hld up: hdwy 5th: chsd wnr appr 3 out: r.o flat)	1¼	**2**	16/1	67	—
4650[6]	**Romantic Warrior** (KSBridgwater) **4-10-5**(3) RMassey (prom: outpcd 8th: styd on one pce fr 3 out)	16	**3**	16/1	58	—
4567[2]	**Real Madrid (97)** (GPEnright) **6-11-7** NWilliamson (hld up: hdwy appr 7th: 3rd & wkng whn mstke 2 out: eased whn btn appr last)	9	**4**	15/8[2]	59	—
4405[4]	**Arioso (64)** (JLNeedham) **9-10-9** BFenton (hld up & plld hrd: hdwy after 6th: wknd appr 3 out)	4	**5**	9/1[3]	43	—
4628[8]	**Westcoast (55)** (MTate) **6-11-0** CLlewellyn (hld up & bhd: hdwy 8th: wknd appr 3 out)	4	**6**	66/1	45	—
4561[3]	**Be In Space** (MissPMWhittle) **6-10-2**(7) MrOMcPhail (a bhd)	14	**7**	16/1	28	—
4242[4]	**Westfield** (AJChamberlain) **5-11-0** BPowell (bhd fr 7th: t.o)	dist	**8**	25/1	—	—
1569[5]	**Trouble At Mill** (JLBrown) **7-11-0** MrDSJones (plld hrd: led to 5th: wknd appr 7th: t.o)	dist	**9**	66/1	—	—

3284[16] **Trianna** (RBrotherton) **4-10-3** SCurran (prom to 6th: t.o whn p.u bef last) .... P 66/1 — —
(SP 126.3%) **10 Rn**

4m 47.1 (16.10) CSF £16.95 TOTE £1.80: £1.10 £2.90 £2.60 (£9.20) Trio £67.00 OWNER Mr T. M. Morris (HAVERFORDWEST) BRED Thomas P. Tatham
WEIGHT FOR AGE 4yo-5lb
4628 Name of Our Father (USA) did not have much to beat with Real Madrid proving a disappointment. (4/5: 4/7-10/11)
3670 Pedaltothemetal (IRE), bought out of Philip Mitchell's stable for 3,000 guineas, ran much better than when well beaten in a seller on her debut for her new connections. (16/1)
4567 Real Madrid may have found this trip beyond his best. (15/8)

4763 THE EDWARDIAN (S) H'CAP CHASE (0-95) (5-Y.O+) (Class G)
7-00 (7-02) **3m 1f 110y (18 fncs)** £2,780.00 (£780.00: £380.00) GOING: 0.03 sec per fur (G)

				SP	RR	SF
957[2]	**Raglan Road (86)** (MissAEEmbiricos) **13-11-5** KGaule (hld up: hdwy 11th: led 2 out: drvn out)	—	1	8/1 2	94	22
4330[U]	**Spring to it (90)** (MCPipe) **11-11-9** APMcCoy (a.p: reminders after 1st: led 6th: hit 14th: hit & hdd 2 out: hrd rdn: r.o)	1½	2	3/1 1	97	25
4727[9]	**Pandora's Prize (67)** (TWall) **11-10-0** SWynne (a.p: r.o one pce fr 2 out)	3	3	25/1	72	—
4344[4]	**Turpin's Green (71)** (JSKing) **14-10-4** TJMurphy (a.p: 3rd whn mstke 2 out: sn wknd)	17	4	8/1 2	66	—
4524[4]	**Loughdoo (IRE) (67)** (RLee) **9-10-0** BFenton (nt j.w: blnd 7th: a bhd: t.o)	17	5	3/1 1	51	—
4389[S]	**Cool Luke (IRE) (72)** (FMurphy) **8-10-5** NWilliamson (sme hdwy 12th: wknd 13th: t.o)	nk	6	8/1 2	56	—
4721[7]	**Boxing Match (71)** (JMBradley) **10-10-4** RJohnson (prom tl wknd 4 out: t.o)	9	7	14/1	49	—
4659[8]	**Desert Run (IRE) (94)** (PRRodford) **9-11-13** SBurrough (fell 1st)		F	33/1	—	—
3812[3]	**Napoleon's Gold (IRE) (67)** (AGFoster) **7-10-0v[1]** DMorris (fell 3rd)		F	25/1	—	—
4442[U]	**Aeolian (67)** (MissPMWhittle) **6-10-0** JCulloty (a bhd: t.o whn p.u bef 3 out)		P	20/1	—	—
4621[4]	**Little Elliot (IRE) (70)** (SEarle) **9-10-3**ow3 CMaude (a bhd: t.o whn p.u bef 12th)		P	12/1 3	—	—
	Rustino (76) (SBClark) **11-10-2**(7) MissRClark (a bhd: t.o whn p.u bef 2 out)		P	14/1	—	—
4721[5]	**Rustic Gent (IRE) (67)** (DBurchell) **9-10-0b** DJBurchell (bdly hmpd 1st: sn t.o: p.u bef 13th)		P	14/1	—	—
4293[3]	**L'Uomo Piu (77)** (ABarrow) **13-10-3**(7) MrOMcPhail (led to 6th: wknd 11th: t.o whn p.u bef 3 out)		P	8/1 2	—	—
4463[4]	**Woodlands Genhire (77)** (PAPritchard) **12-10-10b** CLlewellyn (hmpd & uns rdr 3rd)		U	20/1	—	—
				(SP 142.3%)	**15 Rn**	

6m 26.7 (16.70) CSF £33.62 CT £584.05 TOTE £18.60: £3.60 £1.90 £3.90 (£13.80) Trio £134.10; £113.33 to 30/5/97 OWNER Mr Mark Johnson (NEWMARKET) BRED M. Bowe
LONG HANDICAP Pandora's Prize 9-8 Aeolian 9-10 Napoleon's Gold (IRE) 9-7
No bid
957 Raglan Road, 2lb higher than when second in a similar event at Plumpton last October, had been pulled up in his only point-to-point this season in February. (8/1)
4330 Spring to it, 2lb lower than when last in a handicap, was again inclined to make the odd jumping error. (3/1)
4072 Pandora's Prize, 6lb out of the handicap, had been beaten over thirty lengths in a similar event over hurdles here on Monday. (25/1)

4764 CHAIRMAN'S 80TH BIRTHDAY NOVICES' CHASE (5-Y.O+) (Class D)
7-30 (7-31) **2m (12 fncs)** £3,452.50 (£1,045.00: £510.00: £242.50) GOING: 0.03 sec per fur (G)

				SP	RR	SF
4272[F]	**Sleazey (76)** (JGO'Neill) **6-11-6** SCurran (mde all: rdn 2 out: r.o wl)	—	1	9/4 2	83	14
4512[9]	**Kumari King (IRE)** (AWCarroll) **7-11-0** BPowell (hld up: hdwy 4 out: outpcd & mstke 3 out: hrd rdn & rallied flat: nt trble wnr)	4	2	20/1	73	4
4523*	**Tight Fist (IRE)** (MissHCKnight) **7-11-6** JFTitley (a.p: chsd wnr fr 6th: ev ch 2 out: wknd flat)	1¾	3	4/5 1	77	8
4526[6]	**Hugh Daniels (65)** (CJHemsley) **9-10-7**(7) MissADudley (hld up: wknd appr 3 out)	7	4	40/1	64	—
4574[F]	**Sunkala Shine** (SBClark) **9-10-7**(7) MissRClark (hld up: hit 2nd: bhd whn mstke 4 out: sn t.o)	dist	5	10/1 3	—	—
4444[P]	**Quarter Marker (IRE) (60)** (RLee) **9-11-0** RJohnson (chsd wnr to 6th: sn wknd: t.o fr 4 out)	26	6	12/1	—	—
4523[4]	**Steer Point** (RGFrost) **6-11-0** JFrost (hld up: 5th whn fell 6th (water))		F	10/1 3	—	—
				(SP 119.4%)	**7 Rn**	

4m 3.6 (12.60) CSF £36.16 TOTE £3.20: £2.10 £5.80 (£84.10) OWNER Mr J. G. O'Neill (BICESTER) BRED Finbar O'Neill
4157 Sleazey responded well when challenged by the favourite at the penultimate fence. (9/4: op 4/1)
Kumari King (IRE) fared a lot better on his chasing debut than he had done previously over hurdles. (20/1)
4523* Tight Fist (IRE) could not retain his grip on the winner from the penultimate fence. (4/5: 1/2-10/11)

4765 RICHARD DAVIS MEMORIAL CONDITIONAL H'CAP HURDLE (0-105) (4-Y.O+) (Class F)
8-00 (8-00) **2m 1f (9 hdls)** £2,640.00 (£740.00: £360.00) GOING: 0.03 sec per fur (G)

				SP	RR	SF
4556*	**Fleet Cadet (91)** (MCPipe) **6-11-7v**(3) GSupple (a.gng wl: led appr 5th: clr 3 out: easily)	—	1	5/4 1	74+	38
4723*	**Zingibar (87)** (JMBradley) **5-11-6** 6x TDascombe (rdn after 3rd: outpcd 5th: mstke 2 out: wnt 2nd appr last: no ch w wnr)	8	2	7/2 3	63	27
4162[4]	**Salman (USA) (88)** (MrsVCWard) **11-11-7** PHenley (led tl after 1st: hrd rdn after 6th: btn whn hit 2 out: sn wknd)	13	3	7/1	51	15
4558[6]	**Roc Age (67)** (GWDavies) **6-9-9**(5) LSuthern (led after 1st tl appr 5th: wknd qckly: t.o)	dist	4	10/1	—	—
4510[6]	**Pair of Jacks (IRE) (89)** (PJHobbs) **7-11-8** DJKavanagh (mstke & uns rdr 1st)		U	5/2 2	—	—
				(SP 116.8%)	**5 Rn**	

4m 0.8 (7.80) CSF £6.09 TOTE £2.20: £1.10 £1.90 (£2.60) OWNER Sir John Swaine (WELLINGTON) BRED R. D. Hollingsworth
LONG HANDICAP Roc Age 9-9
4556* Fleet Cadet, stepping-up from selling company, was 5lb higher than when winning at Taunton a month ago. (5/4)
4723* Zingibar, attempting a quick follow-up, certainly made his rider earn his fee over this inadequate trip. (7/2)
4162 Salman (USA) had been dropped 5lb. (7/1)

4766 GARNSTONE NOVICES' H'CAP CHASE (0-100) (5-Y.O+) (Class E)
8-30 (8-30) **2m 3f (14 fncs)** £2,983.00 (£904.00: £442.00: £211.00) GOING: 0.03 sec per fur (G)

				SP	RR	SF
4291[2]	**Castleconner (IRE) (82)** (RGFrost) **6-11-1b** JFrost (hld up: wnt 2nd 9th: led appr 3 out: clr appr last: r.o wl)	—	1	3/1 1	93	3
4383*	**Call Me Albi (IRE) (84)** (MrsLRichards) **6-11-3b** MRichards (rdn after 5th: lost pl 8th: styd on flat)	8	2	4/1 3	88	—

				SP	RR	SF
4699[4]	**Gerry's Pride (IRE) (67)** (JWMullins) **6-10-0** SCurran (hld up & bhd: hdwy 9th: ev ch whn mstke 2 out: sn wknd)	hd	**3**	14/1	71	—
4402*	**Dubelle (87)** (JSKing) **7-11-6** TJMurphy (chsd ldr: led 6th: hit 10th: hdd appr 3 out: sn wknd: t.o)	30	**4**	3/1[1]	66	—
4742[3]	**Miners Rest (76)** (PJHobbs) **9-10-2**(7) MrRWidger (hld up: hdwy 9th: j.slowly 4 out: sn wknd: t.o)	4	**5**	12/1	52	—
4662[P]	**Vallingale (IRE) (73)** (MissHCKnight) **6-10-6** JCulloty (bhd whn p.u after 4 out)		**P**	9/1	—	—
4279[3]	**Inch Emperor (IRE) (92)** (AWCarroll) **7-11-11** BPowell (led to 6th: wknd 8th: bhd whn p.u bef 4 out)		**P**	7/2[2]	—	—

(SP 116.6%) **7 Rn**

4m 46.4 (16.40) CSF £14.85 TOTE £4.20: £1.80 £2.60 (£5.80) OWNER Mrs G. A. Robarts (BUCKFASTLEIGH) BRED Niall Langan
LONG HANDICAP Gerry's Pride (IRE) 9-12
4291 Castleconner (IRE), 7lb higher than when winning a selling chase at Exeter in December, was always travelling well. (3/1)
4383* Call Me Albi (IRE), raised 7lb for his hard-fought win last time, again looked a hard ride. (4/1)
Gerry's Pride (IRE), 2lb out of the handicap, did not appear to be going as well as the winner when an error at the tricky fence two out settled it. (14/1)
4742 Miners Rest (12/1: op 5/1)

4767 LEDGEMOOR 'N.H.' NOVICES' HURDLE (5-Y.O+) (Class E)

9-00 (9-00) **3m 2f (13 hdls)** £2,304.00 (£644.00: £312.00) GOING: 0.03 sec per fur (G)

				SP	RR	SF
4429[3]	**Decyborg (FR) (82)** (MCPipe) **6-11-0** APMcCoy (mde all: rdn 3 out: lft clr after 2 out: r.o)	—	**1**	4/7[1]	66	—
4650[6]	**Pamalyn** (SABrookshaw) **5-10-9** CMaude (a.p: chsd wnr fr 7th: mstke 10th: ev ch whn hung lft & rn wd bnd after 2 out: nt rcvr)	2	**2**	5/1[3]	60	—
	Step In Line (IRE) (GMMcCourt) **5-10-11**(3) DFortt (hld up: hdwy appr 3 out: mstke last: one pce)	2½	**3**	10/1	63	—
3328[P]	**Reluckino (80)** (JGMO'Shea) **7-11-0v** MAFitzgerald (chsd wnr to 7th: wknd appr 9th: t.o)	dist	**4**	7/2[2]	—	—
	True Fred (MrsAPrice) **8-11-0** GaryLyons (prom to 8th: t.o)	3½	**5**	14/1	—	—
4626[12]	**Lady Rosebury** (RJPrice) **7-10-9** TJMurphy (hdwy 4th: wknd appr 9th: t.o)	8	**6**	33/1	—	—
	Animosity (SGKnight) **7-10-9** TDascombe (a bhd: t.o fr 8th: j.slowly 9th: p.u bef 10th)		**P**	20/1	—	—

(SP 126.0%) **7 Rn**

6m 38.3 (35.30) CSF £4.66 TOTE £1.40: £1.20 £1.70 (£3.90) OWNER Mr Terry Neill (WELLINGTON) BRED Bernard Touillon
OFFICIAL EXPLANATION **Decyborg (FR): finished distressed.**
4429 Decyborg (FR), reverting to hurdles, was a fortunate winner. (4/7: 4/11-8/13)
Pamalyn, relishing this stamina test, seemed just about to get on top when taking the scenic route on the adverse camber of the home turn. She stayed on up the run-in but the damage had been done. (5/1: op 10/1)
Step In Line (IRE), a winner between the flags in Ireland, could not sustain his run after an awkward jump at the final hurdle. (10/1)

T/Plpt: £29.80 (278.23 Tckts). T/Qdpt: £13.10 (32.39 Tckts) KH

4738-UTTOXETER (L-H) (Good to firm)

Thursday May 29th

WEATHER: fine & sunny

4768 BRITANNIA UNISON NOVICES' HURDLE (4-Y.O+) (Class D)

2-00 (2-00) **2m 4f 110y (10 hdls)** £2,927.00 (£822.00: £401.00) GOING minus 0.26 sec per fur (GF)

				SP	RR	SF
4708*	**Acajou III (FR)** (GRichards) **9-11-7** PCarberry (mde all: clr appr 2 out: eased flat)	—	**1**	5/4[1]	79+	38
4608[3]	**Give And Take (100)** (MCPipe) **4-11-1b** APMcCoy (sn chsng ldrs: rdn & wnt 2nd 3 out: no imp)	4	**2**	8/1	76	29
4376[5]	**Riverbank Rose (86)** (WClay) **6-11-2v** GTormey (chsd wnr: rdn appr 7th: outpcd next: styd on flat)	6	**3**	20/1	66	25
4608[2]	**Samanid (IRE) (108)** (MissLCSiddall) **5-12-0** RDunwoody (hld up: hdwy 5th: hrd drvn 3 out: sn btn)	4	**4**	9/2[2]	75	34
4171[4]	**Elite Governor (IRE)** (NMLampard) **8-10-11**(3) ChrisWebb (lost pl 4th: t.o fr 6th)	14	**5**	66/1	50	9
4166[4]	**Seabrook Lad (90)** (MJWilkinson) **6-11-7** WMarston (trckd ldrs: hit 7th: wknd next: t.o)	6	**6**	5/1[3]	53	12
4450[4]	**Poppy's Dream (84)** (JWharton) **7-10-9** NWilliamson (a bhd: t.o)	13	**7**	10/1	30	—
4534[5]	**Mollie Silvers (70)** (JKCresswell) **5-10-9** WMcFarland (a bhd: rdn 5th: t.o whn mstke 7th)	dist	**8**	25/1	—	—
4645[6]	**Trentside Major** (CSmith) **5-11-0** MRanger (lost tch 5th: t.o whn p.u bef 7th)		**P**	100/1	—	—

(SP 110.6%) **9 Rn**

4m 46.8 (2.80) CSF £9.98 TOTE £2.10: £1.40 £1.20 £2.70 (£3.90) Trio £23.80 OWNER Mr Robert Ogden (PENRITH) BRED Philippe Achard
WEIGHT FOR AGE 4yo-6lb
4708* Acajou III (FR) is enjoying a new lease of life since being switched back to the smaller obstacles, and he followed up his facile win six days ago with another equally impressive success. (5/4: tchd evens)
3996 Give And Take has trained up very light and, looking ill at ease on this firm ground, could never get the winner off the bridle. (8/1: 6/1-9/1)
4376 Riverbank Rose looked to have shot her bolt when losing touch on the home turn, but she does not lack anything in the stamina stakes, and was getting back into it in the closing stages. (20/1)
4608 Samanid (IRE), close enough to threaten danger turning in, was hard at work approaching the third last but, with top weight taking its toll, dropped away tamely. (9/2)

4769 WELLMAN PLC NOVICES' CHASE (5-Y.O+) (Class D)

2-30 (2-30) **3m 2f (20 fncs)** £3,436.25 (£1,040.00: £507.50: £241.25) GOING minus 0.26 sec per fur (GF)

				SP	RR	SF
4649[4]	**Master Crusader (73)** (DLWilliams) **11-10-9**(7) MrSDurack (lw: chsd ldrs: led 16th: hrd rdn 2 out: drifted rt flat: all out)	—	**1**	11/2[2]	77	—
4546[3]	**Grizzly Bear (IRE) (83)** (RMStronge) **7-11-8** APMcCoy (a.p: reminders 7th: led 11th to 16th: ev ch whn hit 3 out: hrd rdn next: fin tired)	2	**2**	Evens[1]	82	2
4745[U]	**Quixall Crossett (56)** (EMCaine) **12-11-2** GaryLyons (prom tl dropped rr 8th: rallied appr 2 out: rdn & r.o wl flat)	1	**3**	33/1	75	—
4699[P]	**Thunder Road (IRE) (75)** (MissHCKnight) **6-11-8b[1]** JCulloty (swtg: j.rt: led to 11th: rdn 16th: sn wknd)	15	**4**	11/2[2]	72	—
4447[P]	**Doctor Dunklin (USA)** (MrsVCWard) **8-11-2** JRKavanagh (hdwy 7th: wknd 13th: sn t.o)	dist	**5**	33/1	—	—
	Themoreyouknow (MHWeston) **8-11-2** MrMHarris (hld up: hdwy 10th: 4th whn fell 13th)		**F**	11/1	—	—
	Pops Academy (IRE) (CWeedon) **6-11-2** MRichards (lw: hld up in rr: fell 12th)		**F**	6/1[3]	—	—

	Horse / details	Dist	Pos	SP	RR	SF
4699[5]	**Musical Hit (60)** (PAPritchard) **6-11-2b** RSupple (hld up in tch: rdn 8th: sn bhd: t.o whn p.u bef 13th)		P	33/1	—	—
				(SP 112.2%)	**8 Rn**	

6m 45.8 (18.80) CSF £10.58 TOTE £7.70: £2.00 £1.10 £5.60 (£3.10) OWNER Mr D. L. Williams (NEWBURY) BRED Frank and Oliver Lehane

4649 Master Crusader, the paddock pick, had to work to win this mediocre contest but, for the last half-mile, always looked to have the measure of the favourite. (11/2)

4546 Grizzly Bear (IRE), a winner over course and distance two months ago, was given the full treatment here, but he is only moderate and, despite all McCoy could do, he was just not good enough. (Evens)

4058 Quixall Crossett has never won a race and he is reaching the veteran stage, but he made up a tremendous amount of ground in the last half-mile and would definitely have won with another fifty yards to travel. (33/1)

4330* Thunder Road (IRE) had the blinds on this time and was allowed to force the pace, but he lost ground by jumping right and was at the end of his tether jumping the fifth last. (11/2)

4770 BRITANNIA FIVE YEAR FIXED NOVICES' H'CAP HURDLE (0-100) (4-Y.O+) (Class E)

3-00 (3-00) **2m (9 hdls)** £2,400.00 (£675.00: £330.00) GOING minus 0.26 sec per fur (GF)

	Horse / details	Dist	Pos	SP	RR	SF
4514[2]	**Silver Minx (96)** (MrsMReveley) **5-11-10** PNiven (j.lft: led 2nd: clr 2 out: unchal)	—	1	7/1	79	32
4558[7]	**Freno (IRE) (72)** (KCBailey) **6-10-0** NWilliamson (lw: hld up: hdwy 5th: ev ch 3 out: rdn next: sn btn)	6	2	25/1	49	2
3983[W]	**Apollono (72)** (RLee) **5-10-0** RJohnson (prom tl outpcd after 6th: styd on u.p appr last)	½	3	5/1[2]	49	2
4477*	**Oversman (90)** (JGFitzGerald) **4-10-13** PCarberry (lw: hld up: stdy hdwy 6th: rdn & outpcd appr 2 out)	2½	4	11/2[3]	64	12
4711[3]	**Radmore Brandy (90)** (GRichards) **4-10-13** RDunwoody (lw: trckd ldrs: effrt & rdn 3 out: sn btn)	4	5	3/1[1]	60	8
4466[2]	**Alpha Leather (72)** (LPGrassick) **6-10-0** MrJGrassick (led to 2nd: wkng whn hmpd 6th: nt rcvr)	1¼	6	12/1	41	—
4633[3]	**Blotoft (79)** (SGollings) **5-10-7** MAFitzgerald (hld up: a bhd: t.o)	20	7	7/1	28	—
4548[6]	**Red Viper (76)** (NMLampard) **5-10-1**(3) ChrisWebb (hld up: hdwy 4th: prom whn fell 6th: dead)		F	25/1	—	—
4414[4]	**Society Girl (80)** (JGMO'Shea) **4-10-3** RSupple (lw: chsd ldrs: rdn 3 out: poor 2nd whn fell last)		F	11/1	52?	—
4175[2]	**Time Leader (72)** (RDickin) **5-10-0** JCulloty (hld up in rr: bdly hmpd 6th: sn t.o: p.u bef 3 out)		P	11/1	—	—
				(SP 114.1%)	**10 Rn**	

3m 45.2 (4.20) CSF £135.10 CT £858.47 TOTE £6.60: £2.00 £8.60 £2.50 (£93.70) Trio £164.20; £129.57 to Ayr 30/5/97 OWNER Mrs E. A. Kettlewell (SALTBURN) BRED T. E. Phillips

LONG HANDICAP Freno (IRE) 9-7 Apollono 9-12 Alpha Leather 9-9

WEIGHT FOR AGE 4yo-5lb

4514 Silver Minx again jumped left but that was an advantage on this track and, in control from early in the straight, he only had to keep going to score. (7/1)

2893 Freno (IRE) is taking time to find his way, but he produced an improved performance, and all is not lost yet. (25/1)

3733 Apollono has won on the firm ground on the Flat but he never looked to be enjoying himself and, though he renewed his effort after getting outpaced on the long home turn, the winner had gone beyond recall. (5/1)

4477* Oversman moved poorly to post and, though he reached a prominent position entering the straight, he was galloping on the spot on the run to the penultimate flight. (11/2)

4711 Radmore Brandy, successful in a seller here in March, was struggling to stay in touch soon after entering the straight. (3/1)

4466 Alpha Leather (12/1: 8/1-14/1)

4414 Society Girl, ridden along from some way out, would have touched down in second place had she not crumpled up on landing at the last. She would never have given the winner any cause for concern. (11/1: 8/1-12/1)

4175 Time Leader (11/1: 8/1-12/1)

4771 BRITANNIA SIMPLY MORTGAGES H'CAP CHASE (0-115) (5-Y.O+) (Class E)

3-30 (3-30) **2m 5f (16 fncs)** £2,937.50 (£890.00: £435.00: £207.50) GOING minus 0.26 sec per fur (GF)

	Horse / details	Dist	Pos	SP	RR	SF
4659[2]	**Blazer Moriniere (FR) (93)** (PCRitchens) **8-10-7** SFox (swtg: chsd ldrs gng wl: led 2 out: drvn out)	—	1	11/8[1]	100	33
4549[3]	**Nordic Valley (IRE) (91)** (MCPipe) **6-10-5** APMcCoy (hld up & bhd: hdwy 11th: led 3 out to 2 out: rallied u.p flat)	1½	2	5/2[2]	97	30
4429[4]	**Henley Regatta (100)** (PRRodford) **9-11-0** MAFitzgerald (lw: hld up & bhd: hdwy 12th: ev ch next: sn outpcd)	20	3	9/2[3]	91	24
4629[6]	**Earlymorning Light (IRE) (114)** (GRichards) **8-12-0** RDunwoody (prom: ev ch 4 out: sn wknd)	9	4	7/1	98	31
4659[7]	**Brimpton Bertie (86)** (MajorDNChappell) **8-10-0** RJohnson (bit bkwd: j.w: led to 3 out: sn rdn & wknd)	7	5	33/1	64	—
4404[P]	**Northern Optimist (87)** (BJLlewellyn) **9-10-1** NWilliamson (lw: chsd ldr to 10th: wknd appr 12th: p.u bef 4 out)		P	14/1	—	—
				(SP 111.0%)	**6 Rn**	

5m 6.0 (1.00) CSF £4.88 TOTE £2.40: £1.40 £1.40 (£1.90) OWNER Mr John Pearl (TIDWORTH) BRED Robert Jeffroy

4659 Blazer Moriniere (FR) has enjoyed quite a rewarding spring and, always travelling like a winner, won with more in hand than the margin suggests. (11/8)

4549 Nordic Valley (IRE), taking a step down in distance, was the only one able to make a race of it from the third last, but he was only there on sufferance until the winner really got down to work. (5/2)

4429 Henley Regatta gave the impression that he did not see out the trip, for he was on the heels of the leaders four out before the leading pair drew right away. (9/2)

4629 Earlymorning Light (IRE) was a winner first time out this term but he has steadily gone backwards since, and he will probably need to be dropped a few pounds in the handicap if he is to succeed again. (7/1: op 4/1)

4772 BRITANNIA MEMBERS LOYALTY BONUS H'CAP HURDLE (0-130) (4-Y.O+) (Class C)

4-00 (4-00) **3m 110y (12 hdls)** £3,485.00 (£1,055.00: £515.00: £245.00) GOING minus 0.26 sec per fur (GF)

	Horse / details	Dist	Pos	SP	RR	SF
4397[9]	**Edelweis du Moulin (FR) (130)** (GRichards) **5-12-0** PCarberry (hld up & bhd: stdy hdwy 9th: led last: v.easily)	—	1	3/1[2]	111+	58
4536*	**The Toiseach (IRE) (121)** (JRFanshawe) **6-11-5v** JOsborne (led & lft wl clr 4th: pushed along 2 out: hdd last: no ch w wnr)	2½	2	7/4[1]	100	47
4610[F]	**Tragic Hero (129)** (MCPipe) **5-11-13b** APMcCoy (lw: hld up in rr: hdwy 9th: rdn 3 out: no imp whn mstke last)	6	3	5/1[3]	104	51
4476[2]	**Beechfield Flyer (102)** (WClay) **6-10-0** GTormey (swtg: mstke 2nd: rdn & outpcd 7th: wnt 2nd next: wknd 3 out: t.o)	14	4	11/1	68	15
1447*	**Don du Cadran (FR) (104)** (CaptTAForster) **8-10-2**ow2 AThornton (bkwd: chsd ldrs: rdn after 7th: wknd 9th: t.o)	dist	5	10/1	—	—
4521[2]	**Moving Out (107)** (MissHCKnight) **9-10-5** JFTitley (lw: led tl hdd & fell 4th)		F	7/1	—	—

	Horse			SP	RR	SF
4185[P]	**Northern Squire (110)** (JMJefferson) **9-10-8** LWyer (lw: lft 2nd 4th: wknd 8th: sn rdn: t.o whn p.u bef 3 out)......		P	33/1	—	—

(SP 110.9%) **7 Rn**

5m 41.0 (-1.00) CSF £7.64 TOTE £3.20: £1.90 £1.60 (£2.70) OWNER Mr Robert Ogden (PENRITH) BRED Simon Philibert
LONG HANDICAP Don du Cadran (FR) 9-10 Beechfield Flyer 9-8

4397 Edelweis du Moulin (FR), having his first try at such an extended trip, was dropped in at the start. Beginning to creep closer at the end of the back straight, he had five lengths to make up from the penultimate flight but, still cruising when touching down with a slight advantage at the last, did not need to be let down to score. It was rather surprising to hear his trainer say that it would be doubtful if he would stay the trip in a truly-run race. (3/1)

4536* The Toiseach (IRE) attempted to put his undoubted stamina to good use and, for most of the way, promised to come home unchallenged but, as in the past, he finds very little off the bridle and the winner made him look moderate. (7/4)

4397 Tragic Hero, patiently ridden to make sure he got the trip, followed the winner through, but he was under pressure early in the straight, and was already destined for third prize when he made an untidy mistake at the last. (5/1)

4773 BRITANNIA BRIGHTER SAVERS NOVICES' HUNTERS' CHASE (5,6,7 & 8-Y.O) (Class H)

4-30 (4-30) **2m 5f (16 fncs)** £1,127.50 (£340.00: £165.00: £77.50) GOING minus 0.26 sec per fur (GF)

	Horse	Dist	Pos	SP	RR	SF
4522*	**King Torus (IRE)** (VictorDartnall) **7-12-1**(5) MrJJukes (a chsng ldrs: led appr 4 out: clr last: eased nr fin)	—	1	10/11[1]	111	30
4704[F]	**True Fortune** (JohnMoore) **7-11-7**(7) MrDSJones (lw: hld up: hdwy 10th: chsd wnr fr 4 out: styd on flat).......	1½	2	8/1[3]	104	23
4618*	**Muskerry Moya (IRE)** (JWDufosee) **8-11-8**(7) MissAGoschen (lw: j.rt: led 2nd tl appr 4 out: sn btn: fin lame)	28	3	11/4[2]	84	3
4637[3]	**Tellaporky** (THind) **8-11-8**(7)ow1 MrAMiddleton (lw: wl bhd tl styd on fr 3 out: nvr nrr)	11	4	25/1	75	—
	Everso Irish (JPTulloch) **8-11-7**(7) MrJBarnes (lw: nvr plcd to chal: t.o)................................	14	5	33/1	64	—
4607[3]	**Very Daring** (JulianHunt) **7-11-7**(7) MissSSharratt (a in rr: rdn after 8th: t.o)................................	25	6	50/1	44	—
	Beyond the Stars (IPWilliams) **6-11-11**(3) MrMRimell (lw: mstke 2nd: prom tl fell 7th)........................		F	14/1	—	—
4569[P]	**Dragons Bay (IRE)** (MrsMReveley) **8-12-0** MrSSwiers (s.s: wl bhd: hdwy 11th: no ch whn p.u bef 3 out)..........		P	14/1	—	—
4637[P]	**Dark Rhytham** (GACoombe) **8-11-7**(7) MrTLane (led to 2nd: mstke 11th: wknd next: t.o whn p.u bef 2 out)		P	25/1	—	—
	Christmas Thyne (IRE) (MrsPGrainger) **5-11-0**(7) MrAPhillips (mstke 5th: t.o fr 11th: p.u bef 4 out)		P	100/1	—	—
4406[F]	**Thornhill** (FLMatthews) **7-11-2**(7) MrRWidger (s.s: t.o whn p.u bef 11th)..		P	200/1	—	—

(SP 117.6%) **11 Rn**

5m 14.3 (9.30) CSF £7.99 TOTE £1.90: £1.50 £1.50 £1.40 (£8.00) Trio £4.10 OWNER Mr Nick Viney (BARNSTAPLE) BRED Mrs M. McCullagh
WEIGHT FOR AGE 5yo-7lb

4522* King Torus (IRE) had no trouble making it two out of two under Rules and, as he is still a comparative youngster, his future looks bright. (10/11)

4704 True Fortune has not yet won under Rules, and he appears to need far more cut in the ground than he had here. He is a trier and certainly lost no caste in defeat. (8/1)

4618* Muskerry Moya (IRE) goes a right good gallop and tried to put the emphasis on stamina, but she looked none too happy striding to post on this ever-firming ground and, though she held the call to the fourth last, she finished very lame and her future on the racetrack could now be in doubt. (11/4)

4774 BRITANNIA MULTIGUARD MAIDEN OPEN N.H. FLAT RACE (4, 5 & 6-Y.O) (Class H)

5-00 (5-00) **2m** £1,287.00 (£357.00: £171.00)

	Horse	Dist	Pos	SP	RR	SF
4657[2]	**Stormhill Stag** (PBowen) **5-10-12**(7) LCummins (a chsng ldrs: led over 2f out: r.o wl)..............................	—	1	5/2[2]	72 f	—
4531[4]	**Oi Mother (IRE)** (DNicholson) **5-10-11**(3) RMassey (chsd ldrs: ev ch 2f out: rdn & hung lft: rn green)...............	2	2	7/4[1]	65 f	—
3561[4]	**Amlwch** (JBerry) **4-11-0** DParker (hld up in tch: effrt 4f out: one pce fnl 2f)..	7	3	7/1[3]	63 f	—
4656[7]	**Hill's Electric (IRE)** (TKeddy) **5-11-5** RJohnson (hld up: hdwy ½-wy: led over 5f out tl over 2f out: grad wknd)	5	4	16/1	58 f	—
4531[6]	**Dark Horse (IRE)** (CPEBrooks) **5-10-12**(7) MBerry (hld up mid div: effrt 4f out: hung lft: nt rch ldrs)	11	5	8/1	47 f	—
4657[6]	**Minibelle** (DLWilliams) **5-10-7**(7) MrSDurack (prom tl wknd 3f out)	2	6	20/1	40 f	—
4539[4]	**Sweet Little Briar (IRE)** (GCBravery) **6-11-0** RDunwoody (hld up: hdwy 6f out: wknd 3f out)...........................	nk	7	7/1[3]	40 f	—
4531[9]	**Sumo** (OBrennan) **4-10-11**(3) EHusband (chsd ldr: led 7f out tl over 5f out: wknd fnl 3f)................................	1½	8	16/1	43 f	—
4632[11]	**Cahermone Lady (IRE)** (RMWhitaker) **6-11-0** OPears (nvr nr to chal)	7	9	33/1	31 f	—
4288[10]	**The Chase** (JMJefferson) **6-11-5** LWyer (a bhd)	3	10	40/1	33 f	—
4388[6]	**Twelve Club** (KCBailey) **4-11-0** NWilliamson (hld up: hdwy 6f out: wknd over 3f out: t.o)	10	11	12/1	23 f	—
4531[19]	**Postlip Royale** (LPGrassick) **4-10-9** MrJGrassick (a in rr: t.o fr ½-wy)..	dist	12	66/1	—	—
4301[9]	**Spanish Secret (IRE)** (NPLittmoden) **5-11-5** MAFitzgerald (led 9f: wknd 4f out: t.o)..	¾	13	16/1	—	—
4538[P]	**Be Broadminded** (MissPMWhittle) **5-11-5** PNiven (a bhd: t.o)..	dist	14	66/1	—	—
3626[9]	**Denstar (IRE)** (JWhite) **4-10-7**(7) FQuinlan (a bhd: t.o)	dist	15	50/1	—	—

(SP 141.5%) **15 Rn**

3m 37.9 CSF £7.63 TOTE £4.70: £2.00 £1.40 £2.00 (£3.90) Trio £10.50 OWNER Mr R. Taylor (HAVERFORDWEST) BRED Mrs A. E. Ratcliff
WEIGHT FOR AGE 4yo-5lb

4657 Stormhill Stag confirmed the promise shown on his debut with a smoothly-gained success, and he looks to have a future. (5/2)

4531 Oi Mother (IRE), almost upsides entering the last quarter-mile, had to admit the winner always going that bit better, but she was inclined to show signs of greenness and could still be in the process of learning. (7/4)

3561 Amlwch ran on soft ground when making his debut early in March, and he had much faster ground to contend with here. In the end he just could not find sufficient speed to compete with the principals. (7/1)

4433 Hill's Electric (IRE) is getting to know what the game is all about and, in producing by far his best performance yet, should not have much trouble in making his mark. (16/1)

4531 Dark Horse (IRE) looked to be getting himself into the action entering the straight, but he continually hung left and, with his jockey unable to get the best out of him, he just had to accept the situation. (8/1)

4657 Minibelle appears to be doing too much too soon, for once again she was going in reverse when the battle to the post really got under way. (20/1)

T/Plpt: £11.90 (1,113.57 Tckts). T/Qdpt: £6.60 (87.33 Tckts) IM

4775a - 4788a (IrishRacing) - See Computer Raceform

4620-STRATFORD-ON-AVON (L-H) (Good, Hdles Good to firm patches)

Friday May 30th

Race 6: second last flight omitted.
WEATHER: warm & sunny

4789 BAILEYS ORIGINAL IRISH CREAM (S) H'CAP HURDLE (0-95) (4-Y.O+) (Class G)

6-35 (6-35) **2m 110y (9 hdls)** £2,122.00 (£592.00: £286.00) GOING: 0.15 sec per fur (G)

	Horse	Dist	Pos	SP	RR	SF
4290^{P}	**Night Time (70)** (AGHobbs) **5-10-3**(7) MrGShenkin (hdwy 5th: led appr last: rdn out)	—	**1**	16/1	53	19
4633^{*}	**Hever Golf Diamond (83)** (JRBest) **4-10-11b**(7) MrPO'Keeffe (chsd clr ldrs: led 6th: hdd & unable qckn appr last)	3½	**2**	11/2^{3}	63	24
1072^{P}	**Milzig (USA) (64)** (JJoseph) **8-10-4** CLlewellyn (hdwy 6th: one pce fr 2 out)	2	**3**	25/1	42	8
4648^{5}	**Our Eddie (77)** (KGWingrove) **8-11-3v** JRyan (hdwy 6th: no imp appr 2 out)	¾	**4**	12/1	54	20
4648^{7}	**Blatant Outburst (74)** (MissSJWilton) **7-11-0v** APMcCoy (hld up: hit 2nd: hdwy 6th: nvr rchd ldrs)	7	**5**	9/2^{1}	44	10
4276^{P}	**Just Andy (60)** (BPreece) **6-9-7b**(7) JMogford (bhd: blnd 1st: rdn & hdwy 3 out: nvr nrr)	8	**6**	66/1	22	—
76^{6}	**Striding Edge (62)** (THind) **12-10-2**ow1 RDunwoody (bit bkwd: prom to 3 out)	1½	**7**	14/1	23	—
4765^{3}	**Salman (USA) (88)** (MrsVCWard) **11-11-11**(3) MrRThornton (swtg: chsd ldrs: rdn 6th: btn whn hmpd 2 out)	hd	**8**	12/1	49	15
1993^{P}	**My Harvinski (65)** (IRJones) **7-10-5** DJBurchell (hdwy 4th: wkng whn mstke 3 out)	4	**9**	20/1	22	—
4633^{7}	**Tug Your Forelock (60)** (GFJohnsonHoughton) **6-9-9**(5) XAizpuru (nvr trbld ldrs)	½	**10**	20/1	17	—
4648^{8}	**Verro (USA) (60)** (KBishop) **10-9-7v**(7) MGriffiths (w ldr: led 3rd to 4th: wknd 6th)	hd	**11**	50/1	16	—
4658^{8}	**Red Tel (IRE) (78)** (MCPipe) **5-10-13v**[1](5) GSupple (lw: rdn 5th: nvr nr ldrs)	5	**12**	12/1	30	—
888^{P}	**Fame And Fantasy (IRE) (76)** (NoelChance) **6-11-2** RJohnson (chsd ldrs tl wknd 6th)	10	**13**	10/1	18	—
4620^{10}	**Lizium (61)** (JCFox) **5-10-1**ow1 SFox (lw: mstkes 3rd & 4th: a bhd)	12	**14**	33/1	—	—
4648^{9}	**Soccer Ball (60)** (TRWatson) **7-10-0** WMarston (lw: led to 3rd: led 4th tl hdd & fell 3 out)		**F**	33/1	—	—
4633^{2}	**Captain Tandy (IRE) (72)** (CSmith) **8-10-12** PMcLoughlin (hdwy 4th: 5th & btn whn fell 2 out)		**F**	5/1^{2}	—	—
4620^{*}	**Persian Butterfly (74)** (RMStronge) **5-11-0** JCulloty (in tch tl lost pl qckly & p.u appr 5th)		**P**	5/1^{2}	—	—
4648^{10}	**Premier Star (60)** (KGWingrove) **7-9-7**(7) MrSDurack (prom to 4th: bhd whn p.u bef last)		**P**	50/1	—	—
				(SP 136.3%)	**18 Rn**	

3m 58.0 (11.00) CSF £96.11 CT £2,084.33 TOTE £19.50: £4.00 £3.20 £3.10 £2.20 (£171.40) Trio £250.60; £176.52 to 2/6/97 OWNER Mrs Maureen Shenkin (KINGSBRIDGE) BRED Mrs J. Johnson
LONG HANDICAP Tug Your Forelock 9-9 Just Andy 9-3 Verro (USA) 9-9 Lizium 9-10 Premier Star 9-9
WEIGHT FOR AGE 4yo-5lb
No bid
OFFICIAL EXPLANATION **Persian Butterfly: was never travelling.**

393 Night Time moved down well and, with his tongue tied-down, looked a different proposition. (16/1)
4633* Hever Golf Diamond, unable to dominate from the off, still ran his race, and it was the 6lb he was raised for his Fakenham win that made the difference. (11/2: op 5/2)
101* Milzig (USA) looked fit despite his lay-off, and ran respectably over too short a trip. (25/1)
4648 Our Eddie, with his tongue tied-down as usual, could not find anything in the straight (12/1)
3362 Blatant Outburst stays further than this but needs to be restrained, so the way this race was run was far from ideal. He has been a disappointment since winning his bumper. (9/2)
Just Andy did little but stay on past beaten horses, but even that represents a considerable improvement. (66/1)
Striding Edge (14/1: op 8/1)
4765 Salman (USA) (12/1: op 6/1)

4790 JEAN AND TONY HIBBERT 40TH WEDDING ANNIVERSARY NOVICES' H'CAP CHASE (0-110) (5-Y.O+) (Class D)

7-05 (7-05) **2m 5f 110y (16 fncs)** £3,548.00 (£1,064.00: £512.00: £236.00) GOING minus 0.43 sec per fur (GF)

	Horse	Dist	Pos	SP	RR	SF
4627^{2}	**Dandie Imp (73)** (AWCarroll) **9-10-2** BPowell (swtg: mde all: hit 3 out: easily)	—	**1**	9/4^{2}	87+	20
4557^{4}	**Distant Memory (95)** (PJHobbs) **8-11-10b** APMcCoy (chsd wnr to 2nd: chsd wnr 7th: rdn & hit 11th: no imp appr 2 out)	15	**2**	5/2^{3}	98	31
2708^{13}	**Legal Artist (IRE) (79)** (MissCJohnsey) **7-10-8** RichardGuest (mstkes: effrt 9th: nvr nr ldrs)	20	**3**	8/1	67	—
4385^{3}	**Spring to Glory (84)** (PHayward) **10-10-13v** MAFitzgerald (lw: chsd wnr 2nd to 7th: sn rdn: hit 10th & 12th: sn bhd)	6	**4**	13/8^{1}	68	1
				(SP 108.5%)	**4 Rn**	

5m 11.9 (-0.10) CSF £7.36 TOTE £3.20: (£3.30) OWNER Miss A. Clift (WORCESTER) BRED D. Holdway

4627 Dandie Imp, able to dictate, jumped beautifully except for getting in too close at the third last. (9/4)
4557 Distant Memory, continually outjumped by the winner, was done-with by the second last. He probably needs further these days. (5/2)
1472 Legal Artist (IRE), back over fences, did not jump fluently enough to give himself a chance. (8/1: op 5/1)
4385 Spring to Glory has not been running badly, but his confidence at his fences seemed to fade after a slight peck at the sixth.(13/8)

4791 TARMAC CONSTRUCTION H'CAP HURDLE (0-135) (4-Y.O+) (Class C)

7-35 (7-35) **2m 110y (9 hdls)** £3,626.00 (£1,088.00: £524.00: £242.00) GOING: 0.15 sec per fur (G)

	Horse	Dist	Pos	SP	RR	SF
4701^{3}	**Ballet Royal (USA) (104)** (HJManners) **8-9-7**(7) ADowling (hld up: hdwy 5th: ev ch 2 out: rdn & 2l 2nd whn lft clr last)	—	**1**	12/1	80	43
4610^{*}	**Yubralee (USA) (132)** (MCPipe) **5-12-0** APMcCoy (led: clr whn blnd 4th: hdd 2 out: sn btn)	12	**2**	5/4^{1}	96	59
3917^{5}	**Castle Secret (120)** (DBurchell) **11-11-2** DJBurchell (bhd: rdn 4th: hit 6th: r.o fr 2 out)	6	**3**	4/1^{3}	79	42
4397^{12}	**Kadastrof (FR) (132)** (RDickin) **7-11-9**(5) XAizpuru (chsd ldr tl after 4th: wknd 6th)	8	**4**	14/1	83	46
4630^{4}	**Kino's Cross (105)** (AJWilson) **8-10-1** LHarvey (pushed along 4th: a bhd)	5	**5**	25/1	51	14
4141^{*}	**Hay Dance (113)** (PJHobbs) **6-10-9** NWilliamson (lw: trckd ldrs: led 2 out: qckng whn fell last)		**F**	2/1^{2}	89?	—
				(SP 116.0%)	**6 Rn**	

3m 50.6 (3.60) CSF £27.12 TOTE £13.40: £3.20 £2.20 (£18.10) OWNER Mr H. J. Manners (SWINDON) BRED Flaxman Holdings Ltd
LONG HANDICAP Ballet Royal (USA) 9-13

4701 Ballet Royal (USA) confirmed recent promise but, after travelling well, was in the process of being outpaced when presented with the race at the last. (12/1)

4610* Yubralee (USA) might have had a different tale to tell had a bad mistake at the fourth not taken the wind out of his sails. (5/4)
3917 Castle Secret won this race twelve months ago off this mark, but has had only one run over hurdles since and took too long to get going. (4/1: 3/1-9/2)
4117a Kadastrof (FR), forced to chase Yubralee at a respectable distance, failed to run his race as a result. (14/1: op 8/1)
4141* Hay Dance let the two leaders cut each other's throats and quickened well when let down from the second last. Asked for a long one at the last, he flicked the top bar and paid the penalty. (2/1)

4792 HORSE AND HOUND (JOHN CORBET CUP) CHAMPION NOVICES' HUNTERS' CHASE (5-Y.O+) (Class H)
8-05 (8-05) **3m 4f (21 fncs)** £4,272.50 (£1,280.00: £615.00: £282.50) GOING minus 0.43 sec per fur (GF)

				SP	RR	SF
4551*	**Earthmover (IRE)** (RBarber) **6-11-7**(7) MissPGundry (lw: mstkes: hld up: blnd 13th: hdwy 15th: led appr 2 out: sn pushed clr)	—	1	7/4[1]	125+	41
4319*	**Struggles Glory (IRE)** (DCRobinson) **6-11-13**(7)ow6 MrDCRobinson (j.w: led tl appr 2 out: one pce)	4	2	2/1[2]	129	39
	Shuil's Star (IRE) (MrsDHamer) **6-11-7**(7) MrPHamer (lw: hld up: blnd 6th: hdwy 15th: one pce appr 2 out)	9	3	16/1	117	33
4530*	**Prince Buck (IRE)** (MJRoberts) **7-11-11**(3) MrPHacking (prom: ev ch 17th: wknd appr 2 out)	12	4	9/2[3]	110	26
4504*	**Greenmount Lad (IRE)** (JCornforth) **9-11-7**(7) MrPCornforth (mstkes 7th & next: sn t.o)	dist	5	33/1	—	—
4640[3]	**Tom's Gemini Star** (OJCarter) **9-11-7**(7) MissVRoberts (lw: mstke 2nd & 4th: t.o whn fell 4 out)		F	50/1	—	—
4640[5]	**Phar Too Touchy** (VictorDartnall) **10-11-2**(7) MrNHarris (prom: mstke 2nd: hit 13th: sn wknd: p.u bef 16th)		P	11/2	—	—
4457[4]	**Taura's Rascal** (FJBrennan) **8-11-7**(7) MrFBrennan (swtg: prom: hit 3rd & 10th: blnd & wknd 15th: p.u bef 17th)		P	50/1	—	—
4522[4]	**Mister Horatio** (WDLewis) **7-11-7**(7) MrMLewis (prom: 2nd & ev ch whn blnd & uns rdr 4 out)		U	33/1	—	—
				(SP 118.9%)	**9 Rn**	

7m 1.6 (1.60) CSF £5.42 TOTE £2.70: £1.40 £1.60 £2.10 (£3.50) Trio £14.70 OWNER Mr R. M. Penny (BEAMINSTER) BRED Brian McSweeney
4551* Earthmover (IRE), a rangy gelding led round by two handlers in the paddock, may well have found the ground too fast, for he never looked to be travelling that well and fiddled his fences. Once the chips were down, he showed himself to be a very decent prospect. (7/4)
4319* Struggles Glory (IRE) met his match, but gave his rivals a jumping lesson and lost nothing in defeat. (2/1)
Shuil's Star (IRE) won two point-to-points earlier in the month and ran a great race on his debut under Rules. On this evidence, a novice hunter chase should be easy to find next season. (16/1)
4530* Prince Buck (IRE), whose Warwick win is working out well, may have just failed to last out the trip, as he was travelling as strongly as anything with half-a-mile left. (9/2)
4522 Mister Horatio was in the process of running a terrific race when, upsides the leader, he made a dreadful blunder at the last open ditch, giving his jockey no chance. (33/1)

4793 WEATHERBYS YOUNG HORSE AWARDS H'CAP CHASE (0-125) (5-Y.O+) (Class D)
8-35 (8-36) **2m 1f 110y (13 fncs)** £3,418.00 (£1,024.00: £492.00: £226.00) GOING minus 0.43 sec per fur (GF)

				SP	RR	SF
4757*	**Indian Jockey (124)** (MCPipe) **5-11-9** 7x APMcCoy (led: rdn 8th: hdd 3 out: hmpd appr next: rallied appr last: led flat)	—	1	8/11[1]	139	37
2741a[7]	**Fiftysevenchannels (IRE) (123)** (MissHCKnight) **8-12-0** GBradley (lw: chsd wnr: led 3 out tl wknd & hdd flat)	4	2	11/2[3]	134	38
4700[4]	**Society Guest (120)** (AndrewTurnell) **11-11-11** LHarvey (lw: chsd ldrs: mstke 2nd: j.slowly next: rdn & wknd appr 3 out)	10	3	9/1	122	26
4612[2]	**Storm Falcon (USA) (111)** (SMellor) **7-11-2** RDunwoody (t: hld up: hit 8th: no imp fr 4 out)	8	4	5/2[2]	106	10
				(SP 111.9%)	**4 Rn**	

4m 9.5 (0.50) CSF £4.72 TOTE £1.90: (£3.00) OWNER Mr Stuart Mercer (WELLINGTON) BRED John Hayter
WEIGHT FOR AGE 5yo-6lb
4757* Indian Jockey gained his tenth win of the season and his third in a week in the gamest fashion, battling back gallantly after losing two or three lengths when hampered on the home turn. (8/11: 4/9-4/5)
2346a Fiftysevenchannels (IRE), who in the last two years has now had four different trainers and two separate spells with Enda Bolger, was second to Saluter in the Marlborough Cup last time after looking sure to win. Quickening in good style to lead three from home, he repeated the process by stopping alarmingly after the last. (11/2: 4/1-6/1)
4700 Society Guest (9/1: 8/1-12/1)
4612 Storm Falcon (USA) was a front-runner at his peak, and these tactics seem to do little but hinder his jumping. (5/2)

4794 GRANDSTAND CONSULTANTS NOVICES' HURDLE (4-Y.O+) (Class D)
9-05 (9-05) **2m 110y (8 hdls)** £3,020.00 (£845.00: £410.00) GOING: 0.15 sec per fur (G)

				SP	RR	SF
4395[2]	**Fairly Sharp (IRE) (108)** (GraemeRoe) **4-10-8** RDunwoody (a.p: led 6th: clr after next: easily)	—	1	10/11[1]	80+	17
4625[9]	**Irene's Pet** (JCFox) **7-10-12** SFox (bhd: hdwy appr 2 out: r.o flat)	13	2	66/1	66	8
4650[5]	**Camp Head (IRE)** (OSherwood) **6-10-12** JAMcCarthy (trckd ldrs: rdn 2 out: sn btn)	2½	3	5/1[3]	64	6
	Alaflak (IRE) (MajorWRHern) **6-10-12** BPowell (lw: chsd ldrs: hit 5th: wknd 2 out)	12	4	11/2	52	—
3946[6]	**Night Escapade (IRE)** (CWeedon) **5-10-7** MRichards (lw: bhd: blnd 4th: nvr rchd ldrs)	1¼	5	33/1	46	—
4696[11]	**Friar's Oak** (PButler) **5-10-5**(7) MrOMcPhail (lw: bhd fr 5th)	8	6	100/1	43	—
4519[4]	**Press Again** (PHayward) **5-10-7** BFenton (lw: nvr trbld ldrs)	4	7	100/1	35	—
	Eau Benite (NEBerry) **6-10-12** RJohnson (swtg: prom to 4th)	5	8	100/1	35	—
4651*	**Melt The Clouds (CAN) (108)** (MCPipe) **4-11-5b** APMcCoy (led tl hdd & wknd 6th)	12	9	100/30[2]	35	—
4304[11]	**Blue Havana (60)** (GraemeRoe) **5-10-7** JCulloty (prom to 3rd: wkng whn blnd 5th: t.o whn p.u bef next)		P	100/1	—	—
	Damarita (JRBest) **6-10-1**(7)ow1 MrPO'Keeffe (bhd: blnd 2nd: blnd & uns rdr next)		U	66/1	—	—
				(SP 117.4%)	**11 Rn**	

3m 58.0 (11.00) CSF £68.06 TOTE £1.90: £1.10 £6.20 £1.90 (£36.90) Trio £99.70 OWNER Ms Caroline Breay (CHALFORD)
WEIGHT FOR AGE 4yo-5lb
4395 Fairly Sharp (IRE), second in her last four races, found an easy race and took it in style. This should help her confidence no end. (10/11: evens-4/5)
Irene's Pet, who did not appear to stay two and three-quarter miles last time, was having only his third race after a break of more than two years. Staying on strongly in the closing stages, he snatched second place after the last. (66/1)
4650 Camp Head (IRE) was travelling ominously well on the heels of the leaders four from home but did not find much once let down. This trip seems too sharp for him. (5/1)
Alaflak (IRE), who looked fitter for a run on the Flat earlier in the month, recovered well from a mistake four out to be in a challenging position at the next, but was soon done with. (11/2: 3/1-6/1)
3946 Night Escapade (IRE) found everything happening far too quickly, and surely needs a stiffer test than this. (33/1)

Friar's Oak is a poor mover, but this was an improvement on what he had previously achieved. (100/1)

T/Plpt: £178.00 (86.29 Tckts). T/Qdpt: £5.60 (184.64 Tckts) Dk

4295-MARKET RASEN (R-H) (Good to firm, Good patches)
Saturday May 31st
WEATHER: fine & sunny

4795 'END OF SEASON' (S) H'CAP HURDLE (0-90) (4, 5 & 6-Y.O) (Class G)
6-35 (6-35) **2m 1f 110y (8 hdls)** £1,852.50 (£515.00: £247.50) GOING minus 0.17 sec per fur (G)

	Horse	Dist	Pos	SP	RR	SF
3940[5]	**Lucy Tufty (71)** (JPearce) **6-11-6** PCarberry (trckd ldrs: led 2 out: drvn out)	—	1	7/2[3]	54	7
4556[4]	**Master Showman (IRE) (58)** (DJWintle) **6-10-7** RichardGuest (chsd ldrs: rdn 3 out: ev ch next: nt qckn towards fin)	½	2	20/1	41	—
4651[4]	**Hawanafa (71)** (MissKMGeorge) **4-11-1v[1]** RDunwoody (led to 2 out: ev ch last: kpt on same pce)	nk	3	3/1[2]	53	1
4451[2]	**Irie Mon (IRE) (78)** (MPBielby) **5-11-13** JRailton (hld up: hdwy 5th: sn chsng ldrs: rdn appr 2 out: sn btn)	5	4	7/1	56	9
4732[5]	**Summer Villa (73)** (KGWingrove) **5-11-8b** JRyan (hld up: effrt 5th: nvr nr ldrs)	9	5	8/1	43	—
4732*	**Ajdar (72)** (OBrennan) **6-11-4**(3) RMassey (lw: chsd ldrs: rdn 5th: sn wknd)	4	6	9/4[1]	38	—
4468[10]	**Catwalker (IRE) (51)** (HJMWebb) **6-10-0b** MRichards (chsd ldrs tl wknd after 3 out)	9	7	20/1	9	—
4645[5]	**Woodlands Lad Too (51)** (PAPritchard) **5-10-0b[1]** TJMurphy (hld up & bhd: drvn along 4th: sn t.o: p.u bef 2 out)		P	33/1	—	—
				(SP 114.1%)		**8 Rn**

4m 14.3 (11.30) CSF £57.50 CT £211.29 TOTE £4.90: £1.40 £4.80 £1.20 (£78.70) OWNER Mr G. H. Tufts (NEWMARKET) BRED C. R. Franks
LONG HANDICAP Catwalker (IRE) 9-13 Woodlands Lad Too 9-8
WEIGHT FOR AGE 4yo-5lb
Bt in 3,000 gns
3940 Lucy Tufty, third in a selling handicap on the All-Weather seven days earlier, responded to Carberry's tender handling. He never picked up his whip on the run-in even though three were almost in line, and persuaded her to do just enough near the finish. (7/2)
4453 Master Showman (IRE) ran easily his best race so far over hurldes. (20/1)
3590* Hawanafa, dropped in class, set out to make all and battled on when headed. (3/1)
4451 Irie Mon (IRE) as usual wore a tongue-strap. (7/1)
4732* Ajdar, who is not very big, suddenly came under pressure at the fifth and soon called it a day. (9/4: op 6/4)

4796 ROGER JOHNSTONE & PARTNERS NOVICES' CHASE (5-Y.O+) (Class D)
7-05 (7-05) **2m 4f (15 fncs)** £3,803.00 (£1,139.00: £547.00: £251.00) GOING minus 0.17 sec per fur (G)

	Horse	Dist	Pos	SP	RR	SF
4611[2]	**Eid (USA)** (MrsSJSmith) **8-11-0** RichardGuest (trckd ldrs: led 4 out: clr last: pushed out)	—	1	4/7[1]	84	2
1083[5]	**Osgathorpe** (RTate) **10-11-0** MrsFNeedham (lw: trckd ldrs: shkn up 10th: ev ch 3 out: j.lft & outpcd 2 out)	12	2	11/4[2]	74	—
4769[3]	**Quixall Crossett (56)** (EMCaine) **12-11-0** GaryLyons (led to 4 out: sn drvn along: one pce)	1½	3	10/1[3]	73	—
4159[P]	**Morcat (70)** (CIRatcliffe) **8-10-9** MrCMulhall (chsd ldrs: hit 5th: lost pl 11th)	28	4	12/1	46	—
				(SP 107.1%)		**4 Rn**

5m 4.6 (13.60) CSF £2.33 TOTE £1.40 (£1.70) OWNER Mr N. Wilby (BINGLEY) BRED Ralph C. Wilson, Jr.
4611 Eid (USA), who loves this fast ground, proved much too good for these slow horses. (4/7: op 4/11)
1083 Osgathorpe, who has won four point-to-points this time, proved no match once the race began in earnest. (11/4)
4769 Quixall Crossett is still a maiden after fifty-eight starts. He jumps and stays but has nothing in the way of finishing speed. (10/1)

4797 LINCOLNSHIRE BUSINESS DEVELOPMENT CENTRE H'CAP CHASE (0-110) (5-Y.O+) (Class E)
7-35 (7-35) **2m 1f 110y (13 fncs)** £2,880.25 (£862.00: £413.50: £189.25) GOING minus 0.17 sec per fur (G)

	Horse	Dist	Pos	SP	RR	SF
4629[4]	**Tapatch (IRE) (87)** (MWEasterby) **9-11-10b** PCarberry (trckd ldrs: hrd rdn & kpt on flat: led post)	—	1	6/4[1]	95	27
4520[2]	**Thats the Life (78)** (TRGeorge) **12-11-1** RJohnson (t: mde most to 4 out: led 2 out: jst ct)	s.h	2	9/4[2]	86	18
4297[5]	**Dash To The Phone (USA) (71)** (KAMorgan) **5-10-2** RSupple (w ldr: led 4 out to 2 out: wknd appr last)	8	3	10/1	72	—
4254[3]	**Fichu (USA) (82)** (MrsLRichards) **9-11-5** MRichards (outpcd 6th: lost pl 9th: fin lame)	dist	4	5/1[3]	—	—
883[2]	**The Yokel (70)** (BPJBaugh) **11-10-4**(3) PHenley (outpcd 7th: sn drvn along: p.u lame bef 3 out)		P	6/1	—	—
				(SP 110.8%)		**5 Rn**

4m 22.8 (7.80) CSF £5.05 TOTE £2.50: £1.40 £1.80 (£2.40) OWNER Miss V. Foster (SHERIFF HUTTON) BRED London T'bred Services & M. McCalmont in Ireland
WEIGHT FOR AGE 5yo-6lb
4629 Tapatch (IRE) had everything bar the kitchen sink thrown at him on the run-in, and his brilliant jockey forced his head in front right on the line. (6/4)
4520 Thats the Life seemed to hang fire on the run-in, and was just caught. (9/4)
4297 Dash To The Phone (USA) was jumping without any confidence. (10/1)
4254 Fichu (USA) dropped right away over the last three and finished lame. (5/1)

4798 H. & L. GARAGES H'CAP HURDLE (0-120) (4-Y.O+) (Class D)
8-05 (8-05) **2m 3f 110y (10 hdls)** £2,951.75 (£884.00: £424.50: £194.75) GOING minus 0.17 sec per fur (G)

	Horse	Dist	Pos	SP	RR	SF
4696*	**Jamaican Flight (USA) (100)** (MrsSLamyman) **4-10-8** JRailton (mde most: j.big: mstke 3rd: blnd last: styd on wl)	—	1	9/4[1]	82	16
4510[2]	**Out on a Promise (IRE) (110)** (LLungo) **5-11-9** RSupple (hld up & plld hrd: hdwy 6th: chal 3 out: nt qckn appr last)	3½	2	3/1[2]	89	28
4510[4]	**Nashville Star (USA) (92)** (RMathew) **6-10-5v** AThornton (chsd ldr: outpcd fr 3 out)	8	3	14/1	65	4
4501[7]	**Red Jam Jar (91)** (SBBell) **12-10-4** KJohnson (lw: rdn: w ldr: rdn & outpcd 3 out: n.d)	1¾	4	14/1	62	1
4550[5]	**El Don (112)** (MJRyan) **5-11-11** JRyan (hld up: effrt 6th: sn drvn along: no imp)	8	5	5/1	77	16
4708[3]	**Boston Man (88)** (RDEWoodhouse) **6-10-1** PCarberry (prom: drvn along 6th: lost pl after next)	22	6	9/2[3]	35	—

Runner	Dist	Pos	SP		
4550[7] **Mim-Lou-and (106)** (MissHCKnight) **5-11-5** JCulloty (drvn along 5th: sn wl outpcd: lost pl 7th: bhd whn blnd 2 out: p.u bef last)		P	8/1	—	—

(SP 115.1%) **7 Rn**

4m 40.3 (7.30) CSF £9.00 TOTE £3.00: £2.00 £1.80 (£3.10) OWNER Mr P. Lamyman (LINCOLN) BRED Foxfield
WEIGHT FOR AGE 4yo-5lb
IN-FOCUS: **This was a winner on his last ride for Jamie Railton. In a ten year career he managed two hundred and twenty-five winners, his best tally being thirty-three in 1992-3.**
4696* Jamaican Flight (USA) gave his hurdles plenty of air but, three lengths up, he almost threw it away when blundering at the last. (9/4)
4510 Out on a Promise (IRE), having his first outing for his new trainer, would not settle. A stronger run-race would have suited him much better. (3/1)
4510 Nashville Star (USA), who wore a cross-noseband, could not dominate. (14/1)

4799 GEOSTAR HUNTERS' CHASE (5-Y.O+) (Class H)

8-35 (8-36) **2m 6f 110y (15 fncs)** £1,954.00 (£544.00: £262.00) GOING minus 0.17 sec per fur (G)

Runner	Dist	Pos	SP	RR	SF
4713[2] **Cumberland Blues (IRE)** (MrsALockwood) **8-11-11**(7) MissADeniel (led to 4 out: styd on to ld flat: hld on towards fin)	—	1	11/8[1]	94	27
4748[6] **Indie Rock** (RTate) **7-11-3**(7) MrsFNeedham (sn trckng ldrs: hit 7th: led 4 out: hit last: sn hdd: kpt on wl)	½	2	9/2[3]	86	19
4449[2] **Kambalda Rambler** (MrsHelenHarvey) **13-12-3**(7) MrRArmson (wnt prom 8th: ev ch & hrd rdn 4 out: outpcd fr 2 out)	10	3	9/2[3]	93	26
4748[2] **Shuil Saor** (MissPFitton) **10-11-3**(7) MrCMulhall (hdwy u.p 10th: 4th & hrd rdn whn blnd 3 out)	5	4	4/1[2]	75	8
Earl Gray (MrsALockwood) **10-11-3b**(7) MissJEastwood (in tch: wl outpcd 10th: n.d)	16	5	33/1	64	—
4758[P] **Alpha One** (DFBassett) **12-12-0**(7) MissKDiMarte (chsd ldrs: drvn along 7th: sn lost pl: t.o)	dist	6	33/1	—	—
Needwood Joker (RGreen) **6-11-3**(7) MrKGreen (unruly s: a bhd: t.o 4 out)	1¼	7	40/1	—	—
4545[P] **Secret Truth** (AndrewMartin) **8-10-12**(7) MrAndrewMartin (mstkes: trckd ldrs: 4th & wkng whn hit 10th: sn bhd: p.u bef 3 out)		P	33/1	—	—
4607[U] **Ship the Builder** (PeterMaddison) **8-11-3**(7) MrSBrisby (j.b: lost tch 7th: t.o whn p.u bef 2 out)		P	16/1	—	—
Auntie Chris (MrsRGee) **7-10-12**(7) MrPGee (w.r.s & uns rdr)		U	25/1	—	—

(SP 119.5%) **10 Rn**

5m 39.5 (12.50) CSF £7.23 TOTE £2.00: £1.10 £1.90 £1.70 (£5.10) OWNER Mr John Holdroyd (MALTON) BRED P. Browne
4713 Cumberland Blues (IRE) looked cooked when overtaken four out but, most capably handled, he regained the advantage at the last and did just enough. He really needs further. (11/8)
Indie Rock, who had finished well behind Shuil Saor at Wetherby five days earlier, set sail for home four out. Under pressure when hitting the last, the winning combination proved too strong near the line. (9/2)
4449 Kambalda Rambler, now a veteran, moved upsides four out. Despite his rider's over-enthusiastic use of the whip, he was left behind over the last two. (9/2)
4748 Shuil Saor ran out of his skin when runner-up at Wetherby, but was already in trouble when he blundered at the third last. Time may show that his Wetherby effort was a fluke. (4/1)

4800 'SUMMER FESTIVAL COMES NEXT' MAIDEN HURDLE (4-Y.O+) (Class E)

9-05 (9-05) **2m 1f 110y (8 hdls)** £2,547.50 (£710.00: £342.50) GOING minus 0.17 sec per fur (G)

Runner	Dist	Pos	SP	RR	SF
2898[16] **Rushen Raider** (KWHogg) **5-11-5** RGaritty (hld up: hdwy 4th: effrt 3 out: led after last: rdn out)	—	1	5/1[2]	69	24
2825[5] **Fresh Fruit Daily** (PAKelleway) **5-11-0** KGaule (lw: led: hit 3 out: hdd & jumped path after last: no ex)	2½	2	8/11[1]	62	17
337[3] **Silverdale Lad** (KWHogg) **6-11-5** MFoster (hld up: hdwy 4th: ev ch 3 out: one pce appr next)	8	3	11/2[3]	59	14
4696[5] **Orchard King (83)** (OBrennan) **7-11-2**(3) RMassey (chsd ldrs: ev ch & rdn 3 out: wknd appr next)	8	4	5/1[2]	52	7
4638[4] **Can She Can Can** (CSmith) **5-11-0** MRanger (lw: chsd ldrs: rdn 5th: wknd next)	3	5	14/1	44	—
4719[P] **Dramatic Pass (IRE)** (MCChapman) **8-11-5** WWorthington (sn bhd: t.o fr 3 out)	dist	6	66/1	—	—
3324[P] **Good Venture** (LRLloyd-James) **6-11-0** NSmith (nt j.w: sn bhd: t.o 3 out)	dist	7	50/1	—	—
Ilikehim (RFMarvin) **10-11-5** MrNKent (trckd ldrs tl wknd qckly 4th: sn bhd: t.o whn p.u bef last)		P	66/1	—	—

(SP 118.2%) **8 Rn**

4m 9.9 (6.90) CSF £8.90 TOTE £5.90: £1.40 £1.10 £1.20 (£5.40) OWNER Mrs Thelma White (ISLE OF MAN) BRED M. H. D. Madden and Partners
730 Rushen Raider, who won four staying handicaps on the Flat last year, enjoyed a change of luck over hurdles, and boosted his ultra-reliable jockey's final score to sixty-two, easily his best ever. (5/1)
2825 Fresh Fruit Daily was taken the long way down to the start. Flattening the third-last, her measure had been taken when she jumped a crossing after the final flight. (8/11: 4/5-evens)
337 Silverdale Lad possibly needed the outing after an absence of two hundred and ninety-four days. (11/2)

T/Plpt: £8.00 (1,099.67 Tckts). T/Qdpt: £1.70 (257.83 Tckts) WG

4789-STRATFORD-ON-AVON (L-H) (Good to firm, Chases Good patches)

Saturday May 31st

WEATHER: warm & sunny

4801 J. P. SEAFOODS NOVICES' HURDLE (4-Y.O+) (Class D)

2-25 (2-31) **2m 6f 110y (12 hdls)** £3,183.00 (£888.00: £429.00) GOING minus 0.17 sec per fur (G)

Runner	Dist	Pos	SP	RR	SF
4650[2] **Bullens Bay (IRE) (98)** (BJLlewellyn) **8-10-13** MrJLLlewellyn (lw: hld up & bhd: hdwy appr 9th: led 2 out: rdn out)	—	1	4/1[2]	67	17
4651[3] **Santella Cape** (NJHawke) **4-10-7** JRailton (lw: hld up: hdwy appr 8th: mstke 3 out: one pce fr 2 out)	3½	2	15/2[3]	65	9
4625[10] **Faithlegg (IRE)** (NJHenderson) **6-10-8** MAFitzgerald (a.p: led appr 8th to 9th: led 3 out to 2 out: one pce)	3	3	33/1	57	7
157[3] **Mountain Leader** (DMHyde) **7-10-13** BPowell (led tl appr 8th: led 9th to 3 out: wknd appr 2 out)	2	4	33/1	61	11
4290[5] **Rapid Liner (51)** (RJBaker) **4-10-7** VSlattery (hld up: rdn appr 8th: bhd fr 9th)	9	5	100/1	55	—
4625[4] **Cool Harry (USA) (75)** (HEHaynes) **6-10-6**(7) MrSDurack (prom tl wknd after 3 out)	2½	6	12/1	53	3
4638[7] **Derring Well** (JWPayne) **7-10-8** KGaule (hdwy after 7th: wknd 9th: t.o)	24	7	100/1	31	—
4403* **Eau de Cologne (111)** (MrsLRichards) **5-11-11** MRichards (lw: prom: w ldr whn fell 7th)		F	4/5[1]	—	—
Royal Silver (BPreece) **6-10-6**(7) JMogford (bkwd: hld up & plld hrd: fell 4th)		F	16/1	—	—

				SP		
289P	**Five From Home (IRE)** (JJoseph) **9-10-13** DSkyrme (bkwd: dropped rr 5th: sn t.o: p.u bef 8th)		**P**	33/1	—	—
4704U	**Bunny Hare (IRE)** (JJBirkett) **9-10-13** LO'Hara (bhd: rdn after 7th: sn t.o: p.u bef 9th)		**P**	100/1	—	—
42306	***Lord Cool (IRE)*** (CPEBrooks) **6-10-13** GBradley (Withdrawn not under Starter's orders: unruly s)		**W**	10/1	—	—

(SP 121.8%) **11 Rn**

5m 25.5 (9.50) CSF £26.29 TOTE £4.70: £1.20 £1.40 £5.10 (£10.40) OWNER Mr J. Milton (BARGOED) BRED John Lordan
WEIGHT FOR AGE 4yo-6lb
4650 Bullens Bay (IRE) did not mind this extra quarter-mile, and showed no tendency to hang on this occasion. (4/1: op 5/2)
4651 Santella Cape seems to be going the right way. (15/2: 9/2-8/1)
Faithlegg (IRE), who had shown ability in a Down Royal bumper over two years ago, ran by far her best race since coming to this country. (33/1)
157 Mountain Leader made a satisfactory comeback on his first outing for almost a year. (33/1)
4625 Cool Harry (USA) (12/1: op 7/1)

4802 DEVELOPER OF THE YEAR 1997 RICHARDSONS H'CAP CHASE (0-135) (5-Y.O+) (Class C)

2-55 (3-00) **2m 5f 110y (16 fncs)** £4,532.50 (£1,360.00: £655.00: £302.50) GOING minus 0.54 sec per fur (GF)

				SP	RR	SF
4541F	**Stately Home (IRE) (135)** (PBowen) **6-12-0** NWilliamson (j.w: led 4th: clr 2 out: easily)	—	**1**	8/1	146+	60
4621*	**Formal Invitation (IRE) (122)** (DNicholson) **8-11-1** RJohnson (lw: hld up: mstke 5th: hdwy 8th: hit 11th & 12th: sn hrd rdn: ev ch 3 out: no imp)	3½	**2**	13/8 1	130	44
46094	**Seod Rioga (IRE) (114)** (SMellor) **8-10-7** RDunwoody (hld up: hdwy 11th: ev ch 3 out: one pce)	1½	**3**	9/1	121	35
42393	**All for Luck (119)** (MCPipe) **12-10-12** APMcCoy (bhd: rdn 9th: nvr nr to chal)	3½	**4**	15/2 3	124	38
4379F	**Over the Pole (110)** (PRChamings) **10-10-0**(3)ow3 MrCBonner (lw: hld up: hdwy 8th: wknd 3 out)	3½	**5**	8/1	112	23
45095	**Strong Medicine (129)** (KCBailey) **10-11-8** AThornton (lw: prom to 3 out)	13	**6**	20/1	121	35
4747*	**Glemot (IRE) (136)** (KCBailey) **9-11-10**(5) 6x MrRWakley (led: hit 1st: hdd 4th: cl 3rd whn fell 3 out)		**F**	8/1	—	—
46242	**Factor Ten (IRE) (122)** (MissHCKnight) **9-11-1** JFTitley (hld up: hdwy 8th: hit 10th: wknd 12th: t.o whn p.u bef 2 out)		**P**	11/2 2	—	—

(SP 113.3%) **8 Rn**

5m 4.9 (-7.10) CSF £20.14 CT £109.69 TOTE £6.80: £1.70 £1.50 £1.90 (£6.90) Trio £28.10 OWNER Mr P. Bowen (HAVERFORDWEST) BRED Ash Hill Stud
4541 Stately Home (IRE) lifted the Channel 4 Trophy by recording his tenth win of the season from twenty-three starts. A credit to all concerned, he will not rest on his laurels and will go to Market Rasen in a fortnight, before a possible tilt at the Galway Plate. (8/1)
4621* Formal Invitation (IRE), 12lb higher than his previous handicap win, did not jump anywhere near as well as the winner. (13/8)
4247 Seod Rioga (IRE), 4lb higher than when winning at Chepstow, has taken time to get his jumping together since his fall at Ayr. (9/1)
4239 All for Luck had slipped to a mark 11lb lower than when winning this race last season. (15/2: 5/1-8/1)
4747* Glemot (IRE) (8/1: op 5/1)

4803 A. C. LLOYD H'CAP HURDLE (0-115) (5-Y.O+) (Class E)

3-25 (3-26) **3m 3f (14 hdls)** £2,430.00 (£680.00: £330.00) GOING minus 0.17 sec per fur (G)

				SP	RR	SF
4740*	**Doualago (FR) (107)** (MCPipe) **7-11-11b** APMcCoy (led: reminders after 5th: rdn & qcknd appr 10th: clr 3 out: eased flat)	—	**1**	2/1 1	91+	39
41785	**Holy Joe (98)** (DBurchell) **15-11-2** DJBurchell (hld up: hdwy 6th: chsd wnr appr 3 out: no imp: fin lame)	4	**2**	14/1	80	28
45362	**Derring Bridge (93)** (MrsSMJohnson) **7-10-11** RJohnson (hld up & bhd: stdy hdwy 6th: one pce fr 11th)	6	**3**	8/1	71	19
46223	**St Ville (109)** (RHBuckler) **11-11-13** BPowell (hld up: hdwy 9th: wknd 11th)	nk	**4**	9/1	87	35
45632	**Stormy Session (84)** (NATwiston-Davies) **7-10-2** CLlewellyn (chsd wnr tl hit 4th: hit 9th: wnt 2nd 10th: wknd appr 3 out)	s.h	**5**	5/1 3	62	10
4622*	**Jimbalou (90)** (RGBrazington) **14-10-5**(3) RMassey (hld up & bhd: mstke 6th: wknd appr 3 out: p.u bef 2 out)		**P**	7/2 2	—	—
46305	**Albertito (FR) (87)** (RHollinshead) **10-10-5** SWynne (hld up & bhd: sme hdwy appr 8th: wknd 11th: p.u after 3 out)		**P**	33/1	—	—
4524*	**Apachee Flower (87)** (HSHowe) **7-10-5**ow2 MAFitzgerald (dropped rr 5th: t.o 8th: p.u & dismntd bef 10th)		**P**	7/1	—	—
44186	**Uluru (IRE) (94)** (CPMorlock) **9-10-12** JAMcCarthy (prom: chsd wnr 4th to 10th: wkng whn mstke 11th: p.u after 3 out)		**P**	16/1	—	—
46297	**Nickle Joe (85)** (MTate) **11-9-10**(7)ow2 MrOMcPhail (s.s: bhd: rdn appr 8th: sn t.o: p.u bef 11th)		**P**	50/1	—	—
46467	**Little Tincture (IRE) (84)** (MrsTJMcInnesSkinner) **7-10-2**ow2 GUpton (a bhd: t.o 9th: p.u bef 2 out)		**P**	50/1	—	—

(SP 125.2%) **11 Rn**

6m 26.3 (7.30) CSF £29.63 CT £181.53 TOTE £3.20: £1.60 £2.80 £1.90 (£28.60) Trio £54.20 OWNER Martin Pipe Racing Club (WELLINGTON) BRED Monsieur et Madame Bernard le Douarin
LONG HANDICAP Little Tincture (IRE) 8-11
4740* Doualago (FR) was reverting to timber off a mark 18lb lower than when completing a hat-trick over fences at Uttoxeter five days ago. (2/1)
3915 Holy Joe unfortunately finished lame, and one can only hope we have not seen the last of this grand old servant. (14/1)
4536 Derring Bridge could make no impression on the runner-up over the last four flights, let alone the winner. (8/1)
4622 St Ville looked in the Handicapper's grip here. (9/1)
4563 Stormy Session had been raised 6lb for his narrow defeat at Huntingdon. (5/1)

4804 SPILLERS HORSE FEEDS LADIES' HUNTERS' CHASE (5-Y.O+) (Class H)

3-55 (4-01) **3m (18 fncs)** £2,136.00 (£596.00: £288.00) GOING minus 0.54 sec per fur (GF)

				SP	RR	SF
4713F	**Thank U Jim** (MrsGSunter) **9-10-7**(7) MissTJackson (led to 4th: led appr 14th: clr 2 out: r.o)	—	**1**	16/1	107	20
4241*	**Final Pride** (MrsCHiggon) **11-10-9**(3) MissPJones (lw: led 4th tl appr 14th: mstke 4 out: one pce fr 3 out)	3½	**2**	5/6 1	103	16
42414	**Wake Up Luv** (RWilliams) **12-10-7**(7) MissPCooper (wl bhd tl styd on fr 2 out: fin wl)	4	**3**	33/1	102	15
4551P	**Mister Gebo** (MrsDJDyson) **12-10-7**(7) MissCDyson (wl bhd whn mstkes 6th & hit 7th: wnt poor 3rd 3 out: j.lft 2 out: nt rch ldrs)	½	**4**	50/1	102	15
	Old Mill Stream (RBarber) **11-10-7**(7) MissPGundry (lw: s.s: hit 3rd: wl bhd whn mstke 7th: t.o)	20	**5**	5/1 3	88	1
45042	**What Chance (IRE)** (MrsHMobley) **9-10-5**(7) MrsKSunderland (wl bhd whn mstke 11th: t.o)	24	**6**	16/1	70	—
4560U	**No Panic** (CRJohnson) **13-10-7**(7) MissAMeakins (t.o fr 5th: virtually p.u flat)	dist	**7**	66/1	—	—
45512	**Sams Heritage** (RTBaimbridge) **13-10-9**(5) MissADare (lw: chsd ldrs: 3rd whn p.u lame bef 12th)		**P**	11/4 2	—	—
4543P	**Hickelton Lad** (DLWilliams) **13-10-10**(7) MissSDuckett (s.s: wl bhd whn mstke 7th: t.o whn p.u bef 2 out)		**P**	50/1	—	—

Celtic Daughter (HWLavis) **8-10-2**(7) MissEJJones (Withdrawn not under Starter's orders: vet's advice at s).... **W** 16/1 — —
(SP 123.9%) **9 Rn**

5m 53.1 (1.10) CSF £29.46 TOTE £15.00: £1.90 £1.10 £5.00 (£18.60) Trio £63.80 OWNER Mrs G. Sunter (FERRYHILL) BRED G. T. Sunter
Thank U Jim, twice a winner between the flags, had failed to complete in his two previous starts under Rules. Never putting a foot wrong, he showed how well he stays by simply refusing to leave the front-running favourite alone. (16/1)
4241* Final Pride did not have things all her own way this time and, after missing out at the final ditch, was always finding it a bit of a struggle.(5/6)
4241 Wake Up Luv again finished closer to the runner-up, and fairly flew from the final fence to snatch third place. (33/1)
Mister Gebo, like most of the field, did not attempt to go the furious pace set by the two leaders. (50/1)
Old Mill Stream (5/1: 4/1-6/1)

4805 HORSE AND HOUND CUP FINAL CHAMPION HUNTERS' CHASE (5-Y.O+) (Class B)

4-30 (4-30) **3m 4f (21 fncs)** £12,575.00 (£3,800.00: £1,850.00: £875.00) GOING minus 0.54 sec per fur (GF)

				SP	RR	SF
4325*	**Celtic Abbey** (MissVenetiaWilliams) **9-12-0** MrDSJones (sn chsng ldr: led 10th: qckND clr 15th: r.o wl fr 3 out)	—	**1**	13/8 1	129	62
4380*	**Bitofamixup (IRE)** (MJRoberts) **6-12-0** MrPHacking (hld up: hdwy 13th: mstke 14th: wnt 2nd after 16th: ev ch 3 out: no imp)	8	**2**	9/4 2	124	57
4647²	**Mr Boston** (MrsMReveley) **12-12-0** MrNWilson (lw: hld up: hdwy 10th: wknd 16th)	17	**3**	8/1	114	47
4617*	**Glen Oak** (DGDuggan) **12-12-0** MrJMPritchard (prom to 15th)	10	**4**	40/1	108	41
4213ᴾ	**Cab on Target** (MrsMReveley) **11-12-0** MrSSwiers (lw: hld up: hdwy 6th: 5th whn blnd 16th: nt rcvr)	8	**5**	7/2 3	103	36
4616ᴮ	**Cape Cottage** (DJCaro) **13-12-0** MrAPhillips (hdwy 10th: wknd 15th)	1¼	**6**	40/1	102	35
4560³	**Rusty Bridge** (MrsSMJohnson) **10-12-0** MrRBurton (led to 10th: wknd qckly after 13th: sn t.o)	22	**7**	33/1	89	22
4617²	**Sirisat** (MissTOBlazey) **13-12-0** MissTBlazey (prom to 15th: t.o)	6	**8**	66/1	86	19
4545*	**Magnolia Man** (MsDCole) **11-12-0** MrNHarris (bhd: hit 9th: t.o whn p.u bef 4 out)		**P**	16/1	—	—
4634⁵	**Abbotsham** (OJCarter) **12-12-0** MrRThornton (hit 1st & 3rd: hdwy 11th: wknd 15th: t.o: p.u bef 17th)		**P**	50/1	—	—
4545²	**Lucky Christopher** (GJTarry) **12-12-0** MrGTarry (mid div: blnd 7th: mstke 8th: sn bhd: t.o whn p.u bef last)		**P**	25/1	—	—

(SP 123.2%) **11 Rn**

6m 50.2 (-9.80) CSF £5.32 TOTE £2.80: £1.30 £1.50 £2.50 (£4.40) Trio £10.50 OWNER Mr G. J. Powell (HEREFORD) BRED J. P. Powell
4325* Celtic Abbey, given a breather in the back straight, pulled away from the third last having allowed the runner-up to close the gap. (13/8)
4380* Bitofamixup (IRE) got within a length of the winner three out, but his rival had been given a breather and there was no answer when Celtic Abbey kicked again. This trip might be beyond his best at this stage of his career. (9/4)
4647 Mr Boston was already feeling the pace turning into the back straight for the final time. (8/1)

4806 WILLIAM YOUNGER H'CAP CHASE (0-125) (5-Y.O+) (Class D)

5-05 (5-05) **3m 4f (21 fncs)** £3,626.00 (£1,088.00: £524.00: £242.00) GOING minus 0.54 sec per fur (GF)

				SP	RR	SF
4557³	**Diamond Fort (95)** (JCMcConnochie) **12-10-5** MAFitzgerald (lost pl 6th: hdwy 17th: wnt 2nd 2 out: styd on to ld nr fin)	—	**1**	7/1	106	34
3699⁶	**Special Account (94)** (CRBarwell) **11-10-4** BFenton (hld up: hdwy 17th: led appr 3 out: clr 2 out: hung lft & wknd flat: ct nr fin)	½	**2**	10/1	105	33
4467⁴	**Don't Light Up (110)** (MissVenetiaWilliams) **11-11-3v**(3) MrRThornton (sn prom: j.slowly 7th: mstkes 15th & 16th: led briefly after 4 out: wknd appr 2 out)	13	**3**	20/1	113	41
4609³	**Peruvian Gale (IRE) (90)** (MrsSJSmith) **8-9-11**(3) GFRyan (lw: a.p: led 15th: mstke 4 out: sn hdd: wknd 3 out)	3	**4**	7/1	91	19
4418³	**Smith Too (IRE) (102)** (MrsJPitman) **9-10-12** DLeahy (hld up: hdwy 17th: wknd 3 out)	nk	**5**	5/1 2	103	31
4722³	**Banntown Bill (IRE) (97)** (MCPipe) **8-10-7v** APMcCoy (w ldr: led 10th to 15th: wknd qckly 3 out: t.o)	dist	**6**	6/1 3	—	—
4697²	**Harristown Lady (101)** (GBBalding) **10-10-11b** BClifford (mid div: j.slowly 16th: sn t.o: p.u bef 3 out)		**P**	7/1	—	—
4557*	**Bally Clover (114)** (MissVenetiaWilliams) **10-11-10** NWilliamson (nvr gng wl: a bhd: t.o whn p.u bef 14th)		**P**	4/1 1	—	—
4344⁶	**Merivel (110)** (RRowe) **10-11-6** DO'Sullivan (bhd: mstke 14th: t.o whn p.u & dismntd bef 17th)		**P**	25/1	—	—
4640²	**Fight to Win (USA) (93)** (LPGrassick) **9-9-10**(7)ow3 MrOMcPhail (a bhd: hit 9th: t.o whn p.u bef 2 out)		**P**	33/1	—	—
4655ᴾ	**Balasani (FR) (90)** (JGO'Neill) **11-10-0** SCurran (bhd whn j.lft 5th: mstke 12th: t.o whn p.u bef 15th)		**P**	33/1	—	—
4763ᵁ	**Woodlands Genhire (90)** (PAPritchard) **12-10-0b** CLlewellyn (led to 10th: wknd 12th: mstke 14th: t.o whn p.u bef 4 out)		**P**	33/1	—	—

(SP 115.0%) **12 Rn**

6m 52.5 (-7.50) CSF £60.09 CT £1,199.18 TOTE £8.30: £2.30 £2.90 £6.70 (£33.50) Trio £56.70 OWNER Mrs R. E. Stocks (STRATFORD) BRED Mrs M. Lowry
LONG HANDICAP Fight to Win (USA) 9-4 Balasani (FR) 9-1 Woodlands Genhire 9-1
4557 Diamond Fort again had to contend with fast ground, but relished every yard of this longer trip. (7/1)
3153 Special Account seemed to have this in the bag until becoming leg-weary on the run-in. (10/1)
Don't Light Up was back down the mark from which he won at Towcester in March last year. (20/1)
4448 Peruvian Gale (IRE) found an error at the final ditch the beginning of the end, and may have found this trip beyond him. (7/1)
4418 Smith Too (IRE) was by no means disgraced on this return to fences. (5/1)
4557* Bally Clover failed to handle the fast ground. (4/1: op 9/4)

4807 JONES SPRING'S DARLASTON NOVICES' H'CAP HURDLE (0-100) (4-Y.O+) (Class E)

5-35 (5-35) **2m 110y (9 hdls)** £2,556.00 (£716.00: £348.00) GOING minus 0.17 sec per fur (G)

				SP	RR	SF
4552²	**Cuillin Caper (72)** (TRWatson) **5-10-5**ow2 MAFitzgerald (lw: a.p: led 2 out: all out)	—	**1**	8/1 3	53	15
3663⁴	**Happy Brave (77)** (PDCundell) **5-10-10** LHarvey (hld up: hdwy 5th: hrd rdn appr last: r.o one pce flat)	2	**2**	16/1	56	20
4532²	**Tiutchev (93)** (MissHCKnight) **4-11-4**(3) MrRThornton (lw: hld up: hdwy 6th: led after 3 out to 2 out: one pce)	4	**3**	4/1 1	68	27
4743³	**Khalikhoum (IRE) (83)** (SirJohnBarlowBt) **4-10-6**(5) DJKavanagh (a.p: led 6th tl after 3 out: one pce)	hd	**4**	11/1	58	17
4558ᶠ	**Reverse Thrust (79)** (PRHedger) **6-10-5**(7) MClinton (s.s: stdy hdwy fr 4th: wknd appr 2 out)	6	**5**	13/2 2	48	12
4226⁷	**Anif (USA) (68)** (JJoseph) **6-10-1**ow1 DSkyrme (rdn & hdwy appr 3 out: wknd appr 2 out)	14	**6**	25/1	24	—
4636³	**Holkham Bay (67)** (LWordingham) **5-9-9b**(5) XAizpuru (led to 6th: wknd after 3 out)	½	**7**	25/1	22	—
4403⁷	**Bay Fair (85)** (MRBosley) **5-11-4** SMcNeill (nvr nr ldrs)	8	**8**	16/1	32	—
4401³	**Scalp 'em (IRE) (67)** (DrPPritchard) **9-10-0** DrPPritchard (hdwy 4th: wknd appr 6th)	2	**9**	25/1	13	—
4003⁶	**Kevasingo (84)** (RJBaker) **5-11-3** VSlattery (a bhd)	¾	**10**	16/1	29	—
4443³	**Tango Man (IRE) (73)** (JGMO'Shea) **5-10-6** APMcCoy (prom: eased whn btn after 3 out)	3½	**11**	4/1 1	14	—
4525⁶	**Lucky Archer (90)** (PJHobbs) **4-11-4** NWilliamson (sme hdwy whn mstke 3 out: sn wknd: t.o)	10	**12**	13/2 2	22	—

4620[4] **Bold Time Monkey (67)** (MTate) **6-10-0** CLlewellyn (a bhd: t.o)......26	**13**	20/1	—	—
4512[7] **Andsome Boy (84)** (CRBarwell) **4-10-12** BFenton (w.r.s: t.o tl p.u bef 3 out)......	**P**	11/1	—	—
4743[6] **Amazon Heights (70)** (LPGrassick) **5-9-10**(7)ow3 MrOMcPhail (a bhd: t.o whn p.u bef 3 out)......	**P**	33/1	—	—

(SP 131.3%) **15 Rn**

3m 52.5 (5.50) CSF £116.41 CT £553.21 TOTE £8.60: £2.40 £6.30 £2.30 (£86.90) Trio £60.90 OWNER Manor Farm Stud (Rutland) (FORD) BRED W. A. Bromley
LONG HANDICAP Anif (USA) 9-7 Scalp 'em (IRE) 9-9 Holkham Bay 9-8 Amazon Heights 9-1
WEIGHT FOR AGE 4yo-5lb
IN-FOCUS: **This was David Skyrme's final ride. He rode ninety-seven winners during his career.**
4552 Cuillin Caper, a shade more aggressively ridden this time, found what was required to keep the second at bay in the closing stages. (8/1: op 5/1)
3663 Happy Brave could not quite sustain his effort towards the finish. (16/1)
4532 Tiutchev seemed set to go very close on the home turn, but failed to deliver the goods. (4/1: op 5/2)
4743 Khalikhoum (IRE) produced another good run following his third on Monday. (11/1: 7/1-12/1)
4558 Reverse Thrust rather overdid the waiting tactics at the start. (13/2)

T/Plpt: £251.20 (70.93 Tckts). T/Qdpt: £30.20 (31.59 Tckts) KH

INDEX TO STEEPLECHASING & HURDLE RACING

Figure following the horses name indicates it's **age**. The figures following the pedigree refer to the numbers of the races (steeplechases are in **bold**) in which the horse has run; parentheses () indicate a win; small figures ^{2,3,4} etc denote other placings. Foreign races are denoted by the suffix 'a'. Horses withdrawn (not under orders) are shown with the suffix 'w'. The figure within arrows eg. **>100<** indicate Raceform Private Handicap MASTER rating. The ratings are based on a scale of 0-175. The following symbols are used: 'h' hurdle rating, 'c' chase rating, '+' on the upgrade, 'd' disappointing, '?' questionable form, 't' tentative rating based on time.

Alabang 6 ch g Valiyar-Seleter (Hotfoot) (1208) (1687) >75+h<

Alaflak (IRE) 6 b h Caerleon (USA)-Safe Haven (Blakeney) 4794^{4} >52h<

Alana's Ballad (IRE) 4 b f Be My Native (USA)-Radalgo (Ballad Rock) 2925^{P}

Alan's Pride (IRE) 6 b m 1692^{10} 2047^{13} 2539^{9} 2917^{6} 3026^{P} 3325^{5} 3478^{13} 3908^{7} >38h<

Alapa 10 b g Alzao (USA)-Gay Folly (Wolver Hollow) 3799^{U} 4637^{U}

Alarico (FR) 4 ch g Kadrou (FR)-Calabria (FR) (Vitiges (FR)) 1370^{9} 1872^{7} >44h<

Alasad 7 ch g 318a^{7} >100h< (DEAD)

Alaskan Heir 6 b g 1860^{F} 1984^{10} 2842^{10} 3002^{5} 3201^{5} 3732^{6} 3945^{3} 4221^{2} 4447^{2} 4742^{5} >73h 86c<

Albaha (USA) 4 br g Woodman (USA)-Linda's Magic (USA) (Far North (CAN)) 1953^{R}

Albeit 7 ch m 1330^{8} >45h<

Albemine (USA) 8 b g 1567^{5} 1832^{2} (2114) 2779^{9} 2929^{3} 3177^{6} 4130^{3} 4271^{7} 4741^{5} >101h<

Albermarle (IRE) 6 ch g (4528) >79h<

Albert Blake 10 b g 14^{3} >100c<

Albertina 5 b m Phardante (FR)-Rambling Gold (Little Buskins) 4407^{16}

Albertito (FR) 10 b g 2062^{6} 2780^{6} 4630^{5} 4803^{P} >42h<

Albert's Fancy (IRE) 11 b g Furry Glen-Bride To Be 1003a^{P}

Albert The Lion (IRE) 5 gr g 593^{P}

Al Billal 9 b h 4560^{P} >46h<

Albury Grey 10 gr m Petong-Infelice (Nishapour (FR)) 1708^{4} 2910^{P} 3179^{P} >51c<

Al Capone II (FR) 9 b g 92a^{2} (717a) (1498a) >104h 156?c<

Alcove 6 ch g 675^{6} >79h<

Aldington Chapple 9 b g 188^{4} >62h 82c<

Aldwick Colonnade 10 ch m 1836^{5} 2792^{14} 3110^{13} 3207^{9} 3632^{5} 3811^{6} (4096) >40h<

Algan (FR) 9 b g 1498a^{4} >166?c<

Al Haal (USA) 8 b g Northern Baby (CAN)-Kit's Double (USA) (Spring Double) 1198^{5} 1836^{4} 2946^{12} 3207^{7} >35h< (DEAD)

Al Hashimi 13 b g 2944^{F} 3439^{5} 3744^{10} 4543^{6} >82c<

Al Helal 5 b h 1132^{5} 1276^{F} 1413^{F} 1537^{5} 1830^{12} >33h< (DEAD)

Alicat (IRE) 6 b g 1309^{P} 2549^{3} 3097^{3} 3367^{3} 4149^{4} 4515^{P}

Alice Sheer Thorn (IRE) 7 ch m Sheer Grit-Rugged Thorn (Rugged Man) 99^{10}

Alice Shorelark 6 ch m 1177^{12} 2656^{P} 2875^{7} 3340^{P}

Alice's Mirror 8 gr m 1198^{2} 1446^{5} 2838^{P} 3112^{6} 3338^{U} (3632) >48h<

Alice Smith 10 gr m 3185^{2} 3361^{6} >71dh 88c<

Alicharger 7 ch g 1022^{P} 1138^{5} 1311^{6} 1672^{P} 2506^{P} >34h 53c<

Alicia Lea (IRE) 5 b m Cyrano de Bergerac-Sasha Lea (Cawston's Clown) 4737^{10}

Ali's Alibi 10 br g 869^{2} 1162^{4} 1655^{3} 1806^{2} 2542^{2} 2765^{3} 3414^{P} >83h 127c<

Alisande (IRE) 5 b m King's Ride-Enchanted Evening (Warpath) 2675^{3} 3203^{3} 3440^{4} >52fh<

Ali's Delight 6 br g Idiot's Delight-Almelikeh (Neltino) 1180^{P} 1581^{P} 4403^{P} (DEAD)

Alistover 4 b f Zalazl (USA)-Song of Gold (Song) 2566^{7} 2840^{10} 3184^{8} >49h<

Aljadeer (USA) 8 b or br g 1128^{2} 1657^{3} 2674^{3} 3101^{2} (3198) 3349^{2} (3694) >103h 125c<

Al Jawwal 7 ch g Lead on Time (USA)-Littlefield (Bay Express) 4637^{P}

Al Jinn 6 ch g Hadeer-Mrs Musgrove (Jalmood (USA)) 3100^{P} 3727^{P}

Alka International 5 b g 3228^{2} 3623^{4} 3955^{2} 4097^{P} >63h<

Allahrakha 6 ch g 971^{P} 1993^{P} 3891^{U} 4139^{3}

Allatrim (IRE) 7 b m Montelimar (USA)-Robertina (USA) 1751a^{3} >90h<

All Clear (IRE) 6 b g 2631^{16} 2764^{6} 3137^{8} 3478^{P} 4151^{2} 4574^{3} 4703^{2} >41h 68c<

All Done 4 ch f Northern State (USA)-Doogali (Doon) 3006^{2} 3290^{2} 3425^{3} 3685^{7} >61fh<

Allegation 7 b g 1645^{6} (3267) 3615^{2} 4053^{5} >126h<

Allerbank 6 b g Meadowbrook-Allerdale (Chebs Lad) 2787^{4} 3066^{6} 3449^{F} 3644^{5} >59h<

Allerbeck 7 br m Meadowbrook-Allerdale (Chebs Lad) 3029^{12} 3324^{11}

Allerby 9 gr g 3475^{9} 3883^{7} 4081^{6} 4152^{F} 4708^{6} >45h<

Aller Moor (IRE) 6 b g (4623) >50h 90c<

Allexton Lad 6 b g 1050^{11} >38h<

Allez Cyrano (IRE) 6 b g Alzao (USA)-Miss Bergerac (Bold Lad (IRE)) 4176^{5} >43h<

Allez Pablo 7 b g Crisp-Countess Mariga (Amboise) 818^{5} 956^{P} 1077^{8} 1390^{P} >47dh<

All for Luck 12 b g 1917^{7} 3039^{4} 3230^{6} 3599^{4} 4054^{6} 4239^{3} 4802^{4} >130c<

Allforus (IRE) 5 gr m Sula Bula-Kissing Gate (Realm) 3142^{13} >13fh<

Allimac Nomis 8 b g 4300^{6} 4733^{3} >74h 88c< (DEAD)

All In Good Time 4 b g Shadeed (USA)-Good Thinking (USA) (Raja Baba (USA)) 282^{7}

All In The Game (IRE) 9 b g 4351a^{3} >95c<

Allo George 11 ch g 1949^{4} 3629^{4} 4529^{4} 4642^{2} >116c<

All On 6 ch m 16^{U} 131^{6} 3045^{4} 3309^{2} 3351^{3} >90h<

All Or Nothing 9 ch m Scorpio (FR)-Kelton Lass (Lord Nelson (FR)) 3913^{5} 4155^{U} 4704^{U} >74c<

All Over Red Rover 5 b g 1451^{U} 1580^{7} >57h<

Allow (IRE) 6 b g 788^{5} (1174) 1429^{4} (1638) 2817^{4} 3013^{2} 3108^{5} 3423^{4} >74h<

All Sewn Up 5 ch g 653^{10} 915^{6} 1065^{3} 1333^{9} 1695^{P} >55?h<

Allstars Express 4 b g Rambo Dancer (CAN)-Aligote (Nebbiolo) 3301^{10} 4382^{2} >76h<

All the Aces 10 br g 1361^{5} 1805^{5} 2011^{P} (3160) 3618^{2} >140c<

All The Colours (IRE) 4 br g Classic Secret (USA)-Rainbow Vision (Prince Tenderfoot (USA)) 3619^{3} >92fh<

All the Vowels (IRE) 6 g 2347a^{5} >75h<

Alltime Dancer (IRE) 5 b g 790^{5} 1017^{4} 1125^{5} 1661^{8} 2059^{7} 2644^{11} 2780^{3} 3430^{6} 4130^{5} (4345) >98h<

Almapa 5 ch g Absalom-More Fun (Malicious) 300^{2} 408^{3} 481^{3} 603^{4} (749) 913^{3} 1091^{3} 2578^{8} 2818^{2} 2874^{2} 3050^{6} 3338^{3} 3979^{3} 4069^{3} >67h<

Alnbrook 6 ch g 1349^{5} 3529^{6} >54h<

Alone Home (IRE) 6 b br g Lancastrian-Party Tricks (USA) (Tom Fool) 1200^{P} 1541^{P} 1811^{5}

Alongwaydown (IRE) 8 b g Supreme Leader-Trident Missile (Vulgan Slave) 1810^{F} 2010^{12} 2663^{P} 2826^{P} >9h<

Alosaili 10 ch g 1007^{3} 1166^{5} 1332^{6} 1861^{6} 3921^{7} 4526^{3} >46h 77c<

Alotawanna (IRE) 4 gr g Scenic-Aluda Queen (Alzao (USA)) 4118a^{11} >70fh<

Alpha Leather 6 b g 1663^{B} 1772^{6} 2806^{8} 3049^{5} 3431^{5} 3989^{5} 4226^{5} 4466^{2} 4770^{6} >52h<

Alpha One 12 ch g 4640^{P} 4748^{8} 4758^{P} 4799^{6} >80c<

Alpheton Prince 4 b g Prince of Cill Dara-Batsam Lady (Battle Hymn) 3544^{P} 4299^{9} >43h<

Alpine Joker 4 b g Tirol-Whitstar (Whitstead) 2655^{7} 3109^{7} 3404^{5} 3632^{2} 4209^{7} >59h<

Alpine Mist (IRE) 5 br g (498) 630^{5} 781^{F} 1034^{2} 1183^{5} 3473^{P} 3983^{13} (4526) >72dh 83c<

Alpine Song 12 b m 2656^{P} 3054^{6} 3178^{6} 3538^{2} 3738^{3} >15h 104c<

Alqairawaan 8 b g (390) 946^{3} >108+h 118c<

Alright Guvnor 7 br m 1685^{P} 2090^{P}

Alsahib (USA) 4 b g Slew O' Gold (USA)-Khwlah (USA) (Best Turn (USA)) 3494^{10}

Al Skeet (USA) 11 b g 339^{6} 456^{5} >54h<

Althrey Aristocrat (IRE) 7 ch g 1448^{P} 1683^{P} 3073^{5} 3331^{P} 3470^{P} >23h<

Althrey Blue (IRE) 8 b g 2691^{6} 3086^{F} 4221^{6} >40h 64c<

Althrey Gale (IRE) 6 b g Supreme Leader-Greek Gale (Strong Gale) 1768^{P} 3000^{P}

Althrey Lord (IRE) 7 b g 3470^{P}

Althrey Mist (IRE) 5 ch g Zaffaran (USA)-Clearing Mist (Double Jump) 3468^{P}

Althrey Pilot (IRE) 6 br g Torus-Black Pilot (Linacre) 3000^{4} 3500^{10} 3802^{9} >60h<

Alwarqa 4 b f Old Vic-Ostora (USA) (Blushing Groom (FR)) 1205^{8} 1526^{2} 1700^{4} 2509^{8} >51h<

Always Greener (IRE) 6 gr m (488) 891^{5} (1251) 1959^{3} 3583^{2} 3760^{2} >63h<

Always Happy 4 ch f Sharrood (USA)-Convivial (Nordance (USA)) (294) 358^{2} (1184) 1387^{2} 1675^{2} 2755^{4} (3234) 3634^{16} >75h<

Always in Trouble 10 b g 4350a^{F} >92h 88c<

Always Remember 10 b g 1330^{9} >110dc<

Aly Daley (IRE) 9 ch g (1162) 1307^{2} 1670^{5} 2542^{3} 2765^{5} 3308^{2} 4013^{4} 4392^{B} >116c<

Alzotic (IRE) 4 b g Alzao (USA)-Exotic Bride (USA) (Blushing Groom (FR)) 906^{12} >17h<

Alzulu (IRE) 6 b g 1777^{2} (2064) (2619) (3139) >99fh<

Amadeus (FR) 9 b g 3089^{P} 3357^{P} 4135^{P} >56h 88c<

Amancio (USA) 6 b g 947^{2} 1270^{2} (2549) (2793) (2933) 4012^{4} >105h 126c<

Amany (IRE) 5 b m Waajib-Treeline (High Top) 3677^{P}

Amari King 13 b g 3107^{5} 3273^{P} >108?c<

Amaze 8 b g 473^{3} (723) 810^{2} >94h<

Amazing Sail (IRE) 4 b g Alzao (USA)-Amazer (USA) (Vaguely Noble) 1940^{10} 3031^{2} 3287^{8} (4055) 4296^{2} 4477^{F} 4705^{F} >72h<

Amazon Express 8 b g 103^{4} 159^{F} 255^{5} (422) (465) 605^{P} >77h<

Amazon Heights 5 b m 1905^{P} 2034^{P} 4625^{13} 4743^{6} 4807^{P}

Amazon Lily 10 ch m 2951^{F} >89c<

Ambassador Royale (IRE) 9 gr g (889) 1018^{3} 1328^{P} >84h 85c<

Amber Holly 8 ch m 786^{P} 854^{4} 939^{3} 1020^{4} 1853^{F} 3641^{7} 4075^{7} 4152^{6} 4335^{7} 4514^{3} >41h<

Amber Lily 5 ch m Librate-Just Bluffing (Green Shoon) 483^{7} 600^{9} >26h<

Amber Ring 4 ch f Belmez (USA)-Ring of Pearl (Auction Ring (USA)) 331^{4} 471^{2} 654^{F} 881^{3} 1131^{2} 3088^{P} 3431^{3} 3592^{7} >49h<

Amber Spark (IRE) 8 ch g 1199^{3} 1423^{2} 1694^{F} 1829^{3} 2679^{3} 3538^{U} (3688) >71h 101c<

Amber Valley (USA) 6 ch g 1831^{2} 1987^{4} 2885^{3} 3427^{4} 3749^{4} 3797^{3} >128?h 102c<

Ambidextrous (IRE) 5 b h 1796^{2} (2006) (2692) 2842^{3} 3429^{5} 4313^{3} >64h<

Ambleside (IRE) 6 b g 1698^{3} (1933) 2884^{2} 3231^{4} 3640^{10} 4053^{3} >107h<

Amble Speedy (IRE) 7 b g 1405a^{6} 2345a^{5} 2856a^{2} 3389a^{5} 4110a^{2} 4356a^{10} >98h 135c<

Ambrosia (IRE) 4 b f Strong Gale-Scotsman Ice (Deep Run) 4414^{5}

Ameer Alfayaafi (IRE) 4 b g Mujtahid (USA)-Sharp Circle (IRE) (Sure Blade (USA)) 4726^{R}

Amercius 5 ch g 31^{3} 139^{5} **>71h<**

American Eyre 12 gr g **3553^{P} 4617^{4} 4724^{P} >79c<**

American Hero 9 ch g **(3790) (4183) (4334) >102h 122+c<**

Ami Bleu (FR) 5 ch g Bikala-Note Bleue (Posse (USA)) 4082^{3} 4559^{F} **>67h< (DEAD)**

Amillionmemories 7 br g 2929^{4} 3269^{9} 3415^{6} 3604^{P} 4418^{5} 4524^{2} **>63h<**

A Million Watts 6 b g Belfort (FR)-Peters Pet Girl (Norwick (USA)) 2815^{B} 3054^{13}

Amlah (USA) 5 gr g 456^{3} 4061^{9} (4246) (4425) 4741^{3} **>92h<**

Amlwch 4 b g Weld-Connaughts' Trump (Connaught) 3561^{4} 4774^{3} **>63fh<**

Amothebambo (IRE) 4 b g Martin John-Twilight In Paris (Kampala) 4554^{3} **>58fh<**

Amtrak Express 10 ch g 4131^{3} **>152c<**

Amylou 4 b f Dunbeath (USA)-La Chiquita 646^{P}

Anabatic (IRE) 9 b g **314a^{P} 763a^{2} (1231a) 1366^{4} 1917^{6} >147c<**

Anabranch 6 br m 400^{2} (593) 743^{F} 871^{3} 1204^{2} (1577) 1852^{2} 2543^{U} 2952^{5} 3995^{2} 4246^{5} **>94h<**

Analogical 4 br f Teenoso (USA)-The Howlet (New Brig) 1980^{5} 3029^{5} 3471^{9} 3730^{3} 3940^{7} 4620^{5} 4756^{F} **>57h<**

Analogue (IRE) 5 b g 1772^{11} 2036^{P} **>40h<**

Anastasia Windsor 6 b m 3305^{C} 3416^{6} **>46h< (DEAD)**

A N C Express 9 gr g **1697^{3} 2869^{2} 3153^{8} >74h 119c<**

Anchorena 5 b m Slip Anchor-Canna (Caerleon (USA)) (528) 632^{P} 1807^{12} 2003^{P} 2509^{5} **>59h<**

Andalucian Sun (IRE) 9 ch g **4730^{U} >54c<**

Andanito (IRE) 6 b g 3041^{4} **>95fh<**

Andermatt 10 b g **3804^{6} 4185^{9} 4475^{2} 4629^{2} >105dh 119c<**

Andrea Cova (IRE) 5 bb m Strong Gale-Blue Suede Shoes (Bargello) 4360a^{13} **>78h<**

Andre Laval (IRE) 8 ch g **(1473) 1765^{6} >117c<**

Andrelot 10 b g **130^{3} 180^{2} 215^{2} 298^{4} (487) 550^{4} (689) 797^{3} 1063^{2} 1167^{P} 1631^{3} 1957^{6} 2568^{7} >83h 121c<**

Andretti's Heir 11 ch g **4160^{F} >78c<**

Andros Prince 12 b g **797^{2} 1122^{7} 1513^{U} 3046^{6} >96c<**

Andsome Boy 4 ch g Out of Hand-My Home (Homing) 458^{3} 736^{3} 912^{5} 4512^{7} 4807^{P} **>60h<**

Andsuephi (IRE) 5 b g Montelimar (USA)-Butler's Daughter (Rhett Butler) (4531) (4657) **>58fh<**

And Why Not 9 ro g **30^{6} 4618^{F} >72h 64c<**

Andy Clyde 4 b g Rambo Dancer (CAN)-Leprechaun Lady (Royal Blend) 2770^{5} **>40fh<**

Andy Coin 6 ch m 829^{4} **>48h<**

Angelo's Double (IRE) 9 b g **3086^{2} 3422^{F} 3576^{2} >117h 97c<**

Anglesey Sea View 8 gr m 1438^{3} (1523) 3004^{7} 3611^{5} **>59h<**

Angry Native (IRE) 5 b g Be My Native (USA)-An Grianan (Ballymore) 4301^{14} **>15fh<**

Angus McCoatup (IRE) 4 ch c Mac's Imp (USA)-In For More (Don) 1953^{9} 2669^{7} 2859^{9} 4732^{6} **>66h<**

Anif (USA) 6 b or br g 3084^{P} 3172^{P} 3674^{5} 3757^{4} (3959) 4226^{7} 4807^{6} **>50h<**

Anika's Gem (IRE) 4 b f Buckskin (FR)-Picton Lass (Rymer) 3394^{2} 3789^{9} 4570^{3} **>16h<**

Animosity 7 b m Latest Model-Perplexity (Pony Express) 4767^{P}

Anjubi 12 b g **4432^{4} 4730^{2} >96c<**

Anlace 8 b m 1034^{7} 1181^{S} 1381^{6} **1552^{6} 1875^{P}** 3741^{3} 3904^{8} 4187^{14} 4259^{4} 4440^{F} **>57?h 62c<**

An Maineach (IRE) 8 b g **314a^{U} >108h 115c<**

Anna Bannanna 5 b m 600^{P} **>37h<**

Annabel's Baby (IRE) 8 b m 2838^{10} 3674^{8} **>6h<**

Anna Soleil (IRE) 4 b g Red Sunset-Flying Anna (Roan Rocket) 2751^{3} 3075^{U} 3287^{5} (3953) 4170^{2} 4434^{3} 4720^{3} **>72h<**

Annie Ruth (IRE) 6 ch m 2875^{5} 3226^{16} 4458^{4} 4662^{5} **>34h<**

Annio Chilone 11 b g **3062^{4} 3446^{6} >85c<**

Ann's Ambition 10 b g **4070^{5} 4308^{3} 4522^{P} 4730^{3} >94c<**

Anorak (USA) 7 b g 505^{3} 1047^{7} 1249^{5} 1701^{4} 1990^{6} 2629^{2} 2862^{7} 3031^{9} 3448^{6} 4018^{2} **>54h<**

Another Bula (IRE) 6 b g Cardinal Flower-Celtic Lace (Celtic Cone) 24^{13}

Another Cockpit 5 b g 1329^{2} 1673^{3} **>72h<**

Another Comedy 7 b g El Conquistador-Miss Comedy (Comedy Star (USA)) **359^{2} 477^{P} 3470^{4} 3732^{3}** 3932^{P} 4226^{8} **4437^{W} >34h 64c<**

Another Coq Hardi (IRE) 9 ch g **323a^{P} >97c<**

Another Fiddle (IRE) 7 b g 2678^{14} 3057^{P} **>5h<**

Another George 7 b g 3910^{13} 4500^{8} **>51h<**

Another Grouse 10 b m **314a^{8} 323a^{2} >78h 111c<**

Another Hubblick 6 ch g 915^{F} 1036^{10} **4643^{3} >19h 82c<**

Another Meadow 9 b g **4569^{P} >54h<**

Another Nick 11 ch g **423^{F} 454^{F}** 805^{6} 893^{P} **>37c<**

Anotherone to Note 6 ch g 488^{P} 2882^{14} 3429^{6} **>38h<**

Another Point (IRE) 9 ch g **1758a^{4} >60h 101c<**

Another Quarter (IRE) 4 b f Distinctly North (USA)-Numidia (Sallust) 291^{5} 1205^{9} 1370^{7} 4707^{5} 4718^{3} **>56h<**

Another Rumpus 5 b g Mr Fluorocarbon-Premier Susan (Murrayfield) 3821^{8} 4420^{14} **>56fh<**

Another Venture (IRE) 7 br g **1563^{6} 1831^{4} 2544^{P} 4072^{F} 4149^{2} >77h 89c<**

An Spailpin Fanach (IRE) 8 b g 3499^{13} 3958^{4} 4233^{P} **>58h< (DEAD)**

Anstey Gadabout 11 ch g 605^{P}

Ansuro Again 8 b g **2788^{P} 2954^{P}** 3157^{7} 3358^{P} (3481) **>60h<**

Antapoura (IRE) 5 b m 1647^{2} 2361a^{2} 3126a^{2} 4365a^{6} **>130h<**

Antarctica (USA) 5 ch m Arctic Tern (USA)-Loved Etsu (USA) (Liloy (FR)) 2663^{P} 2898^{14} 3283^{6} **>38h<**

Antarctic Wind (IRE) 7 b g Kambalda-Green Arctic (Green Shoon) 693^{2} 910^{2} (1139) 1689^{3} 2701^{7} 3307^{4} **>71h<**

Antartictern (USA) 7 b g 27^{5} 1247^{3} 1628^{10} 1825^{R} 4236^{U} **>56dh<**

Anthony Bell 11 b g 642^{8} **783^{D} 895^{P} 4410^{P} >68h 98dc<**

Antiguan Flyer 8 b g Shirley Heights-Fleet Girl (Habitat) 355^{2} 488^{4} 655^{4} 1072^{7} 2006^{10} (3663) 3923^{2} (4236) (4565) **>69h<**

Antigua's Treasure (IRE) 8 ch g Treasure Hunter-Sans Culotte (FR) (Roi Dagobert) 1594^{8} **>24h<**

Antonin (FR) 9 ch g **1397a^{5} 2348a^{5} (3261a) 4074^{11} >136c<**

Antonio Mariano (SWE) 6 b g 552^{6} **>76+h<**

Anusha 7 b m 3254a^{8} 3523a^{11} **>81h<**

Any Port (IRE) 7 b m **323a^{U} >90c<**

Anythingyoulike 8 b g **1468^{3} 2039^{3} 2658^{P} 3003^{3} >58h 92c<**

Anzum 6 b g (1645) 3150^{3} 3635^{2} **>124h<**

Apachee Flower 7 ch m 1256^{5} 1553^{8} 3112^{2} 3499^{5} 3737^{4} 4310^{6} 4470^{2} (4524) 4803^{P} **>62h<**

Apache Len (USA) 4 br g Rahy (USA)-Shining Skin (USA) (Fappiano (USA)) 2784^{5} 4184^{11} 4299^{P} 4714^{4} **>40h<**

Apache Park (USA) 4 b g Alleged (USA)-Fairly Magic (USA) (Raise A Native) 1634^{9} 2668^{6} 2925^{P} (3072) 3752^{4} 3923^{5} 4534^{6} 4548^{2} 4723^{F} **>68h<**

Apache Raider 5 br g Dancing Brave (USA)-Calandra (USA) (Sir Ivor) 60^{6} **>63h<**

Apache Twist (IRE) 4 b g Digamist (USA)-Mystery Treat 2333a^{13} **>77h<**

Apartments Abroad 4 b f Prince Sabo-La Graciosa (Comedy Star (USA)) 1935^{P}

Apatura Hati 8 br m **1711^{P} 2039^{4} 3060^{3} (3409) 3675^{5} >98c<**

Apatura King 7 ch g Button Bright (USA)-Apatura Iris (Space King) **4135^{7} >89c<**

Apollo Colosso 7 br g Sunyboy-Culinary (Tower Walk) 2766^{P} **4260^{P}**

Apollono 5 b g Cyrano de Bergerac-Daima (Dominion) 1905^{F} 2939^{10} 3406^{7} 3733^{5} 3983^{W} 4770^{3} **>49h<**

Apollo's Daughter 9 b m (1249) 3035^{9} 3485^{6} (3641) 3822^{7} **>53h<**

Appeal Again (IRE) 4 br g Mujtahid (USA)-Diva Encore (Star Appeal) 1184^{16} 1595^{F} 2050^{9} **>24h<**

Appearance Money (IRE) 6 b m 1523^{3} 1686^{7} 1992^{12} 2629^{4} **2799^{2} 3092^{F}** 3325^{7} **3938^{3} (4446) 4703^{F} >53h 81c<**

Apple John 8 b g Sula Bula-Hazelwain (Hard Fact) **1456^{3} 1771^{F}**

Applianceofscience 10 b g 2038^{9} **3966^{P} 4277^{F} 4448^{P} >34h 56?c<**

April Cruise 10 ch m **72^{P}**

April Seventh (IRE) 6 br g 1431^{3} 2619^{8} 3133^{6} **>61h<**

Aqua Amber 5 ch g 1336^{9} 2034^{P} 3342^{U} 3918^{4} 4226^{P} 4405^{P} **>41h<**

Aqua Star (IRE) 4 br g Village Star (FR)-First Water (FR) (Margouillat (FR)) 3535^{W}

Arabian Bold (IRE) 9 br g 1288^{7} 1828^{P} **2091^{3} 2571^{7} >70?c<**

Arabian Design 5 b g Shareef Dancer (USA)-Classic Design (Busted) 3072^{P}

Arabian Heights 4 ch g Persian Heights-Arabian Rose (USA) (Lyphard (USA)) 1776^{7} 2060^{5} 2859^{3} 3049^{4} 3438^{5} 3932^{6} **>71h<**

Arabian Sultan 10 b g Muscatite-Church Bay (Reliance II) 1645^{P} 3180^{P} 3402^{P}

Aradia's Diamond 6 ch m Naskracker (USA)-Eight of Diamonds (Silent Spring) 968^{5} 1523^{2} 3964^{5} **>53h<**

Ar Aghaidh Abhaile (IRE) 6 ch g Henbit (USA)-Gaoth Na Bride (Strong Gale) 1263^{9} 1713^{7} 1854^{P} **>1h<**

Aragon Ayr 9 b or br g 2617^{7} 3398^{8} **3530^{P}** 3791^{8} **>82h<**

Aramon 7 b g 552^{F} **>66h< (DEAD)**

Arch Angel (IRE) 4 ch f Archway (IRE)-Saintly Guest (What A Guest) 1413^{U} 1908^{6} 2050^{8} 2678^{3} 3284^{4} 3663^{3} 3921^{3} **>56h<**

Arch Enemy (IRE) 4 gr c Archway (IRE)-Rosserk (Roan Rocket) 358^{3}

Archer (IRE) 9 b g **4469^{3} >77h 80c<**

Archies Oats 8 ch g Oats-Archetype (Over The River (FR)) **(3568) 3837^{5} >91c<**

Arctic Affair (IRE) 4 b f Glacial Storm (USA)-Moonlight Romance (Teenoso (USA)) 4656^{10} **>32fh<**

Arctic Baron 12 b g **4022^{4} >99c<**

Arctic Bloom 11 gr m **3608^{6}** 4163^{4} **4419^{3} >22h 56c<**

Arctic Camper 5 b g Arctic Lord-Mayotte (Little Buskins) 3304^{2} 3619^{2} (4360a) **>94f+h<**

Arctic Chanter 5 b g Arctic Lord-Callope (USA) (Recitation (USA)) 25^{9} 1203^{4} **>37fh<**
Arctic Charmer (USA) 5 ch g Arctic Tern (USA)-Bunch of Smiles (USA) (Graustark) 3798^{P} 4698^{P}
Arctic Chill (IRE) 7 b g **3455^{4}**
Arctic Flame 6 b m Arctic Lord-Rekindle (Relkino) 865^{5}
Arctic Fox (IRE) 5 b g Glacial Storm (USA)-Fleeting Vixen (Paddy's Stream) 3297^{4} 3808^{10} 4102^{7} 4188^{9} **>29h<**
Arctic Fusilier 6 gr g 1329^{15} **>25fh<**
Arctic Kinsman 9 gr g **3037^{U} 3299^{2} 3614^{W} 4062^{F} 4349a^{6} >119+h 148c<**
Arctic Life (IRE) 8 b g **180^{4}** 208^{4} **286^{P} >86h 104c<**
Arctic Madam 8 b m Town And Country-Arctic Servant (Goldhill) **1468^{5} 1811^{4} 1947^{9} >75c<**
Arctic Muse 6 b m Arctic Lord-Vacuna (Bargello) 3052^{6} **>9h< (DEAD)**
Arctic Red River (IRE) 8 ch g 327^{4} **>46h<**
Arctic Sandy (IRE) 7 ch g 2177^{4} **2799^{3} 3436^{3}** 4075^{8} **>70h 86c<**
Arctic Triumph 6 b g 1551^{5} 2891^{5} 3133^{4} 4427^{2} **>60h<**
Arctic Venture 5 b m 4388^{9} **>18fh<**
Arctic Weather (IRE) 8 b g **1737a^{4} 2741a^{2} 4123a^{5} >95h 118c<**
Arcus (IRE) 4 ch g Archway (IRE)-Precision Chop (Hard Fought) 3575^{9} **>5h<**
Ardarroch Prince 6 b g (1362) 2785^{2} 3366^{5} 3973^{2} 4184^{5} **>77h<**
Ardbrennan 10 b g **3799^{2} 4015^{3} 4322^{2} >101c<**
Ardcroney Chief 11 ch g **1122^{4} 1338^{2}**
Ardearned 10 b m Ardross-Divine Penny (Divine Gift) 66^{19} 156^{P} 739^{7}
Ardenbar 5 b m Ardross-Barwell (Barolo) 679^{2} 865^{6} 1013^{4}
Ardent Love (IRE) 8 b m **1947^{6} 2614^{2} 2841^{3} 3020^{5}** 3488^{2} (4458) (4563) **>60h 94c<**
Ardent Step (IRE) 4 b f Brush Aside (USA)-Ardelle Grey (Ardross) 4433^{8} **>17fh<**
Ardesee 17 ch g **3432^{3} 4208^{P} >75c<**
Ardleigh Venture 4 br f Daring March-Miss Adventure (Adonijah) 2696^{19}
Ardrina 6 ch m 1296^{3} 1685^{3} 2861^{6} 3226^{2} (3483) (3910) 4355a^{4} **>72h<**
Ardrom 5 ch m Ardross-Drom Lady (Royalty) 1913^{5} 2757^{7} (3440) **>58fh<**
Ardronan (IRE) 7 b g Roselier (FR)-Molly Coddle (Belfalas) 1362^{3} 3883^{2} **>71+h<**
Ardscud 10 b g Le Bavard (FR)-Tudor Lady (Green Shoon) **3489^{8} >43h<**
Areal (IRE) 8 br m Roselier (FR)-Stream Flyer (Paddy's Stream) 3764^{9} **>21h<**
Arenice (FR) 9 ch g **(92a) >166c<**
Arfer Mole (IRE) 9 b g **(2843) (3145) 3356^{3} >102h 119c<**
Arian Spirit (IRE) 6 b m 1821^{2} 2800^{5} 3157^{9} **>57h<**
Arioso 9 b m 1448^{4} 3054^{2} 3364^{12} 4405^{4} 4762^{5} **>43h<**
Arise (IRE) 8 b g Rising-What's The Point (Major Point) **3135^{2} 3664^{5} >114?c<**
Aristodemus 8 b g **1668^{F} 2912^{P} 3138^{6} 3393^{7} 3826^{P} 4057^{8} 4153^{3} 4502^{6} 4751^{7} >53c<**
Arithmetic 7 ch g 1039^{10} 1372^{2} (2078) 3045^{7} 3600^{P} **>92h<**
Arkley Royal 6 b g Ardross-Lady Geneva (Royalty) (2073) (2682) 3042^{3} **>79fh<**
Arklow King (IRE) 5 br g King's Ride-Lantern Lass (Monksfield) 1329^{21} 3054^{P}
Armala 12 ch g **470^{3} 814^{2} 1570^{F} 2621^{6} 2823^{6} >112c<**
Armateur (FR) 9 b g 3628^{2} 4230^{7} **>64h 76c<**
Around The Gale (IRE) 6 b g **(1120) 1326^{2} (1981) 3300^{2} 3805^{3} >86h 136c<**
Around the Horn 10 b g **1637^{2} 2058^{3} 2783^{4} 3039^{P} 3585^{U} 4225^{P} >132c<**
Arrange 5 b g Deploy-Willowbed (Wollow) 99^{2} 3235^{11} 3606^{8}
Arrange A Game 10 ch g 354^{5} 489^{2} 642^{7} (673) 824^{2} **1357^{5}** 1562^{7} **1778^{R}** 4452^{P} 4563^{5} 4727^{P} **>32h 65c<**
Arr Eff Bee 10 b g **70^{P} 1371^{7} 2809^{4} >75h 48c<**
Arrogant Boy 8 b or br g 101^{P} 183^{U} 288^{8} **>26h<**
Arrogant Heir 4 b g Henbit (USA)-Quiet Arrogance (USA) (Greek Sky (USA)) 699^{P} 906^{8} 1064^{R} 1900^{8} 3965^{2} 4169^{3} **>60h<**
Artful Arthur 11 b g **23^{5} 70^{F} 130^{5} 190^{11} 213^{6} 817^{3} 1063^{P} 3593^{4} 3906^{6} 4324^{5} >31h 89c<**
Arthur Bee 10 ch g 1304^{P} 1703^{5} 2629^{3} 2862^{6} 3327^{3} 3448^{2} 3711^{14} 4055^{P} **>42h<**
Arthur's Minstrel 10 ch g **1133^{3} >137c<**
Arthur's Special 7 gr m 890^{6} 1053^{9} 1251^{7} **>24h<**
Artic Meadow 6 ch m Little Wolf-Meadow Maid (Deep Run) 2931^{14} 4003^{P} **>37fh<**
Artic Wings (IRE) 9 b m **2894^{P} (3132) 3413^{6} 3665^{2} 3903^{3} 4235^{F} >95h 105c<**
Artistic Plan (IRE) 5 b g Creative Plan (USA)-North Rose VII (Damsire Unregistered) 3233^{11} 3796^{P} **>46h<**
Art Prince (IRE) 7 b g Aristocracy-Come Now (Prince Hansel) **1646^{F} (1920) (2077) >117+c<**
Arturo 6 b g 1260^{5} 1541^{6} **>56h<**
Artworld (USA) 9 b g 1942^{5} 2862^{8} **>60h<**
As du Trefle (FR) 9 ch g Petit Montmorency (USA)-Gall de Marsalin (FR) (Roi de Perse II) **2867^{3} (3279) 3618^{6} >120c<**
Ashby Hill (IRE) 6 ch m 1471^{3} **>60h<**
Ashgrove Dancer (IRE) 7 ch g 3024^{P} 3159^{2} 3449^{2} **>65h<**
Ashley House 8 b g Ore-Jupiter's Gem (Jupiter Pluvius) 1200^{P} 1507^{P} **1787^{P} 2873^{P}** 3072^{P}
Ashmead Rambler (IRE) 7 b g **1061^{F} 1331^{2} 1449^{C} 2037^{6} >42h 62++c<**
Ashtar (USA) 7 b g 2655^{4} 2875^{6} **>42h< (DEAD)**
Ashwell April (IRE) 5 ch m Denel (FR)-Paiukiri (Ballyciptic) 4118a^{17} **>56fh<**
Ashwell Boy (IRE) 6 b g 1919^{4} 2059^{P} 2645^{F} 3816^{2} 4053^{6} (4240) 4397^{P} **>110h<**
A S Jim 6 b g Welsh Captain-Cawston's Arms (Cawston's Clown) 865^{12} 1303^{2} 1659^{8} 3471^{3} 3590^{2} (4002) 4544^{4} 4652^{5} **>56h<**
Ask Antony (IRE) 7 gr g Roselier (FR)-Lady Casita (Paddy's Stream) **3357^{2} 3913^{2} >117dc<**
Asked To Leave 5 ch m Montelimar (USA)-The Parson Fox (The Parson) 3440^{7} 3611^{9} **>29fh<**
Ask Harry (IRE) 6 b or br g 837^{3} 934^{F} 1390^{P} **>40h<**
Ask In Time (IRE) 5 br g Jeu de Paille (FR)-C B M Girl (Diamonds Are Trump (USA)) 3365^{16}
Ask Me In (IRE) 6 ch m Orchestra-Olimpus Lady (Furry Glen) 4217^{9} 4405^{F} **>73h<**
Ask Me Later (IRE) 8 b g **2767^{4} 2954^{2} (3141) 3560^{2} (4078) 4245^{2} >82h 106c<**
Ask The Butler (IRE) 6 ch g (319a) 2359a^{2} 2596a^{P} 3396^{5} 4352a^{9} **>109h<**
Ask Tom (IRE) 8 b g **(1650) 2058^{2} (2646) 3614^{2} 4049^{4} >76h 167c<**
Aslan (IRE) 9 gr g **1803^{F} 1944^{7} 2548^{F} >109h< (DEAD)**
Aslar (IRE) 8 ch g (969) 1135^{P} **>46h<**
Asterix 9 ch g 341^{6} 399^{3} **>74h<**
Astings (FR) 9 b g **1806^{U} 1941^{2} 2616^{6} >120c<**
Astound (IRE) 7 ch g Avocat-Clement Queen (Lucifer (USA)) **3208^{4} >88c< (DEAD)**
Astounded 10 ch g Radical-Swinging Ears VII (Damsire Unregistered) **222^{5} 349^{5} 457^{F} >68c<**
Astraleon (IRE) 9 b g 4079^{4} 4246^{P} 4337^{7} **4709^{2} >82h 84c<**
Astral Invader (IRE) 5 ch g Astronef-Numidia (Sallust) 1788^{P} 1873^{8} **>33h<**
Astral Invasion (USA) 6 ch g 1256^{P} 1542^{6} 2567^{2} 2943^{13} **3111^{5} 3472^{F} 3732^{4} 3966^{2} 4402^{P} 4533^{F} 4649^{5} >64h 72c<**
Astrolabe 5 b g 65^{P} 4468^{14} **>47h<**
Aswamedh 9 ro g **3113^{P} >88h<**
Atavistic (IRE) 5 b g 1476^{3} 1870^{P} (2875) 3342^{3} 3920^{F} **>76h<**
Ath Cheannaithe (FR) 5 ch g 812^{3} (915) 974^{4} 1168^{P} 1333^{6} 1715^{4} 2578^{3} 3050^{11} 3979^{2} (4289) (4430) 4660^{5} **>73h<**
Athenian Alliance 8 ch m 396^{6} 461^{7} 648^{W} 729^{P}
Atlantic Sunrise 5 ch m Super Sunrise-Camden (David Jack) 1827^{6} 2804^{6} **>28fh<**
At Liberty (IRE) 5 b h Danehill (USA)-Music of The Night (USA) (Blushing Groom (FR)) 2624^{9} 2822^{5} **>52h<**
Attadale 9 b g 1265^{4} **>101dh<**
At The Acorn (IRE) 6 b g 219^{5} **>72h<**
At The Grove (IRE) 7 b g **1472^{3} 1833^{F} >97c<**
Auburn Boy 10 ch g **1164^{4}** 1577^{5} 1686^{2} 1942^{3} 2631^{4} 2932^{P} **>83h 80c<**
Audrey Grace 6 b m Infantry-Fair Nic (Romancero) 1770^{P}
August Twelfth 9 b g 1585^{3} 1732^{4} 1960^{4} 2828^{2} 3087^{2} 3209^{4} 3577^{5} **>76h<**
Auntie Alice 7 b m 1500^{3} 1807^{10} 2920^{3} 3031^{3} **3200^{4}** 3478^{12} **>69h 78c<**
Auntie Chris 7 ch m **4799^{U} >22h<**
Auntie Lorna 8 b m **746^{P} 964^{F}** 1069^{P}
Aunt Piquee 8 ch m Import-Meggies Dene (Apollo Eight) 2649^{16} 2785^{13} **>13h<**
Aut Even (IRE) 7 b g 1683^{3} 2053^{6} 3004^{9} **>70h<**
Autobabble (IRE) 4 b g Glenstal (USA)-Almalat (Darshaan) 1747a^{9} **>77h<**
Autofyr 4 br f Autobird (FR)-Fyrish (Mr Fluorocarbon) 906^{P}
Auto Pilot (NZ) 9 b g **4270^{7} >33h 111c<**
Autumn Flame (IRE) 6 ch m 679^{12} 1337^{7} 2946^{10} 3284^{9} 3620^{7} **>26h<**
Autumn Lord 4 b g Lord Bud-Naturally Autumn (Hello Gorgeous (USA)) (2633) (3203) **>73fh<**
Auvillar (USA) 9 br g 480^{6} 587^{8} 725^{7} **869^{3}** 899^{4} **1122^{5} 1445^{8} >78h 90c<**
Avanti Express (IRE) 7 b g 2547^{2} 2791^{2} (3184) 3536^{P} **>85h<**
A Verse To Order 6 b g Rymer-Born Bossy (Eborneezer) 4539^{8} 4656^{12} **>41fh<**
Avoncliff 4 ch f Sharp Deal-Dusty Run (Deep Run) 4008^{17} **>18fh<**
Avostar 10 ch g **3089^{2} 3458^{P} 3906^{2} 4222^{F} >105c<**
Avowhat (IRE) 7 ch g **1850^{P} >54h 75c< (DEAD)**
Avril Etoile 7 ch m 288^{6} 600^{P} **>46h< (DEAD)**
Avro Anson 9 b g **2636^{3} 2887^{U} 4074^{6} 4303^{5} >150dh 152c<**
Award (IRE) 6 b g Executive Perk-Stage Debut (Decent Fellow) 1867^{4} 2663^{F} 3272^{2} **>83h<**
Awestruck 7 b g 825^{5} 950^{9} 1040^{3} 1251^{5} 1814^{8} 2570^{6} 3834^{4} (4281) 4727^{7} **>47h<**
A Windy Citizen (IRE) 8 ch m **(3460) 3852^{F} >101c< (DEAD)**
Aws Contracts 6 br g 26^{13} **>1h<**
Axo Sport (IRE) 5 ch g Orchestra-Zaydeen (Sassafras (FR)) 2812^{14} **>17h<**
Aydisun 5 gr g 718^{7} 1663^{R} 1992^{13} **>57h<**

Aylesbury Lad (IRE) 8 ch g **1246^{7} 1574^{5} 1845^{2} 2788^{P} >51h 80c< (DEAD)**
Aztec Warrior 6 b g El Conquistador-Jaunty Slave (Le Johnstan) 1275^{5} 1774^{9} **>57fh< (DEAD)**

B

Baasm 4 br g Polar Falcon (USA)-Sariah (Kris) 1205^{6} 1776^{4} 2060^{4} 2692^{4} 3102^{6} **>57h<**
Baba Au Rhum (IRE) 5 b g Baba Karam-Spring About (Hard Fought) 476^{P} 1369^{6} **>52h<**
Baba Sam (IRE) 6 b g Detroit Sam (FR)-Bluehel (Bluerullah) 865^{10} 1033^{9} 2093^{7} 2574^{9} 2907^{13} 3205^{P} **>27h<**
Babbling Brook (IRE) 5 ch g Meneval (USA)-Sparkling Stream (Paddy's Stream) 4538^{14}
Babil 12 b g **3586^{P} 3984^{P} >97c<**
Baby Jake (IRE) 7 ch g 319a^{2} **>61c<**
Baby Lancaster 6 b g Shaab-Lancaster Rose (Canadel II) 1573^{11} 2661^{15} 3895^{7} 4388^{10} **>47fh<**
Baccarat Collonges (FR) 8 b g Olmeto-Mariane Collonge (FR) (Cap Martin (FR)) **1498a^{2} >147?c<**
Bache Dingle 6 b g 4082^{P} 4441^{6} 4626^{P}
Back Bar (IRE) 9 b g **2348a^{4} 2848a^{7} 4074^{F} 4362a^{4} >104c<**
Backhander (IRE) 5 b g Cadeaux Genereux-Chevrefeuille (Ile de Bourbon (USA)) 939^{11} 3072^{P} 3471^{P} **>44h<**
Back On The Lash (IRE) 5 b g Supreme Leader-Avida Dancer (Ballymore) 2066^{10} **>15fh<**
Back The Road (IRE) 9 ch g **4160^{5} >83c<**
Backview 5 ch g 186^{5} 3184^{6} **>51h<**
Badastan (IRE) 8 b g **(1674) 2575^{5} >109h 117c<**
Badger Hill 4 ch g Nalchik (USA)-Cutler Heights (Galivanter) 3031^{F}
Badger's Lane 6 b g 2066^{9} **>34fh<**
Bagareur (BEL) 8 b h Bacalao (USA)-Louitonne (BEL) (Bel Baraka) (579a) **>100h<**
Bahamian Sunshine (USA) 6 ch g Sunshine Forever (USA)-Pride of Darby (USA) (Danzig (USA)) 2055^{4} **>61h<**
Baher (USA) 8 b g 1050^{2} 1292^{2} 2654^{F} **>77h<**
Bahrain Queen (IRE) 9 ch m 184^{4} **>75h<**
Baile Na Gcloch (IRE) 8 ch g **3389a^{7} >71h 101c<**
Baileys Bridge (IRE) 6 ch g **2856a^{8} >82c<**
Bailiwick 4 b g Dominion-Lady Barkley (Habitat) 2070^{11} 2622^{13} **>15h<**
Balanak (USA) 6 b g 1039^{3} 1429^{5} (1661) 1906^{F} **>107?h<**
Bala Pyjama 4 b g Henbit (USA)-Rodney's Sister (Leading Man) 4215^{9} **>65fh<**
Balasani (FR) 11 b g **4135^{4} 4471^{B} 4655^{P} 4806^{P} >113h 89c<**
Balawhar (IRE) 7 b g 2345a^{13} **>116h<**
Balcony Boy 5 b g Palm Track-Energia (Alias Smith (USA)) 2550^{P}
Baldhu Chance 9 ch g **3631^{P} >42h<**
Bald Joker 12 b g **2^{5} 9^{4} 323a^{P} >82c<**
Bali Tender 6 ch g **4157^{P} 4297^{2} 4446^{3} >47h 73c<**
Ballad Minstrel (IRE) 5 gr g 2640^{2} 3619^{22} **>47fh<**
Ballad Ruler 11 ch g 479^{3} 553^{5} **3333^{P} 3622^{P} >84c<**
Ballad Song 14 br g Ballad Rock-Apt (Ragusa) 4280^{P}
Balladur (USA) 4 b c Nureyev (USA)-Ballinderry (Irish River (FR)) 2840^{P} 4014^{8} **>75h<**
Balleswhidden 5 b g 1768^{3} 3084^{7} **>71h<**
Ballet Royal (USA) 8 b h 3584^{P} 4006^{10} 4550^{4} 4701^{3} (4791) **>80h<**
Ballina 5 b g Ayyabaan-Nicolene (Nice Music) 1820^{6} 4008^{18} 4554^{7} **>56fh<**
Ballinaboola Grove (IRE) 10 b g 1492a^{6} **>70h 83c<**
Ballindoo 8 ch g 465^{3} 805^{2} 878^{3} 1080^{2} 1256^{2} 1528^{3} 1849^{2} (4470) 4754^{2} **>68h<**
Ballinlammy Rose (IRE) 7 ch g 1751a^{6} **>90h<**
Ballochan Linn 5 ch g Denel (FR)-Kawarau Queen (Taufan (USA)) 4259^{P}
Ballpoint 4 ch g Indian Ridge-Ballaquine (Martinmas) 803^{3} **>23h<**
Ballyallia Castle (IRE) 8 ch g 1^{3} **4319^{4} 4614^{F} >59h 87c<**
Ballyandrew 12 b g **3580^{P} >61c<**
Ballyboden (IRE) 10 ch g Over The River (FR)-Dadooronron (Deep Run) **1003a^{P} >78c<**
Ballybriken Castle (IRE) 10 bb m **314a^{P} >67c<**
Bally Clover 10 ch g **1122^{2} (1391) 1598^{3} (1961) 4306^{2} (4557) 4806^{P} >111h 118c<**
Bally Cruise 10 br m Cruise Missile-Ballynore (News Item) **4291^{W}**
Ballydougan (IRE) 9 ch g 2076^{P} **2658^{P} 2841^{8} 3155^{8} 3489^{3} 3700^{P} 3848^{3} 4203^{5} 4312^{6} 4404^{4} (4546) >80h 89c<**
Ballyea Boy (IRE) 7 gr g **(1338) (1765) 2758^{6} 3018^{5} 3617^{8} 3969^{2} >85h 116c<**
Ballyedward (IRE) 7 b g **1318^{P} 1728^{4} >81c<**
Ballyhamage (IRE) 9 br g **4308^{F} >73h<**
Ballyhays (IRE) 8 ch g Glow (USA)-Relanca (Relic) 727^{P} 902^{9} 1770^{F}
Ballyhire Lad (IRE) 8 b g **1750a^{6} 2348a^{13} >98h 123c<**
Ballykissangel 4 ro g Hadeer-April Wind (Windjammer (USA)) 1184^{14} 1526^{P} 1908^{P}
Ballyline (IRE) 6 b g **30^{2} 70^{9} (1051) 1248^{2} 1311^{2} 1557^{F} 2638^{2} 2767^{3} 3068^{P} 3616^{P} 3972^{2} 4186^{4} >101c<**
Ballymacool 5 ch g Ballacashtal (CAN)-Storm of Plenty (Billion (USA)) *3846^{3}* **>39fh<**
Ballymacrevan (IRE) 7 ch g **4356a^{P} >60h 112c<**
Ballymana Boy (IRE) 4 b g Commanche Run-Spring Chimes (Slippered) 4287^{6} **>51fh<**
Ballymgyr (IRE) 8 ch g 2067^{P} **2679^{P} 2819^{4} >49?h 92?c<**
Bally Parson 11 b g **56^{5} 742^{4} 862^{U}** 1060^{4} 1183^{4} **1660^{2} 1957^{4} 2621^{5} 2821^{9}** 4226^{6} **4300^{5} 4456^{U} 4635^{3} >59h 105c<**
Ballyquintet (IRE) 6 ch m 1555^{12} 1830^{15} 3084^{P}
Ballyranebow (IRE) 9 ch m **160^{7} >30c<**
Ballyranter 8 ch g Bold Owl-Whipalash (Stephen George) 2074^{11} 2697^{6} 2898^{6} 3818^{12} **>58h<**
Ballyrihy Boy (IRE) 6 b g Farhaan-Ceoil Eireann (Tudor Music) 3615^{7} **>103h<**
Ballysokerry (IRE) 6 b h 743^{R}
Bally Wonder 5 b m Music Boy-Salacious (Sallust) 2840^{P} 3226^{P} 3416^{P} 3752^{9} 4163^{7} 4236^{8}
Balmaha 6 b m Absalom-Mo Ceri (Kampala) 7^{P}
Balmoral Princess 4 b f Thethingaboutitis (USA)-Fair Balmoral (Hasty Word) 282^{3} (388) 458^{4} 640^{6} 1953^{6} 3473^{6} 4091^{P} **>44h<**
Balyara (IRE) 7 ch g The Noble Player (USA)-Puss Moth (Hotfoot) **323a^{4} 1142^{5} >105c<**
Bandit Boy 4 gr g Robellino (USA)-Patraana (Nishapour (FR)) 3621^{P}
Bangabunny 7 ch g **4350a^{5} >76h 86c<**
Bang in Trouble (IRE) 6 b g 3028^{7} 3269^{P} 3317^{6} 3531^{3} 3885^{P} **>67h< (DEAD)**
Banjo (FR) 7 b g **3636^{P} 4206^{6} >143c<**
Bank Avenue 6 b g 1795^{6} 2550^{10} 3541^{U} **>61h<**
Banker Count 5 b g Lord Bud-Gilzie Bank (New Brig) 1926^{6} 2904^{6} 3366^{3} 3691^{2} **>76h<**
Bankhead (IRE) 8 gr g **(1538) (1632) 1936^{P} 2658^{P}** (3013) (3156) 3415^{4} 3731^{2} 4005^{4} **>105h 109c<**
Bank On Inland 4 ch f Rakaposhi King-Blakesware Gift (Dominion) 1652^{17} 1940^{12} 2859^{14} **>32h<**
Bankonit (IRE) 9 b g **1572^{7} 1771^{P}** 2006^{P} **>67h<**
Banks of The Bride 7 ch g 549^{6} 649^{9}
Bank Statement (IRE) 6 ch g 4117a^{8} **>92h<**
Banner Year (IRE) 6 b g Lancastrian-Stunted Reina (Reformed Character) 2047^{15} **3097^{P}** 3823^{17} 4144^{9} **4408^{3} 4751^{3} >69c<**
Bannkipour (IRE) 8 b g **92a^{3}**
Banntown Bill (IRE) 8 gr g **550^{P} 683^{P} 726^{P} 833^{5} 1961^{2} (2671) (2876) 3003^{5} 3444^{5} 4078^{6} 4387^{2} 4467^{2} 4722^{3} 4806^{6} >106c<**
Banny Hill Lad 7 gr g Pragmatic-Four M'S (Majestic Maharaj) 2074^{6} 2663^{4} 3048^{3} 3355^{2} 4476^{5} **>82h<**
Baranov (IRE) 4 b g Mulhollande (USA)-Silojoka (Home Guard (USA)) 1872^{3} 2622^{P} **>68h<**
Baraqueta 5 b h Sayf El Arab (USA)-Coqueta (Coquelin (USA)) 910^{15} **>14h<**
Barbara's Jewel 5 b g Rakaposhi King-Aston Lass (Headin' Up) 3084^{P}
Barbary Falcon 7 b g 2791^{6} 2961^{3} 3295^{2} **>76h<**
Barbrallen 5 b m 956^{P}
Bardaros 8 b g Lighter-Suttons Hill (Le Bavard (FR)) **704^{2} 875^{3} 1160^{P}** (2654) 2918^{3} **>66h 77c<**
Barefoot Landing (USA) 6 b m 2541^{3} 2790^{7} 3325^{P} **>52h<**
Barford Sovereign 5 b m 952^{2} 1088^{5} 1418^{4} (1866) 2644^{4} 2929^{2} 3286^{4} (3666) 4005^{2} (4229) 4425^{2} **>92h<**
Bargash 5 ch g Sharpo-Anchor Inn (Be My Guest (USA)) 974^{10} **>6h<**
Bargin Inn 7 b g 2931^{2}
Barichste 9 ch g **4457^{P} >55dc<**
Barik (IRE) 7 b g 1141^{7} 1305^{P} 1666^{11} 1824^{6} 1969^{8} **>38h<**
Barkisland 13 b g **3005^{P} >74?c<**
Bark'n'bite 5 b g 1143^{7} 1796^{8} 3157^{P} 3313^{8} 3620^{3} 3711^{P} **>62h<**
Barley Meadow (IRE) 5 ch g Phardante (FR)-Foredefine (Bonne Noel) 1485a^{8} **>54h<**
Barlot 5 b m Sayf El Arab (USA)-Biding Time (Bellypha) 872^{15} 1124^{18}
Barnabe Lad 7 ch g Rabdan-Literary Lady (Class Distinction) 3437^{P}
Barna Boy (IRE) 9 b g 948^{4} 1137^{3} 1365^{3} 1793^{6} 3011^{4} (3640) 4397^{4} **>116h 136?c<**
Barnageera Boy (IRE) 8 b g **3526a^{3} >80h 112c<**
Barn Elms 10 ch g **4615^{3} >85c<**
Barnetts Boy 5 b g Librate-Guilty Sparkle (Roc Imp) 980^{10} 1124^{15}
Barney Rubble 12 b or br g 2042^{11} **3560^{P} >63h 75?c<**
Barneys Gold (IRE) 8 ch g **4623^{3} >78c<**
Barnstormer 11 ch g 1050^{9} 1139^{7} 1304^{5} (1822) 3887^{8} 4147^{6} 4283^{7} 4389^{5} 4760^{6} **>47h<**
Baronburn 7 b m 872^{16} **(DEAD)**
Baroncelli 7 ch g **2077^{3} 2679^{5} >63h 60c<**
Baronet (IRE) 7 ro g **(1192) (1503) 2883^{3} 3616^{8} 4213^{3} >82h 132c<**
Baron Hrabovsky 4 ch g Prince Sabo-Joli's Girl (Mansingh (USA)) 3404^{P} 3918^{6} 4095^{6} **>23h<**
Baron's Heir 10 b g **3739^{6} 3934^{2} 4442^{6} 4738^{P} >88dc<**
Barrie Stir 5 b g 1013^{7} 1581^{P} 4719^{4} **>53h<**
Barrigan's Hill (IRE) 7 b g 319a^{6} **>69h<**
Barrington (IRE) 4 b g Warrshan (USA)-Chez Nous (Habitat) 4360a^{19} **>17fh<**

Barristers Boy 7 b g 1539^{9} >**57h**<

Barrow Street 7 b g Sula Bula-Kerry Street (Dairialatan) **4462^{4} 4522^{P}** >**72?c**<

Barryben 8 b or br g (1418) 1767^{6} >**72+h**<

Bartholomew Fair 6 b g Sadler's Wells (USA)-Barada (USA) (Damascus (USA)) 2012^{11} 2696^{18}

Barton Bank 11 br g **1157^{2} 1366^{5} 2115^{3} 2775^{2} 3636^{2} (4011) 4303^{F}** >**166c**<

Barton Blade (IRE) 5 b g 865^{15} 974^{11} 1065^{4} >**37h**<

Barton Bulldozer (IRE) 7 b g 25^{12}

Barton Heights 5 b g 1686^{3} 1945^{7} 2178^{5} 2864^{4} 3448^{3} (3971) 4389^{2} 4501^{2} 4754^{4} >**66h**<

Barton Lil 5 ch m Nicholas Bill-Lily Mab (FR) (Prince Mab (FR)) 4538^{8}

Barton Scamp 5 ch g 1276^{4} 2669^{6} 3158^{6} 3733^{7} 4006^{4} >**69h**<

Barton Ward 6 b g 1250^{5} 1802^{3} 2053^{3} (2759) 3048^{2} 3269^{2} >**85h**<

Bart Owen 12 br g **2848a^{9}** >**127h 101c**<

Barty Boy (IRE) 5 b g Buckskin (FR)-Black Tulip (Pals Passage) 3703^{9}

Bas de Laine (FR) 11 b g **809^{4} (940) 1142^{3} (1315) (1501) 2821^{3} 4609^{2} 4716^{U}** >**83h 130c**<

Basher Bill 14 b g **4320^{P}** >**69c**<

Basilicus (FR) 8 b g **(1122) 1293^{9}** >**75dh 113c**<

Basil Street (IRE) 5 b g 630^{2} 727^{4} >**74h**<

Basincroft 7 b g 1842^{3} 2627^{B} 3100^{P} >**40h**<

Bassenhally 7 ch g (1253) **1563^{7} 2679^{U} 2947^{P}** 3371^{3} 3612^{11} 3923^{6} >**63h 74c**<

Bath Knight 4 b g Full Extent (USA)-Mybella Ann (Anfield) 501^{4} 640^{3} 831^{4} 3447^{12} 3898^{2} 4137^{2} 4313^{8} >**53h**<

Bath Times 5 ch m 603^{11} 3445^{7}

Bathwick Bobbie 10 b g **1773^{P} 2679^{P} 2823^{7} 3051^{9} 3331^{8}** 4318^{5} >**47h 78c**<

Battery Fired 8 ch g K-Battery-Party Cloak (New Member) 3691^{5} 3887^{6} 4714^{2} >**55h**<

Battle Creek (IRE) 7 b g 3295^{7} >**35h**<

Battleship Bruce 5 b g 1380^{2} 1729^{3} 2624^{8} 2818^{F} 3057^{P} 3352^{3} 3583^{5} 3757^{5} >**68h**<

Battuta 8 ch m Ballacashtal (CAN)-Valpolicella (Lorenzaccio) 1703^{20}

Batty's Island 8 b g 71^{12} 223^{6} 285^{7} 391^{U} 413^{5} 641^{11} 868^{3} 1121^{3} 1256^{6} 2694^{P} 2877^{4} **3436^{P}** >**53h 85dc**<

Bavard Dieu (IRE) 9 g **946^{4} 1277^{3} 1366^{8} 3598^{11} 3916^{5} 4306^{3} (4624)** >**132c**<

Bavardier (IRE) 6 ch g Le Bavard (FR)-Clairellen (Ashmore (FR)) 1289^{8} 1800^{4} >**48fh**<

Bavario (USA) 4 ch g Theatrical-Hawaiian Miss (USA) 2993a^{10} >**62h**<

Baxworthy Lord 6 b g 885^{P} **1449^{U} 1596^{P} 2873^{F}** 4276^{P}

Bayerd (IRE) 6 b g (1165) 1638^{7} 2676^{P} 3004^{10} 4292^{3} 4453^{2} 4658^{3} >**73h**<

Bay Fair 5 b m 1453^{5} 1855^{5} 4403^{7} 4807^{8} >**61h**<

Bayline Star (IRE) 7 b g 1541^{P} **1981^{2} 2947^{5} 4621^{2}** >**81dh 102c**<

Baylord Prince (IRE) 9 b g 3760^{6} 3958^{7} 4096^{2} 4524^{8} 4727^{3} >**42h**<

Bay Lough (IRE) 6 b m Lancastrian-Cauriedator (Laurence O) 4273^{4}

Bayrak (USA) 7 b g Bering-Phydilla (FR) (Lyphard (USA)) **2068^{4}**

Beach Bum 11 gr g **4254^{P}** >**36h 90?c**<

Beachy Head 9 gr g 1645^{7} 2078^{6} **3025^{4} (3349)** >**80h 126c**<

Beacon Flight (IRE) 6 br g (1044) 1516^{2} 1905^{3} 2673^{5} >**71h**<

Beacon Hill Lady 4 b f Golden Lahab (USA)-Homing Hill (Homing) 1940^{P} 2859^{16} 3031^{12} 3313^{7} 3908^{11} 4055^{9} >**46h**<

Beacon Lane (IRE) 4 br g Strong Gale-Sharpaway (Royal Highway) 4531^{10} 4657^{5} >**34fh**<

Beakstown (IRE) 8 b g **763a^{7} 1216a^{4} 1486a^{4} 2335a^{3} 2739a^{2} 3260a^{P} 3596^{7} 4123a^{4} 4366a^{4}** >**107h 127c**<

Beam Me Up Scotty (IRE) 8 br g 71^{11} 187^{6} 301^{3} 362^{4} 407^{F} >**57h**<

Bear Claw 8 br g **3334^{F} (3537) 4050^{U} 4203^{3}** >**100h 104c**<

Beatson (IRE) 8 gr g **1284^{F} (1837) (1902) (2009) 2647^{4} 2962^{2} 3986^{3}** >**92h 111c**<

Beat The Rap 11 b g **72^{4} 180^{5} 206^{4}** >**84c**<

Beat The Second (IRE) 9 gr g **1003a^{6} 2348a^{9}** >**106c**<

Beau Babillard 10 b g **(1167) 1570^{2} 1837^{3} 2660^{P} 2823^{9} 3410^{3} 4140^{4} 4520^{5}** >**116h 108dc**<

Beaucadeau 11 b g **464^{2} 583^{4} (702)** >**117h 111c**< **(DEAD)**

Beau Dandy 10 ch g **(2944) 3460^{4}** >**105c**<

Beaufan 10 br g 339^{9} **1122^{P} 1684^{P}** >**26h**<

Beauman 7 b g 3031^{8} >**66h**<

Beau Matelot 5 ch g 871^{6} 2631^{P} 3612^{6} 4249^{3} 4505^{4} 4755^{2} >**57h**<

Beaumont (IRE) 7 br g 2806^{3} 3166^{2} 3438^{3} >**76h**<

Beau Noir (FR) 7 br g Alluvia-Brave Paix (BEL) (Premier Violon) **(580a)**

Beaurepaire (IRE) 9 b g **1473^{2} 1662^{P} 2754^{5} 3018^{4} 3428^{2} 3699^{7}** >**71dh 113c**<

Bebe Grey 6 b m Pragmatic-Dawn Magic (Cleon) 2073^{6} 2757^{6} 3090^{8} >**35fh**<

Be Brave 7 b g **1680^{P} 2052^{3} 2699^{4} 3370^{F}** >**61h 87c**<

Be Broadminded 5 b g Broadsword (USA)-Random Romance (Eric) 4538^{P} 4774^{14}

Beccy Brown 9 b m **8^{5}** >**62c**<

Beckamere 5 b m Rushmere-Dela Moon (Algora) 2682^{18}

Beck and Call (IRE) 8 ch g 4224^{4} 4479^{4} >**69h**<

Becky Boo 7 b m 66^{7} >**58h**<

Becky's Girl 7 br m Sweet Monday-Bransford (Hallodri (AUT)) 1470^{13} 1679^{9} 1959^{11} 2546^{15} **3043^{10} 3489^{U}** >**55h 46c**<

Becky's Lad 7 ch g 1151^{3} 1329^{17} 2875^{9}

Beech Brook 8 b g **4637^{4}** >**61h 71c**<

Beechfield Flyer 6 ch g 1857^{2} (2813) 3076^{3} 3283^{2} 3733^{6} 3967^{2} 4476^{2} 4772^{4} >**69h**<

Beet Statement (IRE) 8 br m Strong Statement (USA)-Cora Swan (Tarqogan) **(323a)** >**85c**<

Beggars Banquet (IRE) 7 b g 1050^{3} (1245) (1689) >**92h**<

Begger's Opera 5 ch g North Briton-Operelle (Music Boy) 1908^{P}

Be Home Early (IRE) 7 ch g Arapahos (FR)-Dara's Last 3650a^{7} 4352a^{3} >**97h**<

Beinn Mohr 10 b m **4241^{6}**

Be In Space 6 b m Gunner B-Spaced Out (Space King) 3006^{11} 3808^{7} 4561^{3} 4762^{7} >**28h**<

Belarus (IRE) 5 b g Waajib-Kavali (Blakeney) 4547^{5} 4696^{7} >**55h**<

Bel-de-Moor 5 br m 1036^{11} 1341^{9} 2959^{4} >**40h**<

Beldine 12 b g **537^{2} 702^{2} 855^{3} 895^{3}** >**106c**< **(DEAD)**

Belgran (USA) 8 b g 2663^{P} 3184^{P}

Believe It 8 g 4056^{F} 4714^{7} >**9h**<

Bella Sedona 5 ch m 1165^{4} 1451^{6} (2678) 3352^{P} >**56h**<

Bellator 4 b g Simply Great (FR)-Jupiter's Message (Jupiter Island) (1158) (1514) >**102+h**<

Belle Baroness 7 br m 3437^{7} >**28h**<

Belle Perk (IRE) 6 b m Executive Perk-Bellatollah (Bellman (FR)) 344^{5} 2071^{U} 2791^{8} 3057^{P} >**33h**<

Belle Rose (IRE) 7 gr m (1047) (1247) 1849^{3} 2768^{2} 3032^{P} 3557^{P} >**64h**<

Bellidium 5 b m 1275^{12} 1665^{6} 3042^{9} 3734^{6} 4299^{P} 4743^{2} >**55h**<

Bell One (USA) 8 ch g 1996^{3} 2884^{12} 3277^{9} >**70h**<

Bellroi (IRE) 6 b g (641) (692) 1392^{6} 1556^{3} >**92h**<

Bells Bridge (IRE) 7 b g Salluceva-Pollys Flake (Will Somers) 3650a^{4} >**82h**<

Bells Hill Lad 10 ch g **1348^{2}** >**54h 89c**<

Bells Life (IRE) 8 b g **(1570) 1937^{6} 2660^{3} (2879) 3151^{3} 3618^{8} (4013)** >**114h 141c**<

Bell Staffboy (IRE) 8 b g **(2748) (3044) (3285) 3616^{10} 4116a^{F}** >**118h 125c**<

Bells Will Ring (IRE) 7 b g **3713^{4}** >**28h 50c**< **(DEAD)**

Bells Wood 8 br g Sousa-Virtuosity (Reliance II) **602^{P} 720^{P} 1199^{F} 3181^{5} 3339^{5} 3627^{P} 4100^{3} 4314^{U}** >**64c**<

Belmarita (IRE) 4 ch f Belmez (USA)-Congress Lady (General Assembly (USA)) 1370^{2} 1776^{6} 2889^{5} 3226^{8} (3544) 3634^{25} >**60h**<

Belmont King (IRE) 9 b g **(1785) 2997a^{P} 3563^{2} (4213)** >**156c**<

Belmorebruno 7 b g Pitpan-Direct Call (Menelek) 3154^{3} >**71h**<

Below The Red Line 4 b g Reprimand-Good Try (Good Bond) 807^{P}

Beltino 6 gr g Neltino-Thorganby Bella (Porto Bello) 3100^{P} 3823^{18}

Belvederian 10 b g **1397a^{2} 1737a^{3} 1917^{U} 2362a^{4} 2741a^{4} 3526a^{4}** >**129h 139c**<

Belvento (IRE) 5 b g Strong Gale-Salufair (Salluceva) 2012^{9} 3143^{9}

Be My Romany (IRE) 5 ch m Be My Native (USA)-Romany Fortune (Sunyboy) 4407^{3} >**62fh**<

Ben Bowden 4 br g Sharrood (USA)-Elegant Rose (Noalto) 294^{3} (358) 501^{2} 599^{W} 736^{4} 836^{2} 912^{2} 1064^{2} 1387^{3} 1706^{3} 1935^{4} 3301^{7} 3953^{3} 4341^{3} >**67h**<

Benbulbin (IRE) 7 b g **1632^{P} 2072^{P} 2841^{U}**

Ben Connan (IRE) 7 b g 1007^{7} 4562^{F} >**3h**<

Ben Cruachan (IRE) 7 b g 1290^{2} (1802) >**66h**<

Bendor Mark 8 b g **1122^{P} (2665) 2928^{2}** >**68h 102c**<

Ben Doula 5 b g Dunbeath (USA)-Singing High (Julio Mariner) 3914^{6} 4580^{6} >**47fh**<

Bend Sable (IRE) 7 b g 1360^{P} 1804^{9} 2631^{F} 3137^{3} 3346^{13} 3728^{5} >**88?h**<

Benefit-In-Kind (IRE) 5 br g Executive Perk-Tanarpa (Dusky Boy) 2080^{2} >**60fh**<

Ben Eiger (IRE) 5 ch g Good Thyne (USA)-Priscilla's Pride (Laurence O) 2066^{5} 3304^{11} >**55fh**<

Benfleet 6 ch g Dominion-Penultimate (Final Straw) 2634^{10} 2945^{3} 3184^{4} 3628^{P} >**62h**<

Bengazee (IRE) 9 b g **70^{U}** >**22h**<

Benjamin Jones 5 b g Teenoso (USA)-Mizzie Lizzie (Netherkelly) 2012^{14} 4088^{7} >**27fh**<

Benjamin Lancaster 13 b g **(1257) 1570^{3} 1696^{4} 2657^{P} 2879^{7} 3113^{P} 3567^{3}** >**99c**<

Benji 6 ch g High Kicker (USA)-Snap Tin (Jimmy Reppin) 1966^{8} 2677^{12} 3019^{P} **3356^{U} 3582^{F}** 3755^{7} 4102^{5} 4233^{P} >**44h**<

Benkarosam 4 b g Full Extent (USA)-Discreet Charm (Moorestyle) 1900^{11} 2705^{9} >**14h**<

Bentley Manor 8 ch g **4530^{P}** >**74h**<

Benvenuto 6 b g Neltino-Rydewells Daughter (Celtic Cone) 1834^{6} (3365) 4216^{P} >**65fh**<

Bernera 5 br g Rakaposhi King-Isle Maree (Star Appeal) 4538^{13} 4561^{10} >**16fh**<

Berrings Dasher 10 ch g **3568^{3} 4135^{5} 4322^{P}** >**88c**<

Bertie 7 b g 679^{11}

Bertie Bavard 5 ch g Le Bavard (FR)-Acushla Macree (Mansingh (USA)) 4008^{14} **>40fh<**

Bertone (IRE) 8 b g (799) 946^{2} 1155^{3} 1520^{4} 1917^{4} 4054^{3} (4131) 4311^{6} **>96h 139+c<**

Berts Choice 6 b g 2664^{6} 2813^{6} **>29h<**

Berude Not to (IRE) 8 b g (1456) (1909) 2883^{4} (3274) 3616^{4} **>117h 144c<**

Bervie House (IRE) 9 br g 3476^{7} **>74h 67c<**

Bessie Browne (IRE) 5 b m Strong Gale-Shuil Ub (Le Moss) 1834^{3} (3548) 3821^{4} **>68fh<**

Best Friend 5 b m Lord Bud-Sand Kit (Saucy Kit) 686^{4} 858^{5} 1208^{11} 1523^{5} 2566^{6} 2920^{7} 3611^{6} **>50h<**

Best of All (IRE) 5 b m Try My Best (USA)-Skisette (Malinowski (USA)) (2503) 2798^{2} 3325^{6} 4711^{6} **>73h<**

Best of Bold 5 ch g 73^{8} **>15h<**

Best of Friends (IRE) 7 ch g 1581^{2} 2880^{10} 3582^{P} **>76h< (DEAD)**

Be Surprised 11 ch g 959^{P} 1934^{P} 2823^{5} 3176^{4} 3675^{P} 3899^{2} 4344^{5} **>78c<**

Betabetcorbett 6 b g 67^{2} 183^{10} 219^{4} 339^{2} 419^{3} 652^{4} 1120^{7} 1254^{P} 1664^{5} **>65h 78c<**

Beths Wish 8 br m 871^{10} 1090^{6} 1251^{8} 2088^{10} 3190^{P} **>48h<**

Better Bythe Glass (IRE) 8 br g (725) 1429^{6} 3013^{12} 3362^{12} 4220^{U} 4470^{7} 4562^{P} **>50h<**

Better Future (IRE) 8 br g Good Thyne (USA)-Little Else (Abednego) 3155^{9} 3334^{6} 4537^{6} 4699^{P} **>52c<**

Better Times Ahead 11 ro g 1359^{5} 1647^{10} 3025^{5} 3160^{6} 3267^{P} 4016^{P} 4207^{11} **>107h 136c<**

Betty's Boy (IRE) 8 b g 1273^{3} 1558^{2} 2782^{5} 3046^{5} **>103h 135c<**

Bet Wiltshire 5 b g Arctic Lord-Solhoon (Tycoon II) 4161^{6} 4528^{P} **>41h<**

Beweldered 5 ch g Weld-Bush Radio (Hot Grove) 1289^{17} 3500^{15} 3735^{P}

Beyond Our Reach 9 br g 1599^{2} 1767^{5} **>81h<**

Beyond the Stars 6 b g 4773^{F} **>52h<**

B Fifty Two (IRE) 6 b g 954^{P}

Bickleigh Belle 7 ch m Gunner B-Deep Coach (Deep Run) 900^{P} 1056^{P}

Bide Our Time (USA) 5 b h 67^{F} **>37h<**

Bid For Tools (IRE) 5 b g 1200^{P}

Bietschhorn Bard 7 b g (1036) 1323^{4} 1791^{7} 2040^{2} 2692^{7} 3012^{3} 3740^{F} **>67h<**

Big Archie 7 br g El Conquistador-Royal Declaration (Breeders Dream) 1797^{F} 1829^{P} 2896^{5} (4227) **>112?c<**

Big Ben Dun 11 b g (809) 1089^{3} 1287^{U} 2011^{P} 2758^{5} 2928^{U} 3175^{2} 4270^{8} 4529^{7} **>110c<**

Big Matt (IRE) 9 b g 1134^{2} 1366^{6} 1917^{P} 2646^{3} 2935^{4} 4311^{7} 4349a^{2} **>121h 151?c<**

Big Perks (IRE) 5 ch g Executive Perk-Secret Ocean (Most Secret) 898^{2} (2811) **>57fh<**

Bigsound (IRE) 5 b g Little Bighorn-Lightfoot Lady (Tekoah) 2682^{5} **>48fh<**

Big Stan's Boy 6 b g Lighter-Shelleys Rocky Gem (Kemal (FR)) 1013^{3} 1801^{8} 3690^{5} 4376^{P} **>34fh<**

Big Strand (IRE) 8 b g (1681) 1952^{2} (3269) (3615) 4016^{2} **>110h 100c<**

Big Theo 6 br g 2576^{P}

Big Treat (IRE) 5 b g 60^{3} 218^{4} 1050^{5} **>71h<**

Bigwheel Bill (IRE) 8 br g 2694^{7} 2952^{4} 3228^{3} 3570^{5} 4345^{3} **>57h<**

Bigwig (IRE) 4 ch c Thatching-Sabaah (USA) (Nureyev (USA)) 1935^{6} 2070^{5} 2865^{8} 3953^{4} 4434^{4} **>52h<**

Bikalamoun (FR) 7 b g Bikala-Zabriskie Point (FR) (Sword Dancer (USA)) 2496a^{2}

Bilbo Baggins (IRE) 9 ch g 4135^{8} **>63c<**

Bill and Win 6 b g 1034^{P} 1299^{13} 2006^{P} 2882^{16} 3201^{12} **>15h<**

Billingsgate 5 ch g Nicholas Bill-Polly Washdish (Oats) (1685) 2012^{2} 3042^{4} **>74fh<**

Billion Dollarbill 9 ch g 4317^{P} **>76c<**

Bill of Rights 9 b g 791^{W} 933^{3}

Billsbrook 7 b g (1160) **>56h 96c<**

Bill's Pride 6 gr m 1343^{3} 1666^{5} 3064^{P} 3313^{5} 3534^{6} 3641^{U} 3908^{10} 4259^{14} **>55h<**

Billy Bathgate 11 ch g 2944^{3} **>132dc<**

Billy Box 5 gr g Lord Bud-Counter Coup (Busted) (3574) **>72fh<**

Billy Buckskin 5 ch g Buckskin (FR)-Money Run (Deep Run) 1692^{3} 2066^{4} 2633^{2} 3021^{6} **>66fh<**

Billy Buoyant 8 b g 4751^{P} **>60dh<**

Billy Bushwacker 6 b g Most Welcome-Secret Valentine (Wollow) 2953^{3} 3197^{6} **>63h<**

Billygoat Gruff 8 b g 1324^{2} 1784^{U} **>91h 129c<**

Bimsey (IRE) 7 b h 1916^{2} 2635^{3} 3597^{13} (4063) **>136h<**

Bingley Bank (IRE) 5 br g Mandalus-Royal Reliance (Rymer) 4215^{19} **>41fh<**

Birchall Boy 9 br g 3010^{P} **>51h<**

Birdietoo 5 ch m Nad Elshiba (USA)-Wylie Hill VII (Damsire Unregistered) 2012^{15}

Birequest 6 ch g 1^{2} 1118^{4} **>62h< (DEAD)**

Birkdale (IRE) 6 gr g Roselier (FR)-Clonroche Lady (Charlottesvilles Flyer) 4188^{7} 4249^{2} **>69h<**

Bironi 8 b g 1252^{2} 1472^{2} 1817^{F} **>105+c<**

Birthday Boy (IRE) 5 b g (26) 105^{2} 189^{9} **>74h<**

Birthplace (IRE) 7 b or br g 3035^{F} 3327^{P} 3448^{P} 4236^{6} 4409^{F} 4714^{F}

Bishopdale 16 ch g 1846^{6} 2179^{P} 2923^{8} (4153) 4410^{3} **>78c<**

Bishops Castle (IRE) 9 ch g 411^{2} 595^{2} (903) 1449^{U} 2873^{5} (3538) 4000^{4} 4331^{2} 4520^{6} **>65h 94c<**

Bishops Hall 11 br g 314a^{2} (763a) 3563^{P} 4074^{P} 4303^{P} **>148c<**

Bishops Tale 7 b g 4618^{5} **>73h 41c<**

Bitacrack 10 ch g 9^{2} 68^{3} 136^{3} 190^{8} 696^{3} 4753^{5} **>80c<**

Bites 4 b f Risk Me (FR)-Sundaysport Splash (Lord Gayle (USA)) 1149^{11} 2815^{11} 3072^{9} 3985^{4} **>50h<**

Bite the Bullet 6 ch g 820^{4} 900^{7} 969^{6} 1322^{4} 1638^{11} 2088^{15} **>47h<**

Bit Of A Citizen (IRE) 6 b m 4623^{U} **>61c<**

Bit of A Dream (IRE) 7 b g 13^{7} 188^{2} 254^{4} 4314^{3} 4446^{5} (4715) **>37h 74c<**

Bitofamixup (IRE) 6 br g Strong Gale-Geeaway (Gala Performance (USA)) 954^{14} (3357) (4015) (4380) 4805^{2} **>124c<**

Bit of A Touch 11 b br g Touching Wood (USA)-Edelliette (FR) (Edellic) 362^{P} 482^{2} (547) (728) (835) 1951^{5} 3044^{5} 3629^{3} 3843^{3} 4385^{2} **>92c<**

Bit of Rough (IRE) 7 b g 3471^{12} 3803^{P}

Bit 'o' Sunshine 6 ch m Tout Ensemble-Bit 'o' Sun (Laurence O) 1685^{18} 2008^{P}

Biya (IRE) 5 ch g 871^{8} 1628^{9} 1816^{7} 1984^{5} 3228^{4} 4626^{5} **>47h<**

Blaaziing Joe (IRE) 6 b g Alzao (USA)-Beijing (USA) (Northjet) 1351^{5} **(DEAD)**

Black Brook (IRE) 8 br g Royal Fountain-Ski Cap (Beau Chapeau) 1803^{5} 2061^{4} 2912^{3} 3347^{P} **>89c<**

Black Church 11 ch g 20^{6} 814^{5} 959^{3} 1284^{5} 1420^{U} 1837^{4} 2681^{3} (2910) 3182^{P} 3496^{4} (3759) (3899) (4085) 4467^{3} **>114c<**

Black Hero (FR) 8 br h Lashkari-Damasquine (USA) (Damascus (USA)) (53a) (851a) **>111c<**

Black Ice (IRE) 6 b g 1672^{3} 2649^{9} 3032^{5} 3481^{9} **>61h<**

Black Ice Boy (IRE) 6 b g 2701^{P}

Black Queen (IRE) 6 b m 2603a^{2} 3640^{4} **>103h<**

Black Spur 15 br g 4716^{U} **>66?c<**

Black Statement (IRE) 7 br g 1476^{P} 1867^{10} 2053^{13} 3172^{9} 3443^{2} **>50h 64?c<**

Blade of Fortune 9 b g Beldale Flutter (USA)-Foil 'em (USA) (Blade (USA)) 1950^{4} 2655^{6} 3054^{8} (3338) 3594^{11} 3890^{2} 4466^{5} (4548) (4644) **>71h<**

Blair Castle (IRE) 6 b g 2691^{F} 2892^{2} 3167^{4} 3417^{F} 3571^{4} 3816^{6} 4061^{15} 4240^{3} 4430^{2} **>100?h 116?c<**

Blake's Oemin 5 b g Baron Blakeney-Marjoemin (Import) 4215^{16} **>58fh<**

Blakeway 10 gr m Baron Blakeney-Provoking (Sharp Edge) 1200^{P} 1874^{P}

Blameless 5 b m Little Wolf-Hitting Supreme (Supreme Sovereign) 1555^{11} 2696^{20}

Blanc Seing (FR) 10 b g 643^{5} 876^{6} 1152^{9} 1304^{3} 1854^{4} 2045^{P} **>57h<**

Blasket Hero 9 gr g (485) 605^{2} (810) 1286^{3} (1376) 1635^{P} 4279^{2} 4383^{2} 4521^{P} **>86h 98c< (DEAD)**

Blasted 5 ch g 3955^{8} **>9h< (DEAD)**

Blaster Watson 6 ch g Kind of Hush-Economy Pep (Jimmy Reppin) 2675^{7} 2904^{13} 4450^{6} 4613^{3} 4737^{4} **>57h<**

Blast Freeze (IRE) 8 b m 2780^{F} 3231^{3} 3615^{15} **>104h<**

Blatant Outburst 7 b g 3362^{5} 3621^{9} 3831^{4} 4648^{7} 4789^{5} **>44h<**

Blaze Away (USA) 6 b h 1067^{3} (1556) (1922) 2056^{F} **>117?h< (DEAD)**

Blaze Of Honour (IRE) 6 ch m 3697^{7} **>97+h 99+c<**

Blaze of Oak (USA) 6 ch g 885^{2} 955^{6} 1250^{11} 1394^{P} **>70h<**

Blaze of Song 5 ch h Jester-Intellect (Frimley Park) 2937^{6} 3148^{4} 3359^{10} 3594^{6} **>54h<**

Blazer 4 b g Lighter-Australia Fair (AUS) (Without Fear (FR)) 4657^{7}

Blazer Moriniere (FR) 8 b g 1556^{4} 1783^{7} 2657^{7} 3053^{3} 3354^{3} 3843^{F} (4254) (4438) 4659^{2} (4771) **>56h 102c<**

Blazing Batman 4 ch g Shaab-Cottage Blaze (Sunyboy) 3606^{5} 3853^{10} **>41fh<**

Blazing Dawn 10 b g 9^{3} 420^{2} 464^{3} 702^{5} 896^{P} (1082) (1164) 1307^{6} 1657^{9} 1846^{P} 1941^{5} 3452^{3} 3692^{2} 3886^{11} 4392^{2} 4503^{P} 4716^{3} 4757^{2} **>99c<**

Blazing Dove 6 ch g 3798^{P} 4528^{P}

Blazing Imp (USA) 4 ch g Imp Society (USA)-Marital (USA) (Marine Patrol (USA)) 1940^{P}

Blazing Miracle 5 b m 1327^{4} 1568^{7} 1995^{5} 2620^{2} 2891^{8} 3190^{F} 3541^{5} **>50h<**

Blazing Storm (IRE) 5 ch g 2759^{7} 3019^{6} 3408^{4} **>64h<**

Blazing Trail (IRE) 9 gr g 537^{3} 2790^{5} 3069^{F} 3101^{3} 3482^{P} **>57h 98c<**

Blennerville (IRE) 7 ch m 69^{5} 137^{9} **>67h<**

Blomberg (IRE) 5 b h Indian Ridge-Daniella Drive (USA) (Shelter Half (USA)) 2624^{7} 2937^{P} **>64h< (DEAD)**

Blond Moss 7 b g 1654^{P} 1999^{12}

Blood Brother 5 ch g 1084^{2} 1362^{5} 1827^{7} 2785^{17} 2953^{P} 3305^{P} 3448^{7} 4409^{9} **>4h<**

Blooming Spring (IRE) 8 b m (10) 533^{3} 536^{2} 693^{4} 2922^{8} 3096^{6} 4147^{3} 4248^{14} 4575^{3} 4760^{7} **>51h<**

Bloom'in Junes (IRE) 5 gr m Celio Rufo-Flat Out (Random Shot) 1026^{10}

Blossom Dearie 4 b f Landyap (USA)-Jose Collins (Singing Bede) 1172^{5} 1595^{P}

Blotoft 5 b g 3438^{16} 3542^{6} (3921) 4089^{4} (4472) 4633^{3} 4770^{7} **>62h<**

Blow Dry (IRE) 7 b g Glenstal (USA)-Haco (Tribal Chief) 1851[P]
Blowing Rock (IRE) 5 b g Strong Gale-Poor Elsie (Crash Course) 2080[5] 2572[6] 4329[2] 4528[P] 4726[2] >70h<
Blown Wind (IRE) 6 b g (634) >76h<
Blue And Royal (IRE) 5 b g 1517[5] 1959[9] 3587[P] >44h<
Blue Bit (IRE) 4 b g Bluebird (USA)-Minnie Habit (Habitat) 1747a[P] >57h<
Blue Charm (IRE) 7 b g (694) 897[2] 1264[3] 1348[F] 1653[3] (2176) >78h 104c<
Blue Cheek 11 b or br g (3744) (4051) >117c<
Blue Chequer 6 gr m Rakaposhi King-Mount St Mary's (Lochnager) 1827[8] 2619[P] >23fh<
Blue Domain 6 b g 2505[4] 3313[12] 3663[6] >48h<
Blue Havana 5 br m 24[7] 2690[P] 3275[10] 4304[11] 4794[P]
Blue Lugana 5 b g Lugana Beach-Two Friendly (Be Friendly) 1118[7] 1276[6] >51h<
Blue Raven 6 ch g 16[3] 285[5] 351[2] 503[2] 602[3] (752) 828[F] >81h 93+c<
Bluntswood Hall 4 b g Governor General-Miss Sarajane (Skyliner) 1149[4] 1413[2] 2815[2] 2946[6] 3284[11] 3985[9] >62h<
Blurred (IRE) 4 ch g Al Hareb (USA)-I'll Take Paris (USA) (Vaguely Noble) 1519[2] >85h<
Blurred Image (IRE) 6 ch g 961[3] 1168[4] 1332[2] 3921[6] >47h<
Blushing Sand (IRE) 7 ch g 2857a[6] 3126a[5] (3650a) 4124a[3] >93+h<
Boardroom Shuffle (IRE) 6 b g (1551) (2071) (2771) (3152) >108h<
Bobby Grant 6 ch g Gunner B-Goldaw (Gala Performance (USA)) 1579[3] (2047) (2701) (3159) 3702[5] >74+h<
Bobbyjo (IRE) 7 b g 1486a[2] 4356a[2] >78h 109+c<
Bobby Socks 11 b or br g (56) >121c< (DEAD)
Bob Nelson 10 b g 4186[P]
Bob's Ploy 5 b g 1830[10] 2842[4] 3076[7] 3750[3] 4233[4] >62h<
Bob Treacy (IRE) 8 b g Over The River (FR)-Banish Misfortune (Master Owen) 3391a[3] >98c<
Bodantree 6 b g 4162[6] 4384[F] 4525[4] 4739[2] >72h<
Boddington Hill 9 b m St Columbus-Dane Hole (Past Petition) 3055[P]
Boethius (USA) 8 ch g 4[P] 423[R] 505[7] 681[3] 873[6] >51h 71c<
Bo Knows Best (IRE) 8 ch g 1454[F] 1650[P] 1934[U] 2879[P] 4438[P] 4653[4] >119h 106dc<
Bolaney Girl (IRE) 8 b m 647[3] (684) 856[4] 1346[7] 1576[S] 1702[R] 1846[F] 2543[7] 2799[R] >60h 79?c<
Bold Account (IRE) 7 b g 1022[4] 1160[2] 1357[4] 1850[3] 2650[2] 2923[3] (3138) 3477[5] 3695[3] 4334[3] >80h 92c<
Bold Acre 7 ch g 1199[6] 1300[5] 1708[5] 2037[4] 2569[2] 2752[F] 3001[P] 3343[6] >94h 82+c<
Bold Action (IRE) 6 b g 1926[3] 2673[13] 3159[6] >58h<
Bold Boss 8 b g 1346[2] 1644[5] 1780[2] 2628[2] (2786) (2914) 3161[2] 3350[2] 3558[3] >134h 109c<
Bold Buster 4 b g Bustino-Truly Bold (Bold Lad (IRE)) 3007[P]
Bold Charlie 5 ch g 1168[P] 1339[7] 1663[9] 2038[11] 2664[7] 4089[10] >16h<
Bold Classic (IRE) 4 b c Persian Bold-Bay Street (Grundy) 1652[5] 3345[9] 3789[2] 3887[3] >71h<
Bold Echo 5 b m Silly Prices-Fair Echo (Quality Fair) 4249[P]
Bold Fountain (IRE) 6 b g 1349[2] >62h<
Bold Leap 5 b g Bold Owl-Thabeh (Shareef Dancer (USA)) 2682[7] 3170[3] 3425[2] 3821[3] >78fh<
Bold Look 6 b g 96[P] >33h<
Bold'n 10 ch g Ardross-Princess Dina (Huntercombe) 1689[P] 1802[P] 1854[P]
Bold Reine (FR) 8 b or br m 3110[P] 3764[P] (DEAD)
Bold Start Lady 4 b f Nicholas Bill-La Comedienne (Comedy Star (USA)) 1706[F] 2705[P]
Bold Statement 5 ch g 1296[7] (1579) 2785[U] 3315[4] 3483[5] (3823) 4244[2] (4514) (4707) >85h<
Bold Street (IRE) 7 ch g Shy Groom (USA)-Ferry Lane (Dom Racine (FR)) 1499[P]
Bold Time Monkey 6 ch m Bold Owl-Play For Time (Comedy Star (USA)) 3583[11] 3741[7] 4067[3] 4276[8] 4620[4] 4807[13] >33h<
Bold Top 5 ch g 1908[5] 2629[8] >47h<
Bolino Star (IRE) 6 b m 1752a[4] 3254a[6] 3523a[5] >109h<
Bolivar (IRE) 5 b g 1636[5] 2777[2] 3011[6] >100h<
Bollin Frank 5 b h Rambo Dancer (CAN)-Bollin Emily (Lochnager) 1305[4] 2649[12] 2898[12] >58h<
Bollinger 11 ch g 3446[4] 3753[3] >71h 91c<
Boll Weevil 11 b g 4619[P] >120?c<
Bolshie Baron 8 b g Baron Blakeney-Contrary Lady (Conwyn) 1829[6] 2054[6] 2704[2] 2816[8] 2940[4] 3354[2] 3719[2] >87c<
Boltrose 7 b g 21[3] >78h< (DEAD)
Bomba Charger 5 b g Prince of Peace-Lady Guinevere (Tormento) 2844[12] 3895[6] >53fh<
Bombadil 5 b g Gunner B-Sugar Token (Record Token) 865[3] 3171[4] >67?h<
Bond Jnr (IRE) 8 ch g (1202) 1784[P] 3671[3] >87h 117dc<
Bonita Blakeney 7 gr m 1998[12] 2819[8] 3719[F] >61h<
Bonjour 7 br g 2763[3] >75h<
Bon Luck (IRE) 5 ch g Waajib-Elle Va Bon (Tanfirion) 2868[9] 3818[13] >3h<
Bonnifer (IRE) 8 ch g 1447[F] 1680[8] 2679[4] 2947[7] 3472[P] 4007[P] 4628[9] >66c<
Bonny Johnny 7 b g Welsh Captain-Very Merry (Lord of Verona) 853[4] 1525[F] 1576[4] 1853[3] 2043[F] 2861[8] >48h 79c<
Bonny Rigg (IRE) 5 b m 2697[P] 2898[20] 3159[14] 3888[8] 4184[8] >47h 49c<
Bon Voyage (USA) 5 b g 815[3] 1045[4] 1709[5] 2797[8] 3958[2] >75h<
Book of Dreams (IRE) 9 b g 2746[P] 3416[P]
Boost 5 b g 105[11] 183[7] 259[6] 490[7] >40h<
Boot Jack (IRE) 8 b g Rhoman Rule (USA)-Dusty Foot (Simbir) 3677[P] 4069[P]
Boots Madden (IRE) 7 b g The Parson-Little Welly (Little Buskins) (1013) (1329) (1768) 2550[4] >93h<
Boots N All (IRE) 7 bl g 1994[6] 2693[9] 3051[2] 3819[2] 4007[5] (4168) (4272) 4659[4] >49h 90c<
Boozys Dream 6 b g 1336[7] 2965[5] 3233[P] 3342[12] 3628[P] 3977[8]
Border Glory 6 ch g Derrylin-Boreen's Glory (Boreen (FR)) 4256[U]
Border Image 6 b g Derring Rose-Border Gambler (Strong Gale) 2924[10] 3066[P] 3483[13] 3990[6] 4244[9] >59h<
Boreen Owen 13 b g 4059[4] >87c<
Boring (USA) 8 ch g 4[3] 507[5] >60h 80c<
Boris Brook 6 ch g 1579[8] 1854[14] 2619[6] 2787[P] 3307[6] >70dh<
Borjito (SPA) 6 b h 1993[5] 3740[P] >64h< (DEAD)
Born At Kings 4 ch g Jupiter Island-My Coquette (Coquelin (USA)) 3853[11] 4088[4] >43fh<
Born to Please (IRE) 5 ch g 22[2] (218) 343[3] 410[2] 528[2] (539) 741[6] (861) (936) 4172[5] 4252[4] >85h<
Boro Bow (IRE) 6 b m Buckskin (FR)-Boro Quarter (Normandy) 4355a[3] >110h<
Borodino (IRE) 5 b g Strong Gale-Boro Quarter (Normandy) 1289[10] 2938[2] >58fh<
Boro Vacation (IRE) 8 b g 314a[9] 1016[U] 4225[6] 4553[P] >110c<
Bossa Nova 4 b f Teenoso (USA)-Out of Range (Faraway Times (USA)) 4407[9] 4561[7] >41fh<
Boss Doyle (IRE) 5 b g Lapierre-Prolific Scot (Northern Guest (USA)) 3613[11] >87h<
Bossymoss (IRE) 8 b g 1378[4] 1773[F] 2052[P] 2632[U] 3362[10] >55h<
Boston Bomber 6 b g Wonderful Surprise-Miss Anax (Anax) 3480[8]
Boston Man 6 b g 700[P] 1030[P] 1689[9] 2042[3] 2507[6] 2654[P] (3201) 3351[5] 3825[7] 4188[4] 4479[2] 4708[3] 4798[6] >71h<
Bosworth Field (IRE) 9 br g 1209[8] 1668[P] 1845[P] (2000) 2632[F] >84c< (DEAD)
Bottle Black 10 b g 3633[P] 3925[P] 4404[F] 4476[P] 4697[U]
Boulevard Bay (IRE) 6 b g Royal Fountain-Cairita (Pitcairn) 3476[8]
Bound For Gold 6 b g 1036[8] >50h<
Boundtohonour (IRE) 5 b g Rashar (USA)-Densidal (Tanfirion) 24[3] 2844[14] 3365[7] 3621[6] >58h<
Bourbon Dynasty (FR) 4 b g Rainbow Quest (USA)-Bourbon Girl (Ile de Bourbon (USA)) 3555[3] 3789[4] 3883[3] >72h<
Bourdonner 5 b g (5) 65[4] (343) 391[2] (533) 695[5] 3904[2] (4261) >85h<
Bournel 9 ch m 1582[9] 1947[7] 3043[9] 3181[4] 3633[3] >77h 78c<
Bowcliffe 6 b g 1343[4] 1524[3] 1848[3] 1992[7] 2697[5] 3064[P] >60h<
Bowcliffe Court (IRE) 5 b g Slip Anchor-Res Nova (USA) (Blushing Groom (FR)) 1651[P] (1788) 2055[3] 3041[7] >74h<
Bowden Surprise 7 ch g 1946[P] (3949) 4233[5] >44h<
Bow Handy Man 15 ch g 4256[6] >88c<
Bowland Park 6 b m 218[U] 450[4] 585[P] 642[5] >37h<
Bowles Patrol (IRE) 5 gr g 961[7] 2842[8] 3049[9] 3941[2] 4298[2] 4442[3] >35h 102dc<
Bowl of Oats 11 ch g 3928[3] >107dc<
Boxgrove Man (IRE) 7 br g 4184[P] 4547[P]
Boxing Match 10 b g 158[7] 256[5] 395[5] 457[F] 597[3] 726[6] 4404[5] 4535[F] 4721[7] 4763[7] >55h 59c<
Boxit Again 7 b g 866[P] 1118[P]
Boy Blakeney 4 b g Blakeney-Sarah Bear (Mansingh (USA)) 1205[7] 1413[4] 1652[21] 2050[2] 2629[13] 3284[5] 3748[3] 4231[4] >57h<
Boyfriend 7 b g 2666[14] 3447[4] >65h<
Boyo (IRE) 6 ch g Phardante (FR)-Bobs My Uncle (Deep Run) 450[P] 510[5] 593[R] >46h< (DEAD)
Boyzontoowa (IRE) 5 b g Beau Sher-Lindabell (Over The River (FR)) 1296[19] 1842[6] 2673[8] 2958[7] 3607[14] >37h<
Bozo (IRE) 6 b g Kefaah (USA)-Hossvend (Malinowski (USA)) 1774[3] 3619[11] 4388[3] >85fh<
Brabazon (USA) 12 b g Cresta Rider (USA)-Brilliant Touch (USA) (Gleaming (USA)) 3739[5] >78c<
Brackenfield 11 ch g (3553) 3837[F] >125?c<
Brackenheath (IRE) 6 b g Le Moss-Stable Lass (Golden Love) 1422[7] 3178[2] 3603[2] 4005[11] >80h<
Brackenthwaite 7 ch g 2913[2] >69h<
Bracker (IRE) 5 ch g 316a[10] >41h<
Bradbury Star 12 b g 1869[3] 2057[F] 2773[7] 3036[P] 3599[7] >122c<
Braes of Mar 7 b g 1342[6] 2075[4] 2869[F] 3146[8] >87h 110c<

Bramblehill Buck (IRE) 8 gr g 1197^{3} 1428^{2} (1697) 1951^{6} 3185^{5} >68h 119dc<
Brambles Way 8 ch g (505) (1305) (2815) 3396^{6} (3714) 4146^{3} >90h<
Bramley May 7 b g 22^{3} 2034^{8} >68h< (DEAD)
Bramshaw Wood (IRE) 5 b g Brush Aside (USA)-Lovely Sanara (Proverb) (4433) >51fh<
Brancher 6 gr g 1121^{F} 1945^{2} 2694^{6} 3709^{F} >75?h<
Brandon Bridge 6 b g 3548^{11} 3802^{P} >15fh<
Brandon Magic 4 ch c Primo Dominie-Silk Stocking (Pardao) 1387^{5} 1900^{5} 2622^{9} >74h<
Brandsby Minster 6 gr g Minster Son-Courting Day (Right Boy) 2005^{6} >31fh<
Brandy Cross (IRE) 8 br g 2540^{2} 2936^{F} 3314^{P} 3705^{2} >98c<
Brass Band (IRE) 6 b m 3650a^{11} >79h<
Brassic Lint 7 gr g (557) >61h< (DEAD)
Brave and Tender (IRE) 8 b g 1807^{P} (DEAD)
Brave Buccaneer 10 ch g 2011^{P} (2681) (3018) >106h 118c<
Brave Edwin (IRE) 7 ch h 2661^{9} 3085^{6} 3355^{8} >60h<
Brave Fountain (IRE) 9 b g 2856a^{9} >98h 99c<
Brave Patriarch (IRE) 6 gr g (22) 73^{2} (506) >82h<
Brave Spy 6 b g Law Society (USA)-Contralto (Busted) 4002^{2} >49h<
Brave Tornado 6 ch g 2884^{5} (3150) 4016^{10} (4521) >116h<
Bravo Star (USA) 12 b g 23^{4} 101^{7} 190^{9} 317a^{8} 323a^{7} 480^{2} 587^{6} 3892^{P} 4429^{6} >50dh 75c<
Braydon Forest 5 b g Presidium-Sleekit (Blakeney) 955^{F} 1380^{P} 1729^{9} 2870^{P} 3447^{14} >8h< (DEAD)
Brazil Or Bust (IRE) 6 b g (1179) 1552^{F} 1831^{6} 2745^{3} 2810^{2} >72h 111c<
Break the Rules 5 b g Dominion-Surf Bird (Shareef Dancer (USA)) 1470^{8} 2566^{4} 2872^{2} (3109) (3271) 3564^{3} 4082^{2} >79h<
Breath of Scandal (IRE) 6 br g Strong Gale-Her Name Was Lola (Pitskelly) 2066^{6} 3798^{9} >35h<
Brecon 4 b br c High Estate-No Can Tell (USA) (Clev Er Tell (USA)) 2622^{10} 2925^{6} (4282) >72+h<
Bred For Pleasure 4 b f Niniski (USA)-The Fink Sisters (Tap On Wood) 4301^{12} >18fh<
Bree Hill (IRE) 9 b g Pollerton-Just Our Luck (London Gazette) 4361a^{3} >99c<
Brensham Folly 6 b g 129^{P} 156^{P}
Bresil (USA) 8 ch g 1166^{3} 1299^{7} 1446^{6} 4472^{4} 4552^{4} >25h<
Breydon 4 ch g Be My Guest (USA)-Palmella (USA) (Grundy) (4570) >43?h<
Briar's Delight 9 b g (1140) 1527^{2} >70h 99c<
Brick Court (IRE) 5 ch m 3072^{B} >45h<
Briden 5 gr m 872^{12}
Bridepark Rose (IRE) 9 b m 870^{3} 1252^{U} 1475^{2} 1856^{2} 2007^{3} 2577^{5} 4649^{U} >75h 96dc<
Bridge Delight 8 b m 1341^{4} 1958^{8} >53h<
Bridie's Pride 6 b g 3628^{P} >24h<
Bridled Tern 6 b m 1190^{4} 1438^{F} 1795^{5} >51h<
Bridle Path (IRE) 6 b g (805) >66h<
Bridlington Bay 4 b g Roscoe Blake-City Sound (On Your Mark) 906^{F} 1526^{11} 2503^{7} 2859^{15} 3310^{4} >48h<
Brief Suspence (IRE) 4 b g Distinctly North (USA)-Edwinarowe (Blakeney) 2750^{10} >34fh<
Briery Gale 7 b m 1565^{P} 1958^{4} >48h<
Brigadier John (IRE) 8 ch g Sheer Grit-Deep Toi (Deep Run) 2000^{2} >79c< (DEAD)
Brigadier Supreme (IRE) 8 b br g 327^{P} 406^{3} 2752^{6} 2793^{4} 3059^{8}
Bright Destiny 6 br g 696^{8} 802^{4} 938^{4} 1138^{6} 1845^{P} 2630^{7} 2788^{5} 3067^{P} 3306^{9} 3607^{3} (3824) 3975^{F} 4203^{6} 4503^{6} 4576^{4} 4710^{6} >38h 88c<
Bright Eclipse (USA) 4 br g Sunny's Halo (CAN)-Miss Lantana (USA) (Danzig Connection (USA)) 402^{2} 1634^{P} 1862^{P} 1953^{11} 2939^{8} 3438^{11} (4440) >61h<
Brighter Shade (IRE) 7 b g Sheer Grit-Shady Doorknocker (Mon Capitaine) (1084) 1296^{6} (3314) 3695^{2} (3972) 4480^{3} 4649^{2} >64fh 113c<
Bright Flame (IRE) 5 b g Over The River (FR)-Shreelane (Laurence O) 3621^{11} 4182^{5} >67?h<
Bright Hour 12 ro g 4614^{P} >65c<
Brightling Fair 5 b m Ivor's Lad (USA)-Mop Fair (Fair Season) 2805^{18}
Brighton Road (IRE) 4 b br g Pennine Walk-Share The Vision (Vision (USA)) 2070^{4} (DEAD)
Bright Sapphire 11 b g 902^{2} 971^{5} 1256^{7} 1466^{2} 1962^{10} 2088^{3} >64h<
Bright Season 9 b g 3810^{P} 3954^{F} 4100^{P} >49h<
Brilliant Red 4 b c Royal Academy (USA)-Red Comes Up (USA) (Blushing Groom (FR)) 2622^{6} 2872^{4} >70h<
Brimpton Bertie 8 ch g 4438^{P} 4659^{7} 4771^{5} >68h 94?c<
Brindley House 10 b g 14^{5} 70^{P} 957^{3} 1122^{P} 2570^{2} (4562) 4723^{2} >80h 86c<
Brin-Lodge (IRE) 4 b f Doubletour (USA)-Nordico's Dream (Nordico (USA)) 912^{10} 1149^{P}
Bristol Gold 4 b g Golden Heights-The Bristol Flyer (True Song) 4531^{20} 4656^{13}
Britannia Mills 6 gr m 1816^{P} 3743^{5} 4089^{6} >45h<
Broad Steane 8 b g 3357^{3} 3906^{4} 4322^{F} >75h 107c<
Brockley Court 10 b g 1410a^{3} >112h 138c<
Brockville Bairn 4 b g Tina's Pet-Snow Chief (Tribal Chief) 2953^{P}
Brodessa 11 gr g (697) >95+h<
Brogans Brush 4 ch c Jendali (USA)-Sweet 'n' Sharp (Sharpo) 1526^{7} 2175^{P} >8h<
Brogeen Lady (IRE) 7 br m 1797^{4} 2039^{2} 2660^{6} 3173^{F} 3339^{F} 3489^{5} (3667) 4546^{2} (4647) >74h 92+c<
Broken Rites (IRE) 4 b g Broken Hearted-Lady Wise (Lord Gayle (USA)) 1747a^{10} >90h<
Brook Bee 5 br g Meadowbrook-Brown Bee III (Marcus Superbus) 3090^{6} 3581^{3} 4403^{5} 4559^{P} >47h<
Brookhampton Lane (IRE) 6 b g Balinger-Deerpark Rose (Arapaho) 1800^{3} 2012^{6} 2677^{8} 3172^{4} 3364^{4} 4309^{10} 4427^{F} >63h<
Brook House 6 ro m Colway Radial-Move Ahead (Move Off) 1296^{17} 2005^{7} 3330^{12} 4156^{5} >26fh<
Broomhill Boy 8 b g 100^{F} >70h<
Broomhill Duker (IRE) 7 br g 1160^{4} 1691^{U} 1845^{U} 1989^{P} 2803^{P} 4055^{7} 4515^{4} >33h 74c<
Brora Rose (IRE) 9 b m 70^{P} 482^{4} >57dh 72c<
Brother Harry 5 ch g Rakaposhi King-Magic (Sweet Revenge) 3203^{5} *3846*^{4} >35fh<
Brother Nero (NZ) 5 br g Roman Empire-End of The Road (NZ) (Double Nearco (CAN)) 4143^{3} 4433^{4} >44fh<
Brother of Iris (IRE) 4 b g Decent Fellow-Granita Cafe (FR) (Arctic Tern (USA)) (3914) >65fh<
Broughtons Relish 4 b f Nomination-Mosso (Ercolano (USA)) 2946^{13} >8h<
Browjoshy (IRE) 4 b g Zaffaran (USA)-Keeping Company (King's Company) 3821^{5} >66fh<
Brown And Mild 6 b g 1180^{6} 2547^{15} 3222^{P} >46h<
Brown Baby 11 br m 4623^{4} >60c<
Brownes Hill Lad (IRE) 5 ch g King of Clubs-Record Finish (Record Token) 1966^{2} 3619^{8} >89fh<
Brown Eyed Girl 5 ch m Sharpo-Ella Mon Amour (Ela-Mana-Mou) 1337^{6} >28h<
Brown Robber 9 gr g 1328^{4} 1646^{P} 1875^{2} 2841^{P} 3339^{P} 3602^{2} 3848^{U} 4100^{2} >43h 79c<
Brownscroft 9 b m Dubassoff (USA)-Keino (Kautokeino (FR)) 2550^{11} 2926^{P} 3054^{9} 3364^{8} >36h<
Brown Wren 6 b m 1998^{10} 2576^{6} 2875^{4} 3112^{10} 3683^{4} >46h<
Brumon (IRE) 6 b g (2044) 3559^{4} 3888^{2} 4285^{7} >72h 72c<
Brunida 5 b m Newski (USA)-Arvida (Bruni) 4407^{15} >3fh<
Brush With Fame (IRE) 5 b g Brush Aside (USA)-Cheeney's Gift (Quayside) 4009^{3} >60fh<
Bryan Robson (USA) 6 b g Topsider (USA)-Queen's Visit (Top Command (USA)) 1427^{P} 1651^{15}
Bryanston Square (IRE) 4 b g Taufan (USA)-Noble Treasure (USA) (Vaguely Noble) 1172^{2} >63h<
Bryn's Story 10 b g Push On-Lido Legend (Good Light) 3631^{P}
B The One 6 b g 1152^{P} (1263) 1705^{2} >71h<
Buabhall Mor 4 ch g Nishapour (FR)-Share a Friend (Ascertain (USA)) 4215^{18} >54fh<
Buckaneer Bay 10 b g 135^{3} 179^{P} 4504^{4} 4713^{P} >53h 73c<
Buckbee Flyer 5 ch m Jupiter Island-Buckbe (Ragstone) 3764^{P}
Buckboard Bounce 11 br g 3563^{P} 3885^{8} 4074^{4} 4213^{P} >81h 143?c<
Bucket of Gold 7 b g 2007^{P} 3015^{5} 3227^{P} 3941^{P} >83h 86c<
Buckhouse Boy 7 b g 1259^{3} (1646) 1936^{F} 2113^{F} 3040^{2} 3155^{2} 3616^{P} 4050^{F} 4213^{9} >100h 135c<
Buckland Lad (IRE) 6 ch g 3059^{3} (3206) 3686^{2} (3810) >59h 86+c<
Buckley Boys 6 gr m 641^{P} >66h<
Buckley House 5 b g Buckley-Reperage (USA) (Key To Content (USA)) 4156^{4} 4420^{10} 4514^{4} 4750^{P} >36h<
Buck's Delight (IRE) 9 br g Buckskin (FR)-Ethel's Delight (Tiepolo II) 3397^{P} (3913) >101c<
Bucks Reef 5 b g Buckley-Coral Delight (Idiot's Delight) 2811^{12} 3297^{11} >29fh<
Buddleia 4 b f Lord Bud-Cap That (Derek H) 2633^{5} 2804^{11} 3828^{10} 4390^{6} >46fh<
Buddy Diver 4 br g Revlow-Rely-On-Pearl (Deep Diver) 4433^{11}
Bud's Bet (IRE) 9 b g 32^{9} 2505^{8} 2629^{7} 3091^{9} 3803^{11} >46h<
Buggsy Blade (IRE) 11 b g 317a^{3} >78h 75c<
Buggy (IRE) 8 b g 2359a^{3} 2857a^{4} 3382a^{P} 3523a^{10} >101h<
Buglet 7 b m Taufan (USA)-Blue Bell Girl (Blakeney) 21^{7} (407) 598^{2} 684^{P} 741^{P} 899^{6} >69h<
Bugsy Moran (IRE) 7 b g Buckskin (FR)-Rusheen's Girl (Dusky Boy) 4736^{3}
Bugsysiegel 7 ch g 59^{11}
Bukhari (IRE) 5 b g Shahrastani (USA)-Balance (USA) 4348a^{7} >93h<
Bula Vogue (IRE) 7 b m Phardante (FR)-Bulabos (Proverb) (1555) 2794^{3} (3061) 3411^{3} 3817^{5} >73h<
Bulko Boy (NZ) 5 br g Pandemonium-Comedy of Errors (NZ) (Sobig) 2811^{10} 3853^{7} >47fh<
Bullanguero (IRE) 8 ch g 1994^{P} 3339^{P}
Bullens Bay (IRE) 8 b g 4536^{5} 4650^{2} (4801) >67h<
Bullpen Belle 4 b f Relief Pitcher-Hopeful Waters (Forlorn River) 294^{2} >55h<
Bulwark Hill (IRE) 7 br g Dromod Hill-Farina

(Raise You Ten) 316a[9] **>78h<**
Bungee Jumper 7 b g 75[11] **>87h<**
Bunny Buck (IRE) 7 ch g Buckskin (FR)-Kassina (Laurence O) 2918[P] 3727[7]
Bunny Hare (IRE) 9 ch g Callernish-Maggie Pickens (Beau Chapeau) **4704[U]** 4801[P]
Bures (IRE) 6 b g 62[10] (419) 505[2] 692[4] 806[2] 1163[3] 3995[5] 4246[7] 4702[8] **>88dh<**
Burfords For Scrap 5 b g Bedford (USA)-Headstrong Miss (Le Bavard (FR)) 1071[6] 1685[14] 2546[13] 3054[12] **>40h<**
Burlington Sam (NZ) 9 b g (1072) (1299) (1762) 2573[2] 3932[3] (4139) 4660[2] **>72h<**
Burn Out 5 b g 2791[7] 3564[4] 3798[6] 3937[2] **>64h<**
Burnt Imp (USA) 7 ch g (1127) (1360) 1645[2] 2888[9] 3267[5] **>104h<**
Burnt Sienna (IRE) 5 b m 295[5] 350[2] (469) 555[2] 600[6] 749[7] 879[2] 905[4] **>67h<**
Burntwood Melody 6 gr g 1250[9] 1536[5] 1768[5] 2076[6] 2759[8] **3001[5] 3188[5] 3472[4] 3966[5]** **>57h 66c<**
Busman (IRE) 8 ch g **3457[3] (3721) 4241[3]** **>73h 103c<**
Buster 9 br g 3621[14] 4231[7] 4378[13] **>28h< (DEAD)**
Buster Two (IRE) 4 ch g Bustomi-Revida Girl (Habat) 2804[S]
Bus Way Girl 4 ch f Itsu (USA)-Ridgeway Girl (Mr Bigmore) 1172[P]
Busy Boy 10 b g 2654[P] 2787[P] 3328[11] 3449[6] 3727[5] 3795[13] 3910[14] 4248[17] 4572[R] 4760[P] **>13h 57c<**
Butchers Minstrel 5 ch g Brotherly (USA)-Flash Bunny (Flashback) 1639[P]
Buttercup Joe 7 b g **1326[P]** **>99h<**
Butterwick King (IRE) 5 br g 2539[3] 2917[10] 3271[6] **>75h<**
Buyers Dream (IRE) 7 b g 212[6] 465[6] **508[2] 584[2] 685[3] 897[4] (1244) (1578) 1902[2] 3094[2] 3308[4]** **>61h 96c<**
Buzz O'The Crowd 10 br g **(4640)** >115?c<
Byhookorbycrook (IRE) 5 b m Cardinal Flower-Frisky Matron (On Your Mark) 1665[12] 2675[15]

C

Caballus (USA) 4 b g Danzig Connection (USA)-Rutledge Place (USA) (Caro) 3224[7]
Cabbery Rose (IRE) 9 ch m **8[2] 1291[F] 3503a[4] 4351a[4]** **>64h 89c<**
Cabin Hill 11 ch g 976[4] **>44h<**
Cable Beach (IRE) 8 ch g **3638[9] 4123a[2] 4349a[7]** **>129c<**
Cabochon 10 b g 657[3] 810[4] 3750[5] 3962[3] 4101[F] **>64h 117?c<**
Cab on Target 11 br g **(2903) (3135) 3637[2] 4054[2] 4213[P] 4805[5]** **>147h 139dc<**
Caddy Man (IRE) 8 ch g **2998a[6]** **>89c<**
Caddy's First 5 b g 603[2] 675[9] 818[3] 956[5] 1818[2] 3663[5] 4453[4] 4732[7] **>66h<**
Cader Idris 8 b g St Columbus-Llanon (Owen Dudley) **1028[3] (1308) 1578[8] 1850[F]** **>85c<**
Cades Bay 6 b g 1830[14] 2547[11] 2897[F] 3222[3] **>63h<**
Cadougold (FR) 6 b g 1201[3] 1636[4] (1783) 3150[4] (4053) **>115h<**
Caherass Court (IRE) 6 b m 871[F]
Caherlow (IRE) 6 ch g Kambalda-Wrens Lass (Wrens Hill) 1926[11] 3203[19]
Cahermone Lady (IRE) 6 ch m Cardinal Flower-Altaghaderry Rose (Ete Indien (USA)) 4301[10] 4632[11] 4774[9] **>37fh<**
Cahonis (IRE) 5 bb g Strong Gale-Alix (Malinowski (USA)) 1485a[10] **>33h<**
Cailin Supreme (IRE) 6 b m 4360a[P]
Cairncross (IRE) 6 b g 3382a[5] **>101h<**
Cairo Prince (IRE) 7 b h Darshaan-Sphinx (GER) (Alpenkonig (GER)) 1802[P] 2041[4] **>63h<**
Caitriona's Choice (IRE) 6 b g 1233a[2] 1752a[3] **>95h<**
Caldebrook (IRE) 6 ch g Cardinal Flower-Frisky Matron (On Your Mark) 2682[13] 2911[4] 3304[12] 4255[F] **>48fh<**
Calder King 6 ch g 1666[6] 2041[5] 3324[7] **>63h<**
Calder's Grove 7 b g 700[8] **853[2] 938[5]** **>53h 69c<**
Calgary Girl 5 ch m 4382[9] 4552[9] 4739[5] **>36h<**
Call Equiname 7 gr g **(791) (1037)** **>102h 124c<**
Callermine 8 ch m 3226[10] 3761[9] 4620[2] 4731[5] **>44h<**
Callernish Dan (IRE) 7 ch g 1312[6] 1802[2] **>61h<**
Calleva Star (IRE) 6 b g 965[4] **1596[4] 1920[2] 2816[3] 3173[4] 3472[2]** **>42h 91c<**
Call Home (IRE) 9 b g **1540[7]** **>90h 121?c<**
Callindoe (IRE) 7 b m Callernish-Winsome Doe (Buckskin (FR)) 1124[4] 1986[2] 3184[5] **>47h<**
Calling The Tune 6 ch g 4288[6] 4568[P]
Callisoe Bay (IRE) 8 b or br g **(1087) 1509[2] 1910[2] 2646[U] 2783[8]** 3286[8] **3986[2] 4225[5]** **>107dh 139c<**
Call it a Day (IRE) 7 b g **(1277) 2741a[3] (3036) 3302[4] 3598[5] 4054[4]** **>99h 148c<**
Call Me Albi (IRE) 6 ch g **13[2] 102[P] 330[3] 472[2] 887[P] 1300[4] 3925[3]** (4383) 4766[2] **>76h 93c<**
Call Me Black (IRE) 8 b m **2614[3] 2919[4] 3393[P]** **>48h 81c< (DEAD)**
Call-Me-Dinky 13 ch m Mart Lane-Call-Me-Sally (Hul A Hul) **4308[P]**
Call Me Early 12 ch g **1731[P] 2665[U] 2923[P] 3132[7] 4159[8] 4300[P]** **>70h 66c<**
Call Me River (IRE) 9 ch g **887[6] 1285[2] (1582) (1877) 2665[3] 3113[4] 3956[F]** **>89c<**
Call My Guest (IRE) 7 b g 796[2] 948[2] 1982[7] 2644[8] 3045[8] 3562[5] 3920[F] 4084[4] **>80h<**
Callonescy (IRE) 5 b g 1729[P] 2866[6] **>18h<**
Call the Guv'nor 8 b g 21[2] 71[3] 187[7] **>79h<**
Call the Shots (IRE) 8 br g **1307[4] 2671[2] (3451)** **>50h 111c<**
Calm Down (IRE) 6 b g Phardante (FR)-Extra Chance (Pollerton) 2677[18] 3014[8] 3275[6] 3569[5] **>70h<**
Calogan 10 br g Callernish-Lady Tarsel (Tarqogan) 902[6] **(DEAD)**
Calon Lan (IRE) 6 b g 1651[F]
Calvaro (IRE) 6 b g 1471[2] 1867[11] **>56h<**
Caman 10 br g **4748[5]** **>90c<**
Cambo (USA) 11 b g 1732[8] 2666[10] 2895[3] 3429[4] (3709) 3923[4] 4296[P] 4455[3] 4544[3] 4723[P] **>64h 77c<**
Camden's Ransom (USA) 10 b g Hostage (USA)-Camden Court (USA) (Inverness Drive (USA)) 634[7] **>59h<**
Camelot Knight 11 br g **3018[2] 3266[4] 3599[6] 4074[3]** **>141c<**
Camera Man 7 ch g 2891[4] 3552[7] 4309[9] 4625[2] **>64h<**
Camillas Legacy 6 br m Newski (USA)-Just Certain (Sula Bula) 2656[P] 2959[P] 3342[7] **>47h<**
Camino 10 b g 1536[P] 1673[P] **>91dc<**
Camitrov (FR) 7 b g **3266[5] 3804[5]** **>122?c<**
Campaign 6 b g 2900[3] 4207[9] **>89h<**
Camp Bank 7 b g **746[3] 1153[7]** **>67h 81?c<**
Campeche Bay (IRE) 8 b g **3422[W] 3495[F] 3806[2]** **>77h 115dc<**
Camp Head (IRE) 6 ch g Camden Town-Poll's Best (Pollerton) 1774[10] 4547[R] 4650[5] 4794[3] **>64h<**
Camptosaurus (IRE) 8 br g **1826[U] 2632[8] 3608[5] 3826[5]** **>64h 68c<**
Canaan Valley 9 ch g 2177[6] 2509[10] **>62h<**
Canary Blue (IRE) 6 b m 587[10] 1047[8] **>55h<**
Canary Falcon 6 ch g 262[5] 327[2] 557[2] 834[2] (961) (1451) 1911[6] **>69h<**
Canaver 11 b g Callernish-Golden Lucy (Lucifer (USA)) **3472[P]** **>86?c<**
Can Can Charlie 7 gr g 2932[2] 3105[3] 3430[5] **>82h<**
Candid Lad 10 b g 3[P] 505[5] 731[8] 1703[18] **>63h<**
Candle Glow 9 ch m **4094[4] 4228[P] 4320[6]** **>94?c<**
Candy Gale (IRE) 5 b m Strong Gale-Sweet Start (Candy Cane) 4118a[18] **>56fh<**
Canestrelli (USA) 12 b g 262[8] 963[5] **>34h<**
Canister Castle 9 b g **4076[P] 4704[10]**
Canny Chronicle 9 b or br g **3533[F]**
Canonbiebothered 6 ch m Liberated-Play Mount (Spur On) 782[2] 1245[4] 1851[9] 3096[P] 3328[10] **>41h<**
Canons Park 4 ch g Keen-Low Line (High Line) 807[R]
Can She Can Can 5 b m Sulaafah (USA)-Dominance (Dominion) 4299[11] 4451[P] 4638[4] 4800[5] **>48h<**
Cantantivy 12 b m **158[P]** **>80c<**
Canton Venture 5 ch g Arctic Tern (USA)-Ski Michaela (USA) (Devil's Bag (USA)) 735[2] 876[3] (1069) 1322[F] 1639[10] **>76h<**
Cantoris Frater 10 ch g **2660[P] 3332[P] 3969[U]** >101+c<
Cape Cottage 13 ch g **3055[2] (3363) 3469[3] 4094[2] 4280[2] 4616[B] 4805[6]** **>110c<**
Capo Castanum 8 ch g **880[U] (957) 1068[2] 3165[F] (3446) 3617[U] 4135[3] 4404[P]** **>67h 110c<**
Cappajune (IRE) 9 b m Codebreaker-Hainault (Hardicanute) **3432[U] 3460[P]**
Capsoff (IRE) 4 b f Mazaad-Minerstown (IRE) (Miner's Lamp) 3433[3] 3946[11] 4301[4] **>69fh<**
Captain Brandy 12 ch g **4361a[5]** **>84c<**
Captain Coe 7 b g 816[6] **>66h<**
Captain Culpepper (IRE) 6 b g Supreme Leader-Publicola (Furry Glen) 3170[12] **>30fh<**
Captain Felix (NZ) 7 br g Captain Jason (NZ)-Pulka (NZ) (North Pole) 653[5] 1203[9] 1695[P] **>25fh< (DEAD)**
Captain Jack 7 b g 1476[2] 1964[P] (2620) 3405[4] **>78h<**
Captain Khedive 9 ch g **592[2] (633) (742) 811[F] 943[3] 1352[4]** **>90h 130c<**
Captain Marmalade 8 ch g 3131[3] 4633[4] **>59h<**
Captain My Captain (IRE) 9 ch g 187[P] 1859[P] **3546[7]** **>64c<**
Captain Navar (IRE) 7 gr g 679[6] 865[16] 2822[6] 2945[4] 3283[P] 3985[P] **>61h<**
Captain Stockford 10 b g **1120[P] 1414[2] 1664[P] 1763[P] (2037)** **>77c<**
Captain Tandy (IRE) 8 ch g 1045[P] 1775[7] 2006[11] 3959[3] 4089[2] 4633[2] 4789[F] **>54h 89c<**
Captain Walter (IRE) 7 b h 2010[7] 3019[5] 4547[4] **>58h<**
Captiva Bay 8 b m **1819[5] 3043[6] 3472[5] (3830) 4158[6]** **>86c<**
Caracol 8 b g **1680[P] 2037[F] 2752[F]** (3054) (3674) (4223) **>59h<**
Caractacus Potts 5 ch g Mr Fluorocarbon-Raglan Rose (Roselier (FR)) 3021[11] **>12fh<**
Caras Rose (IRE) 5 gr g Roselier (FR)-Glencara (Sallust) 3425[11] **>38fh<**
Cardan 11 b g **330[6] 417[2]** **>70dc<**
Cardea Castle (IRE) 9 b m 101[13] 134[10] **>55h<**
Cardenden (IRE) 9 b g **11[4]** 531[6] **975[2] (1972) 2769[7] 4258[6] 4410[2] 4517[3] 4721[U] 4757[3]** **>56h**

74c<

Cardinal Black 11 br g Cardinal Flower-Clockonocra (Shall We Dance) 3922^{P}

Cardinal Gayle (IRE) 7 b g 2620^{3} 2820^{15} 3189^{2} 3488^{8} 3736^{2} 4251^{3} >48h 74c<

Cardinal Red 10 b g 4317^{P} 4634^{P} >102h 93c<

Cardinal Richelieu 10 ch g Cardinal Flower-Knockane Rose (Giolla Mear) 3551^{4} 4616^{P}

Cardinal Rule (IRE) 8 ch g 1038^{U} 1285^{P} 1447^{3} 1582^{3} (2795) (3051) (3188) 3400^{5} 3617^{P} 4272^{2} 4566^{W} (4699) >62h 110c<

Cardinal Sinner (IRE) 8 br g 584^{3} 733^{5} 1083^{P} 1525^{R} 1780^{P} 2000^{P} 2628^{F} 3450^{3} 4298^{P} >49c<

Carey's Cottage (IRE) 7 ch g 954^{9} 1274^{7} 1772^{12} 1963^{9} 2905^{P} >46h 52c<

Careysville (IRE) 6 b g 1683^{10} 4249^{6} 4537^{5} 4655^{F} >50h 71c<

Caribbean Prince 9 ch g 4307^{12} >4h<

Cariboo (IRE) 5 b g King's Ride-Back To Bahrain (Mandalus) 3365^{11} >6fh<

Cariboo Gold (USA) 8 b g Slew O' Gold (USA)-Selket's Treasure (USA) (Gleaming (USA)) 2061^{3} 2778^{2} (2947) (3354) (3472) 4185^{3} (4541) >131c<

Carlingford Gale (IRE) 6 ch m Carlingford Castle-Vul Gale (Strong Gale) 872^{10} 3364^{5} 3592^{P} 4304^{6} 4458^{P} 4643^{6} >41h 42c<

Carlingford Lakes (IRE) 9 ch m 1564^{P} 2075^{3} 2681^{4} (3492) (3969) >102c<

Carlingford Tyke (IRE) 5 b g Carlingford Castle-Athenian Primrose (Tower Walk) 3418^{2} 4216^{7} >64fh<

Carlisle Bandito's (IRE) 5 b g (1827) (1973) 2953^{F} 3282^{3} 3529^{2} (4335) 4702^{5} >69h<

Carlito Brigante 5 b g Robellino (USA)-Norpella (Northfields (USA)) 1517^{2} 1905^{4} 2624^{4} (2805) 2948^{4} (3345) (3572) 3640^{2} >103h<

Carly Brrin 12 br g 3543^{2} >93c<

Carly-J 6 b m 1713^{4} 2053^{10} 2552^{P} 3029^{8} 3325^{10} 3844^{4} 4233^{P} >51h<

Carmel's Joy (IRE) 8 ch m 1947^{8} 3402^{6} >76h<

Carnanee (IRE) 7 ch g Toravich (USA)-Running Line (Deep Run) 1362^{16}

Carnival Clown 5 b g 25^{5} 133^{6} 218^{7} 4173^{3} 4461^{3} 4663^{P} >45h< (DEAD)

Carnmoney (IRE) 9 gr g 1854^{9} 2627^{P} 2802^{6} 4144^{4} 4513^{4} >57h 69c<

Carnmore Castle (IRE) 9 ch g 319a^{19} >4h<

Carole's Crusader 6 ch m (1085) (1507) 1915^{3} (3165) 3537^{D} 3882^{2} 4356a^{5} >84h 113c<

Carrigeen Kerria (IRE) 9 b m 1750a^{5} 3261a^{3} >74h 112c<

Carson City 10 ch g 907^{6} >72h 83c<

Casey Jane (IRE) 6 b m 2345a^{3} >94h<

Cashaplenty 4 ch g Ballacashtal (CAN)-Storm of Plenty (Billion (USA)) 589^{P} 906^{10} >41h<

Cash Box (IRE) 9 ch g 1316^{3} 1672^{2} 3096^{F} 3328^{6} (3794) 4081^{3} 4296^{5} >76h<

Cashel Quay (IRE) 7 ch g 1504^{10} 1986^{13}

Cashflow Crisis (IRE) 5 ch g 297^{3} 468^{4} 737^{2} (899) 969^{U} >65h<

Caspian Beluga 9 b g (132) >52h 110c<

Caspian Dawn 7 b m Governor General-Parijoun (Manado) 872^{18}

Cassio's Boy 6 b g (1121) 1392^{2} 1710^{6} 2666^{4} 3146^{7} 3269^{5} 3630^{2} 3807^{F} (3920) 4310^{4} >78h<

Cast A Fly (IRE) 4 b f Cyrano de Bergerac-Leaping Salmon (Salmon Leap (USA)) 1014^{P}

Castalino 11 b m 323a^{3} >103+c<

Castle Bay (IRE) 6 ch g Castle Keep-Castle Pearl (Welsh Term) 2804^{5} 2924^{11} >34fh<

Castlebay Lad 14 br g 3089^{R} 3709^{P} 3892^{P} 3949^{5} 4093^{5} 4340^{P} 4622^{P} >32h<

Castle Chief (IRE) 8 b or br g 1041^{4} 1192^{2} >80h 86c<

Castle Clear (IRE) 4 b g Castle Keep-Rose Of Allendale (Green Shoon) (3561) >72fh<

Castleconner (IRE) 6 b g Orchestra-Elle Et Lui (Dike (USA)) 900^{4} 1197^{5} 1426^{P} 1569^{3} (1763) 2068^{U} 2906^{4} 3051^{8} 4001^{3} 4172^{4} 4291^{2} (4766) >65h 93c<

Castle Courageous 10 b g Castle Keep-Peteona (Welsh Saint) 1661^{7} 1922^{4} >102h<

Castlekellyleader (IRE) 8 b g 1326^{F} 1759a^{4} 1994^{P} 3303^{4} 4210^{P} >119h<

Castle King 10 b g 20^{P} 68^{P} >111c<

Castle Lynch (IRE) 5 b m Castle Keep-Shirowen (Master Owen) 1555^{9} 2959^{8} 3764^{6} 3982^{7} >41h<

Castle Mews (IRE) 6 b m Persian Mews-Ladycastle (Pitpan) 2931^{3} 3437^{4} 3621^{7} 3937^{4} 4458^{5} >53h<

Castle of Light 6 b g 4538^{9} >1fh<

Castle Owen (IRE) 5 b g Castle Keep-Lady Owenette (IRE) (Salluceva) (4561) >71fh<

Castle Red (IRE) 6 b g 1161^{8} 3453^{2} >64h<

Castleroyal (IRE) 8 br g Royal Fountain-Dicklers Niece (Golden Love) 319a^{9} 528^{3} 1022^{2} 1346^{5} >71h 118c<

Castle Secret 11 b g 3917^{5} 4791^{3} >105h<

Castle Sweep (IRE) 6 b g (1258) 1656^{2} 2774^{3} 3615^{3} 4053^{B} >134+h<

Cast of Thousands 6 b g 1683^{8} 2673^{P} >44h< (DEAD)

Cast the Line 7 b g 469^{P} >80h<

Catchapenny 12 br g 3055^{5} >116c<

Catch the Cross 11 gr g 4087^{5} >79c<

Catch the Pigeon 8 b m 3641^{F} 4060^{6} 4144^{2} (4393) 4500^{2} >68h<

Catch The Wind 7 b m Afzal-Watch Her Go (Beldale Flutter (USA)) 865^{18} (DEAD)

Cathay (IRE) 5 gr g Roselier (FR)-Coolentallagh (Perhapsburg) 3235^{13} 3821^{17} >41fh<

Catherine's Choice 4 ch g Primo Dominie-Bambolona (Bustino) 2175^{5} 2649^{4} 2918^{2} 3139^{4} >64h<

Catherine's Way (IRE) 5 b g Mandalus-Sharp Approach (Crash Course) 3399^{8} >35h<

Cats Run (IRE) 9 ch g 29^{3} 131^{2} (333) (602) (691) 797^{4} >99h 117c<

Cattly Hang (IRE) 7 b g 1803^{4} 2699^{3} (2899) 3198^{7} >75h 107?c<

Catton Lady 7 b m 289^{10} 1078^{3} 1247^{5} 1703^{12} 1969^{3} 2505^{3} 4055^{3} 4163^{8} 4501^{8} >39h<

Catwalker (IRE) 6 b g 648^{7} 879^{8} 899^{3} 969^{4} 1378^{6} 1786^{6} 2088^{8} 3959^{7} 4468^{10} 4795^{7} >21h<

Caught At Last (IRE) 6 b g 1827^{5} 2861^{9} 3307^{3} 3453^{5} 4144^{3} 4335^{2} 4752^{4} >64h<

Caulker 4 ch g Noblissimo (FR)-Cape Farewell (Record Run) 3789^{10} 4075^{10} >36h<

Caulkin (IRE) 6 b g 718^{10} 1165^{6} 1541^{P} >46h<

Cavalero 8 b g 4323^{4} >78?h 84?c<

Cavallo (FR) 7 b g 2360a^{4} >71c<

Cavil 5 b g 65^{7} 1276^{3} >62h<

Cavina 7 b m 810^{5} 1678^{4} >83h<

Cavo Greco (USA) 8 b g 159^{9} 1072^{5} 3063^{P} 3811^{P} >41h<

Cawarra Boy 9 b g 1567^{4} 1860^{4} 2666^{11} 3001^{8} 3336^{5} 3538^{U} >83h 89c<

Caxton (USA) 10 b g 255^{6} 349^{4} 532^{2} 681^{2} 808^{P} >36h 74c<

Ceannaire (IRE) 7 b g 1036^{P}

Cedar Square (IRE) 6 b g Dancing Dissident (USA)-Friendly Ann (Artaius (USA)) 3631^{F}

Cedric Tudor 4 b g Picea-English Mint (Jalmood (USA)) 4531^{15} >19fh<

Ceejayell 4 b f Say Primula-Spring Garden (Silly Prices) 2904^{16} 3290^{9}

Ceeyou At Midnight 6 b g Seymour Hicks (FR)-Midnight Affair (Mandamus) 3676^{8} *3846^{6}* >49fh<

Ceilidh Boy 11 b g 2^{P} 1162^{2} 1655^{6} 2616^{8} 2765^{4} 3162^{U} 3395^{2} 3486^{2} 3694^{4} >119c<

Celcius 13 b g 66^{15} 899^{7} 2088^{14} >59dh<

Celestial Choir 7 b m 2779^{F} 2902^{3} (3163) 3584^{4} (3992) 4210^{8} >107h<

Celestial Dollar 6 b g 634^{12} >37h<

Celestial Fire 5 gr g 301^{2} 404^{4} 469^{2} >54h<

Celibate (IRE) 6 ch g 579a^{2} (652) (808) (1066) (1386) 3296^{2} 3596^{3} 4062^{F} 4366a^{2} >109h 137c<

Celio Lucy (IRE) 7 gr m Celio Rufo-Cahore (Quayside) 316a^{7} >87h<

Celtic Abbey 9 b g 3055^{P} 3637^{4} 4074^{U} (4325) (4805) >129c<

Celtic Barle 13 ch g 2011^{P} 2754^{6} (3223) 3492^{U} >120?c<

Celtic Buck (IRE) 11 b g 4361a^{F} >81c<

Celtic Carrot 5 b g Rustingo-Celtic Princess (Celtic Cone) 3170^{15} 3365^{13} >26fh<

Celtic Comma 6 b m 1821^{P} 1967^{4} >38h<

Celtic Daughter 8 b m 4804^{W} >54h<

Celtic Duke 5 b g Strong Gale-Celtic Cygnet (Celtic Cone) 1802^{7} 2787^{3} 3644^{7} >60h<

Celtic Emerald 9 ch m 1693^{4} 3166^{P} >10h<

Celtic Firefly 5 ch m Cruise Missile-Celtic Art (Celtic Cone) 653^{6}

Celtic Giant 7 ch g 1944^{F} 2043^{2} 2912^{5} 3556^{3} >75h 88c<

Celtic Laird 9 ch g 342^{7} 500^{3} 3209^{P} 3622^{P} 4165^{4} >49h 66c<

Celtic Lilley 7 ch m 2678^{7} 3088^{8} 3207^{6} >41h<

Celtic Lore 5 b g 3640^{19} >80h<

Celtic Season 5 b g Vital Season-Welsh Flower (Welsh Saint) 3425^{6} >62fh<

Celtic Silver 9 gr g 966^{3} 1142^{2} 1338^{3} 1778^{4} 1934^{5} (2916) 2956^{4} >58dh 105c<

Celtic Town 9 ch g 1415^{2} 1839^{3} 2075^{5} 2754^{4} 3003^{P} 3444^{P} >84h 111c<

Celtino 9 ch g 1039^{7} 1717^{F} 2092^{P} 2894^{4} 3113^{6} 3622^{P} >75h 100c< (DEAD)

Centaur Express 5 b g (1123) (1779) 2603a^{20} 3034^{3} 3421^{10} >96h<

Centre Stage 11 b g 3089^{4} 3208^{7} 4614^{5}

Ceridwen 7 ch m 1285^{5} (1773) (3003) 3617^{W} >60h 91c<

Certain Angle 8 ch g (28) 719^{3} 789^{F} 953^{3} 1194^{4} 1598^{P} 1876^{P} >90h 106c<

Certainly Strong (IRE) 7 b m (2890) 3144^{F} 3638^{8} >93h 140+c<

Certain Shot 6 b g Little Wolf-Duckdown (Blast) 2572^{4} 3606^{2} 4008^{3} >67fh<

Cesar du Manoir (FR) 7 ch g 2856a^{U} >79h 82c<

C'Est Tres Bien (FR) 7 ch g Azimut (FR)-Miss Ascot (FR) (Ascot Heath (FR)) 387a^{3}

Chabrol (CAN) 4 b c El Gran Senor (USA)-Off The Record (USA) (Chas Conerly (USA)) 2865^{4} 3301^{4} >83h<

Chadleigh Walk (IRE) 5 b or br g Pennine Walk-Safiya (USA) (Riverman (USA)) 353^{4} 490^{P} 675^{12} 892^{P} >38h<

Chadwick's Ginger 9 ch m 1310^{4} (3200) (4159) 4448^{4} >76h 102c<

Chain Line 7 br g 2953^{9} 3888^{P} 4075^{12} >31h<

Chain Shot 12 b g 794^{12} 1298^{5} 1696^{P} 4157^{P} >51h 51c<

Chai-Yo 7 b h (1188) (1502) 1636^{2} (1903) 2114^{2} 3572^{F} >105h<

Chalcuchima 4 gr g Reprimand-Ica (Great Nephew) 2655^{P} 2872^{12} 3590^{P} 3735^{U}

Challenger du Luc (FR) 7 b g (1366) 1649^{F} 2773^{6} (2962) 3636^{5} 4011^{4} >87h 160c<

Champagne Friend 6 b m 3425^{13}

Champs-Girl (IRE) 4 b f Yashgan-Ramy's Gayle (Strong Gale) 2640^{6} 3070^{11}

Chance Coffey 12 b g 3126a^{7} **>103h 85c<**

Chancey Fella 6 ch g 186^{3} (262) (416) 675^{5} **>70h<**

Change the Act 12 b g **3800^{2} 4379^{2} >118h 122c<**

Change the Reign 10 b g **(74) 864^{3} 1089^{4} 2671^{3} 3414^{2} 4013^{B} 4098^{P} >114c<**

Chan Move 5 b g Move Off-Kanisa (Chantro) 3070^{12} 3330^{9} 3487^{11} 4580^{10} 4708^{F}

Channel Pastime 13 b g **56^{4} 136^{2} 256^{3} 342^{4} 882^{4} 1070^{4} 1284^{2} 1465^{3} 2092^{4} 2756^{4} 2962^{3} 3232^{4} >98c<**

Chan The Man 6 b g 1065^{5} **4070^{4} (4728)** >77c<

Chantro Bay 9 b g 1278^{8} 1369^{P} **>34h< (DEAD)**

Chantry Beath 6 ch g 2579^{5} 2838^{F} **>69h< (DEAD)**

Chaos And Order 5 b g Petoski-Chez Nous (Habitat) 1820^{8} **>48fh< (DEAD)**

Chapel of Barras (IRE) 8 b g **826^{W}** 950^{F} 1086^{6} 1207^{7} 3447^{17} **4100^{4}** >12h<

Chapilliere (FR) 7 b g 1938^{9} 2663^{P} 3171^{6} **3582^{5} 3968^{P} 4426^{4} >56h 47c<**

Chaprassi (IRE) 8 ch g 1455^{4} 2884^{10} **>91h<**

Chaps 7 b g 216^{3} **>64h<**

Charged 8 ch g **23^{3} 728^{7}** 837^{4} **>80h 96c<**

Chariot Man (IRE) 5 b br g Mandalus-Mum's Chariot (Callernish) 4450^{5} 4514^{F} 4696^{10} **>33h<**

Charley Lambert (IRE) 6 b g 2812^{11} 3159^{4} 3437^{2} 3734^{B} 3990^{P} 4204^{8} **>71h<**

Charlie Banker (IRE) 5 b g Supreme Leader-Hack Along (Little Buskins) 1457^{7} 3143^{7} **>46fh<**

Charlie Bee 8 b g 3178^{P} **3736^{7} 4004^{P} >48c<**

Charlie Bigtime 7 b g Norwick (USA)-Sea Aura (Roi Soleil) 3431^{P}

Charlie Foxtrot (IRE) 5 b g 1757a^{4} **>94fh<**

Charlie Keay (IRE) 5 br g Supreme Leader-View of The Hills (Croghan Hill) *3846^{5}* **>30fh<**

Charlie Parrot (IRE) 7 gr g 1059^{2} 1283^{3} 1507^{5} 2875^{3} **3073^{3} 3617^{P}** 4096^{P} **>80h 80c<**

Charlie Pip 5 b g Rakaposhi King-Gilberts Choice (My Swanee) 3235^{17}

Charlies Delight (IRE) 9 b g **3010^{8} 3270^{F} 3753^{4} 4218^{U} >46h 88?c<**

Charlie's Folly 6 ch g Capitano-Cavity (True Song) 1551^{4} 2677^{6} 3085^{P} 3685^{6} **>60?h<**

Charlistiona 6 ch m 5^{3} 1703^{P} **1853^{B}** (4259) 4409^{2} 4578^{3} **>60h<**

Charlvic 7 ch g 1822^{P} 2768^{6} 2913^{7} 3313^{10} 3971^{6} **4751^{U} >30h<**

Charming Gale 10 b or br m **9^{5} 732^{2} (855) 1268^{2} (1823) 1970^{6} 2801^{3} >106c<**

Charming Girl (USA) 6 b m 1137^{4} 1510^{2} 1793^{13} 2779^{6} 3412^{5} 3987^{F} **>107h<**

Charter Lane (IRE) 7 b g 1394^{8} **1856^{6} 2827^{8} 3134^{3} 3667^{3} >17h 80c<**

Chasing Dreams 6 b g St Columbus-Into Song (True Song) 2750^{8} 3158^{13} 3795^{5} **>60h<**

Chasing The Moon (IRE) 5 b g Yashgan-Super Cailin (Brave Invader (USA)) 1986^{3} 2696^{16} **>54fh<**

Chatergold (IRE) 5 b g Posen (USA)-Fiodoir (Weavers' Hall) 1639^{12} 2053^{12} 2812^{P} **>28h<**

Chatter Box 5 ch m Backchat (USA)-Vulgan's Bella (Vulgan Slave) 4008^{19} **>8fh<**

Cheap Metal 12 br g 356^{5} **>58h<**

Cheater (IRE) 6 b g 1296^{5} 1672^{5} 2177^{2} 2627^{5} (2802) 3309^{6} 4147^{5} 4257^{P} **>71h<**

Checks And Stripes (IRE) 6 ch g 1191^{8}

Cheeka 8 ch g **1066^{3} 1248^{P} 1714^{5} 3571^{5} 4159^{2} 4300^{4} 4611^{P} >74h 91dc<**

Cheeky Charlie 5 b g Jupiter Island-Double Shuffle (Tachypous) 3084^{9} 3445^{2} 3685^{4} **>63h<**

Cheerful Aspect (IRE) 4 b g Cadeaux Genereux-Strike Home (Be My Guest (USA)) (2865) 3426^{2} 3685^{2} **>84h<**

Cheer's Baby 7 b g 129^{6} 343^{4} 499^{P} **>39h< (DEAD)**

Chef Comedien (IRE) 7 ch g Commanche Run-Clipper Queen (Balidar) 1567^{3} 3421^{P} **>80h<**

Chelworth Wolf 5 ch g 407^{6} 476^{5} **>28h<**

Chemin-de-Fer 5 b g Darshaan-Whitehaven (Top Ville) 2073^{9}

Cherokee Chief 6 ch g 2701^{3} 3364^{2} 4217^{2} **>72h<**

Cherry Chap 12 b g **3924^{2} >95c<**

Cherry Dee 6 ch m 1692^{2} 2701^{9} 3066^{5} 3348^{3} (3557) (3887) 4188^{P} **>68h<**

Cherry Island (IRE) 9 ch g King Persian-Tamar di Bulgaria (ITY) (Duke of Marmalade (USA)) **3455^{2} >92c<**

Cherrymore (IRE) 6 br g Cataldi-Cherry Bow (Beau Chapeau) (2080) 2690^{7} 4184^{4} **>77+h<**

Cherrynut 8 b g **(1324) 3230^{F} 3599^{P} >123c<**

Cherry Orchid 10 b br g Callernish-Cherry Token (Prince Hansel) **1189^{P} 1449^{7} >23c<**

Cheryl's Lad (IRE) 7 b g **1815^{2} 2054^{4}** 3640^{11} 4357a^{10} 4610^{3} **>113dh 117c<**

Cheslock (IRE) 8 b g **3255a^{3}**

Chester Ben 8 ro g Alias Smith (USA)-Saleander (Leander) **4637^{8} >32c<**

Chesters Quest 5 ch g Domynsky-Chess Mistress (USA) (Run The Gantlet (USA)) 497^{9} **>34h<**

Chiappelli (IRE) 5 b m Buckskin (FR)-Lean Over (Over The River (FR)) 1913^{10} **>38fh< (DEAD)**

Chiappucci (IRE) 7 b g **2007^{9} 3836^{2} 4158^{P} 4232^{4} 4298^{5} 4549^{7} 4736^{F} >80h 72c<**

Chickabiddy 9 b m **547^{3} 738^{3} 903^{2} 972^{2} (1331) >77h 92c<**

Chickawicka (IRE) 6 b h (1178) 1470^{3} 3850^{R} **>81?h<**

Chicodari 5 b g 1325^{3} 1559^{3} 2777^{4} 3164^{3} **>111h<**

Chief Chippie 4 b g Mandalus-Little Katrina (Little Buskins) 2804^{12} 3070^{10} 3789^{P} 4152^{8}

Chief Gale (IRE) 5 b g 653^{4} 787^{2} 931^{3} 1505^{6} 4450^{P} **>53h<**

Chief Joseph 10 b m **3232^{F} >83h 92c< (DEAD)**

Chief Minister (IRE) 8 br g **2653^{2} 2899^{2} (3161) 4211^{4} >128h 124c<**

Chief Mouse 4 b g Be My Chief (USA)-Top Mouse (High Top) (458) 736^{2} (1205) 1634^{10} 2872^{6} 3184^{P} (3741) (4169) (4313) 4527^{5} **>83h<**

Chief of Khorassan (FR) 5 br g 59^{9} 2804^{8} 4150^{8} **>42fh<**

Chief Rager 8 ch g **1799^{6} 2063^{P} 2681^{P}** 3016^{P} 3166^{6} **>60h 96c<**

Chief's Lady 5 b m Reprimand-Pussy Foot (Red Sunset) 400^{6} 603^{8} **>26h<**

Chief's Song 7 b g (945) 1365^{6} 2645^{5} 2886^{2} 3038^{14} 3572^{9} **>120h<**

Chieftain's Crown (USA) 6 ch g 208^{5} 2952^{6} 3063^{4} (4725) **>67h<**

Childhay Chocolate 9 b g **797^{R} 1063^{3} 1391^{F} 1839^{F} 2876^{3} 3280^{3} 3605^{P} >105c<**

Children's Choice (IRE) 6 b m 1417^{6} 3438^{8} **>54h<**

Childsway 9 b g Salmon Leap (USA)-Tharita (Thatch (USA)) **584^{8} 2628^{8} 3030^{F} 3314^{5} 3450^{F} 3608^{F} 4502^{P} 4751^{P} >49c<**

Chili Heights 7 gr g 1768^{P} 1948^{5} 2578^{10} **3538^{U}** 4086^{7} 4175^{4} 4328^{3} **>51h<**

Chilipour 10 gr g **4051^{F} (4432) 4634^{6} >120dc<**

Chilled (IRE) 5 b g 1422^{4} **>62h<**

Chill Factor 7 br g 1026^{3} 1290^{4} 1654^{8} 2627^{3} 3100^{4} 4147^{8} 4513^{6} 4646^{6} **>43h<**

Chillington 4 gr g Chilibang-Saskia's Pride (Giacometti) 831^{7} 1149^{13} 1980^{11} **>20h<**

Chill Wind 8 gr or gr g 2817^{10} 3076^{4} **3336^{2} (3482) 3645^{F}** 3827^{3} **3886^{F} 4247^{5} 4456^{3}** 4577^{2} **>65h 74c<**

Chilly Lad 6 ch g 2838^{P} **>54h<**

China Castle 4 b g Sayf El Arab (USA)-Honey Plum (Kind of Hush) 3345^{5} **>61h<**

China Gem (IRE) 6 b g 1317^{11} 1541^{2} **>66h<**

China King (IRE) 6 b g 3914^{5} 4288^{2} 4479^{8} 4752^{2} **>64h<**

China Lal 5 b m Rakaposhi King-Doris Blake (Roscoe Blake) 4645^{7}

China Mail (IRE) 5 b g 337^{2} (413) (499) 549^{3} 690^{4} 813^{4} 1322^{6} 1569^{7} 4464^{3} 4662^{7} **>48h<**

Chinese Gordon (IRE) 7 2613a^{3}

Chinook's Daughter (IRE) 5 b m Strong Gale-Lulu's Daughter (Levanter) 1362^{11} 1579^{11} 4244^{P} **>19fh<**

Chipalata 4 b g Derrylin-Kirsheda (Busted) 881^{4} **>33h<**

Chip'n'run 11 gr g **3680^{3} >86c<**

Chipped Out 7 gr g **1653^{4} 1981^{5}** 3885^{4} 4261^{P} **>82h 83c<**

Chism (IRE) 6 br g Euphemism-Melody Gayle VII (Damsire Unregistered) **4462^{3} >92?c<**

Chocolate Drum (IRE) 6 br g Orchestra-Precious Petra (Bing II) 4216^{9} 4420^{8} **>63fh<**

Chocolate Ice 4 b g Shareef Dancer (USA)-Creake (Derring-Do) 2753^{2} **>52h<**

Choisty (IRE) 7 ch g **1629^{U} 1845^{F} (2540) (2698) 3033^{U} >112?c<**

Choosey's Treasure (IRE) 4 gr f Treasure Kay-Catherine Linton (USA) 1747a^{11} 2333a^{4} **>100h<**

Chopwell Curtains 7 ch g **1129^{2} (1574) (3805) 4050^{P} (4203) 4245^{F} >94h 121c<**

Chopwell Drapes (IRE) 7 br g 2898^{4} 3437^{3} 3794^{4} **>69h<**

Chorus Line (IRE) 8 b m **1051^{3} 1126^{2} 2628^{4} 2799^{U} 3030^{F} 3200^{5} (3842) 4157^{U} 4446^{U} >85++c<**

Chris's Glen 8 ch g 55^{7} (815) 936^{3} **1038^{6} 1252^{5} 1629^{W} 1875^{4} 2577^{4} 3051^{3} 3188^{3} 3588^{3} 3717^{3}** 4006^{11} 4381^{6} **>63h 72c<**

Christchurch (FR) 7 b g Highlanders (FR)-Olchany (FR) (Labus (FR)) 1966^{7} 3441^{3} 3796^{8} **>75h<**

Christian Soldier 10 b g Tickled Pink-Super Princess (Falcon) 1040^{P} **>52h<**

Christian Warrior 8 gr g Primo Dominie-Rashah (Blakeney) 794^{13}

Christmas Gorse 11 b g **(1662) 2063^{F} 2928^{U} 3599^{9} >125dc<**

Christmas Thyne (IRE) 5 b g Good Thyne (USA)-Shady Lady (Proverb) **4773^{P}**

Chuck (IRE) 7 b g Kamehameha (USA)-Kill A Dawn 317a^{6} **>76h<**

Chucklestone 14 b g 598^{4} **>86h<**

Chukkario 11 b g **738^{9} 972^{P} 1009^{P}**

Chummy's Saga 7 ch g 1247^{4} 1344^{6} 1703^{2} 2629^{5} 3327^{2} 3704^{4} **>58h<**

Church Law 10 br g **(1089) 1428^{P} 1662^{2} 1871^{2} 2758^{9} 3046^{P} (3585) 4110a^{10} >113c<**

Churchtown Port (IRE) 7 gr g **2796^{7} 3009^{F} 3176^{F} 3336^{P} >44h 81c<**

Churchtown Spirit 6 b m Town And Country-Kindled Spirit (Little Buskins) 813^{P} 1422^{P} 1707^{5}

Churchworth 6 b g Damister (USA)-Be Tuneful (Be Friendly) 3359^{17} 3592^{P} 3704^{F} **>1h<**

Ciara's Prince (IRE) 6 b g 3523a^{3} **>102+h<**

Cinnamon Club 5 b m Derrylin-Cinnamon Run (Deep Run) 3149^{9} 3433^{5} 4561^{2} **>63fh<**

Cinq Frank (IRE) 7 gr g Buckskin (FR)-Clever Milly (Precipice Wood) 4360a^{17} **>51fh<**
Cipisek (CZE) 9 b h Val II (CZE)-Cecilka (USA) (Porterhouse) **(930a) >115?c<**
Cipriani Queen (IRE) 7 b m (1132) **>56h<**
Circle Boy 10 b g 1247^{F} 1344^{10} 1942^{P} 2045^{8} **>48h<**
Circled (USA) 4 gr f Cozzene (USA)-Hold The Hula (USA) (Hawaii) 3075^{16}
Circulation 11 b g **207^{4} 292^{4} 475^{2} 742^{3} (895) 1146^{2} 1306^{F} 1584^{5} 1864^{F} >88c<**
Circus Colours 7 b g 16^{6} 264^{3} 348^{4} (473) 657^{2} 816^{9} 2755^{6} 2946^{7} (4340) 4527^{6} 4732^{8} **>72h<**
Circus Line 6 ch g 1439^{2} (1658) (1860) (2670) 2817^{P} **>97h<**
Circus Star 4 b g Soviet Star (USA)-Circus Act (Shirley Heights) 1014^{4} 1935^{2} 2697^{P} 3075^{2} 3404^{2} 3634^{2} 4014^{3} 4364a^{3} **>100h<**
Cittadino 7 b g 1358^{4} 1658^{6} 2543^{2} (2817) 3028^{4} 3885^{P} 4187^{11} **>82h<**
Civil Law (IRE) 7 b g Law Society (USA)-Senane (Vitiges (FR)) 3575^{P}
Clady Boy (IRE) 6 ch g 3382a^{9} **>72h<**
Clairabell (IRE) 6 b m 1021^{P} 2920^{5} 3887^{5} (4188) **>69h<**
Claire's Dancer (IRE) 4 b g Classic Music (USA)-Midnight Patrol (Ashmore (FR)) 1634^{13} 2751^{7} **>23h<**
Claireswan (IRE) 5 ch g (1394) 1586^{5} 2797^{4} 3351^{4} (3722) 4415^{2} **>77h<**
Clancy's Express 6 b g 212^{4} 295^{4} **>49h<**
Clan Ross (IRE) 6 ch m Ardross-Rozifer (Lucifer (USA)) 3821^{16} **>42fh<**
Claregary (IRE) 4 b f Brush Aside (USA)-Adare Lady (Varano) 2911^{6} **>30fh<**
Clare Maid (IRE) 8 b m (1345) 1854^{7} **>67h<**
Clares Own 13 b g **583^{5} 689^{5} 1082^{4} >85c<**
Clare's Spring (IRE) 4 ch g King Luthier-Do We Know (Derrylin) 3574^{16} **>25fh<**
Clarkes Gorse (IRE) 6 b g Miner's Lamp-Mo Storeen (Abednego) 2676^{4} 3178^{P} 3796^{4} **>75h<**
Clashawan (IRE) 7 b m 58^{P} 3133^{P}
Clash of Cymbals 8 gr g 502^{P} **>60h<**
Clash of Swords 4 b g Shaadi (USA)-Swept Away (Kris) 3022^{2} (3394) 3789^{3} 4209^{3} 4395^{7} **>70h<**
Classic Account 9 ch g Pharly (FR)-Money Supply (Brigadier Gerard) 3803^{F}
Classicaction (IRE) 6 b g King's Ride-Laurestown Rose (Derring Rose) 1317^{P}
Classical Joker 4 b f Old Jocus-Classy Miss (Homeboy) 1014^{8}
Classic Chat 5 b g 1685^{9} 2656^{P} 3048^{7} **>41h<**
Classic Colours (USA) 4 ch g Blushing John (USA)-All Agleam (USA) (Gleaming (USA)) 2784^{8} 3058^{5} **>4h<**
Classic Crest (IRE) 6 ch g 60^{9} 585^{5} 642^{F} 693^{P} **892^{2} 2803^{U} 2954^{P} 4408^{P} >63h<**
Classic Daisy 4 b f Prince Sabo-Bloom of Youth (IRE) (Last Tycoon) 1370^{B} 1776^{P}
Classic Defence (IRE) 4 b c Cyrano de Bergerac-My Alanna (Dalsaan) (944) **>72+h<**
Classic Delight (USA) 4 b f Green Forest (USA)-Weather Girl (USA) (One For All (USA)) 2818^{7} 2946^{14} 3670^{9} **>30h<**
Classic Exhibit 8 b g 75^{4} 103^{5} **>76h<**
Classic Image (IRE) 7 b g 17^{5} 66^{10} 134^{8} **>62h<**
Classic Jenny (IRE) 4 b f Green Desert (USA)-Eileen Jenny (IRE) (Kris) 3548^{2} **>41fh<**
Classic Jester (IRE) 6 b g 69^{P} 2627^{P} **>32h<**
Classic Model 6 b g High Line-Fast Car (FR) (Carwhite) 2805^{14} 3494^{9} 3761^{12} 4181^{P} **>39h<**
Classic Pal (USA) 6 b g 1767^{P} 2755^{2} 3234^{2} 4006^{F} 4534^{3} 4654^{2} 4725^{3} **>56h<**
Classic Silk (IRE) 5 b m 316a^{3} **>83h<**
Classic Statement 11 ch g 6^{P} **>74h<**
Classic Victory 4 b g Puissance-Seattle Mama (USA) (Seattle Song (USA)) 3404^{10}
Class of Ninetytwo (IRE) 8 b g **1175^{2} (1469) 1643^{2} >127c<**
Classy Chief 4 b g Be My Chief (USA)-Jalopy (Jalmood (USA)) 1712^{5} 1900^{7} **>69h<**
Classy Kahyasi (IRE) 7 b m 531^{4} **>56h<**
Classy Lad (NZ) 7 b br g Golden Elder-Barrel (NZ) (The Monk) 3298^{5} 3820^{2} **>80h<**
Claverhouse (IRE) 8 b g **3202^{P} 3546^{4} (3705) >89h 100c<**
Clavering (IRE) 7 br g 1689^{P} 2539^{4} 2917^{4} 3307^{2} 3612^{P} **>71h<**
Claxton Greene 13 b g **2821^{7} 3003^{P} >90c<**
Clay And Wattles (IRE) 6 br g Alzao (USA)-Inisfree (USA) (Hoist The Flag (USA)) 4360a^{20} **>79fh<**
Clay County 12 b g **943^{2} 2646^{2} >73h 151c< (DEAD)**
Claymore Lad 7 b g **1635^{P} 2693^{5} 2947^{4} 3736^{3} >83c<**
Clean Edge (USA) 5 ch g 139^{2} (347) 493^{2} (894) 1031^{5} 1342^{P} **>89h< (DEAD)**
Clear Home 11 ch g (326a) **>64h<**
Clear Idea (IRE) 9 ch g **604^{3} 750^{U} >80h 106c< (DEAD)**
Cleasby Hill 12 ch g Avocat-Strandhill (Bargello) **4022^{P} >90c<**
Cleric on Broadway (IRE) 9 b m 3431^{U} 4318^{6} 4562^{5} **>33h<**
Clever Boy (IRE) 6 b g 1152^{10} (1316) 1575^{3} 2550^{8} 2746^{6} 3100^{2} 3557^{5} 3967^{P} **>71h< (DEAD)**
Cliburnel News (IRE) 7 b m Horage-Dublin Millennium (Dalsaan) 1187^{11} 1438^{4} 1818^{3} 3325^{4} 3733^{4} 3967^{3} **>58h<**
Clifdon Fog (IRE) 6 b g 2603a^{17} **>107+h<**
Clifton 8 b g 675^{P} **(DEAD)**
Clifton Beat (USA) 6 b h 3038^{P} 4061^{4} 4212^{10} **>124h<**
Clifton Game 7 b g **1018^{2} 1386^{4} 2892^{3} >43h 95c<**
Clifton Match 5 gr m 3342^{9} **>38h<**
Clifton Set 6 b g **(482) 631^{2} >108h 115c<**
Clinking 6 b g 1800^{5} (2648) 2938^{4} **>53fh<**
Clinton (IRE) 6 b g 1830^{8} 2690^{2} 3133^{2} 3399^{2} **>85h<**
Clobracken Lad 9 ch g **3403^{3} 3637^{P} 4322^{3} (4462) >96c<**
Clock Watchers 9 b g 2624^{10} 2791^{5} 3084^{P} 3755^{6} 3955^{4} 4097^{2} 4341^{6} **>58h<**
Clod Hopper (IRE) 7 br g (1135) 1322^{7} 1448^{3} (2708) 2820^{2} **>63h<**
Clonagam (IRE) 8 b g (316a) 4355a^{7} **>89h<**
Clonattin Lady (IRE) 8 b m Sandalay-Cold Arctic (Bargello) **860^{P} 1075^{P}**
Clongour (IRE) 7 ch g 1654^{12} 2042^{10} 2627^{7} (4073) 4147^{B} **>64h<**
Clonroche Lucky (IRE) 7 b g Strong Statement (USA)-Clonroche Artic (Pauper) **875^{P}** 1689^{12} **1845^{7} 1989^{4} 2540^{10} 2698^{3} 3067^{4} 3347^{P} 3824^{6} >20h 61dc<**
Clonrosh Slave 10 br g Tesoro Mio-Clonroche Artic (Pauper) **3637^{8} >98c<**
Clontoura (IRE) 9 b g Salluceva-Clara Novello (Maclver (USA)) 1854^{5} **3155^{7} 3409^{F} >54h 70c<**
Cloone Bridge (IRE) 5 b g Phardante (FR)-Carney's Hill 4360a^{2} **>88fh<**
Close Harmony 5 ch m 3154^{6} 3569^{8} **>34h<**
Cloudy Bill 5 ch g Nicholas Bill-Welsh Cloud (Welsh Saint) 4538^{15}
Cloudy House 8 gr m Grey Desire-Scenic Villa (Top Ville) 4230^{P} 4304^{P}
Clover Girl 6 bl m 463^{2} 647^{5} 731^{4} (893) 1078^{2} **>50h<**
Club Caribbean 5 br m Strong Gale-Murex (Royalty) 1180^{5} 2634^{8} 3052^{8} **>42h<**
Club Elite 5 b m 401^{4} **>47h<**
Coast Along (IRE) 5 b g 32^{5} (187) 347^{3} **>74h<**
Coasting 11 b g **1684^{P} 2823^{11} 3332^{P} 3622^{4} 4429^{5} 4557^{2} >90c<**
Coble Lane 5 ch g Minster Son-Preziosa (Homing) 1827^{2} 2811^{3} 3021^{5} 4009^{2} **>62fh<**
Cockney Lad (IRE) 8 ch g 1234a^{4} (1487a) 1759a^{2} 2461a^{3} (2740a) 3597^{9} **>130h<**
Cockpit (IRE) 6 b g Henbit (USA)-Forthetimebeing (Prince Regent (FR)) 3798^{11} 3982^{6} **>54h<**
Code Red 4 b c Warning-For Action (USA) (Assert) 1953^{7} 2678^{8} 3284^{U} 3620^{2} **>59h<**
Coeur Battant (FR) 7 ch g 185^{12} 301^{F} 407^{4} 480^{4} 546^{4} 598^{5} 725^{P} **>45h<**
Coeur Francais (FR) 5 b g Hero's Honor (USA)-Marie d'Anjou (FR) (Free Round (USA)) 2649^{R} 3311^{8} 3474^{U} **>12h<**
Cointosser (IRE) 4 b f Nordico (USA)-Sure Flyer (IRE) (Sure Blade (USA)) (753) (836) (912) 4381^{5} **>74h<**
Cokenny Boy 12 b g **719^{5}** (1794) 1952^{5} (2625) 2934^{3} **>89h 109dc<**
Cold Feet 0 D Arctic Lord-Hammerhill (Grisaille) 3853^{5} **>47fh<**
Colebrook Willie 4 br g Dowsing (USA)-A Little Hot (Petong) 753^{4} 831^{6} 1377^{12} 1595^{6} **>52h<**
Colette's Choice (IRE) 8 b m **1199^{U} 1426^{5} 1694^{3} 2657^{8} 2896^{P}** 3112^{7} **3538^{U} >42h 70c<**
Colin's Pride 6 b m 603^{6} 812^{8} 913^{8} 973^{P} **>50h<**
Collier Bay 7 b g (3017) 3597^{P} **>164h<**
Collon Leader (IRE) 8 b m 2345a^{2} 3523a^{8} **>88h<**
Colm's Rock (IRE) 6 ch g 4348a^{5} **>110h<**
Colonel Blazer 5 b g 2053^{7} (3342) 4204^{P} (4329) **>82h<**
Colonel Colt 6 b g **3051^{P} 3188^{P} 3602^{3} 4735^{2} >45dh 79c<**
Colonel In Chief (IRE) 7 br g **1646^{P} 2899^{3} (3068) 3314^{2} (3882) (4245) (4481) >86h 116c<**
Colonel Jack 5 b g Tragic Role (USA)-Cedar Lady (Telsmoss) 1966^{17} 2815^{12} **>9h<**
Colonel Kenson 11 ch g **3062^{F} >53c<**
Colonial Kelly 9 ch g **3089^{P} 3353^{3} 3637^{P} (3813) 4724^{P} >101c<**
Colorful Ambition 7 b g 1630^{4} 1779^{3} 1852^{3} (4339) (4712) **>86h<**
Colossus of Roads 8 br g 3177^{3} 3570^{P} **>75h<**
Colour Code 5 ch g Polish Precedent (USA)-Reprocolor (Jimmy Reppin) (1296) (2640) **>100fh<**
Colour Counsellor 4 gr g Touch of Grey-Bourton Downs (Philip of Spain) 962^{7} 1149^{F} 1377^{4} 1663^{4} 4313^{4} **>67h<**
Colour Scheme 10 ch g Rainbow Quest (USA)-Much Pleasure (Morston (FR)) 899^{P} 1198^{R} 1332^{8} 1466^{P} **>29h<**
Colt D'Or 5 ch g 262^{P} **(DEAD)**
Coltibuono (IRE) 5 ch g Orchestra-Baby Birch (Le Moss) 2844^{11} **>16fh<**
Colwall 6 br g 1327^{6} (1814) 2036^{2} 2552^{6} 2820^{3} 3831^{5} 4181^{U} 4470^{8} 4731^{2} **>53h<**
Colway Prince (IRE) 9 b g **61^{F}** 339^{3} 697^{7} **>65h<**
Comedy Gayle 10 b g Lir-Follifoot's Folly (Comedy Star (USA)) **4522^{P}**
Comedy Road 13 br g **(68) 342^{3} (500) 799^{F} 953^{4} 1284^{4} 1704^{5} 2092^{5} >97dc<**
Come on Dancer (IRE) 9 ch g **4733^{4} >29h 80c<**

Come On In 4 b g Most Welcome-Lominda (IRE) (Lomond (USA)) 1444^{F} 2050^{4} 2840^{6} 3054^{4} 3222^{6} 3566^{5} 4453^{F} 4636^{2} **>42h<**

Come On Penny 6 b m (718) **>66h<**

Comeonup 6 b g Most Welcome-Scarlet Veil (Tyrnavos) 1770^{4} 1874^{6} 2038^{4} **>52h<**

Come on Winn 5 ch m Handsome Sailor-Ragusa Girl (Morston (FR)) 105^{R}

Commanche Court (IRE) 4 ch c Commanche Run-Sorceress (FR) (Fabulous Dancer (USA)) (2993a) (3258a) (3634) **>101h<**

Commanche Creek 7 b g 75^{2} 128^{6} 214^{P} 299^{5} 3740^{3} 4175^{3} 4401^{6} **>60h<**

Commanche Cup (IRE) 4 b g Commanche Run-Royal Cup (Politico (USA)) 3747^{9} **>43fh<**

Commanche Storm (IRE) 5 b g 963^{6} 1251^{P}

Commandeer (IRE) 7 b g **696^{5} 907^{2} 1129^{4} 1246^{2} >45h 85c< (DEAD)**

Commander Glen (IRE) 5 b g Glenstal (USA)-Une Parisienne (FR) (Bolkonski) 450^{2} 700^{5} (801) 1081^{3} 1360^{5} (1825) **>73h<**

Commando Dancer (IRE) 5 b g Zaffaran (USA)-Laricina (Tarboosh (USA)) 191^{10} 418^{7}

Commercial Artist 11 b g **1016^{3} 1133^{4} >140c<**

Common Sound (IRE) 6 b g 1314^{5} 2617^{8} 2764^{4} 3065^{5} 3398^{9} 4246^{P} **>44h<**

Community Service (IRE) 6 b m Homo Sapien-Perpetue (Proverb) 3440^{6} *3846^{8}* 4632^{12} **>34fh<**

Commuter Country 6 gr g 2927^{6} 3535^{6} 3761^{11} **>49h<**

Conchobor (IRE) 5 b br g Supreme Leader-Nights Crack (Callernish) (4538) **>74fh<**

Concinnity (USA) 8 b g 2874^{8} 3234^{P} 3344^{5} 3499^{11} 3589^{6} 3740^{U} 3949^{7} **>34h<**

Coneygree 5 b m 65^{8} **>71h<**

Coney Road 8 gr g **1468^{6} 1773^{P} 2665^{F}** 3004^{P}

Conna Moss (IRE) 8 b g Le Moss-Glitter On (Even Money) **3341^{U}**

Connaught's Pride 6 ch m 900^{9} 2759^{14} 3337^{6} 3628^{P} (3894) 4445^{P} 4663^{5} **>47h<**

Connel's Croft 5 ch g Rich Charlie-Technology (FR) (Top Ville) 2750^{13} 4156^{2} **>41fh<**

Connie Leathart 6 b m 3440^{12} 3823^{13} 3908^{6} 4259^{P} **>23h<**

Conquering Leader (IRE) 8 b m **1963^{2} 2827^{F}** 3303^{2} 3635^{F} 4396^{4} **>118h 103c<**

Conquer The Kilt 6 b g 3425^{9} 3798^{F} **>52fh<**

Consharon (IRE) 9 br m **4110a^{P} 4116a^{3} >84c<**

Conti D'Estruval (FR) 7 b g **496^{2} 811^{3} 1272^{U} 1373^{P} 1869^{5} 2065^{3} 2879^{4} 3413^{3} 3701^{5} >75h 122c<**

Contract Bridge (IRE) 4 b f Contract Law (USA)-Mystery Bid (Auction Ring (USA)) 2574^{5} 2840^{12} 3406^{6} 3764^{8} (4069) (4294) 4333^{5} 4548^{4} **>57?h<**

Contrafire (IRE) 5 b g Contract Law (USA)-Fiery Song (Ballad Rock) (871) (1020) 1305^{2} 4746^{4} **>75h<**

Convamore Queen (IRE) 8 b m Carlingford Castle-Santa Ponsa (Wishing Star) **2926^{U} 3173^{10}** 3352^{12} **>27c<**

Coolafinka (IRE) 8 b m Strong Statement (USA)-Petaluma Pet (Callernish) **3389a^{2} 3617^{7} >93c<**

Cool As A Cucumber (IRE) 6 ch g 2844^{6} 3271^{8} **>28h<**

Cool Bandit (IRE) 7 b g Lancastrian-Madam Owen (Master Owen) **4317^{2} 4615^{U}**

Cool Cat (IRE) 6 b g Cataldi-Arctic Sue (Arctic Slave) 3337^{P} 4217^{P}

Cool Character (IRE) 9 b g **190^{10} 1385^{4} 1773^{6} 1877^{2} 2706^{4} 2876^{4} 3181^{P} >88c<**

Cool Dawn (IRE) 9 br g **1273^{4} >143c<**

Coole Cherry 7 b g Buckley-Cherry Opal (Saint Denys) 1507^{6} 2053^{8} 2822^{4} 3048^{11} 3541^{4} 3683^{12} **>60h<**

Coolegale 11 br g 156^{6} 813^{3} 960^{7} 1077^{9} 1322^{8} 3811^{8} **>40h<**

Coole Hill (IRE) 6 b br m 1174^{5} 1384^{3} 1654^{4} 2076^{2} 2746^{4} **3360^{2} >75h 95c<**

Coolest By Phar (IRE) 5 ch g Phardante (FR)-Gemma's Fridge (Frigid Aire) 3021^{U} 4657^{12}

Cooley's Valve (IRE) 9 b g 299^{6} 483^{4} (635) 723^{2} 863^{3} 1123^{3} 4307^{4} 4644^{2} **>78h<**

Cool Game 7 b g 2918^{5} 4744^{F} **>39h<**

Coolgreen (IRE) 9 ch g Andretti-Emanuela (Lorenzaccio) **3455^{P} >89c<**

Cool Gunner 7 b g 1427^{6} (1995) 2680^{U} 3019^{4} (3539) (3740) 4204^{9} **>77+h<**

Cool Harry (USA) 6 b br g 1774^{12} 3184^{9} 3431^{4} 3628^{5} 3796^{6} 4427^{U} 4625^{4} 4801^{6} **>63h<**

Cool Kevin 4 b g Sharkskin Suit (USA)-Cool Snipe (Dynastic) 3070^{6} 3330^{6} 3487^{4} 3914^{8} **>34fh<**

Cool Luke (IRE) 8 b g 1188^{6} 1360^{6} 1658^{8} 2957^{5} **3326^{5}** 3693^{5} 4389^{S} **4763^{6} >73h 70c<**

Cool Mandy 6 b m 1251^{P} **>2h<**

Coolmoreen (IRE) 9 ch g Carlingford Castle-Sirrahdis (Bally Joy) 129^{10} 181^{5} **>18h<**

Cool Norman (NZ) 5 b g First Norman (USA)-Ice Flake (NZ) (Icelandic) 4433^{7} **>38fh<**

Coolree (IRE) 9 b g **(979) 1350^{2} 1731^{3} 2568^{5} (2942) 3151^{P} 3800^{4} >115c<**

Coolreny (IRE) 8 ch g **1943^{U} 3030^{4} 3138^{P} >66?c< (DEAD)**

Cool Runner 7 b g **1326^{F} 3020^{7} 3223^{P} >78h 97c<**

Cool Spot (IRE) 9 ch g 3685^{P} **>58h<**

Cool Steel (IRE) 5 gr g 911^{5} 1654^{11} 1849^{11} 1990^{5} 2913^{8} 3031^{7} 3327^{6} 3542^{F} **>57h< (DEAD)**

Coolteen Hero (IRE) 7 b g King Luthier-Running Stream (Paddy's Stream) **738^{6} (917) 1169^{2} 1414^{U} 1552^{5} 2810^{U} (3059) 3673^{2} 3832^{2} (4174) 4344^{2} 4659^{F} >100c<**

Coolvawn Lady (IRE) 8 b m **3357^{7} 4411^{2} 4637^{2} >81c<**

Cool Virtue (IRE) 6 b m 3500^{U} 3592^{9} **>42h<**

Cool Weather (IRE) 9 b g **907^{5} 1153^{5} 1313^{5} 1778^{F} 2540^{6} 2671^{6} 2954^{5} 3724^{2} 3975^{3} 4077^{4} 4260^{2} 4446^{2} >80c<**

Cool Yule (IRE) 9 ch g Good Thyne (USA)-Sleigh Lady (Lord Gayle (USA)) **4076^{4} 4155^{3} 4411^{4} 4704^{4} >86c<**

Coome Hill (IRE) 8 b g **(1063) (1287) (1649) 2887^{F} (3230) 3636^{7} >160+c<**

Coonawara 11 b g **4013^{P} >145c< (DEAD)**

Copper Boy 8 ch g (1586) (3011) 3615^{24} **>94h<**

Copper Cable 10 ch g **1179^{5} 1340^{4} 1717^{2} 2674^{P} 3842^{4} 3960^{3} 4297^{4} 4566^{6} >64c<**

Copper Coil 7 ch g 934^{2} 1077^{3} 1197^{4} 1334^{2} 1673^{5} (1840) 3048^{5} 3683^{3} 3834^{3} 4073^{P} **>68h<**

Copper Diamond 4 ch f So Careful-Lady Abbott (Grey Love) 458^{P} 589^{10} 881^{6}

Copperhurst (IRE) 6 ch m 509^{F} 878^{P} **>63dh<**

Copper Mine 11 b g **1147^{2} 1367^{2} 1558^{3} 2758^{10} 4167^{3} (4424) 4740^{3} >126c<**

Copper Thistle (IRE) 9 b g **(3459) 3637^{9} 4457^{3} >91c<**

Coq Hardi Affair (IRE) 9 b g **4110a^{F} >118h 118c< (DEAD)**

Coq Hardi Venture (IRE) 6 b g Roselier (FR)-Big Polly 3382a^{7} 3650a^{6} **>92h<**

Coquet Gold 6 b m 5^{8} 1524^{8} 2541^{8} 2913^{15} 3313^{P} **>11h<**

Coquettish 4 b f Precocious-Cold Line (Exdirectory) 2904^{15} 4420^{13} **>7fh<**

Coqui Lane 10 ch g 1669^{3} **2767^{P} 3023^{3} 3138^{2} (3558) 3792^{2} 4077^{F} 4186^{P}** 4339^{3} **>98h 103c<**

Coralcious (IRE) 6 b g Precocious-Coral Heights (Shirley Heights) 262^{9}

Coralette (IRE) 7 ch g **3339^{P} >79h<**

Corbleu (IRE) 7 b g 1208^{10} 1807^{9} 2045^{3} 3328^{5} (3646) 3825^{6} **>53h<**

Core Business 6 b g 1077^{4} **>64h<**

Corkers Flame (IRE) 6 b g Corvaro (USA)-Preflame 319a^{16} **>59h<**

Corket (IRE) 7 b g **(3380a) 3616^{5} 4356a^{F} >79h 138c<**

Corly Special 10 b g **3460^{3} 3721^{5} >75h 93c<**

Corn Abbey (IRE) 4 b c Runnett-Connaught Rose (Connaught) 1747a^{6} 2333a^{10} **>81h<**

Corner Boy 10 br g **3458^{4} 4551^{3} >100h 90c<**

Cornet 11 b g **1823^{U} >108dc<**

Corn Exchange 9 b g **2930^{U} 3055^{P} 3469^{U} 4730^{P} >29h<**

Corns Little Fella 9 ch g 2838^{P} **>51h<**

Coromandel 5 b m Prince Sabo-Jandell (NZ) (Shifnal) 2750^{9} 3433^{18} 3939^{6} **>35fh<**

Corporal Kirkwood (IRE) 7 br g **1691^{4} 1968^{U} 2954^{P}** 4243^{P} **>64h 81c<**

Corporate Image 7 ch g Executive Man-Robis (Roan Rocket) 3677^{8} 4002^{6} 4162^{10} **>27h<**

Corpus 8 ch g **3678^{4} (3981) 4157^{F} >93c<**

Corrarder 13 ch g **799^{P} 1302^{4} 2092^{2} >69h 109c<**

Corrib Song 8 b g **3356^{4} 3671^{4} >48h<**

Corrimulzie (IRE) 6 ch g 2701^{14} 3754^{4} **>12h<**

Corrin Hill 10 b g 648^{2} 729^{3} 751^{3} 936^{2} **>79h 79c<**

Corston Dancer (IRE) 9 b m **1231a^{3} 3245a^{4} >73c<**

Corston Joker 7 b g 1292^{F} 1848^{8} **2786^{7} 3530^{3} (3695) 3909^{3} 4186^{P} >62h 90c<**

Corymandel (IRE) 8 b g **2848a^{2} 3261a^{P} 3503a^{P} 4110a^{9} >124c<**

Cosa Fuair (IRE) 7 b g 954^{5} 1181^{2} **>65h<**

Cosmic Force (NZ) 13 b g **57^{3} >73dh 88c<**

Cosmic Star 7 gr m Siberian Express (USA)-Miss Bunty (Song) 1727^{6} 1861^{2} 2567^{3} 3663^{10} **>45h<**

Cosy Ride (IRE) 5 b g King's Ride-Fortysumthin (IRE) (Forties Field (FR)) 1834^{5} 2640^{5} **>49fh<**

Co-Tack 12 ch g Connaught-Dulcidene (Behistoun) (4018) **>53h<**

Cotswold Castle 11 ch g **4426^{P} 4735^{P} >50h 69?c<**

Cottage Joker 7 b g 1795^{P} 2006^{P}

Cottage Prince (IRE) 4 b g Classic Secret (USA)-Susan's Blues (Cure The Blues (USA)) 646^{2} (1011) 1205^{5} 1652^{8} (4755) **>68h<**

Cotteir Chief (IRE) 6 b g Chief Singer-Hasty Key (USA) (Key To The Mint (USA)) 2794^{2} 3197^{5} **>78+h<**

Cottesmore 6 b g 2547^{14} **>49h<**

Cotton Eyed Jimmy (IRE) 6 b g 4360a^{18} **>32fh<**

Cottstown Boy (IRE) 6 ch g King Luthier-Ballyanihan (Le Moss) 2770^{9} 2804^{10} 3311^{3} 3529^{7} 4205^{4} 4249^{5} **>53h<**

Couldnt Be Better 10 br g **1440^{2} 1649^{8} (2848a) 3294^{4} >165c<**

Coulton 10 ch g (1055) 1173^{2} **>170c<**

Count Balios (IRE) 8 b g Trojan Fen-Soyez Sage (FR) (Grundy) **3455^{5}**

Count Barachois (USA) 9 b g **1660^{7} 1833^{4} 2009^{4} 2621^{7} 2695^{3} 2843^{4} 3071^{7} 3839^{3} 4157^{4} 4235^{5} >61h 78c<**

Counter Attack (IRE) 6 b br m 1013^{8} 3355^{10} 3706^{6} 3937^{6} 4099^{5} **>46h<**

Counterbalance 10 b m **28^{3} (3843) >108c<**

Counterbid 10 gr g **4320^{2} 4619^{2} >111c<**

Countess Millie 5 ch m 1336^{8} 1659^{U} 3000^{F}

Countess of Cadiz (USA) 4 b f Badger Land

(USA)-Cokebutton (Be My Guest (USA)) 906^{P}

Count Karmuski 5 b g Ardross-Trimar Gold (Goldhill) 3365^{4} 4420^{5} **>65fh<**

Count of Flanders (IRE) 7 b g 219^{3} 393^{3} 687^{3} (1027) 1327^{7} **>56h<**

Country Beau 5 b g Town And Country-Chanelle (The Parson) 2661^{6} (3304) (3821) **>89fh<**

Country Blue 6 b g Town And Country-Blue Breeze (USA) (Blue Times (USA)) 1261^{4}

Country Cousin 5 b g Town And Country-Archie's Niece (Sagaro) 2965^{4} 4328^{P} **(DEAD)**

Country House 6 b m Town And Country-Mearlin (Giolla Mear) 3690^{2} 4539^{2} **>59fh<**

Country Keeper 9 b g **1038^{U} 1199^{F} 1426^{3} 1697^{P} 1951^{2} 2657^{4} 3086^{F} 3400^{P} 3948^{2}** 4250^{P} **>74c<**

Country Kris 5 b g Town And Country-Mariban (Mummy's Pet) 1573^{10} 3895^{4} 4143^{2} **>57fh<**

Country Lover 6 ch g Thatching-Fair Country (Town And Country) 2655^{3} 2805^{3} 3197^{4} 3592^{4} (4001) (4173) (4242) (4315) 4399^{P} **>83+h<**

Countryman (IRE) 6 ch g Henbit (USA)-Riancoir Alainn (Strong Gale) 1071^{2} 3149^{4} **>63fh<**

Country Minstrel (IRE) 6 b g 636^{2} 718^{F} 1448^{P} 1772^{4} 1984^{3} 2578^{F} 2771^{F} 3186^{P} 3733^{2} 3983^{12} **>52h<**

Country Orchid 6 b m Town And Country-Star Flower (Star Appeal) 1190^{2} 1913^{6} (2804) 3290^{4} 3611^{2} 4390^{2} 4737^{2} **>63h<**

Country Star (IRE) 6 b g (299) (527a) 717a^{2} (1015) 1365^{4} **1925^{U} 2054^{5} >106h 111c<**

Country Store 8 ch m 1170^{3} 1443^{3} **1947^{2} 3489^{P} 3697^{F}** 4248^{3} 4470^{5} **4699^{3} >74h 89c<**

Country Style 8 ch m Town And Country-Win Green Hill (National Trust) 1998^{6} 3178^{P} **3978^{P} >64dh<**

Country Tarquin 5 b h 1431^{4} 1594^{9} 2642^{5} 2891^{9} (3499) 4521^{3} **>76h<**

Country Tarrogen 8 b g **3270^{2} 3458^{B} 4051^{F} >114c< (DEAD)**

Country Town 7 b m 1998^{11} **3173^{5} 3360^{4} >23h 72c<**

Countrywide Lad 8 ch g 128^{10} 217^{7} **>39h<**

Count Surveyor 10 ch g **3713^{P} >86?c<**

Coup de Vent 7 ch g 3434^{8} 4296^{7} **>24h<**

Courage-Mon-Brave 9 gr g 3110^{P} **(DEAD)**

Courageous Knight 8 gr g (128) 159^{7} 304^{4} 3814^{3} 3904^{10} 4071^{R} (4443) 4654^{4} **>63h<**

Courbaril 5 b g Warrshan (USA)-Free on Board (Free State) (555) 675^{2} (739) (837) (900) (1067) 1351^{F} 1556^{2} 2642^{3} (2937) 4048^{2} (4178) **>95h<**

Coureur 8 b g (73) (253) 876^{7} **>77h< (DEAD)**

Court Circular 8 b g 95^{8} **>77h<**

Courting Danger 4 b g Tina's Pet-Court Town (Camden Town) 2825^{P} 3075^{P}

Court Jester 6 gr g 293^{8} 343^{5} 461^{6} 476^{4} **>55h<**

Court Joker (IRE) 5 b g 698^{P} 735^{3} 876^{5} 1292^{P} 1577^{3} (1848) 2509^{4} 3035^{B} 3346^{3} 3478^{P} 3822^{3} **>60h<**

Court Master (IRE) 9 b or br g **1320^{3} 1646^{4} 1994^{2} 2827^{5} 3407^{2} 3567^{2} (3627) 4007^{8} 4350a^{4} 4535^{4} 4659^{3} >104h 97dc<**

Court Melody (IRE) 9 b g **1089^{2} 1799^{4} (2754) 3046^{3} 3451^{U} 4213^{5} (4416) 4541^{3} >134c<**

Court Nap (IRE) 5 ch g 1933^{F} 2884^{13} 3105^{U} 3554^{6} **>65h<**

Coven Moon 7 ch m Crofthall-Mayspark (Stanford) 3668^{6}

Coverdale Lane 10 ch m **1037^{3} 1291^{2} 1773^{U} (2052) 2788^{3} (3370) 3697^{8} (3884) >114+c<**

Cover Point (IRE) 6 b g **1943^{2} 2810^{4} (3097) 3288^{6} >82h 93c<**

Cowboy Dreams (IRE) 4 b g Nashamaa-Shahrazad (Young Emperor) 291^{6} **>31h<**

Coxwell Steptoe 7 b g 1466^{F} **>69h<**

Crabbie's Pride 4 ch g Red Sunset-Free Rein (Sagaro) 1205^{2} 1700^{7} 2649^{8} 3004^{P} 3555^{2} 3888^{3} **>59h 58c<**

Cracking Idea (IRE) 9 b g **70^{7} 4634^{3} >82h 106c<**

Cracking Prospect 6 ch g 1174^{3} **1472^{U} 1875^{3} 2873^{2} >67h 87c<**

Crackling Frost (IRE) 9 b br g **583^{3} (830) 1012^{2} 1465^{P} 4235^{2} (4456) (4733) >96+c<**

Crack On 7 ch g (904) (1271) 1365^{7} **2691^{3}** 4130^{7} **>107h 112c<**

Crackon Jake (IRE) 4 br g Jolly Jake (NZ)-Antiflo (Furry Glen) 2844^{3} 3090^{7} 4118a^{R}

Craftsman 11 b g Balinger-Crafty Look (Don't Look) **3455^{U}**

Crafty Chaplain 11 ch g **728^{6} 867^{2} (1012) 1244^{2} 1641^{4} 1957^{3} 2674^{7} >105c<**

Cragnabuoy (IRE) 7 b g 1654^{P} 2042^{12} **>56h<**

Craigary 6 b g 4451^{3} **>54h<**

Craighill (IRE) 8 br g Dromod Hill-Walnut Hill (Pry) **3335^{P}**

Craigie Boy 7 b g Crofthall-Lady Carol (Lord Gayle (USA)) 3158^{14} **>23h<**

Craigie Rambler (IRE) 8 b m 3529^{F} **>17h<**

Craigmore Magic (USA) 4 br g Simply Majestic (USA)-Some Rehearsal (USA) (Halo (USA)) 1205^{10} 1526^{P} **>34h<**

Crambella (IRE) 5 b m 65^{P} **>56h<**

Crampscastle (IRE) 7 ch g 2794^{P} 3399^{12} **>1h<**

Cranbrook Lad 5 b g 1013^{5} 1551^{P}

Crandon Boulevard 4 b c Niniski (USA)-Last Clear Chance (USA) (Alleged (USA)) 3233^{3} 3535^{3} (3745) 4010^{P} **>77h<**

Crane Hill 7 b g 1938^{3} 2659^{6} **3806^{4} 4533^{4} >86h 81c<**

Crashballoo (IRE) 6 ch g 1672^{7} 2042^{13} 3557^{P} 3887^{P}

Cravate (FR) 7 ch m 1814^{P} 2570^{5} 2905^{5} 3190^{2} 3683^{7} **3978^{P} 4138^{U} >41h<**

Crazy Horse Dancer (USA) 9 b g (27) 465^{4} 582^{4} 3545^{9} 3985^{6} **>54h 63c<**

Cream O The Border 5 b m Meadowbrook-Spring-Ann (Workboy) 3024^{P} 3529^{5} 3823^{7} **>39h<**

Credit Call (IRE) 9 br g 157^{P} 4091^{10}

Credit Controller (IRE) 8 b g 655^{2} 824^{3} 958^{2} 1072^{3} 1419^{6} 1707^{4} 1946^{4} **>52h<**

Credite Risque 4 b f Risk Me (FR)-Lompoa (Lomond (USA)) 3669^{F}

Credo Boy 8 ch g 1171^{F} 1323^{P} 3085^{3} 3340^{5} 4405^{6} **>61h<**

Credo Is King (IRE) 7 b g Le Moss-Merendas Sister (Pauper) **(1797) 2883^{5} 3155^{P} (3347) >110c<**

Credon 9 b g **1420^{3} 1674^{P} 1839^{P} 1961^{4} 3182^{3} 3444^{4} (3605) 3838^{2} (4098) >74h 107c<**

Crehelp Express (IRE) 7 br m **1240a^{3} 1405a^{5} 3389a^{P} >90c<**

Criminal Record (USA) 7 b g 463^{6} **>53h 78c<**

Crimson King (IRE) 6 b g (1633) 2812^{3} **>90h<**

Cristys Picnic (IRE) 7 b g 1485a^{9} **>53h 94c<**

Croagh Patrick 5 b g Faustus (USA)-Pink Pumpkin (Tickled Pink) 1651^{P}

Crockalawn (IRE) 9 ch g Arapahos (FR)-Naomi Night VII (Damsire Unregistered) 939^{12} **1576^{3} >27h 78c<**

Crocknamohill (IRE) 6 br g 1774^{6} 4528^{6} 4650^{8} **>49h<**

Crofton Lake 9 ch g (782) 878^{2} 942^{3} 1080^{4} 1854^{11} 2768^{5} 3096^{4} **>48h 72c<**

Crohane Quay (IRE) 8 b g 792^{4} 3499^{9} **>70h<**

Cromaboo Crown 6 b m 55^{6} 101^{5} 345^{4} 4163^{2} **>52h<**

Cropredy Lad 10 b g **1147^{3} 1350^{4} 2814^{5} 3071^{5} 3280^{6} 4013^{F} >95c<**

Cross Cannon 11 b g **2^{F} 56^{7} 732^{3} 909^{4} 1142^{F} 1268^{3} 1970^{5} 3160^{4} 3369^{3} (3610) 3725^{2} 4300^{7} 4392^{F} >88h 117c<**

Crossfarnogue (IRE) 8 bb g Brewery Boy (AUS)-Rozmeen (FR) (Relko) 318a^{17} **1405a^{2} 2335a^{F} >107+h 87c<**

Crosshot 10 b g **1346^{9} (1943) 2786^{4} 3161^{4} (3350) (3692) >104c<**

Crossing The Styx 11 b g Lucifer (USA)-Glad Rain (Bahrain) 397^{P}

Cross Talk (IRE) 5 b g Darshaan-Liaison (USA) (Blushing Groom (FR)) 1337^{3} **>56h<**

Crosula 9 br g **104^{F} (DEAD)**

Crown And Cushion 4 b g High Adventure-Soulieana (Manado) (1444) 1953^{10} 3004^{P} 3184^{P} **>56h<**

Crown Equerry (IRE) 7 b br g **1357^{P} (2650) 2767^{P} (2919) 3347^{2} 4050^{P} 4211^{6} 4447^{F} 4503^{P} >84h 111dc<**

Crownhill Cross 6 ch g Dutch Treat-Royal Cross (Royal Smoke) 594^{6} 788^{10} 900^{8} **>12h<**

Crown Ivory (NZ) 9 br g Ivory Hunter (USA)-Spotless (NZ) (Regalis) 31^{8} 360^{3} 489^{3} 649^{6} 900^{3} (978) 1638^{6} **1819^{P}** 3962^{6} 4341^{5} 4563^{6} **>50dh<**

Cruise Control 11 b g **1423^{P} 1965^{4} 2756^{P} 3173^{6} 3444^{P} 3719^{3} 3900^{3} (4100) >38h 75c<**

Cruise Free 8 b g Cruise Missile-Lyons Charity (Impecunious) 489^{4}

Cruisinforabruisin 7 b g 931^{4} 1253^{7} **>43h<**

Cruising Kate 9 b m 854^{P} **>6h<**

Crustygun 7 b g 99^{7} 1726^{15} **>5h<**

Cry Baby 4 b g Baim (USA)-Estonia (Kings Lake (USA)) 1356^{8} 2615^{8} (3022) 3394^{3} 3887^{11} **>68h<**

Crystal Gift 5 b g 1360^{2} 1654^{6} **>79h<**

Crystal Jewel 5 b m Lir-Crystal Comet (Cosmo) 3006^{4} 3425^{4} 4287^{7} **>57fh<**

Crystal Spirit 10 b g **1910^{3} >144c<**

Cuban Nights (USA) 5 b g 96^{2} 3115^{6} **>60h<**

Cuchullains Gold (IRE) 9 ch g **135^{5} 179^{2} (417) 581^{U} 685^{2} >79h 92c<**

Cue Call (IRE) 4 br f In The Wings-Arousal (Rousillon (USA)) 3676^{4} 3939^{2} **>56fh<**

Cuillin 5 b m Emarati (USA)-Eyry (Falcon) 2805^{16} 3536^{P} 3818^{P} 4086^{P} **>17h<**

Cuillin Caper 5 b m 1207^{6} 1417^{9} 1988^{6} 2654^{11} (3448) 4401^{4} 4552^{2} (4807) **>53h<**

Cullane Lake (IRE) 7 b m Strong Statement (USA)-Gusserane Lark (Napoleon Bonaparte) **1944^{5} 2614^{4} 3141^{4} (3645) 3886^{10} 4417^{2} 4569^{3} >78c<**

Cullenstown Lady (IRE) 6 gr m (317a) **>105h 78c<**

Culpeppers Dish 6 b g Lochnager-Faint Praise (Lepanto (GER)) **4241^{P}**

Culrain 6 b g 794^{3} (965) 1180^{3} 1309^{5} 3284^{13} **>56dh<**

Cultural Icon (USA) 5 b g 812^{9} **>34h<**

Cumberland Blues (IRE) 8 b g **(4411) 4551^{P} 4713^{2} (4799) >52h 108c<**

Cumberland Youth 6 b g 2893^{P} 3283^{P} **4526^{P} 4564^{4} 4655^{P}**

Cumbrian Challenge (IRE) 8 ch g 945^{5} 1154^{5} **1520^{7} 1805^{2} (1910) 3804^{2} 4206^{5} (4311) 4478^{4} >116h 135c<**

Cumbrian Maestro 4 b g Puissance-Flicker Toa Flame (USA) (Empery (USA)) 2539^{2} (3324) (3475) **>76h<**

Cunninghams Ford (IRE) 9 b g 3016^{P} 3180^{P} 3358^{P} **>99c<**

Cupronickel (IRE) 5 b m 1679^{P} **>10h<**

Curraduff Moll (IRE) 6 b m Good Thyne (USA)-Running Tide (Deep Run) (1177) 3090^{2} 3619^{12} **>77fh<**
Curragh Peter 10 b g Orchestra-Slaney Valley (Even Money) 978^{5} 1256^{P} 1500^{4} **1856^{3} 2628^{9} 2778^{3} 2892^{U} 3732^{P} 3843^{2} 4221^{4} >36h 80c<**
Curra Minstral (IRE) 7 ch m 3748^{7} 4508^{P} **>15h<**
Currency Basket (IRE) 8 b g **3260a^{F} >141h 95c<**
Current Attraction 11 b m Paddy's Stream-Chorabelle (Choral Society) **4319^{P}**
Currer Bell 4 b f Belmez (USA)-Hello Cuddles (He Loves Me) 2648^{4} **>26fh<**
Curtis The Second 4 b f Thowra (FR)-Bay Jade (Ardross) 3433^{8} 4009^{18} **>53fh<**
Cush Supreme (IRE) 8 b g **1853^{2} 2000^{4} (2803) 2923^{2} (3094) >96c<**
Cuthill Hope (IRE) 6 gr g Peacock (FR)-Sicilian Princess (Sicilian Prince) 1938^{4} 3024^{4} (3575) **>73h<**
Cutthroat Kid (IRE) 7 b g 3434^{3} (3704) 3915^{4} 4220^{10} **>80h<**
Cyber King 4 ch g Rakaposhi King-Leabrannagh Lass (Ballad Rock) 2510^{7} **>60fh<**
Cyborgo (FR) 7 b g **(2658) (3040) (3155) 3636^{8} (4050) >156h 136c<**
Cyphratis (IRE) 6 b g Le Bavard (FR)-Torus Light (Torus) 1044^{4} 2677^{9} 2961^{9} 3983^{10} **>57h<**
Cypress Avenue (IRE) 5 b g Law Society (USA)-Flying Diva (Chief Singer) 1278^{4} 1689^{5} 1907^{4} 2546^{9} 3328^{3} 3967^{9} 4476^{4} **>60h<**
Cyrill Henry (IRE) 8 b g **222^{4} >59h 88c<**
Cyrus the Great (IRE) 5 ch g 976^{2} **>85h<**

D

Dacelo (FR) 6 b g 593^{2} 675^{4} 818^{2} 1180^{R} 1297^{2} 1507^{3} 2961^{4} 3621^{8} **>74h<**
Dad's Army Two (IRE) 4 b g Dancing Dissident (USA)-Checkers (Habat) 3626^{2} **>66fh<**
Dad's Pipe 7 b g Nearly A Hand-Paddy's Pipe (Paddy's Stream) **3357^{F}**
Dahlia's Best (USA) 7 br g Dahar (USA)-Eleanor's Best (USA) (Full Partner (USA)) 1123^{6} 1342^{4} 1732^{11} 2694^{F} **>75h< (DEAD)**
Daily Sport Girl 8 b m 1630^{P} 1727^{5} 1948^{3} 2871^{3} 3056^{6} 3234^{16} 3623^{P} 4006^{8} (4163) 4381^{4} 4534^{U} 4654^{3} **>58h<**
Daisy Days (IRE) 7 ch m 1849^{12} (2920) 3348^{7} 3817^{7} 4394^{P} **>77h<**
Dajraan (IRE) 8 b h 792^{7} **>64h<**
Dakota III (FR) 6 ch g Bad Conduct (USA)-Manolette (FR) (Signani (FR)) 3808^{8} **>36fh<**
Dakyns Boy 12 ch g **1784^{2} 2881^{4} 3153^{11} 4074^{8} 4213^{6} >127c<**
Dalametre 10 b g **1041^{2} 4070^{3} 4218^{2} 4543^{P} >86c<**
Dally Boy 5 b g 952^{4} 1127^{3} (1528) 1645^{3} 2078^{2} 2702^{5} 3163^{5} 3317^{3} 3600^{20} **>95h<**
Dalusman (IRE) 9 b g 3^{4} 1021^{9} 3096^{7} 3711^{6} **3886^{P}** 4389^{7} **>35h 86dc<**
Damarita 6 ch m Starry Night (USA)-Sirenivo (USA) (Sir Ivor) 4794^{U}
Damas (FR) 6 b br g 69^{3} **136^{P} 740^{4} 914^{U} >74h 99c<**
Damcada (IRE) 9 b or br g 1072^{8} **1376^{2} 1582^{P} 3279^{P} 4447^{P} 4735^{7} >50h 69?c<**
Dame Prospect 6 br m 3284^{6} 3434^{6} **>47h<**
Damers Treasure 11 ch g **4530^{5} >77c<**
Damien's Choice (IRE) 5 b g Erins Hope-Reenoga (Tug of War) 705^{3} 3149^{2} 3821^{6} 4008^{4} **>72fh<**
Dana Point (IRE) 5 br g Phardante (FR)-Wallpark Princess (Balidar) 1412^{2} (1667) 2840^{2} 3139^{2} 3396^{3} **>81h<**
Danbys Gorse 5 ch g 1701^{8} 2545^{7} 2842^{2} 3137^{2} (3351) 3827^{5} 3912^{3} 4261^{7} **>72h<**
Dance Beat (IRE) 6 b m 318a^{8} **1486a^{P} >100h 92c< (DEAD)**
Dance King 5 b g 3148^{2} **>79h<**
Dances With Hooves 5 b h Dancing Dissident (USA)-Princesse Legere (USA) (Alleged (USA)) 2055^{U}
Dancetillyoudrop (IRE) 6 b g 1394^{2} 1683^{5} 3085^{2} 3408^{2} **>74h<**
Dancing At Laharn (IRE) 7 b g 26^{9} 77^{U} 100^{4} 216^{2} **977^{2} >71h 77c<**
Dancing Dancer 8 b m 1047^{6} 3088^{P} **>59h<**
Dancing Dove (IRE) 9 ch m 285^{2} **>98h<**
Dancing Holly 10 br g 3976^{P} **(DEAD)**
Dancing In Rio (IRE) 5 b m Lord Americo-Carnival Blossom (Carnival Night) 4088^{6} 4539^{15} **>33fh<**
Dancing Paddy 9 b g **1509^{3} (1914) 2646^{F} 3037^{2} 3638^{10}** 4130^{4} 4271^{4} 4610^{2} **>114h 148c<**
Dancing Ranger 6 b g 1986^{10} **>35fh<**
Dancing Vision (IRE) 7 br g Vision (USA)-Dewan's Niece (USA) (Dewan (USA)) **(1350) 2348a^{6} >78h 112c<**
Dande Dove 6 gr g Baron Blakeney-Ryans Dove (Rustingo) 4009^{11} 4547^{P}
Dan de Lyon 9 ch g 98^{P} 253^{U} 259^{F} **>61h 84c<**
Dan de Man (IRE) 6 br g 2064^{6} 2917^{13} 3345^{F} 3734^{5} **>58h<**
Dandie Imp 9 b g **2926^{P} 3278^{B} 3582^{3} 3806^{R} 4007^{4} 4377^{4} 4627^{2} (4790) >87+c<**
Dandy des Plauts (FR) 6 b g Cap Martin (FR)-Pagode (FR) (Saumon (FR)) **2628^{F} 2914^{6} 3326^{4} 3909^{9} >77c<**
Danegold (IRE) 5 b g 1375^{2} (1726) 2771^{3} 3572^{15} **>87h<**
Dane Rose 11 b m Full of Hope-Roella (Gold Rod) 630^{7} 725^{6} 825^{4} **>52h<**
Danger Baby 7 ch g **1934^{3} 2821^{4} 2928^{U} 3182^{P} 3428^{6} 3599^{5} 3961^{3} 4085^{2} 4270^{4} >73h 107c<**
Danjing (IRE) 5 b g 1319^{R} 1353^{R} 3600^{3} 4016^{12} **>106h<**
Dannicus 6 b g 1782^{3} 2746^{10} **3073^{C} 3343^{10} >62h 46c<**
Danny Gale (IRE) 6 b g (636) 859^{P} 3204^{8} 3438^{12} 3583^{4} 4309^{8} **>46h<**
Danoli (IRE) 9 b g **(1405a) 1758a^{F} (2335a) 2739a^{F} (2997a) 3636^{F} >154h 170c<**
Dantean 5 b g Warning-Danthonia (USA) (Northern Dancer) 396^{3} 634^{2} **>68h<**
Dantes Amour (IRE) 6 b g 1504^{11} 2005^{8} 2180^{4} 2918^{P} 3940^{3} 4075^{6} 4296^{4} 4759^{3} **>58h<**
Dante's Battle (IRE) 5 bb g Phardante (FR)-No Battle (Khalkis) 4118a^{23} **>55fh<**
Dantes Cavalier (IRE) 7 b g 1422^{2} 1683^{2} (1810) 2071^{4} 3146^{2} **>87h<**
Dante's Gold (IRE) 6 ch g Phardante (FR)-Gold Bank (Over The River (FR)) 2682^{9} 2830^{2} 3330^{11}
Dante's Rubicon (IRE) 6 ch g 885^{P} 3344^{P}
Dante's View (USA) 9 ch g **1994^{3} 2569^{5} 2795^{3} >71h 92c<**
Danucha 5 ch m Derrylin-Connaught Queen (Connaught) 4097^{P} 4259^{F} **(DEAD)**
Danzante (IRE) 5 b g Ajraas (USA)-Baliana (CAN) (Riverman (USA)) (1151) 1964^{6} 2822^{P} 2945^{5} 4376^{8} **>59h<**
Danzig Island (IRE) 6 b g 1039^{11} **1300^{F} >78h<**
Dara Knight (IRE) 8 br g Dara Monarch-Queen of The Dance (Dancers Image (USA)) 1345^{8} **>29fh<**
Darakshan (IRE) 5 b g 1044^{3} 1301^{2} 1583^{2} 2673^{3} (3000) (3468) 4271^{2} 4474^{3} **>84h<**
Dara's Course (IRE) 8 b m **2569^{7} 2896^{F} 3188^{P} 4738^{3} >77c<**
Daraydan (IRE) 5 b g Kahyasi-Delsy (FR) (Abdos) (1412) 1568^{6} (1905) 2624^{3} 2771^{7} 3613^{3} 3917^{2} (4134) **>107+h<**
D'Arblay Street (IRE) 8 b g 1143^{5} 1304^{4} 1671^{7} 1844^{4} 1971^{2} 2178^{2} 2507^{5} **2803^{U} (2954) 3067^{3} 3370^{4} 3724^{P} 3975^{P} >75h 89?c<**
Dardjini (USA) 7 b g Nijinsky (CAN)-Darara (Top Ville) (1752a) 2740a^{3} 3254a^{4} 3597^{12} **>127h<**
Daring Hen (IRE) 7 b m 129^{11} 1663^{P} 1786^{4} 2088^{12} 2838^{P} **3360^{P} >35h<**
Daring King 7 b g 1170^{4} 1586^{P} 1710^{2} 3180^{P} 3499^{4} 3923^{P} **>74h<**
Daringly 8 b g **(64) 135^{2}** 221^{P} **>50h 92c<**
Daring Magic 5 b m Daring March-Magic Chat (Le Bavard (FR)) 2627^{P}
Daring Past 7 b g **(1853) 2628^{F} 2914^{4} 3943^{2} 4183^{5} (4297) 4540^{F} (4703) >102h 101+c<**
Daring Ryde 6 b g Daring March-Mini Myra (Homing) 1278^{7} 1369^{P} 1770^{6} 2692^{6} **>49h<**
Dark Age (IRE) 4 b c Darshaan-Sarela (USA) (Danzig (USA)) 1808^{7}
Dark Buoy 8 b g **1576^{5} 1853^{4} 2650^{P} 3138^{P} >64h 78c<**
Dark Challenger (IRE) 5 b br g Brush Aside (USA)-Great Aunt Emily (Traditionalist (USA)) 1289^{9} 1580^{3} 2550^{7} **>73h<**
Dark Dawn 13 b g **4080^{4} 4256^{5} >101c<**
Dark Honey 12 b g 1196^{6} 1647^{11} 1794^{5} 2817^{U} 3146^{6} **>85h 118c<**
Dark Horse (IRE) 5 br g Kambalda-Laurence Lady (Laurence O) 4531^{6} 4774^{5} **>47fh<**
Dark Midnight (IRE) 8 br g 586^{12} 642^{6} 784^{6} 893^{7} 1304^{P} 1703^{13} 1969^{7} 4259^{13} 4409^{7} 4759^{P} **>20h<**
Dark Nightingale 7 br m (1058) 1176^{2} 1727^{7} **>79h<**
Dark Oak 11 br g **689^{4} 857^{2} (1029) 1315^{3} 1806^{5} 2568^{3} 3033^{4} 3560^{P} 3969^{3} >114dc<**
Dark Orchard (IRE) 6 b g 1685^{2} 2677^{4} 3143^{8} **>67h<**
Dark Phoenix (IRE) 7 b m 1341^{6} 1536^{11} 1777^{4} 2744^{5} 2917^{2} 3315^{3} 3621^{10} 3983^{14} 4427^{P} **>63dh<**
Dark Rhytham 8 br g True Song-Crozanna (Crozier) **3455^{6} 4637^{P} 4773^{P}**
Dark Silhouette (IRE) 8 br g 55^{F} **>72h<**
Dark Swan (IRE) 7 br g Soughaan (USA)-Last Stop 2345a^{11} **>89h<**
Dark Truffle 4 br f Deploy-River Dove (USA) (Riverman (USA)) 1413^{3} 1595^{3} 2865^{9} 3186^{P} **>47h<**
Darleyfordbay 8 b g **64^{P} >79?c<**
Darra (FR) 6 ch m Jefferson-Miss Darras (FR) (D'Arras (FR)) 527a^{3} **>87h<**
Darren the Brave 9 ch g **2681^{5} 3132^{3} 3815^{4} 4185^{4} >65h 108c<**
Darton Ri 14 b g Abednego-Boogie Woogie (No Argument) **4530^{3} >83c<**
Daru (USA) 8 gr g 3438^{6} **>57h<**
Dashanti 6 b g 1504^{6} 1830^{6} **>59h<**
Dashboard Light 7 b g Idiot's Delight-Good Lady (Deep Run) **3208^{P} 3455^{7}**
Dashing Dancer (IRE) 6 ch g Conquering Hero (USA)-Santa Maria (GER) (Literat) 950^{8} 1276^{7} 1628^{11} **>48h<**
Dashing Dollar (IRE) 6 b g 1752a^{11} **>85h<**
Dashmar 10 b g 1575^{2} 2045^{5} 2654^{5} 3481^{10} 3711^{10} **3909^{P}** 4283^{9} **>29h<**
Dash On By 4 ch g Daster-Blue Condor (Condorcet (FR)) 3330^{10} 4088^{11} **>16fh<**
Dash To The Phone (USA) 5 b br g 794^{5} 1049^{6} 1253^{9} **3030^{F} 3842^{U} 4297^{5} 4797^{3} >53h 72c<**

Datem (IRE) 5 b g Beau Sher-Comeragh Heather 4118a^{25} **>44fh<**
Dato Star (IRE) 6 br g 1656^{3} 2635^{2} **>142h<**
Daunt 5 b g Darshaan-Minute Waltz (Sadler's Wells (USA)) 2035^{8} 2668^{7} 2886^{6} 3424^{7} 3594^{12} **>56h<**
Davy Blake 10 b g **(2956) 3316^{4}** **>118c<**
Dawn Caller (IRE) 6 b g Derrylin-Raise the Dawn (Rymer) 319a^{11} **>48h<**
Dawn Chance 11 gr g **740^{F} 883^{4} (1421) 1965^{6} 3954^{3} 4142^{P}** **>85c<**
Dawn Flight 8 b g (184) **>74h<**
Dawn Lad (IRE) 8 b g Lancastrian-Lek Dawn (Menelek) **1022^{5} 1308^{U} 1574^{4} (1847) 2923^{7} 3726^{3}** **>85c<**
Dawn Leader (IRE) 6 b g (3149) 3619^{13} **>79fh<**
Dawn Mission 5 b g 1125^{7} 1804^{7} 1922^{3} 3545^{8} 3885^{7} **>81h<**
Dawn Spinner 5 gr m Arctic Lord-Madame Russe (Bally Russe) (4407) **>65fh<**
Daydream Believer 5 b m Rakaposhi King-Petite Mirage (Hittite Glory) 1303^{4} 1685^{7} 2822^{8} 2959^{6} 4002^{4} 4226^{P} 4276^{2} 4466^{6} **>40h<**
Daydreamer (USA) 4 b c Alleged (USA)-Stardusk (USA) (Stage Door Johnny) 2751^{6} 3075^{7} 3575^{3} **>69h<**
Days of Thunder 9 ch g **328^{4} 475^{P}** 3429^{13} **3897^{4}** 4142^{7} 4472^{9} **4721^{P}** **>25h 72c<**
Daytime Dawn (IRE) 6 b g 5^{9} **>57h<**
Daytona Beach (IRE) 7 ch g 967^{P} **>79h<**
Dazzle Me 5 ch m 483^{P}
Deano's Beeno 5 b g Far North (CAN)-Sans Dot (Busted) (1950) 3595^{7} 4048^{5} **>93h<**
Dear Chris (IRE) 6 bb m Supreme Leader-Our Chrisy (Carlburg) 319a^{7}
Dear Do 10 b g **1393^{2} 1730^{2} 2621^{4} 2906^{2} 3336^{4}** **>72h 111c<**
Dear Emily 9 b m **61^{3} 135^{4} 206^{5} 873^{5} 3439^{P}** **>63h 71c<**
Dear Jean 7 ch m Exorbitant-High Jean (Arrigle Valley) **1308^{P} 1574^{8} 2860^{4} 3334^{P}** 3449^{4} **>43c<**
Debonair Dude (IRE) 7 b g Lafontaine (USA)-Debonair Dolly (Cidrax (FR)) **3688^{3} 4227^{P} 4546^{P}** **>84c<**
Deceit the Second 5 ch g 1873^{11} 2550^{P} 2763^{9} 2907^{P} 3057^{P} 3541^{7} 3735^{7} 4173^{4} **>37h<**
Decent Penny (IRE) 8 b m 2504^{7} 2787^{7} 3325^{3} 3478^{14} **>43h<**
Decide Yourself (IRE) 7 b g 51a^{P} 1996^{P} 3164^{8} 3286^{6} 3722^{2} **>80h<**
Decision Maker (IRE) 4 b g Taufan (USA)-Vain Deb (Gay Fandango (USA)) 1953^{12} 3103^{10}
Decor (IRE) 7 ch g 885^{P} 968^{4} 1165^{5} **>52h<**
Decoupage 5 b g Bustino-Collage (Ela-Mana-Mou) (4216) **>81fh<**
Decyborg (FR) 6 ch g Cyborg (FR)-Kelinda (FR) (Pot d'Or (FR)) **1981^{4} 2549^{2}** 2878^{2} **(3948) 4168^{2} (4251) 4429^{3}** (4767) **>66h 107c<**
Dee Dee 5 b m Buckskin (FR)-Special Venture (Giolla Mear) 4632^{9} **>28fh<**
Dee Ell 11 b g 2361a^{4} **3503a^{P}** **>104h 102c<**
Dee Light 8 ch m Scorpio (FR)-Francis Lane (Broxted) **3347^{P} 3806^{3} 4219^{F}** **>77c<**
Deel Quay (IRE) 6 b g 1639^{7} **2816^{2}** **>71h 90c<**
Deep C Diva (IRE) 5 b m Supreme Leader-Deep Adventure (Deep Run) 4632^{4} **>48fh<**
Deep Decision 11 b g **1029^{2} 1209^{7} 1657^{2} 2765^{7} 3694^{2} 3974^{2} 4247^{4} 4480^{4}** **>105c<**
Deependable 10 ch g **1554^{P} 1934^{4} 2756^{P} 3176^{P}** **>62c<**
Deep Fair 10 br g 18^{6} **>60h<**
Deep Isle 11 ch g 2882^{15} 3362^{P} **>12h 58c<**
Deep Refrain (IRE) 7 b g 316a^{11} **>37h 67c<**
Deep Song 7 ch g **3335^{4} 3625^{3} 4442^{P}** **>65c<**
Deerhunter 6 b br g Gunner B-Royal Scarlet (Royal Fountain) 1692^{8} 1827^{4} **>45fh<**
Defendtherealm 6 br g Derring Rose-Armagnac Princess (Armagnac Monarch) 1203^{5} 1431^{10} 1695^{3} 2656^{2} 3337^{3} (3628) 4639^{3} **>69h<**
Deference Due (IRE) 6 b g 980^{13} 1301^{5}
Definite Maybe (IRE) 7 b g **421^{2} (466) 639^{2} 720^{5} 1054^{P}** **>100c<**
Deise Marshall (IRE) 9 b g **691^{2} 907^{3} 1246^{6} 2540^{7}** **>83c<**
De Jordaan 10 br g **909^{3} 1070^{F} 3991^{4} 4159^{9}** **>70h 110c<**
Delightfool 6 gr m Idiot's Delight-Parselle (Pardigras) 2804^{3} 3070^{9} 3440^{5} 3691^{13} 4243^{P} **>36fh<**
Delire d'Estruval (FR) 6 b g Synefos (USA)-Magie (FR) (Ardale (ITY)) 1085^{P} **1423^{6} 1538^{U}** **>69c<**
Dellen Walker (IRE) 4 b g Pennine Walk-Lady Ellen (Horage) 3548^{16}
Dellone 5 b g Gunner B-Coire Vannich (Celtic Cone) 4450^{R}
Delos (NZ) 7 b g Famous Star-Take All (NZ) (Kazakstaan) 3441^{U}
Delphi Lodge (IRE) 7 gr g 2347a^{3} 2857a^{5} (3382a) **>109h<**
Del Piero (IRE) 6 b g (1312) 1667^{6} 2631^{P} **>66h<** **(DEAD)**
Denfield (IRE) 6 ch g Denel (FR)-Shirley's Sis **4361a^{U}** **>80c<**
Denham Hill (IRE) 6 ch g 1323^{2} 1683^{4} 2812^{2} (3178) **>81h<**
Denim Blue 8 ch g Mandrake Major-Delphinium (Tin King) **(3533) (3994) 4256^{F} 4579^{P}** **>72h 84c<**
Denis Compton 6 b g Lighter-Dyna Drueni (Law of The Wise) 865^{11}
Denise's Profiles 7 b g 1197^{2} **>78h<**
Denomination (USA) 5 br g 98^{P} (183) (217) 304^{5} 407^{3} 555^{3} 879^{3} 1425^{5} 1628^{8} 1693^{F} 2567^{7} 2815^{8} 3338^{8} 3590^{3} 4175^{5} **>56h<**
Denstar (IRE) 4 b g Thatching-Bone China (IRE) (Sadler's Wells (USA)) 3021^{10} 3626^{9} 4774^{15}
Denticulata 9 ch g 2003^{6} 3157^{P} 3313^{6} 3607^{6} **>49h<**
Denver Bay 10 b g **1373^{6} 1805^{3} 2879^{5} (3147) 3573^{4} (3838) 4167^{P}** **>82h 125c<**
Departure 10 ch m Gorytus (USA)-La Gravotte (FR) (Habitat) **4022^{P}**
Deptford Belle 7 b m 961^{6} 3057^{6} 3207^{12} **>26h<**
Deputy Leader (IRE) 5 b g Florida Son-Larne (Giolla Mear) 4538^{5} **>35fh<**
Derannie (IRE) 5 b g 2047^{6} 3024^{3} (3529) 3794^{10} **>75h<**
Derby Haven (IRE) 10 b g 317a^{P} **>77h<**
Derisbay (IRE) 9 b g 2067^{6} 2792^{8} 2866^{4} 3057^{3} 3207^{5} 3447^{3} (3579) 3811^{3} (3896) 4101^{7} **>71h<**
Derring Bridge 7 b g (95) 131^{U} 184^{6} 257^{5} 2570^{4} 2761^{3} 3013^{7} 3362^{8} 3737^{6} 3962^{4} 4220^{2} 4418^{2} 4536^{2} 4803^{3} **>73h<**
Derring Court 7 b m 24^{14} 504^{8}
Derring Dove 5 b g Derring Rose-Shadey Dove (Deadly Nightshade) 4301^{13} **>25fh<**
Derring Floss 7 b m Derring Rose-Win Green Hill (National Trust) 1913^{2} 2673^{6} 3029^{4} 3226^{9} 3937^{5} 4528^{7} 4756^{5} **>45h<**
Derring Jack 6 b g 1453^{F} 1683^{U} 3761^{8} **>53h<**
Derring Knight 7 b g Derring Rose-Arctic Servant (Goldhill) 980^{11} 1071^{5}
Derring Well 7 b m 4450^{P} 4638^{7} 4801^{7} **>32h<**
Derrybelle 6 ch m 25^{8} 1337^{8} 1679^{8} 3085^{P} (3748) 3959^{4} 4086^{6} 4439^{7} 4727^{P} **>45h<**
Derrymoyle (IRE) 8 b g 1487a^{6} 3126a^{3} 3635^{10} 4365a^{3} **>125h 78c<**
Derrys Prerogative 7 b g Nearly A Hand-Derrycreha Lass (Precipice Wood) 1457^{16} 1683^{14} 2093^{6} 2576^{7} 2838^{9} **3173^{P} 4232^{3} 4546^{P}** **>45h 80c<**
Desert Brave (IRE) 7 b g **1083^{7} 1252^{3} 1702^{F} 3941^{3} 4183^{6} 4377^{3} 4533^{5} 4745^{3}** **>70h 89c<**
Desert Calm (IRE) 8 br g Glow (USA)-Lancette (Double Jump) 253^{5} 915^{5} 1058^{3} 3570^{4} 3743^{3} 3983^{11} **>69h<**
Desert Challenger (IRE) 7 b g 217^{3} 354^{2} 677^{5} **1009^{F}** **>71h 34c<**
Desert Devil 5 b h Green Desert (USA)-Jolie Pelouse (USA) (Riverman (USA)) 1052^{7} 1667^{13} **>11h<**
Desert Fighter 6 b g (908) 1154^{4} 1439^{3} 1658^{7} 1924^{2} 2779^{5} 2902^{5} 3034^{2} 3286^{3} 3412^{F} (3995) **>98h<**
Desert Force (IRE) 8 b g (1181) 1443^{2} 1718^{2} 3362^{9} 3589^{2} 3709^{2} 3885^{10} 4296^{P} 4527^{2} **>73h<**
Desert Green (FR) 8 b g Green Desert (USA)-Green Leaf (USA) (Alydar (USA)) 1729^{2} 2112^{P} **>86h<**
Desert Lore 6 b g Green Desert (USA)-Chinese Justice (USA) (Diesis) 2503^{11} 2798^{12}
Desert Mountain (IRE) 4 b g Alzao (USA)-Curie Point (USA) (Sharpen Up) 1862^{2} (2751) 3007^{7} (3584) **>93h<**
Desert Run (IRE) 9 ch g **4659^{8} 4763^{F}** **>74h 100dc<**
Desert Scout 4 b g Picea-Queens Pearl (Queen's Hussar) 881^{P}
Desert Way (IRE) 4 b g Waajib-Cactus Road (FR) (Iron Duke (FR)) 3574^{5} 4009^{P} 4421^{P}
Design (IRE) 7 b m 1178^{U} **(DEAD)**
Desmond Gold (IRE) 9 b g **4380^{4}** **>85h<**
Desperate 9 ch g **1428^{P} 1662^{4} 1983^{P}** **>106h 110dc<**
Desperate Days (IRE) 8 b g **1850^{7} 2672^{6} 3068^{3} 3393^{2} 3667^{4}** **>80c<**
Destin d'Estruval (FR) 6 b g Port Etienne (FR)-Vocation (FR) (Toujours Pret (USA)) 1964^{2} 2550^{3} 2880^{4} **3266^{3} 3639^{5} (4206) 4480^{2} (4653)** **>97h 135c<**
Destiny Calls 7 ch g **3413^{2} 3618^{5} 4206^{2} 4509^{4}** **>99h 135c<**
Deux Carr (USA) 4 b c Carr de Naskra (USA)-Deux Chance (USA) (Vaguely Noble) 1269^{7} 1444^{F}
De-Veers Currie (IRE) 5 b m Glenstal (USA)-Regent Star (Prince Regent (FR)) 3026^{7} 3611^{8} 3908^{12} 4259^{11} 4719^{5} **>38h<**
Devilry 7 b g 745^{5} **(1009) 1346^{12} 2506^{2} 3001^{11} 3436^{5}** **>82h 89c<**
Devon Peasant 5 b m Deploy-Serration (Kris) 890^{2} 1171^{2} 1427^{2} 1788^{4} 3109^{2} 3539^{2} **>73h<**
Dextra (IRE) 7 b g 1323^{P} 1639^{11} **2883^{P} 3409^{F} 3537^{P} 3797^{P}**
Dextra Dove 10 gr g **1649^{5} 2057^{P} (2623) (2887) 3147^{4} 3302^{P} 4074^{P}** **>145c<**
Deymiar (IRE) 5 b g (1255) **>94h<**
Dia Georgy 6 b h Reesh-Carpadia (Icecapade (USA)) 3084^{P} 3282^{P}
Diamond Beach 4 b g Lugana Beach-Cannon Boy (USA) (Canonero II (USA)) 1700^{9} 2859^{U} 3158^{8} 3612^{2} (3822) 4056^{2} 4390^{5} **>71h<**
Diamond Cut (FR) 9 b g (285) 362^{3} 394^{F} **>99h<** **(DEAD)**
Diamond Double (IRE) 6 ch m Orchestra-Betty Sue (Menelek) 319a^{4} 3650a^{8} **>72h<**
Diamond Fort 12 b g **1643^{4} 1961^{5} 2063^{2} 2754^{P} 3185^{P} 3893^{2} 4270^{6} 4387^{3} 4557^{3} (4806)** **>106c<**
Diamond Hall 4 b g Lapierre-Willitwin (Majestic Maharaj) 3747^{5} (4088) **>66fh<**

Diamond Lady 5 ch m Nicholas Bill-Charossa (Ardross) 1275[8] **>43fh<**

Diamond Light 10 ch g Roman Warrior-Another Jo (Hotfoot) **4072[4] 4237[U] 4305[2] 4402[U] 4728[P] >64c<**

Diamond Sprite (USA) 10 b g **1348[3] >64c<**

Diamond Time 6 b m 3006[12] 3226[13]

Diamond Wind (USA) 9 b m Wind And Wuthering (USA)-Diamond Oyster (Formidable (USA)) **3455[8]**

Dibloom 9 b g 16[4] 97[2] **>69h<**

Dickies Girl 7 b m Saxon Farm-Menel Arctic (Menelek) 69[7] 189[8] 260[5] 341[5] 461[5] **>52h<**

Dictation (USA) 5 b g Dayjur (USA)-Mofida (Right Tack) 1276[9] 1499[P] **>42h<**

Dictum (IRE) 6 ch g 1422[6] 3441[F] (3734) **>82?h<**

Diddy Rymer 7 b m **2628[F]** 2838[11] 3098[3] 3325[9] 3481[4] 3644[8] (4479) 4628[P] 4705[B] **>61?h<**

Difficult Decision (IRE) 6 ch g John French-Lady Mala (So Blessed) 634[5] 718[3] 954[10] 1840[P] 2509[14] **>66h<**

Difficult Times (IRE) 5 ch g 1156[3] 3126a[6] 3382a[3] 3613[7] **>118h<**

Dig Deeper 10 b g 1347[5] 1671[4] 3157[P] 4248[15] **>64h<**

Dig For Gold 4 ch g Digamist (USA)-Formidable Task (Formidable (USA)) 2675[9] 3418[4] 3946[9] **>54fh<**

Dingle Wood (IRE) 7 ch g 1795[8] 1964[8] 2927[7] **>45h<**

Dinky Dora 4 ch f Gunner B-Will Be Wanton (Palm Track) 3548[7] 3808[2] 4088[12] **>45fh<**

Dino Malta (FR) 6 ch g **213[5] >85h 89c<**

Diorraing (IRE) 7 b g Tremblant-Seskin Bridge (Laurence O) **3503a[10] 4351a[U] >80c<**

Direct 14 b g **3490[4] 4256[P] >99dc<**

Direct Route (IRE) 6 b g 908[4] (1154) (1267) 1793[5] (2617) 3038[3] 3615[P] 4061[2] **>122h<**

Disallowed (IRE) 4 b f Distinctly North (USA)-Miss Allowed (USA) (Alleged (USA)) (1900) 2622[7] 2805[2] (3287) 3847[3] (4428) **>86+h<**

Disco des Mottes (FR) 6 b g 2702[6] 2900[5] **(3452) (3532) (3701) 4509[2] >89h 140c<**

Disco's Well 6 ro h 133[8] 287[5] 498[6]

Dish The Dosh 4 b f Superpower-Taxitilly (Formidable (USA)) 1014[11] 1172[R]

Di's Last 7 ch m 1958[5] 2090[3] 2576[4] **>65h<**

Dispol Conqueror (IRE) 4 b g Conquering Hero (USA)-Country Niece (Great Nephew) 1908[P]

Dispol Dancer 6 ch g Salse (USA)-High Quail (USA) (Blushing Groom (FR)) **2551[P] 2672[P]**

Dissolve 5 gr m 1638[12] (3110) 3204[2] 3594[4] (3752) 3904[P] 4071[3] 4139[2] **>59h<**

Distant Echo (IRE) 7 b g 745[4] **>100h<**

Distant Hills 5 gr m 872[8]

Distant Memory 8 gr g **254[2] (359) 411[3] (535) 658[2] 817[2] 1057[4] 4385[6] 4557[4] 4790[2]** >99?h **99c<**

Distant Storm 4 ch g Pharly (FR)-Candle in the Wind (Thatching) 3730[2] 4176[3] **>66h<**

Distillation 12 b g **2575[P] 2881[P] 3113[P]** >56h **69dc<**

Distillery Hill (IRE) 9 ch g **1691[7] 1850[F] 1944[6] 3141[P]** 3306[8] **3479[6] 3642[U] 3724[6] 4057[7]** >65c<

Distinctive (IRE) 8 ch g **1564[3] (1985) 2762[U] (2894) (2949) 3198[P] 3919[4] >59h 114dc<**

Ditopero 5 b g Teenoso (USA)-Al Zoud (USA) (Sharpen Up) 1151[2] 1303[6] **>50fh<**

Diwali Dancer 7 gr g 1859[2] 2625[3] 2817[7] 3267[8] 3600[10] 3942[6] (4398) (4550) (4734) **>98h<**

Dixon Varner (IRE) 7 b g **3391a[F] (4361a) >107c<**

Djais (FR) 8 ch g 103[F] 1148[3] 1319[3] **1521[3] 1856[P]** 2644[9] 2950[9] **>92h 86?c<**

Djeddah (FR) 6 b g Shafoun (FR)-Union Jack III (FR) (Mister Jack (FR)) **(2113) (2936) 3616[3] >145c<**

D'naan (IRE) 4 b g Royal Academy (USA)-Festive Season (USA) (Lypheor) (1980) 2574[2] 2705[2] (2874) 3110[2] 3344[3] 3473[P] **>76h<**

Do Be Ware 7 b g 579a[8] (819) 1040[P] 1419[4] 1841[4] (2792) 2905[2] 3577[2] 4552[10] 4633[6] 4725[5] **>55h<**

Docklands Courier 5 b g Dominion-High Quail (USA) (Blushing Groom (FR)) 956[3] 1424[2] 1905[6] 3204[10] **>69h<**

Dockline (IRE) 5 ch g Dry Dock-Grease Proof 4118a[22] **>70fh<**

Dockmaster 6 b g 1031[P] 1294[9] 2651[5] 2915[8] (3157) 3358[4] 3646[7] 4081[2] (4452) **>77h<**

Docs Boy 7 b g 3295[9] 4506[4] **>57h<**

Doc's Coat 12 b g 879[14] 1072[10] **>46dh<**

Doc Spot 7 b g Doc Marten-Detonate (Derring-Do) 4755[9] **>6h<**

Doctoor (USA) 7 ch g Cozzene (USA)-To The Top (USA) (Bold Hour) 2884[3] (3105) 3572[2] **>106h<**

Doctor Death (IRE) 6 ch g 3579[P]

Doctor Dunklin (USA) 8 b g 3545[7] **4158[P] 4447[P] 4769[5] >47h<**

Doctor Green (FR) 4 b g Green Desert (USA)-Highbrow (Shirley Heights) (730) (962) (1064) 1269[4] 1519[3] 2872[5] 3566[4] 3737[P] **>91h<**

Doctor-J (IRE) 7 ch g 66[14] 259[5] 531[5] **744[5] 1009[5] >68h 59c<**

Dodgy Dancer 7 b g 1663[10] 1818[8] 2746[P] 2945[7] 3282[5] **>47dh<**

Dodgy Dealer (IRE) 7 ch g **1994[5] 3015[P] 4402[P] >48c<**

Dolce Notte (IRE) 7 b m 1177[7] 1695[P] 1998[P] 2090[4] **>57h<**

Dolikos 10 b g **1985[P] 3018[7] 3198[6] 3333[3] 3456[2] 3804[4] 3886[P] >93c<**

Dolliver (USA) 5 b g Northern Baby (CAN)-Mabira (Habitat) 2946[11] 3205[P] **>14h<**

Dolly Prices 12 b m 2862[P] **>37h<**

Domaine de Pron (FR) 6 ch g Brezzo (FR)-Pasiphae (FR) (Signani (FR)) **1680[7] 1920[3] 2778[U] (2896) (4004) 4227[2] 4312[3] >117?c<**

Domappel 5 b g (1467) 1661[5] 1956[3] 2780[2] (3698) 3992[3] **>100h<**

Dom Beltrano (FR) 5 b g Dom Pasquini (FR)-Famous Horse (FR) (Labus (FR)) 1431[5] (1774) 2661[2] 3042[2] 3619[16] **>72fh<**

Domindross 5 ch g Ardross-Plum Tree (Dominion) 1329[6] **>50fh<**

Dominie (IRE) 9 b g **1038[P] 1252[6] 2052[6]** 2507[7] **>82h 67c<**

Dominion's Dream 5 ch m 741[9] 971[8] 1642[4] (1767) 1956[4] 2909[5] **>80h<**

Domino Night (IRE) 7 b g **4471[F] >54h< (DEAD)**

Dominos Ring (IRE) 8 b g 1191[6] 1542[2] **3015[3] >78h 103c<**

Dom Samourai (FR) 6 gr g **1175[3] 1428[3] 1997[5] 2869[7] 3153[5] >121c<**

Don du Cadran (FR) 8 b g 638[5] 703[4] 827[3] **(1281) (1447)** 4772[5] **>79h 110c<**

Doneraile Park (IRE) 10 ch g Floriferous-Southfields 317a[10] **>65h<**

Done Well (USA) 5 b g 908[5] 1163[2] 1267[5] 1502[6] 1658[2] 1852[5] 4079[3] **>97h<**

Donjuan Collonges (FR) 6 ch g **(3567) 4185[2] >124+c<**

Donna Del Lago 11 b m **74[4] >59dh 112c<**

Donnegale (IRE) 5 b g Strong Gale-Marys Gift (Monksfield) 2675[6] 2861[10] 3453[4] 3823[10] 4299[6] 4626[4] **>56h<**

Donnington (IRE) 7 b g 1651[5] (2763) 3041[5] 3569[4] 3918[P] 4205[2] **>80h<**

Donnybrook (IRE) 4 ch c Riot Helmet-Evening Bun (Baragoi) 3297[8] 4215[8] 4420[4] **>68fh<**

Donovans Reef 11 b g **421[3] 466[4] 581[4] 1138[3] 3824[P] 4149[5] >66c<**

Donside 9 gr g **4411[S] 4504[6]**

Don't Argue 6 ch g Whistlefield-Kara Star (Whistlewood) 918[8] 1056[P]

Don'tcallmegeorge 6 b g Lighter-Pennulli (Sir Nulli) 2830[8] 3090[12]

Dontdressfordinner 7 b g 1381[2] (1585) 1732[10] 2824[6] 3056[2] 3234[8] 3766[4] 4071[5] **>70h<**

Dont Forget Curtis (IRE) 5 b g 1152[F] 1807[3] 2509[7] 2662[4] 3004[5] 3371[4] 3711[9] 4055[11] 4152[4] 4335[8] 4518[4] 4638[5] 4712[5] 4754[3] **>51h<**

Dontleavethenest (IRE) 7 b g 1036[3] **>64h<**

Don't Light Up 11 b g **4074[F] 4467[4] 4806[3] >113c<**

Don't Mind If I Do (IRE) 6 gr g 1470[11] 1683[9] 2663[P] 3818[9] 4242[3] **>62h<**

Don Tocino 7 b g 156[9] 304[6] **389[F] >45h<**

Don't Tell Judy (IRE) 9 b g **3097[U]** 3328[9] 3607[11] 4283[P] 4572[5] 4760[3] **>55h<**

Dont Tell Marie 7 b m K-Battery-Waminda (Native Prince) 1781[9]

Dont Tell the Wife 11 br g 1586[11] **(1863) 2004[4] 2758[11] 3074[7] 3361[3] 3729[P] 4148[5] 4270[F] 4404[P] 4535[P] >86h 112dc<**

Don't Tell Tom (IRE) 7 b g 1999[4] 2539[8] 2701[6] 3035[6] 3159[9] 3711[2] **>62h<**

Doolar (USA) 10 b g 1282[2] 1701[7] 2913[11] 3807[F] **>62h<**

Doone Braes (IRE) 7 b g 1757a[7] **>59h<**

Doonloughan 12 b g **74[3] >112c<**

Doon Ridge 6 ch g 1686[P] 1824[7] 3711[P]

Dorans Pride (IRE) 8 ch g **(1240a) (1758a) (2360a) (2994a) 3245a[F] 3636[3] (4116a) >157h 165+c<**

Dorans Way (IRE) 6 b g **720[F]** 816[7] **>54h 87c<**

Dorlin Castle 9 b g **1989[F]** 2915[P] **3347[3] 3882[4]** 4248[7] **>68h 102c<**

Dormston Boyo 7 b g **13[8] 1300[3] 1629[P] 1819[6] >60h 67c<**

Dormy Three 7 b g 3115[4] 3233[13] 3594[P] 3949[8] **>57h<**

Dotterel (IRE) 9 b g 129[12] **>61h<**

Doualago (FR) 7 b g 3166[8] **(4019) 4140[3] (4463) (4609) (4740)** (4803) **>93h 140+c<**

Double Achievement (IRE) 7 gr g 2677[16] 3337[P]

Double Agent 4 ch g Niniski (USA)-Rexana (Relko) 2615[6] (3093) (3310) 3634[F] 3912[8] 4282[3] 4395[5] **>77h<**

Doubleback (IRE) 4 b f Simply Great (FR)-Wonder Woman (Horage) 3525a[9] **>65h<**

Double Collect 11 b br g **3439[3] 3712[F] 3984[U] >89c<**

Double Colour (IRE) 5 br g Doyoun-Calaloo Sioux (USA) (Our Native (USA)) 3525a[5] **>79h<**

Double Dash (IRE) 4 gr g Darshaan-Safka (USA) (Irish River (FR)) (852) 1159[3] 1700[6] 2615[9] 3066[7] 3310[2] 3555[5] 4376[10] 4705[B] **>53h<**

Double Pendant (IRE) 6 b g 26[4] 295[3] **>61h<**

Double Silk 13 b g **(2964) 3637[5] (4179) 4325[2] >124c<**

Double Star 6 b g Soviet Star (USA)-Startino (Bustino) 3946[3] 4301[2] 4656[5] **>67fh<**

Double Symphony (IRE) 9 ch m (2886) **(3037) 3639[P]** 4063[P] **>102h 144c<**

Double the Stakes (USA) 8 b g **3928[P] >77h 80c< (DEAD)**

Double Thriller 7 b g Dubassoff (USA)-Cape Thriller (Thriller) **4322[4] >95c<**

Double Trouble 6 b g 133^{7} 3205^{8}

Double Vintage (IRE) 4 b g Double Schwartz-Great Alexandra (Runnett) 3741^{8} 3940^{11} 4477^{4} 4705^{P} 4717^{5}

Doubling Dice 6 b g 1667^{4} 1848^{6} 2505^{7} 2800^{8} 2913^{6} 3091^{3} **>58h<**

Doubting Donna 11 gr m Tom Noddy-Dewy's Quince (Quorum) **3593^{U} 4241^{P} >80c<**

Dougal 6 b g 1777^{P} 1907^{P} 2898^{10} 3102^{P} 3437^{P} **>50h<**

Doug Eng (IRE) 4 b g King's Ride-Euroville Lady (Light Brigade) 4531^{12} **>29fh<**

Dovetto 8 ch g 3594^{3} 4296^{8} 4512^{8} 4558^{4} **>53h<**

Down the Fell 8 b g 894^{4} **(1032) 1264^{2} (1511) 1790^{3} 2641^{4} 2901^{3} (4062) >98h 137c<**

Down The Yard 4 b f Batshoof-Sequin Lady (Star Appeal) 462^{4} 589^{3} 3544^{6} 3745^{5} 4718^{2} **>57h<**

Dowshi 6 b m Baron Blakeney-Molinello (Balinger) 3794^{7} 4182^{P} **>53h<**

Do Ye Know Wha (IRE) 5 bb g Ajraas (USA)-Norton Princess (Wolver Hollow) 4118a^{3} 4360a^{8} **>92fh<**

Dragon Fly (IRE) 6 ch g 133^{4} 306^{6}

Dragon King 5 b g Rakaposhi King-Dunsilly Bell (London Bells (CAN)) 3853^{2} **>63fh<**

Dragonmist (IRE) 7 b m 649^{5} 725^{3} 905^{2} 1251^{2} 1334^{3} (1569) 2897^{4} 3112^{P} **>57h<**

Dragons Bay (IRE) 8 b g Radical-Logical View (Mandalus) **4481^{3} 4569^{P} 4773^{P}**

Drakestone 6 b g 974^{3} 1323^{9} 1568^{8} 1788^{3} 2034^{3} **>68h<**

Drakewrath (IRE) 7 b g 7^{P} 1667^{5} 3066^{4} 3307^{U} **>58h<**

Dramatic Act 4 gr f Tragic Role (USA)-Curious Feeling (Nishapour (FR)) 1172^{P}

Dramatic Pass (IRE) 8 ch g 4707^{F} 4719^{P} 4800^{6}

Dramatic Venture (IRE) 8 g **1758a^{F} >96h 117c<**

Dr Bones (IRE) 4 bb g Durgam (USA)-Rose Deer (Whistling Deer) 1747a^{12} (2738a) 3258a^{8} **>92h<**

Dr Dave (IRE) 6 b g 210^{F} 295^{7} 2678^{11} 2943^{3} 3131^{7} 3741^{4} **>49h<**

Dream Here 9 b g 69^{4} (297) **>77h<**

Dream Leader (IRE) 7 b g 1077^{2} (1378) 1581^{5} 1962^{6} **2819^{P} 3227^{4} 3546^{5} (3956) 4234^{4} 4342^{3} >78h 90c<**

Dream Ride (IRE) 7 b g **1521^{2} 1787^{2} (2807) 3015^{4} 3427^{U} 3762^{3} (4158) 4537^{2} 4655^{B} >88h 115c<**

Dreams End 9 ch h 318a^{6} (1288) 1365^{8} 1793^{14} 2645^{8} 2884^{6} (3231) 3597^{14} 4061^{3} 4212^{5} (4397) **>130h<**

Dr Edgar 5 b g Most Welcome-African Dancer (Nijinsky (CAN)) 698^{3} 1030^{10} 1667^{8} 1992^{8} **>64h<**

Dress Dance (IRE) 7 b g **1328^{5} 1572^{4} 1708^{6} 3059^{4} 3339^{F} 3495^{F} 4007^{P} >79h 73c<**

Dressed In Style (IRE) 5 ch m Meneval (USA)-Inundated (Raise You Ten) 3433^{6} **>56fh<**

Drewitts Dancer 10 b g **3206^{U}** 3338^{P} **>86?c<**

Driving Force 11 ch g **3005^{4} 3439^{2} 3840^{3} 4543^{P} >83h 102dc<**

Dr King (IRE) 5 b g Broken Hearted-Joanns Goddess (Godswalk (USA)) 4360a^{10} **>85fh<**

Dr Leunt (IRE) 6 ch g 1258^{7} 2078^{5} 2777^{6} 3038^{10} 3150^{5} 3615^{6} 4016^{5} 4210^{7} **>107h<**

Dromhana (IRE) 7 ch g Le Bavard (FR)-Honey Come Back (Master Owen) **(1468) 1819^{2} (2551) 2706^{2} 2936^{2} 3617^{5} 3978^{2} >115dc<**

Dromineer (IRE) 6 b g 4348a^{6} **>105h<**

Dromin Leader 12 b g **(3924) 4316^{3} (4634) >110c<**

Dromore Dream (IRE) 8 ch g Black Minstrel-Vickies Rambler (Wrekin Rambler) 2917^{9} 3368^{P} 3910^{5} **>57h<**

Dr Rocket 12 b g **15^{3}** 1796^{5} **1864^{2} 2009^{3} 2674^{5} 3053^{2} 3336^{7} (3588) 3678^{3} (4157) 4733^{2} >44h 91c<**

Druid's Brook 8 b g Meadowbrook-Struide (Guide) **(2841) 3162^{4} >105c<**

Drum Battle 5 ch g 1639^{P} 2676^{6} (2945) 3178^{4} 3831^{2} 4250^{2} **>70h<**

Drumcairn (IRE) 9 b g **3713^{8} 4758^{P} >9c<**

Drumcullen (IRE) 8 gr g **94^{7} 597^{2} (678) (833) 914^{2} (1194) 1338^{4} 4270^{2} 4463^{P} 4722^{2} >69h 111c<**

Drummond Warrior (IRE) 8 b g 4415^{3} **4564^{F}** **>77h<**

Drumstick 11 ch g **68^{6} 136^{7} (292) 335^{2} 414^{2} 656^{2} 830^{2} 959^{4} (1182) >76h 103c<**

Dry Hill Lad 6 b g Cruise Missile-Arctic Lee (Arctic Judge) 1713^{2} **2540^{F} 2860^{F}** 3032^{P} 3283^{5} 3706^{5} 3844^{5} **>55h<**

Dry Sea 6 b g 481^{4} 600^{P} **>60h< (DEAD)**

Dtoto 5 b g 727^{F} **>53h<**

Dual Image 10 b g 1658^{10} 1945^{6} (2780) 2957^{4} **(3140) 3289^{3} 3547^{2} 3692^{4} >88h 113c<**

Dubai Dolly (IRE) 4 b f Law Society (USA)-Lola Sharp (Sharpen Up) 3601^{6} 4176^{4} 4465^{B} 4720^{4} **>59?h<**

Dubelle 7 b m **(411) 595^{3} 722^{7} 901^{3} 3697^{9} 3950^{P} (4402) 4766^{4} >60h 92dc<**

Dublin Flyer 11 b g **1366^{S} (1566) (2773) 3636^{P} >171c<**

Dublin Freddy 6 b g 2661^{5} 3587^{2} **>68h<**

Dublin River (USA) 4 b g Irish River (FR)-Vivre Libre (USA) (Honest Pleasure (USA)) 4737^{6} **>31h<**

Dudley Do Right (IRE) 5 b g Be My Native (USA)-Speedy Debbie (Pollerton) 2995a^{5} **>102h<**

Dudwell Valley (IRE) 5 ch m Zaffaran (USA)-Chosen Flight (Selko) 553^{P}

Duet 4 b f Loch Pearl-Double Song (Double Form) 1413^{11} **>21h<**

Duffertoes 5 ch g High Kicker (USA)-Miss Poll Flinders (Swing Easy (USA)) 4567^{8} **>28h<**

Dugort Strand (IRE) 6 b or br g 2838^{P} 4055^{P}

Duhallow Lodge 10 ch g **1284^{F} 1379^{3} (1598) 1997^{P} 2782^{8} 3113^{2} 3551^{5}** 3600^{15} **>72h 117c<**

Duke of Aprolon 10 ch g **887^{5} 1420^{4} (1708) >94+c<**

Duke of Dreams 7 gr g **72^{6} 132^{4} 188^{5} 296^{3} (361) 484^{2} 547^{2} 886^{P} (4072) 4291^{P} >65h 84+c< (DEAD)**

Duke of Lancaster (IRE) 8 br g **302^{3} 417^{3} 494^{3} 658^{P} >49h 82?c<**

Duke of Perth 6 ch g 1852^{4} 1988^{2} 2543^{5} 2915^{F} 3351^{2} 3827^{2} 4577^{3} **>74h<**

Dukes Castle (IRE) 6 b g Buckskin (FR)-Arctic Lucy (Lucifer (USA)) 1203^{8} 1334^{F} 3154^{9} **3495^{P}** **>35h<**

Dukes Meadow (IRE) 7 ch g 1422^{5} **1728^{F} 1920^{5} 2693^{8} 2940^{F} >67h 71c<**

Dunabrattin 4 b c Blakeney-Relatively Smart (Great Nephew) 4538^{6} **>20fh<**

Dun Belle (IRE) 8 b m **(2341a) 2848a^{4} 2994a^{3} >74h 123c<**

Dungannon Lad 6 b g Skyliner-Sarphele Larches (Gay Fandango (USA)) 4433^{9} 4656^{11} **>20fh<**

Dunlir 7 bl g **1716^{6} 2760^{5} 2908^{F} 3060^{4} 3736^{U} 3892^{U} 4138^{2} 4330^{U} 4661^{5} >61h 66c<**

Dunnellie 4 br f Dunbeath (USA)-Miss Gallant (Gallo Gallante) 4156^{7} 4335^{13} **>15fh<**

Dunnicks Country 7 ch m 1260^{P} **1680^{P}** 2959^{5} 3499^{16} **>58h<**

Dunnicks Dolittle 4 b g Sulaafah (USA)-Field Chance (Whistlefield) 3767^{13}

Dunnicks Town 5 b g Town And Country-Country Magic (National Trust) 1336^{5} **>50fh<**

Dunnicks View 8 b g **2037^{P} 3111^{4} 3565^{3} >31h 67dc<**

Dunnicks Well 8 ch g 3535^{9}

Dunsfold Dolly 4 b f Strong Gale-Rositary (FR) (Trenel) 3690^{4} 4407^{6} **>58fh<**

Dunston Knight 4 ch g Proud Knight (USA)-Lucy Johnston's (IRE) (Burslem) 4217^{P} 4376^{12} 4650^{11} **>14h<**

Dunston Queen 4 ch f Proud Knight (USA)-Alto Dancer (Noalto) 4645^{P}

Dunston Slick 4 ch g Weld-Havrin Princess (Scallywag) 4531^{18}

Duntalkin 4 b f Dunbeath (USA)-Melody Moon (Philip of Spain) 1159^{P} 1699^{10} **>11h< (DEAD)**

Duraid (IRE) 5 ch g (686) (898) (1052) 1309^{2} 1666^{4} **>63h<**

Duralock Fencer 4 b g General Wade-Madame Laffitte (Welsh Pageant) 1377^{F} **(DEAD)**

Durano 6 b g 1030^{F} 1152^{4} 1848^{10} 2697^{2} (2898) 3158^{3} (3346) 3584^{2} 4246^{2} 4398^{7} **>90h<**

Durham Hornet 10 ch g **584^{U} 691^{3}**

Durrington 11 b g **1076^{F} >79c< (DEAD)**

Durshan (USA) 8 ch g 958^{5} 1732^{6} 1866^{5} 1962^{11} **>64h<**

Dustys Trail (IRE) 8 b g Seclude (USA)-Another Coup (Le Patron) **70^{4} 102^{4} 179^{4} 213^{7} 421^{P} 581^{3} 2039^{P} >71c<**

Duty Free 4 b g El Conquistador-Golden Medina (Cornuto) 4008^{5} **>61fh<**

E

Eager Beaver 5 gr g Petoski-Strathdearn (Saritamer (USA)) 3703^{7} **>48h<**

Eagle Bid (IRE) 9 b g **3721^{4} >89?c<**

Eagle Dancer 5 b g Persian Bold-Stealthy (Kind of Hush) 3574^{10} 3808^{U} **>50fh<**

Eagles Rest (IRE) 6 ch g 2055^{2} 2662^{6} 2937^{2} **>92h<**

Ealing Court 8 ch g 2117^{3} 2659^{2} 3013^{3} (3415) 3635^{12} **>92h<**

Earl Grant (FR) 8 dk g Cadoudal (FR)-Halloween (FR) (Gairloch) 52a^{3} (155a) **>156h<**

Earl Gray 10 gr g Baron Blakeney-Conveyor Belle (Gunner B) **4799^{5} >64c<**

Early Drinker 9 gr g **1584^{10} 1812^{3} >76h 94c<**

Early Man 10 b g **4617^{P} >91h 90?c<**

Earlymorning Light (IRE) 8 gr g **(420) 588^{4} 1315^{4} 1655^{P} 1941^{3} 4629^{6} 4771^{4} >80h 99c<**

Early Peace (IRE) 5 b g Bluebird (USA)-Everything Nice (Sovereign Path) 1030^{4} **>66h<**

Early Warning 4 br f Warning-Ile de Danse (Ile de Bourbon (USA)) 688^{9} **>28h<**

Earthmover (IRE) 6 ch g Mister Lord (USA)-Clare's Crystal (Tekoah) **(4551) (4792) >125+c<**

Easby Blue 5 b g Teenoso (USA)-Mellie (Impecunious) 3070^{5} (3480) 4288^{3} **>61fh<**

Easby Joker 9 b g **(1268) (1657) 2782^{P} 3160^{P} >74h 135c<**

Eastcliffe (IRE) 5 ch g Zaffaran (USA)-Missing Note (Rarity) 1926^{R} 2633^{7} 2924^{4} 3480^{3} 3823^{3} 4075^{4} (4152) 4513^{F} **>64h<**

Eastern Charly (BEL) 7 br g Ishamo-Sarah Bear (Mansingh (USA)) 54^{4} **>52h<**

Eastern Magic 9 b g **(951) (1186) 1912^{3} (2700) 3009^{5} 3225^{U} >58h 107c<**

Eastern Pleasure 10 gr g **4228^{3} 4748^{F} >63h 62c<**

Eastern River 11 ch g **(1465) 1684^{2} 2681^{2} 3223^{2} (3456) >34h 97c<**

Easter Oats 10 b m **4185^{P} >105c<**

Easter Ross 4 ch g Ardross-Caserta (Royal

Palace) (4388) **>74fh<**
Easthorpe 9 b g **1016^{2} 1366^{9} 1869^{4} 2639^{2} 3039^{2} 3638^{P}** >99h 142c<
East Houston 8 b g **2^{3} (57)** 131^{9} **799^{3} 1029^{4} 1293^{8} 1527^{F} 1657^{7} (1833) (4576) >70h 115c<**
Eastlands Hi-Light 8 ch g **3476^{4} >85c<**
Easy Breezy 7 b g **1680^{U} 2760^{4} 3060^{2} 3279^{4} 4203^{U} >67h 109c<**
Easy Listening (USA) 5 b g Easy Goer (USA)-Queen of Song (USA) (His Majesty (USA)) 1873^{3} 2669^{15} (2872) 3766^{2} 4048^{P} 4307^{7} **>78h<**
Easy Over (USA) 11 ch g 55^{5} 95^{3} 134^{7} 587^{5} **>50h 73c<**
Eau Benite 6 br g 4794^{8} **>35h<**
Eau de Cologne 5 b g Persian Bold-No More Rosies (Warpath) 2791^{3} 3084^{2} (3755) 4273^{2} (4403) 4801^{F} **>78h<**
Eau So Sloe 6 b g 1938^{12} 2676^{P} **3059^{F} 3407^{4} 3576^{F} 3810^{4} 4272^{P} 4437^{2} >27h 55c<**
Eccentric Dancer 4 b f Rambo Dancer (CAN)-Lady Eccentric (IRE) (Magical Wonder (USA)) 688^{P}
Echo de Janser (FR) 5 b g Courtroom (FR)-Joueuse de Luth (FR) (Fabulous Dancer (USA)) 721^{6} 904^{4} 4521^{F} **(DEAD)**
Ecu de France (IRE) 7 ch g 1171^{10} 1537^{8} 2036^{3} 2792^{10} 3205^{6} 4089^{8} 4233^{3} 4439^{4} 4562^{U} 4662^{6} **>56dh<**
Edelweis du Moulin (FR) 5 b g 1636^{F} (2902) 3038^{6} 4212^{3} 4397^{9} (4772) **>117+h<**
Eden Dancer 5 b g 538^{3} 745^{3} 941^{3} 1144^{7} 1832^{8} 4259^{3} 4505^{2} **>85h<**
Eden Roc 7 b g 4315^{7} **>63h<**
Eden Stream 10 b g **4083^{F}** 4445^{7} 4563^{7} **>27h 66?c<**
Edge Ahead (IRE) 7 b g Le Bavard (FR)-Blackrath Beauty (Le Tricolore) (2510) 4528^{8} **>13h<**
Edgemoor Prince 6 b g (968) 1351^{P} (1996) 2576^{2} 2880^{9} (3430) 3698^{4} **>82h<**
Edge of Night 8 b g 3706^{7} **>48h<**
Edipo Re 5 b h Slip Anchor-Lady Barrister (Law Society (USA)) 2635^{7} **>83?h<**
Editorial 5 b g Bustino-Deep Line (Deep Run) 3149^{11} **>37fh<**
Edmond (FR) 5 b g Video Rock (FR)-Galia III (FR) (Baraban) 2682^{2} **>55fh<**
Edredon Bleu (FR) 5 b g Grand Tresor (FR)-Nuit Bleue III (FR) (Le Pontet (FR)) 2663^{2} 2948^{8} **4214^{P} >75h<**
Edstone (IRE) 5 b g Mandalus-Smashing Run (Deep Run) 1687^{10} 1999^{13} 2627^{P} 3366^{7} 4514^{6} **>57h<**
Edward Seymour (USA) 10 b g 3471^{2} (3620) 3985^{2} 4378^{2} 4739^{4} **>60h 76c<**
Efaad (IRE) 6 b g 1208^{4} **>47h<**
Efharisto 8 b g 26^{3} (137) 557^{4} **>75h<**
Egypt Mill Prince 11 b g **1016^{P} >155dc<**
Ehtefaal (USA) 6 b g 1418^{3} 1798^{2} 2659^{4} 3016^{2} 3358^{2} 3499^{3} 3737^{3} (4455) 4550^{2} **>78h<**
Eid (USA) 8 b g (16) **4402^{2} 4611^{2} (4796) >96h 84c<**
Eilid Anoir 8 ch g **3713^{7} >68dc<**
Eirespray (IRE) 6 ch g Executive Perk-Shannon Spray (Le Bavard (FR)) 1692^{9} 2064^{4} **>51h<**
Ekeus (IRE) 7 ch g 2010^{8} **2807^{3} 3188^{P} 3339^{4} 3550^{2} >38h 72c<**
Ela Agapi Mou (USA) 4 b g Storm Bird (CAN)-Vaguar (USA) (Vaguely Noble) 2865^{2} 3174^{5} (3601) (3685) (4434) 4701^{7} **>84h<**
Ela Man Howa 6 b g 794^{2} 871^{4} 1030^{6} 1500^{5} 1628^{2} 3471^{11} **>65h<**
Ela Mata 5 br g (866) 1021^{2} (1309) (1807) (2651) 3615^{13} **>101+h<**
Elastic 11 b m 2041^{2} 3137^{4} **>71h 101c<**
Elation 5 b g 1804^{11} 2062^{7} 2651^{6} 3137^{5} 3398^{2} 3559^{7} 4261^{2} 4398^{3} **>91h<**
El Bardador (IRE) 4 b g Thatching-Osmunda (Mill Reef (USA)) 2705^{4} 3471^{F} 3677^{4} 3730^{6} 3953^{6} **>48h<**
Elburg (IRE) 7 b g 1031^{3} (1256) (1372) (1906) **>94h<**
El Cordobes (IRE) 6 b g 718^{11} **>41h<**
El Crank Senor 5 b g Scallywag-Spuggie (Ancient Monro) 865^{4} **2628^{3}** 3802^{P} **>92c< (DEAD)**
El Don 5 b g 1053^{2} (1125) 1791^{4} 2771^{P} (4084) 4178^{3} 4550^{5} 4798^{5} **>91h<**
Eleanora Muse 7 b m 21^{6} 1471^{4} 1762^{4} 2576^{5} **3360^{F} >47h<**
Electric Committee (IRE) 7 ch g **3568^{4} (3840) >82h 93c<**
Element of Risk (IRE) 7 b g 1654^{14} 1999^{11} **>54h<**
Elflaa (IRE) 6 b or br g 182^{5} **>95h<**
El Freddie 7 b g 1274^{3} 1536^{3} 1962^{P} (2891) 3431^{2} (3967) (4310) **>80h<**
Elgintorus (IRE) 7 b g Torus-Marble Owen (Master Owen) 2893^{4} 3426^{12} 3982^{5} **>56h<**
El Grando 7 b g 159^{2} 223^{2} 551^{P} 3087^{4} 3234^{13} **>65h<**
Eli Peckanpah (IRE) 7 b g **3533^{R} >58?h<**
Elite Force (IRE) 4 b g Fairy King (USA)-La Petruschka (Ballad Rock) 2751^{P}
Elite Governor (IRE) 8 b g **964^{2} 1150^{3} 1909^{P} 2926^{F} 3797^{4} 4085^{3} 4171^{4}** 4768^{5} **>50h 90dc<**
Elite Justice 5 ch g 54^{2} 334^{3} 1703^{8} 1861^{3} **>63h<**
Elite Reg 8 b g (257) 495^{2} **>91h 130+c<**
Ellen Gail (IRE) 5 b m Strong Gale-Kemchee (Kemal (FR)) 4428^{4} 4737^{9} **>50?h<**
Ell Gee 7 ch m **3089^{F} 3208^{6} 3667^{5} 3836^{F} 4100^{P}**
Elliott's Wish (IRE) 6 b g 1046^{P} 1316^{6} **(1576) 2043^{P} 2506^{4}** 3100^{3} **3477^{P} 4149^{7} >50h 81dc<**
Elliott The Butler 5 b g Lord Bud-Comarch (Ancient Monro) 3914^{19} 4514^{U}
Elltee-Ess 12 ch g 731^{6} 1040^{P} **1147^{4} >46h<**
Elly Fleetfoot (IRE) 5 b m Elmaamul (USA)-Fleetwood Fancy (Taufan (USA)) 137^{3} 156^{4} **>63h<**
Elly's Dream 6 b m El Conquistador-Laura's Dream (Royal Blend) 1820^{9} 2661^{14} 3052^{P} 4255^{P} **>43fh<**
Elmore 10 ch g Le Moss-Be Nice (Bowsprit) **3459^{2} 4135^{P} >84c<**
Elpidos 5 ch g 1125^{3} 1512^{5} 1804^{4} 1924^{3} 2644^{7} 2902^{7} 3034^{P} 3269^{P} **>98h<**
Elraas (USA) 5 b g Gulch (USA)-Full Card (USA) (Damascus (USA)) 3233^{16} **>9h<**
Ely's Harbour (IRE) 6 gr g Roselier (FR)-Sweet Run (Deep Run) 1412^{3} 1802^{4} 2812^{9} 3355^{P} **>60h<**
Elzoba (FR) 5 b g Un Desperado (FR)-Izoba (FR) (Bamako III) **3073^{F} (3187) 3638^{2} 4062^{F} >143c<**
Emallen (IRE) 9 b g 404^{5} 552^{5} **>60dh 60c<**
Embankment (IRE) 7 b or br g Tate Gallery (USA)-Great Leighs (Vaigly Great) 3233^{4} 3500^{4} 3761^{2} (4441) (4519) **>83+h<**
Embargo (IRE) 5 gr g Roselier (FR)-Honey Dream (Orchestra) 2648^{5} 2844^{15} 3425^{5} 3626^{5} **>62fh<**
Embellished (IRE) 5 b g 1793^{9} 4357a^{9} **>112h<**
Ember 4 b f Nicholas (USA)-Cinderwench (Crooner) 1712^{6} 3058^{P} **>44h<**
Embley Buoy 9 ch g 412^{2} (792) 1135^{B} 1274^{4} 1767^{3} **>55h 66dc<**
Embroidered 4 br f Charmer-Emblazon (Wolver Hollow) 962^{U} 1377^{13} 1712^{7} 2070^{7} 3057^{9} **>44h<**
Emerald Charm (IRE) 9 b m **4280^{P} >65h<**
Emerald Knight (IRE) 7 ch g Sandalay-Fort Etna (Be Friendly) **901^{6}**
Emerald Lamp (IRE) 6 b g Miner's Lamp-Mary Kate (Callernish) 4008^{10} **>45fh<**
Emerald Moon 10 b g **15^{4} 93^{4}** 483^{8} **3446^{U} 4619^{5} >71h 82c<**
Emerald Ruler 10 b g **4228^{P} 4543^{7} >74h 81c<**
Emerald Sea (USA) 10 ch g **2786^{10} 3069^{P}** 3474^{7}
Emerald Statement (IRE) 7 b g Strong Statement (USA)-Popsi's Darling (Le Bavard (FR)) (1550) (1835) 2676^{2} 2948^{3} 3552^{3} **>91h<**
Emerald Venture 10 b g 3131^{5} 3471^{U} 3921^{9} 4162^{P} 4633^{9} 4739^{3} **>46h 61c<**
Emilymoore 6 ch m 1021^{7} **>56h<**
Emma's Jewel (IRE) 6 b m Duky-Stand In (Star Moss) 418^{12}
Emnala (IRE) 5 b m Contract Law (USA)-African Light (Kalaglow) 1788^{6}
Emperor Chang (USA) 10 b g 641^{9} 798^{2} 916^{5} 1023^{4} **>60h<**
Emperor's Magic (IRE) 6 ch g 4750^{2} **>55h<**
Emperors Wood 6 b g 156^{10} **>27h<**
Emrys 14 ch g **3928^{P} >83?c<**
Emsee-H 12 b g **3135^{6} >69c<**
Emu Park 9 gr g **4411^{5} 4704^{7} >68c<**
Enchanted Cottage 5 b g (3102) 3371^{2} 3485^{2} (3825) 4248^{6} **>69h<**
Enchanted Man 13 b g **3928^{P} >76c<**
Encore Un Peu (FR) 10 ch g **3302^{6} >109h 146?c<**
Endeavour (FR) 5 b br g Video Rock (FR)-Ogigy (FR) (Quart de Vin (FR)) 1289^{7} 1801^{3} (3021) 3619^{20} **>66fh<**
Endowment 5 ch g Cadeaux Genereux-Palm Springs (Top Ville) 1152^{2} (1343) 1921^{4} (2541) 2764^{5} **>81h<**
English Invader 6 b h Rainbow Quest (USA)-Modica (Persian Bold) 1651^{12} 1835^{4} **>33h<**
Enigma Bell 4 b c Rambo Dancer (CAN)-Skelton (Derrylin) 2938^{5} **>29fh<**
Ennel Gale (IRE) 7 br m 2857a^{7} **>62h<**
Ennistymon (IRE) 6 b m **590^{P} 817^{U} 1076^{5} 1445^{F} 3456^{6} 3837^{6} >34h 66c<**
Ensign Ewart (IRE) 6 ch g Buckskin (FR)-Clonea Fog (Laurence O) **4076^{2} (4256) >112c<**
Environmental Law 6 b g 1025^{7} 1292^{6} 1575^{5} 1992^{2} 2629^{9} **>53h<**
Envocamanda (IRE) 8 b g 2825^{8} **>20h<**
Eoins Lad (IRE) 6 ch g The Noble Player (USA)-Dulcet Dido (Dike (USA)) 319a^{13} **>56h<**
Eostre 8 b g Saxon Farm-Herald The Dawn (Dubassoff (USA)) **3913^{P}**
Equity Player 12 ch g **(3175) 3573^{P} >115c<**
Equity's Darling (IRE) 5 b m 1840^{6} 1962^{B} 2797^{10} (2870) 3088^{P} 3687^{4} 4181^{8} **>57h<**
Eric's Bett 4 b g Chilibang-Mira Lady (Henbit (USA)) 906^{6} 1652^{18} 1700^{2} **>63h<**
Eric The King 6 ch g Seymour Hicks (FR)-Friendly Marina (Be Friendly) 3583^{10}
Erin's Lad 6 br g (3983) **>63h<**
Erintante (IRE) 4 b f Denel (FR)-Glen of Erin (Furry Glen) (2931) 3619^{10} **>91fh<**
Eriny (USA) 8 br g 97^{P} 3666^{7} 4060^{4} 4154^{2} 4278^{6} 4505^{P} **>66h<**
Erlemo 8 b g 101^{2} 587^{11} **4228^{7} >61h 68c<**
Erlking (IRE) 7 b g 1860^{9} 2824^{8} 3056^{7} 3429^{12} 3915^{P} **>42h<**
Ermyns Pet 6 gr g 865^{7} 1317^{16} **>11h<**
Ernest Aragorn 8 b g **1771^{P} 2628^{R} 2867^{P}** 3072^{7} 3677^{P} 3959^{P} **>29h<**
Ernest William (IRE) 5 b br g 859^{F} 1132^{4} 1339^{5} 1777^{8} **>32h<**
Erni (FR) 5 b g Un Numide (FR)-Quianoa (FR) (Beaugency (FR)) 1843^{3} 2627^{6} 3727^{3} 4393^{W} 4500^{5} 4698^{2} **>66h<**

Erzadjan (IRE) 7 b g 1906^7 2702^2 2888^4 3600^U 4016^7 4207^3 **>110h<**

Escadaro (USA) 8 b g 2008^P 3328^F **(DEAD)**

Escartefigue (FR) 5 b g 2740a^5 3017^3 3303^3 3635^5 (4016) 4365a^2 **>134+h<**

Es Go 4 ch g Dunbeath (USA)-Track Angel (Ardoon) 2804^2 3365^3 **>55fh<**

Eskimo Kiss (IRE) 4 b f Distinctly North (USA)-Felicitas (Mr Fluorocarbon) 2070^{12} 2705^3 3054^{11} 3704^2 3953^P **>61h<**

Eskimo Nel (IRE) 6 ch m 1288^5 1793^{11} 2059^2 2635^6 3038^{12} **>116h<**

Eskleybrook 4 b g Arzanni-Crystal Run VII (Damsire Unregistered) 4388^{11} **>12fh<**

Esperanza IV (FR) 5 b m Quart de Vin (FR)-Relizane III (FR) (Diaghilev) 4656^6 **>46fh<**

Espla 6 b g Sure Blade (USA)-Morica (Moorestyle) 2818^9 3072^F 4542^R **>25h<**

Establish (IRE) 9 b m 8^P 1968^U 2176^B 2614^F 2919^P (3449) 3794^{12} **>60h 53c<**

Eternal City 6 b g (467) 636^5 1999^9 3096^2 3485^{10} 3803^5 4283^4 4513^3 **>64h<**

Ethbaat (USA) 6 b or br g 1663^P 2040^7 3234^{17} **>70dh<**

Ethical Note (IRE) 6 ch g 1139^6 1349^6 1576^F 1714^6 2789^P **>49h 43c<**

Eton Gale (IRE) 8 b g 3615^8 **>103h<**

Etta Dove 6 b m Olympic Casino-Clifford's Dove (Rustingo) 3895^{12}

Eudipe (FR) 5 b g Useful (FR)-Toskaninie (FR) (Kashnil (FR)) (2892) 3008^2 (3268) 3616^2 **>148c<**

Eulogy (FR) 10 b or br g 1828^4 2091^2 3051^6 3331^9 **>74h 70c<**

Eulogy (IRE) 7 ch g 1392^3 1870^3 2666^9 2880^7 3145^2 3550^F 4207^{12} **>89?h 101+c<**

Euphonic 7 br g Elegant Air-Monalda (FR) (Claude) (1342) **>75h<**

Eurobox Boy 4 ch g Savahra Sound-Princess Poquito (Hard Fought) 1011^5 1370^{13} **>57h<**

Eurochief 6 ch g 1966^{12} 2696^8 **>42fh<**

Euro Express 4 ch g Domynsky-Teresa Deevey (Runnett) 688^{10} 803^4 **>31h<**

Eurofast Pet (IRE) 7 b g Supreme Leader-Inagh's Image (Menelek) 1329^7 2763^7 3271^5 3703^5 **>56h<**

Eurolink Shadow 5 b g 794^6 1282^3 2035^9 3829^5 4219^4 4444^2 **>53h 69?c<**

Eurolink the Lad 10 b g 1828^6 2048^7 2946^F **>59h<**

Eurolink the Rebel (USA) 5 ch g 2651^P 3327^P 3542^4 3976^4 4236^7 (4295) 4381^9 4729^2 **>64h<**

Euro Singer 5 br g 1860^7 1954^4 2573^4 (3904) (4071) 4307^5 4534^F **>74?h<**

Euro Thyne (IRE) 7 ch g 910^8 **>32h<**

Eurotwist 8 b g 1439^5 1642^3 2670^9 2946^3 3346^7 **>87h<**

Evangelica (USA) 7 b m (158) (220) 342^5 485^3 789^2 (966) (1367) 1789^4 2575^2 4074^{17} **>87h 129c<**

Even Blue (IRE) 9 b g 1631^2 2011^5 3071^4 **>78h 126c<**

Evening Dancer 4 b g Nearly A Hand-Laval (Cheval) 2938^7 **>15fh<**

Evening Dusk (IRE) 5 b m Phardante (FR)-Red Dusk (Deep Run) 2953^P 3315^{10} 3691^{17} **>15h<**

Evening Rain 11 b g 190^5 3981^U (4142) (4520) 4721^F **>90c<**

Evening Rush 11 ch g 3972^4 4391^4 4745^7 **>79?c<**

Eventsinternashnal 8 ch g Funny Man-Tamorina (Quayside) 1037^P 1261^P 2926^P

Ever Blessed (IRE) 5 b g 1317^3 **>78+h<**

Everso Irish 8 b g 4773^5 **>49h 85?c<**

Evezio Rufo 5 b g Blakeney-Empress Corina (Free State) 910^{12} 1470^5 1659^4 1959^5 2076^4 2570^{10} 3488^P (3933) 4086^5 4223^5 4295^{10} **>56h<**

Evriza (IRE) 4 b f Kahyasi-Evrana (USA) (Nureyev (USA)) 1747a^5 2333a^F 2738a^{12} 2993a^5 3634^{18} **>69h<**

Ewar Bold 4 b c Bold Arrangement-Monaneigue Lady (Julio Mariner) 1595^U 2678^9 2818^6 3088^6 3205^5 3442^5 3689^P 4250^4 4340^3 4658^7 **>61h<**

Ewar Imperial 5 b g Legend of France (USA)-Monaneigue Lady (Julio Mariner) 156^5 218^2 **>63h< (DEAD)**

Exalted (IRE) 4 b g High Estate-Heavenward (USA) (Conquistador Cielo (USA)) 2925^2 3224^4 3634^{20} **>67h<**

Excise Man 9 ch g 4^F **>89c<**

Exclusion 8 ch g 132^9 188^3 389^2 423^F 647^8 822^4 **>54h 77c<**

Excuse Me (IRE) 8 b g 1^4 **>43h<**

Executive (IRE) 5 ch g Polish Precedent (USA)-Red Comes Up (USA) (Blushing Groom (FR)) 3445^P

Executive Design 5 b g (1510) 2603a^7 3615^{17} 4210^5 **>110h<**

Executive Options (IRE) 8 br g 1758a^3 2856a^4 3261a^U 3389a^3 **>99c<**

Exemplar (IRE) 9 b g 894^5 1023^3 (1143) 1945^5 2651^7 2915^9 3201^7 3642^2 3826^3 4219^2 4447^U 4515^3 (4753) **>81h 96c<**

Expedient Option (IRE) 7 b g 317a^P **>86h 43c< (DEAD)**

Express Again 5 b g Then Again-Before Long (Longleat (USA)) 3574^{13} 3690^7 **>42fh<**

Express Gift 8 br g 2078^3 2603a^{16} 2888^{11} (3148) 3572^3 4212^{11} 4397^8 **>113h<**

Expressment 13 br g 3341^5 3799^5 4640^7 **>95c<**

Express Travel (IRE) 9 b g (1038) 1773^U 2829^3 **>59h 86c<**

Exterior Profiles (IRE) 7 b g 1664^F 2867^4 3044^U 3427^3 3848^F **>88h 124c<**

Extra Hour (IRE) 4 b g Cyrano de Bergerac-Renzola (Dragonara Palace (USA)) 1953^P

Extremely Friendly 4 ch g Generous (IRE)-Water Woo (USA) (Tom Rolfe) 1205^P 1776^{10} **>38h<**

Eye of The Storm (IRE) 6 b g 653^{12}

Ezanak (IRE) 4 b g Darshaan-Ezana (Ela-Mana-Mou) 3075^9 3364^3 3965^3 **>58h<**

F

Fabbl Approved 5 br g Newski (USA)-What An Experiance (Chance Meeting) 4388^{14}

Fabulous Francy (IRE) 9 ch g 860^4 1012^3 1423^P

Fabulous Mtoto 7 b h 1878^3 **>67h<**

Factor Ten (IRE) 9 b g (30) 809^P (869) 1354^2 4416^P 4624^2 4802^P **>130c<**

Fair Ally 7 gr g Scallywag-Fair Kitty (Saucy Kit) 1206^5 1576^F 1780^5 2000^3 2672^P 3436^6 3724^4 3945^P 4151^F **>76c<**

Fair and Fancy (FR) 6 b g 4261^P (4451) 4744^5 **>65h<**

Fair Attraction 5 ch g Charmer-Fairfields (Sharpen Up) 603^{10} **>2h<**

Fair Crossing 11 ch g 4222^P **>98?c<**

Fairelaine 5 b m Zalazl (USA)-Blue and White (Busted) 1679^4 1838^2 2907^3 3054^5 3752^8 4285^2 4405^{10} 4512^{11} **>66h<**

Fair Haul 6 gr g 1289^{14} 1594^P 1766^P 2907^{14} **>8fh<**

Fairies Farewell 7 ch m 1327^5 1840^P 4559^4 **>43h<**

Fairly Sharp (IRE) 4 b f Glenstal (USA)-Bengala (FR) (Hard To Beat) 3301^6 3544^2 3801^2 4136^2 4395^2 (4794) **>80+h<**

Fairy Knight 5 b h Fairy King (USA)-Vestal Flame (Habitat) 1651^7 1726^3 3233^6 **>70h<**

Fairy-Land (IRE) 5 ch m Executive Perk-Season's Delight (Idiot's Delight) 1821^7 3029^{14} **>6h<**

Fairy Mist (IRE) 9 gr g 3503a^3 **>91c<**

Fairy Park 12 ch g 604^P 678^2 797^P 1122^P 1817^2 2089^6 3053^U 3623^7 3824^P 3891^P 3966^3 4159^7 **>81c<**

Faithful Hand 7 ch g Nearly A Hand-Allende (Grand Roi) 718^4 1079^4 1263^2 1705^3 1911^2 3976^3 4162^5 **>64h<**

Faithlegg (IRE) 6 b m Bold Owl-Combe Hill (Crozier) 3052^P 4625^{10} 4801^3 **>57h<**

Falcons Dawn 10 b g 408^5 481^5 **>70dh<**

Falcon's Flame (USA) 4 b br g Hawkster (USA)-Staunch Flame (USA) (Bold Forbes (USA)) 906^2 2503^3 2798^3 3093^4 3315^7 3612^8 **>71dh<**

False Economy 12 ch g Torus-Vulvic (Vulgan) 4551^R **>100?c<**

Fame And Fantasy (IRE) 6 b m 888^P 4789^{13} **>32h<**

Familiar Art 6 b m 1358^8 1703^7 2044^P 2629^{14} **>39h<**

Familiar Friend 11 gr g 3744^{11} 3852^P 3928^2 4327^4 4406^2 4543^P **>102dc<**

Family Project (IRE) 4 b f Project Manager-Favourite Niece (Busted) 2738a^8 **>70h<**

Family Way 10 b g 1752a^2 2603a^4 3615^P **>108h<**

Fanadiyr (IRE) 5 b g 2913^{16} 4283^6 4714^3 **>35h<**

Fancy Nancy (IRE) 6 b m 1250^7 2662^7 (3189) 3488^P **>53h<**

Fancytalkintinker (IRE) 7 b g Bold Owl-Our Ena (Tower Walk) 4743^5 **>42h<**

Fane Park (IRE) 9 br g 2708^F 3234^{14} 3442^{17} 3810^F **>55h< (DEAD)**

Fantastic Fleet (IRE) 5 b g 485^4 651^B 3586^U 4327^3 **>76h 76c<**

Fantasy Line 6 b m Master Willie-Transcendence (USA) (Sham (USA)) 1551^3 1855^6 2547^8 2870^4 (3348) 3817^2 3970^F 4166^F **>78h< (DEAD)**

Fantus 10 b g (3637) **>145c<**

Far Ahead 5 b g Soviet Star (USA)-Cut Ahead (Kalaglow) 3158^4 (3311) (3691) 4048^4 4204^6 **>94h<**

Far Dawn (USA) 4 b c Sunshine Forever (USA)-Dawn's Reality (USA) (In Reality) (1377) (1872) 2622^4 3174^2 4014^2 **>99h<**

Far East (NZ) 8 gr g (475) **>39h 86c<**

Faringo 12 b g 3089^P 3446^7 4051^9 4511^3 4616^2 **>96c<**

Farleyer Rose (IRE) 8 b m 2820^{10} 3108^9 3441^5 **>39h<**

Farmers Subsidy 5 ch g 787^4 1021^P 1713^6 2042^7 2654^P 2915^P **>64h<**

Farmer's Tern (IRE) 5 ch m 961^{10} **>71h<**

Farm Talk 5 ch g Palm Track-Kilkenny Gorge (Deep Run) 2675^{13} 3203^{14} 3449^P

Farney Glen 10 b g Furry Glen-Windara (Double-U-Jay) 2545^{10} 2922^6 3198^5 (3332) 3560^3 3911^U 4535^3 **>43h 96c<**

Far Out 11 b g 29^P **>70h 68c<**

Far Pasture 5 br m Meadowbrook-Farm Consultation (Farm Walk) 2804^P

Farriers Fantasy 5 ch m Alias Smith (USA)-Little Hut (Royal Palace) 1084^4

Far Senior 11 ch g 1415^3 1662^P 2630^P 2817^{11} 3332^P 3807^P **>110c<**

Far Springs (IRE) 6 b g 1453^4 **>69h<**

Fashion Leader (IRE) 6 br g Supreme Leader-Record Halmony (Record Token) 866^P 1077^P 3085^P 4096^P

Fashion Maker (IRE) 7 b g 1539^3 3423^5 3754^3

>59h<
Fasil (IRE) 4 ch g Polish Patriot (USA)-Apple Peel (Pall Mall) 3174[8] 3359[3] (3592) 4136[4] >83h<
Fassan (IRE) 5 br g 1305[5] 1804[2] 2041[3] 2670[8] 3345[2] 3883[4] >78h<
Faster Ron (IRE) 6 b g 1026[6] 1139[8] 3795[9] >49h<
Fast Forward Fred 6 gr g Sharrood (USA)-Sun Street (Ile de Bourbon (USA)) 1191[P]
Fast Fun 9 b g 4411[P] >61c<
Fastini Gold 5 b g Weldnaas (USA)-La Carlotta (Ela-Mana-Mou) 1276[5] 1425[3] 1857[4] 1980[3] (2567) 2806[2] 3050[5] 3186[5] 3594[5] 3834[2] 4091[7] >57h<
Fast Run (IRE) 9 ch g 1562[P] >63h 81c<
Fast Study 12 b g 3609[5] >73?c<
Fast Thoughts 10 b g 1428[P] 1681[4] 2761[4] 3013[6] 3175[4] 3444[2] 3751[2] 3892[P] >68dh 95c< (DEAD)
Fatack 8 b g 3303[10] 3615[22] 3920[P] >69h<
Fatehalkhair (IRE) 5 ch g Kris-Midway Lady (USA) (Alleged (USA)) 467[3] 506[2] 643[3] 801[2] (4390) (4505) 4702[10] >76h<
Father Dowling 10 br g 130[2] 158[13] 190[6] 4722[P] >44h 83c<
Father Gerard 6 ch g 1921[10]
Father Henry (IRE) 6 b g The Parson-Little Sloop (Balinger) 3143[5] 3798[8] >69h<
Father O'Brien 10 b g 3915[7] 4248[11] 4283[8] 4622[5] >44h<
Father Power (IRE) 9 b g 360[6] 590[P] 2067[7] >79dh 93c<
Father Rector (IRE) 8 b g 4350a[6] >98h 102c<
Father Sky 6 b g (631) (795) 1054[3] 1302[2] 1923[2] 2749[2] (3280) (3414) (3841) 3993[3] 4227[5] >97h 131dc<
Fattash (USA) 5 ch g 327[5] 394[6] 469[5] 3684[3] 3954[P] 4083[U] 4442[P] >8h<
Faustino 5 gr g 255[2] 341[7] (459) 790[9] 3640[20] 4130[2] 4278[2] 4660[4] >94h<
Fawley Flyer 8 ch g 899[2] (958) (1170) 1419[2] (1718) 1988[3] 2797[2] 3114[3] 3362[4] 3746[2] 3830[3] 4252[3] >74h 89c< (DEAD)
Fawn Prince (IRE) 4 b g Electric-Regent Star (Prince Regent (FR)) 3619[24] >25fh<
Fayette County (IRE) 6 b g Executive Perk-Lady Kas (Pollerton) 3066[8] 3295[10] >44h<
Fearless Hussar 7 b g 4003[9] 4230[P] 4403[U] >51h<
Fearless Wonder 6 b g 1330[P] >93h<
Feathered Gale 10 b g 1216a[2] 1649[6] 2348a[7] 3526a[5] 4074[P] 4303[4] >131c<
Fed on Oats 9 b g Oats-Fedelm (Celtic Cone) 4220[P] 4455[F]
Feebee Five 5 b m State Trooper-Idiot's Beauty (Idiot's Delight) 1457[13] 1834[2] >51fh<
Feeling Foolish (IRE) 8 ch g (468) >64h<
Feel the Power (IRE) 9 b g 1452[3] 1771[2] 2760[2] 3047[6] >93h 113c<
Felloo (IRE) 8 br g 1320[4] 2076[5] 2870[P] 3565[P] >65h 77c<
Fellow Countryman 10 b g 1937[2] >134c<
Fellow Sioux 10 ch g Sunley Builds-Sue Lark (Sir Lark) 4522[P]
Feltham Mistress 7 ch m Sula Bula-Tycoons Belle (Tycoon II) 3721[P] 4070[F] 4543[4] >83c<
Fencer's Quest (IRE) 4 ch c Bluebird (USA)-Fighting Run (Runnett) 2655[5] 3075[13] 3359[14] 3983[3] 4226[4] 4405[5] >57h<
Fenian Court (IRE) 6 b m 1027[U] 1078[5] 1345[3] 1857[5] 4089[9] (4423) 4620[3] >57h<
Fenloe Rambler (IRE) 6 b g 1292[7] 1654[18] 2654[7] 3644[4] >65h<
Fen Terrier 5 b m 893[2] 1025[4] (1144) 1658[5] 1824[2] (2001) 4187[6] 4261[5] >81h<
Fenwick 10 b g 361[4] 457[2] 601[2] 728[4] 886[4] (975) 1298[2] 1430[4] 1696[3] 1763[3] 2657[U] 2962[4] 3053[4] 3206[2] 3588[U] 3832[3] (3897) 4090[3] 4140[2] >91c<
Fenwick's Brother 7 ch g 186[7] 424[4] 1576[F] 1780[4] 1987[3] 2628[F] 2653[5] 2786[5] >48h 90c<
Ferens Hall 10 b g 675[11] 749[4] 813[2] >55h<
Fergal (USA) 4 ch g Inishpour-Campus (USA) (Minnesota Mac) 688[13] >14h<
Fern Grove 5 ch g 26[P]
Fern Leader (IRE) 7 b g Supreme Leader-Mossbrook (Le Moss) 2510[6] 3608[3] 3715[2] 3882[U] 4447[3] 4569[2] >63fh 95c<
Ferny Ball (IRE) 9 b g 1472[F] 1814[10] 2008[P] >53dh<
Ferrers 6 b g 1208[8] 1777[5] 2010[3] 2690[14] 2861[7] 3019[F] 3366[6] 3612[4] 3752[5] >68h<
Ferrino Fruits (IRE) 6 b g The Parson-Starry Karen (Joshua) 2924[12] 3297[12]
Ferrycarrigcrystal (IRE) 9 b g 2856a[6] >141h 96c<
Ferrycarrig Hotel (IRE) 8 b g 4352a[22] >90h 65c<
Festival (FR) 4 gr g Mourtazam-Oseille (FR) (Le Pontet (FR)) 3767[8] >27fh<
Festival Fancy 10 ch m Le Coq d'Or-Rabbit Patrol (Guide) 3398[6] 3531[7] 3882[7] 4078[F] 4248[16] 4515[7] 4569[P] >64h 65c<
Fiasco 4 ch f Dunbeath (USA)-Rainbow Trout (Comedy Star (USA)) 1205[11] 1526[8] 3474[3] 3711[4] 3971[P] >45h<
Fibreguide Tech 14 b g 4222[P] 4631[F] >79?c<
Fichu (USA) 9 b g 1076[4] (1298) 1584[3] 1769[2] 1965[3] 3686[4] (3832) 4254[3] 4797[4] >67h 88dc<
Fiddlers Bow VI (IRE) 9 b g 4352a[7] >100h<
Fiddler's Leap (IRE) 5 br g Phardante (FR)-Chief Dilke (Saulingo) 1457[15] 1834[4] 2696[14] >50fh<
Fiddlers Pike 16 b g 3055[P] 3490[2] 3739[B] 4098[5] >98?c<
Fiddling The Facts (IRE) 6 b br m Orchestra-Facts 'n Fancies (Furry Glen) 1998[2] (2826) 3152[4] 3423[2] 3817[3] (4182) >82h<
Field Of Destiny (IRE) 8 b m 4351a[P] >61c<
Field of Vision (IRE) 7 b g Vision (USA)-Bold Meadows (Persian Bold) (293) 455[3] (643) 745[2] 941[5] (1025) 1314[3] 3398[4] 3559[3] 4060[5] >84h<
Fieldridge 8 ch g 214[3] (362) (651) 721[2] 1019[7] 1196[2] 1508[3] >101h<
Fierce 9 ch g 76[5] 723[5] 862[4] 949[5] 1007[P] >73h 101dc<
Fiery Footsteps 5 ro m Chilibang-Dancing Daughter (Dance In Time (CAN)) 743[P] 3115[13] 3590[10]
Fiery Sun 12 b g 3822[8] 4147[F] 4389[P] 4744[7] >44h<
Fifth Amendment 12 b g 3089[3] 3273[U] 3580[R] 4256[P] 4449[3] >78c<
Fiftysevenchannels (IRE) 8 b g (1410a) 2346a[3] 2741a[7] 4793[2] >134c<
Fighting Days (USA) 11 ch g 957[6] 1812[P] 3179[P] >67c< (DEAD)
Fight to Win (USA) 9 b g 4270[9] 4326[5] 4640[2] 4806[P] >43h 94c<
Fijon (IRE) 4 b f Doyoun-Tasskeen (FR) (Lyphard (USA)) 1149[5] (1370) 1862[7] 2815[B] >63h<
Filch 6 ch m Precocious-Pilfer (Vaigly Great) 1171[12] 1568[P] 1768[P]
Fill The Boot (IRE) 7 br g Mandalus-Lady O' The Grange (Stanford) 4738[P]
Filscot 5 b h Scottish Reel-Fililode (Mossberry) 3235[2] 3365[6] (4143) >66fh<
Fils de Cresson (IRE) 7 b g 1343[F] 1999[5] 2785[4] 3064[P] 3703[3] 4183[4] >75h 91c<
Final Ace 10 ch g 456[P] >41h 42c< (DEAD)
Final Beat (IRE) 8 ch g 746[4] 1153[8] 1308[2] 1691[F] 1845[5] 2551[2] 2919[5] 3201[15] 3435[2] 3968[3] >80c<
Final Express 9 ch m 3341[6] >31h<
Final Hope (IRE) 9 ch g (3712) >97c<
Final Pride 11 b m 68[4] 3637[6] (4241) 4804[2] >77h 108c<
Final Rose 7 b m Derring Rose-Final Flirtation (Clear Run) 3491[P] 3970[P] 4224[9]
Final Score (IRE) 7 ch m Orchestra-Bailieboro (Bonne Noel) 133[12] 191[12] 3889[P] 4519[3] 4641[6] >31h<
Final Tub 14 ch g 317a[4] 3503a[P] >83h 102c<
Fin Bec (FR) 4 b g Tip Moss (FR)-Tourbrune (FR) (Pamponi (FR)) 3090[3] 3425[7] >56fh<
Fine De Claire 4 b f Teenoso (USA)-Princess Florine (USA) 4360a[16] >75fh<
Fine Harvest 11 b g (862) 1035[F] (1660) 1912[W] 2621[2] 3738[4] >132c<
Fine Sir 7 b g 1536[2] 1795[2] 2676[P] >76h<
Fine Spirit 5 b m Brush Aside (USA)-Our Chrisy (Carlburg) 1573[5] 1913[9] 2931[16] 3342[11] >19h<
Fine Thyne (IRE) 8 ch g (591) 1037[2] (1195) (1456) (2643) 3300[4] 4302[F] >96h 123c<
Fine Timing 10 b g 210[P] >21c<
Fine Tune (IRE) 7 br g 1248[U] 1346[13] 1576[7] 2176[3] 2789[F] 3306[5] 3393[4] 3695[4] 4077[6] >59h 75c<
Fingerhill (IRE) 8 b g 1161[5] 1308[3] 1525[4] 1653[U] 1853[6] 1968[2] 2176[4] >54h 83c<
Finkle Street (IRE) 9 b or br g 678[F] >46h 92+c< (DEAD)
Finlana 4 b f Alzao (USA)-Insaf (USA) (Raise A Native) 3061[4] >48h<
Finnegais 10 b g Floriferous-Marline (Captain James) 3407[5] 3671[P]
Finnegan's Hollow (IRE) 7 b g 2857a[2] 2995a[2] 3595[F] 4109a[5] >118h<
Finnigan Free 7 ch g 3166[11] 3627[2] 3765[P] 4507[4] 4643[2] >30h 85c<
Fionans Flutter (IRE) 9 gr g 2680[3] 2867[F] >94?h< (DEAD)
Fion Corn 10 br g 794[P] >54?h<
Fire and Reign (IRE) 9 b g Sandhurst Prince-Fine Form (USA) (Fachendon) 3353[F]
Firecrown 7 b g Royal Vulcan-Grouse (March Past) 1329[12] 2662[P] >29fh<
Fired Earth (IRE) 9 b g (948) 1522[W] 2888[8] 3415[5] 3992[2] >109h<
Fire on Ice (IRE) 5 b h Sadler's Wells (USA)-Foolish Lady (USA) (Foolish Pleasure (USA)) 3014[6] 3324[3] 3672[2] 3923[3] >66h<
Fire Opal 5 ch g Fire Rocket-Australia Fair (AUS) (Without Fear (FR)) 3149[15]
First Bee 6 b m 392[3] (1818) 3471[P] >56h<
First Century (IRE) 8 b g 1767[9] 2579[6] >85h 102c<
First Class 7 b g 71[4] 557[P] 1392[5] 1599[5] 1814[2] 2708[5] 3166[3] 3998[F] 4402[3] >61h 80c<
First Command (NZ) 10 b g 4623[P] >41dh 41c<
First Crack 12 b m 29[8] 187[4] 285[3] 347[2] (502) 641[2] 1121[P] 1718[4] 2570[3] 2941[2] 3362[3] (3831) 4093[2] (4220) >67h<
First Gold 8 gr g Absalom-Cindys Gold (Sonnen Gold) 2815[13] 2946[8] 3197[9] >50h<
First Harvest 10 b g 3680[5] >81dc<
First Instance (IRE) 7 b g 961[4] 1378[7] >51h<
First in the Field 6 ch m 1851[U] (3325) 3478[4] 3888[P] >47h<
First Light 5 b g Lord Bud-New Dawning (Deep Run) 1013[2] 1504[2] 2047[5] 3330[2] >51fh<
Fiscal Policy 9 b g Politico (USA)-Moschata (Star Moss) 4471[U]

Fishin Joella (IRE) 5 ch m 3525a^{2} **>85h<**
Fish Quay 14 ch g **3095^{4} 3543^{R} 4059^{P} 4320^{10} 4635^{6} >63c<**
Fisio Sands 8 b m (75) 159^{P} **>77h<**
Fissure Seal 11 ch g **1495a^{6} 2602a^{U} 2848a^{8} 3261a^{F} 3503a^{5} 4110a^{8} 4362a^{6} >135h 120c<**
Fitzwilliam (USA) 4 b g Rahy (USA)-Early Lunch (USA) (Noble Table (USA)) 1872^{2} 2566^{2} (2925) 3287^{3} **>84h<**
Five Boys (IRE) 5 b h King Luthier-Riverside Willow (Callernish) 3767^{9} 3895^{P} **>25fh<**
Five Flags (IRE) 9 ch g 2922^{4} 3646^{2} 3971^{4} **4158^{5} 4537^{P}** (4717) **>68h<**
Five From Home (IRE) 9 gr g 289^{P} 4801^{P}
Fiveleigh Builds 10 b g **1048^{4} 1315^{2} 1501^{2} 2568^{4} (2765) 3160^{2} 3451^{2} 4054^{5} 4213^{7} (4716) >72h 135c<**
Five to Seven (USA) 8 br g **1676^{2} 1934^{2} 2647^{2} 2821^{2} 3232^{F} >104h 126c< (DEAD)**
Fixed Assets 10 b m **323a^{5} >88c<**
Fizzy Boy (IRE) 4 b g Contract Law (USA)-Generation Gap (Young Generation) 646^{P}
Flair Lady 6 gr m 400^{5} 498^{4} **>30h<**
Flaked Oats 8 b g Oats-Polly Toodle (Kabale) **(1711) 2658^{F} (3182) >111c<**
Flame of Dance 6 b g Dancing Brave (USA)-Samya's Flame (Artaius (USA)) 59^{5} 133^{9} 161^{9}
Flame O'Frensi 11 b m **3010^{6} >98dc<**
Flaming Hope (IRE) 7 ch m (1079) 1524^{7} 2800^{13} **>64h<**
Flaming Miracle (IRE) 7 b g **1038^{P} 1254^{2} 1714^{P} (2810) 3278^{F} >57h 93c<**
Flamingo Flower (IRE) 9 b m 1751a^{2} **>89h<**
Flaming Rose (IRE) 7 b m 1422^{P} 1707^{8} 2820^{P}
Flapjack Lad 8 b g **740^{3} 1119^{2} 1465^{2} 2762^{2} 2949^{4} 3701^{P} >82dh 95c<**
Flash Chick (IRE) 8 ch m Denel (FR)-Tara Run (Deep Run) 4440^{3} 4731^{P} **>29h<**
Flashing Sabre 5 b g Statoblest-Placid Pet (Mummy's Pet) 260^{P} 400^{P} 490^{P} 634^{P} 749^{11}
Flash In The Pan (IRE) 4 ch f Bluebird (USA)-Tomona (Linacre) 1172^{3} 2050^{F} 2678^{12} (3670) 3959^{6} **>60h<**
Flashman 7 b g 3050^{12} 3541^{P} **>61h<**
Flashmans Mistress 10 b m Stan Flashman-Blue Mist (New Member) 727^{P}
Flash of Realm (FR) 11 b g **855^{4} 1140^{4} 1306^{5} 1972^{4} >94h 94c<**
Flashthecash 11 b g **1806^{6} 2754^{P} >119c<**
Flashy Lad (IRE) 6 gr g Step Together (USA)-Lakefield Lady (Over The River (FR)) **4110a^{11} >44h 108c<**
Flat Top 6 b g **1126^{F}** 1443^{4} **1803^{P}** 1849^{7} 1988^{4} 3157^{2} 3317^{P} 3807^{4} **>76h<**
Flaxley Wood 6 b br g 1766^{6} 1964^{5} 2634^{4} (2797) 3405^{P} **>65h<**
Fleet Cadet 6 ch h Bairn (USA)-Pirogue (Reliance II) 253^{4} 293^{7} 408^{2} 749^{2} 913^{4} (1857) 2038^{2} (2664) 2813^{3} 3050^{8} (3735) 3979^{4} (4290) 4468^{6} (4556) (4765) **>76+h<**
Fleeting Mandate (IRE) 5 br g Mandalus-Mistress Sarah (Ashford (USA)) 3275^{7} **>62h<**
Fleur de Tal 6 b m 741^{3} 884^{2} 971^{7} 1330^{F} 1553^{3} 1599^{3} 2573^{3} 2941^{3} 3112^{3} **>80h<**
Flic Royal (FR) 4 gr g Royal Charter (FR)-Flika d'Or (FR) (Pot d'Or (FR)) (4737) **>69h<**
Flight Lieutenant (USA) 8 b g **(1664) 1925^{2} 2776^{6} 2926^{2} (3422) (3758) >93h 120c<**
Flimsy Truth 11 b g **1122^{P} 1364^{2} 1557^{2} (1901) 2638^{3} (2809) 3047^{4} (3617) 4013^{F} 4167^{P} >126c<**
Flint And Steel 4 b g Rock City-Brassy Nell (Dunbeath (USA)) 1370^{11} **>39h<**
Flinters 10 b g 1090^{P} **>56h 26c<**

Flintlock (IRE) 7 ch g 12^{4} 211^{7} 453^{5} 647^{4} 695^{4} 734^{5} 892^{6} 1027^{3} (4389) 4501^{4} **>52h<**
Flippance 7 b g **1764^{4} 2827^{4} (3134) (3671) >75h 117+c<**
Flood's Fancy 4 b gr f Then Again-Port Na Blath (On Your Mark) 640^{8} 881^{2} 962^{5} **>57h<**
Floosy 6 b m 1820^{4} 3061^{6} 4441^{2} 4626^{13} **>70h<**
Floral Reef 6 ch m Jupiter Island-Spartan Daisy (Spartan General) 4407^{4} **>60fh<**
Florid (USA) 6 ch h The Minstrel (CAN)-Kenanga (Kris) 2886^{4} 3231^{R} 3359^{8} (3668) (3802) **>92+h<**
Florida Pearl (IRE) 5 b g Florida Son-Ice Pearl (Flatbush) (3619) **>99fh<**
Florida Sky 10 b g **789^{F} 1279^{5} 1697^{P} 3701^{P} 3893^{4} >103dc<**
Florrie Gunner 7 b m Gunner B-Precipice Moss (Precipice Wood) 2861^{U} 3197^{P} 3437^{6} 3823^{14} **>32h<**
Florrie'm 4 ch f Tina's Pet-Rosie Dickins (Blue Cashmere) 688^{16}
Flossie Hands (IRE) 5 b m Northern State (USA)-Piropo (Impecunious) 4407^{11} **>39fh<**
Floss The Boss 4 gr f Weld-Summer Path (Warpath) 3914^{11} **>1fh<**
Flow 8 b m **(1428) (1728) 2754^{P} >70h 101c<**
Flow Back 5 gr g 2909^{3} 3204^{7} 4313^{6} 4558^{2} **>49h<**
Flowing River (USA) 11 b g **3010^{4} 3343^{F} 3852^{4} 4083^{4} 4326^{9} 4522^{P} 4721^{4} >86h 83c<**
Fluidity (USA) 9 b g 66^{2} **72^{5}** (182) **>71h 82c<**
Flutterbud 5 b m Lord Bud-Spartan Flutter (Spartan General) 3468^{5} 3970^{5} **>36h<**
Flyaway Blues 5 b g Bluebird (USA)-Voltigeuse (USA) (Filiberto (USA)) 698^{F} 743^{6} 939^{4} 1141^{2} (1703) 2509^{2} 2957^{2} 4393^{3} **>73h<**
Flyer's Nap 11 b g 2659^{P} **(2881) 3046^{P} (3598) 4303^{2} >79h 146c<**
Fly Executive 6 b g Executive Perk-March Fly (Sousa) 1692^{21} 3315^{11}
Fly Fishing (USA) 4 ch c Miswaki (USA)-Sharp Flick (USA) (Sharpen Up) 3007^{6} **>62+h<**
Flying Eagle 6 b g 2824^{9} **>87h<**
Flying Fiddler (IRE) 6 ch g 955^{3} 1165^{2} 1394^{4} 1710^{4} (2932) 3497^{2} 3847^{6} **>82?h<**
Flying Green (FR) 4 ch g Persian Bold-Flying Sauce (Sauce Boat (USA)) 640^{2} 1370^{12} 1634^{16} **>64h<**
Flying Gunner 6 ch g 1085^{2} (1261) 1507^{2} 2546^{2} (3355) 4052^{5} **>88h<**
Flying Instructor 7 gr g 1793^{10} **3167^{3} (3296) 3596^{4} 3835^{3} 4012^{F} 4366a^{3} (4627) >88h 135c<**
Flying Ziad (CAN) 14 ch g **76^{2} 104^{3} 215^{8} 261^{3} 305^{3} 398^{2} >90c<**
Flynn's Girl (IRE) 8 b m 649^{4} **>50h 65c<**
Fly the Wind 12 b m **(70) 102^{2} >91c<**
Fly to the End (USA) 7 b g 647^{9} 893^{5} 1027^{8} (1078) 1577^{9} 1703^{16} 1942^{8} 4389^{10} **>51h<**
Folding 6 b g Rymer-Dealers Dream (Whistlefield) 2696^{11} **>37fh<**
Folesclave (IRE) 5 b m Brush Aside (USA)-Strong Slave (IRE) (Strong Gale) 2757^{8} 3433^{16} 3889^{9} **>27fh<**
Follow de Call 7 b g 636^{3} **933^{F}** 1537^{9} 1772^{13} 2818^{11} 2943^{7} 4162^{3} 4443^{5} 4648^{4} **>47h<**
Folly Road (IRE) 7 b g Mister Lord (USA)-Lady Can (Cantab) **2856a^{5} >71h 97c<**
Fontaine Lodge (IRE) 7 b m Lafontaine (USA)-Cambridge Lodge (Tower Walk) 2603a^{15} **>90h<**
Fontainerouge (IRE) 7 gr g 1767^{7} 1952^{4} 2897^{11} 3088^{P} **>57h<**
Fontanays (IRE) 9 b g 1828^{2} 1960^{3} 2882^{2} 3056^{3} 3447^{2} (3589) 3915^{5} 4162^{2} 4534^{4} 4701^{5} **>72h<**

Font Romeu (FR) 4 b g Start Fast (FR)-Ile d'Amour (FR) (Montevideo) (3075) 3291^{3} (3535) **>85h<**
Foodbroker Star (IRE) 7 gr g **1646^{2} (1936) 2883^{6} 3155^{6} >84h 123?c<**
Fools Errand (IRE) 7 b g **(1175) (1540) 1985^{2} 2660^{5} 2821^{P} 3496^{3} (3763) 3916^{4} >87h 120c<**
Fools Future 8 b g 4230^{8} 4329^{3} **>63?h<**
Fools Nook 6 gr g 24^{6}
Fools of Pride (IRE) 5 ch m 326a^{2} **>62h<**
Forbes (IRE) 6 b g 939^{8} **>60h<**
Forbidden Time (IRE) 9 b g **3312^{3} >88h 116c<**
Forbidden Waters (IRE) 6 b g 2844^{9} (4161) 4563^{3} **>58h<**
Forburies (IRE) 8 b m 1448^{P} 1679^{P}
For Cathal (IRE) 6 b g Legal Circles (USA)-Noble For Stamps (Deep Run) 1579^{2} **2540^{3} (2912) >51fh 97c<**
Forcing Two (USA) 6 b h 879^{5} **>46h<**
Fordstown (IRE) 8 ch g **2903^{4} 3397^{5} 3609^{3} 4051^{8} 4256^{4} 4724^{3} 4758^{2} >101c<**
Foreign Judgement (USA) 4 b g El Gran Senor (USA)-Numeral (USA) (Alleged (USA)) 3352^{U} 3730^{10} **>22h<**
Forestal 5 b g 1512^{3} 1903^{4} (2777) 3572^{5} 4061^{7} 4240^{4} **>97h<**
Forest Boy 4 b g Komaite (USA)-Khadine (Astec) 1862^{4} **>67h<**
Forest Feather (IRE) 9 b g **263^{4} 286^{3} 2756^{P} >103h 89c<**
Forest Fountain (IRE) 6 b br g Royal Fountain-Forest Gale (Strong Gale) **3055^{P}**
Forest Ivory (NZ) 6 ch g (1536) (1683) 2948^{2} 3613^{4} (4052) **>97h<**
Forest Mill 5 ch m 3085^{7} 3222^{P}
Forest Musk (IRE) 6 b g Strong Gale-Brown Forest (Brave Invader (USA)) 1275^{4} 1550^{2} **1829^{5} >60h 86c<**
Forest Rose 7 b m Derring Rose-Star of Corrie (Ballynockan) 3918^{7} 4082^{8}
Forest Sun 12 ch g **3039^{5} 3302^{P} >115c<**
Foresworn (USA) 5 b g Alleged (USA)-Sybilline (FR) (Satingo) (3026) 3345^{P} **>82+h< (DEAD)**
Forever Noble (IRE) 4 b g Forzando-Pagan Queen (Vaguely Noble) 2649^{3} 2898^{2} **>74h<**
Forever Shy (IRE) 9 b g Sandalay-Cill Damhnait (Double-U-Jay) **897^{F} >2c<**
Forgetful 8 br m **138^{4} 188^{6}** 284^{3} 347^{4} 538^{4} **>48h 93dc<**
Forgiveness (IRE) 7 b g The Parson-Panel Pin (Menelek) 319a^{15}
Forgotten Empress 5 b m Dowsing (USA)-Vynz Girl (Tower Walk) 7^{2} 293^{3} (350) 585^{3} **>70h<**
Formal Invitation (IRE) 8 ch g Be My Guest (USA)-Clarista (USA) (Riva Ridge (USA)) **1714^{2} (3941) (4180) (4475) (4621) 4802^{2} >130c<**
Formentiere 4 gr f Sharrood (USA)-Me Spede (Valiyar) 831^{5} 1444^{P} **>44h<**
Formidable Partner 4 b g Formidable (USA)-Brush Away (Ahonoora) 2859^{6} 3093^{3} 3359^{5} 3668^{3} 3965^{4} **>75h<**
Forofivetwohundred (IRE) 7 b g Convinced-Goldend (Goldhill) 1303^{3} 1569^{10} **>37fh<**
Fort Deely (IRE) 6 ch g 1384^{F} **>68h<**
Fort Gale (IRE) 6 b br g **556^{U} 595^{4} 720^{7} >78c<**
Fortria Rosie Dawn 7 b m **2704^{F} 4158^{3} 4314^{F}** 4458^{P} **>89c<**
Fortuitious (IRE) 4 b f Polish Patriot (USA)-Echo Cove (Slip Anchor) 4343^{P}
Fortunes Course (IRE) 8 b m 1088^{2} 1342^{3} 1571^{5} 2069^{2} **2568^{2}** 3281^{8} 3554^{5} **(3893) 4697^{3} >91h 107c<**

Fortunes Flight (IRE) 4 b g Tremblant-Night Rose (Sovereign Gleam) 3574^{2} 4009^{7} **>67fh<**

Fortunes Gleam (IRE) 6 b m 1573^{14} 2676^{P} 2959^{P}

Fortunes Rose (IRE) 5 b m 1417^{7} 1569^{4} 1993^{3} 2838^{5} 3442^{15} 4340^{4} **>44h<**

Fortytwo Dee (IRE) 7 b m Amazing Bust-Maggie's Way (Decent Fellow) **2841^{10} 3020^{6} 3279^{P} 3409^{3} >93c<**

Fort Zeddaan (IRE) 7 b g Trojan Fort-Jasminia (Zeddaan) 1999^{10} **3479^{F} 3608^{4} 3806^{F} (4751)** >5h **75c<**

Forward Glen 10 br g **(696) 896^{5} 1244^{3} 1578^{10} 1704^{4} 2179^{2} 2652^{F} 3094^{5} 4078^{4} 4336^{6} >76h 92c<**

Four From Home (IRE) 5 ch g Carlingford Castle-Loving Way (Golden Love) 686^{5} 1504^{7} 1705^{7} 2787^{6} **>44h<**

Fourth in Line (IRE) 9 b g 1154^{2} 1416^{5} 1783^{4} 2777^{5} 3850^{3} 3992^{4} (4474) **>102h<**

Four Weddings (USA) 4 b g Runaway Groom (CAN)-Kitty's Best (USA) (Amen (FR)) 282^{2} 548^{P} 1413^{P} 1675^{7} 2792^{16} **>28h<**

Foxbow (IRE) 7 b g **3664^{F} 4616^{F} >75h<**

Fox Chapel 10 b g 415^{2} 725^{P} 3442^{6} 3731^{4} **3968^{P} >68h 84?c< (DEAD)**

Foxgrove 11 b m **726^{5} 833^{3} 932^{3} 1063^{4} 1307^{P} 1445^{P} 2089^{4} (3742) 4167^{6} 4293^{4} 4463^{P} >93c<**

Foxies Lad 6 b g 1368^{4} 1640^{9} 2010^{10} 3535^{2} 3798^{3} 4001^{2} 4275^{3} 4376^{4} **>78h<**

Fox on the Run 10 b g **1022^{P} >44h<**

Fox Pointer 12 b g **3363^{2} (3799) 4094^{3} 4228^{4} >113dc<**

Fox Sparrow 7 b g 2764^{7} 3137^{7} 3346^{9} 3485^{11} 3995^{6} 4482^{4} 4573^{7} **>53h<**

Foxtrot Romeo 7 ch g **1426^{2} 2658^{P} 2947^{3} (3339) 3700^{2} >84h 115c<**

Foxwoods Valley (IRE) 8 b g Crash Course-Victor's Valley (Deep Run) **3334^{F} 3805^{U}**

Fradicant 8 b g 3283^{P}

Frank Be Lucky 11 b g **3984^{P} 4228^{P} 4326^{6} >108?c<**

Frankie Harry 5 ch g 22^{9} 67^{8} **>38h<**

Frankie Muck 5 ch g Gunner B-Muckertoo (Sagaro) 1203^{10} 2682^{12} 4561^{4} 4656^{8} **>51fh<**

Frankie Willow (IRE) 4 ch g Lanfranco-Winnie Willow (Kambalda) 3619^{23} **>77h<**

Frank Knows 7 ch g **3073^{2} 3296^{4} >35h 96c<**

Frank Naylar 6 b g 1334^{5} 2008^{5} 3178^{P} **>51h<**

Franks Jester 6 b g 1424^{P} 2678^{16}

Frans Lad 5 ch g 4423^{6} 4626^{11} **>36h<**

Fraser Carey (IRE) 5 b g 4443^{4} 4726^{3} **>82h<**

Frau Dante (IRE) 7 bb m 4352a^{18} **>87h<**

Frazer Island (IRE) 8 br g Phardante (FR)-Avransha (Random Shot) **901^{2} 2827^{2} (3227) 3495^{2} 3849^{2} 4133^{U} (4342) >120c<**

Freddie Fox 11 b g **3586^{P} >92dc<**

Freddie Muck 7 b g (721) (747) 1067^{2} (1982) 3045^{3} 3600^{6} 4016^{3} 4210^{9} **>110h<**

Fred Fuggles 5 ch g 3000^{8} 3337^{8} **>43h<**

Fred Jeffrey (IRE) 6 b g 2805^{10} 3222^{9} **>54h<**

Fred Moth 4 b g Cisto (FR)-Calypso Gold (Gulf of Salerno) 2682^{10} 3090^{5} **>37fh<**

Fred's Delight (IRE) 6 b g 1779^{7} 2001^{4} **>48h<**

Freeline Fontaine (IRE) 5 b br g Lafontaine (USA)-Mandavard (IRE) (Mandalus) 3233^{14} 4224^{U} 4506^{5} **>57h<**

Freeline Lustre (IRE) 7 b g 1174^{P} **4072^{P}**

Free Transfer (IRE) 8 b g **3095^{3} 3439^{U} 3712^{5} >64h 94c<**

Free Tyson 6 b g 54^{11} **>35h<**

French Buck (IRE) 7 br g 1174^{8} **>66h<**

French County (IRE) 5 b g Executive Perk-Donegal Moss (Le Moss) 3939^{3} 4420^{9} 4567^{7} **>38h<**

French Holly (USA) 6 b g 3619^{6} 4360a^{3} **>90fh<**

French Project (IRE) 5 b m 4573^{5} 4711^{4} **>37h<**

Freno (IRE) 6 ch g 1275^{11} 1583^{8} 2893^{3} 3989^{8} 4558^{7} 4770^{2} **>49h<**

Fresh Fruit Daily 5 b m Reprimand-Dalmally (Sharpen Up) 2825^{5} 4800^{2} **>62h<**

Fresh Rose Mary (IRE) 5 b m Welsh Term-Clare's Sheen (Choral Society) 3907^{7} **>49fh<**

Fret (USA) 7 b g 3933^{8} 4409^{5} 4562^{6} 4744^{6} **>46h<**

Friar's Oak 5 b g Absalom-Sunset Ray (Hotfoot) 4436^{P} 4696^{11} 4794^{6} **>43h<**

Frickley 11 br g 3286^{7} **(3413) (3804)** 4053^{8} **4206^{4} 4379^{3} >90h 123c<**

Friday Thirteenth (IRE) 8 b g Torus-Liffey's Choice (Little Buskins) **1240a^{5} >87c<**

Friendly Coast 11 b g Blakeney-Noreena (Nonoalco (USA)) 2946^{16}

Friendly Dreams (IRE) 4 gr f Midyan (USA)-Friendly Thoughts (USA) (Al Hattab (USA)) (282) 388^{5} 599^{2} **>52h<**

Friendly House (IRE) 8 b g (1948) 2871^{5} 3539^{3} 3632^{3} **>73h<**

Friendly Knight 7 b g 1701^{9} **1987^{F} 2786^{8} 2914^{2} 3326^{R} (3826) 4203^{R} >65h 79c<**

Friendly Society 11 ch g Le Moss-Panetta (USA) (Pantene) **4389^{F} 4513^{P} >44c<**

Friendly Viking 7 ch g **4522^{P}**

Friendship (IRE) 5 b g 1867^{3} 2812^{4} (3171) (3552) 4166^{F} **>85h<**

Frisky Thyne (IRE) 8 b g 3096^{8} 4248^{12} 4568^{3} **>69h<**

Frizzball (IRE) 5 br m 418^{13}

Fro 4 b f Salse (USA)-Silent Sun (Blakeney) 1699^{2} 1940^{5} 3029^{6} 3328^{8} **>60h<**

Frogmarch (USA) 7 ch g 1201^{5} 3164^{5} **>105h<**

Frome Lad 5 ch g Buzzards Bay-Groundsel (Reform) 900^{10} 2034^{4} 2655^{P} **>40h<**

Front Cover 7 b m Sunyboy-Roman Lilly (Romany Air) **(4471) (4607) >103+c<**

Frontier Flight (USA) 7 b g 21^{F} (491) 539^{F} 690^{5} 734^{6} 942^{4} 1060^{2} **1629^{P} (1875) 4221^{5} 4460^{3} 4635^{P} 4742^{6} >74+h 78c<**

Front Line 10 ch g **1655^{4} 1983^{P} 3162^{10} >104c<**

Front Street 10 b g **1650^{P} 3039^{P} >92h 119dc<**

Frown 7 ch g 3589^{5} 4147^{10} **>50h<**

Frozen Drop 10 b g **(658) 823^{2} 1057^{2} 1383^{3} 1871^{3} 2575^{3} 2706^{P} 4239^{2} 4463^{3} 4722^{P} >57h 111dc<**

Frozen Sea (USA) 6 ch h 3722^{4} 4061^{8} **>83h<**

Frozen Stiff (IRE) 9 ro g Carlingford Castle-Run Wardasha (Run The Gantlet (USA)) **3533^{3} 3913^{P} 4607^{U} 4713^{P} >62c<**

Frugal 4 b g Dunbeath (USA)-Sum Music (Music Boy) 3203^{18} 4150^{14} **>20fh<**

Fruitation 6 b m Tuam-Kenn Towy Streak (Streak) 2931^{8} 3203^{6} **>64fh<**

Fruit Town (IRE) 8 b g Camden Town-Fruitful (Oats) 1836^{6} **3758^{4} 3957^{F} >29h<**

Frys No Fool 7 b g 3084^{5} 3399^{U} **>58h<**

Fryup Satellite 6 br g 1701^{6} (1988) 2509^{13} 3035^{3} 3102^{3} 3478^{2} 3728^{2} 3976^{5} **>63h<**

Full Alirt 9 ch m **(3593) 3739^{P} 4522^{3} >97c<**

Full of Bounce (IRE) 6 b g Corvaro (USA)-Keep The Link (Takawalk II) 1966^{11} 2656^{6} 3171^{9} **(3495) 3736^{U} 3978^{U} 4302^{3} >49h 107c<**

Full of Fire 10 b g **(1997) 3573^{2} >65h 131c<**

Full of Oats 11 b g **1784^{3} 2616^{F} 2881^{3} 3428^{3} 4074^{F} >125c<**

Full of Tricks 9 ch g 961^{8} **1270^{3} 1389^{P}** 1585^{7} **1708^{7} 2752^{P} 2867^{7} 3897^{3} 4100^{F}** 4255^{7} **(4437) >58c<**

Full O'Praise (NZ) 10 br g **15^{6} 207^{2} 1035^{4} (1306) 1702^{3} 2700^{5} >109c<**

Full Shilling (USA) 8 b or br g **1829^{F} 2704^{P} 2823^{10} 3073^{4} 3179^{6} 3343^{5} 3684^{U} 3960^{2} 4083^{2} 4232^{P} 4274^{3} >56h 70c<**

Full Throttle 4 br g Daring March-Wheatley (Town Crier) 3007^{8} 3324^{F} **>53h<**

Funcheon Gale 10 b g **(23) 130^{U} 158^{8} 1194^{3} (1554) 3550^{P} (3903) (4467) 4697^{4} >110c<**

Funny Old Game 10 ch g **9^{P} 1991^{F} 2769^{4} 3069^{4} 3560^{P} >85c<**

Funny Rose 7 b m 586^{4} 647^{7} **>48h<**

Funny Spirit (FR) 8 b h Esprit du Nord (USA)-Funny Reef (FR) (Mill Reef (USA)) 2495a^{3} **>81h<**

Fun While It Lasts 6 b m Idiot's Delight-Henry's True Love (Random Shot) 1450^{7} 3052^{5} 3491^{4} 4304^{3} **>62h<**

Furietto (IRE) 7 b g 1047^{2} 1569^{F} 1990^{2} 2753^{3} **>82h<**

Furnitureville (IRE) 5 ch g 3619^{17} **>84fh<**

Furry Fox (IRE) 9 b g Furry Glen-Pillow Chat (Le Bavard (FR)) **2007^{7} 2793^{3} 2926^{6} (3181) 3354^{5} 4234^{3} 4404^{P} 4442^{2} >86c<**

Furry Knowe 12 b g **2964^{F} >102?c<**

Fursan (USA) 4 b g Fred Astaire (USA)-Ancient Art (USA) (Tell (USA)) 1444^{P} 2772^{P}

Furtado (FR) 8 b g Mistigri-Little Virtue (FR) (Kouban (FR)) **1385^{P}**

Further Future (IRE) 4 br g Doubletour (USA)-Tamara's Reef (Main Reef) 654^{6} **>44h<**

Future Health 7 b g Royal Vulcan-Jupiter's Gem (Jupiter Pluvius) 24^{9}

Future's Trader 4 b g Alzao (USA)-Awatef (Ela-Mana-Mou) 2697^{4} **>50h<**

G

Gabish 12 b g **305^{4} 361^{5} 457^{3}** 551^{6} **597^{P} 728^{5} 750^{3} 835^{3} 975^{5}** 4294^{3} 4384^{6} 4430^{3} **(4721) >25h 82c<**

Gabrielle Gerard 5 ch m Roaring Riva-Mr Chris Cakemaker (Hotfoot) 504^{3} 872^{13} 4620^{11} 4756^{6} **>41h<**

Gaelic Blue 7 ch g **1944^{2} 2650^{U} 2699^{F} (3546) (3708) 3975^{F} (4186) 4312^{2} >63h 104c<**

Gaelic Charm (IRE) 9 b m 2539^{6} 3313^{P} **>61h<**

Gaelic Million (IRE) 6 b m 739^{6} 954^{7} **>26h<**

Gaelic Warrior 10 b g **4748^{P} >74?c<**

Gaf 5 b g 1665^{9} 3468^{6} 3802^{P} **>29h<**

Galafron 5 ch h Nashwan (USA)-Gayane (Nureyev (USA)) 871^{P}

Galatasori Jane (IRE) 7 b m Mister Lord (USA)-Ardsallagh (Gala Performance (USA)) 832^{2} 1334^{4} (1673) 1915^{6} 2090^{2} (2959) 3499^{7} (4250) (4464) **>83h<**

Gala Water 11 ch m **1142^{7} 1307^{P} 1578^{7} 1670^{6} 2046^{2} >95c<**

Galaxy High 10 b g 4384^{7} **>100dc<**

Gale Ahead (IRE) 7 br g **57^{8} 1024^{3} 1162^{U} 1293^{7} 1704^{2} 2630^{9} 2916^{2} 3710^{5} 3911^{2} 4078^{5} 4336^{F} >74h 107c<**

Gale Force (IRE) 6 b g Strong Gale-Stay As You Are (Buckskin (FR)) 1052^{6} 1362^{15} 1689^{10} **>38h<**

Galen (IRE) 6 br g 1187^{4} 2064^{5} 2634^{9} 2915^{6} 3201^{3} **>63h<**

Gales Cavalier (IRE) 9 b g **1055^{2} 1440^{3} 1566^{2}** 2645^{2} **2890^{3}** 4053^{9} **4165^{2} >111h 157c<**

Galeshan (IRE) 5 b g Strong Gale-Shan's Pal (Pals Passage) 3808^{3} **>48fh<**

Gales of Laughter 8 br g 1250^{F} **>73+h<**

Gale Spring (IRE) 5 br m 1283^{6} 2872^{F} 3172^{8} **>22h<**

Gale Wargame (IRE) 6 br g 1659^{10} 1867^{12} 2808^{P} >31h<

Gallant Major 5 ch g 1343^{P}

Gallants Delight 7 b m (4076) 4623^{U} >64h 87c<

Gallant Taffy 5 b g Bold Fox-Emlyn Princess (Julio Mariner) 3365^{10} 3828^{14} >34fh<

Gallardini (IRE) 8 b g 1628^{P} 2631^{13} 3822^{6} 4187^{5} 4378^{8} >57h 87c<

Gallic Girl (IRE) 7 br m 1038^{U} 1335^{3} 1421^{3} 1877^{P} >54h 77c<

Gallopen Garry (IRE) 7 ch g 1492a^{3} >95h<

Galloping Guns (IRE) 5 ch g Conquering Hero (USA)-Jillette (Fine Blade (USA)) 300^{5} 400^{7} 416^{2} 648^{3} 879^{6} 969^{7} 1253^{8} 1299^{11} >50h<

Galway Blade 4 b g Faustus (USA)-Slipperose (Persepolis (FR)) (331) >57h<

Galway Boss (IRE) 5 b g Good Thyne (USA)-Galway Shawl (Cure The Blues (USA)) 1424^{7} 1873^{7} 2805^{9} (3429) 3733^{3} >56h<

Galzig 9 b g 3476^{P} 3664^{2} 3840^{P} 3922^{3} 4218^{4} >85c<

Gamay 7 b g Rymer-Darling Rose (Darling Boy) 4528^{5} 4650^{4} >65h<

Gambling Royal 14 ch g 3089^{P} 3446^{3} 3852^{3} 4087^{3} >91c<

Game Dilemma 6 b m 303^{3} 356^{2} 483^{2} 1145^{6} 1390^{5} >59h<

Game Drive (IRE) 5 b g 1781^{5} 3704^{P}

Game Point 8 b m 2614^{F} 3908^{9} >29h<

Gan Awry 10 b m 1085^{7}

Garabagh (IRE) 8 b g 2360a^{3} 2600a^{5} >69h 69c<

Garaiyba (IRE) 6 bb m Doyoun-Glowing Halo (Grundy) 2666^{F} (DEAD)

Garbo's Boy 7 br g 911^{4} 1653^{6} (1944) 2632^{6} 2788^{4} 3141^{6} 3370^{3} >68h 82c<

Garcall 11 b g 1022^{P} >70?c<

Gardenia's Song 6 ch g True Song-Gardenia Lady (Mummy's Game) 4708^{P}

Garethson (IRE) 6 b g Cataldi-Tartan Sash (Crofter (USA)) 1728^{3} 2841^{2} 3268^{3} 3705^{3} >102dc<

Garnwin (IRE) 7 b g 1646^{B} 1981^{3} (2548) (2926) (3427) (3849) 4133^{2} 4302^{5} >80h 131+c<

Garolo (FR) 7 b g 1644^{3} (2079) 2495a^{2} (2496a) 2613a^{7} 2867^{2} 3111^{2} 3638^{P} 4183^{F} >110?h 116dc<

Garrison Savannah 14 b g 1287^{P} >145c<

Garrylough (IRE) 8 ch m 953^{2} 1119^{6} 1765^{7} (2647) 3106^{F} 3701^{4} (4270) 4529^{6} >90dh 127c<

Garrylucas 11 ch g Bishop of Orange-Susy Carne (Woodville II) 3459^{4} >73c<

Garrynisk (IRE) 7 b g 727^{3} 3441^{2} >76h<

Garrys Lock (IRE) 8 b g Fools Holme (USA)-Tale of Intrigue (USA) (Alleged (USA)) 4360a^{5} >83fh<

Gatflax (IRE) 5 b g Supreme Leader-Polly's Slipper (Pollerton) (3853) >75fh<

Gathering Time 11 ch g 3712^{7} 3824^{U} >57c<

Gautby Henpecked 4 ch f Henbit (USA)-Mervins (Foggy Bell) 1699^{8} 2547^{18} 3029^{7} >37h<

Gavaskar (IRE) 8 b g 334^{4} >63h 68c<

Gawn Inn (IRE) 7 b g 1^{P} (DEAD)

Gaye Fame 6 ch m (1565) 1998^{4} 2746^{5} 3817^{9} >74h<

Gay Ruffian 11 b g 3353^{5} 3680^{4} >94h 76c<

Gay Time 5 ch m Nearly A Hand-Gay Edition (New Member) 2959^{10}

Gazalani (IRE) 5 b g 3382a^{6} (4109a) 4348a^{3} >101h<

Gazanali (IRE) 6 b g Asir-Miss Cali (Young Man (FR)) 898^{3} 1084^{3} 1633^{3} 1999^{7} 2503^{5} 3000^{9} 3723^{8} >43h<

Geallainnban (IRE) 7 ch g 4366a^{6} >76h 98c<

Geegee Emmarr 4 b f Rakaposhi King-Fair Sara (McIndoe) 4288^{7} >17fh<

Geisha 0 D Royal Vulcan-Maycrest (Imperial Fling (USA)) 2931^{13} >38fh<

Geisway (CAN) 7 br g 2825^{6} 3283^{4} 3359^{9} 3594^{2} (3926) (4333) 4466^{4} >66h<

Gemini Dream 4 br g Green Ruby (USA)-Dream Again (Blue Cashmere) 3075^{P}

Gemini Mist 6 b m 1707^{P} 1938^{13} 3111^{P} 3538^{5} 3998^{4} >22h 26c<

Gemma's Wager (IRE) 7 b m 1536^{6} 1797^{U} 2072^{3} 2841^{6} 3335^{3} (4417) >44h 89c<

Gem of Holly 4 b f Holly Buoy-Stuart's Gem (Meldrum) 4216^{19}

Gems Lad 10 ch g 1028^{4} (1246) 1716^{F} (1989) 4203^{4} 4699^{2} >99c<

Gems Lass 6 gr m Neltino-Dolben Gem (Mandamus) 2931^{12} >45fh<

Gem's Precious 6 b g Precious Metal-Masami (King Log) 2080^{14} 2939^{P} (DEAD)

General Command (IRE) 9 b g (909) (1024) (2065) (2782) 3598^{3} >69h 148c<

General Crack (IRE) 8 ch g (789) (946) 1649^{P} >78h 136c<

General Delight 10 gr g General Ironside-Mistress Anna (Arapaho) 3713^{2} 3913^{6} >78c<

General Giggs (IRE) 9 br g 2672^{P} >98?c<

General Henry 4 b g Belmez (USA)-Western Star (Alcide) 1377^{U} 1808^{6}

General Killiney (IRE) 5 ch g General Ironside-Just Killiney (Bargello) 3235^{14} 4088^{8} >27fh<

General Manager (USA) 5 b h Criminal Type (USA)-Best Decision (USA) (Best Turn (USA)) 4287^{13}

General Monty 5 b g Vague Shot-State Free (Free State) 59^{4} 679^{10}

General Mouktar 7 ch g Hadeer-Fly The Coop (Kris) 748^{3} 973^{3} 1085^{3} (1250) (1678) (1813) 1841^{3} 2552^{4} 2708^{4} 3013^{4} 3600^{9} 4005^{7} 4536^{3} >86h<

General Muck (IRE) 8 b g 876^{8} >38h<

General Parker 6 b g Governor General-Dancing Clara (Billion (USA)) 1296^{13} 1689^{P} 4161^{3} 4450^{3} >56h<

General Pershing 11 br g 2879^{8} 3169^{3} (3276) 3804^{F} 4185^{P} >135c<

General Pongo 8 b g 1364^{3} (1629) 1918^{2} (3047) 3617^{P} 4356a^{P} >65h 111c<

General Shirley (IRE) 6 b g 22^{4} 186^{6} 3110^{10} 3447^{8} 3663^{2} (3757) >58h< (DEAD)

General Tonic 10 ch g 1418^{2} (1571) 1982^{4} >85h<

General Wolfe 8 ch g (3266) 3563^{4} 4074^{16} >96?h 152c<

Genereux 4 ch g Generous (IRE)-Flo Russell (USA) (Round Table) 3500^{P} 3669^{4} 3947^{3} 4445^{3} 4663^{3} >62h<

Generous Streak (FR) 4 ch g Generous (IRE)-Riverstreak (USA) (Irish River (FR)) 2904^{3} 3142^{4} 3418^{3} 3907^{6} >61fh<

Genesis Four 7 b g Dreams to Reality (USA)-Relma (Relko) 505^{4} 586^{3} 675^{13} >55h<

Gentle Breeze (IRE) 5 b m 1171^{6} 1565^{P} 2680^{4} >55h<

Gentle Buck (IRE) 8 ch g 1234a^{6} >122h 61c<

Gentleman James (IRE) 7 gr g Euphemism-Lucy Grey (Lucifer (USA)) 3014^{P}

Gentleman Jim 7 b g Nearly A Hand-Jerpoint Jessy (Tula Rocket) 4182^{F} 4508^{2} >61h<

Gentleman Sid 7 b g 3720^{4} >60h< (DEAD)

Gentle Tune (IRE) 7 b g Paean-Gentle Maggie (Tarqogan) 2826^{P} 3085^{P}

Genuine John (IRE) 4 b g High Estate-Fiscal Folly (USA) (Foolish Pleasure (USA)) 1776^{11} >21h<

George Ashford (IRE) 7 b g 182^{7} 289^{3} (351) 487^{3} 581^{2} 644^{4} 827^{6} 2052^{7} 2896^{6} 4566^{4} >82h 88c<

George Bull 5 b g Petoski-Firgrove (Relkino) 890^{F}

George Lane 9 b g 132^{U} 188^{U} 286^{U} 339^{7} >56h<

Georgetown 6 ch g Ballacashtal (CAN)-Wessex Kingdom (Vaigly Great) 3399^{13} 3761^{13} >34h<

Gergaash 5 gr g 980^{5}

German Legend 7 br g (685) 802^{3} 875^{6} 3909^{8} 4077^{3} 4149^{P} 4391^{3} >69h 86dc<

Gerry's Pride (IRE) 6 b g 973^{5} 1378^{8} 1875^{F} 2795^{F} 3181^{P} 4537^{P} 4699^{4} 4766^{3} >63h 71c<

Gesnera 9 br m 15^{2} (93) >92h 99c< (DEAD)

Get Even (IRE) 5 b g Beau Sher-Bell Walks Breeze (Flaming Breeze (CAN)) 4118a^{15} >65fh<

Get Real (IRE) 6 br g 3041^{6} 3399^{5} 3818^{4} >71h<

Get Tough 4 b c Petong-Mrs Waddilove (Bustino) 1900^{10}

Ghedi (POL) 6 b g 290^{3} 346^{3} 597^{F} 658^{U}

Ghia Gneuiagh 11 b or br g 1765^{9} 2011^{P} >118dc<

Ghostly Apparition 4 gr g Gods Solution-Tawny (Grey Ghost) 688^{15} 753^{3} 831^{2} >56h<

Gift Star (USA) 4 b g Star de Naskra (USA)-Super Kitten (USA) (Cougar (CHI)) 2626^{9}

Gikongoro 4 ch g Dominion-Sea Charm (Julio Mariner) 4150^{7} >48fh<

Gilbert (IRE) 9 br g 2882^{P} >26h 63c<

Gildoran Palace 6 ch g Gildoran-Hyperion Palace (Dragonara Palace (USA)) 3426^{P}

Gillan Cove (IRE) 8 b g 3303^{9} >120h<

Gillie's Fountain 6 b g Baron Blakeney-Florella (Royal Fountain) 4471^{3}

Gilling Dancer (IRE) 4 b g Dancing Dissident (USA)-Rahwah (Northern Baby (CAN)) 906^{14} >8h<

Gilpa Valu 8 ch g 864^{F} >74h 122c< (DEAD)

Gilsan Star 4 b f High Kicker (USA)-Gilsan Grey (Grey Ghost) 4156^{6} 4420^{11} >37fh<

Gilston Lass 10 b m 158^{14} 342^{6} 550^{2} 726^{2} >100c<

Gimme (IRE) 7 b g Sheer Grit-Barrow Breeze (Laurence O) 132^{F} (208) 3045^{P} 3417^{3} 3842^{U} 4452^{W} (4564) >77h 100c<

Gi Moss 10 b m Le Moss-Kay's Gi Gi (General Ironside) 2090^{5} 2815^{7} 3072^{6} 3189^{3} 4162^{7} 4289^{2} 4318^{7} 4452^{5} 4562^{7} 4755^{6} >49h<

Ginger Fox (USA) 4 ch c Diesis-Over Your Shoulder (USA) (Graustark) 3404^{4} 4014^{P} >73h<

Ginger Maid 9 ch m Push On-Dial Direct (Peacock (FR)) 1810^{P} 1998^{7} 3541^{P} >14h<

Ginger Watt (IRE) 5 ch g Electric-Deirdre Oge (Pontifex (USA)) 3170^{21} 3365^{17}

Giorgione (FR) 8 b g Zino-Restless Nell (Northern Baby (CAN)) 631^{P} 1042^{P}

Gipsy Geof (IRE) 6 b g 3964^{4} 4299^{3} 4512^{F} >74h<

Gipsy Rambler 12 gr g 2548^{4} 3188^{P} 3436^{P} >77?c<

Give And Take 4 ch g Generous (IRE)-Starlet (Teenoso (USA)) 3115^{3} 3233^{2} (3536) 3996^{2} 4169^{4} 4608^{3} 4768^{2} >76h<

Give Best 6 ch g 1645^{9} 3157^{3} 3600^{12} >80h<

Give it a Bash (IRE) 9 b m Gianchi-Marzia Fabbricotti (Ribero) 4319^{P}

Giventime 9 ch g 1951^{4} (2869) (3153) (3563) 4110a^{P} >106h 127c<

Givry (IRE) 7 b g Remainder Man-Beyond The Rainbow (Royal Palace) 2634^{P} 3115^{5} 3342^{8} 3588^{F} 4007^{P} 4446^{4} >53h 65c<

Givus a Call (IRE) 7 ch g 948^{3} 1196^{4} 1963^{5} 2819^{U} 3060^{P} 3762^{U} 4253^{3} 4439^{6} >82h 93c<

Glacial Girl (IRE) 5 m 2619^{17} >10h<
Gladys Emmanuel 10 b m 3234^{12} 3764^{4} 4304^{7} 4520^{3} 4659^{R} >57h 82c<
Glaisnock Lad (IRE) 5 b g Andretti-Owenette (Master Owen) 3426^{9} 3603^{P} >43h<
Glamanglitz 7 ch g 870^{F} 964^{U} 1920^{4} 2914^{3} 3288^{3} 3436^{F} 3988^{3} 4168^{U} (4738) >68h 97c<
Glanmerin (IRE) 6 b g 1832^{5} 2670^{7} 2952^{2} 3412^{4} >101h<
Glebe Lad (IRE) 5 b g 4355a^{6} >90h<
Glemot (IRE) 9 br g (811) 909^{2} 1287^{2} 1513^{3} 1904^{2} 4074^{U} 4206^{7} 4541^{P} (4747) 4802^{F} >67h 139c<
Glenalla Star (IRE) 8 b g 1557^{3} >102c<
Glenbower 5 ch g Primitive Rising (USA)-My Muszka (Viking (USA)) 1640^{6} 2042^{4} 2701^{5} 3032^{P} >67h<
Glenbricken 11 b g 4447^{5} 4699^{7} >80dc<
Glendine (IRE) 7 b g 2704^{3} 3020^{P} 3667^{F} 3848^{5} 4099^{3} >44h 84c<
Glendoe (IRE) 6 b g 1091^{5} 1572^{5} 3001^{6} 3331^{F} >13h 78c<
Glendronach 5 b m Seymour Hicks (FR)-Irini (USA) (Gregorian (USA)) 1124^{14} 1986^{14} 2931^{20} 4620^{14}
Glenfields Castle (IRE) 7 ch g 4352a^{5} >84h<
Glenfinn Princess 9 ch m 503^{U} 631^{3} (880) 1029^{5} 1684^{4} 1983^{2} (4239) 4312^{P} >80h 107+c<
Glen Garnock (IRE) 5 gr g Danehill (USA)-Inanna (Persian Bold) 1770^{10} 2939^{6} 3359^{13} 4069^{4} 4276^{5} >26h<
Glengarrif Girl (IRE) 7 b m 317a^{2} (415) 605^{3} 1363^{2} 1571^{B} 1906^{4} 3156^{3} 4084^{2} 4537^{P} 4661^{P} >89h<
Glenmavis 10 b g 2079^{U} 2690^{13} 3050^{P} 4002^{5} 4089^{12} >50h<
Glen Mirage 12 b g 1330^{6} 1553^{2} 1817^{4} 1961^{3} 2708^{6} 2876^{P} 3132^{6} 3456^{F} 3919^{5} 4006^{6} >56h 66c<
Glen Oak 12 b g Glenstal (USA)-Neeran (Wollow) 3270^{3} 3458^{3} (3609) 3906^{5} 4323^{2} (4617) 4805^{4} >108c<
Glenreef Boy (IRE) 8 b g Orange Reef-Lajnata (Nishapour (FR)) 319a^{5} 4352a^{17} >76h<
Glenrowan (IRE) 9 b g Euphemism-Deity (Red God) 4631^{7} >71c<
Glentower (IRE) 9 b g Furry Glen-Helens Tower (Dual) 1192^{F} 1763^{4} 2876^{P} >92h 85c<
Glenugie 6 b g 62^{6} 1945^{8} 2545^{6} 2651^{3} 3028^{8} 3309^{4} 3485^{5} (3728) (4060) (4154) 4337^{3} 4702^{7} >84h<
Glenvally 6 gr m (353) 455^{4} 1027^{2} (1775) 2670^{3} >75h<
Glevum 5 gr m Town And Country-Peggy Wig (Counsel) 3821^{9} 4216^{6} >59fh<
Glide Path (USA) 8 ch g Stalwart (USA)-Jolly Polka (USA) (Nice Dancer (CAN)) 3103^{2} 3298^{7} 3847^{P} 4318^{9} >62h<
Glint of Ayr 7 b m 1667^{F} 2786^{P} >41h<
Glint Of Eagles (IRE) 8 b g 2603a^{S} >103h 83c< (DEAD)
Glistening Dawn 7 ch m 973^{4} (1417) 1681^{5} 2552^{12} 2708^{11} 4181^{P} >73h< (DEAD)
Glitter Isle (IRE) 7 gr g 1568^{2} (2867) (3086) 3616^{6} >77h 134c<
Global Dancer 6 b g Night Shift (USA)-Early Call (Kind of Hush) 3955^{P} 4082^{4} 4255^{3} >43h<
Globe Runner 4 b c Adbass (USA)-Scenic Villa (Top Ville) 699^{2} 906^{4} 1184^{2} 1356^{P} (3049) 3291^{2} >76h<
Gloriana 5 b m Formidable (USA)-Tudor Pilgrim (Welsh Pageant) (1388) 1679^{6} >65h<
Glowing Moon 4 b f Kalaglow-Julia Flyte (Drone) 3433^{19} >13fh<
Glowing Path 7 b g 879^{4} 969^{2} (1145) 1198^{3} (1446) 1816^{2} 1984^{2} 2579^{3} 2866^{5} 3110^{6} 3896^{3} 4141^{5} >67h<
Goatsfut (IRE) 7 ch g 1042^{U} 1921^{R} 2759^{P} 3426^{11} >21h<
Gobalino Girl (IRE) 5 b m Over The River (FR)-Ogan Spa (Tarqogan) 865^{9} 3764^{7} >39h<
Go Ballistic 8 br g 1039^{4} (1133) 1518^{2} (2057) 2887^{F} 3636^{4} 4074^{P} >103h 162c<
Go Cahoots (USA) 4 gr g Sunshine Forever (USA)-Puss In Cahoots (USA) (The Axe II) (3808) >50fh<
God Speed You (IRE) 8 gr g (1285) (1819) 2089^{2} 2568^{6} (2749) 3047^{P} 4167^{2} (4387) >53h 119c<
Gods Squad 5 ro g 3000^{2} (3366) 3564^{P} >87h< (DEAD)
Go For The Doctor 7 b g 2080^{10} >26fh<
Go Frolic 9 ch m 2941^{8} 3932^{4} 4181^{6} 4625^{P} >31h<
Go-Go-Power-Ranger 4 ch g Golden Lahab (USA)-Nibelunga (Miami Springs) 462^{2} (646) >71h<
Going Primitive 6 b g Primitive Rising (USA)-Good Going Girl (Import) 3480^{2} 3828^{4} 4150^{3} 4539^{3} 4749^{2} >59h<
Going Public 10 br g 2957^{10} 4259^{P} 4482^{6} >33h<
Gold Bits (IRE) 6 b g 4568^{F} >4h<
Golden Drops (NZ) 9 b g Dorchester (FR)-Super Maric (NZ) (Super Gray (USA)) 2658^{P} 3155^{5} >58h 92c<
Golden Drum (IRE) 7 ch g 1252^{4} 1773^{7} 2704^{P} 4237^{3} 4699^{U} >21h 69c<
Golden Eagle 5 b g Ardross-Leading Line (Leading Man) 3574^{4} 3821^{2} >81fh<
Golden Fiddle (IRE) 9 b g 1142^{6} 1266^{7} 2769^{3} 3027^{5} (3710) >107c<
Golden Hello 6 b g (1126) 1264^{F} 1576^{U} 1780^{3} (1925) 2641^{F} 2745^{2} 2899^{4} 3546^{2} 3972^{3} 4214^{4} 4480^{F} >110h 108c<
Golden Lily 4 ch f Interrex (CAN)-Gold Risk (Mansingh (USA)) 2965^{3} 3433^{7} 3676^{12} >54fh<
Golden Mac 10 ch g 3341^{7} 3553^{U} >86?c<
Golden Madjambo 11 ch g 68^{P} >71h 101c<
Golden Opal 12 ch g 1697^{P} 1951^{P} 2660^{P} 3179^{2} 3410^{B} 3578^{U} 3891^{2} 4385^{7} 4535^{P} 4721^{P} >88c<
Golden Savannah 7 b g 13^{6} 733^{4} 875^{5} >78dh 67c<
Golden Spinner 10 ch g 1272^{2} (1637) 2782^{3} (3039) 3618^{P} 4013^{9} >86dh 141c<
Goldenswift (IRE) 7 ch m 970^{2} (1318) 1797^{5} 2947^{2} 3697^{2} 4302^{4} >89h 107c<
Goldingo 10 ch g 2963^{2} (3164) 3421^{6} 3584^{5} >86h<
Gold Lance (USA) 4 ch g Seeking the Gold (USA)-Lucky State (USA) (State Dinner (USA)) 1014^{10} 1706^{P}
Gold Medal (FR) 9 gr g Saint Cyrien (FR)-Golden Glance (FR) (Crystal Palace (FR)) 551^{F} 741^{11} (DEAD)
Gold of Arabia (USA) 4 b g Seeking the Gold (USA)-Twitchet (USA) (Roberto (USA)) 3544^{F} 4282^{7}
Gold Pigeon (IRE) 8 b m 1632^{4} 1850^{P} (3099) 3370^{2} 3643^{3} 4576^{5} >59h 88c<
Golf Ball 7 b g 586^{11} >60?h<
Golf Land (IRE) 5 ch g 705^{2} 1079^{3} 1345^{6} 2541^{5} 3983^{9} 4295^{14} >44h<
Go Mary 11 b m 3582^{6} >98?h 31c<
Gonalston Percy 9 gr g Dawn Johnny (USA)-Porto Louise (Porto Bello) 4160^{P}
Go Native (IRE) 5 br g Be My Native (USA)-Terrama Sioux (Relkino) (3716) 4216^{2} (4613) >87fh<
Gone Ashore (IRE) 6 b g 1249^{7} 1987^{U} 2506^{3} 2628^{P} 4057^{10} (4151) 4502^{P} >69c<
Gone Away (IRE) 8 b g 2650^{4} 3268^{5} 4149^{P} >48h<
Gone by (IRE) 9 ch g 11^{2} 64^{3} 182^{6} 391^{3} (404) (478) 635^{3} 682^{2} 815^{4} 861^{3} >91h 91c<
Gone For Lunch 6 br g 555^{9} 3664^{P} 3760^{P} >62h<
Go Now (IRE) 7 b g 3650a^{5} >89h<
Good (IRE) 5 b g 497^{10} 634^{16} >25h<
Good for a Laugh 13 b g 789^{P} 886^{3} 1035^{7} 1328^{7} 2657^{3} 2823^{2} 3132^{5} 3891^{4} (3966) 4174^{P} 4535^{6} >92c<
Good Hand (USA) 11 ch g Northjet-Ribonette (USA) (Ribot) (424) (536) 4146^{6} (4760) >76h<
Goodheavens Mrtony 10 b g 4748^{9} >45dh 65c<
Good Job 5 b m King's Ride-Oh So Ripe (Deep Run) 2931^{4} >77fh<
Good King Henry 11 b g 3631^{3} 4022^{P} >96c<
Good Lord Murphy (IRE) 5 br g Montelimar (USA)-Semiwild (USA) (Rumbo (USA)) 3365^{2} >55fh<
Goodnight Vienna (IRE) 7 ch m 189^{10} 394^{P}
Good Old Chips 10 b g 1863^{P}
Good Team 12 b g 695^{7} >43h 104c<
Good Thyne Girl 5 ch m Good Thyne (USA)-Kentucky Calling (Pry) 1555^{5} >16fh<
Good Time Dancer 5 ch m Good Times (ITY)-Linpac Mapleleaf (Dominion) 2682^{15} 3170^{10} 4421^{6} >41fh<
Good Venture 6 b m 2920^{P} 3324^{P} 4800^{7}
Good Vibes 5 b g Ardross-Harmoney Jane (Hardboy) 1052^{2} 1296^{2} (1504) (1777) 2064^{2} 3139^{3} 3366^{2} (3973) 4166^{3} >90h<
Gorby's Myth 7 b g 64^{4} 3546^{3} 3705^{F} >72h 79c<
Gordon 6 b g 1572^{3} 2007^{P} 2577^{6} 3051^{P} 3278^{3} 3422^{3} >53h 95c<
Gorman (IRE) 5 b g Lord Americo-Alcmena's Last (Pauper) 3235^{5} 4118a^{19} >58fh<
Gorodenka Boy 7 ch g Then Again-Simply Jane (Sharpen Up) 7^{P}
Gort 9 b g 185^{11} 257^{P} >48h<
Go Sasha (IRE) 4 b g Magical Strike (USA)-Miss Flirt (Welsh Pageant) 2333a^{11} >102h<
Go Silly 11 b g 644^{P} 857^{P} 1024^{5} >106c<
Gospel Song 5 ch g 3158^{7} 3324^{2} 3691^{3} >68h<
Go Universal (IRE) 9 br g 1637^{F} 1917^{2} 2647^{P} 2773^{4} >57h 137c<
Governor Daniel 6 b g 105^{4} 182^{4} >74h<
Governor's Bid 4 b g Governor General-Maiden Bidder (Shack (USA)) 402^{P}
Gower-Slave 5 b g Mandalus-Slave's Bangle (Prince Rheingold) 1986^{4} 2911^{2} 3149^{10} 3676^{9} 4217^{5} 4376^{3} (4508) >68h<
Go With The Wind 4 b c Unfuwain (USA)-Cominna (Dominion) 1872^{6} 2889^{4} 3103^{8} 3942^{5} 4395^{8} (4718) >68h<
Grace And Favour 6 b m Respect-Little Hut (Royal Palace) 686^{6} 937^{P}
Grace Card 11 b g 3201^{16} 3646^{9} >87c<
Graceland 5 ch m Buckley-Ina's Farewell (Random Shot) 3914^{17}
Gracious Imp (USA) 4 ch f Imp Society (USA)-Lady Limbo (USA) (Dance Spell (USA)) 3304^{13} 3433^{12} >35fh<
Grampsawinna 9 b m Peter Wrekin-Seabright Smile (Pitpan) 2917^{14} 3449^{P} >21h<
Grand Applause (IRE) 7 gr g 1148^{P} >87h 93c<
Grand as Owt 7 b g 1346^{11} 1853^{8} 2000^{5} 2789^{P} >53?h 69c<
Grand Crack (IRE) 5 b g Runnett-Foston Bridge

(Relkino) 1651^{14} **>19h<**
Grand Cru 6 ch g 1640^{8} 1842^{2} 2552^{13} 3201^{13} **>58h<**
Granderise (IRE) 7 b g 801^{5} **>60h<**
Grand Fiasco 4 gr f Zambrano-Lady Crusty (Golden Dipper) 2931^{P} **(DEAD)**
Grandinare (USA) 5 b or br g 1187^{3} 1343^{2} 1654^{5} **>73h<**
Grandman (IRE) 6 b g 1360^{8} 1630^{7} 2631^{11} 2915^{14} 3940^{6} 4378^{6} **>61h<**
Grand Scenery (IRE) 9 ch g **696^{4} 896^{3} 1578^{3} 1823^{5} 2508^{4} 2801^{U} 2923^{4} 3452^{F} 3645^{7} 4058^{4} >50h 84c< (DEAD)**
Grange Brake 11 b g **789^{4} 1266^{5} 1649^{U} 1785^{5} 2636^{P} 3598^{10} 4074^{R} >126c<**
Granham Pride (IRE) 7 ch g 3048^{P} 4249^{4} >55h<
Granstown Lake (IRE) 6 b g Clearly Bust-More Hassel (Torenaga) 4097^{P}
Granville Again 11 ch g 1656^{P}
Granville Guest 11 ch g **3353^{2} 3593^{2} 4473^{P}** >102c<
Graphic Equaliser (IRE) 5 b g 2857a^{3} 3595^{5} **>103h<**
Grasshopper 4 b g Petoski-Mistral's Dancer (Shareef Dancer (USA)) 1184^{12} 1444^{8} **>16h<**
Grassington (IRE) 8 gr g **4319^{6} 4616^{F}** >52h **79c< (DEAD)**
Grate Deel (IRE) 7 ch g 1023^{2} **>68h<**
Gratomi (IRE) 7 b g Bustomi-Granny Grumble (Politico (USA)) 3423^{P} 4528^{2} **>74h<**
Greatest Friend (IRE) 4 b f Mandalus-Miss Ranova (Giacometti) 4632^{8} **>32fh<**
Great Gable (IRE) 6 b g 2619^{15} **3030^{F} 3417^{5} >46h 39c<**
Great Gusto 11 b g **3744^{5} (4280) 4748^{7}** >111c<
Great Pokey 12 b or br g **3593^{P} 3744^{12} 3840^{2} 4051^{7} 4326^{10}** >91c<
Great Simplicity 10 ch g **3446^{P}**
Great Uncle 9 b g **296^{5} 359^{5} 547^{5} >46c<**
Greek Gold (IRE) 8 b g 1666^{7} 1969^{6} **>29h<**
Greenacres Star 7 ch m 3282^{P} **>47h<**
Green An Castle 7 ch m Gypsy Castle-Vultop (Vulgan Slave) 686^{11} 787^{5} **(DEAD)**
Green Archer 14 b g **3458^{5} >108dc<**
Greenback (BEL) 6 b g **808^{2} 947^{3} 1195^{F} (1596) (1809) (2116) 3300^{3} 3849^{3} (4133) 4180^{3} 4507^{5} >104h 131c<**
Green Bopper (USA) 4 b g Green Dancer (USA)-Wayage (USA) (Mr Prospector (USA)) 2925^{12} 3494^{8} 3745^{6} 3951^{P} **>46h<**
Greenfield George (IRE) 6 b g Royal Fountain-Meenia (Black Minstrel) 1431^{6} 1683^{13} **2039^{7} 3155^{P} >13h<**
Greenfield Manor 10 ch g 2800^{14} 3328^{7} (3607) **>48h 93dc<**
Greenfinch (CAN) 6 gr g 3158^{12} 3371^{P} 3711^{5} 4055^{6} **>41h<**
Green Green Desert (FR) 6 b g Green Desert (USA)-Green Leaf (USA) (Alydar (USA)) (1276) 1368^{3} 2747^{3} (3359) 4010^{6} 4397^{10} **>95h<**
Greenhill Raffles 11 ch g **1024^{6} 1162^{6} 1513^{F} 1823^{7} 2616^{P}** >104c<
Greenhue (IRE) 4 ch g Soviet Lad (USA)-Vaguely Jade (Corvaro (USA)) 1747a^{3} 2333a^{2} **>93h<**
Green King 5 b g Green Adventure (USA)-Devine Lady (The Parson) 2696^{13} 3284^{7} 4224^{7} 4436^{5} 4542^{P} **>45h<**
Green Lane (USA) 9 ch g 103^{7} 221^{3} 2952^{9} 3177^{9} 4654^{5} >70h<
Greenmount Lad (IRE) 9 ch g Fidel-Deep Chariot (Deep Run) **3476^{2} (4059) 4160^{2} (4504) 4792^{5} >100c<**
Green Sheen (IRE) 9 ch g Green Shoon-Hill Sixty (Slippered) **3913^{P} >95dc<**
Greenside Chat (IRE) 7 b g 813^{P} **>64h<**
Greens Pride 5 br g 99^{13}
Green's Seago (USA) 9 ch g 284^{2} **340^{2} (389) 423^{F} >47h 71c<**
Green's Van Goyen (IRE) 9 b g **2951^{P}**
Green Times 12 ch g **4208^{5} 4338^{4}** >77c<
Greenwich Again 5 b g Exodal (USA)-What a Challenge (Sallust) 956^{4} **>41h<**
Greenwine (USA) 11 br g **4326^{4} >67h 97c<**
Greg's Profiles 6 b br g 3085^{5} 3272^{P} 4318^{4} **>48h<**
Grematic 6 gr g Pragmatic-Greendown Lass (Decoy Boy) 2648^{7} 2811^{13} 3337^{P} **>23fh<**
Greybury Lane (IRE) 9 b g Roselier (FR)-Troyside (Quayside) **3208^{U}**
Greybury Star (IRE) 9 b g **4319^{5} >81c<**
Greycoat Boy 5 br g Pragmatic-Sirdar Girl (Milford) 129^{2} **>68h<**
Grey Dante (IRE) 6 gr m 872^{11}
Grey Gorden (IRE) 9 gr g Mister Lord (USA)-Grey Squirrell (Golden Gorden) **1075^{2} 1376^{F} 1711^{3} >90c<**
Grey Guy (IRE) 5 gr g 3525a^{3} 4109a^{3} **>89h<**
Grey Smoke 7 ch g **1273^{2} 1558^{4} 2623^{F}** >136dc<
Grief (IRE) 4 ch g Broken Hearted-Crecora (Royal Captive) 2825^{2} 3301^{9} **>79?h<**
Griffins Bar 9 b g **(1209) 1778^{P} 2052^{P} 2665^{P} 3223^{5} 4013^{U} >56h 91dc<**
Griffin's Girl 5 ch m Bairn (USA)-All That Crack (Stanford) 950^{4} 1086^{2} 1413^{10} 1707^{7} 4290^{4} 4658^{9} **>45h<**
Grimes 4 b g Reprimand-Diva Madonna (Chief Singer) 1747a^{15} (2333a) 2993a^{8} 3258a^{2} (4364a) **>104+h<**
Grinnell 7 ch g 5^{11} 7^{6} 1343^{8} **>36h 41c<**
Grizzly Bear (IRE) 7 b g Orchestra-Grilse (Raga Navarro (ITY)) 3171^{10} 3426^{10} **3805^{6} (3968) 4312^{P} 4546^{3} 4769^{2} >42h 94dc<**
Grooving (IRE) 8 b g **1270^{F} (1994) 2691^{F} 2885^{F} (3749) 4438^{2} >99h 112c<**
Grosvenor (IRE) 6 b g 1580^{5} 2958^{2} 3295^{5} 3795^{3} 4248^{2} 4452^{P} 4719^{2} **>77dh<**
Ground Nut (IRE) 7 ch g 1288^{3} 1510^{5} 2886^{3} 3231^{6} 3572^{14} 3640^{8} 3850^{4} 4352a^{21} **>103+h 110c<**
Grouseman 11 gr g 1467^{3} (3183) 3698^{P} **>96h 97c<**
Grouse-N-Heather 8 gr m **(11) 3312^{5} 3482^{3} 3692^{3} (3991) (4145) (4258) >56h 109c<**
Grove Victor (IRE) 6 ch g Abednego-Lobelia's Last 316a^{12} **>48h<**
Grundon (IRE) 8 br g **1153^{6} >74h 67c<**
Grunge (IRE) 9 b or br g 1798^{7} 2659^{3} (3016) **>74h<**
Guards Brigade 6 b g Bustino-Light Duty (Queen's Hussar) 105^{8} **>35h<**
Guest Performance (IRE) 5 ch g 2461a^{U} 2603a^{8} 3254a^{2} 3597^{15} **>104h<**
Guido (IRE) 6 b g (1966) 3203^{2} **>77fh<**
Guile Point 6 b m Bybicello-Abergeen (Abwah) 1579^{10} 2041^{P} 4243^{P} 4575^{P}
Guinda (IRE) 7 b m **(1764) 2691^{2} 3043^{2} 3300^{5} 3596^{U} 4211^{P} >90h 114dc<**
Gulf of Siam 4 ch g Prince Sabo-Jussoli (Don) 1158^{P} 2925^{8} 3287^{9} 3733^{11} **>50h<**
Gulliver 4 b g Rainbow Quest (USA)-Minskip (USA) (The Minstrel (CAN)) 2865^{P} 3224^{P}
Gunmaker 8 ch g 184^{8} 303^{P} 357^{4} 725^{2} 1466^{7} 2088^{9} (2570) 2877^{5} **>56h<**
Gunner Be Good 7 b m 4510^{5} **>65h<**
Gunner Boon 7 b g Gunner B-Miss Boon (Road House II) **4160^{U}**
Gunner John 6 b g 1042^{P} **4100^{U}**
Gunner Sid 6 ch g 980^{2}
Gunner Stream 13 ch g **3551^{F} >92?c<**
Gunny's Girl 6 ch m 3468^{B} **>29h<**
Gutteridge (IRE) 7 b g 1090^{P} 1683^{P} 1907^{6} 2074^{7} 2820^{P} 3032^{7} **3746^{F} >49h<**
Gwithian 5 b g Shaab-Jerpoint Jessy (Tula Rocket) 1873^{10} 2642^{8} 3734^{P} **>33h<**
Gymcrak Cyrano (IRE) 8 b m 1849^{6} 4717^{U} 4761^{4} **>70h<**
Gymcrak-Gypsy 5 b m Teenoso (USA)-My Purple Prose (Rymer) 2675^{11} 3487^{12}
Gymcrak Pharoah 4 b g Flying Tyke-Hatshepsut (Ardross) 2510^{16}
Gymcrak Sovereign 9 b g 1796^{9} 1988^{8} **>38h 99c<**
Gymcrak Tiger (IRE) 7 b g 1207^{4} 2670^{6} 3201^{B} **>72h<**
Gypsy King (IRE) 9 b g **3208^{5} 3664^{3} >87c<**
Gysart (IRE) 8 br g (1286) 1522^{3} **(1955) 2551^{F}** 3615^{21} **>100h 88+c<**

H

Habasha (IRE) 7 b m 154a^{2} **>86h<**
Haberdasher 6 ch g Dubassoff (USA)-Vonnage (Levanter) 3170^{17} 3365^{14} 4161^{F} 4556^{P}
Hacketts Cross (IRE) 9 b g 75^{10} 103^{6} 182^{P} 264^{5} 419^{2} 493^{3} (553) (600) 697^{4} 749^{3} 1123^{8} 1299^{2} 1466^{5} 1816^{9} 2088^{P} (4714) **>79h<**
Hack On 5 b m Good Thyne (USA)-Wing On (Quayside) 4216^{12} 4421^{9} **>36fh<**
Hadaway Lad 5 ch g 1705^{6} 3449^{5} 3644^{P} 3910^{12} >10h<
Haido'hart 5 b g 1118^{P}
Haile Derring 7 br g (1294) (1443) 1798^{8} (2761) (2934) 3600^{4} 3851^{4} **>100h<**
Halam Bell 5 b m Kalaglow-Mevlevi (Shareef Dancer (USA)) 504^{5} 872^{9} 1177^{13} 1336^{4} 1713^{U} 1835^{R} **>50fh<**
Half An Inch (IRE) 4 gr g Petoski-Inch (English Prince) 1377^{14} 2070^{9} 2678^{13} **>31h<**
Half Moon Girl 5 ch m Los Cerrillos (ARG)-Moon Girl (Impersonator) 1998^{8} **>4h<**
Halham Tarn (IRE) 7 b g **1902^{U}** 2038^{5} **2796^{F} 3053^{P}** 3228^{5} 3352^{2} 3471^{6} 3748^{P} 4006^{7} 4086^{4} **>58h 93dc<**
Hal Hoo Yaroom 4 b c Belmez (USA)-Princess Nawaal (USA) (Seattle Slew (USA)) 962^{3} **>67h<**
Halkopous 11 b g **2672^{P} 4004^{F} 4661^{P} >142dh<**
Halona 7 b m 1453^{3} 2840^{3} (3052) 3423^{P} **>73h<**
Hamadryad (IRE) 9 b g 96^{5} 723^{4} (879) (1007) 4223^{7} **>73h<**
Hamilton Silk 5 b g (790) (967) 1271^{3} 1474^{3} 3038^{2} 3640^{14} 3816^{F} 4061^{13} **>106h<**
Ham N'Eggs 6 b g 75^{5} 453^{2} 2902^{4} 3346^{2} 3791^{6} **>92h<**
Hamper 14 ch g **68^{5} 158^{10} >88dc<**
Hanaford Point (IRE) 8 ch m Celtic Cone-Mid-Day Milli (Midsummer Night II) 1683^{P}
Hanakham (IRE) 8 b g Phardante (FR)-Evas Charm (Carlburg) **(1054) 1560^{U} 3230^{3} (3616) >153c<**
Hanbitooh (USA) 4 b g Hansel (USA)-Bitooh (Seattle Slew (USA)) 1269^{6} 1706^{4} 2070^{8} 3672^{4} **>62h<**
Hancock 5 b g **1563^{F}** 3201^{2} 3488^{3} 3967^{4} 4233^{2} (4296) 4445^{P} **>66h<**
Hand of Straw (IRE) 5 b g 186^{9} 4244^{5} 4335^{3} 4568^{2} 4707^{6} 4719^{3} **>60h<**
Hands Off Millie 6 b m Nearly A Hand-Model Milly

(Latest Model) 1820[11] 3433[S]
Handson 5 ch g 971[3] 1145[8] (1382) 1767[4] 2824[2] 2932[3] 3344[2] 3740[2] 4386[3] **>72h<**
Hand Woven 5 b g (727) 790[4] 1258[4] 1654[2] 2546[3] 2746[8] 3613[10] 4052[7] **>99h<**
Handy Lass 8 b m 2069[3] 2666[5] 2797[11] (4006) 4164[2] 4229[2] 4474[5] **>79h<**
Hang'em Out To Dry (IRE) 6 b g **674[P]** **>52h<**
Hanging Grove (IRE) 7 b g 2870[10] 3186[7] 3499[12] (3677) 3748[2] 4006[9] **>60h<**
Hangover 11 b or br g **1684[3] 1773[P] 2795[5] 3331[3] (3684) 4377[W] 4533[P] 4742[4]** **>28h 79c<**
Han Line 9 ch g Capricorn Line-Nine Hans (Prince Hansel) 3541[P]
Hannahs Bay 4 b f Buzzards Bay-Hi-Hannah (Red Sunset) 688[5] 852[P] **>55h< (DEAD)**
Hannies Girl (IRE) 8 b m Invited (USA)-Star Mill (Milan) **1737a[P]** **>113c<**
Hansel's Streak 5 br g Majestic Streak-Hansel's Meadow VII (Damsire Unregistered) 4288[9] 4580[9] 4749[7]
Hanson Street (NZ) 10 br g **2657[F] 2795[P]** **>27h<**
Happy Blake 6 b g Blakelight-Happy To Play (Knave To Play) 4150[6] **>48fh<**
Happy Brave 5 b g 3050[9] 3663[4] 4807[2] **>56h<**
Happy Days Bill 5 ch g 3548[4] 3940[10] **>49fh<**
Happy Henry (IRE) 7 ch g Arapahos (FR)-Pike Run (Deep Run) 3798[12] 3982[8] **>11h<**
Happy Jack 6 b g 1568[P] 1795[P]
Happy Paddy 14 ch g **3460[7] 4070[8]** **>64dc<**
Harbet House (FR) 4 b g Bikala-Light of Hope (USA) (Lyphard (USA)) 2865[F] (3084) 3634[F] 4184[6] **>82h<**
Harbour Island 5 b g Rainbow Quest (USA)-Quay Line (High Line) (2634) 2808[U] 3152[6] 3613[6] **>84h<**
Harcon (IRE) 9 ch g **3255a[F]** **>154c<**
Harden Glen 6 b g Respect-Polly Peril (Politico (USA)) **4579[6]**
Harding 6 b g 1196[5] **>85h<**
Hard News (USA) 4 b g Lyphard (USA)-Social Column (USA) (Swoon's Son) 2333a[7] 2993a[2] 4014[10] 4364a[7] **>66h<**
Hard To Break 6 b g 1086[P]
Hard to Figure 11 gr g Telsmoss-Count On Me (No Mercy) 1288[P]
Hardy Breeze (IRE) 6 b g Henbit (USA)-Chake-Chake (Goldhill) 956[P] 1810[5] 2826[6] 3355[7] **4007[6]** **>60h 80c<**
Hardy Weather (IRE) 8 br g **738[2]** **>68h 81c<**
Harfdecent 6 b g 1362[9] 2005[3] 2673[9] 3066[P] 3324[4] (3727) 4204[3] **>67h<**
Harington Hundreds 7 ch g 4528[P]
Harlequin Chorus 7 ch g 2690[9] 3014[5] 3493[2] 4315[6] **>71h<**
Harlequin Walk (IRE) 6 ch m 751[5] 4401[5] **>54h<**
Harris Croft Star (IRE) 6 b g Euphemism-Beau Lady (Beau Chapeau) (3297) 3821[18] **>65fh<**
Harristown (IRE) 9 b g Orchestra-Maynooth Belle (Busted) **3882[6]** **>80c<**
Harristown Lady 10 b m **256[9] 2089[3] 2758[7] 3605[2] (3751) 3838[U] 3961[8] 4270[3] 4424[2] 4529[3] 4697[2] 4806[P]** **>110c<**
Harrow Way (IRE) 7 b g **349[3] (472) (554) 722[5]** **>89c<**
Harry 7 ch g (1537) (1770) (1874) **>80h<**
Harry Heaney (IRE) 8 ch g 2857a[9] **>51h<**
Harry the Horse 9 ch g 1568[11] **2827[6]** **>60h 76c< (DEAD)**
Harvest Reaper 5 gr g Bairn (USA)-Real Silver (Silly Season) 4638[8] 4737[7] **>27h<**
Harvest View (IRE) 7 b m **(3043) 3232[3] 3697[4] 4221[P]** **>68h 106c<**
Harwell Lad (IRE) 8 b g **1175[P] (1799) 3916[2] (4303)** **>141c<**
Hatcham Boy (IRE) 7 br g **(1635) 2113[U] 2698[2] 3047[P] 3797[2]** **>82h 112?c<**
Hatta Breeze 5 b m 1017[2] 2617[F] 3038[9] **>96h<**
Hatta River (USA) 7 b g Irish River (FR)-Fallacieuse (Habitat) 26[10] 397[3] 497[6] 687[8] 950[15] 1371[P] **>42h<**
Haughton Lad (IRE) 8 b g 455[5] 586[9] 642[2] 854[2] 1292[4] 1775[6] 2654[3] 2915[P] 3607[4] **>52h<**
Haunting Music (IRE) 9 b g **1563[4] 1811[3] 2548[5]** **>83h 110dc<**
Haute Cuisine 4 b g Petong-Nevis (Connaught) 1862[5] 2678[P] **>46h<**
Havana Express 5 b g Cigar-On the Rocks (Julio Mariner) 679[9] 1013[10]
Have a Nightcap 8 ch g 21[P] (453) 638[6] 751[F] **>67h 108c< (DEAD)**
Have to Think 9 b g **719[2] 1937[3] 2575[P] 3153[P] 4239[4]** **>79h 127c<**
Hawaiian Goddess (USA) 10 b m **14[P]** **>30h<**
Hawaiian Sam (IRE) 7 b g **1150[2] 1538[3] 2819[2] (3104) 3616[7] 3961[6]** **>84h 124?c<**
Hawaiian Youth (IRE) 9 ch g **1696[2] (2823) (3176) 3496[2] 3665[4] 4159[5] (4306) 4541[4]** **>98h 116c<**
Hawanafa 4 b f Tirol-Woodland View (Precipice Wood) 1377[8] 1634[17] 1872[11] 2680[10] 2882[4] 3058[2] 3284[10] (3590) 4651[4] 4795[3] **>53h<**
Hawker Hunter (USA) 6 b or br g **2672[U] 2867[U] 3015[7]** **>98dh 77tc<**
Hawkers Deal 4 b g K-Battery-Boreen Geal (Boreen (FR)) 2633[18]
Hawk Hill Boy 6 b g Meadowbrook-Hawkes Hill Flyer (Nicholas Bill) 1687[12] 2541[P] 2787[P] **>5h<**
Hawthorne Glen 10 b g 1933[4] 2067[4] **>75h<**
Hawwam 11 b g Glenstal (USA)-Hone (Sharpen Up) 1502[4] **>48h<**
Hayaain 4 b c Shirley Heights-Littlefield (Bay Express) (2889) 3174[4] 3634[5] (3965) **>94h<**
Hay Dance 6 b g Shareef Dancer (USA)-Hay Reef (Mill Reef (USA)) 1382[3] (1597) 1791[2] (2040) (2703) 2771[5] 2963[3] (4141) 4791[F] **>95+h<**
Haydown (IRE) 5 b or br g 4559[P]
Hayling-Billy 4 ch c Captain Webster-Mistress Royal (Royalty) 1595[4] 2946[U] **>49h< (DEAD)**
Hazaaf (USA) 8 ch h Woodman (USA)-Solo Disco (USA) (Solo Landing (USA)) 1380[3] 1726[10] **>63h<**
Hazel Crest 10 b g **873[4] 1051[2] 1248[5]** **>66h 75c<**
Hazle Wand 10 b g **4004[U]**
Headbanger 10 b g **1405a[4] 2335a[4] 2739a[5] 4350a[2]** **>89h 102c<**
Heading North 6 ch g North Street-Penny Change (Money Business) 161[7]
Heads Or Tails (IRE) 6 br m Spin of a Coin-Moyadam Lady (Cherubino) 3883[11] **>22h<**
Headwind (IRE) 6 b g **1389[2]** **>84h 112c<**
Heart 4 ch f Cadeaux Genereux-Recipe (Bustino) 2889[P] 4434[5] 4651[P] **>42h<**
Heathview 10 b g **4724[2]** **>70h 103c<**
Heathyards Boy 7 b g **1120[6] 1629[P] 2077[R] 2810[5] 3187[2] 3296[3] 3571[6] 3732[2] 3941[4] 4221[F]** **>60h 81tc< (DEAD)**
Heathyards Jade 4 b f Damister (USA)-French Cooking (Royal And Regal (USA)) 4304[12] 4620[P]
Heaton (NZ) 10 b g 549[5] 649[8] **>27h<**
Heavenly Citizen (IRE) 9 ch g **(2004) 2630[5] 3033[2] 3395[7] 3643[4] 3911[6]** **>98c<**
Heavens Above 5 br g 892[P] 1703[6] 1990[3] 2692[3] (2800) 3096[3] **>55h<**
Heavy Hustler (IRE) 6 br g 3650a[9] **>78h<**
Hebridean 10 b g 1647[9] 3156[8] 4550[6] **>103h 101+c<**
Heddon Haugh (IRE) 9 br g 693[P] 911[6] **1826[2] (1968) 2176[P]** **>57h 83c< (DEAD)**
Hedgehopper (IRE) 9 b g **1386[3]** **>80h 109c<**
Hee's a Dancer 5 b g 538[6] 1824[4] 2957[8] **3092[2] 3450[F] 4057[5] 4502[2]** **>78h 87c<**
Heidiqueenofclubs (IRE) 6 b m Phardante (FR)-Affordthe Queen (Pitpan) 2661[7] 4215[14] **>55fh<**
Heighth of Fame 6 b g 1187[7] **>44h<**
Heist 8 ch g **1003a[F] 1495a[2] 2348a[8] 4110a[7] 4362a[2]** **>112h 120c<**
He Knows The Rules 5 b g 3103[5] 3761[6] 4255[2] 4382[5] **>65h<**
Helens Bay (IRE) 7 b m 1247[6] 1310[6] 1849[9] 2178[4] 3478[10] 3607[5] **>52h<**
Hello Me Man (IRE) 9 b g Asir-Tide Gate (Dike (USA)) 1039[P] 1427[5] 1695[2] 1952[P] 2870[P] **3051[P]** 3442[3] 3577[4] 4309[4] (4468) (4652) **>62h<**
Helperby (IRE) 5 b br g Brush Aside (USA)-Kings de Lema (IRE) (King's Ride) 2633[11] 3098[6] 3311[5] 3823[15] **>41h<**
Henbrig 7 b m Henbit (USA)-Malozza Brig (New Brig) 2005[13] 2917[15] 3611[P] **>15h<**
Henley Regatta 9 br g **20[3] 68[2] 215[3] 298[2] (409) 604[4] 851a[3] 4174[2] (4331) 4429[4] 4771[3]** **>105c<**
Henley Wood 12 b g **(470) 656[U] 814[3] 914[3] 1335[2] 1465[P]** **>104c<**
Hennerwood Oak 7 b m **2944[2] 3744[P]** **>36h 93c<**
Henpecked (IRE) 6 b g Henbit (USA)-Desmond Lady (Maculata) 686[3] 1052[9] 1705[F]
Henrietta Howard (IRE) 7 b m (1374) 1727[4] (2666) (2950) 3600[7] 4178[P] **>102h<**
Henry Cone 8 br g 3920[6] **>94h<**
Henry Hoolet 8 b g 2649[10] 2785[8] 2913[12] 3091[4] **>71h<**
Henrys Port 7 b g 1583[3] 1907[F] 2690[6] 3012[6] 4382[3] **>72h<**
Herbalist 8 b g **4709[P]** **>56h<**
Herballistic 5 ch m 1190[7] **>51fh<**
Herbert Buchanan (IRE) 7 ch g **(604) 728[F] 835[2] (1076) 1284[U] 1335[4] 1598[4] 4000[3] 4019[2] 4277[2]** **>61h 104c<**
Herbert Lodge (IRE) 8 b g (1059) 1368[2] 1639[3] 1907[2] **2506[U]** 2747[5] **>90h<**
Herbidacious (IRE) 7 br m **1075[P]**
Here Comes Herbie 5 ch g 506[3] 2044[3] 2631[10] 2800[3] (3035) (3309) 3696[F] **>72?h<**
Heresthedeal (IRE) 8 b g **296[4] 554[2] 652[2]** 731[7] **889[P]** **>88h 108c< (DEAD)**
Heretical Miss 7 br m 183[8] 259[3] 579a[5] **>54h<**
Herhorse 10 ch m Royal Vulcan-Ditchling Beacon (High Line) **(3631) 4522[5]** **>101c<**
He's a King (USA) 7 b g **724[3] 889[P]** **>88h 79c< (DEAD)**
Hever Golf Diamond 4 b g Nomination-Cadi Ha (Welsh Pageant) (831) 912[4] 1158[3] 1519[5] 3177[7] 3601[7] 4082[5] 4313[P] 4451[4] (4633) 4789[2] **>63h<**
Hever Golf Eagle 4 b g Aragon-Elkie Brooks (Relkino) 3898[6] **>21h<**
Hey Sam (IRE) 4 b g Samhoi (USA)-Beswick Paper Lady (Giolla Mear) 3828[16]
Hey Zoe 4 ch f Hey Romeo-Whichford Lass (Indian Ruler) 4009[P]
Hickelton Lad 13 ch g **2944[4] 3568[5] 3753[2] 3963[3] 4543[P] 4804[P]** **>96?c<**
Hidden Flower 8 b m 19[P] 100[6] 4662[9] **>48dh<**
Hidden Pleasure 11 b g Furry Glen-Baloney (Balidar) **1708[F] 1812[F] 2752[P]**
Hidden Valley 5 b g St Columbus-Leven Valley (Ragstone) 918[9]
High Alltitude (IRE) 9 b g **1321[F] 3009[2] 3401[2] 3800[3] 4225[P]** **>124h 111c<**

Highbank 5 b g 1125^{2} 1358^{2} >82h<

Highbeath 6 b g 910^{3} (1046) 1807^{8} 2789^{5} 3202^{4} (3436) (4300) >73h 98+c<

High Burnshot 10 br g 3603^{P} 3757^{7} >20h<

High Celleste (IRE) 6 b m Fat-Taak-Saulest (Saulingo) 3561^{8} 3828^{15} 4244^{P} >30fh<

Highest Call (IRE) 6 b g Buckley-Call Me Anna (Giolla Mear) 319a^{8}

High Flown (USA) 5 b g 17^{4} 183^{5} 892^{5} >71h<

High Grade 9 b g 1255^{2} 1455^{2} 3277^{2} >96h<

High Handed (IRE) 6 ch g Roselier (FR)-Slaney Pride (Busted) 1124^{10} 1308^{U} 1771^{P} 1920^{U} 3364^{6} >38h<

High Holme 6 ch g Fools Holme (USA)-Corn Seed (Nicholas Bill) 788^{12} (DEAD)

High Hope Henry (USA) 4 b g Known Fact (USA)-Parquill (USA) (One For All (USA)) 2798^{4} >64h<

High In The Clouds (IRE) 5 b g Scenic-Miracle Drug (USA) (Seattle Slew (USA)) 2668^{2} (2939) 3359^{2} 4010^{3} >95h<

High In The Sky 4 b g Ilium-Sweet Canyon (NZ) (Headland II) 4531^{11} >33fh<

Highland Flame 8 ch g 3623^{P} 3842^{F} 3960^{4} 4157^{P} 4314^{P} >56dc<

Highland Jack 7 ch g (1472) 1728^{5} >57h 93c<

Highlandman 11 b g 2903^{7} (3458) 3712^{2} 4051^{2} 4213^{P} >48h 100c<

Highland Park 11 ch g 1047^{3} 1344^{3} (2507) 2802^{2} 3711^{16} >68h<

Highland Prince 5 ch g Le Moss-Rose of the Glen (Respighi) 3907^{10}

Highland Spin 6 ch g 4423^{S} >19h<

Highland Way (IRE) 9 b g 870^{F} 1032^{2} 1576^{F} 1826^{F} 2044^{5} 3485^{7} 3822^{2} 4060^{3} 4154^{3} 4482^{3} 4518^{2} 4712^{2} (4761) >74h 87?c<

High Learie 7 b g (3060) 3356^{2} 3671^{2} 4004^{2} >87h 112c<

High Low (USA) 9 b g 1328^{P} 2946^{5} 3072^{5} 4573^{4} 4702^{3} >66h 80c<

Highly Charming (IRE) 5 b g 634^{9} 739^{4} 963^{2} 1178^{4} 1772^{7} 1992^{3} 2669^{13} 3102^{5} 3623^{2} >60h<

Highly Decorated 12 b g 1952^{10} 2792^{13} 2905^{9} >12h 85c<

Highly Motivated 4 b f Midyan (USA)-Spin Dry (High Top) 1747a^{2} 2333a^{B} 2738a^{7} 2993a^{11} 3258a^{6} >86h<

Highly Reputable (IRE) 7 ch g (66) >63h<

High Mind (FR) 8 br g 4187^{13} >81h<

High Mood 7 b g 1536^{7} 3085^{8} 3479^{4} 4260^{U} >39h 67c<

High Padre 11 b g 1162^{5} 1643^{3} >126c<

High Patriarch (IRE) 5 b g 3172^{3} >67h<

High Penhowe 9 ch m 1988^{5} 2864^{3} 3200^{7} 3545^{10} >66h<

High Pitch 5 bl g Orchestra-Combe Hill (Crozier) 4547^{8} >8h<

High Post 8 b g 19^{2} 77^{3} 2897^{6} 3050^{F} 3186^{P} >57h< (DEAD)

High Statesman 5 b g High Kicker (USA)-Avenita Lady (Free State) 1329^{19}

High Summer 7 b g Green Desert (USA)-Beacon Hill (Bustino) 3798^{5} 4134^{3} 4403^{4} >64h<

Hightech Touch 7 b g Sunley Builds-Caribs Love (Caliban) 3154^{7} 4273^{F} >38h<

Highway Five (IRE) 9 ch g (3469) 3680^{P} 4051^{F} 4222^{P} >94c<

Hi Hedley (IRE) 7 b g 4227^{P} (4418) >68h<

Hijack 6 b g Cigar-Ballirumba (Balliol) 2844^{8} 3170^{13} >29fh<

Hi Jamie (IRE) 5 b g 4361a^{F} >84c<

Hildens Memory 7 ch m 161^{11}

Hill Island 10 br g Strong Gale-Affordalot (Fordham (USA)) 4323^{3} 4511^{F} >103c<

Hill of Tullow (IRE) 8 b br g 1155^{F} 1789^{3} 2773^{3} 3147^{2} >144c< (DEAD)

Hill's Electric (IRE) 5 br g Electric-Turvey (Royal Buck) 4433^{5} 4656^{7} 4774^{4} >58fh<

Hills Gamble 7 b g 1329^{11} 2546^{12} 3014^{7} 3468^{4} >52h<

Hill Society (IRE) 5 br g 1487a^{2} 2461a^{2} 2603a^{10} 3597^{5} 4357a^{5} >136?h<

Hill Sprite 6 b m Lighter-Belsprit Lady (Belfalas) 3433^{15} >28fh<

Hill Trix 11 b g 3420^{4} >124dc<

Hillwalk 11 b g (2) 74^{2} (342) 452^{3} 550^{3} 1029^{6} >124c<

Hiltons Travel (IRE) 6 b g Red Sunset-Free Rein (Sagaro) 2539^{P} 4626^{P}

Hi Marble (IRE) 6 ch m Wylfa-Red Marble (Le Bavard (FR)) 1651^{10} 1938^{11} 3672^{5} 4073^{3} >47h<

Him of Praise (IRE) 7 b g 2760^{3} 3155^{3} (3489) >85+h 103c<

Hisar (IRE) 4 br c Doyoun-Himaya (IRE) (Mouktar) 3174^{9} 3404^{7} 3818^{2} 4414^{2} >81h<

Hit The Bid (IRE) 6 b g Buckskin (FR)-Dont Call Me Lady (Le Bavard (FR)) 1536^{10} 2812^{13} 3587^{6} >41h<

Hizal 8 b g 13^{4} 70^{6} 102^{P} 213^{2} (290) 359^{3} 460^{3} 486^{3} 556^{U} 595^{5} 658^{4} 4435^{P} >66c<

Hobbs Choice 4 b f Superpower-Excavator Lady (Most Secret) 646^{5} (874) 1158^{8} 1652^{20} 2539^{10} 2859^{11} >60h<

Hobkirk 8 b g 2922^{2} >71h<

Hobnobber 10 br g 3010^{3} >90c<

Hoh Warrior (IRE) 6 b g (1651) 2010^{9} (2547) 2781^{3} >92h<

Holders Hill (IRE) 5 b g 1125^{6} 1439^{F} 2902^{8} 3412^{2} 3584^{7} 3995^{F} >79h<

Holdimclose 7 b g 1201^{4} 1429^{2} 2807^{F} 3952 4643^{4} >87h 57c<

Hold My Hand 6 b g Nearly A Hand-Harts Lane (Record Run) 3090^{13} 3606^{12}

Hold The Fort 6 b g 1036^{P} 1171^{P}

Hold Your Ranks 10 b g 3229^{U} (3630) >94h 82dc<

Holkham Bay 5 b g Blakeney-Occatillo (Maris Piper) 1013^{9} 2626^{11} 3133^{5} 3355^{11} 3669^{5} 3921^{10} 4636^{3} 4807^{7} >34h<

Holland House 11 b g 3089^{U} (3403) 3637^{P} 4473^{F} >123c<

Holloa Away (IRE) 5 b g Red Sunset-Lili Bengam (Welsh Saint) (4539) >65fh<

Hollow Palm (IRE) 6 b g Hollow Hand-Meneroyal (Menelek) 3142^{12} 3914^{9} >36fh<

Hollow Wood (IRE) 6 b g 818^{7} 1376^{4}

Hollybank Buck (IRE) 7 b g Buckskin (FR)-Mayrhofen 1485a^{5} 3650a^{3} >85h<

Holy Joe 15 b g 71^{9} 264^{7} (587) 721^{3} (827) 3915^{2} 4178^{5} 4803^{2} >80h<

Holy Sting (IRE) 8 b g 1293^{3} 1778^{B} 1983^{5} 2671^{5} 3153^{7} 3492^{3} >75h 99c<

Holy Wanderer (USA) 8 b g 652^{F} 674^{D} 808^{3} 826^{3} 1864^{4} 2091^{U} 2569^{6} 4130^{P} 4639^{F} >94dc<

Home Cookin' 4 b f Salse (USA)-Home Fire (Firestreak) 291^{2} 402^{3} 688^{2} 1172^{4} >58h<

Home Counties (IRE) 8 ch g 945^{3} 1267^{F} 1656^{4} 2617^{5} 3150^{8} 4212^{8} 4398^{4} >109h<

Homecrest 5 b g 1020^{6} 1305^{P} 1703^{15} >6h<

Homeville (IRE) 5 b g Homo Sapien-Golden Ingot (Prince Hansel) 4118a^{9} >69h<

Homme de Fer 5 b g Arctic Lord-Florence May (Grange Melody) 3574^{6} 3747^{6} 4420^{6} >64fh<

Honest Dave 7 b g 2642^{9} 4250^{P}

Honest George 6 b g Cruise Missile-Colourful Girl (Blue Streak) 1151^{7} 3170^{22} 4161^{P}

Honeybed Wood 9 ch m 1536^{P} 1772^{9} 2838^{12} 4401^{2} (4552) >49h<

Honey Mount 6 b g (1334) 1638^{5} 1840^{4} (4099) >67h<

Honeyschoice (IRE) 4 b c Distinctly North (USA)-Indian Honey (Indian King (USA)) 2175^{2} 2669^{12} 3789^{7} >75dh<

Honeyshan 5 b m Warrshan (USA)-Divissima (Music Boy) 3494^{P} 3820^{6} 4548^{10} >42h<

Honeysuckle Rose 0 D Palm Track-O My Honey VII (Damsire Unregistered) 4301^{19} 4749^{P}

Hooded Hawk (IRE) 6 b g 1661^{4} 2932^{P} 3166^{5} 3402^{3} 4220^{3} >92h<

Hoodwinker (IRE) 8 b g 2666^{P} 3269^{10} 3362^{P} >87h<

Hopeful Lord (IRE) 5 b g Lord Americo-Billie Gibb (Cavo Doro) 1152^{F} 3823^{12} 4205^{5} 4578^{2} 4749^{5} >59h<

Hopperdante (IRE) 7 ch m Phardante (FR)-Cherry Lodge (Charlottesvilles Flyer) 1197^{P} 1565^{4}

Hops and Pops 10 b m 948^{F} 1288^{6} 1363^{4} >110dh 99c<

Hornblower 10 b g Noalto-Hot Lips Moll (Firestreak) (4758) >101+c<

Horrible Hatta (IRE) 9 dk g Horage-Atropine (Beldale Flutter (USA)) 53a^{3} >97c<

Hostile Witness (IRE) 7 br g 187^{2} 657^{P} >82h< (DEAD)

Hot Dogging 4 b f Petoski-Mehtab (Touching Wood (USA)) 646^{11} >30h<

Hotel Casino (NZ) 5 b g Dorchester (FR)-Against The Odds (NZ) (Harbor Prince (USA)) 4008^{20} >4fh<

Hot 'n Saucy 5 b m El Conquistador-Hot 'n Scopey (Hot Brandy) 2661^{4} 3006^{3} 3606^{3} >58fh<

Hotspur Street 5 b g 1046^{4} 1161^{4} 1807^{5} 2076^{U} 2915^{11} 3102^{4} >64h<

Houghton 11 b g 633^{2} 689^{6} 867^{4} 979^{3} 1717^{3} 2665^{F} 3002^{7} 4277^{3} >74c<

Hour Horse 6 b g Derrylin-Fille de Soleil (Sunyboy) 3304^{14} 3798^{P} >38fh<

House Captain 8 br g 2062^{3} 3045^{2} 4016^{P} (4210) >105h<

Houselope Spring 5 ch g Dancing High-Hallo Cheeky (Flatbush) 2047^{9} 3100^{5} 3453^{P}

Howaryadoon 11 b g Good Thyne (USA)-Butler's Daughter (Rhett Butler) 4724^{P} >90c<

Howaryasun (IRE) 9 b g 3107^{2} >110c<

Howayman 7 b g (3095) 3397^{3} 4015^{2} 4256^{2} 4579^{2} (4713) >117c<

Howcleuch 10 b m 1293^{10} 1778^{P} >64dh 109c<

How Could-I (IRE) 4 br f Don't Forget Me-Shikari Rose (Kala Shikari) 654^{2} 699^{8} 807^{3} 962^{6} 1149^{3} 2050^{3} 3730^{7} 4620^{7} >52h< (DEAD)

Howesshecutting (IRE) 7 ch m Over The River (FR)-Diplomat's Tam (Tamariscifolia) 319a^{18}

How Friendly 7 ch g Gabitat-Bucks Fizz Music (Be Friendly) 3460^{F}

Howgill 11 b g 23^{2} 2814^{6} 3071^{3} 3929^{2} >37h 96c<

How's it Goin (IRE) 6 ch g 21^{5} 71^{F} >88h< (DEAD)

How To Run (IRE) 4 b g Commanche Run-How Hostile (Tumble Wind (USA)) 4657^{9}

Hudson Bay Trader (USA) 10 b g 1080^{3} (1849) 2915^{5} 3157^{6} 3358^{5} 3531^{5} (3643) 3911^{P} 4153^{4} >60h 99dc<

Huge Mistake 8 b g 2007^{F} 2658^{U} 3016^{P} 3499^{P} >75h<

Hugh Daniels 9 b g 66^{17} 222^{6} 975^{6} 1120^{P} 2664^{P} 4235^{P} 4444^{3} 4526^{6} 4764^{4} >14h 64c<

Huish (IRE) 6 br g 2073^{7} 2626^{10} 3275^{8} 3569^{6} 4257^{P} >61h<

Hula 9 b g Broadsword (USA)-Blakes Lass (Blakeney) 4076^{B}

Hulalea (NZ) 5 ch g Hula Town (NZ)-Larilea (NZ) (Music Teacher (USA)) 2911[5] 3399[10] 3761[10] **>43h<**

Hullo Mary Doll 8 br m (888) 1121[P] 1181[3] 1382[5] 1948[4] **>66h<**

Humbel (USA) 5 b h Theatrical-Claxton's Slew (USA) (Seattle Slew (USA)) 3595[P] 4109a[2] **>103h<**

Humminbirdprincess 6 b m Interrex (CAN)-Under the Wing (Aragon) 1077[P]

Hunters Rock (IRE) 8 ch g Treasure Hunter-Ring Twice (Prince Hansel) 812[7] (934) (1062) 1476[5] 3013[11] **>95+h<**

Hunting Lore (IRE) 6 b br g (1351) **>87h<**

Hunting Slane 5 b g Move Off-Singing Slane (Cree Song) 2005[9] 2633[12] 3475[12] 3973[P] 4244[14] 4514[9]

Hurdante (IRE) 7 ch g 1260[2] 1640[7] (2662) 2880[6] 3613[15] 4048[3] **>94h<**

Hurricane Andrew (IRE) 9 ch g **1209[P] 1578[6] (2179) 2671[P] 3094[P] 4078[3] 4336[5] 4716[2]** **>55h 103c<**

Hurricane Jane (IRE) 5 br m Strong Gale-Jane Bond (Good Bond) 1966[5] 2757[5] 4561[5] **>43fh<**

Hurricane Lamp 6 b g (1470) (1867) 2747[2] 3569[F] **>96+h<**

Hurryup 10 b g **28[P] 130[6] (190) 342[8] 395[P] 2665[F]** **>99c<**

Hurst Flyer 5 br gr m 1190[3] (1913) **>61fh<**

Huso 9 ch g (451) 509[2] 1347[2] 1844[5] **>78h<**

Hutcel Bell 6 b m 293[11] 337[6] 1027[P]

Hutcel Loch 6 b m 872[3] 1999[P] (2504) 2861[11] **3200[2]** **>67h 96c<**

Hutchies Lady 5 b m Efisio-Keep Mum (Mummy's Pet) 1821[5] **>33h<**

Hydemilla 7 b m 630[8] 792[11] 905[3] 1088[P] 1323[3] 1638[8] **>66h<**

Hydro (IRE) 6 b g 1516[3] 2861[5] **>63h<**

Hydropic 10 b g 4249[8] **>25h 60c<**

Hylters Chance (IRE) 6 ch g 632[2] (824) 891[P] 1274[2] 1384[5] 4181[10] **>66h<**

Hymoss 6 b m 636[7] **>28h<**

Hyperion Lad 5 gr g Dawn Johnny (USA)-Hyperion Princess (Dragonara Palace (USA)) 2510[13]

I

Iacchus (IRE) 4 br c Mac's Imp (USA)-Burkina (African Sky) 1747a[13] 2333a[9] **>92h<**

Iades Boy (NZ) 6 b g Iades (FR)-Phero's Bay (NZ) (Brazen Boy (AUS)) 1810[P]

Ibn Sina (USA) 10 b g Dr Blum (USA)-Two On One (CAN) (Lord Durham (CAN)) 641[12] **870[6]** **>54c<**

Icantelya (IRE) 8 b g **860[2] 964[4] 1694[6]** 2694[12] **2910[R] 3551[P] 3837[F] 4100[R]** 4470[6] **>63dh 49c<**

Icarus (USA) 11 b g **3135[F]** **>43h 111c< (DEAD)**

Ice Magic 10 ch g **947[5] 1179[F] 2569[8] 2816[R]** **>68h 53tc<**

Ickford Okey 5 b g Broadsword (USA)-Running Kiss (Deep Run) 3821[10] 4008[12] **>53fh<**

Ideal Partner (IRE) 8 ch g **3357[4] 3586[3]** **>103c<**

Idiom 10 b g 258[4] 297[2] (360) 549[2] 727[P] **903[F]** **>66h<**

Idiomatic 8 b g Idiot's Delight-Young Mistress (Young Emperor) **3984[P]**

Idiotic 9 br g **3010[F] 3135[5] (3984) 4179[4] 4316[2]** **>112c<**

Idiot's Lady 8 b m **(1279) 1469[2]** **>105h 131c<**

Idiots Venture 10 ch g **2362a[U] 2602a[5] 2848a[F] 2997a[P] 3128a[2] 3383a[F] (4123a) 4349a[3]** **>135h 140c<**

I Don't Think So 6 b m 69[6] 100[10]

Ifafa Beach (IRE) 5 b g Le Moss-Greenpeace (Master Owen) 2510[15]

Ifallelsefails 9 b g 1642[5] 1849[5] 2003[3] 2178[3] 3398[3] (3485) 3822[4] (4283) **>81h<**

Iffeee 10 b g **(719) 789[3] 953[5]** **>130c<**

If Only 7 b g 3989[6] 4161[2] **>56h<**

'iggins (IRE) 7 br g 3421[9] **>73h<**

I Have Him 10 b g 253[3] **336[R]** **>81dh 110dc<**

Ihtimaam (FR) 5 b g Polish Precedent (USA)-Haebeh (USA) (Alydar (USA)) 506[7] 4568[7] **>53h<**

Ijab (CAN) 7 b g 2862[5] 3607[15] 4389[3] **>47h<**

Ikhtiraa (USA) 7 b g 329[4] 473[5] 635[2] 741[7] **>72h<**

Iktasab 5 ch g 790[F] 968[2] 1873[F] **>81h< (DEAD)**

Ilandra (IRE) 5 b m 1726[5] 3061[5] 3955[6] **>55h<**

Il Bambino 9 ch g **1680[P] 2037[8]** **>74h 43c<**

Ilengar (IRE) 8 b g Spanish Place (USA)-Ilen (Pitskelly) (937) 1844[P] **>57h<**

Ilewin 10 br g 641[4] **(783)** 2862[11] 4552[7] **4721[3]** **>66h 92c<**

Ilewinit (IRE) 8 b g Rising-Brave Dorney (Brave Invader (USA)) 2677[17] 3171[P] 3892[P] 4528[P]

Ilewin Janine (IRE) 6 b m 26[5] 1583[6] 2680[11] 3061[F] 3207[4] 4002[P] 4238[2] 4645[2] **>58h<**

Ilikehim 10 b g Orange Reef-Coffee (Warpath) 4800[P]

Illegally Yours 4 br f Be My Chief (USA)-Legal Precedent (Star Appeal) 1377[9] 1706[8] **>51h<**

Illuminate 4 b g Marju (IRE)-Light Bee (USA) (Majestic Light (USA)) 2751[5] 3809[P] 3898[4] **>60h<**

Ilsley Star 7 ch g 1729[10]

Il Trastevere (FR) 5 b g 1950[P] **>58h<**

I'm A Chippy (IRE) 7 ch g 1639[6] 1915[4] **>76h<**

I'm a Dreamer (IRE) 7 b g 73[4] 1729[5] 2001[3] (2744) 3438[9] 3983[8] (4130) 4271[5] **>95?h<**

Image Maker (IRE) 4 gr f Nordico (USA)-Dream Trader (Auction Ring (USA)) 282[U]

Imalight 8 b m 1427[F] 3234[10] 3499[8] **3627[3]** **>62h 62c<**

I'm in Clover (IRE) 8 ch g **2630[U] 3202[P]** **>72dh 53c<**

Imlak (IRE) 5 ch g 26[2] **>74h<**

Immense (IRE) 7 br g 3041[14] **>32h<**

Impending Danger 4 ch g Fearless Action (USA)-Crimson Sol (Crimson Beau) 1377[11] 1953[4] 2668[5] 2925[P] **>66h<**

Imperial Bid (FR) 9 b or br g 4505[6]

Imperial Call (IRE) 8 b or br g **1889a[4] 2997a[3] 3636[P]** **>172dc<**

Imperial Honors (IRE) 6 ch g 1056[4] 2008[P] 3798[13] 3902[5] 4445[6] **>9h<**

Imperial Vintage (IRE) 7 ch g **(102) (724) 880[2] (977) (1189) (1415) (1560) 1858[F] (1918) (2568) 2776[4] 3969[U] (4090) 4298[3] 4621[3] 4740[P]** **>68h 123?c<**

I'm Supposin (IRE) 5 b h Posen (USA)-Robinia (USA) (Roberto (USA)) (2857a) 3597[4] 4212[7] **>140+h<**

I'm The Man 6 ro g 698[5] 801[4] 939[7] 1139[3] **>63h<**

I'm Toby 10 b g **4208[F]** **>60h<**

I'm Tyson (NZ) 9 br g 3474[6] 3723[5] 4060[U] 4146[8] 4335[9] **>53h<**

In a Moment (USA) 6 ch g 1577[6] 1775[5] 1990[4] 2862[4] 3313[2] 3711[8] 3912[7] 4409[8] 4516[7] 4714[5] **>56dh<**

In A Tizzy 4 b f Sizzling Melody-Tizzy (Formidable (USA)) (688) 803[5] 1526[9] **>64h<**

Inca Bird 4 b f Inca Chief (USA)-Polly Oligant (Prince Tenderfoot (USA)) 282[6]

In Cahoots 4 gr c Kalaglow-Royal Celerity (USA) (Riverman (USA)) 1149[6] 1377[6] 1595[7] 3234[P] **>60h<**

Inchcailloch (IRE) 8 b g **(1273) (1518) (1871) 2057[6]** **>100h 135c<**

Inch Emperor (IRE) 7 b g Torus-Pamrina (Pamroy) **1068[4] 1326[P] 1468[P] (2571) 2940[3] (4092) 4279[3] 4766[P]** **>87c<**

Inch Maid 11 b m **(3005) 3363[3]** **>123c<**

Inchydoney Boy (IRE) 8 b g 4096[U] 4231[5] **>48h<**

Inculcate (IRE) 6 br g 1325[6] 1585[P] **>82dh< (DEAD)**

Indestructible (IRE) 9 ch g **(4362a)** **>73h 111+c<**

Indian Arrow (NZ) 9 b g **(2657) 3001[7] (3407) 3567[4]** **>82dh 104c<**

Indian Crown 7 b m 834[R] 905[R] 1388[10] 4255[6]

Indian Delight 7 br g **3086[3] 3339[3] 3537[3]** **>74c<**

Indian Jockey 5 b g (751) (963) 1193[3] 1502[7] 2670[5] **(2873) (3229) (3470) (4219) (4274)** (4702) **(4757) (4793)** **>86h 139c<**

Indian Knight 12 b g **4432[6] 4730[U]** **>91?c<**

Indian Minor 13 b g Jimsun-Indian Whistle (Rugantino) 259[2] 357[5] 749[P] 1198[7] **>41h<**

Indian Quest 8 b g 1661[9] 1813[3] 2797[6] 3554[3] 3807[F] **>81h<**

Indian Sunset 4 ch c Indian Ridge-Alanood (Northfields (USA)) 501[7] 2050[P]

Indian Temple 6 ch g 1448[11] 1767[8] 2664[2] 2943[6] **3538[4] 4021[3] 4402[4]** **>47h 67c<**

Indian Tracker 7 b g **(2039) 2883[2] 3616[11]** **>132c<**

Indian Wolf 4 ch c Indian Ridge-Red Riding Hood (FR) (Mummy's Pet) 881[5] 962[F] 1980[P] **>8h<**

Indicator 5 b g 2669[8] 3032[2] **>77h<**

Indie Rock 7 b g **4748[6] 4799[2]** **>83h 86c<**

Indira 4 b f Indian Ridge-Princess Rosananti (IRE) (Shareef Dancer (USA)) 753[2] 836[3] 912[3] (1149) 1332[U] 1526[13] 1675[5] **>62h<**

Indrapura (IRE) 5 b g Gallic League-Stella Ann (Ahonoora) (295) (300) (687) (834) (1118) (1327) **>81h<**

Induna Mkubwa 4 ch c Be My Chief (USA)-Hyatti (Habitat) 2070[14] 2925[11] **>34h<**

Infamous (USA) 4 ch g Diesis-Name And Fame (USA) (Arts And Letters) 3174[3] 3404[F] 3601[2] **>79h<**

Influence Pedler 4 b g Keen-La Vie En Primrose (Henbit (USA)) 1900[6] (3168) 3566[2] 4048[8] 4273[3] 4532[3] **>86h<**

Ingletonian 8 b g 2617[4] (2957) (3398) (3559) 3791[2] 4212[4] 4397[7] **>115?h 89dc<**

In Good Faith 5 b g 794[4] 1666[F] 4749[4] (4759) **>72h<**

Ingram Valley 7 b m 467[4] **>58h<**

In Harmony 5 ch m Nicholas Bill-Precociously (Precocious) 4433[12]

Inishmann (IRE) 6 ch g Soughaan (USA)-Danova (FR) (Dan Cupid) 4231[6] 4698[P] **>34h<**

Injunction (IRE) 6 ch g 101[14] **>62h<**

Inn At the Top 5 b g Top Ville-Woolpack (Golden Fleece (USA)) 871[2] (1042) 1689[2] (1907) (2781) **>92h<**

Inner Temple 7 b g 954[2] **>63h< (DEAD)**

Inniscein (IRE) 9 b g **4351a[U]** **>56h 84c<**

Innocent George 8 b g 1439[6] 1779[4] 3035[4] 3346[5] 4223[10] 4415[4] 4534[P] **>55h<**

Innovate (IRE) 5 b m Posen (USA)-Innate (Be My Native (USA)) 4580[7] **>35fh<**

Innovative (IRE) 6 br g 4352a[12] **>73h<**

Insiouxbordinate 5 ch g 718[P]

Instantaneous 5 b m Rock City-Mainmast (Bustino) 137[8] **>40h<**

Inteabadun 5 ch g 287[R]

Intendant 5 b g 1187[P]

Intermagic 7 ch g 1636[3] 2777[12] **3008[3]** 3421[11]

3562^P 4386^4 **>61dh<**
In The Future (IRE) 6 b m Phardante (FR)-Chief Dilke (Saulingo) 686^{10}
In The Rough (IRE) 6 b g 3275^4 **>80h<**
In The Van 5 b g Bedford (USA)-Sea Countess (Ercolano (USA)) 2510^2 3042^7 **>71fh<**
Into The Black (IRE) 6 ch g Over The River (FR)-Legal Fortune (Cash And Courage) 2640^3 3142^2 (3828) **>68fh<**
Into the Red 13 ch g **(1266) (1513) 2616^4 3294^2 >137c<**
Into The Web (IRE) 6 br g Noalto-Elena's Beauty (Tarqogan) 3184^2 3406^3 **>64h<**
Into the West (IRE) 8 b or br g (3371) 3483^2 3910^4 **>80+h<**
In Truth 9 ch g **2748^3 2901^4 3292^U 3413^5 >74h 111c<**
Invasion 13 b g **3018^P 3223^P >102dc<**
Invercargill (NZ) 5 b g Sound Reason (CAN)-Szabo (NZ) (Imperial March (CAN)) (2675) **>55fh< (DEAD)**
Invest Wisely 5 ch g Dashing Blade-Saniette (Crystal Palace (FR)) (1967) 2802^4 **>76h<**
Inyougoblue (IRE) 5 b g Fools Holme (USA)-Blue Parrot (FR) (Lyphard (USA)) 3691^P
Ionio (USA) 6 ch g Silver Hawk (USA)-Private View (USA) (Mr Prospector (USA)) (1659) 1921^2 2781^4 2886^5 (3364) 3796^7 **>79h<**
Iranos (FR) 5 b g Labus (FR)-Misvaria (FR) (On My Way (USA)) (1431) (2661) 3042^5 3619^{14} **>72fh<**
Irbee 5 b g Gunner B-Cupids Bower (Owen Dudley) 58^5
I Recall (IRE) 6 b g 1394^7 1651^9 3012^4 3234^7 3424^4 3818^5 **>54h<**
I Remember You (IRE) 7 ch g **738^5 903^3 >60h 54c<**
Irene's Pet 7 ch g 4382^7 4625^9 4794^2 **>66h<**
Irie Mon (IRE) 5 b g 137^{11} 183^3 (288) 353^2 490^6 687^5 743^4 4295^{12} 4451^2 4795^4 **>60h<**
Irish Buzz (IRE) 5 b g 1843^6 2898^{18} 3032^P **>58h<**
Irish Delight 5 gr g Pragmatic-Kelly's Delight (IRE) (Never Got A Chance) 133^5 1685^6 2073^4 4224^5 4625^7 **>62h<**
Irish Dominion 7 b g 3894^P 4289^3 4548^7 4731^3 **>38h<**
Irish Emerald 10 b g Taufan (USA)-Gaelic Jewel (Scottish Rifle) 3136^4 **>42h<**
Irish Kinsman 4 b g Distant Relative-Inesdela (Wolver Hollow) 1444^7 2060^9 2815^{10} 3583^9 **>20h<**
Irish Light (IRE) 9 ch g Orchestra-Lets Cruise (Deep Run) **3617^4 >107c<**
Irish Mist 5 b g Cardinal Flower-Solent Express (Undulate (USA)) 4554^8 **>30fh<**
Irish Oasis (IRE) 4 b g Mazaad-Alpenwind (Tumble Wind (USA)) 4477^F
Irish Peace (IRE) 9 ch g Hold Your Peace (USA)-Tajniak (USA) (Irish River (FR)) **2341a^4 2856a^7 >79h 100c<**
Irish Perry 10 b m 1118^9 1568^{13} **1771^7 1955^2 >53h<**
Irish Stamp (IRE) 8 b g **580a^2 930a^2 1385^2 >80h 119c<**
Irish Stout (IRE) 6 b g Buckskin (FR)-Winning Nora **3391a^2 >98c<**
Irish Wildcard (NZ) 9 b g 73^5 1178^6 1772^3 1848^4 **>59h<**
Iron N Gold 5 b g (955) 1709^2 2771^P 3272^9 3570^3 (3623) 3904^4 4101^5 **>72h<**
Irrepressible (IRE) 6 b g 788^8 **>43h<**
Isaiah 8 gr g 1715^P 1954^3 2670^2 3183^5 3666^5 4510^F **>89h<**
I Say Dancer (IRE) 4 b f Distinctly North (USA)-Lady Marigot (Lord Gayle (USA)) 962^9
Ishma (IRE) 6 b g **860^P 1009^P 4449^R 4618^P**
Isis Dawn 5 b m Rakaposhi King-Dawn Encounter (Rymer) 3494^7 (4224) 4528^3 **>79h<**
Island Chief (IRE) 8 b g **(1806) >84h 126+c<**
Island Gale 12 br g **3027^P**
Island Jewel 9 ch g **1632^P** 4207^P
Islandreagh (IRE) 6 gr m **532^P 733^3 1248^6 1943^4 3092^P >62c<**
Island Vision (IRE) 7 b g 97^D 128^2 (211) **>80h<**
Islawen Lady 4 b f Relief Pitcher-Thorngirl (Reformed Character) 3290^7 **>39fh< (DEAD)**
Ismeno 6 b g (1841) 2666^2 **>89h<**
Istabraq (IRE) 5 b g Sadler's Wells (USA)-Betty's Secret (USA) (Secretariat (USA)) 1485a^2 (1757a) (2347a) (2995a) (3613) (4355a) **>101++h<**
Itani 5 b g Tuam-Kenn Towy Streak (Streak) 2624^P 4097^P
Ita's Fellow (IRE) 9 ch g Decent Fellow-Castle Ita (Midland Gayle) **4471^U 4631^4 >83c<**
Its a Deal 11 b g **4057^P 4576^P >69dc<**
It's A Gem 8 ch g (1171) **>78h<**
Itsahardlife (IRE) 6 ch g Air Display (USA)-Clauin Cearaban (Orchestra) 2572^7 2917^{17} 3910^{15} **>8h<**
Itsajungleoutthere (IRE) 7 ch g **3617^P >21h 90c<**
Its A Myth 8 b m Itsu (USA)-Laputum (Rage Royal) 218^P
Its a Snip 12 ch g **726^4 930a^3 1385^P >51h 100?c<**
It's Dawan 4 b g Siberian Express (USA)-Diami (Swing Easy (USA)) 1011^B 1377^{10} 2705^P **>55h<**
Itsgoneoff 8 br g **3353^P >122c< (DEAD)**
Itsgonnashine 8 ch m Itsu (USA)-Shesheen (Lauso) 4376^{13} **>9h<**
Its Grand 8 b g **64^P 1038^5 1285^4 1426^4 1582^8** 1962^8 2088^5 **3339^P** 3892^5 4096^3 4378^9 **>60h 81c<**
Itspenshams 8 ch m Itsu (USA)-Pensham's Lawyer (Spanish Lawyer) 2550^{12} **>30h<**
It'sthebusiness 5 b g Most Welcome-Douceur (USA) (Shadeed (USA)) 2668^F **(DEAD)**
Its Unbelievable 7 ch g **136^6 >77h 103dc<**
Ivory Coaster (NZ) 6 b g 1203^3 1581^7 2791^4 3084^3 3847^2 4188^2 **>74h<**
Ivy Boy (IRE) 7 ch g **2007^8 >79h 72c<**
Ivy Edith 7 b m 75^7 (103) (255) **>97h<**
Ivy House (IRE) 9 b g **1038^2 1122^U (1307) (1778)** 3162^2 **3993^P >109h 110c<**
Izza 6 b m 1645^5 2702^F **>78h< (DEAD)**

J

Jaazim 7 ch g 812^5 1053^7 **>60h<**
Jabaroot (IRE) 6 b g 700^2 805^5 3309^P
Jac Del Prince 7 b g **1206^P 1582^2 2704^4 2947^{10} 3181^2 3409^F 4245^5 4383^4 >47h 88dc<**
Jack (IRE) 5 br g Be My Native (USA)-Martialette (Welsh Saint) 1774^7 2938^6 **>43fh<**
Jackamus (IRE) 6 b br g Noalto-Mel's Day (Dominion Day) 24^8 133^{15} 1950^P 3628^P
Jack Button (IRE) 8 b g 1019^2 1647^8 **>115h<**
Jack Doyle (IRE) 6 ch g **1346^3 1525^F 1780^P 3001^2 3329^P >88h 109c<**
Jack Gallagher 6 gr g 1457^2 1800^2 2822^2 3552^8 **>69h<**
Jackho 5 b g Welsh Captain-Celdeed (Celtic Cone) 1033^7 1362^{14} 1457^{14} 1777^7 **>21h<**
Jack of Diamonds 9 ch g True Song-Fiesta Day (Weathercock) 1835^P **2704^F** 2907^P
Jack Robbo (IRE) 5 br g Montelimar (USA)-Derring Lass (Derring Rose) 2750^4 3142^9 **>50fh<**
Jackson Flint 9 b g 1586^6 1813^2 3146^3 (3362) 4439^3 **>77h 106c<**
Jackson Park 4 gr g Domynsky-Hysteria (Prince Bee) 906^5 1158^2 (1652) 1940^3 2615^3 (2784) 3291^6 **>87h<**
Jacksons Bay 7 b g 961^9 **1073^6 1552^F 1708^3 1812^F >60c< (DEAD)**
Jack Sound 11 b g **4560^4 >100?c<**
Jack Tanner (IRE) 8 b br g (1090) (1280) 1870^2 **>100h<**
Jack the Td (IRE) 8 b g **3460^U >54h<**
Jacob's Wife 7 br m **2009^F 2660^P 3198^4 3567^F (4379) 4629^5 >67h 111c<**
Jadidh 9 b m 1196^7 1286^4 1429^F 1586^9 2659^P 2877^6 **>52h<**
Jailbreaker 10 ch g **1697^4 1951^3 2823^4 3113^3 3333^F 3629^2 4535^P 4659^5 >89?c<**
Jaime's Joy 7 b m 794^{10} 954^{11} 1261^P 4273^5 4458^6 4556^5
Jakes Justice (IRE) 6 b g 1388^3 1938^8 2677^3 3549^7 **>68h<**
Jalapeno (IRE) 6 b g 788^2 **>70h<**
Jalcanto 7 ch g 747^2 **>105h<**
Jalmaid 5 ch m Jalmood (USA)-Misowni (Niniski (USA)) 1666^8 1821^6 2503^6 2629^6 2862^2 (3711) 3971^2 **>55h<**
Jamaican Flight (USA) 4 b c Sunshine Forever (USA)-Kalamona (USA) (Hawaii) 3158^U 3305^R 3544^5 3964^2 (4696) (4798) **>82h<**
Jamarsam (IRE) 9 b g **802^P 1022^P**
James Pigg 10 b g **3147^6 3598^P 4167^5 4463^2 4647^4 >67h 121dc<**
James the First 9 ch g **886^5 1169^3 1430^2 (1949) 3009^P 3401^4 (3919) 4379^4 4553^4 >92h 121dc<**
Jameswick 7 b g **132^6 263^5 472^4 602^4 >45h 65c<**
Jamies First (IRE) 4 ch c Commanche Run-Avionne (Derrylin) 2070^{13} 2751^P 3755^9 **>30h<**
Jammy Jenny 4 ch f Rakaposhi King-Moaning Jenny (Privy Seal) 1595^2 1953^P **>48h< (DEAD)**
Japodene 9 b m **4748^P**
Jari (USA) 6 b g 859^P **>10h<**
Jarrow 6 ch g 1345^F 1667^{10} 1992^F 2541^6 2744^{10} 2953^5 3091^7 3803^9 **>43h<**
Jarvey (IRE) 5 ch g 455^7 **>24h<**
Jasilu 7 ch m **(1865) 2658^P 3043^3 3360^3 3617^P (3934) (4279) 4417^P >98c<**
Jason's Boy 7 b g **3113^5 3289^2 3452^4 3707^3 3929^P >66h 92c<**
Jasons Farm 7 ch g **3470^P 3682^F** 3989^{10}
Jassu 11 br g **314a^P 763a^5 846a^3 1750a^3 2346a^4 2848a^{11} >125c<**
Jathib (CAN) 6 ch g **(744) (860) 1066^2 (2745) 2933^2 4062^P >122h 125+c<**
Jaunty General 6 b g 1345^2 1689^8 2177^P 4187^{10} 4335^5 **>47h<**
Jaunty Gig 11 b g **3886^9 4148^U 4336^9 4503^2 >95c<**
Java Red (IRE) 5 b g Red Sunset-Coffee Bean (Doulab (USA)) 743^3 **>60h<**
Java Shrine (USA) 6 b g 21^F 183^{11} 600^5 749^8 879^7 1299^8 1569^P 1861^8 **>51dh<**
Javelin Cool (IRE) 6 gr g 1085^5 1323^7 **>20h<**
Jawani (IRE) 9 b g 221^4 **>105h<**
Jayandoubleu (IRE) 8 b g Buckskin (FR)-Lucky House (Pollerton) **4704^2 >88c<**
Jaydeebee 6 b m Buckley-Miss Poker Face (Raise You Ten) 1177^5 1966^6 2757^4 **>49fh<**
Jay Em Ess (NZ) 8 b g 2820^6 3442^4 3949^3 4652^4 **>64h<**
Jayfcee 5 b g 1801^4 2673^{11} 2927^3 3483^{12} 3967^8 **>69h<**
Jay Jay's Voyage 14 b g **(3891) 4142^4 >84c<**
Jazilah (FR) 9 br g 1267^7 1656^6 1804^{10} 1942^4 2617^P **>85h<**

Jazz Duke 4 ch g Rising-Gone (Whistling Wind) 4008^{8} **>59fh<**
Jazzman (IRE) 5 b g Black Minstrel-Carbery Star (Kemal (FR)) 1867^{9} 2812^{6} (3172) 3552^{4} **>78h<**
J B Lad 11 b g **3055^{P} 3363^{4} 4022^{3} 4323^{P} 4560^{6} 4640^{U}** **>90c<**
Jean de Florette (USA) 6 b g 630^{6} 910^{10} **>59h< (DEAD)**
Jebi (USA) 7 b g Phone Trick (USA)-Smokey Legend (USA) (Hawaii) 344^{3} **>55h<**
Jed Abbey 5 gr m Alias Smith (USA)-Lurdenlaw Rose (New Brig) 858^{R} 1026^{8} 2504^{8} 4152^{P} **>29h<**
Jeffell 7 gr g **(1486a) 2335a^{6} (3260a) 4116a^{2} (4366a) >99h 128+c<**
Jefferies 8 br g (1542) 1767^{2} 2817^{6} (3114) 3554^{2} **>84h<**
Jelali (IRE) 4 b g Last Tycoon-Lautreamont (Auction Ring (USA)) (1712) 2865^{P} 3283^{P} **>65dh<**
Jemaro (IRE) 6 b g Tidaro (USA)-Jeremique (Sunny Way) 1124^{11} 2938^{W} 3170^{7} 4217^{P} **>56fh<**
Jemima Puddleduck 6 ch m 1282^{U} 1832^{7} 2631^{3} 3035^{F} **>74h<**
Jendee (IRE) 9 b g **645^{4} 683^{P} (896) 1082^{3}** 1304^{P} **2046^{4} 2630^{P} 2956^{5} 3824^{5} 4503^{3}** **>91c<**
Jendorcet 7 b m 3612^{3} 3825^{12} 4163^{5} 4390^{4} 4505^{3} **>52h<**
Jennie's Prospect 6 b g Rakaposhi King-Jennie Pat (Rymer) 1296^{15} 1926^{8} 3330^{3} 3483^{9} **>40h<**
Jennyellen (IRE) 8 b m 55^{3} (185) 301^{F} 394^{F} 4727^{8} **>73h<**
Jenzsoph (IRE) 6 br m (264) 362^{2} 502^{F} 651^{F} 4340^{U} (4436) (4639) **>82h<**
Jerevan (CZE) 8 b g Patcher (CZE)-Jistota (CZE) (Seal (CZE)) 154a^{3}
Jervaulx (IRE) 6 b g Le Bavard (FR)-Saltee Star (Arapaho) 1296^{12} (2785) 3026^{2} 3265^{7} 3534^{2} 3807^{7} 4204^{10} (4450) 4750^{3} **>82h<**
Jessica One (IRE) 6 b m Supreme Leader-Lochadoo (Lochnager) 1296^{11} 2675^{4} 3440^{2} **>55fh<**
Jessolle 5 gr m Scallywag-Dark City (Sweet Monday) 1296^{14} 2924^{5} 3158^{9} 3271^{9} 3802^{3} (4075) 4285^{P} (4399) (4628) 4760^{2} **>81+h<**
Jet Boys (IRE) 7 b g 1261^{2} 1541^{5} 3845^{3} **>75dh<**
Jet Files (IRE) 6 ro g 1801^{5} 2759^{11} 3355^{P} **>48h<**
Jet Rules (IRE) 7 b g 1258^{9} **(3020) 3165^{3} >104h 115c<**
Jet Specials (IRE) 4 b g Be My Native (USA)-Glencuragh (Deep Run) 3304^{10} **>49fh<**
Jewel Thief 7 b g 551^{7} **972^{3} 1328^{8} 1763^{8}** 4071^{6} 4236^{9} 4401^{8} 4658^{6} **>59h<**
Jewel Trader 5 b g 1938^{16} **>25h<**
Jhal Frezi 9 b g 954^{4} 1200^{6} **1763^{5} (4083) >68h 85c<**
Jigginstown 10 b g 1349^{8} 1654^{10} 2076^{P} 2915^{3} 3157^{8} 3807^{5} 4309^{13} 4575^{4} **>58h 89++c<**
Jigtime 8 b m **(3397) (3793) (4208) >111c<**
Jills Joy (IRE) 6 b g 866^{4} 1309^{3} 1539^{2} 1842^{F} 2627^{8} **>62h<**
Jimbalou 14 b g 4005^{9} (4622) 4803^{P} **>60+h<**
Jimmy O'Dea 10 br g **94^{6} 158^{P} 256^{8} (4503) 4740^{2} >62h 107c<**
Jimmy's Cross (IRE) 7 ch g 810^{P} **>93h<**
Jimmy Sprite 6 b g Silly Prices-Little Mittens (Little Buskins) 2180^{6} **>15fh<**
Jimmy the Jackdaw 10 b g **330^{5} 405^{2} >57c<**
Jims Choice 10 ch g Abednego-Dikaro Lady (Dike (USA)) **2^{P}**
Jim's Quest 4 ch g Charmer-Salt of The Earth (Sterling Bay (SWE)) 2572^{3} 3821^{7} 3895^{8} 4433^{6} **>69fh<**
Jimsue 6 gr g Afzal-Gentian (Roan Rocket) 2572^{12}
Jim Valentine 11 br g **158^{5} 190^{4} 298^{5} (597) (823) 1209^{3} 4234^{U} 4697^{P} >106c<**
J J Baboo (IRE) 4 b g Be My Guest (USA)-Maricica (Ahonoora) 1940^{4} 2615^{4} 2859^{2} **>78h<**
Jobber's Fiddle 5 b m 27^{7} 2678^{10} 2818^{5} 2943^{14} 3442^{13} **>42h<**
Jobie 7 b g Precocious-Lingering (Kind of Hush) 3109^{P} 3500^{14}
Jobsagoodun 6 b g 1639^{4} 2546^{8} 3048^{8} 4309^{P} 4662^{4} **>55h<**
Jock 5 b g Scottish Reel-Northern Lady (The Brianstan) 2539^{P}
Jocks Cross (IRE) 6 ch g (1023) (1265) 2702^{4} 2900^{7} 3415^{7} **>97h<**
Joctor Don (IRE) 5 b br g Pitpan-Thats Irish (Furry Glen) **3208^{F}** 4001^{P}
Jodami 12 b g **1359^{2} (2636) 2997a^{2} >173c<**
Jodesi (IRE) 7 bl g Sandalay-Neasham (Nishapour (FR)) 3382a^{8} **>91h<**
Joe Jagger (IRE) 6 b g 1161^{6} 1524^{4} 1807^{11} **>52h<**
Joe Luke (IRE) 5 b g 1079^{7} 1633^{9} 1999^{8} **>45h<**
Joe's Bit of Gold 5 gr m Gold Song-Katie Grey (Pongee) 686^{8} 858^{4}
Joe Shaw 4 ch g Interrex (CAN)-Super Lady (Averof) 1652^{15} 2060^{F} 2898^{7} 3064^{2} 3310^{F} **>66h<**
Joe White 11 ch g **1155^{2} 1266^{4} 1513^{F} 1805^{6} 2179^{P} >115c<**
John Drumm 6 gr g 1651^{8} 2071^{5} 3154^{2} (3820) 4048^{9} (4136) 4271^{6} 4701^{4} **>87h<**
John Naman (IRE) 8 b g 1088^{7} 1466^{8} **>33h<**
Johnneys Spirit 5 b g Kala Shikari-Summerhill Spirit (Daring March) 2047^{12} 3828^{11} 4707^{7} **>39h<**
Johnny-K (IRE) 6 b g (1124) 1633^{5} **>83fh<**
Johnny Kelly 10 ch g 2545^{P} **3099^{P} 3316^{P}**
Johnny Setaside (IRE) 8 b g **1495a^{3} (1750a) (2362a) >100h 145c< (DEAD)**
Johnny's Turn 12 b g Buckskin (FR)-Lovely Tyrone (Peacock (FR)) 2864^{F} 3016^{P} 3281^{P}
Johnny The Fox (IRE) 9 ch g **4015^{U} 4308^{P} >96dc<**
Johnny Will 12 b g 131^{5} 187^{P} **>95h 108c<**
Johnstons Buck (IRE) 8 b g 3624^{5} **>53h<**
John-T 4 b c Thatching-Ower (IRE) (Lomond (USA)) 1184^{13} **>8h<**
John Tufty 6 ch g 334^{2} 478^{2} **>66h<**
Johnymoss (IRE) 8 ch g Le Moss-Deep Pride (Deep Run) 3796^{P}
Jo Jo Boy (IRE) 8 ch g 1752a^{F} **>90h 97c<**
Joker Jack 12 ch g **1008^{3} 1075^{4} 1169^{4} 1421^{2} 1554^{3} 1837^{5} 1863^{5} 1961^{P} 3134^{5} 3675^{P} 3759^{2} 3899^{4} >56dh 75c<**
Jo Lightning (IRE) 4 b g Electric-Santa Jo (Pitpan) 2633^{15} 3142^{15} 4150^{13} 4288^{8} **>27fh<**
Jolis Absent 7 b m (1056) 1130^{5} 1417^{2} **3173^{P} 3356^{5} >75h<**
Joli's Great 9 ch m 134^{9} (289) (474) 1040^{P} **>71h<**
Jolly Boat 10 br g Lord Ha Ha-Mariner's Dash (Master Buck) **1771^{4} 2039^{U} 2571^{2} 2841^{9} 3051^{7} 3436^{2} 3667^{2} 3833^{P} >91c<**
Jolly Heart (IRE) 7 b g Kambalda-Wrens Lass (Wrens Hill) 2012^{7} 4479^{P} **>6fh<**
Jolson 6 ch g Black Minstrel-Pearly Lady (Tycoon II) 4008^{15} **>37fh<**
Jolto 8 b g Noalto-Joytime (John de Coombe) 1938^{P}
Jonaem (IRE) 7 b g 700^{4} (854) 942^{2} 1081^{6} 1992^{10} 3481^{7} 3795^{10} **3909^{6} 4151^{3} 4408^{F}** 4705^{5} **>55h 58c<**
Jonbel 9 b g Norwick (USA)-Two Shots (Dom Racine (FR)) 3352^{9} 3672^{7} **>13h<**
Jonjas Chudleigh 10 ch g 1390^{6} 2882^{9} 3442^{P} **3842^{5} 3998^{3} 4171^{2} 4431^{2} 4661^{6} >45h 87dc<**
Jon's Choice 9 b g 829^{3} 1297^{5} **>67h<**
Josephine Grey 6 gr m Malaspina-Khareedah (Tender King) 918^{11}
Joshua's Vision (IRE) 6 b g 2093^{2} **>71h<**
Josifina 6 b m **1677^{2} 1994^{7}** 3681^{4} 4425^{3} 4701^{9} **>72h 81c<**
Joss Bay 5 ch g Nearly A Hand-Maranzi (Jimmy Reppin) 2701^{F}
Jo's Wedding 6 ch g Newski (USA)-Meant (Menelek) 4539^{10} **>24fh<**
Jovial Man (IRE) 8 b g **1596^{2} 1963^{6} 2867^{6} 3176^{2} 3427^{U} 3756^{3} 4007^{P} >88h 105c<**
Jovie King (IRE) 5 ch g Salt Dome (USA)-Jovial Josie (USA) (Sea Bird II) 1726^{7} (2907) (3570) 3920^{3} 4275^{2} 4725^{4} **>72h<**
Jowoody 4 ch f Gunner B-Maskwood (Precipice Wood) 4215^{13} **>57fh<**
Joy For Life (IRE) 6 b m 1539^{P} 1958^{2} 2694^{9} 2941^{7} 3817^{6} **4227^{4} 4417^{P}** 4622^{P} **>33h<**
Joyful Pabs 5 b m 2661^{12} 2959^{9}
Joyrider 6 b g 1047^{11} 1577^{7} 1942^{F} 2862^{12} **>68dh<**
Jubran (USA) 11 b g 693^{3} 3559^{6} 3696^{5} 3887^{P} **>32h<**
Judgeroger 11 b g Decent Fellow-Carnation Cruise (Dual) **3455^{P} 4160^{P}**
Judicial Field (IRE) 8 b g **1833^{2} 1972^{3} 2769^{2} 3027^{2} (3308) >105c<**
Judicious Captain 10 b g **2789^{3} (3067) 3395^{F} (3700) 4050^{3} >107c<**
Judicious Charlie (IRE) 5 bl g Strong Gale-Miss Spike (Tarqogan) 3418^{10} **>8fh<**
Judicious Norman (IRE) 6 br g 1345^{U} 1633^{11} 2619^{5} 2766^{P} **>71h<**
Judy Line 8 b m Funny Man-Deirdre's Choice (Golden Love) **3055^{P} 4094^{P} >47h<**
Juke Box Billy (IRE) 9 ch g **1209^{5} 1578^{4} 1847^{2} 1991^{5} 2769^{5} 3707^{4} 4300^{8} >68h 91c<**
Juleit Jones (IRE) 8 ch m **2009^{2} 2679^{6} 3145^{4} 3333^{2} 3571^{2} >76h 107c<**
Julian Oliver 5 ch g Sylvan Express-Lottie Rose (Blakeney) 2939^{12}
Jultara (IRE) 8 ch g **1447^{U} 2809^{2} 3551^{2} (3848) (4312) >82h 126+c<**
Jumbeau 12 ch g **1284^{P} 1554^{P} >108c<**
Jumbo's Dream 6 b g Jumbo Hirt (USA)-Joyful Star (Rubor) 2924^{9} 3487^{8} **>23fh<**
Jumbo Star 7 ch g 1025^{6} 4518^{3} 4712^{8} 4761^{6} **>63?h<**
Jungle Fresh 4 b g Rambo Dancer (CAN)-Report 'em (USA) (Staff Writer (USA)) 3139^{P} 3555^{P}
Jungle Highway 8 b m 54^{12} **>50h<**
Jungle Knife 11 b g Kris-Jungle Queen (Twilight Alley) 2670^{P}
Jungle Patrol (IRE) 5 ch g Night Shift (USA)-Jungle Rose (Shirley Heights) 3888^{P}
Juniper Hill 5 b g Dragonara (FR)-Sombreuil (Bold Lad (IRE)) 2675^{5} 3548^{8} 3946^{4} 4287^{8} **>64fh<**
Jupiter Moon 8 b g **2964^{P} 3446^{2} (3580) 4179^{U} 4222^{3} >64h 101c<**
Jupiter Probe (IRE) 6 br g Phardante (FR)-Bramble Hill (Goldhill) 2844^{7} 3423^{F} **>30fh<**
Jurassic Classic 10 gr g **1420^{6} (1839) 2869^{5} (3428) >73dh 119c<**
Just a Beau 6 b g 961^{11} 1390^{P} 1861^{10} 2907^{12}
Just A Guess (IRE) 6 ch g 1^{P} 10^{4}
Just Andy 6 b g 1986^{12} 2572^{10} 2690^{P} 4002^{U} 4276^{P} 4789^{6} **>22h<**
Just Bayard (IRE) 5 b g Kambalda-Whistling Doe (Whistling Deer) 1774^{5} 2830^{6} 4554^{6} **>47fh<**

Just Because (IRE) 5 ch g Sharp Charter-Lakefield Lady (Over The River (FR)) 865[17] 4441[9] 4626[10] 4726[F] >14h<
Just Ben 9 br g Oats-Kayella (Fine Blade (USA)) 4640[6]
Just Bruce 8 ch g 18[4] 2547[3] 2691[5] (3073) 3417[2] 3749[3] (3835) 4133[3] >79h 117?c<
Just Eve 10 gr m 3066[P] 3393[P]
Just Flamenco 6 ch g 2818[13] 2946[15]
Just for a Reason 5 b g 1039[P] 1337[5] 1816[4] 2943[4] 3933[6] 4290[2] 4556[3] >51h<
Just For Me (IRE) 8 b g 3824[2] 3913[7] 4515[6] 4704[5] >85c<
Just Jack 11 br g 3135[4] 3924[5] 4619[4] >93c<
Just Jasmine 5 ch m 1177[3] 1450[5] 3337[4] 4403[3] >64h<
Justjim 5 b g Derring Rose-Crystal Run VII (Damsire Unregistered) 2080[8] 2696[21] 3587[8] >21h<
Just Like Dad 5 ch g 866[P]
Justlikejim 6 ch g Say Primula-Trois Filles (French Mamy) 1800[6] 2080[7] >43fh<
Just Little 5 b m 318a[3] (1353) 1365[F] 4357a[7] >110h<
Just-Mana-Mou (IRE) 5 b g 546[5] 2907[9] >64h<
Just Marmalade 8 ch g 4471[B] >63h<
Just 'n Ace (IRE) 6 b br g 1423[F] 3040[4] >81h 92c<
Just Ned 6 b g Gunner B-Heckley Loch (Lochnager) 2804[4] 3070[7] 3487[7] 3823[9] >34fh<
Just Nip 4 b g Lord Bud-Popping on (Sonnen Gold) (4150) >57fh<
Just Norman 6 b g Sunley Builds-Gameover Lady (Aragon) 3821[21] >32fh<
Just One Canaletto 9 ch g 1817[3] 2665[5] 2947[P] (3929) 4404[3] 4735[P] >82h 83c<
Just One Question (IRE) 7 b g 1774[8] 2066[12] 3000[P] 3795[2] >69h<
Just Polly 5 b m Meadowbrook-Dajopede (Lighter) 2627[P] 3794[13] >31h<
Just Rory 4 b g Skyliner-Judys Girl (IRE) (Simply Great (FR)) 1652[P]
Just Supposen (IRE) 6 b g 1031[P] 2778[F] 2899[P] 3031[F] 3201[14] 3434[2] 3704[3] >54?h<
Just Whistle 5 gr m Absalom-Aunt Blue (Blue Refrain) 3888[F] 4244[11] 4390[F] >12h<
Juyush (USA) 5 b h Silver Hawk (USA)-Silken Doll (USA) (Chieftain II) (2655) (2840) (3103) (3293) >116h<
Jymjam Johnny (IRE) 8 b g 1120[P] 1348[4] 1831[3] 2544[5] 3790[6] 3886[2] 4261[8] >82h 108c<

K

Kabylie Ouest (FR) 4 ch f Franc Parler-Kadastra (FR) (Stradavinsky) 3574[7] 3821[14] >51fh<
Kadari 8 b m 1642[6] 1860[5] 1984[4] 2838[4] 3002[2] 3201[6] 3281[3] (3681) 3915[3] 4417[4] 4744[3] >76h 68c<
Kadastrof (FR) 7 ch h 1933[2] 2777[9] (2884) 3150[7] 3572[6] (3816) 4117a[6] 4212[6] 4397[12] 4791[4] >118h<
Kadi (GER) 8 b g 1566[3] 2741a[5] 2901[2] 3230[5] 3598[8] 4013[3] >124h 145c<
Kadiri (IRE) 6 b g Darshaan-Kadissya (USA) (Blushing Groom (FR)) 1569[9]
Kaifoon (USA) 8 b g 1388[7] 4567[6] >43h<
Kailash (USA) 6 b g (25) (161) (306) (885) (1065) (1368) 2112[4] 3275[2] 3595[F] >94h<
Kai's Lady (IRE) 4 b f Jareer (USA)-Rathnaleen (Scorpio (FR)) 688[7] 874[3] 1149[12] 4017[2] 4137[5] 4290[6] >35h<
Kaitak (IRE) 6 ch g 1154[3] 1510[4] 1804[3] 2603a[11] 2779[4] 3163[4] 3267[2] 4061[18] 4397[F] >99h<
Kajostar 7 ch m 210[P] 259[8] 687[7] 743[P] 1027[10] 1247[7] >38h<
Kaladross 6 ch g 1323[F] >46fh<
Kalajo 7 b g Kala Shikari-Greenacres Joy (Tycoon II) 2803[4] 3141[7] (3393) (3556) (3715) 4245[P] 4576[6] >99c<
Kalakate 12 gr g 1419[7] >73h<
Kalao Tua (IRE) 4 b f Shaadi (USA)-Lisa's Favourite (Gorytus (USA)) 807[F] 962[2] >65h<
Kalasadi (USA) 6 b g (657) 1074[2] 1392[P] 1586[2] 1859[5] 2644[5] 3013[8] >92h<
Kaldan Khan 6 b g 2994a[4] >101h 80c<
Kalisko (FR) 7 b g (2509) >59h<
Kaloore 8 ch g Ore-Cool Straight (Straight Lad) 3631[2] >97c<
Kalzari (USA) 12 b g 32[2] 103[3] 159[4] 967[2] 1060[3] 1382[6] 1585[P] 2943[9] (4089) 4278[P] 4732[9] >59h 78c<
Kama Simba 5 b g 26[8] 300[F] 406[P] >59h< (DEAD)
Kambalda Rambler 13 b or br g 3457[4] 4320[4] 4449[2] 4799[3] >56h 95c<
Kambletree (IRE) 6 ch m Kambalda-Spindle Tree (Laurence O) 2627[P] 3100[P] 3611[P]
Kamikaze 7 gr g (2672) 3020[4] 3700[F] 4213[8] 4537[4] >111h 125dc<
Kandyson 6 gr g Neltino-Kandy Belle (Hot Brandy) 3626[3] >64fh<
Kanona 6 ch g 586[10] 730[3] >23h<
Kano Warrior 10 b g 3429[P] 3620[9] 4220[11] 4727[P] >24h<
Kapco (IRE) 5 b g Be My Native (USA)-Shake Up (Paico) 3574[9] 3853[4] >52fh<
Karar (IRE) 7 b g 816[5] 1074[4] 1571[2] 2667[4] 3047[5] 3600[16] 4310[3] 4549[4] 4722[4] >92h 97c<
Karena's Prince 5 b g Rakaposhi King-Karena Park (Hot Spark) 1296[18] 1777[9]
Karenastino 6 b g 897[U] 1032[4] 1629[P] 1847[11] 1991[2] 2632[4] 3097[U] 3289[4] (3477) 3945[2] 4481[4] >14h 78c<
Karen's Typhoon (IRE) 6 b g 649[7] 792[5] 978[4] 1762[3] 2820[8] 3088[S] 3488[4] 3958[5] 4439[S] 4563[F] >44h<
Karibu (GER) 6 b g 3677[F] >8h< (DEAD)
Karicleigh Man 7 b g 1197[P] 1683[P]
Karinska 7 b m (65) 253[2] 4702[9] >72h<
Kariver (FR) 6 b g River Mist (USA)-The Equal Skies (USA) (Sir Gaylord) 2496a[3]
Karline Ka (FR) 6 ch m 2842[11] 3056[F] 3493[4]
Karlovac 11 ch g Stanford-Croatia (Sharpen Up) 738[7] 870[4] (935) 1252[P] 4297[7] 4408[8] 4703[3] >45c<
Karshi 7 b g 1319[W] 1661[2] (1919) 3011[3] (3635) >126h<
Kaselectric (IRE) 6 b g Electric-Susan's Blues (Cure The Blues (USA)) 4352a[14] >104h<
Kashan (IRE) 9 b g 1390[2] 2006[5] 3110[5] 3442[9] 4727[4] >40h 84c<
Kashana (IRE) 5 b m Shahrastani (USA)-Kashna (USA) (Blushing Groom (FR)) 586[R] 643[6] 1141[3] 3325[P] >53h<
Kasirama (IRE) 6 b g 1316[2] 1672[P] 2790[8] 4204[P] 4516[P] >65h<
Katballou 8 b g 1466[3] 1562[3] 1861[7] 3222[4] 3442[11] 3625[2] 3934[R] 4646[P] >43dh 76c<
Kates Castle 10 b m 4614[4] >84c<
Katharine's Song (IRE) 7 br m Millfontaine-Country Niece (Great Nephew) 161[14] 306[3] 418[4] 504[4] 1036[P] 1178[9] 1334[7] 1795[P] >30h<
Katsar (IRE) 5 b g Castle Keep-Welsh Partner (Welsh Saint) 2804[13] >7fh<
Katy-Belle 5 b m Newski (USA)-Kutati's Belle (NZ) (Kutati (NZ)) 4388[7] >43fh<
Kawa-Kawa 10 b m 318a[16] >86h<
Kaye's Secret 4 b f Failiq (FR)-Another-Kaye (Jimmy The Singer) 2815[9] 3029[10] 3426[8] >41h<
Kayfaat (USA) 9 b g 1256[10] 1630[6] (1836) 2905[P] 3442[P] >72h<
Kaytu's Carousel 8 ch m 3970[2] >59h<
Kazaran (IRE) 4 bb g Shardari-Khatima (Relko) 4118a[13] >77fh<
Kaz Kalem (IRE) 5 b g Lancastrian-Kilclare Lass (Pitpan) 2682[14]
K C'S Dancer 12 ch g 57[7] 823[3] 1063[5] 4051[4] 4324[P] >96c<
Keal Ryan (IRE) 4 b g 2993a[6] >89h<
Keano (IRE) 8 ch g 2681[8] 3003[6] 3633[4] >81h 98dc<
Kedge Anchor Man 6 b g 1260[F]
Kedwick (IRE) 8 b g 3500[3] >82h<
Keen Bid (IRE) 6 b g Alzao (USA)-Gaychimes (Steel Heart) 3103[3] 3592[5] 4003[7] >60h<
Keen To The Last (FR) 5 ch g (1050) 1207[3] 1945[4] 2651[4] 3942[2] >78h<
Keep Battling 7 b g (12) >74h<
Keep it Zipped (IRE) 7 gr g 887[2] (1075) 1711[4] 1983[F] 2908[2] 3185[P] 4251[2] (4435) >89h 94+c<
Keep Me in Mind (IRE) 8 b g 2963[4] 3850[5] 3920[5] 4307[8] 4510[7] >78h<
Keep-On 9 b m Castle Keep-Gale Flash (News Item) 813[5]
Kellsboro Queen 6 ch m Rakaposhi King-Kellsboro' Joan (Rymer) 3767[P]
Kelly Mac 7 b g 1381[3] 1860[6] 2824[5] 3177[4] 3570[2] 3579[3] (3760) 3958[6] >71h<
Kelly's Pearl 10 b m 314a[7] >115c<
Kellytino 8 gr m Neltino-Kelly's Maid (Netherkelly) 4530[U] 4655[R]
Kelpie the Celt 10 b or br g 530[P] 2923[P] >88?c<
Kemo Sabo 5 b g 1144[2] (1686) 2044[2] 2651[2] 3028[5] 3534[4] 3888[10] >71h 41c<
Kendal Cavalier 7 gr g 973[2] (1197) 1798[5] 2072[2] 2658[4] 2883[7] 3400[4] 3551[F] 3737[7] >83h 92c<
Kenilworth Lad 9 br g 3646[P] 3827[7] >12h 93c<
Kenmare River (IRE) 7 b g 1083[3] 1629[3] 1845[P] 2630[2] 2954[7] >63h 89c<
Kenmore-Speed 10 gr g 1022[7] 1206[3] 1503[2] (1704) 2004[2] 3288[2] (3484) 3701[2] (3974) (4185) (4302) 4541[2] >89+h 120c<
Kennett Square (IRE) 8 ro g 2870[9] 3473[P]
Kentavrus Way (IRE) 6 b g 1073[U] 1708[P] 2068[R] 2866[3] (3057) 3204[9] 3577[R] >43h<
Kentford Conquista 4 b f El Conquistador-Notinhand (Nearly A Hand) 589[7] >24h<
Kentford Tina 6 b m 1317[9] >64h<
Kentucky Gold (IRE) 8 b g 1633[8] 1854[10] 2701[12] 3015[P] 3279[P] 3683[13] 3882[P] >42dh<
Kenyatta (USA) 8 b g 210[4] >56h< (DEAD)
Kerawi 4 b g Warning-Kerali (High Line) (1014) 1158[4] 1935[B] (3007) 3301[2] 3634[13] 4364a[12] >101h<
Keriali (USA) 4 b c Irish River (FR)-Kerita (Formidable (USA)) 3480[4] >33fh<
Kernof (IRE) 4 b g Rambo Dancer (CAN)-Empress Wu (High Line) (291) 540[2] (803) 1158[P] >67h<
Kerrier (IRE) 5 ch h Nashwan (USA)-Kerrera (Diesis) 360[P] 3583[P] 3918[P]
Kerry's Oats 5 b m Derrylin-Kerry's Web (Oats) 4656[3] >57fh<
Kesanta 7 b m The Dissident-Nicaline (High Line) 553[U] 727[2] 832[F] 905[5] 1786[P] 2905[6] >56h< (DEAD)
Ketabi (USA) 6 ch g Alydar (USA)-Ivory Fields (USA) (Sir Ivor) 186[10]
Ketchican 5 b g 3343[P] 3717[5] 4021[2] 4226[9] 4294[2] 4382[6] >60h 70c<

Kettles 10 b m 3055[U] 3341[3] 4324[7] >94c<

Kevasingo 5 b g Superpower-Katharina (Frankincense) 1782[8] 2035[3] 2655[8] 4003[6] 4807[10] >74h<

Keynote (IRE) 5 ch g Orchestra-St Moritz (Linacre) 3821[13] >50fh<

Key Player (IRE) 8 ch g (2752) 3176[3] 3578[3] 3836[F] 3925[P] >41h 88dc< (DEAD)

Key To Moyade (IRE) 7 bl g 1195[C] 1340[2] 1680[6] 1909[2] 2551[3] 3288[4] 4168[3] 4312[5] >68h 103dc< (DEAD)

Khalidi (IRE) 8 b g 1325[4] 1794[3] 1996[4] (2695) 3044[4] (4454) 4653[2] >94h 104c<

Khalikhoum (IRE) 4 b g Darshaan-Khalisiyn (Shakapour) 2697[3] 3014[P] 3544[10] 3691[14] 4217[4] 4743[3] 4807[4] >63h<

Kharasar (IRE) 7 b g 2335a[F] 2739a[4] 3260a[3] 4366a[5] >132h 103c<

Khatir (CAN) 6 gr g 1876[7] 1993[4] 2882[7] >62dh<

Khayrawani (IRE) 5 b g 318a[4] 2603a[6] (4117a) 4357a[6] >124+h<

Khazari (USA) 9 ch g 131[P] 185[P] 3072[8] 3442[2] 4468[3] 4727[P] >50h 52c<

Kibreet 10 ch g 1366[10] 1914[2] 2646[5] 2884[4] 3638[7] >93h 144c<

Ki Chi Saga (USA) 5 ch g Miswaki (USA)-Cedilla (USA) (Caro) 1729[11] 2010[P]

Kickcashtal 8 b g Ballacashtal (CAN)-Teenager (Never Say Die) 2746[P] 3100[P]

Kierchem (IRE) 6 b g 1666[13] (2629) 2913[5] 3327[9] 3474[5] (3976) 4223[3] 4482[2] 4746[2] >55h<

Kilcarne Bay (IRE) 7 b g 1470[4] 2663[P] 3103[6] >70h<

Kilcolgan 10 ch g 1266[3] 1670[F] 2916[4] 3025[2] 3162[5] (3560) 3792[U] 3884[3] 4185[6] >120c<

Kilcoran Bay 5 b g 1698[R] 2797[7] 3063[5] 3499[P] >62h<

Kildrummy Castle 5 b g 1687[7] 1921[8] 2918[9] 3102[7] (3733) 3983[2] 4285[5] >62h<

Killbally Boy (IRE) 7 b g 1500[2] 2653[F] 3326[3] 3691[9] 4079[2] 4337[2] >75?h 79c<

Killelan Lad 15 br g Kambalda-Dusky Glory (Dusky Boy) 4432[P] 4560[P]

Killeshin 11 bl g 1643[5] 2575[P] 2881[5] 3162[3] 3428[4] 3699[4] 4074[7] 4213[10] >134c<

Killimor Lad 10 b g 4320[9] 4543[8] >74c<

Killing Time 6 b g (594) 1448[5] 2838[P] 2943[11] (3207) 3338[U] 3488[7] 4181[5] (4328) 4468[7] >59+h<

Killmessan-Town (IRE) 4 ch g Jareer (USA)-Perfect Chance (Petorius) 291[3] 388[4] >51h<

Killmurray Buck (IRE) 9 b m Buckskin (FR)-Larrys Glen (Laurence O) 3391a[P] 4361a[B] >64c<

Killy's Filly 7 b m 64[6] >49h 70c<

Kilminfoyle 10 b g 3095[U] >65h 102c<

Kilmington (IRE) 8 gr g 1053[4] (1476) 1673[6] 3146[5] (3982) >80+h<

Kilnamartyra Girl 7 b m 1030[5] 1312[2] 1524[6] 1667[9] (1821) (4162) >76h<

Kilshey 6 gr m 1966[9] 3061[3] 3575[5] 4097[5] >65h<

Kiltulla (IRE) 7 br g 853[3] 1126[3] 1248[3] 1847[3] 2632[3] 3138[3] 3331[4] 3909[2] 4221[3] 4481[2] 4706[F] 4745[4] >56h 90c<

Kimanicky (IRE) 7 b g 1994[P] >97h< (DEAD)

Kimdaloo (IRE) 5 b g Mandalus-Kimin (Kibenka) 4216[14] >57fh<

Kincardine Bridge (USA) 8 b g 704[3] 938[F] 4245[P] 4334[U] 4574[2] 4709[P] >73c<

Kinda Groovy 8 b g 3693[6] 3992[6] 4296[11] (4518) 4712[6] >66h<

Kind Cleric 6 b g 1203[12] 1568[3] (2676) 3541[P] >75h< (DEAD)

Kindergarten Boy (IRE) 6 b g 137[7] (304) >71+h<

Kindle's Delight 9 b g 814[6] 1379[4] 1765[P] 2674[9] >94h 99c<

Kindly Lady 9 b m Kind of Hush-Welcome Honey (Be Friendly) 887[P] 1068[5] >58c<

King Athelstan (USA) 9 b g 1502[2] 1715[P] >92h 65c<

King Credo 12 b g 1272[4] 1730[P] >145h 122dc<

King Curan (USA) 6 b g 4403[P] 4626[7] >32h<

Kingdom of Shades (USA) 7 ch g 1416[2] 1783[6] 3011[2] 3267[3] 3562[2] 4016[9] >107h<

Kingfisher Bay 12 b g 3363[6] 3680[P] 4241[7] >51c<

Kingfisher Blues (IRE) 9 ch g 98[5] >43h<

Kingfisher Brave 4 b g Rock City-Lambada Style (IRE) (Dancing Brave (USA)) 1184[4] 1370[6] 1776[5] 3825[13] 4707[4] >63h<

King Fly 7 ch g Saxon Farm-Deep Goddess (Deep Run) 2627[9] 3159[P] 3324[8] 3727[2] 3910[6] 4144[5] >66h<

King High 10 b g Shirley Heights-Regal Twin (USA) (Majestic Prince (USA)) 3208[3] >91c<

King Lucifer (IRE) 8 b g 1324[3] 1799[3] 2782[2] 3302[2] (3599) >96h 145c<

King Mole 6 b g Rakaposhi King-Sayshar (Sayfar) 2012[3] (2696) 3021[2] 3619[15] >72fh<

King of Babylon (IRE) 5 b g 212[3] 259[4] 461[3] 587[2] 673[6] (825) 899[F] 1466[9] 2088[13] >68h<

King of Camelot (IRE) 7 b g King's Ride-Radical Review (Radical) (1926) (2893) 3168[4] >74h<

King Of Kerry (IRE) 6 b g 2603a[12] >82h<

King of Shadows 10 b or br g 3005[B] 3363[P] 3744[8] 3984[4] 4218[P] 4543[P] >84c<

King of Sparta 4 b g Kefaah (USA)-Khaizaraan (CAN) (Sham (USA)) 2697[P] (3989) 4176[2] >74h<

King of Steel 11 b g Kemal (FR)-Black Spangle (Black Tarquin) 3370[U] 3882[P]

King of Swing (IRE) 5 b g Lancastrian-Romantic Rhapsody (Ovac (ITY)) 3676[14] 3939[10] >4fh<

King of The Blues 5 b g Rakaposhi King-Colonial Princess (Roscoe Blake) 1336[3] 1820[2] 2572[5] 4388[12] >62fh<

King of the Gales 10 b or br g 1397a[6] 2362a[2] 2602a[3] 2997a[5] 3261a[2] >143c<

King of the Horse (IRE) 6 ch g 4389[8] >71h<

King Pin 5 b g 1263[4] 1666[3] (1999) (2766) 3168[3] 4204[5] >92h<

King Rat (IRE) 6 ch g King of Clubs-Mrs Tittlemouse (Nonoalco (USA)) 876[4] 974[5] 2034[2] 2806[11] 3324[5] 3471[F] >66h<

Kings Adventure 5 ch g Rakaposhi King-Mendick Adventure (Mandrake Major) 4075[13]

King's Affair 7 b g 3085[P] 3445[P] 3755[P]

Kings Cay (IRE) 6 b g 1499[P]

Kings Cherry (IRE) 9 b g 1568[5] 1952[8] 2796[2] 2949[2] (3401) 3567[5] 4013[F] >60h 112c<

King's Courtier (IRE) 8 b g 1260[7] 1819[P] 1961[P] 2665[U] 2820[13] 3176[P] 3354[P] 3736[P] >30h<

Kingsfold Pet 8 b g 1271[F] 1636[7] 3293[6] 3572[11] >95h<

King's Gold 7 b g 889[P] 1073[P] 1771[6] 2068[U] 2680[5] 3411[5] 3760[3] >51h<

Kings High (IRE) 7 br g 2503[8] 2619[P] >36h<

Kingsland Taverner 6 ch g 479[2] >58h<

Kings Lane 8 b g 1849[8] 2042[5] 2654[10] 2915[2] 3157[10] 3557[3] 3646[4] 3887[7] (4147) >64h<

Kings Measure (IRE) 4 b g King's Ride-Snoqualmie (Warpath) (4215) >84fh<

Kingsmill Quay 8 b m 1947[P]

Kings Minstral (IRE) 7 ch g 1247[2] (1575) 1825[3] 2509[9] 2790[P] 3646[10] 3727[6] 4152[5] 4408[5] 4706[R] >44h 52c<

Kings Nightclub 4 b f Shareef Dancer (USA)-Troy Moon (Troy) 331[S] 471[4] 654[7] 912[6] >43h<

King Spring 12 br g Royal Fountain-K-King (Fury Royal) 4579[P] 4704[P]

King's Rainbow (IRE) 8 b m King's Ride-Royalement (Little Buskins) 3491[5] 3902[4] 4476[6] 4699[6] >54h 62c<

Kings Return (IRE) 6 b g 3382a[4] 3650a[13] >108h<

Kings Sermon (IRE) 8 br g 1357[3] 1845[6] (2788) 3202[F] 3477[2] (3975) 4186[3] 4245[4] >71h 103c<

King's Shilling (USA) 10 b g 159[6] 223[4] 285[4] 641[6] 724[5] 935[2] 1041[5] 1449[4] 1771[P] 2940[2] 3051[F] 3622[5] 4007[P] 4321[4] >66h 91c<

Kings Token 7 b g Rakaposhi King-Pro-Token (Proverb) 4713[P]

Kingston Way 11 b or br g 323a[B] >110c< (DEAD)

King's Treasure (USA) 8 b g 3586[2] 3765[F] >90h 116+c<

Kings Vision 5 gr g 1327[P] 2806[12] 3471[8] 3741[6] 4472[5] 4652[P] >26h<

Kingswell Boy 11 ch g Floriferous-Tide Gate (Dike (USA)) 492[R] 553[3] >58h<

Kings Witness (USA) 4 b g Lear Fan (USA)-Allison's Deeds (Sassafras (FR)) 2825[4] (3224) 3634[P] 4414[3] >80h<

Kingswood Imperial 4 ch g Absalom-Allied Newcastle (Crooner) 2911[3] 3304[15] 3606[10]

Kingswood Manor 5 b g 2826[5] 3902[3] 4073[2] 4662[8] >67h<

King Torus (IRE) 7 b g Torus-Kam A Dusk (Kambalda) (4522) (4773) >111c<

King Ubad (USA) 8 ch g 387a[5] >84dh<

King Wah Glory (IRE) 8 b g 314a[3] 763a[U] >135h 139c<

King William 12 b g 677[4] >89h<

Kinnescash (IRE) 4 ch g Persian Heights-Gayla Orchestra (Lord Gayle (USA)) 3109[3] 3233[8] 3592[2] 3802[2] (3898) (4082) 4395[4] (4532) 4630[3] (4729) >92h<

Kino 10 b g Niniski (USA)-Relkina (FR) (Relkino) 3005[P] 3744[9] 4316[4] (4511) 4640[P] >85c<

Kino's Cross 8 b g 1179[4] 1764[P] 2657[P] 2892[F] 3164[6] 3402[9] 3584[6] 3766[3] 4006[3] (4307) 4630[4] 4791[5] >72h 62c<

Kintavi 7 b g 1630[3] 1860[2] (1984) 3076[2] (3136) 3584[3] 3666[2] >81h<

Kippanour (USA) 5 b g 71[7] 1903[2] 2666[12] 2817[8] 2932[7] 3281[5] >87h<

Kir (IRE) 9 ch g 3454[P] 3607[12] >25h<

Kirby Moorside 6 b g 900[P] 1085[P] 3431[F] 3590[P]

Kirchwyn Lad 9 b g Kirchner-Gowyn (Goldhill) 1021[P]

Kirkie Cross 5 b m Efisio-Balgownie (Prince Tenderfoot (USA)) 476[P] 2678[P]

Kirov Royale 6 b m Rambo Dancer (CAN)-Gay Princess (Lord Gayle (USA)) 965[3] 3426[6] 3672[P] >49h<

Kirstenbosch 10 b g 3028[P] 3485[4] 3711[3] (4572) (4744) >75h<

Kirtle Monstar 6 ch g 1290[P] 2785[16] 2918[P]

Kismetim 7 b g 2862[9] 3091[5] 3803[7] >38h<

Kissair (IRE) 6 b g 2645[9] 3038[8] 3293[3] 3615[20] >97h<

Kit Smartie (IRE) 5 b g Be My Native (USA)-Smart Cookie (Lord Gayle (USA)) 3716[6] 3914[3] >57fh<

Kitzberg (IRE) 6 br m 1[5] >46h<

Kiwi Crystal (NZ) 8 b m 3999[2] 4172[2] 4661[3] >71h 85c<

Klairon Davis (FR) 8 b or br g 1410a[2] 1889a[F] 2346a[2] (3128a) 3614[4] (4349a) >158h 173?c<

Klosters 5 ch m Royal Match-Snowy Autumn

(Deep Run) 653^{11} 1333^{8} 2655^{P}
Knave 4 b g Prince Sabo-Royal Agnes (Royal Palace) 2798^{8} 3093^{5} 3394^{5} **>40h<**
Knave of Diamonds 5 b h Bustomi-Kohinoor Diamond (Roman Warrior) 1276^{11}
Knifeboard 11 b g Kris-Catalpa (Reform) **3739^{P} 4326^{2} 4640^{4} >105c<**
Knight in Side 11 ch g 793^{5} (3471) 4141^{2} **>75h< (DEAD)**
Knighton 6 b g 99^{8}
Knightsbridge Girl (IRE) 6 ch m Buckskin (FR)-Solo Guest (Northern Guest (USA)) 4008^{9} 4184^{10} **>44fh<**
Knight's Crest (IRE) 7 ch g The Parson-Sno-Cat (Arctic Slave) 1275^{9} 1774^{4} 1915^{7} **>67h<**
Knockaulin (IRE) 6 ch g Buckley-Two Shares 1233a^{3} 1485a^{6} **>79h<**
Knockaverry (IRE) 9 b m **1420^{7} 1799^{P} 2821^{8} 3223^{U} >91dh 78c<**
Knockbride (IRE) 8 b g 1654^{P} 2662^{P}
Knockbrit Lady (IRE) 6 b m 2668^{11} **>28h<**
Knockreigh Cross (IRE) 8 b m Lancastrian-Futurum Lady VII (Damsire Unregistered) **3200^{6} 3331^{5} 3477^{F} >52c<**
Knock Star (IRE) 6 gr g Celio Rufo-Star of Monroe (Derring Rose) 3569^{P} 3989^{11} **4745^{5}**
Knockumshin 14 ch g **57^{2} 130^{P} >96c<**
Knot True 7 b m True Song-Ganglion (Martinmas) 3061^{B} 3575^{7} 3755^{10} **>22h<**
Knowe Head 13 b g **4504^{3} 4713^{P} >98c<**
Knowing 10 gr m **1449^{6} 1771^{5} 1947^{P} 3746^{P} 3931^{4} >46c<**
Know-No-No (IRE) 8 ch g **2632^{F} 2786^{6} 3092^{3} (4574) (4709) >100c<**
Known Secret (USA) 4 ch g Known Fact (USA)-Loa (USA) (Hawaii) 3022^{5} 3311^{4} 3555^{6} 3789^{6} 3888^{11} **>54h 21c<**
Knucklebuster (IRE) 7 b g (492) **>80h<**
Komaseph 5 b g Komaite (USA)-Starkist (So Blessed) 679^{8}
Komiamaite 5 b g 1086^{P} **>63h<**
Kongies Melody 6 b m 727^{5} 1425^{4} 1786^{2} 2838^{P} 3112^{P} **>43h<**
Konvekta King (IRE) 9 br g **1128^{4} (1352) 1682^{W} (2639) (2901) 3618^{P} >93h 135c<**
Konvekta Queen (IRE) 6 b m 1679^{P} (1958) 2634^{5} 3186^{2} (3491) 3817^{8} **>76h< (DEAD)**
Koo's Promise 6 bl m 1176^{6} **(1475) 1677^{3} 1875^{5} 2795^{7} (2960) 3288^{5} 3697^{3} 3819^{5} >66h 89c<**
Korbell (IRE) 8 ch m Roselier (FR)-Chipmunk (Apollo Eight) 1810^{2} (2546) 2880^{2} 2950^{2} 3156^{F} **>97h< (DEAD)**
Kosheen (IRE) 6 br m Supreme Leader-Koshear (Hardgreen (USA)) 1177^{4} 1450^{3} 1685^{8} 3052^{3} 3491^{3} 3970^{4} **>59h<**
Kota 4 b c Kris-Lady Be Mine (USA) (Sir Ivor) 3548^{6} **>39fh<**
Kralingen 5 ch m 536^{3} **>50h<**
Krasnik (IRE) 4 br g Roi Danzig (USA)-Kermesse (IRE) (Reference Point) 640^{9} 1413^{6} **>38h<**
Kraton Garden (USA) 5 b g 1191^{7} **>61h<**
Kreator (POL) 5 b h Babant-Kodina (CZE) (Dipol (CZE)) (154a)
Kulshi Momken 4 ch g In The Wings-Gesedeh (Ela-Mana-Mou) 1011^{F} 1370^{U}
Kumada 10 b g **4615^{P} >88c<**
Kumari King (IRE) 7 ch g 1375^{8} 1782^{6} 4405^{8} 4512^{9} **4764^{2} >44h 73c<**
Kushbaloo 12 b g **4524^{4} 683^{2} (857) 1024^{4} 2903^{9} 3609^{2} 4080^{3} (4316) >106c<**
Kutan (IRE) 7 ch g 22^{F} 66^{12} 396^{2} 480^{3} (546) **>53h< (DEAD)**
Kutman (USA) 4 b c Seattle Slew (USA)-Ouro Verde (USA) (Cool Moon (CAN)) 3007^{11} 3927^{P} **>37h< (DEAD)**
Kybo's Revenge (IRE) 6 ch g Carlingford Castle-Mettle Kettle (Cut Above) 1835^{U} 1964^{7} 2690^{10} 3063^{6} 3408^{P} 3755^{5} 4099^{2} **>50h<**
Kylami (NZ) 5 ch g Veloso (NZ)-Lady Comique (NZ) (Funny Fellow) 1289^{5} 1820^{7} 2965^{2} 3364^{F} 3536^{6} **>13h<**
Kyle David (IRE) 5 gr g Peacock (FR)-Aunty Babs (Sexton Blake) 1124^{17} 2546^{R} 3189^{P} 3734^{P}
Kymin (IRE) 5 b m Kahyasi-Akila (FR) (Top Ville) 497^{2} (832) (3932) 4091^{2} **>65h<**
Kytton Castle 10 ch m **1393^{F} 1682^{P} 1934^{F}** 2817^{P} **>97?c< (DEAD)**

L

La Bella Villa 7 b m 1085^{P} **>21h<**
Laburnum Gold (IRE) 6 b g 1178^{F} 1375^{4} 2547^{9} 3989^{4} 4528^{F} **>67h<**
Lac de Gras (IRE) 6 gr g 5^{5} 77^{P} 297^{5} 406^{2} 655^{P} 825^{2} **>47h<**
La Chance 7 b g Lafontaine (USA)-Lucky Omen (Queen's Hussar) 1261^{5} 1539^{11} 3100^{6} 3368^{6} **>15h<**
Lackendara 10 ch g 936^{4} **1454^{3} 2647^{3} 3276^{2} 3905^{3} 4331^{4} >86h 112dc<**
Lady Arpel (IRE) 5 b m 318a^{19} 1487a^{3} 1752a^{10} 2603a^{21} 3523a^{9} **>103h<**
Lady Blakeney 11 gr m **14^{P} >93c<**
Lady Boco 4 b f Roscoe Blake-Bella Banus (Rapid River) 3290^{8} 4539^{11} 4657^{10} **>27fh<**
Lady Callernish 7 b m Callernish-Lady Vulmid (Sir Lark) 3764^{U} 3889^{4} 4658^{F} **>31h<**
Lady Confess 7 ch m (32) 75^{3} 159^{5} 214^{4} **>72h<**
Lady Daisy (IRE) 8 br m 3254a^{3} 3572^{4} 3640^{12} (4357a) **>128h<**
Lady Eclat 4 b f Nomination-Romantic Saga (Prince Tenderfoot (USA)) 4069^{5}
Lady Foley (IRE) 5 b m Doubletour (USA)-Ice Baby (Grundy) 679^{5} 872^{7} 1071^{3} 1329^{16} 1855^{7} **>26h<**
Lady High Sheriff (IRE) 7 b m 1341^{3} 1565^{3} 2870^{2} (3222) 3491^{2} **>72h<**
Lady Khadija 11 b m 1703^{P}
Lady Lois 6 b m 27^{11} 4378^{12} 4648^{11} **>8h<**
Lady Magnum (IRE) 4 b f Eve's Error-Illiney Girl (Lochnager) 912^{9} 1149^{2} 1444^{5} (1675) 1953^{8} (2705) 3050^{P} **>65h<**
Ladymalord 5 br m 718^{8} 890^{P} **>23h<**
Lady Ness 6 gr m 837^{P} **>6h<**
Lady Noso 6 b m 1090^{P} 3889^{P} **>67h<**
Lady of Mine 7 gr m Cruise Missile-Native Star (Go Native) 2656^{P} 3052^{9} 3364^{7} 3683^{6} 4073^{4} 4091^{5} **>33h<**
Lady Peta (IRE) 7 b g (1301) (1580) 1791^{5} 2961^{2} 4052^{6} **>96h<**
Lady Poly 9 b m 469^{3} **>39h<**
Lady Rebecca 5 b m (872) (1289) (1573) **>76fh<**
Lady Rosebury 7 b m Derring Rose-Foxbury (Healaugh Fox) 1190^{8} 1450^{8} 3052^{P} **3806^{P} 4305^{4} 4526^{R}** 4626^{12} 4767^{6} **>4h 52c<**
Lady's Pet 6 b g Tina's Pet-Northern Lady (The Brianstan) 2904^{12} **>14fh<**
Lady Swift 6 ch m Jalmood (USA)-Appealing (Star Appeal) 1030^{11} 4393^{5} **>31h<**
La Fontainbleau (IRE) 9 gr g 29^{6} 95^{5} **3357^{P}** 3545^{3} **>64h 84dc<**
Lagan 4 b g Shareef Dancer (USA)-Lagta (Kris) (906) 1158^{5} 1575^{6} (4749) **>78h<**
Lagen Bridge (IRE) 8 gr g (1705) 1999^{2} (3024) 3152^{5} (3453) 4204^{U} (4257) 4761^{2} **>102h<**
Lagham Lad 8 b g 3012^{9} **3819^{6} >66dh<**
Lago Lago (IRE) 5 b m 54^{6} 98^{3} **>66h< (DEAD)**
La Gougouline (FR) 5 ch m Tip Moss (FR)-Sanhia (Sanhedrin (USA)) (2495a) **>98h<**
Laird O'Rhynie 5 gr g Scallywag-Kinsham Dene (Kampala) 1151^{4} **>40fh<**
Lajadhal (FR) 8 gr g 2038^{6} 2567^{8} 2792^{7} 3063^{2} 3209^{6} 3442^{7} **>47h<**
Lake Aria 4 b f Rambo Dancer (CAN)-Hinge (Import) 4301^{18}
Lake Kariba 6 b g (788) 1171^{3} (1427) 1757a^{6} 1950^{2} 3402^{5} 3562^{6} **>92h<**
Lake of Loughrea (IRE) 7 ch g **740^{F} 835^{U} 932^{4} 1284^{W} 1379^{2} 1660^{4} 1957^{5} 3843^{4} 4385^{4} >111h 101c<**
Lakeside Lad 5 b g St Columbus-Beyond The Trimm (Trimmingham) 653^{8} 737^{R}
La Maja (IRE) 8 b m Lafontaine (USA)-Eiger Sanctions (St Alphage) **4059^{2} >58c<**
Lambrini (IRE) 7 b m **3043^{8} 3360^{5} 3830^{4} 3966^{8} 4417^{3} 4706^{F} >34h 75c<**
Lambson 10 b g 289^{8} **>52h<**
La Menorquina (USA) 7 b m 459^{2} 884^{3} 1039^{6} 1176^{F} 1342^{5} 3630^{3} 3935^{3} **>73h<**
La Mezeray 9 b m **887^{7} 1068^{3} (1335) 1582^{7} 2638^{4} 2776^{5} 2940^{5} >81c<**
La Mode Lady 12 b or br m Mandalus-Indictment (Desert Call) **321a^{7} >71c<**
La Mon Dere (IRE) 6 b g Lafontaine (USA)-Brown Foam (Horage) 2634^{12} 4188^{8}
Lancastrian Pride (IRE) 7 b g Lancastrian-Another Pride 4124a^{4} **>95h<**
Lance Armstrong (IRE) 7 ch g (1713) 2552^{2} 2766^{3} **(3333) (3540)** 4166^{6} **>84h 114c<**
Lancer (USA) 5 ch g 67^{5} 210^{3} (287) 344^{2} 348^{2} 455^{2} 497^{4} 741^{10} **>69h<**
Land Afar 10 b g **(947) 1386^{2} 1790^{2} 2335a^{2} (2641) 2885^{2} (3300) >125h 142c<**
Landa's Counsel 6 b m 1685^{4} **>49fh<**
Landfall 4 b g Most Welcome-Sextant (Star Appeal) 1205^{P}
Landler 4 b g Shareef Dancer (USA)-Les Dancelles (Pas de Seul) 3203^{16} (3418) 3716^{3} 4150^{2} **>63fh<**
Landlord 5 b g Be My Chief (USA)-Pubby (Doctor Wall) 603^{7} 1594^{10} **>40h<**
Landsker Missile 8 b m **3744^{2} (3928) 4406^{3} >106c<**
Landsker Star 7 b m 2878^{5} 4384^{5} **>7h<**
Lanesra Breeze 5 b g Petoski-Constant Companion (Pas de Seul) 1380^{P} 1569^{6} 1707^{2} 2006^{9} **>56h<**
Langtonian 8 br g Primo Dominie-Yankee Special (Bold Lad (IRE)) 3115^{9} 3233^{10} 3535^{8} 3890^{5} **>47h<**
Langton Parmill 12 b g Pardigras-Millie Langton (Langton Heath) **1711^{F} 2039^{P}**
Lansborough 7 gr g **1632^{2} 1803^{6} 2789^{2} 3023^{2} >84h 104c<**
Lansdowne 9 b g **724^{2}** (1019) 1286^{2} 1571^{4} 2659^{8} 2888^{13} 3731^{3} **>100h 97c<**
Laredo (IRE) 4 b c Accordion-Amelita (Strong Gale) (3946) **>71fh<**
Large Action (IRE) 9 b g (1759a) (1916) (2774) 3597^{P} 4063^{P} **>160+h 97+c<**
La Riviera (IRE) 5 ch g Over The River (FR)-La Gloriosa (Ardross) 1672^{10} 2917^{7} 3529^{3} 3823^{P} **>58h<**
Larkshill (IRE) 6 b g Phardante (FR)-Fairy Hollow (Furry Glen) 1124^{9} 1296^{8} 1802^{5} 2701^{11} 3706^{2} 4299^{10} **>71h<**
Larks Tail 9 b m **821^{3} 917^{F} 964^{3} 1179^{6} 1414^{3} >35h 71?c<**
Larry's Lord (IRE) 8 ch g **(953) >126+c<**
Las Animas (USA) 6 b m Imperial Falcon (CAN)-

Awe (USA) (Le Fabuleux) 3818^{14} 4102^{R}
Lasata 12 b g **943^{4} 1584^{2} 1769^{3} 2674^{8} 3588^{2} 3673^{3}** **>103dc<**
Laser Light Lady 5 b m Tragic Role (USA)-Raina Perera (Tyrnavos) 22^{8} 67^{9} 129^{8} 212^{5} 355^{3} 401^{5} **>26h<**
Last Action 4 gr f Lyphento (USA)-Sunlit (Warpath) 3297^{9} 3440^{11} **>27fh<**
Last But Not Least 4 b f Dominion-Almadaniyah (Dunbeath (USA)) 331^{P}
Last Corner 5 b h Weldnaas (USA)-Shadha (Shirley Heights) (50a) **>88h<**
Last Laugh (IRE) 5 b m 350^{5} 634^{3} 739^{5} (905) 974^{9} 1193^{4} **>60h<**
Lasto Adree (IRE) 6 b g 2034^{6} **>9h<**
Lastoftheidiots 8 b g 1250^{14} 3004^{P} **>34h<**
Last Penny 5 b m Scorpio (FR)-Penny Princess (Normandy) 3676^{P}
Last Refuge (IRE) 8 b g **1847^{10}** 3032^{4} **3452^{2}** 3645^{5} 3825^{11} **4336^{8} 4753^{4}** **>57h 91c<**
Last Roundup 5 b g Good Times (ITY)-Washita (Valiyar) 1851^{4} **>60h<**
Last Try (IRE) 6 ch g 1050^{10} 1152^{6} (1524) (1992) 3475^{4} 3995^{3} 4285^{11} **>78h<**
Latahaab (USA) 6 b h Lyphard (USA)-Eye Drop (USA) (Irish River (FR)) 2055^{P} 2663^{5} 3272^{4} 3613^{16} 3847^{4} **>76h<**
Late Encounter 6 ch g Ra Nova-Kadelian (Rustingo) 306^{5} 418^{10} 727^{P} 788^{P}
Latest Thyne (IRE) 7 b or br g 1830^{11} **3001^{3} 3188^{P}** **>78h 104c<**
Latin Leader 7 b g 453^{4} 701^{3} 856^{3} 1025^{3} (1344) 1971^{4} (3313) 3912^{6} 4187^{3} **>69h<**
Latvian 10 gr g (781) 856^{5} 1344^{11} **>63dh<**
Laughing Buccaneer 4 ch g Weldnaas (USA)-Atlantic Line (Capricorn Line) 1014^{5} 1634^{12} 1908^{2} 2806^{10} 2874^{4} 3471^{4} 3915^{P} **>52h< (DEAD)**
Laughing Fontaine (IRE) 7 b g 1687^{8} 3305^{2} 3416^{5} **>72h<**
Laughing Gas (IRE) 8 ch g 131^{8} 1255^{P} **>62h< (DEAD)**
Laura Lye (IRE) 7 b m **722^{P} 826^{R} 903^{F}** 1086^{P} 1334^{8} 1786^{3} 2678^{4} 3670^{2} 3933^{5} 4162^{9} (4292) 4548^{5} 4739^{7} **>63h<**
Lauren's Treasure (IRE) 6 b g 2878^{4} 3405^{P}
Laurie-O 13 b g **645^{5} 785^{F}** 1021^{12} 1822^{P} **>65c<**
Lavalight 10 b g **328^{U} 403^{3} 470^{F} 554^{4}** **>55h 51c<**
Lawbuster (IRE) 5 b g 480^{5} 659^{2} 1077^{5} 1500^{P} **>67h<**
Lawful Love (IRE) 7 b g 208^{3} 4381^{8} **>67h<**
Lawnswood Junior 10 gr g 128^{8} 1446^{2} **>67h<**
Layham Low (IRE) 6 b g 478^{4} 651^{P} 692^{P} 798^{4} 4020^{2} 4220^{7} 4439^{8} **>64h<**
Lay it Off (IRE) 8 br m **1839^{5} 2665^{6} 3729^{3} 3961^{2} 4234^{2} (4535)** **>78?h 99c<**
Layston d'Or 8 ch g Le Coq d'Or-Water Crescent (No Mercy) **4560^{7}** **>79c<**
Lazzaretto 9 b g Ballacashtal (CAN)-Florence Mary (Mandamus) **3341^{P}**
Leading Prospect 10 b g 1690^{2} 2802^{7} 3531^{2} 3693^{4} **>74h 97c<**
Leading Spirit (IRE) 5 b g Fairy King (USA)-Shopping (FR) (Sheshoon) 2112^{5} 2937^{3} **>80h<**
Le Amber (IRE) 8 ch m Le Bavard (FR)-Amber Ballad (Ballad Rock) 1020^{9}
Leamhog (IRE) 7 b g The Parson-Corun Girl 1751a^{5} **>87h 95c<**
Leannes Man (IRE) 8 b g Tale Quale-Spring of Patricia (High Top) **4076^{F}**
Leap Frog 6 ch g 1766^{4} 3672^{3} 4003^{5} 4315^{4} 4698^{5} **>70h<**
Leap in the Dark (IRE) 8 br h 31^{6} 586^{6} 630^{3} 1161^{3} 1292^{3} 1351^{3} 1825^{2} 2634^{7} 2897^{3} 3416^{3} 3621^{5} 3845^{4} **>68h<**
Lear Dancer (USA) 6 b or br g Lear Fan (USA)-Green Gown (Green Dancer (USA)) 498^{2} 649^{2} 700^{3} 859^{4} **>60h<**
Lear Jet (USA) 4 b c Lear Fan (USA)-Lajna (Be My Guest (USA)) (1519) 2772^{5} 2937^{P} **>87h<**
Le Baron 6 br g 866^{5} 1251^{3} 1786^{P} 2088^{4} (3930) **>55h<**
Lebedinski (IRE) 4 ch f Soviet Lad (USA)-Excavate (Nishapour (FR)) 501^{3} 1149^{7} 1370^{8} 2050^{10} 3921^{4} 4295^{4} 4633^{8} **>53h<**
Ledburian 7 br g Primitive Rising (USA)-Pretty Lass (Workboy) 2080^{6} 3190^{P} **3582^{P} 3806^{P} 4004^{U} 4158^{P}** **>44fh<**
Le Denstan 10 b g **4^{P} (897) 1083^{2} 1311^{3} 1653^{5} 3023^{4} 3138^{4} 3726^{4} (3886) 4186^{6}** **>92c<**
Lees Please (IRE) 5 b g 1950^{P} 3442^{P} **>25h<**
Leeswood 9 b g **3928^{4}** **>54h 83dc<**
Legal Artist (IRE) 7 b g **72^{3} 160^{4} 889^{5} 1254^{5} (1300) 1472^{4} 1875^{P}** 2708^{13} **4790^{3}** **>77h 74c<**
Legal Drama (USA) 5 ch m 17^{7} **>43h<**
Legatee 6 ch m 21^{4} **>62h<**
Leggies Legacy 6 b g Jupiter Island-Hit The Line (Saulingo) 3676^{10} **>48fh<**
Legible 9 b g 2010^{11} (2690) **>85h<**
Le Ginno (FR) 10 ch g **2360a^{2} 2856a^{3} 3255a^{2} 3380a^{2}** **>88h 113c<**
L'Eglise Belle 5 b m 1050^{7} **>37h< (DEAD)**
Le Grand Loup 8 ch g **3495^{P} 3978^{F}**
Leigh Boy (USA) 11 b g Bates Motel (USA)-Afasheen (Sheshoon) **4326^{P} (DEAD)**
Leighten Lass (IRE) 6 b m 1245^{7} 1689^{P}
Leinthall Princess 11 b m **1122^{3} 1684^{5} 1983^{F} 3053^{P}** **>42h 84dc<**
Le Khoumf (FR) 6 ch g (2579) 2779^{P} **>89h<**
Le Meille (IRE) 8 ch g **1473^{4} 2623^{4} 3036^{3} 3414^{5} (4167) 4416^{2}** **>72h 121c<**
Le Mirabeau (FR) 7 b g Fabulous Dancer (USA)-Danseuse Etoile (FR) (Green Dancer (USA)) 579a^{3} **>64h<**
Lemon's Mill (USA) 8 b m **28^{2} 130^{P}** **>88h 130c<**
Leon Des Perrets (FR) 6 ch g Son of Silver-Leonie Des Champs (FR) (Crystal Palace (FR)) 527a^{2} 717a^{3} **>92h<**
Leopard Lady 5 b m Sulaafah (USA)-Swift Turtle (Le Bavard (FR)) 653^{13} 918^{6} 980^{9}
Leotard 10 b g **4206^{3} 4478^{3}** **>129h 140c<**
Lepton (IRE) 6 gr g 1033^{3} 1312^{8} 1689^{P} 1802^{P} **2628^{P} 2672^{P} 3030^{B} (4502) (4745)** **>42h 99c<**
L'Equipe (IRE) 7 b g 1152^{7} 1375^{7} 1796^{3} **>63h<**
Lessons Lass (IRE) 5 b m 741^{8} 1586^{3} 2069^{5} (2909) (3277) **>93h<**
Le Teteu (FR) 4 b c Saint Andrews (FR)-Nouvelle Star (USA) (Star de Naskra (USA)) 1014^{2} 1634^{5} (1862) (2747) **>85h<**
Letmo Warrior (IRE) 5 ch g Orchestra-Cherry Jubilee (Le Bavard (FR)) 2676^{P} 3445^{3} **>58h<**
Lets Be Frank 6 b g 1091^{2} 1327^{2} (1448) (1732) (1959) 3045^{5} (3166) 3430^{2} **>86h<**
Lets Go Now (IRE) 7 b g **1073^{P} 1371^{P} 1552^{7}** 1786^{P} 1962^{5} 2694^{P} **>53dh<**
Let You Know (IRE) 7 b m 1177^{14} 1450^{13} 1818^{11}
Level Edge 6 b m 3^{2} 139^{P} 208^{6} **>72h<**
Lewesdon Manor 6 b g Broadsword (USA)-Lewesdon View (Dubassoff (USA)) (4656) **>68fh<**
Liability Order 8 b g 12^{6} 185^{P} **>29h 79c<**
Liam's Loss (IRE) 8 ch g **1845^{P}** 2627^{P} 2958^{6} 3313^{11} **>28h<**
Liam's River (IRE) 5 b g Over The River (FR)-Just A Maid (Rarity) 3828^{13} **>39fh<**
Libertarian (IRE) 7 b g 2690^{12} 3004^{P} **4221^{P}** **>61h<**
Liberty James 10 ch g 218^{P} **302^{P} 411^{P}** **>57h 73c<**
Lie Detector 9 b g **1244^{4} 1655^{7}** **>88h 108dc<**
Lien de Famille (IRE) 7 b g **(2043) 2632^{7} 3068^{P} 4186^{9} 4537^{3}** **>83h 96c<**
Lifebuoy (IRE) 6 b g 910^{9} 1021^{5} (1292) 1575^{4} 2790^{2} 3032^{P} **>64h<**
Life of a King (IRE) 9 b g **2998a^{4} 3391a^{F}** **>94c<**
Life of a Lord 11 b g **(314a) 763a^{P}** **>174c< (DEAD)**
Life of Brian (IRE) 6 b g Meneval (USA)-Miss de Jager (Lord Gayle (USA)) 59^{10}
Lift and Load (USA) 10 b g **1963^{P}** **>77c<**
Lift The Latch (IRE) 5 b g Strong Gale-Pallastown Run (Deep Run) 3574^{19}
Lightening Lad 9 b g 1271^{2} **(2691) (3015) 3596^{5}** **>107h 133c<**
Lightening Steel 6 gr g Sulaafah (USA)-Wotusay (Lighter) 4009^{9} 4539^{5} **>55fh<**
Lighten the Load 10 b g **3055^{P}** **>73?c<**
Light The Fuse (IRE) 5 b g Electric-Celtic Bombshell (Celtic Cone) 3170^{2} (4288) **>70fh<**
Light Veneer 12 ch g **3585^{6}** **>115?h 123?c<**
Lilac Rain 5 b m Petong-Dame Corley (L'Enjoleur (CAN)) 396^{P} 737^{6} 965^{5} **>23h<**
Lilly The Filly 6 br m 492^{F} 954^{13} 968^{6} 1062^{P} 1766^{P} 1998^{P} 2576^{8} 2746^{P} 3621^{15} **>34h<**
Lime Street Blues (IRE) 6 b g 793^{9} 1091^{6} 1770^{2} 1980^{2} 2664^{8} 2882^{6} 3110^{8} **>67h<**
Limited Liability 7 b g 65^{P} **>73h<**
Limonaire (FR) 11 b g **2928^{F}** **>109?c<**
Limosa 6 b m 19^{5} 100^{5} (327) 468^{3} **>68h<**
Limyski 4 b g Petoski-Hachimitsu (Vaigly Great) 291^{8} **>28h<**
Lindajane (IRE) 5 b m Erins Hope-Tempo Rose (Crash Course) 787^{3} 858^{3}
Linden's Lotto (IRE) 8 b g **1902^{3} 2748^{4} 2894^{8}** 3177^{8} 3430^{8} **3905^{4} 4085^{F} (4344) 4635^{5}** **>56h 110c<**
Lindon Run 8 b g Cruise Missile-Trial Run (Deep Run) **3713^{U} 4076^{F}**
Lineker (IRE) 10 g **2998a^{P}** **>88c<**
Line Lawyer (FR) 6 b m Sky Lawyer (FR)-Skara (FR) (Carmarthen (FR)) **580a^{3}**
Line of Conquest 7 b g 1453^{9} **>53h<**
Linford (IRE) 7 b g 954^{12} 1090^{5} **>9h<**
Linger Balinda 11 ch m Balinger-Artalinda (Indiaro) **4614^{P}**
Link Copper 8 ch g **4462^{2} 4730^{P}** **>95?c<**
Linkside 12 b g 2922^{5} **>57h<**
Linlathen 7 ch g 3693^{2} 4261^{4} (4577) 4734^{4} **>95h<**
Linngate 8 b m 3559^{5} 3791^{7} **>56h<**
Linton Rocks 8 b g 3045^{6} 3281^{2} 3600^{8} **(3797) (4350a)** **>97h 105+c<**
Linwood 6 gr m Ardross-Silva Linda (Precipice Wood) 3070^{4} 3297^{7} (3487) **>56fh<**
Lippy Louise 5 b m Buckley-Kersti Dunn (Doctor Wall) 872^{5} 1190^{6} 1654^{15} 2920^{2} 3348^{2} **>57h<**
Liscahill Fort (IRE) 8 gr g Roselier (FR)-Carlow Highway 2345a^{9} **>93h<**
Lislaughtin Abbey 5 ch g Nicholas Bill-Kates Fling (USA) (Quiet Fling (USA)) 3946^{10} **>38fh<**
Lisnavaragh 11 b g **3279^{P}** **>64c<**
Liss De Paor (IRE) 6 b m 1233a^{F} 1492a^{F} (2596a) 2995a^{7} 4048^{6} 4355a^{P} **>90h<**
Lisselan Prince (IRE) 9 b g **1003a^{F}** **>118c< (DEAD)**
Little Beau 6 b g Idiot's Delight-Saxon Belle (Deep Run) 3767^{11}

Little Buck (IRE) 9 b g 1319[2] 1647[5] **>126h<**
Little By Little 7 b g **637[3] 828[2] 977[3]** **>65c<**
Little Court 6 b g 19[8] (77) 157[4] 4731[P] **>40h<**
Little Crumplin 5 b g Pablond-Speckyfoureyes (Blue Cashmere) 1052[3] 3149[5] **>59fh<**
Little Derring 6 b m Derring Rose-Little Khan (Maystreak) 99[14] 416[4]
Little Earn 7 b g Little Wolf-Strathdearn (Saritamer (USA)) 1422[8] 1683[15] **>26h<**
Little Elliot (IRE) 9 b g 3500[7] 3894[2] **4227[P] 4621[4] 4763[P]** **>61h<**
Little Embers 5 ch m Librate-Seasoned Ember (Royal Smoke) 918[10] 980[14] 1118[8] 1388[U]
Little Gains 8 b g **3188[P] 3334[4] 4507[3] 4738[2]** **>46h 91c<**
Little General 14 ch g **3397[6]** **>93c<**
Little Gunner 7 ch g 1441[W] 1571[B] 1783[8] 1982[5] 2625[6] 3166[10] **>80h<**
Little Hooligan 6 b or br g 483[6] 551[5] 596[3] 741[2] 904[3] 971[4] 1181[5] (1332) 1599[4] 1841[7] 2567[5] 2882[8] 3110[14] **>64h<**
Little Jake (IRE) 7 b g Callernish-Fugue (Le Prince) 1336[2] 3154[8] 3340[4] 3587[7] **>66h<**
Little Kenny 4 b f Warning-Tarvie (Swing Easy (USA)) 589[8] 831[3] 1444[P] **>51h<**
Little Luke (IRE) 6 b h 1388[8] 1707[9]
Little Martina (IRE) 9 b m **1538[2] (1811) 2754[2] 3047[P] 3617[U] 3812[2] (4149)** **>114c<**
Little Murray 4 b g Mon Tresor-Highland Daisy (He Loves Me) 2784[9] **>47h<**
Little-Nipper 12 ch g Derrylin-Emily Kent (Royal Palace) **2681[7] 3333[P] 4535[P] 4653[3]** **>79c<**
Little Notice (IRE) 6 b g Cheval-A Weeks Notice (IRE) (Ovac (ITY)) 1085[4] 1539[7] **3806[F]** **>59h<**
Little Redwing 5 ch m Be My Chief (USA)-Forward Rally (Formidable (USA)) 293[6] 528[4] 585[7] 784[3] 1027[5] 1141[4] 1703[3] 1822[3] 2177[3] 2800[6] 2922[7] 3096[5] **>53h<**
Little Rousillon 9 b g 105[6] 217[4] **>44h<**
Little Rowley 8 ch g **1711[P] 2681[P] 2908[P] 3675[P] 3833[3] (4460)** **>65c<**
Little Shefford 5 ch g 1380[4] (2578) 2897[2] 3186[6] 3829[2] 4020[3] 4278[4] **>68?h<**
Little Thyne 12 br g Good Thyne (USA)-You Never Know (Brave Invader (USA)) **64[7] 135[F]** 257[P] **>75dh<**
Little Time 5 b m Arctic Lord-Olympian Princess (Master Owen) 4088[4] **>38fh<**
Little Tincture (IRE) 7 ch g 65[5] (157) 338[2] 499[3] (632) 792[6] 911[3] 4646[7] 4803[P] **>41h<**
Little Wenlock 13 b g **3095[P] 3397[4] 3712[2] 4080[P]** **>107?c<**
Live Action 10 b g Alzao (USA)-Brig O'Doon (Shantung) 3743[6] 4101[P]
Lively Encounter (IRE) 6 b g 1457[11] (1800) 2503[4] 2677[5] 3143[2] 3569[B] 3798[2] **>79h<**
Lively Knight (IRE) 8 b g **(1371) 1764[2] 2007[5] 2776[3] 3334[2] (3576) 3900[2]** **>81h 117dc<**
Liver Bird (IRE) 7 b g 4124a[2] 4355a[5] **>102h<**
Livin It Up (IRE) 7 b g **4356a[7]** **>84h 110c<**
Livio (USA) 6 b g (1945) (2545) **>99+h<**
Lixos 6 b g 3474[8] 4337[5] **>66h<**
Lizium 5 b m Ilium-Lizaway (Casino Boy) 1132[U] 1651[13] 3818[P] 4620[10] 4789[14] **>19h<**
Lizzys First 5 b g Town And Country-Lizzy Longstocking (Jimsun) 3154[10] 4329[P] **>8h<**
Lobster Cottage 9 b g **1298[F] 1714[3] 2569[3] 2926[3] 3343[P] 4007[3]** **>103c<**
Loch Dancer 4 br f Lochnager-Cute Dancer (Remainder Man) 1953[14]
Loch Garman (IRE) 7 b g 1830[13] 2690[P] **(DEAD)**
Loch Garman Hotel (IRE) 8 b g **1281[2] 1538[U] 1856[4] 2758[8] 2816[4] 3003[2] 3185[P] 3617[9] 3968[2]** **>89c<**
Lochnagrain (IRE) 9 b or br g **11[3] 909[P]** (1207) (1347) (1671) 1906[U] 2545[2] 2888[10] 3415[3] **3707[2]** **>103h 118c<**
Loch Na Keal 5 b m 1329[10] 1867[7] 3233[9] 3621[2] 3817[10] (4427) **>60h<**
Locket 4 b f Precocious-Bracelet (Balidar) 1014[P]
Lock Tight (USA) 7 b g 1007[8] 1562[P]
Lodestone Lad (IRE) 7 br g **883[P]** 2620[4] 2820[16] **3332[P] 3665[P]** **>28h 92dc<**
Lo-Flying Missile 9 br g **64[P]** **>79c<**
Loftus Lad (IRE) 9 b g **314a[10] 4351a[6]** **>92c<**
Lofty Deed (USA) 7 b g **132[8] 188[7]** 289[2] 339[5] **>54h 54c<**
Logani 7 b m 698[7] 801[7] **>42h<**
Logical Step (IRE) 7 b g 1260[6] 3014[3] 3265[4] 3541[P] **>70h<**
Lomond Lassie (USA) 4 b f Lomond (USA)-Herbivorous (USA) (Northern Jove (CAN)) 852[3] 1699[9] 3031[13] **>15h<**
Lonesome Train (USA) 8 ch g 1271[5] **>109h<**
Lonesome Traveller (NZ) 8 b g **4551[4]**
Longcroft 5 ch m Weldnaas (USA)-Najariya (Northfields (USA)) (354) 450[5] 4146[7] 4712[7] **>56h<**
Longshore 4 ch g Lord Bud-Milly Kelly (Murrayfield) 4009[12] **>18fh<**
Longstone Lad 5 b g Pittacus (USA)-Fatu Hiva (GER) (Marduk (GER)) 3767[6] 3895[5] **>54fh<**
Lonicera 7 br m 915[2] 2874[5] 3977[5] **>67h<**
Lookingforarainbow (IRE) 9 ch g Godswalk (USA)-Bridget Folly (Crofter (USA)) 1369[5] 1639[P] 1866[8] **>53h<**
Look In The Mirror 6 b g Rakaposhi King-Moaning Jenny (Privy Seal) 1329[13] 1504[9] 3184[7] 3340[6] 3796[P] 4468[4] 4556[2] 4727[P] **>57h<**
Look Sharpe 6 b g Looking Glass-Washburn Flyer (Owen Dudley) 858[2] 1026[7]
L'Opera (FR) 4 ch g Old Vic-Ma Pavlova (USA) (Irish River (FR)) (3301) 3634[4] 4014[F] **>99+h<**
Lorcanjo 6 b m 264[P] **>52h<**
Lord Antrim (IRE) 8 b g **460[P] 590[P] 1728[P] 2819[P] 2940[U]**
Lordan Velvet (IRE) 5 br g Lord Americo-Danny's Miracle (Superlative) 4451[F]
Lord Cool (IRE) 6 b g Lord Americo-Coolbawn Lady (Laurence O) 4230[6] 4801[W] **>41h<**
Lord Dorcet (IRE) 7 b g **1352[3] 1792[F] 2618[3] (2783) 3144[2] 3614[6] 4062[2] 4349a[4]** **>94h 145tc<**
Lord Ellangowan (IRE) 4 ch c Astronef-Gossip (Sharp Edge) 654[4] 2865[P] **>57h<**
Lord Foley (NZ) 5 b g Cache of Gold (USA)-Gay Beat (NZ) (Gay Apollo) 1203[2] (1665) 2811[7] 3170[5] 4559[3]
Lord Fortune (IRE) 7 b g 3366[4] **>69h<**
Lord Gyllene (NZ) 9 b g **1277[2] 1806[3] (2075) (2758) (3046) 3699[2] (4074)** **>157+c<**
Lord Khalice (IRE) 6 b g King's Ride-Khalice (Khalkis) 1090[2] 1550[4] 2891[7] 3108[2] 3405[2] **>60h<**
Lord Kilton 9 ch g Crested Lark-Kilton Jill (Adropejo) **4228[W] (4422)** **>64?c<**
Lord Knows (IRE) 6 b g Nearly a Nose (USA)-Roaming Free (Monsanto (FR)) 3142[7] 3561[6] 3828[2] **>64fh<**
Lord Lamb 5 gr g (2180) (3626) 4360a[4] **>89fh<**
Lord Love (IRE) 5 b g 3178[P] 3703[F] 3847[8] 4097[3] 4255[B] 4725[2] **>58h<**
Lord Mcmurrough (IRE) 7 b g 1188[3] 1374[2] 1859[3] 1956[2] 3136[3] (3402) 3698[3] 4248[13] (4527) 4550[3] **>93h<**
Lord Mills (IRE) 6 b g 3592[3] 3755[2] **>75h<**
Lord Muff (IRE) 8 b g Mister Lord (USA)-Any Wonder (Hardboy) **3616[9] 4356a[F]** **>123c<**
Lord Nitrogen (USA) 7 b or br g **889[3] 972[4] 1254[U] 1331[3] 2039[F]** 3683[9] 3894[3] 4452[4] (4663) **>59+h 81dc<**
Lord of The Loch (IRE) 6 b br g Lord Americo-Loughamaire (Brave Invader (USA)) 1033[U] 1362[2] 1579[4] 1827[3] 4568[4] **>43h<**
Lord of The Mill (IRE) 6 b g 129[13]
Lord of The Rings 5 b g Arctic Lord-Sister of Gold (The Parson) 3142[11] 3418[6] 3939[4] **>47fh<**
Lord Of The River (IRE) 5 br g Lord Americo-Well Over (Over The River (FR)) 4215[5] **>74fh<**
Lord of the West (IRE) 8 b g **(1302) (1684) (1858) 1901[3] 2767[P] 3047[2] 3599[F]** **>75h 117c<**
Lord Pat (IRE) 6 ch g Mister Lord (USA)-Arianrhod (L'Homme Arme) 3794[11] 4243[5] 4479[7] **>40h<**
Lord Podgski (IRE) 6 b g (2770) 3561[3] (4287) **>71fh<**
Lord Regal (IRE) 6 b g 2655[W]
Lord Relic (NZ) 11 b g **3005[2] (3270) 3432[2] 3637[P] 4416[4]** **>126c<**
Lord Rooble (IRE) 6 b g 890[4] 1042[3] 1422[3] 1810[3] 2694[5] 3088[2] (3445) 3754[2] 3901[4] **>75h<**
Lord Singapore (IRE) 9 ch g **763a[F] 1003a[2] (1495a) 2348a[12] 4110a[6]** **>129c<**
Lord Tomanico (FR) 5 b g Tirol-Lady Beauvallon (Coquelin (USA)) (344) 413[3] 2825[P] **>69h<**
Lord Vick (IRE) 8 ch g **2749[5]** **>56c<**
Lorna-Gail 11 b m **1947[5] 3182[F]** **>86c<**
Lost In The Post (IRE) 4 ch g Don't Forget Me-Postie (Sharpo) 2510[9] 2675[8] 4335[6] **>42h<**
Lo Stregone 11 b g **1649[3] 2616[3] 3294[5] 4074[P]** **>157?c<**
Lostris (IRE) 6 b m Pennine Walk-Herila (FR) (Bold Lad (USA)) 1689[7] 2541[2] 2787[8] 3696[4] **>64h<**
Lothian Commander 5 ch g 1536[8] 1640[14] 2806[7] 3004[4] 3473[4] 3628[7] 3967[6] **>50h<**
Lothian Commodore 7 gr g **4076[5]** **>53h 68c<**
Lothian Jem 8 b m **1414[F] 1664[P]** 2552[P] 2664[P] **>49h<**
Lotschberg Express 5 ch m 1177[8] **>10fh<**
Lottery Ticket (IRE) 8 b g **1318[2] 3279[U] 3400[P]** 4257[5] 4476[3] 4622[2] **>69h 108c<**
Lottover (IRE) 8 b m **4361a[U]** **>11h 74c<**
Loughdoo (IRE) 9 ch g Avocat-Balmy Grove (Virginia Boy) 1683[7] 2093[8] 2945[6] 4309[11] 4524[4] **4763[5]** **>56h 51c<**
Lough Slania (IRE) 4 b c Pennine Walk-Sister Ursula 2738a[11] **>59h<**
Lough Tully (IRE) 7 ch g Denel (FR)-Lough Hill Lady (Cantab) 788[6] 1090[4] 1539[5] 1840[2] 2552[3] (3108) (3473) **>75+h<**
Love and Porter (IRE) 9 b m **1397a[7] 1495a[P] 2348a[15]** 3126a[9] **>87h 114c<**
Lovelark 8 b m 27[13] 648[8] 737[3] 2088[2] 2838[6] 3488[P] 3997[4] 4091[8] **>25h<**
Lovely Outlook 5 b g Teenoso (USA)-Black Penny (West Partisan) 3574[P]
Lovely Rascal 5 gr m Scallywag-Owen Belle (Master Owen) 1190[5] 1450[2] 1834[7] 2047[7] 2920[6] **>29h<**
Love The Blues 5 ch m 790[7] 2701[2] 3048[6] 3295[4] **>78h<**
Love the Lord (IRE) 7 b m **1003a[7] 1397a[3] 1495a[5] 1737a[5] 1889a[P]** **>88h 119c<**
Loveyoumillions (IRE) 5 b g Law Society (USA)-Warning Sound (Red Alert) 1343[7] **>4h<**
Lowawatha 9 b g **61[4] 592[6] 862[2] 1066[4] 3225[P] 4564[2] 4733[P]** **>70h 93c<**
Lower Bitham 10 ch m **1199[P]** **>38h< (DEAD)**
Loyal Gait (NZ) 9 ch g **3813[P] 4135[P] 4317[P]**

Loyal Note 9 ch g **(3062) 3353[4] 3580[2] 4324[4]** **>107c<**

Lucayan Cay (IRE) 6 ch g 2952[7] 3234[4] 3499[P] **>69h<**

Lucayan Gold 13 br g 729[5] **>77+h 75c<**

Lucia Forte 6 b m (1516) 1873[2] 2090[F] 2763[4] (2961) (3817) **>84h<**

Lucker 10 b g 3714[3] 4162[P] **>39h<**

Lucknam Dreamer 9 b g **1150[P]** **>70c< (DEAD)**

Lucky Archer 4 b g North Briton-Preobrajenska (Double Form) 3820[4] 4095[3] 4382[U] 4525[6] 4807[12] **>59h<**

Lucky Bea 4 b g Lochnager-Knocksharry (Palm Track) 906[9] 1159[F] 1652[11] 2744[4] 2859[13] (3031) **>62h<**

Lucky Blue 10 b g 2644[P] 2950[8] 4053[10] **>82h<**

Lucky Bust (IRE) 7 b g **4351a[5]** **>76h 102c<**

Lucky Call (NZ) 6 b g Lucky Ring-Afrea (NZ) (Imposing (AUS)) 1203[7] 1568[12] **3086[U]** 4625[3] **>64h<**

Lucky Christopher 12 b g **4545[2] 4805[P]** **>100c<**

Lucky Dollar (IRE) 9 ch g **(503) 602[2] 720[3] 1008[2] 1318[3] 1506[2] 1716[3] 2054[F] (2940) 3599[3] (3837) 4148[4]** **>90h 111c<**

Lucky Domino 7 b g 555[5] 913[12] **>38h<**

Lucky Eddie (IRE) 6 b g 1709[6] 1878[2] **2810[6] 3111[3] 3591[3] 3931[2] (4305) 4523[5]** **>85h 76dc<**

Lucky Escape 6 b g Then Again-Lucky Love (Mummy's Pet) 3184[10] 3829[6]

Lucky Hoof 4 b f Batshoof-Lucky Omen (Queen's Hussar) 4056[P]

Lucky Landing (IRE) 8 b g **4320[P] 4543[P]**

Lucky Lane 13 b g 1571[P] **1937[7] 3018[P]** **>85h 106c<**

Lucky Mo 7 ch m 306[4] 504[7] 737[R] 885[R]

Lucky Tanner 6 b g 1633[10] 2676[P] **3111[F]** 3426[13] **>24h<**

Lucky Touch 4 ch g Broadsword (USA)-Solatia (Kalydon) 4539[7] **>51fh<**

Lucrative Perk (IRE) 5 b m Executive Perk-Lucrative (Wolverlife) 1800[9] 2811[11] 3226[11] 4304[9] 4506[3] **>58?h<**

Lucy Glitters 5 b m Ardross-Henry's True Love (Random Shot) 4531[2] **>53fh<**

Lucy's Choice 6 b m 2090[P]

Lucys Red Slipper 5 ch m Newski (USA)-Slipalong (Slippered) 4009[17]

Lucy Tufty 6 b m 1374[8] 1861[9] 2792[11] 3352[5] 3666[6] 3940[5] (4795) **>59h<**

Ludo's Orchestra (IRE) 6 ch g 2844[10] 3021[8] 4450[P] 4726[5] **>43h<**

Lugs Brannigan (IRE) 8 b g 1876[3] **>74h<**

Luker Boy (IRE) 7 b g 1541[P]

Luke Warm 7 ch g 891[2] 1174[4] 2694[3] 3473[3] 4544[2] **>58h 82c<**

Lumback Lady 7 b m State Diplomacy (USA)-Jalome (Uncle Pokey) 939[10] 1312[4] 2504[4] 2649[5] 2953[2] 3325[2] 3529[4] 4244[13] 4335[4] **>65h<**

Lumo (IRE) 6 ch g 1071[U] 1795[P] 3431[P] **(DEAD)**

Lunar Dancer 5 b g Dancing High-Pauper Moon (Pauper) (4156) **>61fh<**

Lunar Gris 4 gr f Absalom-Sliprail (USA) (Our Native (USA)) 912[7] 3764[P] 4238[4]

L'Uomo Piu 13 b g 605[5] **658[3] 726[P] 833[4] 957[P] (4022) 4179[P] 4293[3] 4763[P]** **>84c<**

Lupy Minstrel 12 br g **4545[3] 4758[5]** **>100c<**

Lurriga Glitter (IRE) 9 gr g General Ironside-Glitter On (Even Money) **2951[2] 3357[6] 3490[3] 4015[5] 4135[2] 4324[6] 4730[P]** **>102dc<**

Lustreman 10 ch g 641[P] 868[P] 1299[12]

Lyford Cay (IRE) 7 ch g Waajib-Island Goddess (Godswalk (USA)) 1672[P] 2918[P] 3159[P] **3393[F] 4149[F]** 4283[16] **>57h<**

Lying Eyes 6 ch m 3150[6] 3615[19] 3920[4] **>89h< (DEAD)**

Lyme Gold (IRE) 8 ch g **3924[P] 4634[7]** **>85dh 90c<**

Lyphantastic (USA) 8 b g 4310[P]

Lyphard's Fable (USA) 6 b g 1135[F] 1638[10] 2036[6] 4333[4] 4652[2] 4731[F] **>43h<**

Lysander 5 ch g Takachiho-Apple At Night (Carnival Night) 133[16]

M

Maamur (USA) 9 gr g **3230[4] 3598[P]** **>135?h 150+c< (DEAD)**

Mabthul (USA) 9 b g 459[3] **>39dh 77c<**

Macallister (IRE) 7 br g **1758a[U] 2362a[6] 4351a[P]** **>103h 119c<**

Macaunta (IRE) 7 b g Mandalus-Laois Story (Royal Match) **3617[P]** **>43h 87c<**

Macedonas 9 b g 29[7] 958[6] **>39h 98c<**

Macgeorge (IRE) 7 b g **1320[U] 1680[5] 1981[F] (2699) (3071) 3335[2] 4211[2] (4537)** **>77h 125c<**

Mack a Day 10 b g Niels-Soothamona (Beau Charmeur (FR)) **4361a[6]** **>82c<**

Macmorris (USA) 4 b c Silver Hawk (USA)-Andover Cottage (USA) (Affiliate (USA)) 2772[P] 2889[F]

Macnamarasband (IRE) 8 b g **4350a[9]** **>122h 95c<**

Mac'smyuncle 6 b g Derring Rose-Magelka (Relkino) 3235[16] 3590[7] 4382[8] **>32h<**

Mac's Supreme (IRE) 5 b g Supreme Leader-Merry Breeze (Strong Gale) 1504[5] (3142) 3561[5] **>67fh<**

Mac's Taxi 5 b g 7[5]

Macy (IRE) 4 ch g Sharp Charter-Lumax (Maximilian) (2911) 3203[4] 3606[4] 4118a[12] **>74fh<**

Madam Cora 5 b m Gildoran-Lawnswood Miss (Grey Mirage) 4304[P] **(DEAD)**

Madame Beck 8 b m **3913[P]**

Madame President (IRE) 6 b m 958[P] 1586[4] (2694) 2941[4] 3358[7] **>65h<**

Madam Muck 6 ch m 1768[10] **>26h<**

Madam Polly 5 b m 1820[3] 2656[P] 3052[7] 3587[P] **>53fh<**

Madam Rose (IRE) 7 b m 1550[9] 1762[5] 2036[7] **2873[6] 3188[6] 3684[2] 4157[U]** 4468[16]

Madam's Walk 7 ch m 1090[3] 2759[P] 3355[9] 3798[4] 4304[5] 4458[2] **>67h<**

Maddie 5 b m Primitive Rising (USA)-Dubavarna (Dubassoff (USA)) 4301[7] **>45fh<**

Mademist Sam 5 b g Lord Bud-Mademist Susie (French Vine) 3828[8] 3914[16] **>49fh<**

Madge McSplash 5 ch m 800[3] **>58h<**

Mad Harry 5 b g Dunbeath (USA)-Hannie Caulder (Workboy) (3939) **>61fh<**

Madhaze (IRE) 6 ch g Zaffaran (USA)-Canhaar (Sparkler) 653[2]

Madison County (IRE) 7 b g **1320[2] 1635[5] 2660[P] 3422[2]** **>108h 101c<**

Madraj (IRE) 9 b or br g 303[7] **>69h 51c<**

Maenad 6 gr m 3143[P] **>45fh<**

Maestro Paul 11 b g **1812[2] 2665[4] 2829[4] (3232) 3496[5]** **>102h 103c<**

Maeterlinck (IRE) 5 b g Bluebird (USA)-Entracte (Henbit (USA)) 1873[F] 2822[7] 3441[6] 3820[3] 4136[5] 4313[7] **>60h<**

Mafuta (IRE) 5 b m 22[7] **>30h<**

Maggies Lad 9 b g 4259[8] 4732[4] **>56h<**

Maggie Strait 5 b m 1986[6] 2757[11]

Maggots Green 10 ch m **57[5] 207[3] (222) 292[3] (352) (414) (484) (588) 650[2] 689[3] 4379[5] 4553[5]** **>33h 100c<**

Magical Blues (IRE) 5 b g Magical Strike (USA)-Blue Bell Girl (Blakeney) 3284[F] 3901[P] 4069[2] (4405) (4731) **>68h<**

Magical Lady (IRE) 5 b m 2603a[9] 3254a[5] 4357a[8] **>116h 102c<**

Magic Bloom 11 br m **94[P] 215[4] 256[2] (335) 487[2] (583) 645[P] (732) 857[4] 1029[3] 1415[4]** **>77h 109c<**

Magic Combination (IRE) 4 b g Scenic-Etage (Ile de Bourbon (USA)) 2868[3] 3075[11] **>60h<**

Magic Role 4 b g Tragic Role (USA)-Athens by Night (USA) (London Bells (CAN)) 1862[8] 2622[12] 2889[P] 3224[6] **>24h<**

Magic Times 6 b g Good Times (ITY)-Young Wilkie (Callernish) 1689[P] 2697[P]

Magic Wizard 6 b g 1333[3] **>62h<**

Magnolia Man 11 b g **(4545) 4805[P]** **>98c<**

Magnum Force (IRE) 6 br g Strong Gale-Innocent Choice (Deep Run) 25[P] **(DEAD)**

Magnus Maximus 5 b g Takachiho-L'Oraz (Ile de Bourbon (USA)) 2675[14]

Magpie Melody (IRE) 6 ch g Orchestra-Judysway (Deep Run) 1296[9] 2047[2] 2770[2] (3644) 3910[3] 4182[6] **>71h<**

Magslad 7 ch g 62[3] **>91h<**

Magslass 5 b m 1579[14] 1774[15]

Magsood 12 ch g **190[13]** **>69h 101c<**

Mahler 7 b g (2036) 2552[7] 2676[5] 3108[4] (3587) (4204) **>69h<**

Maid Equal 6 gr m (2659) (2877) (3112) 3737[5] **>89h<**

Maid For Adventure (IRE) 6 br m 1317[6] (2090) 2927[4] 4304[2] (4506) **>73h<**

Maid For Dancing (IRE) 8 b m Crash Course-La Flemenca **3380a[3]** **>94c<**

Maine Marie 5 b m Northern State (USA)-Marie Galante (Shirley Heights) 3676[6] **>50fh<**

Maitre de Musique (FR) 6 ch g 1843[5] 2785[5] 3703[4] 3825[2] 4081[8] **>75h<**

Majestic Ride 13 b g **4730[P]** **>78c<**

Majic Belle 9 b m Majestic Maharaj-Ankerdine Belle (Paddy Boy) **3744[U]**

Major Bell 9 br g **(1119) 1520[2] 2057[3] 3292[3] 3639[2]** **>115h 151c<**

Major Dundee (IRE) 4 b g Distinctly North (USA)-Indigo Blue (IRE) (Bluebird (USA)) 2865[6] 3918[2] (4097) (4170) (4720) **>90?h<**

Major Hage (IRE) 6 gr g Over The River (FR)-Kilross (Menelek) 3142[5] 3727[4] **>44h<**

Major Harris (IRE) 5 b g Lord Americo-Bamtown (Belfalas) 1999[3] 2785[7] 3794[2] (3990) 4257[4] **>75h<**

Majority Major (IRE) 8 b g **(1691) 2954[6] 3141[3] 3556[P] 3882[5] 4447[4] 4576[7]** **>54h 86c<**

Major Jamie (IRE) 6 b g 1752a[6] **>97h<**

Major Look (NZ) 9 gr g **2049[3] 2672[4] 3047[P] 3268[4]** **>104c<**

Major Mac 10 b g **3089[P] 3341[P] 3490[5] 3837[P]**

Major Nova 8 b g 1681[P] 1952[P] **2883[P] 3020[10] 3334[5] 3489[2] 3848[4]** **>77h 97c<**

Major's Law (IRE) 8 b g **4732[2]** **>66h 66c<**

Majors Legacy (IRE) 8 b br g **1538[5] 1773[4] 2052[2] 3400[2]** **>53h 93c<**

Major Summit (IRE) 8 b or br g **1637[U] 1789[2] 2887[F]** **>98h 137c< (DEAD)**

Major Yaasi (USA) 7 b g 2670[F] 2842[7] 3201[9] (3478) 3709[5] 3942[4] **>69h<**

Majra (USA) 5 b g Alleged (USA)-Miss Tusculum (USA) (Boldnesian) 3668[5] **>43h<**

Make A Buck 7 ch g 1705[11] **2000[F]** 2619[16] **>9h<**

Make a Stand 6 ch g (952) 1280[2] 1365[5] (1793) (2055) (2645) (3038) (3597) 4063[3] **>147h<**

Makes Me Goosey (IRE) 9 b g **1540[6] 1799[7] 2869[6] 3074[P]** **>67h 100c< (DEAD)**

Making Time 10 gr m **4135[P] 4320[P]** **>65?h 78c<**

Malacca King (IRE) 6 b g 4352a^{8} >91h 80c<
Malta Man (IRE) 7 b g 1667^{2} 2619^{4} 2958^{5} 3159^{8} 3790^{5} (4286) 4745^{P} >71h 103dc<
Malwood Castle (IRE) 7 b g 3443^{F} 3537^{2} (3762) 3919^{3} 4342^{2} (4549) 4735^{6} >76h 107c<
Malzoom 5 b g Statoblest-Plum Bold (Be My Guest (USA)) 137^{P}
Mamica 7 b g 1574^{2} 1850^{F} 2540^{4} 2788^{P} 2919^{P} 4077^{7} >68h 89c<
Mammy's Choice (IRE) 7 br m (1423) (1812) 2660^{P} 3043^{7} 3410^{B} 3540^{2} 3819^{3} 4174^{P} >67dh 99c<
Mamnoon (USA) 6 b g 4623^{P} >63h<
Manabar 5 b g Reprimand-Ring of Pearl (Auction Ring (USA)) 3072^{U}
Manaboutthehouse 10 b g 22^{6} 132^{11} >76h 87dc<
Manamour 10 br g 158^{6} 215^{5} (305) 361^{2} 414^{3} (656) 4438^{P} >93c<
Manasis (NZ) 6 b g Tom's Shu (USA)-Ruakiwi Nymph (NZ) (Sea Anchor) 1280^{3} 2074^{10} (3431) >76h<
Mandys Mantino 7 br g (1319) (1559) 1919^{2} 2641^{3} 3227^{2} 3615^{10} >128h 115c<
Mandys Royal Lad 9 b g Royal Vulcan-Mandy's Melody (Highland Melody) 675^{10} >41h<
Maneree 10 b m 1271^{6} 1567^{6} 1813^{4} 2694^{P} >76h 113c<
Manetti 5 b h Reference Point-Bex (USA) (Explodent (USA)) 317a^{9} >99h<
Manettia (IRE) 8 b m 1081^{5} 1844^{2} 2922^{3} 3157^{P} >66h<
Manhattan Castle (IRE) 8 br g (2741a) 3639^{P} >114h 136c<
Mankind 6 b g (4228) 4406^{P} >107c<
Man Mood (FR) 6 b g 1035^{5} 1182^{P} 1350^{3} 1660^{3} 2695^{P} >110dc<
Mannagar (IRE) 5 ch g Irish River (FR)-Meadow Glen Lady (USA) (Believe It (USA)) 812^{10} 1942^{9} 2798^{11} >16h<
Man of Arran (IRE) 7 ch g 2600a^{4} >104h 87c<
Man of The Match 7 b g Vital Season-Kate The Shrew (Comedy Star (USA)) 2668^{13} 3171^{7} 3734^{3} >65h<
Man of Wisley (IRE) 7 b g 3704^{P}
Manolete 6 b g 1681^{P} 2670^{10} 2884^{11} 3051^{5} >60h<
Manor Bound 7 ch m 482^{3} 631^{4} 726^{3} 957^{4} 3683^{10} >16h 79c<
Manor Court (IRE) 9 ch g 2698^{P} 3317^{P} >82?c<
Manor Mieo 11 b g 860^{3} 1075^{5} 1716^{U} (4635) >100c<
Manor Rhyme 10 b g 30^{5} 70^{3} (135) 283^{4} >90c<
Manoy 4 b g Precocious-Redcross Miss (Tower Walk) 462^{3} 4744^{P} >56h<
Mansur (IRE) 5 b g Be My Chief (USA)-Moorish Idol (Aragon) 1726^{11} 2112^{7} >38h<
Manvulane (IRE) 7 b g 1633^{P} 2093^{3} 2927^{P} >64h<
Mapengo 6 b g 1053^{10} >18h<
Maple Bay (IRE) 8 b g Bold Arrangement-Cannon Boy (USA) (Canonero II (USA)) 1992^{9} 2504^{2} (2798) 2957^{7} 3396^{7} 4056^{7} 4244^{10} 4285^{12} >73dh<
Maple Dancer 11 b g (215) (256) (395) 588^{3} >112c<
Mapleton 4 br g Skyliner-Maple Syrup (Charlottown) 1356^{6} 2615^{12} 2785^{6} 3265^{6} 3612^{12} 3888^{5} 4223^{P} >59h 55c<
Marble Man (IRE) 7 ch g 337^{4} (939) 1525^{2} 1826^{3} 2674^{2} (2921) 3350^{3} >73h 100c<
Marchant Ming (IRE) 5 br g 1267^{3} 1656^{5} 2062^{4} 2617^{6} 3163^{8} 3293^{P} >105h<
Marchaway (IRE) 4 b g Magical Strike (USA)-Milly Whiteway (Great White Way (USA)) 2993a^{13} >52h<
Marchies Magic 7 b g 3399^{9} >20h<
Marching Marquis (IRE) 6 b g 1059^{U} 1171^{U} 1938^{2} (2927) 3152^{3} 3613^{8} >90h<
Marchman 12 b g Daring March-Saltation (Sallust) 551^{2} 596^{4} >63h 81c<
Marchwood 10 ch g 1347^{6} 1704^{F} 2004^{F} 2630^{8} >51h 88c<
Marco Magnifico (USA) 7 b or br g 697^{8} 893^{6} 1047^{5} 1078^{6} 1822^{P} >64h<
Mardood 12 b g 1562^{5} 1849^{10} 2915^{10} 3607^{8} 3971^{3} 4378^{7} 4572^{2} (4727) >44h<
Marello 6 br m (1190) (1438) (3158) (3396) (4205) >90+h<
Maremma Gale (IRE) 9 b g 833^{P} >106c<
Margier 7 br m Queen's Soldier (USA)-Princess Impala (Damsire Unregistered) 4082^{7}
Margot's Boy 6 ch g 4152^{P}
Marie's Pride (IRE) 6 b m 319a^{10} >21h<
Marigliano (USA) 4 b c Riverman (USA)-Mount Holyoke (Golden Fleece (USA)) 3197^{P} 3544^{8} >28h<
Mariners Cove 9 br g 13^{5} 132^{7} >55h 71c<
Mariners Memory 9 b g 4508^{F}
Mariners Mirror 10 b m 1176^{3} (1291) (1771) (2072) 2879^{3} 3165^{2} >85h 127c<
Mariners Reef (IRE) 6 gr m 4352a^{6} >82h<
Mario's Dream (IRE) 9 ch g Boyne Valley-Its All A Dream (Le Moss) 253^{6} 300^{R} 594^{3} 899^{5} 969^{F} >24h<
Marius (IRE) 7 b g 1567^{2} 1832^{4} (2828) 3183^{2} 3562^{4} 3814^{2} 4271^{3} >91h<
Marjimel 6 b m Backchat (USA)-Mary's Double (Majetta) 3029^{9} >15h<
Market Gossip 7 b g 1285^{P} 1773^{3} >56dh 75c<
Marketing Man 7 b g 98^{P} 217^{U} 393^{5} >57h<
Market Mayhem 7 b g 1633^{2} 1938^{P} 3000^{5} 3186^{P} 3627^{4} >56h<
Marketplace (IRE) 6 b h Runnett-Ordinary Fare (USA) (What A Pleasure (USA)) 1385^{6} >90c<
Marksman Sparks 7 b g 1452^{4} 3443^{F} >60?h 97+c<
Marks Refrain 13 b g Blue Refrain-Markup (Appiani II) 1672^{P} >38h< (DEAD)
Marlast (IRE) 6 ch m 317a^{7} >62h 78c<
Marlies Gohr 5 b m Arctic Bronze VII-Miss Carvin (Carvin (FR)) 4403^{P}
Marlingford 10 ch g 1143^{6} 1358^{7} 1653^{7} (2632) 2699^{5} 3030^{3} 3299^{3} 3329^{4} 3886^{8} >41h 79c<
Marlonette (IRE) 4 ch f Jareer (USA)-Marlova (FR) (Salvo) 2738a^{5} 2993a^{4} 3634^{6} 4014^{7} >88h<
Marlousion (IRE) 5 ch m Montelimar (USA)-Ware Princess (Crash Course) 161^{2} 504^{2} 594^{P} 630^{4} 1341^{2} 1565^{2} 3172^{P} >64h<
Marnies Wolf 6 ch g 1033^{6}
Maronetta 5 ch m 219^{P} >54h<
Marrowfat Lady (IRE) 6 b m 2692^{F} 2818^{10} 3110^{11} >11h<
Marsden Rock 10 b or br m 893^{3} 1121^{6} 1310^{2} >63h 85?c<
Marsh's Law 10 br g 32^{7} 1249^{6} 3434^{7} 3976^{8} 4296^{10} >31h 69c<
Martell Boy (NZ) 10 b g 4535^{2} (4697) >91h 114c<
Martello Girl (IRE) 5 b m Buckskin (FR)-Moss Gale (Strong Gale) 344^{P}
Martha Buckle 8 br m 2539^{12} 2790^{P} >28h<
Martha's Daughter 8 br m 634^{11} 722^{4} 821^{2} 935^{4} >68h 93dc<
Martha's Son 10 b g 3299^{F} (3614) (4049) >121h 173c<
Martomick 10 br m 1055^{3} 1367^{3} 2775^{4} >138c<
Maryjo (IRE) 8 b m 101^{8} 185^{9} >60h<
Mary's Case (IRE) 7 b g 1141^{8} >37h<
Masimara Music 6 ch m Almushmmir-Native Chant (Gone Native) 600^{10} 788^{11} >6h<
Masked Martin 6 b g 1875^{7} 2551^{5} 2575^{P} 2704^{F} >25h<
Mason Dixon 8 b or br g 27^{P} >56h<
Masruf (IRE) 5 b g Taufan (USA)-Queen's Share (Main Reef) 498^{P} 2815^{P}
Masrur (USA) 8 b g Mt Livermore (USA)-Presto Youth (USA) (Youth (USA)) 4273^{P}
Master Art 7 b g Scorpio (FR)-The Huyton Girls (Master Sing) 160^{5} 263^{P} >60c<
Master Beveled 7 b g 1512^{2} 1793^{2} 2645^{7} 4212^{9} 4397^{13} >112h<
Master Bomber (IRE) 6 b g Lancastrian-London Anne (London Bells (CAN)) 1766^{7} 1964^{P}
Master Boston (IRE) 9 gr g 953^{P} 3349^{P} 3451^{4} 4013^{U} >94h 125dc<
Master Bradan 4 ch c Genuine Gift (CAN)-Lady Lily (Quiet Fling (USA)) 4156^{3} >40fh<
Master Comedy 13 b g 1076^{2} 1554^{4} 2910^{2} 3179^{4} 3605^{3} 4098^{3} 4438^{5} 4722^{5} >87c<
Master Crozina 9 br g 3460^{P} 3713^{5} >34c<
Master Crusader 11 b g Mandalus-Abi's Dream (Paddy's Stream) 4327^{2} 4435^{2} 4649^{4} (4769) >81c<
Master Donnington 9 br g Julio Mariner-Lor Damie (Dumbarnie) 3765^{5} >87c<
Master Flashman 8 ch g 2917^{12} 3306^{P} 3608^{2} 3726^{5} 4149^{P} 4408^{7} >59h 79c<
Master Goodenough (IRE) 6 ch g 859^{P} 1663^{F} 1729^{8} 2680^{13} 2905^{F} 4018^{3} >34h<
Master-H 4 ch g Ballacashtal (CAN)-Edith Rose (Cheval) 3109^{12} 3898^{5} >25h<
Master Harry (IRE) 5 b g Strong Gale-Another Miller (Gala Performance (USA)) 1665^{10} >18fh<
Master Hope (IRE) 8 b g 1371^{5} 1829^{4} 2816^{F} >97c< (DEAD)
Master Hyde (USA) 8 gr g 1127^{4} 1658^{9} 1852^{6} 2631^{12} 3827^{6} 4081^{F} >76h<
Master Jolson 9 b g 1997^{P} 2829^{7} 3185^{P} >79c<
Master Kit (IRE) 8 b g 3095^{F} 3270^{U} 3617^{F} 4256^{8} 4579^{3} 4713^{3} >103c<
Master Kiwi (NZ) 10 b g 482^{P}
Master Oats 11 ch g 3261a^{P} 4074^{5} >167c<
Master Ofthe House 11 b g 3^{3} 422^{4} >69h<
Master of the Rock 8 b g 747^{4} 1418^{7} 3454^{3} >87dh 81c<
Master of Troy 9 b g 2699^{6} 3306^{4} 3484^{4} 4081^{5} 4261^{3} 4744^{4} >75h 87c<
Master Orchestra (IRE) 8 ch g 1194^{P} >110c<
Master Pangloss (IRE) 7 b g 1073^{4} 1472^{U} 1582^{F} 2752^{B} 3343^{7} 3810^{2} >59c<
Master Pilgrim 5 b g Supreme Leader-Patterdon (Precipice Wood) 2071^{3} 2868^{5} 3337^{2} >70h<
Master Pip 5 ch g Risk Me (FR)-Whose Lady (USA) (Master Willie) 2811^{5} 3149^{P} (DEAD)
Master Rupert 5 gr g Colway Radial-Maybella (Quiet Fling (USA)) 4205^{P}
Master Salesman 14 b g 15^{P} 975^{4} 1306^{4} 1846^{5} >66c<
Master Showman (IRE) 6 b g 4453^{5} 4556^{4} 4795^{2} >43h<
Master Toby 7 b g (3334) 3849^{4} 4227^{U} 4546^{P} >75h 108dc<
Master Tribe (IRE) 7 ch g 1636^{8} 2048^{2} (2603a) 2635^{P} 3187^{P} >101h<
Master Upex 5 b g Aragon-Little Egret (Carwhite) 1337^{9} 1550^{P} 1810^{P}
Matachon 7 ro g 31^{P} 1999^{14} 2918^{P} 4144^{S} >17h<

Matamoros 5 gr h 634^4 1390^P 3722^P **>64h<**
Match The Colour 4 b g Full Extent (USA)-Matching Lines (Thatching) 2859^P
Matt Reid 13 ch g **2903^3 3162^6 3543^3 4051^F >103c<**
Matts Dilemma (IRE) 9 gr g **4351a^P >87h 90c<**
Maurachas (IRE) 7 ch g 1639^9 **>63h<**
Maxxum Express (IRE) 9 b g **1284^6 1564^5 1877^5 3551^3 3837^4 4404^7 >90c<**
Mayasta (IRE) 7 br m 1487a^4 2461a^5 3254a^9 3523a^6 **>100h<**
Maybe O'Grady (IRE) 8 b g 1294^{10} 1690^4 **>43h<**
Mayb-Mayb 7 ch g 934^5 (3063) 3201^F (3411) (3577) (4309) **>72h<**
Mayday Lauren 5 b m Scottish Reel-Real Claire (Dreams to Reality (USA)) (3747) *(3846)* **>66fh<**
Maylin Magic 6 b m 1341^8 1958^3 2642^P 3061^2 3755^4 3902^2 4099^4 **>68h<**
May Rose 7 ch m Ayres Rock-Misty Morn III (Mount Sherwood) 2080^{13}
May Sunset (IRE) 7 b g Tremblant-Donegal Queen (Quayside) 3406^5 4188^6 **>59h<**
Mazamet (USA) 4 b g Elmaamul (USA)-Miss Mazepah (USA) (Nijinsky (CAN)) 1900^4 2772^4 4299^2 4651^2 **>76h<**
Mazileo 4 b g Mazilier (USA)-Embroglio (USA) (Empery (USA)) 3747^4 (3895) **>67fh<**
Mazirah 6 b g Mazilier (USA)-Barbary Court (Grundy) 1659^5 1835^3 2547^{17} 3012^8 3760^7 3933^9 **>41h<**
Mazzelmo 4 gr f Thethingaboutitis (USA)-Nattfari (Tyrnavos) 3808^5 3914^{15} 4421^5 **>43fh<**
Mazzini (IRE) 6 b g (812) 961^2 (1283) 1791^8 2755^3 3105^4 4101^4 **>75h<**
M'Bebe 7 b or br h 65^P 96^P **>8h<**
Mccartney 11 b g **4637^7 >67dc<**
Mc Clatchey (IRE) 6 b g 319a^{12} **>27h<**
Mcgillycuddy Reeks (IRE) 6 b m 97^7 505^6 **>63h<**
McGregor The Third 11 ch g **(645) (797) 1048^2 (1385) 3266^2 3699^5 4303^3 >142c<**
Mead Court (IRE) 7 ch g **933^2 >82h<**
Meadow Bee 5 b g Meadowbrook-Regal Bee (Royal Fountain) 2539^{11} 2861^P
Meadow Hymn (IRE) 6 b g Hymns On High-Nevada Run (Deep Run) 1504^3 1692^7 2066^2 2510^3 (2958) (3100) 3910^2 (4146) 4257^2 **>92h<**
Meadowleck 8 b m 1247^8 1349^9 1851^{11} 2768^4 2913^{10} 3024^7 3066^F 3529^8 3641^B 3825^5 4055^{10} 4283^{13} 4513^P 4572^P 4711^8 4756^9 **>30h<**
Meanus Miller (IRE) 9 ch m 793^F **>68h< (DEAD)**
Mecado 10 b g **3631^R** 4472^2 4552^6 4739^P **>60h<**
Mederic (IRE) 7 b g Strong Gale-Our Gale (Dusky Boy) 1854^P
Medford 7 b g (1297) 1541^7 1768^8 **>74h<**
Media Express 5 b g 4259^7 **>32h<**
Mediane (USA) 12 b g **2951^P 3273^2 3403^R 3498^R >105h 93?c<**
Meditator 13 ch g 1258^{10} 1783^5 2659^P (4207) 4310^2 **>90h<**
Meesonette 5 ch m Hubbly Bubbly (USA)-Iron Lass (Thatch (USA)) 1438^8 1687^{14} 1851^7 1990^P 3908^{13} **4151^F 4502^7 4751^5 >28h 54c<**
Meesons Express 7 ch g 1999^P
Mega Gale (IRE) 5 br g Strong Gale-Doneraile's Joy 4118a^{20} **>67fh<**
Megamunch (IRE) 9 ch g 424^3 **>64?h<**
Mega Tid 5 b g Old Vic-Dunoof (Shirley Heights) 3575^{10} 4453^7
Meggie Scott 4 ch f Dunbeath (USA)-Abigails Portrait (Absalom) 3561^9 3828^{19} 4287^{10}
Meg's Memory (IRE) 4 b f Superlative-Meanz Beanz (High Top) 2566^5 (3029) 3745^4 4628^5 **>67h<**
Mel (IRE) 7 ch g 1810^6 2634^6 **2795^8 3051^P 4383^3 4738^5 >60h 82c<**
Mellow Master 4 b g Royal Academy (USA)-Upward Trend (Salmon Leap (USA)) 2939^{11} (3352) (3951) 4137^P **>65h<**
Mellow Yellow 6 b g 392^4 497^7 743^5 **>51h<**
Melnik 6 ch g **(1963) 2693^P 3060^P 4227^3 4537^P >99h 109dc<**
Melody Dancer 6 b g 5^{10} **>27h<**
Melody Maid 5 b m Strong Gale-Ribo Melody (Riboboy (USA)) 2931^2 (3433) (4009) 4360a^6 **>88fh<**
Melstock Meggie 7 ch m (1450) (1679) 1855^3 2552^5 3186^3 **>68h<**
Meltemison 4 b g Charmer-Salchow (Niniski (USA)) 1184^8 1652^4 2615^5 3093^2 3291^5 4209^2 **>75h<**
Melton Made (IRE) 4 br g Strong Gale-Pamela's Princess (Black Minstrel) 4531^7 **>42fh<**
Melt The Clouds (CAN) 4 ch g Diesis-Population (General Assembly (USA)) 2751^2 2872^7 (3947) 4395^6 4555^2 (4651) 4794^9 **>77h<**
Mely Moss (FR) 6 ch g Tip Moss (FR)-The Exception (FR) (Melyno) **(2762) 3018^3 3419^2 >141c<**
Memory's Music 5 b h 1424^4 1707^F 2753^P 3057^P **>64h<**
Memsahib Ofesteem 6 gr m Neltino-Occatillo (Maris Piper) (3290) 3440^3 3619^{25} **>64fh<**
Menaldi (IRE) 7 b g Meneval (USA)-Top Riggin (Jupiter Pluvius) 1208^6 1654^9 2673^{10} 2917^3 3139^5 3534^5 3794^9 4243^2 **>72h<**
Menature (IRE) 8 ch g Meneval (USA)-Speedy Venture (Bargello) **102^3 158^3 4637^5 >85dc<**
Mendip Prince (IRE) 7 b g 1261^3 2550^6 3016^P **3736^4 >75h 79c<**
Mendip Son 7 b g 54^7 **>82h<**
Menelave (IRE) 7 b m (1045) 1374^6 1832^3 3136^5 3679^4 **>71h<**
Menesonic (IRE) 7 b g 1476^4 1639^2 2880^3 3156^5 (3541) 3796^3 **>81h<**
Men Of Ninetyeight (IRE) 5 b g King's Ride-Penny Holder 4118a^7 **>78fh<**
Menshaar (USA) 5 b g 1292^5 1807^6 (1854) (2076) 2768^3 3646^6 **>78h<**
Mentmore Towers (IRE) 5 gr g 1369^2 2662^2 (3048) 4052^3 **>94h<**
Merawang (IRE) 4 b g Shahrastani (USA)-Modiyna (Nishapour (FR)) 2872^3 3184^3 3634^{23} **>70+h<**
Merely Mortal 6 b g 73^P 287^4 **>46h<**
Merilena (IRE) 7 b m 1342^7 1779^5 **3134^U 3200^3** 3358^8 **>58h 89c<**
Merivel 10 b g **23^P 4344^6 4806^P >63?h 98c<**
Merlins Dream (IRE) 8 ch g **500^2 689^2 864^2 (1043) (3074) 3585^2 (3961) 4270^5 >92h 125c<**
Merlins Wish (USA) 8 ch g **222^P** 255^7 394^5 483^9 600^7 913^7 **>94h 99?c<**
Merry Gale (IRE) 9 b g **1397a^4 1889a^2 (2346a) 2997a^4 (3245a) 3383a^2 4011^2 >111++h 155c<**
Merryhill Gold 6 b g 687^6 854^3 **1083^U 1206^6 2571^5 2698^4 >49h 54c<**
Merryhill Madam 8 b m 725^P **>50h<**
Merry Major 4 br g K-Battery-Merry Missus (Bargello) 3716^7 **>45fh<**
Merry Masquerade (IRE) 6 b g King's Ride-Merry Madness (Raise You Ten) 2066^3 2696^4 (3070) **>59fh<**
Merry Master 13 br g **1655^F 2782^{10} 3414^P >120dc<**
Merry Mermaid 7 ch m 3065^2 3346^{10} 3485^{12} 4573^6 **>57h<**
Merry Panto (IRE) 8 ch g **(886) 1321^2 1731^F 2894^5 4225^3 4300^3 4529^5 >29dh 106c<**
Merry People (IRE) 9 b g 4352a^{15} **>101h 107c<**
Mesp (IRE) 6 br m 1036^6 1250^6 1565^P 1907^5 2746^7 **>57h<**
Metastasio 5 b g 1752a^5 2603a^5 3615^{11} **>109h<**
Methodius (IRE) 5 b g Venetian Gate-Heaven Bound (Fine Blade (USA)) 4450^P **4736^U**
Mheanmetoo 6 ch g **2691^P 2926^P 3443^3 3758^3** 4231^8 **>24h 81c<**
Mhemeanles 7 br g **3270^P 3744^U >64h 72dc<**
Miami Splash 10 ch g **1035^P >108h 90c< (DEAD)**
Michandra Boy 4 b g Skyliner-Magdalene (IRE) (Runnett) 3142^{18}
Michelles Crystal 6 b m **3460^U 4070^F**
Michelles Gold (IRE) 5 b m Buckskin (FR)-Blue Rainbow (Balinger) 4118a^{24} **>40fh<**
Micherado (FR) 7 ch g **61^2 222^3 390^F (496) 799^2 (1252) >108c<**
Michigan Blue 5 b g Rakaposhi King-Starquin (IRE) (Strong Gale) 3808^{11} 4421^{15} **>13fh<**
Mickleover 7 b g Executive Man-Mickley Vulstar (Sea Moss) 3468^P
Micks Delight (IRE) 7 ch g **323a^P >55h 103c< (DEAD)**
Micksdilemma 10 b g Mick The Lark (USA)-Lovely Sister (Menelek) 10^2 **>61h<**
Mick The Yank (IRE) 7 b g 2882^{11} 3110^{12} 3338^6 3620^5 4055^5 **4158^4 >38h<**
Micky Brown 6 b g 3148^6
Midas 6 b g Rambo Dancer (CAN)-Curzon House (Green God) (1336) 1986^{11} 2804^9 3042^{11} **>70fh<**
Mid Day Chaser (IRE) 6 b m (2035) **>82+h<**
Middle Moggs (IRE) 5 b m 316a^8 **>76h<**
Midnight Bob 6 b g Derring Rose-Anner Amanda (Mandamus) 866^6 1030^{15}
Midnight Caller 11 br g **1649^4 >80h 145?c<**
Midnight Hour (IRE) 8 gr g **323a^P >74h 106c< (DEAD)**
Midnight Jestor (IRE) 9 b m 67^6 **>44h<**
Midnight Legend 6 b h Night Shift (USA)-Myth (Troy) 3359^4 (3761) (4010) (4348a) **>100+h<**
M-I-Five (IRE) 6 ch g 3973^4 4299^7 **>63h<**
Mighty Falcon 12 b g **4432^2 (4724) >105c<**
Mighty Frolic 10 b m **1420^P 1839^4 2681^P 3223^P**
Mighty Keen 4 ch c Keen-Mary Martin (Be My Guest (USA)) 2784^6 2925^{10} 3075^{10} **>47h<**
Mighty Merc 9 ch g **4649^6 >58c<**
Mighty Moss (IRE) 6 b g (1323) (1568) 2053^2 2781^2 3152^2 3613^2 **>100h<**
Mike's Music (IRE) 6 br g Orchestra-Seaville (Charlottesvilles Flyer) 1457^{10} 1966^3 2830^4 3441^8 **>49fh<**
Mike Stan (IRE) 6 b g Rontino-Fair Pirouette (Fair Turn) 3315^5 3483^4 3795^8 **>63h<**
Milenberg Joys 5 ch g 1692^{14} 3098^5 3475^6 4056^5 4479^9 **>56h<**
Miles More Fun 8 b m Idiot's Delight-Mary Mile (Athenius) **3739^P**
Milestone 5 b g 3592^P
Miletrian City 4 gr g Petong-Blueit (FR) (Bold Lad (IRE)) 2175^7 2649^B 3031^{14} **>30h<**
Milford Sound 4 b g Batshoof-Nafis (USA) (Nodouble (USA)) 2547^4 **>73h<**
Military Academy 8 ch g (1290) 1654^3 (3066) 3368^3 3531^6 (4575) **>88+h<**
Military Law 6 ch g Infantry-Sister-in-Law (Legal Tender) 1457^4 3399^6 **>47h<**
Mill Bay Sam 6 b g 3418^R 3574^{15} 4224^8 **>27fh<**
Millcroft Regatta (IRE) 5 br g Miner's Lamp-

Stradbally Bay (Shackleton) 1317^{15} 3178^{P} 3535^{7} **>28h<**

Millcroft Riviera (IRE) 6 b g 593^{5} 1597^{3} 1878^{4} (2878) 3171^{8} **>68h<**

Mill Dancer (IRE) 5 b m Broken Hearted-Theatral (Orchestra) 1818^{7} 3072^{11} 3284^{14} **>28h<**

Mill-Dot 5 b g Petoski-Bright-One (Electric) 3914^{10} **>6fh<**

Millenium Lass (IRE) 9 ch m Viking (USA)-Sandford Star (Sandford Lad) 2692^{9} 2897^{9} 3429^{P} 3733^{8} **3842^{P} >56h< (DEAD)**

Millennium Man 6 b g Silly Prices-Socher (Anax) 99^{4} 910^{13} 1139^{10} **>32h<**

Millers Action 4 b f Fearless Action (USA)-Miller's Gait (Mill Reef (USA)) 3425^{12}

Millersford 6 b g (1191) 1581^{4} 2961^{5} 3272^{5} 3552^{2} **>85h<**

Millers Goldengirl (IRE) 6 ch m 2649^{15} 2840^{14} 3641^{4} 3752^{6} 4163^{9} 4233^{6} **>27h<**

Millfield Miss 8 ch m 812^{P}

Millfrone (IRE) 7 ch g **1037^{P} 1389^{P} 1839^{P} 2819^{6} 3181^{F} >31h<**

Mill House Boy (IRE) 4 b g Astronef-Avantage Service (IRE) (Exactly Sharp (USA)) 388^{F}

Millies Image 6 ch m 1310^{5} 2509^{12} **2860^{3} 3393^{6}** >49h<

Millies Own 10 ch g **869^{4} 1445^{P} 4174^{P} >66h 72c<**

Milling Brook 5 b g 980^{6} 1118^{3} 1633^{7} 2035^{6} 2578^{6} 2806^{6} (3004) 3186^{P} 3932^{F} 4226^{P} **>54h<**

Million Dancer 5 b g Rambo Dancer (CAN)-Tea-Pot (Ragstone) (219) 287^{2} 481^{2} (497) 680^{3} (737) 891^{P} 1174^{2} **>78h<**

Millmount (IRE) 7 ch m 1810^{4} 2797^{9} 3063^{3} (3209) 4622^{P} **>73h<**

Mill O'The Rags (IRE) 8 b g **(556) 637^{2} (821) (1041) 1557^{5} 4254^{2} 4566^{2} 4700^{2} >65h 111c<**

Millstone Hill 5 b g Meadowbrook-Bromley Rose (Rubor) 3716^{9} **>14fh<**

Mill Thyme 5 b m 1204^{P} 1701^{10} 3166^{12} 3641^{6} 4220^{P} **>22h<**

Milly le Moss (IRE) 8 b m 934^{7} 1562^{8} 3189^{P} 3358^{P}

Milngavie (IRE) 7 ch g Pharly (FR)-Wig And Gown (Mandamus) 69^{2} 100^{3} **>81h<**

Mils Mij 12 br g **4410^{5} 4753^{7} >101dc<**

Miltonfield 8 ch g (2345a) 3523a^{4} 3600^{5} **>102h<**

Milwaukee (IRE) 8 ch m Over The River (FR)-Loch Gorman (Bargello) 2010^{14} **2841^{P} 3134^{4} 3472^{P} 3708^{2} >72c<**

Milzig (USA) 8 b g 66^{3} (101) 184^{9} 264^{4} 394^{4} 655^{6} 1072^{P} 4789^{3} **>42h<**

Mim-Lou-and 5 b g 790^{2} 1125^{4} 1353^{2} 2670^{12} 3430^{3} 3816^{4} 4550^{7} 4798^{P} **>78h<**

Mindyerownbusiness (IRE) 8 gr m **3188^{F} 3909^{P} 4417^{P} >70h<**

Minella Derby (IRE) 7 br g (1260) 2676^{7} 2945^{R} **>74—h<**

Minella Express (IRE) 8 b g **3457^{2} 3744^{3} >106c<**

Minella Gold (IRE) 8 b g **2341a^{F} >137h 68c<**

Minella Hotel (IRE) 5 b g Be My Native (USA)-Due Consideration (Sir Herbert) 4118a^{4} **>80fh<**

Minella Lad 11 b g **1003a^{5} >148h 110c<**

Minella Man 10 b g 1647^{4} **>126h<**

Mineral Water 4 ch g Weldnaas (USA)-Joud (Dancing Brave (USA)) 699^{P}

Miners Rest 9 b m Sula Bula-Miners Lodge (Ebomeezer) **286^{2}** 297^{4} **(457) (529) 597^{5} 752^{F} 4460^{2} 4742^{3} 4766^{5} >33h 80c<**

Miner's Rose (IRE) 6 b m Miner's Lamp-Ballinarose (Arctic Slave) 4008^{16} **>30fh<**

Mine's an Ace (NZ) 10 br g **959^{2} 1985^{F}** 2797^{P} **4456^{2} (4700) >106c<**

Mingay 6 b g 1203^{14} 1573^{15} 2878^{6} 3190^{P}

Mingus (USA) 10 b g **970^{3} 1285^{P} 1447^{P} 1582^{4} 2910^{F} 3113^{U} >86dh 85c<**

Minibelle 5 br m Macmillion-Pokey's Belle (Uncle Pokey) 4554^{5} 4657^{6} 4774^{6} **>46fh<**

Minidia 5 b m 262^{P} 396^{P}

Mini Fete (FR) 8 br m 1707^{6} 2664^{P} **3043^{11} 3331^{6} >40c<**

Minisioux 4 ch g Mandrake Major-Siouxsie (Warpath) 3561^{2} **>64fh<**

Minister for Fun (IRE) 9 b g **314a^{P} >62h 117c<**

Miniture Melody (IRE) 9 b m 27^{12} **>34h<**

Minneola 5 ch m Midyan (USA)-High Halo (High Top) 885^{P} 1333^{P} 4658^{P}

Minnesota Fats (IRE) 5 b br g 67^{3} 183^{4} 212^{2} 300^{4} 400^{3} 490^{2} (648) 697^{6} **>57h<**

Minnie (IRE) 4 b f Mandalus-Minnies Dipper (Royal Captive) 3606^{9} 3889^{10}

Minnies Turn 6 br m 4184^{P} 4244^{15}

Minnisam 4 ch g Niniski (USA)-Wise Speculation (USA) (Mr Prospector (USA)) 4423^{P} 4548^{8} 4658^{U} **>21h<**

Minor Key (IRE) 7 b g Orchestra-Maid of Moyode (Giolla Mear) 859^{3} 954^{F} **1136^{2} 1354^{F} 1506^{3} 2795^{P} 3086^{P}** 3408^{P} **>68h 75?c<**

Minster Boy 6 b g Minster Son-Rigton Sally (Joshua) 1777^{6} 2053^{11} 2550^{14} **>34h<**

Minster's Madam 6 ch m 793^{8} 888^{4} (1166) **1714^{F} 1809^{3}** 2792^{6} 3057^{8} 3338^{9} 3670^{8} **>75?h 89?c<**

Mintulyar 6 br g Broadsword (USA)-Minimint (Menelek) 4708^{7} **>15h<**

Miracle Man 9 b g **2600a^{2} >112h 108c<**

Mirador 6 b m (1710) 2950^{6} 3180^{4} 3554^{7} **>80dh<**

Mirage Dancer 14 b g **507^{4} 1012^{F} >75c< (DEAD)**

Mirage of Windsor (IRE) 9 b g Bulldozer-Lucky Favour (Ballyciptic) 3674^{P}

Miramare 7 br g 129^{4} 189^{7} 262^{4} 360^{4} **556^{P}** 655^{3} 837^{2} 913^{9} 1200^{P} 1419^{3} 1786^{5} 1874^{P} **2704^{P} 3891^{P}** 4091^{6} 4328^{2} (4384) 4658^{2} **>65h<**

Miry Leader 4 ch f Polar Falcon (USA)-Mrs Leader (USA) (Mr Leader (USA)) *3846^{2}* **>55fh<**

Mischief Star 4 b f Be My Chief (USA)-Star Face (African Sky) 4003^{2} **>71h<**

Mischievous Girl 9 ch m **4234^{6} 4503^{P} 4710^{8}** >39h 67?c<

Miss Bartholomew 7 b m 1275^{13} **>12fh<**

Miss Blues Singer 4 b f Sula Bula-Lady Blues Singer (Chief Singer) 4009^{8} 4657^{11} **>27fh<**

Miss Colette 9 b m Meadowbrook-Miss Colonnette (Flatbush) **1291^{3} 1845^{8} 3393^{5} (3724) 4077^{5} 4391^{2} >80c<**

Miss Diskin (IRE) 8 b m 1571^{3} **1811^{2} (1947) 2658^{5} 3697^{6} 3916^{P} 4351a^{2} (4529) >90h 112c<**

Miss Dotty 7 gr m **61^{5} 72^{8} 417^{P} 482^{P} >83dc<**

Missed the Boat (IRE) 7 b g 303^{2} **>64h<**

Missed The Match 7 ch g Royal Match-Miss Levantine (Levanter) 1289^{13} 1573^{13} 2576^{9} **>21h<**

Miss Enrico 11 b m **14^{4} 94^{P} 420^{4} 507^{6}** >86dc<

Miss Foley 4 b f Thethingaboutitis (USA)-Rue de Remarque (The Noble Player (USA)) 3170^{16} 4632^{15} **>22fh<**

Miss Fortina 5 b m Belfort (FR)-Lady Martina (Martinmas) 1692^{23} 2633^{19}

Miss Foxy 7 br m (408) 2878^{3} 4292^{P} **>59h<**

Miss Gee-Ell 5 br m Lyphento (USA)-Miss Black Glama (Derrylin) 3340^{P} 3603^{P} 4017^{3} 4102^{6} 4289^{5} **>32h<**

Miss Greenyards 6 b m 1358^{3} 1686^{6} 3822^{5} **>65h<**

Miss Impulse 4 b f Precocious-Dingle Belle (Dominion) 540^{S} 646^{12} **>20h<**

Miss Kilworth (IRE) 6 b m Lord Americo-Frozen Ground (Arctic Slave) 3433^{20} 3747^{10} **>24fh<**

Miss Lamplight 7 b m 700^{6} **802^{F} 1845^{F} 1968^{3} 2954^{8} 3326^{P} 3909^{P} >57h 76c<**

Miss Magic 12 b m **3721^{6} >73c<**

Miss Marigold 8 b m **1284^{F} 1584^{8} 2657^{P}** 2824^{4} 3112^{U} 3362^{11} 3589^{3} 3980^{2} 4093^{4} **>69h 99?c<**

Miss Match 0 D Lighter-Designer (Celtic Cone) 2931^{6} 3365^{5} 3592^{8} **>43h<**

Miss Matchmaker 5 b m Lighter-Precious Sue (Malicious) 4632^{16}

Miss Mighty 4 b f Bigivor-Fancy Blue (Fine Blue) 2811^{18} 3365^{18} 4441^{P}

Miss Millbrook 9 b m **(3055) 3403^{2} 3637^{P} 4241^{2} (4323) (4560) >110c<**

Miss Moneypenny 5 b m Silly Prices-Edenburt (Bargello) 3142^{6} 3440^{9} **>42fh<**

Miss Mont 8 ch m 1438^{6} 1575^{P} 1821^{4} 1969^{U} 2505^{P} **3092^{P} >44h<**

Miss Mouse 5 br m Arctic Lord-Gypsy's Barn Rat (Balliol) 4301^{6} 4561^{9} **>46fh<**

Miss Mylette (IRE) 6 b m 1341^{10} 1683^{P} 3088^{7} 3491^{P} **>26h<**

Miss Night Owl 6 ch m Bold Owl-Regal Flame (Royalty) 1177^{9} 1336^{10} 2655^{P} 3590^{8} 3889^{6} **>23h<**

Miss Nonnie 5 b m High Kicker (USA)-Miss Cragg (Monsanto (FR)) 653^{B} 705^{7} 872^{14} 3416^{7} 3603^{P} **>26h<**

Miss Norwait 7 b m 357^{6}

Miss Optimist 7 b m **2672^{3} >84h 89c<**

Miss Pennyhill (IRE) 4 b f 1747a^{4} 2333a^{5} 2993a^{7} 3258a^{7} **>82h<**

Miss Pimpernel 7 b m 27^{6} 95^{4} 131^{4} 257^{3} 657^{P} **>59h<**

Miss Pravda 4 ch f Soviet Star (USA)-Miss Paige (AUS) (Luskin Star (AUS)) 1675^{8}

Miss Roberto (IRE) 4 ch f Don Roberto (USA)-Frau Ahuyentante (ARG) (Frari (ARG)) 2333a^{6} 2993a^{9} 3258a^{3} 3634^{22} **>19h<**

Miss Secret 7 b m 1200^{5} 1476^{6} 1840^{3} 3112^{5} **>48h<**

Miss Souter 8 b m 101^{4} 184^{5} 345^{3} 546^{2} 4332^{3} 4644^{3} **>47h<**

Miss Spent Youth 6 ch m 69^{P} **>28h<**

Miss Starteam 7 br m Teamwork-Stars and Stripes (Royalty) 1177^{10} 3052^{P} **>8fh<**

Miss The Beat 5 b m 1380^{P} 1788^{P} 1980^{10} **>20h<**

Miss Tino 9 b m **1291^{4} >13h<**

Mister Audi (IRE) 5 br g Good Thyne (USA)-Symphony Orchestra 4118a^{16} **>53h<**

Mister Black (IRE) 9 ch g **4^{5} >57h 68c<**

Mister Blake 7 b g (649) 934^{3} 1130^{2} (1384) 1906^{6} 2076^{P} 2570^{P} 3016^{4} 3408^{3} 3600^{11} 3851^{7} 4309^{P} **>61h<**

Mister Casual 8 br g 5^{6} **8^{4} 1576^{8} 1968^{P} >65h 77dc<**

Mister Chippy (IRE) 5 b g 4352a^{20} **>90h<**

Mister Chips 6 b g Macmillion-Nikali (Siliconn) 1573^{6} **>27fh<**

Mister Drum (IRE) 8 gr g (62) **1371^{2} (1563) (1780) 2116^{2} 2641^{2} 2885^{F} (3111) 3835^{2} 3936^{U} 4298^{4} (4736) >101h 122c<**

Mister Ermyn 4 ch g Minster Son-Rosana Park (Music Boy) 2682^{3} (2938) 3304^{8} **>67fh<**

Mister Gebo 12 b g **4551^{P} 4804^{4} >102c<**

Mister Generosity (IRE) 6 b g 216^{4} 3272^{10} 3552^{P}

Mister Gigi (IRE) 6 b g 634^{14} **>31h<**
Mister Goodguy (IRE) 8 b g Supreme Leader-Mislay (Henbit (USA)) 3041^{12} 3364^{11} 4134^{P} **(4566) (4735) >30h 86c<**
Mister Horatio 7 b g **(4160) 4380^{2} 4522^{4} 4792^{U} >102c<**
Mister Main Man (IRE) 9 ch g Remainder Man-Mainstown Belle (Peacock (FR)) **3568^{2} (4614) >95c<**
Mister Morose (IRE) 7 b g (1636) 3038^{7} 3267^{6} **>123h<**
Mister Oddy 11 b g **(1682) 2051^{2} (3009) (3144) 3401^{3} 3638^{U} 4062^{4} 4214^{2} 4311^{3} 4478^{2} >76h 136c<**
Mister River (IRE) 6 ch g Over The River (FR)-Miss Redmarshall (Most Secret) 3767^{5} **>38fh<**
Mister Rm 5 b g Dominion-La Cabrilla (Carwhite) (743) (1060) 1171^{5} 1382^{4} (2074) 2747^{4} 3298^{2} 3595^{F} 3850^{2} 4010^{4} 4397^{2} **>101h<**
Mister Ross (IRE) 7 b g Mister Lord (USA)-Ross Rag (Ragapan) (1666) (2649) 2937^{5} 3396^{4} (3795) 4261^{9} **>87h<**
Mister Spectator (IRE) 8 br g Mandalus-Focal Point (Hawaiian Sound (USA)) **4319^{2} 4615^{P} >97c<**
Mister Trick (IRE) 7 br g **1138^{F} (1845) 2788^{F} 2954^{4} (3306) 3708^{P} (3993)** 4513^{2} **>55h 93c<**
Mistinguett (IRE) 5 b m (1017) 1288^{4} 1508^{2} (2059) (2635) 3038^{4} 3293^{2} 3597^{10} 3917^{3} **>122h<**
Mistress Rosie 10 b m **1677^{4} 1947^{P} 2657^{P} (3950) 4142^{3} 4291^{5} 4431^{P} >58h 72c<**
Mistress Tudor 6 b m Scallywag-Tudor Mischief (Mister Tudor) 1665^{8} 1986^{7} 2757^{9} 3006^{6} 3226^{14} 3423^{P} 3734^{8} **>29h<**
Mistroy 7 gr m 289^{7} **870^{5} 1028^{5} >54h 64c< (DEAD)**
Misty (NZ) 10 b g **3341^{P} >74c<**
Misty Class (IRE) 5 gr g Roselier (FR)-Toevarro (Raga Navarro (ITY)) 3907^{4} **>61fh<**
Misty Grey 8 gr g **30^{9} >36h 70c<**
Misty View 8 ch m Absalom-Long View (Persian Bold) 401^{2} 950^{6} **>58h<**
Mitchells Best 11 br g True Song-Emmalina (Doubtless II) **3459^{3} >76c<**
Mithraic (IRE) 5 b g (698) 1049^{2} 1152^{3} 1312^{3} 2631^{15} 3345^{3} 3691^{4} **>80h<**
Mizyan (IRE) 9 b g 1416^{3} **>109h<**
Mobile Messenger (NZ) 9 b g **746^{2} 1075^{P} 3270^{F} 3476^{6} 4324^{P} >73h 82c<**
Mock Trial (IRE) 4 b g Old Vic-Test Case (Busted) 1205^{3} 1652^{6} 1940^{F} (2552) 3696^{2} **>73h<**
Modajjaj 5 ch g Polish Precedent (USA)-Upend (Main Reef) 3103^{7} 3441^{7} **>40h<**
Model Tee (IRE) 8 b g Teofane-Carraigaloe (Little Buskins) 3423^{P}
Mollie Silvers 5 b m 161^{12} 2805^{13} 3226^{15} 4304^{8} 4534^{5} 4768^{8} **>51h<**
Molly Grey (IRE) 6 gr m Boreen (FR)-Golden Robe (Yankee Gold) **3533^{P}**
Molonys Dram 6 b g 3946^{8} 4095^{7} **>54fh<**
Moment of Glory (IRE) 6 ch g 1262^{4} (1392) 1522^{4} 2817^{2} 3011^{7} **>96h< (DEAD)**
Monaco Gold (IRE) 5 b g 801^{3} 1020^{2} **>63h<**
Monalee River (IRE) 9 b g **3128a^{4} 3526a^{2} >106h 137c<**
Mon Amie 7 ch g Right Regent-Woodcourt Gold (Goldhill) 4001^{4} (4625) **>65h<**
Monaughty Man 11 br g **1164^{U} 1311^{7} 1442^{R} 1566^{6} 1657^{10} 1815^{3} 1833^{F} 1943^{5} 2002^{R} 2914^{P} 3023^{5} 3069^{6} >70dc<**
Monday Club 13 ch g 1204^{P} **1660^{5} 3678^{2} 3832^{5} 4142^{6} >81dh 95c<**
Mon Domino 8 ch h Dominion-Arderelle (FR) (Pharly (FR)) 2613a^{2}
Monicas Buzz 7 b m Buzzards Bay-Duellist (Town Crier) 1026^{9}
Monica's Choice (IRE) 6 b g 3065^{3} 3345^{6} **>86h<**
Monicasman (IRE) 7 br g 1262^{6} 1416^{6} 1922^{2} **3173^{3} 3435^{3} >91h 94dc<**
Monkey Ago 10 b g **2848a^{6} 3503a^{9} 4351a^{P} >111c<**
Monkey's Wedding 6 b g 950^{14} **(DEAD)**
Monkey Wench (IRE) 6 b m **3479^{3} 3790^{8}** 4259^{5} 4409^{4} 4572^{6} **>57h 67c<**
Monksaan (IRE) 8 b g **1574^{F} 1668^{4} >61c<**
Monks Jay (IRE) 8 br g **20^{4} (1284) 1379^{5} 1769^{4} 3053^{P}** 3362^{P} **(4000) 4235^{3} >100c<**
Monks Soham (IRE) 9 b g 2948^{6} 3209^{5} 3402^{P} **3941^{F} (4298) (4507) 4635^{P} >75h 114c<**
Monmouth Way (IRE) 5 b g King's Ride-Mimmsie Starr (Pitskelly) 3090^{9} 3425^{14}
Monnaie Forte (IRE) 7 b g **(1348) 1629^{P} (2632) 2921^{F} 3140^{F} 3413^{F}** (3791) (3912) (4271) 4397^{P} **>87h 99c<**
Monnedell (IRE) 5 b g 3100^{P}
Monsieur Darcy (IRE) 6 b g Phardante (FR)-Ballycurnane Lady (Orchestra) 2005^{5} 2640^{4} 3024^{5} 3794^{6} **>63h<**
Monsieur Dupont (IRE) 7 b g Alzao (USA)-Katie Koo (Persian Bold) 1492a^{P}
Monsieur Pink 5 gr g Nishapour (FR)-Charter Belle (Runnymede) 705^{6} 1820^{10} **>44fh<**
Montagnard 13 b g 2659^{P} **>76?h<**
Montebel (IRE) 9 br g **2660^{2} 3036^{P} >125c<**
Montecot (FR) 8 b g Le Riverain (FR)-Pour Ta Pomme (FR) (Stratege (USA)) 2550^{2} 2642^{2} 2759^{6} **3151^{4} 3573^{P} >97h<**
Montein 6 b g Ovac (ITY)-River Bark (Rapid River) 2047^{18} 2541^{9} 2917^{20} 3483^{14} 3910^{P}
Montel Express (IRE) 5 b g (859) 1274^{8} (2820) 3157^{P} **>79h< (DEAD)**
Montezumas Revenge (IRE) 9 b g 3473^{P}
Montperle (FR) 8 dk g Tip Moss (FR)-La Vernigeole (FR) (Chateau Du Diable (FR)) (52a) 155a^{3} **>154h<**
Montrave 8 ch g **1361^{4} (1970) 2508^{F} (2769) 3308^{5} 3532^{4} >84h 112c<**
Montroe (IRE) 5 gr g Roselier (FR)-Cathedral Street (Boreen Beag) 3304^{5} 4008^{6} **>69fh<**
Monty 5 ch g Colmore Row-Sussarando (Music Boy) 1276^{10} 1770^{9} 3072^{10} **>35h<**
Monyman (IRE) 7 b g 1049^{5} **(1311) 1511^{2} (1987) (2506) 2700^{3} (4214) 4258^{4} >79h 122c<**
Monymax (IRE) 8 b g **1206^{7} 1574^{9} 1691^{5} 2698^{F} >61c<**
Monymoss (IRE) 8 b g **1120^{3} 1189^{2} 1629^{4} (1850) 2672^{2} 3285^{2} 3700^{P} 3805^{4} >59h 108c<**
Mony-Skip (IRE) 8 b g **(907) (1068) 1326^{3} (1506) 1670^{2} 2616^{2} 2936^{F} >55h 135c< (DEAD)**
Moobakkr (USA) 6 b or br g 95^{P} 690^{P} 2003^{4} 2694^{P} 3545^{4} 3709^{U} 4093^{3} 4296^{U} 4734^{5} **>61h<**
Moofaji 6 b g 1141^{6} **>45h<**
Moonax (IRE) 6 ch h Caerleon (USA)-Moonsilk (Solinus) 1830^{2} 2668^{3} 3359^{6} **>90h<**
Moon Castle (IRE) 9 ch g 1689^{P} **>72c<**
Moon Devil (IRE) 7 br g 2510^{10} 3042^{8} 3399^{4} 4003^{3} 4400^{3} **>72h<**
Moon-Frog (IRE) 10 ch g Tesoro Mio-Willya Pauper **4350a^{P} >77h<**
Moonlight Calypso 6 ch m Jupiter Island-Moonlight Bay (Palm Track) 1821^{P} **(DEAD)**
Moonlighter 7 b m 1541^{P} 1998^{3} 3052^{2} 3405^{P} **>71h<**
Moonlight Escapade (IRE) 6 b g Executive Perk-Baybush (Boreen (FR)) 918^{3} 1056^{5} 1695^{5} 3337^{5} 3594^{9} 3733^{9} 3951^{3} 4095^{4} **>49h<**
Moonlight Venture 5 b g 4479^{P} 4708^{5} **>39h<**
Moon Monkey (IRE) 9 b g **3459^{U} >49dh 46c<**
Moonraker's Mirage 6 b g Idiot's Delight-Save it Lass (Nicholas Bill) 3235^{6} 3574^{12} 3853^{6} **>49fh<**
Moonshine Dancer 7 b g 2915^{P} 3351^{6} 3478^{11} **>62h<**
Moor Dance Man 7 b g 1665^{11} 2550^{P} 4299^{12} 4450^{7} **4540^{U} >35h<**
Moor Dutch 6 br g Dutch Treat-Moorland Nell (Neltino) 3115^{P} 3233^{15} 4328^{F} **>9h<**
Moor Hall Lady 6 gr m 1341^{5} 1679^{2} 2112^{6} 2744^{8} 3114^{4} **>58h<**
Moor Hall Prince 7 b g 4476^{P} 4650^{9} **>46h<**
Moorish 7 b g 1916^{7} 3150^{2} 3293^{4} 3597^{8} **>133h< (DEAD)**
Morcat 8 ch m **93^{2} 3200^{P} 4159^{P} 4796^{4} >73dc<**
Morceli (IRE) 9 gr g **1359^{3} >127h 158c<**
Mordros 7 b g Interrex (CAN)-Jay Jays Dream (Shaab) 4003^{10} 4641^{4} **>38h<**
More Bills (IRE) 5 b g 555^{7} 4069^{F} 4290^{P} 4384^{P} 4552^{11}
Moreceva (IRE) 7 ch g Salluceva-Moredee (Morston (FR)) 161^{6} 319a^{17} 418^{6} 1200^{P} 2875^{10} 4173^{5} 4548^{P} 4662^{P} **>15h<**
More Champagne 7 ch m 1672^{4} 2509^{P} **>55h<**
More Dash Thancash (IRE) 7 ch g 1939^{3} (2952) (3177) (3412) 3572^{7} **>92h<**
Moreflash 5 b m 3611^{W} 3794^{P} 4144^{8} 4257^{P}
More Joy 9 b g **507^{P} 685^{4} 875^{4} 1246^{5} 1653^{9} 3824^{P} 3911^{5} 4149^{6} 4408^{4} 4735^{P} >60c<**
More Manners 12 b g **3739^{P} >92c<**
Moreof a Gunner 7 ch g 4261^{P} 4518^{6} **>47h<**
More to Life 8 b m 3844^{U} 3970^{6}
Morgans Harbour 11 b g **1359^{4} >110+h 141c<**
Morning Blush (IRE) 7 ch m (29) 95^{P} **135^{P} 190^{U} 256^{P} 597^{P}** 4253^{P} **>82h<**
Morning Sir 4 b g Southern Music-Morning Miss (Golden Dipper) 4555^{6} **>25h<**
Morpheus 8 b g 2547^{7} 3041^{10} 3197^{3} 3468^{3} 3944^{2} 4204^{2} 4625^{5} (4650) **>68h<**
Morstock 7 gr g 741^{4} **1037^{U}** 1148^{2} 1201^{2} (1474) 1678^{2} 2644^{3} 2703^{2} 2932^{6} 3497^{3} 3640^{6} **>99?h<**
Mo's Boy 6 b g Sulaafah (USA)-Ridans Girl (Ridan (USA)) 1289^{12} **>36fh<**
Mo's Chorister 11 b g Lir-Revelstoke (North Stoke) **3593^{F}**
Moscow Express (IRE) 5 ch g (4124a) **>105h<**
Mosephine (IRE) 7 b m The Parson-Run Madam (Deep Run) 4376^{14}
Moss Bee 10 br g **3645^{P} >91dc<**
Moss Pageant 7 b g Then Again-Water Pageant (Welsh Pageant) **2786^{P} 2914^{F} 3329^{2} 3450^{2} 3790^{4} 4502^{5} 4709^{4} >88dc<**
Mossy Buck (IRE) 5 b g Buckskin (FR)-Mollamoss (Le Moss) 4657^{8}
Most Equal 7 ch g (1832) 2048^{3} 2777^{8} 4061^{14} (4510) **>95h<**
Most Interesting 12 b m 66^{4} 101^{9} **>43h 64c<**
Most Respectful 4 ch g Respect-Active Movement (Music Boy) 906^{13} 2504^{9} **>15h<**
Most Rich (IRE) 9 b g **2632^{P} 3030^{U} 3092^{U} 3306^{6} 3479^{5} 3726^{2} 3909^{P} >80c<**
Most Wanted (IRE) 4 ch f Priolo (USA)-Dewan's Niece (USA) (Dewan (USA)) 874^{4}
Motoqua 5 b m Mtoto-Neeran (Wollow) 2010^{F} 2655^{2} (2808) 3564^{2} (3764) (3970) **>74h<**
Moubeed (USA) 7 ch g Secretariat (USA)-Hanoof (USA) (Northern Dancer) 1692^{19} **>1fh<**
Mountain Dream 4 b c Batshoof-Echoing (Formidable (USA)) 2175^{6} 2615^{11} **>47h<**
Mountain Fox (IRE) 7 b g **1248^{8} 1826^{5} >60c<**

Mountain Leader 7 b g 157^{3} 4801^{4} **>61h<**

Mountain Path 7 b g Rakaposhi King-Donna Farina (Little Buskins) 1191^{3} (3340) 4230^{2} 4544^{5} **>74h<**

Mountain Reach 7 b g 2659^{P} 3016^{6} 3499^{10} **>63h<**

Mountain Storm (IRE) 5 b g Strong Gale-Luminous Run (Deep Run) (2572) **>76fh<**

Mount Keen 5 b g Takachiho-Make a Bee Line (Prince Bee) 585^{P}

Mount Lodge (IRE) 6 b g 1810^{P}

Mount Serrath (IRE) 9 b or br g **1447^{2} 1829^{U} 2039^{P} >99c<**

Mouse Bird (IRE) 7 b g (1201) 1325^{2} **1572^{F} 2867^{5} >103h 103c<**

Moussahim (USA) 7 ch g **2341a^{5} >79h 101c<**

Movac (IRE) 8 br g **4^{2} 102^{5} 1022^{6} 1138^{U} 1578^{9} 2653^{P} 2799^{4} 3306^{10} >59h 89c<**

Movie Man 5 ch g 1046^{2} 1316^{4} 2654^{6} 2787^{10} 4147^{7} 4393^{4} **4745^{2} >56h 90c<**

Moving Out 9 b g 2048^{5} **2679^{8} 2926^{7}** 3421^{5} 3702^{4} 4398^{6} 4521^{2} 4772^{F} **>89h 82dc<**

Movisa 7 b m Move Off-Kanisa (Chantro) 1362^{19} 1781^{7} 2005^{12}

Moylough Rebel 4 ch g Hotfoot-Stellajoe (Le Dauphin) 1377^{S}

Moymet 11 b g 159^{10} **>72h<**

Moynsha House (IRE) 9 b g 3674^{P} **>68h<**

Mozemo 10 ch g **2876^{2} 3188^{U} 3591^{2} 3736^{P} 3998^{2} 4083^{3} 4291^{3} 4314^{5} 4735^{4} >75dh 72c<**

Mr Agriwise 6 gr g Newski (USA)-Stars and Stripes (Royalty) 1431^{8} 2661^{8} 2805^{12} **>40h<**

Mr Bean 7 b g **2752^{2} 3001^{9} 3179^{U} 3278^{7} 3954^{2} >83h 87c<**

Mr Boal (IRE) 8 ch g Simply Great (FR)-Lady Moorfield (Sallust) 2345a^{15} **>114h<**

Mr Bobbit (IRE) 7 b g Over The River (FR)-Orient Breeze (Deep Run) **4623^{P}**

Mr Bojangles (IRE) 6 b g 3853^{8} 4528^{P}

Mr Boston 12 b g **(3107) (3353) (3543) 4051^{F} 4361a^{4} 4647^{2} 4805^{3} >114c<**

Mr Bruno 4 ch g Primitive Rising (USA)-Thelmas Secret (Secret Ace) 4477^{3} 4570^{4} 4708^{U} **>15h<**

Mr Bureaucrat (NZ) 8 b br g 1441^{4} 1804^{5} 2048^{4} 2779^{7} **3161^{P} 3443^{U}** 3987^{4} **>94h<**

Mr Busker (IRE) 8 b g **4222^{2} >57h 90c<**

Mr Campus (IRE) 6 b g Noalto-Bluebell Avenue (Boreen Beag) **4655^{P}**

Mr Celebration 6 br g Hubbly Bubbly (USA)-Westerlands Finis (Owen Anthony) 4329^{4}

Mr Christie 5 b g 1049^{7} 1499^{4} 1687^{5} 1848^{5} 2509^{3} 2634^{2} 2820^{5} (3096) 3328^{4} 3644^{6} 3967^{5} 4181^{7} 4309^{2} (4476) 4646^{2} **>76h<**

Mr C-I-P (IRE) 6 ch g 980^{8}

Mr Clancy (IRE) 9 b g **957^{P} >61h<**

Mr Conductor (IRE) 6 ch g **652^{3} 870^{2} (1150) 1389^{3} 2823^{3} (3625) 3936^{2} 4331^{3} >77h 109c<**

Mr Copyforce 7 gr g 810^{3} **>83h<**

Mr Cotton Socks 9 ch g 1200^{2} **>75h<**

Mr Cube (IRE) 7 ch h Tate Gallery (USA)-Truly Thankful (CAN) (Graustark) 915^{10} **>21h<**

Mr Darcy 5 b g Dominion-Rose Chanelle (Welsh Pageant) 1470^{7} 1905^{2} 2566^{3} 2868^{4} 3431^{F} 3964^{6} **>67h<**

Mr Edgar (IRE) 6 b g (818) **>93h<**

Mr Flutts 11 b g 971^{6} 1256^{3} (1562) **>57h<**

Mr Geneaology (USA) 7 b g 16^{7} 404^{3} 673^{2} **>77h 95c<**

Mr Gold (IRE) 4 b g Toledo (USA)-Liangold (Rheingold) 1776^{9} 2060^{6} 2541^{4} 4295^{6} **>53h<**

Mr Golightly 10 gr g **3637^{P} >125c<**

Mr Goonhilly 7 b g 1317^{14} 1583^{P} 2812^{P} **3229^{F} >38h<**

Mr Gordon Bennett 6 b g 1059^{4} 1278^{11} 1959^{P} 2692^{13} 2806^{13} **>9h<**

Mr Hacker 4 b g Shannon Cottage (USA)-Aosta (Shack (USA)) 2622^{15}

Mr Hatchet (IRE) 6 ch g 898^{4}

Mr Hemp 5 b g Town And Country-Straw Castle (Final Straw) 1453^{10} 1726^{9} 2034^{7} **>45h<**

Mr Invader 10 br g **1765^{10} 1961^{6} 2665^{8} 2821^{5} 3132^{9} (3444) 4404^{2} >101?c<**

Mr Jamboree 11 b g **3800^{5} >93c<**

Mr Jasper 5 b g Colmore Row-Spic And Span (Crisp And Even) 915^{11} 968^{7} 1056^{6} 1476^{P}

Mr Jervis (IRE) 8 b g **1195^{P} >76h<**

Mr Kermit 6 b g 1019^{6} 2888^{12} **>99h<**

Mr Knitwit 10 ch g 1360^{4} 1669^{2} **(2789) 3068^{2} 3558^{2} 3790^{2} >95h 113c<**

Mr K's Winterblues (IRE) 7 br m **2998a^{3} >89c<**

Mr Lovely (IRE) 6 b g General View-Woldowa (Wolver Hollow) **2039^{F}** 3085^{P} 3340^{7} 3536^{U} 3760^{4} 4652^{B} **>49h< (DEAD)**

Mr Lowry 5 b g 3802^{8} 4381^{P} 4534^{P} (4626) 4743^{4} **>66h<**

Mr Lurpak 5 b g 191^{2} (1692) (2750) 3619^{19} **>84fh<**

Mr Markham (IRE) 5 b g Naheez (USA)-Brighter Gail (Bustineto) (1275) (3042) 3619^{5} **>90fh<**

Mr Matt (IRE) 9 b g **1167^{3} 1420^{2} 1837^{2} >104h 111c< (DEAD)**

Mr Medley 5 b g Merdon Melody-Hsian (Shantung) 3026^{P}

Mr Montague (IRE) 5 b g Pennine Walk-Ballyewry (Prince Tenderfoot (USA)) 2080^{4} 3626^{7} **>57fh<**

Mr Moonlight (IRE) 5 ch g Orchestra-Midnight Mistress (Midsummer Night II) 2012^{4} 2696^{3} 3271^{4} **>50h<**

Mr Moriarty (IRE) 6 ch g (2631) 3076^{5} 4746^{3} **>75h<**

Mr Motivator 7 b g 1323^{10} 1768^{P} **2549^{F} 2691^{7} 3285^{U}**

Mr Moylan 5 b g Ardross-Belle Bavard (Le Bavard (FR)) 4360a^{15} **>49fh<**

Mr Mulligan (IRE) 9 ch g **1785^{4} 2115^{F} (3636) >87+h 171c<**

Mr Oriental 7 b g **290^{4} 581^{P} 4615^{F} 4724^{U}**

Mr Percy (IRE) 6 ch g (675) (1369) 1648^{F} 2059^{3} 3041^{2} 3572^{12} **>104h<**

Mr Pickpocket (IRE) 9 b g **1206^{2} 1538^{6} 1797^{3} 2072^{F} 2693^{4} (3113)** 3700^{3} **4312^{4} 4546^{4} >95h 117dc<**

Mr Pinball 10 b g Balinger-Pin Hole (Parthia) **4317^{P}**

Mr Playfull 7 br g **889^{4} (970) 1199^{4} 2657^{2} 3339^{2} 3540^{U} 4174^{3} 4429^{2} (4659) >65h 100c<**

Mr Poppleton 8 ch g 19^{6} 360^{5} 461^{2} 1183^{3} 1339^{2} 1663^{3} 3424^{2} 3752^{3} 4466^{3} **>55h<**

Mr President (IRE) 8 b g **1373^{2} 1641^{2} 1957^{2} >59h 111c<**

Mr Primetime (IRE) 7 b g **979^{F} >67h 90c<**

Mr Reiner (IRE) 9 br g **873^{2} 1022^{P} 1138^{2} 4502^{4} 4710^{9} >86h 86dc<**

Mr Robstee 6 b g Pragmatic-Miss Northwick (Remezzo) 2012^{13} 3690^{6} 4242^{5} **>10fh<**

Mr Rough 6 b g Fayruz-Rheinbloom (Rheingold) 1470^{P}

Mrs Barty (IRE) 7 b or br m 3172^{P}

Mrs Em 5 b m Nicholas Bill-Sleepline Comfort (Tickled Pink) (918) (1820) 2510^{4} 2878^{F} 3226^{4} (3977) (4175) (4238) (4459) 4613^{2} **>82+h<**

Mrs Jawleyford (USA) 9 b m 2842^{P} 3056^{5} 3234^{5} 3478^{3} 3904^{P} 4163^{F} **>54h<**

Mr Sloan 7 b g 2045^{6} **2540^{8} 2788^{F} 2954^{F}** 3157^{P} 3825^{14} 3971^{7} **>21h 62c<**

Mrs Molotoff 6 b m Dubassoff (USA)-Ml Cottage (Mljet) 133^{14}

Mr Snaggle (IRE) 8 ch g Pollerton-Truly Deep (Deep Run) 223^{3} 303^{5} **477^{2} 590^{3}** 816^{3} 1074^{7} 1681^{3} **3582^{F} (3746) (3905)** (3999) **(4235) >78h 98+c<**

Mr Sox 6 ch g **206^{F} >62h<**

Mrs Robinson (IRE) 6 b m 31^{5} 3004^{3} 3201^{8} 3481^{2} 4188^{5} **>55h<**

Mr Strong Gale (IRE) 6 b g 954^{3} 1388^{6} 1673^{P} 2708^{2} 2877^{2} (3281) 3982^{4} (4461) **>73+h<**

Mr Titch 4 b g Totem (USA)-Empress Nicki (Nicholas Bill) 3474^{F}

Mr Wild (USA) 4 b g Wild Again (USA)-Minstress (USA) (The Minstrel (CAN)) 1519^{U} 1935^{F} 2622^{2} 2751^{4} 3174^{7} 3634^{8} 4014^{5} **>90h<**

Ms Jones (IRE) 4 ch f Headin' Up-Deep Joy (Deep Run) 3583^{P}

Muallaf (IRE) 5 b g Unfuwain (USA)-Honourable Sheba (USA) (Roberto (USA)) 3090^{14} 3626^{10} 4088^{2} **>49fh<**

Mua-Tab 4 ch f Polish Precedent (USA)-Alsabiha (Lord Gayle (USA)) 1652^{12} **>53h< (DEAD)**

Mubariz (IRE) 5 b g Royal Academy (USA)-Ringtail (Auction Ring (USA)) 1208^{P} 2898^{P}

Mudahim 11 b g 2637^{4} **3046^{2} (3302) 3598^{6} (4110a) >126h 140c<**

Mudlark 5 b g Salse (USA)-Mortal Sin (USA) (Green Forest (USA)) 1369^{9} 1908^{7} 2898^{4} 3371^{6} 3940^{8} 4648^{2} **>59h<**

Mugoni Beach 12 b g **2814^{7} 3074^{4} 3280^{5} 4074^{P} 4293^{5} >116c<**

Muhandam (IRE) 4 b g Common Grounds-Unbidden Melody (USA) (Chieftain II) (3669) 3898^{3} **>67h<**

Muhtadi (IRE) 4 br g Marju (IRE)-Moon Parade (Welsh Pageant) 3007^{9} (3500) 3802^{5} 4209^{6} **>86h<**

Muhtashim (IRE) 7 b g 1381^{5} 1709^{7} 1948^{2} 2909^{6} **>67h<**

Muizenberg 10 b g 1123^{P} 3346^{8} 3743^{2} 4381^{2} (4525) **>69+h<**

Mull House 10 b g 2905^{3} **>60h<**

Mulligan (IRE) 7 ch g **(1254) (1452) (1790) (2739a) (3167) 3596^{F} 4012^{F} >96h 141++c<**

Mullingar (IRE) 8 b g **1704^{P}** 4081^{7} **>43h 69c<**

Mullins (IRE) 6 b g 7^{3} 1021^{10} 1345^{4} 1524^{5} 1848^{7} **>58h<**

Mullintor (IRE) 6 b g 1424^{3} 1782^{4} 2677^{13} 2907^{2} 3209^{P} 3674^{2} 3896^{2} 4102^{2} (4255) **>65h<**

Mullover 6 ch g 1492a^{4} 1751a^{4} 2596a^{2} **>96h<**

Multan 5 b g Indian Ridge-Patchinia (Patch) 1651^{P}

Multi Line 7 ch m High Line-Waterford Cream (Proverb) **3173^{9} 3357^{8} >46c<**

Multy (IRE) 5 b br g 50a^{2} **>88h<**

Mummy's Mole 6 gr g 4069^{P} 4506^{P}

Muntafi 6 b g 1074^{9} **>91h<**

Murberry (IRE) 7 b br m Strong Statement (USA)-Lady Tarsel (Tarqogan) 129^{3} 218^{3} 260^{2} **>57h<**

Murchan Tyne (IRE) 4 ch f Good Thyne (USA)-Ardnamurchan (Ardross) 3907^{2} (4421) 4632^{2} **>65fh<**

Murder Moss (IRE) 7 ch g Doulab (USA)-Northern Wind (Northfields (USA)) **3095^{2} >102c<**

Murphaideez 10 b g 3157^{P} 3607^{10} **>46h<**

Murphy's Gold (IRE) 6 ch g Salt Dome (USA)-Winter Harvest (Grundy) 1208^{5} 1369^{11} **>35h<**

Murphy's Malt (IRE) 5 ch g 1651^{6} 3525a^{8} **>82h<**

Murphy's Run (IRE) 7 b g 700^{P} 1394^{P} 1726^{14} 2680^{15} 3442^{12} **>27h<**

Murray's Million 5 b g Macmillion-Random Select (Random Shot) 1203^{13} 1774^{11} 2791^{9} 4508^{P} **>21h<**

Muse 10 ch g 1258^{5} (1508) 1916^{4} 2774^{4}

>143h<

Museum (IRE) 6 b g 1375^{6} 1663^{6} 2067^{2} 2680^{8} (3204) 3549^{2} >68h<

Musical Hit 6 ch g 800^{P} 1085^{6} 1541^{P} 1795^{P} 2809^{3} 3020^{P} 3334^{7} 3968^{P} 4546^{P} 4699^{5} 4769^{P} >58c<

Musical Mayhem (IRE) 4 b g Shernazar-Minstrels Folly (USA) (The Minstrel (CAN)) 3619^{9} >87fh<

Musical Monarch (NZ) 11 ch g 2666^{13} >50h<

Musical Vocation (IRE) 6 ch m 72^{P} >38h<

Music Blitz 6 b g 694^{P} 910^{7} 1346^{4} 1847^{4} 3790^{7} 3909^{7} >71h 84dc<

Music Class (IRE) 6 ch g 3019^{9} 3222^{11} 3552^{6} 3819^{7} 4073^{P} 4662^{P} >51dh<

Music Master (IRE) 7 ch g 2546^{5} 2826^{4} 3355^{4} 3667^{P} >69h<

Music Please 5 ch g Music Boy-Ask Mama (Mummy's Pet) 1726^{6} 2504^{5} 2805^{5} 2939^{4} 3926^{2} 4441^{3} >73h<

Music Score 11 ch g 30^{4} 102^{P} 460^{P} 494^{2} 631^{P} >51h 79c< (DEAD)

Muskerry Moya (IRE) 8 ch m Rising-Muskerry Mary (Mon Capitaine) (4618) 4773^{3} >90c<

Muskora (IRE) 8 b g 20^{5} 298^{3} 496^{U} 588^{P} >106h 121?c<

Musthaveaswig 11 gr g 1279^{3} 1501^{P} (1923) 2758^{4} (2928) 3414^{4} 3699^{P} 4167^{4} 4424^{P} >124?c<

Mu-Tadil 5 ch g 891^{4} 1197^{P} 1334^{6} 1678^{5} 3234^{P} 3541^{6} 3892^{7} >41h<

Mutanassib (IRE) 4 b g Mtoto-Lightning Legacy (USA) (Super Concorde (USA)) 2868^{2} 3084^{8} 3271^{3} 3634^{12} >82h<

Mutawali (IRE) 7 ch g (913) 1198^{6} 1332^{3} 1818^{6} >54h<

Mutazz (USA) 5 b h 916^{3} 1255^{5} 3497^{4} >84h<

Mutley 7 b g 69^{P} 156^{2} 258^{3} 304^{3} 408^{6} 546^{P} 4466^{7} 4652^{P} >35h<

Mutual Agreement 10 ch m 417^{F} >67dh 75c<

Mutual Memories 9 b g 343^{P} 4618^{3} >43h 59c<

Mutual Trust 13 ch g 28^{P} 799^{4} 1057^{F} 1302^{P} >88c< (DEAD)

Muzrak (CAN) 6 ch g (1) 58^{2} 4500^{4} 4708^{2} >80h<

Mweenish 15 b g 2011^{P} 2681^{P} >93c<

My Beautiful Dream 4 gr f Kalaglow-Cinderella Derek (Hittite Glory) 458^{5} 753^{P}

Myblackthorn (IRE) 7 br m 792^{3} 3112^{P} >68h 110dc<

My Buster 5 ch g 2750^{7} >44fh<

My Cheeky Man 6 ch g (3019) (3197) (3942) >93h<

My Friend Billy (IRE) 5 ch g Yashgan-Super Boreen (Boreen (FR)) 4531^{17}

Myhamet 10 b g 4522^{6} >101h 95c<

My Handsome Prince 5 b g Handsome Sailor-My Serenade (USA) (Sensitive Prince (USA)) 1276^{P}

My Handy Man 6 ch g 1703^{9} >57h<

My Harvinski 7 b g 594^{4} 788^{9} 902^{5} 1086^{3} 1337^{4} 1446^{4} 1628^{14} 1993^{P} 4789^{9} >46dh<

My Kind 4 ch f Mon Tresor-Kind of Shy (Kind of Hush) 282^{4} 534^{5} >41h<

Mykon Gold (IRE) 4 b g Montekin-Yukon Lil (Yankee Gold) 4118a^{8} >69fh<

Mylink (IRE) 7 br g 1766^{9}

Mylordmayor 10 ch g 66^{5} 185^{3} 339^{4} 913^{2} 978^{P} >39h<

My Main Man 9 b g 2075^{P} 2839^{P} >96c<

My Man in Dundalk (IRE) 8 ch g Orchestra-Marla (Hul A Hul) (2038) 2870^{P} 3088^{W} >64h<

My Mavourneen 5 b m Ardross-Queen's Darling (Le Moss) 2619^{13} 2785^{10} 3795^{4} 4182^{4} >65?h<

My Micky 6 br g 4433^{3} >45fh<

My Missile 7 ch m 1312^{9} 1851^{6} 2042^{8} 3825^{4} 4705^{4} >47h<

My Nad Knows 4 b g Derrylin-Early Run (Deep Run) 3406^{F} 3575^{8} 3809^{P} >16h<

My Nominee 9 b g 3005^{3} 3270^{4} 3637^{P} 3984^{2} (4094) (4218) 4326^{3} 4560^{8} (4748) >111c<

My Rossini 8 b g 3156^{4} >97h 73c<

My Shenandoah (IRE) 6 br g Derrylin-Edwina's Dawn (Space King) 1124^{6} 1453^{14} 1568^{10} 1768^{6} 1992^{11} 3426^{U} >55fh<

Mysilv 7 ch m 52a^{2} 155a^{2} >151h< (DEAD)

Mystical City (IRE) 7 ch m (318a) 1365^{2} 1759a^{6} 1793^{7} 3615^{9} 4117a^{3} 4357a^{4} >128h<

Mystical Mind 4 gr g Emarati (USA)-Spanish Chestnut (Philip of Spain) 3789^{P}

Mystical Rye (IRE) 6 ch m Henbit (USA)-Maugherow Invader 319a^{21}

Mystic Court (IRE) 6 br g 1572^{6} 3173^{U} 3488^{P} >58h 49c<

Mystic Hill 6 b g Shirley Heights-Nuryana (Nureyev (USA)) 2872^{9} 3109^{4} 3535^{4} (4017) 4181^{2} (4332) 4644^{4} >69h<

Mystic Isle (IRE) 7 b g 1195^{2} 3020^{9} 3565^{2} 3805^{2} >79?h 114c<

Mystic Legend (IRE) 5 gr g Standaan (FR)-Mandy Girl (Manado) 915^{9} >21h<

Mystic Manna 11 b g 2819^{P} 3155^{P} 3489^{U} >91dc<

Mythical Approach (IRE) 7 ch g 1036^{2} 1938^{5} 2619^{3} (4611) >72h 90+c<

Mytton's Choice (IRE) 6 b g (793) 1015^{2} 1258^{2} 1441^{2} 1661^{3} 2117^{4} 2645^{6} 3640^{9} >108h<

My Vantage 4 ch g Be My Guest (USA)-Sarajill (High Line) 2675^{10} 3203^{12}

My Warrior 9 b g 1563^{8} 3173^{U} 3582^{P} >67?c<

Mywend's (IRE) 7 ch g (1278) 1507^{P} >79h< (DEAD)

My Young Man 12 b g Young Man (FR)-Hampsruth (Sea Hawk II) 3005^{P} 3432^{P} 4320^{3} 4406^{U} 4543^{2} 4733^{5} >98c<

My Young Pet 8 ch g Young Man (FR)-Tierna's Pet (Laurence O) 2627^{P}

N

Nadiad 11 b g 4218^{5} 4380^{3} 4715^{F} >67c<

Nadjati (USA) 8 ch g 20^{P} (72) 4235^{6} 4611^{5} >93h 97dc<

Nafertiti (IRE) 5 b m 1980^{12}

Nagara Sound 6 b g 955^{F} 2692^{11} 2874^{7} 3049^{6} 3438^{10} 4223^{12} >39h<

Nagobelia 9 b or br g 1374^{9} 1562^{10} 1866^{7} 3131^{2} 3429^{3} 3663^{7} 3933^{4} 4633^{11} >58h 61c<

Nahla 7 b m 4226^{3} 4405^{2} 4512^{2} 4646^{5} >60h<

Nahrawali (IRE) 6 b g (655) (1380) >90h<

Nahri (USA) 6 ch g 1039^{2} (1416) >92h<

Nahthen Lad (IRE) 8 b g 1982^{6} 2636^{P} 3151^{2} 3636^{P} 4074^{9} >109h 150c<

Naiysari (IRE) 9 gr g 32^{4} 1120^{4} 1257^{3} 1644^{2} (1934) >91h 119c<

Naked Feelings 5 b g Feelings (FR)-Meg's Mantle (New Brig) 871^{7} 1030^{14} >25h<

Nakir (FR) 9 b g 1173^{5} 1650^{2} >116h 127c<

Name of Our Father (USA) 4 b g Northern Baby (CAN)-Ten Hail Marys (USA) (Halo (USA)) (1953) 2889^{3} 3075^{6} 4095^{2} 4242^{2} 4434^{F} 4628^{2} (4762) >79h<

Namoodaj 4 b g Polish Precedent (USA)-Leipzig (Relkino) 2738a^{6} 2898^{8} >74h<

Nancys Choice 7 b g 2798^{6} 3064^{4} >54h<

Nandura 6 b m 54^{5} 101^{P} >50h<

Nangeo Brae (IRE) 6 br m Touch Boy-Xiara (Callernish) 3440^{13}

Nanjizal 5 b g Right Regent-Kaltezza Cross (Altezza) 653^{15} 918^{12} 1151^{6} 2035^{7} 3184^{P} 3829^{7}

Nantgarw 4 b f Teamster-Dikay (IRE) (Anita's Prince) 1595^{10}

Napoleon's Gold (IRE) 7 ch g 2819^{9} 3472^{P} 3812^{3} 4763^{F} >16h<

Narrow Focus (USA) 4 b g Deputy Minister (CAN)-Starushka (USA) (Sham (USA)) 1747a^{7} >93h< (DEAD)

Nasayer (IRE) 7 b g 3324^{6} 3483^{3} 3825^{8} >64h<

Nascimento (USA) 4 b g Green Dancer (USA)-Miss Pele (USA) (Sea Bird II) 2738a^{13} 2993a^{12} >57h<

Nashaat (USA) 9 b g El Gran Senor (USA)-Absentia (USA) (Raise A Cup (USA)) 675^{3} 743^{2} 1030^{3} 1204^{4} 1369^{7} 1818^{5} 4567^{U} 4737^{5} >56h<

Nashville Star (USA) 6 ch g 1439^{4} 1793^{15} 2040^{5} 2703^{4} 2777^{11} (3002) 3234^{9} 3904^{6} 4130^{6} 4187^{9} 4381^{3} 4510^{4} 4798^{3} >68h<

Nasone (IRE) 6 b g 1651^{4} 1867^{2} 2690^{5} 3613^{13} 4204^{13} >86+h<

Nathan Blake 12 gr g 827^{2} >72h 101c<

National Choice 11 b g 535^{3}

National Fiasco 4 b g Pragmatic-Lady Barunbe (Deep Run) 4009^{16} 4388^{8} >26fh<

National Flag (FR) 7 b g 1390^{10} 1552^{3} 1864^{7} 3057^{P} >77c<

Native-Darrig (IRE) 6 br g 4109a^{6} 4352a^{4} >106+h<

Native Estates (IRE) 5 b g Be My Native (USA)-Sesetta (Lucky Brief) 4118a^{2} >85fh<

Native Fleck (IRE) 7 b g Be My Native (USA)-Rare Find (Rarity) 4352a^{10} >86h<

Native Mission 10 ch g 2051^{3} 2783^{2} 3009^{3} >142c<

Native Rambler (IRE) 7 ch g 977^{4} 3005^{F} >35h 60c<

Native Venture (IRE) 9 b g 4098^{6} >80c<

Natural Talent 5 ch g Kris-Tropicaro (FR) (Caro) 1026^{2} 1296^{10} >41fh<

Naughty Future 8 ch g (1357) 1632^{U} 1981^{P} 2540^{5} 2954^{F} 3067^{2} 3882^{8} >92h 102c<

Nautical George (IRE) 7 b g 1664^{4} 1875^{6} 3810^{3} 3956^{U} 4235^{U} 4468^{15} >8h 76c<

Nautical Jewel 5 b g 1537^{6} (4067) (4231) 4427^{3} 4562^{2} >70h<

Nautilus The Third (IRE) 6 b g 1296^{16} 1579^{5} 2746^{P} 4182^{P} >39fh< (DEAD)

Nawtinookey 7 gr m 1344^{5} 1523^{F} 2045^{7} 3066^{9} 3313^{P} 3642^{4} 3826^{2} 4057^{4} 4260^{5} >42h 71+c<

Nazzaro 8 b g 1784^{F} 2616^{7} 3153^{P} 3428^{P} 3605^{4} >83h 120dc<

Ndaba 6 b g 3590^{9} 4423^{P} >19h<

Nearly All Right 8 ch g Nearly A Hand-Solhoon (Tycoon II) 3535^{F} 3755^{11} 3892^{P} >9h<

Nearly A Score 5 b m Nearly A Hand-Boherash (Boreen (FR)) 2931^{9} 3433^{14} 4519^{5} >2h<

Nearly At Sea 8 ch m Nearly A Hand-Culm Port (Port Corsair) 4623^{P} >46h<

Nearly Splendid 12 br g 3341^{P} >109c<

Neat Feat (IRE) 6 b g 1283^{2} 1583^{4} 1867^{5} 2909^{2} 3012^{2} 3569^{3} 3718^{2} 3977^{3} >73h<

Nebaal (USA) 7 ch g 3282^{4} 4299^{P} 4648^{P}

Nebraska 11 b g 323a^{8} >89c<

Nectanebo (IRE) 9 b br g Persian Bold-Dancing Sally (Sallust) (4070) 4327^{U} 4543^{3} >92c<

Needle Match 4 ch c Royal Academy (USA)-Miss Tatting (USA) (Miswaki (USA)) 1699^{7} 2649^{F} 2918^{P} >43h<

Needle Thread 5 gr m Henbit (USA)-Linen Thread (Broxted) 4216^{16} >44fh<

Needwood Cube 6 b g 54^{10} >39h<

Needwood Joker 6 b g 4799^{7} >53h<

Needwood Muppet 10 b g 1039^{9} 1429^{P} >112h<

Needwood Poppy 9 b m Rolfe (USA)-Needwood

Nap (Some Hand) 3166^{9} 3545^{5} 3807^{6} 4418^{4} 4536^{4} **>68h<**

Nell Valley 6 b m 4238^{3} 4318^{8} **4533^{P}** **>39h<**

Nelly Blanche 6 b m 2757^{12}

Nelson Must 7 b g Pollerton-Needs Supporting (Home Guard (USA)) 910^{14} **>20h<**

Nenagh Gunner 7 ch m Gunner B-Lulagh Bird (Weathercock) 99^{3} 872^{6} 1208^{7} 1672^{8} 1990^{7} **>41h<**

Neptunes Miss 5 ch m 1855^{10} 3889^{7} **>21h<**

Nero's Gem 6 b m 1536^{P} 1958^{7}

Nescaf (NZ) 7 b g **30^{3}** 95^{9} **>72h 75c<**

Netherby Said 7 b g **(1717) (2674) 3069^{3} 3198^{3} (3547) (3707) (3943) 4258^{5}** **>52h 122c<**

Nevada Gold 11 ch g **946^{5} 1194^{5} 3185^{3} 4535^{P} 4740^{P}** **>101c<**

Never Forgotten 12 ch g The Parson-Our Gale (Dusky Boy) 1939^{W} 2792^{12} 3183^{4} 3720^{P} 3896^{5} **>39h<**

Never In Debt 5 ch g Nicholas Bill-Deep In Debt (Deep Run) (653) 1431^{2} 1801^{9} 4657^{3} **>53fh<**

Never Say so 5 ch m 18^{P} 96^{P}

Never so Blue (IRE) 6 b g 1984^{8} 2882^{10} 3031^{6} 3234^{15} 3803^{3} 3940^{4} 4223^{6} 4423^{4} 4648^{6} 4714^{U} **>47h<**

Never Time (IRE) 5 b g Simply Great (FR)-Islet Time (Burslem) 2547^{P}

New Capricorn (USA) 7 ch g 700^{7} **>54h<**

New Century (USA) 5 gr g Manila (USA)-Casessa (USA) (Caro) 2898^{3} **>73h<**

New Charges 10 b g 3028^{6} 3157^{B} 3646^{8} 4248^{P} **>62h<**

New Co (IRE) 9 ch g 1234a^{2} 1759a^{F} **(2348a) 2848a^{3}** 3254a^{7} **3618^{10} 4074^{15}** **>125h 129c<**

Newgate Pixie (IRE) 4 b br f Accordion-Newgate Fairy (Flair Path) 3433^{21}

New Ghost 12 ch g **3837^{F} 4270^{P}** **>97?c<**

Newhall Prince 9 b g **702^{3} 951^{P}** 1145^{3} 1204^{3} **1527^{4} 1912^{2} 3329^{3} 3943^{3}** 4223^{9} **>71h 110dc<**

New Inn 6 b g 1779^{6} (1924) 2062^{2} 2543^{3} 2779^{2} 3164^{4} **>99h<**

Newlands-General 11 ch g **951^{4} 1035^{2} 1257^{2} (1393) 1682^{4} 2660^{U} (2707) 3419^{3} 3673^{F} 3981^{U} 4177^{2}** **>126c<**

New Leaf (IRE) 5 b g Brush Aside (USA)-Page of Gold (Goldhill) 1329^{8} 2696^{2} 3042^{6} (3888) **>78+h 78c<**

New Regime (IRE) 4 b f Glenstal (USA)-Gay Refrain (Furry Glen) 3583^{P} 4162^{11}

New Ross (IRE) 5 gr g Roselier (FR)-Miss Lucille (Fine Blade (USA)) 4301^{15} 4441^{5} 4625^{12} **>59h<**

News Flash (IRE) 5 b g Strong Gale-Gale Flash (News Item) 3399^{7} **>39h<**

News From Afar 6 b g 1561^{4}

Newski Express 12 bl or br m Newski (USA)-Mint Express (Pony Express) **4522^{F}**

Newski Lass 5 ch m Newski (USA)-Vitapep (Vital Season) 3170^{19}

Newton Point 8 b g 1019^{4} **>119h 91c<**

Newtown Rosie (IRE) 8 gr m Roselier (FR)-Sicilian Princess (Sicilian Prince) **795^{4} 1447^{4} 1635^{P}** **>76c<**

Nexsis Star 4 ch g Absalom-The High Dancer (High Line) 1652^{10} 1940^{9} 2669^{3} 2859^{12} 3197^{8} **>76h<**

Nicanjon 6 ch g Nicholas Bill-Rosalina (Porto Bello) 1685^{11} 3853^{9} 4506^{F} 4625^{8} **>47h<**

Nicholas Plant 8 ch g 6^{2} 695^{6} (942) 1143^{3} 1360^{3} 1671^{5} 2545^{5} **2769^{U} (3027) 3069^{2} 3312^{2} 3556^{2} 4186^{2} 4247^{2} (4480) 4571^{3}** **>83h 112c<**

Nickle Joe 11 ro g **1641^{5} 1957^{7}** 4178^{7} **4467^{U} 4629^{7}** 4803^{P} **>80c<**

Nicklup 10 ch m **1338^{F} 1540^{2}** **>110c<**

Nick Ross 6 b g 1263^{3} 1667^{3} 3396^{8} 3823^{11} 4075^{2} 4188^{3} **>72h<**

Nick the Beak (IRE) 8 ch g 1031^{6} (1553) 1783^{3} (2702) 3045^{9} 3281^{7} 4005^{10} **>88h<**

Nick the Bill 6 b g 1078^{9} 1247^{9} **>54h<**

Nick the Biscuit 6 b g 77^{P} 156^{12} **>77dh<**

Nick the Dreamer 12 ch g **484^{7} 823^{5} 914^{F} 1057^{F}** 1528^{4} 3892^{P} 4096^{4} 4253^{5} 4524^{10} **>54h 97c<**

Nickys Peril 5 ch m Nicholas Bill-Priceless Peril (Silly Prices) 3828^{17} 4156^{8} **>14fh<**

Nicky Wilde 7 br g Strong Gale-Dark Trix (Peacock (FR)) 2805^{15} 3054^{3} 4231^{P} **>46h<**

Nicola Marie (IRE) 8 ch m 4048^{7} **>71h<**

Nifaaf (USA) 5 b m 1033^{2} 2005^{2} **>38fh<**

Nigel's Boy 5 b g 1289^{6} **>49fh<**

Nigels Choice 5 gr g Teenoso (USA)-Warm Winter (Kalaglow) 1333^{P}

Nigel's Lad (IRE) 5 b g Dominion Royale-Back To Earth (FR) (Vayrann) 3158^{2} (3315) (3416) 4010^{5} (4608) **>90h<**

Night Boat 6 b g 17^{9} 794^{7} 1118^{2} 1980^{9} 2943^{U} 3741^{2} (3803) 3983^{4} **4419^{U}** **>62h<**

Night City 6 b g Kris-Night Secret (Nijinsky (CAN)) 1726^{4} 2034^{5} **>64h<**

Night Dance 5 ch h Weldnaas (USA)-Shift Over (USA) (Night Shift (USA)) 1830^{4} (2669) 3034^{5} **>78h<**

Night Escapade (IRE) 5 b m Be My Native (USA)-Right Dark (Buckskin (FR)) 872^{4} 1504^{8} 2931^{10} 3946^{6} 4794^{5} **>46h<**

Night Fancy 9 ch g **1963^{7} 3051^{10} 3332^{4} 3622^{3} 3934^{4} 4083^{P}** **>48?h 73c<**

Night Flare (FR) 5 ch g Night Shift (USA)-Gold Flair (Tap On Wood) 1517^{P} 1726^{13} 2868^{6} **>44h<**

Night in a Million 6 br g **808^{4} 1073^{5}** 1193^{5} 2907^{4} 3447^{7} 3603^{4} (3958) 4101^{3} 4345^{2} **>66h 47c<**

Night Thyne (IRE) 5 b g 960^{P} 1713^{F}

Night Time 5 b g (67) 210^{2} 300^{3} 348^{3} 393^{6} 596^{5} 749^{6} 879^{12} 4290^{P} (4789) **>53h<**

Nijmegen 9 b g 2779^{8} 2950^{5} 3163^{7} 3615^{18} **>98h<**

Nijway 7 b g **1248^{7} 1346^{6} 1574^{U} 2653^{4} 3314^{F} 3450^{U} 3484^{3} (3608)** 3695^{U} **(3911)** 4078^{2} **4245^{P} (4336)** 4576^{3} **(4710)** **>68h 102c<**

Niki Dee (IRE) 7 b g **1691^{F} 1803^{2}** **>77h 109c<**

Nikkis Pet 10 ch m **3060^{P} 3409^{4} 3675^{P}** **>77c<**

Nine O Three (IRE) 8 b g (71) 2579^{2} 3114^{2} 3277^{6} **>87h<**

Nine Pipes (IRE) 6 b g 3714^{F} 3883^{9} 4259^{12} 4626^{P} **>29h<**

Nipper Reed 7 b g 3002^{6} (3087) 3421^{3} 3579^{2} **>83h<**

Nirvana Prince 8 ch g (495) 4207^{2} **>97h<**

Nirvana Princess 5 ch m Glacial Storm (USA)-Princess Sunshine (Busted) 3626^{8} 3808^{R} 4420^{12} 4632^{14} **>35fh<**

Nishaman 6 gr g 1583^{9} 1938^{15} 2868^{8} 3757^{9} 3921^{11} **>4h<**

Nishamira (IRE) 5 gr m (705) 872^{2} 3029^{3} (3226) 4204^{4} **>65h<**

Nita's Choice 7 b m 1198^{P}

Nite Sprite 7 b m 4055^{2} 4394^{5} 4501^{5} (4754) **>53h<**

Niyaka 10 b g 2634^{P}

Nizaal (USA) 6 ch h Diesis-Shicklah (USA) (The Minstrel (CAN)) 1666^{9} 1967^{3} **>59h<**

Noble Act (IRE) 6 br g Parliament-Vellgrove Lady (Torus) 191^{11}

Noble Angel (IRE) 9 b g **3455^{F} 4631^{P}**

Noble Canonire 5 b m Gunner B-Lucky Candy (Lucky Wednesday) 2697^{7} **>21h<**

Noble Colours 4 b g Distinctly North (USA)-Kentucky Tears (USA) (Cougar (CHI)) 1444^{B} 1900^{9} 3054^{10} 3424^{3} 3745^{3} (3927) 4169^{F} 4395^{9} 4555^{3} **>88?h<**

Noble Lord 4 ch g Lord Bud-Chasers' Bar (Oats) (548) (599) (1387) 1514^{2} 2772^{2} 3007^{3} 3917^{4} 4014^{9} 4720^{2} **>93h<**

Noblely (USA) 10 b g **(76) 138^{3} (207) 261^{2} 305^{2} 352^{2} (403) 470^{2} (592) 633^{U}** **>103h 112c<**

Noble Monarch (IRE) 8 br g Strong Gale-Perusia (Pirate King) 1161^{7} 1312^{7} 1687^{9} **>52h<**

Noble Norman 6 b g Grey Desire-Pokey's Pet (Uncle Pokey) 4719^{6}

Noble Society 9 b g 210^{P} 4071^{7} **>81h<**

Noblesse Oblige 0 G Salse (USA)-Fair Rosamunda (Try My Best (USA)) 3058^{P} 3359^{15} **>19h<**

Noble Thyne (IRE) 7 b g (1485a) 1757a^{3} (2359a) **>106+h<**

Noble Tom (IRE) 5 b g The Noble Player (USA)-Hospitality (Homing) 2675^{2} 2904^{10} 3548^{9} 4580^{4} **>54fh<**

Nobodys Flame (IRE) 9 b g **1688^{P} 3608^{8} 4057^{9} 4334^{4} 4502^{P}** **>51c<**

Nobodys Son 11 gr g Nobody Knows-Fine Performance (Gala Performance (USA)) **314a^{11}** **>98c< (DEAD)**

Nocatchim 8 b g (17) (97) **(180) 256^{7} 352^{3} 645^{3}** **>84h 101c<**

Noddadante (IRE) 7 b g Phardante (FR)-Loughcopple (Over The River (FR)) 1077^{7} 1539^{12} 2907^{8} (3442) 3683^{U} 4001^{5} **>56h<**

Nodform Wonder 10 b g **(4222) (4631)** **>87h 116+c<**

No Fiddling (IRE) 6 br g 3166^{7} 3545^{6} 3750^{4} **(4007) 4157^{3} 4535^{F} 4742^{2}** **>66h 95c<**

No Finer Man (IRE) 6 b g Lord Americo-Ballaroe Bar (Bargello) 2066^{7} 2917^{5} 3159^{5} **>70h<**

No Gimmicks (IRE) 5 b g Lord Americo-Catspaw (Laurence O) 3070^{3} 3794^{3} **>73h<**

No Inhibitions 10 ch g **4619^{3} 4724^{P}** **>92c<**

Noir Esprit 4 br g Prince Daniel (USA)-Danse D'Esprit (Lidhame) 1526^{R} 1700^{3} 2175^{3} 2859^{7} 3287^{6} 3474^{2} 4162^{8} 4295^{P} 4516^{2} **>62h<**

Noisy Miner (IRE) 5 b g Kambalda-Furry Lady (Furry Glen) (3235) (3767) **>75fh<**

Noisy Welcome 11 b g The Parson-Lady Pitpan (Pitpan) **3341^{F}**

No Joker (IRE) 9 b g **2951^{U} 3553^{5} 3837^{2} 4308^{P} 4614^{2} (4730)** **>98c<**

No Light 10 gr g 62^{5} 75^{8} 329^{2} 404^{2} 677^{6} 4381^{7} 4701^{6} **>59h 100c<**

No Matter (IRE) 6 br g Roselier (FR)-Nataf (Whistling Deer) 1938^{14} 2668^{P} 3818^{7} **>42h<**

No Mistake VI (IRE) 9 ch g **2998a^{7}** **>106c<**

No Morals 6 b g 2552^{P} **>32h<**

No More Hassle (IRE) 4 ch g Magical Wonder (USA)-Friendly Ann (Artaius (USA)) 646^{7} (1776) (2842) (3291) 3634^{10} **>84h<**

No More the Fool 11 ch g **4631^{P}** **>43c<**

No More Trix 11 b g **3135^{U}** **>112c<**

None Stirred (IRE) 7 b g 1581^{3} (2680) **>80h<**

Nonios (IRE) 6 b g 731^{2} 856^{2} 941^{2} 1144^{4} 1577^{4} 1942^{6} 4259^{10} 4516^{5} **>62dh<**

Non Non Joesephine 6 b m Dunbeath (USA)-Go Lightly (Galivanter) 4287^{12}

Non Vintage (IRE) 6 ch g 62^{4} (745) 1156^{4} 1271^{4} 1510^{F} 1656^{R} 1804^{6} 1924^{6} 2059^{5} 2777^{10} 2950^{7} (3199) 3615^{16} **>105h<**

Nooran 6 b g 1144^{6} 1316^{9} **2786^{2} 3161^{3} 3530^{U} 3826^{4} 4260^{3}** **>43h 97dc<**

Noosa Sound (IRE) 7 br g **1850^{5} 2788^{2} 3067^{F} 3370^{P}** **>50h 83c<**

No Pain No Gain (IRE) 9 ch g **1186[F] 1937[5] 3106[2] 3349[3] 3585[4] 4013[5] 4214[8] >99h 117c<**

No Panic 13 b g **4560[U] 4804[7]** >87?c<

No Pattern 5 ch g 1375[3] (2794) 3298[3] 3564[6] 4010[P] 4275[4] **>84h<**

Noquita (NZ) 10 ch g Nassipour (USA)-Memphis (AUS) (Boldest Melody (USA)) 1640[15] 1964[P] 3677[9] 4231[P] 4382[P] 4737[8] **>19h<**

Nordance Prince (IRE) 6 b g 1427[3] 1651[3] 2624[5] 2840[5] 3494[3] 3761[4] (4382) (4567) 4696[2] **>86h<**

Nordansk 8 ch g **947[6] 1195[F] >89h 45tc<**

Nordic Breeze (IRE) 5 b or br g (794) 1053[3] 1187[2] 2573[U] 3595[3] 4010[7] 4397[F] (4641) (4743) **>98++h<**

Nordic Crown (IRE) 6 b m 134[4] 185[5] 407[2] 888[2] 969[3] **>55h<**

Nordic Flight 9 b or br g 2038[7] 2546[14] 2838[7] **3334[8] 3472[P]** 3683[P] **>40dh<**

Nordic Hero (IRE) 4 b g Nordico (USA)-Postscript (Final Straw) 1011[B] 1413[P] 2050[P]

Nordic Prince (IRE) 6 b g 2619[7] 2861[3] **>69h<**

Nordic Spree (IRE) 5 b g Nordico (USA)-Moonsilk (Solinus) 1388[2] 2820[7] 3178[P] 3689[5] 3901[3] 4250[3] 4341[2] (4544) 4698[P] **>70h<**

Nordic Sun (IRE) 9 gr g **(136) 215[7]** 4746[5] **>64h 121c<**

Nordic Thorn (IRE) 7 b g **321a[4] 1361[2] >107h 123c<**

Nordic Valley (IRE) 6 b g 97[4] **160[3] 296[2] 333[2] (595) (740) 1331[F] 1696[5] 1875[F] 2548[2] 2873[3] 3343[8] 3602[4] 4237[2] (4442) 4549[3] 4771[2] >93h 97c<**

Nordisk Legend 5 b g Colmore Row-Nordic Rose (DEN) (Drumhead) 3026[6] 3311[6] 4244[6] 4568[5] **>47h<**

Nord Lys (IRE) 6 b g (357) 2866[7] 3110[9] 3803[2] **>50h<**

Norfolk Glory 5 ch g Weldnaas (USA)-Caviar Blini (What A Guest) 1413[F] 1569[P] 1993[U] 2574[U]

Norlandic (NZ) 5 ch g First Norman (USA)-April Snow (NZ) (Icelandic) 2682[11] 3342[6] **>53h<**

Normandy Duke (NZ) 5 ch g First Norman (USA)-Royal Step (NZ) (Ring Round The Moon) 1457[12] 1834[12] **>29fh<**

Normania (NZ) 5 b g First Norman (USA)-Brigania (NZ) (Brigand (USA)) 3767[2] 4216[10] **>60fh<**

Normarange (IRE) 7 ch g **2827[3] 3409[2] 3688[2] (3957) 4168[U] >67h 98c<**

Normead Lass 9 b m 54[9] **>46h<**

Norse Raider 7 gr g **2942[3] 3638[F] 3839[4] >87h 95c<**

Northants 11 b g **3025[3] 3266[P] >111h 125c<**

North Bannister 10 br g 134[2] (480) **556[3] >55h 66c<**

North Bear 5 b g North Briton-Sarah Bear (Mansingh (USA)) 1208[3] **>56h<**

North End Lady 6 b m North Briton-Nibelunga (Miami Springs) (504) 705[5] 1052[13] 1821[F] 3098[P]

Northern Charmer 5 b g 3904[5] **>62h<**

Northern Clan 4 b g Clantime-Northern Line (Camden Town) 1634[15] **>17h<**

Northern Diamond (IRE) 4 b g Distinctly North (USA)-Mitsubishi Diamond (Tender King) 1700[11] 4069[P] 4440[P] **>22h<**

Northern Falcon 4 gr f Polar Falcon (USA)-Bishah (USA) (Balzac (USA)) 291[4] 646[4] 1652[7] 1776[P] 2744[9] 2913[4] **>56h<**

Northern Fancy (IRE) 6 b g 318a[5] **>82h<**

Northern Fleet 4 b c Slip Anchor-Kamkova (USA) (Northern Dancer) 1808[2] 2668[4] 2889[2] 3075[4] 3801[4] **>77h<**

Northern Fusilier 5 ch g (858) (1026) 1412[F] **(DEAD)**

Northern Grey 5 gr g Puissance-Sharp Anne (Belfort (FR)) 4423[3] **>46h<**

Northern Hide 11 b g **1917[3] 2887[2] 3618[9] 4074[12] >133c<**

Northern Law 5 gr h Law Society (USA)-Pharland (FR) (Bellypha) 634[10] 819[P] **>45h<**

Northern Motto 4 b g Mtoto-Soulful (FR) (Zino) 1356[U]

Northern Nation 9 b g 97[P] **286[4] 389[F]** 488[3] 648[10] **>75h 88dc<**

Northern Optimist 9 b m **728[3] (883) 951[3] 1146[3] 1257[6] 1445[6] 3678[5] 3843[U] 4177[6] 4404[P] 4771[P] >75dh 72dc<**

Northern Saddler 10 ch g **1257[4] 1321[3] >101h 118c<**

Northern Singer 7 ch g **1449[3] 2037[3] (2569) 2873[U] 3053[P] (3343) 3682[F] 3981[P] (4021) >55h 89c<**

Northern Spruce (IRE) 5 ch g Astronef-Perle's Fashion (Sallust) 1375[12]

Northern Squire 9 b g (2922) 3317[2] **(3486) 3710[2] 3884[2] 3911[P] 4185[P]** 4772[P] **>81h 117c<**

Northern Star 6 ch g 1800[8] (3621) 3990[U] 4217[7] 4393[2] 4563[4] 4760[4] **>66h<**

Northern Starlight 6 b g (2963) (3497) (3766) (3890) (4172) 4397[F] (4741) **>103+h<**

Northern Trial (USA) 9 b g 32[6] 211[4] 326a[F] **>82h 62c< (DEAD)**

Northern Union (CAN) 6 b g 2649[2] 3026[3] **>69h<**

Northern Village 10 ch g 1088[4] **3580[4] 3765[3] (3906) 4135[6] >92h 105c<**

North Pride (USA) 12 ch g **4410[4] >50c<**

No Sacrifice 5 b m Revlow-Cool Brae (Rymer) 161[10]

Nosam 7 b g 2633[6] (4719) **>72+h<**

Nosmo King (IRE) 6 b g 2913[9] 3327[7] 3483[7] 3711[13] 4055[F] **>42h<**

Notable Exception 8 b g **(179) (733)** 894[2] **(1083)** 1265[3] **>91dh 99c<**

No Tag (IRE) 9 b g 318a[13] **>127h 94c<**

No Takers 10 b m Carlingford Castle-La Perla (Majority Blue) 3711[P] 4711[9] 4756[7] **>34h<**

Notary-Nowell 11 b g **4317[4] >78c<**

Notcomplainingbut (IRE) 6 b m 1234a[3] 2603a[18] 2740a[6] 3126a[4] **>113h<**

Noted Strain (IRE) 9 b g 288[5] 4755[8] **>37h<**

Not For Turning (IRE) 6 b g (1453) 1915[P] **>73h<**

Nothing Doing (IRE) 8 b g 1451[7] **>44h<**

Nothingtodowithme 7 ch g 1262[3] 1542[5] 1816[5] **>69h<**

Nothing To It 6 b g Lyphento (USA)-Corniche Rose (Punchinello) 3418[8] **>37fh<**

Nothing Ventured 8 b g Sonnen Gold-Dream Venture (Giolla Mear) **4631[2] >97c<**

No Time To Wait 6 b g Dubassoff (USA)-Flopsy Mopsy (Full of Hope) 4150[11] 4421[12] **>32fh<**

Not My Line (IRE) 8 gr g Entre Nous-Uno Navarro (Raga Navarro (ITY)) **2951[P] 3055[4] 3586[6] (3922) 4160[4] 4320[5] (4543) 4748[4] >109c<**

Not So Prim 5 b m Primitive Rising (USA)-Sobriquet (Roan Rocket) 1084[6]

Not To Panic (IRE) 7 ch m 1168[5] 1726[12] 1959[8] 2800[7] 3621[4] **>56h<**

Nova Champ 9 ch g **(4404) 4535[5] >77h 95c<**

Nova Run 8 ch g (1330) **>90h<**

Nowhiski 9 b g **3460[2] >97c<**

No Word 10 b or br g **2903[P] 3439[6] 4543[10] 4748[P] >21h 50c<**

Now We Know (IRE) 9 ch g **1038[3] >77h 93c<**

Now Young Man (IRE) 8 br g **(4080) 4208[4] 4745[6] >74dh 101dc<**

Noyan 7 ch g **(1826) 2176[F] (2628) 3044[2] (3288) 3618[4] (4356a) >110h 129c<**

Nuaffe 12 b g **1397a[8] 1495a[P] 2348a[U] 2848a[10] (3255a) 3503a[P] 4074[F] 4362a[P] >46h 117c<**

Nuclear Express 10 b g **261[4] 328[3] 457[4] >81dc<**

Nukud (USA) 5 b g Topsider (USA)-Summer Silence (USA) (Stop The Music (USA)) 794[11] 1278[9] 1413[P] **>34h<**

Nuns Cone 9 ch g 1681[P] 3269[11] 3499[15] **>36h<**

Nuns Lucy 6 ch m 1448[P] 1693[P] 2805[17] 3621[13] 4073[P] **4444[P] >14h<**

Nunson 8 ch g Celtic Cone-Nunswalk (The Parson) 871[11] 1580[4] 1768[11] 2076[P] **2569[P] >50h<**

Nutty Solera 7 ch g Henbit (USA)-Friendly Cherry (Bargello) 1692[4] 1973[3] 2180[2] 2504[3] 2918[6] 3315[6] 3887[12] **>63h<**

O

Oakbury (IRE) 5 ch g 58[6] 1251[4] 1628[15] 1908[3] 2913[3] 3091[2] 3284[8] 3542[3] 3711[11] 3985[10] **>51h<**

Oaklands Billy 8 b g Silly Prices-Fishermans Lass (Articulate) **3479[P] 3724[5] >65c<**

Oakley 8 ch g **3094[F] >82h 83+c<**

Oat Couture 9 b g **(1644) 2061[F] 2789[4]** (3028) 3269[8] 3559[2] **>99h 100dc<**

Oatis Regrets 9 b g **1175[4] 1997[3] >130c<**

Oatis Rose 7 b m 1429[3] 1571[F] 1798[4] 1952[6] 2659[7] (3146) 3402[2] 4005[3] 4132[5] 4418[8] **>84h<**

Oats For Notes 7 b m Oats-Run in Tune (Deep Run) 99[6] 161[8] 191[4] 4070[7] **>33c<**

Oats N Barley 8 b g **2052[F] 2681[10] 2883[P] 3537[P] >71h 57c<**

Oban 7 ch g **(1389) (2049) 3274[2] >77h 125c<**

Obsidian 5 b g Prince of Peace-Barosca (Bargello) 4539[16]

Obvious Risk 6 b g 1666[12] 2787[9] 2953[6] 3026[5] 3313[3] 3371[5] 3448[4] **3642[U]** 4501[P] **>34h<**

Occold (IRE) 6 b g Over The River (FR)-My Puttens (David Jack) 4224[3] **>82h<**

Ocean Hawk (USA) 5 b g (1196) 1522[2] (2056) (2637) 3303[8] 3635[11] **>140h<**

Ocean Leader 10 b g **(1716) 2052[5] 2671[P] 3472[P] (3945) >100c<**

October Brew (USA) 7 ch g Seattle Dancer (USA)-Princess Fager (USA) (Dr Fager) **411[5] 1763[6] 2873[4]** 3338[P] 3949[4] 4294[R] 4384[4] 4658[5] **>64h<**

Odda's Chapel 4 b g Little Wolf-Pity's Pet (Stanford) 4554[4] **>54fh<**

Odell (IRE) 7 br g **1664[6] (3938) >74c<**

Office Hours 5 b g Danehill (USA)-Charmina (FR) (Nonoalco (USA)) 1594[6] 1770[F] 1818[P] 2753[P] **>32h<**

Off Piste Sally 5 b m Newski (USA)-Sols Joker (Comedy Star (USA)) 1565[P] 2627[P]

Off The Bru 12 b g **2[P] 696[7] 804[2] 940[U] 1266[8] 1704[3] (2046) 2956[2] (3395) 3643[2] >73h 106c<**

Ogulla 5 b m Crowning Honors (CAN)-Home Sweet Home (Royal Palace) 4088[10] 4441[P] 4567[9] **>9h<**

Oh Brother 4 br g Move Off-Scally's Girl (Scallywag) 3480[7]

Oh Dear Me 6 b m Northern State (USA)-Canvas Shoe (Hotfoot) 24[2] 133[2] 161[4]

Oh So Cosy (IRE) 4 br g Mandalus-Milan Pride (Northern Guest (USA)) 4215[7] **>69fh<**

Oh So Grumpy 9 br g **4123a[3] >103h 118c<**

Oh So Risky 10 b g 1015[3] **(1521) 2054[3] 4012[2] >135?h 129c<**

Oi Mother (IRE) 5 b m Strong Gale-Pops Girl (Deep Run) 4531[4] 4774[2] **>65fh<**

O K Kealy 7 gr g Absalom-Constanza (Sun Prince) 3197[P] 3345[W]

Old Archives (IRE) 8 b g 1074[5] 1384[4] 1553[6]

>76h<

Old Betsy 7 b m 2614^{5} 2841^{11} >52h 71c<

Old Bombay (IRE) 5 br g Be My Native (USA)-Zelamere (Le Bavard (FR)) 4150^{4} 4580^{3} >57fh<

Old Bridge (IRE) 9 ch g 1454^{2} 1649^{7} 1917^{8} 3039^{F} 3916^{3} 4206^{F} >140+c<

Old Cavalier 6 b g 1026^{4} 1768^{7} 2042^{6} 3048^{9} 4220^{5} >64h<

Old Dundalk 13 b g Derrylin-Georgiana (Never Say Die) 3664^{P}

Olden Days 5 b g 1036^{P} 1337^{P}

Old Gold N Tan 4 ch g Ballacashtal (CAN)-Raleigh Gazelle (Absalom) 471^{5} >33h<

Old Habits (IRE) 8 b g 2545^{8} 2802^{5} 3163^{6} 3309^{3} 3885^{6} 4081^{4} 4248^{5} >78h<

Old Hush Wing (IRE) 4 b g Tirol-Saneena (Kris) 3345^{4} >75h<

Old Man of Ramas 5 b g Lochnager-Ramas Silk (Amber Rama (USA)) 2844^{13} 4531^{21}

Old Master (IRE) 6 b g 749^{10} 915^{7} 1174^{9} 1299^{5} 1874^{5} >48h<

Old Mill Stream 11 br g 4804^{5} >88c<

Old Money 11 b g 9^{6} >68h 95c<

Old Mortality 11 b g 138^{P} 419^{5} 463^{7} >63h 71?c<

Old Redwood 10 b or br g 1563^{P} 1920^{P} 3015^{6} 3278^{6} 3826^{6} 4305^{3} 4454^{3} 4526^{5} 4627^{6} >63c<

Ole Ole 11 br g 911^{P} 1082^{2} 1307^{3} 2630^{P} >93c<

Oliver-J 6 b g 101^{12} >51h<

Olivipet 8 b m 2907^{7} 3670^{6} 3896^{4} 4436^{4} >39h<

Ollardale (IRE) 9 b g Abednego-Kauai-Ka-Zum (Kauai King) 3459^{P}

Olliver Duckett 8 b g 1257^{5} (2577) 2796^{3} 3051^{4} 3343^{9} 3981^{2} >64dh 89dc<

Olympian 10 ch g 796^{4} (1031) 1196^{3} (1522) 1906^{3} 2625^{2} 3600^{21} 4132^{4} 4310^{5} >98h 85c<

Olympic D'Or (IRE) 9 ch g Boreen (FR)-Brook Lady 3503a^{7} >84c<

O My Love 6 b m 1583^{7} 1998^{5} 2680^{6} 3050^{4} 3983^{6} >58h<

Once More for Luck (IRE) 6 b g 1163^{5} 2543^{6} 2946^{2} >95h<

One Boy 5 gr g Scallywag-Saucy Eater (Saucy Kit) *3846^{7}* 4217^{P}

One For Navigation (IRE) 5 b g Tremblant-Rossnagran (Ardross) 1200^{3} 2656^{P} 2961^{P} >46fh<

One for the Pot 12 ch g 1361^{6} 1688^{4} 1846^{4} 2618^{4} 3069^{5} >81h 108c<

One In The Eye 4 br c Arrasas (USA)-Mingalles (Prince de Galles) 2678^{2} >61h<

One Man (IRE) 9 gr g (1157) (2115) (2775) 2935^{2} 3636^{6} 4011^{P} >173c<

One More Bill 7 b g 1079^{5} 1245^{5} >41h<

One More Dime (IRE) 7 b m 77^{4} 978^{3} 1297^{3} 3189^{4} 3488^{P} 3831^{3} 3967^{10} (4445) 4705^{3} >50h<

One More Man (IRE) 6 b g 1077^{11} 1505^{5} 1809^{U} >45h<

One More Rupee 6 b g Presidium-Little Token (Shack (USA)) 1774^{13} 2746^{12} 3364^{P}

Oneoftheoldones 5 b g 1305^{F} 1659^{9} 1848^{F} >34h<

Oneofus 8 b g 2679^{P} 3104^{U} 3181^{S} 3688^{4} 4314^{4} >40h 50c<

One Stop 4 b f Silly Prices-Allerdale (Chebs Lad) 2924^{2} 3142^{10} 3529^{F} 3883^{10} >25h<

Only A Sioux 5 b g 1579^{12} 2701^{P} 2861^{13} 3315^{9} 4472^{8} >10h<

Only One (IRE) 7 ch g 3391a^{4}

On My Toes 6 b m 410^{3} 546^{P} (3997) 4384^{2} (4662) >50+h<

On The Home Run 4 b f Governor General-In the Papers (Aragon) 688^{8} >29h<

On the Ledge (USA) 7 b g 137^{P} 212^{F} 300^{P} 396^{P} 555^{8} 596^{P} 655^{5} 749^{9} >20h<

On The Move 6 b m 5^{P} 463^{4} 1078^{7} >54h<

On The Off Chance 5 ch g French Gondolier (USA)-Off and on (Touching Wood (USA)) 2798^{10} 2898^{21} 3158^{15} 3534^{F} >21h<

On the Tear 11 br g 637^{4} (828) 1041^{P} 1300^{2} 1629^{P} >74c<

Onyourown (IRE) 4 b g Treasure Kay-Mursuma (Rarity) 1514^{3} 1652^{13} 1700^{5} 3691^{10} 3825^{15} >46h<

Oozlem (IRE) 8 b g 1086^{P} >60h<

Opal's Tenspot 10 b g 957^{5} 1122^{6} 1445^{5} (1817) 2665^{P} 2756^{6} (3179) 3456^{F} 3684^{P} >80c<

Open Affair 4 ch f Bold Arrangement-Key to Enchantment (Key To Content (USA)) 1413^{13} >20h<

Open Fairway 4 ch g Opening Run (USA)-Golfe (Idiot's Delight) 3828^{7} 4216^{11} >59fh<

Open Market (USA) 8 b g Northern Baby (CAN)-Spiranthes (USA) 314a^{F} >95h 101c<

Opera Fan (IRE) 5 b g 2001^{2} 2631^{2} 3035^{7} >66h<

Opera Hat (IRE) 9 br m 763a^{4} 1216a^{3} 2362a^{3} 2741a^{6} (3383a) 4349a^{5} >131h 153c<

Operatic Dancer 6 b g Germont-Indian Dancer (Streak) 3026^{P}

Operetto (IRE) 7 b g 1180^{F} 1351^{4} 1581^{6} 3050^{2} 3362^{2} 4403^{9} >62h<

Optimistic Affair 6 b g 1301^{4} 1713^{5} >56h<

Orange Imp 4 ch f Kind of Hush-Sip of Orange (Celtic Cone) 4632^{3} >52fh<

Orange Order (IRE) 4 ch g Generous (IRE)-Fleur D'Oranger (Northfields (USA)) 589^{6} 807^{P} 4718^{6} >40h<

Orange Ragusa 11 ch g 3793^{3} 4222^{5} >101dc<

Orchard Generation 6 b m Joligeneration-Miss Orchard (Latest Model) 504^{9}

Orchard King 7 ch g 3019^{10} 3438^{13} 4512^{4} 4696^{5} 4800^{4} >60h<

Orchestral Designs (IRE) 6 b g 66^{18} 129^{P} 4739^{P}

Orchestral Suite (IRE) 9 br g Orchestra-Sweetly Stung (Master Rocky) (2951) (3586) 4015^{F} >117+c<

Orchid House 5 b m Town And Country-Tudor Orchid (Tudor Rhythm) 3061^{U} 3337^{P} 3494^{U} 3977^{7}

Ordog Mor (IRE) 8 ch g 18^{2} 100^{2} (181) (260) (489) 690^{2} 747^{3} 3473^{7} 3709^{P} >81h<

Oriental Boy (IRE) 5 b g Boreen (FR)-Arctic Sue (Arctic Slave) 2844^{16} 3365^{15}

Orinoco Venture (IRE) 6 br g 498^{P} 600^{8} 4217^{P} 4472^{7} 4648^{12} >23h<

Or Royal (FR) 6 gr g Kendor (FR)-Pomme Royale (FR) (Shergar) (1572) (1787) 2054^{2} (3596) 3639^{3} >147c<

Orswell Lad 8 b g (1426) 1765^{4} (2660) 3047^{P} (3629) >82h 123c<

Orton House 10 b g 3469^{4} 3680^{P} 4222^{4} 4322^{5} 4704^{8} >65h 79c<

Orujo (IRE) 9 b g 3010^{7} 4326^{P} >67dh 61c<

Oscail An Doras (IRE) 8 ch g 63^{6} 979^{2} 1350^{5} >76h 112dc<

Oscilights Gift 5 b m Chauve Souris-Oscilight (Swing Easy (USA)) 3761^{P} 4017^{4} 4255^{P} >23h<

Osgathorpe 10 ch g 1083^{5} 4796^{2} >74c<

Otago Heights (NZ) 5 b g Gold and Ivory (USA)-Mountain Heights (NZ) (Rocky Mountain (FR)) 1685^{10} 4420^{2} >69fh<

Ottadini (IRE) 5 br m Cardinal Flower-Anniversary Waltz (Carnival Dancer) 1692^{18} 2047^{16} 2627^{F} 2920^{P} 3315^{8} 3611^{7} 4152^{7} 4575^{P} >39h<

Ottavio Farnese 5 ch g Scottish Reel-Sense of Pride (Welsh Pageant) 293^{4} 1369^{4} 1729^{6} 2692^{8} >73h<

Otter Prince 8 b g 1030^{13} 1200^{4} 1448^{8} 2870^{8} 3190^{3} 3488^{P} 4330^{2} >32h 77?c<

Otter River 8 ch g 3403^{P}

Otto E Mezzo 5 bl g Persian Bold-Carolside (Music Maestro) 3084^{10} (3282) 3549^{5} 3926^{3} >74h<

Our Adventure 4 ch f Green Adventure (USA)-Honey Dipper (Golden Dipper) 294^{P} 881^{P}

Our Barny 5 b g Wuzo (USA)-Speed Baby (USA) (Diplomat Way) 189^{P}

Our Bid (IRE) 6 b g Electric-Aplomb (Ballymore) 3619^{18} >67fh<

Our Carol (IRE) 5 br m Buckskin (FR)-Hampton Grange (Boreen (FR)) 2626^{7} 2904^{9} 3914^{14} >18fh<

Our Eddie 8 ch g Gabitat-Ragusa Girl (Morston (FR)) 3933^{7} 4231^{2} 4453^{3} 4567^{5} 4648^{5} 4789^{4} >57h<

Our Emma 8 b m Precocious-Miller's Daughter (Mill Reef (USA)) 3061^{P} 3226^{P}

Our Kris 5 b g 790^{P} 945^{4} 1156^{6} 1267^{6} 2780^{5} 3199^{3} 3728^{3} 3942^{3} >92dh<

Our Laughter 7 ch m 3706^{8}

Our Man Flin (IRE) 4 br g Mandalus-Flinging (Good Times (ITY)) 4009^{10} >31fh<

Our Mica 7 gr g 284^{4} >41h<

Our Nikki 7 gr m 132^{10} 411^{4} 556^{2} 720^{2} 901^{4} 970^{4} 1285^{6} 1389^{U} >42h 89dc<

Ourownfellow (IRE) 8 ch g Arapahos (FR)-Dara's March (March Parade) 1192^{3} 1456^{4} 2551^{P} >90dh 81c<

Our Pete 6 b g 1317^{W}

Our Rainbow 5 b m 1050^{4} 1250^{4} 1562^{P} 3222^{10} 3607^{13} >61dh<

Our Robert 5 b g 3065^{4} 3346^{4} 3485^{8} 3791^{3} (3940) 4295^{P} 4534^{2} 4630^{2} >69h<

Our Tom 5 br g Petong-Boa (Mandrake Major) 1659^{P} 2074^{9} 2815^{6} 2946^{9} >56h<

Our Wilma 8 ch m 2503^{9} 3727^{P} >27h<

Ousefleet Boy 5 b g 59^{7} 293^{10} 585^{P} 680^{P}

Out For A Duck 6 b g 22^{5} 2840^{P} 3342^{10} 3820^{P} >48h<

Out For Fun 11 ch g 2930^{2} >76+c<

Out of The Blue 5 b m 1145^{9} 1448^{7} 1816^{10} 3049^{U} 3429^{8} 3473^{5} 3733^{12} 4223^{P} >32h<

Out on a Promise (IRE) 5 b g 1333^{F} 1594^{3} (1911) (4101) 4386^{2} 4510^{2} 4798^{2} >89h<

Outrageous Affair 5 b m Idiot's Delight-Lac Royale (Lochnager) 3808^{14} 4421^{14} 4538^{11} >21fh<

Out Ranking (FR) 5 b m 159^{3} (223) (596) (741) 904^{2} 1176^{4} (1642) (1878) 2666^{8} (3915) 4141^{3} 4307^{9} 4510^{F} >92h<

Outset (IRE) 7 ch g 1645^{4} 2078^{4} 2888^{3} 3267^{4} 4053^{4} 4210^{6} >106h<

Over and Under (IRE) 4 ch g Over The River (FR)-Silver Gala (Gala Performance (USA)) 4547^{9} 4696^{P}

Overflowing River (IRE) 8 ch g 3886^{P} >99c<

Overrunning 5 ch m Over The River (FR)-Flo-Jo (DEN) (Pelton Lad) 3090^{10} 3433^{11} >39fh<

Overseas Invader (IRE) 5 b g Mansooj-Sniggy (Belfort (FR)) 161^{15} 418^{14}

Oversman 4 b g Keen-Jamaican Punch (IRE) (Shareef Dancer (USA)) 1652^{22} 3475^{2} 3789^{5} (4477) 4770^{4} >64h<

Over Stated (IRE) 7 b g 510^{3} 1703^{11} 1851^{3} 2913^{13} 3711^{12} 4056^{9} 4409^{B} 4516^{6} >37h<

Over the Deel 11 ch g 940^{F} >119c<

Over the Edge 11 ch g 3089^{P} 3553^{3} >97c<

Over The Maine (IRE) 7 b g 3503a^{8} >63h 90c<

Over the Pole 10 b g 1769^{P} 2894^{3} (3289) 3701^{3} 4225^{F} 4379^{F} 4802^{5} >95h 120dc<

Over the Stream 11 b g 2916^{6} 3710^{7} 4148^{F} 4503^{P} >67h 95c<

Over The Water (IRE) 5 gr g Over The River (FR)-

Shanacloon Lass (General Ironside) 1964[P] 2875[2] 3172[6] 3761[7] >65h<

Over The Way (IRE) 7 b br g Over The River (FR)-Biddy The Crow (Bargello) 4134[2] 4315[5] >70h<

Over The Wrekin 10 ch g 1632[P] 3472[P] >86c<

Overwhelm (IRE) 9 br g 937[6] 1304[7] 1826[4] 1968[4] 3314[4] 3608[P] 3824[P] >73c<

Over Zealous (IRE) 5 ch g Over The River (FR)-Chatty Di (Le Bavard (FR)) 2840[8] 3283[7] 3823[8] 4257[8] >29h<

Owenduff (USA) 7 ch g 4350a[U] >94h<

Owens Quest (IRE) 7 b m 1291[F] >66h<

Owes the Till 7 br m 3971[P]

Oxbridge Lady 6 b m Impecunious-White African (Carwhite) 1665[5] 3433[13] >49fh<

Oxford Quill 10 b g 1331[F] 1582[6] 1819[4] (2756) 2949[U] 3206[P] 3756[4] 4159[6] >50h 79c<

Oxgang (IRE) 4 b g Taufan (USA)-Casla (Lomond (USA)) 646[10] >41h<

Oykel River (IRE) 9 b g 3141[8] >58c<

Oyster Delight (IRE) 6 b m Miner's Lamp-Levitstown Lady (Paddy's Stream) 3889[8] >19h<

Ozzie Jones 6 b g 187[5] 495[3] >85h<

P

Pacific Overture 5 br m 183[9] >46h<

Pacific Power 7 b or br g 179[P] >45h<

Pacific Ridge (IRE) 6 gr g Roselier (FR)-Pacific Ocean (Optimistic Pirate) 718[9] >27h<

Pacifist 6 ch m 865[P]

Packitin Parky 4 b g Rakaposhi King-Divine Affair (IRE) (The Parson) 4301[16] 4441[7]

Padashpan (USA) 8 b g 1487a[5] 1759a[5] 2345a[6] >134h 105+c<

Padditate (IRE) 8 b g Supreme Leader-Ballyoran Princess (The Parson) 649[P] 885[F] (DEAD)

Paddy Burke (IRE) 7 bl g Ovac (ITY)-Another Space (Brave Invader (USA)) 1199[P] 1596[P] 2816[F]

Paddy's Return (IRE) 5 b g 1017[3] 2059[F] 3038[11] 3635[3] (4365a) >125+h<

Paddysway 10 b g 1553[5] 1876[2] (3180) 3499[14] 3720[P] >70h<

Page Royale (FR) 7 ch m Le Page-Dafka (FR) (Laniste) 4435[P]

Pagliaccio 9 b g 1295[2] 1657[4] 1823[2] 1970[3] >75h 108c<

Paid Elation 12 br m 66[P] 132[W] 160[6] >53c<

Paint Your Wagon 7 b g 1346[U] 1687[11] >6h<

Pair of Jacks (IRE) 7 ch g 223[5] (329) 473[2] 552[2] 793[2] 949[2] (1010) 1145[5] (1193) 1381[4] 1585[2] 1866[6] 4510[6] 4765[U] >73h<

Palacegate King 8 ch g 1347[4] 1510[6] 2603a[13] 3028[3] 3398[7] 3885[3] >94h<

Palace of Gold 7 b g 854[5] 2701[P] (2913) (3091) 3313[4] 3803[4] (4516) (4646) >66h<

Palace Parade (USA) 7 ch g 19[4] 157[2] >55h<

Palace River (IRE) 9 b m (4756) >55h<

Palace Yard 15 ch g 190[P] >69c<

Palafico 7 b g Broken Hearted-Supercube (USA) (Master Willie) 3295[P] 3468[7] 3820[8] >20h<

Palamon (USA) 4 ch c Sanglamore (USA)-Gantlette (Run The Gantlet (USA)) 2060[7] 2805[8] 2925[5] 3174[10] 3634[19] 3953[2] >57h<

Palette (IRE) 5 b m 1757a[2] 2347a[2] 2995a[3] 4117a[2] 4348a[8] >112h<

Paliapour (IRE) 6 br g 461[8]

Palladium Boy 7 b g 1427[8] 1766[P] 2771[6] 3424[6] 4226[10] >63h<

Pallium (IRE) 9 b g Try My Best (USA)-Jungle Gardenia (Nonoalco (USA)) 506[P]

Palm Reader 13 b g Palm Track-Carbia (Escart III) 3005[P] >106dc<

Palosanto (IRE) 7 b g (1185) 1441[5] 1645[8] (1946) (2819) 2960[F] 3600[14] (3892) >89h 113dc<

Pamalyn 5 b m Derrylin-Cute Pam (Pamroy) 4539[6] 4650[6] 4767[2] >60h<

Pamela's Lad 11 ch g 3455[9] 4631[3] >89c<

Pampajim (FR) 8 (2613a)

Panda Shandy 9 b m Nearly A Hand-Panda Pops (Cornuto) 3498[F]

Pandora's Prize 11 ch m Royal Vulcan-Semi-Colon (Colonist II) 2037[7] 3202[P] 3227[5] 3966[9] 4072[2] 4090[4] 4279[4] 4442[4] 4727[9] 4763[3] >23h 72c<

Pangeran (USA) 5 ch g Forty Niner (USA)-Smart Heiress (USA) (Vaguely Noble) 680[4] 781[2] 910[6] 1249[2] 1848[2] 2001[5] 2800[9] 3612[5] >66h<

Pantara Prince (IRE) 8 b g Ovac (ITY)-Clara Girl (Fine Blade (USA)) 1246[3] 1357[2] 1944[4] 2540[P] 2912[2] 3141[5] 3934[3] 4515[8] >93dc<

Pant Llin 11 b g 2089[5] 2665[P] 3185[4] 3354[6] 3742[4] 3929[P] >67h 71c<

Paparazzo 6 b g 2918[7] 3159[13] 3691[6] 4285[8] >54h<

Papa's Boy (IRE) 6 b g 18[7] 730[U] 892[F] 1247[F] >49h< (DEAD)

Paper Cloud 5 b m Lugana Beach-Sweet Enough (Caerleon (USA)) 555[4] >53h<

Paperising 5 b g 1245[2] 1640[4] (1843) (2042) 2766[2] (2918) 3885[5] 4257[P] >90h<

Paperprince (NZ) 5 gr g Lord Triad (NZ)-Sleigh Song (NZ) (Reindeer) 3090[11] 4539[13] >16fh<

Paper Star 10 br m 395[6] 932[2] 959[P] 1194[2] 1383[5] 1518[3] 1877[3] 2063[3] 4344[3] 4557[5] >93c<

Paper Tigress (IRE) 6 b m 2931[P]

Paperwork Pete (IRE) 5 b g Kahyasi-Palitana (Nonoalco (USA)) 679[7] 4580[11]

Papillon (IRE) 6 b g 3260a[2] (3389a) 4110a[4] 4356a[6] >144h 131c<

Pappa Charlie (USA) 6 b g 1687[4] 2958[F] 3159[7] 3485[3] 3825[3] 4152[2] (4513) (4750) >60h<

Paprika (IRE) 8 ch m 3085[P] 3628[P]

Parade Racer 6 b g 885[P] 1171[P] 1427[4] 1569[2] 2578[F] (2838) 3481[5] 4309[3] >57h<

Paradise Road 8 gr g Teenoso (USA)-Fair Melys (FR) (Welsh Pageant) 4351a[P] >85c<

Parahandy (IRE) 7 b g Lancastrian-Dishcloth (Fury Royal) 1711[2] 2896[2] 3155[4] 3617[6] >101c<

Paramount Leader 5 b g Presidium-Dragusa (Dara Monarch) 1283[P]

Pariah (IRE) 8 b g 2790[3] 3028[2] 3398[5] 3482[2] 3645[F] (3827) 3886[3] 4248[8] 4573[2] 4577[4] >74h 105c<

Paris Fashion (FR) 6 br m 2550[5] 3152[P] >78h 104c<

Parish Walk (IRE) 6 ch g 17[2] 66[13] 697[3] 819[2] 1775[3] 1857[3] 4283[5] >52h<

Parisian 12 b g 1448[9] 1562[P] 3207[2] 3674[4] >44h<

Park Drift 11 ch g 4155[4] >79c<

Park End 5 ch g Bairn (USA)-Abdera (Ahonoora) 2080[12] >14fh<

Parklife (IRE) 5 ch g 910[4] 3714[2] >64h<

Parliamentarian (IRE) 8 br g 1192[4] 1468[7] 2679[P] (3550) 3756[5] 3905[2] 4235[P] >51dh 84c<

Parrot's Hill (IRE) 4 b g Nashamaa-Cryptic Gold (Glint of Gold) 1776[3] 2784[4] 3022[4] 3224[3] >64h<

Parry 5 b m 1687[13] 3098[F] 3940[9]

Parsons Belle (IRE) 9 b m 3546[8] 3726[P] >56c<

Parsons Boy 8 ch g (1293) (1643) 3162[9] 3451[3] >59h 127c<

Parsons Brig 11 b g 4213[P] 4339[6] >110c<

Parson's Lodge (IRE) 9 ch m 1306[F] 2785[3] 2920[4] 3325[8] 4187[2] 4285[4] 4711[2] >66h 106?c<

Party Lady (IRE) 8 ch m 2840[15] 3054[P]

Pashto 10 b g 2773[5] 3618[11] 4624[4] >125c<

Pasja (IRE) 6 b m 55[2] >72h<

Pas Possible (IRE) 5 b h The Bart (USA)-Pollette 3254a[10] >92h<

Passed Pawn 10 b g Blakeney-Miss Millicent (Milesian) 485[5] 2877[P] 3201[17] >66h<

Past Master (USA) 9 b g 1030[12] 1156[P] 1911[3] 1992[5] 2744[7] 3076[6] 3327[10] >63h<

Pastoral Pride (USA) 13 b g 2944[P] 3928[P] >87?c<

Pat Buckley 6 b g Buckley-Raheny (Sir Herbert) 4230[3] 4315[8] >63h<

Pat Hartigan (IRE) 7 ch g Orchestra-Oriental Star (Falcon) 3650a[2] >84h<

Patong Beach 7 ch m Infantry-Winter Resort (Miami Springs) 3204[P] 3352[8] 3997[7] 4401[10] 4643[P] >25h<

Patscilla 6 b or br m 60[8] >6h<

Pats Cross (IRE) 8 b g 5[7] 4390[P] >67h<

Pats Folly 6 bl m Macmillion-Cavo Varka (Cavo Doro) 67[11] 156[7] 416[3] 1027[11] >37h<

Pats Minstrel 12 b g 1186[3] 1660[6] 1863[3] 2046[5] (3665) >101c<

Patter Merchant 8 ch g 7[R] >27h<

Pattern Arms 5 b g 455[6] 586[F] 1020[5] >35h<

Paula Jane (IRE) 4 b f Orchestra-Parsonetta 4118a[21] >52fh<

Paula's Boy (IRE) 7 br g 3228[7] 3748[4] 4001[6] >49h<

Paulton 4 b g Lugana Beach-Runcina (Runnett) 1172[P] 1444[4] 2050[6] 2574[3] 2813[8] 3590[4] 3959[2] 4231[3] (4658) >67h<

Pause For Thought 4 b g Bairn (USA)-Mill D'Art (Artaius (USA)) 3203[7] 4421[13] >29fh<

Pavi's Brother 9 ch g 2643[2] 2947[6] 4004[P] >95c<

Pavlova (IRE) 7 ch m 792[9] 1710[3] 2756[5] 2908[U] (3410) 3700[4] 4098[4] >66h 93dc<

Paypnutsgetmonkeys (IRE) 4 b f Prince Rupert (FR)-Sweet Finale (Sallust) 3170[14] 3914[13] >22fh<

Peace Initiative 5 b g Hadeer-Rostova (Blakeney) 2073[5] 3690[3] >52fh<

Peace Lord (IRE) 7 ch g 1044[2] 1369[3] 2673[2] (3133) 3423[3] (3844) >77h<

Peace Officer 11 br g 3843[P] 4721[P] >112?c<

Peajade 13 b g 2903[6] 3458[2] 3906[3] 4473[P] >101c<

Peak A Boo 6 b m Le Coq d'Or-Peak Princess (Charlottown) 3483[10] 3883[12] >28h<

Pealings (IRE) 5 gr g Wood Chanter-Ten-Cents (Taste of Honey) 1800[7] 3103[U] 3818[6] 3944[4] 4134[4] 4528[9] 4638[3] >63h<

Pearla Dubh (IRE) 8 b g Over The River (FR)-Canverb (Proverb) 4403[P]

Pearl Epee 8 b m 1563[5] 1829[F] 2077[4] 2693[P] 3279[3] (3806) 3988[2] 4159[4] (4629) >60h 101c<

Pearl Hart 5 b m Puissance-Pearl Pet (Mummy's Pet) 3115[8] 3494[P] 3955[7] >33h<

Pearl's Choice (IRE) 9 b br m 1557[4] 1947[3] 2756[3] 3043[4] 3279[2] >92c<

Pearl Silk 4 br f Cigar-Purrlea Atoll (Gulf Pearl) 2750[12] 3006[8] >38fh<

Pearls of Thought (IRE) 4 b f Persian Bold-Miss Loving (Northfields (USA)) 2953[11] 3305[3] 3908[3] >48h<

Peatsville (IRE) 5 b g Ela-Mana-Mou-Windy Cheyenne (USA) (Tumble Wind (USA)) 1069[2] 1425[P]

Peatswood 9 ch g 1067[4] 2117[2] 2934[5] >99h 104c<

Pebble Beach (IRE) 7 gr g (911) 1130[3] 1290[3] 2654[2] 2787[F] 3644[2] 4257[7] >71h<

Pecan Princess (IRE) 4 b f Prince Rupert (FR)-Route Royale (Roi Soleil) 3747[11] >18fh<

Pedaltothemetal (IRE) 5 b m 1727^{3} 1866^{2} 2067^{5} 2897^{5} 3148^{3} 3447^{6} 3670^{3} 4620^{9} 4762^{2} **>67h<**

Pedlar's Cross (IRE) 5 b g Lancastrian-Fine Debut (Fine Blade (USA)) 2696^{10} 3418^{5} **>50fh<**

Peep O Day 6 b m 2545^{11} **>72h<**

Peers Folly (IRE) 7 ch g Remainder Man-Bola Stream (Paddy's Stream) 3818^{8} 4134^{P} **>41h<**

Peetsie (IRE) 5 b m 2624^{6} **>69fh<**

Pegasus Bay 6 b g 18^{5} 105^{5} (209) 859^{5} (974) 1145^{7} 1374^{7} **1563^{F}** **>75h<**

Peggy Gordon 6 b m (695) 1081^{7} 1824^{3} 3309^{5} 3641^{3} 3912^{4} (4248) 4394^{3} 4761^{5} **>69?h<**

Pegmarine (USA) 14 b g **1584^{7} (1965) 2796^{9} 3053^{5} 3336^{6}** **>89c<**

Pembridge Place 6 b g 31^{2} 60^{5} 258^{6} **>69h<**

Pendil's Delight 8 b m **179^{P}** **>35h<**

Peniarth 11 b m 345^{2} 510^{4} 587^{P} **>44h 70c< (DEAD)**

Penlea Lady 10 b m **(3680)** **>54h 92c<**

Penlet 9 b g Kinglet-Pensun (Jimsun) **3459^{5}** **>72c<**

Pennant Cottage (IRE) 9 b m 824^{4} 1197^{6} **1865^{5} 2667^{F} 3003^{P}** 3683^{11} **>28h<**

Penncaler (IRE) 7 ch g **1811^{F} 2551^{4} 2883^{8} 3400^{3} 3848^{P}** **>80h 95c<**

Penndara (IRE) 8 gr g Pennine Walk-Adaraya (FR) (Zeddaan) **2335a^{7} 2739a^{3} 3260a^{F} 3596^{6} 4116a^{P}** **>102h 115c<**

Pennine Pride 10 b g **1293^{4} 1778^{5} (1983) 2542^{F} 3162^{7} 3643^{P}** **>106c<**

Pennine View 10 ch g **3713^{3} 4076^{3}** **>83c<**

Penny a Day (IRE) 7 b g (1804) 2603a^{3} 3640^{3} 4053^{F} **>122+h< (DEAD)**

Pennyahei 6 b m Malaspina-Pennyazena (Pamroy) 3052^{P}

Penny Bride (IRE) 8 ch m **4350a^{7}** **>55h 83c<**

Pennybridge (IRE) 8 ch g **3503a^{6}** **>79h 107c<**

Pennybryn 4 br f Teenoso (USA)-Be Bold (Bustino) 3808^{4} **>42fh<**

Pennymoor Prince 8 b g 1952^{P} 2884^{7} 3156^{6} 3539^{6} **>76h<**

Penny Peppermint 5 b br m 2177^{7} 3098^{8} 3475^{5} 4056^{C} **>40h<**

Penny Pot 5 br m Lord Bud-Karmelanna (Silly Season) **2856a^{P}** **>28c<**

Penny's Wishing 5 b m Clantime-Lady Pennington (Blue Cashmere) 1659^{P}

Penrose Lad (NZ) 7 b g 1152^{8} 1499^{3} 1830^{3} 2662^{3} 3166^{4} 4205^{3} **>77h<**

Pentlands Flyer (IRE) 6 b g 1036^{5} 1187^{8} 2918^{4} 3159^{12} 4075^{3} (4243) 4575^{2} **>64h<**

Pentland Squire 6 b g 794^{9} 1020^{3} 1687^{2} 2064^{3} 3823^{5} 4075^{5} **>62h<**

Pepper Pot Boy (IRE) 5 b g Lapierre-That's it (Adropejo) 3828^{5} **>64fh<**

Peptic Lady (IRE) 7 b m **1468^{4}** **>80c<**

Percy Braithwaite (IRE) 5 b g Kahyasi-Nasseem (FR) (Zeddaan) 2074^{4} (2566) 2937^{7} 3564^{7} (4095) 4307^{U} 4443^{2} 4741^{2} **>86h<**

Percy Parrot 5 b g Lochnager-Soltago (Touching Wood (USA)) 1343^{6} 1667^{12} 1942^{P} **>31h<**

Percy Pit 8 b g **4713^{P}** **>40h<**

Percy's Joy 5 b g Strong Gale-Knockeevan Girl (Tarqogan) 3548^{10} 4150^{9} **>40fh<**

Percy Smollett 9 br g **3302^{3} 4110a^{P}** **>152dc<**

Percy Thrower 10 gr g 1322^{3} 1639^{8} **>81h 119c<**

Perfect Answer 4 ch f Keen-Hasty Key (USA) (Key To The Mint (USA)) 3626^{11}

Perfect Bertie (IRE) 5 b g 1874^{F} 2088^{6} **>30h<**

Perfect Pal (IRE) 6 ch g 2055^{U} 2791^{11} 3041^{11} **>32h<**

Periroyal 7 ch g **2000^{F}** **>34h<**

Perknapp 10 b g **3638^{3}** **>126c<**

Perky Too (IRE) 5 b g Executive Perk-Laud (Dual) 3366^{P} 3823^{P}

Perpetual Light 4 b f Petoski-Butosky (Busted) 1700^{8} 1940^{6} 2615^{10} 3310^{3} **>43h<**

Perryman (IRE) 6 ch g Good Thyne (USA)-Poetic Lady (Rymer) 4215^{17} **>58fh<**

Persian Bud (IRE) 9 b or br g 1836^{8} **>53h<**

Persian Butterfly 5 b m Dancing Dissident (USA)-Butterfly Kiss (Beldale Flutter (USA)) 1470^{P} 1679^{7} 1857^{P} 2692^{12} 2818^{4} 2943^{12} (4620) 4789^{P} **>48h<**

Persian Dawn 4 br f Anshan-Visible Form (Formidable (USA)) 1980^{P} 4086^{8} 4343^{2} 4620^{6} **>49?h<**

Persian Elite (IRE) 6 ch g Persian Heights-Late Sally (Sallust) 2794^{4} 3178^{3} (3845) 4217^{U} (4341) (4638) **>79+h<**

Persian Grange (IRE) 7 ch g 2701^{15} 2958^{F} 3100^{P} 3453^{3} 3711^{P} 3794^{8} 4257^{P} **4515^{P} 4715^{3}** **>60h 55c<**

Persian House 10 ch g 1294^{5} **>71h 120c< (DEAD)**

Persian Mystic (IRE) 5 ch g 3344^{7} 3579^{4} 4101^{2} **>63h<**

Persian Power (IRE) 9 b g **1405a^{8}** **>111c<**

Persian Sunset (IRE) 5 b m Persian Mews-Fifth Gear (Red Sunset) 1457^{18} 1679^{P} 3029^{13}

Persian Sword 11 b g **3567^{U}** **>105?c<**

Persian Tactics 8 b g **63^{7}** **>115c<**

Persian View (IRE) 7 ch g 4248^{R} 4321^{3} 4524^{5} **4699^{8}** **>74h 71c<**

Persistent Gunner 7 ch m 4332^{5} **>33h<**

Persuasive Talent (IRE) 6 ch g 939^{9} 1263^{7} 1843^{7} 2619^{9} 3096^{9} **>54h<**

Pertemps Flyer 6 b g 354^{3} **>47h<**

Pertemps Zola 8 b m Oats-Little Buskinbelle (Little Buskins) 129^{P}

Peruvian Gale (IRE) 8 b g **4159^{3} 4448^{2} 4609^{3} 4806^{4}** **>58h 95c<**

Peter 9 b g **3027^{U} 3532^{F} 3886^{5}** **>62h 90c<**

Peter Monamy 5 ch g (284) (399) (483) 591^{2} 692^{7} (916) 1058^{2} (1413) 1715^{3} 1993^{2} 2946^{4} 4006^{2} 4340^{2} 4436^{2} 4639^{2} **>82h<**

Pete's Sake 12 b g Scorpio (FR)-Pete's Money (USA) (Caucasus (USA)) **4308^{P}** **>89?c<**

Petit Flora 5 b m (59) 99^{5}

Petitjean (IRE) 6 b g 976^{F} **>84h< (DEAD)**

Petrico 5 b g Petong-Balearica (Bustino) 2697^{9} 3345^{11} 3691^{18} 3976^{6} 4295^{13} **>26h<**

Petros Gem 4 br f Sulaafah (USA)-Dancing Ballerina (Record Run) 1014^{9} 1712^{P} 3058^{3} 3601^{P} **>54h<**

Petros Pride 4 b f Safawan-Hala (Persian Bold) 1634^{P} 3058^{P}

Pettaugh (IRE) 9 b g 1088^{6} 1553^{4} 1798^{9} **>76h<**

Pett Lad 9 b g Remainder Man-Winter Lodge (Super Slip) 1964^{P}

Petty Bridge 13 b g **74^{P} 130^{P}** **>98c<**

Peutetre 5 ch h 262^{7} **>50h<**

Peyton Jones 4 b g Presidium-York Street (USA) (Diamond Shoal) 640^{P} 736^{8} 912^{11}

P Grayco Choice 4 b f Bold Fox-Unjha (Grey Desire) 4720^{5}

Phaedair 7 b g **795^{3}**

Phairy Miracles (IRE) 8 b m **323a^{F}** **>65h 89c<**

Phalarope (IRE) 9 b g (21) 55^{4} **>65h 65dc<**

Phantom Dancer (IRE) 4 b g Distinctly North (USA)-Angel of Music (Burslem) 646^{13} 906^{7} 1158^{P} 1526^{12} 1776^{14} 2862^{P} **>44h<**

Phantom Haze 4 gr g Absalom-Caroline Lamb (Hotfoot) 906^{3} 3022^{3} 3555^{4} **>65h<**

Pharanear (IRE) 7 b g **1281^{3} (1680) 1936^{F}** (3303) (3600) **>127h 119c<**

Pharare (IRE) 7 ch g 868^{2} 1255^{3} 1347^{3} (2003) 2702^{7} 3281^{4} 3454^{4} 4220^{6} 4452^{3} **>70h 79c<**

Phar Better Off (IRE) 6 b m Phardante (FR)-Quids In (Brave Invader (USA)) 3821^{20} **>28fh<**

Phar Closer 4 br f Phardante (FR)-Forever Together (Hawaiian Return (USA)) 534^{3} **>55h<**

Phardy (IRE) 6 b g 318a^{9} **846a^{2}** **>74h 115c<**

Phar Echo (IRE) 6 b g 1349^{3} 1654^{7} 2627^{4} (2790) 3265^{3} (3534) 3887^{10} 4204^{P} **>80h<**

Phar Enough (IRE) 5 b g Phardante (FR)-Avise La Fin (Scottish Rifle) 1033^{5} 1781^{8} 1990^{P} **>5fh<**

Phar From Funny 6 ch g 1262^{2} 1474^{2} **1764^{5}** **>88h 94++c<**

Phargold (IRE) 8 ch g **4446^{P}** 4714^{6} **>10h 77?c<**

Pharly Reef 5 b g 1091^{8} 1390^{7} 1628^{6} (1861) 2792^{2} **>59h<**

Pharmistice (IRE) 6 b g (1672) 1854^{8} **>66h<**

Pharmony (IRE) 7 b br g Phardante (FR)-Richest (Richboy) 4217^{10}

Pharmorefun (IRE) 5 ch m Phardante (FR)-Sacajawea (Tanfirion) 1177^{11} 1998^{14} 3052^{P} **>6fh<**

Pharrago (IRE) 8 ch g 129^{5} **190^{2} 283^{2} 346^{2} 597^{P} 3055^{P}** **>40h 85c<**

Pharrambling (IRE) 6 b m 1802^{P} 3348^{6} 3481^{3} **>57h<**

Pharsilk (IRE) 8 ch g **2949^{P} 3919^{2}** **>104c<**

Phar Smoother (IRE) 5 br g Phardante (FR)-Loughaderra (IRE) (Strong Gale) 1926^{7} 2633^{3} (2904) (3944) **>74h<**

Phar Too Touchy 10 ch m Mister Lord (USA)-Bridgitte Browne (Mon Fetiche) **(4308) (4469) 4640^{5} 4792^{P}** **>95c<**

Philatelic (IRE) 6 br g **3736^{P} 3830^{2}** **>69h 90c<**

Philbecky 6 b m 1523^{4} 1999^{P} **>37h<**

Phileas Fogg (IRE) 8 gr g 1842^{5} **>29h<**

Philip's Woody 9 b g **(882) 1070^{2} 1383^{2} 1858^{2} 2623^{2} 2942^{F} (4225) (4509) 4642^{3}** **>83h 130?c<**

Philisitate 8 ch m Tinoco-Kitty Royal (Kinglet) 3755^{8} 4638^{9} **>34h<**

Phoebe The Freebee (IRE) 6 ch m Phardante (FR)-Stormy Night (Deep Run) 3433^{9} **>52fh<**

Phone The Pipeline 4 b g Dunbeath (USA)-Grand Occasion (Great Nephew) 3203^{10} 3895^{11} 4143^{5} **>4fh<**

Physical Fun 6 b g 1453^{11} 1867^{6} 2690^{8} 2891^{2} 3108^{3} 4315^{3} 4547^{3} **>70h<**

Piccolina 5 ch m Phardante (FR)-Highland Chain (Furry Glen) 2576^{10} 4292^{4} **>16h<**

Pickens (USA) 5 b g 65^{2} 137^{5} 156^{3} (950) 1086^{4} **>75h<**

Picketstone 10 b g **1447^{P}** **>84dc<**

Pilkington (IRE) 7 b g 1802^{6} 2898^{13} 3102^{2} (3328) 3887^{13} **>68h<**

Pillow Talk (IRE) 6 b m 210^{5} **>68h<**

Pimberley Place (IRE) 9 b g **1173^{3} 1520^{6} 3639^{7} 4177^{4} 4467^{5}** **>113h 129dc<**

Pimsboy 10 b g 96^{6} 137^{P} 284^{S} 497^{5} 585^{6} 642^{4} 781^{3} 1047^{P} **>53dh<**

Pims Gunner (IRE) 9 b g **180^{3} 1048^{5} 1670^{4} 1923^{U} 2004^{5} 2782^{9} 3033^{3} 3414^{6}** **>78h 112c<**

Pinkerton's Pal 6 ch g Dominion-White Domino (Sharpen Up) 2939^{5} 3282^{2} **>70h<**

Pink Gin 10 ch g **(2063) 2616^{11} 3162^{P} 3395^{6} 4074^{14}** **>115dc<**

Pinkpinkfizz (IRE) 6 b g King's Ride-Coforta (The Parson) 3650a^{12} **>70h<**

Pink Sunset (IRE) 9 ch g **70^{F}** **>49h<**

Pinoccio 10 b g **1075^{P}** 1423^{5} **1708^{P} 3060^{P} 3759^{3} 3956^{3} 4180^{4}** **>68h 52c<**

Pinxton Penny 5 ch m Crowning Honors (CAN)-Penwood (Precipice Wood) 3491^{P} 4376^{9} **>39h<**

Pioneer Princess 5 b or br m 549^{P} **>15h<**

Piper O'Drummond 10 ch g Ardross-Skelbrooke

(Mummy's Pet) **3712^{4}** **>95c<**
Piper's Rock (IRE) **6** ch g 2655^{9} 3205^{P} 3500^{5} 3761^{5} 3977^{4} (4091) 4333^{3} 4662^{2} **>70h<**
Pip's Dream **6** b m 1030^{2} 1855^{2} 2669^{5} **>63h<**
Pirate Minstrel (IRE) **5** bl g Black Minstrel-Ailwee Lady (USA) (Nikoli) 3939^{7} **>22fh<**
Pitarry **7** b g Pitpan-Servilia (Calpurnius) 2073^{8} 3581^{F} 4250^{P}
Pitsburgh **6** b g Pitpan-Faraway Flirt (Bali Dancer) 3910^{P}
Plaid Maid (IRE) **5** b m Executive Perk-Tipperary Tartan (Rarity) 1555^{3} **>25fh<**
Plan-A (IRE) **7** br g Creative Plan (USA)-Faravaun Rose (Good Thyne (USA)) **(4237) 4426^{2}** **>88c<**
Planning Gain **6** b g **3533^{F}** **>45h<**
Plas-Hendy **11** ch g Celtic Cone-Little Cindy II (Nine One) **4241^{8}**
Plassy Boy (IRE) **8** ch g 1840^{7} **2077^{2} 2704^{5} 3181^{3} 3370^{P} 3472^{P} 3617^{P} 4168^{P}** **>77?c< (DEAD)**
Plastic Spaceage **14** b g **2869^{3} 3153^{6}** **>91h 121c<**
Playful Juliet (CAN) **9** b m 97^{3} 285^{6} (509) 3607^{P} 4283^{14} 4472^{3} 4572^{P} **>58h 82dc<**
Play Games (USA) **9** ch g 2828^{P} 3447^{9} **>46h<**
Playing Truant **9** b g **(972) 1629^{5} 1833^{U} 2756^{2}** **>68h 90c<**
Pleasant Surprise (FR) **5** ch h 67^{4} **>85h<**
Please Call (IRE) **8** b g Flair Path-Javana (Levanter) 641^{10} 1040^{2} **>52h<**
Pleasure Cruise **7** b g **3073^{F} 3546^{P}** **>50h<**
Pleasureland (IRE) **4** ch g Don't Forget Me-Elminya (IRE) (Sure Blade (USA)) 1269^{2} 1634^{6} 1900^{3} 2634^{11} 2865^{3} (3441) 3634^{11} (3902) 4132^{2} **>98?h<**
Pleasure Shared (IRE) **9** ch g **(1326) 1936^{F}** 2056^{3} 2637^{2} **3274^{F} 3537^{F}** **>140h 137?c<**
Plinth **6** b g 65^{3} (338) 468^{2} 641^{3} 1174^{10} 4181^{3} 4439^{9} **>58dh<**
Plumbob (IRE) **8** br g 1294^{4} 1528^{2} 1844^{6} **4515^{2} (4649) 4715^{U}** **>71h 101c<**
Plumbridge **9** ch g Oats-Hayley (Indian Ruler (USA)) **3086^{4} 3409^{P} 3688^{5}**
Plumpton Wood (IRE) **5** br m Phardante (FR)-The Furnituremaker (Mandalus) 3574^{18} 3946^{13}
Plunder Bay (USA) **6** b g **(1018) 1270^{F} 1520^{5} 2814^{4} 3175^{U} 3427^{6} (3986) 4302^{F} 4475^{4}** **>93h 118c<**
Poacher's Delight **11** ch g High Line-Moonlight Night (FR) (Levmoss) **215^{P}** **>100?c<**
Pocaire Gaoithe (IRE) **7** gr g Roselier (FR)-Ervamoira (Energist) 1349^{4} 1654^{16} 1689^{11} 2654^{9} **2912^{6} 3067^{P} 3762^{4}** **>56h 43c<**
Pocono Knight **7** gr g 456^{6} 600^{4} 879^{11} 3131^{F} **>52h<**
Poetry (IRE) **4** gr f Treasure Kay-Silver Heart (Yankee Gold) 1862^{6} 3075^{P} **>36h<**
Point Duty **7** b g 2953^{10} 3098^{P} 3723^{6} 4144^{P} **>49h<**
Point Reyes (IRE) **5** b g Brush Aside (USA)-Lady's Wager (Girandole) (2005) **>43fh<**
Pokey Grange **9** b g **3455^{10}** **>73c<**
Polar Ana (IRE) **8** b m Pollerton-O Ana (Laurence O) **4614^{3}** **>82c<**
Polar King (IRE) **4** b g Glacial Storm (USA)-Our Little Lamb (Prince Regent (FR)) 3716^{4} 4150^{5} **>55fh<**
Polar Region **11** br g **823^{P} 932^{5}** **>111dc<**
Polar Wind **8** ch g El Gran Senor (USA)-Tundra Goose (Habitat) 3989^{9} 4162^{P} 4626^{P} **>6h<**
Polden Pride **9** b g **20^{2} 3738^{2} 4000^{2} (4140) 4225^{4} 4438^{3} (4642)** **>64h 124c<**
Policemans Pride (FR) **8** bl g 1053^{5} 1174^{P} 1732^{5} **2068^{3} 2752^{3} 2910^{3}** **>59h 67c<**
Polish Consul **6** ch g Polish Precedent (USA)-Consolation (Troy) 189^{3} **>68h<**
Polish Rider (USA) **9** ch g 4729^{3} **>42h<**
Political Bill **6** ch g Politico (USA)-Trial Run (Deep Run) 1666^{10} 2627^{P} **>12h<**
Political Issue **13** b g **3095^{P}** **>92c<**
Political Mandate **4** br f Respect-Political Mill (Politico (USA)) 3142^{16} 3394^{6} 4075^{9} 4282^{6} 4477^{2} 4718^{7} **>42h<**
Political Millstar **5** b g Leading Star-Political Mill (Politico (USA)) 1362^{12} 1692^{15} 2539^{5} 3794^{5} **>69h<**
Political Panto (IRE) **6** b g 139^{3} 739^{2} 1056^{2} **>83h<**
Political Power **6** b g Politico (USA)-Pauper Moon (Pauper) 3297^{6} 3914^{12} **>48fh<**
Political Sam **8** ch g Politico (USA)-Samonia (Rolfe (USA)) **3476^{5}** **>76c<**
Political Skirmish **8** b m 60^{P} **>1h<**
Political Tower **10** b g **855^{2} 1128^{3} (1361) (1688) 2639^{3} 2783^{5} 3064^{3} (3369) 3638^{6} 4062^{F} 4214^{6} 4258^{3} (4478)** **>69h 134c<**
Pollerman **7** b g Pollerton-Lady Redhaven (Red Man) 3541^{P}
Pollerton's Dream **7** b m Pollerton-Dream World (Quadrangle) 1450^{11} 1569^{P}
Pollifumas **7** b m Pollerton-Fumarole (USA) (Sensitive Prince (USA)) 653^{14} 1124^{13}
Polli Pui **5** b m Puissance-Wing of Freedom (Troy) 1537^{F} 1818^{10} **>3h<**
Pollyanna **6** ch m 360^{P} **(DEAD)**
Polly Cinders **6** gr m 680^{7}
Pollys Sister **5** b m Green Adventure (USA)-Fly Blackie (Dear Gazelle) 2931^{19}
Polly Star **7** b m 1079^{P}
Polo Kit (IRE) **6** b g Trempolino (USA)-Nikitina (Nijinsky (CAN)) 885^{P} 960^{5} **>47h<**
Polo Pony (IRE) **5** b g 1050^{8} 1536^{9} 2006^{2} 2694^{8} 2838^{8} (3985) 4233^{P} **>46h<**
Polo Ridge (IRE) **5** gr g Phardante (FR)-Fane Bridge (Random Shot) 2750^{6} 3676^{7} **>51fh<**
Polydamas **5** b h Last Tycoon-Graecia Magna (USA) (Private Account (USA)) 3041^{3} 3298^{4} 3595^{8} **>83h<**
Polydeuces **11** b g **4530^{P}** **>52dh<**
Polynth **8** b g Politico (USA)-Miss Trixie (Le Tricolore) **3609^{P}**
Pomme Secret (FR) **4** b c Assert-Thalestria (FR) (Mill Reef (USA)) (2791) 3075^{15} 3634^{17} **>89dh<**
Pond House (IRE) **8** b g **254^{P} (286) (330) 409^{P} 4013^{U} 4174^{4} (4377) (4612) 4733^{F}** **>40h 112+c<**
Pongo Waring (IRE) **8** b g **724^{P} (738) (901) 1061^{2} (1557)** **>86h 112c<**
Pontevedra (IRE) **4** b f Belmez (USA)-Pretoria (Habitat) 1370^{10} 1776^{8} 2669^{10} 3032^{3} (3611) 3990^{4} 4281^{2} **>67h<**
Pontoon Bridge **10** ch g **160^{2} (3836)** **>96h 95c<**
Pontynyswen **9** b g **20^{U}** **>114h 112c<**
Pooh Stick **7** b g 3338^{5} 3632^{6} **>46h<**
Poors Wood **10** b g **3107^{4} 3273^{3} (3852) 4135^{P}** **>98h 97c<**
Popeshall **10** b g **2544^{8}** **>120c<**
Pop In There (IRE) **9** br g **4^{P}** **>46h<**
Poplin **6** b m 139^{F} 288^{3} **>54h<**
Poppets Pet **10** b g **(1445)** **>95c<**
Poppy's Dream **7** b m Dreams to Reality (USA)-Poppy's Pride (Uncle Pokey) (1303) 1781^{3} 4095^{5} 4299^{4} 4450^{4} 4768^{7} **>65h<**
Pops Academy (IRE) **6** b g Roselier (FR)-Al's Niece (Al Sirat (USA)) **4769^{F}**
Popsi's Cloggs **5** ch g Joli Wasfi (USA)-Popsi's Poppet (Hill Clown (USA)) 25^{3} 133^{U}
Porphyrios **6** b g 1045^{5} **(1328) 1809^{F}** **>84h 105c<**
Port in a Storm **8** b g **1306^{6} 1527^{3} 1704^{P} 2002^{2} 2863^{P}** **>80?h 94c< (DEAD)**
Portman **5** b g Sulaafah (USA)-Bride (Remainder Man) 2770^{4} 3297^{5} **>52fh<**
Portscatho (IRE) **5** b g (1183) 1333^{2} **>71h<**
Port Valenska (IRE) **4** b g Roi Danzig (USA)-Silvera (Ribero) 2510^{11} 3031^{10} 3287^{P} 3964^{10} 4295^{11} 4718^{5} **>36h<**
Positive Action **11** b g **2^{7} 1702^{4} 2002^{3} 2921^{4}** **>89dc<**
Positivo **6** br g 105^{7} 137^{4} 189^{5} 506^{6} 557^{3} 1135^{3} 1274^{5} 1378^{3} 1539^{4} 1959^{10} 3752^{2} 3904^{7} 4236^{3} 4512^{3} 4652^{F} 4696^{4} **>52h<**
Postage Stamp **10** ch g **56^{6}** **>128c<**
Posted Abroad (IRE) **5** b g 2041^{7} 4152^{9} **>58h<**
Postlip Royale **4** b f Zambrano-Wilhemina Crusty (Jester) 4531^{19} 4774^{12}
Postman's Path **11** ch g **2762^{P} 3585^{5} 3903^{2} 4234^{P}** **>99c<**
Potato Man **11** gr g **1295^{6} 1442^{4} 1985^{P} 2630^{P} 3140^{3} 3312^{6} 3419^{5}** **>87c<**
Pot Blackbird **8** ch m 26^{7} 3431^{B} 3802^{6} 3910^{11} **>61h<**
Pot Black Uk **6** b g Joligeneration-Golden Home (Homing) 1289^{3} 2080^{3} 2805^{6} 3734^{4} **>63h<**
Potentate (USA) **6** b or br g (1262) 1933^{3} 3231^{7} (3562) (3917) **>120h<**
Potter Again (IRE) **5** b m Brush Aside (USA)-Polly Puttens (Pollerton) 2750^{2} (3006) 3433^{4} **>73fh<**
Potter's Bay (IRE) **8** br g **(1153) (1364) (1868) 2116^{3} 2776^{2} 2936^{F}** **>82h 126c<**
Potter's Gale (IRE) **6** br m 1177^{2} (1341) (1855) 2771^{2} 3168^{2} 3817^{4} **>85h<**
Poucher (IRE) **7** b g **1449^{2} (1694) 2896^{3} (3185)** **>112c<**
Powder Boy **12** ch g **750^{P}** **>108c<**
Powder Monkey **7** ch m 3889^{2} 4468^{5} 4552^{5} 4658^{4} **>56h<**
Powerful Spirit **5** b g Presidium-Spiritofaffection (Raga Navarro (ITY)) 161^{3} 418^{3} 636^{8} 1036^{P}
Power Pack (IRE) **9** b g 3523a^{7} **4183^{3}** **>96h 107+c<**
Praise Be (FR) **7** b g Baillamont (USA)-Louange (Green Dancer (USA)) 3271^{10} 3475^{7} 3691^{11} 3990^{P} 4479^{6} 4759^{4} **>48h<**
Prate Box (IRE) **7** b g **4356a^{F}** **>86h 101c<**
Preceptor (IRE) **8** ch g 316a^{6} **>85h 86c<**
Precious Girl **4** ch f Precious Metal-Oh My Oh My (Ballacashtal (CAN)) 1356^{9}
Precious Island **4** b f Jupiter Island-Burmese Ruby (Good Times (ITY)) 1370^{5} 3075^{8} 3287^{4} 3681^{5} **>68h<**
Precious Wonder **8** b g **1073^{F}** 1390^{11} 3057^{5} 3207^{3} 3447^{16} 3674^{P} **>43h 57c<**
Precipice Run **12** ch g 1718^{6} (2045) **3886^{F}** 4283^{11} 4572^{3} **>61h<**
Precis **9** b m **30^{P}**
Prelude To Fame (USA) **4** b g Affirmed (USA)-Dance Call (USA) (Nijinsky (CAN)) (462) 646^{3} 1158^{6} 1652^{19} 2800^{2} **>71h<**
Premier Generation (IRE) **4** b g Cadeaux Genereux-Bristle (Thatch (USA)) 944^{8} 1634^{19} **>36h<**
Premier League (IRE) **7** gr g 3549^{4} **>54h<**
Premier Son **4** b g Presidium-Snow Child (Mandrake Major) 548^{4}
Premier Star **7** ch g 4648^{10} 4789^{P} **>7h<**
Prerogative **7** ch g 341^{4} (493) 651^{3} 741^{5} **(964) 4272^{P} 4549^{6}** 4701^{8} **>69h 93c<**
Press Again **5** ch m Then Again-Silver Empress (Octavo (USA)) 4519^{4} 4794^{7} **>35h<**
Press for Action **12** b g **4218^{P} 4504^{5}** **>67c<**

Prestige Lady 6 b m 600^{3} 749^{5} 969^{8} **>54h<**

Prestigious Man (IRE) 6 b g Sandalay-Loch Gorman (Bargello) 3399^{14} 3754^{5}

Price's Hill 10 gr g **1674^{2} (2011)** **>116c<**

Priddy Fair 4 b f North Briton-Rainbow Ring (Rainbow Quest (USA)) (1699) 1940^{8} 2175^{4} 2859^{5} 4282^{4} **>73?h<**

Pride of May (IRE) 6 b g 533^{4} 1121^{4} 1294^{8} **>82dh< (DEAD)**

Pride of Pennker (IRE) 4 b f Glacial Storm (USA)-Quitrentina (Green Shoon) 4561^{8} **>24fh<**

Pridewood Fuggle 7 b g Little Wolf-Quick Reply (Tarqogan) 191^{3} 418^{8} 4067^{2} **>25h<**

Pridewood Picker 10 b g 1123^{7} 1325^{5} 1502^{5} (1816) 1954^{2} 2579^{F} **4444^{F}** **>69h<**

Pridwell 7 b g 1916^{5} 2635^{4} 2774^{2} 3597^{7} 3635^{8} 4063^{2} (4164) 4240^{2} (4396) **>136h 115dc<**

Priesthill (IRE) 8 ch g 129^{9} **179^{P} 213^{F} 405^{P}** **>19h<**

Prime Course (IRE) 8 b g **4730^{P}** **>51h<**

Prime Display (USA) 11 ch g Golden Act (USA)-Great Display (FR) (Great Nephew) 4220^{P} 4321^{6} 4717^{2} **>65h 65c<**

Prime Example (IRE) 6 ch g Orchestra-Vanessa's Princess (Laurence O) 3070^{2} 3483^{6} 3823^{4} **>48h<**

Prime of Life (IRE) 7 b g 1451^{4} 4527^{4} 4652^{3} **>65h<**

Primitive Heart 5 b g 1033^{4} 1263^{6} 1705^{9} 2798^{9} 3474^{9} 4144^{P} **>44h<**

Primitive Light 7 ch m Primitive Rising (USA)-Ring of Flowers (Nicholas Bill) 1913^{8} 2066^{8} 3029^{F} 3704^{P} **>48fh<**

Primitive Penny 6 ch m Primitive Rising (USA)-Penny Pink (Spartan General) 1565^{P} **2667^{6} (2816) 3708^{P}** **>85c<**

Primitive Singer 9 b g **3492^{P}** **>90?c<**

Prince Baltasar 8 ch g 2697^{8} 2915^{P} **3331^{F} 3642^{5} 3826^{P}** 4243^{P} 4578^{6} **>17h 34c<**

Prince Buck (IRE) 7 b g Buckskin (FR)-Rechime (Prince Regent (FR)) **3813^{F} (4447) (4530) 4792^{4}** **>110c<**

Prince Canute 7 b g **3020^{P}**

Prince de Berry 6 ch g 396^{U} 1597^{4} **>61?h<**

Prince Equiname 5 gr g 4018^{4} 4290^{P}

Princeful (IRE) 6 b g (2012) 2812^{5} (3154) 3595^{2} 4109a^{P} **>98h<**

Princely Affair 4 b g Prince Sabo-Shillay (Lomond (USA)) 1706^{6} 3115^{7} **>43h<**

Princely Charm (IRE) 5 bl g Royal Fountain-Constant Rose (Confusion) 191^{13}

Prince Nepal 13 b g Kinglet-Nepal (Indian Ruler) **3593^{5}** **>72c<**

Prince of Prey 9 ch g Buzzards Bay-Sleepline Princess (Royal Palace) 1788^{P} 1995^{8}

Prince of Saints (IRE) 6 ch g 1687^{6} 2627^{10} 2917^{8} 3265^{5} **>56h<**

Prince of Spades 5 ch g 217^{6} 3760^{5} 3951^{4} 4384^{3} **>40h<**

Prince of Thyne (IRE) 8 b br g Good Thyne (USA)-Ryehill Rose (Prince Hansel) 3529^{P} 3795^{7} **>51h<**

Prince of Verona 10 b br g Zambrano-Verona Queen (Majestic Streak) **3680^{P}**

Prince Rico 6 b g 820^{5}

Prince Rockaway (IRE) 9 b g **13^{P} 72^{9}** 101^{15} **>72dc<**

Prince Rudolf (IRE) 5 b g Cyrano de Bergerac-Princess Raisa (Indian King (USA)) 2574^{F} 2791^{12}

Prince Skyburd 6 b g **(508) (722) (867) 1140^{3} 1521^{F} 2843^{3}** **>54h 95c<**

Princess Helen (IRE) 4 ch f Glacial Storm (USA)-Princess Umm (Duky) 4407^{17}

Princess Wenllyan 12 b m White Prince (USA)-Prince's Daughter (Black Prince) **3341^{P}**

Prince Teeton 8 b g 1286^{F} **>82h<**

Principal Boy (IRE) 4 br g Cyrano de Bergerac-Shenley Lass (Prince Tenderfoot (USA)) 2859^{P} 3394^{4} 3544^{7} 3926^{4} 4223^{11} **>53h<**

Principle Music (USA) 9 ch g **3010^{2} 3403^{U}** **>95h 108c<**

Prinzal 10 b br g 96^{4} **3135^{U} 3446^{U}** 3844^{3} **3925^{P} 4228^{P}** **>58h 97dc<**

Priory Piper 8 b g **4758^{6}** **>20dh 81c<**

Priory Rose 10 br m Cardinal Flower-The Priory (Oats) **791^{P} 889^{P} 977^{F}** **(DEAD)**

Private Memories 7 b g 1457^{20} 1685^{17} 2093^{9}

Private Peace (IRE) 7 gr g 4052^{2} 4365a^{F} **>97h<**

Private Percival 4 b c Arrasas (USA)-Romacina (Roman Warrior) 1706^{9}

Prizefighter 6 b g (677) (806) 908^{3} 2952^{3} 4061^{6} 4565^{2} **>98h<**

Prize Match 8 ch m 641^{5} 1732^{9} **1865^{3} 2756^{F} 2910^{6} 3456^{3} 3746^{3} 3833^{4}** 4468^{13} **>55dh 65c<**

Pro Bono (IRE) 7 ch g **3010^{F} 3135^{3} 3457^{P} 3813^{U} 3984^{3} 4228^{2} (4327)** **>106c<**

Profession 6 b h 973^{P} 1550^{7} 1710^{P} 2905^{P}

Professor Page (IRE) 7 b g 3172^{5} 3423^{6} 3683^{8} 4445^{5} **4627^{3} 4735^{3}** **>42h 75c<**

Professor Strong (IRE) 9 b g **2681^{P}** **>87c<**

Profit And Loss 6 ch m 25^{4} 392^{2} 1139^{5} 1349^{P} **>52h<**

Profluent (USA) 6 ch g Sunshine Forever (USA)-Proflare (USA) (Mr Prospector (USA)) (387a)

Promalee (IRE) 5 b g Homo Sapien-Oralee 4360a^{7} **>94fh<**

Promise To Try (IRE) 5 b m 1245^{6} 1438^{9} 3313^{P} 3612^{13} **>14h<**

Propaganda 9 b g Nishapour (FR)-Mrs Moss (Reform) 3920^{7}

Proper Primitive 4 b f Primitive Rising (USA)-Nidd Bridges (Grey Ghost) 3170^{9} 3433^{17} **>49fh<**

Propolis Power (IRE) 4 ch g Simply Great (FR)-Now Then (Sandford Lad) 906^{15} 1526^{5} 1776^{12} **>36h<**

Prospero 4 b g Petong-Pennies to Pounds (Ile de Bourbon (USA)) 2751^{P}

Proton 7 b g Sure Blade (USA)-Banket (Glint of Gold) (1729) 2112^{3} 2937^{4} **>95h<**

Prototype 6 b g Governor General-Sweet Enough (Caerleon (USA)) (679) 1275^{3} 2750^{11} 3233^{12} 3500^{8} 3755^{3} 3901^{2} **>70h<**

Proud Image 5 b g Zalazl (USA)-Fleur de Foret (USA) (Green Forest (USA)) 1770^{3} (2818) 3110^{3} 3284^{2} 3677^{2} (3979) 4313^{5} **>63h<**

Proud Toby (IRE) 7 b br g Lancastrian-Lady Conkers (Domenico Fuoco) **1646^{P} 1797^{P}** 3798^{10} **>29h<**

Provence 10 ch g 1256^{9} 1372^{5} 1562^{6} 4468^{9} 4727^{2} **>42h<**

Prove The Point (IRE) 4 b f Maelstrom Lake-In Review (Ela-Mana-Mou) 836^{4} 1184^{15} 1413^{5} 1675^{P} 3499^{P} 3735^{4} 3997^{3} **>39h<**

Province 4 b g Dominion-Shih Ching (USA) (Secreto (USA)) 1712^{3} 1935^{5} 3301^{8} 3801^{3} **>59h<**

Prudent Peggy 10 br m **305^{6} 484^{5} 601^{4}** 725^{5} **1445^{2} 1696^{6} 3053^{U} 3456^{7}** **>45h 77c<**

Pru's Profiles (IRE) 6 b g 1250^{3} 1507^{P} **>67h<**

Prussia 6 b g 105^{3} (189) 1253^{3} 2074^{3} 2759^{9} 3049^{7} 3613^{14} 3807^{2} 4220^{8} **>75h<**

Prussian Eagle (IRE) 5 b m Strong Gale-Court Session (Seymour Hicks (FR)) 1438^{7} 1673^{P} 3670^{P}

Prussian Steel (IRE) 6 gr g Torus-Lady Barnaby (Young Barnaby) 3021^{4} 3172^{P} **>63fh<**

Prussian Storm (IRE) 8 b m **1252^{F}** **>33h<**

Public Way (IRE) 7 b g Common Grounds-Kilpeacon (Florescence) 1343^{5} **>34h<**

Punch 5 b g 634^{15} **>38h<**

Punch's Hotel 12 ch g 816^{8} 3180^{P} 3604^{4} **>91h 97c<**

Punters Overhead (IRE) 9 b g **(1199) 1936^{P}** **>86h 117c<**

Punting Pete (IRE) 7 ch g **1405a^{7}** 1648^{3} **>124?h 43c<**

Purbeck Cavalier 8 ch g **1199^{5} 1764^{6} 2793^{U} 3059^{2} 3187^{F} 3407^{3}** **>84h 77c<**

Purbeck Polly 7 ch m 4524^{9} **>60h<**

Purbeck Rambler 6 b g **1472^{6} 1694^{5} 2795^{6} 3400^{P} 3495^{F} 3736^{6}** **>61h 63c<**

Pure Swing 4 b g Shareef Dancer (USA)-Mrs Warren (USA) (Hail To Reason) 3676^{13} **>16fh<**

Purevalue (IRE) 6 b br g 1945^{3} 2780^{4} (2900) 3269^{6} (3693) **>91h<**

Puritan (CAN) 8 b g **1373^{5} 1657^{5} 1823^{3} 1970^{2} 2508^{2} 2748^{2} 2801^{U}** **>119c<**

Purple Ace (IRE) 5 b g King's Ride-The Best I Can (Derring Rose) 3425^{8} **>52fh<**

Purple Splash 7 b g 3277^{7} 3562^{P} **>86h<**

Pusey Street Boy 10 ch g 299^{4} 339^{F} 723^{9} 1007^{6} **>67h 67c<**

Push On Polly (IRE) 7 b m Salluceva-Brave Polly (Brave Invader (USA)) 1781^{4} 2005^{10} 3283^{U} 3355^{P} 3910^{10} 4476^{8} **>25h<**

Pyramis Prince (IRE) 7 b g 1342^{P} **>83h<**

Pyr Four 10 b g **2346a^{5} 3585^{3} 3815^{2}** **>71h 127c<**

Pyrrhic Dance 7 b g Sovereign Dancer (USA)-Cherubim (USA) (Stevward) 1732^{12} 2114^{4} 3663^{P} **>7h<**

Pytchley Dawn 7 b m Welsh Captain-Cawston's Arms (Cawston's Clown) 498^{3} 788^{F} 950^{10} 1086^{5} 1299^{9} **>38h<**

Q

Qattara (IRE) 7 b g 1026^{5} 1687^{3} (2041) 2541^{P} **>82h< (DEAD)**

Quabmatic 4 b g Pragmatic-Good Skills (Bustino) 4009^{4} **>58fh<**

Quaff (IRE) 7 b g 1191^{2} 1639^{P} **>74h<**

Quaker Bob 12 b g **3181^{P}** **>60?c<**

Quakers Field 4 b c Anshan-Nosey (Nebbiolo) 3809^{2} (4014) 4364a^{5} **>104+h<**

Quaker Waltz 7 br m Faustus (USA)-Silent Dancer (Quiet Fling (USA)) 885^{3} 1369^{10} 1679^{5} 2753^{4} 3997^{2} 4086^{3} **>64h<**

Qualitair Pride 5 b m 1855^{8} 3641^{5} 4737^{3} **>58h<**

Quality (IRE) 4 b c Rock City-Queens Welcome (Northfields (USA)) 2622^{3} 3494^{4} (3818) 4014^{6} (4414) **>89h<**

Quango 5 b g Charmer-Quaranta (Hotfoot) (2539) 2898^{15} 3158^{5} **>79h<**

Qu'appelle 4 ch g Teamster-Gay Rhythm (Quiet Fling (USA)) 2872^{10} 3041^{13} **>20h<**

Quare Dream's (IRE) 6 b m 1044^{5} 1191^{P} **>39h<**

Quarter Marker (IRE) 9 br g **3460^{6} 3826^{6} 3931^{3} 4092^{F} 4444^{P} 4764^{6}** **>51c<**

Quartz Hill (USA) 8 b g 643^{F} **>46h 52c<**

Queen Buzzard 9 b m 3035^{P} **3941^{P}**

Queen of Shannon (IRE) 9 b m 1380^{P}

Queen of Spades (IRE) 7 b or br m (1152) 1438^{2} 1651^{2} (3143) 3595^{9} **>94h<**

Queen Of The Suir (IRE) 8 ch m 1260^{P} 1835^{P} 2959^{P} 3764^{P}

Queen's Award (IRE) 8 ch g 792^{10} (1130) (1322) 1384^{2} 1915^{8} 3013^{P} **>62h 89dc<**

Queens Brigade 5 b h K-Battery-Queen of Dara (Dara Monarch) 1579^{9} 2047^{11} **>34fh<**

Queen's Counsel (IRE) 4 b f Law Society (USA)-Mo Pheata (Petorius) 3475^{8} 3789^{8} 4056^{8} 4295^{8}

4389[4] 4756[3] **>52h<**

Queens Curate 10 b m 1948[7] **3443[4] 3682[P]**

Queens Fancy 4 ch f Infantry-Sagareina (Sagaro) 2751[P]

Queensway (IRE) 5 b g Pennine Walk-Polaregina (FR) (Rex Magna (FR)) (4580) **>71fh<**

Quelque Chose 7 b g 2708[7] (2905) 3499[6] **>76h<**

Query Line 6 ch m 2844[17] 3626[4] **>57fh<**

Questan 5 b g Rainbow Quest (USA)-Vallee Dansante (USA) (Lyphard (USA)) 1333[5] 2566[8] **>47h<**

Quick Bowler (IRE) 5 b g 1457[8] **>43fh<**

Quick Decision (IRE) 6 ch g **93[P]** 949[7] 1299[4] 1770[7] 2088[7] **2807[4] 3682[5] >45h 57?c<**

Quick Quote 7 b m 1855[4] 2870[5] 3052[4] **(3443) (3682) 3938[2] 4417[6] >61h 79c<**

Quiet Arch (IRE) 4 b g Archway (IRE)-My Natalie (Rheingold) 3500[13]

Quiet Confidence (IRE) 7 b m Pennine Walk-Northern Wisdom (Northfields (USA)) **3446[U] 3852[2] >90c<**

Quiet Dawn 11 b m 221[P] **>64h 72?c<**

Quiet Mistress 7 b m 1294[6] 1562[2] 2008[3] 2915[12] 3358[6] **>61h 89c<**

Quiet Moments (IRE) 4 b g Ron's Victory (USA)-Saint Cynthia (Welsh Saint) 1064[5] 1444[P] 1706[5] 2808[5] 3411[7] 3985[3] **>69h<**

Quillwork (USA) 5 b m 1828[5] 2008[P] **>53h<**

Quinag 6 ch m 1417[4] 1673[4] 1840[5] 2826[7] 3325[11] 3764[5] 4458[3] **>56h<**

Quince Bay 5 b g My Treasure Chest-Quince Wine (Malt) 1834[9] **>36fh<**

Quini Eagle (FR) 5 gr g Dom Pasquini (FR)-Miss Eagle (FR) (Staunch Eagle (USA)) 1289[2] (1457) 1766[5] 2546[4] 2676[3] (3798) **>80h<**

Quinta Royale 10 b g **132[3] >67h 77c<**

Quistaquay 5 b m El Conquistador-Busy Quay (Quayside) 1801[6] 2757[3] (3690) **>50fh<**

Quisti 7 b g El Conquistador-May Moss (Sea Moss) 1388[9] 1673[P]

Quite A Man 9 ch g 1814[5] 2076[7] **3051[P] (3732) (3833) (3988) (4221) (4277)** 4646[3] **>58+h 122+c<**

Quixall Crossett 12 b g **135[P]** 181[P] 288[7] **351[3] 508[3] 581[5] 802[2] 907[4] 1130[6] 1160[5] 1311[4] 1440[4] 1566[4] 1829[9] 2063[F] 2788[7] 2954[U] 3027[6] 3067[F] 3370[P] 3482[6] 3643[P] 3824[U] 4058[5] 4151[5] 4408[6] 4481[5] 4611[4] 4745[U] 4769[3] 4796[3] >16h 75c<**

Quixotry 6 ro g 3284[15] 3471[5] 3803[8] **>40h<**

R

Raahin (USA) 12 ch g 1709[P] 1841[5] 1962[7] 2824[10] 2905[4] 3442[18] 3604[3] 3720[P] **>45dh<**

Raba Riba 12 gr g **(3936) 4090[2] 4700[3] >124c<**

Rachael's Dawn 7 b m 3159[P] **>39h<**

Rachael's Owen 7 ch g 1166[2] 1732[2] **3001[P]** 3687[3] 4187[4] 4246[3] (4573) 4702[4] **>72h<**

Rachel Louise 5 ch m Beveled (USA)-Andrea Dawn (Run The Gantlet (USA)) 1329[3] 1913[3] 2696[15] 3290[3] 4382[4] 4428[2] **>61h<**

Racing Hawk (USA) 5 ch g Silver Hawk (USA)-Lorn Lady (Lorenzaccio) 1594[U]

Racing Telegraph 7 b g 955[12] 2074[P] **>17h<**

Racketball 4 ch g Green Adventure (USA)-Hylton Road (Kinglet) 3235[4] 3853[14] **>61fh<**

Radanpour (IRE) 5 b g (1233a) 1492a[2] 1759a[F] 2361a[F] 2596a[3] 3816[5] 4246[8] 4398[9] **>78h<**

Radiant River (IRE) 7 b g **2600a[6] 2856a[P] >48h 50c<**

Radical Exception (IRE) 7 b g Radical-A Stoir (Camden Town) 555[P]

Radical Storm (IRE) 6 ch g Radical-On The Dry (Over The River (FR)) 4215[20] **>38fh<**

Radmore Brandy 4 b f Derrylin-Emerin (King Emperor (USA)) 1184[10] 1699[6] 2859[10] 3031[5] (3474) (3730) 4711[3] 4770[5] **>68h<**

Raffles Rooster 5 ch g Galetto (FR)-Singapore Girl (FR) (Lyphard (USA)) 1950[3] 3426[5] **>58+h<**

Rafter-J 6 b or br g 3352[10] 3663[11]

Rafters 8 b g 952[P] **1037[F] 1120[2] >85h 104c<**

Ragamuffin Romeo 8 b g 183[P] (259) 338[3] 687[2] 822[2] 1007[4] (1091) 1253[2] 1451[3] 4337[6] 4755[3] **>60h<**

Ragazzo (IRE) 7 b g 1703[14] 1911[7] **>13h<**

Rag Doll 5 b m Buckskin (FR)-Nightlinger (Radical) 3914[20]

Ragdon 6 b g 1052[12] 1297[4] 1683[P] 2840[13] **>12h<**

Ragged Kingdom (IRE) 8 b g **1773[F] 2052[F] >43h<**

Raglan Road 13 b g **53a[6] 957[2] (4763) >94c<**

Ragosa 6 ch m 636[4] 1090[P] **>47h<**

Ragtime Boy 9 b g **3593[3] >70h 82c<**

Ragtime Song 8 b g Dunbeath (USA)-Kelowna (USA) (Master Derby (USA)) 634[F] 675[14] 820[3] 956[8] 1072[9] **>57h<**

Rah Wan (USA) 11 ch g 31[7] **>95?c<**

Raider (FR) 8 ch h Vacarme (USA)-Red At Night (FR) (Ela-Mana-Mou) 387a[2]

Rainbow Castle 10 b g **(550) (726) 1057[3] 1302[3] 1473[3] 1674[F] 1877[F] 4387[5] >73h 109c<**

Rainbow Fountain 10 b m 1200[P] **1538[P] 2039[6] 2910[P] >72c<**

Rainbow Victor (IRE) 4 b g Sharp Victor (USA)-Little Helen 3525a[7] 4364a[13] **>87h<**

Raincheck 6 b g **3495[5] 3762[2] 4007[P] >76c<**

Raining Stairs (IRE) 6 b g 1854[6] 4243[4] **>54h<**

Rain-N-Sun 11 gr g 1718[8] 2842[6] **3030[P]** 3429[10] **>48h<**

Raise A Dollar 7 br m 3348[4] 3691[8] 3944[3] 4152[3] 4299[5] 4394[2] **>61h<**

Rajadora 5 b m 3747[3] **>62fh<**

Rakaposhi Imp 7 ch m 2676[P] 3748[U] 4002[P] 4440[4] 4556[P]

Rakazona Beau 7 b g 2659[5] **>86h<**

Raki Crazy 6 ch g Lyphento (USA)-Tom's Nap Hand (Some Hand) **4637[6] >55c<**

Ralitsa (IRE) 5 b g 1143[4] 1658[4] 1701[2] 2780[P] 2955[P] 3995[R] **>88h<**

Rallegio 8 b g (2543) **2786[3] (3069) (3642) 4214[5] 4574[4] >83h 103dc<**

Rallying Cry (IRE) 9 b g **4758[P] >51h 84dc<**

Ramallah 8 b g **1596[3] 2007[2] >73h 101c<**

Rambling Lane 8 ch g Germont-Panbel (Dragonara Palace (USA)) 2917[18] 3794[P]

Rambling Lord (IRE) 9 b g Mister Lord (USA)-Vickies Gold (Golden Love) **3586[7] >73c<**

Rambling On 7 b g 1673[P] **>33h<**

Rambling Rajah 5 ch g Rakaposhi King-Red Rambler (Rymer) 3691[12] 4243[F] 4568[P] **>39h<**

Rambollina 6 b m 1049[9] **>65h<**

Ramillion 5 b m Macmillion-Annie Ra (Ra (USA)) 3808[15]

Ramozra 4 b f Rambo Dancer (CAN)-Ozra (Red Alert) 1940[P]

Rampant Rosie (IRE) 9 b m (345) 451[2] 465[5] **>58h<**

Ramsdens (IRE) 5 b g 793[4] 1121[P] 1355[2] 2666[P] 3471[10] 3915[6] **>81dh<**

Ramstar 9 ch g **15[5] 305[7]** 497[3] 603[5] **(676) (750) 862[3] 951[6] 1076[3] 3010[P] 3744[7] 4438[4] >64h 104dc<**

Ramstown Lad (IRE) 8 b g **1423[3] 1955[F] 2039[P] 2949[5]** 3937[7] 4244[8] **>39h 79c<**

Random Assault (NZ) 8 b g Random Chance (NZ)-Lady Frisco (NZ) (Uncle Remus (NZ)) **1682[3] 2051[4] 2700[4] 3225[F] >130c<**

Random Harvest (IRE) 8 br g **1153[2] 1506[4] (2544) 2699[2] (3202) 3617[P] 3974[U] >119c<**

Ranger Sloane 5 ch g 950[3] 1027[6] 1183[6] 1992[6] (3050) 3186[F] 3594[8] 3706[4] 3887[9] **>74h<**

Rangitikei (NZ) 6 b g 788[4] (1030) (1339) 1640[3] 2771[4] (3012) 3421[2] 3703[2] **>93h<**

Rapid Fire (IRE) 9 ch g Good Thyne (USA)-Princess Pixie (Royal Captive) **590[F] 733[P] 897[B]** 1046[3] 1292[P] **>52h<**

Rapid Liner 4 b g Skyliner-Stellaris (Star Appeal) 589[11] 3115[12] 3536[P] 3735[6] 4069[7] 4137[3] 4290[5] 4801[5] **>55h<**

Rapid Mover 10 ch g 1824[5] **1972[2] 2508[5] 2801[4] >69h 97c<**

Raqib 6 b g 1586[7] **>88h<**

Rare Gift (USA) 6 ch g Bounding Basque (USA)-Cherie's Hope (USA) (Flying Paster (USA)) 4538[10] 4696[8] **>23h<**

Rare Occurance 7 b g 2744[3] 3004[8] 3416[4] **3988[4] >54h 77c<**

Rare Paddy 8 b m 289[6] 393[4] **>41h<**

Rare Spread (IRE) 7 b g Rare One-Wide Spread (Sparkler) 133[R] 418[2] 594[2] 1197[P] 1561[3] 1962[2] 2570[7] (3205) 3340[2] 4281[F] **>76h< (DEAD)**

Rarfy's Dream 9 b g 1267[F] 1358[P]

Rasak 5 b g Kris-Lypharita (FR) (Lightning (FR)) 2682[4] (3090) 4216[18] **>66fh< (DEAD)**

Rascally 7 gr m 3827[4] (4081) 4518[5] **>67h<**

Rasin Luck 7 b m 1705[8]

Rasin Standards 7 b g Relkino-Growing Wild (Free State) 1926[10] 3305[4] 3474[4] 3888[6] **>61h<**

Rather Sharp 11 b g **20[P] 4218[P] >74c<**

Rathfardon (IRE) 9 b g Callernish-Our June (Tarqogan) **1563[9] 1944[3] 2540[9] 3477[P] >73c<**

Rathgibbon (IRE) 6 br g 2361a[3] **>114h<**

Rathkeal (IRE) 6 gr g 1317[13] 1683[6] 2550[9] 3108[8] **3537[P] >61h<**

Rattle 4 b g Mazilier (USA)-Snake Song (Mansingh (USA)) 1159[4] 1356[5] 1652[14] 1980[8] 2505[9] **>46h<**

Raven's Roost (IRE) 6 b g 344[4] (393) (461) 591[5] 1448[2] 1772[5] **>66h<**

Ravus 7 gr g 818[6] 1077[P]

Rawy (USA) 5 b g 3615[14] **>104h< (DEAD)**

Rayman (IRE) 9 ch g **3664[7] >91dc<**

Ray River 5 b g 71[5] 211[5] 264[6] 355[4] 474[3] 648[4] 1145[10] 1466[6] **>77h<**

Reach The Clouds (IRE) 5 b g Lord Americo-Dusky Stream (Paddy's Stream) 1583[10] 2690[P] 2840[11] 3802[F] 3823[6] 4285[3] **>60h<**

Ready Money Creek (IRE) 6 ch g (1583) 2642[4] 3014[2] 3272[3] (3796) **>86h<**

Reaganesque (USA) 5 b g 790[8] 952[3] 1286[5] 1681[2] (1956) 2666[6] (2929) 3430[4] 3920[2] **>96h<**

Real Glee (IRE) 8 ch g **1119[7] (1527)** 1843[2] **2674[4] 3413[7]** 4001[P] **>70h 109c<**

Real Lucille 5 b m Idiot's Delight-La Verite (Vitiges (FR)) 1555[13]

Really a Rascal 10 b g **1167[P] 1540[3] 1799[2] 1985[3] 2821[6] 3113[F] 3280[4] 3884[P] >109c<**

Really Neat 11 gr m Alias Smith (USA)-Tiddley (Filiberto (USA)) 67[10] 129[P] **>39h<**

Really Useful (IRE) 5 b g Strong Gale-Arctic Match (Royal Match) 4215[10] **>65fh<**

Real Madrid 6 b g Dreams to Reality (USA)-Spanish Princess (King of Spain) 3820[5] 3955[3] 4102[4] (4318) 4567[2] 4762[4] **>73h<**

Real Progress (IRE) 9 ch g **530[2] 797[5] >110c<**

Real Tonic 7 br g **3138[F] (3450)** 3530[2] **3790[3] (4077) 4186[7] (4515) >70h 110c<**

Reapers Rock 10 br g **3332[2] 3622[U] 3751[3] 3911[3] 4234[5] >89c<**

Reasilvia (IRE) 7 br m 2603a[22] **>91h<**
Rebel King 7 b g **645[2] 696[6] 1442[3] 1846[2] 1991[3] 2508[6] 2923[6] 3140[2] 3329[P] 3482[5] 3991[2] 4145[3] 4247[6] 4392[3] 4753[2] >85h 92c<**
Rebel Priest (IRE) 7 b g **3339[P] 3966[P]**
Rebounder 4 b g Reprimand-So Bold (Never so Bold) 2050[P]
Recall To Mind 4 b g Don't Forget Me-Northern Notion (USA) (Northern Baby (CAN)) 291[7] 388[3] 462[6] 688[6] 874[5] **>43h<**
Recca (IRE) 5 b g Detroit Sam (FR)-French Note (Eton Rambler) 2005[11] 2633[13] **>8fh<**
Recluse 6 b g 4712[9] **>36h<**
Record Lover (IRE) 7 b g 465[2] 587[3] 673[3] **744[4] 1028[2] 1206[4] 1371[6] 1716[2] 1819[3] 2671[P] 2947[8] 3278[2] 3547[3] 3708[3] >68h 80dc<**
Recruitment 4 b g Lord Bud-Mab (Morston (FR)) 1700[10] 2649[7] 3287[7] 4399[3] 4744[F] **>52h<**
Rectory Garden (IRE) 8 b g **1279[2] 1799[5] 2758[3] (3361) 4284[2] >58h 121c<**
Red Beacon 10 b g 1701[11] **>71h<**
Red Bean 9 ch g **1584[4] 1934[6] 2906[5] 3206[4] (3686) (3839) 4177[3] >67h 97c<**
Red Blazer 6 ch g (2010) (2812) 4184[2] **>93h<**
Red Branch (IRE) 8 ch g Remainder Man-Run With Rosie (Deep Run) 1568[9] 1840[P] **2807[2] 3145[U] (3331) (3602) (3717) (3819) 4186[5] (4385) (4553) (4722) >46h 115c<**
Red Bronze (IRE) 6 b g Phardante (FR)-Gorryelm (Arctic Slave) 1476[8] 1795[4] 2891[6] **>56h<**
Red Brook 5 ch g Weld-Scrambird (Dubassoff (USA)) (1801) (2844) **>68fh<**
Red Channel (IRE) 7 b g **4618[4] >30h 60c<**
Red Curate (IRE) 6 b g Radical-Parsfield (The Parson) (3425) 4215[4] **>81fh<**
Redeemyourself (IRE) 8 b g **(1320) >114h 111+c<**
Red Eikon 6 ch g 19[P] **70[2] 135[P] >56h 89c<**
Redgrave Wolf 4 ch f Little Wolf-Redgrave Rose (Tug of War) 3235[3] 4407[13] **>58fh<**
Red Hot Prince 6 b g 3973[7] 4243[P]
Red Jam Jar 12 ch g (134) 509[3] 690[3] 805[U] (892) 1047[4] 4060[7] 4501[7] 4798[4] **>77h<**
Red Lane 7 ch g Rustingo-Caubeen (Scottish Rifle) 2566[9] 3364[13] **>7h<**
Red Light 5 b g 65[P] 1010[3] 1183[2] 1451[8] 1959[7] 2692[5] 3222[12] 4341[4] 4638[2] **>62h<**
Red Lighter 8 ch g 3088[5] (3358) 3689[2] **>72h<**
Red March Hare 6 b m 463[3] 731[3] 3803[P] **>48h<**
Red Match 12 ch g **883[P] 975[P]** 1166[7] **>37h 75dc<**
Red Oassis 6 ch g Rymer-Heron's Mirage (Grey Mirage) 2626[12] 3203[9] 3703[8] 4161[F] **>17fh<**
Red Parade (NZ) 9 b g **1765[3] 2658[P] 2839[3] 3020[U] >82h 103c<**
Red Phantom (IRE) 5 ch g Kefaah (USA)-Highland Culture (Lomond (USA)) 2035[10] 2668[15] 2818[B] 3338[11] **>20h<**
Red Raja 4 b g Persian Heights-Jenny Splendid (John Splendid) 1634[8] (1808) 2070[2] 2865[5] (3174) 3301[5] (3801) 4364a[9] **>96h<**
Red River (IRE) 6 ch m 3014[P] 3491[6] **>42h<**
Red Rusty (USA) 4 ch g The Carpenter (USA)-Super Sisters (AUS) (Call Report (USA)) 1712[P] 4555[5] **>28h<**
Red Spectacle (IRE) 5 b g (450) **>58h<**
Red-Stoat (IRE) 8 ch m Oats-Rednael (Leander) 3098[P]
Red Tel (IRE) 5 b g Alzao (USA)-Arbour (USA) (Graustark) 306[2] (418) 918[5] 1124[8] 1453[13] 1713[3] 4292[2] 4459[2] 4552[P] 4658[8] 4789[12] **>67h<**
Red Tie Affair (USA) 4 b c Miswaki (USA)-Quiet Rendezvous (USA) (Nureyev (USA)) 1953[13]
Red Time 4 br g Timeless Times (USA)-Crimson Dawn (Manado) 912[8] 1595[8] 2705[8] **>24h<**
Red Trix 5 ch m 505[P]
Red Valerian 6 b g 16[2] (582) 638[3] (734) 894[P] **>101h< (DEAD)**
Red Viper 5 b g 3964[8] 4441[4] 4548[6] 4770[F] **>63h<**
Redwood Lad 7 b g 2673[P] 2861[W]
Reed 12 b g **4579[5] 4713[4] >53h 79c<**
Reefa's Mill (IRE) 5 b g 65[6] 483[5] 555[6] 879[10] 913[10] **1664[3] 1920[P] >63h 79c<**
Reem Fever (IRE) 4 b f Fairy King (USA)-Jungle Jezebel (Thatching) 1712[8] 1953[17]
Reeshloch 8 b g **1328[2] 1552[2] 1994[F] 2679[7] 3086[5] 3495[4] >73h 81c<**
Reflex Hammer 6 b g 1030[9] 1633[6] 1796[6] **>56h<**
Regal Aura (IRE) 7 ch g **3059[6] (3578) (3756) 4168[4] >85dh 92dc<**
Regal Bluff 5 ch g 4561[6] **>43fh<**
Regal Domain (IRE) 6 ro g Dominion Royale-Adaraya (FR) (Zeddaan) 1020[8] 1312[10] 1667[P] **4260[4] 4574[6] 4703[6] >32c<**
Regal Eagle 4 b g Shirley Heights-On The Tiles (Thatch (USA)) 4184[7] 4477[F] **>62h<**
Regal Gem (IRE) 6 ch m (24) (133) 191[6] 350[3] 408[4] 492[2] 792[8] 2961[10] 3764[2] 3982[3] 4506[2] 4663[U] **>67h<**
Regal Jest 7 gr m 3029[P] 3803[P] 4144[U]
Regal Pursuit (IRE) 6 b m (956) 1505[2] 3549[6] 4136[6] 4304[4] **>67h<**
Regal Romper (IRE) 9 b g **867[3] (1128) (1295) 1361[3] 1688[3] 2618[2] 2921[2] 3225[2] 3369[2] 3610[4] 3991[3] >93h 108c<**
Regal Splendour (CAN) 4 ch g Vice Regent (CAN)-Seattle Princess (USA) (Seattle Slew (USA)) 3494[6] 3818[11] **>54h<**
Regal Spring (IRE) 5 b g Royal Fountain-Ride The Rapids (Bulldozer) 4009[5] **>57fh<**
Regardless 15 b g Quayside-Bel Arbre (Beau Chapeau) **57[9] 94[4] 190[14] 335[P] >74c<**
Regency Leisure 5 ch g Mr Fluorocarbon-Pixie's Party (Celtic Cone) 3021[7] **>34fh<**
Registano (GER) 10 b g Tauchsport (GER)-Reklame (GER) (Immer (GER)) (51a)
Reimei 8 b g Top Ville-Brilliant Reay (Ribero) 1782[5] 2668[9] **>53h<**
Reine de La Chasse (FR) 5 ch m 748[4] 1261[P] **>63h<**
Relative Chance 8 b g 971[2] 1732[3] **>55h<**
Relaxed Lad 8 ro g **3187[3] 3470[U] 3682[3] 4627[4] >54h 54c<**
Relkander 7 b g 3399[11] **>9h<**
Relkeel 8 b g 3017[2] **>132+h<**
Relkowen 7 ch m **1677[F] 2752[F] 3343[P]** 4006[13] **>11h<**
Reluckino 7 b g 1640[11] 2820[9] 3180[2] 3328[P] 4767[4] **>63h<**
Remember Star 4 ch f Don't Forget Me-Star Girl Gay (Lord Gayle (USA)) 501[6] 688[14] 836[6] 1332[7] 2664[4] 2905[P] **>41h<**
Reno's Treasure (USA) 4 ch f Beau Genius (CAN)-Ligia M (USA) (Noholme Jr (USA)) 3284[17] 4423[5] 4542[5] 4719[P] **>28h<**
Rent Day 8 b m **639[3] 970[U] 2816[9] 3360[6] >61?h 67c<**
Repeat Offer 5 b g Then Again-Bloffa (Derrylin) 1573[4] 2073[3] **>52fh<**
Re Roi (IRE) 5 b g 299[3] (400) (481) 591[3] 815[2] 936[P] 2815[5] 2952[10] 3741[5] 3979[5] **>54h<**
Rescue Time (IRE) 4 b g Mtoto-Tamassos (Dance In Time (CAN)) 2333a[3] 2603a[14] 3258a[5] **>96h<**
Reservation Rock (IRE) 6 ch g Ballad Rock-Crazyfoot (Luthier) 3669[6] **>33h<**
Resist the Force (USA) 7 br g Shadeed (USA)-Countess Tully (Hotfoot) (1517) 1791[6] 2624[P] **>87h<**
Respecting 4 b g Respect-Pricey (Silly Prices) 2175[8] 3475[10] 4335[12] **>29h<**
Restandbejoyful 5 ch m 1913[11] **>33fh<**
Restate (IRE) 6 b m 1523[8] **>41h<**
Retail Runner 12 b g **2756[P] 3206[3] 3622[P] >104?c<**
Ret Frem (IRE) 4 b g Posen (USA)-New Light (Reform) 534[2] 699[6] 852[2] **>61h<**
Reve de Valse (USA) 10 ch g **4[4] (454) 529[2] 694[3] 873[3] 1051[4] (1702) 1846[3] 2674[6] 3610[3] 4058[3] 4145[4] 4297[6] 4753[8] >70h 91c<**
Reveillon (GER) 5 b h 50a[3] **>85h<**
Reverend Brown (IRE) 7 b g **3922[4] 4618[2] >66h 80c<**
Reverse Thrust 6 b g 1729[7] 2690[11] 3012[5] 3494[P] (3955) 4226[2] 4558[F] 4807[5] **>63h<**
Revolt 5 b g Primitive Rising (USA)-Fit For A King (Royalty) 1692[6] 1926[5] 2619[2] **>73h<**
Rex to the Rescue (IRE) 9 ch g **592[3] 740[2] 882[3] 1430[3] 1731[2] (1957) 2814[2] >112c<**
Rhoman Fun (IRE) 8 b g **1335[P] 1445[7] 1554[2] 3179[5] >59h 76c<**
Rhossili Bay 9 b g **(138) 292[F] >46h 111c<**
Rhyming Thomas 9 ch g 3711[15] **>55h<**
Rhythm And Blues 7 b g 1036[4] 1171[7] 3154[5] (3406) 3718[3] 4166[5] 4521[U] 4625[6] **>75h<**
Rhythmic Dancer 9 b g Music Boy-Stepping Gaily (Gay Fandango (USA)) 643[P] 698[P]
Richard Hunt 13 b g **3353[P] >108c<**
Rich Desire 8 b m **1291[P] >92+h<**
Rich Life (IRE) 7 b g **4533[P] >93h 95c<**
Richmond (IRE) 9 ch g **532[3] 584[7] 681[4]** 806[6] **>69h 54c<**
Rich Tycoon (IRE) 8 b g 3628[3] 3798[P] **>60h<**
Riding Crop (IRE) 7 b g 1132[2] 1639[5] 2891[3] **4007[P] >78h<**
Rifawan (USA) 6 b g **2789[F] >103h< (DEAD)**
Right Ron Run 5 b g Primitive Rising (USA)-Sheshells (Zino) 4538[12]
Right Win (IRE) 7 br h 1916[6] 2635[5] 3011[5] **>127?h<**
Rimouski 9 b h 2761[2] 3013[13] 3281[6] 3646[5] 3962[7] **>70h<**
Ri Na Mara (IRE) 6 b g 3431[7]
Ring Corbitts 9 b g **1716[5] 1839[2] 2795[U] 3020[8] >76h 91c<**
Ring For Rosie 6 br m Derrylin-Clear the Course (Crash Course) 3226[6] (4304) **>63h<**
Ring of Vision (IRE) 5 br g Scenic-Circus Lady (High Top) 3500[2] 3761[3] (3964) 4217[3] **>84h<**
Ringrone (IRE) 8 ch m Lancastrian-Naomi Night VII (Damsire Unregistered) 1523[7] 1851[13] 2177[8] **3608[P] 3726[P] >11h<**
Rinus Majestic (IRE) 5 b g Gallic League-Deepwater Blues (Gulf Pearl) 705[12] 1013[11] 1633[P]
Rinus Major (IRE) 6 b g **3278[F]** 3802[10] **>55h<**
Rio Haina 12 ch g **3444[P] 3925[4] >90c<**
Riot Leader (IRE) 7 b g 3171[2] **>75?h<**
Riparius (USA) 6 b g Riverman (USA)-Sweet Simone (FR) (Green Dancer (USA)) 3818[3] (4003) 4400[4] (4630) **>85h<**
Riseupwilliereilly 11 ch g Deep Run-Sinarga (Even Money) **3684[F] 3954[U]**
Rising Dawn (IRE) 5 ch g Rising-Bawnard Lady (Ragapan) 4580[8] **>32fh<**
Rising Dough (IRE) 5 br g 790[6] 3084[4] 3424[5] 3964[3] **>81h<**
Rising Man 6 b g 1921[7] 3672[6] **>50h<**
Rising Mill 6 b g Primitive Rising (USA)-Milly

L'Attaque (Military) 3716^{10}

Rising Sap 7 ch g Brotherly (USA)-Miss Kewmill (Billion (USA)) **2951^{P} 3341^{P} 3586^{8} 3984^{P} >71c<**

Rising's Lass (IRE) 7 ch m 3894^{4} 4524^{7} **>48h<**

Risky Dee 8 b g **1847^{7} 1970^{4} 2179^{4} 3094^{3} 3308^{3} 3452^{W} 3645^{4} 3725^{W} >84c<**

Risky Romeo 5 b g Charmer-Chances Are (He Loves Me) 400^{4} **>53h<**

Risky Rose 5 b m Risk Me (FR)-Moharabuiee (Pas de Seul) 902^{8}

Risky Tu 6 ch m Risk Me (FR)-Sarah Gillian (USA) (Zen (USA)) 3282^{P} 3445^{6} **>37h<**

Ritto 7 b g Arctic Tern (USA)-Melodrama (Busted) 739^{3} (890) 1053^{P} (1424) 3630^{P} 4226^{F} 4405^{P} 4548^{P}

Riva Rock 7 b g 187^{P} **>63+h<**

Riva's Book (USA) 6 b g 101^{6} 184^{10} 394^{3} 488^{2} **>67h<**

Riveaux (IRE) 7 b g 3271^{7} 3449^{3} 3888^{7} 4479^{3} **>64h 45c<**

Riverbank Red 6 ch m 1412^{P} 1628^{13} 2939^{9} **3200^{P} 3746^{F} >54h<**

Riverbank Rose 6 b m 800^{4} 1256^{4} 1417^{3} 2076^{P} 3284^{3} (3583) 3730^{4} 3970^{3} 4376^{5} 4768^{3} **>72h<**

River Bay (IRE) 6 b m 1341^{7} 1580^{2} (1998) 2822^{3} 3817^{P} 4182^{3} **>71h<**

River Bounty 11 ch g **1637^{B} 2762^{3} 3039^{3} 3266^{P} >88h 123?c<**

Rivercare (IRE) 4 b c Alzao (USA)-Still River (Kings Lake (USA)) 1014^{6}

River Challenge (IRE) 6 ch g 338^{P} **>68h<**

River Dawn (IRE) 5 ch g Over The River (FR)-Morning Susan (Status Seeker) 3170^{6} 3425^{15}

River Gala (IRE) 7 ch g **724^{4} 752^{U} 3736^{P} 3957^{2} >75c<**

River Island (USA) 9 b g 2040^{6} 2828^{4} 3076^{P} **>49h<**

River Leven 8 b g **(1831) 2068^{2} 2752^{4} 3686^{3} 4535^{P} >77h 93c<**

River Mandate 10 b or br g **(1631) 2011^{2} 2839^{2} 3036^{2} 3420^{3} 3598^{F} 4074^{P} >72+h 134c<**

River Monarch 6 b h Just A Monarch-Costa Beck (Forlorn River) 1517^{8} **>22h<**

River Mulligan (IRE) 5 ch g Over The River (FR)-Miss Manhattan (Bally Joy) 4215^{12} **>63fh<**

River Red 11 ch g **1465^{4} 2548^{6} 4159^{10} >73h 66c<**

River Rock (IRE) 4 ch g Classic Music (USA)-Borough Counsel 1747a^{14} **>52h<**

River Room 7 ch g (58) (139) 181^{2} 1031^{4} (1274) 1322^{5} 1870^{5} **>87h<**

Rivers Magic 4 b g Dominion-Rivers Maid (Rarity) 1808^{5} 2705^{F}

River Unshion (IRE) 7 ch g **1803^{3} 3141^{2} (3367) (3726) 4245^{3} >87h 105c<**

River Wye (IRE) 5 b g 868^{8} (2897) 3186^{P} **>76+h<**

Rizal (USA) 5 ch g Zilzal (USA)-Sigy (FR) (Habitat) 955^{F} 1059^{R} 1178^{P}

R N Commander 11 b g **3543^{4} 3994^{5}**

Road by the River (IRE) 9 ch g **1655^{2} 2046^{3} 2544^{4} 2916^{5} >100c<**

Roadrunner 7 ch g Sunley Builds-Derraleena (Derrylin) **3407^{F}** 3796^{P}

Road to Au Bon (USA) 9 b g (1599) 1996^{5} 2708^{12} **>59h<**

Roadway Joker 6 b g 1362^{18} 1851^{F} **(DEAD)**

Roaming Shadow 10 gr g Rymer-Silver Shadow (Birdbrook) **4457^{P}**

Robara 7 b or br g 2041^{9} **2914^{5} 3138^{5} 3826^{7} >62h 64c<**

Robert Samuel 6 b g Another Sam-Dracons Girl (Cave of Dracan) 99^{9} 4097^{4}

Robert's Toy (IRE) 6 b g **(61) 93^{F} 411^{6}** 638^{4} 798^{3} 1382^{2} 2040^{8} 3199^{6} 4430^{F} **(4643) >89h 111c<**

Robert The Brave 5 b g 1705^{4} 1990^{8} 3158^{P} **>32h< (DEAD)**

Roberty Lea 9 b g 1642^{2} (2008) 2702^{P} **(3030) 3326^{2} (3479) 3909^{5} >115h 99c<**

Robin Island 5 b g 1838^{3} 1993^{P} **>22h<**

Robins Pride (IRE) 7 b g **1764^{P} 2079^{2} 2793^{2} 3001^{P} 3229^{3} 3443^{U} 3758^{2} >80h 104c<**

Robsand (IRE) 8 b g **1538^{4} 1773^{8} 2841^{4} 3020^{2} 3617^{3} >49h 115c<**

Robsera (IRE) 6 b g 506^{4} 643^{2} 701^{4} 786^{2} 1010^{4} 1278^{6} 1628^{3} (1851) 2631^{8} 3031^{4} 3327^{5} **>68h<**

Roc Age 6 ch m 24^{5} 963^{4} 1178^{7} 1594^{7} 3364^{10} 3583^{7} 4468^{8} 4558^{6} 4765^{4} **>30h<**

Roca Murada (IRE) 8 br g 299^{2} 4307^{6} 4443^{7} **4643^{P} >79dh<**

Roche Mentor (IRE) 7 bb g Yashgan-African Bloom **1486a^{F} >53h 75c<**

Rockange (IRE) 8 b m Ballad Rock-Ange de Feu (Double Form) 186^{8}

Rockcliffe Lad 8 b g (1939) 2656^{7} 3168^{P} **>82h<**

Rocket Ron 5 b g 59^{3}

Rocket Run (IRE) 9 b g **2^{4} 940^{2} >56h 114c<**

Rocketts Castle (IRE) 7 ch g **3260a^{P} 4350a^{U} >67h 80c<**

Rockville Pike (IRE) 5 b g Glenstal (USA)-Sound Pet (Runnett) 2818^{F}

Rocky Balboa 5 b g Buckley-Midnight Pansy (Deadly Nightshade) 3808^{13} **>17fh<**

Rocky Park 11 ch g **1202^{2} 1428^{4} 1765^{2} 1983^{U} 2829^{2} 3153^{2} 3428^{5} 4185^{U} 4404^{F} >77h 108c<**

Rodeo Star (USA) 11 ch g **(63) >105dh 113c<**

Roderick Hudson 5 b g Elmaamul (USA)-Moviegoer (Pharly (FR)) 1594^{4} **>62h<**

Roger de Mowbray 7 b g 4726^{P} **>35h<**

Rogerson 9 ch g Green-Fingered-Town Belle (Town Crier) 4001^{P} 4175^{8} **>10h<**

Roger's Pal 10 ch g 553^{4} 655^{U} 816^{4} 1074^{3} 1390^{4} 1710^{5} 2905^{8} 3209^{3} 3442^{10} 3604^{2} 4096^{6} **>45h<**

Roi du Nord (FR) 5 b g 908^{7} 1010^{2} **>83h<**

Roker Joker 6 b g Jupiter Island-Trikkala Star (Tachypous) 4538^{2} **>52fh<**

Rolfe (NZ) 7 b g (31) 214^{5} **1340^{P} 2079^{3}** 4415^{P} **>86h<**

Roll a Dollar 11 b g 2645^{10} 2777^{7} 3038^{13} **>101h<**

Roll Again 6 b g Tragic Role (USA)-Land of Ginger (Young Man (FR)) 2626^{5} 3085^{P} 3342^{4} 3592^{10} **>69h<**

Rolled Gold 8 b g **1711^{P} 1829^{8} 2816^{F} 4431^{4} >56c<**

Rolleston Blade 10 ch g **2795^{9} 3134^{2} 3409^{F} >88c<**

Roly Prior 8 b g **3913^{4} >52h 80c<**

Romaldkirk 5 b g Jalmood (USA)-Palace Tor (Dominion) 3142^{17} 3305^{5} 3475^{13} 3727^{P}

Romalito 7 b g **3688^{W} >69h<**

Roman Actor 5 b g Tragic Role (USA)-Christines Lady (Roman Warrior) 1966^{10} **>17fh<**

Romancer (IRE) 6 br g 3038^{16} 3231^{2} 3640^{16} 4396^{3} **>116h<**

Roman Outlaw 5 gr g Alias Smith (USA)-Roman Moor (Owen Anthony) 2047^{3} 2904^{4} 3914^{4} **>52fh<**

Romantic Warrior 4 b g Welsh Captain-Romantic Melody (Battle Hymn) 4465^{U} 4532^{4} 4650^{6} 4762^{3} **>58h<**

Romany Ark 11 b g Arkan-Romany Charm (Romany Air) **3924^{4} >84c<**

Romany Blues 8 b m **1582^{U} 1819^{U} 2052^{4} 2704^{U} 2823^{F}** 3752^{7} 3894^{U} **>40h 69c<**

Romany Creek (IRE) 8 b g **1043^{2} 1279^{4} 1863^{2} 2782^{U} 3074^{2} 3361^{2} 3598^{4} 4013^{P} >127c<**

Romany King 13 br g **57^{P} >112c<**

Ronans Glen 10 b or br g 1798^{10} **2077^{F} 2548^{3} 2749^{4} 3181^{P}** 3935^{P} **>78c<**

Rood Music 6 ro g Sharrood (USA)-Rose Music (Luthier) 1187^{9} 1369^{8} 2074^{8} 3473^{P} 3967^{7} **>49h<**

Roo's Leap (IRE) 9 b m **4406^{P} >58h<**

Rory 6 b g Dowsing (USA)-Crymlyn (Welsh Pageant) 2939^{3} **>81h<**

Rory'm (IRE) 8 ch g Remainder Man-First In (Over The River (FR)) 69^{P} 2878^{P} 3340^{P} 3536^{5} 3740^{4} 3949^{9} 4333^{P} **>14h<**

Rosalee Royale 5 ch m 1857^{7}

Ros Castle 6 b g 318a^{18} 2645^{11} 2884^{8} 2963^{5} 3177^{5} 3421^{7} **>93h< (DEAD)**

Roscolvin (IRE) 5 b g Prince Rupert (FR)-Chepstow House (USA) (Northern Baby (CAN)) **4615^{P} >70h<**

Roscommon Lad (IRE) 5 b g 27^{P} **>43h<**

Roseberry Avenue (IRE) 4 b c Sadler's Wells (USA)-Lady's Bridge (USA) (Sir Ivor) (2070) 2772^{3} **>91h<**

Rose Chime (IRE) 5 b or br m Tirol-Repicado Rose (USA) (Repicado (CHI)) 490^{5} 634^{6} 735^{4} 965^{2} **>54h<**

Rosehall 6 b br m 653^{9} 955^{11} (1180) 1467^{5} 1958^{P} 2932^{5} 3272^{7} 3488^{6} **>63h<**

Rose King 10 b g **2623^{3} 2910^{5}** 4016^{P} **>83h 88tc<**

Rosencrantz (IRE) 5 b g (1053) (1333) 1597^{2} 2644^{F} 2817^{3} 3180^{P} (3850) 4061^{10} **>95+h<**

Rose of Glenn 6 b m 2574^{4} 2678^{5} 2818^{F} 3590^{6} 3735^{2} 3997^{6} **>51h<**

Roses Niece (IRE) 4 br f Jeu de Paille (FR)-Pollyville 4118a^{26} **>9fh<**

Rosglinn (IRE) 5 gr m Roselier (FR)-Over The Pond (IRE) (Over The River (FR)) 4009^{14} 4620^{12}

Rosie (IRE) 7 gr m (98) **>38h<**

Rosie-B 7 b m (891) (1876) 3146^{4} 3358^{9} **4699^{9} >63h 51c<**

Roskeen Bridge (IRE) 6 br g Black Minstrel-Miss Lou (Levanter) 397^{2} 954^{8} 1541^{P} 1962^{3} 3088^{3} (3408) 3689^{4} **>49h<**

Ross Dancer (IRE) 5 b g Ajraas (USA)-Crimson Crown (Lord Gayle (USA)) 1171^{4} 1394^{5} 1550^{3} 2820^{11} 3488^{5} (3962) 4084^{3} **>66h<**

Rossel (USA) 4 b g Blushing John (USA)-Northern Aspen (USA) (Northern Dancer) (534) 699^{4} (1356) 1652^{3} 1940^{2} (2175) (2615) 3291^{7} 4209^{5} **>92h<**

Rossell Island (IRE) 6 br g 1369^{B} 1867^{8} 2546^{7} 2820^{P} **>60h<**

Rosslayne Serenade 6 b m Northern State (USA)-Trojan Melody (Troy) 25^{10} 1042^{P} 1369^{F}

Ross Venture 12 b g **3055^{P} >113?c<**

Rostino (IRE) 8 b g 4055^{P} 4389^{9} **4751^{4} >11h 60c<**

Rothari 5 b g 1052^{4} 1640^{5} 1921^{9} 3345^{8} (3612) 3883^{8} **>64h<**

Rough Diamond (IRE) 5 b g King's Ride-Casaurina (IRE) (Le Moss) 4003^{11} **>8h<**

Rough Edge 9 b g Broadsword (USA)-Mini Gazette (London Gazette) **(4637) >90c<**

Rough Quest 11 b g (1964) **2115^{2} >97+h 170c<**

Route One (IRE) 4 br g Welsh Term-Skylin (Skyliner) (4301) **>68fh<**

Routing 9 b g (159) 2147 **>92h<**

Rouyan 11 b g **4011^{3} 4206^{P} >154c<**

Rovestar 6 b g 1274^{6} (1663) 2552^{10} 2870^{7} **3343^{3} >72h 93c<**

Rowbet Jack 5 b g Colmore Row-Bet Oliver (Kala

Shikari) 918[P]
Rowhedge 11 ch g 480[P] **>73h<**
Roxy Hicks 5 b m Seymour Hicks (FR)-Damsong (Petong) 4009[15] 4276[P]
Royal Action 4 b c Royal Academy (USA)-Ivor's Honey (Sir Ivor) 1862[3] 2784[2] **>80h<**
Royal Ag Nag 7 b m 4440[P] **>79h<**
Royal Albert (IRE) 8 b g 318a[S] **>103h<**
Royal Banker (IRE) 7 b g **3556[F] 3882[P]** 4260[U] **4569[4] 4715[2] >57c<**
Royal Chip 5 br g Rakaposhi King-Up Cooke (Deep Run) 3480[5] **>15fh<**
Royal Circus 8 b g (391) 491[4] 582[6] 657[P] 868[4] 942[5] 1181[6] **>75h<**
Royal Citizen (IRE) 8 b g 1360[P] 1859[P] 4734[3] **>71h<**
Royal Crimson 6 b g **2628[5] 3030[2] 3417[P] >76h 81c<**
Royal Diversion (IRE) 4 b f Marju (IRE)-Royal Recreation (USA) (His Majesty (USA)) 1808[4] 2547[16] **>46h<**
Royal Divide (IRE) 5 b g Lord Americo-Divided Loyalties (Balidar) 1801[10] 2073[10]
Royal Event 6 ch g 1453[2] 1659[2] 1964[3] (2824) 3105[2] 4204[12] **>79h<**
Royal Glint 8 b m 75[P] 128[7] 1772[10] 2680[14] 2874[6] 3429[9] 3632[P] 4405[9] **>21h<**
Royal Hand 7 b g **821[U] 917[2] 1920[F] 2000[F] 2816[7] 3020[P]** 3100[F] 3748[5] 4055[4] 4289[4] 4501[3] 4636[F] **>51h 69c<**
Royal Irish 13 ch g **3107[P] 3580[P] >60c<**
Royal Jester 13 b g **3397[2] 3793[2] 4080[2] 4208[2] 4473[4] >108c<**
Royal Member 4 ch f Seven Hearts-Little Member (New Member) 3606[11] 3889[U] 4170[3] 4304[P]
Royal Midyan 4 b c Midyan (USA)-Royal Agreement (USA) (Vaguely Noble) 4364a[11] **>76h<**
Royal Mile 12 b g **14[P] >55c<**
Royal Mint 4 b g Bustino-Royal Seal (Privy Seal) 4301[5] **>48fh<**
Royal Mist (IRE) 6 b g Hays-Kings Perhaps (King's Ride) 2811[14] 3937[P]
Royal Mountbrowne 9 b g **763a[6] 1003a[P] (1216a) (1397a) 1495a[7] 1737a[2] (1889a) 1917[5] 2602a[6] 2741a[8] 3245a[2] 3383a[3] >154c<**
Royal Oasis (IRE) 6 b g Royal Fountain-Progello **4350a[F] >54h 80c<**
Royal Oats 12 b m Oats-Knights Queen (Arctic Chevalier) **4241[F]**
Royal Palm 5 b g Palm Track-Royal Export (Import) 1245[8] 1666[U] 1967[6]
Royal Paris (IRE) 9 b g Beau Charmeur (FR)-Raised-in-Paris (Raise You Ten) **1189[3] 1357[F] 1845[P] 2698[5] 2841[7] 3141[P] 3333[4] >78c<**
Royal Piper (NZ) 10 br g 1571[9] 1876[4] 2644[2] 3013[5] 3277[3] 3702[3] (4005) **>86h 46c<**
Royal Pot Black (IRE) 6 b br g Royal Fountain-Polly-Glide (Pollerton) 2661[3] 2844[2] 3090[4] 3853[3] **>60fh<**
Royal Rank (USA) 7 ch g 2958[9] **>53h<**
Royal Rapport 4 ch g Rich Charlie-Miss Camellia (Sonnen Gold) 458[2] (540) **>65h<**
Royal Raven (IRE) 6 b g (1505) 2010[4] 2826[2] 3108[P] **>74h<**
Royal Rosy (IRE) 6 b m **3389a[4] 4356a[P] >93h 95c<**
Royal Ruler (IRE) 6 b m 1555[4] 1998[P] 2868[7] 3977[2] 4466[8] **>68h<**
Royal Salute 5 ch g Royal Vulcan-Nuns Royal (Royal Boxer) 306[7] 865[20]
Royal Santal (IRE) 5 br m Royal Fountain-Santal Air (Ballycipitic) 3525a[11] **>71h<**
Royal Saxon 11 b g **1877[P] 2910[P] 3175[3] 3361[4] (3675) 3899[3] (4068) 4148[2] 4234[P] >106c<**
Royal Scimitar (USA) 5 ch h Diesis-Princess of Man (Green God) 3271[2] 3564[5] **>69h<**
Royal Segos 10 b g **3586[4] 4471[2] >77?h 90c<**
Royal Silver 6 gr g 4801[F] **>66h<**
Royal Spruce (IRE) 6 b g Step Together (USA)-Lacken Lady (Le Moss) 2770[7] 3066[P] 3910[8] **>32h<**
Royal Square (CAN) 11 ch g **2665[P] 2894[7] 3622[6] 3966[6] (4448) 4629[3] >108h 96c<**
Royal Standard 10 b g (1198) 1693[3] 1861[5] **>61h<**
Royal Surprise 10 b g **802[5] 875[2] 1246[4] 1574[7] 1691[3] 2043[4] 2540[P] >56h 83c<**
Royal Team 5 ch g Royal Vulcan-Avado (Cleon) 2696[9] 3820[S] **>42fh<**
Royal Then (FR) 4 ch g Garde Royale-Miss Then (FR) (Carmarthen (FR)) 881[F] 1184[6] 1370[P] 2865[7] **>52h<**
Royal Thimble (IRE) 6 b m (348) (456) 591[4] **>85h<**
Royaltino (IRE) 5 b h (3272) 3613[9] **>93h<**
Royal Toast (IRE) 5 b g Supreme Leader-Hats Off (Manado) 4656[4] **>60fh<**
Royal Vacation 8 b g **(14) (452) 588[2] 650[3] (804) 946[P] (1142) 1266[2] 3974[3] 4167[7] 4336[4] 4710[7] >86h 120c<**
Royal York 5 b m Bustino-Rustle of Silk (General Assembly (USA)) 2898[9] 3315[F] (4249) 4500[3] (4711) (4752) **>75+h<**
Royrace 5 b g Wace (USA)-Royal Tycoon (Tycoon II) 1187[12] 1810[P] 2035[5] 3204[P] 3932[5] 4558[5] 4646[4] 4760[P] **>36h<**
Rozel Bay 4 ch f Beveled (USA)-Salinas (Bay Express) 1205[P]
Rub Al Khali 6 br g Green Ruby (USA)-Nullah (Riverman (USA)) 950[F] 1818[9] **>9h<**
Ruber 10 b g **135[P]** 1290[5] 1654[17] 1854[13] 2507[4] 2654[4] (3032) 3328[2] 3607[9] 4572[7] 4717[4] **>58h 69c<**
Rubins Boy 11 ch g 1372[4] 1798[11] **2829[5] 3176[6] 3472[3] 3675[4] >59h 86c<**
Rubislaw 5 ch g 1687[15] 1825[4] 1988[9] 2800[15] 2957[11] 3311[7] 3612[10] 3976[9] 4296[13] 4500[6] 4708[4] 4755[5] **>41h<**
Ruby Rosa 5 b m Idiot's Delight-Whey (Sallust) 4531[5] **>43fh<**
Rudi's Pride (IRE) 6 b g (356) 582[P] 3942[7] **>77h<**
Rudolphine (IRE) 6 ch g Persian Bold-Ruffling Point (Gorytus (USA)) 2626[4] **>40fh<**
Rule Out The Rest 6 ch g 586[8] (730) 910[5] 1021[3] 1081[4] 3990[F] 4146[5] **>73h<**
Ruling (USA) 11 b g Alleged (USA)-All Dance (USA) (Northern Dancer) 1647[7] 2637[5] 3045[P] **>116h<**
Rumble (USA) 9 ch g **1812[4] 2827[P]**
Rum Customer 6 b g 900[2] 1056[W] **>64h<**
Rumi 6 ch m 157[P] **>67h<**
Rumpelstiltskin 5 ch g Sharpo-Ouija (Silly Season) 3109[6] 3918[3] **>55h<**
Runaway Pete (USA) 7 b g (1148) 1258[6] 1467[2] 1698[2] 1906[2] 2888[6] 3600[19] 3851[2] 4253[2] **>103h 85c<**
Run For Cover (IRE) 5 b m 3895[3] 4388[5] **>57fh<**
Run for Free 13 b g **3813[2] >149dc<**
Run For The Mill 5 b g Primitive Rising (USA)-Brydonna (Good Times (ITY)) 1579[6] 1834[13] 4287[9]
Runhim 5 b g Runton-Lady Ever-so-Sure (Malicious) 3716[8] 3914[18] **>32fh<**
Runic Symbol 6 b g 3344[4] 3632[8] **>50h<**
Running Green 6 b g 3064[P]
Run Up the Flag 10 ch g **1287[4] 2782[7] >127c<**
Runwell Hall 5 b m Celestial Storm (USA)-Two Shots (Dom Racine (FR)) 4161[P]
Run With Joy (IRE) 6 b g **4291[4] 4523[3] 4643[7] 4728[3] >53h 67dc<**
Rupert Belle (IRE) 6 b g 318a[12] **>98h<**
Rupert Blues 5 b g Thowra (FR)-Atlantic Line (Capricorn Line) (4008) 4554[2] **>68fh<**
Rupples 10 b g **63[3] 138[5]** 463[5] **>58h 86c<**
Rushaway 6 b g 4403[6] 4559[2] **>40h<**
Rushen Raider 5 br g Reprimand-Travel Storm (Lord Gayle (USA)) 693[S] 730[P] 2746[11] 2898[16] (4800) **>69h<**
Rushhome 10 gr m **13[R]**
Rushing Burn 11 b m Royal Fountain-Money Penny (Even Money) **3913[8] 4704[9] >50h 68c<**
Rush Me Not (IRE) 4 b g Treasure Kay-Elegant Act (USA) (Shecky Greene (USA)) 2510[14]
Russells Runner 6 ch g 915[8] **>22h<**
Russian Castle (IRE) 8 b g **2544[3] 2630[6] >72h 108c<**
Russian Rascal (IRE) 4 b g Soviet Lad (USA)-Anglo Irish (Busted) 462[5] 1526[3] (1700) 2631[6] (2859) 3002[3] 3995[P] **>87h<**
Rustic Air 10 ch g **1119[3] 1373[4] 1657[8] 2544[2] 2814[3] 3198[2] 3710[4] (4058) 4300[2] >114c<**
Rustic Flight 10 ch g Rustingo-Emerald Flight (Cantab) **3111[P] 3591[4] 3948[3] 4138[D] 4330[4] 4523[6] >53h 44c<**
Rustic Gent (IRE) 9 gr g **1864[P]** 2692[15] **2796[8] 3053[P] 3206[5] 3547[5]** 3674[7] **(3954) 4177[5] 4331[5] 4721[5] 4763[P] >8h 72c<**
Rustic Miss 6 b m Town And Country-Miss Chikara (Majestic Maharaj) 4388[13]
Rustic Ramble 11 br g **4614[P]**
Rustic Warrior 7 b g 1309[P] 2041[10]
Rustino 11 ch g **4763[P] >74h 86dc<**
Rusty Blade 8 b g **3094[P] 3645[9] 3824[3] 4256[P] 4338[3] 4576[2] 4710[3] >61h 101c<**
Rusty Bridge 10 b g **94[5] 158[4] 190[7] 256[U] 3055[3] (3341) 3739[4] 4022[2] 4087[2] 4179[3] (4324) 4473[3] 4560[3] 4805[7] >111c<**
Ruth's Gamble 9 b g 1072[6] 1390[8] 1861[4] 2006[7] 2792[9] 2943[2] (3131) 3663[9] (3811) 3921[2] 4089[11] **>51h<**
Ryder Cup (IRE) 5 b g Orchestra-Vaghe Stelle (ITY) (Looking For) 2676[P] 2927[2] 3845[2] **>71h<**
Ryders Wells 10 gr g **4160[P] 4471[U] >91dc<**
Rye Crossing (IRE) 7 b g **1153[3] >84h 89c<**
Rye Rum (IRE) 6 br g 2958[P] 3453[P] 3723[P] 4513[P]
Ryming Cuplet 12 b g **(3498) 3799[3] 4325[3] 4473[2] >113c<**
Rysanshyn 5 b m Primitive Rising (USA)-Shining Bann (Bargello) 1079[6] **>30h<**
Rythm Rock (IRE) 8 ch g 4547[2] 4650[3] **>75h<**
Ryton Guard 12 br g **130[P] >99dc<**
Ryton Run 12 b g **674[3] 738[P] 826[2] 935[3] 1073[7] 3833[2] 3966[P] 4140[P] 4272[P] 4426[3] >67c<**

S

Saafi (IRE) 6 b g 902[3] 1171[9] 1427[U] 3050[10] 3234[11] 3338[2] 3594[7] 3829[4] 4089[13] 4468[S] 4663[4] **>45h<**
Saahi (USA) 8 b g **4218[3] >71h 84c<**
Saboteuse 5 b m 59[6] 1044[6] 1333[P] 2753[P] 3896[8] 4259[15] **>35h<**
Sabrecool (IRE) 6 b g Lord Americo-Minerstown (IRE) (Miner's Lamp) 1329[20]
Sabu 5 gr g Jumbo Hirt (USA)-Shankhouse Girl (General Ironside) 2924[8] 3939[5] 4288[5] **>43fh<**
Sadler's Pearl 5 b m Thowra (FR)-Queens Pearl (Queen's Hussar) 350[4] **>45h<**
Sadler's Realm 4 b g Sadler's Wells (USA)-Rensaler (USA) (Stop The Music (USA)) 3820[7]

4282[2] 4626[2] **>68h<**
Safecracker 4 ch g Sayf El Arab (USA)-My Polished Corner (IRE) (Tate Gallery (USA)) 3359[16] 3601[P] 3927[3] (4137) 4333[2] 4663[6] **>53h<**
Safeglide (IRE) 7 b g 1317[7] 1964[4] **2841[5] 3145[5] >73h 94c<**
Safe Secret 6 b m 888[P] **>48dh<**
Safety (USA) 10 b g **(328) 403[2]** 552[3] 751[2] **975[3] >73h 95?c<**
Safety Factor (IRE) 9 gr g Strong Gale-Myra Grey (Upper Case (USA)) **3393[F] 3608[F]**
Safety Tip 5 b m Damister (USA)-Unexpected Guest (Be My Guest (USA)) 1084[5] 1579[13] 1687[16] 1851[P]
Saffaah (USA) 10 ch g **470[P] >93?c<**
Safwan 5 b g Primo Dominie-French Plait (Thatching) 4506[P] 4650[10]
Sahel (IRE) 9 b g Green Desert (USA)-Fremanche (FR) (Jim French (USA)) 1132[3] 1375[9] 1873[6] 2578[9] **>55h<**
Sahhar 4 ch c Sayf El Arab (USA)-Native Magic (Be My Native (USA)) 2815[4] **>59h<**
Sail by the Stars 8 b m (1176) (1698) (2069) **(3173) 3697[U] >97h 97+c<**
Sailep (FR) 5 ch g 834[3] (1168) 1451[2] 1726[2] 2040[3] 2680[2] **>77h<**
Sailor Jim 10 gr g **1119[4] 1279[F] 1641[3] 2075[2] 2762[4] 3071[2] 3349[4] 3729[2] 4013[8] 4475[3] >108c<**
Sailormaite 6 ch g Komaite (USA)-Marina Plata (Julio Mariner) 4749[3] **>55h<**
Sails Legend 6 b h 1388[5] **>81h<**
Saint Amigo 5 gr g Presidium-Little Token (Shack (USA)) 262[6] 396[5] 1276[8] 1413[12] **>46h<**
Saint Bene't (IRE) 9 b g **206[3] 351[5] 494[4] 957[8] 3924[3] 4324[P] 4735[5] >75h 88dc<**
Saint Ciel (USA) 9 b h 1188[2] (1439) 2048[6] 2779[10] 3164[7] 3421[12] 4187[12] 4307[11] 4474[4] 4525[5] **>69h<**
Saint Keyne 7 b h **2007[P] 2693[P] >88dh<**
Sakbah (USA) 8 b m 17[F] 474[2] 587[4] 642[3] 673[4] 1417[8] **1829[7] 2672[P] 3015[8] >49h 59c<**
Salaman (FR) 5 b g Saumarez-Merry Sharp (Sharpen Up) 2825[7] 3171[3] **>71?h<**
Salcombe Harbour (NZ) 13 ch g **68[P] 975[7] 1445[P] 3179[7] 3456[4] 3756[P] >57c<**
Salem Beach 5 b m Strong Gale-Ellen Greaves (Deep Run) 1692[17] 1973[4] 2180[3] 3098[9] 4075[11] 4144[6] 4514[7] **>25h<**
Salisong 8 gr g 1010[7] **>62h<**
Salix 5 ch g Vital Season-Last Ditch (Ben Novus) 3235[12] 3895[13]
Salkeld King (IRE) 5 b g 735[6] 893[8] 4390[3] 4759[2] **>56h<**
Sallow Glen 11 b g 4552[8] 4726[4] **>59h<**
Sally Scally 5 ch m Scallywag-Petite Cone (Celtic Cone) 3767[3] 4388[4] **>58fh<**
Sally Smith 8 b m Alias Smith (USA)-Salira (Double Jump) 10[P]
Sally's Twins 4 b f Dowsing (USA)-Bird of Love (Ela-Mana-Mou) 1935[3] 2772[6] 3628[4] **>65h<**
Salman (USA) 11 b g 3666[4] 4162[4] 4765[3] 4789[8] **>67h 105c<**
Salmon Breeze (IRE) 6 ch g 1042[2] (1539) (2746) 4052[P] (4698) **>92h<**
Salmon Cellar (IRE) 4 ch g Roselier (FR)-Perfect Excuse (Certingo) 3716[5] 3914[7] 4421[4] **>60fh<**
Salmon Poutcher 8 ch m Brando-Heythrop VII (Damsire Unregistered) **4730[P]**
Salsian 4 b f Salse (USA)-Phylae (Habitat) 4343[3] 4620[13]
Saltis (IRE) 5 ch g Salt Dome (USA)-Mrs Tittlemouse (Nonoalco (USA)) 156[11] 649[3] 819[3] 978[2] 1256[8] 1814[3] 3985[11] 4091[3] **>58h<**
Salty Girl (IRE) 4 b f Scenic-Sodium's Niece (Northfields (USA)) 3174[6] 3404[3] 3601[5] **>69h<**
Salvo 6 ch g **3765[U] >72h<**
Samakaan (IRE) 4 b c Darshaan-Samarzana (USA) (Blushing Groom (FR)) 1634[4] **>77+h<**
Samaka Hara (IRE) 5 b g 812[4] 955[8] 1042[4] 1471[5] **>74h<**
Samanid (IRE) 5 b h 341[2] 1152[5] 1353[3] 2074[5] 2771[8] 3049[2] (3137) 3572[10] 3995[4] 4187[7] 4315[2] 4608[2] 4768[4] **>82h<**
Samara Song 4 ch g Savahra Sound-Hosting (Thatching) 1377[3] 1526[6] 1595[9] **>67h<**
Samba Sharply 6 b g Rambo Dancer (CAN)-Sharper Still (Sharpen Up) 262[2] 955[2] 1059[3] **>72h<**
Sam Champagne (IRE) 5 b g Lafontaine (USA)-Bumps A Daisy (Windjammer (USA)) 1692[16] **>22fh<**
Same Difference (IRE) 9 b g 221[5] 3737[P] **>76c<**
Samite (IRE) 6 br g Detroit Sam (FR)-French Note (Eton Rambler) 1296[20] 1692[24] 2042[P]
Samlee (IRE) 8 b g (800) (973) **1287[3] 1662[U] (1784) 2758[2] 3046[4] (3573) 4213[2] >91h 131c<**
Sammorello (IRE) 6 b g 1323[6] 1795[9] 2746[9] (3190) 3355[P] 3683[2] (3834) 4309[5] 4563[P] **>56h<**
Sam Rockett 4 b g Petong-Art Deco (Artaius (USA)) 1519[6] 1872[10] 2070[10] (2574) 2692[14] 2897[8] **>73+h<**
Sams Heritage 13 b g **4551[2] 4804[P] >106c<**
Samsword 8 ch g Broadsword (USA)-True Divine (True Song) **3455[P]**
Samuel Scott 4 b g Shareef Dancer (USA)-Revisit (Busted) 3494[2] **>84h<**
Samuel Wilderspin 5 b g Henbit (USA)-Littoral (Crash Course) (3170) 3619[7] 4215[6] **>89fh<**
Sandford Thyne (IRE) 7 ch m Good Thyne (USA)-Dippy Girl (Sandford Lad) 69[U] 129[7] 185[8] **>24h<**
San Diego Charger (IRE) 6 ch g 949[6] 1145[11] 1262[5] 1330[4] 1599[6] **1875[U] 2037[5] 3762[F] >63h 56c<**
Sand King (NZ) 11 gr g **421[P] 685[P] >50h 80c< (DEAD)**
Sandrift 8 ch m 2920[P] 3481[6] 3908[5] 4283[2] **>59h<**
Sandro 8 b g **472[P]** 655[P] 950[13] **>50h<**
Sands of Gold (IRE) 9 ch g **3208[2] 3357[5] 4015[4] (4704) >97c<**
Sands Point 7 b g 792[P] 1174[P] **>69h<**
Sandville Lad 5 gr g 2811[15] 3747[2] 3977[P] 4403[P] 4559[P]
Sandybraes 12 ch g **4634[2] 4748[P] >107?c<**
Sandy Forest Lady (IRE) 8 b m **321a[6] >66h 88c<**
Sandys Girl (IRE) 9 b m **846a[4] >29h 82c<**
San Giorgio 8 b g **639[4] 726[P]** 1031[2] 1363[3] **>72h 94dc<**
Sanmartino (IRE) 5 b h Salse (USA)-Oscura (USA) (Caro) (2112) (2668) (3298) 3597[6] (4048) **>136h<**
San Remo 10 b g **4607[4] >72c<**
Sans Pere 4 b g Shadow Minister (USA)-Creetown Sally (Creetown) 501[8]
Santa Barbara (IRE) 6 b m Henbit (USA)-Fiery Rose (Boreen (FR)) 1692[11] 1913[7] **>54fh<**
Santa Concerto (IRE) 8 ch g **(2767) 2919[2] >94h 110c<**
Santaray 11 ch g **3470[3] 3842[3] 3988[5] >76h 72c<**
Santella Boy (USA) 5 b g (60) 131[3] 257[2] (479) (598) 721[4] 3702[2] 3980[F] 4178[4] **(4661) >85h 96+c<**
Santella Cape 4 b g Alzao (USA)-Kijafa (USA) (Chief's Crown (USA)) 4465[F] 4651[3] 4801[2] **>65h<**
Sapphire Son (IRE) 5 ch g Maelstrom Lake-Gluhwein (Ballymoss) 4441[8] 4567[4] 4645[4] **>51h<**
Saracen Prince (USA) 5 ch g 7[4] 137[6] 209[4] 1537[4] 1874[3] **>65h<**
Saracen's Boy (IRE) 9 gr g **359[4] 503[3] 547[U] >60c< (DEAD)**
Sarah Supreme (IRE) 6 b m Supreme Leader-Rusheen's Girl (Dusky Boy) 4360a[11] **>68fh<**
Saras Delight 5 b g Idiot's Delight-Lady Bess (Straight Lad) 1966[16] 4009[6] **>41fh<**
Sarenacare (IRE) 5 b g Lafontaine (USA)-Brown Foam (Horage) 25[6] 1820[5] 2642[7] **>56fh<**
Sarmatian (USA) 6 br g 12[2] 214[2] (538) 638[2] (701) 908[2] (1358) 1502[3] 4246[6] 4482[5] 4702[2] **>90h<**
Sarona Smith 10 ch m **4716[4]**
Sartorius 11 b g **(20) >110c<**
Saskia's Hero 10 ch g **(15) 63[2] (104) 215[F] >119+c<**
Sassiver (USA) 7 b g 62[7] **(206) 290[2] 333[3] 1371[4] 1582[P]** 2670[4] 2828[3] 3201[10] (3545) 3709[3] (3935) 4132[3] **>98?h 84c<**
Sassy Street (IRE) 4 b g Danehill (USA)-Sassy Lane (Sassafras (FR)) 3007[P] 3964[7] 4465[5] **>44h<**
Satcotino (IRE) 6 b m Satco (FR)-Autumn Bounty (Plano (FR)) 1505[4] 2746[3] 3355[3] (3603) **>76h<**
Satellite Express (IRE) 4 b g Henbit (USA)-Waffling (Lomond (USA)) 3574[8] 3895[9] **>54fh<**
Satpura 5 b h Nishapour (FR)-Madiyla (Darshaan) 4156[9]
Saturiba (USA) 4 b g Fighting Fit (USA)-My Popsicle (USA) (Raja Baba (USA)) 3544[13]
Saucy Dancer 4 ch f Chilibang-Silent Dancer (Quiet Fling (USA)) 1953[15] 2622[14] 3468[8] 4137[4] **>3h<**
Saucy Nun (IRE) 5 ch m Orchestra-Port Flyer (Yashgan) 1275[6] 3006[9] 4508[4] 4625[11] **>26h<**
Saucy Soul 4 ch g Ballacashtal (CAN)-Ninotchka (Niniski (USA)) 294[P]
Saucy's Wolf 7 ch g 1573[12] **1787[F] 2039[P] 3565[P] 3891[R]**
Sausalito Boy 9 b g **1787[F]** 2659[P] 2797[P] 3114[P] **4232[R]**
Saving Bond (IRE) 5 ch g 1485a[3] 4117a[4] **>110h<**
Savoy 10 ch g **3397[F] 4469[2] (4579) >93h 112c<**
Savuti (IRE) 8 ch g **846a[6] >66h 110c<**
Sawaab (USA) 5 b g Storm Cat (USA)-Sweet Valentine (USA) (Honey Jay (USA)) 3946[2] **>68fh<**
Saxon Blade 9 b g 69[P] **213[P] 254[U] 652[6] 738[8] 860[6] >52c<**
Saxon Magic 7 ch m **206[2]** 4163[6] **>37dh 79c<**
Saxon Mead 7 ch g Saxon Farm-Great Chance (General Ironside) 788[7] 1171[8] 1427[P] **1875[F] 2795[F] 3188[F]** 3932[2] 4243[3] **>55h<**
Sayin Nowt 9 b m Nicholas Bill-Greyburn (Saintly Song) **(3476) >89c<**
Sayitagain 5 b g Bering-Casey (Caerleon (USA)) 73[P] 2678[15] 2753[P]
Saymore 11 ch g 868[7] 952[6] 1121[5] 1299[10] 2006[3] 2862[3] **(3001) 3278[5] 3966[4] >52h 91c<**
Sayraf Dancer (IRE) 8 b g 1049[12] 1344[9] **>66h< (DEAD)**
Scale Down (IRE) 8 b g Lancastrian-Willie Pat (Pitpan) **3459[F]** 4376[P] 4476[P]
Scally Beau 6 ch g Scallywag-Torobelle (Torus) 4205[6] 4575[6]
Scally Blue 6 gr g Scallywag-Blue Gift (Hasty Word) 4538[4] **>36fh<**
Scally Hicks 6 ch m 1438[5] 2053[9] 2763[8] 3004[6] 3222[8] **>36h<**
Scallymill 7 gr m Scallywag-Melfio Miss (Town Crier) 293[9] 337[5] 680[6]
Scalp 'em (IRE) 9 b g Commanche Run-

Supremely Royal (Crowned Prince (USA)) 469^{4} 594^{5} 879^{9} 913^{6} 1198^{4} 1446^{3} 2567^{P} 2820^{12} 3442^{16} 3757^{2} 3921^{5} 4401^{3} 4807^{9} **>41h<**

Scamallach (IRE) 7 gr m 18^{3} 77^{2} (401) 593^{4} 659^{3} (813) 1062^{3} **1320^{F} 1865^{2}** 2941^{6} **>65h 86c< (DEAD)**

Scaraben 9 b g **349^{2} >79dh 95c<**

Scarba 9 b g 734^{2} 894^{3} 1849^{4} (2915) 3157^{F} 4147^{4} **>80h<**

Scarra Darragh (IRE) 7 b m Phardante (FR)-The Black Rattler (Black Minstrel) **4618^{6} >27c<**

Scathebury 4 b g Aragon-Lady Bequick (Sharpen Up) 2622^{11} 2705^{10} **>24h<**

Scboo 8 b g 1276^{P} 2805^{P}

Scene Stealer 4 b f Scenic-Sindos (Busted) 654^{P}

Scenic Waters 5 b m Scenic-Money Supply (Brigadier Gerard) 3552^{5} 3764^{3} 3937^{3} 4181^{9} **>59h<**

Schnozzle (IRE) 6 b g 1663^{7} 1816^{3} 1984^{6} 3679^{3} 4226^{P} 4525^{3} **>64h<**

Scholar Green 5 b g Green Adventure (USA)-Quelle Chemise (Night Shift (USA)) 1124^{16} 1665^{7} 2066^{14}

School of Science 7 b g 1969^{5} 2505^{5} 2800^{11} **>43h<**

Schwartzndigger (IRE) 7 b g 1178^{8} 1369^{P} **>21h<**

Scobie Boy (IRE) 9 ch g **3638^{5} >95h 122c<**

Scoresheet (IRE) 7 ch g **(1552) 2679^{2} 3331^{2} 3565^{F} >67h 111c<**

Scoring Pedigree (IRE) 5 b g King Luthier-Quick Romance (Lucky Brief) 1336^{D} (1986) 3304^{3} 3619^{4} 4360a^{14} **>92fh<**

Scorpion Bay 9 b g **1320^{F} 1563^{U}** 2905^{7} 3205^{2} 3442^{P} **>35h< (DEAD)**

Scotby (BEL) 7 gr g (1422) 1568^{4} 1835^{F} (2656) 2880^{8} 3156^{2} 3541^{2} 4005^{5} **>89h<**

Scotoni 11 ch g **1202^{5} 1598^{2} 1951^{P} 2894^{6} 3232^{2} 3742^{3} 4385^{5} >87h 99dc<**

Scottish Bambi 9 ch g **1254^{3} (1449) 1664^{2} (1815) 2037^{2} 2569^{P} (3336) 3571^{3} (3678) >69h 116c<**

Scottish Hero 4 b c North Briton-Tartan Pimpernel (Blakeney) 2070^{6}

Scottish Park 8 ch m Scottish Reel-Moss Agate (Alias Smith (USA)) 408^{W} 902^{7} 1857^{6} 3889^{5} 4548^{P} **>26h<**

Scottish Wedding 7 b m 1034^{4} 1630^{8} 2038^{3} (2882) (2941) 3112^{4} 3615^{25} 4093^{P} **>64h<**

Scotton Banks (IRE) 8 b g **1157^{4} 1513^{4} 1923^{3} 2636^{4}** 2900^{6} **>88dh 153dc<**

Scotton Green 6 ch g 1263^{5} 1524^{2} **>54h<**

Scott's Risk 7 b g Risk Me (FR)-Madam de Seul (Pas de Seul) 1187^{P}

Scoundrel 6 gr g (865) (980) (2822) **>69h<**

Scrabble 8 ch m **1038^{P} >72h< (DEAD)**

Scrabo View (IRE) 9 ch g 6^{3} 95^{7} 184^{3} **283^{3} (421) 535^{2} (875) 1307^{5} 1778^{U} 4503^{5} 4710^{5} >80h 100c<**

Scraptastic 6 ch g Scallywag-Rusty To Reign (General Ironside) **3922^{F}**

Scribbler 11 ch g **3153^{12} 3492^{5} 3699^{F} 4074^{P} 4306^{4} >83h 120dc<**

Script 6 b g 502^{3} 552^{4} **722^{6} 828^{3}** 1040^{8} 1962^{9} 2792^{4} (2866) 3207^{10} 3411^{4} 3577^{3} 3811^{5} 4321^{5} 4562^{3} **>43h 66c<**

Scud Missile (IRE) 6 b or gr g 692^{3} 816^{10} 1074^{6} 1207^{5} 3935^{2} (4252) 4439^{2} 4734^{2} **>75h<**

Sea Barn 14 ch g 3722^{6} 3949^{6} **>52h<**

Sea Breaker (IRE) 9 b g **14^{2} >79h 102c<**

Seabright Saga 7 b g Ra Nova-Seabright Smile (Pitpan) **3546^{P} 3667^{F}** 3944^{5}

Seabrook Lad 6 b g 2053^{4} 2662^{F} 2812^{7} 3222^{2} (3937) 4166^{4} 4768^{6} **>67h<**

Seachange 8 gr g **1326^{P} >85?h 94c< (DEAD)**

Seachest 8 ch m **1300^{6} 4330^{3} >68?c<**

Sea God 6 ch g 137^{2} 293^{5} 467^{2} 687^{4} 1027^{4} 3346^{11} **>68h<**

Seahawk Retriever 8 ch g **(423) 486^{2} 590^{2} 601^{3} 722^{3} >23h 82c<**

Seal King 12 ch g **130^{P} 180^{P} 484^{4} 604^{5} 728^{F} >83c<**

Sea Patrol 10 b g **(4314) 4549^{5} >61h 83c<**

Searchlight (IRE) 9 ch g (129) 189^{4} **>75h<**

Seasamacamile 10 b m **554^{3} 595^{6} (817) 1038^{7} 1075^{3} 1385^{3} >87c<**

Sea Search 10 ch g **70^{8} >78h 94c<**

Seasonal Splendour (IRE) 7 b m 1188^{5} 1727^{2} **>96h<**

Sea Tarth 6 gr m Nicholas Bill-Seajan (Mandamus) (4632) **>61fh<**

Seattle Alley (USA) 4 b g Seattle Dancer (USA)-Alyanaabi (USA) (Roberto (USA)) 1387^{6} 2622^{8} 2784^{3} 3566^{3} 3634^{7} (3809) 3927^{2} (4395) **>90h<**

Sea Victor 5 b g Slip Anchor-Victoriana (USA) (Storm Bird (CAN)) (1921) (2642) 3163^{9} 3412^{3} 3615^{26} **>97h<**

Second Call 8 ch m **(1340) 1475^{4} (1677) 2843^{2} 3227^{3} 3697^{5} >108h 115c<**

Second Colours (USA) 7 b or br g Timeless Moment (USA)-Ruffled Silk (USA) (Our Hero (USA)) 603^{3} 748^{2} 915^{3} **>67h<**

Second Fiddle (IRE) 7 ch m 3366^{9} **>26h<**

Seconds Away 6 b g 1047^{12} 1141^{5} 1703^{10} 1969^{2} 2629^{11} 2800^{12} 3091^{10} 4259^{P} **>46h<**

Second Schedual 12 b g **314a^{4} 763a^{3} 1003a^{4} 1495a^{4} 2348a^{10} 3261a^{P} >132c<**

Second Step (IRE) 6 b g 1165^{3} 1424^{6} 1726^{8} 4205^{F} **>71h< (DEAD)**

Secretary of State 11 b g **(4) 93^{3} >76h 91c<**

Secret Bay 8 b g Zambrano-Secret Storm (Secret Ace) **(4155) (4317) >110++c<**

Secret Bid (IRE) 7 ch g **1728^{2} 2819^{7} 3537^{U}** 3737^{P} **>98c<**

Secret Castle 9 b g 128^{P} **4228^{P} >51h< (DEAD)**

Secret Gift 4 ch f Cadeaux Genereux-Triste Oeil (USA) (Raise A Cup (USA)) 1444^{P} (3889) 4229^{5} **>54h<**

Secret Serenade 6 b g 737^{4} 1251^{P} **>30h< (DEAD)**

Secret Service (IRE) 5 b g Classic Secret (USA)-Mystery Bid (Auction Ring (USA)) (2953) 3416^{2} 3912^{5} **>73h<**

Secret Spring (FR) 5 b g (1375) 1594^{2} 2112^{2} (2624) 4061^{12} 4275^{F} **>100h<**

Secret Truth 8 ch m Nestor-Another Nitty (Country Retreat) **4545^{P} 4799^{P}**

Securon Gale (IRE) 5 br g Strong Gale-Thousand Flowers (Take A Reef) 3574^{14} **>36fh<**

Sedvicta 5 b g (1690) **>80h<**

See Enough 9 ch g **2007^{4} 2658^{3} 2881^{F} 3162^{8} 3563^{P} >144dh 99dc<**

Seeking Destiny (IRE) 4 b g Two Timing (USA)-Heads We Called (IRE) (Bluebird (USA)) 688^{12} **>43h<**

Seeking Gold (IRE) 8 b m **(1138) 1313^{4} (1668) 1850^{2} (2614) 2767^{2} 2956^{3} 3395^{4} >100c<**

Seek The Faith (USA) 8 ch g **1682^{5} 2879^{2} (4177) 4553^{3} >116c<**

See Minnow 4 b f Riverwise (USA)-Shepani (New Member) 2911^{8} 3433^{10} 3895^{10} **>41fh<**

See More Angels 6 br m 3808^{12} **>18fh<**

See More Business (IRE) 7 b g **(1259) 1758a^{2} 2994a^{2} 3302^{F} >101+h 143c<**

See More Ghosts (IRE) 6 ch g 1654^{13} 1842^{4} **>55h<**

See Prosperity 5 b g Impecunious-Shepani (New Member) 3767^{7} 4143^{4} 4433^{10} **>31fh<**

See You Always (IRE) 7 b g 463^{8} **584^{5} 704^{4} 1051^{P} 1348^{U} 1578^{13}** 2505^{11} 2629^{10} **2786^{9}** 3485^{13} **>27h 59c<**

Segala (IRE) 6 b g Petorius-Cerosia (Pitskelly) 1030^{8} 1187^{10} 1499^{5} 1772^{8} 2044^{4} 3064^{5} **>59h<**

Selatan (IRE) 5 ch g 2666^{7} 3269^{3} 3562^{3} (3807) **>89h<**

Seldom But Severe (IRE) 7 br g 1139^{9} **1653^{8} 2919^{6} 3067^{P} 3306^{3} 3715^{5} >33h 72c<**

Selectric (IRE) 6 b g 1052^{11} 1305^{P} 2697^{P}

Seminole Wind 6 gr g 1375^{10} 1729^{12} 2008^{P} 3442^{8} 3683^{14} 3735^{3} **>51h<**

Senna Blue 12 ch g **3489^{7} >57c<**

Senora d'Or 7 br m Le Coq d'Or-Eustacia Vye (Viking Chief) **1574^{6} 1845^{3} >69c<**

Senor El Betrutti (IRE) 8 gr g **1133^{5} 1520^{P} 2621^{3} 2879^{6} (3169) (3496) (3815) 4013^{6} >94h 144c<**

Sense of Value 8 br m **1252^{7} 2795^{10} >77h 75?c<**

Sentosa Star (IRE) 6 b g 3523a^{2} 4109a^{4} **>114h<**

Seod Rioga (IRE) 8 br g **1035^{3} 1934^{P}** 2644^{10} **2894^{2} (3916) 4185^{F} 4247^{3} 4609^{4} 4802^{3} >89h 121c<**

September Breeze (IRE) 6 b m 1341^{F} 1777^{3} 2861^{4} 3355^{5} 3706^{3} **>72h<**

Serafin (POL) 13 b g Frombork-Secesja (POL) (Antiquarian) **53a^{2} 851a^{2} >112c<**

Serenity Prayer (USA) 7 ch g Private Thoughts (USA)-Three Nymphs (USA) (Three Bagger) 1559^{2} 1919^{3} **>117h<**

Serenus (USA) 4 b c Sunshine Forever (USA)-Curl And Set (USA) (Nijinsky (CAN)) 1014^{3} 1269^{5} (1706) (1935) 3174^{F} 3298^{6} 3634^{14} **>86h<**

Sergent Kay 7 b g K-Battery-Kindly Night (Midsummer Night II) 2546^{10} **2672^{5} >48h 78c<**

Serious 7 b g **1831^{7}** (3987) 4130^{F} 4271^{8} 4741^{4} **>87h 51c<**

Serious Money (USA) 12 ch g Plugged Nickle (USA)-Broadway Hit (Hittite Glory) **4614^{R}**

Serious Option (IRE) 6 b g 2547^{19} 3205^{P} 4226^{P} 4440^{2} **>42h< (DEAD)**

Sesame Seed (IRE) 9 b g 3286^{5} 3615^{23} **>90h<**

Set-Em-Alight 7 b g 17^{F} (212) 259^{7} **>50h<**

Set the Fashion 8 br g Green Desert (USA)-Prelude (Troy) 1059^{F} 1297^{P}

Seven Brooks 7 ch g 73^{7} 890^{7} **>56h<**

Seven Crowns (USA) 4 b c Chief's Crown (USA)-Ivory Dance (USA) (Sir Ivor) 736^{6} 1014^{7} 2705^{P} 3205^{P} 3442^{P} 3735^{8} **>34h<**

Seven Four Seven 6 b m Jumbo Hirt (USA)-Star of the Ocean (Callernish) 2750^{16} 3021^{12} 3364^{14}

Seven Potato More (IRE) 7 b g Salluceva-Why Don't Ye (Illa Laudo) 1250^{12} 1640^{12} 4376^{11} **>44h<**

Seventeens Lucky 5 gr g Touch of Grey-Westminster Waltz (Dance In Time (CAN)) 1517^{7} **>42h<**

Seventh Lock 11 b g Oats-Barge Mistress (Bargello) **3631^{P}**

Seven Towers (IRE) 8 b g **1293^{5} (1670) (2616) (3162) (3699) >105+h 150c<**

Seven Wells 5 ch g 24^{4} 133^{10} 287^{3} 492^{3} 718^{6} 931^{2} **>60h<**

Severn Gale 7 br m 641^{7} 888^{3} (1086) 1330^{2} (1727) (1954) 2779^{3} 2952^{F} 4510^{3} 4729^{F} **>71h<**

Severn Invader 12 b g **(4457) >93+c<**

Sevso 8 b m 3344^{6} 3681^{3} (3980) 4172^{3} 4464^{2} **>71h<**

Seymour Fiddles 6 b m King's Holt-Kidcello (Bybicello) **4076^{F}**

Seymour's Double **6** b g 1412^{5} 1795^{7} 2064^{7} >**39h**<

Seymour Spy **8** b g **1038^{8} 3285^{P}** >**56h 98c**<

Seymours Secret **5** b m Seymour Hicks (FR)-Stanton Queen (Most Secret) 4407^{12} >**28fh**<

Seymourswift **7** b m (1200) 1565^{F} >**70h**<

Seymour Who **4** b g Seymour Hicks (FR)-Normazoo (Rhodomantade) 3853^{12} >**27fh**<

Shaagni Ana (USA) **6** ch g 2669^{17} 2905^{P}

Shaarid (USA) **9** b g **56^{P} 1272^{3} 1515^{2}** >**80dh 113c**<

Shaa Spin **5** b m Shaadi (USA)-Tight Spin (High Top) 467^{5} >**41h**<

Shabo Shabo **5** ch m Soldier Rose-Shaenas Girl VII (Damsire Unregistered) 3970^{P}

Shadirwan (IRE) **6** b h 1905^{5} 2624^{F} >**54h**<

Shadow Leader **6** br g Tragic Role (USA)-Hush it Up (Tina's Pet) (2825) (3041) (3595) (4212) >**126+h**<

Shadows of Silver **9** gr m Carwhite-Mimika (Lorenzaccio) 2898^{F}

Shady Emma **5** ch m 636^{6} 1250^{P} 2034^{P} >**38h**<

Shahgram (IRE) **9** gr g 2631^{5} **3001^{10}** >**76h 87c**<

Shahrani **5** b g Lear Fan (USA)-Windmill Princess (Gorytus (USA)) (105) (186) (337) (410) (682) (902) 1196^{P} 1418^{6} 2932^{8} 3549^{3} 3589^{4} 3999^{3} 4181^{4} >**83h**<

Shalholme **7** ch m 813^{6} 913^{11} >**35h**<

Shalik (IRE) **7** ch g 327^{S} 353^{3} (406) 632^{P} **674^{2} 744^{6}** 950^{12} **1009^{2} 1714^{4} 1965^{5} 2054^{P}** >**41h 82dc**<

Shallow River (IRE) **6** b g 1294^{7} **1632^{3} 1850^{6}** 2915^{15} >**74h 81c**<

Shamarphil **11** b m **1202^{3} 1385^{5} 1697^{6} 1983^{4} 3153^{9} 3492^{4} 3675^{2}** >**95c**<

Shanagarry (IRE) **8** b g **2848a^{P} 3128a^{3} 4362a^{3}** >**142c**<

Shanagore Hill (IRE) **7** ch g Torus-Port La Joie (Charlottown) **3957^{F}**

Shanagore Warrior (IRE) **5** b g Arapahos (FR)-Our Linda (Proverb) 1695^{4} 2071^{6} 2656^{3} 3088^{4} 3689^{3} >**66h**<

Shanakee **10** b g 3110^{7} 3338^{4} 3620^{P} >**47h**<

Shanavogh **6** b g (1021) 1161^{2} (1640) 2766^{4} (3307) 3696^{3} >**81h**<

Shanes Hero (IRE) **7** ch g 2603a^{19} >**99h**<

Shankar (IRE) **6** gr g **3229^{F}** 3572^{16} 3816^{3} (4061) 4357a^{2} 4397^{3} >**124h**<

Shankorak **10** b g **321a^{8}** 2345a^{14} >**125h 95c**<

Shannon Gale (IRE) **5** b g 1485a^{7} >**77fh**<

Shannon Glen **11** b g **28^{5}** >**93h 105c**<

Shannon Lad (IRE) **7** ch g 1065^{2} 1453^{12} 1814^{7} 4091^{4} >**65h**<

Shannon Shoon (IRE) **5** b g Zaffaran (USA)-Carrick Shannon (Green Shoon) 2904^{11} 3142^{14} 3330^{7} >**18fh**<

Shanoora (IRE) **4** gr f Don't Forget Me-Shalara (Dancers Image (USA)) 1149^{8} 1413^{7} 1908^{8} >**36h**<

Shared Risk **5** ch g Risk Me (FR)-Late Idea (Tumble Wind (USA)) 1030^{7} 1208^{2} 3014^{4} 3159^{3} >**63h**<

Shareef Star **9** b g **3928^{P} 4457^{F}**

Share Options (IRE) **6** b br g (910) 1802^{F} 2053^{5} (2627) 2900^{2} 3368^{4} 4204^{P} 4418^{P} >**82h**<

Shariakanndi (FR) **5** b g 1329^{9} 2073^{2} 2656^{4} 3171^{5} 4182^{7} >**65h**<

Sharley Cop **5** ch m Lord Bud-Buckby Folly (Netherkelly) 3691^{15} >**26h**<

[illegible]armoor **5** b m 1417^{10} 1628^{4} 2006^{P} 2818^{8} [illegible]^{6} 3284^{12} 3313^{14} >**47h**<

[illegible]mand **4** ch g Sharpo-Bluish (USA) [illegible] 2060^{U} 3359^{7} 3544^{4} (4144) 4220^{4} (4233) 4508^{P} >**83h**<

Sharp Elver (IRE) **5** ch m Sharp Victor (USA)-Blue Elver (Kings Lake (USA)) 1394^{P} 1594^{11} >**6h**<

Sharp Holly (IRE) **5** b m 497^{8} 600^{P} >**31h**<

Sharpical **5** b g Sharpo-Magical Spirit (Top Ville) (1830) 2624^{2} (3672) 4010^{2} 4348a^{F} 4400^{2} >**98h**<

Sharp Sand **7** ch g 2785^{11} 3024^{P} >**57h**<

Sharp Sensation **7** ch g 684^{5} **744^{3}** 4505^{5} 4712^{4} >**67h 77c**<

Sharp Thrill **6** ch g 603^{9} 913^{5} 1072^{2} 1390^{3} 3677^{3} 3933^{2} >**53h**<

Sharp Thyne (IRE) **7** b g Good Thyne (USA)-Cornamucla (Lucky Guy) 4001^{P} (4376) 4622^{4} >**74h**<

Sharp to Oblige **10** ch g Dublin Taxi-Please Oblige (Le Levanstell) 4389^{B}

Sharrow Bay (NZ) **10** ch g **3134^{F} 3759^{P}**

Shavano **5** ch g 2648^{8}

Shawkey (IRE) **4** ch g Nashwan (USA)-Rosia Bay (High Top) 3297^{10} 3703^{F} 4414^{P} >**24fh**<

Shawwell **10** ro g **1022^{3} 1264^{4} 1691^{2} 1989^{3} 3314^{3} 4153^{2} 4408^{2} 4753^{6}** >**65h 80c**<

Sheath Kefaah **4** ch c Kefaah (USA)-Wasslaweyeh (USA) (Damascus (USA)) (501) 640^{7} 1953^{3} >**59h**<

Shebang (IRE) **5** b g Be My Native (USA)-Polly's Cottage (Pollerton) 1926^{2} 2572^{2} 3149^{3} 3676^{2} >**71fh**<

Shedansar (IRE) **5** b g 648^{11} 3668^{7} 3921^{12} >**23h**<

Sheecky **6** b g 1860^{8} 2813^{2} 3072^{F} 3985^{5} (4086) >**67?h**<

Sheelin Lad (IRE) **9** ch g **2011^{P} 2681^{P} 3223^{6} (3622) (3729) 3961^{4}** >**98c**<

Sheemore (IRE) **4** b g Don't Forget Me-Curie Abu (Crofter (USA)) 4570^{2} 4718^{4} >**43?h**<

Sheepcote Hill (IRE) **6** b g Corvaro (USA)-Misty Boosh (Tarboosh (USA)) 2811^{4} >**48fh**<

Sheephaven **13** b g **3729^{P}** >**105?c**<

Sheep Stealer **9** gr g 1984^{7} 3589^{7} 4332^{2} >**58h 95?c**<

Sheer Ability **11** b g **1937^{P} 2754^{7} 3153^{P}** >**113?c**<

Sheer Jest **12** b g **3439^{P}** >**127c**<

Sheet Lightning **5** b g Lightning Dealer-White Linen (Nishapour (FR)) 2012^{10} 2811^{9} 3149^{14}

Shekels (IRE) **6** ch g 1457^{3} 2690^{4} (3703) 4224^{2} 4734^{W} >**90h**<

Shellhouse (IRE) **9** ch g 97^{P} 128^{9} 211^{6} >**78h**<

Shelton Abbey **11** br g 509^{4} (878) 892^{3} 3478^{8} 3607^{2} 4296^{6} (4501) 4712^{3} >**53h 61dc**<

Shepherds Rest (IRE) **5** b g 1860^{3} (2067) 2755^{U} 2871^{2} 3177^{2} 3421^{8} >**83h**<

Sheriff **6** b g 493^{4} >**95h**<

Sheriffmuir **8** b g **1728^{P} 1963^{8}** (3076) (3228) (3421) 4053^{2} 4210^{2} 4398^{2} >**108h 62c**<

Shers Delight (IRE) **7** b g 31^{9} 1339^{4} 1542^{3} 1779^{2} >**67h**<

Sherwood Boy **8** ch g **61^{P} 389^{3}** >**81h**<

She Said No **5** ch m Beveled (USA)-She Said Yes (Local Suitor (USA)) 2868^{P}

She's All Heart **4** b f Broken Hearted-Tina's Brig (Majestic Streak) 4580^{12}

She's Simply Great (IRE) **4** b f Simply Great (FR)-Petrine (IRE) (Petorius) 282^{5} 803^{2} >**28h**<

She's The Governor **6** b m 1431^{P}

Sheyl Seymour **6** b m Seymour Hicks (FR)-Shemust (Deadly Nightshade) 4340^{P}

Shift Again (IRE) **5** b m 890^{3} 1053^{6} 1168^{2} 1451^{5} (1693) 2578^{4} 4223^{8} >**65h**<

Shifting Moon **5** b g 159^{11} 214^{P} 1123^{P} 1715^{2} 2631^{14} 3002^{4} 3429^{7} 3623^{3} (4020) 4294^{F} >**53h**<

Shikaree (IRE) **6** b g 71^{2} 182^{3} **263^{2} 738^{4} 791^{F} 880^{3}** 1088^{8} **4721^{2}** >**89h 101c**<

Shildon (IRE) **9** b g 1245^{P}

Shimmy Dancing **4** b f Rambo Dancer (CAN)-Sharp Lady (Sharpen Up) 4088^{3} 4407^{10} >**38fh**<

Shine A Light **7** ch g K-Battery-Lady Jay (Double Jump) **4338^{P}**

Shinerolla **5** b g Thatching-Primrolla (Relko) 1666^{2} 2503^{2} 2798^{5} 4285^{10} >**71h**<

Shining Edge **5** ch g 908^{6} 1163^{4} 1658^{3} (1852) (2062) 2543^{4} (2779) (3286) 3572^{13} 4061^{17} >**100h**<

Shining Light (IRE) **8** b g **(1373) 1997^{2} (2814) 3074^{5} 3540^{3} 4300^{P}** >**87h 118c**<

Shining Penny **10** b g **4449^{P}** >**80c**<

Shining Willow **7** b m **3389a^{6} 4356a^{9}** >**79h 110c**<

Ship the Builder **8** ch g **4449^{F} 4607^{U} 4799^{P}** >**18h**<

Shirley's Time **6** b br g 2541^{W} 2669^{18} 3158^{P} >**28h**<

Shisoma (IRE) **7** b g **3380a^{4}** >**79h 105c**<

Shoja **4** ch g Persian Bold-Dancing Berry (Sadler's Wells (USA)) 1776^{13}

Shonara's Way **6** b m (700) >**71h**<

Shoofe (USA) **9** ch g 3201^{11} **3436^{4} 3945^{5}** >**18h 79c**<

Shoofk **6** ch g 591^{6} 863^{4} 1137^{2} 1510^{3} >**99h**<

Shooting Light (IRE) **4** b g Shernazar-Church Light (Caerleon (USA)) (1269) 1634^{2} (2772) 3634^{3} >**99h**<

Shore Party (IRE) **5** b g Strong Gale-Ariannrun (Deep Run) 1573^{2} 2012^{5} 3149^{7} >**58fh**<

Shortstaff (IRE) **8** b g Strong Gale-Earn More (Prince Hansel) 4184^{3} >**81?h**<

Shouldhavesaidno (IRE) **6** br m Orchestra-Corbal-Lis (Tumble Gold) 2677^{P} 3226^{P}

Show Faith (IRE) **7** ch g 1873^{4} 2578^{7} 2703^{3} **3059^{5}** >**83h 54c**<

Show Your Hand (IRE) **9** ch g Aristocracy-Sister's Prize (Pry) **(853) 1051^{U} 1248^{4} 1348^{F} 1943^{F} 1991^{P} 2650^{P}** >**63+c**<

Shrewd John **11** b g **138^{6} 592^{F} 702^{4} 951^{5} 1306^{P} 2796^{6} (2906)** >**62h 101c**<

Shrimp **6** b m Buzzards Bay-Deep Ocean (Deep Run) 1053^{12} 1766^{8} 3190^{P}

Shropshire Gale (IRE) **6** b g Strong Gale-Willow Fashion (Quayside) 3297^{2} 3808^{9} 4008^{11} >**63fh**<

Shu Gaa (IRE) **4** ch g Salse (USA)-River Reem (USA) (Irish River (FR)) (2060) 2759^{12} 3291^{4} (3566) (4209) 4395^{3} >**85h**<

Shuil Saor **10** b g **4543^{9} 4748^{2} 4799^{4}** >**93c**<

Shuil's Star (IRE) **6** b g Henbit (USA)-Shuil Run (Deep Run) **4792^{3}** >**117c**<

Shultan (IRE) **8** ch m 3611^{P} 3883^{13} >**29c**<

Shuttlecock **6** ch g Pharly (FR)-Upper Sister (Upper Case (USA)) 675^{7} (731) 950^{2} 1466^{10} 1848^{9} >**69h**<

Shut Up **8** b m 1078^{10} 1703^{17} **3092^{F} 3530^{4} 3695^{5} 3826^{P} 4157^{U}** 4283^{10} 4409^{U} 4754^{5} >**13h 16c**<

Sian Wyn **7** ch m (54) 128^{5} 183^{2} 551^{4} >**65h**<

Siberian Henry **4** b g Siberian Express (USA)-Semperflorens (Don) 1712^{2} 3075^{5} >**73h**<

Siberian Mystic **4** gr f Siberian Express (USA)-Mystic Crystal (IRE) (Caerleon (USA)) (589) 1064^{4} 1444^{2} 1675^{4} (3594) 4229^{3} 4512^{10} >**65h**<

Siberian Tale (IRE) **7** ch g 4352a^{16} >**85h**<

Sibton Abbey **12** b g **3147^{5} 3302^{P} 3598^{9} 4416^{3}** >**127c**<

Sicarian **5** b g Kris-Sharka (Shareef Dancer (USA)) 3989^{3} 4403^{8} >**65h**<

Sidanora (IRE) **7** ch g Montekin-Lady of Eilat (Cut Above) 1457^{9} >**37fh**<

Side Bar **7** b g 66^{16} 3207^{11} **3956^{2} 4232^{P} 4442^{5}**

4721^{6} >56h 60c<
Side Brace (NZ) 13 gr g **3609^{6} >73?c<**
Side By Side (IRE) 4 b f Brush Aside (USA)-Jupiter Miss (USA) (Hawaii) 3006^{5} 3290^{5} 3487^{3} 3888^{9} **>48fh<**
Side of Hill 12 b g 937^{3} **1266^{6} 1578^{12} 2616^{10} 2956^{P} 4336^{7} >42h 93c<**
Sidney 8 b g 3734^{7} 4224^{6} 4476^{7} **>61h<**
Sierra Bay (IRE) 7 b g 2690^{3} 2937^{P} **>83h<**
Sierra Nevada 6 ch g 418^{5} 1036^{12} 2576^{11} **>17h<**
Siesta Time (USA) 7 ch m 17^{10} 401^{3} 737^{R} 825^{R} **>37?h<**
Sigma Run (IRE) 8 b g (829) 900^{5} **1179^{3} (1414) 2745^{F} 3001^{P} 3417^{4} (4444) 4736^{2} >70h 84c<**
Sigma Wireless (IRE) 8 b g (69) 189^{6} (216) 343^{2} 499^{2} **720^{6} >85h 75c<**
Signe de Mars (FR) 6 b g Synefos (USA)-L'Eclipse (FR) (Lightning (FR)) **213^{P} 333^{P} 454^{2} 466^{2} 1248^{P} >76c<**
Signor Nortone 5 b g 1021^{8} 1247^{10} **>60h<**
Silent Cracker 5 br g Teenoso (USA)-Silent Surrender (Nearly A Hand) 2811^{6} 3170^{11} 4450^{2} 4626^{6} **>63h<**
Silent Guest (IRE) 4 b g Don't Forget Me-Guest House (What A Guest) 874^{2} (1159) 4056^{6} 4146^{4} 4479^{5} **>60h<**
Silent Sovereign 8 ch g 3228^{R}
Sille Me (IRE) 5 ch g Over The River (FR)-Alamo Bay (Torenaga) 3431^{6}
Silly Money 6 b g 955^{4} 1049^{4} 1309^{4} 2744^{2} 3035^{5} 3265^{2} (3438) **>72h<**
Silly Point 5 ch m 3901^{P}
Silver Age (USA) 11 b g **3739^{U} >76h 74c<**
Silver Bird (IRE) 5 b m 100^{7} 134^{6} **>60h<**
Silverdale Knight 4 b c Nomination-Its My Turn (Palm Track) (640) 699^{3} 2859^{4} **>77h<**
Silverdale Lad 6 b h 293^{2} 337^{3} 4800^{3} **>76h<**
Silver Groom (IRE) 7 gr g (1137) 1793^{4} 2645^{3} 3038^{5} 3572^{8} **>117h<**
Silver Grove 7 gr g Pollerton-Silver Shadow (Birdbrook) 1640^{U} 3295^{P} **(DEAD)**
Silver Gull (IRE) 6 gr g Step Together (USA)-Popsi's Darling (Le Bavard (FR)) 2510^{12}
Silver Hill 7 b m Pragmatic-Rare Game (Raise You Ten) **3339^{F} 3537^{P}**
Silverino 11 gr g **2660^{P} 2910^{P} (3633) 3893^{3} >90c<**
Silver Minx 5 gr g 898^{5} (1033) 1705^{5} 1999^{6} 2917^{16} 3098^{4} (3327) (4056) 4146^{F} 4514^{2} (4770) **>79h<**
Silver Quill 6 br m Sharp Deal-Bird Stream (Birdbrook) 1450^{12} 1685^{15} **>7fh<**
Silver Shred 6 gr m 1258^{3} 2069^{4} 3430^{B} 4016^{P} **>109h< (DEAD)**
Silver Sirocco (IRE) 5 gr g Razzo Forte-Oronocco Gift (Camden Town) 3676^{3} 3907^{3} **>65fh<**
Silver Sleeve (IRE) 5 b g (258) 288^{2} 338^{4} 419^{4} 531^{3} 684^{7} **>62h<**
Silver Spinney 6 gr m 3754^{P}
Silver Standard 7 b g 1088^{3} 1342^{2} 1678^{3} 2666^{3} (2895) 3430^{F} **>84h<**
Silver Stick 10 gr g **1048^{3} >133c<**
Silver Thyne (IRE) 5 br g 1283^{4} 2547^{5} 2961^{7} (3426) 3734^{2} 4052^{P} 4166^{2} **>89h<**
Silver Treasure (IRE) 6 gr g Cataldi-Languid (English Prince) 3821^{19} 4009^{13} **>37fh<**
Silvretta (IRE) 4 br f Tirol-Lepoushka (Salmon Leap (USA)) 2889^{6} 3224^{5} 3601^{8} 3809^{4} **>73?h<**
Simand 5 b m (490) 648^{6} 697^{2} 893^{4} 1628^{12} 1851^{5} 1992^{4} 2505^{10} 3908^{4} 4295^{7} 4389^{6} **>51h<**
Simone's Son (IRE) 9 ch g Hatim (USA)-Simone's Luck (Malinowski (USA)) (949) **>60h<**
Simon Says 7 b g Giacometti-Mrs Scattercash (Northfields (USA)) 58^{4}
Simons Castle (IRE) 4 b g Scenic-Miss Toot (Ardross) 4215^{3} **>88fh<**
Simply (IRE) 8 b g **72^{2} 330^{2}** 483^{3} 3493^{3} **3756^{P} >88h 98c<**
Simply Dashing (IRE) 6 br g **(1028) (1206) 1511^{F} (1803) (2054) (2638) 2885^{F} 3268^{2} >103h 137c<**
Simply George 8 b g 4714^{P} **>63h 117c<**
Simply Perfect 11 b g **3744^{6} 4218^{U} 4326^{8} 4631^{5} 4748^{3} >97c<**
Simply Seven 4 b g Seven Hearts-Simply Spim (Simply Great (FR)) 3058^{P}
Simpson 12 ch g **(2829) 3332^{3} 3492^{2} 3884^{5} >127dh 99c<**
Singers Corner 5 br m Sharpo-Guest Singer (Chief Singer) 2857a^{10} **>44h<**
Singh Song 7 b m True Song-Regal Ranee (Indian Ruler) 4161^{5} **4751^{9} >37h<**
Singing Sand 7 b g **1346^{10} 1943^{3} 2653^{3} 2789^{F} (3092) (3530) 4183^{2} 4334^{2} >66h 117c<**
Singlesole 12 ch g 1207^{2} 1372^{6} 1798^{P} 2838^{P} **>70h 107c<**
Single Sourcing (IRE) 6 b g 2677^{P} 4547^{P} (4645) **>65+h<**
Sioux To Speak 5 b g 1835^{2} 2662^{9} 2878^{F} 3186^{P} 3844^{2} 4508^{3} 4663^{W} 4731^{4} **>60h<**
Sioux Warrior 5 br g 686^{2} (787) 1973^{2} 2785^{14} 2917^{11} 3158^{11} 3438^{15} **>30h<**
Sir Bob (IRE) 5 br g 2047^{4} 3024^{2} 3295^{8} 3483^{11} **>72h<**
Sir Boston 4 b g Kalaglow-Pride of Paris (Troy) 2626^{3} 2770^{8} 3203^{13} 3828^{9} **>49fh<**
Sir Dante (IRE) 6 ch g 1036^{9} 1453^{8} 1766^{3} 2680^{9} 3222^{P} (3549) (3923) (4166) **>83+h<**
Siren Song (IRE) 6 b g Warning-Nazwa (Tarboosh (USA)) 4215^{2} 4301^{3} **>93fh<**
Sireric (IRE) 7 b g **1803^{7} 2043^{3} >71?h 85c<**
Sir Galeforce (IRE) 7 br g Mister Lord (USA)-Forest Gale (Strong Gale) 327^{3} **>59h<**
Sir Harry Rinus 11 ch g Golden Love-Teresa Jane (My Swanee) **3476^{P} 3913^{P}**
Sirisat 13 ch g **2930^{3} 3341^{4} 3739^{2} 4617^{2} 4805^{8} >100c<**
Sir John (IRE) 8 gr g Roselier (FR)-Dame Of St John 2345a^{7} **>85h<**
Sir Leonard (IRE) 7 b g **1963^{3} (2693) 3047^{7} 3671^{P} >85h 104dc<**
Sir Lunchalot (IRE) 4 b g Homo Sapien-Halpin (Yashgan) (3907) **>70fh<**
Sir Oliver (IRE) 8 b g 1838^{P}
Sir Pageant 8 b g 587^{9} 673^{P} 1088^{9} 1299^{6} (1466) 2006^{4} **>52h<**
Sir Peter Lely 10 b g **946^{6} >137c<**
Sir Prize (IRE) 4 b g Prince Rupert (FR)-Banasiya (Mill Reef (USA)) 3021^{3} 3304^{7} 3574^{11} **>64fh<**
Sirtelimar (IRE) 8 b g 303^{4} 399^{2} 456^{4} 551^{3} (729) 751^{4} **>81h<**
Sissinghurst Flyer (IRE) 5 gr m Celio Rufo-Jeanarie (Reformed Character) 3606^{13} 4304^{F}
Sister Gale 5 br m Strong Gale-Saffron's Daughter (Prince Hansel) 866^{7} 1021^{4} **>42h<**
Sister Jane 4 b f Fine Blue-Bell Cord (Beldale Flutter (USA)) 3203^{11}
Sister Jim 7 b m 26^{P} 350^{6}
Sister Rosza (IRE) 9 b m **1584^{6} (1769) 1985^{F} 2630^{4} 2869^{4} >102c<**
Sister Stephanie (IRE) 8 b or br m **1785^{6} (2839) 3420^{2} 3699^{3} 4110a^{R} 4213^{U} >60+h 136c<**
Six Clerks (IRE) 4 b g Shadeed (USA)-Skidmore Girl (USA) (Vaguely Noble) 1158^{7} 1370^{4} 1776^{2} (3098) 3544^{3} 4056^{3} 4285^{9} 4578^{5} **>71h<**
Sizzling Serenade 4 gr f Sizzling Melody-Trynova (Tyrnavos) 688^{11} **>19h<**
Sizzling Symphony 4 b g Sizzling Melody-Polly Worth (Wolver Hollow) 1158^{9}
Skane River (IRE) 6 ch g 1344^{4} 3534^{7} 3825^{9} 4283^{3} (4378) 4572^{4} 4705^{P} **>49h<**
Skerry Meadow 13 b g **4634^{P} >92c<**
Skiddaw Knight (IRE) 6 br g 1362^{7} 3366^{10} **>27h<**
Skiddaw Samba 8 b m Viking (USA)-Gavea (African Sky) 1686^{5} 2913^{U} 3137^{6} 4060^{2} 4187^{8} 4409^{3} 4573^{3} 4711^{5} **>61h<**
Skillwise 5 b g Buckley-Calametta (Oats) 4216^{8} 4420^{7} **>63fh<**
Ski Path 8 ch m 1807^{14} 1988^{7} 3032^{6} 3157^{11} 3481^{P} 3641^{2} 3825^{16} **>36h<**
Skiplam Wood 11 b m 354^{4} 463^{9} **>39h<**
Skip to Somerfield 5 ch m Shavian-St Isadora (Lyphard (USA)) 2669^{11} 3029^{11} 3226^{P} **>50dh<**
Skittle Alley 11 b g 27^{14} **>88dh<**
Skram 4 b g Rambo Dancer (CAN)-Skarberg (FR) (Noir Et Or) 388^{F} (471) 589^{4} 654^{5} 1253^{5} 1663^{2} 1772^{P} 2578^{2} 2897^{7} **>71h<**
Sky Burst 7 ch m 4230^{5} **>49h<**
Skycab (IRE) 5 b g Montelimar (USA)-Sams Money (Pry) 2844^{4} **>46fh<**
Skylight 4 ch g Domynsky-Indian Flower (Mansingh (USA)) 534^{4} **>47h<**
Slack Alice 6 ro m Derring Rose-Fonmon (Blast) 2661^{10} 3226^{12}
Slaney Glow (IRE) 6 b m 2461a^{4} **>106h<**
Slaney Rasher 10 br g Strong Gale-Gala Noon (Gala Performance (USA)) 3677^{11} **>9h<**
Slaught Son (IRE) 9 br g 6^{4} 95^{2} **>74h<**
Sleazey 6 b g 1959^{P} 2668^{16} 3000^{6} 3441^{4} **3749^{2} (3960) 4157^{2} 4272^{F} (4764) >37h 86c<**
Sleeptite (FR) 7 gr g (960) 1072^{4} 1148^{4} 1537^{7} 1874^{2} (2088) **>67h<**
Sleepy Boy 4 br g Zero Watt (USA)-Furnace Lass VII (Damsire Unregistered) 646^{8} **>49h<**
Sleepy River (IRE) 6 ch g 4352a^{19} **>86h<**
Sleetmore Gale (IRE) 7 b m Strong Gale-Lena's Reign (Quayside) **1963^{4} 3173^{8} >66h 90c<**
Slew Man (FR) 6 b g 1996^{6} 2884^{9} 3421^{4} 3640^{13} 3920^{9} **>91h<**
Slideofhill (IRE) 8 ch g **1829^{2} 2007^{6} 3202^{2} 3617^{P} 4203^{7} >98c<**
Slide On 7 b g (2066) 2510^{5} 2626^{2} 3197^{P} **>76fh<**
Slievenamon Mist 11 ch g **(3010) (3439) (4320) (4619) >125c<**
Slightly Special (IRE) 5 ch g 105^{10} 185^{10} 960^{6} 1040^{7} 1836^{2} 2006^{6} 2664^{3} 2866^{2} 3057^{7} 3447^{15} 3620^{8} **>39h<**
Slightly Speedy (IRE) 4 b c Prince Rupert (FR)-Moutalina (Ela-Mana-Mou) 2333a^{B} **>75h<**
Slight Panic 9 b m Lighter-Midnight Panic (Panco) 934^{6} **>35h<**
Slingsby (IRE) 7 b g **1179^{2} 1563^{3} (1856) (2667) 3145^{F} >74h 113c< (DEAD)**
Slipmatic 8 b m 1034^{5} 1378^{2} 1673^{2} **2049^{F} 3086^{F} >69h<**
Slippery Fin 5 b m Slip Anchor-Finyska (FR) (Niniski (USA)) 1679^{3} 3359^{11} 3930^{4} **>52h<**
Slippery Max 13 b g 413^{2} 488^{P} 648^{9} **750^{2} 914^{4} >49h 83c<**
Sloe Brandy 7 b m 955^{10} 1438^{F} **>43h<**
Slotamatique (IRE) 8 b g **1503^{3} 1850^{4} (2061) 2652^{3} 2916^{3} 4186^{10} (4569) (4706) >108c<**
Small Flame (IRE) 6 b m Camden Town-Hazel Gig (Captain's Gig (USA)) 1329^{14} 1537^{10} **>22fh<**
Small N Smart 7 b g Germont-Sanjo (Kafu) **1246^{F} 1574^{10} >38c<**
Smart Act 8 br g 1090^{P} 1251^{P}

Smart Approach (IRE) 7 br m (693) 911^{2} 1130^{4} 1310^{3} 2003^{2} 2627^{2} 3368^{2} (3454) **>76h<**

Smart Casanova 8 br g 1412^{7} **2548^{B} 2752^{U} 3331^{7} 4232^{6} 4549^{P} >42h 49c<**

Smart Guy 5 ch g Gildoran-Talahache Bridge (New Brig) 3676^{15}

Smart In Satin 7 ch g Scorpio (FR)-Smart In Amber (Sagaro) 1349^{P} 1705^{10} 2785^{15} **>14h<**

Smart in Silk 8 gr m **4183^{P} 4260^{F}**

Smart In Socks 6 ch g Jupiter Island-Cool Down (Warpath) 705^{10} 1343^{9} 4184^{P} 4249^{9}

Smart In Velvet 7 gr m Scorpio (FR)-Cool Down (Warpath) 885^{5} 1422^{P} **>56h<**

Smart Lord 6 br g 593^{3} 955^{7} 1178^{3} 1663^{5} 1959^{4} 3437^{5} 3894^{P} **>67h<**

Smart Pal 12 b g Balinger-Smart Bird (Stephen George) **4317^{5} >49c<**

Smart Rebal (IRE) 9 b g 1638^{P} **(DEAD)**

Smart Remark 5 b g Broadsword (USA)-Miss Cervinia (Memling) 133^{3} 191^{8} 2840^{9} 3275^{9} 3918^{5} **>38h<**

Smart Rookie (IRE) 7 b or br g 3272^{F}

Smiddy Lad 6 ch g 1692^{12} 2619^{10} 2787^{2} 2958^{3} 3317^{5} 3531^{8} **>71h<**

Smile Pleeze (IRE) 5 b g Naheez (USA)-Harkin Park (Pollerton) 3487^{6} 3795^{6} 4144^{F} **>54h<**

Smiley Face 5 b g 1770^{8} 1980^{4} 2574^{7} 2813^{7} **>47h<**

Smiling Always (IRE) 4 b f Montelimar (USA)-Always Smiling (Prominer (FR)) 4118a^{P} **>64fh<**

Smith's Band (IRE) 9 b g **3420^{P} 4074^{F} >67h 148?c<**

Smith Too (IRE) 9 br g 2761^{6} 2895^{2} 3415^{2} (3731) 4016^{11} 4418^{3} **4806^{5} >86h 103c<**

Smocking 7 ch m Night Shift (USA)-Sue Grundy (Grundy) 137^{10} 209^{5} **>36h<**

Smokey Track 12 b m 488^{P} **584^{6} 645^{6} 785^{U} 875^{7} >57c<**

Smolensk (IRE) 5 b g 1278^{3} 1470^{2} 1967^{2} (2177) 3283^{3} 3595^{P} (4400) 4707^{3} **>80h<**

Smuggler's Point (USA) 7 b g 1392^{4} 1709^{3} 2644^{6} 2797^{5} 2932^{4} 3554^{4} (3720) 3851^{6} 3958^{3} 4439^{5} **>82h<**

Sniper 5 ch g Gunner B-Highfrith (Deep Run) 3324^{9} 3691^{16} 3883^{P} **>29h<**

Snitton Lane 11 b m **261^{5} >105c<**

Snook Point 10 b g **1704^{P} 2046^{P} 2630^{3} 2916^{P} 3099^{P} 3645^{3} 4078^{P} 4284^{P} >76c<**

Snooty Eskimo (IRE) 5 ch g Aristocracy-Over The Arctic (Over The River (FR)) 2047^{10} 2633^{14} 3487^{5} 3828^{12} **>41fh<**

Snow Board 8 gr g (822) (971) (1798) 2507^{2} 3016^{3} 3600^{18} (3737) 4253^{P} **>74h<**

Snow Domino (IRE) 4 ch g Habyom-Magic Picture (Deep Diver) 1184^{11} 1413^{P} **>45h<**

Snowdon Lily 6 br m Town And Country-Welsh Flower (Welsh Saint) **1447^{B} 1797^{7} 1909^{3} 2571^{4} 2667^{F} >50c<**

Snow Falcon 4 b g Polar Falcon (USA)-Cameroun 2738a^{4} 4364a^{2} **>98h<**

Snowshill Harvest (IRE) 6 b g Strong Gale-Slave-Lady (Menelek) 1317^{10} 1788^{5} 3041^{F} **>68h<**

Snowshill Shaker 8 b g Son of Shaka-Knight Hunter (Skyliner) 2552^{8} 2870^{6} 3049^{8} 3473^{2} (4226) 4321^{2} (4512) **>74+h<**

Snowy Lane (IRE) 9 ch g 1040^{6} 1304^{2} 2008^{4} 3892^{6} 4501^{6} **>58h 88c<**

Snowy Petrel (IRE) 5 b g 1077^{6} 1550^{6} 1814^{6} [illegible]^{3} **3278^{4} 4092^{2} 4437^{U} 4526^{4} >65h 87dc<**

[illegible]nd 8 b g 2578^{11} 2806^{15} 4558^{9} 4731^{P}

[illegible]344^{P} 3691^{19} 3823^{16} 4405^{7}

Social Insecurity (IRE) 6 b g Mandalus-Credo Park (Sunley Builds) 1685^{12} 1834^{10} 2066^{13} 2750^{14}

Society Girl 4 b f Shavian-Sirene Bleu Marine (USA) (Secreto (USA)) 2784^{7} 2939^{7} 3634^{21} 4414^{4} 4770^{F} **>60h<**

Society Guest 11 ch g 1325^{U} 2824^{7} **4311^{5} 4700^{4} 4793^{3} >93h 122c<**

Society Magic (USA) 4 b g Imp Society (USA)-Lady Kirtling (USA) (Kirtling) 1776^{U} 1900^{2} 2889^{7} **>87h<**

Society Times (USA) 4 b g Imp Society (USA)-Mauna Loa (USA) (Hawaii) 2572^{8} (2965) 4215^{15} **>65fh<**

So Far Bold (IRE) 7 br g 2550^{13} **3018^{P} 3599^{8}** **>34h 114?c<**

Sohail (USA) 14 ch g **(298) 395^{3} >106c<**

Sohrab (IRE) 9 ch g 3635^{4} **>122h<**

Solar Gem 10 b g Easter Topic-River Gem (Arctic Judge) **3490^{U} 3906^{P}**

Solar Moon 6 b m Nearly A Hand-Solhoon (Tycoon II) 653^{3} 1177^{6} 1555^{6} **>41fh<**

Solar Warrior 7 b g 1077^{10} **>39h 49c<**

Solazzi (FR) 5 b m Saint Cyrien (FR)-Sunclad (FR) (Tennyson (FR)) 3536^{2} **>64h<**

Solba (USA) 8 b g **1295^{3} 1985^{4} 2544^{7} 2765^{6} 3027^{4} (3312) 3532^{2} 3886^{6} 3911^{4}** 4210^{10} **>45h 109c<**

Soldat (USA) 4 b g Bering-Sans Prix (USA) (Vaguely Noble) 2615^{2} 3007^{4} 3152^{P} 3613^{5} 4355a^{2} **>92h<**

Soldier-B 7 ch g 4188^{P} 4250^{5} 4445^{8} **>32h<**

Soldier Blue 4 ch g Infantry-Greenhil Jazz Time (Music Boy) 807^{5} 944^{7} 1064^{6} 1332^{9} **>37h<**

Soldier Cove (USA) 7 ch g Manila (USA)-Secret Form (Formidable (USA)) 3109^{8} **>45h<**

Soldier Mak 4 ch g Infantry-Truly Blest (So Blessed) 1370^{3} 1872^{5} 2705^{7} **>64h<**

Soleil Dancer (IRE) 9 b g 1170^{5} **1965^{2} 2796^{P} >93c<**

Solo Gent 8 br g **696^{2} (1564) 1877^{4} 2665^{7} 3106^{P} 3223^{3} 3492^{6} 3929^{P} >115h 102dc<**

Soloman Springs (USA) 7 ch g **1008^{P}** 1718^{7} 2864^{2} 3454^{2} 4147^{9} 4452^{2} **4740^{4} >56h 95c<**

Solomon's Dancer (USA) 7 b or br g **(1022) (1264) 1653^{2} 2113^{2} 3484^{2} 4203^{2} 4286^{2} >88h 111c<**

Solo Volumes 8 ch g 555^{P} 600^{11} 1053^{8} 1171^{11} **>15h<**

Solsgirth 6 br g 2619^{11} (3064) 3534^{3} 3887^{P} **>62h<**

Solvang (IRE) 5 b g Carlingford Castle-Bramble Bird 4360a^{12} **>62fh 90c<**

Solway King 7 b g Germont-Copper Tinsell (Crooner) 2953^{F} 3315^{P} 3691^{P}

Solwaysands 7 b g Germont-Castle Point (Majestic Streak) **3913^{P}**

Some Day Soon 12 b g **395^{2} (932) >111c<**

Somerset Dancer (USA) 10 br g 1585^{6} 1710^{P}

Something Catchy (IRE) 7 b m Toravich (USA)-Spring Flower II (Ozymandias) **4072^{3} 4330^{P} >44c<**

Something Speedy (IRE) 5 b m Sayf El Arab (USA)-Fabulous Pet (Somethingfabulous (USA)) 1821^{3} 2177^{5} 2898^{17} 3325^{P} 3908^{8} **>47h<**

Some Tourist (IRE) 9 b g Torus-Noellespir (Bargello) **4319^{P}**

Some-Toy 11 ch g **3055^{6} 3765^{4} (4087) 4179^{2} 4325^{4} 4640^{P} >113c<**

Sommersby (IRE) 6 b g 218^{6} **>60h<**

Song For Jess (IRE) 4 b f Accordion-Ritual Girl (Ballad Rock) 282^{U} 388^{F} 501^{5} 589^{2} 640^{4} 753^{P} 881^{7} 1908^{4} 2705^{6} 3352^{6} 3620^{4} 3930^{2} 4281^{3} 4727^{5} **>51h<**

Song of Kenda 5 b m Rolfe (USA)-Kenda (Bargello) 3115^{10} 3590^{5} 3889^{3} **>34h<**

Song Of The Sword 4 b g Kris-Melodist (USA) (The Minstrel (CAN)) (4465) (4555) (4726) **>85+h<**

Sonic Star (IRE) 8 b g **(263) (590) (637) 791^{2} >83h 106+c<**

Sonofagipsy 13 b g **2964^{3} 3446^{5} 3837^{3} 4087^{6} >102dc<**

Son of Anshan 4 b g Anshan-Anhaar (Ela-Mana-Mou) 906^{11} 1184^{3} 1652^{2} (1940) 2541^{F} (3555) (3789) **>88+h<**

Son of Iris 9 br g **1029^{P} 1209^{6} 1847^{5} (2652) (2923) (3792) >74h 120c<**

Son of Tempo (IRE) 8 b g Sandhurst Prince-Top Love (USA) (Topsider (USA)) 4154^{4}

Son Of War 10 gr g **1750a^{2} 2362a^{5} 3261a^{U} >146c<**

Sonrisa (IRE) 5 b g 24^{11} 1795^{11}

Sophie May 6 b m 816^{2} 1074^{8} **1552^{4} 1865^{4} (2679) 3176^{F} 3400^{P} >78h 98c<**

Sophies Dream 6 ch g 1289^{15} 1633^{P} 1873^{9} **>33h<**

So Proud 12 b g 3430^{U} 4178^{P} 4536^{6} **>105c<**

Sorbiere 10 b g **1043^{4} 1194^{F} 1391^{2} 1684^{P} 1961^{F}** 2625^{5} 3013^{9} 3720^{3} **>67h 87dc<**

Sorciere 6 ch m **(3998) 4232^{5} 4728^{P} >58h 77c<**

Sorisky 5 ch g Risk Me (FR)-Minabella (Dance In Time (CAN)) 186^{4} 262^{3} 950^{F} 1091^{7} **>70h<**

Sorrel Hill 10 b g **1428^{5} 1694^{4} 2658^{P} >90c<**

Sound Carrier (USA) 9 br g Lord Gaylord (USA)-Bright Choice (USA) (Best Turn (USA)) **3155^{P} 3891^{5} 4237^{F} >82dh 86c< (DEAD)**

Sound Man (IRE) 9 b g **(846a) 1231a^{2} (1737a) (1792) 2935^{3} >144h 167c<**

Soundpost 5 b g Shareef Dancer (USA)-Cheerful Note (Cure The Blues (USA)) 1124^{7} 1362^{13} 1842^{7} 4217^{P} **>16h<**

Sound Reveille 9 b g **1650^{4} 1914^{3} 2639^{5} 2879^{U} >69h 136c<**

Sounds Devious 4 ch f Savahra Sound-Trust Ann (Capistrano) 1356^{7} 1940^{P} 2785^{U} 3093^{P} **>20h<**

Sounds Golden 9 br g **1864^{5} 2667^{7} >62?h 62c<**

Sounds Like Fun 6 b g (931) 2093^{4} 2771^{P} (3569) (4275) **>93h<**

Sounds Strong (IRE) 8 br g **(1048) 1469^{F} (1937) 2782^{6} 3428^{P} 4529^{2} 4747^{2} >138c<**

Sound Statement (IRE) 8 ch g Strong Statement (USA)-Coolishall Again (Push On) **3086^{P} 4183^{7} >49c<**

Soupreme 5 ch m 101^{P} **>40h< (DEAD)**

Souson (IRE) 9 b g 539^{4} 684^{3} 892^{4} **>75h 71c<**

Sou Sou Westerly (IRE) 6 b g Strong Gale-Fair Fashion (Miner's Lamp) 1457^{19}

Sousse 4 b f Warrshan (USA)-Mona (Auction Ring (USA)) 1184^{9} 1940^{7} 2615^{7} 3131^{4} (3284) (3908) 4209^{4} 4399^{2} 4744^{2} **>72h<**

Southampton 7 b g **1087^{2} 1352^{2} 1520^{3} 3169^{2} 3618^{7} 3804^{3} >93h 124c<**

South Coast Star (IRE) 7 b h Good Thyne (USA)-Sun Chimes (Roi Soleil) 1290^{6} 1654^{19} 2042^{9} **2628^{P}** 3031^{11} **>50h<**

Southerly Gale 10 b g **64^{2} (94) 302^{2} 833^{F} >91h 111c< (DEAD)**

Southern Cross 5 ch g 1692^{5} 2673^{4} 3644^{3} 3823^{2} 3990^{3} **>73h<**

Southerncrosspatch 6 ch g 679^{4} 865^{13}

Southernhay Boy 6 b g 1782^{9} 2872^{8} 3337^{P} 3982^{2} **>62h<**

Southern Minstrel 14 ch g **2903^{5} 3793^{4} 4208^{3} 4449^{4} 4758^{4} >106dc<**

Southern Nights 7 ch g 1036^{P} 1278^{2} (1541) (1795) 1915^{2} 3600^{P} **>87h<**

Southern Ridge 6 b g 304[2] 357[2] (603) 915[4] 1330[5] **>80h<**

Southsea Scandals (IRE) 6 ch g 885[4] 1541[P] 3048[P] **>64h<**

South Westerly (IRE) 9 br g 29[2] 131[7] **>93h<**

South West Express (IRE) 5 ch g 2093[5] 3109[10] 3364[9] **>50h<**

Sovereign Grit (IRE) 7 ch g 1250[13] **>44h<**

Sovereign Niche (IRE) 9 gr g 27[2] 101[11] 134[5] 185[7] 969[R] 1198[R] **>74h 99dc<**

Sovereign Pass 5 b g Rakaposhi King-Pro-Token (Proverb) 2546[P] 2701[13] 3295[6] 3449[P] **>43h< (DEAD)**

Sovereigns Match 9 b g Royal Match-Sovereign's Folly (Sovereign Bill) **3994[2] 4338[5] 4611[3] 4709[3] 4751[6] >76dc<**

Sovereigns Parade 5 ch g 1510[7] 1903[3] 2929[5] **>81h<**

Soviet Bride (IRE) 5 b m Soviet Star (USA)-Nihad (Alleged (USA)) 1368[5] **>57h<**

So Welcome 5 b m 4008[P]

Spaceage Gold 8 b g 1322[2] 1541[4] (1561) 1915[5] 3108[7] 3541[3] 3851[5] **>81h<**

Space Cappa 9 br g **3153[10] 3354[4] 3633[P] >71c<**

Space Molly 8 b m **4070[P] 4317[F]**

Space Trucker (IRE) 6 b g 318a[2] 1288[2] (1365) (1656) (3523a) 3597[3] 4063[4] 4357a[3] **>143+h<**

Spanish Arch (IRE) 8 ch g Ovac (ITY)-Castile's Rose (Ballyciptic) 2943[8] **>35h<**

Spanish Blaze (IRE) 9 b g 19[7] 77[U] 258[5] **351[F] >44h<**

Spanish Light (IRE) 8 b g **1350[P] 1442[2] 1631[4] 2942[2] 3292[5] >80h 120c<**

Spanish Money 10 gr g **93[F]** 139[P] **179[P]**

Spanish Secret (IRE) 5 bl g Executive Perk-Tarahumara (Soldier Rose) 4301[9] 4774[13]

Spankers Hill (IRE) 8 b g **1495a[8] 1750a[7] >78h 120c<**

Sparkling Buck 5 gr m 1594[5] 2701[8] 2959[7] 4641[2] **>42h<**

Sparkling Cone 8 gr g 2761[5] 3150[P] **>86h<**

Sparkling Spring (IRE) 6 b g Strong Gale-Cherry Jubilee (Le Bavard (FR)) (1581) 2759[2] 3172[2] (3901) 4257[6] **>84h<**

Sparkling Yasmin 5 b m 796[3] (1429) 1783[2] 2934[2] **>105h<**

Sparky Gayle (IRE) 7 b g **(1346) (1653) (2653) (3023) (3639) (4211) >115h 152+c<**

Sparrow Hall 10 b g **1209[4] 1778[3] 2004[3] 2671[4] 3099[3] >79dh 99c<**

Spartan Silver 11 ch g **3135[P] >120dc<**

Sparts Fault (IRE) 7 ch g 73[P] (156) 258[2] 260[4] **>69h 42c<**

Speaker's House (USA) 8 b g 17[6] **(532) 694[P] 4151[P] (4410) 4757[4] >78h 94c<**

Speaker Weatherill (IRE) 8 b g **1863[F] >70h 115+c<**

Spearhead Again (IRE) 8 b g **1038[P]** 1174[6] 1539[8] **2077[F] 3071[6] >65h 87c<**

Special Account 11 b g **(1057) 1765[8] 2011[4] 3153[4] 3699[6] 4806[2] >86h 105c<**

Special Beat 5 b m Bustino-Special Guest (Be My Guest (USA)) (2663) 3108[10] (4217) (4559) **>80+h<**

Specialize 5 b g 105[9] 209[6] **>58h<**

Special Topic 7 ch m 1289[16] 1958[P] 2907[11] 3670[7] **>1h<**

Spectacle Jim 8 b g Mummy's Game-Welsh Blossom (Welsh Saint) 3820[9] 3955[10]

Spectre Brown 7 b g 2541[W] **3092[4] 4419[2] 4574[5] 4709[P] >66c<**

Speedwell Prince (IRE) 7 ch g **1644[4]** 3286[9] **>102h<**

Speedy Snapsgem (IRE) 7 ch g **903[4] 2704[F] >61h< (DEAD)**

Speedy Snaps Image 6 ch g **3343[2] 3717[2] >59h 78c<**

Speedy Snaps Pride 5 gr g Hallgate-Pineapple's Pride (John de Coombe) 2794[9] **>30h<**

Spencer Stallone 4 b g Rambo Dancer (CAN)-Armour of Light (Hot Spark) 3544[12] 3927[4] 4170[4] 4465[4]

Spendid (IRE) 5 b g Tidaro (USA)-Spendapromise (Goldhill) (2673) (3014) **>82+h<**

Sperrin View 11 ch m Fidel-Baroness Vimy (Barrons Court) **3922[5] >72c<**

Spikey (NZ) 11 b g **487[4] 2681[P] >95?c<**

Spin Echo (IRE) 8 b g **3422[4] 4004[F] >53h 89c<**

Spinnaker 7 gr g 1586[8] **2061[2] 2760[F] >73h 107c< (DEAD)**

Spinning Steel 10 b g **1298[4] 1509[F] 2092[3] 4142[5] (4293) 4463[P] >104?c<**

Spiral Flyer (IRE) 4 b br f Contract Law (USA)-Souveniers (Relko) 1872[4] 2050[5] 2818[P] **>48h<**

Spirit Dancer (IRE) 4 ch g Carmelite House (USA)-Theatral (Orchestra) (1747a) 2333a[8] 2738a[3] 3258a[4] 4364a[6] **>102h<**

Spirit Level 9 ch m 1950[5] 3156[10] 3536[4] 3628[6] 3997[5] 4382[U] 4552[3] 4662[3] **>37h<**

Spirit of Steel 4 gr g Arzanni-Miss Redlands (Dubassoff (USA)) (3330) 3853[13] **>55fh<**

Spirit of Success 7 b g Rakaposhi King-Sweet Linda (Saucy Kit) 1685[16] 1966[13] 3796[P] **>4fh<**

Spitfire Bridge (IRE) 5 b g Cyrano de Bergerac-Maria Renata (Jaazeiro (USA)) 1168[P] 1980[7] 2668[10] 2943[5] (3542) 3683[5] 4562[P] **>48h<**

Spitfire Jubilee 11 b g **3721[3] 4432[5] >88c<**

Splash of Blakeney 6 b m Blakeney Point-Upper Persuasion (Hard Fact) 2661[11] 2965[6] 3767[12]

Splendid Thyne 5 ch g 1551[2] (2677) 3143[3] (3399) 3685[3] **>93h<**

Splicethemainbrace 5 b m Broadsword (USA)-Mellfell (Silly Season) 4632[13]

Split The Wind 11 br m Strong Gale-Dane-Jor's (Take A Reef) 4708[F]

Sporting Fixture (IRE) 6 b g **860[5] 1150[F]** 1550[8] **3746[4] >66c<**

Spread The Word 5 b m Deploy-Apply (Kings Lake (USA)) 3233[5] 3535[5] **>67h<**

Sprightley Pip (IRE) 6 gr g Roselier (FR)-Owen's Rose (Master Owen) 2904[5] 3042[10] 3418[9] **>36fh<**

Sprig Muslin 5 br m 1431[7] 1781[2] 3205[3] 3748[6] 4002[P] **>37h<**

Spring Blade 5 b g Jester-Runfawit Pet (Welsh Saint) 1457[17]

Spring Campaign (IRE) 4 b g Sayaarr (USA)-March The Second (Millfontaine) 548[3] 3601[4] 4003[4] 4465[3] **>71h<**

Spring Double (IRE) 6 br g 1191[4] 1683[12] 2662[5] (3186) (3423) 4052[P] 4182[2] **>89h<**

Springfield Dancer 6 b m (301) 605[P] **>76+h<**

Springfield Rhyme 6 b m 4299[13]

Springfort Lady (IRE) 8 b m **323a[6] >94c<**

Spring Gale (IRE) 6 b g (1077) 1807[2] (2576) 2948[5] (3437) 4166[P] **>82h<**

Spring Hebe 7 b m 1571[P] 3499[2] **>69?h<**

Springhill Quay (IRE) 8 br g Quayside-Home Rejoicing (Carlburg) **1845[4] 2000[P] 3067[P] >64c<**

Springlea Tower 4 b g Meadowbrook-Tringa (GER) (Kaiseradler) 4182[P] 4568[6] **>16h<**

Spring Loaded 6 b g 634[8] 784[2] **(873) 975[U] 1009[4]** 1816[8] 2813[5] **3179[F] >56h 81c<**

Spring Saint 8 ch g 1996[2] 2817[P] 3114[P] **>84dh<**

Spring to Glory 10 b g 1039[8] 3114[F] 3277[4] 3687[2] **3819[4] 4007[7] 4272[3] 4385[3] 4790[4] >78h 96dc<**

Spring to it 11 ch g **3113[P] 3763[3] 3891[3] (4171) 4330[U] 4763[2] >97c<**

Sprintfayre 9 b g (1390) 1537[3] (1796) 2010[2] 3687[5] **>76h<**

Spritzer (IRE) 5 ch m 1807[4] (2861) 3029[2] 3348[5] 3990[5] **>73h<**

Sprowston Boy 14 ch g **(1008) 1778[6] 2671[U] >95h 91c<**

Spruce Lodge 4 b g Full Extent (USA)-Miss Ticklemouse (Rhodomantade) 3235[8] **>33fh<**

Spuffington 9 b g **1175[5] 1540[4] 1765[5] 2011[3] 2754[3] 2881[B] 3153[3] 3563[3] 4074[U] 4213[P] >79h 120c<**

Spumante 5 ch g 675[8] 900[6] 974[8] **>60h<**

Spunkie 4 ch g Jupiter Island-Super Sol (Rolfe (USA)) 2811[2] (3606) **>70fh<**

Spy Dessa 9 br g **70[5] 2756[P] 3086[P] >82c<**

Spy's Delight 11 b g **3005[U] 4631[8] >72c<**

Squaddie 5 ch g Infantry-Mendelita (King's Company) 2830[3] 4421[2] **>65fh<**

Squealing Jeanie 8 b m 4378[3] 4727[P] **>32h<**

Squire Silk 8 b g **1764[7] (3008) 3167[2] 3596[2] (4012) >153h 143c<**

Squire's Occasion (CAN) 4 b g Black Tie Affair-Tayana (USA) (Wajima (USA)) 944[3] (1131) 1269[3] 1519[4] 2781[5] 3007[10] 4169[U] **>86h<**

Squirrellsdaughter 10 gr m 492[5] **>13h 90dc<**

Stac-Pollaidh 7 b m 1176[5] 1698[U] 2008[2] 2708[3] 2941[5] 3624[4] 3962[2] 4248[10] 4470[3] **>57h<**

Stage Fright 6 b g 189[2] **>71h<**

Stage Player 11 b g **1566[5] 1797[6] (2068) 2892[4] 3288[7] 4446[6] 4566[5] 4699[P] >63h 74c<**

Stags Fell 12 gr g 684[2] 731[5] 4060[8] 4409[6] 4746[6] **>46h 93c<**

Staigue Fort (IRE) 9 b g **507[2] 583[2] 644[2] >95c<**

Stamp Duty 10 b g Sunyboy-Royal Seal (Privy Seal) **4007[P]**

Stanmore (IRE) 5 b g Aristocracy-Lady Go Marching (USA) (Go Marching (USA)) 1457[5] 2811[8] 3149[8] **>54fh<**

Stan's Pride 5 b g Lord Bud-Kilkilanne (Brave Invader (USA)) 2904[14] 3203[17]

Stan's Your Man 7 b g Young Man (FR)-Charlotte's Festival (Gala Performance (USA)) (1161) 1689[4] (3696) **>74h<**

Stanwick Hall 5 b g Poetic Justice-Allez Stanwick (Goldhill) 3480[6] **>15fh<**

Stapleford Lady 9 ch m 128[4] 187[3] **(296) 336[2] 472[3] 601[8]** 4101[6] 4229[4] **4454[2] >65h 84c<**

Star Adventure 5 b g Green Adventure (USA)-Lady Martha (Sidon) 3808[6] 4008[2] 4656[9] **>67fh<**

Star Blakeney 4 b g Blakeney-Trikkala Star (Tachypous) 1184[7] 2805[7] **>58h<**

Stardante (IRE) 5 b g Phardante (FR)-Borecca (Boreen (FR)) 4531[16] 4657[13] **>5fh<**

Star Island 4 b g Jupiter Island-Gippeswyck Lady (Pas de Seul) 2648[6] 2830[7] **>25fh<**

Stark Lomond (USA) 4 b g Lomond (USA)-Stark Home (USA) (Graustark) 2818[P]

Starlight Fool 8 b g **2807[F] 2947[P]** 3569[P] 3733[14] **>17h<**

Starlin Sam 8 b g Alias Smith (USA)-Czarosa (Czarist) 3973[3] 4514[8] 4759[P] **>52h<**

Star Market 7 b g (214) 255[3] 341[3] (638) 796[R] (863) **>113h<**

Star Master 6 b g Rainbow Quest (USA)-Chellita (Habitat) 1499[6] 1802[U] 2041[8] 4184[12] 4285[6] **>55h<**

Star Mystery 6 b g 3143[4] 3342[5] **>73h<**

Star Oats 11 ch g **3363[P] (3753) 3852[P] 4228[P] >95dc<**

Star of David (IRE) 9 b g 815[P] 2670[11] **>82h 96c<**

Star of Italy 10 b g **1769[P] 1949[3]** >94?c<
Star Performer (IRE) 6 b g 1946[2] 3362[6] 3583[3] 3892[4] 4468[2] 4660[3] 4723[4] >76h<
Star Rage (IRE) 7 b g 2777[3] (3034) 3286[2] 3572[P] 3640[17] 3987[3] >108h<
Star Selection 6 b g Rainbow Quest (USA)-Selection Board (Welsh Pageant) 1187[6] 1659[3] (2034) 2631[9] (3065) 3396[2] (3883) 4397[5] >103h<
Starshadow 8 br g Swing Easy (USA)-Sahara Shadow (Formidable (USA)) 407[5]
Startingo 4 b c Rustingo-Spartan's Girl (Spartan General) 1064[P] 3927[F] 4082[6] 4555[4] >43h<
Stash the Cash (IRE) 6 b g 1314[2] (1669) (1824) (2764) 4246[4] (4337) >101h<
Stately Home (IRE) 6 b or br g 128[3] **(160) (254) (261) (340) (398) (464) 592[4] 676[U] 886[2] 951[2] 1055[4] (1155) 1186[2] (1869) (2885) 3300[P] 3639[6] 4211[3] 4302[2] 4507[2] 4541[F] (4802)** >82h 146+c<
State Princess (IRE) 7 b m 318a[20] >113h<
Station Express (IRE) 9 b g 27[9] 4175[7] 4464[4] 4739[6] >41h<
Staunch Rival (USA) 10 b g **650[4] 1175[6]** 1355[3] 1876[5] **2821[10] 3903[4] 4293[2]** >100h 99c<
Stay Happy (FR) 8 b g 66[8] 212[F] >40h< (DEAD)
Stay In Touch (IRE) 7 ch g **2998a[5] (3391a) 4361a[2]** >112c<
Stay Lucky (NZ) 8 b g Sir Sydney (NZ)-Against The Odds (NZ) (Harbor Prince (USA)) **1680[4] 1936[2] 4350a[3]** >122c<
Stay With Me (FR) 7 b g 97[6] 211[3] 303[6] 473[4] 596[P] 692[6] (868) 976[3] 1145[4] 1630[2] (1715) (4534) (4654) >86+h<
Steadfast Elite (IRE) 6 b m (463) 531[2] 701[5] (798) (1034) 1282[F] >77h<
Stealing Home (IRE) 7 ch m **3097[2]** >44h 60c<
Steals Yer Thunder (IRE) 5 b g Celio Rufo-Midsummer Blends (IRE) (Duky) 4216[17]
Stede Quarter 10 b g **2951[4]** >87c< (DEAD)
Steel Chimes (IRE) 8 ch g Burslem-Gaychimes (Steel Heart) 4476[P] **4627[5] 4738[4]**
Steel Dawn 10 b g 317a[P] >107h 96c<
Steel Gem (IRE) 8 b g 1448[6] 2870[3] 3344[8] >50h<
Steel Gold 7 gr g **4305[P] 4533[P] 4706[3]**
Steeple Jack 10 b g **1202[4] 1697[5] 2876[5] 3961[5]** >86c<
Steer Point 6 b g 968[3] 1174[7] 3110[4] 3536[3] 3844[7] **4523[4] 4764[F]** >55h 63c<
Stellar Force (IRE) 6 br g Strong Gale-Glenroe Star (Furry Glen) 1289[11] 1810[P] 3587[P] >41fh<
Stellar Line (USA) 4 ch g Zilzal (USA)-Stellaria (USA) (Roberto (USA)) 3494[P]
Stencil 5 ch h Nashwan (USA)-Colorspin (FR) (High Top) 1275[10] >37fh<
Stepdaughter 11 b m 2958[8] 3557[4] 3795[11] 4147[P] >36?h<
Step In Line (IRE) 5 gr g Step Together (USA)-Ballycahan Girl (Bargello) 4767[3] >63h<
Step On Eyre (IRE) 7 b g 4124a[5] >91h<
Sterling Fellow 4 b c Pharly (FR)-Favorable Exchange (USA) (Exceller (USA)) 1269[8] 1377[2] 1634[7] 2070[3] 2820[18] 3075[12] 3962[5] 4169[2] 4434[2] 4542[2] 4731[6] >57h<
Steve Ford 8 gr g 3429[U] 3623[6] 3904[3] 4236[2] (4415) >69h<
Stevie's Wonder (IRE) 7 ch g Don't Forget Me-Azurai (Dance In Time (CAN)) 1782[7] 2038[8] 2566[R] >24h<
Stickwiththehand 6 b g Nearly A Hand-Royal Rushes (Royal Palace) 1071[7]
Sticky Money 9 b m 71[6] **(213) (283) (346)** >78h 105++c<
Still Here (IRE) 4 b g Astronef-Covey's Quick Step (Godswalk (USA)) 388[2] 589[9] 736[7] 2925[9] 3594[10] 3677[5] 3803[10] >37h<
Still In Business 9 b g **3637[U]** >110dc<
Stilltodo 10 gr m **4511[5]** >75c<
Stinging Bee 6 b g 1020[7] >10h<
Stingray City (USA) 8 b g Raft (USA)-Out of This World (High Top) 3309[P] 3559[8] >9h<
Stipple 6 ch m Blushing Scribe (USA)-April (Silly Season) 3583[8] 3730[12]
St Kitts 6 b m 499[P] >62h<
St Mabyn Inn Boy 5 b g Lir-Weiss Rose (FR) (Pilgrim (USA)) 2661[13] 3592[P]
St Mellion Drive 7 b g 2656[5] 3000[3] >60h<
St Mellion Fairway (IRE) 8 b g **1785[3] 2616[5] 3294[3] 4110a[5]** >84h 134c<
St Mellion Leisure (IRE) 5 b g Lord Americo-Forthetimebeing (Prince Regent (FR)) 1573[7] 1966[14] 2673[12] 3205[P] >10h<
Stoleamarch 4 br g Daring March-Pennine Star (IRE) (Pennine Walk) 646[6] 1011[3] 1184[P] >61h<
Stompin 6 b g 3640[18] 4061[16] 4397[11] >122h<
Stonecrop 6 br g 19[P] 100[P] >54h<
Stone Cross (IRE) 5 b g Pennine Walk-Micro Mover (Artaius (USA)) 467[6] 4759[5] >38h<
Stonecutter 4 b br g Warning-South Shore (Caerleon (USA)) 1377[5] 1675[3] (2050) 4512[5] >68h<
Stonehenge Sam (IRE) 5 b g Asir-Astrina's Daughter (Pry) 2696[17] 3494[F] 4161[F]
Stone Island 4 b g Rambo Dancer (CAN)-Single Gal (Mansingh (USA)) (1172) 1595[5] 1675[6] 2668[14] 3131[6] 3666[U] 3926[5] 4453[6] (4636) >49?h<
Stonesby (IRE) 5 b g The Bart (USA)-Maid In The Mist (Pry) 2633[10] 3548[3] >49fh<
Stone The Crows (IRE) 7 b g 2626[6] >24fh<
Stoney Burke (IRE) 8 b or br g **2956[P] 3316[2] 3643[P]** >118dc<
Stoney Valley 7 b g 952[5] 1137[5] 1355[F] 1841[2] 1939[2] 3148[5] >83h<
Stop the Waller (IRE) 8 b g **1142[4] 1293[6] 1662[3] 1983[3]** >67h 123c<
Storm Alert 11 b g **(1134) (1509) 1792[3] (2058) 2646[6] 4131[4]** >155dc<
Storm Alive (IRE) 6 b g Electric-Gaileen (Boreen (FR)) **4076[6]**
Storm Call 6 b m 2041[6] 2785[9] 3024[6] >58h<
Storm Damage (IRE) 5 b g 3038[17] 3150[10] >89h<
Storm Dance 6 b g 100[9] >62h<
Storm Drum 8 ch g 415[3] 605[4] 725[4] 827[5] 1040[5] >79h<
Storm Dust 8 b g 1832[6] (2644) 4398[8] (4660) >94h<
Storm Falcon (USA) 7 ch g 2952[8] **3638[12] 4214[7] 4258[2] 4612[2] 4793[4]** >62dh 121dc<
Storm Forecast (IRE) 5 b g Strong Gale-Cooleogan (Proverb) 4433[2] >51fh<
Stormhill Harpie 6 b m Nearly A Hand-Kelpie (Import) 1673[P]
Stormhill Pilgrim 8 b g **1032[3] 1285[3] 1472[5] (3900) 4158[2] 4344[F]** >102c<
Stormhill Stag 5 b g Buckley-Sweet Sirenia (Al Sirat (USA)) 4657[2] (4774) >72fh<
Stormhill Warrior 6 b g Welsh Captain-Port'n Lemon (Hot Brandy) **3830[P]**
Storm Home 5 gr g Little Wolf-Persian Water (Waterfall) 4531[14] 4626[14] >19fh<
Stormin Gift 6 ch g Germont-God's Gift (Green God) 99[12]
Storming Lady 7 b m Strong Gale-Drom Lady (Royalty) **(4615)** >94++c<
Storming Lorna (IRE) 7 b m 1049[8] 1310[P] 2913[14] 3327[4] 3448[5] >34h<
Storm Queen (IRE) 6 b m Le Bavard (FR)-Strong Willed (Strong Gale) 2931[15] >26fh<
Storm Run (IRE) 7 b g (549) 3342[F] >78h<
Storm Tiger (IRE) 6 b g 1036[13] 1317[12] 1796[4] 2692[2] 3050[P] (3447) >57h<
Stormtracker (IRE) 8 br g (221) **(720) 1054[2] (1354) 3598[2] 4213[P] 4661[2]** >86?h 128?c<
Storm Warrior 12 b g **57[4] 94[P] 158[P] 213[U]** 257[6] **460[4]** >61h 80dc<
Storm Wind (IRE) 4 ch g Digamist (USA)-Hilton Gateway (Hello Gorgeous (USA)) 1149[10] 2753[P] >27h<
Stormy Coral (IRE) 7 br g 1294[3] **(1941) (2542) 3316[3] 4185[5]** >70h 117c<
Stormyfairweather (IRE) 5 b g Strong Gale-Game Sunset (Menelek) 1457[6] 2808[2] 3172[7] (3754) (4181) (4547) >95+h<
Stormy Passage (IRE) 7 b g 1260[4] (1695) 2074[2] (3405) (3581) 4052[8] >91h<
Stormy Session 7 b g 3048[4] 3295[12] 3689[P] 4309[6] 4563[2] 4803[5] >63h<
Stormy Sunset 10 br m **547[4] 887[4] 1199[F] (2704) 3537[P]** >61dh 88c<
Straight Laced (USA) 10 b g **556[4]** >83h<
Straight Talk 10 b g **809[2] 1133[2] 1287[5] 1513[U] 4074[F]** >136dc<
Strange Ways 9 b g **1179[U] 1445[P]** 1537[P] >64c<
Strategic Ploy 4 b f Deploy-Wryneck (Niniski (USA)) 2993a[3] 3525a[4] 4364a[10] >87h<
Strathminster 6 gr g Minster Son-Strathdearn (Saritamer (USA)) 1317[8] 2010[6] 3621[P] >71h< (DEAD)
Strathmore Lodge 8 b m **3556[P]** 3827[P] 4283[P] >62h<
Strath Royal 11 b g **3316[5] 3751[4]** >114h 139?c<
Strathtore Dream (IRE) 6 b or br m **694[P]** 1078[8] >37h<
Stratton Flyer 7 b m **3456[5] 4523[2] 4643[5]** >26h 62dc<
Stray Harmony 7 ch m 3112[8] **4537[U] (4655)** >29h 49?c<
Strephon (IRE) 7 b g 1775[8]
Stretching (IRE) 4 br g Contract Law (USA)-Mrs Mutton (Dancers Image (USA)) 1514[4]
Striding Edge 12 ch g **76[6]** 4789[7] >31h 82c<
Striffolino 5 b g 3921[P] >35h< (DEAD)
Strike A Light (IRE) 5 b g 980[4] 3337[P]
Strike-a-Pose 7 ch m 1569[8] 1770[5] 1946[3] 2882[3] 3112[9] 3803[6] 4002[3] 4468[11] (4648) (4739) >54h<
Strokesaver (IRE) 7 ch g 1586[10] 1798[6] **2007[P] 2693[P] 2908[3] 3173[2] 3427[5] 3717[6] (3978)** >75?h 97+c<
Stroll Home (IRE) 7 ch g Tale Quale-Sales Centre (Deep Run) **4116a[F] 4356a[11]** >26h 97+c<
Strongalong (IRE) 7 b g **1313[6] 1668[F] 2912[4] 3306[2] 3715[3]** 4481[P] 4575[5] **4706[2]** >48h 81c<
Strong Approach 12 br g **63[F]** >113c< (DEAD)
Strong Case (IRE) 9 gr g Strong Gale-Sunshot (Candy Cane) **179[F]** >105h<
Strong Character 11 b g Torus-La'bavette (Le Bavard (FR)) 3032[P] 3481[8] 4147[P] 4393[7] 4500[7] 4705[P] >35h<
Strong Deel (IRE) 9 b g **1162[3] 1315[U] 1655[5] 1806[P]** >73h 122c< (DEAD)
Strong Glen (IRE) 9 br g **3334[P]** >26h<
Strong John (IRE) 9 b g 95[P] 184[11] 208[2] 264[2] 582[3] (647) >65h 85c<
Strong Magic (IRE) 5 br g Strong Gale-Baybush (Boreen (FR)) 2904[8] 3365[12] >30fh<
Strong Medicine 10 b g **(1016) (1272) 1366[7] 1637[F] 1869[2] 2057[5] 2647[5] 4509[5] 4802[6]** >108h 124c<
Strong Mint (IRE) 6 br g Strong Gale-Derrygold

(Derrylin) 1052[5] 1362[4] (1834) 2066[11] 3366[8] >45h<

Strong Paladin (IRE) 6 b g 1453[6] 1938[7] (3337) (3718) >84h<

Strong Promise (IRE) 6 b or br g (674) 744[2] (1061) (1136) 1366[2] (1520) 2115[4] (2935) 3614[5] 4049[2] (4165) >155h 171c<

Strong Sound 10 b g 56[P] 136[5] 3710[3] >109c<

Strong Stuff (IRE) 7 b g Strong Gale-Must Rain (Raincheck) 1371[F]

Strong Tarquin (IRE) 7 br g (887) 1038[4] 1426[6] 3339[P] >110c<

Strong Tel (IRE) 7 b g 1573[3] 3399[3] 3734[F] >75h<

Struggles Glory (IRE) 6 b g Kamehameha (USA)-Another Struggle (Cheval) (4135) (4319) 4792[2] >129c<

Studio Thirty 5 gr g Rock City-Chepstow Vale (USA) (Key To The Mint (USA)) 871[5] 1059[F] 1208[9] 1597[P] >34h<

St Ville 11 b g 1571[8] 1952[7] 2659[10] 3016[7] 3180[3] 3411[2] (3604) 3737[2] 3892[2] (4253) (4439) 4622[3] 4803[4] >87h<

Stylish Allure (USA) 4 b g Topsider (USA)-Excellent Fettle (USA) (State Dinner (USA)) (3525a) 3634[15] 4364a[4] >89h<

Stylish Gent 10 br g 3744[U] 4280[3] >48h<

Stylish Interval 5 ch g 806[5] 1049[11] (1141) 1942[7] 2509[11] (3723) 3983[7] 4146[2] 4339[5] 4628[3] (4705) >67h<

Stylish Rose (IRE) 7 b m 4163[3] >48h<

Suas Leat (IRE) 7 b br g 96[3] (586) 647[2] (735) 876[2] (1049) 1305[3] 2701[4] 3992[7] 4204[11] >77h<

Sublime Fellow (IRE) 7 b g (933) 1120[5] (1714) 2116[4] 2783[6] (3417) (3571) 4012[3] 4274[2] (4540) >102h 124c<

Sudanor (IRE) 8 b g Khartoum (USA)-Alencon (Northfields (USA)) 4406[P] >70h<

Sudden Spin 7 b g 1701[3] 1988[F] 2545[9] 3693[3] >71h<

Sudden Storm (IRE) 6 br m 317a[5] >89h<

Suffolk Girl 5 ch m 25[7]

Suffolk Road 10 br g 3756[2] 4167[P] >110c<

Sugar Hill (IRE) 7 b g 1073[2] 1318[5] 1564[2] (1829) 2681[6] 3675[P] 4098[2] >34h 96c<

Suilven 5 b m Teenoso (USA)-Erica Superba (Langton Heath) 2931[7] 3440[8] >68fh<

Suivez 7 b g 62[2] 103[2] 318a[11] 651[F] 4271[P] 4398[5] >87h<

Sujud (IRE) 5 b br m 60[4] (585) (680) 3709[4] >77h<

Sukaab 12 gr g 413[4] 3949[2] >58h 81c<

Sula's Dream 8 b m Sula Bula-Gallic Dream (French Vine) 1323[P] 2875[8] 3052[P] 3541[P]

Sulawesi (IRE) 4 b f In The Wings-Royal Loft (Homing) 2622[5] 2925[F] 3224[2] 3745[2] (3996) (4093) >82h<

Sullamell 6 b g 1964[P] 2678[P] 4451[P] 4707[S]

Sultan's Son 11 b g 4308[U] 4469[4] >72?h 68c<

Summer Haven 8 b m 934[4] 1798[P] 1962[4] 3112[F] 3360[7] 3671[5] 3962[P] >46h<

Summerhill Special (IRE) 6 b m 2957[3] 3199[5] 3351[7] 3728[4] >93dh<

Summer Princess 4 ch f Prince Sabo-Lafrowda (Crimson Beau) 3226[7] 3544[P] 4532[5] 4756[2] >53h<

Summer Spell (USA) 4 b br c Alleged (USA)-Summertime Lady (USA) (No Robbery) 1634[3] (2622) 3007[5] 3301[3] 4014[4] (4273) >93h<

Summer Villa 5 b m 490[3] 2792[3] 3057[2] 3131[9] 3542[2] 3730[5] 3933[3] 4295[2] 4423[2] 4542[3] 4732[5] 4795[5] >50h<

Summerway Legend 5 b m Then Again-Bit of a Lass (Wassl) 191[5] 918[4]

Summit Else 6 b m 2656[P] 3431[P] 4508[P]

Sumo 4 ch g Superlative-Model Lady (Le Bavard (FR)) 4531[9] 4774[8] >43fh<

Sunday Venture (NZ) 5 b g Lucky Ring-Guimpe (NZ) (Bold Venture (NZ)) 1774[2] 3626[W] (3676) >68fh<

Sungia (IRE) 8 b g 935[F] 1041[P] >51h<

Sunkala Shine 9 ch g 4502[3] 4574[F] 4764[5] >51h 78dc<

Sunley Bay 11 gr g 1997[4] 2575[4] 2881[2] 3036[P] 3763[2] >126c<

Sunley Secure 4 b g Warrshan (USA)-Brown Velvet (Mansingh (USA)) 944[5] 1011[2] 1634[14] >66h<

Sun Mark (IRE) 6 ch g Red Sunset-Vivungi (USA) (Exbury) 3031[15]

Sunny Leith 6 b g Feelings (FR)-Pinkie Hill (Le Coq d'Or) 1345[5] 1667[7] 2619[12] 2790[4] 3066[2] 3531[4] >69h<

Sunny Mount 11 b g 3062[3] >99c<

Sun of Spring 7 b g Green Desert (USA)-Unsuspected (Above Suspicion) 1659[7] 1905[7] 3587[4] 3955[5] >57h<

Sunrise Sensation 4 ch g Super Sunrise-Gilzie's Touch (Feelings (FR)) 2804[7] 3142[8] >44fh<

Sunrise Special (IRE) 4 b g Petorius-Break of Day (On Your Mark) 4382[11]

Sunset and Vine 10 gr g Norwick (USA)-Starky's Pet (Mummy's Pet) 1195[3] 1809[2] 2049[2] 2643[4] >104dc<

Sunset Flash 5 b g Good Times (ITY)-Political Prospect (Politico (USA)) 2770[10] >15fh<

Sunset Run 11 b g 3922[P] (DEAD)

Sunstrike 5 ch g Super Sunrise-Gilzie's Touch (Feelings (FR)) 2633[8] 2953[8] >33h<

Sun Surfer (FR) 9 ch g 1661[6] 1982[3] >122h 84+c<

Sunsword 6 b m Broadsword (USA)-Suntino (Rugantino) 2931[17] 3703[P] >19fh<

Suny Bay (IRE) 8 gr g 1454[5] (3294) 4074[2] >80+h 155c<

Super Brush (IRE) 5 br m 1085[P] 1278[10]

Super Coin 9 b g 1199[2] 1572[2] 1787[F] (2091) 3015[2] 3638[11] 4225[2] 4624[3] >122c<

Superensis 7 ch g Sayf El Arab (USA)-Superlife (USA) (Super Concorde (USA)) 829[2] 974[6] >68h<

Superexalt 5 ch g Exorbitant-Super Sue (Lochnager) 2924[7] 3487[9] 3973[6] >30h<

Supergold (IRE) 4 ch g Keen-Superflash (Superlative) 1953[16] 2678[P]

Super Guy 5 b g Exodal (USA)-Custard Pie (Castle Keep) 705[9] 939[13] 1667[11] 1967[5] 4249[P] 4409[P] >41h<

Super High 5 b g Superlative-Nell of The North (USA) (Canadian Gil (CAN)) 2055[6] >50h<

Superhoo 6 b g (55) 182[2] 734[3] >70h<

Superior Finish 11 br g 3147[3] >143c<

Superior Risk (IRE) 8 b g 1645[P] >103h 105c<

Supermarine 11 b g Noalto-Lucky Love (Mummy's Pet) 3882[P] 4151[4] 4334[U] 4517[5] 4751[U] >45c<

Supermick 6 ch g 1145[2] (1381) 1599[7] 2824[3] 3056[4] >66h<

Supermister 4 br g Damister (USA)-Superfina (USA) (Fluorescent Light (USA)) 589[P]

Supermodel 5 ch m 31[4] 139[4] 219[2] 1351[2] 1870[4] 4743[P] >69h<

Super Nova 6 b g Ra Nova-Windrush Song (True Song) 2811[17] 3939[9]

Super Rapier (IRE) 5 b g Strong Gale-Misty Venture (Foggy Bell) 1329[4] 1551[6] 3133[3] 3445[4] 3942[W] 4136[3] 4527[3] >62h<

Super Ritchart 9 b g 1418[5] 1732[7] 2667[3] 2819[3] 3188[2] 3331[U] >59h 89c<

Super Saffron 7 b m 2510[8] >39fh<

Super Sandy 10 ch m 1295[5] 1578[11] 2544[6] 3069[7] 3482[4] 4013[7] 4517[2] >92c<

Super Sharp (NZ) 9 ch g 63[4] 76[3] (537) (601) 676[2] 883[3] (1146) 3547[4] 3832[4] >53dh 93c<

Super Tactics (IRE) 9 b g 811[2] (943) (1321) 1454[4] (2051) (2621) 2890[F] 3999[4] 4131[2] >90h 143c<

Supertop 9 b or br g 698[2] (784) (876) 1025[2] (1500) 1701[5] (1971) 2507[3] 2802[3] 4339[2] 4761[3] >93h 102c<

Supposin 9 b g 857[3] 1024[2] 1209[9] 1578[14] 2652[4] 3223[P] 3645[8] 3886[7] (4234) 4404[6] 4710[2] >62h 107c<

Supreme Charm (IRE) 5 b g 1507[4] 2055[5] 2690[16] 2961[6] 4403[2] >69h<

Supreme Comfort (IRE) 5 b m Supreme Leader-Malozza Brig (New Brig) 59[2] 1052[P]

Supreme Crusader (IRE) 6 br g 1685[P] 3535[P] 3685[8]

Supreme Dealer 12 ch g 4615[4] >75c<

Supreme Flyer (IRE) 7 b g 1768[2] 2759[3] (3706) (4230) 4376[2] >80h<

Supreme Genotin (IRE) 8 b g 1788[2] 1995[2] 2552[9] 3424[U] >79h<

Supreme Illusion (AUS) 4 ch f Rory's Jester (AUS)-Counterfeit Coin (AUS) (Comeram (FR)) (3058) 3542[5] 3689[P] 4129a[2] >54h<

Supreme Kellycarra (IRE) 6 b m 1260[8] >24h<

Supreme Lady (IRE) 6 b m (1709) (3045) 3615[12] 4210[4] >104h<

Supreme Rambler (IRE) 8 b g 3796[9] >35h<

Supreme Soviet 7 ch g 2764[2] 2958[4] 3315[2] 3485[9] 3791[4] (4568) 4702[6] >67h<

Supreme Star (USA) 6 b g (659) 960[2] 1378[5] 1599[8] >68h<

Supreme Target (IRE) 5 b m 2633[4] 3006[7] 3611[4] >58h<

Supreme Troglodyte (IRE) 5 b m Supreme Leader-Clontinty Queen (Laurence O) 1555[2] 1966[4] 2677[11] 3226[5] 3581[2] 4528[4] 4628[4] >58h<

Supremo (IRE) 8 b g Cataldi-Sanctify (Joshua) 1250[8] 2663[6] 3295[11] 4233[P] >57h<

Suranom (IRE) 5 b h Alzao (USA)-Gracieuse Majeste (FR) (Saint Cyrien (FR)) 2669[14] 3575[2] (3829) 4236[5] >68h<

Sure Metal 14 b g 702[F] >95dc<

Sure Pride (USA) 9 b g 4619[5] >86?h 82c<

Surgical Spirit 7 b m 54[8] >39h<

Surprise City 6 b g Wonderful Surprise-Better Try Again (Try My Best (USA)) 1774[14] 3548[14] 4528[W]

Surprise Guest (IRE) 6 ch g 1539[10] >58h<

Surrey Dancer 9 b g 1512[4] (1828) >110?h<

Sursum Corda 6 b g 2677[2] >79h<

Suselja (IRE) 6 b m 4259[2] 4516[3] >51h<

Sutherland Moss 6 b g (1842) 2546[11] 3159[10] 3644[F] >77fh< (DEAD)

Sutton Boy 8 b g 4161[P] 4450[U]

Suvalu (USA) 5 b g Woodman (USA)-Danlu (USA) (Danzig (USA)) 743[7] 3723[2] 3989[7] >60h<

Suvla Bay (IRE) 9 b g 2915[13] 3281[9] (3435) 3945[4] >38h 81c<

Swahili Run 9 ch g 3053[F] 3229[F] 3743[P] 4443[6] 4732[P] >28h<

Swallows Nest 10 ch g 314a[6] >119c< (DEAD)

Swanbister (IRE) 7 b g 1290[U] 1640[2] 2042[2] (2787) 3317[4] 3557[2] (3885) 4207[10] >88h<

Swandale Flyer 5 ch g Weldnaas (USA)-Misfire (Gunner B) 3888[4] 4244[3] >65h 72c<

Swank Gilbert 11 b g 784[8] 3976[7] 4755[7] >12h<

Swansea Gold (IRE) 6 ch m Torus-Show M How (Ashmore (FR)) 4623[2] >85c<

Swan Street (NZ) 6 b g 955^{5} 1276^{2} 1394^{6} 1873^{5} 2694^{4} 3604^{5} 3818^{10} 4255^{4} **>53h<**
Swarf (IRE) 7 ch g 3295^{P}
Swedish Invader 6 b g 212^{7} 474^{4} **>66h<**
Sweepaway (IRE) 4 b f Brush Aside (USA)-Her Name Was Lola (Pitskelly) 3548^{P} **(DEAD)**
Sweep Clean (IRE) 5 b g Brush Aside (USA)-Quay Blues (Quayside) 3425^{10} 3676^{5} **>56fh<**
Sweet Buck 8 br g 1472^{7} 3732^{U} 3968^{P} 4158^{P} **>30c<**
Sweet Disorder (IRE) 7 br m 217^{5} 295^{6} **>62h<**
Sweet Glow (FR) 10 b g 2950^{P}
Sweet Little Briar (IRE) 6 gr m Celio Rufo-Mandias Slave (Ozymandias) 4301^{11} 4539^{4} 4774^{7} **>52fh<**
Sweet Lord (IRE) 6 ch g Aristocracy-Sweet And Fleet (Whistling Deer) 2808^{4} **>74h<**
Sweetly Disposed (IRE) 9 b g 1962^{F} 3424^{P}
Sweet Mount (IRE) 5 b m Mandalus-Sweet Slievenamon (Arctic Slave) 1800^{10} 2572^{9} 3226^{P} **>42fh<**
Sweet Noble (IRE) 8 ch g 27^{4} 71^{10} 4378^{5} **>55h<**
Sweet Perry 6 b g Sweet Monday-La Charmit (Nearly A Hand) 3170^{20}
Sweet Talker (IRE) 5 b g Le Bavard (FR)-Vultellobar (Bargello) 25^{W} 99^{11} 181^{P}
Sweet Trentino (IRE) 6 b g 1327^{P} 1642^{7} 1959^{6} 2808^{6} 3269^{7} (3434) **>60h<**
Swiftly Supreme (IRE) 4 b f Supreme Leader-Malozza Brig (New Brig) 4150^{10} **>32fh<**
Swift Move 5 ch m Move Off-Phyl's Pet (Aberdeen) 1821^{P}
Swift Pokey 7 b g 2883^{P} 3334^{R} 3489^{R} 3964^{9} 4233^{P} 4437^{3} **>30h<**
Swift Riposte (IRE) 6 b g 2953^{4} (3305) 3883^{6} 4244^{12} **>62h<**
Swinging Sixties (IRE) 6 b g 3204^{5} 3674^{3} 3811^{4} **>57h<**
Swing Lucky 12 b g 1339^{6} 1537^{P} 1828^{P} **>52h<**
Swing Quartet (IRE) 7 b or br m 887^{F} 1037^{4} 1447^{P} 1906^{8} 2694^{11} (3554) 3681^{2} 3920^{8} 4178^{6} **>73h<**
Swings'N'Things (USA) 5 b m 723^{7} (748) **>69h<**
Swiss Account 8 ch m Alias Smith (USA)-Chubby Ears (Burglar) 4548^{9}
Swiss Comfort (IRE) 6 b m 60^{P}
Swiss Gold 7 ch g 1080^{5} **>55h< (DEAD)**
Swiss Mountain 7 b or br m 54^{3} 66^{11} **>64h<**
Swiss Tactic (IRE) 8 br g 1829^{U} 2926^{4} 3274^{P} 3729^{P} **>46h 82c<**
Sword Beach 13 ch g 2^{6} 56^{3} 104^{2} 136^{4} 180^{F} **>117dc<**
Swynford King 5 b g 161^{5}
Swynford Supreme 4 ch g Statoblest-Comtec Princess (Gulf Pearl) 1356^{3} 1699^{5} 2669^{16} **>54h<**
Syban 6 ch g 980^{12} 1303^{5}
Sybillin 11 b g 2058^{4} 2618^{5} 2783^{7} **>121?c<**
Sydillium 5 b g Ilium-Blue Mischief (Precocious) 865^{21}
Sydmonton 11 ch g Deep Run-Inaghmose (Pitpan) 263^{3} (477) **>81c<**
Sydney Barry (NZ) 12 b g 63^{5} 187^{8} 222^{2} 457^{P} **>83h 96c< (DEAD)**
Sydney Boon 6 ch g Newski (USA)-Bassinet (Sagaro) 3111^{P}
Sylvan Celebration 6 b m 3^{P} **>52h<**
Sylvan Sabre (IRE) 8 b g 62^{8} **>89h<**
Sylvester (IRE) 7 ch g 1036^{7} 1327^{P} 3050^{3} 3186^{P} 3429^{2} **>57h<**
Symbol of Success (IRE) 6 b g 2951^{3} **>77h 101?c<**
Symphony's Son (IRE) 6 b g 1329^{5} 1830^{9} 2663^{3} 3272^{6} (3847) **>83+h<**
Synieyourmissed (IRE) 8 b g $321a^{5}$ **>44h 85c<**
Syrus P Turntable 11 b g 3994^{3} 4545^{P} 4748^{10} **>57c<**

T

Taarish (IRE) 4 b g Priolo (USA)-Strike It Rich (FR) (Rheingold) 3445^{5} 3668^{2} **>70h<**
Tabbitts Hill 5 gr m Kalaglow-Woodfold (Saritamer (USA)) 1555^{14} 3170^{18} 4420^{15} **(DEAD)**
Tablets of Stone (IRE) 4 b g Contract Law (USA)-Remember Mulvilla (Ballad Rock) 548^{2} 688^{3} 736^{5} **>62h<**
Tabriz 4 b f Persian Heights-Faisalah (Gay Mecene (USA)) 3802^{7} 3908^{2} **>53h<**
Tabu Lady (IRE) 6 b m (3) 12^{3} **>84h<**
Tactix 7 gr m 1716^{4} 2803^{F} 3094^{4} 3306^{7} 3724^{3} 4149^{3} 4515^{5} 4751^{8} **>42h 67c<**
Tadellal (IRE) 6 ch m 1299^{P} **>77h< (DEAD)**
Tadpole (IRE) 5 gr g Wood Chanter-Iora Rua (King of Clubs) 1362^{17}
Tafzal 6 br g Afzal-Taffidale (Welsh Pageant) 980^{3}
Tafzalette 5 ch m Afzal-Taffidale (Welsh Pageant) 3006^{13} **>18fh<**
Tagatay 4 b g Nomination-Salala (Connaught) 2060^{3} 2859^{8} 3287^{10} **>66h<**
Tailormade 5 ch g Broadsword (USA)-Blades (Supreme Sovereign) 2696^{7} **>43fh<**
Tailormade Future 5 b g Starch Reduced-Miss Admington (Double Jump) 418^{11} 653^{17} 1118^{P}
Tain Ton 5 ch g Green Adventure (USA)-Hylton Road (Kinglet) 1203^{6} 1685^{5} **>53fh<**
Tajar (USA) 5 b g Slew O' Gold (USA)-Mashaarif (USA) (Mr Prospector (USA)) 1851^{10} **>29h<**
Take a Flyer (IRE) 7 b g 916^{4} 971^{P} **>62h<**
Takeamemo (IRE) 4 ch f Don't Forget Me-Persian Myth (Persian Bold) 2925^{3} 3226^{3} (3404) **>78+h<**
Take Cover (IRE) 6 b g 1517^{3} 1807^{7} 2861^{2} 3049^{3} **>69h<**
Take the Buckskin 10 b g 1646^{3} 2049^{4} 3104^{2} **>103h 98c<**
Take Two 9 b g 422^{2} 539^{3} 684^{6} **>74h 84c<**
Talathath (FR) 5 b g Soviet Star (USA)-Mashmoon (USA) (Habitat) 1921^{3} 2939^{2} (3494) 3802^{4} (4176) (4299) 4701^{2} **>89h<**
Tales Of Hearsay (GER) 7 gr g 3735^{9} **>24h<**
Talina's Law (IRE) 5 b m $318a^{14}$ $1752a^{8}$ **>99h<**
Talk Back (IRE) 5 br g 1659^{P} 1830^{P} 3536^{P} **>78dh<**
Tall Measure 11 b g 805^{3} 1344^{2} 1988^{F} 4077^{2} 4286^{P} **>70h 93c<**
Tallulah Belle 4 b f Crowning Honors (CAN)-Fine a Leau (USA) (Youth (USA)) 640^{F} 807^{2} 906^{U} **>59h<**
Tallywagger 10 b g 29^{4} 495^{F} (690) 827^{4} 1143^{2} 1265^{2} 1671^{6} 1971^{3} 2507^{8} **>105h 90dc<**
Tamandu 7 b m 1337^{2} 1466^{4} **>58h<**
Tamarpour (USA) 10 b g Sir Ivor-Tarsila (High Top) 3615^{5} 3851^{3} 4016^{8} **>106h<**
Tamars Cousin 7 b g Ascendant-Hurricane Lizzie (Kalimnos) 549^{P}
Tammy's Friend 10 b g 3924^{U} 4316^{U} 4634^{4} 4724^{5} **>100c<**
Tamsin's Gem 6 ch m Most Welcome-Sea Power (Welsh Pageant) 59^{8}
Tancred Mischief 6 b m 1822^{6} 3641^{B} **>65h<**
Tangle Baron 9 gr g 3586^{5} 4015^{6} **>89c<**
Tanglefoot Tipple 6 b g 25^{2} 2648^{2} 2794^{7} 3340^{8} **>37h<**
Tango Man (IRE) 5 ch g 1814^{P} 1984^{9} 2813^{4} (2943) 3429^{11} 4443^{3} 4807^{11} **>56h<**
Tango's Delight 9 b g 76^{4} 190^{P} 305^{5} 411^{F} 740^{P} 903^{5} 4174^{F} 4520^{4} 4659^{P} **>68h 69c<**
Tanseeq 6 b g 1123^{2} 1374^{5} (1630) **>70+h<**
Tantara Lodge (IRE) 6 b g Import-Fashion Blade (Tanfirion) 2035^{4} 2763^{5} 2945^{2} 3967^{P} **>74?h<**
Tapageur 12 b g Tap On Wood-Ravenshead (Charlottown) 1202^{P} 1763^{P} 2660^{P} 3179^{P}
Tapatch (IRE) 9 b g 2631^{7} 2799^{F} 3034^{4} 3199^{4} 3479^{2} 3642^{3} (4057) 4297^{3} (4517) 4629^{4} (4797) **>75h 97c<**
Tapestry Rose 6 ch m 3061^{P} 3811^{7} 3896^{7} **>16h<**
Tap On Tootsie 5 b m 502^{2} 792^{2} 1135^{2} **>70h<**
Tappers Knapp (IRE) 5 b g Brush Aside (USA)-Gales Money (Strong Gale) 2696^{5} **>57fh<**
Tap Shoes (IRE) 7 b g 1693^{2} 1995^{7} 4071^{4} **>49h<**
Ta-Ra-Abit (IRE) 4 br f Tornabuoni-Frigid Lady (Frigid Aire) 3006^{10} 3365^{8} **>30fh<**
Tara Boy 12 b g Rusticaro (FR)-Flosshilde (Rheingold) 4326^{7} 4511^{2} 4631^{6} **>88c<**
Tara Gale (IRE) 5 b m Phardante (FR)-Smashing Gale (Lord Gayle (USA)) (2757) 4287^{4} 4407^{5} **>66fh<**
Taramoss 10 b g 3492^{P} **>120?c<**
Tara Rambler (IRE) 8 ch g 1127^{2} 1794^{4} **>98h<**
Target Line 7 b g 1718^{5} 1853^{5} **>57h 71c<**
Tarragon (IRE) 7 ch g Good Thyne (USA)-Vanda (Florescence) 4519^{2} 4737^{P} **>60?h<**
Tarrock 7 ch g 1933^{P} **>86h< (DEAD)**
Tarrs Bridge (IRE) 6 gr g Riberetto-Grey Tor (Ahonoora) (954) (1088) 1561^{2} (1915) 2888^{5} 3303^{5} 3635^{9} 4052^{U} **>102h<**
Tarry 4 b f Salse (USA)-Waitingformargaret (Kris) (699) 944^{6} 1253^{4} 1699^{4} 2763^{6} 3434^{P} **>60h<**
Tarry Awhile 11 ch g 4319^{7} **>85c<**
Tartan Joy (IRE) 6 b g Good Thyne (USA)-Liscarton (Le Bavard (FR)) 1579^{7} 1926^{9} 3644^{P} 4144^{P} 4513^{P} 4705^{6} **>19h<**
Tartan Mix (IRE) 6 b g 1050^{6} 1316^{5} **>52h<**
Tartan Tornado 11 b g 3609^{4} 3793^{5} **>100c<**
Tartan Tradewinds 10 b g (650) 789^{5} **>130c<**
Tarthooth (IRE) 6 ch g $316a^{2}$ (1492a) (1751a) $2359a^{F}$ $2995a^{6}$ $3382a^{2}$ **>111h<**
Tashreef 7 b g 453^{6} 539^{2} 641^{8} 695^{3} 1249^{4} 1718^{R} 2044^{P} 4259^{R}
Tathmin 4 b g Weldnaas (USA)-Alcassa (FR) (Satingo) 1706^{7} 2050^{7} 2705^{5} 3204^{3} (4558) **>53h<**
Tatibag 5 ch g Gabitat-Hadera (Northfields (USA)) 1665^{13} 3574^{17} 4069^{6} 4231^{P}
Tau 12 ch g 4317^{3} 4617^{3} **>79c<**
Taura's Rascal 8 b g Scallywag-Centaura (Centaurus) 3357^{F} 4319^{3} 4457^{4} 4792^{P} **>91c<**
Taurean Fire 4 ch g Tina's Pet-Golden Decoy (Decoy Boy) 548^{P}
Taurean Tycoon 13 b g 130^{P} 3568^{6} 3837^{U} **>67c< (DEAD)**
Tauten (IRE) 7 br m Taufan (USA)-Pitaka (Pitskelly) 2818^{12} **>5h<**
Tawafij (USA) 8 ch g 393^{2} 586^{2} 698^{4} 3098^{2} 3324^{U} (4244) 4578^{4} **>69h<**
Tawny Warbler 5 b m Teenoso (USA)-Arctic Warbler (Deep Run) 1555^{8}
Tax Reform (USA) 4 b c Deputy Minister (CAN)-Epicure's Garden (USA) (Affirmed (USA)) $1747a^{8}$ $2333a^{12}$ **>78h<**
Tbilisi 10 b g 3460^{P}
Tea Cee Kay 7 ch g 3010^{5} 3721^{2} 3922^{6} 4308^{2} 4457^{2} **>89c<**
Teacher (IRE) 7 b g Caerleon (USA)-Clunk Click (Star Appeal) 937^{2} 1312^{5} **>57h<**
Teal Bay 5 b m Scallywag-Centaura (Centaurus) 3747^{7} **>46fh<**

Teal Bridge (IRE) 12 b g (3503a) 4110a^{F} 4362a^{5} >109c<

Te Amo (IRE) 5 b h Waajib-Avebury Ring (Auction Ring (USA)) 1874^{4} 3340^{3} >67+h<

Team Princess 7 ch m Prince of Peace-Meant (Menelek) 2812^{P}

Teaplanter 14 b g 2903^{2} 3273^{4} (3490) (3963) >129?c<

Tearaway King (IRE) 7 b g 3637^{P} >85c<

Tearful Prince 13 b g 1057^{U} 1285^{P} >39h 98c<

Teatrader 11 b g 3469^{2} 3680^{P} 3799^{4} 3906^{7} 4323^{P} 4616^{3} 4730^{5} >88c<

Technical Move (IRE) 6 br m Move Off-Technical Merit (Gala Performance (USA)) 3767^{10} 4304^{P} 4641^{3} >22h<

Teddy Edward 7 b g Governor General-Marcee (Rouser) 653^{S} 705^{8} 1052^{8} 1263^{8} 4335^{10} 4516^{P} >20h<

Tedross 6 b br h Ardross-Town Fair (Town Crier) 2682^{17} 2911^{7} 4737^{11}

Teejay'n'aitch (IRE) 5 b g 5^{2} 1049^{3} 1144^{3} 1911^{5} 2790^{6} 3064^{P} 3558^{4} 3826^{U} 3976^{2} (4187) (4285) (4482) (4578) (4746) >74h 76c<

Teejay's Future (IRE) 6 b m 3626^{6} 3907^{5} 4299^{8} 4423^{P} 4638^{6} >44h<

Teelin Bay (IRE) 5 b g Be My Native (USA)-Fahy Quay (Quayside) 1362^{10} 2047^{17}

Teen Jay 7 b g (1039) 1258^{8} 1467^{F} >100h< (DEAD)

Tee Tee Too (IRE) 5 ch g 1413^{9} 1818^{4} 2567^{6} 2882^{12} 4089^{7} 4276^{4} 4558^{3} 4732^{3} >45h<

Teeter The Peeth 7 gr g Dawn Johnny (USA)-Ferndalis (Legal Eagle) 139^{R} 189^{P}

Teeton Mill 8 b g Neltino-Celtic Well (Celtic Cone) (3455) >94+c<

Teeton Two 6 br g Joligeneration-Princess Teeton (Dairialatan) 980^{15} (DEAD)

Teinein (FR) 6 b g (1325) (1567) 1793^{12} 2867^{F} (3356) (3582) >108h 107++c<

Tejano Gold (USA) 7 ch g 1374^{4} (2048) 2779^{F} 3987^{2} 4061^{11} 4307^{3} 4425^{4} 4630^{6} >90h<

Tel E Thon 10 b g 491^{2} (552) >69h<

Telf 17 ch g 957^{U}

Tellaporky 8 b g 3586^{U} 3664^{4} 3852^{6} 4228^{6} 4406^{4} 4637^{3} 4773^{4} >80c<

Tellicherry 8 br m 1423^{4} 1994^{4} 2614^{U} 3040^{5} (3360) (3697) >79h 101c<

Tell The Nipper (IRE) 6 b g 2345a^{4} 4356a^{4} >101h 94c<

Telmar Systems 8 b g 132^{5} 254^{3} 330^{4} 477^{3} 752^{2} 4564^{3} >53h 66c<

Teluk (IRE) 6 ch g 1453^{P}

Temple Garth 8 b g (8) 1082^{F} 4284^{3} 4503^{4} 4609^{P} >87h 109c<

Templemary Lad (IRE) 5 ch g Glacial Storm (USA)-Rhumb Line 4118a^{5} >80fh<

Tempted (IRE) 9 ch m Invited (USA)-Fauvette (USA) (Youth (USA)) (455) >59h<

Tenayestelign 9 gr m (826) 917^{U} 1449^{5} 3352^{4} 3682^{2} 3842^{2} (3931) 4092^{3} 4305^{F} >63h 81c<

Tenbit (IRE) 7 b g 14^{6} 158^{P} >56h 68c<

Ten More Singhas 7 b g Reesh-Legal Darling (Legal Tender) 4399^{P}

Tennessee Twist (IRE) 7 b g 1326^{P} (2883) >89h 128+c<

Tennyson Bay 5 b g Allazzaz-Richards Folly (Hotfoot) 2753^{P}

Ten Past Six 5 ch g Kris-Tashinsky (USA) (Nijinsky (CAN)) 1921^{6} 2539^{7} 2701^{P} 3102^{P} 3612^{9} >36h<

Ten Times (USA) 4 b g On To Glory (USA)-Third And Ten (USA) (Pass Catcher (USA)) 2648^{3} >37fh<

Teoroma 7 ch h Teofane-Poppy Kelly (Netherkelly) 3205^{4} 3621^{12} 3748^{8} >28h<

Terao 11 b g 1173^{6} 1785^{P} 1937^{4} 2879^{9} 3292^{2} (3618) (3800) >141c<

Terrano Star (IRE) 6 ch g Phardante (FR)-Sovereign Sox (Don) 653^{7} 977^{F}

Test Match 10 ch g 3987^{P} >85h 92c<

Texan Baby (BEL) 8 b g 1952^{3} 2659^{9} 3156^{9} >85h 91c<

Thai Electric (IRE) 6 ch m 4352a^{2} >94h<

Thaleros 7 b g 586^{7} 680^{2} 786^{3} 878^{4} 1021^{11} >70h<

Thank U Jim 9 b g 4256^{U} 4713^{F} (4804) >107c<

Tharsis 12 ch g 289^{9} 1304^{6} 1562^{9} 1775^{4} 1822^{4} 2045^{4} >62h<

That Big Baby (IRE) 7 b g Lancastrian-More Chat (Torenaga) 4382^{10} >13h<

That Man Carter (IRE) 6 b g Persian Mews-Jeanarie (Reformed Character) 1834^{15} 2965^{7}

That Old Feeling (IRE) 5 b g 1278^{F} 1663^{8} 2680^{7} 2897^{10} 3689^{P} >41h<

Thats the Life 12 ch g 1328^{3} 1696^{P} (3053) 3336^{3} 4520^{2} 4797^{2} >86c<

The Alamo (IRE) 6 b g 1802^{P} >35h< (DEAD)

Theatreworld (IRE) 5 b g 1759a^{3} 1916^{3} (2461a) 2740a^{2} (3254a) 3597^{2} 4117a^{5} 4365a^{4} >145h<

The Bargeman (NZ) 9 b g 2759^{5} 3539^{5} 4204^{7} 4533^{3} >67h 88c<

The Bird O'Donnell 11 b g 1357^{P} 2693^{6} 2860^{2} >95c<

The Bizzo 6 b m 2791^{10} 3447^{10} 4275^{5} 4547^{6} 4696^{9} >47h<

The Black Dubh (IRE) 4 b g Classic Secret (USA)-Coral Cave (Ashmore (FR)) 646^{9} >47h<

The Black Monk (IRE) 9 ch g 221^{2} 301^{4} 480^{7} >76h<

The Blue Boy (IRE) 9 ch g 23^{P} 158^{2} 190^{3} 256^{P} 395^{4} 452^{2} 583^{D} 644^{3} (683) 732^{4} (914) 1335^{F} >111c< (DEAD)

The Bodhran (IRE) 7 b g 3799^{F}

The Bombers Moon 4 br g Lord Bud-Oakington (Henry The Seventh) 4301^{17} 4554^{9} >7fh<

The Booley House (IRE) 7 b g 1680^{F} 1856^{5} 2749^{3} 3165^{4} 3489^{6} >91c<

The Boozing Brief (USA) 4 b g Turkoman (USA)-Evening Silk (USA) (Damascus (USA)) 1159^{2} 1356^{2} 1652^{U} >58h<

The Bratpack (IRE) 7 b m 133^{11}

The Breaser Fawl (IRE) 9 b g Mississippi-Bandera 319a^{20}

The Brewer 5 ch g 1178^{10} 1476^{9} 1768^{9} 2692^{10} 3234^{3} 3733^{10} 3951^{2} 4223^{2} 4405^{3} >54h<

The Brewmaster (IRE) 5 ch g Torus-Bonne Bouche (Bonne Noel) 865^{2} 1275^{7} 1659^{6} 2808^{3} 2961^{8} (3424) >74h<

The Brud 9 b g 1468^{U} 1582^{5} 2052^{P} >76c<

The Bug 0 G Germont-La Maraichere (Welsh Captain) 2080^{11} 4161^{7} >27h<

The Burglar (IRE) 5 b g Denel (FR)-Night Invader (Brave Invader (USA)) 2047^{14}

The Butterwick Kid 4 ch g Interrex (CAN)-Ville Air (Town Crier) 1205^{4} >56h<

The Campdonian (IRE) 6 ch g 73^{6} >50h<

The Captain's Wish 6 ch g 1317^{4} 1638^{2} 1959^{2} 2759^{4} 3145^{3} 3582^{2} >91h 101c<

The Carrig Rua (IRE) 7 b g 2335a^{5} 2600a^{3} >111c<

The Carrot Man 9 ch g 1393^{3} 3050^{7} 3232^{5} (3673) 3839^{2} 4235^{4} 4553^{2} >50h 111c<

The Caumrue (IRE) 9 b g 1035^{6} 1284^{3} (1515) 1676^{F} 2762^{6} 2894^{F} 3176^{P} 4006^{P} >108dc<

The Chase 6 gr g Komaite (USA)-Torrington's Hope (Rambah) 3548^{17} 4288^{10} 4774^{10} >33fh<

The Cheese Baron 6 b g 890^{8} 1260^{P} 1814^{9} 2036^{P} >37h<

The Clarsach 5 ch m Nicholas Bill-Celtic Slave (Celtic Cone) 2696^{6} >52fh<

The Communicator 11 b g 3439^{P} 3744^{P} 4070^{6} >85?c<

The Cottonwool Kid 5 b g 506^{8} >36h<

The Country Don 5 ch g Town And Country-Huntless (Songedor) 3203^{8} >19fh<

The Country Trader 11 br g 352^{4} >71+h 95c<

The Crazy Bishop (IRE) 9 b g 2602a^{4} 2848a^{5} 3383a^{5} >135+c<

The Crooked Oak 5 ch g 1296^{4} 1801^{7} 2673^{7} 4217^{P} >57h<

The Croppy Boy 5 b g Arctic Lord-Deep Cut (Deep Run) 1124^{5} 1665^{4} 1986^{8} 3676^{11} >59fh<

The Deaconess 6 b m Minster Son-Haddon Anna (Dragonara Palace (USA)) 963^{3} 1178^{5} 1470^{9} 1772^{2} >55h<

The Difference 10 b g Cruise Missile-Brandy's Honour (Hot Brandy) 3459^{6} >68c<

The Early Bird 6 b m Bold Owl-Monsoon (Royal Palace) 2180^{5} >20fh<

The Eens 5 b g Rakaposhi King-Snippet (Ragstone) 1986^{5} 3000^{7} 3703^{6} 4161^{4} 4445^{2} 4628^{6} 4759^{P} >55h<

The Eloper 9 b g 3227^{P}

The Energiser 11 ch g 1022^{P} 1083^{6} 1308^{4} 1691^{6} 1968^{5} 4569^{P} 4751^{P} >63c<

The Executor 7 ch g 66^{6} 183^{6} >72dh<

The Fence Shrinker 6 b g 1118^{6} 1449^{8} 1644^{F} 1815^{4} 3030^{5} 3832^{7} 4419^{4} 4540^{2} 4703^{4} >18h 44c<

Thefieldsofathenry (IRE) 7 b g King Persian-Clodianus (Bay Express) 2828^{5} 3136^{6} 3352^{7} >44h<

The Final Spark 6 b m 1628^{5} 1851^{8} 2649^{13} 3313^{9} >45h<

The Flying Doctor (IRE) 7 b g 3041^{8} 3569^{7} 3718^{5} 4003^{8} (4453) (4542) 4723^{F} >74h<

The Flying Fiddle 5 ch m Northern State (USA)-Miss Flossa (FR) (Big John (FR)) 4304^{P}

The Flying Footman 11 b g 1584^{9} 2695^{P} 3198^{P} >80c<

The Flying Phantom 6 gr g Sharrood (USA)-Miss Flossa (FR) (Big John (FR)) (3233) 3595^{F} 3847^{7} >83h<

The Foolish One 10 b m Idiot's Delight-The Ceiriog (Deep Diver) 72^{7} 158^{P} >68c<

The Frog Prince (IRE) 9 b g 3419^{4} 4013^{P} >84h 136?c<

The Gadfly 5 br g Welsh Captain-Spartan Imp (Spartan General) 2844^{18}

The Gallopin'major (IRE) 7 ch g 179^{P} 351^{P} 424^{2} 510^{2} (581) (644) (746) 896^{2} 3945^{F} >65h 101c< (DEAD)

The General's Drum 10 b g 4545^{4} >98?c<

The Glow (IRE) 9 b g 2817^{9} 3074^{6} >71h 104c<

The Gnome (IRE) 5 b g Polish Precedent (USA)-Argon Laser (Kris) 3330^{4} 3548^{13} 4421^{11} >37fh<

The Go Ahead (IRE) 7 b g 1038^{P} 1318^{4} 2947^{P} >41h 98c<

The Gopher (IRE) 8 ch g General View-Egg Shells 4356a^{P} >97+c<

The Great Flood 4 ch g Risk Me (FR)-Yukosan (Absalom) 1011^{4} (1526) >55h<

The Grey Monk (IRE) 9 gr g (1359) 1649^{2} 2997a^{F} (3292) 4110a^{3} >79h 162+c<

The Grey Texan 8 gr g 3313^{13} 3474^{10} 3723^{9} 4436^{3} 4723^{P} >61h<

The Grey Weaver 4 gr c Touch of Grey-Foggy Dew (Smoggy) 962^{8} 1149^{9} 1377^{15} >31h< (DEAD)

The Herbivore (IRE) 8 b g 1376^{3} 1728^{P} >61c<

The Jogger 12 b g (3273) 3637^{7} >109c<

The Keek (IRE) 5 b m Brush Aside (USA)-Fairgoi (Baragoi) 4580^{14}

The Kerry Ledgend (IRE) 4 b g Phardante (FR)-I'm Grannie (Perspex) 4539^{9} >39fh<

The Khoinoa (IRE) 7 b g (2626) 2787^{5} 3483^{8} 3883^{P} >46h<

The Knitter 5 ch g Derrylin-Meryett (BEL) (Le Grand Meaulnes) 686^{7} 858^{6} 939^{14} 1059^{F} >17h<

The Lad 8 b g Bold Owl-Solbella (Starch Reduced) 859^{2} 1056^{3} >74h<

The Lady Captain 5 b m Neltino-Lady Seville (Orange Bay) (1781) 2844^{5} 3133^{P} >46fh<

The Lady Scores (IRE) 5 br m Orchestra-Lysanders Lady (Saulingo) 4407^{8} >55fh<

The Lancer (IRE) 8 b g 889^{2} 1073^{3} (1696) (1864) 2657^{5} 2949^{3} 4512^{6} >67h 99c<

The Land Agent 6 b g 1766^{2} 2812^{8} >64h<

The Last Fling (IRE) 7 ch g (870) (1129) 1354^{U} (1805) 1936^{3} 2901^{F} 3160^{3} 3616^{U} 4050^{2} >104h 137c<

The Last Mistress 10 b m 549^{4} 901^{7} 4241^{5} >87c<

The Latvian Lark (IRE) 9 b g 4110a^{F} >113h 95+c<

The Legions Pride 4 b c Rambo Dancer (CAN)-Immaculate Girl (Habat) (654) >65h<

The Lightmaker (IRE) 4 b g Mac's Imp (USA)-Lady's Turn (Rymer) 3304^{4} >77fh<

The Little Ferret 7 ch g 209^{3} >52h< (DEAD)

The Lorryman (IRE) 9 ch g 68^{P} 158^{12} 298^{P} 395^{P} 4320^{8} >63h 75dc<

The Major General 10 b g 3270^{P} 4511^{4} >34h 100c<

The Malakarma 11 b g (2930) (3432) 3739^{3} 4179^{6} 4324^{2} (4473) >117c<

The Marmalade Cat 8 ch g Escapism (USA)-Garrison Girl (Queen's Hussar) 1829^{P} 1955^{F}

Theme Arena 4 b f Tragic Role (USA)-Sea Siesta (Vaigly Great) (1595) 1953^{2} 3204^{4} 3447^{11} 3940^{2} 4086^{2} (4276) (4343) >66h<

The Mexicans Gone 9 b g 3156^{P} 3402^{8} >78h<

The Mickletonian 6 ch g 1843^{8} 4056^{4} >62h<

The Mill Height (IRE) 7 ch g Callernish-Cherry Gamble (Meadsville) 3840^{P}

The Millmaster (IRE) 6 b g 1580^{6} 1795^{10} 2816^{5} 2947^{9} 3181^{P} 3945^{P} >33h 70c<

The Millstone 6 b g Welsh Captain-Blue Mint (Bilsborrow) 3907^{9} >24fh<

The Minder (FR) 10 b or br g 485^{2} >86h<

The Mine Captain 10 b g 1676^{3} 2577^{2} (2776) >72h 107c<

The Minister (IRE) 8 br g 1328^{P} 1864^{6} >52h 82c<

Themoreyouknow 8 b g 4769^{F}

The Motcombe Oak 11 ch g 1420^{P} >99?c<

Them Times (IRE) 8 b m 1446^{7} 1816^{6} 2567^{4} 2943^{10} 3338^{7} 3733^{13} 3997^{F} >25h<

The Muckle Quine 6 b m Hubbly Bubbly (USA)-Blessed Damsel (So Blessed) 2080^{15} 2633^{16}

The Naughty Vicar 7 ch g 4217^{6} 4376^{6} >53h<

The Next Waltz (IRE) 6 b g 1245^{3} 1672^{6} 2654^{8} 2800^{10} 4751^{P} >56h<

The Oddfellow 4 b g Efisio-Agnes Jane (Sweet Monday) 2815^{15} 3075^{14} >6h< (DEAD)

The Oozler (IRE) 4 b g Montelimar (USA)-Tikrara (USA) (Assert) (4118a) >85fh<

The Operator (IRE) 6 b g Kefaah (USA)-Come In (Be My Guest (USA)) 4215^{11} 4626^{8} >17h<

The Other Man (IRE) 7 b g 1640^{13} 1807^{13} 2701^{10} 2915^{7} 3368^{5} 3646^{3} >52h<

The Outback Way (IRE) 7 br g 1486a^{3} 1758a^{R} 2848a^{P} 4356a^{8} >91h 93c<

The Parsons Fox 5 ch g Scallywag-Arctic Mission (The Parson) 3592^{6} >54h<

The Phantom Farmer (IRE) 6 b g Phardante (FR)-Good Calx (Khalkis) 3149^{12} 4315^{9} >36fh<

The Point Is 10 ch g Major Point-Babble (Forlorn River) 4160^{P}

The Proms (IRE) 6 b g 890^{5} (1938) 3019^{2} (3265) 3613^{12} >89h<

The Real Article (IRE) 8 gr g 3245a^{3} >123c<

The Reverend Bert (IRE) 9 b g 1260^{3} 1429^{7} 1680^{U} 2693^{2} (2827) 3427^{F} 3639^{8} 3805^{5} 4186^{8} 4211^{5} >81h 117c<

The Ridge Boreen 13 b g 321a^{2} >119c<

Thermal Warrior 9 ch g 1936^{4} 2795^{4} 3060^{U} 3489^{4} 3882^{3} 4549^{2} 4647^{3} >87h 92dc<

Thermecon (IRE) 6 ch g Phardante (FR)-Brosna Girl (Le Moss) 865^{14}

The Road West (IRE) 8 b g Where To Dance (USA)-Cameo Dancer (Jukebox) 2898^{19} 3990^{2} >75h<

The Rum Mariner 10 gr g Julio Mariner-Decorum (Quorum) 3055^{P} 3680^{2} 4607^{2} 4730^{4} >96c<

The Secret Grey 6 gr g 1124^{12} 1633^{12} 2892^{5} 3073^{F} 3470^{2} 3627^{P} 4219^{3} 4377^{2} >7fh 82c<

The Secret Seven 7 ch m 27^{10} >65dh<

The Sharrow Legend (IRE) 5 ch g 1926^{4} 2619^{14} 2798^{7} 3307^{5} 3438^{7} 3727^{P} >52h<

The Shy Padre (IRE) 8 br g 1468^{2} 1858^{F} 2693^{7} 3700^{P} >71h 90c<

The Snow Burn 4 ch g River God (USA)-Rose Rambler (Scallywag) 2750^{3} 3828^{3} >68fh<

The Stager (IRE) 5 b h Danehill (USA)-Wedgewood Blue (USA) (Sir Ivor) 1517^{4} 1830^{7} >62h<

The Stitcher (IRE) 7 b g 1023^{5} >65h<

The Stuffed Puffin (IRE) 5 b g Cataldi-Proud Fairy (Prefairy) 1362^{8} 2005^{4} 2633^{9} 3026^{4} 3494^{5} 3668^{4} 4244^{7} 4285^{P} 4450^{P} >62h<

The Subbie (IRE) 8 b g 1240a^{2} 4350a^{8} >123h 93c<

The Swan 4 ch f Old Vic-El Vino (Habitat) 2738a^{9} >64h<

The Toaster 10 b g 138^{2} 420^{3} 1823^{6} 1991^{4} 2630^{P} 2956^{P} (3725) 4058^{2} 4753^{3} >84h 106c<

The Toiseach (IRE) 6 b g 1455^{3} 2702^{3} 3013^{10} 3402^{4} (3750) 4178^{2} (4536) 4772^{2} >100h<

The True Miller 6 b g Silly Prices-Shankhouse Girl (General Ironside) 3828^{18} 4287^{11}

Thetwokays 6 b br g Pragmatic-Tender Soul (Prince Tenderfoot (USA)) 2012^{12} 3434^{P}

The Vale (IRE) 5 b g Satco (FR)-Lady Kasbah (Lord Gayle (USA)) 705^{11} 2770^{11} >5fh<

The Village Way (IRE) 6 b g Jamesmead-Rydal Way (Roscoe Blake) 4216^{4} (4554) 4656^{2} >74fh<

The Wasp (IRE) 5 gr g Lancastrian-Moll of Kintire (Politico (USA)) 3416^{8}

The Wayward Bishop (IRE) 8 b g 1423^{7} 1572^{U} 2037^{F} 3048^{P} 3688^{F} >35h< (DEAD)

The Weatherman 9 b g 1423^{U} 3173^{F} 4296^{12} >10h<

The West's Asleep 12 ch g 179^{3} 957^{9} >87c<

The Whole Hog (IRE) 8 b g 1582^{U} 1763^{2} (3719) 3993^{2} (4138) (4391) >71h 89c<

The Widget Man 11 b g 1391^{P} 1934^{P} >56h<

The Wise Knight (IRE) 6 b g 4352a^{11} >79h<

They All Forgot Me 10 b g 101^{10} 184^{7} 185^{4} 465^{7} 598^{3} 673^{7} 825^{3} 979^{U} >45h 84c<

The Yank 11 b or br g 2^{2} 342^{2} (530) 678^{3} 804^{3} >108dc<

Theydon Pride 8 ch g 950^{11} 1153^{9} >50h 53c<

The Yokel 11 b g 722^{2} 742^{2} 883^{2} 4797^{P} >29h 88?c<

Thinking Twice (USA) 8 ch g 1340^{3} 1636^{9} 2777^{13} 3150^{9} 3430^{7} >99h 64c<

Thirty Below (IRE) 8 b g Strong Gale-Arctic Bavard (Le Bavard (FR)) 2677^{15} 2948^{7} 3143^{6} 3887^{P} >51h<

This Is My Life (IRE) 8 ch g General View-Bluemore (Morston (FR)) 4630^{7} >28h<

This Nettle Danger 13 b g 3317^{7} 3624^{2} 3750^{6} 4220^{9} >56h<

This Time Lucky 7 b g Ilium-Lac Royale (Lochnager) 3295^{P}

Thomas Rand 8 b g 3973^{5} >42h<

Thornhill 7 b m 4218^{P} 4406^{F} 4773^{P} >52h<

Thornton Gate 8 b g 1032^{F} 1267^{4} 1512^{F} 1804^{8} 1924^{5} 2617^{3} 2902^{6} 3164^{2} 3412^{F} >101h< (DEAD)

Thorntoun Estate (IRE) 4 b g Durgam (USA)-Furry Friend (USA) (Bold Bidder) 699^{7} 1356^{4} 1526^{4} 2060^{8} 2800^{4} 4513^{5} >49h<

Thorntoun House (IRE) 4 b g Durgam (USA)-Commanche Song (Commanche Run) 3910^{7} 4184^{9} 4282^{5} >52h<

Thornwood (IRE) 5 ch g Phardante (FR)-Arctic Mistress (Quayside) 3315^{F} 3883^{5} >60h<

Three Brownies 10 b g (1003a) 1750a^{F} >134c< (DEAD)

Three Farthings 7 b g 1782^{2} 2071^{2} (2868) >68h<

Three Jays 10 b g 4476^{P} >22h<

Three Philosophers (IRE) 8 b or br g 1680^{3} 2667^{F} 2940^{U} >79h 115c< (DEAD)

Three Saints (IRE) 8 b g 1540^{5} 1697^{2} 2869^{U} 3003^{4} >70h 103dc<

Three Scholars 6 b g 1757a^{5} 2347a^{4} 2995a^{4} 3595^{6} 4117a^{9} 4124a^{6} >100h<

Threesocks 4 ch f Weldnaas (USA)-Jeethgaya (USA) (Critique (USA)) 3072^{2} 3226^{F} 4343^{P} >65?h<

Three Wild Days 5 b g 1187^{5} 1499^{2} 2177^{F} >78h< (DEAD)

Thromedownsometing 7 b m 3024^{P} 3483^{P}

Thuhool 9 b g 1034^{6} >68h<

Thumbs Up 11 b g 851a^{4} 1087^{3} 1134^{3} (1442) 1682^{2} 2707^{2} 3009^{4} 3144^{3} (3225) (3738) 4311^{2} >131h 135c<

Thunderbird 5 b m Funny Man-Carlton Valley (Barolo) 3149^{13} 4506^{P}

Thunderpoint (IRE) 5 b g Glacial Storm (USA)-Urdite (FR) (Concertino (FR)) 2904^{7} 3142^{3} 3330^{5} >62fh<

Thunder Road (IRE) 6 b br g Cardinal Flower-Ann Advancer (Even Money) 1275^{14} 2039^{5} 2816^{6} 2908^{F} (4330) 4699^{P} 4769^{4} >7fh 80c<

Thunderstruck 11 b g 895^{2} 1164^{2} 1306^{3} 1702^{P} 1847^{8} >91dc<

Thursday Night (IRE) 6 ch g 1188^{4} 1780^{F} 2049^{F} 2545^{3} 3545^{2} 3698^{2} 3992^{5} 4261^{6} >89h<

Tibbi Blues 10 b m Cure The Blues (USA)-Tiberly (FR) (Lyphard (USA)) 1161^{P}

Tibbs Inn 8 ch g 723^{8} 834^{S} 879^{13} 958^{3} 1251^{R} 1332^{4} 1680^{R} 2038^{P} >42h< (DEAD)

Tibetan 5 b g 2059^{4} 2900^{4} 3267^{7} >104h<

Tickerty's Gift 7 b g 1585^{5} 1709^{4} 1939^{4} 2067^{3} (2871) 3087^{3} (3687) (3814) >92+h<

Ticket To The Moon 7 b m Pollerton-Spring Rocket (Harwell) 4522^{2} >97c<

Tico Gold 9 ch g 1153^{4} 1574^{3} 1691^{F} 1989^{2} 2650^{3} (2860) 3099^{2} 3367^{2} 3477^{3} 3643^{5} 3975^{2} >73h 96c<

Tidal Force (IRE) 6 br g Strong Gale-Liffey Travel (Le Bavard (FR)) (1071) 2547^{13} 2690^{15} 3977^{6} >69h<

Tidal Race (IRE) 5 b g Homo Sapien-Flowing Tide (Main Reef) 1692^{22} 2633^{17} 4288^{11}

Tidebrook 7 ch h 2927^{5} (4260) (4419) >65h

95+c<
Tidjani (IRE) 5 b g 1752a^{7} 1793^{3} 3640^{5} **>99h<**
Tied For Time (IRE) 5 b g Montelimar (USA)-Cornamucla (Lucky Guy) 4216^{15} **>55fh<**
Tigana 5 b m 3352^{11} 3670^{P} 3757^{10} 3811^{P}
Tiger Bee 6 br m 24^{10}
Tiger Claw (USA) 11 b g (1040) **1285^{P}** 1562^{4} 1876^{6} 2570^{8} 2877^{3} 3624^{3} 3892^{3} 4220^{P} 4524^{3} 4727^{6} **>55h<**
Tigh-Na-Mara 9 b m 396^{4} 585^{R} 730^{2} 866^{2} 1046^{U} (1310) 1417^{5} **>71h<**
Tighter Budget (USA) 10 b g **(704) (802) (938) 1142^{8} 1313^{2} 1668^{3} 1823^{4} 3645^{6} 3792^{3} 3911^{P} >95h 108c<**
Tight Fist (IRE) 7 b g 1255^{4} **1664^{U}** 4307^{10} **(4523) 4764^{3} >85h 77c<**
Tilaal (USA) 5 ch h 2806^{4} 3311^{2} **>64h<**
Tilt Tech Flyer 12 b g 1948^{6} 3207^{P} 3632^{7} 3915^{P} **>22h 57c<**
Tilty (USA) 7 b g Linkage (USA)-En Tiempo (USA) (Bold Hour) 2076^{3} (2864) 3358^{3} (3624) 4207^{5} **>77h<**
Tim (IRE) 7 b g 884^{5} 1374^{3} (1455) 1794^{2} (2117) 2625^{4} 2888^{7} 2950^{3} 3277^{5} 3600^{13} **>94h<**
Timbucktoo 10 b g **1688^{2} 2801^{5} 2921^{3} 3692^{5} >121c<**
Time And Charges (IRE) 7 b g **1405a^{F} >32h 97c<**
Time Enough (IRE) 8 ch g **604^{2} 966^{2} (1147) (1383) 1784^{4}** **>53h 116c<**
Time for a Run 10 b g **1889a^{3} 2348a^{3} (2602a) 3383a^{4} 3599^{2} >133dh 143c<**
Time Goes On 5 b m Latest Model-Impromptu (My Swanee) 2566^{10} 2872^{11}
Time Leader 5 ch g 1253^{6} 1327^{3} 1638^{4} 1762^{2} 2036^{5} 2552^{11} 2806^{5} 4175^{2} 4770^{P} **>55h<**
Timely Affair (IRE) 8 b m **323a^{B} >44h 75c<**
Timely Example (USA) 6 ch g 794^{8} 950^{7} 3959^{5} 4276^{7} **>48h<**
Timely Magic (IRE) 5 b g Good Thyne (USA)-Magic Quiz (Quisling) 3574^{3} **>65fh<**
Time To Parlez 6 b g Amboise-Image of War (Warpath) 2840^{7} 3272^{8} **>47h<**
Time Warrior (IRE) 6 ch g Decent Fellow-Oonagh's Teddy (Quayside) 3828^{6} 4287^{2} **>61fh<**
Time Won't Wait (IRE) 8 b g **2639^{4} 2783^{3} 3638^{4} 4062^{U} 4311^{4}** 4565^{3} **>139c<**
Timidjar (IRE) 4 b g Doyoun-Timissara (USA) (Shahrastani (USA)) 3404^{6} 3601^{9} 3996^{3} 4465^{2} 4645^{3} **>71h<**
Tim Soldier (FR) 10 ch g **1564^{P}** 1798^{P} **(1991) (2630) 2863^{2} 3223^{4} 3622^{2} (3925)** 4452^{P} **4635^{4} >59dh 101c<**
Timur's Star 8 b m 60^{P}
Tingrith Lad 5 b g 2811^{16} 3606^{6} **>17fh<**
Tinker's Cuss 6 ch m 1450^{10} 1810^{P} 2576^{12} **3360^{P} >9h<**
Tinklers Folly 5 ch g 586^{P} **>23h<**
Tinotops 7 br g Neltino-Topte (Copte (FR)) **(3739) (4326) >107c<**
Tin Pan Alley 8 b g 1938^{10} 3178^{5} **3758^{U} >47h<**
Tiotao (IRE) 7 b g 1249^{3} 1911^{4} 2505^{2} 2913^{R} 3091^{6} 3327^{8} 4409^{B} 4516^{4} **>45h<**
Tip it In 8 gr g 356^{6} 908^{8} (1204) 1577^{2} (1701) 3035^{8} 3199^{2} 3478^{7} 4296^{9} **>71h<**
Tipp Down 14 ch g **3439^{F} >64c< (DEAD)**
Tipping Along (IRE) 8 ch g **503^{B}** 649^{P} 891^{3} 1040^{4} **>70h<**
Tipping The Line 7 b g 60^{2} (131) 181^{P} 800^{2} 1062^{2} 1384^{6} **>94h<**
Tipp Mariner 12 ch g **1089^{P} 1554^{P} >107c<**
Tipsy Queen 6 b m 133^{13} 287^{6}
Tirley Missile 11 ch g **3185^{P}** 4698^{3} **>64h 72c<**
Tirmizi (USA) 6 b g 1628^{7} (1990) 3478^{9} 3885^{9} **>64h<**
Tissisat (USA) 8 ch g 3234^{6} 3447^{5} **>73h<**
Titan Empress 8 b m 1170^{2} **1420^{5} 1684^{6} 1839^{P} (1951) 2756^{B} >65h 94c< (DEAD)**
Titanium Honda (IRE) 6 gr g Doulab (USA)-Cumbrian Melody (Petong) 675^{P}
Titus Andronicus 10 b g **823^{4} >101c<**
Tiutchev 4 b g Soviet Star (USA)-Cut Ahead (Kalaglow) 2925^{4} 3404^{F} 4003^{U} 4395^{U} 4532^{2} 4807^{3} **>68h<**
T'Niel 6 ch m Librate-Classy Colleen (St Paddy) 3184^{P} 4304^{R} 4423^{R}
Toast The Spreece (IRE) 5 b g Nordance (USA)-Pamphylia (Known Fact (USA)) 3640^{15} 4348a^{4} **>104+h<**
Toat Chieftain 5 b g Puissance-Tribal Lady (Absalom) 3730^{13} 3937^{8} **>1h<**
To Be Fair 10 ch g Adonijah-Aquarula (Dominion) 587^{7} 969^{5} 1332^{5} **>51h<**
Toberlone 4 b g K-Battery-Elisetta (Monsanto (FR)) 4288^{12}
To Be the Best 7 ch g **(681) 694^{2} >51h 91c<**
Toby 4 b g Jendali (USA)-Au Revoir Sailor (Julio Mariner) 4288^{4} **>47fh<**
Toby Brown 4 b g Arzanni-Forest Nymph (NZ) (Oak Ridge (FR)) 1953^{F} 2669^{2} 2925^{7} 3222^{5} 3587^{3} **>78h<**
Todd (USA) 6 b g Theatrical-Boldara (USA) (Alydar (USA)) 974^{2} 2547^{12} 2805^{11} 3222^{P} **>64h<**
Toddling Inn 10 b m **3551^{P} 3837^{P}**
Toddys Lass 5 b m Rakaposhi King-Heaven And Earth (Midsummer Night II) 1665^{15} 1834^{14}
Tod Law 9 b m Le Moss-Owenburn (Menelek) **4411^{6}**
Toejam 4 ch g Move Off-Cheeky Pigeon (Brave Invader (USA)) 4150^{12} **>32fh<**
Tolcarne Lady 8 b m 1200^{P} 2815^{P}
Tolepa (IRE) 4 b f Contract Law (USA)-Our Investment (Crofter (USA)) 4756^{8} **>31h<**
Toll Booth 8 b m 419^{P} **>64h<**
Tomal 5 b g 820^{2} 915^{W} 1337^{W} 1470^{10} 1663^{U} 1796^{7} 2866^{F} 3757^{8} **>61h<**
Tom Brodie 7 b g (941) (1163) (1512) 1924^{4} 2645^{4} 2902^{2} 3163^{3} 3640^{7} 4397^{14} **>108h<**
Tom Diamond 5 ch g Right Regent-Shavegreen Holly VII (Damsire Unregistered) 3235^{15}
Tom Furze 10 b g **3852^{5} 4422^{2} >89?c<**
Tom Log 10 ch g **2903^{8} 3994^{4} >78?c<**
Tommy Cooper 6 br h 4173^{2} 4309^{P} 4376^{7} 4521^{P} **>52h<**
Tommys Webb (IRE) 9 b g Asir-Coleman Lass (Pry) **3439^{4} >80c<**
Tommy Tickle 5 b g Rustingo-Ruths Magic (Current Magic) 3767^{4} 4088^{9} **>39fh<**
Tomorrows Harvest 5 b m Thowra (FR)-Gold Risk (Mansingh (USA)) 1450^{9} 1770^{P} 2678^{P} 3054^{P}
Tompetoo (IRE) 6 ch g 1317^{5} (1782) 2547^{6} 3154^{4} **>78h<**
Tom Pinch (IRE) 8 b g 3569^{9} 3798^{7} **>72h<**
Tom's Apache 8 br g Sula Bula-Tom's Nap Hand (Some Hand) **3631^{P} 4070^{2} 4302^{P} 4523^{P} >85c<**
Toms Choice (IRE) 8 gr g Mandalus-Prior Engagement (Push On) **4383^{6}**
Tom's Gemini Star 9 ch g Celtic Cone-Je Dit (I Say) 26^{6} 129^{P} **3498^{F} 3631^{U} (3765) 4015^{F} 4135^{U} 4303^{P} 4522^{P} 4640^{3} 4792^{F} >41h 104dc<**
Tom's River (IRE) 5 ch g Over The River (FR)-Nesford (Walshford) (2924) 3487^{2} 3910^{9} **>60fh<**
Tom Tugg (IRE) 7 b g 2080^{9} 2812^{12} **>40h<**
Tondres (USA) 6 br g 1007^{5} **>40h<**
Tonka 5 b g Mazilier (USA)-Royal Meeting (Dara Monarch) 3019^{3} 3406^{2} **>69h<**
Tonto 4 b g Nomination-Brigado (Brigadier Gerard) 3197^{7} 3544^{P} **>30h< (DEAD)**
Tony's Delight (IRE) 9 b g 209^{P} **>66h<**
Tony's Feelings 9 b g 451^{3} **584^{4} 704^{F} 802^{6} 897^{P} >59dh 69c<**
Tonys Gift 5 b m 3411^{6} **>81h<**
Tony's Mist 7 b g 288^{4} (339) 461^{4} **>71h<**
Toogood to Be True 9 br g **1048^{6} 3974^{P} >112h 135c<**
Toomuch Toosoon (IRE) 9 b g **361^{3} 484^{6} 601^{7}** 793^{7} **4142^{2} 4254^{P} >85h 96c<**
Too Plush 8 b g **1119^{5} (1379) (1676) (3106) (3419) 4013^{F} >60h 119c<**
Too Sharp 9 b m 1542^{4} **(2092) 2762^{5} 3176^{5} 3742^{P} 3843^{5} >75h 100c<**
Top Ace 5 b g Statoblest-Innes House (Great Nephew) 1692^{13} 2047^{8} **>43fh<**
Topaglow (IRE) 4 ch g Topanoora-River Glow (River Knight (FR)) 962^{4} 1387^{4} 1699^{3} 1900^{F} 2759^{10} 3075^{3} 3287^{2} 3601^{3} **>79h<**
Topanga 5 b g 890^{P} 1170^{6} 1388^{4} 2680^{12} 3722^{3} **>64h<**
Top Bank 9 b g Rymer-Domtony (Martinmas) 1051^{3} 210^{P}
Top Brass (IRE) 9 ch g **2754^{P} 3153^{P} 3573^{5} 3729^{P} 4306^{P} 4379^{P} >81h 99c< (DEAD)**
Top Fella (USA) 5 b or br g 642^{9} 784^{5} **>61h<**
Topformer 10 gr g 16^{5} **>68h<**
Topical Tip (IRE) 8 b g **1750a^{4} 2348a^{14} >119c<**
Top it All 9 b g Song-National Dress (Welsh Pageant) **3165^{P} 4007^{P} 4703^{5} >39c<**
Top Javalin (NZ) 10 ch g 1571^{6} (1952) **2660^{4} 2896^{4} (3400) 3633^{2} >82h 100c<**
Top Miss 8 b m **656^{R} 1073^{P} >43h 31c<**
Top Note (IRE) 5 ch g Orchestra-Clarrie (Ballycipitic) (2830) 3619^{21} **>56fh<**
Topsawyer 9 b g 3035^{2} 3269^{4} 3698^{P} **>78h<**
Top Skipper (IRE) 5 b g Nordico (USA)-Scarlet Slipper (Gay Mecene (USA)) 735^{5} 784^{4} 910^{11} 1027^{7} 1078^{4} (1304) (1993) 2708^{9} 3892^{P} **>49h<**
Top Spin 8 b g **13^{3} 70^{P}** 1647^{6} 2056^{4} 2637^{3} 2934^{4} 3303^{6} 3635^{13} 4016^{13} **>104h 81c<**
Topup 4 b g Weldnaas (USA)-Daisy Topper (Top Ville) 4056^{C} 4335^{11}
Top Wave 9 br g 1058^{4} 1553^{9} **>92h<**
Toraja 5 b g Petoski-Helvetique (FR) (Val de Loir) 3359^{12} 3685^{5} 4645^{F} **>65?h<**
Torch Vert (IRE) 5 b g 2870^{P} 3222^{7} 3426^{4} 3603^{P} **>70h<**
Tordo (IRE) 6 ch g 729^{4} 868^{5} **>67h<**
Toro Loco (IRE) 5 b g Torus-Welsh Folly (Welsh Saint) 865^{19} 1665^{14} 3548^{15}
To Say The Least 7 ch g Sayyaf-Little Hut (Royal Palace) 1021^{13} 1654^{P}
Toscanini (IRE) 4 bb g Homo Sapien-Maria Tudor (Sassafras (FR)) 4118a^{10} **>68fh<**
Toshiba House (IRE) 6 ch m Le Moss-Santa Jo (Pitpan) 898^{7} 1052^{10} 1907^{7} 2042^{P} 3423^{P}
Toshiba Talk (IRE) 5 ch g 1921^{P} 3158^{10} 3309^{7} 3424^{8} (4500) 4705^{2} **>74h<**
Total Asset 7 b g 955^{9} 1007^{2} **1254^{4} 1831^{5} 3582^{4} 3732^{F} 3988^{6} >50h 66c<**
Total Confusion 10 b g 2345a^{12} **>87h<**
Total Joy (IRE) 6 gr g 1830^{5} 2035^{2} 2669^{4} 2797^{3} (3088) (3283) **>78h<**
Total Success (IRE) 5 b g King's Ride-Mullaun (Deep Run) 4118a^{14} **>32h<**
Totem Fole 4 gr g Totem (USA)-Tenez la Corde (Boco (USA)) 3946^{5} 4420^{3} **>66fh<**
Touch Silver 7 ch g 1198^{8} **>75?h<**
Tough Character (IRE) 9 b g 1775^{P} 2629^{15} 2669^{P}
Tough Test (IRE) 7 ch g (6) 533^{F} 582^{2} 703^{3}

734[4] 1313[3] 1668[F] 2176[P] 2803[2] 2954[3] (3909) 4245[P] (4408) 4571[2] 4710[U] >77h 110c<

Toulston Lady (IRE) 5 b m Handsome Sailor-Rainbow Lady (Jaazeiro (USA)) (1908) 3049[F] 3438[14] >51?h<

Toureen Gale (IRE) 8 gr m 3650a[10] >91h<

Tour Leader (NZ) 8 ch g 64[5] 220[3] 302[U] 460[2] 597[P] >82h 86c<

Toute Bagaille (FR) 5 b m 32[3] >60h<

Tout Va Bien 9 b g 3503a[2] >73h 94c<

Tower Street 6 br g Idiot's Delight-Premier Nell (Mandamus) 1317[2] 3143[P] >79h<

Tracey Trooper 6 br m 1077[12] >25h<

Trade Wind 6 br g (210) 295[2] (355) 1185[2] >73h<

Tragic Hero 5 b g 2059[6] 2635[8] 3293[5] 3635[R] 4053[7] 4397[6] 4610[F] 4772[3] >110h<

Trail Boss (IRE) 6 b g 900[F] 1274[9] 3538[P] 3746[P] >64?h<

Trainglot 10 ch g (1156) 1647[3] 2056[2] 3635[7] (4132) >138h<

Trap Dancer 9 gr g 1021[6] 1139[2] (1349) 1671[2] 1822[2] >67h<

Trauma (IRE) 5 b m Broken Hearted-Remoosh (Glint of Gold) 902[4] 1333[7]

Travado 11 br g 1173[4] 2057[P] >144c<

Travel Bound 12 b g 3270[5] >40h 87dc<

Tread the Boards 6 br m 1786[P] 2678[6] 2818[3] 3054[7] >52h<

Treasure Again (IRE) 8 b g 1156[5] 1680[2] 1936[U] >123h 119c<

Treble Bob (IRE) 7 b g 318a[15] >124h<

Trecento 6 b m 1681[P] >76h<

Tree Creeper (IRE) 5 b g King's Ride-Lispatrick Lass (Kambalda) 1583[5] 2805[4] 3275[3] >82h<

Trehane 5 b m Rock City-Trelissick (Electric) 1380[5] 1855[9] 2010[13] 2820[17] 3442[19] >37h<

Tremble 8 b g 60[P] 98[2] 134[3] 181[4] >47h<

Tremendisto 7 b g (1499) 1689[6] 2634[3] 2898[11] 3887[P] 4608[5] >73h<

Tremplin (IRE) 6 b m Tremblant-Sweet Slievenamon (Arctic Slave) 1453[7] 2959[2] 3295[3] 3796[5] >66h<

Trench Hill Lass (IRE) 8 b m 3503a[P] 4110a[P] >66h 108c<

Trendy Auctioneer (IRE) 9 b g 1836[7] 2664[5] >44dh<

Trentside Major 5 b g Country Classic-Trent Lane (Park Lane) 4476[P] 4645[6] 4768[P]

Tresidder 15 b g 507[3] 895[4] >62h 103c<

Trevveethan (IRE) 8 ch g 4322[U] >65h<

Trianna 4 b f General Holme (USA)-Triemma (IRE) (M Double M (USA)) 753[5] 1387[P] 1595[P] 2815[14] 3284[16] 4762[P] >32h<

Tribal Ruler 12 b g 2823[8] 3071[P] >67c<

Tribune 6 ch g (1081) (2955) (3317) (3531) (3851) 4207[4] >94h<

Trickle Lad (IRE) 8 b g 1160[3] (1313) >118h 90c<

Triennium (USA) 8 ch g 5[4] 1358[5] 1686[4] (1969) (2505) 2764[P] >68h<

Trifast Lad 12 ch g Scallywag-Cilla (Highland Melody) 3062[2] (3208) (3457) 4051[6] (4449) 4560[2] 4724[4] >113c<

Trina's Cottage (IRE) 8 br g 26[11] >43h<

Triona's Hope (IRE) 8 br g Rising-Quinpool (Royal Highway) 1654[P] 2649[14] 2785[12] 2918[8] 3024[8] 3327[11] 3477[4] 3608[7] 3825[10] 4057[3] 4148[P] >34h 86c<

Triple Tie (USA) 6 ch m 498[5] 603[P] >47h<

Triple Witching 11 b g 1868[2] 3040[3] 3274[4] >144h 104c<

Triptodicks (IRE) 7 br m (4351a) >95c<

Tristan's Comet 10 br g 30[7] >73h 83c<

Tristram's Image (NZ) 6 b g 1665[3] 2547[10] (3115) 3342[2] >78h<

Troodos 11 b g (1080) 1294[2] 1528[F] (1844) 4147[2] >78h<

Tropwen Marroy 8 b m 129[P]

Trouble Ahead (IRE) 6 b g Cataldi-Why 'o' Why (Giolla Mear) 4287[5] 4421[3] >64fh<

Trouble At Mill 7 ch g 1053[11] 1569[5] 4762[9] >20h<

Trouble's Brewing 6 gr m 105[12]

Trouvaille (IRE) 6 b g (2806) 3084[6] 3539[4] >71h<

Troy's Dream 6 b g 1344[8] 1775[P] 1969[4] 2505[6] 2913[P] >53h<

Troystar 6 b g 3939[8] >19fh<

Truancy 4 b g Polar Falcon (USA)-Zalfa (Luthier) (807) >80h<

True Fortune 7 b g True Song-Cost A Fortune (Silver Cloud) 3469[F] 4530[2] 4704[F] 4773[2] >104c<

True Fred 8 ch g 4767[5]

True Rhyme 7 b m 31[P]

True Scot (IRE) 7 b g 3885[2] >75h<

True Steel 11 b g 3357[P] 3553[4] 3840[4] >78c<

Trumble 5 b g 490[4] 784[7] >65h<

Trump 8 b g 1671[3] (2178) 2545[4] 2803[3] 2919[3] 3909[4] 4481[P] >98h 91c<

Trumped (IRE) 5 b m Last Tycoon-Sweetbird (Ela-Mana-Mou) 586[5] 643[4] 939[5] >64h<

Trumpet 8 ch g 491[5] (785) 896[4] 1008[4] 1244[5] 1564[4] 3742[2] 3841[F] >78h 102c< (DEAD)

Truss 10 b g 14[F] 94[2] 158[11] 180[P] 335[4] 451[4] >96dc<

Trust Deed (USA) 9 ch g 158[9] 3495[3] (3736) 3929[3] 4171[3] (4429) 4535[P] 4722[U] >81h 91c<

Truthfully 4 ch f Weldnaas (USA)-Persian Express (Persian Bold) 4531[8] 4632[7] >33fh<

Tryfirion (IRE) 8 b g 314a[5] (321a) 1752a[9] 2348a[F] 2602a[U] >124+h 127c<

Try God 10 gr g Godswalk (USA)-Are You Sure (Lepanto (GER)) 3664[6] >61c<

Trying Again 9 b g (1454) 1785[2] >136h 149c<

Try it Alone 15 b g 4432[P] >59?c<

Trymyply 5 b g 1834[8] 4421[10] 4657[4] >40fh<

Tryph 5 b m 339[8] >61h<

Tsanga 5 b g 2541[7] 2861[12] 3098[7] 3723[4] 4295[3] (4409) 4752[3] >60h<

Tuckers Town (IRE) 5 br g Strong Gale-Moate Gypsy (Fine Blade (USA)) 2938[3] >48fh<

Tudor Fable (IRE) 9 b g 4228[5] 4320[7] >86c<

Tudor Falcon 4 b g Midyan (USA)-Tudorealm (USA) (Palace Music (USA)) 3019[11] 3730[11] >16h<

Tudor Flight 6 b m 27[8] >39h<

Tudor Town 9 b g 1995[4] 3189[7] 4399[4] 4524[P] 4663[W] >52h<

Tuffnut George 10 ch g (13) 3744[4] 3963[2] 4228[P] 4406[P] >100c<

Tug of Peace 10 b g 1067[5] 1287[P] 2706[3] 2928[3] >80h 119dc<

Tug Your Forelock 6 b g 260[3] 492[4] 553[2] 673[8] 1814[4] 2088[11] 2905[U] 3179[U] 3546[6] 3806[P] 4096[5] 4231[9] 4633[7] 4789[10] >35h 66c<

Tukano (CAN) 6 ch g (7) 58[3] (392) 630[P] >75h<

Tukum 9 ch g 98[P] >74h<

Tullabawn (IRE) 5 b g Rontino-Reliant Nell (Reliance II) 1485a[4] >74h<

Tullow Lady (IRE) 6 b m 1913[4] 2690[17] 4528[10] 4698[4]

Tullymurry Toff (IRE) 6 b g (796) (1441) (2888) 3615[4] 4210[3] >118h<

Tulu 6 ch m 3072[3] 3346[6] >71h<

Tumlin Oot (IRE) 8 b g 3460[5] 3713[6] 4076[P] >34h 83c<

Tungsten (IRE) 6 gr g 1178[P]

Tupenny Smoke 5 b m 2696[22] 3304[16]

Turf Scorcher 6 ch g 4539[17]

Turkish Tower 6 b g 2955[2] 3157[5] >67h<

Turning Trix 10 b g (1655) 2057[4] 2782[4] (3420) 4074[13] >137c<

Turnpole (IRE) 6 br g 1441[3] 2912[U] 3163[2] >108h<

Turpin's Green 14 b g 190[12] (507) 597[4] 732[5] 833[2] 3966[7] 4344[4] 4763[4] >76c<

Turrill House 5 b m 4295[5] (4401) >55+h<

Tursal (IRE) 8 b g 3426[7] 3621[3] 3844[6] >62h<

Twablade (IRE) 9 gr m 3475[11] >41h<

Tweedswood (IRE) 7 b g 1316[8] 1907[3] 3696[F] 3990[7] 4479[U] 4608[4] >72dh<

Twelve Club 4 ch g Sharrood (USA)-Persian Victory (IRE) (Persian Bold) 4008[13] 4388[6] 4774[11] >57fh<

Twice Shy (IRE) 6 gr g 1120[P]

Twice the Groom (IRE) 7 b g 71[F] 600[2] 950[5] 1166[6] 1299[3] >69h<

Twin Falls (IRE) 6 b g 703[2] 1081[2] 1311[5] (1525) 1987[2] (2002) 2632[5] 2863[3] (3326) 3532[3] 3725[3] 4057[6] 4408[F] 4517[6] >77h 97dc<

Twin Rainbow (IRE) 10 ch g 1003a[3] 1495a[P] >118c<

Twin States 8 b g 1704[U] 2630[P] >64h 101dc<

Twist 'n' Scu 9 ch g Prince Sabo-Oranella (Orange Bay) 4406[P] >69dh<

Two For One (IRE) 8 b br g 3393[3] 3824[P] 4245[P] 4751[2] >75c<

Two Hearts 5 ch m Nearly A Hand-Tinsel Rose (Porto Bello) 191[7] 555[P]

Two John's (IRE) 8 b or br g 1646[F] 1680[P] >58h< (DEAD)

Two Lords 5 b g Arctic Lord-Doddycross (Deep Run) 3235[10] 3365[9] >24fh<

Two Step Rhythm 13 gr g 14[7]

Tycoon Prince 4 b g Last Tycoon-Princesse Vali (FR) (Val de L'Ome (FR)) 2675[12] >6fh<

Typhoon (IRE) 7 br g 1856[U] 2807[5] 2926[R] 3587[P] 3901[P]

Typhoon Eight (IRE) 5 b h High Estate-Dance Date (IRE) (Sadler's Wells (USA)) 1950[P]

Typhoon Lad 4 ch c Risk Me (FR)-Muninga 944[4] >61h<

U

Ubu Val (FR) 11 b g 1293[2] 1799[P] 2542[4] 3486[4] >119dc<

Uckerby Lad 6 b g 3171[P] >20h<

Uk Hygiene (IRE) 7 br g 1346[8] 1576[2] 1780[P] 2569[4] 4145[2] >80h 91c<

Ultimate Smoothie 5 b g Highest Honor (FR)-Baino Charm (USA) (Diesis) (99) (191) 679[3] (1203) 1633[4] (2093) 2578[5] 2874[3] (4466) 4628[7] >83h<

Ultimate Warrior 7 b g Master Willie-Fighting Lady (Chebs Lad) 4542[4] >41h<

Ultra Flutter 10 b g 1234a[5] 2341a[2] (2600a) (2856a) >119c<

Ultrason IV (FR) 11 b g Quart de Vin (FR)-Jivati (FR) (Laniste) 4631[P]

Uluru (IRE) 9 b g 1372[3] 1906[5] 2117[5] 3013[P] 4005[6] 4253[4] 4418[6] 4803[P] >80dh<

Umberston (IRE) 4 b g Nabeel Dancer (USA)-Pivotal Walk (IRE) (Pennine Walk) 3041[9] >52h<

Uncle Algy 8 ch g 1994[P] 2667[2] 2947[P] 3040[P] 4314[2] >67h 92dc<

Uncle Bert (IRE) 7 b g 867[5] (1169) 1702[2] 2618[6] >48h 103c<

Uncle Doug 6 b g 1690[5] 2617[2] 2902[P] 3412[6] 3791[5] >102h<

Uncle Ernie 12 b g 1134[4] 1650[3] 3292[4] (3638)

>149c<

Uncle George 4 ch g Anshan-Son Et Lumiere (Rainbow Quest (USA)) 589^{5} 688^{4} >62h<

Uncle Keeny (IRE) 7 b g 1028^{U} 1308^{P} >100h<

Undawaterscubadiva 5 ch g Keen-Northern Scene (Habitat) 3475^{3} 3723^{3} 4318^{3} 4567^{3} >60h<

Unforgetable 5 ch g Scottish Reel-Shercol (Monseigneur (USA)) 2830^{9} >6fh<

Unguided Missile (IRE) 9 br g (1440) 2057^{2} 2636^{2} 3230^{2} 3636^{F} (4054) (4284) >167c<

United Front 5 br g 1123^{4} 1325^{7} 1630^{F} >73h<

Unor (FR) 11 b g (9) 732^{P} >112?c<

Un Poco Loco 5 b g Lord Bud-Trailing Rose (Undulate (USA)) 1263^{10} 2917^{19} 3324^{10}

Unprejudice 6 b g 2504^{6} >63h<

Unsinkable Boxer (IRE) 8 b g 2826^{3} 3405^{3} >71h<

Uoni 4 ch f Minster Son-Maid of Essex (Bustino) 3670^{5} >38h<

Up For Ransome (IRE) 8 b g 897^{5} 1083^{4} 3455^{3} 3713^{F} 3922^{2} 4155^{2} >89c<

Upham Close 11 ch m 2964^{F} >101?c<

Upham Rascal 6 ch g 1165^{7} 1340^{F} 1563^{P} 1762^{U} 2806^{9} 3689^{P} >45h<

Upham Surprise 9 b g 2826^{P} 4476^{9}

Upper Club (IRE) 5 b m Taufan (USA)-Sixpenny (English Prince) 1412^{6} >15h<

Uprising (IRE) 7 ch g 2677^{7} >51h<

Upshepops (IRE) 9 b m The Parson-Avocan (Avocat) 3391a^{F} >53c<

Up The Creek (IRE) 5 br m Supreme Leader-Jacob's Creek (IRE) (Buckskin (FR)) 954^{6} >35h<

Up the Tempo (IRE) 8 ch m 19^{P} 218^{5} 316a^{5} 360^{2} 499^{4} 1197^{P} 1475^{3} 1677^{P} 1763^{P} 4175^{6} 4428^{3} 4663^{2} 4727^{10} >17h<

Upward Surge (IRE) 7 ch g 3897^{5} 4254^{4} 4320^{P} 4721^{8} >46h 58c<

Upwell 13 b g 94^{3} 452^{5} 683^{3} 785^{2} 804^{4} 896^{6} 3824^{4} 4059^{3} 4148^{6} >50h 84c<

Uranus Collonges (FR) 11 b g 1806^{P} 2063^{4} 2916^{P} 3729^{4} 4148^{P} >100c<

Urban Dancing (USA) 8 ch g 894^{P} 1144^{8} 1267^{2} 1793^{8} 2628^{7} (2799) >93h 86c<

Urban Lily 7 ch m (1425) 1762^{U} (1838) 2036^{4} 2708^{8} 2882^{5} 3632^{4} >54h<

Ur Only Young Once 7 b m 4547^{7} 4696^{6} >33h<

Uron V (FR) 11 b g 2950^{4} 3402^{7} 3600^{17} >101h 101dc<

Urshi-Jade 9 b m Pennine Walk-Treeline (High Top) 2806^{14} 3325^{P}

Urubande (IRE) 7 ch g (1234a) 1648^{2} 2740a^{4} 3126a^{8} 3635^{F} 4063^{5} >130h<

V

Vadlawys (FR) 6 b g Always Fair (USA)-Vadlava (FR) (Bikala) 3426^{3} 3802^{F} 3989^{2} >67h<

Vague Hope (IRE) 5 b g Strong Gale-Misty's Wish (Furry Glen) 4388^{2} >72fh<

Vain Prince 10 b g 255^{4} 356^{3} 478^{3} 538^{5} 702^{P} 806^{3} 941^{4} >84h<

Valamir (IRE) 7 ch g 317a^{11} >35h<

Val D'Alene (FR) 10 b g 1498a^{3} >171c<

Val de Rama (IRE) 8 b g (584) 733^{2} 897^{3} 1083^{U} 1306^{2} 1525^{3} 2508^{3} >83h 97c<

Vale of Oak 6 b m Meadowbrook-Farm Consultation (Farm Walk) 686^{9}

Vales Ales 4 b g Dominion Royale-Keep Mum (Mummy's Pet) 874^{P}

Valhalla (IRE) 4 b g Brush Aside (USA)-Eimers Pet (Paddy's Stream) 4216^{3} (4420) >77fh<

Valiant Dash 11 b g 422^{3} 533^{2} (703) 805^{F} 3971^{5} 4248^{4} 4717^{3} >64h<

Valianthe (USA) 9 b g 3207^{8} 3630^{P} >44h<

Valiant Warrior 9 br g 2065^{2} 2901^{5} 3160^{5} 3815^{3} 4074^{10} >130c<

Valisky 7 gr m (19) 157^{F} >58h<

Valley Erne (IRE) 6 b g 4117a^{7} (4352a) >97h<

Valley Garden 7 b g 1981^{P} 2788^{P} 3023^{P} >70h<

Vallingale (IRE) 6 b m 718^{5} 866^{3} 3004^{2} 3473^{P} 4309^{7} 4445^{4} 4662^{P} 4766^{P} >58h<

Valnau (FR) 10 b g Grandchant (FR)-Matale (FR) (Danoso) 2681^{F} 3891^{6} >84?c<

Vanborough Lad 8 b g Precocious-Lustrous (Golden Act (USA)) 3109^{9} 3500^{9} 3757^{3} 3921^{P} 4259^{6} >54h<

Vancouver Lad (IRE) 8 ch g 2656^{P} 3551^{P}

Van Der Grass 8 ch g 19^{P} >43h<

Vansell 6 b m Rambo Dancer (CAN)-Firmiter (Royal Palace) 1573^{9} 1998^{9} >10fh<

Vareck II (FR) 10 b g Brezzo (FR)-Kavala II (FR) (Danoso) 887^{P} 970^{P} 1068^{P} 1285^{P} 1426^{7}

Va Utu 9 b g 3338^{10} (3679) 3890^{3} 4071^{2} 4236^{4} >67h<

Vazon Express 11 b g 94^{P} >57?h 78c<

Vendoon (IRE) 7 b g 1278^{5} 1638^{9} >63h<

Venice Beach 5 b g Shirley Heights-Bold and Beautiful (Bold Lad (IRE)) 3109^{11} >29h<

Verde Luna 5 b g 211^{2} (303) 491^{3} 723^{3} 822^{F} 3890^{4} 4141^{4} 4278^{5} 4526^{2} >64h 82c<

Veronica Franco 4 b f Darshaan-Maiden Eileen (Stradavinsky) 1712^{4} 1872^{9} 2070^{15} 3623^{5} 3809^{3} 3953^{5} 4102^{3} 4255^{5} >74?h<

Verro (USA) 10 ch g 3471^{7} 4648^{8} 4789^{11} >23h<

Verulam (IRE) 4 b br c Marju (IRE)-Hot Curry (USA) (Sharpen Up) 331^{2} (402) 654^{F} 881^{8} 1011^{7} >56h<

Very Daring 7 b g 4322^{6} 4471^{B} 4530^{4} 4607^{3} 4773^{6} >44c<

Very Evident (IRE) 8 b g 4339^{4} >63h 94c<

Veryvel (CZE) 6 b or br g 2754^{U} 2869^{8} 3156^{7} >54h 99dc<

Vexford Lucy 4 b f Latest Model-Suchong (No Mercy) 3895^{P}

Vexford Model 7 b m 185^{6} >48h<

Viaggio 9 b g 1010^{5} 1328^{P} 1833^{3} >64h 75c<

Viardot (IRE) 8 b g (394) 3163^{10} 3351^{8} >54h<

Vicaridge 10 b g 1164^{3} 1657^{6} 1941^{4} 2801^{2} 3710^{6} >100c<

Vicar of Bray 10 b g 23^{P} 1961^{P} 4309^{12} 4424^{3} 4697^{P} >75dc<

Vicar Street (IRE) 7 b g 2345a^{10} >97h< (DEAD)

Vicar's Vase 4 b f Montelimar (USA)-Church Leap (Pollerton) 4407^{2} >65fh<

Vicompt de Valmont 12 b g (3089) 3341^{2} 3580^{3} >113dc<

Vicosa (IRE) 8 gr g 809^{3} 1043^{3} 1383^{4} 3444^{3} 3605^{F} >81h 99c<

Victor Bravo (NZ) 10 br g (816) (1074) (1363) 4016^{6} 4207^{6} 4418^{7} >95h 95c<

Victoria Day 5 b m 1250^{2} 2074^{12} 2759^{13} >62h<

Victor Laszlo 5 b g Ilium-Report 'em (USA) (Staff Writer (USA)) 939^{6} >62h<

Victory Anthem 11 ch g 23^{6} 256^{6} 328^{U} 403^{4} >80h 71dc<

Victory Bound (USA) 4 ch c Bering-Furajet (USA) (The Minstrel (CAN)) 2738a^{10} >85h<

Victory Gate (USA) 12 b g 1389^{P} 1863^{4} 2679^{P} 2910^{4} 3132^{8} 3550^{P} 3717^{4} >63c<

Viking Dream (IRE) 5 b m 3500^{11} 4652^{P} >38h<

Viking Flagship 10 b g 1792^{2} 2646^{4} (3299) 3614^{3} 4049^{3} 4165^{3} >166c<

Village Opera 4 gr f Rock City-Lucky Song (Lucky Wednesday) 462^{7} >8h<

Village Reindeer (NZ) 10 b g 1645^{P} 3027^{3} 3312^{4} 3560^{U} >99h 112c< (DEAD)

Vilprano 6 b g 10^{3} >62h<

Vintage Claret 8 gr g 3108^{6} 3423^{F} 3720^{2} 3980^{3} >74h<

Vintage Red 7 b g (531) 701^{2} (786) 1049^{10} 1848^{11} 2957^{9} 3091^{8} >76h<

Vintage Taittinger (IRE) 5 b g 1703^{19} 3674^{9} >29h<

Virbazar (FR) 10 br g 2752^{5} 3073^{F} >61c< (DEAD)

Viridian 12 b g (4616) >55h 110c<

Visaga 11 b g 2964^{2} >105c<

Viscount Tully 12 b g 1859^{4} 2838^{3} 3362^{7} 3620^{6} 4332^{4} >56h<

Vision of Freedom (IRE) 9 b g 1474^{4} 2573^{5} 2929^{F} 3743^{F} 4401^{7} >57h<

Vital Song 10 b g Vital Season-Tia Song (Acrania) 3765^{2} (4322) 4560^{5} >104c<

Vital Wonder 9 ch g 3677^{7} 3741^{U} 4401^{9} 4558^{8} >30h<

Vitaman (IRE) 8 b g 2010^{5} >65h<

Vita Nuova (IRE) 6 ch m 2572^{11} 3468^{9} 3677^{6} 4002^{U} 4276^{6} 4445^{9} >26h<

Voila Premiere (IRE) 5 b g Roi Danzig (USA)-Salustrina (Sallust) 2794^{6} >46h<

Volleyball (IRE) 8 b g 2007^{P} 2643^{3} 2819^{5} 3173^{7} 3736^{8} 4232^{2} >62+h 88c<

Vol Par Nuit (USA) 6 b h Cozzene (USA)-Hedonic (USA) (Fappiano (USA)) (2908) 3617^{2} >122c<

Vosne Romanee II (FR) 10 b g Torvay (FR)-Ossiane II (FR) (Quart de Vin (FR)) 1199^{F}

Vulpin de Laugere (FR) 10 b g 1240a^{4} >92c<

W

Waaza (USA) 8 b g 66^{20} >54h 78c<

Wacko Jacko (IRE) 8 b g 3383a^{P} >42h 87c<

Wadada 6 b or br g (341) 651^{2} 1866^{3} 2040^{4} >84h<

Wade Road (IRE) 6 b g 1275^{2} (1766) 2763^{2} (3275) 3595^{4} >95h<

Waipiro 7 ch g 2704^{P} >50dh<

Wait You There (USA) 12 b g 4392^{P} >87dc<

Wakeel (USA) 5 b g Gulch (USA)-Raahia (CAN) (Vice Regent (CAN)) 956^{2} >59h<

Wake Up Luv 12 ch g Some Hand-Arctic Ander (Leander) 292^{F} 335^{3} 457^{P} 4241^{4} 4804^{3} >102c<

Wakt 7 b m 102^{F} 213^{3} (302) (405) (460) 639^{U} 795^{2} >66h 96c<

Walkers Lady (IRE) 9 b m 763a^{F} >84c<

Walking Tall (IRE) 6 ch g 3183^{3} 3720^{P} 4307^{2} >80h<

Walk In The Wild 5 b m 801^{6} 937^{5} 1141^{9} >28h<

Walk in the Woods 10 b m Elegant Air-Red Roses (FR) (Roi Dagobert) 3627^{5} 3950^{2} 4383^{5} >61?c<

Walls Court 10 ch g 1847^{9} 2077^{P} 4286^{3} (4426) >81c<

Walter's Destiny 5 ch g 1427^{7} 3109^{5} 3337^{7} 3847^{5} >53h<

Wamdha (IRE) 7 b m 62^{9} 103^{F} 159^{8} 214^{6} (334) 538^{2} 692^{5} 863^{2} 1045^{3} >81h<

Wandering Light (IRE) 8 b g 2039^{8} 3155^{10} >45h 45c<

Wandering Thoughts (IRE) 8 ch g Boyne Valley-Moves Well (Green God) 4649a^{5}

Wang How 9 b g Nishapour (FR)-Killifreth (Jimmy Reppin) 4704^{6} >52h 73c<

Wanstead (IRE) 5 ch g 476^{2} 634^{13} 812^{2} 960^{3} 1180^{2} 1791^{3} 2620^{5} 3935^{4} 4313^{9} >50h<

War Flower (IRE) 9 ch m 720^{U} 795^{5} 1089^{W} >77?c<

Warm Spell 7 b g 945^{2} >119h<

Warner For Players (IRE) 6 br g 1323^{5} 1768^{4}

2880[5] (3085) **>91h<**

Warner Forpleasure 11 b g **188[8] 286[P]** **>63c<**

Warner's Sports 8 b g **(494) (639) 3929[P]** **>3h 84c<**

Warning Reef 4 b g Warning-Horseshoe Reef (Mill Reef (USA)) 1444[3] 1634[11] 1953[5] 3204[6] 3634[24] **>36h<**

War Paint (IRE) 5 gr g Zaffaran (USA)-Rosy Posy (IRE) (Roselier (FR)) 3170[4] 3821[12] **>67fh<**

War Requiem (IRE) 7 b g Don't Forget Me-Ladiz (Persian Bold) 890[P]

Warrio 7 b g 865[8] 1013[6] 1412[4] 1673[8] 3798[14] **>42h<**

Warspite 7 b g Slip Anchor-Valkyrie (Bold Lad (IRE)) 1838[4] **2691[8] 2892[6] 3179[P]**

War Whoop 5 ch g 209[2] (510) 680[5] 3159[P] 3825[P] **4709[P]** **>66h<**

Washakie 12 gr g **3712[6] (4338)** **>92c<**

Wassl Street (IRE) 5 b g (1859) 2702[P] 3201[4] (3493) 3750[2] **>80h<**

Watchit Lad 7 b g **4730[P]**

Watch My Lips 5 b g 1010[6] 2062[5] 2909[4] **>77h<**

Watch Sooty 6 br m 26[12] **>16h<**

Water Font (IRE) 5 b g Lafontaine (USA)-Belle Savenay (Coquelin (USA)) 705[4] 898[P] 1986[9] 2924[3] 3100[P]

Waterford Castle 10 b g **(130) 220[2] 588[P]** **>108c< (DEAD)**

Water Hazard (IRE) 5 b g 812[6] 961[5] 1145[F] 1390[9] 1707[3] 1836[3] 2792[5] **>55h<**

Water Music Melody 4 b f Sizzling Melody-Raintree Venture (Good Times (ITY)) 358[P] 807[4] 881[9] 4163[P]

Waver Lane 4 ch f Jumbo Hirt (USA)-Kelly's Move (Lord Nelson (FR)) 4514[P]

Wayfarers Way (USA) 6 ch g 723[6] 1091[4] (1471) (1772) 1960[2] **>81+h<**

Wayuphill 10 b m **1445[3] 1578[5] (1641) 2179[3] (2508) (2801) 2923[5]** 3611[3] **>61h 112c<**

Weapons Free 6 b g Idiot's Delight-Sea Kestrel (Sea Hawk II) 3170[8] 3418[7] 3723[P] 4390[B] 4514[5] 4750[4] **>35h<**

Weather Alert (IRE) 6 b g 1775[2] 2629[12] 3607[7] 4283[P] 4562[4] **>49h<**

Weather Wise 5 b g Town And Country-Sunshine Gal (Alto Volante) 918[7] 980[7] 1536[4] 2576[3] **>68h<**

Weaver George (IRE) 7 b g **1140[2] 1295[4] (1846) 2700[2] (2863) (3101) (3329) 3610[2] 4214[3] (4392) (4571)** **>87h 122c<**

Weaver Square (IRE) 8 b g 319a[14] **>75h<**

Web of Steel 7 gr g Regal Steel-Wenreb VII (Damsire Unregistered) 1178[P] 1380[P] 1659[P] 1952[9] 3748[F]

Wednesdays Auction (IRE) 9 b g **4615[2]** **>60dh 76c<**

Weeheby (USA) 8 ch g 949[4] **1714[U] 1925[3] 2628[6] 2926[5] (3278)** **>83h 94c<**

Weejumpawud 7 b m Jumbo Hirt (USA)-Weewumpawud (King Log) **2614[F]** 2958[10] 3795[12] 4249[7] **>24h<**

Wee River (IRE) 8 b g **1805[4] (2618) 2890[2] 3413[4] 4062[3]** **>86h 134c<**

Wee Tam 8 b g Silver Season-Bishop's Song (Bishop's Move) 937[4] **>39h<**

Wee Windy (IRE) 8 b g **1259[2] 1563[2] 1901[2] 2693[3] 3104[U]** 3303[7] **(3812) 4180[2] 4312[P]** **>87h 113c<**

Wee Wizard (IRE) 8 b g 647[6] **694[4] 897[6]** 1047[10] **1576[6] 1853[7] 2632[9] 2788[P]** **>92h 72c<**

Weissenstein (IRE) 6 b g Strong Gale-Wladislawa (GER) (Windwurf (GER)) 51a[2]

Welburn Boy 5 b g 698[6] 2503[10] 2627[P] **>39h<**

Welcome Call (IRE) 7 ch g **1635[2]** **>81+h 111c<**

Welcome Parade 4 b g Generous (IRE)-Jubilee Trail (Shareef Dancer (USA)) 3525a[6]

Welcome Royale (IRE) 4 ch g Be My Guest (USA)-Kirsova (Absalom) 640[5] **>32h< (DEAD)**

Well Appointed (IRE) 8 b g 12[5] 684[4] 806[4] (856) 1025[5] 1144[5] 1314[4] 1577[8] 3912[2] (4079) 4337[4] **>78h<**

Well Armed (IRE) 6 b g 316a[4] 3159[11] 3345[7] 4091[9] **>55h<**

Well Bank 10 b g **4322[F]** **>4h 71c<**

Well Briefed 10 br g **1287[P] 1637[3] 1858[3] 2568[P] 3074[8]** **>115c<**

Well Suited 7 b g Elegant Air-Gay Appeal (Star Appeal) 73[9] **>8h<**

Wellswood (IRE) 4 ch g Montelimar (USA)-Many Views (Bargello) 2770[6] 4287[3] **>59fh<**

Well Timed 7 ch g **(1430) 1694[2] 2658[2] 3047[P]** **>64dh 113dc<**

Welsh Asset 6 ch g Bedford (USA)-Wild Asset (Welsh Pageant) 2682[8] 3548[12] 3730[8] **>47h<**

Welsh Cottage 10 b g **2827[7]** **>52h 76c< (DEAD)**

Welsh Daisy 5 b m Welsh Captain-Singing Hills (Crash Course) 2931[18] **>9fh<**

Welsh Lightning 9 b br g Lighter-Welsh Log (King Log) **3363[5]**

Welsh Loot (IRE) 6 b g 1301[3] 3283[F] **>57h<**

Welshman 11 ch g 1455[5] 1678[P] **>103c<**

Welsh's Gamble 8 b g **30[8] 70[10]** **>8h 61c<**

Welsh Silk 5 b g Weld-Purple Silk (Belfalas) 1124[2] 1801[2] 2668[8] 2812[10] 3019[8] 3887[2] **>56h<**

Welsh Spinner (IRE) 6 b g 1033[8]

Welsh Wizzard 5 b g Robellino (USA)-My Greatest Star (Great Nephew) 3406[4] 3575[6] 3955[9] **>52h<**

Welton Arsenal 5 b g Statoblest-Miller's Gait (Mill Reef (USA)) 3115[2] 3233[P] **>63h<**

Welton Rambler 10 b m 905[7] 969[9] **>19h<**

Wentworth (USA) 5 b g 1289[4] 2750[5] 3275[5] 3669[2] 4134[5] **>77h<**

We're in the Money 13 ch m 1344[7] 1718[3] 2694[10] 3281[10] 4633[10] **>21h 59c<**

Were's Me Money 7 b m Lightning Dealer-Seven Year Itch (Jimsun) 686[12]

Wessex Milord 12 ch g **2809[P]** **>38h<**

Wesshaun 7 b m **4728[2]** **>14h 54c<**

West Bay Breeze 5 br m Town And Country-Arctic Granada (Arctic Slave) 1283[5] 1683[11] 3399[F] 3500[12] 4006[12] **>35h<**

Westcoast 6 b g 4002[8] 4468[12] 4628[8] 4762[6] **>45h<**

Westcote Lad 8 b g Adonijah-Lady Lynx (USA) (Stop The Music (USA)) 2662[8] 3048[10] **3746[P]** **>35h<**

Westerly (IRE) 6 b br g 3946[7] **>57fh<**

Westerly Gale (IRE) 7 br g **720[4] 901[5] 1041[U] 1318[U] 1582[F]** 2570[9] 3434[4] **>70h 91dc<**

Western General 6 ch g 2953[7] 3438[4] 4244[4] 4626[3] 4749[6] **>62h<**

Western Playboy 5 b g Law Society (USA)-Reine D'Beaute (Caerleon (USA)) 1873[P] 4519[F]

Western Sun 7 b g Sunyboy-Running Valley (Buckskin (FR)) 4217[8] 4403[10] **>18h<**

Western Venture (IRE) 4 ch g Two Timing (USA)-Star Gazing (IRE) (Caerleon (USA)) 1940[11] 2175[9] **>25h<**

Westfield 5 b g Lyphento (USA)-Wessex Flyer (Pony Express) 4242[4] 4762[8] **>52h<**

West Lutton 5 b g Scorpio (FR)-Crammond Brig (New Brig) 3946[12] 4144[7] **>34fh<**

West On Bridge St (IRE) 7 b g 318a[10] 4352a[13] **>86h<**

West Quay 11 b g **3765[P]** **>101c<**

Westwell Boy 11 b g **1209[2] 1670[3] 2046[U] 2652[2] 3033[F] 3694[3] 4148[3] 4336[3]** **>71h 112c<**

Westwood Treat 5 b m Dutch Treat-Lucky Ripple (Panco) 2959[P]

Wet Patch (IRE) 5 b or br g 219[6] **>5h<**

Whaat Fettle 12 br g **1501[P] 2616[9] 3027[P] 3395[3] 3792[4] 4078[7] 4336[2] 4517[4] 4710[4]** **>115dc<**

Whale of a Knight (IRE) 8 b g **2348a[11] 2602a[2]** **>117c<**

What A Choice (IRE) 7 ch m Lancastrian-Ursula's Choice (Cracksman) **846a[5]** **>75c<**

What A Difference (IRE) 8 ch g 509[P]

What A Fiddler (IRE) 4 ch g Orchestra-Crowenstown Miss (Over The River (FR)) 3914[2] **>60fh<**

What A Hand 9 ch g **(2998a) 3637[3] 4361a[F]** **>128+c<**

What a Question (IRE) 9 b m 1156[2] (1647) 2056[5] (2361a) (3126a) 3635[6] 4016[4] 4365a[5] **>132h<**

Whatashot 7 ch g 3932[P] 4231[P] **>37h<**

What A Tale (IRE) 5 b g Tale Quale-Cherish (Bargello) 2924[6] **>41fh<**

What a to Do 13 b g **3490[U] 4087[4]** **>99?c<**

What Chance (IRE) 9 ch m Buckskin (FR)-Grainne Geal (General Ironside) **(3664) 4504[2] 4804[6]** **>94c<**

What It Is (IRE) 8 b m **1405a[3]** **>48h 71c<**

What Jim Wants (IRE) 4 b g Magical Strike (USA)-Sally Gone (IRE) (Last Tycoon) 699[5] 1652[9] 2060[2] 2509[6] 2654[P] 3157[4] **>64h<**

What's Secreto (USA) 5 gr g 450[3] 506[5] 585[2] (642) 3545[P] **>65h<**

What's the Joke 8 b m 655[P] 737[5] 891[P] **>45h<**

What's the Verdict (IRE) 5 b g Law Society (USA)-Cecina (Welsh Saint) (3564) 4348a[2] **>98h<**

What's Your Story (IRE) 8 ch g **1447[F] 2658[F] 3047[3] 3347[4]** 4207[7] **>86h 117dc<**

Whattabob (IRE) 8 ch g **(2007) 2841[U] 3202[3]** **>100h 103c<**

What The Devil 4 ch f Devil to Play-Whats Yours Called (Windjammer (USA)) 3290[6] 3747[8] 4421[8] **>38fh<**

Whatyeronabout (IRE) 5 b m Doubletour (USA)-Calcine (Roan Rocket) 1692[20] 2920[P]

Where's Miranda 5 ch m Carlingford Castle-Cindie Girl (Orchestra) 1450[4] 2757[2] 2931[11] **>53fh<**

Wheres Sarah 7 br m 191[9]

Where's Willie (FR) 8 br g **1445[4]** **>57h 97c<**

Whinholme Lass (IRE) 5 b m Mister Lord (USA)-Deep Down (Deep Run) 3480[9]

Whip Hand (IRE) 6 br g 1504[4] (2697) (2917) 3197[2] 3595[10] **>88h<**

Whippers Delight (IRE) 9 ch g **1167[P] 1321[P] 1420[P]** 1731[5] **(2796) 2906[3] 3132[2] 3665[3] 3925[2] 4635[2]** **>86h 100c<**

Whirlwind Romance (IRE) 6 br m 585[P] 876[P] 1047[9] 1139[4] 1316[7] **>56h<**

Whirly (IRE) 8 b g **1472[U] 1629[2] 3001[4] 3427[2]** **>75h 110c<**

Whisky Wilma 5 b m Gildoran-Danny D'Albi (Wrens Hill) 3690[8] 4539[12] **>15fh<**

Whispering Dawn 4 b f Then Again-Summer Sky (Skyliner) 1872[8] 2815[3] 3058[4] 3549[F] 3670[4] **>63h<**

Whispering Steel 11 b g **2765[2] (3025) 3414[3] 4185[7]** **>133c<**

Whistling Buck (IRE) 9 br g 21[8] 788[3] 958[4] (1419) 1553[P] 1841[6] **2796[5] 3179[3]** **>69h 83c<**

Whistling Gipsy 12 ch g 27[3] 101[3] 289[4] **>63h<**

Whistling Jake (IRE) 6 b g Jolly Jake (NZ)-Hibiscus (Green Shoon) 4538[3] **>41fh<**

Whistling Rufus (IRE) 5 gr g Celio Rufo-Aryumad

(Goldhill) 3821^{11} **>51fh<**

White Axle (IRE) 7 ch g Denel (FR)-Bluehel (Bluerullah) 653^{16}

Whitebonnet (IRE) 7 b g 1553^{7} 2838^{2} 3016^{5} 3442^{14} 3807^{8} 4378^{11} 4524^{6} 4622^{P} **>50h<**

White Claret 5 b g Alzao (USA)-Vivid Impression (Cure The Blues (USA)) 1470^{12} **>26h<**

White Diamond 9 b g 8^{3} 466^{3} 529^{3} 938^{3} 1138^{4} 1826^{6} 2571^{6} 3395^{5} 4248^{18} **>93c<**

Whitegatesprincess (IRE) 6 b m 4055^{8} 4283^{12} (4394) 4572^{8} 4711^{7} 4755^{4} **>53h<**

Whitegates Willie 5 b g 1843^{P} 3159^{15} 3723^{7} 4057^{2} 4146^{P} **>44h 94c<**

White In Front 6 ch g Tina's Pet-Lyaaric (Privy Seal) 1422^{P}

Whitemoss Leader (IRE) 7 b br m 1079^{P} **>37h<**

White Plains (IRE) 4 b g Nordico (USA)-Flying Diva (Chief Singer) 2669^{9} 3500^{6} 3745^{7} 3947^{2} **>76h<**

Whiter Morn 7 b m 3265^{8} 3587^{5} **>38h<**

White Sea (IRE) 4 ch f Soviet Lad (USA)-Bilander (High Line) (1634) 3007^{2} 3634^{9} **>94h<**

White Willow 8 br g (1942) 2884^{14} 3072^{4} 3434^{5} 3807^{9} 3985^{8} **>53h<**

Who Am I (IRE) 7 b g 1328^{6} 1550^{5} (4533) **>74h 98c<**

Whod of Thought It (IRE) 6 b g Cataldi-Granalice (Giolla Mear) 2682^{16} 3073^{F} 3682^{4} 4092^{4} 4526^{U} **>43c<**

Who Is Ed (IRE) 6 b g Idiot's Delight-Matilda Mile (Pardigras) 1492a^{7} **>57h<**

Who Is Equiname (IRE) 7 b g 2691^{4} 3044^{3} 3334^{3} 3848^{2} (4232) 4655^{F} **>78h 105c<**

Who's to Say 11 b g 321a^{3} 464^{4} 814^{4} 1070^{3} 1379^{6} 1730^{3} **>121c<**

Who's Your Man (IRE) 7 br g Strong Statement (USA)-Pennies River (Over The River (FR)) 4308^{P}

Whothehellisharry 4 ch g Rich Charlie-Ballagarrow Girl (North Stoke) 1184^{5} 1652^{16} 2649^{11} **>56h<**

Wickens One 7 ch m 2006^{8} 3189^{5} 3488^{P} **>49h<**

Wicklow Boy (IRE) 6 b g 3921^{8} 4723^{3} **>50h<**

Wide Support 12 b g Be My Guest (USA)-Riva Ring (USA) (Riva Ridge (USA)) 2067^{F} 2792^{15} 2882^{13} **>35h<**

Wild Brook (IRE) 7 b g 4410^{6} 4502^{P} **>46h 70c<**

Wild Cat Bay 5 b g 898^{6}

Wilde Music (IRE) 7 b g 947^{4} 1009^{3} 1452^{2} 3849^{5} **>119c<**

Wild Game (IRE) 6 b g 2540^{P} 2899^{P} 3097^{P}

Wild Illusion 13 ch g 3107^{3} 3498^{2} 4094^{P} **>112c<**

Wild Native (IRE) 5 br g Be My Native (USA)-Wild Justice (Sweet Revenge) 3235^{7} **>36fh<**

Wild West Wind (IRE) 7 br g 1371^{3} 1764^{3} (2760) (3335) 3639^{4} **>82h 134c<**

Wilkins 8 b g 887^{3} (1073) 1731^{4} 4659^{6} **>91h 86c<**

Willchris 10 b g 9^{P} **>37h 102c<**

William of Orange 5 ch g Nicholas Bill-Armonit (Town Crier) 4216^{13} **>57fh<**

Willie Makeit (IRE) 7 b g 64^{P} 132^{2} (188) (349) (486) 601^{6} 1041^{3} 1298^{3} 1708^{2} 1965^{U} **>91c<**

Willie Sparkle 11 b g 696^{P} 877^{2} 1244^{U} 1578^{2} 1847^{6} 2179^{5} 2769^{6} 2955^{3} 3645^{2} 4336^{P} **>114h 82c<**

Willie Wannabe (IRE) 7 gr g 910^{16} 1349^{7} 1654^{20} 3481^{P} 3644^{P} **>43h<**

Will it Last 11 b m 3270^{P} 3432^{U}

Will James 11 ch g 21^{P} 793^{10} 1034^{8} 1181^{4} 1381^{7} 1732^{13} **>33h<**

Willows Roulette 5 b g High Season-Willows Casino (Olympic Casino) 1071^{4} 1573^{8} 2012^{8} 3085^{4} 4230^{4} 4461^{2} **>57h<**

Willsford 14 b g 1273^{5} 1367^{P} **>101h 148?c< (DEAD)**

Will Travel (IRE) 8 b g Mandalus-Kenga (Roman Warrior) 4411^{3} 4579^{4} 4758^{7} **>82c<**

Willy Star (BEL) 7 b g Minstrel Star-Landing Power (Hill's Forecast) (1337) 1537^{2} (1628) 1851^{2} 2744^{6} (2946) 3228^{6} **>84h<**

Wilma's Choice 6 ch m Gildoran-Miss Colleen (Joshua) 3021^{9} **>16fh<**

Win a Hand 7 b m 1062^{P} 2892^{U} 3111^{R} **>52h<**

Windle Brook 5 b g Gildoran-Minigale (Strong Gale) 4008^{7} **>60fh<**

Windward Ariom 11 ch g 591^{U} 638^{F} 2703^{5} 3059^{7} **>96h 23c<**

Windy Bee (IRE) 6 ch m Aristocracy-Dozing Sinead 4365a^{P} **>82h<**

Windyedge (USA) 4 ch g Woodman (USA)-Abeesh (USA) (Nijinsky (CAN)) 3345^{10} 3544^{11} **>12h<**

Wings Cove 7 b g 2817^{5} 3277^{8} 3554^{8} **>94h<**

Wingspan (USA) 13 b g 484^{3} 592^{5} 728^{2} 814^{7} **>98c<**

Win I Did (IRE) 7 ch m Camden Town-Ask The Boss (Gulf Pearl) 2655^{P} 2959^{3} 3603^{3} 3834^{5} **>61h<**

Winn Caley 4 ch f Beveled (USA)-Responder (Vitiges (FR)) 1526^{10}

Winnetka Gal (IRE) 5 br m Phardante (FR)-Asigh Glen (Furry Glen) 1450^{6} 1685^{13} **>44fh<**

Winnie Lorraine 12 b m 57^{P} 342^{P} 550^{U} **>102c<**

Winnow 7 ch m 1191^{5} 1539^{6} 1995^{3} 2577^{3} 2795^{2} 3188^{4} 3736^{5} 4007^{2} 4221^{7} **>54h 86c<**

Winn's Pride (IRE) 6 b g (3702) 3807^{3} **>83h<**

Winsford Hill 6 ch g 1467^{4} 2842^{5} 3087^{5} (4381) **>63h<**

Winspit (IRE) 7 b g 1769^{U} 1864^{3} 2796^{4} 3053^{U} 3410^{2} 3578^{2} 3897^{2} **>54h 91c<**

Winston Run 5 ch g Derrylin-Craftsmans Made (Jimsun) 4531^{3} **>55fh<**

Winter Belle (USA) 9 b g 340^{U} 1668^{2} 2176^{2} **>99+h 93c<**

Winter Gem 8 b m Hasty Word-Masami (King Log) 26^{P}

Winter Rose 6 br g 19^{P} 718^{2} 868^{6} 971^{9} 2893^{2} 3186^{4} (3488) **>68h<**

Winter's Lane 13 ch g 3744^{P} **>84c<**

Win The Toss 5 b g 4421^{7} **>43fh<**

Wise Advice (IRE) 7 b g 9^{7} 215^{6} 256^{4} 336^{3} 398^{3} 645^{F} 689^{F} (877) 4571^{5} **>72h 101c<**

Wise Approach 10 bl g 56^{2} 719^{4} (864) 882^{2} (1070) 1454^{F} **>138c< (DEAD)**

Wise Gunner 4 ch f Gunner B-Edelweiss (Kemal (FR)) 2931^{5} 3297^{3} 3433^{2} **>74fh<**

Wise King 7 b g 2825^{3} 3154^{F} 3569^{2} 4474^{2} 4696^{3} **>79h<**

Wise 'n' Shine 6 ch m Sunley Builds-More Wise (Ballymore) 1053^{13} 1180^{4} 1323^{8} 1958^{6} 3205^{7} **>44h<**

Wishing William (IRE) 5 b g Riot Helmet-Forest Gale (Strong Gale) 3907^{8} **>53fh<**

Wisley Warrior 6 b g Derring Rose-Miss Topem (Mossberry) 2682^{6} 3304^{6} **>67fh<**

Wisley Wonder (IRE) 7 ch g 1189^{U} 1326^{4} 1635^{3} 1797^{2} 2551^{U} 3020^{3} 3635^{14} 4005^{8} **>98h 127?c<**

Wissywis (IRE) 5 b m 412^{3}

Witherkay 4 b g Safawan-High Heather (Shirley Heights) 3404^{8} 3730^{9} 4276^{3} 4548^{3} 4648^{3} **>68?h<**

With Impunity 8 br g 3086^{F} (3565) 4211^{7} 4533^{2} 4649^{3} **>104h 104c<**

With Intent 5 b g Governor General-Don't Loiter (Town And Country) 4641^{5} **>25h<**

Without a Flag (USA) 7 ch g 13^{9} **>65h 56c<**

With Respect 6 ch g Respect-Satinanda (Leander) 4750^{P}

Withy Close (IRE) 4 b g Petorius-Tender Pearl (Prince Tenderfoot (USA)) 3203^{15}

Withycombe Hill 7 b g Nearly A Hand-Gay Park (Pardigras) 2704^{6} 2908^{R} 4661^{4} **>85c<**

Witney-de-Bergerac (IRE) 5 b g 476^{3} 1339^{3} 1663^{F} **>71h<**

Wixoe Wonder (IRE) 7 ch h 1195^{F} 1596^{5} 1773^{2} 3132^{4} 3617^{P} (4431) 4549^{F} 4659^{P} **>55h 90dc<**

Woldsman 7 b h Tout Ensemble-Savanna Lady VII (Damsire Unregistered) 3189^{P} 4067^{R} 4506^{P}

Wollboll 7 b g 596^{2} 692^{2} 822^{3} (4129a) **>85?h<**

Wolver's Pet (IRE) 9 ch g Tina's Pet-Wolviston (Wolverlife) 4160^{3} **>84c<**

Woman From Hell 7 b m Buckley-Vipsania (General Ironside) 3718^{P} 4255^{P}

Wonderfull Polly (IRE) 9 ch m 1947^{4} 2657^{6} 3043^{5} 4417^{5} **>72h 88c<**

Woodbine 7 b g Idiot's Delight-Grange Hill Girl (Workboy) 137^{F} 293^{P}

Woodbridge (IRE) 8 b g (2778) **>95c<**

Wooden Dance (IRE) 4 b f Al Hareb (USA)-Bella Blue 3525a^{10} **>72h<**

Woodfield Vision (IRE) 6 ch g Castle Keep-Comeragh Vision (Golden Vision) 2770^{3} 3548^{5} 4216^{5} **>71fh<**

Woodford Gale (IRE) 7 b g 938^{2} 2540^{11} **>77h 82c<**

Woodhouse Lane 5 ch g Say Primula-Kerosa (Keren) 2750^{15} 3487^{10} 3795^{14} 4393^{6} 4760^{5} **>47h<**

Woodlands Boy (IRE) 9 b g (1420) 1778^{2} 2575^{P} 3018^{6} 3182^{2} **>79h 111c<**

Woodlands Electric 7 b g 555^{P}

Woodlands Energy 6 b m 17^{8} 67^{7} 1086^{P} 1828^{P} 2038^{10} 2574^{P} 2892^{P} 4620^{8} **>28h<**

Woodlands Genhire 12 ch g 823^{6} 957^{7} 1799^{8} 1871^{4} (2575) 3046^{P} 3428^{P} 3961^{7} 4234^{P} 4463^{4} 4763^{U} 4806^{P} **>70?c<**

Woodlands Lad Too 5 b g 1091^{P} 1830^{P} 2034^{P} 2943^{15} 3542^{7} 4512^{12} 4645^{5} 4795^{P}

Woodstock Lodge (USA) 9 ch g 1672^{9} 1854^{12} **>36h<**

Woodstock Wanderer (IRE) 5 b g Mandalus-Minnies Dipper (Royal Captive) 918^{2} 3304^{17} 4531^{13} 4626^{9} **>15h<**

Woodville Star (IRE) 8 b m 2341a^{3} 4356a^{3} **>98h 114+c<**

Woody Dare 7 b g Phardante (FR)-Woodland Pit (Pitpan) 3533^{2} (3713) **>75c<**

Woody Will 11 b g Mandalus-Woodville Grove (Harwell) 4316^{5} **>97?c<**

Wordsmith (IRE) 7 b g 32^{8} 356^{4} 648^{5} 1027^{9} 3663^{8} 3985^{P} 4089^{5} 4472^{6} **>53h<**

Wordy's Wind 8 br m 98^{4} 184^{2} 257^{4} 355^{U} 3131^{8} **>50h<**

Workingforpeanuts (IRE) 7 ch m Entitled-Tracy's Sundown (Red Sunset) (3689) 3887^{4} **>56+h<**

World Express (IRE) 7 b g 1201^{6} (1355) **>86h<**

World Without End (USA) 8 ch g 1844^{P} 2632^{F} 2672^{U} 2862^{10} 3704^{5} **>54h 80dc<**

Worleston Farrier 9 b g Looking Glass-Madame Serenity (What A Man) 4704^{3} **>87c<**

Worth The Bill 4 ch g Afzal-Rectory Rose (Rustingo) 1444^{6} 2060^{P} 2668^{12} 3468^{P} 3927^{P} **>29h<**

Worth the Wait 6 ch m 905^{6}

Worthy Memories 8 b m Don't Forget Me-Intrinsic (Troy) 2794^{5} 3019^{7} 3829^{3} 3983^{5} 4233^{P} **>54h<**

Wotanite 7 b g Nesselrode (USA)-Melinite

(Milesian) 25^{11} 161^{13} **652^{5}** >**54c**<
Wot No Gin 8 b g **1449^{F} 1771^{F} 2667^{5} 2926^{8} 4431^{3} 4566^{3} (4742)** >**53h 87c**<
Wotstheproblem 5 b g Rymer-Alfie's Own (New Brig) 4580^{5} >**45fh**<
Wottashambles 6 b or br g (476) (630) 721^{5} (884) 1039^{5} 1196^{P} >**92h**<
Wreckless Man 10 b g 1638^{3} 2694^{2} >**73h 95c**<
Wrekengale (IRE) 7 br g **797^{P}** >**75h 109?c**<
Wren Warbler 7 ch m **1032^{F}** >**71h**<
Wristburn 7 ch g 1938^{6} 3355^{6} >**68h**<
Written (IRE) 7 ch g Le Bavard (FR)-Pencil (Crash Course) 319a^{3}
Written Agreement 9 ch g 499^{F} >**47h**<
Wudimp 8 b g **4054^{P} 4185^{8} 4475^{5}** >**101c**<
Wye Oats 8 b m 100^{8} >**47h**<
Wylde Hide 10 b g **2348a^{2} (3526a) 4074^{U}** >**139h 144+c**<
Wynberg 6 b g 19^{3} (100) 181^{3} (397) 415^{F} 632^{3} >75h< (DEAD)
Wynyard Knight 5 b g Silly Prices-The White Lion (Flying Tyke) 2904^{2} 3418^{R} 3716^{2} >**58fh**<

X

X-Ray (IRE) 4 gr g Actinium (FR)-Charter Lights (Kalaglow) 2682^{19} 3352^{13}

Y

Yaakum 8 b g **292^{2} (336) 475^{U}** >**77h 99c**<
Yacht 5 ch g 75^{9} >**75h**<
Yacht Club 15 b g 185^{2} 289^{5} 673^{5} 805^{4} 1047^{U} 1822^{5} 2045^{2} (2862) 3478^{6} 3711^{7} >**52h**<
Yahmi (IRE) 7 b g (1639) (1870) 2888^{2} 3600^{2} 4052^{4} 4396^{2} >**111h**<
Yarsley Jester 5 b m Phardante (FR)-Thank Yourself (Le Bavard (FR)) 1555^{7} 2794^{8} 3718^{4} >**59h**<
Yeenoso (IRE) 5 b m Teenoso (USA)-Yellow Ring (Auction Ring (USA)) 4580^{13}
Yellow Dragon (IRE) 4 b g Kefaah (USA)-Veldt (High Top) 471^{3} 654^{3} 836^{5} (2753) 2871^{F} 3063^{7} 3583^{6} 3811^{2} 3953^{R} 4101^{R} >**61h**<
Yeoman Warrior 10 b g **1902^{U} 2665^{2} 2829^{6} 3223^{7} 3675^{3} 4013^{2}** >**124c**<
Yes Man (IRE) 8 b g 1019^{3} 1571^{10} 1982^{2} >**88h**< **(DEAD)**
Yes We Are 11 br m **970^{P} 1038^{P}** >**24h**<
Yet Again 5 ch g Weldnaas (USA)-Brightelmstone (Prince Regent (FR)) 1425^{2} (1594) (1873) 2114^{3} >**89h**<
Yewcroft Boy 6 ch g Meadowbrook-Another Joyful (Rubor) 1843^{4} 2649^{6} >**59h**<
Yezza (IRE) 4 b f Distinctly North (USA)-Small Paradise (Habat) 1064^{3} >**46h**<
Yonder Star 5 b g 2938^{8} 3425^{16} 4726^{U}
Yorkshire Gale 11 br g **(1558) 1806^{4} (1904) 2775^{3} 3598^{7} 4303^{F}** >**147c**<
Youbetterbelieveit (IRE) 8 ch g 1045^{2} >**90h**<
Young Alfie 12 b g **2796^{P} 3756^{P} 3839^{5} 4131^{5} 4235^{P} 4456^{4}** >**40c**<
Young At Heart (IRE) 6 ch g 1832^{F}
Young Benson 5 b g Zalazl (USA)-Impala Lass (Kampala) 871^{9} 974^{7} 1118^{5} 1499^{7} >**36h**<
Young Brave 11 b g **3498^{3} 4179^{5} 4324^{3}** >**110c**<
Young Dubliner (IRE) 8 br g **1129^{3}** >**85h 108c**<
Young Endeavour 5 b g Nashwan (USA)-Just Class (Dominion) 1362^{P} **(DEAD)**
Young Hustler 10 ch g **1157^{3} 1513^{2}** >**159c**<
Young Kenny 6 b g 60^{7} 1046^{F} 1290^{U} 1541^{3} 1854^{2} (2550) (2880) (3368) 4207^{8} 4257^{3} >**103h**<
Young Manny 6 ch g 1966^{15} 3606^{7} >**2fh**<
Young Mazaad (IRE) 4 b g Mazaad-Lucky Charm (IRE) (Pennine Walk) 1377^{7} >**58h**<
Young Miner 11 ch g **3280^{2}** >**108?c**<
Young Mrs Kelly (IRE) 7 b m Boreen (FR)-Murs Girl (Deep Run) 2345a^{8} **3617^{F}** >**77h 87c**<
Young Nimrod 10 b g **3457^{5} 4051^{5} 4619^{U}** >**93c**<
Young Radical (IRE) 5 b g (820) 1060^{5} >**70h**<
Young Rose 5 b m Aragon-Primrose Way (Young Generation) 1830^{16}
Young Semele 5 b m Teenoso (USA)-Polly Verry (Politico (USA)) 3070^{8} 4259^{9} >**17h**<
Young Steven 6 b g 585^{4} 1360^{7} >**62h**<
Young Tess 7 b m 824^{5} 1448^{10} (3683) >**61h**<
Young Tomo (IRE) 5 b g Lafontaine (USA)-Siege Queen (Tarqogan) 4580^{2} >**65fh**<
Young Tycoon (NZ) 6 br g 1327^{P} 1476^{7} 1673^{7} 2820^{14} >**51h**<
Your Fellow (IRE) 5 b g Phardante (FR)-Cousin Gretel (Prince Hansel) 2830^{5} >**39fh**<
Your Opinion 11 gr g Cut Above-Dance Mistress (Javelot) **4615^{U}**
Your Risk (IRE) 7 b g 4307^{13} >**79h**<
Yquem (IRE) 7 ch g Henbit (USA)-Silent Run (Deep Run) **(4406) 4543^{5}** >**108c**<
Yubralee (USA) 5 ch g 75^{6} 677^{2} 790^{3} (976) (1282) 1416^{4} 1585^{4} 2579^{4} (4278) (4386) (4610) 4791^{2} >**107+h**<

Z

Zabadi (IRE) 5 b g (1648) 2740a^{7} 3038^{15} 3231^{5} 3597^{11} 4061^{5} 4212^{2} >**124h**<
Zabargar (USA) 6 ch g 329^{3} >**86h**<
Zabari (IRE) 4 b g Soviet Star (USA)-Zafadola (IRE) (Darshaan) 3821^{15} >**48fh**<
Zacaroon 6 b m Last Tycoon-Samaza (USA) (Arctic Tern (USA)) 1168^{3} 1424^{5} >**59h**<
Zadok 5 ch g Exodal (USA)-Glenfinlass (Lomond (USA)) 956^{7} 1729^{4} 2676^{P} 2907^{10} 3057^{4} 3575^{4} 3757^{6} >**45h**<
Zaggy Lane 5 b g 1203^{11} 1431^{9} 3189^{6} >**15h**<
Zahid (USA) 6 ch g (18) (96) 217^{2} 3012^{7} >**76h**<
Zaisan (IRE) 4 b br g Executive Perk-Belace (Belfalas) 2677^{14} 3404^{9} 3809^{5} >**67?h**<
Zaitoon (IRE) 6 b g 793^{6} **1472^{U} 1771^{3} 2049^{F}** >**89h 84c**<
Zajira (IRE) 7 b m 453^{3} >**93h 113c**<
Zajko (USA) 7 b g Nureyev (USA)-Hope For All (USA) (Secretariat (USA)) 1729^{P}
Zamalek (USA) 5 b g 956^{6}
Zambezi Spirit (IRE) 8 br g **(959) 1167^{2} 1717^{P} 2681^{9} (2821) 3175^{P} 3841^{2}** >**63dh 106dc**<
Zamorston 8 b g Morston (FR)-Zamandra (Foggy Bell) 1250^{10} 1802^{P} >**55h**<
Zander 5 ch g Mr Fluorocarbon-Frieda's Joy (Proverb) 1124^{3} 1665^{2} 2677^{10} 3468^{2} 3820^{U} (3918) (4184) >**88h**<
Zen Or 6 b m 1695^{P} 1998^{13} 2878^{7}
Zeny The Nesta 5 ch m Afzal-Free Clare (Free State) 4538^{7} 4632^{10} >**22fh**<
Zephyrelle (IRE) 5 gr br m Celio Rufo-No Honey (Dual) 3149^{6} 3440^{10} >**53fh**<
Zeredar (NZ) 7 b g **(1035) 1146^{P} (1584) (1730) (1912) 2058^{F}** >**92h 122+c**<
Zesti 5 br g Charmer-Lutine Royal (Formidable (USA)) (1707) 2755^{7} 2907^{6} 3674^{6} 3921^{U} 4226^{P} >**49h**<
Zidac 5 b or br g 3233^{7} 3494^{11} >**58h**<
Zimulante (IRE) 6 ch g 1233a^{F} **(DEAD)**
Zine Lane 5 ch g 73^{3} 186^{2} (396) (551) 677^{3} 1567^{7} 3743^{4} **4419^{F}** >**80h**<
Zingibar 5 b g 729^{2} 793^{3} 916^{2} 949^{3} 1034^{3} 1121^{2} 1330^{3} 1630^{5} (1960) (2573) 2755^{5} 2871^{4} 4278^{3} 4470^{4} (4723) 4765^{2} >**65h**<
Zipalong 6 b g Idiot's Delight-Evening Song (True Song) 3103^{9} 3847^{P}
Zip Your Lip 7 b g 1185^{3} 1330^{7} 1952^{P} 2820^{4} >**58h**<
Zoot Money 5 gr m Scallywag-Moonduster (Sparkler) 4243^{P}
Zuno Flyer (USA) 5 br g 818^{4} 960^{4} 1191^{9} 1419^{5} >**65h**<

INDEX TO MEETINGS

† abandoned

LEADING JUMP TRAINERS

	Runners Since wnr	Total W-R	Chase	Hurdle	NH Flat	Per cent	£1 Level stake
M. C. Pipe	1	212-820	54-209	146-575	12-36	25.9	+ **20.30**
D. Nicholson	7	100-391	46-183	45-177	9-31	25.6	- 5.29
Mrs M. Reveley	3	87-386	28-91	41-229	15-59	22.5	- 46.36
K. C. Bailey	6	77-382	44-185	27-167	6-30	20.2	- 56.77
G. Richards	0	74-292	41-131	31-139	1-17	25.3	- 50.38
P. J. Hobbs	11	64-384	25-144	38-209	1-31	16.7	- 73.76
N. J. Henderson	1	58-303	19-106	33-174	6-23	19.1	- 73.33
P. F. Nicholls	11	56-279	36-183	18-85	2-8	20.1	- 72.72
N. A. Twiston-Davies	11	52-362	8-100	41-216	3-46	14.4	- 52.77
O. Sherwood	10	49-243	23-87	26-146	0-10	20.2	- 60.20
Miss H. C. Knight	12	47-306	17-102	30-174	0-29	15.4	- 63.12
M. D. Hammond	7	47-364	18-111	29-239	0-14	12.9	- 184.25
Mrs S. J. Smith	1	42-274	31-185	10-84	1-5	15.3	- 26.59
J. T. Gifford	16	41-254	17-119	21-121	3-14	16.1	- 20.22
Capt T. A. Forster	3	36-187	19-94	16-84	1-9	19.3	- 32.00
Miss Venetia Williams	2	33-115	17-64	8-35	6-14	28.7	+ **11.96**
P. Bowen	0	33-158	18-75	13-73	2-10	20.9	+ **67.46**
T. D. Easterby	5	32-153	12-41	19-98	1-14	20.9	- 11.07
G. M. Moore	2	32-221	11-62	20-148	1-11	14.5	- 77.08
J. A. B. Old	0	30-125	4-22	22-90	4-13	24.0	- 11.67
D. R. Gandolfo	2	30-201	16-84	14-106	0-11	14.9	- 41.17
J. G. FitzGerald	3	29-169	5-51	22-93	2-25	17.2	+ **0.85**
L. Lungo	3	28-188	8-42	20-131	0-15	14.9	+ **7.66**
J. S. King	2	28-134	20-64	5-51	3-19	20.9	+ **52.24**
C. P. E. Brooks	2	27-208	14-115	10-66	3-23	13.0	- 27.07
P. R. Webber	1	27-151	13-63	11-71	3-16	17.9	- 11.32
P. Monteith	4	27-132	12-46	13-79	2-4	20.5	- 14.97
R. H. Buckler	10	26-192	9-89	17-96	0-7	13.5	- 45.92
Mrs A. Swinbank	3	25-96	3-17	18-71	3-6	26.0	+ **34.02**
P. Beaumont	28	25-127	13-55	10-62	2-10	19.7	- 0.23
J. M. Jefferson	13	24-124	4-19	15-88	5-17	19.4	+ **4.51**
R. H. Alner	3	24-208	21-134	2-71	1-3	11.5	- 14.66
C. J. Mann	0	24-137	7-32	15-90	2-12	17.5	- 29.51
Howard Johnson	18	23-217	8-72	15-132	0-13	10.6	- 73.33
R. J. Hodges	2	22-207	12-64	10-133	0-10	10.6	- 33.22
G. M. McCourt	13	22-125	12-54	8-57	2-12	17.6	- 24.78
J. Neville	5	22-127	0-14	21-103	1-10	17.3	+ **9.83**
G. B. Balding	8	21-224	12-139	9-71	0-14	9.4	- 139.42
R. G. Frost	0	19-150	10-59	9-79	0-12	12.7	- 1.78
C. Parker	0	19-128	12-39	6-77	0-10	14.8	- 58.52
J. G. M. O'Shea	8	19-138	11-40	8-84	0-14	13.8	- 56.34
R. Rowe	7	18-151	9-63	8-80	1-8	11.9	- 11.94
R. Curtis	1	18-128	14-53	4-66	0-9	14.1	+ **9.06**
Mrs J. Pitman	25	17-159	4-41	10-100	3-18	10.7	- 49.84
C. R. Egerton	1	17-100	2-26	14-68	1-6	17.0	- 32.31
J. J. O'Neill	1	17-180	13-69	4-88	0-23	9.4	- 87.75
Mrs D. Haine	0	16-63	9-26	7-31	0-6	25.4	+ **27.85**
J. R. Jenkins	12	16-200	0-29	16-162	0-9	8.0	- 118.17
Andrew Turnell	7	15-103	13-67	1-35	1-1	14.6	- 3.62
S. A. Brookshaw	8	15-76	12-30	2-34	0-10	19.7	+ **28.93**

LEADING JUMP JOCKEYS

	Mounts Since wnr	Win £	1st	2nd	3rd	Unpl	Total Mts	Per cent		£1 Level stake
A. P. McCoy	2	1025946	190	130	78	266	664	28.6	+	3.28
J. Osborne	4	847233	131	82	63	254	530	24.7	+	64.31
R. Dunwoody	2	779999	111	101	70	276	558	19.9	-	134.80
R. Johnson	10	414173	102	78	91	293	564	18.1	-	24.53
N. Williamson	2	507958	85	71	66	308	530	16.0	-	53.76
P. Niven	1	316186	84	57	50	188	379	22.2	-	15.85
M. A. Fitzgerald	0	315946	82	62	52	248	444	18.5	-	82.69
A. Maguire	1	367732	81	72	61	183	397	20.4	-	103.76
A. Dobbin	1	474961	73	52	46	224	395	18.5	-	16.28
D. Bridgwater	4	255010	69	47	49	224	389	17.7	-	25.52
R. Garritty	0	221605	62	66	51	176	355	17.5	-	92.63
P. Carberry	1	240296	61	40	29	120	250	24.4	+	47.67
C. Llewellyn	17	297037	57	42	48	265	412	13.8	+	17.29
C. Maude	4	238007	56	45	38	222	361	15.5	-	96.88
Richard Guest	0	173088	50	47	41	180	318	15.7	-	51.91
R. Supple	14	163498	49	39	43	206	337	14.5	-	9.99
B. Storey	7	225553	48	48	49	253	398	12.1	-	131.14
A. Thornton	8	117260	38	66	54	295	453	8.4	-	166.84
B. Powell	3	160261	36	43	49	323	451	8.0	-	248.90
D. Walsh	1	133471	35	25	26	185	271	12.9	-	85.03
P. Hide	3	130976	35	39	26	174	274	12.8	-	87.15
B. Fenton	6	113702	35	55	44	271	405	8.6	-	149.43
G. Bradley	16	136067	33	40	37	152	262	12.6	-	38.02
J. Culloty	11	108080	32	22	24	162	240	13.3	-	13.27
Mr R. Thornton	11	159337	30	41	50	182	303	9.9	-	53.42
C. O'Dwyer	4	121240	28	23	14	84	149	18.8	-	36.97
T. J. Murphy	6	112866	28	28	33	192	281	10.0	-	81.97
J. F. Titley	10	90665	28	22	14	102	166	16.9	-	26.30
S. Wynne	6	71158	27	33	31	156	247	10.9	-	14.01
M. Foster	2	85193	27	21	19	145	212	12.7	-	15.22
J. Railton	1	82972	26	27	26	147	226	11.5	-	63.16
Michael Brennan	0	77458	26	19	23	158	226	11.5	-	71.55
R. Farrant	2	213278	26	16	22	104	168	15.5	+	48.55
Derek Byrne	12	87455	26	22	21	124	193	13.5	-	82.34
G. Cahill	3	60898	24	39	28	192	283	8.5	-	129.91
L. Wyer	10	82144	23	15	15	100	153	15.0	-	36.97
J. R. Kavanagh	20	80274	23	33	27	185	268	8.6	-	173.55
L. Aspell	11	103485	23	29	18	123	193	11.9	+	25.98
T. Dascombe	11	59185	22	28	37	182	269	8.2	-	69.50
M. Richards	17	75530	22	26	27	158	233	9.4	-	58.15
E. Callaghan	10	78552	21	21	15	93	150	14.0	+	7.88
A. S. Smith	15	61883	21	39	30	213	303	6.9	-	142.76
G. Tormey	4	116393	20	14	20	104	158	12.7	+	3.55
J. Supple	2	46893	20	9	12	94	135	14.8	-	28.44
P. Henley	11	58603	20	33	26	126	205	9.8	-	48.48
D. Gallagher	41	79026	19	32	26	189	266	7.1	-	134.64
R. Massey	7	36176	19	9	7	127	162	11.7	-	61.21
D. Morris	3	62928	19	13	25	104	161	11.8	-	29.98
X. Aizpuru	12	45693	18	21	11	87	137	13.1	+	2.28
W. Marston	27	60738	18	37	29	271	355	5.1	-	255.98

REVIEW OF THE SEASON
by Richard Onslow

The sensation of the season was the postponement of the 150th Grand National on 5th April. Just as the jockeys were putting on their caps, a message saying that a bomb had been planted on the course was received, giving the Stewards no option but to abandon the remainder of the card. An estimated 60,000 people streamed away from the course and, with no option but to leave their cars overnight, many were forced to seek temporary accommodation. Admirably cool and collected throughout the crisis, Charles Barnett, Clerk of the Course and Managing Director, organised the evacuation of the stands and enclosures, and announced that the Grand National would be run at 5.00p.m. on the Monday. Although the warning of the bomb had been accompanied by an authenticated IRA codeword, it proved to be a hoax as an extensive police search revealed no explosives.

Charles Barnett (left) and Sir Peter O'Sullevan, principal players in the Grand National saga

No further outrage, though more threats were received, prevented the postponed race starting on schedule on the Monday, when Lord Gyllene became the first horse to make all the running in the Grand National since Troytown in 1920, the winning margin being twenty-five lengths, the same as that by which Red Rum obtained his third success in the race twenty years ago. One man particularly pleased that the race finally went ahead was the great Peter O'Sullevan, commentating on his fiftieth and last National.

Lord Gyllene is owned by Stan Clarke, Chairman of the courses at Newcastle and Uttoxeter, is trained by Steve Brookshaw and was ridden by Tony Dobbin. It was no coincidence that the horse should have matched the wide winning margin of Red Rum as Clarke bought him because of his great resemblance to the legendary triple Grand National winner.

Steve Brookshaw is a member of a well-known sporting family from Shropshire, as he is a nephew of the late Tim Brookshaw, who was second in the Grand National of 1959 on Wyndburgh, beaten two lengths after riding without stirrups from Becher's Brook second time round. After training and riding with considerable success in point-to-points, Steve Brookshaw was persuaded by Stan Clarke to take out a full trainer's licence just two years ago.

Lord Gyllene leads the Grand National field over Becher's Brook

On the first day of the Aintree meeting, Bells Life, ridden by Glenn Tormey, had to overcome obstacles other than the eighteen fences in the John Hughes Memorial Trophy. As he established clear authority on the long run-in, two loose horses carried him relentlessly toward the wings of the Chair, until Tormey brought his mount back on to the course. Hardly was Bells Life on an even keel again than he was carried towards the stands' rails, while Yeoman Warrior went to the front. Once again Tormey extricated Bells Life, and drove him back into a lead that he most-deservedly retained.

Ken Higson, born within six miles of Aintree, achieved his heart's desire when leading Quakers Field into the winner's enclosure following the success of the four-year-old in the Glenlivet Hurdle. Four years earlier, Higson had won with Roll a Dollar on the course, but was sitting in a gridlock on the M6 when the race was run.

Forest Ivory, who won the Belle Epoque Sefton Novices' Hurdle, is in a very different sort of ownership. The chestnut carries the colours of the Old Foresters Partnership. The members of the syndicate all attended the Forest School at Snaresbrook in East London.

Blue Cheek chases Mr Boston on his way to Foxhunters' victory

There could hardly be a bigger difference in the ages of Robert Thornton and Jim Mahon, rider and trainer respectively of Blue Cheek, winner of the Martell Fox Hunters' Chase. Thornton is eighteen years old, whereas eighty-year-old Mahon rode his first point-to-point winner in Ireland sixty-five years ago. Thornton, surely a professional star of the future, went on to secure the amateurs' championship with thirty winners.

An ugly duckling completed the transition into swan when Mr Mulligan won the Cheltenham Gold Cup. Noel Chance, who trains him at Lambourn, was somewhat less than impressed when he first clapped eyes on the large light chestnut with a lot of white about him.

Mr Mulligan (centre) on his way to Cheltenham Gold Cup glory

Mr Mulligan had been off the course for seventy-seven days as he seemed to have damaged a ligament in his back when falling in the King George VI Chase. A haematoma, a tumour of partially clotted blood, developed, and he spent ten days in the care of Mary Bromiley. Formerly a point-to-pointer in Ireland, Mr Mulligan was bought for £18,000 by Michael Worcester who manufactures ice-cream at Bristol.

Twenty-two-year-old Tony McCoy also landed the Champion Hurdle on Make a Stand. Entirely in his element on ground that was very much on the fast side, Make a Stand made all the running to win in a time that was over a second faster than the course and distance record set by Shadow Leader earlier in the afternoon.

Tony McCoy celebrates Champion Hurdle success on Make a Stand

The steady improvement of Make a Stand has been another tribute to the skill and judgement of Martin Pipe, who claimed him for £8,000 after he had won for Henry Candy's stable at Leicester in August 1995. At the time he seemed very far from an attractive acquisition as his temperament had become unsatisfactory following castration, and he only entered the stalls with the greatest reluctance. Pipe was to retain his trainers' championship, earning his owners more than a million pounds in win prizemoney alone.

Captain Tim Forster also performed a wonderful feat of training when winning the Queen Mother Champion Chase with Martha's Son. As a result of being continually plagued by leg trouble, Martha's Son had only jumped one fence in public successfully during the previous sixteen months. Although his troubles were behind him, his trainer was nevertheless characteristically pessimistic about the prospects of success in this case, because he thought his horse unlikely to be suited by the course as he jumps low and flat. Martha's Son went on to land the Mumm

Melling Chase at Aintree, handing out a five-length beating to another of the season's stars, Strong Promise.

The Queen Mother presents her Champion Chase trophy to Rodney Farrant

Mary Bromiley, who made such an enormous contribution to ensuring that Mr Mulligan could do justice to himself in the Gold Cup, also deserved some of the credit for the success of Hanakham in the Royal SunAlliance Chase. When unseating at the ditch on the course earlier in the season, Hanakham had suffered injury to his back and had been sent to her for physiotherapy. Earlier in his career Hanakham had made his mark in point-to-points and, rather interestingly, was rated a little above Coome Hill, of whom more later.

When winning the National Hunt Handicap Chase, Flyer's Nap gained his second success at Cheltenham's Festival for Jim and Ann Tory, two of the most stalwart and best-liked supporters of steeplechasing and hunting. Two years earlier Flyer's Nap had won the Fulke Walwyn/Kim Muir Challenge Cup.

Lord Vestey, a director of Cheltenham for twenty-one years, had his first winner at the Festival when Karshi came out best in the Bonusprint Stayers' Hurdle. Whereas Australian professional jockeys have been winning races of the highest class throughout the century, none had ridden a winner at the Festival until twenty-seven-year-old Jamie Evans, three times champion jockey in his own country, brought Big Strand home in the Coral Cup Handicap Hurdle. Evans's compatriot Mr Laurie Morgan won the Foxhunters' on Colledge Master in 1961 and 1962.

Charles Egerton also enjoyed a first success at the Festival as he saddled Shadow Leader, who briefly held the record time for the course and distance after he had triumphed in the Citroen Supreme Novices' Hurdle. A versatile performer with more than useful form on the Flat, Shadow Leader was third in the Bessborough Handicap, beaten less than two lengths, at Royal Ascot in 1995.

Two of the runners declared for the Grand National, Over the Stream and Belmont King were withdrawn as a result of the postponement. The ordeal of long confinement to strange stabling badly affected the nerves of Over the Stream, who did not eat up for some time, while Belmont King was found to have lost twenty kilos on his return to Somerset, and the going had become too firm for him by the Monday.

Saving Belmont King to fight another day paid off in spades when he carried top weight in the Scottish Grand National. Forcing tactics, so greatly favoured by Martin Pipe, seem very much in vogue, and like Make a Stand in the Champion Hurdle and Lord Gyllene in the Grand National, Belmont King led from start to finish. Belmont King was bought in Ireland by his trainer Paul Nicholls on behalf of seventy-five-year-old Mrs Billie Bond of Truro, Cornwall, who wanted to see her colours being carried while watching television on Saturdays. The gratification of that desire was somewhat delayed as a result of Belmont King being afflicted by leg trouble so that he had been off the course for no less than five hundred and ninety days before winning the Rehearsal Chase at Chepstow in December.

During the early hours of 16th September flames swept through the Upper Herdswick Farm Stables of Jim Old, trainer of Champion Hurdler Collier Bay, near Wroughton in Wiltshire. Four horses were killed and others injured. Old's string gradually came into form, but the trainer was forced to swallow another bitter pill when his grand servant Mole Board died on the gallops later in the season.

Martin Pipe made another attempt to become the first trainer to win all six races on a card at Exeter in early October, but the disappointing performance of Shikaree in the third put paid to the bid. The champion trainer had also won five races on the course on 23rd August 1991.

In early November Storm Alert won the United House Construction Handicap Chase again at Ascot after having prevailed in 1993 and 1994. That third success in the race was of particular poignancy to Mrs Dawn Perrett as it occurred on the anniversary of the death of her father Colonel Bill Weatherly, from whom she inherited Storm Alert.

Challenger du Luc won an exciting Murphy's Gold Cup

Challenger du Luc justified massive ante-post support from 16/1 when winning the Murphy's Gold Cup on going that was distinctly hard to handle at Cheltenham. Dublin Flyer, bidding to repeat his success in the race twelve months earlier, had been going very comfortably within himself as he made the left-hand turn at the top of the hill, when his hind legs gave way beneath him as he slipped.

The Hennessy Cognac Gold Cup at Newbury produced the sort of result that is always popular with grass roots National Hunt enthusiasts as it was won by Coome Hill, one of only five horses trained under a permit by Walter Dennis on his farm near Bude in Cornwall. Dennis, well known in point-to-point circles, bought Coome Hill as a four-year-old in Ireland. It was on the strength of what Coome Hill achieved between the flags that Walter Dennis finally took out a permit to enable the horse to prove himself under Rules.

When Mulligan beat Land Afar in the Henry VIII Novices' Chase at Sandown Park in early December, David Nicholson was winning the race for the fourth time in five years. At the next Sandown meeting the Cesarewitch winner Inchcailloch gained his fourth success on the Esher course when he tackled three miles and five furlongs for the first time in the P&O Handicap Chase.

When One Man won the King George VI Chase for the second time at Kempton Park on Boxing Day, he set a new record for the course and distance and provided Richard Dunwoody with a record fourth success in the race. Kempton, incidentally, was the only one of ten scheduled Boxing Day jumping fixtures to beat the weather.

Few successes have given David Nicholson greater satisfaction than that of Dream Ride in the inaugural running of the Roscoe Harvey Memorial Chase at Warwick in late January. Nicholson enjoyed a close friendship with Brigadier Harvey, and at Warwick almost exactly a year earlier had sent out Chicodari to become the last winner to be owned by the distinguished war hero. The Brigadier, then aged ninety-five, was present at Warwick that day and died a few weeks later.

The lack of rain and consequent firm ground, that had decimated so many fields in the autumn, continued to affect trainers' plans well after the turn of the year. Thus it was not until the 7th February that Jim Old was able to give Collier Bay his first race of the season by sending him to Towcester to win *The Sporting Life* Champion Hurdle Trial, the race having been arranged by the paper in association with The British Horseracing Board. Collier Bay started second favourite to retain his crown at Cheltenham, but was pulled up on ground too fast for him.

After surviving a far wider variety of vicissitudes than most horses, Suny Bay emerged as a serious challenger for Grand National honours by beating his stable companion Couldnt Be Better in the Greenalls Trial Handicap Chase at Haydock Park towards the end of February. As well as having legs that give rise to problems and a tendency to break blood-vessels, Suny Bay had had his jaw smashed when kicked at Sandown Park. Moreover training him is made no easier by his refusal to put his back into his work. In the only strong gallop he had done since breaking a blood-vessel on his seasonal reappearance at Kempton Park he had been beaten twenty lengths by Couldnt Be Better, so it was hardly surprising that stable jockey Graham Bradley elected to ride the latter.

Suny Bay's task was certainly eased by the withdrawal of Avro Anson because he was coughing, Belmont King with an infected foot and Buckboard Bounce because the ground was drying up again, while Lo Stregone, who had won the race twelve months previously, seemed to take little interest in proceedings and was never going well. All the same, Suny Bay deserved credit for having put up the performance of a brave and dour stayer.

The limitless patience brought into play by Jenny Pitman when bringing staying chasers back to their best paid rich dividends again when Mudahim won the *Racing Post* Chase at Kempton Park. After being bought out of Chris Broad's stable for 26,000 guineas at Ascot in June 1996, Mudahim lost his confidence until schooling with the retired Gold Cup winner Garrison Savannah had the desired effect. Mudahim went on to win the Irish Grand National by the width of a cigarette paper.

The former champion point-to-point rider Robert Alner became the first trainer to saddle the first and second in the Whitbread Gold Cup when Harwell Lad won from Flyer's Nap. Until comparably recently the prospects of Harwell Lad winning such a prestigious race seemed remote in the extreme, as his temperament was a cause for grave concern. In November 1995 he pulled himself up when going out on the final circuit at Wincanton, but got going again and went on to win by fifteen lengths.

Alner gave most of the credit for making Harwell Lad a more amenable character to the winning rider Rupert Nuttall, a thirty-seven-year-old Old Etonian, who is joint-master of the Blackmore Vale. He rides Harwell Lad all the time, and the diversity of interests to be found in hunting have done much to improve the horse's attitude.

The campaign ended on a memorable note when Stately Home became the first novice this century to win ten chases in a season by beating Formal Invitation at Stratford. The gelding's phenomenal rise through the ranks reflects great credit on his trainer Peter Bowen. Two other horses to have prolific seasons were Indian Jockey, also successful ten times, and Imperial Vintage, nine times a winner over fences. Jockeys made the news in one way or another throughout the season. Tony McCoy completed the fastest hundred with a double at Warwick on 21st November. The Irishman duly went on to secure his second riders' championship with one hundred and ninety winners, an excellent tally considering he missed a month of the season with a cracked collar-bone and three more weeks, including Aintree, after a bout of concussion. The conditional jockeys' title was won by Barry Fenton, with thirty-five winners. David Walsh rode the same number, despite ending the season suspended after testing positive for Ecstacy, but Fenton rode more seconds. The stylish Sophie Mitchell was the leading woman professional.

Adrian Maguire rode five winners at Kempton Park on 22nd February, but had the misfortune to miss his third consecutive Cheltenham Festival, and the remainder of the season, after breaking an arm. Other leading riders to suffer lengthy spells of inaction due to injury were Mark Dwyer, Lorcan Wyer and David Bridgwater. Riding Jervaulx at Southwell on 5th May, Richard Dunwoody became the first jump jockey to partner one hundred winners in eight consecutive seasons, while Jamie Osborne and Richard Johnson also topped the century.

John Edwards, who trained Pearlyman to win the Queen Mother Champion Chase in 1987 and 1988, retired in November. Pearlyman died during the season, as did those other fine two-milers Tingle Creek and Sound Man. John Bosley announced his retirement in January. He trained some useful chasers including Eyecatcher, third to both Rag Trade and Red Rum in the Grand National. Gee Armytage, one of our most successful woman jump jockeys, retired at the age of thirty-one in October, nineteen months after breaking her back at Huntingdon. Other riders to hang up their boots were Jamie Railton, David Skyrme, Roger Marley, Kevin Jones and Eamon Murphy.

Captain Neville Crump, who won the Grand National with Sheila's Cottage (1948), Teal (1952) and Merryman II (1960), died at the age of eighty-six in January. Paddy Sleator, trainer of the 1960 Champion Hurdler Another Flash, was also eighty-six on his death in June. Colin Davies, who died suddenly in November, won the Champion Hurdle with Persian War in 1968, 1969 and 1970. Major Verly Bewicke, who won the Gold Cup with Kerstin in 1958, was eighty-two when he died in February.

Captain Bobby Petre died aged eighty-four in August. After being champion amateur before the war, he won the Grand National on Lovely Cottage in 1946. Alex Marsh, another pre-war amateur champion and later Jockey Club starter, was eighty-eight when he died in November.

Captain Miles Gosling, who died at the age of eighty-nine in February, was an energetic administrator and Chairman at Cheltenham during the vital stages of the development of the course.

Mysilv, one of the most popular and courageous mares of recent years, fractured a pelvis while at exercise in early January and sadly had to be put down. Among the races she won were the Triumph Hurdle in 1994 and the Tote Gold Trophy at Newbury in 1995. Spanish Steps, one of the best chasers of the seventies, died in May at the great age of thirty-four. Aldaniti, on whom Bob Champion won the Grand National in 1981, died at the age of twenty-seven in March. Perhaps the saddest loss of all occurred on July 19th when jockey Richard Davis died as a result of a fall at Southwell. The death of hugely-popular Davis, who was twenty-six, led to widespread concern over safety issues, while the risks run by jump jockeys were starkly underlined when Irish riders Shane Broderick and Trevor Horgan suffered life-threatening injuries in the spring.

CHASEFORM RECORD TIMES

AINTREE

Distance	Time	Age	Weight	Going	Horse	Date	
2m C	3m 45.2	9	10-7		Nohalmdun	Apr 7,	1990
2m 110y H	3m 44.6	6	10-7		Spinning	Apr 3,	1993
2m 4f C	4m 47.5	8	11-6		Wind Force	Apr 2,	1993
2m 4f H	4m 37.1	5	10-11		Gallateen	Apr 2,	1993
2m 6f C	5m 26.7	9	12-0		Double Silk	Apr 2,	1993
3m 110y H	5m 50.6	6	10-2		Andrew's First	Apr 1,	1993
3m 1f C	6m 3.4	7	11-3		Cab on Target	Apr 2,	1993
3m 3f C	6m 54.4	8	12-0		Young Hustler	Nov 18,	1995
4m 4f C	8m 47.8	11	10-6		Mr Frisk	Apr 7,	1990

ASCOT

Distance	Time	Age	Weight	Going	Horse	Date	
2m C	3m 45.8	6	10-3		With Gods Help	May 1,	1990
2m 110y H	3m 43.4	6	10-3		Fred the Tread	Apr 13,	1988
2m 3f 110y C	4m 41.4	6	10-1		Sword Beach	Apr 11,	1990
2m 4f H	4m 38.5	5	11-7		Babil	Mar 31,	1990
3m H	5m 33.0	9	11-7	Firm	Cab on Target	Apr 1,	1995
3m 110y C	6m 2.5	8	10-0		Golden Fox	May 1,	1990
3m 1f 110y H	6m 6.4	10	11-7		Floyd	Dec 15,	1990

AYR

Distance	Time	Age	Weight	Going	Horse	Date	
2m H	3m 27.4	6	10-7		Secret Ballot	Apr 19,	1980
2m C	3m 38.7	6	11-0		Clay County	Oct 12,	1991
2m 4f C	4m 44.1	8	12-2		Chandigar	May 15,	1972
2m 4f H	4m 35.0	8	9-10		Moss Royal	Apr 19,	1974
2m 5f 110y C	5m 25.9	5	11-0		Blazing Walker	Oct 14,	1989
2m 6f H	5m 6.8	11	10-0		Any Second	Apr 19,	1980
3m 110y C	5m 52.7	6	11-10	Good	St Mellion Fairway (IRE)	Apr 21,	1995
3m 110y H	5m 42.0	13	10-11		Nautical Lad	Apr 6,	1964
3m 1f C	5m 57.7	9	11-0		Top 'N' Tale	May 12,	1982
3m 2f 110y H	6m 27.5	6	12-0	Good	Loch Scavaig (IRE)	Apr 20,	1995
3m 3f 110y C	6m 51.4	8	10-8		Straight Vulgan	Nov 18,	1974
4m 1f C	8m 0.4	7	10-2		Young Ash Leaf	Apr 17,	1971

BANGOR-ON-DEE

Distance	Time	Age	Weight	Going	Horse	Date	
2m 1f H	3m 44.5	9	10-2		Andy Rew	Apr 24,	1982
2m 1f 110y C	4m 7.7	5	11-0		Bunrannoch House	Aug 16,	1986
2m 4f H	4m 34.1	5	11-13		Smithy's Choice	Apr 25,	1987
2m 4f 110y C	4m 57.8	8	11-4		Peace Officer	Aug 13,	1994
3m H	5m 39.0	5	12-0		Selatan (IRE)	Mar 22,	1997
3m 110y C	5m 57.7	8	11-0		Tartan Trademark	Spt 15,	1990
4m 1f C	8m 50.7	6	10-11		Nazzaro	Dec 13,	1995

CARLISLE

Distance	Time	Age	Weight	Going	Horse	Date	
2m C	3m 55.8	8	11-2		Cape Felix	Apr 20,	1981
2m 1f H	4m 5.8	4	10-4		Tasmim	Spt 28,	1991
2m 4f 110y H	4m 45.4	4	10-12	Firm	Sujud (IRE)	Spt 21,	1996
2m 4f 110y C	5m 4.2	8	10-11		Flying Dancer	Spt 29,	1990
3m C	5m 59.9	8	10-8	Firm	The Blue Boy (IRE)	Spt 21,	1996
3m 110y H	5m 53.5	7	9-11		Fingers Crossed	Spt 30,	1991
3m 2f C	6m 51.3	7	11-0		Zam Bee	Nov 8,	1993

CARTMEL

Distance	Time	Age	Weight	Going	Horse	Date	
2m 1f 110y C	4m 22.6	10	11-1	Good	Precipice Run	May 31,	1995
2m 1f 110y H	3m 57.9	6	11-11		Kalshan	May 26,	1990
2m 5f 110y C	5m 6.1	10	10-10		Corrarder	May 30,	1994
2m 6f H	5m 16.1	5	11-6		Stylish Interval	May 24,	1997
3m 2f C	6m 27.2	7	11-6		Tribal Ruler	May 23,	1992
3m 2f H	5m 57.9	10	11-3		Portonia	May 30,	1994

CATTERICK

Distance	Time	Age	Weight	Going	Horse	Date	
2m C	3m 44.6	6	10-0		Preston Deal	Dec 18,	1971
2m H	3m 36.5	7	11-3		Lunar Wind	Apr 22,	1982
2m 3f C	4m 48.5	15	11-12		Vulrory's Clown	Mar 15,	1993
2m 3f H	4m 39.1	8	10-5		Marsden Rock	Nov 18,	1995
3m 1f 110y C	6m 14.0	10	10-1		Clever General	Nov 7 ,	1981
3m 1f 110y H	6m 3.8	6	10-9		Seamus O'Flynn	Nov 7 ,	1981

CHELTENHAM

Distance	Time	Age	Weight	Going	Horse	Date	
2mOldC	3m 48.3	10	10-2		Captain Dawn	Oct 8 ,	1986
2m 110yNwC	3m 56.0	11	11-4		Clever Folly	Oct 3 ,	1991
2m 110yOldC	3m 48.4	6	12-0	Good	Make a Stand	Mar 11,	1997
2m 110yNwC	3m 53.4	8	11-5		Spring Spirit	Spt 22,	1971
2m 110y PkC	3m 53.8	5	11-9		Bo Knows Best	Oct 7 ,	1994
2m 1f NwH	3m 51.2	5	11-2		Moody Man	Mar 15,	1990
2m 4f NwH	5m 7.1	6	11-8	Soft	Bear Claw	Mar 17,	1995
2m 4f 110OC	4m 58.0	8	11-7		Half Free	Oct 10,	1984
2m 5f PkC	5m 5.8	7	11-2		Tri Folene	Spt 29,	1993
2m 5f OldH	4m 56.2	6	11-7		Regal Ambition	Mar 14,	1990
2m 5f NwC	5m 1.6	9	11-10		Barnbrook Again	Apr 18,	1990
2m 5f 110PkH	5m 6.3	9	11-10		Tipping Tim	Oct 7 ,	1994
2m 7f 110PkH	5m 33.5	7	10-4		Hurricane Blake	Spt 28,	1995
3m 110y NwH	5m 36.9	6	11-4		Mandavi	Apr 23,	1987
3m 1f OldC	6m 6.6	9	11-4		Miinnehoma	Mar 11,	1992
3m 1f 110PC	6m 16.4	7	11-2		Mere Class	Spt 29,	1993
3m 1f 110NC	6m 13.4	9	10-11		Bigsun	Mar 15,	1990
3m 2f OldH	6m 18.7	7	11-9		Henry Mann	Mar 14,	1990
3m 2f 110yNC	6m 30.9	9	10-11		Norton's Coin	Mar 15,	1990
3m 3f 110yNC	7m 3.9	10	11-7		Run and Skip	Nov 12,	1988
4m OldC	8m 11.9	11	12-7		Flimsey Truth	Mar 12,	1997
4m 1f NewC	8m 37.6	12	12-0		Tartevie	May 2 ,	1990

CHEPSTOW

Distance	Time	Age	Weight	Going	Horse	Date	
2m 110y H	3m 43.2	4	10-1		Tingle Bell	Oct 4 ,	1986
2m 110y C	3m 54.1	8	12-0		Panto Prince	May 9 ,	1989
2m 3f 110y C	4m 46.2	11	12-0		Guiburn's Nephew	Mar 20,	1993
2m 4f 110y H	4m 36.2	9	11-3		Aileen's Cacador	Apr 23,	1957
3m H	5m 33.5	10	10-0		Chucklestone	May 11,	1993
3m C	5m 47.9	9	10-11		Broadheath	Oct 4 ,	1986
3m 2f 110y C	6m 39.4	7	12-0		Jaunty Jane	May 26,	1975
3m 5f 110y C	7m 24.0	9	10-5		Creeola	Apr 27,	1957

DONCASTER

Distance	Time	Age	Weight	Going	Horse	Date	
2m 110y H	3m 46.6	6	10-0		Good for a Loan	Feb 24,	1993
2m 110y C	3m 51.9	12	10-9		Itsgottabealright	Jan 28,	1989
2m 3f 110y C	4m 45.4	8	10-0		Powder Horn	Feb 25,	1985
2m 4f H	4m 34.6	6	12-7		Magic Court	Nov 21,	1964
3m C	5m 52.4	8	10-9		Dalkey Sound	Jan 26,	1991
3m 110y H	5m 45.3	6	10-12		Pandolfi	Nov 4 ,	1972
3m 2f C	6m 18.4	7	10-0		Saggarts Choice	Mar 25,	1970

EXETER

Distance	Time	Age	Weight	Going	Horse	Date	
2m 1f 110y H	3m 53.8	5	10-0		Valtaki	Aug 24,	1990
2m 1f 110y C	4m 6.8	8	11-5		Some Jinks	Aug 23,	1984
2m 2f H	4m 3.6	4	10-12	Firm	Serious Danger (IRE)	Apr 12,	1995
2m 2f C	4m 13.9	7	11-0		Travado	Nov 2 ,	1993
2m 3f H	4m 17.9	7	10-9	Firm	Charlafrivola	May 25,	1995
2m 3f C	4m 31.4	8	10-8	Hard	James Pigg	Aug 25,	1995
2m 3f 110y H	4m 30.1	9	10-0	Firm	Green Island (USA)	Apr 12,	1995
2m 3f 110y C	4m 39.9	11	10-9	Firm	Abu Muslab	Apr 12,	1995
2m 6f H	4m 59.9	10	11-11		Owenius	Aug 21,	1980
2m 6f 110y C	5m 22.8	8	12-0	Hard	James Pigg	Spt 6 ,	1995
2m 7f 110y H	5m 34.9	12	11-10		Running Comment (USA)	Oct 7 ,	1986
3m 1f C	6m 17.1	8	9-9		Royle Speedmaster	Spt 16,	1992
3m 1f 110y H	5m 56.6	6	11-7	Firm	Tour Leader (NZ)	May 25,	1995
3m 2f C	6m 30.6	10	11-10		The Leggett	Mar 24,	1993
3m 2f H	6m 26.9	9	12-1	Good to soft	Rufus	Mar 22,	1995

FAKENHAM

Distance	Time	Age	Weight	Going	Horse	Date	
2m H	3m 47.1	4	10-1	Good	Lorcanjo	May 20,	1995
2m 110y C	3m 44.9	11	12-4		Cheekio Ora	Apr 23,	1984
2m 4f H	4m 54.5	5	10-12	Good	Dark Nightingale	May 20,	1995
2m 5f 110yC	5m 10.1	13	12-2		Skipping Tim	May 25,	1992
2m 7f 110yH	5m 37.1	6	11-3	Good	Laughing Gas (IRE)	May 20,	1995
3m 110y C	6m 21.8	10	12-8	Good	Duncan	May 20,	1995

FOLKESTONE

Distance	Time	Age	Weight	Going	Horse	Date	
2m C	3m 52.0	7	11-7		Zaccio	Apr 30,	1985
2m 1f 110y H	3m 56.2	5	11-5		Super Tek	Nov 14,	1983
2m 5f C	5m 6.4	11	11-12		Silver Buck	Nov 11,	1983
2m 6f 110y H	5m 18.2	6	10-0		Royalty Miss	Apr 30,	1985
3m 2f C	6m 23.1	9	10-13		Bolt Hole	Apr 26,	1988
3m 7f C	8m 7.3	10	12-0	Good	Doonloughan	May 18,	1995

FONTWELL

Distance	Time	Age	Weight	Going	Horse	Date	
2m 2f H	4m 6.0	4	10-13		Fighting Days (USA)	Aug 14,	1990
2m 2f C	4m 17.6	8	11-13		St Athan's Lad	May 31,	1993
2m 3f C	4m 35.9	8	11-10		St Athan's Lad	May 3 ,	1993
2m 6f H	5m 3.2	5	11-8	Firm	Doualago (FR)	May 29,	1995
3m 2f 110y C	6m 27.4	9	10-11		Donaghmoyne	Oct 21,	1986
3m 2f 110y H	6m 14.8	10	10-0	Firm	Punch's Hotel	Apr 27,	1995

HAYDOCK

Distance	Time	Age	Weight	Going	Horse	Date	
2m H	3m 33.3	6	11-0		Spinning	May 3 ,	1993
2m C	3m 55.4	9	10-0		Teddy Bear II	Mar 5 ,	1976
2m 4f C	4m 56.5	6	10-0		Hallo Dandy	May 5 ,	1980
2m 4f H	4m 35.3	7	10-10	Good to firm	Moving Out	May 6 ,	1995
2m 6f H	5m 12.7	5	10-10		Peter the Butcher	May 3 ,	1982
2m 7f 110y H	5m 32.3	9	11-0		Boscean Chieftain	May 3 ,	1993
3m C	6m 3.5	12	11-10		Jodami	Jan 18,	1997
3m 4f 110y C	7m 17.9	8	10-0		Rubstic	Dec 1 ,	1977
4m 110y C	8m 37.4	8	10-4		Jer (USA)	Nov 19,	1979

HEREFORD

Distance	Time	Age	Weight	Going	Horse	Date	
2m C	3m 48.8	9	10-5		Dan'l Widden	Oct 7 ,	1975
2m 1f H	3m 42.2	10	10-1		Tasty Son	Spt 11,	1973

2m 3f C	4m 32.2	14	10-6		Lor Moss	May 30, 1994
2m 3f 110y H	4m 22.2	7	11-3	Good to firm	Rolden Pride	May 6, 1995
3m 1f 110y C	6m 10.7	8	10-10	Good to firm	Gilston Lass	Apr 8, 1995
3m 2f H	6m 5.6	4	11-11	Good to firm	Clifton Set	Apr 8, 1995

HEXHAM

Distance	Time	Age	Weight	Going	Horse	Date
2m H	3m 46.5	9	11-1		Any Second	May 27, 1978
2m 110y C	4m 2.4	11	11-8	Firm	Golden Isle	May 6, 1995
2m 4f 110y H	4m 47.0	5	10-1		Mendaleak	May 31, 1982
2m 4f 110y C	4m 57.8	7	10-4		Peacework	Spt 2, 1991
3m H	5m 45.4	7	9-9		Fingers Crossed	Apr 29, 1991
3m 1f C	6m 10.3	6	11-7		The Fencer	May 29, 1978
4m C	8m 37.6	7	11-3		Rubika	Mar 15, 1990

HUNTINGDON

Distance	Time	Age	Weight	Going	Horse	Date
2m 110y H	3m 42.1	9	10-13	Firm	Golden Madjambo	Apr 17, 1995
2m 110y C	3m 55.6	9	11-3	Firm	Fine Harvest	May 29, 1995
2m 4f 110y C	4m 53.6	11	10-7		Guildway	May 11, 1994
2m 5f 110y H	4m 45.8	6	11-5		Sound of Laughter	Apr 14, 1984
3m C	5m 56.1	9	12-0	Firm	Donna Del Lago	May 29, 1995
3m 2f H	6m 4.1	7	12-0		Happy Horse (NZ)	May 11, 1994

KELSO

Distance	Time	Age	Weight	Going	Horse	Date
2m 110y H	3m 39.6	5	10-0	Firm	The Premier Expres	May 2, 1995
2m 1f C	4m 2.6	8	11-9		Mr Coggy	May 2, 1984
2m 2f H	4m 11.5	7	11-0		All Welcome	Oct 15, 1994
2m 6f 110y H	5m 12.9	7	10-7	Firm	Dancing Dove (IRE)	May 2, 1995
2m 6f 110y C	5m 33.3	7	10-9		Misty Rascal	Spt 11, 1982
3m 1f C	6m 2.0	10	11-2	Firm	Bas de Laine (FR)	Oct 19, 1996
3m 4f C	7m 2.3	7	10-6		Seven Towers (IRE)	Dec 2, 1996

KEMPTON

Distance	Time	Age	Weight	Going	Horse	Date
2m C	3m 49.3	6	10-13		Oh So Grumpy (IRE)	Oct 15, 1994
2m H	3m 37.0	5	11-8		Freight Forwarder	Oct 20, 1979
2m 4f 110y C	4m 55.8	8	10-6		Mr Entertainer	Dec 27, 1991
2m 5f H	4m 51.6	7	11-8		Grand Canyon (NZ)	Oct 15, 1977
3m C	5m 45.3	8	11-10	Good to firm	One Man (IRE)	Dec 26, 1996
3m 110y H	5m 45.6	7	10-6		Esmenella	Oct 17, 1964

LEICESTER

Distance	Time	Age	Weight	Going	Horse	Date
2m H	3m 39.6	6	10-11		Ryde Again	Nov 20, 1989
2m 1f C	4m 10.2	4	10-2		Noon	Nov 2, 1971
2m 4f 110y C	5m 4.4	5	11-8		Sire Nantais (FR)	Dec 5, 1989
2m 4f 110y H	4m 45.5	4	11-7		Prince of Rheims	Dec 5, 1989
3m C	5m 55.4	10	10-7		Sorbus	Apr 24, 1967
3m H	5m 48.0	5	10-6		King Tarquin	Apr 1, 1967

LINGFIELD

Distance	Time	Age	Weight	Going	Horse	Date
2m C	3m 51.9	8	11-1		Cotapaxi	Mar 19, 1993
2m 110y H	3m 47.2	5	11-0		Va Utu	Mar 19, 1993
2m 3f 110y H	4m 37.4	6	10-3		Bellezza	Mar 20, 1993
2m 4f 110y C	5m 9.2	6	11-3		Kisu Kali	Mar 20, 1993
2m 7f H	6m 37.4	6	11-10	Heavy	Holy Sting (IRE)	Mar 18, 1995
3m C	5m 58.4	6	11-3		Mighty Frolic	Mar 19, 1993

LUDLOW

Distance	Time	Age	Weight	Going	Horse	Date	
2m H	3m 30.9	5	10-13		British Grenadier	Apr 16,	1980
2m C	3m 50.4	10	12-4		Mighty Marine	Oct 2,	1979
2m 4f C	4m 48.4	9	10-3	Firm	Dark Oak	Apr 5,	1995
2m 5f 110y H	4m 56.2	5	10-8		Rahiib	May 14,	1987
3m C	5m 48.8	8	11-2	Good to firm	Act of Parliament (IRE)	Dec 23,	1996

MARKET RASEN

Distance	Time	Age	Weight	Going	Horse	Date	
2m 1f 110y H	3m 54.4	4	10-9		Border River	Jly 30,	1977
2m 1f 110y C	4m 11.9	9	12-7		Cape Felix	Aug 14,	1982
2m 3f 110y H	4m 34.7	7	10-13		Momser	May 7,	1993
2m 4f C	4m 51.4	10	10-8	Good to firm	Bobby Socks	Jun 14,	1996
2m 5f 110y H	5m 3.8	4	10-0		Pandolfi	Oct 3,	1970
2m 6f 110y C	5m 24.2	8	11-9		Annas Prince	Oct 19,	1979
3m H	5m 38.8	6	12-5		Trustful	May 21,	1977
3m 1f C	6m 1.0	7	11-8		Allerlea	May 1,	1985
4m 1f C	8m 51.2	8	10-0		Barkin	Nov 23,	1991

MUSSELBURGH

Distance	Time	Age	Weight	Going	Horse	Date	
2m H	3m 35.9	3	10-7		Joe Bumpas	Dec 11,	1989
2m C	3m 48.1	8	10-12		Sonsie Mo	Dec 6,	1993
2m 4f C	4m 53.0	6	11-3		Sir Peter Lely	Dec 20,	1993
2m 4f H	4m 43.4	5	10-1		Juke Box Billy (IRE)	Dec 6,	1993
3m C	5m 50.7	9	10-2		Charming Gale	Dec 9,	1996
3m H	5m 39.1	8	11-5		Supertop	Dec 17,	1996

NEWBURY

Distance	Time	Age	Weight	Going	Horse	Date	
2m 110y H	3m 45.2	5	10-2		Dhofar	Oct 25,	1985
2m 1f C	3m 58.2	8	12-0		Barnbrook Again	Nov 25,	1989
2m 4f C	4m 47.9	8	11-12		Espy	Oct 25,	1991
2m 5f H	4m 56.2	6	10-3		Northern Jinks	Apr 1,	1989
3m C	5m 47.6	8	10-4		Royal Cedar	Oct 27,	1989
3m 110y H	5m 45.4	8	10-9		Lansdowne	Oct 25,	1996
3m 2f 110y C	6m 27.1	10	12-0		Topsham Bay	Mar 26,	1993

NEWCASTLE

Distance	Time	Age	Weight	Going	Horse	Date	
2m H	3m 51.8	6	10-8	Good to firm	Classic Exhibit	May 13,	1995
2m 110y C	3m 56.7	7	11-12		Greenheart	May 7,	1990
2m 4f C	4m 46.7	7	9-13		Snow Blessed	May 19,	1984
2m 4f H	4m 42.0	4	10-10		Mils Mij	May 13,	1989
3m C	5m 48.1	8	10-4		Even Swell	Oct 30,	1975
3m H	5m 40.1	4	10-5		Withy Bank	Nov 29,	1986
3m 6f C	7m 30.0	8	12-0		Charlie Potheen	Apr 28,	1973
4m 1f C	8m 32.5	8	11-8		Seven Towers (IRE)	Feb 15,	1997

NEWTON ABBOT

Distance	Time	Age	Weight	Going	Horse	Date	
2m 110y C	3m 53.3	7	10-0		Peter Anthony	May 10,	1985
2m 1f H	3m 45.0	5	11-0		Windbound Lass	Aug 1,	1988
2m 5f C	4m 56.5	5	11-5		Rahiib	Aug 13,	1987
2m 6f H	4m 55.4	7	10-0		Virbian	Jun 30,	1983
3m 2f 110y C	6m 21.9	7	10-9		Parcelstown	Aug 16,	1984
3m 3f H	6m 17.6	7	12-0		Le Carotte	Jly 31,	1989

PERTH

Distance	Time	Age	Weight	Going	Horse	Date	
2m C	3m 50.2	8	12-2		Clareman	Apr 27,	1967
2m 110y H	3m 40.4	4	11-8		Molly Fay	Spt 23,	1971
2m 4f 110y H	4m 41.2	8	10-2		Valiant Dash	May 19,	1994
2m 4f 110y C	4m 56.3	9	11-12		General Chandos	Aug 17,	1990
3m C	5m 55.8	9	12-5		Chandigar	Apr 17,	1973
3m 110y H	5m 43.1	5	12-0		Mystic Memory	Aug 20,	1994

PLUMPTON

Distance	Time	Age	Weight	Going	Horse	Date	
2m C	3m 47.1	15	11-13		Brinkwater	Aug 8 ,	1991
2m 1f H	3m 58.7	7	10-2		Striding Edge	Aug 7 ,	1992
2m 2f C	4m 24.1	10	11-9	Firm	Pats Minstrel	Apr 15,	1995
2m 4f H	4m 37.5	9	10-2		Director's Choice	Apr 30,	1994
2m 5f C	5m 4.8	6	11-0	Firm	Preenka Girl (FR)	Aug 4 ,	1995
3m 1f 110y C	6m 9.2	9	12-7		Betton Gorse	Apr 29,	1982

SANDOWN

Distance	Time	Age	Weight	Going	Horse	Date	
2m C	3m 44.3	8	12-0		News King	Apr 23,	1982
2m 110y H	3m 42.0	6	10-0		Olympian	Mar 13,	1993
2m 4f 110y C	4m 57.2	8	11-7	Good to firm	Coulton	Apr 29,	1995
2m 6f H	5m 5.6	8	11-3		Kintbury	Nov 5 ,	1983
3m 110y C	5m 59.0	8	12-7		Arkle	Nov 6 ,	1965
3m 5f 110y	7m 9.1	9	10-0	Good to firm	Cache Fleur (FR)	Apr 29,	1995

SEDGEFIELD

Distance	Time	Age	Weight	Going	Horse	Date	
2m 1f C	4m 0.3	8	10-10		Stay Awake	May 18,	1994
2m 1f 110y H	3m 51.7	4	10-13		Byzantine	Spt 4 ,	1992
2m 5f C	4m 59.8	10	11-0	Good to firm	Magic Bloom	Spt 6 ,	1996
2m 5f 110y H	4m 46.3	7	10-0		Palm House	Spt 4 ,	1992
3m 3f C	6m 39.1	9	11-4	Good to firm	Little Martina (IRE)	Apr 12,	1997
3m 3f 110y H	6m 30.5	8	11-6		Stated Case	May 6 ,	1993
3m 4f C	7m 11.6	10	9-8		Bow Handy Man	Mar 3 ,	1992

SOUTHWELL

Distance	Time	Age	Weight	Going	Horse	Date	
2m C	3m 51.0	8	11-1		Stay Awake	May 11,	1994
2m H	3m 36.2	5	11-8		Merlins Wish (USA)	May 2 ,	1994
2m 2f H	4 n 19.5	6	11-2	Good to firm	Heresthedeal (IRE)	May 8 ,	1995
2m 4f 110y C	5m 2.8	9	10-0	Good to firm	Bally Parson	May 8 ,	1995
2m 4f 110y H	4m 47.8	8	11-13		Man of the Grange	May 2 ,	1994
3m 110y H	5m 46.5	5	10-0	Good to firm	Soloman Springs (USA)	May 8 ,	1995
3m 110y C	6m 9.0	7	11-8		Strong Medicine	May 2 ,	1994

STRATFORD-ON-AVON

Distance	Time	Age	Weight	Going	Horse	Date	
2m 110y H	3m 40.4	6	11-12		Chusan	May 7 ,	1956
2m 1f 110y C	4m 0.2	7	11-8		Money In	Spt 5 ,	1981
2m 4f C	4m 47.9	8	10-2		Air Commander	Mar 25,	1993
2m 5f 110y C	5m 8.9	9	11-0		Gaelic Frolic	Spt 5 ,	1992
2m 6f 110y H	5m 6.8	6	11-0		Broken Wing	May 31,	1986
3m C	5m 45.9	12	10-5		The Nigelstan	Jun 5 ,	1993
3m 2f H	6m 21.3	8	10-5		Space Kate	Jun 3 ,	1989
3m 4f C	6m 44.8	8	10-0		Gold Castle	Jun 1 ,	1985

TAUNTON

Distance	Time	Age	Weight	Going	Horse	Date	
2m 110y C	3m 49.5	8	10-9	Firm	I Have Him	Apr 28,	1995
2m 1f H	3m 41.2	5	10-0		Va Utu	Spt 23,	1993
2m 3f C	4m 31.1	12	10-1	Good to firm	Wickfield Lad	Spt 21,	1995
2m 3f 110y H	4m 22.4	10	10-11	Firm	Glen Mirage	Apr 28,	1995
3m C	5m 43.2	8	11-8	Good to firm	The Blue Boy (IRE)	Oct 17,	1996
3m 110y H	5m 36.0	5	11-4		Cairncastle	Oct 18,	1990
3m 3f C	6m 53.1	9	11-7		En Gounasi Theon	Apr 12,	1990
4m 2f 110y C	9m 1.5	12	10-0	Good to firm	Woodlands Genhire	Jan 16,	1997

TOWCESTER

Distance	Time	Age	Weight	Going	Horse	Date	
2mH	3m 39.5	4	10-0		Nascracker (USA)	May 22,	1987
2m 110y C	3m 59.0	6	10-1		Silver Knight	May 25,	1974
2m 5f H	5m 0.9	7	11-2		Mailcom	May 3 ,	1993
2m 6f C	5m 30.0	7	11-13		Whiskey Eyes	May 10,	1988
3m H	5m 44.0	9	9-10		Dropshot	May 25,	1984
3m 1f C	6m 12.3	9	10-8		Veleso	May 22,	1987

UTTOXETER

Distance	Time	Age	Weight	Going	Horse	Date	
2m H	3m 37.2	4	10-9	Good to firm	Flying Eagle	Jun 11,	1995
2m C	3m 49.0	7	11-0		Large Action (IRE)	Nov 3 ,	1995
2m 4f 110y H	4m 39.1	8	10-9	Good to firm	Chicago's Best	Jun 11,	1995
2m 5f C	4m 54.2	8	11-8		McKenzie	Apr 27,	1974
2m 6f 110y H	5m 17.7	8	11-0		Garston La Gaffe	May 6 ,	1993
2m 7f C	5m 26.8	7	10-13	Good to firm	Certain Angle	Jun 9 ,	1996
3m 110y H	5m 35.3	5	10-4		Volcanic Dancer	Spt 19,	1991
3m 2f C	6m 23.5	10	11-13	Good to firm	McGregor the Third	Oct 5 ,	1996
4m 2f C	8m 33.7	8	11-4		Seven Towers (IRE)	Mar 15,	1997

WARWICK

Distance	Time	Age	Weight	Going	Horse	Date	
2m H	3m 34.6	5	11-4		Arabian Bold	May 22,	1993
2mC	3m 49.1	8	11-0		Super Sharp (NZ)	Nov 2 ,	1996
2m 4f 110y C	4m 53.3	9	9-12		Dudie	May 16,	1987
2m 4f 110y H	4m 43.0	7	10-0		Carrymore	Spt 19,	1970
3m 2f C	6m 16.1	12	10-12		Castle Warden	May 6 ,	1989
3m 5f C	7m 13.2	8	11-0		Purple Haze	Spt 18,	1982
4m 1f 110y C	8m 36.4	10	10-6		Jolly's Clump	Jan 24,	1976

WETHERBY

Distance	Time	Age	Weight	Going	Horse	Date	
2m H	3m 39.2	5	10-1		Able Player	Oct 14,	1992
2m C	3m 47.3	6	11-0		Cumbriam Challenge (IRE)	Oct 22,	1996
2m 4f 110y H	4m 45.5	7	11-10		Lumen	Apr 13,	1982
2m 4f 110y C	5m 5.5	9	12-0	Good to firm	Mr Jamboree	May 10,	1995
2m 7f 110y H	5m 43.7	7	11-10	Good to firm	Five Flags (IRE)	Apr 17,	1995
3m 110y C	6m 10.5	7	11-2		Barton Bank	Oct 30,	1993
3m 1f H	5m 58.1	9	11-0		Trainglot	Nov 2 ,	1996
3m 5f C	7m 45.8	8	10-9	Good	Snook Point	Apr 18,	1995

WINCANTON

Distance	Time	Age	Weight	Going	Horse	Date	
2m H	3m 28.3	6	10-10		Mulciber	May 6 ,	1994
2m C	3m 43.7	8	12-7		Kescast	May 11,	1988
2m 5f C	4m 59.7	8	11-10	Firm	Coulton	Oct 22,	1995
2m 6f H	5m 1.9	6	11-0	Firm	St Mellion Green (IRE)	May 9 ,	1995
3m 1f 110y C	6m 12.3	8	11-6	Firm	Straight Talk	May 9 ,	1995

WINDSOR

Distance	Time	Age	Weight	Going	Horse	Date	
2m H	3m 41.8	4	10-12		Skylander	Nov 21,	1983
2m C	3m 54.0	7	10-10		Guiburns Nephew	Nov 20,	1989
2m 4f H	5m 32.6	4	10-7	Heavy	Cadougold (FR)	Mar 6 ,	1995
2m 5f C	5m 13.1	5	10-7		Fight To Win (USA)	Mar 8 ,	1993
2m 6f 110y H	5m 19.1	5	10-9		Qannaas	Nov 20,	1989
3m C	5m 56.2	9	12-0		Acarine	Nov 18,	1985
3m 4f 110y C	7m 7.6	9	10-9		Brave Defender	Mar 8 ,	1993

WORCESTER

Distance	Time	Age	Weight	Going	Horse	Date	
2m H	3m 35.3	6	11-7		Santopadre	May 11,	1988
2m C	3m 47.6	7	11-7	Good to firm	Regal Romper (IRE)	Aug 5 ,	1995
2m 2f H	4m 7.1	5	12-2		Molly Fay	Aug 19,	1972
2m 4f H	4m 38.6	8	11-7	Good to firm	Chicago's Best	Jly 27,	1995
2m 4f 110y C	4m 56.5	7	11-11		Copper Mine	May 8 ,	1993
2m 5f 110y H	4m 48.4	4	12-2		Elite Reg	May 19,	1993
2m 7f C	5m 37.6	12	10-7		Tanora	May 5 ,	1981
3m H	5m 35.9	5	11-7		High Renown	Spt 14,	1985

KEY TO RACEREADERS' INITIALS

(AA) Alan Amies
(AK) Anthony Kemp
(AR) Ashley Rumney
(CR) Colin Roberts
(DB) David Bellingham
(Dk) David Dickinson
(DO) Darren Owen
(DS) Desmond Stoneham
(GB) Gordon Brown
(GM) Gary Millard
(Hn) John Hanmer
(IM) Ivor Markham
(KH) Keith Hewitt
(LM) Louise Mackinlay
(LMc) Lee McKenzie
(NB) Nicola Bowen
(NR) Neville Ring
(O'R) Tom O'Ryan
(RL) Richard Lowther
(SC) Steven Clarke
(SM) Stephen Mellish
(T) Mary Trueman
(WG) Walter Glynn

CHASEFORM STANDARD TIMES

AINTREE

HURDLES

2m 110y 3m 54.0
2m 4f 4m 42.0
3m 110y 5m 51.0

CHASES

2m 1f 110y 4m 18.0
2m 6f 5m 30.0
3m 3f 6m 45.0
4m 4f 9m 2.0

MILDMAY CHASE

2m 3m 58.0
2m 4f 4m 58.0
3m 1f 6m 17.0

ASCOT

HURDLES

2m 110y 3m 50.0
2m 4f 4m 42.0
3m 5m 39.0
3m 1f 110y 6m 1.0

CHASES

2m 3m 51.0
2m 3f 110y 4m 47.0
3m 110y 6m 5.0

AYR

HURDLES

2m 3m 37.0
2m 4f 4m 41.0
2m 6f 5m 11.0
3m 110y 5m 46.0
3m 2f 110y 6m 11.0

CHASES

2m 3m 45.0
2m 4f 4m 55.0
2m 5f 110y 5m 12.0
3m 1f 6m 7.0
3m 3f 110y 6m 43.0
4m 1f 8m 6.0

BANGOR-ON-DEE

HURDLES

2m 1f 3m 55.0
2m 4f 4m 36.0
3m 5m 39.0

CHASES

2m 1f 110y 4m 10.0
2m 4f 110y 5m 0.0
3m 110y 6m 2.0
4m 1f 8m 11.0

CARLISLE

HURDLES

2m 1f 4m 1.0
2m 4f 110y 4m 51.0
3m 110y 5m 44.0

CHASES

2m 3m 54.0
2m 4f 110y 5m 3.0
3m 5m 52.0
3m 2f 6m 28.0

CARTMEL

HURDLES

2m 1f 110y 4m 1.0
2m 6f 5m 11.0
3m 2f 6m 7.0

CHASES

2m 1f 110y 4m 11.0
2m 5f 110y 5m 12.0
3m 2f 6m 24.0

CATTERICK

HURDLES

2m 3m 43.0
2m 3f 4m 25.0
3m 1f 110y 6m 7.0

CHASES

2m 3m 52.0
2m 3f 4m 39.0
3m 1f 110y 6m 18.0

CHELTENHAM

Old Course

HURDLES

2m 110y 3m 51.0
2m 5f 4m 58.0
3m 2f 6m 17.0

CHASES

2m 3m 53.0
2m 4f 110y 5m 2.0
3m 1f 6m 13.0
3m 3f 110y 6m 50.0
4m 7m 56.0

New Course

2m 1f..3m 57.0
2m 4f..4m 40.0
2m 5f 110y..................................5m 0.0
3m 110y.....................................5m 42.0

2m 110y.....................................3m 57.0
2m 5f..5m 9.0
3m 1f 110y.................................6m 21.0
3m 2f 110y.................................6m 35.0
4m 1f..8m 11.0

Park Course

2m 110y.....................................3m 52.0
2m 5f 110y..................................5m 2.0
2m 7f 110y..................................5m 31.0

2m 110y.....................................4m 1.0
2m 5f..5m 7.0
3m 1f 110y.................................6m 18.0

CHEPSTOW

HURDLES

2m 110y.....................................3m 49.0
2m 4f 110y..................................4m 47.0
3m...5m 40.0

CHASES

2m 110y.....................................3m 58.0
2m 3f 110y..................................4m 49.0
3m...5m 53.0
3m 2f 110y..................................6m 30.0
3m 5f 110y..................................7m 20.0

DONCASTER

HURDLES

2m 110y.....................................3m 50.0
2m 4f..4m 40.0
3m 110y.....................................5m 43.0

CHASES

2m 110y.....................................3m 55.0
2m 3f 110y..................................4m 47.0
3m...5m 54.0
3m 2f..6m 22.0

EXETER

HURDLES

2m 1f 110y..................................4m 4.0
2m 2f..4m 10.0
2m 3f..4m 26.0
2m 3f 110y..................................4m 32.0
2m 6f..5m 10.0
3m 2f..6m 10.0

CHASES

2m 1f 110y..................................4m 16.0
2m 2f..4m 21.0
2m 3f..4m 40.0
2m 3f 110y..................................4m 45.0
2m 6f 110y..................................5m 31.0
2m 7f 110y..................................5m 47.0
3m 2f..6m 27.0

FAKENHAM

HURDLES

2m...3m 44.0
2m 4f..4m 45.0
2m 7f 110y..................................5m 31.0

CHASES

2m 110y.....................................4m
2m 5f 110y..................................5m 15.0
3m 110y.....................................6m 3.0

FOLKESTONE

HURDLES

2m 1f 110y..................................4m 6.0
2m 6f 110y..................................5m 17.0
....

CHASES

2m...3m 52.0
2m 5f..5m 8.0
3m 2f..6m 20.0
3m 7f..7m 37.0

FONTWELL

HURDLES

2m 2f..4m 9.0
2m 6f..5m 10.0
3m 2f 110y..................................6m 13.0

CHASES

2m 2f..4m 22.0
2m 3f..4m 39.0
3m 2f 110y..................................6m 40.0

HAYDOCK

HURDLES

2m...3m 42.0
2m 4f..4m 37.0
2m 6f..5m 10.0
2m 7f 110y..................................5m 32.0

CHASES

2m...3m 55.0
2m 4f..4m 57.0
3m...5m 58.0
3m 4f 110y..................................7m 5.0
4m 110y.....................................8m 6.0

HEREFORD

HURDLES

2m 1f....3m 53.0
2m 3f 110y....4m 31.0
3m 2f....6m 3.0

CHASES

2m....3m 51.0
2m 3f....4m 30.0
3m 1f 110y....6m 10.0

HEXHAM

HURDLES

2m....3m 48.0
2m 4f 110y....4m 48.0
3m....5m 40.0

CHASES

2m 110y....3m 57.0
2m 4f 110y....4m 57.0
3m 1f....6m 11.0
4m....8m

HUNTINGDON

HURDLES

2m 110y....3m 48.0
2m 5f 110y....5m 0.0
3m 2f....6m 6.0

CHASES

2m 110y....4m 2.0
2m 4f 110y....5m
3m....5m 57.0

KELSO

HURDLES

2m 110y....3m 46.0
2m 2f....4m 13.0
2m 6f 110y....5m 17.0

CHASES

2m 1f....4m 7.0
2m 6f 110y....5m 32.0
3m 1f....6m 10.0
3m 4f....6m 56.0

KEMPTON

HURDLES

2m....3m 42.0
2m 5f....4m 52.0
3m 110y....5m 46.0

CHASES

2m....3m 44.0
2m 4f 110y....5m 1.0
3m....5m 55.0

LEICESTER

HURDLES

2m....3m 45.0
2m 4f 110y....4m 49.0
3m....5m 41.0

CHASES

2m 1f....4m 10.0
2m 4f 110y....5m 1.0
3m....5m 54.0

LINGFIELD

HURDLES

2m 110y....3m 45.0
2m 3f 110y....4m 34.0
2m 7f....5m 23.0

CHASES

2m....3m 52.0
2m 4f 110y....4m 59.0
3m....5m 54.0

LUDLOW

HURDLES

2m....3m 37.0
2m 5f 110y....5m 1.0
3m 2f 110y....5m 59.0

CHASES

2m....3m 52.0
2m 4f....4m 52.0
3m....6m

MARKET RASEN

HURDLES

2m 1f 110y....4m 3.0
2m 3f 110y....4m 33.0
2m 5f 110y....5m 4.0
3m....5m 39.0

CHASES

2m 1f 110y....4m 15.0
2m 4f....4m 51.0
2m 6f 110y....5m 27.0
3m 1f....6m 11.0
4m 1f....8m 9.0

MUSSELBURGH

HURDLES

2m....3m 39.0
2m 4f....4m 42.0
3m....5m 40.0

CHASES

2m....3m 54.0
2m 4f....4m 56.0
3m....5m 53.0

NEWBURY

HURDLES		CHASES	
2m 110y	3m 50.0	2m 1f	4m 4.0
2m 5f	4m 54.0	2m 4f	4m 55.0
3m 110y	5m 35.0	3m	5m 50.0
		3m 2f 110y	6m 35.0

NEWCASTLE

HURDLES		CHASES	
2m	3m 52.0	2m 110y	3m 58.0
2m 4f	4m 48.0	2m 4f	4m 53.0
3m	5m 42.0	3m	5m 52.0
		3m 6f	7m 30.0
		4m 1f	8m 16.0

NEWTON ABBOT

HURDLES		CHASES	
2m 1f	3m 53.0	2m 110y	4m 0.0
2m 6f	5m 12.0	2m 5f 110y	5m 17.0
3m 3f	6m 23.0	3m 2f 110y	6m 34.0

PERTH

HURDLES		CHASES	
2m 110y	3m 46.0	2m	3m 51.0
2m 4f 110y	4m 48.0	2m 4f 110y	4m 59.0
3m 110y	5m 46.0	3m	5m 58.0

PLUMPTON

HURDLES		CHASES	
2m 1f	4m	2m	3m 52.0
2m 4f	4m 47.0	2m 2f	4m 18.0
		2m 5f	5m 13.0
		3m 1f 110y	6m 20.0

SANDOWN

HURDLES		CHASES	
2m 110y	3m 51.0	2m	3m 51.0
2m 6f	5m 13.0	2m 4f 110y	4m 59.0
		3m 110y	6m 2.0
		3m 5f 110y	7m 15.0

SEDGEFIELD

HURDLES		CHASES	
2m 1f	3m 55.0	2m 100y	3m 58.0
2m 1f 110y	4m 4.0	2m 1f	4m 7.0
2m 5f 110y	5m	2m 5f	5m 11.0
3m 3f 110y	6m 35.0	3m 3f	6m 46.0
		3m 4f	7m 5

SOUTHWELL

HURDLES		CHASES	
2m	3m 42.0	2m	3m 53.0
2m 2f	4m 11.0	2m 4f 110y	5m 4.0
2m 4f 110y	4m 46.0	3m 110y	6m 7.0
3m 110y	5m 46.0		

STRATFORD-ON-AVON

HURDLES		CHASES	
2m 110y	3m 47.0	2m 1f 110y	4m 9.0
2m 3f	4m 18.0	2m 4f	4m 56.0
2m 6f 110y	5m 16.0	2m 5f 110y	5m 52.0
		3m	5m 50.0
		3m 4f	7m

TAUNTON

HURDLES		CHASES	
2m 1f	3m 53.0	2m 110y	4m
2m 3f 110y	4m 31.0	2m 3f	4m 42.0
3m 110y	5m 52.0	3m	5m 57.0
		3m 3f	6m 38.0
		4m 2f 110y	8m 45.0

TOWCESTER

HURDLES		CHASES	
2m	3m 46.0	2m 110y	4m 2.0
2m 5f	5m 2.0	2m 6f	5m 29.0
3m	5m 40.0	3m 1f	6m 15.0

UTTOXETER

HURDLES		CHASES	
2m	3m 41.0	2m	3m 50.0
2m 4f 110y	4m 44.0	2m 5f	5m 5.0
2m 6f 110y	5m 17.0	2m 7f	5m 36.0
3m 110y	5m 42.0	3m 2f	6m 27.0
		4m 2f	8m 25.0

WARWICK

HURDLES		CHASES	
2m	3m 42.0	2m	3m 54.0
2m 4f 110y	4m 47.0	2m 4f 110y	5m 4.0
		3m 2f	6m 25.0
		3m 5f	7m 20.0
		4m 1f 110y	8m 22.0

WETHERBY

HURDLES		CHASES	
2m	3m 42.0	2m	3m 52.0
2m 4f 110y	4m 47.0	2m 4f 110y	5m 7.0
2m 7f	5m 30.0	3m 1f	6m 10.0
3m 1f	5m 53.0	3m 5f	7m 6.0

WINCANTON

HURDLES		CHASES	
2m	3m 40.0	2m	3m 53.0
2m 6f	5m 9.0	2m 5f	5m 8.0
		3m 1f 110y	6m 19.0

WINDSOR

HURDLES		CHASES	
2m	3m 48.0	2m	3m 50.0
2m 4f	4m 46.0	2m 5f	5m 9.0
2m 6f 110y	5m 23.0	3m	5m 55.0
		3m 4f 110y	7m 2.0

WOLVERHAMPTON

No figures available as yet

WORCESTER

HURDLES		CHASES	
2m	3m 40.0	2m	3m 51.0
2m 2f	4m 10.0	2m 4f 110y	5m 1.0
2m 4f	4m 38.0	2m 7f	5m 38.0
2m 5f 110y	5m 2.0		
3m	5m 36.0		

MURPHY'S GOLD CUP (HANDICAP CHASE)
formerly Mackeson Gold Cup
Cheltenham 2m 4f 110y

1986	Very Promising	8-11-13	11
1987	Beau Ranger	9-10-12	14
1988	Pegwell Bay	7-11-02	13
1989	Joint Sovereignty	9-10-04	15
1990	Multum In Parvo	7-11-02	13
1991	Another Coral	8-10-01	15
1992	Tipping Tim	7-10-10	16
1993	Bradbury Star	8-11-08	15
1994	Bradbury Star	9-11-11	14
1995	Dublin Flyer	9-11-08	12
1996	Challenger du Luc	6-10-02	12

FIRST NATIONAL BANK GOLD CUP (HANDICAP CHASE)
formerly H & T WALKER GOLD CUP
Ascot 2m 4f

1986	Church Warden	7-10-07	6
1987	Weather The Storm	7-11-00	11
1988	Saffron Lord	6-11-03	5
1989	Man O'Magic	8-11-05	11
1990	Blazing Walker	6-11-06	5
1991	Kings Fountain	8-11-01	8
1992	Deep Sensation	7-11-02	10
1993	*Abandoned due to frost*		
1994	Raymylette	7-11-10	11
1995	Sound Man	7-12-00	5
1996	Strong Promise	5-10-05	8

HENNESSY COGNAC GOLD CUP (HANDICAP CHASE)
Newbury 3m 2f 110y

1986	Broadheath	9-10-05	15
1987	Playschool	9-10-08	12
1988	Strands Of Gold	9-10-00	12
1989	Ghofar	6-10-02	8
1990	Arctic Call	7-11-00	13
1991	Chatam	7-10-06	15
1992	Sibton Abbey	7-10-00	13
1993	Cogent	9-10-01	9
1994	One Man	6-10-00	16
1995	Couldnt Be Better	8-10-08	11
1996	Coome Hill	7-10-00	11

TRIPLEPRINT GOLD CUP (HANDICAP CHASE)
Cheltenham 2m 4f

1986	Oregon Trail	6-10-07	6
1987	Bishop's Yarn	8-10-07	5
1988	Pegwell Bay	7-10-13	10
1989	Clever Folly	9-10-04	6
1990	*Abandoned due to snow*		
1991	Kings Fountain	8-11-10	8
1992	Another Coral	9-11-04	10
1993	Fragrant Dawn	9-10-02	11
1994	Dublin Flyer	8-10-02	11
1995	*Abandoned due to frost*		
1996	Addington Boy	8-11-10	10

BONUSPRINT CHRISTMAS HURDLE
Kempton 2m

1986	Nohalmdun	5-11-03	7
1987	Osric	4-11-03	8
1988	Kribensis	4-11-03	7
1989	Kribensis	5-11-03	8
1990	Fidway	5-11-07	8
1991	Gran Alba	5-11-07	7
1992	Mighty Mogul	5-11-07	8
1993	Muse	6-11-07	5
1994	Absaloms's Lady	6-11-02	6
1995	*Abandoned due to frost*		
1996	*Abandoned due to frost*		

KING GEORGE VI CHASE
Kempton 3m

1986	Desert Orchid	7-11-10	8
1987	Nupsala (FR)	8-11-10	9
1988	Desert Orchid	9-11-10	5
1989	Desert Orchid	10-11-10	6
1990	Desert Orchid	11-11-10	9
1991	The Fellow (FR)	6-11-10	8
1992	The Fellow (FR)	7-11-10	8
1993	Barton Bank	7-11-10	10
1994	Algan (FR)	6-11-10	9
1995	*One Man	8-11-10	11
1996	One Man	8-11-10	5
	(*Run at Sandown Jan 6th 1996)		

CORAL WELSH NATIONAL (HANDICAP CHASE)
Chepstow 3m 6f

1986	Stearsby	7-11-05	17
1987	Playschool	9-10-11	13
1988	Bonanza Boy	7-10-01	12
1989	Bonanza Boy	8-11-11	12
1990	Cool Ground	11-10-00	9
1991	Carvill's Hill	9-11-12	17
1992	Run For Free	8-10-09	11
1993	Riverside Boy	10-10-00	8
1994	*Master Oats	8-11-06	8
1995	*Abandoned due to frost*		
1996	*Abandoned due to frost*		
	(*Run at Newbury)		

LADBROKE HANDICAP HURDLE
Leopardstown 2m

1986	Bonalma	6-10-13	22
1987	Barnbrook Again	6-11-08	22
1988	Roark	6-11-11	15
1989	Redundant Pal	6-10-00	17
1990	Redundant Pal	7-11-05	27
1991	The Illiad	10-10-13	17
1992	How's The Boss	6-10-02	20
1993	Glencloud	5-10-13	25
1994	Atone	7-10-08	25
1995	Anusha	5-10-02	17
1996	Dance Beat	5-09-12	22
1997	Master Tribe	7-10-04	23

VICTOR CHANDLER (HANDICAP CHASE)
Ascot 2m

1987	*Abandoned due to frost*		
1988	*Abandoned due to fog*		
1989	Desert Orchid	10-12-00	5
1990	Blitzkreig	8-10-04	5
1991	Meikleour	11-10-00	10
1992	Waterloo Boy	9-11-10	5
1993	Sybillin	7-10-10	11
1994	*Viking Flagship	7-10-10	4
1995	Martha's Son	8-10-09	8
1996	Big Matt	9-10-04	11
1997	**Ask Tom	8-10-10	8

(* Run at Warwick)
(**Run at Kempton Jan 18th)

AGFA DIAMOND (HANDICAP) CHASE
Sandown 3m 110y

1986	Burrough Hill Lad	10-12-00	6
1987	Desert Orchid	8-11-10	6
1988	Charter Party	10-10-11	11
1989	Desert Orchid	10-12-00	4
1990	*Abandoned due to waterlogging*		
1991	Desert Orchid	12-12-00	4
1992	Espy	9-10-07	9
1993	Country Member	8-10-07	3
1994	Second Schedual	9-10-07	5
1995	Deep Bramble	8-11-10	11
1996	Amtrak Express	9-10-07	3
1997	Dextra Dove	10-11-02	6

TOTE GOLD TROPHY (HANDICAP HURDLE)
Newbury 2m 110y

1986	*Abandoned due to snow*		
1987	Neblin	8-10-00	21
1988	Jamesmead	7-10-00	19
1989	Grey Salute	6-11-05	10
1990	Deep Sensation	5-11-03	17
1991	*Abandoned due to frost*		
1992	Rodeo Star	6-10-10	15
1993	King Credo	8-10-00	16
1994	Large Action	6-10-08	11
1995	Mysilv	5-10-08	8
1996	Squire Silk	7-10-12	18
1997	Make a Stand	6-11-07	18

HENNESSY COGNAC GOLD CUP
Leopardstown 3m

1988	Playschool	10-12-00	5
1989	Carvill's Hill	7-12-00	9
1990	Nick The Brief	8-12-00	6
1991	Nick The Brief	9-12-00	6
1992	Carvill's Hill	10-12-00	10
1993	Jodami	8-12-00	7
1994	Jodami	9-12-00	6
1995	Jodami	10-12-00	6
1996	Imperial Call	7-12-00	8
1997	Danoli	9-12-00	8

RACING POST HANDICAP CHASE
Kempton 3m

1988	Rhyme 'n' Reason	9-10-11	12
1989	Bonanza Boy	8-11-01	11
1990	Desert Orchid	11-12-03	8
1991	Docklands Express	9-10-07	9
1992	Docklands Express	10-11-10	11
1993	Zeta's Lad	10-10-10	12
1994	Antonin	6-10-04	16
1995	Val D'Alene	8-11-02	9
1996	Rough Quest	10-10-08	9
1997	Mudahim	11-10-02	9

SUNDERLANDS IMPERIAL CUP (HANDICAP) HURDLE
Sandown 2m 110y

1986	Insular	6-9-10	19
1987	Inlander	6-10-03	23
1988	Sprowston Boy	5-10-11	15
1989	Travel Mystery	6-10-08	8
1990	Moody Man	5-10-13	15
1991	Precious Boy	5-10-06	13
1992	King Credo	7-10-04	10
1993	Olympian	6-10-00	15
1994	Precious Boy	8-11-07	13
1995	Collier Bay	5-10-02	10
1996	Amancio	5-10-08	11
1997	Carlito Brigante	5-10-00	18

GUINNESS ARKLE CHALLENGE TROPHY (NOVICES) CHASE
Cheltenham 2m

1986	Oregon Trail	6-11-08	14
1987	Gala's Image	7-11-08	19
1988	Danish Flight	9-11-08	12
1989	Waterloo Boy	6-11-08	14
1990	Comandante	8-11-08	14
1991	Remittance Man	7-11-08	14
1992	Young Pokey	7-11-08	11
1993	Travado	7-11-08	8
1994	Nakir	6-11-08	11
1995	Klairon Davis	6-11-08	11
1996	Ventana Canyon	7-11-08	16
1997	Or Royal	6-11-08	9

SMURFIT CHAMPION HURDLE
Cheltenham 2m 110y

1986	See You Then	6-12-00	23
1987	See You Then	7-12-00	18
1988	Celtic Shot	6-12-00	21
1989	Beech Road	7-12-00	15
1990	Kribensis	6-12-00	19
1991	Morley Street	7-12-00	24
1992	Royal Gait	9-12-00	16
1993	Granville Again	7-12-00	18
1994	Flakey Dove	8-11-09	15
1995	Alderbrook	6-12-00	14
1996	Collier Bay	6-12-00	16
1997	Make a Stand	6-12-00	17

Winners of Principal Races

QUEEN MOTHER CHAMPION CHASE
Cheltenham 2m

1986	Buck House	8-12-00	11
1987	Pearlyman	8-12-00	8
1988	Pearlyman	9-12-00	8
1989	Barnbrook Again	8-12-00	8
1990	Barnbrook Again	9-12-00	9
1991	Katabatic	8-12-00	7
1992	Remittance Man	8-12-00	6
1993	Deep Sensation	8-12-00	9
1994	Viking Flagship	7-12-00	8
1995	Viking Flagship	8-12-00	10
1996	Klairon Davis	7-12-00	7
1997	Martha's Son	10-12-00	6

ROYAL SUNALLIANCE NOVICES' CHASE
Cheltenham 3m

1986	Cross Master	9-11-04	30
1987	Kildimo	7-11-04	18
1988	The West Awake	7-11-04	14
1989	Envopak Token	8-11-04	15
1990	Garrison Savannah	7-11-04	9
1991	Rolling Ball	8-11-04	20
1992	Miinnehoma	9-11-04	18
1993	Young Hustler	6-11-04	8
1994	Monsieur Le Cure	8-11-04	18
1995	Brief Gale	8-10-13	13
1996	Nahthen Lad	7-11-04	12
1997	Hanakham	8-11-04	14

ELITE RACING CLUB TRIUMPH HURDLE (4-y-o)
formerly Daily Express Triumph Hurdle
Cheltenham 2m 1f

1986	Solar Cloud	11-00	28
1987	Alone Success	11-00	29
1988	Kribensis	11-00	26
1989	Ikdam	11-00	27
1990	Rare Holiday	11-00	30
1991	Oh So Risky	11-00	27
1992	Duke Of Monmouth	11-00	30
1993	Shawiya	10-09	25
1994	Mysilv	10-09	28
1995	Kissair	11-00	26
1996	Paddy's Return	11-00	29
1997	Commanche Court	11-00	28

TOTE CHELTENHAM GOLD CUP (CHASE)
Cheltenham 3m 2f

1986	Dawn Run	8-11-09	11
1987	The Thinker	9-12-00	12
1988	Charter Party	10-12-00	15
1989	Desert Orchid	10-12-00	13
1990	Norton's Coin	9-12-00	12
1991	Garrison Savannah	8-12-00	14
1992	Cool Ground	10-12-00	8
1993	Jodami	8-12-00	16
1994	The Fellow	9-12-00	15
1995	Master Oats	9-12-00	15
1996	Imperial Call	7-12-00	10
1997	Mr Mulligan	9-12-00	14

MARTELL CUP CHASE
Aintree 3m 1f

1986	Beau Ranger	8-11-05	4
1987	Wayward Lad	12-11-05	6
1988	Desert Orchid	9-11-05	4
1989	Yahoo	8-11-05	8
1990	Toby Tobias	8-11-09	5
1991	Aquilifer	11-11-05	5
1992	Kings Fountain	9-11-09	8
1993	Docklands Express	11-11-05	4
1994	Docklands Express	12-11-05	4
1995	Merry Gale	7-11-09	6
1996	Scotton Banks	7-11-05	6
1997	Barton Bank	11-11-05	5

GLENLIVET ANNIVERSARY HURDLE (4-y-o)
Aintree 2m 110y

1986	Dark Raven	11-00	16
1987	Aldino	11-00	13
1988	Royal Illusion	11-00	14
1989	Vayrua	11-00	9
1990	Sybillin	11-00	18
1991	Montpelier Lad	11-05	14
1992	Salwan	11-00	13
1993	Titled Dancer	10-09	8
1994	Tropical Lake	10-09	12
1995	Stompin	11-00	18
1996	Zabadi	11-00	11
1997	Quakers Field	11-00	12

MUMM MELLING CHASE
Aintree 2m 4f

1991	Blazing Walker	7-11-10	7
1992	Remittance Man	8-11-10	4
1993	Deep Sensation	8-11-10	4
1994	Katabatic	11-11-10	5
1995	Viking Flagship	8-11-10	6
1996	Viking Flagship	9-11-10	4
1997	Martha's Son	10-11-10	4

MARTELL AINTREE CHASE (LIMITED HANDICAP)
Aintree 2m

1986	Kathies Lad	9-10-13	6
1987	Sea Merchant	10-10-07	9
1988	Prideaux Boy	10-10-07	13
1989	Feroda	8-10-07	9
1990	Nohalmdun	9-10-07	12
1991	Blitzkreig	8-10-13	11
1992	Katabatic	9-12-00	4
1993	Boutzdaroff	11-10-07	6
1994	Uncle Ernie	9-10-08	8
1995	Coulton	8-11-08	12
1996	Arctic Kinsman	8-11-00	10
1997	Down the Fell	8-10-07	10

MARTELL AINTREE HURDLE
Aintree 2m 4f

1985	Bajan Sunshine	6-11-06	7
1986	Aonoch	7-11-09	9
1987	Aonoch	8-11-09	7
1988	Celtic Chief	5-11-06	9
1989	Beech Road	7-11-09	12
1990	Morley Street	6-11-06	6
1991	Morley Street	7-11-07	9
1992	Morley Street	8-11-07	6
1993	Morley Street	9-11-07	6
1994	Danoli	6-11-07	9
1995	Danoli	7-11-07	6
1996	Urubande	6-11-07	8
1997	Bimsey	7-11-07	7

MARTELL GRAND NATIONAL (HANDICAP CHASE)
4m 4f

1970	Gay Trip	8-11-05	28
1971	Specify	9-10-13	42
1972	Well To Do	9-10-01	42
1973	Red Rum	8-10-05	38
1974	Red Rum	9-12-00	42
1975	L'Escargot	12-11-03	31
1976	Rag Trade	10-10-12	32
1977	Red Rum	12-11-08	42
1978	Lucius	9-10-09	37
1979	Rubstic	10-10-00	34
1980	Ben Nevis	12-10-12	30
1981	Aldaniti	11-10-13	39
1982	Grittar	9-11-05	39
1983	Corbiere	8-11-04	41
1984	Hallo Dandy	10-10-02	40
1985	Last Suspect	11-10-05	40
1986	West Tip	9-10-11	40
1987	Maori Venture	11-10-13	40
1988	Rhyme 'N Reason	9-11-00	40
1989	Little Polveir	12-10-03	40
1990	Mr Frisk	11-10-06	38
1991	Seagram	11-10-06	40
1992	Party Politics	8-10-07	40
1993	*Void Race*		
1994	Miinnehoma	11-10-08	36
1995	Royal Athlete	12-10-06	35
1996	Rough Quest	10-10-07	27
1997	Lord Gyllene	9-10-00	36

STAKIS SCOTTISH GRAND NATIONAL (HANDICAP CHASE)
Ayr 4m 1f

1986	Hardy Lad	9-10-00	24
1987	Little Polveir	9-10-00	11
1988	Mighty Mark	9-10-04	17
1989	Roll-A-Joint	11-10-00	11
1990	Four Trix	9-10-00	28
1991	Killone Abbey	8-10-00	18
1992	Captain Dibble	7-11-00	21
1993	Run For Free	9-11-10	21
1994	Earth Summit	6-10-00	22
1995	Willsford	12-10-12	22
1996	Moorcroft Boy	11-10-02	20
1997	Belmont King	9-11-10	17

WHITBREAD GOLD CUP (HANDICAP CHASE)
Sandown 3m 5f 110y

1986	Plundering	9-10-06	16
1987	Lean Ar Aghaidh	10- 9-10	9
1988	Desert Orchid	9-11-11	12
1989	Brown Windsor	7-10-00	18
1990	Mr Frisk	11-10-05	13
1991	*Docklands Express	9-10-03	10
1992	Topsham Bay	9-10-01	11
1993	**Topsham Bay	10-10-01	13
1994	Ushers Island	8-10-00	12
1995	Cache Fleur	9-10-01	14
1996	Life of a Lord	10-11-10	17
1997	Harwell Lad	8-10-0	9

(* Cahervillahow 7-11-02 disqualified from 1st)
(** Givus A Buck 10-10-00 disqualified from 1st)

CROWTHER HOMES SWINTON (HANDICAP HURDLE)
Haydock 2m

1986	Prideaux Boy	8-11-02	20
1987	Inlander	6-10-08	8
1988	Past Glories	5-11-09	23
1989	State Jester	6-10-00	18
1990	Sybillin	4-10-01	14
1991	Winnie The Witch	7-10-02	12
1992	Bitofabanter	5-11-11	22
1993	Spinning	6-11-00	17
1994	Dreams End	6-11-04	18
1995	Chief Minister	6-11-06	13
1996	Tragic Hero	4-10-09	19
1997	Dreams End	9-11-11	19

Special offer to Chaseform Annual Purchasers !
*Use this order form and **save £5.50** on the normal price of £21.00*
You pay just £15.50!!

£5.50 OFF!!

Racehorse Record Jumps 1996-97

Chaseform
1996-97 JUMPS ANNUAL
THE OFFICIAL FORM BOOK
Raceform

A superb and lasting record of the past season and a great guide to future winners, *Racehorse Record* is a complete A-Z directory by horse (rather than race) of every runner from June 1996 to June 1997.

As a purchaser of Chaseform Annual you can save £5.50 bringing the price down to just £15.50 by using this order form (normal price £21.00).

IMPERIAL VINTAGE (IRE) BHB 84h121c **RR 68h123?c4621**[3]
6 ch g Aristocracy - Monasootha (Paddy's Stream)
Form - 44043FF31121111F114U133
Record 1995/6 - 1st:9 2nd:1 3rd:4 Ran:23
Win Prizemoney £39,024 *Total Prizemoney* £42,388

Wins								
• 1997	Apr	Ludlow	(FRM)	HCh	20f	118	123+	<
• 1997	Jan	Ludlow	(G-F)	HCh	24f	115	118	
• 1996	Dec	Chelte	(G-F)	Ch	21f		116	
• 1996	Nov	Chelte	(G-F)	Ch	25f		115	
• 1996	Nov	Leices	(G-F)	HCh	24f	110	115	
• 1996	Nov	Haydoc	(GD)	Ch	24f		114	
• 1996	Oct	Ludlow	(FRM)	Ch	20f		102	
• 1996	Spt	Newton	(G-F)	Ch	21.5f		102+	
1996	Jun	Uttoxe	(G-F)	Ch	23f		96	

1995/6 Hurdle 0-5: (18f, 20f, 21f, 23f, 25f) (hvy, g-s 2, gd 2) 1995/6 Chase 9-18: (20f 2-3, 21f 1-3, 22f 1-3, 23f 1-2, 24f 3-5, 25f 1-2) (g-s 2-4, gd 3-9, g-f 2-3, frm 2-2)
Fair hurdler decent chaser, effective 20 to 25f, acts on g-s to frm, likes right handed tracks, excels at Ludlow and Cheltenham. Hurdle high 68. Chase high 123 (began May) - 1st of 4 getting 10lb from Raba Riba (9 Apr Ludlow RF 4090) - also 1st of 8 giving 19lb to Fortunes Course (16 Jan Ludlow RF 2568). He won for Kim Bailey during the summer jumping season, but joined Venetia Williams afterwards and was a good advert for her, winning a further eight times in thirteen starts. He is very useful in the early part of the season, although he may find things more difficult in handicap company.
**Miss Venetia Williams [8-14] David Williams (from K C Bailey [1-9] Jun 96).*

Its 900 pages give details of each horse (as opposite) showing its full race history, breeding details, Raceform and Official ratings and winning performances. Our team of expert comment-writers have compiled reports and a unique descriptive comment on each horse, showing its going, distance, course requirements and other pertinent facts.

Liberally illustrated with action photographs from the season, plus leading statistics by course for Jockeys and Trainers, Course Maps and details, Racehorse Record is a must for all Jump enthusiasts.

Racehorse Record is designed to stand alone *or* beside Chaseform Annual as a permanent and quality reference guide to last season, as well as pointing the way to future winners.

See over for reviews of Racehorse Record Flat for the 1997 Flat Season.

Return this form ✂

I wish to purchase .... copies of Racehorse Record Jumps 1996-97 and have already purchased Chaseform Jumps Annual 1996-97. I enclose a cheque/p.o. @ £15.50 each (normal price £21.00) or
I wish to pay by Visa/Mastercard Switch/Delta. My card number is:

SPECIAL OFFER!
SAVE £5.50!

.... Expiry Date: .... Iss No: ....

Name:..

Address: ....

....Postcode......................

Return to: (no stamp required) Freepost, Raceform Ltd, Compton, Newbury, Berkshire, RG20 6NL
Tel: 01635 578080 Fax: 01635 578101

SAVE £5.50!!

Some Recent Press Comments and Reviews

"... a useful time-saver addition to the punter's armoury and it deserves to do well."
Melvyn Collier, RACING POST 25. 1.97

"... A useful reference book for punters ... it succeeds admirably."
Malcolm Heyhoe, SPORTING LIFE WEEKENDER 25. 1.97

"... Its practicality and adaptability make it an indispensable workbench ... the most reliable and instantly informative short-cut I have seen. It is genuinely good ... it is difficult to know how the profiles could be improved...."

Derek Mitchell, ODDS ON, March 1997

"... thought provoking reading ... a highly promising newcomer with scope to reach the top."
Weatherby's BULLETIN, December 1996

"... an absolute gem ... a thoroughly good read - an absolute mine of information and all for £21.00."
Ray Webster, SMART, 4. 2.97

"Everything about this publication is right and in my humble opinion deserves the highest accolade..."

Customer A.W., Warwickshire